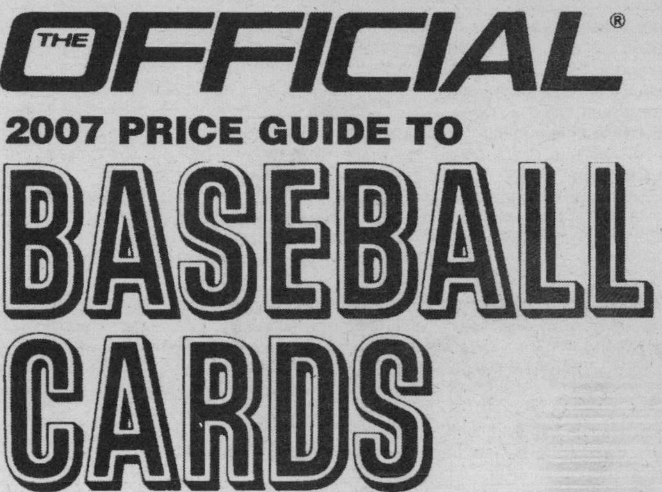

DR. JAMES BECKETT

TWENTY-SEVENTH EDITION

House of Collectibles
New York

Important Notice: All of the information, including valuations, in this book has been compiled from reliable sources, and efforts have been made to eliminate errors and questionable data. Nevertheless, the possibility of error, in a work of such immense scope, always exists. The publisher will not be held responsible for losses that may occur in the purchase, sale, or other transaction of items because of information contained herein. Readers who feel they have discovered errors are invited to *write* and inform us, so they may be corrected in subsequent editions. Those seeking further information on the topics covered in this book are advised to refer to the complete line of *Official Price Guides* published by the House of Collectibles.

House of Collectibles and colophon
are trademarks of Random House, Inc.

Published by:
House of Collectibles
Random House Reference
New York, New York

Distributed by Random House Reference,
an imprint of Random House, Inc.,
New York, and simultaneously in Canada by
Random House of Canada Limited, Toronto.

www.houseofcollectibles.com

Manufactured in the United States of America

ISSN: 1062-7138

ISBN: 978-0-375-72208-0

10 9 8 7 6 5 4 3 2 1

Twenty-Seventh Edition: April 2007

Table of Contents

About the Author 7
How to Use This Book 7
How to Collect 8
- Obtaining Cards 8
- Preserving Your Cards 9
- Collecting vs. Investing 9

Terminology 9
Glossary/Legend 10
Understanding Card Values 15
- Determining Value 15
- Regional Variation 15
- Set Prices 16
- Scarce Series 16

Grading Your Cards 17
- Centering 17
- Corner Wear 17
- Creases 18
- Alterations 18
- Categorization of Defects 18

Condition Guide 18
- Grades 18

Selling Your Cards 19
Interesting Notes 20
History of Baseball Cards 20
- Increasing Popularity 22
- Intensified Competition 25
- Sharing the Pie 26

Additional Reading 33
Prices in This Guide 34
Acknowledgments 34, 619

2005 Artifacts 35
2006 Artifacts 36
2005 Bazooka 36
2006 Bazooka 37
1948 Bowman 38
1949 Bowman 38
1950 Bowman 39
1951 Bowman 41
1952 Bowman 42
1953 Bowman Color 43
1954 Bowman 44
1955 Bowman 45
1989 Bowman 46
1990 Bowman 48
1991 Bowman 50
1992 Bowman 53
1993 Bowman 56
1994 Bowman 59
1995 Bowman 61
1996 Bowman 63
1997 Bowman 65
1998 Bowman 67
1999 Bowman 68
2000 Bowman 70
2000 Bowman Draft Picks 72
2001 Bowman 72
2001 Bowman Draft Picks 74
2002 Bowman 75
2002 Bowman Draft 77
2003 Bowman 77
2003 Bowman Draft 79
2004 Bowman 79
2004 Bowman Draft 81
2005 Bowman 81
2005 Bowman Draft 83
2006 Bowman 84
1997 Bowman Chrome 85
1998 Bowman Chrome 86
1999 Bowman Chrome 88
2000 Bowman Chrome 90
2000 Bowman Chrome Draft Picks 91
2001 Bowman Chrome 92
2002 Bowman Chrome 93
2002 Bowman Chrome Draft 95
2003 Bowman Chrome 96
2003 Bowman Chrome Draft 97
2004 Bowman Chrome 98
2004 Bowman Chrome Draft 99
2005 Bowman Chrome 100
2005 Bowman Chrome Draft 102
2006 Bowman Chrome 103
2001 Bowman Heritage 104
2002 Bowman Heritage 105
2003 Bowman Heritage 107
2004 Bowman Heritage 108
2005 Bowman Heritage 110
2004 Bowman Sterling 111
2005 Bowman Sterling 112
1914 Cracker Jack 113
1915 Cracker Jack 113
1981 Donruss 114
1982 Donruss 117
1983 Donruss 120
1984 Donruss 122
1985 Donruss 125
1986 Donruss 128
1986 Donruss Rookies 131
1987 Donruss 131

1987 Donruss Rookies 134
1988 Donruss 134
1988 Donruss Rookies 137
1989 Donruss 137
1989 Donruss Rookies 140
1990 Donruss 140
1991 Donruss 143
1992 Donruss 146
1992 Donruss Rookies 150
1993 Donruss 150
1994 Donruss 153
1995 Donruss 156
1996 Donruss 158
1997 Donruss 160
1998 Donruss 162
2001 Donruss 164
2002 Donruss 165
2003 Donruss 166
2003 Donruss Rookies 168
2004 Donruss 168
2005 Donruss 170
2001 eTopps 171
1993 Finest 172
1996 Finest 172
1999 Finest 174
2000 Finest 175
2001 Finest 176
2002 Finest 177
2003 Finest 178
2004 Finest 178
2005 Finest 179
2006 Finest 179
1994 Flair 180
2003 Flair 182
2005 Flair 183
1997 Flair Showcase Row 2 183
2006 Flair Showcase 184
1960 Fleer 185
1961 Fleer 185
1963 Fleer 186
1981 Fleer 186
1982 Fleer 189
1983 Fleer 192
1984 Fleer 194
1984 Fleer Update 197
1985 Fleer 198
1985 Fleer Update 201
1986 Fleer 201
1986 Fleer Update 204
1987 Fleer 204
1987 Fleer Update 207
1988 Fleer 208
1988 Fleer Update 211
1989 Fleer 211
1989 Fleer Update 214
1990 Fleer 215
1991 Fleer 217
1992 Fleer 221
1992 Fleer Update 224
1993 Fleer 224
1993 Fleer Final Edition 227
1994 Fleer 228
1994 Fleer Update 231
1995 Fleer 232
1996 Fleer 234
1997 Fleer 237
2002 Fleer 240
2006 Fleer 242
2001 Fleer Showcase 244
2003 Fleer Showcase 245
2005 Fleer Showcase 245
1998 Fleer Tradition Update 246
1999 Fleer Tradition Update 246
2000 Fleer Tradition 247
2000 Fleer Tradition Update 249
2001 Fleer Tradition 250
2003 Fleer Tradition Update 252
2004 Fleer Tradition 253
2005 Fleer Tradition 255
2006 Fleer Tradition 257
1933 Goudey 258
1934 Goudey 259
2004 Greats of the Game 259
2006 Greats of the Game 260
1949 Leaf 260
1990 Leaf 261
1993 Leaf 263
2003 Leaf 265
2005 Leaf 267
1998 Leaf Rookies and Stars 268
2001 Leaf Rookies and Stars 269
1939 Play Ball 270
1940 Play Ball 271
1941 Play Ball 272
1988 Score 273
1988 Score Rookie/Traded 275
1989 Score Rookie/Traded 276
1990 Score 276

1991 Score 279
1992 Score 283
1992 Score Rookie/Traded 287
1993 Score 288
1994 Score 290
1994 Score Rookie/Traded 293
1993 SP 294
1994 SP 295
2000 SP Authentic 296
2001 SP Authentic 297
2002 SP Authentic 298
2003 SP Authentic 299
2004 SP Authentic 300
2005 SP Authentic 300
2004 SP Legendary Cuts 301
2005 SP Legendary Cuts 302
2006 SP Legendary Cuts 302
2004 SP Prospects 303
1996 SPx 305
1998 SPx Finite 305
1999 SPx 307
2000 SPx 307
2001 SPx 308
2002 SPx 309
2003 SPx 310
2004 SPx 311
2005 SPx 312
2006 SPx 313
2001 Sweet Spot 314
2002 Sweet Spot 314
2003 Sweet Spot 315
2004 Sweet Spot 316
2005 Sweet Spot 317
2006 Sweet Spot 318
2003 Sweet Spot Classics 319
2005 Sweet Spot Classic 320
1911 T205 320
1909 T206 321
1952 Topps 323
1953 Topps 325
1954 Topps 326
1955 Topps 328
1956 Topps 328
1957 Topps 330
1958 Topps 332
1959 Topps 334
1960 Topps 336
1961 Topps 339
1962 Topps 341
1963 Topps 344
1964 Topps 346
1965 Topps 348
1966 Topps 351
1967 Topps 353
1968 Topps 356
1969 Topps 358
1970 Topps 361
1971 Topps 364
1972 Topps 367
1973 Topps 370
1974 Topps 373
1975 Topps 376
1976 Topps 378
1977 Topps 381
1978 Topps 384
1979 Topps 387
1980 Topps 389
1981 Topps 392
1981 Topps Traded 395
1982 Topps 396
1982 Topps Traded 399
1983 Topps 400
1983 Topps Traded 403
1984 Topps 404
1984 Topps Traded 407
1985 Topps 408
1985 Topps Traded 411
1986 Topps 412
1986 Topps Traded 415
1987 Topps 415
1987 Topps Traded 419
1988 Topps 420
1988 Topps Traded 423
1989 Topps 423
1989 Topps Traded 427
1990 Topps 427
1991 Topps 431
1991 Topps Traded 434
1992 Topps 435
1992 Topps Traded 438
1993 Topps 439
1993 Topps Traded 442
1994 Topps 443
1994 Topps Traded 446
1995 Topps 446
1995 Topps Traded 449
1996 Topps 450
1997 Topps 451

1998 Topps 453
1999 Topps 456
1999 Topps Traded 458
2000 Topps 459
2000 Topps Traded 461
2001 Topps 461
2001 Topps Traded 464
2002 Topps 466
2002 Topps Traded 469
2003 Topps 470
2003 Topps Traded 473
2004 Topps 474
2004 Topps Traded 477
2005 Topps 478
2005 Topps Factory Set Draft Picks Bonus ..481
2005 Topps Update 481
2006 Topps 482
2003 Topps 205 485
2002 Topps 206 486
2006 Topps Allen and Ginter 489
1998 Topps Chrome 490
1999 Topps Chrome 492
1999 Topps Chrome Traded 495
2000 Topps Chrome Traded 495
2001 Topps Chrome 496
2001 Topps Chrome Traded 498
2002 Topps Chrome 500
2002 Topps Chrome Traded 502
2003 Topps Chrome 503
2003 Topps Chrome Traded 505
2004 Topps Chrome 506
2004 Topps Chrome Traded 508
2005 Topps Chrome 509
2005 Topps Chrome Update 511
2006 Topps Chrome 512
2006 Topps Co-Signers 514
2001 Topps Heritage 514
2002 Topps Heritage 516
2003 Topps Heritage 518
2004 Topps Heritage 520
2005 Topps Heritage 522
2006 Topps Heritage 524
2005 Topps Opening Day 526
2006 Topps Opening Day 527
2006 Topps Sterling 528
2002 Topps Total 528
2003 Topps Total 532
2004 Topps Total 536
2005 Topps Total 539
2006 Topps Triple Threads 542
2006 Topps Turkey Red 543
2006 Topps Update and Highlights 544
2001 Ultimate Collection 546
2002 Ultimate Collection 546
2003 Ultimate Collection 547
2004 Ultimate Collection 548
2005 Ultimate Collection 549
1991 Ultra Update 550
1993 Ultra 550
1997 Ultra 553
1998 Ultra 555
2001 Ultra 557
2003 Ultra 558
2004 Ultra 560
2005 Ultra 561
2006 Ultra 562
1989 Upper Deck 563
1990 Upper Deck 567
1991 Upper Deck 570
1991 Upper Deck Final Edition 573
1992 Upper Deck 574
1993 Upper Deck 577
1994 Upper Deck 580
1995 Upper Deck 583
1996 Upper Deck 585
1997 Upper Deck 587
1998 Upper Deck 589
1999 Upper Deck 592
2000 Upper Deck 594
2001 Upper Deck 596
2002 Upper Deck 598
2003 Upper Deck 601
2004 Upper Deck 604
2005 Upper Deck 606
2006 Upper Deck 608
2006 Upper Deck Epic 612
2006 Upper Deck First Pitch 614
2001 Upper Deck Ovation 615
2006 Upper Deck Ovation 615
2001 Upper Deck Prospect Premieres 616
2002 Upper Deck Prospect Premieres 616
2003 Upper Deck Prospect Premieres 617
2005 Upper Deck Update 618
Acknowledgments....................................619

About the Author

Jim Beckett, the leading authority on sports card values in the United States, maintains a wide range of activities in the world of sports. He possesses one of the finest collections of sports cards and autographs in the world, has made numerous appearances on radio and television, and has been frequently cited in many national publications. He was awarded the first "Special Achievement Award" for Contributions to the Hobby by the National Sports Collectors Convention in 1980, the "Jock Jaspersen Award" for Hobby Dedication in 1983, and the "Buck Barker, Spirit of the Hobby" award in 1991.

Dr. Beckett is the author of *Beckett Baseball Card Price Guide, The Official Price Guide to Baseball Cards, Price Guide to Baseball Collectibles, The Sport Americana Baseball Memorabilia and Autograph Price Guide, Beckett Almanac of Baseball Cards and Collectibles, Beckett Football Card Price Guide, The Official Price Guide to Football Cards, Beckett Hockey Card Price Guide, The Official Price Guide to Hockey Cards, Beckett Basketball Card Price Guide, The Official Price Guide to Basketball Cards, The Beckett Baseball Card Alphabetical Checklist, The Beckett Basketball Card Alphabetical Checklist,* and *The Beckett Football Card Alphabetical Checklist.* In addition, he is the founder, publisher, and editor of *Beckett Baseball Card Monthly, Beckett Basketball Monthly, Beckett Football Card Monthly, Beckett Hockey Collector, Beckett Sports Collectibles,* and *Beckett Racing and Motorsports Marketplace.*

Jim Beckett received his Ph.D. in Statistics from Southern Methodist University in 1975. Prior to starting Beckett Publications in 1984, Dr. Beckett served as an Associate Professor of Statistics at Bowling Green State University and as a vice president of a consulting firm in Dallas, Texas.

How to Use This Book

Isn't it great? Every year this book gets better with all the new sets coming out. But even more exciting is that every year there are more options in collecting the cards we love so much. This edition has been enhanced and expanded from the previous edition. The cards you collect — who appears on them, what they look like, where they are from, and (most important to most of you) what their current values are — are enumerated within. Many of the features contained in the other *Beckett Price Guides* have been incorporated into this volume since condition grading, terminology, and many other aspects of collecting are common to the card hobby in general. We hope you find the book both interesting and useful in your collecting pursuits.

The Beckett Guide has been successful where other attempts have failed because it is complete, current, and valid. This price guide contains not just one, but three prices by condition for all the baseball cards listed. The prices were added to the card lists just prior to printing and reflect not the author's opinions or desires but the going retail prices for each card, based on the marketplace (sports memorabilia conventions and shows, sports card shops, hobby papers, current mail-order catalogs, local club meetings, auction results, and other firsthand reportings of actually realized prices).

What is the best price guide available on the market today? Of course, card sellers prefer the price guide with the highest prices, while card buyers naturally prefer the one with the lowest prices. Accuracy, however, is the true test. Use the price guide trusted by more collectors and dealers than all the others combined. Look for the Beckett® name. I won't put my name on anything I won't stake my reputation on. Not the lowest and not the highest — but the most accurate, with integrity.

To facilitate your use of this book, read the complete introductory section on the following pages before going to the pricing pages. Every collectible field has its own terminology; we've tried to capture most of these terms and definitions in our glossary. Please read carefully the section on grading and the condition of your cards, as you cannot determine which price column is appropriate for a given card without first knowing its condition.

Welcome to the world of baseball cards.

How to Collect

Each collection is personal and reflects the individuality of its owner. There are no set rules on how to collect cards. Since card collecting is a hobby or leisure pastime, what you collect, how much you collect, and how much time and money you spend collecting are entirely up to you. The funds you have available for collecting and your own personal tàste should determine how you collect. Information and ideas presented here are intended to help you get the most enjoyment from this hobby.

It is impossible to collect every card ever produced. Therefore, beginners as well as intermediate and advanced collectors usually specialize in some way. One of the reasons this hobby is popular is that individual collectors can define and tailor their collecting methods to match their own tastes. To give you some idea of the various approaches to collecting, we will list some of the more popular areas of specialization.

Many collectors select complete sets from particular years. For example, they may concentrate on assembling complete sets from all the years since their birth or since they became avid sports fans. They may try to collect a card for every player during that specified period of time.

Many others wish to acquire only certain players. Usually such players are the superstars of the sport, but occasionally collectors will specialize in all the cards of players who attended a particular college or came from a certain town. Some collectors are interested in only the first cards or Rookie Cards of certain players. A handy guide for collectors interested in pursuing the hobby this way is *The Sport Americana Baseball Card Alphabetical Checklist.*

Another fun way to collect cards is by team. Most fans have a favorite team, and it is natural for that loyalty to be translated into a desire for cards of the players on that favorite team. For most of the recent years, team sets (all the cards from a given team for that year) are readily available at a reasonable price. The Sport *Americana Team Baseball Card Checklist* will open up this field to the collector.

Obtaining Cards

Several avenues are open to card collectors. Cards still can be purchased in the traditional way: by the pack at the local candy, grocery, drug, or major discount store.

But there are also thousands of card shops across the country that specialize in selling cards individually or by the pack, box, or set. Another alternative are the thousands of card shows held each month around the country, which feature anywhere from 8 to 800 tables of sports cards and memorabilia for sale.

For many years, it has been possible to purchase complete sets of baseball cards through mail-order advertisers found in traditional sports media publications, such as the *Sporting News, Baseball Digest*, and, *Street & Smith* yearbooks. These sets also are advertised in the card collecting periodicals. Many collectors will begin by subscribing to at least one of the hobby periodicals, all with good up-to-date information. In fact, subscription offers can be found in the advertising section of this book.

Most serious card collectors obtain old (and new) cards from one or more of several main sources: (1) trading or buying from other collectors or dealers; (2) responding to sale or auction ads in the hobby publications; (3) buying at a local hobby store; (4) attending sports collectibles shows or conventions; and (5) purchasing cards over the Internet.

We advise that you try all five methods since each has its own distinct advantages: (1) trading is a great way to make new friends; (2) hobby periodicals help you keep up with what´s going on in the hobby (including when and where the conventions are happening); (3) stores provide the opportunity to enjoy personalized service and consider a great diversity of material in a relaxed sports-oriented atmosphere; (4) shows allow you to choose from multiple dealers and thousands of cards under one roof in a competitive situation; and (5) the Internet allows one to purchase cards in a convenient manner from almost anywhere in the world.

Preserving Your Cards

Cards are fragile. They must be handled properly in order to retain their value. Careless handling can easily result in creased or bent cards. It is, however, not recommended that tweezers or tongs be used to pick up your cards since such utensils might mar or indent card surfaces and thus reduce those cards´ conditions and values.

In general, your cards should be handled directly as little as possible. This is sometimes easier to say than to do.

Although there are still many who use custom boxes, storage trays, or even shoe boxes, plastic sheets are the preferred method of many collectors for storing cards.

A collection stored in plastic pages in a three-ring album allows you to view your collection at any time without the need to touch the card itself. Cards can also be kept in single holders (of various types and thicknesses) designed for the enjoyment of each card individually.

For a large collection, some collectors may use a combination of the above methods. When purchasing plastic sheets for your cards, be sure that you find the pocket size that fits the cards snugly. Don´t put your 1951 Bowman in a sheet designed to fit 1981 Topps.

Most hobby and collectibles shops and virtually all collectors´ conventions will have these plastic pages available in quantity for the various sizes offered, or you can purchase them directly from the advertisers in this book.

Also, remember that pocket size isn´t the only factor to consider when looking for plastic sheets. Other factors such as safety, economy, appearance, availability, or personal preference also may influence which types of sheets a collector may want to buy.

Damp, sunny, and/or hot conditions — no, this is not a weather forecast — are three elements to avoid in extremes if you are interested in preserving your collection. Too much (or too little) humidity can cause the gradual deterioration of a card. Direct, bright sun (or fluorescent light) over time will bleach out the color of a card. Extreme heat accelerates the decomposition of the card. On the other hand, many cards have lasted more than 75 years without much scientific intervention. So be cautious, even if the above factors typically present a problem only when present in the extreme. It never hurts to be prudent.

Collecting vs. Investing

Collecting individual players and collecting complete sets are both popular vehicles for investment and speculation.

Most investors and speculators stock up on complete sets or on quantities of players they think have good investment potential.

There is obviously no guarantee in this book, or anywhere else for that matter, that cards will outperform the stock market or other investment alternatives in the future. After all, baseball cards do not pay quarterly dividends and cards cannot be sold at their "current values" as easily as stocks or bonds.

Nevertheless, investors have noticed a favorable long-term trend in the past performance of baseball and other sports collectibles, and certain cards and sets have outperformed just about any other investment in some years.

Many hobbyists maintain that the best investment is and always will be the building of a collection, which traditionally has held up better than outright speculation.

Some of the obvious questions are: Which cards? When to buy? When to sell? The best investment you can make is in your own education.

The more you know about your collection and the hobby, the more informed the decisions you will be able to make. We´re not selling investment tips. We´re selling information about the current value of baseball cards. It´s up to you to use that information to your best advantage.

Terminology

Each hobby has its own language to describe its area of interest. The nomenclature traditionally used for trading cards is derived from the American Card Catalog, published in 1960 by Nostalgia Press. That catalog, written by Jefferson Burdick (who is called the "Father of Card Collecting" for his pioneering work), uses letter and number designations for each separate set of cards. The letter used in the ACC designation refers to the generic type of card. While both sport and nonsport issues are classified in the ACC, we shall confine ourselves to the sport issues. The following list defines the letters and their meanings as used by the American Card Catalog.

(none) or N - 19th Century U.S. Tobacco.

B - Blankets.

D - Bakery Inserts Including Bread.

E - Early Candy and Gum.

F - Food Inserts.

H - Advertising.

M - Periodicals.

PC - Postcards.

R - Candy and Gum since 1930.

T - Tobacco.

Following the letter prefix and an optional hyphen are one-, two-, or three-digit numbers, R(-)999. These typically represent the company or entity issuing the cards. In several cases, the ACC number is extended by an additional hyphen and another one- or two-digit numerical suffix. For example, the 1957 Topps regular-series baseball card issue carries an ACC designation of R414-11. The "R" indicates a Candy or Gum card produced since 1930. The "414" is the ACC designation for Topps Chewing Gum baseball card issues, and the "11" is the ACC designation for the 1957 regular issue (Topps´ eleventh baseball set). Like other traditional methods of identification, this system provides order to the process of cataloging cards; however, most serious collectors learn the ACC designation of the popular sets by repetition and familiarity, rather than by attempting to "figure out" what they might or should be. From 1948 forward, collectors and dealers commonly refer to all sets by their year, maker, type of issue, and any other distinguishing characteristic. For example, such a characteristic could be an unusual issue or one of several regular issues put out by a specific maker in a single year. Regional issues are usually referred to by year, maker, and sometimes by title or theme of the set.

Glossary/Legend

Our glossary defines terms used in the card collecting hobby and in this book. Many of these terms are also common to other types of sports memorabilia collecting. Some terms may have several meanings depending on use and context.

ACETATE—A transparent plastic.

AS—All-Star card. A card portraying an All-Star Player of the previous year that says "All-Star" on its face.

ATG—All-Time Great card.

ATL—All-Time Leaders card.

AU(TO)—Autographed card.

AW—Award Winner.

BB—Building Blocks.

BC—Bonus Card.

BF—Bright Futures.

BL—Blue Letters.

BNR—Banner Season

BOX CARD—Card issued on a box (e.g., 1987 Topps Box Bottoms).

BRICK—A group of 50 or more cards having common characteristics that is intended to be bought, sold, or traded as a unit.

CABINETS—Popular and highly valuable photographs on thick card stock produced in the 19th and early 20th century.

CC—Curtain Call.

CG—Cornerstones of the Game.

CHECKLIST—A list of the cards contained in a particular set. The list is always in numerical order if the cards are numbered. Some unnumbered sets are artificially numbered in alphabetical order, by team and alphabetically within the team, or by uniform number for convenience.
CL—Checklist card. A card that lists in order the cards and players in the set or series. Older checklist cards in Mint condition that have not been marked are very desirable and command premiums.
CP—Changing Places.
CO—Coach.
COMM—Commissioner.
COMMON CARD—The typical card of any set; it has no premium value accruing from subject matter, numerical scarcity, popular demand, or anomaly.
CONVENTION—A gathering of dealers and collectors at a single location for the purpose of buying, selling, and trading sports memorabilia items. Conventions are open to the public and sometimes feature autograph guests, door prizes, contests, seminars, etc. They are frequently referred to simply as "shows."
COOP—Cooperstown.
COR—Corrected card.
CT—Cooperstown.
CY—Cy Young Award.
DD—Decade of Dominance.
DEALER—A person who engages in buying, selling, and trading sports collectibles or supplies. A dealer may also be a collector, but as a dealer, his main goal is to earn a profit.
DIE-CUT—A card with part of its stock partially cut, allowing one or more parts to be folded or removed. After removal or appropriate folding, the remaining part of the card can frequently be made to stand up.
DK—Diamond King.
DL—Division Leaders.
DP—Double Print (a card that was printed in double the quantity compared to the other cards in the same series) or a Draft Pick card.
DT—Dream Team.
DUFEX—A method of card manufacturing technology patented by Pinnacle Brands, Inc. It involves a refractive quality to a card with a foil coating.
ERA—Earned Run Average.
ERR—Error card. A card with erroneous information, spelling, or depiction on either side of the card. Most errors are not corrected by the producing card company.
FC—Fan Club.
FDP—First or First-Round Draft Pick.
FF—Future Foundation.
FOIL—Foil embossed stamp on card.
FOLD—Foldout.
FP—Franchise Player.
Fr—Franchise.
FS—Father/son card.
FS—Future Star.
FUN—Fun cards.
FY—First Year.
GL—Green Letters.
GLOSS—A card with luster; a shiny finish as in a card with UV coating.
HG—Heroes of the Game.
HIGH NUMBER—The cards in the last series of numbers in a year in which

such higher-numbered cards were printed or distributed in significantly lesser amounts than the lower-numbered cards. The high-number designation refers to a scarcity of the high-numbered cards. Not all years have high numbers in terms of this definition.

HL—Highlight card.

HOF—Hall of Fame, or a card that portrays a Hall of Famer (HOFer).

HOLOGRAM—A three-dimensional photographic image.

HH—Hometown Heroes.

HOR—Horizontal pose on card as opposed to the standard vertical orientation found on most cards.

IA—In Action card.

IF—Infielder.

INSERT—A card of a different type or any other sports collectible (typically a poster or sticker) contained and sold in the same package along with a card or cards of a major set. An insert card is either unnumbered or not numbered in the same sequence as the major set. Sometimes the inserts are randomly distributed and are not found in every pack.

INTERACTIVE—A concept that involves collector participation.

IRT—International Road Trip.

ISSUE—Synonymous with set, but usually used in conjunction with a manufacturer, e.g., a Topps issue.

JSY—means Jersey.

KM—K-Men.

LHP—Left-handed pitcher.

LL—League Leaders or large letters on card.

LUM—Lumberjack.

MAJOR SET—A set produced by a national manufacturer of cards containing a large number of cards. Usually 100 or more different cards constitute a major set.

MB—Master Blasters.

MEM—Memorial card. For example, the 1990 Donruss and Topps Bart Giamatti cards.

METALLIC—A glossy design method that enhances card features.

MG—Manager.

MI—Maximum Impact.

MINI—A small card; for example, a 1975 Topps card of identical design but smaller dimensions than the regular Topps issue of 1975.

ML—Major League.

MM—Memorable Moments.

MULTI-PLAYER CARD—A single card depicting two or more players (but not a team card).

MVP—Most Valuable Player.

NAU—No autograph on card.

NG—Next Game.

NH—No-Hitter.

NNOF—No name on front.

NOF—Name on front.

NOTCHING—The grooving of the card, usually caused by fingernails, rubber bands, or bumping card edges against other objects.

NT—Now and Then.

NV—Novato.

OF—Outfield or Outfielder.

OLY—Olympics Card.

P—Pitcher or Pitching pose.

P1—First Printing.
P2—Second Printing.
P3—Third Printing.
PACKS—A means by which cards are issued in terms of pack type (wax, cello, foil, rack, etc.) and channel of distribution (hobby, retail, etc.).
PARALLEL— A card that is similar in design to its counterpart from a basic set but offers a distinguishing quality.
PF—Profiles.
PG—Postseason Glory.
PLASTIC SHEET—A clear, plastic page that is punched for insertion into a binder (with standard three-ring spacing) containing pockets for displaying cards. Many different styles of sheets exist with pockets of varying sizes to hold the many differing card formats. Also called a display sheet or storage sheet.
PP—Power Passion.
PLATINUM—A metallic element used in the process of creating a glossy card.
PR—Printed name on back.
PREMIUM—A card, sometimes on photographic stock, that is purchased or obtained in conjunction with, or redemption for, another card or product. The premium is not packaged in the same unit as the primary item.
PRES—President.
PRISMATIC/PRISM—A glossy or bright design that refracts or disperses light.
PS—Pace Setters.
PT—Power Tools.
PUZZLE CARD—A card whose back contains a part of a picture which, when joined correctly with other puzzle cards, forms the completed picture.
PUZZLE PIECE—A die-cut piece designed to interlock with similar pieces (e.g., early 1980s Donruss).
PVC—Polyvinyl chloride, a substance used to make many of the popular card display protective sheets. Non-PVC sheets are considered preferable for long-term storage of cards by many.
RARE—A card or series of cards of very limited availability. Unfortunately, "rare" is a subjective term frequently used indiscriminately to hype value. "Rare" cards are harder to obtain than "scarce" cards.
RB—Record Breaker.
RC—Rookie Card.
REDEMPTION—A program established by multiple card manufacturers that allows collectors to mail in a special card (usually a random insert) in return for special cards, sets, or other prizes not available through conventional channels.
REFRACTORS—A card that features a design element that enhances (distorts) its color/appearance through deflecting light.
REV NEG—Reversed or flopped photo side of the card. This is a major type of error card, but only some are corrected.
RHP—Right-handed pitcher.
RHW—Rookie Home Whites.
RIF—Rifleman.
RPM—Rookie Premiere Materials.
RR—Rated Rookie.
ROO—Rookie.
ROY—Rookie of the Year.
RP—Relief pitcher.
RTC—Rookie True Colors.
SA—Super Action card.
SASE—Self-Addressed, Stamped Envelope.

SB—Scrapbook.
SB—Stolen Bases.
SCARCE—A card or series of cards of limited availability. This subjective term is sometimes used indiscriminately to hype value. "Scarce" cards are not as difficult to obtain as "rare" cards.
SCR—Script name on back.
SD—San Diego Padres.
SEMI-HIGH—A card from the next-to-last series of a sequentially issued set. It has more value than an average card and generally less value than a high number. A card is not called a semi-high unless the next-to-last series in which it exists has an additional premium attached to it.
SERIES—The entire set of cards issued by a particular producer in a particular year; e.g., the 1971 Topps series. Also, within a particular set, series can refer to a group of (consecutively numbered) cards printed at the same time, e.g., the first series of the 1957 Topps issue (#1 through #88).
SET—One each of the entire run of cards of the same type produced by a particular manufacturer during a single year. In other words, if you have a complete set of 1976 Topps then you have every card from #1 up to and including #660; i.e., all the different cards that were produced.
SF—Starflics.
SH—Season Highlight.
SHEEN—Brightness or luster emitted by card.
SKIP-NUMBERED—A set that has many unissued card numbers between the lowest number in the set and the highest number in the set, e.g., the 1948 Leaf baseball set contains 98 cards skip-numbered from #1 to #168. A major set in which a few numbers were not printed is not considered to be skip-numbered.
SP—Single or Short Print (a card that was printed in lesser quantity compared to the other cards in the same series; see also DP and TP).
SPECIAL CARD—A card that portrays something other than a single player or team, for example, a card that portrays the previous year's statistical leaders or the results from the previous year's World Series.
SS—Shortstop.
STANDARD SIZE—Most modern sports cards measure 2-1/2 by 3-1/2 inches. Exceptions are noted in card descriptions throughout this book.
STAR CARD—A card that portrays a player of some repute, usually determined by his ability; but sometimes referring to sheer popularity.
STOCK—The cardboard or paper on which the card is printed.
SUPERIMPOSED—To be affixed on top of something; i.e., a player photo over a solid background.
SUPERSTAR CARD—A card that portrays a superstar, e.g., a Hall of Famer or player with strong Hall of Fame potential.
TC—Team Checklist.
TEAM CARD—A card that depicts an entire team.
THREE-DIMENSIONAL (3D)—A visual image that provides an illusion of depth and perspective.
TOPICAL—A subset or group of cards that have a common theme (e.g., MVP award winners).
TP—Triple Print (a card that was printed in triple the quantity compared to the other cards in the same series).
TR—Trade reference on card.
TRANSPARENT—Clear, see-through.
UDCA—Upper Deck Classic Alumni.
UER—Uncorrected Error.
UMP—Umpire.

USA—Team USA.
UV—Ultraviolet, a glossy coating used in producing cards.
VAR—Variation card. One of two or more cards from the same series with the same number (or player with identical pose if the series is unnumbered) differing from one another by some aspect, the different feature stemming from the printing or stock of the card. This can be caused when the manufacturer of the cards notices an error in one or more of the cards, makes the changes, and then resumes the print run. In this case there will be two versions or variations of the same card. Sometimes one of the variations is relatively scarce.
VERT—Vertical pose on card.
WAS—Washington National League (1974 Topps).
WC—What´s the Call?
WL—White letters on front.
WS—World Series card.
YL—Yellow letters on front.
YT—Yellow team name on front.
*—to denote multi-sport sets.

Understanding Card Values

Determining Value

Why are some cards more valuable than others? Obviously, the economic laws of supply and demand are applicable to card collecting just as they are to any other field where a commodity is bought, sold, or traded in a free, unregulated market.

Supply (the number of cards available on the market) is less than the total number of cards originally produced since attrition diminishes that original quantity. Each year a percentage of cards is typically thrown away, destroyed, or otherwise lost to collectors. This percentage is much, much smaller today than it was in the past because more and more people have become increasingly aware of the value of their cards.

For those who collect only Mint condition cards, the supply of older cards can be quite small indeed. Until recently, collectors were not so conscious of the need to preserve the condition of their cards. For this reason, it is difficult to know exactly how many 1953 Topps are currently available, Mint or otherwise. It is generally accepted that there are fewer 1953 Topps available than 1963, 1973, or 1983 Topps cards. If demand were equal for each of these sets, the law of supply and demand would increase the price for the least available sets. Demand, however, is never equal for all sets, so price correlations can be complicated. The demand for a card is influenced by many factors. These include: (1) the age of the card; (2) the number of cards printed; (3) the player(s) portrayed on the card; (4) the attractiveness and popularity of the set; and (5) the physical condition of the card.

In general, (1) the older the card, (2) the fewer the number of the cards printed, (3) the more famous, popular, and talented the player, (4) the more attractive and popular the set, and (5) the better the condition of the card, the higher the value of the card will be. There are exceptions to all but one of these factors: the condition of the card. Given two cards similar in all respects except condition, the one in the best condition will always be valued higher.

While those guidelines help to establish the value of a card, the countless exceptions and peculiarities make any simple, direct mathematical formula to determine card values impossible.

Regional Variation

Since the market varies from region to region, card prices of local players may be higher. This is known as a regional premium. How significant the premium is — and if there is any premium at all — depends on the local popularity of the team and the player.

The largest regional premiums usually do not apply to superstars, who often are so well known nationwide that the prices of their key cards are too high for local dealers to realize a premium.

Lesser stars often command the strongest premiums. Their popularity is concentrated in their home region, creating local demand that greatly exceeds overall demand.

Regional premiums can apply to popular retired players and sometimes can be found in the areas where the players grew up or starred in college.

A regional discount is the converse of a regional premium. Regional discounts occur when a player has been so popular in his region for so long that local collectors and dealers have accumulated quantities of his key cards. The abundant supply may make the cards available in that area at the lowest prices anywhere.

Set Prices

A somewhat paradoxical situation exists in the price of a complete set versus the combined cost of the individual cards in the set. In nearly every case, the sum of the prices for the individual cards is higher than the cost for the complete set. This is prevalent especially in the cards of the last few years. The reasons for this apparent anomaly stem from the habits of collectors and from the carrying costs to dealers. Today, each card in a set normally is produced in the same quantity as all other cards in its set.

Many collectors pick up only stars, superstars, and particular teams. As a result, the dealer is left with a shortage of certain player cards and an abundance of others. He therefore incurs an expense in simply "carrying" these less desirable cards in stock. On the other hand, if he sells a complete set, he gets rid of large numbers of cards at one time. For this reason, he generally is willing to receive less money for a complete set. By doing this, he recovers all of his costs and also makes a profit.

The disparity between the price of the complete set and the sum of the individual cards also has been influenced by the fact that some of the major manufacturers now are pre-collating card sets. Since "pulling" individual cards from the sets involves a specific type of labor (and cost), the singles or star card market is not affected significantly by pre-collation.

Set prices also do not include rare card varieties, unless specifically stated. Of course, the prices for sets do include one example of each type for the given set, but this is the least expensive variety.

Scarce Series

Scarce series occur because cards issued before 1974 were made available to the public each year in several series of finite numbers of cards, rather than all cards of the set being available for purchase at one time. At some point during the year, usually toward the end of the baseball season, interest in current year baseball cards waned. Consequently, the manufacturers produced smaller numbers of these later-series cards.

Nearly all nationwide issues from post–World War II manufacturers (1948 to 1970) exhibit these series variations. In the past, Topps, for example, may have issued series consisting of many different numbers of cards, including 55, 66, 80, 88, and others. Recently, Topps has settled on what is now its standard sheet size of 132 cards, six of which constitute its 792-card set.

While the number of cards within a given series is usually the same as the number of cards on one printed sheet, this is not always the case. For example, Bowman used 36 cards on its standard printed sheets, but in 1948 substituted 12 cards during later print runs of that year's baseball cards. Twelve of the cards from the initial sheet of 36 cards were removed and replaced by 12 different cards, giving, in effect, a first series of 36 cards and a second series of 12 new cards. This replacement produced a scarcity of 24 cards — the 12 cards removed from the original sheet and the 12 new cards added to the sheet. A full sheet of 1948 Bowman cards (second printing) shows that card numbers 37 through 48 have replaced 12 of the cards on the first printing sheet.

The Topps Company also has created scarcities and/or excesses of certain cards in many of its sets. Topps, however, has most frequently gone the other direction by double printing some of the cards. Double printing causes an abundance of cards of the players who are on the same sheet more than one time. During the years from 1978 to 1981, Topps double printed 66 cards out of their large 726-card set. The Topps practice of double printing cards in earlier years is the most logical explanation for the known scarcities of particular cards in some of these Topps sets.

From 1988 through 1990, Donruss short printed and double printed certain cards in its major sets. Ostensibly this was because of its addition of bonus team MVP cards in its regular-issue wax packs.

We are always looking for information or photographs of printing sheets of cards for research. Each year, we try to update the hobby´s knowledge of distribution anomalies. Please let us know at the address in this book if you have firsthand knowledge that would be helpful in this pursuit.

Grading Your Cards

Each hobby has its own grading terminology — stamps, coins, comic books, record collecting, etc. Collectors of sports cards are no exception. The one invariable criterion for determining the value of a card is its condition: The better the condition of the card, the more valuable it is. Condition grading, however, is subjective. Individual card dealers and collectors differ in the strictness of their grading, but the stated condition of a card should be determined without regard to whether it is being bought or sold.

No allowance is made for age. A 1952 card is judged by the same standards as a 1992 card. But there are specific sets and cards that are condition-sensitive (marked with "!" in the Price Guide) because of their border color, consistently poor centering, etc. Such cards and sets sometimes command premiums above the listed percentages in Mint condition.

Centering

Current centering terminology uses numbers representing the percentage of border on either side of the main design. Obviously, centering is diminished in importance for borderless cards such as Stadium Club.

Slightly Off-Center (60/40): A slightly off-center card is one that, upon close inspection, is found to have one border bigger than the opposite border. This degree once was offensive only to purists, but now some hobbyists try to avoid cards that are anything other than perfectly centered.

Off-Center (70/30): An off-center card has one border that is noticeably more than twice as wide as the opposite border.

Badly Off-Center (80/20 or worse): A badly off-center card has virtually no border on one side of the card.

Miscut: A miscut card actually shows part of the adjacent card in its larger border and consequently a corresponding amount of its card is cut off.

Corner Wear

Corner wear is the most scrutinized grading criteria in the hobby. These are the major categories of corner wear:

Corner with a slight touch of wear: The corner still is sharp, but there is a slight touch of wear showing. On a dark-bordered card, this shows as a dot of white.

Fuzzy corner: The corner still comes to a point, but the point has just begun to fray. A slightly "dinged" corner is considered the same as a fuzzy corner.

Slightly rounded corner: The fraying of the corner has increased to where there is only a hint of a point. Mild layering may be evident. A "dinged" corner is considered the same as a slightly rounded corner.

Rounded corner: The point is completely gone. Some layering is noticeable.

Badly rounded corner: The corner is completely round and rough. Severe layering is evident.

Creases

A third common defect is the crease. The degree of creasing in a card is difficult to show in a drawing or picture. On giving the specific condition of an expensive card for sale, the seller should note any creases additionally. Creases can be categorized as to severity according to the following scale:

Light Crease: A light crease is a crease that is barely noticeable upon close inspection. In fact, when cards are in plastic sheets or holders, a light crease may not be seen (until the card is taken out of the holder). A light crease on the front is much more serious than a light crease on the card back only.

Medium Crease: A medium crease is noticeable when held and studied at arm´s length by the naked eye, but does not overly detract from the appearance of the card. It is an obvious crease, but not one that breaks the picture surface of the card.

Heavy Crease: A heavy crease is one that has torn or broken through the card´s picture surface; i.e., puts a tear in the photo surface.

Alterations

Deceptive Trimming: This occurs when someone alters the card in order (1) to shave off edge wear, (2) to improve the sharpness of the corners, or (3) to improve centering — obviously their objective is to falsely increase the perceived value of the card to an unsuspecting buyer. The shrinkage usually is evident only if the trimmed card is compared to an adjacent full-size card or if the trimmed card is itself measured.

Obvious Trimming: Obvious trimming is noticeable and unfortunate. It is usually performed by noncollectors who give no thought to the present or future value of their cards.

Deceptively Retouched Borders: This occurs when the borders (especially on those cards with dark borders) are touched up on the edges and corners with magic marker or crayons of appropriate color in order to make the card appear Mint.

Categorization of Defects—Miscellaneous Flaws

The following are common minor flaws that, depending on severity, lower a card´s condition by one to four grades and often render it no better than Excellent-Mint: bubbles (lumps in surface), gum and wax stains, diamond cutting (slanted borders), notching, off-centered backs, paper wrinkles, scratched-off cartoons or puzzles on back, rubber band marks, scratches, surface impressions, and warping.

The following are common serious flaws that, depending on severity, lower a card´s condition at least four grades and often render it no better than Good: chemical or sun fading, erasure marks, mildew, miscutting (severe off-centering), holes, bleached or retouched borders, tape marks, tears, trimming, water or coffee stains, and writing.

Condition Guide

Grades

Mint (Mt)—A card with no flaws or wear. The card has four perfect corners, 60/40 or better centering from top to bottom and from left to right, original gloss, smooth edges, and original color borders. A Mint card does not have print spots or color or focus imperfections.

Near Mint-Mint (NrMt-Mt)—A card with one minor flaw. Any one of the following would lower a Mint card to Near Mint-Mint: one corner with a slight touch of wear, barely noticeable print spots, or color or focus imperfections. The card must have

60/40 or better centering in both directions, original gloss, smooth edges, and original color borders.

Near Mint (NrMt)—A card with one minor flaw. Any one of the following would lower a Mint card to Near Mint: one fuzzy corner or two to four corners with slight touches of wear, 70/30 to 60/40 centering, slightly rough edges, minor print spots, color or focus imperfections. The card must have original gloss and original color borders.

Excellent-Mint (ExMt)—A card with two or three fuzzy, but not rounded, corners and centering no worse than 80/20. The card may have no more than two of the following: slightly rough edges, very slightly discolored borders, minor print spots, color or focus imperfections. The card must have original gloss.

Excellent (Ex)—A card with four fuzzy but definitely not rounded corners and centering no worse than 80/20. The card may have a small amount of original gloss lost, rough edges, slightly discolored borders, and minor print spots or color or focus imperfections.

Very Good (Vg)—A card that has been handled but not abused: slightly rounded corners with slight layering, slight notching on edges, a significant amount of gloss lost from the surface (but no scuffing) and moderate discoloration of borders. The card may have a few light creases.

Good (G), Fair (F), Poor (P)—A well-worn, mishandled, or abused card: badly rounded and layered corners, scuffing, most or all original gloss missing, seriously discolored borders, moderate or heavy creases, and one or more serious flaws. The grade of Good, Fair, or Poor depends on the severity of wear and flaws. Good, Fair, and Poor cards generally are used only as fillers.

The most widely used grades are defined above. Obviously, many cards will not perfectly fit one of the definitions.

Therefore, categories between the major grades known as in-between grades are used, such as Good to Very Good (G-Vg), Very Good to Excellent (VgEx), and Excellent-Mint to Near Mint (ExMt-NrMt). Such grades indicate a card with all qualities of the lower category but with at least a few qualities of the higher category.

Beckett Baseball Card Price Guide lists each card and set in two grades, with the middle grade valued at about 40%–45% of the top grade.

The value of cards that fall between the listed columns can also be calculated using a percentage of the top grade. For example, a card that falls between the top and middle grades (Ex, ExMt, or NrMt in most cases) will generally be valued at anywhere from 50% to 90% of the top grade.

Similarly, a card that falls between the middle and bottom grades (G-Vg, Vg, or VgEx in most cases) will generally be valued at anywhere from 20%–40% of the top grade.

There are also cases where cards are in better condition than the top grade or worse than the bottom grade. Cards that grade worse than the lowest grade are generally valued at 5%–10% of the top grade.

When a card exceeds the top grade by one — such as NrMt-Mt when the top grade is NrMt, or Mint when the top grade is NrMt-Mt — a premium of up to 50% is possible, with 10%–20% the usual norm.

When a card exceeds the top grade by two — such as Mint when the top grade is NrMt, or NrMt-Mt when the top grade is ExMt — a premium of 25%–50% is the usual norm. But certain condition-sensitive cards or sets, particularly those from the pre-war era, can bring premiums of up to 100% or even more.

Unopened packs, boxes, and factory-collated sets are considered Mint in their unknown (and presumed perfect) state. Once opened, however, each card can be graded (and valued) in its own right by taking into account any defects that may be present in spite of the fact that the card has never been handled.

Selling Your Cards

Just about every collector sells cards or will sell cards eventually. Someday you may be interested in selling your duplicates or maybe even your whole collection. You may sell to other collectors, friends, or dealers. You may even sell cards you purchased from a certain dealer back to that same dealer. In any event, it helps to know some of the mechanics of the typical transaction between buyer and seller.

Dealers will buy cards in order to resell them to other collectors who are interested in the cards. Dealers will always pay a higher percentage for items that (in their opinion) can be resold quickly, and a much lower percentage for those Items that are perceived as having low demand and hence are slow moving. In either case, dealers must buy at a price that allows for the expense of doing business and a margin for profit.

If you have cards for sale, the best advice we can give is that you get several offers for your cards — either from card shops or at a card show — and take the best offer, all things considered. Note, the "best" offer may not be the one for the highest amount. And remember, if a dealer really wants your cards, he won´t let you get away without making his best competitive offer. Another alternative is to place your cards in an auction as one or several lots.

Many people think nothing of going into a department store and paying $15 for an item of clothing for which the store paid $5. But if you were selling your $15 card to a dealer and he offered you $5 for it, you might consider his markup unreasonable. To complete the analogy: Most department stores (and card dealers) that consistently pay $10 for $15 items eventually go out of business. An exception is when the dealer has lined up a willing buyer for the item(s) you are attempting to sell, or if the cards are so hot that it´s likely he´ll have to hold the cards for just a short period of time.

In those cases, an offer of up to 75% of book value still will allow the dealer to make a reasonable profit considering the short time he will need to hold the merchandise. In general, however, most cards and collections will bring offers in the range of 25%–50% of retail price. Also consider that most material from the last 5 to 10 years is plentiful. If that´s what you´re selling, don´t be surprised if your best offer is well below that range.

Interesting Notes

The first card numerically of an issue is the single card most likely to obtain excessive wear.

Consequently, you typically will find the price on the #1 card (in NrMt or Mint condition) somewhat higher than might otherwise be the case.

Similarly, but to a lesser extent (because normally the less important, reverse side of the card is the one exposed), the last card numerically in an issue also is prone to abnormal wear. This extra wear and tear occurs because the first and last cards are exposed to the elements (human element included) more than any of the other cards. They are generally end cards in any brick formations and are subject to rubber bandings, stackings on wet surfaces, and like activities.

Sports cards have no intrinsic value. The value of a card, like the value of other collectibles, can be determined only by you and your enjoyment in viewing and possessing these cardboard treasures.

Remember, the buyer ultimately determines the price of each baseball card. You are the determining price factor because you have the ability to say "No" to the price of any card by not exchanging your hard-earned money for a given issue. When the cost of a trading card exceeds the enjoyment you will receive from it, your answer should be "No." We assess and report the prices. You set them!

We are always interested in receiving the price input of collectors and dealers. We happily credit major contributors.

We welcome your opinions, since your contributions assist us in ensuring a better guide each year.

If you would like to join our survey list for the next editions of this book and others authored by Dr. Beckett, please send your name and address to Dr. James Beckett, 15850 Dallas Parkway, Dallas, TX 75248.

History of Baseball Cards

Today´s version of the baseball card, with its colorful and oftentimes high-tech front and back, is a far cry from its earliest predecessors. The issue remains cloudy as to which was the very first baseball card ever produced, but the institution of base-

Centering

Well-centered

Slightly Off-centered

Off-centered

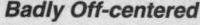

Badly Off-centered

Miscut

ball cards dates from the latter half of the 19th century, more than 100 years ago. Early issues, generally printed on heavy cardboard, were of poor quality, with photographs, drawings, and printing far short of today's standards.

Goodwin & Co., of New York, makers of Gypsy Queen, Old Judge, and other cigarette brands, is considered by many to be the first issuer of baseball and other sports cards. Its issues, predominantly sized 1-1/2 by 2-1/2 inches, generally consisted of photographs of baseball players, boxers, wrestlers, and other subjects mounted on stiff cardboard. More than 2,000 different photos of baseball players alone have been identified. These "Old Judges," a collective name commonly used for the Goodwin & Co. cards, were issued from 1886 to 1890 and are treasured parts of many collections today.

Among the other cigarette companies that issued baseball cards still attracting attention today are Allen & Ginter, D. Buchner & Co. (Gold Coin Chewing Tobacco), and P. H. Mayo & Brother. Cards from the first two companies bear colored line drawings, while the Mayos are sepia photographs on black cardboard. In addition to the small-size cards from this era, several tobacco companies issued cabinet-size baseball cards. These "cabinets" were considerably larger than the small cards, usually about 4-1/4 by 6-1/2 inches, and were printed on heavy stock. Goodwin & Co.'s Old Judge cabinets and the National Tobacco Works' "Newsboy" baseball photos are two that remain popular today.

By 1895, the American Tobacco Company began to dominate its competition. They discontinued baseball card inserts in their cigarette packages (actually slide boxes in those days). The lack of competition in the cigarette market had made these inserts unnecessary. This marked the end of the first era of baseball cards. At the dawn of the 20th century, few baseball cards were being issued. But once again, it was the cigarette companies, particularly, the American Tobacco Company, followed to a lesser extent by the candy and gum makers that revived the practice of including baseball cards with their products. The bulk of these cards, identified in the American Card Catalog (designated hereafter as ACC) as T or E cards for 20th century "Tobacco" or "Early Candy and Gum" issues, respectively, were released from 1909 to 1915.

This romantic and popular era of baseball card collecting produced many desirable items. The most outstanding is the fabled T-206 Honus Wagner card. Other perennial favorites among collectors are the T-206 Eddie Plank card, and the T-206 Magee error card. The former was once the second most valuable card and only recently relinquished that position to a more distinctive and aesthetically pleasing Napoleon Lajoie card from the 1933–34 Goudey Gum series. The latter misspells the player's name as "Magie"; the most famous and most valuable blooper card.

The ingenuity and distinctiveness of this era has yet to be surpassed. Highlights include:

- The T-202 Hassan triple-folders, one of the best looking and the most distinctive cards ever issued;
- The durable T-201 Mecca double-folders, one of the first sets with players' records on the reverse;
- The T-3 Turkey Reds, the hobby's most popular cabinet card;
- The E-145 Cracker Jacks, the only major set containing Federal League player cards; and
- The T-204 Ramlys, with their distinctive black-and-white oval photos and ornate gold borders.

These are but a few of the varieties issued during this period.

Increasing Popularity

While the American Tobacco Company dominated the field, several other tobacco companies, as well as clothing manufacturers, newspapers and periodicals, game makers, and companies whose identities remain anonymous, also issued cards during this period. In fact, the Collins-McCarthy Candy Company, makers of Zeenuts Pacific Coast League baseball cards, issued cards yearly from 1911 to 1938. Its record for continuous annual card production has been exceeded only by the Topps Chewing Gum Company. The era of the tobacco card issues closed with the onset of World War I, with the exception of the Red Man chewing tobacco sets produced from 1952 to 1955.

Corner Wear

The partial cards here have been photographed at 300%. This was done in order to magnify each card's corner wear to such a degree that differences could be shown on a printed page.

The 1962 Topps Mickey Mantle card definitely has a rounded corner. Some may say that this card is badly rounded, but that is a judgment call.

The 1962 Topps Hank Aaron card has a slightly rounded corner. Note that there is definite corner wear evident by the fraying and that the corner no longer sports a sharp point.

The 1962 Topps Gil Hodges card has corner wear; it is slightly better than the Aaron card above. Nevertheless, some collectors might classify this Hodges corner as slightly rounded.

The 1962 Topps Manager's Dream card showing Mantle and Mays has slight corner wear. This is not a fuzzy corner as very slight wear is noticeable on the card's photo surface.

The 1962 Topps Don Mossi card has very slight corner wear such that it might be called a fuzzy corner. A close look at the original card shows the corner is not perfect, but almost. However, note that corner wear is somewhat academic on this card. As you can plainly see, the heavy crease going across his name breaks through the photo surface.

The next flurry of card issues broke out in the roaring and prosperous 1920s, the era of the E card. The caramel companies (National Caramel, American Caramel, York Caramel) were the leading distributors of these E cards. In addition, the strip card, a continuous strip with several cards divided by dotted lines or other sectioning features, flourished during this time. While the E cards and the strip cards generally are considered less imaginative than the T cards or the recent candy and gum issues, they still are pursued by many advanced collectors.

Another significant event of the 1920s was the introduction of the arcade card. Taking its designation from its issuer, the Exhibit Supply Company of Chicago, it is usually known as the "Exhibit" card. Once a trademark of the penny arcades, amusement parks, and county fairs across the country, Exhibit machines dispensed nearly postcard-size photos on thick stock for one penny. These picture cards bore likenesses of a favorite cowboy, actor, actress, or baseball player. Exhibit Supply and its associated companies produced baseball cards during a longer time span, although discontinuous, than any other manufacturer. Its first cards appeared in 1921, while its last issue was in 1966. In 1979, the Exhibit Supply Company was bought and somewhat revived by a collector/dealer who has since reprinted Exhibit photos of the past.

If the T card period, from 1909 to 1915, can be designated the "Golden Age" of baseball card collecting, then perhaps the "Silver Age" commenced with the introduction of the Big League Gum series of 239 cards in 1933 (a 240th card was added in 1934). These are the forerunners of today´s baseball gum cards, and the Goudey Gum Company of Boston is responsible for their success. This era spanned the period from the Depression days of 1933 to America´s formal involvement in World War II in 1941.

Goudey´s attractive designs, with full-color line drawings on thick card stock, greatly influenced other cards being issued at that time. As a result, the most attractive and popular vintage cards in history were produced in this "Silver Age." The 1933 Goudey Big League Gum series also owes its popularity to the more than 40 Hall of Fame players in the set. These include four cards of Babe Ruth and two of Lou Gehrig. Goudey´s reign continued in 1934, when it issued a 96-card set in color, together with the single remaining card from the 1933 series, #106, the Napoleon Lajoie card.

In addition to Goudey, several other bubblegum manufacturers issued baseball cards during this era. DeLong Gum Company issued an extremely attractive set in 1933. National Chicle Company´s 192-card "Batter-Up" series of 1934-36 became the largest die-cut set in card history. In addition, that company offered the popular "Diamond Stars" series during the same period. Other popular sets included the "Tattoo Orbit" set of 60 color cards issued in 1933 and Gum Products´ 75-card "Double Play" set, featuring sepia depictions of two players per card.

In 1939, Gum Inc., which later became Bowman Gum, replaced Goudey Gum as the leading baseball card producer. In 1939 and the following year, it issued two important sets of black-and-white cards. In 1939, its "Play Ball America" set consisted of 162 cards. The larger, 240-card "Play Ball" set of 1940 still is considered by many to be the most attractive black-and-white cards ever produced. That firm introduced its only color set in 1941, consisting of 72 cards titled "Play Ball Sports Hall of Fame." Many of these were colored repeats of poses from the black-and-white 1940 series.

In addition to regular gum cards, many manufacturers distributed premium issues during the 1930s. These premiums were printed on paper or photographic stock, rather than card stock. They were much larger than the regular cards and were sold for a penny across the counter with gum (which was packaged separately from the premium). They often were redeemed at the store or through the mail in exchange for the wrappers of previously purchased gum cards, like proof-of-purchase box-top premiums today. The gum premiums are scarcer than the card issues of the 1930s and in most cases no manufacturer´s name is present.

World War II brought an end to this popular era of card collecting when paper and rubber shortages curtailed the production of bubblegum baseball cards. They were resurrected again in 1948 by the Bowman Gum Company (the direct descendent of Gum Inc.). This marked the beginning of the modern era of card collecting.

In 1948, Bowman Gum issued a 48-card set in black and white consisting of one card and one slab of gum in every 1-cent pack. That same year, the Leaf Gum Company also issued a set of cards. Although rather poor in quality, these cards were issued in color. A squabble over the rights to use players´ pictures developed between Bowman and Leaf. Eventually Leaf dropped out of the card market, but not before it had left a lasting heritage to the hobby by issuing some of the rarest cards now in existence. Leaf´s baseball card series of 1948-49 contained 98 cards, skip numbered to #168 (not all numbers were printed). Of these 98 cards, 49 are relatively plentiful; the other 49, however, are rare and quite valuable.

Bowman continued its production of cards in 1949 with a color series of 240 cards. Because there are many scarce "high numbers," this series remains the most difficult Bowman regular issue to complete. Although the set was printed in color and commands great interest due to its scarcity, it is considered aesthetically inferior to the Goudey and National Chicle issues of the 1930s. In addition to the regular issue of 1949, Bowman also produced a set of 36 Pacific Coast League players. Although this was not a regular issue, it still is prized by collectors. In fact, it has become the most valuable Bowman series.

In 1950 (representing Bowman´s one-year monopoly of the baseball card market), the company began a string of top-quality cards that continued until its demise in 1955. The 1950 series was itself something of an oddity because the low numbers, rather than the traditional high numbers, were the more difficult cards to obtain.

The year 1951 marked the beginning of the most competitive and perhaps the highest quality period of baseball card production. In that year, Topps Chewing Gum Company of Brooklyn entered the market. Topps´ 1951 series consisted of two sets of 52 cards each, one set with red backs and the other with blue backs. In addition, Topps also issued 31 insert cards, three of which remain the rarest Topps cards ("Current All-Stars" Konstanty, Roberts, and Stanky). The 1951 Topps cards were unattractive and paled in comparison to the 1951 Bowman issues. They were successful, however, and Topps has continued to produce cards ever since.

Intensified Competition

Topps issued a larger and more attractive card set in 1952. This larger size became standard for the next five years. (Bowman followed with larger-size baseball cards in 1953.) This 1952 Topps set has become, like the 1933 Goudey series and the T-206 white border series, the classic set of its era. The 407-card set is a collector´s dream of scarcities, rarities, errors, and variations. It also contains the first Topps issues of Mickey Mantle and Willie Mays.

As with Bowman and Leaf in the late 1940s, competition over player rights arose. Ensuing court battles occurred between Topps and Bowman. The market split due to stiff competition, and in January 1956, Topps bought out Bowman. (Topps, using the Bowman name, resurrected Bowman as a label in 1989.) Topps remained essentially unchallenged as the primary producer of baseball cards through 1980. So, the story of major baseball card sets from 1956 through 1980 is by and large the story of Topps´ issues. Notable exceptions include the small sets produced by Fleer Gum in 1959, 1960, 1961, and 1963, and the Kellogg´s Cereal and Hostess Cakes baseball cards issued to promote their products.

A court decision in 1980 paved the way for two other large gum companies to enter (or reenter, in Fleer´s case) the baseball card arena. Fleer, which had last made photo cards in 1963, and the Donruss Company (then a division of General Mills) secured rights to produce baseball cards of current players, thus breaking Topps´ monopoly. Each company issued major card sets in 1981 with bubblegum products.

Then a higher court decision in that year overturned the lower court ruling against Topps. It appeared that Topps had regained its sole position as a producer of baseball cards. Undaunted by the revocation ruling, Fleer and Donruss continued to issue cards in 1982 but without bubblegum or any other edible product. Fleer issued its current player baseball cards with "team logo stickers," while Donruss issued its cards with a piece of a baseball jigsaw puzzle.

Sharing the Pie

Since 1981, these three major baseball card producers all have thrived, sharing relatively equal recognition. Each has steadily increased its involvement in terms of numbers of issues per year. To the delight of collectors, their competition has generated novel, and in some cases exceptional, issues of current Major League Baseball players. Collectors also eagerly accepted the debut efforts of Score (1988) and Upper Deck (1989). These five companies were about to embark on a wild ride through the 1990s.

Upper Deck's successful entry into the market turned out to be very important. The company's card stock, photography, packaging, and marketing gave baseball cards a new standard for quality and began the "premium card" trend that continues today. The second premium baseball card set to be issued was the 1990 Leaf set, named for and issued by the parent company of Donruss. To gauge the significance of the premium card trend, one need only note that two of the most valuable post-1986 regular-issue cards in the hobby are the 1989 Upper Deck Ken Griffey Jr. and 1990 Leaf Frank Thomas Rookie Cards.

The impressive debut of Leaf in 1990 was followed by Studio, Ultra, and Stadium Club in 1991. Of those, Stadium Club with its dramatic borderless photo, uncoated card fronts made the biggest impact. In 1992, Bowman and Pinnacle joined the premium fray. In 1992, Donruss and Fleer abandoned the traditional 50-cent pack market and instead produced premium sets comparable to (and presumably designed to compete against) Upper Deck's set. Those moves, combined with the almost instantaneous spread of premium cards to the other major team sports cards, serve as strong indicators that premium cards were here to stay. Bowman had been a lower-level product from 1989 to 1991.

In 1993, Fleer, Topps, and Upper Deck produced the first "super premium" cards with Flair, Finest, and SP, respectively. The success of all three products was an indication the baseball card market was headed toward even higher price levels, and that turned out to be the case in 1994 with the introduction of Bowman's Best (a Topps hybrid of prospect-oriented Bowman and the superpremium Finest) and Leaf Limited. Other 1994 debuts included Upper Deck's entry-level Collector's Choice and Pinnacle's hobby-only Select.

Overall, inserts continued to dominate the hobby scene. Specifically, the parallel chase cards introduced in 1992 with Topps Gold became the latest major hobby trend. Topps Gold was followed by 1993 Finest Refractors (at the time the scarcest insert ever produced and still a landmark set) and the one-per-box Stadium Club First Day Issue.

Of course, the biggest on-field news of 1994 was the owner-provoked players' strike that halted the season prematurely. While the baseball card hobby suffered noticeably from the strike, there was no catastrophic market crash as some had feared. However, the strike drastically slowed down a market that was both strong and growing and contributed to a serious hobby contraction that continues to this day.

By 1995, parallel insert sets were commonplace and had taken on a new complexion: the most popular ones were those that had announced (or at least suspected) print runs of 500 or less, such as Finest Refractors and Select Artist's Proofs.

This trend continued in 1996, with several parallel inserts that were printed in quantities of 250 or less, such as Finest Gold Refractors, Fleer Circa Rave, Studio Silver Press Proofs, and three of the six Select Certified parallels. It could be argued that the high price tags on these extremely limited parallel cards (many exceeded the $1,000 plateau) were driving many single-player collectors to frustration, and even completely out of the hobby. At the same time, average pack prices soared while average number of cards per pack dropped, making the baseball card hobby increasingly expensive.

On the positive side, two trends from 1996 clearly brought in new collectors: Topps' Mickey Mantle retrospective inserts in both series of Topps and Stadium Club and Leaf's Signature Series, which included one certified autograph per pack. Although the Mantle craze following his passing seemed to be a short-term phenomenon, the inclusion of autographs in packs seemed to have more long-term significance.

In 1997 the print runs in selected sets got even lower. Both Fleer/SkyBox and Pinnacle brands issued cards of which only one exists.

The growth in popularity of autographs also continued. Many products had autographed cards in their packs. A very positive trend was a return to basics. Many collectors bought Rookie Cards, as they understood that concept, and worked on finishing sets.

There was also an increase in international players collecting. Hideo Nomo was incredibly popular in Japan while Chan Ho Park was in demand in Korea. This bodes well for an international growth in the hobby.

Clearly, 1998 was a year of rebirth and growth for the hobby. The big boost came from the home run chase being conducted by Mark McGwire and Sammy Sosa, as well as the continued brilliance of stalwarts like Ken Griffey Jr. and Roger Clemens. The baseball card hobby received a great deal of positive publicity from the renewed interest in the game.

Rookie Cards of the key players of 1998 made significant gains in value as the hobby once again turned to Rookie Cards as the collectible of choice. Also, cards professionally graded by companies such as PSA and SGC were becoming more heavily traded in both older and newer material.

In addition, the Internet and various services such as eBay contributed to the strong growth in collecting interest over the year.

There were downsides in 1998, though. Pinnacle Brands folded, leaving a legacy of innovation and promotions not seen by other companies. In addition, there still was the problem of collectors being frustrated by the extremely short printed cards of their favorite players, making set completion almost impossible.

During 1998, Pacific received a full baseball license and added many innovations to the card market. Their 1998 OnLine set is the most comprehensive set issued in the last five years and many veteran collectors applauded Pacific´s continuing attempts to get as many players as possible into their sets.

In the last couple of years, card companies have been printing specific subsets (usually young players or Rookie Cards) in shorter supply than the regular cards. This is not in every set, but in many sets produced since 1998.

In 1999, many of the trends of the last couple of years continued to gain strength. Buying, selling, and trading cards over the Internet became a dominant factor in the secondary market. Beckett Media LP began its own Marketplace, offering the collectors a chance to search across inventory from many of the finest dealers nationwide in one comprehensive on-line database; eBay continued to flourish, while many other parties began to reap the benefits of the burgeoning online auction market. The Barry Halper collection was auctioned off, bringing many museum quality items to the market and giving the older memorabilia market a significant boost as many treasures were made available to collectors.

Also, the boom in Internet trading created a perfect fit for professionally graded cards, as buyers and sellers traded cards sight unseen with the confidence established by a third-party grader.

From a field of almost a dozen contenders, three companies emerged in 1999 to dominate the field of professional grading, BGS (Beckett Grading Services), PSA (Professional Sports Authenticator), and SGC (Sportscard Guaranty L.L.C.). In 1999 these companies made dramatic expansions in on-site grading and submissions at card shows throughout the nation. In response to the widespread acceptance of graded cards, the line of monthly Beckett Price Guides each added a separate section within the price guide area for professionally graded cards.

Similar to 1998, four licensed manufacturers (Fleer/SkyBox, Pacific, Topps, and Upper Deck) produced slightly more than fifty different products for 1999.

Perhaps the biggest hit of the 1999 card season was created by Topps. Card #220 within the basic issue first series 1999 Topps brand featured Home Run King Mark McGwire in 70 variations, one for each homer he slugged in 1998, and many collectors went after the whole set. Continuing a legacy as strong as the Yankees, the basic Topps issue was one of the most popular sets released in 1999.

Closely trailing the Topps McGwire promotion was Upper Deck´s dynamic A Piece of History bat card promotion. The card that kicked off the frenzy was the Babe Ruth A Piece of History distributed in 1999 Upper Deck series 1 packs. Upper Deck actually purchased a cracked game-used Babe Ruth bat for $24,000 and proceeded to cut it up into approximately 350-400 chips of wood to create the now famous Ruth bat card. The card instantly created polar opposites of opinion among hobbyists. Traditional collectors howled at the sacrilegious act of destroying such a historic piece of memorabilia while more open-minded collectors jumped at the opportunity to chase such an important card. The Ruth card was followed up by the cross-brand "500 Club" bat card promotion, whereby UD produced bat cards from every major league ballplayer who hit 500 or more home runs in their career (except for Mark McGwire, who hit his 500th in the midst of the 1999 season and promptly stated that he did not support Upper Deck´s promotion).

More memorabilia cards than ever were offered to collectors in 1999 as Fleer/SkyBox kicked up their efforts to match the standards set by Upper Deck in previous years. Batting gloves, hats, and shoes joined the typical bats and jerseys as pieces of game-used equipment to be featured on trading cards. Sets like E-X Century Authen-Kicks and Fleer Mystique Feel the Game typified the new offerings.

Topps only dabbled with memorabilia cards in 1999, but continued to offer some of the hottest autographed inserts, highlighted by the Topps Stars Rookie Reprint Autographs and the Topps Nolan Ryan Autographs.

Pacific made a clear decision to steer free of memorabilia and autograph inserts, instead focusing on offering collectors a wide selection of beautifully designed insert and parallel cards. Those themes worked beautifully with their established presence for making comprehensive sets, providing collectors with the necessary challenge to pursue regional stars and a favorite team in addition to the typical superstars.

An astounding total of 264 players made their first appearance on a major league licensed trading card in 1999. What may go down as the deepest class of Rookie Cards of all time features a cornucopia of talented youngsters led by Rick Ankiel, Josh Beckett, Pat Burrell, Josh Hamilton, Eric Munson, Corey Patterson, and Alfonso Soriano.

As in years past, Topps continued to provide collectors with a fistful of Rookie Cards within their Bowman, Bowman Chrome, and Bowman´s Best brands. In a trend established in 1998 by Fleer when they released their Fleer Update set (fueled largely by a J. D. Drew Rookie Card), hobbyists enjoyed a bevy of late-season sets chock full of RC´s. Fleer/SkyBox made an all-out effort by stuffing more than 100 Rookie Cards into their 1999 Fleer Update set. Topps produced their first boxed Traded set since 1994. Each 1999 Topps Traded set contained 1 of 75 different cards autographed by a rookie prospect. Considering how much wider the selection of Rookie Cards became in 1999, it´s amazing to see that so few of these RC´s were serial numbered. When one looks at the success established with serial numbered Rookie Cards in the basketball and football card markets with brands like SP Authentic and SPx Finite, one can only scratch his head when realizing that Fleer Mystique was the only brand to offer baseball collectors serial numbered RC´s. Thus, it´s not surprising to see that despite having 25 different Rookie Cards issued in 1999, Pat Burrell´s Fleer Mystique RC (#´d of 2,999) had been established as his "best" RC by year´s end.

Youngsters weren´t the only players in the limelight in 1999 as retired stars and Hall of Famers were featured on more cards than any other year in the 1990s. Upper Deck´s Century Legends brand, featuring the top 50 active and top 50 retired players of the decade as chosen by the Sporting News was a runaway hit.

Perhaps the most popular insert set of the year, outpacing all of the dazzling high-dollar memorabilia cards, was Topps Gallery Heritage. Utilizing the design and painting style of artist Gerry Dvorak from the classic 1953 Topps set, these modern masterpieces proved that insert cards can still be a hot commodity in the secondary market, albeit assuming they´re well conceived and well made, an unfortunate rarity these days.

The spate of basic issue sets with short-printed subsets continued across many brands in 1999. In reaction to many frustrated dealers and collectors struggling to complete these sets, Fleer/SkyBox created dual versions of each prospect card for the 1999 SkyBox Premium set, an action shot was short-printed and a posed shot was seeded at the same rate as other basic issue cards. The idea was well received by collectors but enjoyed a surprisingly short-lived period of active trading in the secondary market.

The year 2000 was marked by several major developments that would continue shaping the future of our hobby. First off, Pacific decided to forfeit their baseball card license on January 1st, 2000, in an effort to more sharply focus their production expenditures into football and hockey.

In a separate development, Wizards of the Coast (primarily known for their non-sport gaming cards) was granted a license to produce baseball trading cards and debuted their MLB Showdown brand. The cards proved to be quite successful in that they were collected as a set by veteran collectors and played as a game by children (and some adults) both inside and outside of the typical collecting community.

By year´s end, Fleer fazed out their SkyBox and Flair brand names in an effort to take full advantage of the historic significance and brand recognition of their flagship Fleer sets issued sporadically during the late 1950s-1970s and consistently from 1981 to the present.

Almost sixty brands of MLB-licensed cards, issued by five manufacturers, were produced in 2000. In addition, Just Minors and Team Best produced a variety of attractive minor league products. Most shop owners continued to generate their income primarily through the sales of packs and boxes of new product, and, as in years past, they had to make careful decisions as to what to keep in stock for customers and what to pass up in fear of a low sell through.

Vintage (or retro-themed) sets dominated the market highlighted by Fleer Greats of the Game, Upper Deck Yankees Legends, and the run of 3,000 hit club and Joe DiMaggio game-used cards issued by Fleer and Upper Deck. In 2001, Topps Heritage (mimicking the style of the classic ´52 Topps cards), Upper Deck Vintage (in an homage to ´63 Topps baseball), and the return of Topps Archives (after a six-year hiatus) added fuel to the fire.

Using the vintage-theme to tap into a base of wealthy consumers, Upper Deck rolled out their line of Master Collection products (which debuted in basketball a year prior with a Michael Jordan set). Both the Yankees Master Collection and Brooklyn Dodgers Master Collection sets carried initial SRP´s of $4,000 or more, marking the most expensive "factory set" of all-time. Each of these sets was serial numbered (500 Yankees and 250 Dodgers), came in a stylish wood box and contained an assortment of game-used and autograph cards from legends of days gone by.

Game-used memorabilia cards became more abundant in all products to the point where a few early 2001 releases (2001 Pacific Private Stock and 2001 SP Game Bat Edition both carrying SRP´s in the $15-$20 range) included them at a rate of one per pack. Both products enjoyed a dynamic sell through and proved to be very popular in the secondary market. The result, however, on the secondary market values of game-used memorabilia cards has been dramatic. An Alex Rodriguez or Ken Griffey Jr. game bat or game jersey card that sold for $200+ in 1999 could be had for as little as $25-$50 in early 2001.

Patch cards (a swatch of jersey that contains part of a multi-colored patch) really caught on by year´s end as the market formalized premium values on these cards. Upper Deck was the first to create separate "super-premium" jersey Patch inserts within 2000 Upper Deck 1 and 2000 Upper Deck Game Jersey Edition (aka series 2). Pacific followed suit with their Game Gear patch subset within the invincible brand.

By early 2001, Major League Baseball Properties had gotten involved with the trading card autograph and memorabilia programs. From 2001 on, all MLB-licensed trading cards produced by the manufacturers that involved an autograph or game-used memorabilia item had to have the procurement of the item witnessed by a representative of Andersen Consulting, a firm hired by MLB to oversee this historic program. Never before had consumers been provided such an effort by the league and manufacturers to be offered autographed or game-used memorabilia trading cards of such authentic provenance.

Short-printed subset cards, a trend started in 1999, continued to be a common element in most basic sets. The trend, however, evolved to the point where these short prints were now being serial numbered, autographed by the player, or incorporating an element of game-used material onto the card. The result was higher values on the key singles, but lower odds of actually finding a good RC in a pack. By year´s end, a general sentiment of frustration over not being able to pull good Rookie Cards from a box was beginning to be heard more and more often from collectors.

Rookie Cards incorporating game-used material debuted at year´s end in 2000 Black Diamond Rookie Edition. Also, Rookie Cards signed by the player, introduced within the basketball and football card markets in 1999 (with Upper Deck´s SPx brand), made their baseball debut in 2000 SPx. Serial-numbered Rookie Cards grew in total usage, but shrank in print run numbers as production figures reached an all-time low of 999 copies for a basic issue RC within the 2000 Pacific Omega set.

Year-end boxed sets, a trend brought back from a four-year hiatus by Fleer in 1998 with their Fleer Update set, continued to expand as Topps issued their Bowman Draft Picks and Bowman Chrome Draft Picks sets to cap the now single-series accompanying standard Bowman and Bowman Chrome products.

Fleer broke new ground by blending a 1980s "old-school" concept with some postmodern angles in their 2000 Fleer Glossy boxed set. Harkening back to the run of Glossy parallel factory sets produced from 1987 to 1989, the 2000 Fleer Glossy set included a parallel version of the complete 400-card basic 2000 Fleer set. In addition, 50 new cards (card #´s 401-450, each serial numbered to 1,000 copies) featuring a selection of prospects and rookies were created. Each Glossy factory set contained 5 of the 50 new cards, making it a real challenge to complete the Glossy set.

In a first of its kind for the baseball market, Upper Deck issued a product in December 2000 called Rookie Update that incorporated new cards for three separate popular brands (SP Authentic, SPx, and UD Pros and Prospects) into each pack of cards.

Upper Deck came to terms with Major League Baseball for a license to produce cards featuring members of past and present Team USA squads (bringing back a run of cards last seen in 1993 Topps Traded). That allowed Upper Deck the opportunity to radically expand their production of "true" Rookie Cards in year-end 2000 products, adding a spate of cards featuring heroes from the Olympics in Sydney, Australia, like Ben Sheets. Not surprisingly, the number of prospects making their Rookie Card debut in 2000 sets jumped from about 280 players in 1999 to slightly more than 350 players in 2000.

The influence of sports card dealers and collectors from the Far East (and most noticeably Japan) continued to grow in 2000 as stateside buying approached frenzied levels over scarce Hideo Nomo and Kazuhiro Sasaki cards. A much-traveled starter these days, Nomo´s first-ever certified autograph card (issued within the Fleer Mystique Fresh Ink insert set) was the hottest card in the hobby for two months (initially trading for as much as $600-$800).

Not all trends were met with success this year. In particular, low-end products geared towards the youth audience (like 2000 Impact by Fleer) were roundly ignored. The hobby still faces a tough road ahead to keep new waves of collectors involved from generation to generation. Part of the Catch-22 with creating affordable brands catered to youths is that the same customers are most interested in the high-end, expensive material.

Also, Upper Deck´s PowerDeck product faced an indifferent audience for a second year in a row, as collectors and even general sports enthusiasts outside the hobby failed to get excited over the CD-ROM cards. More success was met by UD´s e-Card insert program, whereby collectors who pulled an e-Card from a pack of UD cards had to go to UD´s Website and check the serial number printed on the card to see whether it could evolve into an autograph, game jersey, or game jersey autograph exchange.

The Internet continued to have profound ramifications on shaping the destiny of sports card collecting. By 2000, nearly every dealer (and hard-core collector) was buying or selling cards to some degree in on-line auctions. Auction sales had become so prolific that they were now having a strong effect on the secondary market sales levels of trading cards in arenas entirely outside of cyberspace, like shops, shows, and mail order.

The eBay site continued to dominate the on-line auction action, introducing what appears to be a popular "Buy It Now" option to their already established auction format. The Pit.com opened in mid-year with their concept of buying and selling a portfolio of professionally graded sports cards through their Web site. The concept is based almost exactly upon the methodology used for buying and selling stocks through a brokerage house, with daily ebbs and flows in posted buy and sell prices on your inventory.

Beckett.com made radical improvements to their Marketplace search engines and expanded their inventory of sports cards to the point where they were providing both a wider and a deeper selection of trading cards than any site on the Internet. In addition, a company-wide effort to provide daily news content on their site (coupled with a weekly newsletter sent to over 400,000 collectors) began at year´s end, and the hobby has reaped the benefits ever since.

As the 2001 season approached, hobbyists waited with bated breath for seven-time Japanese batting champ Ichiro Suzuki to make his debut in the Seattle Mariner´s outfield. And what a stunning debut it was. Ichiro led the league in hitting, led the Mariners to their best record ever, and walked off with the A.L. Rookie of the Year and Most Valuable Player awards. Upper Deck obtained the exclusive rights to produce his autograph cards and they hit a grand slam in midsummer by releasing his SPx Rookie Card, featuring a game jersey swatch and a cut signature autograph. In a year studded with notable cards, this one was likely the most memorable.

In the National League, 37-year-old San Francisco Giants superstar Barry Bonds captivated the nation by bashing a jaw-dropping 73 home runs, shattering Mark McGwire´s 1998 single-season home run record.

Cardinals´ rookie Albert Pujols emerged out of the low minor leagues to become an instant hobby superstar and walk away with N.L. Rookie of the Year honors.

The year 2001 was a tumultuous one for sports cards. Topps started the year off with a bang by celebrating their 50th anniversary producing baseball cards. Pacific forfeited its license to make baseball cards after an eight-year run to focus on football and hockey cards. Playoff, a company based out of Grand Prairie, Texas, that had earned its stripes by producing football cards in the late 1990s, purchased the rights to the much-hallowed Donruss corporate name and became a formal MLB licensee in the spring of 2001. Their entrance into the baseball card market heralded the return of benchmark brands like Donruss, Donruss Signature, and Leaf.

Competition was fiercer than ever amongst the four primary licensees (Donruss-Playoff, Fleer, Topps, and Upper Deck) as they cranked out almost 80 different products over the course of 2001.

Of all these, likely the most historically important product, Upper Deck Prospect Premieres, was widely overlooked upon release. In a bold move, Upper Deck created a set of 102 prospects, none of which had played a day in the majors. Each player was pictured, however, in the major league uniforms of their parent ballclubs and signed to individual contracts. Because no active major leaguers were featured, Upper Deck did not have to include licensing rights from the MLB Players Association, though they did get licensing from Major League Properties. The industry had never seen a major release featuring active ballplayers marketed to the mainstream audience that lacked licensing from the MLBPA. Because of its lack of historical predecessors and a mixed reception from collectors, the cards were tagged by Beckett Baseball Card Monthly as XRC´s (or Extended Rookie Cards), a term that had not been used since 1989.

UD´s Prospect Premieres was the first major effort by a manufacturer to level the playing field between Topps and everyone else in that Topps has exclusive rights from the MLBPA to include minor leaguers in their basic brands.

Rookie Cards continued to fascinate collectors, especially in a year with talents like Ichiro and Albert Pujols. The number of players featured on Rookie Cards in 2001 ballooned to an almost absurd figure of 505.

Exchange cards became more prevalent than ever, as manufacturers expanded their use from autograph cards that didn´t get returned in time for pack out to slots within basic sets left open in brands released early in the year to fill in with late-season rookie call-ups.

Certified autograph cards remained a huge player in how brands were structured, but the quality of the players suffered greatly as autograph fees continued to spiral out of control. Signatures from superstars like Barry Bonds and Derek Jeter were now being featured on cards with miniscule print runs of 25 or 50 copies while unknown (and often aging and talentless) prospects signed their serial-numbered Rookies Cards by the hundred count.

More serial-numbered Rookie Cards were produced than ever before, but the quantities produced kept sinking lower and lower as companies tried to create secondary market value by simply limiting supply, a dangerous move to say the least. Donruss-Playoff produced the scarcest Rookie Cards of the year, a handful of Game Base cards (including Ichiro) each serial #'d to a scant 100 copies, within their Leaf Limited set.

After a six-month delay, Topps released their much awaited e-Topps program, a product sold entirely on their Web site whereby trading is conducted in a similar fashion to the buying and selling of stocks, in September.

Several products incorporated non-card memorabilia such as signed caps, bobbing head dolls, and signed baseballs with mixed results.

Memorabilia cards continued their slide into mediocrity as the number of cards featuring various bits and pieces of balls, bases, bats, jerseys, pants, shoes, seats, and whatever else could be dreamt up continued to be offered to consumers, who found the cards less appealing with each passing month. To battle consumer apathy, companies often started to offer combination memorabilia cards featuring notable teammates or several pieces of equipment from a notable star.

Retro-themed cards continued to grow in popularity, and some of the innovations seen in these sets were remarkable. Of particular note was Upper Deck's SP Legendary Cuts Autographs set, featuring 84 deceased players. The set required UD to purchase more than 3,300 autograph cuts, which were then incorporated into a windowpane card design. The result was the first certified autograph cards for legends like Roger Maris, Satchell Paige, and Jackie Robinson. Also, Topps Tribute released at year's end and carrying a hefty $40 per pack suggested retail was widely hailed as one of the most beautiful retro-themed cards ever designed, with their crystal-board fronts encasing full-color, razor-sharp photos.

Pack prices continued to escalate, but surprisingly, the public did not balk as long as they delivered value. The most notable high-end product to hit the market in 2001 was Upper Deck Ultimate Collection with a suggested retail of $100 per pack.

September 11th, 2001, is a day that will go down as one of the most devastating in the history of the United States of America. The game of baseball and the hobby of collecting sports cards were rightfully cast aside as the nation mourned the tragic loss of lives in New York, Pennsylvania, and Washington, D.C. America's economy tumbled as airline traveling ground to a near halt and threats of anthrax crippled the mail system. An economy threatening to slip into recession at the beginning of the year dove headlong into it. The sports card market, along with many other industries, felt the hit for several months. Slowly, Americans looked to move past the grief and the sports card industry, steeped in American nostalgia, provided an ideal retreat for many.

The Arizona Diamondbacks beat the New York Yankees in one of the finest World Series ever played, a much-needed diversion for a grief-stricken nation and a calling card for the dramatic power and glory of our National Pastime.

Last year was a relatively quiet one for baseball cards. Dodger's rookie pitcher Kazuhisa Ishii got off to a blazing first half start and his cards carried many releases through to the All-Star break. Ishii stumbled badly in the second half and no notable rookies were in place to pick up market interest. Cubs hurler Mark Prior created a stir, and his 2001 Rookie Cards were red hot at mid-season. For the second straight season, Barry Bonds was the most dominant star in our sport. His early cards continued to outpace all others in volume trading and professional grading submissions.

The number of players featured on Rookie Cards (or Extended Rookie Cards) reached an all-time high of 524 in 2002 as the manufacturers continued to push the envelope toward more immediate coverage of the current year draft. Though few collectors took notice at the time of release, Upper Deck's incorporation of collegiate Team USA athletes into several year-end brands may take hold and grow into a more prominent position in our industry for collegiate ballplayers. The results of these trends, however, are cards that feature a lot of talented youngsters whom most collectors, unfortunately, have never heard of and won't see in a major league uniform for several years.

To make up for the void in excitement generated by rookies and prospects, the manufacturers made some interesting innovations in product distribution and brand development. In general, base sets got noticeably bigger (including Upper Deck's 1,182 card 40-Man brand and Topps 990-card Topps Total brand). In addition, brands like Topps 206, Leaf Rookies and Stars, and Fleer Fall Classics started to incorporate variations of the base cards directly into the basic issue set (different images, switched out teams, etc.).

One of the bigger surprise hits of the year was the aforementioned Topps 206 brand, which borrowed design elements and set composition from the legendary T-206 tobacco set. Other brands continued to successfully mine from cards and eras long since passed.

Donruss continued to push the creative envelope by incorporating 8½" by 11" framed signature pieces directly into boxes of their Playoff Absolute brand. After a four-year hiatus, Fleer brought back their eponymous "Fleer" name brand with a 540-card set. Donruss introduced their wildly successful Diamond Kings brand, which featured a 150-card painted set. Fleer's Box Score brand was also a popular debut utilizing a unique box-inside-a-box distribution concept. Popular brands like SP Legendary Cuts, Leaf Certified, Topps Heritage, and Topps Tribute all received warm welcomes for their follow-ups to their successes achieved the prior year.

The 2004 season continued to bring us again a growing number of sets with price points ranging from $1.29 to $150. There were also many new heroes during the 2003 season as players such as Josh Beckett, Miguel Cabrera, and Dontrelle Willis of the World Champion Florida Marlins were very strong sellers.

Hideki Matsui, who was the most anticipated rookie for the 2003 season, had a very fine year for the American League Champion Yankees but did not draw the same interest from collectors as Ichiro Suzuki did during the 2001 season.

The 2005 season was most notable for the departure of both Fleer and Donruss/Playoff from the ranks of major manufacturers. One of the issues in recent years has been the staggering amount of sets as well as the complexities of those sets. With some direction from the licensors, the baseball card market was reduced and a maximum of 40 products are expected to be released during the 2006 calendar year.

Despite the struggles the sport of baseball has endured; in recent years, the baseball card market has stepped back to the forefront of the card-collecting hobby, outpacing football, basketball, hockey, golf, and motor sports in volume dollars. As the hobby of collecting baseball cards evolves, we continue to face a market that is blessed with bold creativity and superlative quality; and also challenged with the need to reach new consumers both in mass retail and in cyberspace to continue its growth.

Additional Reading

Each year Beckett Media LP produces comprehensive annual price guides for several sports: *Beckett Baseball Card Price Guide, Beckett Basketball Card Price Guide, Beckett Football Card Price Guide, Beckett Hockey Card Price Guide, Beckett Racing Price Guide,* and a line of *Beckett Alphabetical Checklists Books* have been released as well. The aim of these annual guides is to provide information and accurate pricing on a wide array of sports cards, ranging from main issues by the major card manufacturers to various regional, promotional, and food issues. Alphabetical checklist books are published to assist the collector in identifying all the cards of any particular player. The seasoned collector will find these tools valuable sources of information that will enable him to pursue his hobby interests.

In addition, abridged editions of the *Beckett Price Guides* have been published for each of these major sports as part of the House of Collectibles series: *The Official Price Guide to Baseball Cards*, *The Official Price Guide to Football Cards,* and *The Official Price Guide to Basketball Cards*. Published in a convenient mass-market paperback format, these price guides provide information and accurate pricing on all the main issues by the major card manufacturers.

Prices in This Guide

Prices found in this guide reflect current retail rates just prior to the printing of this book. They do not reflect the FOR SALE prices of the author, the publisher, the distributors, the advertisers, or any card dealers associated with this guide. No one is obligated in any way to buy, sell, or trade his or her cards based on these prices. The price listings were compiled by the author from actual buy/sell transactions at sports conventions, sports card shops, buy/sell advertisements in the hobby papers, for sale prices from dealer catalogs and price lists, and discussions with leading hobbyists in the United States and Canada. All prices are in U.S. dollars.

Acknowledgments

A great deal of diligence, hard work, and dedicated effort went into this year´s volume. However, the high standards to which we hold ourselves could not have been met without the expert input and generous amount of time contributed by many people. Our sincere thanks are extended to each and every one of you.

A complete list of these invaluable contributors appears after the **Price Guide** section.

2005 Artifacts

	COMP.SET w/o SP's (100)	40.00	15.00
	COMMON CARD (1-100)	.50	.20
	COMMON CARD (101-150)	3.00	1.25
	COMMON CARD (151-200)	3.00	1.25
	COMMON CARD (201-285)	3.00	1.25
	201-285 ISSUED IN 05 UD UPDATE PACKS		
	201-285: ONE #'d CARD OR AU PER PACK		
	201-285 PRINT RUN 799 SERIAL #'d SETS		
1	Adam Dunn	.50	.20
2	Adrian Beltre	.50	.20
3	Albert Pujols	2.50	1.00
4	Alex Rodriguez	2.00	.75
5	Alfonso Soriano	.50	.20
6	Andruw Jones	.75	.30
7	Andy Pettitte	.75	.30
8	Aramis Ramirez	.50	.20
9	Aubrey Huff	.50	.20
10	Barry Larkin	.75	.30
11	Ben Sheets	.50	.20
12	Bernie Williams	.75	.30
13	Bobby Abreu	.50	.20
14	Brad Penny	.50	.20
15	Bret Boone	.50	.20
16	Brian Giles	.50	.20
17	Carl Crawford	.50	.20
18	Carl Pavano	.50	.20
19	Carlos Beltran	.50	.20
20	Carlos Delgado	.50	.20
21	Carlos Guillen	.50	.20
22	Carlos Lee	.50	.20
23	Carlos Zambrano	.50	.20
24	Chipper Jones	1.25	.50
25	Craig Biggio	.75	.30
26	Craig Wilson	.50	.20
27	Curt Schilling	.75	.30
28	David Ortiz	1.25	.50
29	Derek Jeter	2.50	1.00
30	Eric Chavez	.50	.20
31	Eric Gagne	.50	.20
32	Frank Thomas	1.25	.50
33	Garret Anderson	.50	.20
34	Gary Sheffield	.50	.20
35	Greg Maddux	2.00	.75
36	Hank Blalock	.50	.20
37	Hideki Matsui	2.00	.75
38	Ichiro Suzuki	2.50	1.00
39	Ivan Rodriguez	.75	.30
40	J.D. Drew	.50	.20
41	Jake Peavy	.50	.20
42	Jason Kendall	.50	.20
43	Jason Schmidt	.50	.20
44	Jeff Bagwell	.75	.30
45	Jeff Kent	.50	.20
46	Jim Edmonds	.50	.20
47	Jim Thome	.75	.30
48	Joe Mauer	1.25	.50
49	Johan Santana	1.25	.50
50	John Smoltz	.75	.30
51	Jose Reyes	.50	.20
52	Jose Vidro	.50	.20
53	Josh Beckett	.50	.20
54	Ken Griffey Jr.	2.00	.75
55	Kerry Wood	.50	.20
56	Kevin Brown	.50	.20
57	Lance Berkman	.50	.20
58	Larry Walker	.75	.30
59	Livan Hernandez	.50	.20
60	Luis Gonzalez	.50	.20
61	Lyle Overbay	.50	.20
62	Magglio Ordonez	.50	.20
63	Manny Ramirez	.75	.30
64	Mark Mulder	.50	.20
65	Mark Prior	.75	.30
66	Mark Teixeira	.75	.30
67	Melvin Mora	.50	.20
68	Michael Young	.50	.20
69	Miguel Cabrera	.75	.30
70	Miguel Tejada	.50	.20
71	Mike Lowell	.50	.20
72	Mike Mussina	.75	.30
73	Mike Piazza	1.25	.50
74	Mike Sweeney	.50	.20
75	Nomar Garciaparra	1.25	.50
76	Oliver Perez	.50	.20
77	Paul Konerko	.50	.20
78	Pedro Martinez	.75	.30
79	Preston Wilson	.50	.20
80	Rafael Furcal	.50	.20
81	Rafael Palmeiro	.75	.30
82	Randy Johnson	1.25	.50
83	Richie Sexson	.50	.20
84	Roger Clemens	2.00	.75
85	Roy Halladay	.50	.20
86	Roy Oswalt	.50	.20
87	Sammy Sosa	1.25	.50
88	Scott Podsednik	.50	.20
89	Scott Rolen	.75	.30
90	Shawn Green	.50	.20
91	Steve Finley	.50	.20
92	Tim Hudson	.50	.20
93	Todd Helton	.75	.30
94	Tom Glavine	.75	.30
95	Torii Hunter	.50	.20
96	Travis Hafner	.50	.20
97	Troy Glaus	.50	.20
98	Vernon Wells	.50	.20
99	Victor Martinez	.50	.20
100	Vladimir Guerrero	1.25	.50
101	Aaron Rowand FS	3.00	1.25
102	Adam LaRoche FS	3.00	1.25
103	Adrian Gonzalez FS	3.00	1.25
104	Alexis Rios FS	3.00	1.25
105	Angel Guzman FS	3.00	1.25
106	B.J. Upton FS	3.00	1.25
107	Bobby Crosby FS	3.00	1.25
108	Bobby Madritsch FS	3.00	1.25
109	Brandon Claussen FS	3.00	1.25
110	Bucky Jacobsen FS	3.00	1.25
111	Casey Kotchman FS	3.00	1.25
112	Chad Cordero FS	3.00	1.25
113	Chase Utley FS	4.00	1.50
114	Chris Burke FS	3.00	1.25
115	Dallas McPherson FS	3.00	1.25
116	Daniel Cabrera FS	3.00	1.25
117	David DeJesus FS	3.00	1.25
118	David Wright FS	8.00	3.00
119	Eddy Rodriguez FS	3.00	1.25
120	Edwin Jackson FS	3.00	1.25
121	Gabe Gross FS	3.00	1.25
122	Garrett Atkins FS	3.00	1.25
123	Gavin Floyd FS	3.00	1.25
124	Gerald Laird FS	3.00	1.25
125	Guillermo Quiroz FS	3.00	1.25
126	J.D. Closser FS	3.00	1.25
127	Jason Bay FS	3.00	1.25
128	Jason DuBois FS	3.00	1.25
129	Jason Lane FS	3.00	1.25
130	Jayson Werth FS	3.00	1.25
131	Jeff Francis FS	3.00	1.25
132	Jesse Crain FS	3.00	1.25
133	Joe Blanton FS	3.00	1.25
134	Joe Mauer FS	5.00	2.00
135	Jose Capellan FS	3.00	1.25
136	Kevin Youkilis FS	3.00	1.25
137	Khalil Greene FS	4.00	1.50
138	Laynce Nix FS	3.00	1.25
139	Nick Swisher FS	3.00	1.25
140	Oliver Perez FS	3.00	1.25
141	Rickie Weeks FS	3.00	1.25
142	Robb Quinlan FS	3.00	1.25
143	Roman Colon FS	3.00	1.25
144	Ryan Howard FS	5.00	2.00
145	Ryan Wagner FS	3.00	1.25
146	Scott Kazmir FS	3.00	1.25
147	Scott Proctor FS	3.00	1.25
148	Wily Mo Pena FS	3.00	1.25
149	Yhency Brazoban FS	3.00	1.25
150	Zack Greinke FS	3.00	1.25
151	Al Kaline LGD	4.00	1.50
152	Babe Ruth LGD	10.00	4.00
153	Billy Williams LGD	3.00	1.25
154	Bob Feller LGD	3.00	1.25
155	Bob Gibson LGD	3.00	1.25
156	Bob Lemon LGD	3.00	1.25
157	Bobby Doerr LGD	3.00	1.25
158	Brooks Robinson LGD	3.00	1.25
159	Cal Ripken LGD	10.00	4.00
160	Christy Mathewson LGD	4.00	1.50
161	Cy Young LGD	4.00	1.50
162	Dizzy Dean LGD	3.00	1.25
163	Don Drysdale LGD	3.00	1.25
164	Eddie Mathews LGD	4.00	1.50
165	Enos Slaughter LGD	3.00	1.25
166	Ernie Banks LGD	4.00	1.50
167	Fergie Jenkins LGD	3.00	1.25
168	George Sisler LGD	3.00	1.25
169	Harmon Killebrew LGD	4.00	1.50
170	Honus Wagner LGD	4.00	1.50
171	Jackie Robinson LGD	4.00	1.50
172	Jimmie Foxx LGD	4.00	1.50
173	Joe DiMaggio LGD	5.00	2.00
174	Joe Morgan LGD	3.00	1.25
175	Juan Marichal LGD	3.00	1.25
176	Lou Brock LGD	3.00	1.25
177	Lou Gehrig LGD	5.00	2.00
178	Luis Aparicio LGD	3.00	1.25
179	Mel Ott LGD	3.00	1.25
180	Mickey Cochrane LGD	3.00	1.25
181	Mickey Mantle LGD	15.00	6.00
182	Mike Schmidt LGD	5.00	2.00
183	Nolan Ryan LGD	8.00	3.00
184	Pee Wee Reese LGD	3.00	1.25
185	Phil Rizzuto LGD	3.00	1.25
186	Ralph Kiner LGD	3.00	1.25
187	Rogers Hornsby LGD	3.00	1.25
188	Roy Campanella LGD	4.00	1.50
189	Satchel Paige LGD	4.00	1.50
190	Stan Musial LGD	4.00	1.50
191	Rick Ferrell LGD	3.00	1.25
192	Thurman Munson LGD	4.00	1.50
193	Tom Seaver LGD	3.00	1.25
194	Ty Cobb LGD	4.00	1.50
195	Walter Johnson LGD	4.00	1.50
196	Warren Spahn LGD	3.00	1.25
197	Whitey Ford LGD	3.00	1.25
198	Willie McCovey LGD	3.00	1.25
199	Willie Stargell LGD	3.00	1.25
200	Yogi Berra LGD	4.00	1.50
201	Adam Shabala FS RC	3.00	1.25
202	Ambiorix Burgos FS RC	3.00	1.25
203	Ambiorix Concepcion FS RC	3.00	1.25
204	Anibal Sanchez FS RC	8.00	3.00
205	Bill McCarthy FS RC	3.00	1.25
206	Brandon McCarthy FS RC	4.00	1.50
207	Brian Burres FS RC	3.00	1.25
208	Carlos Ruiz FS RC	3.00	1.25
209	Casey Rogowski FS RC	4.00	1.50
210	Chad Orvella FS RC	3.00	1.25
211	Chris Resop FS RC	3.00	1.25
212	Chris Roberson FS RC	3.00	1.25
213	Chris Seddon FS RC	3.00	1.25
214	Colter Bean FS RC	3.00	1.25
215	Dae-Sung Koo FS RC	3.00	1.25
216	Dave Gassner FS RC	3.00	1.25
217	Brian Anderson FS RC	4.00	1.50
218	D.J. Houlton FS RC	3.00	1.25
219	Derek Wathan FS RC	3.00	1.25
220	Devon Lowery FS RC	3.00	1.25
221	Enrique Gonzalez FS RC	3.00	1.25
222	Eude Brito FS RC	3.00	1.25
223	Francisco Butto FS RC	3.00	1.25
224	Franquelis Osoria FS RC	3.00	1.25
225	Garrett Jones FS RC	3.00	1.25
226	Geovany Soto FS RC	3.00	1.25
227	Hayden Penn FS RC	4.00	1.50
228	Ismael Ramirez FS RC	3.00	1.25
229	Jared Gothreaux FS RC	3.00	1.25
230	Jason Hammel FS RC	3.00	1.25

❑ 231 Jeff Miller FS RC	3.00	1.25
❑ 232 Jeff Niemann FS RC	4.00	1.50
❑ 233 Joel Peralta FS RC	3.00	1.25
❑ 234 John Hattig FS RC	3.00	1.25
❑ 235 Jorge Campillo FS RC	3.00	1.25
❑ 236 Juan Morillo FS RC	3.00	1.25
❑ 237 Justin Verlander FS RC	10.00	4.00
❑ 238 Ryan Garko FS RC	5.00	2.00
❑ 239 Keiichi Yabu FS RC	3.00	1.25
❑ 240 Kendry Morales FS RC	5.00	2.00
❑ 241 Luis Hernandez FS RC	3.00	1.25
❑ 242 Luis Pena FS RC	3.00	1.25
❑ 243 Luis O.Rodriguez FS RC	3.00	1.25
❑ 244 Luke Scott FS RC	5.00	2.00
❑ 245 Marcos Carvajal FS RC	3.00	1.25
❑ 246 Mark Woodyard FS RC	3.00	1.25
❑ 247 Matt A.Smith FS RC	3.00	1.25
❑ 248 Matthew Lindstrom FS RC	3.00	1.25
❑ 249 Miguel Negron FS RC	4.00	1.50
❑ 250 Mike Morse FS RC	3.00	1.25
❑ 251 Nate McLouth FS RC	4.00	1.50
❑ 252 Nelson Cruz FS RC	5.00	2.00
❑ 253 Nick Masset FS RC	3.00	1.25
❑ 254 Oscar Robles FS RC	3.00	1.25
❑ 255 Paulino Reynoso FS RC	3.00	1.25
❑ 256 Pedro Lopez FS RC	3.00	1.25
❑ 257 Pete Orr FS RC	3.00	1.25
❑ 258 Philip Humber FS RC	4.00	1.50
❑ 259 Prince Fielder FS RC	10.00	4.00
❑ 260 Randy Messenger FS RC	3.00	1.25
❑ 261 Randy Williams FS RC	3.00	1.25
❑ 262 Raul Tablado FS RC	3.00	1.25
❑ 263 Ronny Paulino FS RC	4.00	1.50
❑ 264 Russ Rohlicek FS RC	3.00	1.25
❑ 265 Russell Martin FS RC	5.00	2.00
❑ 266 Scott Baker FS RC	4.00	1.50
❑ 267 Scott Munter FS RC	3.00	1.25
❑ 268 Sean Thompson FS RC	3.00	1.25
❑ 269 Sean Tracey FS RC	3.00	1.25
❑ 270 Shane Costa FS RC	3.00	1.25
❑ 271 Stephen Drew FS RC	10.00	4.00
❑ 272 Steve Schmoll FS RC	3.00	1.25
❑ 273 Tadahito Iguchi FS RC	5.00	2.00
❑ 274 Tony Giarratano FS RC	3.00	1.25
❑ 275 Tony Pena FS RC	3.00	1.25
❑ 276 Travis Bowyer FS RC	3.00	1.25
❑ 277 Ubaldo Jimenez FS RC	3.00	1.25
❑ 278 Wladimir Balentien FS RC	4.00	1.50
❑ 279 Yorman Bazardo FS RC	3.00	1.25
❑ 280 Yuniesky Betancourt FS RC	5.00	2.00
❑ 281 Ryan Zimmerman FS RC	15.00	6.00
❑ 282 Chris Denorfia FS RC	4.00	1.50
❑ 283 Dana Eveland FS RC	3.00	1.25
❑ 284 Jermaine Van Buren FS	3.00	1.25
❑ 285 Mark McLemore FS RC	3.00	1.25

2006 Artifacts

❑ COMPLETE SET (100)	40.00	15.00
❑ COMMON CARD (1-100)	.50	.20
❑ COMMON ROOKIE	.75	.30
❑ 1 Luis Gonzalez	.50	.20
❑ 2 Conor Jackson (RC)	1.25	.50
❑ 3 Joey Devine RC	.75	.30
❑ 4 Andruw Jones	.75	.30
❑ 5 Chipper Jones	1.25	.50
❑ 6 John Smoltz	.75	.30
❑ 7 Jeff Francoeur	1.25	.50
❑ 8 Brian Roberts	.50	.20
❑ 9 Miguel Tejada	.50	.20
❑ 10 Nick Markakis (RC)	1.25	.50
❑ 11 Curt Schilling	.75	.30
❑ 12 David Ortiz	1.25	.50
❑ 13 Johnny Damon	.75	.30
❑ 14 Manny Ramirez	.75	.30
❑ 15 Jonathan Papelbon (RC)	4.00	1.50
❑ 16 Aramis Ramirez	.50	.20
❑ 17 Carlos Zambrano	.50	.20
❑ 18 Derrek Lee	.50	.20
❑ 19 Greg Maddux	2.00	.75
❑ 20 Mark Prior	.75	.30
❑ 21 Mark Buehrle	.50	.20
❑ 22 Paul Konerko	.50	.20
❑ 23 Adam Dunn	.50	.20
❑ 24 Ken Griffey Jr.	2.00	.75
❑ 25 Travis Hafner	.50	.20
❑ 26 Victor Martinez	.50	.20
❑ 27 Todd Helton	.75	.30
❑ 28 Ivan Rodriguez	.75	.30
❑ 29 Jeremy Bonderman	.50	.20
❑ 30 Jeremy Hermida (RC)	1.25	.50
❑ 31 Carlos Delgado	.50	.20
❑ 32 Dontrelle Willis	.50	.20
❑ 33 Josh Beckett	.50	.20
❑ 34 Miguel Cabrera	.75	.30
❑ 35 Craig Biggio	.75	.30
❑ 36 Lance Berkman	.50	.20
❑ 37 Roger Clemens	2.50	1.00
❑ 38 Roy Oswalt	.50	.20
❑ 39 Josh Willingham (RC)	.75	.30
❑ 40 Hanley Ramirez (RC)	2.00	.75
❑ 41 Prince Fielder (RC)	3.00	1.25
❑ 42 Zack Greinke	.50	.20
❑ 43 Francisco Rodriguez	.50	.20
❑ 44 Vladimir Guerrero	1.25	.50
❑ 45 Tim Hamulack (RC)	.75	.30
❑ 46 Jeff Kent	.50	.20
❑ 47 Ben Sheets	.50	.20
❑ 48 Rickie Weeks	.50	.20
❑ 49 Francisco Liriano (RC)	4.00	1.50
❑ 50 Joe Mauer	.75	.30
❑ 51 Johan Santana	.75	.30
❑ 52 Justin Morneau	.50	.20
❑ 53 Torii Hunter	.50	.20
❑ 54 Carlos Beltran	.50	.20
❑ 55 David Wright	2.00	.75
❑ 56 Jose Reyes	.50	.20
❑ 57 Mike Piazza	1.25	.50
❑ 58 Pedro Martinez	.75	.30
❑ 59 Alex Rodriguez	2.00	.75
❑ 60 Derek Jeter	3.00	1.25
❑ 61 Hideki Matsui	1.25	.50
❑ 62 Randy Johnson	1.25	.50
❑ 63 Justin Verlander (RC)	3.00	1.25
❑ 64 Bobby Crosby	.50	.20
❑ 65 Eric Chavez	.50	.20
❑ 66 Brian Anderson (RC)	.75	.30
❑ 67 Bobby Abreu	.50	.20
❑ 68 Pat Burrell	.50	.20
❑ 69 Jason Bay	.50	.20
❑ 70 Oliver Perez	.50	.20
❑ 71 Chuck James (RC)	1.25	.50
❑ 72 Brian Giles	.50	.20
❑ 73 Jake Peavy	.50	.20
❑ 74 Khalil Greene	.75	.30
❑ 75 Jason Schmidt	.50	.20
❑ 76 Kenji Johjima RC	4.00	1.50
❑ 77 Jeremy Accardo RC	.75	.30
❑ 78 Adrian Beltre	.50	.20
❑ 79 Ichiro Suzuki	2.00	.75
❑ 80 Jeff Harris RC	.75	.30
❑ 81 Felix Hernandez	.75	.30
❑ 82 Albert Pujols	2.50	1.00
❑ 83 Chris Carpenter	.50	.20
❑ 84 Jim Edmonds	.75	.30
❑ 85 Scott Rolen	.75	.30
❑ 86 Mike Jacobs (RC)	.75	.30
❑ 87 Carl Crawford	.50	.20
❑ 88 Anderson Hernandez (RC)	.75	.30
❑ 89 Scott Kazmir	.75	.30
❑ 90 Josh Rupe (RC)	.75	.30
❑ 91 Scott Feldman RC	.75	.30
❑ 92 Alfonso Soriano	.50	.20
❑ 93 Hank Blalock	.50	.20
❑ 94 Mark Teixeira	.75	.30
❑ 95 Michael Young	.50	.20
❑ 96 Roy Halladay	.50	.20
❑ 97 Vernon Wells	.50	.20
❑ 98 Jason Bergmann RC	.75	.30
❑ 99 Ryan Zimmerman (RC)	5.00	2.00
❑ 100 Jose Vidro	.50	.20

2005 Bazooka

❑ COMPLETE SET (220)	60.00	30.00
❑ COMMON CARD (1-170)	.40	.15
❑ COMMON CARD (171-190)	.50	.20
❑ COMMON CARD (191-220)	.50	.20
❑ 1 Eric Gagne	.40	.15
❑ 2 Aramis Ramirez	.40	.15
❑ 3 Hank Blalock	.40	.15
❑ 4 Jason Kendall	.40	.15
❑ 5 Jeromy Burnitz	.40	.15
❑ 6 Jose Guillen	.40	.15
❑ 7 Tom Glavine	.60	.25
❑ 8 Adrian Beltre	.40	.15
❑ 9 Jason Bay	.40	.15
❑ 10 Mark Teixeira	.60	.25
❑ 11 Moises Alou	.40	.15
❑ 12 Ronnie Belliard	.40	.15
❑ 13 Aaron Guiel	.40	.15
❑ 14 Vladimir Guerrero	1.00	.40
❑ 15 Scott Podsednik	.40	.15
❑ 16 Alfonso Soriano	.40	.15
❑ 17 Craig Wilson	.40	.15
❑ 18 Jose Reyes	.40	.15
❑ 19 Mark Prior	.60	.25
❑ 20 Preston Wilson	.40	.15
❑ 21 Shawn Green	.40	.15
❑ 22 Troy Glaus	.40	.15
❑ 23 Dmitri Young	.40	.15
❑ 24 Garret Anderson	.40	.15
❑ 25 Kazuo Matsui	.40	.15
❑ 26 Kerry Wood	.40	.15
❑ 27 Michael Young	.40	.15
❑ 28 Oliver Perez	.40	.15
❑ 29 Bartolo Colon	.40	.15
❑ 30 Richie Sexson	.40	.15
❑ 31 Brad Penny	.40	.15
❑ 32 Carlos Guillen	.40	.15
❑ 33 Carlos Zambrano	.40	.15
❑ 34 David Wright	1.50	.60
❑ 35 Al Leiter	.40	.15
❑ 36 Jack Wilson	.40	.15
❑ 37 Ryan Drese	.40	.15
❑ 38 Darin Erstad	.40	.15
❑ 39 Derrek Lee	.60	.25
❑ 40 Ivan Rodriguez	.60	.25
❑ 41 Kenny Rogers	.40	.15
❑ 42 Mike Piazza	1.00	.40
❑ 43 Phil Nevin	.40	.15
❑ 44 Geoff Jenkins	.40	.15
❑ 45 Jorge Posada	.60	.25
❑ 46 Khalil Greene	.60	.25
❑ 47 Randy Johnson	1.00	.40
❑ 48 Rondell White	.40	.15
❑ 49 Sammy Sosa	1.00	.40
❑ 50 Vernon Wells	.40	.15
❑ 51 Ben Sheets	.40	.15
❑ 52 Brian Giles	.40	.15
❑ 53 Carlos Delgado	.40	.15
❑ 54 Derek Jeter	2.00	.75
❑ 55 Jeremy Bonderman	.40	.15
❑ 56 Magglio Ordonez	.40	.15

❑ 57 Chad Tracy .40 .15
❑ 58 Kevin Brown .40 .15
❑ 59 Luis Castillo .40 .15
❑ 60 Lyle Overbay .40 .15
❑ 61 Mark Buehrle .40 .15
❑ 62 Mark Loretta .40 .15
❑ 63 Orlando Hudson .40 .15
❑ 64 Adam Dunn .40 .15
❑ 65 Frank Thomas 1.00 .40
❑ 66 Jake Peavy .40 .15
❑ 67 Jason Giambi .40 .15
❑ 68 Joe Mauer 1.00 .40
❑ 69 Marcus Giles .40 .15
❑ 70 Mike Lowell .40 .15
❑ 71 Roy Halladay .40 .15
❑ 72 Aaron Rowand .40 .15
❑ 73 Alex Rodriguez 1.50 .60
❑ 74 Brian Lawrence .40 .15
❑ 75 Gabe Gross .40 .15
❑ 76 Johnny Estrada .40 .15
❑ 77 Justin Morneau .40 .15
❑ 78 Miguel Cabrera .60 .25
❑ 79 Alex Rios .40 .15
❑ 80 Gary Sheffield .40 .15
❑ 81 Jason Schmidt .40 .15
❑ 82 Juan Pierre .40 .15
❑ 83 Paul Konerko .40 .15
❑ 84 Jermaine Dye .40 .15
❑ 85 Rafael Furcal .40 .15
❑ 86 Torii Hunter .40 .15
❑ 87 A.J. Pierzynski .40 .15
❑ 88 Carl Pavano .40 .15
❑ 89 Carlos Lee .40 .15
❑ 90 J.D. Drew .40 .15
❑ 91 Javier Vazquez .40 .15
❑ 92 Lew Ford .40 .15
❑ 93 Ted Lilly .40 .15
❑ 94 Austin Kearns .40 .15
❑ 95 Chipper Jones 1.00 .40
❑ 96 Erubiel Durazo .40 .15
❑ 97 Johan Santana 1.00 .40
❑ 98 Josh Beckett .40 .15
❑ 99 Mariano Rivera 1.00 .40
❑ 100 Mark Mulder .40 .15
❑ 101 Andruw Jones .60 .25
❑ 102 Barry Zito .40 .15
❑ 103 Bret Boone .40 .15
❑ 104 Paul LoDuca .40 .15
❑ 105 Shannon Stewart .40 .15
❑ 106 Wily Mo Pena .40 .15
❑ 107 Dontrelle Willis .40 .15
❑ 108 Eric Chavez .40 .15
❑ 109 Jamie Moyer .40 .15
❑ 110 Joe Nathan .40 .15
❑ 111 Sidney Ponson .40 .15
❑ 112 John Smoltz .60 .25
❑ 113 Ichiro Suzuki 2.00 .75
❑ 114 Javy Lopez .40 .15
❑ 115 Victor Martinez .40 .15
❑ 116 Ken Griffey Jr. 1.50 .60
❑ 117 Lance Berkman .40 .15
❑ 118 Scott Hatteberg .40 .15
❑ 119 Jim Edmonds .40 .15
❑ 120 Kazuhisa Ishii .40 .15
❑ 121 Miguel Tejada .40 .15
❑ 122 Roger Clemens 1.50 .60
❑ 123 Ryan Freel .40 .15
❑ 124 Albert Pujols 2.00 .75
❑ 125 Hideo Nomo 1.00 .40
❑ 126 Mark Kotsay .40 .15
❑ 127 Melvin Mora .40 .15
❑ 128 Roy Oswalt .40 .15
❑ 129 Sean Casey .40 .15
❑ 130 Casey Blake .40 .15
❑ 131 Edgar Renteria .40 .15
❑ 132 Jeff Kent .40 .15
❑ 133 Rafael Palmeiro .60 .25
❑ 134 Tim Hudson .40 .15
❑ 135 Barry Bonds 2.50 1.00
❑ 136 Andy Pettitte .60 .25
❑ 137 Brian Roberts .40 .15
❑ 138 Jose Vidro .40 .15
❑ 139 Omar Vizquel .60 .25
❑ 140 Rich Harden .40 .15
❑ 141 Scott Rolen .60 .25
❑ 142 Carlos Beltran .40 .15
❑ 143 Chris Carpenter .40 .15
❑ 144 Manny Ramirez .60 .25
❑ 145 Nick Johnson .40 .15
❑ 146 Pat Burrell .40 .15
❑ 147 C.C. Sabathia .40 .15
❑ 148 Johnny Damon .60 .25
❑ 149 Juan Rivera .40 .15
❑ 150 Ken Harvey .40 .15
❑ 151 Kevin Millwood .40 .15
❑ 152 Larry Walker .60 .25
❑ 153 Aubrey Huff .40 .15
❑ 154 Curt Schilling .60 .25
❑ 155 Jake Westbrook .40 .15
❑ 156 Randy Wolf .40 .15
❑ 157 Zach Day .40 .15
❑ 158 Zack Greinke .40 .15
❑ 159 Brad Wilkerson .40 .15
❑ 160 Carl Crawford .40 .15
❑ 161 Jim Thome .60 .25
❑ 162 Mike Sweeney .40 .15
❑ 163 Pedro Martinez .60 .25
❑ 164 Travis Hafner .40 .15
❑ 165 Bobby Abreu .40 .15
❑ 166 Cliff Floyd .40 .15
❑ 167 David DeJesus .40 .15
❑ 168 David Ortiz 1.00 .40
❑ 169 Rocco Baldelli .40 .15
❑ 170 Todd Helton .60 .25
❑ 171 Dallas McPherson PROS .50 .20
❑ 172 Kevin Youkilis PROS .50 .20
❑ 173 Val Majewski PROS .50 .20
❑ 174 Grady Sizemore PROS .75 .30
❑ 175 Joey Gathright PROS .50 .20
❑ 176 Rickie Weeks PROS .50 .20
❑ 177 Jason Kubel PROS .50 .20
❑ 178 Robinson Cano PROS .75 .30
❑ 179 Nick Swisher PROS .75 .30
❑ 180 Ryan Howard PROS 2.50 1.00
❑ 181 Tim Stauffer PROS .50 .20
❑ 182 Merkin Valdez PROS .50 .20
❑ 183 B.J. Upton PROS .75 .30
❑ 184 Scott Kazmir PROS 1.00 .40
❑ 185 Chris Burke PROS .50 .20
❑ 186 Felix Hernandez PROS 2.00 .75
❑ 187 Freddy Guzman PROS .50 .20
❑ 188 Josh Labandeira PROS .50 .20
❑ 189 Willy Taveras PROS .50 .20
❑ 190 Casey Kotchman PROS .50 .20
❑ 191 Steve Doetsch FY RC .75 .30
❑ 192 Melky Cabrera FY RC 2.00 .75
❑ 193 Luis Ramirez FY RC .50 .20
❑ 194 Chris Seddon FY RC .50 .20
❑ 195 Chad Orvella FY RC .50 .20
❑ 196 Ian Kinsler FY RC 2.00 .75
❑ 197 Brandon Moss FY RC 2.00 .75
❑ 198 Chadd Blasko FY RC .75 .30
❑ 199 Jeremy West FY RC .75 .30
❑ 200 Sean Marshall FY RC 2.00 .75
❑ 201 Matt DeSalvo FY RC .75 .30
❑ 202 Ryan Sweeney FY RC 1.00 .40
❑ 203 Matthew Lindstrom FY RC .50 .20
❑ 204 Ryan Goleski FY RC .75 .30
❑ 205 Brett Harper FY RC .75 .30
❑ 206 Chris Roberson FY RC .50 .20
❑ 207 Andre Ethier FY RC 5.00 2.00
❑ 208 Chris Denorfia FY RC 1.00 .40
❑ 209 Darren Fenster FY RC .50 .20
❑ 210 Elvys Quezada FY RC .50 .20
❑ 211 Kevin West FY RC .50 .20
❑ 212 Chaz Lytle FY RC .75 .30
❑ 213 James Jurries FY RC .75 .30
❑ 214 Matt Rogelstad FY RC .50 .20
❑ 215 Wade Robinson FY RC .50 .20
❑ 216 Ian Bladergroen FY RC .75 .30
❑ 217 Jake Dittler FY .50 .20
❑ 218 Nate McLouth FY RC .75 .30
❑ 219 Kole Strayhorn FY RC .50 .20
❑ 220 Jose Vaquedano FY RC .50 .20

2006 Bazooka

❑ COMPLETE SET (220) 40.00 15.00
❑ COMMON CARD (1-200) .40 .15
❑ COMMON CARD (201-220) .40 .15
❑ 1 Josh Gibson 1.50 .60
❑ 2 Scott Podsednik .40 .15
❑ 3 Sammy Sosa 1.00 .40
❑ 4 Ivan Rodriguez .60 .25
❑ 5 Derek Jeter 2.50 1.00
❑ 6 Manny Ramirez .60 .25
❑ 7 Nook Logan .40 .15
❑ 8 Adam Dunn .40 .15
❑ 9 Travis Hafner .40 .15
❑ 10 Felix Hernandez .60 .25
❑ 11 Larry Bigbie .40 .15
❑ 12 Magglio Ordonez .40 .15
❑ 13 Josh Beckett .40 .15
❑ 14 Mike Sweeney .40 .15
❑ 15 Mickey Mantle 5.00 2.00
❑ 16 Grady Sizemore .60 .25
❑ 17 Brian Fuentes .40 .15
❑ 18 Wily Mo Pena .40 .15
❑ 19 Morgan Ensberg .40 .15
❑ 20 Tim Hudson .40 .15
❑ 21 Justin Verlander 1.50 .60
❑ 22 Jermaine Dye .40 .15
❑ 23 Miguel Cabrera .40 .15
❑ 24 Greg Maddux 1.50 .60
❑ 25 Jason Giambi .40 .15
❑ 26 Ben Sheets .40 .15
❑ 27 Brad Radke .40 .15
❑ 28 Torii Hunter .40 .15
❑ 29 Mike Piazza 1.00 .40
❑ 30 Jason Kendall .40 .15
❑ 31 Pat Burrell .40 .15
❑ 32 Khalil Greene .60 .25
❑ 33 Brian Roberts .40 .15
❑ 34 C.C. Sabathia .40 .15
❑ 35 Mike Mussina .60 .25
❑ 36 Bob Wickman .40 .15
❑ 37 Dmitri Young .40 .15
❑ 38 Dontrelle Willis .40 .15
❑ 39 David DeJesus .40 .15
❑ 40 J.D. Drew .40 .15
❑ 41 Chad Tracy .40 .15
❑ 42 Joe Mauer 1.00 .40
❑ 43 Melvin Mora .40 .15
❑ 44 Carlos Zambrano .40 .15
❑ 45 Mariano Rivera 1.00 .40
❑ 46 Coco Crisp .40 .15
❑ 47 Derrek Lee .60 .25
❑ 48 Cliff Floyd .40 .15
❑ 49 Willy Taveras .40 .15
❑ 50 Albert Pujols 2.00 .75
❑ 51 Aaron Boone .40 .15
❑ 52 Mark Mulder .40 .15
❑ 53 Brad Wilkerson .40 .15
❑ 54 Hank Blalock .40 .15
❑ 55 Hideki Matsui 1.00 .40
❑ 56 Victor Martinez .40 .15
❑ 57 Jeremy Bonderman .40 .15
❑ 58 Felipe Lopez .40 .15
❑ 59 Paul Lo Duca .40 .15
❑ 60 Derek Lowe .40 .15
❑ 61 Luis Gonzalez .40 .15
❑ 62 Paul Konerko .40 .15
❑ 63 Miguel Tejada .40 .15
❑ 64 Jeromy Burnitz .40 .15
❑ 65 Orlando Hernandez .40 .15
❑ 66 Curt Schilling .60 .25
❑ 67 Joe Nathan .40 .15
❑ 68 Jose Reyes .40 .15
❑ 69 David Wright 1.00 .40
❑ 70 Eric Chavez .40 .15

❑ 71 Rich Harden .40 .15
❑ 72 A.J. Pierzynski .40 .15
❑ 73 Trevor Hoffman .40 .15
❑ 74 Adrian Beltre .40 .15
❑ 75 Alex Rodriguez 1.50 .60
❑ 76 Jonathan Papelbon 2.00 .75
❑ 77 Jorge Cantu .40 .15
❑ 78 Mark Teixeira .60 .25
❑ 79 Chien-Ming Wang 1.50 .60
❑ 80 Jeff Francoeur 1.00 .40
❑ 81 Ichiro Suzuki 1.50 .60
❑ 82 Jhonny Peralta .40 .15
❑ 83 Todd Helton .60 .25
❑ 84 Brad Penny .40 .15
❑ 85 Shawn Chacon .40 .15
❑ 86 Billy Wagner .40 .15
❑ 87 Jason Schmidt .40 .15
❑ 88 Austin Kearns .40 .15
❑ 89 Chris Carpenter .40 .15
❑ 90 Chipper Jones 1.00 .40
❑ 91 Shawn Green .40 .15
❑ 92 A.J. Burnett .40 .15
❑ 93 Joe Crede .40 .15
❑ 94 Mark Prior .60 .25
❑ 95 Andy Pettitte .60 .25
❑ 96 Edgar Renteria .40 .15
❑ 97 Roy Halladay .40 .15
❑ 98 Eric Milton .40 .15
❑ 99 Craig Biggio .60 .25
❑ 100 Barry Bonds 2.50 1.00
❑ 101 Troy Glaus .40 .15
❑ 102 Aaron Rowand .40 .15
❑ 103 Aramis Ramirez .40 .15
❑ 104 Nomar Garciaparra 1.00 .40
❑ 105 Randy Johnson 1.00 .40
❑ 106 David Ortiz 1.00 .40
❑ 107 Vinny Castilla .40 .15
❑ 108 Carl Crawford .40 .15
❑ 109 Zach Duke .40 .15
❑ 110 Barry Zito .40 .15
❑ 111 Darin Erstad .40 .15
❑ 112 Chris Capuano .40 .15
❑ 113 Javy Lopez .40 .15
❑ 114 Lew Ford .40 .15
❑ 115 Robinson Cano .60 .25
❑ 116 Ronnie Belliard .40 .15
❑ 117 Placido Polanco .40 .15
❑ 118 Rickie Weeks .40 .15
❑ 119 Brad Lidge .40 .15
❑ 120 Andruw Jones .60 .25
❑ 121 Nick Swisher .40 .15
❑ 122 Bartolo Colon .40 .15
❑ 123 Juan Pierre .40 .15
❑ 124 Johan Santana 1.00 .40
❑ 125 Jorge Posada .60 .25
❑ 126 Jeff Francis .40 .15
❑ 127 Matt Holliday .40 .15
❑ 128 Carlos Delgado .40 .15
❑ 129 Zack Greinke .40 .15
❑ 130 Lyle Overbay .40 .15
❑ 131 Conor Jackson .40 .15
❑ 132 Mark Buehrle .40 .15
❑ 133 Chone Figgins .40 .15
❑ 134 Pedro Martinez .60 .25
❑ 135 Roger Clemens 2.00 .75
❑ 136 Raul Ibanez .40 .15
❑ 137 Jim Edmonds .40 .15
❑ 138 Michael Young .40 .15
❑ 139 Preston Wilson .40 .15
❑ 140 Rafael Furcal .40 .15
❑ 141 Bobby Abreu .40 .15
❑ 142 Tadahito Iguchi .40 .15
❑ 143 B.J. Ryan .40 .15
❑ 144 Francisco Rodriguez .40 .15
❑ 145 J.T. Snow .40 .15
❑ 146 Aubrey Huff .40 .15
❑ 147 Mike Morse .40 .15
❑ 148 Jason Bay .40 .15
❑ 149 Roy Oswalt .40 .15
❑ 150 Carlos Beltran .40 .15
❑ 151 Carlos Lee .40 .15
❑ 152 Emil Brown .40 .15
❑ 153 Craig Monroe .40 .15
❑ 154 Kris Benson .40 .15
❑ 155 Gary Sheffield .40 .15
❑ 156 Jake Peavy .40 .15
❑ 157 David Eckstein .40 .15
❑ 158 Tom Glavine .60 .25
❑ 159 Jeff Kent .40 .15
❑ 160 Livan Hernandez .40 .15
❑ 161 Orlando Hudson .40 .15
❑ 162 Randy Winn .40 .15
❑ 163 Jimmy Rollins .40 .15
❑ 164 Luis Castillo .40 .15
❑ 165 Nick Johnson .40 .15
❑ 166 Johnny Damon .60 .25
❑ 167 Eric Gagne .40 .15
❑ 168 Geoff Jenkins .40 .15
❑ 169 Mike Cameron .40 .15
❑ 170 Marcus Giles .40 .15
❑ 171 Huston Street .40 .15
❑ 172 Moises Alou .40 .15
❑ 173 Scott Rolen .60 .25
❑ 174 Jose Vidro .40 .15
❑ 175 Alfonso Soriano .40 .15
❑ 176 Toby Hall .40 .15
❑ 177 Orlando Cabrera .40 .15
❑ 178 Brian Giles .40 .15
❑ 179 Erubiel Durazo .40 .15
❑ 180 Matt Morris .40 .15
❑ 181 Jack Wilson .40 .15
❑ 182 Brady Clark .40 .15
❑ 183 Shannon Stewart .40 .15
❑ 184 Kerry Wood .40 .15
❑ 185 Carl Pavano .40 .15
❑ 186 Chase Utley .60 .25
❑ 187 Omar Vizquel .60 .25
❑ 188 Vladimir Guerrero 1.00 .40
❑ 189 Richie Sexson .40 .15
❑ 190 John Smoltz .60 .25
❑ 191 Garret Anderson .40 .15
❑ 192 Jon Garland .40 .15
❑ 193 Julio Lugo .40 .15
❑ 194 Rocco Baldelli .40 .15
❑ 195 Jaret Wright .40 .15
❑ 196 Matt Clement .40 .15
❑ 197 Vernon Wells .40 .15
❑ 198 Sean Casey .40 .15
❑ 199 Lance Berkman .40 .15
❑ 200 Justin Morneau .40 .15
❑ 201 Shaun Marcum (RC) .40 .15
❑ 202 Chuck James (RC) .40 .15
❑ 203 Hong-Chih Kuo (RC) 1.00 .40
❑ 204 Darrell Rasner (RC) .40 .15
❑ 205 Anthony Reyes (RC) .60 .25
❑ 206 Francisco Liriano (RC) 2.00 .75
❑ 207 Joe Saunders (RC) .40 .15
❑ 208 Fausto Carmona (RC) .40 .15
❑ 209 Charlton Jimerson (RC) .40 .15
❑ 210 Bryan Bullington (RC) .40 .15
❑ 211 Tom Gorzelanny (RC) .40 .15
❑ 212 Anderson Hernandez (RC) .40 .15
❑ 213 Ryan Garko (RC) .40 .15
❑ 214 John Koronka (RC) .40 .15
❑ 215 Chris Denorfia (RC) .40 .15
❑ 216 Jeff Mathis (RC) .40 .15
❑ 217 Jose Bautista (RC) .40 .15
❑ 218 Danny Sandoval RC .40 .15
❑ 219 Robert Andino RC .40 .15
❑ 220 Justin Huber (RC) .40 .15

1948 Bowman

❑ COMPLETE SET (48) 3600.00 2500.00
❑ COMMON CARD (1-36) 20.00 10.00
❑ COMMON CARD (37-48) 30.00 15.00
❑ WRAPPER (5-CENT) 700.00 600.00
❑ WRAPPER (1-CENT)
❑ 1 Bob Elliott RC 125.00 75.00
❑ 2 Ewell Blackwell RC 60.00 35.00
❑ 3 Ralph Kiner RC 250.00 150.00
❑ 4 Johnny Mize RC 125.00 75.00
❑ 5 Bob Feller RC 250.00 150.00
❑ 6 Yogi Berra RC 800.00 500.00
❑ 7 Pete Reiser SP RC 125.00 75.00
❑ 8 Phil Rizzuto SP RC 350.00 200.00
❑ 9 Walker Cooper RC 20.00 10.00
❑ 10 Buddy Rosar RC 20.00 10.00
❑ 11 Johnny Lindell RC 25.00 12.50
❑ 12 Johnny Sain RC 80.00 50.00
❑ 13 Willard Marshall SP RC 40.00 20.00
❑ 14 Allie Reynolds RC 60.00 35.00
❑ 15 Eddie Joost 20.00 10.00
❑ 16 Jack Lohrke SP RC 40.00 20.00
❑ 17 Enos Slaughter RC 100.00 60.00
❑ 18 Warren Spahn RC 300.00 175.00
❑ 19 Tommy Henrich 60.00 35.00
❑ 20 Buddy Kerr SP RC 40.00 20.00
❑ 21 Ferris Fain RC 40.00 20.00
❑ 22 Floyd Bevens SP RC 50.00 30.00
❑ 23 Larry Jansen RC 25.00 12.50
❑ 24 Dutch Leonard SP 40.00 20.00
❑ 25 Barney McCosky 20.00 10.00
❑ 26 Frank Shea SP RC 50.00 30.00
❑ 27 Sid Gordon RC 25.00 12.50
❑ 28 Emil Verban SP RC 40.00 20.00
❑ 29 Joe Page SP RC 80.00 50.00
❑ 30 Whitey Lockman SP RC 50.00 30.00
❑ 31 Bill McCahan RC 20.00 10.00
❑ 32 Bill Rigney RC 20.00 10.00
❑ 33 Bill Johnson RC 25.00 12.50
❑ 34 Sheldon Jones SP RC 40.00 20.00
❑ 35 Snuffy Stirnweiss RC 40.00 20.00
❑ 36 Stan Musial RC 800.00 500.00
❑ 37 Clint Hartung RC 30.00 15.00
❑ 38 Red Schoendienst RC 200.00 125.00
❑ 39 Augie Galan RC 30.00 15.00
❑ 40 Marty Marion RC 80.00 50.00
❑ 41 Rex Barney RC 60.00 35.00
❑ 42 Ray Poat RC 30.00 15.00
❑ 43 Bruce Edwards RC 40.00 20.00
❑ 44 Johnny Wyrostek RC 30.00 15.00
❑ 45 Hank Sauer RC 60.00 35.00
❑ 46 Herman Wehmeier RC 30.00 15.00
❑ 47 Bobby Thomson RC 100.00 60.00
❑ 48 Dave Koslo RC 80.00 50.00

1949 Bowman

❑ COMP. MASTER SET (252) 16000.00 10000.00
❑ COMPLETE SET (240) 15000.00 10000.00
❑ COMMON CARD (1-144) 15.00 7.50
❑ COMMON CARD (145-240) 50.00 30.00
❑ WRAPPER (1-CENT,Rd,Wh,Bl)
❑ WRAPPER (5-CENT, GR.) 250.00 200.00
❑ WRAPPER (5-CENT, BL.) 200.00 150.00
❑ 1 Vern Bickford RC 125.00 75.00
❑ 2 Whitey Lockman 40.00 20.00
❑ 3 Bob Porterfield RC 15.00 7.50
❑ 4A Jerry Priddy NNOF RC 15.00 7.50
❑ 4B Jerry Priddy NOF 50.00 30.00
❑ 5 Hank Sauer 40.00 20.00

❑ 6 Phil Cavarretta RC 40.00 20.00
❑ 7 Joe Dobson RC 15.00 7.50
❑ 8 Murry Dickson RC 15.00 7.50
❑ 9 Ferris Fain 40.00 20.00
❑ 10 Ted Gray RC 15.00 7.50
❑ 11 Lou Boudreau MG RC 80.00 50.00
❑ 12 Cass Michaels RC 15.00 7.50
❑ 13 Bob Chesnes RC 15.00 7.50
❑ 14 Curt Simmons RC 40.00 20.00
❑ 15 Ned Garver RC 15.00 7.50
❑ 16 Al Kozar RC 15.00 7.50
❑ 17 Earl Torgeson RC 15.00 7.50
❑ 18 Bobby Thomson 40.00 20.00
❑ 19 Bobby Brown RC 60.00 35.00
❑ 20 Gene Hermanski RC 15.00 7.50
❑ 21 Frank Baumholtz RC 25.00 12.50
❑ 22 Peanuts Lowrey RC 15.00 7.50
❑ 23 Bobby Doerr 80.00 50.00
❑ 24 Stan Musial 600.00 350.00
❑ 25 Carl Scheib RC 15.00 7.50
❑ 26 George Kell RC 80.00 50.00
❑ 27 Bob Feller 300.00 200.00
❑ 28 Don Kolloway RC 15.00 7.50
❑ 29 Ralph Kiner 125.00 75.00
❑ 30 Andy Seminick 40.00 20.00
❑ 31 Dick Kokos RC 15.00 7.50
❑ 32 Eddie Yost RC 60.00 35.00
❑ 33 Warren Spahn 200.00 125.00
❑ 34 Dave Koslo 15.00 7.50
❑ 35 Vic Raschi RC 60.00 35.00
❑ 36 Pee Wee Reese 200.00 125.00
❑ 37 Johnny Wyrostek 15.00 7.50
❑ 38 Emil Verban 15.00 7.50
❑ 39 Billy Goodman RC 25.00 12.50
❑ 40 George Munger RC 15.00 7.50
❑ 41 Lou Brissie RC 15.00 7.50
❑ 42 Hoot Evers RC 15.00 7.50
❑ 43 Dale Mitchell RC 40.00 20.00
❑ 44 Dave Philley RC 15.00 7.50
❑ 45 Wally Westlake RC 15.00 7.50
❑ 46 Robin Roberts RC 250.00 150.00
❑ 47 Johnny Sain 60.00 35.00
❑ 48 Willard Marshall 15.00 7.50
❑ 49 Frank Shea 25.00 12.50
❑ 50 Jackie Robinson RC 1200.00 700.00
❑ 51 Herman Wehmeier 15.00 7.50
❑ 52 Johnny Schmitz RC 15.00 7.50
❑ 53 Jack Kramer RC 15.00 7.50
❑ 54 Marty Marion 60.00 35.00
❑ 55 Eddie Joost 15.00 7.50
❑ 56 Pat Mullin RC 15.00 7.50
❑ 57 Gene Bearden RC 40.00 20.00
❑ 58 Bob Elliott 40.00 20.00
❑ 59 Jack Lohrke 15.00 7.50
❑ 60 Yogi Berra 300.00 175.00
❑ 61 Rex Barney 40.00 20.00
❑ 62 Grady Hatton RC 15.00 7.50
❑ 63 Andy Pafko RC 40.00 20.00
❑ 64 Dom DiMaggio 60.00 35.00
❑ 65 Enos Slaughter 80.00 50.00
❑ 66 Elmer Valo RC 15.00 7.50
❑ 67 Alvin Dark RC 40.00 20.00
❑ 68 Sheldon Jones 15.00 7.50
❑ 69 Tommy Henrich 40.00 20.00
❑ 70 Carl Furillo RC 150.00 90.00
❑ 71 Vern Stephens RC 15.00 7.50
❑ 72 Tommy Holmes RC 40.00 20.00
❑ 73 Billy Cox RC 40.00 20.00
❑ 74 Tom McBride RC 15.00 7.50
❑ 75 Eddie Mayo RC 15.00 7.50
❑ 76 Bill Nicholson RC 25.00 12.50
❑ 77 Ernie Bonham RC 15.00 7.50
❑ 78A Sam Zoldak NNOF RC 15.00 7.50
❑ 78B Sam Zoldak NOF 50.00 30.00
❑ 79 Ron Northey RC 15.00 7.50
❑ 80 Bill McCahan 15.00 7.50
❑ 81 Virgil Stallcup RC 15.00 7.50
❑ 82 Joe Page 60.00 35.00
❑ 83A Bob Scheffing NNOF RC 15.00 7.50
❑ 83B Bob Scheffing NOF 50.00 30.00
❑ 84 Roy Campanella RC 800.00 500.00
❑ 85A Johnny Mize NNOF 100.00 60.00
❑ 85B Johnny Mize NOF 150.00 90.00
❑ 86 Johnny Pesky RC 60.00 35.00
❑ 87 Randy Gumpert RC 15.00 7.50
❑ 88A Bill Salkeld NNOF RC 15.00 7.50
❑ 88B Bill Salkeld NOF 50.00 30.00
❑ 89 Mizell Platt RC 15.00 7.50
❑ 90 Gil Coan RC 15.00 7.50
❑ 91 Dick Wakefield RC 15.00 7.50
❑ 92 Willie Jones RC 40.00 20.00
❑ 93 Ed Stevens RC 15.00 7.50
❑ 94 Mickey Vernon RC 40.00 20.00
❑ 95 Howie Pollet RC 15.00 7.50
❑ 96 Taft Wright 15.00 7.50
❑ 97 Danny Litwhiler RC 15.00 7.50
❑ 98A Phil Rizzuto NNOF 200.00 125.00
❑ 98B Phil Rizzuto NOF 250.00 150.00
❑ 99 Frank Gustine RC 15.00 7.50
❑ 100 Gil Hodges RC 250.00 150.00
❑ 101 Sid Gordon 15.00 7.50
❑ 102 Stan Spence RC 15.00 7.50
❑ 103 Joe Tipton RC 15.00 7.50
❑ 104 Eddie Stanky RC 40.00 20.00
❑ 105 Bill Kennedy RC 15.00 7.50
❑ 106 Jake Early RC 15.00 7.50
❑ 107 Eddie Lake RC 15.00 7.50
❑ 108 Ken Heintzelman RC 15.00 7.50
❑ 109A Ed Fitzgerald SCR RC 15.00 7.50
❑ 109B Ed Fitzgerald PR 60.00 35.00
❑ 110 Early Wynn RC 150.00 90.00
❑ 111 Red Schoendienst 100.00 60.00
❑ 112 Sam Chapman 40.00 20.00
❑ 113 Ray LaManno RC 15.00 7.50
❑ 114 Allie Reynolds 60.00 35.00
❑ 115 Dutch Leonard 15.00 7.50
❑ 116 Joe Hatten RC 15.00 7.50
❑ 117 Walker Cooper 15.00 7.50
❑ 118 Sam Mele RC 15.00 7.50
❑ 119 Floyd Baker RC 15.00 7.50
❑ 120 Cliff Fannin RC 15.00 7.50
❑ 121 Mark Christman RC 15.00 7.50
❑ 122 George Vico RC 15.00 7.50
❑ 123 Johnny Blatnick 15.00 7.50
❑ 124A D.Murtaugh SCR RC 40.00 20.00
❑ 124B D.Murtaugh PR 60.00 35.00
❑ 125 Ken Keltner RC 25.00 12.50
❑ 126A Al Brazle SCR RC 15.00 7.50
❑ 126B Al Brazle PR 60.00 35.00
❑ 127A Hank Majeski SCR RC 15.00 7.50
❑ 127B Hank Majeski PR 60.00 35.00
❑ 128 Johnny VanderMeer 60.00 35.00
❑ 129 Bill Johnson 40.00 20.00
❑ 130 Harry Walker RC 15.00 7.50
❑ 131 Paul Lehner RC 15.00 7.50
❑ 132A Al Evans SCR RC 15.00 7.50
❑ 132B Al Evans PR 60.00 35.00
❑ 133 Aaron Robinson RC 15.00 7.50
❑ 134 Hank Borowy RC 15.00 7.50
❑ 135 Stan Rojek RC 15.00 7.50
❑ 136 Hank Edwards RC 15.00 7.50
❑ 137 Ted Wilks RC 15.00 7.50
❑ 138 Buddy Rosar 15.00 7.50
❑ 139 Hank Arft RC 15.00 7.50
❑ 140 Ray Scarborough RC 15.00 7.50
❑ 141 Tony Lupien RC 15.00 7.50
❑ 142 Eddie Waitkus RC 40.00 20.00
❑ 143A Bob Dillinger PR RC 25.00 12.50
❑ 143B Bob Dillinger SC 60.00 35.00
❑ 144 Mickey Haefner RC 15.00 7.50
❑ 145 Sylvester Donnelly RC 50.00 30.00
❑ 146 Mike McCormick RC 50.00 30.00
❑ 147 Bert Singleton RC 50.00 30.00
❑ 148 Bob Swift RC 50.00 30.00
❑ 149 Roy Partee RC 50.00 30.00
❑ 150 Allie Clark RC 50.00 30.00
❑ 151 Mickey Harris RC 50.00 30.00
❑ 152 Clarence Maddern RC 50.00 30.00
❑ 153 Phil Masi RC 50.00 30.00
❑ 154 Clint Hartung 60.00 35.00
❑ 155 Mickey Guerra RC 50.00 30.00
❑ 156 Al Zarilla RC 50.00 30.00
❑ 157 Walt Masterson RC 50.00 30.00
❑ 158 Harry Brecheen RC 60.00 35.00
❑ 159 Glen Moulder RC 50.00 30.00
❑ 160 Jim Blackburn RC 50.00 30.00
❑ 161 Jocko Thompson RC 50.00 30.00
❑ 162 Preacher Roe RC 125.00 75.00
❑ 163 Clyde McCullough RC 50.00 30.00
❑ 164 Vic Wertz RC 80.00 50.00
❑ 165 Snuffy Stirnweiss 80.00 50.00
❑ 166 Mike Tresh RC 50.00 30.00
❑ 167 Babe Martin RC 50.00 30.00
❑ 168 Doyle Lade RC 50.00 30.00
❑ 169 Jeff Heath RC 60.00 35.00
❑ 170 Bill Rigney 60.00 35.00
❑ 171 Dick Fowler RC 50.00 30.00
❑ 172 Eddie Pellagrini RC 50.00 30.00
❑ 173 Eddie Stewart RC 50.00 30.00
❑ 174 Terry Moore RC 80.00 50.00
❑ 175 Luke Appling 150.00 90.00
❑ 176 Ken Raffensberger RC 50.00 30.00
❑ 177 Stan Lopata RC 60.00 35.00
❑ 178 Tom Brown RC 60.00 35.00
❑ 179 Hugh Casey 80.00 50.00
❑ 180 Connie Berry 50.00 30.00
❑ 181 Gus Niarhos RC 50.00 30.00
❑ 182 Hal Peck RC 50.00 30.00
❑ 183 Lou Stringer RC 50.00 30.00
❑ 184 Bob Chipman RC 50.00 30.00
❑ 185 Pete Reiser 80.00 50.00
❑ 186 Buddy Kerr 50.00 30.00
❑ 187 Phil Marchildon RC 50.00 30.00
❑ 188 Karl Drews RC 50.00 30.00
❑ 189 Earl Wooten RC 50.00 30.00
❑ 190 Jim Hearn RC 50.00 30.00
❑ 191 Joe Haynes RC 50.00 30.00
❑ 192 Harry Gumbert 50.00 30.00
❑ 193 Ken Trinkle RC 50.00 30.00
❑ 194 Ralph Branca RC 100.00 60.00
❑ 195 Eddie Bockman RC 50.00 30.00
❑ 196 Fred Hutchinson RC 60.00 35.00
❑ 197 Johnny Lindell 60.00 35.00
❑ 198 Steve Gromek RC 50.00 30.00
❑ 199 Tex Hughson RC 50.00 30.00
❑ 200 Jess Dobernic RC 50.00 30.00
❑ 201 Sibby Sisti RC 50.00 30.00
❑ 202 Larry Jansen 60.00 35.00
❑ 203 Barney McCosky 50.00 30.00
❑ 204 Bob Savage RC 50.00 30.00
❑ 205 Dick Sisler RC 60.00 35.00
❑ 206 Bruce Edwards 50.00 30.00
❑ 207 Johnny Hopp RC 50.00 30.00
❑ 208 Dizzy Trout 60.00 35.00
❑ 209 Charlie Keller 80.00 50.00
❑ 210 Joe Gordon RC 80.00 50.00
❑ 211 Boo Ferriss RC 50.00 30.00
❑ 212 Ralph Hamner RC 50.00 30.00
❑ 213 Red Barrett RC 50.00 30.00
❑ 214 Richie Ashburn RC 600.00 350.00
❑ 215 Kirby Higbe 50.00 30.00
❑ 216 Schoolboy Rowe 60.00 35.00
❑ 217 Marino Pieretti RC 50.00 30.00
❑ 218 Dick Kryhoski RC 50.00 30.00
❑ 219 Virgil Trucks RC 60.00 35.00
❑ 220 Johnny McCarthy 50.00 30.00
❑ 221 Bob Muncrief RC 50.00 30.00
❑ 222 Alex Kellner RC 50.00 30.00
❑ 223 Bobby Hofman RC 50.00 30.00
❑ 224 Satchel Paige RC 1500.001000.00
❑ 225 Jerry Coleman RC 80.00 50.00
❑ 226 Duke Snider RC 1000.00 600.00
❑ 227 Fritz Ostermueller 50.00 30.00
❑ 228 Jackie Mayo RC 50.00 30.00
❑ 229 Ed Lopat RC 150.00 90.00
❑ 230 Augie Galan 60.00 35.00
❑ 231 Earl Johnson RC 50.00 30.00
❑ 232 George McQuinn 60.00 35.00
❑ 233 Larry Doby RC 300.00 175.00
❑ 234 Rip Sewell RC 50.00 30.00
❑ 235 Jim Russell RC 50.00 30.00
❑ 236 Fred Sanford RC 50.00 30.00
❑ 237 Monte Kennedy RC 50.00 30.00
❑ 238 Bob Lemon RC 200.00 125.00
❑ 239 Frank McCormick 50.00 30.00
❑ 240 Babe Young UER 100.00 60.00

1950 Bowman

❑ COMPLETE SET (252) 8500.006000.00
❑ COMMON CARD (1-72) 50.00 30.00
❑ COMMON CARD (73-252) 15.00 7.50
❑ WRAPPER (1-CENT) 250.00 200.00
❑ WRAPPER (5-CENT) 250.00 200.00
❑ 1 Mel Parnell RC 150.00 90.00
❑ 2 Vern Stephens 60.00 35.00
❑ 3 Dom DiMaggio 80.00 50.00
❑ 4 Gus Zernial RC 60.00 35.00

❑	5	Bob Kuzava RC	50.00	30.00
❑	6	Bob Feller	300.00	175.00
❑	7	Jim Hegan	60.00	35.00
❑	8	George Kell	80.00	50.00
❑	9	Vic Wertz	60.00	35.00
❑	10	Tommy Henrich	80.00	50.00
❑	11	Phil Rizzuto	300.00	175.00
❑	12	Joe Page	80.00	50.00
❑	13	Ferris Fain	60.00	35.00
❑	14	Alex Kellner	50.00	30.00
❑	15	Al Kozar	50.00	30.00
❑	16	Roy Sievers RC	80.00	50.00
❑	17	Sid Hudson	50.00	30.00
❑	18	Eddie Robinson RC	50.00	30.00
❑	19	Warren Spahn	300.00	175.00
❑	20	Bob Elliott	60.00	35.00
❑	21	Pee Wee Reese	300.00	175.00
❑	22	Jackie Robinson	1200.00	700.00
❑	23	Don Newcombe RC	150.00	90.00
❑	24	Johnny Schmitz	50.00	30.00
❑	25	Hank Sauer	60.00	35.00
❑	26	Grady Hatton	50.00	30.00
❑	27	Herman Wehmeier	50.00	30.00
❑	28	Bobby Thomson	80.00	50.00
❑	29	Eddie Stanky	60.00	35.00
❑	30	Eddie Waitkus	60.00	35.00
❑	31	Del Ennis	80.00	50.00
❑	32	Robin Roberts	150.00	90.00
❑	33	Ralph Kiner	100.00	60.00
❑	34	Murry Dickson	50.00	30.00
❑	35	Enos Slaughter	100.00	60.00
❑	36	Eddie Kazak RC	60.00	35.00
❑	37	Luke Appling	80.00	50.00
❑	38	Bill Wight RC	50.00	30.00
❑	39	Larry Doby	100.00	60.00
❑	40	Bob Lemon	80.00	50.00
❑	41	Hoot Evers	50.00	30.00
❑	42	Art Houtteman RC	50.00	30.00
❑	43	Bobby Doerr	80.00	50.00
❑	44	Joe Dobson	50.00	30.00
❑	45	Al Zarilla	50.00	30.00
❑	46	Yogi Berra	400.00	250.00
❑	47	Jerry Coleman	80.00	50.00
❑	48	Lou Brissie	50.00	30.00
❑	49	Elmer Valo	50.00	30.00
❑	50	Dick Kokos	50.00	30.00
❑	51	Ned Garver	60.00	35.00
❑	52	Sam Mele	50.00	30.00
❑	53	Clyde Vollmer RC	50.00	30.00
❑	54	Gil Coan	50.00	30.00
❑	55	Buddy Kerr	50.00	30.00
❑	56	Del Crandall RC	60.00	35.00
❑	57	Vern Bickford	50.00	30.00
❑	58	Carl Furillo	80.00	50.00
❑	59	Ralph Branca	80.00	50.00
❑	60	Andy Pafko	60.00	35.00
❑	61	Bob Rush RC	50.00	30.00
❑	62	Ted Kluszewski	125.00	75.00
❑	63	Ewell Blackwell	60.00	35.00
❑	64	Alvin Dark	60.00	35.00
❑	65	Dave Koslo	50.00	30.00
❑	66	Larry Jansen	60.00	35.00
❑	67	Willie Jones	60.00	35.00
❑	68	Curt Simmons	60.00	35.00
❑	69	Wally Westlake	50.00	30.00
❑	70	Bob Chesnes	50.00	30.00
❑	71	Red Schoendienst	80.00	50.00
❑	72	Howie Pollet	50.00	30.00
❑	73	Willard Marshall	15.00	7.50
❑	74	Johnny Antonelli RC	60.00	35.00
❑	75	Roy Campanella	300.00	175.00
❑	76	Rex Barney	40.00	20.00
❑	77	Duke Snider	300.00	175.00
❑	78	Mickey Owen	25.00	12.50
❑	79	Johnny VanderMeer	40.00	20.00
❑	80	Howard Fox RC	15.00	7.50
❑	81	Ron Northey	15.00	7.50
❑	82	Whitey Lockman	25.00	12.50
❑	83	Sheldon Jones	15.00	7.50
❑	84	Richie Ashburn	125.00	75.00
❑	85	Ken Heintzelman	15.00	7.50
❑	86	Stan Rojek	15.00	7.50
❑	87	Bill Werle RC	15.00	7.50
❑	88	Marty Marion	40.00	20.00
❑	89	George Munger	15.00	7.50
❑	90	Harry Brecheen	40.00	20.00
❑	91	Cass Michaels	15.00	7.50
❑	92	Hank Majeski	15.00	7.50
❑	93	Gene Bearden	40.00	20.00
❑	94	Lou Boudreau MG	60.00	35.00
❑	95	Aaron Robinson	15.00	7.50
❑	96	Virgil Trucks	25.00	12.50
❑	97	Maurice McDermott RC	15.00	7.50
❑	98	Ted Williams	1000.00	600.00
❑	99	Billy Goodman	25.00	12.50
❑	100	Vic Raschi	60.00	35.00
❑	101	Bobby Brown	60.00	35.00
❑	102	Billy Johnson	25.00	12.50
❑	103	Eddie Joost	15.00	7.50
❑	104	Sam Chapman	15.00	7.50
❑	105	Bob Dillinger	15.00	7.50
❑	106	Cliff Fannin	15.00	7.50
❑	107	Sam Dente RC	15.00	7.50
❑	108	Ray Scarborough	15.00	7.50
❑	109	Sid Gordon	15.00	7.50
❑	110	Tommy Holmes	25.00	12.50
❑	111	Walker Cooper	15.00	7.50
❑	112	Gil Hodges	125.00	75.00
❑	113	Gene Hermanski	15.00	7.50
❑	114	Wayne Terwilliger RC	15.00	7.50
❑	115	Roy Smalley	15.00	7.50
❑	116	Virgil Stallcup	15.00	7.50
❑	117	Bill Rigney	15.00	7.50
❑	118	Clint Hartung	15.00	7.50
❑	119	Dick Sisler	25.00	12.50
❑	120	John Thompson	15.00	7.50
❑	121	Andy Seminick	25.00	12.50
❑	122	Johnny Hopp	25.00	12.50
❑	123	Dino Restelli RC	15.00	7.50
❑	124	Clyde McCullough	15.00	7.50
❑	125	Del Rice RC	15.00	7.50
❑	126	Al Brazle	15.00	7.50
❑	127	Dave Philley	15.00	7.50
❑	128	Phil Masi	15.00	7.50
❑	129	Joe Gordon	25.00	12.50
❑	130	Dale Mitchell	25.00	12.50
❑	131	Steve Gromek	15.00	7.50
❑	132	Mickey Vernon	25.00	12.50
❑	133	Don Kolloway	15.00	7.50
❑	134	Paul Trout	15.00	7.50
❑	135	Pat Mullin	15.00	7.50
❑	136	Buddy Rosar	15.00	7.50
❑	137	Johnny Pesky	25.00	12.50
❑	138	Allie Reynolds	60.00	35.00
❑	139	Johnny Mize	80.00	50.00
❑	140	Pete Suder RC	15.00	7.50
❑	141	Joe Coleman RC	25.00	12.50
❑	142	Sherman Lollar RC	40.00	20.00
❑	143	Eddie Stewart	15.00	7.50
❑	144	Al Evans	15.00	7.50
❑	145	Jack Graham RC	15.00	7.50
❑	146	Floyd Baker	15.00	7.50
❑	147	Mike Garcia RC	40.00	20.00
❑	148	Early Wynn	80.00	50.00
❑	149	Bob Swift	15.00	7.50
❑	150	George Vico	15.00	7.50
❑	151	Fred Hutchinson	25.00	12.50
❑	152	Ellis Kinder RC	15.00	7.50
❑	153	Walt Masterson	15.00	7.50
❑	154	Gus Niarhos	15.00	7.50
❑	155	Frank Shea	25.00	12.50
❑	156	Fred Sanford	25.00	12.50
❑	157	Mike Guerra	15.00	7.50
❑	158	Paul Lehner	15.00	7.50
❑	159	Joe Tipton	15.00	7.50
❑	160	Mickey Harris	15.00	7.50
❑	161	Sherry Robertson RC	15.00	7.50
❑	162	Eddie Yost	25.00	12.50
❑	163	Earl Torgeson	15.00	7.50
❑	164	Sibby Sisti	15.00	7.50
❑	165	Bruce Edwards	15.00	7.50
❑	166	Joe Hatton	15.00	7.50
❑	167	Preacher Roe	60.00	35.00
❑	168	Bob Scheffing	15.00	7.50
❑	169	Hank Edwards	15.00	7.50
❑	170	Dutch Leonard	15.00	7.50
❑	171	Harry Gumbert	15.00	7.50
❑	172	Peanuts Lowrey	15.00	7.50
❑	173	Lloyd Merriman RC	15.00	7.50
❑	174	Hank Thompson RC	40.00	20.00
❑	175	Monte Kennedy	15.00	7.50
❑	176	Sylvester Donnelly	15.00	7.50
❑	177	Hank Borowy	15.00	7.50
❑	178	Ed Fitzgerald	15.00	7.50
❑	179	Chuck Diering RC	15.00	7.50
❑	180	Harry Walker	25.00	12.50
❑	181	Marino Pieretti	15.00	7.50
❑	182	Sam Zoldak	15.00	7.50
❑	183	Mickey Haefner	15.00	7.50
❑	184	Randy Gumpert	15.00	7.50
❑	185	Howie Judson RC	15.00	7.50
❑	186	Ken Keltner	25.00	12.50
❑	187	Lou Stringer	15.00	7.50
❑	188	Earl Johnson	15.00	7.50
❑	189	Owen Friend RC	15.00	7.50
❑	190	Ken Wood RC	15.00	7.50
❑	191	Dick Starr RC	15.00	7.50
❑	192	Bob Chipman	15.00	7.50
❑	193	Pete Reiser	40.00	20.00
❑	194	Billy Cox	60.00	35.00
❑	195	Phil Cavarretta	40.00	20.00
❑	196	Doyle Lade	15.00	7.50
❑	197	Johnny Wyrostek	15.00	7.50
❑	198	Danny Litwhiler	15.00	7.50
❑	199	Jack Kramer	15.00	7.50
❑	200	Kirby Higbe	25.00	12.50
❑	201	Pete Castiglione RC	15.00	7.50
❑	202	Cliff Chambers RC	15.00	7.50
❑	203	Danny Murtaugh	25.00	12.50
❑	204	Granny Hamner RC	40.00	20.00
❑	205	Mike Goliat RC	15.00	7.50
❑	206	Stan Lopata	25.00	12.50
❑	207	Max Lanier RC	15.00	7.50
❑	208	Jim Hearn	15.00	7.50
❑	209	Johnny Lindell	15.00	7.50
❑	210	Ted Gray	15.00	7.50
❑	211	Charlie Keller	40.00	20.00
❑	212	Jerry Priddy	15.00	7.50
❑	213	Carl Scheib	15.00	7.50
❑	214	Dick Fowler	15.00	7.50
❑	215	Ed Lopat	60.00	35.00
❑	216	Bob Porterfield	25.00	12.50
❑	217	Casey Stengel MG	125.00	75.00
❑	218	Cliff Mapes RC	25.00	12.50
❑	219	Hank Bauer RC	100.00	60.00
❑	220	Leo Durocher MG	60.00	35.00
❑	221	Don Mueller RC	40.00	20.00
❑	222	Bobby Morgan RC	15.00	7.50
❑	223	Jim Russell	15.00	7.50
❑	224	Jack Banta RC	15.00	7.50
❑	225	Eddie Sawyer MG RC	25.00	12.50
❑	226	Jim Konstanty RC	60.00	35.00
❑	227	Bob Miller RC	25.00	12.50
❑	228	Bill Nicholson	25.00	12.50
❑	229	Frankie Frisch MG	60.00	35.00
❑	230	Bill Serena RC	15.00	7.50
❑	231	Preston Ward RC	15.00	7.50
❑	232	Al Rosen RC	60.00	35.00
❑	233	Allie Clark	15.00	7.50
❑	234	Bobby Shantz RC	60.00	35.00
❑	235	Harold Gilbert RC	15.00	7.50
❑	236	Bob Cain RC	15.00	7.50
❑	237	Bill Salkeld	15.00	7.50
❑	238	Nippy Jones RC	15.00	7.50
❑	239	Bill Howerton RC	15.00	7.50
❑	240	Eddie Lake	15.00	7.50
❑	241	Neil Berry RC	15.00	7.50
❑	242	Dick Kryhoski	15.00	7.50
❑	243	Johnny Groth RC	15.00	7.50
❑	244	Dale Coogan RC	15.00	7.50
❑	245	Al Papai RC	15.00	7.50
❑	246	Walt Dropo RC	40.00	20.00

❑ 247 Irv Noren RC 25.00 12.50
❑ 248 Sam Jethroe RC 60.00 35.00
❑ 249 Snuffy Stirnweiss 25.00 12.50
❑ 250 Ray Coleman RC 15.00 7.50
❑ 251 Les Moss RC 15.00 7.50
❑ 252 Billy DeMars RC 60.00 35.00
❑ 252A Billy DeMars NC

1951 Bowman

❑ COMPLETE SET (324) 20000.00 15000.00
❑ COMMON CARD (1-252) 20.00 10.00
❑ COMMON CARD (253-324) 50.00 30.00
❑ WRAPPER (1-CENT) 200.00 150.00
❑ WRAPPER (5-CENT) 250.00 200.00
❑ 1 Whitey Ford RC 2500.00 1500.00
❑ 2 Yogi Berra 400.00 250.00
❑ 3 Robin Roberts 100.00 60.00
❑ 4 Del Ennis 25.00 12.50
❑ 5 Dale Mitchell 25.00 12.50
❑ 6 Don Newcombe 60.00 35.00
❑ 7 Gil Hodges 125.00 75.00
❑ 8 Paul Lehner 20.00 10.00
❑ 9 Sam Chapman 20.00 10.00
❑ 10 Red Schoendienst 60.00 35.00
❑ 11 George Munger 20.00 10.00
❑ 12 Hank Majeski 20.00 10.00
❑ 13 Eddie Stanky 25.00 12.50
❑ 14 Alvin Dark 40.00 20.00
❑ 15 Johnny Pesky 25.00 12.50
❑ 16 Maurice McDermott 20.00 10.00
❑ 17 Pete Castiglione 20.00 10.00
❑ 18 Gil Coan 20.00 10.00
❑ 19 Sid Gordon 20.00 10.00
❑ 20 Del Crandall UER 25.00 12.50
❑ 21 Snuffy Stirnweiss 25.00 12.50
❑ 22 Hank Sauer 25.00 12.50
❑ 23 Hoot Evers 20.00 10.00
❑ 24 Ewell Blackwell 40.00 20.00
❑ 25 Vic Raschi 60.00 35.00
❑ 26 Phil Rizzuto 150.00 90.00
❑ 27 Jim Konstanty 25.00 12.50
❑ 28 Eddie Waitkus 20.00 10.00
❑ 29 Allie Clark 20.00 10.00
❑ 30 Bob Feller 125.00 75.00
❑ 31 Roy Campanella 300.00 175.00
❑ 32 Duke Snider 250.00 150.00
❑ 33 Bob Hooper RC 20.00 10.00
❑ 34 Marty Marion MG 40.00 20.00
❑ 35 Al Zarilla 20.00 10.00
❑ 36 Joe Dobson 20.00 10.00
❑ 37 Whitey Lockman 40.00 20.00
❑ 38 Al Evans 20.00 10.00
❑ 39 Ray Scarborough 20.00 10.00
❑ 40 Gus Bell RC 60.00 35.00
❑ 41 Eddie Yost 25.00 12.50
❑ 42 Vern Bickford 20.00 10.00
❑ 43 Billy DeMars 20.00 10.00
❑ 44 Roy Smalley 20.00 10.00
❑ 45 Art Houtteman 20.00 10.00
❑ 46 George Kell UER 60.00 35.00
❑ 47 Grady Hatton 20.00 10.00
❑ 48 Ken Raffensberger 20.00 10.00
❑ 49 Jerry Coleman 25.00 12.50
❑ 50 Johnny Mize 80.00 50.00
❑ 51 Andy Seminick 20.00 10.00
❑ 52 Dick Sisler 40.00 20.00
❑ 53 Bob Lemon 60.00 35.00
❑ 54 Ray Boone RC 40.00 20.00
❑ 55 Gene Hermanski 20.00 10.00
❑ 56 Ralph Branca 60.00 35.00
❑ 57 Alex Kellner 20.00 10.00
❑ 58 Enos Slaughter 60.00 35.00
❑ 59 Randy Gumpert 20.00 10.00
❑ 60 Chico Carrasquel RC 60.00 35.00
❑ 61 Jim Hearn 25.00 12.50
❑ 62 Lou Boudreau MG 60.00 35.00
❑ 63 Bob Dillinger 20.00 10.00
❑ 64 Bill Werle 20.00 10.00
❑ 65 Mickey Vernon 40.00 20.00
❑ 66 Bob Elliott 25.00 12.50
❑ 67 Roy Sievers 25.00 12.50
❑ 68 Dick Kokos 20.00 10.00
❑ 69 Johnny Schmitz 20.00 10.00
❑ 70 Ron Northey 20.00 10.00
❑ 71 Jerry Priddy 20.00 10.00
❑ 72 Lloyd Merriman 20.00 10.00
❑ 73 Tommy Byrne RC 20.00 10.00
❑ 74 Billy Johnson 25.00 12.50
❑ 75 Russ Meyer RC 25.00 12.50
❑ 76 Stan Lopata 25.00 12.50
❑ 77 Mike Goliat 20.00 10.00
❑ 78 Early Wynn 60.00 35.00
❑ 79 Jim Hegan 25.00 12.50
❑ 80 Pee Wee Reese 200.00 125.00
❑ 81 Carl Furillo 60.00 35.00
❑ 82 Joe Tipton 20.00 10.00
❑ 83 Carl Scheib 20.00 10.00
❑ 84 Barney McCosky 20.00 10.00
❑ 85 Eddie Kazak 20.00 10.00
❑ 86 Harry Brecheen 25.00 12.50
❑ 87 Floyd Baker 20.00 10.00
❑ 88 Eddie Robinson 20.00 10.00
❑ 89 Hank Thompson 25.00 12.50
❑ 90 Dave Koslo 20.00 10.00
❑ 91 Clyde Vollmer 20.00 10.00
❑ 92 Vern Stephens 25.00 12.50
❑ 93 Danny O'Connell RC 20.00 10.00
❑ 94 Clyde McCullough 20.00 10.00
❑ 95 Sherry Robertson 20.00 10.00
❑ 96 Sandy Consuegra RC 20.00 10.00
❑ 97 Bob Kuzava 20.00 10.00
❑ 98 Willard Marshall 20.00 10.00
❑ 99 Earl Torgeson 20.00 10.00
❑ 100 Sherm Lollar 25.00 12.50
❑ 101 Owen Friend 20.00 10.00
❑ 102 Dutch Leonard 20.00 10.00
❑ 103 Andy Pafko 40.00 20.00
❑ 104 Virgil Trucks 25.00 12.50
❑ 105 Don Kolloway 20.00 10.00
❑ 106 Pat Mullin 20.00 10.00
❑ 107 Johnny Wyrostek 20.00 10.00
❑ 108 Virgil Stallcup 20.00 10.00
❑ 109 Allie Reynolds 60.00 35.00
❑ 110 Bobby Brown 40.00 20.00
❑ 111 Curt Simmons 25.00 12.50
❑ 112 Willie Jones 20.00 10.00
❑ 113 Bill Nicholson 20.00 10.00
❑ 114 Sam Zoldak 20.00 10.00
❑ 115 Steve Gromek 20.00 10.00
❑ 116 Bruce Edwards 20.00 10.00
❑ 117 Eddie Miksis RC 20.00 10.00
❑ 118 Preacher Roe 60.00 35.00
❑ 119 Eddie Joost 20.00 10.00
❑ 120 Joe Coleman 25.00 12.50
❑ 121 Gerry Staley RC 20.00 10.00
❑ 122 Joe Garagiola RC 100.00 60.00
❑ 123 Howie Judson 20.00 10.00
❑ 124 Gus Niarhos 20.00 10.00
❑ 125 Bill Rigney 25.00 12.50
❑ 126 Bobby Thomson 60.00 35.00
❑ 127 Sal Maglie RC 60.00 35.00
❑ 128 Ellis Kinder 20.00 10.00
❑ 129 Matt Batts 20.00 10.00
❑ 130 Tom Saffell RC 20.00 10.00
❑ 131 Cliff Chambers 20.00 10.00
❑ 132 Cass Michaels 20.00 10.00
❑ 133 Sam Dente 20.00 10.00
❑ 134 Warren Spahn 150.00 90.00
❑ 135 Walker Cooper 20.00 10.00
❑ 136 Ray Coleman 20.00 10.00
❑ 137 Dick Starr 20.00 10.00
❑ 138 Phil Cavarretta 25.00 12.50
❑ 139 Doyle Lade 20.00 10.00
❑ 140 Eddie Lake 20.00 10.00
❑ 141 Fred Hutchinson 25.00 12.50
❑ 142 Aaron Robinson 20.00 10.00
❑ 143 Ted Kluszewski 80.00 50.00
❑ 144 Herman Wehmeier 20.00 10.00
❑ 145 Fred Sanford 25.00 12.50
❑ 146 Johnny Hopp 25.00 12.50
❑ 147 Ken Heintzelman 20.00 10.00
❑ 148 Granny Hamner 20.00 10.00
❑ 149 Bubba Church RC 20.00 10.00
❑ 150 Mike Garcia 25.00 12.50
❑ 151 Larry Doby 60.00 35.00
❑ 152 Cal Abrams RC 20.00 10.00
❑ 153 Rex Barney 25.00 12.50
❑ 154 Pete Suder 20.00 10.00
❑ 155 Lou Brissie 20.00 10.00
❑ 156 Del Rice 20.00 10.00
❑ 157 Al Brazle 20.00 10.00
❑ 158 Chuck Diering 20.00 10.00
❑ 159 Eddie Stewart 20.00 10.00
❑ 160 Phil Masi 20.00 10.00
❑ 161 Wes Westrum RC 20.00 10.00
❑ 162 Larry Jansen 25.00 12.50
❑ 163 Monte Kennedy 20.00 10.00
❑ 164 Bill Wight 20.00 10.00
❑ 165 Ted Williams UER 800.00 500.00
❑ 166 Stan Rojek 20.00 10.00
❑ 167 Murry Dickson 20.00 10.00
❑ 168 Sam Mele 20.00 10.00
❑ 169 Sid Hudson 20.00 10.00
❑ 170 Sibby Sisti 20.00 10.00
❑ 171 Buddy Kerr 20.00 10.00
❑ 172 Ned Garver 20.00 10.00
❑ 173 Hank Arft 20.00 10.00
❑ 174 Mickey Owen 25.00 12.50
❑ 175 Wayne Terwilliger 20.00 10.00
❑ 176 Vic Wertz 40.00 20.00
❑ 177 Charlie Keller 25.00 12.50
❑ 178 Ted Gray 20.00 10.00
❑ 179 Danny Litwhiler 20.00 10.00
❑ 180 Howie Fox 20.00 10.00
❑ 181 Casey Stengel MG 80.00 50.00
❑ 182 Tom Ferrick RC 20.00 10.00
❑ 183 Hank Bauer 60.00 35.00
❑ 184 Eddie Sawyer MG 40.00 20.00
❑ 185 Jimmy Bloodworth 20.00 10.00
❑ 186 Richie Ashburn 100.00 60.00
❑ 187 Al Rosen 40.00 20.00
❑ 188 Bobby Avila RC 25.00 12.50
❑ 189 Erv Palica RC 20.00 10.00
❑ 190 Joe Hatten 20.00 10.00
❑ 191 Billy Hitchcock RC 20.00 10.00
❑ 192 Hank Wyse RC 20.00 10.00
❑ 193 Ted Wilks 20.00 10.00
❑ 194 Peanuts Lowrey 20.00 10.00
❑ 195 Paul Richards MG 25.00 12.50
❑ 196 Billy Pierce RC 60.00 35.00
❑ 197 Bob Cain 20.00 10.00
❑ 198 Monte Irvin RC 125.00 75.00
❑ 199 Sheldon Jones 20.00 10.00
❑ 200 Jack Kramer 20.00 10.00
❑ 201 Steve O'Neill MG RC 20.00 10.00
❑ 202 Mike Guerra 20.00 10.00
❑ 203 Vern Law RC 60.00 35.00
❑ 204 Vic Lombardi RC 20.00 10.00
❑ 205 Mickey Grasso RC 20.00 10.00
❑ 206 Conrado Marrero RC 20.00 10.00
❑ 207 Billy Southworth MG RC 20.00 10.00
❑ 208 Blix Donnelly 20.00 10.00
❑ 209 Ken Wood 20.00 10.00
❑ 210 Les Moss 20.00 10.00
❑ 211 Hal Jeffcoat RC 20.00 10.00
❑ 212 Bob Rush 20.00 10.00
❑ 213 Neil Berry 20.00 10.00
❑ 214 Bob Swift 20.00 10.00
❑ 215 Ken Peterson 20.00 10.00
❑ 216 Connie Ryan RC 20.00 10.00
❑ 217 Joe Page 25.00 12.50
❑ 218 Ed Lopat 60.00 35.00
❑ 219 Gene Woodling RC 60.00 35.00
❑ 220 Bob Miller 20.00 10.00
❑ 221 Dick Whitman RC 20.00 10.00
❑ 222 Thurman Tucker RC 20.00 10.00
❑ 223 Johnny VanderMeer 40.00 20.00
❑ 224 Billy Cox 25.00 12.50
❑ 225 Dan Bankhead RC 40.00 20.00

226	Jimmie Dykes MG	20.00	10.00
227	Bobby Shantz UER	25.00	12.50
228	Cloyd Boyer RC	25.00	12.50
229	Bill Howerton	20.00	10.00
230	Max Lanier	20.00	10.00
231	Luis Aloma RC	20.00	10.00
232	Nellie Fox RC	250.00	150.00
233	Leo Durocher MG	60.00	35.00
234	Clint Hartung	25.00	12.50
235	Jack Lohrke	20.00	10.00
236	Buddy Rosar	20.00	10.00
237	Billy Goodman	25.00	12.50
238	Pete Reiser	40.00	20.00
239	Bill MacDonald RC	20.00	10.00
240	Joe Haynes	20.00	10.00
241	Irv Noren	25.00	12.50
242	Sam Jethroe	25.00	12.50
243	Johnny Antonelli	25.00	12.50
244	Cliff Fannin	20.00	10.00
245	John Berardino RC	60.00	35.00
246	Bill Serena	20.00	10.00
247	Bob Ramazzotti RC	20.00	10.00
248	Johnny Klippstein RC	20.00	10.00
249	Johnny Groth	20.00	10.00
250	Hank Borowy	20.00	10.00
251	Willard Ramsdell RC	20.00	10.00
252	Dixie Howell RC	20.00	10.00
253	Mickey Mantle RC	8000.00	5000.00
254	Jackie Jensen RC	100.00	60.00
255	Milo Candini RC	50.00	30.00
256	Ken Silvestri RC	50.00	30.00
257	Birdie Tebbetts RC	60.00	35.00
258	Luke Easter RC	60.00	35.00
259	Chuck Dressen MG	60.00	35.00
260	Carl Erskine RC	100.00	60.00
261	Wally Moses	60.00	35.00
262	Gus Zernial	60.00	35.00
263	Howie Pollet	60.00	35.00
264	Don Richmond RC	50.00	30.00
265	Steve Bilko RC	50.00	30.00
266	Harry Dorish RC	50.00	30.00
267	Ken Holcombe RC	50.00	30.00
268	Don Mueller	60.00	35.00
269	Ray Noble RC	50.00	30.00
270	Willard Nixon RC	50.00	30.00
271	Tommy Wright RC	50.00	30.00
272	Billy Meyer MG RC	50.00	30.00
273	Danny Murtaugh	60.00	35.00
274	George Metkovich RC	50.00	30.00
275	Bucky Harris MG	80.00	50.00
276	Frank Quinn RC	50.00	30.00
277	Roy Hartsfield RC	50.00	30.00
278	Norman Roy RC	50.00	30.00
279	Jim Delsing RC	50.00	30.00
280	Frank Overmire	50.00	30.00
281	Al Widmar RC	50.00	30.00
282	Frankie Frisch MG	100.00	60.00
283	Walt Dubiel RC	50.00	30.00
284	Gene Bearden	60.00	35.00
285	Johnny Lipon RC	50.00	30.00
286	Bob Usher RC	50.00	30.00
287	Jim Blackburn	50.00	30.00
288	Bobby Adams	50.00	30.00
289	Cliff Mapes	60.00	35.00
290	Bill Dickey CO	150.00	90.00
291	Tommy Henrich CO	80.00	50.00
292	Eddie Pellagrini	50.00	30.00
293	Ken Johnson RC	50.00	30.00
294	Jocko Thompson	50.00	30.00
295	Al Lopez MG RC	125.00	75.00
296	Bob Kennedy RC	60.00	35.00
297	Dave Philley	50.00	30.00
298	Joe Astroth RC	50.00	30.00
299	Clyde King RC	50.00	30.00
300	Hal Rice RC	50.00	30.00
301	Tommy Glaviano RC	50.00	30.00
302	Jim Busby RC	50.00	30.00
303	Marv Rotblatt RC	50.00	30.00
304	Al Gettell RC	50.00	30.00
305	Willie Mays RC	2500.00	1800.00
306	Jimmy Piersall RC	125.00	75.00
307	Walt Masterson	50.00	30.00
308	Ted Beard RC	50.00	30.00
309	Mel Queen RC	50.00	30.00
310	Erv Dusak RC	50.00	30.00
311	Mickey Harris	50.00	30.00
312	Gene Mauch RC	60.00	35.00
313	Ray Mueller RC	50.00	30.00
314	Johnny Sain	80.00	50.00
315	Zack Taylor MG	50.00	30.00
316	Duane Pillette RC	50.00	30.00
317	Smoky Burgess RC	80.00	50.00
318	Warren Hacker RC	50.00	30.00
319	Red Rolfe MG	60.00	35.00
320	Hal White RC	50.00	30.00
321	Earl Johnson	50.00	30.00
322	Luke Sewell MG	60.00	35.00
323	Joe Adcock RC	80.00	50.00
324	Johnny Pramesa RC	125.00	75.00

1952 Bowman

	COMPLETE SET (252)	8500.00	5500.00
	COMMON CARD (1-216)	15.00	7.50
	COMMON CARD (217-252)	60.00	35.00
	WRAPPER (1-CENT)	200.00	150.00
	WRAPPER (5-CENT)	100.00	75.00
1	Yogi Berra	600.00	350.00
2	Bobby Thomson	40.00	20.00
3	Fred Hutchinson	25.00	12.50
4	Robin Roberts	80.00	50.00
5	Minnie Minoso RC	125.00	75.00
6	Virgil Stallcup	15.00	7.50
7	Mike Garcia	25.00	12.50
8	Pee Wee Reese	150.00	90.00
9	Vern Stephens	25.00	12.50
10	Bob Hooper	15.00	7.50
11	Ralph Kiner	60.00	35.00
12	Max Surkont RC	15.00	7.50
13	Cliff Mapes	15.00	7.50
14	Cliff Chambers	15.00	7.50
15	Sam Mele	15.00	7.50
16	Turk Lown RC	15.00	7.50
17	Ed Lopat	40.00	20.00
18	Don Mueller	25.00	12.50
19	Bob Cain	15.00	7.50
20	Willie Jones	15.00	7.50
21	Nellie Fox	100.00	60.00
22	Willard Ramsdell	15.00	7.50
23	Bob Lemon	60.00	35.00
24	Carl Furillo	40.00	20.00
25	Mickey McDermott	15.00	7.50
26	Eddie Joost	15.00	7.50
27	Joe Garagiola	40.00	20.00
28	Roy Hartsfield	15.00	7.50
29	Ned Garver	15.00	7.50
30	Red Schoendienst	60.00	35.00
31	Eddie Yost	25.00	12.50
32	Eddie Miksis	15.00	7.50
33	Gil McDougald RC	80.00	50.00
34	Alvin Dark	25.00	12.50
35	Granny Hamner	15.00	7.50
36	Cass Michaels	15.00	7.50
37	Vic Raschi	25.00	12.50
38	Whitey Lockman	25.00	12.50
39	Vic Wertz	25.00	12.50
40	Bubba Church	15.00	7.50
41	Chico Carrasquel	25.00	12.50
42	Johnny Wyrostek	15.00	7.50
43	Bob Feller	150.00	90.00
44	Roy Campanella	250.00	150.00
45	Johnny Pesky	25.00	12.50
46	Carl Scheib	15.00	7.50
47	Pete Castiglione	15.00	7.50
48	Vern Bickford	15.00	7.50
49	Jim Hearn	15.00	7.50
50	Gerry Staley	15.00	7.50
51	Gil Coan	15.00	7.50
52	Phil Rizzuto	150.00	90.00
53	Richie Ashburn	125.00	75.00
54	Billy Pierce	25.00	12.50
55	Ken Raffensberger	15.00	7.50
56	Clyde King	25.00	12.50
57	Clyde Vollmer	15.00	7.50
58	Hank Majeski	15.00	7.50
59	Murry Dickson	15.00	7.50
60	Sid Gordon	15.00	7.50
61	Tommy Byrne	15.00	7.50
62	Joe Presko RC	15.00	7.50
63	Irv Noren	15.00	7.50
64	Roy Smalley	15.00	7.50
65	Hank Bauer	40.00	20.00
66	Sal Maglie	25.00	12.50
67	Johnny Groth	15.00	7.50
68	Jim Busby	15.00	7.50
69	Joe Adcock	25.00	12.50
70	Carl Erskine	40.00	20.00
71	Vern Law	25.00	12.50
72	Earl Torgeson	15.00	7.50
73	Jerry Coleman	25.00	12.50
74	Wes Westrum	25.00	12.50
75	George Kell	60.00	35.00
76	Del Ennis	25.00	12.50
77	Eddie Robinson	15.00	7.50
78	Lloyd Merriman	15.00	7.50
79	Lou Brissie	15.00	7.50
80	Gil Hodges	100.00	60.00
81	Billy Goodman	25.00	12.50
82	Gus Zernial	25.00	12.50
83	Howie Pollet	15.00	7.50
84	Sam Jethroe	25.00	12.50
85	Marty Marion CO	25.00	12.50
86	Cal Abrams	15.00	7.50
87	Mickey Vernon	25.00	12.50
88	Bruce Edwards	15.00	7.50
89	Billy Hitchcock	15.00	7.50
90	Larry Jansen	25.00	12.50
91	Don Kolloway	15.00	7.50
92	Eddie Waitkus	25.00	12.50
93	Paul Richards MG	25.00	12.50
94	Luke Sewell MG	25.00	12.50
95	Luke Easter	25.00	12.50
96	Ralph Branca	25.00	12.50
97	Willard Marshall	15.00	7.50
98	Jimmie Dykes MG	25.00	12.50
99	Clyde McCullough	15.00	7.50
100	Sibby Sisti	15.00	7.50
101	Mickey Mantle	2500.00	1500.00
102	Peanuts Lowrey	15.00	7.50
103	Joe Haynes	15.00	7.50
104	Hal Jeffcoat	15.00	7.50
105	Bobby Brown	25.00	12.50
106	Randy Gumpert	15.00	7.50
107	Del Rice	15.00	7.50
108	George Metkovich	15.00	7.50
109	Tom Morgan RC	15.00	7.50
110	Max Lanier	15.00	7.50
111	Hoot Evers	15.00	7.50
112	Smoky Burgess	25.00	12.50
113	Al Zarilla	15.00	7.50
114	Frank Hiller RC	15.00	7.50
115	Larry Doby	60.00	35.00
116	Duke Snider	200.00	125.00
117	Bill Wight	15.00	7.50
118	Ray Murray RC	15.00	7.50
119	Bill Howerton	15.00	7.50
120	Chet Nichols RC	15.00	7.50
121	Al Corwin RC	15.00	7.50
122	Billy Johnson	15.00	7.50
123	Sid Hudson	15.00	7.50
124	Birdie Tebbetts	15.00	7.50
125	Howie Fox	15.00	7.50
126	Phil Cavarretta	25.00	12.50
127	Dick Sisler	15.00	7.50
128	Don Newcombe	60.00	35.00
129	Gus Niarhos	15.00	7.50
130	Allie Clark	15.00	7.50
131	Bob Swift	15.00	7.50
132	Dave Cole RC	15.00	7.50
133	Dick Kryhoski	15.00	7.50
134	Al Brazle	15.00	7.50

❑ 135	Mickey Harris	15.00	7.50
❑ 136	Gene Hermanski	15.00	7.50
❑ 137	Stan Rojek	15.00	7.50
❑ 138	Ted Wilks	15.00	7.50
❑ 139	Jerry Priddy	15.00	7.50
❑ 140	Ray Scarborough	15.00	7.50
❑ 141	Hank Edwards	15.00	7.50
❑ 142	Early Wynn	60.00	35.00
❑ 143	Sandy Consuegra	15.00	7.50
❑ 144	Joe Hatton	15.00	7.50
❑ 145	Johnny Mize	60.00	35.00
❑ 146	Leo Durocher MG	60.00	35.00
❑ 147	Marlin Stuart RC	15.00	7.50
❑ 148	Ken Heintzelman	15.00	7.50
❑ 149	Howie Judson	15.00	7.50
❑ 150	Herman Wehmeier	15.00	7.50
❑ 151	Al Rosen	25.00	12.50
❑ 152	Billy Cox	15.00	7.50
❑ 153	Fred Hatfield RC	15.00	7.50
❑ 154	Ferris Fain	25.00	12.50
❑ 155	Billy Meyer MG	15.00	7.50
❑ 156	Warren Spahn	125.00	75.00
❑ 157	Jim Delsing	15.00	7.50
❑ 158	Bucky Harris MG	40.00	20.00
❑ 159	Dutch Leonard	15.00	7.50
❑ 160	Eddie Stanky	25.00	12.50
❑ 161	Jackie Jensen	40.00	20.00
❑ 162	Monte Irvin	60.00	35.00
❑ 163	Johnny Lipon	15.00	7.50
❑ 164	Connie Ryan	15.00	7.50
❑ 165	Saul Rogovin RC	15.00	7.50
❑ 166	Bobby Adams	15.00	7.50
❑ 167	Bobby Avila	25.00	12.50
❑ 168	Preacher Roe	25.00	12.50
❑ 169	Walt Dropo	25.00	12.50
❑ 170	Joe Astroth	15.00	7.50
❑ 171	Mel Queen	15.00	7.50
❑ 172	Ebba St.Claire RC	15.00	7.50
❑ 173	Gene Bearden	15.00	7.50
❑ 174	Mickey Grasso	15.00	7.50
❑ 175	Randy Jackson RC	15.00	7.50
❑ 176	Harry Brecheen	25.00	12.50
❑ 177	Gene Woodling	25.00	12.50
❑ 178	Dave Williams RC	25.00	12.50
❑ 179	Pete Suder	15.00	7.50
❑ 180	Ed Fitzgerald	15.00	7.50
❑ 181	Joe Collins RC	25.00	12.50
❑ 182	Dave Koslo	15.00	7.50
❑ 183	Pat Mullin	15.00	7.50
❑ 184	Curt Simmons	25.00	12.50
❑ 185	Eddie Stewart	15.00	7.50
❑ 186	Frank Smith RC	15.00	7.50
❑ 187	Jim Hegan	25.00	12.50
❑ 188	Chuck Dressen MG	25.00	12.50
❑ 189	Jimmy Piersall	25.00	12.50
❑ 190	Dick Fowler	15.00	7.50
❑ 191	Bob Friend RC	40.00	20.00
❑ 192	John Cusick RC	15.00	7.50
❑ 193	Bobby Young RC	15.00	7.50
❑ 194	Bob Porterfield	15.00	7.50
❑ 195	Frank Baumholtz	15.00	7.50
❑ 196	Stan Musial	500.00	300.00
❑ 197	Charlie Silvera RC	15.00	7.50
❑ 198	Chuck Diering	15.00	7.50
❑ 199	Ted Gray	15.00	7.50
❑ 200	Ken Silvestri	15.00	7.50
❑ 201	Ray Coleman	15.00	7.50
❑ 202	Harry Perkowski RC	15.00	7.50
❑ 203	Steve Gromek	15.00	7.50
❑ 204	Andy Pafko	25.00	12.50
❑ 205	Walt Masterson	15.00	7.50
❑ 206	Elmer Valo	15.00	7.50
❑ 207	George Strickland RC	15.00	7.50
❑ 208	Walker Cooper	15.00	7.50
❑ 209	Dick Littlefield RC	15.00	7.50
❑ 210	Archie Wilson RC	15.00	7.50
❑ 211	Paul Minner RC	15.00	7.50
❑ 212	Solly Hemus RC	15.00	7.50
❑ 213	Monte Kennedy	15.00	7.50
❑ 214	Ray Boone	15.00	7.50
❑ 215	Sheldon Jones	15.00	7.50
❑ 216	Matt Batts	15.00	7.50
❑ 217	Casey Stengel MG	150.00	90.00
❑ 218	Willie Mays	1500.00	900.00
❑ 219	Neil Berry	60.00	35.00
❑ 220	Russ Meyer	60.00	35.00
❑ 221	Lou Kretlow RC	60.00	35.00
❑ 222	Dixie Howell	60.00	35.00
❑ 223	Harry Simpson RC	60.00	35.00
❑ 224	Johnny Schmitz	60.00	35.00
❑ 225	Del Wilber RC	60.00	35.00
❑ 226	Alex Kellner	60.00	35.00
❑ 227	Clyde Sukeforth CO RC	60.00	35.00
❑ 228	Bob Chipman	60.00	35.00
❑ 229	Hank Arft	60.00	35.00
❑ 230	Frank Shea	60.00	35.00
❑ 231	Dee Fondy RC	60.00	35.00
❑ 232	Enos Slaughter	100.00	60.00
❑ 233	Bob Kuzava	60.00	35.00
❑ 234	Fred Fitzsimmons CO	60.00	35.00
❑ 235	Steve Souchock RC	60.00	35.00
❑ 236	Tommy Brown	60.00	35.00
❑ 237	Sherm Lollar	60.00	35.00
❑ 238	Roy McMillan RC	60.00	35.00
❑ 239	Dale Mitchell	60.00	35.00
❑ 240	Billy Loes RC	60.00	35.00
❑ 241	Mel Parnell	60.00	35.00
❑ 242	Everett Kell RC	60.00	35.00
❑ 243	George Munger	60.00	35.00
❑ 244	Lew Burdette RC	80.00	50.00
❑ 245	George Schmees RC	60.00	35.00
❑ 246	Jerry Snyder RC	60.00	35.00
❑ 247	Johnny Pramesa	60.00	35.00
❑ 248	Bill Werle Full Name	60.00	35.00
❑ 248A	Bill Werle No W	60.00	35.00
❑ 249	Hank Thompson	60.00	35.00
❑ 250	Ike Delock RC	60.00	35.00
❑ 251	Jack Lohrke	60.00	35.00
❑ 252	Frank Crosetti CO	125.00	75.00

1953 Bowman Color

❑	COMPLETE SET (160)	15000.00	9000.00
❑	COMMON CARD (1-112)	40.00	20.00
❑	COMMON CARD (113-128)	80.00	50.00
❑	COMMON CARD (129-160)	75.00	45.00
❑	WRAPPER (1-CENT)	400.00	300.00
❑	WRAPPER (5-CENT)	300.00	250.00
❑ 1	Davey Williams	175.00	100.00
❑ 2	Vic Wertz	50.00	30.00
❑ 3	Sam Jethroe	50.00	30.00
❑ 4	Art Houtteman	40.00	20.00
❑ 5	Sid Gordon	40.00	20.00
❑ 6	Joe Ginsberg	40.00	20.00
❑ 7	Harry Chiti RC	40.00	20.00
❑ 8	Al Rosen	50.00	30.00
❑ 9	Phil Rizzuto	225.00	150.00
❑ 10	Richie Ashburn	150.00	90.00
❑ 11	Bobby Shantz	50.00	30.00
❑ 12	Carl Erskine	60.00	35.00
❑ 13	Gus Zernial	50.00	30.00
❑ 14	Billy Loes	50.00	30.00
❑ 15	Jim Busby	40.00	20.00
❑ 16	Bob Friend	50.00	30.00
❑ 17	Gerry Staley	40.00	20.00
❑ 18	Nellie Fox	150.00	90.00
❑ 19	Alvin Dark	50.00	30.00
❑ 20	Don Lenhardt	40.00	20.00
❑ 21	Joe Garagiola	60.00	35.00
❑ 22	Bob Porterfield	40.00	20.00
❑ 23	Herman Wehmeier	40.00	20.00
❑ 24	Jackie Jensen	60.00	35.00
❑ 25	Hoot Evers	40.00	20.00
❑ 26	Roy McMillan	50.00	30.00
❑ 27	Vic Raschi	60.00	35.00
❑ 28	Smoky Burgess	50.00	30.00
❑ 29	Bobby Avila	50.00	30.00
❑ 30	Phil Cavarretta	50.00	30.00
❑ 31	Jimmy Dykes MG	50.00	30.00
❑ 32	Stan Musial	600.00	350.00
❑ 33	Pee Wee Reese	1000.00	500.00
❑ 34	Gil Coan	40.00	20.00
❑ 35	Maurice McDermott	40.00	20.00
❑ 36	Minnie Minoso	80.00	50.00
❑ 37	Jim Wilson	40.00	20.00
❑ 38	Harry Byrd RC	40.00	20.00
❑ 39	Paul Richards MG	50.00	30.00
❑ 40	Larry Doby	100.00	60.00
❑ 41	Sammy White	40.00	20.00
❑ 42	Tommy Brown	40.00	20.00
❑ 43	Mike Garcia	50.00	30.00
❑ 44	Bauer/Berra/Mantle	800.00	500.00
❑ 45	Walt Dropo	50.00	30.00
❑ 46	Roy Campanella	350.00	200.00
❑ 47	Ned Garver	40.00	20.00
❑ 48	Hank Sauer	50.00	30.00
❑ 49	Eddie Stanky MG	50.00	30.00
❑ 50	Lou Kretlow	40.00	20.00
❑ 51	Monte Irvin	80.00	50.00
❑ 52	Marty Marion MG	50.00	30.00
❑ 53	Del Rice	40.00	20.00
❑ 54	Chico Carrasquel	40.00	20.00
❑ 55	Leo Durocher MG	80.00	50.00
❑ 56	Bob Cain	40.00	20.00
❑ 57	Lou Boudreau MG	80.00	50.00
❑ 58	Willard Marshall	40.00	20.00
❑ 59	Mickey Mantle	2000.00	1200.00
❑ 60	Granny Hamner	40.00	20.00
❑ 61	George Kell	80.00	50.00
❑ 62	Ted Kluszewski	100.00	60.00
❑ 63	Gil McDougald	80.00	50.00
❑ 64	Curt Simmons	50.00	30.00
❑ 65	Robin Roberts	125.00	75.00
❑ 66	Mel Parnell	50.00	30.00
❑ 67	Mel Clark RC	40.00	20.00
❑ 68	Allie Reynolds	60.00	35.00
❑ 69	Charlie Grimm MG	50.00	30.00
❑ 70	Clint Courtney RC	40.00	20.00
❑ 71	Paul Minner	40.00	20.00
❑ 72	Ted Gray	40.00	20.00
❑ 73	Billy Pierce	50.00	30.00
❑ 74	Don Mueller	50.00	30.00
❑ 75	Saul Rogovin	40.00	20.00
❑ 76	Jim Hearn	40.00	20.00
❑ 77	Mickey Grasso	40.00	20.00
❑ 78	Carl Furillo	60.00	35.00
❑ 79	Ray Boone	50.00	30.00
❑ 80	Ralph Kiner	100.00	60.00
❑ 81	Enos Slaughter	100.00	60.00
❑ 82	Joe Astroth	40.00	20.00
❑ 83	Jack Daniels RC	40.00	20.00
❑ 84	Hank Bauer	60.00	35.00
❑ 85	Solly Hemus	40.00	20.00
❑ 86	Harry Simpson	40.00	20.00
❑ 87	Harry Perkowski	40.00	20.00
❑ 88	Joe Dobson	40.00	20.00
❑ 89	Sandy Consuegra	40.00	20.00
❑ 90	Joe Nuxhall	50.00	30.00
❑ 91	Steve Souchock	40.00	20.00
❑ 92	Gil Hodges	300.00	175.00
❑ 93	P.Rizzuto/B.Martin	300.00	175.00
❑ 94	Bob Addis	40.00	20.00
❑ 95	Wally Moses CO	50.00	30.00
❑ 96	Sal Maglie	50.00	30.00
❑ 97	Eddie Mathews	350.00	200.00
❑ 98	Hector Rodriguez RC	40.00	20.00
❑ 99	Warren Spahn	350.00	200.00
❑ 100	Bill Wight	40.00	20.00
❑ 101	Red Schoendienst	80.00	50.00
❑ 102	Jim Hegan	50.00	30.00
❑ 103	Del Ennis	50.00	30.00
❑ 104	Luke Easter	50.00	30.00
❑ 105	Eddie Joost	40.00	20.00
❑ 106	Ken Raffensberger	40.00	20.00
❑ 107	Alex Kellner	40.00	20.00
❑ 108	Bobby Adams	40.00	20.00
❑ 109	Ken Wood	40.00	20.00
❑ 110	Bob Rush	40.00	20.00
❑ 111	Jim Dyck RC	40.00	20.00
❑ 112	Toby Atwell	40.00	20.00
❑ 113	Karl Drews	80.00	50.00

❑ 114 Bob Feller 500.00 350.00
❑ 115 Cloyd Boyer 80.00 50.00
❑ 116 Eddie Yost 100.00 60.00
❑ 117 Duke Snider 600.00 350.00
❑ 118 Billy Martin 400.00 250.00
❑ 119 Dale Mitchell 100.00 60.00
❑ 120 Marlin Stuart 80.00 50.00
❑ 121 Yogi Berra 800.00 500.00
❑ 122 Bill Serena 80.00 50.00
❑ 123 Johnny Lipon 80.00 50.00
❑ 124 Chuck Dressen MG 100.00 60.00
❑ 125 Fred Hatfield 80.00 50.00
❑ 126 Al Corwin 80.00 50.00
❑ 127 Dick Kryhoski 80.00 50.00
❑ 128 Whitey Lockman 100.00 60.00
❑ 129 Russ Meyer 75.00 45.00
❑ 130 Cass Michaels 75.00 45.00
❑ 131 Connie Ryan 75.00 45.00
❑ 132 Fred Hutchinson 90.00 60.00
❑ 133 Willie Jones 75.00 45.00
❑ 134 Johnny Pesky 90.00 60.00
❑ 135 Bobby Morgan 75.00 45.00
❑ 136 Jim Brideweser RC 75.00 45.00
❑ 137 Sam Dente 75.00 45.00
❑ 138 Bubba Church 75.00 45.00
❑ 139 Pete Runnels 90.00 60.00
❑ 140 Al Brazle 75.00 45.00
❑ 141 Frank Shea 75.00 45.00
❑ 142 Larry Miggins RC 75.00 45.00
❑ 143 Al Lopez MG 110.00 70.00
❑ 144 Warren Hacker 75.00 45.00
❑ 145 George Shuba 90.00 60.00
❑ 146 Early Wynn 200.00 125.00
❑ 147 Clem Koshorek 75.00 45.00
❑ 148 Billy Goodman 90.00 60.00
❑ 149 Al Corwin 75.00 45.00
❑ 150 Carl Scheib 75.00 45.00
❑ 151 Joe Adcock 110.00 70.00
❑ 152 Clyde Vollmer 75.00 45.00
❑ 153 Whitey Ford 800.00 500.00
❑ 154 Turk Lown 75.00 45.00
❑ 155 Allie Clark 75.00 45.00
❑ 156 Max Surkont 75.00 45.00
❑ 157 Sherm Lollar 90.00 60.00
❑ 158 Howard Fox 75.00 45.00
❑ 159 Mickey Vernon UER 90.00 60.00
❑ 160 Cal Abrams 500.00 300.00

1954 Bowman

❑ COMPLETE SET (224) 4000.00 2500.00
❑ WRAP.(1-CENT, DATED) 150.00 100.00
❑ WRAP.(1-CENT, UNDAT) 200.00 150.00
❑ WRAP.(5-CENT, DATED) 150.00 100.00
❑ WRAP.(5-CENT, UNDAT) 60.00 50.00
❑ 1 Phil Rizzuto 175.00 100.00
❑ 2 Jackie Jensen 30.00 15.00
❑ 3 Marion Fricano 12.00 6.00
❑ 4 Bob Hooper 12.00 6.00
❑ 5 Billy Hunter 12.00 6.00
❑ 6 Nellie Fox 80.00 50.00
❑ 7 Walt Dropo 20.00 10.00
❑ 8 Jim Busby 12.00 6.00
❑ 9 Dave Williams 12.00 6.00
❑ 10 Carl Erskine 20.00 10.00
❑ 11 Sid Gordon 12.00 6.00
❑ 12 Roy McMillan 20.00 10.00
❑ 13 Paul Minner 12.00 6.00
❑ 14 Gerry Staley 12.00 6.00
❑ 15 Richie Ashburn 80.00 50.00
❑ 16 Jim Wilson 12.00 6.00
❑ 17 Tom Gorman 12.00 6.00
❑ 18 Hoot Evers 12.00 6.00
❑ 19 Bobby Shantz 20.00 10.00
❑ 20 Art Houtteman 12.00 6.00
❑ 21 Vic Wertz 20.00 10.00
❑ 22 Sam Mele 12.00 6.00
❑ 23 Harvey Kuenn RC 30.00 15.00
❑ 24 Bob Porterfield 12.00 6.00
❑ 25 Wes Westrum 20.00 10.00
❑ 26 Billy Cox 20.00 10.00
❑ 27 Dick Cole RC 12.00 6.00
❑ 28 Jim Greengrass 12.00 6.00
❑ 29 Johnny Klippstein 12.00 6.00
❑ 30 Del Rice 12.00 6.00
❑ 31 Smoky Burgess 20.00 10.00
❑ 32 Del Crandall 20.00 10.00
❑ 33A Vic Raschi NTR 20.00 10.00
❑ 33B Vic Raschi TR 30.00 15.00
❑ 34 Sammy White 12.00 6.00
❑ 35 Eddie Joost 12.00 6.00
❑ 36 George Strickland 12.00 6.00
❑ 37 Dick Kokos 12.00 6.00
❑ 38 Minnie Minoso 30.00 15.00
❑ 39 Ned Garver 12.00 6.00
❑ 40 Gil Coan 12.00 6.00
❑ 41 Alvin Dark 20.00 10.00
❑ 42 Billy Loes 20.00 10.00
❑ 43 Bob Friend 20.00 10.00
❑ 44 Harry Perkowski 12.00 6.00
❑ 45 Ralph Kiner 50.00 25.00
❑ 46 Rip Repulski 12.00 6.00
❑ 47 Granny Hamner 12.00 6.00
❑ 48 Jack Dittmer 12.00 6.00
❑ 49 Harry Byrd 12.00 6.00
❑ 50 George Kell 50.00 25.00
❑ 51 Alex Kellner 12.00 6.00
❑ 52 Joe Ginsberg 12.00 6.00
❑ 53 Don Lenhardt 12.00 6.00
❑ 54 Chico Carrasquel 12.00 6.00
❑ 55 Jim Delsing 12.00 6.00
❑ 56 Maurice McDermott 12.00 6.00
❑ 57 Hoyt Wilhelm 50.00 25.00
❑ 58 Pee Wee Reese 80.00 50.00
❑ 59 Bob Schultz 12.00 6.00
❑ 60 Fred Baczewski RC 12.00 6.00
❑ 61 Eddie Miksis 12.00 6.00
❑ 62 Enos Slaughter 50.00 25.00
❑ 63 Earl Torgeson 12.00 6.00
❑ 64 Eddie Mathews 80.00 50.00
❑ 65 Mickey Mantle 1500.00 900.00
❑ 66A Ted Williams 3000.00 1800.00
❑ 66B Jimmy Piersall 80.00 50.00
❑ 67 Carl Scheib 12.00 6.00
❑ 68 Bobby Avila 20.00 10.00
❑ 69 Clint Courtney 12.00 6.00
❑ 70 Willard Marshall 12.00 6.00
❑ 71 Ted Gray 12.00 6.00
❑ 72 Eddie Yost 20.00 10.00
❑ 73 Don Mueller 20.00 10.00
❑ 74 Jim Gilliam 30.00 15.00
❑ 75 Max Surkont 12.00 6.00
❑ 76 Joe Nuxhall 20.00 10.00
❑ 77 Bob Rush 12.00 6.00
❑ 78 Sal Yvars 12.00 6.00
❑ 79 Curt Simmons 20.00 10.00
❑ 80 Johnny Logan 12.00 6.00
❑ 81 Jerry Coleman 20.00 10.00
❑ 82 Billy Goodman 20.00 10.00
❑ 83 Ray Murray 12.00 6.00
❑ 84 Larry Doby 50.00 25.00
❑ 85 Jim Dyck 12.00 6.00
❑ 86 Harry Dorish 12.00 6.00
❑ 87 Don Lund 12.00 6.00
❑ 88 Tom Umphlett RC 12.00 6.00
❑ 89 Willie Mays 500.00 300.00
❑ 90 Roy Campanella 150.00 90.00
❑ 91 Cal Abrams 12.00 6.00
❑ 92 Ken Raffensberger 12.00 6.00
❑ 93 Bill Serena 12.00 6.00
❑ 94 Solly Hemus 12.00 6.00
❑ 95 Robin Roberts 50.00 25.00
❑ 96 Joe Adcock 20.00 10.00
❑ 97 Gil McDougald 20.00 10.00
❑ 98 Ellis Kinder 12.00 6.00
❑ 99 Pete Suder 12.00 6.00
❑ 100 Mike Garcia 20.00 10.00
❑ 101 Don Larsen RC 80.00 50.00
❑ 102 Billy Pierce 20.00 10.00
❑ 103 Steve Souchock 12.00 6.00
❑ 104 Frank Shea 12.00 6.00
❑ 105 Sal Maglie 20.00 10.00
❑ 106 Clem Labine 20.00 10.00
❑ 107 Paul LaPalme 12.00 6.00
❑ 108 Bobby Adams 12.00 6.00
❑ 109 Roy Smalley 12.00 6.00
❑ 110 Red Schoendienst 50.00 25.00
❑ 111 Murry Dickson 12.00 6.00
❑ 112 Andy Pafko 20.00 10.00
❑ 113 Allie Reynolds 20.00 10.00
❑ 114 Willard Nixon 12.00 6.00
❑ 115 Don Bollweg 12.00 6.00
❑ 116 Luke Easter 20.00 10.00
❑ 117 Dick Kryhoski 12.00 6.00
❑ 118 Bob Boyd 12.00 6.00
❑ 119 Fred Hatfield 12.00 6.00
❑ 120 Mel Hoderlein RC 12.00 6.00
❑ 121 Ray Katt RC 12.00 6.00
❑ 122 Carl Furillo 30.00 15.00
❑ 123 Toby Atwell 12.00 6.00
❑ 124 Gus Bell 20.00 10.00
❑ 125 Warren Hacker 12.00 6.00
❑ 126 Cliff Chambers 12.00 6.00
❑ 127 Del Ennis 20.00 10.00
❑ 128 Ebba St.Claire 12.00 6.00
❑ 129 Hank Bauer 30.00 15.00
❑ 130 Milt Bolling 12.00 6.00
❑ 131 Joe Astroth 12.00 6.00
❑ 132 Bob Feller 80.00 50.00
❑ 133 Duane Pillette 12.00 6.00
❑ 134 Luis Aloma 12.00 6.00
❑ 135 Johnny Pesky 20.00 10.00
❑ 136 Clyde Vollmer 12.00 6.00
❑ 137 Al Corwin 12.00 6.00
❑ 138 Gil Hodges 80.00 50.00
❑ 139 Preston Ward 12.00 6.00
❑ 140 Saul Rogovin 12.00 6.00
❑ 141 Joe Garagiola 30.00 15.00
❑ 142 Al Brazle 12.00 6.00
❑ 143 Willie Jones 12.00 6.00
❑ 144 Ernie Johnson RC 30.00 15.00
❑ 145 Billy Martin 80.00 50.00
❑ 146 Dick Gernert 12.00 6.00
❑ 147 Joe DeMaestri 12.00 6.00
❑ 148 Dale Mitchell 20.00 10.00
❑ 149 Bob Young 12.00 6.00
❑ 150 Cass Michaels 12.00 6.00
❑ 151 Pat Mullin 12.00 6.00
❑ 152 Mickey Vernon 20.00 10.00
❑ 153 Whitey Lockman 20.00 10.00
❑ 154 Don Newcombe 30.00 15.00
❑ 155 Frank Thomas RC 20.00 10.00
❑ 156 Rocky Bridges 12.00 6.00
❑ 157 Turk Lown 12.00 6.00
❑ 158 Stu Miller 20.00 10.00
❑ 159 Johnny Lindell 12.00 6.00
❑ 160 Danny O'Connell 12.00 6.00
❑ 161 Yogi Berra 175.00 100.00
❑ 162 Ted Lepcio 12.00 6.00
❑ 163A Dave Philley NTR 20.00 10.00
❑ 163B Dave Philley TR 30.00 15.00
❑ 164 Early Wynn 50.00 25.00
❑ 165 Johnny Groth 12.00 6.00
❑ 166 Sandy Consuegra 12.00 6.00
❑ 167 Billy Hoeft 12.00 6.00
❑ 168 Ed Fitzgerald 12.00 6.00
❑ 169 Larry Jansen 20.00 10.00
❑ 170 Duke Snider 250.00 150.00
❑ 171 Carlos Bernier 12.00 6.00
❑ 172 Andy Seminick 12.00 6.00
❑ 173 Dee Fondy 12.00 6.00
❑ 174 Pete Castiglione 12.00 6.00
❑ 175 Mel Clark 12.00 6.00
❑ 176 Vern Bickford 12.00 6.00
❑ 177 Whitey Ford 100.00 60.00
❑ 178 Del Wilber 12.00 6.00
❑ 179 Morrie Martin 12.00 6.00
❑ 180 Joe Tipton 12.00 6.00
❑ 181 Les Moss 12.00 6.00
❑ 182 Sherm Lollar 20.00 10.00
❑ 183 Matt Batts 12.00 6.00

❑ 184 Mickey Grasso 12.00 6.00
❑ 185 Daryl Spencer RC 12.00 6.00
❑ 186 Russ Meyer 12.00 6.00
❑ 187 Vern Law 20.00 10.00
❑ 188 Frank Smith 12.00 6.00
❑ 189 Randy Jackson 12.00 6.00
❑ 190 Joe Presko 12.00 6.00
❑ 191 Karl Drews 12.00 6.00
❑ 192 Lew Burdette 20.00 10.00
❑ 193 Eddie Robinson 12.00 6.00
❑ 194 Sid Hudson 12.00 6.00
❑ 195 Bob Cain 12.00 6.00
❑ 196 Bob Lemon 50.00 25.00
❑ 197 Lou Kretlow 12.00 6.00
❑ 198 Virgil Trucks 12.00 6.00
❑ 199 Steve Gromek 12.00 6.00
❑ 200 Conrado Marrero 12.00 6.00
❑ 201 Bobby Thomson 30.00 15.00
❑ 202 George Shuba 20.00 10.00
❑ 203 Vic Janowicz 20.00 10.00
❑ 204 Jack Collum RC 12.00 6.00
❑ 205 Hal Jeffcoat 12.00 6.00
❑ 206 Steve Bilko 12.00 6.00
❑ 207 Stan Lopata 12.00 6.00
❑ 208 Johnny Antonelli 20.00 10.00
❑ 209 Gene Woodling 12.00 6.00
❑ 210 Jimmy Piersall 30.00 15.00
❑ 211 Al Robertson RC 12.00 6.00
❑ 212 Owen Friend 12.00 6.00
❑ 213 Dick Littlefield 12.00 6.00
❑ 214 Ferris Fain 20.00 10.00
❑ 215 Johnny Bucha 12.00 6.00
❑ 216 Jerry Snyder 12.00 6.00
❑ 217 Hank Thompson 20.00 10.00
❑ 218 Preacher Roe 20.00 10.00
❑ 219 Hal Rice 12.00 6.00
❑ 220 Hobie Landrith RC 12.00 6.00
❑ 221 Frank Baumholtz 12.00 6.00
❑ 222 Memo Luna RC 12.00 6.00
❑ 223 Steve Ridzik 12.00 6.00
❑ 224 Bill Bruton 50.00 25.00

1955 Bowman

❑ COMPLETE SET (320) 5000.00 3000.00
❑ COMMON CARD (1-96) 12.00 6.00
❑ COM. CARD (97-224) 10.00 5.00
❑ COM. CARD (225-320) 15.00 7.50
❑ COM. UMPIRE (225-320) 30.00 18.00
❑ WRAPPER (1-CENT) 60.00 50.00
❑ WRAPPER (5-CENT) 60.00 50.00
❑ 1 Hoyt Wilhelm 100.00 60.00
❑ 2 Alvin Dark 15.00 7.50
❑ 3 Joe Coleman 15.00 7.50
❑ 4 Eddie Waitkus 15.00 7.50
❑ 5 Jim Robertson 12.00 6.00
❑ 6 Pete Suder 12.00 6.00
❑ 7 Gene Baker RC 12.00 6.00
❑ 8 Warren Hacker 12.00 6.00
❑ 9 Gil McDougald 20.00 10.00
❑ 10 Phil Rizzuto 125.00 75.00
❑ 11 Bill Bruton 15.00 7.50
❑ 12 Andy Pafko 15.00 7.50
❑ 13 Clyde Vollmer 12.00 6.00
❑ 14 Gus Keriazakos RC 12.00 6.00
❑ 15 Frank Sullivan RC 12.00 6.00
❑ 16 Jimmy Piersall 20.00 10.00
❑ 17 Del Ennis 15.00 7.50
❑ 18 Stan Lopata 12.00 6.00
❑ 19 Bobby Avila 15.00 7.50
❑ 20 Al Smith 15.00 7.50
❑ 21 Don Hoak 12.00 6.00
❑ 22 Roy Campanella 125.00 75.00
❑ 23 Al Kaline 150.00 90.00
❑ 24 Al Aber 12.00 6.00
❑ 25 Minnie Minoso 30.00 15.00
❑ 26 Virgil Trucks 15.00 7.50
❑ 27 Preston Ward 12.00 6.00
❑ 28 Dick Cole 12.00 6.00
❑ 29 Red Schoendienst 30.00 15.00
❑ 30 Bill Sarni 12.00 6.00
❑ 31 Johnny Temple RC 15.00 7.50
❑ 32 Wally Post 15.00 7.50
❑ 33 Nellie Fox 50.00 30.00
❑ 34 Clint Courtney 12.00 6.00
❑ 35 Bill Tuttle RC 12.00 6.00
❑ 36 Wayne Belardi RC 12.00 6.00
❑ 37 Pee Wee Reese 100.00 60.00
❑ 38 Early Wynn 30.00 15.00
❑ 39 Bob Darnell RC 15.00 7.50
❑ 40 Vic Wertz 15.00 7.50
❑ 41 Mel Clark 12.00 6.00
❑ 42 Bob Greenwood RC 12.00 6.00
❑ 43 Bob Buhl 15.00 7.50
❑ 44 Danny O'Connell 12.00 6.00
❑ 45 Tom Umphlett 12.00 6.00
❑ 46 Mickey Vernon 15.00 7.50
❑ 47 Sammy White 12.00 6.00
❑ 48A Milt Bolling ERR 20.00 10.00
❑ 48B Milt Bolling COR 20.00 10.00
❑ 49 Jim Greengrass 12.00 6.00
❑ 50 Hobie Landrith 12.00 6.00
❑ 51 Elvin Tappe RC 12.00 6.00
❑ 52 Hal Rice 12.00 6.00
❑ 53 Alex Kellner 12.00 6.00
❑ 54 Don Bollweg 12.00 6.00
❑ 55 Cal Abrams 12.00 6.00
❑ 56 Billy Cox 15.00 7.50
❑ 57 Bob Friend 15.00 7.50
❑ 58 Frank Thomas 15.00 7.50
❑ 59 Whitey Ford 100.00 60.00
❑ 60 Enos Slaughter 30.00 15.00
❑ 61 Paul LaPalme 12.00 6.00
❑ 62 Royce Lint RC 12.00 6.00
❑ 63 Irv Noren 15.00 7.50
❑ 64 Curt Simmons 15.00 7.50
❑ 65 Don Zimmer RC 20.00 10.00
❑ 66 George Shuba 20.00 10.00
❑ 67 Don Larsen 20.00 10.00
❑ 68 Elston Howard RC 80.00 50.00
❑ 69 Billy Hunter 12.00 6.00
❑ 70 Lew Burdette 20.00 10.00
❑ 71 Dave Jolly 12.00 6.00
❑ 72 Chet Nichols 12.00 6.00
❑ 73 Eddie Yost 15.00 7.50
❑ 74 Jerry Snyder 12.00 6.00
❑ 75 Brooks Lawrence RC 12.00 6.00
❑ 76 Tom Poholsky 12.00 6.00
❑ 77 Jim McDonald RC 12.00 6.00
❑ 78 Gil Coan 12.00 6.00
❑ 79 Willie Miranda 12.00 6.00
❑ 80 Lou Limmer 12.00 6.00
❑ 81 Bobby Morgan 12.00 6.00
❑ 82 Lee Walls RC 12.00 6.00
❑ 83 Max Surkont 12.00 6.00
❑ 84 George Freese RC 12.00 6.00
❑ 85 Cass Michaels 12.00 6.00
❑ 86 Ted Gray 12.00 6.00
❑ 87 Randy Jackson 12.00 6.00
❑ 88 Steve Bilko 12.00 6.00
❑ 89 Lou Boudreau MG 30.00 15.00
❑ 90 Art RC 12.00 6.00
❑ 91 Dick Marlowe RC 12.00 6.00
❑ 92 George Zuverink 12.00 6.00
❑ 93 Andy Seminick 12.00 6.00
❑ 94 Hank Thompson 15.00 7.50
❑ 95 Sal Maglie 15.00 7.50
❑ 96 Ray Narleski RC 12.00 6.00
❑ 97 Johnny Podres 30.00 15.00
❑ 98 Jim Gilliam 20.00 10.00
❑ 99 Jerry Coleman 15.00 7.50
❑ 100 Tom Morgan 10.00 5.00
❑ 101A Don Johnson ERR 20.00 10.00
❑ 101B Don Johnson COR 20.00 10.00
❑ 102 Bobby Thomson 15.00 7.50
❑ 103 Eddie Mathews 80.00 50.00
❑ 104 Bob Porterfield 10.00 5.00
❑ 105 Johnny Schmitz 10.00 5.00
❑ 106 Del Rice 10.00 5.00
❑ 107 Solly Hemus 10.00 5.00
❑ 108 Lou Kretlow 10.00 5.00
❑ 109 Vern Stephens 15.00 7.50
❑ 110 Bob Miller 10.00 5.00
❑ 111 Steve Ridzik 10.00 5.00
❑ 112 Granny Hamner 10.00 5.00
❑ 113 Bob Hall RC 10.00 5.00
❑ 114 Vic Janowicz 15.00 7.50
❑ 115 Roger Bowman RC 10.00 5.00
❑ 116 Sandy Consuegra 10.00 5.00
❑ 117 Johnny Groth 10.00 5.00
❑ 118 Bobby Adams 10.00 5.00
❑ 119 Joe Astroth 10.00 5.00
❑ 120 Ed Burtschy RC 10.00 5.00
❑ 121 Rufus Crawford RC 10.00 5.00
❑ 122 Al Corwin 10.00 5.00
❑ 123 Marv Grissom RC 10.00 5.00
❑ 124 Johnny Antonelli 15.00 7.50
❑ 125 Paul Giel RC 15.00 7.50
❑ 126 Billy Goodman 15.00 7.50
❑ 127 Hank Majeski 10.00 5.00
❑ 128 Mike Garcia 15.00 7.50
❑ 129 Hal Naragon RC 10.00 5.00
❑ 130 Richie Ashburn 50.00 30.00
❑ 131 Willard Marshall 10.00 5.00
❑ 132A Harvey Kueen ERR 50.00 30.00
❑ 132B Harvey Kuenn COR 30.00 15.00
❑ 133 Charles King RC 10.00 5.00
❑ 134 Bob Feller 80.00 50.00
❑ 135 Lloyd Merriman 10.00 5.00
❑ 136 Rocky Bridges 10.00 5.00
❑ 137 Bob Talbot 10.00 5.00
❑ 138 Davey Williams 15.00 7.50
❑ 139 W.Shantz/B.Shantz 15.00 7.50
❑ 140 Bobby Shantz 15.00 7.50
❑ 141 Wes Westrum 15.00 7.50
❑ 142 Rudy Regalado RC 10.00 5.00
❑ 143 Don Newcombe 30.00 15.00
❑ 144 Art Houtteman 10.00 5.00
❑ 145 Bob Nieman RC 10.00 5.00
❑ 146 Don Liddle 10.00 5.00
❑ 147 Sam Mele 10.00 5.00
❑ 148 Bob Chakales 10.00 5.00
❑ 149 Cloyd Boyer 10.00 5.00
❑ 150 Billy Klaus RC 10.00 5.00
❑ 151 Jim Brideweser 10.00 5.00
❑ 152 Johnny Klippstein 10.00 5.00
❑ 153 Eddie Robinson 10.00 5.00
❑ 154 Frank Lary RC 15.00 7.50
❑ 155 Gerry Staley 10.00 5.00
❑ 156 Jim Hughes 15.00 7.50
❑ 157A Ernie Johnson ERR 20.00 10.00
❑ 157B Ernie Johnson COR 20.00 10.00
❑ 158 Gil Hodges 50.00 30.00
❑ 159 Harry Byrd 10.00 5.00
❑ 160 Bill Skowron 20.00 10.00
❑ 161 Matt Batts 10.00 5.00
❑ 162 Charlie Maxwell 10.00 5.00
❑ 163 Sid Gordon 15.00 7.50
❑ 164 Toby Atwell 10.00 5.00
❑ 165 Maurice McDermott 10.00 5.00
❑ 166 Jim Busby 10.00 5.00
❑ 167 Bob Grim RC 20.00 10.00
❑ 168 Yogi Berra 125.00 75.00
❑ 169 Carl Furillo 30.00 15.00
❑ 170 Carl Erskine 20.00 10.00
❑ 171 Robin Roberts 50.00 30.00
❑ 172 Willie Jones 10.00 5.00
❑ 173 Chico Carrasquel 10.00 5.00
❑ 174 Sherm Lollar 15.00 7.50
❑ 175 Wilmer Shantz RC 10.00 5.00
❑ 176 Joe DeMaestri 10.00 5.00
❑ 177 Willard Nixon 10.00 5.00
❑ 178 Tom Brewer RC 10.00 5.00
❑ 179 Hank Aaron 250.00 150.00
❑ 180 Johnny Logan 15.00 7.50
❑ 181 Eddie Miksis 10.00 5.00
❑ 182 Bob Rush 10.00 5.00
❑ 183 Ray Katt 10.00 5.00
❑ 184 Willie Mays 250.00 150.00
❑ 185 Vic Raschi 10.00 5.00
❑ 186 Alex Grammas 10.00 5.00

❑ 187 Fred Hatfield 10.00 5.00
❑ 188 Ned Garver 10.00 5.00
❑ 189 Jack Collum 10.00 5.00
❑ 190 Fred Baczewski 10.00 5.00
❑ 191 Bob Lemon 30.00 15.00
❑ 192 George Strickland 10.00 5.00
❑ 193 Howie Judson 10.00 5.00
❑ 194 Joe Nuxhall 15.00 7.50
❑ 195A Erv Palica 15.00 7.50
❑ 195B Erv Palica TR 40.00 20.00
❑ 196 Russ Meyer 15.00 7.50
❑ 197 Ralph Kiner 30.00 15.00
❑ 198 Dave Pope RC 10.00 5.00
❑ 199 Vern Law 15.00 7.50
❑ 200 Dick Littlefield 10.00 5.00
❑ 201 Allie Reynolds 20.00 10.00
❑ 202 Mickey Mantle UER 800.00 500.00
❑ 203 Steve Gromek 10.00 5.00
❑ 204A Frank Bolling ERR RC 20.00 10.00
❑ 204B Frank Bolling COR 20.00 10.00
❑ 205 Rip Repulski 10.00 5.00
❑ 206 Ralph Beard RC 10.00 5.00
❑ 207 Frank Shea 10.00 5.00
❑ 208 Ed Fitzgerald 10.00 5.00
❑ 209 Smoky Burgess 15.00 7.50
❑ 210 Earl Torgeson 10.00 5.00
❑ 211 Sonny Dixon RC 10.00 5.00
❑ 212 Jack Dittmer 10.00 5.00
❑ 213 George Kell 30.00 15.00
❑ 214 Billy Pierce 15.00 7.50
❑ 215 Bob Kuzava 10.00 5.00
❑ 216 Preacher Roe 20.00 10.00
❑ 217 Del Crandall 15.00 7.50
❑ 218 Joe Adcock 15.00 7.50
❑ 219 Whitey Lockman 15.00 7.50
❑ 220 Jim Hearn 10.00 5.00
❑ 221 Hector Brown 10.00 5.00
❑ 222 Russ Kemmerer RC 10.00 5.00
❑ 223 Hal Jeffcoat 10.00 5.00
❑ 224 Dee Fondy 10.00 5.00
❑ 225 Paul Richards MG 15.00 7.50
❑ 226 Bill McKinley UMP 30.00 18.00
❑ 227 Frank Baumholtz 15.00 7.50
❑ 228 John Phillips RC 15.00 7.50
❑ 229 Jim Brosnan RC 20.00 10.00
❑ 230 Al Brazle 15.00 7.50
❑ 231 Jim Konstanty 20.00 10.00
❑ 232 Birdie Tebbetts MG 20.00 10.00
❑ 233 Bill Serena 15.00 7.50
❑ 234 Dick Bartell CO 20.00 10.00
❑ 235 Joe Paparella UMP 30.00 18.00
❑ 236 Murry Dickson 15.00 7.50
❑ 237 Johnny Wyrostek 15.00 7.50
❑ 238 Eddie Stanky MG 20.00 10.00
❑ 239 Edwin Rommel UMP 40.00 20.00
❑ 240 Billy Loes 20.00 10.00
❑ 241 Johnny Pesky 20.00 10.00
❑ 242 Ernie Banks 350.00 200.00
❑ 243 Gus Bell 20.00 10.00
❑ 244 Duane Pillette 15.00 7.50
❑ 245 Bill Miller 15.00 7.50
❑ 246 Hank Bauer 30.00 15.00
❑ 247 Dutch Leonard CO 15.00 7.50
❑ 248 Harry Dorish 15.00 7.50
❑ 249 Billy Gardner RC 20.00 10.00
❑ 250 Larry Napp UMP 30.00 18.00
❑ 251 Stan Jok 15.00 7.50
❑ 252 Roy Smalley 15.00 7.50
❑ 253 Jim Wilson 15.00 7.50
❑ 254 Bennett Flowers RC 15.00 7.50
❑ 255 Pete Runnels 20.00 10.00
❑ 256 Owen Friend 15.00 7.50
❑ 257 Tom Alston RC 15.00 7.50
❑ 258 John Stevens UMP 30.00 18.00
❑ 259 Don Mossi RC 30.00 15.00
❑ 260 Edwin Hurley UMP 30.00 18.00
❑ 261 Walt Moryn RC 20.00 10.00
❑ 262 Jim Lemon FBC 15.00 7.50
❑ 263 Eddie Joost 15.00 7.50
❑ 264 Bill Henry RC 15.00 7.50
❑ 265 Al Barlick UMP 80.00 50.00
❑ 266 Mike Fornieles 15.00 7.50
❑ 267 J.Honochick UMP 80.00 50.00
❑ 268 Roy Lee Hawes RC 15.00 7.50
❑ 269 Joe Amalfitano RC 20.00 10.00
❑ 270 Chico Fernandez RC 20.00 10.00
❑ 271 Bob Hooper 15.00 7.50
❑ 272 John Flaherty UMP 30.00 18.00
❑ 273 Bubba Church 15.00 7.50
❑ 274 Jim Delsing 15.00 7.50
❑ 275 William Grieve UMP 30.00 18.00
❑ 276 Ike Delock 15.00 7.50
❑ 277 Ed Runge UMP 30.00 18.00
❑ 278 Charlie Neal RC 40.00 20.00
❑ 279 Hank Soar UMP 40.00 20.00
❑ 280 Clyde McCullough 15.00 7.50
❑ 281 Charles Berry UMP 40.00 20.00
❑ 282 Phil Cavarretta MG 20.00 10.00
❑ 283 Nestor Chylak UMP 80.00 50.00
❑ 284 Bill Jackowski UMP 30.00 18.00
❑ 285 Walt Dropo 20.00 10.00
❑ 286 Frank Secory UMP 30.00 18.00
❑ 287 Ron Mrozinski RC 15.00 7.50
❑ 288 Dick Smith RC 15.00 7.50
❑ 289 Arthur Gore UMP 30.00 18.00
❑ 290 Hershell Freeman RC 15.00 7.50
❑ 291 Frank Dascoli UMP 30.00 18.00
❑ 292 Marv Blaylock RC 15.00 7.50
❑ 293 Thomas Gorman UMP 40.00 20.00
❑ 294 Wally Moses CO 15.00 7.50
❑ 295 Lee Ballanfant UMP 30.00 18.00
❑ 296 Bill Virdon RC 30.00 15.00
❑ 297 Dusty Boggess UMP 30.00 18.00
❑ 298 Charlie Grimm 20.00 10.00
❑ 299 Lon Warneke UMP 40.00 20.00
❑ 300 Tommy Byrne 20.00 10.00
❑ 301 William Engeln UMP 30.00 18.00
❑ 302 Frank Malzone RC 30.00 15.00
❑ 303 Jocko Conlan UMP 80.00 50.00
❑ 304 Harry Chiti 15.00 7.50
❑ 305 Frank Umont UMP 30.00 18.00
❑ 306 Bob Cerv 20.00 10.00
❑ 307 Babe Pinelli UMP 40.00 20.00
❑ 308 Al Lopez MG 50.00 30.00
❑ 309 Hal Dixon UMP 30.00 18.00
❑ 310 Ken Lehman RC 15.00 7.50
❑ 311 Lawrence Goetz UMP 30.00 18.00
❑ 312 Bill Wight 15.00 7.50
❑ 313 Augie Donatelli UMP 50.00 30.00
❑ 314 Dale Mitchell 20.00 10.00
❑ 315 Cal Hubbard UMP 80.00 50.00
❑ 316 Marion Fricano 15.00 7.50
❑ 317 William Summers UMP 20.00 10.00
❑ 318 Sid Hudson 15.00 7.50
❑ 319 Al Schroll RC 15.00 7.50
❑ 320 George Susce RC 50.00 30.00

1989 Bowman

❑ COMPLETE SET (484) 25.00 10.00
❑ COMP.FACT.SET (484) 25.00 10.00
❑ 1 Oswald Peraza .05 .01
❑ 2 Brian Holton .05 .01
❑ 3 Jose Bautista RC .10 .02
❑ 4 Pete Harnisch RC .25 .08
❑ 5 Dave Schmidt .05 .01
❑ 6 Gregg Olson RC .25 .08
❑ 7 Jeff Ballard .05 .01
❑ 8 Bob Melvin .05 .01
❑ 9 Cal Ripken .75 .30
❑ 10 Randy Milligan .05 .01
❑ 11 Juan Bell RC .10 .02
❑ 12 Billy Ripken .05 .01
❑ 13 Jim Traber .05 .01
❑ 14 Pete Stanicek .05 .01
❑ 15 Steve Finley RC .75 .30
❑ 16 Larry Sheets .05 .01
❑ 17 Phil Bradley .05 .01
❑ 18 Brady Anderson RC .40 .15
❑ 19 Lee Smith .10 .02
❑ 20 Tom Fischer .05 .01
❑ 21 Mike Boddicker .05 .01
❑ 22 Rob Murphy .05 .01
❑ 23 Wes Gardner .05 .01
❑ 24 John Dopson .05 .01
❑ 25 Bob Stanley .05 .01
❑ 26 Roger Clemens 1.00 .40
❑ 27 Rich Gedman .05 .01
❑ 28 Marty Barrett .05 .01
❑ 29 Luis Rivera .05 .01
❑ 30 Jody Reed .05 .01
❑ 31 Nick Esasky .05 .01
❑ 32 Wade Boggs .15 .05
❑ 33 Jim Rice .10 .02
❑ 34 Mike Greenwell .05 .01
❑ 35 Dwight Evans .15 .05
❑ 36 Ellis Burks .10 .02
❑ 37 Chuck Finley .10 .02
❑ 38 Kirk McCaskill .05 .01
❑ 39 Jim Abbott RC 1.00 .40
❑ 40 Bryan Harvey RC * .25 .08
❑ 41 Bert Blyleven .10 .02
❑ 42 Mike Witt .05 .01
❑ 43 Bob McClure .05 .01
❑ 44 Bill Schroeder .05 .01
❑ 45 Lance Parrish .10 .02
❑ 46 Dick Schofield .05 .01
❑ 47 Wally Joyner .10 .02
❑ 48 Jack Howell .05 .01
❑ 49 Johnny Ray .05 .01
❑ 50 Chili Davis .10 .02
❑ 51 Tony Armas .10 .02
❑ 52 Claudell Washington .05 .01
❑ 53 Brian Downing .10 .02
❑ 54 Devon White .10 .02
❑ 55 Bobby Thigpen .05 .01
❑ 56 Bill Long .05 .01
❑ 57 Jerry Reuss .05 .01
❑ 58 Shawn Hillegas .05 .01
❑ 59 Melido Perez .05 .01
❑ 60 Jeff Bittiger .05 .01
❑ 61 Jack McDowell .10 .02
❑ 62 Carlton Fisk .15 .05
❑ 63 Steve Lyons .05 .01
❑ 64 Ozzie Guillen .10 .02
❑ 65 Robin Ventura RC .75 .30
❑ 66 Fred Manrique .05 .01
❑ 67 Dan Pasqua .05 .01
❑ 68 Ivan Calderon .05 .01
❑ 69 Ron Kittle .05 .01
❑ 70 Daryl Boston .05 .01
❑ 71 Dave Gallagher .05 .01
❑ 72 Harold Baines .10 .02
❑ 73 Charles Nagy RC .25 .08
❑ 74 John Farrell .05 .01
❑ 75 Kevin Wickander .05 .01
❑ 76 Greg Swindell .05 .01
❑ 77 Mike Walker .05 .01
❑ 78 Doug Jones .05 .01
❑ 79 Rich Yett .05 .01
❑ 80 Tom Candiotti .05 .01
❑ 81 Jesse Orosco .05 .01
❑ 82 Bud Black .05 .01
❑ 83 Andy Allanson .05 .01
❑ 84 Pete O'Brien .05 .01
❑ 85 Jerry Browne .05 .01
❑ 86 Brook Jacoby .05 .01
❑ 87 Mark Lewis RC .25 .08
❑ 88 Luis Aguayo .05 .01
❑ 89 Cory Snyder .05 .01
❑ 90 Oddibe McDowell .05 .01
❑ 91 Joe Carter .10 .02
❑ 92 Frank Tanana .10 .02
❑ 93 Jack Morris .10 .02
❑ 94 Doyle Alexander .05 .01
❑ 95 Steve Searcy .05 .01
❑ 96 Randy Bockus .05 .01
❑ 97 Jeff M. Robinson .05 .01
❑ 98 Mike Henneman .05 .01
❑ 99 Paul Gibson .05 .01
❑ 100 Frank Williams .05 .01

❑	101	Matt Nokes	.05	.01
❑	102	Rico Brogna RC	.40	.15
❑	103	Lou Whitaker	.10	.02
❑	104	Al Pedrique	.05	.01
❑	105	Alan Trammell	.10	.02
❑	106	Chris Brown	.05	.01
❑	107	Pat Sheridan	.05	.01
❑	108	Chet Lemon	.10	.02
❑	109	Keith Moreland	.05	.01
❑	110	Mel Stottlemyre Jr.	.05	.01
❑	111	Bret Saberhagen	.10	.02
❑	112	Floyd Bannister	.05	.01
❑	113	Jeff Montgomery	.05	.01
❑	114	Steve Farr	.05	.01
❑	115	Tom Gordon UER RC	.40	.15
❑	116	Charlie Leibrandt	.05	.01
❑	117	Mark Gubicza	.05	.01
❑	118	Mike Macfarlane RC *	.25	.08
❑	119	Bob Boone	.10	.02
❑	120	Kurt Stillwell	.05	.01
❑	121	George Brett	.60	.25
❑	122	Frank White	.10	.02
❑	123	Kevin Seitzer	.05	.01
❑	124	Willie Wilson	.10	.02
❑	125	Pat Tabler	.05	.01
❑	126	Bo Jackson	.25	.08
❑	127	Hugh Walker RC	.10	.02
❑	128	Danny Tartabull	.05	.01
❑	129	Teddy Higuera	.05	.01
❑	130	Don August	.05	.01
❑	131	Juan Nieves	.05	.01
❑	132	Mike Birkbeck	.05	.01
❑	133	Dan Plesac	.05	.01
❑	134	Chris Bosio	.05	.01
❑	135	Bill Wegman	.05	.01
❑	136	Chuck Crim	.05	.01
❑	137	B.J. Surhoff	.10	.02
❑	138	Joey Meyer	.05	.01
❑	139	Dale Sveum	.05	.01
❑	140	Paul Molitor	.10	.02
❑	141	Jim Gantner	.05	.01
❑	142	Gary Sheffield RC	1.50	.60
❑	143	Greg Brock	.05	.01
❑	144	Robin Yount	.40	.15
❑	145	Glenn Braggs	.05	.01
❑	146	Rob Deer	.05	.01
❑	147	Fred Toliver	.05	.01
❑	148	Jeff Reardon	.10	.02
❑	149	Allan Anderson	.05	.01
❑	150	Frank Viola	.10	.02
❑	151	Shane Rawley	.05	.01
❑	152	Juan Berenguer	.05	.01
❑	153	Johnny Ard	.05	.01
❑	154	Tim Laudner	.05	.01
❑	155	Brian Harper	.05	.01
❑	156	Al Newman	.05	.01
❑	157	Kent Hrbek	.10	.02
❑	158	Gary Gaetti	.10	.02
❑	159	Wally Backman	.05	.01
❑	160	Gene Larkin	.05	.01
❑	161	Greg Gagne	.05	.01
❑	162	Kirby Puckett	.25	.08
❑	163	Dan Gladden	.05	.01
❑	164	Randy Bush	.05	.01
❑	165	Dave LaPoint	.05	.01
❑	166	Andy Hawkins	.05	.01
❑	167	Dave Righetti	.10	.02
❑	168	Lance McCullers	.05	.01
❑	169	Jimmy Jones	.05	.01
❑	170	Al Leiter	.25	.08
❑	171	John Candelaria	.05	.01
❑	172	Don Slaught	.05	.01
❑	173	Jamie Quirk	.05	.01
❑	174	Rafael Santana	.05	.01
❑	175	Mike Pagliarulo	.05	.01
❑	176	Don Mattingly	.60	.25
❑	177	Ken Phelps	.05	.01
❑	178	Steve Sax	.05	.01
❑	179	Dave Winfield	.10	.02
❑	180	Stan Jefferson	.05	.01
❑	181	Rickey Henderson	.25	.08
❑	182	Bob Brower	.05	.01
❑	183	Roberto Kelly	.05	.01
❑	184	Curt Young	.05	.01
❑	185	Gene Nelson	.05	.01
❑	186	Bob Welch	.10	.02
❑	187	Rick Honeycutt	.05	.01
❑	188	Dave Stewart	.10	.02
❑	189	Mike Moore	.05	.01
❑	190	Dennis Eckersley	.15	.05
❑	191	Eric Plunk	.05	.01
❑	192	Storm Davis	.05	.01
❑	193	Terry Steinbach	.10	.02
❑	194	Ron Hassey	.05	.01
❑	195	Stan Royer RC	.10	.02
❑	196	Walt Weiss	.05	.01
❑	197	Mark McGwire	1.00	.40
❑	198	Carney Lansford	.10	.02
❑	199	Glenn Hubbard	.05	.01
❑	200	Dave Henderson	.05	.01
❑	201	Jose Canseco	.25	.08
❑	202	Dave Parker	.10	.02
❑	203	Scott Bankhead	.05	.01
❑	204	Tom Niedenfuer	.05	.01
❑	205	Mark Langston	.05	.01
❑	206	Erik Hanson RC	.25	.08
❑	207	Mike Jackson	.05	.01
❑	208	Dave Valle	.05	.01
❑	209	Scott Bradley	.05	.01
❑	210	Harold Reynolds	.10	.02
❑	211	Tino Martinez RC	2.00	.75
❑	212	Rich Renteria	.05	.01
❑	213	Rey Quinones	.05	.01
❑	214	Jim Presley	.05	.01
❑	215	Alvin Davis	.05	.01
❑	216	Edgar Martinez	.25	.08
❑	217	Darnell Coles	.05	.01
❑	218	Jeffrey Leonard	.05	.01
❑	219	Jay Buhner	.10	.02
❑	220	Ken Griffey Jr. RC	8.00	3.00
❑	221	Drew Hall	.05	.01
❑	222	Bobby Witt	.05	.01
❑	223	Jamie Moyer	.10	.02
❑	224	Charlie Hough	.10	.02
❑	225	Nolan Ryan	1.00	.40
❑	226	Jeff Russell	.05	.01
❑	227	Jim Sundberg	.10	.02
❑	228	Julio Franco	.10	.02
❑	229	Buddy Bell	.10	.02
❑	230	Scott Fletcher	.05	.01
❑	231	Jeff Kunkel	.05	.01
❑	232	Steve Buechele	.05	.01
❑	233	Monty Fariss	.05	.01
❑	234	Rick Leach	.05	.01
❑	235	Ruben Sierra	.10	.02
❑	236	Cecil Espy	.05	.01
❑	237	Rafael Palmeiro	.25	.08
❑	238	Pete Incaviglia	.05	.01
❑	239	Dave Stieb	.10	.02
❑	240	Jeff Musselman	.05	.01
❑	241	Mike Flanagan	.05	.01
❑	242	Todd Stottlemyre	.05	.01
❑	243	Jimmy Key	.10	.02
❑	244	Tony Castillo RC	.10	.02
❑	245	Alex Sanchez RC	.05	.01
❑	246	Tom Henke	.05	.01
❑	247	John Cerutti	.05	.01
❑	248	Ernie Whitt	.05	.01
❑	249	Bob Brenly	.05	.01
❑	250	Rance Mulliniks	.05	.01
❑	251	Kelly Gruber	.05	.01
❑	252	Ed Sprague RC	.25	.08
❑	253	Fred McGriff	.15	.05
❑	254	Tony Fernandez	.05	.01
❑	255	Tom Lawless	.05	.01
❑	256	George Bell	.10	.02
❑	257	Jesse Barfield	.10	.02
❑	258	Roberto Alomar w/Dad	.15	.05
❑	259	Ken Griffey Sr./Jr.	1.00	.40
❑	260	Cal Ripken Sr./Jr.	.25	.08
❑	261	M.Stottlemyre Jr./Sr.	.05	.01
❑	262	Zane Smith	.05	.01
❑	263	Charlie Puleo	.05	.01
❑	264	Derek Lilliquist RC	.10	.02
❑	265	Paul Assenmacher	.05	.01
❑	266	John Smoltz RC	1.50	.60
❑	267	Tom Glavine	.25	.08
❑	268	Steve Avery RC	.25	.08
❑	269	Pete Smith	.05	.01
❑	270	Jody Davis	.05	.01
❑	271	Bruce Benedict	.05	.01
❑	272	Andres Thomas	.05	.01
❑	273	Gerald Perry	.05	.01
❑	274	Ron Gant	.10	.02
❑	275	Darrell Evans	.10	.02
❑	276	Dale Murphy	.15	.05
❑	277	Dion James	.05	.01
❑	278	Lonnie Smith	.05	.01
❑	279	Geronimo Berroa	.05	.01
❑	280	Steve Wilson RC	.10	.02
❑	281	Rick Sutcliffe	.10	.02
❑	282	Kevin Coffman	.05	.01
❑	283	Mitch Williams	.05	.01
❑	284	Greg Maddux	.50	.20
❑	285	Paul Kilgus	.05	.01
❑	286	Mike Harkey RC	.10	.02
❑	287	Lloyd McClendon	.05	.01
❑	288	Damon Berryhill	.05	.01
❑	289	Ty Griffin	.05	.01
❑	290	Ryne Sandberg	.40	.15
❑	291	Mark Grace	.25	.08
❑	292	Curt Wilkerson	.05	.01
❑	293	Vance Law	.05	.01
❑	294	Shawon Dunston	.05	.01
❑	295	Jerome Walton RC	.25	.08
❑	296	Mitch Webster	.05	.01
❑	297	Dwight Smith RC	.25	.08
❑	298	Andre Dawson	.10	.02
❑	299	Jeff Sellers	.05	.01
❑	300	Jose Rijo	.10	.02
❑	301	John Franco	.10	.02
❑	302	Rick Mahler	.05	.01
❑	303	Ron Robinson	.05	.01
❑	304	Danny Jackson	.05	.01
❑	305	Rob Dibble RC	.40	.15
❑	306	Tom Browning	.05	.01
❑	307	Bo Diaz	.05	.01
❑	308	Manny Trillo	.05	.01
❑	309	Chris Sabo RC *	.40	.15
❑	310	Ron Oester	.05	.01
❑	311	Barry Larkin	.15	.05
❑	312	Todd Benzinger	.05	.01
❑	313	Paul O'Neill	.15	.05
❑	314	Kal Daniels	.05	.01
❑	315	Joel Youngblood	.05	.01
❑	316	Eric Davis	.10	.02
❑	317	Dave Smith	.05	.01
❑	318	Mark Portugal	.05	.01
❑	319	Brian Meyer	.05	.01
❑	320	Jim Deshaies	.05	.01
❑	321	Juan Agosto	.05	.01
❑	322	Mike Scott	.10	.02
❑	323	Rick Rhoden	.05	.01
❑	324	Jim Clancy	.05	.01
❑	325	Larry Andersen	.05	.01
❑	326	Alex Trevino	.05	.01
❑	327	Alan Ashby	.05	.01
❑	328	Craig Reynolds	.05	.01
❑	329	Bill Doran	.05	.01
❑	330	Rafael Ramirez	.05	.01
❑	331	Glenn Davis	.05	.01
❑	332	Willie Ansley RC	.10	.02
❑	333	Gerald Young	.05	.01
❑	334	Cameron Drew	.05	.01
❑	335	Jay Howell	.05	.01
❑	336	Tim Belcher	.05	.01
❑	337	Fernando Valenzuela	.10	.02
❑	338	Ricky Horton	.05	.01
❑	339	Tim Leary	.05	.01
❑	340	Bill Bene	.05	.01
❑	341	Orel Hershiser	.10	.02
❑	342	Mike Scioscia	.10	.02
❑	343	Rick Dempsey	.05	.01
❑	344	Willie Randolph	.10	.02
❑	345	Alfredo Griffin	.05	.01
❑	346	Eddie Murray	.25	.08
❑	347	Mickey Hatcher	.05	.01
❑	348	Mike Sharperson	.05	.01
❑	349	John Shelby	.05	.01
❑	350	Mike Marshall	.05	.01
❑	351	Kirk Gibson	.10	.02
❑	352	Mike Davis	.05	.01
❑	353	Bryn Smith	.05	.01
❑	354	Pascual Perez	.05	.01
❑	355	Kevin Gross	.05	.01
❑	356	Andy McGaffigan	.05	.01
❑	357	Brian Holman RC *	.10	.02
❑	358	Dave Wainhouse RC	.10	.02

❑ 359 Dennis Martinez .10 .02
❑ 360 Tim Burke .05 .01
❑ 361 Nelson Santovenia .05 .01
❑ 362 Tim Wallach .05 .01
❑ 363 Spike Owen .05 .01
❑ 364 Rex Hudler .05 .01
❑ 365 Andres Galarraga .10 .02
❑ 366 Otis Nixon .05 .01
❑ 367 Hubie Brooks .05 .01
❑ 368 Mike Aldrete .05 .01
❑ 369 Tim Raines .10 .02
❑ 370 Dave Martinez .05 .01
❑ 371 Bob Ojeda .05 .01
❑ 372 Ron Darling .10 .02
❑ 373 Wally Whitehurst RC .10 .02
❑ 374 Randy Myers .10 .02
❑ 375 David Cone .10 .02
❑ 376 Dwight Gooden .10 .02
❑ 377 Sid Fernandez .05 .01
❑ 378 Dave Proctor .05 .01
❑ 379 Gary Carter .10 .02
❑ 380 Keith Miller .05 .01
❑ 381 Gregg Jefferies .05 .01
❑ 382 Tim Teufel .05 .01
❑ 383 Kevin Elster .05 .01
❑ 384 Dave Magadan .05 .01
❑ 385 Keith Hernandez .10 .02
❑ 386 Mookie Wilson .10 .02
❑ 387 Darryl Strawberry .10 .02
❑ 388 Kevin McReynolds .05 .01
❑ 389 Mark Carreon .05 .01
❑ 390 Jeff Parrett .05 .01
❑ 391 Mike Maddux .05 .01
❑ 392 Don Carman .05 .01
❑ 393 Bruce Ruffin .05 .01
❑ 394 Ken Howell .05 .01
❑ 395 Steve Bedrosian .05 .01
❑ 396 Floyd Youmans .05 .01
❑ 397 Larry McWilliams .05 .01
❑ 398 Pat Combs RC * .10 .02
❑ 399 Steve Lake .05 .01
❑ 400 Dickie Thon .05 .01
❑ 401 Ricky Jordan RC * .25 .08
❑ 402 Mike Schmidt .50 .20
❑ 403 Tom Herr .05 .01
❑ 404 Chris James .05 .01
❑ 405 Juan Samuel .05 .01
❑ 406 Von Hayes .05 .01
❑ 407 Ron Jones .10 .02
❑ 408 Curt Ford .05 .01
❑ 409 Bob Walk .05 .01
❑ 410 Jeff D. Robinson .05 .01
❑ 411 Jim Gott .05 .01
❑ 412 Scott Medvin .05 .01
❑ 413 John Smiley .05 .01
❑ 414 Bob Kipper .05 .01
❑ 415 Brian Fisher .05 .01
❑ 416 Doug Drabek .05 .01
❑ 417 Mike LaValliere .05 .01
❑ 418 Ken Oberkfell .05 .01
❑ 419 Sid Bream .05 .01
❑ 420 Austin Manahan .05 .01
❑ 421 Jose Lind .05 .01
❑ 422 Bobby Bonilla .10 .02
❑ 423 Glenn Wilson .05 .01
❑ 424 Andy Van Slyke .15 .05
❑ 425 Gary Redus .05 .01
❑ 426 Barry Bonds 1.50 .60
❑ 427 Don Heinkel .05 .01
❑ 428 Ken Dayley .05 .01
❑ 429 Todd Worrell .05 .01
❑ 430 Brad DuVall .05 .01
❑ 431 Jose DeLeon .05 .01
❑ 432 Joe Magrane .05 .01
❑ 433 John Ericks .05 .01
❑ 434 Frank DiPino .05 .01
❑ 435 Tony Pena .05 .01
❑ 436 Ozzie Smith .40 .15
❑ 437 Terry Pendleton .10 .02
❑ 438 Jose Oquendo .05 .01
❑ 439 Tim Jones .05 .01
❑ 440 Pedro Guerrero .10 .02
❑ 441 Milt Thompson .05 .01
❑ 442 Willie McGee .10 .02
❑ 443 Vince Coleman .05 .01
❑ 444 Tom Brunansky .05 .01
❑ 445 Walt Terrell .05 .01
❑ 446 Eric Show .05 .01
❑ 447 Mark Davis .05 .01
❑ 448 Andy Benes RC .40 .15
❑ 449 Ed Whitson .05 .01
❑ 450 Dennis Rasmussen .05 .01
❑ 451 Bruce Hurst .05 .01
❑ 452 Pat Clements .05 .01
❑ 453 Benito Santiago .10 .02
❑ 454 Sandy Alomar Jr. RC .40 .15
❑ 455 Garry Templeton .10 .02
❑ 456 Jack Clark .10 .02
❑ 457 Tim Flannery .05 .01
❑ 458 Roberto Alomar .25 .08
❑ 459 Carmelo Martinez .05 .01
❑ 460 John Kruk .10 .02
❑ 461 Tony Gwynn .30 .10
❑ 462 Jerald Clark RC .10 .02
❑ 463 Don Robinson .05 .01
❑ 464 Craig Lefferts .05 .01
❑ 465 Kelly Downs .05 .01
❑ 466 Rick Reuschel .10 .02
❑ 467 Scott Garrelts .05 .01
❑ 468 Wil Tejada .05 .01
❑ 469 Kirt Manwaring .05 .01
❑ 470 Terry Kennedy .05 .01
❑ 471 Jose Uribe .05 .01
❑ 472 Royce Clayton RC .40 .15
❑ 473 Robby Thompson .05 .01
❑ 474 Kevin Mitchell .10 .02
❑ 475 Ernie Riles .05 .01
❑ 476 Will Clark .15 .05
❑ 477 Donell Nixon .05 .01
❑ 478 Candy Maldonado .05 .01
❑ 479 Tracy Jones .05 .01
❑ 480 Brett Butler .10 .02
❑ 481 Checklist 1-121 .05 .01
❑ 482 Checklist 122-242 .05 .01
❑ 483 Checklist 243-363 .05 .01
❑ 484 Checklist 364-484 .05 .01

1990 Bowman

❑ COMPLETE SET (528) 25.00 10.00
❑ COMP.FACT.SET (528) 25.00 10.00
❑ 1 Tommy Greene RC .10 .02
❑ 2 Tom Glavine .15 .05
❑ 3 Andy Nezelek .05 .01
❑ 4 Mike Stanton RC .25 .08
❑ 5 Rick Luecken RC .05 .01
❑ 6 Kent Mercker RC .25 .08
❑ 7 Derek Lilliquist .05 .01
❑ 8 Charlie Leibrandt .05 .01
❑ 9 Steve Avery .05 .01
❑ 10 John Smoltz .25 .08
❑ 11 Mark Lemke .05 .01
❑ 12 Lonnie Smith .05 .01
❑ 13 Oddibe McDowell .05 .01
❑ 14 Tyler Houston RC .25 .08
❑ 15 Jeff Blauser .05 .01
❑ 16 Ernie Whitt .05 .01
❑ 17 Alexis Infante .05 .01
❑ 18 Jim Presley .05 .01
❑ 19 Dale Murphy .15 .05
❑ 20 Nick Esasky .05 .01
❑ 21 Rick Sutcliffe .10 .02
❑ 22 Mike Bielecki .05 .01
❑ 23 Steve Wilson .05 .01
❑ 24 Kevin Blankenship .05 .01
❑ 25 Mitch Williams .05 .01
❑ 26 Dean Wilkins RC .05 .01
❑ 27 Greg Maddux .40 .15
❑ 28 Mike Harkey .05 .01
❑ 29 Mark Grace .15 .05
❑ 30 Ryne Sandberg .40 .15
❑ 31 Greg Smith RC .05 .01
❑ 32 Dwight Smith .05 .01
❑ 33 Damon Berryhill .05 .01
❑ 34 Earl Cunningham UER RC .10 .02
❑ 35 Jerome Walton .05 .01
❑ 36 Lloyd McClendon .05 .01
❑ 37 Ty Griffin .05 .01
❑ 38 Shawon Dunston .05 .01
❑ 39 Andre Dawson .10 .02
❑ 40 Luis Salazar .05 .01
❑ 41 Tim Layana RC .05 .01
❑ 42 Rob Dibble .10 .02
❑ 43 Tom Browning .05 .01
❑ 44 Danny Jackson .05 .01
❑ 45 Jose Rijo .05 .01
❑ 46 Scott Scudder .05 .01
❑ 47 Randy Myers UER (Career ERA .274, should be 2.74 .10 .02
❑ 48 Brian Lane RC .10 .02
❑ 49 Paul O'Neill .15 .05
❑ 50 Barry Larkin .15 .05
❑ 51 Reggie Jefferson RC .25 .08
❑ 52 Jeff Branson RC .10 .02
❑ 53 Chris Sabo .05 .01
❑ 54 Joe Oliver .05 .01
❑ 55 Todd Benzinger .05 .01
❑ 56 Rolando Roomes .05 .01
❑ 57 Hal Morris .05 .01
❑ 58 Eric Davis .10 .02
❑ 59 Scott Bryant RC .05 .01
❑ 60 Ken Griffey Sr. .10 .02
❑ 61 Darryl Kile RC .50 .20
❑ 62 Dave Smith .05 .01
❑ 63 Mark Portugal .05 .01
❑ 64 Jeff Juden RC .10 .02
❑ 65 Bill Gullickson .05 .01
❑ 66 Danny Darwin .05 .01
❑ 67 Larry Andersen .05 .01
❑ 68 Jose Cano RC .05 .01
❑ 69 Dan Schatzeder .05 .01
❑ 70 Jim Deshaies .05 .01
❑ 71 Mike Scott .05 .01
❑ 72 Gerald Young .05 .01
❑ 73 Ken Caminiti .10 .02
❑ 74 Ken Oberkfell .05 .01
❑ 75 Dave Rohde RC .05 .01
❑ 76 Bill Doran .05 .01
❑ 77 Andujar Cedeno RC .10 .02
❑ 78 Craig Biggio .25 .08
❑ 79 Karl Rhodes RC .25 .08
❑ 80 Glenn Davis .05 .01
❑ 81 Eric Anthony RC .10 .02
❑ 82 John Wetteland .25 .08
❑ 83 Jay Howell .05 .01
❑ 84 Orel Hershiser .10 .02
❑ 85 Tim Belcher .05 .01
❑ 86 Kiki Jones RC .05 .01
❑ 87 Mike Hartley RC .05 .01
❑ 88 Ramon Martinez .05 .01
❑ 89 Mike Scioscia .05 .01
❑ 90 Willie Randolph .10 .02
❑ 91 Juan Samuel .05 .01
❑ 92 Jose Offerman RC .25 .08
❑ 93 Dave Hansen RC .25 .08
❑ 94 Jeff Hamilton .05 .01
❑ 95 Alfredo Griffin .05 .01
❑ 96 Tom Goodwin RC .25 .08
❑ 97 Kirk Gibson .10 .02
❑ 98 Jose Vizcaino RC .25 .08
❑ 99 Kal Daniels .05 .01
❑ 100 Hubie Brooks .05 .01
❑ 101 Eddie Murray .25 .08
❑ 102 Dennis Boyd .05 .01
❑ 103 Tim Burke .05 .01
❑ 104 Bill Sampen RC .05 .01
❑ 105 Brett Gideon .05 .01
❑ 106 Mark Gardner RC .10 .02
❑ 107 Howard Farmer RC .05 .01
❑ 108 Mel Rojas RC .10 .02

❑ 109 Kevin Gross .05 .01
❑ 110 Dave Schmidt .05 .01
❑ 111 Dennis Martinez .10 .02
❑ 112 Jerry Goff RC .05 .01
❑ 113 Andres Galarraga .10 .02
❑ 114 Tim Wallach .05 .01
❑ 115 Marquis Grissom RC .50 .20
❑ 116 Spike Owen .05 .01
❑ 117 Larry Walker RC 1.00 .40
❑ 118 Tim Raines .10 .02
❑ 119 Delino DeShields RC .25 .08
❑ 120 Tom Foley .05 .01
❑ 121 Dave Martinez .05 .01
❑ 122 Frank Viola UER
(Career ERA .384
should be 3.84 .05 .01
❑ 123 Julio Valera RC .05 .01
❑ 124 Alejandro Pena .05 .01
❑ 125 David Cone .10 .02
❑ 126 Dwight Gooden .10 .02
❑ 127 Kevin D. Brown RC .05 .01
❑ 128 John Franco .10 .02
❑ 129 Terry Bross RC .05 .01
❑ 130 Blaine Beatty RC .05 .01
❑ 131 Sid Fernandez .05 .01
❑ 132 Mike Marshall .05 .01
❑ 133 Howard Johnson .05 .01
❑ 134 Jaime Roseboro RC .05 .01
❑ 135 Alan Zinter RC .10 .02
❑ 136 Keith Miller .05 .01
❑ 137 Kevin Elster .05 .01
❑ 138 Kevin McReynolds .05 .01
❑ 139 Barry Lyons .05 .01
❑ 140 Gregg Jefferies .10 .02
❑ 141 Darryl Strawberry .10 .02
❑ 142 Todd Hundley RC .25 .08
❑ 143 Scott Service .05 .01
❑ 144 Chuck Malone RC .05 .01
❑ 145 Steve Ontiveros .05 .01
❑ 146 Roger McDowell .05 .01
❑ 147 Ken Howell .05 .01
❑ 148 Pat Combs .05 .01
❑ 149 Jeff Parrett .05 .01
❑ 150 Chuck McElroy RC .10 .02
❑ 151 Jason Grimsley RC .10 .02
❑ 152 Len Dykstra .10 .02
❑ 153 Mickey Morandini RC .25 .08
❑ 154 John Kruk .10 .02
❑ 155 Dickie Thon .05 .01
❑ 156 Ricky Jordan .05 .01
❑ 157 Jeff Jackson RC .10 .02
❑ 158 Darren Daulton .10 .02
❑ 159 Tom Herr .05 .01
❑ 160 Von Hayes .05 .01
❑ 161 Dave Hollins RC .25 .08
❑ 162 Carmelo Martinez .05 .01
❑ 163 Bob Walk .05 .01
❑ 164 Doug Drabek .05 .01
❑ 165 Walt Terrell .05 .01
❑ 166 Bill Landrum .05 .01
❑ 167 Scott Ruskin RC .05 .01
❑ 168 Bob Patterson .05 .01
❑ 169 Bobby Bonilla .10 .02
❑ 170 Jose Lind .05 .01
❑ 171 Andy Van Slyke .15 .05
❑ 172 Mike LaValliere .05 .01
❑ 173 Willie Greene RC .10 .02
❑ 174 Jay Bell .10 .02
❑ 175 Sid Bream .05 .01
❑ 176 Tom Prince .05 .01
❑ 177 Wally Backman .05 .01
❑ 178 Moises Alou RC .75 .30
❑ 179 Steve Carter .05 .01
❑ 180 Gary Redus .05 .01
❑ 181 Barry Bonds 1.00 .40
❑ 182 Don Slaught UER
(Card back shows
headings for a .05 .01
❑ 183 Joe Magrane .05 .01
❑ 184 Bryn Smith .05 .01
❑ 185 Todd Worrell .05 .01
❑ 186 Jose DeLeon .05 .01
❑ 187 Frank DiPino .05 .01
❑ 188 John Tudor .05 .01
❑ 189 Howard Hilton RC .05 .01
❑ 190 John Ericks .05 .01
❑ 191 Ken Dayley .05 .01
❑ 192 Ray Lankford RC .50 .20
❑ 193 Todd Zeile .10 .02
❑ 194 Willie McGee .10 .02
❑ 195 Ozzie Smith .40 .15
❑ 196 Milt Thompson .05 .01
❑ 197 Terry Pendleton .10 .02
❑ 198 Vince Coleman .05 .01
❑ 199 Paul Coleman RC .10 .02
❑ 200 Jose Oquendo .05 .01
❑ 201 Pedro Guerrero .05 .01
❑ 202 Tom Brunansky .05 .01
❑ 203 Roger Smithberg RC .05 .01
❑ 204 Eddie Whitson .05 .01
❑ 205 Dennis Rasmussen .05 .01
❑ 206 Craig Lefferts .05 .01
❑ 207 Andy Benes .10 .02
❑ 208 Bruce Hurst .05 .01
❑ 209 Eric Show .05 .01
❑ 210 Rafael Valdez RC .05 .01
❑ 211 Joey Cora .10 .02
❑ 212 Thomas Howard .05 .01
❑ 213 Rob Nelson .05 .01
❑ 214 Jack Clark .10 .02
❑ 215 Garry Templeton .05 .01
❑ 216 Fred Lynn .05 .01
❑ 217 Tony Gwynn .30 .10
❑ 218 Benito Santiago .10 .02
❑ 219 Mike Pagliarulo .05 .01
❑ 220 Joe Carter .10 .02
❑ 221 Roberto Alomar .15 .05
❑ 222 Bip Roberts .05 .01
❑ 223 Rick Reuschel .05 .01
❑ 224 Russ Swan RC .05 .01
❑ 225 Eric Gunderson RC .05 .01
❑ 226 Steve Bedrosian .05 .01
❑ 227 Mike Remlinger RC .05 .01
❑ 228 Scott Garrelts .05 .01
❑ 229 Ernie Camacho .05 .01
❑ 230 Andres Santana RC .10 .02
❑ 231 Will Clark .15 .05
❑ 232 Kevin Mitchell .05 .01
❑ 233 Robby Thompson .05 .01
❑ 234 Bill Bathe .05 .01
❑ 235 Tony Perezchica .05 .01
❑ 236 Gary Carter .10 .02
❑ 237 Brett Butler .10 .02
❑ 238 Matt Williams .10 .02
❑ 239 Earnie Riles .05 .01
❑ 240 Kevin Bass .05 .01
❑ 241 Terry Kennedy .05 .01
❑ 242 Steve Hosey RC .10 .02
❑ 243 Ben McDonald RC .25 .08
❑ 244 Jeff Ballard .05 .01
❑ 245 Joe Price .05 .01
❑ 246 Curt Schilling 1.00 .40
❑ 247 Pete Harnisch .05 .01
❑ 248 Mark Williamson .05 .01
❑ 249 Gregg Olson .10 .02
❑ 250 Chris Myers RC .05 .01
❑ 251A David Segui ERR .50 .20
❑ 251B David Segui COR RC .50 .20
❑ 252 Joe Orsulak .05 .01
❑ 253 Craig Worthington .05 .01
❑ 254 Mickey Tettleton .05 .01
❑ 255 Cal Ripken .75 .30
❑ 256 Bill Ripken .05 .01
❑ 257 Randy Milligan .05 .01
❑ 258 Brady Anderson .10 .02
❑ 259 Chris Hoiles RC .25 .08
❑ 260 Mike Devereaux .05 .01
❑ 261 Phil Bradley .05 .01
❑ 262 Leo Gomez RC .10 .02
❑ 263 Lee Smith .10 .02
❑ 264 Mike Rochford .05 .01
❑ 265 Jeff Reardon .10 .02
❑ 266 Wes Gardner .05 .01
❑ 267 Mike Boddicker .05 .01
❑ 268 Roger Clemens 1.00 .40
❑ 269 Rob Murphy .05 .01
❑ 270 Mickey Pina RC .05 .01
❑ 271 Tony Pena .05 .01
❑ 272 Jody Reed .05 .01
❑ 273 Kevin Romine .05 .01
❑ 274 Mike Greenwell .05 .01
❑ 275 Mo Vaughn RC 1.00 .40
❑ 276 Danny Heep .05 .01
❑ 277 Scott Cooper RC .10 .02
❑ 278 Greg Blosser RC .10 .02
❑ 279 Dwight Evans UER
(* by "1990 Team
Breakdown") .15 .05
❑ 280 Ellis Burks .15 .05
❑ 281 Wade Boggs .15 .05
❑ 282 Marty Barrett .05 .01
❑ 283 Kirk McCaskill .05 .01
❑ 284 Mark Langston .05 .01
❑ 285 Bert Blyleven .10 .02
❑ 286 Mike Fetters RC .25 .08
❑ 287 Kyle Abbott RC .05 .01
❑ 288 Jim Abbott .15 .05
❑ 289 Chuck Finley .10 .02
❑ 290 Gary DiSarcina RC .25 .08
❑ 291 Dick Schofield .05 .01
❑ 292 Devon White .10 .02
❑ 293 Bobby Rose .05 .01
❑ 294 Brian Downing .05 .01
❑ 295 Lance Parrish .05 .01
❑ 296 Jack Howell .05 .01
❑ 297 Claudell Washington .05 .01
❑ 298 John Orton RC .10 .02
❑ 299 Wally Joyner .10 .02
❑ 300 Lee Stevens .10 .02
❑ 301 Chili Davis .10 .02
❑ 302 Johnny Ray .05 .01
❑ 303 Greg Hibbard RC .10 .02
❑ 304 Eric King .05 .01
❑ 305 Jack McDowell .05 .01
❑ 306 Bobby Thigpen .05 .01
❑ 307 Adam Peterson .05 .01
❑ 308 Scott Radinsky RC .25 .08
❑ 309 Wayne Edwards RC .05 .01
❑ 310 Melido Perez .05 .01
❑ 311 Robin Ventura .25 .08
❑ 312 Sammy Sosa RC 3.00 1.25
❑ 313 Dan Pasqua .05 .01
❑ 314 Carlton Fisk .15 .05
❑ 315 Ozzie Guillen .10 .02
❑ 316 Ivan Calderon .05 .01
❑ 317 Daryl Boston .05 .01
❑ 318 Craig Grebeck RC .25 .08
❑ 319 Scott Fletcher .05 .01
❑ 320 Frank Thomas RC 2.00 .75
❑ 321 Steve Lyons .05 .01
❑ 322 Carlos Martinez .05 .01
❑ 323 Joe Skalski .05 .01
❑ 324 Tom Candiotti .05 .01
❑ 325 Greg Swindell .05 .01
❑ 326 Steve Olin RC .25 .08
❑ 327 Kevin Wickander .05 .01
❑ 328 Doug Jones .05 .01
❑ 329 Jeff Shaw .05 .01
❑ 330 Kevin Bearse RC .05 .01
❑ 331 Dion James .05 .01
❑ 332 Jerry Browne .05 .01
❑ 333 Albert Belle .25 .08
❑ 334 Felix Fermin .05 .01
❑ 335 Candy Maldonado .05 .01
❑ 336 Cory Snyder .05 .01
❑ 337 Sandy Alomar Jr. .10 .02
❑ 338 Mark Lewis .05 .01
❑ 339 Carlos Baerga RC .25 .08
❑ 340 Chris James .05 .01
❑ 341 Brook Jacoby .05 .01
❑ 342 Keith Hernandez .10 .02
❑ 343 Frank Tanana .05 .01
❑ 344 Scott Aldred RC .05 .01
❑ 345 Mike Henneman .05 .01
❑ 346 Steve Wapnick RC .05 .01
❑ 347 Greg Gohr RC .10 .02
❑ 348 Eric Stone RC .05 .01
❑ 349 Brian DuBois RC .05 .01
❑ 350 Kevin Ritz RC .05 .01
❑ 351 Rico Brogna .25 .08
❑ 352 Mike Heath .05 .01
❑ 353 Alan Trammell .10 .02
❑ 354 Chet Lemon .05 .01
❑ 355 Dave Bergman .05 .01
❑ 356 Lou Whitaker .10 .02
❑ 357 Cecil Fielder UER .10 .02
❑ 358 Milt Cuyler RC .10 .02
❑ 359 Tony Phillips .05 .01

❑	360	Travis Fryman RC	.50	.20
❑	361	Ed Romero	.05	.01
❑	362	Lloyd Moseby	.05	.01
❑	363	Mark Gubicza	.05	.01
❑	364	Bret Saberhagen	.10	.02
❑	365	Tom Gordon	.10	.02
❑	366	Steve Farr	.05	.01
❑	367	Kevin Appier	.10	.02
❑	368	Storm Davis	.05	.01
❑	369	Mark Davis	.05	.01
❑	370	Jeff Montgomery	.10	.02
❑	371	Frank White	.10	.02
❑	372	Brent Mayne RC	.25	.08
❑	373	Bob Boone	.10	.02
❑	374	Jim Eisenreich	.05	.01
❑	375	Danny Tartabull	.05	.01
❑	376	Kurt Stillwell	.05	.01
❑	377	Bill Pecota	.05	.01
❑	378	Bo Jackson	.25	.08
❑	379	Bob Hamelin RC	.25	.08
❑	380	Kevin Seitzer	.05	.01
❑	381	Rey Palacios	.05	.01
❑	382	George Brett	.60	.25
❑	383	Gerald Perry	.05	.01
❑	384	Teddy Higuera	.05	.01
❑	385	Tom Filer	.05	.01
❑	386	Dan Plesac	.05	.01
❑	387	Cal Eldred RC	.25	.08
❑	388	Jaime Navarro	.05	.01
❑	389	Chris Bosio	.05	.01
❑	390	Randy Veres	.05	.01
❑	391	Gary Sheffield	.25	.08
❑	392	George Canale RC	.05	.01
❑	393	B.J. Surhoff	.10	.02
❑	394	Tim McIntosh RC	.05	.01
❑	395	Greg Brock	.05	.01
❑	396	Greg Vaughn	.05	.01
❑	397	Darryl Hamilton	.05	.01
❑	398	Dave Parker	.10	.02
❑	399	Paul Molitor	.10	.02
❑	400	Jim Gantner	.05	.01
❑	401	Rob Deer	.05	.01
❑	402	Billy Spiers	.05	.01
❑	403	Glenn Braggs	.05	.01
❑	404	Robin Yount	.40	.15
❑	405	Rick Aguilera	.10	.02
❑	406	Johnny Ard	.05	.01
❑	407	Kevin Tapani RC	.25	.08
❑	408	Park Pittman RC	.05	.01
❑	409	Allan Anderson	.05	.01
❑	410	Juan Berenguer	.05	.01
❑	411	Willie Banks RC	.10	.02
❑	412	Rich Yett	.05	.01
❑	413	Dave West	.05	.01
❑	414	Greg Gagne	.05	.01
❑	415	Chuck Knoblauch RC	.50	.20
❑	416	Randy Bush	.05	.01
❑	417	Gary Gaetti	.10	.02
❑	418	Kent Hrbek	.10	.02
❑	419	Al Newman	.05	.01
❑	420	Danny Gladden	.05	.01
❑	421	Paul Sorrento RC	.25	.08
❑	422	Derek Parks RC	.10	.02
❑	423	Scott Leius RC	.10	.02
❑	424	Kirby Puckett	.25	.08
❑	425	Willie Smith	.05	.01
❑	426	Dave Righetti	.05	.01
❑	427	Jeff D. Robinson	.05	.01
❑	428	Alan Mills RC	.10	.02
❑	429	Tim Leary	.05	.01
❑	430	Pascual Perez	.05	.01
❑	431	Alvaro Espinoza	.05	.01
❑	432	Dave Winfield	.10	.02
❑	433	Jesse Barfield	.05	.01
❑	434	Randy Velarde	.05	.01
❑	435	Rick Cerone	.05	.01
❑	436	Steve Balboni	.05	.01
❑	437	Mel Hall	.05	.01
❑	438	Bob Geren	.05	.01
❑	439	Bernie Williams RC	1.50	.60
❑	440	Kevin Maas RC	.25	.08
❑	441	Mike Blowers RC	.10	.02
❑	442	Steve Sax	.05	.01
❑	443	Don Mattingly	.60	.25
❑	444	Roberto Kelly	.05	.01
❑	445	Mike Moore	.05	.01
❑	446	Reggie Harris RC	.10	.02
❑	447	Scott Sanderson	.05	.01
❑	448	Dave Otto	.05	.01
❑	449	Dave Stewart	.10	.02
❑	450	Rick Honeycutt	.05	.01
❑	451	Dennis Eckersley	.10	.02
❑	452	Carney Lansford	.10	.02
❑	453	Scott Hemond RC	.10	.02
❑	454	Mark McGwire	1.00	.40
❑	455	Felix Jose	.05	.01
❑	456	Terry Steinbach	.05	.01
❑	457	Rickey Henderson	.25	.08
❑	458	Dave Henderson	.05	.01
❑	459	Mike Gallego	.05	.01
❑	460	Jose Canseco	.15	.05
❑	461	Walt Weiss	.05	.01
❑	462	Ken Phelps	.05	.01
❑	463	Darren Lewis RC	.10	.02
❑	464	Ron Hassey	.05	.01
❑	465	Roger Salkeld RC	.10	.02
❑	466	Scott Bankhead	.05	.01
❑	467	Keith Comstock	.05	.01
❑	468	Randy Johnson	.50	.20
❑	469	Erik Hanson	.05	.01
❑	470	Mike Schooler	.05	.01
❑	471	Gary Eave RC	.05	.01
❑	472	Jeffrey Leonard	.05	.01
❑	473	Dave Valle	.05	.01
❑	474	Omar Vizquel	.25	.08
❑	475	Pete O'Brien	.05	.01
❑	476	Henry Cotto	.05	.01
❑	477	Jay Buhner	.10	.02
❑	478	Harold Reynolds	.10	.02
❑	479	Alvin Davis	.05	.01
❑	480	Darnell Coles	.05	.01
❑	481	Ken Griffey Jr.	.75	.30
❑	482	Greg Briley	.05	.01
❑	483	Scott Bradley	.05	.01
❑	484	Tino Martinez	.50	.20
❑	485	Jeff Russell	.05	.01
❑	486	Nolan Ryan	1.00	.40
❑	487	Robb Nen RC	.50	.20
❑	488	Kevin Brown	.10	.02
❑	489	Brian Bohanon RC	.10	.02
❑	490	Ruben Sierra	.10	.02
❑	491	Pete Incaviglia	.05	.01
❑	492	Juan Gonzalez RC	1.00	.40
❑	493	Steve Buechele	.05	.01
❑	494	Scott Coolbaugh	.05	.01
❑	495	Geno Petralli	.05	.01
❑	496	Rafael Palmeiro	.15	.05
❑	497	Julio Franco	.10	.02
❑	498	Gary Pettis	.05	.01
❑	499	Donald Harris RC	.05	.01
❑	500	Monty Fariss	.05	.01
❑	501	Harold Baines	.10	.02
❑	502	Cecil Espy	.05	.01
❑	503	Jack Daugherty RC	.05	.01
❑	504	Willie Blair RC	.10	.02
❑	505	Dave Stieb	.10	.02
❑	506	Tom Henke	.05	.01
❑	507	John Cerutti	.05	.01
❑	508	Paul Kilgus	.05	.01
❑	509	Jimmy Key	.10	.02
❑	510	John Olerud RC	1.00	.40
❑	511	Ed Sprague	.10	.02
❑	512	Manuel Lee	.05	.01
❑	513	Fred McGriff	.25	.08
❑	514	Glenallen Hill	.05	.01
❑	515	George Bell	.05	.01
❑	516	Mookie Wilson	.10	.02
❑	517	Luis Sojo RC	.25	.08
❑	518	Nelson Liriano	.05	.01
❑	519	Kelly Gruber	.05	.01
❑	520	Greg Myers	.05	.01
❑	521	Pat Borders	.05	.01
❑	522	Junior Felix	.05	.01
❑	523	Eddie Zosky RC	.10	.02
❑	524	Tony Fernandez	.05	.01
❑	525	Checklist 1-132 UER (No copyright mark on the ba	.05	.01
❑	526	Checklist 133-264	.05	.01
❑	527	Checklist 265-396	.05	.01
❑	528	Checklist 397-528	.05	.01

1991 Bowman

❑		COMPLETE SET (704)	40.00	15.00
❑		COMP.FACT.SET (704)	40.00	15.00
❑	1	Rod Carew I	.15	.05
❑	2	Rod Carew II	.15	.05
❑	3	Rod Carew III	.15	.05
❑	4	Rod Carew IV	.15	.05
❑	5	Rod Carew V	.15	.05
❑	6	Willie Fraser	.05	.01
❑	7	John Olerud	.10	.02
❑	8	William Suero RC	.05	.01
❑	9	Roberto Alomar	.15	.05
❑	10	Todd Stottlemyre	.05	.01
❑	11	Joe Carter	.10	.02
❑	12	Steve Karsay RC	.50	.20
❑	13	Mark Whiten	.05	.01
❑	14	Pat Borders	.05	.01
❑	15	Mike Timlin RC	.50	.20
❑	16	Tom Henke	.05	.01
❑	17	Eddie Zosky	.05	.01
❑	18	Kelly Gruber	.05	.01
❑	19	Jimmy Key	.10	.02
❑	20	Jerry Schunk RC	.05	.01
❑	21	Manuel Lee	.05	.01
❑	22	Dave Stieb	.05	.01
❑	23	Pat Hentgen RC	.50	.20
❑	24	Glenallen Hill	.05	.01
❑	25	Rene Gonzales	.05	.01
❑	26	Ed Sprague	.05	.01
❑	27	Ken Dayley	.05	.01
❑	28	Pat Tabler	.05	.01
❑	29	Denis Boucher RC	.15	.05
❑	30	Devon White	.10	.02
❑	31	Dante Bichette	.10	.02
❑	32	Paul Molitor	.10	.02
❑	33	Greg Vaughn	.05	.01
❑	34	Dan Plesac	.05	.01
❑	35	Chris George RC	.15	.05
❑	36	Tim McIntosh	.05	.01
❑	37	Franklin Stubbs	.05	.01
❑	38	Bo Dodson RC	.15	.05
❑	39	Ron Robinson	.05	.01
❑	40	Ed Nunez	.05	.01
❑	41	Greg Brock	.05	.01
❑	42	Jaime Navarro	.05	.01
❑	43	Chris Bosio	.05	.01
❑	44	B.J. Surhoff	.10	.02
❑	45	Chris Johnson RC	.05	.01
❑	46	Willie Randolph	.10	.02
❑	47	Narciso Elvira RC	.05	.01
❑	48	Jim Gantner	.05	.01
❑	49	Kevin Brown	.05	.01
❑	50	Julio Machado	.05	.01
❑	51	Chuck Crim	.05	.01
❑	52	Gary Sheffield	.10	.02
❑	53	Angel Miranda RC	.15	.05
❑	54	Ted Higuera	.05	.01
❑	55	Robin Yount	.40	.15
❑	56	Cal Eldred	.05	.01
❑	57	Sandy Alomar Jr.	.05	.01
❑	58	Greg Swindell	.05	.01
❑	59	Brook Jacoby	.05	.01
❑	60	Efrain Valdez RC	.05	.01
❑	61	Ever Magallanes RC	.05	.01
❑	62	Tom Candiotti	.05	.01
❑	63	Eric King	.05	.01
❑	64	Alex Cole	.05	.01

❑ 65	Charles Nagy	.05	.01
❑ 66	Mitch Webster	.05	.01
❑ 67	Chris James	.05	.01
❑ 68	Jim Thome RC	5.00	2.00
❑ 69	Carlos Baerga	.05	.01
❑ 70	Mark Lewis	.05	.01
❑ 71	Jerry Browne	.05	.01
❑ 72	Jesse Orosco	.05	.01
❑ 73	Mike Huff	.05	.01
❑ 74	Jose Escobar RC	.05	.01
❑ 75	Jeff Manto	.05	.01
❑ 76	Turner Ward RC	.15	.05
❑ 77	Doug Jones	.05	.01
❑ 78	Bruce Egloff RC	.05	.01
❑ 79	Tim Costo RC	.15	.05
❑ 80	Beau Allred	.05	.01
❑ 81	Albert Belle	.10	.02
❑ 82	John Farrell	.05	.01
❑ 83	Glenn Davis	.05	.01
❑ 84	Joe Orsulak	.05	.01
❑ 85	Mark Williamson	.05	.01
❑ 86	Ben McDonald	.05	.01
❑ 87	Billy Ripken	.05	.01
❑ 88	Leo Gomez	.05	.01
❑ 89	Bob Melvin	.05	.01
❑ 90	Jeff M. Robinson	.05	.01
❑ 91	Jose Mesa	.05	.01
❑ 92	Gregg Olson	.05	.01
❑ 93	Mike Devereaux	.05	.01
❑ 94	Luis Mercedes RC	.15	.05
❑ 95	Arthur Rhodes RC	.50	.20
❑ 96	Juan Bell	.05	.01
❑ 97	Mike Mussina RC	4.00	1.50
❑ 98	Jeff Ballard	.05	.01
❑ 99	Chris Hoiles	.05	.01
❑ 100	Brady Anderson	.10	.02
❑ 101	Bob Milacki	.05	.01
❑ 102	David Segui	.05	.01
❑ 103	Dwight Evans	.15	.05
❑ 104	Cal Ripken	.75	.30
❑ 105	Mike Linskey RC	.05	.01
❑ 106	Jeff Tackett RC	.15	.05
❑ 107	Jeff Reardon	.10	.02
❑ 108	Dana Kiecker	.05	.01
❑ 109	Ellis Burks	.10	.02
❑ 110	Dave Owen	.05	.01
❑ 111	Danny Darwin	.05	.01
❑ 112	Mo Vaughn	.10	.02
❑ 113	Jeff McNeely RC	.15	.05
❑ 114	Tom Bolton	.05	.01
❑ 115	Greg Blosser	.05	.01
❑ 116	Mike Greenwell	.05	.01
❑ 117	Phil Plantier RC	.15	.05
❑ 118	Roger Clemens	.75	.30
❑ 119	John Marzano	.05	.01
❑ 120	Jody Reed	.05	.01
❑ 121	Scott Taylor RC	.15	.05
❑ 122	Jack Clark	.10	.02
❑ 123	Derek Livernois RC	.05	.01
❑ 124	Tony Pena	.05	.01
❑ 125	Tom Brunansky	.05	.01
❑ 126	Carlos Quintana	.05	.01
❑ 127	Tim Naehring	.05	.01
❑ 128	Matt Young	.05	.01
❑ 129	Wade Boggs	.15	.05
❑ 130	Kevin Morton RC	.05	.01
❑ 131	Pete Incaviglia	.05	.01
❑ 132	Rob Deer	.05	.01
❑ 133	Bill Gullickson	.05	.01
❑ 134	Rico Brogna	.05	.01
❑ 135	Lloyd Moseby	.05	.01
❑ 136	Cecil Fielder	.10	.02
❑ 137	Tony Phillips	.05	.01
❑ 138	Mark Leiter RC	.15	.05
❑ 139	John Cerutti	.05	.01
❑ 140	Mickey Tettleton	.05	.01
❑ 141	Milt Cuyler	.05	.01
❑ 142	Greg Gohr	.05	.01
❑ 143	Tony Bernazard	.05	.01
❑ 144	Dan Gakeler RC	.05	.01
❑ 145	Travis Fryman	.10	.02
❑ 146	Dan Petry	.05	.01
❑ 147	Scott Aldred	.05	.01
❑ 148	John DeSilva RC	.05	.01
❑ 149	Rusty Meacham RC	.15	.05
❑ 150	Lou Whitaker	.10	.02
❑ 151	Dave Haas RC	.05	.01
❑ 152	Luis de los Santos	.05	.01
❑ 153	Ivan Cruz RC	.05	.01
❑ 154	Alan Trammell	.10	.02
❑ 155	Pat Kelly RC	.05	.01
❑ 156	Carl Everett RC	1.50	.60
❑ 157	Greg Cadaret	.05	.01
❑ 158	Kevin Maas	.05	.01
❑ 159	Jeff Johnson RC	.05	.01
❑ 160	Willie Smith	.05	.01
❑ 161	Gerald Williams RC	.50	.20
❑ 162	Mike Humphreys RC	.15	.05
❑ 163	Alvaro Espinoza	.05	.01
❑ 164	Matt Nokes	.05	.01
❑ 165	Wade Taylor RC	.05	.01
❑ 166	Roberto Kelly	.05	.01
❑ 167	John Habyan	.05	.01
❑ 168	Steve Farr	.05	.01
❑ 169	Jesse Barfield	.05	.01
❑ 170	Steve Sax	.05	.01
❑ 171	Jim Leyritz	.05	.01
❑ 172	Robert Eenhoorn RC	.15	.05
❑ 173	Bernie Williams	.25	.08
❑ 174	Scott Lusader	.05	.01
❑ 175	Torey Lovullo	.05	.01
❑ 176	Chuck Cary	.05	.01
❑ 177	Scott Sanderson	.05	.01
❑ 178	Don Mattingly	.60	.25
❑ 179	Mel Hall	.05	.01
❑ 180	Juan Gonzalez	.25	.08
❑ 181	Hensley Meulens	.05	.01
❑ 182	Jose Offerman	.05	.01
❑ 183	Jeff Bagwell RC	4.00	1.50
❑ 184	Jeff Conine RC	1.00	.40
❑ 185	Henry Rodriguez RC	.50	.20
❑ 186	Jimmy Reese CO	.10	.02
❑ 187	Kyle Abbott	.05	.01
❑ 188	Lance Parrish	.10	.02
❑ 189	Rafael Montalvo RC	.05	.01
❑ 190	Floyd Bannister	.05	.01
❑ 191	Dick Schofield	.05	.01
❑ 192	Scott Lewis RC	.05	.01
❑ 193	Jeff D. Robinson	.05	.01
❑ 194	Kent Anderson	.05	.01
❑ 195	Wally Joyner	.10	.02
❑ 196	Chuck Finley	.10	.02
❑ 197	Luis Sojo	.05	.01
❑ 198	Jeff Richardson RC	.05	.01
❑ 199	Dave Parker	.10	.02
❑ 200	Jim Abbott	.15	.05
❑ 201	Junior Felix	.05	.01
❑ 202	Mark Langston	.05	.01
❑ 203	Tim Salmon RC	1.50	.60
❑ 204	Cliff Young	.05	.01
❑ 205	Scott Bailes	.05	.01
❑ 206	Bobby Rose	.05	.01
❑ 207	Gary Gaetti	.10	.02
❑ 208	Ruben Amaro RC	.15	.05
❑ 209	Luis Polonia	.05	.01
❑ 210	Dave Winfield	.10	.02
❑ 211	Bryan Harvey	.05	.01
❑ 212	Mike Moore	.05	.01
❑ 213	Rickey Henderson	.25	.08
❑ 214	Steve Chitren RC	.05	.01
❑ 215	Bob Welch	.05	.01
❑ 216	Terry Steinbach	.05	.01
❑ 217	Earnest Riles	.05	.01
❑ 218	Todd Van Poppel RC	.50	.20
❑ 219	Mike Gallego	.05	.01
❑ 220	Curt Young	.05	.01
❑ 221	Todd Burns	.05	.01
❑ 222	Vance Law	.05	.01
❑ 223	Eric Show	.05	.01
❑ 224	Don Peters RC	.05	.01
❑ 225	Dave Stewart	.10	.02
❑ 226	Dave Henderson	.05	.01
❑ 227	Jose Canseco	.15	.05
❑ 228	Walt Weiss	.05	.01
❑ 229	Dann Howitt	.05	.01
❑ 230	Willie Wilson	.05	.01
❑ 231	Harold Baines	.10	.02
❑ 232	Scott Hemond	.05	.01
❑ 233	Joe Slusarski RC	.05	.01
❑ 234	Mark McGwire	.75	.30
❑ 235	Kirk Dressendorfer RC	.15	.05
❑ 236	Craig Paquette RC	.50	.20
❑ 237	Dennis Eckersley	.10	.02
❑ 238	Dana Allison RC	.05	.01
❑ 239	Scott Bradley	.05	.01
❑ 240	Brian Holman	.05	.01
❑ 241	Mike Schooler	.05	.01
❑ 242	Rich DeLucia RC	.05	.01
❑ 243	Edgar Martinez	.15	.05
❑ 244	Henry Cotto	.05	.01
❑ 245	Omar Vizquel	.15	.05
❑ 246	Ken Griffey Jr.	.50	.20
❑ 247	Jay Buhner	.10	.02
❑ 248	Bill Krueger	.05	.01
❑ 249	Dave Fleming RC	.15	.05
❑ 250	Patrick Lennon RC	.05	.01
❑ 251	Dave Valle	.05	.01
❑ 252	Harold Reynolds	.10	.02
❑ 253	Randy Johnson	.30	.10
❑ 254	Scott Bankhead	.05	.01
❑ 255	Ken Griffey Sr. UER 246	.05	.01
❑ 256	Greg Briley	.05	.01
❑ 257	Tino Martinez	.25	.08
❑ 258	Alvin Davis	.05	.01
❑ 259	Pete O'Brien	.05	.01
❑ 260	Erik Hanson	.05	.01
❑ 261	Bret Boone RC	1.50	.60
❑ 262	Roger Salkeld	.05	.01
❑ 263	Dave Burba RC	.50	.20
❑ 264	Kerry Woodson RC	.15	.05
❑ 265	Julio Franco	.10	.02
❑ 266	Dan Peltier RC	.15	.05
❑ 267	Jeff Russell	.05	.01
❑ 268	Steve Buechele	.05	.01
❑ 269	Donald Harris	.05	.01
❑ 270	Robb Nen	.15	.05
❑ 271	Rich Gossage	.10	.02
❑ 272	Ivan Rodriguez RC	4.00	1.50
❑ 273	Jeff Huson	.05	.01
❑ 274	Kevin Brown	.10	.02
❑ 275	Dan Smith RC	.15	.05
❑ 276	Gary Pettis	.05	.01
❑ 277	Jack Daugherty	.05	.01
❑ 278	Mike Jeffcoat	.05	.01
❑ 279	Brad Arnsberg	.05	.01
❑ 280	Nolan Ryan	1.00	.40
❑ 281	Eric McCray RC	.05	.01
❑ 282	Scott Chiamparino	.05	.01
❑ 283	Ruben Sierra	.10	.02
❑ 284	Geno Petralli	.05	.01
❑ 285	Monty Fariss	.05	.01
❑ 286	Rafael Palmeiro	.15	.05
❑ 287	Bobby Witt	.05	.01
❑ 288	Dean Palmer UER	.10	.02
❑ 289	Tony Scruggs RC	.05	.01
❑ 290	Kenny Rogers	.10	.02
❑ 291	Bret Saberhagen	.10	.02
❑ 292	Brian McRae RC	.50	.20
❑ 293	Storm Davis	.05	.01
❑ 294	Danny Tartabull	.05	.01
❑ 295	David Howard RC	.05	.01
❑ 296	Mike Boddicker	.05	.01
❑ 297	Joel Johnston RC	.15	.05
❑ 298	Tim Spehr RC	.05	.01
❑ 299	Hector Wagner RC	.05	.01
❑ 300	George Brett	.60	.25
❑ 301	Mike Macfarlane	.05	.01
❑ 302	Kirk Gibson	.10	.02
❑ 303	Harvey Pulliam RC	.15	.05
❑ 304	Jim Eisenreich	.05	.01
❑ 305	Kevin Seitzer	.05	.01
❑ 306	Mark Davis	.05	.01
❑ 307	Kurt Stillwell	.05	.01
❑ 308	Jeff Montgomery	.05	.01
❑ 309	Kevin Appier	.10	.02
❑ 310	Bob Hamelin	.05	.01
❑ 311	Tom Gordon	.05	.01
❑ 312	Kerwin Moore RC	.15	.05
❑ 313	Hugh Walker	.05	.01
❑ 314	Terry Shumpert	.05	.01
❑ 315	Warren Cromartie	.05	.01
❑ 316	Gary Thurman	.05	.01
❑ 317	Steve Bedrosian	.05	.01
❑ 318	Danny Gladden	.05	.01
❑ 319	Jack Morris	.10	.02
❑ 320	Kirby Puckett	.25	.08
❑ 321	Kent Hrbek	.10	.02
❑ 322	Kevin Tapani	.05	.01

❑ 323 Denny Neagle RC	.50	.20
❑ 324 Rich Garces RC	.15	.05
❑ 325 Larry Caslan RC	.05	.01
❑ 326 Shane Mack	.05	.01
❑ 327 Allan Anderson	.05	.01
❑ 328 Junior Ortiz	.05	.01
❑ 329 Paul Abbott RC	.15	.05
❑ 330 Chuck Knoblauch	.10	.02
❑ 331 Chili Davis	.10	.02
❑ 332 Todd Ritchie RC	.50	.20
❑ 333 Brian Harper	.05	.01
❑ 334 Rick Aguilera	.10	.02
❑ 335 Scott Erickson	.05	.01
❑ 336 Pedro Munoz RC	.15	.05
❑ 337 Scott Leius	.05	.01
❑ 338 Greg Gagne	.05	.01
❑ 339 Mike Pagliarulo	.05	.01
❑ 340 Terry Leach	.05	.01
❑ 341 Willie Banks	.05	.01
❑ 342 Bobby Thigpen	.05	.01
❑ 343 Roberto Hernandez RC	.50	.20
❑ 344 Melido Perez	.05	.01
❑ 345 Carlton Fisk	.15	.05
❑ 346 Norberto Martin RC	.05	.01
❑ 347 Johnny Ruffin RC	.15	.05
❑ 348 Jeff Carter	.05	.01
❑ 349 Lance Johnson	.05	.01
❑ 350 Sammy Sosa	.25	.08
❑ 351 Alex Fernandez	.05	.01
❑ 352 Jack McDowell	.05	.01
❑ 353 Bob Wickman RC	1.50	.60
❑ 354 Wilson Alvarez	.05	.01
❑ 355 Charlie Hough	.10	.02
❑ 356 Ozzie Guillen	.10	.02
❑ 357 Cory Snyder	.05	.01
❑ 358 Robin Ventura	.10	.02
❑ 359 Scott Fletcher	.05	.01
❑ 360 Cesar Bernhardt RC	.05	.01
❑ 361 Dan Pasqua	.05	.01
❑ 362 Tim Raines	.10	.02
❑ 363 Brian Drahman RC	.05	.01
❑ 364 Wayne Edwards	.05	.01
❑ 365 Scott Radinsky	.05	.01
❑ 366 Frank Thomas	.25	.08
❑ 367 Cecil Fielder SLUG	.05	.01
❑ 368 Julio Franco SLUG	.05	.01
❑ 369 Kelly Gruber SLUG	.05	.01
❑ 370 Alan Trammell SLUG	.10	.02
❑ 371 Rickey Henderson SLUG	.15	.05
❑ 372 Jose Canseco SLUG	.10	.02
❑ 373 Ellis Burks SLUG	.05	.01
❑ 374 Lance Parrish SLUG	.05	.01
❑ 375 Dave Parker SLUG	.05	.01
❑ 376 Eddie Murray SLUG	.15	.05
❑ 377 Ryne Sandberg SLUG	.25	.08
❑ 378 Matt Williams SLUG	.05	.01
❑ 379 Barry Larkin SLUG	.10	.02
❑ 380 Barry Bonds SLUG	.50	.20
❑ 381 Bobby Bonilla SLUG	.05	.01
❑ 382 Darryl Strawberry SLUG	.05	.01
❑ 383 Benny Santiago SLUG	.05	.01
❑ 384 Don Robinson SLUG	.05	.01
❑ 385 Paul Coleman	.05	.01
❑ 386 Milt Thompson	.05	.01
❑ 387 Lee Smith	.10	.02
❑ 388 Ray Lankford	.10	.02
❑ 389 Tom Pagnozzi	.05	.01
❑ 390 Ken Hill	.05	.01
❑ 391 Jamie Moyer	.10	.02
❑ 392 Greg Carmona RC	.05	.01
❑ 393 John Ericks	.05	.01
❑ 394 Bob Tewksbury	.05	.01
❑ 395 Jose Oquendo	.05	.01
❑ 396 Rheal Cormier RC	.15	.05
❑ 397 Mike Milchin RC	.05	.01
❑ 398 Ozzie Smith	.40	.15
❑ 399 Aaron Holbert RC	.15	.05
❑ 400 Jose DeLeon	.05	.01
❑ 401 Felix Jose	.05	.01
❑ 402 Juan Agosto	.05	.01
❑ 403 Pedro Guerrero	.10	.02
❑ 404 Todd Zeile	.05	.01
❑ 405 Gerald Perry	.05	.01
❑ 406 Donovan Osborne UER RC	.15	.05
❑ 407 Bryn Smith	.05	.01
❑ 408 Bernard Gilkey	.05	.01
❑ 409 Rex Hudler	.05	.01
❑ 410 Thomson/Branca FOIL	.25	.08
❑ 411 Lance Dickson RC	.15	.05
❑ 412 Danny Jackson	.05	.01
❑ 413 Jerome Walton	.05	.01
❑ 414 Sean Cheetham RC	.05	.01
❑ 415 Joe Girardi	.05	.01
❑ 416 Ryne Sandberg	.40	.15
❑ 417 Mike Harkey	.05	.01
❑ 418 George Bell	.05	.01
❑ 419 Rick Wilkins RC	.15	.05
❑ 420 Earl Cunningham	.05	.01
❑ 421 Heathcliff Slocumb RC	.15	.05
❑ 422 Mike Bielecki	.05	.01
❑ 423 Jessie Hollins RC	.15	.05
❑ 424 Shawon Dunston	.05	.01
❑ 425 Dave Smith	.05	.01
❑ 426 Greg Maddux	.40	.15
❑ 427 Jose Vizcaino	.05	.01
❑ 428 Luis Salazar	.05	.01
❑ 429 Andre Dawson	.10	.02
❑ 430 Rick Sutcliffe	.10	.02
❑ 431 Paul Assenmacher	.05	.01
❑ 432 Erik Pappas RC	.05	.01
❑ 433 Mark Grace	.15	.05
❑ 434 Dennis Martinez	.10	.02
❑ 435 Marquis Grissom	.10	.02
❑ 436 Wil Cordero RC	.50	.20
❑ 437 Tim Wallach	.05	.01
❑ 438 Brian Barnes RC	.05	.01
❑ 439 Barry Jones	.05	.01
❑ 440 Ivan Calderon	.05	.01
❑ 441 Stan Spencer RC	.05	.01
❑ 442 Larry Walker	.25	.08
❑ 443 Chris Haney RC	.15	.05
❑ 444 Hector Rivera RC	.05	.01
❑ 445 Delino DeShields	.10	.02
❑ 446 Andres Galarraga	.10	.02
❑ 447 Gilberto Reyes	.05	.01
❑ 448 Willie Greene	.05	.01
❑ 449 Greg Colbrunn RC	.50	.20
❑ 450 Rondell White RC	1.00	.40
❑ 451 Steve Frey	.05	.01
❑ 452 Shane Andrews RC	.15	.05
❑ 453 Mike Fitzgerald	.05	.01
❑ 454 Spike Owen	.05	.01
❑ 455 Dave Martinez	.05	.01
❑ 456 Dennis Boyd	.05	.01
❑ 457 Eric Bullock	.05	.01
❑ 458 Reid Cornelius RC	.15	.05
❑ 459 Chris Nabholz	.05	.01
❑ 460 David Cone	.10	.02
❑ 461 Hubie Brooks	.05	.01
❑ 462 Sid Fernandez	.05	.01
❑ 463 Doug Simons RC	.05	.01
❑ 464 Howard Johnson	.05	.01
❑ 465 Chris Donnels RC	.05	.01
❑ 466 Anthony Young RC	.15	.05
❑ 467 Todd Hundley	.05	.01
❑ 468 Rick Cerone	.05	.01
❑ 469 Kevin Elster	.05	.01
❑ 470 Wally Whitehurst	.05	.01
❑ 471 Vince Coleman	.05	.01
❑ 472 Dwight Gooden	.10	.02
❑ 473 Charlie O'Brien	.05	.01
❑ 474 Jeromy Burnitz RC	1.00	.40
❑ 475 John Franco	.10	.02
❑ 476 Daryl Boston	.05	.01
❑ 477 Frank Viola	.10	.02
❑ 478 D.J. Dozier	.05	.01
❑ 479 Kevin McReynolds	.05	.01
❑ 480 Tom Herr	.05	.01
❑ 481 Gregg Jefferies	.05	.01
❑ 482 Pete Schourek RC	.15	.05
❑ 483 Ron Darling	.05	.01
❑ 484 Dave Magadan	.05	.01
❑ 485 Andy Ashby RC	.50	.20
❑ 486 Dale Murphy	.15	.05
❑ 487 Von Hayes	.05	.01
❑ 488 Kim Batiste RC	.15	.05
❑ 489 Tony Longmire RC	.15	.05
❑ 490 Wally Backman	.05	.01
❑ 491 Jeff Jackson	.05	.01
❑ 492 Mickey Morandini	.05	.01
❑ 493 Darrel Akerfelds	.05	.01
❑ 494 Ricky Jordan	.05	.01
❑ 495 Randy Ready	.05	.01
❑ 496 Darrin Fletcher	.05	.01
❑ 497 Chuck Malone	.05	.01
❑ 498 Pat Combs	.05	.01
❑ 499 Dickie Thon	.05	.01
❑ 500 Roger McDowell	.05	.01
❑ 501 Len Dykstra	.10	.02
❑ 502 Joe Boever	.05	.01
❑ 503 John Kruk	.10	.02
❑ 504 Terry Mulholland	.05	.01
❑ 505 Wes Chamberlain RC	.15	.05
❑ 506 Mike Lieberthal RC	1.00	.40
❑ 507 Darren Daulton	.10	.02
❑ 508 Charlie Hayes	.05	.01
❑ 509 John Smiley	.05	.01
❑ 510 Gary Varsho	.05	.01
❑ 511 Curt Wilkerson	.05	.01
❑ 512 Orlando Merced RC	.15	.05
❑ 513 Barry Bonds	1.00	.40
❑ 514 Mike LaValliere	.05	.01
❑ 515 Doug Drabek	.05	.01
❑ 516 Gary Redus	.05	.01
❑ 517 William Pennyfeather RC	.15	.05
❑ 518 Randy Tomlin RC	.05	.01
❑ 519 Mike Zimmerman RC	.15	.05
❑ 520 Jeff King	.05	.01
❑ 521 Kurt Miller RC	.15	.05
❑ 522 Jay Bell	.10	.02
❑ 523 Bill Landrum	.05	.01
❑ 524 Zane Smith	.05	.01
❑ 525 Bobby Bonilla	.10	.02
❑ 526 Bob Walk	.05	.01
❑ 527 Austin Manahan	.05	.01
❑ 528 Joe Ausanio RC	.05	.01
❑ 529 Andy Van Slyke	.15	.05
❑ 530 Jose Lind	.05	.01
❑ 531 Carlos Garcia RC	.15	.05
❑ 532 Don Slaught	.05	.01
❑ 533 Gen.Colin Powell	.50	.20
❑ 534 Frank Bolick RC	.15	.05
❑ 535 Gary Scott RC	.05	.01
❑ 536 Nikco Riesgo RC	.05	.01
❑ 537 Reggie Sanders RC	1.50	.60
❑ 538 Tim Howard RC	.15	.05
❑ 539 Ryan Bowen RC	.15	.05
❑ 540 Eric Anthony	.05	.01
❑ 541 Jim Deshaies	.05	.01
❑ 542 Tom Nevers RC	.15	.05
❑ 543 Ken Caminiti	.10	.02
❑ 544 Karl Rhodes	.05	.01
❑ 545 Xavier Hernandez	.05	.01
❑ 546 Mike Scott	.05	.01
❑ 547 Jeff Juden	.05	.01
❑ 548 Darryl Kile	.10	.02
❑ 549 Willie Ansley	.05	.01
❑ 550 Luis Gonzalez RC	1.50	.60
❑ 551 Mike Simms RC	.05	.01
❑ 552 Mark Portugal	.05	.01
❑ 553 Jimmy Jones	.05	.01
❑ 554 Jim Clancy	.05	.01
❑ 555 Pete Harnisch	.05	.01
❑ 556 Craig Biggio	.15	.05
❑ 557 Eric Yelding	.05	.01
❑ 558 Dave Rohde	.05	.01
❑ 559 Casey Candaele	.05	.01
❑ 560 Curt Schilling	.25	.08
❑ 561 Steve Finley	.10	.02
❑ 562 Javier Ortiz	.05	.01
❑ 563 Andujar Cedeno	.05	.01
❑ 564 Rafael Ramirez	.05	.01
❑ 565 Kenny Lofton RC	1.50	.60
❑ 566 Steve Avery	.05	.01
❑ 567 Lonnie Smith	.05	.01
❑ 568 Kent Mercker	.05	.01
❑ 569 Chipper Jones RC	5.00	2.00
❑ 570 Terry Pendleton	.10	.02
❑ 571 Otis Nixon	.05	.01
❑ 572 Juan Berenguer	.05	.01
❑ 573 Charlie Leibrandt	.05	.01
❑ 574 David Justice	.10	.02
❑ 575 Keith Mitchell RC	.15	.05
❑ 576 Tom Glavine	.15	.05
❑ 577 Greg Olson	.05	.01
❑ 578 Rafael Belliard	.05	.01
❑ 579 Ben Rivera RC	.15	.05
❑ 580 John Smoltz	.15	.05

❑	581 Tyler Houston	.05	.01
❑	582 Mark Wohlers RC	.50	.20
❑	583 Ron Gant	.10	.02
❑	584 Ramon Caraballo RC	.15	.05
❑	585 Sid Bream	.05	.01
❑	586 Jeff Treadway	.05	.01
❑	587 Javy Lopez RC	3.00	1.25
❑	588 Deion Sanders	.15	.05
❑	589 Mike Heath	.05	.01
❑	590 Ryan Klesko RC	1.00	.40
❑	591 Bob Ojeda	.05	.01
❑	592 Alfredo Griffin	.05	.01
❑	593 Raul Mondesi RC	1.00	.40
❑	594 Greg Smith	.05	.01
❑	595 Orel Hershiser	.10	.02
❑	596 Juan Samuel	.05	.01
❑	597 Brett Butler	.10	.02
❑	598 Gary Carter	.10	.02
❑	599 Stan Javier	.05	.01
❑	600 Kal Daniels	.05	.01
❑	601 Jamie McAndrew RC	.15	.05
❑	602 Mike Sharperson	.05	.01
❑	603 Jay Howell	.05	.01
❑	604 Eric Karros RC	1.50	.60
❑	605 Tim Belcher	.05	.01
❑	606 Dan Opperman RC	.05	.01
❑	607 Lenny Harris	.05	.01
❑	608 Tom Goodwin	.05	.01
❑	609 Darryl Strawberry	.10	.02
❑	610 Ramon Martinez	.05	.01
❑	611 Kevin Gross	.05	.01
❑	612 Zakary Shinall RC	.05	.01
❑	613 Mike Scioscia	.05	.01
❑	614 Eddie Murray	.25	.08
❑	615 Ronnie Walden RC	.15	.05
❑	616 Will Clark	.15	.05
❑	617 Adam Hyzdu RC	.50	.20
❑	618 Matt Williams	.10	.02
❑	619 Don Robinson	.05	.01
❑	620 Jeff Brantley	.05	.01
❑	621 Greg Litton	.05	.01
❑	622 Steve Decker RC	.05	.01
❑	623 Robby Thompson	.05	.01
❑	624 Mark Leonard RC	.05	.01
❑	625 Kevin Bass	.05	.01
❑	626 Scott Garrelts	.05	.01
❑	627 Jose Uribe	.05	.01
❑	628 Eric Gunderson	.05	.01
❑	629 Steve Hosey	.05	.01
❑	630 Trevor Wilson	.05	.01
❑	631 Terry Kennedy	.05	.01
❑	632 Dave Righetti	.10	.02
❑	633 Kelly Downs	.05	.01
❑	634 Johnny Ard	.05	.01
❑	635 Eric Christopherson RC	.15	.05
❑	636 Kevin Mitchell	.05	.01
❑	637 John Burkett	.05	.01
❑	638 Kevin Rogers RC	.15	.05
❑	639 Bud Black	.05	.01
❑	640 Willie McGee	.10	.02
❑	641 Royce Clayton	.05	.01
❑	642 Tony Fernandez	.05	.01
❑	643 Ricky Bones RC	.15	.05
❑	644 Thomas Howard	.05	.01
❑	645 Dave Staton RC	.15	.05
❑	646 Jim Presley	.05	.01
❑	647 Tony Gwynn	.30	.10
❑	648 Marty Barrett	.05	.01
❑	649 Scott Coolbaugh	.05	.01
❑	650 Craig Lefferts	.05	.01
❑	651 Eddie Whitson	.05	.01
❑	652 Oscar Azocar	.05	.01
❑	653 Wes Gardner	.05	.01
❑	654 Bip Roberts	.05	.01
❑	655 Robbie Beckett RC	.15	.05
❑	656 Benito Santiago	.10	.02
❑	657 Greg W.Harris	.05	.01
❑	658 Jerald Clark	.05	.01
❑	659 Fred McGriff	.15	.05
❑	660 Larry Andersen	.05	.01
❑	661 Bruce Hurst	.05	.01
❑	662 Steve Martin UER RC	.15	.05
❑	663 Rafael Valdez	.05	.01
❑	664 Paul Faries RC	.05	.01
❑	665 Andy Benes	.05	.01
❑	666 Randy Myers	.05	.01
❑	667 Rob Dibble	.10	.02
❑	668 Glenn Sutko RC	.05	.01
❑	669 Glenn Braggs	.05	.01
❑	670 Billy Hatcher	.05	.01
❑	671 Joe Oliver	.05	.01
❑	672 Freddie Benavides RC	.15	.05
❑	673 Barry Larkin	.15	.05
❑	674 Chris Sabo	.05	.01
❑	675 Mariano Duncan	.05	.01
❑	676 Chris Jones RC	.05	.01
❑	677 Gino Minutelli RC	.05	.01
❑	678 Reggie Jefferson	.05	.01
❑	679 Jack Armstrong	.05	.01
❑	680 Chris Hammond	.05	.01
❑	681 Jose Rijo	.05	.01
❑	682 Bill Doran	.05	.01
❑	683 Terry Lee RC	.05	.01
❑	684 Tom Browning	.05	.01
❑	685 Paul O'Neill	.15	.05
❑	686 Eric Davis	.10	.02
❑	687 Dan Wilson RC	.50	.20
❑	688 Ted Power	.05	.01
❑	689 Tim Layana	.05	.01
❑	690 Norm Charlton	.05	.01
❑	691 Hal Morris	.05	.01
❑	692 Rickey Henderson RB	.15	.05
❑	693 Sam Militello RC	.15	.05
❑	694 Matt Mieske RC	.15	.05
❑	695 Paul Russo RC	.15	.05
❑	696 Domingo Mota MVP	.05	.01
❑	697 Todd Guggiana RC	.15	.05
❑	698 Marc Newfield RC	.15	.05
❑	699 Checklist 1-122	.05	.01
❑	700 Checklist 123-244	.05	.01
❑	701 Checklist 245-366	.05	.01
❑	702 Checklist 367-471	.05	.01
❑	703 Checklist 472-593	.05	.01
❑	704 Checklist 594-704	.05	.01

1992 Bowman

❑	COMPLETE SET (705)	150.00	75.00
❑	1 Ivan Rodriguez	1.25	.50
❑	2 Kirk McCaskill	.50	.20
❑	3 Scott Livingstone	.50	.20
❑	4 Salomon Torres RC	.50	.20
❑	5 Carlos Hernandez	.50	.20
❑	6 Dave Hollins	.50	.20
❑	7 Scott Fletcher	.50	.20
❑	8 Jorge Fabregas RC	.50	.20
❑	9 Andujar Cedeno	.50	.20
❑	10 Howard Johnson	.50	.20
❑	11 Trevor Hoffman RC	10.00	4.00
❑	12 Roberto Kelly	.50	.20
❑	13 Gregg Jefferies	.50	.20
❑	14 Marquis Grissom	.50	.20
❑	15 Mike Ignasiak	.50	.20
❑	16 Jack Morris	.50	.20
❑	17 William Pennyfeather	.50	.20
❑	18 Todd Stottlemyre	.50	.20
❑	19 Chito Martinez	.50	.20
❑	20 Roberto Alomar	.75	.30
❑	21 Sam Militello	.50	.20
❑	22 Hector Fajardo RC	.50	.20
❑	23 Paul Quantrill RC	.50	.20
❑	24 Chuck Knoblauch	.50	.20
❑	25 Reggie Jefferson	.50	.20
❑	26 Jeremy McGarity RC	.50	.20
❑	27 Jerome Walton	.50	.20
❑	28 Chipper Jones	10.00	4.00
❑	29 Brian Barber RC	.50	.20
❑	30 Ron Darling	.50	.20
❑	31 Roberto Petagine RC	.50	.20
❑	32 Chuck Finley	.50	.20
❑	33 Edgar Martinez	.75	.30
❑	34 Napoleon Robinson	.50	.20
❑	35 Andy Van Slyke	.75	.30
❑	36 Bobby Thigpen	.50	.20
❑	37 Travis Fryman	.50	.20
❑	38 Eric Christopherson	.50	.20
❑	39 Terry Mulholland	.50	.20
❑	40 Darryl Strawberry	.50	.20
❑	41 Manny Alexander RC	.50	.20
❑	42 Tracy Sanders RC	.50	.20
❑	43 Pete Incaviglia	.50	.20
❑	44 Kim Batiste	.50	.20
❑	45 Frank Rodriguez	.50	.20
❑	46 Greg Swindell	.50	.20
❑	47 Delino DeShields	.50	.20
❑	48 John Ericks	.50	.20
❑	49 Franklin Stubbs	.50	.20
❑	50 Tony Gwynn	1.50	.60
❑	51 Clifton Garrett RC	.50	.20
❑	52 Mike Gardella	.50	.20
❑	53 Scott Erickson	.50	.20
❑	54 Gary Caraballo RC	.50	.20
❑	55 Jose Oliva RC	.50	.20
❑	56 Brook Fordyce	.50	.20
❑	57 Mark Whiten	.50	.20
❑	58 Joe Slusarski	.50	.20
❑	59 J.R. Phillips RC	.50	.20
❑	60 Barry Bonds	4.00	1.50
❑	61 Bob Milacki	.50	.20
❑	62 Keith Mitchell	.50	.20
❑	63 Angel Miranda	.50	.20
❑	64 Raul Mondesi	.50	.20
❑	65 Brian Koelling RC	.50	.20
❑	66 Brian McRae	.50	.20
❑	67 John Patterson RC	.50	.20
❑	68 John Wetteland	.50	.20
❑	69 Wilson Alvarez	.50	.20
❑	70 Wade Boggs	.75	.30
❑	71 Darryl Ratliff RC	.50	.20
❑	72 Jeff Jackson	.50	.20
❑	73 Jeremy Hernandez RC	.50	.20
❑	74 Darryl Hamilton	.50	.20
❑	75 Rafael Belliard	.50	.20
❑	76 Rick Trlicek RC	.50	.20
❑	77 Felipe Crespo RC	.50	.20
❑	78 Carney Lansford	.50	.20
❑	79 Ryan Long RC	.50	.20
❑	80 Kirby Puckett	1.25	.50
❑	81 Earl Cunningham	.50	.20
❑	82 Pedro Martinez	10.00	4.00
❑	83 Scott Hatteberg RC	1.00	.40
❑	84 Juan Gonzalez	.75	.30
❑	85 Robert Nutting RC	.50	.20
❑	86 Pokey Reese RC	1.00	.40
❑	87 Dave Silvestri	.50	.20
❑	88 Scott Ruffcorn RC	.50	.20
❑	89 Rick Aguilera	.50	.20
❑	90 Cecil Fielder	.50	.20
❑	91 Kirk Dressendorfer	.50	.20
❑	92 Jerry DiPoto RC	.50	.20
❑	93 Mike Felder	.50	.20
❑	94 Craig Paquette	.50	.20
❑	95 Elvin Paulino RC	.50	.20
❑	96 Donovan Osborne	.50	.20
❑	97 Hubie Brooks	.50	.20
❑	98 Derek Lowe RC	4.00	1.50
❑	99 David Zancanaro	.50	.20
❑	100 Ken Griffey Jr.	2.00	.75
❑	101 Todd Hundley	.50	.20
❑	102 Mike Trombley RC	.50	.20
❑	103 Ricky Gutierrez RC	1.00	.40
❑	104 Braulio Castillo	.50	.20
❑	105 Craig Lefferts	.50	.20
❑	106 Rick Sutcliffe	.50	.20
❑	107 Dean Palmer	.50	.20
❑	108 Henry Rodriguez	.50	.20
❑	109 Mark Clark RC	1.00	.40
❑	110 Kenny Lofton	.75	.30
❑	111 Mark Carreon	.50	.20
❑	112 J.T. Bruett	.50	.20
❑	113 Gerald Williams	.50	.20

❑ 114 Frank Thomas 1.25 .50
❑ 115 Kevin Reimer .50 .20
❑ 116 Sammy Sosa 1.25 .50
❑ 117 Mickey Tettleton .50 .20
❑ 118 Reggie Sanders .50 .20
❑ 119 Trevor Wilson .50 .20
❑ 120 Cliff Brantley .50 .20
❑ 121 Spike Owen .50 .20
❑ 122 Jeff Montgomery .50 .20
❑ 123 Alex Sutherland .50 .20
❑ 124 Brien Taylor RC 1.00 .40
❑ 125 Brian Williams RC .50 .20
❑ 126 Kevin Seitzer .50 .20
❑ 127 Carlos Delgado RC 12.00 5.00
❑ 128 Gary Scott .50 .20
❑ 129 Scott Cooper .50 .20
❑ 130 Domingo Jean RC .50 .20
❑ 131 Pat Mahomes RC 1.00 .40
❑ 132 Mike Boddicker .50 .20
❑ 133 Roberto Hernandez .50 .20
❑ 134 Dave Valle .50 .20
❑ 135 Kurt Stillwell .50 .20
❑ 136 Brad Pennington RC .50 .20
❑ 137 Jermaine Swinton RC .50 .20
❑ 138 Ryan Hawblitzel RC .50 .20
❑ 139 Tito Navarro RC .50 .20
❑ 140 Sandy Alomar Jr. .50 .20
❑ 141 Todd Benzinger .50 .20
❑ 142 Danny Jackson .50 .20
❑ 143 Melvin Nieves RC .50 .20
❑ 144 Jim Campanis .50 .20
❑ 145 Luis Gonzalez .50 .20
❑ 146 Dave Doorneweerd RC .50 .20
❑ 147 Charlie Hayes .50 .20
❑ 148 Greg Maddux 2.00 .75
❑ 149 Brian Harper .50 .20
❑ 150 Brent Miller RC .50 .20
❑ 151 Shawn Estes RC 1.00 .40
❑ 152 Mike Williams RC 1.00 .40
❑ 153 Charlie Hough .50 .20
❑ 154 Randy Myers .50 .20
❑ 155 Kevin Young RC 1.00 .40
❑ 156 Rick Wilkins .50 .20
❑ 157 Terry Shumpert .50 .20
❑ 158 Steve Karsay .50 .20
❑ 159 Gary DiSarcina .50 .20
❑ 160 Deion Sanders .75 .30
❑ 161 Tom Browning .50 .20
❑ 162 Dickie Thon .50 .20
❑ 163 Luis Mercedes .50 .20
❑ 164 Riccardo Ingram .50 .20
❑ 165 Tavo Alvarez RC .50 .20
❑ 166 Rickey Henderson 1.25 .50
❑ 167 Jaime Navarro .50 .20
❑ 168 Billy Ashley RC .50 .20
❑ 169 Phil Dauphin RC .50 .20
❑ 170 Ivan Cruz .50 .20
❑ 171 Harold Baines .50 .20
❑ 172 Bryan Harvey .50 .20
❑ 173 Alex Cole .50 .20
❑ 174 Curtis Shaw RC .50 .20
❑ 175 Matt Williams .50 .20
❑ 176 Felix Jose .50 .20
❑ 177 Sam Horn .50 .20
❑ 178 Randy Johnson 1.25 .50
❑ 179 Ivan Calderon .50 .20
❑ 180 Steve Avery .50 .20
❑ 181 William Suero .50 .20
❑ 182 Bill Swift .50 .20
❑ 183 Howard Battle RC .50 .20
❑ 184 Ruben Amaro .50 .20
❑ 185 Jim Abbott .75 .30
❑ 186 Mike Fitzgerald .50 .20
❑ 187 Bruce Hurst .50 .20
❑ 188 Jeff Juden .50 .20
❑ 189 Jeromy Burnitz .50 .20
❑ 190 Dave Burba .50 .20
❑ 191 Kevin Brown .50 .20
❑ 192 Patrick Lennon .50 .20
❑ 193 Jeff McNeely .50 .20
❑ 194 Wil Cordero .50 .20
❑ 195 Chili Davis .50 .20
❑ 196 Milt Cuyler .50 .20
❑ 197 Von Hayes .50 .20
❑ 198 Todd Revenig RC .50 .20
❑ 199 Joel Johnston .50 .20
❑ 200 Jeff Bagwell 1.25 .50
❑ 201 Alex Fernandez .50 .20
❑ 202 Todd Jones RC 2.50 1.00
❑ 203 Charles Nagy .50 .20
❑ 204 Tim Raines .50 .20
❑ 205 Kevin Maas .50 .20
❑ 206 Julio Franco .50 .20
❑ 207 Randy Velarde .50 .20
❑ 208 Lance Johnson .50 .20
❑ 209 Scott Leius .50 .20
❑ 210 Derek Lee .50 .20
❑ 211 Joe Sondrini RC .50 .20
❑ 212 Royce Clayton .50 .20
❑ 213 Chris George .50 .20
❑ 214 Gary Sheffield .50 .20
❑ 215 Mark Gubicza .50 .20
❑ 216 Mike Moore .50 .20
❑ 217 Rick Huisman RC .50 .20
❑ 218 Jeff Russell .50 .20
❑ 219 D.J. Dozier .50 .20
❑ 220 Dave Martinez .50 .20
❑ 221 Alan Newman RC .50 .20
❑ 222 Nolan Ryan 4.00 1.50
❑ 223 Teddy Higuera .50 .20
❑ 224 Damon Buford RC .50 .20
❑ 225 Ruben Sierra .50 .20
❑ 226 Tom Nevers .50 .20
❑ 227 Tommy Greene .50 .20
❑ 228 Nigel Wilson RC .50 .20
❑ 229 John DeSilva .50 .20
❑ 230 Bobby Witt .50 .20
❑ 231 Greg Cadaret .50 .20
❑ 232 John Vander Wal RC 1.00 .40
❑ 233 Jack Clark .50 .20
❑ 234 Bill Doran .50 .20
❑ 235 Bobby Bonilla .50 .20
❑ 236 Steve Olin .50 .20
❑ 237 Derek Bell .50 .20
❑ 238 David Cone .50 .20
❑ 239 Victor Cole .50 .20
❑ 240 Rod Bolton RC .50 .20
❑ 241 Tom Pagnozzi .50 .20
❑ 242 Rob Dibble .50 .20
❑ 243 Michael Carter RC .50 .20
❑ 244 Don Peters .50 .20
❑ 245 Mike LaValliere .50 .20
❑ 246 Joe Perona RC .50 .20
❑ 247 Mitch Williams .50 .20
❑ 248 Jay Buhner .50 .20
❑ 249 Andy Benes .50 .20
❑ 250 Alex Ochoa RC .50 .20
❑ 251 Greg Blosser .50 .20
❑ 252 Jack Armstrong .50 .20
❑ 253 Juan Samuel .50 .20
❑ 254 Terry Pendleton .50 .20
❑ 255 Ramon Martinez .50 .20
❑ 256 Rico Brogna .50 .20
❑ 257 John Smiley .50 .20
❑ 258 Carl Everett .75 .30
❑ 259 Tim Salmon .75 .30
❑ 260 Will Clark .75 .30
❑ 261 Ugueth Urbina RC 1.00 .40
❑ 262 Jason Wood RC .50 .20
❑ 263 Dave Magadan .50 .20
❑ 264 Dante Bichette .50 .20
❑ 265 Jose DeLeon .50 .20
❑ 266 Mike Neill RC 1.00 .40
❑ 267 Paul O'Neill .75 .30
❑ 268 Anthony Young .50 .20
❑ 269 Greg W. Harris .50 .20
❑ 270 Todd Van Poppel .50 .20
❑ 271 Pedro Castellano RC .50 .20
❑ 272 Tony Phillips .50 .20
❑ 273 Mike Gallego .50 .20
❑ 274 Steve Cooke RC .50 .20
❑ 275 Robin Ventura .50 .20
❑ 276 Kevin Mitchell .50 .20
❑ 277 Doug Linton RC .50 .20
❑ 278 Robert Eenhoorn .50 .20
❑ 279 Gabe White RC .50 .20
❑ 280 Dave Stewart .50 .20
❑ 281 Mo Sanford .50 .20
❑ 282 Greg Perschke .50 .20
❑ 283 Kevin Flora RC .50 .20
❑ 284 Jeff Williams RC 1.00 .40
❑ 285 Keith Miller .50 .20
❑ 286 Andy Ashby .50 .20
❑ 287 Doug Dascenzo .50 .20
❑ 288 Eric Karros .50 .20
❑ 289 Glenn Murray RC .50 .20
❑ 290 Troy Percival RC 3.00 1.25
❑ 291 Orlando Merced .50 .20
❑ 292 Peter Hoy .50 .20
❑ 293 Tony Fernandez .50 .20
❑ 294 Juan Guzman .50 .20
❑ 295 Jesse Barfield .50 .20
❑ 296 Sid Fernandez .50 .20
❑ 297 Scott Cepicky .50 .20
❑ 298 Garret Anderson RC 8.00 3.00
❑ 299 Cal Eldred .50 .20
❑ 300 Ryne Sandberg 2.50 1.00
❑ 301 Jim Gantner .50 .20
❑ 302 Mariano Rivera RC 25.00 10.00
❑ 303 Ron Lockett RC .50 .20
❑ 304 Jose Offerman .50 .20
❑ 305 Dennis Martinez .50 .20
❑ 306 Luis Ortiz RC .50 .20
❑ 307 David Howard .50 .20
❑ 308 Russ Springer RC 1.00 .40
❑ 309 Chris Howard .50 .20
❑ 310 Kyle Abbott .50 .20
❑ 311 Aaron Sele RC 1.00 .40
❑ 312 David Justice .50 .20
❑ 313 Pete O'Brien .50 .20
❑ 314 Greg Hansell RC .50 .20
❑ 315 Dave Winfield .50 .20
❑ 316 Lance Dickson .50 .20
❑ 317 Eric King .50 .20
❑ 318 Vaughn Eshelman RC .50 .20
❑ 319 Tim Belcher .50 .20
❑ 320 Andres Galarraga .50 .20
❑ 321 Scott Bullett RC .50 .20
❑ 322 Doug Strange .50 .20
❑ 323 Jerald Clark .50 .20
❑ 324 Dave Righetti .50 .20
❑ 325 Greg Hibbard .50 .20
❑ 326 Eric Hillman RC .50 .20
❑ 327 Shane Reynolds RC 1.00 .40
❑ 328 Chris Hammond .50 .20
❑ 329 Albert Belle .50 .20
❑ 330 Rich Becker RC .50 .20
❑ 331 Ed Williams .50 .20
❑ 332 Donald Harris .50 .20
❑ 333 Dave Smith .50 .20
❑ 334 Steve Fireovid .50 .20
❑ 335 Steve Buechele .50 .20
❑ 336 Mike Schooler .50 .20
❑ 337 Kevin McReynolds .50 .20
❑ 338 Hensley Meulens .50 .20
❑ 339 Benji Gil RC 1.00 .40
❑ 340 Don Mattingly 3.00 1.25
❑ 341 Alvin Davis .50 .20
❑ 342 Alan Mills .50 .20
❑ 343 Kelly Downs .50 .20
❑ 344 Leo Gomez .50 .20
❑ 345 Tarrik Brock RC .50 .20
❑ 346 Ryan Turner RC .50 .20
❑ 347 John Smoltz .75 .30
❑ 348 Bill Sampen .50 .20
❑ 349 Paul Byrd RC 3.00 1.25
❑ 350 Mike Bordick .50 .20
❑ 351 Jose Lind .50 .20
❑ 352 David Wells .50 .20
❑ 353 Barry Larkin .75 .30
❑ 354 Bruce Ruffin .50 .20
❑ 355 Luis Rivera .50 .20
❑ 356 Sid Bream .50 .20
❑ 357 Julian Vasquez RC .50 .20
❑ 358 Jason Bere RC 1.00 .40
❑ 359 Ben McDonald .50 .20
❑ 360 Scott Stahoviak RC .50 .20
❑ 361 Kirt Manwaring .50 .20
❑ 362 Jeff Johnson .50 .20
❑ 363 Rob Deer .50 .20
❑ 364 Tony Pena .50 .20
❑ 365 Melido Perez .50 .20
❑ 366 Clay Parker .50 .20
❑ 367 Dale Sveum .50 .20
❑ 368 Mike Scioscia .50 .20
❑ 369 Roger Salkeld .50 .20
❑ 370 Mike Stanley .50 .20
❑ 371 Jack McDowell .50 .20

❑ 372	Tim Wallach	.50	.20
❑ 373	Billy Ripken	.50	.20
❑ 374	Mike Christopher	.50	.20
❑ 375	Paul Molitor	.50	.20
❑ 376	Dave Stieb	.50	.20
❑ 377	Pedro Guerrero	.50	.20
❑ 378	Russ Swan	.50	.20
❑ 379	Bob Ojeda	.50	.20
❑ 380	Donn Pall	.50	.20
❑ 381	Eddie Zosky	.50	.20
❑ 382	Darnell Coles	.50	.20
❑ 383	Tom Smith RC	.50	.20
❑ 384	Mark McGwire	3.00	1.25
❑ 385	Gary Carter	.50	.20
❑ 386	Rich Amaral RC	.50	.20
❑ 387	Alan Embree RC	1.00	.40
❑ 388	Jonathan Hurst RC	.50	.20
❑ 389	Bobby Jones RC	1.00	.40
❑ 390	Rico Rossy	.50	.20
❑ 391	Dan Smith	.50	.20
❑ 392	Terry Steinbach	.50	.20
❑ 393	Jon Farrell RC	.50	.20
❑ 394	Dave Anderson	.50	.20
❑ 395	Benny Santiago	.50	.20
❑ 396	Mark Wohlers	.50	.20
❑ 397	Mo Vaughn	.50	.20
❑ 398	Randy Kramer	.50	.20
❑ 399	John Jaha RC	1.00	.40
❑ 400	Cal Ripken	4.00	1.50
❑ 401	Ryan Bowen	.50	.20
❑ 402	Tim McIntosh	.50	.20
❑ 403	Bernard Gilkey	.50	.20
❑ 404	Junior Felix	.50	.20
❑ 405	Cris Colon RC	.50	.20
❑ 406	Marc Newfield	.50	.20
❑ 407	Bernie Williams	.75	.30
❑ 408	Jay Howell	.50	.20
❑ 409	Zane Smith	.50	.20
❑ 410	Jeff Shaw	.50	.20
❑ 411	Kerry Woodson	.50	.20
❑ 412	Wes Chamberlain	.50	.20
❑ 413	Dave Mlicki RC	1.00	.40
❑ 414	Benny Distefano	.50	.20
❑ 415	Kevin Rogers	.50	.20
❑ 416	Tim Naehring	.50	.20
❑ 417	Clemente Nunez RC	.50	.20
❑ 418	Luis Sojo	.50	.20
❑ 419	Kevin Ritz	.50	.20
❑ 420	Omar Olivares	.50	.20
❑ 421	Manuel Lee	.50	.20
❑ 422	Julio Valera	.50	.20
❑ 423	Omar Vizquel	.75	.30
❑ 424	Darren Burton RC	.50	.20
❑ 425	Mel Hall	.50	.20
❑ 426	Dennis Powell	.50	.20
❑ 427	Lee Stevens	.50	.20
❑ 428	Glenn Davis	.50	.20
❑ 429	Willie Greene	.50	.20
❑ 430	Kevin Wickander	.50	.20
❑ 431	Dennis Eckersley	.50	.20
❑ 432	Joe Orsulak	.50	.20
❑ 433	Eddie Murray	1.25	.50
❑ 434	Matt Stairs RC	1.00	.40
❑ 435	Wally Joyner	.50	.20
❑ 436	Rondell White	.50	.20
❑ 437	Rob Maurer	.50	.20
❑ 438	Joe Redfield	.50	.20
❑ 439	Mark Lewis	.50	.20
❑ 440	Darren Daulton	.50	.20
❑ 441	Mike Henneman	.50	.20
❑ 442	John Cangelosi	.50	.20
❑ 443	Vincent Moore RC	.50	.20
❑ 444	John Wehner	.50	.20
❑ 445	Kent Hrbek	.50	.20
❑ 446	Mark McLemore	.50	.20
❑ 447	Bill Wegman	.50	.20
❑ 448	Robby Thompson	.50	.20
❑ 449	Mark Anthony RC	.50	.20
❑ 450	Archi Cianfrocco RC	.50	.20
❑ 451	Johnny Ruffin	.50	.20
❑ 452	Javy Lopez	2.00	.75
❑ 453	Greg Gohr	.50	.20
❑ 454	Tim Scott	.50	.20
❑ 455	Stan Belinda	.50	.20
❑ 456	Darrin Jackson	.50	.20
❑ 457	Chris Gardner	.50	.20
❑ 458	Esteban Beltre	.50	.20
❑ 459	Phil Plantier	.50	.20
❑ 460	Jim Thome	8.00	3.00
❑ 461	Mike Piazza RC	40.00	15.00
❑ 462	Matt Sinatro	.50	.20
❑ 463	Scott Servais	.50	.20
❑ 464	Brian Jordan RC	2.00	.75
❑ 465	Doug Drabek	.50	.20
❑ 466	Carl Willis	.50	.20
❑ 467	Bret Barberie	.50	.20
❑ 468	Hal Morris	.50	.20
❑ 469	Steve Sax	.50	.20
❑ 470	Jerry Willard	.50	.20
❑ 471	Dan Wilson	.50	.20
❑ 472	Chris Hoiles	.50	.20
❑ 473	Rheal Cormier	.50	.20
❑ 474	John Morris	.50	.20
❑ 475	Jeff Reardon	.50	.20
❑ 476	Mark Leiter	.50	.20
❑ 477	Tom Gordon	.50	.20
❑ 478	Kent Bottenfield RC	1.00	.40
❑ 479	Gene Larkin	.50	.20
❑ 480	Dwight Gooden	.50	.20
❑ 481	B.J. Surhoff	.50	.20
❑ 482	Andy Stankiewicz	.50	.20
❑ 483	Tino Martinez	.75	.30
❑ 484	Craig Biggio	.75	.30
❑ 485	Denny Neagle	.50	.20
❑ 486	Rusty Meacham	.50	.20
❑ 487	Kal Daniels	.50	.20
❑ 488	Dave Henderson	.50	.20
❑ 489	Tim Costo	.50	.20
❑ 490	Doug Davis	.50	.20
❑ 491	Frank Viola	.50	.20
❑ 492	Cory Snyder	.50	.20
❑ 493	Chris Martin	.50	.20
❑ 494	Dion James	.50	.20
❑ 495	Randy Tomlin	.50	.20
❑ 496	Greg Vaughn	.50	.20
❑ 497	Dennis Cook	.50	.20
❑ 498	Rosario Rodriguez	.50	.20
❑ 499	Dave Staton	.50	.20
❑ 500	George Brett	3.00	1.25
❑ 501	Brian Barnes	.50	.20
❑ 502	Butch Henry RC	.50	.20
❑ 503	Harold Reynolds	.50	.20
❑ 504	David Nied RC	.50	.20
❑ 505	Lee Smith	.50	.20
❑ 506	Steve Chitren	.50	.20
❑ 507	Ken Hill	.50	.20
❑ 508	Robbie Beckett	.50	.20
❑ 509	Troy Afenir	.50	.20
❑ 510	Kelly Gruber	.50	.20
❑ 511	Bret Boone	.75	.30
❑ 512	Jeff Branson	.50	.20
❑ 513	Mike Jackson	.50	.20
❑ 514	Pete Harnisch	.50	.20
❑ 515	Chad Kreuter	.50	.20
❑ 516	Joe Vitko RC	.50	.20
❑ 517	Orel Hershiser	.50	.20
❑ 518	John Doherty RC	.50	.20
❑ 519	Jay Bell	.50	.20
❑ 520	Mark Langston	.50	.20
❑ 521	Dann Howitt	.50	.20
❑ 522	Bobby Reed RC	.50	.20
❑ 523	Bobby Munoz RC	.50	.20
❑ 524	Todd Ritchie	.50	.20
❑ 525	Bip Roberts	.50	.20
❑ 526	Pat Listach RC	1.00	.40
❑ 527	Scott Brosius RC	2.00	.75
❑ 528	John Roper RC	.50	.20
❑ 529	Phil Hiatt RC	.50	.20
❑ 530	Denny Walling	.50	.20
❑ 531	Carlos Baerga	.50	.20
❑ 532	Manny Ramirez RC	25.00	10.00
❑ 533	Pat Clements UER	.50	.20
❑ 534	Ron Gant	.50	.20
❑ 535	Pat Kelly	.50	.20
❑ 536	Bill Spiers	.50	.20
❑ 537	Darren Reed	.50	.20
❑ 538	Ken Caminiti	.50	.20
❑ 539	Butch Huskey RC	.50	.20
❑ 540	Matt Nokes	.50	.20
❑ 541	John Kruk	.50	.20
❑ 542	John Jaha FOIL	.50	.20
❑ 543	Justin Thompson RC	.50	.20
❑ 544	Steve Hosey	.50	.20
❑ 545	Joe Kmak	.50	.20
❑ 546	John Franco	.50	.20
❑ 547	Devon White	.50	.20
❑ 548	Elston Hansen FOIL SP RC	.50	.20
❑ 549	Ryan Klesko	.50	.20
❑ 550	Danny Tartabull	.50	.20
❑ 551	Frank Thomas FOIL	1.25	.50
❑ 552	Kevin Tapani	.50	.20
❑ 553	Willie Banks	.50	.20
❑ 554	B.J.Wallace FOIL RC	.50	.20
❑ 555	Orlando Miller RC	.50	.20
❑ 556	Mark Smith RC	.50	.20
❑ 557	Tim Wallach FOIL	.50	.20
❑ 558	Bill Gullickson	.50	.20
❑ 559	Derek Bell FOIL	.50	.20
❑ 560	Joe Randa FOIL RC	3.00	1.25
❑ 561	Frank Seminara RC	.50	.20
❑ 562	Mark Gardner	.50	.20
❑ 563	Rick Greene FOIL RC	.50	.20
❑ 564	Gary Gaetti	.50	.20
❑ 565	Ozzie Guillen	.50	.20
❑ 566	Charles Nagy FOIL	.50	.20
❑ 567	Mike Milchin	.50	.20
❑ 568	Ben Shelton RC	.50	.20
❑ 569	Chris Roberts FOIL	.50	.20
❑ 570	Ellis Burks	.50	.20
❑ 571	Scott Scudder	.50	.20
❑ 572	Jim Abbott FOIL	.75	.30
❑ 573	Joe Carter	.50	.20
❑ 574	Steve Finley	.50	.20
❑ 575	Jim Olander FOIL	.50	.20
❑ 576	Carlos Garcia	.50	.20
❑ 577	Gregg Olson	.50	.20
❑ 578	Greg Swindell FOIL	.50	.20
❑ 579	Matt Williams FOIL	.50	.20
❑ 580	Mark Grace	.75	.30
❑ 581	Howard House FOIL RC	.50	.20
❑ 582	Luis Polonia	.50	.20
❑ 583	Erik Hanson	.50	.20
❑ 584	Salomon Torres FOIL	.50	.20
❑ 585	Carlton Fisk	.75	.30
❑ 586	Bret Saberhagen	.50	.20
❑ 587	Chad McConnell FOIL RC	.50	.20
❑ 588	Jimmy Key	.50	.20
❑ 589	Mike Macfarlane	.50	.20
❑ 590	Barry Bonds FOIL	4.00	1.50
❑ 591	Jamie McAndrew	.50	.20
❑ 592	Shane Mack	.50	.20
❑ 593	Kerwin Moore	.50	.20
❑ 594	Joe Oliver	.50	.20
❑ 595	Chris Sabo	.50	.20
❑ 596	Alex Gonzalez RC	1.00	.40
❑ 597	Brett Butler	.50	.20
❑ 598	Mark Hutton RC	.50	.20
❑ 599	Andy Benes FOIL	.50	.20
❑ 600	Jose Canseco	.75	.30
❑ 601	Darryl Kile	.50	.20
❑ 602	Matt Stairs FOIL	.50	.20
❑ 603	Rob Butler FOIL RC	.50	.20
❑ 604	Willie McGee	.50	.20
❑ 605	Jack McDowell FOIL	.50	.20
❑ 606	Tom Candiotti	.50	.20
❑ 607	Ed Martel RC	.50	.20
❑ 608	Matt Mieske FOIL	.50	.20
❑ 609	Darrin Fletcher	.50	.20
❑ 610	Rafael Palmeiro	.75	.30
❑ 611	Bill Swift FOIL	.50	.20
❑ 612	Mike Mussina	1.25	.50
❑ 613	Vince Coleman	.50	.20
❑ 614	Scott Cepicky COR	.50	.20
❑ 614A	Scott Cepicky FOIL UER	.50	.20
❑ 615	Mike Greenwell	.50	.20
❑ 616	Kevin McGehee RC	.50	.20
❑ 617	Jeffrey Hammonds FOIL	.50	.20
❑ 618	Scott Taylor	.50	.20
❑ 619	Dave Otto	.50	.20
❑ 620	Mark McGwire FOIL	3.00	1.25
❑ 621	Kevin Tatar RC	.50	.20
❑ 622	Steve Farr	.50	.20
❑ 623	Ryan Klesko FOIL	.50	.20
❑ 624	Dave Fleming	.50	.20
❑ 625	Andre Dawson	.50	.20
❑ 626	Tino Martinez FOIL SP	.75	.30
❑ 627	Chad Curtis RC	1.00	.40
❑ 628	Mickey Morandini	.50	.20

❑ 629 Gregg Olson FOIL SP .50 .20
❑ 630 Lou Whitaker .50 .20
❑ 631 Arthur Rhodes .60 .20
❑ 632 Brandon Wilson RC .50 .20
❑ 633 Lance Jennings RC .50 .20
❑ 634 Allen Watson RC .50 .20
❑ 635 Len Dykstra .50 .20
❑ 636 Joe Girardi .50 .20
❑ 637 Kiki Hernandez FOIL RC .50 .20
❑ 638 Mike Hampton RC 2.00 .75
❑ 639 Al Osuna .50 .20
❑ 640 Kevin Appier .50 .20
❑ 641 Rick Helling FOIL .50 .20
❑ 642 Jody Reed .50 .20
❑ 643 Ray Lankford .50 .20
❑ 644 John Olerud .50 .20
❑ 645 Paul Molitor FOIL .50 .20
❑ 646 Pat Borders .50 .20
❑ 647 Mike Morgan .50 .20
❑ 648 Larry Walker .75 .30
❑ 649 Pedro Castellano FOIL .50 .20
❑ 650 Fred McGriff .75 .30
❑ 651 Walt Weiss .50 .20
❑ 652 Calvin Murray FOIL RC 1.00 .40
❑ 653 Dave Nilsson .50 .20
❑ 654 Greg Pirkl RC .50 .20
❑ 655 Robin Ventura FOIL .50 .20
❑ 656 Mark Portugal .50 .20
❑ 657 Roger McDowell .50 .20
❑ 658 Rick Hirtensteiner FOIL RC .50 .20
❑ 659 Glenallen Hill .50 .20
❑ 660 Greg Gagne .50 .20
❑ 661 Charles Johnson FOIL .50 .20
❑ 662 Brian Hunter .50 .20
❑ 663 Mark Lemke .50 .20
❑ 664 Tim Belcher FOIL SP .50 .20
❑ 665 Rich DeLucia .50 .20
❑ 666 Bob Walk .50 .20
❑ 667 Joe Carter FOIL .50 .20
❑ 668 Jose Guzman .50 .20
❑ 669 Otis Nixon .50 .20
❑ 670 Phil Nevin FOIL .50 .20
❑ 671 Eric Davis .50 .20
❑ 672 Damion Easley RC 1.00 .40
❑ 673 Will Clark FOIL .75 .30
❑ 674 Mark Kiefer RC .50 .20
❑ 675 Ozzie Smith 2.00 .75
❑ 676 Manny Ramirez FOIL 6.00 2.50
❑ 677 Gregg Olson .50 .20
❑ 678 Cliff Floyd RC 3.00 1.25
❑ 679 Duane Singleton RC .50 .20
❑ 680 Jose Rijo .50 .20
❑ 681 Willie Randolph .50 .20
❑ 682 Michael Tucker FOIL RC 1.00 .40
❑ 683 Darren Lewis .50 .20
❑ 684 Dale Murphy .75 .30
❑ 685 Mike Pagliarulo .50 .20
❑ 686 Paul Miller RC .50 .20
❑ 687 Mike Robertson RC .50 .20
❑ 688 Mike Devereaux .50 .20
❑ 689 Pedro Astacio RC 1.00 .40
❑ 690 Alan Trammell .50 .20
❑ 691 Roger Clemens 2.50 1.00
❑ 692 Bud Black .50 .20
❑ 693 Turk Wendell RC 1.00 .40
❑ 694 Barry Larkin FOIL .75 .30
❑ 695 Todd Zeile .50 .20
❑ 696 Pat Hentgen .50 .20
❑ 697 Eddie Taubensee RC 1.00 .40
❑ 698 Guillermo Velasquez RC .50 .20
❑ 699 Tom Glavine .75 .30
❑ 700 Robin Yount 2.00 .75
❑ 701 Checklist 1-141 .50 .20
❑ 702 Checklist 142-282 .50 .20
❑ 703 Checklist 283-423 .50 .20
❑ 704 Checklist 424-564 .50 .20
❑ 705 Checklist 565-705 .50 .20

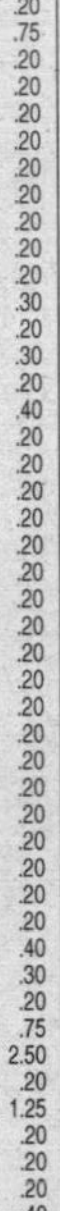

1993 Bowman

❑ COMPLETE SET (708) 50.00 25.00
❑ 1 Glenn Davis .15 .05
❑ 2 Hector Roa RC .25 .08
❑ 3 Ken Ryan RC .25 .08
❑ 4 Derek Wallace RC .25 .08
❑ 5 Jorge Fabregas .15 .05

❑ 6 Joe Oliver .15 .05
❑ 7 Brandon Wilson .15 .05
❑ 8 Mark Thompson RC .25 .08
❑ 9 Tracy Sanders .15 .05
❑ 10 Rich Renteria .15 .05
❑ 11 Lou Whitaker .30 .10
❑ 12 Brian L. Hunter RC .50 .20
❑ 13 Joe Vitiello .15 .05
❑ 14 Eric Karros .30 .10
❑ 15 Joe Kmak .15 .05
❑ 16 Tavo Alvarez .15 .05
❑ 17 Steve Dunn RC .25 .08
❑ 18 Tony Fernandez .15 .05
❑ 19 Melido Perez .15 .05
❑ 20 Mike Lieberthal .30 .10
❑ 21 Terry Steinbach .15 .05
❑ 22 Stan Belinda .15 .05
❑ 23 Jay Buhner .30 .10
❑ 24 Allen Watson .15 .05
❑ 25 Daryl Henderson RC .25 .08
❑ 26 Ray McDavid RC .25 .08
❑ 27 Shawn Green 1.00 .40
❑ 28 Bud Black .15 .05
❑ 29 Sherman Obando RC .25 .08
❑ 30 Mike Hostetler RC .25 .08
❑ 31 Nate Minchey RC .25 .08
❑ 32 Randy Myers .15 .05
❑ 33 Brian Grebeck .15 .05
❑ 34 John Roper .15 .05
❑ 35 Larry Thomas .15 .05
❑ 36 Alex Cole .15 .05
❑ 37 Tom Kramer RC .25 .08
❑ 38 Matt Whisenant RC .25 .08
❑ 39 Chris Gomez RC .50 .20
❑ 40 Luis Gonzalez .30 .10
❑ 41 Kevin Appier .30 .10
❑ 42 Omar Daal RC .25 .08
❑ 43 Duane Singleton .15 .05
❑ 44 Bill Risley .15 .05
❑ 45 Pat Meares RC .50 .20
❑ 46 Butch Huskey .15 .05
❑ 47 Bobby Munoz .15 .05
❑ 48 Juan Bell .15 .05
❑ 49 Scott Lydy RC .25 .08
❑ 50 Dennis Moeller .15 .05
❑ 51 Marc Newfield .15 .05
❑ 52 Tripp Cromer RC .25 .08
❑ 53 Kurt Miller .15 .05
❑ 54 Jim Pena .15 .05
❑ 55 Juan Guzman .15 .05
❑ 56 Matt Williams .30 .10
❑ 57 Harold Reynolds .30 .10
❑ 58 Donnie Elliott RC .25 .08
❑ 59 Jon Shave RC .25 .08
❑ 60 Kevin Roberson RC .25 .08
❑ 61 Hilly Hathaway RC .25 .08
❑ 62 Jose Rijo .15 .05
❑ 63 Kerry Taylor RC .15 .05
❑ 64 Ryan Hawblitzel .15 .05
❑ 65 Glenallen Hill .15 .05
❑ 66 Ramon D. Martinez RC .25 .08
❑ 67 Travis Fryman .30 .10
❑ 68 Tom Nevers .15 .05
❑ 69 Phil Hiatt .15 .05
❑ 70 Tim Wallach .15 .05
❑ 71 B.J. Surhoff .30 .10
❑ 72 Rondell White .30 .10
❑ 73 Denny Hocking RC .50 .20

❑ 74 Mike Oquist RC .25 .08
❑ 75 Paul O'Neill .50 .20
❑ 76 Willie Banks .15 .05
❑ 77 Bob Welch .15 .05
❑ 78 Jose Sandoval RC .25 .08
❑ 79 Bill Haselman .15 .05
❑ 80 Rheal Cormier .15 .05
❑ 81 Dean Palmer .30 .10
❑ 82 Pat Gomez RC .25 .08
❑ 83 Steve Karsay .15 .05
❑ 84 Carl Hanselman RC .25 .08
❑ 85 T.R. Lewis RC .25 .08
❑ 86 Chipper Jones .75 .30
❑ 87 Scott Hatteberg .15 .05
❑ 88 Greg Hibbard .15 .05
❑ 89 Lance Painter RC .25 .08
❑ 90 Chad Mottola RC .50 .20
❑ 91 Jason Bere .15 .05
❑ 92 Dante Bichette .30 .10
❑ 93 Sandy Alomar Jr. .15 .05
❑ 94 Carl Everett .30 .10
❑ 95 Danny Bautista RC .50 .20
❑ 96 Steve Finley .30 .10
❑ 97 David Cone .30 .10
❑ 98 Todd Hollandsworth .15 .05
❑ 99 Matt Mieske .15 .05
❑ 100 Larry Walker .30 .10
❑ 101 Shane Mack .15 .05
❑ 102 Aaron Ledesma RC .25 .08
❑ 103 Andy Pettitte RC 8.00 3.00
❑ 104 Kevin Stocker .15 .05
❑ 105 Mike Mohler RC .25 .08
❑ 106 Tony Menendez .15 .05
❑ 107 Derek Lowe .30 .10
❑ 108 Basil Shabazz .15 .05
❑ 109 Dan Smith .15 .05
❑ 110 Scott Sanders RC .50 .20
❑ 111 Todd Stottlemyre .15 .05
❑ 112 Benji Simonton RC .25 .08
❑ 113 Rick Sutcliffe .30 .10
❑ 114 Lee Heath RC .25 .08
❑ 115 Jeff Russell .15 .05
❑ 116 Dave Stevens RC .25 .08
❑ 117 Mark Holzemer RC .25 .08
❑ 118 Tim Belcher .15 .05
❑ 119 Bobby Thigpen .15 .05
❑ 120 Roger Bailey RC .25 .08
❑ 121 Tony Mitchell RC .25 .08
❑ 122 Junior Felix .15 .05
❑ 123 Rich Robertson RC .25 .08
❑ 124 Andy Cook RC .25 .08
❑ 125 Brian Bevil RC .25 .08
❑ 126 Darryl Strawberry .30 .10
❑ 127 Cal Eldred .15 .05
❑ 128 Cliff Floyd .30 .10
❑ 129 Alan Newman .15 .05
❑ 130 Howard Johnson .15 .05
❑ 131 Jim Abbott .50 .20
❑ 132 Chad McConnell .15 .05
❑ 133 Miguel Jimenez RC .25 .08
❑ 134 Brett Backlund RC .25 .08
❑ 135 John Cummings RC .25 .08
❑ 136 Brian Barber .15 .05
❑ 137 Rafael Palmeiro .50 .20
❑ 138 Tim Worrell RC .25 .08
❑ 139 Jose Pett RC .25 .08
❑ 140 Barry Bonds 2.00 .75
❑ 141 Damon Buford .15 .05
❑ 142 Jeff Blauser .15 .05
❑ 143 Frankie Rodriguez .15 .05
❑ 144 Mike Morgan .15 .05
❑ 145 Gary DiSarcina .15 .05
❑ 146 Pokey Reese .15 .05
❑ 147 Johnny Ruffin .15 .05
❑ 148 David Nied .15 .05
❑ 149 Charles Nagy .15 .05
❑ 150 Mike Myers RC .25 .08
❑ 151 Kenny Carlyle RC .25 .08
❑ 152 Eric Anthony .15 .05
❑ 153 Jose Lind .15 .05
❑ 154 Pedro Martinez 1.50 .60
❑ 155 Mark Kiefer .15 .05
❑ 156 Tim Laker RC .25 .08
❑ 157 Pat Mahomes .15 .05
❑ 158 Bobby Bonilla .30 .10
❑ 159 Domingo Jean .15 .05

❑ 160 Darren Daulton .30 .10
❑ 161 Mark McGwire 2.00 .75
❑ 162 Jason Kendall RC 2.00 .75
❑ 163 Desi Relaford .15 .05
❑ 164 Ozzie Canseco .15 .05
❑ 165 Rick Helling .15 .05
❑ 166 Steve Pegues RC .25 .08
❑ 167 Paul Molitor .30 .10
❑ 168 Larry Carter RC .15 .05
❑ 169 Arthur Rhodes .15 .05
❑ 170 Damon Hollins RC .50 .20
❑ 171 Frank Viola .30 .10
❑ 172 Steve Trachsel RC 1.00 .40
❑ 173 J.T.Snow RC 1.00 .40
❑ 174 Keith Gordon RC .25 .08
❑ 175 Carlton Fisk .50 .20
❑ 176 Jason Bates RC .25 .08
❑ 177 Mike Crosby RC .25 .08
❑ 178 Benny Santiago .30 .10
❑ 179 Mike Moore .15 .05
❑ 180 Jeff Juden .15 .05
❑ 181 Darren Burton .15 .05
❑ 182 Todd Williams RC .50 .20
❑ 183 John Jaha .15 .05
❑ 184 Mike Lansing RC .50 .20
❑ 185 Pedro Grifol RC .25 .08
❑ 186 Vince Coleman .15 .05
❑ 187 Pat Kelly .15 .05
❑ 188 Clemente Alvarez RC .25 .08
❑ 189 Ron Darling .15 .05
❑ 190 Orlando Merced .15 .05
❑ 191 Chris Bosio .15 .05
❑ 192 Steve Dixon RC .25 .08
❑ 193 Doug Dascenzo .15 .05
❑ 194 Ray Holbert RC .25 .08
❑ 195 Howard Battle .15 .05
❑ 196 Willie McGee .30 .10
❑ 197 John O'Donoghue RC .25 .08
❑ 198 Steve Avery .15 .05
❑ 199 Greg Blosser .15 .05
❑ 200 Ryne Sandberg 1.25 .50
❑ 201 Joe Grahe .15 .05
❑ 202 Dan Wilson .30 .10
❑ 203 Domingo Martinez RC .25 .08
❑ 204 Andres Galarraga .30 .10
❑ 205 Jamie Taylor RC .25 .08
❑ 206 Darrell Whitmore RC .25 .08
❑ 207 Ben Blomdahl RC .25 .08
❑ 208 Doug Drabek .15 .05
❑ 209 Keith Miller .15 .05
❑ 210 Billy Ashley .15 .05
❑ 211 Mike Farrell RC .25 .08
❑ 212 John Wetteland .30 .10
❑ 213 Randy Tomlin .15 .05
❑ 214 Sid Fernandez .15 .05
❑ 215 Quilvio Veras RC .50 .20
❑ 216 Dave Hollins .15 .05
❑ 217 Mike Neill .15 .05
❑ 218 Andy Van Slyke .50 .20
❑ 219 Bret Boone .30 .10
❑ 220 Tom Pagnozzi .15 .05
❑ 221 Mike Welch RC .25 .08
❑ 222 Frank Seminara .15 .05
❑ 223 Ron Villone .15 .05
❑ 224 D.J.Thielen RC .25 .08
❑ 225 Cal Ripken 2.50 1.00
❑ 226 Pedro Borbon Jr. RC .25 .08
❑ 227 Carlos Quintana .15 .05
❑ 228 Tommy Shields .15 .05
❑ 229 Tim Salmon .50 .20
❑ 230 John Smiley .15 .05
❑ 231 Ellis Burks .30 .10
❑ 232 Pedro Castellano .15 .05
❑ 233 Paul Byrd .30 .10
❑ 234 Bryan Harvey .15 .05
❑ 235 Scott Livingstone .15 .05
❑ 236 James Mouton RC .25 .08
❑ 237 Joe Randa .30 .10
❑ 238 Pedro Astacio .15 .05
❑ 239 Darryl Hamilton .15 .05
❑ 240 Joey Eischen RC .25 .08
❑ 241 Edgar Herrera RC .25 .08
❑ 242 Dwight Gooden .30 .10
❑ 243 Sam Militello .15 .05
❑ 244 Ron Blazier RC .25 .08
❑ 245 Ruben Sierra .30 .10
❑ 246 Al Martin .15 .05
❑ 247 Mike Felder .15 .05
❑ 248 Bob Tewksbury .15 .05
❑ 249 Craig Lefferts .15 .05
❑ 250 Luis Lopez RC .25 .08
❑ 251 Devon White .30 .10
❑ 252 Will Clark .50 .20
❑ 253 Mark Smith .15 .05
❑ 254 Terry Pendleton .30 .10
❑ 255 Aaron Sele .15 .05
❑ 256 Jose Viera RC .25 .08
❑ 257 Damion Easley .15 .05
❑ 258 Rod Lofton RC .25 .08
❑ 259 Chris Snopek RC .25 .08
❑ 260 Quinton McCracken RC .50 .20
❑ 261 Mike Matthews RC .25 .08
❑ 262 Hector Carrasco RC .25 .08
❑ 263 Rick Greene .15 .05
❑ 264 Chris Holt RC .50 .20
❑ 265 George Brett 2.00 .75
❑ 266 Rick Gorecki RC .25 .08
❑ 267 Francisco Gamez RC .25 .08
❑ 268 Marquis Grissom .30 .10
❑ 269 Kevin Tapani UER .15 .05
❑ 270 Ryan Thompson .15 .05
❑ 271 Gerald Williams .15 .05
❑ 272 Paul Fletcher RC .25 .08
❑ 273 Lance Blankenship .15 .05
❑ 274 Marty Neff RC .25 .08
❑ 275 Shawn Estes .15 .05
❑ 276 Rene Arocha RC .50 .20
❑ 277 Scott Eyre RC .25 .08
❑ 278 Phil Plantier .15 .05
❑ 279 Paul Spoljaric RC .25 .08
❑ 280 Chris Gambs .15 .05
❑ 281 Harold Baines .30 .10
❑ 282 Jose Oliva .15 .05
❑ 283 Matt Whiteside RC .25 .08
❑ 284 Brant Brown RC .50 .20
❑ 285 Russ Springer .15 .05
❑ 286 Chris Sabo .15 .05
❑ 287 Ozzie Guillen .30 .10
❑ 288 Marcus Moore RC .25 .08
❑ 289 Chad Ogea .15 .05
❑ 290 Walt Weiss .15 .05
❑ 291 Brian Edmondson .15 .05
❑ 292 Jimmy Gonzalez .15 .05
❑ 293 Danny Miceli RC .50 .20
❑ 294 Jose Offerman .15 .05
❑ 295 Greg Vaughn .15 .05
❑ 296 Frank Bolick .15 .05
❑ 297 Mike Maksudian RC .25 .08
❑ 298 John Franco .30 .10
❑ 299 Danny Tartabull .15 .05
❑ 300 Len Dykstra .30 .10
❑ 301 Bobby Witt .15 .05
❑ 302 Trey Beamon RC .25 .08
❑ 303 Tino Martinez .50 .20
❑ 304 Aaron Holbert .15 .05
❑ 305 Juan Gonzalez .30 .10
❑ 306 Billy Hall RC .25 .08
❑ 307 Duane Ward .15 .05
❑ 308 Rod Beck .15 .05
❑ 309 Jose Mercedes RC .25 .08
❑ 310 Otis Nixon .15 .05
❑ 311 Gettys Glaze RC .25 .08
❑ 312 Candy Maldonado .15 .05
❑ 313 Chad Curtis .15 .05
❑ 314 Tim Costo .15 .05
❑ 315 Mike Robertson .15 .05
❑ 316 Nigel Wilson .15 .05
❑ 317 Greg McMichael RC .50 .20
❑ 318 Scott Pose RC .25 .08
❑ 319 Ivan Cruz .15 .05
❑ 320 Greg Swindell .15 .05
❑ 321 Kevin McReynolds .15 .05
❑ 322 Tom Candiotti .15 .05
❑ 323 Rob Wishnevski RC .25 .08
❑ 324 Ken Hill .15 .05
❑ 325 Kirby Puckett .75 .30
❑ 326 Tim Bogar RC .25 .08
❑ 327 Mariano Rivera 2.50 1.00
❑ 328 Mitch Williams .15 .05
❑ 329 Craig Paquette .15 .05
❑ 330 Jay Bell .30 .10
❑ 331 Jose Martinez RC .25 .08
❑ 332 Rob Deer .15 .05
❑ 333 Brook Fordyce .15 .05
❑ 334 Matt Nokes .15 .05
❑ 335 Derek Lee .15 .05
❑ 336 Paul Ellis RC .25 .08
❑ 337 Desi Wilson RC .25 .08
❑ 338 Roberto Alomar .50 .20
❑ 339 Jim Tatum FOIL RC .25 .08
❑ 340 J.T.Snow FOIL 1.00 .40
❑ 341 Tim Salmon FOIL .50 .20
❑ 342 Russ Davis FOIL RC .50 .20
❑ 343 Javy Lopez FOIL .50 .20
❑ 344 Troy O'Leary FOIL RC .50 .20
❑ 345 Marty Cordova FOIL RC .50 .20
❑ 346 Bubba Smith RC FOIL .25 .08
❑ 347 Chipper Jones FOIL .75 .30
❑ 348 Jessie Hollins FOIL .15 .05
❑ 349 Willie Greene FOIL .15 .05
❑ 350 Mark Thompson FOIL .15 .05
❑ 351 Nigel Wilson FOIL .15 .05
❑ 352 Todd Jones FOIL .30 .10
❑ 353 Raul Mondesi FOIL .30 .10
❑ 354 Cliff Floyd FOIL .30 .10
❑ 355 Bobby Jones FOIL .30 .10
❑ 356 Kevin Stocker FOIL .15 .05
❑ 357 Midre Cummings FOIL .15 .05
❑ 358 Allen Watson FOIL .15 .05
❑ 359 Ray McDavid FOIL .15 .05
❑ 360 Steve Hosey FOIL .15 .05
❑ 361 Brad Pennington FOIL .15 .05
❑ 362 Frankie Rodriguez FOIL .15 .05
❑ 363 Troy Percival FOIL .50 .20
❑ 364 Jason Bere FOIL .15 .05
❑ 365 Manny Ramirez FOIL 1.25 .50
❑ 366 Justin Thompson FOIL .15 .05
❑ 367 Joe Vitiello FOIL .15 .05
❑ 368 Tyrone Hill FOIL .15 .05
❑ 369 David McCarty FOIL .15 .05
❑ 370 Brien Taylor FOIL .15 .05
❑ 371 Todd Van Poppel FOIL .15 .05
❑ 372 Marc Newfield FOIL .15 .05
❑ 373 Terrell Lowery FOIL RC .50 .20
❑ 374 Alex Gonzalez FOIL .15 .05
❑ 375 Ken Griffey Jr. 1.25 .50
❑ 376 Donovan Osborne .15 .05
❑ 377 Ritchie Moody RC .25 .08
❑ 378 Shane Andrews .15 .05
❑ 379 Carlos Delgado .75 .30
❑ 380 Bill Swift .15 .05
❑ 381 Leo Gomez .15 .05
❑ 382 Ron Gant .30 .10
❑ 383 Scott Fletcher .15 .05
❑ 384 Matt Walbeck RC .50 .20
❑ 385 Chuck Finley .30 .10
❑ 386 Kevin Mitchell .15 .05
❑ 387 Wilson Alvarez UER .15 .05
❑ 388 John Burke RC .25 .08
❑ 389 Alan Embree .15 .05
❑ 390 Trevor Hoffman .75 .30
❑ 391 Alan Trammell .30 .10
❑ 392 Todd Jones .30 .10
❑ 393 Felix Jose .15 .05
❑ 394 Orel Hershiser .30 .10
❑ 395 Pat Listach .15 .05
❑ 396 Gabe White .15 .05
❑ 397 Dan Serafini RC .25 .08
❑ 398 Todd Hundley .15 .05
❑ 399 Wade Boggs .50 .20
❑ 400 Tyler Green .15 .05
❑ 401 Mike Bordick .15 .05
❑ 402 Scott Bullett .15 .05
❑ 403 LaGrande Russell RC .25 .08
❑ 404 Ray Lankford .30 .10
❑ 405 Nolan Ryan 3.00 1.25
❑ 406 Robbie Beckett .15 .05
❑ 407 Brent Bowers RC .25 .08
❑ 408 Adell Davenport RC .25 .08
❑ 409 Brady Anderson .30 .10
❑ 410 Tom Glavine .50 .20
❑ 411 Doug Hecker RC .25 .08
❑ 412 Jose Guzman .15 .05
❑ 413 Luis Polonia .15 .05
❑ 414 Brian Williams .15 .05
❑ 415 Bo Jackson .75 .30
❑ 416 Eric Young .15 .05
❑ 417 Kenny Lofton .30 .10

❑ 418 Orestes Destrade .15 .05
❑ 419 Tony Phillips .15 .05
❑ 420 Jeff Bagwell .50 .20
❑ 421 Mark Gardner .15 .05
❑ 422 Brett Butler .30 .10
❑ 423 Graeme Lloyd RC .50 .20
❑ 424 Delino DeShields .15 .05
❑ 425 Scott Erickson .15 .05
❑ 426 Jeff Kent .75 .30
❑ 427 Jimmy Key .30 .10
❑ 428 Mickey Morandini .15 .05
❑ 429 Marcos Armas RC .25 .08
❑ 430 Don Slaught .15 .05
❑ 431 Randy Johnson .75 .30
❑ 432 Omar Olivares .15 .05
❑ 433 Charlie Leibrandt .15 .05
❑ 434 Kurt Stillwell .15 .05
❑ 435 Scott Brow RC .25 .08
❑ 436 Robby Thompson .15 .05
❑ 437 Ben McDonald .15 .05
❑ 438 Deion Sanders .50 .20
❑ 439 Tony Pena .15 .05
❑ 440 Mark Grace .50 .20
❑ 441 Eduardo Perez .15 .05
❑ 442 Tim Pugh RC .25 .08
❑ 443 Scott Ruffcorn .15 .05
❑ 444 Jay Gainer RC .25 .08
❑ 445 Albert Belle .30 .10
❑ 446 Bret Barberie .15 .05
❑ 447 Justin Mashore .15 .05
❑ 448 Pete Harnisch .15 .05
❑ 449 Greg Gagne .15 .05
❑ 450 Eric Davis .30 .10
❑ 451 Dave Mlicki .15 .05
❑ 452 Moises Alou .30 .10
❑ 453 Rick Aguilera .15 .05
❑ 454 Eddie Murray .75 .30
❑ 455 Bob Wickman .15 .05
❑ 456 Wes Chamberlain .15 .05
❑ 457 Brent Gates .15 .05
❑ 458 Paul Wagner .15 .05
❑ 459 Mike Hampton .30 .10
❑ 460 Ozzie Smith 1.25 .50
❑ 461 Tom Henke .15 .05
❑ 462 Ricky Gutierrez .15 .05
❑ 463 Jack Morris .30 .10
❑ 464 Joel Chimelis .15 .05
❑ 465 Gregg Olson .15 .05
❑ 466 Javy Lopez .50 .20
❑ 467 Scott Cooper .15 .05
❑ 468 Willie Wilson .15 .05
❑ 469 Mark Langston .15 .05
❑ 470 Barry Larkin .50 .20
❑ 471 Rod Bolton .15 .05
❑ 472 Freddie Benavides .15 .05
❑ 473 Ken Ramos RC .25 .08
❑ 474 Chuck Carr .15 .05
❑ 475 Cecil Fielder .30 .10
❑ 476 Eddie Taubensee .15 .05
❑ 477 Chris Eddy RC .25 .08
❑ 478 Greg Hansell .15 .05
❑ 479 Kevin Reimer .15 .05
❑ 480 Dennis Martinez .30 .10
❑ 481 Chuck Knoblauch .30 .10
❑ 482 Mike Draper .15 .05
❑ 483 Spike Owen .15 .05
❑ 484 Terry Mulholland .15 .05
❑ 485 Dennis Eckersley .30 .10
❑ 486 Blas Minor .15 .05
❑ 487 Dave Fleming .15 .05
❑ 488 Dan Cholowsky .15 .05
❑ 489 Ivan Rodriguez .50 .20
❑ 490 Gary Sheffield .30 .10
❑ 491 Ed Sprague .15 .05
❑ 492 Steve Hosey .15 .05
❑ 493 Jimmy Haynes RC .50 .20
❑ 494 John Smoltz .50 .20
❑ 495 Andre Dawson .30 .10
❑ 496 Rey Sanchez .15 .05
❑ 497 Ty Van Burkleo .15 .05
❑ 498 Bobby Ayala RC .25 .08
❑ 499 Tim Raines .30 .10
❑ 500 Charlie Hayes .15 .05
❑ 501 Paul Sorrento .15 .05
❑ 502 Richie Lewis RC .25 .08
❑ 503 Jason Pfaff RC .25 .08
❑ 504 Ken Caminiti .30 .10
❑ 505 Mike Macfarlane .15 .05
❑ 506 Jody Reed .15 .05
❑ 507 Bobby Hughes RC .25 .08
❑ 508 Wil Cordero .15 .05
❑ 509 George Tsamis RC .25 .08
❑ 510 Bret Saberhagen .30 .10
❑ 511 Derek Jeter RC 20.00 8.00
❑ 512 Gene Schall .15 .05
❑ 513 Curtis Shaw .15 .05
❑ 514 Steve Cooke .15 .05
❑ 515 Edgar Martinez .50 .20
❑ 516 Mike Milchin .15 .05
❑ 517 Billy Ripken .15 .05
❑ 518 Andy Benes .15 .05
❑ 519 Juan de la Rosa RC .25 .08
❑ 520 John Burkett .15 .05
❑ 521 Alex Ochoa .15 .05
❑ 522 Tony Tarasco RC .50 .20
❑ 523 Luis Ortiz .15 .05
❑ 524 Rick Wilkins .15 .05
❑ 525 Chris Turner RC .25 .08
❑ 526 Rob Dibble .30 .10
❑ 527 Jack McDowell .15 .05
❑ 528 Daryl Boston .15 .05
❑ 529 Bill Wertz RC .25 .08
❑ 530 Charlie Hough .30 .10
❑ 531 Sean Bergman .15 .05
❑ 532 Doug Jones .15 .05
❑ 533 Jeff Montgomery .15 .05
❑ 534 Roger Cedeno RC .50 .20
❑ 535 Robin Yount 1.25 .50
❑ 536 Mo Vaughn .30 .10
❑ 537 Brian Harper .15 .05
❑ 538 Juan Castillo RC .15 .05
❑ 539 Steve Farr .15 .05
❑ 540 John Kruk .30 .10
❑ 541 Troy Neel .15 .05
❑ 542 Danny Clyburn RC .25 .08
❑ 543 Jim Converse RC .25 .08
❑ 544 Gregg Jefferies .15 .05
❑ 545 Jose Canseco .50 .20
❑ 546 Julio Bruno RC .25 .08
❑ 547 Rob Butler .15 .05
❑ 548 Royce Clayton .15 .05
❑ 549 Chris Hoiles .15 .05
❑ 550 Greg Maddux 1.25 .50
❑ 551 Joe Ciccarella RC .25 .08
❑ 552 Ozzie Timmons .15 .05
❑ 553 Chili Davis .30 .10
❑ 554 Brian Koelling .15 .05
❑ 555 Frank Thomas .75 .30
❑ 556 Vinny Castilla .75 .30
❑ 557 Reggie Jefferson .15 .05
❑ 558 Rob Natal .15 .05
❑ 559 Mike Henneman .15 .05
❑ 560 Craig Biggio .50 .20
❑ 561 Billy Brewer .15 .05
❑ 562 Dan Melendez .15 .05
❑ 563 Kenny Felder RC .25 .08
❑ 564 Miguel Batista RC 1.00 .40
❑ 565 Dave Winfield .30 .10
❑ 566 Al Shirley .15 .05
❑ 567 Robert Eenhoorn .15 .05
❑ 568 Mike Williams .15 .05
❑ 569 Tanyon Sturtze RC .50 .20
❑ 570 Tim Wakefield .75 .30
❑ 571 Greg Pirkl .15 .05
❑ 572 Sean Lowe RC .25 .08
❑ 573 Terry Burrows RC .25 .08
❑ 574 Kevin Higgins .15 .05
❑ 575 Joe Carter .30 .10
❑ 576 Kevin Rogers .15 .05
❑ 577 Manny Alexander .15 .05
❑ 578 David Justice .30 .10
❑ 579 Brian Conroy RC .25 .08
❑ 580 Jessie Hollins .15 .05
❑ 581 Ron Watson RC .25 .08
❑ 582 Bip Roberts .15 .05
❑ 583 Tom Urbani RC .25 .08
❑ 584 Jason Hutchins RC .25 .08
❑ 585 Carlos Baerga .15 .05
❑ 586 Jeff Mutis .15 .05
❑ 587 Justin Thompson .15 .05
❑ 588 Orlando Miller .15 .05
❑ 589 Brian McRae .15 .05
❑ 590 Ramon Martinez .15 .05
❑ 591 Dave Nilsson .15 .05
❑ 592 Jose Vidro RC 2.00 .75
❑ 593 Rich Becker .15 .05
❑ 594 Preston Wilson RC 1.50 .60
❑ 595 Don Mattingly 2.00 .75
❑ 596 Tony Longmire .15 .05
❑ 597 Kevin Seitzer .15 .05
❑ 598 Midre Cummings RC .25 .08
❑ 599 Omar Vizquel .50 .20
❑ 600 Lee Smith .30 .10
❑ 601 David Hulse RC .25 .08
❑ 602 Darrell Sherman RC .25 .08
❑ 603 Alex Gonzalez .15 .05
❑ 604 Geronimo Pena .15 .05
❑ 605 Mike Devereaux .15 .05
❑ 606 Sterling Hitchcock RC .50 .20
❑ 607 Mike Greenwell .15 .05
❑ 608 Steve Buechele .15 .05
❑ 609 Troy Percival .50 .20
❑ 610 Roberto Kelly .15 .05
❑ 611 James Baldwin RC .50 .20
❑ 612 Jerald Clark .15 .05
❑ 613 Albie Lopez RC .25 .08
❑ 614 Dave Magadan .15 .05
❑ 615 Mickey Tettleton .15 .05
❑ 616 Sean Runyan RC .25 .08
❑ 617 Bob Hamelin .15 .05
❑ 618 Raul Mondesi .30 .10
❑ 619 Tyrone Hill .15 .05
❑ 620 Darrin Fletcher .15 .05
❑ 621 Mike Trombley .15 .05
❑ 622 Jeromy Burnitz .30 .10
❑ 623 Bernie Williams .50 .20
❑ 624 Mike Farmer RC .25 .08
❑ 625 Rickey Henderson .75 .30
❑ 626 Carlos Garcia .15 .05
❑ 627 Jeff Darwin RC .25 .08
❑ 628 Todd Zeile .15 .05
❑ 629 Benji Gil .15 .05
❑ 630 Tony Gwynn 1.00 .40
❑ 631 Aaron Small RC 1.00 .40
❑ 632 Joe Rosselli RC .25 .08
❑ 633 Mike Mussina .50 .20
❑ 634 Ryan Klesko .30 .10
❑ 635 Roger Clemens 1.50 .60
❑ 636 Sammy Sosa .75 .30
❑ 637 Orlando Palmeiro RC .25 .08
❑ 638 Willie Greene .15 .05
❑ 639 George Bell .15 .05
❑ 640 Garvin Alston RC .25 .08
❑ 641 Pete Janicki RC .25 .08
❑ 642 Chris Sheff RC .25 .08
❑ 643 Felipe Lira RC .25 .08
❑ 644 Roberto Petagine .15 .05
❑ 645 Wally Joyner .30 .10
❑ 646 Mike Piazza 3.00 1.25
❑ 647 Jaime Navarro .15 .05
❑ 648 Jeff Hartsock .15 .05
❑ 649 David McCarty .15 .05
❑ 650 Bobby Jones .30 .10
❑ 651 Mark Hutton .15 .05
❑ 652 Kyle Abbott .15 .05
❑ 653 Steve Cox RC .25 .08
❑ 654 Jeff King .15 .05
❑ 655 Norm Charlton .15 .05
❑ 656 Mike Gulan RC .25 .08
❑ 657 Julio Franco .30 .10
❑ 658 Cameron Cairncross RC .25 .08
❑ 659 John Olerud .30 .10
❑ 660 Salomon Torres .15 .05
❑ 661 Brad Pennington .15 .05
❑ 662 Melvin Nieves .15 .05
❑ 663 Ivan Calderon .15 .05
❑ 664 Turk Wendell .15 .05
❑ 665 Chris Pritchett .15 .05
❑ 666 Reggie Sanders .30 .10
❑ 667 Robin Ventura .30 .10
❑ 668 Joe Girardi .15 .05
❑ 669 Manny Ramirez 1.25 .50
❑ 670 Jeff Conine .30 .10
❑ 671 Greg Gohr .15 .05
❑ 672 Andujar Cedeno .15 .05
❑ 673 Les Norman RC .25 .08
❑ 674 Mike James RC .25 .08
❑ 675 Marshall Boze RC .25 .08

❑ 676 B.J.Wallace .15 .05
❑ 677 Kent Hrbek .30 .10
❑ 678 Jack Voigt RC .25 .08
❑ 679 Brien Taylor .15 .05
❑ 680 Curt Schilling .30 .10
❑ 681 Todd Van Poppel .15 .05
❑ 682 Kevin Young .30 .10
❑ 683 Tommy Adams .15 .05
❑ 684 Bernard Gilkey .15 .05
❑ 685 Kevin Brown .30 .10
❑ 686 Fred McGriff .50 .20
❑ 687 Pat Borders .15 .05
❑ 688 Kirt Manwaring .15 .05
❑ 689 Sid Bream .15 .05
❑ 690 John Valentin .15 .05
❑ 691 Steve Olsen RC .25 .08
❑ 692 Roberto Mejia RC .25 .08
❑ 693 Carlos Delgado FOIL .75 .30
❑ 694 Steve Gibralter FOIL RC .25 .08
❑ 695 Gary Mota FOIL RC .25 .08
❑ 696 Jose Malave FOIL RC .25 .08
❑ 697 Larry Sutton FOIL RC .25 .08
❑ 698 Dan Frye FOIL RC .25 .08
❑ 699 Tim Clark FOIL RC .25 .08
❑ 700 Brian Rupp FOIL RC .25 .08
❑ 701 Felipe/Moises Alou FOIL .30 .10
❑ 702 Barry/Bobby Bonds FOIL 1.00 .40
❑ 703 Ken Griffey Jr./Sr. FOIL .75 .30
❑ 704 Brian/Hal McRae FOIL .15 .05
❑ 705 Checklist 1 .15 .05
❑ 706 Checklist 2 .15 .05
❑ 707 Checklist 3 .15 .05
❑ 708 Checklist 4 .15 .05

1994 Bowman

❑ COMPLETE SET (682) 60.00 30.00
❑ 1 Joe Carter .40 .15
❑ 2 Marcus Moore .25 .08
❑ 3 Doug Creek RC .40 .15
❑ 4 Pedro Martinez 1.00 .40
❑ 5 Ken Griffey Jr. 1.50 .60
❑ 6 Greg Swindell .25 .08
❑ 7 J.J. Johnson .25 .08
❑ 8 Homer Bush RC .40 .15
❑ 9 Arquimedez Pozo RC .40 .15
❑ 10 Bryan Harvey .25 .08
❑ 11 J.T. Snow .40 .15
❑ 12 Alan Benes RC 1.00 .40
❑ 13 Chad Kreuter .25 .08
❑ 14 Eric Karros .40 .15
❑ 15 Frank Thomas 1.00 .40
❑ 16 Bret Saberhagen .40 .15
❑ 17 Terrell Lowery .25 .08
❑ 18 Rod Bolton .25 .08
❑ 19 Harold Baines .40 .15
❑ 20 Matt Walbeck .25 .08
❑ 21 Tom Glavine .60 .25
❑ 22 Todd Jones .25 .08
❑ 23 Alberto Castillo RC .40 .15
❑ 24 Ruben Sierra .40 .15
❑ 25 Don Mattingly 2.50 1.00
❑ 26 Mike Morgan .25 .08
❑ 27 Jim Musselwhite RC .40 .15
❑ 28 Matt Brunson RC .40 .15
❑ 29 Adam Meinershagen RC .40 .15
❑ 30 Joe Girardi .25 .08
❑ 31 Shane Halter .25 .08
❑ 32 Jose Paniagua RC 1.00 .40
❑ 33 Paul Perkins RC .40 .15
❑ 34 John Hudek RC .40 .15
❑ 35 Frank Viola .40 .15
❑ 36 David Lamb RC .40 .15
❑ 37 Marshall Boze .25 .08
❑ 38 Jorge Posada RC 8.00 3.00
❑ 39 Brian Anderson RC 1.00 .40
❑ 40 Mark Whiten .25 .08
❑ 41 Sean Bergman .25 .08
❑ 42 Jose Parra RC .40 .15
❑ 43 Mike Robertson .25 .08
❑ 44 Pete Walker RC .40 .15
❑ 45 Juan Gonzalez .40 .15
❑ 46 Cleveland Ladell RC .40 .15
❑ 47 Mark Smith .25 .08
❑ 48 Kevin Jarvis RC UER .40 .15
❑ 49 Amaury Telemaco RC .40 .15
❑ 50 Andy Van Slyke .60 .25
❑ 51 Rikkert Faneyte RC .40 .15
❑ 52 Curtis Shaw .25 .08
❑ 53 Matt Drews RC .40 .15
❑ 54 Wilson Alvarez .25 .08
❑ 55 Manny Ramirez 1.00 .40
❑ 56 Bobby Munoz .25 .08
❑ 57 Ed Sprague .25 .08
❑ 58 Jamey Wright RC 1.00 .40
❑ 59 Jeff Montgomery .25 .08
❑ 60 Kirk Rueter .25 .08
❑ 61 Edgar Martinez .60 .25
❑ 62 Luis Gonzalez .40 .15
❑ 63 Tim Vanegmond RC .40 .15
❑ 64 Bip Roberts .25 .08
❑ 65 John Jaha .25 .08
❑ 66 Chuck Carr .25 .08
❑ 67 Chuck Finley .40 .15
❑ 68 Aaron Holbert .25 .08
❑ 69 Cecil Fielder .40 .15
❑ 70 Tom Engle RC .40 .15
❑ 71 Ron Karkovice .25 .08
❑ 72 Joe Orsulak .25 .08
❑ 73 Duff Brumley RC .40 .15
❑ 74 Craig Clayton RC .40 .15
❑ 75 Cal Ripken 3.00 1.25
❑ 76 Brad Fullmer RC 1.00 .40
❑ 77 Tony Tarasco .25 .08
❑ 78 Terry Farrar RC .40 .15
❑ 79 Matt Williams .40 .15
❑ 80 Rickey Henderson 1.00 .40
❑ 81 Terry Mulholland .25 .08
❑ 82 Sammy Sosa 1.00 .40
❑ 83 Paul Sorrento .25 .08
❑ 84 Pete Incaviglia .25 .08
❑ 85 Darren Hall RC .40 .15
❑ 86 Scott Klingenbeck .25 .08
❑ 87 Dario Perez RC .40 .15
❑ 88 Ugueth Urbina .25 .08
❑ 89 Dave Vanhof RC .40 .15
❑ 90 Domingo Jean .25 .08
❑ 91 Otis Nixon .25 .08
❑ 92 Andres Berumen .25 .08
❑ 93 Jose Valentin .25 .08
❑ 94 Edgar Renteria RC 5.00 2.00
❑ 95 Chris Turner .25 .08
❑ 96 Ray Lankford .40 .15
❑ 97 Danny Bautista .25 .08
❑ 98 Chan Ho Park RC 1.50 .60
❑ 99 Glenn DiSarcina RC .40 .15
❑ 100 Butch Huskey .25 .08
❑ 101 Ivan Rodriguez .60 .25
❑ 102 Johnny Ruffin .25 .08
❑ 103 Alex Ochoa .25 .08
❑ 104 Torii Hunter RC 5.00 2.00
❑ 105 Ryan Klesko .40 .15
❑ 106 Jay Bell .40 .15
❑ 107 Kurt Peltzer RC .40 .15
❑ 108 Miguel Jimenez .25 .08
❑ 109 Russ Davis .25 .08
❑ 110 Derek Wallace .25 .08
❑ 111 Keith Lockhart RC 1.00 .40
❑ 112 Mike Lieberthal .40 .15
❑ 113 Dave Stewart .40 .15
❑ 114 Tom Schmidt .25 .08
❑ 115 Brian McRae .25 .08
❑ 116 Moises Alou .40 .15
❑ 117 Dave Fleming .25 .08
❑ 118 Jeff Bagwell .60 .25
❑ 119 Luis Ortiz .25 .08
❑ 120 Tony Gwynn 1.25 .50
❑ 121 Jaime Navarro .25 .08
❑ 122 Benito Santiago .40 .15
❑ 123 Darrell Whitmore .25 .08
❑ 124 John Mabry RC 1.00 .40
❑ 125 Mickey Tettleton .25 .08
❑ 126 Tom Candiotti .25 .08
❑ 127 Tim Raines .40 .15
❑ 128 Bobby Bonilla .40 .15
❑ 129 John Dettmer .25 .08
❑ 130 Hector Carrasco .25 .08
❑ 131 Chris Hoiles .25 .08
❑ 132 Rick Aguilera .25 .08
❑ 133 David Justice .40 .15
❑ 134 Esteban Loaiza RC 1.50 .60
❑ 135 Barry Bonds 2.50 1.00
❑ 136 Bob Welch .25 .08
❑ 137 Mike Stanley .25 .08
❑ 138 Roberto Hernandez .25 .08
❑ 139 Sandy Alomar Jr. .25 .08
❑ 140 Darren Daulton .40 .15
❑ 141 Angel Martinez RC .40 .15
❑ 142 Howard Johnson .25 .08
❑ 143 Bob Hamelin .25 .08
❑ 144 J.J.Thobe RC .40 .15
❑ 145 Roger Salkeld .25 .08
❑ 146 Orlando Miller .25 .08
❑ 147 Dmitri Young .40 .15
❑ 148 Tim Hyers RC .40 .15
❑ 149 Mark Loretta RC 5.00 2.00
❑ 150 Chris Hammond .25 .08
❑ 151 Joel Moore RC .40 .15
❑ 152 Todd Zeile .25 .08
❑ 153 Wil Cordero .25 .08
❑ 154 Chris Smith .25 .08
❑ 155 James Baldwin .25 .08
❑ 156 Edgardo Alfonzo RC 1.00 .40
❑ 157 Kym Ashworth RC .40 .15
❑ 158 Paul Bako RC .40 .15
❑ 159 Rick Krivda RC .40 .15
❑ 160 Pat Mahomes .25 .08
❑ 161 Damon Hollins .25 .08
❑ 162 Felix Martinez RC .40 .15
❑ 163 Jason Myers RC .40 .15
❑ 164 Izzy Molina RC .40 .15
❑ 165 Brien Taylor .25 .08
❑ 166 Kevin Orie RC .40 .15
❑ 167 Casey Whitten RC .40 .15
❑ 168 Tony Longmire .25 .08
❑ 169 John Olerud .40 .15
❑ 170 Mark Thompson .25 .08
❑ 171 Jorge Fabregas .25 .08
❑ 172 John Wetteland .40 .15
❑ 173 Dan Wilson .25 .08
❑ 174 Doug Drabek .25 .08
❑ 175 Jeff McNeely .25 .08
❑ 176 Melvin Nieves .25 .08
❑ 177 Doug Glanville RC 1.00 .40
❑ 178 Javier De La Hoya RC .40 .15
❑ 179 Chad Curtis .25 .08
❑ 180 Brian Barber .25 .08
❑ 181 Mike Henneman .25 .08
❑ 182 Jose Offerman .25 .08
❑ 183 Robert Ellis RC .40 .15
❑ 184 John Franco .40 .15
❑ 185 Benji Gil .25 .08
❑ 186 Hal Morris .25 .08
❑ 187 Chris Sabo .25 .08
❑ 188 Blaise Ilsley RC .40 .15
❑ 189 Steve Avery .25 .08
❑ 190 Rick White RC .40 .15
❑ 191 Rod Beck .25 .08
❑ 192 Mark McGwire UER NNO 2.50 1.00
❑ 193 Jim Abbott .60 .25
❑ 194 Randy Myers .25 .08
❑ 195 Kenny Lofton .40 .15
❑ 196 Mariano Duncan .25 .08
❑ 197 Lee Daniels RC .40 .15
❑ 198 Armando Reynoso .25 .08
❑ 199 Joe Randa .40 .15
❑ 200 Cliff Floyd .40 .15
❑ 201 Tim Harkrider RC .40 .15
❑ 202 Kevin Gallaher RC .40 .15
❑ 203 Scott Cooper .25 .08
❑ 204 Phil Stidham RC .40 .15

❑ 205 Jeff D'Amico RC .40 .15
❑ 206 Matt Whisenant .25 .08
❑ 207 DeShawn Warren .25 .08
❑ 208 Rene Arocha .25 .08
❑ 209 Tony Clark RC 1.50 .60
❑ 210 Jason Jacome RC .40 .15
❑ 211 Scott Christman RC .40 .15
❑ 212 Bill Pulsipher .40 .15
❑ 213 Dean Palmer .40 .15
❑ 214 Chad Mottola .25 .08
❑ 215 Manny Alexander .25 .08
❑ 216 Rich Becker .25 .08
❑ 217 Andre King RC .40 .15
❑ 218 Carlos Garcia .25 .08
❑ 219 Ron Pezzoni RC .40 .15
❑ 220 Steve Karsay .25 .08
❑ 221 Jose Musset RC .40 .15
❑ 222 Karl Rhodes .25 .08
❑ 223 Frank Cimorelli RC .40 .15
❑ 224 Kevin Jordan RC .40 .15
❑ 225 Duane Ward .25 .08
❑ 226 John Burke .25 .08
❑ 227 Mike Macfarlane .25 .08
❑ 228 Mike Lansing .25 .08
❑ 229 Chuck Knoblauch .40 .15
❑ 230 Ken Caminiti .40 .15
❑ 231 Gar Finnvold RC .40 .15
❑ 232 Derrek Lee RC 10.00 4.00
❑ 233 Brady Anderson .40 .15
❑ 234 Vic Darensbourg RC .40 .15
❑ 235 Mark Langston .25 .08
❑ 236 T.J.Mathews RC .40 .15
❑ 237 Lou Whitaker .40 .15
❑ 238 Roger Cedeno .25 .08
❑ 239 Alex Fernandez .25 .08
❑ 240 Ryan Thompson .25 .08
❑ 241 Kerry Lacy RC .40 .15
❑ 242 Reggie Sanders .40 .15
❑ 243 Brad Pennington .25 .08
❑ 244 Bryan Eversgerd RC .40 .15
❑ 245 Greg Maddux 1.50 .60
❑ 246 Jason Kendall .40 .15
❑ 247 J.R. Phillips .25 .08
❑ 248 Bobby Witt .25 .08
❑ 249 Paul O'Neill .60 .25
❑ 250 Ryne Sandberg 1.50 .60
❑ 251 Charles Nagy .25 .08
❑ 252 Kevin Stocker .25 .08
❑ 253 Shawn Green 1.00 .40
❑ 254 Charlie Hayes .25 .08
❑ 255 Donnie Elliott .25 .08
❑ 256 Rob Fitzpatrick RC .40 .15
❑ 257 Tim Davis .25 .08
❑ 258 James Mouton .25 .08
❑ 259 Mike Greenwell .25 .08
❑ 260 Ray McDavid .25 .08
❑ 261 Mike Kelly .25 .08
❑ 262 Andy Larkin RC .40 .15
❑ 263 Marquis Riley UER .25 .08
❑ 264 Bob Tewksbury .25 .08
❑ 265 Brian Edmondson .25 .08
❑ 266 Eduardo Lantigua RC .40 .15
❑ 267 Brandon Wilson .25 .08
❑ 268 Mike Welch .25 .08
❑ 269 Tom Henke .25 .08
❑ 270 Pokey Reese .25 .08
❑ 271 Gregg Zaun RC 1.00 .40
❑ 272 Todd Ritchie .25 .08
❑ 273 Javier Lopez .40 .15
❑ 274 Kevin Young .25 .08
❑ 275 Kirt Manwaring .25 .08
❑ 276 Bill Taylor RC .40 .15
❑ 277 Robert Eenhoorn .25 .08
❑ 278 Jessie Hollins .25 .08
❑ 279 Julian Tavarez RC 1.00 .40
❑ 280 Gene Schall .25 .08
❑ 281 Paul Molitor .40 .15
❑ 282 Neifi Perez RC 1.00 .40
❑ 283 Greg Gagne .25 .08
❑ 284 Marquis Grissom .40 .15
❑ 285 Randy Johnson 1.00 .40
❑ 286 Pete Harnisch .25 .08
❑ 287 Joel Bennett RC .40 .15
❑ 288 Derek Bell .25 .08
❑ 289 Darryl Hamilton .25 .08
❑ 290 Gary Sheffield .40 .15
❑ 291 Eduardo Perez .25 .08
❑ 292 Basil Shabazz .25 .08
❑ 293 Eric Davis .40 .15
❑ 294 Pedro Astacio .25 .08
❑ 295 Robin Ventura .40 .15
❑ 296 Jeff Kent .60 .25
❑ 297 Rick Helling .25 .08
❑ 298 Joe Oliver .25 .08
❑ 299 Lee Smith .40 .15
❑ 300 Dave Winfield .40 .15
❑ 301 Deion Sanders .60 .25
❑ 302 Ravelo Manzanillo RC .40 .15
❑ 303 Mark Portugal .25 .08
❑ 304 Brent Gates .25 .08
❑ 305 Wade Boggs .60 .25
❑ 306 Rick Wilkins .25 .08
❑ 307 Carlos Baerga .25 .08
❑ 308 Curt Schilling .40 .15
❑ 309 Shannon Stewart 1.00 .40
❑ 310 Darren Holmes .25 .08
❑ 311 Robert Toth RC .40 .15
❑ 312 Gabe White .25 .08
❑ 313 Mac Suzuki RC 1.00 .40
❑ 314 Alvin Morman RC .40 .15
❑ 315 Mo Vaughn .40 .15
❑ 316 Bryce Florie RC .40 .15
❑ 317 Gabby Martinez RC .40 .15
❑ 318 Carl Everett .40 .15
❑ 319 Kerwin Moore .25 .08
❑ 320 Tom Pagnozzi .25 .08
❑ 321 Chris Gomez .25 .08
❑ 322 Todd Williams .25 .08
❑ 323 Pat Hentgen .25 .08
❑ 324 Kirk Presley RC .40 .15
❑ 325 Kevin Brown .40 .15
❑ 326 Jason Isringhausen RC 3.00 1.25
❑ 327 Rick Forney RC .40 .15
❑ 328 Carlos Pulido RC .40 .15
❑ 329 Terrell Wade RC .40 .15
❑ 330 Al Martin .25 .08
❑ 331 Dan Carlson RC .40 .15
❑ 332 Mark Acre RC .40 .15
❑ 333 Sterling Hitchcock .25 .08
❑ 334 Jon Ratliff RC .40 .15
❑ 335 Alex Ramirez RC .40 .15
❑ 336 Phil Geisler RC .25 .08
❑ 337 Eddie Zambrano FOIL RC .40 .15
❑ 338 Jim Thome FOIL .60 .25
❑ 339 James Mouton FOIL .25 .08
❑ 340 Cliff Floyd FOIL .40 .15
❑ 341 Carlos Delgado FOIL .60 .25
❑ 342 Roberto Petagine FOIL .25 .08
❑ 343 Tim Clark FOIL .25 .08
❑ 344 Bubba Smith FOIL .25 .08
❑ 345 Randy Curtis FOIL RC .40 .15
❑ 346 Joe Biasucci FOIL RC .40 .15
❑ 347 D.J. Boston FOIL RC .40 .15
❑ 348 Ruben Rivera FOIL RC .40 .15
❑ 349 Bryan Link FOIL RC .40 .15
❑ 350 Mike Bell FOIL RC .40 .15
❑ 351 Marty Watson FOIL RC .40 .15
❑ 352 Jason Myers FOIL .25 .08
❑ 353 Chipper Jones FOIL 1.00 .40
❑ 354 Brooks Kieschnick FOIL .40 .15
❑ 355 Pokey Reese FOIL .25 .08
❑ 356 John Burke FOIL .25 .08
❑ 357 Kurt Miller FOIL .25 .08
❑ 358 Orlando Miller FOIL .25 .08
❑ 359 Todd Hollandsworth FOIL .25 .08
❑ 360 Rondell White FOIL .40 .15
❑ 361 Bill Pulsipher FOIL .40 .15
❑ 362 Tyler Green FOIL .25 .08
❑ 363 Midre Cummings FOIL .25 .08
❑ 364 Brian Barber FOIL .25 .08
❑ 365 Melvin Nieves FOIL .25 .08
❑ 366 Salomon Torres FOIL .25 .08
❑ 367 Alex Ochoa FOIL .25 .08
❑ 368 Frankie Rodriguez FOIL .25 .08
❑ 369 Brian Anderson FOIL .40 .15
❑ 370 James Baldwin FOIL .25 .08
❑ 371 Manny Ramirez FOIL 1.00 .40
❑ 372 Justin Thompson FOIL .25 .08
❑ 373 Johnny Damon FOIL .60 .25
❑ 374 Jeff D'Amico FOIL .40 .15
❑ 375 Rich Becker FOIL .25 .08
❑ 376 Derek Jeter FOIL 3.00 1.25
❑ 377 Steve Karsay FOIL .25 .08
❑ 378 Mac Suzuki FOIL .40 .15
❑ 379 Benji Gil FOIL .25 .08
❑ 380 Alex Gonzalez FOIL .25 .08
❑ 381 Jason Bere FOIL .25 .08
❑ 382 Brett Butler FOIL .40 .15
❑ 383 Jeff Conine FOIL .40 .15
❑ 384 Darren Daulton FOIL .40 .15
❑ 385 Jeff Kent FOIL .60 .25
❑ 386 Don Mattingly FOIL 2.50 1.00
❑ 387 Mike Piazza FOIL 2.00 .75
❑ 388 Ryne Sandberg FOIL 1.50 .60
❑ 389 Rich Amaral .25 .08
❑ 390 Craig Biggio .60 .25
❑ 391 Jeff Suppan RC 2.00 .75
❑ 392 Andy Benes .25 .08
❑ 393 Cal Eldred .25 .08
❑ 394 Jeff Conine .40 .15
❑ 395 Tim Salmon .60 .25
❑ 396 Ray Suplee RC .40 .15
❑ 397 Tony Phillips .25 .08
❑ 398 Ramon Martinez .25 .08
❑ 399 Julio Franco .40 .15
❑ 400 Dwight Gooden .40 .15
❑ 401 Kevin Loman RC .40 .15
❑ 402 Jose Rijo .25 .08
❑ 403 Mike Devereaux .25 .08
❑ 404 Mike Zolecki RC .40 .15
❑ 405 Fred McGriff .60 .25
❑ 406 Danny Clyburn .25 .08
❑ 407 Robby Thompson .25 .08
❑ 408 Terry Steinbach .25 .08
❑ 409 Luis Polonia .25 .08
❑ 410 Mark Grace .60 .25
❑ 411 Albert Belle .40 .15
❑ 412 John Kruk .40 .15
❑ 413 Scott Spiezio RC 1.00 .40
❑ 414 Ellis Burks UER .40 .15
❑ 415 Joe Vitiello .25 .08
❑ 416 Tim Costo .25 .08
❑ 417 Marc Newfield .25 .08
❑ 418 Oscar Henriquez RC .40 .15
❑ 419 Matt Perisho RC .40 .15
❑ 420 Julio Bruno .25 .08
❑ 421 Kenny Felder .25 .08
❑ 422 Tyler Green .25 .08
❑ 423 Jim Edmonds 1.00 .40
❑ 424 Ozzie Smith 1.50 .60
❑ 425 Rick Greene .25 .08
❑ 426 Todd Hollandsworth .25 .08
❑ 427 Eddie Pearson RC .40 .15
❑ 428 Quilvio Veras .25 .08
❑ 429 Kenny Rogers .40 .15
❑ 430 Willie Greene .25 .08
❑ 431 Vaughn Eshelman .25 .08
❑ 432 Pat Meares .25 .08
❑ 433 Jermaine Dye RC 8.00 3.00
❑ 434 Steve Cooke .25 .08
❑ 435 Bill Swift .25 .08
❑ 436 Fausto Cruz RC .40 .15
❑ 437 Mark Hutton .25 .08
❑ 438 Brooks Kieschnick RC .40 .15
❑ 439 Yorkis Perez .25 .08
❑ 440 Len Dykstra .40 .15
❑ 441 Pat Borders .25 .08
❑ 442 Doug Walls RC .40 .15
❑ 443 Wally Joyner .40 .15
❑ 444 Ken Hill .25 .08
❑ 445 Eric Anthony .25 .08
❑ 446 Mitch Williams .25 .08
❑ 447 Cory Bailey RC .40 .15
❑ 448 Dave Staton .25 .08
❑ 449 Greg Vaughn .25 .08
❑ 450 Dave Magadan .25 .08
❑ 451 Chili Davis .40 .15
❑ 452 Gerald Santos RC .40 .15
❑ 453 Joe Perona .25 .08
❑ 454 Delino DeShields .25 .08
❑ 455 Jack McDowell .25 .08
❑ 456 Todd Hundley .25 .08
❑ 457 Ritchie Moody .25 .08
❑ 458 Bret Boone .40 .15
❑ 459 Ben McDonald .25 .08
❑ 460 Kirby Puckett 1.00 .40
❑ 461 Gregg Olson .25 .08
❑ 462 Rich Aude RC .40 .15

❑ 463	John Burkett	.25	.08
❑ 464	Troy Neel	.25	.08
❑ 465	Jimmy Key	.40	.15
❑ 466	Ozzie Timmons	.25	.08
❑ 467	Eddie Murray	1.00	.40
❑ 468	Mark Tranberg RC	.40	.15
❑ 469	Alex Gonzalez	.25	.08
❑ 470	David Nied	.25	.08
❑ 471	Barry Larkin	.60	.25
❑ 472	Brian Looney RC	.40	.15
❑ 473	Shawn Estes	.25	.08
❑ 474	A.J.Sager RC	.40	.15
❑ 475	Roger Clemens	2.00	.75
❑ 476	Vince Moore	.25	.08
❑ 477	Scott Karl RC	.40	.15
❑ 478	Kurt Miller	.25	.08
❑ 479	Garret Anderson	1.00	.40
❑ 480	Allen Watson	.25	.08
❑ 481	Jose Lima RC	1.00	.40
❑ 482	Rick Gorecki	.25	.08
❑ 483	Jimmy Hurst RC	.40	.15
❑ 484	Preston Wilson	.40	.15
❑ 485	Will Clark	.60	.25
❑ 486	Mike Ferry RC	.40	.15
❑ 487	Curtis Goodwin RC	.40	.15
❑ 488	Mike Myers	.25	.08
❑ 489	Chipper Jones	1.00	.40
❑ 490	Jeff King	.25	.08
❑ 491	W.VanLandingham RC	.40	.15
❑ 492	Carlos Reyes RC	.40	.15
❑ 493	Andy Pettitte	1.00	.40
❑ 494	Brant Brown	.25	.08
❑ 495	Daron Kirkreit	.25	.08
❑ 496	Ricky Bottalico RC	.40	.15
❑ 497	Devon White	.40	.15
❑ 498	Jason Johnson RC	1.00	.40
❑ 499	Vince Coleman	.25	.08
❑ 500	Larry Walker	.40	.15
❑ 501	Bobby Ayala	.25	.08
❑ 502	Steve Finley	.40	.15
❑ 503	Scott Fletcher	.25	.08
❑ 504	Brad Ausmus	.60	.25
❑ 505	Scott Talanoa RC	.40	.15
❑ 506	Orestes Destrade	.25	.08
❑ 507	Gary DiSarcina	.25	.08
❑ 508	Willie Smith RC	.40	.15
❑ 509	Alan Trammell	.40	.15
❑ 510	Mike Piazza	2.00	.75
❑ 511	Ozzie Guillen	.40	.15
❑ 512	Jeromy Burnitz	.40	.15
❑ 513	Darren Oliver RC	1.00	.40
❑ 514	Kevin Mitchell	.25	.08
❑ 515	Rafael Palmeiro	.60	.25
❑ 516	David McCarty	.25	.08
❑ 517	Jeff Blauser	.25	.08
❑ 518	Trey Beamon	.25	.08
❑ 519	Royce Clayton	.25	.08
❑ 520	Dennis Eckersley	.40	.15
❑ 521	Bernie Williams	.60	.25
❑ 522	Steve Buechele	.25	.08
❑ 523	Dennis Martinez	.40	.15
❑ 524	Dave Hollins	.25	.08
❑ 525	Joey Hamilton	.25	.08
❑ 526	Andres Galarraga	.40	.15
❑ 527	Jeff Granger	.25	.08
❑ 528	Joey Eischen	.25	.08
❑ 529	Desi Relaford	.25	.08
❑ 530	Roberto Petagine	.25	.08
❑ 531	Andre Dawson	.40	.15
❑ 532	Ray Holbert	.25	.08
❑ 533	Duane Singleton	.25	.08
❑ 534	Kurt Abbott RC	.40	.15
❑ 535	Bo Jackson	1.00	.40
❑ 536	Gregg Jefferies	.25	.08
❑ 537	David Mysel	.25	.08
❑ 538	Raul Mondesi	.40	.15
❑ 539	Chris Snopek	.25	.08
❑ 540	Brook Fordyce	.25	.08
❑ 541	Ron Frazier RC	.40	.15
❑ 542	Brian Koelling	.25	.08
❑ 543	Jimmy Haynes	.25	.08
❑ 544	Marty Cordova	.25	.08
❑ 545	Jason Green RC	.40	.15
❑ 546	Orlando Merced	.25	.08
❑ 547	Lou Pote RC	.40	.15
❑ 548	Todd Van Poppel	.25	.08
❑ 549	Pat Kelly	.25	.08
❑ 550	Turk Wendell	.25	.08
❑ 551	Herbert Perry RC	.40	.15
❑ 552	Ryan Karp RC	.40	.15
❑ 553	Juan Guzman	.25	.08
❑ 554	Bryan Rekar RC	.40	.15
❑ 555	Kevin Appier	.40	.15
❑ 556	Chris Schwab RC	.40	.15
❑ 557	Jay Buhner	.40	.15
❑ 558	Andujar Cedeno	.25	.08
❑ 559	Ryan McGuire RC	.40	.15
❑ 560	Ricky Gutierrez	.25	.08
❑ 561	Keith Kimsey RC	.40	.15
❑ 562	Tim Clark	.25	.08
❑ 563	Damion Easley	.25	.08
❑ 564	Clint Davis RC	.40	.15
❑ 565	Mike Moore	.25	.08
❑ 566	Orel Hershiser	.40	.15
❑ 567	Jason Bere	.25	.08
❑ 568	Kevin McReynolds	.25	.08
❑ 569	Leland Macon RC	.40	.15
❑ 570	John Courtright RC	.40	.15
❑ 571	Sid Fernandez	.25	.08
❑ 572	Chad Roper	.25	.08
❑ 573	Terry Pendleton	.40	.15
❑ 574	Danny Miceli	.25	.08
❑ 575	Joe Rosselli	.25	.08
❑ 576	Mike Bordick	.25	.08
❑ 577	Danny Tartabull	.25	.08
❑ 578	Jose Guzman	.25	.08
❑ 579	Omar Vizquel	.60	.25
❑ 580	Tommy Greene	.25	.08
❑ 581	Paul Spoljaric	.25	.08
❑ 582	Walt Weiss	.25	.08
❑ 583	Oscar Jimenez RC	.40	.15
❑ 584	Rod Henderson	.25	.08
❑ 585	Derek Lowe	.40	.15
❑ 586	Richard Hidalgo RC	1.00	.40
❑ 587	Shayne Bennett RC	.40	.15
❑ 588	Tim Belk RC	.40	.15
❑ 589	Matt Mieske	.25	.08
❑ 590	Nigel Wilson	.25	.08
❑ 591	Jeff Knox RC	.40	.15
❑ 592	Bernard Gilkey	.25	.08
❑ 593	David Cone	.40	.15
❑ 594	Paul LoDuca RC	5.00	2.00
❑ 595	Scott Ruffcorn	.25	.08
❑ 596	Chris Roberts	.25	.08
❑ 597	Oscar Munoz RC	.40	.15
❑ 598	Scott Sullivan RC	.40	.15
❑ 599	Matt Jarvis RC	.40	.15
❑ 600	Jose Canseco	.60	.25
❑ 601	Tony Graffanino RC	1.50	.60
❑ 602	Don Slaught	.25	.08
❑ 603	Brett King RC	.40	.15
❑ 604	Jose Herrera RC	.40	.15
❑ 605	Melido Perez	.25	.08
❑ 606	Mike Hubbard RC	.40	.15
❑ 607	Chad Ogea	.25	.08
❑ 608	Wayne Gomes RC	1.00	.40
❑ 609	Roberto Alomar	.60	.25
❑ 610	Angel Echevarria RC	.40	.15
❑ 611	Jose Lind	.25	.08
❑ 612	Darrin Fletcher	.25	.08
❑ 613	Chris Bosio	.25	.08
❑ 614	Darryl Kile	.40	.15
❑ 615	Frankie Rodriguez	.25	.08
❑ 616	Phil Plantier	.25	.08
❑ 617	Pat Listach	.25	.08
❑ 618	Charlie Hough	.40	.15
❑ 619	Ryan Hancock RC	.40	.15
❑ 620	Darrel Deak RC	.40	.15
❑ 621	Travis Fryman	.40	.15
❑ 622	Brett Butler	.40	.15
❑ 623	Lance Johnson	.25	.08
❑ 624	Pete Smith	.25	.08
❑ 625	James Hurst RC	.40	.15
❑ 626	Roberto Kelly	.25	.08
❑ 627	Mike Mussina	.60	.25
❑ 628	Kevin Tapani	.25	.08
❑ 629	John Smoltz	.60	.25
❑ 630	Midre Cummings	.25	.08
❑ 631	Salomon Torres	.25	.08
❑ 632	Willie Adams	.25	.08
❑ 633	Derek Jeter	3.00	1.25
❑ 634	Steve Trachsel	.25	.08
❑ 635	Albie Lopez	.25	.08
❑ 636	Jason Moler	.25	.08
❑ 637	Carlos Delgado	.60	.25
❑ 638	Roberto Mejia	.25	.08
❑ 639	Darren Burton	.25	.08
❑ 640	B.J. Wallace	.25	.08
❑ 641	Brad Clontz RC	.40	.15
❑ 642	Billy Wagner RC	5.00	2.00
❑ 643	Aaron Sele	.25	.08
❑ 644	Cameron Cairncross	.25	.08
❑ 645	Brian Harper	.25	.08
❑ 646	Marc Valdes UER NNO	.25	.08
❑ 647	Mark Ratekin	.25	.08
❑ 648	Terry Bradshaw RC	.40	.15
❑ 649	Justin Thompson	.25	.08
❑ 650	Mike Busch RC	.40	.15
❑ 651	Joe Hall RC	.40	.15
❑ 652	Bobby Jones	.25	.08
❑ 653	Kelly Stinnett RC	1.00	.40
❑ 654	Rod Steph RC	.40	.15
❑ 655	Jay Powell RC	1.00	.40
❑ 656	Keith Garagozzo RC	.40	.15
❑ 657	Todd Dunn	.25	.08
❑ 658	Charles Peterson RC	.40	.15
❑ 659	Darren Lewis	.25	.08
❑ 660	John Wasdin RC	.40	.15
❑ 661	Tate Seefried RC	.40	.15
❑ 662	Hector Trinidad RC	.40	.15
❑ 663	John Carter RC	.25	.08
❑ 664	Larry Mitchell	.25	.08
❑ 665	David Catlett RC	.40	.15
❑ 666	Dante Bichette	.40	.15
❑ 667	Felix Jose	.25	.08
❑ 668	Rondell White	.40	.15
❑ 669	Tino Martinez	.60	.25
❑ 670	Brian L.Hunter	.25	.08
❑ 671	Jose Malave	.25	.08
❑ 672	Archi Cianfrocco	.25	.08
❑ 673	Mike Matheny RC	1.50	.60
❑ 674	Bret Barberie	.25	.08
❑ 675	Andrew Lorraine RC	.40	.15
❑ 676	Brian Jordan	.40	.15
❑ 677	Tim Belcher	.25	.08
❑ 678	Antonio Osuna RC	.40	.15
❑ 679	Checklist	.25	.08
❑ 680	Checklist	.25	.08
❑ 681	Checklist	.25	.08
❑ 682	Checklist	.25	.08

1995 Bowman

❑	COMPLETE SET (439)	150.00	90.00
❑ 1	Billy Wagner	.75	.30
❑ 2	Chris Widger	.25	.08
❑ 3	Brent Bowers	.25	.08
❑ 4	Bob Abreu RC	8.00	3.00
❑ 5	Lou Collier RC	1.00	.40
❑ 6	Juan Acevedo RC	.50	.20
❑ 7	Jason Kelley RC	.50	.20
❑ 8	Brian Sackinsky	.25	.08
❑ 9	Scott Christman	.25	.08
❑ 10	Damon Hollins	.25	.08
❑ 11	Willis Otanez RC	.50	.20
❑ 12	Jason Ryan RC	.50	.20
❑ 13	Jason Giambi	.75	.30
❑ 14	Andy Taulbee RC	.50	.20
❑ 15	Mark Thompson	.25	.08
❑ 16	Hugo Pivaral RC	.50	.20
❑ 17	Brien Taylor	.25	.08

❑ 18	Antonio Osuna	.25	.08
❑ 19	Edgardo Alfonzo	.25	.08
❑ 20	Carl Everett	.50	.20
❑ 21	Matt Drews	.25	.08
❑ 22	Bartolo Colon RC	5.00	2.00
❑ 23	Andruw Jones RC	30.00	15.00
❑ 24	Robert Person RC	1.00	.40
❑ 25	Derrek Lee	1.25	.50
❑ 26	John Ambrose RC	.50	.20
❑ 27	Eric Knowles RC	.50	.20
❑ 28	Chris Roberts	.25	.08
❑ 29	Don Wengert	.25	.08
❑ 30	Marcus Jensen RC	1.00	.40
❑ 31	Brian Barber	.25	.08
❑ 32	Kevin Brown C	.50	.20
❑ 33	Benji Gil	.25	.08
❑ 34	Mike Hubbard	.25	.08
❑ 35	Bart Evans RC	.50	.20
❑ 36	Enrique Wilson RC	.50	.20
❑ 37	Brian Buchanan RC	.50	.20
❑ 38	Ken Ray RC	.50	.20
❑ 39	Micah Franklin RC	.50	.20
❑ 40	Ricky Otero RC	.50	.20
❑ 41	Jason Kendall	.50	.20
❑ 42	Jimmy Hurst	.25	.08
❑ 43	Jerry Wolak RC	.50	.20
❑ 44	Jayson Peterson RC	.50	.20
❑ 45	Allen Battle RC	.50	.20
❑ 46	Scott Stahoviak	.25	.08
❑ 47	Steve Schrenk RC	.50	.20
❑ 48	Travis Miller RC	.50	.20
❑ 49	Eddie Rios RC	.50	.20
❑ 50	Mike Hampton	.50	.20
❑ 51	Chad Frontera RC	.50	.20
❑ 52	Tom Evans	.25	.08
❑ 53	C.J. Nitkowski	.25	.08
❑ 54	Clay Caruthers RC	.50	.20
❑ 55	Shannon Stewart	.50	.20
❑ 56	Jorge Posada	1.25	.50
❑ 57	Aaron Holbert	.25	.08
❑ 58	Harry Berrios RC	.50	.20
❑ 59	Steve Rodriguez	.25	.08
❑ 60	Shane Andrews	.25	.08
❑ 61	Will Cunnane RC	.50	.20
❑ 62	Richard Hidalgo	.25	.08
❑ 63	Bill Selby RC	.50	.20
❑ 64	Jay Cranford RC	.50	.20
❑ 65	Jeff Suppan	.50	.20
❑ 66	Curtis Goodwin	.25	.08
❑ 67	John Thomson RC	1.00	.40
❑ 68	Justin Thompson	.25	.08
❑ 69	Troy Porcival	.50	.20
❑ 70	Matt Wagner RC	.50	.20
❑ 71	Terry Bradshaw	.25	.08
❑ 72	Greg Hansell	.25	.08
❑ 73	John Burke	.25	.08
❑ 74	Jeff D'Amico	.25	.08
❑ 75	Ernie Young	.25	.08
❑ 76	Jason Bates	.25	.08
❑ 77	Chris Stynes	.25	.08
❑ 78	Cade Gaspar RC	.50	.20
❑ 79	Melvin Nieves	.25	.08
❑ 80	Rick Gorecki	.25	.08
❑ 81	Felix Rodriguez RC	.50	.20
❑ 82	Ryan Hancock	.25	.08
❑ 83	Chris Carpenter RC	8.00	3.00
❑ 84	Ray McDavid	.25	.08
❑ 85	Chris Wimmer	.25	.08
❑ 86	Doug Glanville	.25	.08
❑ 87	DeShawn Warren	.25	.08
❑ 88	Damian Moss RC	.50	.20
❑ 89	Rafael Orellano RC	.50	.20
❑ 90	Vladimir Guerrero RC !	40.00	20.00
❑ 91	Raul Casanova RC	.50	.20
❑ 92	Karim Garcia RC	.50	.20
❑ 93	Bryce Florie	.25	.08
❑ 94	Kevin Orie	.25	.08
❑ 95	Ryan Nye RC	.50	.20
❑ 96	Matt Sachse RC	.50	.20
❑ 97	Ivan Arteaga RC	.50	.20
❑ 98	Glenn Murray	.25	.08
❑ 99	Stacy Hollins RC	.50	.20
❑ 100	Jim Pittsley	.25	.08
❑ 101	Craig Mattson RC	.50	.20
❑ 102	Neifi Perez	.25	.08
❑ 103	Keith Williams	.25	.08
❑ 104	Roger Cedeno	.25	.08
❑ 105	Tony Terry RC	.50	.20
❑ 106	Jose Malave	.25	.08
❑ 107	Joe Rosselli	.25	.08
❑ 108	Kevin Jordan	.25	.08
❑ 109	Sid Roberson RC	.50	.20
❑ 110	Alan Embree	.25	.08
❑ 111	Terrell Wade	.25	.08
❑ 112	Bob Wolcott	.25	.08
❑ 113	Carlos Perez RC	1.00	.40
❑ 114	Mike Bovee RC	.50	.20
❑ 115	Tommy Davis RC	.50	.20
❑ 116	Jeremey Kendall RC	.50	.20
❑ 117	Rich Aude	.25	.08
❑ 118	Rick Huisman	.25	.08
❑ 119	Tim Belk	.25	.08
❑ 120	Edgar Renteria	.50	.20
❑ 121	Calvin Maduro RC	.50	.20
❑ 122	Jerry Martin RC	.50	.20
❑ 123	Ramon Fermin RC	.50	.20
❑ 124	Kimera Bartee RC	.50	.20
❑ 125	Mark Farris	.25	.08
❑ 126	Frank Rodriguez	.25	.08
❑ 127	Bob Higginson RC	2.00	.75
❑ 128	Bret Wagner	.25	.08
❑ 129	Edwin Diaz RC	.50	.20
❑ 130	Jimmy Haynes	.25	.08
❑ 131	Chris Weinke RC QB	1.00	.40
❑ 132	Damian Jackson RC	.50	.20
❑ 133	Felix Martinez	.25	.08
❑ 134	Edwin Hurtado RC	.50	.20
❑ 135	Matt Raleigh RC	.50	.20
❑ 136	Paul Wilson	.25	.08
❑ 137	Ron Villone	.25	.08
❑ 138	Eric Stuckenschneider RC	.50	.20
❑ 139	Tate Seefried	.25	.08
❑ 140	Rey Ordonez RC	2.00	.75
❑ 141	Eddie Pearson	.25	.08
❑ 142	Kevin Gallaher	.25	.08
❑ 143	Torii Hunter	.75	.30
❑ 144	Daron Kirkreit	.25	.08
❑ 145	Craig Wilson	.25	.08
❑ 146	Ugueth Urbina	.25	.08
❑ 147	Chris Snopek	.25	.08
❑ 148	Kym Ashworth	.25	.08
❑ 149	Wayne Gomes	.25	.08
❑ 150	Mark Loretta	.50	.20
❑ 151	Ramon Morel RC	.50	.20
❑ 152	Trot Nixon	.50	.20
❑ 153	Desi Relaford	.25	.08
❑ 154	Scott Sullivan	.25	.08
❑ 155	Marc Barcelo	.25	.08
❑ 156	Willie Adams	.25	.08
❑ 157	Derrick Gibson RC	.50	.20
❑ 158	Brian Meadows RC	.50	.20
❑ 159	Julian Tavarez	.25	.08
❑ 160	Bryan Rekar	.25	.08
❑ 161	Steve Gibralter	.25	.08
❑ 162	Esteban Loaiza	.25	.08
❑ 163	John Wasdin	.25	.08
❑ 164	Kirk Presley	.25	.08
❑ 165	Mariano Rivera	1.50	.60
❑ 166	Andy Larkin	.25	.08
❑ 167	Sean Whiteside RC	.50	.20
❑ 168	Matt Apana RC	.50	.20
❑ 169	Shawn Senior RC	.50	.20
❑ 170	Scott Gentile	.25	.08
❑ 171	Quilvio Veras	.25	.08
❑ 172	Eli Marrero RC	1.50	.60
❑ 173	Mendy Lopez RC	.50	.20
❑ 174	Homer Bush	.25	.08
❑ 175	Brian Stephenson RC	.50	.20
❑ 176	Jon Nunnally	.25	.08
❑ 177	Jose Herrera	.25	.08
❑ 178	Corey Avrard RC	.50	.20
❑ 179	David Bell	.25	.08
❑ 180	Jason Isringhausen	.50	.20
❑ 181	Jamey Wright	.25	.08
❑ 182	Lonell Roberts RC	.25	.08
❑ 183	Marty Cordova	.25	.08
❑ 184	Amaury Telemaco	.25	.08
❑ 185	John Mabry	.25	.08
❑ 186	Andrew Vessel RC	.50	.20
❑ 187	Jim Cole RC	.50	.20
❑ 188	Marquis Riley	.25	.08
❑ 189	Todd Dunn	.25	.08
❑ 190	John Carter	.25	.08
❑ 191	Donnie Sadler RC	1.00	.40
❑ 192	Mike Bell	.25	.08
❑ 193	Chris Cumberland RC	.50	.20
❑ 194	Jason Schmidt	1.25	.50
❑ 195	Matt Brunson	.25	.08
❑ 196	James Baldwin	.25	.08
❑ 197	Bill Simas RC	.50	.20
❑ 198	Gus Gandarillas	.25	.08
❑ 199	Mac Suzuki	.25	.08
❑ 200	Rick Holifield RC	.50	.20
❑ 201	Fernando Lunar RC	.50	.20
❑ 202	Kevin Jarvis	.25	.08
❑ 203	Everett Stull	.25	.08
❑ 204	Steve Wojciechowski	.25	.08
❑ 205	Shawn Estes	.25	.08
❑ 206	Jermaine Dye	.50	.20
❑ 207	Marc Kroon	.25	.08
❑ 208	Peter Munro RC	1.00	.40
❑ 209	Pat Watkins	.25	.08
❑ 210	Matt Smith	.25	.08
❑ 211	Joe Vitiello	.25	.08
❑ 212	Gerald Witasick Jr.	.25	.08
❑ 213	Freddy Adrian Garcia RC	.50	.20
❑ 214	Glenn Dishman RC	.50	.20
❑ 215	Jay Canizaro RC	.50	.20
❑ 216	Angel Martinez	.25	.08
❑ 217	Yamil Benitez RC	.50	.20
❑ 218	Fausto Macey RC	.50	.20
❑ 219	Eric Owens	.25	.08
❑ 220	Checklist	.25	.08
❑ 221	Dwayne Hosey FOIL RC	.50	.20
❑ 222	Brad Woodall FOIL RC	.50	.20
❑ 223	Billy Ashley FOIL	.25	.08
❑ 224	Mark Grudzielanek FOIL RC	2.00	.75
❑ 225	Mark Johnson FOIL RC	1.00	.40
❑ 226	Tim Unroe FOIL RC	.50	.20
❑ 227	Todd Greene FOIL	.25	.08
❑ 228	Larry Sutton FOIL	.25	.08
❑ 229	Derek Jeter FOIL	4.00	1.50
❑ 230	Sal Fasano FOIL RC	.50	.20
❑ 231	Ruben Rivera FOIL	.25	.08
❑ 232	Chris Truby FOIL RC	.50	.20
❑ 233	John Donati FOIL	.25	.08
❑ 234	Decomba Conner FOIL RC	.50	.20
❑ 235	Sergio Nunez FOIL RC	.50	.20
❑ 236	Ray Brown FOIL RC	.50	.20
❑ 237	Juan Melo FOIL RC	.50	.20
❑ 238	Hideo Nomo FOIL RC	5.00	2.00
❑ 239	Jaime Bluma RC FOIL	.50	.20
❑ 240	Jay Payton FOIL RC	2.00	.75
❑ 241	Paul Konerko FOIL	4.00	1.50
❑ 242	Scott Elarton FOIL RC	1.00	.40
❑ 243	Jeff Abbott FOIL RC	1.00	.40
❑ 244	Jim Brower FOIL RC	.50	.20
❑ 245	Geoff Blum FOIL RC	2.00	.75
❑ 246	Aaron Boone FOIL RC	2.00	.75
❑ 247	J.R. Phillips FOIL	.25	.08
❑ 248	Alex Ochoa FOIL	.25	.08
❑ 249	Nomar Garciaparra FOIL	4.00	1.50
❑ 250	Garret Anderson FOIL	.50	.20
❑ 251	Ray Durham FOIL	.50	.20
❑ 252	Paul Shuey FOIL	.25	.08
❑ 253	Tony Clark FOIL	.25	.08
❑ 254	Johnny Damon FOIL	.75	.30
❑ 255	Duane Singleton FOIL	.25	.08
❑ 256	LaTroy Hawkins FOIL	.25	.08
❑ 257	Andy Pettitte FOIL	.75	.30
❑ 258	Ben Grieve FOIL	.25	.08
❑ 259	Marc Newfield FOIL	.25	.08
❑ 260	Terrell Lowery FOIL	.25	.08
❑ 261	Shawn Green FOIL	.50	.20
❑ 262	Chipper Jones FOIL	1.25	.50
❑ 263	Brooks Kieschnick FOIL	.25	.08
❑ 264	Pokey Reese FOIL	.25	.08
❑ 265	Doug Million FOIL	.25	.08
❑ 266	Marc Valdes FOIL	.25	.08
❑ 267	Brian L.Hunter FOIL	.25	.08
❑ 268	Todd Hollandsworth FOIL	.25	.08
❑ 269	Rod Henderson FOIL	.25	.08
❑ 270	Bill Pulsipher FOIL	.25	.08
❑ 271	Scott Rolen FOIL RC	15.00	6.00
❑ 272	Trey Beamon FOIL	.25	.08
❑ 273	Alan Benes FOIL	.25	.08
❑ 274	Dustin Hermanson FOIL	.25	.08
❑ 275	Ricky Bottalico	.25	.08

❑	276	Albert Belle	.50	.20
❑	277	Deion Sanders	.75	.30
❑	278	Matt Williams	.50	.20
❑	279	Jeff Bagwell	.75	.30
❑	280	Kirby Puckett	1.25	.50
❑	281	Dave Hollins	.25	.08
❑	282	Don Mattingly	3.00	1.25
❑	283	Joey Hamilton	.25	.08
❑	284	Bobby Bonilla	.50	.20
❑	285	Moises Alou	.50	.20
❑	286	Tom Glavine	.75	.30
❑	287	Brett Butler	.50	.20
❑	288	Chris Hoiles	.25	.08
❑	289	Kenny Rogers	.50	.20
❑	290	Larry Walker	.50	.20
❑	291	Tim Raines	.50	.20
❑	292	Kevin Appier	.50	.20
❑	293	Roger Clemens	2.50	1.00
❑	294	Chuck Carr	.25	.08
❑	295	Randy Myers	.25	.08
❑	296	Dave Nilsson	.25	.08
❑	297	Joe Carter	.50	.20
❑	298	Chuck Finley	.50	.20
❑	299	Ray Lankford	.50	.20
❑	300	Roberto Kelly	.25	.08
❑	301	Jon Lieber	.25	.08
❑	302	Travis Fryman	.50	.20
❑	303	Mark McGwire	3.00	1.25
❑	304	Tony Gwynn	1.50	.60
❑	305	Kenny Lofton	.50	.20
❑	306	Mark Whiten	.25	.08
❑	307	Doug Drabek	.25	.08
❑	308	Terry Steinbach	.25	.08
❑	309	Ryan Klesko	.50	.20
❑	310	Mike Piazza	2.00	.75
❑	311	Ben McDonald	.25	.08
❑	312	Reggie Sanders	.50	.20
❑	313	Alex Fernandez	.25	.08
❑	314	Aaron Sele	.25	.08
❑	315	Gregg Jefferies	.25	.08
❑	316	Rickey Henderson	1.25	.50
❑	317	Brian Anderson	.25	.08
❑	318	Jose Valentin	.25	.08
❑	319	Rod Beck	.25	.08
❑	320	Marquis Grissom	.50	.20
❑	321	Ken Griffey Jr.	2.00	.75
❑	322	Bret Saberhagen	.50	.20
❑	323	Juan Gonzalez	.50	.20
❑	324	Paul Molitor	.50	.20
❑	325	Gary Sheffield	.50	.20
❑	326	Darren Daulton	.50	.20
❑	327	Bill Swift	.25	.08
❑	328	Brian McRae	.25	.08
❑	329	Robin Ventura	.50	.20
❑	330	Lee Smith	.50	.20
❑	331	Fred McGriff	.75	.30
❑	332	Delino DeShields	.25	.08
❑	333	Edgar Martinez	.75	.30
❑	334	Mike Mussina	.75	.30
❑	335	Orlando Merced	.25	.08
❑	336	Carlos Baerga	.25	.08
❑	337	Wil Cordero	.25	.08
❑	338	Tom Pagnozzi	.25	.08
❑	339	Pat Hentgen	.25	.08
❑	340	Chad Curtis	.25	.08
❑	341	Darren Lewis	.25	.08
❑	342	Jeff Kent	.50	.20
❑	343	Bip Roberts	.25	.08
❑	344	Ivan Rodriguez	.75	.30
❑	345	Jeff Montgomery	.25	.08
❑	346	Hal Morris	.25	.08
❑	347	Danny Tartabull	.25	.08
❑	348	Raul Mondesi	.50	.20
❑	349	Ken Hill	.25	.08
❑	350	Pedro Martinez	.75	.30
❑	351	Frank Thomas	1.25	.50
❑	352	Manny Ramirez	.75	.30
❑	353	Tim Salmon	.75	.30
❑	354	W. VanLandingham	.25	.08
❑	355	Andres Galarraga	.50	.20
❑	356	Paul O'Neill	.75	.30
❑	357	Brady Anderson	.50	.20
❑	358	Ramon Martinez	.25	.08
❑	359	John Olerud	.50	.20
❑	360	Ruben Sierra	.50	.20
❑	361	Cal Eldred	.25	.08
❑	362	Jay Buhner	.50	.20
❑	363	Jay Bell	.50	.20
❑	364	Wally Joyner	.50	.20
❑	365	Chuck Knoblauch	.50	.20
❑	366	Len Dykstra	.50	.20
❑	367	John Wetteland	.50	.20
❑	368	Roberto Alomar	.75	.30
❑	369	Craig Biggio	.75	.30
❑	370	Ozzie Smith	2.00	.75
❑	371	Terry Pendleton	.50	.20
❑	372	Sammy Sosa	1.25	.50
❑	373	Carlos Garcia	.25	.08
❑	374	Jose Rijo	.25	.08
❑	375	Chris Gomez	.25	.08
❑	376	Barry Bonds	3.00	1.25
❑	377	Steve Avery	.25	.08
❑	378	Rick Wilkins	.25	.08
❑	379	Pete Harnisch	.25	.08
❑	380	Dean Palmer	.50	.20
❑	381	Bob Hamelin	.25	.08
❑	382	Jason Bere	.25	.08
❑	383	Jimmy Key	.50	.20
❑	384	Dante Bichette	.50	.20
❑	385	Rafael Palmeiro	.75	.30
❑	386	David Justice	.50	.20
❑	387	Chili Davis	.50	.20
❑	388	Mike Greenwell	.25	.08
❑	389	Todd Zeile	.25	.08
❑	390	Jeff Conine	.50	.20
❑	391	Rick Aguilera	.25	.08
❑	392	Eddie Murray	1.25	.50
❑	393	Mike Stanley	.25	.08
❑	394	Cliff Floyd UER	.50	.20
❑	395	Randy Johnson	1.25	.50
❑	396	David Nied	.25	.08
❑	397	Devon White	.50	.20
❑	398	Royce Clayton	.25	.08
❑	399	Andy Benes	.25	.08
❑	400	John Hudek	.25	.08
❑	401	Bobby Jones	.25	.08
❑	402	Eric Karros	.50	.20
❑	403	Will Clark	.75	.30
❑	404	Mark Langston	.25	.08
❑	405	Kevin Brown	.50	.20
❑	406	Greg Maddux	2.00	.75
❑	407	David Cone	.50	.20
❑	408	Wade Boggs	.75	.30
❑	409	Steve Trachsel	.25	.08
❑	410	Greg Vaughn	.25	.08
❑	411	Mo Vaughn	.50	.20
❑	412	Wilson Alvarez	.25	.08
❑	413	Cal Ripken	4.00	1.50
❑	414	Rico Brogna	.25	.08
❑	415	Barry Larkin	.75	.30
❑	416	Cecil Fielder	.50	.20
❑	417	Jose Canseco	.75	.30
❑	418	Jack McDowell	.25	.08
❑	419	Mike Lieberthal	.50	.20
❑	420	Andrew Lorraine	.25	.08
❑	421	Rich Becker	.25	.08
❑	422	Tony Phillips	.25	.08
❑	423	Scott Ruffcorn	.25	.08
❑	424	Jeff Granger	.25	.08
❑	425	Greg Pirkl	.25	.08
❑	426	Dennis Eckersley	.50	.20
❑	427	Jose Lima	.25	.08
❑	428	Russ Davis	.25	.08
❑	429	Armando Benitez	.25	.08
❑	430	Alex Gonzalez	.25	.08
❑	431	Carlos Delgado	.50	.20
❑	432	Chan Ho Park	.50	.20
❑	433	Mickey Tettleton	.25	.08
❑	434	Dave Winfield	.50	.20
❑	435	John Burkett	.25	.08
❑	436	Orlando Miller	.25	.08
❑	437	Rondell White	.50	.20
❑	438	Jose Oliva	.25	.08
❑	439	Checklist	.25	.08

1996 Bowman

❑		COMPLETE SET (385)	50.00	20.00
❑	1	Cal Ripken	2.50	1.00
❑	2	Ray Durham	.30	.10
❑	3	Ivan Rodriguez	.50	.20
❑	4	Fred McGriff	.50	.20
❑	5	Hideo Nomo	.75	.30
❑	6	Troy Percival	.30	.10
❑	7	Moises Alou	.30	.10
❑	8	Mike Stanley	.30	.10
❑	9	Jay Buhner	.30	.10
❑	10	Shawn Green	.30	.10
❑	11	Ryan Klesko	.30	.10
❑	12	Andres Galarraga	.30	.10
❑	13	Dean Palmer	.30	.10
❑	14	Jeff Conine	.30	.10
❑	15	Brian L.Hunter	.30	.10
❑	16	J.T. Snow	.30	.10
❑	17	Larry Walker	.30	.10
❑	18	Barry Larkin	.50	.20
❑	19	Alex Gonzalez	.30	.10
❑	20	Edgar Martinez	.50	.20
❑	21	Mo Vaughn	.30	.10
❑	22	Mark McGwire	2.00	.75
❑	23	Jose Canseco	.50	.20
❑	24	Jack McDowell	.30	.10
❑	25	Dante Bichette	.30	.10
❑	26	Wade Boggs	.50	.20
❑	27	Mike Piazza	1.25	.50
❑	28	Ray Lankford	.30	.10
❑	29	Craig Biggio	.50	.20
❑	30	Rafael Palmeiro	.50	.20
❑	31	Ron Gant	.30	.10
❑	32	Javy Lopez	.30	.10
❑	33	Brian Jordan	.30	.10
❑	34	Paul O'Neill	.50	.20
❑	35	Mark Grace	.50	.20
❑	36	Matt Williams	.30	.10
❑	37	Pedro Martinez	.50	.20
❑	38	Rickey Henderson	.75	.30
❑	39	Bobby Bonilla	.30	.10
❑	40	Todd Hollandsworth	.30	.10
❑	41	Jim Thome	.50	.20
❑	42	Gary Sheffield	.75	.30
❑	43	Tim Salmon	.50	.20
❑	44	Gregg Jefferies	.30	.10
❑	45	Roberto Alomar	.50	.20
❑	46	Carlos Baerga	.30	.10
❑	47	Mark Grudzielanek	.30	.10
❑	48	Randy Johnson	.75	.30
❑	49	Tino Martinez	.50	.20
❑	50	Robin Ventura	.30	.10
❑	51	Ryne Sandberg	1.25	.50
❑	52	Jay Bell	.30	.10
❑	53	Jason Schmidt	.50	.20
❑	54	Frank Thomas	.75	.30
❑	55	Kenny Lofton	.30	.10
❑	56	Ariel Prieto	.30	.10
❑	57	David Cone	.30	.10
❑	58	Reggie Sanders	.30	.10
❑	59	Michael Tucker	.30	.10
❑	60	Vinny Castilla	.30	.10
❑	61	Len Dykstra	.30	.10
❑	62	Todd Hundley	.30	.10
❑	63	Brian McRae	.30	.10
❑	64	Dennis Eckersley	.30	.10
❑	65	Rondell White	.30	.10
❑	66	Eric Karros	.30	.10
❑	67	Greg Maddux	1.25	.50
❑	68	Kevin Appier	.30	.10
❑	69	Eddie Murray	.75	.30
❑	70	John Olerud	.30	.10
❑	71	Tony Gwynn	1.00	.40
❑	72	David Justice	.30	.10
❑	73	Ken Caminiti	.30	.10

❑ 74 Terry Steinbach .30 .10
❑ 75 Alan Benes .30 .10
❑ 76 Chipper Jones .75 .30
❑ 77 Jeff Bagwell .50 .20
❑ 78 Barry Bonds 2.00 .75
❑ 79 Ken Griffey Jr. 1.50 .60
❑ 80 Roger Cedeno .30 .10
❑ 81 Joe Carter .30 .10
❑ 82 Henry Rodriguez .30 .10
❑ 83 Jason Isringhausen .30 .10
❑ 84 Chuck Knoblauch .30 .10
❑ 85 Manny Ramirez .50 .20
❑ 86 Tom Glavine .50 .20
❑ 87 Jeffrey Hammonds .30 .10
❑ 88 Paul Molitor .30 .10
❑ 89 Roger Clemens 1.50 .60
❑ 90 Greg Vaughn .30 .10
❑ 91 Marty Cordova .30 .10
❑ 92 Albert Belle .30 .10
❑ 93 Mike Mussina .50 .20
❑ 94 Garret Anderson .30 .10
❑ 95 Juan Gonzalez .30 .10
❑ 96 John Valentin .30 .10
❑ 97 Jason Giambi .30 .10
❑ 98 Kirby Puckett .75 .30
❑ 99 Jim Edmonds .30 .10
❑ 100 Cecil Fielder .30 .10
❑ 101 Mike Aldrete .30 .10
❑ 102 Marquis Grissom .30 .10
❑ 103 Derek Bell .30 .10
❑ 104 Raul Mondesi .30 .10
❑ 105 Sammy Sosa .75 .30
❑ 106 Travis Fryman .30 .10
❑ 107 Rico Brogna .30 .10
❑ 108 Will Clark .50 .20
❑ 109 Bernie Williams .50 .20
❑ 110 Brady Anderson .30 .10
❑ 111 Torii Hunter .30 .10
❑ 112 Derek Jeter 2.00 .75
❑ 113 Mike Kusiewicz RC .50 .20
❑ 114 Scott Rolen .75 .30
❑ 115 Ramon Castro .30 .10
❑ 116 Jose Guillen RC 3.00 1.25
❑ 117 Wade Walker RC .50 .20
❑ 118 Shawn Senior .30 .10
❑ 119 Onan Masaoka RC 1.00 .40
❑ 120 Marlon Anderson RC 1.00 .40
❑ 121 Katsuhiro Maeda RC 1.00 .40
❑ 122 Garrett Stephenson RC .50 .20
❑ 123 Butch Huskey .30 .10
❑ 124 D'Angelo Jimenez RC 1.00 .40
❑ 125 Tony Mounce RC .50 .20
❑ 126 Jay Canizaro .30 .10
❑ 127 Juan Melo .30 .10
❑ 128 Steve Gibralter .30 .10
❑ 129 Freddy Adrian Garcia .30 .10
❑ 130 Julio Santana .30 .10
❑ 131 Richard Hidalgo .30 .10
❑ 132 Jermaine Dye .30 .10
❑ 133 Willie Adams .30 .10
❑ 134 Everett Stull .30 .10
❑ 135 Ramon Morel .30 .10
❑ 136 Chan Ho Park .30 .10
❑ 137 Jamey Wright .30 .10
❑ 138 Luis R.Garcia RC .50 .20
❑ 139 Dan Serafini .30 .10
❑ 140 Ryan Dempster RC 2.00 .75
❑ 141 Tate Seefried .30 .10
❑ 142 Jimmy Hurst .30 .10
❑ 143 Travis Miller .30 .10
❑ 144 Curtis Goodwin .30 .10
❑ 145 Rocky Coppinger RC .50 .20
❑ 146 Enrique Wilson .30 .10
❑ 147 Jaime Bluma .30 .10
❑ 148 Andrew Vessel .30 .10
❑ 149 Damian Moss .30 .10
❑ 150 Shawn Gallagher RC .50 .20
❑ 151 Pat Watkins .30 .10
❑ 152 Jose Paniagua .30 .10
❑ 153 Danny Graves .30 .10
❑ 154 Bryon Gainey RC .50 .20
❑ 155 Steve Soderstrom .30 .10
❑ 156 Cliff Brumbaugh RC .50 .20
❑ 157 Eugene Kingsale RC .50 .20
❑ 158 Lou Collier .30 .10
❑ 159 Todd Walker .30 .10
❑ 160 Kris Detmers RC .50 .20
❑ 161 Josh Booty RC .50 .20
❑ 162 Greg Whiteman RC .50 .20
❑ 163 Damian Jackson .30 .10
❑ 164 Tony Clark .30 .10
❑ 165 Jeff D'Amico .30 .10
❑ 166 Johnny Damon .50 .20
❑ 167 Rafael Orellano .30 .10
❑ 168 Ruben Rivera .30 .10
❑ 169 Alex Ochoa .30 .10
❑ 170 Jay Powell .30 .10
❑ 171 Tom Evans .30 .10
❑ 172 Ron Villone .30 .10
❑ 173 Shawn Estes .30 .10
❑ 174 John Wasdin .30 .10
❑ 175 Bill Simas .30 .10
❑ 176 Kevin Brown .30 .10
❑ 177 Shannon Stewart .30 .10
❑ 178 Todd Greene .30 .10
❑ 179 Bob Wolcott .30 .10
❑ 180 Chris Snopek .30 .10
❑ 181 Nomar Garciaparra 1.50 .60
❑ 182 Cameron Smith RC .50 .20
❑ 183 Matt Drews .30 .10
❑ 184 Jimmy Haynes .30 .10
❑ 185 Chris Carpenter .50 .20
❑ 186 Desi Relaford .30 .10
❑ 187 Ben Grieve .30 .10
❑ 188 Mike Bell .30 .10
❑ 189 Luis Castillo RC 1.50 .60
❑ 190 Ugueth Urbina .30 .10
❑ 191 Paul Wilson .30 .10
❑ 192 Andruw Jones 1.25 .50
❑ 193 Wayne Gomes .30 .10
❑ 194 Craig Counsell RC 1.50 .60
❑ 195 Jim Cole .30 .10
❑ 196 Brooks Kieschnick .30 .10
❑ 197 Trey Beamon .30 .10
❑ 198 Marino Santana RC .50 .20
❑ 199 Bob Abreu .75 .30
❑ 200 Pokey Reese .30 .10
❑ 201 Dante Powell .30 .10
❑ 202 George Arias .30 .10
❑ 203 Jorge Velandia RC .50 .20
❑ 204 George Lombard RC .50 .20
❑ 205 Byron Browne RC .50 .20
❑ 206 John Frascatore .30 .10
❑ 207 Terry Adams .30 .10
❑ 208 Wilson Delgado RC .50 .20
❑ 209 Billy McMillon .30 .10
❑ 210 Jeff Abbott .30 .10
❑ 211 Trot Nixon .30 .10
❑ 212 Amaury Telemaco .30 .10
❑ 213 Scott Sullivan .30 .10
❑ 214 Justin Thompson .30 .10
❑ 215 Decomba Conner .30 .10
❑ 216 Ryan McGuire .30 .10
❑ 217 Matt Luke .30 .10
❑ 218 Doug Million .30 .10
❑ 219 Jason Dickson RC .50 .20
❑ 220 Ramon Hernandez RC 2.00 .75
❑ 221 Mark Bellhorn RC 2.00 .75
❑ 222 Eric Ludwick RC .50 .20
❑ 223 Luke Wilcox RC .50 .20
❑ 224 Marty Malloy RC .50 .20
❑ 225 Gary Coffee RC .50 .20
❑ 226 Wendell Magee RC .50 .20
❑ 227 Brett Tomko RC 1.00 .40
❑ 228 Derek Lowe .30 .10
❑ 229 Jose Rosado RC .50 .20
❑ 230 Steve Bourgeois RC .50 .20
❑ 231 Neil Weber RC .50 .20
❑ 232 Jeff Ware .30 .10
❑ 233 Edwin Diaz .30 .10
❑ 234 Greg Norton .30 .10
❑ 235 Aaron Boone .30 .10
❑ 236 Jeff Suppan .30 .10
❑ 237 Bret Wagner .30 .10
❑ 238 Elieser Marrero .30 .10
❑ 239 Will Cunnane .30 .10
❑ 240 Brian Barkley RC .50 .20
❑ 241 Jay Payton .30 .10
❑ 242 Marcus Jensen .30 .10
❑ 243 Ryan Nye .30 .10
❑ 244 Chad Mottola .30 .10
❑ 245 Scott McClain RC .50 .20
❑ 246 Jesse Ibarra RC .50 .20
❑ 247 Mike Darr RC .50 .20
❑ 248 Bobby Estalella RC .50 .20
❑ 249 Michael Barrett .30 .10
❑ 250 Jamie Lopiccolo RC .50 .20
❑ 251 Shane Spencer RC 1.00 .40
❑ 252 Ben Petrick RC .50 .20
❑ 253 Jason Bell RC .50 .20
❑ 254 Arnold Gooch RC .50 .20
❑ 255 T.J. Mathews .30 .10
❑ 256 Jason Ryan .30 .10
❑ 257 Pat Cline RC .50 .20
❑ 258 Rafael Carmona RC .50 .20
❑ 259 Carl Pavano RC 2.00 .75
❑ 260 Ben Davis .30 .10
❑ 261 Matt Lawton RC 1.00 .40
❑ 262 Kevin Sefcik RC .50 .20
❑ 263 Chris Fussell RC .50 .20
❑ 264 Mike Cameron RC 1.50 .60
❑ 265 Marty Janzen RC .50 .20
❑ 266 Livan Hernandez RC 2.00 .75
❑ 267 Raul Ibanez RC 2.00 .75
❑ 268 Juan Encarnacion .30 .10
❑ 269 David Yocum RC .50 .20
❑ 270 Jonathan Johnson RC .50 .20
❑ 271 Reggie Taylor .30 .10
❑ 272 Danny Buxbaum RC .50 .20
❑ 273 Jacob Cruz .30 .10
❑ 274 Bobby Morris RC .50 .20
❑ 275 Andy Fox RC .50 .20
❑ 276 Greg Keagle .30 .10
❑ 277 Charles Peterson .30 .10
❑ 278 Derrek Lee .50 .20
❑ 279 Bryant Nelson RC .50 .20
❑ 280 Antone Williamson .30 .10
❑ 281 Scott Elarton .30 .10
❑ 282 Shad Williams RC .50 .20
❑ 283 Rich Hunter RC .50 .20
❑ 284 Chris Sheff .30 .10
❑ 285 Derrick Gibson .30 .10
❑ 286 Felix Rodriguez .30 .10
❑ 287 Brian Banks RC .50 .20
❑ 288 Jason McDonald .30 .10
❑ 289 Glendon Rusch RC 1.00 .40
❑ 290 Gary Rath .30 .10
❑ 291 Peter Munro .30 .10
❑ 292 Tom Fordham .30 .10
❑ 293 Jason Kendall .30 .10
❑ 294 Russ Johnson .30 .10
❑ 295 Joe Long .30 .10
❑ 296 Robert Smith RC .50 .20
❑ 297 Jarrod Washburn RC 1.50 .60
❑ 298 Dave Coggin RC .50 .20
❑ 299 Jeff Yoder RC .50 .20
❑ 300 Jed Hansen RC .50 .20
❑ 301 Matt Morris RC 3.00 1.25
❑ 302 Josh Bishop RC .50 .20
❑ 303 Dustin Hermanson .30 .10
❑ 304 Mike Gulan .30 .10
❑ 305 Felipe Crespo .30 .10
❑ 306 Quinton McCracken .30 .10
❑ 307 Jim Bonnici RC .50 .20
❑ 308 Sal Fasano .30 .10
❑ 309 Gabe Alvarez RC .50 .20
❑ 310 Heath Murray RC .50 .20
❑ 311 Javier Valentin RC .50 .20
❑ 312 Bartolo Colon .75 .30
❑ 313 Olmedo Saenz .30 .10
❑ 314 Norm Hutchins RC .50 .20
❑ 315 Chris Holt .30 .10
❑ 316 David Doster RC .50 .20
❑ 317 Robert Person .30 .10
❑ 318 Donne Wall RC .50 .20
❑ 319 Adam Riggs RC .50 .20
❑ 320 Homer Bush .30 .10
❑ 321 Brad Rigby RC .50 .20
❑ 322 Lou Merloni RC .50 .20
❑ 323 Neifi Perez .30 .10
❑ 324 Chris Cumberland .30 .10
❑ 325 Alvie Shepherd RC .50 .20
❑ 326 Jarrod Patterson RC .50 .20
❑ 327 Ray Ricken RC .50 .20
❑ 328 Danny Klassen RC .50 .20
❑ 329 David Miller RC .50 .20
❑ 330 Chad Alexander RC .50 .20
❑ 331 Matt Beaumont .30 .10

❑ 332 Damon Hollins .30 .10
❑ 333 Todd Dunn .30 .10
❑ 334 Mike Sweeney RC 2.00 .75
❑ 335 Richie Sexson .50 .20
❑ 336 Billy Wagner .30 .10
❑ 337 Ron Wright RC .50 .20
❑ 338 Paul Konerko .75 .30
❑ 339 Tommy Phelps RC .50 .20
❑ 340 Karim Garcia .30 .10
❑ 341 Mike Grace RC .50 .20
❑ 342 Russell Branyan RC 1.00 .40
❑ 343 Randy Winn RC 1.50 .60
❑ 344 A.J. Pierzynski RC 4.00 1.50
❑ 345 Mike Busby RC .50 .20
❑ 346 Matt Beech RC .50 .20
❑ 347 Jose Cepeda RC .50 .20
❑ 348 Brian Stephenson .30 .10
❑ 349 Rey Ordonez .30 .10
❑ 350 Rich Aurilia RC 1.00 .40
❑ 351 Edgard Velazquez RC .50 .20
❑ 352 Raul Casanova .30 .10
❑ 353 Carlos Guillen RC 2.00 .75
❑ 354 Bruce Aven RC .50 .20
❑ 355 Ryan Jones RC .50 .20
❑ 356 Derek Aucoin RC .50 .20
❑ 357 Brian Rose RC .50 .20
❑ 358 Richard Almanzar RC .50 .20
❑ 359 Fletcher Bates RC .50 .20
❑ 360 Russ Ortiz RC 1.50 .60
❑ 361 Wilton Guerrero RC .50 .20
❑ 362 Geoff Jenkins RC 1.50 .60
❑ 363 Pete Janicki .30 .10
❑ 364 Yamil Benitez .30 .10
❑ 365 Aaron Holbert .30 .10
❑ 366 Tim Belk .30 .10
❑ 367 Terrell Wade .30 .10
❑ 368 Terrence Long .30 .10
❑ 369 Brad Fullmer .30 .10
❑ 370 Matt Wagner .30 .10
❑ 371 Craig Wilson RC .50 .20
❑ 372 Mark Loretta .30 .10
❑ 373 Eric Owens .30 .10
❑ 374 Vladimir Guerrero 1.50 .60
❑ 375 Tommy Davis .30 .10
❑ 376 Donnie Sadler .30 .10
❑ 377 Edgar Renteria .30 .10
❑ 378 Todd Helton 1.50 .60
❑ 379 Ralph Milliard RC .50 .20
❑ 380 Darin Blood RC .50 .20
❑ 381 Shayne Bennett .30 .10
❑ 382 Mark Redman .30 .10
❑ 383 Felix Martinez .30 .10
❑ 384 Sean Watkins RC .50 .20
❑ 385 Oscar Henriquez .30 .10
❑ M20 52 Bowman Mantle 5.00 2.00
❑ NNO Unnumbered Checklists .30 .10

1997 Bowman

❑ COMPLETE SET (441) 60.00 25.00
❑ COMPLETE SERIES 1 (221) 30.00 12.50
❑ COMPLETE SERIES 2 (220) 30.00 12.50
❑ 1 Derek Jeter 2.00 .75
❑ 2 Edgar Renteria .30 .10
❑ 3 Chipper Jones .75 .30
❑ 4 Hideo Nomo .75 .30
❑ 5 Tim Salmon .50 .20
❑ 6 Jason Giambi .30 .10
❑ 7 Robin Ventura .30 .10
❑ 8 Tony Clark .30 .10
❑ 9 Barry Larkin .50 .20
❑ 10 Paul Molitor .30 .10
❑ 11 Bernard Gilkey .30 .10
❑ 12 Jack McDowell .30 .10
❑ 13 Andy Benes .30 .10
❑ 14 Ryan Klesko .30 .10
❑ 15 Mark McGwire 2.00 .75
❑ 16 Ken Griffey Jr. 1.25 .50
❑ 17 Robb Nen .30 .10
❑ 18 Cal Ripken 2.50 1.00
❑ 19 John Valentin .30 .10
❑ 20 Ricky Bottalico .30 .10
❑ 21 Mike Lansing .30 .10
❑ 22 Ryne Sandberg 1.25 .50
❑ 23 Carlos Delgado .30 .10
❑ 24 Craig Biggio .50 .20
❑ 25 Eric Karros .30 .10
❑ 26 Kevin Appier .30 .10
❑ 27 Mariano Rivera .75 .30
❑ 28 Vinny Castilla .30 .10
❑ 29 Juan Gonzalez .30 .10
❑ 30 Al Martin .30 .10
❑ 31 Jeff Cirillo .30 .10
❑ 32 Eddie Murray .75 .30
❑ 33 Ray Lankford .30 .10
❑ 34 Manny Ramirez .50 .20
❑ 35 Roberto Alomar .50 .20
❑ 36 Will Clark .50 .20
❑ 37 Chuck Knoblauch .30 .10
❑ 38 Harold Baines .30 .10
❑ 39 Trevor Hoffman .30 .10
❑ 40 Edgar Martinez .50 .20
❑ 41 Geronimo Berroa .30 .10
❑ 42 Rey Ordonez .30 .10
❑ 43 Mike Stanley .30 .10
❑ 44 Mike Mussina .50 .20
❑ 45 Kevin Brown .30 .10
❑ 46 Dennis Eckersley .30 .10
❑ 47 Henry Rodriguez .30 .10
❑ 48 Tino Martinez .50 .20
❑ 49 Eric Young .30 .10
❑ 50 Bret Boone .30 .10
❑ 51 Raul Mondesi .30 .10
❑ 52 Sammy Sosa .75 .30
❑ 53 John Smoltz .50 .20
❑ 54 Billy Wagner .30 .10
❑ 55 Jeff D'Amico .30 .10
❑ 56 Ken Caminiti .30 .10
❑ 57 Jason Kendall .30 .10
❑ 58 Wade Boggs .50 .20
❑ 59 Andres Galarraga .30 .10
❑ 60 Jeff Brantley .30 .10
❑ 61 Mel Rojas .30 .10
❑ 62 Brian L. Hunter .30 .10
❑ 63 Bobby Bonilla .30 .10
❑ 64 Roger Clemens 1.50 .60
❑ 65 Jeff Kent .30 .10
❑ 66 Matt Williams .30 .10
❑ 67 Albert Belle .30 .10
❑ 68 Jeff King .30 .10
❑ 69 John Wetteland .30 .10
❑ 70 Deion Sanders .50 .20
❑ 71 Bubba Trammell RC .60 .25
❑ 72 Felix Heredia RC .40 .15
❑ 73 Billy Koch RC 1.00 .40
❑ 74 Sidney Ponson RC 1.00 .40
❑ 75 Ricky Ledee RC .60 .25
❑ 76 Brett Tomko .30 .10
❑ 77 Braden Looper RC .40 .15
❑ 78 Damian Jackson .30 .10
❑ 79 Jason Dickson .30 .10
❑ 80 Chad Green RC .40 .15
❑ 81 R.A. Dickey RC .40 .15
❑ 82 Jeff Liefer .30 .10
❑ 83 Matt Wagner .30 .10
❑ 84 Richard Hidalgo .30 .10
❑ 85 Adam Riggs .30 .10
❑ 86 Robert Smith .30 .10
❑ 87 Chad Hermansen RC .40 .15
❑ 88 Felix Martinez .30 .10
❑ 89 J.J. Johnson .30 .10
❑ 90 Todd Dunwoody .30 .10
❑ 91 Katsuhiro Maeda .30 .10
❑ 92 Darin Erstad .30 .10
❑ 93 Elieser Marrero .30 .10
❑ 94 Bartolo Colon .30 .10
❑ 95 Chris Fussell .30 .10
❑ 96 Ugueth Urbina .30 .10
❑ 97 Josh Paul RC .40 .15
❑ 98 Jaime Bluma .30 .10
❑ 99 Seth Greisinger RC .40 .15
❑ 100 Jose Cruz Jr. RC .60 .25
❑ 101 Todd Dunn .30 .10
❑ 102 Joe Young RC .40 .15
❑ 103 Jonathan Johnson .30 .10
❑ 104 Justin Towle RC .40 .15
❑ 105 Brian Rose .30 .10
❑ 106 Jose Guillen .30 .10
❑ 107 Andruw Jones .50 .20
❑ 108 Mark Kotsay RC 1.50 .60
❑ 109 Wilton Guerrero .30 .10
❑ 110 Jacob Cruz .30 .10
❑ 111 Mike Sweeney .30 .10
❑ 112 Julio Mosquera .30 .10
❑ 113 Matt Morris .30 .10
❑ 114 Wendell Magee .30 .10
❑ 115 John Thomson .30 .10
❑ 116 Javier Valentin .30 .10
❑ 117 Tom Fordham .30 .10
❑ 118 Ruben Rivera .30 .10
❑ 119 Mike Drumright RC .40 .15
❑ 120 Chris Holt .30 .10
❑ 121 Sean Maloney .30 .10
❑ 122 Michael Barrett .30 .10
❑ 123 Tony Saunders RC .40 .15
❑ 124 Kevin Brown C .30 .10
❑ 125 Richard Almanzar .30 .10
❑ 126 Mark Redman .30 .10
❑ 127 Anthony Sanders RC .40 .15
❑ 128 Jeff Abbott .30 .10
❑ 129 Eugene Kingsale .30 .10
❑ 130 Paul Konerko .50 .20
❑ 131 Randall Simon RC .60 .25
❑ 132 Andy Larkin .30 .10
❑ 133 Rafael Medina .30 .10
❑ 134 Mendy Lopez .30 .10
❑ 135 Freddy Adrian Garcia .30 .10
❑ 136 Karim Garcia .30 .10
❑ 137 Larry Rodriguez RC .40 .15
❑ 138 Carlos Guillen .30 .10
❑ 139 Aaron Boone .30 .10
❑ 140 Donnie Sadler .30 .10
❑ 141 Brooks Kieschnick .30 .10
❑ 142 Scott Spiezio .30 .10
❑ 143 Everett Stull .30 .10
❑ 144 Enrique Wilson .30 .10
❑ 145 Milton Bradley RC 2.00 .75
❑ 146 Kevin Orie .30 .10
❑ 147 Derek Wallace .30 .10
❑ 148 Russ Johnson .30 .10
❑ 149 Joe Lagarde RC .40 .15
❑ 150 Luis Castillo .30 .10
❑ 151 Jay Payton .30 .10
❑ 152 Joe Long .30 .10
❑ 153 Livan Hernandez .30 .10
❑ 154 Vladimir Nunez RC .60 .25
❑ 155 Pokey Reese UER .30 .10
❑ 156 George Arias .30 .10
❑ 157 Homer Bush .30 .10
❑ 158 Chris Carpenter UER .30 .10
❑ 159 Eric Milton RC .60 .25
❑ 160 Richie Sexson .30 .10
❑ 161 Carl Pavano .30 .10
❑ 162 Chris Gissell RC .40 .15
❑ 163 Mac Suzuki .30 .10
❑ 164 Pat Cline .30 .10
❑ 165 Ron Wright .30 .10
❑ 166 Dante Powell .30 .10
❑ 167 Mark Bellhorn .30 .10
❑ 168 George Lombard .30 .10
❑ 169 Pee Wee Lopez RC .40 .15
❑ 170 Paul Wilder RC .40 .15
❑ 171 Brad Fullmer .30 .10
❑ 172 Willie Martinez RC .40 .15
❑ 173 Dario Veras RC .40 .15
❑ 174 Dave Coggin .30 .10
❑ 175 Kris Benson RC 1.00 .40
❑ 176 Torii Hunter .30 .10
❑ 177 D.T. Cromer .30 .10
❑ 178 Nelson Figueroa RC .40 .15
❑ 179 Hiram Bocachica RC .40 .15

❑	180	Shane Monahan	.30	.10
❑	181	Jimmy Anderson RC	.40	.15
❑	182	Juan Melo	.30	.10
❑	183	Pablo Ortega RC	.40	.15
❑	184	Calvin Pickering RC	.40	.15
❑	185	Reggie Taylor	.30	.10
❑	186	Jeff Farnsworth RC	.40	.15
❑	187	Terrence Long	.30	.10
❑	188	Geoff Jenkins	.30	.10
❑	189	Steve Rain RC	.40	.15
❑	190	Nerio Rodriguez RC	.40	.15
❑	191	Derrick Gibson	.30	.10
❑	192	Darin Blood	.30	.10
❑	193	Ben Davis	.30	.10
❑	194	Adrian Beltre RC	3.00	1.25
❑	195	Damian Sapp RC UER	.40	.15
❑	196	Kerry Wood RC	5.00	2.00
❑	197	Nate Rolison RC	.40	.15
❑	198	Fernando Tatis RC	.40	.15
❑	199	Brad Penny RC	2.50	1.00
❑	200	Jake Westbrook RC	1.00	.40
❑	201	Edwin Diaz	.30	.10
❑	202	Joe Fontenot RC	.60	.25
❑	203	Matt Halloran RC	.40	.15
❑	204	Blake Stein RC	.40	.15
❑	205	Onan Masaoka	.30	.10
❑	206	Ben Petrick	.30	.10
❑	207	Matt Clement RC	1.00	.40
❑	208	Todd Greene	.30	.10
❑	209	Ray Ricken	.30	.10
❑	210	Eric Chavez RC	4.00	1.50
❑	211	Edgard Velazquez	.30	.10
❑	212	Bruce Chen RC	1.00	.40
❑	213	Danny Patterson	.30	.10
❑	214	Jeff Yoder	.30	.10
❑	215	Luis Ordaz RC	.40	.15
❑	216	Chris Widger	.30	.10
❑	217	Jason Brester	.30	.10
❑	218	Carlton Loewer	.30	.10
❑	219	Chris Reitsma RC	.60	.25
❑	220	Neifi Perez	.30	.10
❑	221	Hideki Irabu RC	.60	.25
❑	222	Ellis Burks	.30	.10
❑	223	Pedro Martinez	.50	.20
❑	224	Kenny Lofton	.30	.10
❑	225	Randy Johnson	.75	.30
❑	226	Terry Steinbach	.30	.10
❑	227	Bernie Williams	.50	.20
❑	228	Dean Palmer	.30	.10
❑	229	Alan Benes	.30	.10
❑	230	Marquis Grissom	.30	.10
❑	231	Gary Sheffield	.30	.10
❑	232	Curt Schilling	.30	.10
❑	233	Reggie Sanders	.30	.10
❑	234	Bobby Higginson	.30	.10
❑	235	Moises Alou	.30	.10
❑	236	Tom Glavine	.50	.20
❑	237	Mark Grace	.50	.20
❑	238	Ramon Martinez	.30	.10
❑	239	Rafael Palmeiro	.50	.20
❑	240	John Olerud	.30	.10
❑	241	Dante Bichette	.30	.10
❑	242	Greg Vaughn	.30	.10
❑	243	Jeff Bagwell	.50	.20
❑	244	Barry Bonds	2.00	.75
❑	245	Pat Hentgen	.30	.10
❑	246	Jim Thome	.50	.20
❑	247	Jermaine Allensworth	.30	.10
❑	248	Andy Pettitte	.50	.20
❑	249	Jay Bell	.30	.10
❑	250	John Jaha	.30	.10
❑	251	Jim Edmonds	.30	.10
❑	252	Ron Gant	.30	.10
❑	253	David Cone	.30	.10
❑	254	Jose Canseco	.50	.20
❑	255	Jay Buhner	.30	.10
❑	256	Greg Maddux	1.25	.50
❑	257	Brian McRae	.30	.10
❑	258	Lance Johnson	.30	.10
❑	259	Travis Fryman	.30	.10
❑	260	Paul O'Neill	.50	.20
❑	261	Ivan Rodriguez	.50	.20
❑	262	Gregg Jefferies	.30	.10
❑	263	Fred McGriff	.50	.20
❑	264	Derek Bell	.30	.10
❑	265	Jeff Conine	.30	.10
❑	266	Mike Piazza	1.25	.50
❑	267	Mark Grudzielanek	.30	.10
❑	268	Brady Anderson	.30	.10
❑	269	Marty Cordova	.30	.10
❑	270	Ray Durham	.30	.10
❑	271	Joe Carter	.30	.10
❑	272	Brian Jordan	.30	.10
❑	273	David Justice	.30	.10
❑	274	Tony Gwynn	1.00	.40
❑	275	Larry Walker	.30	.10
❑	276	Cecil Fielder	.30	.10
❑	277	Mo Vaughn	.30	.10
❑	278	Alex Fernandez	.30	.10
❑	279	Michael Tucker	.30	.10
❑	280	Jose Valentin	.30	.10
❑	281	Sandy Alomar Jr.	.30	.10
❑	282	Todd Hollandsworth	.30	.10
❑	283	Rico Brogna	.30	.10
❑	284	Rusty Greer	.30	.10
❑	285	Roberto Hernandez	.30	.10
❑	286	Hal Morris	.30	.10
❑	287	Johnny Damon	.50	.20
❑	288	Todd Hundley	.30	.10
❑	289	Rondell White	.30	.10
❑	290	Frank Thomas	.75	.30
❑	291	Don Denbow RC	.40	.15
❑	292	Derrek Lee	.50	.20
❑	293	Todd Walker	.30	.10
❑	294	Scott Rolen	.50	.20
❑	295	Wes Helms	.30	.10
❑	296	Bob Abreu	.50	.20
❑	297	John Patterson RC	1.50	.60
❑	298	Alex Gonzalez RC	1.00	.40
❑	299	Grant Roberts RC	.40	.15
❑	300	Jeff Suppan	.30	.10
❑	301	Luke Wilcox	.30	.10
❑	302	Marlon Anderson	.30	.10
❑	303	Ray Brown	.30	.10
❑	304	Mike Caruso RC	.40	.15
❑	305	Sam Marsonek RC	.40	.15
❑	306	Brady Raggio RC	.40	.15
❑	307	Kevin McGlinchy RC	.60	.25
❑	308	Roy Halladay RC	5.00	2.00
❑	309	Jeremi Gonzalez RC	.40	.15
❑	310	Aramis Ramirez RC	4.00	1.50
❑	311	Dee Brown RC	.40	.15
❑	312	Justin Thompson	.30	.10
❑	313	Jay Tessmer RC	.40	.15
❑	314	Mike Johnson RC	.40	.15
❑	315	Danny Clyburn	.30	.10
❑	316	Bruce Aven	.30	.10
❑	317	Keith Foulke RC	1.50	.60
❑	318	Jimmy Osting RC	.60	.25
❑	319	Valerio De Los Santos RC	.40	.15
❑	320	Shannon Stewart	.30	.10
❑	321	Willie Adams	.30	.10
❑	322	Larry Barnes RC	.40	.15
❑	323	Mark Johnson RC	.40	.15
❑	324	Chris Stowers RC	.40	.15
❑	325	Brandon Reed	.30	.10
❑	326	Randy Winn	.30	.10
❑	327	Steve Chavez RC	.40	.15
❑	328	Nomar Garciaparra	1.25	.50
❑	329	Jacque Jones RC	1.50	.60
❑	330	Chris Clemons	.30	.10
❑	331	Todd Helton	.75	.30
❑	332	Ryan Brannan RC	.40	.15
❑	333	Alex Sanchez RC	.60	.25
❑	334	Arnold Gooch	.30	.10
❑	335	Russell Branyan	.30	.10
❑	336	Daryle Ward	.40	.15
❑	337	John LeRoy RC	.40	.15
❑	338	Steve Cox	.30	.10
❑	339	Kevin Witt	.30	.10
❑	340	Norm Hutchins	.30	.10
❑	341	Gabby Martinez	.30	.10
❑	342	Kris Detmers	.30	.10
❑	343	Mike Villano RC	.40	.15
❑	344	Preston Wilson	.30	.10
❑	345	James Manias RC	.40	.15
❑	346	Deivi Cruz RC	.60	.25
❑	347	Donzell McDonald RC	.40	.15
❑	348	Rod Myers RC	.40	.15
❑	349	Shawn Chacon RC	1.00	.40
❑	350	Elvin Hernandez RC	.60	.25
❑	351	Orlando Cabrera RC	1.50	.60
❑	352	Brian Banks	.30	.10
❑	353	Robbie Bell	.40	.15
❑	354	Brad Rigby	.30	.10
❑	355	Scott Elarton	.30	.10
❑	356	Kevin Sweeney RC	.40	.15
❑	357	Steve Soderstrom	.30	.10
❑	358	Ryan Nye	.30	.10
❑	359	Marlon Allen RC	.40	.15
❑	360	Donny Leon RC	.40	.15
❑	361	Garrett Neubart RC	.60	.25
❑	362	Abraham Nunez RC	.60	.25
❑	363	Adam Eaton RC	1.00	.40
❑	364	Octavio Dotel RC	.60	.25
❑	365	Dean Crow RC	.40	.15
❑	366	Jason Baker RC	.40	.15
❑	367	Sean Casey	1.00	.40
❑	368	Joe Lawrence RC	.40	.15
❑	369	Adam Johnson RC	.40	.15
❑	370	Scott Schoeneweis RC	.60	.25
❑	371	Gerald Witasick Jr.	.30	.10
❑	372	Ronnie Belliard RC	1.25	.50
❑	373	Russ Ortiz	.30	.10
❑	374	Robert Stratton RC	.60	.25
❑	375	Bobby Estalella	.30	.10
❑	376	Corey Lee RC	.40	.15
❑	377	Carlos Beltran	2.00	.75
❑	378	Mike Cameron	.30	.10
❑	379	Scott Randall RC	.40	.15
❑	380	Corey Erickson RC	.40	.15
❑	381	Jay Canizaro	.30	.10
❑	382	Kerry Robinson RC	.40	.15
❑	383	Todd Noel RC	.40	.15
❑	384	A.J. Zapp RC	.40	.15
❑	385	Jarrod Washburn	.30	.10
❑	386	Ben Grieve	.30	.10
❑	387	Javier Vazquez RC	1.50	.60
❑	388	Tony Graffanino	.30	.10
❑	389	Travis Lee RC	.60	.25
❑	390	DaRond Stovall	.30	.10
❑	391	Dennis Reyes RC	.60	.25
❑	392	Danny Buxbaum	.30	.10
❑	393	Marc Lewis RC	.40	.15
❑	394	Kelvim Escobar RC	1.00	.40
❑	395	Danny Klassen	.30	.10
❑	396	Ken Cloude RC	.40	.15
❑	397	Gabe Alvarez	.30	.10
❑	398	Jaret Wright RC	.60	.25
❑	399	Raul Casanova	.30	.10
❑	400	Clayton Bruner RC	.40	.15
❑	401	Jason Marquis RC	1.00	.40
❑	402	Marc Kroon	.30	.10
❑	403	Jamey Wright	.30	.10
❑	404	Matt Snyder RC	.40	.15
❑	405	Josh Garrett RC	.40	.15
❑	406	Juan Encarnacion	.30	.10
❑	407	Heath Murray	.30	.10
❑	408	Brett Herbison RC	.60	.25
❑	409	Brent Butler RC	.40	.15
❑	410	Danny Peoples RC	.40	.15
❑	411	Miguel Tejada RC	8.00	3.00
❑	412	Damian Moss	.30	.10
❑	413	Jim Pittsley	.30	.10
❑	414	Dmitri Young	.30	.10
❑	415	Glendon Rusch	.30	.10
❑	416	Vladimir Guerrero	.75	.30
❑	417	Cole Liniak RC	.60	.25
❑	418	Ramon Hernandez	.30	.10
❑	419	Cliff Politte RC	.40	.15
❑	420	Mel Rosario RC	.40	.15
❑	421	Jorge Carrion RC	.40	.15
❑	422	John Barnes RC	.40	.15
❑	423	Chris Stowe RC	.40	.15
❑	424	Vernon Wells RC	5.00	2.00
❑	425	Brett Caradonna RC	.40	.15
❑	426	Scott Hodges RC	.60	.25
❑	427	Jon Garland RC	2.50	1.00
❑	428	Nathan Haynes RC	.40	.15
❑	429	Geoff Goetz RC	.40	.15
❑	430	Adam Kennedy RC	1.00	.40
❑	431	T.J. Tucker RC	.40	.15
❑	432	Aaron Akin RC	.40	.15
❑	433	Jayson Werth RC	1.00	.40
❑	434	Glenn Davis RC	.40	.15
❑	435	Mark Mangum RC	.40	.15
❑	436	Troy Cameron RC	.40	.15
❑	437	J.J. Davis RC	.40	.15

❑ 438 Lance Berkman RC 6.00 2.50
❑ 439 Jason Standridge RC .40 .15
❑ 440 Jason Dellaero RC .60 .25
❑ 441 Hideki Irabu .60 .25

1998 Bowman

❑ COMPLETE SET (441) 50.00 20.00
❑ COMPLETE SERIES 1 (221) 25.00 10.00
❑ COMPLETE SERIES 2 (220) 25.00 10.00
❑ 1 Nomar Garciaparra 1.25 .50
❑ 2 Scott Rolen .50 .20
❑ 3 Andy Pettitte .50 .20
❑ 4 Ivan Rodriguez .50 .20
❑ 5 Mark McGwire 2.00 .75
❑ 6 Jason Dickson .30 .10
❑ 7 Jose Cruz Jr. .30 .10
❑ 8 Jeff Kent .30 .10
❑ 9 Mike Mussina .50 .20
❑ 10 Jason Kendall .30 .10
❑ 11 Brett Tomko .30 .10
❑ 12 Jeff King .30 .10
❑ 13 Brad Radke .30 .10
❑ 14 Robin Ventura .30 .10
❑ 15 Jeff Bagwell .50 .20
❑ 16 Greg Maddux 1.25 .50
❑ 17 John Jaha .30 .10
❑ 18 Mike Piazza 1.25 .50
❑ 19 Edgar Martinez .50 .20
❑ 20 David Justice .30 .10
❑ 21 Todd Hundley .30 .10
❑ 22 Tony Gwynn 1.00 .40
❑ 23 Larry Walker .30 .10
❑ 24 Bernie Williams .50 .20
❑ 25 Edgar Renteria .30 .10
❑ 26 Rafael Palmeiro .50 .20
❑ 27 Tim Salmon .50 .20
❑ 28 Matt Morris .30 .10
❑ 29 Shawn Estes .30 .10
❑ 30 Vladimir Guerrero .75 .30
❑ 31 Fernando Tatis .30 .10
❑ 32 Justin Thompson .30 .10
❑ 33 Ken Griffey Jr. 1.25 .50
❑ 34 Edgardo Alfonzo .30 .10
❑ 35 Mo Vaughn .30 .10
❑ 36 Marty Cordova .30 .10
❑ 37 Craig Biggio .50 .20
❑ 38 Roger Clemens 1.50 .60
❑ 39 Mark Grace .50 .20
❑ 40 Ken Caminiti .30 .10
❑ 41 Tony Womack .30 .10
❑ 42 Albert Belle .30 .10
❑ 43 Tino Martinez .50 .20
❑ 44 Sandy Alomar Jr. .30 .10
❑ 45 Jeff Cirillo .30 .10
❑ 46 Jason Giambi .30 .10
❑ 47 Darin Erstad .30 .10
❑ 48 Livan Hernandez .30 .10
❑ 49 Mark Grudzielanek .30 .10
❑ 50 Sammy Sosa .75 .30
❑ 51 Curt Schilling .30 .10
❑ 52 Brian Hunter .30 .10
❑ 53 Neifi Perez .30 .10
❑ 54 Todd Walker .30 .10
❑ 55 Jose Guillen .30 .10
❑ 56 Jim Thome .50 .20
❑ 57 Tom Glavine .50 .20
❑ 58 Todd Greene .30 .10
❑ 59 Rondell White .30 .10
❑ 60 Roberto Alomar .50 .20
❑ 61 Tony Clark .30 .10
❑ 62 Vinny Castilla .30 .10
❑ 63 Barry Larkin .50 .20
❑ 64 Hideki Irabu .30 .10
❑ 65 Johnny Damon .50 .20
❑ 66 Juan Gonzalez .30 .10
❑ 67 John Olerud .30 .10
❑ 68 Gary Sheffield .30 .10
❑ 69 Raul Mondesi .30 .10
❑ 70 Chipper Jones .75 .30
❑ 71 David Ortiz 2.50 1.00
❑ 72 Warren Morris RC .40 .15
❑ 73 Alex Gonzalez .30 .10
❑ 74 Nick Bierbrodt .30 .10
❑ 75 Roy Halladay .30 .10
❑ 76 Danny Buxbaum .30 .10
❑ 77 Adam Kennedy .30 .10
❑ 78 Jared Sandberg .30 .10
❑ 79 Michael Barrett .30 .10
❑ 80 Gil Meche .60 .25
❑ 81 Jayson Werth .30 .10
❑ 82 Abraham Nunez .30 .10
❑ 83 Ben Petrick .30 .10
❑ 84 Brett Caradonna .30 .10
❑ 85 Mike Lowell RC 2.00 .75
❑ 86 Clayton Bruner .30 .10
❑ 87 John Curtice RC .60 .25
❑ 88 Bobby Estalella .30 .10
❑ 89 Juan Melo .30 .10
❑ 90 Arnold Gooch .30 .10
❑ 91 Kevin Millwood RC 1.50 .60
❑ 92 Richie Sexson .30 .10
❑ 93 Orlando Cabrera .30 .10
❑ 94 Pat Cline .30 .10
❑ 95 Anthony Sanders .30 .10
❑ 96 Russ Johnson .30 .10
❑ 97 Ben Grieve .30 .10
❑ 98 Kevin McGlinchy .30 .10
❑ 99 Paul Wilder .30 .10
❑ 100 Russ Ortiz .30 .10
❑ 101 Ryan Jackson RC .40 .15
❑ 102 Heath Murray .30 .10
❑ 103 Brian Rose .30 .10
❑ 104 Ryan Radmanovich RC .40 .15
❑ 105 Ricky Ledee .30 .10
❑ 106 Jeff Wallace RC .40 .15
❑ 107 Ryan Minor RC .40 .15
❑ 108 Dennis Reyes .30 .10
❑ 109 James Manias .30 .10
❑ 110 Chris Carpenter .30 .10
❑ 111 Daryle Ward .30 .10
❑ 112 Vernon Wells .30 .10
❑ 113 Chad Green .30 .10
❑ 114 Mike Stoner RC .40 .15
❑ 115 Brad Fullmer .30 .10
❑ 116 Adam Eaton .30 .10
❑ 117 Jeff Liefer .30 .10
❑ 118 Corey Koskie RC 1.00 .40
❑ 119 Todd Helton .50 .20
❑ 120 Jaime Jones RC .40 .15
❑ 121 Mel Rosario .30 .10
❑ 122 Geoff Goetz .30 .10
❑ 123 Adrian Beltre .30 .10
❑ 124 Jason Dellaero .30 .10
❑ 125 Gabe Kapler RC 1.00 .40
❑ 126 Scott Schoeneweis .30 .10
❑ 127 Ryan Brannan .30 .10
❑ 128 Aaron Akin .30 .10
❑ 129 Ryan Anderson RC .40 .15
❑ 130 Brad Penny .30 .10
❑ 131 Bruce Chen .30 .10
❑ 132 Eli Marrero .30 .10
❑ 133 Eric Chavez .30 .10
❑ 134 Troy Glaus RC 4.00 1.50
❑ 135 Troy Cameron .30 .10
❑ 136 Brian Sikorski RC .40 .15
❑ 137 Mike Kinkade RC .40 .15
❑ 138 Braden Looper .30 .10
❑ 139 Mark Mangum .30 .10
❑ 140 Danny Peoples .30 .10
❑ 141 J.J. Davis .30 .10
❑ 142 Ben Davis .30 .10
❑ 143 Jacque Jones .30 .10
❑ 144 Derrick Gibson .30 .10
❑ 145 Bronson Arroyo 1.50 .60
❑ 146 Luis De Los Santos RC .40 .15
❑ 147 Jeff Abbott .30 .10
❑ 148 Mike Cuddyer RC 1.50 .60
❑ 149 Jason Romano .30 .10
❑ 150 Shane Monahan .30 .10
❑ 151 Ntema Ndungidi RC .40 .15
❑ 152 Alex Sanchez .30 .10
❑ 153 Jack Cust RC .60 .25
❑ 154 Brent Butler .30 .10
❑ 155 Ramon Hernandez .30 .10
❑ 156 Norm Hutchins .30 .10
❑ 157 Jason Marquis .30 .10
❑ 158 Jacob Cruz .30 .10
❑ 159 Rob Burger RC .40 .15
❑ 160 Dave Coggin .30 .10
❑ 161 Preston Wilson .30 .10
❑ 162 Jason Fitzgerald RC .40 .15
❑ 163 Dan Serafini .30 .10
❑ 164 Peter Munro .30 .10
❑ 165 Trot Nixon .30 .10
❑ 166 Homer Bush .30 .10
❑ 167 Dermal Brown .30 .10
❑ 168 Chad Hermansen .30 .10
❑ 169 Julio Moreno RC .40 .15
❑ 170 John Roskos RC .40 .15
❑ 171 Grant Roberts .30 .10
❑ 172 Ken Cloude .30 .10
❑ 173 Jason Brester .30 .10
❑ 174 Jason Conti .30 .10
❑ 175 Jon Garland .30 .10
❑ 176 Robbie Bell .30 .10
❑ 177 Nathan Haynes .30 .10
❑ 178 Ramon Ortiz RC .60 .25
❑ 179 Shannon Stewart .30 .10
❑ 180 Pablo Ortega .30 .10
❑ 181 Jimmy Rollins RC 2.50 1.00
❑ 182 Sean Casey .30 .10
❑ 183 Ted Lilly RC 1.00 .40
❑ 184 Chris Enochs RC .40 .15
❑ 185 Magglio Ordonez UER RC 4.00 1.50
❑ 186 Mike Drumright .30 .10
❑ 187 Aaron Boone .30 .10
❑ 188 Matt Clement .30 .10
❑ 189 Todd Dunwoody .30 .10
❑ 190 Larry Rodriguez .30 .10
❑ 191 Todd Noel .30 .10
❑ 192 Geoff Jenkins .30 .10
❑ 193 George Lombard .30 .10
❑ 194 Lance Berkman .30 .10
❑ 195 Marcus McCain .30 .10
❑ 196 Ryan McGuire .30 .10
❑ 197 Jhensy Sandoval .30 .10
❑ 198 Corey Lee .30 .10
❑ 199 Mario Valdez .30 .10
❑ 200 Robert Fick RC .60 .25
❑ 201 Donnie Sadler .30 .10
❑ 202 Marc Kroon .30 .10
❑ 203 David Miller .30 .10
❑ 204 Jarrod Washburn .30 .10
❑ 205 Miguel Tejada .75 .30
❑ 206 Raul Ibanez .30 .10
❑ 207 John Patterson .30 .10
❑ 208 Calvin Pickering .30 .10
❑ 209 Felix Martinez .30 .10
❑ 210 Mark Redman .30 .10
❑ 211 Scott Elarton .30 .10
❑ 212 Jose Amado RC .40 .15
❑ 213 Kerry Wood .30 .10
❑ 214 Dante Powell .30 .10
❑ 215 Aramis Ramirez .30 .10
❑ 216 A.J. Hinch .30 .10
❑ 217 Dustin Carr RC .40 .15
❑ 218 Mark Kotsay .30 .10
❑ 219 Jason Standridge .30 .10
❑ 220 Luis Ordaz .30 .10
❑ 221 Orlando Hernandez RC 2.00 .75
❑ 222 Cal Ripken 2.50 1.00
❑ 223 Paul Molitor .30 .10
❑ 224 Derek Jeter 2.00 .75
❑ 225 Barry Bonds 2.00 .75
❑ 226 Jim Edmonds .30 .10
❑ 227 John Smoltz .50 .20
❑ 228 Eric Karros .30 .10
❑ 229 Ray Lankford .30 .10
❑ 230 Rey Ordonez .30 .10
❑ 231 Kenny Lofton .30 .10

No.	Player	Price	Price
232	Alex Rodriguez	1.25	.50
233	Dante Bichette	.30	.10
234	Pedro Martinez	.50	.20
235	Carlos Delgado	.30	.10
236	Rod Beck	.30	.10
237	Matt Williams	.30	.10
238	Charles Johnson	.30	.10
239	Rico Brogna	.30	.10
240	Frank Thomas	.75	.30
241	Paul O'Neill	.50	.20
242	Jaret Wright	.30	.10
243	Brant Brown	.30	.10
244	Ryan Klesko	.30	.10
245	Chuck Finley	.30	.10
246	Derek Bell	.30	.10
247	Delino DeShields	.30	.10
248	Chan Ho Park	.30	.10
249	Wade Boggs	.50	.20
250	Jay Buhner	.30	.10
251	Butch Huskey	.30	.10
252	Steve Finley	.30	.10
253	Will Clark	.50	.20
254	John Valentin	.30	.10
255	Bobby Higginson	.30	.10
256	Darryl Strawberry	.30	.10
257	Randy Johnson	.75	.30
258	Al Martin	.30	.10
259	Travis Fryman	.30	.10
260	Fred McGriff	.50	.20
261	Jose Valentin	.30	.10
262	Andruw Jones	.50	.20
263	Kenny Rogers	.30	.10
264	Moises Alou	.30	.10
265	Denny Neagle	.30	.10
266	Ugueth Urbina	.30	.10
267	Derrek Lee	.50	.20
268	Ellis Burks	.30	.10
269	Mariano Rivera	.75	.30
270	Dean Palmer	.30	.10
271	Eddie Taubensee	.30	.10
272	Brady Anderson	.30	.10
273	Brian Giles	.30	.10
274	Quinton McCracken	.30	.10
275	Henry Rodriguez	.30	.10
276	Andres Galarraga	.30	.10
277	Jose Canseco	.50	.20
278	David Segui	.30	.10
279	Bret Saberhagen	.30	.10
280	Kevin Brown	.50	.20
281	Chuck Knoblauch	.30	.10
282	Jeromy Burnitz	.30	.10
283	Jay Bell	.30	.10
284	Manny Ramirez	.50	.20
285	Rick Helling	.30	.10
286	Francisco Cordova	.30	.10
287	Bob Abreu	.30	.10
288	J.T. Snow	.30	.10
289	Hideo Nomo	.75	.30
290	Brian Jordan	.30	.10
291	Javy Lopez	.30	.10
292	Travis Lee	.30	.10
293	Russell Branyan	.30	.10
294	Paul Konerko	.30	.10
295	Masato Yoshii RC	.60	.25
296	Kris Benson	.30	.10
297	Juan Encarnacion	.30	.10
298	Eric Milton	.30	.10
299	Mike Caruso	.30	.10
300	Ricardo Aramboles RC	.40	.15
301	Bobby Smith	.30	.10
302	Billy Koch	.30	.10
303	Richard Hidalgo	.30	.10
304	Justin Baughman RC	.40	.15
305	Chris Gissell	.30	.10
306	Donnie Bridges RC	.40	.15
307	Nelson Lara RC	.40	.15
308	Randy Wolf RC	.60	.25
309	Jason LaRue RC	.60	.25
310	Jason Gooding RC	.40	.15
311	Edgard Clemente	.30	.10
312	Andrew Vessel	.30	.10
313	Chris Reitsma	.30	.10
314	Jesus Sanchez RC	.40	.15
315	Buddy Carlyle RC	.40	.15
316	Randy Winn	.30	.10
317	Luis Rivera RC	.40	.15
318	Marcus Thames RC	2.50	1.00
319	A.J. Pierzynski	.30	.10
320	Scott Randall	.30	.10
321	Damian Sapp	.30	.10
322	Ed Yarnall RC	.40	.15
323	Luke Allen RC	.40	.15
324	J.D. Smart	.30	.10
325	Willie Martinez	.30	.10
326	Alex Ramirez	.30	.10
327	Eric DuBose RC	.40	.15
328	Kevin Witt	.30	.10
329	Dan McKinley RC	.40	.15
330	Cliff Politte	.30	.10
331	Vladimir Nunez	.30	.10
332	John Halama RC	.40	.15
333	Nerio Rodriguez	.30	.10
334	Desi Relaford	.30	.10
335	Robinson Checo	.30	.10
336	John Nicholson	.50	.20
337	Tom LaRosa RC	.40	.15
338	Kevin Nicholson RC	.40	.15
339	Javier Vazquez	.30	.10
340	A.J. Zapp	.30	.10
341	Tom Evans	.30	.10
342	Kerry Robinson	.30	.10
343	Gabe Gonzalez RC	.40	.15
344	Ralph Milliard	.30	.10
345	Enrique Wilson	.30	.10
346	Elvin Hernandez	.30	.10
347	Mike Lincoln RC	.40	.15
348	Cesar King RC	.40	.15
349	Cristian Guzman RC	.60	.25
350	Donzell McDonald	.30	.10
351	Jim Parque RC	.40	.15
352	Mike Saipe RC	.40	.15
353	Carlos Febles RC	.60	.25
354	Dernell Stenson RC	.40	.15
355	Mark Osborne RC	.40	.15
356	Odalis Perez RC	1.50	.60
357	Jason Dewey RC	.40	.15
358	Joe Fontenot	.30	.10
359	Jason Grilli RC	.40	.15
360	Kevin Haverbusch RC	.40	.15
361	Jay Yennaco RC	.40	.15
362	Brian Buchanan	.30	.10
363	John Barnes	.30	.10
364	Chris Fussell	.30	.10
365	Kevin Gibbs RC	.40	.15
366	Joe Lawrence	.30	.10
367	DaRond Stovall	.30	.10
368	Brian Fuentes RC	.40	.15
369	Jimmy Anderson	.30	.10
370	Lariel Gonzalez RC	.40	.15
371	Scott Williamson RC	.40	.15
372	Milton Bradley	.30	.10
373	Jason Halper RC	.40	.15
374	Brent Billingsley RC	.40	.15
375	Joe DePastino RC	.40	.15
376	Jake Westbrook	.30	.10
377	Octavio Dotel	.30	.10
378	Jason Williams RC	.40	.15
379	Julio Ramirez RC	.40	.15
380	Seth Greisinger	.30	.10
381	Mike Judd RC	.40	.15
382	Ben Ford RC	.40	.15
383	Tom Bennett RC	.40	.15
384	Adam Butler RC	.40	.15
385	Wade Miller RC	1.00	.40
386	Kyle Peterson RC	.40	.15
387	Tommy Peterman RC	.40	.15
388	Onan Masaoka	.30	.10
389	Jason Rakers RC	.40	.15
390	Rafael Medina	.30	.10
391	Luis Lopez RC	.40	.15
392	Jeff Yoder	.30	.10
393	Vance Wilson RC	.40	.15
394	Fernando Seguignol RC	.40	.15
395	Ron Wright	.30	.10
396	Ruben Mateo RC	.40	.15
397	Steve Lomasney RC	.60	.25
398	Damian Jackson	.30	.10
399	Mike Jerzembeck RC	.40	.15
400	Luis Rivas RC	1.00	.40
401	Kevin Burford RC	.40	.15
402	Glenn Davis	.30	.10
403	Robert Luce RC	.40	.15
404	Cole Liniak	.30	.10
405	Matt LeCroy RC	.60	.25
406	Jeremy Giambi RC	.60	.25
407	Shawn Chacon	.30	.10
408	Dewayne Wise RC	.40	.15
409	Steve Woodard	.30	.10
410	Francisco Cordero RC	1.00	.40
411	Damon Minor RC	.40	.15
412	Lou Collier	.30	.10
413	Justin Towle	.30	.10
414	Juan LeBron	.30	.10
415	Michael Coleman	.30	.10
416	Felix Rodriguez	.30	.10
417	Paul Ah Yat RC	.40	.15
418	Kevin Barker RC	.40	.15
419	Brian Meadows	.30	.10
420	Darnell McDonald RC	.40	.15
421	Matt Kinney RC	.40	.15
422	Mike Vavrek RC	.40	.15
423	Courtney Duncan RC	.40	.15
424	Kevin Millar RC	1.50	.60
425	Ruben Rivera	.30	.10
426	Steve Shoemaker RC	.40	.15
427	Dan Reichert RC	.40	.15
428	Carlos Lee RC	3.00	1.25
429	Rod Barajas	1.00	.40
430	Pablo Ozuna RC	.60	.25
431	Todd Belitz RC	.40	.15
432	Sidney Ponson	.30	.10
433	Steve Carver RC	.40	.15
434	Esteban Yan RC	.60	.25
435	Cedrick Bowers	.30	.10
436	Marlon Anderson	.30	.10
437	Carl Pavano	.30	.10
438	Jae Weong Seo RC	.60	.25
439	Jose Taveras RC	.40	.15
440	Matt Anderson RC	.40	.15
441	Darron Ingram RC	.40	.15
NNO	S.Hasegawa '91 BBM	10.00	4.00
NNO	H.Irabu '91 BBM	10.00	4.00
NNO	H.Nomo '91 BBM	25.00	10.00

1999 Bowman

No.	Player	Price	Price
	COMPLETE SET (440)	80.00	30.00
	COMPLETE SERIES 1 (220)	30.00	12.50
	COMPLETE SERIES 2 (220)	50.00	20.00
1	Ben Grieve	.30	.10
2	Kerry Wood	.30	.10
3	Ruben Rivera	.30	.10
4	Sandy Alomar Jr.	.30	.10
5	Cal Ripken	2.50	1.00
6	Mark McGwire	2.00	.75
7	Vladimir Guerrero	.75	.30
8	Moises Alou	.30	.10
9	Jim Edmonds	.30	.10
10	Greg Maddux	1.25	.50
11	Gary Sheffield	.30	.10
12	John Valentin	.30	.10
13	Chuck Knoblauch	.30	.10
14	Tony Clark	.30	.10
15	Rusty Greer	.30	.10
16	Al Leiter	.30	.10
17	Travis Lee	.30	.10
18	Jose Cruz Jr.	.30	.10
19	Pedro Martinez	.50	.10
20	Paul O'Neill	.50	.10
21	Todd Walker	.30	.10
22	Vinny Castilla	.30	.10

❑	23	Barry Larkin	.50	.10
❑	24	Curt Schilling	.30	.10
❑	25	Jason Kendall	.30	.10
❑	26	Scott Erickson	.30	.10
❑	27	Andres Galarraga	.30	.10
❑	28	Jeff Shaw	.30	.10
❑	29	John Olerud	.30	.10
❑	30	Orlando Hernandez	.30	.10
❑	31	Larry Walker	.30	.10
❑	32	Andruw Jones	.50	.10
❑	33	Jeff Cirillo	.30	.10
❑	34	Barry Bonds	2.00	.75
❑	35	Manny Ramirez	.50	.10
❑	36	Mark Kotsay	.30	.10
❑	37	Ivan Rodriguez	.50	.10
❑	38	Jeff King	.30	.10
❑	39	Brian Hunter	.30	.10
❑	40	Ray Durham	.30	.10
❑	41	Bernie Williams	.50	.10
❑	42	Darin Erstad	.30	.10
❑	43	Chipper Jones	.75	.30
❑	44	Pat Hentgen	.30	.10
❑	45	Eric Young	.30	.10
❑	46	Jaret Wright	.30	.10
❑	47	Juan Guzman	.30	.10
❑	48	Jorge Posada	.50	.10
❑	49	Bobby Higginson	.30	.10
❑	50	Jose Guillen	.30	.10
❑	51	Trevor Hoffman	.30	.10
❑	52	Ken Griffey Jr.	1.25	.50
❑	53	David Justice	.30	.10
❑	54	Matt Williams	.30	.10
❑	55	Eric Karros	.30	.10
❑	56	Derek Bell	.30	.10
❑	57	Ray Lankford	.30	.10
❑	58	Mariano Rivera	.75	.30
❑	59	Brett Tomko	.30	.10
❑	60	Mike Mussina	.50	.10
❑	61	Kenny Lofton	.30	.10
❑	62	Chuck Finley	.30	.10
❑	63	Alex Gonzalez	.30	.10
❑	64	Mark Grace	.50	.10
❑	65	Raul Mondesi	.30	.10
❑	66	David Cone	.30	.10
❑	67	Brad Fullmer	.30	.10
❑	68	Andy Benes	.30	.10
❑	69	John Smoltz	.50	.10
❑	70	Shane Reynolds	.30	.10
❑	71	Bruce Chen	.30	.10
❑	72	Adam Kennedy	.30	.10
❑	73	Jack Cust	.30	.10
❑	74	Matt Clement	.30	.10
❑	75	Derrick Gibson	.30	.10
❑	76	Darnell McDonald	.30	.10
❑	77	Adam Everett RC	1.00	.40
❑	78	Ricardo Aramboles	.30	.10
❑	79	Mark Quinn RC	.40	.15
❑	80	Jason Rakers	.30	.10
❑	81	Seth Etherton RC	.40	.15
❑	82	Jeff Urban RC	.60	.25
❑	83	Manny Aybar	.30	.10
❑	84	Mike Nannini RC	.40	.15
❑	85	Onan Masaoka	.30	.10
❑	86	Rod Barajas	.30	.10
❑	87	Mike Frank	.30	.10
❑	88	Scott Randall	.30	.10
❑	89	Justin Bowles RC	.40	.15
❑	90	Chris Haas	.30	.10
❑	91	Arturo McDowell RC	.40	.15
❑	92	Matt Belisle RC	.40	.15
❑	93	Scott Elarton	.30	.10
❑	94	Vernon Wells	.30	.10
❑	95	Pat Cline	.30	.10
❑	96	Ryan Anderson	.30	.10
❑	97	Kevin Barker	.30	.10
❑	98	Ruben Mateo	.30	.10
❑	99	Robert Fick	.30	.10
❑	100	Corey Koskie	.30	.10
❑	101	Ricky Ledee	.30	.10
❑	102	Rick Elder RC	.40	.15
❑	103	Jack Cressend RC	.40	.15
❑	104	Joe Lawrence	.30	.10
❑	105	Mike Lincoln	.30	.10
❑	106	Kit Pellow RC	.40	.15
❑	107	Matt Burch RC	.60	.25
❑	108	Cole Liniak	.30	.10
❑	109	Jason Dewey	.30	.10
❑	110	Cesar King	.30	.10
❑	111	Julio Ramirez	.30	.10
❑	112	Jake Westbrook	.30	.10
❑	113	Eric Valent RC	.60	.25
❑	114	Roosevelt Brown RC	.40	.15
❑	115	Choo Freeman RC	.60	.25
❑	116	Juan Melo	.30	.10
❑	117	Jason Grilli	.30	.10
❑	118	Jared Sandberg	.30	.10
❑	119	Glenn Davis	.30	.10
❑	120	David Riske RC	.40	.15
❑	121	Jacque Jones	.30	.10
❑	122	Corey Lee	.30	.10
❑	123	Michael Barrett	.30	.10
❑	124	Lariel Gonzalez	.30	.10
❑	125	Mitch Meluskey	.30	.10
❑	126	F.Adrian Garcia	.30	.10
❑	127	Tony Torcato RC	.40	.15
❑	128	Jeff Liefer	.30	.10
❑	129	Ntema Ndungidi	.30	.10
❑	130	Andy Brown RC	.40	.15
❑	131	Ryan Mills RC	.40	.15
❑	132	Andy Abad RC	.40	.15
❑	133	Carlos Febles	.30	.10
❑	134	Jason Tyner RC	.40	.15
❑	135	Mark Osborne	.30	.10
❑	136	Phil Norton RC	.40	.15
❑	137	Nathan Haynes	.30	.10
❑	138	Roy Halladay	.30	.10
❑	139	Juan Encarnacion	.30	.10
❑	140	Brad Penny	.30	.10
❑	141	Grant Roberts	.30	.10
❑	142	Aramis Ramirez	.30	.10
❑	143	Cristian Guzman	.30	.10
❑	144	Mamon Tucker RC	.40	.15
❑	145	Ryan Bradley	.30	.10
❑	146	Brian Simmons	.30	.10
❑	147	Dan Reichert	.30	.10
❑	148	Russ Branyan	.30	.10
❑	149	Victor Valencia RC	.50	.20
❑	150	Scott Schoeneweis	.30	.10
❑	151	Sean Spencer RC	.40	.15
❑	152	Odalis Perez	.30	.10
❑	153	Joe Fontenot	.30	.10
❑	154	Milton Bradley	.30	.10
❑	155	Josh McKinley RC	.40	.15
❑	156	Terrence Long	.30	.10
❑	157	Danny Klassen	.30	.10
❑	158	Paul Hoover RC	.60	.25
❑	159	Ron Belliard	.30	.10
❑	160	Armando Rios	.30	.10
❑	161	Ramon Hernandez	.30	.10
❑	162	Jason Conti	.30	.10
❑	163	Chad Hermansen	.30	.10
❑	164	Jason Standridge	.30	.10
❑	165	Jason Dellaero	.30	.10
❑	166	John Curtice	.30	.10
❑	167	Clayton Andrews RC	.40	.15
❑	168	Jeremy Giambi	.30	.10
❑	169	Alex Ramirez	.30	.10
❑	170	Gabe Molina RC	.40	.15
❑	171	Mario Encarnacion RC	.40	.15
❑	172	Mike Zywica RC	.40	.15
❑	173	Chip Ambres RC	.40	.15
❑	174	Trot Nixon	.30	.10
❑	175	Pat Burrell RC	3.00	1.25
❑	176	Jeff Yoder	.30	.10
❑	177	Chris Jones RC	.40	.15
❑	178	Kevin Witt	.30	.10
❑	179	Keith Luuloa RC	.40	.15
❑	180	Billy Koch	.30	.10
❑	181	Damaso Marte RC	.40	.15
❑	182	Ryan Glynn RC	.40	.15
❑	183	Calvin Pickering	.30	.10
❑	184	Michael Cuddyer	.30	.10
❑	185	Nick Johnson RC	2.00	.75
❑	186	Doug Mientkiewicz RC	1.00	.40
❑	187	Nate Cornejo RC	.40	.15
❑	188	Octavio Dotel	.30	.10
❑	189	Wes Helms	.30	.10
❑	190	Nelson Lara	.30	.10
❑	191	Chuck Abbott RC	.40	.15
❑	192	Tony Armas Jr.	.30	.10
❑	193	Gil Meche	.30	.10
❑	194	Ben Petrick	.30	.10
❑	195	Chris George RC	.40	.15
❑	196	Scott Hunter RC	.40	.15
❑	197	Ryan Brannan	.30	.10
❑	198	Amaury Garcia RC	.60	.25
❑	199	Chris Gissell	.30	.10
❑	200	Austin Kearns RC	3.00	1.25
❑	201	Alex Gonzalez	.30	.10
❑	202	Wade Miller	.30	.10
❑	203	Scott Williamson	.30	.10
❑	204	Chris Enochs	.30	.10
❑	205	Fernando Seguignol	.30	.10
❑	206	Marlon Anderson	.30	.10
❑	207	Todd Sears RC	.40	.15
❑	208	Nate Bump RC	.40	.15
❑	209	J.M. Gold RC	.40	.15
❑	210	Matt LeCroy	.30	.10
❑	211	Alex Hernandez	.30	.10
❑	212	Luis Rivera	.30	.10
❑	213	Troy Cameron	.30	.10
❑	214	Alex Escobar RC	.60	.25
❑	215	Jason LaRue	.30	.10
❑	216	Kyle Peterson	.30	.10
❑	217	Brent Butler	.30	.10
❑	218	Dernell Stenson	.30	.10
❑	219	Adrian Beltre	.30	.10
❑	220	Daryle Ward	.30	.10
❑	221	Jim Thome	.50	.10
❑	222	Cliff Floyd	.30	.10
❑	223	Rickey Henderson	.75	.30
❑	224	Garret Anderson	.30	.10
❑	225	Ken Caminiti	.30	.10
❑	226	Bret Boone	.30	.10
❑	227	Jeromy Burnitz	.30	.10
❑	228	Steve Finley	.30	.10
❑	229	Miguel Tejada	.30	.10
❑	230	Greg Vaughn	.30	.10
❑	231	Jose Offerman	.30	.10
❑	232	Andy Ashby	.30	.10
❑	233	Albert Belle	.30	.10
❑	234	Fernando Tatis	.30	.10
❑	235	Todd Helton	.50	.10
❑	236	Sean Casey	.30	.10
❑	237	Brian Giles	.30	.10
❑	238	Andy Pettitte	.50	.10
❑	239	Fred McGriff	.50	.10
❑	240	Roberto Alomar	.50	.10
❑	241	Edgar Martinez	.50	.10
❑	242	Lee Stevens	.30	.10
❑	243	Shawn Green	.30	.10
❑	244	Ryan Klesko	.30	.10
❑	245	Sammy Sosa	.75	.30
❑	246	Todd Hundley	.30	.10
❑	247	Shannon Stewart	.30	.10
❑	248	Randy Johnson	.75	.30
❑	249	Rondell White	.30	.10
❑	250	Mike Piazza	1.25	.50
❑	251	Craig Biggio	.50	.10
❑	252	David Wells	.30	.10
❑	253	Brian Jordan	.30	.10
❑	254	Edgar Renteria	.30	.10
❑	255	Bartolo Colon	.30	.10
❑	256	Frank Thomas	.75	.30
❑	257	Will Clark	.50	.10
❑	258	Dean Palmer	.30	.10
❑	259	Dmitri Young	.30	.10
❑	260	Scott Rolen	.50	.10
❑	261	Jeff Kent	.30	.10
❑	262	Dante Bichette	.30	.10
❑	263	Nomar Garciaparra	1.25	.50
❑	264	Tony Gwynn	1.00	.40
❑	265	Alex Rodriguez	1.25	.50
❑	266	Jose Canseco	.50	.10
❑	267	Jason Giambi	.30	.10
❑	268	Jeff Bagwell	.50	.10
❑	269	Carlos Delgado	.30	.10
❑	270	Tom Glavine	.50	.10
❑	271	Eric Davis	.30	.10
❑	272	Edgardo Alfonzo	.30	.10
❑	273	Tim Salmon	.50	.10
❑	274	Johnny Damon	.50	.10
❑	275	Rafael Palmeiro	.50	.10
❑	276	Denny Neagle	.30	.10
❑	277	Neifi Perez	.30	.10
❑	278	Roger Clemens	1.50	.60
❑	279	Brant Brown	.30	.10
❑	280	Kevin Brown	.50	.10

❑ 281	Jay Bell	.30	.10
❑ 282	Jay Buhner	.30	.10
❑ 283	Matt Lawton	.30	.10
❑ 284	Robin Ventura	.30	.10
❑ 285	Juan Gonzalez	.30	.10
❑ 286	Mo Vaughn	.30	.10
❑ 287	Kevin Millwood	.30	.10
❑ 288	Tino Martinez	.50	.10
❑ 289	Justin Thompson	.30	.10
❑ 290	Derek Jeter	2.00	.75
❑ 291	Ben Davis	.30	.10
❑ 292	Mike Lowell	.30	.10
❑ 293	Calvin Murray	.30	.10
❑ 294	Micah Bowie RC	.40	.15
❑ 295	Lance Berkman	.30	.10
❑ 296	Jason Marquis	.30	.10
❑ 297	Chad Green	.30	.10
❑ 298	Dee Brown	.30	.10
❑ 299	Jerry Hairston Jr.	.30	.10
❑ 300	Gabe Kapler	.30	.10
❑ 301	Brent Stentz RC	.60	.25
❑ 302	Scott Mullen RC	.40	.15
❑ 303	Brandon Reed	.30	.10
❑ 304	Shea Hillenbrand RC	1.50	.60
❑ 305	J.D. Closser RC	.60	.25
❑ 306	Gary Matthews Jr.	.30	.10
❑ 307	Toby Hall RC	.60	.25
❑ 308	Jason Phillips RC	.40	.15
❑ 309	Jose Macias RC	.40	.15
❑ 310	Jung Bong RC	.40	.15
❑ 311	Ramon Soler RC	.40	.15
❑ 312	Kelly Dransfeldt RC	.40	.15
❑ 313	Carlos E. Hernandez RC	.60	.25
❑ 314	Kevin Haverbusch	.30	.10
❑ 315	Aaron Myette RC	.40	.15
❑ 316	Chad Harville RC	.40	.15
❑ 317	Kyle Farnsworth RC	.60	.25
❑ 318	Gookie Dawkins RC	.60	.25
❑ 319	Willie Martinez	.30	.10
❑ 320	Carlos Lee	.30	.10
❑ 321	Carlos Pena RC	.60	.25
❑ 322	Peter Bergeron RC	.40	.15
❑ 323	A.J. Burnett RC	1.50	.60
❑ 324	Bucky Jacobsen RC	.60	.25
❑ 325	Mo Bruce RC	.40	.15
❑ 326	Reggie Taylor	.30	.10
❑ 327	Jackie Rexrode	.30	.10
❑ 328	Alvin Morrow RC	.40	.15
❑ 329	Carlos Beltran	.50	.10
❑ 330	Eric Chavez	.30	.10
❑ 331	John Patterson	.30	.10
❑ 332	Jayson Werth	.30	.10
❑ 333	Richie Sexson	.30	.10
❑ 334	Randy Wolf	.30	.10
❑ 335	Eli Marrero	.30	.10
❑ 336	Paul LoDuca	.30	.10
❑ 337	J.D Smart	.30	.10
❑ 338	Ryan Minor	.30	.10
❑ 339	Kris Benson	.30	.10
❑ 340	George Lombard	.30	.10
❑ 341	Troy Glaus	.50	.10
❑ 342	Eddie Yarnall	.30	.10
❑ 343	Kip Wells RC	.60	.25
❑ 344	C.C. Sabathia RC	2.00	.75
❑ 345	Sean Burroughs RC	1.00	.40
❑ 346	Felipe Lopez RC	2.50	1.00
❑ 347	Ryan Rupe RC	.40	.15
❑ 348	Orber Moreno RC	.40	.15
❑ 349	Rafael Roque RC	.40	.15
❑ 350	Alfonso Soriano RC	8.00	3.00
❑ 351	Pablo Ozuna	.30	.10
❑ 352	Corey Patterson RC	1.50	.60
❑ 353	Braden Looper	.30	.10
❑ 354	Robbie Bell	.30	.10
❑ 355	Mark Mulder RC	2.50	1.00
❑ 356	Angel Pena	.30	.10
❑ 357	Kevin McGlinchy	.30	.10
❑ 358	Michael Restovich RC	.60	.25
❑ 359	Eric DuBose	.30	.10
❑ 360	Geoff Jenkins	.30	.10
❑ 361	Mark Harriger RC	.40	.15
❑ 362	Junior Herndon RC	.40	.15
❑ 363	Tim Raines Jr. RC	.40	.15
❑ 364	Rafael Furcal RC	2.00	.75
❑ 365	Marcus Giles RC	1.50	.60
❑ 366	Ted Lilly	.30	.10
❑ 367	Jorge Toca RC	.60	.25
❑ 368	David Kelton RC	.40	.15
❑ 369	Adam Dunn RC	6.00	2.50
❑ 370	Guillermo Mota RC	.40	.15
❑ 371	Brett Laxton RC	.40	.15
❑ 372	Travis Harper RC	.60	.25
❑ 373	Tom Davey RC	.40	.15
❑ 374	Darren Blakely RC	.40	.15
❑ 375	Tim Hudson RC	3.00	1.25
❑ 376	Jason Romano	.30	.10
❑ 377	Dan Reichert	.30	.10
❑ 378	Julio Lugo RC	1.00	.40
❑ 379	Jose Garcia RC	.40	.15
❑ 380	Erubiel Durazo RC	.60	.25
❑ 381	Jose Jimenez	.30	.10
❑ 382	Chris Fussell	.30	.10
❑ 383	Steve Lomasney	.30	.10
❑ 384	Juan Pena RC	.60	.25
❑ 385	Allen Levrault RC	.40	.15
❑ 386	Juan Rivera RC	1.50	.60
❑ 387	Steve Colyer RC	.40	.15
❑ 388	Joe Nathan RC	2.00	.75
❑ 389	Ron Walker RC	.40	.15
❑ 390	Nick Bierbrodt	.30	.10
❑ 391	Luke Prokopec RC	.40	.15
❑ 392	Dave Roberts RC	1.00	.40
❑ 393	Mike Darr	.30	.10
❑ 394	Abraham Nunez RC	.60	.25
❑ 395	Giuseppe Chiaramonte RC	.40	.15
❑ 396	Jermaine Van Buren RC	.40	.15
❑ 397	Mike Kusiewicz	.30	.10
❑ 398	Matt Wise RC	.40	.15
❑ 399	Joe McEwing RC	.60	.25
❑ 400	Matt Holliday RC	3.00	1.25
❑ 401	Willi Mo Pena RC	5.00	2.00
❑ 402	Ruben Quevedo RC	.40	.15
❑ 403	Rob Ryan RC	.40	.15
❑ 404	Freddy Garcia RC	1.50	.60
❑ 405	Kevin Eberwein RC	.40	.15
❑ 406	Jesus Colome RC	.40	.15
❑ 407	Chris Singleton	.30	.10
❑ 408	Bubba Crosby RC	1.00	.40
❑ 409	Jesus Cordero RC	.40	.15
❑ 410	Donny Leon	.30	.10
❑ 411	Goefrey Tomlinson RC	.60	.25
❑ 412	Jeff Winchester RC	.40	.15
❑ 413	Adam Piatt RC	.40	.15
❑ 414	Robert Stratton	.30	.10
❑ 415	T.J. Tucker	.30	.10
❑ 416	Ryan Langerhans RC	1.00	.40
❑ 417	Anthony Shumaker RC	.40	.15
❑ 418	Matt Miller RC	.40	.15
❑ 419	Doug Clark RC	.40	.15
❑ 420	Kory DeHaan RC	.40	.15
❑ 421	David Eckstein RC	3.00	1.25
❑ 422	Brian Cooper RC	.40	.15
❑ 423	Brady Clark RC	1.50	.60
❑ 424	Chris Magruder RC	.60	.25
❑ 425	Bobby Seay RC	.40	.15
❑ 426	Aubrey Huff RC	2.00	.75
❑ 427	Mike Jerzembeck	.30	.10
❑ 428	Matt Blank RC	.60	.25
❑ 429	Benny Agbayani RC	.60	.25
❑ 430	Kevin Beirne RC	.40	.15
❑ 431	Josh Hamilton RC	.60	.25
❑ 432	Josh Girdley RC	.40	.15
❑ 433	Kyle Snyder RC	.40	.15
❑ 434	Mike Paradis RC	.40	.15
❑ 435	Jason Jennings RC	1.00	.40
❑ 436	David Walling RC	.40	.15
❑ 437	Omar Ortiz RC	.60	.25
❑ 438	Jay Gehrke RC	.60	.25
❑ 439	Casey Burns RC	.60	.25
❑ 440	Carl Crawford RC	5.00	2.00

2000 Bowman

❑ COMPLETE SET (440)		60.00	25.00
❑ 1	Vladimir Guerrero	.75	.30
❑ 2	Chipper Jones	.75	.30
❑ 3	Todd Walker	.30	.10
❑ 4	Barry Larkin	.50	.20
❑ 5	Bernie Williams	.50	.20
❑ 6	Todd Helton	.50	.20
❑ 7	Jermaine Dye	.30	.10
❑ 8	Brian Giles	.30	.10
❑ 9	Freddy Garcia	.30	.10
❑ 10	Greg Vaughn	.30	.10
❑ 11	Alex Gonzalez	.30	.10
❑ 12	Luis Gonzalez	.30	.10
❑ 13	Ron Belliard	.30	.10
❑ 14	Ben Grieve	.30	.10
❑ 15	Carlos Delgado	.30	.10
❑ 16	Brian Jordan	.30	.10
❑ 17	Fernando Tatis	.30	.10
❑ 18	Ryan Rupe	.30	.10
❑ 19	Miguel Tejada	.30	.10
❑ 20	Mark Grace	.50	.20
❑ 21	Kenny Lofton	.30	.10
❑ 22	Eric Karros	.30	.10
❑ 23	Cliff Floyd	.30	.10
❑ 24	John Halama	.30	.10
❑ 25	Cristian Guzman	.30	.10
❑ 26	Scott Williamson	.30	.10
❑ 27	Mike Lieberthal	.30	.10
❑ 28	Tim Hudson	.30	.10
❑ 29	Warren Morris	.30	.10
❑ 30	Pedro Martinez	.50	.20
❑ 31	John Smoltz	.50	.20
❑ 32	Ray Durham	.30	.10
❑ 33	Chad Allen	.30	.10
❑ 34	Tony Clark	.30	.10
❑ 35	Tino Martinez	.50	.20
❑ 36	J.T. Snow	.30	.10
❑ 37	Kevin Brown	.30	.10
❑ 38	Bartolo Colon	.30	.10
❑ 39	Rey Ordonez	.30	.10
❑ 40	Jeff Bagwell	.50	.20
❑ 41	Ivan Rodriguez	.50	.20
❑ 42	Eric Chavez	.30	.10
❑ 43	Eric Milton	.30	.10
❑ 44	Jose Canseco	.50	.20
❑ 45	Shawn Green	.30	.10
❑ 46	Rich Aurilia	.30	.10
❑ 47	Roberto Alomar	.50	.20
❑ 48	Brian Daubach	.30	.10
❑ 49	Magglio Ordonez	.30	.10
❑ 50	Derek Jeter	2.00	.75
❑ 51	Kris Benson	.30	.10
❑ 52	Albert Belle	.30	.10
❑ 53	Rondell White	.30	.10
❑ 54	Justin Thompson	.30	.10
❑ 55	Nomar Garciaparra	1.25	.50
❑ 56	Chuck Finley	.30	.10
❑ 57	Omar Vizquel	.50	.20
❑ 58	Luis Castillo	.30	.10
❑ 59	Richard Hidalgo	.30	.10
❑ 60	Barry Bonds	2.00	.75
❑ 61	Craig Biggio	.50	.20
❑ 62	Doug Glanville	.30	.10
❑ 63	Gabe Kapler	.30	.10
❑ 64	Johnny Damon	.50	.20
❑ 65	Pokey Reese	.30	.10
❑ 66	Andy Pettitte	.50	.20
❑ 67	B.J. Surhoff	.30	.10
❑ 68	Richie Sexson	.30	.10
❑ 69	Javy Lopez	.30	.10
❑ 70	Raul Mondesi	.30	.10
❑ 71	Darin Erstad	.30	.10
❑ 72	Kevin Millwood	.30	.10
❑ 73	Ricky Ledee	.30	.10
❑ 74	John Olerud	.30	.10
❑ 75	Sean Casey	.30	.10
❑ 76	Carlos Febles	.30	.10

❑ 77 Paul O'Neill .50 .20
❑ 78 Bob Abreu .30 .10
❑ 79 Neifi Perez .30 .10
❑ 80 Tony Gwynn 1.00 .40
❑ 81 Russ Ortiz .30 .10
❑ 82 Matt Williams .30 .10
❑ 83 Chris Carpenter .30 .10
❑ 84 Roger Cedeno .30 .10
❑ 85 Tim Salmon .50 .20
❑ 86 Billy Koch .30 .10
❑ 87 Jeromy Burnitz .30 .10
❑ 88 Edgardo Alfonzo .30 .10
❑ 89 Jay Bell .30 .10
❑ 90 Manny Ramirez .50 .20
❑ 91 Frank Thomas .75 .30
❑ 92 Mike Mussina .50 .20
❑ 93 J.D. Drew .30 .10
❑ 94 Adrian Beltre .30 .10
❑ 95 Alex Rodriguez 1.25 .50
❑ 96 Larry Walker .30 .10
❑ 97 Juan Encarnacion .30 .10
❑ 98 Mike Sweeney .30 .10
❑ 99 Rusty Greer .30 .10
❑ 100 Randy Johnson .75 .30
❑ 101 Jose Vidro .30 .10
❑ 102 Preston Wilson .30 .10
❑ 103 Greg Maddux 1.25 .50
❑ 104 Jason Giambi .30 .10
❑ 105 Cal Ripken 2.50 1.00
❑ 106 Carlos Beltran .30 .10
❑ 107 Vinny Castilla .30 .10
❑ 108 Mariano Rivera .75 .30
❑ 109 Mo Vaughn .30 .10
❑ 110 Rafael Palmeiro .50 .20
❑ 111 Shannon Stewart .30 .10
❑ 112 Mike Hampton .30 .10
❑ 113 Joe Nathan .30 .10
❑ 114 Ben Davis .30 .10
❑ 115 Andruw Jones .50 .20
❑ 116 Robin Ventura .30 .10
❑ 117 Damion Easley .30 .10
❑ 118 Jeff Cirillo .30 .10
❑ 119 Kerry Wood .30 .10
❑ 120 Scott Rolen .50 .20
❑ 121 Sammy Sosa .75 .30
❑ 122 Ken Griffey Jr. 1.25 .50
❑ 123 Shane Reynolds .30 .10
❑ 124 Troy Glaus .30 .10
❑ 125 Tom Glavine .50 .20
❑ 126 Michael Barrett .30 .10
❑ 127 Al Leiter .30 .10
❑ 128 Jason Kendall .30 .10
❑ 129 Roger Clemens 1.50 .60
❑ 130 Juan Gonzalez .30 .10
❑ 131 Corey Koskie .30 .10
❑ 132 Curt Schilling .30 .10
❑ 133 Mike Piazza 1.25 .50
❑ 134 Gary Sheffield .30 .10
❑ 135 Jim Thome .50 .20
❑ 136 Orlando Hernandez .30 .10
❑ 137 Ray Lankford .30 .10
❑ 138 Geoff Jenkins .30 .10
❑ 139 Jose Lima .30 .10
❑ 140 Mark McGwire 2.00 .75
❑ 141 Adam Piatt .30 .10
❑ 142 Pat Manning RC .30 .10
❑ 143 Marcos Castillo RC .30 .10
❑ 144 Lesli Brea RC .30 .10
❑ 145 Humberto Cota RC .50 .20
❑ 146 Ben Petrick .30 .10
❑ 147 Kip Wells .30 .10
❑ 148 Wily Pena .30 .10
❑ 149 Chris Wakeland RC .30 .10
❑ 150 Brad Baker RC .30 .10
❑ 151 Robbie Morrison RC .30 .10
❑ 152 Reggie Taylor .30 .10
❑ 153 Matt Ginter RC .30 .10
❑ 154 Peter Bergeron .30 .10
❑ 155 Roosevelt Brown .30 .10
❑ 156 Matt Cepicky RC .30 .10
❑ 157 Ramon Castro .30 .10
❑ 158 Brad Baisley RC .30 .10
❑ 159 Jeff Goldbach RC .30 .10
❑ 160 Mitch Meluskey .30 .10
❑ 161 Chad Harville .30 .10
❑ 162 Brian Cooper .30 .10
❑ 163 Marcus Giles .30 .10
❑ 164 Jim Morris .75 .30
❑ 165 Geoff Goetz .30 .10
❑ 166 Bobby Bradley RC .30 .10
❑ 167 Rob Bell .30 .10
❑ 168 Joe Crede 1.50 .60
❑ 169 Michael Restovich .30 .10
❑ 170 Quincy Foster RC .30 .10
❑ 171 Enrique Cruz RC .30 .10
❑ 172 Mark Quinn .30 .10
❑ 173 Nick Johnson .30 .10
❑ 174 Jeff Liefer .30 .10
❑ 175 Kevin Mench RC 2.00 .75
❑ 176 Steve Lomasney .30 .10
❑ 177 Jayson Werth .30 .10
❑ 178 Tim Drew .30 .10
❑ 179 Chip Ambres .30 .10
❑ 180 Ryan Anderson .30 .10
❑ 181 Matt Blank .30 .10
❑ 182 Giuseppe Chiaramonte .30 .10
❑ 183 Corey Myers RC .30 .10
❑ 184 Jeff Yoder .30 .10
❑ 185 Craig Dingman RC .30 .10
❑ 186 Jon Hamilton RC .30 .10
❑ 187 Toby Hall .30 .10
❑ 188 Russell Branyan .30 .10
❑ 189 Brian Falkenborg RC .30 .10
❑ 190 Aaron Harang RC 1.50 .60
❑ 191 Juan Pena .30 .10
❑ 192 Travis Thompson RC .30 .10
❑ 193 Alfonso Soriano .75 .30
❑ 194 Alejandro Diaz RC .30 .10
❑ 195 Carlos Pena .30 .10
❑ 196 Kevin Nicholson .30 .10
❑ 197 Mo Bruce .30 .10
❑ 198 C.C. Sabathia .30 .10
❑ 199 Carl Crawford .30 .10
❑ 200 Rafael Furcal .30 .10
❑ 201 Andrew Beinbrink RC .30 .10
❑ 202 Jimmy Osting .30 .10
❑ 203 Aaron McNeal RC .30 .10
❑ 204 Brett Laxton .30 .10
❑ 205 Chris George .30 .10
❑ 206 Felipe Lopez .30 .10
❑ 207 Ben Sheets RC 2.50 1.00
❑ 208 Mike Meyers RC .50 .20
❑ 209 Jason Conti .30 .10
❑ 210 Milton Bradley .30 .10
❑ 211 Chris Mears RC .30 .10
❑ 212 Carlos Hernandez RC .75 .30
❑ 213 Jason Romano .30 .10
❑ 214 Geofrey Tomlinson .30 .10
❑ 215 Jimmy Rollins .30 .10
❑ 216 Pablo Ozuna .30 .10
❑ 217 Steve Cox .30 .10
❑ 218 Terrence Long .30 .10
❑ 219 Jeff DaVanon RC .50 .20
❑ 220 Rick Ankiel .30 .10
❑ 221 Jason Standridge .30 .10
❑ 222 Tony Armas Jr. .30 .10
❑ 223 Jason Tyner .30 .10
❑ 224 Ramon Ortiz .30 .10
❑ 225 Daryle Ward .30 .10
❑ 226 Enger Veras RC .30 .10
❑ 227 Chris Jones .30 .10
❑ 228 Eric Cammack RC .30 .10
❑ 229 Ruben Mateo .30 .10
❑ 230 Ken Harvey RC .50 .20
❑ 231 Jake Westbrook .30 .10
❑ 232 Rob Purvis RC .30 .10
❑ 233 Choo Freeman .30 .10
❑ 234 Aramis Ramirez .30 .10
❑ 235 A.J. Burnett .30 .10
❑ 236 Kevin Barker .30 .10
❑ 237 Chance Caple RC .30 .10
❑ 238 Jarrod Washburn .30 .10
❑ 239 Lance Berkman .30 .10
❑ 240 Michael Wenner RC .30 .10
❑ 241 Alex Sanchez .30 .10
❑ 242 Pat Daneker .30 .10
❑ 243 Grant Roberts .30 .10
❑ 244 Mark Ellis RC .50 .20
❑ 245 Donny Leon .30 .10
❑ 246 David Eckstein .30 .10
❑ 247 Dicky Gonzalez RC .30 .10
❑ 248 John Patterson .30 .10
❑ 249 Chad Green .30 .10
❑ 250 Scot Shields RC .30 .10
❑ 251 Troy Cameron .30 .10
❑ 252 Jose Molina .30 .10
❑ 253 Rob Pugmire RC .30 .10
❑ 254 Rick Elder .30 .10
❑ 255 Sean Burroughs .30 .10
❑ 256 Josh Kalinowski RC .30 .10
❑ 257 Matt LeCroy .30 .10
❑ 258 Alex Graman RC .30 .10
❑ 259 Tomo Ohka RC .50 .20
❑ 260 Brady Clark .30 .10
❑ 261 Rico Washington RC .30 .10
❑ 262 Gary Matthews Jr. .30 .10
❑ 263 Matt Wise .30 .10
❑ 264 Keith Reed RC .30 .10
❑ 265 Santiago Ramirez RC .30 .10
❑ 266 Ben Broussard RC 1.25 .50
❑ 267 Ryan Langerhans .30 .10
❑ 268 Juan Rivera .30 .10
❑ 269 Shawn Gallagher .30 .10
❑ 270 Jorge Toca .30 .10
❑ 271 Brad Lidge .50 .20
❑ 272 Leoncio Estrella RC .30 .10
❑ 273 Ruben Quevedo .30 .10
❑ 274 Jack Cust .30 .10
❑ 275 T.J. Tucker .30 .10
❑ 276 Mike Colangelo .30 .10
❑ 277 Brian Schneider .30 .10
❑ 278 Calvin Murray .30 .10
❑ 279 Josh Girdley .30 .10
❑ 280 Mike Paradis .30 .10
❑ 281 Chad Hermansen .30 .10
❑ 282 Ty Howington RC .30 .10
❑ 283 Aaron Myette .30 .10
❑ 284 D'Angelo Jimenez .30 .10
❑ 285 Dernell Stenson .30 .10
❑ 286 Jerry Hairston Jr. .30 .10
❑ 287 Gary Majewski RC .50 .20
❑ 288 Derrin Ebert .30 .10
❑ 289 Steve Fish RC .30 .10
❑ 290 Carlos E. Hernandez .30 .10
❑ 291 Allen Levrault .30 .10
❑ 292 Sean McNally RC .30 .10
❑ 293 Randey Dorame RC .30 .10
❑ 294 Wes Anderson RC .30 .10
❑ 295 B.J. Ryan .30 .10
❑ 296 Alan Webb RC .30 .10
❑ 297 Brandon Inge RC 2.00 .75
❑ 298 David Walling .30 .10
❑ 299 Sun Woo Kim RC .30 .10
❑ 300 Pat Burrell .30 .10
❑ 301 Rick Guttormson RC .30 .10
❑ 302 Gil Meche .30 .10
❑ 303 Carlos Zambrano RC 5.00 2.00
❑ 304 Eric Byrnes UER RC .50 .20
❑ 305 Robb Quinlan RC .50 .20
❑ 306 Jackie Rexrode .30 .10
❑ 307 Nate Bump .30 .10
❑ 308 Sean DePaula RC .30 .10
❑ 309 Matt Riley .30 .10
❑ 310 Ryan Minor .30 .10
❑ 311 J.J. Davis .30 .10
❑ 312 Randy Wolf .30 .10
❑ 313 Jason Jennings .30 .10
❑ 314 Scott Seabol RC .30 .10
❑ 315 Doug Davis .30 .10
❑ 316 Todd Moser RC .30 .10
❑ 317 Rob Ryan .30 .10
❑ 318 Bubba Crosby .30 .10
❑ 319 Lyle Overbay RC 1.25 .50
❑ 320 Mario Encarnacion .30 .10
❑ 321 Francisco Rodriguez RC 2.50 1.00
❑ 322 Michael Cuddyer .30 .10
❑ 323 Ed Yarnall .30 .10
❑ 324 Cesar Saba RC .30 .10
❑ 325 Gookie Dawkins .30 .10
❑ 326 Alex Escobar .30 .10
❑ 327 Julio Zuleta RC .30 .10
❑ 328 Josh Hamilton .30 .10
❑ 329 Nick Neugebauer RC .30 .10
❑ 330 Matt Belisle .30 .10
❑ 331 Kurt Ainsworth RC .30 .10
❑ 332 Tim Raines Jr. .30 .10
❑ 333 Eric Munson .30 .10
❑ 334 Donzell McDonald .30 .10

❑ 335	Larry Bigbie RC	.75	.30
❑ 336	Matt Watson RC	.30	.10
❑ 337	Aubrey Huff	.30	.10
❑ 338	Julio Ramirez	.30	.10
❑ 339	Jason Grabowski RC	.30	.10
❑ 340	Jon Garland	.30	.10
❑ 341	Austin Kearns	.30	.10
❑ 342	Josh Pressley RC	.30	.10
❑ 343	Miguel Olivo RC	.75	.30
❑ 344	Julio Lugo	.30	.10
❑ 345	Roberto Vaz	.30	.10
❑ 346	Ramon Soler	.30	.10
❑ 347	Brandon Phillips RC	1.50	.60
❑ 348	Vince Faison RC	.30	.10
❑ 349	Mike Venafro	.30	.10
❑ 350	Rick Asadoorian RC	.50	.20
❑ 351	B.J. Garbe RC	.30	.10
❑ 352	Dan Reichert	.30	.10
❑ 353	Jason Stumm RC	.30	.10
❑ 354	Ruben Salazar RC	.30	.10
❑ 355	Francisco Cordero	.30	.10
❑ 356	Juan Guzman RC	.30	.10
❑ 357	Mike Bacsik RC	.30	.10
❑ 358	Jared Sandberg	.30	.10
❑ 359	Rod Barajas	.30	.10
❑ 360	Junior Brignac RC	.30	.10
❑ 361	J.M. Gold	.30	.10
❑ 362	Octavio Dotel	.30	.10
❑ 363	David Kelton	.30	.10
❑ 364	Scott Morgan	.30	.10
❑ 365	Wascar Serrano RC	.30	.10
❑ 366	Wilton Veras	.30	.10
❑ 367	Eugene Kingsale	.30	.10
❑ 368	Ted Lilly	.30	.10
❑ 369	George Lombard	.30	.10
❑ 370	Chris Haas	.30	.10
❑ 371	Wilton Pena RC	.30	.10
❑ 372	Vernon Wells	.30	.10
❑ 373	Jason Royer RC	.30	.10
❑ 374	Jeff Heaverlo RC	.30	.10
❑ 375	Calvin Pickering	.30	.10
❑ 376	Mike Lamb RC	.75	.30
❑ 377	Kyle Snyder	.30	.10
❑ 378	Javier Cardona RC	.30	.10
❑ 379	Aaron Rowand RC	2.00	.75
❑ 380	Dee Brown	.30	.10
❑ 381	Brett Myers RC	2.00	.75
❑ 382	Abraham Nunez	.30	.10
❑ 383	Eric Valent	.30	.10
❑ 384	Jody Gerut RC	.50	.20
❑ 385	Adam Dunn	.75	.30
❑ 386	Jay Gehrke	.30	.10
❑ 387	Omar Ortiz	.30	.10
❑ 388	Darnell McDonald	.30	.10
❑ 389	Tony Schrager RC	.30	.10
❑ 390	J.D. Closser	.30	.10
❑ 391	Ben Christensen RC	.30	.10
❑ 392	Adam Kennedy	.30	.10
❑ 393	Nick Green RC	.30	.10
❑ 394	Ramon Hernandez	.30	.10
❑ 395	Roy Oswalt RC	12.00	5.00
❑ 396	Andy Tracy RC	.30	.10
❑ 397	Eric Gagne	.75	.30
❑ 398	Michael Tejera RC	.30	.10
❑ 399	Adam Everett	.30	.10
❑ 400	Corey Patterson	.30	.10
❑ 401	Gary Knotts RC	.30	.10
❑ 402	Ryan Christianson RC	.30	.10
❑ 403	Eric Ireland RC	.30	.10
❑ 404	Andrew Good RC	.30	.10
❑ 405	Brad Penny	.30	.10
❑ 406	Jason LaRue	.30	.10
❑ 407	Kit Pellow	.30	.10
❑ 408	Kevin Beirne	.30	.10
❑ 409	Kelly Dransfeldt	.30	.10
❑ 410	Jason Grilli	.30	.10
❑ 411	Scott Downs RC	.30	.10
❑ 412	Jesus Colome	.30	.10
❑ 413	John Sneed RC	.30	.10
❑ 414	Tony McKnight	.30	.10
❑ 415	Luis Rivera	.30	.10
❑ 416	Adam Eaton	.30	.10
❑ 417	Mike MacDougal RC	.50	.20
❑ 418	Mike Nannini	.30	.10
❑ 419	Barry Zito RC	4.00	1.50
❑ 420	DeWayne Wise	.30	.10
❑ 421	Jason Dellaero	.30	.10
❑ 422	Chad Moeller	.30	.10
❑ 423	Jason Marquis	.30	.10
❑ 424	Tim Redding RC	.50	.20
❑ 425	Mark Mulder	.30	.10
❑ 426	Josh Paul	.30	.10
❑ 427	Chris Enochs	.30	.10
❑ 428	Wilfredo Rodriguez RC	.30	.10
❑ 429	Kevin Witt	.30	.10
❑ 430	Scott Sobkowiak RC	.30	.10
❑ 431	McKay Christensen	.30	.10
❑ 432	Jung Bong	.30	.10
❑ 433	Keith Evans RC	.30	.10
❑ 434	Garry Maddox Jr. RC	.30	.10
❑ 435	Ramon Santiago RC	.30	.10
❑ 436	Alex Cora	.30	.10
❑ 437	Carlos Lee	.30	.10
❑ 438	Jason Repko RC	.75	.30
❑ 439	Matt Burch	.30	.10
❑ 440	Shawn Sonnier RC	.30	.10

2000 Bowman Draft Picks

❑	COMP.FACT.SET (111)	40.00	20.00
❑	COMPLETE SET (110)	20.00	8.00
❑ 1	Pat Burrell	.30	.10
❑ 2	Rafael Furcal	.30	.10
❑ 3	Grant Roberts	.30	.10
❑ 4	Barry Zito	1.50	.60
❑ 5	Julio Zuleta	.30	.10
❑ 6	Mark Mulder	.30	.10
❑ 7	Rob Bell	.30	.10
❑ 8	Adam Piatt	.30	.10
❑ 9	Mike Lamb	.60	.25
❑ 10	Pablo Ozuna	.30	.10
❑ 11	Jason Tyner	.30	.10
❑ 12	Jason Marquis	.30	.10
❑ 13	Eric Munson	.30	.10
❑ 14	Seth Etherton	.30	.10
❑ 15	Milton Bradley	.30	.10
❑ 16	Nick Green	.30	.10
❑ 17	Chin-Feng Chen RC	.60	.25
❑ 18	Matt Boone RC	.30	.10
❑ 19	Kevin Gregg RC	.30	.10
❑ 20	Eddy Garabito RC	.30	.10
❑ 21	Aaron Capista RC	.30	.10
❑ 22	Esteban German RC	.30	.10
❑ 23	Derek Thompson RC	.30	.10
❑ 24	Phil Merrell RC	.30	.10
❑ 25	Brian O'Connor RC	.30	.10
❑ 26	Yamid Haad	.30	.10
❑ 27	Hector Mercado RC	.30	.10
❑ 28	Jason Woolf RC	.30	.10
❑ 29	Eddy Furniss RC	.30	.10
❑ 30	Cha Sueng Baek RC	.30	.10
❑ 31	Colby Lewis RC	.30	.10
❑ 32	Pasqual Coco RC	.30	.10
❑ 33	Jorge Cantu RC	2.50	1.00
❑ 34	Erasmo Ramirez RC	.30	.10
❑ 35	Bobby Kielty RC	.40	.15
❑ 36	Joaquin Benoit RC	.30	.10
❑ 37	Brian Esposito RC	.30	.10
❑ 38	Michael Wenner	.30	.10
❑ 39	Juan Rincon RC	.30	.10
❑ 40	Yorvit Torrealba RC	.30	.10
❑ 41	Chad Durham RC	.30	.10
❑ 42	Jim Mann RC	.30	.10
❑ 43	Shane Loux RC	.30	.10
❑ 44	Luis Rivas	.30	.10
❑ 45	Ken Chenard RC	.30	.10
❑ 46	Mike Lockwood RC	.30	.10
❑ 47	Yovanny Lara RC	.30	.10
❑ 48	Bubba Carpenter RC	.30	.10
❑ 49	Ryan Dittfurth RC	.30	.10
❑ 50	John Stephens RC	.30	.10
❑ 51	Pedro Feliz RC	1.00	.40
❑ 52	Kenny Kelly RC	.30	.10
❑ 53	Neil Jenkins RC	.30	.10
❑ 54	Mike Glendenning RC	.30	.10
❑ 55	Bo Porter	.30	.10
❑ 56	Eric Byrnes	.30	.10
❑ 57	Tony Alvarez RC	.30	.10
❑ 58	Kazuhiro Sasaki RC	.60	.25
❑ 59	Chad Durbin RC	.30	.10
❑ 60	Mike Bynum RC	.30	.10
❑ 61	Travis Wilson RC	.30	.10
❑ 62	Jose Leon RC	.30	.10
❑ 63	Ryan Vogelsong RC	.30	.10
❑ 64	Geraldo Guzman RC	.30	.10
❑ 65	Craig Anderson RC	.30	.10
❑ 66	Carlos Silva RC	.40	.15
❑ 67	Brad Thomas RC	.30	.10
❑ 68	Chin-Hui Tsao RC	2.00	.75
❑ 69	Mark Buehrle RC	3.00	1.25
❑ 70	Juan Salas RC	.30	.10
❑ 71	Denny Abreu RC	.30	.10
❑ 72	Keith McDonald RC	.30	.10
❑ 73	Chris Richard RC	.30	.10
❑ 74	Tomas De la Rosa RC	.30	.10
❑ 75	Vicente Padilla RC	.40	.15
❑ 76	Justin Brunette RC	.30	.10
❑ 77	Scott Linebrink RC	.30	.10
❑ 78	Jeff Sparks RC	.30	.10
❑ 79	Tike Redman RC	.60	.25
❑ 80	John Lackey RC	2.50	1.00
❑ 81	Joe Strong RC	.30	.10
❑ 82	Brian Tollberg RC	.30	.10
❑ 83	Steve Sisco RC	.30	.10
❑ 84	Chris Clapinski RC	.30	.10
❑ 85	Augie Ojeda RC	.30	.10
❑ 86	Adrian Gonzalez RC	2.50	1.00
❑ 87	Mike Stodolka RC	.30	.10
❑ 88	Adam Johnson RC	.30	.10
❑ 89	Matt Wheatland RC	.30	.10
❑ 90	Corey Smith RC	.30	.10
❑ 91	Rocco Baldelli RC	2.50	1.00
❑ 92	Keith Bucktrot RC	.30	.10
❑ 93	Adam Wainwright RC	1.00	.40
❑ 94	Blaine Boyer RC	.30	.10
❑ 95	Aaron Herr RC	.40	.15
❑ 96	Scott Thorman RC	1.00	.40
❑ 97	Bryan Digby RC	.30	.10
❑ 98	Josh Shortslef RC	.30	.10
❑ 99	Sean Smith RC	.30	.10
❑ 100	Alex Cruz RC	.30	.10
❑ 101	Marc Love RC	.30	.10
❑ 102	Kevin Lee RC	.30	.10
❑ 103	Victor Ramos RC	.30	.10
❑ 104	Jason Kaanoi RC	.30	.10
❑ 105	Luis Escobar RC	.30	.10
❑ 106	Tripper Johnson RC	.30	.10
❑ 107	Phil Dumatrait RC	.30	.10
❑ 108	Bryan Edwards RC	.30	.10
❑ 109	Grady Sizemore RC	15.00	6.00
❑ 110	Thomas Mitchell RC	.30	.10

2001 Bowman

COMPLETE SET (440)	150.00	90.00
COMMON CARD (1-440)	.30	.10
COMMON RC	.40	.15
1 Jason Giambi	.30	.10
2 Rafael Furcal	.30	.10
3 Rick Ankiel	.30	.10
4 Freddy Garcia	.30	.10
5 Maggio Ordonez	.30	.10
6 Bernie Williams	.50	.20
7 Kenny Lofton	.30	.10
8 Al Leiter	.30	.10
9 Albert Belle	.30	.10
10 Craig Biggio	.50	.20
11 Mark Mulder	.30	.10
12 Carlos Delgado	.30	.10
13 Darin Erstad	.30	.10
14 Richie Sexson	.30	.10
15 Randy Johnson	.75	.30
16 Greg Maddux	1.25	.50
17 Cliff Floyd	.30	.10
18 Mark Buehrle	.50	.20
19 Chris Singleton	.30	.10
20 Orlando Hernandez	.30	.10
21 Javier Vazquez	.30	.10
22 Jeff Kent	.30	.10
23 Jim Thome	.50	.20
24 John Olerud	.30	.10
25 Jason Kendall	.30	.10
26 Scott Rolen	.50	.20
27 Tony Gwynn	1.00	.40
28 Edgardo Alfonzo	.30	.10
29 Pokey Reese	.30	.10
30 Todd Helton	.50	.20
31 Mark Quinn	.30	.10
32 Dan Tosca RC	.40	.15
33 Dean Palmer	.30	.10
34 Jacque Jones	.30	.10
35 Ray Durham	.30	.10
36 Rafael Palmeiro	.50	.20
37 Carl Everett	.30	.10
38 Ryan Dempster	.30	.10
39 Randy Wolf	.30	.10
40 Vladimir Guerrero	.75	.30
41 Livan Hernandez	.30	.10
42 Mo Vaughn	.30	.10
43 Shannon Stewart	.30	.10
44 Preston Wilson	.30	.10
45 Jose Vidro	.30	.10
46 Fred McGriff	.50	.20
47 Kevin Brown	.30	.10
48 Peter Bergeron	.30	.10
49 Miguel Tejada	.30	.10
50 Chipper Jones	.75	.30
51 Edgar Martinez	.50	.20
52 Tony Batista	.30	.10
53 Jorge Posada	.50	.20
54 Ricky Ledee	.30	.10
55 Sammy Sosa	.75	.30
56 Steve Cox	.30	.10
57 Tony Armas Jr.	.30	.10
58 Gary Sheffield	.30	.10
59 Bartolo Colon	.30	.10
60 Pat Burrell	.30	.10
61 Jay Payton	.30	.10
62 Sean Casey	.30	.10
63 Larry Walker	.30	.10
64 Mike Mussina	.50	.20
65 Nomar Garciaparra	1.25	.50
66 Darren Dreifort	.30	.10
67 Richard Hidalgo	.30	.10
68 Troy Glaus	.30	.10
69 Ben Grieve	.30	.10
70 Jim Edmonds	.30	.10
71 Raul Mondesi	.30	.10
72 Andruw Jones	.50	.20
73 Luis Castillo	.30	.10
74 Mike Sweeney	.30	.10
75 Derek Jeter	2.00	.75
76 Ruben Mateo	.30	.10
77 Carlos Lee	.30	.10
78 Cristian Guzman	.30	.10
79 Mike Hampton	.30	.10
80 J.D. Drew	.30	.10
81 Matt Lawton	.30	.10
82 Moises Alou	.30	.10
83 Terrence Long	.30	.10
84 Geoff Jenkins	.30	.10
85 Manny Ramirez Sox	.50	.20
86 Johnny Damon	.50	.20
87 Barry Larkin	.50	.20
88 Pedro Martinez	.50	.20
89 Juan Gonzalez	.30	.10
90 Roger Clemens	1.50	.60
91 Carlos Beltran	.30	.10
92 Brad Radke	.30	.10
93 Orlando Cabrera	.30	.10
94 Roberto Alomar	.50	.20
95 Barry Bonds	2.00	.75
96 Tim Hudson	.30	.10
97 Tom Glavine	.50	.20
98 Jeromy Burnitz	.30	.10
99 Adrian Beltre	.30	.10
100 Mike Piazza	1.25	.50
101 Kerry Wood	.30	.10
102 Steve Finley	.30	.10
103 Alex Cora	.30	.10
104 Bob Abreu	.30	.10
105 Neifi Perez	.30	.10
106 Mark Redman	.30	.10
107 Paul Konerko	.30	.10
108 Jermaine Dye	.30	.10
109 Brian Giles	.30	.10
110 Ivan Rodriguez	.50	.20
111 Vinny Castilla	.30	.10
112 Adam Kennedy	.30	.10
113 Eric Chavez	.30	.10
114 Billy Koch	.30	.10
115 Shawn Green	.30	.10
116 Matt Williams	.30	.10
117 Greg Vaughn	.30	.10
118 Gabe Kapler	.30	.10
119 Jeff Cirillo	.30	.10
120 Frank Thomas	.75	.30
121 David Justice	.30	.10
122 Cal Ripken	2.50	1.00
123 Rich Aurilia	.30	.10
124 Curt Schilling	.30	.10
125 Barry Zito	.50	.20
126 Brian Jordan	.30	.10
127 Chan Ho Park	.30	.10
128 J.T. Snow	.30	.10
129 Kazuhiro Sasaki	.30	.10
130 Alex Rodriguez	1.25	.50
131 Mariano Rivera	.75	.30
132 Eric Milton	.30	.10
133 Andy Pettitte	.50	.20
134 Scott Elarton	.30	.10
135 Ken Griffey Jr.	1.25	.50
136 Bengie Molina	.30	.10
137 Jeff Bagwell	.50	.20
138 Kevin Millwood	.30	.10
139 Tino Martinez	.50	.20
140 Mark McGwire	2.00	.75
141 Larry Barnes	.30	.10
142 John Buck RC	1.00	.40
143 Freddie Bynum RC	.40	.15
144 Abraham Nunez	.30	.10
145 Felix Diaz RC	.40	.15
146 Horacio Estrada	.30	.10
147 Ben Diggins	.30	.10
148 Tsuyoshi Shinjo RC	1.00	.40
149 Rocco Baldelli	.30	.10
150 Rod Barajas	.30	.10
151 Luis Terrero	.30	.10
152 Milton Bradley	.30	.10
153 Kurt Ainsworth	.30	.10
154 Russell Branyan	.30	.10
155 Ryan Anderson	.30	.10
156 Mitch Jones RC	.60	.25
157 Chip Ambres	.30	.10
158 Steve Bennett RC	.40	.15
159 Ivanon Coffie	.30	.10
160 Sean Burroughs	.30	.10
161 Keith Bucktrot	.30	.10
162 Tony Alvarez	.30	.10
163 Joaquin Benoit	.30	.10
164 Rick Asadoorian	.30	.10
165 Ben Broussard	.30	.10
166 Ryan Madson RC	1.25	.50
167 Dee Brown	.30	.10
168 Sergio Contreras RC	.60	.25
169 John Barnes	.30	.10
170 Ben Washburn RC	.40	.15
171 Erick Almonte RC	.40	.15
172 Shawn Fagan RC	.40	.15
173 Gary Johnson RC	.40	.15
174 Brady Clark	.30	.10
175 Grant Roberts	.30	.10
176 Tony Torcato	.30	.10
177 Ramon Castro	.30	.10
178 Esteban German	.30	.10
179 Joe Hamer RC	.60	.25
180 Nick Neugebauer	.30	.10
181 Dernell Stenson	.30	.10
182 Yhency Brazoban RC	1.00	.40
183 Aaron Myette	.30	.10
184 Juan Sosa	.30	.10
185 Brandon Inge	.30	.10
186 Domingo Guante RC	.40	.15
187 Adrian Brown	.30	.10
188 Deivi Mendez RC	.40	.15
189 Luis Matos	.30	.10
190 Pedro Liriano RC	.60	.25
191 Donnie Bridges	.30	.10
192 Alex Cintron	.30	.10
193 Jace Brewer	.30	.10
194 Ron Davenport RC	.60	.25
195 Jason Belcher RC	.40	.15
196 Adrian Hernandez RC	.40	.15
197 Bobby Kielty	.30	.10
198 Reggie Griggs RC	.60	.25
199 Reggie Abercrombie RC	1.00	.40
200 Troy Farnsworth RC	.60	.25
201 Matt Belisle	.30	.10
202 Miguel Villilo RC	.60	.25
203 Adam Everett	.30	.10
204 John Lackey	.30	.10
205 Pasqual Coco	.30	.10
206 Adam Wainwright	.30	.10
207 Matt White RC	.60	.25
208 Chin-Feng Chen	.30	.10
209 Jeff Andra RC	.40	.15
210 Willie Bloomquist	.30	.10
211 Wes Anderson	.30	.10
212 Enrique Cruz	.30	.10
213 Jerry Hairston Jr.	.30	.10
214 Mike Bynum	.30	.10
215 Brian Hitchcox RC	.40	.15
216 Ryan Christianson	.30	.10
217 J.J. Davis	.30	.10
218 Jovanny Cedeno	.30	.10
219 Elvin Nina	.30	.10
220 Alex Graman	.30	.10
221 Arturo McDowell	.30	.10
222 Deivis Santos RC	.40	.15
223 Jody Gerut	.30	.10
224 Sun Woo Kim	.30	.10
225 Jimmy Rollins	.30	.10
226 Ntema Ndungidi	.30	.10
227 Ruben Salazar	.30	.10
228 Josh Girdley	.30	.10
229 Carl Crawford	.30	.10
230 Luis Montanez RC	.60	.25
231 Ramon Carvajal RC	.60	.25
232 Matt Riley	.30	.10
233 Ben Davis	.30	.10
234 Jason Grabowski	.30	.10
235 Chris George	.30	.10
236 Hank Blalock RC	5.00	2.00
237 Roy Oswalt	.75	.30
238 Eric Reynolds RC	.40	.15
239 Brian Cole	.30	.10
240 Denny Bautista RC	1.00	.40
241 Hector Garcia RC	.40	.15
242 Joe Thurston RC	.60	.25
243 Brad Cresse	.30	.10
244 Corey Patterson	.30	.10
245 Brett Evert RC	.40	.15
246 Elpidio Guzman RC	.40	.15
247 Vernon Wells	.30	.10
248 Roberto Miniel RC	.60	.25
249 Brian Bass RC	.40	.15
250 Mark Burnett RC	.60	.25
251 Juan Silvestre	.30	.10
252 Pablo Ozuna	.30	.10
253 Jayson Werth	.30	.10
254 Russ Jacobson	.30	.10
255 Chad Hermansen	.30	.10

❑ 256 Travis Hafner RC 10.00 4.00
❑ 257 Brad Baker .30 .10
❑ 258 Gookie Dawkins .30 .10
❑ 259 Michael Cuddyer .30 .10
❑ 260 Mark Buehrle .50 .20
❑ 261 Ricardo Aramboles .30 .10
❑ 262 Esix Snead RC .40 .15
❑ 263 Wilson Betemit RC 3.00 1.25
❑ 264 Albert Pujols RC 100.00 50.00
❑ 265 Joe Lawrence .30 .10
❑ 266 Ramon Ortiz .30 .10
❑ 267 Ben Sheets .50 .20
❑ 268 Luke Lockwood RC .60 .25
❑ 269 Toby Hall .30 .10
❑ 270 Jack Cust .30 .10
❑ 271 Pedro Feliz .30 .10
❑ 272 Noel Devarez RC .60 .25
❑ 273 Josh Beckett .50 .20
❑ 274 Alex Escobar .30 .10
❑ 275 Doug Gredvig RC .40 .15
❑ 276 Marcus Giles .30 .10
❑ 277 Jon Rauch .30 .10
❑ 278 Brian Schmitt RC .40 .15
❑ 279 Seung Song RC .60 .25
❑ 280 Kevin Mench .30 .10
❑ 281 Adam Eaton .30 .10
❑ 282 Shawn Sonnier .30 .10
❑ 283 Andy Van Hekken RC .40 .15
❑ 284 Aaron Rowand .30 .10
❑ 285 Tony Blanco RC .60 .25
❑ 286 Ryan Kohlmeier .30 .10
❑ 287 C.C. Sabathia .30 .10
❑ 288 Bubba Crosby .30 .10
❑ 289 Josh Hamilton .30 .10
❑ 290 Dee Haynes RC .40 .15
❑ 291 Jason Marquis .30 .10
❑ 292 Julio Zuleta .30 .10
❑ 293 Carlos Hernandez .30 .10
❑ 294 Matt Lecroy .30 .10
❑ 295 Andy Beal RC .40 .15
❑ 296 Carlos Pena .30 .10
❑ 297 Reggie Taylor .30 .10
❑ 298 Bob Keppel RC .40 .15
❑ 299 Miguel Cabrera 1.50 .60
❑ 300 Ryan Franklin .30 .10
❑ 301 Brandon Phillips .30 .10
❑ 302 Victor Hall RC .60 .25
❑ 303 Tony Pena Jr. .30 .10
❑ 304 Jim Journell RC .60 .25
❑ 305 Cristian Guerrero .30 .10
❑ 306 Miguel Olivo .30 .10
❑ 307 Jin Ho Cho .30 .10
❑ 308 Choo Freeman .30 .10
❑ 309 Danny Borrell RC .40 .15
❑ 310 Doug Mientkiewicz .30 .10
❑ 311 Aaron Herr .30 .10
❑ 312 Keith Ginter .30 .10
❑ 313 Felipe Lopez .30 .10
❑ 314 Jeff Goldbach .30 .10
❑ 315 Travis Harper .30 .10
❑ 316 Paul LoDuca .30 .10
❑ 317 Joe Torres .30 .10
❑ 318 Eric Byrnes .30 .10
❑ 319 George Lombard .30 .10
❑ 320 Dave Krynzel .30 .10
❑ 321 Ben Christensen .30 .10
❑ 322 Aubrey Huff .30 .10
❑ 323 Lyle Overbay .30 .10
❑ 324 Sean McGowan .30 .10
❑ 325 Jeff Heaverlo .30 .10
❑ 326 Timo Perez .30 .10
❑ 327 Octavio Martinez RC .60 .25
❑ 328 Vince Faison .30 .10
❑ 329 David Parrish RC .40 .15
❑ 330 Bobby Bradley .30 .10
❑ 331 Jason Miller RC .40 .15
❑ 332 Corey Spencer RC .40 .15
❑ 333 Craig House .30 .10
❑ 334 Maxim St. Pierre RC .60 .25
❑ 335 Adam Johnson .30 .10
❑ 336 Joe Crede .75 .30
❑ 337 Greg Nash RC .40 .15
❑ 338 Chad Durbin .30 .10
❑ 339 Pat Magness RC .60 .25
❑ 340 Matt Wheatland .30 .10
❑ 341 Julio Lugo .30 .10
❑ 342 Grady Sizemore 1.00 .40
❑ 343 Adrian Gonzalez .30 .10
❑ 344 Tim Raines Jr. .30 .10
❑ 345 Ranier Olmedo RC .60 .25
❑ 346 Phil Dumatrait .30 .10
❑ 347 Brandon Mims RC .40 .15
❑ 348 Jason Jennings .30 .10
❑ 349 Phil Wilson RC .60 .25
❑ 350 Jason Hart .30 .10
❑ 351 Cesar Izturis .30 .10
❑ 352 Matt Butler RC .60 .25
❑ 353 David Kelton .30 .10
❑ 354 Luke Prokopec .30 .10
❑ 355 Corey Smith .30 .10
❑ 356 Joel Pineiro .60 .25
❑ 357 Ken Chenard .30 .10
❑ 358 Keith Reed .30 .10
❑ 359 David Walling .30 .10
❑ 360 Alexis Gomez RC .40 .15
❑ 361 Justin Morneau RC 10.00 4.00
❑ 362 Josh Fogg RC .60 .25
❑ 363 J.R. House .30 .10
❑ 364 Andy Tracy .30 .10
❑ 365 Kenny Kelly .30 .10
❑ 366 Aaron McNeal .30 .10
❑ 367 Nick Johnson .30 .10
❑ 368 Brian Esposito .30 .10
❑ 369 Charles Frazier RC .40 .15
❑ 370 Scott Heard .30 .10
❑ 371 Pat Strange .30 .10
❑ 372 Mike Meyers .30 .10
❑ 373 Ryan Ludwick RC .60 .25
❑ 374 Brad Wilkerson .30 .10
❑ 375 Allen Levrault .30 .10
❑ 376 Seth McClung RC .60 .25
❑ 377 Joe Nathan .30 .10
❑ 378 Rafael Soriano RC .60 .25
❑ 379 Chris Richard .30 .10
❑ 380 Jared Sandberg .30 .10
❑ 381 Tike Redman .30 .10
❑ 382 Adam Dunn .50 .20
❑ 383 Jared Abruzzo RC .40 .15
❑ 384 Jason Richardson RC .40 .15
❑ 385 Matt Holliday .30 .10
❑ 386 Darwin Cubillan RC .40 .15
❑ 387 Mike Nannini .30 .10
❑ 388 Blake Williams RC .40 .15
❑ 389 Valentino Pascucci RC .60 .25
❑ 390 Jon Garland .30 .10
❑ 391 Josh Pressley .30 .10
❑ 392 Jose Ortiz .30 .10
❑ 393 Ryan Hannaman RC .60 .25
❑ 394 Steve Smyth RC .60 .25
❑ 395 John Patterson .30 .10
❑ 396 Chad Petty RC .40 .15
❑ 397 Jake Peavy UER RC 5.00 2.00
❑ 398 Onix Mercado RC .60 .25
❑ 399 Jason Romano .30 .10
❑ 400 Luis Torres RC .60 .25
❑ 401 Casey Fossum RC .40 .15
❑ 402 Eduardo Figueroa RC .40 .15
❑ 403 Bryan Barnowski RC .40 .15
❑ 404 Tim Redding .30 .10
❑ 405 Jason Standridge .30 .10
❑ 406 Marvin Seale RC .60 .25
❑ 407 Todd Moser .30 .10
❑ 408 Alex Gordon .30 .10
❑ 409 Steve Smitherman RC .60 .25
❑ 410 Ben Petrick .30 .10
❑ 411 Eric Munson .30 .10
❑ 412 Luis Rivas .30 .10
❑ 413 Matt Ginter .30 .10
❑ 414 Alfonso Soriano .50 .20
❑ 415 Rafael Boitel RC .40 .15
❑ 416 Dany Morban RC .40 .15
❑ 417 Justin Woodrow RC .60 .25
❑ 418 Wilfredo Rodriguez .30 .10
❑ 419 Derrick Van Dusen RC .40 .15
❑ 420 Josh Spoerl RC .60 .25
❑ 421 Juan Pierre .30 .10
❑ 422 J.C. Romero .30 .10
❑ 423 Ed Rogers RC .40 .15
❑ 424 Tomo Ohka .30 .10
❑ 425 Ben Hendrickson RC .40 .15
❑ 426 Carlos Zambrano .50 .20
❑ 427 Brett Myers .30 .10
❑ 428 Scott Seabol .30 .10
❑ 429 Thomas Mitchell .30 .10
❑ 430 Jose Reyes RC 15.00 6.00
❑ 431 Kip Wells .30 .10
❑ 432 Donzell McDonald .30 .10
❑ 433 Adam Pettyjohn RC .40 .15
❑ 434 Austin Kearns .30 .10
❑ 435 Rico Washington .30 .10
❑ 436 Doug Nickle RC .40 .15
❑ 437 Steve Lomasney .30 .10
❑ 438 Jason Jones RC .40 .15
❑ 439 Bobby Seay .30 .10
❑ 440 Justin Wayne RC .60 .25
❑ ROYR Sasaki/Furcal ROY Jsy 15.00 6.00
❑ NNO Sean Burroughs Ball/80 15.00 6.00

2001 Bowman Draft Picks

❑ COMP.FACT.SET (112) 40.00 20.00
❑ COMPLETE SET (110) 30.00 15.00
❑ BDP1 Alfredo Amezaga RC .30 .10
❑ BDP2 Andrew Good .30 .10
❑ BDP3 Kelly Johnson RC 1.50 .60
❑ BDP4 Larry Bigbie .30 .10
❑ BDP5 Matt Thompson RC .40 .15
❑ BDP6 Wilton Chavez RC .40 .15
❑ BDP7 Joe Borchard RC .40 .15
❑ BDP8 David Espinosa .30 .10
❑ BDP9 Zach Day RC .40 .15
❑ BDP10 Brad Hawpe RC 4.00 1.50
❑ BDP11 Nate Cornejo .30 .10
❑ BDP12 Matt Cooper RC .40 .15
❑ BDP13 Brad Lidge .30 .10
❑ BDP14 Angel Berroa RC .60 .25
❑ BDP15 Lamont Matthews RC .40 .15
❑ BDP16 Jose Garcia .30 .10
❑ BDP17 Grant Balfour RC .30 .10
❑ BDP18 Ron Chiavacci RC .30 .10
❑ BDP19 Jae Seo .30 .10
❑ BDP20 Juan Rivera .30 .10
❑ BDP21 D'Angelo Jimenez .30 .10
❑ BDP22 Juan A.Pena RC .40 .15
❑ BDP23 Marlon Byrd RC .40 .15
❑ BDP24 Sean Burnett .30 .10
❑ BDP25 Josh Pearce RC .40 .15
❑ BDP26 Brandon Duckworth RC .30 .10
❑ BDP27 Jack Taschner RC .30 .10
❑ BDP28 Marcus Thames .30 .10
❑ BDP29 Brent Abernathy .30 .10
❑ BDP30 David Elder RC .30 .10
❑ BDP31 Scott Cassidy RC .40 .15
❑ BDP32 Dennis Tankersley RC .30 .10
❑ BDP33 Denny Stark .30 .10
❑ BDP34 Dave Williams RC .30 .10
❑ BDP35 Boof Bonser RC .30 .10
❑ BDP36 Kris Foster RC .30 .10
❑ BDP37 Luis Garcia RC .40 .15
❑ BDP38 Shawn Chacon .30 .10
❑ BDP39 Mike Rivera RC .40 .15
❑ BDP40 Will Smith RC .40 .15
❑ BDP41 Morgan Ensberg RC 2.00 .75
❑ BDP42 Ken Harvey .30 .10
❑ BDP43 Ricardo Rodriguez RC .40 .15
❑ BDP44 Jose Mieses RC .40 .15
❑ BDP45 Luis Maza RC .30 .10
❑ BDP46 Julio Perez RC .40 .15
❑ BDP47 Dustan Mohr RC .40 .15
❑ BDP48 Randy Flores RC .30 .10
❑ BDP49 Covelli Crisp RC 8.00 3.00

❑ BDP50 Kevin Reese RC .40 .15
❑ BDP51 Brad Thomas UER .30 .10
❑ BDP52 Xavier Nady .30 .10
❑ BDP53 Ryan Vogelsong .30 .10
❑ BDP54 Carlos Silva .30 .10
❑ BDP55 Dan Wright .30 .10
❑ BDP56 Brent Butler .30 .10
❑ BDP57 Brandon Knight RC .30 .10
❑ BDP58 Brian Reith RC .30 .10
❑ BDP59 Mario Valenzuela RC .40 .15
❑ BDP60 Bobby Hill RC .40 .15
❑ BDP61 Rich Rundles RC .40 .15
❑ BDP62 Rick Elder .30 .10
❑ BDP63 J.D. Closser .30 .10
❑ BDP64 Scot Shields .30 .10
❑ BDP65 Miguel Olivo .30 .10
❑ BDP66 Stubby Clapp RC .30 .10
❑ BDP67 Jerome Williams RC .60 .25
❑ BDP68 Jason Lane RC .60 .25
❑ BDP69 Chase Utley RC 15.00 6.00
❑ BDP70 Erik Bedard RC 5.00 2.00
❑ BDP71 Alex Herrera UER RC .30 .10
❑ BDP72 Juan Cruz RC .40 .15
❑ BDP73 Billy Martin RC .30 .10
❑ BDP74 Ronnie Merrill RC .40 .15
❑ BDP75 Jason Kinchen RC .30 .10
❑ BDP76 Wilkin Ruan RC .40 .15
❑ BDP77 Cody Ransom RC .30 .10
❑ BDP78 Bud Smith RC .30 .10
❑ BDP79 Wily Mo Pena .30 .10
❑ BDP80 Jeff Nettles RC .40 .15
❑ BDP81 Jamal Strong RC .30 .10
❑ BDP82 Bill Ortega RC .30 .10
❑ BDP83 Mike Bell .30 .10
❑ BDP84 Ichiro Suzuki RC 8.00 3.00
❑ BDP85 Fernando Rodney RC .30 .10
❑ BDP86 Chris Smith RC .30 .10
❑ BDP87 John VanBenschoten RC .40 .15
❑ BDP88 Bobby Crosby RC 4.00 1.50
❑ BDP89 Kenny Baugh RC .30 .10
❑ BDP90 Jake Gautreau RC .30 .10
❑ BDP91 Gabe Gross RC .60 .25
❑ BDP92 Kris Honel RC .40 .15
❑ BDP93 Dan Denham RC .30 .10
❑ BDP94 Aaron Heilman RC .40 .15
❑ BDP95 Irvin Guzman RC 4.00 1.50
❑ BDP96 Mike Jones RC .60 .25
❑ BDP97 John-Ford Griffin RC .40 .15
❑ BDP98 Macay McBride RC 1.00 .40
❑ BDP99 John Rheinecker RC 1.00 .40
❑ BDP100 Bronson Sardinha RC .30 .10
❑ BDP101 Jason Weintraub RC .30 .10
❑ BDP102 J.D. Martin RC .30 .10
❑ BDP103 Jayson Nix RC .40 .15
❑ BDP104 Noah Lowry RC 2.50 1.00
❑ BDP105 Richard Lewis RC .40 .15
❑ BDP106 Brad Hennessey RC .60 .25
❑ BDP107 Jeff Mathis RC .60 .25
❑ BDP108 Jon Skaggs RC .40 .15
❑ BDP109 Justin Pope RC .40 .15
❑ BDP110 Josh Burrus RC .40 .15

2002 Bowman

❑ COMPLETE SET (440) 80.00 40.00
❑ COMMON CARD (1-110) .30 .10
❑ COMMON CARD (111-440) .30 .10
❑ 1 Adam Dunn .30 .10
❑ 2 Derek Jeter 2.00 .75
❑ 3 Alex Rodriguez 1.25 .50
❑ 4 Miguel Tejada .30 .10
❑ 5 Nomar Garciaparra 1.25 .50
❑ 6 Toby Hall .30 .10
❑ 7 Brandon Duckworth .30 .10
❑ 8 Paul LoDuca .30 .10
❑ 9 Brian Giles .30 .10
❑ 10 C.C. Sabathia .30 .10
❑ 11 Curt Schilling .30 .10
❑ 12 Tsuyoshi Shinjo .30 .10
❑ 13 Ramon Hernandez .30 .10
❑ 14 Jose Cruz Jr. .30 .10
❑ 15 Albert Pujols 1.50 .60
❑ 16 Joe Mays .30 .10
❑ 17 Javy Lopez .30 .10
❑ 18 J.T. Snow .30 .10
❑ 19 David Segui .30 .10
❑ 20 Jorge Posada .50 .20
❑ 21 Doug Mientkiewicz .30 .10
❑ 22 Jerry Hairston Jr. .30 .10
❑ 23 Bernie Williams .50 .20
❑ 24 Mike Sweeney .30 .10
❑ 25 Jason Giambi .30 .10
❑ 26 Ryan Dempster .30 .10
❑ 27 Ryan Klesko .30 .10
❑ 28 Mark Quinn .30 .10
❑ 29 Jeff Kent .30 .10
❑ 30 Eric Chavez .30 .10
❑ 31 Adrian Beltre .30 .10
❑ 32 Andruw Jones .50 .20
❑ 33 Alfonso Soriano .30 .10
❑ 34 Aramis Ramirez .30 .10
❑ 35 Greg Maddux 1.25 .50
❑ 36 Andy Pettitte .50 .20
❑ 37 Bartolo Colon .30 .10
❑ 38 Ben Sheets .30 .10
❑ 39 Bobby Higginson .30 .10
❑ 40 Ivan Rodriguez .50 .20
❑ 41 Brad Penny .30 .10
❑ 42 Carlos Lee .30 .10
❑ 43 Damion Easley .30 .10
❑ 44 Preston Wilson .30 .10
❑ 45 Jeff Bagwell .50 .20
❑ 46 Eric Milton .30 .10
❑ 47 Rafael Palmeiro .50 .20
❑ 48 Gary Sheffield .30 .10
❑ 49 J.D. Drew .30 .10
❑ 50 Jim Thome .50 .20
❑ 51 Ichiro Suzuki 1.50 .60
❑ 52 Bud Smith .30 .10
❑ 53 Chan Ho Park .30 .10
❑ 54 D'Angelo Jimenez .30 .10
❑ 55 Ken Griffey Jr. 1.25 .50
❑ 56 Wade Miller .30 .10
❑ 57 Vladimir Guerrero .75 .30
❑ 58 Troy Glaus .30 .10
❑ 59 Shawn Green .30 .10
❑ 60 Kerry Wood .30 .10
❑ 61 Jack Wilson .30 .10
❑ 62 Kevin Brown .30 .10
❑ 63 Marcus Giles .30 .10
❑ 64 Pat Burrell .30 .10
❑ 65 Larry Walker .30 .10
❑ 66 Sammy Sosa .75 .30
❑ 67 Raul Mondesi .30 .10
❑ 68 Tim Hudson .30 .10
❑ 69 Lance Berkman .30 .10
❑ 70 Mike Mussina .50 .20
❑ 71 Barry Zito .30 .10
❑ 72 Jimmy Rollins .30 .10
❑ 73 Barry Bonds 2.00 .75
❑ 74 Craig Biggio .50 .20
❑ 75 Todd Helton .50 .20
❑ 76 Roger Clemens 1.50 .60
❑ 77 Frank Catalanotto .30 .10
❑ 78 Josh Towers .30 .10
❑ 79 Roy Oswalt .30 .10
❑ 80 Chipper Jones .75 .30
❑ 81 Cristian Guzman .30 .10
❑ 82 Darin Erstad .30 .10
❑ 83 Freddy Garcia .30 .10
❑ 84 Jason Tyner .30 .10
❑ 85 Carlos Delgado .30 .10
❑ 86 Jon Lieber .30 .10
❑ 87 Juan Pierre .30 .10
❑ 88 Matt Morris .30 .10
❑ 89 Phil Nevin .30 .10
❑ 90 Jim Edmonds .30 .10
❑ 91 Maggio Ordonez .30 .10
❑ 92 Mike Hampton .30 .10
❑ 93 Rafael Furcal .30 .10
❑ 94 Richie Sexson .30 .10
❑ 95 Luis Gonzalez .30 .10
❑ 96 Scott Rolen .50 .20
❑ 97 Tim Redding .30 .10
❑ 98 Moises Alou .30 .10
❑ 99 Jose Vidro .30 .10
❑ 100 Mike Piazza 1.25 .50
❑ 101 Pedro Martinez .50 .20
❑ 102 Geoff Jenkins .30 .10
❑ 103 Johnny Damon Sox .50 .20
❑ 104 Mike Cameron .30 .10
❑ 105 Randy Johnson .75 .30
❑ 106 David Eckstein .30 .10
❑ 107 Javier Vazquez .30 .10
❑ 108 Mark Mulder .30 .10
❑ 109 Robert Fick .30 .10
❑ 110 Roberto Alomar .50 .20
❑ 111 Wilson Betemit .30 .10
❑ 112 Chris Tritle RC .30 .10
❑ 113 Ed Rogers .30 .10
❑ 114 Juan Pena .30 .10
❑ 115 Josh Beckett .40 .15
❑ 116 Juan Cruz .30 .10
❑ 117 Noochie Varner RC .40 .15
❑ 118 Taylor Buchholz RC .60 .25
❑ 119 Mike Rivera .30 .10
❑ 120 Hank Blalock .60 .25
❑ 121 Hansel Izquierdo RC .40 .15
❑ 122 Orlando Hudson .30 .10
❑ 123 Bill Hall .40 .15
❑ 124 Jose Reyes .60 .25
❑ 125 Juan Rivera .30 .10
❑ 126 Eric Valent .30 .10
❑ 127 Scotty Layfield RC .40 .15
❑ 128 Austin Kearns .30 .10
❑ 129 Nic Jackson RC .40 .15
❑ 130 Chris Baker RC .40 .15
❑ 131 Chad Qualls RC .50 .20
❑ 132 Marcus Thames .30 .10
❑ 133 Nathan Haynes .30 .10
❑ 134 Brett Evert .30 .10
❑ 135 Joe Borchard .30 .10
❑ 136 Ryan Christianson .30 .10
❑ 137 Josh Hamilton .30 .10
❑ 138 Corey Patterson .30 .10
❑ 139 Travis Wilson .30 .10
❑ 140 Alex Escobar .30 .10
❑ 141 Alexis Gomez .30 .10
❑ 142 Nick Johnson .40 .15
❑ 143 Kenny Kelly .30 .10
❑ 144 Marlon Byrd .30 .10
❑ 145 Kory DeHaan .30 .10
❑ 146 Matt Belisle .30 .10
❑ 147 Carlos Hernandez .30 .10
❑ 148 Sean Burroughs .30 .10
❑ 149 Angel Berroa .30 .10
❑ 150 Aubrey Huff .40 .15
❑ 151 Travis Hafner .40 .15
❑ 152 Brandon Berger .30 .10
❑ 153 David Krynzel .30 .10
❑ 154 Ruben Salazar .30 .10
❑ 155 J.H. House .30 .10
❑ 156 Juan Silvestre .30 .10
❑ 157 Dewon Brazelton .30 .10
❑ 158 Jayson Werth .30 .10
❑ 159 Larry Barnes .30 .10
❑ 160 Elvis Pena .30 .10
❑ 161 Ruben Gotay RC .50 .20
❑ 162 Tommy Marx RC .40 .15
❑ 163 John Suomi RC .40 .15
❑ 164 Javier Colina .30 .10
❑ 165 Greg Sain RC .40 .15
❑ 166 Robert Cosby RC .40 .15
❑ 167 Angel Pagan RC 1.00 .40
❑ 168 Ralph Santana RC .40 .15
❑ 169 Joe Orloski RC .40 .15
❑ 170 Shayne Wright RC .40 .15
❑ 171 Jay Caligiuri RC .40 .15
❑ 172 Greg Montalbano RC .40 .15
❑ 173 Rich Harden RC 3.00 1.25
❑ 174 Rich Thompson RC .40 .15

❑ 175 Fred Bastardo RC .40 .15
❑ 176 Alejandro Giron RC .40 .15
❑ 177 Jesus Medrano RC .40 .15
❑ 178 Kevin Deaton RC .40 .15
❑ 179 Mike Rosamond RC .40 .15
❑ 180 Jon Guzman RC .40 .15
❑ 181 Gerard Oakes RC .40 .15
❑ 182 Francisco Liriano RC 10.00 4.00
❑ 183 Matt Allegra RC .40 .15
❑ 184 Mike Snyder RC .40 .15
❑ 185 James Shanks RC .40 .15
❑ 186 Anderson Hernandez RC .40 .15
❑ 187 Dan Trumble RC .40 .15
❑ 188 Luis DePaula RC .40 .15
❑ 189 Randall Shelley RC .40 .15
❑ 190 Richard Lane RC .40 .15
❑ 191 Antwon Rollins RC .40 .15
❑ 192 Ryan Bukvich RC .40 .15
❑ 193 Derrick Lewis .30 .10
❑ 194 Eric Miller RC .40 .15
❑ 195 Justin Schuda RC .40 .15
❑ 196 Brian West RC .40 .15
❑ 197 Adam Roller RC .40 .15
❑ 198 Neal Frendling RC .40 .15
❑ 199 Jeremy Hill RC .40 .15
❑ 200 James Barrett RC .40 .15
❑ 201 Brett Kay RC .40 .15
❑ 202 Ryan Mottl RC .40 .15
❑ 203 Brad Nelson RC .40 .15
❑ 204 Juan M. Gonzalez RC .40 .15
❑ 205 Curtis Legendre RC .40 .15
❑ 206 Ronald Acuna RC .40 .15
❑ 207 Chris Flinn RC .40 .15
❑ 208 Nick Alvarez RC .40 .15
❑ 209 Jason Ellison RC .75 .30
❑ 210 Blake McGinley RC .40 .15
❑ 211 Dan Phillips RC .40 .15
❑ 212 Demetrius Heath RC .40 .15
❑ 213 Eric Bruntlett RC .40 .15
❑ 214 Joe Jiannetti RC .40 .15
❑ 215 Mike Hill RC .40 .15
❑ 216 Ricardo Cordova RC .40 .15
❑ 217 Mark Hamilton RC .40 .15
❑ 218 David Mattox RC .40 .15
❑ 219 Jose Morban RC .40 .15
❑ 220 Scott Wiggins RC .30 .10
❑ 221 Steve Green .30 .10
❑ 222 Brian Rogers .30 .10
❑ 223 Chin-Hui Tsao .40 .15
❑ 224 Kenny Baugh .30 .10
❑ 225 Nate Teut .30 .10
❑ 226 Josh Wilson RC .40 .15
❑ 227 Christian Parker .30 .10
❑ 228 Tim Raines Jr. .30 .10
❑ 229 Anastacio Martinez RC .40 .15
❑ 230 Richard Lewis .30 .10
❑ 231 Tim Kalita RC .40 .15
❑ 232 Edwin Almonte RC .40 .15
❑ 233 Hee-Seop Choi .30 .10
❑ 234 Ty Howington .30 .10
❑ 235 Victor Alvarez RC .40 .15
❑ 236 Morgan Ensberg .40 .15
❑ 237 Jeff Austin RC .40 .15
❑ 238 Luis Terrero .30 .10
❑ 239 Adam Wainwright .30 .10
❑ 240 Clint Weibl RC .30 .10
❑ 241 Eric Cyr .30 .10
❑ 242 Marlyn Tisdale RC .40 .15
❑ 243 John VanBenschoten .30 .10
❑ 244 Ryan Raburn RC .40 .15
❑ 245 Miguel Cabrera 1.50 .60
❑ 246 Jung Bong .30 .10
❑ 247 Raul Chavez RC .30 .10
❑ 248 Erik Bedard .40 .15
❑ 249 Chris Snelling RC .60 .25
❑ 250 Joe Rogers RC .40 .15
❑ 251 Nate Field RC .40 .15
❑ 252 Matt Herges RC .30 .10
❑ 253 Matt Childers RC .40 .15
❑ 254 Erick Almonte .30 .10
❑ 255 Nick Neugebauer .30 .10
❑ 256 Ron Calloway RC .40 .15
❑ 257 Seung Song .30 .10
❑ 258 Brandon Phillips .30 .10
❑ 259 Cole Barthel RC .30 .10
❑ 260 Jason Lane .40 .15
❑ 261 Jae Seo .30 .10
❑ 262 Randy Flores .30 .10
❑ 263 Scott Chiasson .30 .10
❑ 264 Chase Utley 2.50 1.00
❑ 265 Tony Alvarez .30 .10
❑ 266 Ben Howard RC .40 .15
❑ 267 Nelson Castro RC .40 .15
❑ 268 Mark Lukasiewicz .30 .10
❑ 269 Eric Glaser RC .40 .15
❑ 270 Rob Henkel RC .40 .15
❑ 271 Jose Valverde RC .40 .15
❑ 272 Ricardo Rodriguez .30 .10
❑ 273 Chris Smith .30 .10
❑ 274 Mark Prior .60 .25
❑ 275 Miguel Olivo .30 .10
❑ 276 Ben Broussard .30 .10
❑ 277 Zach Sorensen .30 .10
❑ 278 Brian Mallette RC .30 .10
❑ 279 Brad Wilkerson .30 .10
❑ 280 Carl Crawford .40 .15
❑ 281 Chone Figgins RC 1.50 .60
❑ 282 Jimmy Alvarez RC .40 .15
❑ 283 Gavin Floyd RC 1.00 .40
❑ 284 Josh Bonifay RC .40 .15
❑ 285 Garrett Guzman RC .40 .15
❑ 286 Blake Williams .30 .10
❑ 287 Matt Holliday .30 .10
❑ 288 Ryan Madson .30 .10
❑ 289 Luis Torres .30 .10
❑ 290 Jeff Verplancke RC .40 .15
❑ 291 Nate Espy RC .40 .15
❑ 292 Jeff Lincoln RC .40 .15
❑ 293 Ryan Snare RC .40 .15
❑ 294 Jose Ortiz .30 .10
❑ 295 Eric Munson .30 .10
❑ 296 Denny Bautista .30 .10
❑ 297 Willy Aybar .40 .15
❑ 298 Kelly Johnson .60 .25
❑ 299 Justin Morneau .40 .15
❑ 300 Derrick Van Dusen .30 .10
❑ 301 Chad Petty .30 .10
❑ 302 Mike Restovich .30 .10
❑ 303 Shawn Fagan .30 .10
❑ 304 Yurendell DeCaster RC .40 .15
❑ 305 Justin Wayne .30 .10
❑ 306 Mike Peeples RC .30 .10
❑ 307 Joel Guzman 1.00 .40
❑ 308 Ryan Vogelsong .30 .10
❑ 309 Jorge Padilla RC .40 .15
❑ 310 Grady Sizemore 1.00 .40
❑ 311 Joe Jester RC .40 .15
❑ 312 Jim Journell .30 .10
❑ 313 Bobby Seay .30 .10
❑ 314 Ryan Church RC 1.00 .40
❑ 315 Grant Balfour .30 .10
❑ 316 Mitch Jones .30 .10
❑ 317 Travis Foley RC .40 .15
❑ 318 Bobby Crosby 1.00 .40
❑ 319 Adrian Gonzalez .30 .10
❑ 320 Ronnie Merrill .30 .10
❑ 321 Joel Pineiro .30 .10
❑ 322 John-Ford Griffin .30 .10
❑ 323 Brian Forystek RC .40 .15
❑ 324 Sean Douglass .30 .10
❑ 325 Manny Delcarmen RC .50 .20
❑ 326 Donnie Bridges .30 .10
❑ 327 Jim Kavourias RC .40 .15
❑ 328 Gabe Gross .30 .10
❑ 329 Jon Rauch .30 .10
❑ 330 Bill Ortega .30 .10
❑ 331 Joey Hammond RC .40 .15
❑ 332 Ramon Moreta RC .40 .15
❑ 333 Ron Davenport .30 .10
❑ 334 Brett Myers .40 .15
❑ 335 Carlos Pena .30 .10
❑ 336 Ezequiel Astacio RC .40 .15
❑ 337 Edwin Yan RC .40 .15
❑ 338 Josh Girdley .30 .10
❑ 339 Shaun Boyd .30 .10
❑ 340 Juan Rincon .30 .10
❑ 341 Chris Duffy RC 1.00 .40
❑ 342 Jason Kinchen .30 .10
❑ 343 Brad Thomas .30 .10
❑ 344 David Kelton .30 .10
❑ 345 Rafael Soriano .30 .10
❑ 346 Colin Young RC .40 .15
❑ 347 Eric Byrnes .30 .10
❑ 348 Chris Narveson RC .50 .20
❑ 349 John Rheinecker .30 .10
❑ 350 Mike Wilson RC .40 .15
❑ 351 Justin Sherrod RC .40 .15
❑ 352 Deivi Mendez .30 .10
❑ 353 Wily Mo Pena .40 .15
❑ 354 Brett Roneberg RC .40 .15
❑ 355 Trey Lunsford RC .40 .15
❑ 356 Jimmy Gobble RC .40 .15
❑ 357 Brent Butler .30 .10
❑ 358 Aaron Heilman .30 .10
❑ 359 Wilkin Ruan .30 .10
❑ 360 Brian Wolfe RC .40 .15
❑ 361 Cody Ransom .30 .10
❑ 362 Koyie Hill .30 .10
❑ 363 Scott Cassidy .30 .10
❑ 364 Tony Fontana RC .40 .15
❑ 365 Mark Teixeira 1.50 .60
❑ 366 Doug Sessions RC .40 .15
❑ 367 Victor Hall .30 .10
❑ 368 Josh Cisneros RC .40 .15
❑ 369 Kevin Mench .30 .10
❑ 370 Tike Redman .30 .10
❑ 371 Jeff Heaverlo .30 .10
❑ 372 Carlos Brackley RC .40 .15
❑ 373 Brad Hawpe .30 .10
❑ 374 Jesus Colome .30 .10
❑ 375 David Espinosa .30 .10
❑ 376 Jesse Foppert RC .50 .20
❑ 377 Ross Peeples RC .40 .15
❑ 378 Alex Requena RC .40 .15
❑ 379 Joe Mauer RC 12.00 5.00
❑ 380 Carlos Silva .30 .10
❑ 381 David Wright RC 40.00 15.00
❑ 382 Craig Kuzmic RC .40 .15
❑ 383 Pete Zamora RC .40 .15
❑ 384 Matt Parker RC .40 .15
❑ 385 Keith Ginter .30 .10
❑ 386 Gary Cates Jr. RC .40 .15
❑ 387 Justin Reid RC .40 .15
❑ 388 Jake Mauer RC .40 .15
❑ 389 Dennis Tankersley .30 .10
❑ 390 Josh Barfield RC 2.50 1.00
❑ 391 Luis Maza .30 .10
❑ 392 Henry Pichardo RC .40 .15
❑ 393 Michael Floyd RC .40 .15
❑ 394 Clint Nageotte RC .50 .20
❑ 395 Raymond Cabrera RC .40 .15
❑ 396 Mauricio Lara RC .40 .15
❑ 397 Alejandro Cadena RC .40 .15
❑ 398 Jonny Gomes RC 2.50 1.00
❑ 399 Jason Bulger RC .40 .15
❑ 400 Bobby Jenks RC 1.50 .60
❑ 401 David Gil RC .40 .15
❑ 402 Joel Crump RC .40 .15
❑ 403 Kazuhisa Ishii RC .75 .30
❑ 404 So Taguchi RC .75 .30
❑ 405 Ryan Doumit RC .60 .25
❑ 406 Macay McBride .40 .15
❑ 407 Brandon Claussen .30 .10
❑ 408 Chin-Feng Chen .40 .15
❑ 409 Josh Phelps .30 .10
❑ 410 Freddie Money RC .50 .20
❑ 411 Cliff Bartosh RC .40 .15
❑ 412 Josh Pearce .30 .10
❑ 413 Lyle Overbay .30 .10
❑ 414 Ryan Anderson .30 .10
❑ 415 Terrance Hill RC .40 .15
❑ 416 John Rodriguez RC .50 .20
❑ 417 Richard Stahl .30 .10
❑ 418 Brian Specht .30 .10
❑ 419 Chris Latham RC .30 .10
❑ 420 Carlos Cabrera RC .40 .15
❑ 421 Jose Bautista RC 1.00 .40
❑ 422 Kevin Frederick RC .40 .15
❑ 423 Jerome Williams .30 .10
❑ 424 Napoleon Calzado RC .40 .15
❑ 425 Benito Baez .30 .10
❑ 426 Xavier Nady .30 .10
❑ 427 Jason Botts RC .60 .25
❑ 428 Steve Bechler RC .40 .15
❑ 429 Reed Johnson RC .50 .20
❑ 430 Mark Outlaw RC .40 .15
❑ 431 Billy Sylvester .30 .10
❑ 432 Luke Lockwood .30 .10

❑ 433 Jake Peavy .60 .25
❑ 434 Alfredo Amezaga .30 .10
❑ 435 Aaron Cook RC .40 .15
❑ 436 Josh Shaffer RC .40 .15
❑ 437 Dan Wright .30 .10
❑ 438 Ryan Gripp RC .40 .15
❑ 439 Alex Herrera .30 .10
❑ 440 Jason Bay RC 5.00 2.00

2002 Bowman Draft

❑ COMPLETE SET (165) 50.00 25.00
❑ BDP1 Clint Everts RC .50 .20
❑ BDP2 Fred Lewis RC .40 .15
❑ BDP3 Jon Broxton RC 1.00 .40
❑ BDP4 Jason Anderson RC .40 .15
❑ BDP5 Mike Eusebio RC .40 .15
❑ BDP6 Zack Greinke RC 2.00 .75
❑ BDP7 Joe Blanton RC 2.00 .75
❑ BDP8 Sergio Santos RC .50 .20
❑ BDP9 Jason Cooper RC .40 .15
❑ BDP10 Delwyn Young RC 1.00 .40
❑ BDP11 Jeremy Hermida RC 5.00 2.00
❑ BDP12 Dan Ortmeier RC .50 .20
❑ BDP13 Kevin Jepsen RC .50 .20
❑ BDP14 Russ Adams RC .50 .20
❑ BDP15 Mike Nixon RC .40 .15
❑ BDP16 Nick Swisher RC 5.00 2.00
❑ BDP17 Cole Hamels RC 10.00 4.00
❑ BDP18 Brian Dopirak RC 1.00 .40
❑ BDP19 James Loney RC 6.00 2.50
❑ BDP20 Denard Span RC .50 .20
❑ BDP21 Billy Petrick RC .40 .15
❑ BDP22 Jared Doyle RC .40 .15
❑ BDP23 Jeff Francoeur RC 15.00 6.00
❑ BDP24 Nick Bourgeois RC .40 .15
❑ BDP25 Matt Cain RC 8.00 3.00
❑ BDP26 John McCurdy RC .40 .15
❑ BDP27 Mark Kiger RC .40 .15
❑ BDP28 Bill Murphy RC .40 .15
❑ BDP29 Matt Craig RC .50 .20
❑ BDP30 Mike Megrew RC .40 .15
❑ BDP31 Ben Crockett RC .40 .15
❑ BDP32 Luke Hagerty RC .40 .15
❑ BDP33 Matt Whitney RC .40 .15
❑ BDP34 Dan Meyer RC .50 .20
❑ BDP35 Jeremy Brown RC .40 .15
❑ BDP36 Doug Johnson RC .40 .15
❑ BDP37 Steve Obenchain RC .40 .15
❑ BDP38 Matt Clanton RC .40 .15
❑ BDP39 Mark Teahen RC 1.00 .40
❑ BDP40 Tom Carrow RC .40 .15
❑ BDP41 Micah Schilling RC .40 .15
❑ BDP42 Blair Johnson RC .40 .15
❑ BDP43 Jason Pridie RC .40 .15
❑ BDP44 Joey Votto RC 2.50 1.00
❑ BDP45 Taber Lee RC .40 .15
❑ BDP46 Adam Peterson RC .40 .15
❑ BDP47 Adam Donachie RC .40 .15
❑ BDP48 Josh Murray RC .40 .15
❑ BDP49 Brent Clevlen RC 2.00 .75
❑ BDP50 Chad Pleiness RC .40 .15
❑ BDP51 Zach Hammes RC .40 .15
❑ BDP52 Chris Snyder RC .50 .20
❑ BDP53 Chris Smith RC .40 .15
❑ BDP54 Justin Maureau RC .40 .15
❑ BDP55 David Bush RC 1.00 .40
❑ BDP56 Tim Gilhooly RC .40 .15
❑ BDP57 Blair Barbier RC .40 .15
❑ BDP58 Zach Segovia RC .40 .15
❑ BDP59 Jeremy Reed RC 1.00 .40
❑ BDP60 Matt Pender RC .40 .15
❑ BDP61 Eric Thomas RC .40 .15
❑ BDP62 Justin Jones RC .50 .20
❑ BDP63 Brian Slocum RC .40 .15
❑ BDP64 Larry Broadway RC .40 .15
❑ BDP65 Bo Flowers RC .40 .15
❑ BDP66 Scott White RC .40 .15
❑ BDP67 Steve Stanley RC .40 .15
❑ BDP68 Alex Merricks RC .40 .15
❑ BDP69 Josh Womack RC .40 .15
❑ BDP70 Dave Jensen RC .40 .15
❑ BDP71 Curtis Granderson RC 3.00 1.25
❑ BDP72 Pat Osborn RC .40 .15
❑ BDP73 Nic Carter RC .40 .15
❑ BDP74 Mitch Talbot RC .40 .15
❑ BDP75 Don Murphy RC .40 .15
❑ BDP76 Val Majewski RC .40 .15
❑ BDP77 Javy Rodriguez RC .40 .15
❑ BDP78 Fernando Pacheco RC .40 .15
❑ BDP79 Steve Russell RC .40 .15
❑ BDP80 Jon Slack RC .40 .15
❑ BDP81 John Baker RC .40 .15
❑ BDP82 Aaron Coonrod RC .40 .15
❑ BDP83 Josh Johnson RC 5.00 2.00
❑ BDP84 Jake Blalock RC .50 2.00
❑ BDP85 Alex Hart RC .40 .15
❑ BDP86 Wes Bankston RC 2.00 .75
❑ BDP87 Josh Rupe RC .40 .15
❑ BDP88 Dan Cevette RC .40 .15
❑ BDP89 Kiel Fisher RC .50 .20
❑ BDP90 Alan Rick RC .40 .15
❑ BDP91 Charlie Morton RC .40 .15
❑ BDP92 Chad Spann RC .40 .15
❑ BDP93 Kyle Boyer RC .40 .15
❑ BDP94 Bob Malek RC .40 .15
❑ BDP95 Ryan Rodriguez RC .40 .15
❑ BDP96 Jordan Renz RC .40 .15
❑ BDP97 Randy Frye RC .40 .15
❑ BDP98 Rich Hill RC 2.50 1.00
❑ BDP99 B.J. Upton RC 5.00 2.00
❑ BDP100 Dan Christensen RC .40 .15
❑ BDP101 Casey Kotchman RC 1.00 .40
❑ BDP102 Eric Good RC .30 .10
❑ BDP103 Mike Fontenot RC .40 .15
❑ BDP104 John Webb RC .40 .15
❑ BDP105 Jason Dubois RC .50 .20
❑ BDP106 Ryan Kibler RC .40 .15
❑ BDP107 Jhonny Peralta RC 2.50 1.00
❑ BDP108 Kirk Saarloos RC .40 .15
❑ BDP109 Rhett Parrott RC .40 .15
❑ BDP110 Jason Grove RC .40 .15
❑ BDP111 Colt Griffin RC .40 .15
❑ BDP112 Dallas McPherson RC 1.00 .40
❑ BDP113 Oliver Perez RC 1.00 .40
❑ BDP114 Marshall McDougall RC .40 .15
❑ BDP115 Mike Wood RC .40 .15
❑ BDP116 Scott Hairston RC .50 .20
❑ BDP117 Jason Simontacchi RC .40 .15
❑ BDP118 Taggert Bozied RC .50 .20
❑ BDP119 Shelley Duncan RC .40 .15
❑ BDP120 Dontrelle Willis RC 5.00 2.00
❑ BDP121 Sean Burnett .30 .10
❑ BDP122 Aaron Cook .30 .10
❑ BDP123 Brett Evert .30 .10
❑ BDP124 Jimmy Journell .30 .10
❑ BDP125 Brett Myers .30 .10
❑ BDP126 Brad Baker .30 .10
❑ BDP127 Billy Traber RC .40 .15
❑ BDP128 Adam Wainwright .30 .10
❑ BDP129 Jason Young RC .30 .10
❑ BDP130 John Buck .30 .10
❑ BDP131 Kevin Cash RC .40 .15
❑ BDP132 Jason Stokes RC .50 .20
❑ BDP133 Drew Henson .30 .10
❑ BDP134 Chad Tracy RC 1.00 .40
❑ BDP135 Orlando Hudson .30 .10
❑ BDP136 Brandon Phillips .30 .10
❑ BDP137 Joe Borchard .30 .10
❑ BDP138 Marlon Byrd .30 .10
❑ BDP139 Carl Crawford .30 .10
❑ BDP140 Michael Restovich .30 .10
❑ BDP141 Corey Hart RC 1.50 .60
❑ BDP142 Edwin Almonte .30 .10
❑ BDP143 Francis Beltran RC .40 .15
❑ BDP144 Jorge De La Rosa RC .40 .15
❑ BDP145 Gerardo Garcia RC .40 .15
❑ BDP146 Franklyn German RC .40 .15
❑ BDP147 Francisco Liriano 4.00 1.50
❑ BDP148 Francisco Rodriguez .30 .10
❑ BDP149 Ricardo Rodriguez .30 .10
❑ BDP150 Seung Song .30 .10
❑ BDP151 John Stephens .30 .10
❑ BDP152 Justin Huber RC .75 .30
❑ BDP153 Victor Martinez .75 .30
❑ BDP154 Hee Seop Choi .30 .10
❑ BDP155 Justin Morneau .30 .10
❑ BDP156 Miguel Cabrera 1.25 .50
❑ BDP157 Victor Diaz RC .75 .30
❑ BDP158 Jose Reyes .50 .20
❑ BDP159 Omar Infante .30 .10
❑ BDP160 Angel Berroa .30 .10
❑ BDP161 Tony Alvarez .30 .10
❑ BDP162 Shin Soo Choo RC .75 .30
❑ BDP163 Wily Mo Pena .30 .10
❑ BDP164 Andres Torres .30 .10
❑ BDP165 Jose Lopez RC 2.00 .75

2003 Bowman

❑ COMPLETE SET (330) 60.00 25.00
❑ COMMON CARD (1-155) .30 .10
❑ COMMON CARD (156-330) .30 .10
❑ 1 Garret Anderson .30 .10
❑ 2 Derek Jeter 2.00 .75
❑ 3 Gary Sheffield .30 .10
❑ 4 Matt Morris .30 .10
❑ 5 Derek Lowe .30 .10
❑ 6 Andy Van Hekken .30 .10
❑ 7 Sammy Sosa .75 .30
❑ 8 Ken Griffey Jr. 1.25 .50
❑ 9 Omar Vizquel .50 .20
❑ 10 Jorge Posada .50 .20
❑ 11 Lance Berkman .30 .10
❑ 12 Mike Sweeney .30 .10
❑ 13 Adrian Beltre .30 .10
❑ 14 Richie Sexson .30 .10
❑ 15 A.J. Pierzynski .30 .10
❑ 16 Bartolo Colon .30 .10
❑ 17 Mike Mussina .50 .20
❑ 18 Paul Byrd .30 .10
❑ 19 Bobby Abreu .30 .10
❑ 20 Miguel Tejada .30 .10
❑ 21 Aramis Ramirez .30 .10
❑ 22 Edgardo Alfonzo .30 .10
❑ 23 Edgar Martinez .50 .20
❑ 24 Albert Pujols 1.50 .60
❑ 25 Carl Crawford .30 .10
❑ 26 Eric Hinske .30 .10
❑ 27 Tim Salmon .50 .20
❑ 28 Luis Gonzalez .30 .10
❑ 29 Jay Gibbons .30 .10
❑ 30 John Smoltz .50 .20
❑ 31 Tim Wakefield .30 .10
❑ 32 Mark Prior .50 .20
❑ 33 Magglio Ordonez .30 .10
❑ 34 Adam Dunn .30 .10
❑ 35 Larry Walker .30 .10
❑ 36 Luis Castillo .30 .10
❑ 37 Wade Miller .30 .10
❑ 38 Carlos Beltran .30 .10
❑ 39 Odalis Perez .30 .10
❑ 40 Alex Sanchez .30 .10
❑ 41 Torii Hunter .30 .10

❑ 42 Cliff Floyd .30 .10
❑ 43 Andy Pettitte .50 .20
❑ 44 Francisco Rodriguez .30 .10
❑ 45 Eric Chavez .30 .10
❑ 46 Kevin Millwood .30 .10
❑ 47 Dennis Tankersley .30 .10
❑ 48 Hideo Nomo .75 .30
❑ 49 Freddy Garcia .30 .10
❑ 50 Randy Johnson .75 .30
❑ 51 Aubrey Huff .30 .10
❑ 52 Carlos Delgado .30 .10
❑ 53 Troy Glaus .30 .10
❑ 54 Junior Spivey .30 .10
❑ 55 Mike Hampton .30 .10
❑ 56 Sidney Ponson .30 .10
❑ 57 Aaron Boone .30 .10
❑ 58 Kerry Wood .30 .10
❑ 59 Runelvys Hernandez .30 .10
❑ 60 Nomar Garciaparra 1.25 .50
❑ 61 Todd Helton .50 .20
❑ 62 Mike Lowell .30 .10
❑ 63 Roy Oswalt .30 .10
❑ 64 Raul Ibanez .30 .10
❑ 65 Brian Jordan .30 .10
❑ 66 Geoff Jenkins .30 .10
❑ 67 Jermaine Dye .30 .10
❑ 68 Tom Glavine .50 .20
❑ 69 Bernie Williams .50 .20
❑ 70 Vladimir Guerrero .75 .30
❑ 71 Mark Mulder .30 .10
❑ 72 Jimmy Rollins .30 .10
❑ 73 Oliver Perez .30 .10
❑ 74 Rich Aurilia .30 .10
❑ 75 Joel Pineiro .30 .10
❑ 76 J.D. Drew .30 .10
❑ 77 Ivan Rodriguez .50 .20
❑ 78 Josh Phelps .30 .10
❑ 79 Darin Erstad .30 .10
❑ 80 Curt Schilling .30 .10
❑ 81 Paul Lo Duca .30 .10
❑ 82 Marty Cordova .30 .10
❑ 83 Manny Ramirez .50 .20
❑ 84 Bobby Hill .30 .10
❑ 85 Paul Konerko .30 .10
❑ 86 Austin Kearns .30 .10
❑ 87 Jason Jennings .30 .10
❑ 88 Brad Penny .30 .10
❑ 89 Jeff Bagwell .50 .20
❑ 90 Shawn Green .30 .10
❑ 91 Jason Schmidt .30 .10
❑ 92 Doug Mientkiewicz .30 .10
❑ 93 Jose Vidro .30 .10
❑ 94 Bret Boone .30 .10
❑ 95 Jason Giambi .30 .10
❑ 96 Barry Zito .30 .10
❑ 97 Roy Halladay .30 .10
❑ 98 Pat Burrell .30 .10
❑ 99 Sean Burroughs .30 .10
❑ 100 Barry Bonds 2.00 .75
❑ 101 Kazuhiro Sasaki .30 .10
❑ 102 Fernando Vina .30 .10
❑ 103 Chan Ho Park .30 .10
❑ 104 Andruw Jones .50 .20
❑ 105 Adam Kennedy .30 .10
❑ 106 Shea Hillenbrand .30 .10
❑ 107 Greg Maddux 1.25 .50
❑ 108 Jim Edmonds .30 .10
❑ 109 Pedro Martinez .50 .20
❑ 110 Moises Alou .30 .10
❑ 111 Jeff Weaver .30 .10
❑ 112 C.C. Sabathia .30 .10
❑ 113 Robert Fick .30 .10
❑ 114 A.J. Burnett .30 .10
❑ 115 Jeff Kent .30 .10
❑ 116 Kevin Brown .30 .10
❑ 117 Rafael Furcal .30 .10
❑ 118 Cristian Guzman .30 .10
❑ 119 Brad Wilkerson .30 .10
❑ 120 Mike Piazza 1.25 .50
❑ 121 Alfonso Soriano .30 .10
❑ 122 Mark Ellis .30 .10
❑ 123 Vicente Padilla .30 .10
❑ 124 Eric Gagne .30 .10
❑ 125 Ryan Klesko .30 .10
❑ 126 Ichiro Suzuki 1.50 .60
❑ 127 Tony Batista .30 .10
❑ 128 Roberto Alomar .50 .20
❑ 129 Alex Rodriguez 1.25 .50
❑ 130 Jim Thome .50 .20
❑ 131 Jarrod Washburn .30 .10
❑ 132 Orlando Hudson .30 .10
❑ 133 Chipper Jones .75 .30
❑ 134 Rodrigo Lopez .30 .10
❑ 135 Johnny Damon .50 .20
❑ 136 Matt Clement .30 .10
❑ 137 Frank Thomas .75 .30
❑ 138 Ellis Burks .30 .10
❑ 139 Carlos Pena .30 .10
❑ 140 Josh Beckett .30 .10
❑ 141 Joe Randa .30 .10
❑ 142 Brian Giles .30 .10
❑ 143 Kazuhisa Ishii .30 .10
❑ 144 Corey Koskie .30 .10
❑ 145 Orlando Cabrera .30 .10
❑ 146 Mark Buehrle .30 .10
❑ 147 Roger Clemens 1.50 .60
❑ 148 Tim Hudson .30 .10
❑ 149 Randy Wolf .30 .10
❑ 150 Josh Fogg .30 .10
❑ 151 Phil Nevin .30 .10
❑ 152 John Olerud .30 .10
❑ 153 Scott Rolen .50 .20
❑ 154 Joe Kennedy .30 .10
❑ 155 Rafael Palmeiro .50 .20
❑ 156 Chad Hutchinson .30 .10
❑ 157 Quincy Carter XRC .40 .15
❑ 158 Hee Seop Choi .30 .10
❑ 159 Joe Borchard .30 .10
❑ 160 Brandon Phillips .30 .10
❑ 161 Wily Mo Pena .30 .10
❑ 162 Victor Martinez .50 .20
❑ 163 Jason Stokes .30 .10
❑ 164 Ken Harvey .30 .10
❑ 165 Juan Rivera .30 .10
❑ 166 Jose Contreras RC 1.50 .60
❑ 167 Dan Haren RC .75 .30
❑ 168 Michel Hernandez RC .40 .15
❑ 169 Eider Torres RC .40 .15
❑ 170 Chris De La Cruz RC .40 .15
❑ 171 Ramon Nivar-Martinez RC .40 .15
❑ 172 Mike Adams RC .40 .15
❑ 173 Justin Arneson RC .40 .15
❑ 174 Jamie Athas RC .40 .15
❑ 175 Dwaine Bacon RC .40 .15
❑ 176 Clint Barmes RC 1.00 .40
❑ 177 B.J. Barns RC .40 .15
❑ 178 Tyler Johnson RC .40 .15
❑ 179 Bobby Basham RC .40 .15
❑ 180 T.J. Bohn RC .40 .15
❑ 181 J.D. Durbin RC .40 .15
❑ 182 Brandon Bowe RC .40 .15
❑ 183 Craig Brazell RC .40 .15
❑ 184 Dusty Brown RC .40 .15
❑ 185 Brian Bruney RC .50 .20
❑ 186 Greg Bruso RC .40 .15
❑ 187 Jaime Bubela RC .40 .15
❑ 188 Bryan Bullington RC .40 .15
❑ 189 Brian Burgamy RC .40 .15
❑ 190 Eny Cabreja RC 1.25 .50
❑ 191 Daniel Cabrera RC .75 .30
❑ 192 Ryan Cameron RC .40 .15
❑ 193 Lance Caraccioli RC .40 .15
❑ 194 David Cash RC .40 .15
❑ 195 Bernie Castro RC .40 .15
❑ 196 Ismael Castro RC .50 .20
❑ 197 Daryl Clark RC .40 .15
❑ 198 Jeff Clark RC .40 .15
❑ 199 Chris Colton RC .40 .15
❑ 200 Dexter Cooper RC .40 .15
❑ 201 Callix Crabbe RC .50 .20
❑ 202 Chien-Ming Wang RC 5.00 2.00
❑ 203 Eric Crozier RC .50 .20
❑ 204 Nook Logan RC .50 .20
❑ 205 David DeJesus RC .75 .30
❑ 206 Matt DeMarco RC .40 .15
❑ 207 Chris Duncan RC 3.00 1.25
❑ 208 Eric Eckenstahler .30 .10
❑ 209 Willie Eyre RC .40 .15
❑ 210 Evel Bastida-Martinez RC .40 .15
❑ 211 Chris Fallon RC .40 .15
❑ 212 Mike Flannery RC .40 .15
❑ 213 Mike Oâ ™Keefe RC .40 .15
❑ 214 Ben Francisco RC .40 .15
❑ 215 Kason Gabbard RC .40 .15
❑ 216 Mike Gallo RC .40 .15
❑ 217 Jairo Garcia RC .50 .20
❑ 218 Angel Garcia RC .50 .20
❑ 219 Michael Garciaparra RC .30 .10
❑ 220 Joey Gomes RC .40 .15
❑ 221 Dusty Gomon RC .50 .20
❑ 222 Bryan Grace RC .40 .15
❑ 223 Tyson Graham RC .40 .15
❑ 224 Henry Guerrero RC .40 .15
❑ 225 Franklin Gutierrez RC 1.00 .40
❑ 226 Carlos Guzman RC .50 .20
❑ 227 Matthew Hagen RC .40 .15
❑ 228 Josh Hall RC .40 .15
❑ 229 Rob Hammock RC .40 .15
❑ 230 Brendan Harris RC .50 .20
❑ 231 Gary Harris RC .40 .15
❑ 232 Clay Hensley RC .40 .15
❑ 233 Michael Hinckley RC .50 .20
❑ 234 Luis Hodge RC .40 .15
❑ 235 Donnie Hood RC .50 .20
❑ 236 Travis Ishikawa RC 1.00 .40
❑ 237 Edwin Jackson RC .50 .20
❑ 238 Ardley Jansen RC .50 .20
❑ 239 Ferenc Jongejan RC .40 .15
❑ 240 Matt Kata RC .40 .15
❑ 241 Kazuhiro Takeoka RC .40 .15
❑ 242 Beau Kemp RC .40 .15
❑ 243 Il Kim RC .40 .15
❑ 244 Brennan King RC .40 .15
❑ 245 Chris Kroski RC .40 .15
❑ 246 Jason Kubel RC 2.00 .75
❑ 247 Pete LaForest RC .40 .15
❑ 248 Wil Ledezma RC .40 .15
❑ 249 Jeremy Bonderman RC 3.00 1.25
❑ 250 Gonzalo Lopez RC .40 .15
❑ 251 Brian Luderer RC .40 .15
❑ 252 Ruddy Lugo RC .40 .15
❑ 253 Wayne Lydon RC .40 .15
❑ 254 Mark Malaska RC .40 .15
❑ 255 Andy Marte RC 3.00 1.25
❑ 256 Tyler Martin RC .40 .15
❑ 257 Branden Florence RC .40 .15
❑ 258 Aneudis Mateo RC .40 .15
❑ 259 Derell McCall RC .40 .15
❑ 260 Brian McCann RC 5.00 2.00
❑ 261 Mike McNutt RC .40 .15
❑ 262 Jacabo Meque RC .40 .15
❑ 263 Derek Michaelis RC .40 .15
❑ 264 Aaron Miles RC .50 .20
❑ 265 Jose Morales RC .40 .15
❑ 266 Dustin Moseley RC .40 .15
❑ 267 Adrian Myers RC .40 .15
❑ 268 Dan Neil RC .40 .15
❑ 269 Jon Nelson RC .50 .20
❑ 270 Mike Neu RC .40 .15
❑ 271 Leigh Neuage RC .40 .15
❑ 272 Wes O'Brien RC .40 .15
❑ 273 Trent Oeltjen RC .50 .20
❑ 274 Tim Olson RC .40 .15
❑ 275 David Pahucki RC .40 .15
❑ 276 Nathan Panther RC .40 .15
❑ 277 Arnie Munoz RC .40 .15
❑ 278 Dave Pember RC .40 .15
❑ 279 Jason Perry RC .50 .20
❑ 280 Matthew Peterson RC .40 .15
❑ 281 Ryan Shealy RC 2.50 1.00
❑ 282 Jorge Piedra RC .50 .20
❑ 283 Simon Pond RC .40 .15
❑ 284 Aaron Rakers RC .40 .15
❑ 285 Hanley Ramirez RC 5.00 2.00
❑ 286 Manuel Ramirez RC .50 .20
❑ 287 Kevin Randel RC .40 .15
❑ 288 Darrell Rasner RC .40 .15
❑ 289 Prentice Redman RC .40 .15
❑ 290 Eric Reed RC .40 .15
❑ 291 Wilton Reynolds RC .50 .20
❑ 292 Eric Riggs RC .50 .20
❑ 293 Carlos Rijo RC .40 .15
❑ 294 Rajai Davis RC .40 .15
❑ 295 Aron Weston RC .40 .15
❑ 296 Arturo Rivas RC .40 .15
❑ 297 Kyle Roat RC .40 .15
❑ 298 Bubba Nelson RC .50 .20
❑ 299 Levi Robinson RC .40 .15

❑ 300 Ray Sadler RC .40 .15
❑ 301 Gary Schneidmiller RC .40 .15
❑ 302 Jon Schuerholz RC .40 .15
❑ 303 Corey Shafer RC .40 .15
❑ 304 Brian Shackelford RC .40 .15
❑ 305 Bill Simon RC .40 .15
❑ 306 Haj Turay RC .30 .10
❑ 307 Sean Smith RC .50 .20
❑ 308 Ryan Spataro RC .40 .15
❑ 309 Jemel Spearman RC .40 .15
❑ 310 Keith Stamler RC .40 .15
❑ 311 Luke Steidlmayer RC .40 .15
❑ 312 Adam Stern RC .30 .10
❑ 313 Jay Sitzman RC .40 .15
❑ 314 Thomari Story-Harden RC .50 .20
❑ 315 Terry Tiffee RC .40 .15
❑ 316 Nick Trzesniak RC .40 .15
❑ 317 Denny Tussen RC .40 .15
❑ 318 Scott Tyler RC .50 .20
❑ 319 Shane Victorino RC .75 .30
❑ 320 Doug Waechter RC .50 .20
❑ 321 Brandon Watson RC .40 .15
❑ 322 Todd Wellemeyer RC .40 .15
❑ 323 Eli Whiteside RC .40 .15
❑ 324 Josh Willingham RC 1.00 .40
❑ 325 Travis Wong RC .50 .20
❑ 326 Brian Wright RC .40 .15
❑ 327 Kevin Youkilis RC 2.00 .75
❑ 328 Andy Sisco RC .30 .10
❑ 329 Dustin Yount RC .50 .20
❑ 330 Andrew Dominique RC .40 .15
❑ NNO Hinske/Jennings ROY Relic 15.00 6.00

2003 Bowman Draft

❑ COMPLETE SET (165) 50.00 20.00
❑ 1 Dontrelle Willis .75 .30
❑ 2 Freddy Sanchez .30 .10
❑ 3 Miguel Cabrera .75 .30
❑ 4 Ryan Ludwick .30 .10
❑ 5 Ty Wigginton .30 .10
❑ 6 Mark Teixeira .50 .20
❑ 7 Trey Hodges .30 .10
❑ 8 Laynce Nix .30 .10
❑ 9 Antonio Perez .30 .10
❑ 10 Jody Gerut .30 .10
❑ 11 Jae Weong Seo .30 .10
❑ 12 Erick Almonte .30 .10
❑ 13 Lyle Overbay .30 .10
❑ 14 Billy Traber .30 .10
❑ 15 Andres Torres .30 .10
❑ 16 Jose Valverde .30 .10
❑ 17 Aaron Heilman .30 .10
❑ 18 Brandon Larson .30 .10
❑ 19 Jung Bong .30 .10
❑ 20 Jesse Foppert .30 .10
❑ 21 Angel Berroa .30 .10
❑ 22 Jeff DaVanon .30 .10
❑ 23 Kurt Ainsworth .30 .10
❑ 24 Brandon Claussen .30 .10
❑ 25 Xavier Nady .30 .10
❑ 26 Travis Hafner .30 .10
❑ 27 Jerome Williams .30 .10
❑ 28 Jose Reyes .30 .10
❑ 29 Sergio Mitre RC .50 .20
❑ 30 Bo Hart RC .40 .15
❑ 31 Adam Miller RC 2.00 .75
❑ 32 Brian Finch RC .40 .15
❑ 33 Taylor Mattingly RC .50 .20
❑ 34 Daric Barton RC 2.50 1.00
❑ 35 Chris Ray RC 1.00 .40
❑ 36 Jarrod Saltalamacchia RC 5.00 2.00
❑ 37 Dennis Dove RC .50 .20
❑ 38 James Houser RC .50 .20
❑ 39 Clint King RC .50 .20
❑ 40 Lou Palmisano RC .50 .20
❑ 41 Dan Moore RC .40 .15
❑ 42 Craig Stansberry RC .50 .20
❑ 43 Jo Jo Reyes RC 1.25 .50
❑ 44 Jake Stevens RC .50 .20
❑ 45 Tom Gorzelanny RC 1.25 .50
❑ 46 Brian Marshall RC .40 .15
❑ 47 Scott Beerer RC .40 .15
❑ 48 Javi Herrera RC .50 .20
❑ 49 Steve LeRud RC .50 .20
❑ 50 Josh Banks RC .75 .30
❑ 51 Jon Papelbon RC 12.00 5.00
❑ 52 Juan Valdes RC .50 .20
❑ 53 Beau Vaughan RC .50 .20
❑ 54 Matt Chico RC .50 .20
❑ 55 Todd Jennings RC .50 .20
❑ 56 Anthony Gwynn RC 1.25 .50
❑ 57 Matt Harrison RC .75 .30
❑ 58 Aaron Marsden RC .50 .20
❑ 59 Casey Abrams RC .40 .15
❑ 60 Cory Stuart RC .40 .15
❑ 61 Mike Wagner RC .40 .15
❑ 62 Jordan Pratt RC .50 .20
❑ 63 Andre Randolph RC .50 .20
❑ 64 Blake Balkcom RC .50 .20
❑ 65 Josh Muecke RC .40 .15
❑ 66 Jamie D'Antona RC .75 .30
❑ 67 Cole Seifrig RC .40 .15
❑ 68 Josh Anderson RC .50 .20
❑ 69 Matt Lorenzo RC .50 .20
❑ 70 Nate Spears RC .50 .20
❑ 71 Chris Goodman RC .40 .15
❑ 72 Brian McFall RC .40 .15
❑ 73 Billy Hogan RC .50 .20
❑ 74 Jamie Romak RC .50 .20
❑ 75 Jeff Cook RC .50 .20
❑ 76 Brooks McNiven RC .40 .15
❑ 77 Xavier Paul RC .50 .20
❑ 78 Bob Zimmerman RC .40 .15
❑ 79 Mickey Hall RC .50 .20
❑ 80 Shaun Marcum RC .50 .20
❑ 81 Matt Nachreiner RC .50 .20
❑ 82 Chris Kinsey RC .40 .15
❑ 83 Jonathan Fulton RC .50 .20
❑ 84 Edgardo Baez RC .50 .20
❑ 85 Robert Valido RC .50 .20
❑ 86 Kenny Lewis RC .50 .20
❑ 87 Trent Peterson RC .40 .15
❑ 88 Johnny Woodard RC .50 .20
❑ 89 Wes Littleton RC .50 .20
❑ 90 Sean Rodriguez RC 1.50 .60
❑ 91 Kyle Pearson RC .40 .15
❑ 92 Josh Rainwater RC .50 .20
❑ 93 Travis Schlichting RC .50 .20
❑ 94 Tim Battle RC .75 .30
❑ 95 Aaron Hill RC .75 .30
❑ 96 Bob McCrory RC .40 .15
❑ 97 Rick Guarno RC .50 .20
❑ 98 Brandon Yarbrough RC .40 .15
❑ 99 Peter Stonard RC .40 .15
❑ 100 Darin Downs RC .50 .20
❑ 101 Matt Bruback RC .30 .10
❑ 102 Danny Garcia RC .40 .15
❑ 103 Cory Stewart RC .40 .15
❑ 104 Ferdin Tejeda RC .40 .15
❑ 105 Kade Johnson RC .40 .15
❑ 106 Andrew Brown RC .50 .20
❑ 107 Aquilino Lopez RC .40 .15
❑ 108 Stephen Randolph RC .40 .15
❑ 109 Dave Matranga RC .40 .15
❑ 110 Dustin McGowan RC .50 .20
❑ 111 Juan Camacho RC .40 .15
❑ 112 Cliff Lee .30 .10
❑ 113 Jeff Duncan RC .40 .15
❑ 114 C.J. Wilson .30 .10
❑ 115 Brandon Roberson RC .40 .15
❑ 116 David Corrente RC .40 .15
❑ 117 Kevin Beavers RC .40 .15
❑ 118 Anthony Webster RC .50 .20
❑ 119 Oscar Villarreal RC .40 .15
❑ 120 Hong-Chih Kuo RC 2.50 1.00
❑ 121 Josh Barfield .30 .10
❑ 122 Denny Bautista .30 .10
❑ 123 Chris Burke RC 1.25 .50
❑ 124 Robinson Cano RC 6.00 2.50
❑ 125 Jose Castillo .30 .10
❑ 126 Neal Cotts .30 .10
❑ 127 Jorge De La Rosa .30 .10
❑ 128 J.D. Durbin .40 .15
❑ 129 Edwin Encarnacion 1.00 .40
❑ 130 Gavin Floyd .30 .10
❑ 131 Alexis Gomez .30 .10
❑ 132 Edgar Gonzalez RC .40 .15
❑ 133 Khalil Greene .75 .30
❑ 134 Zack Greinke .30 .10
❑ 135 Franklin Gutierrez .50 .20
❑ 136 Rich Harden .50 .20
❑ 137 J.J. Hardy RC 1.50 .60
❑ 138 Ryan Howard RC 30.00 12.50
❑ 139 Justin Huber .30 .10
❑ 140 David Kelton .30 .10
❑ 141 Dave Krynzel .30 .10
❑ 142 Pete LaForest .40 .15
❑ 143 Adam LaRoche .30 .10
❑ 144 Preston Larrison RC .50 .20
❑ 145 John Maine RC 3.00 1.25
❑ 146 Andy Marte 1.25 .50
❑ 147 Jeff Mathis .30 .10
❑ 148 Joe Mauer .75 .30
❑ 149 Clint Nageotte .30 .10
❑ 150 Chris Narveson .30 .10
❑ 151 Ramon Nivar .40 .15
❑ 152 Felix Pie RC 4.00 1.50
❑ 153 Guillermo Quiroz RC .40 .15
❑ 154 Rene Reyes .30 .10
❑ 155 Royce Ring .30 .10
❑ 156 Alexis Rios 1.00 .40
❑ 157 Grady Sizemore .75 .30
❑ 158 Stephen Smitherman .30 .10
❑ 159 Seung Song .30 .10
❑ 160 Scott Thorman .30 .10
❑ 161 Chad Tracy .30 .10
❑ 162 Chin-Hui Tsao .30 .10
❑ 163 John VanBenschoten .30 .10
❑ 164 Kevin Youkilis 1.50 .60
❑ 165 Chien-Ming Wang 5.00 2.00

2004 Bowman

❑ COMPLETE SET (330) 80.00 40.00
❑ ROY ODDS 1:829 H, 1:284 HTA, 1:1632 R

❑ 1 Garret Anderson .30 .10
❑ 2 Larry Walker .30 .10
❑ 3 Derek Jeter 1.50 .60
❑ 4 Curt Schilling .50 .20
❑ 5 Carlos Zambrano .30 .10
❑ 6 Shawn Green .30 .10
❑ 7 Manny Ramirez .50 .20
❑ 8 Randy Johnson .75 .30
❑ 9 Jeremy Bonderman .30 .10
❑ 10 Alfonso Soriano .30 .10
❑ 11 Scott Rolen .50 .20
❑ 12 Kerry Wood .30 .10
❑ 13 Eric Gagne .30 .10
❑ 14 Ryan Klesko .30 .10
❑ 15 Kevin Millar .30 .10
❑ 16 Ty Wigginton .30 .10
❑ 17 David Ortiz .75 .30

❑ 18 Luis Castillo .30 .10
❑ 19 Bernie Williams .50 .20
❑ 20 Edgar Renteria .30 .10
❑ 21 Matt Kata .30 .10
❑ 22 Bartolo Colon .30 .10
❑ 23 Derrek Lee .50 .20
❑ 24 Gary Sheffield .30 .10
❑ 25 Nomar Garciaparra 1.25 .50
❑ 26 Kevin Millwood .30 .10
❑ 27 Corey Patterson .30 .10
❑ 28 Carlos Beltran .30 .10
❑ 29 Mike Lieberthal .30 .10
❑ 30 Troy Glaus .30 .10
❑ 31 Preston Wilson .30 .10
❑ 32 Jorge Posada .50 .20
❑ 33 Bo Hart .30 .10
❑ 34 Mark Prior .50 .20
❑ 35 Hideo Nomo .75 .30
❑ 36 Jason Kendall .30 .10
❑ 37 Roger Clemens 1.50 .60
❑ 38 Dmitri Young .30 .10
❑ 39 Jason Giambi .30 .10
❑ 40 Jim Edmonds .30 .10
❑ 41 Ryan Ludwick .30 .10
❑ 42 Brandon Webb .30 .10
❑ 43 Todd Helton .50 .20
❑ 44 Jacque Jones .30 .10
❑ 45 Jamie Moyer .30 .10
❑ 46 Tim Salmon .50 .20
❑ 47 Kelvim Escobar .30 .10
❑ 48 Tony Batista .30 .10
❑ 49 Nick Johnson .30 .10
❑ 50 Jim Thome .50 .20
❑ 51 Casey Blake .30 .10
❑ 52 Trot Nixon .30 .10
❑ 53 Luis Gonzalez .30 .10
❑ 54 Dontrelle Willis .50 .20
❑ 55 Mike Mussina .50 .20
❑ 56 Carl Crawford .30 .10
❑ 57 Mark Buehrle .30 .10
❑ 58 Scott Podsednik .30 .10
❑ 59 Brian Giles .30 .10
❑ 60 Rafael Furcal .30 .10
❑ 61 Miguel Cabrera .50 .20
❑ 62 Rich Harden .30 .10
❑ 63 Mark Teixeira .50 .20
❑ 64 Frank Thomas .75 .30
❑ 65 Johan Santana .75 .30
❑ 66 Jason Schmidt .30 .10
❑ 67 Aramis Ramirez .30 .10
❑ 68 Jose Reyes .30 .10
❑ 69 Magglio Ordonez .30 .10
❑ 70 Mike Sweeney .30 .10
❑ 71 Eric Chavez .30 .10
❑ 72 Rocco Baldelli .30 .10
❑ 73 Sammy Sosa .75 .30
❑ 74 Javy Lopez .30 .10
❑ 75 Roy Oswalt .30 .10
❑ 76 Raul Ibanez .30 .10
❑ 77 Ivan Rodriguez .50 .20
❑ 78 Jerome Williams .30 .10
❑ 79 Carlos Lee .30 .10
❑ 80 Geoff Jenkins .30 .10
❑ 81 Sean Burroughs .30 .10
❑ 82 Marcus Giles .30 .10
❑ 83 Mike Lowell .30 .10
❑ 84 Barry Zito .30 .10
❑ 85 Aubrey Huff .30 .10
❑ 86 Esteban Loaiza .30 .10
❑ 87 Torii Hunter .30 .10
❑ 88 Phil Nevin .30 .10
❑ 89 Andruw Jones .50 .20
❑ 90 Josh Beckett .30 .10
❑ 91 Mark Mulder .30 .10
❑ 92 Hank Blalock .30 .10
❑ 93 Jason Phillips .30 .10
❑ 94 Russ Ortiz .30 .10
❑ 95 Juan Pierre .30 .10
❑ 96 Tom Glavine .50 .20
❑ 97 Gil Meche .30 .10
❑ 98 Ramon Ortiz .30 .10
❑ 99 Richie Sexson .30 .10
❑ 100 Albert Pujols 1.50 .60
❑ 101 Javier Vazquez .30 .10
❑ 102 Johnny Damon .50 .20
❑ 103 Alex Rodriguez Yanks 1.25 .50
❑ 104 Omar Vizquel .50 .20
❑ 105 Chipper Jones .75 .30
❑ 106 Lance Berkman .30 .10
❑ 107 Tim Hudson .30 .10
❑ 108 Carlos Delgado .30 .10
❑ 109 Austin Kearns .30 .10
❑ 110 Orlando Cabrera .30 .10
❑ 111 Edgar Martinez .50 .20
❑ 112 Melvin Mora .30 .10
❑ 113 Jeff Bagwell .50 .20
❑ 114 Marlon Byrd .30 .10
❑ 115 Vernon Wells .30 .10
❑ 116 C.C. Sabathia .30 .10
❑ 117 Cliff Floyd .30 .10
❑ 118 Ichiro Suzuki 1.50 .60
❑ 119 Miguel Olivo .30 .10
❑ 120 Mike Piazza 1.25 .50
❑ 121 Adam Dunn .30 .10
❑ 122 Paul Lo Duca .30 .10
❑ 123 Brett Myers .30 .10
❑ 124 Michael Young .30 .10
❑ 125 Sidney Ponson .30 .10
❑ 126 Greg Maddux 1.25 .50
❑ 127 Vladimir Guerrero .75 .30
❑ 128 Miguel Tejada .30 .10
❑ 129 Andy Pettitte .50 .20
❑ 130 Rafael Palmeiro .50 .20
❑ 131 Ken Griffey Jr. 1.25 .50
❑ 132 Shannon Stewart .30 .10
❑ 133 Joel Pineiro .30 .10
❑ 134 Luis Matos .30 .10
❑ 135 Jeff Kent .30 .10
❑ 136 Randy Wolf .30 .10
❑ 137 Chris Woodward .30 .10
❑ 138 Jody Gerut .30 .10
❑ 139 Jose Vidro .30 .10
❑ 140 Bret Boone .30 .10
❑ 141 Bill Mueller .30 .10
❑ 142 Angel Berroa .30 .10
❑ 143 Bobby Abreu .30 .10
❑ 144 Roy Halladay .30 .10
❑ 145 Delmon Young .50 .20
❑ 146 Jonny Gomes .30 .10
❑ 147 Rickie Weeks .30 .10
❑ 148 Edwin Jackson .30 .10
❑ 149 Neal Cotts .30 .10
❑ 150 Jason Bay .30 .10
❑ 151 Khalil Greene .50 .20
❑ 152 Joe Mauer .75 .30
❑ 153 Bobby Jenks .30 .10
❑ 154 Chin-Feng Chen .30 .10
❑ 155 Chien-Ming Wang 1.00 .40
❑ 156 Mickey Hall .30 .10
❑ 157 James Houser .30 .10
❑ 158 Jay Sborz .30 .10
❑ 159 Jonathan Fulton .30 .10
❑ 160 Steven Lerud .30 .10
❑ 161 Grady Sizemore .75 .30
❑ 162 Felix Pie .50 .20
❑ 163 Dustin McGowan .30 .10
❑ 164 Chris Lubanski .30 .10
❑ 165 Tom Gorzelanny .30 .10
❑ 166 Rudy Guillen FY RC .75 .30
❑ 167 Bobby Brownlie FY RC 1.00 .40
❑ 168 Conor Jackson FY RC 3.00 1.25
❑ 169 Matt Moses FY RC 1.00 .40
❑ 170 Ervin Santana FY RC 1.50 .60
❑ 171 Merkin Valdez FY RC .50 .20
❑ 172 Erick Aybar FY RC 1.00 .40
❑ 173 Brad Sullivan FY RC .50 .20
❑ 174 David Aardsma FY RC .50 .20
❑ 175 Brad Snyder FY RC 1.00 .40
❑ 176 Alberto Callaspo FY RC .75 .30
❑ 177 Brandon Medders FY RC .40 .15
❑ 178 Zach Miner FY RC 1.25 .50
❑ 179 Charlie Zink FY RC .30 .10
❑ 180 Adam Greenberg FY RC .75 .30
❑ 181 Kevin Howard FY RC .50 .20
❑ 182 Wanell Severino FY RC .30 .10
❑ 183 Kevin Kouzmanoff FY RC 2.00 .75
❑ 184 Joel Zumaya FY RC 5.00 2.00
❑ 185 Skip Schumaker FY RC .40 .15
❑ 186 Nic Ungs FY RC .40 .15
❑ 187 Todd Self FY RC .50 .20
❑ 188 Brian Steffek FY RC .30 .10
❑ 189 Brock Peterson FY RC .40 .15
❑ 190 Greg Thissen FY RC .40 .15
❑ 191 Frank Brooks FY RC .30 .10
❑ 192 Estee Harris FY RC .50 .20
❑ 193 Chris Mabeus FY RC .40 .15
❑ 194 Dan Giese FY RC .40 .15
❑ 195 Jared Wells FY RC .30 .10
❑ 196 Carlos Sosa FY RC .40 .15
❑ 197 Bobby Madritsch FY .30 .10
❑ 198 Calvin Hayes FY RC .50 .20
❑ 199 Omar Quintanilla FY RC .50 .20
❑ 200 Chris O'Riordan FY RC .40 .15
❑ 201 Tim Hutting FY RC .30 .10
❑ 202 Carlos Quentin FY RC 2.50 1.00
❑ 203 Brayan Pena FY RC .40 .15
❑ 204 Jeff Salazar FY RC 1.00 .40
❑ 205 David Murphy FY RC .75 .30
❑ 206 Alberto Garcia FY RC .50 .20
❑ 207 Ramon Ramirez FY RC .40 .15
❑ 208 Luis Bolivar FY RC .50 .20
❑ 209 Rodney Choy Foo FY RC .30 .10
❑ 210 Kyle Sleeth FY RC .50 .20
❑ 211 Anthony Acevedo FY RC .40 .15
❑ 212 Chad Santos FY RC .40 .15
❑ 213 Jason Frasor FY RC .40 .15
❑ 214 Jesse Roman FY RC .30 .10
❑ 215 James Tomlin FY RC .40 .15
❑ 216 Josh Labandeira FY RC .40 .15
❑ 217 Joaquin Arias FY RC .75 .30
❑ 218 Don Sutton FY UER RC 1.00 .40
❑ 219 Danny Gonzalez FY RC .30 .10
❑ 220 Javier Guzman FY RC .50 .20
❑ 221 Anthony Lerew FY RC .75 .30
❑ 222 Jon Knott FY RC .40 .15
❑ 223 Jesse English FY RC .40 .15
❑ 224 Felix Hernandez FY RC 6.00 2.50
❑ 225 Travis Hanson FY RC .50 .20
❑ 226 Jesse Floyd FY RC .40 .15
❑ 227 Nick Gorneault FY RC .50 .20
❑ 228 Craig Ansman FY RC .40 .15
❑ 229 Wardell Starling FY RC .40 .15
❑ 230 Carl Loadenthal FY RC .50 .20
❑ 231 Dave Crouthers FY RC .30 .10
❑ 232 Harvey Garcia FY RC .30 .10
❑ 233 Casey Kopitzke FY RC .30 .10
❑ 234 Ricky Nolasco FY RC 1.25 .50
❑ 235 Miguel Perez FY RC .40 .15
❑ 236 Ryan Mulhern FY RC .40 .15
❑ 237 Chris Aguila FY RC .40 .15
❑ 238 Brooks Conrad FY RC .50 .20
❑ 239 Damaso Espino FY RC .30 .10
❑ 240 Jereme Milons FY RC .50 .20
❑ 241 Luke Hughes FY RC .30 .10
❑ 242 Kory Casto FY RC .50 .20
❑ 243 Jose Valdez FY RC .40 .15
❑ 244 J.T. Stotts FY RC .30 .10
❑ 245 Lee Gwaltney FY RC .30 .10
❑ 246 Yoann Torrealba FY RC .30 .10
❑ 247 Omar Falcon FY RC .40 .15
❑ 248 Jon Coutlangus FY RC .30 .10
❑ 249 George Sherrill FY RC .40 .15
❑ 250 John Santor FY RC .30 .10
❑ 251 Tony Richie FY RC .40 .15
❑ 252 Kevin Richardson FY RC .30 .10
❑ 253 Tim Bittner FY RC .40 .15
❑ 254 Dustin Nippert FY RC 1.25 .50
❑ 255 Jose Capellan FY RC .50 .20
❑ 256 Donald Levinski FY RC .30 .10
❑ 257 Jerome Gamble FY RC .30 .10
❑ 258 Jeff Keppinger FY RC .40 .15
❑ 259 Jason Szuminski FY RC .30 .10
❑ 260 Akinori Otsuka FY RC .40 .15
❑ 261 Ryan Budde FY RC .40 .15
❑ 262 Shingo Takatsu FY RC .75 .30
❑ 263 Jeff Allison FY RC .40 .15
❑ 264 Hector Gimenez FY RC .30 .10
❑ 265 Tim Frend FY RC .40 .15
❑ 266 Tom Farmer FY RC .40 .15
❑ 267 Shawn Hill FY RC .40 .15
❑ 268 Lastings Milledge FY RC 5.00 2.00
❑ 269 Scott Proctor FY RC .50 .20
❑ 270 Jorge Mejia FY RC .40 .15
❑ 271 Terry Jones FY RC .50 .20
❑ 272 Zach Duke FY RC 2.00 .75
❑ 273 Tim Stauffer FY RC .75 .30
❑ 274 Luke Anderson FY RC .30 .10
❑ 275 Hunter Brown FY RC .30 .10

❑ 276	Matt Lemanczyk FY RC	.40	.15
❑ 277	Fernando Cortez FY RC	.30	.10
❑ 278	Vince Perkins FY RC	.50	.20
❑ 279	Tommy Murphy FY RC	.40	.15
❑ 280	Mike Gosling FY RC	.30	.10
❑ 281	Paul Bacot FY RC	.50	.20
❑ 282	Matt Capps FY RC	.40	.15
❑ 283	Juan Gutierrez FY RC	.40	.15
❑ 284	Teodoro Encarnacion FY RC	.50	.20
❑ 285	Juan Cedeno FY RC	.40	.15
❑ 286	Matt Creighton FY RC	.40	.15
❑ 287	Ryan Hankins FY RC	.30	.10
❑ 288	Leo Nunez FY RC	.40	.15
❑ 289	Dave Wallace FY RC	.40	.15
❑ 290	Rob Tejeda FY RC	.75	.30
❑ 291	Lincoln Holdzkom FY RC	.40	.15
❑ 292	Jason Hirsh FY RC	1.50	.60
❑ 293	Tydus Meadows FY RC	.40	.15
❑ 294	Khalid Ballouli FY RC	.30	.10
❑ 295	Benji DeQuin FY RC	.30	.10
❑ 296	Tyler Davidson FY RC	1.50	.60
❑ 297	Brant Colamarino FY RC	.75	.30
❑ 298	Marcus McBeth FY RC	.30	.10
❑ 299	Brad Eldred FY RC	.60	.25
❑ 300	David Pauley FY RC	1.25	.50
❑ 301	Yadier Molina FY RC	1.50	.60
❑ 302	Chris Shelton FY RC	1.25	.50
❑ 303	Travis Blackley FY RC	.40	.15
❑ 304	Jon DeVries FY RC	.40	.15
❑ 305	Sheldon Fulse FY RC	.30	.10
❑ 306	Vito Chiaravalloti FY RC	.40	.15
❑ 307	Warner Madrigal FY RC	.75	.30
❑ 308	Reid Gorecki FY RC	.40	.15
❑ 309	Sung Jung FY RC	.30	.10
❑ 310	Pete Shier FY RC	.30	.10
❑ 311	Michael Mooney FY RC	.40	.15
❑ 312	Kenny Perez FY RC	.40	.15
❑ 313	Michael Mallory FY RC	.40	.15
❑ 314	Ben Himes FY RC	.30	.10
❑ 315	Ivan Ochoa FY RC	.40	.15
❑ 316	Donald Kelly FY RC	.40	.15
❑ 317	Logan Kensing FY RC	.40	.15
❑ 318	Kevin Davidson FY RC	.30	.10
❑ 319	Brian Pilkington FY RC	.30	.10
❑ 320	Alex Romero FY RC	.40	.15
❑ 321	Chad Chop FY RC	.40	.15
❑ 322	Dioner Navarro FY RC	.75	.30
❑ 323	Casey Myers FY RC	.30	.10
❑ 324	Mike Rouse FY RC	.40	.15
❑ 325	Sergio Silva FY RC	.30	.10
❑ 326	J.J. Furmaniak FY RC	.75	.30
❑ 327	Brad Vericker FY RC	.40	.15
❑ 328	Blake Hawksworth FY RC	.50	.20
❑ 329	Brock Jacobsen FY RC	.30	.10
❑ 330	Alec Zumwalt FY RC	.30	.10
❑ BW	Berroa Bat/Willis Jsy ROY	15.00	6.00

2004 Bowman Draft

❑ COMPLETE SET (165)	40.00	15.00
❑ COMMON CARD (1-165)	.30	.10
❑ COMMON RC (1-165)	.30	.10
❑ COMMON RC YR	.30	.10
❑ PLATES ODDS 1:559 HOBBY		
❑ PLATES PRINT RUN 1 SERIAL #'d SET		
❑ BLACK-CYAN-MAGENTA-YELLOW EXIST		
❑ NO PLATES PRICING DUE TO SCARCITY		

❑ 1	Lyle Overbay	.30	.10
❑ 2	David Newhan	.30	.10
❑ 3	J.R. House	.30	.10
❑ 4	Chad Tracy	.30	.10
❑ 5	Humberto Quintero	.30	.10
❑ 6	Dave Bush	.30	.10
❑ 7	Scott Hairston	.30	.10
❑ 8	Mike Wood	.30	.10
❑ 9	Alexis Rios	.30	.10
❑ 10	Sean Burnett	.30	.10
❑ 11	Wilson Valdez	.30	.10
❑ 12	Lew Ford	.30	.10
❑ 13	Freddy Thon RC	.40	.15
❑ 14	Zack Greinke	.30	.10
❑ 15	Bucky Jacobsen	.30	.10
❑ 16	Kevin Youkilis	.30	.10
❑ 17	Grady Sizemore	.75	.30
❑ 18	Denny Bautista	.30	.10
❑ 19	David DeJesus	.30	.10
❑ 20	Casey Kotchman	.30	.10
❑ 21	David Kelton	.30	.10
❑ 22	Charles Thomas RC	.40	.15
❑ 23	Kazuhito Tadano RC	.50	.20
❑ 24	Justin Leone RC	.50	.20
❑ 25	Eduardo Villacis RC	.40	.15
❑ 26	Brian Dallimore RC	.30	.10
❑ 27	Nick Green	.30	.10
❑ 28	Sam McConnell RC	.40	.15
❑ 29	Brad Halsey RC	.50	.20
❑ 30	Roman Colon RC	.30	.10
❑ 31	Josh Fields RC	2.00	.75
❑ 32	Cody Bunkelman RC	.50	.20
❑ 33	Jay Rainville RC	1.25	.50
❑ 34	Richie Robnett RC	1.00	.40
❑ 35	Jon Poterson RC	.75	.30
❑ 36	Huston Street RC	2.00	.75
❑ 37	Erick San Pedro RC	.40	.15
❑ 38	Cory Dunlap RC	1.25	.50
❑ 39	Kurt Suzuki RC	1.00	.40
❑ 40	Anthony Swarzak RC	.75	.30
❑ 41	Ian Desmond RC	1.25	.50
❑ 42	Chris Covington RC	.50	.20
❑ 43	Christian Garcia RC	.75	.30
❑ 44	Gaby Hernandez RC	1.25	.50
❑ 45	Steven Register RC	.40	.15
❑ 46	Eduardo Morlan RC	.75	.30
❑ 47	Collin Balester RC	.50	.20
❑ 48	Nathan Phillips RC	.50	.20
❑ 49	Dan Schwartzbauer RC	.50	.20
❑ 50	Rafael Gonzalez RC	.40	.15
❑ 51	K.C. Herren RC	.75	.30
❑ 52	William Susdorf RC	.40	.15
❑ 53	Rob Johnson RC	.50	.20
❑ 54	Louis Marson RC	.75	.30
❑ 55	Joe Koshansky RC	2.00	.75
❑ 56	Jamar Walton RC	.75	.30
❑ 57	Mark Lowe RC	1.50	.60
❑ 58	Matt Macri RC	1.00	.40
❑ 59	Donny Lucy RC	.40	.15
❑ 60	Mike Ferris RC	.50	.20
❑ 61	Mike Nickeas RC	.50	.20
❑ 62	Eric Hurley RC	1.00	.40
❑ 63	Scott Elbert RC	1.00	.40
❑ 64	Blake DeWitt RC	1.50	.60
❑ 65	Danny Putnam RC	.75	.30
❑ 66	J.P. Howell RC	1.00	.40
❑ 67	John Wiggins RC	.40	.15
❑ 68	Justin Orenduff RC	.75	.30
❑ 69	Ray Liotta RC	1.25	.50
❑ 70	Billy Buckner RC	.50	.20
❑ 71	Eric Campbell RC	2.00	.75
❑ 72	Olin Wick RC	.75	.30
❑ 73	Sean Gamble RC	.50	.20
❑ 74	Seth Smith RC	1.00	.40
❑ 75	Wade Davis RC	1.50	.60
❑ 76	Joe Jacobitz RC	.40	.15
❑ 77	J.A. Happ RC	.75	.30
❑ 78	Eric Ridener RC	.40	.15
❑ 79	Matt Tuiasosopo RC	2.00	.75
❑ 80	Brad Bergesen RC	.40	.15
❑ 81	Javy Guerra RC	.50	.20
❑ 82	Buck Shaw RC	.50	.20
❑ 83	Paul Janish RC	.75	.30
❑ 84	Sean Kazmar RC	.40	.15
❑ 85	Josh Johnson RC	.50	.20
❑ 86	Angel Salome RC	1.25	.50
❑ 87	Jordan Parraz RC	.75	.30
❑ 88	Kelvin Vazquez RC	.40	.15
❑ 89	Grant Hansen RC	.40	.15
❑ 90	Matt Fox RC	.40	.15
❑ 91	Trevor Plouffe RC	1.25	.50
❑ 92	Wes Whisler RC	.40	.15
❑ 93	Curtis Thigpen RC	.75	.30
❑ 94	Donnie Smith RC	.50	.20
❑ 95	Luis Rivera RC	.50	.20
❑ 96	Jesse Hoover RC	.50	.20
❑ 97	Jason Vargas RC	1.50	.60
❑ 98	Clary Carlsen RC	.40	.15
❑ 99	Mark Robinson RC	.40	.15
❑ 100	J.C. Holt RC	.50	.20
❑ 101	Chad Blackwell RC	.40	.15
❑ 102	Daryl Jones RC	1.00	.40
❑ 103	Jonathan Tierce RC	.40	.15
❑ 104	Patrick Bryant RC	.40	.15
❑ 105	Eddie Prasch RC	.50	.20
❑ 106	Mitch Einertson RC	.50	.20
❑ 107	Kyle Waldrop RC	1.00	.40
❑ 108	Jeff Marquez RC	.50	.20
❑ 109	Zach Jackson RC	.75	.30
❑ 110	Josh Wahpepah RC	.40	.15
❑ 111	Adam Lind RC	2.00	.75
❑ 112	Kyle Bloom RC	.50	.20
❑ 113	Ben Harrison RC	.40	.15
❑ 114	Taylor Tankersley RC	.50	.20
❑ 115	Steven Jackson RC	.40	.15
❑ 116	David Purcey RC	.75	.30
❑ 117	Jacob McGee RC	1.00	.40
❑ 118	Lucas Harrell RC	.40	.15
❑ 119	Brandon Allen RC	1.00	.40
❑ 120	Van Pope RC	.50	.20
❑ 121	Jeff Francis	.30	.10
❑ 122	Joe Blanton	.30	.10
❑ 123	Wil Ledezma	.30	.10
❑ 124	Bryan Bullington	.30	.10
❑ 125	Jairo Garcia	.30	.10
❑ 126	Matt Cain	1.00	.40
❑ 127	Arnie Munoz	.30	.10
❑ 128	Clint Everts	.30	.10
❑ 129	Jesus Cota	.30	.10
❑ 130	Gavin Floyd	.30	.10
❑ 131	Edwin Encarnacion	.30	.10
❑ 132	Koyie Hill	.30	.10
❑ 133	Ruben Gotay	.30	.10
❑ 134	Jeff Mathis	.30	.10
❑ 135	Andy Marte	.50	.20
❑ 136	Dallas McPherson	.30	.10
❑ 137	Justin Morneau	.30	.10
❑ 138	Rickie Weeks	.30	.10
❑ 139	Joel Guzman	.50	.20
❑ 140	Shin Soo Choo	.30	.10
❑ 141	Yusmeiro Petit RC	2.00	.75
❑ 142	Jorge Cortes RC	.40	.15
❑ 143	Val Majewski	.30	.10
❑ 144	Felix Pie	.50	.20
❑ 145	Aaron Hill	.30	.10
❑ 146	Jose Capellan	.30	.10
❑ 147	Dioner Navarro	.50	.20
❑ 148	Fausto Carmona RC	1.25	.50
❑ 149	Robinzon Diaz RC	.40	.15
❑ 150	Felix Hernandez	3.00	1.25
❑ 151	Andres Blanco RC	.40	.15
❑ 152	Jason Kubel	.30	.10
❑ 153	Willy Taveras RC	1.00	.40
❑ 154	Merkin Valdez	.50	.20
❑ 155	Robinson Cano	.75	.30
❑ 156	Bill Murphy	.30	.10
❑ 157	Chris Burke	.30	.10
❑ 158	Kyle Sleeth	.30	.10
❑ 159	B.J. Upton	.50	.20
❑ 160	Tim Stauffer	.50	.20
❑ 161	David Wright	2.00	.75
❑ 162	Conor Jackson	1.25	.50
❑ 163	Brad Thompson RC	.75	.30
❑ 164	Delmon Young	.50	.20
❑ 165	Jeremy Reed	.30	.10

2005 Bowman

❑ COMPLETE SET (330)	80.00	40.00
❑ COMMON CARD (1-140)	.30	.10
❑ COMMON CARD (141-165)	.40	.15
❑ COMMON CARD (166-330)	.40	.15
❑ PLATE ODDS 1:695 HOBBY, 1:177 HTA		
❑ PLATE PRINT RUN 1 SET PER COLOR		

❑ BLACK-CYAN-MAGENTA-YELLOW ISSUED
❑ NO PLATE PRICING DUE TO SCARCITY
❑ ROY ODDS 1:668 H, 1:248 HTA, 1:1535 R

❑	1	Gavin Floyd	.30	.10
❑	2	Eric Chavez	.30	.10
❑	3	Miguel Tejada	.30	.10
❑	4	Dmitri Young	.30	.10
❑	5	Hank Blalock	.30	.10
❑	6	Kerry Wood	.30	.10
❑	7	Andy Pettitte	.50	.20
❑	8	Pat Burrell	.30	.10
❑	9	Johnny Estrada	.30	.10
❑	10	Frank Thomas	.75	.30
❑	11	Juan Pierre	.30	.10
❑	12	Tom Glavine	.50	.20
❑	13	Lyle Overbay	.30	.10
❑	14	Jim Edmonds	.30	.10
❑	15	Steve Finley	.30	.10
❑	16	Jermaine Dye	.30	.10
❑	17	Omar Vizquel	.50	.20
❑	18	Nick Johnson	.30	.10
❑	19	Brian Giles	.30	.10
❑	20	Justin Morneau	.30	.10
❑	21	Preston Wilson	.30	.10
❑	22	Wily Mo Pena	.30	.10
❑	23	Rafael Palmeiro	.50	.20
❑	24	Scott Kazmir	.30	.10
❑	25	Derek Jeter	1.50	.60
❑	26	Barry Zito	.30	.10
❑	27	Mike Lowell	.30	.10
❑	28	Jason Bay	.30	.10
❑	29	Ken Harvey	.30	.10
❑	30	Nomar Garciaparra	.75	.30
❑	31	Roy Halladay	.30	.10
❑	32	Todd Helton	.50	.20
❑	33	Mark Kotsay	.30	.10
❑	34	Jake Peavy	.30	.10
❑	35	David Wright	1.25	.50
❑	36	Dontrelle Willis	.30	.10
❑	37	Marcus Giles	.30	.10
❑	38	Chone Figgins	.30	.10
❑	39	Sidney Ponson	.30	.10
❑	40	Randy Johnson	.75	.30
❑	41	John Smoltz	.50	.20
❑	42	Kevin Millar	.30	.10
❑	43	Mark Teixeira	.50	.20
❑	44	Alex Rios	.30	.10
❑	45	Mike Piazza	.75	.30
❑	46	Victor Martinez	.30	.10
❑	47	Jeff Bagwell	.50	.20
❑	48	Shawn Green	.30	.10
❑	49	Ivan Rodriguez	.50	.20
❑	50	Alex Rodriguez	1.25	.50
❑	51	Kazuo Matsui	.30	.10
❑	52	Mark Mulder	.30	.10
❑	53	Michael Young	.30	.10
❑	54	Javy Lopez	.30	.10
❑	55	Johnny Damon	.50	.20
❑	56	Jeff Francis	.30	.10
❑	57	Rich Harden	.30	.10
❑	58	Bobby Abreu	.30	.10
❑	59	Mark Loretta	.30	.10
❑	60	Gary Sheffield	.30	.10
❑	61	Jamie Moyer	.30	.10
❑	62	Garret Anderson	.30	.10
❑	63	Vernon Wells	.30	.10
❑	64	Orlando Cabrera	.30	.10
❑	65	Magglio Ordonez	.30	.10
❑	66	Ronnie Belliard	.30	.10
❑	67	Carlos Lee	.30	.10
❑	68	Carl Pavano	.30	.10
❑	69	Jon Lieber	.30	.10
❑	70	Aubrey Huff	.30	.10
❑	71	Rocco Baldelli	.30	.10
❑	72	Jason Schmidt	.30	.10
❑	73	Bernie Williams	.50	.20
❑	74	Hideki Matsui	1.25	.50
❑	75	Ken Griffey Jr.	1.25	.50
❑	76	Josh Beckett	.30	.10
❑	77	Mark Buehrle	.30	.10
❑	78	David Ortiz	.75	.30
❑	79	Luis Gonzalez	.30	.10
❑	80	Scott Rolen	.50	.20
❑	81	Joe Mauer	.75	.30
❑	82	Jose Reyes	.30	.10
❑	83	Adam Dunn	.30	.10
❑	84	Greg Maddux	1.25	.50
❑	85	Bartolo Colon	.30	.10
❑	86	Bret Boone	.30	.10
❑	87	Mike Mussina	.50	.20
❑	88	Ben Sheets	.30	.10
❑	89	Lance Berkman	.30	.10
❑	90	Miguel Cabrera	.50	.20
❑	91	C.C. Sabathia	.30	.10
❑	92	Mike Maroth	.30	.10
❑	93	Andruw Jones	.50	.20
❑	94	Jack Wilson	.30	.10
❑	95	Ichiro Suzuki	1.50	.60
❑	96	Geoff Jenkins	.30	.10
❑	97	Zack Greinke	.30	.10
❑	98	Jorge Posada	.50	.20
❑	99	Travis Hafner	.30	.10
❑	100	Barry Bonds	2.00	.75
❑	101	Aaron Rowand	.30	.10
❑	102	Aramis Ramirez	.30	.10
❑	103	Curt Schilling	.50	.20
❑	104	Melvin Mora	.30	.10
❑	105	Albert Pujols	1.50	.60
❑	106	Austin Kearns	.30	.10
❑	107	Shannon Stewart	.30	.10
❑	108	Carl Crawford	.30	.10
❑	109	Carlos Zambrano	.30	.10
❑	110	Roger Clemens	1.25	.50
❑	111	Javier Vazquez	.30	.10
❑	112	Randy Wolf	.30	.10
❑	113	Chipper Jones	.75	.30
❑	114	Larry Walker	.50	.20
❑	115	Alfonso Soriano	.30	.10
❑	116	Brad Wilkerson	.30	.10
❑	117	Bobby Crosby	.30	.10
❑	118	Jim Thome	.50	.20
❑	119	Oliver Perez	.30	.10
❑	120	Vladimir Guerrero	.75	.30
❑	121	Roy Oswalt	.30	.10
❑	122	Torii Hunter	.30	.10
❑	123	Rafael Furcal	.30	.10
❑	124	Luis Castillo	.30	.10
❑	125	Carlos Beltran	.30	.10
❑	126	Mike Sweeney	.30	.10
❑	127	Johan Santana	.75	.30
❑	128	Tim Hudson	.30	.10
❑	129	Troy Glaus	.30	.10
❑	130	Manny Ramirez	.50	.20
❑	131	Jeff Kent	.30	.10
❑	132	Jose Vidro	.30	.10
❑	133	Edgar Renteria	.30	.10
❑	134	Russ Ortiz	.30	.10
❑	135	Sammy Sosa	.75	.30
❑	136	Carlos Delgado	.30	.10
❑	137	Richie Sexson	.30	.10
❑	138	Pedro Martinez	.50	.20
❑	139	Adrian Beltre	.30	.10
❑	140	Mark Prior	.50	.20
❑	141	Omar Quintanilla	.40	.15
❑	142	Carlos Quentin	.50	.20
❑	143	Dan Johnson	.50	.20
❑	144	Jake Stevens	.40	.15
❑	145	Nate Schierholtz	.50	.20
❑	146	Neil Walker	.40	.15
❑	147	Bill Bray	.40	.15
❑	148	Taylor Tankersley	.40	.15
❑	149	Trevor Plouffe	.50	.20
❑	150	Felix Hernandez	2.00	.75
❑	151	Philip Hughes	.50	.20
❑	152	James Houser	.40	.15
❑	153	David Murphy	.40	.15
❑	154	Ervin Santana	.40	.15
❑	155	Anthony Whittington	.40	.15
❑	156	Chris Lambert	.40	.15
❑	157	Jeremy Sowers	.50	.20
❑	158	Giovanny Gonzalez	.40	.15
❑	159	Blake DeWitt	.50	.20
❑	160	Thomas Diamond	.50	.20
❑	161	Greg Golson	.40	.15
❑	162	David Aardsma	.40	.15
❑	163	Paul Maholm	.40	.15
❑	164	Mark Rogers	.50	.20
❑	165	Homer Bailey	.50	.20
❑	166	Chip Cannon FY RC	1.00	.40
❑	167	Tony Giarratano FY RC	.50	.20
❑	168	Darren Fenster FY RC	.50	.20
❑	169	Elvys Quezada FY RC	.50	.20
❑	170	Glen Perkins FY RC	1.00	.40
❑	171	Ian Kinsler FY RC	2.50	1.00
❑	172	Mike Bourn FY RC	1.00	.40
❑	173	Jeremy West FY RC	.75	.30
❑	174	Justin Verlander FY RC	4.00	1.50
❑	175	Kevin West FY RC	.50	.20
❑	176	Luis Hernandez FY RC	.50	.20
❑	177	Matt Campbell FY RC	.50	.20
❑	178	Nate McLouth FY RC	.75	.30
❑	179	Ryan Goleski FY RC	.75	.30
❑	180	Matthew Lindstrom FY RC	.50	.20
❑	181	Matt DeSalvo FY RC	.75	.30
❑	182	Kole Strayhorn FY RC	.50	.20
❑	183	Jose Vaquedano FY RC	.50	.20
❑	184	James Jurries FY RC	.75	.30
❑	185	Ian Bladergroen FY RC	.75	.30
❑	186	Eric Nielsen FY RC	.50	.20
❑	187	Chris Vines FY RC	.50	.20
❑	188	Chris Denorfia FY RC	1.00	.40
❑	189	Kevin Melillo FY RC	1.00	.40
❑	190	Melky Cabrera FY RC	2.50	1.00
❑	191	Ryan Sweeney FY RC	1.25	.50
❑	192	Sean Marshall FY RC	2.00	.75
❑	193	Andy LaRoche FY RC	4.00	1.50
❑	194	Tyler Pelland FY RC	.75	.30
❑	195	Mike Morse FY RC	.60	.25
❑	196	Wes Swackhamer FY RC	.50	.20
❑	197	Wade Robinson FY RC	.50	.20
❑	198	Dan Santin FY RC	.50	.20
❑	199	Steve Doetsch FY RC	.75	.30
❑	200	Shane Costa FY RC	.50	.20
❑	201	Scott Mathieson FY RC	1.00	.40
❑	202	Ben Jones FY RC	1.00	.40
❑	203	Michael Rogers FY RC	.50	.20
❑	204	Matt Hogelstad FY RC	.50	.20
❑	205	Luis Ramirez FY RC	.50	.20
❑	206	Landon Powell FY RC	.75	.30
❑	207	Erik Cordier FY RC	.50	.20
❑	208	Chris Seddon FY RC	.50	.20
❑	209	Chris Roberson FY RC	.50	.20
❑	210	Thomas Oldham FY RC	.50	.20
❑	211	Dana Eveland FY RC	.50	.20
❑	212	Cody Haerther FY RC	.50	.20
❑	213	Danny Core FY RC	.50	.20
❑	214	Craig Tatum FY RC	.50	.20
❑	215	Elliot Johnson FY RC	.50	.20
❑	216	Ender Chavez FY RC	.50	.20
❑	217	Errol Simonitsch FY RC	.75	.30
❑	218	Matt Van Der Bosch FY RC	.50	.20
❑	219	Eulogio de la Cruz FY RC	.50	.20
❑	220	C.J. Smith FY RC	.50	.20
❑	221	Adam Boeve FY RC	.50	.20
❑	222	Adam Harben FY RC	.75	.30
❑	223	Baltazar Lopez FY RC	.50	.20
❑	224	Russ Martin FY RC	1.50	.60
❑	225	Brian Bannister FY RC	1.00	.40
❑	226	Brian Miller FY RC	.50	.20
❑	227	Casey McGehee FY RC	.50	.20
❑	228	Humberto Sanchez FY RC	2.00	.75
❑	229	Javon Moran FY RC	.50	.20
❑	230	Brandon McCarthy FY RC	1.50	.60
❑	231	Danny Zell FY RC	.50	.20
❑	232	Jake Postlewait FY RC	.50	.20
❑	233	Juan Tejeda FY RC	.50	.20
❑	234	Keith Ramsey FY RC	.50	.20
❑	235	Lorenzo Scott FY RC	.50	.20
❑	236	Wladimir Balentien FY RC	1.00	.40
❑	237	Martin Prado FY RC	.50	.20

❑ 238 Matt Albers FY RC 1.25 .50
❑ 239 Brian Schweiger FY RC .50 .20
❑ 240 Brian Stavisky FY RC .50 .20
❑ 241 Pat Misch FY RC .50 .20
❑ 242 Pat Osborn FY .40 .15
❑ 243 Ryan Feierabend FY RC .50 .20
❑ 244 Shaun Marcum FY .40 .15
❑ 245 Kevin Collins FY RC .50 .20
❑ 246 Stuart Pomeranz FY RC .50 .20
❑ 247 Tetsu Yofu FY RC .50 .20
❑ 248 Hernan Iribarren FY RC .75 .30
❑ 249 Mike Spidale FY RC .50 .20
❑ 250 Tony Arnerich FY RC .50 .20
❑ 251 Manny Parra FY RC .50 .20
❑ 252 Drew Anderson FY RC .50 .20
❑ 253 T.J. Beam FY RC 1.00 .40
❑ 254 Pedro Lopez FY RC .50 .20
❑ 255 Andy Sides FY RC .50 .20
❑ 256 Bear Bay FY RC .75 .30
❑ 257 Bill McCarthy FY RC .50 .20
❑ 258 Daniel Haigwood FY RC 1.00 .40
❑ 259 Brian Sprout FY RC 1.00 .40
❑ 260 Bryan Triplett FY RC .50 .20
❑ 261 Steven Bondurant FY RC .50 .20
❑ 262 Darwinson Salazar FY RC .50 .20
❑ 263 David Shepard FY RC .50 .20
❑ 264 Johan Silva FY RC .50 .20
❑ 265 J.B. Thurmond FY RC .50 .20
❑ 266 Brandon Moorhead FY RC .50 .20
❑ 267 Kyle Nichols FY RC .75 .30
❑ 268 Jonathan Sanchez FY RC 1.25 .50
❑ 269 Mike Esposito FY RC .50 .20
❑ 270 Erik Schindewolf FY RC .50 .20
❑ 271 Peeter Ramos FY RC .50 .20
❑ 272 Juan Senreiso FY RC .50 .20
❑ 273 Matthew Kemp FY RC 4.00 1.50
❑ 274 Vinny Rottino FY RC .50 .20
❑ 275 Micah Furtado FY RC .50 .20
❑ 276 George Kottaras FY RC 1.00 .40
❑ 277 Billy Butler FY RC 4.00 1.50
❑ 278 Buck Coats FY RC .50 .20
❑ 279 Kenny Durost FY RC .50 .20
❑ 280 Nick Touchstone FY RC .50 .20
❑ 281 Jerry Owens FY RC .75 .30
❑ 282 Stefan Bailie FY RC .50 .20
❑ 283 Jesse Gutierrez FY RC .50 .20
❑ 284 Chuck Tiffany FY RC 1.25 .50
❑ 285 Brendan Ryan FY RC .50 .20
❑ 286 Hayden Penn FY RC 1.00 .40
❑ 287 Shawn Bowman FY RC .75 .30
❑ 288 Alexander Smit FY RC .50 .20
❑ 289 Micah Schnurstein FY RC .50 .20
❑ 290 Jared Gothreaux FY RC .50 .20
❑ 291 Jair Jurrjens FY RC 1.25 .50
❑ 292 Bobby Livingston FY RC .50 .20
❑ 293 Ryan Speier FY RC .50 .20
❑ 294 Zach Parker FY RC .50 .20
❑ 295 Christian Colonel FY RC .50 .20
❑ 296 Scott Mitchinson FY RC .50 .20
❑ 297 Neil Wilson FY RC .50 .20
❑ 298 Chuck James FY RC 2.00 .75
❑ 299 Heath Totten FY RC .50 .20
❑ 300 Sean Tracey FY RC .50 .20
❑ 301 Ismael Ramirez FY RC .50 .20
❑ 302 Matt Brown FY RC .50 .20
❑ 303 Franklin Morales FY RC .75 .30
❑ 304 Brandon Sing FY RC .75 .30
❑ 305 D.J. Houlton FY RC .50 .20
❑ 306 Jayce Tingler FY RC .50 .20
❑ 307 Mitchell Arnold FY RC .50 .20
❑ 308 Jim Burt FY RC .50 .20
❑ 309 Jason Motte FY RC .50 .20
❑ 310 David Gassner FY RC .50 .20
❑ 311 Andy Santana FY RC .50 .20
❑ 312 Kelvin Pichardo FY RC .50 .20
❑ 313 Carlos Carrasco FY RC 1.25 .50
❑ 314 Willy Mota FY RC .50 .20
❑ 315 Frank Mata FY RC .50 .20
❑ 316 Carlos Gonzalez FY RC 4.00 1.50
❑ 317 Jeff Niemann FY RC 1.00 .40
❑ 318 Chris B.Young FY RC 2.50 1.00
❑ 319 Billy Sadler FY RC .50 .20
❑ 320 Ricky Barrett FY RC .50 .20
❑ 321 Ben Harrison FY .40 .15
❑ 322 Steve Nelson FY RC .50 .20
❑ 323 Daryl Thompson FY RC .50 .20
❑ 324 Philip Humber FY RC 1.00 .40
❑ 325 Jeremy Harts FY RC .50 .20
❑ 326 Nick Masset FY RC .50 .20
❑ 327 Mike Rodriguez FY RC .50 .20
❑ 328 Mike Garber FY RC .50 .20
❑ 329 Kennard Bibbs FY RC .50 .20
❑ 330 Ryan Garko FY RC 1.50 .60
❑ BC Bay Bat/Crosby Bat ROY 15.00 6.00

2005 Bowman Draft

❑ COMPLETE SET (165) 40.00 15.00
❑ COMMON CARD (1-165) .30 .10
❑ COMMON RC .30 .10
❑ COMMON RC YR .30 .10
❑ OVERALL PLATE ODDS 1:826 HOBBY
❑ PLATE PRINT RUN 1 SET PER COLOR
❑ BLACK-CYAN-MAGENTA-YELLOW ISSUED
❑ NO PLATE PRICING DUE TO SCARCITY
❑ 1 Rickie Weeks .30 .10
❑ 2 Kyle Davies .30 .10
❑ 3 Garrett Atkins .30 .10
❑ 4 Chien-Ming Wang 1.00 .40
❑ 5 Dallas McPherson .30 .10
❑ 6 Dan Johnson .30 .10
❑ 7 Andy Sisco .30 .10
❑ 8 Ryan Doumit .30 .10
❑ 9 J.P. Howell .30 .10
❑ 10 Tim Stauffer .30 .10
❑ 11 Willy Taveras .30 .10
❑ 12 Aaron Hill .30 .10
❑ 13 Victor Diaz .30 .10
❑ 14 Wilson Betemit .30 .10
❑ 15 Ervin Santana .30 .10
❑ 16 Mike Morse .30 .10
❑ 17 Yadier Molina .30 .10
❑ 18 Kelly Johnson .30 .10
❑ 19 Clint Barmes .30 .10
❑ 20 Robinson Cano .50 .20
❑ 21 Brad Thompson .30 .10
❑ 22 Jorge Cantu .30 .10
❑ 23 Brad Halsey .30 .10
❑ 24 Lance Niekro .30 .10
❑ 25 D.J. Houlton .30 .10
❑ 26 Ryan Church .30 .10
❑ 27 Hayden Penn .75 .30
❑ 28 Chris Young .30 .10
❑ 29 Chad Orvella RC .30 .10
❑ 30 Mark Teahen .30 .10
❑ 31 Mark McCormick FY RC .50 .20
❑ 32 Jay Bruce FY RC 2.50 1.00
❑ 33 Beau Jones FY RC .75 .30
❑ 34 Tyler Greene FY RC .75 .30
❑ 35 Zach Ward FY RC .30 .10
❑ 36 Josh Bell FY RC .75 .30
❑ 37 Josh Wall FY RC .50 .20
❑ 38 Nick Webber FY RC .30 .10
❑ 39 Travis Buck FY RC 1.00 .40
❑ 40 Kyle Winters FY RC .50 .20
❑ 41 Mitch Boggs FY RC .30 .10
❑ 42 Tommy Mendoza FY RC .75 .30
❑ 43 Brad Corley FY RC .50 .20
❑ 44 Drew Butera FY RC .30 .10
❑ 45 Ryan Mount FY RC .75 .30
❑ 46 Tyler Herron FY RC .50 .20
❑ 47 Nick Weglarz FY RC .75 .30
❑ 48 Brandon Erbe FY RC 1.00 .40
❑ 49 Cody Allen FY RC .30 .10
❑ 50 Eric Fowler FY RC .30 .10
❑ 51 James Boone FY RC .50 .20
❑ 52 Josh Flores FY RC 1.25 .50
❑ 53 Brandon Monk FY RC .50 .20
❑ 54 Kieron Pope FY RC .75 .30
❑ 55 Kyle Cofield FY RC .30 .10
❑ 56 Brent Lillibridge FY RC .30 .10
❑ 57 Daryl Jones FY .30 .10
❑ 58 Eli Iorg FY RC .50 .20
❑ 59 Brett Hayes FY RC .30 .10
❑ 60 Mike Durant FY RC .75 .30
❑ 61 Michael Bowden FY RC 1.50 .60
❑ 62 Paul Kelly FY RC .50 .20
❑ 63 Andrew McCutchen FY RC 2.00 .75
❑ 64 Travis Wood FY RC 1.00 .40
❑ 65 Cesar Ramos FY RC .50 .20
❑ 66 Chaz Roe FY RC .50 .20
❑ 67 Matt Torra FY RC .50 .20
❑ 68 Kevin Slowey FY RC 1.25 .50
❑ 69 Trayvon Robinson FY RC .50 .20
❑ 70 Reid Engel FY RC .30 .10
❑ 71 Kris Harvey FY RC .75 .30
❑ 72 Craig Italiano FY RC .75 .30
❑ 73 Matt Maloney FY RC 1.00 .40
❑ 74 Sean West FY RC 1.25 .50
❑ 75 Henry Sanchez FY RC .75 .30
❑ 76 Scott Blue FY RC .30 .10
❑ 77 Jordan Schafer FY RC .50 .20
❑ 78 Chris Robinson FY RC .50 .20
❑ 79 Chris Hobdy FY RC .30 .10
❑ 80 Brandon Durden FY RC .30 .10
❑ 81 Clay Buchholz FY RC 1.25 .50
❑ 82 Josh Geer FY RC .30 .10
❑ 83 Sam LeCure FY RC .30 .10
❑ 84 Justin Thomas FY RC .30 .10
❑ 85 Brett Gardner FY RC .50 .20
❑ 86 Tommy Manzella FY RC .30 .10
❑ 87 Matt Green FY RC .30 .10
❑ 88 Yunel Escobar FY RC 1.00 .40
❑ 89 Mike Costanzo FY RC 1.00 .40
❑ 90 Nick Hundley FY RC .30 .10
❑ 91 Zach Simons FY RC .30 .10
❑ 92 Jacob Marceaux FY RC .30 .10
❑ 93 Jed Lowrie FY RC .75 .30
❑ 94 Brandon Snyder FY RC 1.25 .50
❑ 95 Matt Goyen FY RC .30 .10
❑ 96 Jon Egan FY RC .50 .20
❑ 97 Drew Thompson FY RC .50 .20
❑ 98 Bryan Anderson FY RC 1.00 .40
❑ 99 Clayton Richard FY RC .30 .10
❑ 100 Jimmy Shull FY RC .50 .20
❑ 101 Mark Pawelek FY RC 1.50 .60
❑ 102 P.J. Phillips FY RC .75 .30
❑ 103 John Drennen FY RC 1.25 .50
❑ 104 Nolan Reimold FY RC 1.00 .40
❑ 105 Troy Tulowitzki FY RC 2.00 .75
❑ 106 Kevin Whelan FY RC .40 .15
❑ 107 Wade Townsend FY RC .50 .20
❑ 108 Micah Owings FY RC .75 .30
❑ 109 Ryan Tucker FY RC .50 .20
❑ 110 Jeff Clement FY RC 2.50 1.00
❑ 111 Josh Sullivan FY RC .30 .10
❑ 112 Jeff Lyman FY RC .50 .20
❑ 113 Brian Bogusevic FY RC .30 .10
❑ 114 Trevor Bell FY RC .75 .30
❑ 115 Brent Cox FY RC .50 .20
❑ 116 Michael Billek FY RC .30 .10
❑ 117 Garrett Olson FY RC .75 .30
❑ 118 Steven Johnson FY RC .30 .10
❑ 119 Chase Headley FY RC .50 .20
❑ 120 Daniel Carte FY RC .75 .30
❑ 121 Francisco Liriano PROS 1.50 .60
❑ 122 Fausto Carmona PROS .30 .10
❑ 123 Zach Jackson PROS .30 .10
❑ 124 Adam Loewen PROS .30 .10
❑ 125 Chris Lambert PROS .30 .10
❑ 126 Scott Mathieson FY .30 .10
❑ 127 Paul Maholm PROS .30 .10
❑ 128 Fernando Nieve PROS .30 .10
❑ 129 Justin Verlander FY 1.50 .60
❑ 130 Yusmeiro Petit PROS .50 .20
❑ 131 Joel Zumaya PROS .30 .10
❑ 132 Merkin Valdez PROS .30 .10
❑ 133 Ryan Garko FY .75 .30
❑ 134 Edison Volquez FY RC .75 .30
❑ 135 Russ Martin FY .75 .30
❑ 136 Conor Jackson PROS .30 .10

❑ 137 Miguel Montero FY RC 1.00 .40
❑ 138 Josh Barfield PROS .30 .10
❑ 139 Delmon Young PROS .50 .20
❑ 140 Andy LaRoche FY .75 .30
❑ 141 William Bergolla PROS .30 .10
❑ 142 B.J. Upton PROS .30 .10
❑ 143 Hernan Iribarren FY .30 .10
❑ 144 Brandon Wood PROS .75 .30
❑ 145 Jose Bautista PROS .30 .10
❑ 146 Edwin Encarnacion PROS .30 .10
❑ 147 Javier Herrera FY RC 1.25 .50
❑ 148 Jeremy Hermida PROS .75 .30
❑ 149 Frank Diaz PROS RC .30 .10
❑ 150 Chris B.Young FY 1.00 .40
❑ 151 Shin-Soo Choo PROS .30 .10
❑ 152 Kevin Thompson PROS RC .30 .10
❑ 153 Hanley Ramirez PROS .50 .20
❑ 154 Lastings Milledge PROS .30 .10
❑ 155 Luis Montanez PROS .30 .10
❑ 156 Justin Huber PROS .30 .10
❑ 157 Zach Duke PROS .50 .20
❑ 158 Jeff Francoeur PROS .75 .30
❑ 159 Melky Cabrera FY 1.00 .40
❑ 160 Bobby Jenks PROS .30 .10
❑ 161 Ian Snell PROS .30 .10
❑ 162 Fernando Cabrera PROS .30 .10
❑ 163 Troy Patton PROS .50 .20
❑ 164 Anthony Lerew PROS .30 .10
❑ 165 Nelson Cruz FY RC 1.25 .50

2006 Bowman

❑ COMP.SET w/o AU's (220) 40.00 15.00
❑ COMP.SET w/PROS (330) 80.00 40.00
❑ COMMON CARD (1-200) .30 .10
❑ SEMISTARS 1-220 .50 .20
❑ UNLISTED STARS 1-220 .75 .30
❑ COMMON ROOKIE (201-220) .40 .15
❑ ROOKIE SEMIS 201-220 .60 .25
❑ 219-220 AU ODDS 1:1150 HOBBY, 1:699 HTA
❑ COMMON AUTO (221-231) 10.00 4.00
❑ 221-231 AU ODDS 1:82 HOBBY, 1:40 HTA
❑ 1-220 PLATE ODDS 1:588 HOBBY, 1:575 HTA
❑ 221-231 AU PLATES 1:15,700 H, 1:4100 HTA
❑ PLATE PRINT RUN 1 SET PER COLOR
❑ BLACK-CYAN-MAGENTA-YELLOW ISSUED
❑ NO PLATE PRICING DUE TO SCARCITY
❑ 1 Nick Swisher .30 .12
❑ 2 Ted Lilly .30 .12
❑ 3 John Smoltz .50 .20
❑ 4 Lyle Overbay .30 .12
❑ 5 Alfonso Soriano .30 .12
❑ 6 Javier Vazquez .30 .12
❑ 7 Ronnie Belliard .30 .12
❑ 8 Jose Reyes .30 .12
❑ 9 Brian Roberts .30 .12
❑ 10 Curt Schilling .50 .20
❑ 11 Adam Dunn .30 .12
❑ 12 Zack Greinke .30 .12
❑ 13 Carlos Guillen .30 .12
❑ 14 Jon Garland .30 .12
❑ 15 Robinson Cano .50 .20
❑ 16 Chris Burke .30 .10
❑ 17 Barry Zito .30 .10
❑ 18 Russ Adams .30 .10
❑ 19 Chris Capuano .30 .10
❑ 20 Scott Rolen .50 .20
❑ 21 Kerry Wood .30 .10
❑ 22 Scott Kazmir .50 .20
❑ 23 Brandon Webb .30 .10
❑ 24 Jeff Kent .30 .10
❑ 25 Albert Pujols 1.50 .00
❑ 26 C.C. Sabathia .30 .10
❑ 27 Adrian Beltre .30 .10
❑ 28 Brad Wilkerson .30 .10
❑ 29 Randy Wolf .30 .10
❑ 30 Jason Bay .30 .10
❑ 31 Austin Kearns .30 .10
❑ 32 Clint Barmes .30 .10
❑ 33 Mike Sweeney .30 .10
❑ 34 Justin Verlander 1.25 .50
❑ 35 Justin Morneau .30 .10
❑ 36 Scott Podsednik .30 .10
❑ 37 Jason Giambi .30 .10
❑ 38 Steve Finley .30 .10
❑ 39 Morgan Ensberg .30 .10
❑ 40 Eric Chavez .30 .10
❑ 41 Roy Halladay .30 .10
❑ 42 Horacio Ramirez .30 .10
❑ 43 Ben Sheets .30 .10
❑ 44 Chris Carpenter .30 .10
❑ 45 Andruw Jones .50 .20
❑ 46 Carlos Zambrano .30 .10
❑ 47 Jonny Gomes .30 .10
❑ 48 Shawn Green .30 .10
❑ 49 Moises Alou .30 .10
❑ 50 Ichiro Suzuki 1.25 .50
❑ 51 Juan Pierre .30 .10
❑ 52 Grady Sizemore .50 .20
❑ 53 Kazuo Matsui .30 .10
❑ 54 Jose Vidro .30 .10
❑ 55 Jake Peavy .30 .10
❑ 56 Dallas Mcpherson .30 .10
❑ 57 Ryan Howard 1.25 .50
❑ 58 Zach Duke .30 .10
❑ 59 Michael Young .30 .10
❑ 60 Todd Helton .50 .20
❑ 61 David Dejesus .30 .10
❑ 62 Ivan Rodriguez .50 .20
❑ 63 Johan Santana .50 .20
❑ 64 Danny Haren .30 .10
❑ 65 Derek Jeter 2.00 .75
❑ 66 Greg Maddux 1.25 .50
❑ 67 Jorge Cantu .30 .10
❑ 68 Conor Jackson .30 .10
❑ 69 Victor Martinez .30 .10
❑ 70 David Wright 1.25 .50
❑ 71 Ryan Church .30 .10
❑ 72 Khalil Greene .50 .20
❑ 73 Jimmy Rollins .30 .10
❑ 74 Hank Blalock .30 .10
❑ 75 Pedro Martinez .50 .20
❑ 76 Jon Papelbon 2.00 .75
❑ 77 Felipe Lopez .30 .10
❑ 78 Jeff Francis .30 .10
❑ 79 Andy Sisco .30 .10
❑ 80 Hideki Matsui 1.25 .50
❑ 81 Ken Griffey Jr. 1.25 .50
❑ 82 Nomar Garciaparra .75 .30
❑ 83 Kevin Millwood .30 .10
❑ 84 Paul Konerko .30 .10
❑ 85 A.J. Burnett .30 .10
❑ 86 Mike Piazza .75 .30
❑ 87 Brian Giles .30 .10
❑ 88 Johnny Damon .50 .20
❑ 89 Jim Thome .50 .20
❑ 90 Roger Clemens 1.50 .60
❑ 91 Aaron Rowand .30 .10
❑ 92 Rafael Furcal .30 .10
❑ 93 Gary Sheffield .30 .10
❑ 94 Mike Cameron .30 .10
❑ 95 Carlos Delgado .30 .10
❑ 96 Jorge Posada .50 .20
❑ 97 Denny Bautista .30 .10
❑ 98 Mike Maroth .30 .10
❑ 99 Brad Radke .30 .10
❑ 100 Alex Rodriguez 1.25 .50
❑ 101 Freddy Garcia .30 .10
❑ 102 Oliver Perez .30 .10
❑ 103 Jon Lieber .30 .10
❑ 104 Melvin Mora .30 .10
❑ 105 Travis Hafner .30 .10
❑ 106 Matt Cain .50 .20
❑ 107 Derek Lowe .30 .10
❑ 108 Luis Castillo .30 .10
❑ 109 Livan Hernandez .30 .10
❑ 110 Tadahilo Iguchi .30 .10
❑ 111 Shawn Chacon .00 .10
❑ 112 Frank Thomas .75 .30
❑ 113 Josh Beckett .30 .10
❑ 114 Aubrey Huff .30 .10
❑ 115 Derrek Lee .30 .10
❑ 116 Chien-Ming Wang 1.25 .50
❑ 117 Joe Crede .30 .10
❑ 118 Torii Hunter .30 .10
❑ 119 J.D. Drew .30 .10
❑ 120 Troy Glaus .30 .10
❑ 121 Sean Casey .30 .10
❑ 122 Edgar Renteria .30 .10
❑ 123 Craig Wilson .30 .10
❑ 124 Adam Eaton .30 .10
❑ 125 Jeff Francoeur .75 .30
❑ 126 Bruce Chen .30 .10
❑ 127 Cliff Floyd .30 .10
❑ 128 Jeremy Reed .30 .10
❑ 129 Jake Westbrook .30 .10
❑ 130 Wily Mo Pena .30 .10
❑ 131 Toby Hall .30 .10
❑ 132 David Ortiz .75 .30
❑ 133 David Eckstein .30 .10
❑ 134 Brady Clark .30 .10
❑ 135 Marcus Giles .30 .10
❑ 136 Aaron Hill .30 .10
❑ 137 Mark Kotsay .30 .10
❑ 138 Carlos Lee .30 .10
❑ 139 Roy Oswalt .30 .10
❑ 140 Chone Figgins .30 .10
❑ 141 Mike Mussina .50 .20
❑ 142 Orlando Hernandez .30 .10
❑ 143 Magglio Ordonez .30 .10
❑ 144 Jim Edmonds .50 .20
❑ 145 Bobby Abreu .30 .10
❑ 146 Nick Johnson .30 .10
❑ 147 Carlos Beltran .30 .10
❑ 148 Jhonny Peralta .30 .10
❑ 149 Pedro Feliz .30 .10
❑ 150 Miguel Tejada .30 .10
❑ 151 Luis Gonzalez .30 .10
❑ 152 Carl Crawford .30 .10
❑ 153 Yadier Molina .30 .10
❑ 154 Rich Harden .30 .10
❑ 155 Tim Wakefield .30 .10
❑ 156 Rickie Weeks .30 .10
❑ 157 Johnny Estrada .30 .10
❑ 158 Gustavo Chacin .30 .10
❑ 159 Dan Johnson .30 .10
❑ 160 Willy Taveras .30 .10
❑ 161 Garret Anderson .30 .10
❑ 162 Randy Johnson .75 .30
❑ 163 Jermaine Dye .30 .10
❑ 164 Joe Mauer .50 .20
❑ 165 Ervin Santana .30 .10
❑ 166 Jeremy Bonderman .30 .10
❑ 167 Garrett Atkins .30 .10
❑ 168 Manny Ramirez .50 .20
❑ 169 Brad Eldred .30 .10
❑ 170 Chase Utley .75 .30
❑ 171 Mark Loretta .30 .10
❑ 172 John Patterson .30 .10
❑ 173 Tom Glavine .50 .20
❑ 174 Dontrelle Willis .30 .10
❑ 175 Mark Teixeira .50 .20
❑ 176 Felix Hernandez .50 .20
❑ 177 Cliff Lee .30 .10
❑ 178 Jason Schmidt .30 .10
❑ 179 Chad Tracy .30 .10
❑ 180 Rocco Baldelli .30 .10
❑ 181 Aramis Ramirez .30 .10
❑ 182 Andy Pettitte .30 .10
❑ 183 Mark Mulder .30 .10
❑ 184 Geoff Jenkins .30 .10
❑ 185 Chipper Jones .75 .30
❑ 186 Vernon Wells .30 .10
❑ 187 Bobby Crosby .30 .10
❑ 188 Lance Berkman .30 .10
❑ 189 Vladimir Guerrero .75 .30
❑ 190 Jose Capellan .30 .10
❑ 191 Brad Penny .30 .10
❑ 192 Jose Guillen .30 .10
❑ 193 Brett Myers .30 .10
❑ 194 Miguel Cabrera .50 .20

❑ 195 Bartolo Colon	.30	.10
❑ 196 Craig Biggio	.50	.20
❑ 197 Tim Hudson	.30	.10
❑ 198 Mark Prior	.50	.20
❑ 199 Mark Buehrle	.30	.10
❑ 200 Barry Bonds	2.00	.75
❑ 201 Anderson Hernandez (RC)	.40	.15
❑ 202 Charlton Jimerson (RC)	.40	.15
❑ 203 Jeremy Accardo RC	.40	.15
❑ 204 Hanley Ramirez (RC)	1.00	.40
❑ 205 Matt Capps (RC)	.40	.15
❑ 206 John-Ford Griffin (RC)	.40	.15
❑ 207 Chuck James (RC)	.60	.25
❑ 208 Jaime Bubela (RC)	.40	.15
❑ 209 Mark Woodyard (RC)	.40	.15
❑ 210 Jason Botts (RC)	.40	.15
❑ 211 Chris Demaria RC	.40	.15
❑ 212 Miguel Perez (RC)	.40	.15
❑ 213 Tom Gorzelanny (RC)	.40	.15
❑ 214 Adam Wainwright (RC)	.40	.15
❑ 215 Ryan Garko (RC)	.40	.15
❑ 216 Jason Bergmann RC	.40	.15
❑ 217 J.J. Furmaniak (RC)	.40	.15
❑ 218 Francisco Liriano (RC)	2.00	.75
❑ 219 Kenji Johjima RC	2.00	.75
❑ 219a Kenji Johjima AU	150.00	75.00
❑ 220 Craig Hansen RC	1.50	.60
❑ 220a Craig Hansen AU	50.00	20.00
❑ 221 Ryan Zimmerman AU (RC)	50.00	20.00
❑ 222 Joey Devine AU RC	10.00	4.00
❑ 223 Scott Olsen AU (RC)	10.00	4.00
❑ 224 Darrel Rasner AU (RC)	10.00	4.00
❑ 225 Craig Breslow AU RC	10.00	4.00
❑ 226 Reggie Abercrombie AU (RC)	10.00	4.00
❑ 227 Dan Uggla AU (RC)	40.00	15.00
❑ 228 Willie Eyre AU (RC)	10.00	4.00
❑ 229 Joel Zumaya AU (RC)	30.00	12.50
❑ 230 Ricky Nolasco AU (RC)	10.00	4.00
❑ 231 Ian Kinsler AU (RC)	15.00	6.00

1997 Bowman Chrome

❑ COMPLETE SET (300)	150.00	75.00
❑ 1 Derek Jeter	3.00	1.25
❑ 2 Chipper Jones	1.25	.50
❑ 3 Hideo Nomo	1.25	.50
❑ 4 Tim Salmon	.75	.30
❑ 5 Robin Ventura	.50	.20
❑ 6 Tony Clark	.50	.20
❑ 7 Barry Larkin	.75	.30
❑ 8 Paul Molitor	.50	.20
❑ 9 Andy Benes	.50	.20
❑ 10 Ryan Klesko	.50	.20
❑ 11 Mark McGwire	3.00	1.25
❑ 12 Ken Griffey Jr.	2.00	.75
❑ 13 Robb Nen	.50	.20
❑ 14 Cal Ripken	4.00	1.50
❑ 15 John Valentin	.50	.20
❑ 16 Ricky Bottalico	.50	.20
❑ 17 Mike Lansing	.50	.20
❑ 18 Ryne Sandberg	2.00	.75
❑ 19 Carlos Delgado	.50	.20
❑ 20 Craig Biggio	.75	.30
❑ 21 Eric Karros	.50	.20
❑ 22 Kevin Appier	.50	.20
❑ 23 Mariano Rivera	1.25	.50
❑ 24 Vinny Castilla	.50	.20
❑ 25 Juan Gonzalez	.50	.20
❑ 26 Al Martin	.50	.20
❑ 27 Jeff Cirillo	.50	.20
❑ 28 Ray Lankford	.50	.20
❑ 29 Manny Ramirez	.75	.30
❑ 30 Roberto Alomar	.75	.30
❑ 31 Will Clark	.75	.30
❑ 32 Chuck Knoblauch	.50	.20
❑ 33 Harold Baines	.50	.20
❑ 34 Edgar Martinez	.75	.30
❑ 35 Mike Mussina	.75	.30
❑ 36 Kevin Brown	.50	.20
❑ 37 Dennis Eckersley	.50	.20
❑ 38 Tino Martinez	.75	.30
❑ 39 Raul Mondesi	.50	.20
❑ 40 Sammy Sosa	1.25	.50
❑ 41 John Smoltz	.75	.30
❑ 42 Billy Wagner	.50	.20
❑ 43 Ken Caminiti	.50	.20
❑ 44 Wade Boggs	.75	.30
❑ 45 Andres Galarraga	.50	.20
❑ 46 Roger Clemens	2.50	1.00
❑ 47 Matt Williams	.50	.20
❑ 48 Albert Belle	.50	.20
❑ 49 Jeff King	.50	.20
❑ 50 John Wetteland	.50	.20
❑ 51 Deion Sanders	.75	.30
❑ 52 Ellis Burks	.50	.20
❑ 53 Pedro Martinez	.75	.30
❑ 54 Kenny Lofton	.50	.20
❑ 55 Randy Johnson	1.25	.50
❑ 56 Bernie Williams	.75	.30
❑ 57 Marquis Grissom	.50	.20
❑ 58 Gary Sheffield	.50	.20
❑ 59 Curt Schilling	.50	.20
❑ 60 Reggie Sanders	.50	.20
❑ 61 Bobby Higginson	.50	.20
❑ 62 Moises Alou	.50	.20
❑ 63 Tom Glavine	.75	.30
❑ 64 Mark Grace	.75	.30
❑ 65 Rafael Palmeiro	.75	.30
❑ 66 John Olerud	.50	.20
❑ 67 Dante Bichette	.50	.20
❑ 68 Jeff Bagwell	.75	.30
❑ 69 Barry Bonds	3.00	1.25
❑ 70 Pat Hentgen	.50	.20
❑ 71 Jim Thome	.75	.30
❑ 72 Andy Pettitte	.75	.30
❑ 73 Jay Bell	.50	.20
❑ 74 Jim Edmonds	.50	.20
❑ 75 Ron Gant	.50	.20
❑ 76 David Cone	.50	.20
❑ 77 Jose Canseco	.75	.30
❑ 78 Jay Buhner	.50	.20
❑ 79 Greg Maddux	2.00	.75
❑ 80 Lance Johnson	.50	.20
❑ 81 Travis Fryman	.50	.20
❑ 82 Paul O'Neill	.75	.30
❑ 83 Ivan Rodriguez	.75	.30
❑ 84 Fred McGriff	.75	.30
❑ 85 Mike Piazza	2.00	.75
❑ 86 Brady Anderson	.50	.20
❑ 87 Marty Cordova	.50	.20
❑ 88 Joe Carter	.50	.20
❑ 89 Brian Jordan	.50	.20
❑ 90 David Justice	.50	.20
❑ 91 Tony Gwynn	1.50	.60
❑ 92 Larry Walker	.50	.20
❑ 93 Mo Vaughn	.50	.20
❑ 94 Sandy Alomar Jr.	.50	.20
❑ 95 Rusty Greer	.50	.20
❑ 96 Roberto Hernandez	.50	.20
❑ 97 Hal Morris	.50	.20
❑ 98 Todd Hundley	.50	.20
❑ 99 Rondell White	.50	.20
❑ 100 Frank Thomas	1.25	.50
❑ 101 Bubba Trammell RC	1.50	.60
❑ 102 Sidney Ponson RC	2.50	1.00
❑ 103 Ricky Ledee RC	1.50	.60
❑ 104 Brett Tomko	.50	.20
❑ 105 Braden Looper RC	1.00	.40
❑ 106 Jason Dickson	.50	.20
❑ 107 Chad Green RC	1.00	.40
❑ 108 R.A. Dickey RC	1.00	.40
❑ 109 Jeff Liefer	.50	.20
❑ 110 Richard Hidalgo	.50	.20
❑ 111 Chad Hermansen RC	1.00	.40
❑ 112 Felix Martinez	.50	.20
❑ 113 J.J. Johnson	.50	.20
❑ 114 Todd Dunwoody	.50	.20
❑ 115 Katsuhiro Maeda	.50	.20
❑ 116 Darin Erstad	.50	.20
❑ 117 Elieser Marrero	.50	.20
❑ 118 Bartolo Colon	.50	.20
❑ 119 Ugueth Urbina	.50	.20
❑ 120 Jaime Bluma	.50	.20
❑ 121 Seth Greisinger RC	1.00	.40
❑ 122 Jose Cruz Jr. RC	1.50	.60
❑ 123 Todd Dunn	.50	.20
❑ 124 Justin Towle RC	1.00	.40
❑ 125 Brian Rose	.50	.20
❑ 126 Jose Guillen	.50	.20
❑ 127 Andruw Jones	.75	.30
❑ 128 Mark Kotsay RC	4.00	1.50
❑ 129 Wilton Guerrero	.50	.20
❑ 130 Jacob Cruz	.50	.20
❑ 131 Mike Sweeney	.50	.20
❑ 132 Matt Morris	.50	.20
❑ 133 John Thomson	.50	.20
❑ 134 Javier Valentin	.50	.20
❑ 135 Mike Drumright RC	1.00	.40
❑ 136 Michael Barrett	.50	.20
❑ 137 Tony Saunders RC	1.00	.40
❑ 138 Kevin Brown	.50	.20
❑ 139 Anthony Sanders RC	1.00	.40
❑ 140 Jeff Abbott	.50	.20
❑ 141 Eugene Kingsale	.50	.20
❑ 142 Paul Konerko	.75	.30
❑ 143 Randall Simon RC	1.50	.60
❑ 144 Freddy Adrian Garcia	.50	.20
❑ 145 Karim Garcia	.50	.20
❑ 146 Carlos Guillen	.50	.20
❑ 147 Aaron Boone	.50	.20
❑ 148 Donnie Sadler	.50	.20
❑ 149 Brooks Kieschnick	.50	.20
❑ 150 Scott Spiezio	.50	.20
❑ 151 Kevin Orie	.50	.20
❑ 152 Russ Johnson	.50	.20
❑ 153 Livan Hernandez	.50	.20
❑ 154 Vladimir Nunez RC	1.00	.40
❑ 155 Pokey Reese	.50	.20
❑ 156 Chris Carpenter	.50	.20
❑ 157 Eric Milton RC	1.50	.60
❑ 158 Richie Sexson	.50	.20
❑ 159 Carl Pavano	.50	.20
❑ 160 Pat Cline	.50	.20
❑ 161 Ron Wright	.50	.20
❑ 162 Dante Powell	.50	.20
❑ 163 Mark Bellhorn	.50	.20
❑ 164 George Lombard	.50	.20
❑ 165 Paul Wilder RC	1.00	.40
❑ 166 Brad Fullmer	.50	.20
❑ 167 Kris Benson RC	2.50	1.00
❑ 168 Torii Hunter	.50	.20
❑ 169 D.T. Cromer RC	1.00	.40
❑ 170 Nelson Figueroa RC	1.00	.40
❑ 171 Hiram Bocachica RC	1.00	.40
❑ 172 Shane Monahan	.50	.20
❑ 173 Juan Melo	.50	.20
❑ 174 Calvin Pickering RC	1.00	.40
❑ 175 Reggie Taylor	.50	.20
❑ 176 Geoff Jenkins	.50	.20
❑ 177 Steve Rain RC	1.00	.40
❑ 178 Nerio Rodriguez RC	1.00	.40
❑ 179 Derrick Gibson	.50	.20
❑ 180 Darin Blood	.50	.20
❑ 181 Ben Davis	.50	.20
❑ 182 Adrian Beltre RC	8.00	3.00
❑ 183 Kerry Wood RC	12.00	5.00
❑ 184 Nate Rolison RC	1.00	.40
❑ 185 Fernando Tatis RC	1.00	.40
❑ 186 Jake Westbrook RC	2.50	1.00
❑ 187 Edwin Diaz	.50	.20
❑ 188 Joe Fontenot RC	1.00	.40
❑ 189 Matt Halloran RC	1.00	.40
❑ 190 Matt Clement RC	2.50	1.00
❑ 191 Todd Greene	.50	.20
❑ 192 Eric Chavez RC	10.00	4.00
❑ 193 Edgard Velazquez	.50	.20
❑ 194 Bruce Chen RC	2.50	1.00
❑ 195 Jason Brester	.50	.20
❑ 196 Chris Reitsma RC	1.50	.60
❑ 197 Neifi Perez	.50	.20
❑ 198 Hideki Irabu RC	1.50	.60

❑ 199	Don Denbow RC	1.00	.40
❑ 200	Derrek Lee	.75	.30
❑ 201	Todd Walker	.50	.20
❑ 202	Scott Rolen	.75	.30
❑ 203	Wes Helms	.50	.20
❑ 204	Bob Abreu	.75	.30
❑ 205	John Patterson RC	4.00	1.50
❑ 206	Alex Gonzalez RC	2.50	1.00
❑ 207	Grant Roberts RC	1.00	.40
❑ 208	Jeff Suppan	.50	.20
❑ 209	Luke Wilcox	.50	.20
❑ 210	Marlon Anderson	.50	.20
❑ 211	Mike Caruso RC	1.00	.40
❑ 212	Roy Halladay RC	12.00	5.00
❑ 213	Jeremi Gonzalez RC	1.00	.40
❑ 214	Aramis Ramirez RC	10.00	4.00
❑ 215	Dee Brown RC	1.00	.40
❑ 216	Justin Thompson	.50	.20
❑ 217	Danny Clyburn	.50	.20
❑ 218	Bruce Aven	.50	.20
❑ 219	Keith Foulke RC	4.00	1.50
❑ 220	Shannon Stewart	.50	.20
❑ 221	Larry Barnes RC	1.00	.40
❑ 222	Mark Johnson RC	1.00	.40
❑ 223	Randy Winn	.50	.20
❑ 224	Nomar Garciaparra	2.00	.75
❑ 225	Jacque Jones RC	4.00	1.50
❑ 226	Chris Clemons	.50	.20
❑ 227	Todd Helton	1.25	.50
❑ 228	Ryan Brannan RC	1.00	.40
❑ 229	Alex Sanchez RC	1.50	.60
❑ 230	Russell Branyan	.50	.20
❑ 231	Daryle Ward	1.00	.40
❑ 232	Kevin Witt	.50	.20
❑ 233	Gabby Martinez	.50	.20
❑ 234	Preston Wilson	.50	.20
❑ 235	Donzell McDonald RC	1.00	.40
❑ 236	Orlando Cabrera RC	4.00	1.50
❑ 237	Brian Banks	.50	.20
❑ 238	Robbie Bell	1.00	.40
❑ 239	Brad Rigby	.50	.20
❑ 240	Scott Elarton	.50	.20
❑ 241	Donny Leon RC	1.00	.40
❑ 242	Abraham Nunez RC	1.00	.40
❑ 243	Adam Eaton RC	2.50	1.00
❑ 244	Octavio Dotel RC	1.50	.60
❑ 245	Sean Casey	2.50	1.00
❑ 246	Joe Lawrence RC	1.00	.40
❑ 247	Adam Johnson RC	1.00	.40
❑ 248	Ronnie Belliard RC	3.00	1.25
❑ 249	Bobby Estalella	.50	.20
❑ 250	Corey Lee RC	1.00	.40
❑ 251	Mike Cameron	.50	.20
❑ 252	Kerry Robinson RC	1.00	.40
❑ 253	A.J. Zapp RC	1.00	.40
❑ 254	Jarrod Washburn	.50	.20
❑ 255	Ben Grieve	.50	.20
❑ 256	Javier Vazquez RC	4.00	1.50
❑ 257	Travis Lee RC	1.50	.60
❑ 258	Dennis Reyes RC	1.00	.40
❑ 259	Danny Buxbaum	.50	.20
❑ 260	Kelvim Escobar RC	2.50	1.00
❑ 261	Danny Klassen	.50	.20
❑ 262	Ken Cloude RC	1.00	.40
❑ 263	Gabe Alvarez	.50	.20
❑ 264	Clayton Bruner RC	1.00	.40
❑ 265	Jason Marquis RC	2.50	1.00
❑ 266	Jamey Wright	.50	.20
❑ 267	Matt Snyder RC	1.00	.40
❑ 268	Josh Garrett RC	1.00	.40
❑ 269	Juan Encarnacion	.50	.20
❑ 270	Heath Murray	.50	.20
❑ 271	Brent Butler RC	1.00	.40
❑ 272	Danny Peoples RC	1.00	.40
❑ 273	Miguel Tejada RC	20.00	8.00
❑ 274	Jim Pittsley	.50	.20
❑ 275	Dmitri Young	.50	.20
❑ 276	Vladimir Guerrero	1.25	.50
❑ 277	Cole Liniak RC	1.00	.40
❑ 278	Ramon Hernandez	.50	.20
❑ 279	Cliff Politte RC	1.00	.40
❑ 280	Mel Rosario RC	1.00	.40
❑ 281	Jorge Carrion RC	1.00	.40
❑ 282	John Barnes RC	1.00	.40
❑ 283	Chris Stowe RC	1.00	.40
❑ 284	Vernon Wells RC	12.00	5.00
❑ 285	Brett Caradonna RC	1.00	.40
❑ 286	Scott Hodges RC	1.00	.40
❑ 287	Jon Garland RC	6.00	2.50
❑ 288	Nathan Haynes RC	1.00	.40
❑ 289	Geoff Goetz RC	1.00	.40
❑ 290	Adam Kennedy RC	2.50	1.00
❑ 291	T.J. Tucker RC	1.00	.40
❑ 292	Aaron Akin RC	1.00	.40
❑ 293	Jayson Werth RC	2.50	1.00
❑ 294	Glenn Davis RC	1.00	.40
❑ 295	Mark Mangum RC	1.00	.40
❑ 296	Troy Cameron RC	1.00	.40
❑ 297	J.J. Davis RC	1.00	.40
❑ 298	Lance Berkman RC	15.00	6.00
❑ 299	Jason Standridge RC	1.00	.40
❑ 300	Jason Dellaero RC	1.00	.40

1998 Bowman Chrome

❑	COMPLETE SET (441)	160.00	60.00
❑	COMPLETE SERIES 1 (221)	80.00	30.00
❑	COMPLETE SERIES 2 (220)	80.00	30.00
❑ 1	Nomar Garciaparra	2.00	.75
❑ 2	Scott Rolen	.75	.30
❑ 3	Andy Pettitte	.75	.30
❑ 4	Ivan Rodriguez	.75	.30
❑ 5	Mark McGwire	3.00	1.25
❑ 6	Jason Dickson	.50	.20
❑ 7	Jose Cruz Jr.	.50	.20
❑ 8	Jeff Kent	.50	.20
❑ 9	Mike Mussina	.75	.30
❑ 10	Jason Kendall	.50	.20
❑ 11	Brett Tomko	.50	.20
❑ 12	Jeff King	.50	.20
❑ 13	Brad Radke	.50	.20
❑ 14	Robin Ventura	.50	.20
❑ 15	Jeff Bagwell	.75	.30
❑ 16	Greg Maddux	2.00	.75
❑ 17	John Jaha	.50	.20
❑ 18	Mike Piazza	2.00	.75
❑ 19	Edgar Martinez	.75	.30
❑ 20	David Justice	.50	.20
❑ 21	Todd Hundley	.50	.20
❑ 22	Tony Gwynn	1.50	.60
❑ 23	Larry Walker	.50	.20
❑ 24	Bernie Williams	.75	.30
❑ 25	Edgar Renteria	.50	.20
❑ 26	Rafael Palmeiro	.75	.30
❑ 27	Tim Salmon	.75	.30
❑ 28	Matt Morris	.50	.20
❑ 29	Shawn Estes	.50	.20
❑ 30	Vladimir Guerrero	1.25	.50
❑ 31	Fernando Tatis	.50	.20
❑ 32	Justin Thompson	.50	.20
❑ 33	Ken Griffey Jr.	2.00	.75
❑ 34	Edgardo Alfonzo	.50	.20
❑ 35	Mo Vaughn	.50	.20
❑ 36	Marty Cordova	.50	.20
❑ 37	Craig Biggio	.75	.30
❑ 38	Roger Clemens	2.50	1.00
❑ 39	Mark Grace	.75	.30
❑ 40	Ken Caminiti	.50	.20
❑ 41	Tony Womack	.50	.20
❑ 42	Albert Belle	.50	.20
❑ 43	Tino Martinez	.75	.30
❑ 44	Sandy Alomar Jr.	.50	.20
❑ 45	Jeff Cirillo	.50	.20
❑ 46	Jason Giambi	.50	.20
❑ 47	Darin Erstad	.50	.20
❑ 48	Livan Hernandez	.50	.20
❑ 49	Mark Grudzielanek	.50	.20
❑ 50	Sammy Sosa	1.25	.50
❑ 51	Curt Schilling	.50	.20
❑ 52	Brian Hunter	.50	.20
❑ 53	Neifi Perez	.50	.20
❑ 54	Todd Walker	.50	.20
❑ 55	Jose Guillen	.50	.20
❑ 56	Jim Thome	.75	.30
❑ 57	Tom Glavine	.75	.30
❑ 58	Todd Greene	.50	.20
❑ 59	Rondell White	.50	.20
❑ 60	Roberto Alomar	.75	.30
❑ 61	Tony Clark	.50	.20
❑ 62	Vinny Castilla	.50	.20
❑ 63	Barry Larkin	.75	.30
❑ 64	Hideki Irabu	.50	.20
❑ 65	Johnny Damon	.75	.30
❑ 66	Juan Gonzalez	.50	.20
❑ 67	John Olerud	.50	.20
❑ 68	Gary Sheffield	.50	.20
❑ 69	Raul Mondesi	.50	.20
❑ 70	Chipper Jones	1.25	.50
❑ 71	David Ortiz	6.00	2.50
❑ 72	Warren Morris RC	1.00	.40
❑ 73	Alex Gonzalez	.50	.20
❑ 74	Nick Bierbrodt	.50	.20
❑ 75	Roy Halladay	.50	.20
❑ 76	Danny Buxbaum	.50	.20
❑ 77	Adam Kennedy	.50	.20
❑ 78	Jared Sandberg	.50	.20
❑ 79	Michael Barrett	.50	.20
❑ 80	Gil Meche	1.50	.60
❑ 81	Jayson Werth	.50	.20
❑ 82	Abraham Nunez	.50	.20
❑ 83	Ben Petrick	.50	.20
❑ 84	Brett Caradonna	.50	.20
❑ 85	Mike Lowell RC	5.00	2.00
❑ 86	Clay Bruner	.50	.20
❑ 87	John Curtice RC	1.50	.60
❑ 88	Bobby Estalella	.50	.20
❑ 89	Juan Melo	.50	.20
❑ 90	Arnold Gooch	.50	.20
❑ 91	Kevin Millwood RC	4.00	1.50
❑ 92	Richie Sexson	.50	.20
❑ 93	Orlando Cabrera	.50	.20
❑ 94	Pat Cline	.50	.20
❑ 95	Anthony Sanders	.50	.20
❑ 96	Russ Johnson	.50	.20
❑ 97	Ben Grieve	.50	.20
❑ 98	Kevin McGlinchy	.50	.20
❑ 99	Paul Wilder	.50	.20
❑ 100	Russ Ortiz	.50	.20
❑ 101	Ryan Jackson RC	1.00	.40
❑ 102	Heath Murray	.50	.20
❑ 103	Brian Rose	.50	.20
❑ 104	Ryan Radmanovich RC	1.00	.40
❑ 105	Ricky Ledee	.50	.20
❑ 106	Jeff Wallace RC	1.00	.40
❑ 107	Ryan Minor RC	1.00	.40
❑ 108	Dennis Reyes	.50	.20
❑ 109	James Manias	.50	.20
❑ 110	Chris Carpenter	.50	.20
❑ 111	Daryle Ward	.50	.20
❑ 112	Vernon Wells	.50	.20
❑ 113	Chad Green	.50	.20
❑ 114	Mike Stoner RC	1.00	.40
❑ 115	Brad Fullmer	.50	.20
❑ 116	Adam Eaton	.50	.20
❑ 117	Jeff Liefer	.50	.20
❑ 118	Corey Koskie RC	2.50	1.00
❑ 119	Todd Helton	.75	.30
❑ 120	Jaime Jones RC	1.00	.40
❑ 121	Mel Rosario	.50	.20
❑ 122	Geoff Goetz	.50	.20
❑ 123	Adrian Beltre	.50	.20
❑ 124	Jason Dellaero	.50	.20
❑ 125	Gabe Kapler RC	2.50	1.00
❑ 126	Scott Schoeneweis	.50	.20
❑ 127	Ryan Brannan	.50	.20
❑ 128	Aaron Akin	.50	.20
❑ 129	Ryan Anderson RC	1.00	.40
❑ 130	Brad Penny	.50	.20
❑ 131	Bruce Chen	.50	.20
❑ 132	Eli Marrero	.50	.20
❑ 133	Eric Chavez	.50	.20

- ❑ 134 Troy Glaus RC 10.00 4.00
- ❑ 135 Troy Cameron .50 .20
- ❑ 136 Brian Sikorski RC 1.00 .40
- ❑ 137 Mike Kinkade RC 1.00 .40
- ❑ 138 Braden Looper .50 .20
- ❑ 139 Mark Mangum .50 .20
- ❑ 140 Danny Peoples .50 .20
- ❑ 141 J.J. Davis .50 .20
- ❑ 142 Ben Davis .50 .20
- ❑ 143 Jacque Jones .50 .20
- ❑ 144 Derrick Gibson .50 .20
- ❑ 145 Bronson Arroyo 4.00 1.50
- ❑ 146 Luis De Los Santos RC 1.00 .40
- ❑ 147 Jeff Abbott .50 .20
- ❑ 148 Mike Cuddyer RC 4.00 1.50
- ❑ 149 Jason Romano .50 .20
- ❑ 150 Shane Monahan .50 .20
- ❑ 151 Ntema Ndungidi RC 1.00 .40
- ❑ 152 Alex Sanchez .50 .20
- ❑ 153 Jack Cust RC 1.50 .60
- ❑ 154 Brent Butler .50 .20
- ❑ 155 Ramon Hernandez .50 .20
- ❑ 156 Norm Hutchins .50 .20
- ❑ 157 Jason Marquis .50 .20
- ❑ 158 Jacob Cruz .50 .20
- ❑ 159 Rob Burger RC 1.00 .40
- ❑ 160 Dave Coggin .50 .20
- ❑ 161 Preston Wilson .50 .20
- ❑ 162 Jason Fitzgerald RC 1.00 .40
- ❑ 163 Dan Serafini .50 .20
- ❑ 164 Pete Munro .50 .20
- ❑ 165 Trot Nixon .50 .20
- ❑ 166 Homer Bush .50 .20
- ❑ 167 Dermal Brown .50 .20
- ❑ 168 Chad Hermansen .50 .20
- ❑ 169 Julio Moreno RC 1.00 .40
- ❑ 170 John Roskos RC 1.00 .40
- ❑ 171 Grant Roberts .50 .20
- ❑ 172 Ken Cloude .50 .20
- ❑ 173 Jason Brester .50 .20
- ❑ 174 Jason Conti .50 .20
- ❑ 175 Jon Garland .50 .20
- ❑ 176 Robbie Bell .50 .20
- ❑ 177 Nathan Haynes .50 .20
- ❑ 178 Ramon Ortiz RC 1.50 .60
- ❑ 179 Shannon Stewart .50 .20
- ❑ 180 Pablo Ortega .50 .20
- ❑ 181 Jimmy Rollins RC 6.00 2.50
- ❑ 182 Sean Casey .50 .20
- ❑ 183 Ted Lilly RC 2.50 1.00
- ❑ 184 Chris Enochs RC 1.00 .40
- ❑ 185 Magglio Ordonez UER RC 10.00 4.00
- ❑ 186 Mike Drumright .50 .20
- ❑ 187 Aaron Boone .50 .20
- ❑ 188 Matt Clement .50 .20
- ❑ 189 Todd Dunwoody .50 .20
- ❑ 190 Larry Rodriguez .50 .20
- ❑ 191 Todd Noel .50 .20
- ❑ 192 Geoff Jenkins .50 .20
- ❑ 193 George Lombard .50 .20
- ❑ 194 Lance Berkman .50 .20
- ❑ 195 Marcus McCain .50 .20
- ❑ 196 Ryan McGuire .50 .20
- ❑ 197 Jhensy Sandoval .50 .20
- ❑ 198 Corey Lee .50 .20
- ❑ 199 Mario Valdez .50 .20
- ❑ 200 Robert Fick RC 1.50 .60
- ❑ 201 Donnie Sadler .50 .20
- ❑ 202 Marc Kroon .50 .20
- ❑ 203 David Miller .50 .20
- ❑ 204 Jarrod Washburn .50 .20
- ❑ 205 Miguel Tejada 1.25 .50
- ❑ 206 Raul Ibanez .50 .20
- ❑ 207 John Patterson .50 .20
- ❑ 208 Calvin Pickering .50 .20
- ❑ 209 Felix Martinez .50 .20
- ❑ 210 Mark Redman .50 .20
- ❑ 211 Scott Elarton .50 .20
- ❑ 212 Jose Amado RC 1.00 .40
- ❑ 213 Kerry Wood .50 .20
- ❑ 214 Dante Powell .50 .20
- ❑ 215 Aramis Ramirez .50 .20
- ❑ 216 A.J. Hinch .50 .20
- ❑ 217 Dustin Carr RC 1.00 .40
- ❑ 218 Mark Kotsay .50 .20
- ❑ 219 Jason Standridge .50 .20
- ❑ 220 Luis Ordaz .50 .20
- ❑ 221 Orlando Hernandez RC 5.00 2.00
- ❑ 222 Cal Ripken 4.00 1.50
- ❑ 223 Paul Molitor .50 .20
- ❑ 224 Derek Jeter 3.00 1.25
- ❑ 225 Barry Bonds 3.00 1.25
- ❑ 226 Jim Edmonds .50 .20
- ❑ 227 John Smoltz .75 .30
- ❑ 228 Eric Karros .50 .20
- ❑ 229 Ray Lankford .50 .20
- ❑ 230 Rey Ordonez .50 .20
- ❑ 231 Kenny Lofton .50 .20
- ❑ 232 Alex Rodriguez 2.00 .75
- ❑ 233 Dante Bichette .50 .20
- ❑ 234 Pedro Martinez .75 .30
- ❑ 235 Carlos Delgado .50 .20
- ❑ 236 Rod Beck .50 .20
- ❑ 237 Matt Williams .50 .20
- ❑ 238 Charles Johnson .50 .20
- ❑ 239 Rico Brogna .50 .20
- ❑ 240 Frank Thomas 1.25 .50
- ❑ 241 Paul O'Neill .75 .30
- ❑ 242 Jaret Wright .50 .20
- ❑ 243 Brant Brown .50 .20
- ❑ 244 Ryan Klesko .50 .20
- ❑ 245 Chuck Finley .50 .20
- ❑ 246 Derek Bell .50 .20
- ❑ 247 Delino DeShields .50 .20
- ❑ 248 Chan Ho Park .50 .20
- ❑ 249 Wade Boggs .75 .30
- ❑ 250 Jay Buhner .50 .20
- ❑ 251 Butch Huskey .50 .20
- ❑ 252 Steve Finley .50 .20
- ❑ 253 Will Clark .75 .30
- ❑ 254 John Valentin .50 .20
- ❑ 255 Bobby Higginson .50 .20
- ❑ 256 Darryl Strawberry .50 .20
- ❑ 257 Randy Johnson 1.25 .50
- ❑ 258 Al Martin .50 .20
- ❑ 259 Travis Fryman .50 .20
- ❑ 260 Fred McGriff .75 .30
- ❑ 261 Jose Valentin .50 .20
- ❑ 262 Andruw Jones .75 .30
- ❑ 263 Kenny Rogers .50 .20
- ❑ 264 Moises Alou .50 .20
- ❑ 265 Denny Neagle .50 .20
- ❑ 266 Ugueth Urbina .50 .20
- ❑ 267 Derrek Lee .75 .30
- ❑ 268 Ellis Burks .50 .20
- ❑ 269 Mariano Rivera 1.25 .50
- ❑ 270 Dean Palmer .50 .20
- ❑ 271 Eddie Taubensee .50 .20
- ❑ 272 Brady Anderson .50 .20
- ❑ 273 Brian Giles .50 .20
- ❑ 274 Quinton McCracken .50 .20
- ❑ 275 Henry Rodriguez .50 .20
- ❑ 276 Andres Galarraga .50 .20
- ❑ 277 Jose Canseco .75 .30
- ❑ 278 David Segui .50 .20
- ❑ 279 Bret Saberhagen .50 .20
- ❑ 280 Kevin Brown .75 .30
- ❑ 281 Chuck Knoblauch .50 .20
- ❑ 282 Jeromy Burnitz .50 .20
- ❑ 283 Jay Bell .50 .20
- ❑ 284 Manny Ramirez .75 .30
- ❑ 285 Rick Helling .50 .20
- ❑ 286 Francisco Cordova .50 .20
- ❑ 287 Bob Abreu .50 .20
- ❑ 288 J.T. Snow .50 .20
- ❑ 289 Hideo Nomo 1.25 .50
- ❑ 290 Brian Jordan .50 .20
- ❑ 291 Javy Lopez .50 .20
- ❑ 292 Travis Lee .50 .20
- ❑ 293 Russell Branyan .50 .20
- ❑ 294 Paul Konerko .50 .20
- ❑ 295 Masato Yoshii RC 1.50 .60
- ❑ 296 Kris Benson .50 .20
- ❑ 297 Juan Encarnacion .50 .20
- ❑ 298 Eric Milton .50 .20
- ❑ 299 Mike Caruso .50 .20
- ❑ 300 Ricardo Aramboles RC 1.00 .40
- ❑ 301 Bobby Smith .50 .20
- ❑ 302 Billy Koch .50 .20
- ❑ 303 Richard Hidalgo .50 .20
- ❑ 304 Justin Baughman RC 1.00 .40
- ❑ 305 Chris Gissell .50 .20
- ❑ 306 Donnie Bridges RC 1.00 .40
- ❑ 307 Nelson Lara RC 1.00 .40
- ❑ 308 Randy Wolf RC 1.50 .60
- ❑ 309 Jason LaRue RC 1.50 .60
- ❑ 310 Jason Gooding RC 1.00 .40
- ❑ 311 Edgard Clemente .50 .20
- ❑ 312 Andrew Vessel .50 .20
- ❑ 313 Chris Reitsma .50 .20
- ❑ 314 Jesus Sanchez RC 1.00 .40
- ❑ 315 Buddy Carlyle RC 1.00 .40
- ❑ 316 Randy Winn .50 .20
- ❑ 317 Luis Rivera RC 1.00 .40
- ❑ 318 Marcus Thames RC 6.00 2.50
- ❑ 319 A.J. Pierzynski .50 .20
- ❑ 320 Scott Randall .50 .20
- ❑ 321 Damian Sapp .50 .20
- ❑ 322 Ed Yarnall RC 1.00 .40
- ❑ 323 Luke Allen RC 1.00 .40
- ❑ 324 J.D. Smart .50 .20
- ❑ 325 Willie Martinez .50 .20
- ❑ 326 Alex Ramirez .50 .20
- ❑ 327 Eric DuBose RC 1.00 .40
- ❑ 328 Kevin Witt .50 .20
- ❑ 329 Dan McKinley RC 1.00 .40
- ❑ 330 Cliff Politte .50 .20
- ❑ 331 Vladimir Nunez .50 .20
- ❑ 332 John Halama RC 1.00 .40
- ❑ 333 Nerio Rodriguez .50 .20
- ❑ 334 Desi Relaford .50 .20
- ❑ 335 Robinson Checo .50 .20
- ❑ 336 John Nicholson .75 .30
- ❑ 337 Tom LaRosa RC 1.00 .40
- ❑ 338 Kevin Nicholson RC 1.00 .40
- ❑ 339 Javier Vazquez .50 .20
- ❑ 340 A.J. Zapp .50 .20
- ❑ 341 Tom Evans .50 .20
- ❑ 342 Kerry Robinson .50 .20
- ❑ 343 Gabe Gonzalez RC 1.00 .40
- ❑ 344 Ralph Milliard .50 .20
- ❑ 345 Enrique Wilson .50 .20
- ❑ 346 Elvin Hernandez .50 .20
- ❑ 347 Mike Lincoln RC 1.00 .40
- ❑ 348 Cesar King RC 1.00 .40
- ❑ 349 Cristian Guzman RC 1.50 .60
- ❑ 350 Donzell McDonald .50 .20
- ❑ 351 Jim Parque RC 1.00 .40
- ❑ 352 Mike Saipe RC 1.00 .40
- ❑ 353 Carlos Febles RC 1.50 .60
- ❑ 354 Dernell Stenson RC 1.00 .40
- ❑ 355 Mark Osborne RC 1.00 .40
- ❑ 356 Odalis Perez RC 4.00 1.50
- ❑ 357 Jason Dewey RC 1.00 .40
- ❑ 358 Joe Fontenot .50 .20
- ❑ 359 Jason Grilli RC 1.00 .40
- ❑ 360 Kevin Haverbusch RC 1.00 .40
- ❑ 361 Jay Yennaco RC 1.00 .40
- ❑ 362 Brian Buchanan .50 .20
- ❑ 363 John Barnes .50 .20
- ❑ 364 Chris Fussell .50 .20
- ❑ 365 Kevin Gibbs RC 1.00 .40
- ❑ 366 Joe Lawrence .50 .20
- ❑ 367 DaRond Stovall .50 .20
- ❑ 368 Brian Fuentes RC 1.00 .40
- ❑ 369 Jimmy Anderson .50 .20
- ❑ 370 Lariel Gonzalez RC 1.00 .40
- ❑ 371 Scott Williamson RC 1.00 .40
- ❑ 372 Milton Bradley .50 .20
- ❑ 373 Jason Halper RC 1.00 .40
- ❑ 374 Brent Billingsley RC 1.00 .40
- ❑ 375 Joe DePastino RC 1.00 .40
- ❑ 376 Jake Westbrook .50 .20
- ❑ 377 Octavio Dotel .50 .20
- ❑ 378 Jason Williams RC 1.00 .40
- ❑ 379 Julio Ramirez RC 1.00 .40
- ❑ 380 Seth Greisinger .50 .20
- ❑ 381 Mike Judd RC 1.00 .40
- ❑ 382 Ben Ford RC 1.00 .40
- ❑ 383 Tom Bennett RC 1.00 .40
- ❑ 384 Adam Butler RC 1.00 .40
- ❑ 385 Wade Miller RC 2.50 1.00
- ❑ 386 Kyle Peterson RC 1.00 .40
- ❑ 387 Tommy Peterman RC 1.00 .40
- ❑ 388 Onan Masaoka .50 .20
- ❑ 389 Jason Rakers RC 1.00 .40
- ❑ 390 Rafael Medina .50 .20
- ❑ 391 Luis Lopez RC 1.00 .40

	Card	Player	Price	Price
❑	392	Jeff Yoder	.50	.20
❑	393	Vance Wilson RC	1.00	.40
❑	394	Fernando Seguignol RC	1.00	.40
❑	395	Ron Wright	.50	.20
❑	396	Ruben Mateo RC	1.00	.40
❑	397	Steve Lomasney RC	1.50	.60
❑	398	Damian Jackson	.50	.20
❑	399	Mike Jerzembeck RC	1.00	.40
❑	400	Luis Rivas RC	2.50	1.00
❑	401	Kevin Burford RC	1.00	.40
❑	402	Glenn Davis	.50	.20
❑	403	Robert Luce RC	1.00	.40
❑	404	Cole Liniak	.50	.20
❑	405	Matt LeCroy RC	1.50	.60
❑	406	Jeremy Giambi RC	1.50	.60
❑	407	Shawn Chacon	.50	.20
❑	408	Dewayne Wise RC	1.00	.40
❑	409	Steve Woodard	.50	.20
❑	410	Francisco Cordero RC	2.50	1.00
❑	411	Damon Minor RC	1.00	.40
❑	412	Lou Collier	.50	.20
❑	413	Justin Towle	.50	.20
❑	414	Juan LeBron	.50	.20
❑	415	Michael Coleman	.50	.20
❑	416	Felix Rodriguez	.50	.20
❑	417	Paul Ah Yat RC	1.00	.40
❑	418	Kevin Barker RC	1.00	.40
❑	419	Brian Meadows	.50	.20
❑	420	Darnell McDonald RC	1.00	.40
❑	421	Matt Kinney RC	1.00	.40
❑	422	Mike Vavrek RC	1.00	.40
❑	423	Courtney Duncan RC	1.00	.40
❑	424	Kevin Millar RC	4.00	1.50
❑	425	Ruben Rivera	.50	.20
❑	426	Steve Shoemaker RC	1.00	.40
❑	427	Dan Reichert RC	1.00	.40
❑	428	Carlos Lee RC	8.00	3.00
❑	429	Rod Barajas	2.50	1.00
❑	430	Pablo Ozuna RC	1.50	.60
❑	431	Todd Belitz RC	1.00	.40
❑	432	Sidney Ponson	.50	.20
❑	433	Steve Carver RC	1.00	.40
❑	434	Esteban Yan RC	1.50	.60
❑	435	Cedrick Bowers	.50	.20
❑	436	Marlon Anderson	.50	.20
❑	437	Carl Pavano	.50	.20
❑	438	Jae Weong Seo RC	1.50	.60
❑	439	Jose Taveras RC	1.00	.40
❑	440	Matt Anderson RC	1.00	.40
❑	441	Darron Ingram RC	1.00	.40

1999 Bowman Chrome

	Card	Player	Price	Price
❑		COMPLETE SET (440)	200.00	100.00
❑		COMPLETE SERIES 1 (220)	80.00	40.00
❑		COMPLETE SERIES 2 (220)	120.00	60.00
❑	1	Ben Grieve	.50	.20
❑	2	Kerry Wood	.50	.20
❑	3	Ruben Rivera	.50	.20
❑	4	Sandy Alomar Jr.	.50	.20
❑	5	Cal Ripken	4.00	1.50
❑	6	Mark McGwire	3.00	1.25
❑	7	Vladimir Guerrero	1.25	.50
❑	8	Moises Alou	.50	.20
❑	9	Jim Edmonds	.50	.20
❑	10	Greg Maddux	2.00	.75
❑	11	Gary Sheffield	.50	.20
❑	12	John Valentin	.50	.20
❑	13	Chuck Knoblauch	.50	.20
❑	14	Tony Clark	.50	.20
❑	15	Rusty Greer	.50	.20
❑	16	Al Leiter	.50	.20
❑	17	Travis Lee	.50	.20
❑	18	Jose Cruz Jr.	.50	.20
❑	19	Pedro Martinez	.75	.30
❑	20	Paul O'Neill	.75	.30
❑	21	Todd Walker	.50	.20
❑	22	Vinny Castilla	.50	.20
❑	23	Barry Larkin	.75	.30
❑	24	Curt Schilling	.50	.20
❑	25	Jason Kendall	.50	.20
❑	26	Scott Erickson	.50	.20
❑	27	Andres Galarraga	.50	.20
❑	28	Jeff Shaw	.50	.20
❑	29	John Olerud	.50	.20
❑	30	Orlando Hernandez	.50	.20
❑	31	Larry Walker	.50	.20
❑	32	Andruw Jones	.75	.30
❑	33	Jeff Cirillo	.50	.20
❑	34	Barry Bonds	3.00	1.25
❑	35	Manny Ramirez	.75	.30
❑	36	Mark Kotsay	.50	.20
❑	37	Ivan Rodriguez	.75	.30
❑	38	Jeff King	.50	.20
❑	39	Brian Hunter	.50	.20
❑	40	Ray Durham	.50	.20
❑	41	Bernie Williams	.75	.30
❑	42	Darin Erstad	.50	.20
❑	43	Chipper Jones	1.25	.50
❑	44	Pat Hentgen	.50	.20
❑	45	Eric Young	.50	.20
❑	46	Jaret Wright	.50	.20
❑	47	Juan Guzman	.50	.20
❑	48	Jorge Posada	.75	.30
❑	49	Bobby Higginson	.50	.20
❑	50	Jose Guillen	.50	.20
❑	51	Trevor Hoffman	.50	.20
❑	52	Ken Griffey Jr.	2.00	.75
❑	53	David Justice	.50	.20
❑	54	Matt Williams	.50	.20
❑	55	Eric Karros	.50	.20
❑	56	Derek Bell	.50	.20
❑	57	Ray Lankford	.50	.20
❑	58	Mariano Rivera	1.25	.50
❑	59	Brett Tomko	.50	.20
❑	60	Mike Mussina	.75	.30
❑	61	Kenny Lofton	.50	.20
❑	62	Chuck Finley	.50	.20
❑	63	Alex Gonzalez	.50	.20
❑	64	Mark Grace	.75	.30
❑	65	Raul Mondesi	.50	.20
❑	66	David Cone	.50	.20
❑	67	Brad Fullmer	.50	.20
❑	68	Andy Benes	.50	.20
❑	69	John Smoltz	.75	.30
❑	70	Shane Reynolds	.50	.20
❑	71	Bruce Chen	.50	.20
❑	72	Adam Kennedy	.50	.20
❑	73	Jack Cust	.50	.20
❑	74	Matt Clement	.50	.20
❑	75	Derrick Gibson	.50	.20
❑	76	Darnell McDonald	.50	.20
❑	77	Adam Everett RC	2.50	1.00
❑	78	Ricardo Aramboles	.50	.20
❑	79	Mark Quinn RC	1.00	.40
❑	80	Jason Rakers	.50	.20
❑	81	Seth Etherton RC	1.00	.40
❑	82	Jeff Urban RC	1.00	.40
❑	83	Manny Aybar	.50	.20
❑	84	Mike Nannini RC	1.00	.40
❑	85	Onan Masaoka	.50	.20
❑	86	Rod Barajas	.50	.20
❑	87	Mike Frank	.50	.20
❑	88	Scott Randall	.50	.20
❑	89	Justin Bowles RC	1.00	.40
❑	90	Chris Haas	.50	.20
❑	91	Arturo McDowell RC	1.00	.40
❑	92	Matt Belisle RC	1.00	.40
❑	93	Scott Elarton	.50	.20
❑	94	Vernon Wells	.50	.20
❑	95	Pat Cline	.50	.20
❑	96	Ryan Anderson	.50	.20
❑	97	Kevin Barker	.50	.20
❑	98	Ruben Mateo	.50	.20
❑	99	Robert Fick	.50	.20
❑	100	Corey Koskie	.50	.20
❑	101	Ricky Ledee	.50	.20
❑	102	Rick Elder RC	1.00	.40
❑	103	Jack Cressend RC	1.00	.40
❑	104	Joe Lawrence	.50	.20
❑	105	Mike Lincoln	.50	.20
❑	106	Kit Pellow RC	1.00	.40
❑	107	Matt Burch RC	1.00	.40
❑	108	Cole Liniak	.50	.20
❑	109	Jason Dewey	.50	.20
❑	110	Cesar King	.50	.20
❑	111	Julio Ramirez	.50	.20
❑	112	Jake Westbrook	.50	.20
❑	113	Eric Valent RC	1.50	.60
❑	114	Roosevelt Brown RC	1.00	.40
❑	115	Choo Freeman RC	1.50	.60
❑	116	Juan Melo	.50	.20
❑	117	Jason Grilli	.50	.20
❑	118	Jared Sandberg	.50	.20
❑	119	Glenn Davis	.50	.20
❑	120	David Riske RC	1.00	.40
❑	121	Jacque Jones	.50	.20
❑	122	Corey Lee	.50	.20
❑	123	Michael Barrett	.50	.20
❑	124	Lariel Gonzalez	.50	.20
❑	125	Mitch Meluskey	.50	.20
❑	126	F.Adrian Garcia	.50	.20
❑	127	Tony Torcato RC	1.00	.40
❑	128	Jeff Liefer	.50	.20
❑	129	Ntema Ndungidi	.50	.20
❑	130	Andy Brown RC	1.00	.40
❑	131	Ryan Mills RC	1.00	.40
❑	132	Andy Abad RC	1.00	.40
❑	133	Carlos Febles	.50	.20
❑	134	Jason Tyner RC	1.00	.40
❑	135	Mark Osborne	.50	.20
❑	136	Phil Norton RC	1.00	.40
❑	137	Nathan Haynes	.50	.20
❑	138	Roy Halladay	.50	.20
❑	139	Juan Encarnacion	.50	.20
❑	140	Brad Penny	.50	.20
❑	141	Grant Roberts	.50	.20
❑	142	Aramis Ramirez	.50	.20
❑	143	Cristian Guzman	.50	.20
❑	144	Mamon Tucker RC	1.00	.40
❑	145	Ryan Bradley	.50	.20
❑	146	Brian Simmons	.50	.20
❑	147	Dan Reichert	.50	.20
❑	148	Russell Branyan	.50	.20
❑	149	Victor Valencia RC	1.00	.40
❑	150	Scott Schoeneweis	.50	.20
❑	151	Sean Spencer RC	1.00	.40
❑	152	Odalis Perez	.50	.20
❑	153	Joe Fontenot	.50	.20
❑	154	Milton Bradley	.50	.20
❑	155	Josh McKinley RC	1.00	.40
❑	156	Terrence Long	.50	.20
❑	157	Danny Klassen	.50	.20
❑	158	Paul Hoover RC	1.00	.40
❑	159	Ron Belliard	.50	.20
❑	160	Armando Rios	.50	.20
❑	161	Ramon Hernandez	.50	.20
❑	162	Jason Conti	.50	.20
❑	163	Chad Hermansen	.50	.20
❑	164	Jason Standridge	.50	.20
❑	165	Jason Dellaero	.50	.20
❑	166	John Curtice	.50	.20
❑	167	Clayton Andrews RC	1.00	.40
❑	168	Jeremy Giambi	.50	.20
❑	169	Alex Ramirez	.50	.20
❑	170	Gabe Molina RC	1.00	.40
❑	171	Mario Encarnacion RC	1.00	.40
❑	172	Mike Zywica RC	1.00	.40
❑	173	Chip Ambres RC	1.00	.40
❑	174	Trot Nixon	.50	.20
❑	175	Pat Burrell RC	8.00	3.00
❑	176	Jeff Yoder	.50	.20
❑	177	Chris Jones RC	1.00	.40
❑	178	Kevin Witt	.50	.20
❑	179	Keith Luuloa RC	1.00	.40
❑	180	Billy Koch	.50	.20
❑	181	Damaso Marte RC	1.00	.40
❑	182	Ryan Glynn RC	1.00	.40
❑	183	Calvin Pickering	.50	.20
❑	184	Michael Cuddyer	.50	.20
❑	185	Nick Johnson RC	5.00	2.00

❑ 186 Doug Mientkiewicz RC 2.50 1.00
❑ 187 Nate Cornejo RC 1.00 .40
❑ 188 Octavio Dotel .50 .20
❑ 189 Wes Helms .50 .20
❑ 190 Nelson Lara .50 .20
❑ 191 Chuck Abbott RC 1.00 .40
❑ 192 Tony Armas Jr. .50 .20
❑ 193 Gil Meche .50 .20
❑ 194 Ben Petrick .50 .20
❑ 195 Chris George RC 1.00 .40
❑ 196 Scott Hunter RC 1.00 .40
❑ 197 Ryan Brannan .50 .20
❑ 198 Amaury Garcia RC 1.00 .40
❑ 199 Chris Gissell .50 .20
❑ 200 Austin Kearns RC 8.00 3.00
❑ 201 Alex Gonzalez .50 .20
❑ 202 Wade Miller .50 .20
❑ 203 Scott Williamson .50 .20
❑ 204 Chris Enochs .50 .20
❑ 205 Fernando Seguignol .50 .20
❑ 206 Marlon Anderson .50 .20
❑ 207 Todd Sears RC 1.00 .40
❑ 208 Nate Bump RC 1.00 .40
❑ 209 J.M. Gold RC 1.00 .40
❑ 210 Matt LeCroy .50 .20
❑ 211 Alex Hernandez .50 .20
❑ 212 Luis Rivera .50 .20
❑ 213 Troy Cameron .50 .20
❑ 214 Alex Escobar RC 1.50 .60
❑ 215 Jason LaRue .50 .20
❑ 216 Kyle Peterson .50 .20
❑ 217 Brent Butler .50 .20
❑ 218 Dernell Stenson .50 .20
❑ 219 Adrian Beltre .50 .20
❑ 220 Daryle Ward .50 .20
❑ 221 Jim Thome .75 .30
❑ 222 Cliff Floyd .50 .20
❑ 223 Rickey Henderson 1.25 .50
❑ 224 Garret Anderson .50 .20
❑ 225 Ken Caminiti .50 .20
❑ 226 Bret Boone .50 .20
❑ 227 Jeromy Burnitz .50 .20
❑ 228 Steve Finley .50 .20
❑ 229 Miguel Tejada .50 .20
❑ 230 Greg Vaughn .50 .20
❑ 231 Jose Offerman .50 .20
❑ 232 Andy Ashby .50 .20
❑ 233 Albert Belle .50 .20
❑ 234 Fernando Tatis .50 .20
❑ 235 Todd Helton .75 .30
❑ 236 Sean Casey .50 .20
❑ 237 Brian Giles .50 .20
❑ 238 Andy Pettitte .75 .30
❑ 239 Fred McGriff .75 .30
❑ 240 Roberto Alomar .75 .30
❑ 241 Edgar Martinez .75 .30
❑ 242 Lee Stevens .50 .20
❑ 243 Shawn Green .50 .20
❑ 244 Ryan Klesko .50 .20
❑ 245 Sammy Sosa 1.25 .50
❑ 246 Todd Hundley .50 .20
❑ 247 Shannon Stewart .50 .20
❑ 248 Randy Johnson 1.25 .50
❑ 249 Rondell White .50 .20
❑ 250 Mike Piazza 2.00 .75
❑ 251 Craig Biggio .75 .30
❑ 252 David Wells .50 .20
❑ 253 Brian Jordan .50 .20
❑ 254 Edgar Renteria .50 .20
❑ 255 Bartolo Colon .50 .20
❑ 256 Frank Thomas 1.25 .50
❑ 257 Will Clark .75 .30
❑ 258 Dean Palmer .50 .20
❑ 259 Dmitri Young .50 .20
❑ 260 Scott Rolen .75 .30
❑ 261 Jeff Kent .50 .20
❑ 262 Dante Bichette .50 .20
❑ 263 Nomar Garciaparra 2.00 .75
❑ 264 Tony Gwynn 1.50 .60
❑ 265 Alex Rodriguez 2.00 .75
❑ 266 Jose Canseco .75 .30
❑ 267 Jason Giambi .50 .20
❑ 268 Jeff Bagwell .75 .30
❑ 269 Carlos Delgado .50 .20
❑ 270 Tom Glavine .75 .30
❑ 271 Eric Davis .50 .20
❑ 272 Edgardo Alfonzo .50 .20
❑ 273 Tim Salmon .75 .30
❑ 274 Johnny Damon .75 .30
❑ 275 Rafael Palmeiro .75 .30
❑ 276 Denny Neagle .50 .20
❑ 277 Neifi Perez .50 .20
❑ 278 Roger Clemens 2.50 1.00
❑ 279 Brant Brown .50 .20
❑ 280 Kevin Brown .75 .30
❑ 281 Jay Bell .50 .20
❑ 282 Jay Buhner .50 .20
❑ 283 Matt Lawton .50 .20
❑ 284 Robin Ventura .50 .20
❑ 285 Juan Gonzalez .50 .20
❑ 286 Mo Vaughn .50 .20
❑ 287 Kevin Millwood .50 .20
❑ 288 Tino Martinez .75 .30
❑ 289 Justin Thompson .50 .20
❑ 290 Derek Jeter 3.00 1.25
❑ 291 Ben Davis .50 .20
❑ 292 Mike Lowell .50 .20
❑ 293 Calvin Murray .50 .20
❑ 294 Micah Bowie RC 1.00 .40
❑ 295 Lance Berkman .50 .20
❑ 296 Jason Marquis .50 .20
❑ 297 Chad Green .50 .20
❑ 298 Dee Brown .50 .20
❑ 299 Jerry Hairston Jr. .50 .20
❑ 300 Gabe Kapler .50 .20
❑ 301 Brent Stentz RC 1.00 .40
❑ 302 Scott Mullen RC 1.00 .40
❑ 303 Brandon Reed .50 .20
❑ 304 Shea Hillenbrand RC 4.00 1.50
❑ 305 J.D. Closser RC 1.50 .60
❑ 306 Gary Matthews Jr. .50 .20
❑ 307 Toby Hall RC 1.50 .60
❑ 308 Jason Phillips RC 1.00 .40
❑ 309 Jose Macias RC 1.00 .40
❑ 310 Jung Bong RC 1.00 .40
❑ 311 Ramon Soler RC 1.00 .40
❑ 312 Kelly Dransfeldt RC 1.00 .40
❑ 313 Carlos E. Hernandez RC 1.50 .60
❑ 314 Kevin Haverbusch .50 .20
❑ 315 Aaron Myette RC 1.00 .40
❑ 316 Chad Harville RC 1.00 .40
❑ 317 Kyle Farnsworth RC 1.50 .60
❑ 318 Gookie Dawkins RC 1.50 .60
❑ 319 Willie Martinez .50 .20
❑ 320 Carlos Lee .50 .20
❑ 321 Carlos Pena RC 1.50 .60
❑ 322 Peter Bergeron RC 1.00 .40
❑ 323 A.J. Burnett RC 4.00 1.50
❑ 324 Bucky Jacobsen RC 1.50 .60
❑ 325 Mo Bruce RC 1.00 .40
❑ 326 Reggie Taylor .50 .20
❑ 327 Jackie Rexrode .50 .20
❑ 328 Alvin Morrow RC 1.00 .40
❑ 329 Carlos Beltran .75 .30
❑ 330 Eric Chavez .50 .20
❑ 331 John Patterson .50 .20
❑ 332 Jayson Werth .50 .20
❑ 333 Richie Sexson .50 .20
❑ 334 Randy Wolf .50 .20
❑ 335 Eli Marrero .50 .20
❑ 336 Paul LoDuca .50 .20
❑ 337 J.D Smart .50 .20
❑ 338 Ryan Minor .50 .20
❑ 339 Kris Benson .50 .20
❑ 340 George Lombard .50 .20
❑ 341 Troy Glaus .75 .30
❑ 342 Eddie Yarnall .50 .20
❑ 343 Kip Wells RC 1.50 .60
❑ 344 C.C. Sabathia RC 5.00 2.00
❑ 345 Sean Burroughs RC 2.50 1.00
❑ 346 Felipe Lopez RC 6.00 2.50
❑ 347 Ryan Rupe RC 1.00 .40
❑ 348 Orber Moreno RC 1.00 .40
❑ 349 Rafael Roque RC 1.00 .40
❑ 350 Alfonso Soriano RC 25.00 10.00
❑ 351 Pablo Ozuna .50 .20
❑ 352 Corey Patterson RC 4.00 1.50
❑ 353 Braden Looper .50 .20
❑ 354 Robbie Bell .50 .20
❑ 355 Mark Mulder RC 6.00 2.50
❑ 356 Angel Pena .50 .20
❑ 357 Kevin McGlinchy .50 .20
❑ 358 Michael Restovich RC 1.50 .60
❑ 359 Eric DuBose .50 .20
❑ 360 Geoff Jenkins .50 .20
❑ 361 Mark Harriger RC 1.00 .40
❑ 362 Junior Herndon RC 1.00 .40
❑ 363 Tim Raines Jr. RC 1.00 .40
❑ 364 Rafael Furcal RC 5.00 2.00
❑ 365 Marcus Giles RC 4.00 1.50
❑ 366 Ted Lilly .50 .20
❑ 367 Jorge Toca RC 1.50 .60
❑ 368 David Kelton RC 1.00 .40
❑ 369 Adam Dunn RC 20.00 8.00
❑ 370 Guillermo Mota RC 1.00 .40
❑ 371 Brett Laxton RC 1.00 .40
❑ 372 Travis Harper RC 1.00 .40
❑ 373 Tom Davey RC 1.00 .40
❑ 374 Darren Blakely RC 1.00 .40
❑ 375 Tim Hudson RC 8.00 3.00
❑ 376 Jason Romano .50 .20
❑ 377 Dan Reichert .50 .20
❑ 378 Julio Lugo RC 2.50 1.00
❑ 379 Jose Garcia RC 1.00 .40
❑ 380 Erubiel Durazo RC 1.50 .60
❑ 381 Jose Jimenez .50 .20
❑ 382 Chris Fussell .50 .20
❑ 383 Steve Lomasney .50 .20
❑ 384 Juan Pena RC 1.00 .40
❑ 385 Allen Levrault RC 1.00 .40
❑ 386 Juan Rivera RC 4.00 1.50
❑ 387 Steve Colyer RC 1.00 .40
❑ 388 Joe Nathan RC 5.00 2.00
❑ 389 Ron Walker RC 1.00 .40
❑ 390 Nick Bierbrodt .50 .20
❑ 391 Luke Prokopec RC 1.00 .40
❑ 392 Dave Roberts RC 2.50 1.00
❑ 393 Mike Darr .50 .20
❑ 394 Abraham Nunez RC 1.50 .60
❑ 395 Giuseppe Chiaramonte RC 1.00 .40
❑ 396 Jermaine Van Buren RC 1.00 .40
❑ 397 Mike Kusiewicz .50 .20
❑ 398 Matt Wise RC 1.00 .40
❑ 399 Joe McEwing RC 1.50 .60
❑ 400 Matt Holliday RC 8.00 3.00
❑ 401 Willi Mo Pena RC 12.00 5.00
❑ 402 Ruben Quevedo RC 1.00 .40
❑ 403 Rob Ryan RC 1.00 .40
❑ 404 Freddy Garcia RC 4.00 1.50
❑ 405 Kevin Eberwein RC 1.00 .40
❑ 406 Jesus Colome RC 1.00 .40
❑ 407 Chris Singleton .50 .20
❑ 408 Bubba Crosby RC 2.50 1.00
❑ 409 Jesus Cordero RC 1.00 .40
❑ 410 Donny Leon .50 .20
❑ 411 Goefrey Tomlinson RC 1.00 .40
❑ 412 Jeff Winchester RC 1.00 .40
❑ 413 Adam Piatt RC 1.00 .40
❑ 414 Robert Stratton .50 .20
❑ 415 T.J. Tucker .50 .20
❑ 416 Ryan Langerhans RC 2.50 1.00
❑ 417 Anthony Shumaker RC 1.00 .40
❑ 418 Matt Miller RC 1.00 .40
❑ 419 Doug Clark RC 1.00 .40
❑ 420 Kory DeHaan RC 1.00 .40
❑ 421 David Eckstein RC 8.00 3.00
❑ 422 Brian Cooper RC 1.00 .40
❑ 423 Brady Clark RC 4.00 1.50
❑ 424 Chris Magruder RC 1.00 .40
❑ 425 Bobby Seay RC 1.00 .40
❑ 426 Aubrey Huff RC 5.00 2.00
❑ 427 Mike Jerzembeck .50 .20
❑ 428 Matt Blank RC 1.00 .40
❑ 429 Benny Agbayani RC 1.50 .60
❑ 430 Kevin Beirne RC 1.00 .40
❑ 431 Josh Hamilton RC 1.50 .60
❑ 432 Josh Girdley RC 1.00 .40
❑ 433 Kyle Snyder RC 1.00 .40
❑ 434 Mike Paradis RC 1.00 .40
❑ 435 Jason Jennings RC 2.50 1.00
❑ 436 David Walling RC 1.00 .40
❑ 437 Omar Ortiz RC 1.00 .40
❑ 438 Jay Gehrke RC 1.50 .60
❑ 439 Casey Burns RC 1.00 .40
❑ 440 Carl Crawford RC 12.00 5.00

2000 Bowman Chrome

❑	COMPLETE SET (440)	120.00	60.00
❑ 1	Vladimir Guerrero	1.25	.50
❑ 2	Chipper Jones	1.25	.50
❑ 3	Todd Walker	.50	.20
❑ 4	Barry Larkin	.75	.30
❑ 5	Bernie Williams	.75	.30
❑ 6	Todd Helton	.75	.30
❑ 7	Jermaine Dye	.50	.20
❑ 8	Brian Giles	.50	.20
❑ 9	Freddy Garcia	.50	.20
❑ 10	Greg Vaughn	.50	.20
❑ 11	Alex Gonzalez	.50	.20
❑ 12	Luis Gonzalez	.50	.20
❑ 13	Ron Belliard	.50	.20
❑ 14	Ben Grieve	.50	.20
❑ 15	Carlos Delgado	.50	.20
❑ 16	Brian Jordan	.50	.20
❑ 17	Fernando Tatis	.50	.20
❑ 18	Ryan Rupe	.50	.20
❑ 19	Miguel Tejada	.50	.20
❑ 20	Mark Grace	.75	.30
❑ 21	Kenny Lofton	.50	.20
❑ 22	Eric Karros	.50	.20
❑ 23	Cliff Floyd	.50	.20
❑ 24	John Halama	.50	.20
❑ 25	Cristian Guzman	.50	.20
❑ 26	Scott Williamson	.50	.20
❑ 27	Mike Lieberthal	.50	.20
❑ 28	Tim Hudson	.50	.20
❑ 29	Warren Morris	.50	.20
❑ 30	Pedro Martinez	.75	.30
❑ 31	John Smoltz	.75	.30
❑ 32	Ray Durham	.50	.20
❑ 33	Chad Allen	.50	.20
❑ 34	Tony Clark	.50	.20
❑ 35	Tino Martinez	.75	.30
❑ 36	J.T. Snow	.50	.20
❑ 37	Kevin Brown	.75	.30
❑ 38	Bartolo Colon	.50	.20
❑ 39	Rey Ordonez	.50	.20
❑ 40	Jeff Bagwell	.75	.30
❑ 41	Ivan Rodriguez	.75	.30
❑ 42	Eric Chavez	.50	.20
❑ 43	Eric Milton	.50	.20
❑ 44	Jose Canseco	.75	.30
❑ 45	Shawn Green	.50	.20
❑ 46	Rich Aurilia	.50	.20
❑ 47	Roberto Alomar	.75	.30
❑ 48	Brian Daubach	.50	.20
❑ 49	Magglio Ordonez	.50	.20
❑ 50	Derek Jeter	3.00	1.25
❑ 51	Kris Benson	.50	.20
❑ 52	Albert Belle	.50	.20
❑ 53	Rondell White	.50	.20
❑ 54	Justin Thompson	.50	.20
❑ 55	Nomar Garciaparra	2.00	.75
❑ 56	Chuck Finley	.50	.20
❑ 57	Omar Vizquel	.75	.30
❑ 58	Luis Castillo	.50	.20
❑ 59	Richard Hidalgo	.50	.20
❑ 60	Barry Bonds	3.00	1.25
❑ 61	Craig Biggio	.75	.30
❑ 62	Doug Glanville	.50	.20
❑ 63	Gabe Kapler	.50	.20
❑ 64	Johnny Damon	.75	.30
❑ 65	Pokey Reese	.50	.20
❑ 66	Andy Pettitte	.75	.30
❑ 67	B.J. Surhoff	.50	.20
❑ 68	Richie Sexson	.50	.20
❑ 69	Javy Lopez	.50	.20
❑ 70	Raul Mondesi	.50	.20
❑ 71	Darin Erstad	.50	.20
❑ 72	Kevin Millwood	.50	.20
❑ 73	Ricky Ledee	.50	.20
❑ 74	John Olerud	.50	.20
❑ 75	Sean Casey	.50	.20
❑ 76	Carlos Febles	.50	.20
❑ 77	Paul O'Neill	.75	.30
❑ 78	Bob Abreu	.50	.20
❑ 79	Neifi Perez	.50	.20
❑ 80	Tony Gwynn	1.50	.60
❑ 81	Russ Ortiz	.50	.20
❑ 82	Matt Williams	.50	.20
❑ 83	Chris Carpenter	.50	.20
❑ 84	Roger Cedeno	.50	.20
❑ 85	Tim Salmon	.75	.30
❑ 86	Billy Koch	.50	.20
❑ 87	Jeromy Burnitz	.50	.20
❑ 88	Edgardo Alfonzo	.50	.20
❑ 89	Jay Bell	.50	.20
❑ 90	Manny Ramirez	.75	.30
❑ 91	Frank Thomas	1.25	.50
❑ 92	Mike Mussina	.75	.30
❑ 93	J.D. Drew	.50	.20
❑ 94	Adrian Beltre	.50	.20
❑ 95	Alex Rodriguez	2.00	.75
❑ 96	Larry Walker	.50	.20
❑ 97	Juan Encarnacion	.50	.20
❑ 98	Mike Sweeney	.50	.20
❑ 99	Rusty Greer	.50	.20
❑ 100	Randy Johnson	1.25	.50
❑ 101	Jose Vidro	.50	.20
❑ 102	Preston Wilson	.50	.20
❑ 103	Greg Maddux	2.00	.75
❑ 104	Jason Giambi	.50	.20
❑ 105	Cal Ripken	4.00	1.50
❑ 106	Carlos Beltran	.50	.20
❑ 107	Vinny Castilla	.50	.20
❑ 108	Mariano Rivera	1.25	.50
❑ 109	Mo Vaughn	.50	.20
❑ 110	Rafael Palmeiro	.75	.30
❑ 111	Shannon Stewart	.50	.20
❑ 112	Mike Hampton	.50	.20
❑ 113	Joe Nathan	.50	.20
❑ 114	Ben Davis	.50	.20
❑ 115	Andruw Jones	.75	.30
❑ 116	Robin Ventura	.50	.20
❑ 117	Damion Easley	.50	.20
❑ 118	Jeff Cirillo	.50	.20
❑ 119	Kerry Wood	.50	.20
❑ 120	Scott Rolen	.75	.30
❑ 121	Sammy Sosa	1.25	.50
❑ 122	Ken Griffey Jr.	2.00	.75
❑ 123	Shane Reynolds	.50	.20
❑ 124	Troy Glaus	.50	.20
❑ 125	Tom Glavine	.75	.30
❑ 126	Michael Barrett	.50	.20
❑ 127	Al Leiter	.50	.20
❑ 128	Jason Kendall	.50	.20
❑ 129	Roger Clemens	2.50	1.00
❑ 130	Juan Gonzalez	.50	.20
❑ 131	Corey Koskie	.50	.20
❑ 132	Curt Schilling	.50	.20
❑ 133	Mike Piazza	2.00	.75
❑ 134	Gary Sheffield	.50	.20
❑ 135	Jim Thome	.75	.30
❑ 136	Orlando Hernandez	.50	.20
❑ 137	Ray Lankford	.50	.20
❑ 138	Geoff Jenkins	.50	.20
❑ 139	Jose Lima	.50	.20
❑ 140	Mark McGwire	3.00	1.25
❑ 141	Adam Piatt	.50	.20
❑ 142	Pat Manning RC	.75	.30
❑ 143	Marcos Castillo RC	.75	.30
❑ 144	Lesli Brea RC	.75	.30
❑ 145	Humberto Cota RC	1.25	.50
❑ 146	Ben Petrick	.50	.20
❑ 147	Kip Wells	.50	.20
❑ 148	Wily Pena	.50	.20
❑ 149	Chris Wakeland RC	.75	.30
❑ 150	Brad Baker RC	.75	.30
❑ 151	Robbie Morrison RC	.75	.30
❑ 152	Reggie Taylor	.50	.20
❑ 153	Matt Ginter RC	.75	.30
❑ 154	Peter Bergeron	.50	.20
❑ 155	Roosevelt Brown	.50	.20
❑ 156	Matt Cepicky RC	.75	.30
❑ 157	Ramon Castro	.50	.20
❑ 158	Brad Baisley RC	.75	.30
❑ 159	Jason Hart RC	.75	.30
❑ 160	Mitch Meluskey	.50	.20
❑ 161	Chad Harville	.50	.20
❑ 162	Brian Cooper	.50	.20
❑ 163	Marcus Giles	.50	.20
❑ 164	Jim Morris	1.25	.50
❑ 165	Geoff Goetz	.50	.20
❑ 166	Bobby Bradley RC	.75	.30
❑ 167	Rob Bell	.50	.20
❑ 168	Joe Crede	2.50	1.00
❑ 169	Michael Restovich	.50	.20
❑ 170	Quincy Foster RC	.75	.30
❑ 171	Enrique Cruz RC	.75	.30
❑ 172	Mark Quinn	.50	.20
❑ 173	Nick Johnson	.50	.20
❑ 174	Jeff Liefer	.50	.20
❑ 175	Kevin Mench RC	5.00	2.00
❑ 176	Steve Lomasney	.50	.20
❑ 177	Jayson Werth	.50	.20
❑ 178	Tim Drew	.50	.20
❑ 179	Chip Ambres	.50	.20
❑ 180	Ryan Anderson	.50	.20
❑ 181	Matt Blank	.50	.20
❑ 182	Giuseppe Chiaramonte	.50	.20
❑ 183	Corey Myers RC	.75	.30
❑ 184	Jeff Yoder	.50	.20
❑ 185	Craig Dingman RC	.75	.30
❑ 186	Jon Hamilton RC	.75	.30
❑ 187	Toby Hall	.50	.20
❑ 188	Russell Branyan	.50	.20
❑ 189	Brian Falkenborg RC	.75	.30
❑ 190	Aaron Harang RC	4.00	1.50
❑ 191	Juan Pena	.50	.20
❑ 192	Chin-Hui Tsao RC	5.00	2.00
❑ 193	Alfonso Soriano	1.25	.50
❑ 194	Alejandro Diaz RC	.75	.30
❑ 195	Carlos Pena	.50	.20
❑ 196	Kevin Nicholson	.50	.20
❑ 197	Mo Bruce	.50	.20
❑ 198	C.C. Sabathia	.50	.20
❑ 199	Carl Crawford	.50	.20
❑ 200	Rafael Furcal	.50	.20
❑ 201	Andrew Beinbrink RC	.75	.30
❑ 202	Jimmy Osting	.50	.20
❑ 203	Aaron McNeal RC	.75	.30
❑ 204	Brett Laxton	.50	.20
❑ 205	Chris George	.50	.20
❑ 206	Felipe Lopez	.50	.20
❑ 207	Ben Sheets RC	6.00	2.50
❑ 208	Mike Meyers RC	1.25	.50
❑ 209	Jason Conti	.50	.20
❑ 210	Milton Bradley	.50	.20
❑ 211	Chris Mears RC	.75	.30
❑ 212	Carlos Hernandez RC	1.25	.50
❑ 213	Jason Romano	.50	.20
❑ 214	Geofrey Tomlinson	.50	.20
❑ 215	Jimmy Rollins	.50	.20
❑ 216	Pablo Ozuna	.50	.20
❑ 217	Steve Cox	.50	.20
❑ 218	Terrence Long	.50	.20
❑ 219	Jeff DaVanon RC	1.25	.50
❑ 220	Rick Ankiel	.50	.20
❑ 221	Jason Standridge	.50	.20
❑ 222	Tony Armas Jr.	.50	.20
❑ 223	Jason Tyner	.50	.20
❑ 224	Ramon Ortiz	.50	.20
❑ 225	Daryle Ward	.50	.20
❑ 226	Enger Veras RC	.75	.30
❑ 227	Chris Jones	.50	.20
❑ 228	Eric Cammack RC	.75	.30
❑ 229	Ruben Mateo	.50	.20
❑ 230	Ken Harvey RC	1.25	.50
❑ 231	Jake Westbrook	.50	.20
❑ 232	Rob Purvis RC	.75	.30
❑ 233	Choo Freeman	.50	.20
❑ 234	Aramis Ramirez	.50	.20
❑ 235	A.J. Burnett	.50	.20
❑ 236	Kevin Barker	.50	.20
❑ 237	Chance Caple RC	.75	.30

❑ 238 Jarrod Washburn	.50	.20
❑ 239 Lance Berkman	.50	.20
❑ 240 Michael Wenner RC	.75	.30
❑ 241 Alex Sanchez	.50	.20
❑ 242 Pat Daneker	.50	.20
❑ 243 Grant Roberts	.50	.20
❑ 244 Mark Ellis RC	1.25	.50
❑ 245 Donny Leon	.50	.20
❑ 246 David Eckstein	.50	.20
❑ 247 Dicky Gonzalez RC	.75	.30
❑ 248 John Patterson	.50	.20
❑ 249 Chad Green	.50	.20
❑ 250 Scot Shields RC	.75	.30
❑ 251 Troy Cameron	.50	.20
❑ 252 Jose Molina	.50	.20
❑ 253 Rob Pugmire RC	.75	.30
❑ 254 Rick Elder	.50	.20
❑ 255 Sean Burroughs	.50	.20
❑ 256 Josh Kalinowski RC	.75	.30
❑ 257 Matt LeCroy	.50	.20
❑ 258 Alex Graman RC	.75	.30
❑ 259 Juan Silvestre RC	.75	.30
❑ 260 Brady Clark	.50	.20
❑ 261 Rico Washington RC	.75	.30
❑ 262 Gary Matthews Jr.	.50	.20
❑ 263 Matt Wise	.50	.20
❑ 264 Keith Reed RC	.75	.30
❑ 265 Santiago Ramirez RC	.75	.30
❑ 266 Ben Broussard RC	3.00	1.25
❑ 267 Ryan Langerhans	.50	.20
❑ 268 Juan Rivera	.50	.20
❑ 269 Shawn Gallagher	.50	.20
❑ 270 Jorge Toca	.50	.20
❑ 271 Brad Lidge	.75	.30
❑ 272 Leoncio Estrella RC	.75	.30
❑ 273 Ruben Quevedo	.50	.20
❑ 274 Jack Cust	.50	.20
❑ 275 T.J. Tucker	.50	.20
❑ 276 Mike Colangelo	.50	.20
❑ 277 Brian Schneider	.50	.20
❑ 278 Calvin Murray	.50	.20
❑ 279 Josh Girdley	.50	.20
❑ 280 Mike Paradis	.50	.20
❑ 281 Chad Hermansen	.50	.20
❑ 282 Ty Howington RC	.75	.30
❑ 283 Aaron Myette	.50	.20
❑ 284 D'Angelo Jimenez	.50	.20
❑ 285 Dernell Stenson	.50	.20
❑ 286 Jerry Hairston Jr.	.50	.20
❑ 287 Gary Majewski RC	1.25	.50
❑ 288 Derrin Ebert	.50	.20
❑ 289 Steve Fish RC	.75	.30
❑ 290 Carlos E. Hernandez	.50	.20
❑ 291 Allen Levrault	.50	.20
❑ 292 Sean McNally RC	.75	.30
❑ 293 Randey Dorame RC	.75	.30
❑ 294 Wes Anderson RC	.75	.30
❑ 295 B.J. Ryan	.50	.20
❑ 296 Alan Webb RC	.75	.30
❑ 297 Brandon Inge RC	5.00	2.00
❑ 298 David Walling	.50	.20
❑ 299 Sun Woo Kim RC	.75	.30
❑ 300 Pat Burrell	.50	.20
❑ 301 Rick Guttormson RC	.75	.30
❑ 302 Gil Meche	.50	.20
❑ 303 Carlos Zambrano RC	12.00	5.00
❑ 304 Eric Byrnes UER RC	1.25	.50
❑ 305 Robb Quinlan RC	1.25	.50
❑ 306 Jackie Rexrode	.50	.20
❑ 307 Nate Bump	.50	.20
❑ 308 Sean DePaula RC	.75	.30
❑ 309 Matt Riley	.50	.20
❑ 310 Ryan Minor	.50	.20
❑ 311 J.J. Davis	.50	.20
❑ 312 Randy Wolf	.50	.20
❑ 313 Jason Jennings	.50	.20
❑ 314 Scott Seabol RC	.75	.30
❑ 315 Doug Davis	.50	.20
❑ 316 Todd Moser RC	.75	.30
❑ 317 Rob Ryan	.50	.20
❑ 318 Bubba Crosby	.50	.20
❑ 319 Lyle Overbay RC	3.00	1.25
❑ 320 Mario Encarnacion	.50	.20
❑ 321 Francisco Rodriguez RC	6.00	2.50
❑ 322 Michael Cuddyer	.50	.20
❑ 323 Ed Yarnall	.50	.20

❑ 324 Cesar Saba RC	.75	.30
❑ 325 Gookie Dawkins	.50	.20
❑ 326 Alex Escobar	.50	.20
❑ 327 Julio Zuleta RC	.75	.30
❑ 328 Josh Hamilton	.50	.20
❑ 329 Carlos Urquiola RC	.75	.30
❑ 330 Matt Belisle	.50	.20
❑ 331 Kurt Ainsworth RC	.75	.30
❑ 332 Tim Raines Jr.	.50	.20
❑ 333 Eric Munson	.50	.20
❑ 334 Donzell McDonald	.50	.20
❑ 335 Larry Bigbie RC	2.00	.75
❑ 336 Matt Watson RC	.75	.30
❑ 337 Aubrey Huff	.50	.20
❑ 338 Julio Ramirez	.50	.20
❑ 339 Jason Grabowski RC	.75	.30
❑ 340 Jon Garland	.50	.20
❑ 341 Austin Kearns	.50	.20
❑ 342 Josh Pressley RC	.75	.30
❑ 343 Miguel Olivo RC	2.00	.75
❑ 344 Julio Lugo	.50	.20
❑ 345 Roberto Vaz	.50	.20
❑ 346 Ramon Soler	.50	.20
❑ 347 Brandon Phillips RC	4.00	1.50
❑ 348 Vince Faison RC	.75	.30
❑ 349 Mike Venafro	.50	.20
❑ 350 Rick Asadoorian RC	1.25	.50
❑ 351 B.J. Garbe RC	.75	.30
❑ 352 Dan Reichert	.50	.20
❑ 353 Jason Stumm RC	.75	.30
❑ 354 Ruben Salazar RC	.75	.30
❑ 355 Francisco Cordero	.50	.20
❑ 356 Juan Guzman RC	.75	.30
❑ 357 Mike Bacsik RC	.75	.30
❑ 358 Jared Sandberg	.50	.20
❑ 359 Rod Barajas	.50	.20
❑ 360 Junior Brignac RC	.75	.30
❑ 361 J.M. Gold	.50	.20
❑ 362 Octavio Dotel	.50	.20
❑ 363 David Kelton	.50	.20
❑ 364 Scott Morgan	.50	.20
❑ 365 Wascar Serrano RC	.75	.30
❑ 366 Wilton Veras	.50	.20
❑ 367 Eugene Kingsale	.50	.20
❑ 368 Ted Lilly	.50	.20
❑ 369 George Lombard	.50	.20
❑ 370 Chris Haas	.50	.20
❑ 371 Wilton Pena RC	.75	.30
❑ 372 Vernon Wells	.50	.20
❑ 373 Keith Ginter RC	.75	.30
❑ 374 Jeff Heaverlo RC	.75	.30
❑ 375 Calvin Pickering	.50	.20
❑ 376 Mike Lamb RC	2.00	.75
❑ 377 Kyle Snyder	.50	.20
❑ 378 Javier Cardona RC	.75	.30
❑ 379 Aaron Rowand RC	5.00	2.00
❑ 380 Dee Brown	.50	.20
❑ 381 Brett Myers RC	5.00	2.00
❑ 382 Abraham Nunez	.50	.20
❑ 383 Eric Valent	.50	.20
❑ 384 Jody Gerut RC	1.25	.50
❑ 385 Adam Dunn	1.25	.50
❑ 386 Jay Gehrke	.50	.20
❑ 387 Omar Ortiz	.50	.20
❑ 388 Darnell McDonald	.50	.20
❑ 389 Tony Schrager RC	.75	.30
❑ 390 J.D. Closser	.50	.20
❑ 391 Ben Christensen RC	.75	.30
❑ 392 Adam Kennedy	.50	.20
❑ 393 Nick Green RC	.75	.30
❑ 394 Ramon Hernandez	.50	.20
❑ 395 Roy Oswalt RC	25.00	10.00
❑ 396 Andy Tracy RC	.75	.30
❑ 397 Eric Gagne	1.25	.50
❑ 398 Michael Tejera RC	.75	.30
❑ 399 Adam Everett	.50	.20
❑ 400 Corey Patterson	.50	.20
❑ 401 Gary Knotts RC	.75	.30
❑ 402 Ryan Christianson RC	.75	.30
❑ 403 Eric Ireland RC	.75	.30
❑ 404 Andrew Good RC	.75	.30
❑ 405 Brad Penny	.50	.20
❑ 406 Jason LaRue	.50	.20
❑ 407 Kit Pellow	.50	.20
❑ 408 Kevin Beirne	.50	.20
❑ 409 Kelly Dransfeldt	.50	.20

❑ 410 Jason Grilli	.50	.20
❑ 411 Scott Downs RC	.75	.30
❑ 412 Jesus Colome	.50	.20
❑ 413 John Sneed RC	.75	.30
❑ 414 Tony McKnight	.50	.20
❑ 415 Luis Rivera	.50	.20
❑ 416 Adam Eaton	.50	.20
❑ 417 Mike MacDougal RC	1.25	.50
❑ 418 Mike Nannini	.50	.20
❑ 419 Barry Zito RC	10.00	4.00
❑ 420 DeWayne Wise	.50	.20
❑ 421 Jason Dellaero	.50	.20
❑ 422 Chad Moeller	.50	.20
❑ 423 Jason Marquis	.50	.20
❑ 424 Tim Redding RC	1.25	.50
❑ 425 Mark Mulder	.50	.20
❑ 426 Josh Paul	.50	.20
❑ 427 Chris Enochs	.50	.20
❑ 428 Wilfredo Rodriguez RC	.75	.30
❑ 429 Kevin Witt	.50	.20
❑ 430 Scott Sobkowiak RC	.75	.30
❑ 431 McKay Christensen	.50	.20
❑ 432 Jung Bong	.50	.20
❑ 433 Keith Evans RC	.75	.30
❑ 434 Garry Maddox Jr. RC	.75	.30
❑ 435 Ramon Santiago RC	.75	.30
❑ 436 Alex Cora	.50	.20
❑ 437 Carlos Lee	.50	.20
❑ 438 Jason Repko RC	2.00	.75
❑ 439 Matt Burch	.50	.20
❑ 440 Shawn Sonnier RC	.75	.30

2000 Bowman Chrome Draft Picks

❑ COMP.FACT.SET (110)	50.00	20.00
❑ 1 Pat Burrell	.50	.20
❑ 2 Rafael Furcal	.50	.20
❑ 3 Grant Roberts	.50	.20
❑ 4 Barry Zito	4.00	1.50
❑ 5 Julio Zuleta	.50	.20
❑ 6 Mark Mulder	.50	.20
❑ 7 Rob Bell	.50	.20
❑ 8 Adam Piatt	.50	.20
❑ 9 Mike Lamb	.75	.30
❑ 10 Pablo Ozuna	.50	.20
❑ 11 Jason Tyner	.50	.20
❑ 12 Jason Marquis	.50	.20
❑ 13 Eric Munson	.50	.20
❑ 14 Seth Etherton	.50	.20
❑ 15 Milton Bradley	.50	.20
❑ 16 Nick Green	.50	.20
❑ 17 Chin-Feng Chen RC	1.50	.60
❑ 18 Matt Boone RC	.50	.20
❑ 19 Kevin Gregg RC	.50	.20
❑ 20 Eddy Garabito RC	.50	.20
❑ 21 Aaron Capista RC	.50	.20
❑ 22 Esteban German RC	.50	.20
❑ 23 Derek Thompson RC	.50	.20
❑ 24 Phil Merrell RC	.50	.20
❑ 25 Brian O'Connor RC	.50	.20
❑ 26 Yamid Haad	.50	.20
❑ 27 Hector Mercado RC	.50	.20
❑ 28 Jason Woolf RC	.50	.20
❑ 29 Eddy Furniss RC	.50	.20
❑ 30 Cha Sueng Baek RC	.50	.20
❑ 31 Colby Lewis RC	.50	.20
❑ 32 Pasqual Coco RC	.50	.20
❑ 33 Jorge Cantu RC	5.00	2.00

❑ 34 Erasmo Ramirez RC	.50	.20
❑ 35 Bobby Kielty RC	1.00	.40
❑ 36 Joaquin Benoit RC	.50	.20
❑ 37 Brian Esposito RC	.50	.20
❑ 38 Michael Wenner	.50	.20
❑ 39 Juan Rincon RC	.50	.20
❑ 40 Yorvit Torrealba RC	.50	.20
❑ 41 Chad Durham RC	.50	.20
❑ 42 Jim Mann RC	.50	.20
❑ 43 Shane Loux RC	.50	.20
❑ 44 Luis Rivas	.50	.20
❑ 45 Ken Chenard RC	.50	.20
❑ 46 Mike Lockwood RC	.50	.20
❑ 47 Yovanny Lara RC	.50	.20
❑ 48 Bubba Carpenter RC	.50	.20
❑ 49 Ryan Dittfurth RC	.50	.20
❑ 50 John Stephens RC	.50	.20
❑ 51 Pedro Feliz RC	2.50	1.00
❑ 52 Kenny Kelly RC	.50	.20
❑ 53 Neil Jenkins RC	.50	.20
❑ 54 Mike Glendenning RC	.50	.20
❑ 55 Bo Porter	.50	.20
❑ 56 Eric Byrnes	.50	.20
❑ 57 Tony Alvarez RC	.50	.20
❑ 58 Kazuhiro Sasaki RC	1.50	.60
❑ 59 Chad Durbin RC	.50	.20
❑ 60 Mike Bynum RC	.50	.20
❑ 61 Travis Wilson RC	.50	.20
❑ 62 Jose Leon RC	.50	.20
❑ 63 Ryan Vogelsong RC	.50	.20
❑ 64 Geraldo Guzman RC	.50	.20
❑ 65 Craig Anderson RC	.50	.20
❑ 66 Carlos Silva RC	1.00	.40
❑ 67 Brad Thomas RC	.50	.20
❑ 68 Chin-Hui Tsao	1.50	.60
❑ 69 Mark Buehrle RC	8.00	3.00
❑ 70 Juan Salas RC	.50	.20
❑ 71 Denny Abreu RC	.50	.20
❑ 72 Keith McDonald RC	.50	.20
❑ 73 Chris Richard RC	.50	.20
❑ 74 Tomas De la Rosa RC	.50	.20
❑ 75 Vicente Padilla RC	1.00	.40
❑ 76 Justin Brunette RC	.50	.20
❑ 77 Scott Linebrink RC	.50	.20
❑ 78 Jeff Sparks RC	.50	.20
❑ 79 Tike Redman RC	1.50	.60
❑ 80 John Lackey RC	5.00	2.00
❑ 81 Joe Strong RC	.50	.20
❑ 82 Brian Tollberg RC	.50	.20
❑ 83 Steve Sisco RC	.50	.20
❑ 84 Chris Clapinski RC	.50	.20
❑ 85 Augie Ojeda RC	.50	.20
❑ 86 Adrian Gonzalez RC	5.00	2.00
❑ 87 Mike Stodolka RC	.50	.20
❑ 88 Adam Johnson RC	.50	.20
❑ 89 Matt Wheatland RC	.50	.20
❑ 90 Corey Smith RC	.50	.20
❑ 91 Rocco Baldelli RC	5.00	2.00
❑ 92 Keith Bucktrot RC	.50	.20
❑ 93 Adam Wainwright RC	2.50	1.00
❑ 94 Blaine Boyer RC	.50	.20
❑ 95 Aaron Herr RC	1.00	.40
❑ 96 Scott Thorman RC	2.50	1.00
❑ 97 Bryan Digby RC	.50	.20
❑ 98 Josh Shortslef RC	.50	.20
❑ 99 Sean Smith RC	.50	.20
❑ 100 Alex Cruz RC	.50	.20
❑ 101 Marc Love RC	.50	.20
❑ 102 Kevin Lee RC	.50	.20
❑ 103 Timo Perez RC	1.00	.40
❑ 104 Alex Cabrera RC	1.00	.40
❑ 105 Shane Heams RC	.50	.20
❑ 106 Tripper Johnson RC	.50	.20
❑ 107 Brent Abernathy RC	.50	.20
❑ 108 John Cotton RC	.50	.20
❑ 109 Brad Wilkerson RC	2.50	1.00
❑ 110 Jon Rauch RC	.50	.20

2001 Bowman Chrome

❑ COMP.SET w/o SP's (220)	50.00	20.00
❑ COMMON (1-110/201-310)	.50	.20
❑ COM.REF (111-200/311-330)	5.00	2.00
❑ COMMON AU REF (331-350)	50.00	20.00
❑ 1 Jason Giambi	.50	.20
❑ 2 Rafael Furcal	.50	.20

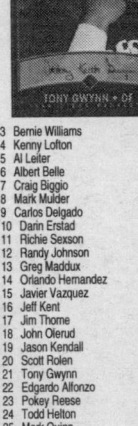

❑ 3 Bernie Williams	.75	.30
❑ 4 Kenny Lofton	.50	.20
❑ 5 Al Leiter	.50	.20
❑ 6 Albert Belle	.50	.20
❑ 7 Craig Biggio	.75	.30
❑ 8 Mark Mulder	.50	.20
❑ 9 Carlos Delgado	.50	.20
❑ 10 Darin Erstad	.50	.20
❑ 11 Richie Sexson	.50	.20
❑ 12 Randy Johnson	1.25	.50
❑ 13 Greg Maddux	2.00	.75
❑ 14 Orlando Hernandez	.50	.20
❑ 15 Javier Vazquez	.50	.20
❑ 16 Jeff Kent	.50	.20
❑ 17 Jim Thome	.75	.30
❑ 18 John Olerud	.50	.20
❑ 19 Jason Kendall	.50	.20
❑ 20 Scott Rolen	.75	.30
❑ 21 Tony Gwynn	1.50	.60
❑ 22 Edgardo Alfonzo	.50	.20
❑ 23 Pokey Reese	.50	.20
❑ 24 Todd Helton	.75	.30
❑ 25 Mark Quinn	.50	.20
❑ 26 Dean Palmer	.50	.20
❑ 27 Ray Durham	.50	.20
❑ 28 Rafael Palmeiro	.75	.30
❑ 29 Carl Everett	.50	.20
❑ 30 Vladimir Guerrero	1.25	.50
❑ 31 Livan Hernandez	.50	.20
❑ 32 Preston Wilson	.50	.20
❑ 33 Jose Vidro	.50	.20
❑ 34 Fred McGriff	.75	.30
❑ 35 Kevin Brown	.50	.20
❑ 36 Miguel Tejada	.50	.20
❑ 37 Chipper Jones	1.25	.50
❑ 38 Edgar Martinez	.75	.30
❑ 39 Tony Batista	.50	.20
❑ 40 Jorge Posada	.75	.30
❑ 41 Sammy Sosa	1.25	.50
❑ 42 Gary Sheffield	.50	.20
❑ 43 Bartolo Colon	.50	.20
❑ 44 Pat Burrell	.50	.20
❑ 45 Jay Payton	.50	.20
❑ 46 Mike Mussina	.75	.30
❑ 47 Nomar Garciaparra	2.00	.75
❑ 48 Darren Dreifort	.50	.20
❑ 49 Richard Hidalgo	.50	.20
❑ 50 Troy Glaus	.50	.20
❑ 51 Ben Grieve	.50	.20
❑ 52 Jim Edmonds	.50	.20
❑ 53 Raul Mondesi	.50	.20
❑ 54 Andruw Jones	.75	.30
❑ 55 Mike Sweeney	.50	.20
❑ 56 Derek Jeter	3.00	1.25
❑ 57 Ruben Mateo	.50	.20
❑ 58 Cristian Guzman	.50	.20
❑ 59 Mike Hampton	.50	.20
❑ 60 J.D. Drew	.50	.20
❑ 61 Matt Lawton	.50	.20
❑ 62 Moises Alou	.50	.20
❑ 63 Terrence Long	.50	.20
❑ 64 Geoff Jenkins	.50	.20
❑ 65 Manny Ramirez Sox	.75	.30
❑ 66 Johnny Damon	.75	.30
❑ 67 Pedro Martinez	.75	.30
❑ 68 Juan Gonzalez	.50	.20
❑ 69 Roger Clemens	2.50	1.00
❑ 70 Carlos Beltran	.50	.20
❑ 71 Roberto Alomar	.75	.30
❑ 72 Barry Bonds	3.00	1.25
❑ 73 Tim Hudson	.50	.20
❑ 74 Tom Glavine	.75	.30
❑ 75 Jeromy Burnitz	.50	.20
❑ 76 Adrian Beltre	.50	.20
❑ 77 Mike Piazza	2.00	.75
❑ 78 Kerry Wood	.50	.20
❑ 79 Steve Finley	.50	.20
❑ 80 Bob Abreu	.50	.20
❑ 81 Neifi Perez	.50	.20
❑ 82 Mark Redman	.50	.20
❑ 83 Paul Konerko	.50	.20
❑ 84 Jermaine Dye	.50	.20
❑ 85 Brian Giles	.50	.20
❑ 86 Ivan Rodriguez	.75	.30
❑ 87 Adam Kennedy	.50	.20
❑ 88 Eric Chavez	.50	.20
❑ 89 Billy Koch	.50	.20
❑ 90 Shawn Green	.50	.20
❑ 91 Matt Williams	.50	.20
❑ 92 Greg Vaughn	.50	.20
❑ 93 Jeff Cirillo	.50	.20
❑ 94 Frank Thomas	1.25	.50
❑ 95 David Justice	.50	.20
❑ 96 Cal Ripken	4.00	1.50
❑ 97 Curt Schilling	.50	.20
❑ 98 Barry Zito	.75	.30
❑ 99 Brian Jordan	.50	.20
❑ 100 Chan Ho Park	.50	.20
❑ 101 J.T. Snow	.50	.20
❑ 102 Kazuhiro Sasaki	.50	.20
❑ 103 Alex Rodriguez	2.00	.75
❑ 104 Mariano Rivera	1.25	.50
❑ 105 Eric Milton	.50	.20
❑ 106 Andy Pettitte	.75	.30
❑ 107 Ken Griffey Jr.	2.00	.75
❑ 108 Bengie Molina	.50	.20
❑ 109 Jeff Bagwell	.75	.30
❑ 110 Mark McGwire	3.00	1.25
❑ 111 Dan Tosca RC	5.00	2.00
❑ 112 Sergio Contreras RC	8.00	3.00
❑ 113 Mitch Jones RC	8.00	3.00
❑ 114 Ramon Carvajal RC	8.00	3.00
❑ 115 Ryan Madson RC	10.00	4.00
❑ 116 Hank Blalock RC	40.00	20.00
❑ 117 Ben Washburn RC	5.00	2.00
❑ 118 Erick Almonte RC	5.00	2.00
❑ 119 Shawn Fagan RC	8.00	3.00
❑ 120 Gary Johnson RC	5.00	2.00
❑ 121 Brett Evert RC	5.00	2.00
❑ 122 Joe Hamer RC	8.00	3.00
❑ 123 Yhency Brazoban RC	10.00	4.00
❑ 124 Domingo Guante RC	5.00	2.00
❑ 125 Deivi Mendez RC	5.00	2.00
❑ 126 Adrian Hernandez RC	5.00	2.00
❑ 127 Reggie Abercrombie RC	10.00	4.00
❑ 128 Steve Bennett RC	5.00	2.00
❑ 129 Matt White RC	8.00	3.00
❑ 130 Brian Hitchcox RC	5.00	2.00
❑ 131 Deivis Santos RC	5.00	2.00
❑ 132 Luis Montanez RC	8.00	3.00
❑ 133 Eric Reynolds RC	5.00	2.00
❑ 134 Denny Bautista RC	10.00	4.00
❑ 135 Hector Garcia RC	5.00	2.00
❑ 136 Joe Thurston RC	8.00	3.00
❑ 137 Tsuyoshi Shinjo RC	10.00	4.00
❑ 138 Elpidio Guzman RC	5.00	2.00
❑ 139 Brian Bass RC	5.00	2.00
❑ 140 Mark Burnett RC	8.00	3.00
❑ 141 Russ Jacobson UER	5.00	2.00
❑ 142 Travis Hafner RC	60.00	35.00
❑ 143 Wilson Betemit RC	15.00	6.00
❑ 144 Luke Lockwood RC	8.00	3.00
❑ 145 Noel Devarez RC	8.00	3.00
❑ 146 Doug Gredvig RC	5.00	2.00
❑ 147 Seung Song RC	8.00	3.00
❑ 148 Andy Van Hekken RC	5.00	2.00
❑ 149 Ryan Kohlmeier	5.00	2.00
❑ 150 Dee Haynes RC	5.00	2.00
❑ 151 Jim Journell RC	8.00	3.00
❑ 152 Chad Petty RC	5.00	2.00
❑ 153 Danny Borrell RC	5.00	2.00
❑ 154 Dave Krynzel	5.00	2.00
❑ 155 Octavio Martinez RC	8.00	3.00
❑ 156 David Parrish RC	5.00	2.00

157	Jason Miller RC	5.00	2.00
158	Corey Spencer RC	5.00	2.00
159	Maxim St. Pierre RC	8.00	3.00
160	Pat Magness RC	8.00	3.00
161	Ranier Olmedo RC	8.00	3.00
162	Brandon Mims RC	5.00	2.00
163	Phil Wilson RC	8.00	3.00
164	Jose Reyes RC	100.00	50.00
165	Matt Butler RC	8.00	3.00
166	Joel Pineiro	8.00	3.00
167	Ken Chenard	5.00	2.00
168	Alexis Gomez RC	5.00	2.00
169	Justin Morneau RC	60.00	35.00
170	Josh Fogg RC	8.00	3.00
171	Charles Frazier RC	5.00	2.00
172	Ryan Ludwick RC	8.00	3.00
173	Seth McClung RC	8.00	3.00
174	Justin Wayne RC	8.00	3.00
175	Rafael Soriano RC	8.00	3.00
176	Jared Abruzzo RC	5.00	2.00
177	Jason Richardson RC	5.00	2.00
178	Darwin Cubillan RC	5.00	2.00
179	Blake Williams RC	5.00	2.00
180	Valentino Pascucci RC	8.00	3.00
181	Ryan Hannaman RC	8.00	3.00
182	Steve Smyth RC	8.00	3.00
183	Jake Peavy RC	40.00	20.00
184	Onix Mercado RC	8.00	3.00
185	Luis Torres RC	8.00	3.00
186	Casey Fossum RC	5.00	2.00
187	Eduardo Figueroa RC	5.00	2.00
188	Bryan Barnowski RC	5.00	2.00
189	Jason Standridge	5.00	2.00
190	Marvin Seale RC	8.00	3.00
191	Steve Smitherman RC	8.00	3.00
192	Rafael Boitel RC	5.00	2.00
193	Dany Morban RC	5.00	2.00
194	Justin Woodrow RC	8.00	3.00
195	Ed Rogers RC	5.00	2.00
196	Ben Hendrickson RC	5.00	2.00
197	Thomas Mitchell	5.00	2.00
198	Adam Pettyjohn RC	5.00	2.00
199	Doug Nickle RC	5.00	2.00
200	Jason Jones RC	5.00	2.00
201	Larry Barnes	.50	.20
202	Ben Diggins	.50	.20
203	Dee Brown	.50	.20
204	Rocco Baldelli	.50	.20
205	Luis Terrero	.50	.20
206	Milton Bradley	.50	.20
207	Kurt Ainsworth	.50	.20
208	Sean Burroughs	.50	.20
209	Rick Asadoorian	.50	.20
210	Ramon Castro	.50	.20
211	Nick Neugebauer	.50	.20
212	Aaron Myette	.50	.20
213	Luis Matos	.50	.20
214	Donnie Bridges	.50	.20
215	Alex Cintron	.50	.20
216	Bobby Kielty	.50	.20
217	Matt Belisle	.50	.20
218	Adam Everett	.50	.20
219	John Lackey	.50	.20
220	Adam Wainwright	.50	.20
221	Jerry Hairston Jr.	.50	.20
222	Mike Bynum	.50	.20
223	Ryan Christianson	.50	.20
224	J.J. Davis	.50	.20
225	Alex Graman	.50	.20
226	Abraham Nunez	.50	.20
227	Sun Woo Kim	.50	.20
228	Jimmy Rollins	.50	.20
229	Ruben Salazar	.50	.20
230	Josh Girdley	.50	.20
231	Carl Crawford	.50	.20
232	Ben Davis	.50	.20
233	Jason Grabowski	.50	.20
234	Chris George	.50	.20
235	Roy Oswalt	1.25	.50
236	Brian Cole	.50	.20
237	Corey Patterson	.50	.20
238	Vernon Wells	.50	.20
239	Brad Baker	.50	.20
240	Gookie Dawkins	.50	.20
241	Michael Cuddyer	.50	.20
242	Ricardo Aramboles	.50	.20
243	Ben Sheets	.75	.30
244	Toby Hall	.50	.20
245	Jack Cust	.50	.20
246	Pedro Feliz	.50	.20
247	Josh Beckett	.75	.30
248	Alex Escobar	.50	.20
249	Marcus Giles	.50	.20
250	Jon Rauch	.50	.20
251	Kevin Mench	.50	.20
252	Shawn Sonnier	.50	.20
253	Aaron Rowand	.50	.20
254	C.C. Sabathia	.50	.20
255	Bubba Crosby	.50	.20
256	Josh Hamilton	.50	.20
257	Carlos Hernandez	.50	.20
258	Carlos Pena	.50	.20
259	Miguel Cabrera	4.00	1.50
260	Brandon Phillips	.50	.20
261	Tony Pena Jr.	.50	.20
262	Cristian Guerrero	.50	.20
263	Jin Ho Cho	.50	.20
264	Aaron Herr	.50	.20
265	Keith Ginter	.50	.20
266	Felipe Lopez	.50	.20
267	Travis Harper	.50	.20
268	Joe Torres	.50	.20
269	Eric Byrnes	.50	.20
270	Ben Christensen	.50	.20
271	Aubrey Huff	.50	.20
272	Lyle Overbay	.50	.20
273	Vince Faison	.50	.20
274	Bobby Bradley	.50	.20
275	Joe Crede	1.25	.50
276	Matt Wheatland	.50	.20
277	Grady Sizemore	1.50	.60
278	Adrian Gonzalez	.50	.20
279	Tim Raines Jr.	.50	.20
280	Phil Dumatrait	.50	.20
281	Jason Hart	.50	.20
282	David Kelton	.50	.20
283	David Walling	.50	.20
284	J.R. House	.50	.20
285	Kenny Kelly	.50	.20
286	Aaron McNeal	.50	.20
287	Nick Johnson	.50	.20
288	Scott Heard	.50	.20
289	Brad Wilkerson	.50	.20
290	Allen Levrault	.50	.20
291	Chris Richard	.50	.20
292	Jared Sandberg	.50	.20
293	Tike Redman	.50	.20
294	Adam Dunn	.75	.30
295	Josh Pressley	.50	.20
296	Jose Ortiz	.50	.20
297	Jason Romano	.50	.20
298	Tim Redding	.50	.20
299	Alex Gordon	.50	.20
300	Ben Petrick	.50	.20
301	Eric Munson	.50	.20
302	Luis Rivas	.50	.20
303	Matt Ginter	.50	.20
304	Alfonso Soriano	.75	.30
305	Wilfredo Rodriguez	.50	.20
306	Brett Myers	.50	.20
307	Scott Seabol	.50	.20
308	Tony Alvarez	.50	.20
309	Donzell McDonald	.50	.20
310	Austin Kearns	.50	.20
311	Will Ohman RC	8.00	3.00
312	Ryan Soules RC	5.00	2.00
313	Cody Ross RC	5.00	2.00
314	Bill Whitecotton RC	5.00	2.00
315	Mike Burns RC	8.00	3.00
316	Manuel Acosta RC	5.00	2.00
317	Lance Niekro RC	10.00	4.00
318	Travis Thompson RC	8.00	3.00
319	Zach Sorensen RC	8.00	3.00
320	Austin Evans RC	5.00	2.00
321	Brad Stiles RC	5.00	2.00
322	Joe Kennedy RC	10.00	4.00
323	Luke Martin RC	8.00	3.00
324	Juan Diaz RC	8.00	3.00
325	Pat Hallmark RC	5.00	2.00
326	Christian Parker RC	5.00	2.00
327	Ronny Corona RC	8.00	3.00
328	Jermaine Clark RC	5.00	2.00
329	Scott Dunn RC	8.00	3.00
330	Scott Chiasson RC	8.00	3.00
331	Greg Nash AU RC	50.00	20.00
332	Brad Cresse AU	50.00	20.00
333	John Buck AU RC	80.00	40.00
334	Freddie Bynum AU RC	50.00	20.00
335	Felix Diaz AU RC	50.00	20.00
336	Jason Belcher AU RC	50.00	20.00
337	Troy Farnsworth AU RC	50.00	20.00
338	Roberto Miniel AU RC	50.00	20.00
339	Esix Snead AU RC	50.00	20.00
340	Albert Pujols AU RC	3500.00	3000.00
341	Jeff Andra AU RC	50.00	20.00
342	Victor Hall AU RC	50.00	20.00
343	Pedro Liriano AU RC	50.00	20.00
344	Andy Beal AU RC	50.00	20.00
345	Bob Keppel AU RC	50.00	20.00
346	Brian Schmitt AU RC	50.00	20.00
347	Ron Davenport AU RC	150.00	90.00
348	Tony Blanco AU RC	50.00	20.00
349	Reggie Griggs AU RC	50.00	20.00
350	Derrick Van Dusen AU RC	50.00	20.00
351A	Ichiro Suzuki English RC	100.00	60.00
351B	Ichiro Suzuki Japan RC	100.00	60.00

2002 Bowman Chrome

	COMP.RED SET (110)	40.00	15.00
	COMP.BLUE w/o SP's (110)	40.00	15.00
	COMMON RED (1-110)	.50	.20
	COMMON BLUE (111-383)	.75	.30
	COMMON AU (324B/384-405)	10.00	4.00
	324B/384-405 GROUP A AUTO ODDS 1:28		
	403-404 GROUP B AUTO ODDS 1:1290		
	324B/384-405 OVERALL AUTO ODDS 1:27		
1	Adam Dunn	.50	.20
2	Derek Jeter	3.00	1.25
3	Alex Rodriguez	2.00	.75
4	Miguel Tejada	.50	.20
5	Nomar Garciaparra	2.00	.75
6	Toby Hall	.50	.20
7	Brandon Duckworth	.50	.20
8	Paul LoDuca	.50	.20
9	Brian Giles	.50	.20
10	C.C. Sabathia	.50	.20
11	Curt Schilling	.50	.20
12	Tsuyoshi Shinjo	.50	.20
13	Ramon Hernandez	.50	.20
14	Jose Cruz Jr.	.50	.20
15	Albert Pujols	2.50	1.00
16	Joe Mays	.50	.20
17	Javy Lopez	.50	.20
18	J.T. Snow	.50	.20
19	David Segui	.50	.20
20	Jorge Posada	.75	.30
21	Doug Mientkiewicz	.50	.20
22	Jerry Hairston Jr.	.50	.20
23	Bernie Williams	.75	.30
24	Mike Sweeney	.50	.20
25	Jason Giambi	.50	.20
26	Ryan Dempster	.50	.20
27	Ryan Klesko	.50	.20
28	Mark Quinn	.50	.20
29	Jeff Kent	.50	.20
30	Eric Chavez	.50	.20
31	Adrian Beltre	.50	.20
32	Andruw Jones	.75	.30
33	Alfonso Soriano	.50	.20
34	Aramis Ramirez	.50	.20

❑	35	Greg Maddux	2.00	.75
❑	36	Andy Pettitte	.75	.30
❑	37	Bartolo Colon	.50	.20
❑	38	Ben Sheets	.50	.20
❑	39	Bobby Higginson	.50	.20
❑	40	Ivan Rodriguez	.75	.30
❑	41	Brad Penny	.50	.20
❑	42	Carlos Lee	.50	.20
❑	43	Damion Easley	.50	.20
❑	44	Preston Wilson	.50	.20
❑	45	Jeff Bagwell	.75	.30
❑	46	Eric Milton	.50	.20
❑	47	Rafael Palmeiro	.75	.30
❑	48	Gary Sheffield	.50	.20
❑	49	J.D. Drew	.50	.20
❑	50	Jim Thome	.75	.30
❑	51	Ichiro Suzuki	2.50	1.00
❑	52	Bud Smith	.50	.20
❑	53	Chan Ho Park	.50	.20
❑	54	D'Angelo Jimenez	.50	.20
❑	55	Ken Griffey Jr.	2.00	.75
❑	56	Wade Miller	.50	.20
❑	57	Vladimir Guerrero	1.25	.50
❑	58	Troy Glaus	.50	.20
❑	59	Shawn Green	.50	.20
❑	60	Kerry Wood	.50	.20
❑	61	Jack Wilson	.50	.20
❑	62	Kevin Brown	.50	.20
❑	63	Marcus Giles	.50	.20
❑	64	Pat Burrell	.50	.20
❑	65	Larry Walker	.50	.20
❑	66	Sammy Sosa	1.25	.50
❑	67	Raul Mondesi	.50	.20
❑	68	Tim Hudson	.50	.20
❑	69	Lance Berkman	.50	.20
❑	70	Mike Mussina	.75	.30
❑	71	Barry Zito	.50	.20
❑	72	Jimmy Rollins	.50	.20
❑	73	Barry Bonds	3.00	1.25
❑	74	Craig Biggio	.75	.30
❑	75	Todd Helton	.75	.30
❑	76	Roger Clemens	2.50	1.00
❑	77	Frank Catalanotto	.50	.20
❑	78	Josh Towers	.50	.20
❑	79	Roy Oswalt	.50	.20
❑	80	Chipper Jones	1.25	.50
❑	81	Cristian Guzman	.50	.20
❑	82	Darin Erstad	.50	.20
❑	83	Freddy Garcia	.50	.20
❑	84	Jason Tyner	.50	.20
❑	85	Carlos Delgado	.50	.20
❑	86	Jon Lieber	.50	.20
❑	87	Juan Pierre	.50	.20
❑	88	Matt Morris	.50	.20
❑	89	Phil Nevin	.50	.20
❑	90	Jim Edmonds	.50	.20
❑	91	Magglio Ordonez	.50	.20
❑	92	Mike Hampton	.50	.20
❑	93	Rafael Furcal	.50	.20
❑	94	Richie Sexson	.50	.20
❑	95	Luis Gonzalez	.50	.20
❑	96	Scott Rolen	.75	.30
❑	97	Tim Redding	.50	.20
❑	98	Moises Alou	.50	.20
❑	99	Jose Vidro	.50	.20
❑	100	Mike Piazza	2.00	.75
❑	101	Pedro Martinez	.75	.30
❑	102	Geoff Jenkins	.50	.20
❑	103	Johnny Damon Sox	.75	.30
❑	104	Mike Cameron	.50	.20
❑	105	Randy Johnson	1.25	.50
❑	106	David Eckstein	.50	.20
❑	107	Javier Vazquez	.50	.20
❑	108	Mark Mulder	.50	.20
❑	109	Robert Fick	.50	.20
❑	110	Roberto Alomar	.75	.30
❑	111	Wilson Betemit	.75	.30
❑	112	Chris Tritle SP RC	5.00	2.00
❑	113	Ed Rogers	.75	.30
❑	114	Juan Pena	.75	.30
❑	115	Josh Beckett	1.25	.50
❑	116	Juan Cruz	.75	.30
❑	117	Noochie Varner SP RC	5.00	2.00
❑	118	Blake Williams	.75	.30
❑	119	Mike Rivera	.75	.30
❑	120	Hank Blalock	2.00	.75
❑	121	Hansel Izquierdo SP RC	5.00	2.00
❑	122	Orlando Hudson	.75	.30
❑	123	Bill Hall SP	5.00	2.00
❑	124	Jose Reyes	2.00	.75
❑	125	Juan Rivera	.75	.30
❑	126	Eric Valent	.75	.30
❑	127	Scotty Layfield SP RC	5.00	2.00
❑	128	Austin Kearns	.75	.30
❑	129	Nic Jackson SP RC	5.00	2.00
❑	130	Scott Chiasson	.75	.30
❑	131	Chad Qualls SP RC	8.00	3.00
❑	132	Marcus Thames	.75	.30
❑	133	Nathan Haynes	.75	.30
❑	134	Joe Borchard	.75	.30
❑	135	Josh Hamilton	.75	.30
❑	136	Corey Patterson	.75	.30
❑	137	Travis Wilson	.75	.30
❑	138	Alex Escobar	.75	.30
❑	139	Alexis Gomez	.75	.30
❑	140	Nick Johnson	1.25	.50
❑	141	Marlon Byrd	.75	.30
❑	142	Kory DeHaan	.75	.30
❑	143	Carlos Hernandez	.75	.30
❑	144	Sean Burroughs	.75	.30
❑	145	Angel Berroa	.75	.30
❑	146	Aubrey Huff	1.25	.50
❑	147	Travis Hafner	1.25	.50
❑	148	Brandon Berger	.75	.30
❑	149	J.R. House	.75	.30
❑	150	Dewon Brazelton	.75	.30
❑	151	Jayson Werth	.75	.30
❑	152	Larry Barnes	.75	.30
❑	153	Ruben Gotay SP RC	8.00	3.00
❑	154	Tommy Marx SP RC	5.00	2.00
❑	155	John Suomi SP RC	5.00	2.00
❑	156	Javier Colina SP	5.00	2.00
❑	157	Greg Sain SP RC	5.00	2.00
❑	158	Robert Cosby SP RC	5.00	2.00
❑	159	Angel Pagan SP RC	10.00	4.00
❑	160	Ralph Santana RC	1.25	.50
❑	161	Joe Orloski RC	1.25	.50
❑	162	Shayne Wright SP RC	5.00	2.00
❑	163	Jay Caligiuri SP RC	5.00	2.00
❑	164	Greg Montalbano SP RC	5.00	2.00
❑	165	Rich Harden SP RC	25.00	10.00
❑	166	Rich Thompson SP RC	5.00	2.00
❑	167	Fred Bastardo SP RC	5.00	2.00
❑	168	Alejandro Giron SP RC	5.00	2.00
❑	169	Jesus Medrano SP RC	5.00	2.00
❑	170	Kevin Deaton SP RC	5.00	2.00
❑	171	Mike Rosamond RC	1.25	.50
❑	172	Jon Guzman SP RC	5.00	2.00
❑	173	Gerard Oakes SP RC	5.00	2.00
❑	174	Francisco Liriano SP RC	50.00	20.00
❑	175	Matt Allegra SP RC	5.00	2.00
❑	176	Mike Snyder SP RC	5.00	2.00
❑	177	James Shanks SP RC	5.00	2.00
❑	178	Anderson Hernandez SP RC	5.00	2.00
❑	179	Dan Trumble SP RC	5.00	2.00
❑	180	Luis DePaula SP RC	5.00	2.00
❑	181	Randall Shelley SP RC	5.00	2.00
❑	182	Richard Lane SP RC	5.00	2.00
❑	183	Antwon Rollins SP RC	5.00	2.00
❑	184	Ryan Bukvich SP RC	5.00	2.00
❑	185	Derrick Lewis SP	5.00	2.00
❑	186	Eric Miller SP RC	5.00	2.00
❑	187	Justin Schuda SP RC	5.00	2.00
❑	188	Brian West SP RC	5.00	2.00
❑	189	Brad Wilkerson	.75	.30
❑	190	Neal Frendling SP RC	5.00	2.00
❑	191	Jeremy Hill SP RC	5.00	2.00
❑	192	James Barrett SP RC	5.00	2.00
❑	193	Brett Kay SP RC	5.00	2.00
❑	194	Ryan Mottl SP RC	5.00	2.00
❑	195	Brad Nelson SP RC	5.00	2.00
❑	196	Juan M. Gonzalez SP RC	5.00	2.00
❑	197	Curtis Legendre SP RC	5.00	2.00
❑	198	Ronald Acuna SP RC	5.00	2.00
❑	199	Chris Flinn SP RC	5.00	2.00
❑	200	Nick Alvarez SP RC	5.00	2.00
❑	201	Jason Ellison SP RC	10.00	4.00
❑	202	Blake McGinley SP RC	5.00	2.00
❑	203	Dan Phillips SP RC	5.00	2.00
❑	204	Demetrius Heath SP RC	5.00	2.00
❑	205	Eric Bruntlett SP RC	5.00	2.00
❑	206	Joe Jiannetti SP RC	5.00	2.00
❑	207	Mike Hill SP RC	5.00	2.00
❑	208	Ricardo Cordova SP RC	5.00	2.00
❑	209	Mark Hamilton SP RC	5.00	2.00
❑	210	David Mattox SP RC	5.00	2.00
❑	211	Jose Morban SP RC	5.00	2.00
❑	212	Scott Wiggins SP RC	5.00	2.00
❑	213	Steve Green	.75	.30
❑	214	Brian Rogers SP	5.00	2.00
❑	215	Kenny Baugh	.75	.30
❑	216	Anastacio Martinez SP RC	5.00	2.00
❑	217	Richard Lewis	.75	.30
❑	218	Tim Kalita SP RC	5.00	2.00
❑	219	Edwin Almonte SP RC	5.00	2.00
❑	220	Hee Seop Choi	.75	.30
❑	221	Ty Howington	.75	.30
❑	222	Victor Alvarez SP RC	5.00	2.00
❑	223	Morgan Ensberg	1.25	.50
❑	224	Jeff Austin SP RC	5.00	2.00
❑	225	Clint Weibl SP RC	5.00	2.00
❑	226	Eric Cyr	.75	.30
❑	227	Marlyn Tisdale SP RC	5.00	2.00
❑	228	John VanBenschoten	.75	.30
❑	229	David Krynzel	.75	.30
❑	230	Raul Chavez SP RC	5.00	2.00
❑	231	Brett Evert	.75	.30
❑	232	Joe Rogers SP RC	5.00	2.00
❑	233	Adam Wainwright	.75	.30
❑	234	Matt Herges RC	.75	.30
❑	235	Matt Childers SP RC	5.00	2.00
❑	236	Nick Neugebauer	.75	.30
❑	237	Carl Crawford	1.25	.50
❑	238	Seung Song	.75	.30
❑	239	Randy Flores	.75	.30
❑	240	Jason Lane	1.25	.50
❑	241	Chase Utley	8.00	3.00
❑	242	Ben Howard SP RC	5.00	2.00
❑	243	Eric Glaser SP RC	5.00	2.00
❑	244	Josh Wilson RC	1.25	.50
❑	245	Jose Valverde SP RC	5.00	2.00
❑	246	Chris Smith	.75	.30
❑	247	Mark Prior	2.00	.75
❑	248	Brian Mallette SP RC	5.00	2.00
❑	249	Chone Figgins SP RC	8.00	3.00
❑	250	Jimmy Alvarez SP RC	5.00	2.00
❑	251	Luis Terrero	.75	.30
❑	252	Josh Bonifay SP RC	5.00	2.00
❑	253	Garrett Guzman SP RC	5.00	2.00
❑	254	Jeff Verplancke SP RC	5.00	2.00
❑	255	Nate Espy SP RC	5.00	2.00
❑	256	Jeff Lincoln SP RC	5.00	2.00
❑	257	Ryan Snare SP RC	5.00	2.00
❑	258	Jose Ortiz	.75	.30
❑	259	Denny Bautista	.75	.30
❑	260	Willy Aybar	.75	.30
❑	261	Kelly Johnson	3.00	1.25
❑	262	Shawn Fagan	.75	.30
❑	263	Yurendell DeCaster SP RC	5.00	2.00
❑	264	Mike Peeples SP RC	5.00	2.00
❑	265	Joel Guzman	3.00	1.25
❑	266	Ryan Vogelsong	.75	.30
❑	267	Jorge Padilla SP RC	5.00	2.00
❑	268	Joe Jester SP RC	5.00	2.00
❑	269	Ryan Church SP RC	10.00	4.00
❑	270	Mitch Jones	.75	.30
❑	271	Travis Foley SP RC	5.00	2.00
❑	272	Bobby Crosby	3.00	1.25
❑	273	Adrian Gonzalez	.75	.30
❑	274	Ronnie Merrill	.75	.30
❑	275	Joel Pineiro	.75	.30
❑	276	John-Ford Griffin	.75	.30
❑	277	Brian Forystek SP RC	5.00	2.00
❑	278	Sean Douglass	.75	.30
❑	279	Manny Delcarmen SP RC	8.00	3.00
❑	280	Jim Kavourias SP RC	5.00	2.00
❑	281	Gabe Gross	.75	.30
❑	282	Bill Ortega	.75	.30
❑	283	Joey Hammond SP RC	5.00	2.00
❑	284	Brett Myers	1.25	.50
❑	285	Carlos Pena	.75	.30
❑	286	Ezequiel Astacio SP RC	5.00	2.00
❑	287	Edwin Yan SP RC	5.00	2.00
❑	288	Chris Duffy SP RC	10.00	4.00
❑	289	Jason Kinchen	.75	.30
❑	290	Rafael Soriano	.75	.30
❑	291	Colin Young RC	5.00	2.00
❑	292	Eric Byrnes	.75	.30

❑ 293 Chris Narveson SP RC 8.00 3.00
❑ 294 John Rheinecker .75 .30
❑ 295 Mike Wilson SP RC 5.00 2.00
❑ 296 Justin Sherrod SP RC 5.00 2.00
❑ 297 Deivi Mendez .75 .30
❑ 298 Wily Mo Pena 1.25 .50
❑ 299 Brett Roneberg SP RC 5.00 2.00
❑ 300 Trey Lunsford SP RC 5.00 2.00
❑ 301 Christian Parker .75 .30
❑ 302 Brent Butler .75 .30
❑ 303 Aaron Heilman .75 .30
❑ 304 Wilkin Ruan .75 .30
❑ 305 Kenny Kelly .75 .30
❑ 306 Cody Ransom .75 .30
❑ 307 Koyie Hill SP 5.00 2.00
❑ 308 Tony Fontana SP RC 5.00 2.00
❑ 309 Mark Teixeira 5.00 2.00
❑ 310 Doug Sessions SP RC 5.00 2.00
❑ 311 Josh Cisneros SP RC 5.00 2.00
❑ 312 Carlos Brackley SP RC 5.00 2.00
❑ 313 Tim Raines Jr. .75 .30
❑ 314 Ross Peeples SP RC 5.00 2.00
❑ 315 Alex Requena SP RC 5.00 2.00
❑ 316 Chin-Hui Tsao 1.25 .50
❑ 317 Tony Alvarez .75 .30
❑ 318 Craig Kuzmic SP RC 5.00 2.00
❑ 319 Pete Zamora SP RC 5.00 2.00
❑ 320 Matt Parker SP RC 5.00 2.00
❑ 321 Keith Ginter .75 .30
❑ 322 Gary Cates Jr. SP RC 5.00 2.00
❑ 323 Matt Belisle .75 .30
❑ 324A Ben Broussard .75 .30
❑ 324B Jake Mauer AU A RC 10.00 4.00
❑ 325 Dennis Tankersley .75 .30
❑ 326 Juan Silvestre .75 .30
❑ 327 Henry Pichardo SP RC 5.00 2.00
❑ 328 Michael Floyd SP RC 5.00 2.00
❑ 329 Clint Nageotte SP RC 8.00 3.00
❑ 330 Raymond Cabrera SP RC 5.00 2.00
❑ 331 Mauricio Lara SP RC 5.00 2.00
❑ 332 Alejandro Cadena SP RC 5.00 2.00
❑ 333 Jonny Gomes SP RC 15.00 6.00
❑ 334 Jason Bulger SP RC 5.00 2.00
❑ 335 Nate Teut .75 .30
❑ 336 David Gil SP RC 5.00 2.00
❑ 337 Joel Crump SP RC 5.00 2.00
❑ 338 Brandon Phillips .75 .30
❑ 339 Macay McBride 1.25 .50
❑ 340 Brandon Claussen .75 .30
❑ 341 Josh Phelps .75 .30
❑ 342 Freddie Money SP RC 5.00 2.00
❑ 343 Cliff Bartosh SP RC 5.00 2.00
❑ 344 Terrance Hill SP RC 5.00 2.00
❑ 345 John Rodriguez SP RC 8.00 3.00
❑ 346 Chris Latham SP RC 5.00 2.00
❑ 347 Carlos Cabrera SP RC 5.00 2.00
❑ 348 Jose Bautista SP RC 10.00 4.00
❑ 349 Kevin Frederick SP RC 5.00 2.00
❑ 350 Jerome Williams .75 .30
❑ 351 Napoleon Calzado SP RC 5.00 2.00
❑ 352 Benito Baez SP 5.00 2.00
❑ 353 Xavier Nady .75 .30
❑ 354 Jason Botts SP RC 8.00 3.00
❑ 355 Steve Bechler SP RC 5.00 2.00
❑ 356 Reed Johnson SP RC 8.00 3.00
❑ 357 Mark Outlaw SP RC 5.00 2.00
❑ 358 Jake Peavy 2.00 .75
❑ 359 Josh Shaffer SP RC 5.00 2.00
❑ 360 Dan Wright SP 5.00 2.00
❑ 361 Ryan Gripp SP RC 5.00 2.00
❑ 362 Nelson Castro SP RC 5.00 2.00
❑ 363 Jason Bay SP RC 25.00 10.00
❑ 364 Franklyn German SP RC 5.00 2.00
❑ 365 Corwin Malone SP RC 5.00 2.00
❑ 366 Kelly Ramos SP RC 5.00 2.00
❑ 367 John Ennis SP RC 5.00 2.00
❑ 368 George Perez SP 5.00 2.00
❑ 369 Rene Reyes SP RC 5.00 2.00
❑ 370 Rolando Viera SP RC 5.00 2.00
❑ 371 Earl Snyder SP RC 5.00 2.00
❑ 372 Kyle Kane SP RC 5.00 2.00
❑ 373 Mario Ramos SP RC 5.00 2.00
❑ 374 Tyler Yates SP RC 5.00 2.00
❑ 375 Jason Young SP RC 5.00 2.00
❑ 376 Chris Bootcheck SP RC 5.00 2.00
❑ 377 Jesus Cota SP RC 5.00 2.00
❑ 378 Corky Miller SP 5.00 2.00
❑ 379 Matt Erickson SP RC 5.00 2.00
❑ 380 Justin Huber SP RC 10.00 4.00
❑ 381 Felix Escalona SP RC 5.00 2.00
❑ 382 Kevin Cash SP RC 5.00 2.00
❑ 383 J.J. Putz SP RC 8.00 3.00
❑ 384 Chris Snelling AU A RC 20.00 8.00
❑ 385 David Wright AU A RC 600.00 400.00
❑ 386 Brian Wolfe AU A RC 10.00 4.00
❑ 387 Justin Reid AU A RC 10.00 4.00
❑ 389 Ryan Raburn AU A RC 10.00 4.00
❑ 390 Josh Barfield AU A RC 50.00 25.00
❑ 391 Joe Mauer AU A RC 200.00 125.00
❑ 392 Bobby Jenks AU A RC 25.00 10.00
❑ 393 Rob Henkel AU A RC 10.00 4.00
❑ 394 Jimmy Gobble AU A RC 10.00 4.00
❑ 395 Jesse Foppert AU A RC 15.00 6.00
❑ 396 Gavin Floyd AU A RC 25.00 10.00
❑ 397 Nate Field AU A RC 10.00 4.00
❑ 398 Ryan Doumit AU A RC 20.00 8.00
❑ 399 Ron Calloway AU A RC 10.00 4.00
❑ 400 Taylor Buchholz AU A RC 15.00 6.00
❑ 401 Adam Roller AU A RC 10.00 4.00
❑ 402 Cole Barthel AU A RC 10.00 4.00
❑ 403 Kazuhisa Ishii SP RC 8.00 3.00
❑ 403A Kazuhisa Ishii AU B 50.00 30.00
❑ 404 So Taguchi SP RC 8.00 3.00
❑ 404A So Taguchi AU B 50.00 30.00
❑ 405 Chris Baker AU A RC 10.00 4.00

2002 Bowman Chrome Draft

❑ COMPLETE SET (175) 350.00 200.00
❑ COMP.SET w/o AU's (165) 200.00 135.00
❑ COMMON CARD (1-165) .40 .15
❑ COMMON CARD (166-175) 10.00 4.00
❑ 1 Clint Everts RC 1.50 .60
❑ 2 Fred Lewis RC 1.00 .40
❑ 3 Jon Broxton RC 3.00 1.25
❑ 4 Jason Anderson RC 1.00 .40
❑ 5 Mike Eusebio RC 1.00 .40
❑ 6 Zack Greinke RC 6.00 2.50
❑ 7 Joe Blanton RC 6.00 2.50
❑ 8 Sergio Santos RC 1.50 .60
❑ 9 Jason Cooper RC 1.00 .40
❑ 10 Delwyn Young RC 3.00 1.25
❑ 11 Jeremy Hermida RC 15.00 6.00
❑ 12 Dan Ortmeier RC 1.50 .60
❑ 13 Kevin Jepsen RC 1.50 .60
❑ 14 Russ Adams RC 1.50 .60
❑ 15 Mike Nixon RC 1.00 .40
❑ 16 Nick Swisher RC 15.00 6.00
❑ 17 Cole Hamels RC 25.00 10.00
❑ 18 Brian Dopirak RC 3.00 1.25
❑ 19 James Loney RC 20.00 8.00
❑ 20 Denard Span RC 1.50 .60
❑ 21 Billy Petrick RC 1.00 .40
❑ 22 Jared Doyle RC 1.00 .40
❑ 23 Jeff Francoeur RC 50.00 20.00
❑ 24 Nick Bourgeois RC 1.00 .40
❑ 25 Matt Cain RC 20.00 8.00
❑ 26 John McCurdy RC 1.00 .40
❑ 27 Mark Kiger RC 1.00 .40
❑ 28 Bill Murphy RC 1.00 .40
❑ 29 Matt Craig RC 1.50 .60
❑ 30 Mike Megrew RC 1.00 .40
❑ 31 Ben Crockett RC 1.00 .40
❑ 32 Luke Hagerty RC 1.00 .40
❑ 33 Matt Whitney RC 1.00 .40
❑ 34 Dan Meyer RC 1.50 .60
❑ 35 Jeremy Brown RC 1.00 .40
❑ 36 Doug Johnson RC 1.00 .40
❑ 37 Steve Obenchain RC 1.00 .40
❑ 38 Matt Clanton RC 1.00 .40
❑ 39 Mark Teahen RC 3.00 1.25
❑ 40 Tom Carrow RC 1.00 .40
❑ 41 Micah Schilling RC 1.00 .40
❑ 42 Blair Johnson RC 1.00 .40
❑ 43 Jason Pridie RC 1.00 .40
❑ 44 Joey Votto RC 8.00 3.00
❑ 45 Taber Lee RC 1.00 .40
❑ 46 Adam Peterson RC 1.00 .40
❑ 47 Adam Donachie RC 1.00 .40
❑ 48 Josh Murray RC 1.00 .40
❑ 49 Brent Clevlen RC 6.00 2.50
❑ 50 Chad Pleiness RC 1.00 .40
❑ 51 Zach Hammes RC 1.00 .40
❑ 52 Chris Snyder RC 1.50 .60
❑ 53 Chris Smith RC 1.00 .40
❑ 54 Justin Maureau RC 1.00 .40
❑ 55 David Bush RC 3.00 1.25
❑ 56 Tim Gilhooly RC 1.00 .40
❑ 57 Blair Barbier RC 1.00 .40
❑ 58 Zach Segovia RC 1.00 .40
❑ 59 Jeremy Reed RC 3.00 1.25
❑ 60 Matt Pender RC 1.00 .40
❑ 61 Eric Thomas RC 1.00 .40
❑ 62 Justin Jones RC 1.50 .60
❑ 63 Brian Slocum RC 1.00 .40
❑ 64 Larry Broadway RC 1.00 .40
❑ 65 Bo Flowers RC 1.00 .40
❑ 66 Scott White RC 1.00 .40
❑ 67 Steve Stanley RC 1.00 .40
❑ 68 Alex Merricks RC 1.00 .40
❑ 69 Josh Womack RC 1.00 .40
❑ 70 Dave Jensen RC 1.00 .40
❑ 71 Curtis Granderson RC 8.00 3.00
❑ 72 Pat Osborn RC 1.00 .40
❑ 73 Nic Carter RC 1.00 .40
❑ 74 Mitch Talbot RC 1.00 .40
❑ 75 Don Murphy RC 1.00 .40
❑ 76 Val Majewski RC 1.00 .40
❑ 77 Javy Rodriguez RC 1.00 .40
❑ 78 Fernando Pacheco RC 1.00 .40
❑ 79 Steve Russell RC 1.00 .40
❑ 80 Jon Slack RC 1.00 .40
❑ 81 John Baker RC 1.00 .40
❑ 82 Aaron Coonrod RC 1.00 .40
❑ 83 Josh Johnson RC 10.00 4.00
❑ 84 Jake Blalock RC 1.50 .60
❑ 85 Alex Hart RC 1.00 .40
❑ 86 Wes Bankston RC 6.00 2.50
❑ 87 Josh Rupe RC 1.00 .40
❑ 88 Dan Cevette RC 1.00 .40
❑ 89 Kiel Fisher RC 1.50 .60
❑ 90 Alan Rick RC 1.00 .40
❑ 91 Charlie Morton RC 1.00 .40
❑ 92 Chad Spann RC 1.00 .40
❑ 93 Kyle Boyer RC 1.00 .40
❑ 94 Bob Malek RC 1.00 .40
❑ 95 Ryan Rodriguez RC 1.00 .40
❑ 96 Jordan Renz RC 1.00 .40
❑ 97 Randy Frye RC 1.00 .40
❑ 98 Rich Hill RC 8.00 3.00
❑ 99 B.J. Upton RC 15.00 6.00
❑ 100 Dan Christensen RC 1.00 .40
❑ 101 Casey Kotchman RC 5.00 2.00
❑ 102 Eric Good RC 1.00 .40
❑ 103 Mike Fontenot RC 1.00 .40
❑ 104 John Webb RC 1.00 .40
❑ 105 Jason Dubois RC 1.50 .60
❑ 106 Ryan Kibler RC 1.00 .40
❑ 107 Jhonny Peralta RC 8.00 3.00
❑ 108 Kirk Saarloos RC 1.00 .40
❑ 109 Rhett Parrott RC 1.00 .40
❑ 110 Jason Grove RC 1.00 .40
❑ 111 Colt Griffin RC 1.00 .40
❑ 112 Dallas McPherson RC 3.00 1.25
❑ 113 Oliver Perez RC 3.00 1.25
❑ 114 Marshall McDougall RC 1.00 .40
❑ 115 Mike Wood RC 1.00 .40
❑ 116 Scott Hairston RC 1.50 .60
❑ 117 Jason Simontacchi RC 1.00 .40
❑ 118 Taggert Bozied RC 1.50 .60

❑ 119	Shelley Duncan RC	1.00	.40
❑ 120	Dontrelle Willis RC	15.00	6.00
❑ 121	Sean Burnett	.40	.15
❑ 122	Aaron Cook	.60	.25
❑ 123	Brett Evert	.40	.15
❑ 124	Jimmy Journell	.40	.15
❑ 125	Brett Myers	.60	.25
❑ 126	Brad Baker	.40	.15
❑ 127	Billy Traber RC	1.00	.40
❑ 128	Adam Wainwright	.40	.15
❑ 129	Jason Young	1.00	.40
❑ 130	John Buck	.40	.15
❑ 131	Kevin Cash	1.00	.40
❑ 132	Jason Stokes RC	1.50	.60
❑ 133	Drew Henson	.40	.15
❑ 134	Chad Tracy RC	5.00	2.00
❑ 135	Orlando Hudson	.40	.15
❑ 136	Brandon Phillips	.40	.15
❑ 137	Joe Borchard	.40	.15
❑ 138	Marlon Byrd	.40	.15
❑ 139	Carl Crawford	.60	.25
❑ 140	Michael Restovich	.40	.15
❑ 141	Corey Hart RC	5.00	2.00
❑ 142	Edwin Almonte	.60	.25
❑ 143	Francis Beltran RC	1.00	.40
❑ 144	Jorge De La Rosa RC	1.00	.40
❑ 145	Gerardo Garcia RC	1.00	.40
❑ 146	Franklyn German RC	1.00	.40
❑ 147	Francisco Liriano	12.00	5.00
❑ 148	Francisco Rodriguez	.60	.25
❑ 149	Ricardo Rodriguez	.40	.15
❑ 150	Seung Song	.40	.15
❑ 151	John Stephens	.40	.15
❑ 152	Justin Huber RC	2.50	1.00
❑ 153	Victor Martinez	1.50	.60
❑ 154	Hee Seop Choi	.40	.15
❑ 155	Justin Morneau	.60	.25
❑ 156	Miguel Cabrera	2.50	1.00
❑ 157	Victor Diaz RC	2.50	1.00
❑ 158	Jose Reyes	1.00	.40
❑ 159	Omar Infante	.40	.15
❑ 160	Angel Berroa	.40	.15
❑ 161	Tony Alvarez	.40	.15
❑ 162	Shin Soo Choo RC	2.50	1.00
❑ 163	Wily Mo Pena	.60	.25
❑ 164	Andres Torres	.40	.15
❑ 165	Jose Lopez RC	6.00	2.50
❑ 166	Scott Moore AU RC	15.00	6.00
❑ 167	Chris Gruler AU RC	10.00	4.00
❑ 168	Joe Saunders AU RC	20.00	8.00
❑ 169	Jeff Francis AU RC	25.00	10.00
❑ 170	Royce Ring AU RC	10.00	4.00
❑ 171	Greg Miller AU RC	15.00	6.00
❑ 172	Brandon Weeden AU RC	10.00	4.00
❑ 173	Drew Meyer AU RC	10.00	4.00
❑ 174	Khalil Greene AU RC	60.00	30.00
❑ 175	Mark Schramek AU RC	10.00	4.00

2003 Bowman Chrome

❑ COMPLETE SET (351)	500.00	300.00
❑ COMP.SET w/o AU's (331)	150.00	75.00
❑ COMMON CARD (1-165)	.50	.20
❑ COMMON CARD (166-330)	.50	.20
❑ COMMON RC (156-330)	1.00	.40

❑ COMP.SET w/o AU'S INCLUDES 351 MAYS
❑ MAYS AU IS NOT PART OF 351-CARD SET

❑ 1	Garret Anderson	.50	.20
❑ 2	Derek Jeter	3.00	1.25
❑ 3	Gary Sheffield	.50	.20
❑ 4	Matt Morris	.50	.20
❑ 5	Derek Lowe	.50	.20
❑ 6	Andy Van Hekken	.50	.20
❑ 7	Sammy Sosa	1.25	.50
❑ 8	Ken Griffey Jr.	2.00	.75
❑ 9	Omar Vizquel	.75	.30
❑ 10	Jorge Posada	.75	.30
❑ 11	Lance Berkman	.50	.20
❑ 12	Mike Sweeney	.50	.20
❑ 13	Adrian Beltre	.50	.20
❑ 14	Richie Sexson	.50	.20
❑ 15	A.J. Pierzynski	.50	.20
❑ 16	Bartolo Colon	.50	.20
❑ 17	Mike Mussina	.75	.30
❑ 18	Paul Byrd	.50	.20
❑ 19	Bobby Abreu	.50	.20
❑ 20	Miguel Tejada	.50	.20
❑ 21	Aramis Ramirez	.50	.20
❑ 22	Edgardo Alfonzo	.50	.20
❑ 23	Edgar Martinez	.75	.30
❑ 24	Albert Pujols	2.50	1.00
❑ 25	Carl Crawford	.50	.20
❑ 26	Eric Hinske	.50	.20
❑ 27	Tim Salmon	.75	.30
❑ 28	Luis Gonzalez	.50	.20
❑ 29	Jay Gibbons	.50	.20
❑ 30	John Smoltz	.50	.20
❑ 31	Tim Wakefield	.50	.20
❑ 32	Mark Prior	.75	.30
❑ 33	Magglio Ordonez	.50	.20
❑ 34	Adam Dunn	.50	.20
❑ 35	Larry Walker	.50	.20
❑ 36	Luis Castillo	.50	.20
❑ 37	Wade Miller	.50	.20
❑ 38	Carlos Beltran	.50	.20
❑ 39	Odalis Perez	.50	.20
❑ 40	Alex Sanchez	.50	.20
❑ 41	Torii Hunter	.50	.20
❑ 42	Cliff Floyd	.50	.20
❑ 43	Andy Pettitte	.75	.30
❑ 44	Francisco Rodriguez	.50	.20
❑ 45	Eric Chavez	.50	.20
❑ 46	Kevin Millwood	.50	.20
❑ 47	Dennis Tankersley	.50	.20
❑ 48	Hideo Nomo	1.25	.50
❑ 49	Freddy Garcia	.50	.20
❑ 50	Randy Johnson	1.25	.50
❑ 51	Aubrey Huff	.50	.20
❑ 52	Carlos Delgado	.50	.20
❑ 53	Troy Glaus	.50	.20
❑ 54	Junior Spivey	.50	.20
❑ 55	Mike Hampton	.50	.20
❑ 56	Sidney Ponson	.50	.20
❑ 57	Aaron Boone	.50	.20
❑ 58	Kerry Wood	.50	.20
❑ 59	Willie Harris	.50	.20
❑ 60	Nomar Garciaparra	2.00	.75
❑ 61	Todd Helton	.75	.30
❑ 62	Mike Lowell	.50	.20
❑ 63	Roy Oswalt	.50	.20
❑ 64	Raul Ibanez	.50	.20
❑ 65	Brian Jordan	.50	.20
❑ 66	Geoff Jenkins	.50	.20
❑ 67	Jermaine Dye	.50	.20
❑ 68	Tom Glavine	.75	.30
❑ 69	Bernie Williams	.75	.30
❑ 70	Vladimir Guerrero	1.25	.50
❑ 71	Mark Mulder	.50	.20
❑ 72	Jimmy Rollins	.50	.20
❑ 73	Oliver Perez	.50	.20
❑ 74	Rich Aurilia	.50	.20
❑ 75	Joel Pineiro	.50	.20
❑ 76	J.D. Drew	.50	.20
❑ 77	Ivan Rodriguez	.75	.30
❑ 78	Josh Phelps	.50	.20
❑ 79	Darin Erstad	.50	.20
❑ 80	Curt Schilling	.50	.20
❑ 81	Paul Lo Duca	.50	.20
❑ 82	Marty Cordova	.50	.20
❑ 83	Manny Ramirez	.75	.30
❑ 84	Bobby Hill	.50	.20
❑ 85	Paul Konerko	.50	.20
❑ 86	Austin Kearns	.50	.20
❑ 87	Jason Jennings	.50	.20
❑ 88	Brad Penny	.50	.20
❑ 89	Jeff Bagwell	.75	.30
❑ 90	Shawn Green	.50	.20
❑ 91	Jason Schmidt	.50	.20
❑ 92	Doug Mientkiewicz	.50	.20
❑ 93	Jose Vidro	.50	.20
❑ 94	Bret Boone	.50	.20
❑ 95	Jason Giambi	.50	.20
❑ 96	Barry Zito	.50	.20
❑ 97	Roy Halladay	.50	.20
❑ 98	Pat Burrell	.50	.20
❑ 99	Sean Burroughs	.50	.20
❑ 100	Barry Bonds	3.00	1.25
❑ 101	Kazuhiro Sasaki	.50	.20
❑ 102	Fernando Vina	.50	.20
❑ 103	Chan Ho Park	.50	.20
❑ 104	Andruw Jones	.75	.30
❑ 105	Adam Kennedy	.50	.20
❑ 106	Shea Hillenbrand	.50	.20
❑ 107	Greg Maddux	2.00	.75
❑ 108	Jim Edmonds	.50	.20
❑ 109	Pedro Martinez	.75	.30
❑ 110	Moises Alou	.50	.20
❑ 111	Jeff Weaver	.50	.20
❑ 112	C.C. Sabathia	.50	.20
❑ 113	Robert Fick	.50	.20
❑ 114	A.J. Burnett	.50	.20
❑ 115	Jeff Kent	.50	.20
❑ 116	Kevin Brown	.50	.20
❑ 117	Rafael Furcal	.50	.20
❑ 118	Cristian Guzman	.50	.20
❑ 119	Brad Wilkerson	.50	.20
❑ 120	Mike Piazza	2.00	.75
❑ 121	Alfonso Soriano	.50	.20
❑ 122	Mark Ellis	.50	.20
❑ 123	Vicente Padilla	.50	.20
❑ 124	Eric Gagne	.50	.20
❑ 125	Ryan Klesko	.50	.20
❑ 126	Ichiro Suzuki	2.50	1.00
❑ 127	Tony Batista	.50	.20
❑ 128	Roberto Alomar	.75	.30
❑ 129	Alex Rodriguez	2.00	.75
❑ 130	Jim Thome	.75	.30
❑ 131	Jarrod Washburn	.50	.20
❑ 132	Orlando Hudson	.50	.20
❑ 133	Chipper Jones	1.25	.50
❑ 134	Rodrigo Lopez	.50	.20
❑ 135	Johnny Damon	.75	.30
❑ 136	Matt Clement	.50	.20
❑ 137	Frank Thomas	1.25	.50
❑ 138	Ellis Burks	.50	.20
❑ 139	Carlos Pena	.50	.20
❑ 140	Josh Beckett	.50	.20
❑ 141	Joe Randa	.50	.20
❑ 142	Brian Giles	.50	.20
❑ 143	Kazuhisa Ishii	.50	.20
❑ 144	Corey Koskie	.50	.20
❑ 145	Orlando Cabrera	.50	.20
❑ 146	Mark Buehrle	.50	.20
❑ 147	Roger Clemens	2.50	1.00
❑ 148	Tim Hudson	.50	.20
❑ 149	Randy Wolf	.50	.20
❑ 150	Josh Fogg	.50	.20
❑ 151	Phil Nevin	.50	.20
❑ 152	John Olerud	.50	.20
❑ 153	Scott Rolen	.75	.30
❑ 154	Joe Kennedy	.50	.20
❑ 155	Rafael Palmeiro	.75	.30
❑ 156	Chad Hutchinson	.50	.20
❑ 157	Quincy Carter XRC	1.50	.60
❑ 158	Hee Seop Choi	.50	.20
❑ 159	Joe Borchard	.50	.20
❑ 160	Brandon Phillips	.50	.20
❑ 161	Wily Mo Pena	.50	.20
❑ 162	Victor Martinez	.75	.30
❑ 163	Jason Stokes	.50	.20
❑ 164	Ken Harvey	.50	.20
❑ 165	Juan Rivera	.50	.20
❑ 166	Joe Valentine RC	1.50	.60
❑ 167	Dan Haren RC	3.00	1.25
❑ 168	Michel Hernandez RC	1.50	.60
❑ 169	Eider Torres RC	1.50	.60
❑ 170	Chris De La Cruz RC	1.50	.60
❑ 171	Ramon Nivar-Martinez RC	1.50	.60
❑ 172	Mike Adams RC	1.50	.60
❑ 173	Justin Arneson RC	1.50	.60
❑ 174	Jamie Athas RC	1.50	.60

❑ 175 Dwaine Bacon RC 1.50 .60
❑ 176 Clint Barmes RC 4.00 1.50
❑ 177 B.J. Barns RC 1.50 .60
❑ 178 Tyler Johnson RC 1.50 .60
❑ 179 Brandon Webb RC 10.00 4.00
❑ 180 T.J. Bohn RC 1.50 .60
❑ 181 Ozzie Chavez RC 1.50 .60
❑ 182 Brandon Bowe RC 1.50 .60
❑ 183 Craig Brazell RC 1.50 .60
❑ 184 Dusty Brown RC 1.50 .60
❑ 185 Brian Bruney RC 2.00 .75
❑ 186 Greg Bruso RC 1.50 .60
❑ 187 Jaime Bubela RC 1.50 .60
❑ 188 Matt Diaz RC 3.00 1.25
❑ 189 Brian Burgamy RC 1.50 .60
❑ 190 Eny Cabreja RC 5.00 2.00
❑ 191 Daniel Cabrera RC 3.00 1.25
❑ 192 Ryan Cameron RC 1.50 .60
❑ 193 Lance Caraccioli RC 1.50 .60
❑ 194 David Cash RC 1.50 .60
❑ 195 Bernie Castro RC 1.50 .60
❑ 196 Ismael Castro RC 2.00 .75
❑ 197 Cory Doyne RC 1.50 .60
❑ 198 Jeff Clark RC 1.50 .60
❑ 199 Chris Colton RC 1.50 .60
❑ 200 Dexter Cooper RC 1.50 .60
❑ 201 Callix Crabbe RC 2.00 .75
❑ 202 Chien-Ming Wang RC 15.00 6.00
❑ 203 Eric Crozier RC 2.00 .75
❑ 204 Nook Logan RC 2.00 .75
❑ 205 David DeJesus RC 3.00 1.25
❑ 206 Matt DeMarco RC 1.50 .60
❑ 207 Chris Duncan RC 12.00 5.00
❑ 208 Eric Eckenstahler .50 .20
❑ 209 Willie Eyre RC 1.50 .60
❑ 210 Evel Bastida-Martinez RC 1.50 .60
❑ 211 Chris Fallon RC 1.50 .60
❑ 212 Mike Flannery RC 1.50 .60
❑ 213 Mike Oâ ™Keefe RC 1.50 .60
❑ 214 Lew Ford RC 2.00 .75
❑ 215 Kason Gabbard RC 1.50 .60
❑ 216 Mike Gallo RC 1.50 .60
❑ 217 Jairo Garcia RC 2.00 .75
❑ 218 Angel Garcia RC 2.00 .75
❑ 219 Michael Garciaparra RC 1.50 .60
❑ 220 Jeremy Griffiths RC 1.50 .60
❑ 221 Dusty Gomon RC 2.00 .75
❑ 222 Bryan Grace RC 1.50 .60
❑ 223 Tyson Graham RC 1.50 .60
❑ 224 Henry Guerrero RC 1.50 .60
❑ 225 Franklin Gutierrez RC 4.00 1.50
❑ 226 Carlos Guzman RC 2.00 .75
❑ 227 Matthew Hagen RC 1.50 .60
❑ 228 Josh Hall RC 1.50 .60
❑ 229 Rob Hammock RC 1.50 .60
❑ 230 Brendan Harris RC 2.00 .75
❑ 231 Gary Harris RC 1.50 .60
❑ 232 Clay Hensley RC 1.50 .60
❑ 233 Michael Hinckley RC 2.00 .75
❑ 234 Luis Hodge RC 1.50 .60
❑ 235 Donnie Hood RC 2.00 .75
❑ 236 Matt Hensley RC 1.50 .60
❑ 237 Edwin Jackson RC 2.00 .75
❑ 238 Ardley Jansen RC 2.00 .75
❑ 239 Ferenc Jongejan RC 1.50 .60
❑ 240 Matt Kata RC 1.50 .60
❑ 241 Kazuhiro Takeoka RC 1.50 .60
❑ 242 Charlie Manning RC 1.50 .60
❑ 243 Il Kim RC 1.50 .60
❑ 244 Brennan King RC 1.50 .60
❑ 245 Chris Kroski RC 1.50 .60
❑ 246 David Martinez RC 1.50 .60
❑ 247 Pete LaForest RC 1.50 .60
❑ 248 Wil Ledezma RC 1.50 .60
❑ 249 Jeremy Bonderman RC 10.00 4.00
❑ 250 Gonzalo Lopez RC 1.50 .60
❑ 251 Brian Luderer RC 1.50 .60
❑ 252 Ruddy Lugo RC 1.50 .60
❑ 253 Wayne Lydon RC 1.50 .60
❑ 254 Mark Malaska RC 1.50 .60
❑ 255 Andy Marte RC 12.00 5.00
❑ 256 Tyler Martin RC 1.50 .60
❑ 257 Branden Florence RC 1.50 .60
❑ 258 Aneudis Mateo RC 1.50 .60
❑ 259 Derell McCall RC 1.50 .60
❑ 260 Elizardo Ramirez RC 2.00 .75
❑ 261 Mike McNutt RC 1.50 .60
❑ 262 Jacobo Meque RC 1.50 .60
❑ 263 Derek Michaelis RC 1.50 .60
❑ 264 Aaron Miles RC 2.00 .75
❑ 265 Jose Morales RC 1.50 .60
❑ 266 Dustin Moseley RC 1.50 .60
❑ 267 Adrian Myers RC 1.50 .60
❑ 268 Dan Neil RC 1.50 .60
❑ 269 Jon Nelson RC 2.00 .75
❑ 270 Mike Neu RC 1.50 .60
❑ 271 Leigh Neuage RC 1.50 .60
❑ 272 Wes O'Brien RC 1.50 .60
❑ 273 Trent Oeltjen RC 2.00 .75
❑ 274 Tim Olson RC 1.50 .60
❑ 275 David Pahucki RC 1.50 .60
❑ 276 Nathan Panther RC 1.50 .60
❑ 277 Arnie Munoz RC 1.50 .60
❑ 278 Dave Pember RC 1.50 .60
❑ 279 Jason Perry RC 2.00 .75
❑ 280 Matthew Peterson RC 1.50 .60
❑ 281 Greg Aquino RC 1.50 .60
❑ 282 Jorge Piedra RC 2.00 .75
❑ 283 Simon Pond RC 1.50 .60
❑ 284 Aaron Rakers RC 1.50 .60
❑ 285 Felix Sanchez RC 1.50 .60
❑ 286 Manuel Ramirez RC 2.00 .75
❑ 287 Kevin Randel RC 1.50 .60
❑ 288 Kelly Shoppach RC 3.00 1.25
❑ 289 Prentice Redman RC 1.50 .60
❑ 290 Eric Reed RC 1.50 .60
❑ 291 Wilton Reynolds RC 2.00 .75
❑ 292 Eric Riggs RC 2.00 .75
❑ 293 Carlos Rijo RC 1.50 .60
❑ 294 Tyler Adamczyk RC 1.50 .60
❑ 295 Jon-Mark Sprowl RC 1.50 .60
❑ 296 Arturo Rivas RC 1.50 .60
❑ 297 Kyle Roat RC 1.50 .60
❑ 298 Bubba Nelson RC .75 .30
❑ 299 Levi Robinson RC 1.50 .60
❑ 300 Ray Sadler RC 1.50 .60
❑ 301 Rylan Reed RC 1.50 .60
❑ 302 Jon Schuerholz RC 1.50 .60
❑ 303 Nobuaki Yoshida RC 1.50 .60
❑ 304 Brian Shackelford RC 1.50 .60
❑ 305 Bill Simon RC 1.50 .60
❑ 306 Haj Turay RC 1.00 .40
❑ 307 Sean Smith RC 2.00 .75
❑ 308 Ryan Spataro RC 1.50 .60
❑ 309 Jemel Spearman RC 1.50 .60
❑ 310 Keith Stamler RC 1.50 .60
❑ 311 Luke Steidlmayer RC 1.50 .60
❑ 312 Adam Stern RC 1.00 .40
❑ 313 Jay Sitzman RC 1.50 .60
❑ 314 Mike Wodnicki RC 1.50 .60
❑ 315 Terry Tiffee RC 1.50 .60
❑ 316 Nick Trzesniak RC 1.50 .60
❑ 317 Denny Tussen RC 1.50 .60
❑ 318 Scott Tyler RC 2.00 .75
❑ 319 Shane Victorino RC 3.00 1.25
❑ 320 Doug Waechter RC 2.00 .75
❑ 321 Brandon Watson RC 1.50 .60
❑ 322 Todd Wellemeyer RC 1.50 .60
❑ 323 Eli Whiteside RC 1.50 .60
❑ 324 Josh Willingham RC 4.00 1.50
❑ 325 Travis Wong RC 2.00 .75
❑ 326 Brian Wright RC 1.50 .60
❑ 327 Felix Pie RC 15.00 6.00
❑ 328 Andy Sisco RC .50 .20
❑ 329 Dustin Yount RC 2.00 .75
❑ 330 Andrew Dominique RC 1.50 .60
❑ 331 Brian McCann AU A RC 70.00 40.00
❑ 332 Jose Contreras AU B RC 150.00 90.00
❑ 333 Corey Shafer AU A RC 10.00 4.00
❑ 334 Hanley Ramirez AU A RC 80.00 40.00
❑ 335 Ryan Shealy AU A RC 40.00 15.00
❑ 336 Kevin Youkilis AU A RC 40.00 20.00
❑ 337 Jason Kubel AU A RC 30.00 12.50
❑ 338 Aron Weston AU A RC 10.00 4.00
❑ 338B Rajai Davis AU A ERR
❑ 339 J.D. Durbin AU A RC 10.00 4.00
❑ 340 Gary Schneidmiller AU A RC 10.00 4.00
❑ 341 Travis Ishikawa AU A RC 15.00 6.00
❑ 342 Ben Francisco AU A RC 10.00 4.00
❑ 343 Bobby Basham AU A RC 10.00 4.00
❑ 344 Joey Gomes AU A RC 10.00 4.00
❑ 345 Beau Kemp AU A RC 10.00 4.00
❑ 346 T.Story-Harden AU A RC 10.00 4.00
❑ 347 Daryl Clark AU A RC 10.00 4.00
❑ 348 Bryan Bullington AU A RC 10.00 4.00
❑ 349 Rajai Davis AU A RC 10.00 4.00
❑ 350 Darrell Rasner AU A RC 10.00 4.00
❑ 351 Willie Mays 2.00 .75
❑ 351AU Willie Mays AU 250.00 150.00

2003 Bowman Chrome Draft

❑ COMPLETE SET (176) 550.00 400.00
❑ COMP.SET w/o AU's (165) 100.00 50.00
❑ COMMON CARD (1-165) .40 .15
❑ 1-165 TWO PER BOWMAN DRAFT PACK
❑ COMMON CARD (166-176) 10.00 4.00
❑ 166-176 STATED ODDS 1:41 H/R
❑ LUBANSKI IS AN SP BY 1000 COPIES
❑ 1 Dontrelle Willis 1.50 .60
❑ 2 Freddy Sanchez .40 .15
❑ 3 Miguel Cabrera 1.50 .60
❑ 4 Ryan Ludwick .40 .15
❑ 5 Ty Wigginton .40 .15
❑ 6 Mark Teixeira 1.00 .40
❑ 7 Trey Hodges .40 .15
❑ 8 Laynce Nix .60 .25
❑ 9 Antonio Perez .40 .15
❑ 10 Jody Gerut .40 .15
❑ 11 Jae Weong Seo .40 .15
❑ 12 Erick Almonte .40 .15
❑ 13 Lyle Overbay .40 .15
❑ 14 Billy Traber .40 .15
❑ 15 Andres Torres .40 .15
❑ 16 Jose Valverde .40 .15
❑ 17 Aaron Heilman .40 .15
❑ 18 Brandon Larson .40 .15
❑ 19 Jung Bong .40 .15
❑ 20 Jesse Foppert .40 .15
❑ 21 Angel Berroa .40 .15
❑ 22 Jeff DaVanon .40 .15
❑ 23 Kurt Ainsworth .40 .15
❑ 24 Brandon Claussen .40 .15
❑ 25 Xavier Nady .40 .15
❑ 26 Travis Hafner .60 .25
❑ 27 Jerome Williams .40 .15
❑ 28 Jose Reyes .60 .25
❑ 29 Sergio Mitre RC 1.50 .60
❑ 30 Bo Hart RC 1.00 .40
❑ 31 Adam Miller RC 8.00 3.00
❑ 32 Brian Finch RC 1.00 .40
❑ 33 Taylor Mattingly RC 1.50 .60
❑ 34 Daric Barton RC 8.00 3.00
❑ 35 Chris Ray RC 3.00 1.25
❑ 36 Jarrod Saltalamacchia RC 15.00 6.00
❑ 37 Dennis Dove RC 1.50 .60
❑ 38 James Houser RC 1.50 .60
❑ 39 Clint King RC 1.50 .60
❑ 40 Lou Palmisano RC 1.50 .60
❑ 41 Dan Moore RC 1.00 .40
❑ 42 Craig Stansberry RC 1.50 .60
❑ 43 Jo Jo Reyes RC 3.00 1.25
❑ 44 Jake Stevens RC 1.50 .60
❑ 45 Tom Gorzelanny RC 4.00 1.50
❑ 46 Brian Marshall RC 1.00 .40
❑ 47 Scott Beerer RC 1.00 .40
❑ 48 Javi Herrera RC 1.50 .60
❑ 49 Steve LeRud RC 1.50 .60
❑ 50 Josh Banks RC 2.50 1.00
❑ 51 Jon Papelbon RC 25.00 10.00

❑	52	Juan Valdes RC	1.50	.60
❑	53	Beau Vaughan RC	1.50	.60
❑	54	Matt Chico RC	1.50	.60
❑	55	Todd Jennings RC	1.50	.60
❑	56	Anthony Gwynn RC	3.00	1.25
❑	57	Matt Harrison RC	2.50	1.00
❑	58	Aaron Marsden RC	1.50	.60
❑	59	Casey Abrams RC	1.00	.40
❑	60	Cory Stuart RC	1.00	.40
❑	61	Mike Wagner RC	1.00	.40
❑	62	Jordan Pratt RC	1.50	.60
❑	63	Andre Randolph RC	1.50	.60
❑	64	Blake Balkcom RC	1.50	.60
❑	65	Josh Muecke RC	1.00	.40
❑	66	Jamie D'Antona RC	2.50	1.00
❑	67	Cole Seifrig RC	1.00	.40
❑	68	Josh Anderson RC	1.50	.60
❑	69	Matt Lorenzo RC	1.50	.60
❑	70	Nate Spears RC	1.50	.60
❑	71	Chris Goodman RC	1.00	.40
❑	72	Brian McFall RC	1.00	.40
❑	73	Billy Hogan RC	1.50	.60
❑	74	Jamie Romak RC	1.50	.60
❑	75	Jeff Cook RC	1.50	.60
❑	76	Brooks McNiven RC	1.00	.40
❑	77	Xavier Paul RC	1.50	.60
❑	78	Bob Zimmerman RC	1.00	.40
❑	79	Mickey Hall RC	1.50	.60
❑	80	Shaun Marcum RC	1.50	.60
❑	81	Matt Nachreiner RC	1.50	.60
❑	82	Chris Kinsey RC	1.00	.40
❑	83	Jonathan Fulton RC	1.50	.60
❑	84	Edgardo Baez RC	1.50	.60
❑	85	Robert Valido RC	1.50	.60
❑	86	Kenny Lewis RC	1.50	.60
❑	87	Trent Peterson RC	1.00	.40
❑	88	Johnny Woodard RC	1.50	.60
❑	89	Wes Littleton RC	1.50	.60
❑	90	Sean Rodriguez RC	5.00	2.00
❑	91	Kyle Pearson RC	1.00	.40
❑	92	Josh Rainwater RC	1.50	.60
❑	93	Travis Schlichting RC	1.50	.60
❑	94	Tim Battle RC	2.50	1.00
❑	95	Aaron Hill RC	2.50	1.00
❑	96	Bob McCrory RC	1.00	.40
❑	97	Rick Guarno RC	1.50	.60
❑	98	Brandon Yarbrough RC	1.00	.40
❑	99	Peter Stonard RC	1.00	.40
❑	100	Darin Downs RC	1.50	.60
❑	101	Matt Bruback RC	1.00	.40
❑	102	Danny Garcia RC	1.00	.40
❑	103	Cory Stewart RC	1.00	.40
❑	104	Ferdin Tejeda RC	1.00	.40
❑	105	Kade Johnson RC	1.00	.40
❑	106	Andrew Brown RC	1.50	.60
❑	107	Aquilino Lopez RC	1.00	.40
❑	108	Stephen Randolph RC	1.00	.40
❑	109	Dave Matranga RC	1.00	.40
❑	110	Dustin McGowan RC	1.50	.60
❑	111	Juan Camacho RC	1.00	.40
❑	112	Cliff Lee	.40	.15
❑	113	Jeff Duncan RC	1.00	.40
❑	114	C.J. Wilson	.40	.15
❑	115	Brandon Roberson RC	1.00	.40
❑	116	David Corrente RC	1.00	.40
❑	117	Kevin Beavers RC	1.00	.40
❑	118	Anthony Webster RC	1.50	.60
❑	119	Oscar Villarreal RC	1.00	.40
❑	120	Hong-Chih Kuo RC	8.00	3.00
❑	121	Josh Barfield	.60	.25
❑	122	Denny Bautista	.40	.15
❑	123	Chris Burke RC	4.00	1.50
❑	124	Robinson Cano RC	20.00	8.00
❑	125	Jose Castillo	.40	.15
❑	126	Neal Cotts	.40	.15
❑	127	Jorge De La Rosa	.40	.15
❑	128	J.D. Durbin	.50	.20
❑	129	Edwin Encarnacion	2.00	.75
❑	130	Gavin Floyd	.40	.15
❑	131	Alexis Gomez	.40	.15
❑	132	Edgar Gonzalez RC	1.00	.40
❑	133	Khalil Greene	1.50	.60
❑	134	Zack Greinke	.60	.25
❑	135	Franklin Gutierrez	1.50	.60
❑	136	Rich Harden	1.00	.40
❑	137	J.J. Hardy RC	5.00	2.00
❑	138	Ryan Howard RC	70.00	40.00
❑	139	Justin Huber	.40	.15
❑	140	David Kelton	.40	.15
❑	141	Dave Krynzel	.40	.15
❑	142	Pete LaForest	.50	.20
❑	143	Adam LaRoche	.40	.15
❑	144	Preston Larrison RC	1.00	.40
❑	145	John Maine RC	6.00	2.50
❑	146	Andy Marte	4.00	1.50
❑	147	Jeff Mathis	.40	.15
❑	148	Joe Mauer	1.50	.60
❑	149	Clint Nageotte	.40	.15
❑	150	Chris Narveson	.40	.15
❑	151	Ramon Nivar	.50	.20
❑	152	Felix Pie	6.00	2.50
❑	153	Guillermo Quiroz RC	1.00	.40
❑	154	Rene Reyes	.40	.15
❑	155	Royce Ring	.40	.15
❑	156	Alexis Rios	3.00	1.25
❑	157	Grady Sizemore	1.50	.60
❑	158	Stephen Smitherman	.40	.15
❑	159	Seung Song	.40	.15
❑	160	Scott Thorman	.40	.15
❑	161	Chad Tracy	.40	.15
❑	162	Chin-Hui Tsao	.60	.25
❑	163	John VanBenschoten	.40	.15
❑	164	Kevin Youkilis	4.00	1.50
❑	165	Chien-Ming Wang	6.00	2.50
❑	166	Chris Lubanski AU SP RC	40.00	20.00
❑	167	Ryan Harvey AU RC	30.00	15.00
❑	168	Matt Murton AU RC	30.00	15.00
❑	169	Jay Sborz AU RC	10.00	4.00
❑	170	Brandon Wood AU RC	100.00	70.00
❑	171	Nick Markakis AU RC	60.00	30.00
❑	172	Rickie Weeks AU RC	60.00	35.00
❑	173	Eric Duncan AU RC	25.00	10.00
❑	174	Chad Billingsley AU RC	50.00	30.00
❑	175	Ryan Wagner AU RC	10.00	4.00
❑	176	Delmon Young AU RC	150.00	100.00

2004 Bowman Chrome

❑		COMPLETE SET (350)	400.00	250.00
❑		COMP.SET w/o AU's (330)	120.00	60.00
❑		COMMON CARD (1-150)	.50	.20
❑		COMMON CARD (151-165)	.50	.20
❑		COMMON AUTO (331-350)	10.00	4.00
❑		331-350 AU'S ARE NOT SERIAL-NUMBERED		
❑		331-350 PRINT RUN PROVIDED BY TOPPS		
❑	1	Garret Anderson	.50	.20
❑	2	Larry Walker	.50	.20
❑	3	Derek Jeter	2.50	1.00
❑	4	Curt Schilling	.75	.30
❑	5	Carlos Zambrano	.50	.20
❑	6	Shawn Green	.50	.20
❑	7	Manny Ramirez	.75	.30
❑	8	Randy Johnson	1.25	.50
❑	9	Jeremy Bonderman	.50	.20
❑	10	Alfonso Soriano	.50	.20
❑	11	Scott Rolen	.75	.30
❑	12	Kerry Wood	.50	.20
❑	13	Eric Gagne	.50	.20
❑	14	Ryan Klesko	.50	.20
❑	15	Kevin Millar	.50	.20
❑	16	Ty Wigginton	.50	.20
❑	17	David Ortiz	1.25	.50
❑	18	Luis Castillo	.50	.20
❑	19	Bernie Williams	.75	.30
❑	20	Edgar Renteria	.50	.20
❑	21	Matt Kata	.50	.20
❑	22	Bartolo Colon	.50	.20
❑	23	Derrek Lee	.75	.30
❑	24	Gary Sheffield	.50	.20
❑	25	Nomar Garciaparra	2.00	.75
❑	26	Kevin Millwood	.50	.20
❑	27	Corey Patterson	.50	.20
❑	28	Carlos Beltran	.50	.20
❑	29	Mike Lieberthal	.50	.20
❑	30	Troy Glaus	.50	.20
❑	31	Preston Wilson	.50	.20
❑	32	Jorge Posada	.75	.30
❑	33	Bo Hart	.50	.20
❑	34	Mark Prior	.75	.30
❑	35	Hideo Nomo	1.25	.50
❑	36	Jason Kendall	.50	.20
❑	37	Roger Clemens	2.50	1.00
❑	38	Dmitri Young	.50	.20
❑	39	Jason Giambi	.50	.20
❑	40	Jim Edmonds	.50	.20
❑	41	Ryan Ludwick	.50	.20
❑	42	Brandon Webb	.50	.20
❑	43	Todd Helton	.75	.30
❑	44	Jacque Jones	.50	.20
❑	45	Jamie Moyer	.50	.20
❑	46	Tim Salmon	.75	.30
❑	47	Kelvim Escobar	.50	.20
❑	48	Tony Batista	.50	.20
❑	49	Nick Johnson	.50	.20
❑	50	Jim Thome	.75	.30
❑	51	Casey Blake	.50	.20
❑	52	Trot Nixon	.50	.20
❑	53	Luis Gonzalez	.50	.20
❑	54	Dontrelle Willis	.75	.30
❑	55	Mike Mussina	.75	.30
❑	56	Carl Crawford	.50	.20
❑	57	Mark Buehrle	.50	.20
❑	58	Scott Podsednik	.50	.20
❑	59	Brian Giles	.50	.20
❑	60	Rafael Furcal	.50	.20
❑	61	Miguel Cabrera	.75	.30
❑	62	Rich Harden	.50	.20
❑	63	Mark Teixeira	.75	.30
❑	64	Frank Thomas	1.25	.50
❑	65	Johan Santana	1.25	.50
❑	66	Jason Schmidt	.50	.20
❑	67	Aramis Ramirez	.50	.20
❑	68	Jose Reyes	.50	.20
❑	69	Magglio Ordonez	.50	.20
❑	70	Mike Sweeney	.50	.20
❑	71	Eric Chavez	.50	.20
❑	72	Rocco Baldelli	.50	.20
❑	73	Sammy Sosa	1.25	.50
❑	74	Javy Lopez	.50	.20
❑	75	Roy Oswalt	.50	.20
❑	76	Raul Ibanez	.50	.20
❑	77	Ivan Rodriguez	.75	.30
❑	78	Jerome Williams	.50	.20
❑	79	Carlos Lee	.50	.20
❑	80	Geoff Jenkins	.50	.20
❑	81	Sean Burroughs	.50	.20
❑	82	Marcus Giles	.50	.20
❑	83	Mike Lowell	.50	.20
❑	84	Barry Zito	.50	.20
❑	85	Aubrey Huff	.50	.20
❑	86	Esteban Loaiza	.50	.20
❑	87	Torii Hunter	.50	.20
❑	88	Phil Nevin	.50	.20
❑	89	Andruw Jones	.75	.30
❑	90	Josh Beckett	.50	.20
❑	91	Mark Mulder	.50	.20
❑	92	Hank Blalock	.50	.20
❑	93	Jason Phillips	.50	.20
❑	94	Russ Ortiz	.50	.20
❑	95	Juan Pierre	.50	.20
❑	96	Tom Glavine	.75	.30
❑	97	Gil Meche	.50	.20
❑	98	Ramon Ortiz	.50	.20
❑	99	Richie Sexson	.50	.20
❑	100	Albert Pujols	2.50	1.00
❑	101	Javier Vazquez	.50	.20
❑	102	Johnny Damon	.75	.30
❑	103	Alex Rodriguez	2.00	.75
❑	104	Omar Vizquel	.75	.30
❑	105	Chipper Jones	1.25	.50
❑	106	Lance Berkman	.50	.20

❑	107	Tim Hudson	.50	.20
❑	108	Carlos Delgado	.50	.20
❑	109	Austin Kearns	.50	.20
❑	110	Orlando Cabrera	.50	.20
❑	111	Edgar Martinez	.75	.30
❑	112	Melvin Mora	.50	.20
❑	113	Jeff Bagwell	.75	.30
❑	114	Marlon Byrd	.50	.20
❑	115	Vernon Wells	.50	.20
❑	116	C.C. Sabathia	.50	.20
❑	117	Cliff Floyd	.50	.20
❑	118	Ichiro Suzuki	2.50	1.00
❑	119	Miguel Olivo	.50	.20
❑	120	Mike Piazza	2.00	.75
❑	121	Adam Dunn	.50	.20
❑	122	Paul Lo Duca	.50	.20
❑	123	Brett Myers	.50	.20
❑	124	Michael Young	.50	.20
❑	125	Sidney Ponson	.50	.20
❑	126	Greg Maddux	2.00	.75
❑	127	Vladimir Guerrero	1.25	.50
❑	128	Miguel Tejada	.50	.20
❑	129	Andy Pettitte	.75	.30
❑	130	Rafael Palmeiro	.75	.30
❑	131	Ken Griffey Jr.	2.00	.75
❑	132	Shannon Stewart	.50	.20
❑	133	Joel Pineiro	.50	.20
❑	134	Luis Matos	.50	.20
❑	135	Jeff Kent	.50	.20
❑	136	Randy Wolf	.50	.20
❑	137	Chris Woodward	.50	.20
❑	138	Jody Gerut	.50	.20
❑	139	Jose Vidro	.50	.20
❑	140	Bret Boone	.50	.20
❑	141	Bill Mueller	.50	.20
❑	142	Angel Berroa	.50	.20
❑	143	Bobby Abreu	.50	.20
❑	144	Roy Halladay	.50	.20
❑	145	Delmon Young	.75	.30
❑	146	Jonny Gomes	.50	.20
❑	147	Rickie Weeks	.50	.20
❑	148	Edwin Jackson	.50	.20
❑	149	Neal Cotts	.50	.20
❑	150	Jason Bay	.50	.20
❑	151	Khalil Greene	1.00	.40
❑	152	Joe Mauer	1.25	.50
❑	153	Bobby Jenks	.75	.30
❑	154	Chin-Feng Chen	.50	.20
❑	155	Chien-Ming Wang	2.00	.75
❑	156	Mickey Hall	.50	.20
❑	157	James Houser	.50	.20
❑	158	Jay Sborz	.50	.20
❑	159	Jonathan Fulton	.50	.20
❑	160	Steven Lerud	.50	.20
❑	161	Grady Sizemore	1.50	.60
❑	162	Felix Pie	2.00	.75
❑	163	Dustin McGowan	.50	.20
❑	164	Chris Lubanski	.75	.30
❑	165	Tom Gorzelanny	.50	.20
❑	166	Rudy Guillen RC	3.00	1.25
❑	167	Aarom Baldiris RC	2.00	.75
❑	168	Conor Jackson RC	10.00	4.00
❑	169	Matt Moses RC	4.00	1.50
❑	170	Ervin Santana RC	6.00	2.50
❑	171	Merkin Valdez RC	2.00	.75
❑	172	Erick Aybar RC	3.00	1.25
❑	173	Brad Sullivan RC	2.00	.75
❑	174	Joey Gathright RC	4.00	1.50
❑	175	Brad Snyder RC	4.00	1.50
❑	176	Alberto Callaspo RC	3.00	1.25
❑	177	Brandon Medders RC	1.50	.60
❑	178	Zach Miner RC	5.00	2.00
❑	179	Charlie Zink RC	1.00	.40
❑	180	Adam Greenberg RC	3.00	1.25
❑	181	Kevin Howard RC	2.00	.75
❑	182	Wanell Severino RC	1.00	.40
❑	183	Chin-Lung Hu RC	5.00	2.00
❑	184	Joel Zumaya RC	12.00	5.00
❑	185	Skip Schumaker RC	1.50	.60
❑	186	Nic Ungs RC	1.50	.60
❑	187	Todd Self RC	2.00	.75
❑	188	Brian Steffek RC	1.00	.40
❑	189	Brock Peterson RC	1.50	.60
❑	190	Greg Thissen RC	1.50	.60
❑	191	Frank Brooks RC	1.00	.40
❑	192	Scott Olsen RC	6.00	2.50
❑	193	Chris Mabeus RC	1.50	.60
❑	194	Dan Giese RC	1.50	.60
❑	195	Jared Wells RC	1.00	.40
❑	196	Carlos Sosa RC	1.50	.60
❑	197	Bobby Madritsch	1.00	.40
❑	198	Calvin Hayes RC	2.00	.75
❑	199	Omar Quintanilla RC	2.00	.75
❑	200	Chris O'Riordan RC	1.50	.60
❑	201	Tim Hutting RC	1.00	.40
❑	202	Carlos Quentin RC	10.00	4.00
❑	203	Brayan Pena RC	1.50	.60
❑	204	Jeff Salazar RC	4.00	1.50
❑	205	David Murphy RC	3.00	1.25
❑	206	Alberto Garcia RC	2.00	.75
❑	207	Ramon Ramirez RC	1.50	.60
❑	208	Luis Bolivar RC	1.50	.60
❑	209	Rodney Choy Foo RC	1.00	.40
❑	210	Fausto Carmona RC	5.00	2.00
❑	211	Anthony Acevedo RC	1.50	.60
❑	212	Chad Santos RC	1.50	.60
❑	213	Jason Frasor RC	1.50	.60
❑	214	Jesse Roman RC	1.00	.40
❑	215	James Tomlin RC	1.50	.60
❑	216	Josh Labandeira RC	1.50	.60
❑	217	Ryan Meaux RC	1.50	.60
❑	218	Don Sutton RC	4.00	1.50
❑	219	Danny Gonzalez RC	1.00	.40
❑	220	Javier Guzman RC	2.00	.75
❑	221	Anthony Lerew RC	3.00	1.25
❑	222	Jon Connolly RC	4.00	1.50
❑	223	Jesse English RC	1.50	.60
❑	224	Hector Made RC	3.00	1.25
❑	225	Travis Hanson RC	2.00	.75
❑	226	Jesse Floyd RC	1.50	.60
❑	227	Nick Gorneault RC	2.00	.75
❑	228	Craig Ansman RC	1.50	.60
❑	229	Paul McAnulty RC	3.00	1.25
❑	230	Carl Loadenthal RC	2.00	.75
❑	231	Dave Crouthers RC	1.00	.40
❑	232	Harvey Garcia RC	1.00	.40
❑	233	Casey Kopitzke RC	1.00	.40
❑	234	Ricky Nolasco RC	5.00	2.00
❑	235	Miguel Perez RC	1.50	.60
❑	236	Ryan Mulhern RC	1.50	.60
❑	237	Chris Aguila RC	1.50	.60
❑	238	Brooks Conrad RC	2.00	.75
❑	239	Damaso Espino RC	1.00	.40
❑	240	Jereme Milons RC	2.00	.75
❑	241	Luke Hughes RC	1.00	.40
❑	242	Kory Casto RC	2.00	.75
❑	243	Jose Valdez RC	1.50	.60
❑	244	J.T. Stotts RC	1.00	.40
❑	245	Lee Gwaltney RC	1.00	.40
❑	246	Yoann Torrealba RC	1.00	.40
❑	247	Omar Falcon RC	1.50	.60
❑	248	Jon Coutlangus RC	1.00	.40
❑	249	George Sherrill RC	1.50	.60
❑	250	John Santor RC	1.00	.40
❑	251	Tony Richie RC	1.50	.60
❑	252	Kevin Richardson RC	1.00	.40
❑	253	Tim Bittner RC	1.50	.60
❑	254	Chris Saenz RC	1.50	.60
❑	255	Jose Capellan RC	2.00	.75
❑	256	Donald Levinski RC	1.00	.40
❑	257	Jerome Gamble RC	1.00	.40
❑	258	Jeff Keppinger RC	1.50	.60
❑	259	Jason Szuminski RC	1.00	.40
❑	260	Akinori Otsuka RC	1.50	.60
❑	261	Ryan Budde RC	1.50	.60
❑	262	Marland Williams RC	2.00	.75
❑	263	Jeff Allison RC	1.50	.60
❑	264	Hector Gimenez RC	1.00	.40
❑	265	Tim Frend RC	1.50	.60
❑	266	Tom Farmer RC	1.50	.60
❑	267	Shawn Hill RC	1.50	.60
❑	268	Mike Huggins RC	1.50	.60
❑	269	Scott Proctor RC	2.00	.75
❑	270	Jorge Mejia RC	1.50	.60
❑	271	Terry Jones RC	2.00	.75
❑	272	Zach Duke RC	8.00	3.00
❑	273	Jesse Crain RC	3.00	1.25
❑	274	Luke Anderson RC	1.00	.40
❑	275	Hunter Brown RC	1.00	.40
❑	276	Matt Lemanczyk RC	1.50	.60
❑	277	Fernando Cortez RC	1.00	.40
❑	278	Vince Perkins RC	2.00	.75
❑	279	Tommy Murphy RC	1.50	.60
❑	280	Mike Gosling RC	1.00	.40
❑	281	Paul Bacot RC	2.00	.75
❑	282	Matt Capps RC	1.50	.60
❑	283	Juan Gutierrez RC	1.50	.60
❑	284	Teodoro Encarnacion RC	2.00	.75
❑	285	Chad Bentz RC	1.50	.60
❑	286	Kazuo Matsui RC	2.00	.75
❑	287	Ryan Hankins RC	1.00	.40
❑	288	Leo Nunez RC	1.50	.60
❑	289	Dave Wallace RC	1.50	.60
❑	290	Rob Tejeda RC	3.00	1.25
❑	291	Paul Maholm RC	4.00	1.50
❑	292	Casey Daigle RC	1.50	.60
❑	293	Tydus Meadows RC	1.00	.40
❑	294	Khalid Ballouli RC	1.00	.40
❑	295	Benji DeQuin RC	1.00	.40
❑	296	Tyler Davidson RC	2.00	.75
❑	297	Brant Colamarino RC	3.00	1.25
❑	298	Marcus McBeth RC	1.00	.40
❑	299	Brad Eldred RC	2.00	.75
❑	300	David Pauley RC	5.00	2.00
❑	301	Yadier Molina RC	6.00	2.50
❑	302	Chris Shelton RC	5.00	2.00
❑	303	Nyjer Morgan RC	1.00	.40
❑	304	Jon DeVries RC	1.50	.60
❑	305	Sheldon Fulse RC	1.00	.40
❑	306	Vito Chiaravalloti RC	1.50	.60
❑	307	Warner Madrigal RC	3.00	1.25
❑	308	Reid Gorecki RC	1.50	.60
❑	309	Sung Jung RC	1.00	.40
❑	310	Pete Shier RC	1.00	.40
❑	311	Michael Mooney RC	1.50	.60
❑	312	Kenny Perez RC	1.50	.60
❑	313	Michael Mallory RC	1.50	.60
❑	314	Ben Himes RC	1.00	.40
❑	315	Ivan Ochoa RC	1.50	.60
❑	316	Donald Kelly RC	1.50	.60
❑	317	Tom Mastny RC	1.50	.60
❑	318	Kevin Davidson RC	1.00	.40
❑	319	Brian Pilkington RC	1.00	.40
❑	320	Alex Romero RC	1.50	.60
❑	321	Chad Chop RC	1.50	.60
❑	322	Kody Kirkland RC	2.00	.75
❑	323	Casey Myers RC	1.00	.40
❑	324	Mike Rouse RC	1.50	.60
❑	325	Sergio Silva RC	1.00	.40
❑	326	J.J. Furmaniak RC	3.00	1.25
❑	327	Brad Vericker RC	1.50	.60
❑	328	Blake Hawksworth RC	2.00	.75
❑	329	Brock Jacobsen RC	1.00	.40
❑	330	Alec Zumwalt RC	1.00	.40
❑	331	Wardell Starling AU RC	10.00	4.00
❑	332	Estee Harris AU RC	10.00	4.00
❑	333	Kyle Sleeth AU RC	10.00	4.00
❑	334	Dioner Navarro AU RC	15.00	6.00
❑	335	Logan Kensing AU RC	10.00	4.00
❑	336	Travis Blackley AU RC	10.00	4.00
❑	337	Lincoln Holdzkom AU RC	10.00	4.00
❑	338	Jason Hirsh AU RC	25.00	10.00
❑	339	Juan Cedeno AU RC	10.00	4.00
❑	340	Matt Creighton AU RC	10.00	4.00
❑	341	Tim Stauffer AU RC	15.00	6.00
❑	342	Shingo Takatsu AU RC	15.00	6.00
❑	343	Lastings Milledge AU RC	80.00	50.00
❑	344	Dustin Nippert AU RC	10.00	4.00
❑	345	Felix Hernandez AU RC	125.00	75.00
❑	346	Joaquin Arias AU RC	15.00	6.00
❑	347	Kevin Kouzmanoff AU RC	50.00	20.00
❑	348	B.Brownlie AU RC EXCH	10.00	4.00
❑	349	David Aardsma AU RC	10.00	4.00
❑	350	Jon Knott AU RC	15.00	6.00

2004 Bowman Chrome Draft

❑	COMPLETE SET (175)	300.00	175.00
❑	COMP.SET w/o SP's (165)	100.00	50.00
❑	COMMON CARD (1-165)	.40	.15
❑	COMMON RC YR	.40	.15

- ❑ 1-165 TWO PER BOWMAN DRAFT PACK
- ❑ 166-175 ODDS 1:60 BOWMAN DRAFT HOBBY
- ❑ 166-175 ODDS 1:60 BOWMAN DRAFT RETAIL
- ❑ 166-175 STATED PRINT RUN 1695 SETS
- ❑ 166-175 ARE NOT SERIAL-NUMBERED
- ❑ 166-175 PRINT RUN PROVIDED BY TOPPS

❑ PLATES 1-165 ODDS 1:559 HOBBY
❑ PLATES 166-175 ODDS 1:18,354 HOBBY
❑ PLATES PRINT RUN 1 SERIAL #'d SET
❑ BLACK-CYAN-MAGENTA-YELLOW EXIST
❑ NO PLATES PRICING DUE TO SCARCITY

❑ 1	Lyle Overbay	.40	.15
❑ 2	David Newhan	.40	.15
❑ 3	J.R. House	.40	.15
❑ 4	Chad Tracy	.40	.15
❑ 5	Humberto Quintero	.40	.15
❑ 6	Dave Bush	.40	.15
❑ 7	Scott Hairston	.40	.15
❑ 8	Mike Wood	.40	.15
❑ 9	Alexis Rios	.60	.25
❑ 10	Sean Burnett	.40	.15
❑ 11	Wilson Valdez	.40	.15
❑ 12	Lew Ford	.40	.15
❑ 13	Freddy Thon RC	1.00	.40
❑ 14	Zack Greinke	.60	.25
❑ 15	Bucky Jacobsen	.40	.15
❑ 16	Kevin Youkilis	.40	.15
❑ 17	Grady Sizemore	1.50	.60
❑ 18	Denny Bautista	.40	.15
❑ 19	David DeJesus	.40	.15
❑ 20	Casey Kotchman	.60	.25
❑ 21	David Kelton	.40	.15
❑ 22	Charles Thomas RC	1.00	.40
❑ 23	Kazuhito Tadano RC	1.50	.60
❑ 24	Justin Leone RC	1.50	.60
❑ 25	Eduardo Villacis RC	1.00	.40
❑ 26	Brian Dallimore RC	1.00	.40
❑ 27	Nick Green	.40	.15
❑ 28	Sam McConnell RC	1.00	.40
❑ 29	Brad Halsey RC	1.50	.60
❑ 30	Roman Colon RC	1.00	.40
❑ 31	Josh Fields RC	6.00	2.50
❑ 32	Cody Bunkelman RC	1.50	.60
❑ 33	Jay Rainville RC	4.00	1.50
❑ 34	Richie Robnett RC	3.00	1.25
❑ 35	Jon Poterson RC	2.50	1.00
❑ 36	Huston Street RC	5.00	2.00
❑ 37	Erick San Pedro RC	1.00	.40
❑ 38	Cory Dunlap RC	3.00	1.25
❑ 39	Kurt Suzuki RC	3.00	1.25
❑ 40	Anthony Swarzak RC	2.50	1.00
❑ 41	Ian Desmond RC	4.00	1.50
❑ 42	Chris Covington RC	1.50	.60
❑ 43	Christian Garcia RC	2.50	1.00
❑ 44	Gaby Hernandez RC	4.00	1.50
❑ 45	Steven Register RC	1.00	.40
❑ 46	Eduardo Morlan RC	3.00	1.25
❑ 47	Collin Balester RC	1.50	.60
❑ 48	Nathan Phillips RC	1.50	.60
❑ 49	Dan Schwartzbauer RC	1.50	.60
❑ 50	Rafael Gonzalez RC	1.00	.40
❑ 51	K.C. Herren RC	2.50	1.00
❑ 52	William Susdorf RC	1.00	.40
❑ 53	Rob Johnson RC	1.50	.60
❑ 54	Louis Marson RC	2.50	1.00
❑ 55	Joe Koshansky RC	6.00	2.50
❑ 56	Jamar Walton RC	2.50	1.00
❑ 57	Mark Lowe RC	5.00	2.00
❑ 58	Matt Macri RC	3.00	1.25
❑ 59	Donny Lucy RC	1.00	.40
❑ 60	Mike Ferris RC	1.50	.60
❑ 61	Mike Nickeas RC	1.50	.60
❑ 62	Eric Hurley RC	3.00	1.25
❑ 63	Scott Elbert RC	3.00	1.25
❑ 64	Blake DeWitt RC	5.00	2.00
❑ 65	Danny Putnam RC	2.50	1.00
❑ 66	J.P. Howell RC	3.00	1.25
❑ 67	John Wiggins RC	1.00	.40
❑ 68	Justin Orenduff RC	2.50	1.00
❑ 69	Ray Liotta RC	3.00	1.25
❑ 70	Billy Buckner RC	1.50	.60
❑ 71	Eric Campbell RC	6.00	2.50
❑ 72	Olin Wick RC	2.50	1.00
❑ 73	Sean Gamble RC	1.50	.60
❑ 74	Seth Smith RC	3.00	1.25
❑ 75	Wade Davis RC	5.00	2.00
❑ 76	Joe Jacobitz RC	1.00	.40
❑ 77	J.A. Happ RC	2.50	1.00
❑ 78	Eric Ridener RC	1.00	.40
❑ 79	Matt Tuiasosopo RC	6.00	2.50
❑ 80	Brad Bergesen RC	1.00	.40
❑ 81	Javy Guerra RC	1.50	.60
❑ 82	Buck Shaw RC	1.50	.60
❑ 83	Paul Janish RC	2.00	.75
❑ 84	Sean Kazmar RC	1.00	.40
❑ 85	Josh Johnson RC	1.50	.60
❑ 86	Angel Salome RC	4.00	1.50
❑ 87	Jordan Parraz RC	2.50	1.00
❑ 88	Kelvin Vazquez RC	1.00	.40
❑ 89	Grant Hansen RC	1.00	.40
❑ 90	Matt Fox RC	1.00	.40
❑ 91	Trevor Plouffe RC	4.00	1.50
❑ 92	Wes Whisler RC	1.00	.40
❑ 93	Curtis Thigpen RC	2.50	1.00
❑ 94	Donnie Smith RC	1.50	.60
❑ 95	Luis Rivera RC	1.50	.60
❑ 96	Jesse Hoover RC	1.50	.60
❑ 97	Jason Vargas RC	4.00	1.50
❑ 98	Clary Carlsen RC	1.00	.40
❑ 99	Mark Robinson RC	1.00	.40
❑ 100	J.C. Holt RC	1.50	.60
❑ 101	Chad Blackwell RC	1.00	.40
❑ 102	Daryl Jones RC	3.00	1.25
❑ 103	Jonathan Tierce RC	1.00	.40
❑ 104	Patrick Bryant RC	1.00	.40
❑ 105	Eddie Prasch RC	1.50	.60
❑ 106	Mitch Einertson RC	1.50	.60
❑ 107	Kyle Waldrop RC	3.00	1.25
❑ 108	Jeff Marquez RC	1.50	.60
❑ 109	Zach Jackson RC	2.50	1.00
❑ 110	Josh Wahpepah RC	1.00	.40
❑ 111	Adam Lind RC	8.00	3.00
❑ 112	Kyle Bloom RC	1.50	.60
❑ 113	Ben Harrison RC	1.00	.40
❑ 114	Taylor Tankersley RC	1.50	.60
❑ 115	Steven Jackson RC	1.00	.40
❑ 116	David Purcey RC	2.50	1.00
❑ 117	Jacob McGee RC	3.00	1.25
❑ 118	Lucas Harrell RC	1.00	.40
❑ 119	Brandon Allen RC	3.00	1.25
❑ 120	Van Pope RC	1.50	.60
❑ 121	Jeff Francis	.60	.25
❑ 122	Joe Blanton	.60	.25
❑ 123	Wil Ledezma	.40	.15
❑ 124	Bryan Bullington	.40	.15
❑ 125	Jairo Garcia	.40	.15
❑ 126	Matt Cain	2.00	.75
❑ 127	Arnie Munoz	.40	.15
❑ 128	Clint Everts	.40	.15
❑ 129	Jesus Cota	.40	.15
❑ 130	Gavin Floyd	.40	.15
❑ 131	Edwin Encarnacion	.60	.25
❑ 132	Koyie Hill	.40	.15
❑ 133	Ruben Gotay	.40	.15
❑ 134	Jeff Mathis	.40	.15
❑ 135	Andy Marte	1.00	.40
❑ 136	Dallas McPherson	.60	.25
❑ 137	Justin Morneau	.60	.25
❑ 138	Rickie Weeks	.60	.25
❑ 139	Joel Guzman	1.00	.40
❑ 140	Shin Soo Choo	.40	.15
❑ 141	Yusmeiro Petit RC	5.00	2.00
❑ 142	Jorge Cortes RC	1.00	.40
❑ 143	Val Majewski	.40	.15
❑ 144	Felix Pie	1.00	.40
❑ 145	Aaron Hill	.40	.15
❑ 146	Jose Capellan	.60	.25
❑ 147	Dioner Navarro	1.00	.40
❑ 148	Fausto Carmona	2.00	.75
❑ 149	Robinzon Diaz RC	1.00	.40
❑ 150	Felix Hernandez	8.00	3.00
❑ 151	Andres Blanco RC	1.00	.40
❑ 152	Jason Kubel	.40	.15
❑ 153	Willy Taveras RC	2.50	1.00
❑ 154	Merkin Valdez	1.00	.40
❑ 155	Robinson Cano	1.50	.60
❑ 156	Bill Murphy	.40	.15
❑ 157	Chris Burke	.60	.25
❑ 158	Kyle Sleeth	.40	.15
❑ 159	B.J. Upton	1.00	.40
❑ 160	Tim Stauffer	1.00	.40
❑ 161	David Wright	4.00	1.50
❑ 162	Conor Jackson	4.00	1.50
❑ 163	Brad Thompson RC	2.50	1.00
❑ 164	Delmon Young	1.00	.40
❑ 165	Jeremy Reed	.60	.25
❑ 166	Matt Bush AU RC	25.00	10.00
❑ 167	Mark Rogers AU RC	20.00	8.00
❑ 168	Thomas Diamond AU RC	25.00	10.00
❑ 169	Greg Golson AU RC	15.00	6.00
❑ 170	Homer Bailey AU RC	60.00	30.00
❑ 171	Chris Lambert AU RC	10.00	4.00
❑ 172	Neil Walker AU RC	25.00	10.00
❑ 173	Bill Bray AU RC	10.00	4.00
❑ 174	Philip Hughes AU RC	150.00	75.00
❑ 175	Gio Gonzalez AU RC	25.00	10.00

2005 Bowman Chrome

❑ COMP.SET w/o AU's (330)	120.00	60.00
❑ COMMON CARD (1-140)	.50	.20
❑ COMMON CARD (141-165)	.50	.20
❑ COMMON CARD (166-330)	1.00	.40
❑ COMMON AUTO (331-353)	10.00	4.00

❑ 1-330 PLATE ODDS 1:779 HOBBY
❑ 331-353 AU PLATE ODDS 1:10,906 HOBBY
❑ PLATE PRINT RUN 1 SET PER COLOR
❑ BLACK-CYAN-MAGENTA-YELLOW ISSUED
❑ NO PLATE PRICING DUE TO SCARCITY

❑ 1	Gavin Floyd	.50	.20
❑ 2	Eric Chavez	.50	.20
❑ 3	Miguel Tejada	.50	.20
❑ 4	Dmitri Young	.50	.20
❑ 5	Hank Blalock	.50	.20
❑ 6	Kerry Wood	.50	.20
❑ 7	Andy Pettitte	.75	.30
❑ 8	Pat Burrell	.50	.20
❑ 9	Johnny Estrada	.50	.20
❑ 10	Frank Thomas	1.25	.50
❑ 11	Juan Pierre	.50	.20
❑ 12	Tom Glavine	.75	.30
❑ 13	Lyle Overbay	.50	.20
❑ 14	Jim Edmonds	.50	.20
❑ 15	Steve Finley	.50	.20
❑ 16	Jermaine Dye	.50	.20
❑ 17	Omar Vizquel	.75	.30
❑ 18	Nick Johnson	.50	.20
❑ 19	Brian Giles	.50	.20
❑ 20	Justin Morneau	.50	.20
❑ 21	Preston Wilson	.50	.20
❑ 22	Wily Mo Pena	.50	.20
❑ 23	Rafael Palmeiro	.75	.30
❑ 24	Scott Kazmir	.50	.20
❑ 25	Derek Jeter	2.50	1.00
❑ 26	Barry Zito	.50	.20
❑ 27	Mike Lowell	.50	.20
❑ 28	Jason Bay	.50	.20
❑ 29	Ken Harvey	.50	.20
❑ 30	Nomar Garciaparra	1.25	.50

❑ 31 Roy Halladay .50 .20
❑ 32 Todd Helton .75 .30
❑ 33 Mark Kotsay .50 .20
❑ 34 Jake Peavy .50 .20
❑ 35 David Wright 2.00 .75
❑ 36 Dontrelle Willis .50 .20
❑ 37 Marcus Giles .50 .20
❑ 38 Chone Figgins .50 .20
❑ 39 Sidney Ponson .50 .20
❑ 40 Randy Johnson 1.25 .50
❑ 41 John Smoltz .75 .30
❑ 42 Kevin Millar .50 .20
❑ 43 Mark Teixeira .75 .30
❑ 44 Alex Rios .50 .20
❑ 45 Mike Piazza 1.25 .50
❑ 46 Victor Martinez .50 .20
❑ 47 Jeff Bagwell .75 .30
❑ 48 Shawn Green .50 .20
❑ 49 Ivan Rodriguez .75 .30
❑ 50 Alex Rodriguez 2.00 .75
❑ 51 Kazuo Matsui .50 .20
❑ 52 Mark Mulder .50 .20
❑ 53 Michael Young .50 .20
❑ 54 Javy Lopez .50 .20
❑ 55 Johnny Damon .75 .30
❑ 56 Jeff Francis .50 .20
❑ 57 Rich Harden .50 .20
❑ 58 Bobby Abreu .50 .20
❑ 59 Mark Loretta .50 .20
❑ 60 Gary Sheffield .50 .20
❑ 61 Jamie Moyer .50 .20
❑ 62 Garret Anderson .50 .20
❑ 63 Vernon Wells .50 .20
❑ 64 Orlando Cabrera .50 .20
❑ 65 Magglio Ordonez .50 .20
❑ 66 Ronnie Belliard .50 .20
❑ 67 Carlos Lee .50 .20
❑ 68 Carl Pavano .50 .20
❑ 69 Jon Lieber .50 .20
❑ 70 Aubrey Huff .50 .20
❑ 71 Rocco Baldelli .50 .20
❑ 72 Jason Schmidt .50 .20
❑ 73 Bernie Williams .75 .30
❑ 74 Hideki Matsui 2.00 .75
❑ 75 Ken Griffey Jr. 2.00 .75
❑ 76 Josh Beckett .50 .20
❑ 77 Mark Buehrle .50 .20
❑ 78 David Ortiz 1.25 .50
❑ 79 Luis Gonzalez .50 .20
❑ 80 Scott Rolen .75 .30
❑ 81 Joe Mauer 1.25 .50
❑ 82 Jose Reyes .50 .20
❑ 83 Adam Dunn .50 .20
❑ 84 Greg Maddux 2.00 .75
❑ 85 Bartolo Colon .50 .20
❑ 86 Bret Boone .50 .20
❑ 87 Mike Mussina .75 .30
❑ 88 Ben Sheets .50 .20
❑ 89 Lance Berkman .50 .20
❑ 90 Miguel Cabrera .75 .30
❑ 91 C.C. Sabathia .50 .20
❑ 92 Mike Maroth .50 .20
❑ 93 Andruw Jones .75 .30
❑ 94 Jack Wilson .50 .20
❑ 95 Ichiro Suzuki 2.50 1.00
❑ 96 Geoff Jenkins .50 .20
❑ 97 Zack Greinke .50 .20
❑ 98 Jorge Posada .75 .30
❑ 99 Travis Hafner .50 .20
❑ 100 Barry Bonds 3.00 1.25
❑ 101 Aaron Rowand .50 .20
❑ 102 Aramis Ramirez .50 .20
❑ 103 Curt Schilling .75 .30
❑ 104 Melvin Mora .50 .20
❑ 105 Albert Pujols 2.50 1.00
❑ 106 Austin Kearns .50 .20
❑ 107 Shannon Stewart .50 .20
❑ 108 Carl Crawford .50 .20
❑ 109 Carlos Zambrano .50 .20
❑ 110 Roger Clemens 2.00 .75
❑ 111 Javier Vazquez .50 .20
❑ 112 Randy Wolf .50 .20
❑ 113 Chipper Jones 1.25 .50
❑ 114 Larry Walker .75 .30
❑ 115 Alfonso Soriano .50 .20
❑ 116 Brad Wilkerson .50 .20
❑ 117 Bobby Crosby .50 .20
❑ 118 Jim Thome .75 .30
❑ 119 Oliver Perez .50 .20
❑ 120 Vladimir Guerrero 1.25 .50
❑ 121 Roy Oswalt .50 .20
❑ 122 Torii Hunter .50 .20
❑ 123 Rafael Furcal .50 .20
❑ 124 Luis Castillo .50 .20
❑ 125 Carlos Beltran .50 .20
❑ 126 Mike Sweeney .50 .20
❑ 127 Johan Santana 1.25 .50
❑ 128 Tim Hudson .50 .20
❑ 129 Troy Glaus .50 .20
❑ 130 Manny Ramirez .75 .30
❑ 131 Jeff Kent .50 .20
❑ 132 Jose Vidro .50 .20
❑ 133 Edgar Renteria .50 .20
❑ 134 Russ Ortiz .50 .20
❑ 135 Sammy Sosa 1.25 .50
❑ 136 Carlos Delgado .50 .20
❑ 137 Richie Sexson .50 .20
❑ 138 Pedro Martinez .75 .30
❑ 139 Adrian Beltre .50 .20
❑ 140 Mark Prior .75 .30
❑ 141 Omar Quintanilla .50 .20
❑ 142 Carlos Quentin .75 .30
❑ 143 Dan Johnson .50 .20
❑ 144 Jake Stevens .50 .20
❑ 145 Nate Schierholtz .75 .30
❑ 146 Neil Walker .50 .20
❑ 147 Bill Bray .50 .20
❑ 148 Taylor Tankersley .50 .20
❑ 149 Trevor Plouffe .75 .30
❑ 150 Felix Hernandez 6.00 2.50
❑ 151 Philip Hughes 2.00 .75
❑ 152 James Houser .50 .20
❑ 153 David Murphy .50 .20
❑ 154 Ervin Santana .75 .30
❑ 155 Anthony Whittington .50 .20
❑ 156 Chris Lambert .50 .20
❑ 157 Jeremy Sowers .75 .30
❑ 158 Giovanny Gonzalez .75 .30
❑ 159 Blake DeWitt .75 .30
❑ 160 Thomas Diamond .75 .30
❑ 161 Greg Golson .75 .30
❑ 162 David Aardsma .50 .20
❑ 163 Paul Maholm .50 .20
❑ 164 Mark Rogers .75 .30
❑ 165 Homer Bailey .75 .30
❑ 166 Elvin Puello RC 1.50 .60
❑ 167 Tony Giarratano RC 1.50 .60
❑ 168 Darren Fenster RC 1.50 .60
❑ 169 Elvys Quezada RC 1.50 .60
❑ 170 Glen Perkins RC 3.00 1.25
❑ 171 Ian Kinsler RC 8.00 3.00
❑ 172 Adam Bostick RC 1.50 .60
❑ 173 Jeremy West RC 2.00 .75
❑ 174 Brett Harper RC 2.00 .75
❑ 175 Kevin West RC 1.50 .60
❑ 176 Luis Hernandez RC 1.50 .60
❑ 177 Matt Campbell RC 1.50 .60
❑ 178 Nate McLouth RC 2.00 .75
❑ 179 Ryan Goleski RC 2.00 .75
❑ 180 Matthew Lindstrom RC 1.50 .60
❑ 181 Matt DeSalvo RC 2.00 .75
❑ 182 Kole Strayhorn RC 1.50 .60
❑ 183 Jose Vaquedano RC 1.50 .60
❑ 184 James Jurries RC 2.00 .75
❑ 185 Ian Bladergroen RC 2.00 .75
❑ 186 Kila Kaaihue RC 4.00 1.50
❑ 187 Luke Scott RC 6.00 2.50
❑ 188 Chris Denorfia RC 4.00 1.50
❑ 189 Jai Miller RC 2.00 .75
❑ 190 Melky Cabrera RC 8.00 3.00
❑ 191 Ryan Sweeney RC 4.00 1.50
❑ 192 Sean Marshall RC 6.00 2.50
❑ 193 Erick Abreu RC 3.00 1.25
❑ 194 Tyler Pelland RC 2.00 .75
❑ 195 Cole Armstrong RC 1.50 .60
❑ 196 John Hudgins RC 1.50 .60
❑ 197 Wade Robinson RC 1.50 .60
❑ 198 Dan Santin RC 1.50 .60
❑ 199 Steve Doetsch RC 1.50 .60
❑ 200 Shane Costa RC 1.50 .60
❑ 201 Scott Mathieson RC 3.00 1.25
❑ 202 Ben Jones RC 2.00 .75
❑ 203 Michael Rogers RC 1.50 .60
❑ 204 Matt Rogelstad RC 1.50 .60
❑ 205 Luis Ramirez RC 1.50 .60
❑ 206 Landon Powell RC 2.00 .75
❑ 207 Erik Cordier RC 1.50 .60
❑ 208 Chris Seddon RC 1.50 .60
❑ 209 Chris Roberson RC 1.50 .60
❑ 210 Thomas Oldham RC 1.50 .60
❑ 211 Dana Eveland RC 1.50 .60
❑ 212 Cody Haerther RC 1.50 .60
❑ 213 Danny Core RC 1.50 .60
❑ 214 Craig Tatum RC 1.50 .60
❑ 215 Elliot Johnson RC 1.50 .60
❑ 216 Ender Chavez RC 1.50 .60
❑ 217 Errol Simonitsch RC 2.00 .75
❑ 218 Matt Van Der Bosch RC 1.50 .60
❑ 219 Eulogio de la Cruz RC 1.50 .60
❑ 220 Drew Toussaint RC 1.50 .60
❑ 221 Adam Boeve RC 1.50 .60
❑ 222 Adam Harben RC 2.00 .75
❑ 223 Baltazar Lopez RC 1.50 .60
❑ 224 Russ Martin RC 5.00 2.00
❑ 225 Brian Bannister RC 4.00 1.50
❑ 226 Chris Walker RC 1.50 .60
❑ 227 Casey McGehee RC 1.50 .60
❑ 228 Humberto Sanchez RC 8.00 3.00
❑ 229 Javon Moran RC 1.50 .60
❑ 230 Brandon McCarthy RC 5.00 2.00
❑ 231 Danny Zell RC 1.50 .60
❑ 232 Kevin Barry RC 1.50 .60
❑ 233 Juan Tejeda RC 1.50 .60
❑ 234 Keith Ramsey RC 1.50 .60
❑ 235 Lorenzo Scott RC 1.50 .60
❑ 236 Jon Barratt RC 1.50 .60
❑ 237 Martin Prado RC 1.50 .60
❑ 238 Matt Albers RC 4.00 1.50
❑ 239 Brian Schweiger RC 1.50 .60
❑ 240 Raul Tablado RC 1.50 .60
❑ 241 Pat Misch RC 1.50 .60
❑ 242 Pat Osborn 1.50 .60
❑ 243 Ryan Feierabend RC 1.50 .60
❑ 244 Shaun Marcum 1.00 .40
❑ 245 Kevin Collins RC 1.50 .60
❑ 246 Stuart Pomeranz RC 1.50 .60
❑ 247 Tetsu Yofu RC 1.50 .60
❑ 248 Hernan Iribarren RC 2.00 .75
❑ 249 Mike Spidale RC 1.50 .60
❑ 250 Tony Arnerich RC 1.50 .60
❑ 251 Manny Parra RC 1.50 .60
❑ 252 Drew Anderson RC 1.50 .60
❑ 253 T.J. Beam RC 3.00 1.25
❑ 254 Claudio Arias RC 2.00 .75
❑ 255 Andy Sides RC 1.50 .60
❑ 256 Bear Bay RC 2.00 .75
❑ 257 Bill McCarthy RC 1.50 .60
❑ 258 Daniel Haigwood RC 3.00 1.25
❑ 259 Brian Sprout RC 2.00 .75
❑ 260 Bryan Triplett RC 1.50 .60
❑ 261 Steven Bondurant RC 1.50 .60
❑ 262 Darwinson Salazar RC 1.50 .60
❑ 263 David Shepard RC 1.50 .60
❑ 264 Johan Silva RC 1.50 .60
❑ 265 J.B. Thurmond RC 1.50 .60
❑ 266 Brandon Moorhead RC 1.50 .60
❑ 267 Kyle Nichols RC 2.00 .75
❑ 268 Jonathan Sanchez RC 5.00 2.00
❑ 269 Mike Esposito RC 1.50 .60
❑ 270 Erik Schindewolf RC 1.50 .60
❑ 271 Peeter Ramos RC 1.50 .60
❑ 272 Juan Senreiso RC 1.50 .60
❑ 273 Travis Chick RC 2.00 .75
❑ 274 Vinny Rottino RC 1.50 .60
❑ 275 Micah Furtado RC 1.50 .60
❑ 276 George Kottaras RC 3.00 1.25
❑ 277 Abel Gomez RC 2.00 .75
❑ 278 Buck Coats RC 1.50 .60
❑ 279 Kenny Durost RC 1.50 .60
❑ 280 Nick Touchstone RC 1.50 .60
❑ 281 Jerry Owens RC 2.00 .75
❑ 282 Stefan Bailie RC 1.50 .60
❑ 283 Jesse Gutierrez RC 1.50 .60
❑ 284 Chuck Tiffany RC 4.00 1.50
❑ 285 Brendan Ryan RC 1.50 .60
❑ 286 Julio Pimentel RC 2.00 .75
❑ 287 Shawn Bowman RC 2.00 .75
❑ 288 Alexander Smit RC 1.50 .60

❑ 289 Micah Schnurstein RC 1.50 .60
❑ 290 Jared Gothreaux RC 1.50 .60
❑ 291 Jair Jurrjens RC 3.00 1.25
❑ 292 Bobby Livingston RC 1.50 .60
❑ 293 Ryan Speier RC 1.50 .60
❑ 294 Zach Parker RC 1.50 .60
❑ 295 Christian Colonel RC 1.50 .60
❑ 296 Scott Mitchinson RC 1.50 .60
❑ 297 Neil Wilson RC 1.50 .60
❑ 298 Chuck James RC 6.00 2.50
❑ 299 Heath Totten RC 1.50 .60
❑ 300 Sean Tracey RC 1.50 .60
❑ 301 Tadahito Iguchi RC 5.00 2.00
❑ 302 Matt Brown RC 1.50 .60
❑ 303 Franklin Morales RC 3.00 1.25
❑ 304 Brandon Sing RC 2.00 .75
❑ 305 D.J. Houlton RC 1.50 .60
❑ 306 Jayce Tingler RC 1.50 .60
❑ 307 Mitchell Arnold RC 1.50 .60
❑ 308 Jim Burt RC 1.50 .60
❑ 309 Jason Motte RC 1.50 .60
❑ 310 David Gassner RC 1.50 .60
❑ 311 Andy Santana RC 1.50 .60
❑ 312 Kelvin Pichardo RC 1.50 .60
❑ 313 Carlos Carrasco RC 5.00 2.00
❑ 314 Willy Mota RC 1.50 .60
❑ 315 Frank Mata RC 1.50 .60
❑ 316 Carlos Gonzalez RC 12.00 5.00
❑ 317 Jesse Floyd 1.00 .40
❑ 318 Chris B.Young RC 8.00 3.00
❑ 319 Billy Sadler RC 1.50 .60
❑ 320 Ricky Barrett RC 1.50 .60
❑ 321 Ben Harrison 1.50 .60
❑ 322 Steve Nelson RC 1.50 .60
❑ 323 Daryl Thompson RC 1.50 .60
❑ 324 Davis Romero RC 1.50 .60
❑ 325 Jeremy Harts RC 1.50 .60
❑ 326 Nick Masset RC 1.50 .60
❑ 327 Thomas Pauly RC 1.50 .60
❑ 328 Mike Garber RC 1.50 .60
❑ 329 Kennard Bibbs RC 1.50 .60
❑ 330 Colter Bean RC 1.50 .60
❑ 331 Justin Verlander AU RC 100.00 50.00
❑ 332 Chip Cannon AU RC 30.00 12.50
❑ 333 Kevin Melillo AU RC 15.00 6.00
❑ 334 Jake Postlewait AU RC 10.00 4.00
❑ 335 Wes Swackhamer AU RC 10.00 4.00
❑ 336 Mike Rodriguez AU RC 10.00 4.00
❑ 337 Philip Humber AU RC 30.00 15.00
❑ 338 Jeff Niemann AU RC 30.00 12.50
❑ 339 Brian Miller AU RC 10.00 4.00
❑ 340 Chris Vines AU RC 10.00 4.00
❑ 341 Andy LaRoche AU RC 70.00 40.00
❑ 342 Mike Bourn AU RC 20.00 8.00
❑ 343 Eric Nielsen AU RC 10.00 4.00
❑ 344 Wladimir Balentien AU RC 20.00 8.00
❑ 345 Ismael Ramirez AU RC 10.00 4.00
❑ 346 Pedro Lopez AU RC 10.00 4.00
❑ 347 Shawn Bowman AU 15.00 6.00
❑ 348 Hayden Penn AU RC 25.00 10.00
❑ 349 Matthew Kemp AU RC 70.00 40.00
❑ 350 Brian Stavisky AU RC 10.00 4.00
❑ 351 C.J. Smith AU RC 10.00 4.00
❑ 352 Mike Morse AU RC 10.00 4.00
❑ 353 Billy Butler AU RC 80.00 50.00

2005 Bowman Chrome Draft

❑ COMP.SET w/o SP's (165) 100.00 50.00
❑ COMMON CARD (1-165) .40 .15
❑ COMMON RC 1.00 .40
❑ COMMON RC YR .40 .15
❑ 1-165 TWO PER BOWMAN DRAFT PACK
❑ 166-180 GROUP A ODDS 1:671 H, 1:643 R
❑ 166-180 GROUP B ODDS 1:69 H, 1:69 R
❑ 1-165 PLATE ODDS 1:826 HOBBY
❑ 166-180 AU PLATE ODDS 1:18,411 HOBBY
❑ PLATE PRINT RUN 1 SET PER COLOR
❑ BLACK-CYAN-MAGENTA-YELLOW ISSUED
❑ NO PLATE PRICING DUE TO SCARCITY
❑ 1 Rickie Weeks .60 .25
❑ 2 Kyle Davies .40 .15
❑ 3 Garrett Atkins .40 .15
❑ 4 Chien-Ming Wang 2.00 .75
❑ 5 Dallas McPherson .40 .15
❑ 6 Dan Johnson .60 .25
❑ 7 Andy Sisco .40 .15
❑ 8 Ryan Doumit .40 .15
❑ 9 J.P. Howell .40 .15
❑ 10 Tim Stauffer .40 .15
❑ 11 Willy Taveras .60 .25
❑ 12 Aaron Hill .40 .15
❑ 13 Victor Diaz .40 .15
❑ 14 Wilson Betemit .40 .15
❑ 15 Ervin Santana .60 .25
❑ 16 Mike Morse .60 .25
❑ 17 Yadier Molina .60 .25
❑ 18 Kelly Johnson .40 .15
❑ 19 Clint Barmes .60 .25
❑ 20 Robinson Cano 1.00 .40
❑ 21 Brad Thompson .40 .15
❑ 22 Jorge Cantu .60 .25
❑ 23 Brad Halsey .40 .15
❑ 24 Lance Niekro .60 .25
❑ 25 D.J. Houlton .40 .15
❑ 26 Ryan Church .40 .15
❑ 27 Hayden Penn 1.50 .60
❑ 28 Chris Young .40 .15
❑ 29 Chad Orvella RC 1.00 .40
❑ 30 Mark Teahen .40 .15
❑ 31 Mark McCormick FY RC 1.50 .60
❑ 32 Jay Bruce FY RC 12.00 5.00
❑ 33 Beau Jones FY RC 3.00 1.25
❑ 34 Tyler Greene FY RC 2.50 1.00
❑ 35 Zach Ward FY RC 1.00 .40
❑ 36 Josh Bell FY RC 4.00 1.50
❑ 37 Josh Wall FY RC 1.50 .60
❑ 38 Nick Webber FY RC 1.00 .40
❑ 39 Travis Buck FY RC 4.00 1.25
❑ 40 Kyle Winters FY RC 1.50 .60
❑ 41 Mitch Boggs FY RC 1.00 .40
❑ 42 Tommy Mendoza FY RC 2.50 1.00
❑ 43 Brad Corley FY RC 1.50 .60
❑ 44 Drew Butera FY RC 1.00 .40
❑ 45 Ryan Mount FY RC 2.50 1.00
❑ 46 Tyler Herron FY RC 1.50 .60
❑ 47 Nick Weglarz FY RC 3.00 1.25
❑ 48 Brandon Erbe FY RC 4.00 1.50
❑ 49 Cody Allen FY RC 1.00 .40
❑ 50 Eric Fowler FY RC 1.00 .40
❑ 51 James Boone FY RC 1.50 .60
❑ 52 Josh Flores FY RC 4.00 1.50
❑ 53 Brandon Monk FY RC 1.50 .60
❑ 54 Kieron Pope FY RC 2.50 1.00
❑ 55 Kyle Cofield FY RC 1.00 .40
❑ 56 Brent Lillibridge FY RC 1.00 .40
❑ 57 Daryl Jones FY 1.00 .40
❑ 58 Eli Iorg FY RC 1.50 .60
❑ 59 Brett Hayes FY RC 1.00 .40
❑ 60 Mike Durant FY RC 3.00 1.25
❑ 61 Michael Bowden FY RC 5.00 2.00
❑ 62 Paul Kelly FY RC 1.50 .60
❑ 63 Andrew McCutchen FY RC 10.00 4.00
❑ 64 Travis Wood FY RC 4.00 1.50
❑ 65 Cesar Ramos FY RC 1.50 .60
❑ 66 Chaz Roe FY RC 1.50 .60
❑ 67 Matt Torra FY RC 1.50 .60
❑ 68 Kevin Slowey FY RC 5.00 2.00
❑ 69 Trayvon Robinson FY RC 1.50 .60
❑ 70 Reid Engel FY RC 1.00 .40
❑ 71 Kris Harvey FY RC 2.50 1.00
❑ 72 Craig Italiano FY RC 2.50 1.00
❑ 73 Matt Maloney FY RC 3.00 1.25
❑ 74 Sean West FY RC 4.00 1.50
❑ 75 Henry Sanchez FY RC 3.00 1.25
❑ 76 Scott Blue FY RC 1.00 .40
❑ 77 Jordan Schafer FY RC 1.50 .60
❑ 78 Chris Robinson FY RC 1.50 .60
❑ 79 Chris Hobdy FY RC 1.00 .40
❑ 80 Brandon Durden FY RC 1.00 .40
❑ 81 Clay Buchholz FY RC 5.00 2.00
❑ 82 Josh Geer FY RC 1.00 .40
❑ 83 Sam LeCure FY RC 1.00 .40
❑ 84 Justin Thomas FY RC 1.00 .40
❑ 85 Brett Gardner FY RC 1.50 .60
❑ 86 Tommy Manzella FY RC 1.00 .40
❑ 87 Matt Green FY RC 1.00 .40
❑ 88 Yunel Escobar FY RC 3.00 1.25
❑ 89 Mike Costanzo FY RC 4.00 1.50
❑ 90 Nick Hundley FY RC 1.00 .40
❑ 91 Zach Simons FY RC 1.00 .40
❑ 92 Jacob Marceaux FY RC 1.00 .40
❑ 93 Jed Lowrie FY RC 2.50 1.00
❑ 94 Brandon Snyder FY RC 5.00 2.00
❑ 95 Matt Goyen FY RC 1.00 .40
❑ 96 Jon Egan FY RC 1.50 .60
❑ 97 Drew Thompson FY RC 1.50 .60
❑ 98 Bryan Anderson FY RC 4.00 1.50
❑ 99 Clayton Richard FY RC 1.00 .40
❑ 100 Jimmy Shull FY RC 1.50 .60
❑ 101 Mark Pawelek FY RC 6.00 2.50
❑ 102 P.J. Phillips FY RC 2.50 1.00
❑ 103 John Drennen FY RC 4.00 1.50
❑ 104 Nolan Reimold FY RC 5.00 2.00
❑ 105 Troy Tulowitzki FY RC 10.00 4.00
❑ 106 Kevin Whelan FY RC 1.25 .50
❑ 107 Wade Townsend FY RC 1.50 .60
❑ 108 Micah Owings FY RC 2.00 .75
❑ 109 Ryan Tucker FY RC 1.50 .60
❑ 110 Jeff Clement FY RC 10.00 4.00
❑ 111 Josh Sullivan FY RC 1.00 .40
❑ 112 Jeff Lyman FY RC 1.50 .60
❑ 113 Brian Bogusevic FY RC 1.00 .40
❑ 114 Trevor Bell FY RC 2.50 1.00
❑ 115 Brent Cox FY RC 1.50 .60
❑ 116 Michael Billek FY RC 1.00 .40
❑ 117 Garrett Olson FY RC 2.50 1.00
❑ 118 Steven Johnson FY RC 1.50 .60
❑ 119 Chase Headley FY RC 1.50 .60
❑ 120 Daniel Carte FY RC 2.50 1.00
❑ 121 Francisco Liriano PROS 2.50 1.00
❑ 122 Fausto Carmona PROS .40 .15
❑ 123 Zach Jackson PROS .40 .15
❑ 124 Adam Loewen PROS .40 .15
❑ 125 Chris Lambert PROS .40 .15
❑ 126 Scott Mathieson FY .60 .25
❑ 127 Paul Maholm PROS .60 .25
❑ 128 Fernando Nieve PROS .40 .15
❑ 129 Justin Verlander FY 6.00 2.50
❑ 130 Yusmeiro Petit PROS 1.00 .40
❑ 131 Joel Zumaya PROS 1.50 .60
❑ 132 Merkin Valdez PROS .40 .15
❑ 133 Ryan Garko FY RC 5.00 2.00
❑ 134 Edison Volquez FY RC 2.50 1.00
❑ 135 Russ Martin FY 1.50 .60
❑ 136 Conor Jackson PROS .60 .25
❑ 137 Miguel Montero FY RC 4.00 1.50
❑ 138 Josh Barfield PROS .60 .25
❑ 139 Delmon Young PROS 1.00 .40
❑ 140 Andy LaRoche FY 1.50 .60
❑ 141 William Bergolla PROS .40 .15
❑ 142 B.J. Upton PROS .60 .25
❑ 143 Hernan Iribarren FY .60 .25
❑ 144 Brandon Wood PROS 1.50 .60
❑ 145 Jose Bautista PROS .40 .15
❑ 146 Edwin Encarnacion PROS .60 .25
❑ 147 Javier Herrera FY RC 3.00 1.25
❑ 148 Jeremy Hermida PROS 1.50 .60
❑ 149 Frank Diaz PROS RC 1.00 .40
❑ 150 Chris B.Young FY 3.00 1.25
❑ 151 Shin-Soo Choo PROS .40 .15
❑ 152 Kevin Thompson PROS RC 1.00 .40
❑ 153 Hanley Ramirez PROS 1.00 .40
❑ 154 Lastings Milledge PROS .60 .25
❑ 155 Luis Montanez PROS .40 .15
❑ 156 Justin Huber PROS .40 .15
❑ 157 Zach Duke PROS .75 .30
❑ 158 Jeff Francoeur PROS 1.25 .50
❑ 159 Melky Cabrera FY 3.00 1.25

❑ 160 Bobby Jenks PROS .60 .25
❑ 161 Ian Snell PROS .40 .15
❑ 162 Fernando Cabrera PROS .40 .15
❑ 163 Troy Patton PROS 1.00 .40
❑ 164 Anthony Lerew PROS .60 .25
❑ 165 Nelson Cruz FY RC 5.00 2.00
❑ 166 Stephen Drew AU A RC 120.00 70.00
❑ 167 Jered Weaver AU A RC 100.00 60.00
❑ 168 Ryan Braun AU B RC 50.00 20.00
❑ 169 John Mayberry Jr. AU B RC 15.00 6.00
❑ 170 Aaron Thompson AU B RC 15.00 6.00
❑ 171 Cesar Carrillo AU B RC 25.00 10.00
❑ 172 Jacoby Ellsbury AU B RC 50.00 20.00
❑ 173 Matt Garza AU B RC 50.00 30.00
❑ 174 Cliff Pennington AU B RC 15.00 6.00
❑ 175 Colby Rasmus AU B RC 50.00 20.00
❑ 176 Chris Volstad AU B RC 20.00 8.00
❑ 177 Ricky Romero AU B RC 15.00 6.00
❑ 178 Ryan Zimmerman AU B RC 125.00 75.00
❑ 179 C.J. Henry AU B RC 25.00 10.00
❑ 180 Eddy Martinez AU B RC 15.00 6.00

2006 Bowman Chrome

❑ COMP.SET w/o AU's (220) 60.00 30.00
❑ COMMON CARD (1-200) .50 .20
❑ COMMON ROOKIE (201-220) .60 .25
❑ 219 AU ODDS 1:2734 HOBBY, 1:6617 RETAIL
❑ 221-224 AU ODDS 1:27 HOBBY, 1:65 RETAIL
❑ 1-220 PLATE ODDS 1:836 HOBBY
❑ 219 AU PLATE ODDS 1:292,536 HOBBY
❑ 221-224 AU PLATES ODDS 1:9,000 HOBBY
❑ PLATE PRINT RUN 1 SET PER COLOR
❑ BLACK-CYAN-MAGENTA-YELLOW ISSUED
❑ NO PLATE PRICING DUE TO SCARCITY
❑ 1 Nick Swisher .50 .20
❑ 2 Ted Lilly .50 .20
❑ 3 John Smoltz .75 .30
❑ 4 Lyle Overbay .50 .20
❑ 5 Alfonso Soriano .50 .20
❑ 6 Javier Vazquez .50 .20
❑ 7 Ronnie Belliard .50 .20
❑ 8 Jose Reyes .50 .20
❑ 9 Brian Roberts .50 .20
❑ 10 Curt Schilling .75 .30
❑ 11 Adam Dunn .50 .20
❑ 12 Zack Greinke .50 .20
❑ 13 Carlos Guillen .50 .20
❑ 14 Jon Garland .50 .20
❑ 15 Robinson Cano .75 .30
❑ 16 Chris Burke .50 .20
❑ 17 Barry Zito .50 .20
❑ 18 Russ Adams .50 .20
❑ 19 Chris Capuano .50 .20
❑ 20 Scott Rolen .75 .30
❑ 21 Kerry Wood .50 .20
❑ 22 Scott Kazmir .75 .30
❑ 23 Brandon Webb .50 .20
❑ 24 Jeff Kent .50 .20
❑ 25 Albert Pujols 2.50 1.00
❑ 26 C.C. Sabathia .50 .20
❑ 27 Adrian Beltre .50 .20
❑ 28 Brad Wilkerson .50 .20
❑ 29 Randy Wolf .50 .20
❑ 30 Jason Bay .50 .20
❑ 31 Austin Kearns .50 .20
❑ 32 Clint Barmes .50 .20
❑ 33 Mike Sweeney .50 .20
❑ 34 Kevin Youkilis .50 .20
❑ 35 Justin Morneau .50 .20
❑ 36 Scott Podsednik .50 .20
❑ 37 Jason Giambi .50 .20
❑ 38 Steve Finley .50 .20
❑ 39 Morgan Ensberg .50 .20
❑ 40 Eric Chavez .50 .20
❑ 41 Roy Halladay .50 .20
❑ 42 Horacio Ramirez .50 .20
❑ 43 Ben Sheets .50 .20
❑ 44 Chris Carpenter .50 .20
❑ 45 Andruw Jones .75 .30
❑ 46 Carlos Zambrano .50 .20
❑ 47 Jonny Gomes .50 .20
❑ 48 Shawn Green .50 .20
❑ 49 Moises Alou .50 .20
❑ 50 Ichiro Suzuki 2.00 .75
❑ 51 Juan Pierre .50 .20
❑ 52 Grady Sizemore .75 .30
❑ 53 Kazuo Matsui .50 .20
❑ 54 Jose Vidro .50 .20
❑ 55 Jake Peavy .50 .20
❑ 56 Dallas McPherson .50 .20
❑ 57 Ryan Howard 2.00 .75
❑ 58 Zach Duke .50 .20
❑ 59 Michael Young .50 .20
❑ 60 Todd Helton .75 .30
❑ 61 David DeJesus .50 .20
❑ 62 Ivan Rodriguez .75 .30
❑ 63 Johan Santana .75 .30
❑ 64 Danny Haren .50 .20
❑ 65 Derek Jeter 3.00 1.25
❑ 66 Greg Maddux 2.00 .75
❑ 67 Jorge Cantu .50 .20
❑ 68 J.J. Hardy .50 .20
❑ 69 Victor Martinez .50 .20
❑ 70 David Wright 2.00 .75
❑ 71 Ryan Church .50 .20
❑ 72 Khalil Greene .75 .30
❑ 73 Jimmy Rollins .50 .20
❑ 74 Hank Blalock .50 .20
❑ 75 Pedro Martinez .75 .30
❑ 76 Chris Shelton .50 .20
❑ 77 Felipe Lopez .50 .20
❑ 78 Jeff Francis .50 .20
❑ 79 Andy Sisco .50 .20
❑ 80 Hideki Matsui 1.25 .50
❑ 81 Ken Griffey Jr. 2.00 .75
❑ 82 Nomar Garciaparra 1.25 .50
❑ 83 Kevin Millwood .50 .20
❑ 84 Paul Konerko .50 .20
❑ 85 A.J. Burnett .50 .20
❑ 86 Mike Piazza 1.25 .50
❑ 87 Brian Giles .50 .20
❑ 88 Johnny Damon .75 .30
❑ 89 Jim Thome .75 .30
❑ 90 Roger Clemens 2.50 1.00
❑ 91 Aaron Rowand .50 .20
❑ 92 Rafael Furcal .50 .20
❑ 93 Gary Sheffield .50 .20
❑ 94 Mike Cameron .50 .20
❑ 95 Carlos Delgado .50 .20
❑ 96 Jorge Posada .75 .30
❑ 97 Denny Bautista .50 .20
❑ 98 Mike Maroth .50 .20
❑ 99 Brad Radke .50 .20
❑ 100 Alex Rodriguez 2.00 .75
❑ 101 Freddy Garcia .50 .20
❑ 102 Oliver Perez .50 .20
❑ 103 Jon Lieber .50 .20
❑ 104 Melvin Mora .50 .20
❑ 105 Travis Hafner .50 .20
❑ 106 Alex Rios .50 .20
❑ 107 Derek Lowe .50 .20
❑ 108 Luis Castillo .50 .20
❑ 109 Livan Hernandez .50 .20
❑ 110 Tadahito Iguchi .50 .20
❑ 111 Shawn Chacon .50 .20
❑ 112 Frank Thomas 1.25 .50
❑ 113 Josh Beckett .50 .20
❑ 114 Aubrey Huff .50 .20
❑ 115 Derrek Lee .50 .20
❑ 116 Chien-Ming Wang 2.00 .75
❑ 117 Joe Crede .50 .20
❑ 118 Torii Hunter .50 .20
❑ 119 J.D. Drew .50 .20
❑ 120 Troy Glaus .50 .20
❑ 121 Sean Casey .50 .20
❑ 122 Edgar Renteria .50 .20
❑ 123 Craig Wilson .50 .20
❑ 124 Adam Eaton .50 .20
❑ 125 Jeff Francoeur 1.25 .50
❑ 126 Bruce Chen .50 .20
❑ 127 Cliff Floyd .50 .20
❑ 128 Jeremy Reed .50 .20
❑ 129 Jake Westbrook .50 .20
❑ 130 Wily Mo Pena .50 .20
❑ 131 Toby Hall .50 .20
❑ 132 David Ortiz 1.25 .50
❑ 133 David Eckstein .50 .20
❑ 134 Brady Clark .50 .20
❑ 135 Marcus Giles .50 .20
❑ 136 Aaron Hill .50 .20
❑ 137 Mark Kotsay .50 .20
❑ 138 Carlos Lee .50 .20
❑ 139 Roy Oswalt .50 .20
❑ 140 Chone Figgins .50 .20
❑ 141 Mike Mussina .75 .30
❑ 142 Orlando Hernandez .50 .20
❑ 143 Magglio Ordonez .50 .20
❑ 144 Jim Edmonds .75 .30
❑ 145 Bobby Abreu .50 .20
❑ 146 Nick Johnson .50 .20
❑ 147 Carlos Beltran .50 .20
❑ 148 Jhonny Peralta .50 .20
❑ 149 Pedro Feliz .50 .20
❑ 150 Miguel Tejada .50 .20
❑ 151 Luis Gonzalez .50 .20
❑ 152 Carl Crawford .50 .20
❑ 153 Yadier Molina .50 .20
❑ 154 Rich Harden .50 .20
❑ 155 Tim Wakefield .50 .20
❑ 156 Rickie Weeks .50 .20
❑ 157 Johnny Estrada .50 .20
❑ 158 Gustavo Chacin .50 .20
❑ 159 Dan Johnson .50 .20
❑ 160 Willy Taveras .50 .20
❑ 161 Garret Anderson .50 .20
❑ 162 Randy Johnson 1.25 .50
❑ 163 Jermaine Dye .50 .20
❑ 164 Joe Mauer .75 .30
❑ 165 Ervin Santana .50 .20
❑ 166 Jeremy Bonderman .50 .20
❑ 167 Garrett Atkins .50 .20
❑ 168 Manny Ramirez .75 .30
❑ 169 Brad Eldred .50 .20
❑ 170 Chase Utley 1.25 .50
❑ 171 Mark Loretta .50 .20
❑ 172 John Patterson .50 .20
❑ 173 Tom Glavine .75 .30
❑ 174 Dontrelle Willis .50 .20
❑ 175 Mark Teixeira .75 .30
❑ 176 Felix Hernandez .75 .30
❑ 177 Cliff Lee .50 .20
❑ 178 Jason Schmidt .50 .20
❑ 179 Chad Tracy .50 .20
❑ 180 Rocco Baldelli .50 .20
❑ 181 Aramis Ramirez .50 .20
❑ 182 Andy Pettitte .50 .20
❑ 183 Mark Mulder .50 .20
❑ 184 Geoff Jenkins .50 .20
❑ 185 Chipper Jones 1.25 .50
❑ 186 Vernon Wells .50 .20
❑ 187 Bobby Crosby .50 .20
❑ 188 Lance Berkman .50 .20
❑ 189 Vladimir Guerrero 1.25 .50
❑ 190 Coco Crisp .50 .20
❑ 191 Brad Penny .50 .20
❑ 192 Jose Guillen .50 .20
❑ 193 Brett Myers .50 .20
❑ 194 Miguel Cabrera .75 .30
❑ 195 Bartolo Colon .50 .20
❑ 196 Craig Biggio .75 .30
❑ 197 Tim Hudson .50 .20
❑ 198 Mark Prior .75 .30
❑ 199 Mark Buehrle .50 .20
❑ 200 Barry Bonds 2.50 1.00
❑ 201 Anderson Hernandez (RC) .60 .25
❑ 202 Jose Capellan (RC) .60 .25
❑ 203 Jeremy Accardo RC .60 .25
❑ 204 Hanley Ramirez (RC) 1.50 .60
❑ 205 Matt Capps (RC) .60 .25
❑ 206 Jonathan Papelbon (RC) 3.00 1.25

❑ 207 Chuck James (RC) 1.00 .40
❑ 208 Matt Cain (RC) 1.00 .40
❑ 209 Cole Hamels (RC) 1.50 .60
❑ 210 Jason Botts (RC) .60 .25
❑ 211 Lastings Milledge (RC) 1.00 .40
❑ 212 Conor Jackson (RC) 1.00 .40
❑ 213 Yusmeiro Petit (RC) .60 .25
❑ 214 Alay Soler RC .60 .25
❑ 215 Willy Aybar (RC) .60 .25
❑ 216 Adam Loewen (RC) .60 .25
❑ 217 Justin Verlander (RC) 2.50 1.00
❑ 218 Francisco Liriano (RC) 3.00 1.25
❑ 219 Kenji Johjima RC 3.00 1.25
❑ 219a Kenji Johjima AU 150.00 70.00
❑ 220 Craig Hansen RC 2.50 1.00
❑ 221 Prince Fielder AU (RC) 40.00 15.00
❑ 222 Josh Barfield AU (RC) 15.00 6.00
❑ 223 Fausto Carmona AU (RC) 15.00 6.00
❑ 224 James Loney AU (RC) 25.00 10.00

2001 Bowman Heritage

❑ COMPLETE SET (440) 200.00 125.00
❑ COMP.SET w/o SP's (330) 50.00 20.00
❑ COMMON CARD (1-330) .40 .15
❑ COMMON RC (1-330) .40 .15
❑ COMMON CARD (331-440) 2.00 .75
❑ 1 Chipper Jones 1.00 .40
❑ 2 Pete Harnisch .40 .15
❑ 3 Brian Giles .40 .15
❑ 4 J.T. Snow .40 .15
❑ 5 Bartolo Colon .40 .15
❑ 6 Jorge Posada .60 .25
❑ 7 Shawn Green .40 .15
❑ 8 Derek Jeter 2.50 1.00
❑ 9 Benito Santiago .40 .15
❑ 10 Ramon Hernandez .40 .15
❑ 11 Bernie Williams .60 .25
❑ 12 Greg Maddux 1.50 .60
❑ 13 Barry Bonds 2.50 1.00
❑ 14 Roger Clemens 2.00 .75
❑ 15 Miguel Tejada .40 .15
❑ 16 Pedro Feliz .40 .15
❑ 17 Jim Edmonds .40 .15
❑ 18 Tom Glavine .60 .25
❑ 19 David Justice .40 .15
❑ 20 Rich Aurilia .40 .15
❑ 21 Jason Giambi .40 .15
❑ 22 Orlando Hernandez .40 .15
❑ 23 Shawn Estes .40 .15
❑ 24 Nelson Figueroa .40 .15
❑ 25 Terrence Long .40 .15
❑ 26 Mike Mussina .60 .25
❑ 27 Eric Davis .40 .15
❑ 28 Jimmy Rollins .40 .15
❑ 29 Andy Pettitte .60 .25
❑ 30 Shawon Dunston .40 .15
❑ 31 Tim Hudson .40 .15
❑ 32 Jeff Kent .40 .15
❑ 33 Scott Brosius .40 .15
❑ 34 Livan Hernandez .40 .15
❑ 35 Alfonso Soriano .60 .25
❑ 36 Mark McGwire 2.50 1.00
❑ 37 Russ Ortiz .40 .15
❑ 38 Fernando Vina .40 .15
❑ 39 Ken Griffey Jr. 1.50 .60
❑ 40 Edgar Renteria .40 .15
❑ 41 Kevin Brown .40 .15
❑ 42 Robb Nen .40 .15
❑ 43 Paul LoDuca .40 .15
❑ 44 Bobby Abreu .40 .15
❑ 45 Adam Dunn .60 .25
❑ 46 Osvaldo Fernandez .40 .15
❑ 47 Marvin Benard .40 .15
❑ 48 Mark Gardner .40 .15
❑ 49 Alex Rodriguez 1.50 .60
❑ 50 Preston Wilson .40 .15
❑ 51 Roberto Alomar .60 .25
❑ 52 Ben Davis .40 .15
❑ 53 Derek Bell .40 .15
❑ 54 Ken Caminiti .40 .15
❑ 55 Barry Zito .60 .25
❑ 56 Scott Rolen .60 .25
❑ 57 Geoff Jenkins .40 .15
❑ 58 Mike Cameron .40 .15
❑ 59 Ben Grieve .40 .15
❑ 60 Chuck Knoblauch .40 .15
❑ 61 Matt Lawton .40 .15
❑ 62 Chan Ho Park .40 .15
❑ 63 Lance Berkman .40 .15
❑ 64 Carlos Beltran .40 .15
❑ 65 Dean Palmer .40 .15
❑ 66 Alex Gonzalez .40 .15
❑ 67 Larry Walker .40 .15
❑ 68 Magglio Ordonez .40 .15
❑ 69 Ellis Burks .40 .15
❑ 70 Mark Mulder .40 .15
❑ 71 Randy Johnson 1.00 .40
❑ 72 John Smoltz .60 .25
❑ 73 Jerry Hairston Jr. .40 .15
❑ 74 Pedro Martinez .60 .25
❑ 75 Fred McGriff .60 .25
❑ 76 Sean Casey .40 .15
❑ 77 C.C. Sabathia .40 .15
❑ 78 Todd Helton .60 .25
❑ 79 Brad Penny .40 .15
❑ 80 Mike Sweeney .40 .15
❑ 81 Billy Wagner .40 .15
❑ 82 Mark Buehrle .60 .25
❑ 83 Cristian Guzman .40 .15
❑ 84 Jose Vidro .40 .15
❑ 85 Pat Burrell .40 .15
❑ 86 Jermaine Dye .40 .15
❑ 87 Brandon Inge .40 .15
❑ 88 David Wells .40 .15
❑ 89 Mike Piazza 1.50 .60
❑ 90 Jose Cabrera .40 .15
❑ 91 Cliff Floyd .40 .15
❑ 92 Matt Morris .40 .15
❑ 93 Raul Mondesi .40 .15
❑ 94 Joe Kennedy RC .60 .25
❑ 95 Jack Wilson RC .60 .25
❑ 96 Andruw Jones .60 .25
❑ 97 Mariano Rivera 1.00 .40
❑ 98 Mike Hampton .40 .15
❑ 99 Roger Cedeno .40 .15
❑ 100 Jose Cruz .40 .15
❑ 101 Mike Lowell .40 .15
❑ 102 Pedro Astacio .40 .15
❑ 103 Joe Mays .40 .15
❑ 104 John Franco .40 .15
❑ 105 Tim Redding .40 .15
❑ 106 Sandy Alomar Jr. .40 .15
❑ 107 Bret Boone .40 .15
❑ 108 Josh Towers RC .60 .25
❑ 109 Matt Stairs .40 .15
❑ 110 Chris Truby .40 .15
❑ 111 Jeff Suppan .40 .15
❑ 112 J.C. Romero .40 .15
❑ 113 Felipe Lopez .40 .15
❑ 114 Ben Sheets .60 .25
❑ 115 Frank Thomas 1.00 .40
❑ 116 A.J. Burnett .40 .15
❑ 117 Tony Clark .40 .15
❑ 118 Mac Suzuki .40 .15
❑ 119 Brad Radke .40 .15
❑ 120 Jeff Shaw .40 .15
❑ 121 Nick Neugebauer .40 .15
❑ 122 Kenny Lofton .40 .15
❑ 123 Jacque Jones .40 .15
❑ 124 Brent Mayne .40 .15
❑ 125 Carlos Hernandez .40 .15
❑ 126 Shane Spencer .40 .15
❑ 127 John Lackey .40 .15
❑ 128 Sterling Hitchcock .40 .15
❑ 129 Darren Dreifort .40 .15
❑ 130 Rusty Greer .40 .15
❑ 131 Michael Cuddyer .40 .15
❑ 132 Tyler Houston .40 .15
❑ 133 Chin-Feng Chen .40 .15
❑ 134 Ken Harvey .40 .15
❑ 135 Marquis Grissom .40 .15
❑ 136 Russell Branyan .40 .15
❑ 137 Eric Karros .40 .15
❑ 138 Josh Beckett .60 .25
❑ 139 Todd Zeile .40 .15
❑ 140 Corey Koskie .40 .15
❑ 141 Steve Sparks .40 .15
❑ 142 Bobby Seay .40 .15
❑ 143 Tim Raines Jr. .40 .15
❑ 144 Julio Zuleta .40 .15
❑ 145 Jose Lima .40 .15
❑ 146 Dante Bichette .40 .15
❑ 147 Randy Keisler .40 .15
❑ 148 Brent Butler .40 .15
❑ 149 Antonio Alfonseca .40 .15
❑ 150 Bryan Rekar .40 .15
❑ 151 Jeffrey Hammonds .40 .15
❑ 152 Larry Bigbie .40 .15
❑ 153 Blake Stein .40 .15
❑ 154 Robin Ventura .40 .15
❑ 155 Rondell White .40 .15
❑ 156 Juan Silvestre .40 .15
❑ 157 Marcus Thames .40 .15
❑ 158 Sidney Ponson .40 .15
❑ 159 Juan A. Pena RC .40 .15
❑ 160 C.J. Nitkowski .40 .15
❑ 161 Adam Everett .40 .15
❑ 162 Eric Munson .40 .15
❑ 163 Jason Isringhausen .40 .15
❑ 164 Brad Fullmer .40 .15
❑ 165 Miguel Olivo .40 .15
❑ 166 Fernando Tatis .40 .15
❑ 167 Freddy Garcia .40 .15
❑ 168 Tom Goodwin .40 .15
❑ 169 Armando Benitez .40 .15
❑ 170 Paul Konerko .40 .15
❑ 171 Jeff Cirillo .40 .15
❑ 172 Shane Reynolds .40 .15
❑ 173 Kevin Tapani .40 .15
❑ 174 Joe Crede 1.00 .40
❑ 175 Omar Infante RC .40 .15
❑ 176 Jake Peavy RC 4.00 1.50
❑ 177 Corey Patterson .40 .15
❑ 178 Mike Penney RC .40 .15
❑ 179 Jeromy Burnitz .40 .15
❑ 180 David Segui .40 .15
❑ 181 Marcus Giles .40 .15
❑ 182 Paul O'Neill .60 .25
❑ 183 John Olerud .40 .15
❑ 184 Andy Benes .40 .15
❑ 185 Brad Cresse .40 .15
❑ 186 Ricky Ledee .40 .15
❑ 187 Allen Levrault UER .40 .15
❑ 188 Royce Clayton .40 .15
❑ 189 Kelly Johnson RC 1.50 .60
❑ 190 Quilvio Veras .40 .15
❑ 191 Mike Williams .40 .15
❑ 192 Jason Lane RC .60 .25
❑ 193 Rick Helling .40 .15
❑ 194 Tim Wakefield .40 .15
❑ 195 James Baldwin .40 .15
❑ 196 Cody Ransom RC .40 .15
❑ 197 Bobby Kielty .40 .15
❑ 198 Bobby Jones .40 .15
❑ 199 Steve Cox .40 .15
❑ 200 Jamal Strong RC .40 .15
❑ 201 Steve Lomasney .40 .15
❑ 202 Brian Cardwell RC .40 .15
❑ 203 Mike Matheny .40 .15
❑ 204 Jeff Randazzo RC .40 .15
❑ 205 Aubrey Huff .40 .15
❑ 206 Chuck Finley .40 .15
❑ 207 Denny Bautista RC .60 .25
❑ 208 Terry Mulholland .40 .15
❑ 209 Rey Ordonez .40 .15
❑ 210 Keith Surkont RC .40 .15
❑ 211 Orlando Cabrera .40 .15
❑ 212 Juan Encarnacion .40 .15
❑ 213 Dustin Hermanson .40 .15
❑ 214 Luis Rivas .40 .15

❑ 215	Mark Quinn	.40	.15
❑ 216	Randy Velarde	.40	.15
❑ 217	Billy Koch	.40	.15
❑ 218	Ryan Rupe	.40	.15
❑ 219	Keith Ginter	.40	.15
❑ 220	Woody Williams	.40	.15
❑ 221	Ryan Franklin	.40	.15
❑ 222	Aaron Myette	.40	.15
❑ 223	Joe Borchard RC	.40	.15
❑ 224	Nate Cornejo	.40	.15
❑ 225	Julian Tavarez	.40	.15
❑ 226	Kevin Millwood	.40	.15
❑ 227	Travis Hafner RC	5.00	2.00
❑ 228	Charles Nagy	.40	.15
❑ 229	Mike Lieberthal	.40	.15
❑ 230	Jeff Nelson	.40	.15
❑ 231	Ryan Dempster	.40	.15
❑ 232	Andres Galarraga	.40	.15
❑ 233	Chad Durbin	.40	.15
❑ 234	Timo Perez	.40	.15
❑ 235	Troy O'Leary	.40	.15
❑ 236	Kevin Young	.40	.15
❑ 237	Gabe Kapler	.40	.15
❑ 238	Juan Cruz RC	.40	.15
❑ 239	Masato Yoshii	.40	.15
❑ 240	Aramis Ramirez	.40	.15
❑ 241	Matt Cooper RC	.40	.15
❑ 242	Randy Flores RC	.40	.15
❑ 243	Rafael Furcal	.40	.15
❑ 244	David Eckstein	.40	.15
❑ 245	Matt Clement	.40	.15
❑ 246	Craig Biggio	.60	.25
❑ 247	Rick Reed	.40	.15
❑ 248	Jose Macias	.40	.15
❑ 249	Alex Escobar	.40	.15
❑ 250	Roberto Hernandez	.40	.15
❑ 251	Andy Ashby	.40	.15
❑ 252	Tony Armas Jr.	.40	.15
❑ 253	Jamie Moyer	.40	.15
❑ 254	Jason Tyner	.40	.15
❑ 255	Charles Kegley RC	.40	.15
❑ 256	Jeff Conine	.40	.15
❑ 257	Francisco Cordova	.40	.15
❑ 258	Ted Lilly	.40	.15
❑ 259	Joe Randa	.40	.15
❑ 260	Jeff D'Amico	.40	.15
❑ 261	Albie Lopez	.40	.15
❑ 262	Kevin Appier	.40	.15
❑ 263	Richard Hidalgo	.40	.15
❑ 264	Omar Daal	.40	.15
❑ 265	Ricky Gutierrez	.40	.15
❑ 266	John Rocker	.40	.15
❑ 267	Ray Lankford	.40	.15
❑ 268	Beau Hale RC	.40	.15
❑ 269	Tony Blanco RC	.40	.15
❑ 270	Derrek Lee UER	.60	.25
❑ 271	Jamey Wright	.40	.15
❑ 272	Alex Gordon	.40	.15
❑ 273	Jeff Weaver	.40	.15
❑ 274	Jaret Wright	.40	.15
❑ 275	Jose Hernandez	.40	.15
❑ 276	Bruce Chen	.40	.15
❑ 277	Todd Hollandsworth	.40	.15
❑ 278	Wade Miller	.40	.15
❑ 279	Luke Prokopec	.40	.15
❑ 280	Rafael Soriano RC	.40	.15
❑ 281	Damion Easley	.40	.15
❑ 282	Darren Oliver	.40	.15
❑ 283	Brandon Duckworth RC	.40	.15
❑ 284	Aaron Herr	.40	.15
❑ 285	Ray Durham	.40	.15
❑ 286	Wilmy Caceras RC	.40	.15
❑ 287	Ugueth Urbina	.40	.15
❑ 288	Scott Seabol	.40	.15
❑ 289	Lance Niekro RC	.60	.25
❑ 290	Trot Nixon	.40	.15
❑ 291	Adam Kennedy	.40	.15
❑ 292	Brian Schmitt RC	.40	.15
❑ 293	Grant Roberts	.40	.15
❑ 294	Benny Agbayani	.40	.15
❑ 295	Travis Lee	.40	.15
❑ 296	Erick Almonte RC	.40	.15
❑ 297	Jim Thome	.60	.25
❑ 298	Eric Young	.40	.15
❑ 299	Dan Denham RC	.40	.15
❑ 300	Boof Bonser RC	.40	.15
❑ 301	Denny Neagle	.40	.15
❑ 302	Kenny Rogers	.40	.15
❑ 303	J.D. Closser	.40	.15
❑ 304	Chase Utley RC	12.00	5.00
❑ 305	Rey Sanchez	.40	.15
❑ 306	Sean McGowan	.40	.15
❑ 307	Justin Pope RC	.40	.15
❑ 308	Torii Hunter	.40	.15
❑ 309	B.J. Surhoff	.40	.15
❑ 310	Aaron Heilman RC	.50	.20
❑ 311	Gabe Gross RC	.60	.25
❑ 312	Lee Stevens	.40	.15
❑ 313	Todd Hundley	.40	.15
❑ 314	Macay McBride RC	1.00	.40
❑ 315	Edgar Martinez	.60	.25
❑ 316	Omar Vizquel	.60	.25
❑ 317	Reggie Sanders	.40	.15
❑ 318	John-Ford Griffin RC	.40	.15
❑ 319	T.Salmon UER Glaus Photo	.40	.15
❑ 320	Pokey Reese	.40	.15
❑ 321	Jay Payton	.40	.15
❑ 322	Doug Glanville	.40	.15
❑ 323	Greg Vaughn	.40	.15
❑ 324	Ruben Sierra	.40	.15
❑ 325	Kip Wells	.40	.15
❑ 326	Carl Everett	.40	.15
❑ 327	Garret Anderson	.40	.15
❑ 328	Jay Bell	.40	.15
❑ 329	Barry Larkin	.60	.25
❑ 330	Jeff Mathis RC	.60	.25
❑ 331	Adrian Gonzalez SP	2.00	.75
❑ 332	Juan Rivera SP	2.00	.75
❑ 333	Tony Alvarez SP	2.00	.75
❑ 334	Xavier Nady SP	2.00	.75
❑ 335	Josh Hamilton SP	2.00	.75
❑ 336	Will Smith SP RC	2.00	.75
❑ 337	Israel Alcantara SP	2.00	.75
❑ 338	Chris George SP	2.00	.75
❑ 339	Sean Burroughs SP	2.00	.75
❑ 340	Jack Cust SP	2.00	.75
❑ 341	Henry Mateo SP RC	2.00	.75
❑ 342	Carlos Pena SP	2.00	.75
❑ 343	J.R. House SP	2.00	.75
❑ 344	Carlos Silva SP	2.00	.75
❑ 345	Mike Rivera SP RC	2.00	.75
❑ 346	Adam Johnson SP	2.00	.75
❑ 347	Scott Heard SP	2.00	.75
❑ 348	Alex Cintron SP	2.00	.75
❑ 349	Miguel Cabrera SP	8.00	3.00
❑ 350	Nick Johnson SP	2.00	.75
❑ 351	Albert Pujols SP RC	80.00	40.00
❑ 352	Ichiro Suzuki SP RC	40.00	15.00
❑ 353	Carlos Delgado SP	2.00	.75
❑ 354	Troy Glaus SP	2.00	.75
❑ 355	Sammy Sosa SP	3.00	1.25
❑ 356	Ivan Rodriguez SP	3.00	1.25
❑ 357	Vladimir Guerrero SP	3.00	1.25
❑ 358	Manny Ramirez Sox SP	3.00	1.25
❑ 359	Luis Gonzalez SP	2.00	.75
❑ 360	Roy Oswalt SP	3.00	1.25
❑ 361	Moises Alou SP	2.00	.75
❑ 362	Juan Gonzalez SP	2.00	.75
❑ 363	Tony Gwynn SP	4.00	1.50
❑ 364	Hideo Nomo SP	3.00	1.25
❑ 365	Tsuyoshi Shinjo SP RC	3.00	1.25
❑ 366	Kazuhiro Sasaki SP	2.00	.75
❑ 367	Cal Ripken SP	10.00	4.00
❑ 368	Rafael Palmeiro SP	3.00	1.25
❑ 369	J.D. Drew SP	2.00	.75
❑ 370	Doug Mientkiewicz SP	2.00	.75
❑ 371	Jeff Bagwell SP	3.00	1.25
❑ 372	Darin Erstad SP	2.00	.75
❑ 373	Tom Gordon SP	2.00	.75
❑ 374	Ben Petrick SP	2.00	.75
❑ 375	Eric Milton SP	2.00	.75
❑ 376	Nomar Garciaparra SP	5.00	2.00
❑ 377	Julio Lugo SP	2.00	.75
❑ 378	Tino Martinez SP	3.00	1.25
❑ 379	Javier Vazquez SP	2.00	.75
❑ 380	Jeremy Giambi SP	2.00	.75
❑ 381	Marty Cordova SP	2.00	.75
❑ 382	Adrian Beltre SP	2.00	.75
❑ 383	John Burkett SP	2.00	.75
❑ 384	Aaron Boone SP	2.00	.75
❑ 385	Eric Chavez SP	2.00	.75
❑ 386	Curt Schilling SP	2.00	.75
❑ 387	Cory Lidle UER SP	2.00	.75
❑ 388	Jason Schmidt SP	2.00	.75
❑ 389	Johnny Damon SP	3.00	1.25
❑ 390	Steve Finley SP	2.00	.75
❑ 391	Edgardo Alfonzo SP	2.00	.75
❑ 392	Jose Valentin SP	2.00	.75
❑ 393	Jose Canseco SP	3.00	1.25
❑ 394	Ryan Klesko SP	2.00	.75
❑ 395	David Cone SP	2.00	.75
❑ 396	Jason Kendall UER SP	2.00	.75
❑ 397	Placido Polanco SP	2.00	.75
❑ 398	Glendon Rusch SP	2.00	.75
❑ 399	Aaron Sele SP	2.00	.75
❑ 400	D'Angelo Jimenez SP	2.00	.75
❑ 401	Mark Grace SP	3.00	1.25
❑ 402	Al Leiter SP	2.00	.75
❑ 403	Brian Jordan SP	2.00	.75
❑ 404	Phil Nevin SP	2.00	.75
❑ 405	Brent Abernathy SP	2.00	.75
❑ 406	Kerry Wood SP	2.00	.75
❑ 407	Alex Gonzalez SP	2.00	.75
❑ 408	Robert Fick SP	2.00	.75
❑ 409	Dmitri Young UER SP	2.00	.75
❑ 410	Wes Helms SP	2.00	.75
❑ 411	Trevor Hoffman SP	2.00	.75
❑ 412	Rickey Henderson SP	3.00	1.25
❑ 413	Bobby Higginson SP	2.00	.75
❑ 414	Gary Sheffield SP	2.00	.75
❑ 415	Darryl Kile SP	2.00	.75
❑ 416	Richie Sexson SP	2.00	.75
❑ 417	Frank Menechino SP RC	2.00	.75
❑ 418	Javy Lopez SP	2.00	.75
❑ 419	Carlos Lee SP	2.00	.75
❑ 420	Jon Lieber SP	2.00	.75
❑ 421	Hank Blalock SP RC	6.00	2.50
❑ 422	Marlon Byrd SP RC	.40	.15
❑ 423	Jason Kinchen SP RC	2.00	.75
❑ 424	Morgan Ensberg SP RC	5.00	2.00
❑ 425	Greg Nash SP RC	2.00	.75
❑ 426	Dennis Tankersley SP RC	2.00	.75
❑ 427	Nate Murphy SP RC	2.00	.75
❑ 428	Chris Smith SP RC	2.00	.75
❑ 429	Jake Gautreau SP RC	2.00	.75
❑ 430	John VanBenschoten SP RC	2.00	.75
❑ 431	Travis Thompson SP RC	2.00	.75
❑ 432	Orlando Hudson SP RC	3.00	1.25
❑ 433	Jerome Williams SP RC	3.00	1.25
❑ 434	Kevin Reese SP RC	2.00	.75
❑ 435	Ed Rogers SP RC	2.00	.75
❑ 436	Ryan Jamison SP RC	2.00	.75
❑ 437	Adam Pettyjohn SP RC	2.00	.75
❑ 438	Hee Seop Choi SP RC	3.00	1.25
❑ 439	Justin Morneau SP RC	12.00	5.00
❑ 440	Mitch Jones SP RC	2.00	.75

2002 Bowman Heritage

❑	COMP.SET w/o SP's (324)	50.00	25.00
❑	COMMON CARD (1-439)	.40	.15
❑	COMMON SP	2.00	.75
❑ 1	Brent Abernathy	.40	.15
❑ 2	Jermaine Dye	.40	.15
❑ 3	James Shanks RC	.40	.15
❑ 4	Chris Flinn RC	.40	.15
❑ 5	Mike Peeples SP RC	2.00	.75
❑ 6	Gary Sheffield	.40	.15
❑ 7	Livan Hernandez SP	2.00	.75
❑ 8	Jeff Austin RC	.40	.15
❑ 9	Jeremy Giambi	.40	.15

❑	10	Adam Roller RC	.40	.15
❑	11	Sandy Alomar Jr. SP	2.00	.75
❑	12	Matt Williams SP	2.00	.75
❑	13	Hee Seop Choi	.40	.15
❑	14	Jose Offerman	.40	.15
❑	15	Robin Ventura	.40	.15
❑	16	Craig Biggio	.60	.25
❑	17	David Wells	.40	.15
❑	18	Rob Henkel RC	.40	.15
❑	19	Edgar Martinez	.60	.25
❑	20	Matt Morris SP	2.00	.75
❑	21	Jose Valentin	.40	.15
❑	22	Barry Bonds	2.50	1.00
❑	23	Justin Schuda RC	.40	.15
❑	24	Josh Phelps	.40	.15
❑	25	John Rodriguez RC	.50	.20
❑	26	Angel Pagan RC	1.00	.40
❑	27	Aramis Ramirez	.40	.15
❑	28	Jack Wilson	.40	.15
❑	29	Roger Clemens	2.00	.75
❑	30	Kazuhisa Ishii RC	.50	.20
❑	31	Carlos Beltran	.40	.15
❑	32	Drew Henson SP	2.00	.75
❑	33	Kevin Young SP	2.00	.75
❑	34	Juan Cruz SP	2.00	.75
❑	35	Curtis Legendre RC	.40	.15
❑	36	Jose Morban RC	.40	.15
❑	37	Ricardo Cordova SP RC	2.00	.75
❑	38	Adam Everett	.40	.15
❑	39	Mark Prior	.60	.25
❑	40	Jose Bautista RC	1.00	.40
❑	41	Travis Foley RC	.40	.15
❑	42	Kerry Wood	.40	.15
❑	43	B.J. Surhoff	.40	.15
❑	44	Moises Alou	.40	.15
❑	45	Joey Hammond	.40	.15
❑	46	Eric Bruntlett RC	.40	.15
❑	47	Carlos Guillen	.40	.15
❑	48	Joe Crede	.40	.15
❑	49	Dan Phillips RC	.40	.15
❑	50	Jason LaRue	.40	.15
❑	51	Javy Lopez	.40	.15
❑	52	Larry Bigbie SP	2.00	.75
❑	53	Chris Baker RC	.40	.15
❑	54	Marty Cordova	.40	.15
❑	55	C.C. Sabathia	.40	.15
❑	56	Mike Piazza	1.50	.60
❑	57	Brian Giles	.40	.15
❑	58	Mike Bordick SP	2.00	.75
❑	59	Tyler Houston SP	2.00	.75
❑	60	Gabe Kapler	.40	.15
❑	61	Ben Broussard	.40	.15
❑	62	Steve Finley SP	2.00	.75
❑	63	Koyie Hill	.40	.15
❑	64	Jeff D'Amico	.40	.15
❑	65	Edwin Almonte RC	.40	.15
❑	66	Pedro Martinez	.60	.25
❑	66B	Nomar Garciaparra 66	1.50	.60
❑	67	Travis Fryman SP	2.00	.75
❑	68	Brady Clark SP	2.00	.75
❑	69	Reed Johnson SP RC	3.00	1.25
❑	70	Mark Grace SP	3.00	1.25
❑	71	Tony Batista SP	2.00	.75
❑	72	Roy Oswalt	.40	.15
❑	73	Pat Burrell SP	2.00	.75
❑	74	Dennis Tankersley	.40	.15
❑	75	Ramon Ortiz	.40	.15
❑	76	Neal Frendling SP RC	2.00	.75
❑	77	Omar Vizquel SP	3.00	1.25
❑	78	Hideo Nomo	1.00	.40
❑	79	Orlando Hernandez SP	2.00	.75
❑	80	Andy Pettitte	.60	.25
❑	81	Cole Barthel RC	.40	.15
❑	82	Bret Boone	.40	.15
❑	83	Alfonso Soriano	.40	.15
❑	84	Brandon Duckworth	.40	.15
❑	85	Ben Grieve	.40	.15
❑	86	Mike Rosamond SP RC	2.00	.75
❑	87	Luke Prokopec	.40	.15
❑	88	Chone Figgins RC	1.50	.60
❑	89	Rick Ankiel SP	2.00	.75
❑	90	David Eckstein	.40	.15
❑	91	Corey Koskie	.40	.15
❑	92	David Justice	.40	.15
❑	93	Jimmy Alvarez RC	.40	.15
❑	94	Jason Schmidt	.40	.15
❑	95	Reggie Sanders	.40	.15
❑	96	Victor Alvarez RC	.40	.15
❑	97	Brett Roneberg RC	.40	.15
❑	98	D'Angelo Jimenez	.40	.15
❑	99	Hank Blalock	.60	.25
❑	100	Juan Rivera	.40	.15
❑	101	Mark Buehrle SP	2.00	.75
❑	102	Juan Uribe	.40	.15
❑	103	Royce Clayton SP	2.00	.75
❑	104	Brett Kay RC	.40	.15
❑	105	John Olerud	.40	.15
❑	106	Richie Sexson	.40	.15
❑	107	Chipper Jones	1.00	.40
❑	108	Adam Dunn	.40	.15
❑	109	Tim Salmon SP	3.00	1.25
❑	110	Eric Karros	.40	.15
❑	111	Jose Vidro	.40	.15
❑	112	Jerry Hairston Jr.	.40	.15
❑	113	Anastacio Martinez RC	.40	.15
❑	114	Robert Fick SP	2.00	.75
❑	115	Randy Johnson	1.00	.40
❑	116	Trot Nixon SP	2.00	.75
❑	117	Nick Bierbrodt SP	2.00	.75
❑	118	Jim Edmonds	.40	.15
❑	119	Rafael Palmeiro	.60	.25
❑	120	Jose Macias	.40	.15
❑	121	Josh Beckett	.40	.15
❑	122	Sean Douglass	.40	.15
❑	123	Jeff Kent	.40	.15
❑	124	Tim Redding	.40	.15
❑	125	Xavier Nady	.40	.15
❑	126	Carl Everett	.40	.15
❑	127	Joe Randa	.40	.15
❑	128	Luke Hudson SP	2.00	.75
❑	129	Eric Miller RC	.40	.15
❑	130	Melvin Mora	.40	.15
❑	131	Adrian Gonzalez	.40	.15
❑	132	Larry Walker SP	2.00	.75
❑	133	Nic Jackson SP RC	2.00	.75
❑	134	Mike Lowell SP	2.00	.75
❑	135	Jim Thome	.60	.25
❑	136	Eric Milton	.40	.15
❑	137	Rich Thompson SP RC	2.00	.75
❑	138	Placido Polanco SP	2.00	.75
❑	139	Juan Pierre	.40	.15
❑	140	David Segui	.40	.15
❑	141	Chuck Finley	.40	.15
❑	142	Felipe Lopez	.40	.15
❑	143	Toby Hall	.40	.15
❑	144	Fred Bastardo RC	.40	.15
❑	145	Troy Glaus	.40	.15
❑	146	Todd Helton	.60	.25
❑	147	Ruben Gotay SP RC	3.00	1.25
❑	148	Darin Erstad	.40	.15
❑	149	Ryan Gripp SP RC	2.00	.75
❑	150	Orlando Cabrera	.40	.15
❑	151	Jason Young RC	.40	.15
❑	152	Sterling Hitchcock SP	2.00	.75
❑	153	Miguel Tejada	.40	.15
❑	154	Al Leiter	.40	.15
❑	155	Taylor Buchholz RC	.50	.20
❑	156	Juan M. Gonzalez RC	.40	.15
❑	157	Damion Easley	.40	.15
❑	158	Jimmy Gobble RC	.40	.15
❑	159	Dennis Ulacia SP RC	2.00	.75
❑	160	Shane Reynolds SP	2.00	.75
❑	161	Javier Colina	.40	.15
❑	162	Frank Thomas	1.00	.40
❑	163	Chuck Knoblauch	.40	.15
❑	164	Sean Burroughs	.40	.15
❑	165	Greg Maddux	1.50	.60
❑	166	Jason Ellison RC	.75	.30
❑	167	Tony Womack	.40	.15
❑	168	Randall Shelley SP RC	2.00	.75
❑	169	Jason Marquis	.40	.15
❑	170	Brian Jordan	.40	.15
❑	171	Vicente Padilla	.40	.15
❑	172	Barry Zito	.40	.15
❑	173	Matt Allegra SP RC	2.00	.75
❑	174	Ralph Santana SP RC	2.00	.75
❑	175	Carlos Lee	.40	.15
❑	176	Richard Hidalgo SP	2.00	.75
❑	177	Kevin Deaton RC	.40	.15
❑	178	Juan Encarnacion	.40	.15
❑	179	Mark Quinn	.40	.15
❑	180	Rafael Furcal	.40	.15
❑	181	G.Anderson UER Figgins	.40	.15
❑	182	David Wright RC	25.00	10.00
❑	183	Jose Reyes	.60	.25
❑	184	Mario Ramos SP RC	2.00	.75
❑	185	J.D. Drew	.40	.15
❑	186	Juan Gonzalez	.40	.15
❑	187	Nick Neugebauer	.40	.15
❑	188	Alejandro Giron RC	.40	.15
❑	189	John Burkett	.40	.15
❑	190	Ben Sheets	.40	.15
❑	191	Vinny Castilla SP	2.00	.75
❑	192	Cory Lidle	.40	.15
❑	193	Fernando Vina	.40	.15
❑	194	Russell Branyan SP	2.00	.75
❑	195	Ben Davis	.40	.15
❑	196	Angel Berroa	.40	.15
❑	197	Alex Gonzalez	.40	.15
❑	198	Jared Sandberg	.40	.15
❑	199	Travis Lee SP	2.00	.75
❑	200	Luis DePaula SP RC	2.00	.75
❑	201	Ramon Hernandez SP	2.00	.75
❑	202	Brandon Inge	.40	.15
❑	203	Aubrey Huff	.40	.15
❑	204	Mike Rivera	.40	.15
❑	205	Brad Nelson RC	.40	.15
❑	206	Colt Griffin SP RC	2.00	.75
❑	207	Joel Pineiro	.40	.15
❑	208	Adam Pettyjohn	.40	.15
❑	209	Mark Redman	.40	.15
❑	210	Roberto Alomar SP	3.00	1.25
❑	211	Denny Neagle	.40	.15
❑	212	Adam Kennedy	.40	.15
❑	213	Jason Arnold SP RC	2.00	.75
❑	214	Jamie Moyer	.40	.15
❑	215	Aaron Boone	.40	.15
❑	216	Doug Glanville	.40	.15
❑	217	Nick Johnson SP	2.00	.75
❑	218	Mike Cameron SP	2.00	.75
❑	219	Tim Wakefield SP	2.00	.75
❑	220	Todd Stottlemyre SP	2.00	.75
❑	221	Mo Vaughn SP	2.00	.75
❑	222	Vladimir Guerrero	1.00	.40
❑	223	Bill Ortega	.40	.15
❑	224	Kevin Brown	.40	.15
❑	225	Peter Bergeron SP	2.00	.75
❑	226	Shannon Stewart SP	2.00	.75
❑	227	Eric Chavez	.40	.15
❑	228	Clint Weibl RC	.40	.15
❑	229	Todd Hollandsworth SP	2.00	.75
❑	230	Jeff Bagwell	.60	.25
❑	231	Chad Qualls RC	.50	.20
❑	232	Ben Howard RC	.40	.15
❑	233	Rondell White SP	2.00	.75
❑	234	Fred McGriff	.60	.25
❑	235	Steve Cox SP	2.00	.75
❑	236	Chris Tritle RC	.40	.15
❑	237	Eric Valent	.40	.15
❑	238	Joe Mauer RC	8.00	3.00
❑	239	Shawn Green	.40	.15
❑	240	Jimmy Rollins	.40	.15
❑	241	Edgar Renteria	.40	.15
❑	242	Edwin Yan RC	.40	.15
❑	243	Noochie Varner RC	.40	.15
❑	244	Kris Benson SP	2.00	.75
❑	245	Mike Hampton	.40	.15
❑	246	So Taguchi RC	.50	.20
❑	247	Sammy Sosa	1.00	.40
❑	248	Terrence Long	.40	.15
❑	249	Jason Bay RC	5.00	2.00
❑	250	Kevin Millar SP	2.00	.75
❑	251	Albert Pujols	2.00	.75
❑	252	Chris Latham RC	.40	.15
❑	253	Eric Byrnes	.40	.15
❑	254	Napoleon Calzado SP RC	2.00	.75
❑	255	Bobby Higginson	.40	.15
❑	256	Ben Molina	.40	.15
❑	257	Torii Hunter SP	2.00	.75
❑	258	Jason Giambi	.40	.15
❑	259	Bartolo Colon	.40	.15
❑	260	Benito Baez	.40	.15
❑	261	Ichiro Suzuki	2.00	.75
❑	262	Mike Sweeney	.40	.15
❑	263	Brian West RC	.40	.15
❑	264	Brad Penny	.40	.15
❑	265	Kevin Millwood SP	2.00	.75
❑	266	Orlando Hudson	.40	.15

❑ 267 Doug Mientkiewicz .40 .15
❑ 268 Luis Gonzalez SP 2.00 .75
❑ 269 Jay Caligiuri RC .40 .15
❑ 270 Nate Cornejo SP 2.00 .75
❑ 271 Lee Stevens .40 .15
❑ 272 Eric Hinske .40 .15
❑ 273 Antwon Rollins RC .40 .15
❑ 274 Bobby Jenks RC 1.50 .60
❑ 275 Joe Mays .40 .15
❑ 276 Josh Shaffer RC .40 .15
❑ 277 Jonny Gomes RC 2.50 1.00
❑ 278 Bernie Williams .60 .25
❑ 279 Ed Rogers .40 .15
❑ 280 Carlos Delgado .40 .15
❑ 281 Raul Mondesi SP 2.00 .75
❑ 282 Jose Ortiz .40 .15
❑ 283 Cesar Izturis .40 .15
❑ 284 Ryan Dempster SP 2.00 .75
❑ 285 Brian Daubach .40 .15
❑ 286 Hansel Izquierdo RC .40 .15
❑ 287 Mike Lieberthal SP 2.00 .75
❑ 288 Marcus Thames .40 .15
❑ 289 Nomar Garciaparra 1.50 .60
❑ 290 Brad Fullmer .40 .15
❑ 291 Tino Martinez .60 .25
❑ 292 James Barrett RC .40 .15
❑ 293 Jacque Jones .40 .15
❑ 294 Nick Alvarez SP RC 2.00 .75
❑ 295 Jason Grove SP RC 2.00 .75
❑ 296 Mike Wilson SP RC 2.00 .75
❑ 297 J.T. Snow .40 .15
❑ 298 Cliff Floyd .40 .15
❑ 299 Todd Hundley SP 2.00 .75
❑ 300 Tony Clark SP 2.00 .75
❑ 301 Demetrius Heath RC .40 .15
❑ 302 Morgan Ensberg .40 .15
❑ 303 Cristian Guzman .40 .15
❑ 304 Frank Catalanotto .40 .15
❑ 305 Jeff Weaver .40 .15
❑ 306 Tim Hudson .40 .15
❑ 307 Scott Wiggins SP RC 2.00 .75
❑ 308 Shea Hillenbrand SP 2.00 .75
❑ 309 Todd Walker SP 2.00 .75
❑ 310 Tsuyoshi Shinjo .40 .15
❑ 311 Adrian Beltre .40 .15
❑ 312 Craig Kuzmic RC .40 .15
❑ 313 Paul Konerko .40 .15
❑ 314 Scott Hairston RC .50 .20
❑ 315 Chan Ho Park .40 .15
❑ 316 Jorge Posada .60 .25
❑ 317 Chris Snelling RC .75 .30
❑ 318 Keith Foulke .40 .15
❑ 319 John Smoltz .60 .25
❑ 320 Ryan Church SP RC 4.00 1.50
❑ 321 Mike Mussina .60 .25
❑ 322 Tony Armas Jr. SP 2.00 .75
❑ 323 Craig Counsell .40 .15
❑ 324 Marcus Giles .40 .15
❑ 325 Greg Vaughn .40 .15
❑ 326 Curt Schilling .40 .15
❑ 327 Jeromy Burnitz .40 .15
❑ 328 Eric Byrnes .40 .15
❑ 329 Johnny Damon Sox .60 .25
❑ 330 Michael Floyd SP RC 2.00 .75
❑ 331 Edgardo Alfonzo .40 .15
❑ 332 Jeremy Hill RC .40 .15
❑ 333 Josh Bonifay RC .40 .15
❑ 334 Byung-Hyun Kim .40 .15
❑ 335 Keith Ginter .40 .15
❑ 336 Ronald Acuna SP RC 2.00 .75
❑ 337 Mike Hill SP RC 2.00 .75
❑ 338 Sean Casey .40 .15
❑ 339 Matt Anderson SP 2.00 .75
❑ 340 Dan Wright .40 .15
❑ 341 Ben Petrick .40 .15
❑ 342 Mike Sirotka SP 2.00 .75
❑ 343 Alex Rodriguez 1.50 .60
❑ 344 Einar Diaz .40 .15
❑ 345 Derek Jeter 2.50 1.00
❑ 346 Jeff Conine .40 .15
❑ 347 Ray Durham SP 2.00 .75
❑ 348 Wilson Betemit SP 2.00 .75
❑ 349 Jeffrey Hammonds .40 .15
❑ 350 Dan Trumble RC .40 .15
❑ 351 Phil Nevin SP 2.00 .75
❑ 352 A.J. Burnett .40 .15
❑ 353 Bill Mueller .40 .15
❑ 354 Charles Nagy .40 .15
❑ 355 Rusty Greer SP 2.00 .75
❑ 356 Jason Botts RC .50 .20
❑ 357 Magglio Ordonez .40 .15
❑ 358 Kevin Appier .40 .15
❑ 359 Brad Radke .40 .15
❑ 360 Chris George .40 .15
❑ 361 Chris Piersoll RC .40 .15
❑ 362 Ivan Rodriguez .60 .25
❑ 363 Jim Kavourias RC .40 .15
❑ 364 Rick Helling SP 2.00 .75
❑ 365 Dean Palmer .40 .15
❑ 366 Rich Aurilia SP 2.00 .75
❑ 367 Ryan Vogelsong .40 .15
❑ 368 Matt Lawton .40 .15
❑ 369 Wade Miller .40 .15
❑ 370 Dustin Hermanson .40 .15
❑ 371 Craig Wilson .40 .15
❑ 372 Todd Zeile SP 2.00 .75
❑ 373 Jon Guzman RC .40 .15
❑ 374 Ellis Burks .40 .15
❑ 375 Robert Cosby SP RC 2.00 .75
❑ 376 Jason Kendall .40 .15
❑ 377 Scott Rolen SP 3.00 1.25
❑ 378 Andruw Jones .60 .25
❑ 379 Greg Sain RC .40 .15
❑ 380 Paul LoDuca .40 .15
❑ 381 Scotty Layfield RC .40 .15
❑ 382 Tomo Ohka .40 .15
❑ 383 Garrett Guzman RC .40 .15
❑ 384 Jack Cust SP 2.00 .75
❑ 385 Shayne Wright RC .40 .15
❑ 386 Derrek Lee .60 .25
❑ 387 Jesus Medrano RC .40 .15
❑ 388 Javier Vazquez .40 .15
❑ 389 Preston Wilson SP 2.00 .75
❑ 390 Gavin Floyd RC 1.00 .40
❑ 391 Sidney Ponson SP 2.00 .75
❑ 392 Jose Hernandez .40 .15
❑ 393 Scott Erickson SP 2.00 .75
❑ 394 Jose Valverde RC .40 .15
❑ 395 Mark Hamilton SP RC 2.00 .75
❑ 396 Brad Cresse .40 .15
❑ 397 Danny Bautista .40 .15
❑ 398 Ray Lankford SP 2.00 .75
❑ 399 Miguel Batista SP 2.00 .75
❑ 400 Brent Butler .40 .15
❑ 401 Manny Delcarmen SP RC 3.00 1.25
❑ 402 Kyle Farnsworth SP 2.00 .75
❑ 403 Freddy Garcia .40 .15
❑ 404 Joe Jiannetti RC .40 .15
❑ 405 Josh Barfield RC 2.50 1.00
❑ 406 Corey Patterson .40 .15
❑ 407 Josh Towers .40 .15
❑ 408 Carlos Pena .40 .15
❑ 409 Jeff Cirillo .40 .15
❑ 410 Jon Lieber .40 .15
❑ 411 Woody Williams SP 2.00 .75
❑ 412 Richard Lane SP RC 2.00 .75
❑ 413 Alex Gonzalez .40 .15
❑ 414 Wilkin Ruan .40 .15
❑ 415 Geoff Jenkins .40 .15
❑ 416 Carlos Hernandez .40 .15
❑ 417 Matt Clement SP 2.00 .75
❑ 418 Jose Cruz Jr. .40 .15
❑ 419 Jake Mauer RC .40 .15
❑ 420 Matt Childers RC .40 .15
❑ 421 Tom Glavine SP 3.00 1.25
❑ 422 Ken Griffey Jr. 1.50 .60
❑ 423 Anderson Hernandez RC .40 .15
❑ 424 John Suomi RC .40 .15
❑ 425 Doug Sessions RC .40 .15
❑ 426 Jaret Wright .40 .15
❑ 427 Rolando Viera SP RC 2.00 .75
❑ 428 Aaron Sele .40 .15
❑ 429 Dmitri Young .40 .15
❑ 430 Ryan Klesko .40 .15
❑ 431 Kevin Tapani SP 2.00 .75
❑ 432 Joe Kennedy .40 .15
❑ 433 Austin Kearns .40 .15
❑ 434 Roger Cedeno SP 2.00 .75
❑ 435 Lance Berkman .40 .15
❑ 436 Frank Menechino .40 .15
❑ 437 Brett Myers .40 .15
❑ 438 Bob Abreu .40 .15
❑ 439 Shawn Estes SP 2.00 .75

2003 Bowman Heritage

❑ COMPLETE SET (300) 120.00 60.00
❑ 1 Jorge Posada .60 .25
❑ 2 Todd Helton .60 .25
❑ 3 Marcus Giles .40 .15
❑ 4 Eric Chavez .40 .15
❑ 5 Edgar Martinez .60 .25
❑ 6 Luis Gonzalez .40 .15
❑ 7 Corey Patterson .40 .15
❑ 8 Preston Wilson .40 .15
❑ 9 Ryan Klesko .40 .15
❑ 10 Randy Johnson 1.00 .40
❑ 11 Jose Guillen .40 .15
❑ 12 Carlos Lee .40 .15
❑ 13 Steve Finley .40 .15
❑ 14 A.J. Pierzynski .40 .15
❑ 15 Troy Glaus .40 .15
❑ 16 Darin Erstad .40 .15
❑ 17 Moises Alou .40 .15
❑ 18 Torii Hunter .40 .15
❑ 19 Marlon Byrd .40 .15
❑ 20 Mark Prior .60 .25
❑ 21 Shannon Stewart .40 .15
❑ 22 Craig Biggio .60 .25
❑ 23 Johnny Damon .60 .25
❑ 24 Robert Fick .40 .15
❑ 25 Jason Giambi .40 .15
❑ 26 Fernando Vina .40 .15
❑ 27 Aubrey Huff .40 .15
❑ 28 Benito Santiago .40 .15
❑ 29 Jay Gibbons .40 .15
❑ 30 Ken Griffey Jr. 1.50 .60
❑ 31 Rocco Baldelli .40 .15
❑ 32 Pat Burrell .40 .15
❑ 33 A.J. Burnett .40 .15
❑ 34 Omar Vizquel .60 .25
❑ 35 Greg Maddux 1.50 .60
❑ 36 Cliff Floyd .40 .15
❑ 37 C.C. Sabathia .40 .15
❑ 38 Geoff Jenkins .40 .15
❑ 39 Ty Wigginton .40 .15
❑ 40 Jeff Kent .40 .15
❑ 41 Orlando Hudson .40 .15
❑ 42 Edgardo Alfonzo .40 .15
❑ 43 Greg Myers .40 .15
❑ 44 Melvin Mora .40 .15
❑ 45 Sammy Sosa 1.00 .40
❑ 46 Russ Ortiz .40 .15
❑ 47 Josh Beckett .40 .15
❑ 48 David Wells .40 .15
❑ 49 Woody Williams .40 .15
❑ 50 Alex Rodriguez 1.50 .60
❑ 51 Randy Wolf .40 .15
❑ 52 Carlos Beltran .40 .15
❑ 53 Austin Kearns .40 .15
❑ 54 Trot Nixon .40 .15
❑ 55 Ivan Rodriguez .60 .25
❑ 56 Shea Hillenbrand .40 .15
❑ 57 Roberto Alomar .60 .25
❑ 58 John Olerud .40 .15
❑ 59 Michael Young .60 .25
❑ 60 Garret Anderson .40 .15
❑ 61 Mike Lieberthal .40 .15
❑ 62 Adam Dunn .40 .15
❑ 63 Raul Ibanez .40 .15

❑ 64 Kenny Lofton .40 .15
❑ 65 Ichiro Suzuki 2.00 .75
❑ 66 Jarrod Washburn .40 .15
❑ 67 Shawn Chacon .40 .15
❑ 68 Alex Gonzalez .40 .15
❑ 69 Roy Halladay .40 .15
❑ 70 Vladimir Guerrero 1.00 .40
❑ 71 Hee Seop Choi .40 .15
❑ 72 Jody Gerut .40 .15
❑ 73 Ray Durham .40 .15
❑ 74 Mark Teixeira .60 .25
❑ 75 Hank Blalock .40 .15
❑ 76 Jerry Hairston Jr. .40 .15
❑ 77 Erubiel Durazo .40 .15
❑ 78 Frank Catalanotto .40 .15
❑ 79 Jacque Jones .40 .15
❑ 80 Bobby Abreu .40 .15
❑ 81 Mike Hampton .40 .15
❑ 82 Zach Day .40 .15
❑ 83 Jimmy Rollins .40 .15
❑ 84 Joel Pineiro .40 .15
❑ 85 Brett Myers .40 .15
❑ 86 Frank Thomas 1.00 .40
❑ 87 Aramis Ramirez .40 .15
❑ 88 Paul Lo Duca .40 .15
❑ 89 Dmitri Young .40 .15
❑ 90 Brian Giles .40 .15
❑ 91 Jose Cruz Jr. .40 .15
❑ 92 Derek Lowe .40 .15
❑ 93 Mark Buehrle .40 .15
❑ 94 Wade Miller .40 .15
❑ 95 Derek Jeter 2.50 1.00
❑ 96 Bret Boone .40 .15
❑ 97 Tony Batista .40 .15
❑ 98 Sean Casey .40 .15
❑ 99 Eric Hinske .40 .15
❑ 100 Albert Pujols 2.00 .75
❑ 101 Runelvys Hernandez .40 .15
❑ 102 Vernon Wells .40 .15
❑ 103 Kerry Wood .40 .15
❑ 104 Lance Berkman .40 .15
❑ 105 Alfonso Soriano .40 .15
❑ 106 Bill Mueller .40 .15
❑ 107 Bartolo Colon .40 .15
❑ 108 Andy Pettitte .60 .25
❑ 109 Rafael Furcal .40 .15
❑ 110 Dontrelle Willis 1.00 .40
❑ 111 Carl Crawford .40 .15
❑ 112 Scott Rolen .60 .25
❑ 113 Chipper Jones 1.00 .40
❑ 114 Magglio Ordonez .40 .15
❑ 115 Bernie Williams .60 .25
❑ 116 Roy Oswalt .40 .15
❑ 117 Kevin Brown .40 .15
❑ 118 Cristian Guzman .40 .15
❑ 119 Kazuhisa Ishii .40 .15
❑ 120 Larry Walker .40 .15
❑ 121 Miguel Tejada .40 .15
❑ 122 Manny Ramirez .60 .25
❑ 123 Mike Mussina .60 .25
❑ 124 Mike Lowell .40 .15
❑ 125 Scott Podsednik .40 .15
❑ 126 Aaron Boone .40 .15
❑ 127 Carlos Delgado .40 .15
❑ 128 Jose Vidro .40 .15
❑ 129 Brad Radke .40 .15
❑ 130 Rafael Palmeiro .60 .25
❑ 131 Mark Mulder .40 .15
❑ 132 Jason Schmidt .40 .15
❑ 133 Gary Sheffield .40 .15
❑ 134 Richie Sexson .40 .15
❑ 135 Barry Zito .40 .15
❑ 136 Tom Glavine .60 .25
❑ 137 Jim Edmonds .40 .15
❑ 138 Andruw Jones .60 .25
❑ 139 Pedro Martinez .60 .25
❑ 140 Curt Schilling .40 .15
❑ 141 Phil Nevin .40 .15
❑ 142 Nomar Garciaparra 1.50 .60
❑ 143 Vicente Padilla .40 .15
❑ 144 Kevin Millwood .40 .15
❑ 145 Shawn Green .40 .15
❑ 146 Jeff Bagwell .60 .25
❑ 147 Hideo Nomo 1.00 .40
❑ 148 Fred McGriff .60 .25
❑ 149 Matt Morris .40 .15
❑ 150 Roger Clemens 2.00 .75
❑ 151 Jerome Williams .40 .15
❑ 152 Orlando Cabrera .40 .15
❑ 153 Tim Hudson .40 .15
❑ 154 Mike Sweeney .40 .15
❑ 155 Jim Thome .60 .25
❑ 156 Rich Aurilia .40 .15
❑ 157 Mike Piazza 1.50 .60
❑ 158 Edgar Renteria .40 .15
❑ 159 Javy Lopez .40 .15
❑ 160 Jamie Moyer .40 .15
❑ 161 Miguel Cabrera DI 1.00 .40
❑ 162 Adam Loewen DI RC 1.00 .40
❑ 163 Jose Reyes DI .40 .15
❑ 164 Zack Greinke DI .40 .15
❑ 165 Gavin Floyd DI .40 .15
❑ 166 Jeremy Guthrie DI .40 .15
❑ 167 Victor Martinez DI .60 .25
❑ 168 Rich Harden DI .60 .25
❑ 169 Joe Mauer DI 1.00 .40
❑ 170 Khalil Greene DI 1.00 .40
❑ 171A Willie Mays 2.00 .75
❑ 171B Willie Mays DI 2.00 .75
❑ 171C Willie Mays KN 2.00 .75
❑ 172A Phil Rizzuto .60 .25
❑ 172B Phil Rizzuto DI .60 .25
❑ 172C Phil Rizzuto KN .60 .25
❑ 173A Al Kaline 1.00 .40
❑ 173B Al Kaline DI 1.00 .40
❑ 173C Al Kaline KN 1.00 .40
❑ 174A Warren Spahn .60 .25
❑ 174B Warren Spahn DI .60 .25
❑ 174C Warren Spahn KN .60 .25
❑ 175A Jimmy Piersall .40 .15
❑ 175B Jimmy Piersall DI .40 .15
❑ 175C Jimmy Piersall KN .40 .15
❑ 176A Luis Aparicio .40 .15
❑ 176B Luis Aparicio DI .40 .15
❑ 176C Luis Aparicio KN .40 .15
❑ 177A Whitey Ford .60 .25
❑ 177B Whitey Ford DI .60 .25
❑ 177C Whitey Ford KN .60 .25
❑ 178A Harmon Killebrew 1.00 .40
❑ 178B Harmon Killebrew DI 1.00 .40
❑ 178C Harmon Killebrew KN 1.00 .40
❑ 179A Duke Snider .60 .25
❑ 179B Duke Snider DI .60 .25
❑ 179C Duke Snider KN .60 .25
❑ 180A Roberto Clemente 2.50 1.00
❑ 180B Roberto Clemente DI 2.50 1.00
❑ 180C Roberto Clemente KN 2.50 1.00
❑ 181 David Martinez KN RC .40 .15
❑ 182 Felix Pie KN RC 4.00 1.50
❑ 183 Kevin Correia KN RC .40 .15
❑ 184 Brandon Webb KN RC 2.50 1.00
❑ 185 Matt Diaz KN RC .75 .30
❑ 186 Lew Ford KN RC .50 .20
❑ 187 Jeremy Griffiths KN RC .40 .15
❑ 188 Matt Hensley KN RC .40 .15
❑ 189 Danny Garcia KN RC .40 .15
❑ 190 Elizardo Ramirez KN RC .50 .20
❑ 191 Greg Aquino KN RC .40 .15
❑ 192 Felix Sanchez KN RC .40 .15
❑ 193 Kelly Shoppach KN RC .75 .30
❑ 194 Bubba Nelson KN RC .50 .20
❑ 195 Mike Oâ ™Keefe KN RC .40 .15
❑ 196 Hanley Ramirez KN RC 4.00 1.50
❑ 197 Todd Wellemeyer KN RC .40 .15
❑ 198 Dustin Moseley KN RC .40 .15
❑ 199 Eric Crozier KN RC .50 .20
❑ 200 Ryan Shealy KN RC 2.50 1.00
❑ 201 Jeremy Bonderman KN RC 2.50 1.00
❑ 202 Bo Hart KN RC .40 .15
❑ 203 Dusty Brown KN RC .40 .15
❑ 204 Rob Hammock KN RC .40 .15
❑ 205 Jorge Piedra KN RC .50 .20
❑ 206 Jason Kubel KN RC 1.50 .60
❑ 207 Stephen Randolph KN RC .40 .15
❑ 208 Andy Sisco KN RC .40 .15
❑ 209 Matt Kata KN RC .40 .15
❑ 210 Robinson Cano KN RC 8.00 3.00
❑ 211 Ben Francisco KN RC .40 .15
❑ 212 Arnie Munoz KN RC .40 .15
❑ 213 Ozzie Chavez KN RC .40 .15
❑ 214 Beau Kemp KN RC .40 .15
❑ 215 Travis Wong KN RC .50 .20
❑ 216 Brian McCann KN RC 5.00 2.00
❑ 217 Aquilino Lopez KN RC .40 .15
❑ 218 Bobby Basham KN RC .40 .15
❑ 219 Tim Olson KN RC .40 .15
❑ 220 Nathan Panther KN RC .40 .15
❑ 221 Wil Ledezma KN RC .40 .15
❑ 222 Josh Willingham KN RC 1.00 .40
❑ 223 David Cash KN RC .40 .15
❑ 224 Oscar Villarreal KN RC .40 .15
❑ 225 Jeff Duncan KN RC .40 .15
❑ 226 Dan Haren KN RC .75 .30
❑ 227 Michel Hernandez KN RC .40 .15
❑ 228 Matt Murton KN RC 2.00 .75
❑ 229 Clay Hensley KN RC .40 .15
❑ 230 Tyler Johnson KN RC .40 .15
❑ 231 Tyler Martin KN RC .40 .15
❑ 232 J.D. Durbin KN RC .40 .15
❑ 233 Shane Victorino KN RC .75 .30
❑ 234 Rajai Davis KN RC .40 .15
❑ 235 Chien-Ming Wang KN RC 5.00 2.00
❑ 236 Travis Ishikawa KN RC .75 .30
❑ 237 Eric Eckenstahler KN .40 .15
❑ 238 Dustin McGowan KN RC .50 .20
❑ 239 Prentice Redman KN RC .40 .15
❑ 240 Haj Turay KN RC .40 .15
❑ 241 Matt DeMarco KN RC .40 .15
❑ 242 Lou Palmisano KN RC .50 .20
❑ 243 Eric Reed KN RC .40 .15
❑ 244 Willie Eyre KN RC .40 .15
❑ 245 Ferdin Tejeda KN RC .40 .15
❑ 246 Michael Garciaparra KN RC .40 .15
❑ 247 Michael Hinckley KN RC .50 .20
❑ 248 Branden Florence KN RC .40 .15
❑ 249 Trent Oeltjen KN RC .50 .20
❑ 250 Mike Neu KN RC .40 .15
❑ 251 Chris Lubanski KN RC 1.00 .40
❑ 252 Brandon Wood KN RC 10.00 4.00
❑ 253 Delmon Young KN RC 5.00 2.00
❑ 254 Matt Harrison KN RC .75 .30
❑ 255 Chad Billingsley KN RC 3.00 1.25
❑ 256 Josh Anderson KN RC .50 .20
❑ 257 Brian McFall KN RC .40 .15
❑ 258 Ryan Wagner KN RC .40 .15
❑ 259 Billy Hogan KN RC .50 .20
❑ 260 Nate Spears KN RC .50 .20
❑ 261 Ryan Harvey KN RC 2.00 .75
❑ 262 Wes Littleton KN RC .50 .20
❑ 263 Xavier Paul KN RC .50 .20
❑ 264 Sean Rodriguez KN RC 2.00 .75
❑ 265 Brian Finch KN RC .40 .15
❑ 266 Josh Rainwater KN RC .50 .20
❑ 267 Brian Snyder KN RC .50 .20
❑ 268 Eric Duncan KN RC 2.00 .75
❑ 269 Rickie Weeks KN RC 3.00 1.25
❑ 270 Tim Battle KN RC .75 .30
❑ 271 Scott Beerer KN RC .40 .15
❑ 272 Aaron Hill KN RC .75 .30
❑ 273 Casey Abrams KN RC .40 .15
❑ 274 Jonathan Fulton KN RC .50 .20
❑ 275 Todd Jennings KN RC .50 .20
❑ 276 Jordan Pratt KN RC .50 .20
❑ 277 Tom Gorzelanny KN RC 1.25 .50
❑ 278 Matt Lorenzo KN RC .50 .20
❑ 279 Jarrod Saltalamacchia KN RC 5.002.00
❑ 280 Mike Wagner KN RC .40 .15

2004 Bowman Heritage

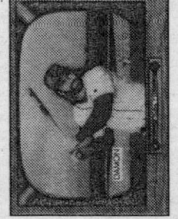

❑ COMPLETE SET (351)	300.00	175.00
❑ COMP.SET w/o SP's (300)	50.00	25.00
❑ SP STATED ODDS 1:3 HOBBY, 1:3 RETAIL		
❑ SP's: 2/9/13/21/25/40B/46/48B/50/55/61		
❑ SP's: 77/80/87/89/95/100/104/109/127/130		
❑ SP's: 132/141/183A/189/204/206/208/210		
❑ SP's: 213/216/220/224/228/234/240/243		
❑ SP's: 246/249/259/268/270-271/282/291		
❑ SP's: 304/318/327/334/342/348		
❑ PLATES STATED ODDS 1:240 HOBBY		
❑ PLATES PRINT RUN 1 #'d SET PER COLOR		
❑ PLATES: BLACK, CYAN, MAGENTA & YELLOW		
❑ NO PLATES PRICING DUE TO SCARCITY		
❑ ROOP BINDER ODDS 1:240 HOBBY		
❑ ROOP BINDER EXCH.DEADLINE 12/31/05		
❑ 1 Tom Glavine	.60	.25
❑ 2 Mike Piazza SP	8.00	3.00
❑ 3 Sidney Ponson	.40	.15
❑ 4 Jerry Hairston Jr.	.40	.15
❑ 5 Jermaine Dye	.40	.15
❑ 6 Bobby Crosby	.40	.15
❑ 7 Carlos Zambrano	.40	.15
❑ 8 Moises Alou	.40	.15
❑ 9 Alex Rodriguez SP	8.00	3.00
❑ 10 Derek Jeter	2.00	.75
❑ 11 Rafael Furcal	.40	.15
❑ 12 J.D. Drew	.40	.15
❑ 13 Joe Mauer SP	6.00	2.50
❑ 14 Brad Radke	.40	.15
❑ 15 Johnny Damon	.60	.25
❑ 16 Derek Lowe	.40	.15
❑ 17 Pat Burrell	.40	.15
❑ 18 Mike Lieberthal	.40	.15
❑ 19 Cliff Lee	.40	.15
❑ 20 Ronnie Belliard	.40	.15
❑ 21 Eric Gagne SP	5.00	2.00
❑ 22 Brad Penny	.40	.15
❑ 23 Al Kaline RET	1.50	.60
❑ 24 Mike Maroth	.40	.15
❑ 25 Magglio Ordonez SP	5.00	2.00
❑ 26 Mark Buehrle	.40	.15
❑ 27 Jack Wilson	.40	.15
❑ 28 Oliver Perez	.40	.15
❑ 29 Red Schoendienst RET	.60	.25
❑ 30 Yadier Molina FY RC	2.00	.75
❑ 31 Ryan Freel	.40	.15
❑ 32 Adam Dunn	.40	.15
❑ 33 Paul Konerko	.40	.15
❑ 34 Esteban Loaiza	.40	.15
❑ 35 Ivan Rodriguez	.60	.25
❑ 36 Carlos Guillen	.40	.15
❑ 37 Adrian Beltre	.40	.15
❑ 38 C.C. Sabathia	.40	.15
❑ 39 Hideo Nomo	1.00	.40
❑ 40A Victor Martinez	.40	.15
❑ 40B V.Martinez Pedro Stats SP	5.00	2.00
❑ 41 Bobby Abreu	.40	.15
❑ 42 Randy Wolf	.40	.15
❑ 43 Johnny Estrada	.40	.15
❑ 44 Russ Ortiz	.40	.15
❑ 45 Kenny Rogers	.40	.15
❑ 46 Hank Blalock SP	5.00	2.00
❑ 47 David Ortiz	1.00	.40
❑ 48A Pedro Martinez	.60	.25
❑ 48B P.Martinez Victor Stats SP	8.00	3.00
❑ 49 Austin Kearns	.40	.15
❑ 50 Ken Griffey Jr. SP	8.00	3.00
❑ 51 Mark Prior	.60	.25
❑ 52 Kerry Wood	.40	.15
❑ 53 Eric Chavez	.40	.15
❑ 54 Tim Hudson	.40	.15
❑ 55 Rafael Palmeiro SP	8.00	3.00
❑ 56 Javy Lopez	.40	.15
❑ 57 Jason Bay	.40	.15
❑ 58 Craig Wilson	.40	.15
❑ 59 Whitey Ford RET	1.00	.40
❑ 60 Jason Giambi	.40	.15
❑ 61 Scott Rolen SP	8.00	3.00
❑ 62 Matt Morris	.40	.15
❑ 63 Javier Vazquez	.40	.15
❑ 64 Jim Thome	.60	.25
❑ 65 Don Zimmer RET	.60	.25
❑ 66 Shawn Green	.40	.15
❑ 67 Don Larsen RET	1.00	.40
❑ 68 Gary Sheffield	.40	.15
❑ 69 Jorge Posada	.60	.25
❑ 70 Bernie Williams	.60	.25
❑ 71 Chipper Jones	1.00	.40
❑ 72 Andruw Jones	.60	.25
❑ 73 John Thomson	.40	.15
❑ 74 Jim Edmonds	.40	.15
❑ 75 Albert Pujols	2.00	.75
❑ 76 Chris Carpenter	.40	.15
❑ 77 Aubrey Huff SP	5.00	2.00
❑ 78 Carl Crawford	.40	.15
❑ 79 Victor Zambrano	.40	.15
❑ 80 Alfonso Soriano SP	5.00	2.00
❑ 81 Lance Berkman	.40	.15
❑ 82 Mike Sweeney	.40	.15
❑ 83 Ken Harvey	.40	.15
❑ 84 Angel Berroa	.40	.15
❑ 85 A.J. Burnett	.40	.15
❑ 86 Mike Lowell	.40	.15
❑ 87 Miguel Cabrera SP	8.00	3.00
❑ 88 Preston Wilson	.40	.15
❑ 89 Todd Helton SP	8.00	3.00
❑ 90 Larry Walker Cards	.60	.25
❑ 91 Vladimir Guerrero	1.00	.40
❑ 92 Garret Anderson	.40	.15
❑ 93 Bartolo Colon	.40	.15
❑ 94 Scott Hairston	.40	.15
❑ 95 Richie Sexson SP	5.00	2.00
❑ 96 Sean Casey	.40	.15
❑ 97 John Podres RET	.60	.25
❑ 98 Andy Pettitte	.60	.25
❑ 99 Roy Oswalt	.40	.15
❑ 100 Roger Clemens SP	8.00	3.00
❑ 101 Scott Podsednik	.40	.15
❑ 102 Ben Sheets	.40	.15
❑ 103 Lyle Overbay	.40	.15
❑ 104 Nick Johnson SP	5.00	2.00
❑ 105 Zach Day	.40	.15
❑ 106 Jose Reyes	.40	.15
❑ 107 Khalil Greene	.60	.25
❑ 108 Sean Burroughs	.40	.15
❑ 109 David Wells SP	5.00	2.00
❑ 110 Jason Schmidt	.40	.15
❑ 111 Neifi Perez	.40	.15
❑ 112 Edgar Renteria	.40	.15
❑ 113 Rich Aurilia	.40	.15
❑ 114 Edgar Martinez	.60	.25
❑ 115 Joel Pineiro	.40	.15
❑ 116 Mark Teixeira	.60	.25
❑ 117 Michael Young	.40	.15
❑ 118 Ricardo Rodriguez	.40	.15
❑ 119 Carlos Delgado	.40	.15
❑ 120 Roy Halladay	.40	.15
❑ 121 Jose Guillen	.40	.15
❑ 122 Troy Glaus	.40	.15
❑ 123 Shea Hillenbrand	.40	.15
❑ 124 Luis Gonzalez	.40	.15
❑ 125 Horacio Ramirez	.40	.15
❑ 126 Melvin Mora	.40	.15
❑ 127 Miguel Tejada SP	5.00	2.00
❑ 128 Manny Ramirez	.60	.25
❑ 129 Tim Wakefield	.40	.15
❑ 130 Curt Schilling SP	8.00	3.00
❑ 131 Aramis Ramirez	.40	.15
❑ 132 Sammy Sosa SP	8.00	3.00
❑ 133 Matt Clement	.40	.15
❑ 134 Juan Uribe	.40	.15
❑ 135 Dontrelle Willis	.60	.25
❑ 136 Paul Lo Duca	.40	.15
❑ 137 Juan Pierre	.40	.15
❑ 138 Kevin Brown	.40	.15
❑ 139 B.Giles/M.Giles	.40	.15
❑ 140 Brian Giles	.40	.15
❑ 141 Nomar Garciaparra SP	8.00	3.00
❑ 142 Cesar Izturis	.40	.15
❑ 143 Don Newcombe RET	.60	.25
❑ 144 Craig Biggio	.60	.25
❑ 145 Carlos Beltran	.40	.15
❑ 146 Torii Hunter	.40	.15
❑ 147 Livan Hernandez	.40	.15
❑ 148 Cliff Floyd	.40	.15
❑ 149 Barry Zito	.40	.15
❑ 150 Mark Mulder	.40	.15
❑ 151 Rocco Baldelli	.40	.15
❑ 152 Bret Boone	.40	.15
❑ 153 Jamie Moyer	.40	.15
❑ 154 Ichiro Suzuki	2.00	.75
❑ 155 Brett Myers	.40	.15
❑ 156 Carl Pavano	.40	.15
❑ 157 Josh Beckett	.40	.15
❑ 158 Randy Johnson	1.00	.40
❑ 159 Trot Nixon	.40	.15
❑ 160 Dmitri Young	.40	.15
❑ 161 Jacque Jones	.40	.15
❑ 162 Lew Ford	.40	.15
❑ 163 Jose Vidro	.40	.15
❑ 164 Mark Kotsay	.40	.15
❑ 165 A.J. Pierzynski	.40	.15
❑ 166 Dewon Brazelton	.40	.15
❑ 167 Jeromy Burnitz	.40	.15
❑ 168 Johan Santana	1.00	.40
❑ 169 Greg Maddux	1.50	.60
❑ 170 Carl Erskine RET	.60	.25
❑ 171 Robin Roberts RET	.60	.25
❑ 172 Freddy Garcia	.40	.15
❑ 173 Carlos Lee	.40	.15
❑ 174 Jeff Bagwell	.60	.25
❑ 175 Jeff Kent	.40	.15
❑ 176 Kazuhisa Ishii	.40	.15
❑ 177 Orlando Cabrera	.40	.15
❑ 178 Shannon Stewart	.40	.15
❑ 179 Mike Cameron	.40	.15
❑ 180 Mike Mussina	.60	.25
❑ 181 Frank Thomas	1.00	.40
❑ 182 Jaret Wright	.40	.15
❑ 183A Alex Gonzalez Marlins SP	5.00	2.00
❑ 183B Alex Gonzalez Padres	.40	.15
❑ 184 Matt Lawton	.40	.15
❑ 185 Derrek Lee	.60	.25
❑ 186 Omar Vizquel	.60	.25
❑ 187 Jeremy Bonderman	.40	.15
❑ 188 Jake Westbrook	.40	.15
❑ 189 Zack Greinke SP	5.00	2.00
❑ 190 Chad Tracy	.40	.15
❑ 191 Rondell White	.40	.15
❑ 192 Alex Gonzalez	.40	.15
❑ 193 Geoff Jenkins	.40	.15
❑ 194 Ralph Kiner RET	1.00	.40
❑ 195 Al Leiter	.40	.15
❑ 196 Kevin Millwood	.40	.15
❑ 197 Jason Kendall	.40	.15
❑ 198 Kris Benson	.40	.15
❑ 199 Ryan Klesko	.40	.15
❑ 200 Mark Loretta	.40	.15
❑ 201 Richard Hidalgo	.40	.15
❑ 202 Reed Johnson	.40	.15
❑ 203 Luis Castillo	.40	.15
❑ 204 Jon Zeringue DP SP RC	5.00	2.00
❑ 205 Matt Bush DP RC	2.50	1.00
❑ 206 Kurt Suzuki DP SP RC	6.00	2.50
❑ 207 Mark Rogers DP RC	2.00	.75
❑ 208 Jason Vargas DP SP RC	5.00	2.00
❑ 209 Homer Bailey DP RC	4.00	1.50
❑ 210 Ray Liotta DP SP RC	5.00	2.00
❑ 211 Eric Campbell DP RC	3.00	1.25
❑ 212 Thomas Diamond DP RC	2.50	1.00
❑ 213 Gaby Hernandez DP SP RC	8.00	3.00
❑ 214 Neil Walker DP RC	2.00	.75
❑ 215 Bill Bray DP RC	.75	.30
❑ 216 Wade Davis DP SP RC	8.00	3.00
❑ 217 David Purcey DP RC	1.50	.60
❑ 218 Scott Elbert DP RC	2.00	.75
❑ 219 Josh Fields DP RC	4.00	1.50
❑ 220 Josh Johnson DP SP RC	5.00	2.00
❑ 221 Chris Lambert DP RC	1.00	.40
❑ 222 Trevor Plouffe DP RC	2.50	1.00
❑ 223 Bruce Froemming UMP	.50	.20
❑ 224 Matt Macri DP SP RC	4.00	1.50
❑ 225 Greg Golson DP RC	2.50	1.00
❑ 226 Philip Hughes DP RC	6.00	2.50
❑ 227 Kyle Waldrop DP RC	2.00	.75
❑ 228 Matt Tuiasosopo DP SP RC	8.00	3.00
❑ 229 Richie Robnett DP RC	2.00	.75
❑ 230 Taylor Tankersley DP RC	1.00	.40
❑ 231 Blake DeWitt DP RC	3.00	1.25
❑ 232 Charlie Reliford UMP	.50	.20
❑ 233 Eric Hurley DP RC	2.00	.75
❑ 234 Jordan Parraz DP SP RC	5.00	2.00
❑ 235 J.P. Howell DP RC	2.00	.75
❑ 236 Dana DeMuth UMP	.50	.20
❑ 237 Zach Jackson DP RC	1.50	.60
❑ 238 Justin Orenduff DP RC	1.50	.00
❑ 239 Brad Thompson FY RC	.75	.30
❑ 240 J.C. Holt DP SP RC	5.00	2.00

❑ 241	Matt Fox DP RC	.75	.30
❑ 242	Danny Putnam DP RC	1.50	.60
❑ 243	Daryl Jones DP SP RC	5.00	2.00
❑ 244	Jon Poterson DP RC	.75	.30
❑ 245	Gio Gonzalez DP RC	2.50	1.00
❑ 246	Lucas Harrell DP SP RC	5.00	2.00
❑ 247	Jerry Crawford UMP	.50	.20
❑ 248	Jay Rainville DP RC	2.50	1.00
❑ 249	Donnie Smith DP SP RC	5.00	2.00
❑ 250	Huston Street DP RC	3.00	1.25
❑ 251	Jeff Marquez DP RC	1.00	.40
❑ 252	Reid Brignac DP RC	3.00	1.25
❑ 253	Yusmeiro Petit FY RC	2.00	.75
❑ 254	K.C. Herren DP RC	1.50	.60
❑ 255	Dale Scott UMP	.50	.20
❑ 256	Erick San Pedro DP RC	.75	.30
❑ 257	Ed Montague UMP	.50	.20
❑ 258	Billy Buckner DP RC	1.00	.40
❑ 259	Mitch Einertson DP SP RC	5.00	2.00
❑ 260	Aarom Baldiris FY RC	.50	.20
❑ 261	Conor Jackson FY RC	3.00	1.25
❑ 262	Rick Reed UMP	.50	.20
❑ 263	Ervin Santana FY RC	2.00	.75
❑ 264	Gerry Davis UMP	.50	.20
❑ 265	Merkin Valdez FY RC	.50	.20
❑ 266	Joey Gathright FY RC	1.00	.40
❑ 267	Alberto Callaspo FY RC	.75	.30
❑ 268	Carlos Quentin FY SP RC	10.00	4.00
❑ 269	Gary Darling UMP	.50	.20
❑ 270	Jeff Salazar FY SP RC	5.00	2.00
❑ 271	Akinori Otsuka FY SP RC	5.00	2.00
❑ 272	Joe Brinkman UMP	.50	.20
❑ 273	Omar Quintanilla FY RC	.50	.20
❑ 274	Brian Runge UMP	.50	.20
❑ 275	Tom Mastny FY RC	.40	.15
❑ 276	John Hirschbeck UMP	.50	.20
❑ 277	Warner Madrigal FY RC	.75	.30
❑ 278	Joe West UMP	.50	.20
❑ 279	Paul Maholm FY RC	1.00	.40
❑ 280	Larry Young UMP	.50	.20
❑ 281	Mike Reilly UMP	.50	.20
❑ 282	Kazuo Matsui FY SP RC	5.00	2.00
❑ 283	Randy Marsh UMP	.50	.20
❑ 284	Frank Francisco FY RC	.40	.15
❑ 285	Zach Duke FY RC	2.00	.75
❑ 286	Tim McClelland UMP	.50	.20
❑ 287	Jesse Crain FY RC	.75	.30
❑ 288	Hector Gimenez FY RC	.40	.15
❑ 289	Marland Williams FY RC	.50	.20
❑ 290	Brian Gorman UMP	.50	.20
❑ 291	Jose Capellan FY SP RC	5.00	2.00
❑ 292	Tim Welke UMP	.50	.20
❑ 293	Javier Guzman FY RC	.50	.20
❑ 294	Paul McAnulty FY RC	.75	.30
❑ 295	Hector Made FY RC	.75	.30
❑ 296	Jon Connolly FY RC	1.00	.40
❑ 297	Don Sutton FY RC	1.00	.40
❑ 298	Fausto Carmona FY RC	1.50	.60
❑ 299	Ramon Ramirez FY RC	.40	.15
❑ 300	Brad Snyder FY RC	1.00	.40
❑ 301	Chin-Lung Hu FY RC	1.25	.50
❑ 302	Rudy Guillen FY RC	.75	.30
❑ 303	Matt Moses FY RC	1.00	.40
❑ 304	Brad Halsey FY SP RC	5.00	2.00
❑ 305	Erick Aybar FY RC	1.00	.40
❑ 306	Brad Sullivan FY RC	.50	.20
❑ 307	Nick Gorneault FY RC	.50	.20
❑ 308	Craig Ansman FY RC	.40	.15
❑ 309	Ricky Nolasco FY RC	1.25	.50
❑ 310	Luke Hughes FY RC	.40	.15
❑ 311	Danny Gonzalez FY RC	.40	.15
❑ 312	Josh Labandeira FY RC	.40	.15
❑ 313	Donald Levinski FY RC	.40	.15
❑ 314	Vince Perkins FY RC	.50	.20
❑ 315	Tommy Murphy FY RC	.40	.15
❑ 316	Chad Bentz FY RC	.40	.15
❑ 317	Chris Shelton FY RC	2.00	.75
❑ 318	Nyjer Morgan FY SP RC	5.00	2.00
❑ 319	Kody Kirkland FY RC	.50	.20
❑ 320	Blake Hawksworth FY RC	.50	.20
❑ 321	Alex Romero FY RC	.40	.15
❑ 322	Mike Gosling FY RC	.40	.15
❑ 323	Ryan Budde FY RC	.40	.15
❑ 324	Kevin Howard FY RC	.50	.20
❑ 325	Wanell Macia FY RC	.40	.15
❑ 326	Travis Blackley FY RC	.40	.15
❑ 327	Kazuhito Tadano FY SP RC	5.00	2.00
❑ 328	Shingo Takatsu FY RC	.75	.30
❑ 329	Joaquin Arias FY RC	.75	.30
❑ 330	Juan Cedeno FY RC	.40	.15
❑ 331	Bobby Brownlie FY RC	1.00	.40
❑ 332	Lastings Milledge FY RC	5.00	2.00
❑ 333	Estee Harris FY RC	.50	.20
❑ 334	Tim Stauffer FY SP RC	5.00	2.00
❑ 335	Jon Knott FY RC	.40	.15
❑ 336	David Aardsma FY RC	.50	.20
❑ 337	Wardell Starling FY RC	.40	.15
❑ 338	Dioner Navarro FY RC	.75	.30
❑ 339	Logan Kensing FY RC	.40	.15
❑ 340	Jason Hirsh FY RC	2.00	.75
❑ 341	Matt Creighton FY RC	.40	.15
❑ 342	Felix Hernandez FY SP RC	15.00	6.00
❑ 343	Kyle Sleeth FY RC	.50	.20
❑ 344	Dustin Nippert FY RC	.50	.20
❑ 345	Anthony Lerew FY RC	.75	.30
❑ 346	Chris Saenz FY RC	.40	.15
❑ 347	Steve Palermo SUP	1.00	.40
❑ 348	Barry Bonds SP	15.00	6.00
❑ MJ	Roop Binder EXCH		

2005 Bowman Heritage

❑ COMPLETE SET (350)	300.00	175.00
❑ COMP.SET w/o SP's (300)	50.00	25.00
❑ COMMON CARD (1-300)	.40	.15
❑ COMMON RC (1-300)	.40	.15
❑ COMMON SP (301-350)	5.00	2.00
❑ COM.SP RC (301-350)	5.00	2.00
❑ 301-350 SP ODDS 1:3 H, 1:3 R		
❑ PLATES STATED ODDS 1:343 HOBBY		
❑ PLATES PRINT RUN 1 #'d SET PER COLOR		
❑ PLATES: BLACK, CYAN, MAGENTA & YELLOW		
❑ NO PLATES PRICING DUE TO SCARCITY		
❑ ROOP BINDER EXCH ODDS 1:240 H		
❑ ROOP BINDER EXCH.DEADLINE 12/31/07		

❑ 1	Steven White FY RC	.40	.15
❑ 2	Jorge Posada	.60	.25
❑ 3	Brett Myers	.40	.15
❑ 4	Pat Burrell	.40	.15
❑ 5	Grady Sizemore	.60	.25
❑ 6	Jeff Weaver	.40	.15
❑ 7	Jeff Kent	.40	.15
❑ 8	Mark Kotsay	.40	.15
❑ 9	Nick Swisher	.60	.25
❑ 10	Scott Rolen	.60	.25
❑ 11	Matt Morris	.40	.15
❑ 12	Luis Castillo	.40	.15
❑ 13	Pedro Feliz	.40	.15
❑ 14	Omar Vizquel	.60	.25
❑ 15	Edgar Renteria	.40	.15
❑ 16	David Wells	.40	.15
❑ 17	Chad Cordero	.40	.15
❑ 18	Brad Wilkerson	.40	.15
❑ 19	Kelly Johnson	.40	.15
❑ 20	Johnny Estrada	.40	.15
❑ 21	Brian Roberts	.40	.15
❑ 22	Jeromy Burnitz	.40	.15
❑ 23	Magglio Ordonez	.40	.15
❑ 24	Adam Dunn	.40	.15
❑ 25	Randy Johnson	1.00	.40
❑ 26	Derek Jeter	2.00	.75
❑ 27	Jon Lieber	.40	.15
❑ 28	Jim Thome	.60	.25
❑ 29	Ronnie Belliard	.40	.15
❑ 30	Jake Westbrook	.40	.15
❑ 31	Bengie Molina	.40	.15
❑ 32	J.D. Drew	.40	.15
❑ 33	Rich Harden	.40	.15
❑ 34	David Eckstein	.40	.15
❑ 35	Scott Podsednik	.40	.15
❑ 36	Mark Buehrle	.40	.15
❑ 37	Barry Bonds	2.50	1.00
❑ 38	Brian Schneider	.40	.15
❑ 39	Tim Wakefield	.40	.15
❑ 40	Craig Wilson	.40	.15
❑ 41	Jose Vidro	.40	.15
❑ 42	Jacque Jones	.40	.15
❑ 43	Felix Hernandez	1.00	.40
❑ 44	Nomar Garciaparra	1.00	.40
❑ 45	Neifi Perez	.40	.15
❑ 46	Brandon Inge	.40	.15
❑ 47	Felipe Lopez	.40	.15
❑ 48	Ken Griffey Jr.	1.50	.60
❑ 49	Robinson Cano	.60	.25
❑ 50	Jason Giambi	.40	.15
❑ 51	Mike Lieberthal	.40	.15
❑ 52	Bobby Abreu	.40	.15
❑ 53	C.C. Sabathia	.40	.15
❑ 54	Aaron Boone	.40	.15
❑ 55	Milton Bradley	.40	.15
❑ 56	Derek Lowe	.40	.15
❑ 57	Barry Zito	.40	.15
❑ 58	Jim Edmonds	.40	.15
❑ 59	Jon Garland	.40	.15
❑ 60	Tadahito Iguchi RC	1.50	.60
❑ 61	Jason Schmidt	.40	.15
❑ 62	David Ortiz	1.00	.40
❑ 63	Matt Lawton	.40	.15
❑ 64	Zach Duke	.60	.25
❑ 65	Gary Sheffield	.40	.15
❑ 66	Chipper Jones	1.00	.40
❑ 67	Sammy Sosa	1.00	.40
❑ 68	Rafael Palmeiro	.60	.25
❑ 69	Carlos Zambrano	.40	.15
❑ 70	Aramis Ramirez	.40	.15
❑ 71	Chris Shelton	.60	.25
❑ 72	Wily Mo Pena	.40	.15
❑ 73	Mike Mussina	.60	.25
❑ 74	Chien-Ming Wang	1.50	.60
❑ 75	Randy Wolf	.40	.15
❑ 76	Jimmy Rollins	.40	.15
❑ 77	Chase Utley	.60	.25
❑ 78	Kevin Millwood	.40	.15
❑ 79	Victor Martinez	.40	.15
❑ 80	Morgan Ensberg	.40	.15
❑ 81	Bartolo Colon	.40	.15
❑ 82	Bobby Crosby	.40	.15
❑ 83	Dan Johnson	.40	.15
❑ 84	Dan Haren	.40	.15
❑ 85	Yadier Molina	.40	.15
❑ 86	Mark Mulder	.40	.15
❑ 87	Russell Branyan	.40	.15
❑ 88	Lyle Overbay	.40	.15
❑ 89	Edgardo Alfonzo	.40	.15
❑ 90	Mike Matheny	.40	.15
❑ 91	J.T. Snow	.40	.15
❑ 92	Curt Schilling	.60	.25
❑ 93	Oliver Perez	.40	.15
❑ 94	Mark Redman	.40	.15
❑ 95	Esteban Loaiza	.40	.15
❑ 96	Livan Hernandez	.40	.15
❑ 97	Ryan Church	.40	.15
❑ 98	Kyle Davies	.40	.15
❑ 99	Mike Hampton	.40	.15
❑ 100	Jeff Francoeur	1.00	.40
❑ 101	Javy Lopez	.40	.15
❑ 102	Mark Prior	.60	.25
❑ 103	Kerry Wood	.40	.15
❑ 104	Carlos Guillen	.40	.15
❑ 105	Dmitri Young	.40	.15
❑ 106	David Wright	1.50	.60
❑ 107	Cliff Floyd	.40	.15
❑ 108	Carlos Beltran	.40	.15
❑ 109	Melky Cabrera RC	2.00	.75
❑ 110	Carl Pavano	.40	.15
❑ 111	Jamie Moyer	.40	.15
❑ 112	Joel Pineiro	.40	.15
❑ 113	Adrian Beltre	.40	.15
❑ 114	Jhonny Peralta	.40	.15
❑ 115	Travis Hafner	.40	.15
❑ 116	Cesar Izturis	.40	.15

❑ 117 Brad Penny .40 .15
❑ 118 Garret Anderson .40 .15
❑ 119 Scott Kazmir .40 .15
❑ 120 Aubrey Huff .40 .15
❑ 121 Larry Walker .60 .25
❑ 122 Albert Pujols 2.00 .75
❑ 123 Paul Konerko .40 .15
❑ 124 Frank Thomas 1.00 .40
❑ 125 Phil Nevin .40 .15
❑ 126 Brian Giles .40 .15
❑ 127 Ramon Hernandez .40 .15
❑ 128 Johnny Damon .60 .25
❑ 129 Trot Nixon .40 .15
❑ 130 Rocco Baldelli .40 .15
❑ 131 Carl Crawford .40 .15
❑ 132 Alfonso Soriano .40 .15
❑ 133 Mark Teixeira .60 .25
❑ 134 Gustavo Chacin .40 .15
❑ 135 Vernon Wells .40 .15
❑ 136 Erik Bedard .40 .15
❑ 137 Daniel Cabrera .40 .15
❑ 138 Michael Barrett .40 .15
❑ 139 Greg Maddux 1.50 .60
❑ 140 Javier Vazquez .40 .15
❑ 141 Chad Tracy .40 .15
❑ 142 Michael Young .40 .15
❑ 143 Kenny Rogers .40 .15
❑ 144 Mike Piazza 1.00 .40
❑ 145 Jose Reyes .40 .15
❑ 146 Geoff Jenkins .40 .15
❑ 147 Carlos Lee .40 .15
❑ 148 Brady Clark .40 .15
❑ 149 Torii Hunter .40 .15
❑ 150 Johan Santana 1.00 .40
❑ 151 Steve Finley .40 .15
❑ 152 Darin Erstad .40 .15
❑ 153 Jake Peavy .40 .15
❑ 154 Xavier Nady .40 .15
❑ 155 Ryan Klesko .40 .15
❑ 156 Ichiro Suzuki 2.00 .75
❑ 157 Richie Sexson .40 .15
❑ 158 Raul Ibanez .40 .15
❑ 159 Freddy Garcia .40 .15
❑ 160 Brad Hawpe .40 .15
❑ 161 Jeff Francis .40 .15
❑ 162 Todd Helton .60 .25
❑ 163 Clint Barmes .40 .15
❑ 164 Rodrigo Lopez .40 .15
❑ 165 Melvin Mora .40 .15
❑ 166 Brandon Webb .40 .15
❑ 167 Shawn Green .40 .15
❑ 168 Moises Alou .40 .15
❑ 169 Matt Clement .40 .15
❑ 170 John Smoltz .60 .25
❑ 171 Rafael Furcal .40 .15
❑ 172 Jeff Bagwell .60 .25
❑ 173 Roger Clemens 1.50 .60
❑ 174 Dontrelle Willis .40 .15
❑ 175 Paul Lo Duca .40 .15
❑ 176 Zack Greinke .40 .15
❑ 177 David DeJesus .40 .15
❑ 178 Mike Sweeney .40 .15
❑ 179 Ben Sheets .40 .15
❑ 180 Doug Davis .40 .15
❑ 181 Mike Cameron .40 .15
❑ 182 Lance Berkman .40 .15
❑ 183 Craig Biggio .60 .25
❑ 184 Shannon Stewart .40 .15
❑ 185 Joe Mauer 1.00 .40
❑ 186 Justin Morneau .40 .15
❑ 187 Mike Maroth .40 .15
❑ 188 Ivan Rodriguez .60 .25
❑ 189 Luis Gonzalez .40 .15
❑ 190 Troy Glaus .40 .15
❑ 191 Adam Eaton .40 .15
❑ 192 Khalil Greene .60 .25
❑ 193 Mike Lowell .40 .15
❑ 194 Miguel Cabrera .60 .25
❑ 195 Roy Halladay .40 .15
❑ 196 Ted Lilly .40 .15
❑ 197 Alex Rios .40 .15
❑ 198 Josh Beckett .40 .15
❑ 199 A.J. Burnett .40 .15
❑ 200 Juan Pierre .40 .15
❑ 201 Marcus Giles .40 .15
❑ 202 Craig Tatum FY RC .40 .15
❑ 203 Hayden Penn FY RC .75 .30
❑ 204 C.J. Smith FY RC .40 .15
❑ 205 Matt Albers FY RC 1.00 .40
❑ 206 Jared Gothreaux FY RC .40 .15
❑ 207 Mike Rodriguez FY RC .40 .15
❑ 208 Hernan Iribarren FY RC .50 .20
❑ 209 Manny Parra FY RC .40 .15
❑ 210 Kevin Collins FY RC .40 .15
❑ 211 Buck Coats FY RC .40 .15
❑ 212 Jeremy West FY RC .75 .30
❑ 213 Ian Bladergroen FY RC .50 .20
❑ 214 Chuck Tiffany FY RC 1.00 .40
❑ 215 Andy LaRoche FY RC 3.00 1.25
❑ 216 Frank Diaz FY RC .40 .15
❑ 217 Jai Miller FY RC .50 .20
❑ 218 Tony Giarratano FY RC .40 .15
❑ 219 Danny Zell FY RC .40 .15
❑ 220 Justin Verlander FY RC 4.00 1.50
❑ 221 Ryan Sweeney FY RC 1.00 .40
❑ 222 Brandon McCarthy FY RC 1.25 .50
❑ 223 Jerry Owens FY RC .50 .20
❑ 224 Glen Perkins FY RC .75 .30
❑ 225 Kevin West FY RC .40 .15
❑ 226 Billy Butler FY RC 4.00 1.50
❑ 227 Shane Costa FY RC .40 .15
❑ 228 Erik Schindewolf FY RC .40 .15
❑ 229 Miguel Montero FY RC 1.25 .50
❑ 230 Stephen Drew FY RC 5.00 2.00
❑ 231 Matt DeSalvo FY RC .50 .20
❑ 232 Ben Jones FY RC .50 .20
❑ 233 Bill McCarthy FY RC .40 .15
❑ 234 Chuck James FY RC 1.50 .60
❑ 235 Brandon Sing FY RC .50 .20
❑ 236 Andy Santana FY RC .40 .15
❑ 237 Brendan Ryan FY RC .40 .15
❑ 238 Wes Swackhamer FY RC .40 .15
❑ 239 Jeff Niemann FY RC .75 .30
❑ 240 Ian Kinsler FY RC 2.00 .75
❑ 241 Micah Furtado FY RC .40 .15
❑ 242 Ryan Mount FY RC .75 .30
❑ 243 P.J. Phillips FY RC .75 .30
❑ 244 Trevor Bell FY RC .75 .30
❑ 245 Jered Weaver FY RC 5.00 2.00
❑ 246 Eddy Martinez FY RC 1.00 .40
❑ 247 Brian Bannister FY RC .75 .30
❑ 248 Philip Humber FY RC .75 .30
❑ 249 Michael Rogers FY RC .40 .15
❑ 250 Landon Powell FY RC .50 .20
❑ 251 Kennard Bibbs FY RC .40 .15
❑ 252 Nelson Cruz FY RC 1.25 .50
❑ 253 Paul Kelly FY RC .50 .20
❑ 254 Kevin Slowey FY RC 1.25 .50
❑ 255 Brandon Snyder FY RC 1.50 .60
❑ 256 Nolan Reimold FY RC 1.25 .50
❑ 257 Brian Stavisky FY RC .40 .15
❑ 258 Javier Herrera FY RC 2.00 .75
❑ 259 Russ Martin FY RC 1.25 .50
❑ 260 Matthew Kemp FY RC 5.00 2.00
❑ 261 Wade Townsend FY RC .50 .20
❑ 262 Nick Touchstone FY RC .40 .15
❑ 263 Ryan Feierabend FY RC .40 .15
❑ 264 Bobby Livingston FY RC .40 .15
❑ 265 Wladimir Balentien FY RC .75 .30
❑ 266 Keiichi Yabu FY RC .40 .15
❑ 267 Craig Italiano FY RC .75 .30
❑ 268 Ryan Golocki FY RC .40 .15
❑ 269 Ryan Garko FY RC 1.25 .50
❑ 270 Mike Bourn FY RC .75 .30
❑ 271 Scott Mathieson FY RC .75 .30
❑ 272 Scott Mitchinson FY RC .40 .15
❑ 273 Tyler Greene FY RC .75 .30
❑ 274 Mark McCormick FY RC .50 .20
❑ 275 Daryl Jones FY .40 .15
❑ 276 Travis Chick FY RC .50 .20
❑ 277 Luis Hernandez FY RC .40 .15
❑ 278 Steve Doetsch FY RC .40 .15
❑ 279 Chris Vines FY RC .40 .15
❑ 280 Mike Costanzo FY RC 1.25 .50
❑ 281 Matt Maloney FY RC 1.00 .40
❑ 282 Matt Goyen FY RC .40 .15
❑ 283 Jacob Marceaux FY RC .40 .15
❑ 284 David Gassner FY RC .40 .15
❑ 285 Ricky Barrett FY RC .40 .15
❑ 286 Jon Egan FY RC .50 .20
❑ 287 Scott Blue FY RC .40 .15
❑ 288 Steven Bondurant FY RC .40 .15
❑ 289 Kevin Melillo FY RC .75 .30
❑ 290 Brad Corley FY RC .50 .20
❑ 291 Brent Lillibridge FY RC .40 .15
❑ 292 Mike Morse FY RC .75 .30
❑ 293 Justin Thomas FY RC .40 .15
❑ 294 Nick Webber FY RC .40 .15
❑ 295 Mitch Boggs FY RC .40 .15
❑ 296 Jeff Lyman FY RC .50 .20
❑ 297 Jordan Schafer FY RC .50 .20
❑ 298 Ismael Ramirez FY RC .40 .15
❑ 299 Chris B.Young FY RC 2.00 .75
❑ 300 Brian Miller FY RC .40 .15
❑ 301 Jason Bay SP 5.00 2.00
❑ 302 Tim Hudson SP 5.00 2.00
❑ 303 Miguel Tejada SP 5.00 2.00
❑ 304 Jeremy Bonderman SP 5.00 2.00
❑ 305 Alex Rodriguez SP 8.00 3.00
❑ 306 Rickie Weeks SP 5.00 2.00
❑ 307 Manny Ramirez SP 8.00 3.00
❑ 308 Nick Johnson SP 5.00 2.00
❑ 309 Andruw Jones SP 8.00 3.00
❑ 310 Hideki Matsui SP 6.00 2.50
❑ 311 Jeremy Reed SP 5.00 2.00
❑ 312 Dallas McPherson SP 5.00 2.00
❑ 313 Vladimir Guerrero SP 8.00 3.00
❑ 314 Eric Chavez SP 5.00 2.00
❑ 315 Chris Carpenter SP 5.00 2.00
❑ 316 Aaron Hill SP 5.00 2.00
❑ 317 Derrek Lee SP 8.00 3.00
❑ 318 Mark Loretta SP 5.00 2.00
❑ 319 Garrett Atkins SP 5.00 2.00
❑ 320 Hank Blalock SP 5.00 2.00
❑ 321 Chris Young SP 5.00 2.00
❑ 322 Roy Oswalt SP 5.00 2.00
❑ 323 Carlos Delgado SP 5.00 2.00
❑ 324 Pedro Martinez SP 8.00 3.00
❑ 325 Jeff Clement FY SP RC 10.00 4.00
❑ 326 Jimmy Shull FY SP RC 5.00 2.00
❑ 327 Daniel Carte FY SP RC 5.00 2.00
❑ 328 Travis Buck FY SP RC 6.00 2.50
❑ 329 Chris Volstad FY SP RC 5.00 2.00
❑ 330 A.McCutchen FY SP RC 10.00 4.00
❑ 331 Cliff Pennington FY SP RC 5.00 2.00
❑ 332 John Mayberry Jr. FY SP RC 5.00 2.00
❑ 333 C.J. Henry FY SP RC 8.00 3.00
❑ 334 Ricky Romero FY SP RC 5.00 2.00
❑ 335 Aaron Thompson FY SP RC 5.00 2.00
❑ 336 Cesar Carrillo FY SP RC 5.00 2.00
❑ 337 Jacoby Ellsbury FY SP RC 6.00 2.50
❑ 338 Matt Garza FY SP RC 8.00 3.00
❑ 339 Colby Rasmus FY SP RC 8.00 3.00
❑ 340 Ryan Zimmerman FY SP RC 15.00 6.00
❑ 341 Ryan Braun FY SP RC 10.00 4.00
❑ 342 Brent Lillibridge FY SP 5.00 2.00
❑ 343 Jay Bruce FY SP RC 12.00 5.00
❑ 344 Matt Green FY SP RC 5.00 2.00
❑ 345 Brent Cox FY SP RC 5.00 2.00
❑ 346 Jed Lowrie FY SP RC 5.00 2.00
❑ 347 Beau Jones FY SP RC 5.00 2.00
❑ 348 Eli Iorg FY SP RC 5.00 2.00
❑ 349 Chaz Roe FY SP RC 5.00 2.00
❑ 350 Mystery Redemption SP 25.00 10.00
❑ NNO Roop Binder Redemption 15.00 6.00

2004 Bowman Sterling

❑ FY ODDS APPX.TWO PER HOBBY PACK
❑ FY AU ODDS APPX.ONE PER HOBBY PACK
❑ AU-GU ODDS APPX.ONE PER HOBBY PACK

- AU-GU 1:2 WRAPPER ODDS IS AN ERROR
- GU ODDS APPX. 1.5 PER HOBBY PACK
- GU 1:2 WRAPPER ODDS IS AN ERROR
- AB Angel Berroa Bat 5.00 2.00
- ABA Aarom Baldiris FY RC 5.00 2.00
- AC Alberto Callaspo FY AU RC 8.00 3.00
- AD Adam Dunn Bat 5.00 2.00
- AER Alex Rodriguez Bat 15.00 6.00
- AJ Andruw Jones Jsy 8.00 3.00
- AK Austin Kearns Jsy 5.00 2.00
- ANR Aramis Ramirez Bat 5.00 2.00
- AP Albert Pujols Jsy 20.00 8.00
- AR Alex Romero FY AU RC 8.00 3.00
- AW Adam Wainwright AU Jsy 10.00 4.00
- AWH A.Whittington FY RC 5.00 2.00
- AZ Alec Zumwalt FY AU RC 8.00 3.00
- BB Brian Bixler AU Jsy RC 10.00 4.00
- BBR Bill Bray FY RC 4.00 1.50
- BBU Billy Buckner FY RC 5.00 2.00
- BC2 Bobby Crosby Jsy 5.00 2.00
- BD Blake DeWitt AU Jsy RC 25.00 10.00
- BE Brad Eldred FY RC 5.00 2.00
- BH B.Hawksworth FY AU RC 10.00 4.00
- BT Brad Thompson FY RC 5.00 2.00
- BU B.J. Upton AU Bat 25.00 10.00
- BW Bernie Williams Jsy 8.00 3.00
- CA Chris Aguila FY AU RC 8.00 3.00
- CB Craig Biggio Jsy 8.00 3.00
- CC Chad Cordero AU Jsy 15.00 6.00
- CG Christian Garcia AU Jsy RC 15.00 6.00
- CH Chin-Lung Hu FY RC 10.00 4.00
- CIB Carlos Beltran Bat 5.00 2.00
- CJ Conor Jackson FY RC 20.00 8.00
- CL Chris Lubanski AU Bat 10.00 4.00
- CLA Chris Lambert FY RC 5.00 2.00
- CN Chris Nelson FY RC 8.00 3.00
- CQ Carlos Quentin FY AU RC 30.00 15.00
- CT Curtis Thigpen FY RC 5.00 2.00
- DD David DeJesus AU Jsy 10.00 4.00
- DP Danny Putnam AU Jsy RC 10.00 4.00
- DPU David Purcey FY RC 5.00 2.00
- DW David Wright AU Jsy 50.00 30.00
- DWW Dontrelle Willis Jsy 8.00 3.00
- DY Delmon Young AU Bat 40.00 15.00
- EG Eric Gagne Jsy 5.00 2.00
- EH Eric Hurley FY RC 5.00 2.00
- ESP Erick San Pedro FY RC 4.00 1.50
- FC Fausto Carmona FY RC 8.00 3.00
- FG Freddy Guzman FY RC 4.00 1.50
- FH Felix Hernandez FY RC 40.00 15.00
- FP Felix Pie AU Jsy 25.00 10.00
- FT Frank Thomas Bat 8.00 3.00
- GG Greg Golson FY RC 8.00 3.00
- GH Gaby Hernandez FY RC 8.00 3.00
- GIG Gio Gonzalez FY RC 8.00 3.00
- GS Gary Sheffield Bat 5.00 2.00
- HB Homer Bailey AU Jsy RC 50.00 20.00
- HC Hee Seop Choi Bat 5.00 2.00
- HG Hector Gimenez FY AU RC 8.00 3.00
- HJB Hank Blalock Bat 5.00 2.00
- HM Hector Made FY RC 5.00 2.00
- HS Huston Street AU Jsy RC 25.00 10.00
- IR Ivan Rodriguez Bat 8.00 3.00
- JB Jeff Bagwell Jsy 8.00 3.00
- JC Jose Capellan FY RC 5.00 2.00
- JCR Jesse Crain FY RC 5.00 2.00
- JD Johnny Damon Bat 8.00 3.00
- JE Johnny Estrada Bat 5.00 2.00
- JFI Josh Fields FY RC 10.00 4.00
- JG Joey Gathright FY RC 5.00 2.00
- JH Jesse Hoover FY RC 5.00 2.00
- JK Jason Kendall Bat 5.00 2.00
- JM Jeff Marquez AU Jsy RC 15.00 6.00
- JO Justin Orenduff FY RC 5.00 2.00
- JP Juan Pierre Bat 5.00 2.00
- JPH J.P. Howell FY RC 5.00 2.00
- JR Jay Rainville FY AU RC 20.00 8.00
- JS Jeremy Sowers FY AU RC 30.00 15.00
- JZ Jon Zeringue FY RC 5.00 2.00
- KCH K.C. Herren FY RC 5.00 2.00
- KS Kurt Suzuki FY RC 6.00 2.50
- KT Kazuhito Tadano FY RC 5.00 2.00
- KW Kerry Wood Jsy 5.00 2.00
- KWA Kyle Waldrop AU Jsy RC 20.00 8.00
- LB Lance Berkman Jsy 5.00 2.00
- LC Luis Castillo Jsy 5.00 2.00
- LH Linc Holdzkom FY AU RC 8.00 3.00
- LN Laynce Nix Bat 5.00 2.00
- MA Moises Alou Bat 5.00 2.00
- MAM Mark Mulder Jsy 5.00 2.00
- MAR Manny Ramirez Bat 8.00 3.00
- MB Matt Bush AU Jsy RC 25.00 10.00
- MC Miguel Cabrera Bat 8.00 3.00
- MCT Mark Teixeira Bat 8.00 3.00
- ME Mitch Einertson FY RC 5.00 2.00
- MF Mike Ferris FY RC 5.00 2.00
- MFO Matt Fox FY RC 4.00 1.50
- MJP Mike Piazza Bat 8.00 3.00
- MM Matt Moses FY AU RC 15.00 6.00
- MMC Matt Macri FY RC 6.00 2.50
- MP Mark Prior Jsy 8.00 3.00
- MR Mike Rouse FY AU RC 8.00 3.00
- MRO Mark Rogers FY RC 8.00 3.00
- MT M.Tuiasosopo AU Bat RC 30.00 15.00
- MT1 Miguel Tejada Bat 5.00 2.00
- MT2 Miguel Tejada Jsy 5.00 2.00
- MW Marland Williams FY RC 5.00 2.00
- MY Michael Young Bat 5.00 2.00
- NJ Nick Johnson Bat 5.00 2.00
- NM Nyjer Morgan FY RC 4.00 1.50
- NS Nate Schierholtz FY RC 8.00 3.00
- NW Neil Walker FY RC 8.00 3.00
- OQ Omar Quintanilla FY RC 5.00 2.00
- PGM Paul Maholm FY RC 8.00 3.00
- PH Philip Hughes FY RC 20.00 8.00
- PL Paul LoDuca Bat 5.00 2.00
- PR Pokey Reese Bat 5.00 2.00
- RB Rocco Baldelli Bat 5.00 2.00
- RBR Reid Brignac FY RC 10.00 4.00
- RC Robinson Cano AU Jsy 50.00 25.00
- RH Ryan Harvey AU Bat 15.00 6.00
- RJH Richard Hidalgo Bat 5.00 2.00
- RM Ryan Meaux FY AU RC 8.00 3.00
- RO Russ Ortiz Jsy 5.00 2.00
- RP Rafael Palmeiro Bat 8.00 3.00
- SK Scott Kazmir AU Jsy RC 50.00 25.00
- SO Scott Olsen AU Jsy RC 30.00 15.00
- SS Sammy Sosa Jsy 8.00 3.00
- SSM Seth Smith FY RC 8.00 3.00
- TD Thomas Diamond FY RC 8.00 3.00
- TG Troy Glaus Bat 5.00 2.00
- TLH Todd Helton Bat 8.00 3.00
- TM Tino Martinez Bat 8.00 3.00
- TMG Tom Glavine Jsy 8.00 3.00
- TP Trevor Plouffe AU Jsy RC 15.00 6.00
- TT T.Tankersley AU Jsy RC 10.00 4.00
- VG Vladimir Guerrero Bat 8.00 3.00
- VP Vince Perkins FY AU RC 10.00 4.00
- YP Yusmeiro Petit FY RC 12.00 5.00
- ZD Zach Duke FY RC 10.00 4.00
- ZJ Zach Jackson FY RC 5.00 2.00

2005 Bowman Sterling

- COMMON CARD 4.00 1.50
- BASIC CARDS APPX.TWO PER HOBBY PACK
- BASIC CARDS APPX.TWO PER RETAIL PACK
- AU GROUP A ODDS 1:2 HOBBY
- AU GROUP B ODDS 1:3 HOBBY
- AU-GU GROUP A ODDS 1:2 H, 1:2 R
- AU-GU GROUP B ODDS 1:37 H, 1:37 R
- AU-GU GROUP C ODDS 1:11 H, 1:11 R
- AU-GU GROUP D ODDS 1:10 H, 1:10 R
- AU-GU GROUP E ODDS 1:27 H, 1:27 R
- AU-GU GROUP F ODDS 1:13 H, 1:13 R
- GU GROUP A ODDS 1:3 H, 1:3 R
- GU GROUP B ODDS 1:5 H, 1:5 R
- GU GROUP C ODDS 1:6 H, 1:6 R
- ACL Andy LaRoche RC 8.00 3.00
- AL Adam Lind AU Bat B 25.00 10.00
- AM A.McCutchen AU Jsy D RC 40.00 20.00
- AP Albert Pujols Jsy B 15.00 6.00
- AR Alex Rodriguez Jsy B UER 15.00 6.00
- ARA Aramis Ramirez Bat A 5.00 2.00
- AS Alfonso Soriano Bat A 5.00 2.00
- AT Aaron Thompson AU A RC 10.00 4.00
- BA Brian Anderson RC 6.00 2.50
- BB Billy Buckner AU Jsy A 10.00 4.00
- BBU Billy Butler RC 12.00 5.00
- BC Brent Cox AU Jsy D RC 15.00 6.00
- BCR Brad Corley RC 5.00 2.00
- BE Brad Eldred AU Jsy C 10.00 4.00
- BH Brett Hayes RC 4.00 1.50
- BJ Beau Jones AU Jsy A RC 20.00 8.00
- BL B.Livingston AU Jsy A RC 10.00 4.00
- BLB Barry Bonds Jsy C 15.00 6.00
- BM B.McCarthy AU Jsy A RC 25.00 10.00
- BMU Bill Mueller Jsy C 5.00 2.00
- BRB Brian Bogusevic RC 4.00 1.50
- BS Brandon Sing AU A RC 10.00 4.00
- BSN Brandon Snyder RC 8.00 3.00
- BZ Barry Zito Uni A 5.00 2.00
- CB Carlos Beltran Bat A 5.00 2.00
- CBU Clay Buchholz RC 8.00 3.00
- CC Cesar Carrillo RC 6.00 2.50
- CD Carlos Delgado Jsy A 5.00 2.00
- CH C.J. Henry AU B RC 20.00 8.00
- CHE Chase Headley RC 5.00 2.00
- CI Craig Italiano RC 5.00 2.00
- CJ Chuck James RC 10.00 4.00
- CLT Chuck Tiffany RC 5.00 2.00
- CN Chris Nelson AU Jsy A 10.00 4.00
- CP Cliff Pennington AU B RC 10.00 4.00
- CPP C.Pignatiello AU Jsy A RC 10.00 4.00
- CR Colby Rasmus AU Jsy A RC 50.00 20.00
- CRA Cesar Ramos RC 5.00 2.00
- CRO Chaz Roe AU Jsy A RC 15.00 6.00
- CS C.J. Smith AU Jsy A RC 10.00 4.00
- CSU Curt Schilling Jsy C 8.00 3.00
- CT Curtis Thigpen AU Jsy A 10.00 4.00
- CV Chris Volstad AU B RC 10.00 4.00
- DC Dan Carte RC 5.00 2.00
- DL Derrek Lee Bat A 8.00 3.00
- DO David Ortiz Bat A 8.00 3.00
- DP Dustin Pedroia AU Jsy A 15.00 6.00
- DT Drew Thompson RC 5.00 2.00
- DW Dontrelle Willis Jsy C 5.00 2.00
- EC Eric Chavez Uni B 5.00 2.00
- EI Eli Iorg AU Jsy C RC 15.00 6.00
- EM Eddy Martinez AU A RC 10.00 4.00
- GK George Kottaras AU A RC 10.00 4.00
- GM Greg Maddux Jsy C 10.00 4.00
- GO Garrett Olson AU A RC 10.00 4.00
- GS Gary Sheffield Bat A 5.00 2.00
- HAS Henry Sanchez RC 6.00 2.50
- HB Hank Blalock Bat A 5.00 2.00
- HI Hernan Iribarren RC 5.00 2.00
- HM Hideki Matsui AS Jsy C 15.00 6.00
- HS Hum Sanchez AU A RC 30.00 12.50
- IR Ivan Rodriguez Bat A 8.00 3.00
- JB Jay Bruce AU Jsy D RC 50.00 25.00
- JBE Josh Beckett Uni A 5.00 2.00
- JC Jeff Clement RC 15.00 6.00
- JCN John Nelson AU Uni A RC 10.00 4.00
- JD Johnny Damon Bat A 8.00 3.00
- JDR John Drennen RC 8.00 3.00
- JE J.Ellsbury AU Jsy E RC 30.00 12.50
- JEG Jon Egan RC 5.00 2.00
- JF Josh Fields AU Jsy A 12.00 5.00
- JG Josh Geer AU Jsy A RC 10.00 4.00
- JGI Josh Gibson Seat C 15.00 6.00
- JL Jed Lowrie AU Jsy F RC 15.00 6.00
- JLY Jeff Lyman RC 5.00 2.00
- JM John Mayberry Jr. AU A RC 15.00 6.00
- JMA Jacob Marceaux RC 4.00 1.50
- JN Jeff Niemann AU Jsy A RC 15.00 6.00
- JO Justin Olson AU Jsy A RC 10.00 4.00
- JP Jorge Posada Bat A 8.00 3.00
- JPE Jim Edmonds Jsy B 5.00 2.00
- JS John Smoltz Jsy A 8.00 3.00
- JV J.Verlander AU Jsy A RC 60.00 35.00
- JW Josh Wall RC 5.00 2.00
- JWE Jered Weaver RC 15.00 6.00
- KG Khalil Greene Jsy B 8.00 3.00
- KM Kevin Millar Bat A 5.00 2.00
- KS Kevin Slowey RC 12.00 5.00
- KW Kevin Whelan RC 5.00 2.00
- LWJ Chipper Jones Bat A 8.00 3.00
- MA Matt Albers AU A RC 10.00 4.00
- MAM Matt Maloney RC 6.00 2.50
- MB M.Bowden AU Jsy A RC 25.00 10.00
- MC Mike Conroy AU Jsy A RC 10.00 4.00
- MCA Miguel Cabrera Jsy A 8.00 3.00
- MCO Mike Costanzo RC 8.00 3.00
- MG Matt Green AU A RC 8.00 3.00
- MGA Matt Garza RC 10.00 4.00
- MGI Marcus Giles AS Jsy B 5.00 2.00
- MM Mark Mulder Uni B 5.00 2.00

❑ MMC Mark McCormick RC	5.00	2.00
❑ MP Mike Piazza Bat A	8.00	3.00
❑ MPR Mark Prior Jsy B	8.00	3.00
❑ MR Manny Ramirez Bat A	8.00	3.00
❑ MT Miguel Tejada Uni A	5.00	2.00
❑ MTE Mark Teixeira Bat A	8.00	3.00
❑ MTO Matt Torra RC	5.00	2.00
❑ MY Michael Young Bat A	5.00	2.00
❑ NH Nick Hundley RC	4.00	1.50
❑ NR Nolan Reimold RC	8.00	3.00
❑ NW Nick Webber RC	4.00	1.50
❑ PH Philip Humber AU Jsy A RC	25.00	10.00
❑ PK Paul Kelly RC	5.00	2.00
❑ PL Paul Lo Duca Bat A	5.00	2.00
❑ PM Pedro Martinez Jsy A	8.00	3.00
❑ PP P.J. Phillips RC	5.00	2.00
❑ RB Ryan Braun AU A RC	25.00	10.00
❑ RBE Ronnie Belliard Bat A	5.00	2.00
❑ RF Rafael Furcal Jsy A	5.00	2.00
❑ RM Russ Martin AU Jsy F RC	25.00	10.00
❑ RMO Ryan Mount RC	5.00	2.00
❑ RR Ricky Romero RC	5.00	2.00
❑ RT Raul Tablado AU Jsy A RC	10.00	4.00
❑ RZ Ryan Zimmerman RC	25.00	10.00
❑ SD Stephen Drew RC	20.00	8.00
❑ SE Scott Elbert AU Jsy A	10.00	4.00
❑ SM Steve Marek AU Jsy A RC	10.00	4.00
❑ SR Scott Rolen Jsy B	8.00	3.00
❑ SS Sammy Sosa Bat A	8.00	3.00
❑ SW Steven White AU B RC	8.00	3.00
❑ TB Trevor Bell AU Jsy C RC	15.00	6.00
❑ TBU Travis Buck RC	6.00	2.50
❑ TC Travis Chick AU A RC	10.00	4.00
❑ TG Tyler Greene RC	5.00	2.00
❑ TH Torii Hunter Bat A	5.00	2.00
❑ THE Tyler Herron RC	5.00	2.00
❑ THU Tim Hudson Uni A	5.00	2.00
❑ TI Tadahito Iguchi RC	5.00	2.00
❑ TLH Todd Helton Jsy B	8.00	3.00
❑ TM Tyler Minges AU Jsy A RC	10.00	4.00
❑ TM Tino Martinez Bat A	8.00	3.00
❑ TN Trot Nixon Bat A	5.00	2.00
❑ TT Troy Tulowitzki RC	12.00	5.00
❑ TW Travis Wood RC	6.00	2.50
❑ VG Vladimir Guerrero Bat A	8.00	3.00
❑ VM Victor Martinez Bat A	5.00	2.00
❑ WT Wade Townsend RC	5.00	2.00
❑ YE Yunel Escobar RC	5.00	2.00
❑ ZS Zach Simons RC	4.00	1.50

1914 Cracker Jack

❑ COMPLETE SET (144)	45000.00	27500.00
❑ 1 Otto Knabe	250.00	150.00
❑ 2 Frank Baker	400.00	250.00
❑ 3 Joe Tinker	400.00	250.00
❑ 4 Larry Doyle	175.00	100.00
❑ 5 Ward Miller	150.00	75.00
❑ 6 Eddie Plank	600.00	350.00
❑ 7 Eddie Collins	450.00	275.00
❑ 8 Rube Oldring	150.00	75.00
❑ 9 Artie Hoffman	150.00	75.00
❑ 10 John McInnis	150.00	75.00
❑ 11 George Stovall	150.00	75.00
❑ 12 Connie Mack MG	500.00	300.00
❑ 13 Art Wilson	150.00	75.00
❑ 14 Sam Crawford	300.00	175.00
❑ 15 Reb Russell	150.00	75.00
❑ 16 Howie Camnitz	150.00	75.00
❑ 17 Roger Bresnahan	350.00	200.00
❑ 18 Johnny Evers	350.00	200.00
❑ 19 Chief Bender	450.00	275.00
❑ 20 Cy Falkenberg	150.00	75.00
❑ 21 Heinie Zimmerman	150.00	75.00
❑ 22 Joe Wood	300.00	175.00
❑ 23 Charles Comiskey	350.00	200.00
❑ 24 George Mullen	150.00	75.00
❑ 25 Michael Simon	150.00	75.00
❑ 26 James Scott	150.00	75.00
❑ 27 Bill Carrigan	150.00	75.00
❑ 28 Jack Barry	150.00	75.00
❑ 29 Vean Gregg Cleveland	200.00	125.00
❑ 30 Ty Cobb	6000.00	3600.00
❑ 31 Heinie Wagner	150.00	75.00
❑ 32 Mordecai Brown	350.00	200.00
❑ 33 Amos Strunk	150.00	75.00
❑ 34 Ira Thomas	150.00	75.00
❑ 35 Harry Hooper	300.00	175.00
❑ 36 Ed Walsh	300.00	175.00
❑ 37 Grover C. Alexander	800.00	500.00
❑ 38 Red Dooin Phila. NL	200.00	125.00
❑ 39 Chick Gandil	350.00	200.00
❑ 40 Jimmy Austin St.L. AL	200.00	125.00
❑ 41 Tommy Leach	150.00	75.00
❑ 42 Al Bridwell	150.00	75.00
❑ 43 Rube Marquard	350.00	200.00
❑ 44 Charles Tesreau	150.00	75.00
❑ 45 Fred Luderus	150.00	75.00
❑ 46 Bob Groom	150.00	75.00
❑ 47 Josh Devore Phila. NL	200.00	125.00
❑ 48 Harry Lord	250.00	150.00
❑ 49 John Miller	150.00	75.00
❑ 50 John Hummell	150.00	75.00
❑ 51 Nap Rucker	175.00	100.00
❑ 52 Zach Wheat	350.00	200.00
❑ 53 Otto Miller	150.00	75.00
❑ 54 Marty O'Toole	150.00	75.00
❑ 55 Dick Hoblitzel Cinc.	200.00	125.00
❑ 56 Clyde Milan	175.00	100.00
❑ 57 Walter Johnson	2000.00	1200.00
❑ 58 Wally Schang	175.00	100.00
❑ 59 Harry Gessler	150.00	75.00
❑ 60 Rollie Zeider	250.00	150.00
❑ 61 Ray Schalk	300.00	175.00
❑ 62 Jay Cashion	300.00	175.00
❑ 63 Babe Adams	175.00	100.00
❑ 64 Jimmy Archer	150.00	75.00
❑ 65 Tris Speaker	700.00	450.00
❑ 66 Napoleon Lajoie	800.00	500.00
❑ 67 Otis Crandall	150.00	75.00
❑ 68 Honus Wagner	2500.00	1800.00
❑ 69 John McGraw	450.00	275.00
❑ 70 Fred Clarke	300.00	175.00
❑ 71 Chief Meyers	175.00	100.00
❑ 72 John Boehling	150.00	75.00
❑ 73 Max Carey	300.00	175.00
❑ 74 Frank Owens	150.00	75.00
❑ 75 Miller Huggins	300.00	175.00
❑ 76 Claude Hendrix	150.00	75.00
❑ 77 Hughie Jennings MG	300.00	175.00
❑ 78 Fred Merkle	200.00	125.00
❑ 79 Ping Bodie	175.00	100.00
❑ 80 Ed Ruelbach	175.00	100.00
❑ 81 Jim C. Delehanty	175.00	100.00
❑ 82 Gavvy Cravath	200.00	125.00
❑ 83 Russ Ford	150.00	75.00
❑ 84 Elmer E. Knetzer	150.00	75.00
❑ 85 Buck Herzog	150.00	75.00
❑ 86 Burt Shotton	150.00	75.00
❑ 87 Forrest Cady	150.00	75.00
❑ 88 Christy Mathewson	3000.00	2000.00
❑ 89 Lawrence Cheney	150.00	75.00
❑ 90 Frank Smith	150.00	75.00
❑ 91 Roger Peckinpaugh	175.00	100.00
❑ 92 Al Demaree N.Y. NL	200.00	125.00
❑ 93 Del Pratt	250.00	150.00
❑ 94 Eddie Cicotte	325.00	175.00
❑ 95 Ray Keating	150.00	75.00
❑ 96 Beals Becker	150.00	75.00
❑ 97 John(Rube) Benton	150.00	75.00
❑ 98 Frank LaPorte	150.00	75.00
❑ 99 Frank Chance	1500.00	1000.00
❑ 100 Thomas Seaton	150.00	75.00
❑ 101 Frank Schulte	150.00	75.00
❑ 102 Ray Fisher	150.00	75.00
❑ 103 Joe Jackson	8000.00	5000.00
❑ 104 Vic Saier	150.00	75.00
❑ 105 James Lavender	150.00	75.00
❑ 106 Joe Birmingham	150.00	75.00
❑ 107 Tom Downey	150.00	75.00
❑ 108 Sherry Magee Phila. NL	200.00	125.00
❑ 109 Fred Blanding	150.00	75.00
❑ 110 Bob Bescher	150.00	75.00
❑ 111 Jim Callahan	300.00	175.00
❑ 112 Ed Sweeney	150.00	75.00
❑ 113 George Suggs	150.00	75.00
❑ 114 Geo.J. Moriarty	175.00	100.00
❑ 115 Addison Brennan	150.00	75.00
❑ 116 Rollie Zeider	150.00	75.00
❑ 117 Ted Easterly	150.00	75.00
❑ 118 Ed Konetchy Pittsburgh	200.00	125.00
❑ 119 George Perring	150.00	75.00
❑ 120 Mike Doolan	150.00	75.00
❑ 121 Hub Perdue Boston NL	200.00	125.00
❑ 122 Owen Bush	150.00	75.00
❑ 123 Slim Sallee	150.00	75.00
❑ 124 Earl Moore	150.00	75.00
❑ 125 Bert Niehoff	200.00	125.00
❑ 126 Walter Blair	150.00	75.00
❑ 127 Butch Schmidt	150.00	75.00
❑ 128 Steve Evans	150.00	75.00
❑ 129 Ray Caldwell	150.00	75.00
❑ 130 Ivy Wingo	150.00	75.00
❑ 131 George Baumgardner	150.00	75.00
❑ 132 Les Nunamaker	150.00	75.00
❑ 133 Branch Rickey MG	450.00	275.00
❑ 134 Armando Marsans Cincinnati	200.00	125.00
❑ 135 Bill Killefer	150.00	75.00
❑ 136 Rabbit Maranville	350.00	200.00
❑ 137 William Rariden	150.00	75.00
❑ 138 Hank Gowdy	150.00	75.00
❑ 139 Rebel Oakes	150.00	75.00
❑ 140 Danny Murphy	150.00	75.00
❑ 141 Cy Barger	150.00	75.00
❑ 142 Eugene Packard	150.00	75.00
❑ 143 Jake Daubert	175.00	100.00
❑ 144 James C. Walsh	200.00	125.00

1915 Cracker Jack

❑ COMPLETE SET (176)	35000.00	20000.00
❑ COMMON CARD (1-144)	100.00	60.00
❑ COMMON CARD(145-176)	125.00	75.00
❑ 1 Otto Knabe	175.00	100.00
❑ 2 Frank Baker	350.00	200.00
❑ 3 Joe Tinker	350.00	200.00
❑ 4 Larry Doyle	100.00	60.00
❑ 5 Ward Miller	100.00	60.00
❑ 6 Eddie Plank	500.00	300.00
❑ 7 Eddie Collins	350.00	200.00
❑ 8 Rube Oldring	100.00	60.00
❑ 9 Artie Hoffman	100.00	60.00
❑ 10 John McInnis	100.00	60.00
❑ 11 George Stovall	100.00	60.00

❑	12 Connie Mack MG	400.00	250.00
❑	13 Art Wilson	100.00	60.00
❑	14 Sam Crawford	300.00	175.00
❑	15 Reb Russell	100.00	60.00
❑	16 Howie Camnitz	100.00	60.00
❑	17 Roger Bresnahan	300.00	175.00
❑	18 Johnny Evers	300.00	175.00
❑	19 Chief Bender	350.00	200.00
❑	20 Cy Falkenberg	100.00	60.00
❑	21 Heinie Zimmerman	100.00	60.00
❑	22 Joe Wood	250.00	150.00
❑	23 C.Comiskey OWN	300.00	200.00
❑	24 George Mullen	100.00	60.00
❑	25 Michael Simon	100.00	60.00
❑	26 James Scott	100.00	60.00
❑	27 Bill Carrigan	100.00	60.00
❑	28 Jack Barry	100.00	60.00
❑	29 Vean Gregg		
	Boston AL	125.00	75.00
❑	30 Ty Cobb	4000.00	3000.00
❑	31 Heinie Wagner	100.00	60.00
❑	32 Mordecai Brown	300.00	175.00
❑	33 Amos Strunk	100.00	60.00
❑	34 Ira Thomas	100.00	60.00
❑	35 Harry Hooper	250.00	150.00
❑	36 Ed Walsh	300.00	175.00
❑	37 Grover C. Alexander	600.00	350.00
❑	38 Red Dooin		
	Cincinnati	125.00	75.00
❑	39 Chick Gandil	300.00	175.00
❑	40 Jimmy Austin		
	Pitts. FED	125.00	75.00
❑	41 Tommy Leach	100.00	60.00
❑	42 Al Bridwell	100.00	60.00
❑	43 Rube Marquard	350.00	200.00
❑	44 Charles(Jeff) Tesreau	100.00	60.00
❑	45 Fred Luderus	100.00	60.00
❑	46 Bob Groom	100.00	60.00
❑	47 Josh Devore		
	Boston NL	125.00	75.00
❑	48 Steve O'Neill	125.00	75.00
❑	49 John Miller	100.00	60.00
❑	50 John Hummell	100.00	60.00
❑	51 Nap Rucker	125.00	75.00
❑	52 Zach Wheat	300.00	175.00
❑	53 Otto Miller	100.00	60.00
❑	54 Marty O'Toole	100.00	60.00
❑	55 Dick Hoblitzel		
	Boston AL	125.00	75.00
❑	56 Clyde Milan	125.00	75.00
❑	57 Walter Johnson	1500.00	1000.00
❑	58 Wally Schang	125.00	75.00
❑	59 Harry Gessler	100.00	60.00
❑	60 Oscar Dugey	125.00	75.00
❑	61 Ray Schalk	250.00	150.00
❑	62 Willie Mitchell	125.00	75.00
❑	63 Babe Adams	125.00	75.00
❑	64 Jimmy Archer	100.00	60.00
❑	65 Tris Speaker	600.00	350.00
❑	66 Napoleon Lajoie	600.00	350.00
❑	67 Otis Crandall	100.00	60.00
❑	68 Honus Wagner	1500.00	1000.00
❑	69 John McGraw MG	300.00	175.00
❑	70 Fred Clarke	250.00	150.00
❑	71 Chief Meyers	100.00	60.00
❑	72 John Boehling	100.00	60.00
❑	73 Max Carey	250.00	150.00
❑	74 Frank Owens	100.00	60.00
❑	75 Miller Huggins	300.00	175.00
❑	76 Claude Hendrix	100.00	60.00
❑	77 Hughie Jennings MG	300.00	175.00
❑	78 Fred Merkle	125.00	75.00
❑	79 Ping Bodie	125.00	75.00
❑	80 Ed Ruelbach	125.00	75.00
❑	81 Jim C. Delehanty	125.00	75.00
❑	82 Gavvy Cravath	125.00	75.00
❑	83 Russ Ford	100.00	60.00
❑	84 Elmer E. Knetzer	100.00	60.00
❑	85 Buck Herzog	100.00	60.00
❑	86 Burt Shotton	100.00	60.00
❑	87 Forrest Cady	100.00	60.00
❑	88 Christy Mathewson	1500.00	1000.00
❑	89 Lawrence Cheney	100.00	60.00
❑	90 Frank Smith	100.00	60.00
❑	91 Roger Peckinpaugh	125.00	75.00
❑	92 Al Demaree		
	Phila. NL	125.00	75.00
❑	93 Del Pratt	175.00	100.00
❑	94 Eddie Cicotte	300.00	175.00
❑	95 Ray Keating	100.00	60.00
❑	96 Beals Becker	100.00	60.00
❑	97 John(Rube) Benton	100.00	60.00
❑	98 Frank LaPorte	100.00	60.00
❑	99 Hal Chase	300.00	175.00
❑	100 Thomas Seaton	100.00	60.00
❑	101 Frank Schulte	100.00	60.00
❑	102 Ray Fisher	100.00	60.00
❑	103 Joe Jackson	8000.00	5000.00
❑	104 Vic Saier	100.00	60.00
❑	105 James Lavender	100.00	60.00
❑	106 Joe Birmingham	100.00	60.00
❑	107 Thomas Downey	100.00	60.00
❑	108 Sherry Magee		
	Boston NL	125.00	75.00
❑	109 Fred Blanding	100.00	60.00
❑	110 Bob Bescher	100.00	60.00
❑	111 Herbie Moran	125.00	75.00
❑	112 Ed Sweeney	100.00	60.00
❑	113 George Suggs	100.00	60.00
❑	114 Geo.J. Moriarty	125.00	75.00
❑	115 Addison Brennan	100.00	60.00
❑	116 Rollie Zeider	100.00	60.00
❑	117 Ted Easterly	100.00	60.00
❑	118 Ed Konetchy		
	Pitts. FED	125.00	75.00
❑	119 George Perring	100.00	60.00
❑	120 Mike Doolan	100.00	60.00
❑	121 Hub Perdue		
	St. Louis NL	125.00	75.00
❑	122 Owen Bush	100.00	60.00
❑	123 Slim Sallee	100.00	60.00
❑	124 Earl Moore	100.00	60.00
❑	125 Bert Niehoff		
	Phila. NL	125.00	75.00
❑	126 Walter Blair	100.00	60.00
❑	127 Butch Schmidt	100.00	60.00
❑	128 Steve Evans	100.00	60.00
❑	129 Ray Caldwell	100.00	60.00
❑	130 Ivy Wingo	100.00	60.00
❑	131 Geo. Baumgardner	100.00	60.00
❑	132 Les Nunamaker	100.00	60.00
❑	133 Branch Rickey MG	300.00	175.00
❑	134 Armando Marsans		
	St.L. FED	125.00	75.00
❑	135 William Killefer	100.00	60.00
❑	136 Rabbit Maranville	250.00	150.00
❑	137 William Rariden	100.00	60.00
❑	138 Hank Gowdy	100.00	60.00
❑	139 Rebel Oakes	100.00	60.00
❑	140 Danny Murphy	100.00	60.00
❑	141 Cy Barger	100.00	60.00
❑	142 Eugene Packard	100.00	60.00
❑	143 Jake Daubert	100.00	60.00
❑	144 James C. Walsh	100.00	60.00
❑	145 Ted Cather	125.00	75.00
❑	146 George Tyler	125.00	75.00
❑	147 Lee Magee	125.00	75.00
❑	148 Owen Wilson	125.00	75.00
❑	149 Hal Janvrin	125.00	75.00
❑	150 Doc Johnston	125.00	75.00
❑	151 George Whitted	125.00	75.00
❑	152 George McQuillen	125.00	75.00
❑	153 Bill James	125.00	75.00
❑	154 Dick Rudolph	125.00	75.00
❑	155 Joe Connolly	125.00	75.00
❑	156 Jean Dubuc	125.00	75.00
❑	157 George Kaiserling	125.00	75.00
❑	158 Fritz Maisel	125.00	75.00
❑	159 Heinie Groh	125.00	75.00
❑	160 Benny Kauff	125.00	75.00
❑	161 Edd Roush	300.00	175.00
❑	162 George Stallings MG	125.00	75.00
❑	163 Bert Whaling	125.00	75.00
❑	164 Bob Shawkey	125.00	75.00
❑	165 Eddie Murphy	125.00	75.00
❑	166 Joe Bush	125.00	75.00
❑	167 Clark Griffith	300.00	175.00
❑	168 Vin Campbell	125.00	75.00
❑	169 Raymond Collins	125.00	75.00
❑	170 Hans Lobert	125.00	75.00
❑	171 Earl Hamilton	125.00	75.00
❑	172 Erskine Mayer	125.00	75.00
❑	173 Tilly Walker	125.00	75.00
❑	174 Robert Veach	125.00	75.00
❑	175 Joseph Benz	125.00	75.00
❑	176 Hippo Vaughn	175.00	100.00

1981 Donruss

❑	COMPLETE SET (605)	40.00	15.00
❑	1 Ozzie Smith	3.00	1.25
❑	2 Rollie Fingers	.25	.08
❑	3 Rick Wise	.10	.02
❑	4 Gene Richards	.10	.02
❑	5 Alan Trammell	.50	.20
❑	6 Tom Brookens	.10	.02
❑	7A Duffy Dyer P1	.25	.08
❑	7B Duffy Dyer P2	.10	.02
❑	8 Mark Fidrych	.25	.08
❑	9 Dave Rozema	.10	.02
❑	10 Ricky Peters RC	.10	.02
❑	11 Mike Schmidt	2.50	1.00
❑	12 Willie Stargell	.50	.20
❑	13 Tim Foli	.10	.02
❑	14 Manny Sanguillen	.25	.08
❑	15 Grant Jackson	.10	.02
❑	16 Eddie Solomon	.10	.02
❑	17 Omar Moreno	.10	.02
❑	18 Joe Morgan	.50	.20
❑	19 Rafael Landestoy	.10	.02
❑	20 Bruce Bochy	.10	.02
❑	21 Joe Sambito	.10	.02
❑	22 Manny Trillo	.10	.02
❑	23A Dave Smith P1	.50	.20
❑	23B Dave Smith P2 RC	.50	.20
❑	24 Terry Puhl	.10	.02
❑	25 Bump Wills	.10	.02
❑	26A John Ellis P1 ERR	.50	.20
❑	26B John Ellis P2 COR	.25	.08
❑	27 Jim Kern	.10	.02
❑	28 Richie Zisk	.10	.02
❑	29 John Mayberry	.10	.02
❑	30 Bob Davis	.10	.02
❑	31 Jackson Todd	.10	.02
❑	32 Alvis Woods	.10	.02
❑	33 Steve Carlton	.50	.20
❑	34 Lee Mazzilli	.25	.08
❑	35 John Stearns	.10	.02
❑	36 Roy Lee Jackson RC	.10	.02
❑	37 Mike Scott	.25	.08
❑	38 Lamar Johnson	.10	.02
❑	39 Kevin Bell	.10	.02
❑	40 Ed Farmer	.10	.02
❑	41 Ross Baumgarten	.10	.02
❑	42 Leo Sutherland RC	.10	.02
❑	43 Dan Meyer	.10	.02
❑	44 Ron Reed	.10	.02
❑	45 Mario Mendoza	.10	.02
❑	46 Rick Honeycutt	.10	.02
❑	47 Glenn Abbott	.10	.02
❑	48 Leon Roberts	.10	.02
❑	49 Rod Carew	.50	.20
❑	50 Bert Campaneris	.25	.08
❑	51A Tom Donahue P1 ERR	.25	.08
❑	51B Tom Donohue P2 RC	.10	.02
❑	52 Dave Frost	.10	.02
❑	53 Ed Halicki	.10	.02
❑	54 Dan Ford	.10	.02
❑	55 Garry Maddox	.10	.02
❑	56A Steve Garvey P1 25HR	.25	.08
❑	56B Steve Garvey P2 21HR	.25	.08

❑ 57 Bill Russell .25 .08
❑ 58 Don Sutton .25 .08
❑ 59 Reggie Smith .25 .08
❑ 60 Rick Monday .25 .08
❑ 61 Ray Knight .25 .08
❑ 62 Johnny Bench 1.00 .40
❑ 63 Mario Soto .25 .08
❑ 64 Doug Bair .10 .02
❑ 65 George Foster .25 .08
❑ 66 Jeff Burroughs .25 .08
❑ 67 Keith Hernandez .25 .08
❑ 68 Tom Herr .10 .02
❑ 69 Bob Forsch .10 .02
❑ 70 John Fulgham .10 .02
❑ 71A Bobby Bonds P1 ERR 1.00 .40
❑ 71B Bobby Bonds P2 COR .50 .20
❑ 72A Rennie Stennett P1 .25 .08
❑ 72B Rennie Stennett P2 .10 .02
❑ 73 Joe Strain .10 .02
❑ 74 Ed Whitson .10 .02
❑ 75 Tom Griffin .10 .02
❑ 76 Billy North .10 .02
❑ 77 Gene Garber .10 .02
❑ 78 Mike Hargrove .10 .02
❑ 79 Dave Rosello .10 .02
❑ 80 Ron Hassey .10 .02
❑ 81 Sid Monge .10 .02
❑ 82A Joe Charboneau P1 1.00 .40
❑ 82B Joe Charboneau P2 RC 1.00 .40
❑ 83 Cecil Cooper .25 .08
❑ 84 Sal Bando .25 .08
❑ 85 Moose Haas .10 .02
❑ 86 Mike Caldwell .10 .02
❑ 87A Larry Hisle P1 .25 .08
❑ 87B Larry Hisle P2 .10 .02
❑ 88 Luis Gomez .10 .02
❑ 89 Larry Parrish .10 .02
❑ 90 Gary Carter .50 .20
❑ 91 Bill Gullickson RC .50 .20
❑ 92 Fred Norman .10 .02
❑ 93 Tommy Hutton .10 .02
❑ 94 Carl Yastrzemski 1.50 .60
❑ 95 Glenn Hoffman RC .10 .02
❑ 96 Dennis Eckersley .50 .20
❑ 97A Tom Burgmeier P1 .25 .08
❑ 97B Tom Burgmeier P2 .10 .02
❑ 98 Win Remmerswaal RC .10 .02
❑ 99 Bob Horner .25 .08
❑ 100 George Brett 2.50 1.00
❑ 101 Dave Chalk .10 .02
❑ 102 Dennis Leonard .10 .02
❑ 103 Renie Martin .10 .02
❑ 104 Amos Otis .25 .08
❑ 105 Graig Nettles .25 .08
❑ 106 Eric Soderholm .10 .02
❑ 107 Tommy John .25 .08
❑ 108 Tom Underwood .10 .02
❑ 109 Lou Piniella .25 .08
❑ 110 Mickey Klutts .10 .02
❑ 111 Bobby Murcer .25 .08
❑ 112 Eddie Murray 1.50 .60
❑ 113 Rick Dempsey .10 .02
❑ 114 Scott McGregor .10 .02
❑ 115 Ken Singleton .25 .08
❑ 116 Gary Roenicke .10 .02
❑ 117 Dave Revering .10 .02
❑ 118 Mike Norris .10 .02
❑ 119 Rickey Henderson 6.00 2.50
❑ 120 Mike Heath .10 .02
❑ 121 Dave Cash .10 .02
❑ 122 Randy Jones .25 .08
❑ 123 Eric Rasmussen .10 .02
❑ 124 Jerry Mumphrey .10 .02
❑ 125 Richie Hebner .10 .02
❑ 126 Mark Wagner .10 .02
❑ 127 Jack Morris .50 .20
❑ 128 Dan Petry .10 .02
❑ 129 Bruce Robbins .10 .02
❑ 130 Champ Summers .10 .02
❑ 131 Pete Rose 3.00 1.25
❑ 131B Pete Rose P2 2.00 .75
❑ 132 Willie Stargell .50 .20
❑ 133 Ed Ott .10 .02
❑ 134 Jim Bibby .10 .02
❑ 135 Bert Blyleven .25 .08
❑ 136 Dave Parker .25 .08
❑ 137 Bill Robinson .10 .02
❑ 138 Enos Cabell .10 .02
❑ 139 Dave Bergman .10 .02
❑ 140 J.R. Richard .25 .08
❑ 141 Ken Forsch .10 .02
❑ 142 Larry Bowa UER .25 .08
❑ 143 Frank LaCorte UER .10 .02
❑ 144 Denny Walling .10 .02
❑ 145 Buddy Bell .25 .08
❑ 146 Fergie Jenkins .25 .08
❑ 147 Dannny Darwin .25 .08
❑ 148 John Grubb .10 .02
❑ 149 Alfredo Griffin .10 .02
❑ 150 Jerry Garvin .10 .02
❑ 151 Paul Mirabella RC .10 .02
❑ 152 Rick Bosetti .10 .02
❑ 153 Dick Ruthven .10 .02
❑ 154 Frank Taveras .10 .02
❑ 155 Craig Swan .10 .02
❑ 156 Jeff Reardon RC 1.00 .40
❑ 157 Steve Henderson .10 .02
❑ 158 Jim Morrison .10 .02
❑ 159 Glenn Borgmann .10 .02
❑ 160 LaMarr Hoyt RC .50 .20
❑ 161 Rich Wortham .10 .02
❑ 162 Thad Bosley .10 .02
❑ 163 Julio Cruz .10 .02
❑ 164A Del Unser P1 .25 .08
❑ 164B Del Unser P2 .10 .02
❑ 165 Jim Anderson .10 .02
❑ 166 Jim Beattie .10 .02
❑ 167 Shane Rawley .10 .02
❑ 168 Joe Simpson .10 .02
❑ 169 Rod Carew .50 .20
❑ 170 Fred Patek .10 .02
❑ 171 Frank Tanana .25 .08
❑ 172 Alfredo Martinez RC .10 .02
❑ 173 Chris Knapp .10 .02
❑ 174 Joe Rudi .25 .08
❑ 175 Greg Luzinski .25 .08
❑ 176 Steve Garvey .50 .20
❑ 177 Joe Ferguson .10 .02
❑ 178 Bob Welch .25 .08
❑ 179 Dusty Baker .25 .08
❑ 180 Rudy Law .10 .02
❑ 181 Dave Concepcion .25 .08
❑ 182 Johnny Bench 1.00 .40
❑ 183 Mike LaCoss .10 .02
❑ 184 Ken Griffey .25 .08
❑ 185 Dave Collins .10 .02
❑ 186 Brian Asselstine .10 .02
❑ 187 Garry Templeton .25 .08
❑ 188 Mike Phillips .10 .02
❑ 189 Pete Vuckovich .10 .02
❑ 190 John Urrea .10 .02
❑ 191 Tony Scott .10 .02
❑ 192 Darrell Evans .25 .08
❑ 193 Milt May .10 .02
❑ 194 Bob Knepper .10 .02
❑ 195 Randy Moffitt .10 .02
❑ 196 Larry Herndon .10 .02
❑ 197 Rick Camp .10 .02
❑ 198 Andre Thornton .25 .08
❑ 199 Tom Veryzer .10 .02
❑ 200 Gary Alexander .10 .02
❑ 201 Rick Waits .10 .02
❑ 202 Rick Manning .10 .02
❑ 203 Paul Molitor 1.00 .40
❑ 204 Jim Gantner .10 .02
❑ 205 Paul Mitchell .10 .02
❑ 206 Reggie Cleveland .10 .02
❑ 207 Sixto Lezcano .10 .02
❑ 208 Bruce Benedict .10 .02
❑ 209 Rodney Scott .10 .02
❑ 210 John Tamargo .10 .02
❑ 211 Bill Lee .25 .08
❑ 212 Andre Dawson .50 .20
❑ 213 Rowland Office .10 .02
❑ 214 Carl Yastrzemski 1.50 .60
❑ 215 Jerry Remy .10 .02
❑ 216 Mike Torrez .10 .02
❑ 217 Skip Lockwood .10 .02
❑ 218 Fred Lynn .25 .08
❑ 219 Chris Chambliss .25 .08
❑ 220 Willie Aikens .10 .02
❑ 221 John Wathan .10 .02
❑ 222 Dan Quisenberry .10 .02
❑ 223 Willie Wilson .25 .08
❑ 224 Clint Hurdle .10 .02
❑ 225 Bob Watson .10 .02
❑ 226 Jim Spencer .10 .02
❑ 227 Ron Guidry .25 .08
❑ 228 Reggie Jackson 1.00 .40
❑ 229 Oscar Gamble .10 .02
❑ 230 Jeff Cox RC .10 .02
❑ 231 Luis Tiant .25 .08
❑ 232 Rich Dauer .10 .02
❑ 233 Dan Graham .10 .02
❑ 234 Mike Flanagan .10 .02
❑ 235 John Lowenstein .10 .02
❑ 236 Benny Ayala .10 .02
❑ 237 Wayne Gross .10 .02
❑ 238 Rick Langford .10 .02
❑ 239 Tony Armas .25 .08
❑ 240A Bob Lacy P1 ERR .50 .20
❑ 240B Bob Lacey P2 COR .10 .02
❑ 241 Gene Tenace .25 .08
❑ 242 Bob Shirley .10 .02
❑ 243 Gary Lucas RC .10 .02
❑ 244 Jerry Turner .10 .02
❑ 245 John Wockenfuss .10 .02
❑ 246 Stan Papi .10 .02
❑ 247 Milt Wilcox .10 .02
❑ 248 Dan Schatzeder .10 .02
❑ 249 Steve Kemp .10 .02
❑ 250 Jim Lentine RC .10 .02
❑ 251 Pete Rose 3.00 1.25
❑ 252 Bill Madlock .25 .08
❑ 253 Dale Berra .10 .02
❑ 254 Kent Tekulve .10 .02
❑ 255 Enrique Romo .10 .02
❑ 256 Mike Easler .10 .02
❑ 257 Chuck Tanner MG .10 .02
❑ 258 Art Howe .10 .02
❑ 259 Alan Ashby .10 .02
❑ 260 Nolan Ryan 5.00 2.00
❑ 261A Vern Ruhle P1 ERR .50 .20
❑ 261B Vern Ruhle P2 COR .25 .08
❑ 262 Bob Boone .25 .08
❑ 263 Cesar Cedeno .25 .08
❑ 264 Jeff Leonard .25 .08
❑ 265 Pat Putnam .10 .02
❑ 266 Jon Matlack .10 .02
❑ 267 Dave Rajsich .10 .02
❑ 268 Billy Sample .10 .02
❑ 269 Damaso Garcia RC .10 .02
❑ 270 Tom Buskey .10 .02
❑ 271 Joey McLaughlin .10 .02
❑ 272 Barry Bonnell .10 .02
❑ 273 Tug McGraw .25 .08
❑ 274 Mike Jorgensen .10 .02
❑ 275 Pat Zachry .10 .02
❑ 276 Neil Allen .10 .02
❑ 277 Joel Youngblood .10 .02
❑ 278 Greg Pryor .10 .02
❑ 279 Britt Burns RC .10 .02
❑ 280 Rich Dotson RC .10 .02
❑ 281 Chet Lemon .25 .08
❑ 282 Rusty Kuntz RC .10 .02
❑ 283 Ted Cox .10 .02
❑ 284 Sparky Lyle .25 .08
❑ 285 Larry Cox .10 .02
❑ 286 Floyd Bannister .10 .02
❑ 287 Byron McLaughlin .10 .02
❑ 288 Rodney Craig .10 .02
❑ 289 Bobby Grich .25 .08
❑ 290 Dickie Thon .10 .02
❑ 291 Mark Clear .10 .02
❑ 292 Dave Lemanczyk .10 .02
❑ 293 Jason Thompson .10 .02
❑ 294 Rick Miller .10 .02
❑ 295 Lonnie Smith .25 .08
❑ 296 Ron Cey .25 .08
❑ 297 Steve Yeager .25 .08
❑ 298 Bobby Castillo .10 .02
❑ 299 Manny Mota .25 .08
❑ 300 Jay Johnstone .10 .02
❑ 301 Dan Driessen .10 .02
❑ 302 Joe Nolan RC .10 .02
❑ 303 Paul Householder RC .10 .02
❑ 304 Harry Spilman .10 .02
❑ 305 Cesar Geronimo .10 .02

❑ 306A Gary Mathews P1 ERR	.50	.20
❑ 306B Gary Matthews P2 COR	.25	.08
❑ 307 Ken Reitz	.10	.02
❑ 308 Ted Simmons	.25	.08
❑ 309 John Littlefield RC	.10	.02
❑ 310 George Frazier	.10	.02
❑ 311 Dane Iorg	.10	.02
❑ 312 Mike Ivie	.10	.02
❑ 313 Dennis Littlejohn	.10	.02
❑ 314 Gary Lavelle	.10	.02
❑ 315 Jack Clark	.25	.08
❑ 316 Jim Wohlford	.10	.02
❑ 317 Rick Matula	.10	.02
❑ 318 Toby Harrah	.25	.08
❑ 319A Dwane Kuiper P1 ERR	.25	.08
❑ 319B Duane Kuiper P2 COR	.10	.02
❑ 320 Len Barker	.25	.08
❑ 321 Victor Cruz	.10	.02
❑ 322 Dell Alston	.10	.02
❑ 323 Robin Yount	1.50	.60
❑ 324 Charlie Moore	.10	.02
❑ 325 Lary Sorensen	.10	.02
❑ 326A Gorman Thomas P1	.50	.20
❑ 326B Gorman Thomas P2	.25	.08
❑ 327 Bob Rodgers MG	.10	.02
❑ 328 Phil Niekro	.25	.08
❑ 329 Chris Speier	.10	.02
❑ 330A Steve Rodgers P1	.25	.08
❑ 330B Steve Rogers P2 COR	.25	.08
❑ 331 Woodie Fryman	.10	.02
❑ 332 Warren Cromartie	.10	.02
❑ 333 Jerry White	.10	.02
❑ 334 Tony Perez	.50	.20
❑ 335 Carlton Fisk	.50	.20
❑ 336 Dick Drago	.10	.02
❑ 337 Steve Renko	.10	.02
❑ 338 Jim Rice	.25	.08
❑ 339 Jerry Royster	.10	.02
❑ 340 Frank White	.25	.08
❑ 341 Jamie Quirk	.10	.02
❑ 342A Paul Spittorff P1 ERR	.25	.08
❑ 342B Paul Splittorff P2 COR	.10	.02
❑ 343 Marty Pattin	.10	.02
❑ 344 Pete LaCock	.10	.02
❑ 345 Willie Randolph	.25	.08
❑ 346 Rick Cerone	.10	.02
❑ 347 Rich Gossage	.25	.08
❑ 348 Reggie Jackson	1.00	.40
❑ 349 Ruppert Jones	.10	.02
❑ 350 Dave McKay RC	.10	.02
❑ 351 Yogi Berra CO	1.00	.40
❑ 352 Doug DeCinces	.10	.02
❑ 353 Jim Palmer	.50	.20
❑ 354 Tippy Martinez	.10	.02
❑ 355 Al Bumbry	.10	.02
❑ 356 Earl Weaver MG	.25	.08
❑ 357A Bob Picciolo P1 ERR	.25	.08
❑ 357B Rob Picciolo P2 COR	.10	.02
❑ 358 Matt Keough	.10	.02
❑ 359 Dwayne Murphy	.10	.02
❑ 360 Brian Kingman	.10	.02
❑ 361 Bill Fahey	.10	.02
❑ 362 Steve Mura	.10	.02
❑ 363 Dennis Kinney RC	.10	.02
❑ 364 Dave Winfield	.50	.20
❑ 365 Lou Whitaker	.50	.20
❑ 366 Lance Parrish	.25	.08
❑ 367 Tim Corcoran	.10	.02
❑ 368 Pat Underwood	.10	.02
❑ 369 Al Cowens	.10	.02
❑ 370 Sparky Anderson MG	.25	.08
❑ 371 Pete Rose	3.00	1.25
❑ 372 Phil Garner	.25	.08
❑ 373 Steve Nicosia	.10	.02
❑ 374 John Candelaria	.25	.08
❑ 375 Don Robinson	.10	.02
❑ 376 Lee Lacy	.10	.02
❑ 377 John Milner	.10	.02
❑ 378 Craig Reynolds	.10	.02
❑ 379A Luis Pujois P1 ERR	.25	.08
❑ 379B Luis Pujols P2 COR	.10	.02
❑ 380 Joe Niekro	.10	.02
❑ 381 Joaquin Andujar	.25	.08
❑ 382 Keith Moreland RC	.10	.02
❑ 383 Jose Cruz	.25	.08
❑ 384 Bill Virdon MG	.10	.02
❑ 385 Jim Sundberg	.25	.08
❑ 386 Doc Medich	.10	.02
❑ 387 Al Oliver	.25	.08
❑ 388 Jim Norris	.10	.02
❑ 389 Bob Bailor	.10	.02
❑ 390 Ernie Whitt	.10	.02
❑ 391 Otto Velez	.10	.02
❑ 392 Roy Howell	.10	.02
❑ 393 Bob Walk RC	.50	.20
❑ 394 Doug Flynn	.10	.02
❑ 395 Pete Falcone	.10	.02
❑ 396 Tom Hausman	.10	.02
❑ 397 Elliott Maddox	.10	.02
❑ 398 Mike Squires	.10	.02
❑ 399 Marvis Foley RC	.10	.02
❑ 400 Steve Trout	.10	.02
❑ 401 Wayne Nordhagen	.10	.02
❑ 402 Tony LaRussa MG	.25	.08
❑ 403 Bruce Bochte	.10	.02
❑ 404 Bake McBride	.25	.08
❑ 405 Jerry Narron	.10	.02
❑ 406 Rob Dressler	.10	.02
❑ 407 Dave Heaverlo	.10	.02
❑ 408 Tom Paciorek	.10	.02
❑ 409 Carney Lansford	.25	.08
❑ 410 Brian Downing	.25	.08
❑ 411 Don Aase	.10	.02
❑ 412 Jim Barr	.10	.02
❑ 413 Don Baylor	.25	.08
❑ 414 Jim Fregosi MG	.10	.02
❑ 415 Dallas Green MG	.10	.02
❑ 416 Dave Lopes	.25	.08
❑ 417 Jerry Reuss	.10	.02
❑ 418 Rick Sutcliffe	.25	.08
❑ 419 Derrel Thomas	.10	.02
❑ 420 Tom Lasorda MG	.50	.20
❑ 421 Charlie Leibrandt RC	.50	.20
❑ 422 Tom Seaver	1.00	.40
❑ 423 Ron Oester	.10	.02
❑ 424 Junior Kennedy	.10	.02
❑ 425 Tom Seaver	1.00	.40
❑ 426 Bobby Cox MG	.25	.08
❑ 427 Leon Durham RC	.50	.20
❑ 428 Terry Kennedy	.10	.02
❑ 429 Silvio Martinez	.10	.02
❑ 430 George Hendrick	.25	.08
❑ 431 Red Schoendienst MG	.50	.20
❑ 432 Johnnie LeMaster	.10	.02
❑ 433 Vida Blue	.25	.08
❑ 434 John Montefusco	.10	.02
❑ 435 Terry Whitfield	.10	.02
❑ 436 Dave Bristol MG	.10	.02
❑ 437 Dale Murphy	.50	.20
❑ 438 Jerry Dybzinski RC	.10	.02
❑ 439 Jorge Orta	.10	.02
❑ 440 Wayne Garland	.10	.02
❑ 441 Miguel Dilone	.10	.02
❑ 442 Dave Garcia MG	.10	.02
❑ 443 Don Money	.10	.02
❑ 444A Buck Martinez P1 ERR	.25	.08
❑ 444B Buck Martinez P2 COR	.10	.02
❑ 445 Jerry Augustine	.10	.02
❑ 446 Ben Oglivie	.25	.08
❑ 447 Jim Slaton	.10	.02
❑ 448 Doyle Alexander	.10	.02
❑ 449 Tony Bernazard	.10	.02
❑ 450 Scott Sanderson	.10	.02
❑ 451 David Palmer	.10	.02
❑ 452 Stan Bahnsen	.10	.02
❑ 453 Dick Williams MG	.10	.02
❑ 454 Rick Burleson	.10	.02
❑ 455 Gary Allenson	.10	.02
❑ 456 Bob Stanley	.10	.02
❑ 457A John Tudor ERR	1.00	.40
❑ 457B John Tudor RC	1.00	.40
❑ 458 Dwight Evans	.50	.20
❑ 459 Glenn Hubbard	.10	.02
❑ 460 U.L. Washington	.10	.02
❑ 461 Larry Gura	.10	.02
❑ 462 Rich Gale	.10	.02
❑ 463 Hal McRae	.25	.08
❑ 464 Jim Frey MG RC	.10	.02
❑ 465 Bucky Dent	.25	.08
❑ 466 Dennis Werth RC	.10	.02
❑ 467 Ron Davis	.10	.02
❑ 468 Reggie Jackson	1.00	.40
❑ 469 Bobby Brown	.10	.02
❑ 470 Mike Davis RC	.50	.20
❑ 471 Gaylord Perry	.25	.08
❑ 472 Mark Belanger	.10	.02
❑ 473 Jim Palmer	.50	.20
❑ 474 Sammy Stewart	.10	.02
❑ 475 Tim Stoddard	.10	.02
❑ 476 Steve Stone	.10	.02
❑ 477 Jeff Newman	.10	.02
❑ 478 Steve McCatty	.10	.02
❑ 479 Billy Martin MG	.50	.20
❑ 480 Mitchell Page	.10	.02
❑ 481 Steve Carlton CY	.25	.08
❑ 482 Bill Buckner	.25	.08
❑ 483A Ivan DeJesus P1 ERR	.25	.08
❑ 483B Ivan DeJesus P2 COR	.10	.02
❑ 484 Cliff Johnson	.10	.02
❑ 485 Lenny Randle	.10	.02
❑ 486 Larry Milbourne	.10	.02
❑ 487 Roy Smalley	.10	.02
❑ 488 John Castino	.10	.02
❑ 489 Ron Jackson	.10	.02
❑ 490A Dave Roberts P1	.25	.08
❑ 490B Dave Roberts P2	.10	.02
❑ 491 George Brett MVP	1.50	.60
❑ 492 Mike Cubbage	.10	.02
❑ 493 Rob Wilfong	.10	.02
❑ 494 Danny Goodwin	.10	.02
❑ 495 Jose Morales	.10	.02
❑ 496 Mickey Rivers	.10	.02
❑ 497 Mike Edwards	.10	.02
❑ 498 Mike Sadek	.10	.02
❑ 499 Lenn Sakata	.10	.02
❑ 500 Gene Michael MG	.10	.02
❑ 501 Dave Roberts	.10	.02
❑ 502 Steve Dillard	.10	.02
❑ 503 Jim Essian	.10	.02
❑ 504 Rance Mulliniks	.10	.02
❑ 505 Darrell Porter	.10	.02
❑ 506 Joe Torre MG	.25	.08
❑ 507 Terry Crowley	.10	.02
❑ 508 Bill Travers	.10	.02
❑ 509 Nelson Norman	.10	.02
❑ 510 Bob McClure	.10	.02
❑ 511 Steve Howe RC	.50	.20
❑ 512 Dave Rader	.10	.02
❑ 513 Mick Kelleher	.10	.02
❑ 514 Kiko Garcia	.10	.02
❑ 515 Larry Biittner	.10	.02
❑ 516A Willie Norwood P1	.25	.08
❑ 516B Willie Norwood P2	.10	.02
❑ 517 Bo Diaz	.10	.02
❑ 518 Juan Beniquez	.10	.02
❑ 519 Scot Thompson	.10	.02
❑ 520 Jim Tracy RC	1.00	.40
❑ 521 Carlos Lezcano RC	.10	.02
❑ 522 Joe Amalfitano MG	.10	.02
❑ 523 Preston Hanna	.10	.02
❑ 524A Ray Burris P1	.25	.08
❑ 524B Ray Burris P2	.10	.02
❑ 525 Broderick Perkins	.10	.02
❑ 526 Mickey Hatcher	.10	.02
❑ 527 John Goryl MG	.10	.02
❑ 528 Dick Davis	.10	.02
❑ 529 Butch Wynegar	.10	.02
❑ 530 Sal Butera RC	.10	.02
❑ 531 Jerry Koosman	.25	.08
❑ 532A Geoff Zahn P1	.25	.08
❑ 532B Geoff Zahn P2	.10	.02
❑ 533 Dennis Martinez	.25	.08
❑ 534 Gary Thomasson	.10	.02
❑ 535 Steve Macko	.10	.02
❑ 536 Jim Kaat	.25	.08
❑ 537 G.Brett/R.Carew	1.50	.60
❑ 538 Tim Raines RC	2.50	1.00
❑ 539 Keith Smith	.10	.02
❑ 540 Ken Macha	.10	.02
❑ 541 Burt Hooton	.10	.02
❑ 542 Butch Hobson	.10	.02
❑ 543 Bill Stein	.10	.02
❑ 544 Dave Stapleton RC	.10	.02
❑ 545 Bob Pate RC	.10	.02
❑ 546 Doug Corbett RC	.10	.02
❑ 547 Darrell Jackson	.10	.02
❑ 548 Pete Redfern	.10	.02
❑ 549 Roger Erickson	.10	.02

❑ 550 Al Hrabosky	.25	.08
❑ 551 Dick Tidrow	.10	.02
❑ 552 Dave Ford RC	.10	.02
❑ 553 Dave Kingman	.25	.08
❑ 554A Mike Vail P1	.25	.08
❑ 554B Mike Vail P2	.10	.02
❑ 555A Jerry Martin P1	.25	.08
❑ 555B Jerry Martin P2	.10	.02
❑ 556A Jesus Figueroa P1	.25	.08
❑ 556B Jesus Figueroa P2 RC	.10	.02
❑ 557 Don Stanhouse	.10	.02
❑ 558 Barry Foote	.10	.02
❑ 559 Tim Blackwell	.10	.02
❑ 560 Bruce Sutter	.50	.20
❑ 561 Rick Reuschel	.25	.08
❑ 562 Lynn McGlothen	.10	.02
❑ 563A Bob Owchinko P1	.25	.08
❑ 563B Bob Owchinko P2	.10	.02
❑ 564 John Verhoeven	.10	.02
❑ 565 Ken Landreaux	.10	.02
❑ 566A Glen Adams P1 ERR	.25	.08
❑ 566B Glenn Adams P2 COR	.10	.02
❑ 567 Hosken Powell	.10	.02
❑ 568 Dick Noles	.10	.02
❑ 569 Danny Ainge RC	3.00	1.25
❑ 570 Bobby Mattick MG RC	.10	.02
❑ 571 Joe Lefebvre RC	.10	.02
❑ 572 Bobby Clark	.10	.02
❑ 573 Dennis Lamp	.10	.02
❑ 574 Randy Lerch	.10	.02
❑ 575 Mookie Wilson RC	3.00	1.25
❑ 576 Ron LeFlore	.25	.08
❑ 577 Jim Dwyer	.10	.02
❑ 578 Bill Castro	.10	.02
❑ 579 Greg Minton	.10	.02
❑ 580 Mark Littell	.10	.02
❑ 581 Andy Hassler	.10	.02
❑ 582 Dave Stieb	.25	.08
❑ 583 Ken Oberkfell	.10	.02
❑ 584 Larry Bradford	.10	.02
❑ 585 Fred Stanley	.10	.02
❑ 586 Bill Caudill	.10	.02
❑ 587 Doug Capilla	.10	.02
❑ 588 George Riley RC	.10	.02
❑ 589 Willie Hernandez	.10	.02
❑ 590 Mike Schmidt MVP	2.50	1.00
❑ 591 Steve Stone CY	.10	.02
❑ 592 Rick Sofield	.10	.02
❑ 593 Bombo Rivera	.10	.02
❑ 594 Gary Ward	.10	.02
❑ 595A Dave Edwards P1	.25	.08
❑ 595B Dave Edwards P2	.10	.02
❑ 596 Mike Proly	.10	.02
❑ 597 Tommy Boggs	.10	.02
❑ 598 Greg Gross	.10	.02
❑ 599 Elias Sosa	.10	.02
❑ 600 Pat Kelly	.10	.02
❑ 601A Checklist 1-120 P1	.25	.08
❑ 601B Checklist 1-120 P2	.50	.20
❑ 602 Checklist 121-240 NNO	.25	.08
❑ 603A Checklist 241-360 P1	.25	.08
❑ 603B Checklist 241-360 P2	.25	.08
❑ 604A Checklist 361-480 P1	.25	.08
❑ 604B Checklist 361-480 P2	.25	.08
❑ 605A Checklist 481-600 P1	.25	.08
❑ 605B Checklist 481-600 P2	.25	.08

1982 Donruss

❑ COMPLETE SET (660)	60.00	30.00
❑ COMP.FACT.SET (660)	60.00	30.00
❑ COMP.RUTH PUZZLE	10.00	5.00
❑ 1 Pete Rose DK	2.50	1.00
❑ 2 Gary Carter DK	.20	.07
❑ 3 Steve Garvey DK	.20	.07
❑ 4 Vida Blue DK	.20	.07
❑ 5 Alan Trammell DK	.20	.07
❑ 5A Alan Trammel DK ERR	.20	.07
❑ 6 Len Barker DK	.10	.02
❑ 7 Dwight Evans DK	.40	.15
❑ 8 Rod Carew DK	.40	.15
❑ 9 George Hendrick DK	.20	.07
❑ 10 Phil Niekro DK	.20	.07
❑ 11 Richie Zisk DK	.10	.02
❑ 12 Dave Parker DK	.20	.07
❑ 13 Nolan Ryan DK	4.00	1.50
❑ 14 Ivan DeJesus DK	.10	.02
❑ 15 George Brett DK	2.00	.75
❑ 16 Tom Seaver DK	.40	.15
❑ 17 Dave Kingman DK	.20	.07
❑ 18 Dave Winfield DK	.20	.07
❑ 19 Mike Norris DK	.10	.02
❑ 20 Carlton Fisk DK	.40	.15
❑ 21 Ozzie Smith DK	1.50	.60
❑ 22 Roy Smalley DK	.10	.02
❑ 23 Buddy Bell DK	.20	.07
❑ 24 Ken Singleton DK	.20	.07
❑ 25 John Mayberry DK	.10	.02
❑ 26 Gorman Thomas DK	.20	.07
❑ 27 Earl Weaver MG	.20	.07
❑ 28 Rollie Fingers	.20	.07
❑ 29 Sparky Anderson MG	.20	.07
❑ 30 Dennis Eckersley	.40	.15
❑ 31 Dave Winfield	.20	.07
❑ 32 Burt Hooton	.10	.02
❑ 33 Rick Waits	.10	.02
❑ 34 George Brett	2.00	.75
❑ 35 Steve McCatty	.10	.02
❑ 36 Steve Rogers	.20	.07
❑ 37 Bill Stein	.10	.02
❑ 38 Steve Renko	.10	.02
❑ 39 Mike Squires	.10	.02
❑ 40 George Hendrick	.20	.07
❑ 41 Bob Knepper	.10	.02
❑ 42 Steve Carlton	.40	.15
❑ 43 Larry Biittner	.10	.02
❑ 44 Chris Welsh	.10	.02
❑ 45 Steve Nicosia	.10	.02
❑ 46 Jack Clark	.20	.07
❑ 47 Chris Chambliss	.20	.07
❑ 48 Ivan DeJesus	.10	.02
❑ 49 Lee Mazzilli	.20	.07
❑ 50 Julio Cruz	.10	.02
❑ 51 Pete Redfern	.10	.02
❑ 52 Dave Stieb	.20	.07
❑ 53 Doug Corbett	.10	.02
❑ 54 George Bell RC	1.00	.40
❑ 55 Joe Simpson	.10	.02
❑ 56 Rusty Staub	.20	.07
❑ 57 Hector Cruz	.10	.02
❑ 58 Claudell Washington	.10	.02
❑ 59 Enrique Romo	.10	.02
❑ 60 Gary Lavelle	.10	.02
❑ 61 Tim Flannery	.10	.02
❑ 62 Joe Nolan	.10	.02
❑ 63 Larry Bowa	.20	.07
❑ 64 Sixto Lezcano	.10	.02
❑ 65 Joe Sambito	.10	.02
❑ 66 Bruce Kison	.10	.02
❑ 67 Wayne Nordhagen	.10	.02
❑ 68 Woodie Fryman	.10	.02
❑ 69 Billy Sample	.10	.02
❑ 70 Amos Otis	.20	.07
❑ 71 Matt Keough	.10	.02
❑ 72 Toby Harrah	.20	.07
❑ 73 Dave Righetti RC	1.50	.60
❑ 74 Carl Yastrzemski	1.25	.50
❑ 75 Bob Welch	.20	.07
❑ 76 Alan Trammell	.20	.07
❑ 76A Alan Trammel ERR	.20	.07
❑ 77 Rick Dempsey	.10	.02
❑ 78 Paul Molitor	.20	.07
❑ 79 Dennis Martinez	.20	.07
❑ 80 Jim Slaton	.10	.02
❑ 81 Champ Summers	.10	.02
❑ 82 Carney Lansford	.20	.07
❑ 83 Barry Foote	.10	.02
❑ 84 Steve Garvey	.20	.07
❑ 85 Rick Manning	.10	.02
❑ 86 John Wathan	.10	.02
❑ 87 Brian Kingman	.10	.02
❑ 88 Andre Dawson	.20	.07
❑ 89 Jim Kern	.10	.02
❑ 90 Bobby Grich	.20	.07
❑ 91 Bob Forsch	.10	.02
❑ 92 Art Howe	.10	.02
❑ 93 Marty Bystrom	.10	.02
❑ 94 Ozzie Smith	1.50	.60
❑ 95 Dave Parker	.20	.07
❑ 96 Doyle Alexander	.10	.02
❑ 97 Al Hrabosky	.10	.02
❑ 98 Frank Taveras	.10	.02
❑ 99 Tim Blackwell	.10	.02
❑ 100 Floyd Bannister	.10	.02
❑ 101 Alfredo Griffin	.10	.02
❑ 102 Dave Engle	.10	.02
❑ 103 Mario Soto	.20	.07
❑ 104 Ross Baumgarten	.10	.02
❑ 105 Ken Singleton	.20	.07
❑ 106 Ted Simmons	.20	.07
❑ 107 Jack Morris	.20	.07
❑ 108 Bob Watson	.10	.02
❑ 109 Dwight Evans	.40	.15
❑ 110 Tom Lasorda MG	.40	.15
❑ 111 Bert Blyleven	.20	.07
❑ 112 Dan Quisenberry	.10	.02
❑ 113 Rickey Henderson	2.50	1.00
❑ 114 Gary Carter	.20	.07
❑ 115 Brian Downing	.20	.07
❑ 116 Al Oliver	.20	.07
❑ 117 LaMarr Hoyt	.10	.02
❑ 118 Cesar Cedeno	.20	.07
❑ 119 Keith Moreland	.10	.02
❑ 120 Bob Shirley	.10	.02
❑ 121 Terry Kennedy	.10	.02
❑ 122 Frank Pastore	.10	.02
❑ 123 Gene Garber	.10	.02
❑ 124 Tony Pena	.20	.07
❑ 125 Allen Ripley	.10	.02
❑ 126 Randy Martz	.10	.02
❑ 127 Richie Zisk	.10	.02
❑ 128 Mike Scott	.20	.07
❑ 129 Lloyd Moseby	.10	.02
❑ 130 Rob Wilfong	.10	.02
❑ 131 Tim Stoddard	.10	.02
❑ 132 Gorman Thomas	.20	.07
❑ 133 Dan Petry	.10	.02
❑ 134 Bob Stanley	.10	.02
❑ 135 Lou Piniella	.20	.07
❑ 136 Pedro Guerrero	.20	.07
❑ 137 Len Barker	.10	.02
❑ 138 Rich Gale	.10	.02
❑ 139 Wayne Gross	.10	.02
❑ 140 Tim Wallach RC	1.00	.40
❑ 141 Gene Mauch MG	.10	.02
❑ 142 Doc Medich	.10	.02
❑ 143 Tony Bernazard	.10	.02
❑ 144 Bill Virdon MG	.10	.02
❑ 145 John Littlefield	.10	.02
❑ 146 Dave Bergman	.10	.02
❑ 147 Dick Davis	.10	.02
❑ 148 Tom Seaver	.75	.30
❑ 149 Matt Sinatro	.10	.02
❑ 150 Chuck Tanner MG	.10	.02
❑ 151 Leon Durham	.10	.02
❑ 152 Gene Tenace	.20	.07
❑ 153 Al Bumbry	.10	.02
❑ 154 Mark Brouhard	.10	.02
❑ 155 Rick Peters	.10	.02
❑ 156 Jerry Remy	.10	.02
❑ 157 Rick Reuschel	.20	.07
❑ 158 Steve Howe	.10	.02
❑ 159 Alan Bannister	.10	.02
❑ 160 U.L. Washington	.10	.02
❑ 161 Rick Langford	.10	.02
❑ 162 Bill Gullickson	.10	.02
❑ 163 Mark Wagner	.10	.02
❑ 164 Geoff Zahn	.10	.02
❑ 165 Ron LeFlore	.20	.07
❑ 166 Dane Iorg	.10	.02
❑ 167 Joe Niekro	.10	.02

❑ 168 Pete Rose	2.50	1.00
❑ 169 Dave Collins	.10	.02
❑ 170 Rick Wise	.10	.02
❑ 171 Jim Bibby	.10	.02
❑ 172 Larry Herndon	.10	.02
❑ 173 Bob Horner	.20	.07
❑ 174 Steve Dillard	.10	.02
❑ 175 Mookie Wilson	.20	.07
❑ 176 Dan Meyer	.10	.02
❑ 177 Fernando Arroyo	.10	.02
❑ 178 Jackson Todd	.10	.02
❑ 179 Darrell Jackson	.10	.02
❑ 180 Alvis Woods	.10	.02
❑ 181 Jim Anderson	.10	.02
❑ 182 Dave Kingman	.20	.07
❑ 183 Steve Henderson	.10	.02
❑ 184 Brian Asselstine	.10	.02
❑ 185 Rod Scurry	.10	.02
❑ 186 Fred Breining	.10	.02
❑ 187 Danny Boone	.10	.02
❑ 188 Junior Kennedy	.10	.02
❑ 189 Sparky Lyle	.20	.07
❑ 190 Whitey Herzog MG	.20	.07
❑ 191 Dave Smith	.10	.02
❑ 192 Ed Ott	.10	.02
❑ 193 Greg Luzinski	.20	.07
❑ 194 Bill Lee	.20	.07
❑ 195 Don Zimmer MG	.20	.07
❑ 196 Hal McRae	.20	.07
❑ 197 Mike Norris	.10	.02
❑ 198 Duane Kuiper	.10	.02
❑ 199 Rick Cerone	.10	.02
❑ 200 Jim Rice	.20	.07
❑ 201 Steve Yeager	.20	.07
❑ 202 Tom Brookens	.10	.02
❑ 203 Jose Morales	.10	.02
❑ 204 Roy Howell	.10	.02
❑ 205 Tippy Martinez	.10	.02
❑ 206 Moose Haas	.10	.02
❑ 207 Al Cowens	.10	.02
❑ 208 Dave Stapleton	.10	.02
❑ 209 Bucky Dent	.20	.07
❑ 210 Ron Cey	.20	.07
❑ 211 Jorge Orta	.10	.02
❑ 212 Jamie Quirk	.10	.02
❑ 213 Jeff Jones	.10	.02
❑ 214 Tim Raines	.40	.15
❑ 215 Jon Matlack	.10	.02
❑ 216 Rod Carew	.40	.15
❑ 217 Jim Kaat	.20	.07
❑ 218 Joe Pittman	.10	.02
❑ 219 Larry Christenson	.10	.02
❑ 220 Juan Bonilla RC	.15	.05
❑ 221 Mike Easler	.10	.02
❑ 222 Vida Blue	.20	.07
❑ 223 Rick Camp	.10	.02
❑ 224 Mike Jorgensen	.10	.02
❑ 225 Jody Davis	.10	.02
❑ 226 Mike Parrott	.10	.02
❑ 227 Jim Clancy	.10	.02
❑ 228 Hosken Powell	.10	.02
❑ 229 Tom Hume	.10	.02
❑ 230 Britt Burns	.10	.02
❑ 231 Jim Palmer	.20	.07
❑ 232 Bob Rodgers MG	.10	.02
❑ 233 Milt Wilcox	.10	.02
❑ 234 Dave Revering	.10	.02
❑ 235 Mike Torrez	.10	.02
❑ 236 Robert Castillo	.10	.02
❑ 237 Von Hayes RC	.50	.20
❑ 238 Renie Martin	.10	.02
❑ 239 Dwayne Murphy	.10	.02
❑ 240 Rodney Scott	.10	.02
❑ 241 Fred Patek	.10	.02
❑ 242 Mickey Rivers	.10	.02
❑ 243 Steve Trout	.10	.02
❑ 244 Jose Cruz	.20	.07
❑ 245 Manny Trillo	.10	.02
❑ 246 Lary Sorensen	.10	.02
❑ 247 Dave Edwards	.10	.02
❑ 248 Dan Driessen	.10	.02
❑ 249 Tommy Boggs	.10	.02
❑ 250 Dale Berra	.10	.02
❑ 251 Ed Whitson	.10	.02
❑ 252 Lee Smith RC	2.00	.75
❑ 253 Tom Paciorek	.10	.02
❑ 254 Pat Zachry	.10	.02
❑ 255 Luis Leal	.10	.02
❑ 256 John Castino	.10	.02
❑ 257 Rich Dauer	.10	.02
❑ 258 Cecil Cooper	.20	.07
❑ 259 Dave Rozema	.10	.02
❑ 260 John Tudor	.20	.07
❑ 261 Jerry Mumphrey	.10	.02
❑ 262 Jay Johnstone	.10	.02
❑ 263 Bo Diaz	.10	.02
❑ 264 Dennis Leonard	.10	.02
❑ 265 Jim Spencer	.10	.02
❑ 266 John Milner	.10	.02
❑ 267 Don Aase	.10	.02
❑ 268 Jim Sundberg	.20	.07
❑ 269 Lamar Johnson	.10	.02
❑ 270 Frank LaCorte	.10	.02
❑ 271 Barry Evans	.10	.02
❑ 272 Enos Cabell	.10	.02
❑ 273 Del Unser	.10	.02
❑ 274 George Foster	.20	.07
❑ 275 Brett Butler RC	1.00	.40
❑ 276 Lee Lacy	.10	.02
❑ 277 Ken Reitz	.10	.02
❑ 278 Keith Hernandez	.20	.07
❑ 279 Doug DeCinces	.10	.02
❑ 280 Charlie Moore	.10	.02
❑ 281 Lance Parrish	.20	.07
❑ 282 Ralph Houk MG	.10	.02
❑ 283 Rich Gossage	.20	.07
❑ 284 Jerry Reuss	.10	.02
❑ 285 Mike Stanton	.10	.02
❑ 286 Frank White	.20	.07
❑ 287 Bob Owchinko	.10	.02
❑ 288 Scott Sanderson	.10	.02
❑ 289 Bump Wills	.10	.02
❑ 290 Dave Frost	.10	.02
❑ 291 Chet Lemon	.20	.07
❑ 292 Tito Landrum	.10	.02
❑ 293 Vern Ruhle	.10	.02
❑ 294 Mike Schmidt	2.00	.75
❑ 295 Sam Mejias	.10	.02
❑ 296 Gary Lucas	.10	.02
❑ 297 John Candelaria	.10	.02
❑ 298 Jerry Martin	.10	.02
❑ 299 Dale Murphy	.40	.15
❑ 300 Mike Lum	.10	.02
❑ 301 Tom Hausman	.10	.02
❑ 302 Glenn Abbott	.10	.02
❑ 303 Roger Erickson	.10	.02
❑ 304 Otto Velez	.10	.02
❑ 305 Danny Goodwin	.10	.02
❑ 306 John Mayberry	.10	.02
❑ 307 Lenny Randle	.10	.02
❑ 308 Bob Bailor	.10	.02
❑ 309 Jerry Morales	.10	.02
❑ 310 Rufino Linares	.10	.02
❑ 311 Kent Tekulve	.10	.02
❑ 312 Joe Morgan	.20	.07
❑ 313 John Urrea	.10	.02
❑ 314 Paul Householder	.10	.02
❑ 315 Garry Maddox	.10	.02
❑ 316 Mike Ramsey	.10	.02
❑ 317 Alan Ashby	.10	.02
❑ 318 Bob Clark	.10	.02
❑ 319 Tony LaRussa MG	.20	.07
❑ 320 Charlie Lea	.10	.02
❑ 321 Danny Darwin	.10	.02
❑ 322 Cesar Geronimo	.10	.02
❑ 323 Tom Underwood	.10	.02
❑ 324 Andre Thornton	.10	.02
❑ 325 Rudy May	.10	.02
❑ 326 Frank Tanana	.20	.07
❑ 327 Dave Lopes	.20	.07
❑ 328 Richie Hebner	.10	.02
❑ 329 Mike Flanagan	.10	.02
❑ 330 Mike Caldwell	.10	.02
❑ 331 Scott McGregor	.10	.02
❑ 332 Jerry Augustine	.10	.02
❑ 333 Stan Papi	.10	.02
❑ 334 Rick Miller	.10	.02
❑ 335 Graig Nettles	.20	.07
❑ 336 Dusty Baker	.20	.07
❑ 337 Dave Garcia MG	.10	.02
❑ 338 Larry Gura	.10	.02
❑ 339 Cliff Johnson	.10	.02
❑ 340 Warren Cromartie	.10	.02
❑ 341 Steve Comer	.10	.02
❑ 342 Rick Burleson	.10	.02
❑ 343 John Martin RC	.15	.05
❑ 344 Craig Reynolds	.10	.02
❑ 345 Mike Proly	.10	.02
❑ 346 Ruppert Jones	.10	.02
❑ 347 Omar Moreno	.10	.02
❑ 348 Greg Minton	.10	.02
❑ 349 Rick Mahler	.10	.02
❑ 350 Alex Trevino	.10	.02
❑ 351 Mike Krukow	.10	.02
❑ 352A Shane Rawley ERR (Photo actually Jim Anderson)	.40	.15
❑ 352B Shane Rawley COR	.10	.02
❑ 353 Garth Iorg	.10	.02
❑ 354 Pete Mackanin	.10	.02
❑ 355 Paul Moskau	.10	.02
❑ 356 Richard Dotson	.10	.02
❑ 357 Steve Stone	.10	.02
❑ 358 Larry Hisle	.10	.02
❑ 359 Aurelio Lopez	.10	.02
❑ 360 Oscar Gamble	.10	.02
❑ 361 Tom Burgmeier	.10	.02
❑ 362 Terry Forster	.20	.07
❑ 363 Joe Charboneau	.20	.07
❑ 364 Ken Brett	.10	.02
❑ 365 Tony Armas	.20	.07
❑ 366 Chris Speier	.10	.02
❑ 367 Fred Lynn	.20	.07
❑ 368 Buddy Bell	.20	.07
❑ 369 Jim Essian	.10	.02
❑ 370 Terry Puhl	.10	.02
❑ 371 Greg Gross	.10	.02
❑ 372 Bruce Sutter	.40	.15
❑ 373 Joe Lefebvre	.10	.02
❑ 374 Ray Knight	.20	.07
❑ 375 Bruce Benedict	.10	.02
❑ 376 Tim Foli	.10	.02
❑ 377 Al Holland	.10	.02
❑ 378 Ken Kravec	.10	.02
❑ 379 Jeff Burroughs	.10	.02
❑ 380 Pete Falcone	.10	.02
❑ 381 Ernie Whitt	.10	.02
❑ 382 Brad Havens	.10	.02
❑ 383 Terry Crowley	.10	.02
❑ 384 Don Money	.10	.02
❑ 385 Dan Schatzeder	.10	.02
❑ 386 Gary Allenson	.10	.02
❑ 387 Yogi Berra CO	.75	.30
❑ 388 Ken Landreaux	.10	.02
❑ 389 Mike Hargrove	.10	.02
❑ 390 Darryl Motley	.10	.02
❑ 391 Dave McKay	.10	.02
❑ 392 Stan Bahnsen	.10	.02
❑ 393 Ken Forsch	.10	.02
❑ 394 Mario Mendoza	.10	.02
❑ 395 Jim Morrison	.10	.02
❑ 396 Mike Ivie	.10	.02
❑ 397 Broderick Perkins	.10	.02
❑ 398 Darrell Evans	.20	.07
❑ 399 Ron Reed	.10	.02
❑ 400 Johnny Bench	.75	.30
❑ 401 Steve Bedrosian RC	.50	.20
❑ 402 Bill Robinson	.10	.02
❑ 403 Bill Buckner	.20	.07
❑ 404 Ken Oberkfell	.10	.02
❑ 405 Cal Ripken RC	40.00	15.00
❑ 406 Jim Gantner	.10	.02
❑ 407 Kirk Gibson	.75	.30
❑ 408 Tony Perez	.40	.15
❑ 409 Tommy John	.20	.07
❑ 410 Dave Stewart RC	1.50	.60
❑ 411 Dan Spillner	.10	.02
❑ 412 Willie Aikens	.10	.02
❑ 413 Mike Heath	.10	.02
❑ 414 Ray Burris	.10	.02
❑ 415 Leon Roberts	.10	.02
❑ 416 Mike Witt	.50	.20
❑ 417 Bob Molinaro	.10	.02
❑ 418 Steve Braun	.10	.02
❑ 419 Nolan Ryan	4.00	1.50
❑ 420 Tug McGraw	.20	.07
❑ 421 Dave Concepcion	.20	.07
❑ 422A Juan Eichelberger		

	ERR (Photo actually		
	Gary Lucas	.40	.15
❑ 422B	Juan Eichelberger		
	COR	.10	.02
❑ 423	Rick Rhoden	.10	.02
❑ 424	Frank Robinson MG	.40	.15
❑ 425	Eddie Miller	.10	.02
❑ 426	Bill Caudill	.10	.02
❑ 427	Doug Flynn	.10	.02
❑ 428	Larry Andersen UER		
	(Misspelled Anderson		
	on card	.10	.02
❑ 429	Al Williams	.10	.02
❑ 430	Jerry Garvin	.10	.02
❑ 431	Glenn Adams	.10	.02
❑ 432	Barry Bonnell	.10	.02
❑ 433	Jerry Narron	.10	.02
❑ 434	John Stearns	.10	.02
❑ 435	Mike Tyson	.10	.02
❑ 436	Glenn Hubbard	.10	.02
❑ 437	Eddie Solomon	.10	.02
❑ 438	Jeff Leonard	.10	.02
❑ 439	Randy Bass	.50	.20
❑ 440	Mike LaCoss	.10	.02
❑ 441	Gary Matthews	.20	.07
❑ 442	Mark Littell	.10	.02
❑ 443	Don Sutton	.20	.07
❑ 444	John Harris	.10	.02
❑ 445	Vada Pinson CO	.20	.07
❑ 446	Elias Sosa	.10	.02
❑ 447	Charlie Hough	.20	.07
❑ 448	Willie Wilson	.20	.07
❑ 449	Fred Stanley	.10	.02
❑ 450	Tom Veryzer	.10	.02
❑ 451	Ron Davis	.10	.02
❑ 452	Mark Clear	.10	.02
❑ 453	Bill Russell	.20	.07
❑ 454	Lou Whitaker	.20	.07
❑ 455	Dan Graham	.10	.02
❑ 456	Reggie Cleveland	.10	.02
❑ 457	Sammy Stewart	.10	.02
❑ 458	Pete Vuckovich	.10	.02
❑ 459	John Wockenfuss	.10	.02
❑ 460	Glenn Hoffman	.10	.02
❑ 461	Willie Randolph	.20	.07
❑ 462	Fernando Valenzuela	.75	.30
❑ 463	Ron Hassey	.10	.02
❑ 464	Paul Splittorff	.10	.02
❑ 465	Rob Picciolo	.10	.02
❑ 466	Larry Parrish	.10	.02
❑ 467	Johnny Grubb	.10	.02
❑ 468	Dan Ford	.10	.02
❑ 469	Silvio Martinez	.10	.02
❑ 470	Kiko Garcia	.10	.02
❑ 471	Bob Boone	.20	.07
❑ 472	Luis Salazar	.10	.02
❑ 473	Randy Niemann	.10	.02
❑ 474	Tom Griffin	.10	.02
❑ 475	Phil Niekro	.20	.07
❑ 476	Hubie Brooks	.10	.02
❑ 477	Dick Tidrow	.10	.02
❑ 478	Jim Beattie	.10	.02
❑ 479	Damaso Garcia	.10	.02
❑ 480	Mickey Hatcher	.10	.02
❑ 481	Joe Price	.10	.02
❑ 482	Ed Farmer	.10	.02
❑ 483	Eddie Murray	.75	.30
❑ 484	Ben Oglivie	.20	.07
❑ 485	Kevin Saucier	.10	.02
❑ 486	Bobby Murcer	.20	.07
❑ 487	Bill Campbell	.10	.02
❑ 488	Reggie Smith	.20	.07
❑ 489	Wayne Garland	.10	.02
❑ 490	Jim Wright	.10	.02
❑ 491	Billy Martin MG	.40	.15
❑ 492	Jim Fanning MG	.10	.02
❑ 493	Don Baylor	.20	.07
❑ 494	Rick Honeycutt	.10	.02
❑ 495	Carlton Fisk	.40	.15
❑ 496	Denny Walling	.10	.02
❑ 497	Bake McBride	.20	.07
❑ 498	Darrell Porter	.10	.02
❑ 499	Gene Richards	.10	.02
❑ 500	Ron Oester	.10	.02
❑ 501	Ken Dayley	.10	.02
❑ 502	Jason Thompson	.10	.02
❑ 503	Milt May	.10	.02
❑ 504	Doug Bird	.10	.02
❑ 505	Bruce Bochte	.10	.02
❑ 506	Neil Allen	.10	.02
❑ 507	Joey McLaughlin	.10	.02
❑ 508	Butch Wynegar	.10	.02
❑ 509	Gary Roenicke	.10	.02
❑ 510	Robin Yount	1.25	.50
❑ 511	Dave Tobik	.10	.02
❑ 512	Rich Gedman	.50	.20
❑ 513	Gene Nelson	.10	.02
❑ 514	Rick Monday	.20	.07
❑ 515	Miguel Dilone	.10	.02
❑ 516	Clint Hurdle	.10	.02
❑ 517	Jeff Newman	.10	.02
❑ 518	Grant Jackson	.10	.02
❑ 519	Andy Hassler	.10	.02
❑ 520	Pat Putnam	.10	.02
❑ 521	Greg Pryor	.10	.02
❑ 522	Tony Scott	.10	.02
❑ 523	Steve Mura	.10	.02
❑ 524	Johnnie LeMaster	.10	.02
❑ 525	Dick Ruthven	.10	.02
❑ 526	John McNamara MG	.10	.02
❑ 527	Larry McWilliams	.10	.02
❑ 528	Johnny Ray RC	.50	.20
❑ 529	Pat Tabler	.10	.02
❑ 530	Tom Herr	.10	.02
❑ 531A	SD Chicken ERR	1.00	.40
❑ 531B	SD Chicken COR	1.00	.40
❑ 532	Sal Butera	.10	.02
❑ 533	Mike Griffin	.10	.02
❑ 534	Kelvin Moore	.10	.02
❑ 535	Reggie Jackson	.40	.15
❑ 536	Ed Romero	.10	.02
❑ 537	Derrel Thomas	.10	.02
❑ 538	Mike O'Berry	.10	.02
❑ 539	Jack O'Connor	.10	.02
❑ 540	Bob Ojeda RC	.50	.20
❑ 541	Roy Lee Jackson	.10	.02
❑ 542	Lynn Jones	.10	.02
❑ 543	Gaylord Perry	.20	.07
❑ 544A	Phil Garner ERR		
	(Reverse negative)	.20	.07
❑ 544B	Phil Garner COR	.20	.07
❑ 545	Garry Templeton	.20	.07
❑ 546	Rafael Ramirez	.10	.02
❑ 547	Jeff Reardon	.20	.07
❑ 548	Ron Guidry	.20	.07
❑ 549	Tim Laudner	.10	.02
❑ 550	John Henry Johnson	.10	.02
❑ 551	Chris Bando	.10	.02
❑ 552	Bobby Brown	.10	.02
❑ 553	Larry Bradford	.10	.02
❑ 554	Scott Fletcher RC	.50	.20
❑ 555	Jerry Royster	.10	.02
❑ 556	Shooty Babitt UER		
	(Spelled Babbitt		
	on front)	.10	.02
❑ 557	Kent Hrbek RC	1.00	.40
❑ 558	R.Guidry/T.John	.20	.07
❑ 559	Mark Bomback	.10	.02
❑ 560	Julio Valdez	.10	.02
❑ 561	Buck Martinez	.10	.02
❑ 562	Mike A. Marshall RC	.50	.20
❑ 563	Rennie Stennett	.10	.02
❑ 564	Steve Crawford	.10	.02
❑ 565	Bob Babcock	.10	.02
❑ 566	Johnny Podres CO	.20	.07
❑ 567	Paul Serna	.10	.02
❑ 568	Harold Baines	.20	.07
❑ 569	Dave LaRoche	.10	.02
❑ 570	Lee May	.10	.02
❑ 571	Gary Ward	.10	.02
❑ 572	John Denny	.10	.02
❑ 573	Roy Smalley	.10	.02
❑ 574	Bob Brenly RC	1.00	.40
❑ 575	R.Jackson/D.Winfield	.20	.07
❑ 576	Luis Pujols	.10	.02
❑ 577	Butch Hobson	.10	.02
❑ 578	Harvey Kuenn MG	.10	.02
❑ 579	Cal Ripken Sr. CO	.20	.07
❑ 580	Juan Berenguer	.10	.02
❑ 581	Benny Ayala	.10	.02
❑ 582	Vance Law	.10	.02
❑ 583	Rick Leach	.10	.02
❑ 584	George Frazier	.10	.02
❑ 585	P.Rose/M.Schmidt	1.50	.60
❑ 586	Joe Rudi	.20	.07
❑ 587	Juan Beniquez	.10	.02
❑ 588	Luis DeLeon	.10	.02
❑ 589	Craig Swan	.10	.02
❑ 590	Dave Chalk	.10	.02
❑ 591	Billy Gardner MG	.10	.02
❑ 592	Sal Bando	.20	.07
❑ 593	Bert Campaneris	.20	.07
❑ 594	Steve Kemp	.10	.02
❑ 595A	Randy Lerch ERR		
	(Braves)	.40	.15
❑ 595B	Randy Lerch COR		
	(Brewers)	.10	.02
❑ 596	Bryan Clark RC	.15	.05
❑ 597	Dave Ford	.10	.02
❑ 598	Mike Scioscia	.20	.07
❑ 599	John Lowenstein	.10	.02
❑ 600	Rene Lachemann MG	.10	.02
❑ 601	Mick Kelleher	.10	.02
❑ 602	Ron Jackson	.10	.02
❑ 603	Jerry Koosman	.20	.07
❑ 604	Dave Goltz	.10	.02
❑ 605	Ellis Valentine	.10	.02
❑ 606	Lonnie Smith	.10	.02
❑ 607	Joaquin Andujar	.20	.07
❑ 608	Garry Hancock	.10	.02
❑ 609	Jerry Turner	.10	.02
❑ 610	Bob Bonner	.10	.02
❑ 611	Jim Dwyer	.10	.02
❑ 612	Terry Bulling	.10	.02
❑ 613	Joel Youngblood	.10	.02
❑ 614	Larry Milbourne	.10	.02
❑ 615	Gene Roof UER		
	(Name on front		
	is Phil Roof)	.10	.02
❑ 616	Keith Drumwright	.10	.02
❑ 617	Dave Rosello	.10	.02
❑ 618	Rickey Keeton	.10	.02
❑ 619	Dennis Lamp	.10	.02
❑ 620	Sid Monge	.10	.02
❑ 621	Jerry White	.10	.02
❑ 622	Luis Aguayo	.10	.02
❑ 623	Jamie Easterly	.10	.02
❑ 624	Steve Sax RC	1.00	.40
❑ 625	Dave Roberts	.10	.02
❑ 626	Rick Bosetti	.10	.02
❑ 627	Terry Francona RC	3.00	1.25
❑ 628	T.Seaver/J.Bench	.75	.30
❑ 629	Paul Mirabella	.10	.02
❑ 630	Rance Mulliniks	.10	.02
❑ 631	Kevin Hickey RC	.15	.05
❑ 632	Reid Nichols	.10	.02
❑ 633	Dave Geisel	.10	.02
❑ 634	Ken Griffey	.20	.07
❑ 635	Bob Lemon MG	.40	.15
❑ 636	Orlando Sanchez	.10	.02
❑ 637	Bill Almon	.10	.02
❑ 638	Danny Ainge	.20	.07
❑ 639	Willie Stargell	.40	.15
❑ 640	Bob Sykes	.10	.02
❑ 641	Ed Lynch	.10	.02
❑ 642	John Ellis	.10	.02
❑ 643	Fergie Jenkins	.20	.07
❑ 644	Lenn Sakata	.10	.02
❑ 645	Julio Gonzalez	.10	.02
❑ 646	Jesse Orosco	.10	.02
❑ 647	Jerry Dybzinski	.10	.02
❑ 648	Tommy Davis CO	.20	.07
❑ 649	Ron Gardenhire RC	.50	.20
❑ 650	Felipe Alou CO	.20	.07
❑ 651	Harvey Haddix CO	.20	.07
❑ 652	Willie Upshaw	.50	.20
❑ 653	Bill Madlock	.20	.07
❑ 654A	DK Checklist 1-26		
	ERR (Unnumbered)		
	(With Trammel	.40	.15
❑ 654B	DK Checklist 1-26		
	COR (Unnumbered)		
	(With Trammel	.20	.07
❑ 655	Checklist 27-130		
	(Unnumbered)	.20	.07
❑ 656	Checklist 131-234		
	(Unnumbered)	.20	.07
❑ 657	Checklist 235-338		

(Unnumbered)	.20	.07
❑ 658 Checklist 339-442 (Unnumbered)	.20	.07
❑ 659 Checklist 443-544 (Unnumbered)	.20	.07
❑ 660 Checklist 545-653 (Unnumbered)	.20	.07

1983 Donruss

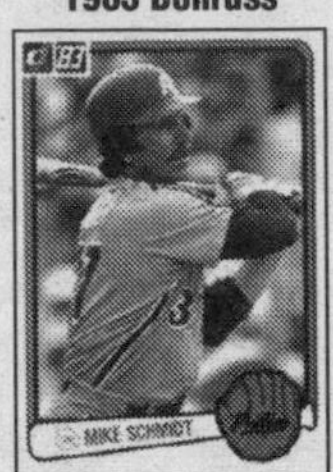

❑ COMPLETE SET (660)	60.00	30.00
❑ COMP.FACT.SET (660)	80.00	40.00
❑ COMP.COBB PUZZLE	5.00	2.00
❑ 1 Fernando Valenzuela DK	.20	.07
❑ 2 Rollie Fingers DK	.20	.07
❑ 3 Reggie Jackson DK	.40	.15
❑ 4 Jim Palmer DK	.20	.07
❑ 5 Jack Morris DK	.20	.07
❑ 6 George Foster DK	.20	.07
❑ 7 Jim Sundberg DK	.20	.07
❑ 8 Willie Stargell DK	.40	.15
❑ 9 Dave Stieb DK	.20	.07
❑ 10 Joe Niekro DK	.10	.02
❑ 11 Rickey Henderson DK	1.50	.60
❑ 12 Dale Murphy DK	.40	.15
❑ 13 Toby Harrah DK	.20	.07
❑ 14 Bill Buckner DK	.20	.07
❑ 15 Willie Wilson DK	.20	.07
❑ 16 Steve Carlton DK	.40	.15
❑ 17 Ron Guidry DK	.20	.07
❑ 18 Steve Rogers DK	.20	.07
❑ 19 Kent Hrbek DK	.20	.07
❑ 20 Keith Hernandez DK	.20	.07
❑ 21 Floyd Bannister DK	.10	.02
❑ 22 Johnny Bench DK	.75	.30
❑ 23 Britt Burns DK	.10	.02
❑ 24 Joe Morgan DK	.20	.07
❑ 25 Carl Yastrzemski DK	.75	.30
❑ 26 Terry Kennedy DK	.10	.02
❑ 27 Gary Roenicke	.10	.02
❑ 28 Dwight Bernard	.10	.02
❑ 29 Pat Underwood	.10	.02
❑ 30 Gary Allenson	.10	.02
❑ 31 Ron Guidry	.20	.07
❑ 32 Burt Hooton	.10	.02
❑ 33 Chris Bando	.10	.02
❑ 34 Vida Blue	.20	.07
❑ 35 Rickey Henderson	1.50	.60
❑ 36 Ray Burris	.10	.02
❑ 37 John Butcher	.10	.02
❑ 38 Don Aase	.10	.02
❑ 39 Jerry Koosman	.20	.07
❑ 40 Bruce Sutter	.40	.15
❑ 41 Jose Cruz	.20	.07
❑ 42 Pete Rose	2.50	1.00
❑ 43 Cesar Cedeno	.20	.07
❑ 44 Floyd Chiffer	.10	.02
❑ 45 Larry McWilliams	.10	.02
❑ 46 Alan Fowlkes	.10	.02
❑ 47 Dale Murphy	.40	.15
❑ 48 Doug Bird	.10	.02
❑ 49 Hubie Brooks	.10	.02
❑ 50 Floyd Bannister	.10	.02
❑ 51 Jack O'Connor	.10	.02
❑ 52 Steve Senteney	.10	.02
❑ 53 Gary Gaetti RC	1.00	.40
❑ 54 Damaso Garcia	.10	.02
❑ 55 Gene Nelson	.10	.02
❑ 56 Mookie Wilson	.20	.07
❑ 57 Allen Ripley	.10	.02
❑ 58 Bob Horner	.20	.07
❑ 59 Tony Pena	.10	.02
❑ 60 Gary Lavelle	.10	.02
❑ 61 Tim Lollar	.10	.02
❑ 62 Frank Pastore	.10	.02
❑ 63 Garry Maddox	.10	.02
❑ 64 Bob Forsch	.10	.02
❑ 65 Harry Spilman	.10	.02
❑ 66 Geoff Zahn	.10	.02
❑ 67 Salome Barojas	.10	.02
❑ 68 David Palmer	.10	.02
❑ 69 Charlie Hough	.20	.07
❑ 70 Dan Quisenberry	.10	.02
❑ 71 Tony Armas	.20	.07
❑ 72 Rick Sutcliffe	.20	.07
❑ 73 Steve Balboni	.10	.02
❑ 74 Jerry Remy	.10	.02
❑ 75 Mike Scioscia	.20	.07
❑ 76 John Wockenfuss	.10	.02
❑ 77 Jim Palmer	.20	.07
❑ 78 Rollie Fingers	.20	.07
❑ 79 Joe Nolan	.10	.02
❑ 80 Pete Vuckovich	.10	.02
❑ 81 Rick Leach	.10	.02
❑ 82 Rick Miller	.10	.02
❑ 83 Graig Nettles	.20	.07
❑ 84 Ron Cey	.20	.07
❑ 85 Miguel Dilone	.10	.02
❑ 86 John Wathan	.10	.02
❑ 87 Kelvin Moore	.10	.02
❑ 88A Bryn Smith FDC Bym	.20	.07
❑ 88B Bryn Smith FDC COR	.40	.15
❑ 89 Dave Hostetler	.10	.02
❑ 90 Rod Carew	.40	.15
❑ 91 Lonnie Smith	.10	.02
❑ 92 Bob Knepper	.10	.02
❑ 93 Marty Bystrom	.10	.02
❑ 94 Chris Welsh	.10	.02
❑ 95 Jason Thompson	.10	.02
❑ 96 Tom O'Malley	.10	.02
❑ 97 Phil Niekro	.20	.07
❑ 98 Neil Allen	.10	.02
❑ 99 Bill Buckner	.20	.07
❑ 100 Ed VandeBerg	.10	.02
❑ 101 Jim Clancy	.10	.02
❑ 102 Robert Castillo	.10	.02
❑ 103 Bruce Berenyi	.10	.02
❑ 104 Carlton Fisk	.40	.15
❑ 105 Mike Flanagan	.10	.02
❑ 106 Cecil Cooper	.20	.07
❑ 107 Jack Morris	.20	.07
❑ 108 Mike Morgan	.10	.02
❑ 109 Luis Aponte	.10	.02
❑ 110 Pedro Guerrero	.20	.07
❑ 111 Len Barker	.10	.02
❑ 112 Willie Wilson	.20	.07
❑ 113 Dave Beard	.10	.02
❑ 114 Mike Gates	.10	.02
❑ 115 Reggie Jackson	.40	.15
❑ 116 George Wright RC	.50	.20
❑ 117 Vance Law	.10	.02
❑ 118 Nolan Ryan	4.00	1.50
❑ 119 Mike Krukow	.10	.02
❑ 120 Ozzie Smith	1.25	.50
❑ 121 Broderick Perkins	.10	.02
❑ 122 Tom Seaver	.75	.30
❑ 123 Chris Chambliss	.20	.07
❑ 124 Chuck Tanner MG	.10	.02
❑ 125 Johnnie LeMaster	.10	.02
❑ 126 Mel Hall RC	.50	.20
❑ 127 Bruce Bochte	.10	.02
❑ 128 Charlie Puleo	.10	.02
❑ 129 Luis Leal	.10	.02
❑ 130 John Pacella	.10	.02
❑ 131 Glenn Gulliver	.10	.02
❑ 132 Don Money	.10	.02
❑ 133 Dave Rozema	.10	.02
❑ 134 Bruce Hurst	.10	.02
❑ 135 Rudy May	.10	.02
❑ 136 Tom Lasorda MG	.40	.15
❑ 137 Dan Spillner UER (Photo actually Ed Whitson)	.10	.02
❑ 138 Jerry Martin	.10	.02
❑ 139 Mike Norris	.10	.02
❑ 140 Al Oliver	.20	.07
❑ 141 Daryl Sconiers	.10	.02
❑ 142 Lamar Johnson	.10	.02
❑ 143 Harold Baines	.20	.07
❑ 144 Alan Ashby	.10	.02
❑ 145 Garry Templeton	.20	.07
❑ 146 Al Holland	.10	.02
❑ 147 Bo Diaz	.10	.02
❑ 148 Dave Concepcion	.20	.07
❑ 149 Rick Camp	.10	.02
❑ 150 Jim Morrison	.10	.02
❑ 151 Randy Martz	.10	.02
❑ 152 Keith Hernandez	.20	.07
❑ 153 John Lowenstein	.10	.02
❑ 154 Mike Caldwell	.10	.02
❑ 155 Milt Wilcox	.10	.02
❑ 156 Rich Gedman	.10	.02
❑ 157 Rich Gossage	.20	.07
❑ 158 Jerry Reuss	.10	.02
❑ 159 Ron Hassey	.10	.02
❑ 160 Larry Gura	.10	.02
❑ 161 Dwayne Murphy	.10	.02
❑ 162 Woodie Fryman	.10	.02
❑ 163 Steve Comer	.10	.02
❑ 164 Ken Forsch	.10	.02
❑ 165 Dennis Lamp	.10	.02
❑ 166 David Green RC	.50	.20
❑ 167 Terry Puhl	.10	.02
❑ 168 Mike Schmidt	2.00	.75
❑ 169 Eddie Milner	.10	.02
❑ 170 John Curtis	.10	.02
❑ 171 Don Robinson	.10	.02
❑ 172 Rich Gale	.10	.02
❑ 173 Steve Bedrosian	.10	.02
❑ 174 Willie Hernandez	.10	.02
❑ 175 Ron Gardenhire	.10	.02
❑ 176 Jim Beattie	.10	.02
❑ 177 Tim Laudner	.10	.02
❑ 178 Buck Martinez	.10	.02
❑ 179 Kent Hrbek	.20	.07
❑ 180 Alfredo Griffin	.10	.02
❑ 181 Larry Andersen	.10	.02
❑ 182 Pete Falcone	.10	.02
❑ 183 Jody Davis	.10	.02
❑ 184 Glenn Hubbard	.10	.02
❑ 185 Dale Berra	.10	.02
❑ 186 Greg Minton	.10	.02
❑ 187 Gary Lucas	.10	.02
❑ 188 Dave Van Gorder	.10	.02
❑ 189 Bob Dernier	.10	.02
❑ 190 Willie McGee RC	1.50	.60
❑ 191 Dickie Thon	.10	.02
❑ 192 Bob Boone	.20	.07
❑ 193 Britt Burns	.10	.02
❑ 194 Jeff Reardon	.20	.07
❑ 195 Jon Matlack	.10	.02
❑ 196 Don Slaught RC	.50	.20
❑ 197 Fred Stanley	.10	.02
❑ 198 Rick Manning	.10	.02
❑ 199 Dave Righetti	.20	.07
❑ 200 Dave Stapleton	.10	.02
❑ 201 Steve Yeager	.20	.07
❑ 202 Enos Cabell	.10	.02
❑ 203 Sammy Stewart	.10	.02
❑ 204 Moose Haas	.10	.02
❑ 205 Lenn Sakata	.10	.02
❑ 206 Charlie Moore	.10	.02
❑ 207 Alan Trammell	.20	.07
❑ 208 Jim Rice	.20	.07
❑ 209 Roy Smalley	.10	.02
❑ 210 Bill Russell	.20	.07
❑ 211 Andre Thornton	.10	.02
❑ 212 Willie Aikens	.10	.02
❑ 213 Dave McKay	.10	.02
❑ 214 Tim Blackwell	.10	.02
❑ 215 Buddy Bell	.20	.07
❑ 216 Doug DeCinces	.10	.02
❑ 217 Tom Herr	.10	.02
❑ 218 Frank LaCorte	.10	.02
❑ 219 Steve Carlton	.40	.15
❑ 220 Terry Kennedy	.10	.02
❑ 221 Mike Easler	.10	.02
❑ 222 Jack Clark	.20	.07
❑ 223 Gene Garber	.10	.02
❑ 224 Scott Holman	.10	.02
❑ 225 Mike Proly	.10	.02

❑ 226 Terry Bulling .10 .02
❑ 227 Jerry Garvin .10 .02
❑ 228 Ron Davis .10 .02
❑ 229 Tom Hume .10 .02
❑ 230 Marc Hill .10 .02
❑ 231 Dennis Martinez .20 .07
❑ 232 Jim Gantner .10 .02
❑ 233 Larry Pashnick .10 .02
❑ 234 Dave Collins .10 .02
❑ 235 Tom Burgmeier .10 .02
❑ 236 Ken Landreaux .10 .02
❑ 237 John Denny .10 .02
❑ 238 Hal McRae .20 .07
❑ 239 Matt Keough .10 .02
❑ 240 Doug Flynn .10 .02
❑ 241 Fred Lynn .20 .07
❑ 242 Billy Sample .10 .02
❑ 243 Tom Paciorek .10 .02
❑ 244 Joe Sambito .10 .02
❑ 245 Sid Monge .10 .02
❑ 246 Ken Oberkfell .10 .02
❑ 247 Joe Pittman UER (Photo actually Juan Eichelberge .10 .02
❑ 248 Mario Soto .20 .07
❑ 249 Claudell Washington .10 .02
❑ 250 Rick Rhoden .10 .02
❑ 251 Darrell Evans .20 .07
❑ 252 Steve Henderson .10 .02
❑ 253 Manny Castillo .10 .02
❑ 254 Craig Swan .10 .02
❑ 255 Joey McLaughlin .10 .02
❑ 256 Pete Redfern .10 .02
❑ 257 Ken Singleton .20 .07
❑ 258 Robin Yount 1.25 .50
❑ 259 Elias Sosa .10 .02
❑ 260 Bob Ojeda .10 .02
❑ 261 Bobby Murcer .20 .07
❑ 262 Candy Maldonado RC .50 .20
❑ 263 Rick Waits .10 .02
❑ 264 Greg Pryor .10 .02
❑ 265 Bob Owchinko .10 .02
❑ 266 Chris Speier .10 .02
❑ 267 Bruce Kison .10 .02
❑ 268 Mark Wagner .10 .02
❑ 269 Steve Kemp .10 .02
❑ 270 Phil Garner .20 .07
❑ 271 Gene Richards .10 .02
❑ 272 Renie Martin .10 .02
❑ 273 Dave Roberts .10 .02
❑ 274 Dan Driessen .10 .02
❑ 275 Rufino Linares .10 .02
❑ 276 Lee Lacy .10 .02
❑ 277 Ryne Sandberg RC 10.00 4.00
❑ 278 Darrell Porter .10 .02
❑ 279 Cal Ripken 6.00 2.50
❑ 280 Jamie Easterly .10 .02
❑ 281 Bill Fahey .10 .02
❑ 282 Glenn Hoffman .10 .02
❑ 283 Willie Randolph .20 .07
❑ 284 Fernando Valenzuela .20 .07
❑ 285 Alan Bannister .10 .02
❑ 286 Paul Splittorff .10 .02
❑ 287 Joe Rudi .20 .07
❑ 288 Bill Gullickson .10 .02
❑ 289 Danny Darwin .10 .02
❑ 290 Andy Hassler .10 .02
❑ 291 Ernesto Escarrega .10 .02
❑ 292 Steve Mura .10 .02
❑ 293 Tony Scott .10 .02
❑ 294 Manny Trillo .10 .02
❑ 295 Greg Harris .10 .02
❑ 296 Luis DeLeon .10 .02
❑ 297 Kent Tekulve .10 .02
❑ 298 Atlee Hammaker .10 .02
❑ 299 Bruce Benedict .10 .02
❑ 300 Fergie Jenkins .20 .07
❑ 301 Dave Kingman .20 .07
❑ 302 Bill Caudill .10 .02
❑ 303 John Castino .10 .02
❑ 304 Ernie Whitt .10 .02
❑ 305 Randy Johnson .10 .02
❑ 306 Garth Iorg .10 .02
❑ 307 Gaylord Perry .20 .07
❑ 308 Ed Lynch .10 .02
❑ 309 Keith Moreland .10 .02
❑ 310 Rafael Ramirez .10 .02
❑ 311 Bill Madlock .20 .07
❑ 312 Milt May .10 .02
❑ 313 John Montefusco .10 .02
❑ 314 Wayne Krenchicki .10 .02
❑ 315 George Vukovich .10 .02
❑ 316 Joaquin Andujar .20 .07
❑ 317 Craig Reynolds .10 .02
❑ 318 Rick Burleson .10 .02
❑ 319 Richard Dotson .10 .02
❑ 320 Steve Rogers .20 .07
❑ 321 Dave Schmidt .10 .02
❑ 322 Bud Black RC .50 .20
❑ 323 Jeff Burroughs .10 .02
❑ 324 Von Hayes .10 .02
❑ 325 Butch Wynegar .10 .02
❑ 326 Carl Yastrzemski 1.25 .50
❑ 327 Ron Roenicke .10 .02
❑ 328 Howard Johnson RC 1.00 .40
❑ 329 Rick Dempsey UER (Posing as a left-handed batte .10 .02
❑ 330A Jim Slaton (Bio printed black on white) .10 .02
❑ 330B Jim Slaton (Bio printed black on yellow) .20 .07
❑ 331 Benny Ayala .10 .02
❑ 332 Ted Simmons .20 .07
❑ 333 Lou Whitaker .20 .07
❑ 334 Chuck Rainey .10 .02
❑ 335 Lou Piniella .20 .07
❑ 336 Steve Sax .20 .07
❑ 337 Toby Harrah .20 .07
❑ 338 George Brett 2.00 .75
❑ 339 Dave Lopes .20 .07
❑ 340 Gary Carter .20 .07
❑ 341 John Grubb .10 .02
❑ 342 Tim Foli .10 .02
❑ 343 Jim Kaat .20 .07
❑ 344 Mike LaCoss .10 .02
❑ 345 Larry Christenson .10 .02
❑ 346 Juan Bonilla .10 .02
❑ 347 Omar Moreno .10 .02
❑ 348 Chili Davis .20 .07
❑ 349 Tommy Boggs .10 .02
❑ 350 Rusty Staub .20 .07
❑ 351 Bump Wills .10 .02
❑ 352 Rick Sweet .10 .02
❑ 353 Jim Gott RC .50 .20
❑ 354 Terry Felton .10 .02
❑ 355 Jim Kern .10 .02
❑ 356 Bill Almon UER (Expos/Mets in 1983, not Padres/M .10 .02
❑ 357 Tippy Martinez .10 .02
❑ 358 Roy Howell .10 .02
❑ 359 Dan Petry .10 .02
❑ 360 Jerry Mumphrey .10 .02
❑ 361 Mark Clear .10 .02
❑ 362 Mike Marshall .10 .02
❑ 363 Lary Sorensen .10 .02
❑ 364 Amos Otis .20 .07
❑ 365 Rick Langford .10 .02
❑ 366 Brad Mills .10 .02
❑ 367 Brian Downing .20 .07
❑ 368 Mike Richardt .10 .02
❑ 369 Aurelio Rodriguez .10 .02
❑ 370 Dave Smith .10 .02
❑ 371 Tug McGraw .20 .07
❑ 372 Doug Bair .10 .02
❑ 373 Ruppert Jones .10 .02
❑ 374 Alex Trevino .10 .02
❑ 375 Ken Dayley .10 .02
❑ 376 Rod Scurry .10 .02
❑ 377 Bob Brenly .10 .02
❑ 378 Scot Thompson .10 .02
❑ 379 Julio Cruz .10 .02
❑ 380 John Stearns .10 .02
❑ 381 Dale Murray .10 .02
❑ 382 Frank Viola RC 1.50 .60
❑ 383 Al Bumbry .10 .02
❑ 384 Ben Oglivie .20 .07
❑ 385 Dave Tobik .10 .02
❑ 386 Bob Stanley .10 .02
❑ 387 Andre Robertson .10 .02
❑ 388 Jorge Orta .10 .02
❑ 389 Ed Whitson .10 .02
❑ 390 Don Hood .10 .02
❑ 391 Tom Underwood .10 .02
❑ 392 Tim Wallach .20 .07
❑ 393 Steve Renko .10 .02
❑ 394 Mickey Rivers .10 .02
❑ 395 Greg Luzinski .20 .07
❑ 396 Art Howe .10 .02
❑ 397 Alan Wiggins .10 .02
❑ 398 Jim Barr .10 .02
❑ 399 Ivan DeJesus .10 .02
❑ 400 Tom Lawless .10 .02
❑ 401 Bob Walk .10 .02
❑ 402 Jimmy Smith .10 .02
❑ 403 Lee Smith .40 .15
❑ 404 George Hendrick .20 .07
❑ 405 Eddie Murray .75 .30
❑ 406 Marshall Edwards .10 .02
❑ 407 Lance Parrish .20 .07
❑ 408 Carney Lansford .20 .07
❑ 409 Dave Winfield .20 .07
❑ 410 Bob Welch .20 .07
❑ 411 Larry Milbourne .10 .02
❑ 412 Dennis Leonard .10 .02
❑ 413 Dan Meyer .10 .02
❑ 414 Charlie Lea .10 .02
❑ 415 Rick Honeycutt .10 .02
❑ 416 Mike Witt .10 .02
❑ 417 Steve Trout .10 .02
❑ 418 Glenn Brummer .10 .02
❑ 419 Denny Walling .10 .02
❑ 420 Gary Matthews .20 .07
❑ 421 Charlie Leibrandt UER (Liebrandt on front of car .10 .02
❑ 422 Juan Eichelberger UER (Photo actually Joe Pittma .10 .02
❑ 423 Cecilio Guante UER (Listed as Matt on card) .10 .02
❑ 424 Bill Laskey .10 .02
❑ 425 Jerry Royster .10 .02
❑ 426 Dickie Noles .10 .02
❑ 427 George Foster .20 .07
❑ 428 Mike Moore RC .50 .20
❑ 429 Gary Ward .10 .02
❑ 430 Barry Bonnell .10 .02
❑ 431 Ron Washington .10 .02
❑ 432 Rance Mulliniks .10 .02
❑ 433 Mike Stanton .10 .02
❑ 434 Jesse Orosco .10 .02
❑ 435 Larry Bowa .20 .07
❑ 436 Biff Pocoroba .10 .02
❑ 437 Johnny Ray .10 .02
❑ 438 Joe Morgan .20 .07
❑ 439 Eric Show RC .50 .20
❑ 440 Larry Biittner .10 .02
❑ 441 Greg Gross .10 .02
❑ 442 Gene Tenace .20 .07
❑ 443 Danny Heep .10 .02
❑ 444 Bobby Clark .10 .02
❑ 445 Kevin Hickey .10 .02
❑ 446 Scott Sanderson .10 .02
❑ 447 Frank Tanana .20 .07
❑ 448 Cesar Geronimo .10 .02
❑ 449 Jimmy Sexton .10 .02
❑ 450 Mike Hargrove .10 .02
❑ 451 Doyle Alexander .10 .02
❑ 452 Dwight Evans .40 .15
❑ 453 Terry Forster .20 .07
❑ 454 Tom Brookens .10 .02
❑ 455 Rich Dauer .10 .02
❑ 456 Rob Picciolo .10 .02
❑ 457 Terry Crowley .10 .02
❑ 458 Ned Yost .10 .02
❑ 459 Kirk Gibson .20 .07
❑ 460 Reid Nichols .10 .02
❑ 461 Oscar Gamble .10 .02
❑ 462 Dusty Baker .20 .07
❑ 463 Jack Perconte .10 .02
❑ 464 Frank White .20 .07
❑ 465 Mickey Klutts .10 .02
❑ 466 Warren Cromartie .10 .02

❑ 467 Larry Parrish .10 .02
❑ 468 Bobby Grich .20 .07
❑ 469 Dane Iorg .10 .02
❑ 470 Joe Niekro .10 .02
❑ 471 Ed Farmer .10 .02
❑ 472 Tim Flannery .10 .02
❑ 473 Dave Parker .20 .07
❑ 474 Jeff Leonard .10 .02
❑ 475 Al Hrabosky .10 .02
❑ 476 Ron Hodges .10 .02
❑ 477 Leon Durham .10 .02
❑ 478 Jim Essian .10 .02
❑ 479 Roy Lee Jackson .10 .02
❑ 480 Brad Havens .10 .02
❑ 481 Joe Price .10 .02
❑ 482 Tony Bernazard .10 .02
❑ 483 Scott McGregor .10 .02
❑ 484 Paul Molitor .20 .07
❑ 485 Mike Ivie .10 .02
❑ 486 Ken Griffey .20 .07
❑ 487 Dennis Eckersley .40 .15
❑ 488 Steve Garvey .20 .07
❑ 489 Mike Fischlin .10 .02
❑ 490 U.L. Washington .10 .02
❑ 491 Steve McCatty .10 .02
❑ 492 Roy Johnson .10 .02
❑ 493 Don Baylor .20 .07
❑ 494 Bobby Johnson .10 .02
❑ 495 Mike Squires .10 .02
❑ 496 Bert Roberge .10 .02
❑ 497 Dick Ruthven .10 .02
❑ 498 Tito Landrum .10 .02
❑ 499 Sixto Lezcano .10 .02
❑ 500 Johnny Bench .75 .30
❑ 501 Larry Whisenton .10 .02
❑ 502 Manny Sarmiento .10 .02
❑ 503 Fred Breining .10 .02
❑ 504 Bill Campbell .10 .02
❑ 505 Todd Cruz .10 .02
❑ 506 Bob Bailor .10 .02
❑ 507 Dave Stieb .20 .07
❑ 508 Al Williams .10 .02
❑ 509 Dan Ford .10 .02
❑ 510 Gorman Thomas .20 .07
❑ 511 Chet Lemon .20 .07
❑ 512 Mike Torrez .10 .02
❑ 513 Shane Rawley .10 .02
❑ 514 Mark Belanger .10 .02
❑ 515 Rodney Craig .10 .02
❑ 516 Onix Concepcion .10 .02
❑ 517 Mike Heath .10 .02
❑ 518 Andre Dawson .20 .07
❑ 519 Luis Sanchez .10 .02
❑ 520 Terry Bogener .10 .02
❑ 521 Rudy Law .10 .02
❑ 522 Ray Knight .20 .07
❑ 523 Joe Lefebvre .10 .02
❑ 524 Jim Wohlford .10 .02
❑ 525 Julio Franco RC 6.00 2.50
❑ 526 Ron Oester .10 .02
❑ 527 Rick Mahler .10 .02
❑ 528 Steve Nicosia .10 .02
❑ 529 Junior Kennedy .10 .02
❑ 530A Whitey Herzog MG (Bio printed black on white) .20 .07
❑ 530B Whitey Herzog MG (Bio printed black on yellow) .20 .07
❑ 531A Don Sutton .20 .07
❑ 531B Don Sutton .20 .07
❑ 532 Mark Brouhard .10 .02
❑ 533A Sparky Anderson MG (Bio printed black on white) .20 .07
❑ 533B Sparky Anderson MG (Bio printed black on yellow) .20 .07
❑ 534 Roger LaFrancois .10 .02
❑ 535 George Frazier .10 .02
❑ 536 Tom Niedenfuer .10 .02
❑ 537 Ed Glynn .10 .02
❑ 538 Lee May .10 .02
❑ 539 Bob Kearney .10 .02
❑ 540 Tim Raines .20 .07
❑ 541 Paul Mirabella .10 .02
❑ 542 Luis Tiant .20 .07
❑ 543 Ron LeFlore .20 .07
❑ 544 Dave LaPoint .10 .02
❑ 545 Randy Moffitt .10 .02
❑ 546 Luis Aguayo .10 .02
❑ 547 Brad Lesley .15 .05
❑ 548 Luis Salazar .10 .02
❑ 549 John Candelaria .10 .02
❑ 550 Dave Bergman .10 .02
❑ 551 Bob Watson .10 .02
❑ 552 Pat Tabler .10 .02
❑ 553 Brent Gaff .10 .02
❑ 554 Al Cowens .10 .02
❑ 555 Tom Brunansky .20 .07
❑ 556 Lloyd Moseby .10 .02
❑ 557A Pascual Perez ERR Twins 2.00 .75
❑ 557B Pascual Perez COR (Braves in glove) .20 .07
❑ 558 Willie Upshaw .10 .02
❑ 559 Richie Zisk .10 .02
❑ 560 Pat Zachry .10 .02
❑ 561 Jay Johnstone .10 .02
❑ 562 Carlos Diaz RC .15 .05
❑ 563 John Tudor .20 .07
❑ 564 Frank Robinson MG .40 .15
❑ 565 Dave Edwards .10 .02
❑ 566 Paul Householder .10 .02
❑ 567 Ron Reed .10 .02
❑ 568 Mike Ramsey .10 .02
❑ 569 Kiko Garcia .10 .02
❑ 570 Tommy John .20 .07
❑ 571 Tony LaRussa MG .20 .07
❑ 572 Joel Youngblood .10 .02
❑ 573 Wayne Tolleson .10 .02
❑ 574 Keith Creel .10 .02
❑ 575 Billy Martin MG .40 .15
❑ 576 Jerry Dybzinski .10 .02
❑ 577 Rick Cerone .10 .02
❑ 578 Tony Perez .40 .15
❑ 579 Greg Brock .10 .02
❑ 580 Glenn Wilson .50 .20
❑ 581 Tim Stoddard .10 .02
❑ 582 Bob McClure .10 .02
❑ 583 Jim Dwyer .10 .02
❑ 584 Ed Romero .10 .02
❑ 585 Larry Herndon .10 .02
❑ 586 Wade Boggs RC 10.00 4.00
❑ 587 Jay Howell .10 .02
❑ 588 Dave Stewart .20 .07
❑ 589 Bert Blyleven .20 .07
❑ 590 Dick Howser MG .10 .02
❑ 591 Wayne Gross .10 .02
❑ 592 Terry Francona .20 .07
❑ 593 Don Werner .10 .02
❑ 594 Bill Stein .10 .02
❑ 595 Jesse Barfield .20 .07
❑ 596 Bob Molinaro .10 .02
❑ 597 Mike Vail .10 .02
❑ 598 Tony Gwynn RC 15.00 6.00
❑ 599 Gary Rajsich .10 .02
❑ 600 Jerry Ujdur .10 .02
❑ 601 Cliff Johnson .10 .02
❑ 602 Jerry White .10 .02
❑ 603 Bryan Clark .10 .02
❑ 604 Joe Ferguson .10 .02
❑ 605 Guy Sularz .10 .02
❑ 606A Ozzie Virgil (Green border on photo) .20 .07
❑ 606B Ozzie Virgil (Orange border on photo) .20 .07
❑ 607 Terry Harper .10 .02
❑ 608 Harvey Kuenn MG .10 .02
❑ 609 Jim Sundberg .20 .07
❑ 610 Willie Stargell .40 .15
❑ 611 Reggie Smith .20 .07
❑ 612 Rob Wilfong .10 .02
❑ 613 Niekro Brothers .20 .07
❑ 614 Lee Elia MG .10 .02
❑ 615 Mickey Hatcher .10 .02
❑ 616 Jerry Hairston .10 .02
❑ 617 John Martin .10 .02
❑ 618 Wally Backman .10 .02
❑ 619 Storm Davis RC .50 .20
❑ 620 Alan Knicely .10 .02
❑ 621 John Stuper .10 .02
❑ 622 Matt Sinatro .10 .02
❑ 623 Geno Petralli .50 .20
❑ 624 Duane Walker .10 .02
❑ 625 Dick Williams MG .10 .02
❑ 626 Pat Corrales MG .10 .02
❑ 627 Vern Ruhle .10 .02
❑ 628 Joe Torre MG .20 .07
❑ 629 Anthony Johnson .10 .02
❑ 630 Steve Howe .10 .02
❑ 631 Gary Woods .10 .02
❑ 632 LaMarr Hoyt .10 .02
❑ 633 Steve Swisher .10 .02
❑ 634 Terry Leach .10 .02
❑ 635 Jeff Newman .10 .02
❑ 636 Brett Butler .20 .07
❑ 637 Gary Gray .10 .02
❑ 638 Lee Mazzilli .20 .07
❑ 639A Ron Jackson ERR A's 20.00 8.00
❑ 639B Ron Jackson COR (Angels in glove, red border on .10 .02
❑ 639C Ron Jackson COR (Angels in glove, green border .40 .15
❑ 640 Juan Beniquez .10 .02
❑ 641 Dave Rucker .10 .02
❑ 642 Luis Pujols .10 .02
❑ 643 Rick Monday .20 .07
❑ 644 Hosken Powell .10 .02
❑ 645 The Chicken .40 .15
❑ 646 Dave Engle .10 .02
❑ 647 Dick Davis .10 .02
❑ 648 F.Robby/V.Blue/J.Morgan .40 .15
❑ 649 Al Chambers .10 .02
❑ 650 Jesus Vega .10 .02
❑ 651 Jeff Jones .10 .02
❑ 652 Marvis Foley .10 .02
❑ 653 Ty Cobb Puzzle .75 .30
❑ 654A Dick Perez/DK CL .40 .15
❑ 654B Dick Perez/DK CL .40 .15
❑ 655 Checklist 27-130 (Unnumbered) .10 .02
❑ 656 Checklist 131-234 (Unnumbered) .10 .02
❑ 657 Checklist 235-338 (Unnumbered) .10 .02
❑ 658 Checklist 339-442 (Unnumbered) .10 .02
❑ 659 Checklist 443-544 (Unnumbered) .10 .02
❑ 660 Checklist 545-653 (Unnumbered) .10 .02

1984 Donruss

❑ COMPLETE SET (660) 80.00 40.00
❑ COMP.FACT.SET (658) 150.00 90.00
❑ COMP.SNIDER PUZZLE 5.00 2.00
❑ 1 Robin Yount DK 2.50 1.00
❑ 1A Robin Yount DK ERR 5.00 2.00
❑ 2 Dave Concepcion DK .75 .30
❑ 2A Dave Concepcion DK ERR .75 .30
❑ 3 Dwayne Murphy DK .25 .08
❑ 3A Dwayne Murphy DK ERR .25 .08
❑ 4 John Castino DK .25 .08
❑ 4A John Castino DK ERR .25 .08

Card	Price 1	Price 2
❑ 5 Leon Durham DK	.75	.30
❑ 5A Leon Durham DK ERR	.25	.08
❑ 6 Rusty Staub DK	.75	.30
❑ 6A Rusty Staub DK ERR	.75	.30
❑ 7 Jack Clark DK	.75	.30
❑ 7A Jack Clark DK ERR	.75	.30
❑ 8 Dave Dravecky DK	.25	.08
❑ 8A Dave Dravecky DK ERR	.25	.08
❑ 9 Al Oliver DK	.75	.30
❑ 9A Al Oliver DK ERR	.75	.30
❑ 10 Dave Righetti DK	.75	.30
❑ 10A Dave Righetti DK ERR	.75	.30
❑ 11 Hal McRae DK	.75	.30
❑ 11A Hal McRae DK ERR	.75	.30
❑ 12 Ray Knight DK	.75	.30
❑ 12A Ray Knight DK ERR	.75	.30
❑ 13 Bruce Sutter DK	1.50	.60
❑ 13A Bruce Sutter DK ERR	1.50	.60
❑ 14 Bob Horner DK	.75	.30
❑ 14A Bob Horner DK ERR	.75	.30
❑ 15 Lance Parrish DK	.75	.30
❑ 15A Lance Parrish DK ERR	.75	.30
❑ 16 Matt Young DK	.75	.30
❑ 16A Matt Young DK ERR	.75	.30
❑ 17 Fred Lynn DK	.75	.30
❑ 17A Fred Lynn DK ERR	.75	.30
❑ 18 Ron Kittle DK	.25	.08
❑ 18A Ron Kittle DK ERR	.25	.08
❑ 19 Jim Clancy DK	.25	.08
❑ 19A Jim Clancy DK ERR	.25	.08
❑ 20 Bill Madlock DK	.75	.30
❑ 20A Bill Madlock DK ERR	.75	.30
❑ 21 Larry Parrish DK	.25	.08
❑ 21A Larry Parrish DK ERR	.25	.08
❑ 22 Eddie Murray DK	3.00	1.25
❑ 22A Eddie Murray DK ERR	3.00	1.25
❑ 23 Mike Schmidt DK	5.00	2.00
❑ 23A Mike Schmidt DK ERR	5.00	2.00
❑ 24 Pedro Guerrero DK	.75	.30
❑ 24A Pedro Guerrero DK ERR	.75	.30
❑ 25 Andre Thornton DK	.25	.08
❑ 25A Andre Thornton DK ERR	.25	.08
❑ 26 Wade Boggs DK	3.00	1.25
❑ 26A Wade Boggs DK ERR	3.00	1.25
❑ 27 Joel Skinner RC	.25	.08
❑ 28 Tommy Dunbar RC	.25	.08
❑ 29A Mike Stenhouse ERR RC	.25	.08
❑ 29B Mike Stenhouse COR	3.00	1.25
❑ 30A Ron Darling ERR RC	2.00	.75
❑ 30B Ron Darling COR	3.00	1.25
❑ 31 Dion James RC	.25	.08
❑ 32 Tony Fernandez RC	2.00	.75
❑ 33 Angel Salazar RC	.25	.08
❑ 34 Kevin McReynolds RC	2.00	.75
❑ 35 Dick Schofield RC	1.00	.40
❑ 36 Brad Komminsk RC	.25	.08
❑ 37 Tim Teufel RC	1.00	.40
❑ 38 Doug Frobel RC	.25	.08
❑ 39 Greg Gagne RC	1.00	.40
❑ 40 Mike Fuentes RC	.25	.08
❑ 41 Joe Carter RC	8.00	3.00
❑ 42 Mike C. Brown RC	.25	.08
❑ 43 Mike Jeffcoat RC	.25	.08
❑ 44 Sid Fernandez RC !	2.00	.75
❑ 45 Brian Dayett RC	.25	.08
❑ 46 Chris Smith RC	.25	.08
❑ 47 Eddie Murray	3.00	1.25
❑ 48 Robin Yount	5.00	2.00
❑ 49 Lance Parrish	1.50	.60
❑ 50 Jim Rice	.75	.30
❑ 51 Dave Winfield	.75	.30
❑ 52 Fernando Valenzuela	.75	.30
❑ 53 George Brett	8.00	3.00
❑ 54 Rickey Henderson	5.00	2.00
❑ 55 Gary Carter	.75	.30
❑ 56 Buddy Bell	.75	.30
❑ 57 Reggie Jackson	1.50	.60
❑ 58 Harold Baines	.75	.30
❑ 59 Ozzie Smith	5.00	2.00
❑ 60 Nolan Ryan	15.00	6.00
❑ 61 Pete Rose	10.00	4.00
❑ 62 Ron Oester	.25	.08
❑ 63 Steve Garvey	.75	.30
❑ 64 Jason Thompson	.25	.08
❑ 65 Jack Clark	.75	.30
❑ 66 Dale Murphy	1.50	.60
❑ 67 Leon Durham	.25	.08
❑ 68 Darryl Strawberry RC	8.00	3.00
❑ 69 Richie Zisk	.25	.08
❑ 70 Kent Hrbek	.75	.30
❑ 71 Dave Stieb	.75	.30
❑ 72 Ken Schrom	.25	.08
❑ 73 George Bell	.75	.30
❑ 74 John Moses	.25	.08
❑ 75 Ed Lynch	.25	.08
❑ 76 Chuck Rainey	.25	.08
❑ 77 Biff Pocoroba	.25	.08
❑ 78 Cecilio Guante	.25	.08
❑ 79 Jim Barr	.25	.08
❑ 80 Kurt Bevacqua	.25	.08
❑ 81 Tom Foley	.25	.08
❑ 82 Joe Lefebvre	.25	.08
❑ 83 Andy Van Slyke RC	4.00	1.50
❑ 84 Bob Lillis MG	.25	.08
❑ 85 Ricky Adams	.25	.08
❑ 86 Jerry Hairston	.25	.08
❑ 87 Bob James	.25	.08
❑ 88 Joe Altobelli MG	.25	.08
❑ 89 Ed Romero	.25	.08
❑ 90 John Grubb	.25	.08
❑ 91 John Henry Johnson	.25	.08
❑ 92 Juan Espino	.25	.08
❑ 93 Candy Maldonado	.25	.08
❑ 94 Andre Thornton	.25	.08
❑ 95 Onix Concepcion	.25	.08
❑ 96 Donnie Hill UER (Listed as P, should be 2B)	.25	.08
❑ 97 Andre Dawson	.75	.30
❑ 98 Frank Tanana	.75	.30
❑ 99 Curt Wilkerson	.25	.08
❑ 100 Larry Gura	.25	.08
❑ 101 Dwayne Murphy	.25	.08
❑ 102 Tom Brennan	.25	.08
❑ 103 Dave Righetti	.75	.30
❑ 104 Steve Sax	.25	.08
❑ 105 Dan Petry	.75	.30
❑ 106 Cal Ripken	20.00	8.00
❑ 107 Paul Molitor	.75	.30
❑ 108 Fred Lynn	.75	.30
❑ 109 Neil Allen	.25	.08
❑ 110 Joe Niekro	.25	.08
❑ 111 Steve Carlton	1.50	.60
❑ 112 Terry Kennedy	.25	.08
❑ 113 Bill Madlock	.75	.30
❑ 114 Chili Davis	.75	.30
❑ 115 Jim Gantner	.25	.08
❑ 116 Tom Seaver	3.00	1.25
❑ 117 Bill Buckner	.75	.30
❑ 118 Bill Caudill	.25	.08
❑ 119 Jim Clancy	.25	.08
❑ 120 John Castino	.25	.08
❑ 121 Dave Concepcion	.75	.30
❑ 122 Greg Luzinski	.75	.30
❑ 123 Mike Boddicker	.25	.08
❑ 124 Pete Ladd	.25	.08
❑ 125 Juan Berenguer	.25	.08
❑ 126 John Montefusco	.25	.08
❑ 127 Ed Jurak	.25	.08
❑ 128 Tom Niedenfuer	.25	.08
❑ 129 Bert Blyleven	.75	.30
❑ 130 Bud Black	.25	.08
❑ 131 Gorman Heimueller	.25	.08
❑ 132 Dan Schatzeder	.25	.08
❑ 133 Ron Jackson	.25	.08
❑ 134 Tom Henke RC	2.00	.75
❑ 135 Kevin Hickey	.25	.08
❑ 136 Mike Scott	.75	.30
❑ 137 Bo Diaz	.25	.08
❑ 138 Glenn Brummer	.25	.08
❑ 139 Sid Monge	.25	.08
❑ 140 Rich Gale	.25	.08
❑ 141 Brett Butler	.75	.30
❑ 142 Brian Harper RC	1.00	.40
❑ 143 John Rabb	.25	.08
❑ 144 Gary Woods	.25	.08
❑ 145 Pat Putnam	.25	.08
❑ 146 Jim Acker	.25	.08
❑ 147 Mickey Hatcher	.25	.08
❑ 148 Todd Cruz	.25	.08
❑ 149 Tom Tellmann	.25	.08
❑ 150 John Wockenfuss	.25	.08
❑ 151 Wade Boggs	8.00	3.00
❑ 152 Don Baylor	.75	.30
❑ 153 Bob Welch	.75	.30
❑ 154 Alan Bannister	.25	.08
❑ 155 Willie Aikens	.25	.08
❑ 156 Jeff Burroughs	.25	.08
❑ 157 Bryan Little	.25	.08
❑ 158 Bob Boone	.75	.30
❑ 159 Dave Hostetler	.25	.08
❑ 160 Jerry Dybzinski	.25	.08
❑ 161 Mike Madden	.25	.08
❑ 162 Luis DeLeon	.25	.08
❑ 163 Willie Hernandez	.25	.08
❑ 164 Frank Pastore	.25	.08
❑ 165 Rick Camp	.25	.08
❑ 166 Lee Mazzilli	.75	.30
❑ 167 Scot Thompson	.25	.08
❑ 168 Bob Forsch	.25	.08
❑ 169 Mike Flanagan	.25	.08
❑ 170 Rick Manning	.25	.08
❑ 171 Chet Lemon	.75	.30
❑ 172 Jerry Remy	.25	.08
❑ 173 Ron Guidry	.75	.30
❑ 174 Pedro Guerrero	.75	.30
❑ 175 Willie Wilson	.75	.30
❑ 176 Carney Lansford	.75	.30
❑ 177 Al Oliver	.75	.30
❑ 178 Jim Sundberg	.75	.30
❑ 179 Bobby Grich	.75	.30
❑ 180 Rich Dotson	.25	.08
❑ 181 Joaquin Andujar	.75	.30
❑ 182 Jose Cruz	.75	.30
❑ 183 Mike Schmidt	8.00	3.00
❑ 184 Gary Redus RC	1.00	.40
❑ 185 Garry Templeton	.75	.30
❑ 186 Tony Pena	.25	.08
❑ 187 Greg Minton	.25	.08
❑ 188 Phil Niekro	.75	.30
❑ 189 Fergie Jenkins	.75	.30
❑ 190 Mookie Wilson	.75	.30
❑ 191 Jim Beattie	.25	.08
❑ 192 Gary Ward	.25	.08
❑ 193 Jesse Barfield	.75	.30
❑ 194 Pete Filson	.25	.08
❑ 195 Roy Lee Jackson	.25	.08
❑ 196 Rick Sweet	.25	.08
❑ 197 Jesse Orosco	.25	.08
❑ 198 Steve Lake	.25	.08
❑ 199 Ken Dayley	.25	.08
❑ 200 Manny Sarmiento	.25	.08
❑ 201 Mark Davis	.25	.08
❑ 202 Tim Flannery	.25	.08
❑ 203 Bill Scherrer	.25	.08
❑ 204 Al Holland	.25	.08
❑ 205 Dave Von Ohlen	.25	.08
❑ 206 Mike LaCoss	.25	.08
❑ 207 Juan Beniquez	.25	.08
❑ 208 Juan Agosto	.25	.08
❑ 209 Bobby Ramos	.25	.08
❑ 210 Al Bumbry	.25	.08
❑ 211 Mark Brouhard	.25	.08
❑ 212 Howard Bailey	.25	.08
❑ 213 Bruce Hurst	.25	.08
❑ 214 Bob Shirley	.25	.08
❑ 215 Pat Zachry	.25	.08
❑ 216 Julio Franco	3.00	1.25
❑ 217 Mike Armstrong	.25	.08
❑ 218 Dave Beard	.25	.08
❑ 219 Steve Rogers	.75	.30
❑ 220 John Butcher	.25	.08
❑ 221 Mike Smithson	.25	.08
❑ 222 Frank White	.75	.30
❑ 223 Mike Heath	.25	.08
❑ 224 Chris Bando	.25	.08
❑ 225 Roy Smalley	.25	.08
❑ 226 Dusty Baker	.75	.30
❑ 227 Lou Whitaker	.75	.30
❑ 228 John Lowenstein	.25	.08
❑ 229 Ben Oglivie	.75	.30
❑ 230 Doug DeCinces	.25	.08
❑ 231 Lonnie Smith	.25	.08
❑ 232 Ray Knight	.75	.30
❑ 233 Gary Matthews	.75	.30
❑ 234 Juan Bonilla	.25	.08
❑ 235 Rod Scurry	.25	.08
❑ 236 Atlee Hammaker	.25	.08

❑ 237 Mike Caldwell	.25	.08
❑ 238 Keith Hernandez	.75	.30
❑ 239 Larry Bowa	.75	.30
❑ 240 Tony Bernazard	.25	.08
❑ 241 Damaso Garcia	.25	.08
❑ 242 Tom Brunansky	.25	.08
❑ 243 Dan Driessen	.25	.08
❑ 244 Ron Kittle	.25	.08
❑ 245 Tim Stoddard	.25	.08
❑ 246 Bob L. Gibson RC (Brewers Pitcher)	.25	.08
❑ 247 Marty Castillo	.25	.08
❑ 248 Don Mattingly RC	40.00	15.00
❑ 249 Jeff Newman	.25	.08
❑ 250 Alejandro Pena RC	2.00	.75
❑ 251 Toby Harrah	.75	.30
❑ 252 Cesar Geronimo	.25	.08
❑ 253 Tom Underwood	.25	.08
❑ 254 Doug Flynn	.25	.08
❑ 255 Andy Hassler	.25	.08
❑ 256 Odell Jones	.25	.08
❑ 257 Rudy Law	.25	.08
❑ 258 Harry Spilman	.25	.08
❑ 259 Marty Bystrom	.25	.08
❑ 260 Dave Rucker	.25	.08
❑ 261 Ruppert Jones	.25	.08
❑ 262 Jeff R. Jones (Reds OF)	.25	.08
❑ 263 Gerald Perry	1.00	.40
❑ 264 Gene Tenace	.75	.30
❑ 265 Brad Wellman	.25	.08
❑ 266 Dickie Noles	.25	.08
❑ 267 Jamie Allen	.25	.08
❑ 268 Jim Gott	.25	.08
❑ 269 Ron Davis	.25	.08
❑ 270 Benny Ayala	.25	.08
❑ 271 Ned Yost	.25	.08
❑ 272 Dave Rozema	.25	.08
❑ 273 Dave Stapleton	.25	.08
❑ 274 Lou Piniella	.75	.30
❑ 275 Jose Morales	.25	.08
❑ 276 Broderick Perkins	.25	.08
❑ 277 Butch Davis RC	.25	.08
❑ 278 Tony Phillips RC	2.00	.75
❑ 279 Jeff Reardon	.75	.30
❑ 280 Ken Forsch	.25	.08
❑ 281 Pete O'Brien RC	1.00	.40
❑ 282 Tom Paciorek	.25	.08
❑ 283 Frank LaCorte	.25	.08
❑ 284 Tim Lollar	.25	.08
❑ 285 Greg Gross	.25	.08
❑ 286 Alex Trevino	.25	.08
❑ 287 Gene Garber	.25	.08
❑ 288 Dave Parker	.75	.30
❑ 289 Lee Smith	.75	.30
❑ 290 Dave LaPoint	.25	.08
❑ 291 John Shelby	.25	.08
❑ 292 Charlie Moore	.25	.08
❑ 293 Alan Trammell	.75	.30
❑ 294 Tony Armas	.75	.30
❑ 295 Shane Rawley	.25	.08
❑ 296 Greg Brock	.25	.08
❑ 297 Hal McRae	.75	.30
❑ 298 Mike Davis	.25	.08
❑ 299 Tim Raines	.75	.30
❑ 300 Bucky Dent	.75	.30
❑ 301 Tommy John	.75	.30
❑ 302 Carlton Fisk	1.50	.60
❑ 303 Darrell Porter	.25	.08
❑ 304 Dickie Thon	.25	.08
❑ 305 Garry Maddox	.25	.08
❑ 306 Cesar Cedeno	.75	.30
❑ 307 Gary Lucas	.25	.08
❑ 308 Johnny Ray	.25	.08
❑ 309 Andy McGaffigan	.25	.08
❑ 310 Claudell Washington	.25	.08
❑ 311 Ryne Sandberg	12.00	5.00
❑ 312 George Foster	.75	.30
❑ 313 Spike Owen RC	1.00	.40
❑ 314 Gary Gaetti	1.50	.60
❑ 315 Willie Upshaw	.25	.08
❑ 316 Al Williams	.25	.08
❑ 317 Jorge Orta	.25	.08
❑ 318 Orlando Mercado	.25	.08
❑ 319 Junior Ortiz	.25	.08
❑ 320 Mike Proly	.25	.08
❑ 321 Randy Johnson UER ('72-'82 stats are from Twins')	.25	.08
❑ 322 Jim Morrison	.25	.08
❑ 323 Max Venable	.25	.08
❑ 324 Tony Gwynn	12.00	5.00
❑ 325 Duane Walker	.25	.08
❑ 326 Ozzie Virgil	.25	.08
❑ 327 Jeff Lahti	.25	.08
❑ 328 Bill Dawley	.25	.08
❑ 329 Rob Wilfong	.25	.08
❑ 330 Marc Hill	.25	.08
❑ 331 Ray Burris	.25	.08
❑ 332 Allan Ramirez	.25	.08
❑ 333 Chuck Porter	.25	.08
❑ 334 Wayne Krenchicki	.25	.08
❑ 335 Gary Allenson	.25	.08
❑ 336 Bobby Meacham	.25	.08
❑ 337 Joe Beckwith	.25	.08
❑ 338 Rick Sutcliffe	.75	.30
❑ 339 Mark Huismann	.25	.08
❑ 340 Tim Conroy	.25	.08
❑ 341 Scott Sanderson	.25	.08
❑ 342 Larry Biittner	.25	.08
❑ 343 Dave Stewart	.75	.30
❑ 344 Darryl Motley	.25	.08
❑ 345 Chris Codiroli	.25	.08
❑ 346 Rich Behenna	.25	.08
❑ 347 Andre Robertson	.25	.08
❑ 348 Mike Marshall	.25	.08
❑ 349 Larry Herndon	.75	.30
❑ 350 Rich Dauer	.25	.08
❑ 351 Cecil Cooper	.75	.30
❑ 352 Rod Carew	1.50	.60
❑ 353 Willie McGee	.75	.30
❑ 354 Phil Garner	.75	.30
❑ 355 Joe Morgan	.75	.30
❑ 356 Luis Salazar	.25	.08
❑ 357 John Candelaria	.25	.08
❑ 358 Bill Laskey	.25	.08
❑ 359 Bob McClure	.25	.08
❑ 360 Dave Kingman	.75	.30
❑ 361 Ron Cey	.75	.30
❑ 362 Matt Young RC	1.00	.40
❑ 363 Lloyd Moseby	.25	.08
❑ 364 Frank Viola	1.50	.60
❑ 365 Eddie Milner	.25	.08
❑ 366 Floyd Bannister	.25	.08
❑ 367 Dan Ford	.25	.08
❑ 368 Moose Haas	.25	.08
❑ 369 Doug Bair	.25	.08
❑ 370 Ray Fontenot	.25	.08
❑ 371 Luis Aponte	.25	.08
❑ 372 Jack Fimple	.25	.08
❑ 373 Neal Heaton	.25	.08
❑ 374 Greg Pryor	.25	.08
❑ 375 Wayne Gross	.25	.08
❑ 376 Charlie Lea	.25	.08
❑ 377 Steve Lubratich	.25	.08
❑ 378 Jon Matlack	.25	.08
❑ 379 Julio Cruz	.25	.08
❑ 380 John Mizerock	.25	.08
❑ 381 Kevin Gross RC	1.00	.40
❑ 382 Mike Ramsey	.25	.08
❑ 383 Doug Gwosdz	.25	.08
❑ 384 Kelly Paris	.25	.08
❑ 385 Pete Falcone	.25	.08
❑ 386 Milt May	.25	.08
❑ 387 Fred Breining	.25	.08
❑ 388 Craig Lefferts RC	.25	.08
❑ 389 Steve Henderson	.25	.08
❑ 390 Randy Moffitt	.25	.08
❑ 391 Ron Washington	.25	.08
❑ 392 Gary Roenicke	.25	.08
❑ 393 Tom Candiotti RC	2.00	.75
❑ 394 Larry Pashnick	.25	.08
❑ 395 Dwight Evans	1.50	.60
❑ 396 Rich Gossage	.75	.30
❑ 397 Derrel Thomas	.25	.08
❑ 398 Juan Eichelberger	.25	.08
❑ 399 Leon Roberts	.25	.08
❑ 400 Dave Lopes	.75	.30
❑ 401 Bill Gullickson	.25	.08
❑ 402 Geoff Zahn	.25	.08
❑ 403 Billy Sample	.25	.08
❑ 404 Mike Squires	.25	.08
❑ 405 Craig Reynolds	.25	.08
❑ 406 Eric Show	.25	.08
❑ 407 John Denny	.25	.08
❑ 408 Dann Bilardello	.25	.08
❑ 409 Bruce Benedict	.25	.08
❑ 410 Kent Tekulve	.25	.08
❑ 411 Mel Hall	.75	.30
❑ 412 John Stuper	.25	.08
❑ 413 Rick Dempsey	.25	.08
❑ 414 Don Sutton	.75	.30
❑ 415 Jack Morris	.75	.30
❑ 416 John Tudor	.75	.30
❑ 417 Willie Randolph	.75	.30
❑ 418 Jerry Reuss	.25	.08
❑ 419 Don Slaught	.75	.30
❑ 420 Steve McCatty	.25	.08
❑ 421 Tim Wallach	.25	.08
❑ 422 Larry Parrish	.25	.08
❑ 423 Brian Downing	.75	.30
❑ 424 Britt Burns	.25	.08
❑ 425 David Green	.25	.08
❑ 426 Jerry Mumphrey	.25	.08
❑ 427 Ivan DeJesus	.25	.08
❑ 428 Mario Soto	.75	.30
❑ 429 Gene Richards	.25	.08
❑ 430 Dale Berra	.25	.08
❑ 431 Darrell Evans	.75	.30
❑ 432 Glenn Hubbard	.25	.08
❑ 433 Jody Davis	.25	.08
❑ 434 Danny Heep	.25	.08
❑ 435 Edwin Nunez RC	.25	.08
❑ 436 Bobby Castillo	.25	.08
❑ 437 Ernie Whitt	.25	.08
❑ 438 Scott Ullger	.25	.08
❑ 439 Doyle Alexander	.25	.08
❑ 440 Domingo Ramos	.25	.08
❑ 441 Craig Swan	.25	.08
❑ 442 Warren Brusstar	.25	.08
❑ 443 Len Barker	.25	.08
❑ 444 Mike Easler	.25	.08
❑ 445 Renie Martin	.25	.08
❑ 446 Dennis Rasmussen RC	1.00	.40
❑ 447 Ted Power	.25	.08
❑ 448 Charles Hudson	.25	.08
❑ 449 Danny Cox RC	.25	.08
❑ 450 Kevin Bass	.25	.08
❑ 451 Daryl Sconiers	.25	.08
❑ 452 Scott Fletcher	.25	.08
❑ 453 Bryn Smith	.25	.08
❑ 454 Jim Dwyer	.25	.08
❑ 455 Rob Picciolo	.25	.08
❑ 456 Enos Cabell	.25	.08
❑ 457 Dennis Boyd	.75	.30
❑ 458 Butch Wynegar	.25	.08
❑ 459 Burt Hooton	.25	.08
❑ 460 Ron Hassey	.25	.08
❑ 461 Danny Jackson RC	1.00	.40
❑ 462 Bob Kearney	.25	.08
❑ 463 Terry Francona	.75	.30
❑ 464 Wayne Tolleson	.25	.08
❑ 465 Mickey Rivers	.25	.08
❑ 466 John Wathan	.25	.08
❑ 467 Bill Almon	.25	.08
❑ 468 George Vukovich	.25	.08
❑ 469 Steve Kemp	.25	.08
❑ 470 Ken Landreaux	.25	.08
❑ 471 Milt Wilcox	.25	.08
❑ 472 Tippy Martinez	.25	.08
❑ 473 Ted Simmons	.75	.30
❑ 474 Tim Foli	.25	.08
❑ 475 George Hendrick	.75	.30
❑ 476 Terry Puhl	.25	.08
❑ 477 Von Hayes	.25	.08
❑ 478 Bobby Brown	.25	.08
❑ 479 Lee Lacy	.25	.08
❑ 480 Joel Youngblood	.25	.08
❑ 481 Jim Slaton	.25	.08
❑ 482 Mike Fitzgerald	.25	.08
❑ 483 Keith Moreland	.25	.08
❑ 484 Ron Roenicke	.25	.08
❑ 485 Luis Leal	.25	.08
❑ 486 Bryan Oelkers	.25	.08
❑ 487 Bruce Berenyi	.25	.08
❑ 488 LaMarr Hoyt	.25	.08
❑ 489 Joe Nolan	.25	.08
❑ 490 Marshall Edwards	.25	.08

❑ 491 Mike Laga .75 .30
❑ 492 Rick Cerone .25 .08
❑ 493 Rick Miller UER (Listed as Mike on card front) .25 .08
❑ 494 Rick Honeycutt .25 .08
❑ 495 Mike Hargrove .25 .08
❑ 496 Joe Simpson .25 .08
❑ 497 Keith Atherton .25 .08
❑ 498 Chris Welsh .25 .08
❑ 499 Bruce Kison .25 .08
❑ 500 Bobby Johnson .25 .08
❑ 501 Jerry Koosman .75 .30
❑ 502 Frank DiPino .25 .08
❑ 503 Tony Perez 1.50 .60
❑ 504 Ken Oberkfell .25 .08
❑ 505 Mark Thurmond .25 .08
❑ 506 Joe Price .25 .08
❑ 507 Pascual Perez .25 .08
❑ 508 Marvell Wynne 1.00 .40
❑ 509 Mike Krukow .25 .08
❑ 510 Dick Ruthven .25 .08
❑ 511 Al Cowens .25 .08
❑ 512 Cliff Johnson .25 .08
❑ 513 Randy Bush .25 .08
❑ 514 Sammy Stewart .25 .08
❑ 515 Bill Schroeder .25 .08
❑ 516 Aurelio Lopez .75 .30
❑ 517 Mike C. Brown .25 .08
❑ 518 Graig Nettles .75 .30
❑ 519 Dave Sax .25 .08
❑ 520 Jerry Willard .25 .08
❑ 521 Paul Splittorff .25 .08
❑ 522 Tom Burgmeier .25 .08
❑ 523 Chris Speier .25 .08
❑ 524 Bobby Clark .25 .08
❑ 525 George Wright .25 .08
❑ 526 Dennis Lamp .25 .08
❑ 527 Tony Scott .25 .08
❑ 528 Ed Whitson .25 .08
❑ 529 Ron Reed .25 .08
❑ 530 Charlie Puleo .25 .08
❑ 531 Jerry Royster .25 .08
❑ 532 Don Robinson .25 .08
❑ 533 Steve Trout .25 .08
❑ 534 Bruce Sutter 1.50 .60
❑ 535 Bob Horner ! .75 .30
❑ 536 Pat Tabler .25 .08
❑ 537 Chris Chambliss .75 .30
❑ 538 Bob Ojeda .25 .08
❑ 539 Alan Ashby .25 .08
❑ 540 Jay Johnstone .25 .08
❑ 541 Bob Dernier .25 .08
❑ 542 Brook Jacoby 1.00 .40
❑ 543 U.L. Washington .25 .08
❑ 544 Danny Darwin .25 .08
❑ 545 Kiko Garcia .25 .08
❑ 546 Vance Law UER (Listed as P on card front) .25 .08
❑ 547 Tug McGraw .75 .30
❑ 548 Dave Smith .25 .08
❑ 549 Len Matuszek .25 .08
❑ 550 Tom Hume .25 .08
❑ 551 Dave Dravecky .25 .08
❑ 552 Rick Rhoden .25 .08
❑ 553 Duane Kuiper .25 .08
❑ 554 Rusty Staub .75 .30
❑ 555 Bill Campbell .25 .08
❑ 556 Mike Torrez .25 .08
❑ 557 Dave Henderson .75 .30
❑ 558 Len Whitehouse .25 .08
❑ 559 Barry Bonnell .25 .08
❑ 560 Rick Lysander .25 .08
❑ 561 Garth Iorg .25 .08
❑ 562 Bryan Clark .25 .08
❑ 563 Brian Giles .25 .08
❑ 564 Vern Ruhle .25 .08
❑ 565 Steve Bedrosian .25 .08
❑ 566 Larry McWilliams .25 .08
❑ 567 Jeff Leonard UER (Listed as P on card front) .25 .08
❑ 568 Alan Wiggins .25 .08
❑ 569 Jeff Russell RC 1.00 .40
❑ 570 Salome Barojas .25 .08
❑ 571 Dane Iorg .25 .08
❑ 572 Bob Knepper .25 .08
❑ 573 Gary Lavelle .25 .08
❑ 574 Gorman Thomas .75 .30
❑ 575 Manny Trillo .25 .08
❑ 576 Jim Palmer .75 .30
❑ 577 Dale Murray .25 .08
❑ 578 Tom Brookens .75 .30
❑ 579 Rich Gedman .25 .08
❑ 580 Bill Doran RC 1.00 .40
❑ 581 Steve Yeager .75 .30
❑ 582 Dan Spillner .25 .08
❑ 583 Dan Quisenberry .25 .08
❑ 584 Rance Mulliniks .25 .08
❑ 585 Storm Davis .25 .08
❑ 586 Dave Schmidt .25 .08
❑ 587 Bill Russell .75 .30
❑ 588 Pat Sheridan .25 .08
❑ 589 Rafael Ramirez UER (A's on front) .25 .08
❑ 590 Bud Anderson .25 .08
❑ 591 George Frazier .25 .08
❑ 592 Lee Tunnell .25 .08
❑ 593 Kirk Gibson 3.00 1.25
❑ 594 Scott McGregor .25 .08
❑ 595 Bob Bailor .25 .08
❑ 596 Tommy Herr .25 .08
❑ 597 Luis Sanchez .25 .08
❑ 598 Dave Engle .25 .08
❑ 599 Craig McMurtry .25 .08
❑ 600 Carlos Diaz .25 .08
❑ 601 Tom O'Malley .25 .08
❑ 602 Nick Esasky .25 .08
❑ 603 Ron Hodges .25 .08
❑ 604 Ed VandeBerg .25 .08
❑ 605 Alfredo Griffin .25 .08
❑ 606 Glenn Hoffman .25 .08
❑ 607 Hubie Brooks .25 .08
❑ 608 Richard Barnes UER (Photo actually Neal Heaton) .25 .08
❑ 609 Greg Walker 1.00 .40
❑ 610 Ken Singleton .75 .30
❑ 611 Mark Clear .25 .08
❑ 612 Buck Martinez .25 .08
❑ 613 Ken Griffey .75 .30
❑ 614 Reid Nichols .25 .08
❑ 615 Doug Sisk .25 .08
❑ 616 Bob Brenly .25 .08
❑ 617 Joey McLaughlin .25 .08
❑ 618 Glenn Wilson .75 .30
❑ 619 Bob Stoddard .25 .08
❑ 620 Lenn Sakata UER (Listed as Len on card front) .25 .08
❑ 621 Mike Young RC .25 .08
❑ 622 John Stefero .25 .08
❑ 623 Carmelo Martinez .25 .08
❑ 624 Dave Bergman .25 .08
❑ 625 Ozzie Smith/W.McGee 3.00 1.25
❑ 626 Rudy May .25 .08
❑ 627 Matt Keough .25 .08
❑ 628 Jose DeLeon RC 1.00 .40
❑ 629 Jim Essian .25 .08
❑ 630 Darnell Coles RC 1.00 .40
❑ 631 Mike Warren .25 .08
❑ 632 Del Crandall MG .25 .08
❑ 633 Dennis Martinez .75 .30
❑ 634 Mike Moore .25 .08
❑ 635 Lary Sorensen .25 .08
❑ 636 Ricky Nelson .25 .08
❑ 637 Omar Moreno .25 .08
❑ 638 Charlie Hough .75 .30
❑ 639 Dennis Eckersley ! 1.50 .60
❑ 640 Walt Terrell .25 .08
❑ 641 Denny Walling .25 .08
❑ 642 Dave Anderson RC .25 .08
❑ 643 Jose Oquendo RC 1.00 .40
❑ 644 Bob Stanley .25 .08
❑ 645 Dave Geisel .25 .08
❑ 646 Scott Garrelts .25 .08
❑ 647 Gary Pettis .25 .08
❑ 648 Duke Snider Puzzle 1.50 .60
❑ 649 Johnnie LeMaster .25 .08
❑ 650 Dave Collins .25 .08
❑ 651 The Chicken 1.50 .60
❑ 652 DK Checklist 1-26 (Unnumbered) .75 .30
❑ 653 Checklist 27-130 (Unnumbered) .25 .08
❑ 654 Checklist 131-234 (Unnumbered) .25 .08
❑ 655 Checklist 235-338 (Unnumbered) .25 .08
❑ 656 Checklist 339-442 (Unnumbered) .25 .08
❑ 657 Checklist 443-546 (Unnumbered) .25 .08
❑ 658 Checklist 547-651 (Unnumbered) .25 .08
❑ A G.Perry/R.Fingers SP 2.50 1.00
❑ B J.Bench/C.Yastrzemski SP 5.00 2.00

1985 Donruss

❑ COMPLETE SET (660) 60.00 30.00
❑ COMP.FACT.SET (660) 100.00 50.00
❑ COMP.GEHRIG PUZZLE 4.00 1.50
❑ 1 Ryne Sandberg DK 1.25 .50
❑ 2 Doug DeCinces DK .15 .05
❑ 3 Richard Dotson DK .15 .05
❑ 4 Bert Blyleven DK .40 .15
❑ 5 Lou Whitaker DK .40 .15
❑ 6 Dan Quisenberry DK .15 .05
❑ 7 Don Mattingly DK 2.50 1.00
❑ 8 Carney Lansford DK .40 .15
❑ 9 Frank Tanana DK .40 .15
❑ 10 Willie Upshaw DK .15 .05
❑ 11 Claudell Washington DK .15 .05
❑ 12 Mike Marshall DK .15 .05
❑ 13 Joaquin Andujar DK .40 .15
❑ 14 Cal Ripken DK 2.50 1.00
❑ 15 Jim Rice DK .40 .15
❑ 16 Don Sutton DK .40 .15
❑ 17 Frank Viola DK .40 .15
❑ 18 Alvin Davis DK .40 .15
❑ 19 Mario Soto DK .40 .15
❑ 20 Jose Cruz DK .40 .15
❑ 21 Charlie Lea DK .15 .05
❑ 22 Jesse Orosco DK .15 .05
❑ 23 Juan Samuel DK .15 .05
❑ 24 Tony Pena DK .15 .05
❑ 25 Tony Gwynn DK 1.25 .50
❑ 26 Bob Brenly DK .15 .05
❑ 27 Danny Tartabull RC 1.00 .40
❑ 28 Mike Bielecki RC .25 .08
❑ 29 Steve Lyons RC .50 .20
❑ 30 Jeff Reed RC .25 .08
❑ 31 Tony Brewer RC .25 .08
❑ 32 John Morris RC .25 .08
❑ 33 Daryl Boston RC .25 .08
❑ 34 Al Pulido RC .25 .08
❑ 35 Steve Kiefer RC .25 .08
❑ 36 Larry Sheets RC .25 .08
❑ 37 Scott Bradley RC .25 .08
❑ 38 Calvin Schiraldi RC .50 .20
❑ 39 Shawon Dunston RC 1.00 .40
❑ 40 Charlie Mitchell RC .25 .08
❑ 41 Billy Hatcher RC .50 .20
❑ 42 Russ Stephans RC .25 .08
❑ 43 Alejandro Sanchez RC .25 .08
❑ 44 Steve Jeltz RC .25 .08
❑ 45 Jim Traber RC .25 .08
❑ 46 Doug Loman RC .25 .08
❑ 47 Eddie Murray 1.25 .50

❑ 48 Robin Yount 2.00 .75
❑ 49 Lance Parrish .40 .15
❑ 50 Jim Rice .40 .15
❑ 51 Dave Winfield .40 .15
❑ 52 Fernando Valenzuela .40 .15
❑ 53 George Brett 3.00 1.25
❑ 54 Dave Kingman .40 .15
❑ 55 Gary Carter .40 .15
❑ 56 Buddy Bell .40 .15
❑ 57 Reggie Jackson .75 .30
❑ 58 Harold Baines .40 .15
❑ 59 Ozzie Smith 2.00 .75
❑ 60 Nolan Ryan 6.00 2.50
❑ 61 Mike Schmidt 3.00 1.25
❑ 62 Dave Parker .40 .15
❑ 63 Tony Gwynn 2.50 1.00
❑ 64 Tony Pena .15 .05
❑ 65 Jack Clark .40 .15
❑ 66 Dale Murphy .75 .30
❑ 67 Ryne Sandberg 2.50 1.00
❑ 68 Keith Hernandez .40 .15
❑ 69 Alvin Davis RC* .50 .20
❑ 70 Kent Hrbek .40 .15
❑ 71 Willie Upshaw .15 .05
❑ 72 Dave Engle .15 .05
❑ 73 Alfredo Griffin .15 .05
❑ 74A Jack Perconte (Career Highlights takes four line .15 .05
❑ 74B Jack Perconte (Career Highlights takes three lin .15 .05
❑ 75 Jesse Orosco .15 .05
❑ 76 Jody Davis .15 .05
❑ 77 Bob Horner .40 .15
❑ 78 Larry McWilliams .15 .05
❑ 79 Joel Youngblood .15 .05
❑ 80 Alan Wiggins .15 .05
❑ 81 Ron Oester .15 .05
❑ 82 Ozzie Virgil .15 .05
❑ 83 Ricky Horton .15 .05
❑ 84 Bill Doran .15 .05
❑ 85 Rod Carew .75 .30
❑ 86 LaMarr Hoyt .15 .05
❑ 87 Tim Wallach .15 .05
❑ 88 Mike Flanagan .15 .05
❑ 89 Jim Sundberg .40 .15
❑ 90 Chet Lemon .40 .15
❑ 91 Bob Stanley .15 .05
❑ 92 Willie Randolph .40 .15
❑ 93 Bill Russell .40 .15
❑ 94 Julio Franco .40 .15
❑ 95 Dan Quisenberry .15 .05
❑ 96 Bill Caudill .15 .05
❑ 97 Bill Gullickson .15 .05
❑ 98 Danny Darwin .15 .05
❑ 99 Curtis Wilkerson .15 .05
❑ 100 Bud Black .15 .05
❑ 101 Tony Phillips .15 .05
❑ 102 Tony Bernazard .15 .05
❑ 103 Jay Howell .15 .05
❑ 104 Burt Hooton .15 .05
❑ 105 Milt Wilcox .15 .05
❑ 106 Rich Dauer .15 .05
❑ 107 Don Sutton .40 .15
❑ 108 Mike Witt .15 .05
❑ 109 Bruce Sutter .40 .15
❑ 110 Enos Cabell .15 .05
❑ 111 John Denny .15 .05
❑ 112 Dave Dravecky .15 .05
❑ 113 Marvell Wynne .15 .05
❑ 114 Johnnie LeMaster .15 .05
❑ 115 Chuck Porter .15 .05
❑ 116 John Gibbons .15 .05
❑ 117 Keith Moreland .15 .05
❑ 118 Darnell Coles .15 .05
❑ 119 Dennis Lamp .15 .05
❑ 120 Ron Davis .15 .05
❑ 121 Nick Esasky .15 .05
❑ 122 Vance Law .15 .05
❑ 123 Gary Roenicke .15 .05
❑ 124 Bill Schroeder .15 .05
❑ 125 Dave Rozema .15 .05
❑ 126 Bobby Meacham .15 .05
❑ 127 Marty Barrett .15 .05
❑ 128 R.J. Reynolds .15 .05
❑ 129 Ernie Camacho UER (Photo actually Rich Thompson) .15 .05
❑ 130 Jorge Orta .15 .05
❑ 131 Lary Sorensen .15 .05
❑ 132 Terry Francona .40 .15
❑ 133 Fred Lynn .40 .15
❑ 134 Bob Jones .15 .05
❑ 135 Jerry Hairston .15 .05
❑ 136 Kevin Bass .15 .05
❑ 137 Garry Maddox .15 .05
❑ 138 Dave LaPoint .15 .05
❑ 139 Kevin McReynolds .40 .15
❑ 140 Wayne Krenchicki .15 .05
❑ 141 Rafael Ramirez .15 .05
❑ 142 Rod Scurry .15 .05
❑ 143 Greg Minton .15 .05
❑ 144 Tim Stoddard .15 .05
❑ 145 Steve Henderson .15 .05
❑ 146 George Bell .40 .15
❑ 147 Dave Meier .15 .05
❑ 148 Sammy Stewart .15 .05
❑ 149 Mark Brouhard .15 .05
❑ 150 Larry Herndon .15 .05
❑ 151 Oil Can Boyd .15 .05
❑ 152 Brian Dayett .15 .05
❑ 153 Tom Niedenfuer .15 .05
❑ 154 Brook Jacoby .15 .05
❑ 155 Onix Concepcion .15 .05
❑ 156 Tim Conroy .15 .05
❑ 157 Joe Hesketh .15 .05
❑ 158 Brian Downing .40 .15
❑ 159 Tommy Dunbar .15 .05
❑ 160 Marc Hill .15 .05
❑ 161 Phil Garner .40 .15
❑ 162 Jerry Davis .15 .05
❑ 163 Bill Campbell .15 .05
❑ 164 John Franco RC 1.00 .40
❑ 165 Len Barker .15 .05
❑ 166 Benny Distefano .15 .05
❑ 167 George Frazier .15 .05
❑ 168 Tito Landrum .15 .05
❑ 169 Cal Ripken 5.00 2.00
❑ 170 Cecil Cooper .40 .15
❑ 171 Alan Trammell .40 .15
❑ 172 Wade Boggs 1.25 .50
❑ 173 Don Baylor .40 .15
❑ 174 Pedro Guerrero .40 .15
❑ 175 Frank White .40 .15
❑ 176 Rickey Henderson 1.50 .60
❑ 177 Charlie Lea .15 .05
❑ 178 Pete O'Brien .15 .05
❑ 179 Doug DeCinces .15 .05
❑ 180 Ron Kittle .15 .05
❑ 181 George Hendrick .40 .15
❑ 182 Joe Niekro .15 .05
❑ 183 Juan Samuel .15 .05
❑ 184 Mario Soto .40 .15
❑ 185 Goose Gossage .40 .15
❑ 186 Johnny Ray .15 .05
❑ 187 Bob Brenly .15 .05
❑ 188 Craig McMurtry .15 .05
❑ 189 Leon Durham .15 .05
❑ 190 Dwight Gooden RC 3.00 1.25
❑ 191 Barry Bonnell .15 .05
❑ 192 Tim Teufel .15 .05
❑ 193 Dave Stieb .40 .15
❑ 194 Mickey Hatcher .15 .05
❑ 195 Jesse Barfield .40 .15
❑ 196 Al Cowens .15 .05
❑ 197 Hubie Brooks .15 .05
❑ 198 Steve Trout .15 .05
❑ 199 Glenn Hubbard .15 .05
❑ 200 Bill Madlock .40 .15
❑ 201 Jeff D. Robinson .15 .05
❑ 202 Eric Show .15 .05
❑ 203 Dave Concepcion .40 .15
❑ 204 Ivan DeJesus .15 .05
❑ 205 Neil Allen .15 .05
❑ 206 Jerry Mumphrey .15 .05
❑ 207 Mike C. Brown .15 .05
❑ 208 Carlton Fisk .75 .30
❑ 209 Bryn Smith .15 .05
❑ 210 Tippy Martinez .15 .05
❑ 211 Dion James .15 .05
❑ 212 Willie Hernandez .15 .05
❑ 213 Mike Easler .15 .05
❑ 214 Ron Guidry .40 .15
❑ 215 Rick Honeycutt .15 .05
❑ 216 Brett Butler .40 .15
❑ 217 Larry Gura .15 .05
❑ 218 Ray Burris .15 .05
❑ 219 Steve Rogers .40 .15
❑ 220 Frank Tanana UER (Bats Left listed twice on card .40 .15
❑ 221 Ned Yost .15 .05
❑ 222 Bret Saberhagen RC 1.50 .60
❑ 223 Mike Davis .15 .05
❑ 224 Bert Blyleven .40 .15
❑ 225 Steve Kemp .15 .05
❑ 226 Jerry Reuss .15 .05
❑ 227 Darrell Evans UER (80 homers in 1980) .40 .15
❑ 228 Wayne Gross .15 .05
❑ 229 Jim Gantner .15 .05
❑ 230 Bob Boone .40 .15
❑ 231 Lonnie Smith .15 .05
❑ 232 Frank DiPino .15 .05
❑ 233 Jerry Koosman .40 .15
❑ 234 Graig Nettles .40 .15
❑ 235 John Tudor .40 .15
❑ 236 John Rabb .15 .05
❑ 237 Rick Manning .15 .05
❑ 238 Mike Fitzgerald .15 .05
❑ 239 Gary Matthews .40 .15
❑ 240 Jim Presley .50 .20
❑ 241 Dave Collins .15 .05
❑ 242 Gary Gaetti .40 .15
❑ 243 Dann Bilardello .15 .05
❑ 244 Rudy Law .15 .05
❑ 245 John Lowenstein .15 .05
❑ 246 Tom Tellmann .15 .05
❑ 247 Howard Johnson .40 .15
❑ 248 Ray Fontenot .15 .05
❑ 249 Tony Armas .40 .15
❑ 250 Candy Maldonado .15 .05
❑ 251 Mike Jeffcoat .15 .05
❑ 252 Dane Iorg .15 .05
❑ 253 Bruce Bochte .15 .05
❑ 254 Pete Rose Expos 4.00 1.50
❑ 255 Don Aase .15 .05
❑ 256 George Wright .15 .05
❑ 257 Britt Burns .15 .05
❑ 258 Mike Scott .40 .15
❑ 259 Len Matuszek .15 .05
❑ 260 Dave Rucker .15 .05
❑ 261 Craig Lefferts .15 .05
❑ 262 Jay Tibbs .15 .05
❑ 263 Bruce Benedict .15 .05
❑ 264 Don Robinson .15 .05
❑ 265 Gary Lavelle .15 .05
❑ 266 Scott Sanderson .15 .05
❑ 267 Matt Young .15 .05
❑ 268 Ernie Whitt .15 .05
❑ 269 Houston Jimenez .15 .05
❑ 270 Ken Dixon .15 .05
❑ 271 Pete Ladd .15 .05
❑ 272 Juan Berenguer .15 .05
❑ 273 Roger Clemens RC 40.00 15.00
❑ 274 Rick Cerone .15 .05
❑ 275 Dave Anderson .15 .05
❑ 276 George Vukovich .15 .05
❑ 277 Greg Pryor .15 .05
❑ 278 Mike Warren .15 .05
❑ 279 Bob James .15 .05
❑ 280 Bobby Grich .40 .15
❑ 281 Mike Mason RC .25 .08
❑ 282 Ron Reed .15 .05
❑ 283 Alan Ashby .15 .05
❑ 284 Mark Thurmond .15 .05
❑ 285 Joe Lefebvre .15 .05
❑ 286 Ted Power .15 .05
❑ 287 Chris Chambliss .40 .15
❑ 288 Lee Tunnell .15 .05
❑ 289 Rich Bordi .15 .05
❑ 290 Glenn Brummer .15 .05
❑ 291 Mike Boddicker .15 .05
❑ 292 Rollie Fingers .40 .15
❑ 293 Lou Whitaker .40 .15
❑ 294 Dwight Evans .75 .30
❑ 295 Don Mattingly 5.00 2.00

❑ 296	Mike Marshall	.15	.05
❑ 297	Willie Wilson	.40	.15
❑ 298	Mike Heath	.15	.05
❑ 299	Tim Raines	.40	.15
❑ 300	Larry Parrish	.15	.05
❑ 301	Geoff Zahn	.15	.05
❑ 302	Rich Dotson	.15	.05
❑ 303	David Green	.15	.05
❑ 304	Jose Cruz	.40	.15
❑ 305	Steve Carlton	.40	.15
❑ 306	Gary Redus	.15	.05
❑ 307	Steve Garvey	.40	.15
❑ 308	Jose DeLeon	.15	.05
❑ 309	Randy Lerch	.15	.05
❑ 310	Claudell Washington	.15	.05
❑ 311	Lee Smith	.40	.15
❑ 312	Darryl Strawberry	1.25	.50
❑ 313	Jim Beattie	.15	.05
❑ 314	John Butcher	.15	.05
❑ 315	Damaso Garcia	.15	.05
❑ 316	Mike Smithson	.15	.05
❑ 317	Luis Leal	.15	.05
❑ 318	Ken Phelps	.15	.05
❑ 319	Wally Backman	.15	.05
❑ 320	Ron Cey	.40	.15
❑ 321	Brad Komminsk	.15	.05
❑ 322	Jason Thompson	.15	.05
❑ 323	Frank Williams	.15	.05
❑ 324	Tim Lollar	.15	.05
❑ 325	Eric Davis RC	3.00	1.25
❑ 326	Von Hayes	.15	.05
❑ 327	Andy Van Slyke	.75	.30
❑ 328	Craig Reynolds	.15	.05
❑ 329	Dick Schofield	.15	.05
❑ 330	Scott Fletcher	.15	.05
❑ 331	Jeff Reardon	.40	.15
❑ 332	Rick Dempsey	.15	.05
❑ 333	Ben Oglivie	.40	.15
❑ 334	Dan Petry	.15	.05
❑ 335	Jackie Gutierrez	.15	.05
❑ 336	Dave Righetti	.40	.15
❑ 337	Alejandro Pena	.15	.05
❑ 338	Mel Hall	.15	.05
❑ 339	Pat Sheridan	.15	.05
❑ 340	Keith Atherton	.15	.05
❑ 341	David Palmer	.15	.05
❑ 342	Gary Ward	.15	.05
❑ 343	Dave Stewart	.40	.15
❑ 344	Mark Gubicza RC*	.50	.20
❑ 345	Carney Lansford	.40	.15
❑ 346	Jerry Willard	.15	.05
❑ 347	Ken Griffey	.40	.15
❑ 348	Franklin Stubbs	.15	.05
❑ 349	Aurelio Lopez	.15	.05
❑ 350	Al Bumbry	.15	.05
❑ 351	Charlie Moore	.15	.05
❑ 352	Luis Sanchez	.15	.05
❑ 353	Darrell Porter	.15	.05
❑ 354	Bill Dawley	.15	.05
❑ 355	Charles Hudson	.15	.05
❑ 356	Garry Templeton	.40	.15
❑ 357	Cecilio Guante	.15	.05
❑ 358	Jeff Leonard	.15	.05
❑ 359	Paul Molitor	.40	.15
❑ 360	Ron Gardenhire	.15	.05
❑ 361	Larry Bowa	.40	.15
❑ 362	Bob Kearney	.15	.05
❑ 363	Garth Iorg	.15	.05
❑ 364	Tom Brunansky	.15	.05
❑ 365	Brad Gulden	.15	.05
❑ 366	Greg Walker	.15	.05
❑ 367	Mike Young	.15	.05
❑ 368	Rick Waits	.15	.05
❑ 369	Doug Bair	.15	.05
❑ 370	Bob Shirley	.15	.05
❑ 371	Bob Ojeda	.15	.05
❑ 372	Bob Welch	.40	.15
❑ 373	Neal Heaton	.15	.05
❑ 374	Danny Jackson UER (Photo actually Frank Wills)	.15	.05
❑ 375	Donnie Hill	.15	.05
❑ 376	Mike Stenhouse	.15	.05
❑ 377	Bruce Kison	.15	.05
❑ 378	Wayne Tolleson	.15	.05
❑ 379	Floyd Bannister	.15	.05
❑ 380	Vern Ruhle	.15	.05
❑ 381	Tim Corcoran	.15	.05
❑ 382	Kurt Kepshire	.15	.05
❑ 383	Bobby Brown	.15	.05
❑ 384	Dave Van Gorder	.15	.05
❑ 385	Rick Mahler	.15	.05
❑ 386	Lee Mazzilli	.40	.15
❑ 387	Bill Laskey	.15	.05
❑ 388	Thad Bosley	.15	.05
❑ 389	Al Chambers	.15	.05
❑ 390	Tony Fernandez	.40	.15
❑ 391	Ron Washington	.15	.05
❑ 392	Bill Swaggerty	.15	.05
❑ 393	Bob L. Gibson	.15	.05
❑ 394	Marty Castillo	.15	.05
❑ 395	Steve Crawford	.15	.05
❑ 396	Clay Christiansen	.15	.05
❑ 397	Bob Bailor	.15	.05
❑ 398	Mike Hargrove	.15	.05
❑ 399	Charlie Leibrandt	.15	.05
❑ 400	Tom Burgmeier	.15	.05
❑ 401	Razor Shines	.15	.05
❑ 402	Rob Wilfong	.15	.05
❑ 403	Tom Henke	.40	.15
❑ 404	Al Jones	.15	.05
❑ 405	Mike LaCoss	.15	.05
❑ 406	Luis DeLeon	.15	.05
❑ 407	Greg Gross	.15	.05
❑ 408	Tom Hume	.15	.05
❑ 409	Rick Camp	.15	.05
❑ 410	Milt May	.15	.05
❑ 411	Henry Cotto RC	.25	.08
❑ 412	David Von Ohlen	.15	.05
❑ 413	Scott McGregor	.15	.05
❑ 414	Ted Simmons	.40	.15
❑ 415	Jack Morris	.40	.15
❑ 416	Bill Buckner	.40	.15
❑ 417	Butch Wynegar	.15	.05
❑ 418	Steve Sax	.15	.05
❑ 419	Steve Balboni	.15	.05
❑ 420	Dwayne Murphy	.15	.05
❑ 421	Andre Dawson	.40	.15
❑ 422	Charlie Hough	.40	.15
❑ 423	Tommy John	.40	.15
❑ 424A	Tom Seaver ERR	.75	.30
❑ 424B	Tom Seaver COR	10.00	4.00
❑ 425	Tommy Herr	.15	.05
❑ 426	Terry Puhl	.15	.05
❑ 427	Al Holland	.15	.05
❑ 428	Eddie Milner	.15	.05
❑ 429	Terry Kennedy	.15	.05
❑ 430	John Candelaria	.15	.05
❑ 431	Manny Trillo	.15	.05
❑ 432	Ken Oberkfell	.15	.05
❑ 433	Rick Sutcliffe	.40	.15
❑ 434	Ron Darling	.40	.15
❑ 435	Spike Owen	.15	.05
❑ 436	Frank Viola	.40	.15
❑ 437	Lloyd Moseby	.15	.05
❑ 438	Kirby Puckett RC	10.00	4.00
❑ 439	Jim Clancy	.15	.05
❑ 440	Mike Moore	.15	.05
❑ 441	Doug Sisk	.15	.05
❑ 442	Dennis Eckersley	.75	.30
❑ 443	Gerald Perry	.15	.05
❑ 444	Dale Berra	.15	.05
❑ 445	Dusty Baker	.40	.15
❑ 446	Ed Whitson	.15	.05
❑ 447	Cesar Cedeno	.40	.15
❑ 448	Rick Schu	.15	.05
❑ 449	Joaquin Andujar	.40	.15
❑ 450	Mark Bailey	.15	.05
❑ 451	Ron Romanick	.15	.05
❑ 452	Julio Cruz	.15	.05
❑ 453	Miguel Dilone	.15	.05
❑ 454	Storm Davis	.15	.05
❑ 455	Jaime Cocanower	.15	.05
❑ 456	Barbaro Garbey	.15	.05
❑ 457	Rich Gedman	.15	.05
❑ 458	Phil Niekro	.40	.15
❑ 459	Mike Scioscia	.40	.15
❑ 460	Pat Tabler	.15	.05
❑ 461	Darryl Motley	.15	.05
❑ 462	Chris Codiroli	.15	.05
❑ 463	Doug Flynn	.15	.05
❑ 464	Billy Sample	.15	.05
❑ 465	Mickey Rivers	.15	.05
❑ 466	John Wathan	.15	.05
❑ 467	Bill Krueger	.15	.05
❑ 468	Andre Thornton	.15	.05
❑ 469	Rex Hudler	.15	.05
❑ 470	Sid Bream RC	.50	.20
❑ 471	Kirk Gibson	.40	.15
❑ 472	John Shelby	.15	.05
❑ 473	Moose Haas	.15	.05
❑ 474	Doug Corbett	.15	.05
❑ 475	Willie McGee	.40	.15
❑ 476	Bob Knepper	.15	.05
❑ 477	Kevin Gross	.15	.05
❑ 478	Carmelo Martinez	.15	.05
❑ 479	Kent Tekulve	.15	.05
❑ 480	Chili Davis	.40	.15
❑ 481	Bobby Clark	.15	.05
❑ 482	Mookie Wilson	.40	.15
❑ 483	Dave Owen	.15	.05
❑ 484	Ed Nunez	.15	.05
❑ 485	Rance Mulliniks	.15	.05
❑ 486	Ken Schrom	.15	.05
❑ 487	Jeff Russell	.15	.05
❑ 488	Tom Paciorek	.15	.05
❑ 489	Dan Ford	.15	.05
❑ 490	Mike Caldwell	.15	.05
❑ 491	Scottie Earl	.15	.05
❑ 492	Jose Rijo RC	1.00	.40
❑ 493	Bruce Hurst	.15	.05
❑ 494	Ken Landreaux	.15	.05
❑ 495	Mike Fischlin	.15	.05
❑ 496	Don Slaught	.15	.05
❑ 497	Steve McCatty	.15	.05
❑ 498	Gary Lucas	.15	.05
❑ 499	Gary Pettis	.15	.05
❑ 500	Marvis Foley	.15	.05
❑ 501	Mike Squires	.15	.05
❑ 502	Jim Pankovits	.15	.05
❑ 503	Luis Aguayo	.15	.05
❑ 504	Ralph Citarella	.15	.05
❑ 505	Bruce Bochy	.15	.05
❑ 506	Bob Owchinko	.15	.05
❑ 507	Pascual Perez	.15	.05
❑ 508	Lee Lacy	.15	.05
❑ 509	Atlee Hammaker	.15	.05
❑ 510	Bob Dernier	.15	.05
❑ 511	Ed VandeBerg	.15	.05
❑ 512	Cliff Johnson	.15	.05
❑ 513	Len Whitehouse	.15	.05
❑ 514	Dennis Martinez	.40	.15
❑ 515	Ed Romero	.15	.05
❑ 516	Rusty Kuntz	.15	.05
❑ 517	Rick Miller	.15	.05
❑ 518	Dennis Rasmussen	.15	.05
❑ 519	Steve Yeager	.40	.15
❑ 520	Chris Bando	.15	.05
❑ 521	U.L. Washington	.15	.05
❑ 522	Curt Young	.15	.05
❑ 523	Angel Salazar	.15	.05
❑ 524	Curt Kaufman	.15	.05
❑ 525	Odell Jones	.15	.05
❑ 526	Juan Agosto	.15	.05
❑ 527	Denny Walling	.15	.05
❑ 528	Andy Hawkins	.15	.05
❑ 529	Sixto Lezcano	.15	.05
❑ 530	Skeeter Barnes RC	.25	.08
❑ 531	Randy Johnson	.15	.05
❑ 532	Jim Morrison	.15	.05
❑ 533	Warren Brusstar	.15	.05
❑ 534A	Jeff Pendleton ERR RC	1.00	.40
❑ 534B	Terry Pendleton COR	1.00	.40
❑ 535	Vic Rodriguez	.15	.05
❑ 536	Bob McClure	.15	.05
❑ 537	Dave Bergman	.15	.05
❑ 538	Mark Clear	.15	.05
❑ 539	Mike Pagliarulo	.15	.05
❑ 540	Terry Whitfield	.15	.05
❑ 541	Joe Beckwith	.15	.05
❑ 542	Jeff Burroughs	.15	.05
❑ 543	Dan Schatzeder	.15	.05
❑ 544	Donnie Scott	.15	.05
❑ 545	Jim Slaton	.15	.05
❑ 546	Greg Luzinski	.40	.15
❑ 547	Mark Salas	.15	.05
❑ 548	Dave Smith	.15	.05
❑ 549	John Wockenfuss	.15	.05

❑ 550 Frank Pastore	.15	.05
❑ 551 Tim Flannery	.15	.05
❑ 552 Rick Rhoden	.15	.05
❑ 553 Mark Davis	.15	.05
❑ 554 Jeff Dedmon	.15	.05
❑ 555 Gary Woods	.15	.05
❑ 556 Danny Heep	.15	.05
❑ 557 Mark Langston RC	1.00	.40
❑ 558 Darrell Brown	.15	.05
❑ 559 Jimmy Key RC	1.00	.40
❑ 560 Rick Lysander	.15	.05
❑ 561 Doyle Alexander	.15	.05
❑ 562 Mike Stanton	.15	.05
❑ 563 Sid Fernandez	.40	.15
❑ 564 Richie Hebner	.15	.05
❑ 565 Alex Trevino	.15	.05
❑ 566 Brian Harper	.15	.05
❑ 567 Dan Gladden RC	.50	.20
❑ 568 Luis Salazar	.15	.05
❑ 569 Tom Foley	.15	.05
❑ 570 Larry Andersen	.15	.05
❑ 571 Danny Cox	.15	.05
❑ 572 Joe Sambito	.15	.05
❑ 573 Juan Beniquez	.15	.05
❑ 574 Joel Skinner	.15	.05
❑ 575 Randy St.Claire	.15	.05
❑ 576 Floyd Rayford	.15	.05
❑ 577 Roy Howell	.15	.05
❑ 578 John Grubb	.15	.05
❑ 579 Ed Jurak	.15	.05
❑ 580 John Montefusco	.15	.05
❑ 581 Orel Hershiser RC	3.00	1.25
❑ 582 Tom Waddell	.15	.05
❑ 583 Mark Huismann	.15	.05
❑ 584 Joe Morgan	.40	.15
❑ 585 Jim Wohlford	.15	.05
❑ 586 Dave Schmidt	.15	.05
❑ 587 Jeff Kunkel	.15	.05
❑ 588 Hal McRae	.40	.15
❑ 589 Bill Almon	.15	.05
❑ 590 Carmelo Castillo	.15	.05
❑ 591 Omar Moreno	.15	.05
❑ 592 Ken Howell	.15	.05
❑ 593 Tom Brookens	.15	.05
❑ 594 Joe Nolan	.15	.05
❑ 595 Willie Lozado	.15	.05
❑ 596 Tom Nieto	.15	.05
❑ 597 Walt Terrell	.15	.05
❑ 598 Al Oliver	.40	.15
❑ 599 Shane Rawley	.15	.05
❑ 600 Denny Gonzalez	.15	.05
❑ 601 Mark Grant	.15	.05
❑ 602 Mike Armstrong	.15	.05
❑ 603 George Foster	.40	.15
❑ 604 Dave Lopes	.40	.15
❑ 605 Salome Barojas	.15	.05
❑ 606 Roy Lee Jackson	.15	.05
❑ 607 Pete Filson	.15	.05
❑ 608 Duane Walker	.15	.05
❑ 609 Glenn Wilson	.15	.05
❑ 610 Rafael Santana	.15	.05
❑ 611 Roy Smith	.15	.05
❑ 612 Ruppert Jones	.15	.05
❑ 613 Joe Cowley	.15	.05
❑ 614 Al Nipper UER (Photo actually Mike Brown)	.15	.05
❑ 615 Gene Nelson	.15	.05
❑ 616 Joe Carter	1.25	.50
❑ 617 Ray Knight	.40	.15
❑ 618 Chuck Rainey	.15	.05
❑ 619 Dan Driessen	.15	.05
❑ 620 Daryl Sconiers	.15	.05
❑ 621 Bill Stein	.15	.05
❑ 622 Roy Smalley	.15	.05
❑ 623 Ed Lynch	.15	.05
❑ 624 Jeff Stone	.15	.05
❑ 625 Bruce Berenyi	.15	.05
❑ 626 Kelvin Chapman	.15	.05
❑ 627 Joe Price	.15	.05
❑ 628 Steve Bedrosian	.15	.05
❑ 629 Vic Mata	.15	.05
❑ 630 Mike Krukow	.15	.05
❑ 631 Phil Bradley	.50	.20
❑ 632 Jim Gott	.15	.05
❑ 633 Randy Bush	.15	.05
❑ 634 Tom Browning RC	.50	.20
❑ 635 Lou Gehrig Puzzle	1.25	.50
❑ 636 Reid Nichols	.15	.05
❑ 637 Dan Pasqua RC	.50	.20
❑ 638 German Rivera	.15	.05
❑ 639 Don Schulze	.15	.05
❑ 640A Mike Jones (Career Highlights, takes five lines)	.15	.05
❑ 640B Mike Jones (Career Highlights, takes four lines)	.15	.05
❑ 641 Pete Rose	4.00	1.50
❑ 642 Wade Rowdon	.15	.05
❑ 643 Jerry Narron	.15	.05
❑ 644 Darrell Miller	.15	.05
❑ 645 Tim Hulett RC	.25	.08
❑ 646 Andy McGaffigan	.15	.05
❑ 647 Kurt Bevacqua	.15	.05
❑ 648 John Russell	.15	.05
❑ 649 Ron Robinson	.15	.05
❑ 650 Donnie Moore	.15	.05
❑ 651A D.Mattingly/D.Winfield YL	2.00	.75
❑ 651B D.Mattingly/D.Winfield WL	5.00	2.00
❑ 652 Tim Laudner	.15	.05
❑ 653 Steve Farr RC	.50	.20
❑ 654 DK Checklist 1-26 (Unnumbered)	.15	.05
❑ 655 Checklist 27-130 (Unnumbered)	.15	.05
❑ 656 Checklist 131-234 (Unnumbered)	.15	.05
❑ 657 Checklist 235-338 (Unnumbered)	.15	.05
❑ 658 Checklist 339-442 (Unnumbered)	.15	.05
❑ 659 Checklist 443-546 (Unnumbered)	.15	.05
❑ 660 Checklist 547-653 (Unnumbered)	.15	.05

1986 Donruss

❑ COMPLETE SET (660)	40.00	15.00
❑ COMP.FACT.SET (660)	40.00	15.00
❑ COMP.AARON PUZZLE	2.00	.75
❑ 1 Kirk Gibson DK	.25	.08
❑ 2 Goose Gossage DK	.25	.08
❑ 3 Willie McGee DK	.25	.08
❑ 4 George Bell DK	.25	.08
❑ 5 Tony Armas DK	.25	.08
❑ 6 Chili Davis DK	.25	.08
❑ 7 Cecil Cooper DK	.25	.08
❑ 8 Mike Boddicker DK	.15	.05
❑ 9 Dave Lopes DK	.25	.08
❑ 10 Bill Doran DK	.15	.05
❑ 11 Bret Saberhagen DK	.25	.08
❑ 12 Brett Butler DK	.25	.08
❑ 13 Harold Baines DK	.25	.08
❑ 14 Mike Davis DK	.15	.05
❑ 15 Tony Perez DK	.50	.20
❑ 16 Willie Randolph DK	.25	.08
❑ 17 Bob Boone DK	.25	.08
❑ 18 Orel Hershiser DK	.50	.20
❑ 19 Johnny Ray DK	.15	.05
❑ 20 Gary Ward DK	.15	.05
❑ 21 Rick Mahler DK	.15	.05
❑ 22 Phil Bradley DK	.15	.05
❑ 23 Jerry Koosman DK	.25	.08
❑ 24 Tom Brunansky DK	.15	.05
❑ 25 Andre Dawson DK	.15	.05
❑ 26 Dwight Gooden DK	.75	.30
❑ 27 Kal Daniels RC	.50	.20
❑ 28 Fred McGriff RC	8.00	3.00
❑ 29 Cory Snyder	.15	.05
❑ 30 Jose Guzman RC	.15	.05
❑ 31 Ty Gainey RC	.15	.05
❑ 32 Johnny Abrego RC	.15	.05
❑ 33A Andres Galarraga RC	1.50	.60
❑ 33B Andre`s Galarraga RC	1.50	.60
❑ 34 Dave Shipanoff RC	.15	.05
❑ 35 Mark McLemore RC	1.00	.40
❑ 36 Marty Clary RC	.15	.05
❑ 37 Paul O'Neill RC	4.00	1.50
❑ 38 Danny Tartabull	.25	.08
❑ 39 Jose Canseco RC	10.00	4.00
❑ 40 Juan Nieves RC	.15	.05
❑ 41 Lance McCullers RC	.15	.05
❑ 42 Rick Surhoff RC	.15	.05
❑ 43 Todd Worrell RC	.50	.20
❑ 44 Bob Kipper RC	.15	.05
❑ 45 John Habyan RC	.15	.05
❑ 46 Mike Woodard RC	.15	.05
❑ 47 Mike Boddicker	.15	.05
❑ 48 Robin Yount	1.25	.50
❑ 49 Lou Whitaker	.25	.08
❑ 50 Oil Can Boyd	.15	.05
❑ 51 Rickey Henderson	.75	.30
❑ 52 Mike Marshall	.15	.05
❑ 53 George Brett	2.00	.75
❑ 54 Dave Kingman	.25	.08
❑ 55 Hubie Brooks	.15	.05
❑ 56 Oddibe McDowell	.15	.05
❑ 57 Doug DeCinces	.15	.05
❑ 58 Britt Burns	.15	.05
❑ 59 Ozzie Smith	1.25	.50
❑ 60 Jose Cruz	.25	.08
❑ 61 Mike Schmidt	2.00	.75
❑ 62 Pete Rose	2.50	1.00
❑ 63 Steve Garvey	.25	.08
❑ 64 Tony Pena	.15	.05
❑ 65 Chili Davis	.25	.08
❑ 66 Dale Murphy	.50	.20
❑ 67 Ryne Sandberg	1.50	.60
❑ 68 Gary Carter	.25	.08
❑ 69 Alvin Davis	.15	.05
❑ 70 Kent Hrbek	.25	.08
❑ 71 George Bell	.25	.08
❑ 72 Kirby Puckett	2.00	.75
❑ 73 Lloyd Moseby	.15	.05
❑ 74 Bob Kearney	.15	.05
❑ 75 Dwight Gooden	.75	.30
❑ 76 Gary Matthews	.25	.08
❑ 77 Rick Mahler	.15	.05
❑ 78 Benny Distefano	.15	.05
❑ 79 Jeff Leonard	.15	.05
❑ 80 Kevin McReynolds	.25	.08
❑ 81 Ron Oester	.15	.05
❑ 82 John Russell	.15	.05
❑ 83 Tommy Herr	.15	.05
❑ 84 Jerry Mumphrey	.15	.05
❑ 85 Ron Romanick	.15	.05
❑ 86 Daryl Boston	.15	.05
❑ 87 Andre Dawson	.25	.08
❑ 88 Eddie Murray	.75	.30
❑ 89 Dion James	.15	.05
❑ 90 Chet Lemon	.25	.08
❑ 91 Bob Stanley	.15	.05
❑ 92 Willie Randolph	.25	.08
❑ 93 Mike Scioscia	.25	.08
❑ 94 Tom Waddell	.15	.05
❑ 95 Danny Jackson	.15	.05
❑ 96 Mike Davis	.15	.05
❑ 97 Mike Fitzgerald	.15	.05
❑ 98 Gary Ward	.15	.05
❑ 99 Pete O'Brien	.15	.05
❑ 100 Bret Saberhagen	.25	.08
❑ 101 Alfredo Griffin	.15	.05
❑ 102 Brett Butler	.25	.08
❑ 103 Ron Guidry	.25	.08
❑ 104 Jerry Reuss	.15	.05
❑ 105 Jack Morris	.25	.08
❑ 106 Rick Dempsey	.15	.05
❑ 107 Ray Burris	.15	.05
❑ 108 Brian Downing	.25	.08

❑	109 Willie McGee	.25	.08
❑	110 Bill Doran	.15	.05
❑	111 Kent Tekulve	.15	.05
❑	112 Tony Gwynn	1.25	.50
❑	113 Marvell Wynne	.15	.05
❑	114 David Green	.15	.05
❑	115 Jim Gantner	.15	.05
❑	116 George Foster	.25	.08
❑	117 Steve Trout	.15	.05
❑	118 Mark Langston	.25	.08
❑	119 Tony Fernandez	.15	.05
❑	120 John Butcher	.15	.05
❑	121 Ron Robinson	.15	.05
❑	122 Dan Spillner	.15	.05
❑	123 Mike Young	.15	.05
❑	124 Paul Molitor	.25	.08
❑	125 Kirk Gibson	.25	.08
❑	126 Ken Griffey	.25	.08
❑	127 Tony Armas	.25	.08
❑	128 Mariano Duncan RC	.50	.20
❑	129 Pat Tabler	.15	.05
❑	130 Frank White	.25	.08
❑	131 Carney Lansford	.25	.08
❑	132 Vance Law	.15	.05
❑	133 Dick Schofield	.15	.05
❑	134 Wayne Tolleson	.15	.05
❑	135 Greg Walker	.15	.05
❑	136 Denny Walling	.15	.05
❑	137 Ozzie Virgil	.15	.05
❑	138 Ricky Horton	.15	.05
❑	139 LaMarr Hoyt	.15	.05
❑	140 Wayne Krenchicki	.15	.05
❑	141 Glenn Hubbard	.15	.05
❑	142 Cecilio Guante	.15	.05
❑	143 Mike Krukow	.15	.05
❑	144 Lee Smith	.25	.08
❑	145 Edwin Nunez	.15	.05
❑	146 Dave Stieb	.25	.08
❑	147 Mike Smithson	.15	.05
❑	148 Ken Dixon	.15	.05
❑	149 Danny Darwin	.15	.05
❑	150 Chris Pittaro	.15	.05
❑	151 Bill Buckner	.25	.08
❑	152 Mike Pagliarulo	.15	.05
❑	153 Bill Russell	.25	.08
❑	154 Brook Jacoby	.15	.05
❑	155 Pat Sheridan	.15	.05
❑	156 Mike Gallego RC	.15	.05
❑	157 Jim Wohlford	.15	.05
❑	158 Gary Pettis	.15	.05
❑	159 Toby Harrah	.25	.08
❑	160 Richard Dotson	.15	.05
❑	161 Bob Knepper	.15	.05
❑	162 Dave Dravecky	.15	.05
❑	163 Greg Gross	.15	.05
❑	164 Eric Davis	.75	.30
❑	165 Gerald Perry	.15	.05
❑	166 Rick Rhoden	.15	.05
❑	167 Keith Moreland	.15	.05
❑	168 Jack Clark	.25	.08
❑	169 Storm Davis	.15	.05
❑	170 Cecil Cooper	.25	.08
❑	171 Alan Trammell	.25	.08
❑	172 Roger Clemens	5.00	2.00
❑	173 Don Mattingly	2.50	1.00
❑	174 Pedro Guerrero	.25	.08
❑	175 Willie Wilson	.25	.08
❑	176 Dwayne Murphy	.15	.05
❑	177 Tim Raines	.25	.08
❑	178 Larry Parrish	.15	.05
❑	179 Mike Witt	.15	.05
❑	180 Harold Baines	.25	.08
❑	181 Vince Coleman UER RC	1.00	.40
❑	182 Jeff Heathcock	.15	.05
❑	183 Steve Carlton	.25	.08
❑	184 Mario Soto	.25	.08
❑	185 Goose Gossage	.25	.08
❑	186 Johnny Ray	.15	.05
❑	187 Dan Gladden	.15	.05
❑	188 Bob Horner	.25	.08
❑	189 Rick Sutcliffe	.25	.08
❑	190 Keith Hernandez	.25	.08
❑	191 Phil Bradley	.15	.05
❑	192 Tom Brunansky	.15	.05
❑	193 Jesse Barfield	.25	.08
❑	194 Frank Viola	.25	.08
❑	195 Willie Upshaw	.15	.05
❑	196 Jim Beattie	.15	.05
❑	197 Darryl Strawberry	.50	.20
❑	198 Ron Cey	.25	.08
❑	199 Steve Bedrosian	.15	.05
❑	200 Steve Kemp	.15	.05
❑	201 Manny Trillo	.15	.05
❑	202 Garry Templeton	.25	.08
❑	203 Dave Parker	.25	.08
❑	204 John Denny	.15	.05
❑	205 Terry Pendleton	.25	.08
❑	206 Terry Puhl	.15	.05
❑	207 Bobby Grich	.25	.08
❑	208 Ozzie Guillen RC	2.00	.75
❑	209 Jeff Reardon	.25	.08
❑	210 Cal Ripken	3.00	1.25
❑	211 Bill Schroeder	.15	.05
❑	212 Dan Petry	.15	.05
❑	213 Jim Rice	.25	.08
❑	214 Dave Righetti	.25	.08
❑	215 Fernando Valenzuela	.25	.08
❑	216 Julio Franco	.25	.08
❑	217 Darryl Motley	.15	.05
❑	218 Dave Collins	.15	.05
❑	219 Tim Wallach	.15	.05
❑	220 George Wright	.15	.05
❑	221 Tommy Dunbar	.15	.05
❑	222 Steve Balboni	.15	.05
❑	223 Jay Howell	.15	.05
❑	224 Joe Carter	.25	.08
❑	225 Ed Whitson	.15	.05
❑	226 Orel Hershiser	.75	.30
❑	227 Willie Hernandez	.15	.05
❑	228 Lee Lacy	.15	.05
❑	229 Rollie Fingers	.25	.08
❑	230 Bob Boone	.25	.08
❑	231 Joaquin Andujar	.25	.08
❑	232 Craig Reynolds	.15	.05
❑	233 Shane Rawley	.15	.05
❑	234 Eric Show	.15	.05
❑	235 Jose DeLeon	.15	.05
❑	236 Jose Uribe	.15	.05
❑	237 Moose Haas	.15	.05
❑	238 Wally Backman	.15	.05
❑	239 Dennis Eckersley	.50	.20
❑	240 Mike Moore	.15	.05
❑	241 Damaso Garcia	.15	.05
❑	242 Tim Teufel	.15	.05
❑	243 Dave Concepcion	.25	.08
❑	244 Floyd Bannister	.15	.05
❑	245 Fred Lynn	.25	.08
❑	246 Charlie Moore	.15	.05
❑	247 Walt Terrell	.15	.05
❑	248 Dave Winfield	.25	.08
❑	249 Dwight Evans	.50	.20
❑	250 Dennis Powell	.15	.05
❑	251 Andre Thornton	.15	.05
❑	252 Onix Concepcion	.15	.05
❑	253 Mike Heath	.15	.05
❑	254A David Palmer ERR (Position 2B)	.15	.05
❑	254B David Palmer COR (Position P)	.50	.20
❑	255 Donnie Moore	.15	.05
❑	256 Curtis Wilkerson	.15	.05
❑	257 Julio Cruz	.15	.05
❑	258 Nolan Ryan	4.00	1.50
❑	259 Jeff Stone	.15	.05
❑	260 John Tudor	.25	.08
❑	261 Mark Thurmond	.15	.05
❑	262 Jay Tibbs	.15	.05
❑	263 Rafael Ramirez	.15	.05
❑	264 Larry McWilliams	.15	.05
❑	265 Mark Davis	.15	.05
❑	266 Bob Dernier	.15	.05
❑	267 Matt Young	.15	.05
❑	268 Jim Clancy	.15	.05
❑	269 Mickey Hatcher	.15	.05
❑	270 Sammy Stewart	.15	.05
❑	271 Bob L. Gibson	.15	.05
❑	272 Nelson Simmons	.15	.05
❑	273 Rich Gedman	.15	.05
❑	274 Butch Wynegar	.15	.05
❑	275 Ken Howell	.15	.05
❑	276 Mel Hall	.15	.05
❑	277 Jim Sundberg	.25	.08
❑	278 Chris Codiroli	.15	.05
❑	279 Herm Winningham	.15	.05
❑	280 Rod Carew	.50	.20
❑	281 Don Slaught	.15	.05
❑	282 Scott Fletcher	.15	.05
❑	283 Bill Dawley	.15	.05
❑	284 Andy Hawkins	.15	.05
❑	285 Glenn Wilson	.15	.05
❑	286 Nick Esasky	.15	.05
❑	287 Claudell Washington	.15	.05
❑	288 Lee Mazzilli	.25	.08
❑	289 Jody Davis	.15	.05
❑	290 Darrell Porter	.15	.05
❑	291 Scott McGregor	.15	.05
❑	292 Ted Simmons	.25	.08
❑	293 Aurelio Lopez	.15	.05
❑	294 Marty Barrett	.15	.05
❑	295 Dale Berra	.15	.05
❑	296 Greg Brock	.15	.05
❑	297 Charlie Leibrandt	.15	.05
❑	298 Bill Krueger	.15	.05
❑	299 Bryn Smith	.15	.05
❑	300 Burt Hooton	.15	.05
❑	301 Stu Cliburn	.15	.05
❑	302 Luis Salazar	.15	.05
❑	303 Ken Dayley	.15	.05
❑	304 Frank DiPino	.15	.05
❑	305 Von Hayes	.15	.05
❑	306 Gary Redus	.15	.05
❑	307 Craig Lefferts	.15	.05
❑	308 Sammy Khalifa	.15	.05
❑	309 Scott Garrelts	.15	.05
❑	310 Rick Cerone	.15	.05
❑	311 Shawon Dunston	.25	.08
❑	312 Howard Johnson	.25	.08
❑	313 Jim Presley	.15	.05
❑	314 Gary Gaetti	.25	.08
❑	315 Luis Leal	.15	.05
❑	316 Mark Salas	.15	.05
❑	317 Bill Caudill	.15	.05
❑	318 Dave Henderson	.15	.05
❑	319 Rafael Santana	.15	.05
❑	320 Leon Durham	.15	.05
❑	321 Bruce Sutter	.25	.08
❑	322 Jason Thompson	.15	.05
❑	323 Bob Brenly	.15	.05
❑	324 Carmelo Martinez	.15	.05
❑	325 Eddie Milner	.15	.05
❑	326 Juan Samuel	.15	.05
❑	327 Tom Nieto	.15	.05
❑	328 Dave Smith	.15	.05
❑	329 Urbano Lugo	.15	.05
❑	330 Joel Skinner	.15	.05
❑	331 Bill Gullickson	.15	.05
❑	332 Floyd Rayford	.15	.05
❑	333 Ben Oglivie	.25	.08
❑	334 Lance Parrish	.25	.08
❑	335 Jackie Gutierrez	.15	.05
❑	336 Dennis Rasmussen	.15	.05
❑	337 Terry Whitfield	.15	.05
❑	338 Neal Heaton	.15	.05
❑	339 Jorge Orta	.15	.05
❑	340 Donnie Hill	.15	.05
❑	341 Joe Hesketh	.15	.05
❑	342 Charlie Hough	.25	.08
❑	343 Dave Rozema	.15	.05
❑	344 Greg Pryor	.15	.05
❑	345 Mickey Tettleton RC	.50	.20
❑	346 George Vukovich	.15	.05
❑	347 Don Baylor	.25	.08
❑	348 Carlos Diaz	.15	.05
❑	349 Barbaro Garbey	.15	.05
❑	350 Larry Sheets	.15	.05
❑	351 Teddy Higuera RC*	.50	.20
❑	352 Juan Beniquez	.15	.05
❑	353 Bob Forsch	.15	.05
❑	354 Mark Bailey	.15	.05
❑	355 Larry Andersen	.15	.05
❑	356 Terry Kennedy	.15	.05
❑	357 Don Robinson	.15	.05
❑	358 Jim Gott	.15	.05
❑	359 Earnie Riles	.15	.05
❑	360 John Christensen	.15	.05
❑	361 Ray Fontenot	.15	.05
❑	362 Spike Owen	.15	.05
❑	363 Jim Acker	.15	.05

❑ 364	Ron Davis	.15	.05
❑ 365	Tom Hume	.15	.05
❑ 366	Carlton Fisk	.50	.20
❑ 367	Nate Snell	.15	.05
❑ 368	Rick Manning	.15	.05
❑ 369	Darrell Evans	.25	.08
❑ 370	Ron Hassey	.15	.05
❑ 371	Wade Boggs	.50	.20
❑ 372	Rick Honeycutt	.15	.05
❑ 373	Chris Bando	.15	.05
❑ 374	Bud Black	.15	.05
❑ 375	Steve Henderson	.15	.05
❑ 376	Charlie Lea	.15	.05
❑ 377	Reggie Jackson	.50	.20
❑ 378	Dave Schmidt	.15	.05
❑ 379	Bob James	.15	.05
❑ 380	Glenn Davis	.15	.05
❑ 381	Tim Corcoran	.15	.05
❑ 382	Danny Cox	.15	.05
❑ 383	Tim Flannery	.15	.05
❑ 384	Tom Browning	.15	.05
❑ 385	Rick Camp	.15	.05
❑ 386	Jim Morrison	.15	.05
❑ 387	Dave LaPoint	.15	.05
❑ 388	Dave Lopes	.25	.08
❑ 389	Al Cowens	.15	.05
❑ 390	Doyle Alexander	.15	.05
❑ 391	Tim Laudner	.15	.05
❑ 392	Don Aase	.15	.05
❑ 393	Jaime Cocanower	.15	.05
❑ 394	Randy O'Neal	.15	.05
❑ 395	Mike Easler	.15	.05
❑ 396	Scott Bradley	.15	.05
❑ 397	Tom Niedenfuer	.15	.05
❑ 398	Jerry Willard	.15	.05
❑ 399	Lonnie Smith	.15	.05
❑ 400	Bruce Bochte	.15	.05
❑ 401	Terry Francona	.25	.08
❑ 402	Jim Slaton	.15	.05
❑ 403	Bill Stein	.15	.05
❑ 404	Tim Hulett	.15	.05
❑ 405	Alan Ashby	.15	.05
❑ 406	Tim Stoddard	.15	.05
❑ 407	Garry Maddox	.15	.05
❑ 408	Ted Power	.15	.05
❑ 409	Len Barker	.15	.05
❑ 410	Denny Gonzalez	.15	.05
❑ 411	George Frazier	.15	.05
❑ 412	Andy Van Slyke	.50	.20
❑ 413	Jim Dwyer	.15	.05
❑ 414	Paul Householder	.15	.05
❑ 415	Alejandro Sanchez	.15	.05
❑ 416	Steve Crawford	.15	.05
❑ 417	Dan Pasqua	.15	.05
❑ 418	Enos Cabell	.15	.05
❑ 419	Mike Jones	.15	.05
❑ 420	Steve Kiefer	.15	.05
❑ 421	Tim Burke	.15	.05
❑ 422	Mike Mason	.15	.05
❑ 423	Ruppert Jones	.15	.05
❑ 424	Jerry Hairston	.15	.05
❑ 425	Tito Landrum	.15	.05
❑ 426	Jeff Calhoun	.15	.05
❑ 427	Don Carman	.15	.05
❑ 428	Tony Perez	.50	.20
❑ 429	Jerry Davis	.15	.05
❑ 430	Bob Walk	.15	.05
❑ 431	Brad Wellman	.15	.05
❑ 432	Terry Forster	.25	.08
❑ 433	Billy Hatcher	.15	.05
❑ 434	Clint Hurdle	.15	.05
❑ 435	Ivan Calderon RC*	.50	.20
❑ 436	Pete Filson	.15	.05
❑ 437	Tom Henke	.25	.08
❑ 438	Dave Engle	.15	.05
❑ 439	Tom Filer	.15	.05
❑ 440	Gorman Thomas	.25	.08
❑ 441	Rick Aguilera RC	.50	.20
❑ 442	Scott Sanderson	.15	.05
❑ 443	Jeff Dedmon	.15	.05
❑ 444	Joe Orsulak RC*	.50	.20
❑ 445	Atlee Hammaker	.15	.05
❑ 446	Jerry Royster	.15	.05
❑ 447	Buddy Bell	.25	.08
❑ 448	Dave Rucker	.15	.05
❑ 449	Ivan DeJesus	.15	.05
❑ 450	Jim Pankovits	.15	.05
❑ 451	Jerry Narron	.15	.05
❑ 452	Bryan Little	.15	.05
❑ 453	Gary Lucas	.15	.05
❑ 454	Dennis Martinez	.25	.08
❑ 455	Ed Romero	.15	.05
❑ 456	Bob Melvin	.15	.05
❑ 457	Glenn Hoffman	.15	.05
❑ 458	Bob Shirley	.15	.05
❑ 459	Bob Welch	.25	.08
❑ 460	Carmen Castillo	.15	.05
❑ 461	Dave Leeper OF	.15	.05
❑ 462	Tim Birtsas	.15	.05
❑ 463	Randy St.Claire	.15	.05
❑ 464	Chris Welsh	.15	.05
❑ 465	Greg Harris	.15	.05
❑ 466	Lynn Jones	.15	.05
❑ 467	Dusty Baker	.25	.08
❑ 468	Roy Smith	.15	.05
❑ 469	Andre Robertson	.15	.05
❑ 470	Ken Landreaux	.15	.05
❑ 471	Dave Bergman	.15	.05
❑ 472	Gary Roenicke	.15	.05
❑ 473	Pete Vuckovich	.15	.05
❑ 474	Kirk McCaskill RC	.50	.20
❑ 475	Jeff Lahti	.15	.05
❑ 476	Mike Scott	.25	.08
❑ 477	Darren Daulton RC	1.00	.40
❑ 478	Graig Nettles	.25	.08
❑ 479	Bill Almon	.15	.05
❑ 480	Greg Minton	.15	.05
❑ 481	Randy Ready	.15	.05
❑ 482	Len Dykstra RC	1.50	.60
❑ 483	Thad Bosley	.15	.05
❑ 484	Harold Reynolds RC	1.50	.60
❑ 485	Al Oliver	.25	.08
❑ 486	Roy Smalley	.15	.05
❑ 487	John Franco	.25	.08
❑ 488	Juan Agosto	.15	.05
❑ 489	Al Pardo	.15	.05
❑ 490	Bill Wegman RC	.15	.05
❑ 491	Frank Tanana	.25	.08
❑ 492	Brian Fisher RC	.15	.05
❑ 493	Mark Clear	.15	.05
❑ 494	Len Matuszek	.15	.05
❑ 495	Ramon Romero	.15	.05
❑ 496	John Wathan	.15	.05
❑ 497	Rob Picciolo	.15	.05
❑ 498	U.L. Washington	.15	.05
❑ 499	John Candelaria	.15	.05
❑ 500	Duane Walker	.15	.05
❑ 501	Gene Nelson	.15	.05
❑ 502	John Mizerock	.15	.05
❑ 503	Luis Aguayo	.15	.05
❑ 504	Kurt Kepshire	.15	.05
❑ 505	Ed Wojna	.15	.05
❑ 506	Joe Price	.15	.05
❑ 507	Milt Thompson RC	.50	.20
❑ 508	Junior Ortiz	.15	.05
❑ 509	Vida Blue	.25	.08
❑ 510	Steve Engel	.15	.05
❑ 511	Karl Best	.15	.05
❑ 512	Cecil Fielder RC	2.00	.75
❑ 513	Frank Eufemia	.15	.05
❑ 514	Tippy Martinez	.15	.05
❑ 515	Billy Joe Robidoux	.15	.05
❑ 516	Bill Scherrer	.15	.05
❑ 517	Bruce Hurst	.15	.05
❑ 518	Rich Bordi	.15	.05
❑ 519	Steve Yeager	.25	.08
❑ 520	Tony Bernazard	.15	.05
❑ 521	Hal McRae	.25	.08
❑ 522	Jose Rijo	.25	.08
❑ 523	Mitch Webster	.15	.05
❑ 524	Jack Howell	.15	.05
❑ 525	Alan Bannister	.15	.05
❑ 526	Ron Kittle	.15	.05
❑ 527	Phil Garner	.25	.08
❑ 528	Kurt Bevacqua	.15	.05
❑ 529	Kevin Gross	.15	.05
❑ 530	Bo Diaz	.15	.05
❑ 531	Ken Oberkfell	.15	.05
❑ 532	Rick Reuschel	.25	.08
❑ 533	Ron Meridith	.15	.05
❑ 534	Steve Braun	.15	.05
❑ 535	Wayne Gross	.15	.05
❑ 536	Ray Searage	.15	.05
❑ 537	Tom Brookens	.15	.05
❑ 538	Al Nipper	.15	.05
❑ 539	Billy Sample	.15	.05
❑ 540	Steve Sax	.15	.05
❑ 541	Dan Quisenberry	.15	.05
❑ 542	Tony Phillips	.15	.05
❑ 543	Floyd Youmans	.15	.05
❑ 544	Steve Buechele RC	.50	.20
❑ 545	Craig Gerber	.15	.05
❑ 546	Joe DeSa	.15	.05
❑ 547	Brian Harper	.15	.05
❑ 548	Kevin Bass	.15	.05
❑ 549	Tom Foley	.15	.05
❑ 550	Dave Van Gorder	.15	.05
❑ 551	Bruce Bochy	.15	.05
❑ 552	R.J. Reynolds	.15	.05
❑ 553	Chris Brown RC	.15	.05
❑ 554	Bruce Benedict	.15	.05
❑ 555	Warren Brusstar	.15	.05
❑ 556	Danny Heep	.15	.05
❑ 557	Darnell Coles	.15	.05
❑ 558	Greg Gagne	.15	.05
❑ 559	Ernie Whitt	.15	.05
❑ 560	Ron Washington	.15	.05
❑ 561	Jimmy Key	.25	.08
❑ 562	Bill Swift	.15	.05
❑ 563	Ron Darling	.25	.08
❑ 564	Dick Ruthven	.15	.05
❑ 565	Zane Smith	.15	.05
❑ 566	Sid Bream	.15	.05
❑ 567A	Joel Youngblood ERR (Position P)	.15	.05
❑ 567B	Joel Youngblood COR (Position IF)	.50	.20
❑ 568	Mario Ramirez	.15	.05
❑ 569	Tom Runnells	.15	.05
❑ 570	Rick Schu	.15	.05
❑ 571	Bill Campbell	.15	.05
❑ 572	Dickie Thon	.15	.05
❑ 573	Al Holland	.15	.05
❑ 574	Reid Nichols	.15	.05
❑ 575	Bert Roberge	.15	.05
❑ 576	Mike Flanagan	.15	.05
❑ 577	Tim Leary	.15	.05
❑ 578	Mike Laga	.15	.05
❑ 579	Steve Lyons	.15	.05
❑ 580	Phil Niekro	.25	.08
❑ 581	Gilberto Reyes	.15	.05
❑ 582	Jamie Easterly	.15	.05
❑ 583	Mark Gubicza	.15	.05
❑ 584	Stan Javier RC	.50	.20
❑ 585	Bill Laskey	.15	.05
❑ 586	Jeff Russell	.15	.05
❑ 587	Dickie Noles	.15	.05
❑ 588	Steve Farr	.15	.05
❑ 589	Steve Ontiveros RC	.15	.05
❑ 590	Mike Hargrove	.15	.05
❑ 591	Marty Bystrom	.15	.05
❑ 592	Franklin Stubbs	.15	.05
❑ 593	Larry Herndon	.15	.05
❑ 594	Bill Swaggerty	.15	.05
❑ 595	Carlos Ponce	.15	.05
❑ 596	Pat Perry	.15	.05
❑ 597	Ray Knight	.25	.08
❑ 598	Steve Lombardozzi	.15	.05
❑ 599	Brad Havens	.15	.05
❑ 600	Pat Clements	.15	.05
❑ 601	Joe Niekro	.15	.05
❑ 602	Hank Aaron Puzzle	.75	.30
❑ 603	Dwayne Henry	.15	.05
❑ 604	Mookie Wilson	.25	.08
❑ 605	Buddy Biancalana	.15	.05
❑ 606	Rance Mulliniks	.15	.05
❑ 607	Alan Wiggins	.15	.05
❑ 608	Joe Cowley	.15	.05
❑ 609	Tom Seaver	.50	.20
❑ 609B	Tom Seaver YL	2.00	.75
❑ 610	Neil Allen	.15	.05
❑ 611	Don Sutton	.25	.08
❑ 612	Fred Toliver	.15	.05
❑ 613	Jay Baller	.15	.05
❑ 614	Marc Sullivan	.15	.05
❑ 615	John Grubb	.15	.05
❑ 616	Bruce Kison	.15	.05
❑ 617	Bill Madlock	.25	.08

Card		
❑ 618 Chris Chambliss	.25	.08
❑ 619 Dave Stewart	.25	.08
❑ 620 Tim Lollar	.15	.05
❑ 621 Gary Lavelle	.15	.05
❑ 622 Charles Hudson	.15	.05
❑ 623 Joel Davis	.15	.05
❑ 624 Joe Johnson	.15	.05
❑ 625 Sid Fernandez	.15	.05
❑ 626 Dennis Lamp	.15	.05
❑ 627 Terry Harper	.15	.05
❑ 628 Jack Lazorko	.15	.05
❑ 629 Roger McDowell RC*	.50	.20
❑ 630 Mark Funderburk	.15	.05
❑ 631 Ed Lynch	.15	.05
❑ 632 Rudy Law	.15	.05
❑ 633 Roger Mason RC	.15	.05
❑ 634 Mike Felder RC	.15	.05
❑ 635 Ken Schrom	.15	.05
❑ 636 Bob Ojeda	.15	.05
❑ 637 Ed VandeBerg	.15	.05
❑ 638 Bobby Meacham	.15	.05
❑ 639 Cliff Johnson	.15	.05
❑ 640 Garth Iorg	.15	.05
❑ 641 Dan Driessen	.15	.05
❑ 642 Mike Brown OF	.15	.05
❑ 643 John Shelby	.15	.05
❑ 644 Pete Rose RB	.75	.30
❑ 645 The Knuckle Brothers	.25	.08
❑ 646 Jesse Orosco	.15	.05
❑ 647 Billy Beane RC	1.00	.40
❑ 648 Cesar Cedeno	.25	.08
❑ 649 Bert Blyleven	.25	.08
❑ 650 Max Venable	.15	.05
❑ 651 Fleet Feet Vince Coleman Willie McGee	.15	.05
❑ 652 Calvin Schiraldi	.15	.05
❑ 653 Pete Rose KING	.75	.30
❑ 654 Diamond Kings CL 1-26 (Unnumbered)	.15	.05
❑ 655A CL 1: 27-130 (Unnumbered) (45 Beane ERR)	.15	.05
❑ 655B CL 1: 27-130 (Unnumbered) (45 Habyan COR)	.15	.05
❑ 656 CL 2: 131-234 (Unnumbered)	.15	.05
❑ 657 CL 3: 235-338 (Unnumbered)	.15	.05
❑ 658 CL 4: 339-442 (Unnumbered)	.15	.05
❑ 659 CL 5: 443-546 (Unnumbered)	.15	.05
❑ 660 CL 6: 547-653 (Unnumbered)	.15	.05

1986 Donruss Rookies

Card		
❑ COMP.FACT.SET (56)	30.00	12.50
❑ 1 Wally Joyner XRC	1.00	.40
❑ 2 Tracy Jones	.15	.05
❑ 3 Allan Anderson XRC	.15	.05
❑ 4 Ed Correa	.15	.05
❑ 5 Reggie Williams	.15	.05
❑ 6 Charlie Kerfeld	.15	.05
❑ 7 Andres Galarraga	1.50	.60
❑ 8 Bob Tewksbury XRC	.50	.20
❑ 9 Al Newman XRC	.25	.08
❑ 10 Andres Thomas	.15	.05
❑ 11 Barry Bonds XRC	20.00	8.00
❑ 12 Juan Nieves	.15	.05
❑ 13 Mark Eichhorn	.15	.05
❑ 14 Dan Plesac XRC	.50	.20
❑ 15 Cory Snyder	.15	.05
❑ 16 Kelly Gruber	.15	.05
❑ 17 Kevin Mitchell XRC	1.00	.40
❑ 18 Steve Lombardozzi	.15	.05
❑ 19 Mitch Williams XRC	.50	.20
❑ 20 John Cerutti	.15	.05
❑ 21 Todd Worrell	.50	.20
❑ 22 Jose Canseco	4.00	1.50
❑ 23 Pete Incaviglia XRC	.50	.20
❑ 24 Jose Guzman	.15	.05
❑ 25 Scott Bailes	.15	.05
❑ 26 Greg Mathews	.15	.05
❑ 27 Eric King	.15	.05
❑ 28 Paul Assenmacher	.50	.20
❑ 29 Jeff Sellers	.15	.05
❑ 30 Bobby Bonilla XRC	1.00	.40
❑ 31 Doug Drabek XRC	1.00	.40
❑ 32 Will Clark XRC	2.00	.75
❑ 33 Bip Roberts XRC	.50	.20
❑ 34 Jim Deshaies XRC	.15	.05
❑ 35 Mike LaValliere XRC	.50	.20
❑ 36 Scott Bankhead	.15	.05
❑ 37 Dale Sveum	.15	.05
❑ 38 Bo Jackson XRC	5.00	2.00
❑ 39 Robby Thompson XRC	.50	.20
❑ 40 Eric Plunk	.15	.05
❑ 41 Bill Bathe	.15	.05
❑ 42 John Kruk XRC	1.50	.60
❑ 43 Andy Allanson XRC	.15	.05
❑ 44 Mark Portugal XRC	.50	.20
❑ 45 Danny Tartabull	.25	.08
❑ 46 Bob Kipper	.15	.05
❑ 47 Gene Walter	.15	.05
❑ 48 Rey Quinones UER (Misspelled Quinonez)	.15	.05
❑ 49 Bobby Witt XRC	.50	.20
❑ 50 Bill Mooneyham	.15	.05
❑ 51 John Cangelosi	.15	.05
❑ 52 Ruben Sierra XRC	1.50	.60
❑ 53 Rob Woodward	.15	.05
❑ 54 Ed Hearn	.15	.05
❑ 55 Joel McKeon	.15	.05
❑ 56 Checklist 1-56	.15	.05

1987 Donruss

Card		
❑ COMPLETE SET (660)	40.00	15.00
❑ COMP.FACT.SET (660)	50.00	20.00
❑ COMP.CLEMENTE PUZZLE	1.50	.60
❑ 1 Wally Joyner DK	.40	.15
❑ 2 Roger Clemens DK	2.00	.75
❑ 3 Dale Murphy DK	.25	.08
❑ 4 Darryl Strawberry DK	.15	.05
❑ 5 Ozzie Smith DK	.60	.25
❑ 6 Jose Canseco DK	1.00	.40
❑ 7 Charlie Hough DK	.15	.05
❑ 8 Brook Jacoby DK	.10	.02
❑ 9 Fred Lynn DK	.15	.05
❑ 10 Rick Rhoden DK	.10	.02
❑ 11 Chris Brown DK	.10	.02
❑ 12 Von Hayes DK	.10	.02
❑ 13 Jack Morris DK	.15	.05
❑ 14A Kevin McReynolds DK ERR	.40	.15
❑ 14B Kevin McReynolds DK COR	.10	.02
❑ 15 George Brett DK	1.00	.40
❑ 16 Ted Higuera DK	.10	.02
❑ 17 Hubie Brooks DK	.10	.02
❑ 18 Mike Scott DK	.15	.05
❑ 19 Kirby Puckett DK	.75	.30
❑ 20 Dave Winfield DK	.15	.05
❑ 21 Lloyd Moseby DK	.10	.02
❑ 22A Eric Davis DK ERR	.40	.15
❑ 22B Eric Davis DK COR	.25	.08
❑ 23 Jim Presley DK	.10	.02
❑ 24 Keith Moreland DK	.10	.02
❑ 25A Greg Walker DK ERR	.40	.15
❑ 25B Greg Walker DK COR	.10	.02
❑ 26 Steve Sax DK	.10	.02
❑ 27 DK Checklist 1-26	.10	.02
❑ 28 B.J. Surhoff RC	.60	.25
❑ 29 Randy Myers RC	.60	.25
❑ 30 Ken Gerhart RC	.15	.05
❑ 31 Benito Santiago	.15	.05
❑ 32 Greg Swindell RC	.40	.15
❑ 33 Mike Birkbeck RC	.15	.05
❑ 34 Terry Steinbach RC	.60	.25
❑ 35 Bo Jackson RC	5.00	2.00
❑ 36 Greg Maddux RC	10.00	4.00
❑ 37 Jim Lindeman RC	.15	.05
❑ 38 Devon White RC	.60	.25
❑ 39 Eric Bell RC	.15	.05
❑ 40 Willie Fraser RC	.15	.05
❑ 41 Jerry Browne RC	.15	.05
❑ 42 Chris James RC *	.15	.05
❑ 43 Rafael Palmeiro RC	5.00	2.00
❑ 44 Pat Dodson RC	.15	.05
❑ 45 Duane Ward RC *	.40	.15
❑ 46 Mark McGwire	8.00	3.00
❑ 47 Bruce Fields UER RC	.15	.05
❑ 48 Eddie Murray	.40	.15
❑ 49 Ted Higuera	.10	.02
❑ 50 Kirk Gibson	.15	.05
❑ 51 Oil Can Boyd	.10	.02
❑ 52 Don Mattingly	1.25	.50
❑ 53 Pedro Guerrero	.15	.05
❑ 54 George Brett	1.00	.40
❑ 55 Jose Rijo	.15	.05
❑ 56 Tim Raines	.15	.05
❑ 57 Ed Correa	.10	.02
❑ 58 Mike Witt	.10	.02
❑ 59 Greg Walker	.10	.02
❑ 60 Ozzie Smith	.60	.25
❑ 61 Glenn Davis	.10	.02
❑ 62 Glenn Wilson	.10	.02
❑ 63 Tom Browning	.10	.02
❑ 64 Tony Gwynn	.60	.25
❑ 65 R.J. Reynolds	.10	.02
❑ 66 Will Clark RC	1.50	.60
❑ 67 Ozzie Virgil	.10	.02
❑ 68 Rick Sutcliffe	.15	.05
❑ 69 Gary Carter	.15	.05
❑ 70 Mike Moore	.10	.02
❑ 71 Bert Blyleven	.15	.05
❑ 72 Tony Fernandez	.10	.02
❑ 73 Kent Hrbek	.15	.05
❑ 74 Lloyd Moseby	.10	.02
❑ 75 Alvin Davis	.10	.02
❑ 76 Keith Hernandez	.15	.05
❑ 77 Ryne Sandberg	.75	.30
❑ 78 Dale Murphy	.25	.08
❑ 79 Sid Bream	.10	.02
❑ 80 Chris Brown	.10	.02
❑ 81 Steve Garvey	.15	.05
❑ 82 Mario Soto	.15	.05
❑ 83 Shane Rawley	.10	.02
❑ 84 Willie McGee	.15	.05
❑ 85 Jose Cruz	.15	.05
❑ 86 Brian Downing	.15	.05
❑ 87 Ozzie Guillen	.25	.08
❑ 88 Hubie Brooks	.10	.02
❑ 89 Cal Ripken	1.50	.60
❑ 90 Juan Nieves	.10	.02
❑ 91 Lance Parrish	.15	.05
❑ 92 Jim Rice	.15	.05
❑ 93 Ron Guidry	.15	.05
❑ 94 Fernando Valenzuela	.15	.05
❑ 95 Andy Allanson RC	.10	.02
❑ 96 Willie Wilson	.15	.05
❑ 97 Jose Canseco	1.00	.40

Card	Player	Nrmt	Exc
❑ 98	Jeff Reardon	.15	.05
❑ 99	Bobby Witt RC	.40	.15
❑ 100	Checklist 28-133	.10	.02
❑ 101	Jose Guzman	.10	.02
❑ 102	Steve Balboni	.10	.02
❑ 103	Tony Phillips	.10	.02
❑ 104	Brook Jacoby	.10	.02
❑ 105	Dave Winfield	.15	.05
❑ 106	Orel Hershiser	.25	.08
❑ 107	Lou Whitaker	.15	.05
❑ 108	Fred Lynn	.15	.05
❑ 109	Bill Wegman	.10	.02
❑ 110	Donnie Moore	.10	.02
❑ 111	Jack Clark	.15	.05
❑ 112	Bob Knepper	.10	.02
❑ 113	Von Hayes	.10	.02
❑ 114	Bip Roberts RC	.40	.15
❑ 115	Tony Pena	.10	.02
❑ 116	Scott Garrelts	.10	.02
❑ 117	Paul Molitor	.15	.05
❑ 118	Darryl Strawberry	.15	.05
❑ 119	Shawon Dunston	.10	.02
❑ 120	Jim Presley	.10	.02
❑ 121	Jesse Barfield	.15	.05
❑ 122	Gary Gaetti	.15	.05
❑ 123	Kurt Stillwell	.10	.02
❑ 124	Joel Davis	.10	.02
❑ 125	Mike Boddicker	.10	.02
❑ 126	Robin Yount	.60	.25
❑ 127	Alan Trammell	.15	.05
❑ 128	Dave Righetti	.15	.05
❑ 129	Dwight Evans	.25	.08
❑ 130	Mike Scioscia	.15	.05
❑ 131	Julio Franco	.15	.05
❑ 132	Bret Saberhagen	.15	.05
❑ 133	Mike Davis	.10	.02
❑ 134	Joe Hesketh	.10	.02
❑ 135	Wally Joyner RC	.60	.25
❑ 136	Don Slaught	.10	.02
❑ 137	Daryl Boston	.10	.02
❑ 138	Nolan Ryan	2.00	.75
❑ 139	Mike Schmidt	1.00	.40
❑ 140	Tommy Herr	.10	.02
❑ 141	Garry Templeton	.15	.05
❑ 142	Kal Daniels	.10	.02
❑ 143	Billy Sample	.10	.02
❑ 144	Johnny Ray	.10	.02
❑ 145	Robby Thompson RC *	.40	.15
❑ 146	Bob Dernier	.10	.02
❑ 147	Danny Tartabull	.10	.02
❑ 148	Ernie Whitt	.10	.02
❑ 149	Kirby Puckett	.75	.30
❑ 150	Mike Young	.10	.02
❑ 151	Ernest Riles	.10	.02
❑ 152	Frank Tanana	.15	.05
❑ 153	Rich Gedman	.10	.02
❑ 154	Willie Randolph	.15	.05
❑ 155	Bill Madlock	.15	.05
❑ 156	Joe Carter	.15	.05
❑ 157	Danny Jackson	.10	.02
❑ 158	Carney Lansford	.15	.05
❑ 159	Bryn Smith	.10	.02
❑ 160	Gary Pettis	.10	.02
❑ 161	Oddibe McDowell	.10	.02
❑ 162	John Cangelosi	.10	.02
❑ 163	Mike Scott	.15	.05
❑ 164	Eric Show	.10	.02
❑ 165	Juan Samuel	.10	.02
❑ 166	Nick Esasky	.10	.02
❑ 167	Zane Smith	.10	.02
❑ 168	Mike C. Brown OF	.10	.02
❑ 169	Keith Moreland	.10	.02
❑ 170	John Tudor	.15	.05
❑ 171	Ken Dixon	.10	.02
❑ 172	Jim Gantner	.10	.02
❑ 173	Jack Morris	.15	.05
❑ 174	Bruce Hurst	.10	.02
❑ 175	Dennis Rasmussen	.10	.02
❑ 176	Mike Marshall	.10	.02
❑ 177	Dan Quisenberry	.10	.02
❑ 178	Eric Plunk	.10	.02
❑ 179	Tim Wallach	.10	.02
❑ 180	Steve Buechele	.10	.02
❑ 181	Don Sutton	.15	.05
❑ 182	Dave Schmidt	.10	.02
❑ 183	Terry Pendleton	.15	.05
❑ 184	Jim Deshaies RC *	.15	.05
❑ 185	Steve Bedrosian	.10	.02
❑ 186	Pete Rose	1.25	.50
❑ 187	Dave Dravecky	.10	.02
❑ 188	Rick Reuschel	.15	.05
❑ 189	Dan Gladden	.10	.02
❑ 190	Rick Mahler	.10	.02
❑ 191	Thad Bosley	.10	.02
❑ 192	Ron Darling	.15	.05
❑ 193	Matt Young	.10	.02
❑ 194	Tom Brunansky	.10	.02
❑ 195	Dave Stieb	.15	.05
❑ 196	Frank Viola	.15	.05
❑ 197	Tom Henke	.10	.02
❑ 198	Karl Best	.10	.02
❑ 199	Dwight Gooden	.25	.08
❑ 200	Checklist 134-239	.10	.02
❑ 201	Steve Trout	.10	.02
❑ 202	Rafael Ramirez	.10	.02
❑ 203	Bob Walk	.10	.02
❑ 204	Roger Mason	.10	.02
❑ 205	Terry Kennedy	.10	.02
❑ 206	Ron Oester	.10	.02
❑ 207	John Russell	.10	.02
❑ 208	Greg Mathews	.10	.02
❑ 209	Charlie Kerfeld	.10	.02
❑ 210	Reggie Jackson	.25	.08
❑ 211	Floyd Bannister	.10	.02
❑ 212	Vance Law	.10	.02
❑ 213	Rich Bordi	.10	.02
❑ 214	Dan Plesac	.10	.02
❑ 215	Dave Collins	.10	.02
❑ 216	Bob Stanley	.10	.02
❑ 217	Joe Niekro	.10	.02
❑ 218	Tom Niedenfuer	.10	.02
❑ 219	Brett Butler	.15	.05
❑ 220	Charlie Leibrandt	.10	.02
❑ 221	Steve Ontiveros	.10	.02
❑ 222	Tim Burke	.10	.02
❑ 223	Curtis Wilkerson	.10	.02
❑ 224	Pete Incaviglia RC *	.40	.15
❑ 225	Lonnie Smith	.10	.02
❑ 226	Chris Codiroli	.10	.02
❑ 227	Scott Bailes	.10	.02
❑ 228	Rickey Henderson	.40	.15
❑ 229	Ken Howell	.10	.02
❑ 230	Darnell Coles	.10	.02
❑ 231	Don Aase	.10	.02
❑ 232	Tim Leary	.10	.02
❑ 233	Bob Boone	.15	.05
❑ 234	Ricky Horton	.10	.02
❑ 235	Mark Bailey	.10	.02
❑ 236	Kevin Gross	.10	.02
❑ 237	Lance McCullers	.10	.02
❑ 238	Cecilio Guante	.10	.02
❑ 239	Bob Melvin	.10	.02
❑ 240	Billy Joe Robidoux	.10	.02
❑ 241	Roger McDowell	.10	.02
❑ 242	Leon Durham	.10	.02
❑ 243	Ed Nunez	.10	.02
❑ 244	Jimmy Key	.15	.05
❑ 245	Mike Smithson	.10	.02
❑ 246	Bo Diaz	.10	.02
❑ 247	Carlton Fisk	.25	.08
❑ 248	Larry Sheets	.10	.02
❑ 249	Juan Castillo RC	.15	.05
❑ 250	Eric King	.10	.02
❑ 251	Doug Drabek RC	.60	.25
❑ 252	Wade Boggs	.25	.08
❑ 253	Mariano Duncan	.10	.02
❑ 254	Pat Tabler	.10	.02
❑ 255	Frank White	.15	.05
❑ 256	Alfredo Griffin	.10	.02
❑ 257	Floyd Youmans	.10	.02
❑ 258	Rob Wilfong	.10	.02
❑ 259	Pete O'Brien	.10	.02
❑ 260	Tim Hulett	.10	.02
❑ 261	Dickie Thon	.10	.02
❑ 262	Darren Daulton	.15	.05
❑ 263	Vince Coleman	.10	.02
❑ 264	Andy Hawkins	.10	.02
❑ 265	Eric Davis	.25	.08
❑ 266	Andres Thomas	.10	.02
❑ 267	Mike Diaz	.10	.02
❑ 268	Chili Davis	.15	.05
❑ 269	Jody Davis	.10	.02
❑ 270	Phil Bradley	.10	.02
❑ 271	George Bell	.15	.05
❑ 272	Keith Atherton	.10	.02
❑ 273	Storm Davis	.10	.02
❑ 274	Rob Deer	.10	.02
❑ 275	Walt Terrell	.10	.02
❑ 276	Roger Clemens	2.00	.75
❑ 277	Mike Easler	.10	.02
❑ 278	Steve Sax	.10	.02
❑ 279	Andre Thornton	.10	.02
❑ 280	Jim Sundberg	.15	.05
❑ 281	Bill Bathe	.10	.02
❑ 282	Jay Tibbs	.10	.02
❑ 283	Dick Schofield	.10	.02
❑ 284	Mike Mason	.10	.02
❑ 285	Jerry Hairston	.10	.02
❑ 286	Bill Doran	.10	.02
❑ 287	Tim Flannery	.10	.02
❑ 288	Gary Redus	.10	.02
❑ 289	John Franco	.15	.05
❑ 290	Paul Assenmacher	.40	.15
❑ 291	Joe Orsulak	.10	.02
❑ 292	Lee Smith	.15	.05
❑ 293	Mike Laga	.10	.02
❑ 294	Rick Dempsey	.10	.02
❑ 295	Mike Felder	.10	.02
❑ 296	Tom Brookens	.10	.02
❑ 297	Al Nipper	.10	.02
❑ 298	Mike Pagliarulo	.10	.02
❑ 299	Franklin Stubbs	.10	.02
❑ 300	Checklist 240-345	.10	.02
❑ 301	Steve Farr	.10	.02
❑ 302	Bill Mooneyham	.10	.02
❑ 303	Andres Galarraga	.15	.05
❑ 304	Scott Fletcher	.10	.02
❑ 305	Jack Howell	.10	.02
❑ 306	Russ Morman	.10	.02
❑ 307	Todd Worrell	.10	.02
❑ 308	Dave Smith	.10	.02
❑ 309	Jeff Stone	.10	.02
❑ 310	Ron Robinson	.10	.02
❑ 311	Bruce Bochy	.10	.02
❑ 312	Jim Winn	.10	.02
❑ 313	Mark Davis	.10	.02
❑ 314	Jeff Dedmon	.10	.02
❑ 315	Jamie Moyer RC	1.00	.40
❑ 316	Wally Backman	.10	.02
❑ 317	Ken Phelps	.10	.02
❑ 318	Steve Lombardozzi	.10	.02
❑ 319	Rance Mulliniks	.10	.02
❑ 320	Tim Laudner	.10	.02
❑ 321	Mark Eichhorn	.10	.02
❑ 322	Lee Guetterman	.10	.02
❑ 323	Sid Fernandez	.10	.02
❑ 324	Jerry Mumphrey	.10	.02
❑ 325	David Palmer	.10	.02
❑ 326	Bill Almon	.10	.02
❑ 327	Candy Maldonado	.10	.02
❑ 328	John Kruk RC	1.00	.40
❑ 329	John Denny	.10	.02
❑ 330	Milt Thompson	.10	.02
❑ 331	Mike LaValliere RC *	.40	.15
❑ 332	Alan Ashby	.10	.02
❑ 333	Doug Corbett	.10	.02
❑ 334	Ron Karkovice RC	.40	.15
❑ 335	Mitch Webster	.10	.02
❑ 336	Lee Lacy	.10	.02
❑ 337	Glenn Braggs RC	.15	.05
❑ 338	Dwight Lowry	.10	.02
❑ 339	Don Baylor	.15	.05
❑ 340	Brian Fisher	.10	.02
❑ 341	Reggie Williams	.10	.02
❑ 342	Tom Candiotti	.10	.02
❑ 343	Rudy Law	.10	.02
❑ 344	Curt Young	.10	.02
❑ 345	Mike Fitzgerald	.10	.02
❑ 346	Ruben Sierra RC	1.00	.40
❑ 347	Mitch Williams RC *	.40	.15
❑ 348	Jorge Orta	.10	.02
❑ 349	Mickey Tettleton	.10	.02
❑ 350	Ernie Camacho	.10	.02
❑ 351	Ron Kittle	.10	.02
❑ 352	Ken Landreaux	.10	.02
❑ 353	Chet Lemon	.15	.05
❑ 354	John Shelby	.10	.02
❑ 355	Mark Clear	.10	.02

❑ 356 Doug DeCinces .10 .02
❑ 357 Ken Dayley .10 .02
❑ 358 Phil Garner .15 .05
❑ 359 Steve Jeltz .10 .02
❑ 360 Ed Whitson .10 .02
❑ 361 Barry Bonds RC 10.00 4.00
❑ 362 Vida Blue .15 .05
❑ 363 Cecil Cooper .15 .05
❑ 364 Bob Ojeda .10 .02
❑ 365 Dennis Eckersley .25 .08
❑ 366 Mike Morgan .10 .02
❑ 367 Willie Upshaw .10 .02
❑ 368 Allan Anderson RC .10 .02
❑ 369 Bill Gullickson .10 .02
❑ 370 Bobby Thigpen RC .40 .15
❑ 371 Juan Beniquez .10 .02
❑ 372 Charlie Moore .10 .02
❑ 373 Dan Petry .10 .02
❑ 374 Rod Scurry .10 .02
❑ 375 Tom Seaver .25 .08
❑ 376 Ed VandeBerg .10 .02
❑ 377 Tony Bernazard .10 .02
❑ 378 Greg Pryor .10 .02
❑ 379 Dwayne Murphy .10 .02
❑ 380 Andy McGaffigan .10 .02
❑ 381 Kirk McCaskill .10 .02
❑ 382 Greg Harris .10 .02
❑ 383 Rich Dotson .10 .02
❑ 384 Craig Reynolds .10 .02
❑ 385 Greg Gross .10 .02
❑ 386 Tito Landrum .10 .02
❑ 387 Craig Lefferts .10 .02
❑ 388 Dave Parker .15 .05
❑ 389 Bob Horner .15 .05
❑ 390 Pat Clements .10 .02
❑ 391 Jeff Leonard .10 .02
❑ 392 Chris Speier .10 .02
❑ 393 John Moses .10 .02
❑ 394 Garth Iorg .10 .02
❑ 395 Greg Gagne .10 .02
❑ 396 Nate Snell .10 .02
❑ 397 Bryan Clutterbuck .10 .02
❑ 398 Darrell Evans .15 .05
❑ 399 Steve Crawford .10 .02
❑ 400 Checklist 346-451 .10 .02
❑ 401 Phil Lombardi .10 .02
❑ 402 Rick Honeycutt .10 .02
❑ 403 Ken Schrom .10 .02
❑ 404 Bud Black .10 .02
❑ 405 Donnie Hill .10 .02
❑ 406 Wayne Krenchicki .10 .02
❑ 407 Chuck Finley RC .60 .25
❑ 408 Toby Harrah .15 .05
❑ 409 Steve Lyons .10 .02
❑ 410 Kevin Bass .10 .02
❑ 411 Marvell Wynne .10 .02
❑ 412 Ron Roenicke .10 .02
❑ 413 Tracy Jones .10 .02
❑ 414 Gene Garber .10 .02
❑ 415 Mike Bielecki .10 .02
❑ 416 Frank DiPino .10 .02
❑ 417 Andy Van Slyke .25 .08
❑ 418 Jim Dwyer .10 .02
❑ 419 Ben Oglivie .15 .05
❑ 420 Dave Bergman .10 .02
❑ 421 Joe Sambito .10 .02
❑ 422 Bob Tewksbury RC * .40 .15
❑ 423 Len Matuszek .10 .02
❑ 424 Mike Kingery RC .15 .05
❑ 425 Dave Kingman .15 .05
❑ 426 Al Newman RC .10 .02
❑ 427 Gary Ward .10 .02
❑ 428 Ruppert Jones .10 .02
❑ 429 Harold Baines .15 .05
❑ 430 Pat Perry .10 .02
❑ 431 Terry Puhl .10 .02
❑ 432 Don Carman .10 .02
❑ 433 Eddie Milner .10 .02
❑ 434 LaMarr Hoyt .10 .02
❑ 435 Rick Rhoden .10 .02
❑ 436 Jose Uribe .10 .02
❑ 437 Ken Oberkfell .10 .02
❑ 438 Ron Davis .10 .02
❑ 439 Jesse Orosco .10 .02
❑ 440 Scott Bradley .10 .02
❑ 441 Randy Bush .10 .02
❑ 442 John Cerutti .10 .02
❑ 443 Roy Smalley .10 .02
❑ 444 Kelly Gruber .10 .02
❑ 445 Bob Kearney .10 .02
❑ 446 Ed Hearn .10 .02
❑ 447 Scott Sanderson .10 .02
❑ 448 Bruce Benedict .10 .02
❑ 449 Junior Ortiz .10 .02
❑ 450 Mike Aldrete .10 .02
❑ 451 Kevin McReynolds .10 .02
❑ 452 Rob Murphy .10 .02
❑ 453 Kent Tekulve .10 .02
❑ 454 Curt Ford .10 .02
❑ 455 Dave Lopes .15 .05
❑ 456 Bob Grich .15 .05
❑ 457 Jose DeLeon .10 .02
❑ 458 Andre Dawson .15 .05
❑ 459 Mike Flanagan .10 .02
❑ 460 Joey Meyer .15 .05
❑ 461 Chuck Cary .10 .02
❑ 462 Bill Buckner .15 .05
❑ 463 Bob Shirley .10 .02
❑ 464 Jeff Hamilton .10 .02
❑ 465 Phil Niekro .15 .05
❑ 466 Mark Gubicza .10 .02
❑ 467 Jerry Willard .10 .02
❑ 468 Bob Sebra .10 .02
❑ 469 Larry Parrish .10 .02
❑ 470 Charlie Hough .15 .05
❑ 471 Hal McRae .15 .05
❑ 472 Dave Leiper .10 .02
❑ 473 Mel Hall .10 .02
❑ 474 Dan Pasqua .10 .02
❑ 475 Bob Welch .15 .05
❑ 476 Johnny Grubb .10 .02
❑ 477 Jim Traber .10 .02
❑ 478 Chris Bosio RC .40 .15
❑ 479 Mark McLemore .15 .05
❑ 480 John Morris .10 .02
❑ 481 Billy Hatcher .10 .02
❑ 482 Dan Schatzeder .10 .02
❑ 483 Rich Gossage .15 .05
❑ 484 Jim Morrison .10 .02
❑ 485 Bob Brenly .10 .02
❑ 486 Bill Schroeder .10 .02
❑ 487 Mookie Wilson .15 .05
❑ 488 Dave Martinez RC .40 .15
❑ 489 Harold Reynolds .15 .05
❑ 490 Jeff Hearron .10 .02
❑ 491 Mickey Hatcher .10 .02
❑ 492 Barry Larkin RC 1.50 .60
❑ 493 Bob James .10 .02
❑ 494 John Habyan .10 .02
❑ 495 Jim Adduci .10 .02
❑ 496 Mike Heath .10 .02
❑ 497 Tim Stoddard .10 .02
❑ 498 Tony Armas .15 .05
❑ 499 Dennis Powell .10 .02
❑ 500 Checklist 452-557 .10 .02
❑ 501 Chris Bando .10 .02
❑ 502 David Cone RC 1.00 .40
❑ 503 Jay Howell .10 .02
❑ 504 Tom Foley .10 .02
❑ 505 Ray Chadwick .10 .02
❑ 506 Mike Loynd RC .15 .05
❑ 507 Neil Allen .10 .02
❑ 508 Danny Darwin .10 .02
❑ 509 Rick Schu .10 .02
❑ 510 Jose Oquendo .10 .02
❑ 511 Gene Walter .10 .02
❑ 512 Terry McGriff .10 .02
❑ 513 Ken Griffey .15 .05
❑ 514 Benny Distefano .10 .02
❑ 515 Terry Mulholland RC .40 .15
❑ 516 Ed Lynch .10 .02
❑ 517 Bill Swift .10 .02
❑ 518 Manny Lee .10 .02
❑ 519 Andre David .10 .02
❑ 520 Scott McGregor .10 .02
❑ 521 Rick Manning .10 .02
❑ 522 Willie Hernandez .10 .02
❑ 523 Marty Barrett .10 .02
❑ 524 Wayne Tolleson .10 .02
❑ 525 Jose Gonzalez RC .15 .05
❑ 526 Cory Snyder .10 .02
❑ 527 Buddy Biancalana .10 .02
❑ 528 Moose Haas .10 .02
❑ 529 Wilfredo Tejada .10 .02
❑ 530 Stu Cliburn .10 .02
❑ 531 Dale Mohorcic .10 .02
❑ 532 Ron Hassey .10 .02
❑ 533 Ty Gainey .10 .02
❑ 534 Jerry Royster .10 .02
❑ 535 Mike Maddux .10 .02
❑ 536 Ted Power .10 .02
❑ 537 Ted Simmons .15 .05
❑ 538 Rafael Belliard RC .40 .15
❑ 539 Chico Walker .10 .02
❑ 540 Bob Forsch .10 .02
❑ 541 John Stefero .10 .02
❑ 542 Dale Sveum .10 .02
❑ 543 Mark Thurmond .10 .02
❑ 544 Jeff Sellers .10 .02
❑ 545 Joel Skinner .10 .02
❑ 546 Alex Trevino .10 .02
❑ 547 Randy Kutcher .10 .02
❑ 548 Joaquin Andujar .15 .05
❑ 549 Casey Candaele .10 .02
❑ 550 Jeff Russell .10 .02
❑ 551 John Candelaria .10 .02
❑ 552 Joe Cowley .10 .02
❑ 553 Danny Cox .10 .02
❑ 554 Denny Walling .10 .02
❑ 555 Bruce Ruffin RC .15 .05
❑ 556 Buddy Bell .15 .05
❑ 557 Jimmy Jones RC .15 .05
❑ 558 Bobby Bonilla RC .60 .25
❑ 559 Jeff D. Robinson .10 .02
❑ 560 Ed Olwine .10 .02
❑ 561 Glenallen Hill RC .40 .15
❑ 562 Lee Mazzilli .15 .05
❑ 563 Mike G. Brown P .10 .02
❑ 564 George Frazier .10 .02
❑ 565 Mike Sharperson RC .15 .05
❑ 566 Mark Portugal RC * .40 .15
❑ 567 Rick Leach .10 .02
❑ 568 Mark Langston .10 .02
❑ 569 Rafael Santana .10 .02
❑ 570 Manny Trillo .10 .02
❑ 571 Cliff Speck .10 .02
❑ 572 Bob Kipper .10 .02
❑ 573 Kelly Downs RC .15 .05
❑ 574 Randy Asadoor .10 .02
❑ 575 Dave Magadan RC .40 .15
❑ 576 Marvin Freeman RC .15 .05
❑ 577 Jeff Lahti .10 .02
❑ 578 Jeff Calhoun .10 .02
❑ 579 Gus Polidor .10 .02
❑ 580 Gene Nelson .10 .02
❑ 581 Tim Teufel .10 .02
❑ 582 Odell Jones .10 .02
❑ 583 Mark Ryal .10 .02
❑ 584 Randy O'Neal .10 .02
❑ 585 Mike Greenwell RC .40 .15
❑ 586 Ray Knight .15 .05
❑ 587 Ralph Bryant .10 .02
❑ 588 Carmen Castillo .10 .02
❑ 589 Ed Wojna .10 .02
❑ 590 Stan Javier .10 .02
❑ 591 Jeff Musselman .10 .02
❑ 592 Mike Stanley RC .40 .15
❑ 593 Darrell Porter .10 .02
❑ 594 Drew Hall .10 .02
❑ 595 Rob Nelson .10 .02
❑ 596 Bryan Oelkers .10 .02
❑ 597 Scott Nielsen .10 .02
❑ 598 Brian Holton .10 .02
❑ 599 Kevin Mitchell RC * .60 .25
❑ 600 Checklist 558-660 .10 .02
❑ 601 Jackie Gutierrez .10 .02
❑ 602 Barry Jones .10 .02
❑ 603 Jerry Narron .10 .02
❑ 604 Steve Lake .10 .02
❑ 605 Jim Pankovits .10 .02
❑ 606 Ed Romero .10 .02
❑ 607 Dave LaPoint .10 .02
❑ 608 Don Robinson .10 .02
❑ 609 Mike Krukow .10 .02
❑ 610 Dave Valle RC ** .15 .05
❑ 611 Len Dykstra .15 .05
❑ 612 Roberto Clemente PUZ .50 .20
❑ 613 Mike Trujillo .10 .02

❑ 614 Damaso Garcia .10 .02
❑ 615 Neal Heaton .10 .02
❑ 616 Juan Berenguer .10 .02
❑ 617 Steve Carlton .15 .05
❑ 618 Gary Lucas .10 .02
❑ 619 Geno Petralli .10 .02
❑ 620 Rick Aguilera .10 .02
❑ 621 Fred McGriff .75 .30
❑ 622 Dave Henderson .10 .02
❑ 623 Dave Clark RC .15 .05
❑ 624 Angel Salazar .10 .02
❑ 625 Randy Hunt .10 .02
❑ 626 John Gibbons .10 .02
❑ 627 Kevin Brown RC 1.50 .60
❑ 628 Bill Dawley .10 .02
❑ 629 Aurelio Lopez .10 .02
❑ 630 Charles Hudson .10 .02
❑ 631 Ray Soff .10 .02
❑ 632 Ray Hayward .10 .02
❑ 633 Spike Owen .10 .02
❑ 634 Glenn Hubbard .10 .02
❑ 635 Kevin Elster RC .40 .15
❑ 636 Mike LaCoss .10 .02
❑ 637 Dwayne Henry .10 .02
❑ 638 Rey Quinones .10 .02
❑ 639 Jim Clancy .10 .02
❑ 640 Larry Andersen .10 .02
❑ 641 Calvin Schiraldi .10 .02
❑ 642 Stan Jefferson .10 .02
❑ 643 Marc Sullivan .10 .02
❑ 644 Mark Grant .10 .02
❑ 645 Cliff Johnson .10 .02
❑ 646 Howard Johnson .15 .05
❑ 647 Dave Sax .10 .02
❑ 648 Dave Stewart .15 .05
❑ 649 Danny Heep .10 .02
❑ 650 Joe Johnson .10 .02
❑ 651 Bob Brower .10 .02
❑ 652 Rob Woodward .10 .02
❑ 653 John Mizerock .10 .02
❑ 654 Tim Pyznarski .10 .02
❑ 655 Luis Aquino .10 .02
❑ 656 Mickey Brantley .10 .02
❑ 657 Doyle Alexander .10 .02
❑ 658 Sammy Stewart .10 .02
❑ 659 Jim Acker .10 .02
❑ 660 Pete Ladd .10 .02

1987 Donruss Rookies

❑ COMP.FACT.SET (56) 25.00 10.00
❑ 1 Mark McGwire 10.00 4.00
❑ 2 Eric Bell .15 .05
❑ 3 Mark Williamson .10 .02
❑ 4 Mike Greenwell .40 .15
❑ 5 Ellis Burks XRC .60 .25
❑ 6 DeWayne Buice .10 .02
❑ 7 Mark McLemore .25 .08
❑ 8 Devon White .60 .25
❑ 9 Willie Fraser .15 .05
❑ 10 Les Lancaster .10 .02
❑ 11 Ken Williams .10 .02
❑ 12 Matt Nokes XRC .40 .15
❑ 13 Jeff M. Robinson .10 .02
❑ 14 Bo Jackson 5.00 2.00
❑ 15 Kevin Seitzer XRC .40 .15
❑ 16 Bill Ripken XRC .40 .15
❑ 17 B.J. Surhoff .60 .25
❑ 18 Chuck Crim .10 .02
❑ 19 Mike Birkbeck .15 .05
❑ 20 Chris Bosio .40 .15
❑ 21 Les Straker .10 .02
❑ 22 Mark Davidson .10 .02
❑ 23 Gene Larkin XRC .40 .15
❑ 24 Ken Gerhart .10 .02
❑ 25 Luis Polonia XRC .40 .15
❑ 26 Terry Steinbach .60 .25
❑ 27 Mickey Brantley .10 .02
❑ 28 Mike Stanley .40 .15
❑ 29 Jerry Browne .15 .05
❑ 30 Todd Benzinger XRC .40 .15
❑ 31 Fred McGriff 1.50 .60
❑ 32 Mike Henneman XRC .40 .15
❑ 33 Casey Candaele .10 .02
❑ 34 Dave Magadan .40 .15
❑ 35 David Cone 1.00 .40
❑ 36 Mike Jackson XRC .40 .15
❑ 37 John Mitchell XRC .15 .05
❑ 38 Mike Dunne .10 .02
❑ 39 John Smiley XRC .40 .15
❑ 40 Joe Magrane XRC .15 .05
❑ 41 Jim Lindeman .15 .05
❑ 42 Shane Mack .10 .02
❑ 43 Stan Jefferson .10 .02
❑ 44 Benito Santiago .25 .08
❑ 45 Matt Williams XRC 2.50 1.00
❑ 46 Dave Meads .10 .02
❑ 47 Rafael Palmeiro 5.00 2.00
❑ 48 Bill Long .10 .02
❑ 49 Bob Brower .10 .02
❑ 50 James Steels .10 .02
❑ 51 Paul Noce .10 .02
❑ 52 Greg Maddux 8.00 3.00
❑ 53 Jeff Musselman .10 .02
❑ 54 Brian Holton .10 .02
❑ 55 Chuck Jackson .10 .02
❑ 56 Checklist 1-56 .10 .02

1988 Donruss

❑ COMPLETE SET (660) 10.00 4.00
❑ COMP.FACT.SET (660) 15.00 6.00
❑ COMMON CARD (1-660) .05 .01
❑ COMMON SP (648-660) .10 .02
❑ 1 Mark McGwire DK .75 .30
❑ 2 Tim Raines DK .10 .02
❑ 3 Benito Santiago DK .10 .02
❑ 4 Alan Trammell DK .10 .02
❑ 5 Danny Tartabull DK .05 .01
❑ 6 Ron Darling DK .10 .02
❑ 7 Paul Molitor DK .10 .02
❑ 8 Devon White DK .10 .02
❑ 9 Andre Dawson DK .05 .01
❑ 10 Julio Franco DK .10 .02
❑ 11 Scott Fletcher DK .05 .01
❑ 12 Tony Fernandez DK .05 .01
❑ 13 Shane Rawley DK .05 .01
❑ 14 Kal Daniels DK .05 .01
❑ 15 Jack Clark DK .10 .02
❑ 16 Dwight Evans DK .15 .05
❑ 17 Tommy John DK .10 .02
❑ 18 Andy Van Slyke DK .15 .05
❑ 19 Gary Gaetti DK .10 .02
❑ 20 Mark Langston DK .05 .01
❑ 21 Will Clark DK .20 .07
❑ 22 Glenn Hubbard DK .05 .01
❑ 23 Billy Hatcher DK .05 .01
❑ 24 Bob Welch DK .10 .02
❑ 25 Ivan Calderon DK .05 .01
❑ 26 Cal Ripken DK .40 .15
❑ 27 DK Checklist 1-26 .05 .01
❑ 28 Mackey Sasser RC .25 .08
❑ 29 Jeff Treadway RC .25 .08
❑ 30 Mike Campbell RR .05 .01
❑ 31 Lance Johnson RC .25 .08
❑ 32 Nelson Liriano RR .05 .01
❑ 33 Shawn Abner RR .05 .01
❑ 34 Roberto Alomar RC 2.00 .75
❑ 35 Shawn Hillegas RR .05 .01
❑ 36 Joey Meyer RR .05 .01
❑ 37 Kevin Elster RR .05 .01
❑ 38 Jose Lind RC .25 .08
❑ 39 Kirt Manwaring RC .25 .08
❑ 40 Mark Grace RC 2.00 .75
❑ 41 Jody Reed RC .25 .08
❑ 42 John Farrell RR RC .10 .02
❑ 43 Al Leiter RC .75 .30
❑ 44 Gary Thurman RR .05 .01
❑ 45 Vicente Palacios RR .05 .01
❑ 46 Eddie Williams RC .10 .02
❑ 47 Jack McDowell RC .40 .15
❑ 48 Ken Dixon .05 .01
❑ 49 Mike Birkbeck .05 .01
❑ 50 Eric King .05 .01
❑ 51 Roger Clemens 1.00 .40
❑ 52 Pat Clements .05 .01
❑ 53 Fernando Valenzuela .10 .02
❑ 54 Mark Gubicza .05 .01
❑ 55 Jay Howell .05 .01
❑ 56 Floyd Youmans .05 .01
❑ 57 Ed Correa .05 .01
❑ 58 DeWayne Buice .05 .01
❑ 59 Jose DeLeon .05 .01
❑ 60 Danny Cox .05 .01
❑ 61 Nolan Ryan 1.00 .40
❑ 62 Steve Bedrosian .05 .01
❑ 63 Tom Browning .05 .01
❑ 64 Mark Davis .05 .01
❑ 65 R.J. Reynolds .05 .01
❑ 66 Kevin Mitchell .10 .02
❑ 67 Ken Oberkfell .05 .01
❑ 68 Rick Sutcliffe .10 .02
❑ 69 Dwight Gooden .10 .02
❑ 70 Scott Bankhead .05 .01
❑ 71 Bert Blyleven .10 .02
❑ 72 Jimmy Key .10 .02
❑ 73 Les Straker .05 .01
❑ 74 Jim Clancy .05 .01
❑ 75 Mike Moore .05 .01
❑ 76 Ron Darling .10 .02
❑ 77 Ed Lynch .05 .01
❑ 78 Dale Murphy .15 .05
❑ 79 Doug Drabek .05 .01
❑ 80 Scott Garrelts .05 .01
❑ 81 Ed Whitson .05 .01
❑ 82 Rob Murphy .05 .01
❑ 83 Shane Rawley .05 .01
❑ 84 Greg Mathews .05 .01
❑ 85 Jim Deshaies .05 .01
❑ 86 Mike Witt .05 .01
❑ 87 Donnie Hill .05 .01
❑ 88 Jeff Reed .05 .01
❑ 89 Mike Boddicker .05 .01
❑ 90 Ted Higuera .05 .01
❑ 91 Walt Terrell .05 .01
❑ 92 Bob Stanley .05 .01
❑ 93 Dave Righetti .10 .02
❑ 94 Orel Hershiser .10 .02
❑ 95 Chris Bando .05 .01
❑ 96 Bret Saberhagen .10 .02
❑ 97 Curt Young .05 .01
❑ 98 Tim Burke .05 .01
❑ 99 Charlie Hough .10 .02
❑ 100A Checklist 28-137 .05 .01
❑ 100B Checklist 28-133 .05 .01
❑ 101 Bobby Witt .05 .01
❑ 102 George Brett .50 .20
❑ 103 Mickey Tettleton .05 .01
❑ 104 Scott Bailes .05 .01
❑ 105 Mike Pagliarulo .05 .01
❑ 106 Mike Scioscia .10 .02
❑ 107 Tom Brookens .05 .01
❑ 108 Ray Knight .10 .02
❑ 109 Dan Plesac .05 .01

❑ 110	Wally Joyner	.10	.02
❑ 111	Bob Forsch	.05	.01
❑ 112	Mike Scott	.10	.02
❑ 113	Kevin Gross	.05	.01
❑ 114	Benito Santiago	.10	.02
❑ 115	Bob Kipper	.05	.01
❑ 116	Mike Krukow	.05	.01
❑ 117	Chris Bosio	.05	.01
❑ 118	Sid Fernandez	.05	.01
❑ 119	Jody Davis	.05	.01
❑ 120	Mike Morgan	.05	.01
❑ 121	Mark Eichhorn	.05	.01
❑ 122	Jeff Reardon	.10	.02
❑ 123	John Franco	.10	.02
❑ 124	Richard Dotson	.05	.01
❑ 125	Eric Bell	.05	.01
❑ 126	Juan Nieves	.05	.01
❑ 127	Jack Morris	.10	.02
❑ 128	Rick Rhoden	.05	.01
❑ 129	Rich Gedman	.05	.01
❑ 130	Ken Howell	.05	.01
❑ 131	Brook Jacoby	.05	.01
❑ 132	Danny Jackson	.05	.01
❑ 133	Gene Nelson	.05	.01
❑ 134	Neal Heaton	.05	.01
❑ 135	Willie Fraser	.05	.01
❑ 136	Jose Guzman	.05	.01
❑ 137	Ozzie Guillen	.10	.02
❑ 138	Bob Knepper	.05	.01
❑ 139	Mike Jackson RC*	.25	.08
❑ 140	Joe Magrane RC*	.25	.08
❑ 141	Jimmy Jones	.05	.01
❑ 142	Ted Power	.05	.01
❑ 143	Ozzie Virgil	.05	.01
❑ 144	Felix Fermin	.05	.01
❑ 145	Kelly Downs	.05	.01
❑ 146	Shawon Dunston	.05	.01
❑ 147	Scott Bradley	.05	.01
❑ 148	Dave Stieb	.10	.02
❑ 149	Frank Viola	.10	.02
❑ 150	Terry Kennedy	.05	.01
❑ 151	Bill Wegman	.05	.01
❑ 152	Matt Nokes RC*	.25	.08
❑ 153	Wade Boggs	.15	.05
❑ 154	Wayne Tolleson	.05	.01
❑ 155	Mariano Duncan	.05	.01
❑ 156	Julio Franco	.10	.02
❑ 157	Charlie Leibrandt	.05	.01
❑ 158	Terry Steinbach	.10	.02
❑ 159	Mike Fitzgerald	.05	.01
❑ 160	Jack Lazorko	.05	.01
❑ 161	Mitch Williams	.05	.01
❑ 162	Greg Walker	.05	.01
❑ 163	Alan Ashby	.05	.01
❑ 164	Tony Gwynn	.30	.10
❑ 165	Bruce Ruffin	.05	.01
❑ 166	Ron Robinson	.05	.01
❑ 167	Zane Smith	.05	.01
❑ 168	Junior Ortiz	.05	.01
❑ 169	Jamie Moyer	.10	.02
❑ 170	Tony Pena	.05	.01
❑ 171	Cal Ripken	.75	.30
❑ 172	B.J. Surhoff	.10	.02
❑ 173	Lou Whitaker	.10	.02
❑ 174	Ellis Burks RC	.40	.15
❑ 175	Ron Guidry	.10	.02
❑ 176	Steve Sax	.05	.01
❑ 177	Danny Tartabull	.05	.01
❑ 178	Carney Lansford	.10	.02
❑ 179	Casey Candaele	.05	.01
❑ 180	Scott Fletcher	.05	.01
❑ 181	Mark McLemore	.05	.01
❑ 182	Ivan Calderon	.05	.01
❑ 183	Jack Clark	.10	.02
❑ 184	Glenn Davis	.05	.01
❑ 185	Luis Aguayo	.05	.01
❑ 186	Bo Diaz	.05	.01
❑ 187	Stan Jefferson	.05	.01
❑ 188	Sid Bream	.05	.01
❑ 189	Bob Brenly	.05	.01
❑ 190	Dion James	.05	.01
❑ 191	Leon Durham	.05	.01
❑ 192	Jesse Orosco	.05	.01
❑ 193	Alvin Davis	.05	.01
❑ 194	Gary Gaetti	.10	.02
❑ 195	Fred McGriff	.20	.07
❑ 196	Steve Lombardozzi	.05	.01
❑ 197	Rance Mulliniks	.05	.01
❑ 198	Rey Quinones	.05	.01
❑ 199	Gary Carter	.10	.02
❑ 200A	Checklist 138-247	.05	.01
❑ 200B	Checklist 134-239	.05	.01
❑ 201	Keith Moreland	.05	.01
❑ 202	Ken Griffey	.10	.02
❑ 203	Tommy Gregg	.05	.01
❑ 204	Will Clark	.20	.07
❑ 205	John Kruk	.10	.02
❑ 206	Buddy Bell	.10	.02
❑ 207	Von Hayes	.05	.01
❑ 208	Tommy Herr	.05	.01
❑ 209	Craig Reynolds	.05	.01
❑ 210	Gary Pettis	.05	.01
❑ 211	Harold Baines	.10	.02
❑ 212	Vance Law	.05	.01
❑ 213	Ken Gerhart	.05	.01
❑ 214	Jim Gantner	.05	.01
❑ 215	Chet Lemon	.10	.02
❑ 216	Dwight Evans	.15	.05
❑ 217	Don Mattingly	.60	.25
❑ 218	Franklin Stubbs	.05	.01
❑ 219	Pat Tabler	.05	.01
❑ 220	Bo Jackson	.20	.07
❑ 221	Tony Phillips	.05	.01
❑ 222	Tim Wallach	.05	.01
❑ 223	Ruben Sierra	.10	.02
❑ 224	Steve Buechele	.05	.01
❑ 225	Frank White	.10	.02
❑ 226	Alfredo Griffin	.05	.01
❑ 227	Greg Swindell	.05	.01
❑ 228	Willie Randolph	.10	.02
❑ 229	Mike Marshall	.05	.01
❑ 230	Alan Trammell	.10	.02
❑ 231	Eddie Murray	.20	.07
❑ 232	Dale Sveum	.05	.01
❑ 233	Dick Schofield	.05	.01
❑ 234	Jose Oquendo	.05	.01
❑ 235	Bill Doran	.05	.01
❑ 236	Milt Thompson	.05	.01
❑ 237	Marvell Wynne	.05	.01
❑ 238	Bobby Bonilla	.10	.02
❑ 239	Chris Speier	.05	.01
❑ 240	Glenn Braggs	.05	.01
❑ 241	Wally Backman	.05	.01
❑ 242	Ryne Sandberg	.40	.15
❑ 243	Phil Bradley	.05	.01
❑ 244	Kelly Gruber	.05	.01
❑ 245	Tom Brunansky	.05	.01
❑ 246	Ron Oester	.05	.01
❑ 247	Bobby Thigpen	.05	.01
❑ 248	Fred Lynn	.10	.02
❑ 249	Paul Molitor	.10	.02
❑ 250	Darrell Evans	.10	.02
❑ 251	Gary Ward	.05	.01
❑ 252	Bruce Hurst	.05	.01
❑ 253	Bob Welch	.10	.02
❑ 254	Joe Carter	.10	.02
❑ 255	Willie Wilson	.10	.02
❑ 256	Mark McGwire	1.50	.60
❑ 257	Mitch Webster	.05	.01
❑ 258	Brian Downing	.10	.02
❑ 259	Mike Stanley	.05	.01
❑ 260	Carlton Fisk	.15	.05
❑ 261	Billy Hatcher	.05	.01
❑ 262	Glenn Wilson	.05	.01
❑ 263	Ozzie Smith	.30	.10
❑ 264	Randy Ready	.05	.01
❑ 265	Kurt Stillwell	.05	.01
❑ 266	David Palmer	.05	.01
❑ 267	Mike Diaz	.05	.01
❑ 268	Robby Thompson	.05	.01
❑ 269	Andre Dawson	.10	.02
❑ 270	Lee Guetterman	.05	.01
❑ 271	Willie Upshaw	.05	.01
❑ 272	Randy Bush	.05	.01
❑ 273	Larry Sheets	.05	.01
❑ 274	Rob Deer	.05	.01
❑ 275	Kirk Gibson	.20	.07
❑ 276	Marty Barrett	.05	.01
❑ 277	Rickey Henderson	.20	.07
❑ 278	Pedro Guerrero	.10	.02
❑ 279	Brett Butler	.10	.02
❑ 280	Kevin Seitzer	.05	.01
❑ 281	Mike Davis	.05	.01
❑ 282	Andres Galarraga	.10	.02
❑ 283	Devon White	.10	.02
❑ 284	Pete O'Brien	.05	.01
❑ 285	Jerry Hairston	.05	.01
❑ 286	Kevin Bass	.05	.01
❑ 287	Carmelo Martinez	.05	.01
❑ 288	Juan Samuel	.05	.01
❑ 289	Kal Daniels	.05	.01
❑ 290	Albert Hall	.05	.01
❑ 291	Andy Van Slyke	.15	.05
❑ 292	Lee Smith	.10	.02
❑ 293	Vince Coleman	.05	.01
❑ 294	Tom Niedenfuer	.05	.01
❑ 295	Robin Yount	.30	.10
❑ 296	Jeff M. Robinson	.05	.01
❑ 297	Todd Benzinger RC*	.25	.08
❑ 298	Dave Winfield	.10	.02
❑ 299	Mickey Hatcher	.05	.01
❑ 300A	Checklist 248-357	.05	.01
❑ 300B	Checklist 240-345	.05	.01
❑ 301	Bud Black	.05	.01
❑ 302	Jose Canseco	.50	.20
❑ 303	Tom Foley	.05	.01
❑ 304	Pete Incaviglia	.05	.01
❑ 305	Bob Boone	.10	.02
❑ 306	Bill Long	.05	.01
❑ 307	Willie McGee	.10	.02
❑ 308	Ken Caminiti RC	2.00	.75
❑ 309	Darren Daulton	.10	.02
❑ 310	Tracy Jones	.05	.01
❑ 311	Greg Booker	.05	.01
❑ 312	Mike LaValliere	.05	.01
❑ 313	Chili Davis	.10	.02
❑ 314	Glenn Hubbard	.05	.01
❑ 315	Paul Noce	.05	.01
❑ 316	Keith Hernandez	.10	.02
❑ 317	Mark Langston	.05	.01
❑ 318	Keith Atherton	.05	.01
❑ 319	Tony Fernandez	.05	.01
❑ 320	Kent Hrbek	.10	.02
❑ 321	John Cerutti	.05	.01
❑ 322	Mike Kingery	.05	.01
❑ 323	Dave Magadan	.05	.01
❑ 324	Rafael Palmeiro	.40	.15
❑ 325	Jeff Dedmon	.05	.01
❑ 326	Barry Bonds	2.00	.75
❑ 327	Jeffrey Leonard	.05	.01
❑ 328	Tim Flannery	.05	.01
❑ 329	Dave Concepcion	.10	.02
❑ 330	Mike Schmidt	.50	.20
❑ 331	Bill Dawley	.05	.01
❑ 332	Larry Andersen	.05	.01
❑ 333	Jack Howell	.05	.01
❑ 334	Ken Williams	.05	.01
❑ 335	Bryn Smith	.05	.01
❑ 336	Bill Ripken RC*	.25	.08
❑ 337	Greg Brock	.05	.01
❑ 338	Mike Heath	.05	.01
❑ 339	Mike Greenwell	.05	.01
❑ 340	Claudell Washington	.05	.01
❑ 341	Jose Gonzalez	.05	.01
❑ 342	Mel Hall	.05	.01
❑ 343	Jim Eisenreich	.05	.01
❑ 344	Tony Bernazard	.05	.01
❑ 345	Tim Raines	.10	.02
❑ 346	Bob Brower	.05	.01
❑ 347	Larry Parrish	.05	.01
❑ 348	Thad Bosley	.05	.01
❑ 349	Dennis Eckersley	.15	.05
❑ 350	Cory Snyder	.05	.01
❑ 351	Rick Cerone	.05	.01
❑ 352	John Shelby	.05	.01
❑ 353	Larry Herndon	.05	.01
❑ 354	John Habyan	.05	.01
❑ 355	Chuck Crim	.05	.01
❑ 356	Gus Polidor	.05	.01
❑ 357	Ken Dayley	.05	.01
❑ 358	Danny Darwin	.05	.01
❑ 359	Lance Parrish	.10	.02
❑ 360	James Steels	.05	.01
❑ 361	Al Pedrique	.05	.01
❑ 362	Mike Aldrete	.05	.01
❑ 363	Juan Castillo	.05	.01
❑ 364	Len Dykstra	.10	.02
❑ 365	Luis Quinones	.05	.01

❑ 366 Jim Presley .05 .01
❑ 367 Lloyd Moseby .05 .01
❑ 368 Kirby Puckett .20 .07
❑ 369 Eric Davis .10 .02
❑ 370 Gary Redus .05 .01
❑ 371 Dave Schmidt .05 .01
❑ 372 Mark Clear .05 .01
❑ 373 Dave Bergman .05 .01
❑ 374 Charles Hudson .05 .01
❑ 375 Calvin Schiraldi .05 .01
❑ 376 Alex Trevino .05 .01
❑ 377 Tom Candiotti .05 .01
❑ 378 Steve Farr .05 .01
❑ 379 Mike Gallego .05 .01
❑ 380 Andy McGaffigan .05 .01
❑ 381 Kirk McCaskill .05 .01
❑ 382 Oddibe McDowell .05 .01
❑ 383 Floyd Bannister .05 .01
❑ 384 Denny Walling .05 .01
❑ 385 Don Carman .05 .01
❑ 386 Todd Worrell .05 .01
❑ 387 Eric Show .05 .01
❑ 388 Dave Parker .10 .02
❑ 389 Rick Mahler .05 .01
❑ 390 Mike Dunne .05 .01
❑ 391 Candy Maldonado .05 .01
❑ 392 Bob Dernier .05 .01
❑ 393 Dave Valle .05 .01
❑ 394 Ernie Whitt .05 .01
❑ 395 Juan Berenguer .05 .01
❑ 396 Mike Young .05 .01
❑ 397 Mike Felder .05 .01
❑ 398 Willie Hernandez .05 .01
❑ 399 Jim Rice .10 .02
❑ 400A Checklist 358-467 .05 .01
❑ 400B Checklist 346-451 .05 .01
❑ 401 Tommy John .10 .02
❑ 402 Brian Holton .05 .01
❑ 403 Carmen Castillo .05 .01
❑ 404 Jamie Quirk .05 .01
❑ 405 Dwayne Murphy .05 .01
❑ 406 Jeff Parrett .05 .01
❑ 407 Don Sutton .10 .02
❑ 408 Jerry Browne .05 .01
❑ 409 Jim Winn .05 .01
❑ 410 Dave Smith .05 .01
❑ 411 Shane Mack .05 .01
❑ 412 Greg Gross .05 .01
❑ 413 Nick Esasky .05 .01
❑ 414 Damaso Garcia .05 .01
❑ 415 Brian Fisher .05 .01
❑ 416 Brian Dayett .05 .01
❑ 417 Curt Ford .05 .01
❑ 418 Mark Williamson .05 .01
❑ 419 Bill Schroeder .05 .01
❑ 420 Mike Henneman RC* .25 .08
❑ 421 John Marzano .05 .01
❑ 422 Ron Kittle .05 .01
❑ 423 Matt Young .05 .01
❑ 424 Steve Balboni .05 .01
❑ 425 Luis Polonia RC* .25 .08
❑ 426 Randy St.Claire .05 .01
❑ 427 Greg Harris .05 .01
❑ 428 Johnny Ray .05 .01
❑ 429 Ray Searage .05 .01
❑ 430 Ricky Horton .05 .01
❑ 431 Gerald Young .05 .01
❑ 432 Rick Schu .05 .01
❑ 433 Paul O'Neill .15 .05
❑ 434 Rich Gossage .10 .02
❑ 435 John Cangelosi .05 .01
❑ 436 Mike LaCoss .05 .01
❑ 437 Gerald Perry .05 .01
❑ 438 Dave Martinez .05 .01
❑ 439 Darryl Strawberry .10 .02
❑ 440 John Moses .05 .01
❑ 441 Greg Gagne .05 .01
❑ 442 Jesse Barfield .10 .02
❑ 443 George Frazier .05 .01
❑ 444 Garth Iorg .05 .01
❑ 445 Ed Nunez .05 .01
❑ 446 Rick Aguilera .05 .01
❑ 447 Jerry Mumphrey .05 .01
❑ 448 Rafael Ramirez .05 .01
❑ 449 John Smiley RC* .25 .08
❑ 450 Atlee Hammaker .05 .01
❑ 451 Lance McCullers .05 .01
❑ 452 Guy Hoffman .05 .01
❑ 453 Chris James .05 .01
❑ 454 Terry Pendleton .10 .02
❑ 455 Dave Meads .05 .01
❑ 456 Bill Buckner .10 .02
❑ 457 John Pawlowski .05 .01
❑ 458 Bob Sebra .05 .01
❑ 459 Jim Dwyer .05 .01
❑ 460 Jay Aldrich .05 .01
❑ 461 Frank Tanana .10 .02
❑ 462 Oil Can Boyd .05 .01
❑ 463 Dan Pasqua .05 .01
❑ 464 Tim Crews RC .25 .08
❑ 465 Andy Allanson .05 .01
❑ 466 Bill Pecota RC* .10 .02
❑ 467 Steve Ontiveros .05 .01
❑ 468 Hubie Brooks .05 .01
❑ 469 Paul Kilgus .05 .01
❑ 470 Dale Mohorcic .05 .01
❑ 471 Dan Quisenberry .05 .01
❑ 472 Dave Stewart .10 .02
❑ 473 Dave Clark .05 .01
❑ 474 Joel Skinner .05 .01
❑ 475 Dave Anderson .05 .01
❑ 476 Dan Petry .05 .01
❑ 477 Carl Nichols .05 .01
❑ 478 Ernest Riles .05 .01
❑ 479 George Hendrick .10 .02
❑ 480 John Morris .05 .01
❑ 481 Manny Hernandez .05 .01
❑ 482 Jeff Stone .05 .01
❑ 483 Chris Brown .05 .01
❑ 484 Mike Bielecki .05 .01
❑ 485 Dave Dravecky .05 .01
❑ 486 Rick Manning .05 .01
❑ 487 Bill Almon .05 .01
❑ 488 Jim Sundberg .10 .02
❑ 489 Ken Phelps .05 .01
❑ 490 Tom Henke .05 .01
❑ 491 Dan Gladden .05 .01
❑ 492 Barry Larkin .15 .05
❑ 493 Fred Manrique .05 .01
❑ 494 Mike Griffin .05 .01
❑ 495 Mark Knudson .05 .01
❑ 496 Bill Madlock .10 .02
❑ 497 Tim Stoddard .05 .01
❑ 498 Sam Horn RC .10 .02
❑ 499 Tracy Woodson RC .10 .02
❑ 500A Checklist 468-577 .05 .01
❑ 500B Checklist 452-557 .05 .01
❑ 501 Ken Schrom .05 .01
❑ 502 Angel Salazar .05 .01
❑ 503 Eric Plunk .05 .01
❑ 504 Joe Hesketh .05 .01
❑ 505 Greg Minton .05 .01
❑ 506 Geno Petralli .05 .01
❑ 507 Bob James .05 .01
❑ 508 Robbie Wine .05 .01
❑ 509 Jeff Calhoun .05 .01
❑ 510 Steve Lake .05 .01
❑ 511 Mark Grant .05 .01
❑ 512 Frank Williams .05 .01
❑ 513 Jeff Blauser RC .25 .08
❑ 514 Bob Walk .05 .01
❑ 515 Craig Lefferts .05 .01
❑ 516 Manny Trillo .05 .01
❑ 517 Jerry Reed .05 .01
❑ 518 Rick Leach .05 .01
❑ 519 Mark Davidson .05 .01
❑ 520 Jeff Ballard .05 .01
❑ 521 Dave Stapleton .05 .01
❑ 522 Pat Sheridan .05 .01
❑ 523 Al Nipper .05 .01
❑ 524 Steve Trout .05 .01
❑ 525 Jeff Hamilton .05 .01
❑ 526 Tommy Hinzo .05 .01
❑ 527 Lonnie Smith .05 .01
❑ 528 Greg Cadaret .05 .01
❑ 529 Bob McClure UER
(%%Rob~ on front) .05 .01
❑ 530 Chuck Finley .10 .02
❑ 531 Jeff Russell .05 .01
❑ 532 Steve Lyons .05 .01
❑ 533 Terry Puhl .05 .01
❑ 534 Eric Nolte .05 .01
❑ 535 Kent Tekulve .05 .01
❑ 536 Pat Pacillo .05 .01
❑ 537 Charlie Puleo .05 .01
❑ 538 Tom Prince .05 .01
❑ 539 Greg Maddux 1.00 .40
❑ 540 Jim Lindeman .05 .01
❑ 541 Pete Stanicek .05 .01
❑ 542 Steve Kiefer .05 .01
❑ 543A Jim Morrison ERR
(No decimal before
lifetime ave .15 .05
❑ 543B Jim Morrison COR .05 .01
❑ 544 Spike Owen .05 .01
❑ 545 Jay Buhner RC .50 .20
❑ 546 Mike Devereaux RC .25 .08
❑ 547 Jerry Don Gleaton .05 .01
❑ 548 Jose Rijo .10 .02
❑ 549 Dennis Martinez .10 .02
❑ 550 Mike Loynd .05 .01
❑ 551 Darrell Miller .05 .01
❑ 552 Dave LaPoint .05 .01
❑ 553 John Tudor .10 .02
❑ 554 Rocky Childress .05 .01
❑ 555 Wally Ritchie .05 .01
❑ 556 Terry McGriff .05 .01
❑ 557 Dave Leiper .05 .01
❑ 558 Jeff D. Robinson .05 .01
❑ 559 Jose Uribe .05 .01
❑ 560 Ted Simmons .10 .02
❑ 561 Les Lancaster .05 .01
❑ 562 Keith Miller RC .25 .08
❑ 563 Harold Reynolds .10 .02
❑ 564 Gene Larkin RC* .25 .08
❑ 565 Cecil Fielder .10 .02
❑ 566 Roy Smalley .05 .01
❑ 567 Duane Ward .05 .01
❑ 568 Bill Wilkinson .05 .01
❑ 569 Howard Johnson .10 .02
❑ 570 Frank DiPino .05 .01
❑ 571 Pete Smith RC .10 .02
❑ 572 Darnell Coles .05 .01
❑ 573 Don Robinson .05 .01
❑ 574 Rob Nelson UER
(Career 0 RBI,
but 1 RBI in '87) .05 .01
❑ 575 Dennis Rasmussen .05 .01
❑ 576 Steve Jeltz UER
(Photo actually Juan
Samuel; Sam .05 .01
❑ 577 Tom Pagnozzi RC .10 .02
❑ 578 Ty Gainey .05 .01
❑ 579 Gary Lucas .05 .01
❑ 580 Ron Hassey .05 .01
❑ 581 Herm Winningham .05 .01
❑ 582 Rene Gonzales RC .10 .02
❑ 583 Brad Komminsk .05 .01
❑ 584 Doyle Alexander .05 .01
❑ 585 Jeff Sellers .05 .01
❑ 586 Bill Gullickson .05 .01
❑ 587 Tim Belcher .05 .01
❑ 588 Doug Jones RC .25 .08
❑ 589 Melido Perez RC .25 .08
❑ 590 Rick Honeycutt .05 .01
❑ 591 Pascual Perez .05 .01
❑ 592 Curt Wilkerson .05 .01
❑ 593 Steve Howe .05 .01
❑ 594 John Davis .05 .01
❑ 595 Storm Davis .05 .01
❑ 596 Sammy Stewart .05 .01
❑ 597 Neil Allen .05 .01
❑ 598 Alejandro Pena .05 .01
❑ 599 Mark Thurmond .05 .01
❑ 600A Checklist 578-660/BC1-BC26 .05 .01
❑ 600B Checklist 558-660 .05 .01
❑ 601 Jose Mesa RC .25 .08
❑ 602 Don August .05 .01
❑ 603 Terry Leach SP .10 .02
❑ 604 Tom Newell .05 .01
❑ 605 Randall Byers SP .10 .02
❑ 606 Jim Gott .05 .01
❑ 607 Harry Spilman .05 .01
❑ 608 John Candelaria .05 .01
❑ 609 Mike Brumley .05 .01
❑ 610 Mickey Brantley .05 .01
❑ 611 Jose Nunez SP .10 .02
❑ 612 Tom Nieto .05 .01

❑ 613 Rick Reuschel .10 .02
❑ 614 Lee Mazzilli SP .10 .02
❑ 615 Scott Lusader .05 .01
❑ 616 Bobby Meacham .05 .01
❑ 617 Kevin McReynolds SP .10 .02
❑ 618 Gene Garber .05 .01
❑ 619 Barry Lyons SP .10 .02
❑ 620 Randy Myers .10 .02
❑ 621 Donnie Moore .05 .01
❑ 622 Domingo Ramos .05 .01
❑ 623 Ed Romero .05 .01
❑ 624 Greg Myers RC .25 .08
❑ 625 The Ripken Family .40 .15
❑ 626 Pat Perry .05 .01
❑ 627 Andres Thomas SP .10 .02
❑ 628 Matt Williams RC .75 .30
❑ 629 Dave Hengel .05 .01
❑ 630 Jeff Musselman SP .10 .02
❑ 631 Tim Laudner .05 .01
❑ 632 Bob Ojeda SP .10 .02
❑ 633 Rafael Santana .05 .01
❑ 634 Wes Gardner .05 .01
❑ 635 Roberto Kelly SP RC .25 .08
❑ 636 Mike Flanagan SP .10 .02
❑ 637 Jay Bell RC .40 .15
❑ 638 Bob Melvin .05 .01
❑ 639 Damon Berryhill RC .25 .08
❑ 640 David Wells RC 1.00 .40
❑ 641 Stan Musial Puzzle .20 .07
❑ 642 Doug Sisk .05 .01
❑ 643 Keith Hughes .05 .01
❑ 644 Tom Glavine RC 2.50 1.00
❑ 645 Al Newman .05 .01
❑ 646 Scott Sanderson .05 .01
❑ 647 Scott Terry .05 .01
❑ 648 Tim Teufel SP .10 .02
❑ 649 Garry Templeton SP .10 .02
❑ 650 Manny Lee SP .10 .02
❑ 651 Roger McDowell SP .10 .02
❑ 652 Mookie Wilson SP .10 .02
❑ 653 David Cone .10 .02
❑ 654 Ron Gant RC .40 .15
❑ 655 Joe Price SP .10 .02
❑ 656 George Bell SP .10 .02
❑ 657 Gregg Jefferies RC .25 .08
❑ 658 Todd Stottlemyre RC .25 .08
❑ 659 Geronimo Berroa RC .25 .08
❑ 660 Jerry Royster SP .10 .02
❑ XX Kirby Puckett
Blister Pack 1.25 .50

1988 Donruss Rookies

❑ COMP.FACT.SET (56) 10.00 4.00
❑ 1 Mark Grace 2.00 .75
❑ 2 Mike Campbell .15 .05
❑ 3 Todd Frohwirth .15 .05
❑ 4 Dave Stapleton .15 .05
❑ 5 Shawn Abner .15 .05
❑ 6 Jose Cecena .15 .05
❑ 7 Dave Gallagher .15 .05
❑ 8 Mark Parent .15 .05
❑ 9 Cecil Espy .15 .05
❑ 10 Pete Smith .15 .05
❑ 11 Jay Buhner 1.00 .40
❑ 12 Pat Borders XRC .50 .20
❑ 13 Doug Jennings .15 .05
❑ 14 Brady Anderson XRC .75 .30
❑ 15 Pete Stanicek .15 .05
❑ 16 Roberto Kelly .50 .20
❑ 17 Jeff Treadway .15 .05
❑ 18 Walt Weiss XRC* .75 .30
❑ 19 Paul Gibson .15 .05
❑ 20 Tim Crews .15 .05
❑ 21 Melido Perez .15 .05
❑ 22 Steve Peters .15 .05
❑ 23 Craig Worthington .15 .05
❑ 24 John Trautwein .15 .05
❑ 25 DeWayne Vaughn .15 .05
❑ 26 David Wells 1.50 .60
❑ 27 Al Leiter 1.00 .40
❑ 28 Tim Belcher .15 .05
❑ 29 Johnny Paredes .15 .05
❑ 30 Chris Sabo XRC .40 .15
❑ 31 Damon Berryhill .15 .05
❑ 32 Randy Milligan XRC* .25 .08
❑ 33 Gary Thurman .15 .05
❑ 34 Kevin Elster .15 .05
❑ 35 Roberto Alomar 4.00 1.50
❑ 36 Edgar Martinez XRC 5.00 2.00
❑ 37 Todd Stottlemyre .15 .05
❑ 38 Joey Meyer .15 .05
❑ 39 Carl Nichols .15 .05
❑ 40 Jack McDowell .75 .30
❑ 41 Jose Bautista XRC .25 .08
❑ 42 Sil Campusano .15 .05
❑ 43 John Dopson .15 .05
❑ 44 Jody Reed .50 .20
❑ 45 Darrin Jackson XRC* .25 .08
❑ 46 Mike Capel .15 .05
❑ 47 Ron Gant .75 .30
❑ 48 John Davis .15 .05
❑ 49 Kevin Coffman .15 .05
❑ 50 Cris Carpenter XRC .25 .08
❑ 51 Mackey Sasser .15 .05
❑ 52 Luis Alicea XRC .50 .20
❑ 53 Bryan Harvey XRC .30 .10
❑ 54 Steve Ellsworth .15 .05
❑ 55 Mike Macfarlane XRC .50 .20
❑ 56 Checklist 1-56 .15 .05

1989 Donruss

❑ COMPLETE SET (660) 25.00 10.00
❑ COMP.FACT.SET (672) 25.00 10.00
❑ 1 Mike Greenwell DK .05 .01
❑ 2 Bobby Bonilla DK DP .10 .02
❑ 3 Pete Incaviglia DK .05 .01
❑ 4 Chris Sabo DK DP .10 .02
❑ 5 Robin Yount DK .40 .15
❑ 6 Tony Gwynn DK DP .15 .05
❑ 7 Carlton Fisk DK UER .15 .05
❑ 8 Cory Snyder DK .05 .01
❑ 9 David Cone DK UER .10 .02
❑ 10 Kevin Seitzer DK .05 .01
❑ 11 Rick Reuschel DK .10 .02
❑ 12 Johnny Ray DK .05 .01
❑ 13 Dave Schmidt DK .05 .01
❑ 14 Andres Galarraga DK .10 .02
❑ 15 Kirk Gibson DK .10 .02
❑ 16 Fred McGriff DK .15 .05
❑ 17 Mark Grace DK .25 .08
❑ 18 Jeff M. Robinson DK .05 .01
❑ 19 Vince Coleman DK DP .05 .01
❑ 20 Dave Henderson DK .05 .01
❑ 21 Harold Reynolds DK .10 .02
❑ 22 Gerald Perry DK .05 .01
❑ 23 Frank Viola DK .10 .02
❑ 24 Steve Bedrosian DK .05 .01
❑ 25 Glenn Davis DK .05 .01
❑ 26 Don Mattingly DK .30 .10
❑ 27 DK Checklist 1-26 DP .05 .01
❑ 28 Sandy Alomar Jr. RC .40 .15
❑ 29 Steve Searcy RR .05 .01
❑ 30 Cameron Drew RR .05 .01
❑ 31 Gary Sheffield RC 1.50 .60
❑ 32 Erik Hanson RC .25 .08
❑ 33 Ken Griffey Jr. RC 8.00 3.00
❑ 34 Greg W.Harris RC .10 .02
❑ 35 Gregg Jefferies .05 .01
❑ 36 Luis Medina RR .05 .01
❑ 37 Carlos Quintana RC .10 .02
❑ 38 Felix Jose RC .10 .02
❑ 39 Cris Carpenter RC * .10 .02
❑ 40 Ron Jones RR .10 .02
❑ 41 Dave West RC .10 .02
❑ 42 Randy Johnson RC 2.50 1.00
❑ 43 Mike Harkey RC .10 .02
❑ 44 Pete Harnisch RC .25 .08
❑ 45 Tom Gordon RC .50 .20
❑ 46 Gregg Olson DP RC .25 .08
❑ 47 Alex Sanchez RC .05 .01
❑ 48 Ruben Sierra .10 .02
❑ 49 Rafael Palmeiro .25 .08
❑ 50 Ron Gant .10 .02
❑ 51 Cal Ripken .75 .30
❑ 52 Wally Joyner .10 .02
❑ 53 Gary Carter .10 .02
❑ 54 Andy Van Slyke .15 .05
❑ 55 Robin Yount .40 .15
❑ 56 Pete Incaviglia .05 .01
❑ 57 Greg Brock .05 .01
❑ 58 Melido Perez .05 .01
❑ 59 Craig Lefferts .05 .01
❑ 60 Gary Pettis .05 .01
❑ 61 Danny Tartabull .05 .01
❑ 62 Guillermo Hernandez .05 .01
❑ 63 Ozzie Smith .40 .15
❑ 64 Gary Gaetti .10 .02
❑ 65 Mark Davis .05 .01
❑ 66 Lee Smith .10 .02
❑ 67 Dennis Eckersley .15 .05
❑ 68 Wade Boggs .15 .05
❑ 69 Mike Scott .10 .02
❑ 70 Fred McGriff .15 .05
❑ 71 Tom Browning .05 .01
❑ 72 Claudell Washington .05 .01
❑ 73 Mel Hall .05 .01
❑ 74 Don Mattingly .60 .25
❑ 75 Steve Bedrosian .05 .01
❑ 76 Juan Samuel .05 .01
❑ 77 Mike Scioscia .10 .02
❑ 78 Dave Righetti .10 .02
❑ 79 Alfredo Griffin .05 .01
❑ 80 Eric Davis UER
(165 games in 1988,
should be 135 .10 .02
❑ 81 Juan Berenguer .05 .01
❑ 82 Todd Worrell .05 .01
❑ 83 Joe Carter .10 .02
❑ 84 Steve Sax .05 .01
❑ 85 Frank White .10 .02
❑ 86 John Kruk .10 .02
❑ 87 Rance Mulliniks .05 .01
❑ 88 Alan Ashby .05 .01
❑ 89 Charlie Leibrandt .05 .01
❑ 90 Frank Tanana .10 .02
❑ 91 Jose Canseco .25 .08
❑ 92 Barry Bonds 1.50 .60
❑ 93 Harold Reynolds .10 .02
❑ 94 Mark McLemore .05 .01
❑ 95 Mark McGwire 1.00 .40
❑ 96 Eddie Murray .25 .08
❑ 97 Tim Raines .10 .02
❑ 98 Robby Thompson .05 .01
❑ 99 Kevin McReynolds .05 .01
❑ 100 Checklist 28-137 .05 .01
❑ 101 Carlton Fisk .15 .05
❑ 102 Dave Martinez .05 .01
❑ 103 Glenn Braggs .05 .01
❑ 104 Dale Murphy .15 .05
❑ 105 Ryne Sandberg .40 .15
❑ 106 Dennis Martinez .10 .02
❑ 107 Pete O'Brien .05 .01

❑ 108 Dick Schofield	.05	.01
❑ 109 Henry Cotto	.05	.01
❑ 110 Mike Marshall	.05	.01
❑ 111 Keith Moreland	.05	.01
❑ 112 Tom Brunansky	.05	.01
❑ 113 Kelly Gruber UER (Wrong birthdate)	.05	.01
❑ 114 Brook Jacoby	.05	.01
❑ 115 Keith Brown	.05	.01
❑ 116 Matt Nokes	.05	.01
❑ 117 Keith Hernandez	.10	.02
❑ 118 Bob Forsch	.05	.01
❑ 119 Bert Blyleven UER (... 3000 strikeouts in 1987,	.10	.02
❑ 120 Willie Wilson	.10	.02
❑ 121 Tommy Gregg	.05	.01
❑ 122 Jim Rice	.10	.02
❑ 123 Bob Knepper	.05	.01
❑ 124 Danny Jackson	.05	.01
❑ 125 Eric Plunk	.05	.01
❑ 126 Brian Fisher	.05	.01
❑ 127 Mike Pagliarulo	.05	.01
❑ 128 Tony Gwynn	.30	.10
❑ 129 Lance McCullers	.05	.01
❑ 130 Andres Galarraga	.10	.02
❑ 131 Jose Uribe	.05	.01
❑ 132 Kirk Gibson UER	.10	.02
❑ 133 David Palmer	.05	.01
❑ 134 R.J. Reynolds	.05	.01
❑ 135 Greg Walker	.05	.01
❑ 136 Kirk McCaskill UER (Wrong birthdate)	.05	.01
❑ 137 Shawon Dunston	.05	.01
❑ 138 Andy Allanson	.05	.01
❑ 139 Rob Murphy	.05	.01
❑ 140 Mike Aldrete	.05	.01
❑ 141 Terry Kennedy	.05	.01
❑ 142 Scott Fletcher	.05	.01
❑ 143 Steve Balboni	.05	.01
❑ 144 Bret Saberhagen	.10	.02
❑ 145 Ozzie Virgil	.05	.01
❑ 146 Dale Sveum	.05	.01
❑ 147 Darryl Strawberry	.10	.02
❑ 148 Harold Baines	.10	.02
❑ 149 George Bell	.10	.02
❑ 150 Dave Parker	.10	.02
❑ 151 Bobby Bonilla	.10	.02
❑ 152 Mookie Wilson	.10	.02
❑ 153 Ted Power	.05	.01
❑ 154 Nolan Ryan	1.00	.40
❑ 155 Jeff Reardon	.10	.02
❑ 156 Tim Wallach	.05	.01
❑ 157 Jamie Moyer	.10	.02
❑ 158 Rich Gossage	.10	.02
❑ 159 Dave Winfield	.10	.02
❑ 160 Von Hayes	.05	.01
❑ 161 Willie McGee	.10	.02
❑ 162 Rich Gedman	.05	.01
❑ 163 Tony Pena	.05	.01
❑ 164 Mike Morgan	.05	.01
❑ 165 Charlie Hough	.10	.02
❑ 166 Mike Stanley	.05	.01
❑ 167 Andre Dawson	.10	.02
❑ 168 Joe Boever	.05	.01
❑ 169 Pete Stanicek	.05	.01
❑ 170 Bob Boone	.10	.02
❑ 171 Ron Darling	.10	.02
❑ 172 Bob Walk	.05	.01
❑ 173 Rob Deer	.05	.01
❑ 174 Steve Buechele	.05	.01
❑ 175 Ted Higuera	.05	.01
❑ 176 Ozzie Guillen	.10	.02
❑ 177 Candy Maldonado	.05	.01
❑ 178 Doyle Alexander	.05	.01
❑ 179 Mark Gubicza	.05	.01
❑ 180 Alan Trammell	.10	.02
❑ 181 Vince Coleman	.05	.01
❑ 182 Kirby Puckett	.25	.08
❑ 183 Chris Brown	.05	.01
❑ 184 Marty Barrett	.05	.01
❑ 185 Stan Javier	.05	.01
❑ 186 Mike Greenwell	.05	.01
❑ 187 Billy Hatcher	.05	.01
❑ 188 Jimmy Key	.10	.02
❑ 189 Nick Esasky	.05	.01
❑ 190 Don Slaught	.05	.01
❑ 191 Cory Snyder	.05	.01
❑ 192 John Candelaria	.05	.01
❑ 193 Mike Schmidt	.50	.20
❑ 194 Kevin Gross	.05	.01
❑ 195 John Tudor	.10	.02
❑ 196 Neil Allen	.05	.01
❑ 197 Orel Hershiser	.10	.02
❑ 198 Kal Daniels	.05	.01
❑ 199 Kent Hrbek	.10	.02
❑ 200 Checklist 138-247	.05	.01
❑ 201 Joe Magrane	.05	.01
❑ 202 Scott Bailes	.05	.01
❑ 203 Tim Belcher	.05	.01
❑ 204 George Brett	.60	.25
❑ 205 Benito Santiago	.10	.02
❑ 206 Tony Fernandez	.05	.01
❑ 207 Gerald Young	.05	.01
❑ 208 Bo Jackson	.25	.08
❑ 209 Chet Lemon	.10	.02
❑ 210 Storm Davis	.05	.01
❑ 211 Doug Drabek	.05	.01
❑ 212 Mickey Brantley UER (Photo actually Nelson Simmo	.05	.01
❑ 213 Devon White	.10	.02
❑ 214 Dave Stewart	.10	.02
❑ 215 Dave Schmidt	.05	.01
❑ 216 Bryn Smith	.05	.01
❑ 217 Brett Butler	.10	.02
❑ 218 Bob Ojeda	.05	.01
❑ 219 Steve Rosenberg	.05	.01
❑ 220 Hubie Brooks	.05	.01
❑ 221 B.J. Surhoff	.10	.02
❑ 222 Rick Mahler	.05	.01
❑ 223 Rick Sutcliffe	.10	.02
❑ 224 Neal Heaton	.05	.01
❑ 225 Mitch Williams	.05	.01
❑ 226 Chuck Finley	.10	.02
❑ 227 Mark Langston	.05	.01
❑ 228 Jesse Orosco	.05	.01
❑ 229 Ed Whitson	.05	.01
❑ 230 Terry Pendleton	.10	.02
❑ 231 Lloyd Moseby	.05	.01
❑ 232 Greg Swindell	.05	.01
❑ 233 John Franco	.10	.02
❑ 234 Jack Morris	.10	.02
❑ 235 Howard Johnson	.10	.02
❑ 236 Glenn Davis	.05	.01
❑ 237 Frank Viola	.10	.02
❑ 238 Kevin Seitzer	.05	.01
❑ 239 Gerald Perry	.05	.01
❑ 240 Dwight Evans	.15	.05
❑ 241 Jim Deshaies	.05	.01
❑ 242 Bo Diaz	.05	.01
❑ 243 Carney Lansford	.10	.02
❑ 244 Mike LaValliere	.05	.01
❑ 245 Rickey Henderson	.25	.08
❑ 246 Roberto Alomar	.25	.08
❑ 247 Jimmy Jones	.05	.01
❑ 248 Pascual Perez	.05	.01
❑ 249 Will Clark	.15	.05
❑ 250 Fernando Valenzuela	.10	.02
❑ 251 Shane Rawley	.05	.01
❑ 252 Sid Bream	.05	.01
❑ 253 Steve Lyons	.05	.01
❑ 254 Brian Downing	.10	.02
❑ 255 Mark Grace	.25	.08
❑ 256 Tom Candiotti	.05	.01
❑ 257 Barry Larkin	.15	.05
❑ 258 Mike Krukow	.05	.01
❑ 259 Billy Ripken	.05	.01
❑ 260 Cecilio Guante	.05	.01
❑ 261 Scott Bradley	.05	.01
❑ 262 Floyd Bannister	.05	.01
❑ 263 Pete Smith	.05	.01
❑ 264 Jim Gantner UER (Wrong birthdate)	.05	.01
❑ 265 Roger McDowell	.05	.01
❑ 266 Bobby Thigpen	.05	.01
❑ 267 Jim Clancy	.05	.01
❑ 268 Terry Steinbach	.10	.02
❑ 269 Mike Dunne	.05	.01
❑ 270 Dwight Gooden	.10	.02
❑ 271 Mike Heath	.05	.01
❑ 272 Dave Smith	.05	.01
❑ 273 Keith Atherton	.05	.01
❑ 274 Tim Burke	.05	.01
❑ 275 Damon Berryhill	.05	.01
❑ 276 Vance Law	.05	.01
❑ 277 Rich Dotson	.05	.01
❑ 278 Lance Parrish	.10	.02
❑ 279 Denny Walling	.05	.01
❑ 280 Roger Clemens	1.00	.40
❑ 281 Greg Mathews	.05	.01
❑ 282 Tom Niedenfuer	.05	.01
❑ 283 Paul Kilgus	.05	.01
❑ 284 Jose Guzman	.05	.01
❑ 285 Calvin Schiraldi	.05	.01
❑ 286 Charlie Puleo UER (Career ERA 4.24, should be 4.	.05	.01
❑ 287 Joe Orsulak	.05	.01
❑ 288 Jack Howell	.05	.01
❑ 289 Kevin Elster	.05	.01
❑ 290 Jose Lind	.05	.01
❑ 291 Paul Molitor	.10	.02
❑ 292 Cecil Espy	.05	.01
❑ 293 Bill Wegman	.05	.01
❑ 294 Dan Pasqua	.05	.01
❑ 295 Scott Garrelts UER (Wrong birthdate)	.05	.01
❑ 296 Walt Terrell	.05	.01
❑ 297 Ed Hearn	.05	.01
❑ 298 Lou Whitaker	.10	.02
❑ 299 Ken Dayley	.05	.01
❑ 300 Checklist 248-357	.05	.01
❑ 301 Tommy Herr	.05	.01
❑ 302 Mike Brumley	.05	.01
❑ 303 Ellis Burks	.10	.02
❑ 304 Curt Young UER (Wrong birthdate)	.05	.01
❑ 305 Jody Reed	.05	.01
❑ 306 Bill Doran	.05	.01
❑ 307 David Wells	.10	.02
❑ 308 Ron Robinson	.05	.01
❑ 309 Rafael Santana	.05	.01
❑ 310 Julio Franco	.10	.02
❑ 311 Jack Clark	.10	.02
❑ 312 Chris James	.05	.01
❑ 313 Milt Thompson	.05	.01
❑ 314 John Shelby	.05	.01
❑ 315 Al Leiter	.25	.08
❑ 316 Mike Davis	.05	.01
❑ 317 Chris Sabo RC *	.40	.15
❑ 318 Greg Gagne	.05	.01
❑ 319 Jose Oquendo	.05	.01
❑ 320 John Farrell	.05	.01
❑ 321 Franklin Stubbs	.05	.01
❑ 322 Kurt Stillwell	.05	.01
❑ 323 Shawn Abner	.05	.01
❑ 324 Mike Flanagan	.05	.01
❑ 325 Kevin Bass	.05	.01
❑ 326 Pat Tabler	.05	.01
❑ 327 Mike Henneman	.05	.01
❑ 328 Rick Honeycutt	.05	.01
❑ 329 John Smiley	.05	.01
❑ 330 Rey Quinones	.05	.01
❑ 331 Johnny Ray	.05	.01
❑ 332 Bob Welch	.10	.02
❑ 333 Larry Sheets	.05	.01
❑ 334 Jeff Parrett	.05	.01
❑ 335 Rick Reuschel UER (For Don Robinson, should be J	.10	.02
❑ 336 Randy Myers	.10	.02
❑ 337 Ken Williams	.05	.01
❑ 338 Andy McGaffigan	.05	.01
❑ 339 Joey Meyer	.05	.01
❑ 340 Dion James	.05	.01
❑ 341 Les Lancaster	.05	.01
❑ 342 Tom Foley	.05	.01
❑ 343 Geno Petralli	.05	.01
❑ 344 Dan Petry	.05	.01
❑ 345 Alvin Davis	.05	.01
❑ 346 Mickey Hatcher	.05	.01
❑ 347 Marvell Wynne	.05	.01
❑ 348 Danny Cox	.05	.01
❑ 349 Dave Stieb	.10	.02
❑ 350 Jay Bell	.10	.02
❑ 351 Jeff Treadway	.05	.01
❑ 352 Luis Salazar	.05	.01

❑ 353 Len Dykstra .10 .02
❑ 354 Juan Agosto .05 .01
❑ 355 Gene Larkin .05 .01
❑ 356 Steve Farr .05 .01
❑ 357 Paul Assenmacher .05 .01
❑ 358 Todd Benzinger .05 .01
❑ 359 Larry Andersen .05 .01
❑ 360 Paul O'Neill .15 .05
❑ 361 Ron Hassey .05 .01
❑ 362 Jim Gott .05 .01
❑ 363 Ken Phelps .05 .01
❑ 364 Tim Flannery .05 .01
❑ 365 Randy Ready .05 .01
❑ 366 Nelson Santovenia .05 .01
❑ 367 Kelly Downs .05 .01
❑ 368 Danny Heep .05 .01
❑ 369 Phil Bradley .05 .01
❑ 370 Jeff D. Robinson .05 .01
❑ 371 Ivan Calderon .05 .01
❑ 372 Mike Witt .05 .01
❑ 373 Greg Maddux .50 .20
❑ 374 Carmen Castillo .05 .01
❑ 375 Jose Rijo .10 .02
❑ 376 Joe Price .05 .01
❑ 377 Rene Gonzales .05 .01
❑ 378 Oddibe McDowell .05 .01
❑ 379 Jim Presley .05 .01
❑ 380 Brad Wellman .05 .01
❑ 381 Tom Glavine .25 .08
❑ 382 Dan Plesac .05 .01
❑ 383 Wally Backman .05 .01
❑ 384 Dave Gallagher .05 .01
❑ 385 Tom Henke .05 .01
❑ 386 Luis Polonia .05 .01
❑ 387 Junior Ortiz .05 .01
❑ 388 David Cone .10 .02
❑ 389 Dave Bergman .05 .01
❑ 390 Danny Darwin .05 .01
❑ 391 Dan Gladden .05 .01
❑ 392 John Dopson .05 .01
❑ 393 Frank DiPino .05 .01
❑ 394 Al Nipper .05 .01
❑ 395 Willie Randolph .10 .02
❑ 396 Don Carman .05 .01
❑ 397 Scott Terry .05 .01
❑ 398 Rick Cerone .05 .01
❑ 399 Tom Pagnozzi .05 .01
❑ 400 Checklist 358-467 .05 .01
❑ 401 Mickey Tettleton .05 .01
❑ 402 Curtis Wilkerson .05 .01
❑ 403 Jeff Russell .05 .01
❑ 404 Pat Perry .05 .01
❑ 405 Jose Alvarez RC .10 .02
❑ 406 Rick Schu .05 .01
❑ 407 Sherman Corbett .05 .01
❑ 408 Dave Magadan .05 .01
❑ 409 Bob Kipper .05 .01
❑ 410 Don August .05 .01
❑ 411 Bob Brower .05 .01
❑ 412 Chris Bosio .05 .01
❑ 413 Jerry Reuss .05 .01
❑ 414 Atlee Hammaker .05 .01
❑ 415 Jim Walewander .05 .01
❑ 416 Mike Macfarlane RC * .25 .08
❑ 417 Pat Sheridan .05 .01
❑ 418 Pedro Guerrero .10 .02
❑ 419 Allan Anderson .05 .01
❑ 420 Mark Parent .05 .01
❑ 421 Bob Stanley .05 .01
❑ 422 Mike Gallego .05 .01
❑ 423 Bruce Hurst .05 .01
❑ 424 Dave Meads .05 .01
❑ 425 Jesse Barfield .10 .02
❑ 426 Rob Dibble RC .40 .15
❑ 427 Joel Skinner .05 .01
❑ 428 Ron Kittle .05 .01
❑ 429 Rick Rhoden .05 .01
❑ 430 Bob Dernier .05 .01
❑ 431 Steve Jeltz .05 .01
❑ 432 Rick Dempsey .05 .01
❑ 433 Roberto Kelly .05 .01
❑ 434 Dave Anderson .05 .01
❑ 435 Herm Winningham .05 .01
❑ 436 Al Newman .05 .01
❑ 437 Jose DeLeon .05 .01
❑ 438 Doug Jones .05 .01
❑ 439 Brian Holton .05 .01
❑ 440 Jeff Montgomery .05 .01
❑ 441 Dickie Thon .05 .01
❑ 442 Cecil Fielder .10 .02
❑ 443 John Fishel .05 .01
❑ 444 Jerry Don Gleaton .05 .01
❑ 445 Paul Gibson .05 .01
❑ 446 Walt Weiss .05 .01
❑ 447 Glenn Wilson .05 .01
❑ 448 Mike Moore .05 .01
❑ 449 Chili Davis .10 .02
❑ 450 Dave Henderson .05 .01
❑ 451 Jose Bautista RC .10 .02
❑ 452 Rex Hudler .05 .01
❑ 453 Bob Brenly .05 .01
❑ 454 Mackey Sasser .05 .01
❑ 455 Daryl Boston .05 .01
❑ 456 Mike R. Fitzgerald .05 .01
❑ 457 Jeffrey Leonard .05 .01
❑ 458 Bruce Sutter .10 .02
❑ 459 Mitch Webster .05 .01
❑ 460 Joe Hesketh .05 .01
❑ 461 Bobby Witt .05 .01
❑ 462 Stu Cliburn .05 .01
❑ 463 Scott Bankhead .05 .01
❑ 464 Ramon Martinez RC .25 .08
❑ 465 Dave Leiper .05 .01
❑ 466 Luis Alicea RC * .25 .08
❑ 467 John Cerutti .05 .01
❑ 468 Ron Washington .05 .01
❑ 469 Jeff Reed .05 .01
❑ 470 Jeff M. Robinson .05 .01
❑ 471 Sid Fernandez .05 .01
❑ 472 Terry Puhl .05 .01
❑ 473 Charlie Lea .05 .01
❑ 474 Israel Sanchez .05 .01
❑ 475 Bruce Benedict .05 .01
❑ 476 Oil Can Boyd .05 .01
❑ 477 Craig Reynolds .05 .01
❑ 478 Frank Williams .05 .01
❑ 479 Greg Cadaret .05 .01
❑ 480 Randy Kramer .05 .01
❑ 481 Dave Eiland .05 .01
❑ 482 Eric Show .05 .01
❑ 483 Garry Templeton .10 .02
❑ 484 Wallace Johnson .05 .01
❑ 485 Kevin Mitchell .10 .02
❑ 486 Tim Crews .05 .01
❑ 487 Mike Maddux .05 .01
❑ 488 Dave LaPoint .05 .01
❑ 489 Fred Manrique .05 .01
❑ 490 Greg Minton .05 .01
❑ 491 Doug Dascenzo UER
(Photo actually
Damon Berryhil .05 .01
❑ 492 Willie Upshaw .05 .01
❑ 493 Jack Armstrong RC * .25 .08
❑ 494 Kirt Manwaring .05 .01
❑ 495 Jeff Ballard .05 .01
❑ 496 Jeff Kunkel .05 .01
❑ 497 Mike Campbell .05 .01
❑ 498 Gary Thurman .05 .01
❑ 499 Zane Smith .05 .01
❑ 500 Checklist 468-577 DP .05 .01
❑ 501 Mike Birkbeck .05 .01
❑ 502 Terry Leach .05 .01
❑ 503 Shawn Hillegas .05 .01
❑ 504 Manny Lee .05 .01
❑ 505 Doug Jennings .05 .01
❑ 506 Ken Oberkfell .05 .01
❑ 507 Tim Teufel .05 .01
❑ 508 Tom Brookens .05 .01
❑ 509 Rafael Ramirez .05 .01
❑ 510 Fred Toliver .05 .01
❑ 511 Brian Holman RC * .10 .02
❑ 512 Mike Bielecki .05 .01
❑ 513 Jeff Pico .05 .01
❑ 514 Charles Hudson .05 .01
❑ 515 Bruce Ruffin .05 .01
❑ 516 Larry McWilliams UER
(New Richland, should
be No .05 .01
❑ 517 Jeff Sellers .05 .01
❑ 518 John Costello .05 .01
❑ 519 Brady Anderson RC .40 .15
❑ 520 Craig McMurtry .05 .01
❑ 521 Ray Hayward DP .05 .01
❑ 522 Drew Hall DP .05 .01
❑ 523 Mark Lemke DP RC .40 .15
❑ 524 Oswald Peraza DP .05 .01
❑ 525 Bryan Harvey DP RC * .25 .08
❑ 526 Rick Aguilera DP .05 .01
❑ 527 Tom Prince DP .05 .01
❑ 528 Mark Clear DP .05 .01
❑ 529 Jerry Browne DP .05 .01
❑ 530 Juan Castillo DP .05 .01
❑ 531 Jack McDowell DP .10 .02
❑ 532 Chris Speier DP .05 .01
❑ 533 Darrell Evans DP .10 .02
❑ 534 Luis Aquino DP .05 .01
❑ 535 Eric King DP .05 .01
❑ 536 Ken Hill DP RC .25 .08
❑ 537 Randy Bush DP .05 .01
❑ 538 Shane Mack DP .05 .01
❑ 539 Tom Bolton DP .05 .01
❑ 540 Gene Nelson DP .05 .01
❑ 541 Wes Gardner DP .05 .01
❑ 542 Ken Caminiti DP .15 .05
❑ 543 Duane Ward DP .05 .01
❑ 544 Norm Charlton DP RC .25 .08
❑ 545 Hal Morris DP RC .25 .08
❑ 546 Rich Yett DP .05 .01
❑ 547 Hensley Meulens DP RC .10 .02
❑ 548 Greg A. Harris DP .05 .01
❑ 549 Darren Daulton .10 .02
❑ 550 Jeff Hamilton DP .05 .01
❑ 551 Luis Aguayo DP .05 .01
❑ 552 Tim Leary DP
(Resembles M.Marshall) .05 .01
❑ 553 Ron Oester DP .05 .01
❑ 554 Steve Lombardozzi DP .05 .01
❑ 555 Tim Jones DP .05 .01
❑ 556 Bud Black DP .05 .01
❑ 557 Alejandro Pena DP .05 .01
❑ 558 Jose DeJesus DP .05 .01
❑ 559 Dennis Rasmussen DP .05 .01
❑ 560 Pat Borders DP RC * .25 .08
❑ 561 Craig Biggio RC 2.00 .75
❑ 562 Luis DeLosSantos DP .05 .01
❑ 563 Fred Lynn DP .10 .02
❑ 564 Todd Burns DP .05 .01
❑ 565 Felix Fermin DP .05 .01
❑ 566 Darnell Coles DP .05 .01
❑ 567 Willie Fraser DP .05 .01
❑ 568 Glenn Hubbard DP .05 .01
❑ 569 Craig Worthington DP .05 .01
❑ 570 Johnny Paredes DP .05 .01
❑ 571 Don Robinson DP .05 .01
❑ 572 Barry Lyons DP .05 .01
❑ 573 Bill Long DP .05 .01
❑ 574 Tracy Jones DP .05 .01
❑ 575 Juan Nieves DP .05 .01
❑ 576 Andres Thomas DP .05 .01
❑ 577 Rolando Roomes DP .05 .01
❑ 578 Luis Rivera UER DP
(Wrong birthdate) .05 .01
❑ 579 Chad Kreuter RC .25 .08
❑ 580 Tony Armas DP .10 .02
❑ 581 Jay Buhner .10 .02
❑ 582 Ricky Horton DP .05 .01
❑ 583 Andy Hawkins DP .05 .01
❑ 584 Sil Campusano .05 .01
❑ 585 Dave Clark .05 .01
❑ 586 Van Snider DP .05 .01
❑ 587 Todd Frohwirth DP .05 .01
❑ 588 Warren Spahn Puzzle DP .15 .05
❑ 589 William Brennan .05 .01
❑ 590 German Gonzalez .05 .01
❑ 591 Ernie Whitt DP .05 .01
❑ 592 Jeff Blauser .05 .01
❑ 593 Spike Owen DP .05 .01
❑ 594 Matt Williams .25 .08
❑ 595 Lloyd McClendon DP .05 .01
❑ 596 Steve Ontiveros .05 .01
❑ 597 Scott Medvin .05 .01
❑ 598 Hipolito Pena DP .05 .01
❑ 599 Jerald Clark DP RC .10 .02
❑ 600A Checklist 578-660 DP .05 .01
❑ 600B Checklist 578-660 DP .05 .01
❑ 600C Checklist 578-660 DP .05 .01
❑ 601 Carmelo Martinez DP .05 .01
❑ 602 Mike LaCoss .05 .01

Card	Player		
603	Mike Devereaux	.05	.01
604	Alex Madrid DP	.05	.01
605	Gary Redus DP	.05	.01
606	Lance Johnson	.05	.01
607	Terry Clark DP	.05	.01
608	Manny Trillo DP	.05	.01
609	Scott Jordan RC	.25	.08
610	Jay Howell DP	.05	.01
611	Francisco Melendez	.05	.01
612	Mike Boddicker	.05	.01
613	Kevin Brown	.25	.08
614	Dave Valle	.05	.01
615	Tim Laudner DP	.05	.01
616	Andy Nezelek UER (Wrong birthdate)	.05	.01
617	Chuck Crim	.05	.01
618	Jack Savage DP	.05	.01
619	Adam Peterson	.05	.01
620	Todd Stottlemyre	.05	.01
621	Lance Blankenship RC	.10	.02
622	Miguel Garcia DP	.05	.01
623	Keith A. Miller DP	.05	.01
624	Ricky Jordan DP RC *	.25	.08
625	Ernest Riles DP	.05	.01
626	John Moses DP	.05	.01
627	Nelson Liriano DP	.05	.01
628	Mike Smithson DP	.05	.01
629	Scott Sanderson	.05	.01
630	Dale Mohorcic	.05	.01
631	Marvin Freeman DP	.05	.01
632	Mike Young DP	.05	.01
633	Dennis Lamp	.05	.01
634	Dante Bichette RC	.40	.15
635	Curt Schilling RC	4.00	1.50
636	Scott May DP	.05	.01
637	Mike Schooler	.05	.01
638	Rick Leach	.05	.01
639	Tom Lampkin UER (Throws Left, should be Throws R	.05	.01
640	Brian Meyer	.05	.01
641	Brian Harper	.05	.01
642	John Smoltz RC	1.50	.60
643	Jose Canseco 40/40	.25	.08
644	Bill Schroeder	.05	.01
645	Edgar Martinez	.25	.08
646	Dennis Cook RC	.25	.08
647	Barry Jones	.05	.01
648	Orel Hershiser (59 and Counting)	.10	.02
649	Rod Nichols	.05	.01
650	Jody Davis	.05	.01
651	Bob Milacki	.05	.01
652	Mike Jackson	.05	.01
653	Derek Lilliquist RC	.10	.02
654	Paul Mirabella	.05	.01
655	Mike Diaz	.05	.01
656	Jeff Musselman	.05	.01
657	Jerry Reed	.05	.01
658	Kevin Blankenship	.05	.01
659	Wayne Tolleson	.05	.01
660	Eric Hetzel	.05	.01
BC	Jose Canseco Blister Pack	2.00	.75

1989 Donruss Rookies

Card	Player		
	COMP.FACT.SET (56)	15.00	6.00
1	Gary Sheffield	2.00	.75
2	Gregg Jefferies	.10	.02
3	Ken Griffey Jr. !	8.00	3.00
4	Tom Gordon	.25	.10
5	Billy Spiers RC	.25	.08
6	Deion Sanders RC	1.50	.60
7	Donn Pall	.05	.01
8	Steve Carter	.05	.01
9	Francisco Oliveras	.05	.01
10	Steve Wilson RC	.10	.02
11	Bob Geren RC	.05	.01
12	Tony Castillo RC	.10	.02
13	Kenny Rogers RC	2.50	1.00
14	Carlos Martinez RC	.10	.02
15	Edgar Martinez	.25	.08
16	Jim Abbott RC	1.00	.40
17	Torey Lovullo RC	.10	.02
18	Mark Carreon	.05	.01
19	Geronimo Berroa	.05	.01
20	Luis Medina	.05	.01
21	Sandy Alomar Jr.	.15	.05
22	Bob Milacki	.05	.01
23	Joe Girardi RC	.40	.15
24	German Gonzalez	.05	.01
25	Craig Worthington	.05	.01
26	Jerome Walton RC	.25	.08
27	Gary Wayne	.05	.01
28	Tim Jones	.05	.01
29	Dante Bichette	.15	.05
30	Alexis Infante RC	.05	.01
31	Ken Hill	.25	.08
32	Dwight Smith RC	.25	.08
33	Luis de los Santos	.05	.01
34	Eric Yelding	.05	.01
35	Gregg Olson	.25	.08
36	Phil Stephenson	.05	.01
37	Ken Patterson	.05	.01
38	Rick Wrona	.05	.01
39	Mike Brumley	.05	.01
40	Cris Carpenter	.05	.01
41	Jeff Brantley RC	.25	.08
42	Ron Jones	.05	.01
43	Randy Johnson	2.00	.75
44	Kevin Brown	.25	.08
45	Ramon Martinez	.10	.02
46	Greg W.Harris	.05	.01
47	Steve Finley RC	.75	.30
48	Randy Kramer	.05	.01
49	Erik Hanson	.10	.02
50	Matt Merullo	.05	.01
51	Mike Devereaux	.05	.01
52	Clay Parker	.05	.01
53	Omar Vizquel RC	1.00	.40
54	Derek Lilliquist	.05	.01
55	Junior Felix RC	.10	.02
56	Checklist 1-56	.05	.01

1990 Donruss

Card	Player		
	COMPLETE SET (716)	15.00	6.00
	COMP.FACT.SET (728)	15.00	6.00
	COMP.YAZ PUZZLE	1.00	.40
1	Bo Jackson DK	.15	.05
2	Steve Sax DK	.05	.01
3A	Ruben Sierra DK ERR	.10	.02
3B	Ruben Sierra DK COR	.10	.02
4	Ken Griffey Jr. DK	.40	.15
5	Mickey Tettleton DK	.05	.01
6	Dave Stewart DK	.05	.01
7	Jim Deshaies DK DP	.05	.01
8	John Smoltz DK	.25	.08
9	Mike Bielecki DK	.05	.01
10A	Brian Downing DK ERR	.15	.05
10B	Brian Downing DK COR	.05	.01
11	Kevin Mitchell DK	.05	.01
12	Kelly Gruber DK	.05	.01
13	Joe Magrane DK	.05	.01
14	John Franco DK	.10	.02
15	Ozzie Guillen DK	.10	.02
16	Lou Whitaker DK	.05	.01
17	John Smiley DK	.05	.01
18	Howard Johnson DK	.05	.01
19	Willie Randolph DK	.10	.02
20	Chris Bosio DK	.05	.01
21	Tommy Herr DK DP	.05	.01
22	Dan Gladden DK	.05	.01
23	Ellis Burks DK	.10	.02
24	Pete O'Brien DK	.05	.01
25	Bryn Smith DK	.05	.01
26	Ed Whitson DK DP	.05	.01
27	DK Checklist 1-27 DP (Comments on Perez-Steele	.05	.01
28	Robin Ventura	.25	.08
29	Todd Zeile	.10	.02
30	Sandy Alomar Jr.	.10	.02
31	Kent Mercker RC	.25	.08
32	Ben McDonald RC	.25	.08
33A	Juan Gonzalez RevNg RC	2.00	.75
33B	Juan Gonzalez COR RC	1.00	.40
34	Eric Anthony RC	.10	.02
35	Mike Fetters RC	.25	.08
36	Marquis Grissom RC	.40	.15
37	Greg Vaughn	.05	.01
38	Brian DuBois RC	.10	.02
39	Steve Avery	.05	.01
40	Mark Gardner RC	.10	.02
41	Andy Benes	.10	.02
42	Delino DeShields RC	.25	.08
43	Scott Coolbaugh RC	.10	.02
44	Pat Combs DP	.05	.01
45	Alex Sanchez DP	.05	.01
46	Kelly Mann DP RC	.10	.02
47	Julio Machado RC	.10	.02
48	Pete Incaviglia	.05	.01
49	Shawon Dunston	.05	.01
50	Jeff Treadway	.05	.01
51	Jeff Ballard	.05	.01
52	Claudell Washington	.05	.01
53	Juan Samuel	.05	.01
54	John Smiley	.05	.01
55	Rob Deer	.05	.01
56	Geno Petralli	.05	.01
57	Chris Bosio	.05	.01
58	Carlton Fisk	.15	.05
59	Kirt Manwaring	.05	.01
60	Chet Lemon	.05	.01
61	Bo Jackson	.25	.08
62	Doyle Alexander	.05	.01
63	Pedro Guerrero	.05	.01
64	Allan Anderson	.05	.01
65	Greg W. Harris	.05	.01
66	Mike Greenwell	.05	.01
67	Walt Weiss	.05	.01
68	Wade Boggs	.15	.05
69	Jim Clancy	.05	.01
70	Junior Felix	.05	.01
71	Barry Larkin	.15	.05
72	Dave LaPoint	.05	.01
73	Joel Skinner	.05	.01
74	Jesse Barfield	.05	.01
75	Tommy Herr	.05	.01
76	Ricky Jordan	.05	.01
77	Eddie Murray	.25	.08
78	Steve Sax	.05	.01
79	Tim Belcher	.05	.01
80	Danny Jackson	.05	.01
81	Kent Hrbek	.10	.02
82	Milt Thompson	.05	.01
83	Brook Jacoby	.05	.01
84	Mike Marshall	.05	.01
85	Kevin Seitzer	.05	.01
86	Tony Gwynn	.30	.10
87	Dave Stieb	.10	.02
88	Dave Smith	.05	.01
89	Bret Saberhagen	.10	.02

Card		
❑ 90 Alan Trammell	.10	.02
❑ 91 Tony Phillips	.05	.01
❑ 92 Doug Drabek	.05	.01
❑ 93 Jeffrey Leonard	.05	.01
❑ 94 Wally Joyner	.10	.02
❑ 95 Carney Lansford	.10	.02
❑ 96 Cal Ripken	.75	.30
❑ 97 Andres Galarraga	.10	.02
❑ 98 Kevin Mitchell	.05	.01
❑ 99 Howard Johnson	.05	.01
❑ 100A Checklist 28-129	.05	.01
❑ 100B Checklist 28-125	.05	.01
❑ 101 Melido Perez	.05	.01
❑ 102 Spike Owen	.05	.01
❑ 103 Paul Molitor	.10	.02
❑ 104 Geronimo Berroa	.05	.01
❑ 105 Ryne Sandberg	.40	.15
❑ 106 Bryn Smith	.05	.01
❑ 107 Steve Buechele	.05	.01
❑ 108 Jim Abbott	.15	.05
❑ 109 Alvin Davis	.05	.01
❑ 110 Lee Smith	.10	.02
❑ 111 Roberto Alomar	.15	.05
❑ 112 Rick Reuschel	.05	.01
❑ 113A Kelly Gruber ERR (Born 2/22)	.05	.01
❑ 113B Kelly Gruber COR (Born 2/26; corrected in factor	.05	.01
❑ 114 Joe Carter	.10	.02
❑ 115 Jose Rijo	.05	.01
❑ 116 Greg Minton	.05	.01
❑ 117 Bob Ojeda	.05	.01
❑ 118 Glenn Davis	.05	.01
❑ 119 Jeff Reardon	.10	.02
❑ 120 Kurt Stillwell	.05	.01
❑ 121 John Smoltz	.25	.08
❑ 122 Dwight Evans	.15	.05
❑ 123 Eric Yelding RC	.05	.01
❑ 124 John Franco	.10	.02
❑ 125 Jose Canseco	.15	.05
❑ 126 Barry Bonds	1.00	.40
❑ 127 Lee Guetterman	.05	.01
❑ 128 Jack Clark	.10	.02
❑ 129 Dave Valle	.05	.01
❑ 130 Hubie Brooks	.05	.01
❑ 131 Ernest Riles	.05	.01
❑ 132 Mike Morgan	.05	.01
❑ 133 Steve Jeltz	.05	.01
❑ 134 Jeff D. Robinson	.05	.01
❑ 135 Ozzie Guillen	.10	.02
❑ 136 Chili Davis	.10	.02
❑ 137 Mitch Webster	.05	.01
❑ 138 Jerry Browne	.05	.01
❑ 139 Bo Diaz	.05	.01
❑ 140 Robby Thompson	.05	.01
❑ 141 Craig Worthington	.05	.01
❑ 142 Julio Franco	.10	.02
❑ 143 Brian Holman	.05	.01
❑ 144 George Brett	.60	.25
❑ 145 Tom Glavine	.15	.05
❑ 146 Robin Yount	.40	.15
❑ 147 Gary Carter	.10	.02
❑ 148 Ron Kittle	.05	.01
❑ 149 Tony Fernandez	.05	.01
❑ 150 Dave Stewart	.10	.02
❑ 151 Gary Gaetti	.10	.02
❑ 152 Kevin Elster	.05	.01
❑ 153 Gerald Perry	.05	.01
❑ 154 Jesse Orosco	.05	.01
❑ 155 Wally Backman	.05	.01
❑ 156 Dennis Martinez	.10	.02
❑ 157 Rick Sutcliffe	.10	.02
❑ 158 Greg Maddux	.40	.15
❑ 159 Andy Hawkins	.05	.01
❑ 160 John Kruk	.10	.02
❑ 161 Jose Oquendo	.05	.01
❑ 162 John Dopson	.05	.01
❑ 163 Joe Magrane	.05	.01
❑ 164 Bill Ripken	.05	.01
❑ 165 Fred Manrique	.05	.01
❑ 166 Nolan Ryan	1.00	.40
❑ 167 Damon Berryhill	.05	.01
❑ 168 Dale Murphy	.15	.05
❑ 169 Mickey Tettleton	.05	.01
❑ 170A Kirk McCaskill ERR (Born 4/19)	.05	.01
❑ 170B Kirk McCaskill COR (Born 4/9; corrected in facto	.05	.01
❑ 171 Dwight Gooden	.10	.02
❑ 172 Jose Lind	.05	.01
❑ 173 B.J. Surhoff	.10	.02
❑ 174 Ruben Sierra	.10	.02
❑ 175 Dan Plesac	.05	.01
❑ 176 Dan Pasqua	.05	.01
❑ 177 Kelly Downs	.05	.01
❑ 178 Matt Nokes	.05	.01
❑ 179 Luis Aquino	.05	.01
❑ 180 Frank Tanana	.05	.01
❑ 181 Tony Pena	.05	.01
❑ 182 Dan Gladden	.05	.01
❑ 183 Bruce Hurst	.05	.01
❑ 184 Roger Clemens	1.00	.40
❑ 185 Mark McGwire	1.00	.40
❑ 186 Rob Murphy	.05	.01
❑ 187 Jim Deshaies	.05	.01
❑ 188 Fred McGriff	.25	.08
❑ 189 Rob Dibble	.10	.02
❑ 190 Don Mattingly	.60	.25
❑ 191 Felix Fermin	.05	.01
❑ 192 Roberto Kelly	.05	.01
❑ 193 Dennis Cook	.05	.01
❑ 194 Darren Daulton	.10	.02
❑ 195 Alfredo Griffin	.05	.01
❑ 196 Eric Plunk	.05	.01
❑ 197 Orel Hershiser	.10	.02
❑ 198 Paul O'Neill	.15	.05
❑ 199 Randy Bush	.05	.01
❑ 200A Checklist 130-231	.05	.01
❑ 200B Checklist 126-223	.05	.01
❑ 201 Ozzie Smith	.40	.15
❑ 202 Pete O'Brien	.05	.01
❑ 203 Jay Howell	.05	.01
❑ 204 Mark Gubicza	.05	.01
❑ 205 Ed Whitson	.05	.01
❑ 206 George Bell	.05	.01
❑ 207 Mike Scott	.05	.01
❑ 208 Charlie Leibrandt	.05	.01
❑ 209 Mike Heath	.05	.01
❑ 210 Dennis Eckersley	.10	.02
❑ 211 Mike LaValliere	.05	.01
❑ 212 Darnell Coles	.05	.01
❑ 213 Lance Parrish	.05	.01
❑ 214 Mike Moore	.05	.01
❑ 215 Steve Finley	.10	.02
❑ 216 Tim Raines	.10	.02
❑ 217A Scott Garrelts ERR (Born 10/20)	.05	.01
❑ 217B Scott Garrelts COR (Born 10/30; corrected in fac	.05	.01
❑ 218 Kevin McReynolds	.05	.01
❑ 219 Dave Gallagher	.05	.01
❑ 220 Tim Wallach	.05	.01
❑ 221 Chuck Crim	.05	.01
❑ 222 Lonnie Smith	.05	.01
❑ 223 Andre Dawson	.10	.02
❑ 224 Nelson Santovenia	.05	.01
❑ 225 Rafael Palmeiro	.15	.05
❑ 226 Devon White	.10	.02
❑ 227 Harold Reynolds	.10	.02
❑ 228 Ellis Burks	.15	.05
❑ 229 Mark Parent	.05	.01
❑ 230 Will Clark	.15	.05
❑ 231 Jimmy Key	.10	.02
❑ 232 John Farrell	.05	.01
❑ 233 Eric Davis	.10	.02
❑ 234 Johnny Ray	.05	.01
❑ 235 Darryl Strawberry	.10	.02
❑ 236 Bill Doran	.05	.01
❑ 237 Greg Gagne	.05	.01
❑ 238 Jim Eisenreich	.05	.01
❑ 239 Tommy Gregg	.05	.01
❑ 240 Marty Barrett	.05	.01
❑ 241 Rafael Ramirez	.05	.01
❑ 242 Chris Sabo	.05	.01
❑ 243 Dave Henderson	.05	.01
❑ 244 Andy Van Slyke	.15	.05
❑ 245 Alvaro Espinoza	.05	.01
❑ 246 Garry Templeton	.05	.01
❑ 247 Gene Harris	.05	.01
❑ 248 Kevin Gross	.05	.01
❑ 249 Brett Butler	.10	.02
❑ 250 Willie Randolph	.10	.02
❑ 251 Roger McDowell	.05	.01
❑ 252 Rafael Belliard	.05	.01
❑ 253 Steve Rosenberg	.05	.01
❑ 254 Jack Howell	.05	.01
❑ 255 Marvell Wynne	.05	.01
❑ 256 Tom Candiotti	.05	.01
❑ 257 Todd Benzinger	.05	.01
❑ 258 Don Robinson	.05	.01
❑ 259 Phil Bradley	.05	.01
❑ 260 Cecil Espy	.05	.01
❑ 261 Scott Bankhead	.05	.01
❑ 262 Frank White	.10	.02
❑ 263 Andres Thomas	.05	.01
❑ 264 Glenn Braggs	.05	.01
❑ 265 David Cone	.10	.02
❑ 266 Bobby Thigpen	.05	.01
❑ 267 Nelson Liriano	.05	.01
❑ 268 Terry Steinbach	.05	.01
❑ 269 Kirby Puckett	.25	.08
❑ 270 Gregg Jefferies	.10	.02
❑ 271 Jeff Blauser	.05	.01
❑ 272 Cory Snyder	.05	.01
❑ 273 Roy Smith	.05	.01
❑ 274 Tom Foley	.05	.01
❑ 275 Mitch Williams	.05	.01
❑ 276 Paul Kilgus	.05	.01
❑ 277 Don Slaught	.05	.01
❑ 278 Von Hayes	.05	.01
❑ 279 Vince Coleman	.05	.01
❑ 280 Mike Boddicker	.05	.01
❑ 281 Ken Dayley	.05	.01
❑ 282 Mike Devereaux	.05	.01
❑ 283 Kenny Rogers	.10	.02
❑ 284 Jeff Russell	.05	.01
❑ 285 Jerome Walton	.05	.01
❑ 286 Derek Lilliquist	.05	.01
❑ 287 Joe Orsulak	.05	.01
❑ 288 Dick Schofield	.05	.01
❑ 289 Ron Darling	.05	.01
❑ 290 Bobby Bonilla	.10	.02
❑ 291 Jim Gantner	.05	.01
❑ 292 Bobby Witt	.05	.01
❑ 293 Greg Brock	.05	.01
❑ 294 Ivan Calderon	.05	.01
❑ 295 Steve Bedrosian	.05	.01
❑ 296 Mike Henneman	.05	.01
❑ 297 Tom Gordon	.10	.02
❑ 298 Lou Whitaker	.10	.02
❑ 299 Terry Pendleton	.10	.02
❑ 300A Checklist 232-333	.05	.01
❑ 300B Checklist 224-321	.05	.01
❑ 301 Juan Berenguer	.05	.01
❑ 302 Mark Davis	.05	.01
❑ 303 Nick Esasky	.05	.01
❑ 304 Rickey Henderson	.25	.08
❑ 305 Rick Cerone	.05	.01
❑ 306 Craig Biggio	.25	.08
❑ 307 Duane Ward	.05	.01
❑ 308 Tom Browning	.05	.01
❑ 309 Walt Terrell	.05	.01
❑ 310 Greg Swindell	.05	.01
❑ 311 Dave Righetti	.05	.01
❑ 312 Mike Maddux	.05	.01
❑ 313 Len Dykstra	.10	.02
❑ 314 Jose Gonzalez	.05	.01
❑ 315 Steve Balboni	.05	.01
❑ 316 Mike Scioscia	.05	.01
❑ 317 Ron Oester	.05	.01
❑ 318 Gary Wayne	.05	.01
❑ 319 Todd Worrell	.05	.01
❑ 320 Doug Jones	.05	.01
❑ 321 Jeff Hamilton	.05	.01
❑ 322 Danny Tartabull	.05	.01
❑ 323 Chris James	.05	.01
❑ 324 Mike Flanagan	.05	.01
❑ 325 Gerald Young	.05	.01
❑ 326 Bob Boone	.10	.02
❑ 327 Frank Williams	.05	.01
❑ 328 Dave Parker	.10	.02
❑ 329 Sid Bream	.05	.01
❑ 330 Mike Schooler	.05	.01
❑ 331 Bert Blyleven	.10	.02
❑ 332 Bob Welch	.05	.01

Card		
❑ 333 Bob Milacki	.05	.01
❑ 334 Tim Burke	.05	.01
❑ 335 Jose Uribe	.05	.01
❑ 336 Randy Myers	.10	.02
❑ 337 Eric King	.05	.01
❑ 338 Mark Langston	.05	.01
❑ 339 Teddy Higuera	.05	.01
❑ 340 Oddibe McDowell	.05	.01
❑ 341 Lloyd McClendon	.05	.01
❑ 342 Pascual Perez	.05	.01
❑ 343 Kevin Brown UER (Signed is misspelled as signeed	.10	.02
❑ 344 Chuck Finley	.10	.02
❑ 345 Erik Hanson	.05	.01
❑ 346 Rich Gedman	.05	.01
❑ 347 Bip Roberts	.05	.01
❑ 348 Matt Williams	.10	.02
❑ 349 Tom Henke	.05	.01
❑ 350 Brad Komminsk	.05	.01
❑ 351 Jeff Reed	.05	.01
❑ 352 Brian Downing	.05	.01
❑ 353 Frank Viola	.05	.01
❑ 354 Terry Puhl	.05	.01
❑ 355 Brian Harper	.05	.01
❑ 356 Steve Farr	.05	.01
❑ 357 Joe Boever	.05	.01
❑ 358 Danny Heep	.05	.01
❑ 359 Larry Andersen	.05	.01
❑ 360 Rolando Roomes	.05	.01
❑ 361 Mike Gallego	.05	.01
❑ 362 Bob Kipper	.05	.01
❑ 363 Clay Parker	.05	.01
❑ 364 Mike Pagliarulo	.05	.01
❑ 365 Ken Griffey Jr.	.75	.30
❑ 366 Rex Hudler	.05	.01
❑ 367 Pat Sheridan	.05	.01
❑ 368 Kirk Gibson	.10	.02
❑ 369 Jeff Parrett	.05	.01
❑ 370 Bob Walk	.05	.01
❑ 371 Ken Patterson	.05	.01
❑ 372 Bryan Harvey	.05	.01
❑ 373 Mike Bielecki	.05	.01
❑ 374 Tom Magrann RC	.05	.01
❑ 375 Rick Mahler	.05	.01
❑ 376 Craig Lefferts	.05	.01
❑ 377 Gregg Olson	.10	.02
❑ 378 Jamie Moyer	.10	.02
❑ 379 Randy Johnson	.50	.20
❑ 380 Jeff Montgomery	.10	.02
❑ 381 Marty Clary	.05	.01
❑ 382 Bill Spiers	.05	.01
❑ 383 Dave Magadan	.05	.01
❑ 384 Greg Hibbard RC	.10	.02
❑ 385 Ernie Whitt	.05	.01
❑ 386 Rick Honeycutt	.05	.01
❑ 387 Dave West	.05	.01
❑ 388 Keith Hernandez	.10	.02
❑ 389 Jose Alvarez	.05	.01
❑ 390 Albert Belle	.25	.08
❑ 391 Rick Aguilera	.10	.02
❑ 392 Mike Fitzgerald	.05	.01
❑ 393 Dwight Smith	.05	.01
❑ 394 Steve Wilson	.05	.01
❑ 395 Bob Geren	.05	.01
❑ 396 Randy Ready	.05	.01
❑ 397 Ken Hill	.10	.02
❑ 398 Jody Reed	.05	.01
❑ 399 Tom Brunansky	.05	.01
❑ 400A Checklist 334-435	.05	.01
❑ 400B Checklist 322-419	.05	.01
❑ 401 Rene Gonzales	.05	.01
❑ 402 Harold Baines	.10	.02
❑ 403 Cecilio Guante	.05	.01
❑ 404 Joe Girardi	.15	.05
❑ 405A Sergio Valdez ERR RC	.05	.01
❑ 405B Sergio Valdez COR RC	.05	.01
❑ 406 Mark Williamson	.05	.01
❑ 407 Glenn Hoffman	.05	.01
❑ 408 Jeff Innis RC	.05	.01
❑ 409 Randy Kramer	.05	.01
❑ 410 Charlie O'Brien	.05	.01
❑ 411 Charlie Hough	.10	.02
❑ 412 Gus Polidor	.05	.01
❑ 413 Ron Karkovice	.05	.01
❑ 414 Trevor Wilson	.05	.01
❑ 415 Kevin Ritz RC	.05	.01
❑ 416 Gary Thurman	.05	.01
❑ 417 Jeff M. Robinson	.05	.01
❑ 418 Scott Terry	.05	.01
❑ 419 Tim Laudner	.05	.01
❑ 420 Dennis Rasmussen	.05	.01
❑ 421 Luis Rivera	.05	.01
❑ 422 Jim Corsi	.05	.01
❑ 423 Dennis Lamp	.05	.01
❑ 424 Ken Caminiti	.10	.02
❑ 425 David Wells	.10	.02
❑ 426 Norm Charlton	.05	.01
❑ 427 Deion Sanders	.25	.08
❑ 428 Dion James	.05	.01
❑ 429 Chuck Cary	.05	.01
❑ 430 Ken Howell	.05	.01
❑ 431 Steve Lake	.05	.01
❑ 432 Kal Daniels	.05	.01
❑ 433 Lance McCullers	.05	.01
❑ 434 Lenny Harris	.05	.01
❑ 435 Scott Scudder	.05	.01
❑ 436 Gene Larkin	.05	.01
❑ 437 Dan Quisenberry	.05	.01
❑ 438 Steve Olin RC	.25	.08
❑ 439 Mickey Hatcher	.05	.01
❑ 440 Willie Wilson	.05	.01
❑ 441 Mark Grant	.05	.01
❑ 442 Mookie Wilson	.10	.02
❑ 443 Alex Trevino	.05	.01
❑ 444 Pat Tabler	.05	.01
❑ 445 Dave Bergman	.05	.01
❑ 446 Todd Burns	.05	.01
❑ 447 R.J. Reynolds	.05	.01
❑ 448 Jay Buhner	.10	.02
❑ 449 Lee Stevens	.10	.02
❑ 450 Ron Hassey	.05	.01
❑ 451 Bob Melvin	.05	.01
❑ 452 Dave Martinez	.05	.01
❑ 453 Greg Litton	.05	.01
❑ 454 Mark Carreon	.05	.01
❑ 455 Scott Fletcher	.05	.01
❑ 456 Otis Nixon	.05	.01
❑ 457 Tony Fossas RC	.05	.01
❑ 458 John Russell	.05	.01
❑ 459 Paul Assenmacher	.05	.01
❑ 460 Zane Smith	.05	.01
❑ 461 Jack Daugherty RC	.05	.01
❑ 462 Rich Monteleone	.05	.01
❑ 463 Greg Briley	.05	.01
❑ 464 Mike Smithson	.05	.01
❑ 465 Benito Santiago	.10	.02
❑ 466 Jeff Brantley	.05	.01
❑ 467 Jose Nunez	.05	.01
❑ 468 Scott Bailes	.05	.01
❑ 469 Ken Griffey Sr.	.10	.02
❑ 470 Bob McClure	.05	.01
❑ 471 Mackey Sasser	.05	.01
❑ 472 Glenn Wilson	.05	.01
❑ 473 Kevin Tapani RC	.25	.08
❑ 474 Bill Buckner	.05	.01
❑ 475 Ron Gant	.10	.02
❑ 476 Kevin Romine	.05	.01
❑ 477 Juan Agosto	.05	.01
❑ 478 Herm Winningham	.05	.01
❑ 479 Storm Davis	.05	.01
❑ 480 Jeff King	.05	.01
❑ 481 Kevin Mmahat RC	.05	.01
❑ 482 Carmelo Martinez	.05	.01
❑ 483 Omar Vizquel	.25	.08
❑ 484 Jim Dwyer	.05	.01
❑ 485 Bob Knepper	.05	.01
❑ 486 Dave Anderson	.05	.01
❑ 487 Ron Jones	.05	.01
❑ 488 Jay Bell	.10	.02
❑ 489 Sammy Sosa RC	2.50	1.00
❑ 490 Kent Anderson	.05	.01
❑ 491 Domingo Ramos	.05	.01
❑ 492 Dave Clark	.05	.01
❑ 493 Tim Birtsas	.05	.01
❑ 494 Ken Oberkfell	.05	.01
❑ 495 Larry Sheets	.05	.01
❑ 496 Jeff Kunkel	.05	.01
❑ 497 Jim Presley	.05	.01
❑ 498 Mike Macfarlane	.05	.01
❑ 499 Pete Smith	.05	.01
❑ 500A Checklist 436-537 DP	.05	.01
❑ 500B Checklist 420-517	.05	.01
❑ 501 Gary Sheffield	.25	.08
❑ 502 Terry Bross RC	.05	.01
❑ 503 Jerry Kutzler RC	.05	.01
❑ 504 Lloyd Moseby	.05	.01
❑ 505 Curt Young	.05	.01
❑ 506 Al Newman	.05	.01
❑ 507 Keith Miller	.05	.01
❑ 508 Mike Stanton RC	.25	.08
❑ 509 Rich Yett	.05	.01
❑ 510 Tim Drummond RC	.05	.01
❑ 511 Joe Hesketh	.05	.01
❑ 512 Rick Wrona	.05	.01
❑ 513 Luis Salazar	.05	.01
❑ 514 Hal Morris	.05	.01
❑ 515 Terry Mulholland	.05	.01
❑ 516 John Morris	.05	.01
❑ 517 Carlos Quintana	.05	.01
❑ 518 Frank DiPino	.05	.01
❑ 519 Randy Milligan	.05	.01
❑ 520 Chad Kreuter	.05	.01
❑ 521 Mike Jeffcoat	.05	.01
❑ 522 Mike Harkey	.05	.01
❑ 523A Andy Nezelek ERR (Wrong birth year)	.05	.01
❑ 523B Andy Nezelek COR (Finally corrected in factory s	.15	.05
❑ 524 Dave Schmidt	.05	.01
❑ 525 Tony Armas	.05	.01
❑ 526 Barry Lyons	.05	.01
❑ 527 Rick Reed RC	.25	.08
❑ 528 Jerry Reuss	.05	.01
❑ 529 Dean Palmer RC	.25	.08
❑ 530 Jeff Peterek RC	.05	.01
❑ 531 Carlos Martinez	.05	.01
❑ 532 Atlee Hammaker	.05	.01
❑ 533 Mike Brumley	.05	.01
❑ 534 Terry Leach	.05	.01
❑ 535 Doug Strange RC	.05	.01
❑ 536 Jose DeLeon	.05	.01
❑ 537 Shane Rawley	.05	.01
❑ 538 Joey Cora	.10	.02
❑ 539 Eric Hetzel	.05	.01
❑ 540 Gene Nelson	.05	.01
❑ 541 Wes Gardner	.05	.01
❑ 542 Mark Portugal	.05	.01
❑ 543 Al Leiter	.25	.08
❑ 544 Jack Armstrong	.05	.01
❑ 545 Greg Cadaret	.05	.01
❑ 546 Rod Nichols	.05	.01
❑ 547 Luis Polonia	.05	.01
❑ 548 Charlie Hayes	.05	.01
❑ 549 Dickie Thon	.05	.01
❑ 550 Tim Crews	.05	.01
❑ 551 Dave Winfield	.10	.02
❑ 552 Mike Davis	.05	.01
❑ 553 Ron Robinson	.05	.01
❑ 554 Carmen Castillo	.05	.01
❑ 555 John Costello	.05	.01
❑ 556 Bud Black	.05	.01
❑ 557 Rick Dempsey	.05	.01
❑ 558 Jim Acker	.05	.01
❑ 559 Eric Show	.05	.01
❑ 560 Pat Borders	.05	.01
❑ 561 Danny Darwin	.05	.01
❑ 562 Rick Luecken RC	.05	.01
❑ 563 Edwin Nunez	.05	.01
❑ 564 Felix Jose	.05	.01
❑ 565 John Cangelosi	.05	.01
❑ 566 Bill Swift	.05	.01
❑ 567 Bill Schroeder	.05	.01
❑ 568 Stan Javier	.05	.01
❑ 569 Jim Traber	.05	.01
❑ 570 Wallace Johnson	.05	.01
❑ 571 Donell Nixon	.05	.01
❑ 572 Sid Fernandez	.05	.01
❑ 573 Lance Johnson	.05	.01
❑ 574 Andy McGaffigan	.05	.01
❑ 575 Mark Knudson	.05	.01
❑ 576 Tommy Greene RC	.10	.02
❑ 577 Mark Grace	.15	.05
❑ 578 Larry Walker RC	1.00	.40
❑ 579 Mike Stanley	.05	.01
❑ 580 Mike Witt DP	.05	.01
❑ 581 Scott Bradley	.05	.01

❑ 582 Greg A. Harris .05 .01
❑ 583A Kevin Hickey ERR .25 .08
❑ 583B Kevin Hickey COR .05 .01
❑ 584 Lee Mazzilli .05 .01
❑ 585 Jeff Pico .05 .01
❑ 586 Joe Oliver .05 .01
❑ 587 Willie Fraser DP .05 .01
❑ 588 Carl Yastrzemski Puzzle .25 .08
❑ 589 Kevin Bass DP .05 .01
❑ 590 John Moses DP .05 .01
❑ 591 Tom Pagnozzi DP .05 .01
❑ 592 Tony Castillo DP .05 .01
❑ 593 Jerald Clark DP .05 .01
❑ 594 Dan Schatzeder .05 .01
❑ 595 Luis Quinones DP .05 .01
❑ 596 Pete Harnisch DP .05 .01
❑ 597 Gary Redus .05 .01
❑ 598 Mel Hall .05 .01
❑ 599 Rick Schu .05 .01
❑ 600A Checklist 538-639 .05 .01
❑ 600B Checklist 518-617 .05 .01
❑ 601 Mike Kingery DP .05 .01
❑ 602 Terry Kennedy DP .05 .01
❑ 603 Mike Sharperson DP .05 .01
❑ 604 Don Carman DP .05 .01
❑ 605 Jim Gott .05 .01
❑ 606 Donn Pall DP .05 .01
❑ 607 Rance Mulliniks .05 .01
❑ 608 Curt Wilkerson DP .05 .01
❑ 609 Mike Felder DP .05 .01
❑ 610 Guillermo Hernandez DP .05 .01
❑ 611 Candy Maldonado DP .05 .01
❑ 612 Mark Thurmond DP .05 .01
❑ 613 Rick Leach DP RC .05 .01
❑ 614 Jerry Reed DP .05 .01
❑ 615 Franklin Stubbs .05 .01
❑ 616 Billy Hatcher DP .05 .01
❑ 617 Don August DP .05 .01
❑ 618 Tim Teufel .05 .01
❑ 619 Shawn Hillegas DP .05 .01
❑ 620 Manny Lee .05 .01
❑ 621 Gary Ward DP .05 .01
❑ 622 Mark Guthrie DP RC .05 .01
❑ 623 Jeff Musselman DP .05 .01
❑ 624 Mark Lemke DP .05 .01
❑ 625 Fernando Valenzuela .10 .02
❑ 626 Paul Sorrento DP RC .25 .08
❑ 627 Glenallen Hill DP .05 .01
❑ 628 Les Lancaster DP .05 .01
❑ 629 Vance Law DP .05 .01
❑ 630 Randy Velarde DP .05 .01
❑ 631 Todd Frohwirth DP .05 .01
❑ 632 Willie McGee .10 .02
❑ 633 Dennis Boyd DP .05 .01
❑ 634 Cris Carpenter DP .05 .01
❑ 635 Brian Holton .05 .01
❑ 636 Tracy Jones DP .05 .01
❑ 637A Terry Steinbach AS (Recent Major League Performa .05 .01
❑ 637B Terry Steinbach AS (All-Star Game Performance) .05 .01
❑ 638 Brady Anderson .10 .02
❑ 639A Jack Morris ERR (Card front shows black line cro .10 .02
❑ 639B Jack Morris COR .10 .02
❑ 640 Jaime Navarro .05 .01
❑ 641 Darrin Jackson .05 .01
❑ 642 Mike Dyer RC .05 .01
❑ 643 Mike Schmidt .50 .20
❑ 644 Henry Cotto .05 .01
❑ 645 John Cerutti .05 .01
❑ 646 Francisco Cabrera .05 .01
❑ 647 Scott Sanderson .05 .01
❑ 648 Brian Meyer .05 .01
❑ 649 Ray Searage .05 .01
❑ 650A Bo Jackson AS ERR .25 .08
❑ 650B Bo Jackson AS COR .25 .08
❑ 651 Steve Lyons .05 .01
❑ 652 Mike LaCoss .05 .01
❑ 653 Ted Power .05 .01
❑ 654A Howard Johnson AS (Recent Major League Performan .05 .01
❑ 654B Howard Johnson AS (All-Star Game Performance) .05 .01
❑ 655 Mauro Gozzo RC .05 .01
❑ 656 Mike Blowers RC .10 .02
❑ 657 Paul Gibson .05 .01
❑ 658 Neal Heaton .05 .01
❑ 659 Nolan Ryan 5000K .50 .20
❑ 659A Nolan Ryan 5000K ERR 1.50 .60
❑ 660A H.Baines AS ERR/ERR .75 .30
❑ 660B H.Baines AS ERR/COR 1.00 .40
❑ 660C H.Baines AS COR/ERR .25 .08
❑ 660D Harold Baines AS (Black line behind star on fron .05 .01
❑ 661 Gary Pettis .05 .01
❑ 662 Clint Zavaras RC .05 .01
❑ 663A Rick Reuschel AS (Recent Major League Performanc .05 .01
❑ 663B Rick Reuschel AS (All-Star Game Performance) .05 .01
❑ 664 Alejandro Pena .05 .01
❑ 665 Nolan Ryan KING .50 .20
❑ 665A Nolan Ryan KING ERR 1.50 .60
❑ 665C Nolan Ryan KING NNO .75 .30
❑ 666 Ricky Horton .05 .01
❑ 667 Curt Schilling 1.00 .40
❑ 668 Bill Landrum .05 .01
❑ 669 Todd Stottlemyre .10 .02
❑ 670 Tim Leary .05 .01
❑ 671 John Wetteland .25 .08
❑ 672 Calvin Schiraldi .05 .01
❑ 673A Ruben Sierra AS ERR .05 .01
❑ 673B Ruben Sierra AS COR .05 .01
❑ 674A Pedro Guerrero AS (Recent Major League Performan .05 .01
❑ 674B Pedro Guerrero AS (All-Star Game Performance) .05 .01
❑ 675 Ken Phelps .05 .01
❑ 676A Cal Ripken AS .40 .15
❑ 676B Cal Ripken AS ERR .75 .30
❑ 677 Denny Walling .05 .01
❑ 678 Goose Gossage .10 .02
❑ 679 Gary Mielke RC .05 .01
❑ 680 Bill Bathe .05 .01
❑ 681 Tom Lawless .05 .01
❑ 682 Xavier Hernandez RC .05 .01
❑ 683A Kirby Puckett AS ERR .15 .05
❑ 683B Kirby Puckett AS COR .15 .05
❑ 684 Mariano Duncan .05 .01
❑ 685 Ramon Martinez .05 .01
❑ 686 Tim Jones .05 .01
❑ 687 Tom Filer .05 .01
❑ 688 Steve Lombardozzi .05 .01
❑ 689 Bernie Williams RC 1.50 .60
❑ 690 Chip Hale RC .05 .01
❑ 691 Beau Allred RC .05 .01
❑ 692A Ryne Sandberg AS ERR .25 .08
❑ 692B Ryne Sandberg AS COR .25 .08
❑ 693 Jeff Huson RC .10 .02
❑ 694 Curt Ford .05 .01
❑ 695A Eric Davis AS (Recent Major League Performance) .05 .01
❑ 695B Eric Davis AS (All-Star Game Performance) .05 .01
❑ 696 Scott Lusader .05 .01
❑ 697A Mark McGwire AS ERR .50 .20
❑ 697B Mark McGwire AS COR .50 .20
❑ 698 Steve Cummings RC .05 .01
❑ 699 George Canale RC .05 .01
❑ 700A Checklist w/out 716 .25 .08
❑ 700B Checklist with 716 .10 .02
❑ 700C Checklist 618-716 .05 .01
❑ 701A Julio Franco AS (Recent Major League Performance .05 .01
❑ 701B Julio Franco AS (All-Star Game Performance) .05 .01
❑ 702 Dave Wayne Johnson RC .05 .01
❑ 703A Dave Stewart AS ERR .05 .01
❑ 703B Dave Stewart AS COR .05 .01
❑ 704 David Justice RC .50 .20
❑ 705 Tony Gwynn AS .15 .05
❑ 705A Tony Gwynn AS ERR .15 .05
❑ 706 Greg Myers .05 .01
❑ 707A Will Clark AS ERR .15 .05
❑ 707B Will Clark AS COR .15 .05
❑ 708A Benito Santiago AS .05 .01
❑ 708B Benito Santiago AS .05 .01
❑ 709 Larry McWilliams .05 .01
❑ 710A Ozzie Smith AS ML Perf .25 .08
❑ 710B Ozzie Smith AS Perf .25 .08
❑ 711 John Olerud RC .50 .20
❑ 712A Wade Boggs AS ERR .10 .02
❑ 712B Wade Boggs AS COR .10 .02
❑ 713 Gary Eave RC .05 .01
❑ 714 Bob Tewksbury .05 .01
❑ 715A Kevin Mitchell AS (Recent Major League Performan .05 .01
❑ 715B Kevin Mitchell AS (All-Star Game Performance) .05 .01
❑ 716 Bart Giamatti MEM .25 .08

1991 Donruss

❑ COMPLETE SET (770) 8.00 3.00
❑ COMP.FACT.w/LEAF PREV 10.00 4.00
❑ COMP.FACT.w/STUDIO PREV 10.00 4.00
❑ COMP.STARGELL PUZZLE 1.00 .40
❑ 1 Dave Stieb DK .05 .01
❑ 2 Craig Biggio DK .10 .02
❑ 3 Cecil Fielder DK .05 .01
❑ 4 Barry Bonds DK .50 .20
❑ 5 Barry Larkin DK .10 .02
❑ 6 Dave Parker DK .05 .01
❑ 7 Len Dykstra DK .05 .01
❑ 8 Bobby Thigpen DK .05 .01
❑ 9 Roger Clemens DK .40 .15
❑ 10 Ron Gant DK UER .10 .02
❑ 11 Delino DeShields DK .05 .01
❑ 12 Roberto Alomar DK UER .10 .02
❑ 13 Sandy Alomar Jr. DK .05 .01
❑ 14 Ryne Sandberg DK UER .25 .08
❑ 15 Ramon Martinez DK .05 .01
❑ 16 Edgar Martinez DK .15 .05
❑ 17 Dave Magadan DK .05 .01
❑ 18 Matt Williams DK .05 .01
❑ 19 Rafael Palmeiro DK UER .10 .02
❑ 20 Bob Welch DK .05 .01
❑ 21 Dave Righetti DK .05 .01
❑ 22 Brian Harper DK .05 .01
❑ 23 Gregg Olson DK .05 .01
❑ 24 Kurt Stillwell DK .05 .01
❑ 25 Pedro Guerrero DK UER .05 .01
❑ 26 Chuck Finley DK UER .10 .02
❑ 27 DK Checklist 1-27 .05 .01
❑ 28 Tino Martinez RR .25 .08
❑ 29 Mark Lewis RR .05 .01
❑ 30 Bernard Gilkey RR .05 .01
❑ 31 Hensley Meulens RR .05 .01
❑ 32 Derek Bell RR .10 .02
❑ 33 Jose Offerman RR .05 .01
❑ 34 Terry Bross RR .05 .01
❑ 35 Leo Gomez RR .05 .01
❑ 36 Derrick May RR .05 .01
❑ 37 Kevin Morton RR RC .05 .01

❑	38 Moises Alou RR	.10	.02
❑	39 Julio Valera RR	.05	.01
❑	40 Milt Cuyler RR	.05	.01
❑	41 Phil Plantier RR RC	.25	.08
❑	42 Scott Chiamparino RR	.05	.01
❑	43 Ray Lankford RR	.10	.02
❑	44 Mickey Morandini RR	.05	.01
❑	45 Dave Hansen RR	.05	.01
❑	46 Kevin Belcher RR RC	.05	.01
❑	47 Darrin Fletcher RR	.05	.01
❑	48 Steve Sax AS	.05	.01
❑	49 Ken Griffey Jr. AS	.25	.08
❑	50A Jose Canseco AS ERR	.10	.02
❑	50B Jose Canseco AS COR	.15	.05
❑	51 Sandy Alomar Jr. AS	.05	.01
❑	52 Cal Ripken AS	.40	.15
❑	53 Rickey Henderson AS	.15	.05
❑	54 Bob Welch AS	.05	.01
❑	55 Wade Boggs AS	.10	.02
❑	56 Mark McGwire AS	.40	.15
❑	57A Jack McDowell ERR	.25	.08
❑	57B Jack McDowell COR	.50	.20
❑	58 Jose Lind	.05	.01
❑	59 Alex Fernandez	.05	.01
❑	60 Pat Combs	.05	.01
❑	61 Mike Walker	.05	.01
❑	62 Juan Samuel	.05	.01
❑	63 Mike Blowers UER	.05	.01
❑	64 Mark Guthrie	.05	.01
❑	65 Mark Salas	.05	.01
❑	66 Tim Jones	.05	.01
❑	67 Tim Leary	.05	.01
❑	68 Andres Galarraga	.10	.02
❑	69 Bob Milacki	.05	.01
❑	70 Tim Belcher	.05	.01
❑	71 Todd Zeile	.05	.01
❑	72 Jerome Walton	.05	.01
❑	73 Kevin Seitzer	.05	.01
❑	74 Jerald Clark	.05	.01
❑	75 John Smoltz UER	.15	.05
❑	76 Mike Henneman	.05	.01
❑	77 Ken Griffey Jr.	.50	.20
❑	78 Jim Abbott	.15	.05
❑	79 Gregg Jefferies	.05	.01
❑	80 Kevin Reimer	.05	.01
❑	81 Roger Clemens	.75	.30
❑	82 Mike Fitzgerald	.05	.01
❑	83 Bruce Hurst UER	.05	.01
❑	84 Eric Davis	.10	.02
❑	85 Paul Molitor	.10	.02
❑	86 Will Clark	.15	.05
❑	87 Mike Bielecki	.05	.01
❑	88 Bret Saberhagen	.10	.02
❑	89 Nolan Ryan	1.00	.40
❑	90 Bobby Thigpen	.05	.01
❑	91 Dickie Thon	.05	.01
❑	92 Duane Ward	.05	.01
❑	93 Luis Polonia	.05	.01
❑	94 Terry Kennedy	.05	.01
❑	95 Kent Hrbek	.10	.02
❑	96 Danny Jackson	.05	.01
❑	97 Sid Fernandez	.05	.01
❑	98 Jimmy Key	.10	.02
❑	99 Franklin Stubbs	.05	.01
❑	100 Checklist 28-103	.05	.01
❑	101 R.J. Reynolds	.05	.01
❑	102 Dave Stewart	.10	.02
❑	103 Dan Pasqua	.05	.01
❑	104 Dan Plesac	.05	.01
❑	105 Mark McGwire	.75	.30
❑	106 John Farrell	.05	.01
❑	107 Don Mattingly	.60	.25
❑	108 Carlton Fisk	.15	.05
❑	109 Ken Oberkfell	.05	.01
❑	110 Darrel Akerfelds	.05	.01
❑	111 Gregg Olson	.05	.01
❑	112 Mike Scioscia	.05	.01
❑	113 Bryn Smith	.05	.01
❑	114 Bob Geren	.05	.01
❑	115 Tom Candiotti	.05	.01
❑	116 Kevin Tapani	.05	.01
❑	117 Jeff Treadway	.05	.01
❑	118 Alan Trammell	.10	.02
❑	119 Pete O'Brien UER	.05	.01
❑	120 Joel Skinner	.05	.01
❑	121 Mike LaValliere	.05	.01
❑	122 Dwight Evans	.15	.05
❑	123 Jody Reed	.05	.01
❑	124 Lee Guetterman	.05	.01
❑	125 Tim Burke	.05	.01
❑	126 Dave Johnson	.05	.01
❑	127 Fernando Valenzuela UER	.10	.02
❑	128 Jose DeLeon	.05	.01
❑	129 Andre Dawson	.10	.02
❑	130 Gerald Perry	.05	.01
❑	131 Greg W. Harris	.05	.01
❑	132 Tom Glavine	.15	.05
❑	133 Lance McCullers	.05	.01
❑	134 Randy Johnson	.30	.10
❑	135 Lance Parrish UER	.10	.02
❑	136 Mackey Sasser	.05	.01
❑	137 Geno Petralli	.05	.01
❑	138 Dennis Lamp	.05	.01
❑	139 Dennis Martinez	.10	.02
❑	140 Mike Pagliarulo	.05	.01
❑	141 Hal Morris	.05	.01
❑	142 Dave Parker	.10	.02
❑	143 Brett Butler	.10	.02
❑	144 Paul Assenmacher	.05	.01
❑	145 Mark Gubicza	.05	.01
❑	146 Charlie Hough	.10	.02
❑	147 Sammy Sosa	.25	.08
❑	148 Randy Ready	.05	.01
❑	149 Kelly Gruber	.05	.01
❑	150 Devon White	.10	.02
❑	151 Gary Carter	.10	.02
❑	152 Gene Larkin	.05	.01
❑	153 Chris Sabo	.05	.01
❑	154 David Cone	.10	.02
❑	155 Todd Stottlemyre	.05	.01
❑	156 Glenn Wilson	.05	.01
❑	157 Bob Walk	.05	.01
❑	158 Mike Gallego	.05	.01
❑	159 Greg Hibbard	.05	.01
❑	160 Chris Bosio	.05	.01
❑	161 Mike Moore	.05	.01
❑	162 Jerry Browne UER	.05	.01
❑	163 Steve Sax UER	.05	.01
❑	164 Melido Perez	.05	.01
❑	165 Danny Darwin	.05	.01
❑	166 Roger McDowell	.05	.01
❑	167 Bill Ripken	.05	.01
❑	168 Mike Sharperson	.05	.01
❑	169 Lee Smith	.10	.02
❑	170 Matt Nokes	.05	.01
❑	171 Jesse Orosco	.05	.01
❑	172 Rick Aguilera	.10	.02
❑	173 Jim Presley	.05	.01
❑	174 Lou Whitaker	.10	.02
❑	175 Harold Reynolds	.10	.02
❑	176 Brook Jacoby	.05	.01
❑	177 Wally Backman	.05	.01
❑	178 Wade Boggs	.15	.05
❑	179 Chuck Cary UER	.05	.01
❑	180 Tom Foley	.05	.01
❑	181 Pete Harnisch	.05	.01
❑	182 Mike Morgan	.05	.01
❑	183 Bob Tewksbury	.05	.01
❑	184 Joe Girardi	.05	.01
❑	185 Storm Davis	.05	.01
❑	186 Ed Whitson	.05	.01
❑	187 Steve Avery UER	.05	.01
❑	188 Lloyd Moseby	.05	.01
❑	189 Scott Bankhead	.05	.01
❑	190 Mark Langston	.05	.01
❑	191 Kevin McReynolds	.05	.01
❑	192 Julio Franco	.10	.02
❑	193 John Dopson	.05	.01
❑	194 Dennis Boyd	.05	.01
❑	195 Bip Roberts	.05	.01
❑	196 Billy Hatcher	.05	.01
❑	197 Edgar Diaz	.05	.01
❑	198 Greg Litton	.05	.01
❑	199 Mark Grace	.15	.05
❑	200 Checklist 104-179	.05	.01
❑	201 George Brett	.60	.25
❑	202 Jeff Russell	.05	.01
❑	203 Ivan Calderon	.05	.01
❑	204 Ken Howell	.05	.01
❑	205 Tom Henke	.05	.01
❑	206 Bryan Harvey	.05	.01
❑	207 Steve Bedrosian	.05	.01
❑	208 Al Newman	.05	.01
❑	209 Randy Myers	.05	.01
❑	210 Daryl Boston	.05	.01
❑	211 Manny Lee	.05	.01
❑	212 Dave Smith	.05	.01
❑	213 Don Slaught	.05	.01
❑	214 Walt Weiss	.05	.01
❑	215 Donn Pall	.05	.01
❑	216 Jaime Navarro	.05	.01
❑	217 Willie Randolph	.10	.02
❑	218 Rudy Seanez	.05	.01
❑	219 Jim Leyritz	.05	.01
❑	220 Ron Karkovice	.05	.01
❑	221 Ken Caminiti	.10	.02
❑	222 Von Hayes	.05	.01
❑	223 Cal Ripken	.75	.30
❑	224 Lenny Harris	.05	.01
❑	225 Milt Thompson	.05	.01
❑	226 Alvaro Espinoza	.05	.01
❑	227 Chris James	.05	.01
❑	228 Dan Gladden	.05	.01
❑	229 Jeff Blauser	.05	.01
❑	230 Mike Heath	.05	.01
❑	231 Omar Vizquel	.15	.05
❑	232 Doug Jones	.05	.01
❑	233 Jeff King	.05	.01
❑	234 Luis Rivera	.05	.01
❑	235 Ellis Burks	.10	.02
❑	236 Greg Cadaret	.05	.01
❑	237 Dave Martinez	.05	.01
❑	238 Mark Williamson	.05	.01
❑	239 Stan Javier	.05	.01
❑	240 Ozzie Smith	.40	.15
❑	241 Shawn Boskie	.05	.01
❑	242 Tom Gordon	.05	.01
❑	243 Tony Gwynn	.30	.10
❑	244 Tommy Gregg	.05	.01
❑	245 Jeff M. Robinson	.05	.01
❑	246 Keith Comstock	.05	.01
❑	247 Jack Howell	.05	.01
❑	248 Keith Miller	.05	.01
❑	249 Bobby Witt	.05	.01
❑	250 Rob Murphy UER	.05	.01
❑	251 Spike Owen	.05	.01
❑	252 Garry Templeton	.05	.01
❑	253 Glenn Braggs	.05	.01
❑	254 Ron Robinson	.05	.01
❑	255 Kevin Mitchell	.05	.01
❑	256 Les Lancaster	.05	.01
❑	257 Mel Stottlemyre Jr.	.05	.01
❑	258 Kenny Rogers UER	.10	.02
❑	259 Lance Johnson	.05	.01
❑	260 John Kruk	.10	.02
❑	261 Fred McGriff	.15	.05
❑	262 Dick Schofield	.05	.01
❑	263 Trevor Wilson	.05	.01
❑	264 David West	.05	.01
❑	265 Scott Scudder	.05	.01
❑	266 Dwight Gooden	.10	.02
❑	267 Willie Blair	.05	.01
❑	268 Mark Portugal	.05	.01
❑	269 Doug Drabek	.05	.01
❑	270 Dennis Eckersley	.10	.02
❑	271 Eric King	.05	.01
❑	272 Robin Yount	.40	.15
❑	273 Carney Lansford	.10	.02
❑	274 Carlos Baerga	.05	.01
❑	275 Dave Righetti	.10	.02
❑	276 Scott Fletcher	.05	.01
❑	277 Eric Yelding	.05	.01
❑	278 Charlie Hayes	.05	.01
❑	279 Jeff Ballard	.05	.01
❑	280 Orel Hershiser	.10	.02
❑	281 Jose Oquendo	.05	.01
❑	282 Mike Witt	.05	.01
❑	283 Mitch Webster	.05	.01
❑	284 Greg Gagne	.05	.01
❑	285 Greg Olson	.05	.01
❑	286 Tony Phillips UER	.05	.01
❑	287 Scott Bradley	.05	.01
❑	288 Cory Snyder UER	.05	.01
❑	289 Jay Bell UER	.10	.02
❑	290 Kevin Romine	.05	.01
❑	291 Jeff D. Robinson	.05	.01
❑	292 Steve Frey UER	.05	.01
❑	293 Craig Worthington	.05	.01

❑ 294 Tim Crews .05 .01
❑ 295 Joe Magrane .05 .01
❑ 296 Hector Villanueva .05 .01
❑ 297 Terry Shumpert .05 .01
❑ 298 Joe Carter .10 .02
❑ 299 Kent Mercker UER .05 .01
❑ 300 Checklist 180-255 .05 .01
❑ 301 Chet Lemon .05 .01
❑ 302 Mike Schooler .05 .01
❑ 303 Dante Bichette .10 .02
❑ 304 Kevin Elster .05 .01
❑ 305 Jeff Huson .05 .01
❑ 306 Greg A. Harris .05 .01
❑ 307 Marquis Grissom UER .10 .02
❑ 308 Calvin Schiraldi .05 .01
❑ 309 Mariano Duncan .05 .01
❑ 310 Bill Spiers .05 .01
❑ 311 Scott Garrelts .05 .01
❑ 312 Mitch Williams .05 .01
❑ 313 Mike Macfarlane .05 .01
❑ 314 Kevin Brown .10 .02
❑ 315 Robin Ventura .10 .02
❑ 316 Darren Daulton .10 .02
❑ 317 Pat Borders .05 .01
❑ 318 Mark Eichhorn .05 .01
❑ 319 Jeff Brantley .05 .01
❑ 320 Shane Mack .05 .01
❑ 321 Rob Dibble .10 .02
❑ 322 John Franco .10 .02
❑ 323 Junior Felix .05 .01
❑ 324 Casey Candaele .05 .01
❑ 325 Bobby Bonilla .10 .02
❑ 326 Dave Henderson .05 .01
❑ 327 Wayne Edwards .05 .01
❑ 328 Mark Knudson .05 .01
❑ 329 Terry Steinbach .05 .01
❑ 330 Colby Ward UER RC .05 .01
❑ 331 Oscar Azocar .05 .01
❑ 332 Scott Radinsky .05 .01
❑ 333 Eric Anthony .05 .01
❑ 334 Steve Lake .05 .01
❑ 335 Bob Melvin .05 .01
❑ 336 Kal Daniels .05 .01
❑ 337 Tom Pagnozzi .05 .01
❑ 338 Alan Mills .05 .01
❑ 339 Steve Olin .05 .01
❑ 340 Juan Berenguer .05 .01
❑ 341 Francisco Cabrera .05 .01
❑ 342 Dave Bergman .05 .01
❑ 343 Henry Cotto .05 .01
❑ 344 Sergio Valdez .05 .01
❑ 345 Bob Patterson .05 .01
❑ 346 John Marzano .05 .01
❑ 347 Dana Kiecker .05 .01
❑ 348 Dion James .05 .01
❑ 349 Hubie Brooks .05 .01
❑ 350 Bill Landrum .05 .01
❑ 351 Bill Sampen .05 .01
❑ 352 Greg Briley .05 .01
❑ 353 Paul Gibson .05 .01
❑ 354 Dave Eiland .05 .01
❑ 355 Steve Finley .10 .02
❑ 356 Bob Boone .10 .02
❑ 357 Steve Buechele .05 .01
❑ 358 Chris Hoiles FDC .05 .01
❑ 359 Larry Walker .25 .08
❑ 360 Frank DiPino .05 .01
❑ 361 Mark Grant .05 .01
❑ 362 Dave Magadan .05 .01
❑ 363 Robby Thompson .05 .01
❑ 364 Lonnie Smith .05 .01
❑ 365 Steve Farr .05 .01
❑ 366 Dave Valle .05 .01
❑ 367 Tim Naehring .05 .01
❑ 368 Jim Acker .05 .01
❑ 369 Jeff Reardon UER .10 .02
❑ 370 Tim Teufel .05 .01
❑ 371 Juan Gonzalez .25 .08
❑ 372 Luis Salazar .05 .01
❑ 373 Rick Honeycutt .05 .01
❑ 374 Greg Maddux .40 .15
❑ 375 Jose Uribe UER .05 .01
❑ 376 Donnie Hill .05 .01
❑ 377 Don Carman .05 .01
❑ 378 Craig Grebeck .05 .01
❑ 379 Willie Fraser .05 .01

❑ 380 Glenallen Hill .05 .01
❑ 381 Joe Oliver .05 .01
❑ 382 Randy Bush .05 .01
❑ 383 Alex Cole .05 .01
❑ 384 Norm Charlton .05 .01
❑ 385 Gene Nelson .05 .01
❑ 386 Checklist 256-331 .05 .01
❑ 387 Rickey Henderson MVP .15 .05
❑ 388 Lance Parrish MVP .05 .01
❑ 389 Fred McGriff MVP .10 .02
❑ 390 Dave Parker MVP .05 .01
❑ 391 Candy Maldonado MVP .05 .01
❑ 392 Ken Griffey Jr. MVP .25 .08
❑ 393 Gregg Olson MVP .05 .01
❑ 394 Rafael Palmeiro MVP .10 .02
❑ 395 Roger Clemens MVP .40 .15
❑ 396 George Brett MVP .25 .08
❑ 397 Cecil Fielder MVP .05 .01
❑ 398 Brian Harper MVP UER .05 .01
❑ 399 Bobby Thigpen MVP .05 .01
❑ 400 Roberto Kelly MVP UER .05 .01
❑ 401 Danny Darwin MVP .05 .01
❑ 402 David Justice MVP .05 .01
❑ 403 Lee Smith MVP .05 .01
❑ 404 Ryne Sandberg MVP .25 .08
❑ 405 Eddie Murray MVP .15 .05
❑ 406 Tim Wallach MVP .05 .01
❑ 407 Kevin Mitchell MVP .05 .01
❑ 408 Darryl Strawberry MVP .05 .01
❑ 409 Joe Carter MVP .05 .01
❑ 410 Len Dykstra MVP .05 .01
❑ 411 Doug Drabek MVP .05 .01
❑ 412 Chris Sabo MVP .05 .01
❑ 413 Paul Marak RR RC .05 .01
❑ 414 Tim McIntosh RR .05 .01
❑ 415 Brian Barnes RR RC .10 .02
❑ 416 Eric Gunderson RR .05 .01
❑ 417 Mike Gardiner RR RC .05 .01
❑ 418 Steve Carter RR .05 .01
❑ 419 Gerald Alexander RR RC .05 .01
❑ 420 Rich Garces RR RC .10 .02
❑ 421 Chuck Knoblauch .10 .02
❑ 422 Scott Aldred RR .05 .01
❑ 423 Wes Chamberlain RR RC .25 .08
❑ 424 Lance Dickson RR RC .10 .02
❑ 425 Greg Colbrunn RR RC .25 .08
❑ 426 Rich DeLucia RR UER RC .05 .01
❑ 427 Jeff Conine RR RC .40 .15
❑ 428 Steve Decker RR RC .05 .01
❑ 429 Turner Ward RR RC .25 .08
❑ 430 Mo Vaughn .10 .02
❑ 431 Steve Chitren RR RC .05 .01
❑ 432 Mike Benjamin RR .05 .01
❑ 433 Ryne Sandberg AS .25 .08
❑ 434 Len Dykstra AS .05 .01
❑ 435 Andre Dawson AS .05 .01
❑ 436A Mike Scioscia AS White .05 .01
❑ 436B Mike Scioscia AS Yellow .05 .01
❑ 437 Ozzie Smith AS .25 .08
❑ 438 Kevin Mitchell AS .05 .01
❑ 439 Jack Armstrong AS .05 .01
❑ 440 Chris Sabo AS .05 .01
❑ 441 Will Clark AS .10 .02
❑ 442 Mel Hall .05 .01
❑ 443 Mark Gardner .05 .01
❑ 444 Mike Devereaux .05 .01
❑ 445 Kirk Gibson .10 .02
❑ 446 Terry Pendleton .10 .02
❑ 447 Mike Harkey .05 .01
❑ 448 Jim Eisenreich .05 .01
❑ 449 Benito Santiago .10 .02
❑ 450 Oddibe McDowell .05 .01
❑ 451 Cecil Fielder .10 .02
❑ 452 Ken Griffey Sr. .10 .02
❑ 453 Bert Blyleven .10 .02
❑ 454 Howard Johnson .05 .01
❑ 455 Monty Fariss UER .05 .01
❑ 456 Tony Pena .05 .01
❑ 457 Tim Raines .10 .02
❑ 458 Dennis Rasmussen .05 .01
❑ 459 Luis Quinones .05 .01
❑ 460 B.J. Surhoff .10 .02
❑ 461 Ernest Riles .05 .01
❑ 462 Rick Sutcliffe .10 .02
❑ 463 Danny Tartabull .05 .01
❑ 464 Pete Incaviglia .05 .01

❑ 465 Carlos Martinez .05 .01
❑ 466 Ricky Jordan .05 .01
❑ 467 John Cerutti .05 .01
❑ 468 Dave Winfield .10 .02
❑ 469 Francisco Oliveras .05 .01
❑ 470 Roy Smith .05 .01
❑ 471 Barry Larkin .15 .05
❑ 472 Ron Darling .05 .01
❑ 473 David Wells .10 .02
❑ 474 Glenn Davis .05 .01
❑ 475 Neal Heaton .05 .01
❑ 476 Ron Hassey .05 .01
❑ 477 Frank Thomas .25 .08
❑ 478 Greg Vaughn .05 .01
❑ 479 Todd Burns .05 .01
❑ 480 Candy Maldonado .05 .01
❑ 481 Dave LaPoint .05 .01
❑ 482 Alvin Davis .05 .01
❑ 483 Mike Scott .05 .01
❑ 484 Dale Murphy .15 .05
❑ 485 Ben McDonald .05 .01
❑ 486 Jay Howell .05 .01
❑ 487 Vince Coleman .05 .01
❑ 488 Alfredo Griffin .05 .01
❑ 489 Sandy Alomar Jr. .05 .01
❑ 490 Kirby Puckett .25 .08
❑ 491 Andres Thomas .05 .01
❑ 492 Jack Morris .10 .02
❑ 493 Matt Young .05 .01
❑ 494 Greg Myers .05 .01
❑ 495 Barry Bonds 1.00 .40
❑ 496 Scott Cooper UER .05 .01
❑ 497 Dan Schatzeder .05 .01
❑ 498 Jesse Barfield .05 .01
❑ 499 Jerry Goff .05 .01
❑ 500 Checklist 332-408 .05 .01
❑ 501 Anthony Telford RC .05 .01
❑ 502 Eddie Murray .25 .08
❑ 503 Omar Olivares RC .25 .08
❑ 504 Ryne Sandberg .40 .15
❑ 505 Jeff Montgomery .05 .01
❑ 506 Mark Parent .05 .01
❑ 507 Ron Gant .10 .02
❑ 508 Frank Tanana .05 .01
❑ 509 Jay Buhner .10 .02
❑ 510 Max Venable .05 .01
❑ 511 Wally Whitehurst .05 .01
❑ 512 Gary Pettis .05 .01
❑ 513 Tom Brunansky .05 .01
❑ 514 Tim Wallach .05 .01
❑ 515 Craig Lefferts .05 .01
❑ 516 Tim Layana .05 .01
❑ 517 Darryl Hamilton .05 .01
❑ 518 Rick Reuschel .05 .01
❑ 519 Steve Wilson .05 .01
❑ 520 Kurt Stillwell .05 .01
❑ 521 Rafael Palmeiro .15 .05
❑ 522 Ken Patterson .05 .01
❑ 523 Len Dykstra .10 .02
❑ 524 Tony Fernandez .05 .01
❑ 525 Kent Anderson .05 .01
❑ 526 Mark Leonard RC .05 .01
❑ 527 Allan Anderson .05 .01
❑ 528 Tom Browning .05 .01
❑ 529 Frank Viola .10 .02
❑ 530 John Olerud .10 .02
❑ 531 Juan Agosto .05 .01
❑ 532 Zane Smith .05 .01
❑ 533 Scott Sanderson .05 .01
❑ 534 Barry Jones .05 .01
❑ 535 Mike Felder .05 .01
❑ 536 Jose Canseco .15 .05
❑ 537 Felix Fermin .05 .01
❑ 538 Roberto Kelly .05 .01
❑ 539 Brian Holman .05 .01
❑ 540 Mark Davidson .05 .01
❑ 541 Terry Mulholland .05 .01
❑ 542 Randy Milligan .05 .01
❑ 543 Jose Gonzalez .05 .01
❑ 544 Craig Wilson RC .05 .01
❑ 545 Mike Hartley .05 .01
❑ 546 Greg Swindell .05 .01
❑ 547 Gary Gaetti .10 .02
❑ 548 David Justice .10 .02
❑ 549 Steve Searcy .05 .01
❑ 550 Erik Hanson .05 .01

❑ 551 Dave Stieb .05 .01
❑ 552 Andy Van Slyke .15 .05
❑ 553 Mike Greenwell .05 .01
❑ 554 Kevin Maas .05 .01
❑ 555 Delino DeShields .10 .02
❑ 556 Curt Schilling .25 .08
❑ 557 Ramon Martinez .05 .01
❑ 558 Pedro Guerrero .10 .02
❑ 559 Dwight Smith .05 .01
❑ 560 Mark Davis .05 .01
❑ 561 Shawn Abner .05 .01
❑ 562 Charlie Leibrandt .05 .01
❑ 563 John Shelby .05 .01
❑ 564 Bill Swift .05 .01
❑ 565 Mike Fetters .05 .01
❑ 566 Alejandro Pena .05 .01
❑ 567 Ruben Sierra .10 .02
❑ 568 Carlos Quintana .05 .01
❑ 569 Kevin Gross .05 .01
❑ 570 Derek Lilliquist .05 .01
❑ 571 Jack Armstrong .05 .01
❑ 572 Greg Brock .05 .01
❑ 573 Mike Kingery .05 .01
❑ 574 Greg Smith .05 .01
❑ 575 Brian McRae RC .25 .08
❑ 576 Jack Daugherty .05 .01
❑ 577 Ozzie Guillen .10 .02
❑ 578 Joe Boever .05 .01
❑ 579 Luis Sojo .05 .01
❑ 580 Chili Davis .10 .02
❑ 581 Don Robinson .05 .01
❑ 582 Brian Harper .05 .01
❑ 583 Paul O'Neill .15 .05
❑ 584 Bob Ojeda .05 .01
❑ 585 Mookie Wilson .10 .02
❑ 586 Rafael Ramirez .05 .01
❑ 587 Gary Redus .05 .01
❑ 588 Jamie Quirk .05 .01
❑ 589 Shawn Hillegas .05 .01
❑ 590 Tom Edens RC .05 .01
❑ 591 Joe Klink .05 .01
❑ 592 Charles Nagy .05 .01
❑ 593 Eric Plunk .05 .01
❑ 594 Tracy Jones .05 .01
❑ 595 Craig Biggio .15 .05
❑ 596 Jose DeJesus .05 .01
❑ 597 Mickey Tettleton .05 .01
❑ 598 Chris Gwynn .05 .01
❑ 599 Rex Hudler .05 .01
❑ 600 Checklist 409-506 .05 .01
❑ 601 Jim Gott .05 .01
❑ 602 Jeff Manto .05 .01
❑ 603 Nelson Liriano .05 .01
❑ 604 Mark Lemke .05 .01
❑ 605 Clay Parker .05 .01
❑ 606 Edgar Martinez .15 .05
❑ 607 Mark Whiten .05 .01
❑ 608 Ted Power .05 .01
❑ 609 Tom Bolton .05 .01
❑ 610 Tom Herr .05 .01
❑ 611 Andy Hawkins UER .05 .01
❑ 612 Scott Ruskin .05 .01
❑ 613 Ron Kittle .05 .01
❑ 614 John Wetteland .10 .02
❑ 615 Mike Perez RC .10 .02
❑ 616 Dave Clark .05 .01
❑ 617 Brent Mayne .05 .01
❑ 618 Jack Clark .10 .02
❑ 619 Marvin Freeman .05 .01
❑ 620 Edwin Nunez .05 .01
❑ 621 Russ Swan .05 .01
❑ 622 Johnny Ray .05 .01
❑ 623 Charlie O'Brien .05 .01
❑ 624 Joe Bitker RC .05 .01
❑ 625 Mike Marshall .05 .01
❑ 626 Otis Nixon .05 .01
❑ 627 Andy Benes .05 .01
❑ 628 Ron Oester .05 .01
❑ 629 Ted Higuera .05 .01
❑ 630 Kevin Bass .05 .01
❑ 631 Damon Berryhill .05 .01
❑ 632 Bo Jackson .25 .08
❑ 633 Brad Arnsberg .05 .01
❑ 634 Jerry Willard .05 .01
❑ 635 Tommy Greene .05 .01
❑ 636 Bob MacDonald RC .05 .01
❑ 637 Kirk McCaskill .05 .01
❑ 638 John Burkett .05 .01
❑ 639 Paul Abbott RC .05 .01
❑ 640 Todd Benzinger .05 .01
❑ 641 Todd Hundley .05 .01
❑ 642 George Bell .05 .01
❑ 643 Javier Ortiz .05 .01
❑ 644 Sid Bream .05 .01
❑ 645 Bob Welch .05 .01
❑ 646 Phil Bradley .05 .01
❑ 647 Bill Krueger .05 .01
❑ 648 Rickey Henderson .25 .08
❑ 649 Kevin Wickander .05 .01
❑ 650 Steve Balboni .05 .01
❑ 651 Gene Harris .05 .01
❑ 652 Jim Deshaies .05 .01
❑ 653 Jason Grimsley .05 .01
❑ 654 Joe Orsulak .05 .01
❑ 655 Jim Poole .05 .01
❑ 656 Felix Jose .05 .01
❑ 657 Denis Cook .05 .01
❑ 658 Tom Brookens .05 .01
❑ 659 Junior Ortiz .05 .01
❑ 660 Jeff Parrett .05 .01
❑ 661 Jerry Don Gleaton .05 .01
❑ 662 Brent Knackert .05 .01
❑ 663 Rance Mulliniks .05 .01
❑ 664 John Smiley .05 .01
❑ 665 Larry Andersen .05 .01
❑ 666 Willie McGee .10 .02
❑ 667 Chris Nabholz .05 .01
❑ 668 Brady Anderson .10 .02
❑ 669 Darren Holmes UER RC .25 .08
❑ 670 Ken Hill .05 .01
❑ 671 Gary Varsho .05 .01
❑ 672 Bill Pecota .05 .01
❑ 673 Fred Lynn .05 .01
❑ 674 Kevin D. Brown .05 .01
❑ 675 Dan Petry .05 .01
❑ 676 Mike Jackson .05 .01
❑ 677 Wally Joyner .10 .02
❑ 678 Danny Jackson .05 .01
❑ 679 Bill Haselman RC .05 .01
❑ 680 Mike Boddicker .05 .01
❑ 681 Mel Rojas .05 .01
❑ 682 Roberto Alomar .15 .05
❑ 683 David Justice ROY .05 .01
❑ 684 Chuck Crim .05 .01
❑ 685 Matt Williams .10 .02
❑ 686 Shawon Dunston .05 .01
❑ 687 Jeff Schulz RC .05 .01
❑ 688 John Barfield .05 .01
❑ 689 Gerald Young .05 .01
❑ 690 Luis Gonzalez RC .50 .20
❑ 691 Frank Wills .05 .01
❑ 692 Chuck Finley .10 .02
❑ 693 Sandy Alomar Jr. ROY .05 .01
❑ 694 Tim Drummond .05 .01
❑ 695 Herm Winningham .05 .01
❑ 696 Darryl Strawberry .10 .02
❑ 697 Al Leiter .10 .02
❑ 698 Karl Rhodes .05 .01
❑ 699 Stan Belinda .05 .01
❑ 700 Checklist 507-604 .05 .01
❑ 701 Lance Blankenship .05 .01
❑ 702 Willie Stargell PUZ .15 .05
❑ 703 Jim Gantner .05 .01
❑ 704 Reggie Harris .05 .01
❑ 705 Rob Ducey .05 .01
❑ 706 Tim Hulett .05 .01
❑ 707 Atlee Hammaker .05 .01
❑ 708 Xavier Hernandez .05 .01
❑ 709 Chuck McElroy .05 .01
❑ 710 John Mitchell .05 .01
❑ 711 Carlos Hernandez .05 .01
❑ 712 Geronimo Pena .05 .01
❑ 713 Jim Neidlinger RC .05 .01
❑ 714 John Orton .05 .01
❑ 715 Terry Leach .05 .01
❑ 716 Mike Stanton .05 .01
❑ 717 Walt Terrell .05 .01
❑ 718 Luis Aquino .05 .01
❑ 719 Bud Black UER .05 .01
❑ 720 Bob Kipper .05 .01
❑ 721 Jeff Gray RC .05 .01
❑ 722 Jose Rijo .05 .01
❑ 723 Curt Young .05 .01
❑ 724 Jose Vizcaino .05 .01
❑ 725 Randy Tomlin RC .10 .02
❑ 726 Junior Noboa .05 .01
❑ 727 Bob Welch CY .05 .01
❑ 728 Gary Ward .05 .01
❑ 729 Rob Deer UER .05 .01
❑ 730 David Segui .05 .01
❑ 731 Mark Carreon .05 .01
❑ 732 Vicente Palacios .05 .01
❑ 733 Sam Horn .05 .01
❑ 734 Howard Farmer .05 .01
❑ 735 Ken Dayley UER .05 .01
❑ 736 Kelly Mann .05 .01
❑ 737 Joe Grahe RC .10 .02
❑ 738 Kelly Downs .05 .01
❑ 739 Jimmy Kremers .05 .01
❑ 740 Kevin Appier .10 .02
❑ 741 Jeff Reed .05 .01
❑ 742 Jose Rijo WS .05 .01
❑ 743 Dave Rohde .05 .01
❑ 744 L.Dykstra/D.Murphy UER .15 .05
❑ 745 Paul Sorrento .05 .01
❑ 746 Thomas Howard .05 .01
❑ 747 Matt Stark RC .05 .01
❑ 748 Harold Baines .10 .02
❑ 749 Doug Dascenzo .05 .01
❑ 750 Doug Drabek CY .05 .01
❑ 751 Gary Sheffield .10 .02
❑ 752 Terry Lee RC .05 .01
❑ 753 Jim Vatcher RC .05 .01
❑ 754 Lee Stevens .05 .01
❑ 755 Randy Veres .05 .01
❑ 756 Bill Doran .05 .01
❑ 757 Gary Wayne .05 .01
❑ 758 Pedro Munoz RC .10 .02
❑ 759 Chris Hammond FDC .05 .01
❑ 760 Checklist 605-702 .05 .01
❑ 761 Rickey Henderson MVP .15 .05
❑ 762 Barry Bonds MVP .50 .20
❑ 763 Billy Hatcher WS UER .05 .01
❑ 764 Julio Machado .05 .01
❑ 765 Jose Mesa .05 .01
❑ 766 Willie Randolph WS .05 .01
❑ 767 Scott Erickson .05 .01
❑ 768 Travis Fryman .10 .02
❑ 769 Rich Rodriguez RC .05 .01
❑ 770 Checklist 703-770/BC1-BC22 .05 .01

1992 Donruss

❑ COMPLETE SET (784) 10.00 4.00
❑ COMP.HOBBY SET (788) 10.00 4.00
❑ COMP.RETAIL SET (788) 10.00 4.00
❑ COMPLETE SERIES 1 (396) 5.00 2.00
❑ COMPLETE SERIES 2 (388) 5.00 2.00
❑ COMP.CAREW PUZZLE 1.00 .40
❑ 1 Mark Wohlers RR .05 .01
❑ 2 Wil Cordero .05 .01
❑ 3 Kyle Abbott RR .05 .01
❑ 4 Dave Nilsson .05 .01
❑ 5 Kenny Lofton .15 .05
❑ 6 Luis Mercedes RR .05 .01
❑ 7 Roger Salkeld RR .05 .01
❑ 8 Eddie Zosky RR .05 .01
❑ 9 Todd Van Poppel .05 .01
❑ 10 Frank Seminara RR RC .10 .02
❑ 11 Andy Ashby .05 .01
❑ 12 Reggie Jefferson RR .05 .01

❑ 13 Ryan Klesko .10 .02
❑ 14 Carlos Garcia .05 .01
❑ 15 John Ramos RR .05 .01
❑ 16 Eric Karros .10 .02
❑ 17 Patrick Lennon RR .05 .01
❑ 18 Eddie Taubensee RR RC .25 .08
❑ 19 Roberto Hernandez RR .05 .01
❑ 20 D.J. Dozier RR .05 .01
❑ 21 Dave Henderson AS .05 .01
❑ 22 Cal Ripken AS .40 .15
❑ 23 Wade Boggs AS .10 .02
❑ 24 Ken Griffey Jr. AS .25 .08
❑ 25 Jack Morris AS .05 .01
❑ 26 Danny Tartabull AS .05 .01
❑ 27 Cecil Fielder AS .05 .01
❑ 28 Roberto Alomar AS .10 .02
❑ 29 Sandy Alomar Jr. AS .05 .01
❑ 30 Rickey Henderson AS .15 .05
❑ 31 Ken Hill .05 .01
❑ 32 John Habyan .05 .01
❑ 33 Otis Nixon HL .05 .01
❑ 34 Tim Wallach .05 .01
❑ 35 Cal Ripken .75 .30
❑ 36 Gary Carter .10 .02
❑ 37 Juan Agosto .05 .01
❑ 38 Doug Dascenzo .05 .01
❑ 39 Kirk Gibson .10 .02
❑ 40 Benito Santiago .10 .02
❑ 41 Otis Nixon .05 .01
❑ 42 Andy Allanson .05 .01
❑ 43 Brian Holman .05 .01
❑ 44 Dick Schofield .05 .01
❑ 45 Dave Magadan .05 .01
❑ 46 Rafael Palmeiro .15 .05
❑ 47 Jody Reed .05 .01
❑ 48 Ivan Calderon .05 .01
❑ 49 Greg W. Harris .05 .01
❑ 50 Chris Sabo .05 .01
❑ 51 Paul Molitor .10 .02
❑ 52 Robby Thompson .05 .01
❑ 53 Dave Smith .05 .01
❑ 54 Mark Davis .05 .01
❑ 55 Kevin Brown .10 .02
❑ 56 Donn Pall .05 .01
❑ 57 Len Dykstra .10 .02
❑ 58 Roberto Alomar .15 .05
❑ 59 Jeff D. Robinson .05 .01
❑ 60 Willie McGee .10 .02
❑ 61 Jay Buhner .10 .02
❑ 62 Mike Pagliarulo .05 .01
❑ 63 Paul O'Neill .15 .05
❑ 64 Hubie Brooks .05 .01
❑ 65 Kelly Gruber .05 .01
❑ 66 Ken Caminiti .10 .02
❑ 67 Gary Redus .05 .01
❑ 68 Harold Baines .10 .02
❑ 69 Charlie Hough .10 .02
❑ 70 B.J. Surhoff .10 .02
❑ 71 Walt Weiss .05 .01
❑ 72 Shawn Hillegas .05 .01
❑ 73 Roberto Kelly .05 .01
❑ 74 Jeff Ballard .05 .01
❑ 75 Craig Biggio .15 .05
❑ 76 Pat Combs .05 .01
❑ 77 Jeff M. Robinson .05 .01
❑ 78 Tim Belcher .05 .01
❑ 79 Cris Carpenter .05 .01
❑ 80 Checklist 1-79 .05 .01
❑ 81 Steve Avery .05 .01
❑ 82 Chris James .05 .01
❑ 83 Brian Harper .05 .01
❑ 84 Charlie Leibrandt .05 .01
❑ 85 Mickey Tettleton .05 .01
❑ 86 Pete O'Brien .05 .01
❑ 87 Danny Darwin .05 .01
❑ 88 Bob Walk .05 .01
❑ 89 Jeff Reardon .10 .02
❑ 90 Bobby Rose .05 .01
❑ 91 Danny Jackson .05 .01
❑ 92 John Morris .05 .01
❑ 93 Bud Black .05 .01
❑ 94 Tommy Greene HL .05 .01
❑ 95 Rick Aguilera .10 .02
❑ 96 Gary Gaetti .10 .02
❑ 97 David Cone .10 .02
❑ 98 John Olerud .10 .02
❑ 99 Joel Skinner .05 .01
❑ 100 Jay Bell .10 .02
❑ 101 Bob Milacki .05 .01
❑ 102 Norm Charlton .05 .01
❑ 103 Chuck Crim .05 .01
❑ 104 Terry Steinbach .05 .01
❑ 105 Juan Samuel .05 .01
❑ 106 Steve Howe .05 .01
❑ 107 Rafael Belliard .05 .01
❑ 108 Joey Cora .05 .01
❑ 109 Tommy Greene .05 .01
❑ 110 Gregg Olson .05 .01
❑ 111 Frank Tanana .05 .01
❑ 112 Lee Smith .10 .02
❑ 113 Greg A. Harris .05 .01
❑ 114 Dwayne Henry .05 .01
❑ 115 Chili Davis .10 .02
❑ 116 Kent Mercker .05 .01
❑ 117 Brian Barnes .05 .01
❑ 118 Rich DeLucia .05 .01
❑ 119 Andre Dawson .10 .02
❑ 120 Carlos Baerga .05 .01
❑ 121 Mike LaValliere .05 .01
❑ 122 Jeff Gray .05 .01
❑ 123 Bruce Hurst .05 .01
❑ 124 Alvin Davis .05 .01
❑ 125 John Candelaria .05 .01
❑ 126 Matt Nokes .05 .01
❑ 127 George Bell .05 .01
❑ 128 Bret Saberhagen .10 .02
❑ 129 Jeff Russell .05 .01
❑ 130 Jim Abbott .15 .05
❑ 131 Bill Gullickson .05 .01
❑ 132 Todd Zeile .05 .01
❑ 133 Dave Winfield .10 .02
❑ 134 Wally Whitehurst .05 .01
❑ 135 Matt Williams .10 .02
❑ 136 Tom Browning .05 .01
❑ 137 Marquis Grissom .10 .02
❑ 138 Erik Hanson .05 .01
❑ 139 Rob Dibble .10 .02
❑ 140 Don August .05 .01
❑ 141 Tom Henke .05 .01
❑ 142 Dan Pasqua .05 .01
❑ 143 George Brett .60 .25
❑ 144 Jerald Clark .05 .01
❑ 145 Robin Ventura .10 .02
❑ 146 Dale Murphy .15 .05
❑ 147 Dennis Eckersley .10 .02
❑ 148 Eric Yelding .05 .01
❑ 149 Mario Diaz .05 .01
❑ 150 Casey Candaele .05 .01
❑ 151 Steve Olin .05 .01
❑ 152 Luis Salazar .05 .01
❑ 153 Kevin Maas .05 .01
❑ 154 Nolan Ryan HL .50 .20
❑ 155 Barry Jones .05 .01
❑ 156 Chris Hoiles .05 .01
❑ 157 Bob Ojeda .05 .01
❑ 158 Pedro Guerrero .10 .02
❑ 159 Paul Assenmacher .05 .01
❑ 160 Checklist 80-157 .05 .01
❑ 161 Mike Macfarlane .05 .01
❑ 162 Craig Lefferts .05 .01
❑ 163 Brian Hunter .05 .01
❑ 164 Alan Trammell .10 .02
❑ 165 Ken Griffey Jr. .40 .15
❑ 166 Lance Parrish .10 .02
❑ 167 Brian Downing .05 .01
❑ 168 John Barfield .05 .01
❑ 169 Jack Clark .10 .02
❑ 170 Chris Nabholz .05 .01
❑ 171 Tim Teufel .05 .01
❑ 172 Chris Hammond .05 .01
❑ 173 Robin Yount .40 .15
❑ 174 Dave Righetti .10 .02
❑ 175 Joe Girardi .05 .01
❑ 176 Mike Boddicker .05 .01
❑ 177 Dean Palmer .10 .02
❑ 178 Greg Hibbard .05 .01
❑ 179 Randy Ready .05 .01
❑ 180 Devon White .10 .02
❑ 181 Mark Eichhorn .05 .01
❑ 182 Mike Felder .05 .01
❑ 183 Joe Klink .05 .01
❑ 184 Steve Bedrosian .05 .01
❑ 185 Barry Larkin .15 .05
❑ 186 John Franco .10 .02
❑ 187 Ed Sprague .05 .01
❑ 188 Mark Portugal .05 .01
❑ 189 Jose Lind .05 .01
❑ 190 Bob Welch .05 .01
❑ 191 Alex Fernandez .05 .01
❑ 192 Gary Sheffield .10 .02
❑ 193 Rickey Henderson .25 .08
❑ 194 Rod Nichols .05 .01
❑ 195 Scott Kamieniecki .05 .01
❑ 196 Mike Flanagan .05 .01
❑ 197 Steve Finley .10 .02
❑ 198 Darren Daulton .10 .02
❑ 199 Leo Gomez .05 .01
❑ 200 Mike Morgan .05 .01
❑ 201 Bob Tewksbury .05 .01
❑ 202 Sid Bream .05 .01
❑ 203 Sandy Alomar Jr. .05 .01
❑ 204 Greg Gagne .05 .01
❑ 205 Juan Berenguer .05 .01
❑ 206 Cecil Fielder .10 .02
❑ 207 Randy Johnson .25 .08
❑ 208 Tony Pena .05 .01
❑ 209 Doug Drabek .05 .01
❑ 210 Wade Boggs .15 .05
❑ 211 Bryan Harvey .05 .01
❑ 212 Jose Vizcaino .05 .01
❑ 213 Alonzo Powell .05 .01
❑ 214 Will Clark .15 .05
❑ 215 Rickey Henderson HL .15 .05
❑ 216 Jack Morris .10 .02
❑ 217 Junior Felix .05 .01
❑ 218 Vince Coleman .05 .01
❑ 219 Jimmy Key .10 .02
❑ 220 Alex Cole .05 .01
❑ 221 Bill Landrum .05 .01
❑ 222 Randy Milligan .05 .01
❑ 223 Jose Rijo .05 .01
❑ 224 Greg Vaughn .05 .01
❑ 225 Dave Stewart .10 .02
❑ 226 Lenny Harris .05 .01
❑ 227 Scott Sanderson .05 .01
❑ 228 Jeff Blauser .05 .01
❑ 229 Ozzie Guillen .10 .02
❑ 230 John Kruk .10 .02
❑ 231 Bob Melvin .05 .01
❑ 232 Milt Cuyler .05 .01
❑ 233 Felix Jose .05 .01
❑ 234 Ellis Burks .10 .02
❑ 235 Pete Harnisch .05 .01
❑ 236 Kevin Tapani .05 .01
❑ 237 Terry Pendleton .10 .02
❑ 238 Mark Gardner .05 .01
❑ 239 Harold Reynolds .10 .02
❑ 240 Checklist 158-237 .05 .01
❑ 241 Mike Harkey .05 .01
❑ 242 Felix Fermin .05 .01
❑ 243 Barry Bonds 1.00 .40
❑ 244 Roger Clemens .50 .20
❑ 245 Dennis Rasmussen .05 .01
❑ 246 Jose DeLeon .05 .01
❑ 247 Orel Hershiser .10 .02
❑ 248 Mel Hall .05 .01
❑ 249 Rick Wilkins .05 .01
❑ 250 Tom Gordon .05 .01
❑ 251 Kevin Reimer .05 .01
❑ 252 Luis Polonia .05 .01
❑ 253 Mike Henneman .05 .01
❑ 254 Tom Pagnozzi .05 .01
❑ 255 Chuck Finley .10 .02
❑ 256 Mackey Sasser .05 .01
❑ 257 John Burkett .05 .01
❑ 258 Hal Morris .05 .01
❑ 259 Larry Walker .15 .05
❑ 260 Bill Swift .05 .01
❑ 261 Joe Oliver .05 .01
❑ 262 Julio Machado .05 .01
❑ 263 Todd Stottlemyre .05 .01
❑ 264 Matt Merullo .05 .01
❑ 265 Brent Mayne .05 .01
❑ 266 Thomas Howard .05 .01
❑ 267 Lance Johnson .05 .01
❑ 268 Terry Mulholland .05 .01
❑ 269 Rick Honeycutt .05 .01
❑ 270 Luis Gonzalez .10 .02

❑ 271 Jose Guzman .05 .01
❑ 272 Jimmy Jones .05 .01
❑ 273 Mark Lewis .05 .01
❑ 274 Rene Gonzales .05 .01
❑ 275 Jeff Johnson .05 .01
❑ 276 Dennis Martinez HL .05 .01
❑ 277 Delino DeShields .05 .01
❑ 278 Sam Horn .05 .01
❑ 279 Kevin Gross .05 .01
❑ 280 Jose Oquendo .05 .01
❑ 281 Mark Grace .15 .05
❑ 282 Mark Gubicza .05 .01
❑ 283 Fred McGriff .15 .05
❑ 284 Ron Gant .10 .02
❑ 285 Lou Whitaker .10 .02
❑ 286 Edgar Martinez .15 .05
❑ 287 Ron Tingley .05 .01
❑ 288 Kevin McReynolds .05 .01
❑ 289 Ivan Rodriguez .25 .08
❑ 290 Mike Gardiner .05 .01
❑ 291 Chris Haney .05 .01
❑ 292 Darrin Jackson .05 .01
❑ 293 Bill Doran .05 .01
❑ 294 Ted Higuera .05 .01
❑ 295 Jeff Brantley .05 .01
❑ 296 Les Lancaster .05 .01
❑ 297 Jim Eisenreich .05 .01
❑ 298 Ruben Sierra .10 .02
❑ 299 Scott Radinsky .05 .01
❑ 300 Jose DeJesus .05 .01
❑ 301 Mike Timlin .05 .01
❑ 302 Luis Sojo .05 .01
❑ 303 Kelly Downs .05 .01
❑ 304 Scott Bankhead .05 .01
❑ 305 Pedro Munoz .05 .01
❑ 306 Scott Scudder .05 .01
❑ 307 Kevin Elster .05 .01
❑ 308 Duane Ward .05 .01
❑ 309 Darryl Kile .10 .02
❑ 310 Orlando Merced .05 .01
❑ 311 Dave Henderson .05 .01
❑ 312 Tim Raines .10 .02
❑ 313 Mark Lee .05 .01
❑ 314 Mike Gallego .05 .01
❑ 315 Charles Nagy .05 .01
❑ 316 Jesse Barfield .05 .01
❑ 317 Todd Frohwirth .05 .01
❑ 318 Al Osuna .05 .01
❑ 319 Darrin Fletcher .05 .01
❑ 320 Checklist 238-316 .05 .01
❑ 321 David Segui .05 .01
❑ 322 Stan Javier .05 .01
❑ 323 Bryn Smith .05 .01
❑ 324 Jeff Treadway .05 .01
❑ 325 Mark Whiten .05 .01
❑ 326 Kent Hrbek .10 .02
❑ 327 David Justice .10 .02
❑ 328 Tony Phillips .05 .01
❑ 329 Rob Murphy .05 .01
❑ 330 Kevin Morton .05 .01
❑ 331 John Smiley .05 .01
❑ 332 Luis Rivera .05 .01
❑ 333 Wally Joyner .10 .02
❑ 334 Heathcliff Slocumb .05 .01
❑ 335 Rick Cerone .05 .01
❑ 336 Mike Remlinger .05 .01
❑ 337 Mike Moore .05 .01
❑ 338 Lloyd McClendon .05 .01
❑ 339 Al Newman .05 .01
❑ 340 Kirk McCaskill .05 .01
❑ 341 Howard Johnson .05 .01
❑ 342 Greg Myers .05 .01
❑ 343 Kal Daniels .05 .01
❑ 344 Bernie Williams .15 .05
❑ 345 Shane Mack .05 .01
❑ 346 Gary Thurman .05 .01
❑ 347 Dante Bichette .10 .02
❑ 348 Mark McGwire .60 .25
❑ 349 Travis Fryman .10 .02
❑ 350 Ray Lankford .10 .02
❑ 351 Mike Jeffcoat .05 .01
❑ 352 Jack McDowell .05 .01
❑ 353 Mitch Williams .05 .01
❑ 354 Mike Devereaux .05 .01
❑ 355 Andres Galarraga .10 .02
❑ 356 Henry Cotto .05 .01
❑ 357 Scott Bailes .05 .01
❑ 358 Jeff Bagwell .25 .08
❑ 359 Scott Leius .05 .01
❑ 360 Zane Smith .05 .01
❑ 361 Bill Pecota .05 .01
❑ 362 Tony Fernandez .05 .01
❑ 363 Glenn Braggs .05 .01
❑ 364 Bill Spiers .05 .01
❑ 365 Vicente Palacios .05 .01
❑ 366 Tim Burke .05 .01
❑ 367 Randy Tomlin .05 .01
❑ 368 Kenny Rogers .10 .02
❑ 369 Brett Butler .10 .02
❑ 370 Pat Kelly .05 .01
❑ 371 Bip Roberts .05 .01
❑ 372 Gregg Jefferies .05 .01
❑ 373 Kevin Bass .05 .01
❑ 374 Ron Karkovice .05 .01
❑ 375 Paul Gibson .05 .01
❑ 376 Bernard Gilkey .05 .01
❑ 377 Dave Gallagher .05 .01
❑ 378 Bill Wegman .05 .01
❑ 379 Pat Borders .05 .01
❑ 380 Ed Whitson .05 .01
❑ 381 Gilberto Reyes .05 .01
❑ 382 Russ Swan .05 .01
❑ 383 Andy Van Slyke .15 .05
❑ 384 Wes Chamberlain .05 .01
❑ 385 Steve Chitren .05 .01
❑ 386 Greg Olson .05 .01
❑ 387 Brian McRae .05 .01
❑ 388 Rich Rodriguez .05 .01
❑ 389 Steve Decker .05 .01
❑ 390 Chuck Knoblauch .10 .02
❑ 391 Bobby Witt .05 .01
❑ 392 Eddie Murray .25 .08
❑ 393 Juan Gonzalez .15 .05
❑ 394 Scott Ruskin .05 .01
❑ 395 Jay Howell .05 .01
❑ 396 Checklist 317-396 .05 .01
❑ 397 Royce Clayton RR .05 .01
❑ 398 John Jaha RR RC .25 .08
❑ 399 Dan Wilson RR .05 .01
❑ 400 Archie Corbin .05 .01
❑ 401 Barry Manuel RR .05 .01
❑ 402 Kim Batiste RR .05 .01
❑ 403 Pat Mahomes RR RC .25 .08
❑ 404 Dave Fleming .05 .01
❑ 405 Jeff Juden RR .05 .01
❑ 406 Jim Thome .25 .08
❑ 407 Sam Militello RR .05 .01
❑ 408 Jeff Nelson RR RC .40 .15
❑ 409 Anthony Young .05 .01
❑ 410 Tino Martinez RR .15 .05
❑ 411 Jeff Mutis RR .05 .01
❑ 412 Rey Sanchez RR RC .25 .08
❑ 413 Chris Gardner RR .05 .01
❑ 414 John Vander Wal RR .05 .01
❑ 415 Reggie Sanders .10 .02
❑ 416 Brian Williams RR RC .10 .02
❑ 417 Mo Sanford RR .05 .01
❑ 418 David Weathers RR RC .40 .15
❑ 419 Hector Fajardo RR RC .10 .02
❑ 420 Steve Foster RR .05 .01
❑ 421 Lance Dickson RR .05 .01
❑ 422 Andre Dawson AS .05 .01
❑ 423 Ozzie Smith AS .25 .08
❑ 424 Chris Sabo AS .05 .01
❑ 425 Tony Gwynn AS .15 .05
❑ 426 Tom Glavine AS .10 .02
❑ 427 Bobby Bonilla AS .05 .01
❑ 428 Will Clark AS .10 .02
❑ 429 Ryne Sandberg AS .25 .08
❑ 430 Benito Santiago AS .05 .01
❑ 431 Ivan Calderon AS .05 .01
❑ 432 Ozzie Smith .40 .15
❑ 433 Tim Leary .05 .01
❑ 434 Bret Saberhagen HL .05 .01
❑ 435 Mel Rojas .05 .01
❑ 436 Ben McDonald .05 .01
❑ 437 Tim Crews .05 .01
❑ 438 Rex Hudler .05 .01
❑ 439 Chico Walker .05 .01
❑ 440 Kurt Stillwell .05 .01
❑ 441 Tony Gwynn .30 .10
❑ 442 John Smoltz .15 .05
❑ 443 Lloyd Moseby .05 .01
❑ 444 Mike Schooler .05 .01
❑ 445 Joe Grahe .05 .01
❑ 446 Dwight Gooden .10 .02
❑ 447 Oil Can Boyd .05 .01
❑ 448 John Marzano .05 .01
❑ 449 Bret Barberie .05 .01
❑ 450 Mike Maddux .05 .01
❑ 451 Jeff Reed .05 .01
❑ 452 Dale Sveum .05 .01
❑ 453 Jose Uribe .05 .01
❑ 454 Bob Scanlan .05 .01
❑ 455 Kevin Appier .10 .02
❑ 456 Jeff Huson .05 .01
❑ 457 Ken Patterson .05 .01
❑ 458 Ricky Jordan .05 .01
❑ 459 Tom Candiotti .05 .01
❑ 460 Lee Stevens .05 .01
❑ 461 Rod Beck RC .25 .08
❑ 462 Dave Valle .05 .01
❑ 463 Scott Erickson .05 .01
❑ 464 Chris Jones .05 .01
❑ 465 Mark Carreon .05 .01
❑ 466 Rob Ducey .05 .01
❑ 467 Jim Corsi .05 .01
❑ 468 Jeff King .05 .01
❑ 469 Curt Young .05 .01
❑ 470 Bo Jackson .25 .08
❑ 471 Chris Bosio .05 .01
❑ 472 Jamie Quirk .05 .01
❑ 473 Jesse Orosco .05 .01
❑ 474 Alvaro Espinoza .05 .01
❑ 475 Joe Orsulak .05 .01
❑ 476 Checklist 397-477 .05 .01
❑ 477 Gerald Young .05 .01
❑ 478 Wally Backman .05 .01
❑ 479 Juan Bell .05 .01
❑ 480 Mike Scioscia .05 .01
❑ 481 Omar Olivares .05 .01
❑ 482 Francisco Cabrera .05 .01
❑ 483 Greg Swindell UER
(Shown on Indians,
but listed .05 .01
❑ 484 Terry Leach .05 .01
❑ 485 Tommy Gregg .05 .01
❑ 486 Scott Aldred .05 .01
❑ 487 Greg Briley .05 .01
❑ 488 Phil Plantier .05 .01
❑ 489 Curtis Wilkerson .05 .01
❑ 490 Tom Brunansky .05 .01
❑ 491 Mike Fetters .05 .01
❑ 492 Frank Castillo .05 .01
❑ 493 Joe Boever .05 .01
❑ 494 Kirt Manwaring .05 .01
❑ 495 Wilson Alvarez HL .05 .01
❑ 496 Gene Larkin .05 .01
❑ 497 Gary DiSarcina .05 .01
❑ 498 Frank Viola .10 .02
❑ 499 Manuel Lee .05 .01
❑ 500 Albert Belle .10 .02
❑ 501 Stan Belinda .05 .01
❑ 502 Dwight Evans .15 .05
❑ 503 Eric Davis .10 .02
❑ 504 Darren Holmes .05 .01
❑ 505 Mike Bordick .05 .01
❑ 506 Dave Hansen .05 .01
❑ 507 Lee Guetterman .05 .01
❑ 508 Keith Mitchell .05 .01
❑ 509 Melido Perez .05 .01
❑ 510 Dickie Thon .05 .01
❑ 511 Mark Williamson .05 .01
❑ 512 Mark Salas .05 .01
❑ 513 Milt Thompson .05 .01
❑ 514 Mo Vaughn .10 .02
❑ 515 Jim Deshaies .05 .01
❑ 516 Rich Garces .05 .01
❑ 517 Lonnie Smith .05 .01
❑ 518 Spike Owen .05 .01
❑ 519 Tracy Jones .05 .01
❑ 520 Greg Maddux .40 .15
❑ 521 Carlos Martinez .05 .01
❑ 522 Neal Heaton .05 .01
❑ 523 Mike Greenwell .05 .01
❑ 524 Andy Benes .05 .01
❑ 525 Jeff Schaefer UER .05 .01
❑ 526 Mike Sharperson .05 .01

❑ 527 Wade Taylor	.05	.01
❑ 528 Jerome Walton	.05	.01
❑ 529 Storm Davis	.05	.01
❑ 530 Jose Hernandez RC	.25	.08
❑ 531 Mark Langston	.05	.01
❑ 532 Rob Deer	.05	.01
❑ 533 Geronimo Pena	.05	.01
❑ 534 Juan Guzman	.05	.01
❑ 535 Pete Schourek	.05	.01
❑ 536 Todd Benzinger	.05	.01
❑ 537 Billy Hatcher	.05	.01
❑ 538 Tom Foley	.05	.01
❑ 539 Dave Cochrane	.05	.01
❑ 540 Mariano Duncan	.05	.01
❑ 541 Edwin Nunez	.05	.01
❑ 542 Rance Mulliniks	.05	.01
❑ 543 Carlton Fisk	.15	.05
❑ 544 Luis Aquino	.05	.01
❑ 545 Ricky Bones	.05	.01
❑ 546 Craig Grebeck	.05	.01
❑ 547 Charlie Hayes	.05	.01
❑ 548 Jose Canseco	.15	.05
❑ 549 Andujar Cedeno	.05	.01
❑ 550 Geno Petralli	.05	.01
❑ 551 Javier Ortiz	.05	.01
❑ 552 Rudy Seanez	.05	.01
❑ 553 Rich Gedman	.05	.01
❑ 554 Eric Plunk	.05	.01
❑ 555 N.Ryan/G.Gossage HL	.40	.15
❑ 556 Checklist 478-555	.05	.01
❑ 557 Greg Colbrunn	.05	.01
❑ 558 Chito Martinez	.05	.01
❑ 559 Darryl Strawberry	.10	.02
❑ 560 Luis Alicea	.05	.01
❑ 561 Dwight Smith	.05	.01
❑ 562 Terry Shumpert	.05	.01
❑ 563 Jim Vatcher	.05	.01
❑ 564 Deion Sanders	.15	.05
❑ 565 Walt Terrell	.05	.01
❑ 566 Dave Burba	.05	.01
❑ 567 Dave Howard	.05	.01
❑ 568 Todd Hundley	.05	.01
❑ 569 Jack Daugherty	.05	.01
❑ 570 Scott Cooper	.05	.01
❑ 571 Bill Sampen	.05	.01
❑ 572 Jose Melendez	.05	.01
❑ 573 Freddie Benavides	.05	.01
❑ 574 Jim Gantner	.05	.01
❑ 575 Trevor Wilson	.05	.01
❑ 576 Ryne Sandberg	.40	.15
❑ 577 Kevin Seitzer	.05	.01
❑ 578 Gerald Alexander	.05	.01
❑ 579 Mike Huff	.05	.01
❑ 580 Von Hayes	.05	.01
❑ 581 Derek Bell	.10	.02
❑ 582 Mike Stanley	.05	.01
❑ 583 Kevin Mitchell	.05	.01
❑ 584 Mike Jackson	.05	.01
❑ 585 Dan Gladden	.05	.01
❑ 586 Ted Power UER (Wrong year given for signing with	.05	.01
❑ 587 Jeff Innis	.05	.01
❑ 588 Bob MacDonald	.05	.01
❑ 589 Jose Tolentino	.05	.01
❑ 590 Bob Patterson	.05	.01
❑ 591 Scott Brosius RC	.40	.15
❑ 592 Frank Thomas	.25	.08
❑ 593 Darryl Hamilton	.05	.01
❑ 594 Kirk Dressendorfer	.05	.01
❑ 595 Jeff Shaw	.05	.01
❑ 596 Don Mattingly	.60	.25
❑ 597 Glenn Davis	.05	.01
❑ 598 Andy Mota	.05	.01
❑ 599 Jason Grimsley	.05	.01
❑ 600 Jim Poole	.05	.01
❑ 601 Jim Gott	.05	.01
❑ 602 Stan Royer	.05	.01
❑ 603 Marvin Freeman	.05	.01
❑ 604 Denis Boucher	.05	.01
❑ 605 Denny Neagle	.10	.02
❑ 606 Mark Lemke	.05	.01
❑ 607 Jerry Don Gleaton	.05	.01
❑ 608 Brent Knackert	.05	.01
❑ 609 Carlos Quintana	.05	.01
❑ 610 Bobby Bonilla	.10	.02
❑ 611 Joe Hesketh	.05	.01
❑ 612 Daryl Boston	.05	.01
❑ 613 Shawon Dunston	.05	.01
❑ 614 Danny Cox	.05	.01
❑ 615 Darren Lewis	.05	.01
❑ 616 Mercker/Pena/Wohlers UER	.05	.01
❑ 617 Kirby Puckett	.25	.08
❑ 618 Franklin Stubbs	.05	.01
❑ 619 Chris Donnels	.05	.01
❑ 620 David Wells UER	.10	.02
❑ 621 Mike Aldrete	.05	.01
❑ 622 Bob Kipper	.05	.01
❑ 623 Anthony Telford	.05	.01
❑ 624 Randy Myers	.05	.01
❑ 625 Willie Randolph	.10	.02
❑ 626 Joe Slusarski	.05	.01
❑ 627 John Wetteland	.10	.02
❑ 628 Greg Cadaret	.05	.01
❑ 629 Tom Glavine	.15	.05
❑ 630 Wilson Alvarez	.05	.01
❑ 631 Wally Ritchie	.05	.01
❑ 632 Mike Mussina	.25	.08
❑ 633 Mark Leiter	.05	.01
❑ 634 Gerald Perry	.05	.01
❑ 635 Matt Young	.05	.01
❑ 636 Checklist 556-635	.05	.01
❑ 637 Scott Hemond	.05	.01
❑ 638 David West	.05	.01
❑ 639 Jim Clancy	.05	.01
❑ 640 Doug Piatt UER (Not born in 1955 as on card; inc	.05	.01
❑ 641 Omar Vizquel	.15	.05
❑ 642 Rick Sutcliffe	.10	.02
❑ 643 Glenallen Hill	.05	.01
❑ 644 Gary Varsho	.05	.01
❑ 645 Tony Fossas	.05	.01
❑ 646 Jack Howell	.05	.01
❑ 647 Jim Campanis	.05	.01
❑ 648 Chris Gwynn	.05	.01
❑ 649 Jim Leyritz	.05	.01
❑ 650 Chuck McElroy	.05	.01
❑ 651 Sean Berry	.05	.01
❑ 652 Donald Harris	.05	.01
❑ 653 Don Slaught	.05	.01
❑ 654 Rusty Meacham	.05	.01
❑ 655 Scott Terry	.05	.01
❑ 656 Ramon Martinez	.05	.01
❑ 657 Keith Miller	.05	.01
❑ 658 Ramon Garcia	.05	.01
❑ 659 Milt Hill	.05	.01
❑ 660 Steve Frey	.05	.01
❑ 661 Bob McClure	.05	.01
❑ 662 Ced Landrum	.05	.01
❑ 663 Doug Henry RC	.10	.02
❑ 664 Candy Maldonado	.05	.01
❑ 665 Carl Willis	.05	.01
❑ 666 Jeff Montgomery	.05	.01
❑ 667 Craig Shipley	.05	.01
❑ 668 Warren Newson	.05	.01
❑ 669 Mickey Morandini	.05	.01
❑ 670 Brook Jacoby	.05	.01
❑ 671 Ryan Bowen	.05	.01
❑ 672 Bill Krueger	.05	.01
❑ 673 Rob Mallicoat	.05	.01
❑ 674 Doug Jones	.05	.01
❑ 675 Scott Livingstone	.05	.01
❑ 676 Danny Tartabull	.05	.01
❑ 677 Joe Carter HL	.05	.01
❑ 678 Cecil Espy	.05	.01
❑ 679 Randy Velarde	.05	.01
❑ 680 Bruce Ruffin	.05	.01
❑ 681 Ted Wood	.05	.01
❑ 682 Dan Plesac	.05	.01
❑ 683 Eric Bullock	.05	.01
❑ 684 Junior Ortiz	.05	.01
❑ 685 Dave Hollins	.05	.01
❑ 686 Dennis Martinez	.10	.02
❑ 687 Larry Andersen	.05	.01
❑ 688 Doug Simons	.05	.01
❑ 689 Tim Spehr	.05	.01
❑ 690 Calvin Jones	.05	.01
❑ 691 Mark Guthrie	.05	.01
❑ 692 Alfredo Griffin	.05	.01
❑ 693 Joe Carter	.10	.02
❑ 694 Terry Mathews	.05	.01
❑ 695 Pascual Perez	.05	.01
❑ 696 Gene Nelson	.05	.01
❑ 697 Gerald Williams	.05	.01
❑ 698 Chris Cron	.05	.01
❑ 699 Steve Buechele	.05	.01
❑ 700 Paul McClellan	.05	.01
❑ 701 Jim Lindeman	.05	.01
❑ 702 Francisco Oliveras	.05	.01
❑ 703 Rob Maurer	.05	.01
❑ 704 Pat Hentgen	.05	.01
❑ 705 Jaime Navarro	.05	.01
❑ 706 Mike Magnante RC	.10	.02
❑ 707 Nolan Ryan	1.00	.40
❑ 708 Bobby Thigpen	.05	.01
❑ 709 John Cerutti	.05	.01
❑ 710 Steve Wilson	.05	.01
❑ 711 Hensley Meulens	.05	.01
❑ 712 Rheal Cormier	.05	.01
❑ 713 Scott Bradley	.05	.01
❑ 714 Mitch Webster	.05	.01
❑ 715 Roger Mason	.05	.01
❑ 716 Checklist 636-716	.05	.01
❑ 717 Jeff Fassero	.05	.01
❑ 718 Cal Eldred	.05	.01
❑ 719 Sid Fernandez	.05	.01
❑ 720 Bob Zupcic RC	.10	.02
❑ 721 Jose Offerman	.05	.01
❑ 722 Cliff Brantley	.05	.01
❑ 723 Ron Darling	.05	.01
❑ 724 Dave Stieb	.05	.01
❑ 725 Hector Villanueva	.05	.01
❑ 726 Mike Hartley	.05	.01
❑ 727 Arthur Rhodes	.05	.01
❑ 728 Randy Bush	.05	.01
❑ 729 Steve Sax	.05	.01
❑ 730 Dave Otto	.05	.01
❑ 731 John Wehner	.05	.01
❑ 732 Dave Martinez	.05	.01
❑ 733 Ruben Amaro	.05	.01
❑ 734 Billy Ripken	.05	.01
❑ 735 Steve Farr	.05	.01
❑ 736 Shawn Abner	.05	.01
❑ 737 Gil Heredia RC	.25	.08
❑ 738 Ron Jones	.05	.01
❑ 739 Tony Castillo	.05	.01
❑ 740 Sammy Sosa	.25	.08
❑ 741 Julio Franco	.10	.02
❑ 742 Tim Naehring	.05	.01
❑ 743 Steve Wapnick	.05	.01
❑ 744 Craig Wilson	.05	.01
❑ 745 Darrin Chapin	.05	.01
❑ 746 Chris George	.05	.01
❑ 747 Mike Simms	.05	.01
❑ 748 Rosario Rodriguez	.05	.01
❑ 749 Skeeter Barnes	.05	.01
❑ 750 Roger McDowell	.05	.01
❑ 751 Dann Howitt	.05	.01
❑ 752 Paul Sorrento	.05	.01
❑ 753 Braulio Castillo	.05	.01
❑ 754 Yorkis Perez	.05	.01
❑ 755 Willie Fraser	.05	.01
❑ 756 Jeremy Hernandez RC	.10	.02
❑ 757 Curt Schilling	.15	.05
❑ 758 Steve Lyons	.05	.01
❑ 759 Dave Anderson	.05	.01
❑ 760 Willie Banks	.05	.01
❑ 761 Mark Leonard	.05	.01
❑ 762 Jack Armstrong (Listed on Indians, but shown on	.05	.01
❑ 763 Scott Servais	.05	.01
❑ 764 Ray Stephens	.05	.01
❑ 765 Junior Noboa	.05	.01
❑ 766 Jim Olander	.05	.01
❑ 767 Joe Magrane	.05	.01
❑ 768 Lance Blankenship	.05	.01
❑ 769 Mike Humphreys	.05	.01
❑ 770 Jarvis Brown	.05	.01
❑ 771 Damon Berryhill	.05	.01
❑ 772 Alejandro Pena	.05	.01
❑ 773 Jose Mesa	.05	.01
❑ 774 Gary Cooper	.05	.01
❑ 775 Carney Lansford	.10	.02
❑ 776 Mike Bielecki (Shown on Cubs, but listed on Brav	.05	.01

❑ 777 Charlie O'Brien	.05	.01
❑ 778 Carlos Hernandez	.05	.01
❑ 779 Howard Farmer	.05	.01
❑ 780 Mike Stanton	.05	.01
❑ 781 Reggie Harris	.05	.01
❑ 782 Xavier Hernandez	.05	.01
❑ 783 Bryan Hickerson RC	.10	.02
❑ 784 Checklist 717-784 and BC1-BC8	.05	.01

1992 Donruss Rookies

❑ COMPLETE SET (132)	10.00	4.00
❑ 1 Kyle Abbott	.05	.01
❑ 2 Troy Afenir	.05	.01
❑ 3 Rich Amaral RC	.10	.02
❑ 4 Ruben Amaro	.05	.01
❑ 5 Billy Ashley RC	.10	.02
❑ 6 Pedro Astacio RC	.25	.08
❑ 7 Jim Austin	.05	.01
❑ 8 Robert Ayrault	.05	.01
❑ 9 Kevin Baez	.05	.01
❑ 10 Esteban Beltre	.05	.01
❑ 11 Brian Bohanon	.05	.01
❑ 12 Kent Bottenfield RC	.25	.08
❑ 13 Jeff Branson	.05	.01
❑ 14 Brad Brink	.05	.01
❑ 15 John Briscoe	.05	.01
❑ 16 Doug Brocail RC	.10	.02
❑ 17 Rico Brogna	.05	.01
❑ 18 J.T. Bruett	.05	.01
❑ 19 Jacob Brumfield	.05	.01
❑ 20 Jim Bullinger	.05	.01
❑ 21 Kevin Campbell	.05	.01
❑ 22 Pedro Castellano RC	.10	.02
❑ 23 Mike Christopher	.05	.01
❑ 24 Archi Cianfrocco RC	.10	.02
❑ 25 Mark Clark RC	.10	.02
❑ 26 Craig Colbert	.05	.01
❑ 27 Victor Cole	.05	.01
❑ 28 Steve Cooke RC	.10	.02
❑ 29 Tim Costo	.05	.01
❑ 30 Chad Curtis RC	.25	.08
❑ 31 Doug Davis	.05	.01
❑ 32 Gary DiSarcina	.05	.01
❑ 33 John Doherty RC	.10	.02
❑ 34 Mike Draper	.05	.01
❑ 35 Monty Fariss	.05	.01
❑ 36 Bien Figueroa	.05	.01
❑ 37 John Flaherty	.05	.01
❑ 38 Tim Fortugno	.05	.01
❑ 39 Eric Fox RC	.10	.02
❑ 40 Jeff Frye RC	.10	.02
❑ 41 Ramon Garcia	.05	.01
❑ 42 Brent Gates RC	.10	.02
❑ 43 Tom Goodwin	.05	.01
❑ 44 Buddy Groom RC	.10	.02
❑ 45 Jeff Grotewold	.05	.01
❑ 46 Juan Guerrero	.05	.01
❑ 47 Johnny Guzman RC	.10	.02
❑ 48 Shawn Hare RC	.10	.02
❑ 49 Ryan Hawblitzel RC	.10	.02
❑ 50 Bert Heffernan	.05	.01
❑ 51 Butch Henry	.05	.01
❑ 52 Cesar Hernandez RC	.10	.02
❑ 53 Vince Horsman	.05	.01
❑ 54 Steve Hosey	.05	.01
❑ 55 Pat Howell	.05	.01
❑ 56 Peter Hoy	.05	.01
❑ 57 Jonathan Hurst RC	.10	.02
❑ 58 Mark Hutton RC	.10	.02
❑ 59 Shawn Jeter RC	.10	.02
❑ 60 Joel Johnston	.05	.01
❑ 61 Jeff Kent RC	2.50	1.00
❑ 62 Kurt Knudsen RC	.10	.02
❑ 63 Kevin Koslofski	.05	.01
❑ 64 Danny Leon	.05	.01
❑ 65 Jesse Levis	.05	.01
❑ 66 Tom Marsh	.05	.01
❑ 67 Ed Martel	.05	.01
❑ 68 Al Martin RC	.25	.08
❑ 69 Pedro Martinez	2.00	.75
❑ 70 Derrick May	.05	.01
❑ 71 Matt Maysey	.05	.01
❑ 72 Russ McGinnis	.05	.01
❑ 73 Tim McIntosh	.05	.01
❑ 74 Jim McNamara	.05	.01
❑ 75 Jeff McNeely	.05	.01
❑ 76 Rusty Meacham	.05	.01
❑ 77 Tony Menendez	.05	.01
❑ 78 Henry Mercedes	.05	.01
❑ 79 Paul Miller	.05	.01
❑ 80 Joe Millette	.05	.01
❑ 81 Blas Minor	.05	.01
❑ 82 Dennis Moeller	.05	.01
❑ 83 Raul Mondesi	.10	.02
❑ 84 Rob Natal	.05	.01
❑ 85 Troy Neel RC	.10	.02
❑ 86 David Nied RC	.10	.02
❑ 87 Jerry Nielson	.05	.01
❑ 88 Donovan Osborne	.05	.01
❑ 89 John Patterson RC	.10	.02
❑ 90 Roger Pavlik RC	.10	.02
❑ 91 Dan Peltier	.05	.01
❑ 92 Jim Pena	.05	.01
❑ 93 William Pennyfeather	.05	.01
❑ 94 Mike Perez	.05	.01
❑ 95 Hipolito Pichardo RC	.10	.02
❑ 96 Greg Pirkl RC	.10	.02
❑ 97 Harvey Pulliam	.05	.01
❑ 98 Manny Ramirez RC	4.00	1.50
❑ 99 Pat Rapp RC	.10	.02
❑ 100 Jeff Reboulet	.05	.01
❑ 101 Darren Reed	.05	.01
❑ 102 Shane Reynolds RC	.25	.08
❑ 103 Bill Risley	.05	.01
❑ 104 Ben Rivera	.05	.01
❑ 105 Henry Rodriguez	.05	.01
❑ 106 Rico Rossy	.05	.01
❑ 107 Johnny Ruffin	.05	.01
❑ 108 Steve Scarsone	.05	.01
❑ 109 Tim Scott	.05	.01
❑ 110 Steve Shifflett	.05	.01
❑ 111 Dave Silvestri	.05	.01
❑ 112 Matt Stairs RC	.25	.08
❑ 113 William Suero	.05	.01
❑ 114 Jeff Tackett	.05	.01
❑ 115 Eddie Taubensee	.10	.02
❑ 116 Rick Trlicek RC	.10	.02
❑ 117 Scooter Tucker	.05	.01
❑ 118 Shane Turner	.05	.01
❑ 119 Julio Valera	.05	.01
❑ 120 Paul Wagner RC	.10	.02
❑ 121 Tim Wakefield RC	3.00	1.25
❑ 122 Mike Walker	.05	.01
❑ 123 Bruce Walton	.05	.01
❑ 124 Lenny Webster	.05	.01
❑ 125 Bob Wickman	.25	.08
❑ 126 Mike Williams RC	.25	.08
❑ 127 Kerry Woodson	.05	.01
❑ 128 Eric Young RC	.25	.08
❑ 129 Kevin Young RC	.25	.08
❑ 130 Pete Young	.05	.01
❑ 131 Checklist 1-66	.05	.01
❑ 132 Checklist 67-132	.05	.01

1993 Donruss

❑ COMPLETE SET (792)	30.00	12.00
❑ COMPLETE SERIES 1 (396)	15.00	6.00
❑ COMPLETE SERIES 2 (396)	15.00	6.00
❑ 1 Craig Lefferts	.10	.02
❑ 2 Kent Mercker	.10	.02
❑ 3 Phil Plantier	.10	.02
❑ 4 Alex Arias	.10	.02
❑ 5 Julio Valera	.10	.02

❑ 6 Dan Wilson	.20	.07
❑ 7 Frank Thomas	.50	.20
❑ 8 Eric Anthony	.10	.02
❑ 9 Derek Lilliquist	.10	.02
❑ 10 Rafael Bournigal	.10	.02
❑ 11 Manny Alexander	.10	.02
❑ 12 Bret Barberie	.10	.02
❑ 13 Mickey Tettleton	.10	.02
❑ 14 Anthony Young	.10	.02
❑ 15 Tim Spehr	.10	.02
❑ 16 Bob Ayrault	.10	.02
❑ 17 Bill Wegman	.10	.02
❑ 18 Jay Bell	.20	.07
❑ 19 Rick Aguilera	.10	.02
❑ 20 Todd Zeile	.10	.02
❑ 21 Steve Farr	.10	.02
❑ 22 Andy Benes	.10	.02
❑ 23 Lance Blankenship	.10	.02
❑ 24 Ted Wood	.10	.02
❑ 25 Omar Vizquel	.30	.10
❑ 26 Steve Avery	.10	.02
❑ 27 Brian Bohanon	.10	.02
❑ 28 Rick Wilkins	.10	.02
❑ 29 Devon White	.20	.07
❑ 30 Bobby Ayala RC	.10	.02
❑ 31 Leo Gomez	.10	.02
❑ 32 Mike Simms	.10	.02
❑ 33 Ellis Burks	.20	.07
❑ 34 Steve Wilson	.10	.02
❑ 35 Jim Abbott	.30	.10
❑ 36 Tim Wallach	.10	.02
❑ 37 Wilson Alvarez	.10	.02
❑ 38 Daryl Boston	.10	.02
❑ 39 Sandy Alomar Jr.	.10	.02
❑ 40 Mitch Williams	.10	.02
❑ 41 Rico Brogna	.10	.02
❑ 42 Gary Varsho	.10	.02
❑ 43 Kevin Appier	.20	.07
❑ 44 Eric Wedge RC	.10	.02
❑ 45 Dante Bichette	.20	.07
❑ 46 Jose Oquendo	.10	.02
❑ 47 Mike Trombley	.10	.02
❑ 48 Dan Walters	.10	.02
❑ 49 Gerald Williams	.10	.02
❑ 50 Bud Black	.10	.02
❑ 51 Bobby Witt	.10	.02
❑ 52 Mark Davis	.10	.02
❑ 53 Shawn Barton RC	.10	.02
❑ 54 Paul Assenmacher	.10	.02
❑ 55 Kevin Reimer	.10	.02
❑ 56 Billy Ashley	.10	.02
❑ 57 Eddie Zosky	.10	.02
❑ 58 Chris Sabo	.10	.02
❑ 59 Billy Ripken	.10	.02
❑ 60 Scooter Tucker	.10	.02
❑ 61 Tim Wakefield	.50	.20
❑ 62 Mitch Webster	.10	.02
❑ 63 Jack Clark	.20	.07
❑ 64 Mark Gardner	.10	.02
❑ 65 Lee Stevens	.10	.02
❑ 66 Todd Hundley	.10	.02
❑ 67 Bobby Thigpen	.10	.02
❑ 68 Dave Hollins	.10	.02
❑ 69 Jack Armstrong	.10	.02
❑ 70 Alex Cole	.10	.02
❑ 71 Mark Carreon	.10	.02
❑ 72 Todd Worrell	.10	.02
❑ 73 Steve Shifflett	.10	.02

❑ 74 Jerald Clark .10 .02
❑ 75 Paul Molitor .20 .07
❑ 76 Larry Carter RC .10 .02
❑ 77 Rich Rowland .10 .02
❑ 78 Damon Berryhill .10 .02
❑ 79 Willie Banks .10 .02
❑ 80 Hector Villanueva .10 .02
❑ 81 Mike Gallego .10 .02
❑ 82 Tim Belcher .10 .02
❑ 83 Mike Bordick .10 .02
❑ 84 Craig Biggio .30 .10
❑ 85 Lance Parrish .20 .07
❑ 86 Brett Butler .20 .07
❑ 87 Mike Timlin .10 .02
❑ 88 Brian Barnes .10 .02
❑ 89 Brady Anderson .20 .07
❑ 90 D.J. Dozier .10 .02
❑ 91 Frank Viola .20 .07
❑ 92 Darren Daulton .20 .07
❑ 93 Chad Curtis .10 .02
❑ 94 Zane Smith .10 .02
❑ 95 George Bell .10 .02
❑ 96 Rex Hudler .10 .02
❑ 97 Mark Whiten .10 .02
❑ 98 Tim Teufel .10 .02
❑ 99 Kevin Ritz .10 .02
❑ 100 Jeff Brantley .10 .02
❑ 101 Jeff Conine .20 .07
❑ 102 Vinny Castilla .50 .20
❑ 103 Greg Vaughn .10 .02
❑ 104 Steve Buechele .10 .02
❑ 105 Darren Reed .10 .02
❑ 106 Bip Roberts .10 .02
❑ 107 John Habyan .10 .02
❑ 108 Scott Servais .10 .02
❑ 109 Walt Weiss .10 .02
❑ 110 J.T.Snow RC .30 .10
❑ 111 Jay Buhner .20 .07
❑ 112 Darryl Strawberry .20 .07
❑ 113 Roger Pavlik .10 .02
❑ 114 Chris Nabholz .10 .02
❑ 115 Pat Borders .10 .02
❑ 116 Pat Howell .10 .02
❑ 117 Gregg Olson .10 .02
❑ 118 Curt Schilling .20 .07
❑ 119 Roger Clemens 1.00 .40
❑ 120 Victor Cole .10 .02
❑ 121 Gary DiSarcina .10 .02
❑ 122 Checklist 1-80
Gary Carter and
Kirt Manwaring .10 .02
❑ 123 Steve Sax .10 .02
❑ 124 Chuck Carr .10 .02
❑ 125 Mark Lewis .10 .02
❑ 126 Tony Gwynn .60 .25
❑ 127 Travis Fryman .20 .07
❑ 128 Dave Burba .10 .02
❑ 129 Wally Joyner .20 .07
❑ 130 John Smoltz .30 .10
❑ 131 Cal Eldred .10 .02
❑ 132 Checklist 81-159
(Roberto Alomar and
Devon White .20 .07
❑ 133 Arthur Rhodes .10 .02
❑ 134 Jeff Blauser .10 .02
❑ 135 Scott Cooper .10 .02
❑ 136 Doug Strange .10 .02
❑ 137 Luis Sojo .10 .02
❑ 138 Jeff Branson .10 .02
❑ 139 Alex Fernandez .10 .02
❑ 140 Ken Caminiti .20 .07
❑ 141 Charles Nagy .10 .02
❑ 142 Tom Candiotti .10 .02
❑ 143 Willie Greene .10 .02
❑ 144 John Vander Wal .10 .02
❑ 145 Kurt Knudsen .10 .02
❑ 146 John Franco .20 .07
❑ 147 Eddie Pierce RC .10 .02
❑ 148 Kim Batiste .10 .02
❑ 149 Darren Holmes .10 .02
❑ 150 Steve Cooke .10 .02
❑ 151 Terry Jorgensen .10 .02
❑ 152 Mark Clark .10 .02
❑ 153 Randy Velarde .10 .02
❑ 154 Greg W. Harris .10 .02
❑ 155 Kevin Campbell .10 .02
❑ 156 John Burkett .10 .02
❑ 157 Kevin Mitchell .10 .02
❑ 158 Deion Sanders .30 .10
❑ 159 Jose Canseco .30 .10
❑ 160 Jeff Hartsock .10 .02
❑ 161 Tom Quinlan RC .10 .02
❑ 162 Tim Pugh RC .10 .02
❑ 163 Glenn Davis .10 .02
❑ 164 Shane Reynolds .10 .02
❑ 165 Jody Reed .10 .02
❑ 166 Mike Sharperson .10 .02
❑ 167 Scott Lewis .10 .02
❑ 168 Dennis Martinez .20 .07
❑ 169 Scott Radinsky .10 .02
❑ 170 Dave Gallagher .10 .02
❑ 171 Jim Thome .30 .10
❑ 172 Terry Mulholland .10 .02
❑ 173 Milt Cuyler .10 .02
❑ 174 Bob Patterson .10 .02
❑ 175 Jeff Montgomery .10 .02
❑ 176 Tim Salmon .30 .10
❑ 177 Franklin Stubbs .10 .02
❑ 178 Donovan Osborne .10 .02
❑ 179 Jeff Reboulet .10 .02
❑ 180 Jeremy Hernandez .10 .02
❑ 181 Charlie Hayes .10 .02
❑ 182 Matt Williams .20 .07
❑ 183 Mike Raczka .10 .02
❑ 184 Francisco Cabrera .10 .02
❑ 185 Rich DeLucia .10 .02
❑ 186 Sammy Sosa .50 .20
❑ 187 Ivan Rodriguez .30 .10
❑ 188 Bret Boone .20 .07
❑ 189 Juan Guzman .10 .02
❑ 190 Tom Browning .10 .02
❑ 191 Randy Milligan .10 .02
❑ 192 Steve Finley .20 .07
❑ 193 John Patterson RR .10 .02
❑ 194 Kip Gross .10 .02
❑ 195 Tony Fossas .10 .02
❑ 196 Ivan Calderon .10 .02
❑ 197 Junior Felix .10 .02
❑ 198 Pete Schourek .10 .02
❑ 199 Craig Grebeck .10 .02
❑ 200 Juan Bell .10 .02
❑ 201 Glenallen Hill .10 .02
❑ 202 Danny Jackson .10 .02
❑ 203 John Kiely .10 .02
❑ 204 Bob Tewksbury .10 .02
❑ 205 Kevin Koslofski .10 .02
❑ 206 Craig Shipley .10 .02
❑ 207 John Jaha .10 .02
❑ 208 Royce Clayton .10 .02
❑ 209 Mike Piazza 3.00 1.25
❑ 210 Ron Gant .20 .07
❑ 211 Scott Erickson .10 .02
❑ 212 Doug Dascenzo .10 .02
❑ 213 Andy Stankiewicz .10 .02
❑ 214 Geronimo Berroa .10 .02
❑ 215 Dennis Eckersley .20 .07
❑ 216 Al Osuna .10 .02
❑ 217 Tino Martinez .30 .10
❑ 218 Henry Rodriguez .10 .02
❑ 219 Ed Sprague .10 .02
❑ 220 Ken Hill .10 .02
❑ 221 Chito Martinez .10 .02
❑ 222 Bret Saberhagen .20 .07
❑ 223 Mike Greenwell .10 .02
❑ 224 Mickey Morandini .10 .02
❑ 225 Chuck Finley .20 .07
❑ 226 Denny Neagle .20 .07
❑ 227 Kirk McCaskill .10 .02
❑ 228 Rheal Cormier .10 .02
❑ 229 Paul Sorrento .10 .02
❑ 230 Darrin Jackson .10 .02
❑ 231 Rob Deer .10 .02
❑ 232 Bill Swift .10 .02
❑ 233 Kevin McReynolds .10 .02
❑ 234 Terry Pendleton .20 .07
❑ 235 Dave Nilsson .10 .02
❑ 236 Chuck McElroy .10 .02
❑ 237 Derek Parks .10 .02
❑ 238 Norm Charlton .10 .02
❑ 239 Matt Nokes .10 .02
❑ 240 Juan Guerrero .10 .02
❑ 241 Jeff Parrett .10 .02
❑ 242 Ryan Thompson .10 .02
❑ 243 Dave Fleming .10 .02
❑ 244 Dave Hansen .10 .02
❑ 245 Monty Fariss .10 .02
❑ 246 Archi Cianfrocco .10 .02
❑ 247 Pat Hentgen .10 .02
❑ 248 Bill Pecota .10 .02
❑ 249 Ben McDonald .10 .02
❑ 250 Cliff Brantley .10 .02
❑ 251 John Valentin .10 .02
❑ 252 Jeff King .10 .02
❑ 253 Reggie Williams .10 .02
❑ 254 Checklist 160-238 .10 .02
❑ 255 Ozzie Guillen .20 .07
❑ 256 Mike Perez .10 .02
❑ 257 Thomas Howard .10 .02
❑ 258 Kurt Stillwell .10 .02
❑ 259 Mike Henneman .10 .02
❑ 260 Steve Decker .10 .02
❑ 261 Brent Mayne .10 .02
❑ 262 Otis Nixon .10 .02
❑ 263 Mark Kiefer .10 .02
❑ 264 Checklist 239-317
(Don Mattingly
and Mike Bordic .30 .10
❑ 265 Richie Lewis RC .10 .02
❑ 266 Pat Gomez RC .10 .02
❑ 267 Scott Taylor .10 .02
❑ 268 Shawon Dunston .10 .02
❑ 269 Greg Myers .10 .02
❑ 270 Tim Costo .10 .02
❑ 271 Greg Hibbard .10 .02
❑ 272 Pete Harnisch .10 .02
❑ 273 Dave Mlicki .10 .02
❑ 274 Orel Hershiser .20 .07
❑ 275 Sean Berry RR .10 .02
❑ 276 Doug Simons .10 .02
❑ 277 John Doherty .10 .02
❑ 278 Eddie Murray .50 .20
❑ 279 Chris Haney .10 .02
❑ 280 Stan Javier .10 .02
❑ 281 Jaime Navarro .10 .02
❑ 282 Orlando Merced .10 .02
❑ 283 Kent Hrbek .20 .07
❑ 284 Bernard Gilkey .10 .02
❑ 285 Russ Springer .10 .02
❑ 286 Mike Maddux .10 .02
❑ 287 Eric Fox .10 .02
❑ 288 Mark Leonard .10 .02
❑ 289 Tim Leary .10 .02
❑ 290 Brian Hunter .10 .02
❑ 291 Donald Harris .10 .02
❑ 292 Bob Scanlan .10 .02
❑ 293 Turner Ward .10 .02
❑ 294 Hal Morris .10 .02
❑ 295 Jimmy Poole .10 .02
❑ 296 Doug Jones .10 .02
❑ 297 Tony Pena .10 .02
❑ 298 Ramon Martinez .10 .02
❑ 299 Tim Fortugno .10 .02
❑ 300 Marquis Grissom .20 .07
❑ 301 Lance Johnson .10 .02
❑ 302 Jeff Kent .50 .20
❑ 303 Reggie Jefferson .10 .02
❑ 304 Wes Chamberlain .10 .02
❑ 305 Shawn Hare .10 .02
❑ 306 Mike LaValliere .10 .02
❑ 307 Gregg Jefferies .10 .02
❑ 308 Troy Neel .10 .02
❑ 309 Pat Listach .10 .02
❑ 310 Geronimo Pena .10 .02
❑ 311 Pedro Munoz .10 .02
❑ 312 Guillermo Velasquez .10 .02
❑ 313 Roberto Kelly .10 .02
❑ 314 Mike Jackson .10 .02
❑ 315 Rickey Henderson .50 .20
❑ 316 Mark Lemke .10 .02
❑ 317 Erik Hanson .10 .02
❑ 318 Derrick May .10 .02
❑ 319 Geno Petralli .10 .02
❑ 320 Melvin Nieves .10 .02
❑ 321 Doug Linton .10 .02
❑ 322 Rob Dibble .20 .07
❑ 323 Chris Hoiles .10 .02
❑ 324 Jimmy Jones .10 .02
❑ 325 Dave Staton .10 .02

❑ 326 Pedro Martinez 1.00 .40
❑ 327 Paul Quantrill .10 .02
❑ 328 Greg Colbrunn .10 .02
❑ 329 Hilly Hathaway RC .10 .02
❑ 330 Jeff Innis .10 .02
❑ 331 Ron Karkovice .10 .02
❑ 332 Keith Shepherd RC .10 .02
❑ 333 Alan Embree .10 .02
❑ 334 Paul Wagner .10 .02
❑ 335 Dave Haas .10 .02
❑ 336 Ozzie Canseco .10 .02
❑ 337 Bill Sampen .10 .02
❑ 338 Rich Rodriguez .10 .02
❑ 339 Dean Palmer .20 .07
❑ 340 Greg Litton .10 .02
❑ 341 Jim Tatum RC .10 .02
❑ 342 Todd Haney RC .10 .02
❑ 343 Larry Casian .10 .02
❑ 344 Ryne Sandberg .75 .30
❑ 345 Sterling Hitchcock RC .20 .07
❑ 346 Chris Hammond .10 .02
❑ 347 Vince Horsman .10 .02
❑ 348 Butch Henry .10 .02
❑ 349 Dann Howitt .10 .02
❑ 350 Roger McDowell .10 .02
❑ 351 Jack Morris .20 .07
❑ 352 Bill Krueger .10 .02
❑ 353 Cris Colon .10 .02
❑ 354 Joe Vitko .10 .02
❑ 355 Willie McGee .20 .07
❑ 356 Jay Baller .10 .02
❑ 357 Pat Mahomes .10 .02
❑ 358 Roger Mason .10 .02
❑ 359 Jerry Nielsen .10 .02
❑ 360 Tom Pagnozzi .10 .02
❑ 361 Kevin Baez .10 .02
❑ 362 Tim Scott .10 .02
❑ 363 Domingo Martinez RC .10 .02
❑ 364 Kirt Manwaring .10 .02
❑ 365 Rafael Palmeiro .30 .10
❑ 366 Ray Lankford .20 .07
❑ 367 Tim McIntosh .10 .02
❑ 368 Jessie Hollins .10 .02
❑ 369 Scott Leius .10 .02
❑ 370 Bill Doran .10 .02
❑ 371 Sam Militello .10 .02
❑ 372 Ryan Bowen .10 .02
❑ 373 Dave Henderson .10 .02
❑ 374 Dan Smith .10 .02
❑ 375 Steve Reed RC .10 .02
❑ 376 Jose Offerman .10 .02
❑ 377 Kevin Brown .20 .07
❑ 378 Darrin Fletcher .10 .02
❑ 379 Duane Ward .10 .02
❑ 380 Wayne Kirby .10 .02
❑ 381 Steve Scarsone .10 .02
❑ 382 Mariano Duncan .10 .02
❑ 383 Ken Ryan RC .10 .02
❑ 384 Lloyd McClendon .10 .02
❑ 385 Brian Holman .10 .02
❑ 386 Braulio Castillo .10 .02
❑ 387 Danny Leon .10 .02
❑ 388 Omar Olivares .10 .02
❑ 389 Kevin Wickander .10 .02
❑ 390 Fred McGriff .30 .10
❑ 391 Phil Clark .10 .02
❑ 392 Darren Lewis .10 .02
❑ 393 Phil Hiatt .10 .02
❑ 394 Mike Morgan .10 .02
❑ 395 Shane Mack .10 .02
❑ 396 Checklist 318-396
(Dennis Eckersley
and Art Kusn .20 .07
❑ 397 David Segui .10 .02
❑ 398 Rafael Belliard .10 .02
❑ 399 Tim Naehring .10 .02
❑ 400 Frank Castillo .10 .02
❑ 401 Joe Grahe .10 .02
❑ 402 Reggie Sanders .20 .07
❑ 403 Roberto Hernandez .10 .02
❑ 404 Luis Gonzalez .20 .07
❑ 405 Carlos Baerga .10 .02
❑ 406 Carlos Hernandez .10 .02
❑ 407 Pedro Astacio .10 .02
❑ 408 Mel Rojas .10 .02
❑ 409 Scott Livingstone .10 .02
❑ 410 Chico Walker .10 .02
❑ 411 Brian McRae .10 .02
❑ 412 Ben Rivera .10 .02
❑ 413 Ricky Bones .10 .02
❑ 414 Andy Van Slyke .30 .10
❑ 415 Chuck Knoblauch .20 .07
❑ 416 Luis Alicea .10 .02
❑ 417 Bob Wickman .10 .02
❑ 418 Doug Brocail .10 .02
❑ 419 Scott Brosius .20 .07
❑ 420 Rod Beck .10 .02
❑ 421 Edgar Martinez .30 .10
❑ 422 Ryan Klesko .20 .07
❑ 423 Nolan Ryan 2.00 .75
❑ 424 Rey Sanchez .10 .02
❑ 425 Roberto Alomar .30 .10
❑ 426 Barry Larkin .30 .10
❑ 427 Mike Mussina .30 .10
❑ 428 Jeff Bagwell .30 .10
❑ 429 Mo Vaughn .20 .07
❑ 430 Eric Karros .20 .07
❑ 431 John Orton .10 .02
❑ 432 Wil Cordero .10 .02
❑ 433 Jack McDowell .10 .02
❑ 434 Howard Johnson .10 .02
❑ 435 Albert Belle .20 .07
❑ 436 John Kruk .20 .07
❑ 437 Skeeter Barnes .10 .02
❑ 438 Don Slaught .10 .02
❑ 439 Rusty Meacham .10 .02
❑ 440 Tim Laker RC .10 .02
❑ 441 Robin Yount .75 .30
❑ 442 Brian Jordan .20 .07
❑ 443 Kevin Tapani .10 .02
❑ 444 Gary Sheffield .20 .07
❑ 445 Rich Monteleone .10 .02
❑ 446 Will Clark .30 .10
❑ 447 Jerry Browne .10 .02
❑ 448 Jeff Treadway .10 .02
❑ 449 Mike Schooler .10 .02
❑ 450 Mike Harkey .10 .02
❑ 451 Julio Franco .20 .07
❑ 452 Kevin Young .20 .07
❑ 453 Kelly Gruber .10 .02
❑ 454 Jose Rijo .10 .02
❑ 455 Mike Devereaux .10 .02
❑ 456 Andujar Cedeno .10 .02
❑ 457 Damion Easley RR .10 .02
❑ 458 Kevin Gross .10 .02
❑ 459 Matt Young .10 .02
❑ 460 Matt Stairs .10 .02
❑ 461 Luis Polonia .10 .02
❑ 462 Dwight Gooden .20 .07
❑ 463 Warren Newson .10 .02
❑ 464 Jose DeLeon .10 .02
❑ 465 Jose Mesa .10 .02
❑ 466 Danny Cox .10 .02
❑ 467 Dan Gladden .10 .02
❑ 468 Gerald Perry .10 .02
❑ 469 Mike Boddicker .10 .02
❑ 470 Jeff Gardner .10 .02
❑ 471 Doug Henry .10 .02
❑ 472 Mike Benjamin .10 .02
❑ 473 Dan Peltier .10 .02
❑ 474 Mike Stanton .10 .02
❑ 475 John Smiley .10 .02
❑ 476 Dwight Smith .10 .02
❑ 477 Jim Leyritz .10 .02
❑ 478 Dwayne Henry .10 .02
❑ 479 Mark McGwire 1.25 .50
❑ 480 Pete Incaviglia .10 .02
❑ 481 Dave Cochrane .10 .02
❑ 482 Eric Davis .20 .07
❑ 483 John Olerud .20 .07
❑ 484 Kent Bottenfield .10 .02
❑ 485 Mark McLemore .10 .02
❑ 486 Dave Magadan .10 .02
❑ 487 John Marzano .10 .02
❑ 488 Ruben Amaro .10 .02
❑ 489 Rob Ducey .10 .02
❑ 490 Stan Belinda .10 .02
❑ 491 Dan Pasqua .10 .02
❑ 492 Joe Magrane .10 .02
❑ 493 Brook Jacoby .10 .02
❑ 494 Gene Harris .10 .02
❑ 495 Mark Leiter .10 .02
❑ 496 Bryan Hickerson .10 .02
❑ 497 Tom Gordon .10 .02
❑ 498 Pete Smith .10 .02
❑ 499 Chris Bosio .10 .02
❑ 500 Shawn Boskie .10 .02
❑ 501 Dave West .10 .02
❑ 502 Milt Hill .10 .02
❑ 503 Pat Kelly .10 .02
❑ 504 Joe Boever .10 .02
❑ 505 Terry Steinbach .10 .02
❑ 506 Butch Huskey .10 .02
❑ 507 David Valle .10 .02
❑ 508 Mike Scioscia .10 .02
❑ 509 Kenny Rogers .20 .07
❑ 510 Moises Alou .20 .07
❑ 511 David Wells .20 .07
❑ 512 Mackey Sasser .10 .02
❑ 513 Todd Frohwirth .10 .02
❑ 514 Ricky Jordan .10 .02
❑ 515 Mike Gardiner .10 .02
❑ 516 Gary Redus .10 .02
❑ 517 Gary Gaetti .20 .07
❑ 518 Checklist .10 .02
❑ 519 Carlton Fisk .30 .10
❑ 520 Ozzie Smith .75 .30
❑ 521 Rod Nichols .10 .02
❑ 522 Benito Santiago .20 .07
❑ 523 Bill Gullickson .10 .02
❑ 524 Robby Thompson .10 .02
❑ 525 Mike Macfarlane .10 .02
❑ 526 Sid Bream .10 .02
❑ 527 Darryl Hamilton .10 .02
❑ 528 Checklist .10 .02
❑ 529 Jeff Tackett .10 .02
❑ 530 Greg Olson .10 .02
❑ 531 Bob Zupcic .10 .02
❑ 532 Mark Grace .30 .10
❑ 533 Steve Frey .10 .02
❑ 534 Dave Martinez .10 .02
❑ 535 Robin Ventura .20 .07
❑ 536 Casey Candaele .10 .02
❑ 537 Kenny Lofton .20 .07
❑ 538 Jay Howell .10 .02
❑ 539 Fernando Ramsey RC .10 .02
❑ 540 Larry Walker .20 .07
❑ 541 Cecil Fielder .20 .07
❑ 542 Lee Guetterman .10 .02
❑ 543 Keith Miller .10 .02
❑ 544 Len Dykstra .20 .07
❑ 545 B.J. Surhoff .20 .07
❑ 546 Bob Walk .10 .02
❑ 547 Brian Harper .10 .02
❑ 548 Lee Smith .20 .07
❑ 549 Danny Tartabull .10 .02
❑ 550 Frank Seminara .10 .02
❑ 551 Henry Mercedes .10 .02
❑ 552 Dave Righetti .20 .07
❑ 553 Ken Griffey Jr. .75 .30
❑ 554 Tom Glavine .30 .10
❑ 555 Juan Gonzalez .20 .07
❑ 556 Jim Bullinger .10 .02
❑ 557 Derek Bell .10 .02
❑ 558 Cesar Hernandez .10 .02
❑ 559 Cal Ripken 1.50 .60
❑ 560 Eddie Taubensee .10 .02
❑ 561 John Flaherty .10 .02
❑ 562 Todd Benzinger .10 .02
❑ 563 Hubie Brooks .10 .02
❑ 564 Delino DeShields .10 .02
❑ 565 Tim Raines .20 .07
❑ 566 Sid Fernandez .10 .02
❑ 567 Steve Olin .10 .02
❑ 568 Tommy Greene .10 .02
❑ 569 Buddy Groom .10 .02
❑ 570 Randy Tomlin .10 .02
❑ 571 Hipolito Pichardo .10 .02
❑ 572 Rene Arocha RC .20 .07
❑ 573 Mike Fetters .10 .02
❑ 574 Felix Jose .10 .02
❑ 575 Gene Larkin .10 .02
❑ 576 Bruce Hurst .10 .02
❑ 577 Bernie Williams .30 .10
❑ 578 Trevor Wilson .10 .02
❑ 579 Bob Welch .10 .02
❑ 580 David Justice .20 .07
❑ 581 Randy Johnson .50 .20

❑ 582 Jose Vizcaino .10 .02
❑ 583 Jeff Huson .10 .02
❑ 584 Rob Maurer .10 .02
❑ 585 Todd Stottlemyre .10 .02
❑ 586 Joe Oliver .10 .02
❑ 587 Bob Milacki .10 .02
❑ 588 Rob Murphy .10 .02
❑ 589 Greg Pirkl .10 .02
❑ 590 Lenny Harris .10 .02
❑ 591 Luis Rivera .10 .02
❑ 592 John Wetteland .20 .07
❑ 593 Mark Langston .10 .02
❑ 594 Bobby Bonilla .20 .07
❑ 595 Esteban Beltre .10 .02
❑ 596 Mike Hartley .10 .02
❑ 597 Felix Fermin .10 .02
❑ 598 Carlos Garcia .10 .02
❑ 599 Frank Tanana .10 .02
❑ 600 Pedro Guerrero .20 .07
❑ 601 Terry Shumpert .10 .02
❑ 602 Wally Whitehurst .10 .02
❑ 603 Kevin Seitzer .10 .02
❑ 604 Chris James .10 .02
❑ 605 Greg Gohr .10 .02
❑ 606 Mark Wohlers .10 .02
❑ 607 Kirby Puckett .50 .20
❑ 608 Greg Maddux .75 .30
❑ 609 Don Mattingly 1.25 .50
❑ 610 Greg Cadaret .10 .02
❑ 611 Dave Stewart .20 .07
❑ 612 Mark Portugal .10 .02
❑ 613 Pete O'Brien .10 .02
❑ 614 Bob Ojeda .10 .02
❑ 615 Joe Carter .20 .07
❑ 616 Pete Young .10 .02
❑ 617 Sam Horn .10 .02
❑ 618 Vince Coleman .10 .02
❑ 619 Wade Boggs .30 .10
❑ 620 Todd Pratt RC .20 .07
❑ 621 Ron Tingley .10 .02
❑ 622 Doug Drabek .10 .02
❑ 623 Scott Hemond .10 .02
❑ 624 Tim Jones .10 .02
❑ 625 Dennis Cook .10 .02
❑ 626 Jose Melendez .10 .02
❑ 627 Mike Munoz .10 .02
❑ 628 Jim Pena .10 .02
❑ 629 Gary Thurman .10 .02
❑ 630 Charlie Leibrandt .10 .02
❑ 631 Scott Fletcher .10 .02
❑ 632 Andre Dawson .20 .07
❑ 633 Greg Gagne .10 .02
❑ 634 Greg Swindell .10 .02
❑ 635 Kevin Maas .10 .02
❑ 636 Xavier Hernandez .10 .02
❑ 637 Ruben Sierra .20 .07
❑ 638 Dmitri Young .20 .07
❑ 639 Harold Reynolds .20 .07
❑ 640 Tom Goodwin .10 .02
❑ 641 Todd Burns .10 .02
❑ 642 Jeff Fassero .10 .02
❑ 643 Dave Winfield .20 .07
❑ 644 Willie Randolph .20 .07
❑ 645 Luis Mercedes .10 .02
❑ 646 Dale Murphy .30 .10
❑ 647 Danny Darwin .10 .02
❑ 648 Dennis Moeller .10 .02
❑ 649 Chuck Crim .10 .02
❑ 650 Checklist .10 .02
❑ 651 Shawn Abner .10 .02
❑ 652 Tracy Woodson .10 .02
❑ 653 Scott Scudder .10 .02
❑ 654 Tom Lampkin .10 .02
❑ 655 Alan Trammell .20 .07
❑ 656 Cory Snyder .10 .02
❑ 657 Chris Gwynn .10 .02
❑ 658 Lonnie Smith .10 .02
❑ 659 Jim Austin .10 .02
❑ 660 Rob Picciolo CL .10 .02
❑ 661 Tim Hulett .10 .02
❑ 662 Marvin Freeman .10 .02
❑ 663 Greg A. Harris .10 .02
❑ 664 Heathcliff Slocumb .10 .02
❑ 665 Mike Butcher .10 .02
❑ 666 Steve Foster .10 .02
❑ 667 Donn Pall .10 .02
❑ 668 Darryl Kile .20 .07
❑ 669 Jesse Levis .10 .02
❑ 670 Jim Gott .10 .02
❑ 671 Mark Hutton .10 .02
❑ 672 Brian Drahman .10 .02
❑ 673 Chad Kreuter .10 .02
❑ 674 Tony Fernandez .10 .02
❑ 675 Jose Lind .10 .02
❑ 676 Kyle Abbott .10 .02
❑ 677 Dan Plesac .10 .02
❑ 678 Barry Bonds 1.50 .60
❑ 679 Chili Davis .20 .07
❑ 680 Stan Royer .10 .02
❑ 681 Scott Kamieniecki .10 .02
❑ 682 Carlos Martinez .10 .02
❑ 683 Mike Moore .10 .02
❑ 684 Candy Maldonado .10 .02
❑ 685 Jeff Nelson .10 .02
❑ 686 Lou Whitaker .20 .07
❑ 687 Jose Guzman .10 .02
❑ 688 Manuel Lee .10 .02
❑ 689 Bob MacDonald .10 .02
❑ 690 Scott Bankhead .10 .02
❑ 691 Alan Mills .10 .02
❑ 692 Brian Williams .10 .02
❑ 693 Tom Brunansky .10 .02
❑ 694 Lenny Webster .10 .02
❑ 695 Greg Briley .10 .02
❑ 696 Paul O'Neill .30 .10
❑ 697 Joey Cora .10 .02
❑ 698 Charlie O'Brien .10 .02
❑ 699 Junior Ortiz .10 .02
❑ 700 Ron Darling .10 .02
❑ 701 Tony Phillips .10 .02
❑ 702 William Pennyfeather .10 .02
❑ 703 Mark Gubicza .10 .02
❑ 704 Steve Hosey .10 .02
❑ 705 Henry Cotto .10 .02
❑ 706 David Hulse RC .10 .02
❑ 707 Mike Pagliarulo .10 .02
❑ 708 Dave Stieb .10 .02
❑ 709 Melido Perez .10 .02
❑ 710 Jimmy Key .20 .07
❑ 711 Jeff Russell .10 .02
❑ 712 David Cone .20 .07
❑ 713 Russ Swan .10 .02
❑ 714 Mark Guthrie .10 .02
❑ 715 Checklist .10 .02
❑ 716 Al Martin .10 .02
❑ 717 Randy Knorr .10 .02
❑ 718 Mike Stanley .10 .02
❑ 719 Rick Sutcliffe .20 .07
❑ 720 Terry Leach .10 .02
❑ 721 Chipper Jones .50 .20
❑ 722 Jim Eisenreich .10 .02
❑ 723 Tom Henke .10 .02
❑ 724 Jeff Frye .10 .02
❑ 725 Harold Baines .20 .07
❑ 726 Scott Sanderson .10 .02
❑ 727 Tom Foley .10 .02
❑ 728 Bryan Harvey .10 .02
❑ 729 Tom Edens .10 .02
❑ 730 Eric Young .10 .02
❑ 731 Dave Weathers .10 .02
❑ 732 Spike Owen .10 .02
❑ 733 Scott Aldred .10 .02
❑ 734 Cris Carpenter .10 .02
❑ 735 Dion James .10 .02
❑ 736 Joe Girardi .10 .02
❑ 737 Nigel Wilson .10 .02
❑ 738 Scott Chiamparino .10 .02
❑ 739 Jeff Reardon .20 .07
❑ 740 Willie Blair .10 .02
❑ 741 Jim Corsi .10 .02
❑ 742 Ken Patterson .10 .02
❑ 743 Andy Ashby .10 .02
❑ 744 Rob Natal .10 .02
❑ 745 Kevin Bass .10 .02
❑ 746 Freddie Benavides .10 .02
❑ 747 Chris Donnels .10 .02
❑ 748 Kerry Woodson .10 .02
❑ 749 Calvin Jones .10 .02
❑ 750 Gary Scott .10 .02
❑ 751 Joe Orsulak .10 .02
❑ 752 Armando Reynoso .10 .02
❑ 753 Monty Fariss .10 .02
❑ 754 Billy Hatcher .10 .02
❑ 755 Denis Boucher .10 .02
❑ 756 Walt Weiss .10 .02
❑ 757 Mike Fitzgerald .10 .02
❑ 758 Rudy Seanez .10 .02
❑ 759 Bret Barberie .10 .02
❑ 760 Mo Sanford .10 .02
❑ 761 Pedro Castellano .10 .02
❑ 762 Chuck Carr .10 .02
❑ 763 Steve Howe .10 .02
❑ 764 Andres Galarraga .20 .07
❑ 765 Jeff Conine .20 .07
❑ 766 Ted Power .10 .02
❑ 767 Butch Henry .10 .02
❑ 768 Steve Decker .10 .02
❑ 769 Storm Davis .10 .02
❑ 770 Vinny Castilla .50 .20
❑ 771 Junior Felix .10 .02
❑ 772 Walt Terrell .10 .02
❑ 773 Brad Ausmus .50 .20
❑ 774 Jamie McAndrew .10 .02
❑ 775 Milt Thompson .10 .02
❑ 776 Charlie Hayes .10 .02
❑ 777 Jack Armstrong .10 .02
❑ 778 Dennis Rasmussen .10 .02
❑ 779 Darren Holmes .10 .02
❑ 780 Alex Arias .10 .02
❑ 781 Randy Bush .10 .02
❑ 782 Javy Lopez .30 .10
❑ 783 Dante Bichette .20 .07
❑ 784 John Johnstone RC .10 .02
❑ 785 Rene Gonzales .10 .02
❑ 786 Alex Cole .10 .02
❑ 787 Jeromy Burnitz .20 .07
❑ 788 Michael Huff .10 .02
❑ 789 Anthony Telford .10 .02
❑ 790 Jerald Clark .10 .02
❑ 791 Joel Johnston .10 .02
❑ 792 David Nied .10 .02

1994 Donruss

❑ COMPLETE SET (660) 30.00 12.00
❑ COMPLETE SERIES 1 (330) 15.00 6.00
❑ COMPLETE SERIES 2 (330) 15.00 6.00
❑ 1 Nolan Ryan Salute 4.00 1.50
❑ 2 Mike Piazza 1.50 .60
❑ 3 Moises Alou .30 .10
❑ 4 Ken Griffey Jr. 1.25 .50
❑ 5 Gary Sheffield .30 .10
❑ 6 Roberto Alomar .50 .20
❑ 7 John Kruk .30 .10
❑ 8 Gregg Olson .15 .05
❑ 9 Gregg Jefferies .15 .05
❑ 10 Tony Gwynn 1.00 .40
❑ 11 Chad Curtis .15 .05
❑ 12 Craig Biggio .50 .20
❑ 13 John Burkett .15 .05
❑ 14 Carlos Baerga .15 .05
❑ 15 Robin Yount 1.25 .50
❑ 16 Dennis Eckersley .30 .10
❑ 17 Dwight Gooden .30 .10
❑ 18 Ryne Sandberg 1.25 .50
❑ 19 Rickey Henderson .75 .30
❑ 20 Jack McDowell .15 .05
❑ 21 Jay Bell .30 .10
❑ 22 Kevin Brown .30 .10
❑ 23 Robin Ventura .30 .10
❑ 24 Paul Molitor .30 .10

❑ 25 David Justice .30 .10
❑ 26 Rafael Palmeiro .50 .20
❑ 27 Cecil Fielder .30 .10
❑ 28 Chuck Knoblauch .30 .10
❑ 29 Dave Hollins .15 .05
❑ 30 Jimmy Key .30 .10
❑ 31 Mark Langston .15 .05
❑ 32 Darryl Kile .30 .10
❑ 33 Ruben Sierra .30 .10
❑ 34 Ron Gant .30 .10
❑ 35 Ozzie Smith 1.25 .50
❑ 36 Wade Boggs .50 .20
❑ 37 Marquis Grissom .30 .10
❑ 38 Will Clark .50 .20
❑ 39 Kenny Lofton .30 .10
❑ 40 Cal Ripken 2.50 1.00
❑ 41 Steve Avery .15 .05
❑ 42 Mo Vaughn .30 .10
❑ 43 Brian McRae .15 .05
❑ 44 Mickey Tettleton .15 .05
❑ 45 Barry Larkin .50 .20
❑ 46 Charlie Hayes .15 .05
❑ 47 Kevin Appier .30 .10
❑ 48 Robby Thompson .15 .05
❑ 49 Juan Gonzalez .30 .10
❑ 50 Paul O'Neill .50 .20
❑ 51 Marcos Armas .15 .05
❑ 52 Mike Butcher .15 .05
❑ 53 Ken Caminiti .30 .10
❑ 54 Pat Borders .15 .05
❑ 55 Pedro Munoz .15 .05
❑ 56 Tim Belcher .15 .05
❑ 57 Paul Assenmacher .15 .05
❑ 58 Damon Berryhill .15 .05
❑ 59 Ricky Bones .15 .05
❑ 60 Rene Arocha .15 .05
❑ 61 Shawn Boskie .15 .05
❑ 62 Pedro Astacio .15 .05
❑ 63 Frank Bolick .15 .05
❑ 64 Bud Black .15 .05
❑ 65 Sandy Alomar Jr. .15 .05
❑ 66 Rich Amaral .15 .05
❑ 67 Luis Aquino .15 .05
❑ 68 Kevin Baez .15 .05
❑ 69 Mike Devereaux .15 .05
❑ 70 Andy Ashby .15 .05
❑ 71 Larry Andersen .15 .05
❑ 72 Steve Cooke .15 .05
❑ 73 Mario Diaz .15 .05
❑ 74 Rob Deer .15 .05
❑ 75 Bobby Ayala .15 .05
❑ 76 Freddie Benavides .15 .05
❑ 77 Stan Belinda .15 .05
❑ 78 John Doherty .15 .05
❑ 79 Willie Banks .15 .05
❑ 80 Spike Owen .15 .05
❑ 81 Mike Bordick .15 .05
❑ 82 Chili Davis .30 .10
❑ 83 Luis Gonzalez .30 .10
❑ 84 Ed Sprague .15 .05
❑ 85 Jeff Reboulet .15 .05
❑ 86 Jason Bere .15 .05
❑ 87 Mark Hutton .15 .05
❑ 88 Jeff Blauser .15 .05
❑ 89 Cal Eldred .15 .05
❑ 90 Bernard Gilkey .15 .05
❑ 91 Frank Castillo .15 .05
❑ 92 Jim Gott .15 .05
❑ 93 Greg Colbrunn .15 .05
❑ 94 Jeff Brantley .15 .05
❑ 95 Jeremy Hernandez .15 .05
❑ 96 Norm Charlton .15 .05
❑ 97 Alex Arias .15 .05
❑ 98 John Franco .30 .10
❑ 99 Chris Hoiles .15 .05
❑ 100 Brad Ausmus .50 .20
❑ 101 Wes Chamberlain .15 .05
❑ 102 Mark Dewey .15 .05
❑ 103 Benji Gil .15 .05
❑ 104 John Dopson .15 .05
❑ 105 John Smiley .15 .05
❑ 106 David Nied .15 .05
❑ 107 George Brett Salute 2.00 .75
❑ 108 Kirk Gibson .30 .10
❑ 109 Larry Casian .15 .05
❑ 110 Ryne Sandberg CL .75 .30
❑ 111 Brent Gates .15 .05
❑ 112 Damion Easley .15 .05
❑ 113 Pete Harnisch .15 .05
❑ 114 Danny Cox .15 .05
❑ 115 Kevin Tapani .15 .05
❑ 116 Roberto Hernandez .15 .05
❑ 117 Domingo Jean .15 .05
❑ 118 Sid Bream .15 .05
❑ 119 Doug Henry .15 .05
❑ 120 Omar Olivares .15 .05
❑ 121 Mike Harkey .15 .05
❑ 122 Carlos Hernandez .15 .05
❑ 123 Jeff Fassero .15 .05
❑ 124 Dave Burba .15 .05
❑ 125 Wayne Kirby .15 .05
❑ 126 John Cummings .15 .05
❑ 127 Bret Barberie .15 .05
❑ 128 Todd Hundley .15 .05
❑ 129 Tim Hulett .15 .05
❑ 130 Phil Clark .15 .05
❑ 131 Danny Jackson .15 .05
❑ 132 Tom Foley .15 .05
❑ 133 Donald Harris .15 .05
❑ 134 Scott Fletcher .15 .05
❑ 135 Johnny Ruffin .15 .05
❑ 136 Jerald Clark .15 .05
❑ 137 Billy Brewer .15 .05
❑ 138 Dan Gladden .15 .05
❑ 139 Eddie Guardado .30 .10
❑ 140 Cal Ripken CL .75 .30
❑ 141 Scott Hemond .15 .05
❑ 142 Steve Frey .15 .05
❑ 143 Xavier Hernandez .15 .05
❑ 144 Mark Eichhorn .15 .05
❑ 145 Ellis Burks .30 .10
❑ 146 Jim Leyritz .15 .05
❑ 147 Mark Lemke .15 .05
❑ 148 Pat Listach .15 .05
❑ 149 Donovan Osborne .15 .05
❑ 150 Glenallen Hill .15 .05
❑ 151 Orel Hershiser .30 .10
❑ 152 Darrin Fletcher .15 .05
❑ 153 Royce Clayton .15 .05
❑ 154 Derek Lilliquist .15 .05
❑ 155 Mike Felder .15 .05
❑ 156 Jeff Conine .30 .10
❑ 157 Ryan Thompson .15 .05
❑ 158 Ben McDonald .15 .05
❑ 159 Ricky Gutierrez .15 .05
❑ 160 Terry Mulholland .15 .05
❑ 161 Carlos Garcia .15 .05
❑ 162 Tom Henke .15 .05
❑ 163 Mike Greenwell .15 .05
❑ 164 Thomas Howard .15 .05
❑ 165 Joe Girardi .15 .05
❑ 166 Hubie Brooks .15 .05
❑ 167 Greg Gohr .15 .05
❑ 168 Chip Hale .15 .05
❑ 169 Rick Honeycutt .15 .05
❑ 170 Hilly Hathaway .15 .05
❑ 171 Todd Jones .15 .05
❑ 172 Tony Fernandez .15 .05
❑ 173 Bo Jackson .75 .30
❑ 174 Bobby Munoz .15 .05
❑ 175 Greg McMichael .15 .05
❑ 176 Graeme Lloyd .15 .05
❑ 177 Tom Pagnozzi .15 .05
❑ 178 Derrick May .15 .05
❑ 179 Pedro Martinez .75 .30
❑ 180 Ken Hill .15 .05
❑ 181 Bryan Hickerson .15 .05
❑ 182 Jose Mesa .15 .05
❑ 183 Dave Fleming .15 .05
❑ 184 Henry Cotto .15 .05
❑ 185 Jeff Kent .50 .20
❑ 186 Mark McLemore .15 .05
❑ 187 Trevor Hoffman .50 .20
❑ 188 Todd Pratt .15 .05
❑ 189 Blas Minor .15 .05
❑ 190 Charlie Leibrandt .15 .05
❑ 191 Tony Pena .15 .05
❑ 192 Larry Luebbers RC .15 .05
❑ 193 Greg W. Harris .15 .05
❑ 194 David Cone .30 .10
❑ 195 Bill Gullickson .15 .05
❑ 196 Brian Harper .15 .05
❑ 197 Steve Karsay .15 .05
❑ 198 Greg Myers .15 .05
❑ 199 Mark Portugal .15 .05
❑ 200 Pat Hentgen .15 .05
❑ 201 Mike LaValliere .15 .05
❑ 202 Mike Stanley .15 .05
❑ 203 Kent Mercker .15 .05
❑ 204 Dave Nilsson .15 .05
❑ 205 Erik Pappas .15 .05
❑ 206 Mike Morgan .15 .05
❑ 207 Roger McDowell .15 .05
❑ 208 Mike Lansing .15 .05
❑ 209 Kirt Manwaring .15 .05
❑ 210 Randy Milligan .15 .05
❑ 211 Erik Hanson .15 .05
❑ 212 Orestes Destrade .15 .05
❑ 213 Mike Maddux .15 .05
❑ 214 Alan Mills .15 .05
❑ 215 Tim Mauser .15 .05
❑ 216 Ben Rivera .15 .05
❑ 217 Don Slaught .15 .05
❑ 218 Bob Patterson .15 .05
❑ 219 Carlos Quintana .15 .05
❑ 220 Tim Raines CL .15 .05
❑ 221 Hal Morris .15 .05
❑ 222 Darren Holmes .15 .05
❑ 223 Chris Gwynn .15 .05
❑ 224 Chad Kreuter .15 .05
❑ 225 Mike Hartley .15 .05
❑ 226 Scott Lydy .15 .05
❑ 227 Eduardo Perez .15 .05
❑ 228 Greg Swindell .15 .05
❑ 229 Al Leiter .30 .10
❑ 230 Scott Radinsky .15 .05
❑ 231 Bob Wickman .15 .05
❑ 232 Otis Nixon .15 .05
❑ 233 Kevin Reimer .15 .05
❑ 234 Geronimo Pena .15 .05
❑ 235 Kevin Roberson .15 .05
❑ 236 Jody Reed .15 .05
❑ 237 Kirk Rueter .15 .05
❑ 238 Willie McGee .30 .10
❑ 239 Charles Nagy .15 .05
❑ 240 Tim Leary .15 .05
❑ 241 Carl Everett .30 .10
❑ 242 Charlie O'Brien .15 .05
❑ 243 Mike Pagliarulo .15 .05
❑ 244 Kerry Taylor .15 .05
❑ 245 Kevin Stocker .15 .05
❑ 246 Joel Johnston .15 .05
❑ 247 Geno Petralli .15 .05
❑ 248 Jeff Russell .15 .05
❑ 249 Joe Oliver .15 .05
❑ 250 Roberto Mejia .15 .05
❑ 251 Chris Haney .15 .05
❑ 252 Bill Krueger .15 .05
❑ 253 Shane Mack .15 .05
❑ 254 Terry Steinbach .15 .05
❑ 255 Luis Polonia .15 .05
❑ 256 Eddie Taubensee .15 .05
❑ 257 Dave Stewart .30 .10
❑ 258 Tim Raines .30 .10
❑ 259 Bernie Williams .50 .20
❑ 260 John Smoltz .50 .20
❑ 261 Kevin Seitzer .15 .05
❑ 262 Bob Tewksbury .15 .05
❑ 263 Bob Scanlan .15 .05
❑ 264 Henry Rodriguez .15 .05
❑ 265 Tim Scott .15 .05
❑ 266 Scott Sanderson .15 .05
❑ 267 Eric Plunk .15 .05
❑ 268 Edgar Martinez .50 .20
❑ 269 Charlie Hough .30 .10
❑ 270 Joe Orsulak .15 .05
❑ 271 Harold Reynolds .30 .10
❑ 272 Tim Teufel .15 .05
❑ 273 Bobby Thigpen .15 .05
❑ 274 Randy Tomlin .15 .05
❑ 275 Gary Redus .15 .05
❑ 276 Ken Ryan .15 .05
❑ 277 Tim Pugh .15 .05
❑ 278 Jayhawk Owens .15 .05
❑ 279 Phil Hiatt .15 .05
❑ 280 Alan Trammell .30 .10
❑ 281 David McCarty .15 .05
❑ 282 Bob Welch .15 .05

❑ 283 J.T.Snow .30 .10
❑ 284 Brian Williams .15 .05
❑ 285 Devon White .30 .10
❑ 286 Steve Sax .15 .05
❑ 287 Tony Tarasco .15 .05
❑ 288 Bill Spiers .15 .05
❑ 289 Allen Watson .15 .05
❑ 290 Rickey Henderson CL .50 .20
❑ 291 Jose Vizcaino .15 .05
❑ 292 Darryl Strawberry .30 .10
❑ 293 John Wetteland .30 .10
❑ 294 Bill Swift .15 .05
❑ 295 Jeff Treadway .15 .05
❑ 296 Tino Martinez .50 .20
❑ 297 Richie Lewis .15 .05
❑ 298 Bret Saberhagen .30 .10
❑ 299 Arthur Rhodes .15 .05
❑ 300 Guillermo Velasquez .15 .05
❑ 301 Milt Thompson .15 .05
❑ 302 Doug Strange .15 .05
❑ 303 Aaron Sele .15 .05
❑ 304 Bip Roberts .15 .05
❑ 305 Bruce Ruffin .15 .05
❑ 306 Jose Lind .15 .05
❑ 307 David Wells .30 .10
❑ 308 Bobby Witt .15 .05
❑ 309 Mark Wohlers .15 .05
❑ 310 B.J. Surhoff .30 .10
❑ 311 Mark Whiten .15 .05
❑ 312 Turk Wendell .15 .05
❑ 313 Raul Mondesi .30 .10
❑ 314 Brian Turang RC .15 .05
❑ 315 Chris Hammond .15 .05
❑ 316 Tim Bogar .15 .05
❑ 317 Brad Pennington .15 .05
❑ 318 Tim Worrell .15 .05
❑ 319 Mitch Williams .15 .05
❑ 320 Rondell White .30 .10
❑ 321 Frank Viola .30 .10
❑ 322 Manny Ramirez .75 .30
❑ 323 Gary Wayne .15 .05
❑ 324 Mike Macfarlane .15 .05
❑ 325 Russ Springer .15 .05
❑ 326 Tim Wallach .15 .05
❑ 327 Salomon Torres .15 .05
❑ 328 Omar Vizquel .50 .20
❑ 329 Andy Tomberlin RC .15 .05
❑ 330 Chris Sabo .15 .05
❑ 331 Mike Mussina .50 .20
❑ 332 Andy Benes .15 .05
❑ 333 Darren Daulton .30 .10
❑ 334 Orlando Merced .15 .05
❑ 335 Mark McGwire 2.00 .75
❑ 336 Dave Winfield .30 .10
❑ 337 Sammy Sosa .75 .30
❑ 338 Eric Karros .30 .10
❑ 339 Greg Vaughn .15 .05
❑ 340 Don Mattingly 2.00 .75
❑ 341 Frank Thomas .75 .30
❑ 342 Fred McGriff .50 .20
❑ 343 Kirby Puckett .75 .30
❑ 344 Roberto Kelly .15 .05
❑ 345 Wally Joyner .30 .10
❑ 346 Andres Galarraga .30 .10
❑ 347 Bobby Bonilla .30 .10
❑ 348 Benito Santiago .30 .10
❑ 349 Barry Bonds 2.00 .75
❑ 350 Delino DeShields .15 .05
❑ 351 Albert Belle .30 .10
❑ 352 Randy Johnson .75 .30
❑ 353 Tim Salmon .50 .20
❑ 354 John Olerud .30 .10
❑ 355 Dean Palmer .30 .10
❑ 356 Roger Clemens 1.50 .60
❑ 357 Jim Abbott .50 .20
❑ 358 Mark Grace .50 .20
❑ 359 Ozzie Guillen .30 .10
❑ 360 Lou Whitaker .30 .10
❑ 361 Jose Rijo .15 .05
❑ 362 Jeff Montgomery .15 .05
❑ 363 Chuck Finley .30 .10
❑ 364 Tom Glavine .50 .20
❑ 365 Jeff Bagwell .50 .20
❑ 366 Joe Carter .30 .10
❑ 367 Ray Lankford .30 .10
❑ 368 Ramon Martinez .15 .05
❑ 369 Jay Buhner .30 .10
❑ 370 Matt Williams .30 .10
❑ 371 Larry Walker .30 .10
❑ 372 Jose Canseco .50 .20
❑ 373 Lenny Dykstra .30 .10
❑ 374 Bryan Harvey .15 .05
❑ 375 Andy Van Slyke .50 .20
❑ 376 Ivan Rodriguez .50 .20
❑ 377 Kevin Mitchell .15 .05
❑ 378 Travis Fryman .30 .10
❑ 379 Duane Ward .15 .05
❑ 380 Greg Maddux 1.25 .50
❑ 381 Scott Servais .15 .05
❑ 382 Greg Olson .15 .05
❑ 383 Rey Sanchez .15 .05
❑ 384 Tom Kramer .15 .05
❑ 385 David Valle .15 .05
❑ 386 Eddie Murray .75 .30
❑ 387 Kevin Higgins .15 .05
❑ 388 Dan Wilson .15 .05
❑ 389 Todd Frohwith .15 .05
❑ 390 Gerald Williams .15 .05
❑ 391 Hipolito Pichardo .15 .05
❑ 392 Pat Meares .15 .05
❑ 393 Luis Lopez .15 .05
❑ 394 Ricky Jordan .15 .05
❑ 395 Bob Walk .15 .05
❑ 396 Sid Fernandez .15 .05
❑ 397 Todd Worrell .15 .05
❑ 398 Darryl Hamilton .15 .05
❑ 399 Randy Myers .15 .05
❑ 400 Rod Brewer .15 .05
❑ 401 Lance Blankenship .15 .05
❑ 402 Steve Finley .30 .10
❑ 403 Phil Leftwich RC .15 .05
❑ 404 Juan Guzman .15 .05
❑ 405 Anthony Young .15 .05
❑ 406 Jeff Gardner .15 .05
❑ 407 Ryan Bowen .15 .05
❑ 408 Fernando Valenzuela .30 .10
❑ 409 David West .15 .05
❑ 410 Kenny Rogers .30 .10
❑ 411 Bob Zupcic .15 .05
❑ 412 Eric Young .15 .05
❑ 413 Bret Boone .30 .10
❑ 414 Danny Tartabull .15 .05
❑ 415 Bob MacDonald .15 .05
❑ 416 Ron Karkovice .15 .05
❑ 417 Scott Cooper .15 .05
❑ 418 Dante Bichette .30 .10
❑ 419 Tripp Cromer .15 .05
❑ 420 Billy Ashley .15 .05
❑ 421 Roger Smithberg .15 .05
❑ 422 Dennis Martinez .30 .10
❑ 423 Mike Blowers .15 .05
❑ 424 Darren Lewis .15 .05
❑ 425 Junior Ortiz .15 .05
❑ 426 Butch Huskey .15 .05
❑ 427 Jimmy Poole .15 .05
❑ 428 Walt Weiss .15 .05
❑ 429 Scott Bankhead .15 .05
❑ 430 Deion Sanders .50 .20
❑ 431 Scott Bullett .15 .05
❑ 432 Jeff Huson .15 .05
❑ 433 Tyler Green .15 .05
❑ 434 Billy Hatcher .15 .05
❑ 435 Bob Hamelin .15 .05
❑ 436 Reggie Sanders .30 .10
❑ 437 Scott Erickson .15 .05
❑ 438 Steve Reed .15 .05
❑ 439 Randy Velarde .15 .05
❑ 440 Tony Gwynn CL .50 .20
❑ 441 Terry Leach .15 .05
❑ 442 Danny Bautista .15 .05
❑ 443 Kent Hrbek .30 .10
❑ 444 Rick Wilkins .15 .05
❑ 445 Tony Phillips .15 .05
❑ 446 Dion James .15 .05
❑ 447 Joey Cora .15 .05
❑ 448 Andre Dawson .30 .10
❑ 449 Pedro Castellano .15 .05
❑ 450 Tom Gordon .15 .05
❑ 451 Rob Dibble .30 .10
❑ 452 Ron Darling .15 .05
❑ 453 Chipper Jones .75 .30
❑ 454 Joe Grahe .15 .05
❑ 455 Domingo Cedeno .15 .05
❑ 456 Tom Edens .15 .05
❑ 457 Mitch Webster .15 .05
❑ 458 Jose Bautista .15 .05
❑ 459 Troy O'Leary .15 .05
❑ 460 Todd Zeile .15 .05
❑ 461 Sean Berry .15 .05
❑ 462 Brad Holman RC .15 .05
❑ 463 Dave Martinez .15 .05
❑ 464 Mark Lewis .15 .05
❑ 465 Paul Carey .15 .05
❑ 466 Jack Armstrong .15 .05
❑ 467 David Telgheder .15 .05
❑ 468 Gene Harris .15 .05
❑ 469 Danny Darwin .15 .05
❑ 470 Kim Batiste .15 .05
❑ 471 Tim Wakefield .50 .20
❑ 472 Craig Lefferts .15 .05
❑ 473 Jacob Brumfield .15 .05
❑ 474 Lance Painter .15 .05
❑ 475 Milt Cuyler .15 .05
❑ 476 Melido Perez .15 .05
❑ 477 Derek Parks .15 .05
❑ 478 Gary DiSarcina .15 .05
❑ 479 Steve Bedrosian .15 .05
❑ 480 Eric Anthony .15 .05
❑ 481 Julio Franco .30 .10
❑ 482 Tommy Greene .15 .05
❑ 483 Pat Kelly .15 .05
❑ 484 Nate Minchey .15 .05
❑ 485 William Pennyfeather .15 .05
❑ 486 Harold Baines .30 .10
❑ 487 Howard Johnson .15 .05
❑ 488 Angel Miranda .15 .05
❑ 489 Scott Sanders .15 .05
❑ 490 Shawon Dunston .15 .05
❑ 491 Mel Rojas .15 .05
❑ 492 Jeff Nelson .15 .05
❑ 493 Archi Cianfrocco .15 .05
❑ 494 Al Martin .15 .05
❑ 495 Mike Gallego .15 .05
❑ 496 Mike Henneman .15 .05
❑ 497 Armando Reynoso .15 .05
❑ 498 Mickey Morandini .15 .05
❑ 499 Rick Renteria .15 .05
❑ 500 Rick Sutcliffe .30 .10
❑ 501 Bobby Jones .15 .05
❑ 502 Gary Gaetti .30 .10
❑ 503 Rick Aguilera .15 .05
❑ 504 Todd Stottlemyre .15 .05
❑ 505 Mike Mohler .15 .05
❑ 506 Mike Stanton .15 .05
❑ 507 Jose Guzman .15 .05
❑ 508 Kevin Rogers .15 .05
❑ 509 Chuck Carr .15 .05
❑ 510 Chris Jones .15 .05
❑ 511 Brent Mayne .15 .05
❑ 512 Greg Harris .15 .05
❑ 513 Dave Henderson .15 .05
❑ 514 Eric Hillman .15 .05
❑ 515 Dan Peltier .15 .05
❑ 516 Craig Shipley .15 .05
❑ 517 John Valentin .15 .05
❑ 518 Wilson Alvarez .15 .05
❑ 519 Andujar Cedeno .15 .05
❑ 520 Troy Neel .15 .05
❑ 521 Tom Candiotti .15 .05
❑ 522 Matt Mieske .15 .05
❑ 523 Jim Thome .50 .20
❑ 524 Lou Frazier .15 .05
❑ 525 Mike Jackson .15 .05
❑ 526 Pedro A.Martinez RC .15 .05
❑ 527 Roger Pavlik .15 .05
❑ 528 Kent Bottenfield .15 .05
❑ 529 Felix Jose .15 .05
❑ 530 Mark Guthrie .15 .05
❑ 531 Steve Farr .15 .05
❑ 532 Craig Paquette .15 .05
❑ 533 Doug Jones .15 .05
❑ 534 Luis Alicea .15 .05
❑ 535 Cory Snyder .15 .05
❑ 536 Paul Sorrento .15 .05
❑ 537 Nigel Wilson .15 .05
❑ 538 Jeff King .15 .05
❑ 539 Willie Greene .15 .05
❑ 540 Kirk McCaskill .15 .05

❑ 541 Al Osuna .15 .05
❑ 542 Greg Hibbard .15 .05
❑ 543 Brett Butler .30 .10
❑ 544 Jose Valentin .15 .05
❑ 545 Wil Cordero .15 .05
❑ 546 Chris Bosio .15 .05
❑ 547 Jamie Moyer .30 .10
❑ 548 Jim Eisenreich .15 .05
❑ 549 Vinny Castilla .30 .10
❑ 550 Dave Winfield CL .15 .05
❑ 551 John Roper .15 .05
❑ 552 Lance Johnson .15 .05
❑ 553 Scott Kamieniecki .15 .05
❑ 554 Mike Moore .15 .05
❑ 555 Steve Buechele .15 .05
❑ 556 Terry Pendleton .30 .10
❑ 557 Todd Van Poppel .15 .05
❑ 558 Rob Butler .15 .05
❑ 559 Zane Smith .15 .05
❑ 560 David Hulse .15 .05
❑ 561 Tim Costo .15 .05
❑ 562 John Habyan .15 .05
❑ 563 Terry Jorgensen .15 .05
❑ 564 Matt Nokes .15 .05
❑ 565 Kevin McReynolds .15 .05
❑ 566 Phil Plantier .15 .05
❑ 567 Chris Turner .15 .05
❑ 568 Carlos Delgado .50 .20
❑ 569 John Jaha .15 .05
❑ 570 Dwight Smith .15 .05
❑ 571 John Vander Wal .15 .05
❑ 572 Trevor Wilson .15 .05
❑ 573 Felix Fermin .15 .05
❑ 574 Marc Newfield .15 .05
❑ 575 Jeromy Burnitz .30 .10
❑ 576 Leo Gomez .15 .05
❑ 577 Curt Schilling .30 .10
❑ 578 Kevin Young .15 .05
❑ 579 Jerry Spradlin RC .15 .05
❑ 580 Curt Leskanic .15 .05
❑ 581 Carl Willis .15 .05
❑ 582 Alex Fernandez .15 .05
❑ 583 Mark Holzemer .15 .05
❑ 584 Domingo Martinez .15 .05
❑ 585 Pete Smith .15 .05
❑ 586 Brian Jordan .30 .10
❑ 587 Kevin Gross .15 .05
❑ 588 J.R. Phillips .15 .05
❑ 589 Chris Nabholz .15 .05
❑ 590 Bill Wertz .15 .05
❑ 591 Derek Bell .15 .05
❑ 592 Brady Anderson .30 .10
❑ 593 Matt Turner .15 .05
❑ 594 Pete Incaviglia .15 .05
❑ 595 Greg Gagne .15 .05
❑ 596 John Flaherty .15 .05
❑ 597 Scott Livingstone .15 .05
❑ 598 Rod Bolton .15 .05
❑ 599 Mike Perez .15 .05
❑ 600 Roger Clemens CL .75 .30
❑ 601 Tony Castillo .15 .05
❑ 602 Henry Mercedes .15 .05
❑ 603 Mike Fetters .15 .05
❑ 604 Rod Beck .15 .05
❑ 605 Damon Buford .15 .05
❑ 606 Matt Whiteside .15 .05
❑ 607 Shawn Green .75 .30
❑ 608 Midre Cummings .15 .05
❑ 609 Jeff McNeely .15 .05
❑ 610 Danny Sheaffer .15 .05
❑ 611 Paul Wagner .15 .05
❑ 612 Torey Lovullo .15 .05
❑ 613 Javier Lopez .30 .10
❑ 614 Mariano Duncan .15 .05
❑ 615 Doug Brocail .15 .05
❑ 616 Dave Hansen .15 .05
❑ 617 Ryan Klesko .30 .10
❑ 618 Eric Davis .30 .10
❑ 619 Scott Ruffcorn .15 .05
❑ 620 Mike Trombley .15 .05
❑ 621 Jaime Navarro .15 .05
❑ 622 Rheal Cormier .15 .05
❑ 623 Jose Offerman .15 .05
❑ 624 David Segui .15 .05
❑ 625 Robb Nen .30 .10
❑ 626 Dave Gallagher .15 .05
❑ 627 Julian Tavarez RC .30 .10
❑ 628 Chris Gomez .15 .05
❑ 629 Jeffrey Hammonds .15 .05
❑ 630 Scott Brosius .30 .10
❑ 631 Willie Blair .15 .05
❑ 632 Doug Drabek .15 .05
❑ 633 Bill Wegman .15 .05
❑ 634 Jeff McKnight .15 .05
❑ 635 Rich Rodriguez .15 .05
❑ 636 Steve Trachsel .15 .05
❑ 637 Buddy Groom .15 .05
❑ 638 Sterling Hitchcock .15 .05
❑ 639 Chuck McElroy .15 .05
❑ 640 Rene Gonzales .15 .05
❑ 641 Dan Plesac .15 .05
❑ 642 Jeff Branson .15 .05
❑ 643 Darrell Whitmore .15 .05
❑ 644 Paul Quantrill .15 .05
❑ 645 Rich Rowland .15 .05
❑ 646 Curtis Pride RC .30 .10
❑ 647 Erik Plantenberg RC .15 .05
❑ 648 Albie Lopez .15 .05
❑ 649 Rich Batchelor RC .15 .05
❑ 650 Lee Smith .30 .10
❑ 651 Cliff Floyd .30 .10
❑ 652 Pete Schourek .15 .05
❑ 653 Reggie Jefferson .15 .05
❑ 654 Bill Haselman .15 .05
❑ 655 Steve Hosey .15 .05
❑ 656 Mark Clark .15 .05
❑ 657 Mark Davis .15 .05
❑ 658 Dave Magadan .15 .05
❑ 659 Candy Maldonado .15 .05
❑ 660 Mark Langston CL .15 .05

1995 Donruss

❑ COMPLETE SET (550) 30.00 12.00
❑ COMPLETE SERIES 1 (330) 20.00 8.00
❑ COMPLETE SERIES 2 (220) 10.00 4.00
❑ 1 David Justice .30 .10
❑ 2 Rene Arocha .15 .05
❑ 3 Sandy Alomar Jr. .15 .05
❑ 4 Luis Lopez .15 .05
❑ 5 Mike Piazza 1.25 .50
❑ 6 Bobby Jones .15 .05
❑ 7 Damion Easley .15 .05
❑ 8 Barry Bonds 2.00 .75
❑ 9 Mike Mussina .50 .20
❑ 10 Kevin Seitzer .15 .05
❑ 11 John Smiley .15 .05
❑ 12 Wm.VanLandingham .15 .05
❑ 13 Ron Darling .15 .05
❑ 14 Walt Weiss .15 .05
❑ 15 Mike Lansing .15 .05
❑ 16 Allen Watson .15 .05
❑ 17 Aaron Sele .15 .05
❑ 18 Randy Johnson .75 .30
❑ 19 Dean Palmer .30 .10
❑ 20 Jeff Bagwell .50 .20
❑ 21 Curt Schilling .30 .10
❑ 22 Darrell Whitmore .15 .05
❑ 23 Steve Trachsel .15 .05
❑ 24 Dan Wilson .15 .05
❑ 25 Steve Finley .30 .10
❑ 26 Bret Boone .30 .10
❑ 27 Charles Johnson .30 .10
❑ 28 Mike Stanton .15 .05
❑ 29 Ismael Valdes .15 .05
❑ 30 Salomon Torres .15 .05
❑ 31 Eric Anthony .15 .05
❑ 32 Spike Owen .15 .05
❑ 33 Joey Cora .15 .05
❑ 34 Robert Eenhoorn .15 .05
❑ 35 Rick White .15 .05
❑ 36 Omar Vizquel .50 .20
❑ 37 Carlos Delgado .30 .10
❑ 38 Eddie Williams .15 .05
❑ 39 Shawon Dunston .15 .05
❑ 40 Darrin Fletcher .15 .05
❑ 41 Leo Gomez .15 .05
❑ 42 Juan Gonzalez .30 .10
❑ 43 Luis Alicea .15 .05
❑ 44 Ken Ryan .15 .05
❑ 45 Lou Whitaker .30 .10
❑ 46 Mike Blowers .15 .05
❑ 47 Willie Blair .15 .05
❑ 48 Todd Van Poppel .15 .05
❑ 49 Roberto Alomar .50 .20
❑ 50 Ozzie Smith 1.25 .50
❑ 51 Sterling Hitchcock .15 .05
❑ 52 Mo Vaughn .30 .10
❑ 53 Rick Aguilera .15 .05
❑ 54 Kent Mercker .15 .05
❑ 55 Don Mattingly 2.00 .75
❑ 56 Bob Scanlan .15 .05
❑ 57 Wilson Alvarez .15 .05
❑ 58 Jose Mesa .15 .05
❑ 59 Scott Kamieniecki .15 .05
❑ 60 Todd Jones .15 .05
❑ 61 John Kruk .30 .10
❑ 62 Mike Stanley .15 .05
❑ 63 Tino Martinez .50 .20
❑ 64 Eddie Zambrano .15 .05
❑ 65 Todd Hundley .15 .05
❑ 66 Jamie Moyer .30 .10
❑ 67 Rich Amaral .15 .05
❑ 68 Jose Valentin .15 .05
❑ 69 Alex Gonzalez .15 .05
❑ 70 Kurt Abbott .15 .05
❑ 71 Delino DeShields .15 .05
❑ 72 Brian Anderson .15 .05
❑ 73 John Vander Wal .15 .05
❑ 74 Turner Ward .15 .05
❑ 75 Tim Raines .30 .10
❑ 76 Mark Acre .15 .05
❑ 77 Jose Offerman .15 .05
❑ 78 Jimmy Key .30 .10
❑ 79 Mark Whiten .15 .05
❑ 80 Mark Gubicza .15 .05
❑ 81 Darren Hall .15 .05
❑ 82 Travis Fryman .30 .10
❑ 83 Cal Ripken 2.50 1.00
❑ 84 Geronimo Berroa .15 .05
❑ 85 Bret Barberie .15 .05
❑ 86 Andy Ashby .15 .05
❑ 87 Steve Avery .15 .05
❑ 88 Rich Becker .15 .05
❑ 89 John Valentin .15 .05
❑ 90 Glenallen Hill .15 .05
❑ 91 Carlos Garcia .15 .05
❑ 92 Dennis Martinez .30 .10
❑ 93 Pat Kelly .15 .05
❑ 94 Orlando Miller .15 .05
❑ 95 Felix Jose .15 .05
❑ 96 Mike Kingery .15 .05
❑ 97 Jeff Kent .30 .10
❑ 98 Pete Incaviglia .15 .05
❑ 99 Chad Curtis .15 .05
❑ 100 Thomas Howard .15 .05
❑ 101 Hector Carrasco .15 .05
❑ 102 Tom Pagnozzi .15 .05
❑ 103 Danny Tartabull .15 .05
❑ 104 Donnie Elliott .15 .05
❑ 105 Danny Jackson .15 .05
❑ 106 Steve Dunn .15 .05
❑ 107 Roger Salkeld .15 .05
❑ 108 Jeff King .15 .05
❑ 109 Cecil Fielder .30 .10
❑ 110 Paul Molitor CL .15 .05
❑ 111 Denny Neagle .30 .10
❑ 112 Troy Neel .15 .05
❑ 113 Rod Beck .15 .05
❑ 114 Alex Rodriguez 2.00 .75
❑ 115 Joey Eischen .15 .05

❑ 116 Tom Candiotti	.15	.05
❑ 117 Ray McDavid	.15	.05
❑ 118 Vince Coleman	.15	.05
❑ 119 Pete Harnisch	.15	.05
❑ 120 David Nied	.15	.05
❑ 121 Pat Rapp	.15	.05
❑ 122 Sammy Sosa	.75	.30
❑ 123 Steve Reed	.15	.05
❑ 124 Jose Oliva	.15	.05
❑ 125 Ricky Bottalico	.15	.05
❑ 126 Jose DeLeon	.15	.05
❑ 127 Pat Hentgen	.15	.05
❑ 128 Will Clark	.50	.20
❑ 129 Mark Dewey	.15	.05
❑ 130 Greg Vaughn	.15	.05
❑ 131 Darren Dreifort	.15	.05
❑ 132 Ed Sprague	.15	.05
❑ 133 Lee Smith	.30	.10
❑ 134 Charles Nagy	.15	.05
❑ 135 Phil Plantier	.15	.05
❑ 136 Jason Jacome	.15	.05
❑ 137 Jose Lima	.15	.05
❑ 138 J.R. Phillips	.15	.05
❑ 139 J.T. Snow	.30	.10
❑ 140 Michael Huff	.15	.05
❑ 141 Billy Brewer	.15	.05
❑ 142 Jeromy Burnitz	.30	.10
❑ 143 Ricky Bones	.15	.05
❑ 144 Carlos Rodriguez	.15	.05
❑ 145 Luis Gonzalez	.30	.10
❑ 146 Mark Lemke	.15	.05
❑ 147 Al Martin	.15	.05
❑ 148 Mike Bordick	.15	.05
❑ 149 Robb Nen	.30	.10
❑ 150 Wil Cordero	.15	.05
❑ 151 Edgar Martinez	.50	.20
❑ 152 Gerald Williams	.15	.05
❑ 153 Esteban Beltre	.15	.05
❑ 154 Mike Moore	.15	.05
❑ 155 Mark Langston	.15	.05
❑ 156 Mark Clark	.15	.05
❑ 157 Bobby Ayala	.15	.05
❑ 158 Rick Wilkins	.15	.05
❑ 159 Bobby Munoz	.15	.05
❑ 160 Brett Butler CL	.15	.05
❑ 161 Scott Erickson	.15	.05
❑ 162 Paul Molitor	.30	.10
❑ 163 Jon Lieber	.15	.05
❑ 164 Jason Grimsley	.15	.05
❑ 165 Norberto Martin	.15	.05
❑ 166 Javier Lopez	.30	.10
❑ 167 Brian McRae	.15	.05
❑ 168 Gary Sheffield	.30	.10
❑ 169 Marcus Moore	.15	.05
❑ 170 John Hudek	.15	.05
❑ 171 Kelly Stinnett	.15	.05
❑ 172 Chris Gomez	.15	.05
❑ 173 Rey Sanchez	.15	.05
❑ 174 Juan Guzman	.15	.05
❑ 175 Chan Ho Park	.30	.10
❑ 176 Terry Shumpert	.15	.05
❑ 177 Steve Ontiveros	.15	.05
❑ 178 Brad Ausmus	.30	.10
❑ 179 Tim Davis	.15	.05
❑ 180 Billy Ashley	.15	.05
❑ 181 Vinny Castilla	.30	.10
❑ 182 Bill Spiers	.15	.05
❑ 183 Randy Knorr	.15	.05
❑ 184 Brian L.Hunter	.15	.05
❑ 185 Pat Meares	.15	.05
❑ 186 Steve Buechele	.15	.05
❑ 187 Kirt Manwaring	.15	.05
❑ 188 Tim Naehring	.15	.05
❑ 189 Matt Mieske	.15	.05
❑ 190 Josias Manzanillo	.15	.05
❑ 191 Greg McMichael	.15	.05
❑ 192 Chuck Carr	.15	.05
❑ 193 Midre Cummings	.15	.05
❑ 194 Darryl Strawberry	.30	.10
❑ 195 Greg Gagne	.15	.05
❑ 196 Steve Cooke	.15	.05
❑ 197 Woody Williams	.15	.05
❑ 198 Ron Karkovice	.15	.05
❑ 199 Phil Leftwich	.15	.05
❑ 200 Jim Thome	.50	.20
❑ 201 Brady Anderson	.30	.10
❑ 202 Pedro A.Martinez	.15	.05
❑ 203 Steve Karsay	.15	.05
❑ 204 Reggie Sanders	.30	.10
❑ 205 Bill Risley	.15	.05
❑ 206 Jay Bell	.30	.10
❑ 207 Kevin Brown	.30	.10
❑ 208 Tim Scott	.15	.05
❑ 209 Lenny Dykstra	.30	.10
❑ 210 Willie Greene	.15	.05
❑ 211 Jim Eisenreich	.15	.05
❑ 212 Cliff Floyd	.30	.10
❑ 213 Otis Nixon	.15	.05
❑ 214 Eduardo Perez	.15	.05
❑ 215 Manuel Lee	.15	.05
❑ 216 Armando Benitez	.15	.05
❑ 217 Dave McCarty	.15	.05
❑ 218 Scott Livingstone	.15	.05
❑ 219 Chad Kreuter	.15	.05
❑ 220 Don Mattingly CL	1.00	.40
❑ 221 Brian Jordan	.30	.10
❑ 222 Matt Whiteside	.15	.05
❑ 223 Jim Edmonds	.50	.20
❑ 224 Tony Gwynn	1.00	.40
❑ 225 Jose Lind	.15	.05
❑ 226 Marvin Freeman	.15	.05
❑ 227 Ken Hill	.15	.05
❑ 228 David Hulse	.15	.05
❑ 229 Joe Hesketh	.15	.05
❑ 230 Roberto Petagine	.15	.05
❑ 231 Jeffrey Hammonds	.15	.05
❑ 232 John Jaha	.15	.05
❑ 233 John Burkett	.15	.05
❑ 234 Hal Morris	.15	.05
❑ 235 Tony Castillo	.15	.05
❑ 236 Ryan Bowen	.15	.05
❑ 237 Wayne Kirby	.15	.05
❑ 238 Brent Mayne	.15	.05
❑ 239 Jim Bullinger	.15	.05
❑ 240 Mike Lieberthal	.30	.10
❑ 241 Barry Larkin	.50	.20
❑ 242 David Segui	.15	.05
❑ 243 Jose Bautista	.15	.05
❑ 244 Hector Fajardo	.15	.05
❑ 245 Orel Hershiser	.30	.10
❑ 246 James Mouton	.15	.05
❑ 247 Scott Leius	.15	.05
❑ 248 Tom Glavine	.50	.20
❑ 249 Danny Bautista	.15	.05
❑ 250 Jose Mercedes	.15	.05
❑ 251 Marquis Grissom	.30	.10
❑ 252 Charlie Hayes	.15	.05
❑ 253 Ryan Klesko	.30	.10
❑ 254 Vicente Palacios	.15	.05
❑ 255 Matias Carrillo	.15	.05
❑ 256 Gary DiSarcina	.15	.05
❑ 257 Kirk Gibson	.30	.10
❑ 258 Garey Ingram	.15	.05
❑ 259 Alex Fernandez	.15	.05
❑ 260 John Mabry	.15	.05
❑ 261 Chris Howard	.15	.05
❑ 262 Miguel Jimenez	.15	.05
❑ 263 Heathcliff Slocumb	.15	.05
❑ 264 Albert Belle	.30	.10
❑ 265 Dave Clark	.15	.05
❑ 266 Joe Orsulak	.15	.05
❑ 267 Joey Hamilton	.15	.05
❑ 268 Mark Portugal	.15	.05
❑ 269 Kevin Tapani	.15	.05
❑ 270 Sid Fernandez	.15	.05
❑ 271 Steve Dreyer	.15	.05
❑ 272 Denny Hocking	.15	.05
❑ 273 Troy O'Leary	.15	.05
❑ 274 Milt Cuyler	.15	.05
❑ 275 Frank Thomas	.75	.30
❑ 276 Jorge Fabregas	.15	.05
❑ 277 Mike Gallego	.15	.05
❑ 278 Mickey Morandini	.15	.05
❑ 279 Roberto Hernandez	.15	.05
❑ 280 Henry Rodriguez	.15	.05
❑ 281 Garret Anderson	.30	.10
❑ 282 Bob Wickman	.15	.05
❑ 283 Gar Finnvold	.15	.05
❑ 284 Paul O'Neill	.50	.20
❑ 285 Royce Clayton	.15	.05
❑ 286 Chuck Knoblauch	.30	.10
❑ 287 Johnny Ruffin	.15	.05
❑ 288 Dave Nilsson	.15	.05
❑ 289 David Cone	.30	.10
❑ 290 Chuck McElroy	.15	.05
❑ 291 Kevin Stocker	.15	.05
❑ 292 Jose Rijo	.15	.05
❑ 293 Sean Berry	.15	.05
❑ 294 Ozzie Guillen	.30	.10
❑ 295 Chris Hoiles	.15	.05
❑ 296 Kevin Foster	.15	.05
❑ 297 Jeff Frye	.15	.05
❑ 298 Lance Johnson	.15	.05
❑ 299 Mike Kelly	.15	.05
❑ 300 Ellis Burks	.30	.10
❑ 301 Roberto Kelly	.15	.05
❑ 302 Dante Bichette	.30	.10
❑ 303 Alvaro Espinoza	.15	.05
❑ 304 Alex Cole	.15	.05
❑ 305 Rickey Henderson	.75	.30
❑ 306 Dave Weathers	.15	.05
❑ 307 Shane Reynolds	.15	.05
❑ 308 Bobby Bonilla	.30	.10
❑ 309 Junior Felix	.15	.05
❑ 310 Jeff Fassero	.15	.05
❑ 311 Darren Lewis	.15	.05
❑ 312 John Doherty	.15	.05
❑ 313 Scott Servais	.15	.05
❑ 314 Rick Helling	.15	.05
❑ 315 Pedro Martinez	.50	.20
❑ 316 Wes Chamberlain	.15	.05
❑ 317 Bryan Eversgerd	.15	.05
❑ 318 Trevor Hoffman	.30	.10
❑ 319 John Patterson	.15	.05
❑ 320 Matt Walbeck	.15	.05
❑ 321 Jeff Montgomery	.15	.05
❑ 322 Mel Rojas	.15	.05
❑ 323 Eddie Taubensee	.15	.05
❑ 324 Ray Lankford	.30	.10
❑ 325 Jose Vizcaino	.15	.05
❑ 326 Carlos Baerga	.15	.05
❑ 327 Jack Voigt	.15	.05
❑ 328 Julio Franco	.30	.10
❑ 329 Brent Gates	.15	.05
❑ 330 Kirby Puckett CL	.50	.20
❑ 331 Greg Maddux	1.25	.50
❑ 332 Jason Bere	.15	.05
❑ 333 Bill Wegman	.15	.05
❑ 334 Tuffy Rhodes	.15	.05
❑ 335 Kevin Young	.15	.05
❑ 336 Andy Benes	.15	.05
❑ 337 Pedro Astacio	.15	.05
❑ 338 Reggie Jefferson	.15	.05
❑ 339 Tim Belcher	.15	.05
❑ 340 Ken Griffey Jr.	1.25	.50
❑ 341 Mariano Duncan	.15	.05
❑ 342 Andres Galarraga	.30	.10
❑ 343 Rondell White	.30	.10
❑ 344 Cory Bailey	.15	.05
❑ 345 Bryan Harvey	.15	.05
❑ 346 John Franco	.30	.10
❑ 347 Greg Swindell	.15	.05
❑ 348 David West	.15	.05
❑ 349 Fred McGriff	.50	.20
❑ 350 Jose Canseco	.50	.20
❑ 351 Orlando Merced	.15	.05
❑ 352 Rheal Cormier	.15	.05
❑ 353 Carlos Pulido	.15	.05
❑ 354 Terry Steinbach	.15	.05
❑ 355 Wade Boggs	.50	.20
❑ 356 B.J. Surhoff	.30	.10
❑ 357 Rafael Palmeiro	.50	.20
❑ 358 Anthony Young	.15	.05
❑ 359 Tom Brunansky	.15	.05
❑ 360 Todd Stottlemyre	.15	.05
❑ 361 Chris Turner	.15	.05
❑ 362 Joe Boever	.15	.05
❑ 363 Jeff Blauser	.15	.05
❑ 364 Derek Bell	.15	.05
❑ 365 Matt Williams	.30	.10
❑ 366 Jeremy Hernandez	.15	.05
❑ 367 Joe Girardi	.15	.05
❑ 368 Mike Devereaux	.15	.05
❑ 369 Jim Abbott	.50	.20
❑ 370 Manny Ramirez	.50	.20
❑ 371 Kenny Lofton	.30	.10
❑ 372 Mark Smith	.15	.05
❑ 373 Dave Fleming	.15	.05

❑	374	Dave Stewart	.30	.10
❑	375	Roger Pavlik	.15	.05
❑	376	Hipolito Pichardo	.15	.05
❑	377	Bill Taylor	.15	.05
❑	378	Robin Ventura	.30	.10
❑	379	Bernard Gilkey	.15	.05
❑	380	Kirby Puckett	.75	.30
❑	381	Steve Howe	.15	.05
❑	382	Devon White	.30	.10
❑	383	Roberto Mejia	.15	.05
❑	384	Darrin Jackson	.15	.05
❑	385	Mike Morgan	.15	.05
❑	386	Rusty Meacham	.15	.05
❑	387	Bill Swift	.15	.05
❑	388	Lou Frazier	.15	.05
❑	389	Andy Van Slyke	.50	.20
❑	390	Brett Butler	.30	.10
❑	391	Bobby Witt	.15	.05
❑	392	Jeff Conine	.30	.10
❑	393	Tim Hyers	.15	.05
❑	394	Terry Pendleton	.30	.10
❑	395	Ricky Jordan	.15	.05
❑	396	Eric Plunk	.15	.05
❑	397	Melido Perez	.15	.05
❑	398	Darryl Kile	.30	.10
❑	399	Mark McLemore	.15	.05
❑	400	Greg W.Harris	.15	.05
❑	401	Jim Leyritz	.15	.05
❑	402	Doug Strange	.15	.05
❑	403	Tim Salmon	.50	.20
❑	404	Terry Mulholland	.15	.05
❑	405	Robby Thompson	.15	.05
❑	406	Ruben Sierra	.30	.10
❑	407	Tony Phillips	.15	.05
❑	408	Moises Alou	.30	.10
❑	409	Felix Fermin	.15	.05
❑	410	Pat Listach	.15	.05
❑	411	Kevin Bass	.15	.05
❑	412	Ben McDonald	.15	.05
❑	413	Scott Cooper	.15	.05
❑	414	Jody Reed	.15	.05
❑	415	Deion Sanders	.50	.20
❑	416	Ricky Gutierrez	.15	.05
❑	417	Gregg Jefferies	.15	.05
❑	418	Jack McDowell	.15	.05
❑	419	Al Leiter	.30	.10
❑	420	Tony Longmire	.15	.05
❑	421	Paul Wagner	.15	.05
❑	422	Geronimo Pena	.15	.05
❑	423	Ivan Rodriguez	.50	.20
❑	424	Kevin Gross	.15	.05
❑	425	Kirk McCaskill	.15	.05
❑	426	Greg Myers	.15	.05
❑	427	Roger Clemens	1.50	.60
❑	428	Chris Hammond	.15	.05
❑	429	Randy Myers	.15	.05
❑	430	Roger Mason	.15	.05
❑	431	Bret Saberhagen	.30	.10
❑	432	Jeff Reboulet	.15	.05
❑	433	John Olerud	.30	.10
❑	434	Bill Gullickson	.15	.05
❑	435	Eddie Murray	.75	.30
❑	436	Pedro Munoz	.15	.05
❑	437	Charlie O'Brien	.15	.05
❑	438	Jeff Nelson	.15	.05
❑	439	Mike Macfarlane	.15	.05
❑	440	Don Mattingly CL	1.00	.40
❑	441	Derrick May	.15	.05
❑	442	John Roper	.15	.05
❑	443	Darryl Hamilton	.15	.05
❑	444	Dan Miceli	.15	.05
❑	445	Tony Eusebio	.15	.05
❑	446	Jerry Browne	.15	.05
❑	447	Wally Joyner	.30	.10
❑	448	Brian Harper	.15	.05
❑	449	Scott Fletcher	.15	.05
❑	450	Bip Roberts	.15	.05
❑	451	Pete Smith	.15	.05
❑	452	Chili Davis	.30	.10
❑	453	Dave Hollins	.15	.05
❑	454	Tony Pena	.15	.05
❑	455	Butch Henry	.15	.05
❑	456	Craig Biggio	.50	.20
❑	457	Zane Smith	.15	.05
❑	458	Ryan Thompson	.15	.05
❑	459	Mike Jackson	.15	.05
❑	460	Mark McGwire	2.00	.75
❑	461	John Smoltz	.50	.20
❑	462	Steve Scarsone	.15	.05
❑	463	Greg Colbrunn	.15	.05
❑	464	Shawn Green	.30	.10
❑	465	David Wells	.30	.10
❑	466	Jose Hernandez	.15	.05
❑	467	Chip Hale	.15	.05
❑	468	Tony Tarasco	.15	.05
❑	469	Kevin Mitchell	.15	.05
❑	470	Billy Hatcher	.15	.05
❑	471	Jay Buhner	.30	.10
❑	472	Ken Caminiti	.30	.10
❑	473	Tom Henke	.15	.05
❑	474	Todd Worrell	.15	.05
❑	475	Mark Eichhorn	.15	.05
❑	476	Bruce Ruffin	.15	.05
❑	477	Chuck Finley	.30	.10
❑	478	Marc Newfield	.15	.05
❑	479	Paul Shuey	.15	.05
❑	480	Bob Tewksbury	.15	.05
❑	481	Ramon J.Martinez	.15	.05
❑	482	Melvin Nieves	.15	.05
❑	483	Todd Zeile	.15	.05
❑	484	Benito Santiago	.30	.10
❑	485	Stan Javier	.15	.05
❑	486	Kirk Rueter	.15	.05
❑	487	Andre Dawson	.30	.10
❑	488	Eric Karros	.30	.10
❑	489	Dave Magadan	.15	.05
❑	490	Joe Carter CL	.15	.05
❑	491	Randy Velarde	.15	.05
❑	492	Larry Walker	.30	.10
❑	493	Cris Carpenter	.15	.05
❑	494	Tom Gordon	.15	.05
❑	495	Dave Burba	.15	.05
❑	496	Darren Bragg	.15	.05
❑	497	Darren Daulton	.30	.10
❑	498	Don Slaught	.15	.05
❑	499	Pat Borders	.15	.05
❑	500	Lenny Harris	.15	.05
❑	501	Joe Ausanio	.15	.05
❑	502	Alan Trammell	.30	.10
❑	503	Mike Fetters	.15	.05
❑	504	Scott Ruffcorn	.15	.05
❑	505	Rich Rowland	.15	.05
❑	506	Juan Samuel	.15	.05
❑	507	Bo Jackson	.75	.30
❑	508	Jeff Branson	.15	.05
❑	509	Bernie Williams	.50	.20
❑	510	Paul Sorrento	.15	.05
❑	511	Dennis Eckersley	.30	.10
❑	512	Pat Mahomes	.15	.05
❑	513	Rusty Greer	.30	.10
❑	514	Luis Polonia	.15	.05
❑	515	Willie Banks	.15	.05
❑	516	John Wetteland	.30	.10
❑	517	Mike LaValliere	.15	.05
❑	518	Tommy Greene	.15	.05
❑	519	Mark Grace	.50	.20
❑	520	Bob Hamelin	.15	.05
❑	521	Scott Sanderson	.15	.05
❑	522	Joe Carter	.30	.10
❑	523	Jeff Brantley	.15	.05
❑	524	Andrew Lorraine	.15	.05
❑	525	Rico Brogna	.15	.05
❑	526	Shane Mack	.15	.05
❑	527	Mark Wohlers	.15	.05
❑	528	Scott Sanders	.15	.05
❑	529	Chris Bosio	.15	.05
❑	530	Andujar Cedeno	.15	.05
❑	531	Kenny Rogers	.30	.10
❑	532	Doug Drabek	.15	.05
❑	533	Curt Leskanic	.15	.05
❑	534	Craig Shipley	.15	.05
❑	535	Craig Grebeck	.15	.05
❑	536	Cal Eldred	.15	.05
❑	537	Mickey Tettleton	.15	.05
❑	538	Harold Baines	.30	.10
❑	539	Tim Wallach	.15	.05
❑	540	Damon Buford	.15	.05
❑	541	Lenny Webster	.15	.05
❑	542	Kevin Appier	.30	.10
❑	543	Raul Mondesi	.30	.10
❑	544	Eric Young	.15	.05
❑	545	Russ Davis	.15	.05
❑	546	Mike Benjamin	.15	.05
❑	547	Mike Greenwell	.15	.05
❑	548	Scott Brosius	.30	.10
❑	549	Brian Dorsett	.15	.05
❑	550	Chili Davis CL	.15	.05

1996 Donruss

❑		COMPLETE SET (550)	40.00	16.00
❑		COMPLETE SERIES 1 (330)	25.00	10.00
❑		COMPLETE SERIES 2 (220)	15.00	6.00
❑	1	Frank Thomas	.75	.30
❑	2	Jason Bates	.30	.10
❑	3	Steve Sparks	.30	.10
❑	4	Scott Servais	.30	.10
❑	5	Angelo Encarnacion RC	.30	.10
❑	6	Scott Sanders	.30	.10
❑	7	Billy Ashley	.30	.10
❑	8	Alex Rodriguez	1.50	.60
❑	9	Sean Bergman	.30	.10
❑	10	Brad Radke	.30	.10
❑	11	Andy Van Slyke	.50	.20
❑	12	Joe Girardi	.30	.10
❑	13	Mark Grudzielanek	.30	.10
❑	14	Rick Aguilera	.30	.10
❑	15	Randy Veres	.30	.10
❑	16	Tim Bogar	.30	.10
❑	17	Dave Veres	.30	.10
❑	18	Kevin Stocker	.30	.10
❑	19	Marquis Grissom	.30	.10
❑	20	Will Clark	.50	.20
❑	21	Jay Bell	.30	.10
❑	22	Allen Battle	.30	.10
❑	23	Frank Rodriguez	.30	.10
❑	24	Terry Steinbach	.30	.10
❑	25	Gerald Williams	.30	.10
❑	26	Sid Roberson	.30	.10
❑	27	Greg Zaun	.30	.10
❑	28	Ozzie Timmons	.30	.10
❑	29	Vaughn Eshelman	.30	.10
❑	30	Ed Sprague	.30	.10
❑	31	Gary DiSarcina	.30	.10
❑	32	Joe Boever	.30	.10
❑	33	Steve Avery	.30	.10
❑	34	Brad Ausmus	.30	.10
❑	35	Kirt Manwaring	.30	.10
❑	36	Gary Sheffield	.30	.10
❑	37	Jason Bere	.30	.10
❑	38	Jeff Manto	.30	.10
❑	39	David Cone	.30	.10
❑	40	Manny Ramirez	.50	.20
❑	41	Sandy Alomar Jr.	.30	.10
❑	42	Curtis Goodwin	.30	.10
❑	43	Tino Martinez	.50	.20
❑	44	Woody Williams	.30	.10
❑	45	Dean Palmer	.30	.10
❑	46	Hipolito Pichardo	.30	.10
❑	47	Jason Giambi	.30	.10
❑	48	Lance Johnson	.30	.10
❑	49	Bernard Gilkey	.30	.10
❑	50	Kirby Puckett	.75	.30
❑	51	Tony Fernandez	.30	.10
❑	52	Alex Gonzalez	.30	.10
❑	53	Bret Saberhagen	.30	.10
❑	54	Lyle Mouton	.30	.10
❑	55	Brian McRae	.30	.10
❑	56	Mark Gubicza	.30	.10
❑	57	Sergio Valdez	.30	.10
❑	58	Darrin Fletcher	.30	.10

❑ 59	Steve Parris	.30	.10
❑ 60	Johnny Damon	.50	.20
❑ 61	Rickey Henderson	.75	.30
❑ 62	Darrell Whitmore	.30	.10
❑ 63	Roberto Petagine	.30	.10
❑ 64	Trenidad Hubbard	.30	.10
❑ 65	Heathcliff Slocumb	.30	.10
❑ 66	Steve Finley	.30	.10
❑ 67	Mariano Rivera	.75	.30
❑ 68	Brian L.Hunter	.30	.10
❑ 69	Jamie Moyer	.30	.10
❑ 70	Ellis Burks	.30	.10
❑ 71	Pat Kelly	.30	.10
❑ 72	Mickey Tettleton	.30	.10
❑ 73	Garret Anderson	.30	.10
❑ 74	Andy Pettitte	.50	.20
❑ 75	Glenallen Hill	.30	.10
❑ 76	Brent Gates	.30	.10
❑ 77	Lou Whitaker	.30	.10
❑ 78	David Segui	.30	.10
❑ 79	Dan Wilson	.30	.10
❑ 80	Pat Listach	.30	.10
❑ 81	Jeff Bagwell	.50	.20
❑ 82	Ben McDonald	.30	.10
❑ 83	John Valentin	.30	.10
❑ 84	John Jaha	.30	.10
❑ 85	Pete Schourek	.30	.10
❑ 86	Bryce Florie	.30	.10
❑ 87	Brian Jordan	.30	.10
❑ 88	Ron Karkovice	.30	.10
❑ 89	Al Leiter	.30	.10
❑ 90	Tony Longmire	.30	.10
❑ 91	Nelson Liriano	.30	.10
❑ 92	David Bell	.30	.10
❑ 93	Kevin Gross	.30	.10
❑ 94	Tom Candiotti	.30	.10
❑ 95	Dave Martinez	.30	.10
❑ 96	Greg Myers	.30	.10
❑ 97	Rheal Cormier	.30	.10
❑ 98	Chris Hammond	.30	.10
❑ 99	Randy Myers	.30	.10
❑ 100	Bill Pulsipher	.30	.10
❑ 101	Jason Isringhausen	.30	.10
❑ 102	Dave Stevens	.30	.10
❑ 103	Roberto Alomar	.50	.20
❑ 104	Bob Higginson	.30	.10
❑ 105	Eddie Murray	.75	.30
❑ 106	Matt Walbeck	.30	.10
❑ 107	Mark Wohlers	.30	.10
❑ 108	Jeff Nelson	.30	.10
❑ 109	Tom Goodwin	.30	.10
❑ 110	Cal Ripken CL	1.25	.50
❑ 111	Rey Sanchez	.30	.10
❑ 112	Hector Carrasco	.30	.10
❑ 113	B.J. Surhoff	.30	.10
❑ 114	Dan Miceli	.30	.10
❑ 115	Dean Hartgraves	.30	.10
❑ 116	John Burkett	.30	.10
❑ 117	Gary Gaetti	.30	.10
❑ 118	Ricky Bones	.30	.10
❑ 119	Mike Macfarlane	.30	.10
❑ 120	Bip Roberts	.30	.10
❑ 121	Dave Mlicki	.30	.10
❑ 122	Chili Davis	.30	.10
❑ 123	Mark Whiten	.30	.10
❑ 124	Herbert Perry	.30	.10
❑ 125	Butch Henry	.30	.10
❑ 126	Derek Bell	.30	.10
❑ 127	Al Martin	.30	.10
❑ 128	John Franco	.30	.10
❑ 129	W. VanLandingham	.30	.10
❑ 130	Mike Bordick	.30	.10
❑ 131	Mike Mordecai	.30	.10
❑ 132	Robby Thompson	.30	.10
❑ 133	Greg Colbrunn	.30	.10
❑ 134	Domingo Cedeno	.30	.10
❑ 135	Chad Curtis	.30	.10
❑ 136	Jose Hernandez	.30	.10
❑ 137	Scott Klingenbeck	.30	.10
❑ 138	Ryan Klesko	.30	.10
❑ 139	John Smiley	.30	.10
❑ 140	Charlie Hayes	.30	.10
❑ 141	Jay Buhner	.30	.10
❑ 142	Doug Drabek	.30	.10
❑ 143	Roger Pavlik	.30	.10
❑ 144	Todd Worrell	.30	.10
❑ 145	Cal Ripken	2.50	1.00
❑ 146	Steve Reed	.30	.10
❑ 147	Chuck Finley	.30	.10
❑ 148	Mike Blowers	.30	.10
❑ 149	Orel Hershiser	.30	.10
❑ 150	Allen Watson	.30	.10
❑ 151	Ramon Martinez	.30	.10
❑ 152	Melvin Nieves	.30	.10
❑ 153	Tripp Cromer	.30	.10
❑ 154	Yorkis Perez	.30	.10
❑ 155	Stan Javier	.30	.10
❑ 156	Mel Rojas	.30	.10
❑ 157	Aaron Sele	.30	.10
❑ 158	Eric Karros	.30	.10
❑ 159	Robb Nen	.30	.10
❑ 160	Raul Mondesi	.30	.10
❑ 161	John Wetteland	.30	.10
❑ 162	Tim Scott	.30	.10
❑ 163	Kenny Rogers	.30	.10
❑ 164	Melvin Bunch	.30	.10
❑ 165	Rod Beck	.30	.10
❑ 166	Andy Benes	.30	.10
❑ 167	Lenny Dykstra	.30	.10
❑ 168	Orlando Merced	.30	.10
❑ 169	Tomas Perez	.30	.10
❑ 170	Xavier Hernandez	.30	.10
❑ 171	Ruben Sierra	.30	.10
❑ 172	Alan Trammell	.30	.10
❑ 173	Mike Fetters	.30	.10
❑ 174	Wilson Alvarez	.30	.10
❑ 175	Erik Hanson	.30	.10
❑ 176	Travis Fryman	.30	.10
❑ 177	Jim Abbott	.50	.20
❑ 178	Bret Boone	.30	.10
❑ 179	Sterling Hitchcock	.30	.10
❑ 180	Pat Mahomes	.30	.10
❑ 181	Mark Acre	.30	.10
❑ 182	Charles Nagy	.30	.10
❑ 183	Rusty Greer	.30	.10
❑ 184	Mike Stanley	.30	.10
❑ 185	Jim Bullinger	.30	.10
❑ 186	Shane Andrews	.30	.10
❑ 187	Brian Keyser	.30	.10
❑ 188	Tyler Green	.30	.10
❑ 189	Mark Grace	.50	.20
❑ 190	Bob Hamelin	.30	.10
❑ 191	Luis Ortiz	.30	.10
❑ 192	Joe Carter	.30	.10
❑ 193	Eddie Taubensee	.30	.10
❑ 194	Brian Anderson	.30	.10
❑ 195	Edgardo Alfonzo	.30	.10
❑ 196	Pedro Munoz	.30	.10
❑ 197	David Justice	.30	.10
❑ 198	Trevor Hoffman	.30	.10
❑ 199	Bobby Ayala	.30	.10
❑ 200	Tony Eusebio	.30	.10
❑ 201	Jeff Russell	.30	.10
❑ 202	Mike Hampton	.30	.10
❑ 203	Walt Weiss	.30	.10
❑ 204	Joey Hamilton	.30	.10
❑ 205	Roberto Hernandez	.30	.10
❑ 206	Greg Vaughn	.30	.10
❑ 207	Felipe Lira	.30	.10
❑ 208	Harold Baines	.30	.10
❑ 209	Tim Wallach	.30	.10
❑ 210	Manny Alexander	.30	.10
❑ 211	Tim Laker	.30	.10
❑ 212	Chris Haney	.30	.10
❑ 213	Brian Maxcy	.30	.10
❑ 214	Eric Young	.30	.10
❑ 215	Darryl Strawberry	.30	.10
❑ 216	Barry Bonds	2.00	.75
❑ 217	Tim Naehring	.30	.10
❑ 218	Scott Brosius	.30	.10
❑ 219	Reggie Sanders	.30	.10
❑ 220	Eddie Murray CL	.50	.20
❑ 221	Luis Alicea	.30	.10
❑ 222	Albert Belle	.30	.10
❑ 223	Benji Gil	.30	.10
❑ 224	Dante Bichette	.30	.10
❑ 225	Bobby Bonilla	.30	.10
❑ 226	Todd Stottlemyre	.30	.10
❑ 227	Jim Edmonds	.30	.10
❑ 228	Todd Jones	.30	.10
❑ 229	Shawn Green	.30	.10
❑ 230	Javier Lopez	.30	.10
❑ 231	Ariel Prieto	.30	.10
❑ 232	Tony Phillips	.30	.10
❑ 233	James Mouton	.30	.10
❑ 234	Jose Oquendo	.30	.10
❑ 235	Royce Clayton	.30	.10
❑ 236	Chuck Carr	.30	.10
❑ 237	Doug Jones	.30	.10
❑ 238	Mark McLemore	.30	.10
❑ 239	Bill Swift	.30	.10
❑ 240	Scott Leius	.30	.10
❑ 241	Russ Davis	.30	.10
❑ 242	Ray Durham	.30	.10
❑ 243	Matt Mieske	.30	.10
❑ 244	Brent Mayne	.30	.10
❑ 245	Thomas Howard	.30	.10
❑ 246	Troy O'Leary	.30	.10
❑ 247	Jacob Brumfield	.30	.10
❑ 248	Mickey Morandini	.30	.10
❑ 249	Todd Hundley	.30	.10
❑ 250	Chris Bosio	.30	.10
❑ 251	Omar Vizquel	.50	.20
❑ 252	Mike Lansing	.30	.10
❑ 253	John Mabry	.30	.10
❑ 254	Mike Perez	.30	.10
❑ 255	Delino DeShields	.30	.10
❑ 256	Wil Cordero	.30	.10
❑ 257	Mike James	.30	.10
❑ 258	Todd Van Poppel	.30	.10
❑ 259	Joey Cora	.30	.10
❑ 260	Andre Dawson	.30	.10
❑ 261	Jerry DiPoto	.30	.10
❑ 262	Rick Krivda	.30	.10
❑ 263	Glenn Dishman	.30	.10
❑ 264	Mike Mimbs	.30	.10
❑ 265	John Ericks	.30	.10
❑ 266	Jose Canseco	.50	.20
❑ 267	Jeff Branson	.30	.10
❑ 268	Curt Leskanic	.30	.10
❑ 269	Jon Nunnally	.30	.10
❑ 270	Scott Stahoviak	.30	.10
❑ 271	Jeff Montgomery	.30	.10
❑ 272	Hal Morris	.30	.10
❑ 273	Esteban Loaiza	.30	.10
❑ 274	Rico Brogna	.30	.10
❑ 275	Dave Winfield	.30	.10
❑ 276	J.R. Phillips	.30	.10
❑ 277	Todd Zeile	.30	.10
❑ 278	Tom Pagnozzi	.30	.10
❑ 279	Mark Lemke	.30	.10
❑ 280	Dave Magadan	.30	.10
❑ 281	Greg McMichael	.30	.10
❑ 282	Mike Morgan	.30	.10
❑ 283	Moises Alou	.30	.10
❑ 284	Dennis Martinez	.30	.10
❑ 285	Jeff Kent	.30	.10
❑ 286	Mark Johnson	.30	.10
❑ 287	Darren Lewis	.30	.10
❑ 288	Brad Clontz	.30	.10
❑ 289	Chad Fonville	.30	.10
❑ 290	Paul Sorrento	.30	.10
❑ 291	Lee Smith	.30	.10
❑ 292	Tom Glavine	.50	.20
❑ 293	Antonio Osuna	.30	.10
❑ 294	Kevin Foster	.30	.10
❑ 295	Sandy Martinez	.30	.10
❑ 296	Mark Leiter	.30	.10
❑ 297	Julian Tavarez	.30	.10
❑ 298	Mike Kelly	.30	.10
❑ 299	Joe Oliver	.30	.10
❑ 300	John Flaherty	.30	.10
❑ 301	Don Mattingly	2.00	.75
❑ 302	Pat Meares	.30	.10
❑ 303	John Doherty	.30	.10
❑ 304	Joe Vitiello	.30	.10
❑ 305	Vinny Castilla	.30	.10
❑ 306	Jeff Brantley	.30	.10
❑ 307	Mike Greenwell	.30	.10
❑ 308	Midre Cummings	.30	.10
❑ 309	Curt Schilling	.30	.10
❑ 310	Ken Caminiti	.30	.10
❑ 311	Scott Erickson	.30	.10
❑ 312	Carl Everett	.30	.10
❑ 313	Charles Johnson	.30	.10
❑ 314	Alex Diaz	.30	.10
❑ 315	Jose Mesa	.30	.10
❑ 316	Mark Carreon	.30	.10

❑ 317	Carlos Perez	.30	.10
❑ 318	Ismael Valdes	.30	.10
❑ 319	Frank Castillo	.30	.10
❑ 320	Tom Henke	.30	.10
❑ 321	Spike Owen	.30	.10
❑ 322	Joe Orsulak	.30	.10
❑ 323	Paul Menhart	.30	.10
❑ 324	Pedro Borbon	.30	.10
❑ 325	Paul Molitor CL	.30	.10
❑ 326	Jeff Cirillo	.30	.10
❑ 327	Edwin Hurtado	.30	.10
❑ 328	Orlando Miller	.30	.10
❑ 329	Steve Ontiveros	.30	.10
❑ 330	Kirby Puckett CL	.50	.20
❑ 331	Scott Bullett	.30	.10
❑ 332	Andres Galarraga	.30	.10
❑ 333	Cal Eldred	.30	.10
❑ 334	Sammy Sosa	.75	.30
❑ 335	Don Slaught	.30	.10
❑ 336	Jody Reed	.30	.10
❑ 337	Roger Cedeno	.30	.10
❑ 338	Ken Griffey Jr.	1.25	.50
❑ 339	Todd Hollandsworth	.30	.10
❑ 340	Mike Trombley	.30	.10
❑ 341	Gregg Jefferies	.30	.10
❑ 342	Larry Walker	.30	.10
❑ 343	Pedro Martinez	.50	.20
❑ 344	Dwayne Hosey	.30	.10
❑ 345	Terry Pendleton	.30	.10
❑ 346	Pete Harnisch	.30	.10
❑ 347	Tony Castillo	.30	.10
❑ 348	Paul Quantrill	.30	.10
❑ 349	Fred McGriff	.50	.20
❑ 350	Ivan Rodriguez	.50	.20
❑ 351	Butch Huskey	.30	.10
❑ 352	Ozzie Smith	1.25	.50
❑ 353	Marty Cordova	.30	.10
❑ 354	John Wasdin	.30	.10
❑ 355	Wade Boggs	.50	.20
❑ 356	Dave Nilsson	.30	.10
❑ 357	Rafael Palmeiro	.50	.20
❑ 358	Luis Gonzalez	.30	.10
❑ 359	Reggie Jefferson	.30	.10
❑ 360	Carlos Delgado	.30	.10
❑ 361	Orlando Palmeiro	.30	.10
❑ 362	Chris Gomez	.30	.10
❑ 363	John Smoltz	.50	.20
❑ 364	Marc Newfield	.30	.10
❑ 365	Matt Williams	.30	.10
❑ 366	Jesus Tavarez	.30	.10
❑ 367	Bruce Ruffin	.30	.10
❑ 368	Sean Berry	.30	.10
❑ 369	Randy Velarde	.30	.10
❑ 370	Tony Pena	.30	.10
❑ 371	Jim Thome	.50	.20
❑ 372	Jeffrey Hammonds	.30	.10
❑ 373	Bob Wolcott	.30	.10
❑ 374	Juan Guzman	.30	.10
❑ 375	Juan Gonzalez	.30	.10
❑ 376	Michael Tucker	.30	.10
❑ 377	Doug Johns	.30	.10
❑ 378	Mike Cameron RC	.60	.25
❑ 379	Ray Lankford	.30	.10
❑ 380	Jose Parra	.30	.10
❑ 381	Jimmy Key	.30	.10
❑ 382	John Olerud	.30	.10
❑ 383	Kevin Ritz	.30	.10
❑ 384	Tim Raines	.30	.10
❑ 385	Rich Amaral	.30	.10
❑ 386	Keith Lockhart	.30	.10
❑ 387	Steve Scarsone	.30	.10
❑ 388	Cliff Floyd	.30	.10
❑ 389	Rich Aude	.30	.10
❑ 390	Hideo Nomo	.75	.30
❑ 391	Geronimo Berroa	.30	.10
❑ 392	Pat Rapp	.30	.10
❑ 393	Dustin Hermanson	.30	.10
❑ 394	Greg Maddux	1.25	.50
❑ 395	Darren Daulton	.30	.10
❑ 396	Kenny Lofton	.30	.10
❑ 397	Ruben Rivera	.30	.10
❑ 398	Billy Wagner	.30	.10
❑ 399	Kevin Brown	.30	.10
❑ 400	Mike Kingery	.30	.10
❑ 401	Bernie Williams	.50	.20
❑ 402	Otis Nixon	.30	.10
❑ 403	Damion Easley	.30	.10
❑ 404	Paul O'Neill	.50	.20
❑ 405	Deion Sanders	.50	.20
❑ 406	Dennis Eckersley	.30	.10
❑ 407	Tony Clark	.30	.10
❑ 408	Rondell White	.30	.10
❑ 409	Luis Sojo	.30	.10
❑ 410	David Hulse	.30	.10
❑ 411	Shane Reynolds	.30	.10
❑ 412	Chris Hoiles	.30	.10
❑ 413	Lee Tinsley	.30	.10
❑ 414	Scott Karl	.30	.10
❑ 415	Ron Gant	.30	.10
❑ 416	Brian Johnson	.30	.10
❑ 417	Jose Oliva	.30	.10
❑ 418	Jack McDowell	.30	.10
❑ 419	Paul Molitor	.30	.10
❑ 420	Ricky Bottalico	.30	.10
❑ 421	Paul Wagner	.30	.10
❑ 422	Terry Bradshaw	.30	.10
❑ 423	Bob Tewksbury	.30	.10
❑ 424	Mike Piazza	1.25	.50
❑ 425	Luis Andujar	.30	.10
❑ 426	Mark Langston	.30	.10
❑ 427	Stan Belinda	.30	.10
❑ 428	Kurt Abbott	.30	.10
❑ 429	Shawon Dunston	.30	.10
❑ 430	Bobby Jones	.30	.10
❑ 431	Jose Vizcaino	.30	.10
❑ 432	Matt Lawton RC	.40	.15
❑ 433	Pat Hentgen	.30	.10
❑ 434	Cecil Fielder	.30	.10
❑ 435	Carlos Baerga	.30	.10
❑ 436	Rich Becker	.30	.10
❑ 437	Chipper Jones	.75	.30
❑ 438	Bill Risley	.30	.10
❑ 439	Kevin Appier	.30	.10
❑ 440	Wade Boggs CL	.30	.10
❑ 441	Jaime Navarro	.30	.10
❑ 442	Barry Larkin	.50	.20
❑ 443	Jose Valentin	.30	.10
❑ 444	Bryan Rekar	.30	.10
❑ 445	Rick Wilkins	.30	.10
❑ 446	Quilvio Veras	.30	.10
❑ 447	Greg Gagne	.30	.10
❑ 448	Mark Kiefer	.30	.10
❑ 449	Bobby Witt	.30	.10
❑ 450	Andy Ashby	.30	.10
❑ 451	Alex Ochoa	.30	.10
❑ 452	Jorge Fabregas	.30	.10
❑ 453	Gene Schall	.30	.10
❑ 454	Ken Hill	.30	.10
❑ 455	Tony Tarasco	.30	.10
❑ 456	Donnie Wall	.30	.10
❑ 457	Carlos Garcia	.30	.10
❑ 458	Ryan Thompson	.30	.10
❑ 459	Marvin Benard RC	.40	.15
❑ 460	Jose Herrera	.30	.10
❑ 461	Jeff Blauser	.30	.10
❑ 462	Chris Hook	.30	.10
❑ 463	Jeff Conine	.30	.10
❑ 464	Devon White	.30	.10
❑ 465	Danny Bautista	.30	.10
❑ 466	Steve Trachsel	.30	.10
❑ 467	C.J. Nitkowski	.30	.10
❑ 468	Mike Devereaux	.30	.10
❑ 469	David Wells	.30	.10
❑ 470	Jim Eisenreich	.30	.10
❑ 471	Edgar Martinez	.50	.20
❑ 472	Craig Biggio	.50	.20
❑ 473	Jeff Frye	.30	.10
❑ 474	Karim Garcia	.30	.10
❑ 475	Jimmy Haynes	.30	.10
❑ 476	Darren Holmes	.30	.10
❑ 477	Tim Salmon	.50	.20
❑ 478	Randy Johnson	.75	.30
❑ 479	Eric Plunk	.30	.10
❑ 480	Scott Cooper	.30	.10
❑ 481	Chan Ho Park	.30	.10
❑ 482	Ray McDavid	.30	.10
❑ 483	Mark Petkovsek	.30	.10
❑ 484	Greg Swindell	.30	.10
❑ 485	George Williams	.30	.10
❑ 486	Yamil Benitez	.30	.10
❑ 487	Tim Wakefield	.30	.10
❑ 488	Kevin Tapani	.30	.10
❑ 489	Derrick May	.30	.10
❑ 490	Ken Griffey Jr. CL	.75	.30
❑ 491	Derek Jeter	2.00	.75
❑ 492	Jeff Fassero	.30	.10
❑ 493	Benito Santiago	.30	.10
❑ 494	Tom Gordon	.30	.10
❑ 495	Jamie Brewington RC	.30	.10
❑ 496	Vince Coleman	.30	.10
❑ 497	Kevin Jordan	.30	.10
❑ 498	Jeff King	.30	.10
❑ 499	Mike Simms	.30	.10
❑ 500	Jose Rijo	.30	.10
❑ 501	Denny Neagle	.30	.10
❑ 502	Jose Lima	.30	.10
❑ 503	Kevin Seitzer	.30	.10
❑ 504	Alex Fernandez	.30	.10
❑ 505	Mo Vaughn	.30	.10
❑ 506	Phil Nevin	.30	.10
❑ 507	J.T. Snow	.30	.10
❑ 508	Andujar Cedeno	.30	.10
❑ 509	Ozzie Guillen	.30	.10
❑ 510	Mark Clark	.30	.10
❑ 511	Mark McGwire	2.00	.75
❑ 512	Jeff Reboulet	.30	.10
❑ 513	Armando Benitez	.30	.10
❑ 514	LaTroy Hawkins	.30	.10
❑ 515	Brett Butler	.30	.10
❑ 516	Tavo Alvarez	.30	.10
❑ 517	Chris Snopek	.30	.10
❑ 518	Mike Mussina	.50	.20
❑ 519	Darryl Kile	.30	.10
❑ 520	Wally Joyner	.30	.10
❑ 521	Willie McGee	.30	.10
❑ 522	Kent Mercker	.30	.10
❑ 523	Mike Jackson	.30	.10
❑ 524	Troy Percival	.30	.10
❑ 525	Tony Gwynn	1.00	.40
❑ 526	Ron Coomer	.30	.10
❑ 527	Darryl Hamilton	.30	.10
❑ 528	Phil Plantier	.30	.10
❑ 529	Norm Charlton	.30	.10
❑ 530	Craig Paquette	.30	.10
❑ 531	Dave Burba	.30	.10
❑ 532	Mike Henneman	.30	.10
❑ 533	Terrell Wade	.30	.10
❑ 534	Eddie Williams	.30	.10
❑ 535	Robin Ventura	.30	.10
❑ 536	Chuck Knoblauch	.30	.10
❑ 537	Les Norman	.30	.10
❑ 538	Brady Anderson	.30	.10
❑ 539	Roger Clemens	1.50	.60
❑ 540	Mark Portugal	.30	.10
❑ 541	Mike Matheny	.30	.10
❑ 542	Jeff Parrett	.30	.10
❑ 543	Roberto Kelly	.30	.10
❑ 544	Damon Buford	.30	.10
❑ 545	Chad Ogea	.30	.10
❑ 546	Jose Offerman	.30	.10
❑ 547	Brian Barber	.30	.10
❑ 548	Danny Tartabull	.30	.10
❑ 549	Duane Singleton	.30	.10
❑ 550	Tony Gwynn CL	.50	.20

1997 Donruss

❑ COMPLETE SET (450)	50.00	20.00
❑ COMPLETE SERIES 1 (270)	25.00	10.00
❑ COMPLETE UPDATE (180)	25.00	10.00
❑ 1 Juan Gonzalez	.30	.10

❑	2	Jim Edmonds	.30	.10
❑	3	Tony Gwynn	1.00	.40
❑	4	Andres Galarraga	.30	.10
❑	5	Joe Carter	.30	.10
❑	6	Raul Mondesi	.30	.10
❑	7	Greg Maddux	1.25	.50
❑	8	Travis Fryman	.30	.10
❑	9	Brian Jordan	.30	.10
❑	10	Henry Rodriguez	.30	.10
❑	11	Manny Ramirez	.50	.20
❑	12	Mark McGwire	2.00	.75
❑	13	Marc Newfield	.30	.10
❑	14	Craig Biggio	.50	.20
❑	15	Sammy Sosa	.75	.30
❑	16	Brady Anderson	.30	.10
❑	17	Wade Boggs	.50	.20
❑	18	Charles Johnson	.30	.10
❑	19	Matt Williams	.30	.10
❑	20	Denny Neagle	.30	.10
❑	21	Ken Griffey Jr.	1.25	.50
❑	22	Robin Ventura	.30	.10
❑	23	Barry Larkin	.50	.20
❑	24	Todd Zeile	.30	.10
❑	25	Chuck Knoblauch	.30	.10
❑	26	Todd Hundley	.30	.10
❑	27	Roger Clemens	1.50	.60
❑	28	Michael Tucker	.30	.10
❑	29	Rondell White	.30	.10
❑	30	Osvaldo Fernandez	.30	.10
❑	31	Ivan Rodriguez	.50	.20
❑	32	Alex Fernandez	.30	.10
❑	33	Jason Isringhausen	.30	.10
❑	34	Chipper Jones	.75	.30
❑	35	Paul O'Neill	.50	.20
❑	36	Hideo Nomo	.75	.30
❑	37	Roberto Alomar	.50	.20
❑	38	Derek Bell	.30	.10
❑	39	Paul Molitor	.30	.10
❑	40	Andy Benes	.30	.10
❑	41	Steve Trachsel	.30	.10
❑	42	J.T. Snow	.30	.10
❑	43	Jason Kendall	.30	.10
❑	44	Alex Rodriguez	1.25	.50
❑	45	Joey Hamilton	.30	.10
❑	46	Carlos Delgado	.30	.10
❑	47	Jason Giambi	.30	.10
❑	48	Larry Walker	.30	.10
❑	49	Derek Jeter	2.00	.75
❑	50	Kenny Lofton	.30	.10
❑	51	Devon White	.30	.10
❑	52	Matt Mieske	.30	.10
❑	53	Melvin Nieves	.30	.10
❑	54	Jose Canseco	.50	.20
❑	55	Tino Martinez	.50	.20
❑	56	Rafael Palmeiro	.50	.20
❑	57	Edgardo Alfonzo	.30	.10
❑	58	Jay Buhner	.30	.10
❑	59	Shane Reynolds	.30	.10
❑	60	Steve Finley	.30	.10
❑	61	Bobby Higginson	.30	.10
❑	62	Dean Palmer	.30	.10
❑	63	Terry Pendleton	.30	.10
❑	64	Marquis Grissom	.30	.10
❑	65	Mike Stanley	.30	.10
❑	66	Moises Alou	.30	.10
❑	67	Ray Lankford	.30	.10
❑	68	Marty Cordova	.30	.10
❑	69	John Olerud	.30	.10
❑	70	David Cone	.30	.10
❑	71	Benito Santiago	.30	.10
❑	72	Ryne Sandberg	1.25	.50
❑	73	Rickey Henderson	.75	.30
❑	74	Roger Cedeno	.30	.10
❑	75	Wilson Alvarez	.30	.10
❑	76	Tim Salmon	.50	.20
❑	77	Orlando Merced	.30	.10
❑	78	Vinny Castilla	.30	.10
❑	79	Ismael Valdes	.30	.10
❑	80	Dante Bichette	.30	.10
❑	81	Kevin Brown	.30	.10
❑	82	Andy Pettitte	.50	.20
❑	83	Scott Stahoviak	.30	.10
❑	84	Mickey Tettleton	.30	.10
❑	85	Jack McDowell	.30	.10
❑	86	Tom Glavine	.50	.20
❑	87	Gregg Jefferies	.30	.10
❑	88	Chili Davis	.30	.10
❑	89	Randy Johnson	.75	.30
❑	90	John Mabry	.30	.10
❑	91	Billy Wagner	.30	.10
❑	92	Jeff Cirillo	.30	.10
❑	93	Trevor Hoffman	.30	.10
❑	94	Juan Guzman	.30	.10
❑	95	Geronimo Berroa	.30	.10
❑	96	Bernard Gilkey	.30	.10
❑	97	Danny Tartabull	.30	.10
❑	98	Johnny Damon	.50	.20
❑	99	Charlie Hayes	.30	.10
❑	100	Reggie Sanders	.30	.10
❑	101	Robby Thompson	.30	.10
❑	102	Bobby Bonilla	.30	.10
❑	103	Reggie Jefferson	.30	.10
❑	104	John Smoltz	.50	.20
❑	105	Jim Thome	.50	.20
❑	106	Ruben Rivera	.30	.10
❑	107	Darren Oliver	.30	.10
❑	108	Mo Vaughn	.30	.10
❑	109	Roger Pavlik	.30	.10
❑	110	Terry Steinbach	.30	.10
❑	111	Jermaine Dye	.30	.10
❑	112	Mark Grudzielanek	.30	.10
❑	113	Rick Aguilera	.30	.10
❑	114	Jamey Wright	.30	.10
❑	115	Eddie Murray	.75	.30
❑	116	Brian L. Hunter	.30	.10
❑	117	Hal Morris	.30	.10
❑	118	Tom Pagnozzi	.30	.10
❑	119	Mike Mussina	.50	.20
❑	120	Mark Grace	.50	.20
❑	121	Cal Ripken	2.50	1.00
❑	122	Tom Goodwin	.30	.10
❑	123	Paul Sorrento	.30	.10
❑	124	Jay Bell	.30	.10
❑	125	Todd Hollandsworth	.30	.10
❑	126	Edgar Martinez	.50	.20
❑	127	George Arias	.30	.10
❑	128	Greg Vaughn	.30	.10
❑	129	Roberto Hernandez	.30	.10
❑	130	Delino DeShields	.30	.10
❑	131	Bill Pulsipher	.30	.10
❑	132	Joey Cora	.30	.10
❑	133	Mariano Rivera	.75	.30
❑	134	Mike Piazza	1.25	.50
❑	135	Carlos Baerga	.30	.10
❑	136	Jose Mesa	.30	.10
❑	137	Will Clark	.50	.20
❑	138	Frank Thomas	.75	.30
❑	139	John Wetteland	.30	.10
❑	140	Shawn Estes	.30	.10
❑	141	Garret Anderson	.30	.10
❑	142	Andre Dawson	.30	.10
❑	143	Eddie Taubensee	.30	.10
❑	144	Ryan Klesko	.30	.10
❑	145	Rocky Coppinger	.30	.10
❑	146	Jeff Bagwell	.50	.20
❑	147	Donovan Osborne	.30	.10
❑	148	Greg Myers	.30	.10
❑	149	Brant Brown	.30	.10
❑	150	Kevin Elster	.30	.10
❑	151	Bob Wells	.30	.10
❑	152	Wally Joyner	.30	.10
❑	153	Rico Brogna	.30	.10
❑	154	Dwight Gooden	.30	.10
❑	155	Jermaine Allensworth	.30	.10
❑	156	Ray Durham	.30	.10
❑	157	Cecil Fielder	.30	.10
❑	158	John Burkett	.30	.10
❑	159	Gary Sheffield	.30	.10
❑	160	Albert Belle	.30	.10
❑	161	Tomas Perez	.30	.10
❑	162	David Doster	.30	.10
❑	163	John Valentin	.30	.10
❑	164	Danny Graves	.30	.10
❑	165	Jose Paniagua	.30	.10
❑	166	Brian Giles RC	1.50	.60
❑	167	Barry Bonds	2.00	.75
❑	168	Sterling Hitchcock	.30	.10
❑	169	Bernie Williams	.50	.20
❑	170	Fred McGriff	.50	.20
❑	171	George Williams	.30	.10
❑	172	Amaury Telemaco	.30	.10
❑	173	Ken Caminiti	.30	.10
❑	174	Ron Gant	.30	.10
❑	175	Dave Justice	.30	.10
❑	176	James Baldwin	.30	.10
❑	177	Pat Hentgen	.30	.10
❑	178	Ben McDonald	.30	.10
❑	179	Tim Naehring	.30	.10
❑	180	Jim Eisenreich	.30	.10
❑	181	Ken Hill	.30	.10
❑	182	Paul Wilson	.30	.10
❑	183	Marvin Benard	.30	.10
❑	184	Alan Benes	.30	.10
❑	185	Ellis Burks	.30	.10
❑	186	Scott Servais	.30	.10
❑	187	David Segui	.30	.10
❑	188	Scott Brosius	.30	.10
❑	189	Jose Offerman	.30	.10
❑	190	Eric Davis	.30	.10
❑	191	Brett Butler	.30	.10
❑	192	Curtis Pride	.30	.10
❑	193	Yamil Benitez	.30	.10
❑	194	Chan Ho Park	.30	.10
❑	195	Bret Boone	.30	.10
❑	196	Omar Vizquel	.50	.20
❑	197	Orlando Miller	.30	.10
❑	198	Ramon Martinez	.30	.10
❑	199	Harold Baines	.30	.10
❑	200	Eric Young	.30	.10
❑	201	Fernando Vina	.30	.10
❑	202	Alex Gonzalez	.30	.10
❑	203	Fernando Valenzuela	.30	.10
❑	204	Steve Avery	.30	.10
❑	205	Ernie Young	.30	.10
❑	206	Kevin Appier	.30	.10
❑	207	Randy Myers	.30	.10
❑	208	Jeff Suppan	.30	.10
❑	209	James Mouton	.30	.10
❑	210	Russ Davis	.30	.10
❑	211	Al Martin	.30	.10
❑	212	Troy Percival	.30	.10
❑	213	Al Leiter	.30	.10
❑	214	Dennis Eckersley	.30	.10
❑	215	Mark Johnson	.30	.10
❑	216	Eric Karros	.30	.10
❑	217	Royce Clayton	.30	.10
❑	218	Tony Phillips	.30	.10
❑	219	Tim Wakefield	.30	.10
❑	220	Alan Trammell	.30	.10
❑	221	Eduardo Perez	.30	.10
❑	222	Butch Huskey	.30	.10
❑	223	Tim Belcher	.30	.10
❑	224	Jamie Moyer	.30	.10
❑	225	F.P. Santangelo	.30	.10
❑	226	Rusty Greer	.30	.10
❑	227	Jeff Brantley	.30	.10
❑	228	Mark Langston	.30	.10
❑	229	Ray Montgomery	.30	.10
❑	230	Rich Becker	.30	.10
❑	231	Ozzie Smith	1.25	.50
❑	232	Rey Ordonez	.30	.10
❑	233	Ricky Otero	.30	.10
❑	234	Mike Cameron	.30	.10
❑	235	Mike Sweeney	.30	.10
❑	236	Mark Lewis	.30	.10
❑	237	Luis Gonzalez	.30	.10
❑	238	Marcus Jensen	.30	.10
❑	239	Ed Sprague	.30	.10
❑	240	Jose Valentin	.30	.10
❑	241	Jeff Frye	.30	.10
❑	242	Charles Nagy	.30	.10
❑	243	Carlos Garcia	.30	.10
❑	244	Mike Hampton	.30	.10
❑	245	B.J. Surhoff	.30	.10
❑	246	Wilton Guerrero	.30	.10
❑	247	Frank Rodriguez	.30	.10
❑	248	Gary Gaetti	.30	.10
❑	249	Lance Johnson	.30	.10
❑	250	Darren Bragg	.30	.10
❑	251	Darryl Hamilton	.30	.10
❑	252	John Jaha	.30	.10
❑	253	Craig Paquette	.30	.10
❑	254	Jaime Navarro	.30	.10
❑	255	Shawon Dunston	.30	.10
❑	256	Mark Loretta	.30	.10
❑	257	Tim Belk	.30	.10
❑	258	Jeff Darwin	.30	.10
❑	259	Ruben Sierra	.30	.10

❑ 260	Chuck Finley	.30	.10
❑ 261	Darryl Strawberry	.30	.10
❑ 262	Shannon Stewart	.30	.10
❑ 263	Pedro Martinez	.50	.20
❑ 264	Neifi Perez	.30	.10
❑ 265	Jeff Conine	.30	.10
❑ 266	Orel Hershiser	.30	.10
❑ 267	Eddie Murray CL	.50	.20
❑ 268	Paul Molitor CL	.30	.10
❑ 269	Barry Bonds CL	1.00	.40
❑ 270	Mark McGwire CL	1.00	.40
❑ 271	Matt Williams	.30	.10
❑ 272	Todd Zeile	.30	.10
❑ 273	Roger Clemens	1.50	.60
❑ 274	Michael Tucker	.30	.10
❑ 275	J.T. Snow	.30	.10
❑ 276	Kenny Lofton	.30	.10
❑ 277	Jose Canseco	.50	.20
❑ 278	Marquis Grissom	.30	.10
❑ 279	Moises Alou	.30	.10
❑ 280	Benito Santiago	.30	.10
❑ 281	Willie McGee	.30	.10
❑ 282	Chili Davis	.30	.10
❑ 283	Ron Coomer	.30	.10
❑ 284	Orlando Merced	.30	.10
❑ 285	Delino DeShields	.30	.10
❑ 286	John Wetteland	.30	.10
❑ 287	Darren Daulton	.30	.10
❑ 288	Lee Stevens	.30	.10
❑ 289	Albert Belle	.30	.10
❑ 290	Sterling Hitchcock	.30	.10
❑ 291	David Justice	.30	.10
❑ 292	Eric Davis	.30	.10
❑ 293	Brian Hunter	.30	.10
❑ 294	Darryl Hamilton	.30	.10
❑ 295	Steve Avery	.30	.10
❑ 296	Joe Vitiello	.30	.10
❑ 297	Jaime Navarro	.30	.10
❑ 298	Eddie Murray	.75	.30
❑ 299	Randy Myers	.30	.10
❑ 300	Francisco Cordova	.30	.10
❑ 301	Javier Lopez	.30	.10
❑ 302	Geronimo Berroa	.30	.10
❑ 303	Jeffrey Hammonds	.30	.10
❑ 304	Deion Sanders	.50	.20
❑ 305	Jeff Fassero	.30	.10
❑ 306	Curt Schilling	.30	.10
❑ 307	Robb Nen	.30	.10
❑ 308	Mark McLemore	.30	.10
❑ 309	Jimmy Key	.30	.10
❑ 310	Quilvio Veras	.30	.10
❑ 311	Bip Roberts	.30	.10
❑ 312	Esteban Loaiza	.30	.10
❑ 313	Andy Ashby	.30	.10
❑ 314	Sandy Alomar Jr.	.30	.10
❑ 315	Shawn Green	.30	.10
❑ 316	Luis Castillo	.30	.10
❑ 317	Benji Gil	.30	.10
❑ 318	Otis Nixon	.30	.10
❑ 319	Aaron Sele	.30	.10
❑ 320	Brad Ausmus	.30	.10
❑ 321	Troy O'Leary	.30	.10
❑ 322	Terrell Wade	.30	.10
❑ 323	Jeff King	.30	.10
❑ 324	Kevin Seitzer	.30	.10
❑ 325	Mark Wohlers	.30	.10
❑ 326	Edgar Renteria	.30	.10
❑ 327	Dan Wilson	.30	.10
❑ 328	Brian McRae	.30	.10
❑ 329	Rod Beck	.30	.10
❑ 330	Julio Franco	.30	.10
❑ 331	Dave Nilsson	.30	.10
❑ 332	Glenallen Hill	.30	.10
❑ 333	Kevin Elster	.30	.10
❑ 334	Joe Girardi	.30	.10
❑ 335	David Wells	.30	.10
❑ 336	Jeff Blauser	.30	.10
❑ 337	Darryl Kile	.30	.10
❑ 338	Jeff Kent	.30	.10
❑ 339	Jim Leyritz	.30	.10
❑ 340	Todd Stottlemyre	.30	.10
❑ 341	Tony Clark	.30	.10
❑ 342	Chris Hoiles	.30	.10
❑ 343	Mike Lieberthal	.30	.10
❑ 344	Matt Lawton	.30	.10
❑ 345	Alex Ochoa	.30	.10
❑ 346	Chris Snopek	.30	.10
❑ 347	Rudy Pemberton	.30	.10
❑ 348	Eric Owens	.30	.10
❑ 349	Joe Randa	.30	.10
❑ 350	John Olerud	.30	.10
❑ 351	Steve Karsay	.30	.10
❑ 352	Mark Whiten	.30	.10
❑ 353	Bob Abreu	.50	.20
❑ 354	Bartolo Colon	.30	.10
❑ 355	Vladimir Guerrero	.75	.30
❑ 356	Darin Erstad	.30	.10
❑ 357	Scott Rolen	.50	.20
❑ 358	Andruw Jones	.50	.20
❑ 359	Scott Spiezio	.30	.10
❑ 360	Karim Garcia	.30	.10
❑ 361	Hideki Irabu RC	.40	.15
❑ 362	Nomar Garciaparra	1.25	.50
❑ 363	Dmitri Young	.30	.10
❑ 364	Bubba Trammell RC	.40	.15
❑ 365	Kevin Orie	.30	.10
❑ 366	Jose Rosado	.30	.10
❑ 367	Jose Guillen	.30	.10
❑ 368	Brooks Kieschnick	.30	.10
❑ 369	Pokey Reese	.30	.10
❑ 370	Glendon Rusch	.30	.10
❑ 371	Jason Dickson	.30	.10
❑ 372	Todd Walker	.30	.10
❑ 373	Justin Thompson	.30	.10
❑ 374	Todd Greene	.30	.10
❑ 375	Jeff Suppan	.30	.10
❑ 376	Trey Beamon	.30	.10
❑ 377	Damon Mashore	.30	.10
❑ 378	Wendell Magee	.30	.10
❑ 379	Shigetoshi Hasegawa RC	.50	.20
❑ 380	Bill Mueller RC	1.25	.50
❑ 381	Chris Widger	.30	.10
❑ 382	Tony Graffanino	.30	.10
❑ 383	Derrek Lee	.50	.20
❑ 384	Brian Moehler RC	.40	.15
❑ 385	Quinton McCracken	.30	.10
❑ 386	Matt Morris	.30	.10
❑ 387	Marvin Benard	.30	.10
❑ 388	Deivi Cruz RC	.40	.15
❑ 389	Javier Valentin	.30	.10
❑ 390	Todd Dunwoody	.30	.10
❑ 391	Derrick Gibson	.30	.10
❑ 392	Raul Casanova	.30	.10
❑ 393	George Arias	.30	.10
❑ 394	Tony Womack RC	.40	.15
❑ 395	Antone Williamson	.30	.10
❑ 396	Jose Cruz Jr. RC	.40	.15
❑ 397	Desi Relaford	.30	.10
❑ 398	Frank Thomas HIT	.50	.20
❑ 399	Ken Griffey Jr. HIT	.75	.30
❑ 400	Cal Ripken HIT	1.25	.50
❑ 401	Chipper Jones HIT	.50	.20
❑ 402	Mike Piazza HIT	.75	.30
❑ 403	Gary Sheffield HIT	.30	.10
❑ 404	Alex Rodriguez HIT	.75	.30
❑ 405	Wade Boggs HIT	.30	.10
❑ 406	Juan Gonzalez HIT	.30	.10
❑ 407	Tony Gwynn HIT	.50	.20
❑ 408	Edgar Martinez HIT	.30	.10
❑ 409	Jeff Bagwell HIT	.30	.10
❑ 410	Larry Walker HIT	.30	.10
❑ 411	Kenny Lofton HIT	.30	.10
❑ 412	Manny Ramirez HIT	.30	.10
❑ 413	Mark McGwire HIT	1.00	.40
❑ 414	Roberto Alomar HIT	.30	.10
❑ 415	Derek Jeter HIT	1.00	.40
❑ 416	Brady Anderson HIT	.30	.10
❑ 417	Paul Molitor HIT	.30	.10
❑ 418	Dante Bichette HIT	.30	.10
❑ 419	Jim Edmonds HIT	.30	.10
❑ 420	Mo Vaughn HIT	.30	.10
❑ 421	Barry Bonds HIT	1.00	.40
❑ 422	Rusty Greer HIT	.30	.10
❑ 423	Greg Maddux KING	.75	.30
❑ 424	Andy Pettitte KING	.30	.10
❑ 425	John Smoltz KING	.30	.10
❑ 426	Randy Johnson KING	.50	.20
❑ 427	Hideo Nomo KING	.30	.10
❑ 428	Roger Clemens KING	.75	.30
❑ 429	Tom Glavine KING	.30	.10
❑ 430	Pat Hentgen KING	.30	.10
❑ 431	Kevin Brown KING	.30	.10
❑ 432	Mike Mussina KING	.30	.10
❑ 433	Alex Fernandez KING	.30	.10
❑ 434	Kevin Appier KING	.30	.10
❑ 435	David Cone KING	.30	.10
❑ 436	Jeff Fassero KING	.30	.10
❑ 437	John Wetteland KING	.30	.10
❑ 438	B.Bonds/I.Rodriguez IS	1.00	.40
❑ 439	K.Griffey Jr./A.Galarraga IS	.75	.30
❑ 440	F.McGriff/R.Palmeiro IS	.30	.10
❑ 441	B.Larkin/J.Thome IS	.50	.20
❑ 442	S.Sosa/A.Belle IS	.50	.20
❑ 443	B.Williams/T.Hundley IS	.30	.10
❑ 444	C.Knoblauch/B.Jordan IS	.30	.10
❑ 445	M.Vaughn/J.Conine IS	.30	.10
❑ 446	K.Caminiti/J.Giambi IS	.30	.10
❑ 447	R.Mondesi/T.Salmon IS	.30	.10
❑ 448	Cal Ripken CL	1.25	.50
❑ 449	Greg Maddux CL	.75	.30
❑ 450	Ken Griffey Jr. CL	.75	.30

1998 Donruss

❑	COMPLETE SET (420)	50.00	20.00
❑	COMPLETE SERIES 1 (170)	20.00	8.00
❑	COMPLETE UPDATE (250)	30.00	12.50
❑ 1	Paul Molitor	.25	.08
❑ 2	Juan Gonzalez	.25	.08
❑ 3	Darryl Kile	.25	.08
❑ 4	Randy Johnson	.60	.25
❑ 5	Tom Glavine	.40	.15
❑ 6	Pat Hentgen	.25	.08
❑ 7	David Justice	.25	.08
❑ 8	Kevin Brown	.40	.15
❑ 9	Mike Mussina	.40	.15
❑ 10	Ken Caminiti	.25	.08
❑ 11	Todd Hundley	.25	.08
❑ 12	Frank Thomas	.60	.25
❑ 13	Ray Lankford	.25	.08
❑ 14	Justin Thompson	.25	.08
❑ 15	Jason Dickson	.25	.08
❑ 16	Kenny Lofton	.25	.08
❑ 17	Ivan Rodriguez	.40	.15
❑ 18	Pedro Martinez	.40	.15
❑ 19	Brady Anderson	.25	.08
❑ 20	Barry Larkin	.40	.15
❑ 21	Chipper Jones	.60	.25
❑ 22	Tony Gwynn	.75	.30
❑ 23	Roger Clemens	1.25	.50
❑ 24	Sandy Alomar Jr.	.25	.08
❑ 25	Tino Martinez	.40	.15
❑ 26	Jeff Bagwell	.40	.15
❑ 27	Shawn Estes	.25	.08
❑ 28	Ken Griffey Jr.	1.00	.40
❑ 29	Javier Lopez	.25	.08
❑ 30	Denny Neagle	.25	.08
❑ 31	Mike Piazza	1.00	.40
❑ 32	Andres Galarraga	.25	.08
❑ 33	Larry Walker	.25	.08
❑ 34	Alex Rodriguez	1.00	.40
❑ 35	Greg Maddux	1.00	.40
❑ 36	Albert Belle	.25	.08
❑ 37	Barry Bonds	1.50	.60
❑ 38	Mo Vaughn	.25	.08
❑ 39	Kevin Appier	.25	.08
❑ 40	Wade Boggs	.40	.15
❑ 41	Garret Anderson	.25	.08
❑ 42	Jeffrey Hammonds	.25	.08
❑ 43	Marquis Grissom	.25	.08
❑ 44	Jim Edmonds	.25	.08

❑ 45	Brian Jordan	.25	.08
❑ 46	Raul Mondesi	.25	.08
❑ 47	John Valentin	.25	.08
❑ 48	Brad Radke	.25	.08
❑ 49	Ismael Valdes	.25	.08
❑ 50	Matt Stairs	.25	.08
❑ 51	Matt Williams	.25	.08
❑ 52	Reggie Jefferson	.25	.08
❑ 53	Alan Benes	.25	.08
❑ 54	Charles Johnson	.25	.08
❑ 55	Chuck Knoblauch	.25	.08
❑ 56	Edgar Martinez	.40	.15
❑ 57	Nomar Garciaparra	1.00	.40
❑ 58	Craig Biggio	.40	.15
❑ 59	Bernie Williams	.40	.15
❑ 60	David Cone	.25	.08
❑ 61	Cal Ripken	2.00	.75
❑ 62	Mark McGwire	1.50	.60
❑ 63	Roberto Alomar	.40	.15
❑ 64	Fred McGriff	.40	.15
❑ 65	Eric Karros	.25	.08
❑ 66	Robin Ventura	.25	.08
❑ 67	Darin Erstad	.25	.08
❑ 68	Michael Tucker	.25	.08
❑ 69	Jim Thome	.40	.15
❑ 70	Mark Grace	.40	.15
❑ 71	Lou Collier	.25	.08
❑ 72	Karim Garcia	.25	.08
❑ 73	Alex Fernandez	.25	.08
❑ 74	J.T. Snow	.25	.08
❑ 75	Reggie Sanders	.25	.08
❑ 76	John Smoltz	.40	.15
❑ 77	Tim Salmon	.40	.15
❑ 78	Paul O'Neill	.40	.15
❑ 79	Vinny Castilla	.25	.08
❑ 80	Rafael Palmeiro	.40	.15
❑ 81	Jaret Wright	.25	.08
❑ 82	Jay Buhner	.25	.08
❑ 83	Brett Butler	.25	.08
❑ 84	Todd Greene	.25	.08
❑ 85	Scott Rolen	.40	.15
❑ 86	Sammy Sosa	.60	.25
❑ 87	Jason Giambi	.25	.08
❑ 88	Carlos Delgado	.25	.08
❑ 89	Deion Sanders	.40	.15
❑ 90	Wilton Guerrero	.25	.08
❑ 91	Andy Pettitte	.40	.15
❑ 92	Brian Giles	.25	.08
❑ 93	Dmitri Young	.25	.08
❑ 94	Ron Coomer	.25	.08
❑ 95	Mike Cameron	.25	.08
❑ 96	Edgardo Alfonzo	.25	.08
❑ 97	Jimmy Key	.25	.08
❑ 98	Ryan Klesko	.25	.08
❑ 99	Andy Benes	.25	.08
❑ 100	Derek Jeter	1.50	.60
❑ 101	Jeff Fassero	.25	.08
❑ 102	Neifi Perez	.25	.08
❑ 103	Hideo Nomo	.60	.25
❑ 104	Andruw Jones	.40	.15
❑ 105	Todd Helton	.40	.15
❑ 106	Livan Hernandez	.25	.08
❑ 107	Brett Tomko	.25	.08
❑ 108	Shannon Stewart	.25	.08
❑ 109	Bartolo Colon	.25	.08
❑ 110	Matt Morris	.25	.08
❑ 111	Miguel Tejada	.60	.25
❑ 112	Pokey Reese	.25	.08
❑ 113	Fernando Tatis	.25	.08
❑ 114	Todd Dunwoody	.25	.08
❑ 115	Jose Cruz Jr.	.25	.08
❑ 116	Chan Ho Park	.25	.08
❑ 117	Kevin Young	.25	.08
❑ 118	Rickey Henderson	.60	.25
❑ 119	Hideki Irabu	.25	.08
❑ 120	Francisco Cordova	.25	.08
❑ 121	Al Martin	.25	.08
❑ 122	Tony Clark	.25	.08
❑ 123	Curt Schilling	.25	.08
❑ 124	Rusty Greer	.25	.08
❑ 125	Jose Canseco	.40	.15
❑ 126	Edgar Renteria	.25	.08
❑ 127	Todd Walker	.25	.08
❑ 128	Wally Joyner	.25	.08
❑ 129	Bill Mueller	.25	.08
❑ 130	Jose Guillen	.25	.08
❑ 131	Manny Ramirez	.40	.15
❑ 132	Bobby Higginson	.25	.08
❑ 133	Kevin Orie	.25	.08
❑ 134	Will Clark	.40	.15
❑ 135	Dave Nilsson	.25	.08
❑ 136	Jason Kendall	.25	.08
❑ 137	Ivan Cruz	.25	.08
❑ 138	Gary Sheffield	.25	.08
❑ 139	Bubba Trammell	.25	.08
❑ 140	Vladimir Guerrero	.60	.25
❑ 141	Dennis Reyes	.25	.08
❑ 142	Bobby Bonilla	.25	.08
❑ 143	Ruben Rivera	.25	.08
❑ 144	Ben Grieve	.25	.08
❑ 145	Moises Alou	.25	.08
❑ 146	Tony Womack	.25	.08
❑ 147	Eric Young	.25	.08
❑ 148	Paul Konerko	.25	.08
❑ 149	Dante Bichette	.25	.08
❑ 150	Joe Carter	.25	.08
❑ 151	Rondell White	.25	.08
❑ 152	Chris Holt	.25	.08
❑ 153	Shawn Green	.25	.08
❑ 154	Mark Grudzielanek	.25	.08
❑ 155	Jermaine Dye	.25	.08
❑ 156	Ken Griffey Jr. FC	.60	.25
❑ 157	Frank Thomas FC	.40	.15
❑ 158	Chipper Jones FC	.40	.15
❑ 159	Mike Piazza FC	.60	.25
❑ 160	Cal Ripken FC	1.00	.40
❑ 161	Greg Maddux FC	.60	.25
❑ 162	Juan Gonzalez FC	.25	.08
❑ 163	Alex Rodriguez FC	.60	.25
❑ 164	Mark McGwire FC	.75	.30
❑ 165	Derek Jeter FC	.75	.30
❑ 166	Larry Walker CL	.25	.08
❑ 167	Tony Gwynn CL	.40	.15
❑ 168	Tino Martinez CL	.25	.08
❑ 169	Scott Rolen CL	.25	.08
❑ 170	Nomar Garciaparra CL	.60	.25
❑ 171	Mike Sweeney	.25	.08
❑ 172	Dustin Hermanson	.25	.08
❑ 173	Darren Dreifort	.25	.08
❑ 174	Ron Gant	.25	.08
❑ 175	Todd Hollandsworth	.25	.08
❑ 176	John Jaha	.25	.08
❑ 177	Kerry Wood	.30	.10
❑ 178	Chris Stynes	.25	.08
❑ 179	Kevin Elster	.25	.08
❑ 180	Derek Bell	.25	.08
❑ 181	Darryl Strawberry	.25	.08
❑ 182	Damion Easley	.25	.08
❑ 183	Jeff Cirillo	.25	.08
❑ 184	John Thomson	.25	.08
❑ 185	Dan Wilson	.25	.08
❑ 186	Jay Bell	.25	.08
❑ 187	Bernard Gilkey	.25	.08
❑ 188	Marc Valdes	.25	.08
❑ 189	Ramon Martinez	.25	.08
❑ 190	Charles Nagy	.25	.08
❑ 191	Derek Lowe	.25	.08
❑ 192	Andy Benes	.25	.08
❑ 193	Delino DeShields	.25	.08
❑ 194	Ryan Jackson RC	.25	.08
❑ 195	Kenny Lofton	.25	.08
❑ 196	Chuck Knoblauch	.25	.08
❑ 197	Andres Galarraga	.25	.08
❑ 198	Jose Canseco	.40	.15
❑ 199	John Olerud	.25	.08
❑ 200	Lance Johnson	.25	.08
❑ 201	Darryl Kile	.25	.08
❑ 202	Luis Castillo	.25	.08
❑ 203	Joe Carter	.25	.08
❑ 204	Dennis Eckersley	.25	.08
❑ 205	Steve Finley	.25	.08
❑ 206	Esteban Loaiza	.25	.08
❑ 207	Ryan Christenson RC	.25	.08
❑ 208	Deivi Cruz	.25	.08
❑ 209	Mariano Rivera	.60	.25
❑ 210	Mike Judd RC	.30	.10
❑ 211	Billy Wagner	.25	.08
❑ 212	Scott Spiezio	.25	.08
❑ 213	Russ Davis	.25	.08
❑ 214	Jeff Suppan	.25	.08
❑ 215	Doug Glanville	.25	.08
❑ 216	Dmitri Young	.25	.08
❑ 217	Rey Ordonez	.25	.08
❑ 218	Cecil Fielder	.25	.08
❑ 219	Masato Yoshii RC	.30	.10
❑ 220	Raul Casanova	.25	.08
❑ 221	Rolando Arrojo RC	.30	.10
❑ 222	Ellis Burks	.25	.08
❑ 223	Butch Huskey	.25	.08
❑ 224	Brian Hunter	.25	.08
❑ 225	Marquis Grissom	.25	.08
❑ 226	Kevin Brown	.40	.15
❑ 227	Joe Randa	.25	.08
❑ 228	Henry Rodriguez	.25	.08
❑ 229	Omar Vizquel	.40	.15
❑ 230	Fred McGriff	.40	.15
❑ 231	Matt Williams	.25	.08
❑ 232	Moises Alou	.25	.08
❑ 233	Travis Fryman	.25	.08
❑ 234	Wade Boggs	.40	.15
❑ 235	Pedro Martinez	.40	.15
❑ 236	Rickey Henderson	.60	.25
❑ 237	Bubba Trammell	.25	.08
❑ 238	Mike Caruso	.25	.08
❑ 239	Wilson Alvarez	.25	.08
❑ 240	Geronimo Berroa	.25	.08
❑ 241	Eric Milton	.25	.08
❑ 242	Scott Erickson	.25	.08
❑ 243	Todd Erdos RC	.25	.08
❑ 244	Bobby Hughes	.25	.08
❑ 245	Dave Hollins	.25	.08
❑ 246	Dean Palmer	.25	.08
❑ 247	Carlos Baerga	.25	.08
❑ 248	Jose Silva	.25	.08
❑ 249	Jose Cabrera RC	.25	.08
❑ 250	Tom Evans	.25	.08
❑ 251	Marty Cordova	.25	.08
❑ 252	Hanley Frias RC	.25	.08
❑ 253	Javier Valentin	.25	.08
❑ 254	Mario Valdez	.25	.08
❑ 255	Joey Cora	.25	.08
❑ 256	Mike Lansing	.25	.08
❑ 257	Jeff Kent	.25	.08
❑ 258	Dave Dellucci RC	.50	.20
❑ 259	Curtis King RC	.25	.08
❑ 260	David Segui	.25	.08
❑ 261	Royce Clayton	.25	.08
❑ 262	Jeff Blauser	.25	.08
❑ 263	Manny Aybar RC	.25	.08
❑ 264	Mike Cather RC	.25	.08
❑ 265	Todd Zeile	.25	.08
❑ 266	Richard Hidalgo	.25	.08
❑ 267	Dante Powell	.25	.08
❑ 268	Mike DeJean RC	.25	.08
❑ 269	Ken Cloude	.25	.08
❑ 270	Danny Klassen	.25	.08
❑ 271	Sean Casey	.25	.08
❑ 272	A.J. Hinch	.25	.08
❑ 273	Rich Butler RC	.25	.08
❑ 274	Ben Ford RC	.25	.08
❑ 275	Billy McMillon	.25	.08
❑ 276	Wilson Delgado	.25	.08
❑ 277	Orlando Cabrera	.25	.08
❑ 278	Geoff Jenkins	.25	.08
❑ 279	Enrique Wilson	.25	.08
❑ 280	Derrek Lee	.40	.15
❑ 281	Marc Pisciotta RC	.25	.08
❑ 282	Abraham Nunez	.25	.08
❑ 283	Aaron Boone	.25	.08
❑ 284	Brad Fullmer	.25	.08
❑ 285	Rob Stanifer RC	.25	.08
❑ 286	Preston Wilson	.25	.08
❑ 287	Greg Norton	.25	.08
❑ 288	Bobby Smith	.25	.08
❑ 289	Josh Booty	.25	.08
❑ 290	Russell Branyan	.25	.08
❑ 291	Jeremi Gonzalez	.25	.08
❑ 292	Michael Coleman	.25	.08
❑ 293	Cliff Politte	.25	.08
❑ 294	Eric Ludwick	.25	.08
❑ 295	Rafael Medina	.25	.08
❑ 296	Jason Varitek	.60	.25
❑ 297	Ron Wright	.25	.08
❑ 298	Mark Kotsay	.25	.08
❑ 299	David Ortiz	.75	.30
❑ 300	Frank Catalanotto RC	.50	.20
❑ 301	Robinson Checo	.25	.08
❑ 302	Kevin Millwood RC	.75	.30

❑ 303 Jacob Cruz .25 .08
❑ 304 Javier Vazquez .25 .08
❑ 305 Magglio Ordonez RC 2.00 .75
❑ 306 Kevin Witt .25 .08
❑ 307 Derrick Gibson .25 .08
❑ 308 Shane Monahan .25 .08
❑ 309 Brian Rose .25 .08
❑ 310 Bobby Estalella .25 .08
❑ 311 Felix Heredia .25 .08
❑ 312 Desi Relaford .25 .08
❑ 313 Esteban Yan RC .30 .10
❑ 314 Ricky Ledee .25 .08
❑ 315 Steve Woodard .25 .08
❑ 316 Pat Watkins .25 .08
❑ 317 Damian Moss .25 .08
❑ 318 Bob Abreu .25 .08
❑ 319 Jeff Abbott .25 .08
❑ 320 Miguel Cairo .25 .08
❑ 321 Rigo Beltran RC .25 .08
❑ 322 Tony Saunders .25 .08
❑ 323 Randall Simon .25 .08
❑ 324 Hiram Bocachica .25 .08
❑ 325 Richie Sexson .25 .08
❑ 326 Karim Garcia .25 .08
❑ 327 Mike Lowell RC 1.00 .40
❑ 328 Pat Cline .25 .08
❑ 329 Matt Clement .25 .08
❑ 330 Scott Elarton .25 .08
❑ 331 Manuel Barrios RC .25 .08
❑ 332 Bruce Chen .25 .08
❑ 333 Juan Encarnacion .25 .08
❑ 334 Travis Lee .25 .08
❑ 335 Wes Helms .25 .08
❑ 336 Chad Fox RC .25 .08
❑ 337 Donnie Sadler .25 .08
❑ 338 Carlos Mendoza RC .25 .08
❑ 339 Damian Jackson .25 .08
❑ 340 Julio Ramirez RC .25 .08
❑ 341 John Halama RC .30 .10
❑ 342 Edwin Diaz .25 .08
❑ 343 Felix Martinez .25 .08
❑ 344 Eli Marrero .25 .08
❑ 345 Carl Pavano .25 .08
❑ 346 Vladimir Guerrero HL .40 .15
❑ 347 Barry Bonds HL .75 .30
❑ 348 Darin Erstad HL .25 .08
❑ 349 Albert Belle HL .25 .08
❑ 350 Kenny Lofton HL .25 .08
❑ 351 Mo Vaughn HL .25 .08
❑ 352 Jose Cruz Jr. HL .25 .08
❑ 353 Tony Clark HL .25 .08
❑ 354 Roberto Alomar HL .25 .08
❑ 355 Manny Ramirez HL .25 .08
❑ 356 Paul Molitor HL .25 .08
❑ 357 Jim Thome HL .25 .08
❑ 358 Tino Martinez HL .25 .08
❑ 359 Tim Salmon HL .25 .08
❑ 360 David Justice HL .25 .08
❑ 361 Raul Mondesi HL .25 .08
❑ 362 Mark Grace HL .25 .08
❑ 363 Craig Biggio HL .25 .08
❑ 364 Larry Walker HL .25 .08
❑ 365 Mark McGwire HL .75 .30
❑ 366 Juan Gonzalez HL .25 .08
❑ 367 Derek Jeter HL .75 .30
❑ 368 Chipper Jones HL .40 .15
❑ 369 Frank Thomas HL .40 .15
❑ 370 Alex Rodriguez HL .60 .25
❑ 371 Mike Piazza HL .60 .25
❑ 372 Tony Gwynn HL .40 .15
❑ 373 Jeff Bagwell HL .25 .08
❑ 374 Nomar Garciaparra HL .60 .25
❑ 375 Ken Griffey Jr. HL .60 .25
❑ 376 Livan Hernandez UN .25 .08
❑ 377 Chan Ho Park UN .25 .08
❑ 378 Mike Mussina UN .25 .08
❑ 379 Andy Pettitte UN .25 .08
❑ 380 Greg Maddux UN .60 .25
❑ 381 Hideo Nomo UN .40 .15
❑ 382 Roger Clemens UN .60 .25
❑ 383 Randy Johnson UN .40 .15
❑ 384 Pedro Martinez UN .40 .15
❑ 385 Jaret Wright UN .25 .08
❑ 386 Ken Griffey Jr. SG .60 .25
❑ 387 Todd Helton SG .25 .08
❑ 388 Paul Konerko SG .25 .08
❑ 389 Cal Ripken SG 1.00 .40
❑ 390 Larry Walker SG .25 .08
❑ 391 Ken Caminiti SG .25 .08
❑ 392 Jose Guillen SG .25 .08
❑ 393 Jim Edmonds SG .25 .08
❑ 394 Barry Larkin SG .25 .08
❑ 395 Bernie Williams SG .25 .08
❑ 396 Tony Clark SG .25 .08
❑ 397 Jose Cruz Jr. SG .25 .08
❑ 398 Ivan Rodriguez SG .25 .08
❑ 399 Darin Erstad SG .25 .08
❑ 400 Scott Rolen SG .25 .08
❑ 401 Mark McGwire SG .75 .30
❑ 402 Andruw Jones SG .25 .08
❑ 403 Juan Gonzalez SG .25 .08
❑ 404 Derek Jeter SG .75 .30
❑ 405 Chipper Jones SG .40 .15
❑ 406 Greg Maddux SG .60 .25
❑ 407 Frank Thomas SG .40 .15
❑ 408 Alex Rodriguez SG .60 .25
❑ 409 Mike Piazza SG .60 .25
❑ 410 Tony Gwynn SG .40 .15
❑ 411 Jeff Bagwell SG .25 .08
❑ 412 Nomar Garciaparra SG .60 .25
❑ 413 Hideo Nomo SG .40 .15
❑ 414 Barry Bonds SG .75 .30
❑ 415 Ben Grieve SG .25 .08
❑ 416 Barry Bonds CL .75 .30
❑ 417 Mark McGwire CL .75 .30
❑ 418 Roger Clemens CL .60 .25
❑ 419 Livan Hernandez CL .25 .08
❑ 420 Ken Griffey Jr. CL .60 .25

2001 Donruss

❑ COMP.SET w/o SP's (150) 25.00 10.00
❑ COMMON CARD (1-150) .30 .10
❑ COMMON CARD (151-200) 8.00 3.00
❑ COMMON CARD (201-220) 2.50 1.00
❑ 1 Alex Rodriguez 1.25 .50
❑ 2 Barry Bonds 2.00 .75
❑ 3 Cal Ripken 2.50 1.00
❑ 4 Chipper Jones .75 .30
❑ 5 Derek Jeter 2.00 .75
❑ 6 Troy Glaus .30 .10
❑ 7 Frank Thomas .75 .30
❑ 8 Greg Maddux 1.25 .50
❑ 9 Ivan Rodriguez .50 .20
❑ 10 Jeff Bagwell .50 .20
❑ 11 Jose Canseco .50 .20
❑ 12 Todd Helton .50 .20
❑ 13 Ken Griffey Jr. 1.25 .50
❑ 14 Manny Ramirez Sox .50 .20
❑ 15 Mark McGwire 2.00 .75
❑ 16 Mike Piazza 1.25 .50
❑ 17 Nomar Garciaparra 1.25 .50
❑ 18 Pedro Martinez .50 .20
❑ 19 Randy Johnson .75 .30
❑ 20 Rick Ankiel .30 .10
❑ 21 Rickey Henderson .75 .30
❑ 22 Roger Clemens 1.50 .60
❑ 23 Sammy Sosa .75 .30
❑ 24 Tony Gwynn 1.00 .40
❑ 25 Vladimir Guerrero .75 .30
❑ 26 Eric Davis .30 .10
❑ 27 Roberto Alomar .30 .10
❑ 28 Mark Mulder .30 .10
❑ 29 Pat Burrell .30 .10
❑ 30 Harold Baines .30 .10
❑ 31 Carlos Delgado .30 .10
❑ 32 J.D. Drew .30 .10
❑ 33 Jim Edmonds .30 .10
❑ 34 Darin Erstad .30 .10
❑ 35 Jason Giambi .30 .10
❑ 36 Tom Glavine .50 .20
❑ 37 Juan Gonzalez .30 .10
❑ 38 Mark Grace .50 .20
❑ 39 Shawn Green .30 .10
❑ 40 Tim Hudson .30 .10
❑ 41 Andruw Jones .50 .20
❑ 42 David Justice .30 .10
❑ 43 Jeff Kent .30 .10
❑ 44 Barry Larkin .50 .20
❑ 45 Pokey Reese .30 .10
❑ 46 Mike Mussina .50 .20
❑ 47 Hideo Nomo .75 .30
❑ 48 Rafael Palmeiro .50 .20
❑ 49 Adam Piatt .30 .10
❑ 50 Scott Rolen .50 .20
❑ 51 Gary Sheffield .30 .10
❑ 52 Bernie Williams .50 .20
❑ 53 Bob Abreu .30 .10
❑ 54 Edgardo Alfonzo .30 .10
❑ 55 Jermaine Clark RC .50 .20
❑ 56 Albert Belle .30 .10
❑ 57 Craig Biggio .50 .20
❑ 58 Andres Galarraga .30 .10
❑ 59 Edgar Martinez .50 .20
❑ 60 Fred McGriff .50 .20
❑ 61 Magglio Ordonez .30 .10
❑ 62 Jim Thome .50 .20
❑ 63 Matt Williams .30 .10
❑ 64 Kerry Wood .30 .10
❑ 65 Moises Alou .30 .10
❑ 66 Brady Anderson .30 .10
❑ 67 Garret Anderson .30 .10
❑ 68 Tony Armas Jr. .30 .10
❑ 69 Tony Batista .30 .10
❑ 70 Jose Cruz Jr. .30 .10
❑ 71 Carlos Beltran .30 .10
❑ 72 Adrian Beltre .30 .10
❑ 73 Kris Benson .30 .10
❑ 74 Lance Berkman .30 .10
❑ 75 Kevin Brown .30 .10
❑ 76 Jay Buhner .30 .10
❑ 77 Jeromy Burnitz .30 .10
❑ 78 Ken Caminiti .30 .10
❑ 79 Sean Casey .30 .10
❑ 80 Luis Castillo .30 .10
❑ 81 Eric Chavez .30 .10
❑ 82 Jeff Cirillo .30 .10
❑ 83 Bartolo Colon .30 .10
❑ 84 David Cone .30 .10
❑ 85 Freddy Garcia .30 .10
❑ 86 Johnny Damon .50 .20
❑ 87 Ray Durham .30 .10
❑ 88 Jermaine Dye .30 .10
❑ 89 Juan Encarnacion .30 .10
❑ 90 Terrence Long .30 .10
❑ 91 Carl Everett .30 .10
❑ 92 Steve Finley .30 .10
❑ 93 Cliff Floyd .30 .10
❑ 94 Brad Fullmer .30 .10
❑ 95 Brian Giles .30 .10
❑ 96 Luis Gonzalez .30 .10
❑ 97 Rusty Greer .30 .10
❑ 98 Jeffrey Hammonds .30 .10
❑ 99 Mike Hampton .30 .10
❑ 100 Orlando Hernandez .30 .10
❑ 101 Richard Hidalgo .30 .10
❑ 102 Geoff Jenkins .30 .10
❑ 103 Jacque Jones .30 .10
❑ 104 Brian Jordan .30 .10
❑ 105 Gabe Kapler .30 .10
❑ 106 Eric Karros .30 .10
❑ 107 Jason Kendall .30 .10
❑ 108 Adam Kennedy .30 .10
❑ 109 Byung-Hyun Kim .30 .10
❑ 110 Ryan Klesko .30 .10
❑ 111 Chuck Knoblauch .30 .10
❑ 112 Paul Konerko .30 .10
❑ 113 Carlos Lee .30 .10
❑ 114 Kenny Lofton .30 .10
❑ 115 Javy Lopez .30 .10
❑ 116 Tino Martinez .50 .20

❑ 117 Ruben Mateo .30 .10
❑ 118 Kevin Millwood .30 .10
❑ 119 Ben Molina .30 .10
❑ 120 Raul Mondesi .30 .10
❑ 121 Trot Nixon .30 .10
❑ 122 John Olerud .30 .10
❑ 123 Paul O'Neill .50 .20
❑ 124 Chan Ho Park .30 .10
❑ 125 Andy Pettitte .50 .20
❑ 126 Jorge Posada .50 .20
❑ 127 Mark Quinn .30 .10
❑ 128 Aramis Ramirez .30 .10
❑ 129 Mariano Rivera .75 .30
❑ 130 Tim Salmon .50 .20
❑ 131 Curt Schilling .30 .10
❑ 132 Richie Sexson .30 .10
❑ 133 John Smoltz .50 .20
❑ 134 J.T. Snow .30 .10
❑ 135 Jay Payton .30 .10
❑ 136 Shannon Stewart .30 .10
❑ 137 B.J. Surhoff .30 .10
❑ 138 Mike Sweeney .30 .10
❑ 139 Fernando Tatis .30 .10
❑ 140 Miguel Tejada .30 .10
❑ 141 Jason Varitek .75 .30
❑ 142 Greg Vaughn .30 .10
❑ 143 Mo Vaughn .30 .10
❑ 144 Robin Ventura .30 .10
❑ 145 Jose Vidro .30 .10
❑ 146 Omar Vizquel .50 .20
❑ 147 Larry Walker .30 .10
❑ 148 David Wells .30 .10
❑ 149 Rondell White .30 .10
❑ 150 Preston Wilson .30 .10
❑ 151 Brent Abernathy RR 8.00 3.00
❑ 152 Cory Aldridge RR RC 8.00 3.00
❑ 153 Gene Altman RR RC 8.00 3.00
❑ 154 Josh Beckett RR 10.00 4.00
❑ 155 Wilson Betemit RR RC 10.00 4.00
❑ 156 Albert Pujols RR/500 RC 250.00 125.00
❑ 157 Joe Crede RR 10.00 4.00
❑ 158 Jack Cust RR 8.00 3.00
❑ 159 Ben Sheets RR/500 40.00 15.00
❑ 160 Alex Escobar RR 8.00 3.00
❑ 161 Adrian Hernandez RR RC 8.00 3.00
❑ 162 Pedro Feliz RR 8.00 3.00
❑ 163 Nate Frese RR RC 8.00 3.00
❑ 164 Carlos Garcia RR RC 8.00 3.00
❑ 165 Marcus Giles RR 8.00 3.00
❑ 166 Alexis Gomez RR RC 8.00 3.00
❑ 167 Jason Hart RR 8.00 3.00
❑ 168 Eric Hinske RR RC 10.00 4.00
❑ 169 Cesar Izturis RR 8.00 3.00
❑ 170 Nick Johnson RR 8.00 3.00
❑ 171 Mike Young RR 10.00 4.00
❑ 172 Brian Lawrence RR RC 8.00 3.00
❑ 173 Steve Lomasney RR 8.00 3.00
❑ 174 Nick Maness RR 8.00 3.00
❑ 175 Jose Mieses RR RC 8.00 3.00
❑ 176 Greg Miller RR RC 8.00 3.00
❑ 177 Eric Munson RR 8.00 3.00
❑ 178 Xavier Nady RR 8.00 3.00
❑ 179 Blaine Neal RR RC 8.00 3.00
❑ 180 Abraham Nunez RR 8.00 3.00
❑ 181 Jose Ortiz RR 8.00 3.00
❑ 182 Jeremy Owens RR RC 8.00 3.00
❑ 183 Pablo Ozuna RR 8.00 3.00
❑ 184 Corey Patterson RR 8.00 3.00
❑ 185 Carlos Pena RR 8.00 3.00
❑ 186 Wily Mo Pena RR 8.00 3.00
❑ 187 Timo Perez RR 8.00 3.00
❑ 188 Adam Pettyjohn RR RC 8.00 3.00
❑ 189 Luis Rivas RR 8.00 3.00
❑ 190 Jackson Melian RR RC 8.00 3.00
❑ 191 Wilken Ruan RR RC 8.00 3.00
❑ 192 Duaner Sanchez RR RC 8.00 3.00
❑ 193 Alfonso Soriano RR 10.00 4.00
❑ 194 Rafael Soriano RR RC 8.00 3.00
❑ 195 Ichiro Suzuki RR RC 60.00 30.00
❑ 196 Billy Sylvester RR RC 8.00 3.00
❑ 197 Juan Uribe RR RC 10.00 4.00
❑ 198 Eric Valent RR 8.00 3.00
❑ 199 Carlos Valderrama RR RC 8.00 3.00
❑ 200 Matt White RR RC 8.00 3.00
❑ 201 Alex Rodriguez FC 6.00 2.50
❑ 202 Barry Bonds FC 10.00 4.00
❑ 203 Cal Ripken FC 12.00 5.00
❑ 204 Chipper Jones FC 4.00 1.50
❑ 205 Derek Jeter FC 10.00 4.00
❑ 206 Troy Glaus FC 2.50 1.00
❑ 207 Frank Thomas FC 4.00 1.50
❑ 208 Greg Maddux FC 6.00 2.50
❑ 209 Ivan Rodriguez FC 2.50 1.00
❑ 210 Jeff Bagwell FC 2.50 1.00
❑ 211 Todd Helton FC 2.50 1.00
❑ 212 Ken Griffey Jr. FC 6.00 2.50
❑ 213 Manny Ramirez Sox FC 2.50 1.00
❑ 214 Mark McGwire FC 10.00 4.00
❑ 215 Mike Piazza FC 6.00 2.50
❑ 216 Pedro Martinez FC 2.50 1.00
❑ 217 Sammy Sosa FC 4.00 1.50
❑ 218 Tony Gwynn FC 5.00 2.00
❑ 219 Vladimir Guerrero FC 4.00 1.50
❑ 220 Nomar Garciaparra FC 6.00 2.50
❑ NNO BB Best Coupon 2.00 .75
❑ NNO The Rookies Coupon .50 .20

2002 Donruss

❑ COMPLETE SET (220) 150.00 60.00
❑ COMP.SET w/o SP'S (150) 25.00 10.00
❑ COMMON CARD (1-150) .30 .10
❑ COMMON CARD (151-200) 3.00 1.25
❑ COMMON CARD (201-220) 1.50 .60
❑ 1 Alex Rodriguez 1.25 .50
❑ 2 Barry Bonds 2.00 .75
❑ 3 Derek Jeter 2.00 .75
❑ 4 Robert Fick .30 .10
❑ 5 Juan Pierre .30 .10
❑ 6 Torii Hunter .30 .10
❑ 7 Todd Helton .50 .20
❑ 8 Cal Ripken 2.50 1.00
❑ 9 Manny Ramirez .50 .20
❑ 10 Johnny Damon .50 .20
❑ 11 Mike Piazza 1.25 .50
❑ 12 Nomar Garciaparra 1.25 .50
❑ 13 Pedro Martinez .50 .20
❑ 14 Brian Giles .30 .10
❑ 15 Albert Pujols 1.50 .60
❑ 16 Roger Clemens 1.50 .60
❑ 17 Sammy Sosa .75 .30
❑ 18 Vladimir Guerrero .75 .30
❑ 19 Tony Gwynn 1.00 .40
❑ 20 Pat Burrell .30 .10
❑ 21 Carlos Delgado .30 .10
❑ 22 Tino Martinez .50 .20
❑ 23 Jim Edmonds .30 .10
❑ 24 Jason Giambi .30 .10
❑ 25 Tom Glavine .50 .20
❑ 26 Mark Grace .50 .20
❑ 27 Tony Armas Jr. .30 .10
❑ 28 Andruw Jones .50 .20
❑ 29 Ben Sheets .30 .10
❑ 30 Jeff Kent .30 .10
❑ 31 Barry Larkin .50 .20
❑ 32 Joe Mays .30 .10
❑ 33 Mike Mussina .50 .20
❑ 34 Hideo Nomo .75 .30
❑ 35 Rafael Palmeiro .50 .20
❑ 36 Scott Brosius .30 .10
❑ 37 Scott Rolen .50 .20
❑ 38 Gary Sheffield .30 .10
❑ 39 Bernie Williams .50 .20
❑ 40 Bob Abreu .30 .10
❑ 41 Edgardo Alfonzo .30 .10
❑ 42 C.C. Sabathia .30 .10
❑ 43 Jeremy Giambi .30 .10
❑ 44 Craig Biggio .50 .20
❑ 45 Andres Galarraga .30 .10
❑ 46 Edgar Martinez .50 .20
❑ 47 Fred McGriff .50 .20
❑ 48 Magglio Ordonez .30 .10
❑ 49 Jim Thome .50 .20
❑ 50 Matt Williams .30 .10
❑ 51 Kerry Wood .30 .10
❑ 52 Moises Alou .30 .10
❑ 53 Brady Anderson .30 .10
❑ 54 Garret Anderson .30 .10
❑ 55 Juan Gonzalez .30 .10
❑ 56 Bret Boone .30 .10
❑ 57 Jose Cruz Jr. .30 .10
❑ 58 Carlos Beltran .30 .10
❑ 59 Adrian Beltre .30 .10
❑ 60 Joe Kennedy .30 .10
❑ 61 Lance Berkman .30 .10
❑ 62 Kevin Brown .30 .10
❑ 63 Tim Hudson .30 .10
❑ 64 Jeromy Burnitz .30 .10
❑ 65 Jarrod Washburn .30 .10
❑ 66 Sean Casey .30 .10
❑ 67 Eric Chavez .30 .10
❑ 68 Bartolo Colon .30 .10
❑ 69 Freddy Garcia .30 .10
❑ 70 Jermaine Dye .30 .10
❑ 71 Terrence Long .30 .10
❑ 72 Cliff Floyd .30 .10
❑ 73 Luis Gonzalez .30 .10
❑ 74 Ichiro Suzuki 1.50 .60
❑ 75 Mike Hampton .30 .10
❑ 76 Richard Hidalgo .30 .10
❑ 77 Geoff Jenkins .30 .10
❑ 78 Gabe Kapler .30 .10
❑ 79 Ken Griffey Jr. 1.25 .50
❑ 80 Jason Kendall .30 .10
❑ 81 Josh Towers .30 .10
❑ 82 Ryan Klesko .30 .10
❑ 83 Paul Konerko .30 .10
❑ 84 Carlos Lee .30 .10
❑ 85 Kenny Lofton .30 .10
❑ 86 Josh Beckett .30 .10
❑ 87 Raul Mondesi .30 .10
❑ 88 Trot Nixon .30 .10
❑ 89 John Olerud .30 .10
❑ 90 Paul O'Neill .50 .20
❑ 91 Chan Ho Park .30 .10
❑ 92 Andy Pettitte .50 .20
❑ 93 Jorge Posada .50 .20
❑ 94 Mark Quinn .30 .10
❑ 95 Aramis Ramirez .30 .10
❑ 96 Curt Schilling .30 .10
❑ 97 Richie Sexson .30 .10
❑ 98 John Smoltz .50 .20
❑ 99 Wilson Betemit .30 .10
❑ 100 Shannon Stewart .30 .10
❑ 101 Alfonso Soriano .30 .10
❑ 102 Mike Sweeney .30 .10
❑ 103 Miguel Tejada .30 .10
❑ 104 Greg Vaughn .30 .10
❑ 105 Robin Ventura .30 .10
❑ 106 Jose Vidro .30 .10
❑ 107 Larry Walker .30 .10
❑ 108 Preston Wilson .30 .10
❑ 109 Corey Patterson .30 .10
❑ 110 Mark Mulder .30 .10
❑ 111 Tony Clark .30 .10
❑ 112 Roy Oswalt .30 .10
❑ 113 Jimmy Rollins .30 .10
❑ 114 Kazuhiro Sasaki .30 .10
❑ 115 Barry Zito .30 .10
❑ 116 Javier Vazquez .30 .10
❑ 117 Mike Cameron .30 .10
❑ 118 Phil Nevin .30 .10
❑ 119 Bud Smith .30 .10
❑ 120 Cristian Guzman .30 .10
❑ 121 Al Leiter .30 .10
❑ 122 Brad Radke .30 .10
❑ 123 Bobby Higginson .30 .10
❑ 124 Robert Person .30 .10
❑ 125 Adam Dunn .30 .10
❑ 126 Ben Grieve .30 .10
❑ 127 Rafael Furcal .30 .10

❑ 128	Jay Gibbons	.30	.10
❑ 129	Paul LoDuca	.30	.10
❑ 130	Wade Miller	.30	.10
❑ 131	Tsuyoshi Shinjo	.30	.10
❑ 132	Eric Milton	.30	.10
❑ 133	Rickey Henderson	.75	.30
❑ 134	Roberto Alomar	.50	.20
❑ 135	Darin Erstad	.30	.10
❑ 136	J.D. Drew	.30	.10
❑ 137	Shawn Green	.30	.10
❑ 138	Randy Johnson	.75	.30
❑ 139	Austin Kearns	.30	.10
❑ 140	Jose Canseco	.50	.20
❑ 141	Jeff Bagwell	.50	.20
❑ 142	Greg Maddux	1.25	.50
❑ 143	Mark Buehrle	.30	.10
❑ 144	Ivan Rodriguez	.50	.20
❑ 145	Frank Thomas	.75	.30
❑ 146	Rich Aurilia	.30	.10
❑ 147	Troy Glaus	.30	.10
❑ 148	Ryan Dempster	.30	.10
❑ 149	Chipper Jones	.75	.30
❑ 150	Matt Morris	.30	.10
❑ 151	Marlon Byrd RR	3.00	1.25
❑ 152	Ben Howard RR RC	3.00	1.25
❑ 153	Brandon Backe RR RC	3.00	1.25
❑ 154	Jorge De La Rosa RR RC	3.00	1.25
❑ 155	Corky Miller RR	3.00	1.25
❑ 156	Dennis Tankersley RR	3.00	1.25
❑ 157	Kyle Kane RR RC	3.00	1.25
❑ 158	Justin Duchscherer RR	3.00	1.25
❑ 159	Brian Mallette RR RC	3.00	1.25
❑ 160	Chris Baker RR RC	3.00	1.25
❑ 161	Jason Lane RR	3.00	1.25
❑ 162	Hee Seop Choi RR	3.00	1.25
❑ 163	Juan Cruz RR	3.00	1.25
❑ 164	Rodrigo Rosario RR RC	3.00	1.25
❑ 165	Matt Guerrier RR	3.00	1.25
❑ 166	Anderson Machado RR RC	3.00	1.25
❑ 167	Geronimo Gil RR	3.00	1.25
❑ 168	Dewon Brazelton RR	3.00	1.25
❑ 169	Mark Prior RR	4.00	1.50
❑ 170	Bill Hall RR	3.00	1.25
❑ 171	Jorge Padilla RR RC	3.00	1.25
❑ 172	Jose Cueto RR	3.00	1.25
❑ 173	Allan Simpson RR RC	3.00	1.25
❑ 174	Doug Devore RR RC	3.00	1.25
❑ 175	Josh Pearce RR	3.00	1.25
❑ 176	Angel Berroa RR	3.00	1.25
❑ 177	Steve Bechler RR RC	3.00	1.25
❑ 178	Antonio Perez RR	3.00	1.25
❑ 179	Mark Teixeira RR	4.00	1.50
❑ 180	Erick Almonte RR	3.00	1.25
❑ 181	Orlando Hudson RR	3.00	1.25
❑ 182	Michael Rivera RR	3.00	1.25
❑ 183	Raul Chavez RR RC	3.00	1.25
❑ 184	Juan Pena RR	3.00	1.25
❑ 185	Travis Hughes RR RC	3.00	1.25
❑ 186	Ryan Ludwick RR	3.00	1.25
❑ 187	Ed Rogers RR	3.00	1.25
❑ 188	Andy Pratt RR RC	3.00	1.25
❑ 189	Nick Neugebauer RR	3.00	1.25
❑ 190	Tom Shearn RR RC	3.00	1.25
❑ 191	Eric Cyr RR	3.00	1.25
❑ 192	Victor Martinez RR	4.00	1.50
❑ 193	Brandon Berger RR	3.00	1.25
❑ 194	Erik Bedard RR	3.00	1.25
❑ 195	Fernando Rodney RR	3.00	1.25
❑ 196	Joe Thurston RR	3.00	1.25
❑ 197	John Buck RR	3.00	1.25
❑ 198	Jeff Deardorff RR	3.00	1.25
❑ 199	Ryan Jamison RR	3.00	1.25
❑ 200	Alfredo Amezaga RR	3.00	1.25
❑ 201	Luis Gonzalez FC	1.50	.60
❑ 202	Roger Clemens FC	5.00	2.00
❑ 203	Barry Zito FC	1.50	.60
❑ 204	Bud Smith FC	1.50	.60
❑ 205	Magglio Ordonez FC	1.50	.60
❑ 206	Kerry Wood FC	1.50	.60
❑ 207	Freddy Garcia FC	1.50	.60
❑ 208	Adam Dunn FC	1.50	.60
❑ 209	Curt Schilling FC	1.50	.60
❑ 210	Lance Berkman FC	1.50	.60
❑ 211	Rafael Palmeiro FC	1.50	.60
❑ 212	Ichiro Suzuki FC	5.00	2.00
❑ 213	Bob Abreu FC	1.50	.60
❑ 214	Mark Mulder FC	1.50	.60
❑ 215	Roy Oswalt FC	1.50	.60
❑ 216	Mike Sweeney FC	1.50	.60
❑ 217	Paul LoDuca FC	1.50	.60
❑ 218	Aramis Ramirez FC	1.50	.60
❑ 219	Randy Johnson FC	2.50	1.00
❑ 220	Albert Pujols FC	5.00	2.00

2003 Donruss

❑	COMPLETE SET (400)	50.00	25.00
❑	COMMON CARD (71-400)	.30	.10
❑	COMMON CARD (1-20)	.50	.20
❑	COMMON CARD (21-70)	.50	.20
❑ 1	Vladimir Guerrero DK	.75	.30
❑ 2	Derek Jeter DK	2.00	.75
❑ 3	Adam Dunn DK	.50	.20
❑ 4	Greg Maddux DK	1.25	.50
❑ 5	Lance Berkman DK	.50	.20
❑ 6	Ichiro Suzuki DK	1.50	.60
❑ 7	Mike Piazza DK	1.25	.50
❑ 8	Alex Rodriguez DK	1.25	.50
❑ 9	Tom Glavine DK	.50	.20
❑ 10	Randy Johnson DK	.75	.30
❑ 11	Nomar Garciaparra DK	1.25	.50
❑ 12	Jason Giambi DK	.50	.20
❑ 13	Sammy Sosa DK	.75	.30
❑ 14	Barry Zito DK	.50	.20
❑ 15	Chipper Jones DK	.75	.30
❑ 16	Magglio Ordonez DK	.50	.20
❑ 17	Larry Walker DK	.50	.20
❑ 18	Alfonso Soriano DK	.50	.20
❑ 19	Curt Schilling DK	.50	.20
❑ 20	Barry Bonds DK	2.00	.75
❑ 21	Joe Borchard RR	.50	.20
❑ 22	Chris Snelling RR	.50	.20
❑ 23	Brian Tallet RR	.50	.20
❑ 24	Cliff Lee RR	.50	.20
❑ 25	Freddy Sanchez RR	.50	.20
❑ 26	Chone Figgans RR	.50	.20
❑ 27	Kevin Cash RR	.50	.20
❑ 28	Josh Bard RR	.50	.20
❑ 29	Jeriome Robertson RR	.50	.20
❑ 30	Jeremy Hill RR	.50	.20
❑ 31	Shane Nance RR	.50	.20
❑ 32	Jake Peavy RR	.50	.20
❑ 33	Trey Hodges RR	.50	.20
❑ 34	Eric Eckenstahler RR	.50	.20
❑ 35	Jim Rushford RR	.50	.20
❑ 36	Oliver Perez RR	.50	.20
❑ 37	Kirk Saarloos RR	.50	.20
❑ 38	Hank Blalock RR	.50	.20
❑ 39	Francisco Rodriguez RR	.50	.20
❑ 40	Runelvys Hernandez RR	.50	.20
❑ 41	Aaron Cook RR	.50	.20
❑ 42	Josh Hancock RR	.50	.20
❑ 43	P.J. Bevis RR	.50	.20
❑ 44	Jon Adkins RR	.50	.20
❑ 45	Tim Kalita RR	.50	.20
❑ 46	Nelson Castro RR	.50	.20
❑ 47	Colin Young RR	.50	.20
❑ 48	Adrian Burnside RR	.50	.20
❑ 49	Luis Martinez RR	.50	.20
❑ 50	Pete Zamora RR	.50	.20
❑ 51	Todd Donovan RR	.50	.20
❑ 52	Jeremy Ward RR	.50	.20
❑ 53	Wilson Valdez RR	.50	.20
❑ 54	Eric Good RR	.50	.20
❑ 55	Jeff Baker RR	.50	.20
❑ 56	Mitch Wylie RR	.50	.20
❑ 57	Ron Calloway RR	.50	.20
❑ 58	Jose Valverde RR	.50	.20
❑ 59	Jason Davis RR	.50	.20
❑ 60	Scotty Layfield RR	.50	.20
❑ 61	Matt Thornton RR	.50	.20
❑ 62	Adam Walker RR	.50	.20
❑ 63	Gustavo Chacin RR	.50	.20
❑ 64	Ron Chiavacci RR	.50	.20
❑ 65	Wiki Nieves RR	.50	.20
❑ 66	Cliff Bartosh RR	.50	.20
❑ 67	Mike Gonzalez RR	.50	.20
❑ 68	Justin Wayne RR	.50	.20
❑ 69	Eric Junge RR	.50	.20
❑ 70	Ben Kozlowski RR	.50	.20
❑ 71	Darin Erstad	.30	.10
❑ 72	Garret Anderson	.30	.10
❑ 73	Troy Glaus	.30	.10
❑ 74	David Eckstein	.30	.10
❑ 75	Adam Kennedy	.30	.10
❑ 76	Kevin Appier	.30	.10
❑ 77	Jarrod Washburn	.30	.10
❑ 78	Scott Spiezio	.30	.10
❑ 79	Tim Salmon	.50	.20
❑ 80	Ramon Ortiz	.30	.10
❑ 81	Bengie Molina	.30	.10
❑ 82	Brad Fullmer	.30	.10
❑ 83	Troy Percival	.30	.10
❑ 84	David Segui	.30	.10
❑ 85	Jay Gibbons	.30	.10
❑ 86	Tony Batista	.30	.10
❑ 87	Scott Erickson	.30	.10
❑ 88	Jeff Conine	.30	.10
❑ 89	Melvin Mora	.30	.10
❑ 90	Buddy Groom	.30	.10
❑ 91	Rodrigo Lopez	.30	.10
❑ 92	Marty Cordova	.30	.10
❑ 93	Geronimo Gil	.30	.10
❑ 94	Kenny Lofton	.30	.10
❑ 95	Shea Hillenbrand	.30	.10
❑ 96	Manny Ramirez	.50	.20
❑ 97	Pedro Martinez	.50	.20
❑ 98	Nomar Garciaparra	1.25	.50
❑ 99	Rickey Henderson	.75	.30
❑ 100	Johnny Damon	.50	.20
❑ 101	Trot Nixon	.30	.10
❑ 102	Derek Lowe	.30	.10
❑ 103	Hee Seop Choi	.30	.10
❑ 104	Mark Teixeira	.50	.20
❑ 105	Tim Wakefield	.30	.10
❑ 106	Jason Varitek	.75	.30
❑ 107	Frank Thomas	.75	.30
❑ 108	Joe Crede	.30	.10
❑ 109	Magglio Ordonez	.30	.10
❑ 110	Ray Durham	.30	.10
❑ 111	Mark Buehrle	.30	.10
❑ 112	Paul Konerko	.30	.10
❑ 113	Jose Valentin	.30	.10
❑ 114	Carlos Lee	.30	.10
❑ 115	Royce Clayton	.30	.10
❑ 116	C.C. Sabathia	.30	.10
❑ 117	Ellis Burks	.30	.10
❑ 118	Omar Vizquel	.50	.20
❑ 119	Jim Thome	.50	.20
❑ 120	Matt Lawton	.30	.10
❑ 121	Travis Fryman	.30	.10
❑ 122	Earl Snyder	.30	.10
❑ 123	Ricky Gutierrez	.30	.10
❑ 124	Einar Diaz	.30	.10
❑ 125	Danys Baez	.30	.10
❑ 126	Robert Fick	.30	.10
❑ 127	Bobby Higginson	.30	.10
❑ 128	Steve Sparks	.30	.10
❑ 129	Mike Rivera	.30	.10
❑ 130	Wendell Magee	.30	.10
❑ 131	Randall Simon	.30	.10
❑ 132	Carlos Pena	.30	.10
❑ 133	Mark Redman	.30	.10
❑ 134	Juan Acevedo	.30	.10
❑ 135	Mike Sweeney	.30	.10
❑ 136	Aaron Guiel	.30	.10
❑ 137	Carlos Beltran	.30	.10
❑ 138	Joe Randa	.30	.10
❑ 139	Paul Byrd	.30	.10
❑ 140	Shawn Sedlacek	.30	.10
❑ 141	Raul Ibanez	.30	.10

	#	Player		
❑	142	Michael Tucker	.30	.10
❑	143	Torii Hunter	.30	.10
❑	144	Jacque Jones	.30	.10
❑	145	David Ortiz	.75	.30
❑	146	Corey Koskie	.30	.10
❑	147	Brad Radke	.30	.10
❑	148	Doug Mientkiewicz	.30	.10
❑	149	A.J. Pierzynski	.30	.10
❑	150	Dustan Mohr	.30	.10
❑	151	Michael Cuddyer	.30	.10
❑	152	Eddie Guardado	.30	.10
❑	153	Cristian Guzman	.30	.10
❑	154	Derek Jeter	2.00	.75
❑	155	Bernie Williams	.50	.20
❑	156	Roger Clemens	1.50	.60
❑	157	Mike Mussina	.50	.20
❑	158	Jorge Posada	.50	.20
❑	159	Alfonso Soriano	.30	.10
❑	160	Jason Giambi	.30	.10
❑	161	Robin Ventura	.30	.10
❑	162	Andy Pettitte	.50	.20
❑	163	David Wells	.30	.10
❑	164	Nick Johnson	.30	.10
❑	165	Jeff Weaver	.30	.10
❑	166	Raul Mondesi	.30	.10
❑	167	Rondell White	.30	.10
❑	168	Tim Hudson	.30	.10
❑	169	Barry Zito	.30	.10
❑	170	Mark Mulder	.30	.10
❑	171	Miguel Tejada	.30	.10
❑	172	Eric Chavez	.30	.10
❑	173	Billy Koch	.30	.10
❑	174	Jermaine Dye	.30	.10
❑	175	Scott Hatteberg	.30	.10
❑	176	Terrence Long	.30	.10
❑	177	David Justice	.30	.10
❑	178	Ramon Hernandez	.30	.10
❑	179	Ted Lilly	.30	.10
❑	180	Ichiro Suzuki	1.50	.60
❑	181	Edgar Martinez	.50	.20
❑	182	Mike Cameron	.30	.10
❑	183	John Olerud	.30	.10
❑	184	Bret Boone	.30	.10
❑	185	Dan Wilson	.30	.10
❑	186	Freddy Garcia	.30	.10
❑	187	Jamie Moyer	.30	.10
❑	188	Carlos Guillen	.30	.10
❑	189	Ruben Sierra	.30	.10
❑	190	Kazuhiro Sasaki	.30	.10
❑	191	Mark McLemore	.30	.10
❑	192	John Halama	.30	.10
❑	193	Joel Pineiro	.30	.10
❑	194	Jeff Cirillo	.30	.10
❑	195	Rafael Soriano	.30	.10
❑	196	Ben Grieve	.30	.10
❑	197	Aubrey Huff	.30	.10
❑	198	Steve Cox	.30	.10
❑	199	Toby Hall	.30	.10
❑	200	Randy Winn	.30	.10
❑	201	Brent Abernathy	.30	.10
❑	202	Chris Gomez	.30	.10
❑	203	John Flaherty	.30	.10
❑	204	Paul Wilson	.30	.10
❑	205	Chan Ho Park	.30	.10
❑	206	Alex Rodriguez	1.25	.50
❑	207	Juan Gonzalez	.30	.10
❑	208	Rafael Palmeiro	.50	.20
❑	209	Ivan Rodriguez	.50	.20
❑	210	Rusty Greer	.30	.10
❑	211	Kenny Rogers	.30	.10
❑	212	Ismael Valdes	.30	.10
❑	213	Frank Catalanotto	.30	.10
❑	214	Hank Blalock	.30	.10
❑	215	Michael Young	.50	.20
❑	216	Kevin Mench	.30	.10
❑	217	Herbert Perry	.30	.10
❑	218	Gabe Kapler	.30	.10
❑	219	Carlos Delgado	.30	.10
❑	220	Shannon Stewart	.30	.10
❑	221	Eric Hinske	.30	.10
❑	222	Roy Halladay	.30	.10
❑	223	Felipe Lopez	.30	.10
❑	224	Vernon Wells	.30	.10
❑	225	Josh Phelps	.30	.10
❑	226	Jose Cruz	.30	.10
❑	227	Curt Schilling	.30	.10
❑	228	Randy Johnson	.75	.30
❑	229	Luis Gonzalez	.30	.10
❑	230	Mark Grace	.50	.20
❑	231	Junior Spivey	.30	.10
❑	232	Tony Womack	.30	.10
❑	233	Matt Williams	.30	.10
❑	234	Steve Finley	.30	.10
❑	235	Byung-Hyun Kim	.30	.10
❑	236	Craig Counsell	.30	.10
❑	237	Greg Maddux	1.25	.50
❑	238	Tom Glavine	.50	.20
❑	239	John Smoltz	.50	.20
❑	240	Chipper Jones	.75	.30
❑	241	Gary Sheffield	.30	.10
❑	242	Andruw Jones	.50	.20
❑	243	Vinny Castilla	.30	.10
❑	244	Damian Moss	.30	.10
❑	245	Rafael Furcal	.30	.10
❑	246	Javy Lopez	.30	.10
❑	247	Kevin Millwood	.30	.10
❑	248	Kerry Wood	.30	.10
❑	249	Fred McGriff	.50	.20
❑	250	Sammy Sosa	.75	.30
❑	251	Alex Gonzalez	.30	.10
❑	252	Corey Patterson	.30	.10
❑	253	Moises Alou	.30	.10
❑	254	Juan Cruz	.30	.10
❑	255	Jon Lieber	.30	.10
❑	256	Matt Clement	.30	.10
❑	257	Mark Prior	.50	.20
❑	258	Ken Griffey Jr.	1.25	.50
❑	259	Barry Larkin	.50	.20
❑	260	Adam Dunn	.30	.10
❑	261	Sean Casey	.30	.10
❑	262	Jose Rijo	.30	.10
❑	263	Elmer Dessens	.30	.10
❑	264	Austin Kearns	.30	.10
❑	265	Corky Miller	.30	.10
❑	266	Todd Walker	.30	.10
❑	267	Chris Reitsma	.30	.10
❑	268	Ryan Dempster	.30	.10
❑	269	Aaron Boone	.30	.10
❑	270	Danny Graves	.30	.10
❑	271	Brandon Larson	.30	.10
❑	272	Larry Walker	.30	.10
❑	273	Todd Helton	.50	.20
❑	274	Juan Uribe	.30	.10
❑	275	Juan Pierre	.30	.10
❑	276	Mike Hampton	.30	.10
❑	277	Todd Zeile	.30	.10
❑	278	Todd Hollandsworth	.30	.10
❑	279	Jason Jennings	.30	.10
❑	280	Josh Beckett	.30	.10
❑	281	Mike Lowell	.30	.10
❑	282	Derrek Lee	.50	.20
❑	283	A.J. Burnett	.30	.10
❑	284	Luis Castillo	.30	.10
❑	285	Tim Raines	.30	.10
❑	286	Preston Wilson	.30	.10
❑	287	Juan Encarnacion	.30	.10
❑	288	Charles Johnson	.30	.10
❑	289	Jeff Bagwell	.50	.20
❑	290	Craig Biggio	.50	.20
❑	291	Lance Berkman	.30	.10
❑	292	Daryle Ward	.30	.10
❑	293	Roy Oswalt	.30	.10
❑	294	Richard Hidalgo	.30	.10
❑	295	Octavio Dotel	.30	.10
❑	296	Wade Miller	.30	.10
❑	297	Julio Lugo	.30	.10
❑	298	Billy Wagner	.30	.10
❑	299	Shawn Green	.30	.10
❑	300	Adrian Beltre	.30	.10
❑	301	Paul Lo Duca	.30	.10
❑	302	Eric Karros	.30	.10
❑	303	Kevin Brown	.30	.10
❑	304	Hideo Nomo	.75	.30
❑	305	Odalis Perez	.30	.10
❑	306	Eric Gagne	.30	.10
❑	307	Brian Jordan	.30	.10
❑	308	Cesar Izturis	.30	.10
❑	309	Mark Grudzielanek	.30	.10
❑	310	Kazuhisa Ishii	.30	.10
❑	311	Geoff Jenkins	.30	.10
❑	312	Richie Sexson	.30	.10
❑	313	Jose Hernandez	.30	.10
❑	314	Ben Sheets	.30	.10
❑	315	Ruben Quevedo	.30	.10
❑	316	Jeffrey Hammonds	.30	.10
❑	317	Alex Sanchez	.30	.10
❑	318	Eric Young	.30	.10
❑	319	Takahito Nomura	.30	.10
❑	320	Vladimir Guerrero	.75	.30
❑	321	Jose Vidro	.30	.10
❑	322	Orlando Cabrera	.30	.10
❑	323	Michael Barrett	.30	.10
❑	324	Javier Vazquez	.30	.10
❑	325	Tony Armas Jr.	.30	.10
❑	326	Andres Galarraga	.30	.10
❑	327	Tomo Ohka	.30	.10
❑	328	Bartolo Colon	.30	.10
❑	329	Fernando Tatis	.30	.10
❑	330	Brad Wilkerson	.30	.10
❑	331	Masato Yoshii	.30	.10
❑	332	Mike Piazza	1.25	.50
❑	333	Jeromy Burnitz	.30	.10
❑	334	Roberto Alomar	.50	.20
❑	335	Mo Vaughn	.30	.10
❑	336	Al Leiter	.30	.10
❑	337	Pedro Astacio	.30	.10
❑	338	Edgardo Alfonzo	.30	.10
❑	339	Armando Benitez	.30	.10
❑	340	Timo Perez	.30	.10
❑	341	Jay Payton	.30	.10
❑	342	Roger Cedeno	.30	.10
❑	343	Rey Ordonez	.30	.10
❑	344	Steve Trachsel	.30	.10
❑	345	Satoru Komiyama	.30	.10
❑	346	Scott Rolen	.50	.20
❑	347	Pat Burrell	.30	.10
❑	348	Bobby Abreu	.30	.10
❑	349	Mike Lieberthal	.30	.10
❑	350	Brandon Duckworth	.30	.10
❑	351	Jimmy Rollins	.30	.10
❑	352	Marlon Anderson	.30	.10
❑	353	Travis Lee	.30	.10
❑	354	Vicente Padilla	.30	.10
❑	355	Randy Wolf	.30	.10
❑	356	Jason Kendall	.30	.10
❑	357	Brian Giles	.30	.10
❑	358	Aramis Ramirez	.30	.10
❑	359	Pokey Reese	.30	.10
❑	360	Kip Wells	.30	.10
❑	361	Josh Fogg	.30	.10
❑	362	Mike Williams	.30	.10
❑	363	Jack Wilson	.30	.10
❑	364	Craig Wilson	.30	.10
❑	365	Kevin Young	.30	.10
❑	366	Ryan Klesko	.30	.10
❑	367	Phil Nevin	.30	.10
❑	368	Brian Lawrence	.30	.10
❑	369	Mark Kotsay	.30	.10
❑	370	Brett Tomko	.30	.10
❑	371	Trevor Hoffman	.30	.10
❑	372	Deivi Cruz	.30	.10
❑	373	Bubba Trammell	.30	.10
❑	374	Sean Burroughs	.30	.10
❑	375	Barry Bonds	2.00	.75
❑	376	Jeff Kent	.30	.10
❑	377	Rich Aurilia	.30	.10
❑	378	Tsuyoshi Shinjo	.30	.10
❑	379	Benito Santiago	.30	.10
❑	380	Kirk Rueter	.30	.10
❑	381	Livan Hernandez	.30	.10
❑	382	Russ Ortiz	.30	.10
❑	383	David Bell	.30	.10
❑	384	Jason Schmidt	.30	.10
❑	385	Reggie Sanders	.30	.10
❑	386	J.T. Snow	.30	.10
❑	387	Robb Nen	.30	.10
❑	388	Ryan Jensen	.30	.10
❑	389	Jim Edmonds	.30	.10
❑	390	J.D. Drew	.30	.10
❑	391	Albert Pujols	1.50	.60
❑	392	Fernando Vina	.30	.10
❑	393	Tino Martinez	.50	.20
❑	394	Edgar Renteria	.30	.10
❑	395	Matt Morris	.30	.10
❑	396	Woody Williams	.30	.10
❑	397	Jason Isringhausen	.30	.10
❑	398	Placido Polanco	.30	.10

- ❑ 399 Eli Marrero .30 .10
- ❑ 400 Jason Simontacchi .30 .10

2003 Donruss Rookies

- ❑ COMPLETE SET (65) 20.00 8.00
- ❑ COMMON CARD (1-65) .20 .07
- ❑ COMMON RC .25 .08
- ❑ 1 Jeremy Bonderman RC 2.00 .75
- ❑ 2 Adam Loewen RC .50 .20
- ❑ 3 Dan Haren RC .50 .20
- ❑ 4 Jose Contreras RC .50 .20
- ❑ 5 Hideki Matsui RC 2.00 .75
- ❑ 6 Arnie Munoz RC .25 .08
- ❑ 7 Miguel Cabrera .50 .20
- ❑ 8 Andrew Brown RC .40 .15
- ❑ 9 Josh Hall RC .25 .08
- ❑ 10 Josh Stewart RC .25 .08
- ❑ 11 Clint Barmes RC .75 .30
- ❑ 12 Luis Ayala RC .25 .08
- ❑ 13 Brandon Webb RC 1.50 .60
- ❑ 14 Greg Aquino RC .25 .08
- ❑ 15 Chien-Ming Wang RC 5.00 2.00
- ❑ 16 Rickie Weeks RC 1.50 .60
- ❑ 17 Edgar Gonzalez RC .25 .08
- ❑ 18 Dontrelle Willis .50 .20
- ❑ 19 Bo Hart RC .25 .08
- ❑ 20 Rosman Garcia RC .25 .08
- ❑ 21 Jeremy Griffiths RC .25 .08
- ❑ 22 Craig Brazell RC .25 .08
- ❑ 23 Daniel Cabrera RC .50 .20
- ❑ 24 Fernando Cabrera RC .25 .08
- ❑ 25 Terrmel Sledge RC .25 .08
- ❑ 26 Ramon Nivar RC .25 .08
- ❑ 27 Rob Hammock RC .25 .08
- ❑ 28 Francisco Rosario RC .25 .08
- ❑ 29 Cory Stewart RC .25 .08
- ❑ 30 Felix Sanchez RC .25 .08
- ❑ 31 Jorge Cordova RC .25 .08
- ❑ 32 Rocco Baldelli .20 .07
- ❑ 33 Beau Kemp RC .25 .08
- ❑ 34 Mike Nakamura RC .25 .08
- ❑ 35 Rett Johnson RC .25 .08
- ❑ 36 Guillermo Quiroz RC .25 .08
- ❑ 37 Hong-Chih Kuo RC 2.00 .75
- ❑ 38 Ian Ferguson RC .25 .08
- ❑ 39 Franklin Perez RC .25 .08
- ❑ 40 Tim Olson RC .25 .08
- ❑ 41 Jerome Williams .20 .07
- ❑ 42 Rich Fischer RC .25 .08
- ❑ 43 Phil Seibel RC .25 .08
- ❑ 44 Aaron Looper RC .25 .08
- ❑ 45 Jae Weong Seo .20 .07
- ❑ 46 Chad Gaudin RC .25 .08
- ❑ 47 Matt Kata RC .25 .08
- ❑ 48 Ryan Wagner RC .25 .08
- ❑ 49 Michel Hernandez RC .25 .08
- ❑ 50 Diegomar Markwell RC .25 .08
- ❑ 51 Doug Waechter RC .40 .15
- ❑ 52 Mike Nicolas RC .25 .08
- ❑ 53 Prentice Redman RC .25 .08
- ❑ 54 Shane Bazzell RC .25 .08
- ❑ 55 Delmon Young RC 3.00 1.25
- ❑ 56 Brian Stokes RC .25 .08
- ❑ 57 Matt Bruback RC .25 .08
- ❑ 58 Nook Logan RC .40 .15
- ❑ 59 Oscar Villarreal RC .25 .08
- ❑ 60 Pete LaForest RC .25 .08
- ❑ 61 Shea Hillenbrand .20 .07
- ❑ 62 Aramis Ramirez .20 .07
- ❑ 63 Aaron Boone .20 .07
- ❑ 64 Roberto Alomar .30 .10
- ❑ 65 Rickey Henderson .50 .20

2004 Donruss

- ❑ COMPLETE SET (400) 150.00 75.00
- ❑ COMP.SET w/o SP's (300) 25.00 10.00
- ❑ COMMON CARD (71-370) .30 .10
- ❑ COMMON CARD (1-25/371-400) 2.00 .75
- ❑ COMMON CARD (26-70) 2.00 .75
- ❑ 1-70/370-400 RANDOM INSERTS IN PACKS
- ❑ 1 Derek Jeter DK 4.00 1.50
- ❑ 2 Greg Maddux DK 3.00 1.25
- ❑ 3 Albert Pujols DK 4.00 1.50
- ❑ 4 Ichiro Suzuki DK 4.00 1.50
- ❑ 5 Alex Rodriguez DK 3.00 1.25
- ❑ 6 Roger Clemens DK 4.00 1.50
- ❑ 7 Andruw Jones DK 2.00 .75
- ❑ 8 Barry Bonds DK 5.00 2.00
- ❑ 9 Jeff Bagwell DK 2.00 .75
- ❑ 10 Randy Johnson DK 2.00 .75
- ❑ 11 Scott Rolen DK 2.00 .75
- ❑ 12 Lance Berkman DK 2.00 .75
- ❑ 13 Barry Zito DK 2.00 .75
- ❑ 14 Manny Ramirez DK 2.00 .75
- ❑ 15 Carlos Delgado DK 2.00 .75
- ❑ 16 Alfonso Soriano DK 2.00 .75
- ❑ 17 Todd Helton DK 2.00 .75
- ❑ 18 Mike Mussina DK 2.00 .75
- ❑ 19 Austin Kearns DK 2.00 .75
- ❑ 20 Nomar Garciaparra DK 3.00 1.25
- ❑ 21 Chipper Jones DK 2.00 .75
- ❑ 22 Mark Prior DK 2.00 .75
- ❑ 23 Jim Thome DK 2.00 .75
- ❑ 24 Vladimir Guerrero DK 2.00 .75
- ❑ 25 Pedro Martinez DK 2.00 .75
- ❑ 26 Sergio Mitre RR 2.00 .75
- ❑ 27 Adam Loewen RR 2.00 .75
- ❑ 28 Alfredo Gonzalez RR 2.00 .75
- ❑ 29 Miguel Ojeda RR 2.00 .75
- ❑ 30 Rosman Garcia RR 2.00 .75
- ❑ 31 Arnie Munoz RR 2.00 .75
- ❑ 32 Andrew Brown RR 2.00 .75
- ❑ 33 Josh Hall RR 2.00 .75
- ❑ 34 Josh Stewart RR 2.00 .75
- ❑ 35 Clint Barmes RR 3.00 1.25
- ❑ 36 Brandon Webb RR 2.00 .75
- ❑ 37 Chien-Ming Wang RR 8.00 3.00
- ❑ 38 Edgar Gonzalez RR 2.00 .75
- ❑ 39 Alejandro Machado RR 2.00 .75
- ❑ 40 Jeremy Griffiths RR 2.00 .75
- ❑ 41 Craig Brazell RR 2.00 .75
- ❑ 42 Daniel Cabrera RR 2.00 .75
- ❑ 43 Fernando Cabrera RR 2.00 .75
- ❑ 44 Terrmel Sledge RR 2.00 .75
- ❑ 45 Rob Hammock RR 2.00 .75
- ❑ 46 Francisco Rosario RR 2.00 .75
- ❑ 47 Francisco Cruceta RR 2.00 .75
- ❑ 48 Rett Johnson RR 2.00 .75
- ❑ 49 Guillermo Quiroz RR 2.00 .75
- ❑ 50 Hong-Chih Kuo RR 3.00 1.25
- ❑ 51 Ian Ferguson RR 2.00 .75
- ❑ 52 Tim Olson RR 2.00 .75
- ❑ 53 Todd Wellemeyer RR 2.00 .75
- ❑ 54 Rich Fischer RR 2.00 .75
- ❑ 55 Phil Seibel RR 2.00 .75
- ❑ 56 Joe Valentine RR 2.00 .75
- ❑ 57 Matt Kata RR 2.00 .75
- ❑ 58 Michael Hessman RR 2.00 .75
- ❑ 59 Michel Hernandez RR 2.00 .75
- ❑ 60 Doug Waechter RR 2.00 .75
- ❑ 61 Prentice Redman RR 2.00 .75
- ❑ 62 Nook Logan RR 2.00 .75
- ❑ 63 Oscar Villarreal RR 2.00 .75
- ❑ 64 Pete LaForest RR 2.00 .75
- ❑ 65 Matt Bruback RR 2.00 .75
- ❑ 66 Dan Haren RR 2.00 .75
- ❑ 67 Greg Aquino RR 2.00 .75
- ❑ 68 Lew Ford RR 2.00 .75
- ❑ 69 Jeff Duncan RR 2.00 .75
- ❑ 70 Ryan Wagner RR 2.00 .75
- ❑ 71 Bengie Molina .30 .10
- ❑ 72 Brad Fullmer .30 .10
- ❑ 73 Darin Erstad .30 .10
- ❑ 74 David Eckstein .30 .10
- ❑ 75 Garret Anderson .30 .10
- ❑ 76 Jarrod Washburn .30 .10
- ❑ 77 Kevin Appier .30 .10
- ❑ 78 Scott Spiezio .30 .10
- ❑ 79 Tim Salmon .50 .20
- ❑ 80 Troy Glaus .30 .10
- ❑ 81 Troy Percival .30 .10
- ❑ 82 Jason Johnson .30 .10
- ❑ 83 Jay Gibbons .30 .10
- ❑ 84 Melvin Mora .30 .10
- ❑ 85 Sidney Ponson .30 .10
- ❑ 86 Tony Batista .30 .10
- ❑ 87 Bill Mueller .30 .10
- ❑ 88 Byung-Hyun Kim .30 .10
- ❑ 89 David Ortiz .75 .30
- ❑ 90 Derek Lowe .30 .10
- ❑ 91 Johnny Damon .50 .20
- ❑ 92 Casey Fossum .30 .10
- ❑ 93 Manny Ramirez .50 .20
- ❑ 94 Nomar Garciaparra 1.25 .50
- ❑ 95 Pedro Martinez .50 .20
- ❑ 96 Todd Walker .30 .10
- ❑ 97 Trot Nixon .30 .10
- ❑ 98 Bartolo Colon .30 .10
- ❑ 99 Carlos Lee .30 .10
- ❑ 100 D'Angelo Jimenez .30 .10
- ❑ 101 Esteban Loaiza .30 .10
- ❑ 102 Frank Thomas .75 .30
- ❑ 103 Joe Crede .30 .10
- ❑ 104 Jose Valentin .30 .10
- ❑ 105 Magglio Ordonez .30 .10
- ❑ 106 Mark Buehrle .30 .10
- ❑ 107 Paul Konerko .30 .10
- ❑ 108 Brandon Phillips .30 .10
- ❑ 109 C.C Sabathia .30 .10
- ❑ 110 Ellis Burks .30 .10
- ❑ 111 Jeremy Guthrie .30 .10
- ❑ 112 Josh Bard .30 .10
- ❑ 113 Matt Lawton .30 .10
- ❑ 114 Milton Bradley .30 .10
- ❑ 115 Omar Vizquel .50 .20
- ❑ 116 Travis Hafner .30 .10
- ❑ 117 Bobby Higginson .30 .10
- ❑ 118 Carlos Pena .30 .10
- ❑ 119 Dmitri Young .30 .10
- ❑ 120 Eric Munson .30 .10
- ❑ 121 Jeremy Bonderman .30 .10
- ❑ 122 Nate Cornejo .30 .10
- ❑ 123 Omar Infante .30 .10
- ❑ 124 Ramon Santiago .30 .10
- ❑ 125 Angel Berroa .30 .10
- ❑ 126 Carlos Beltran .30 .10
- ❑ 127 Desi Relaford .30 .10
- ❑ 128 Jeremy Affeldt .30 .10
- ❑ 129 Joe Randa .30 .10
- ❑ 130 Ken Harvey .30 .10
- ❑ 131 Mike MacDougal .30 .10
- ❑ 132 Michael Tucker .30 .10
- ❑ 133 Mike Sweeney .30 .10
- ❑ 134 Raul Ibanez .30 .10
- ❑ 135 Runelvys Hernandez .30 .10
- ❑ 136 A.J. Pierzynski .30 .10
- ❑ 137 Brad Radke .30 .10
- ❑ 138 Corey Koskie .30 .10
- ❑ 139 Cristian Guzman .30 .10
- ❑ 140 Doug Mientkiewicz .30 .10
- ❑ 141 Dustan Mohr .30 .10
- ❑ 142 Jacque Jones .30 .10

❑	143	Kenny Rogers	.30	.10
❑	144	Bobby Kielty	.30	.10
❑	145	Kyle Lohse	.30	.10
❑	146	Luis Rivas	.30	.10
❑	147	Torii Hunter	.30	.10
❑	148	Alfonso Soriano	.30	.10
❑	149	Andy Pettitte	.50	.20
❑	150	Bernie Williams	.50	.20
❑	151	David Wells	.30	.10
❑	152	Derek Jeter	1.50	.60
❑	153	Hideki Matsui	1.25	.50
❑	154	Jason Giambi	.30	.10
❑	155	Jorge Posada	.50	.20
❑	156	Jose Contreras	.30	.10
❑	157	Mike Mussina	.50	.20
❑	158	Nick Johnson	.30	.10
❑	159	Robin Ventura	.30	.10
❑	160	Roger Clemens	1.50	.60
❑	161	Barry Zito	.30	.10
❑	162	Chris Singleton	.30	.10
❑	163	Eric Byrnes	.30	.10
❑	164	Eric Chavez	.30	.10
❑	165	Erubiel Durazo	.30	.10
❑	166	Keith Foulke	.30	.10
❑	167	Mark Ellis	.30	.10
❑	168	Miguel Tejada	.30	.10
❑	169	Mark Mulder	.30	.10
❑	170	Ramon Hernandez	.30	.10
❑	171	Ted Lilly	.30	.10
❑	172	Terrence Long	.30	.10
❑	173	Tim Hudson	.30	.10
❑	174	Bret Boone	.30	.10
❑	175	Carlos Guillen	.30	.10
❑	176	Dan Wilson	.30	.10
❑	177	Edgar Martinez	.50	.20
❑	178	Freddy Garcia	.30	.10
❑	179	Gil Meche	.30	.10
❑	180	Ichiro Suzuki	1.50	.60
❑	181	Jamie Moyer	.30	.10
❑	182	Joel Pineiro	.30	.10
❑	183	John Olerud	.30	.10
❑	184	Mike Cameron	.30	.10
❑	185	Randy Winn	.30	.10
❑	186	Ryan Franklin	.30	.10
❑	187	Kazuhiro Sasaki	.30	.10
❑	188	Aubrey Huff	.30	.10
❑	189	Carl Crawford	.30	.10
❑	190	Joe Kennedy	.30	.10
❑	191	Marlon Anderson	.30	.10
❑	192	Rey Ordonez	.30	.10
❑	193	Rocco Baldelli	.30	.10
❑	194	Toby Hall	.30	.10
❑	195	Travis Lee	.30	.10
❑	196	Alex Rodriguez	1.25	.50
❑	197	Carl Everett	.30	.10
❑	198	Chan Ho Park	.30	.10
❑	199	Einar Diaz	.30	.10
❑	200	Hank Blalock	.30	.10
❑	201	Ismael Valdes	.30	.10
❑	202	Juan Gonzalez	.30	.10
❑	203	Mark Teixeira	.50	.20
❑	204	Mike Young	.30	.10
❑	205	Rafael Palmeiro	.50	.20
❑	206	Carlos Delgado	.30	.10
❑	207	Kelvim Escobar	.30	.10
❑	208	Eric Hinske	.30	.10
❑	209	Frank Catalanotto	.30	.10
❑	210	Josh Phelps	.30	.10
❑	211	Orlando Hudson	.30	.10
❑	212	Roy Halladay	.30	.10
❑	213	Shannon Stewart	.30	.10
❑	214	Vernon Wells	.30	.10
❑	215	Carlos Baerga	.30	.10
❑	216	Curt Schilling	.30	.10
❑	217	Junior Spivey	.30	.10
❑	218	Luis Gonzalez	.30	.10
❑	219	Lyle Overbay	.30	.10
❑	220	Mark Grace	.50	.20
❑	221	Matt Williams	.30	.10
❑	222	Randy Johnson	.75	.30
❑	223	Shea Hillenbrand	.30	.10
❑	224	Steve Finley	.30	.10
❑	225	Andruw Jones	.50	.20
❑	226	Chipper Jones	.75	.30
❑	227	Gary Sheffield	.30	.10
❑	228	Greg Maddux	1.25	.50
❑	229	Javy Lopez	.30	.10
❑	230	John Smoltz	.50	.20
❑	231	Marcus Giles	.30	.10
❑	232	Mike Hampton	.30	.10
❑	233	Rafael Furcal	.30	.10
❑	234	Robert Fick	.30	.10
❑	235	Russ Ortiz	.30	.10
❑	236	Alex Gonzalez	.30	.10
❑	237	Carlos Zambrano	.30	.10
❑	238	Corey Patterson	.30	.10
❑	239	Hee Seop Choi	.30	.10
❑	240	Kerry Wood	.30	.10
❑	241	Mark Bellhorn	.30	.10
❑	242	Mark Prior	.50	.20
❑	243	Moises Alou	.30	.10
❑	244	Sammy Sosa	.75	.30
❑	245	Aaron Boone	.30	.10
❑	246	Adam Dunn	.30	.10
❑	247	Austin Kearns	.30	.10
❑	248	Barry Larkin	.50	.20
❑	249	Felipe Lopez	.30	.10
❑	250	Jose Guillen	.30	.10
❑	251	Ken Griffey Jr.	1.25	.50
❑	252	Jason LaRue	.30	.10
❑	253	Scott Williamson	.30	.10
❑	254	Sean Casey	.30	.10
❑	255	Shawn Chacon	.30	.10
❑	256	Chris Stynes	.30	.10
❑	257	Jason Jennings	.30	.10
❑	258	Jay Payton	.30	.10
❑	259	Jose Hernandez	.30	.10
❑	260	Larry Walker	.30	.10
❑	261	Preston Wilson	.30	.10
❑	262	Ronnie Belliard	.30	.10
❑	263	Todd Helton	.50	.20
❑	264	A.J. Burnett	.30	.10
❑	265	Alex Gonzalez	.30	.10
❑	266	Brad Penny	.30	.10
❑	267	Derrek Lee	.50	.20
❑	268	Ivan Rodriguez	.50	.20
❑	269	Josh Beckett	.30	.10
❑	270	Juan Encarnacion	.30	.10
❑	271	Juan Pierre	.30	.10
❑	272	Luis Castillo	.30	.10
❑	273	Mike Lowell	.30	.10
❑	274	Todd Hollandsworth	.30	.10
❑	275	Billy Wagner	.30	.10
❑	276	Brad Ausmus	.30	.10
❑	277	Craig Biggio	.50	.20
❑	278	Jeff Bagwell	.50	.20
❑	279	Jeff Kent	.30	.10
❑	280	Lance Berkman	.30	.10
❑	281	Richard Hidalgo	.30	.10
❑	282	Roy Oswalt	.30	.10
❑	283	Wade Miller	.30	.10
❑	284	Adrian Beltre	.30	.10
❑	285	Brian Jordan	.30	.10
❑	286	Cesar Izturis	.30	.10
❑	287	Dave Roberts	.30	.10
❑	288	Eric Gagne	.30	.10
❑	289	Fred McGriff	.50	.20
❑	290	Hideo Nomo	.75	.30
❑	291	Kazuhisa Ishii	.30	.10
❑	292	Kevin Brown	.30	.10
❑	293	Paul Lo Duca	.30	.10
❑	294	Shawn Green	.30	.10
❑	295	Ben Sheets	.30	.10
❑	296	Geoff Jenkins	.30	.10
❑	297	Rey Sanchez	.30	.10
❑	298	Richie Sexson	.30	.10
❑	299	Wes Helms	.30	.10
❑	300	Brad Wilkerson	.30	.10
❑	301	Claudio Vargas	.30	.10
❑	302	Endy Chavez	.30	.10
❑	303	Fernando Tatis	.30	.10
❑	304	Javier Vazquez	.30	.10
❑	305	Jose Vidro	.30	.10
❑	306	Michael Barrett	.30	.10
❑	307	Orlando Cabrera	.30	.10
❑	308	Tony Armas Jr.	.30	.10
❑	309	Vladimir Guerrero	.75	.30
❑	310	Zach Day	.30	.10
❑	311	Al Leiter	.30	.10
❑	312	Cliff Floyd	.30	.10
❑	313	Jae Weong Seo	.30	.10
❑	314	Jeromy Burnitz	.30	.10
❑	315	Mike Piazza	1.25	.50
❑	316	Mo Vaughn	.30	.10
❑	317	Roberto Alomar	.50	.20
❑	318	Roger Cedeno	.30	.10
❑	319	Tom Glavine	.50	.20
❑	320	Jose Reyes	.30	.10
❑	321	Bobby Abreu	.30	.10
❑	322	Brett Myers	.30	.10
❑	323	David Bell	.30	.10
❑	324	Jim Thome	.50	.20
❑	325	Jimmy Rollins	.30	.10
❑	326	Kevin Millwood	.30	.10
❑	327	Marlon Byrd	.30	.10
❑	328	Mike Lieberthal	.30	.10
❑	329	Pat Burrell	.30	.10
❑	330	Randy Wolf	.30	.10
❑	331	Aramis Ramirez	.30	.10
❑	332	Brian Giles	.30	.10
❑	333	Jason Kendall	.30	.10
❑	334	Kenny Lofton	.30	.10
❑	335	Kip Wells	.30	.10
❑	336	Kris Benson	.30	.10
❑	337	Randall Simon	.30	.10
❑	338	Reggie Sanders	.30	.10
❑	339	Albert Pujols	1.50	.60
❑	340	Edgar Renteria	.30	.10
❑	341	Fernando Vina	.30	.10
❑	342	J.D. Drew	.30	.10
❑	343	Jim Edmonds	.30	.10
❑	344	Matt Morris	.30	.10
❑	345	Mike Matheny	.30	.10
❑	346	Scott Rolen	.50	.20
❑	347	Tino Martinez	.50	.20
❑	348	Woody Williams	.30	.10
❑	349	Brian Lawrence	.30	.10
❑	350	Mark Kotsay	.30	.10
❑	351	Mark Loretta	.30	.10
❑	352	Ramon Vazquez	.30	.10
❑	353	Rondell White	.30	.10
❑	354	Ryan Klesko	.30	.10
❑	355	Sean Burroughs	.30	.10
❑	356	Trevor Hoffman	.30	.10
❑	357	Xavier Nady	.30	.10
❑	358	Andres Galarraga	.30	.10
❑	359	Barry Bonds	2.00	.75
❑	360	Benito Santiago	.30	.10
❑	361	Deivi Cruz	.30	.10
❑	362	Edgardo Alfonzo	.30	.10
❑	363	J.T. Snow	.30	.10
❑	364	Jason Schmidt	.30	.10
❑	365	Kirk Rueter	.30	.10
❑	366	Kurt Ainsworth	.30	.10
❑	367	Marquis Grissom	.30	.10
❑	368	Ray Durham	.30	.10
❑	369	Rich Aurilia	.30	.10
❑	370	Tim Worrell	.30	.10
❑	371	Troy Glaus TC	2.00	.75
❑	372	Melvin Mora TC	2.00	.75
❑	373	Nomar Garciaparra TC	3.00	1.25
❑	374	Magglio Ordonez TC	2.00	.75
❑	375	Omar Vizquel TC	2.00	.75
❑	376	Dmitri Young TC	2.00	.75
❑	377	Mike Sweeney TC	2.00	.75
❑	378	Torii Hunter TC	2.00	.75
❑	379	Derek Jeter TC	4.00	1.50
❑	380	Barry Zito TC	2.00	.75
❑	381	Ichiro Suzuki TC	4.00	1.50
❑	382	Rocco Baldelli TC	2.00	.75
❑	383	Alex Rodriguez TC	3.00	1.25
❑	384	Carlos Delgado TC	2.00	.75
❑	385	Randy Johnson TC	2.00	.75
❑	386	Greg Maddux TC	3.00	1.25
❑	387	Sammy Sosa TC	2.00	.75
❑	388	Ken Griffey Jr. TC	3.00	1.25
❑	389	Todd Helton TC	2.00	.75
❑	390	Ivan Rodriguez TC	2.00	.75
❑	391	Jeff Bagwell TC	2.00	.75
❑	392	Hideo Nomo TC	2.00	.75
❑	393	Richie Sexson TC	2.00	.75
❑	394	Vladimir Guerrero TC	2.00	.75
❑	395	Mike Piazza TC	3.00	1.25
❑	396	Jim Thome TC	2.00	.75
❑	397	Jason Kendall TC	2.00	.75
❑	398	Albert Pujols TC	4.00	1.50
❑	399	Ryan Klesko TC	2.00	.75
❑	400	Barry Bonds TC	5.00	2.00

2005 Donruss

Card		
COMPLETE SET (400)	150.00	75.00
COMP.SET w/o SP's (300)	25.00	10.00
COMMON CARD (71-370)	.30	.10
COMMON (1-25/371-400)	2.00	.75
COMMON CARD (26-70)	2.00	.75
1-25 STATED ODDS 1:6		
26-70 STATED ODDS 1:6		
371-400 STATED ODDS 1:6		
1 Garret Anderson DK	2.00	.75
2 Vladimir Guerrero DK	2.00	.75
3 Manny Ramirez DK	2.00	.75
4 Kerry Wood DK	2.00	.75
5 Sammy Sosa DK	2.00	.75
6 Magglio Ordonez DK	2.00	.75
7 Adam Dunn DK	2.00	.75
8 Todd Helton DK	2.00	.75
9 Josh Beckett DK	2.00	.75
10 Miguel Cabrera DK	2.00	.75
11 Lance Berkman DK	2.00	.75
12 Carlos Beltran DK	2.00	.75
13 Shawn Green DK	2.00	.75
14 Roger Clemens DK	3.00	1.25
15 Mike Piazza DK	2.00	.75
16 Alex Rodriguez DK	3.00	1.25
17 Derek Jeter DK	4.00	1.50
18 Mark Mulder DK	2.00	.75
19 Jim Thome DK	2.00	.75
20 Albert Pujols DK	4.00	1.50
21 Scott Rolen DK	2.00	.75
22 Aubrey Huff DK	2.00	.75
23 Alfonso Soriano DK	2.00	.75
24 Hank Blalock DK	2.00	.75
25 Vernon Wells DK	2.00	.75
26 Kazuo Matsui RR	3.00	1.25
27 B.J. Upton RR	5.00	2.00
28 Charles Thomas RR	2.00	.75
29 Akinori Otsuka RR	3.00	1.25
30 David Aardsma RR	2.00	.75
31 Travis Blackley RR	2.00	.75
32 Brad Halsey RR	2.00	.75
33 David Wright RR	8.00	3.00
34 Kazuhito Tadano RR	3.00	1.25
35 Casey Kotchman RR	3.00	1.25
36 Khalil Greene RR	5.00	2.00
37 Adrian Gonzalez RR	2.00	.75
38 Zack Greinke RR	2.00	.75
39 Chad Cordero RR	2.00	.75
40 Scott Kazmir RR	5.00	2.00
41 Jeremy Guthrie RR	2.00	.75
42 Noah Lowry RR	3.00	1.25
43 Chase Utley RR	5.00	2.00
44 Billy Traber RR	2.00	.75
45 Aarom Baldiris RR	2.00	.75
46 Abe Alvarez RR	2.00	.75
47 Angel Chavez RR	2.00	.75
48 Joe Mauer RR	5.00	2.00
49 Joey Gathright RR	3.00	1.25
50 John Gall RR	2.00	.75
51 Ronald Belisario RR	2.00	.75
52 Ryan Wing RR	2.00	.75
53 Scott Proctor RR	2.00	.75
54 Yadier Molina RR	3.00	1.25
55 Carlos Hines RR	2.00	.75
56 Frankie Francisco RR	2.00	.75
57 Graham Koonce RR	2.00	.75
58 Jake Woods RR	2.00	.75
59 Jason Bartlett RR	2.00	.75
60 Mike Rouse RR	2.00	.75
61 Phil Stockman RR	2.00	.75
62 Renyel Pinto RR	2.00	.75
63 Roberto Novoa RR	2.00	.75
64 Ryan Meaux RR	2.00	.75
65 Dave Crouthers RR	2.00	.75
66 Justin Knoedler RR	2.00	.75
67 Justin Leone RR	2.00	.75
68 Nick Regilio RR	2.00	.75
69 Mike Gosling RR	2.00	.75
70 Onil Joseph RR	2.00	.75
71 Bartolo Colon	.30	.10
72 Brad Fullmer	.30	.10
73 Chone Figgins	.30	.10
74 Darin Erstad	.30	.10
75 Francisco Rodriguez	.30	.10
76 Garret Anderson	.30	.10
77 Jarrod Washburn	.30	.10
78 John Lackey	.30	.10
79 Jose Guillen	.30	.10
80 Robb Quinlan	.30	.10
81 Tim Salmon	.50	.20
82 Troy Glaus	.30	.10
83 Troy Percival	.30	.10
84 Vladimir Guerrero	.75	.30
85 Brandon Webb	.30	.10
86 Casey Fossum	.30	.10
87 Luis Gonzalez	.30	.10
88 Randy Johnson	.75	.30
89 Richie Sexson	.30	.10
90 Robby Hammock	.30	.10
91 Roberto Alomar	.50	.20
92 Adam LaRoche	.30	.10
93 Andruw Jones	.50	.20
94 Bubba Nelson	.30	.10
95 Chipper Jones	.75	.30
96 J.D. Drew	.30	.10
97 John Smoltz	.50	.20
98 Johnny Estrada	.30	.10
99 Marcus Giles	.30	.10
100 Mike Hampton	.30	.10
101 Nick Green	.30	.10
102 Rafael Furcal	.30	.10
103 Russ Ortiz	.30	.10
104 Adam Loewen	.30	.10
105 Brian Roberts	.30	.10
106 Javy Lopez	.30	.10
107 Jay Gibbons	.30	.10
108 L.Bigbie UER Roberts	.30	.10
109 Luis Matos	.30	.10
110 Melvin Mora	.30	.10
111 Miguel Tejada	.30	.10
112 Rafael Palmeiro	.50	.20
113 Rodrigo Lopez	.30	.10
114 Sidney Ponson	.30	.10
115 Bill Mueller	.30	.10
116 Byung-Hyun Kim	.30	.10
117 Curt Schilling	.50	.20
118 David Ortiz	.75	.30
119 Derek Lowe	.30	.10
120 Doug Mientkiewicz	.30	.10
121 Jason Varitek	.75	.30
122 Johnny Damon	.50	.20
123 Keith Foulke	.30	.10
124 Kevin Youkilis	.30	.10
125 Manny Ramirez	.50	.20
126 Orlando Cabrera	.30	.10
127 Pedro Martinez	.50	.20
128 Trot Nixon	.30	.10
129 Aramis Ramirez	.30	.10
130 Carlos Zambrano	.30	.10
131 Corey Patterson	.30	.10
132 Derrek Lee	.50	.20
133 Greg Maddux	1.25	.50
134 Kerry Wood	.30	.10
135 Mark Prior	.50	.20
136 Matt Clement	.30	.10
137 Moises Alou	.30	.10
138 Nomar Garciaparra	.75	.30
139 Sammy Sosa	.75	.30
140 Todd Walker	.30	.10
141 Angel Guzman	.30	.10
142 Billy Koch	.30	.10
143 Carlos Lee	.30	.10
144 Frank Thomas	.75	.30
145 Magglio Ordonez	.30	.10
146 Mark Buehrle	.30	.10
147 Paul Konerko	.30	.10
148 Wilson Valdez	.30	.10
149 Adam Dunn	.30	.10
150 Austin Kearns	.30	.10
151 Barry Larkin	.50	.20
152 Benito Santiago	.30	.10
153 Jason LaRue	.30	.10
154 Ken Griffey Jr.	1.25	.50
155 Ryan Wagner	.30	.10
156 Sean Casey	.30	.10
157 Brandon Phillips	.30	.10
158 Brian Tallet	.30	.10
159 C.C. Sabathia	.30	.10
160 Cliff Lee	.30	.10
161 Jeremy Guthrie	.30	.10
162 Jody Gerut	.30	.10
163 Matt Lawton	.30	.10
164 Omar Vizquel	.50	.20
165 Travis Hafner	.30	.10
166 Victor Martinez	.30	.10
167 Charles Johnson	.30	.10
168 Garrett Atkins	.30	.10
169 Jason Jennings	.30	.10
170 Jay Payton	.30	.10
171 Jeromy Burnitz	.30	.10
172 Joe Kennedy	.30	.10
173 Larry Walker	.50	.20
174 Preston Wilson	.30	.10
175 Todd Helton	.50	.20
176 Vinny Castilla	.30	.10
177 Bobby Higginson	.30	.10
178 Brandon Inge	.30	.10
179 Carlos Guillen	.30	.10
180 Carlos Pena	.30	.10
181 Craig Monroe	.30	.10
182 Dmitri Young	.30	.10
183 Eric Munson	.30	.10
184 Fernando Vina	.30	.10
185 Ivan Rodriguez	.50	.20
186 Jeremy Bonderman	.30	.10
187 Rondell White	.30	.10
188 A.J. Burnett	.30	.10
189 Dontrelle Willis	.30	.10
190 Guillermo Mota	.30	.10
191 Hee Seop Choi	.30	.10
192 Jeff Conine	.30	.10
193 Josh Beckett	.30	.10
194 Juan Encarnacion	.30	.10
195 Juan Pierre	.30	.10
196 Luis Castillo	.30	.10
197 Miguel Cabrera	.50	.20
198 Mike Lowell	.30	.10
199 Paul Lo Duca	.30	.10
200 Andy Pettitte	.50	.20
201 Brad Ausmus	.30	.10
202 Carlos Beltran	.30	.10
203 Chris Burke	.30	.10
204 Craig Biggio	.50	.20
205 Jeff Bagwell	.50	.20
206 Jeff Kent	.30	.10
207 Lance Berkman	.30	.10
208 Morgan Ensberg	.30	.10
209 Octavio Dotel	.30	.10
210 Roger Clemens	1.25	.50
211 Roy Oswalt	.30	.10
212 Tim Redding	.30	.10
213 Angel Berroa	.30	.10
214 Juan Gonzalez	.30	.10
215 Ken Harvey	.30	.10
216 Mike Sweeney	.30	.10
217 Adrian Beltre	.30	.10
218 Brad Penny	.30	.10
219 Eric Gagne	.30	.10
220 Hideo Nomo	.75	.30
221 Hong-Chih Kuo	.30	.10
222 Jeff Weaver	.30	.10
223 Kazuhisa Ishii	.30	.10
224 Milton Bradley	.30	.10
225 Shawn Green	.30	.10
226 Steve Finley	.30	.10
227 Danny Kolb	.30	.10
228 Geoff Jenkins	.30	.10
229 Junior Spivey	.30	.10
230 Lyle Overbay	.30	.10

❑ 231	Rickie Weeks	.30	.10
❑ 232	Scott Podsednik	.30	.10
❑ 233	Brad Radke	.30	.10
❑ 234	Corey Koskie	.30	.10
❑ 235	Cristian Guzman	.30	.10
❑ 236	Dustan Mohr	.30	.10
❑ 237	Eddie Guardado	.30	.10
❑ 238	J.D. Durbin	.30	.10
❑ 239	Jacque Jones	.30	.10
❑ 240	Joe Nathan	.30	.10
❑ 241	Johan Santana	.75	.30
❑ 242	Lew Ford	.30	.10
❑ 243	Michael Cuddyer	.30	.10
❑ 244	Shannon Stewart	.30	.10
❑ 245	Torii Hunter	.30	.10
❑ 246	Brad Wilkerson	.30	.10
❑ 247	Carl Everett	.30	.10
❑ 248	Jeff Fassero	.30	.10
❑ 249	Jose Vidro	.30	.10
❑ 250	Livan Hernandez	.30	.10
❑ 251	Michael Barrett	.30	.10
❑ 252	Tony Batista	.30	.10
❑ 253	Zach Day	.30	.10
❑ 254	Al Leiter	.30	.10
❑ 255	Cliff Floyd	.30	.10
❑ 256	Jae Weong Seo	.30	.10
❑ 257	John Olerud	.30	.10
❑ 258	Jose Reyes	.30	.10
❑ 259	Mike Cameron	.30	.10
❑ 260	Mike Piazza	.75	.30
❑ 261	Richard Hidalgo	.30	.10
❑ 262	Tom Glavine	.50	.20
❑ 263	Vance Wilson	.30	.10
❑ 264	Alex Rodriguez	1.25	.50
❑ 265	Armando Benitez	.30	.10
❑ 266	Bernie Williams	.50	.20
❑ 267	Bubba Crosby	.30	.10
❑ 268	Chien-Ming Wang	1.25	.50
❑ 269	Derek Jeter	1.50	.60
❑ 270	Esteban Loaiza	.30	.10
❑ 271	Gary Sheffield	.30	.10
❑ 272	Hideki Matsui	1.25	.50
❑ 273	Jason Giambi	.30	.10
❑ 274	Javier Vazquez	.30	.10
❑ 275	Jorge Posada	.50	.20
❑ 276	Jose Contreras	.30	.10
❑ 277	Kenny Lofton	.30	.10
❑ 278	Kevin Brown	.30	.10
❑ 279	Mariano Rivera	.75	.30
❑ 280	Mike Mussina	.50	.20
❑ 281	Barry Zito	.30	.10
❑ 282	Bobby Crosby	.30	.10
❑ 283	Eric Byrnes	.30	.10
❑ 284	Eric Chavez	.30	.10
❑ 285	Erubiel Durazo	.30	.10
❑ 286	Jermaine Dye	.30	.10
❑ 287	Mark Kotsay	.30	.10
❑ 288	Mark Mulder	.30	.10
❑ 289	Rich Harden	.30	.10
❑ 290	Tim Hudson	.30	.10
❑ 291	Billy Wagner	.30	.10
❑ 292	Bobby Abreu	.30	.10
❑ 293	Brett Myers	.30	.10
❑ 294	Eric Milton	.30	.10
❑ 295	Jim Thome	.50	.20
❑ 296	Jimmy Rollins	.30	.10
❑ 297	Kevin Millwood	.30	.10
❑ 298	Marlon Byrd	.30	.10
❑ 299	Mike Lieberthal	.30	.10
❑ 300	Pat Burrell	.30	.10
❑ 301	Randy Wolf	.30	.10
❑ 302	Craig Wilson	.30	.10
❑ 303	Jack Wilson	.30	.10
❑ 304	Jacob Cruz	.30	.10
❑ 305	Jason Bay	.30	.10
❑ 306	Jason Kendall	.30	.10
❑ 307	Jose Castillo	.30	.10
❑ 308	Kip Wells	.30	.10
❑ 309	Brian Giles	.30	.10
❑ 310	Brian Lawrence	.30	.10
❑ 311	Chris Oxspring	.30	.10
❑ 312	David Wells	.30	.10
❑ 313	Freddy Guzman	.30	.10
❑ 314	Jake Peavy	.30	.10
❑ 315	Mark Loretta	.30	.10
❑ 316	Ryan Klesko	.30	.10
❑ 317	Sean Burroughs	.30	.10
❑ 318	Trevor Hoffman	.30	.10
❑ 319	Xavier Nady	.30	.10
❑ 320	A.J. Pierzynski	.30	.10
❑ 321	Edgardo Alfonzo	.30	.10
❑ 322	J.T. Snow	.30	.10
❑ 323	Jason Schmidt	.30	.10
❑ 324	Jerome Williams	.30	.10
❑ 325	Kirk Rueter	.30	.10
❑ 326	Bret Boone	.30	.10
❑ 327	Bucky Jacobsen	.30	.10
❑ 328	Edgar Martinez	.50	.20
❑ 329	Freddy Garcia	.30	.10
❑ 330	Ichiro Suzuki	1.50	.60
❑ 331	Jamie Moyer	.30	.10
❑ 332	Joel Pineiro	.30	.10
❑ 333	Scott Spiezio	.30	.10
❑ 334	Shigetoshi Hasegawa	.30	.10
❑ 335	Albert Pujols	1.50	.60
❑ 336	Edgar Renteria	.30	.10
❑ 337	Jason Isringhausen	.30	.10
❑ 338	Jim Edmonds	.30	.10
❑ 339	Matt Morris	.30	.10
❑ 340	Mike Matheny	.30	.10
❑ 341	Reggie Sanders	.30	.10
❑ 342	Scott Rolen	.50	.20
❑ 343	Woody Williams	.30	.10
❑ 344	Jeff Suppan	.30	.10
❑ 345	Aubrey Huff	.30	.10
❑ 346	Carl Crawford	.30	.10
❑ 347	Chad Gaudin	.30	.10
❑ 348	Delmon Young	.50	.20
❑ 349	Dewon Brazelton	.30	.10
❑ 350	Jose Cruz Jr.	.30	.10
❑ 351	Rocco Baldelli	.30	.10
❑ 352	Tino Martinez	.50	.20
❑ 353	Toby Hall	.30	.10
❑ 354	Alfonso Soriano	.30	.10
❑ 355	Brian Jordan	.30	.10
❑ 356	Francisco Cordero	.30	.10
❑ 357	Hank Blalock	.30	.10
❑ 358	Kenny Rogers	.30	.10
❑ 359	Kevin Mench	.30	.10
❑ 360	Laynce Nix	.30	.10
❑ 361	Mark Teixeira	.50	.20
❑ 362	Michael Young	.30	.10
❑ 363	Alex S. Gonzalez	.30	.10
❑ 364	Alexis Rios	.30	.10
❑ 365	Carlos Delgado	.30	.10
❑ 366	Eric Hinske	.30	.10
❑ 367	Frank Catalanotto	.30	.10
❑ 368	Josh Phelps	.30	.10
❑ 369	Roy Halladay	.30	.10
❑ 370	Vernon Wells	.30	.10
❑ 371	Vladimir Guerrero TC	2.00	.75
❑ 372	Randy Johnson TC	2.00	.75
❑ 373	Chipper Jones TC	2.00	.75
❑ 374	Miguel Tejada TC	2.00	.75
❑ 375	Pedro Martinez TC	2.00	.75
❑ 376	Sammy Sosa TC	2.00	.75
❑ 377	Frank Thomas TC	2.00	.75
❑ 378	Ken Griffey Jr. TC	3.00	1.25
❑ 379	Victor Martinez TC	2.00	.75
❑ 380	Todd Helton TC	2.00	.75
❑ 381	Ivan Rodriguez TC	2.00	.75
❑ 382	Miguel Cabrera TC	2.00	.75
❑ 383	Roger Clemens TC	3.00	1.25
❑ 384	Ken Harvey TC	2.00	.75
❑ 385	Eric Gagne TC	2.00	.75
❑ 386	Lyle Overbay TC	2.00	.75
❑ 387	Shannon Stewart TC	2.00	.75
❑ 388	Brad Wilkerson TC	2.00	.75
❑ 389	Mike Piazza TC	2.00	.75
❑ 390	Alex Rodriguez TC	3.00	1.25
❑ 391	Mark Mulder TC	2.00	.75
❑ 392	Jim Thome TC	2.00	.75
❑ 393	Jack Wilson TC	2.00	.75
❑ 394	Khalil Greene TC	2.00	.75
❑ 395	Jason Schmidt TC	2.00	.75
❑ 396	Ichiro Suzuki TC	4.00	1.50
❑ 397	Albert Pujols TC	4.00	1.50
❑ 398	Rocco Baldelli TC	2.00	.75
❑ 399	Alfonso Soriano TC	2.00	.75
❑ 400	Vernon Wells TC	2.00	.75

2001 eTopps

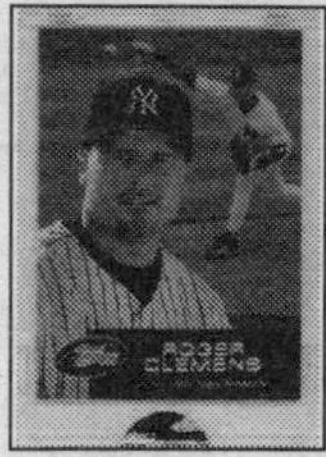

❑ 1	Nomar Garciaparra/1315	20.00	10.00
❑ 2	Chipper Jones/674	125.00	75.00
❑ 3	Jeff Bagwell/485	50.00	25.00
❑ 4	Randy Johnson/1499	30.00	15.00
❑ 7	Adam Dunn/4197	8.00	4.00
❑ 8	J.D. Drew/767	15.00	7.50
❑ 9	Larry Walker/420	40.00	20.00
❑ 10	Edgardo Alfonzo/338	100.00	60.00
❑ 11	Lance Berkman/595	50.00	25.00
❑ 12	Tony Gwynn/828	40.00	20.00
❑ 13	Andruw Jones/908	25.00	12.50
❑ 15	Troy Glaus/862	15.00	7.50
❑ 17	Sammy Sosa/2487	10.00	5.00
❑ 21	Darin Erstad/664	20.00	10.00
❑ 22	Barry Bonds/1567	125.00	75.00
❑ 27	Derek Jeter/1041	60.00	30.00
❑ 29	Curt Schilling/2125	8.00	4.00
❑ 30	Roberto Alomar/448	40.00	20.00
❑ 31	Luis Gonzalez/1104	10.00	5.00
❑ 32	Jimmy Rollins/1307	10.00	5.00
❑ 34	Joe Crede/1050	12.00	6.00
❑ 39	Sean Casey/537	30.00	15.00
❑ 46	Alex Rodriguez/2212	50.00	25.00
❑ 47	Tom Glavine/437	50.00	25.00
❑ 50	Jose Ortiz/738	15.00	7.50
❑ 51	Cal Ripken/2201	40.00	20.00
❑ 52	Bob Abreu/677	30.00	15.00
❑ 55	Alex Escobar/931	10.00	5.00
❑ 56	Ivan Rodriguez/698	20.00	10.00
❑ 59	Jeff Kent/452	40.00	20.00
❑ 62	Rick Ankiel/752	10.00	5.00
❑ 65	Craig Biggio/410	50.00	25.00
❑ 66	Carlos Delgado/398	60.00	30.00
❑ 68	Greg Maddux/1031	25.00	12.50
❑ 69	Kerry Wood/1056	20.00	10.00
❑ 71	Todd Helton/978	30.00	15.00
❑ 72	Mariano Rivera/824	25.00	12.50
❑ 73	Jason Kendall/672	20.00	10.00
❑ 75	Scott Rolen/498	60.00	30.00
❑ 76	Kazuhiro Sasaki/5000	5.00	2.00
❑ 77	Roy Oswalt/915	25.00	12.50
❑ 78	C.C. Sabathia/1974	10.00	5.00
❑ 83	Brian Giles/400	40.00	20.00
❑ 87	Rafael Furcal/646	20.00	10.00
❑ 88	Mike Mussina/793	25.00	12.50
❑ 89	Gary Sheffield/359	80.00	40.00
❑ 92	Mark McGwire/2908	15.00	7.50
❑ 94	Tsuyoshi Shinjo/3000	5.00	2.00
❑ 99	Jose Vidro/443	40.00	20.00
❑ 100	Ichiro Suzuki/10000	20.00	8.00
❑ 105	Manny Ramirez Sox/1074	20.00	10.00
❑ 109	Juan Gonzalez/558	20.00	10.00
❑ 112	Ken Griffey Jr./2398	15.00	7.50
❑ 114	Tim Hudson/663	30.00	15.00
❑ 115	Nick Johnson/1217	10.00	5.00
❑ 118	Jason Giambi/897	15.00	7.50
❑ 122	Rafael Palmeiro/464	50.00	25.00
❑ 124	Vladimir Guerrero/854	40.00	20.00
❑ 125	Vernon Wells/349	150.00	90.00
❑ 127	Roger Clemens/1462	40.00	20.00
❑ 128	Frank Thomas/834	25.00	12.50
❑ 129	Carlos Beltran/489	80.00	40.00
❑ 130	Pat Burrell/1253	25.00	12.50
❑ 131	Pedro Martinez/1038	25.00	12.50
❑ 132	Mike Piazza/1379	15.00	7.50
❑ 135	Luis Montanez/5000	4.00	1.50

❑ 140 Sean Burroughs/5000 4.00 1.50
❑ 141 Barry Zito/843 30.00 15.00
❑ 142 Bobby Bradley/5000 4.00 1.50
❑ 143 Albert Pujols/5000 150.00 90.00
❑ 144 Ben Sheets/1713 12.00 6.00
❑ 145 Alfonso Soriano/1699 25.00 12.50
❑ 146 Josh Hamilton/5000 4.00 1.50
❑ 147 Eric Munson/5000 4.00 1.50
❑ 150 Mark Mulder/4335 5.00 2.00

1993 Finest

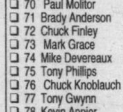

❑ COMPLETE SET (199) 150.00 75.00
❑ 1 David Justice 2.50 1.00
❑ 2 Lou Whitaker 2.50 1.00
❑ 3 Bryan Harvey 1.50 .60
❑ 4 Carlos Garcia 1.50 .60
❑ 5 Sid Fernandez 1.50 .60
❑ 6 Brett Butler 2.50 1.00
❑ 7 Scott Cooper 1.50 .60
❑ 8 B.J. Surhoff 2.50 1.00
❑ 9 Steve Finley 2.50 1.00
❑ 10 Curt Schilling 2.50 1.00
❑ 11 Jeff Bagwell 4.00 1.50
❑ 12 Alex Cole 1.50 .60
❑ 13 John Olerud 2.50 1.00
❑ 14 John Smiley 1.50 .60
❑ 15 Bip Roberts 1.50 .60
❑ 16 Albert Belle 2.50 1.00
❑ 17 Duane Ward 1.50 .60
❑ 18 Alan Trammell 2.50 1.00
❑ 19 Andy Benes 1.50 .60
❑ 20 Reggie Sanders 2.50 1.00
❑ 21 Todd Zeile 1.50 .60
❑ 22 Rick Aguilera 1.50 .60
❑ 23 Dave Hollins 1.50 .60
❑ 24 Jose Rijo 1.50 .60
❑ 25 Matt Williams 2.50 1.00
❑ 26 Sandy Alomar Jr. 1.50 .60
❑ 27 Alex Fernandez 1.50 .60
❑ 28 Ozzie Smith 10.00 4.00
❑ 29 Ramon Martinez 1.50 .60
❑ 30 Bernie Williams 4.00 1.50
❑ 31 Gary Sheffield 2.50 1.00
❑ 32 Eric Karros 2.50 1.00
❑ 33 Frank Viola 2.50 1.00
❑ 34 Kevin Young 2.50 1.00
❑ 35 Ken Hill 1.50 .60
❑ 36 Tony Fernandez 1.50 .60
❑ 37 Tim Wakefield 6.00 2.50
❑ 38 John Kruk 2.50 1.00
❑ 39 Chris Sabo 1.50 .60
❑ 40 Marquis Grissom 2.50 1.00
❑ 41 Glenn Davis 1.50 .60
❑ 42 Jeff Montgomery 1.50 .60
❑ 43 Kenny Lofton 2.50 1.00
❑ 44 John Burkett 1.50 .60
❑ 45 Darryl Hamilton 1.50 .60
❑ 46 Jim Abbott 4.00 1.50
❑ 47 Ivan Rodriguez 4.00 1.50
❑ 48 Eric Young 1.50 .60
❑ 49 Mitch Williams 1.50 .60
❑ 50 Harold Reynolds 2.50 1.00
❑ 51 Brian Harper 1.50 .60
❑ 52 Rafael Palmeiro 4.00 1.50
❑ 53 Bret Saberhagen 2.50 1.00
❑ 54 Jeff Conine 2.50 1.00
❑ 55 Ivan Calderon 1.50 .60
❑ 56 Juan Guzman 1.50 .60

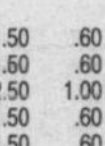
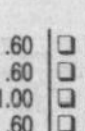

❑ 57 Carlos Baerga 1.50 .60
❑ 58 Charles Nagy 1.50 .60
❑ 59 Wally Joyner 2.50 1.00
❑ 60 Charlie Hayes 1.50 .60
❑ 61 Shane Mack 1.50 .60
❑ 62 Pete Harnisch 1.50 .60
❑ 63 George Brett 15.00 6.00
❑ 64 Lance Johnson 1.50 .60
❑ 65 Ben McDonald 1.50 .60
❑ 66 Bobby Bonilla 2.50 1.00
❑ 67 Terry Steinbach 1.50 .60
❑ 68 Ron Gant 2.50 1.00
❑ 69 Doug Jones 1.50 .60
❑ 70 Paul Molitor 2.50 1.00
❑ 71 Brady Anderson 2.50 1.00
❑ 72 Chuck Finley 2.50 1.00
❑ 73 Mark Grace 4.00 1.50
❑ 74 Mike Devereaux 1.50 .60
❑ 75 Tony Phillips 1.50 .60
❑ 76 Chuck Knoblauch 2.50 1.00
❑ 77 Tony Gwynn 8.00 3.00
❑ 78 Kevin Appier 2.50 1.00
❑ 79 Sammy Sosa 6.00 2.50
❑ 80 Mickey Tettleton 1.50 .60
❑ 81 Felix Jose 1.50 .60
❑ 82 Mark Langston 1.50 .60
❑ 83 Gregg Jefferies 1.50 .60
❑ 84 Andre Dawson AS 2.50 1.00
❑ 85 Greg Maddux AS 10.00 4.00
❑ 86 Rickey Henderson AS 6.00 2.50
❑ 87 Tom Glavine AS 4.00 1.50
❑ 88 Roberto Alomar AS 4.00 1.50
❑ 89 Darryl Strawberry AS 2.50 1.00
❑ 90 Wade Boggs AS 4.00 1.50
❑ 91 Bo Jackson AS 6.00 2.50
❑ 92 Mark McGwire AS 15.00 6.00
❑ 93 Robin Ventura AS 2.50 1.00
❑ 94 Joe Carter AS 2.50 1.00
❑ 95 Lee Smith AS 2.50 1.00
❑ 96 Cal Ripken AS 20.00 8.00
❑ 97 Larry Walker AS 2.50 1.00
❑ 98 Don Mattingly AS 15.00 6.00
❑ 99 Jose Canseco AS 4.00 1.50
❑ 100 Dennis Eckersley AS 2.50 1.00
❑ 101 Terry Pendleton AS 2.50 1.00
❑ 102 Frank Thomas AS 6.00 2.50
❑ 103 Barry Bonds AS 15.00 6.00
❑ 104 Roger Clemens AS 12.00 5.00
❑ 105 Ryne Sandberg AS 10.00 4.00
❑ 106 Fred McGriff AS 4.00 1.50
❑ 107 Nolan Ryan AS 25.00 10.00
❑ 108 Will Clark AS 4.00 1.50
❑ 109 Pat Listach AS 1.50 .60
❑ 110 Ken Griffey Jr. AS 10.00 4.00
❑ 111 Cecil Fielder AS 2.50 1.00
❑ 112 Kirby Puckett AS 6.00 2.50
❑ 113 Dwight Gooden AS 2.50 1.00
❑ 114 Barry Larkin AS 4.00 1.50
❑ 115 David Cone AS 2.50 1.00
❑ 116 Juan Gonzalez AS 2.50 1.00
❑ 117 Kent Hrbek 2.50 1.00
❑ 118 Tim Wallach 1.50 .60
❑ 119 Craig Biggio 4.00 1.50
❑ 120 Roberto Kelly 1.50 .60
❑ 121 Gregg Olson 1.50 .60
❑ 122 Eddie Murray 6.00 2.50
❑ 123 Wil Cordero 1.50 .60
❑ 124 Jay Buhner 2.50 1.00
❑ 125 Carlton Fisk 4.00 1.50
❑ 126 Eric Davis 2.50 1.00
❑ 127 Doug Drabek 1.50 .60
❑ 128 Ozzie Guillen 2.50 1.00
❑ 129 John Wetteland 2.50 1.00
❑ 130 Andres Galarraga 2.50 1.00
❑ 131 Ken Caminiti 2.50 1.00
❑ 132 Tom Candiotti 1.50 .60
❑ 133 Pat Borders 1.50 .60
❑ 134 Kevin Brown 2.50 1.00
❑ 135 Travis Fryman 2.50 1.00
❑ 136 Kevin Mitchell 1.50 .60
❑ 137 Greg Swindell 1.50 .60
❑ 138 Benito Santiago 2.50 1.00
❑ 139 Reggie Jefferson 1.50 .60
❑ 140 Chris Bosio 1.50 .60
❑ 141 Deion Sanders 4.00 1.50
❑ 142 Scott Erickson 1.50 .60

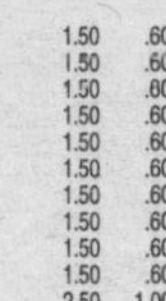

❑ 143 Howard Johnson 1.50 .60
❑ 144 Orestes Destrade 1.50 .60
❑ 145 Jose Guzman 1.50 .60
❑ 146 Chad Curtis 1.50 .60
❑ 147 Cal Eldred 1.50 .60
❑ 148 Willie Greene 1.50 .60
❑ 149 Tommy Greene 1.50 .60
❑ 150 Erik Hanson 1.50 .60
❑ 151 Bob Welch 1.50 .60
❑ 152 John Jaha 1.50 .60
❑ 153 Harold Baines 2.50 1.00
❑ 154 Randy Johnson 6.00 2.50
❑ 155 Al Martin 1.50 .60
❑ 156 J.T.Snow RC 4.00 1.50
❑ 157 Mike Mussina 4.00 1.50
❑ 158 Ruben Sierra 2.50 1.00
❑ 159 Dean Palmer 2.50 1.00
❑ 160 Steve Avery 1.50 .60
❑ 161 Julio Franco 2.50 1.00
❑ 162 Dave Winfield 2.50 1.00
❑ 163 Tim Salmon 4.00 1.50
❑ 164 Tom Henke 1.50 .60
❑ 165 Mo Vaughn 2.50 1.00
❑ 166 John Smoltz 4.00 1.50
❑ 167 Danny Tartabull 1.50 .60
❑ 168 Delino DeShields 1.50 .60
❑ 169 Charlie Hough 2.50 1.00
❑ 170 Paul O'Neill 4.00 1.50
❑ 171 Darren Daulton 2.50 1.00
❑ 172 Jack McDowell 1.50 .60
❑ 173 Junior Felix 1.50 .60
❑ 174 Jimmy Key 2.50 1.00
❑ 175 George Bell 1.50 .60
❑ 176 Mike Stanton 1.50 .60
❑ 177 Len Dykstra 2.50 1.00
❑ 178 Norm Charlton 1.50 .60
❑ 179 Eric Anthony 1.50 .60
❑ 180 Rob Dibble 2.50 1.00
❑ 181 Otis Nixon 1.50 .60
❑ 182 Randy Myers 1.50 .60
❑ 183 Tim Raines 2.50 1.00
❑ 184 Orel Hershiser 2.50 1.00
❑ 185 Andy Van Slyke 4.00 1.50
❑ 186 Mike Lansing RC 2.50 1.00
❑ 187 Ray Lankford 2.50 1.00
❑ 188 Mike Morgan 1.50 .60
❑ 189 Moises Alou 2.50 1.00
❑ 190 Edgar Martinez 4.00 1.50
❑ 191 John Franco 2.50 1.00
❑ 192 Robin Yount 10.00 4.00
❑ 193 Bob Tewksbury 1.50 .60
❑ 194 Jay Bell 2.50 1.00
❑ 195 Luis Gonzalez 2.50 1.00
❑ 196 Dave Fleming 1.50 .60
❑ 197 Mike Greenwell 1.50 .60
❑ 198 David Nied 1.50 .60
❑ 199 Mike Piazza 15.00 6.00

1996 Finest

❑ COMP.BRONZE SER.1 (110) 25.00 10.00
❑ COMP.BRONZE SER.2 (110) 25.00 10.00
❑ COMMON BRONZE .50 .20
❑ COMMON GOLD 5.00 2.00
❑ COMMON G RC 5.00 2.00
❑ COMMON SILVER 2.50 1.00
❑ B5 Roberto Hernandez B .50 .20
❑ B8 Terry Pendleton B .50 .20
❑ B12 Ken Caminiti B .50 .20

Card	Player		
❑ B15	Dan Miceli B	.50	.20
❑ B16	Chipper Jones B	1.25	.50
❑ B17	John Wetteland B	.50	.20
❑ B19	Tim Naehring B	.50	.20
❑ B21	Eddie Murray B	1.25	.50
❑ B23	Kevin Appier B	.50	.20
❑ B24	Ken Griffey Jr. B	2.00	.75
❑ B26	Brian McRae B	.50	.20
❑ B27	Pedro Martinez B	.75	.30
❑ B28	Brian Jordan B	.50	.20
❑ B29	Mike Fetters B	.50	.20
❑ B30	Carlos Delgado B	.50	.20
❑ B31	Shane Reynolds B	.50	.20
❑ B32	Terry Steinbach B	.50	.20
❑ B34	Mark Leiter B	.50	.20
❑ B36	David Segui B	.50	.20
❑ B40	Fred McGriff B	.75	.30
❑ B44	Glenallen Hill B	.50	.20
❑ B45	Brady Anderson B	.50	.20
❑ B47	Jim Thome B	.75	.30
❑ B48	Frank Thomas B	1.25	.50
❑ B49	Chuck Knoblauch B	.50	.20
❑ B50	Len Dykstra B	.50	.20
❑ B53	Tom Pagnozzi B	.50	.20
❑ B55	Ricky Bones B	.50	.20
❑ B56	David Justice B	.50	.20
❑ B57	Steve Avery B	.50	.20
❑ B58	Robby Thompson B	.50	.20
❑ B61	Tony Gwynn B	1.50	.60
❑ B63	Denny Neagle B	.50	.20
❑ B67	Robin Ventura B	.50	.20
❑ B70	Kevin Seitzer B	.50	.20
❑ B71	Ramon Martinez B	.50	.20
❑ B75	Brian L.Hunter B	.50	.20
❑ B76	Alan Benes B	.50	.20
❑ B80	Ozzie Guillen B	.50	.20
❑ B82	Benji Gil B	.50	.20
❑ B85	Todd Hundley B	.50	.20
❑ B87	Pat Hentgen B	.50	.20
❑ B89	Chuck Finley B	.50	.20
❑ B92	Derek Jeter B	3.00	1.25
❑ B93	Paul O'Neill B	.75	.30
❑ B94	Darrin Fletcher B	.50	.20
❑ B96	Delino DeShields B	.50	.20
❑ B97	Tim Salmon B	.75	.30
❑ B98	John Olerud B	.50	.20
❑ B101	Tim Wakefield B	.50	.20
❑ B103	Dave Stevens B	.50	.20
❑ B104	Orlando Merced B	.50	.20
❑ B106	Jay Bell B	.50	.20
❑ B107	John Burkett B	.50	.20
❑ B108	Chris Hoiles B	.50	.20
❑ B110	Dave Nilsson B	.50	.20
❑ B111	Rod Beck B	.50	.20
❑ B113	Mike Piazza B	2.00	.75
❑ B114	Mark Langston B	.50	.20
❑ B116	Rico Brogna B	.50	.20
❑ B118	Tom Goodwin B	.50	.20
❑ B119	Bryan Rekar B	.50	.20
❑ B120	David Cone B	.50	.20
❑ B122	Andy Pettitte B	.75	.30
❑ B123	Chili Davis B	.50	.20
❑ B124	John Smoltz B	.75	.30
❑ B125	Heathcliff Slocumb B	.50	.20
❑ B126	Dante Bichette B	.50	.20
❑ B128	Alex Gonzalez B	.50	.20
❑ B129	Jeff Montgomery B	.50	.20
❑ B131	Denny Martinez B	.50	.20
❑ B132	Mel Rojas B	.50	.20
❑ B133	Derek Bell B	.50	.20
❑ B134	Trevor Hoffman B	.50	.20
❑ B136	Darren Daulton B	.50	.20
❑ B137	Pete Schourek B	.50	.20
❑ B138	Phil Nevin B	.50	.20
❑ B139	Andres Galarraga B	.50	.20
❑ B140	Chad Fonville B	.50	.20
❑ B144	J.T. Snow B	.50	.20
❑ B146	Barry Bonds B	3.00	1.25
❑ B147	Orel Hershiser B	.50	.20
❑ B148	Quilvio Veras B	.50	.20
❑ B149	Will Clark B	.75	.30
❑ B150	Jose Rijo B	.50	.20
❑ B152	Travis Fryman B	.50	.20
❑ B154	Alex Fernandez B	.50	.20
❑ B155	Wade Boggs B	.75	.30
❑ B156	Troy Percival B	.50	.20
❑ B157	Moises Alou B	.50	.20
❑ B158	Javy Lopez B	.50	.20
❑ B159	Jason Giambi B	.50	.20
❑ B162	Mark McGwire B	3.00	1.25
❑ B163	Eric Karros B	.50	.20
❑ B166	Mickey Tettleton B	.50	.20
❑ B167	Barry Larkin B	.75	.30
❑ B169	Ruben Sierra B	.50	.20
❑ B170	Bill Swift B	.50	.20
❑ B172	Chad Curtis B	.50	.20
❑ B173	Dean Palmer B	.50	.20
❑ B175	Bobby Bonilla B	.50	.20
❑ B176	Greg Colbrunn B	.50	.20
❑ B177	Jose Mesa B	.50	.20
❑ B178	Mike Greenwell B	.50	.20
❑ B181	Doug Drabek B	.50	.20
❑ B183	Wilson Alvarez B	.50	.20
❑ B184	Marty Cordova B	.50	.20
❑ B185	Hal Morris B	.50	.20
❑ B187	Carlos Garcia B	.50	.20
❑ B190	Marquis Grissom B	.50	.20
❑ B193	Will Clark B	.75	.30
❑ B194	Paul Molitor B	.50	.20
❑ B195	Kenny Rogers B	.50	.20
❑ B196	Reggie Sanders B	.50	.20
❑ B199	Raul Mondesi B	.50	.20
❑ B200	Lance Johnson B	.50	.20
❑ B201	Alvin Morman B	.50	.20
❑ B203	Jack McDowell B	.50	.20
❑ B204	Randy Myers B	.50	.20
❑ B205	Harold Baines B	.50	.20
❑ B206	Marty Cordova B	.50	.20
❑ B207	Rich Hunter B RC	.50	.20
❑ B208	Al Leiter B	.50	.20
❑ B209	Greg Gagne B	.50	.20
❑ B210	Ben McDonald B	.50	.20
❑ B212	Terry Adams B	.50	.20
❑ B213	Paul Sorrento B	.50	.20
❑ B214	Albert Belle B	.50	.20
❑ B215	Mike Blowers B	.50	.20
❑ B216	Jim Edmonds B	.50	.20
❑ B217	Felipe Crespo B	.50	.20
❑ B219	Shawon Dunston B	.50	.20
❑ B220	Jimmy Haynes B	.50	.20
❑ B221	Jose Canseco B	.75	.30
❑ B222	Eric Davis B	.50	.20
❑ B224	Tim Raines B	.50	.20
❑ B225	Tony Phillips B	.50	.20
❑ B226	Charlie Hayes B	.50	.20
❑ B227	Eric Owens B	.50	.20
❑ B228	Roberto Alomar B	.75	.30
❑ B233	Kenny Lofton B	.50	.20
❑ B236	Mark McGwire B	3.00	1.25
❑ B237	Jay Buhner B	.50	.20
❑ B238	Craig Biggio B	.75	.30
❑ B240	Barry Bonds B	3.00	1.25
❑ B244	Ron Gant B	.50	.20
❑ B245	Paul Wilson B	.50	.20
❑ B246	Todd Hollandsworth B	.50	.20
❑ B247	Todd Zeile B	.50	.20
❑ B248	David Justice B	.50	.20
❑ B250	Moises Alou B	.50	.20
❑ B251	Bob Wolcott B	.50	.20
❑ B252	David Wells B	.50	.20
❑ B253	Juan Gonzalez B	.50	.20
❑ B254	Andres Galarraga B	.50	.20
❑ B255	Dave Hollins B	.50	.20
❑ B257	Sammy Sosa B	1.25	.50
❑ B258	Ivan Rodriguez B	.75	.30
❑ B259	Bip Roberts B	.50	.20
❑ B260	Tino Martinez B	.75	.30
❑ B262	Mike Stanley B	.50	.20
❑ B264	Butch Huskey B	.50	.20
❑ B265	Jeff Conine B	.50	.20
❑ B267	Mark Grace B	.75	.30
❑ B268	Jason Schmidt B	.75	.30
❑ B269	Otis Nixon B	.50	.20
❑ B271	Kirby Puckett B	1.25	.50
❑ B273	Andy Benes B	.50	.20
❑ B275	Mike Piazza B	2.00	.75
❑ B276	Rey Ordonez B	.50	.20
❑ B278	Gary Gaetti B	.50	.20
❑ B280	Robin Ventura B	.50	.20
❑ B281	Cal Ripken B	4.00	1.50
❑ B282	Carlos Baerga B	.50	.20
❑ B283	Roger Cedeno B	.50	.20
❑ B285	Terrell Wade B	.50	.20
❑ B286	Kevin Brown B	.50	.20
❑ B287	Rafael Palmeiro B	.75	.30
❑ B288	Mo Vaughn B	.50	.20
❑ B292	Bob Tewksbury B	.50	.20
❑ B297	T.J. Mathews B	.50	.20
❑ B298	Manny Ramirez B	.75	.30
❑ B299	Jeff Bagwell B	.75	.30
❑ B301	Wade Boggs B	.75	.30
❑ B303	Steve Gibralter B	.50	.20
❑ B304	B.J. Surhoff B	.50	.20
❑ B306	Royce Clayton B	.50	.20
❑ B307	Sal Fasano B	.50	.20
❑ B309	Gary Sheffield B	.50	.20
❑ B310	Ken Hill B	.50	.20
❑ B311	Joe Girardi B	.50	.20
❑ B312	Matt Lawton B RC	.50	.20
❑ B314	Julio Franco B	.50	.20
❑ B315	Joe Carter B	.50	.20
❑ B316	Brooks Kieschnick B	.50	.20
❑ B318	Heathcliff Slocumb B	.50	.20
❑ B319	Barry Larkin B	.75	.30
❑ B320	Tony Gwynn B	1.50	.60
❑ B322	Frank Thomas B	1.25	.50
❑ B323	Edgar Martinez B	.75	.30
❑ B325	Henry Rodriguez B	.50	.20
❑ B326	Marvin Benard B RC	.50	.20
❑ B329	Ugueth Urbina B	.50	.20
❑ B331	Roger Salkeld B	.50	.20
❑ B332	Edgar Renteria B	.50	.20
❑ B333	Ryan Klesko B	.50	.20
❑ B334	Ray Lankford B	.50	.20
❑ B336	Justin Thompson B	.50	.20
❑ B339	Mark Clark B	.50	.20
❑ B340	Ruben Rivera B	.50	.20
❑ B342	Matt Williams B	.50	.20
❑ B343	Francisco Cordova B RC	.50	.20
❑ B344	Cecil Fielder B	.50	.20
❑ B348	Mark Grudzielanek B	.50	.20
❑ B349	Ron Coomer B	.50	.20
❑ B351	Rich Aurilia B RC	.50	.20
❑ B352	Jose Herrera B	.50	.20
❑ B356	Tony Clark B	.50	.20
❑ B358	Dan Naulty B	.50	.20
❑ B359	Checklist B	.50	.20
❑ G4	Marty Cordova G	5.00	2.00
❑ G6	Tony Gwynn G	15.00	6.00
❑ G9	Albert Belle G	5.00	2.00
❑ G18	Kirby Puckett G	12.00	5.00
❑ G20	Karim Garcia G	5.00	2.00
❑ G25	Cal Ripken G	40.00	15.00
❑ G33	Hideo Nomo G	12.00	5.00
❑ G39	Ryne Sandberg G	20.00	8.00
❑ G42	Jeff Bagwell G	4.00	1.50
❑ G51	Jason Isringhausen G	5.00	2.00
❑ G64	Mo Vaughn G	5.00	2.00
❑ G66	Dante Bichette G	5.00	2.00
❑ G74	Mark McGwire G	30.00	12.50
❑ G81	Kenny Lofton G	5.00	2.00
❑ G83	Jim Edmonds G	5.00	2.00
❑ G90	Mike Mussina G	8.00	3.00
❑ G100	Jeff Conine G	5.00	2.00
❑ G102	Johnny Damon G	8.00	3.00
❑ G105	Barry Bonds G	30.00	12.50
❑ G117	Jose Canseco G	8.00	3.00
❑ G135	Ken Griffey Jr. G	20.00	8.00
❑ G141	Chipper Jones G	12.00	5.00
❑ G145	Greg Maddux G	20.00	8.00
❑ G164	Jay Buhner G	5.00	2.00
❑ G186	Frank Thomas G	12.00	5.00
❑ G191	Checklist G	5.00	2.00
❑ G192	Chipper Jones G	12.00	5.00
❑ G197	Roberto Alomar G	8.00	3.00
❑ G198	Dennis Eckersley G	5.00	2.00
❑ G202	George Arias G	5.00	2.00
❑ G232	Hideo Nomo G	12.00	5.00
❑ G243	Chris Snopek G	5.00	2.00
❑ G249	Tim Salmon G	8.00	3.00
❑ G266	Matt Williams G	5.00	2.00
❑ G270	Randy Johnson G	12.00	5.00
❑ G279	Paul Molitor G	5.00	2.00
❑ G290	Cecil Fielder G	5.00	2.00
❑ G294	Livan Hernandez G RC	10.00	4.00
❑ G300	Marty Janzen G RC	5.00	2.00
❑ G308	Ron Gant G	5.00	2.00
❑ G321	Ryan Klesko G	5.00	2.00

❑ G324 Jermaine Dye G 5.00 2.00
❑ G330 Jason Giambi G 5.00 2.00
❑ G335 Edgar Martinez G 8.00 3.00
❑ G338 Rey Ordonez G 5.00 2.00
❑ G347 Sammy Sosa G 12.00 5.00
❑ G354 Juan Gonzalez G 5.00 2.00
❑ G355 Craig Biggio G 8.00 3.00
❑ S1 Greg Maddux S 10.00 4.00
❑ S2 Bernie Williams S 4.00 1.50
❑ S3 Ivan Rodriguez S 4.00 1.50
❑ S7 Barry Larkin S 4.00 1.50
❑ S10 Ray Lankford S 2.50 1.00
❑ S11 Mike Piazza S 10.00 4.00
❑ S13 Larry Walker S 2.50 1.00
❑ S14 Matt Williams S 2.50 1.00
❑ S22 Tim Salmon S 4.00 1.50
❑ S35 Edgar Martinez S 4.00 1.50
❑ S37 Gregg Jefferies S 2.50 1.00
❑ S38 Bill Pulsipher S 2.50 1.00
❑ S41 Shawn Green S 2.50 1.00
❑ S43 Jim Abbott S 4.00 1.50
❑ S46 Roger Clemens S 12.00 5.00
❑ S52 Rondell White S 2.50 1.00
❑ S54 Dennis Eckersley S 2.50 1.00
❑ S59 Hideo Nomo S 6.00 2.50
❑ S60 Gary Sheffield S 2.50 1.00
❑ S62 Will Clark S 4.00 1.50
❑ S65 Bret Boone S 2.50 1.00
❑ S68 Rafael Palmeiro S 4.00 1.50
❑ S69 Carlos Baerga S 2.50 1.00
❑ S72 Tom Glavine S 4.00 1.50
❑ S73 Garret Anderson S 2.50 1.00
❑ S77 Randy Johnson S 6.00 2.50
❑ S78 Jeff King S 2.50 1.00
❑ S79 Kirby Puckett S 6.00 2.50
❑ S84 Cecil Fielder S 2.50 1.00
❑ S86 Reggie Sanders S 2.50 1.00
❑ S88 Ryan Klesko S 2.50 1.00
❑ S91 John Valentin S 2.50 1.00
❑ S95 Manny Ramirez S 4.00 1.50
❑ S99 Vinny Castilla S 2.50 1.00
❑ S109 Carlos Perez S 2.50 1.00
❑ S112 Craig Biggio S 4.00 1.50
❑ S115 Juan Gonzalez S 2.50 1.00
❑ S121 Ray Durham S 2.50 1.00
❑ S127 C.J. Nitkowski S 2.50 1.00
❑ S130 Raul Mondesi S 2.50 1.00
❑ S142 Lee Smith S 2.50 1.00
❑ S143 Joe Carter S 2.50 1.00
❑ S151 Mo Vaughn S 2.50 1.00
❑ S153 Frank Rodriguez S 2.50 1.00
❑ S160 Steve Finley S 2.50 1.00
❑ S161 Jeff Bagwell S 4.00 1.50
❑ S165 Cal Ripken S 20.00 8.00
❑ S168 Lyle Mouton S 2.50 1.00
❑ S171 Sammy Sosa S 6.00 2.50
❑ S174 John Franco S 2.50 1.00
❑ S179 Greg Vaughn S 2.50 1.00
❑ S180 Mark Wohlers S 2.50 1.00
❑ S182 Paul O'Neill S 4.00 1.50
❑ S188 Albert Belle S 2.50 1.00
❑ S189 Mark Grace S 4.00 1.50
❑ S211 Ernie Young S 2.50 1.00
❑ S218 Fred McGriff S 4.00 1.50
❑ S223 Kimera Bartee S 2.50 1.00
❑ S229 Rickey Henderson S 6.00 2.50
❑ S230 Sterling Hitchcock S 2.50 1.00
❑ S231 Bernard Gilkey S 2.50 1.00
❑ S234 Ryne Sandberg S 10.00 4.00
❑ S235 Greg Maddux S 10.00 4.00
❑ S239 Todd Stottlemyre S 2.50 1.00
❑ S241 Jason Kendall S 2.50 1.00
❑ S242 Paul O'Neill S 4.00 1.50
❑ S256 Devon White S 2.50 1.00
❑ S261 Chuck Knoblauch S 2.50 1.00
❑ S263 Wally Joyner S 2.50 1.00
❑ S272 Andy Fox S 2.50 1.00
❑ S274 Sean Berry S 2.50 1.00
❑ S277 Benito Santiago S 2.50 1.00
❑ S284 Chad Mottola S 2.50 1.00
❑ S289 Dante Bichette S 2.50 1.00
❑ S291 Dwight Gooden S 2.50 1.00
❑ S293 Kevin Mitchell S 2.50 1.00
❑ S295 Russ Davis S 2.50 1.00
❑ S296 Chan Ho Park S 2.50 1.00
❑ S302 Larry Walker S 2.50 1.00
❑ S305 Ken Griffey Jr. S 10.00 4.00
❑ S313 Billy Wagner S 2.50 1.00
❑ S317 Mike Grace S RC 2.50 1.00
❑ S327 Kenny Lofton S 2.50 1.00
❑ S328 Derek Bell S 2.50 1.00
❑ S337 Gary Sheffield S 2.50 1.00
❑ S341 Mark Grace S 4.00 1.50
❑ S345 Andres Galarraga S 2.50 1.00
❑ S346 Brady Anderson S 2.50 1.00
❑ S350 Derek Jeter S 12.00 5.00
❑ S353 Jay Buhner S 2.50 1.00
❑ S357 Tino Martinez S 4.00 1.50

1999 Finest

❑ COMPLETE SET (300) 80.00 30.00
❑ COMPLETE SERIES 1 (150) 40.00 15.00
❑ COMPLETE SERIES 2 (150) 40.00 15.00
❑ COMP.SER.1 w/o SP's (100) 15.00 6.00
❑ COMP.SER.2 w/o SP's (100) 15.00 6.00
❑ COMMON (1-100/151-250) .40 .15
❑ COMMON (101-150/251-300) .50 .20
❑ 1 Darin Erstad .40 .15
❑ 2 Javy Lopez .40 .15
❑ 3 Vinny Castilla .40 .15
❑ 4 Jim Thome .60 .25
❑ 5 Tino Martinez .60 .25
❑ 6 Mark Grace .60 .25
❑ 7 Shawn Green .40 .15
❑ 8 Dustin Hermanson .40 .15
❑ 9 Kevin Young .40 .15
❑ 10 Tony Clark .40 .15
❑ 11 Scott Brosius .40 .15
❑ 12 Craig Biggio .60 .25
❑ 13 Brian McRae .40 .15
❑ 14 Chan Ho Park .40 .15
❑ 15 Manny Ramirez .60 .25
❑ 16 Chipper Jones 1.00 .40
❑ 17 Rico Brogna .40 .15
❑ 18 Quinton McCracken .40 .15
❑ 19 J.T. Snow .40 .15
❑ 20 Tony Gwynn 1.25 .50
❑ 21 Juan Guzman .40 .15
❑ 22 John Valentin .40 .15
❑ 23 Rick Helling .40 .15
❑ 24 Sandy Alomar Jr. .40 .15
❑ 25 Frank Thomas 1.00 .40
❑ 26 Jorge Posada .60 .25
❑ 27 Dmitri Young .40 .15
❑ 28 Rick Reed .40 .15
❑ 29 Kevin Tapani .40 .15
❑ 30 Troy Glaus .60 .25
❑ 31 Kenny Rogers .40 .15
❑ 32 Jeromy Burnitz .40 .15
❑ 33 Mark Grudzielanek .40 .15
❑ 34 Mike Mussina .60 .25
❑ 35 Scott Rolen .60 .25
❑ 36 Neifi Perez .40 .15
❑ 37 Brad Radke .40 .15
❑ 38 Darryl Strawberry .40 .15
❑ 39 Robb Nen .40 .15
❑ 40 Moises Alou .40 .15
❑ 41 Eric Young .40 .15
❑ 42 Livan Hernandez .40 .15
❑ 43 John Wetteland .40 .15
❑ 44 Matt Lawton .40 .15
❑ 45 Ben Grieve .40 .15
❑ 46 Fernando Tatis .40 .15
❑ 47 Travis Fryman .40 .15
❑ 48 David Segui .40 .15
❑ 49 Bob Abreu .40 .15
❑ 50 Nomar Garciaparra 1.50 .60
❑ 51 Paul O'Neill .60 .25
❑ 52 Jeff King .40 .15
❑ 53 Francisco Cordova .40 .15
❑ 54 John Olerud .40 .15
❑ 55 Vladimir Guerrero 1.00 .40
❑ 56 Fernando Vina .40 .15
❑ 57 Shane Reynolds .40 .15
❑ 58 Chuck Finley .40 .15
❑ 59 Rondell White .40 .15
❑ 60 Greg Vaughn .40 .15
❑ 61 Ryan Minor .40 .15
❑ 62 Tom Gordon .40 .15
❑ 63 Damion Easley .40 .15
❑ 64 Ray Durham .40 .15
❑ 65 Orlando Hernandez .40 .15
❑ 66 Bartolo Colon .40 .15
❑ 67 Jaret Wright .40 .15
❑ 68 Royce Clayton .40 .15
❑ 69 Tim Salmon .60 .25
❑ 70 Mark McGwire 2.50 1.00
❑ 71 Alex Gonzalez .40 .15
❑ 72 Tom Glavine .60 .25
❑ 73 David Justice .40 .15
❑ 74 Omar Vizquel .60 .25
❑ 75 Juan Gonzalez .40 .15
❑ 76 Bobby Higginson .40 .15
❑ 77 Todd Walker .40 .15
❑ 78 Dante Bichette .40 .15
❑ 79 Kevin Millwood .40 .15
❑ 80 Roger Clemens 2.00 .75
❑ 81 Kerry Wood .40 .15
❑ 82 Cal Ripken 3.00 1.25
❑ 83 Jay Bell .40 .15
❑ 84 Barry Bonds 2.50 1.00
❑ 85 Alex Rodriguez 1.50 .60
❑ 86 Doug Glanville .40 .15
❑ 87 Jason Kendall .40 .15
❑ 88 Sean Casey .40 .15
❑ 89 Aaron Sele .40 .15
❑ 90 Derek Jeter 2.50 1.00
❑ 91 Andy Ashby .40 .15
❑ 92 Rusty Greer .40 .15
❑ 93 Rod Beck .40 .15
❑ 94 Matt Williams .40 .15
❑ 95 Mike Piazza 1.50 .60
❑ 96 Wally Joyner .40 .15
❑ 97 Barry Larkin .60 .25
❑ 98 Eric Milton .40 .15
❑ 99 Gary Sheffield .40 .15
❑ 100 Greg Maddux 1.50 .60
❑ 101 Ken Griffey Jr. GEM 2.50 1.00
❑ 102 Frank Thomas GEM 1.50 .60
❑ 103 Nomar Garciaparra GEM 2.50 1.00
❑ 104 Mark McGwire GEM 4.00 1.50
❑ 105 Alex Rodriguez GEM 2.50 1.00
❑ 106 Tony Gwynn GEM 2.00 .75
❑ 107 Juan Gonzalez GEM .60 .25
❑ 108 Jeff Bagwell GEM 1.00 .40
❑ 109 Sammy Sosa GEM 1.50 .60
❑ 110 Vladimir Guerrero GEM 1.50 .60
❑ 111 Roger Clemens GEM 3.00 1.25
❑ 112 Barry Bonds GEM 4.00 1.50
❑ 113 Darin Erstad GEM .60 .25
❑ 114 Mike Piazza GEM 2.50 1.00
❑ 115 Derek Jeter GEM 4.00 1.50
❑ 116 Chipper Jones GEM 1.50 .60
❑ 117 Larry Walker GEM .60 .25
❑ 118 Scott Rolen GEM 1.00 .40
❑ 119 Cal Ripken GEM 5.00 2.00
❑ 120 Greg Maddux GEM 2.50 1.00
❑ 121 Troy Glaus SENS 1.00 .40
❑ 122 Ben Grieve SENS .50 .20
❑ 123 Ryan Minor SENS .50 .20
❑ 124 Kerry Wood SENS .60 .25
❑ 125 Travis Lee SENS .50 .20
❑ 126 Adrian Beltre SENS .60 .25
❑ 127 Brad Fullmer SENS .50 .20
❑ 128 Aramis Ramirez SENS .60 .25
❑ 129 Eric Chavez SENS .60 .25
❑ 130 Todd Helton SENS 1.00 .40
❑ 131 Pat Burrell RC 3.00 1.25
❑ 132 Ryan Mills RC .50 .20
❑ 133 Austin Kearns RC 3.00 1.25

❑ 134	Josh McKinley RC	.50	.20
❑ 135	Adam Everett RC	1.00	.40
❑ 136	Marlon Anderson	.50	.20
❑ 137	Bruce Chen	.50	.20
❑ 138	Matt Clement	.60	.25
❑ 139	Alex Gonzalez	.50	.20
❑ 140	Roy Halladay	.60	.25
❑ 141	Calvin Pickering	.50	.20
❑ 142	Randy Wolf	.50	.20
❑ 143	Ryan Anderson	.50	.20
❑ 144	Ruben Mateo	.50	.20
❑ 145	Alex Escobar RC	.60	.25
❑ 146	Jeremy Giambi	.50	.20
❑ 147	Lance Berkman	.60	.25
❑ 148	Michael Barrett	.50	.20
❑ 149	Preston Wilson	.60	.25
❑ 150	Gabe Kapler	.60	.25
❑ 151	Roger Clemens	2.00	.75
❑ 152	Jay Buhner	.40	.15
❑ 153	Brad Fullmer	.40	.15
❑ 154	Ray Lankford	.40	.15
❑ 155	Jim Edmonds	.40	.15
❑ 156	Jason Giambi	.40	.15
❑ 157	Bret Boone	.40	.15
❑ 158	Jeff Cirillo	.40	.15
❑ 159	Rickey Henderson	1.00	.40
❑ 160	Edgar Martinez	.60	.25
❑ 161	Ron Gant	.40	.15
❑ 162	Mark Kotsay	.40	.15
❑ 163	Trevor Hoffman	.40	.15
❑ 164	Jason Schmidt	.40	.15
❑ 165	Brett Tomko	.40	.15
❑ 166	David Ortiz	1.00	.40
❑ 167	Dean Palmer	.40	.15
❑ 168	Hideki Irabu	.40	.15
❑ 169	Mike Cameron	.40	.15
❑ 170	Pedro Martinez	.60	.25
❑ 171	Tom Goodwin	.40	.15
❑ 172	Brian Hunter	.40	.15
❑ 173	Al Leiter	.40	.15
❑ 174	Charles Johnson	.40	.15
❑ 175	Curt Schilling	.40	.15
❑ 176	Robin Ventura	.40	.15
❑ 177	Travis Lee	.40	.15
❑ 178	Jeff Shaw	.40	.15
❑ 179	Ugueth Urbina	.40	.15
❑ 180	Roberto Alomar	.60	.25
❑ 181	Cliff Floyd	.40	.15
❑ 182	Adrian Beltre	.40	.15
❑ 183	Tony Womack	.40	.15
❑ 184	Brian Jordan	.40	.15
❑ 185	Randy Johnson	1.00	.40
❑ 186	Mickey Morandini	.40	.15
❑ 187	Todd Hundley	.40	.15
❑ 188	Jose Valentin	.40	.15
❑ 189	Eric Davis	.40	.15
❑ 190	Ken Caminiti	.40	.15
❑ 191	David Wells	.40	.15
❑ 192	Ryan Klesko	.40	.15
❑ 193	Garret Anderson	.40	.15
❑ 194	Eric Karros	.40	.15
❑ 195	Ivan Rodriguez	.60	.25
❑ 196	Aramis Ramirez	.40	.15
❑ 197	Mike Lieberthal	.40	.15
❑ 198	Will Clark	.60	.25
❑ 199	Rey Ordonez	.40	.15
❑ 200	Ken Griffey Jr.	1.50	.60
❑ 201	Jose Guillen	.40	.15
❑ 202	Scott Erickson	.40	.15
❑ 203	Paul Konerko	.40	.15
❑ 204	Johnny Damon	.60	.25
❑ 205	Larry Walker	.40	.15
❑ 206	Denny Neagle	.40	.15
❑ 207	Jose Offerman	.40	.15
❑ 208	Andy Pettitte	.60	.25
❑ 209	Bobby Jones	.40	.15
❑ 210	Kevin Brown	.60	.25
❑ 211	John Smoltz	.60	.25
❑ 212	Henry Rodriguez	.40	.15
❑ 213	Tim Belcher	.40	.15
❑ 214	Carlos Delgado	.40	.15
❑ 215	Andruw Jones	.60	.25
❑ 216	Andy Benes	.40	.15
❑ 217	Fred McGriff	.60	.25
❑ 218	Edgar Renteria	.40	.15
❑ 219	Miguel Tejada	.40	.15
❑ 220	Bernie Williams	.60	.25
❑ 221	Justin Thompson	.40	.15
❑ 222	Marty Cordova	.40	.15
❑ 223	Delino DeShields	.40	.15
❑ 224	Ellis Burks	.40	.15
❑ 225	Kenny Lofton	.40	.15
❑ 226	Steve Finley	.40	.15
❑ 227	Eric Chavez	.40	.15
❑ 228	Jose Cruz Jr.	.40	.15
❑ 229	Marquis Grissom	.40	.15
❑ 230	Jeff Bagwell	.60	.25
❑ 231	Jose Canseco	.60	.25
❑ 232	Edgardo Alfonzo	.40	.15
❑ 233	Richie Sexson	.40	.15
❑ 234	Jeff Kent	.40	.15
❑ 235	Rafael Palmeiro	.60	.25
❑ 236	David Cone	.40	.15
❑ 237	Gregg Jefferies	.40	.15
❑ 238	Mike Lansing	.40	.15
❑ 239	Mariano Rivera	1.00	.40
❑ 240	Albert Belle	.40	.15
❑ 241	Chuck Knoblauch	.40	.15
❑ 242	Derek Bell	.40	.15
❑ 243	Pat Hentgen	.40	.15
❑ 244	Andres Galarraga	.40	.15
❑ 245	Mo Vaughn	.40	.15
❑ 246	Wade Boggs	.60	.25
❑ 247	Devon White	.40	.15
❑ 248	Todd Helton	.60	.25
❑ 249	Raul Mondesi	.40	.15
❑ 250	Sammy Sosa	1.00	.40
❑ 251	Nomar Garciaparra ST	2.50	1.00
❑ 252	Mark McGwire ST	4.00	1.50
❑ 253	Alex Rodriguez ST	2.50	1.00
❑ 254	Juan Gonzalez ST	.60	.25
❑ 255	Vladimir Guerrero ST	1.50	.60
❑ 256	Ken Griffey Jr. ST	2.50	1.00
❑ 257	Mike Piazza ST	2.50	1.00
❑ 258	Derek Jeter ST	4.00	1.50
❑ 259	Albert Belle ST	.60	.25
❑ 260	Greg Vaughn ST	.50	.20
❑ 261	Sammy Sosa ST	1.50	.60
❑ 262	Greg Maddux ST	2.50	1.00
❑ 263	Frank Thomas ST	1.50	.60
❑ 264	Mark Grace ST	1.00	.40
❑ 265	Ivan Rodriguez ST	1.00	.40
❑ 266	Roger Clemens GM	3.00	1.25
❑ 267	Mo Vaughn GM	.60	.25
❑ 268	Jim Thome GM	1.00	.40
❑ 269	Darin Erstad GM	.60	.25
❑ 270	Chipper Jones GM	1.50	.60
❑ 271	Larry Walker GM	.60	.25
❑ 272	Cal Ripken GM	5.00	2.00
❑ 273	Scott Rolen GM	1.00	.40
❑ 274	Randy Johnson GM	1.50	.60
❑ 275	Tony Gwynn GM	2.00	.75
❑ 276	Barry Bonds GM	4.00	1.50
❑ 277	Sean Burroughs RC	1.00	.40
❑ 278	J.M. Gold RC	.50	.20
❑ 279	Carlos Lee	.60	.25
❑ 280	George Lombard	.50	.20
❑ 281	Carlos Beltran	1.00	.40
❑ 282	Fernando Seguignol	.50	.20
❑ 283	Eric Chavez	.60	.25
❑ 284	Carlos Pena RC	.60	.25
❑ 285	Corey Patterson RC	1.50	.60
❑ 286	Alfonso Soriano RC	8.00	3.00
❑ 287	Nick Johnson RC	1.50	.60
❑ 288	Jorge Toca RC	.60	.25
❑ 289	A.J. Burnett RC	1.50	.60
❑ 290	Andy Brown RC	.50	.20
❑ 291	Doug Mientkiewicz RC	1.00	.40
❑ 292	Bobby Seay RC	.50	.20
❑ 293	Chip Ambres RC	.50	.20
❑ 294	C.C. Sabathia RC	2.00	.75
❑ 295	Choo Freeman RC	.60	.25
❑ 296	Eric Valent RC	.60	.25
❑ 297	Matt Belisle RC	.50	.20
❑ 298	Jason Tyner RC	.50	.20
❑ 299	Masao Kida RC	.60	.25
❑ 300	H.Aaron/M.McGwire	3.00	1.25

2000 Finest

❑ COMP.SERIES 1 w/o SP's (100)	25.00	10.00
❑ COMP.SERIES 2 w/o SP's (100)	25.00	10.00
❑ COMMON (1-100/147-246)	.40	.15
❑ COMMON ROOKIE (101-120)	5.00	2.00
❑ COMMON FEATURES (121-135)	1.50	.60
❑ COMM.GEM (136-145/277-286)	2.00	.75
❑ COMMON ROOKIE (247-266)	5.00	2.00
❑ COMMON COUNTER (267-276)	1.00	.40

❑ 1	Nomar Garciaparra	1.50	.60
❑ 2	Chipper Jones	1.00	.40
❑ 3	Erubiel Durazo	.40	.15
❑ 4	Robin Ventura	.60	.25
❑ 5	Garret Anderson	.40	.15
❑ 6	Dean Palmer	.40	.15
❑ 7	Mariano Rivera	1.00	.40
❑ 8	Rusty Greer	.40	.15
❑ 9	Jim Thome	.60	.25
❑ 10	Jeff Bagwell	.60	.25
❑ 11	Jason Giambi	.40	.15
❑ 12	Jeromy Burnitz	.40	.15
❑ 13	Mark Grace	.60	.25
❑ 14	Russ Ortiz	.40	.15
❑ 15	Kevin Brown	.60	.25
❑ 16	Kevin Millwood	.40	.15
❑ 17	Scott Williamson	.40	.15
❑ 18	Orlando Hernandez	.40	.15
❑ 19	Todd Walker	.40	.15
❑ 20	Carlos Beltran	.40	.15
❑ 21	Ruben Rivera	.40	.15
❑ 22	Curt Schilling	.40	.15
❑ 23	Brian Giles	.40	.15
❑ 24	Eric Karros	.40	.15
❑ 25	Preston Wilson	.40	.15
❑ 26	Al Leiter	.40	.15
❑ 27	Juan Encarnacion	.40	.15
❑ 28	Tim Salmon	.60	.25
❑ 29	B.J. Surhoff	.40	.15
❑ 30	Bernie Williams	.60	.25
❑ 31	Lee Stevens	.40	.15
❑ 32	Pokey Reese	.40	.15
❑ 33	Mike Sweeney	.40	.15
❑ 34	Corey Koskie	.40	.15
❑ 35	Roberto Alomar	.60	.25
❑ 36	Tim Hudson	.40	.15
❑ 37	Tom Glavine	.60	.25
❑ 38	Jeff Kent	.40	.15
❑ 39	Mike Lieberthal	.40	.15
❑ 40	Barry Larkin	.60	.25
❑ 41	Paul O'Neill	.60	.25
❑ 42	Rico Brogna	.40	.15
❑ 43	Brian Daubach	.40	.15
❑ 44	Rich Aurilia	.40	.15
❑ 45	Vladimir Guerrero	1.00	.40
❑ 46	Luis Castillo	.40	.15
❑ 47	Bartolo Colon	.40	.15
❑ 48	Kevin Appier	.40	.15
❑ 49	Mo Vaughn	.40	.15
❑ 50	Alex Rodriguez	1.50	.60
❑ 51	Randy Johnson	1.00	.40
❑ 52	Kris Benson	.40	.15
❑ 53	Tony Clark	.40	.15
❑ 54	Chad Allen	.40	.15
❑ 55	Larry Walker	.40	.15
❑ 56	Freddy Garcia	.40	.15
❑ 57	Paul Konerko	.40	.15
❑ 58	Edgardo Alfonzo	.40	.15
❑ 59	Brady Anderson	.40	.15
❑ 60	Derek Jeter	2.50	1.00
❑ 61	John Smoltz	.60	.25
❑ 62	Doug Glanville	.40	.15
❑ 63	Shannon Stewart	.40	.15

❑ 64 Greg Maddux 1.50 .60
❑ 65 Mark McGwire 2.50 1.00
❑ 66 Gary Sheffield .40 .15
❑ 67 Kevin Young .40 .15
❑ 68 Tony Gwynn 1.25 .50
❑ 69 Rey Ordonez .40 .15
❑ 70 Cal Ripken 3.00 1.25
❑ 71 Todd Helton .60 .25
❑ 72 Brian Jordan .40 .15
❑ 73 Jose Canseco .60 .25
❑ 74 Luis Gonzalez .40 .15
❑ 75 Barry Bonds 2.50 1.00
❑ 76 Jermaine Dye .40 .15
❑ 77 Jose Offerman .40 .15
❑ 78 Magglio Ordonez .40 .15
❑ 79 Fred Mcgriff .60 .25
❑ 80 Ivan Rodriguez .60 .25
❑ 81 Josh Hamilton .40 .15
❑ 82 Vernon Wells .40 .15
❑ 83 Mark Mulder .40 .15
❑ 84 John Patterson .40 .15
❑ 85 Nick Johnson .40 .15
❑ 86 Pablo Ozuna .40 .15
❑ 87 A.J. Burnett .40 .15
❑ 88 Jack Cust .40 .15
❑ 89 Adam Piatt .40 .15
❑ 90 Rob Ryan .40 .15
❑ 91 Sean Burroughs .40 .15
❑ 92 D'Angelo Jimenez .40 .15
❑ 93 Chad Hermansen .40 .15
❑ 94 Robert Fick .40 .15
❑ 95 Ruben Mateo .40 .15
❑ 96 Alex Escobar .40 .15
❑ 97 Wily Pena .40 .15
❑ 98 Corey Patterson .40 .15
❑ 99 Eric Munson .40 .15
❑ 100 Pat Burrell .40 .15
❑ 101 Michael Tejera RC 5.00 2.00
❑ 102 Bobby Bradley RC 5.00 2.00
❑ 103 Larry Bigbie RC 8.00 3.00
❑ 104 B.J. Garbe RC 5.00 2.00
❑ 105 Josh Kalinowski RC 5.00 2.00
❑ 106 Brett Myers RC 10.00 4.00
❑ 107 Chris Mears RC 5.00 2.00
❑ 108 Aaron Rowand RC 10.00 4.00
❑ 109 Corey Myers RC 5.00 2.00
❑ 110 John Sneed RC 5.00 2.00
❑ 111 Ryan Christianson RC 5.00 2.00
❑ 112 Kyle Snyder 5.00 2.00
❑ 113 Mike Paradis 5.00 2.00
❑ 114 Chance Caple RC 5.00 2.00
❑ 115 Ben Christensen RC 5.00 2.00
❑ 116 Brad Baker RC 5.00 2.00
❑ 117 Rob Purvis RC 5.00 2.00
❑ 118 Rick Asadoorian RC 5.00 2.00
❑ 119 Ruben Salazar RC 5.00 2.00
❑ 120 Julio Zuleta RC 5.00 2.00
❑ 121 A.Rodriguez/K.Griffey Jr. 2.50 1.00
❑ 122 N.Garciaparra/D.Jeter 3.00 1.25
❑ 123 M.McGwire/S.Sosa 4.00 1.50
❑ 124 R.Johnson/P.Martinez 2.50 1.00
❑ 125 I.Rodriguez/M.Piazza 2.50 1.00
❑ 126 M.Ramirez/R.Alomar 1.50 .60
❑ 127 C.Jones/A.Jones 2.50 1.00
❑ 128 C.Ripken/T.Gwynn 5.00 2.00
❑ 129 J.Bagwell/C.Biggio 1.50 .60
❑ 130 B.Bonds/V.Guerrero 4.00 1.50
❑ 131 N.Johnson/A.Soriano 2.50 1.00
❑ 132 J.Hamilton/P.Burrell 5.00 2.00
❑ 133 C.Patterson/R.Mateo 1.50 .60
❑ 134 L.Walker/T.Helton 1.50 .60
❑ 135 R.Ordonez/E.Alfonzo 1.50 .60
❑ 136 Derek Jeter GEM 8.00 3.00
❑ 137 Alex Rodriguez GEM 5.00 2.00
❑ 138 Chipper Jones GEM 5.00 2.00
❑ 139 Mike Piazza GEM 5.00 2.00
❑ 140 Mark McGwire GEM 8.00 3.00
❑ 141 Ivan Rodriguez GEM 3.00 1.25
❑ 142 Cal Ripken GEM 10.00 4.00
❑ 143 Vladimir Guerrero GEM 5.00 2.00
❑ 144 Randy Johnson GEM 5.00 2.00
❑ 145 Jeff Bagwell GEM 3.00 1.25
❑ 146 Ken Griffey Jr. ACTION 1.50 .60
❑ 146A Ken Griffey Jr. PORT 1.50 .60
❑ 147 Andruw Jones .60 .25
❑ 148 Kerry Wood .40 .15

❑ 149 Jim Edmonds .40 .15
❑ 150 Pedro Martinez .60 .25
❑ 151 Warren Morris .40 .15
❑ 152 Trevor Hoffman .40 .15
❑ 153 Ryan Klesko .40 .15
❑ 154 Andy Pettitte .60 .25
❑ 155 Frank Thomas 1.00 .40
❑ 156 Damion Easley .40 .15
❑ 157 Cliff Floyd .40 .15
❑ 158 Ben Davis .40 .15
❑ 159 John Valentin .40 .15
❑ 160 Rafael Palmeiro .60 .25
❑ 161 Andy Ashby .40 .15
❑ 162 J.D. Drew .40 .15
❑ 163 Jay Bell .40 .15
❑ 164 Adam Kennedy .40 .15
❑ 165 Manny Ramirez .60 .25
❑ 166 John Halama .40 .15
❑ 167 Octavio Dotel .40 .15
❑ 168 Darin Erstad .40 .15
❑ 169 Jose Lima .40 .15
❑ 170 Andres Galarraga .40 .15
❑ 171 Scott Rolen .60 .25
❑ 172 Delino DeShields .40 .15
❑ 173 J.T. Snow .40 .15
❑ 174 Tony Womack .40 .15
❑ 175 John Olerud .40 .15
❑ 176 Jason Kendall .40 .15
❑ 177 Carlos Lee .40 .15
❑ 178 Eric Milton .40 .15
❑ 179 Jeff Cirillo .40 .15
❑ 180 Gabe Kapler .40 .15
❑ 181 Greg Vaughn .40 .15
❑ 182 Denny Neagle .40 .15
❑ 183 Tino Martinez .60 .25
❑ 184 Doug Mientkiewicz .40 .15
❑ 185 Juan Gonzalez .40 .15
❑ 186 Ellis Burks .40 .15
❑ 187 Mike Hampton .40 .15
❑ 188 Royce Clayton .40 .15
❑ 189 Mike Mussina .60 .25
❑ 190 Carlos Delgado .40 .15
❑ 191 Ben Grieve .40 .15
❑ 192 Fernando Tatis .40 .15
❑ 193 Matt Williams .40 .15
❑ 194 Rondell White .40 .15
❑ 195 Shawn Green .40 .15
❑ 196 Hideki Irabu .40 .15
❑ 197 Troy Glaus .40 .15
❑ 198 Roger Cedeno .40 .15
❑ 199 Ray Lankford .40 .15
❑ 200 Sammy Sosa 1.00 .40
❑ 201 Kenny Lofton .40 .15
❑ 202 Edgar Martinez .60 .25
❑ 203 Mark Kotsay .40 .15
❑ 204 David Wells .40 .15
❑ 205 Craig Biggio .60 .25
❑ 206 Ray Durham .40 .15
❑ 207 Troy O'Leary .40 .15
❑ 208 Rickey Henderson 1.00 .40
❑ 209 Bob Abreu .40 .15
❑ 210 Neifi Perez .40 .15
❑ 211 Carlos Febles .40 .15
❑ 212 Chuck Knoblauch .40 .15
❑ 213 Moises Alou .40 .15
❑ 214 Omar Vizquel .60 .25
❑ 215 Vinny Castilla .40 .15
❑ 216 Javy Lopez .40 .15
❑ 217 Johnny Damon .60 .25
❑ 218 Roger Clemens 2.00 .75
❑ 219 Miguel Tejada .40 .15
❑ 220 Carl Everett .40 .15
❑ 221 Matt Lawton .40 .15
❑ 222 Albert Belle .40 .15
❑ 223 Adrian Beltre .40 .15
❑ 224 Dante Bichette .40 .15
❑ 225 Raul Mondesi .40 .15
❑ 226 Mike Piazza 1.50 .60
❑ 227 Brad Penny .40 .15
❑ 228 Kip Wells .40 .15
❑ 229 Adam Everett .40 .15
❑ 230 Eddie Yarnall .40 .15
❑ 231 Matt LeCroy .40 .15
❑ 232 Jason Tyner .40 .15
❑ 233 Rick Ankiel .40 .15
❑ 234 Lance Berkman .40 .15

❑ 235 Rafael Furcal .40 .15
❑ 236 Dee Brown .40 .15
❑ 237 Gookie Dawkins .40 .15
❑ 238 Eric Valent .40 .15
❑ 239 Peter Bergeron .40 .15
❑ 240 Alfonso Soriano 1.00 .40
❑ 241 Adam Dunn 1.00 .40
❑ 242 Jorge Toca .40 .15
❑ 243 Ryan Anderson .40 .15
❑ 244 Jason Dellaero .40 .15
❑ 245 Jason Grilli .40 .15
❑ 246 Milton Bradley .40 .15
❑ 247 Scott Downs RC 5.00 2.00
❑ 248 Keith Reed RC 5.00 2.00
❑ 249 Edgar Cruz RC 5.00 2.00
❑ 250 Wes Anderson RC 5.00 2.00
❑ 251 Lyle Overbay RC 8.00 3.00
❑ 252 Mike Lamb RC 8.00 3.00
❑ 253 Vince Faison RC 5.00 2.00
❑ 254 Chad Alexander 5.00 2.00
❑ 255 Chris Wakeland RC 5.00 2.00
❑ 256 Aaron McNeal RC 5.00 2.00
❑ 257 Tomo Ohka RC 5.00 2.00
❑ 258 Ty Howington RC 5.00 2.00
❑ 259 Javier Colina RC 5.00 2.00
❑ 260 Jason Jennings 5.00 2.00
❑ 261 Ramon Santiago RC 5.00 2.00
❑ 262 Johan Santana RC 80.00 50.00
❑ 263 Quincy Foster RC 5.00 2.00
❑ 264 Junior Brignac RC 5.00 2.00
❑ 265 Rico Washington RC 5.00 2.00
❑ 266 Scott Sobkowiak RC 5.00 2.00
❑ 267 P.Martinez/R.Ankiel 1.50 .60
❑ 268 M.Ramirez/V.Guerrero 2.50 1.00
❑ 269 A.Burnett/M.Mulder 1.00 .40
❑ 270 M.Piazza/E.Munson 2.50 1.00
❑ 271 J.Hamilton/C.Patterson 1.00 .40
❑ 272 K.Griffey Jr./S.Sosa 2.00 .75
❑ 273 D.Jeter/A.Soriano 4.00 1.50
❑ 274 M.McGwire/P.Burrell 4.00 1.50
❑ 275 C.Jones/C.Ripken 4.00 1.50
❑ 276 N.Garciaparra/A.Rodriguez 2.50 1.00
❑ 277 Pedro Martinez GEM 3.00 1.25
❑ 278 Tony Gwynn GEM 4.00 1.50
❑ 279 Barry Bonds GEM 8.00 3.00
❑ 280 Juan Gonzalez GEM 2.00 .75
❑ 281 Larry Walker GEM 2.00 .75
❑ 282 Nomar Garciaparra GEM 5.00 2.00
❑ 283 Ken Griffey Jr. GEM 5.00 2.00
❑ 284 Manny Ramirez GEM 3.00 1.25
❑ 285 Shawn Green GEM 2.00 .75
❑ 286 Sammy Sosa GEM 5.00 2.00
❑ NNO Graded Gems Ser.1 EXCH/10
❑ NNO Graded Gems Ser.2 EXCH/10

2001 Finest

❑ COMP.SET w/o SP's (100) 25.00 10.00
❑ COMMON CARD (1-110) .40 .15
❑ COMMON SP 10.00 4.00
❑ COMMON PROSPECT (111-140) 10.004.00
❑ 1 Mike Piazza SP 20.00 8.00
❑ 2 Andruw Jones .60 .25
❑ 3 Jason Giambi .40 .15
❑ 4 Fred McGriff .60 .25
❑ 5 Vladimir Guerrero SP 10.00 4.00
❑ 6 Adrian Gonzalez .40 .15

Card		
❑ 7 Pedro Martinez	.60	.25
❑ 8 Mike Lieberthal	.40	.15
❑ 9 Warren Morris	.40	.15
❑ 10 Juan Gonzalez	.40	.15
❑ 11 Jose Canseco	.60	.25
❑ 12 Jose Valentin	.40	.15
❑ 13 Jeff Cirillo	.40	.15
❑ 14 Pokey Reese	.40	.15
❑ 15 Scott Rolen	.60	.25
❑ 16 Greg Maddux	1.50	.60
❑ 17 Carlos Delgado	.40	.15
❑ 18 Rick Ankiel	.40	.15
❑ 19 Steve Finley	.40	.15
❑ 20 Shawn Green	.40	.15
❑ 21 Orlando Cabrera	.40	.15
❑ 22 Roberto Alomar	.60	.25
❑ 23 John Olerud	.40	.15
❑ 24 Albert Belle	.40	.15
❑ 25 Edgardo Alfonzo	.40	.15
❑ 26 Rafael Palmeiro	.60	.25
❑ 27 Mike Sweeney	.40	.15
❑ 28 Bernie Williams	.60	.25
❑ 29 Larry Walker	.40	.15
❑ 30 Barry Bonds SP	25.00	10.00
❑ 31 Orlando Hernandez	.40	.15
❑ 32 Randy Johnson	1.00	.40
❑ 33 Shannon Stewart	.40	.15
❑ 34 Mark Grace	.60	.25
❑ 35 Alex Rodriguez SP	25.00	10.00
❑ 36 Tino Martinez	.60	.25
❑ 37 Carlos Febles	.40	.15
❑ 38 Al Leiter	.40	.15
❑ 39 Omar Vizquel	.60	.25
❑ 40 Chuck Knoblauch	.40	.15
❑ 41 Tim Salmon	.60	.25
❑ 42 Brian Jordan	.40	.15
❑ 43 Edgar Renteria	.40	.15
❑ 44 Preston Wilson	.40	.15
❑ 45 Mariano Rivera	1.00	.40
❑ 46 Gabe Kapler	.40	.15
❑ 47 Jason Kendall	.40	.15
❑ 48 Rickey Henderson	1.00	.40
❑ 49 Luis Gonzalez	.40	.15
❑ 50 Tom Glavine	.60	.25
❑ 51 Jeromy Burnitz	.40	.15
❑ 52 Garret Anderson	.40	.15
❑ 53 Craig Biggio	.60	.25
❑ 54 Vinny Castilla	.40	.15
❑ 55 Jeff Kent	.40	.15
❑ 56 Gary Sheffield	.40	.15
❑ 57 Jorge Posada	.60	.25
❑ 58 Sean Casey	.40	.15
❑ 59 Johnny Damon	.60	.25
❑ 60 Dean Palmer	.40	.15
❑ 61 Todd Helton	.60	.25
❑ 62 Barry Larkin	.60	.25
❑ 63 Robin Ventura	.40	.15
❑ 64 Kenny Lofton	.40	.15
❑ 65 Sammy Sosa SP	10.00	4.00
❑ 66 Rafael Furcal	.40	.15
❑ 67 Jay Bell	.40	.15
❑ 68 J.T. Snow	.40	.15
❑ 69 Jose Vidro	.40	.15
❑ 70 Ivan Rodriguez	.60	.25
❑ 71 Jermaine Dye	.40	.15
❑ 72 Chipper Jones SP	10.00	4.00
❑ 73 Fernando Vina	.40	.15
❑ 74 Ben Grieve	.40	.15
❑ 75 Mark McGwire SP	25.00	10.00
❑ 76 Matt Williams	.40	.15
❑ 77 Mark Grudzielanek	.40	.15
❑ 78 Mike Hampton	.40	.15
❑ 79 Brian Giles	.40	.15
❑ 80 Tony Gwynn	1.25	.50
❑ 81 Carlos Beltran	.40	.15
❑ 82 Ray Durham	.40	.15
❑ 83 Brad Radke	.40	.15
❑ 84 David Justice	.40	.15
❑ 85 Frank Thomas	1.00	.40
❑ 86 Todd Zeile	.40	.15
❑ 87 Pat Burrell	.40	.15
❑ 88 Jim Thome	.60	.25
❑ 89 Greg Vaughn	.40	.15
❑ 90 Ken Griffey Jr. SP	15.00	6.00
❑ 91 Mike Mussina	.60	.25
❑ 92 Maggio Ordonez	.40	.15
❑ 93 Bob Abreu	.40	.15
❑ 94 Alex Gonzalez	.40	.15
❑ 95 Kevin Brown	.40	.15
❑ 96 Jay Buhner	.40	.15
❑ 97 Roger Clemens	2.00	.75
❑ 98 Nomar Garciaparra SP	15.00	6.00
❑ 99 Derrek Lee	.60	.25
❑ 100 Derek Jeter SP	25.00	10.00
❑ 101 Adrian Beltre	.40	.15
❑ 102 Geoff Jenkins	.40	.15
❑ 103 Javy Lopez	.40	.15
❑ 104 Raul Mondesi	.40	.15
❑ 105 Troy Glaus	.40	.15
❑ 106 Jeff Bagwell	.60	.25
❑ 107 Eric Karros	.40	.15
❑ 108 Mo Vaughn	.40	.15
❑ 109 Cal Ripken	3.00	1.25
❑ 110 Manny Ramirez Sox	.60	.25
❑ 111 Scott Heard PROS	10.00	4.00
❑ 112 Luis Montanez PROS RC	10.00	4.00
❑ 113 Ben Diggins PROS	10.00	4.00
❑ 114 Shaun Boyd PROS RC	10.00	4.00
❑ 115 Sean Burnett PROS	10.00	4.00
❑ 116 Carmen Cali PROS RC	10.00	4.00
❑ 117 Derek Thompson PROS	10.00	4.00
❑ 118 David Parrish PROS RC	10.00	4.00
❑ 119 Dominic Rich PROS RC	10.00	4.00
❑ 120 Chad Petty PROS RC	10.00	4.00
❑ 121 Steve Smyth PROS RC	10.00	4.00
❑ 122 John Lackey PROS	10.00	4.00
❑ 123 Matt Galante PROS RC	10.00	4.00
❑ 124 Danny Borrell PROS RC	10.00	4.00
❑ 125 Bob Keppel PROS RC	10.00	4.00
❑ 126 Justin Wayne PROS RC	10.00	4.00
❑ 127 J.R. House PROS	10.00	4.00
❑ 128 Brian Sellier PROS RC	10.00	4.00
❑ 129 Dan Moylan PROS RC	10.00	4.00
❑ 130 Scott Pratt PROS RC	10.00	4.00
❑ 131 Victor Hall PROS RC	10.00	4.00
❑ 132 Joel Pineiro PROS	10.00	4.00
❑ 133 Josh Axelson PROS RC	10.00	4.00
❑ 134 Jose Reyes PROS RC	80.00	50.00
❑ 135 Greg Runser PROS RC	10.00	4.00
❑ 136 Bryan Hebson PROS RC	10.00	4.00
❑ 137 Sammy Serrano PROS RC	10.00	4.00
❑ 138 Kevin Joseph PROS RC	10.00	4.00
❑ 139 Juan Richardson PROS RC	10.00	4.00
❑ 140 Mark Fischer PROS RC	10.00	4.00

2002 Finest

Card		
❑ COMP.SET w/o SP's (100)	25.00	10.00
❑ COMMON CARD (1-100)	.50	.20
❑ COMMON CARD (101-110)	10.00	4.00
❑ 1 Mike Mussina	.75	.30
❑ 2 Steve Sparks	.50	.20
❑ 3 Randy Johnson	1.25	.50
❑ 4 Orlando Cabrera	.50	.20
❑ 5 Jeff Kent	.50	.20
❑ 6 Carlos Delgado	.50	.20
❑ 7 Ivan Rodriguez	.75	.30
❑ 8 Jose Cruz	.50	.20
❑ 9 Jason Giambi	.50	.20
❑ 10 Brad Penny	.50	.20
❑ 11 Moises Alou	.50	.20
❑ 12 Mike Piazza	2.00	.75
❑ 13 Ben Grieve	.50	.20
❑ 14 Derek Jeter	3.00	1.25
❑ 15 Roy Oswalt	.50	.20
❑ 16 Pat Burrell	.50	.20
❑ 17 Preston Wilson	.50	.20
❑ 18 Kevin Brown	.50	.20
❑ 19 Barry Bonds	3.00	1.25
❑ 20 Phil Nevin	.50	.20
❑ 21 Aramis Ramirez	.50	.20
❑ 22 Carlos Beltran	.50	.20
❑ 23 Chipper Jones	1.25	.50
❑ 24 Curt Schilling	.50	.20
❑ 25 Jorge Posada	.75	.30
❑ 26 Alfonso Soriano	.50	.20
❑ 27 Cliff Floyd	.50	.20
❑ 28 Rafael Palmeiro	.75	.30
❑ 29 Terrence Long	.50	.20
❑ 30 Ken Griffey Jr.	2.00	.75
❑ 31 Jason Kendall	.50	.20
❑ 32 Jose Vidro	.50	.20
❑ 33 Jermaine Dye	.50	.20
❑ 34 Bobby Higginson	.50	.20
❑ 35 Albert Pujols	2.50	1.00
❑ 36 Miguel Tejada	.50	.20
❑ 37 Jim Edmonds	.50	.20
❑ 38 Barry Zito	.50	.20
❑ 39 Jimmy Rollins	.50	.20
❑ 40 Rafael Furcal	.50	.20
❑ 41 Omar Vizquel	.75	.30
❑ 42 Kazuhiro Sasaki	.50	.20
❑ 43 Brian Giles	.50	.20
❑ 44 Darin Erstad	.50	.20
❑ 45 Mariano Rivera	1.25	.50
❑ 46 Troy Percival	.50	.20
❑ 47 Mike Sweeney	.50	.20
❑ 48 Vladimir Guerrero	1.25	.50
❑ 49 Troy Glaus	.50	.20
❑ 50 So Taguchi RC	2.50	1.00
❑ 51 Edgardo Alfonzo	.50	.20
❑ 52 Roger Clemens	2.50	1.00
❑ 53 Eric Chavez	.50	.20
❑ 54 Alex Rodriguez	2.00	.75
❑ 55 Cristian Guzman	.50	.20
❑ 56 Jeff Bagwell	.75	.30
❑ 57 Bernie Williams	.75	.30
❑ 58 Kerry Wood	.50	.20
❑ 59 Ryan Klesko	.50	.20
❑ 60 Ichiro Suzuki	2.50	1.00
❑ 61 Larry Walker	.50	.20
❑ 62 Nomar Garciaparra	2.00	.75
❑ 63 Craig Biggio	.75	.30
❑ 64 J.D. Drew	.50	.20
❑ 65 Juan Pierre	.50	.20
❑ 66 Roberto Alomar	.75	.30
❑ 67 Luis Gonzalez	.50	.20
❑ 68 Bud Smith	.50	.20
❑ 69 Magglio Ordonez	.50	.20
❑ 70 Scott Rolen	.75	.30
❑ 71 Tsuyoshi Shinjo	.50	.20
❑ 72 Paul Konerko	.50	.20
❑ 73 Garret Anderson	.50	.20
❑ 74 Tim Hudson	.50	.20
❑ 75 Adam Dunn	.50	.20
❑ 76 Gary Sheffield	.50	.20
❑ 77 Johnny Damon Sox	.75	.30
❑ 78 Todd Helton	.75	.30
❑ 79 Geoff Jenkins	.50	.20
❑ 80 Shawn Green	.50	.20
❑ 81 C.C. Sabathia	.50	.20
❑ 82 Kazuhisa Ishii RC	2.50	1.00
❑ 83 Rich Aurilia	.50	.20
❑ 84 Mike Hampton	.50	.20
❑ 85 Ben Sheets	.50	.20
❑ 86 Andruw Jones	.75	.30
❑ 87 Richie Sexson	.50	.20
❑ 88 Jim Thome	.75	.30
❑ 89 Sammy Sosa	1.25	.50
❑ 90 Greg Maddux	2.00	.75
❑ 91 Pedro Martinez	.75	.30
❑ 92 Jeromy Burnitz	.50	.20
❑ 93 Raul Mondesi	.50	.20
❑ 94 Bret Boone	.50	.20
❑ 95 Jerry Hairston	.50	.20
❑ 96 Mike Rivera	.50	.20
❑ 97 Juan Cruz	.50	.20
❑ 98 Morgan Ensberg	.50	.20
❑ 99 Nathan Haynes	.50	.20
❑ 100 Xavier Nady	.50	.20
❑ 101 Nic Jackson FY AU RC	10.00	4.00

❑ 102 Mauricio Lara FY AU RC 10.00 4.00
❑ 103 Freddy Sanchez FY AU RC 30.00 12.50
❑ 104 Clint Nageotte FY AU RC 10.00 4.00
❑ 105 Beltran Perez FY AU RC 10.00 4.00
❑ 106 Garrett Gentry FY AU RC 10.00 4.00
❑ 107 Chad Qualls FY AU RC 10.00 4.00
❑ 108 Jason Bay FY AU RC 40.00 15.00
❑ 109 Michael Hill FY AU RC 10.00 4.00
❑ 110 Brian Tallet FY AU RC 10.00 4.00

2003 Finest

❑ COMP.SET w/o SP's (100) 25.00 10.00
❑ COMMON CARD (1-100) .50 .20
❑ COMMON CARD (101-110) 15.00 6.00
❑ 1 Sammy Sosa 1.25 .50
❑ 2 Paul Konerko .50 .20
❑ 3 Todd Helton .75 .30
❑ 4 Mike Lowell .50 .20
❑ 5 Lance Berkman .50 .20
❑ 6 Kazuhisa Ishii .50 .20
❑ 7 A.J. Pierzynski .50 .20
❑ 8 Jose Vidro .50 .20
❑ 9 Roberto Alomar .75 .30
❑ 10 Derek Jeter 3.00 1.25
❑ 11 Barry Zito .50 .20
❑ 12 Jimmy Rollins .50 .20
❑ 13 Brian Giles .50 .20
❑ 14 Ryan Klesko .50 .20
❑ 15 Rich Aurilia .50 .20
❑ 16 Jim Edmonds .50 .20
❑ 17 Aubrey Huff .50 .20
❑ 18 Ivan Rodriguez .75 .30
❑ 19 Eric Hinske .50 .20
❑ 20 Barry Bonds 3.00 1.25
❑ 21 Darin Erstad .50 .20
❑ 22 Curt Schilling .50 .20
❑ 23 Andruw Jones .75 .30
❑ 24 Jay Gibbons .50 .20
❑ 25 Nomar Garciaparra 2.00 .75
❑ 26 Kerry Wood .50 .20
❑ 27 Magglio Ordonez .50 .20
❑ 28 Austin Kearns .50 .20
❑ 29 Jason Jennings .50 .20
❑ 30 Jason Giambi .50 .20
❑ 31 Tim Hudson .50 .20
❑ 32 Edgar Martinez .75 .30
❑ 33 Carl Crawford .50 .20
❑ 34 Hee Seop Choi .50 .20
❑ 35 Vladimir Guerrero 1.25 .50
❑ 36 Jeff Kent .50 .20
❑ 37 John Smoltz .75 .30
❑ 38 Frank Thomas 1.25 .50
❑ 39 Cliff Floyd .50 .20
❑ 40 Mike Piazza 2.00 .75
❑ 41 Mark Prior .75 .30
❑ 42 Tim Salmon .75 .30
❑ 43 Shawn Green .50 .20
❑ 44 Bernie Williams .75 .30
❑ 45 Jim Thome .75 .30
❑ 46 John Olerud .50 .20
❑ 47 Orlando Hudson .50 .20
❑ 48 Mark Teixeira .75 .30
❑ 49 Gary Sheffield .50 .20
❑ 50 Ichiro Suzuki 2.50 1.00
❑ 51 Tom Glavine .75 .30
❑ 52 Torii Hunter .50 .20
❑ 53 Craig Biggio .75 .30
❑ 54 Carlos Beltran .50 .20
❑ 55 Bartolo Colon .50 .20
❑ 56 Jorge Posada .75 .30
❑ 57 Pat Burrell .50 .20
❑ 58 Edgar Renteria .50 .20
❑ 59 Rafael Palmeiro .75 .30
❑ 60 Alfonso Soriano .50 .20
❑ 61 Brandon Phillips .50 .20
❑ 62 Luis Gonzalez .50 .20
❑ 63 Manny Ramirez .75 .30
❑ 64 Garret Anderson .50 .20
❑ 65 Ken Griffey Jr. 2.00 .75
❑ 66 A.J. Burnett .50 .20
❑ 67 Mike Sweeney .50 .20
❑ 68 Doug Mientkiewicz .50 .20
❑ 69 Eric Chavez .50 .20
❑ 70 Adam Dunn .50 .20
❑ 71 Shea Hillenbrand .50 .20
❑ 72 Troy Glaus .50 .20
❑ 73 Rodrigo Lopez .50 .20
❑ 74 Moises Alou .50 .20
❑ 75 Chipper Jones 1.25 .50
❑ 76 Bobby Abreu .50 .20
❑ 77 Mark Mulder .50 .20
❑ 78 Kevin Brown .50 .20
❑ 79 Josh Beckett .50 .20
❑ 80 Larry Walker .50 .20
❑ 81 Randy Johnson 1.25 .50
❑ 82 Greg Maddux 2.00 .75
❑ 83 Johnny Damon .75 .30
❑ 84 Omar Vizquel .75 .30
❑ 85 Jeff Bagwell .75 .30
❑ 86 Carlos Pena .50 .20
❑ 87 Roy Oswalt .50 .20
❑ 88 Richie Sexson .50 .20
❑ 89 Roger Clemens 2.50 1.00
❑ 90 Miguel Tejada .50 .20
❑ 91 Vicente Padilla .50 .20
❑ 92 Phil Nevin .50 .20
❑ 93 Edgardo Alfonzo .50 .20
❑ 94 Bret Boone .50 .20
❑ 95 Albert Pujols 2.50 1.00
❑ 96 Carlos Delgado .50 .20
❑ 97 Jose Contreras RC 2.00 .75
❑ 98 Scott Rolen .75 .30
❑ 99 Pedro Martinez .75 .30
❑ 100 Alex Rodriguez 2.00 .75
❑ 101 Adam LaRoche AU 15.00 6.00
❑ 102 Andy Marte AU RC 50.00 25.00
❑ 103 Daryl Clark AU RC 10.00 4.00
❑ 104 J.D. Durbin AU RC 10.00 4.00
❑ 105 Craig Brazell AU RC 10.00 4.00
❑ 106 Brian Burgamy AU RC 10.00 4.00
❑ 107 Tylor Johnson AU RC 10.00 4.00
❑ 108 Joey Gomes AU RC 10.00 4.00
❑ 109 Bryan Bullington AU RC 15.00 6.00
❑ 110 Byron Gettis AU RC 10.00 4.00

2004 Finest

❑ COMP.SET w/o SP's (100) 25.00 10.00
❑ COMMON CARD (1-100) .50 .20
❑ COMMON CARD (101-110) 8.00 3.00
❑ 101-110 STATED ODDS 1:7 MINI-BOXES
❑ COMMON CARD (111-122) 10.00 4.00
❑ 111-122 STATED ODDS 1:3 MINI-BOXES
❑ EXCHANGE DEADLINE 04/30/06
❑ CARD 112 EXCH UNABLE TO BE FULFILLED
❑ 04 WS HL B.THOMSON AU SENT INSTEAD
❑ 1 Juan Pierre .50 .20
❑ 2 Derek Jeter 2.50 1.00
❑ 3 Garret Anderson .50 .20
❑ 4 Javy Lopez .50 .20
❑ 5 Corey Patterson .50 .20
❑ 6 Todd Helton .75 .30
❑ 7 Roy Oswalt .50 .20
❑ 8 Shawn Green .50 .20
❑ 9 Vladimir Guerrero 1.25 .50
❑ 10 Jorge Posada .75 .30
❑ 11 Jason Kendall .50 .20
❑ 12 Scott Rolen .75 .30
❑ 13 Randy Johnson 1.25 .50
❑ 14 Bill Mueller .50 .20
❑ 15 Magglio Ordonez .50 .20
❑ 16 Larry Walker .50 .20
❑ 17 Lance Berkman .50 .20
❑ 18 Richie Sexson .50 .20
❑ 19 Orlando Cabrera .50 .20
❑ 20 Alfonso Soriano .50 .20
❑ 21 Kevin Millwood .50 .20
❑ 22 Edgar Martinez .75 .30
❑ 23 Aubrey Huff .50 .20
❑ 24 Carlos Delgado .50 .20
❑ 25 Vernon Wells .50 .20
❑ 26 Mark Teixeira .75 .30
❑ 27 Troy Glaus .50 .20
❑ 28 Jeff Kent .50 .20
❑ 29 Hideo Nomo 1.25 .50
❑ 30 Torii Hunter .50 .20
❑ 31 Hank Blalock .50 .20
❑ 32 Brandon Webb .50 .20
❑ 33 Tony Batista .50 .20
❑ 34 Bret Boone .50 .20
❑ 35 Ryan Klesko .50 .20
❑ 36 Barry Zito .50 .20
❑ 37 Edgar Renteria .50 .20
❑ 38 Geoff Jenkins .50 .20
❑ 39 Jeff Bagwell .75 .30
❑ 40 Dontrelle Willis .75 .30
❑ 41 Adam Dunn .50 .20
❑ 42 Mark Buehrle .50 .20
❑ 43 Esteban Loaiza .50 .20
❑ 44 Angel Berroa .50 .20
❑ 45 Ivan Rodriguez .75 .30
❑ 46 Jose Vidro .50 .20
❑ 47 Mark Mulder .50 .20
❑ 48 Roger Clemens 2.50 1.00
❑ 49 Jim Edmonds .50 .20
❑ 50 Eric Gagne .50 .20
❑ 51 Marcus Giles .50 .20
❑ 52 Curt Schilling .75 .30
❑ 53 Ken Griffey Jr. 2.00 .75
❑ 54 Jason Schmidt .50 .20
❑ 55 Miguel Tejada .50 .20
❑ 56 Dmitri Young .50 .20
❑ 57 Mike Lowell .50 .20
❑ 58 Mike Sweeney .50 .20
❑ 59 Scott Podsednik .50 .20
❑ 60 Miguel Cabrera .75 .30
❑ 61 Johan Santana 1.25 .50
❑ 62 Bernie Williams .75 .30
❑ 63 Eric Chavez .50 .20
❑ 64 Bobby Abreu .50 .20
❑ 65 Brian Giles .50 .20
❑ 66 Michael Young .50 .20
❑ 67 Paul Lo Duca .50 .20
❑ 68 Austin Kearns .50 .20
❑ 69 Jody Gerut .50 .20
❑ 70 Kerry Wood .50 .20
❑ 71 Luis Matos .50 .20
❑ 72 Greg Maddux 2.00 .75
❑ 73 Alex Rodriguez Yanks 2.00 .75
❑ 74 Mike Lieberthal .50 .20
❑ 75 Jim Thome .75 .30
❑ 76 Javier Vazquez .50 .20
❑ 77 Bartolo Colon .50 .20
❑ 78 Manny Ramirez .75 .30
❑ 79 Jacque Jones .50 .20
❑ 80 Johnny Damon .75 .30
❑ 81 Carlos Beltran .50 .20
❑ 82 C.C. Sabathia .50 .20
❑ 83 Preston Wilson .50 .20
❑ 84 Luis Castillo .50 .20
❑ 85 Kevin Brown .50 .20
❑ 86 Shannon Stewart .50 .20
❑ 87 Cliff Floyd .50 .20

❑ 88 Mike Mussina .75 .30
❑ 89 Rafael Furcal .50 .20
❑ 90 Roy Halladay .50 .20
❑ 91 Frank Thomas 1.25 .50
❑ 92 Melvin Mora .50 .20
❑ 93 Andruw Jones .75 .30
❑ 94 Luis Gonzalez .50 .20
❑ 95 David Ortiz 1.25 .50
❑ 96 Gary Sheffield .50 .20
❑ 97 Tim Hudson .50 .20
❑ 98 Phil Nevin .50 .20
❑ 99 Ichiro Suzuki 2.50 1.00
❑ 100 Albert Pujols 2.50 1.00
❑ 101 Nomar Garciaparra SR Jsy 15.00 6.00
❑ 102 Sammy Sosa SR Jsy 10.00 4.00
❑ 103 Josh Beckett SR Jsy 8.00 3.00
❑ 104 Jason Giambi SR Jsy 8.00 3.00
❑ 105 Rocco Baldelli SR Jsy 8.00 3.00
❑ 106 Jose Reyes SR Jsy 8.00 3.00
❑ 107 Chipper Jones SR Jsy 10.00 4.00
❑ 108 Pedro Martinez SR Jsy 10.00 4.00
❑ 109 Mike Piazza SR Jsy 15.00 6.00
❑ 110 Mark Prior SR Jsy 10.00 4.00
❑ 111 Craig Ansman AU RC 10.00 4.00
❑ 113 David Murphy AU RC 10.00 4.00
❑ 114 Jason Hirsh AU RC 25.00 10.00
❑ 115 Matt Moses AU RC 15.00 6.00
❑ 116 Estee Harris AU RC 15.00 6.00
❑ 117 Logan Kensing AU RC 10.00 4.00
❑ 118 L.Milledge AU RC 50.00 20.00
❑ 119 Merkin Valdez AU RC 10.00 4.00
❑ 120 Travis Blackley AU RC 10.00 4.00
❑ 121 Vito Chiaravalloti AU RC 10.00 4.00
❑ 122 Dioner Navarro AU RC 10.00 4.00

2005 Finest

❑ COMP.SET w/o SP's (150) 80.00 40.00
❑ COMMON CARD (1-140) .50 .20
❑ COMMON CARD (157-166) 1.00 .40
❑ AU p/r 970 ODDS 1:3 MINI BOXES
❑ AU p/r 970 PRINT RUN 970 #'d SETS
❑ AU p/r 375 ODDS 1:41 MINI BOXES
❑ AU p/r 375 PRINT RUN 375 #'d SETS
❑ OVERALL PLATE ODDS 1:51 MINI BOX
❑ OVERALL AU PLATE ODDS 1:478 MINI BOX
❑ PLATE PRINT RUN 1 SET PER COLOR
❑ BLACK-CYAN-MAGENTA-YELLOW ISSUED
❑ NO PLATE PRICING DUE TO SCARCITY
❑ 1 Alexis Rios .50 .20
❑ 2 Hank Blalock .50 .20
❑ 3 Bobby Abreu .50 .20
❑ 4 Curt Schilling .75 .30
❑ 5 Albert Pujols 2.50 1.00
❑ 6 Aaron Rowand .50 .20
❑ 7 B.J. Upton .50 .20
❑ 8 Andruw Jones .75 .30
❑ 9 Jeff Francis .50 .20
❑ 10 Sammy Sosa 1.25 .50
❑ 11 Aramis Ramirez .50 .20
❑ 12 Carl Pavano .50 .20
❑ 13 Bartolo Colon .50 .20
❑ 14 Greg Maddux 2.00 .75
❑ 15 Scott Kazmir .50 .20
❑ 16 Melvin Mora .50 .20
❑ 17 Brandon Backe .50 .20
❑ 18 Bobby Crosby .50 .20
❑ 19 Carlos Lee .50 .20
❑ 20 Carl Crawford .50 .20
❑ 21 Brian Giles .50 .20
❑ 22 Jeff Bagwell .75 .30
❑ 23 J.D. Drew .50 .20
❑ 24 C.C. Sabathia .50 .20
❑ 25 Alfonso Soriano .50 .20
❑ 26 Chipper Jones 1.25 .50
❑ 27 Austin Kearns .50 .20
❑ 28 Carlos Delgado .50 .20
❑ 29 Jack Wilson .50 .20
❑ 30 Dmitri Young .50 .20
❑ 31 Carlos Guillen .50 .20
❑ 32 Jim Thome .75 .30
❑ 33 Eric Chavez .50 .20
❑ 34 Jason Schmidt .50 .20
❑ 35 Brad Radke .50 .20
❑ 36 Frank Thomas 1.25 .50
❑ 37 Darin Erstad .50 .20
❑ 38 Javier Vazquez .50 .20
❑ 39 Garret Anderson .50 .20
❑ 40 David Ortiz 1.25 .50
❑ 41 Javy Lopez .50 .20
❑ 42 Geoff Jenkins .50 .20
❑ 43 Jose Vidro .50 .20
❑ 44 Aubrey Huff .50 .20
❑ 45 Bernie Williams .75 .30
❑ 46 Dontrelle Willis .50 .20
❑ 47 Jim Edmonds .50 .20
❑ 48 Ivan Rodriguez .75 .30
❑ 49 Gary Sheffield .50 .20
❑ 50 Alex Rodriguez 2.00 .75
❑ 51 John Buck .50 .20
❑ 52 Andy Pettitte .75 .30
❑ 53 Ichiro Suzuki 2.50 1.00
❑ 54 Johnny Estrada .50 .20
❑ 55 Jake Peavy .50 .20
❑ 56 Carlos Zambrano .50 .20
❑ 57 Jose Reyes .50 .20
❑ 58 Bret Boone .50 .20
❑ 59 Jason Bay .50 .20
❑ 60 David Wright 2.00 .75
❑ 61 Jeromy Burnitz .50 .20
❑ 62 Corey Patterson .50 .20
❑ 63 Juan Pierre .50 .20
❑ 64 Zack Greinke .50 .20
❑ 65 Mike Lowell .50 .20
❑ 66 Ken Griffey Jr. 2.00 .75
❑ 67 Marcus Giles .50 .20
❑ 68 Edgar Renteria .50 .20
❑ 69 Ken Harvey .50 .20
❑ 70 Pedro Martinez .75 .30
❑ 71 Johnny Damon .75 .30
❑ 72 Lyle Overbay .50 .20
❑ 73 Mike Maroth .50 .20
❑ 74 Jorge Posada .75 .30
❑ 75 Carlos Beltran .50 .20
❑ 76 Mark Buehrle .50 .20
❑ 77 Khalil Greene .75 .30
❑ 78 Josh Beckett .50 .20
❑ 79 Mark Loretta .50 .20
❑ 80 Rafael Palmeiro .75 .30
❑ 81 Justin Morneau .50 .20
❑ 82 Rocco Baldelli .50 .20
❑ 83 Ben Sheets .50 .20
❑ 84 Kerry Wood .50 .20
❑ 85 Miguel Tejada .50 .20
❑ 86 Magglio Ordonez .50 .20
❑ 87 Livan Hernandez .50 .20
❑ 88 Kazuo Matsui .50 .20
❑ 89 Manny Ramirez .75 .30
❑ 90 Hideki Matsui 2.00 .75
❑ 91 Jeff Kent .50 .20
❑ 92 Matt Lawton .50 .20
❑ 93 Richie Sexson .50 .20
❑ 94 Mike Mussina .75 .30
❑ 95 Adam Dunn .50 .20
❑ 96 Johan Santana 1.25 .50
❑ 97 Nomar Garciaparra 1.25 .50
❑ 98 Michael Young .50 .20
❑ 99 Victor Martinez .50 .20
❑ 100 Barry Bonds 3.00 1.25
❑ 101 Oliver Perez .50 .20
❑ 102 Randy Johnson 1.25 .50
❑ 103 Mark Mulder .50 .20
❑ 104 Pat Burrell .50 .20
❑ 105 Mike Sweeney .50 .20
❑ 106 Mark Teixeira .75 .30
❑ 107 Paul Lo Duca .50 .20
❑ 108 Jon Lieber .50 .20
❑ 109 Mike Piazza 1.25 .50
❑ 110 Roger Clemens 2.00 .75
❑ 111 Rafael Furcal .50 .20
❑ 112 Troy Glaus .50 .20
❑ 113 Miguel Cabrera .75 .30
❑ 114 Randy Wolf .50 .20
❑ 115 Lance Berkman .50 .20
❑ 116 Mark Prior .75 .30
❑ 117 Rich Harden .50 .20
❑ 118 Preston Wilson .50 .20
❑ 119 Roy Oswalt .50 .20
❑ 120 Luis Gonzalez .50 .20
❑ 121 Ronnie Belliard .50 .20
❑ 122 Sean Casey .50 .20
❑ 123 Barry Zito .50 .20
❑ 124 Larry Walker .75 .30
❑ 125 Derek Jeter 2.50 1.00
❑ 126 Tim Hudson .50 .20
❑ 127 Tom Glavine .75 .30
❑ 128 Scott Rolen .75 .30
❑ 129 Torii Hunter .50 .20
❑ 130 Paul Konerko .50 .20
❑ 131 Shawn Green .50 .20
❑ 132 Travis Hafner .50 .20
❑ 133 Vernon Wells .50 .20
❑ 134 Sidney Ponson .50 .20
❑ 135 Vladimir Guerrero 1.25 .50
❑ 136 Mark Kotsay .50 .20
❑ 137 Todd Helton .75 .30
❑ 138 Adrian Beltre .50 .20
❑ 139 Wily Mo Pena .50 .20
❑ 140 Joe Mauer 1.25 .50
❑ 141 Brian Stavisky AU/970 RC 10.00 4.00
❑ 142 Nate McLouth AU/970 RC 15.00 6.00
❑ 143 Glen Perkins AU/375 RC 20.00 8.00
❑ 144 Chip Cannon AU/970 RC 20.00 8.00
❑ 145 Shane Costa AU/970 RC 10.00 4.00
❑ 146 W.Swackhamer AU/970 RC 10.00 4.00
❑ 147 Kevin Melillo AU/970 RC 15.00 6.00
❑ 148 Billy Butler AU/970 RC 50.00 25.00
❑ 149 Landon Powell AU/970 RC 15.00 6.00
❑ 150 Scott Mathieson AU/970 RC 10.00 4.00
❑ 151 Chris Roberson AU/970 10.00 4.00
❑ 152 Chad Orvella AU/375 RC 15.00 6.00
❑ 153 Eric Nielsen AU/970 RC 10.00 4.00
❑ 154 Matt Campbell AU/970 RC 10.00 4.00
❑ 155 Mike Rogers AU/970 RC 10.00 4.00
❑ 156 Melky Cabrera AU/970 RC 40.00 20.00
❑ 157 Nolan Ryan RET 5.00 2.00
❑ 158 Bo Jackson RET 2.00 .75
❑ 159 Wade Boggs RET 1.50 .60
❑ 160 Andre Dawson RET 1.00 .40
❑ 161 Dave Winfield RET 1.00 .40
❑ 162 Reggie Jackson RET 1.50 .60
❑ 163 David Justice RET 2.00 .75
❑ 164 Dale Murphy RET 1.50 .60
❑ 165 Paul O'Neill RET 1.50 .60
❑ 166 Tom Seaver RET 1.50 .60

2006 Finest

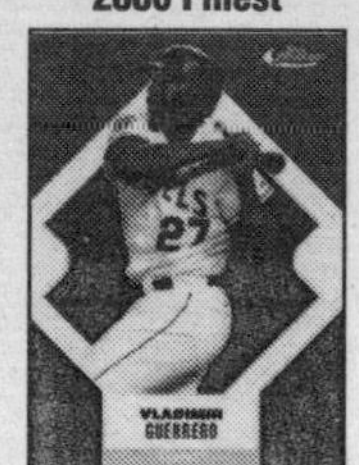

❑ COMPLETE SET (155)
❑ COMP.SET w/o AU's (140) 60.00 30.00
❑ COMMON CARD (1-131) .50 .20
❑ UNLISTED STARS 1-131 1.25 .50
❑ COMMON ROOKIE (132-140) .75 .30
❑ COMMON AUTO (141-155) 10.00 4.00

❑ 141-155 AU ODDS 1:4 MINI BOX
❑ 141-155 AU PRINT RUN 963 SETS
❑ 141-155 AU's NOT SERIAL NUMBERED
❑ PRINT RUN INFO PROVIDED BY TOPPS
❑ 1-140 PLATES RANDOM INSERTS IN PACKS
❑ AU 141-155 PLATE ODDS 1:792 MINI BOX
❑ PLATE PRINT RUN 1 SET PER COLOR
❑ BLACK-CYAN-MAGENTA-YELLOW ISSUED
❑ NO PLATE PRICING DUE TO SCARCITY
❑ 1 Vladimir Guerrero 1.25 .50
❑ 2 Troy Glaus .60 .25
❑ 3 Andruw Jones 1.00 .40
❑ 4 Miguel Tejada .50 .20
❑ 5 Manny Ramirez .75 .30
❑ 6 Curt Schilling .75 .30
❑ 7 Mark Prior .75 .30
❑ 8 Kerry Wood .50 .20
❑ 9 Tadahito Iguchi .50 .20
❑ 10 Freddy Garcia .50 .20
❑ 11 Ryan Howard 2.00 .75
❑ 12 Mark Buehrle .50 .20
❑ 13 Wily Mo Pena .50 .20
❑ 14 C.C. Sabathia .50 .20
❑ 15 Garret Anderson .50 .20
❑ 16 Shawn Green .50 .20
❑ 17 Rafael Furcal .50 .20
❑ 18 Jeff Francoeur 1.25 .50
❑ 19 Ken Griffey Jr. 2.00 .75
❑ 20 Derrek Lee .50 .20
❑ 21 Paul Konerko .50 .20
❑ 22 Rickie Weeks .50 .20
❑ 23 Magglio Ordonez .50 .20
❑ 24 Juan Pierre .50 .20
❑ 25 Felix Hernandez .75 .30
❑ 26 Roger Clemens 2.50 1.00
❑ 27 Zack Greinke .50 .20
❑ 28 Johan Santana .75 .30
❑ 29 Jose Reyes .50 .20
❑ 30 Bobby Crosby .50 .20
❑ 31 Jason Schmidt .50 .20
❑ 32 Khalil Greene .75 .30
❑ 33 Richie Sexson .50 .20
❑ 34 Mark Mulder .50 .20
❑ 35 Mark Teixeira .75 .30
❑ 36 Nick Johnson .50 .20
❑ 37 Vernon Wells .50 .20
❑ 38 Scott Kazmir .75 .30
❑ 39 Jim Edmonds .75 .30
❑ 40 Adrian Beltre .50 .20
❑ 41 Dan Johnson .50 .20
❑ 42 Carlos Lee .50 .20
❑ 43 Lance Berkman .50 .20
❑ 44 Josh Beckett .50 .20
❑ 45 Morgan Ensberg .50 .20
❑ 46 Garrett Atkins .50 .20
❑ 47 Chase Utley 1.25 .50
❑ 48 Joe Mauer .75 .30
❑ 49 Travis Hafner .50 .20
❑ 50 Alex Rodriguez 2.00 .75
❑ 51 Austin Kearns .50 .20
❑ 52 Scott Podsednik .50 .20
❑ 53 Jose Contreras .50 .20
❑ 54 Greg Maddux 2.00 .75
❑ 55 Hideki Matsui 2.00 .75
❑ 56 Matt Clement .50 .20
❑ 57 Javy Lopez .50 .20
❑ 58 Tim Hudson .50 .20
❑ 59 Luis Gonzalez .50 .20
❑ 60 Bartolo Colon .50 .20
❑ 61 Marcus Giles .50 .20
❑ 62 Justin Morneau .50 .20
❑ 63 Nomar Garciaparra 1.25 .50
❑ 64 Robinson Cano .75 .30
❑ 65 Ervin Santana .50 .20
❑ 66 Brady Clark .50 .20
❑ 67 Edgar Renteria .50 .20
❑ 68 Jon Garland .50 .20
❑ 69 Felipe Lopez .50 .20
❑ 70 Ivan Rodriguez .75 .30
❑ 71 Dontrelle Willis .50 .20
❑ 72 Carlos Guillen .50 .20
❑ 73 J.D. Drew .50 .20
❑ 74 Rich Harden .50 .20
❑ 75 Albert Pujols 2.50 1.00
❑ 76 Livan Hernandez .50 .20
❑ 77 Roy Halladay .50 .20
❑ 78 Hank Blalock .50 .20
❑ 79 David Wright 2.00 .75
❑ 80 Jimmy Rollins .50 .20
❑ 81 John Smoltz .75 .30
❑ 82 Miguel Cabrera .75 .30
❑ 83 David DeJesus .50 .20
❑ 83 Zach Duke .50 .20
❑ 84 Torii Hunter .50 .20
❑ 85 Adam Dunn .50 .20
❑ 86 Randy Johnson 1.25 .50
❑ 87 Roy Oswalt .50 .20
❑ 88 Bobby Abreu .50 .20
❑ 89 Rocco Baldelli .50 .20
❑ 90 Ichiro Suzuki 2.00 .75
❑ 91 Jorge Cantu .50 .20
❑ 92 Jack Wilson .50 .20
❑ 93 Jose Vidro .50 .20
❑ 94 Kevin Millwood .50 .20
❑ 95 David Ortiz 1.25 .50
❑ 96 Victor Martinez .50 .20
❑ 97 Jeremy Bonderman .50 .20
❑ 98 Todd Helton .75 .30
❑ 99 Carlos Beltran .50 .20
❑ 100 Barry Bonds 3.00 1.25
❑ 101 Jeff Kent .50 .20
❑ 102 Mike Sweeney .50 .20
❑ 103 Ben Sheets .50 .20
❑ 104 Melvin Mora .50 .20
❑ 105 Gary Sheffield .50 .20
❑ 106 Craig Wilson .50 .20
❑ 107 Chris Carpenter .50 .20
❑ 108 Michael Young .50 .20
❑ 109 Gustavo Chacin .50 .20
❑ 110 Chipper Jones 1.25 .50
❑ 111 Mark Loretta .50 .20
❑ 112 Andy Pettitte .50 .20
❑ 113 Carlos Delgado .50 .20
❑ 114 Pat Burrell .50 .20
❑ 115 Jason Bay .50 .20
❑ 116 Brian Roberts .50 .20
❑ 117 Joe Crede .50 .20
❑ 118 Jake Peavy .50 .20
❑ 119 Aubrey Huff .50 .20
❑ 120 Pedro Martinez .75 .30
❑ 121 Jorge Posada .75 .30
❑ 122 Barry Zito .50 .20
❑ 123 Scott Rolen .75 .30
❑ 124 Brett Myers .50 .20
❑ 125 Derek Jeter 3.00 1.25
❑ 126 Eric Chavez .50 .20
❑ 127 Carl Crawford .50 .20
❑ 128 Jim Thome .75 .30
❑ 129 Johnny Damon .75 .30
❑ 130 Alfonso Soriano .50 .20
❑ 131 Clint Barmes .50 .20
❑ 132 Dustin Nippert (RC) .75 .30
❑ 133 Hanley Ramirez (RC) 2.00 .75
❑ 134 Matt Capps (RC) .75 .30
❑ 135 Miguel Perez (RC) .75 .30
❑ 136 Tom Gorzelanny (RC) .75 .30
❑ 137 Charlton Jimerson (RC) .75 .30
❑ 138 Bryan Bullington (RC) .75 .30
❑ 139 Kenji Johjima RC 4.00 1.50
❑ 140 Craig Hansen RC 3.00 1.25
❑ 141 Craig Breslow AU/963 RC * 10.00 4.00
❑ 142 A.Wainwright AU/963 (RC) * 15.00 6.00
❑ 143 Joey Devine AU/963 RC * 10.00 4.00
❑ 144 H.Kuo AU/963 (RC) * 50.00 20.00
❑ 145 Jason Botts AU/963 (RC) * 10.00 4.00
❑ 146 J.Johnson AU/963 (RC) * 20.00 8.00
❑ 147 J.Bergmann AU/963 RC * 10.00 4.00
❑ 148 Scott Olsen AU/963 (RC) * 15.00 6.00
❑ 149 D.Hasner AU/963 (RC) * 10.00 4.00
❑ 150 Dan Ortmeier AU/963 (RC) * 10.00 4.00
❑ 151 Chuck James AU/963 (RC) * 15.00 6.00
❑ 152 Ryan Garko AU/963 (RC) * 10.00 4.00
❑ 153 Nelson Cruz AU/963 (RC) * 10.00 4.00
❑ 154 A.Lerew AU/963 (RC) * 10.00 4.00
❑ 155 F.Liriano AU/963 (RC) * 50.00 20.00

1994 Flair

❑ COMPLETE SET (450) 80.00 35.00
❑ COMPLETE SERIES 1 (250) 20.00 10.00
❑ COMPLETE SERIES 2 (200) 60.00 25.00
❑ 1 Harold Baines .50 .20
❑ 2 Jeffrey Hammonds .25 .08

❑ 3 Chris Hoiles .25 .08
❑ 4 Ben McDonald .25 .08
❑ 5 Mark McLemore .25 .08
❑ 6 Jamie Moyer .50 .20
❑ 7 Jim Poole .25 .08
❑ 8 Cal Ripken 4.00 1.50
❑ 9 Chris Sabo .25 .08
❑ 10 Scott Bankhead .25 .08
❑ 11 Scott Cooper .25 .08
❑ 12 Danny Darwin .25 .08
❑ 13 Andre Dawson .50 .20
❑ 14 Billy Hatcher .25 .08
❑ 15 Aaron Sele .25 .08
❑ 16 John Valentin .25 .08
❑ 17 Dave Valle .25 .08
❑ 18 Mo Vaughn .50 .20
❑ 19 Brian Anderson RC .50 .20
❑ 20 Gary DiSarcina .25 .08
❑ 21 Jim Edmonds 1.25 .50
❑ 22 Chuck Finley .50 .20
❑ 23 Bo Jackson 1.25 .50
❑ 24 Mark Leiter .25 .08
❑ 25 Greg Myers .25 .08
❑ 26 Eduardo Perez .25 .08
❑ 27 Tim Salmon .75 .30
❑ 28 Wilson Alvarez .25 .08
❑ 29 Jason Bere .25 .08
❑ 30 Alex Fernandez .25 .08
❑ 31 Ozzie Guillen .50 .20
❑ 32 Joe Hall RC .25 .08
❑ 33 Darrin Jackson .25 .08
❑ 34 Kirk McCaskill .25 .08
❑ 35 Tim Raines .50 .20
❑ 36 Frank Thomas 1.25 .50
❑ 37 Carlos Baerga .25 .08
❑ 38 Albert Belle .50 .20
❑ 39 Mark Clark .25 .08
❑ 40 Wayne Kirby .25 .08
❑ 41 Dennis Martinez .50 .20
❑ 42 Charles Nagy .25 .08
❑ 43 Manny Ramirez 1.25 .50
❑ 44 Paul Sorrento .25 .08
❑ 45 Jim Thome .75 .30
❑ 46 Eric Davis .50 .20
❑ 47 John Doherty .25 .08
❑ 48 Junior Felix .25 .08
❑ 49 Cecil Fielder .50 .20
❑ 50 Kirk Gibson .50 .20
❑ 51 Mike Moore .25 .08
❑ 52 Tony Phillips .25 .08
❑ 53 Alan Trammell .50 .20
❑ 54 Kevin Appier .50 .20
❑ 55 Stan Belinda .25 .08
❑ 56 Vince Coleman .25 .08
❑ 57 Greg Gagne .25 .08
❑ 58 Bob Hamelin .25 .08
❑ 59 Dave Henderson .25 .08
❑ 60 Wally Joyner .50 .20
❑ 61 Mike Macfarlane .25 .08
❑ 62 Jeff Montgomery .25 .08
❑ 63 Ricky Bones .25 .08
❑ 64 Jeff Bronkey .25 .08
❑ 65 Alex Diaz RC .25 .08
❑ 66 Cal Eldred .25 .08
❑ 67 Darryl Hamilton .25 .08
❑ 68 John Jaha .25 .08
❑ 69 Mark Kiefer .25 .08
❑ 70 Kevin Seitzer .25 .08

❑ 71 Turner Ward .25 .08
❑ 72 Rich Becker .25 .08
❑ 73 Scott Erickson .25 .08
❑ 74 Keith Garagozzo RC .25 .08
❑ 75 Kent Hrbek .50 .20
❑ 76 Scott Leius .25 .08
❑ 77 Kirby Puckett 1.25 .50
❑ 78 Matt Walbeck .25 .08
❑ 79 Dave Winfield .50 .20
❑ 80 Mike Gallego .25 .08
❑ 81 Xavier Hernandez .25 .08
❑ 82 Jimmy Key .50 .20
❑ 83 Jim Leyritz .25 .08
❑ 84 Don Mattingly 3.00 1.25
❑ 85 Matt Nokes .25 .08
❑ 86 Paul O'Neill .75 .30
❑ 87 Melido Perez .25 .08
❑ 88 Danny Tartabull .25 .08
❑ 89 Mike Bordick .25 .08
❑ 90 Ron Darling .25 .08
❑ 91 Dennis Eckersley .50 .20
❑ 92 Stan Javier .25 .08
❑ 93 Steve Karsay .25 .08
❑ 94 Mark McGwire 3.00 1.25
❑ 95 Troy Neel .25 .08
❑ 96 Terry Steinbach .25 .08
❑ 97 Bill Taylor RC .50 .20
❑ 98 Eric Anthony .25 .08
❑ 99 Chris Bosio .25 .08
❑ 100 Tim Davis .25 .08
❑ 101 Felix Fermin .25 .08
❑ 102 Dave Fleming .25 .08
❑ 103 Ken Griffey Jr. 2.00 .75
❑ 104 Greg Hibbard .25 .08
❑ 105 Reggie Jefferson .25 .08
❑ 106 Tino Martinez .75 .30
❑ 107 Jack Armstrong .25 .08
❑ 108 Will Clark .75 .30
❑ 109 Juan Gonzalez .50 .20
❑ 110 Rick Helling .25 .08
❑ 111 Tom Henke .25 .08
❑ 112 David Hulse .25 .08
❑ 113 Manuel Lee .25 .08
❑ 114 Doug Strange .25 .08
❑ 115 Roberto Alomar .75 .30
❑ 116 Joe Carter .50 .20
❑ 117 Carlos Delgado .75 .30
❑ 118 Pat Hentgen .25 .08
❑ 119 Paul Molitor .50 .20
❑ 120 John Olerud .50 .20
❑ 121 Dave Stewart .50 .20
❑ 122 Todd Stottlemyre .25 .08
❑ 123 Mike Timlin .25 .08
❑ 124 Jeff Blauser .25 .08
❑ 125 Tom Glavine .75 .30
❑ 126 David Justice .50 .20
❑ 127 Mike Kelly .25 .08
❑ 128 Ryan Klesko .50 .20
❑ 129 Javier Lopez .50 .20
❑ 130 Greg Maddux 2.00 .75
❑ 131 Fred McGriff .75 .30
❑ 132 Kent Mercker .25 .08
❑ 133 Mark Wohlers .25 .08
❑ 134 Willie Banks .25 .08
❑ 135 Steve Buechele .25 .08
❑ 136 Shawon Dunston .25 .08
❑ 137 Jose Guzman .25 .08
❑ 138 Glenallen Hill .25 .08
❑ 139 Randy Myers .25 .08
❑ 140 Karl Rhodes .25 .08
❑ 141 Ryne Sandberg 2.00 .75
❑ 142 Steve Trachsel .25 .08
❑ 143 Bret Boone .50 .20
❑ 144 Tom Browning .25 .08
❑ 145 Hector Carrasco .25 .08
❑ 146 Barry Larkin .75 .30
❑ 147 Hal Morris .25 .08
❑ 148 Jose Rijo .25 .08
❑ 149 Reggie Sanders .50 .20
❑ 150 John Smiley .25 .08
❑ 151 Dante Bichette .50 .20
❑ 152 Ellis Burks .50 .20
❑ 153 Joe Girardi .25 .08
❑ 154 Mike Harkey .25 .08
❑ 155 Roberto Mejia .25 .08
❑ 156 Marcus Moore .25 .08
❑ 157 Armando Reynoso .25 .08
❑ 158 Bruce Ruffin .25 .08
❑ 159 Eric Young .25 .08
❑ 160 Kurt Abbott RC .25 .08
❑ 161 Jeff Conine .50 .20
❑ 162 Orestes Destrade .25 .08
❑ 163 Chris Hammond .25 .08
❑ 164 Bryan Harvey .25 .08
❑ 165 Dave Magadan .25 .08
❑ 166 Gary Sheffield .50 .20
❑ 167 David Weathers .25 .08
❑ 168 Andujar Cedeno .25 .08
❑ 169 Tom Edens .25 .08
❑ 170 Luis Gonzalez .50 .20
❑ 171 Pete Harnisch .25 .08
❑ 172 Todd Jones .25 .08
❑ 173 Darryl Kile .50 .20
❑ 174 James Mouton .25 .08
❑ 175 Scott Servais .25 .08
❑ 176 Mitch Williams .25 .08
❑ 177 Pedro Astacio .25 .08
❑ 178 Orel Hershiser .50 .20
❑ 179 Raul Mondesi .50 .20
❑ 180 Jose Offerman .25 .08
❑ 181 Chan Ho Park RC .75 .30
❑ 182 Mike Piazza 2.50 1.00
❑ 183 Cory Snyder .25 .08
❑ 184 Tim Wallach .25 .08
❑ 185 Todd Worrell .25 .08
❑ 186 Sean Berry .25 .08
❑ 187 Wil Cordero .25 .08
❑ 188 Darrin Fletcher .25 .08
❑ 189 Cliff Floyd .50 .20
❑ 190 Marquis Grissom .50 .20
❑ 191 Rod Henderson .25 .08
❑ 192 Ken Hill .25 .08
❑ 193 Pedro Martinez 1.25 .50
❑ 194 Kirk Rueter .25 .08
❑ 195 Jeromy Burnitz .50 .20
❑ 196 John Franco .50 .20
❑ 197 Dwight Gooden .50 .20
❑ 198 Todd Hundley .25 .08
❑ 199 Bobby Jones .25 .08
❑ 200 Jeff Kent .75 .30
❑ 201 Mike Maddux .25 .08
❑ 202 Ryan Thompson .25 .08
❑ 203 Jose Vizcaino .25 .08
❑ 204 Darren Daulton .50 .20
❑ 205 Lenny Dykstra .50 .20
❑ 206 Jim Eisenreich .25 .08
❑ 207 Dave Hollins .25 .08
❑ 208 Danny Jackson .25 .08
❑ 209 Doug Jones .25 .08
❑ 210 Jeff Juden .25 .08
❑ 211 Ben Rivera .25 .08
❑ 212 Kevin Stocker .25 .08
❑ 213 Milt Thompson .25 .08
❑ 214 Jay Bell .50 .20
❑ 215 Steve Cooke .25 .08
❑ 216 Mark Dewey .25 .08
❑ 217 Al Martin .25 .08
❑ 218 Orlando Merced .25 .08
❑ 219 Don Slaught .25 .08
❑ 220 Zane Smith .25 .08
❑ 221 Rick White RC .25 .08
❑ 222 Kevin Young .25 .08
❑ 223 Rene Arocha .25 .08
❑ 224 Rheal Cormier .25 .08
❑ 225 Brian Jordan .50 .20
❑ 226 Ray Lankford .50 .20
❑ 227 Mike Perez .25 .08
❑ 228 Ozzie Smith 2.00 .75
❑ 229 Mark Whiten .25 .08
❑ 230 Todd Zeile .25 .08
❑ 231 Derek Bell .25 .08
❑ 232 Archi Cianfrocco .25 .08
❑ 233 Ricky Gutierrez .25 .08
❑ 234 Trevor Hoffman .75 .30
❑ 235 Phil Plantier .25 .08
❑ 236 Dave Staton .25 .08
❑ 237 Wally Whitehurst .25 .08
❑ 238 Todd Benzinger .25 .08
❑ 239 Barry Bonds 3.00 1.25
❑ 240 John Burkett .25 .08
❑ 241 Royce Clayton .25 .08
❑ 242 Bryan Hickerson .25 .08
❑ 243 Mike Jackson .25 .08
❑ 244 Darren Lewis .25 .08
❑ 245 Kirt Manwaring .25 .08
❑ 246 Mark Portugal .25 .08
❑ 247 Salomon Torres .25 .08
❑ 248 Checklist .25 .08
❑ 249 Checklist .25 .08
❑ 250 Checklist .25 .08
❑ 251 Brady Anderson .50 .20
❑ 252 Mike Devereaux .25 .08
❑ 253 Sid Fernandez .25 .08
❑ 254 Leo Gomez .25 .08
❑ 255 Mike Mussina .75 .30
❑ 256 Mike Oquist .25 .08
❑ 257 Rafael Palmeiro .75 .30
❑ 258 Lee Smith .50 .20
❑ 259 Damon Berryhill .25 .08
❑ 260 Wes Chamberlain .25 .08
❑ 261 Roger Clemens 2.50 1.00
❑ 262 Gar Finnvold RC .25 .08
❑ 263 Mike Greenwell .25 .08
❑ 264 Tim Naehring .25 .08
❑ 265 Otis Nixon .25 .08
❑ 266 Ken Ryan .25 .08
❑ 267 Chad Curtis .25 .08
❑ 268 Chili Davis .50 .20
❑ 269 Damion Easley .25 .08
❑ 270 Jorge Fabregas .25 .08
❑ 271 Mark Langston .25 .08
❑ 272 Phil Leftwich RC .25 .08
❑ 273 Harold Reynolds .50 .20
❑ 274 J.T. Snow .50 .20
❑ 275 Joey Cora .25 .08
❑ 276 Julio Franco .50 .20
❑ 277 Roberto Hernandez .25 .08
❑ 278 Lance Johnson .25 .08
❑ 279 Ron Karkovice .25 .08
❑ 280 Jack McDowell .25 .08
❑ 281 Robin Ventura .50 .20
❑ 282 Sandy Alomar Jr. .25 .08
❑ 283 Kenny Lofton .50 .20
❑ 284 Jose Mesa .25 .08
❑ 285 Jack Morris .50 .20
❑ 286 Eddie Murray 1.25 .50
❑ 287 Chad Ogea .25 .08
❑ 288 Eric Plunk .25 .08
❑ 289 Paul Shuey .25 .08
❑ 290 Omar Vizquel .75 .30
❑ 291 Danny Bautista .25 .08
❑ 292 Travis Fryman .50 .20
❑ 293 Greg Gohr .25 .08
❑ 294 Chris Gomez .25 .08
❑ 295 Mickey Tettleton .25 .08
❑ 296 Lou Whitaker .50 .20
❑ 297 David Cone .50 .20
❑ 298 Gary Gaetti .50 .20
❑ 299 Tom Gordon .25 .08
❑ 300 Felix Jose .25 .08
❑ 301 Jose Lind .25 .08
❑ 302 Brian McRae .25 .08
❑ 303 Mike Fetters .25 .08
❑ 304 Brian Harper .25 .08
❑ 305 Pat Listach .25 .08
❑ 306 Matt Mieske .25 .08
❑ 307 Dave Nilsson .25 .08
❑ 308 Jody Reed .25 .08
❑ 309 Greg Vaughn .25 .08
❑ 310 Bill Wegman .25 .08
❑ 311 Rick Aguilera .25 .08
❑ 312 Alex Cole .25 .08
❑ 313 Denny Hocking .25 .08
❑ 314 Chuck Knoblauch .50 .20
❑ 315 Shane Mack .25 .08
❑ 316 Pat Meares .25 .08
❑ 317 Kevin Tapani .25 .08
❑ 318 Jim Abbott .75 .30
❑ 319 Wade Boggs .75 .30
❑ 320 Sterling Hitchcock .25 .08
❑ 321 Pat Kelly .25 .08
❑ 322 Terry Mulholland .25 .08
❑ 323 Luis Polonia .25 .08
❑ 324 Mike Stanley .25 .08
❑ 325 Bob Wickman .25 .08
❑ 326 Bernie Williams .75 .30
❑ 327 Mark Acre RC .25 .08
❑ 328 Geronimo Berroa .25 .08

❑ 329	Scott Brosius	.50	.20
❑ 330	Brent Gates	.25	.08
❑ 331	Rickey Henderson	1.25	.50
❑ 332	Carlos Reyes RC	.25	.08
❑ 333	Ruben Sierra	.50	.20
❑ 334	Bobby Witt	.25	.08
❑ 335	Bobby Ayala	.25	.08
❑ 336	Jay Buhner	.50	.20
❑ 337	Randy Johnson	1.25	.50
❑ 338	Edgar Martinez	.75	.30
❑ 339	Bill Risley	.25	.08
❑ 340	Alex Rodriguez RC	30.00	12.50
❑ 341	Roger Salkeld	.25	.08
❑ 342	Dan Wilson	.25	.08
❑ 343	Kevin Brown	.50	.20
❑ 344	Jose Canseco	.75	.30
❑ 345	Dean Palmer	.50	.20
❑ 346	Ivan Rodriguez	.75	.30
❑ 347	Kenny Rogers	.50	.20
❑ 348	Pat Borders	.25	.08
❑ 349	Juan Guzman	.25	.08
❑ 350	Ed Sprague	.25	.08
❑ 351	Devon White	.50	.20
❑ 352	Steve Avery	.25	.08
❑ 353	Roberto Kelly	.25	.08
❑ 354	Mark Lemke	.25	.08
❑ 355	Greg McMichael	.25	.08
❑ 356	Terry Pendleton	.50	.20
❑ 357	John Smoltz	.75	.30
❑ 358	Mike Stanton	.25	.08
❑ 359	Tony Tarasco	.25	.08
❑ 360	Mark Grace	.75	.30
❑ 361	Derrick May	.25	.08
❑ 362	Rey Sanchez	.25	.08
❑ 363	Sammy Sosa	1.25	.50
❑ 364	Rick Wilkins	.25	.08
❑ 365	Jeff Brantley	.25	.08
❑ 366	Tony Fernandez	.25	.08
❑ 367	Chuck McElroy	.25	.08
❑ 368	Kevin Mitchell	.25	.08
❑ 369	John Roper	.25	.08
❑ 370	Johnny Ruffin	.25	.08
❑ 371	Deion Sanders	.75	.30
❑ 372	Marvin Freeman	.25	.08
❑ 373	Andres Galarraga	.50	.20
❑ 374	Charlie Hayes	.25	.08
❑ 375	Nelson Liriano	.25	.08
❑ 376	David Nied	.25	.08
❑ 377	Walt Weiss	.25	.08
❑ 378	Bret Barberie	.25	.08
❑ 379	Jerry Browne	.25	.08
❑ 380	Chuck Carr	.25	.08
❑ 381	Greg Colbrunn	.25	.08
❑ 382	Charlie Hough	.50	.20
❑ 383	Kurt Miller	.25	.08
❑ 384	Benito Santiago	.50	.20
❑ 385	Jeff Bagwell	.75	.30
❑ 386	Craig Biggio	.75	.30
❑ 387	Ken Caminiti	.50	.20
❑ 388	Doug Drabek	.25	.08
❑ 389	Steve Finley	.50	.20
❑ 390	John Hudek RC	.25	.08
❑ 391	Orlando Miller	.25	.08
❑ 392	Shane Reynolds	.25	.08
❑ 393	Brett Butler	.50	.20
❑ 394	Tom Candiotti	.25	.08
❑ 395	Delino DeShields	.25	.08
❑ 396	Kevin Gross	.25	.08
❑ 397	Eric Karros	.50	.20
❑ 398	Ramon Martinez	.25	.08
❑ 399	Henry Rodriguez	.25	.08
❑ 400	Moises Alou	.50	.20
❑ 401	Jeff Fassero	.25	.08
❑ 402	Mike Lansing	.25	.08
❑ 403	Mel Rojas	.25	.08
❑ 404	Larry Walker	.50	.20
❑ 405	John Wetteland	.50	.20
❑ 406	Gabe White	.25	.08
❑ 407	Bobby Bonilla	.50	.20
❑ 408	Josias Manzanillo	.25	.08
❑ 409	Bret Saberhagen	.50	.20
❑ 410	David Segui	.25	.08
❑ 411	Mariano Duncan	.25	.08
❑ 412	Tommy Greene	.25	.08
❑ 413	Billy Hatcher	.25	.08
❑ 414	Ricky Jordan	.25	.08
❑ 415	John Kruk	.50	.20
❑ 416	Bobby Munoz	.25	.08
❑ 417	Curt Schilling	.50	.20
❑ 418	Fernando Valenzuela	.50	.20
❑ 419	David West	.25	.08
❑ 420	Carlos Garcia	.25	.08
❑ 421	Brian Hunter	.25	.08
❑ 422	Jeff King	.25	.08
❑ 423	Jon Lieber	.50	.20
❑ 424	Ravelo Manzanillo	.25	.08
❑ 425	Denny Neagle	.50	.20
❑ 426	Andy Van Slyke	.75	.30
❑ 427	Bryan Eversgerd RC	.25	.08
❑ 428	Bernard Gilkey	.25	.08
❑ 429	Gregg Jefferies	.25	.08
❑ 430	Tom Pagnozzi	.25	.08
❑ 431	Bob Tewksbury	.25	.08
❑ 432	Allen Watson	.25	.08
❑ 433	Andy Ashby	.25	.08
❑ 434	Andy Benes	.25	.08
❑ 435	Donnie Elliott	.25	.08
❑ 436	Tony Gwynn	1.50	.60
❑ 437	Joey Hamilton	.25	.08
❑ 438	Tim Hyers RC	.25	.08
❑ 439	Luis Lopez	.25	.08
❑ 440	Bip Roberts	.25	.08
❑ 441	Scott Sanders	.25	.08
❑ 442	Rod Beck	.25	.08
❑ 443	Dave Burba	.25	.08
❑ 444	Darryl Strawberry	.50	.20
❑ 445	Bill Swift	.25	.08
❑ 446	Robby Thompson	.25	.08
❑ 447	W.VanLandingham RC	.25	.08
❑ 448	Matt Williams	.50	.20
❑ 449	Checklist	.25	.08
❑ 450	Checklist	.25	.08
❑ P15	Aaron Sele Promo	1.00	.40

2003 Flair

❑ COMP.LO SET w/o SP's (90)	25.00	10.00
❑ COMMON CARD (1-90)	.50	.20
❑ COMMON CARD (91-135)	4.00	1.50

❑ 1	Hideo Nomo	1.25	.50
❑ 2	Derek Jeter	3.00	1.25
❑ 3	Junior Spivey	.50	.20
❑ 4	Rich Aurilia	.50	.20
❑ 5	Luis Gonzalez	.50	.20
❑ 6	Sean Burroughs	.50	.20
❑ 7	Pedro Martinez	.75	.30
❑ 8	Randy Winn	.50	.20
❑ 9	Carlos Delgado	.50	.20
❑ 10	Pat Burrell	.50	.20
❑ 11	Barry Larkin	.75	.30
❑ 12	Roberto Alomar	.75	.30
❑ 13	Tony Batista	.50	.20
❑ 14	Barry Bonds	3.00	1.25
❑ 15	Craig Biggio	.75	.30
❑ 16	Ivan Rodriguez	.75	.30
❑ 17	Javier Vazquez	.50	.20
❑ 18	Joe Borchard	.50	.20
❑ 19	Josh Phelps	.50	.20
❑ 20	Omar Vizquel	.75	.30
❑ 21	Tom Glavine	.75	.30
❑ 22	Darin Erstad	.50	.20
❑ 23	Hee Seop Choi	.50	.20
❑ 24	Roger Clemens	2.50	1.00
❑ 25	Michael Cuddyer	.50	.20
❑ 26	Mike Sweeney	.50	.20
❑ 27	Phil Nevin	.50	.20
❑ 28	Torii Hunter	.50	.20
❑ 29	Vladimir Guerrero	1.25	.50
❑ 30	Ellis Burks	.50	.20
❑ 31	Jimmy Rollins	.50	.20
❑ 32	Ken Griffey Jr.	2.00	.75
❑ 33	Magglio Ordonez	.50	.20
❑ 34	Mark Prior	.75	.30
❑ 35	Mike Lieberthal	.50	.20
❑ 36	Jorge Posada	.75	.30
❑ 37	Rodrigo Lopez	.50	.20
❑ 38	Todd Helton	.75	.30
❑ 39	Adam Kennedy	.50	.20
❑ 40	Curt Schilling	.50	.20
❑ 41	Jim Thome	.75	.30
❑ 42	Josh Beckett	.50	.20
❑ 43	Carlos Pena	.50	.20
❑ 44	Jason Kendall	.50	.20
❑ 45	Sammy Sosa	1.25	.50
❑ 46	Scott Rolen	.75	.30
❑ 47	Alex Rodriguez	2.00	.75
❑ 48	Aubrey Huff	.50	.20
❑ 49	Bobby Abreu	.50	.20
❑ 50	Jeff Kent	.50	.20
❑ 51	Joe Randa	.50	.20
❑ 52	Lance Berkman	.50	.20
❑ 53	Orlando Cabrera	.50	.20
❑ 54	Richie Sexson	.50	.20
❑ 55	Albert Pujols	2.00	.75
❑ 56	Alfonso Soriano	.50	.20
❑ 57	Greg Maddux	2.00	.75
❑ 58	Jason Giambi	.50	.20
❑ 59	Jeff Bagwell	.75	.30
❑ 60	Kerry Wood	.50	.20
❑ 61	Manny Ramirez	.75	.30
❑ 62	Eric Chavez	.50	.20
❑ 63	Preston Wilson	.50	.20
❑ 64	Shawn Green	.50	.20
❑ 65	Shea Hillenbrand	.50	.20
❑ 66	Austin Kearns	.50	.20
❑ 67	Cliff Floyd	.50	.20
❑ 68	Edgardo Alfonzo	.50	.20
❑ 69	J.D. Drew	.50	.20
❑ 70	Larry Walker	.50	.20
❑ 71	Mike Piazza	2.00	.75
❑ 72	Andruw Jones	.75	.30
❑ 73	Ben Grieve	.50	.20
❑ 74	Eric Hinske	.50	.20
❑ 75	Geoff Jenkins	.50	.20
❑ 76	Kazuhiro Sasaki	.50	.20
❑ 77	Matt Morris	.50	.20
❑ 78	Miguel Tejada	.50	.20
❑ 79	Aramis Ramirez	.50	.20
❑ 80	Troy Glaus	.50	.20
❑ 81	Ichiro Suzuki	2.00	.75
❑ 82	Mark Teixeira	.75	.30
❑ 83	Nomar Garciaparra	2.00	.75
❑ 84	Chipper Jones	1.25	.50
❑ 85	Frank Thomas	1.25	.50
❑ 86	Paul Lo Duca	.50	.20
❑ 87	Bernie Williams	.75	.30
❑ 88	Adam Dunn	.50	.20
❑ 89	Randy Johnson	1.25	.50
❑ 90	Barry Zito	.50	.20
❑ 91	Lew Ford FF RC	6.00	2.50
❑ 92	Joe Valentine FF RC	4.00	1.50
❑ 93	Jhonny Peralta FF	6.00	2.50
❑ 94	Hideki Matsui FF RC	15.00	6.00
❑ 95	Francisco Rosario FF RC	4.00	1.50
❑ 96	Adam LaRoche FF	4.00	1.50
❑ 97	Josh Hall FF RC	4.00	1.50
❑ 98	Chien-Ming Wang FF RC	40.00	15.00
❑ 99	Josh Willingham FF RC	8.00	3.00
❑ 100	Guillermo Quiroz FF RC	4.00	1.50
❑ 101	Termel Sledge FF RC	4.00	1.50
❑ 102	Prentice Redman FF RC	4.00	1.50
❑ 103	Matt Bruback FF RC	4.00	1.50
❑ 104	Alejandro Machado FF RC	4.00	1.50
❑ 105	Shane Victorino FF RC	6.00	2.50
❑ 106	Chris Waters FF RC	4.00	1.50
❑ 107	Jose Contreras FF RC	6.00	2.50
❑ 108	Pete LaForest FF RC	4.00	1.50
❑ 109	Nook Logan FF RC	6.00	2.50
❑ 110	Hector Luna FF RC	4.00	1.50
❑ 111	Daniel Cabrera FF RC	6.00	2.50
❑ 112	Matt Kata FF RC	4.00	1.50

❑ 113 Rontrez Johnson FF RC 4.00 1.50
❑ 114 Josh Stewart FF RC 4.00 1.50
❑ 115 Michael Hessman FF RC 4.00 1.50
❑ 116 Felix Sanchez FF RC 4.00 1.50
❑ 117 Michel Hernandez FF RC 4.00 1.50
❑ 118 Arnaldo Munoz FF RC 4.00 1.50
❑ 119 Ian Ferguson FF RC 4.00 1.50
❑ 120 Clint Barmes FF RC 4.00 1.50
❑ 121 Brian Stokes FF RC 4.00 1.50
❑ 122 Craig Brazell FF RC 4.00 1.50
❑ 123 John Webb FF 4.00 1.50
❑ 124 Tim Olson FF RC 4.00 1.50
❑ 125 Jeremy Bonderman FF RC 12.00 5.00
❑ 126 Jeff Duncan RC 4.00 1.50
❑ 127 Rickie Weeks RC 8.00 3.00
❑ 128 Brandon Webb RC 10.00 4.00
❑ 129 Robby Hammock RC 4.00 1.50
❑ 130 Jon Leicester RC 4.00 1.50
❑ 131 Ryan Wagner RC 4.00 1.50
❑ 132 Bo Hart RC 4.00 1.50
❑ 133 Edwin Jackson RC 6.00 2.50
❑ 134 Sergio Mitre RC 6.00 2.50
❑ 135 Delmon Young RC 20.00 8.00

2005 Flair

❑ COMMON CARD (1-50) 1.50 .60
❑ COMMON CARD (51-80) 4.00 1.50
❑ 51-80 ODDS 1:1 HOBBY, 1:130 RETAIL
❑ 51-80 PRINT RUN 699 SERIAL #'d SETS
❑ COMMON CARD (81-90) 4.00 1.50
❑ 81-90 ODDS 1:2 HOBBY, 1:240 RETAIL
❑ 81-90 PRINT RUN 699 SERIAL #'d SETS
❑ 1 Curt Schilling 2.00 .75
❑ 2 Jim Thome 2.00 .75
❑ 3 Miguel Cabrera 2.00 .75
❑ 4 Randy Johnson 3.00 1.25
❑ 5 David Ortiz 3.00 1.25
❑ 6 Vladimir Guerrero 3.00 1.25
❑ 7 Nomar Garciaparra 3.00 1.25
❑ 8 Ivan Rodriguez 2.00 .75
❑ 9 Jason Schmidt 1.50 .60
❑ 10 Khalil Greene 2.00 .75
❑ 11 Jose Vidro 1.50 .60
❑ 12 Lyle Overbay 1.50 .60
❑ 13 Todd Helton 2.00 .75
❑ 14 Vernon Wells 1.50 .60
❑ 15 B.J. Upton 1.50 .60
❑ 16 Hideki Matsui 5.00 2.00
❑ 17 Pedro Martinez 2.00 .75
❑ 18 Victor Martinez 1.50 .60
❑ 19 Adam Dunn 1.50 .60
❑ 20 Andruw Jones 2.00 .75
❑ 21 Jeff Bagwell 2.00 .75
❑ 22 Mike Sweeney 1.50 .60
❑ 23 Mike Piazza 3.00 1.25
❑ 24 Ben Sheets 1.50 .60
❑ 25 Adrian Beltre 1.50 .60
❑ 26 Chipper Jones 3.00 1.25
❑ 27 Greg Maddux 5.00 2.00
❑ 28 Manny Ramirez 2.00 .75
❑ 29 Roger Clemens 5.00 2.00
❑ 30 Johan Santana 3.00 1.25
❑ 31 Derek Jeter 6.00 2.50
❑ 32 Jason Bay 1.50 .60
❑ 33 Ken Griffey Jr. 5.00 2.00
❑ 34 Miguel Tejada 1.50 .60
❑ 35 Richie Sexson 1.50 .60
❑ 36 Scott Rolen 2.00 .75
❑ 37 Alfonso Soriano 1.50 .60
❑ 38 Ichiro Suzuki 6.00 2.50
❑ 39 Sammy Sosa 3.00 1.25
❑ 40 Barry Zito 1.50 .60
❑ 41 Kaz Matsui 1.50 .60
❑ 42 Mark Teixeira 2.00 .75
❑ 43 Carlos Beltran 1.50 .60
❑ 44 Mark Prior 2.00 .75
❑ 45 Travis Hafner 1.50 .60
❑ 46 Alex Rodriguez 5.00 2.00
❑ 47 Lew Ford 1.50 .60
❑ 48 Albert Pujols 6.00 2.50
❑ 49 Frank Thomas 3.00 1.25
❑ 50 Juan Pierre 1.50 .60
❑ 51 David Aardsma C05 4.00 1.50
❑ 52 J.D. Durbin C05 4.00 1.50
❑ 53 Zack Greinke C05 4.00 1.50
❑ 54 Dioner Navarro C05 4.00 1.50
❑ 55 Edwin Encarnacion C05 4.00 1.50
❑ 56 Luis Hernandez C05 RC 4.00 1.50
❑ 57 Jeff Baker C05 4.00 1.50
❑ 58 Victor Diaz C05 4.00 1.50
❑ 59 Joey Gathright C05 4.00 1.50
❑ 60 Casey Kotchman C05 4.00 1.50
❑ 61 David Wright C05 8.00 3.00
❑ 62 Jon Knott C05 4.00 1.50
❑ 63 Charlton Jimerson C05 4.00 1.50
❑ 64 Nick Swisher C05 4.00 1.50
❑ 65 Ryan Raburn C05 4.00 1.50
❑ 66 Josh Kroeger C05 4.00 1.50
❑ 67 Kelly Johnson C05 4.00 1.50
❑ 68 Justin Verlander C05 RC 8.00 3.00
❑ 69 Taylor Buchholz C05 4.00 1.50
❑ 70 Ubaldo Jimenez C05 RC 5.00 2.00
❑ 71 Russ Adams C05 4.00 1.50
❑ 72 Ronny Cedeno C05 4.00 1.50
❑ 73 Bobby Jenks C05 4.00 1.50
❑ 74 Dan Meyer C05 4.00 1.50
❑ 75 Jeff Francis C05 4.00 1.50
❑ 76 Scott Kazmir C05 4.00 1.50
❑ 77 Sean Burnett C05 4.00 1.50
❑ 78 Jose Lopez C05 4.00 1.50
❑ 79 Andres Blanco C05 4.00 1.50
❑ 80 Gavin Floyd C05 4.00 1.50
❑ 81 Tom Seaver RET 5.00 2.00
❑ 82 Steve Carlton RET 4.00 1.50
❑ 83 Al Kaline RET 5.00 2.00
❑ 84 Cal Ripken RET 15.00 6.00
❑ 85 Willie McCovey RET 5.00 2.00
❑ 86 Johnny Bench RET 5.00 2.00
❑ 87 Nolan Ryan RET 10.00 4.00
❑ 88 Mike Schmidt RET 8.00 3.00
❑ 89 Carlton Fisk RET 5.00 2.00
❑ 90 Don Mattingly RET 8.00 3.00

1997 Flair Showcase Row 2

❑ COMPLETE SET (180) 80.00 40.00
❑ COMMON CARD (1-60) .50 .20
❑ ROW 2 1-60 ODDS 1.5:1
❑ COMMON CARD (61-120) .75 .30
❑ ROW 2 61-120 ODDS 1:1.5
❑ COMMON CARD (121-180) .60 .25
❑ ROW 2 121-180 STATED ODDS 1:1
❑ A.ROD GLOVE EXCH RANDOM IN PACKS
❑ A.ROD GLOVE EXCH.DEADLINE: 8/1/98
❑ 1 Andruw Jones .75 .35
❑ 2 Derek Jeter 3.00 1.25
❑ 3 Alex Rodriguez 2.00 .75
❑ 4 Paul Molitor .50 .20
❑ 5 Jeff Bagwell .75 .35
❑ 6 Scott Rolen .75 .35
❑ 7 Kenny Lofton .50 .20
❑ 8 Cal Ripken 4.00 1.50
❑ 9 Brady Anderson .50 .20
❑ 10 Chipper Jones 1.25 .50
❑ 11 Todd Greene .50 .20
❑ 12 Todd Walker .50 .20
❑ 13 Billy Wagner .50 .20
❑ 14 Craig Biggio .75 .35
❑ 15 Kevin Orie .50 .20
❑ 16 Hideo Nomo 1.25 .50
❑ 17 Kevin Appier .50 .20
❑ 18 Bubba Trammell RC .50 .20
❑ 19 Juan Gonzalez .50 .20
❑ 20 Randy Johnson 1.25 .50
❑ 21 Roger Clemens 2.50 1.00
❑ 22 Johnny Damon .75 .35
❑ 23 Ryne Sandberg 2.00 .75
❑ 24 Ken Griffey Jr. 2.00 .75
❑ 25 Barry Bonds 3.00 1.25
❑ 26 Nomar Garciaparra 2.00 .75
❑ 27 Vladimir Guerrero 1.25 .50
❑ 28 Ron Gant .50 .20
❑ 29 Joe Carter .50 .20
❑ 30 Tim Salmon .75 .35
❑ 31 Mike Piazza 2.00 .75
❑ 32 Barry Larkin .75 .35
❑ 33 Manny Ramirez .75 .35
❑ 34 Sammy Sosa 1.25 .50
❑ 35 Frank Thomas 1.25 .50
❑ 36 Melvin Nieves .50 .20
❑ 37 Tony Gwynn 1.50 .60
❑ 38 Gary Sheffield .50 .20
❑ 39 Darin Erstad .50 .20
❑ 40 Ken Caminiti .50 .20
❑ 41 Jermaine Dye .50 .20
❑ 42 Mo Vaughn .50 .20
❑ 43 Raul Mondesi .50 .20
❑ 44 Greg Maddux 2.00 .75
❑ 45 Chuck Knoblauch .50 .20
❑ 46 Andy Pettitte .75 .35
❑ 47 Deion Sanders .75 .35
❑ 48 Albert Belle .50 .20
❑ 49 Jamey Wright .50 .20
❑ 50 Rey Ordonez .50 .20
❑ 51 Bernie Williams .75 .35
❑ 52 Mark McGwire 3.00 1.25
❑ 53 Mike Mussina .75 .35
❑ 54 Bob Abreu .75 .35
❑ 55 Reggie Sanders .50 .20
❑ 56 Brian Jordan .50 .20
❑ 57 Ivan Rodriguez .75 .35
❑ 58 Roberto Alomar .75 .35
❑ 59 Tim Naehring .50 .20
❑ 60 Edgar Renteria .50 .20
❑ 61 Dean Palmer .75 .30
❑ 62 Benito Santiago .75 .30
❑ 63 David Cone .75 .30
❑ 64 Carlos Delgado .75 .30
❑ 65 Brian Giles RC 2.00 .75
❑ 66 Alex Ochoa .75 .30
❑ 67 Rondell White .75 .30
❑ 68 Robin Ventura .75 .30
❑ 69 Eric Karros .75 .30
❑ 70 Jose Valentin .75 .30
❑ 71 Rafael Palmeiro 1.25 .50
❑ 72 Chris Snopek .75 .30
❑ 73 David Justice .75 .30
❑ 74 Tom Glavine 1.25 .50
❑ 75 Rudy Pemberton .75 .30
❑ 76 Larry Walker .75 .30
❑ 77 Jim Thome 1.25 .50
❑ 78 Charles Johnson .75 .30
❑ 79 Dante Powell .75 .30
❑ 80 Derrek Lee 1.25 .50
❑ 81 Jason Kendall .75 .30
❑ 82 Todd Hollandsworth .75 .30
❑ 83 Bernard Gilkey .75 .30
❑ 84 Mel Rojas .75 .30
❑ 85 Dmitri Young .75 .30
❑ 86 Bret Boone .75 .30
❑ 87 Pat Hentgen .75 .30
❑ 88 Bobby Bonilla .75 .30

❑ 89 John Wetteland .75 .30
❑ 90 Todd Hundley .75 .30
❑ 91 Wilton Guerrero .75 .30
❑ 92 Geronimo Berroa .75 .30
❑ 93 Al Martin .75 .30
❑ 94 Danny Tartabull .75 .30
❑ 95 Brian McRae .75 .30
❑ 96 Steve Finley .75 .30
❑ 97 Todd Stottlemyre .75 .30
❑ 98 John Smoltz 1.25 .50
❑ 99 Matt Williams .75 .30
❑ 100 Eddie Murray 2.00 .75
❑ 101 Henry Rodriguez .75 .30
❑ 102 Marty Cordova .75 .30
❑ 103 Juan Guzman .75 .30
❑ 104 Chili Davis .75 .30
❑ 105 Eric Young .75 .30
❑ 106 Jeff Abbott .75 .30
❑ 107 Shannon Stewart .75 .30
❑ 108 Rocky Coppinger .75 .30
❑ 109 Jose Canseco 1.25 .50
❑ 110 Dante Bichette .75 .30
❑ 111 Dwight Gooden .75 .30
❑ 112 Scott Brosius .75 .30
❑ 113 Steve Avery .75 .30
❑ 114 Andres Galarraga .75 .30
❑ 115 Sandy Alomar Jr. .75 .30
❑ 116 Ray Lankford .75 .30
❑ 117 Jorge Posada 1.25 .50
❑ 118 Ryan Klesko .75 .30
❑ 119 Jay Buhner .75 .30
❑ 120 Jose Guillen .75 .30
❑ 121 Paul O'Neill 1.00 .40
❑ 122 Jimmy Key .60 .25
❑ 123 Hal Morris .60 .25
❑ 124 Travis Fryman .60 .25
❑ 125 Jim Edmonds .60 .25
❑ 126 Jeff Cirillo .60 .25
❑ 127 Fred McGriff 1.00 .40
❑ 128 Alan Benes .60 .25
❑ 129 Derek Bell .60 .25
❑ 130 Tony Graffanino .60 .25
❑ 131 Shawn Green .60 .25
❑ 132 Denny Neagle .60 .25
❑ 133 Alex Fernandez .60 .25
❑ 134 Mickey Morandini .60 .25
❑ 135 Royce Clayton .60 .25
❑ 136 Jose Mesa .60 .25
❑ 137 Edgar Martinez 1.00 .40
❑ 138 Curt Schilling .60 .25
❑ 139 Lance Johnson .60 .25
❑ 140 Andy Benes .60 .25
❑ 141 Charles Nagy .60 .25
❑ 142 Mariano Rivera 1.50 .60
❑ 143 Mark Wohlers .60 .25
❑ 144 Ken Hill .60 .25
❑ 145 Jay Bell .60 .25
❑ 146 Bob Higginson .60 .25
❑ 147 Mark Grudzielanek .60 .25
❑ 148 Ray Durham .60 .25
❑ 149 John Olerud .60 .25
❑ 150 Joey Hamilton .60 .25
❑ 151 Trevor Hoffman .60 .25
❑ 152 Dan Wilson .60 .25
❑ 153 J.T. Snow .60 .25
❑ 154 Marquis Grissom .60 .25
❑ 155 Yamil Benitez .60 .25
❑ 156 Rusty Greer .60 .25
❑ 157 Darryl Kile .60 .25
❑ 158 Ismael Valdes .60 .25
❑ 159 Jeff Conine .60 .25
❑ 160 Darren Daulton .60 .25
❑ 161 Chan Ho Park .60 .25
❑ 162 Troy Percival .60 .25
❑ 163 Wade Boggs 1.00 .40
❑ 164 Dave Nilsson .60 .25
❑ 165 Vinny Castilla .60 .25
❑ 166 Kevin Brown .60 .25
❑ 167 Dennis Eckersley .60 .25
❑ 168 Wendell Magee Jr. .60 .25
❑ 169 John Jaha .60 .25
❑ 170 Garret Anderson .60 .25
❑ 171 Jason Giambi .60 .25
❑ 172 Mark Grace 1.00 .40
❑ 173 Tony Clark .60 .25
❑ 174 Moises Alou .60 .25
❑ 175 Brett Butler .60 .25
❑ 176 Cecil Fielder .60 .25
❑ 177 Chris Widger .60 .25
❑ 178 Doug Drabek .60 .25
❑ 179 Ellis Burks .60 .25
❑ 180 Shigetoshi Hasegawa RC 1.00 .40
❑ NNO A.Rod. Glove EXCH/25 2.00 .75

2006 Flair Showcase

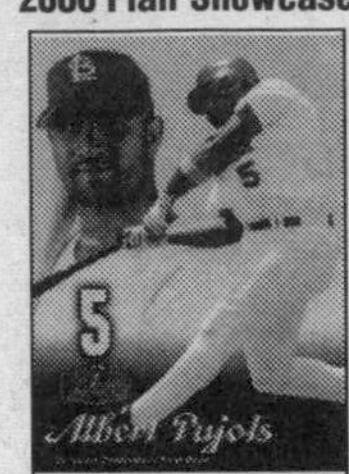

❑ COMP.SET w/o SP's (100) 40.00 15.00
❑ 101-150 STATED ODDS 1:4 H, 1:8 R
❑ 151-200 STATED ODDS 1:8 H, 1:16 R
❑ PLATE ODDS: 1-2 PER HOBBY CASE
❑ PLATE PRINT RUN 1 SET PER COLOR
❑ BLACK-CYAN-MAGENTA-YELLOW ISSUED
❑ NO PLATE PRICING DUE TO SCARCITY
❑ 1 Jeremy Hermida UD (RC) 1.50 .60
❑ 2 Albert Pujols UD 4.00 1.50
❑ 3 Ryan Shealy UD (RC) 1.00 .40
❑ 4 Mark Prior UD 1.25 .50
❑ 5 Chuck James UD (RC) 1.50 .60
❑ 6 Shawn Green UD .75 .30
❑ 7 Rickie Weeks UD .75 .30
❑ 8 Roy Halladay UD .75 .30
❑ 9 Luis Gonzalez UD .75 .30
❑ 10 David Ortiz UD 2.00 .75
❑ 11 Josh Beckett UD .75 .30
❑ 12 Gary Sheffield UD .75 .30
❑ 13 Jose Reyes UD .75 .30
❑ 14 Brandon Watson UD (RC) 1.00 .40
❑ 15 Tadahito Iguchi UD .75 .30
❑ 16 Rich Harden UD .75 .30
❑ 17 Skip Schumaker UD (RC) 1.00 .40
❑ 18 Vladimir Guerrero UD 2.00 .75
❑ 19 Chris Carpenter UD .75 .30
❑ 20 Brian Roberts UD .75 .30
❑ 21 Roy Oswalt UD .75 .30
❑ 22 Ben Johnson UD (RC) 1.00 .40
❑ 23 Todd Helton UD 1.25 .50
❑ 24 Wil Nieves UD (RC) 1.00 .40
❑ 25 Michael Young UD .75 .30
❑ 26 A.J. Burnett UD .75 .30
❑ 27 J.D. Drew UD .75 .30
❑ 28 Adrian Beltre UD .75 .30
❑ 29 Tim Hudson UD .75 .30
❑ 30 Jake Peavy UD .75 .30
❑ 31 Magglio Ordonez UD .75 .30
❑ 32 Brad Wilkerson UD .75 .30
❑ 33 Ryan Freel UD .75 .30
❑ 34 Javier Vazquez UD .75 .30
❑ 35 Tom Glavine UD 1.25 .50
❑ 36 Jason Bergmann UD RC 1.00 .40
❑ 37 Marcus Giles UD .75 .30
❑ 38 Jim Thome UD 1.25 .50
❑ 39 Ichiro Suzuki UD 3.00 1.25
❑ 40 Jeff Harris UD RC .75 .30
❑ 41 Miguel Cabrera UD 1.25 .50
❑ 42 Nomar Garciaparra UD 2.00 .75
❑ 43 Brian Giles UD .75 .30
❑ 44 Jeremy Accardo UD RC 1.00 .40
❑ 45 Taylor Buchholz UD (RC) 1.50 .60
❑ 46 Mike Jacobs UD (RC) 1.00 .40
❑ 47 Chris Denorfia UD (RC) 1.00 .40
❑ 48 Ivan Rodriguez UD 1.25 .50
❑ 49 Mike Piazza UD 2.00 .75
❑ 50 Curt Schilling UD 1.25 .50
❑ 51 Kelly Shoppach UD (RC) 1.00 .40
❑ 52 Jason Kubel UD (RC) 1.00 .40
❑ 53 Craig Biggio UD 1.25 .50
❑ 54 Livan Hernandez UD .75 .30
❑ 55 Joe Mauer UD 1.25 .50
❑ 56 Scott Feldman UD RC 1.00 .40
❑ 57 Garret Anderson UD .75 .30
❑ 58 Steve Stemle UD RC 1.00 .40
❑ 59 Boof Bonser UD (RC) 1.00 .40
❑ 60 Jose Guillen UD .75 .30
❑ 61 Rafael Furcal UD .75 .30
❑ 62 John Van Benschoten UD (RC) 1.00 .40
❑ 63 Dontrelle Willis UD .75 .30
❑ 64 Jose Vidro UD .75 .30
❑ 65 David Wright UD 3.00 1.25
❑ 66 Alfonso Soriano UD .75 .30
❑ 67 Scott Podsednik UD .75 .30
❑ 68 Felix Hernandez UD 1.25 .50
❑ 69 Richie Sexson UD .75 .30
❑ 70 Jeff Francoeur UD 2.00 .75
❑ 71 Conor Jackson UD 1.25 .50
❑ 72 Javy Lopez UD .75 .30
❑ 73 Jonathan Papelbon UD (RC) 5.00 2.00
❑ 74 Frank Thomas UD 2.00 .75
❑ 75 Greg Maddux UD 3.00 1.25
❑ 76 Josh Rupe UD (RC) 1.00 .40
❑ 77 Eric Chavez UD .75 .30
❑ 78 Ben Sheets UD .75 .30
❑ 79 Chase Utley UD 2.00 .75
❑ 80 Derrek Lee UD .75 .30
❑ 81 Manny Ramirez UD 1.25 .50
❑ 82 Pedro Martinez UD 1.25 .50
❑ 83 Hideki Matsui UD 2.00 .75
❑ 84 Jeremy Bonderman UD .75 .30
❑ 85 Ronny Cedeno UD .75 .30
❑ 86 Trevor Hoffman UD .75 .30
❑ 87 Mark Buehrle UD .75 .30
❑ 88 Jason Bay UD .75 .30
❑ 89 Reggie Sanders UD .75 .30
❑ 90 Brian Anderson UD (RC) 1.00 .40
❑ 91 Travis Hafner UD .75 .30
❑ 92 Carlos Beltran UD .75 .30
❑ 93 Cody Ross UD (RC) 1.00 .40
❑ 94 Melvin Mora UD .75 .30
❑ 95 Chris Duffy UD .75 .30
❑ 96 Vernon Wells UD .75 .30
❑ 97 Bartolo Colon UD .75 .30
❑ 98 Aubrey Huff UD .75 .30
❑ 99 Paul Konerko UD .75 .30
❑ 100 Cesar Izturis UD .75 .30
❑ 101 Josh Willingham FB (RC) 2.00 .75
❑ 102 Matt Cain FB (RC) 3.00 1.25
❑ 103 Macay McBride FB (RC) 2.00 .75
❑ 104 Jeff Mathis FB 2.00 .75
❑ 105 Alex Rodriguez FB 8.00 3.00
❑ 106 Justin Morneau FB 2.00 .75
❑ 107 Felipe Lopez FB 2.00 .75
❑ 108 Justin Verlander FB (RC) 8.00 3.00
❑ 109 Ryan Howard FB 8.00 3.00
❑ 110 Mike Sweeney FB 2.00 .75
❑ 111 Scott Rolen FB 3.00 1.25
❑ 112 Hank Blalock FB 2.00 .75
❑ 113 Kerry Wood FB 2.00 .75
❑ 114 B.J. Ryan FB 2.00 .75
❑ 115 Garrett Atkins FB 2.00 .75
❑ 116 Carlos Delgado FB 2.00 .75
❑ 117 Zack Greinke FB 2.00 .75
❑ 118 Chad Cordero FB 2.00 .75
❑ 119 Julio Lugo FB 2.00 .75
❑ 120 Bobby Crosby FB 2.00 .75
❑ 121 Barry Zito FB 2.00 .75
❑ 122 Jhonny Peralta FB 2.00 .75
❑ 123 Miguel Tejada FB 2.00 .75
❑ 124 Grady Sizemore FB 3.00 1.25
❑ 125 Derek Jeter FB 12.00 5.00
❑ 126 Cliff Lee FB 2.00 .75
❑ 127 Khalil Greene FB 3.00 1.25
❑ 128 Lance Berkman FB 2.00 .75
❑ 129 Huston Street FB 2.00 .75
❑ 130 Jermaine Dye FB 2.00 .75
❑ 131 Chone Figgins FB 2.00 .75
❑ 132 Torii Hunter FB 2.00 .75
❑ 133 Jorge Cantu FB 2.00 .75
❑ 134 Jason Giambi FB 2.00 .75
❑ 135 Johan Santana FB 3.00 1.25
❑ 136 Chad Tracy FB 2.00 .75
❑ 137 Troy Glaus FB 2.00 .75
❑ 138 Moises Alou FB 2.00 .75

❑ 139 Jason Schmidt FB 2.00 .75
❑ 140 Ken Griffey Jr. FB 8.00 3.00
❑ 141 Jason Varitek FB 5.00 2.00
❑ 142 John Smoltz FB 3.00 1.25
❑ 143 Andy Pettitte FB 2.00 .75
❑ 144 Jeff Kent FB 2.00 .75
❑ 145 Coco Crisp FB 2.00 .75
❑ 146 Jonny Gomes FB 2.00 .75
❑ 147 Aaron Rowand FB 2.00 .75
❑ 148 Mike Mussina FB 3.00 1.25
❑ 149 Johnny Damon FB 3.00 1.25
❑ 150 Edgar Renteria FB 2.00 .75
❑ 151 Scott Kazmir SL 5.00 2.00
❑ 152 Lyle Overbay SL 3.00 1.25
❑ 153 Placido Polanco SL 3.00 1.25
❑ 154 Mariano Rivera SL 8.00 3.00
❑ 155 Hanley Ramirez SL (RC) 8.00 3.00
❑ 156 Morgan Ensberg SL 3.00 1.25
❑ 157 Kenny Rogers SL 3.00 1.25
❑ 158 Brad Lidge SL 3.00 1.25
❑ 159 A.J. Pierzynski SL 3.00 1.25
❑ 160 Aramis Ramirez SL 3.00 1.25
❑ 161 Mark Teixeira SL 5.00 2.00
❑ 162 Carl Crawford SL 3.00 1.25
❑ 163 Ryan Zimmerman SL (RC) 12.00 5.00
❑ 164 Adam Dunn SL 3.00 1.25
❑ 165 Joe Nathan SL 3.00 1.25
❑ 166 Juan Pierre SL 3.00 1.25
❑ 167 Pat Burrell SL 3.00 1.25
❑ 168 Carlos Lee SL 3.00 1.25
❑ 169 Billy Wagner SL 3.00 1.25
❑ 170 Prince Fielder SL (RC) 8.00 3.00
❑ 171 Randy Johnson SL 8.00 3.00
❑ 172 Andruw Jones SL 5.00 2.00
❑ 173 Francisco Rodriguez SL 3.00 1.25
❑ 174 Robinson Cano SL 5.00 2.00
❑ 175 Matt Holliday SL 3.00 1.25
❑ 176 Jim Edmonds SL 5.00 2.00
❑ 177 Josh Barfield SL (RC) 3.00 1.25
❑ 178 Chipper Jones SL 8.00 3.00
❑ 179 Bobby Jenks SL 3.00 1.25
❑ 180 Carlos Zambrano SL 3.00 1.25
❑ 181 Bobby Abreu SL 3.00 1.25
❑ 182 Brandon Webb SL 3.00 1.25
❑ 183 Kevin Millwood SL 3.00 1.25
❑ 184 Zach Duke SL 3.00 1.25
❑ 185 Randy Winn SL 3.00 1.25
❑ 186 Eric Gagne SL 3.00 1.25
❑ 187 Kenji Johjima SL RC 10.00 4.00
❑ 188 John Patterson SL 3.00 1.25
❑ 189 Mark Loretta SL 3.00 1.25
❑ 190 Anderson Hernandez SL (RC) 3.001.25
❑ 191 Chris Resop SL (RC) 3.00 1.25
❑ 192 Ian Kinsler SL (RC) 5.00 2.00
❑ 193 Francisco Liriano SL (RC) 10.00 4.00
❑ 194 Noah Lowry SL 3.00 1.25
❑ 195 Brett Myers SL 3.00 1.25
❑ 196 Rocco Baldelli SL 3.00 1.25
❑ 197 Cliff Floyd SL 3.00 1.25
❑ 198 Sean Casey SL 3.00 1.25
❑ 199 Geoff Jenkins SL 3.00 1.25
❑ 200 Clint Barmes SL 3.00 1.25

1960 Fleer

❑ COMPLETE SET (79) 600.00 350.00
❑ WRAPPER (5-CENT) 100.00 75.00
❑ 1 Napoleon Lajoie DP 30.00 15.00
❑ 2 Christy Mathewson 15.00 7.50
❑ 3 Babe Ruth 100.00 60.00
❑ 4 Carl Hubbell 8.00 4.00
❑ 5 Grover C. Alexander 8.00 4.00
❑ 6 Walter Johnson DP 10.00 5.00
❑ 7 Chief Bender 4.00 2.00
❑ 8 Roger Bresnahan 4.00 2.00
❑ 9 Mordecai Brown 4.00 2.00
❑ 10 Tris Speaker 8.00 4.00
❑ 11 Arky Vaughan DP 4.00 2.00
❑ 12 Zach Wheat 4.00 2.00
❑ 13 George Sisler 4.00 2.00
❑ 14 Connie Mack 8.00 4.00
❑ 15 Clark Griffith 4.00 2.00
❑ 16 Lou Boudreau DP 8.00 4.00
❑ 17 Ernie Lombardi 4.00 2.00
❑ 18 Heinie Manush 4.00 2.00
❑ 19 Marty Marion 6.00 3.00
❑ 20 Eddie Collins DP 4.00 2.00
❑ 21 Rabbit Maranville DP 4.00 2.00
❑ 22 Joe Medwick 4.00 2.00
❑ 23 Ed Barrow 4.00 2.00
❑ 24 Mickey Cochrane 6.00 3.00
❑ 25 Jimmy Collins 4.00 2.00
❑ 26 Bob Feller DP 15.00 7.50
❑ 27 Luke Appling 6.00 3.00
❑ 28 Lou Gehrig 80.00 50.00
❑ 29 Gabby Hartnett 4.00 2.00
❑ 30 Chuck Klein 4.00 2.00
❑ 31 Tony Lazzeri DP 6.00 3.00
❑ 32 Al Simmons 4.00 2.00
❑ 33 Wilbert Robinson 4.00 2.00
❑ 34 Sam Rice 4.00 2.00
❑ 35 Herb Pennock 4.00 2.00
❑ 36 Mel Ott DP 8.00 4.00
❑ 37 Lefty O'Doul 4.00 2.00
❑ 38 Johnny Mize 8.00 4.00
❑ 39 Edmund (Bing) Miller 4.00 2.00
❑ 40 Joe Tinker 4.00 2.00
❑ 41 Frank Baker DP 4.00 2.00
❑ 42 Ty Cobb 60.00 35.00
❑ 43 Paul Derringer 4.00 2.00
❑ 44 Cap Anson 4.00 2.00
❑ 45 Jim Bottomley 4.00 2.00
❑ 46 Eddie Plank DP 4.00 2.00
❑ 47 Denton (Cy) Young 10.00 5.00
❑ 48 Hack Wilson 6.00 3.00
❑ 49 Ed Walsh UER 4.00 2.00
❑ 50 Frank Chance 4.00 2.00
❑ 51 Dazzy Vance DP 4.00 2.00
❑ 52 Bill Terry 6.00 3.00
❑ 53 Jimmie Foxx 10.00 5.00
❑ 54 Lefty Gomez 8.00 4.00
❑ 55 Branch Rickey 4.00 2.00
❑ 56 Ray Schalk DP 4.00 2.00
❑ 57 Johnny Evers 4.00 2.00
❑ 58 Charley Gehringer 6.00 3.00
❑ 59 Burleigh Grimes 4.00 2.00
❑ 60 Lefty Grove 8.00 4.00
❑ 61 Rube Waddell DP 4.00 2.00
❑ 62 Honus Wagner 15.00 7.50
❑ 63 Red Ruffing 4.00 2.00
❑ 64 Kenesaw M. Landis 4.00 2.00
❑ 65 Harry Heilmann 4.00 2.00
❑ 66 John McGraw DP 4.00 2.00
❑ 67 Hughie Jennings 4.00 2.00
❑ 68 Hal Newhouser 6.00 3.00
❑ 69 Waite Hoyt 4.00 2.00
❑ 70 Bobo Newsom 4.00 2.00
❑ 71 Earl Averill DP 4.00 2.00
❑ 72 Ted Williams 80.00 50.00
❑ 73 Warren Giles 6.00 3.00
❑ 74 Ford Frick 6.00 3.00
❑ 75 Kiki Cuyler 4.00 2.00
❑ 76 Paul Waner DP 6.00 3.00
❑ 77 Pie Traynor 4.00 2.00
❑ 78 Lloyd Waner 4.00 2.00
❑ 79 Ralph Kiner 10.00 5.00
❑ 80A P.Martin SP/Eddie Collins 2500.00 1500.00
❑ 80B P.Martin SP/Lefty Grove 2000.00 1200.00
❑ 80C P.Martin SP/Joe Tinker 2000.00 1200.00

1961 Fleer

❑ COMPLETE SET (154) 1200.00 750.00
❑ COMMON CARD (1-88) 3.00 1.50
❑ COMMON CARD (89-154) 8.00 4.00
❑ WRAPPER (5-CENT) 100.00 75.00
❑ 1 Baker/Cobb/Wheat 50.00 30.00
❑ 2 Grover C. Alexander 6.00 3.00
❑ 3 Nick Altrock 3.00 1.50
❑ 4 Cap Anson 4.00 2.00
❑ 5 Earl Averill 4.00 2.00
❑ 6 Frank Baker 4.00 2.00
❑ 7 Dave Bancroft 4.00 2.00
❑ 8 Chief Bender 4.00 2.00
❑ 9 Jim Bottomley 4.00 2.00
❑ 10 Roger Bresnahan 4.00 2.00
❑ 11 Mordecai Brown 4.00 2.00
❑ 12 Max Carey 4.00 2.00
❑ 13 Jack Chesbro 4.00 2.00
❑ 14 Ty Cobb 50.00 30.00
❑ 15 Mickey Cochrane 4.00 2.00
❑ 16 Eddie Collins 6.00 3.00
❑ 17 Earle Combs 4.00 2.00
❑ 18 Charles Comiskey 4.00 2.00
❑ 19 Kiki Cuyler 4.00 2.00
❑ 20 Paul Derringer 3.00 1.50
❑ 21 Howard Ehmke 3.00 1.50
❑ 22 Billy Evans UMP 4.00 2.00
❑ 23 Johnny Evers 4.00 2.00
❑ 24 Urban Faber 4.00 2.00
❑ 25 Bob Feller 12.00 6.00
❑ 26 Wes Ferrell 3.00 1.50
❑ 27 Lew Fonseca 3.00 1.50
❑ 28 Jimmie Foxx 6.00 3.00
❑ 29 Ford Frick 3.00 1.50
❑ 30 Frankie Frisch 4.00 2.00
❑ 31 Lou Gehrig 80.00 50.00
❑ 32 Charley Gehringer 4.00 2.00
❑ 33 Warren Giles 3.00 1.50
❑ 34 Lefty Gomez 4.00 2.00
❑ 35 Goose Goslin 4.00 2.00
❑ 36 Clark Griffith 4.00 2.00
❑ 37 Burleigh Grimes 4.00 2.00
❑ 38 Lefty Grove 6.00 3.00
❑ 39 Chick Hafey 4.00 2.00
❑ 40 Jesse Haines 4.00 2.00
❑ 41 Gabby Hartnett 4.00 2.00
❑ 42 Harry Heilmann 4.00 2.00
❑ 43 Rogers Hornsby 6.00 3.00
❑ 44 Waite Hoyt 4.00 2.00
❑ 45 Carl Hubbell 6.00 3.00
❑ 46 Miller Huggins 4.00 2.00
❑ 47 Hughie Jennings 4.00 2.00
❑ 48 Ban Johnson 4.00 2.00
❑ 49 Walter Johnson 12.00 6.00
❑ 50 Ralph Kiner 6.00 3.00
❑ 51 Chuck Klein 4.00 2.00
❑ 52 Johnny Kling 3.00 1.50
❑ 53 Kenesaw M. Landis 4.00 2.00
❑ 54 Tony Lazzeri 4.00 2.00
❑ 55 Ernie Lombardi 4.00 2.00
❑ 56 Dolf Luque 3.00 1.50
❑ 57 Heinie Manush 4.00 2.00
❑ 58 Marty Marion 3.00 1.50
❑ 59 Christy Mathewson 12.00 6.00
❑ 60 John McGraw 4.00 2.00
❑ 61 Joe Medwick 4.00 2.00
❑ 62 Edmund (Bing) Miller 3.00 1.50
❑ 63 Johnny Mize 4.00 2.00
❑ 64 John Mostil 3.00 1.50
❑ 65 Art Nehf 3.00 1.50
❑ 66 Hal Newhouser 4.00 2.00
❑ 67 Bobo Newsom 3.00 1.50
❑ 68 Mel Ott 6.00 3.00

❑ 69 Allie Reynolds	3.00	1.50
❑ 70 Sam Rice	4.00	2.00
❑ 71 Eppa Rixey	4.00	2.00
❑ 72 Edd Roush	4.00	2.00
❑ 73 Schoolboy Rowe	3.00	1.50
❑ 74 Red Ruffing	4.00	2.00
❑ 75 Babe Ruth	125.00	75.00
❑ 76 Joe Sewell	4.00	2.00
❑ 77 Al Simmons	4.00	2.00
❑ 78 George Sisler	4.00	2.00
❑ 79 Tris Speaker	4.00	2.00
❑ 80 Fred Toney	3.00	1.50
❑ 81 Dazzy Vance	4.00	2.00
❑ 82 Hippo Vaughn	3.00	1.50
❑ 83 Ed Walsh	4.00	2.00
❑ 84 Lloyd Waner	4.00	2.00
❑ 85 Paul Waner	4.00	2.00
❑ 86 Zack Wheat	4.00	2.00
❑ 87 Hack Wilson	4.00	2.00
❑ 88 Jimmy Wilson	3.00	1.50
❑ 89 G.Sisler/P.Traynor	60.00	35.00
❑ 90 Babe Adams	8.00	4.00
❑ 91 Dale Alexander	8.00	4.00
❑ 92 Jim Bagby	8.00	4.00
❑ 93 Ossie Bluege	8.00	4.00
❑ 94 Lou Boudreau	10.00	5.00
❑ 95 Tommy Bridges	8.00	4.00
❑ 96 Donie Bush	8.00	4.00
❑ 97 Dolph Camilli	8.00	4.00
❑ 98 Frank Chance	10.00	5.00
❑ 99 Jimmy Collins	10.00	5.00
❑ 100 Stan Coveleskie	10.00	5.00
❑ 101 Hugh Critz	8.00	4.00
❑ 102 Alvin Crowder	8.00	4.00
❑ 103 Joe Dugan	8.00	4.00
❑ 104 Bibb Falk	8.00	4.00
❑ 105 Rick Ferrell	10.00	5.00
❑ 106 Art Fletcher	8.00	4.00
❑ 107 Dennis Galehouse	8.00	4.00
❑ 108 Chick Galloway	8.00	4.00
❑ 109 Mule Haas	8.00	4.00
❑ 110 Stan Hack	8.00	4.00
❑ 111 Bump Hadley	8.00	4.00
❑ 112 Billy Hamilton	10.00	5.00
❑ 113 Joe Hauser	8.00	4.00
❑ 114 Babe Herman	8.00	4.00
❑ 115 Travis Jackson	10.00	5.00
❑ 116 Eddie Joost	8.00	4.00
❑ 117 Addie Joss	10.00	5.00
❑ 118 Joe Judge	8.00	4.00
❑ 119 Joe Kuhel	8.00	4.00
❑ 120 Napoleon Lajoie	12.00	6.00
❑ 121 Dutch Leonard	8.00	4.00
❑ 122 Ted Lyons	10.00	5.00
❑ 123 Connie Mack	12.00	6.00
❑ 124 Rabbit Maranville	10.00	5.00
❑ 125 Fred Marberry	8.00	4.00
❑ 126 Joe McGinnity	10.00	5.00
❑ 127 Oscar Melillo	8.00	4.00
❑ 128 Ray Mueller	8.00	4.00
❑ 129 Kid Nichols	10.00	5.00
❑ 130 Lefty O'Doul	10.00	5.00
❑ 131 Bob O'Farrell	8.00	4.00
❑ 132 Roger Peckinpaugh	8.00	4.00
❑ 133 Herb Pennock	10.00	5.00
❑ 134 George Pipgras	8.00	4.00
❑ 135 Eddie Plank	10.00	5.00
❑ 136 Ray Schalk	10.00	5.00
❑ 137 Hal Schumacher	8.00	4.00
❑ 138 Luke Sewell	8.00	4.00
❑ 139 Bob Shawkey	8.00	4.00
❑ 140 Riggs Stephenson	8.00	4.00
❑ 141 Billy Sullivan	8.00	4.00
❑ 142 Bill Terry	12.00	6.00
❑ 143 Joe Tinker	10.00	5.00
❑ 144 Pie Traynor	10.00	5.00
❑ 145 Hal Trosky	8.00	4.00
❑ 146 George Uhle	8.00	4.00
❑ 147 Johnny VanderMeer	10.00	5.00
❑ 148 Arky Vaughan	10.00	5.00
❑ 149 Rube Waddell	10.00	5.00
❑ 150 Honus Wagner	50.00	30.00
❑ 151 Dixie Walker	8.00	4.00
❑ 152 Ted Williams	125.00	75.00
❑ 153 Cy Young	40.00	20.00
❑ 154 Ross Youngs	40.00	20.00

1963 Fleer

❑ COMPLETE SET (67)	1500.00	1000.00
❑ WRAPPER (5-CENT)	100.00	75.00
❑ 1 Steve Barber	25.00	12.50
❑ 2 Ron Hansen	15.00	7.50
❑ 3 Milt Pappas	20.00	10.00
❑ 4 Brooks Robinson	100.00	60.00
❑ 5 Willie Mays	175.00	100.00
❑ 6 Lou Clinton	15.00	7.50
❑ 7 Bill Monbouquette	15.00	7.50
❑ 8 Carl Yastrzemski	100.00	60.00
❑ 9 Ray Herbert	15.00	7.50
❑ 10 Jim Landis	15.00	7.50
❑ 11 Dick Donovan	15.00	7.50
❑ 12 Tito Francona	15.00	7.50
❑ 13 Jerry Kindall	15.00	7.50
❑ 14 Frank Lary	20.00	10.00
❑ 15 Dick Howser	20.00	10.00
❑ 16 Jerry Lumpe	15.00	7.50
❑ 17 Norm Siebern	15.00	7.50
❑ 18 Don Lee	15.00	7.50
❑ 19 Albie Pearson	20.00	10.00
❑ 20 Bob Rodgers	20.00	10.00
❑ 21 Leon Wagner	15.00	7.50
❑ 22 Jim Kaat	25.00	12.50
❑ 23 Vic Power	20.00	10.00
❑ 24 Rich Rollins	20.00	10.00
❑ 25 Bobby Richardson	25.00	12.50
❑ 26 Ralph Terry	20.00	10.00
❑ 27 Tom Cheney	15.00	7.50
❑ 28 Chuck Cottier	15.00	7.50
❑ 29 Jimmy Piersall	20.00	10.00
❑ 30 Dave Stenhouse	15.00	7.50
❑ 31 Glen Hobbie	15.00	7.50
❑ 32 Ron Santo	25.00	12.50
❑ 33 Gene Freese	15.00	7.50
❑ 34 Vada Pinson	25.00	12.50
❑ 35 Bob Purkey	15.00	7.50
❑ 36 Joe Amalfitano	15.00	7.50
❑ 37 Bob Aspromonte	15.00	7.50
❑ 38 Dick Farrell	15.00	7.50
❑ 39 Al Spangler	15.00	7.50
❑ 40 Tommy Davis	20.00	10.00
❑ 41 Don Drysdale	80.00	50.00
❑ 42 Sandy Koufax	200.00	125.00
❑ 43 Maury Wills RC	100.00	60.00
❑ 44 Frank Bolling	15.00	7.50
❑ 45 Warren Spahn	80.00	50.00
❑ 46 Joe Adcock SP	150.00	90.00
❑ 47 Roger Craig	20.00	10.00
❑ 48 Al Jackson	20.00	10.00
❑ 49 Rod Kanehl	20.00	10.00
❑ 50 Ruben Amaro	15.00	7.50
❑ 51 Johnny Callison	20.00	10.00
❑ 52 Clay Dalrymple	15.00	7.50
❑ 53 Don Demeter	15.00	7.50
❑ 54 Art Mahaffey	15.00	7.50
❑ 55 Smoky Burgess	20.00	10.00
❑ 56 Roberto Clemente	175.00	100.00
❑ 57 Roy Face	20.00	10.00
❑ 58 Vern Law	20.00	10.00
❑ 59 Bill Mazeroski	30.00	15.00
❑ 60 Ken Boyer	25.00	12.50
❑ 61 Bob Gibson	80.00	50.00
❑ 62 Gene Oliver	15.00	7.50
❑ 63 Bill White	20.00	10.00
❑ 64 Orlando Cepeda	30.00	15.00
❑ 65 Jim Davenport	15.00	7.50
❑ 66 Billy O'Dell	25.00	12.50
❑ NNO Checklist SP	500.00	300.00

1981 Fleer

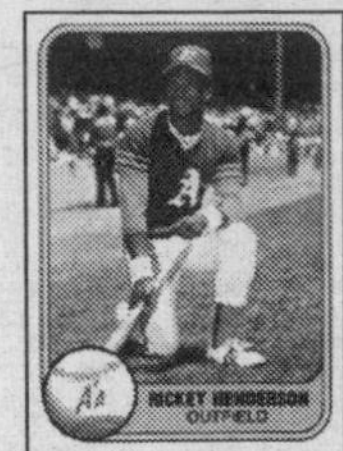

❑ COMPLETE SET (660)	40.00	15.00
❑ 1 Pete Rose	3.00	1.25
❑ 2 Larry Bowa	.25	.08
❑ 3 Manny Trillo	.10	.02
❑ 4 Bob Boone	.25	.08
❑ 5 Mike Schmidt	2.50	1.00
❑ 6 Steve Carlton P1	.50	.20
❑ 6B Steve Carlton P2	1.50	.60
❑ 6C Steve Carlton P3	2.00	.75
❑ 7 Tug McGraw	.25	.08
❑ 8 Larry Christenson	.10	.02
❑ 9 Bake McBride	.25	.08
❑ 10 Greg Luzinski	.25	.08
❑ 11 Ron Reed	.10	.02
❑ 12 Dickie Noles	.10	.02
❑ 13 Keith Moreland RC	.10	.02
❑ 14 Bob Walk RC	.50	.20
❑ 15 Lonnie Smith	.25	.08
❑ 16 Dick Ruthven	.10	.02
❑ 17 Sparky Lyle	.25	.08
❑ 18 Greg Gross	.10	.02
❑ 19 Garry Maddox	.10	.02
❑ 20 Nino Espinosa	.10	.02
❑ 21 George Vukovich RC	.10	.02
❑ 22 John Vukovich	.10	.02
❑ 23 Ramon Aviles	.10	.02
❑ 24A Kevin Saucier P1	.10	.02
❑ 24B Kevin Saucier P2	.10	.02
❑ 24C Kevin Saucier P3	.50	.20
❑ 25 Randy Lerch	.10	.02
❑ 26 Del Unser	.10	.02
❑ 27 Tim McCarver	.25	.08
❑ 28 George Brett	2.50	1.00
❑ 29 Willie Wilson	.25	.08
❑ 30 Paul Splittorff	.10	.02
❑ 31 Dan Quisenberry	.10	.02
❑ 32A Amos Otis P1 Batting	.25	.08
❑ 32B Amos Otis P2	.25	.08
❑ 33 Steve Busby	.10	.02
❑ 34 U.L. Washington	.10	.02
❑ 35 Dave Chalk	.10	.02
❑ 36 Darrell Porter	.10	.02
❑ 37 Marty Pattin	.10	.02
❑ 38 Larry Gura	.10	.02
❑ 39 Renie Martin	.10	.02
❑ 40 Rich Gale	.10	.02
❑ 41A Hal McRae P1	.50	.20
❑ 41B Hal McRae P2	.25	.08
❑ 42 Dennis Leonard	.10	.02
❑ 43 Willie Aikens	.10	.02
❑ 44 Frank White	.25	.08
❑ 45 Clint Hurdle	.10	.02
❑ 46 John Wathan	.10	.02
❑ 47 Pete LaCock	.10	.02
❑ 48 Rance Mulliniks	.10	.02
❑ 49 Jeff Twitty RC	.10	.02
❑ 50 Jamie Quirk	.10	.02
❑ 51 Art Howe	.10	.02
❑ 52 Ken Forsch	.10	.02
❑ 53 Vern Ruhle	.10	.02
❑ 54 Joe Niekro	.10	.02
❑ 55 Frank LaCorte	.10	.02
❑ 56 J.R. Richard	.25	.08
❑ 57 Nolan Ryan	5.00	2.00

☐	58 Enos Cabell	.10	.02
☐	59 Cesar Cedeno	.25	.08
☐	60 Jose Cruz	.25	.08
☐	61 Bill Virdon MG	.10	.02
☐	62 Terry Puhl	.10	.02
☐	63 Joaquin Andujar	.25	.08
☐	64 Alan Ashby	.10	.02
☐	65 Joe Sambito	.10	.02
☐	66 Denny Walling	.10	.02
☐	67 Jeff Leonard	.25	.08
☐	68 Luis Pujols	.10	.02
☐	69 Bruce Bochy	.10	.02
☐	70 Rafael Landestoy	.10	.02
☐	71 Dave Smith RC	.50	.20
☐	72 Danny Heep RC	.10	.02
☐	73 Julio Gonzalez	.10	.02
☐	74 Craig Reynolds	.10	.02
☐	75 Gary Woods	.10	.02
☐	76 Dave Bergman	.10	.02
☐	77 Randy Niemann	.10	.02
☐	78 Joe Morgan	.50	.20
☐	79 Reggie Jackson	1.00	.40
☐	80 Bucky Dent	.25	.08
☐	81 Tommy John	.25	.08
☐	82 Luis Tiant	.25	.08
☐	83 Rick Cerone	.10	.02
☐	84 Dick Howser MG	.10	.02
☐	85 Lou Piniella	.25	.08
☐	86 Ron Davis	.10	.02
☐	87A Craig Nettles P1	5.00	2.00
☐	87B Graig Nettles COR	.25	.08
☐	88 Ron Guidry	.25	.08
☐	89 Rich Gossage	.25	.08
☐	90 Rudy May	.10	.02
☐	91 Gaylord Perry	.25	.08
☐	92 Eric Soderholm	.10	.02
☐	93 Bob Watson	.10	.02
☐	94 Bobby Murcer	.25	.08
☐	95 Bobby Brown	.10	.02
☐	96 Jim Spencer	.10	.02
☐	97 Tom Underwood	.10	.02
☐	98 Oscar Gamble	.10	.02
☐	99 Johnny Oates	.25	.08
☐	100 Fred Stanley	.10	.02
☐	101 Ruppert Jones	.10	.02
☐	102 Dennis Werth RC	.10	.02
☐	103 Joe Lefebvre RC	.10	.02
☐	104 Brian Doyle	.10	.02
☐	105 Aurelio Rodriguez	.10	.02
☐	106 Doug Bird	.10	.02
☐	107 Mike Griffin RC	.15	.05
☐	108 Tim Lollar RC	.10	.02
☐	109 Willie Randolph	.25	.08
☐	110 Steve Garvey	.50	.20
☐	111 Reggie Smith	.25	.08
☐	112 Don Sutton	.25	.08
☐	113 Burt Hooton	.10	.02
☐	114A Dave Lopes P1	.50	.20
☐	114B Dave Lopes P2	.25	.08
☐	115 Dusty Baker	.25	.08
☐	116 Tom Lasorda MG	.50	.20
☐	117 Bill Russell	.25	.08
☐	118 Jerry Reuss UER	.10	.02
☐	119 Terry Forster	.25	.08
☐	120A Bob Welch	.25	.08
☐	120B Bob Welch (Robert)	.25	.08
☐	121 Don Stanhouse	.10	.02
☐	122 Rick Monday	.25	.08
☐	123 Derrel Thomas	.10	.02
☐	124 Joe Ferguson	.10	.02
☐	125 Rick Sutcliffe	.25	.08
☐	126A Ron Cey P1	.25	.08
☐	126B Ron Cey P2	.25	.08
☐	127 Dave Goltz	.10	.02
☐	128 Jay Johnstone	.10	.02
☐	129 Steve Yeager	.25	.08
☐	130 Gary Weiss RC	.10	.02
☐	131 Mike Scioscia RC	1.50	.60
☐	132 Vic Davalillo	.10	.02
☐	133 Doug Rau	.10	.02
☐	134 Pepe Frias	.10	.02
☐	135 Mickey Hatcher	.10	.02
☐	136 Steve Howe RC	.50	.20
☐	137 Robert Castillo RC	.10	.02
☐	138 Gary Thomasson	.10	.02
☐	139 Rudy Law	.10	.02
☐	140 Fernando Valenzuela RC	5.00	2.00
☐	141 Manny Mota	.25	.08
☐	142 Gary Carter	.50	.20
☐	143 Steve Rogers	.25	.08
☐	144 Warren Cromartie	.10	.02
☐	145 Andre Dawson	.50	.20
☐	146 Larry Parrish	.10	.02
☐	147 Rowland Office	.10	.02
☐	148 Ellis Valentine	.10	.02
☐	149 Dick Williams MG	.10	.02
☐	150 Bill Gullickson RC	.50	.20
☐	151 Elias Sosa	.10	.02
☐	152 John Tamargo	.10	.02
☐	153 Chris Speier	.10	.02
☐	154 Ron LeFlore	.25	.08
☐	155 Rodney Scott	.10	.02
☐	156 Stan Bahnsen	.10	.02
☐	157 Bill Lee	.25	.08
☐	158 Fred Norman	.10	.02
☐	159 Woodie Fryman	.10	.02
☐	160 David Palmer	.10	.02
☐	161 Jerry White	.10	.02
☐	162 Roberto Ramos RC	.10	.02
☐	163 John D'Acquisto	.10	.02
☐	164 Tommy Hutton	.10	.02
☐	165 Charlie Lea RC	.10	.02
☐	166 Scott Sanderson	.10	.02
☐	167 Ken Macha	.10	.02
☐	168 Tony Bernazard	.10	.02
☐	169 Jim Palmer	.50	.20
☐	170 Steve Stone	.10	.02
☐	171 Mike Flanagan	.10	.02
☐	172 Al Bumbry	.10	.02
☐	173 Doug DeCinces	.10	.02
☐	174 Scott McGregor	.10	.02
☐	175 Mark Belanger	.10	.02
☐	176 Tim Stoddard	.10	.02
☐	177A Rick Dempsey P1	.25	.08
☐	177B Rick Dempsey P2	.10	.02
☐	178 Earl Weaver MG	.25	.08
☐	179 Tippy Martinez	.10	.02
☐	180 Dennis Martinez	.25	.08
☐	181 Sammy Stewart	.10	.02
☐	182 Rich Dauer	.10	.02
☐	183 Lee May	.10	.02
☐	184 Eddie Murray	1.50	.60
☐	185 Benny Ayala	.10	.02
☐	186 John Lowenstein	.10	.02
☐	187 Gary Roenicke	.10	.02
☐	188 Ken Singleton	.25	.08
☐	189 Dan Graham	.10	.02
☐	190 Terry Crowley	.10	.02
☐	191 Kiko Garcia	.10	.02
☐	192 Dave Ford RC	.10	.02
☐	193 Mark Corey	.10	.02
☐	194 Lenn Sakata	.10	.02
☐	195 Doug DeCinces	.10	.02
☐	196 Johnny Bench	1.00	.40
☐	197 Dave Concepcion	.25	.08
☐	198 Ray Knight	.25	.08
☐	199 Ken Griffey	.25	.08
☐	200 Tom Seaver	1.00	.40
☐	201 Dave Collins	.10	.02
☐	202A George Foster P1	.50	.20
☐	202B George Foster P2	.50	.20
☐	203 Junior Kennedy	.10	.02
☐	204 Frank Pastore	.10	.02
☐	205 Dan Driessen	.10	.02
☐	206 Hector Cruz	.10	.02
☐	207 Paul Moskau	.10	.02
☐	208 Charlie Leibrandt RC	.50	.20
☐	209 Harry Spilman	.10	.02
☐	210 Joe Price RC	.10	.02
☐	211 Tom Hume	.10	.02
☐	212 Joe Nolan RC	.10	.02
☐	213 Doug Bair	.10	.02
☐	214 Mario Soto	.25	.08
☐	215A Bill Bonham P1	.50	.20
☐	215B Bill Bonham P2	.10	.02
☐	216 George Foster SLG	.25	.08
☐	217 Paul Householder RC	.10	.02
☐	218 Ron Oester	.10	.02
☐	219 Sam Mejias	.10	.02
☐	220 Sheldon Burnside RC	.10	.02
☐	221 Carl Yastrzemski	1.50	.60
☐	222 Jim Rice	.25	.08
☐	223 Fred Lynn	.25	.08
☐	224 Carlton Fisk	.50	.20
☐	225 Rick Burleson	.10	.02
☐	226 Dennis Eckersley	.50	.20
☐	227 Butch Hobson	.10	.02
☐	228 Tom Burgmeier	.10	.02
☐	229 Garry Hancock	.10	.02
☐	230 Don Zimmer MG	.25	.08
☐	231 Steve Renko	.10	.02
☐	232 Dwight Evans	.50	.20
☐	233 Mike Torrez	.10	.02
☐	234 Bob Stanley	.10	.02
☐	235 Jim Dwyer	.10	.02
☐	236 Dave Stapleton RC	.10	.02
☐	237 Glenn Hoffman RC	.10	.02
☐	238 Jerry Remy	.10	.02
☐	239 Dick Drago	.10	.02
☐	240 Bill Campbell	.10	.02
☐	241 Tony Perez	.50	.20
☐	242 Phil Niekro	.25	.08
☐	243 Dale Murphy	.50	.20
☐	244 Bob Horner	.25	.08
☐	245 Jeff Burroughs	.25	.08
☐	246 Rick Camp	.10	.02
☐	247 Bobby Cox MG	.25	.08
☐	248 Bruce Benedict	.10	.02
☐	249 Gene Garber	.10	.02
☐	250 Jerry Royster	.10	.02
☐	251A Gary Matthews P1	.50	.20
☐	251B Gary Matthews P2	.25	.08
☐	252 Chris Chambliss	.25	.08
☐	253 Luis Gomez	.10	.02
☐	254 Bill Nahorodny	.10	.02
☐	255 Doyle Alexander	.10	.02
☐	256 Brian Asselstine	.10	.02
☐	257 Biff Pocoroba	.10	.02
☐	258 Mike Lum	.10	.02
☐	259 Charlie Spikes	.10	.02
☐	260 Glenn Hubbard	.10	.02
☐	261 Tommy Boggs	.10	.02
☐	262 Al Hrabosky	.25	.08
☐	263 Rick Matula	.10	.02
☐	264 Preston Hanna	.10	.02
☐	265 Larry Bradford	.10	.02
☐	266 Rafael Ramirez RC	.10	.02
☐	267 Larry McWilliams	.10	.02
☐	268 Rod Carew	.50	.20
☐	269 Bobby Grich	.25	.08
☐	270 Carney Lansford	.25	.08
☐	271 Don Baylor	.25	.08
☐	272 Joe Rudi	.25	.08
☐	273 Dan Ford	.10	.02
☐	274 Jim Fregosi MG	.10	.02
☐	275 Dave Frost	.10	.02
☐	276 Frank Tanana	.25	.08
☐	277 Dickie Thon	.10	.02
☐	278 Jason Thompson	.10	.02
☐	279 Rick Miller	.10	.02
☐	280 Bert Campaneris	.25	.08
☐	281 Tom Donohue	.10	.02
☐	282 Brian Downing	.25	.08
☐	283 Fred Patek	.10	.02
☐	284 Bruce Kison	.10	.02
☐	285 Dave LaRoche	.10	.02
☐	286 Don Aase	.10	.02
☐	287 Jim Barr	.10	.02
☐	288 Alfredo Martinez RC	.10	.02
☐	289 Larry Harlow	.10	.02
☐	290 Andy Hassler	.10	.02
☐	291 Dave Kingman	.25	.08
☐	292 Bill Buckner	.25	.08
☐	293 Rick Reuschel	.25	.08
☐	294 Bruce Sutter	.50	.20
☐	295 Jerry Martin	.10	.02
☐	296 Scot Thompson	.10	.02
☐	297 Ivan DeJesus	.10	.02
☐	298 Steve Dillard	.10	.02
☐	299 Dick Tidrow	.10	.02
☐	300 Randy Martz RC	.10	.02
☐	301 Lenny Randle	.10	.02
☐	302 Lynn McGlothen	.10	.02
☐	303 Cliff Johnson	.10	.02
☐	304 Tim Blackwell	.10	.02
☐	305 Dennis Lamp	.10	.02
☐	306 Bill Caudill	.10	.02
☐	307 Carlos Lezcano RC	.10	.02

❑ 308 Jim Tracy RC 1.00 .40
❑ 309 Doug Capilla UER .10 .02
❑ 310 Willie Hernandez .10 .02
❑ 311 Mike Vail .10 .02
❑ 312 Mike Krukow RC .10 .02
❑ 313 Barry Foote .10 .02
❑ 314 Larry Biittner .10 .02
❑ 315 Mike Tyson .10 .02
❑ 316 Lee Mazzilli .25 .08
❑ 317 John Stearns .10 .02
❑ 318 Alex Trevino .10 .02
❑ 319 Craig Swan .10 .02
❑ 320 Frank Taveras .10 .02
❑ 321 Steve Henderson .10 .02
❑ 322 Neil Allen .10 .02
❑ 323 Mark Bomback RC .10 .02
❑ 324 Mike Jorgensen .10 .02
❑ 325 Joe Torre MG .25 .08
❑ 326 Elliott Maddox .10 .02
❑ 327 Pete Falcone .10 .02
❑ 328 Ray Burris .10 .02
❑ 329 Claudell Washington .10 .02
❑ 330 Doug Flynn .10 .02
❑ 331 Joel Youngblood .10 .02
❑ 332 Bill Almon RC .10 .02
❑ 333 Tom Hausman .10 .02
❑ 334 Pat Zachry .10 .02
❑ 335 Jeff Reardon RC 1.00 .40
❑ 336 Wally Backman RC .50 .20
❑ 337 Dan Norman .10 .02
❑ 338 Jerry Morales .10 .02
❑ 339 Ed Farmer .10 .02
❑ 340 Bob Molinaro .10 .02
❑ 341 Todd Cruz .10 .02
❑ 342A Britt Burns P1 .50 .20
❑ 342B Britt Burns P2 RC .25 .08
❑ 343 Kevin Bell .10 .02
❑ 344 Tony LaRussa MG .25 .08
❑ 345 Steve Trout .10 .02
❑ 346 Harold Baines RC 2.00 .75
❑ 347 Richard Wortham .10 .02
❑ 348 Wayne Nordhagen .10 .02
❑ 349 Mike Squires .10 .02
❑ 350 Lamar Johnson .10 .02
❑ 351 Rickey Henderson SB 3.00 1.25
❑ 352 Francisco Barrios .10 .02
❑ 353 Thad Bosley .10 .02
❑ 354 Chet Lemon .25 .08
❑ 355 Bruce Kimm .10 .02
❑ 356 Richard Dotson RC .10 .02
❑ 357 Jim Morrison .10 .02
❑ 358 Mike Proly .10 .02
❑ 359 Greg Pryor .10 .02
❑ 360 Dave Parker .25 .08
❑ 361 Omar Moreno .10 .02
❑ 362A Kent Tekulve P1 .10 .02
❑ 362B Kent Tekulve P2 .10 .02
❑ 363 Willie Stargell .50 .20
❑ 364 Phil Garner .25 .08
❑ 365 Ed Ott .10 .02
❑ 366 Don Robinson .10 .02
❑ 367 Chuck Tanner MG .10 .02
❑ 368 Jim Rooker .10 .02
❑ 369 Dale Berra .10 .02
❑ 370 Jim Bibby .10 .02
❑ 371 Steve Nicosia .10 .02
❑ 372 Mike Easler .10 .02
❑ 373 Bill Robinson .10 .02
❑ 374 Lee Lacy .10 .02
❑ 375 John Candelaria .25 .08
❑ 376 Manny Sanguillen .25 .08
❑ 377 Rick Rhoden .10 .02
❑ 378 Grant Jackson .10 .02
❑ 379 Tim Foli .10 .02
❑ 380 Rod Scurry RC .10 .02
❑ 381 Bill Madlock .25 .08
❑ 382A Kurt Bevacqua P1 .25 .08
❑ 382B Kurt Bevacqua P2 .10 .02
❑ 383 Bert Blyleven .25 .08
❑ 384 Eddie Solomon .10 .02
❑ 385 Enrique Romo .10 .02
❑ 386 John Milner .10 .02
❑ 387 Mike Hargrove .10 .02
❑ 388 Jorge Orta .10 .02
❑ 389 Toby Harrah .25 .08
❑ 390 Tom Veryzer .10 .02
❑ 391 Miguel Dilone .10 .02
❑ 392 Dan Spillner .10 .02
❑ 393 Jack Brohamer .10 .02
❑ 394 Wayne Garland .10 .02
❑ 395 Sid Monge .10 .02
❑ 396 Rick Waits .10 .02
❑ 397 Joe Charboneau RC 1.00 .40
❑ 398 Gary Alexander .10 .02
❑ 399 Jerry Dybzinski RC .10 .02
❑ 400 Mike Stanton RC .10 .02
❑ 401 Mike Paxton .10 .02
❑ 402 Gary Gray RC .10 .02
❑ 403 Rick Manning .10 .02
❑ 404 Bo Diaz .10 .02
❑ 405 Ron Hassey .10 .02
❑ 406 Ross Grimsley .10 .02
❑ 407 Victor Cruz .10 .02
❑ 408 Len Barker .25 .08
❑ 409 Bob Bailor .10 .02
❑ 410 Otto Velez .10 .02
❑ 411 Ernie Whitt .10 .02
❑ 412 Jim Clancy .10 .02
❑ 413 Barry Bonnell .10 .02
❑ 414 Dave Stieb .25 .08
❑ 415 Damaso Garcia RC .10 .02
❑ 416 John Mayberry .10 .02
❑ 417 Roy Howell .10 .02
❑ 418 Danny Ainge RC 3.00 1.25
❑ 419A Jesse Jefferson P1 .10 .02
❑ 419B Jesse Jefferson P2 .10 .02
❑ 419C Jesse Jefferson P3 .50 .20
❑ 420 Joey McLaughlin .10 .02
❑ 421 Lloyd Moseby RC .50 .20
❑ 422 Alvis Woods .10 .02
❑ 423 Garth Iorg .10 .02
❑ 424 Doug Ault .10 .02
❑ 425 Ken Schrom RC .10 .02
❑ 426 Mike Willis .10 .02
❑ 427 Steve Braun .10 .02
❑ 428 Bob Davis .10 .02
❑ 429 Jerry Garvin .10 .02
❑ 430 Alfredo Griffin .10 .02
❑ 431 Bob Mattick MG RC .10 .02
❑ 432 Vida Blue .25 .08
❑ 433 Jack Clark .25 .08
❑ 434 Willie McCovey .50 .20
❑ 435 Mike Ivie .10 .02
❑ 436A Darrel Evans P1 ERR .50 .20
❑ 436B Darrell Evans P2 COR .50 .20
❑ 437 Terry Whitfield .10 .02
❑ 438 Rennie Stennett .10 .02
❑ 439 John Montefusco .10 .02
❑ 440 Jim Wohlford .10 .02
❑ 441 Bill North .10 .02
❑ 442 Milt May .10 .02
❑ 443 Max Venable RC .10 .02
❑ 444 Ed Whitson .10 .02
❑ 445 Al Holland RC .10 .02
❑ 446 Randy Moffitt .10 .02
❑ 447 Bob Knepper .10 .02
❑ 448 Gary Lavelle .10 .02
❑ 449 Greg Minton .10 .02
❑ 450 Johnnie LeMaster .10 .02
❑ 451 Larry Herndon .10 .02
❑ 452 Rich Murray RC .10 .02
❑ 453 Joe Pettini RC .10 .02
❑ 454 Allen Ripley .10 .02
❑ 455 Dennis Littlejohn .10 .02
❑ 456 Tom Griffin .10 .02
❑ 457 Alan Hargesheimer RC .10 .02
❑ 458 Joe Strain .10 .02
❑ 459 Steve Kemp .10 .02
❑ 460 Sparky Anderson MG .25 .08
❑ 461 Alan Trammell .50 .20
❑ 462 Mark Fidrych .25 .08
❑ 463 Lou Whitaker .50 .20
❑ 464 Dave Rozema .10 .02
❑ 465 Milt Wilcox .10 .02
❑ 466 Champ Summers .10 .02
❑ 467 Lance Parrish .25 .08
❑ 468 Dan Petry .10 .02
❑ 469 Pat Underwood .10 .02
❑ 470 Rick Peters RC .10 .02
❑ 471 Al Cowens .10 .02
❑ 472 John Wockenfuss .10 .02
❑ 473 Tom Brookens .10 .02
❑ 474 Richie Hebner .10 .02
❑ 475 Jack Morris .50 .20
❑ 476 Jim Lentine RC .10 .02
❑ 477 Bruce Robbins .10 .02
❑ 478 Mark Wagner .10 .02
❑ 479 Tim Corcoran .10 .02
❑ 480A Stan Papi P1 .25 .08
❑ 480B Stan Papi P2 .10 .02
❑ 481 Kirk Gibson RC 5.00 2.00
❑ 482 Dan Schatzeder .10 .02
❑ 483A Amos Otis P1 .25 .08
❑ 483B Amos Otis P2 .25 .08
❑ 484 Dave Winfield .50 .20
❑ 485 Rollie Fingers .25 .08
❑ 486 Gene Richards .10 .02
❑ 487 Randy Jones .10 .02
❑ 488 Ozzie Smith 3.00 1.25
❑ 489 Gene Tenace .25 .08
❑ 490 Bill Fahey .10 .02
❑ 491 John Curtis .10 .02
❑ 492 Dave Cash .10 .02
❑ 493A Tim Flannery P1 .25 .08
❑ 493B Tim Flannery P2 .10 .02
❑ 494 Jerry Mumphrey .10 .02
❑ 495 Bob Shirley .10 .02
❑ 496 Steve Mura .10 .02
❑ 497 Eric Rasmussen .10 .02
❑ 498 Broderick Perkins .10 .02
❑ 499 Barry Evans RC .10 .02
❑ 500 Chuck Baker .10 .02
❑ 501 Luis Salazar RC .50 .20
❑ 502 Gary Lucas RC .10 .02
❑ 503 Mike Armstrong RC .10 .02
❑ 504 Jerry Turner .10 .02
❑ 505 Dennis Kinney RC .10 .02
❑ 506 Willie Montanez UER .10 .02
❑ 507 Gorman Thomas .25 .08
❑ 508 Ben Oglivie .25 .08
❑ 509 Larry Hisle .10 .02
❑ 510 Sal Bando .25 .08
❑ 511 Robin Yount 1.50 .60
❑ 512 Mike Caldwell .10 .02
❑ 513 Sixto Lezcano .10 .02
❑ 514A Bill Travers P1 ERR .25 .08
❑ 514B Bill Travers P2 COR .10 .02
❑ 515 Paul Molitor 1.00 .40
❑ 516 Moose Haas .10 .02
❑ 517 Bill Castro .10 .02
❑ 518 Jim Slaton .10 .02
❑ 519 Lary Sorensen .10 .02
❑ 520 Bob McClure .10 .02
❑ 521 Charlie Moore .10 .02
❑ 522 Jim Gantner .10 .02
❑ 523 Reggie Cleveland .10 .02
❑ 524 Don Money .10 .02
❑ 525 Bill Travers .10 .02
❑ 526 Buck Martinez .10 .02
❑ 527 Dick Davis .10 .02
❑ 528 Ted Simmons .25 .08
❑ 529 Garry Templeton .25 .08
❑ 530 Ken Reitz .10 .02
❑ 531 Tony Scott .10 .02
❑ 532 Ken Oberkfell .10 .02
❑ 533 Bob Sykes .10 .02
❑ 534 Keith Smith .10 .02
❑ 535 John Littlefield RC .10 .02
❑ 536 Jim Kaat .25 .08
❑ 537 Bob Forsch .10 .02
❑ 538 Mike Phillips .10 .02
❑ 539 Terry Landrum RC .10 .02
❑ 540 Leon Durham RC .50 .20
❑ 541 Terry Kennedy .10 .02
❑ 542 George Hendrick .25 .08
❑ 543 Dane Iorg .10 .02
❑ 544 Mark Littell .10 .02
❑ 545 Keith Hernandez .25 .08
❑ 546 Silvio Martinez .10 .02
❑ 547A Don Hood P1 ERR .25 .08
❑ 547B Don Hood P2 COR .10 .02
❑ 548 Bobby Bonds .25 .08
❑ 549 Mike Ramsey RC .15 .05
❑ 550 Tom Herr .10 .02
❑ 551 Roy Smalley .10 .02
❑ 552 Jerry Koosman .25 .08
❑ 553 Ken Landreaux .10 .02
❑ 554 John Castino .10 .02

❑	555 Doug Corbett RC	.10	.02
❑	556 Bombo Rivera	.10	.02
❑	557 Ron Jackson	.10	.02
❑	558 Butch Wynegar	.10	.02
❑	559 Hosken Powell	.10	.02
❑	560 Pete Redfern	.10	.02
❑	561 Roger Erickson	.10	.02
❑	562 Glenn Adams	.10	.02
❑	563 Rick Sofield	.10	.02
❑	564 Geoff Zahn	.10	.02
❑	565 Pete Mackanin	.10	.02
❑	566 Mike Cubbage	.10	.02
❑	567 Darrell Jackson	.10	.02
❑	568 Dave Edwards	.10	.02
❑	569 Rob Wilfong	.10	.02
❑	570 Sal Butera RC	.10	.02
❑	571 Jose Morales	.10	.02
❑	572 Rick Langford	.10	.02
❑	573 Mike Norris	.10	.02
❑	574 Rickey Henderson	6.00	2.50
❑	575 Tony Armas	.25	.08
❑	576 Dave Revering	.10	.02
❑	577 Jeff Newman	.10	.02
❑	578 Bob Lacey	.10	.02
❑	579 Brian Kingman	.10	.02
❑	580 Mitchell Page	.10	.02
❑	581 Billy Martin MG	.50	.20
❑	582 Rob Picciolo	.10	.02
❑	583 Mike Heath	.10	.02
❑	584 Mickey Klutts	.10	.02
❑	585 Orlando Gonzalez	.10	.02
❑	586 Mike Davis RC	.50	.20
❑	587 Wayne Gross	.10	.02
❑	588 Matt Keough	.10	.02
❑	589 Steve McCatty	.10	.02
❑	590 Dwayne Murphy	.10	.02
❑	591 Mario Guerrero	.10	.02
❑	592 Dave McKay RC	.10	.02
❑	593 Jim Essian	.10	.02
❑	594 Dave Heaverlo	.10	.02
❑	595 Maury Wills MG	.25	.08
❑	596 Juan Beniquez	.10	.02
❑	597 Rodney Craig	.10	.02
❑	598 Jim Anderson	.10	.02
❑	599 Floyd Bannister	.10	.02
❑	600 Bruce Bochte	.10	.02
❑	601 Julio Cruz	.10	.02
❑	602 Ted Cox	.10	.02
❑	603 Dan Meyer	.10	.02
❑	604 Larry Cox	.10	.02
❑	605 Bill Stein	.10	.02
❑	606 Steve Garvey	.50	.20
❑	607 Dave Roberts	.10	.02
❑	608 Leon Roberts	.10	.02
❑	609 Reggie Walton RC	.10	.02
❑	610 Dave Edler RC	.10	.02
❑	611 Larry Milbourne	.10	.02
❑	612 Kim Allen RC	.10	.02
❑	613 Mario Mendoza	.10	.02
❑	614 Tom Paciorek	.10	.02
❑	615 Glenn Abbott	.10	.02
❑	616 Joe Simpson	.10	.02
❑	617 Mickey Rivers	.10	.02
❑	618 Jim Kern	.10	.02
❑	619 Jim Sundberg	.25	.08
❑	620 Richie Zisk	.10	.02
❑	621 Jon Matlack	.10	.02
❑	622 Fergie Jenkins	.25	.08
❑	623 Pat Corrales MG	.10	.02
❑	624 Ed Figueroa	.10	.02
❑	625 Buddy Bell	.25	.08
❑	626 Al Oliver	.25	.08
❑	627 Doc Medich	.10	.02
❑	628 Bump Wills	.10	.02
❑	629 Rusty Staub	.25	.08
❑	630 Pat Putnam	.10	.02
❑	631 John Grubb	.10	.02
❑	632 Danny Darwin	.10	.02
❑	633 Ken Clay	.10	.02
❑	634 Jim Norris	.10	.02
❑	635 John Butcher RC	.10	.02
❑	636 Dave Roberts	.10	.02
❑	637 Billy Sample	.10	.02
❑	638 Carl Yastrzemski	1.50	.60
❑	639 Cecil Cooper	.25	.08
❑	640 M.Schmidt Portrait P1	2.50	1.00
❑	640B M.Schmidt Portrait P2	2.50	1.00
❑	641A CL: Phils/Royals P1	.25	.08
❑	641B CL: Phils/Royals P2	.25	.08
❑	642 CL: Astros/Yankees	.10	.02
❑	643 CL: Expos/Dodgers	.10	.02
❑	644A CL: Reds/Orioles P1	.25	.08
❑	644B CL: Reds/Orioles P2	.25	.08
❑	645 Rose/Bowa/Schmidt	1.50	.60
❑	645B Rose/Bowa/Schmidt	2.50	1.00
❑	646 CL: Braves/Red Sox	.10	.02
❑	647 CL: Cubs/Angels	.10	.02
❑	648 CL: Mets/White Sox	.10	.02
❑	649 CL: Indians/Pirates	.10	.02
❑	650 Reggie Jackson Mr. BB	1.00	.40
❑	650B R.Jackson Mr. BB P2	.50	.20
❑	651 CL: Giants/Blue Jays	.10	.02
❑	652A CL: Tigers/Padres P1	.25	.08
❑	652B CL: Tigers/Padres P2	.25	.08
❑	653A Willie Wilson Most Hits	.25	.08
❑	653B W.Wilson Hits P2	.25	.08
❑	654A CL:Brewers/Cards P1	.25	.08
❑	654B CL:Brewers/Cards P2	.25	.08
❑	655 George Brett .390 Avg.	2.50	1.00
❑	655B G.Brett .390 Avg. P2	2.50	1.00
❑	656 CL: Twins/Oakland A's	.25	.08
❑	657A Tug McGraw Saver	.25	.08
❑	657B T.McGraw Saver P2	.25	.08
❑	658 CL: Rangers/Mariners	.10	.02
❑	659A Checklist P1	.10	.02
❑	659B Checklist P2	.10	.02
❑	660 S.Carlton Gold Arm P1	.50	.20
❑	660B S.Carlton Golden Arm	2.00	.75

1982 Fleer

❑	COMPLETE SET (660)	50.00	20.00
❑	1 Dusty Baker	.20	.07
❑	2 Robert Castillo	.10	.02
❑	3 Ron Cey	.20	.07
❑	4 Terry Forster	.20	.07
❑	5 Steve Garvey	.20	.07
❑	6 Dave Goltz	.10	.02
❑	7 Pedro Guerrero	.20	.07
❑	8 Burt Hooton	.10	.02
❑	9 Steve Howe	.10	.02
❑	10 Jay Johnstone	.10	.02
❑	11 Ken Landreaux	.10	.02
❑	12 Dave Lopes	.20	.07
❑	13 Mike A. Marshall RC	.50	.20
❑	14 Bobby Mitchell	.10	.02
❑	15 Rick Monday	.20	.07
❑	16 Tom Niedenfuer RC	.50	.20
❑	17 Ted Power RC	.15	.05
❑	18 Jerry Reuss UER (Home:~ omitted)	.10	.02
❑	19 Ron Roenicke	.10	.02
❑	20 Bill Russell	.20	.07
❑	21 Steve Sax RC	1.00	.40
❑	22 Mike Scioscia	.20	.07
❑	23 Reggie Smith	.20	.07
❑	24 Dave Stewart RC	1.50	.60
❑	25 Rick Sutcliffe	.20	.07
❑	26 Derrel Thomas	.10	.02
❑	27 Fernando Valenzuela	.75	.30
❑	28 Bob Welch	.20	.07
❑	29 Steve Yeager	.20	.07
❑	30 Bobby Brown	.10	.02
❑	31 Rick Cerone	.10	.02
❑	32 Ron Davis	.10	.02
❑	33 Bucky Dent	.20	.07
❑	34 Barry Foote	.10	.02
❑	35 George Frazier	.10	.02
❑	36 Oscar Gamble	.10	.02
❑	37 Rich Gossage	.20	.07
❑	38 Ron Guidry	.20	.07
❑	39 Reggie Jackson	.40	.15
❑	40 Tommy John	.20	.07
❑	41 Rudy May	.10	.02
❑	42 Larry Milbourne	.10	.02
❑	43 Jerry Mumphrey	.10	.02
❑	44 Bobby Murcer	.20	.07
❑	45 Gene Nelson	.10	.02
❑	46 Graig Nettles	.20	.07
❑	47 Johnny Oates	.20	.07
❑	48 Lou Piniella	.20	.07
❑	49 Willie Randolph	.20	.07
❑	50 Rick Reuschel	.20	.07
❑	51 Dave Revering	.10	.02
❑	52 Dave Righetti RC	1.50	.60
❑	53 Aurelio Rodriguez	.10	.02
❑	54 Bob Watson	.10	.02
❑	55 Dennis Werth	.10	.02
❑	56 Dave Winfield	.20	.07
❑	57 Johnny Bench	.75	.30
❑	58 Bruce Berenyi	.10	.02
❑	59 Larry Biittner	.10	.02
❑	60 Scott Brown	.10	.02
❑	61 Dave Collins	.10	.02
❑	62 Geoff Combe	.10	.02
❑	63 Dave Concepcion	.20	.07
❑	64 Dan Driessen	.10	.02
❑	65 Joe Edelen	.10	.02
❑	66 George Foster	.20	.07
❑	67 Ken Griffey	.20	.07
❑	68 Paul Householder	.10	.02
❑	69 Tom Hume	.10	.02
❑	70 Junior Kennedy	.10	.02
❑	71 Ray Knight	.20	.07
❑	72 Mike LaCoss	.10	.02
❑	73 Rafael Landestoy	.10	.02
❑	74 Charlie Leibrandt	.10	.02
❑	75 Sam Mejias	.10	.02
❑	76 Paul Moskau	.10	.02
❑	77 Joe Nolan	.10	.02
❑	78 Mike O'Berry	.10	.02
❑	79 Ron Oester	.10	.02
❑	80 Frank Pastore	.10	.02
❑	81 Joe Price	.10	.02
❑	82 Tom Seaver	.75	.30
❑	83 Mario Soto	.20	.07
❑	84 Mike Vail	.10	.02
❑	85 Tony Armas	.20	.07
❑	86 Shooty Babitt	.10	.02
❑	87 Dave Beard	.10	.02
❑	88 Rick Bosetti	.10	.02
❑	89 Keith Drumwright	.10	.02
❑	90 Wayne Gross	.10	.02
❑	91 Mike Heath	.10	.02
❑	92 Rickey Henderson	2.50	1.00
❑	93 Cliff Johnson	.10	.02
❑	94 Jeff Jones	.10	.02
❑	95 Matt Keough	.10	.02
❑	96 Brian Kingman	.10	.02
❑	97 Mickey Klutts	.10	.02
❑	98 Rick Langford	.10	.02
❑	99 Steve McCatty	.10	.02
❑	100 Dave McKay	.10	.02
❑	101 Dwayne Murphy	.10	.02
❑	102 Jeff Newman	.10	.02
❑	103 Mike Norris	.10	.02
❑	104 Bob Owchinko	.10	.02
❑	105 Mitchell Page	.10	.02
❑	106 Rob Picciolo	.10	.02
❑	107 Jim Spencer	.10	.02
❑	108 Fred Stanley	.10	.02
❑	109 Tom Underwood	.10	.02
❑	110 Joaquin Andujar	.20	.07
❑	111 Steve Braun	.10	.02
❑	112 Bob Forsch	.10	.02
❑	113 George Hendrick	.20	.07
❑	114 Keith Hernandez	.20	.07
❑	115 Tom Herr	.10	.02
❑	116 Dane Iorg	.10	.02
❑	117 Jim Kaat	.20	.07
❑	118 Tito Landrum	.10	.02

❑ 119 Sixto Lezcano .10 .02
❑ 120 Mark Littell .10 .02
❑ 121 John Martin RC .15 .05
❑ 122 Silvio Martinez .10 .02
❑ 123 Ken Oberkfell .10 .02
❑ 124 Darrell Porter .10 .02
❑ 125 Mike Ramsey .10 .02
❑ 126 Orlando Sanchez .10 .02
❑ 127 Bob Shirley .10 .02
❑ 128 Lary Sorensen .10 .02
❑ 129 Bruce Sutter .40 .15
❑ 130 Bob Sykes .10 .02
❑ 131 Garry Templeton .20 .07
❑ 132 Gene Tenace .20 .07
❑ 133 Jerry Augustine .10 .02
❑ 134 Sal Bando .20 .07
❑ 135 Mark Brouhard .10 .02
❑ 136 Mike Caldwell .10 .02
❑ 137 Reggie Cleveland .10 .02
❑ 138 Cecil Cooper .20 .07
❑ 139 Jamie Easterly .10 .02
❑ 140 Marshall Edwards .10 .02
❑ 141 Rollie Fingers .20 .07
❑ 142 Jim Gantner .10 .02
❑ 143 Moose Haas .10 .02
❑ 144 Larry Hisle .10 .02
❑ 145 Roy Howell .10 .02
❑ 146 Rickey Keeton .10 .02
❑ 147 Randy Lerch .10 .02
❑ 148 Paul Molitor .20 .07
❑ 149 Don Money .10 .02
❑ 150 Charlie Moore .10 .02
❑ 151 Ben Oglivie .20 .07
❑ 152 Ted Simmons .20 .07
❑ 153 Jim Slaton .10 .02
❑ 154 Gorman Thomas .20 .07
❑ 155 Robin Yount 1.25 .50
❑ 156 Pete Vuckovich
(Should precede Yount
in the team .10 .02
❑ 157 Benny Ayala .10 .02
❑ 158 Mark Belanger .10 .02
❑ 159 Al Bumbry .10 .02
❑ 160 Terry Crowley .10 .02
❑ 161 Rich Dauer .10 .02
❑ 162 Doug DeCinces .10 .02
❑ 163 Rick Dempsey .10 .02
❑ 164 Jim Dwyer .10 .02
❑ 165 Mike Flanagan .10 .02
❑ 166 Dave Ford .10 .02
❑ 167 Dan Graham .10 .02
❑ 168 Wayne Krenchicki .10 .02
❑ 169 John Lowenstein .10 .02
❑ 170 Dennis Martinez .20 .07
❑ 171 Tippy Martinez .10 .02
❑ 172 Scott McGregor .10 .02
❑ 173 Jose Morales .10 .02
❑ 174 Eddie Murray .75 .30
❑ 175 Jim Palmer .20 .07
❑ 176 Cal Ripken RC 40.00 15.00
❑ 177 Gary Roenicke .10 .02
❑ 178 Lenn Sakata .10 .02
❑ 179 Ken Singleton .20 .07
❑ 180 Sammy Stewart .10 .02
❑ 181 Tim Stoddard .10 .02
❑ 182 Steve Stone .10 .02
❑ 183 Stan Bahnsen .10 .02
❑ 184 Ray Burris .10 .02
❑ 185 Gary Carter .20 .07
❑ 186 Warren Cromartie .10 .02
❑ 187 Andre Dawson .20 .07
❑ 188 Terry Francona RC 3.00 1.25
❑ 189 Woodie Fryman .10 .02
❑ 190 Bill Gullickson .10 .02
❑ 191 Grant Jackson .10 .02
❑ 192 Wallace Johnson .10 .02
❑ 193 Charlie Lea .10 .02
❑ 194 Bill Lee .20 .07
❑ 195 Jerry Manuel .10 .02
❑ 196 Brad Mills .10 .02
❑ 197 John Milner .10 .02
❑ 198 Rowland Office .10 .02
❑ 199 David Palmer .10 .02
❑ 200 Larry Parrish .10 .02
❑ 201 Mike Phillips .10 .02
❑ 202 Tim Raines .40 .15
❑ 203 Bobby Ramos .10 .02
❑ 204 Jeff Reardon .20 .07
❑ 205 Steve Rogers .20 .07
❑ 206 Scott Sanderson .10 .02
❑ 207 Rodney Scott UER Raines .40 .15
❑ 208 Elias Sosa .10 .02
❑ 209 Chris Speier .10 .02
❑ 210 Tim Wallach RC 1.00 .40
❑ 211 Jerry White .10 .02
❑ 212 Alan Ashby .10 .02
❑ 213 Cesar Cedeno .20 .07
❑ 214 Jose Cruz .20 .07
❑ 215 Kiko Garcia .10 .02
❑ 216 Phil Garner .20 .07
❑ 217 Danny Heep .10 .02
❑ 218 Art Howe .10 .02
❑ 219 Bob Knepper .10 .02
❑ 220 Frank LaCorte .10 .02
❑ 221 Joe Niekro .10 .02
❑ 222 Joe Pittman .10 .02
❑ 223 Terry Puhl .10 .02
❑ 224 Luis Pujols .10 .02
❑ 225 Craig Reynolds .10 .02
❑ 226 J.R. Richard .20 .07
❑ 227 Dave Roberts .10 .02
❑ 228 Vern Ruhle .10 .02
❑ 229 Nolan Ryan 4.00 1.50
❑ 230 Joe Sambito .10 .02
❑ 231 Tony Scott .10 .02
❑ 232 Dave Smith .10 .02
❑ 233 Harry Spilman .10 .02
❑ 234 Don Sutton .20 .07
❑ 235 Dickie Thon .10 .02
❑ 236 Denny Walling .10 .02
❑ 237 Gary Woods .10 .02
❑ 238 Luis Aguayo .10 .02
❑ 239 Ramon Aviles .10 .02
❑ 240 Bob Boone .20 .07
❑ 241 Larry Bowa .20 .07
❑ 242 Warren Brusstar .10 .02
❑ 243 Steve Carlton .40 .15
❑ 244 Larry Christenson .10 .02
❑ 245 Dick Davis .10 .02
❑ 246 Greg Gross .10 .02
❑ 247 Sparky Lyle .20 .07
❑ 248 Garry Maddox .10 .02
❑ 249 Gary Matthews .20 .07
❑ 250 Bake McBride .20 .07
❑ 251 Tug McGraw .20 .07
❑ 252 Keith Moreland .10 .02
❑ 253 Dickie Noles .10 .02
❑ 254 Mike Proly .10 .02
❑ 255 Ron Reed .10 .02
❑ 256 Pete Rose 2.50 1.00
❑ 257 Dick Ruthven .10 .02
❑ 258 Mike Schmidt 2.00 .75
❑ 259 Lonnie Smith .10 .02
❑ 260 Manny Trillo .10 .02
❑ 261 Del Unser .10 .02
❑ 262 George Vukovich .10 .02
❑ 263 Tom Brookens .10 .02
❑ 264 George Cappuzzello .10 .02
❑ 265 Marty Castillo .10 .02
❑ 266 Al Cowens .10 .02
❑ 267 Kirk Gibson .75 .30
❑ 268 Richie Hebner .10 .02
❑ 269 Ron Jackson .10 .02
❑ 270 Lynn Jones .10 .02
❑ 271 Steve Kemp .10 .02
❑ 272 Rick Leach .10 .02
❑ 273 Aurelio Lopez .10 .02
❑ 274 Jack Morris .20 .07
❑ 275 Kevin Saucier .10 .02
❑ 276 Lance Parrish .20 .07
❑ 277 Rick Peters .10 .02
❑ 278 Dan Petry .10 .02
❑ 279 Dave Rozema .10 .02
❑ 280 Stan Papi .10 .02
❑ 281 Dan Schatzeder .10 .02
❑ 282 Champ Summers .10 .02
❑ 283 Alan Trammell .20 .07
❑ 284 Lou Whitaker .20 .07
❑ 285 Milt Wilcox .10 .02
❑ 286 John Wockenfuss .10 .02
❑ 287 Gary Allenson .10 .02
❑ 288 Tom Burgmeier .10 .02
❑ 289 Bill Campbell .10 .02
❑ 290 Mark Clear .10 .02
❑ 291 Steve Crawford .10 .02
❑ 292 Dennis Eckersley .40 .15
❑ 293 Dwight Evans .40 .15
❑ 294 Rich Gedman .50 .20
❑ 295 Garry Hancock .10 .02
❑ 296 Glenn Hoffman .10 .02
❑ 297 Bruce Hurst .10 .02
❑ 298 Carney Lansford .20 .07
❑ 299 Rick Miller .10 .02
❑ 300 Reid Nichols .10 .02
❑ 301 Bob Ojeda RC .50 .20
❑ 302 Tony Perez .40 .15
❑ 303 Chuck Rainey .10 .02
❑ 304 Jerry Remy .10 .02
❑ 305 Jim Rice .20 .07
❑ 306 Joe Rudi .20 .07
❑ 307 Bob Stanley .10 .02
❑ 308 Dave Stapleton .10 .02
❑ 309 Frank Tanana .20 .07
❑ 310 Mike Torrez .10 .02
❑ 311 John Tudor .20 .07
❑ 312 Carl Yastrzemski 1.25 .50
❑ 313 Buddy Bell .20 .07
❑ 314 Steve Comer .10 .02
❑ 315 Danny Darwin .10 .02
❑ 316 John Ellis .10 .02
❑ 317 John Grubb .10 .02
❑ 318 Rick Honeycutt .10 .02
❑ 319 Charlie Hough .20 .07
❑ 320 Fergie Jenkins .20 .07
❑ 321 John Henry Johnson .10 .02
❑ 322 Jim Kern .10 .02
❑ 323 Jon Matlack .10 .02
❑ 324 Doc Medich .10 .02
❑ 325 Mario Mendoza .10 .02
❑ 326 Al Oliver .20 .07
❑ 327 Pat Putnam .10 .02
❑ 328 Mickey Rivers .10 .02
❑ 329 Leon Roberts .10 .02
❑ 330 Billy Sample .10 .02
❑ 331 Bill Stein .10 .02
❑ 332 Jim Sundberg .20 .07
❑ 333 Mark Wagner .10 .02
❑ 334 Bump Wills .10 .02
❑ 335 Bill Almon .10 .02
❑ 336 Harold Baines .20 .07
❑ 337 Ross Baumgarten .10 .02
❑ 338 Tony Bernazard .10 .02
❑ 339 Britt Burns .10 .02
❑ 340 Richard Dotson .10 .02
❑ 341 Jim Essian .10 .02
❑ 342 Ed Farmer .10 .02
❑ 343 Carlton Fisk .40 .15
❑ 344 Kevin Hickey RC .15 .05
❑ 345 LaMarr Hoyt .10 .02
❑ 346 Lamar Johnson .10 .02
❑ 347 Jerry Koosman .20 .07
❑ 348 Rusty Kuntz .10 .02
❑ 349 Dennis Lamp .10 .02
❑ 350 Ron LeFlore .20 .07
❑ 351 Chet Lemon .20 .07
❑ 352 Greg Luzinski .20 .07
❑ 353 Bob Molinaro .10 .02
❑ 354 Jim Morrison .10 .02
❑ 355 Wayne Nordhagen .10 .02
❑ 356 Greg Pryor .10 .02
❑ 357 Mike Squires .10 .02
❑ 358 Steve Trout .10 .02
❑ 359 Alan Bannister .10 .02
❑ 360 Len Barker .10 .02
❑ 361 Bert Blyleven .20 .07
❑ 362 Joe Charboneau .20 .07
❑ 363 John Denny .10 .02
❑ 364 Bo Diaz .10 .02
❑ 365 Miguel Dilone .10 .02
❑ 366 Jerry Dybzinski .10 .02
❑ 367 Wayne Garland .10 .02
❑ 368 Mike Hargrove .10 .02
❑ 369 Toby Harrah .20 .07
❑ 370 Ron Hassey .10 .02
❑ 371 Von Hayes RC .50 .20
❑ 372 Pat Kelly .10 .02
❑ 373 Duane Kuiper .10 .02
❑ 374 Rick Manning .10 .02

❑ 375 Sid Monge .10 .02
❑ 376 Jorge Orta .10 .02
❑ 377 Dave Rosello .10 .02
❑ 378 Dan Spillner .10 .02
❑ 379 Mike Stanton .10 .02
❑ 380 Andre Thornton .10 .02
❑ 381 Tom Veryzer .10 .02
❑ 382 Rick Waits .10 .02
❑ 383 Doyle Alexander .10 .02
❑ 384 Vida Blue .20 .07
❑ 385 Fred Breining .10 .02
❑ 386 Enos Cabell .10 .02
❑ 387 Jack Clark .20 .07
❑ 388 Darrell Evans .20 .07
❑ 389 Tom Griffin .10 .02
❑ 390 Larry Herndon .10 .02
❑ 391 Al Holland .10 .02
❑ 392 Gary Lavelle .10 .02
❑ 393 Johnnie LeMaster .10 .02
❑ 394 Jerry Martin .10 .02
❑ 395 Milt May .10 .02
❑ 396 Greg Minton .10 .02
❑ 397 Joe Morgan .20 .07
❑ 398 Joe Pettini .10 .02
❑ 399 Allen Ripley .10 .02
❑ 400 Billy Smith .10 .02
❑ 401 Rennie Stennett .10 .02
❑ 402 Ed Whitson .10 .02
❑ 403 Jim Wohlford .10 .02
❑ 404 Willie Aikens .10 .02
❑ 405 George Brett 2.00 .75
❑ 406 Ken Brett .10 .02
❑ 407 Dave Chalk .10 .02
❑ 408 Rich Gale .10 .02
❑ 409 Cesar Geronimo .10 .02
❑ 410 Larry Gura .10 .02
❑ 411 Clint Hurdle .10 .02
❑ 412 Mike Jones .10 .02
❑ 413 Dennis Leonard .10 .02
❑ 414 Renie Martin .10 .02
❑ 415 Lee May .10 .02
❑ 416 Hal McRae .20 .07
❑ 417 Darryl Motley .10 .02
❑ 418 Rance Mulliniks .10 .02
❑ 419 Amos Otis .20 .07
❑ 420 Ken Phelps .10 .02
❑ 421 Jamie Quirk .10 .02
❑ 422 Dan Quisenberry .10 .02
❑ 423 Paul Splittorff .10 .02
❑ 424 U.L. Washington .10 .02
❑ 425 John Wathan .10 .02
❑ 426 Frank White .20 .07
❑ 427 Willie Wilson .20 .07
❑ 428 Brian Asselstine .10 .02
❑ 429 Bruce Benedict .10 .02
❑ 430 Tommy Boggs .10 .02
❑ 431 Larry Bradford .10 .02
❑ 432 Rick Camp .10 .02
❑ 433 Chris Chambliss .20 .07
❑ 434 Gene Garber .10 .02
❑ 435 Preston Hanna .10 .02
❑ 436 Bob Horner .20 .07
❑ 437 Glenn Hubbard .10 .02
❑ 438A All Hrabosky ERR 8.00 4.00
❑ 438B Al Hrabosky ERR (Height 5'1") .40 .15
❑ 438C Al Hrabosky (Height 5'10") .20 .07
❑ 439 Rufino Linares .10 .02
❑ 440 Rick Mahler .10 .02
❑ 441 Ed Miller .10 .02
❑ 442 John Montefusco .10 .02
❑ 443 Dale Murphy .40 .15
❑ 444 Phil Niekro .20 .07
❑ 445 Gaylord Perry .20 .07
❑ 446 Biff Pocoroba .10 .02
❑ 447 Rafael Ramirez .10 .02
❑ 448 Jerry Royster .10 .02
❑ 449 Claudell Washington .10 .02
❑ 450 Don Aase .10 .02
❑ 451 Don Baylor .20 .07
❑ 452 Juan Beniquez .10 .02
❑ 453 Rick Burleson .10 .02
❑ 454 Bert Campaneris .20 .07
❑ 455 Rod Carew .40 .15
❑ 456 Bob Clark .10 .02
❑ 457 Brian Downing .20 .07
❑ 458 Dan Ford .10 .02
❑ 459 Ken Forsch .10 .02
❑ 460A Dave Frost (5 mm space before ERA) .10 .02
❑ 460B Dave Frost (1 mm space) .10 .02
❑ 461 Bobby Grich .20 .07
❑ 462 Larry Harlow .10 .02
❑ 463 John Harris .10 .02
❑ 464 Andy Hassler .10 .02
❑ 465 Butch Hobson .10 .02
❑ 466 Jesse Jefferson .10 .02
❑ 467 Bruce Kison .10 .02
❑ 468 Fred Lynn .20 .07
❑ 469 Angel Moreno .10 .02
❑ 470 Ed Ott .10 .02
❑ 471 Fred Patek .10 .02
❑ 472 Steve Renko .10 .02
❑ 473 Mike Witt .50 .20
❑ 474 Geoff Zahn .10 .02
❑ 475 Gary Alexander .10 .02
❑ 476 Dale Berra .10 .02
❑ 477 Kurt Bevacqua .10 .02
❑ 478 Jim Bibby .10 .02
❑ 479 John Candelaria .10 .02
❑ 480 Victor Cruz .10 .02
❑ 481 Mike Easler .10 .02
❑ 482 Tim Foli .10 .02
❑ 483 Lee Lacy .10 .02
❑ 484 Vance Law .10 .02
❑ 485 Bill Madlock .20 .07
❑ 486 Willie Montanez .10 .02
❑ 487 Omar Moreno .10 .02
❑ 488 Steve Nicosia .10 .02
❑ 489 Dave Parker .20 .07
❑ 490 Tony Pena .20 .07
❑ 491 Pascual Perez .10 .02
❑ 492 Johnny Ray RC .50 .20
❑ 493 Rick Rhoden .10 .02
❑ 494 Bill Robinson .10 .02
❑ 495 Don Robinson .10 .02
❑ 496 Enrique Romo .10 .02
❑ 497 Rod Scurry .10 .02
❑ 498 Eddie Solomon .10 .02
❑ 499 Willie Stargell .40 .15
❑ 500 Kent Tekulve .10 .02
❑ 501 Jason Thompson .10 .02
❑ 502 Glenn Abbott .10 .02
❑ 503 Jim Anderson .10 .02
❑ 504 Floyd Bannister .10 .02
❑ 505 Bruce Bochte .10 .02
❑ 506 Jeff Burroughs .10 .02
❑ 507 Bryan Clark RC .15 .05
❑ 508 Ken Clay .10 .02
❑ 509 Julio Cruz .10 .02
❑ 510 Dick Drago .10 .02
❑ 511 Gary Gray .10 .02
❑ 512 Dan Meyer .10 .02
❑ 513 Jerry Narron .10 .02
❑ 514 Tom Paciorek .10 .02
❑ 515 Casey Parsons .10 .02
❑ 516 Lenny Randle .10 .02
❑ 517 Shane Rawley .10 .02
❑ 518 Joe Simpson .10 .02
❑ 519 Richie Zisk .10 .02
❑ 520 Neil Allen .10 .02
❑ 521 Bob Bailor .10 .02
❑ 522 Hubie Brooks .10 .02
❑ 523 Mike Cubbage .10 .02
❑ 524 Pete Falcone .10 .02
❑ 525 Doug Flynn .10 .02
❑ 526 Tom Hausman .10 .02
❑ 527 Ron Hodges .10 .02
❑ 528 Randy Jones .10 .02
❑ 529 Mike Jorgensen .10 .02
❑ 530 Dave Kingman .20 .07
❑ 531 Ed Lynch .10 .02
❑ 532 Mike G. Marshall .10 .02
❑ 533 Lee Mazzilli .20 .07
❑ 534 Dyar Miller .10 .02
❑ 535 Mike Scott .20 .07
❑ 536 Rusty Staub .20 .07
❑ 537 John Stearns .10 .02
❑ 538 Craig Swan .10 .02
❑ 539 Frank Taveras .10 .02
❑ 540 Alex Trevino .10 .02
❑ 541 Ellis Valentine .10 .02
❑ 542 Mookie Wilson .20 .07
❑ 543 Joel Youngblood .10 .02
❑ 544 Pat Zachry .10 .02
❑ 545 Glenn Adams .10 .02
❑ 546 Fernando Arroyo .10 .02
❑ 547 John Verhoeven .10 .02
❑ 548 Sal Butera .10 .02
❑ 549 John Castino .10 .02
❑ 550 Don Cooper .10 .02
❑ 551 Doug Corbett .10 .02
❑ 552 Dave Engle .10 .02
❑ 553 Roger Erickson .10 .02
❑ 554 Danny Goodwin .10 .02
❑ 555A Darrell Jackson (Black cap) .40 .15
❑ 555B Darrell Jackson (Red cap with T) .20 .07
❑ 555C Darrell Jackson VAR3 3.00 1.25
❑ 556 Pete Mackanin .10 .02
❑ 557 Jack O'Connor .10 .02
❑ 558 Hosken Powell .10 .02
❑ 559 Pete Redfern .10 .02
❑ 560 Roy Smalley .10 .02
❑ 561 Chuck Baker UER (Shortshop on front) .10 .02
❑ 562 Gary Ward .10 .02
❑ 563 Rob Wilfong .10 .02
❑ 564 Al Williams .10 .02
❑ 565 Butch Wynegar .10 .02
❑ 566 Randy Bass .50 .20
❑ 567 Juan Bonilla RC .15 .05
❑ 568 Danny Boone .10 .02
❑ 569 John Curtis .10 .02
❑ 570 Juan Eichelberger .10 .02
❑ 571 Barry Evans .10 .02
❑ 572 Tim Flannery .10 .02
❑ 573 Ruppert Jones .10 .02
❑ 574 Terry Kennedy .10 .02
❑ 575 Joe Lefebvre .10 .02
❑ 576A John Littlefield RevNg 100.00 50.00
❑ 576B John Littlefield COR (Right handed) .20 .07
❑ 577 Gary Lucas .10 .02
❑ 578 Steve Mura .10 .02
❑ 579 Broderick Perkins .10 .02
❑ 580 Gene Richards .10 .02
❑ 581 Luis Salazar .10 .02
❑ 582 Ozzie Smith 1.50 .60
❑ 583 John Urrea .10 .02
❑ 584 Chris Welsh .10 .02
❑ 585 Rick Wise .10 .02
❑ 586 Doug Bird .10 .02
❑ 587 Tim Blackwell .10 .02
❑ 588 Bobby Bonds .20 .07
❑ 589 Bill Buckner .20 .07
❑ 590 Bill Caudill .10 .02
❑ 591 Hector Cruz .10 .02
❑ 592 Jody Davis .10 .02
❑ 593 Ivan DeJesus .10 .02
❑ 594 Steve Dillard .10 .02
❑ 595 Leon Durham .10 .02
❑ 596 Rawly Eastwick .20 .07
❑ 597 Steve Henderson .10 .02
❑ 598 Mike Krukow .10 .02
❑ 599 Mike Lum .10 .02
❑ 600 Randy Martz .10 .02
❑ 601 Jerry Morales .10 .02
❑ 602 Ken Reitz .10 .02
❑ 603 Lee Smith RC 2.00 .75
❑ 603B Lee Smith RC COR 6.00 3.00
❑ 604 Dick Tidrow .10 .02
❑ 605 Jim Tracy .20 .07
❑ 606 Mike Tyson .10 .02
❑ 607 Ty Waller .10 .02
❑ 608 Danny Ainge .20 .07
❑ 609 George Bell RC 1.00 .40
❑ 610 Mark Bomback .10 .02
❑ 611 Barry Bonnell .10 .02
❑ 612 Jim Clancy .10 .02
❑ 613 Damaso Garcia .10 .02
❑ 614 Jerry Garvin .10 .02
❑ 615 Alfredo Griffin .10 .02
❑ 616 Garth Iorg .10 .02
❑ 617 Luis Leal .10 .02

Card		
❑ 618 Ken Macha	.10	.02
❑ 619 John Mayberry	.10	.02
❑ 620 Joey McLaughlin	.10	.02
❑ 621 Lloyd Moseby	.10	.02
❑ 622 Dave Stieb	.20	.07
❑ 623 Jackson Todd	.10	.02
❑ 624 Willie Upshaw	.50	.20
❑ 625 Otto Velez	.10	.02
❑ 626 Ernie Whitt	.10	.02
❑ 627 Alvis Woods	.10	.02
❑ 628 All Star Game		
Cleveland, Ohio	.20	.07
❑ 629 All Star Infielders		
Frank White		
Bucky Dent	.20	.07
❑ 630 Big Red Machine		
Dan Driessen		
Dave Concepcion		
Ge	.20	.07
❑ 631 Bruce Sutter		
Top NL Relief Pitcher	.20	.07
❑ 632 Steve Carlton/C.Fisk	.20	.07
❑ 633 Yaz 3000th Game	.75	.30
❑ 634 J.Bench/T.Seaver	.75	.30
❑ 635 West Meets East		
Fernando Valenzuela		
and Gary Car	.10	.02
❑ 636A Fernando Valenzuela IA	.40	.15
❑ 636B Fernando Valenzuela:		
NL SO King ('the' NL)	.40	.15
❑ 637 Mike Schmidt IA	.75	.30
❑ 638 Gary Carter/D.Parker	.10	.02
❑ 639 Perfect Game UER		
Len Barker and		
Bo Diaz		
(Catche)	.20	.07
❑ 640 Pete and Re-Pete	.75	.30
❑ 641 L.Smith/Schmidt/Carlton	.75	.30
❑ 642 Red Sox Reunion		
Fred Lynn		
Dwight Evans	.40	.15
❑ 643 Rickey Henderson IA	1.25	.50
❑ 644 R.Fingers Most Saves	.20	.07
❑ 645 Tom Seaver Most Wins	.20	.07
❑ 646 R.Jackson/D.Winfield	.20	.07
❑ 646B Reggie/D.Winfield	.20	.07
❑ 647 CL: Yankees/Dodgers	.10	.02
❑ 648 CL: A's/Reds	.10	.02
❑ 649 CL: Cards/Brewers	.10	.02
❑ 650 CL: Expos/Orioles	.10	.02
❑ 651 CL: Astros/Phillies	.10	.02
❑ 652 CL: Tigers/Red Sox	.10	.02
❑ 653 CL: Rangers/White Sox	.10	.02
❑ 654 CL: Giants/Indians	.10	.02
❑ 655 CL: Royals/Braves	.10	.02
❑ 656 CL: Angels/Pirates	.10	.02
❑ 657 CL: Mariners/Mets	.10	.02
❑ 658 CL: Padres/Twins	.10	.02
❑ 659 CL: Blue Jays/Cubs	.10	.02
❑ 660 Specials Checklist	.10	.02

1983 Fleer

Card		
❑ COMPLETE SET (660)	60.00	30.00
❑ 1 Joaquin Andujar	.20	.07
❑ 2 Doug Bair	.10	.02
❑ 3 Steve Braun	.10	.02
❑ 4 Glenn Brummer	.10	.02
❑ 5 Bob Forsch	.10	.02
❑ 6 David Green RC	.50	.20
❑ 7 George Hendrick	.20	.07
❑ 8 Keith Hernandez	.20	.07
❑ 9 Tom Herr	.10	.02
❑ 10 Dane Iorg	.10	.02
❑ 11 Jim Kaat	.20	.07
❑ 12 Jeff Lahti	.10	.02
❑ 13 Tito Landrum	.10	.02
❑ 14 Dave LaPoint	.10	.02
❑ 15 Willie McGee RC	1.50	.60
❑ 16 Steve Mura	.10	.02
❑ 17 Ken Oberkfell	.10	.02
❑ 18 Darrell Porter	.10	.02
❑ 19 Mike Ramsey	.10	.02
❑ 20 Gene Roof	.10	.02
❑ 21 Lonnie Smith	.10	.02
❑ 22 Ozzie Smith	1.25	.50
❑ 23 John Stuper	.10	.02
❑ 24 Bruce Sutter	.40	.15
❑ 25 Gene Tenace	.20	.07
❑ 26 Jerry Augustine	.10	.02
❑ 27 Dwight Bernard	.10	.02
❑ 28 Mark Brouhard	.10	.02
❑ 29 Mike Caldwell	.10	.02
❑ 30 Cecil Cooper	.20	.07
❑ 31 Jamie Easterly	.10	.02
❑ 32 Marshall Edwards	.10	.02
❑ 33 Rollie Fingers	.20	.07
❑ 34 Jim Gantner	.10	.02
❑ 35 Moose Haas	.10	.02
❑ 36 Roy Howell	.10	.02
❑ 37 Pete Ladd	.10	.02
❑ 38 Bob McClure	.10	.02
❑ 39 Doc Medich	.10	.02
❑ 40 Paul Molitor	.20	.07
❑ 41 Don Money	.10	.02
❑ 42 Charlie Moore	.10	.02
❑ 43 Ben Oglivie	.20	.07
❑ 44 Ed Romero	.10	.02
❑ 45 Ted Simmons	.20	.07
❑ 46 Jim Slaton	.10	.02
❑ 47 Don Sutton	.20	.07
❑ 48 Gorman Thomas	.20	.07
❑ 49 Pete Vuckovich	.10	.02
❑ 50 Ned Yost	.10	.02
❑ 51 Robin Yount	1.25	.50
❑ 52 Benny Ayala	.10	.02
❑ 53 Bob Bonner	.10	.02
❑ 54 Al Bumbry	.10	.02
❑ 55 Terry Crowley	.10	.02
❑ 56 Storm Davis RC	.50	.20
❑ 57 Rich Dauer	.10	.02
❑ 58 Rick Dempsey UER	.10	.02
❑ 59 Jim Dwyer	.10	.02
❑ 60 Mike Flanagan	.10	.02
❑ 61 Dan Ford	.10	.02
❑ 62 Glenn Gulliver	.10	.02
❑ 63 John Lowenstein	.10	.02
❑ 64 Dennis Martinez	.20	.07
❑ 65 Tippy Martinez	.10	.02
❑ 66 Scott McGregor	.10	.02
❑ 67 Eddie Murray	.75	.30
❑ 68 Joe Nolan	.10	.02
❑ 69 Jim Palmer	.20	.07
❑ 70 Cal Ripken	6.00	2.50
❑ 71 Gary Roenicke	.10	.02
❑ 72 Lenn Sakata	.10	.02
❑ 73 Ken Singleton	.20	.07
❑ 74 Sammy Stewart	.10	.02
❑ 75 Tim Stoddard	.10	.02
❑ 76 Don Aase	.10	.02
❑ 77 Don Baylor	.20	.07
❑ 78 Juan Beniquez	.10	.02
❑ 79 Bob Boone	.20	.07
❑ 80 Rick Burleson	.10	.02
❑ 81 Rod Carew	.40	.15
❑ 82 Bobby Clark	.10	.02
❑ 83 Doug Corbett	.10	.02
❑ 84 John Curtis	.10	.02
❑ 85 Doug DeCinces	.10	.02
❑ 86 Brian Downing	.20	.07
❑ 87 Joe Ferguson	.10	.02
❑ 88 Tim Foli	.10	.02
❑ 89 Ken Forsch	.10	.02
❑ 90 Dave Goltz	.10	.02
❑ 91 Bobby Grich	.20	.07
❑ 92 Andy Hassler	.10	.02
❑ 93 Reggie Jackson	.40	.15
❑ 94 Ron Jackson	.10	.02
❑ 95 Tommy John	.20	.07
❑ 96 Bruce Kison	.10	.02
❑ 97 Fred Lynn	.20	.07
❑ 98 Ed Ott	.10	.02
❑ 99 Steve Renko	.10	.02
❑ 100 Luis Sanchez	.10	.02
❑ 101 Rob Wilfong	.10	.02
❑ 102 Mike Witt	.10	.02
❑ 103 Geoff Zahn	.10	.02
❑ 104 Willie Aikens	.10	.02
❑ 105 Mike Armstrong	.10	.02
❑ 106 Vida Blue	.20	.07
❑ 107 Bud Black RC	.50	.20
❑ 108 George Brett	2.00	.75
❑ 109 Bill Castro	.10	.02
❑ 110 Onix Concepcion	.10	.02
❑ 111 Dave Frost	.10	.02
❑ 112 Cesar Geronimo	.10	.02
❑ 113 Larry Gura	.10	.02
❑ 114 Steve Hammond	.10	.02
❑ 115 Don Hood	.10	.02
❑ 116 Dennis Leonard	.10	.02
❑ 117 Jerry Martin	.10	.02
❑ 118 Lee May	.10	.02
❑ 119 Hal McRae	.20	.07
❑ 120 Amos Otis	.20	.07
❑ 121 Greg Pryor	.10	.02
❑ 122 Dan Quisenberry	.10	.02
❑ 123 Don Slaught RC	.50	.20
❑ 124 Paul Splittorff	.10	.02
❑ 125 U.L. Washington	.10	.02
❑ 126 John Wathan	.10	.02
❑ 127 Frank White	.20	.07
❑ 128 Willie Wilson	.20	.07
❑ 129 Steve Bedrosian UER		
(Height 6'33")	.10	.02
❑ 130 Bruce Benedict	.10	.02
❑ 131 Tommy Boggs	.10	.02
❑ 132 Brett Butler	.20	.07
❑ 133 Rick Camp	.10	.02
❑ 134 Chris Chambliss	.20	.07
❑ 135 Ken Dayley	.10	.02
❑ 136 Gene Garber	.10	.02
❑ 137 Terry Harper	.10	.02
❑ 138 Bob Horner	.20	.07
❑ 139 Glenn Hubbard	.10	.02
❑ 140 Rufino Linares	.10	.02
❑ 141 Rick Mahler	.10	.02
❑ 142 Dale Murphy	.40	.15
❑ 143 Phil Niekro	.20	.07
❑ 144 Pascual Perez	.10	.02
❑ 145 Biff Pocoroba	.10	.02
❑ 146 Rafael Ramirez	.10	.02
❑ 147 Jerry Royster	.10	.02
❑ 148 Ken Smith	.10	.02
❑ 149 Bob Walk	.10	.02
❑ 150 Claudell Washington	.10	.02
❑ 151 Bob Watson	.10	.02
❑ 152 Larry Whisenton	.10	.02
❑ 153 Porfirio Altamirano	.10	.02
❑ 154 Marty Bystrom	.10	.02
❑ 155 Steve Carlton	.40	.15
❑ 156 Larry Christenson	.10	.02
❑ 157 Ivan DeJesus	.10	.02
❑ 158 John Denny	.10	.02
❑ 159 Bob Dernier	.10	.02
❑ 160 Bo Diaz	.10	.02
❑ 161 Ed Farmer	.10	.02
❑ 162 Greg Gross	.10	.02
❑ 163 Mike Krukow	.10	.02
❑ 164 Garry Maddox	.10	.02
❑ 165 Gary Matthews	.20	.07
❑ 166 Tug McGraw	.20	.07
❑ 167 Bob Molinaro	.10	.02
❑ 168 Sid Monge	.10	.02
❑ 169 Ron Reed	.10	.02
❑ 170 Bill Robinson	.10	.02
❑ 171 Pete Rose	2.50	1.00
❑ 172 Dick Ruthven	.10	.02
❑ 173 Mike Schmidt	2.00	.75
❑ 174 Manny Trillo	.10	.02
❑ 175 Ozzie Virgil	.10	.02
❑ 176 George Vukovich	.10	.02

❑ 177 Gary Allenson .10 .02
❑ 178 Luis Aponte .10 .02
❑ 179 Wade Boggs RC 10.00 4.00
❑ 180 Tom Burgmeier .10 .02
❑ 181 Mark Clear .10 .02
❑ 182 Dennis Eckersley .40 .15
❑ 183 Dwight Evans .40 .15
❑ 184 Rich Gedman .10 .02
❑ 185 Glenn Hoffman .10 .02
❑ 186 Bruce Hurst .10 .02
❑ 187 Carney Lansford .20 .07
❑ 188 Rick Miller .10 .02
❑ 189 Reid Nichols .10 .02
❑ 190 Bob Ojeda .10 .02
❑ 191 Tony Perez .40 .15
❑ 192 Chuck Rainey .10 .02
❑ 193 Jerry Remy .10 .02
❑ 194 Jim Rice .20 .07
❑ 195 Bob Stanley .10 .02
❑ 196 Dave Stapleton .10 .02
❑ 197 Mike Torrez .10 .02
❑ 198 John Tudor .20 .07
❑ 199 Julio Valdez .10 .02
❑ 200 Carl Yastrzemski 1.25 .50
❑ 201 Dusty Baker .20 .07
❑ 202 Joe Beckwith .10 .02
❑ 203 Greg Brock .10 .02
❑ 204 Ron Cey .20 .07
❑ 205 Terry Forster .20 .07
❑ 206 Steve Garvey .20 .07
❑ 207 Pedro Guerrero .20 .07
❑ 208 Burt Hooton .10 .02
❑ 209 Steve Howe .10 .02
❑ 210 Ken Landreaux .10 .02
❑ 211 Mike Marshall .10 .02
❑ 212 Candy Maldonado RC .50 .20
❑ 213 Rick Monday .20 .07
❑ 214 Tom Niedenfuer .10 .02
❑ 215 Jorge Orta .10 .02
❑ 216 Jerry Reuss UER
('Home': omitted) .10 .02
❑ 217 Ron Roenicke .10 .02
❑ 218 Vicente Romo .10 .02
❑ 219 Bill Russell .20 .07
❑ 220 Steve Sax .20 .07
❑ 221 Mike Scioscia .20 .07
❑ 222 Dave Stewart .20 .07
❑ 223 Derrel Thomas .10 .02
❑ 224 Fernando Valenzuela .20 .07
❑ 225 Bob Welch .20 .07
❑ 226 Ricky Wright .10 .02
❑ 227 Steve Yeager .20 .07
❑ 228 Bill Almon .10 .02
❑ 229 Harold Baines .20 .07
❑ 230 Salome Barojas .10 .02
❑ 231 Tony Bernazard .10 .02
❑ 232 Britt Burns .10 .02
❑ 233 Richard Dotson .10 .02
❑ 234 Ernesto Escarrega .10 .02
❑ 235 Carlton Fisk .40 .15
❑ 236 Jerry Hairston .10 .02
❑ 237 Kevin Hickey .10 .02
❑ 238 LaMarr Hoyt .10 .02
❑ 239 Steve Kemp .10 .02
❑ 240 Jim Kern .10 .02
❑ 241 Ron Kittle RC 1.00 .40
❑ 242 Jerry Koosman .20 .07
❑ 243 Dennis Lamp .10 .02
❑ 244 Rudy Law .10 .02
❑ 245 Vance Law .10 .02
❑ 246 Ron LeFlore .20 .07
❑ 247 Greg Luzinski .20 .07
❑ 248 Tom Paciorek .10 .02
❑ 249 Aurelio Rodriguez .10 .02
❑ 250 Mike Squires .10 .02
❑ 251 Steve Trout .10 .02
❑ 252 Jim Barr .10 .02
❑ 253 Dave Bergman .10 .02
❑ 254 Fred Breining .10 .02
❑ 255 Bob Brenly .10 .02
❑ 256 Jack Clark .20 .07
❑ 257 Chili Davis .20 .07
❑ 258 Darrell Evans .20 .07
❑ 259 Alan Fowlkes .10 .02
❑ 260 Rich Gale .10 .02
❑ 261 Atlee Hammaker .10 .02
❑ 262 Al Holland .10 .02
❑ 263 Duane Kuiper .10 .02
❑ 264 Bill Laskey .10 .02
❑ 265 Gary Lavelle .10 .02
❑ 266 Johnnie LeMaster .10 .02
❑ 267 Renie Martin .10 .02
❑ 268 Milt May .10 .02
❑ 269 Greg Minton .10 .02
❑ 270 Joe Morgan .20 .07
❑ 271 Tom O'Malley .10 .02
❑ 272 Reggie Smith .20 .07
❑ 273 Guy Sularz .10 .02
❑ 274 Champ Summers .10 .02
❑ 275 Max Venable .10 .02
❑ 276 Jim Wohlford .10 .02
❑ 277 Ray Burris .10 .02
❑ 278 Gary Carter .20 .07
❑ 279 Warren Cromartie .10 .02
❑ 280 Andre Dawson .20 .07
❑ 281 Terry Francona .20 .07
❑ 282 Doug Flynn .10 .02
❑ 283 Woodie Fryman .10 .02
❑ 284 Bill Gullickson .10 .02
❑ 285 Wallace Johnson .10 .02
❑ 286 Charlie Lea .10 .02
❑ 287 Randy Lerch .10 .02
❑ 288 Brad Mills .10 .02
❑ 289 Dan Norman .10 .02
❑ 290 Al Oliver .20 .07
❑ 291 David Palmer .10 .02
❑ 292 Tim Raines .20 .07
❑ 293 Jeff Reardon .20 .07
❑ 294 Steve Rogers .20 .07
❑ 295 Scott Sanderson .10 .02
❑ 296 Dan Schatzeder .10 .02
❑ 297 Bryn Smith .10 .02
❑ 298 Chris Speier .10 .02
❑ 299 Tim Wallach .20 .07
❑ 300 Jerry White .10 .02
❑ 301 Joel Youngblood .10 .02
❑ 302 Ross Baumgarten .10 .02
❑ 303 Dale Berra .10 .02
❑ 304 John Candelaria .10 .02
❑ 305 Dick Davis .10 .02
❑ 306 Mike Easler .10 .02
❑ 307 Richie Hebner .10 .02
❑ 308 Lee Lacy .10 .02
❑ 309 Bill Madlock .20 .07
❑ 310 Larry McWilliams .10 .02
❑ 311 John Milner .10 .02
❑ 312 Omar Moreno .10 .02
❑ 313 Jim Morrison .10 .02
❑ 314 Steve Nicosia .10 .02
❑ 315 Dave Parker .20 .07
❑ 316 Tony Pena .10 .02
❑ 317 Johnny Ray .10 .02
❑ 318 Rick Rhoden .10 .02
❑ 319 Don Robinson .10 .02
❑ 320 Enrique Romo .10 .02
❑ 321 Manny Sarmiento .10 .02
❑ 322 Rod Scurry .10 .02
❑ 323 Jimmy Smith .10 .02
❑ 324 Willie Stargell .40 .15
❑ 325 Jason Thompson .10 .02
❑ 326 Kent Tekulve .10 .02
❑ 327A Tom Brookens
(Short .375~ brown box
shaded in on) .10 .02
❑ 327B Tom Brookens
(Longer 1.25~ brown box
shaded in o) .10 .02
❑ 328 Enos Cabell .10 .02
❑ 329 Kirk Gibson .20 .07
❑ 330 Larry Herndon .10 .02
❑ 331 Mike Ivie .10 .02
❑ 332 Howard Johnson RC 1.00 .40
❑ 333 Lynn Jones .10 .02
❑ 334 Rick Leach .10 .02
❑ 335 Chet Lemon .20 .07
❑ 336 Jack Morris .20 .07
❑ 337 Lance Parrish .20 .07
❑ 338 Larry Pashnick .10 .02
❑ 339 Dan Petry .10 .02
❑ 340 Dave Rozema .10 .02
❑ 341 Dave Rucker .10 .02
❑ 342 Elias Sosa .10 .02
❑ 343 Dave Tobik .10 .02
❑ 344 Alan Trammell .20 .07
❑ 345 Jerry Turner .10 .02
❑ 346 Jerry Ujdur .10 .02
❑ 347 Pat Underwood .10 .02
❑ 348 Lou Whitaker .20 .07
❑ 349 Milt Wilcox .10 .02
❑ 350 Glenn Wilson .50 .20
❑ 351 John Wockenfuss .10 .02
❑ 352 Kurt Bevacqua .10 .02
❑ 353 Juan Bonilla .10 .02
❑ 354 Floyd Chiffer .10 .02
❑ 355 Luis DeLeon .10 .02
❑ 356 Dave Dravecky RC 1.00 .40
❑ 357 Dave Edwards .10 .02
❑ 358 Juan Eichelberger .10 .02
❑ 359 Tim Flannery .10 .02
❑ 360 Tony Gwynn RC 15.00 6.00
❑ 361 Ruppert Jones .10 .02
❑ 362 Terry Kennedy .10 .02
❑ 363 Joe Lefebvre .10 .02
❑ 364 Sixto Lezcano .10 .02
❑ 365 Tim Lollar .10 .02
❑ 366 Gary Lucas .10 .02
❑ 367 John Montefusco .10 .02
❑ 368 Broderick Perkins .10 .02
❑ 369 Joe Pittman .10 .02
❑ 370 Gene Richards .10 .02
❑ 371 Luis Salazar .10 .02
❑ 372 Eric Show RC .50 .20
❑ 373 Garry Templeton .20 .07
❑ 374 Chris Welsh .10 .02
❑ 375 Alan Wiggins .10 .02
❑ 376 Rick Cerone .10 .02
❑ 377 Dave Collins .10 .02
❑ 378 Roger Erickson .10 .02
❑ 379 George Frazier .10 .02
❑ 380 Oscar Gamble .10 .02
❑ 381 Rich Gossage .20 .07
❑ 382 Ken Griffey .20 .07
❑ 383 Ron Guidry .20 .07
❑ 384 Dave LaRoche .10 .02
❑ 385 Rudy May .10 .02
❑ 386 John Mayberry .10 .02
❑ 387 Lee Mazzilli .20 .07
❑ 388 Mike Morgan .10 .02
❑ 389 Jerry Mumphrey .10 .02
❑ 390 Bobby Murcer .20 .07
❑ 391 Graig Nettles .20 .07
❑ 392 Lou Piniella .20 .07
❑ 393 Willie Randolph .20 .07
❑ 394 Shane Rawley .10 .02
❑ 395 Dave Righetti .20 .07
❑ 396 Andre Robertson .10 .02
❑ 397 Roy Smalley .10 .02
❑ 398 Dave Winfield .20 .07
❑ 399 Butch Wynegar .10 .02
❑ 400 Chris Bando .10 .02
❑ 401 Alan Bannister .10 .02
❑ 402 Len Barker .10 .02
❑ 403 Tom Brennan .10 .02
❑ 404 Carmelo Castillo .10 .02
❑ 405 Miguel Dilone .10 .02
❑ 406 Jerry Dybzinski .10 .02
❑ 407 Mike Fischlin .10 .02
❑ 408 Ed Glynn UER .10 .02
❑ 409 Mike Hargrove .10 .02
❑ 410 Toby Harrah .20 .07
❑ 411 Ron Hassey .10 .02
❑ 412 Von Hayes .10 .02
❑ 413 Rick Manning .10 .02
❑ 414 Bake McBride .20 .07
❑ 415 Larry Milbourne .10 .02
❑ 416 Bill Nahorodny .10 .02
❑ 417 Jack Perconte .10 .02
❑ 418 Lary Sorensen .10 .02
❑ 419 Dan Spillner .10 .02
❑ 420 Rick Sutcliffe .20 .07
❑ 421 Andre Thornton .10 .02
❑ 422 Rick Waits .10 .02
❑ 423 Eddie Whitson .10 .02
❑ 424 Jesse Barfield .20 .07
❑ 425 Barry Bonnell .10 .02
❑ 426 Jim Clancy .10 .02
❑ 427 Damaso Garcia .10 .02
❑ 428 Jerry Garvin .10 .02

❑	429	Alfredo Griffin	.10	.02
❑	430	Garth Iorg	.10	.02
❑	431	Roy Lee Jackson	.10	.02
❑	432	Luis Leal	.10	.02
❑	433	Buck Martinez	.10	.02
❑	434	Joey McLaughlin	.10	.02
❑	435	Lloyd Moseby	.10	.02
❑	436	Rance Mulliniks	.10	.02
❑	437	Dale Murray	.10	.02
❑	438	Wayne Nordhagen	.10	.02
❑	439	Geno Petralli	.50	.20
❑	440	Hosken Powell	.10	.02
❑	441	Dave Stieb	.20	.07
❑	442	Willie Upshaw	.10	.02
❑	443	Ernie Whitt	.10	.02
❑	444	Alvis Woods	.10	.02
❑	445	Alan Ashby	.10	.02
❑	446	Jose Cruz	.20	.07
❑	447	Kiko Garcia	.10	.02
❑	448	Phil Garner	.20	.07
❑	449	Danny Heep	.10	.02
❑	450	Art Howe	.10	.02
❑	451	Bob Knepper	.10	.02
❑	452	Alan Knicely	.10	.02
❑	453	Ray Knight	.20	.07
❑	454	Frank LaCorte	.10	.02
❑	455	Mike LaCoss	.10	.02
❑	456	Randy Moffitt	.10	.02
❑	457	Joe Niekro	.10	.02
❑	458	Terry Puhl	.10	.02
❑	459	Luis Pujols	.10	.02
❑	460	Craig Reynolds	.10	.02
❑	461	Bert Roberge	.10	.02
❑	462	Vern Ruhle	.10	.02
❑	463	Nolan Ryan	4.00	1.50
❑	464	Joe Sambito	.10	.02
❑	465	Tony Scott	.10	.02
❑	466	Dave Smith	.10	.02
❑	467	Harry Spilman	.10	.02
❑	468	Dickie Thon	.10	.02
❑	469	Denny Walling	.10	.02
❑	470	Larry Andersen	.10	.02
❑	471	Floyd Bannister	.10	.02
❑	472	Jim Beattie	.10	.02
❑	473	Bruce Bochte	.10	.02
❑	474	Manny Castillo	.10	.02
❑	475	Bill Caudill	.10	.02
❑	476	Bryan Clark	.10	.02
❑	477	Al Cowens	.10	.02
❑	478	Julio Cruz	.10	.02
❑	479	Todd Cruz	.10	.02
❑	480	Gary Gray	.10	.02
❑	481	Dave Henderson	.10	.02
❑	482	Mike Moore RC	.50	.20
❑	483	Gaylord Perry	.20	.07
❑	484	Dave Revering	.10	.02
❑	485	Joe Simpson	.10	.02
❑	486	Mike Stanton	.10	.02
❑	487	Rick Sweet	.10	.02
❑	488	Ed VandeBerg	.10	.02
❑	489	Richie Zisk	.10	.02
❑	490	Doug Bird	.10	.02
❑	491	Larry Bowa	.20	.07
❑	492	Bill Buckner	.20	.07
❑	493	Bill Campbell	.10	.02
❑	494	Jody Davis	.10	.02
❑	495	Leon Durham	.10	.02
❑	496	Steve Henderson	.10	.02
❑	497	Willie Hernandez	.10	.02
❑	498	Fergie Jenkins	.20	.07
❑	499	Jay Johnstone	.10	.02
❑	500	Junior Kennedy	.10	.02
❑	501	Randy Martz	.10	.02
❑	502	Jerry Morales	.10	.02
❑	503	Keith Moreland	.10	.02
❑	504	Dickie Noles	.10	.02
❑	505	Mike Proly	.10	.02
❑	506	Allen Ripley	.10	.02
❑	507	Ryne Sandberg RC	10.00	4.00
❑	508	Lee Smith	.40	.15
❑	509	Pat Tabler	.10	.02
❑	510	Dick Tidrow	.10	.02
❑	511	Bump Wills	.10	.02
❑	512	Gary Woods	.10	.02
❑	513	Tony Armas	.20	.07
❑	514	Dave Beard	.10	.02
❑	515	Jeff Burroughs	.10	.02
❑	516	John D'Acquisto	.10	.02
❑	517	Wayne Gross	.10	.02
❑	518	Mike Heath	.10	.02
❑	519	Rickey Henderson	1.50	.60
❑	520	Cliff Johnson	.10	.02
❑	521	Matt Keough	.10	.02
❑	522	Brian Kingman	.10	.02
❑	523	Rick Langford	.10	.02
❑	524	Dave Lopes	.20	.07
❑	525	Steve McCatty	.10	.02
❑	526	Dave McKay	.10	.02
❑	527	Dan Meyer	.10	.02
❑	528	Dwayne Murphy	.10	.02
❑	529	Jeff Newman	.10	.02
❑	530	Mike Norris	.10	.02
❑	531	Bob Owchinko	.10	.02
❑	532	Joe Rudi	.20	.07
❑	533	Jimmy Sexton	.10	.02
❑	534	Fred Stanley	.10	.02
❑	535	Tom Underwood	.10	.02
❑	536	Neil Allen	.10	.02
❑	537	Wally Backman	.10	.02
❑	538	Bob Bailor	.10	.02
❑	539	Hubie Brooks	.10	.02
❑	540	Carlos Diaz RC	.25	.08
❑	541	Pete Falcone	.10	.02
❑	542	George Foster	.20	.07
❑	543	Ron Gardenhire	.10	.02
❑	544	Brian Giles	.10	.02
❑	545	Ron Hodges	.10	.02
❑	546	Randy Jones	.10	.02
❑	547	Mike Jorgensen	.10	.02
❑	548	Dave Kingman	.20	.07
❑	549	Ed Lynch	.10	.02
❑	550	Jesse Orosco	.10	.02
❑	551	Rick Ownbey	.10	.02
❑	552	Charlie Puleo	.10	.02
❑	553	Gary Rajsich	.10	.02
❑	554	Mike Scott	.20	.07
❑	555	Rusty Staub	.20	.07
❑	556	John Stearns	.10	.02
❑	557	Craig Swan	.10	.02
❑	558	Ellis Valentine	.10	.02
❑	559	Tom Veryzer	.10	.02
❑	560	Mookie Wilson	.20	.07
❑	561	Pat Zachry	.10	.02
❑	562	Buddy Bell	.20	.07
❑	563	John Butcher	.10	.02
❑	564	Steve Comer	.10	.02
❑	565	Danny Darwin	.10	.02
❑	566	Bucky Dent	.20	.07
❑	567	John Grubb	.10	.02
❑	568	Rick Honeycutt	.10	.02
❑	569	Dave Hostetler	.10	.02
❑	570	Charlie Hough	.20	.07
❑	571	Lamar Johnson	.10	.02
❑	572	Jon Matlack	.10	.02
❑	573	Paul Mirabella	.10	.02
❑	574	Larry Parrish	.10	.02
❑	575	Mike Richardt	.10	.02
❑	576	Mickey Rivers	.10	.02
❑	577	Billy Sample	.10	.02
❑	578	Dave Schmidt	.10	.02
❑	579	Bill Stein	.10	.02
❑	580	Jim Sundberg	.20	.07
❑	581	Frank Tanana	.20	.07
❑	582	Mark Wagner	.10	.02
❑	583	George Wright RC	.50	.20
❑	584	Johnny Bench	.75	.30
❑	585	Bruce Berenyi	.10	.02
❑	586	Larry Biittner	.10	.02
❑	587	Cesar Cedeno	.20	.07
❑	588	Dave Concepcion	.20	.07
❑	589	Dan Driessen	.10	.02
❑	590	Greg Harris	.10	.02
❑	591	Ben Hayes	.10	.02
❑	592	Paul Householder	.10	.02
❑	593	Tom Hume	.10	.02
❑	594	Wayne Krenchicki	.10	.02
❑	595	Rafael Landestoy	.10	.02
❑	596	Charlie Leibrandt	.10	.02
❑	597	Eddie Milner	.10	.02
❑	598	Ron Oester	.10	.02
❑	599	Frank Pastore	.10	.02
❑	600	Joe Price	.10	.02
❑	601	Tom Seaver	.75	.30
❑	602	Bob Shirley	.10	.02
❑	603	Mario Soto	.20	.07
❑	604	Alex Trevino	.10	.02
❑	605	Mike Vail	.10	.02
❑	606	Duane Walker	.10	.02
❑	607	Tom Brunansky	.20	.07
❑	608	Bobby Castillo	.10	.02
❑	609	John Castino	.10	.02
❑	610	Ron Davis	.10	.02
❑	611	Lenny Faedo	.10	.02
❑	612	Terry Felton	.10	.02
❑	613	Gary Gaetti RC	1.00	.40
❑	614	Mickey Hatcher	.10	.02
❑	615	Brad Havens	.10	.02
❑	616	Kent Hrbek	.20	.07
❑	617	Randy Johnson	.10	.02
❑	618	Tim Laudner	.10	.02
❑	619	Jeff Little	.10	.02
❑	620	Bobby Mitchell	.10	.02
❑	621	Jack O'Connor	.10	.02
❑	622	John Pacella	.10	.02
❑	623	Pete Redfern	.10	.02
❑	624	Jesus Vega	.10	.02
❑	625	Frank Viola RC	1.50	.60
❑	626	Ron Washington	.10	.02
❑	627	Gary Ward	.10	.02
❑	628	Al Williams	.10	.02
❑	629	C.Yaz/Eck/M.Clear	.75	.30
❑	630	G.Perry/T.Bulling	.10	.02
❑	631	D.Concepcion/M.Trillo	.20	.07
❑	632	R.Yount/B.Bell	.75	.30
❑	633	D.Winfield/K.Hrbek	.10	.02
❑	634	P.Rose/W.Stargell	.75	.30
❑	635	T.Harrah/A.Thornton	.20	.07
❑	636	O.Smith/Lo.Smith	.75	.30
❑	637	B.Diaz/G.Carter	.10	.02
❑	638	C.Fisk/G.Carter	.20	.07
❑	639	Rickey Henderson IA	.75	.30
❑	640	B.Oglivie/R.Jackson	.40	.15
❑	641	Joel Youngblood	.10	.02
❑	642	R.Hassey/L.Barker	.20	.07
❑	643	V.Blue/Black-Blue	.20	.07
❑	644	B.Black/Black-Blue	.10	.02
❑	645	Reggie Jackson Power	.20	.07
❑	646	Rickey Henderson Speed	.75	.30
❑	647	CL: Cards/Brewers	.10	.02
❑	648	CL: Orioles/Angels	.10	.02
❑	649	CL: Royals/Braves	.10	.02
❑	650	CL: Phillies/Red Sox	.10	.02
❑	651	CL: Dodgers/White Sox	.10	.02
❑	652	CL: Giants/Expos	.10	.02
❑	653	CL: Pirates/Tigers	.10	.02
❑	654	CL: Padres/Yankees	.10	.02
❑	655	CL: Indians/Blue Jays	.10	.02
❑	656	CL: Astros/Mariners	.10	.02
❑	657	CL: Cubs/A's	.10	.02
❑	658	CL: Mets/Rangers	.10	.02
❑	659	CL: Reds/Twins	.10	.02
❑	660	CL: Specials/Teams	.10	.02

1984 Fleer

❑		COMPLETE SET (660)	50.00	25.00
❑	1	Mike Boddicker	.15	.05
❑	2	Al Bumbry	.15	.05
❑	3	Todd Cruz	.15	.05
❑	4	Rich Dauer	.15	.05
❑	5	Storm Davis	.15	.05

Card	Player	Mint	Ex
❑ 6	Rick Dempsey	.15	.05
❑ 7	Jim Dwyer	.15	.05
❑ 8	Mike Flanagan	.15	.05
❑ 9	Dan Ford	.15	.05
❑ 10	John Lowenstein	.15	.05
❑ 11	Dennis Martinez	.40	.15
❑ 12	Tippy Martinez	.15	.05
❑ 13	Scott McGregor	.15	.05
❑ 14	Eddie Murray	1.50	.60
❑ 15	Joe Nolan	.15	.05
❑ 16	Jim Palmer	.40	.15
❑ 17	Cal Ripken	10.00	4.00
❑ 18	Gary Roenicke	.15	.05
❑ 19	Lenn Sakata	.15	.05
❑ 20	John Shelby	.15	.05
❑ 21	Ken Singleton	.40	.15
❑ 22	Sammy Stewart	.15	.05
❑ 23	Tim Stoddard	.15	.05
❑ 24	Marty Bystrom	.15	.05
❑ 25	Steve Carlton	.75	.30
❑ 26	Ivan DeJesus	.15	.05
❑ 27	John Denny	.15	.05
❑ 28	Bob Dernier	.15	.05
❑ 29	Bo Diaz	.15	.05
❑ 30	Kiko Garcia	.15	.05
❑ 31	Greg Gross	.15	.05
❑ 32	Kevin Gross RC	.50	.20
❑ 33	Von Hayes	.15	.05
❑ 34	Willie Hernandez	.15	.05
❑ 35	Al Holland	.15	.05
❑ 36	Charles Hudson	.15	.05
❑ 37	Joe Lefebvre	.15	.05
❑ 38	Sixto Lezcano	.15	.05
❑ 39	Garry Maddox	.15	.05
❑ 40	Gary Matthews	.40	.15
❑ 41	Len Matuszek	.15	.05
❑ 42	Tug McGraw	.40	.15
❑ 43	Joe Morgan	.40	.15
❑ 44	Tony Perez	.75	.30
❑ 45	Ron Reed	.15	.05
❑ 46	Pete Rose	5.00	2.00
❑ 47	Juan Samuel RC	1.00	.40
❑ 48	Mike Schmidt	4.00	1.50
❑ 49	Ozzie Virgil	.15	.05
❑ 50	Juan Agosto	.15	.05
❑ 51	Harold Baines	.40	.15
❑ 52	Floyd Bannister	.15	.05
❑ 53	Salome Barojas	.15	.05
❑ 54	Britt Burns	.15	.05
❑ 55	Julio Cruz	.15	.05
❑ 56	Richard Dotson	.15	.05
❑ 57	Jerry Dybzinski	.15	.05
❑ 58	Carlton Fisk	.75	.30
❑ 59	Scott Fletcher	.15	.05
❑ 60	Jerry Hairston	.15	.05
❑ 61	Kevin Hickey	.15	.05
❑ 62	Marc Hill	.15	.05
❑ 63	LaMarr Hoyt	.15	.05
❑ 64	Ron Kittle	.15	.05
❑ 65	Jerry Koosman	.40	.15
❑ 66	Dennis Lamp	.15	.05
❑ 67	Rudy Law	.15	.05
❑ 68	Vance Law	.15	.05
❑ 69	Greg Luzinski	.40	.15
❑ 70	Tom Paciorek	.15	.05
❑ 71	Mike Squires	.15	.05
❑ 72	Dick Tidrow	.15	.05
❑ 73	Greg Walker	.50	.20
❑ 74	Glenn Abbott	.15	.05
❑ 75	Howard Bailey	.15	.05
❑ 76	Doug Bair	.15	.05
❑ 77	Juan Berenguer	.15	.05
❑ 78	Tom Brookens	.40	.15
❑ 79	Enos Cabell	.15	.05
❑ 80	Kirk Gibson	1.50	.60
❑ 81	John Grubb	.15	.05
❑ 82	Larry Herndon	.40	.15
❑ 83	Wayne Krenchicki	.15	.05
❑ 84	Rick Leach	.15	.05
❑ 85	Chet Lemon	.40	.15
❑ 86	Aurelio Lopez	.40	.15
❑ 87	Jack Morris	.40	.15
❑ 88	Lance Parrish	.75	.30
❑ 89	Dan Petry	.40	.15
❑ 90	Dave Rozema	.15	.05
❑ 91	Alan Trammell	.40	.15
❑ 92	Lou Whitaker	.40	.15
❑ 93	Milt Wilcox	.15	.05
❑ 94	Glenn Wilson	.40	.15
❑ 95	John Wockenfuss	.15	.05
❑ 96	Dusty Baker	.40	.15
❑ 97	Joe Beckwith	.15	.05
❑ 98	Greg Brock	.15	.05
❑ 99	Jack Fimple	.15	.05
❑ 100	Pedro Guerrero	.40	.15
❑ 101	Rick Honeycutt	.15	.05
❑ 102	Burt Hooton	.15	.05
❑ 103	Steve Howe	.15	.05
❑ 104	Ken Landreaux	.15	.05
❑ 105	Mike Marshall	.15	.05
❑ 106	Rick Monday	.40	.15
❑ 107	Jose Morales	.15	.05
❑ 108	Tom Niedenfuer	.15	.05
❑ 109	Alejandro Pena RC*	1.00	.40
❑ 110	Jerry Reuss UER ('Home': omitted)	.15	.05
❑ 111	Bill Russell	.40	.15
❑ 112	Steve Sax	.15	.05
❑ 113	Mike Scioscia	.40	.15
❑ 114	Derrel Thomas	.15	.05
❑ 115	Fernando Valenzuela	.40	.15
❑ 116	Bob Welch	.40	.15
❑ 117	Steve Yeager	.40	.15
❑ 118	Pat Zachry	.15	.05
❑ 119	Don Baylor	.40	.15
❑ 120	Bert Campaneris	.40	.15
❑ 121	Rick Cerone	.15	.05
❑ 122	Ray Fontenot	.15	.05
❑ 123	George Frazier	.15	.05
❑ 124	Oscar Gamble	.15	.05
❑ 125	Rich Gossage	.40	.15
❑ 126	Ken Griffey	.40	.15
❑ 127	Ron Guidry	.40	.15
❑ 128	Jay Howell	.15	.05
❑ 129	Steve Kemp	.15	.05
❑ 130	Matt Keough	.15	.05
❑ 131	Don Mattingly RC	25.00	10.00
❑ 132	John Montefusco	.15	.05
❑ 133	Omar Moreno	.15	.05
❑ 134	Dale Murray	.15	.05
❑ 135	Graig Nettles	.40	.15
❑ 136	Lou Piniella	.40	.15
❑ 137	Willie Randolph	.40	.15
❑ 138	Shane Rawley	.15	.05
❑ 139	Dave Righetti	.40	.15
❑ 140	Andre Robertson	.15	.05
❑ 141	Bob Shirley	.15	.05
❑ 142	Roy Smalley	.15	.05
❑ 143	Dave Winfield	.40	.15
❑ 144	Butch Wynegar	.15	.05
❑ 145	Jim Acker	.15	.05
❑ 146	Doyle Alexander	.15	.05
❑ 147	Jesse Barfield	.40	.15
❑ 148	George Bell	.40	.15
❑ 149	Barry Bonnell	.15	.05
❑ 150	Jim Clancy	.15	.05
❑ 151	Dave Collins	.15	.05
❑ 152	Tony Fernandez RC	1.00	.40
❑ 153	Damaso Garcia	.15	.05
❑ 154	Dave Geisel	.15	.05
❑ 155	Jim Gott	.15	.05
❑ 156	Alfredo Griffin	.15	.05
❑ 157	Garth Iorg	.15	.05
❑ 158	Roy Lee Jackson	.15	.05
❑ 159	Cliff Johnson	.15	.05
❑ 160	Luis Leal	.15	.05
❑ 161	Buck Martinez	.15	.05
❑ 162	Joey McLaughlin	.15	.05
❑ 163	Randy Moffitt	.15	.05
❑ 164	Lloyd Moseby	.15	.05
❑ 165	Rance Mulliniks	.15	.05
❑ 166	Jorge Orta	.15	.05
❑ 167	Dave Stieb	.40	.15
❑ 168	Willie Upshaw	.15	.05
❑ 169	Ernie Whitt	.15	.05
❑ 170	Len Barker	.15	.05
❑ 171	Steve Bedrosian	.15	.05
❑ 172	Bruce Benedict	.15	.05
❑ 173	Brett Butler	.40	.15
❑ 174	Rick Camp	.15	.05
❑ 175	Chris Chambliss	.40	.15
❑ 176	Ken Dayley	.15	.05
❑ 177	Pete Falcone	.15	.05
❑ 178	Terry Forster	.40	.15
❑ 179	Gene Garber	.15	.05
❑ 180	Terry Harper	.15	.05
❑ 181	Bob Horner	.40	.15
❑ 182	Glenn Hubbard	.15	.05
❑ 183	Randy Johnson	.15	.05
❑ 184	Craig McMurtry	.15	.05
❑ 185	Donnie Moore	.15	.05
❑ 186	Dale Murphy	.75	.30
❑ 187	Phil Niekro	.40	.15
❑ 188	Pascual Perez	.15	.05
❑ 189	Biff Pocoroba	.15	.05
❑ 190	Rafael Ramirez	.15	.05
❑ 191	Jerry Royster	.15	.05
❑ 192	Claudell Washington	.15	.05
❑ 193	Bob Watson	.15	.05
❑ 194	Jerry Augustine	.15	.05
❑ 195	Mark Brouhard	.15	.05
❑ 196	Mike Caldwell	.15	.05
❑ 197	Tom Candiotti RC	1.00	.40
❑ 198	Cecil Cooper	.40	.15
❑ 199	Rollie Fingers	.40	.15
❑ 200	Jim Gantner	.15	.05
❑ 201	Bob L. Gibson RC	.25	.08
❑ 202	Moose Haas	.15	.05
❑ 203	Roy Howell	.15	.05
❑ 204	Pete Ladd	.15	.05
❑ 205	Rick Manning	.15	.05
❑ 206	Bob McClure	.15	.05
❑ 207	Paul Molitor	.40	.15
❑ 208	Don Money	.15	.05
❑ 209	Charlie Moore	.15	.05
❑ 210	Ben Oglivie	.40	.15
❑ 211	Chuck Porter	.15	.05
❑ 212	Ed Romero	.15	.05
❑ 213	Ted Simmons	.40	.15
❑ 214	Jim Slaton	.15	.05
❑ 215	Don Sutton	.40	.15
❑ 216	Tom Tellmann	.15	.05
❑ 217	Pete Vuckovich	.15	.05
❑ 218	Ned Yost	.15	.05
❑ 219	Robin Yount	2.50	1.00
❑ 220	Alan Ashby	.15	.05
❑ 221	Kevin Bass	.15	.05
❑ 222	Jose Cruz	.40	.15
❑ 223	Bill Dawley	.15	.05
❑ 224	Frank DiPino	.15	.05
❑ 225	Bill Doran RC*	.50	.20
❑ 226	Phil Garner	.40	.15
❑ 227	Art Howe	.15	.05
❑ 228	Bob Knepper	.15	.05
❑ 229	Ray Knight	.40	.15
❑ 230	Frank LaCorte	.15	.05
❑ 231	Mike LaCoss	.15	.05
❑ 232	Mike Madden	.15	.05
❑ 233	Jerry Mumphrey	.15	.05
❑ 234	Joe Niekro	.15	.05
❑ 235	Terry Puhl	.15	.05
❑ 236	Luis Pujols	.15	.05
❑ 237	Craig Reynolds	.15	.05
❑ 238	Vern Ruhle	.15	.05
❑ 239	Nolan Ryan	8.00	3.00
❑ 240	Mike Scott	.40	.15
❑ 241	Tony Scott	.15	.05
❑ 242	Dave Smith	.15	.05
❑ 243	Dickie Thon	.15	.05
❑ 244	Denny Walling	.15	.05
❑ 245	Dale Berra	.15	.05
❑ 246	Jim Bibby	.15	.05
❑ 247	John Candelaria	.15	.05
❑ 248	Jose DeLeon RC	.50	.20
❑ 249	Mike Easler	.15	.05
❑ 250	Cecilio Guante	.15	.05
❑ 251	Richie Hebner	.15	.05
❑ 252	Lee Lacy	.15	.05
❑ 253	Bill Madlock	.40	.15
❑ 254	Milt May	.15	.05
❑ 255	Lee Mazzilli	.40	.15
❑ 256	Larry McWilliams	.15	.05
❑ 257	Jim Morrison	.15	.05
❑ 258	Dave Parker	.40	.15
❑ 259	Tony Pena	.15	.05
❑ 260	Johnny Ray	.15	.05
❑ 261	Rick Rhoden	.15	.05
❑ 262	Don Robinson	.15	.05

❑ 263 Manny Sarmiento .15 .05
❑ 264 Rod Scurry .15 .05
❑ 265 Kent Tekulve .15 .05
❑ 266 Gene Tenace .40 .15
❑ 267 Jason Thompson .15 .05
❑ 268 Lee Tunnell .15 .05
❑ 269 Marvell Wynne .50 .20
❑ 270 Ray Burris .15 .05
❑ 271 Gary Carter .40 .15
❑ 272 Warren Cromartie .15 .05
❑ 273 Andre Dawson .40 .15
❑ 274 Doug Flynn .15 .05
❑ 275 Terry Francona .40 .15
❑ 276 Bill Gullickson .15 .05
❑ 277 Bob James .15 .05
❑ 278 Charlie Lea .15 .05
❑ 279 Bryan Little .15 .05
❑ 280 Al Oliver .40 .15
❑ 281 Tim Raines .40 .15
❑ 282 Bobby Ramos .15 .05
❑ 283 Jeff Reardon .40 .15
❑ 284 Steve Rogers .40 .15
❑ 285 Scott Sanderson .15 .05
❑ 286 Dan Schatzeder .15 .05
❑ 287 Bryn Smith .15 .05
❑ 288 Chris Speier .15 .05
❑ 289 Manny Trillo .15 .05
❑ 290 Mike Vail .15 .05
❑ 291 Tim Wallach .15 .05
❑ 292 Chris Welsh .15 .05
❑ 293 Jim Wohlford .15 .05
❑ 294 Kurt Bevacqua .15 .05
❑ 295 Juan Bonilla .15 .05
❑ 296 Bobby Brown .15 .05
❑ 297 Luis DeLeon .15 .05
❑ 298 Dave Dravecky .15 .05
❑ 299 Tim Flannery .15 .05
❑ 300 Steve Garvey .40 .15
❑ 301 Tony Gwynn 6.00 2.50
❑ 302 Andy Hawkins .15 .05
❑ 303 Ruppert Jones .15 .05
❑ 304 Terry Kennedy .15 .05
❑ 305 Tim Lollar .15 .05
❑ 306 Gary Lucas .15 .05
❑ 307 Kevin McReynolds RC 1.00 .40
❑ 308 Sid Monge .15 .05
❑ 309 Mario Ramirez .15 .05
❑ 310 Gene Richards .15 .05
❑ 311 Luis Salazar .15 .05
❑ 312 Eric Show .15 .05
❑ 313 Elias Sosa .15 .05
❑ 314 Garry Templeton .40 .15
❑ 315 Mark Thurmond .15 .05
❑ 316 Ed Whitson .15 .05
❑ 317 Alan Wiggins .15 .05
❑ 318 Neil Allen .15 .05
❑ 319 Joaquin Andujar .40 .15
❑ 320 Steve Braun .15 .05
❑ 321 Glenn Brummer .15 .05
❑ 322 Bob Forsch .15 .05
❑ 323 David Green .15 .05
❑ 324 George Hendrick .40 .15
❑ 325 Tom Herr .15 .05
❑ 326 Dane Iorg .15 .05
❑ 327 Jeff Lahti .15 .05
❑ 328 Dave LaPoint .15 .05
❑ 329 Willie McGee .40 .15
❑ 330 Ken Oberkfell .15 .05
❑ 331 Darrell Porter .15 .05
❑ 332 Jamie Quirk .15 .05
❑ 333 Mike Ramsey .15 .05
❑ 334 Floyd Rayford .15 .05
❑ 335 Lonnie Smith .15 .05
❑ 336 Ozzie Smith 2.50 1.00
❑ 337 John Stuper .15 .05
❑ 338 Bruce Sutter .75 .30
❑ 339 Andy Van Slyke RC 2.50 1.00
❑ 340 Dave Von Ohlen .15 .05
❑ 341 Willie Aikens .15 .05
❑ 342 Mike Armstrong .15 .05
❑ 343 Bud Black .15 .05
❑ 344 George Brett 4.00 1.50
❑ 345 Onix Concepcion .15 .05
❑ 346 Keith Creel .15 .05
❑ 347 Larry Gura .15 .05
❑ 348 Don Hood .15 .05
❑ 349 Dennis Leonard .15 .05
❑ 350 Hal McRae .40 .15
❑ 351 Amos Otis .40 .15
❑ 352 Gaylord Perry .40 .15
❑ 353 Greg Pryor .15 .05
❑ 354 Dan Quisenberry .15 .05
❑ 355 Steve Renko .15 .05
❑ 356 Leon Roberts .15 .05
❑ 357 Pat Sheridan .15 .05
❑ 358 Joe Simpson .15 .05
❑ 359 Don Slaught .40 .15
❑ 360 Paul Splittorff .15 .05
❑ 361 U.L. Washington .15 .05
❑ 362 John Wathan .15 .05
❑ 363 Frank White .40 .15
❑ 364 Willie Wilson .40 .15
❑ 365 Jim Barr .15 .05
❑ 366 Dave Bergman .15 .05
❑ 367 Fred Breining .15 .05
❑ 368 Bob Brenly .15 .05
❑ 369 Jack Clark .40 .15
❑ 370 Chili Davis .40 .15
❑ 371 Mark Davis .15 .05
❑ 372 Darrell Evans .40 .15
❑ 373 Atlee Hammaker .15 .05
❑ 374 Mike Krukow .15 .05
❑ 375 Duane Kuiper .15 .05
❑ 376 Bill Laskey .15 .05
❑ 377 Gary Lavelle .15 .05
❑ 378 Johnnie LeMaster .15 .05
❑ 379 Jeff Leonard .15 .05
❑ 380 Randy Lerch .15 .05
❑ 381 Renie Martin .15 .05
❑ 382 Andy McGaffigan .15 .05
❑ 383 Greg Minton .15 .05
❑ 384 Tom O'Malley .15 .05
❑ 385 Max Venable .15 .05
❑ 386 Brad Wellman .15 .05
❑ 387 Joel Youngblood .15 .05
❑ 388 Gary Allenson .15 .05
❑ 389 Luis Aponte .15 .05
❑ 390 Tony Armas .40 .15
❑ 391 Doug Bird .15 .05
❑ 392 Wade Boggs 4.00 1.50
❑ 393 Dennis Boyd .40 .15
❑ 394 Mike G. Brown UER .25 .08
❑ 395 Mark Clear .15 .05
❑ 396 Dennis Eckersley .75 .30
❑ 397 Dwight Evans .75 .30
❑ 398 Rich Gedman .15 .05
❑ 399 Glenn Hoffman .15 .05
❑ 400 Bruce Hurst .15 .05
❑ 401 John Henry Johnson .15 .05
❑ 402 Ed Jurak .15 .05
❑ 403 Rick Miller .15 .05
❑ 404 Jeff Newman .15 .05
❑ 405 Reid Nichols .15 .05
❑ 406 Bob Ojeda .15 .05
❑ 407 Jerry Remy .15 .05
❑ 408 Jim Rice .40 .15
❑ 409 Bob Stanley .15 .05
❑ 410 Dave Stapleton .15 .05
❑ 411 John Tudor .40 .15
❑ 412 Carl Yastrzemski 1.50 .60
❑ 413 Buddy Bell .40 .15
❑ 414 Larry Biittner .15 .05
❑ 415 John Butcher .15 .05
❑ 416 Danny Darwin .15 .05
❑ 417 Bucky Dent .40 .15
❑ 418 Dave Hostetler .15 .05
❑ 419 Charlie Hough .40 .15
❑ 420 Bobby Johnson .15 .05
❑ 421 Odell Jones .15 .05
❑ 422 Jon Matlack .15 .05
❑ 423 Pete O'Brien RC* .50 .20
❑ 424 Larry Parrish .15 .05
❑ 425 Mickey Rivers .15 .05
❑ 426 Billy Sample .15 .05
❑ 427 Dave Schmidt .15 .05
❑ 428 Mike Smithson .15 .05
❑ 429 Bill Stein .15 .05
❑ 430 Dave Stewart .40 .15
❑ 431 Jim Sundberg .40 .15
❑ 432 Frank Tanana .40 .15
❑ 433 Dave Tobik .15 .05
❑ 434 Wayne Tolleson .15 .05
❑ 435 George Wright .15 .05
❑ 436 Bill Almon .15 .05
❑ 437 Keith Atherton .15 .05
❑ 438 Dave Beard .15 .05
❑ 439 Tom Burgmeier .15 .05
❑ 440 Jeff Burroughs .15 .05
❑ 441 Chris Codiroli .15 .05
❑ 442 Tim Conroy .15 .05
❑ 443 Mike Davis .15 .05
❑ 444 Wayne Gross .15 .05
❑ 445 Garry Hancock .15 .05
❑ 446 Mike Heath .15 .05
❑ 447 Rickey Henderson 2.50 1.00
❑ 448 Donnie Hill .15 .05
❑ 449 Bob Kearney .15 .05
❑ 450 Bill Krueger RC .25 .08
❑ 451 Rick Langford .15 .05
❑ 452 Carney Lansford .40 .15
❑ 453 Dave Lopes .40 .15
❑ 454 Steve McCatty .15 .05
❑ 455 Dan Meyer .15 .05
❑ 456 Dwayne Murphy .15 .05
❑ 457 Mike Norris .15 .05
❑ 458 Ricky Peters .15 .05
❑ 459 Tony Phillips RC 1.00 .40
❑ 460 Tom Underwood .15 .05
❑ 461 Mike Warren .15 .05
❑ 462 Johnny Bench 1.50 .60
❑ 463 Bruce Berenyi .15 .05
❑ 464 Dann Bilardello .15 .05
❑ 465 Cesar Cedeno .40 .15
❑ 466 Dave Concepcion .40 .15
❑ 467 Dan Driessen .15 .05
❑ 468 Nick Esasky .15 .05
❑ 469 Rich Gale .15 .05
❑ 470 Ben Hayes .15 .05
❑ 471 Paul Householder .15 .05
❑ 472 Tom Hume .15 .05
❑ 473 Alan Knicely .15 .05
❑ 474 Eddie Milner .15 .05
❑ 475 Ron Oester .15 .05
❑ 476 Kelly Paris .15 .05
❑ 477 Frank Pastore .15 .05
❑ 478 Ted Power .15 .05
❑ 479 Joe Price .15 .05
❑ 480 Charlie Puleo .15 .05
❑ 481 Gary Redus RC* .50 .20
❑ 482 Bill Scherrer .15 .05
❑ 483 Mario Soto .40 .15
❑ 484 Alex Trevino .15 .05
❑ 485 Duane Walker .15 .05
❑ 486 Larry Bowa .40 .15
❑ 487 Warren Brusstar .15 .05
❑ 488 Bill Buckner .40 .15
❑ 489 Bill Campbell .15 .05
❑ 490 Ron Cey .40 .15
❑ 491 Jody Davis .15 .05
❑ 492 Leon Durham .15 .05
❑ 493 Mel Hall .40 .15
❑ 494 Fergie Jenkins .40 .15
❑ 495 Jay Johnstone .15 .05
❑ 496 Craig Lefferts RC .25 .08
❑ 497 Carmelo Martinez .15 .05
❑ 498 Jerry Morales .15 .05
❑ 499 Keith Moreland .15 .05
❑ 500 Dickie Noles .15 .05
❑ 501 Mike Proly .15 .05
❑ 502 Chuck Rainey .15 .05
❑ 503 Dick Ruthven .15 .05
❑ 504 Ryne Sandberg 6.00 2.50
❑ 505 Lee Smith .40 .15
❑ 506 Steve Trout .15 .05
❑ 507 Gary Woods .15 .05
❑ 508 Juan Beniquez .15 .05
❑ 509 Bob Boone .40 .15
❑ 510 Rick Burleson .15 .05
❑ 511 Rod Carew .75 .30
❑ 512 Bobby Clark .15 .05
❑ 513 John Curtis .15 .05
❑ 514 Doug DeCinces .15 .05
❑ 515 Brian Downing .40 .15
❑ 516 Tim Foli .15 .05
❑ 517 Ken Forsch .15 .05
❑ 518 Bobby Grich .40 .15
❑ 519 Andy Hassler .15 .05
❑ 520 Reggie Jackson .75 .30

❑ 521 Ron Jackson .15 .05
❑ 522 Tommy John .40 .15
❑ 523 Bruce Kison .15 .05
❑ 524 Steve Lubratich .15 .05
❑ 525 Fred Lynn .40 .15
❑ 526 Gary Pettis .15 .05
❑ 527 Luis Sanchez .15 .05
❑ 528 Daryl Sconiers .15 .05
❑ 529 Ellis Valentine .15 .05
❑ 530 Rob Wilfong .15 .05
❑ 531 Mike Witt .15 .05
❑ 532 Geoff Zahn .15 .05
❑ 533 Bud Anderson .15 .05
❑ 534 Chris Bando .15 .05
❑ 535 Alan Bannister .15 .05
❑ 536 Bert Blyleven .40 .15
❑ 537 Tom Brennan .15 .05
❑ 538 Jamie Easterly .15 .05
❑ 539 Juan Eichelberger .15 .05
❑ 540 Jim Essian .15 .05
❑ 541 Mike Fischlin .15 .05
❑ 542 Julio Franco .40 .15
❑ 543 Mike Hargrove .15 .05
❑ 544 Toby Harrah .40 .15
❑ 545 Ron Hassey .15 .05
❑ 546 Neal Heaton .15 .05
❑ 547 Bake McBride .40 .15
❑ 548 Broderick Perkins .15 .05
❑ 549 Lary Sorensen .15 .05
❑ 550 Dan Spillner .15 .05
❑ 551 Rick Sutcliffe .40 .15
❑ 552 Pat Tabler .15 .05
❑ 553 Gorman Thomas .40 .15
❑ 554 Andre Thornton .15 .05
❑ 555 George Vukovich .15 .05
❑ 556 Darrell Brown .15 .05
❑ 557 Tom Brunansky .15 .05
❑ 558 Randy Bush .15 .05
❑ 559 Bobby Castillo .15 .05
❑ 560 John Castino .15 .05
❑ 561 Ron Davis .15 .05
❑ 562 Dave Engle .15 .05
❑ 563 Lenny Faedo .15 .05
❑ 564 Pete Filson .15 .05
❑ 565 Gary Gaetti .75 .30
❑ 566 Mickey Hatcher .15 .05
❑ 567 Kent Hrbek .40 .15
❑ 568 Rusty Kuntz .15 .05
❑ 569 Tim Laudner .15 .05
❑ 570 Rick Lysander .15 .05
❑ 571 Bobby Mitchell .15 .05
❑ 572 Ken Schrom .15 .05
❑ 573 Ray Smith .15 .05
❑ 574 Tim Teufel RC .50 .20
❑ 575 Frank Viola .75 .30
❑ 576 Gary Ward .15 .05
❑ 577 Ron Washington .15 .05
❑ 578 Len Whitehouse .15 .05
❑ 579 Al Williams .15 .05
❑ 580 Bob Bailor .15 .05
❑ 581 Mark Bradley .15 .05
❑ 582 Hubie Brooks .15 .05
❑ 583 Carlos Diaz .15 .05
❑ 584 George Foster .40 .15
❑ 585 Brian Giles .15 .05
❑ 586 Danny Heep .15 .05
❑ 587 Keith Hernandez .40 .15
❑ 588 Ron Hodges .15 .05
❑ 589 Scott Holman .15 .05
❑ 590 Dave Kingman .40 .15
❑ 591 Ed Lynch .15 .05
❑ 592 Jose Oquendo RC .50 .20
❑ 593 Jesse Orosco .15 .05
❑ 594 Junior Ortiz .15 .05
❑ 595 Tom Seaver 1.50 .60
❑ 596 Doug Sisk .15 .05
❑ 597 Rusty Staub .40 .15
❑ 598 John Stearns .15 .05
❑ 599 Darryl Strawberry RC 5.00 2.00
❑ 600 Craig Swan .15 .05
❑ 601 Walt Terrell .15 .05
❑ 602 Mike Torrez .15 .05
❑ 603 Mookie Wilson .40 .15
❑ 604 Jamie Allen .15 .05
❑ 605 Jim Beattie .15 .05
❑ 606 Tony Bernazard .15 .05
❑ 607 Manny Castillo .15 .05
❑ 608 Bill Caudill .15 .05
❑ 609 Bryan Clark .15 .05
❑ 610 Al Cowens .15 .05
❑ 611 Dave Henderson .40 .15
❑ 612 Steve Henderson .15 .05
❑ 613 Orlando Mercado .15 .05
❑ 614 Mike Moore .15 .05
❑ 615. Ricky Nelson UER
(Jamie Nelson's
stats on back) .15 .05
❑ 616 Spike Owen RC .50 .20
❑ 617 Pat Putnam .15 .05
❑ 618 Ron Roenicke .15 .05
❑ 619 Mike Stanton .15 .05
❑ 620 Bob Stoddard .15 .05
❑ 621 Rick Sweet .15 .05
❑ 622 Roy Thomas .15 .05
❑ 623 Ed VandeBerg .15 .05
❑ 624 Matt Young RC .50 .20
❑ 625 Richie Zisk .15 .05
❑ 626 Fred Lynn
1982 AS Game RB .40 .15
❑ 627 Manny Trillo
1983 AS Game RB .15 .05
❑ 628 Steve Garvey Iron Man .15 .05
❑ 629 Rod Carew AL RunnerUp .40 .15
❑ 630 Wade Boggs AL Champ 1.50 .60
❑ 631 Tim Raines IA .15 .05
❑ 632 Al Oliver
Double Trouble .40 .15
❑ 633 Steve Sax
AS Second Base .15 .05
❑ 634 Dickie Thon
AS Shortstop .15 .05
❑ 635 Ace Firemen
Dan Quisenberry
and Tippy Martinez .15 .05
❑ 636 J.Morgan/P.Rose/T.Perez 1.50 .60
❑ 637 Backstop Stars
Lance Parrish
Bob Boone .75 .30
❑ 638 G.Brett/G.Perry 2.00 .75
❑ 639 1983 No Hitters
Dave Righetti
Mike Warren
Bob F .75 .30
❑ 640 J.Bench/C.Yastrzemski 1.50 .60
❑ 641 Gaylord Perry Style .15 .05
❑ 642 Steve Carlton IA .40 .15
❑ 643 Joe Altobelli and
Paul Owens
World Series Manage .15 .05
❑ 644 Rick Dempsey
World Series MVP .15 .05
❑ 645 Mike Boddicker
WS Rookie Winner .15 .05
❑ 646 Scott McGregor
WS Clincher .15 .05
❑ 647 CL: Orioles/Royals
Joe Altobelli MG .15 .05
❑ 648 CL: Phillies/Giants
Paul Owens MG .15 .05
❑ 649 CL: White Sox/Red Sox
Tony LaRussa MG .75 .30
❑ 650 CL: Tigers/Rangers
Sparky Anderson MG .75 .30
❑ 651 CL: Dodgers/A's
Tommy Lasorda MG .75 .30
❑ 652 CL: Yankees/Reds
Billy Martin MG .75 .30
❑ 653 CL: Blue Jays/Cubs
Bobby Cox MG .40 .15
❑ 654 CL: Braves/Angels
Joe Torre MG .75 .30
❑ 655 CL: Brewers/Indians
Rene Lachemann MG .15 .05
❑ 656 CL: Astros/Twins
Bob Lillis MG .15 .05
❑ 657 CL: Pirates/Mets
Chuck Tanner MG .15 .05
❑ 658 CL: Expos/Mariners
Bill Virdon MG .15 .05
❑ 659 CL: Padres/Specials
Dick Williams MG .40 .15
❑ 660 CL: Cardinals/Teams
Whitey Herzog MG .75 .30

1984 Fleer Update

❑ COMP.FACT.SET (132) 350.00 200.00
❑ 1 Willie Aikens 1.00 .40
❑ 2 Luis Aponte 1.00 .40
❑ 3 Mark Bailey 1.00 .40
❑ 4 Bob Bailor 1.00 .40
❑ 5 Dusty Baker 1.50 .60
❑ 6 Steve Balboni 1.00 .40
❑ 7 Alan Bannister 1.00 .40
❑ 8 Marty Barrett XRC 2.00 .75
❑ 9 Dave Beard 1.00 .40
❑ 10 Joe Beckwith 1.00 .40
❑ 11 Dave Bergman 1.00 .40
❑ 12 Tony Bernazard 1.00 .40
❑ 13 Bruce Bochte 1.00 .40
❑ 14 Barry Bonnell 1.00 .40
❑ 15 Phil Bradley 2.00 .75
❑ 16 Fred Breining 1.00 .40
❑ 17 Mike C. Brown 1.00 .40
❑ 18 Bill Buckner 1.50 .60
❑ 19 Ray Burris 1.00 .40
❑ 20 John Butcher 1.00 .40
❑ 21 Brett Butler 1.50 .60
❑ 22 Enos Cabell 1.00 .40
❑ 23 Bill Campbell 1.00 .40
❑ 24 Bill Caudill 1.00 .40
❑ 25 Bobby Clark 1.00 .40
❑ 26 Bryan Clark 1.00 .40
❑ 27 Roger Clemens XRC 325.00 225.00
❑ 28 Jaime Cocanower 1.00 .40
❑ 29 Ron Darling XRC 5.00 2.00
❑ 30 Alvin Davis XRC 2.00 .75
❑ 31 Bob Dernier 1.00 .40
❑ 32 Carlos Diaz 1.00 .40
❑ 33 Mike Easler 1.00 .40
❑ 34 Dennis Eckersley 2.50 1.00
❑ 35 Jim Essian 1.00 .40
❑ 36 Darrell Evans 1.50 .60
❑ 37 Mike Fitzgerald 1.00 .40
❑ 38 Tim Foli 1.00 .40
❑ 39 John Franco XRC 5.00 2.00
❑ 40 George Frazier 1.00 .40
❑ 41 Rich Gale 1.00 .40
❑ 42 Barbaro Garbey 1.00 .40
❑ 43 Dwight Gooden XRC 25.00 10.00
❑ 44 Rich Gossage 1.50 .60
❑ 45 Wayne Gross 1.00 .40
❑ 46 Mark Gubicza XRC 2.00 .75
❑ 47 Jackie Gutierrez 1.00 .40
❑ 48 Toby Harrah 1.50 .60
❑ 49 Ron Hassey 1.00 .40
❑ 50 Richie Hebner 1.00 .40
❑ 51 Willie Hernandez 1.00 .40
❑ 52 Ed Hodge 1.00 .40
❑ 53 Ricky Horton 1.00 .40
❑ 54 Art Howe 1.00 .40
❑ 55 Dane Iorg 1.00 .40
❑ 56 Brook Jacoby 2.00 .75
❑ 57 Dion James XRC 1.00 .40
❑ 58 Mike Jeffcoat XRC 1.00 .40
❑ 59 Ruppert Jones 1.00 .40
❑ 60 Bob Kearney 1.00 .40
❑ 61 Jimmy Key XRC 5.00 2.00
❑ 62 Dave Kingman 1.50 .60
❑ 63 Brad Komminsk XRC 1.00 .40

❑ 64 Jerry Koosman 1.50 .60
❑ 65 Wayne Krenchicki 1.00 .40
❑ 66 Rusty Kuntz 1.00 .40
❑ 67 Frank LaCorte 1.00 .40
❑ 68 Dennis Lamp 1.00 .40
❑ 69 Tito Landrum 1.00 .40
❑ 70 Mark Langston XRC 5.00 2.00
❑ 71 Rick Leach 1.00 .40
❑ 72 Craig Lefferts 1.00 .40
❑ 73 Gary Lucas 1.00 .40
❑ 74 Jerry Martin 1.00 .40
❑ 75 Carmelo Martinez 1.00 .40
❑ 76 Mike Mason XRC 1.00 .40
❑ 77 Gary Matthews 1.50 .60
❑ 78 Andy McGaffigan 1.00 .40
❑ 79 Joey McLaughlin 1.00 .40
❑ 80 Joe Morgan 1.50 .60
❑ 81 Darryl Motley 1.00 .40
❑ 82 Graig Nettles 1.50 .60
❑ 83 Phil Niekro 1.50 .60
❑ 84 Ken Oberkfell 1.00 .40
❑ 85 Al Oliver 1.50 .60
❑ 86 Jorge Orta 1.00 .40
❑ 87 Amos Otis 1.50 .60
❑ 88 Bob Owchinko 1.00 .40
❑ 89 Dave Parker 1.50 .60
❑ 90 Jack Perconte 1.00 .40
❑ 91 Tony Perez 2.50 1.00
❑ 92 Gerald Perry 2.00 .75
❑ 93 Kirby Puckett XRC 80.00 40.00
❑ 94 Shane Rawley 1.00 .40
❑ 95 Floyd Rayford 1.00 .40
❑ 96 Ron Reed 1.00 .40
❑ 97 R.J. Reynolds 1.00 .40
❑ 98 Gene Richards 1.00 .40
❑ 99 Jose Rijo XRC 5.00 2.00
❑ 100 Jeff D. Robinson 1.00 .40
❑ 101 Ron Romanick 1.00 .40
❑ 102 Pete Rose 12.00 5.00
❑ 103 Bret Saberhagen XRC 10.00 4.00
❑ 104 Scott Sanderson 1.00 .40
❑ 105 Dick Schofield XRC 2.00 .75
❑ 106 Tom Seaver 4.00 1.50
❑ 107 Jim Slaton 1.00 .40
❑ 108 Mike Smithson 1.00 .40
❑ 109 Lary Sorensen 1.00 .40
❑ 110 Tim Stoddard 1.00 .40
❑ 111 Jeff Stone 1.00 .40
❑ 112 Champ Summers 1.00 .40
❑ 113 Jim Sundberg 1.50 .60
❑ 114 Rick Sutcliffe 1.50 .60
❑ 115 Craig Swan 1.00 .40
❑ 116 Derrel Thomas 1.00 .40
❑ 117 Gorman Thomas 1.50 .60
❑ 118 Alex Trevino 1.00 .40
❑ 119 Manny Trillo 1.00 .40
❑ 120 John Tudor 1.50 .60
❑ 121 Tom Underwood 1.00 .40
❑ 122 Mike Vail 1.00 .40
❑ 123 Tom Waddell 1.00 .40
❑ 124 Gary Ward 1.00 .40
❑ 125 Terry Whitfield 1.00 .40
❑ 126 Curtis Wilkerson 1.00 .40
❑ 127 Frank Williams 1.00 .40
❑ 128 Glenn Wilson 1.50 .60
❑ 129 John Wockenfuss 1.00 .40
❑ 130 Ned Yost 1.00 .40
❑ 131 Mike Young XRC 1.00 .40
❑ 132 Checklist 1-132 1.00 .40

1985 Fleer

❑ COMPLETE SET (660) 60.00 30.00
❑ COMP.FACT.SET (660) 100.00 50.00
❑ 1 Doug Bair .15 .05
❑ 2 Juan Berenguer .15 .05
❑ 3 Dave Bergman .15 .05
❑ 4 Tom Brookens .15 .05
❑ 5 Marty Castillo .15 .05
❑ 6 Darrell Evans .40 .15
❑ 7 Barbaro Garbey .15 .05
❑ 8 Kirk Gibson .40 .15
❑ 9 John Grubb .15 .05
❑ 10 Willie Hernandez .15 .05
❑ 11 Larry Herndon .15 .05
❑ 12 Howard Johnson .40 .15
❑ 13 Ruppert Jones .15 .05

❑ 14 Rusty Kuntz .15 .05
❑ 15 Chet Lemon .40 .15
❑ 16 Aurelio Lopez .15 .05
❑ 17 Sid Monge .15 .05
❑ 18 Jack Morris .40 .15
❑ 19 Lance Parrish .40 .15
❑ 20 Dan Petry .15 .05
❑ 21 Dave Rozema .15 .05
❑ 22 Bill Scherrer .15 .05
❑ 23 Alan Trammell .40 .15
❑ 24 Lou Whitaker .40 .15
❑ 25 Milt Wilcox .15 .05
❑ 26 Kurt Bevacqua .15 .05
❑ 27 Greg Booker .15 .05
❑ 28 Bobby Brown .15 .05
❑ 29 Luis DeLeon .15 .05
❑ 30 Dave Dravecky .15 .05
❑ 31 Tim Flannery .15 .05
❑ 32 Steve Garvey .40 .15
❑ 33 Rich Gossage .40 .15
❑ 34 Tony Gwynn 2.50 1.00
❑ 35 Greg Harris .15 .05
❑ 36 Andy Hawkins .15 .05
❑ 37 Terry Kennedy .15 .05
❑ 38 Craig Lefferts .15 .05
❑ 39 Tim Lollar .15 .05
❑ 40 Carmelo Martinez .15 .05
❑ 41 Kevin McReynolds .40 .15
❑ 42 Graig Nettles .40 .15
❑ 43 Luis Salazar .15 .05
❑ 44 Eric Show .15 .05
❑ 45 Garry Templeton .40 .15
❑ 46 Mark Thurmond .15 .05
❑ 47 Ed Whitson .15 .05
❑ 48 Alan Wiggins .15 .05
❑ 49 Rich Bordi .15 .05
❑ 50 Larry Bowa .40 .15
❑ 51 Warren Brusstar .15 .05
❑ 52 Ron Cey .40 .15
❑ 53 Henry Cotto RC .25 .08
❑ 54 Jody Davis .15 .05
❑ 55 Bob Dernier .15 .05
❑ 56 Leon Durham .15 .05
❑ 57 Dennis Eckersley .75 .30
❑ 58 George Frazier .15 .05
❑ 59 Richie Hebner .15 .05
❑ 60 Dave Lopes .40 .15
❑ 61 Gary Matthews .40 .15
❑ 62 Keith Moreland .15 .05
❑ 63 Rick Reuschel .40 .15
❑ 64 Dick Ruthven .15 .05
❑ 65 Ryne Sandberg 2.50 1.00
❑ 66 Scott Sanderson .15 .05
❑ 67 Lee Smith .40 .15
❑ 68 Tim Stoddard .15 .05
❑ 69 Rick Sutcliffe .40 .15
❑ 70 Steve Trout .15 .05
❑ 71 Gary Woods .15 .05
❑ 72 Wally Backman .15 .05
❑ 73 Bruce Berenyi .15 .05
❑ 74 Hubie Brooks UER
(Kelvin Chapman's
stats on card .15 .05
❑ 75 Kelvin Chapman .15 .05
❑ 76 Ron Darling .40 .15
❑ 77 Sid Fernandez .40 .15
❑ 78 Mike Fitzgerald .15 .05
❑ 79 George Foster .40 .15

❑ 80 Brent Gaff .15 .05
❑ 81 Ron Gardenhire .15 .05
❑ 82 Dwight Gooden RC 3.00 1.25
❑ 83 Tom Gorman .15 .05
❑ 84 Danny Heep .15 .05
❑ 85 Keith Hernandez .40 .15
❑ 86 Ray Knight .40 .15
❑ 87 Ed Lynch .15 .05
❑ 88 Jose Oquendo .15 .05
❑ 89 Jesse Orosco .15 .05
❑ 90 Rafael Santana .15 .05
❑ 91 Doug Sisk .15 .05
❑ 92 Rusty Staub .40 .15
❑ 93 Darryl Strawberry 1.25 .50
❑ 94 Walt Terrell .15 .05
❑ 95 Mookie Wilson .40 .15
❑ 96 Jim Acker .15 .05
❑ 97 Willie Aikens .15 .05
❑ 98 Doyle Alexander .15 .05
❑ 99 Jesse Barfield .40 .15
❑ 100 George Bell .40 .15
❑ 101 Jim Clancy .15 .05
❑ 102 Dave Collins .15 .05
❑ 103 Tony Fernandez .40 .15
❑ 104 Damaso Garcia .15 .05
❑ 105 Jim Gott .15 .05
❑ 106 Alfredo Griffin .15 .05
❑ 107 Garth Iorg .15 .05
❑ 108 Roy Lee Jackson .15 .05
❑ 109 Cliff Johnson .15 .05
❑ 110 Jimmy Key RC 1.00 .40
❑ 111 Dennis Lamp .15 .05
❑ 112 Rick Leach .15 .05
❑ 113 Luis Leal .15 .05
❑ 114 Buck Martinez .15 .05
❑ 115 Lloyd Moseby .15 .05
❑ 116 Rance Mulliniks .15 .05
❑ 117 Dave Stieb .40 .15
❑ 118 Willie Upshaw .15 .05
❑ 119 Ernie Whitt .15 .05
❑ 120 Mike Armstrong .15 .05
❑ 121 Don Baylor .40 .15
❑ 122 Marty Bystrom .15 .05
❑ 123 Rick Cerone .15 .05
❑ 124 Joe Cowley .15 .05
❑ 125 Brian Dayett .15 .05
❑ 126 Tim Foli .15 .05
❑ 127 Ray Fontenot .15 .05
❑ 128 Ken Griffey .40 .15
❑ 129 Ron Guidry .40 .15
❑ 130 Toby Harrah .40 .15
❑ 131 Jay Howell .15 .05
❑ 132 Steve Kemp .15 .05
❑ 133 Don Mattingly 5.00 2.00
❑ 134 Bobby Meacham .15 .05
❑ 135 John Montefusco .15 .05
❑ 136 Omar Moreno .15 .05
❑ 137 Dale Murray .15 .05
❑ 138 Phil Niekro .40 .15
❑ 139 Mike Pagliarulo .15 .05
❑ 140 Willie Randolph .40 .15
❑ 141 Dennis Rasmussen .15 .05
❑ 142 Dave Righetti .40 .15
❑ 143 Jose Rijo RC 1.00 .40
❑ 144 Andre Robertson .15 .05
❑ 145 Bob Shirley .15 .05
❑ 146 Dave Winfield .40 .15
❑ 147 Butch Wynegar .15 .05
❑ 148 Gary Allenson .15 .05
❑ 149 Tony Armas .40 .15
❑ 150 Marty Barrett .15 .05
❑ 151 Wade Boggs 1.25 .50
❑ 152 Dennis Boyd .15 .05
❑ 153 Bill Buckner .40 .15
❑ 154 Mark Clear .15 .05
❑ 155 Roger Clemens RC 40.00 15.00
❑ 156 Steve Crawford .15 .05
❑ 157 Mike Easler .15 .05
❑ 158 Dwight Evans .75 .30
❑ 159 Rich Gedman .15 .05
❑ 160 Jackie Gutierrez w/Boggs .40 .15
❑ 161 Bruce Hurst .15 .05
❑ 162 John Henry Johnson .15 .05
❑ 163 Rick Miller .15 .05
❑ 164 Reid Nichols .15 .05
❑ 165 Al Nipper .15 .05

- ❑ 166 Bob Ojeda .15 .05
- ❑ 167 Jerry Remy .15 .05
- ❑ 168 Jim Rice .40 .15
- ❑ 169 Bob Stanley .15 .05
- ❑ 170 Mike Boddicker .15 .05
- ❑ 171 Al Bumbry .15 .05
- ❑ 172 Todd Cruz .15 .05
- ❑ 173 Rich Dauer .15 .05
- ❑ 174 Storm Davis .15 .05
- ❑ 175 Rick Dempsey .15 .05
- ❑ 176 Jim Dwyer .15 .05
- ❑ 177 Mike Flanagan .15 .05
- ❑ 178 Dan Ford .15 .05
- ❑ 179 Wayne Gross .15 .05
- ❑ 180 John Lowenstein .15 .05
- ❑ 181 Dennis Martinez .40 .15
- ❑ 182 Tippy Martinez .15 .05
- ❑ 183 Scott McGregor .15 .05
- ❑ 184 Eddie Murray 1.25 .50
- ❑ 185 Joe Nolan .15 .05
- ❑ 186 Floyd Rayford .15 .05
- ❑ 187 Cal Ripken 5.00 2.00
- ❑ 188 Gary Roenicke .15 .05
- ❑ 189 Lenn Sakata .15 .05
- ❑ 190 John Shelby .15 .05
- ❑ 191 Ken Singleton .40 .15
- ❑ 192 Sammy Stewart .15 .05
- ❑ 193 Bill Swaggerty .15 .05
- ❑ 194 Tom Underwood .15 .05
- ❑ 195 Mike Young .15 .05
- ❑ 196 Steve Balboni .15 .05
- ❑ 197 Joe Beckwith .15 .05
- ❑ 198 Bud Black .15 .05
- ❑ 199 George Brett 3.00 1.25
- ❑ 200 Onix Concepcion .15 .05
- ❑ 201 Mark Gubicza RC* .50 .20
- ❑ 202 Larry Gura .15 .05
- ❑ 203 Mark Huismann .15 .05
- ❑ 204 Dane Iorg .15 .05
- ❑ 205 Danny Jackson .15 .05
- ❑ 206 Charlie Leibrandt .15 .05
- ❑ 207 Hal McRae .40 .15
- ❑ 208 Darryl Motley .15 .05
- ❑ 209 Jorge Orta .15 .05
- ❑ 210 Greg Pryor .15 .05
- ❑ 211 Dan Quisenberry .15 .05
- ❑ 212 Bret Saberhagen RC 1.50 .60
- ❑ 213 Pat Sheridan .15 .05
- ❑ 214 Don Slaught .15 .05
- ❑ 215 U.L. Washington .15 .05
- ❑ 216 John Wathan .15 .05
- ❑ 217 Frank White .40 .15
- ❑ 218 Willie Wilson .40 .15
- ❑ 219 Neil Allen .15 .05
- ❑ 220 Joaquin Andujar .40 .15
- ❑ 221 Steve Braun .15 .05
- ❑ 222 Danny Cox .15 .05
- ❑ 223 Bob Forsch .15 .05
- ❑ 224 David Green .15 .05
- ❑ 225 George Hendrick .40 .15
- ❑ 226 Tom Herr .15 .05
- ❑ 227 Ricky Horton .15 .05
- ❑ 228 Art Howe .15 .05
- ❑ 229 Mike Jorgensen .15 .05
- ❑ 230 Kurt Kepshire .15 .05
- ❑ 231 Jeff Lahti .15 .05
- ❑ 232 Tito Landrum .15 .05
- ❑ 233 Dave LaPoint .15 .05
- ❑ 234 Willie McGee .40 .15
- ❑ 235 Tom Nieto .15 .05
- ❑ 236 Terry Pendleton RC 1.00 .40
- ❑ 237 Darrell Porter .15 .05
- ❑ 238 Dave Rucker .15 .05
- ❑ 239 Lonnie Smith .15 .05
- ❑ 240 Ozzie Smith 2.00 .75
- ❑ 241 Bruce Sutter .40 .15
- ❑ 242 Andy Van Slyke UER .75 .30
- ❑ 243 Dave Von Ohlen .15 .05
- ❑ 244 Larry Andersen .15 .05
- ❑ 245 Bill Campbell .15 .05
- ❑ 246 Steve Carlton .40 .15
- ❑ 247 Tim Corcoran .15 .05
- ❑ 248 Ivan DeJesus .15 .05
- ❑ 249 John Denny .15 .05
- ❑ 250 Bo Diaz .15 .05
- ❑ 251 Greg Gross .15 .05
- ❑ 252 Kevin Gross .15 .05
- ❑ 253 Von Hayes .15 .05
- ❑ 254 Al Holland .15 .05
- ❑ 255 Charles Hudson .15 .05
- ❑ 256 Jerry Koosman .40 .15
- ❑ 257 Joe Lefebvre .15 .05
- ❑ 258 Sixto Lezcano .15 .05
- ❑ 259 Garry Maddox .15 .05
- ❑ 260 Len Matuszek .15 .05
- ❑ 261 Tug McGraw .40 .15
- ❑ 262 Al Oliver .40 .15
- ❑ 263 Shane Rawley .15 .05
- ❑ 264 Juan Samuel .15 .05
- ❑ 265 Mike Schmidt 3.00 1.25
- ❑ 266 Jeff Stone .15 .05
- ❑ 267 Ozzie Virgil .15 .05
- ❑ 268 Glenn Wilson .15 .05
- ❑ 269 John Wockenfuss .15 .05
- ❑ 270 Darrell Brown .15 .05
- ❑ 271 Tom Brunansky .15 .05
- ❑ 272 Randy Bush .15 .05
- ❑ 273 John Butcher .15 .05
- ❑ 274 Bobby Castillo .15 .05
- ❑ 275 Ron Davis .15 .05
- ❑ 276 Dave Engle .15 .05
- ❑ 277 Pete Filson .15 .05
- ❑ 278 Gary Gaetti .40 .15
- ❑ 279 Mickey Hatcher .15 .05
- ❑ 280 Ed Hodge .15 .05
- ❑ 281 Kent Hrbek .40 .15
- ❑ 282 Houston Jimenez .15 .05
- ❑ 283 Tim Laudner .15 .05
- ❑ 284 Rick Lysander .15 .05
- ❑ 285 Dave Meier .15 .05
- ❑ 286 Kirby Puckett RC 10.00 4.00
- ❑ 287 Pat Putnam .15 .05
- ❑ 288 Ken Schrom .15 .05
- ❑ 289 Mike Smithson .15 .05
- ❑ 290 Tim Teufel .15 .05
- ❑ 291 Frank Viola .40 .15
- ❑ 292 Ron Washington .15 .05
- ❑ 293 Don Aase .15 .05
- ❑ 294 Juan Beniquez .15 .05
- ❑ 295 Bob Boone .40 .15
- ❑ 296 Mike C. Brown .15 .05
- ❑ 297 Rod Carew .75 .30
- ❑ 298 Doug Corbett .15 .05
- ❑ 299 Doug DeCinces .15 .05
- ❑ 300 Brian Downing .40 .15
- ❑ 301 Ken Forsch .15 .05
- ❑ 302 Bobby Grich .40 .15
- ❑ 303 Reggie Jackson .75 .30
- ❑ 304 Tommy John .40 .15
- ❑ 305 Curt Kaufman .15 .05
- ❑ 306 Bruce Kison .15 .05
- ❑ 307 Fred Lynn .40 .15
- ❑ 308 Gary Pettis .15 .05
- ❑ 309 Ron Romanick .15 .05
- ❑ 310 Luis Sanchez .15 .05
- ❑ 311 Dick Schofield .15 .05
- ❑ 312 Daryl Sconiers .15 .05
- ❑ 313 Jim Slaton .15 .05
- ❑ 314 Derrel Thomas .15 .05
- ❑ 315 Rob Wilfong .15 .05
- ❑ 316 Mike Witt .15 .05
- ❑ 317 Geoff Zahn .15 .05
- ❑ 318 Len Barker .15 .05
- ❑ 319 Steve Bedrosian .15 .05
- ❑ 320 Bruce Benedict .15 .05
- ❑ 321 Rick Camp .15 .05
- ❑ 322 Chris Chambliss .40 .15
- ❑ 323 Jeff Dedmon .15 .05
- ❑ 324 Terry Forster .40 .15
- ❑ 325 Gene Garber .15 .05
- ❑ 326 Albert Hall .15 .05
- ❑ 327 Terry Harper .15 .05
- ❑ 328 Bob Horner .40 .15
- ❑ 329 Glenn Hubbard .15 .05
- ❑ 330 Randy Johnson .15 .05
- ❑ 331 Brad Komminsk .15 .05
- ❑ 332 Rick Mahler .15 .05
- ❑ 333 Craig McMurtry .15 .05
- ❑ 334 Donnie Moore .15 .05
- ❑ 335 Dale Murphy .75 .30
- ❑ 336 Ken Oberkfell .15 .05
- ❑ 337 Pascual Perez .15 .05
- ❑ 338 Gerald Perry .15 .05
- ❑ 339 Rafael Ramirez .15 .05
- ❑ 340 Jerry Royster .15 .05
- ❑ 341 Alex Trevino .15 .05
- ❑ 342 Claudell Washington .15 .05
- ❑ 343 Alan Ashby .15 .05
- ❑ 344 Mark Bailey .15 .05
- ❑ 345 Kevin Bass .15 .05
- ❑ 346 Enos Cabell .15 .05
- ❑ 347 Jose Cruz .40 .15
- ❑ 348 Bill Dawley .15 .05
- ❑ 349 Frank DiPino .15 .05
- ❑ 350 Bill Doran .15 .05
- ❑ 351 Phil Garner .40 .15
- ❑ 352 Bob Knepper .15 .05
- ❑ 353 Mike LaCoss .15 .05
- ❑ 354 Jerry Mumphrey .15 .05
- ❑ 355 Joe Niekro .15 .05
- ❑ 356 Terry Puhl .15 .05
- ❑ 357 Craig Reynolds .15 .05
- ❑ 358 Vern Ruhle .15 .05
- ❑ 359 Nolan Ryan 6.00 2.50
- ❑ 360 Joe Sambito .15 .05
- ❑ 361 Mike Scott .40 .15
- ❑ 362 Dave Smith .15 .05
- ❑ 363 Julio Solano .15 .05
- ❑ 364 Dickie Thon .15 .05
- ❑ 365 Denny Walling .15 .05
- ❑ 366 Dave Anderson .15 .05
- ❑ 367 Bob Bailor .15 .05
- ❑ 368 Greg Brock .15 .05
- ❑ 369 Carlos Diaz .15 .05
- ❑ 370 Pedro Guerrero .40 .15
- ❑ 371 Orel Hershiser RC 3.00 1.25
- ❑ 372 Rick Honeycutt .15 .05
- ❑ 373 Burt Hooton .15 .05
- ❑ 374 Ken Howell .15 .05
- ❑ 375 Ken Landreaux .15 .05
- ❑ 376 Candy Maldonado .15 .05
- ❑ 377 Mike Marshall .15 .05
- ❑ 378 Tom Niedenfuer .15 .05
- ❑ 379 Alejandro Pena .15 .05
- ❑ 380 Jerry Reuss UER ('Home': omitted) .15 .05
- ❑ 381 R.J. Reynolds .15 .05
- ❑ 382 German Rivera .15 .05
- ❑ 383 Bill Russell .40 .15
- ❑ 384 Steve Sax .15 .05
- ❑ 385 Mike Scioscia .40 .15
- ❑ 386 Franklin Stubbs .15 .05
- ❑ 387 Fernando Valenzuela .40 .15
- ❑ 388 Bob Welch .40 .15
- ❑ 389 Terry Whitfield .15 .05
- ❑ 390 Steve Yeager .40 .15
- ❑ 391 Pat Zachry .15 .05
- ❑ 392 Fred Breining .15 .05
- ❑ 393 Gary Carter .40 .15
- ❑ 394 Andre Dawson .40 .15
- ❑ 395 Miguel Dilone .15 .05
- ❑ 396 Dan Driessen .15 .05
- ❑ 397 Doug Flynn .15 .05
- ❑ 398 Terry Francona .40 .15
- ❑ 399 Bill Gullickson .15 .05
- ❑ 400 Bob James .15 .05
- ❑ 401 Charlie Lea .15 .05
- ❑ 402 Bryan Little .15 .05
- ❑ 403 Gary Lucas .15 .05
- ❑ 404 David Palmer .15 .05
- ❑ 405 Tim Raines .40 .15
- ❑ 406 Mike Ramsey .15 .05
- ❑ 407 Jeff Reardon .40 .15
- ❑ 408 Steve Rogers .40 .15
- ❑ 409 Dan Schatzeder .15 .05
- ❑ 410 Bryn Smith .15 .05
- ❑ 411 Mike Stenhouse .15 .05
- ❑ 412 Tim Wallach .15 .05
- ❑ 413 Jim Wohlford .15 .05
- ❑ 414 Bill Almon .15 .05
- ❑ 415 Keith Atherton .15 .05
- ❑ 416 Bruce Bochte .15 .05
- ❑ 417 Tom Burgmeier .15 .05
- ❑ 418 Ray Burris .15 .05
- ❑ 419 Bill Caudill .15 .05
- ❑ 420 Chris Codiroli .15 .05
- ❑ 421 Tim Conroy .15 .05
- ❑ 422 Mike Davis .15 .05

❑ 423 Jim Essian .15 .05
❑ 424 Mike Heath .15 .05
❑ 425 Rickey Henderson 1.50 .60
❑ 426 Donnie Hill .15 .05
❑ 427 Dave Kingman .40 .15
❑ 428 Bill Krueger .15 .05
❑ 429 Carney Lansford .40 .15
❑ 430 Steve McCatty .15 .05
❑ 431 Joe Morgan .40 .15
❑ 432 Dwayne Murphy .15 .05
❑ 433 Tony Phillips .15 .05
❑ 434 Lary Sorensen .15 .05
❑ 435 Mike Warren .15 .05
❑ 436 Curt Young .15 .05
❑ 437 Luis Aponte .15 .05
❑ 438 Chris Bando .15 .05
❑ 439 Tony Bernazard .15 .05
❑ 440 Bert Blyleven .40 .15
❑ 441 Brett Butler .40 .15
❑ 442 Ernie Camacho .15 .05
❑ 443 Joe Carter 1.25 .50
❑ 444 Carmelo Castillo .15 .05
❑ 445 Jamie Easterly .15 .05
❑ 446 Steve Farr RC .50 .20
❑ 447 Mike Fischlin .15 .05
❑ 448 Julio Franco .40 .15
❑ 449 Mel Hall .15 .05
❑ 450 Mike Hargrove .15 .05
❑ 451 Neal Heaton .15 .05
❑ 452 Brook Jacoby .15 .05
❑ 453 Mike Jeffcoat .15 .05
❑ 454 Don Schulze .15 .05
❑ 455 Roy Smith .15 .05
❑ 456 Pat Tabler .15 .05
❑ 457 Andre Thornton .15 .05
❑ 458 George Vukovich .15 .05
❑ 459 Tom Waddell .15 .05
❑ 460 Jerry Willard .15 .05
❑ 461 Dale Berra .15 .05
❑ 462 John Candelaria .15 .05
❑ 463 Jose DeLeon .15 .05
❑ 464 Doug Frobel .15 .05
❑ 465 Cecilio Guante .15 .05
❑ 466 Brian Harper .15 .05
❑ 467 Lee Lacy .15 .05
❑ 468 Bill Madlock .40 .15
❑ 469 Lee Mazzilli .40 .15
❑ 470 Larry McWilliams .15 .05
❑ 471 Jim Morrison .15 .05
❑ 472 Tony Pena .15 .05
❑ 473 Johnny Ray .15 .05
❑ 474 Rick Rhoden .15 .05
❑ 475 Don Robinson .15 .05
❑ 476 Rod Scurry .15 .05
❑ 477 Kent Tekulve .15 .05
❑ 478 Jason Thompson .15 .05
❑ 479 John Tudor .40 .15
❑ 480 Lee Tunnell .15 .05
❑ 481 Marvell Wynne .15 .05
❑ 482 Salome Barojas .15 .05
❑ 483 Dave Beard .15 .05
❑ 484 Jim Beattie .15 .05
❑ 485 Barry Bonnell .15 .05
❑ 486 Phil Bradley .50 .20
❑ 487 Al Cowens .15 .05
❑ 488 Alvin Davis RC* .50 .20
❑ 489 Dave Henderson .15 .05
❑ 490 Steve Henderson .15 .05
❑ 491 Bob Kearney .15 .05
❑ 492 Mark Langston RC 1.00 .40
❑ 493 Larry Milbourne .15 .05
❑ 494 Paul Mirabella .15 .05
❑ 495 Mike Moore .15 .05
❑ 496 Edwin Nunez .15 .05
❑ 497 Spike Owen .15 .05
❑ 498 Jack Perconte .15 .05
❑ 499 Ken Phelps .15 .05
❑ 500 Jim Presley .50 .20
❑ 501 Mike Stanton .15 .05
❑ 502 Bob Stoddard .15 .05
❑ 503 Gorman Thomas .40 .15
❑ 504 Ed VandeBerg .15 .05
❑ 505 Matt Young .15 .05
❑ 506 Juan Agosto .15 .05
❑ 507 Harold Baines .40 .15
❑ 508 Floyd Bannister .15 .05
❑ 509 Britt Burns .15 .05
❑ 510 Julio Cruz .15 .05
❑ 511 Richard Dotson .15 .05
❑ 512 Jerry Dybzinski .15 .05
❑ 513 Carlton Fisk .75 .30
❑ 514 Scott Fletcher .15 .05
❑ 515 Jerry Hairston .15 .05
❑ 516 Marc Hill .15 .05
❑ 517 LaMarr Hoyt .15 .05
❑ 518 Ron Kittle .15 .05
❑ 519 Rudy Law .15 .05
❑ 520 Vance Law .15 .05
❑ 521 Greg Luzinski .40 .15
❑ 522 Gene Nelson .15 .05
❑ 523 Tom Paciorek .15 .05
❑ 524 Ron Reed .15 .05
❑ 525 Bert Roberge .15 .05
❑ 526 Tom Seaver .75 .30
❑ 527 Roy Smalley .15 .05
❑ 528 Dan Spillner .15 .05
❑ 529 Mike Squires .15 .05
❑ 530 Greg Walker .15 .05
❑ 531 Cesar Cedeno .40 .15
❑ 532 Dave Concepcion .40 .15
❑ 533 Eric Davis RC 3.00 1.25
❑ 534 Nick Esasky .15 .05
❑ 535 Tom Foley .15 .05
❑ 536 John Franco UER RC 1.00 .40
❑ 537 Brad Gulden .15 .05
❑ 538 Tom Hume .15 .05
❑ 539 Wayne Krenchicki .15 .05
❑ 540 Andy McGaffigan .15 .05
❑ 541 Eddie Milner .15 .05
❑ 542 Ron Oester .15 .05
❑ 543 Bob Owchinko .15 .05
❑ 544 Dave Parker .40 .15
❑ 545 Frank Pastore .15 .05
❑ 546 Tony Perez .75 .30
❑ 547 Ted Power .15 .05
❑ 548 Joe Price .15 .05
❑ 549 Gary Redus .15 .05
❑ 550 Pete Rose 4.00 1.50
❑ 551 Jeff Russell .15 .05
❑ 552 Mario Soto .40 .15
❑ 553 Jay Tibbs .15 .05
❑ 554 Duane Walker .15 .05
❑ 555 Alan Bannister .15 .05
❑ 556 Buddy Bell .40 .15
❑ 557 Danny Darwin .15 .05
❑ 558 Charlie Hough .40 .15
❑ 559 Bobby Jones .15 .05
❑ 560 Odell Jones .15 .05
❑ 561 Jeff Kunkel .15 .05
❑ 562 Mike Mason RC .25 .08
❑ 563 Pete O'Brien .15 .05
❑ 564 Larry Parrish .15 .05
❑ 565 Mickey Rivers .15 .05
❑ 566 Billy Sample .15 .05
❑ 567 Dave Schmidt .15 .05
❑ 568 Donnie Scott .15 .05
❑ 569 Dave Stewart .40 .15
❑ 570 Frank Tanana .40 .15
❑ 571 Wayne Tolleson .15 .05
❑ 572 Gary Ward .15 .05
❑ 573 Curtis Wilkerson .15 .05
❑ 574 George Wright .15 .05
❑ 575 Ned Yost .15 .05
❑ 576 Mark Brouhard .15 .05
❑ 577 Mike Caldwell .15 .05
❑ 578 Bobby Clark .15 .05
❑ 579 Jaime Cocanower .15 .05
❑ 580 Cecil Cooper .40 .15
❑ 581 Rollie Fingers .40 .15
❑ 582 Jim Gantner .15 .05
❑ 583 Moose Haas .15 .05
❑ 584 Dion James .15 .05
❑ 585 Pete Ladd .15 .05
❑ 586 Rick Manning .15 .05
❑ 587 Bob McClure .15 .05
❑ 588 Paul Molitor .40 .15
❑ 589 Charlie Moore .15 .05
❑ 590 Ben Oglivie .40 .15
❑ 591 Chuck Porter .15 .05
❑ 592 Randy Ready RC* .25 .08
❑ 593 Ed Romero .15 .05
❑ 594 Bill Schroeder .15 .05
❑ 595 Ray Searage .15 .05
❑ 596 Ted Simmons .40 .15
❑ 597 Jim Sundberg .40 .15
❑ 598 Don Sutton .40 .15
❑ 599 Tom Tellmann .15 .05
❑ 600 Rick Waits .15 .05
❑ 601 Robin Yount 2.00 .75
❑ 602 Dusty Baker .40 .15
❑ 603 Bob Brenly .15 .05
❑ 604 Jack Clark .40 .15
❑ 605 Chili Davis .40 .15
❑ 606 Mark Davis .15 .05
❑ 607 Dan Gladden RC .50 .20
❑ 608 Atlee Hammaker .15 .05
❑ 609 Mike Krukow .15 .05
❑ 610 Duane Kuiper .15 .05
❑ 611 Bob Lacey .15 .05
❑ 612 Bill Laskey .15 .05
❑ 613 Gary Lavelle .15 .05
❑ 614 Johnnie LeMaster .15 .05
❑ 615 Jeff Leonard .15 .05
❑ 616 Randy Lerch .15 .05
❑ 617 Greg Minton .15 .05
❑ 618 Steve Nicosia .15 .05
❑ 619 Gene Richards .15 .05
❑ 620 Jeff D. Robinson .15 .05
❑ 621 Scot Thompson .15 .05
❑ 622 Manny Trillo .15 .05
❑ 623 Brad Wellman .15 .05
❑ 624 Frank Williams .15 .05
❑ 625 Joel Youngblood .15 .05
❑ 626 Cal Ripken IA 3.00 1.25
❑ 627 Mike Schmidt IA 1.25 .50
❑ 628 Giving The Signs
Sparky Anderson .40 .15
❑ 629 D.Winfield/R.Henderson .40 .15
❑ 630 M.Schmidt/R.Sandberg 2.00 .75
❑ 631 Straw/Carter/Garvey/Oz 1.25 .50
❑ 632 A-S Winning Battery
Gary Carter
Charlie Lea .15 .05
❑ 633 NL Pennant Clinchers
Steve Garvey
Rich Gossage .40 .15
❑ 634 Dwight Gooden/J.Samuel 1.25 .50
❑ 635 Toronto's Big Guns
Willie Upshaw .15 .05
❑ 636 Toronto's Big Guns
Lloyd Moseby .15 .05
❑ 637 HOLLAND: Al Holland .15 .05
❑ 638 TUNNELL: Lee Tunnell .15 .05
❑ 639 Reggie Jackson IA .40 .15
❑ 640 Pete Rose IA 1.25 .50
❑ 641 Cal Ripken Jr./Sr. 3.00 1.25
❑ 642 Cubs: Division Champs .40 .15
❑ 643 Two Perfect Games
and One No-Hitter:
Mike Witt .40 .15
❑ 644 W.Lozado RC/V.Mata RC .15 .05
❑ 645 K.Gruber RC/R.O'Neal RC .50 .20
❑ 646 J.Roman RC/J.Skinner .15 .05
❑ 647 S.Kiefer RC/D.Tartabull RC 1.00 .40
❑ 648 R.Deer RC/A.Sanchez RC .50 .20
❑ 649 B.Hatcher RC/S.Dunston RC 1.00 .40
❑ 650 R.Robinson RC/M.Bielecki RC .15 .05
❑ 651 Z.Smith RC/P.Zuvella RC .50 .20
❑ 652 J.Hesketh RC/G.Davis RC .50 .20
❑ 653 J.Russell RC/S.Jeltz RC .15 .05
❑ 654 CL: Tigers/Padres
and Cubs/Mets .15 .05
❑ 655 CL: Blue Jays/Yankees
and Red Sox/Orioles .15 .05
❑ 656 CL: Royals/Cardinals
and Phillies/Twins .15 .05
❑ 657 CL: Angels/Braves
and Astros/Dodgers .15 .05
❑ 658 CL: Expos/A's
and Indians/Pirates .15 .05
❑ 659 CL: Mariners/White Sox
and Reds/Rangers .15 .05
❑ 660 CL: Brewers/Giants
and Special Cards .15 .05

1985 Fleer Update

❑ COMP.FACT.SET (132) 8.00 3.00
❑ 1 Don Aase .15 .05
❑ 2 Bill Almon .15 .05
❑ 3 Dusty Baker .40 .15
❑ 4 Dale Berra .15 .05
❑ 5 Karl Best .15 .05
❑ 6 Tim Birtsas .15 .05
❑ 7 Vida Blue .40 .15
❑ 8 Rich Bordi .15 .05
❑ 9 Daryl Boston XRC .25 .08
❑ 10 Hubie Brooks .15 .05
❑ 11 Chris Brown XRC .25 .08
❑ 12 Tom Browning XRC .50 .20
❑ 13 Al Bumbry .15 .05
❑ 14 Tim Burke .15 .05
❑ 15 Ray Burris .15 .05
❑ 16 Jeff Burroughs .15 .05
❑ 17 Ivan Calderon XRC .50 .20
❑ 18 Jeff Calhoun .15 .05
❑ 19 Bill Campbell .15 .05
❑ 20 Don Carman .15 .05
❑ 21 Gary Carter .40 .15
❑ 22 Bobby Castillo .15 .05
❑ 23 Bill Caudill .15 .05
❑ 24 Rick Cerone .15 .05
❑ 25 Jack Clark .40 .15
❑ 26 Pat Clements .15 .05
❑ 27 Stu Cliburn .15 .05
❑ 28 Vince Coleman XRC 1.00 .40
❑ 29 Dave Collins .15 .05
❑ 30 Fritz Connally .15 .05
❑ 31 Henry Cotto .25 .08
❑ 32 Danny Darwin .15 .05
❑ 33 Darren Daulton XRC 1.00 .40
❑ 34 Jerry Davis .15 .05
❑ 35 Brian Dayett .15 .05
❑ 36 Ken Dixon .15 .05
❑ 37 Tommy Dunbar .15 .05
❑ 38 Mariano Duncan XRC .50 .20
❑ 39 Bob Fallon .15 .05
❑ 40 Brian Fisher XRC .25 .08
❑ 41 Mike Fitzgerald .15 .05
❑ 42 Ray Fontenot .15 .05
❑ 43 Greg Gagne XRC .50 .20
❑ 44 Oscar Gamble .15 .05
❑ 45 Jim Gott .15 .05
❑ 46 David Green .15 .05
❑ 47 Alfredo Griffin .15 .05
❑ 48 Ozzie Guillen XRC 5.00 2.00
❑ 49 Toby Harrah .40 .15
❑ 50 Ron Hassey .15 .05
❑ 51 Rickey Henderson 2.50 1.00
❑ 52 Steve Henderson .15 .05
❑ 53 George Hendrick .40 .15
❑ 54 Teddy Higuera XRC .50 .20
❑ 55 Al Holland .15 .05
❑ 56 Burt Hooton .15 .05
❑ 57 Jay Howell .15 .05
❑ 58 LaMarr Hoyt .15 .05
❑ 59 Tim Hulett XRC .25 .08
❑ 60 Bob James .15 .05
❑ 61 Cliff Johnson .15 .05
❑ 62 Howard Johnson .40 .15
❑ 63 Ruppert Jones .15 .05
❑ 64 Steve Kemp .15 .05
❑ 65 Bruce Kison .15 .05
❑ 66 Mike LaCoss .15 .05
❑ 67 Lee Lacy .15 .05
❑ 68 Dave LaPoint .15 .05
❑ 69 Gary Lavelle .15 .05
❑ 70 Vance Law .15 .05
❑ 71 Manuel Lee XRC .25 .08
❑ 72 Sixto Lezcano .15 .05
❑ 73 Tim Lollar .15 .05
❑ 74 Urbano Lugo .15 .05
❑ 75 Fred Lynn .40 .15
❑ 76 Steve Lyons XRC .50 .20
❑ 77 Mickey Mahler .15 .05
❑ 78 Ron Mathis .15 .05
❑ 79 Len Matuszek .15 .05
❑ 80 Oddibe McDowell XRC .50 .20
❑ 81 Roger McDowell UER XRC .50 .20
❑ 82 Donnie Moore .15 .05
❑ 83 Ron Musselman .15 .05
❑ 84 Al Oliver .40 .15
❑ 85 Joe Orsulak XRC .50 .20
❑ 86 Dan Pasqua XRC .50 .20
❑ 87 Chris Pittaro .15 .05
❑ 88 Rick Reuschel .40 .15
❑ 89 Earnie Riles .15 .05
❑ 90 Jerry Royster .15 .05
❑ 91 Dave Rozema .15 .05
❑ 92 Dave Rucker .15 .05
❑ 93 Vern Ruhle .15 .05
❑ 94 Mark Salas .15 .05
❑ 95 Luis Salazar .15 .05
❑ 96 Joe Sambito .15 .05
❑ 97 Billy Sample .15 .05
❑ 98 Alejandro Sanchez XRC .25 .08
❑ 99 Calvin Schiraldi XRC .50 .20
❑ 100 Rick Schu .15 .05
❑ 101 Larry Sheets XRC .25 .08
❑ 102 Ron Shephard .15 .05
❑ 103 Nelson Simmons .15 .05
❑ 104 Don Slaught .15 .05
❑ 105 Roy Smalley .15 .05
❑ 106 Lonnie Smith .15 .05
❑ 107 Nate Snell .15 .05
❑ 108 Lary Sorensen .15 .05
❑ 109 Chris Speier .15 .05
❑ 110 Mike Stenhouse .15 .05
❑ 111 Tim Stoddard .15 .05
❑ 112 John Stuper .15 .05
❑ 113 Jim Sundberg .40 .15
❑ 114 Bruce Sutter .40 .15
❑ 115 Don Sutton .40 .15
❑ 116 Bruce Tanner .15 .05
❑ 117 Kent Tekulve .15 .05
❑ 118 Walt Terrell .15 .05
❑ 119 Mickey Tettleton XRC .50 .20
❑ 120 Rich Thompson .15 .05
❑ 121 Louis Thornton .15 .05
❑ 122 Alex Trevino .15 .05
❑ 123 John Tudor .40 .15
❑ 124 Jose Uribe .15 .05
❑ 125 Dave Valle XRC .50 .20
❑ 126 Dave Von Ohlen .15 .05
❑ 127 Curt Wardle .15 .05
❑ 128 U.L. Washington .15 .05
❑ 129 Ed Whitson .15 .05
❑ 130 Herm Winningham .15 .05
❑ 131 Rich Yett .15 .05
❑ 132 Checklist U1-U132 .15 .05

1986 Fleer

❑ COMPLETE SET (660) 40.00 15.00
❑ COMP.FACT.SET (660) 40.00 15.00
❑ 1 Steve Balboni .15 .05
❑ 2 Joe Beckwith .15 .05
❑ 3 Buddy Biancalana .15 .05
❑ 4 Bud Black .15 .05
❑ 5 George Brett 2.00 .75
❑ 6 Onix Concepcion .15 .05
❑ 7 Steve Farr .15 .05
❑ 8 Mark Gubicza .15 .05
❑ 9 Dane Iorg .15 .05
❑ 10 Danny Jackson .15 .05
❑ 11 Lynn Jones .15 .05
❑ 12 Mike Jones .15 .05
❑ 13 Charlie Leibrandt .15 .05
❑ 14 Hal McRae .25 .08
❑ 15 Omar Moreno .15 .05
❑ 16 Darryl Motley .15 .05
❑ 17 Jorge Orta .15 .05
❑ 18 Dan Quisenberry .15 .05
❑ 19 Bret Saberhagen .25 .08
❑ 20 Pat Sheridan .15 .05
❑ 21 Lonnie Smith .15 .05
❑ 22 Jim Sundberg .25 .08
❑ 23 John Wathan .15 .05
❑ 24 Frank White .25 .08
❑ 25 Willie Wilson .25 .08
❑ 26 Joaquin Andujar .25 .08
❑ 27 Steve Braun .15 .05
❑ 28 Bill Campbell .15 .05
❑ 29 Cesar Cedeno .25 .08
❑ 30 Jack Clark .25 .08
❑ 31 Vince Coleman RC 1.00 .40
❑ 32 Danny Cox .15 .05
❑ 33 Ken Dayley .15 .05
❑ 34 Ivan DeJesus .15 .05
❑ 35 Bob Forsch .15 .05
❑ 36 Brian Harper .15 .05
❑ 37 Tom Herr .15 .05
❑ 38 Ricky Horton .15 .05
❑ 39 Kurt Kepshire .15 .05
❑ 40 Jeff Lahti .15 .05
❑ 41 Tito Landrum .15 .05
❑ 42 Willie McGee .25 .08
❑ 43 Tom Nieto .15 .05
❑ 44 Terry Pendleton .25 .08
❑ 45 Darrell Porter .15 .05
❑ 46 Ozzie Smith 1.25 .50
❑ 47 John Tudor .25 .08
❑ 48 Andy Van Slyke .50 .20
❑ 49 Todd Worrell RC .50 .20
❑ 50 Jim Acker .15 .05
❑ 51 Doyle Alexander .15 .05
❑ 52 Jesse Barfield .25 .08
❑ 53 George Bell .25 .08
❑ 54 Jeff Burroughs .15 .05
❑ 55 Bill Caudill .15 .05
❑ 56 Jim Clancy .15 .05
❑ 57 Tony Fernandez .15 .05
❑ 58 Tom Filer .15 .05
❑ 59 Damaso Garcia .15 .05
❑ 60 Tom Henke .25 .08
❑ 61 Garth Iorg .15 .05
❑ 62 Cliff Johnson .15 .05
❑ 63 Jimmy Key .25 .08
❑ 64 Dennis Lamp .15 .05
❑ 65 Gary Lavelle .15 .05
❑ 66 Buck Martinez .15 .05
❑ 67 Lloyd Moseby .15 .05
❑ 68 Rance Mulliniks .15 .05
❑ 69 Al Oliver .25 .08
❑ 70 Dave Stieb .25 .08
❑ 71 Louis Thornton .15 .05
❑ 72 Willie Upshaw .15 .05
❑ 73 Ernie Whitt .15 .05
❑ 74 Rick Aguilera RC .50 .20
❑ 75 Wally Backman .15 .05
❑ 76 Gary Carter .25 .08
❑ 77 Ron Darling .25 .08
❑ 78 Len Dykstra RC 1.50 .60
❑ 79 Sid Fernandez .15 .05
❑ 80 George Foster .25 .08
❑ 81 Dwight Gooden .75 .30
❑ 82 Tom Gorman .15 .05
❑ 83 Danny Heep .15 .05
❑ 84 Keith Hernandez .25 .08

	No.	Player		
❑	85	Howard Johnson	.25	.08
❑	86	Ray Knight	.25	.08
❑	87	Terry Leach	.15	.05
❑	88	Ed Lynch	.15	.05
❑	89	Roger McDowell RC*	.50	.20
❑	90	Jesse Orosco	.15	.05
❑	91	Tom Paciorek	.15	.05
❑	92	Ronn Reynolds	.15	.05
❑	93	Rafael Santana	.15	.05
❑	94	Doug Sisk	.15	.05
❑	95	Rusty Staub	.25	.08
❑	96	Darryl Strawberry	.50	.20
❑	97	Mookie Wilson	.25	.08
❑	98	Neil Allen	.15	.05
❑	99	Don Baylor	.25	.08
❑	100	Dale Berra	.15	.05
❑	101	Rich Bordi	.15	.05
❑	102	Marty Bystrom	.15	.05
❑	103	Joe Cowley	.15	.05
❑	104	Brian Fisher RC	.15	.05
❑	105	Ken Griffey	.25	.08
❑	106	Ron Guidry	.25	.08
❑	107	Ron Hassey	.15	.05
❑	108	Rickey Henderson	.75	.30
❑	109	Don Mattingly	2.50	1.00
❑	110	Bobby Meacham	.15	.05
❑	111	John Montefusco	.15	.05
❑	112	Phil Niekro	.25	.08
❑	113	Mike Pagliarulo	.15	.05
❑	114	Dan Pasqua	.15	.05
❑	115	Willie Randolph	.25	.08
❑	116	Dave Righetti	.25	.08
❑	117	Andre Robertson	.15	.05
❑	118	Billy Sample	.15	.05
❑	119	Bob Shirley	.15	.05
❑	120	Ed Whitson	.15	.05
❑	121	Dave Winfield	.25	.08
❑	122	Butch Wynegar	.15	.05
❑	123	Dave Anderson	.15	.05
❑	124	Bob Bailor	.15	.05
❑	125	Greg Brock	.15	.05
❑	126	Enos Cabell	.15	.05
❑	127	Bobby Castillo	.15	.05
❑	128	Carlos Diaz	.15	.05
❑	129	Mariano Duncan RC	.50	.20
❑	130	Pedro Guerrero	.25	.08
❑	131	Orel Hershiser	.75	.30
❑	132	Rick Honeycutt	.15	.05
❑	133	Ken Howell	.15	.05
❑	134	Ken Landreaux	.15	.05
❑	135	Bill Madlock	.25	.08
❑	136	Candy Maldonado	.15	.05
❑	137	Mike Marshall	.15	.05
❑	138	Len Matuszek	.15	.05
❑	139	Tom Niedenfuer	.15	.05
❑	140	Alejandro Pena	.15	.05
❑	141	Jerry Reuss	.15	.05
❑	142	Bill Russell	.25	.08
❑	143	Steve Sax	.15	.05
❑	144	Mike Scioscia	.25	.08
❑	145	Fernando Valenzuela	.25	.08
❑	146	Bob Welch	.25	.08
❑	147	Terry Whitfield	.15	.05
❑	148	Juan Beniquez	.15	.05
❑	149	Bob Boone	.25	.08
❑	150	John Candelaria	.15	.05
❑	151	Rod Carew	.50	.20
❑	152	Stu Cliburn	.15	.05
❑	153	Doug DeCinces	.15	.05
❑	154	Brian Downing	.25	.08
❑	155	Ken Forsch	.15	.05
❑	156	Craig Gerber	.15	.05
❑	157	Bobby Grich	.25	.08
❑	158	George Hendrick	.25	.08
❑	159	Al Holland	.15	.05
❑	160	Reggie Jackson	.50	.20
❑	161	Ruppert Jones	.15	.05
❑	162	Urbano Lugo	.15	.05
❑	163	Kirk McCaskill RC	.50	.20
❑	164	Donnie Moore	.15	.05
❑	165	Gary Pettis	.15	.05
❑	166	Ron Romanick	.15	.05
❑	167	Dick Schofield	.15	.05
❑	168	Daryl Sconiers	.15	.05
❑	169	Jim Slaton	.15	.05
❑	170	Don Sutton	.25	.08
❑	171	Mike Witt	.15	.05
❑	172	Buddy Bell	.25	.08
❑	173	Tom Browning	.15	.05
❑	174	Dave Concepcion	.25	.08
❑	175	Eric Davis	.75	.30
❑	176	Bo Diaz	.15	.05
❑	177	Nick Esasky	.15	.05
❑	178	John Franco	.25	.08
❑	179	Tom Hume	.15	.05
❑	180	Wayne Krenchicki	.15	.05
❑	181	Andy McGaffigan	.15	.05
❑	182	Eddie Milner	.15	.05
❑	183	Ron Oester	.15	.05
❑	184	Dave Parker	.25	.08
❑	185	Frank Pastore	.15	.05
❑	186	Tony Perez	.50	.20
❑	187	Ted Power	.15	.05
❑	188	Joe Price	.15	.05
❑	189	Gary Redus	.15	.05
❑	190	Ron Robinson	.15	.05
❑	191	Pete Rose	2.50	1.00
❑	192	Mario Soto	.25	.08
❑	193	John Stuper	.15	.05
❑	194	Jay Tibbs	.15	.05
❑	195	Dave Van Gorder	.15	.05
❑	196	Max Venable	.15	.05
❑	197	Juan Agosto	.15	.05
❑	198	Harold Baines	.25	.08
❑	199	Floyd Bannister	.15	.05
❑	200	Britt Burns	.15	.05
❑	201	Julio Cruz	.15	.05
❑	202	Joel Davis	.15	.05
❑	203	Richard Dotson	.15	.05
❑	204	Carlton Fisk	.50	.20
❑	205	Scott Fletcher	.15	.05
❑	206	Ozzie Guillen RC	2.00	.75
❑	207	Jerry Hairston	.15	.05
❑	208	Tim Hulett	.15	.05
❑	209	Bob James	.15	.05
❑	210	Ron Kittle	.15	.05
❑	211	Rudy Law	.15	.05
❑	212	Bryan Little	.15	.05
❑	213	Gene Nelson	.15	.05
❑	214	Reid Nichols	.15	.05
❑	215	Luis Salazar	.15	.05
❑	216	Tom Seaver	.50	.20
❑	217	Dan Spillner	.15	.05
❑	218	Bruce Tanner	.15	.05
❑	219	Greg Walker	.15	.05
❑	220	Dave Wehrmeister	.15	.05
❑	221	Juan Berenguer	.15	.05
❑	222	Dave Bergman	.15	.05
❑	223	Tom Brookens	.15	.05
❑	224	Darrell Evans	.25	.08
❑	225	Barbaro Garbey	.15	.05
❑	226	Kirk Gibson	.25	.08
❑	227	John Grubb	.15	.05
❑	228	Willie Hernandez	.15	.05
❑	229	Larry Herndon	.15	.05
❑	230	Chet Lemon	.25	.08
❑	231	Aurelio Lopez	.15	.05
❑	232	Jack Morris	.25	.08
❑	233	Randy O'Neal	.15	.05
❑	234	Lance Parrish	.25	.08
❑	235	Dan Petry	.15	.05
❑	236	Alejandro Sanchez	.15	.05
❑	237	Bill Scherrer	.15	.05
❑	238	Nelson Simmons	.15	.05
❑	239	Frank Tanana	.25	.08
❑	240	Walt Terrell	.15	.05
❑	241	Alan Trammell	.25	.08
❑	242	Lou Whitaker	.25	.08
❑	243	Milt Wilcox	.15	.05
❑	244	Hubie Brooks	.15	.05
❑	245	Tim Burke	.15	.05
❑	246	Andre Dawson	.25	.08
❑	247	Mike Fitzgerald	.15	.05
❑	248	Terry Francona	.25	.08
❑	249	Bill Gullickson	.15	.05
❑	250	Joe Hesketh	.15	.05
❑	251	Bill Laskey	.15	.05
❑	252	Vance Law	.15	.05
❑	253	Charlie Lea	.15	.05
❑	254	Gary Lucas	.15	.05
❑	255	David Palmer	.15	.05
❑	256	Tim Raines	.25	.08
❑	257	Jeff Reardon	.25	.08
❑	258	Bert Roberge	.15	.05
❑	259	Dan Schatzeder	.15	.05
❑	260	Bryn Smith	.15	.05
❑	261	Randy St.Claire	.15	.05
❑	262	Scot Thompson	.15	.05
❑	263	Tim Wallach	.15	.05
❑	264	U.L. Washington	.15	.05
❑	265	Mitch Webster	.15	.05
❑	266	Herm Winningham	.15	.05
❑	267	Floyd Youmans	.15	.05
❑	268	Don Aase	.15	.05
❑	269	Mike Boddicker	.15	.05
❑	270	Rich Dauer	.15	.05
❑	271	Storm Davis	.15	.05
❑	272	Rick Dempsey	.15	.05
❑	273	Ken Dixon	.15	.05
❑	274	Jim Dwyer	.15	.05
❑	275	Mike Flanagan	.15	.05
❑	276	Wayne Gross	.15	.05
❑	277	Lee Lacy	.15	.05
❑	278	Fred Lynn	.25	.08
❑	279	Tippy Martinez	.15	.05
❑	280	Dennis Martinez	.25	.08
❑	281	Scott McGregor	.15	.05
❑	282	Eddie Murray	.75	.30
❑	283	Floyd Rayford	.15	.05
❑	284	Cal Ripken	3.00	1.25
❑	285	Gary Roenicke	.15	.05
❑	286	Larry Sheets	.15	.05
❑	287	John Shelby	.15	.05
❑	288	Nate Snell	.15	.05
❑	289	Sammy Stewart	.15	.05
❑	290	Alan Wiggins	.15	.05
❑	291	Mike Young	.15	.05
❑	292	Alan Ashby	.15	.05
❑	293	Mark Bailey	.15	.05
❑	294	Kevin Bass	.15	.05
❑	295	Jeff Calhoun	.15	.05
❑	296	Jose Cruz	.25	.08
❑	297	Glenn Davis	.15	.05
❑	298	Bill Dawley	.15	.05
❑	299	Frank DiPino	.15	.05
❑	300	Bill Doran	.15	.05
❑	301	Phil Garner	.25	.08
❑	302	Jeff Heathcock	.15	.05
❑	303	Charlie Kerfeld	.15	.05
❑	304	Bob Knepper	.15	.05
❑	305	Ron Mathis	.15	.05
❑	306	Jerry Mumphrey	.15	.05
❑	307	Jim Pankovits	.15	.05
❑	308	Terry Puhl	.15	.05
❑	309	Craig Reynolds	.15	.05
❑	310	Nolan Ryan	4.00	1.50
❑	311	Mike Scott	.25	.08
❑	312	Dave Smith	.15	.05
❑	313	Dickie Thon	.15	.05
❑	314	Denny Walling	.15	.05
❑	315	Kurt Bevacqua	.15	.05
❑	316	Al Bumbry	.15	.05
❑	317	Jerry Davis	.15	.05
❑	318	Luis DeLeon	.15	.05
❑	319	Dave Dravecky	.15	.05
❑	320	Tim Flannery	.15	.05
❑	321	Steve Garvey	.25	.08
❑	322	Rich Gossage	.25	.08
❑	323	Tony Gwynn	1.25	.50
❑	324	Andy Hawkins	.15	.05
❑	325	LaMarr Hoyt	.15	.05
❑	326	Roy Lee Jackson	.15	.05
❑	327	Terry Kennedy	.15	.05
❑	328	Craig Lefferts	.15	.05
❑	329	Carmelo Martinez	.15	.05
❑	330	Lance McCullers	.15	.05
❑	331	Kevin McReynolds	.15	.05
❑	332	Graig Nettles	.25	.08
❑	333	Jerry Royster	.15	.05
❑	334	Eric Show	.15	.05
❑	335	Tim Stoddard	.15	.05
❑	336	Garry Templeton	.25	.08
❑	337	Mark Thurmond	.15	.05
❑	338	Ed Wojna	.15	.05
❑	339	Tony Armas	.25	.08
❑	340	Marty Barrett	.15	.05
❑	341	Wade Boggs	.50	.20
❑	342	Dennis Boyd	.15	.05

❑ 343 Bill Buckner .25 .08
❑ 344 Mark Clear .15 .05
❑ 345 Roger Clemens 5.00 2.00
❑ 346 Steve Crawford .15 .05
❑ 347 Mike Easler .15 .05
❑ 348 Dwight Evans .50 .20
❑ 349 Rich Gedman .15 .05
❑ 350 Jackie Gutierrez .15 .05
❑ 351 Glenn Hoffman .15 .05
❑ 352 Bruce Hurst .15 .05
❑ 353 Bruce Kison .15 .05
❑ 354 Tim Lollar .15 .05
❑ 355 Steve Lyons .15 .05
❑ 356 Al Nipper .15 .05
❑ 357 Bob Ojeda .15 .05
❑ 358 Jim Rice .25 .08
❑ 359 Bob Stanley .15 .05
❑ 360 Mike Trujillo .15 .05
❑ 361 Thad Bosley .15 .05
❑ 362 Warren Brusstar .15 .05
❑ 363 Ron Cey .25 .08
❑ 364 Jody Davis .15 .05
❑ 365 Bob Dernier .15 .05
❑ 366 Shawon Dunston .25 .08
❑ 367 Leon Durham .15 .05
❑ 368 Dennis Eckersley .50 .20
❑ 369 Ray Fontenot .15 .05
❑ 370 George Frazier .15 .05
❑ 371 Billy Hatcher .15 .05
❑ 372 Dave Lopes .25 .08
❑ 373 Gary Matthews .25 .08
❑ 374 Ron Meridith .15 .05
❑ 375 Keith Moreland .15 .05
❑ 376 Reggie Patterson .15 .05
❑ 377 Dick Ruthven .15 .05
❑ 378 Ryne Sandberg 1.50 .60
❑ 379 Scott Sanderson .15 .05
❑ 380 Lee Smith .25 .08
❑ 381 Lary Sorensen .15 .05
❑ 382 Chris Speier .15 .05
❑ 383 Rick Sutcliffe .25 .08
❑ 384 Steve Trout .15 .05
❑ 385 Gary Woods .15 .05
❑ 386 Bert Blyleven .25 .08
❑ 387 Tom Brunansky .15 .05
❑ 388 Randy Bush .15 .05
❑ 389 John Butcher .15 .05
❑ 390 Ron Davis .15 .05
❑ 391 Dave Engle .15 .05
❑ 392 Frank Eufemia .15 .05
❑ 393 Pete Filson .15 .05
❑ 394 Gary Gaetti .25 .08
❑ 395 Greg Gagne .15 .05
❑ 396 Mickey Hatcher .15 .05
❑ 397 Kent Hrbek .25 .08
❑ 398 Tim Laudner .15 .05
❑ 399 Rick Lysander .15 .05
❑ 400 Dave Meier .15 .05
❑ 401 Kirby Puckett 2.00 .75
❑ 402 Mark Salas .15 .05
❑ 403 Ken Schrom .15 .05
❑ 404 Roy Smalley .15 .05
❑ 405 Mike Smithson .15 .05
❑ 406 Mike Stenhouse .15 .05
❑ 407 Tim Teufel .15 .05
❑ 408 Frank Viola .25 .08
❑ 409 Ron Washington .15 .05
❑ 410 Keith Atherton .15 .05
❑ 411 Dusty Baker .25 .08
❑ 412 Tim Birtsas .15 .05
❑ 413 Bruce Bochte .15 .05
❑ 414 Chris Codiroli .15 .05
❑ 415 Dave Collins .15 .05
❑ 416 Mike Davis .15 .05
❑ 417 Alfredo Griffin .15 .05
❑ 418 Mike Heath .15 .05
❑ 419 Steve Henderson .15 .05
❑ 420 Donnie Hill .15 .05
❑ 421 Jay Howell .15 .05
❑ 422 Tommy John .25 .08
❑ 423 Dave Kingman .25 .08
❑ 424 Bill Krueger .15 .05
❑ 425 Rick Langford .15 .05
❑ 426 Carney Lansford .25 .08
❑ 427 Steve McCatty .15 .05
❑ 428 Dwayne Murphy .15 .05
❑ 429 Steve Ontiveros RC .15 .05
❑ 430 Tony Phillips .15 .05
❑ 431 Jose Rijo .25 .08
❑ 432 Mickey Tettleton RC .50 .20
❑ 433 Luis Aguayo .15 .05
❑ 434 Larry Andersen .15 .05
❑ 435 Steve Carlton .25 .08
❑ 436 Don Carman .15 .05
❑ 437 Tim Corcoran .15 .05
❑ 438 Darren Daulton RC 1.00 .40
❑ 439 John Denny .15 .05
❑ 440 Tom Foley .15 .05
❑ 441 Greg Gross .15 .05
❑ 442 Kevin Gross .15 .05
❑ 443 Von Hayes .15 .05
❑ 444 Charles Hudson .15 .05
❑ 445 Garry Maddox .15 .05
❑ 446 Shane Rawley .15 .05
❑ 447 Dave Rucker .15 .05
❑ 448 John Russell .15 .05
❑ 449 Juan Samuel .15 .05
❑ 450 Mike Schmidt 2.00 .75
❑ 451 Rick Schu .15 .05
❑ 452 Dave Shipanoff .15 .05
❑ 453 Dave Stewart .25 .08
❑ 454 Jeff Stone .15 .05
❑ 455 Kent Tekulve .15 .05
❑ 456 Ozzie Virgil .15 .05
❑ 457 Glenn Wilson .15 .05
❑ 458 Jim Beattie .15 .05
❑ 459 Karl Best .15 .05
❑ 460 Barry Bonnell .15 .05
❑ 461 Phil Bradley .15 .05
❑ 462 Ivan Calderon RC* .50 .20
❑ 463 Al Cowens .15 .05
❑ 464 Alvin Davis .15 .05
❑ 465 Dave Henderson .15 .05
❑ 466 Bob Kearney .15 .05
❑ 467 Mark Langston .25 .08
❑ 468 Bob Long .15 .05
❑ 469 Mike Moore .15 .05
❑ 470 Edwin Nunez .15 .05
❑ 471 Spike Owen .15 .05
❑ 472 Jack Perconte .15 .05
❑ 473 Jim Presley .15 .05
❑ 474 Donnie Scott .15 .05
❑ 475 Bill Swift .15 .05
❑ 476 Danny Tartabull .25 .08
❑ 477 Gorman Thomas .25 .08
❑ 478 Roy Thomas .15 .05
❑ 479 Ed VandeBerg .15 .05
❑ 480 Frank Wills .15 .05
❑ 481 Matt Young .15 .05
❑ 482 Ray Burris .15 .05
❑ 483 Jaime Cocanower .15 .05
❑ 484 Cecil Cooper .25 .08
❑ 485 Danny Darwin .15 .05
❑ 486 Rollie Fingers .25 .08
❑ 487 Jim Gantner .15 .05
❑ 488 Bob L. Gibson .15 .05
❑ 489 Moose Haas .15 .05
❑ 490 Teddy Higuera RC* .50 .20
❑ 491 Paul Householder .15 .05
❑ 492 Pete Ladd .15 .05
❑ 493 Rick Manning .15 .05
❑ 494 Bob McClure .15 .05
❑ 495 Paul Molitor .25 .08
❑ 496 Charlie Moore .15 .05
❑ 497 Ben Oglivie .25 .08
❑ 498 Randy Ready .15 .05
❑ 499 Earnie Riles .15 .05
❑ 500 Ed Romero .15 .05
❑ 501 Bill Schroeder .15 .05
❑ 502 Ray Searage .15 .05
❑ 503 Ted Simmons .25 .08
❑ 504 Pete Vuckovich .15 .05
❑ 505 Rick Waits .15 .05
❑ 506 Robin Yount 1.25 .50
❑ 507 Len Barker .15 .05
❑ 508 Steve Bedrosian .15 .05
❑ 509 Bruce Benedict .15 .05
❑ 510 Rick Camp .15 .05
❑ 511 Rick Cerone .15 .05
❑ 512 Chris Chambliss .25 .08
❑ 513 Jeff Dedmon .15 .05
❑ 514 Terry Forster .25 .08
❑ 515 Gene Garber .15 .05
❑ 516 Terry Harper .15 .05
❑ 517 Bob Horner .25 .08
❑ 518 Glenn Hubbard .15 .05
❑ 519 Joe Johnson .15 .05
❑ 520 Brad Komminsk .15 .05
❑ 521 Rick Mahler .15 .05
❑ 522 Dale Murphy .50 .20
❑ 523 Ken Oberkfell .15 .05
❑ 524 Pascual Perez .15 .05
❑ 525 Gerald Perry .15 .05
❑ 526 Rafael Ramirez .15 .05
❑ 527 Steve Shields .15 .05
❑ 528 Zane Smith .15 .05
❑ 529 Bruce Sutter .25 .08
❑ 530 Milt Thompson RC .50 .20
❑ 531 Claudell Washington .15 .05
❑ 532 Paul Zuvella .15 .05
❑ 533 Vida Blue .25 .08
❑ 534 Bob Brenly .15 .05
❑ 535 Chris Brown RC .15 .05
❑ 536 Chili Davis .25 .08
❑ 537 Mark Davis .15 .05
❑ 538 Rob Deer .15 .05
❑ 539 Dan Driessen .15 .05
❑ 540 Scott Garrelts .15 .05
❑ 541 Dan Gladden .15 .05
❑ 542 Jim Gott .15 .05
❑ 543 David Green .15 .05
❑ 544 Atlee Hammaker .15 .05
❑ 545 Mike Jeffcoat .15 .05
❑ 546 Mike Krukow .15 .05
❑ 547 Dave LaPoint .15 .05
❑ 548 Jeff Leonard .15 .05
❑ 549 Greg Minton .15 .05
❑ 550 Alex Trevino .15 .05
❑ 551 Manny Trillo .15 .05
❑ 552 Jose Uribe .15 .05
❑ 553 Brad Wellman .15 .05
❑ 554 Frank Williams .15 .05
❑ 555 Joel Youngblood .15 .05
❑ 556 Alan Bannister .15 .05
❑ 557 Glenn Brummer .15 .05
❑ 558 Steve Buechele RC .50 .20
❑ 559 Jose Guzman RC .15 .05
❑ 560 Toby Harrah .25 .08
❑ 561 Greg Harris .15 .05
❑ 562 Dwayne Henry .15 .05
❑ 563 Burt Hooton .15 .05
❑ 564 Charlie Hough .25 .08
❑ 565 Mike Mason .15 .05
❑ 566 Oddibe McDowell .15 .05
❑ 567 Dickie Noles .15 .05
❑ 568 Pete O'Brien .15 .05
❑ 569 Larry Parrish .15 .05
❑ 570 Dave Rozema .15 .05
❑ 571 Dave Schmidt .15 .05
❑ 572 Don Slaught .15 .05
❑ 573 Wayne Tolleson .15 .05
❑ 574 Duane Walker .15 .05
❑ 575 Gary Ward .15 .05
❑ 576 Chris Welsh .15 .05
❑ 577 Curtis Wilkerson .15 .05
❑ 578 George Wright .15 .05
❑ 579 Chris Bando .15 .05
❑ 580 Tony Bernazard .15 .05
❑ 581 Brett Butler .25 .08
❑ 582 Ernie Camacho .15 .05
❑ 583 Joe Carter .25 .08
❑ 584 Carmen Castillo .15 .05
❑ 585 Jamie Easterly .15 .05
❑ 586 Julio Franco .25 .08
❑ 587 Mel Hall .15 .05
❑ 588 Mike Hargrove .15 .05
❑ 589 Neal Heaton .15 .05
❑ 590 Brook Jacoby .15 .05
❑ 591 Otis Nixon RC 1.00 .40
❑ 592 Jerry Reed .15 .05
❑ 593 Vern Ruhle .15 .05
❑ 594 Pat Tabler .15 .05
❑ 595 Rich Thompson .15 .05
❑ 596 Andre Thornton .15 .05
❑ 597 Dave Von Ohlen .15 .05
❑ 598 George Vukovich .15 .05
❑ 599 Tom Waddell .15 .05
❑ 600 Curt Wardle .15 .05

❑ 601 Jerry Willard .15 .05
❑ 602 Bill Almon .15 .05
❑ 603 Mike Bielecki .15 .05
❑ 604 Sid Bream .15 .05
❑ 605 Mike C. Brown .15 .05
❑ 606 Pat Clements .15 .05
❑ 607 Jose DeLeon .15 .05
❑ 608 Denny Gonzalez .15 .05
❑ 609 Cecilio Guante .15 .05
❑ 610 Steve Kemp .15 .05
❑ 611 Sammy Khalifa .15 .05
❑ 612 Lee Mazzilli .25 .08
❑ 613 Larry McWilliams .15 .05
❑ 614 Jim Morrison .15 .05
❑ 615 Joe Orsulak RC* .50 .20
❑ 616 Tony Pena .15 .05
❑ 617 Johnny Ray .15 .05
❑ 618 Rick Reuschel .25 .08
❑ 619 R.J. Reynolds .15 .05
❑ 620 Rick Rhoden .15 .05
❑ 621 Don Robinson .15 .05
❑ 622 Jason Thompson .15 .05
❑ 623 Lee Tunnell .15 .05
❑ 624 Jim Winn .15 .05
❑ 625 Marvell Wynne .15 .05
❑ 626 Dwight Gooden IA .50 .20
❑ 627 Don Mattingly IA 1.25 .50
❑ 628 Pete Rose 4192 .50 .20
❑ 629 Rod Carew 3000 Hits .25 .08
❑ 630 T.Seaver/P.Niekro .25 .08
❑ 631 Don Baylor Ouch .25 .08
❑ 632 Tim Raines/Strawberry .25 .08
❑ 633 C.Ripken/A.Trammell 1.50 .60
❑ 634 Wade Boggs/G.Brett 1.00 .40
❑ 635 B.Horner/D.Murphy .50 .20
❑ 636 W.McGee/V.Coleman .25 .08
❑ 637 Vince Coleman IA .25 .08
❑ 638 Pete Rose/D.Gooden .75 .30
❑ 639 Wade Boggs/D.Mattingly 1.25 .50
❑ 640 Murphy/Garvey/Parker .50 .20
❑ 641 D.Gooden/F.Valenzuela .50 .20
❑ 642 Jimmy Key/D.Stieb .25 .08
❑ 643 C.Fisk/R.Gedman .25 .08
❑ 644 Benito Santiago RC 2.00 .75
❑ 645 M.Woodard/C.Ward RC .15 .05
❑ 646 Paul O'Neill RC 4.00 1.50
❑ 647 Andres Galarraga RC 1.50 .60
❑ 648 B.Kipper/C.Ford RC .15 .05
❑ 649 Jose Canseco RC 8.00 3.00
❑ 650 Mark McLemore RC 1.00 .40
❑ 651 R.Woodward/M.Brantley RC .15 .05
❑ 652 B.Robidoux/M.Funderburk RC .15 .05
❑ 653 Cecil Fielder RC 2.00 .75
❑ 654 CL: Royals/Cardinals
Blue Jays/Mets .15 .05
❑ 655 CL: Yankees/Dodgers
Angels/Reds UER
(168 Darly S .15 .05
❑ 656 CL: White Sox/Tigers
Expos/Orioles
(279 Dennis,# .15 .05
❑ 657 CL: Astros/Padres
Red Sox/Cubs .15 .05
❑ 658 CL: Twins/A's
Phillies/Mariners .15 .05
❑ 659 CL: Brewers/Braves
Giants/Rangers .15 .05
❑ 660 CL: Indians/Pirates
Special Cards .15 .05

1986 Fleer Update

❑ COMP.FACT.SET (132) 30.00 12.50
❑ 1 Mike Aldrete XRC .15 .05
❑ 2 Andy Allanson XRC .15 .05
❑ 3 Neil Allen .15 .05
❑ 4 Joaquin Andujar .25 .08
❑ 5 Paul Assenmacher XRC .50 .20
❑ 6 Scott Bailes XRC .15 .05
❑ 7 Jay Baller XRC .15 .05
❑ 8 Scott Bankhead .15 .05
❑ 9 Bill Bathe XRC .15 .05
❑ 10 Don Baylor .25 .08
❑ 11 Billy Beane XRC 1.00 .40
❑ 12 Steve Bedrosian .15 .05
❑ 13 Juan Beniquez .15 .05
❑ 14 Barry Bonds XRC 25.00 10.00

❑ 15 Bobby Bonilla XRC 1.00 .40
❑ 16 Rich Bordi .15 .05
❑ 17 Bill Campbell .15 .05
❑ 18 Tom Candiotti .15 .05
❑ 19 John Cangelosi XRC .50 .20
❑ 20 Jose Canseco 4.00 1.50
❑ 21 Chuck Cary XRC .15 .05
❑ 22 Juan Castillo XRC .15 .05
❑ 23 Rick Cerone .15 .05
❑ 24 John Cerutti XRC .15 .05
❑ 25 Will Clark XRC 2.00 .75
❑ 26 Mark Clear .15 .05
❑ 27 Darnell Coles .15 .05
❑ 28 Dave Collins .15 .05
❑ 29 Tim Conroy .15 .05
❑ 30 Ed Correa .15 .05
❑ 31 Joe Cowley .15 .05
❑ 32 Bill Dawley .15 .05
❑ 33 Rob Deer .15 .05
❑ 34 John Denny .15 .05
❑ 35 Jim Deshaies XRC .15 .05
❑ 36 Doug Drabek XRC 1.00 .40
❑ 37 Mike Easler .15 .05
❑ 38 Mark Eichhorn .15 .05
❑ 39 Dave Engle .15 .05
❑ 40 Mike Fischlin .15 .05
❑ 41 Scott Fletcher .15 .05
❑ 42 Terry Forster .25 .08
❑ 43 Terry Francona .25 .08
❑ 44 Andres Galarraga 1.50 .60
❑ 45 Lee Guetterman .15 .05
❑ 46 Bill Gullickson .15 .05
❑ 47 Jackie Gutierrez .15 .05
❑ 48 Moose Haas .15 .05
❑ 49 Billy Hatcher .15 .05
❑ 50 Mike Heath .15 .05
❑ 51 Guy Hoffman .15 .05
❑ 52 Tom Hume .15 .05
❑ 53 Pete Incaviglia XRC .50 .20
❑ 54 Dane Iorg .15 .05
❑ 55 Chris James XRC .15 .05
❑ 56 Stan Javier XRC* .50 .20
❑ 57 Tommy John .25 .08
❑ 58 Tracy Jones .15 .05
❑ 59 Wally Joyner XRC 1.00 .40
❑ 60 Wayne Krenchicki .15 .05
❑ 61 John Kruk XRC 1.50 .60
❑ 62 Mike LaCoss .15 .05
❑ 63 Pete Ladd .15 .05
❑ 64 Dave LaPoint .15 .05
❑ 65 Mike LaValliere XRC .50 .20
❑ 66 Rudy Law .15 .05
❑ 67 Dennis Leonard .15 .05
❑ 68 Steve Lombardozzi .15 .05
❑ 69 Aurelio Lopez .15 .05
❑ 70 Mickey Mahler .15 .05
❑ 71 Candy Maldonado .15 .05
❑ 72 Roger Mason XRC* .15 .05
❑ 73 Greg Mathews .15 .05
❑ 74 Andy McGaffigan .15 .05
❑ 75 Joel McKeon .15 .05
❑ 76 Kevin Mitchell XRC 1.00 .40
❑ 77 Bill Mooneyham .15 .05
❑ 78 Omar Moreno .15 .05
❑ 79 Jerry Mumphrey .15 .05
❑ 80 Al Newman XRC .25 .08
❑ 81 Phil Niekro .25 .08
❑ 82 Randy Niemann .15 .05
❑ 83 Juan Nieves .15 .05
❑ 84 Bob Ojeda .15 .05
❑ 85 Rick Ownbey .15 .05
❑ 86 Tom Paciorek .15 .05
❑ 87 David Palmer .15 .05
❑ 88 Jeff Parrett XRC .15 .05
❑ 89 Pat Perry .15 .05
❑ 90 Dan Plesac .15 .05
❑ 91 Darrell Porter .15 .05
❑ 92 Luis Quinones .15 .05
❑ 93 Rey Quinones UER
(Misspelled Quinonez) .15 .05
❑ 94 Gary Redus .15 .05
❑ 95 Jeff Reed .15 .05
❑ 96 Bip Roberts XRC .50 .20
❑ 97 Billy Joe Robidoux .15 .05
❑ 98 Gary Roenicke .15 .05
❑ 99 Ron Roenicke .15 .05
❑ 100 Angel Salazar .15 .05
❑ 101 Joe Sambito .15 .05
❑ 102 Billy Sample .15 .05
❑ 103 Dave Schmidt .15 .05
❑ 104 Ken Schrom .15 .05
❑ 105 Ruben Sierra XRC 1.50 .60
❑ 106 Ted Simmons .25 .08
❑ 107 Sammy Stewart .15 .05
❑ 108 Kurt Stillwell .15 .05
❑ 109 Dale Sveum .15 .05
❑ 110 Tim Teufel .15 .05
❑ 111 Bob Tewksbury XRC .50 .20
❑ 112 Andres Thomas .15 .05
❑ 113 Jason Thompson .15 .05
❑ 114 Milt Thompson .50 .20
❑ 115 Robby Thompson XRC .50 .20
❑ 116 Jay Tibbs .15 .05
❑ 117 Fred Toliver .15 .05
❑ 118 Wayne Tolleson .15 .05
❑ 119 Alex Trevino .15 .05
❑ 120 Manny Trillo .15 .05
❑ 121 Ed VandeBerg .15 .05
❑ 122 Ozzie Virgil .15 .05
❑ 123 Tony Walker .15 .05
❑ 124 Gene Walter .15 .05
❑ 125 Duane Ward XRC .50 .20
❑ 126 Jerry Willard .15 .05
❑ 127 Mitch Williams XRC .50 .20
❑ 128 Reggie Williams .15 .05
❑ 129 Bobby Witt XRC .50 .20
❑ 130 Marvell Wynne .15 .05
❑ 131 Steve Yeager .25 .08
❑ 132 Checklist 1-132 .15 .05

1987 Fleer

❑ COMPLETE SET (660) 40.00 20.00
❑ COMP.FACT.SET (672) 50.00 25.00
❑ 1 Rick Aguilera .15 .05
❑ 2 Richard Anderson .15 .05
❑ 3 Wally Backman .15 .05
❑ 4 Gary Carter .25 .08
❑ 5 Ron Darling .25 .08
❑ 6 Len Dykstra .25 .08
❑ 7 Kevin Elster RC .50 .20
❑ 8 Sid Fernandez .15 .05
❑ 9 Dwight Gooden .40 .15
❑ 10 Ed Hearn .15 .05
❑ 11 Danny Heep .15 .05
❑ 12 Keith Hernandez .25 .08
❑ 13 Howard Johnson .25 .08

❑ 14	Ray Knight	.25	.08
❑ 15	Lee Mazzilli	.25	.08
❑ 16	Roger McDowell	.15	.05
❑ 17	Kevin Mitchell RC *	1.25	.50
❑ 18	Randy Niemann	.15	.05
❑ 19	Bob Ojeda	.15	.05
❑ 20	Jesse Orosco	.15	.05
❑ 21	Rafael Santana	.15	.05
❑ 22	Doug Sisk	.15	.05
❑ 23	Darryl Strawberry	.25	.08
❑ 24	Tim Teufel	.15	.05
❑ 25	Mookie Wilson	.25	.08
❑ 26	Tony Armas	.25	.08
❑ 27	Marty Barrett	.15	.05
❑ 28	Don Baylor	.25	.08
❑ 29	Wade Boggs	.40	.15
❑ 30	Oil Can Boyd	.15	.05
❑ 31	Bill Buckner	.25	.08
❑ 32	Roger Clemens	3.00	1.25
❑ 33	Steve Crawford	.15	.05
❑ 34	Dwight Evans	.40	.15
❑ 35	Rich Gedman	.15	.05
❑ 36	Dave Henderson	.15	.05
❑ 37	Bruce Hurst	.15	.05
❑ 38	Tim Lollar	.15	.05
❑ 39	Al Nipper	.15	.05
❑ 40	Spike Owen	.15	.05
❑ 41	Jim Rice	.25	.08
❑ 42	Ed Romero	.15	.05
❑ 43	Joe Sambito	.15	.05
❑ 44	Calvin Schiraldi	.15	.05
❑ 45	Tom Seaver	.40	.15
❑ 46	Jeff Sellers	.15	.05
❑ 47	Bob Stanley	.15	.05
❑ 48	Sammy Stewart	.15	.05
❑ 49	Larry Andersen	.15	.05
❑ 50	Alan Ashby	.15	.05
❑ 51	Kevin Bass	.15	.05
❑ 52	Jeff Calhoun	.15	.05
❑ 53	Jose Cruz	.25	.08
❑ 54	Danny Darwin	.15	.05
❑ 55	Glenn Davis	.15	.05
❑ 56	Jim Deshaies RC *	.25	.08
❑ 57	Bill Doran	.15	.05
❑ 58	Phil Garner	.25	.08
❑ 59	Billy Hatcher	.15	.05
❑ 60	Charlie Kerfeld	.15	.05
❑ 61	Bob Knepper	.15	.05
❑ 62	Dave Lopes	.25	.08
❑ 63	Aurelio Lopez	.15	.05
❑ 64	Jim Pankovits	.15	.05
❑ 65	Terry Puhl	.15	.05
❑ 66	Craig Reynolds	.15	.05
❑ 67	Nolan Ryan	3.00	1.25
❑ 68	Mike Scott	.25	.08
❑ 69	Dave Smith	.15	.05
❑ 70	Dickie Thon	.15	.05
❑ 71	Tony Walker	.15	.05
❑ 72	Denny Walling	.15	.05
❑ 73	Bob Boone	.25	.08
❑ 74	Rick Burleson	.15	.05
❑ 75	John Candelaria	.15	.05
❑ 76	Doug Corbett	.15	.05
❑ 77	Doug DeCinces	.15	.05
❑ 78	Brian Downing	.25	.08
❑ 79	Chuck Finley RC	1.25	.50
❑ 80	Terry Forster	.25	.08
❑ 81	Bob Grich	.25	.08
❑ 82	George Hendrick	.25	.08
❑ 83	Jack Howell	.15	.05
❑ 84	Reggie Jackson	.40	.15
❑ 85	Ruppert Jones	.15	.05
❑ 86	Wally Joyner RC	1.25	.50
❑ 87	Gary Lucas	.15	.05
❑ 88	Kirk McCaskill	.15	.05
❑ 89	Donnie Moore	.15	.05
❑ 90	Gary Pettis	.15	.05
❑ 91	Vern Ruhle	.15	.05
❑ 92	Dick Schofield	.15	.05
❑ 93	Don Sutton	.25	.08
❑ 94	Rob Wilfong	.15	.05
❑ 95	Mike Witt	.15	.05
❑ 96	Doug Drabek RC	1.25	.50
❑ 97	Mike Easler	.15	.05
❑ 98	Mike Fischlin	.15	.05
❑ 99	Brian Fisher	.15	.05
❑ 100	Ron Guidry	.25	.08
❑ 101	Rickey Henderson	.60	.25
❑ 102	Tommy John	.25	.08
❑ 103	Ron Kittle	.15	.05
❑ 104	Don Mattingly	2.00	.75
❑ 105	Bobby Meacham	.15	.05
❑ 106	Joe Niekro	.15	.05
❑ 107	Mike Pagliarulo	.15	.05
❑ 108	Dan Pasqua	.15	.05
❑ 109	Willie Randolph	.25	.08
❑ 110	Dennis Rasmussen	.15	.05
❑ 111	Dave Righetti	.25	.08
❑ 112	Gary Roenicke	.15	.05
❑ 113	Rod Scurry	.15	.05
❑ 114	Bob Shirley	.15	.05
❑ 115	Joel Skinner	.15	.05
❑ 116	Tim Stoddard	.15	.05
❑ 117	Bob Tewksbury RC *	.50	.20
❑ 118	Wayne Tolleson	.15	.05
❑ 119	Claudell Washington	.15	.05
❑ 120	Dave Winfield	.25	.08
❑ 121	Steve Buechele	.15	.05
❑ 122	Ed Correa	.15	.05
❑ 123	Scott Fletcher	.15	.05
❑ 124	Jose Guzman	.15	.05
❑ 125	Toby Harrah	.25	.08
❑ 126	Greg Harris	.15	.05
❑ 127	Charlie Hough	.25	.08
❑ 128	Pete Incaviglia RC *	.50	.20
❑ 129	Mike Mason	.15	.05
❑ 130	Oddibe McDowell	.15	.05
❑ 131	Dale Mohorcic	.15	.05
❑ 132	Pete O'Brien	.15	.05
❑ 133	Tom Paciorek	.15	.05
❑ 134	Larry Parrish	.15	.05
❑ 135	Geno Petralli	.15	.05
❑ 136	Darrell Porter	.15	.05
❑ 137	Jeff Russell	.15	.05
❑ 138	Ruben Sierra RC	2.00	.75
❑ 139	Don Slaught	.15	.05
❑ 140	Gary Ward	.15	.05
❑ 141	Curtis Wilkerson	.15	.05
❑ 142	Mitch Williams RC *	.50	.20
❑ 143	Bobby Witt RC	.50	.20
❑ 144	Dave Bergman	.15	.05
❑ 145	Tom Brookens	.15	.05
❑ 146	Bill Campbell	.15	.05
❑ 147	Chuck Cary	.15	.05
❑ 148	Darnell Coles	.15	.05
❑ 149	Dave Collins	.15	.05
❑ 150	Darrell Evans	.25	.08
❑ 151	Kirk Gibson	.25	.08
❑ 152	John Grubb	.15	.05
❑ 153	Willie Hernandez	.15	.05
❑ 154	Larry Herndon	.15	.05
❑ 155	Eric King	.15	.05
❑ 156	Chet Lemon	.25	.08
❑ 157	Dwight Lowry	.15	.05
❑ 158	Jack Morris	.25	.08
❑ 159	Randy O'Neal	.15	.05
❑ 160	Lance Parrish	.25	.08
❑ 161	Dan Petry	.15	.05
❑ 162	Pat Sheridan	.15	.05
❑ 163	Jim Slaton	.15	.05
❑ 164	Frank Tanana	.25	.08
❑ 165	Walt Terrell	.15	.05
❑ 166	Mark Thurmond	.15	.05
❑ 167	Alan Trammell	.25	.08
❑ 168	Lou Whitaker	.25	.08
❑ 169	Luis Aguayo	.15	.05
❑ 170	Steve Bedrosian	.15	.05
❑ 171	Don Carman	.15	.05
❑ 172	Darren Daulton	.25	.08
❑ 173	Greg Gross	.15	.05
❑ 174	Kevin Gross	.15	.05
❑ 175	Von Hayes	.15	.05
❑ 176	Charles Hudson	.15	.05
❑ 177	Tom Hume	.15	.05
❑ 178	Steve Jeltz	.15	.05
❑ 179	Mike Maddux	.15	.05
❑ 180	Shane Rawley	.15	.05
❑ 181	Gary Redus	.15	.05
❑ 182	Ron Roenicke	.15	.05
❑ 183	Bruce Ruffin RC	.25	.08
❑ 184	John Russell	.15	.05
❑ 185	Juan Samuel	.15	.05
❑ 186	Dan Schatzeder	.15	.05
❑ 187	Mike Schmidt	1.50	.60
❑ 188	Rick Schu	.15	.05
❑ 189	Jeff Stone	.15	.05
❑ 190	Kent Tekulve	.15	.05
❑ 191	Milt Thompson	.15	.05
❑ 192	Glenn Wilson	.15	.05
❑ 193	Buddy Bell	.25	.08
❑ 194	Tom Browning	.15	.05
❑ 195	Sal Butera	.15	.05
❑ 196	Dave Concepcion	.25	.08
❑ 197	Kal Daniels	.15	.05
❑ 198	Eric Davis	.40	.15
❑ 199	John Denny	.15	.05
❑ 200	Bo Diaz	.15	.05
❑ 201	Nick Esasky	.15	.05
❑ 202	John Franco	.25	.08
❑ 203	Bill Gullickson	.15	.05
❑ 204	Barry Larkin RC	3.00	1.25
❑ 205	Eddie Milner	.15	.05
❑ 206	Rob Murphy	.15	.05
❑ 207	Ron Oester	.15	.05
❑ 208	Dave Parker	.25	.08
❑ 209	Tony Perez	.40	.15
❑ 210	Ted Power	.15	.05
❑ 211	Joe Price	.15	.05
❑ 212	Ron Robinson	.15	.05
❑ 213	Pete Rose	2.00	.75
❑ 214	Mario Soto	.25	.08
❑ 215	Kurt Stillwell	.15	.05
❑ 216	Max Venable	.15	.05
❑ 217	Chris Welsh	.15	.05
❑ 218	Carl Willis RC	.25	.08
❑ 219	Jesse Barfield	.25	.08
❑ 220	George Bell	.25	.08
❑ 221	Bill Caudill	.15	.05
❑ 222	John Cerutti	.15	.05
❑ 223	Jim Clancy	.15	.05
❑ 224	Mark Eichhorn	.15	.05
❑ 225	Tony Fernandez	.15	.05
❑ 226	Damaso Garcia	.15	.05
❑ 227	Kelly Gruber ERR (Wrong birth year)	.15	.05
❑ 228	Tom Henke	.15	.05
❑ 229	Garth Iorg	.15	.05
❑ 230	Joe Johnson	.15	.05
❑ 231	Cliff Johnson	.15	.05
❑ 232	Jimmy Key	.25	.08
❑ 233	Dennis Lamp	.15	.05
❑ 234	Rick Leach	.15	.05
❑ 235	Buck Martinez	.15	.05
❑ 236	Lloyd Moseby	.15	.05
❑ 237	Rance Mulliniks	.15	.05
❑ 238	Dave Stieb	.25	.08
❑ 239	Willie Upshaw	.15	.05
❑ 240	Ernie Whitt	.15	.05
❑ 241	Andy Allanson RC	.15	.05
❑ 242	Scott Bailes	.15	.05
❑ 243	Chris Bando	.15	.05
❑ 244	Tony Bernazard	.15	.05
❑ 245	John Butcher	.15	.05
❑ 246	Brett Butler	.25	.08
❑ 247	Ernie Camacho	.15	.05
❑ 248	Tom Candiotti	.15	.05
❑ 249	Joe Carter	.25	.08
❑ 250	Carmen Castillo	.15	.05
❑ 251	Julio Franco	.25	.08
❑ 252	Mel Hall	.15	.05
❑ 253	Brook Jacoby	.15	.05
❑ 254	Phil Niekro	.25	.08
❑ 255	Otis Nixon	.15	.05
❑ 256	Dickie Noles	.15	.05
❑ 257	Bryan Oelkers	.15	.05
❑ 258	Ken Schrom	.15	.05
❑ 259	Don Schulze	.15	.05
❑ 260	Cory Snyder	.15	.05
❑ 261	Pat Tabler	.15	.05
❑ 262	Andre Thornton	.15	.05
❑ 263	Rich Yett	.15	.05
❑ 264	Mike Aldrete	.15	.05
❑ 265	Juan Berenguer	.15	.05
❑ 266	Vida Blue	.25	.08
❑ 267	Bob Brenly	.15	.05
❑ 268	Chris Brown	.15	.05
❑ 269	Will Clark RC	3.00	1.25
❑ 270	Chili Davis	.25	.08

❑ 271 Mark Davis .15 .05
❑ 272 Kelly Downs RC .25 .08
❑ 273 Scott Garrelts .15 .05
❑ 274 Dan Gladden .15 .05
❑ 275 Mike Krukow .15 .05
❑ 276 Randy Kutcher .15 .05
❑ 277 Mike LaCoss .15 .05
❑ 278 Jeff Leonard .15 .05
❑ 279 Candy Maldonado .15 .05
❑ 280 Roger Mason .15 .05
❑ 281 Bob Melvin .15 .05
❑ 282 Greg Minton .15 .05
❑ 283 Jeff D. Robinson .15 .05
❑ 284 Harry Spilman .15 .05
❑ 285 Robby Thompson RC * .50 .20
❑ 286 Jose Uribe .15 .05
❑ 287 Frank Williams .15 .05
❑ 288 Joel Youngblood .15 .05
❑ 289 Jack Clark .25 .08
❑ 290 Vince Coleman .15 .05
❑ 291 Tim Conroy .15 .05
❑ 292 Danny Cox .15 .05
❑ 293 Ken Dayley .15 .05
❑ 294 Curt Ford .15 .05
❑ 295 Bob Forsch .15 .05
❑ 296 Tom Herr .15 .05
❑ 297 Ricky Horton .15 .05
❑ 298 Clint Hurdle .15 .05
❑ 299 Jeff Lahti .15 .05
❑ 300 Steve Lake .15 .05
❑ 301 Tito Landrum .15 .05
❑ 302 Mike LaValliere RC * .50 .20
❑ 303 Greg Mathews .15 .05
❑ 304 Willie McGee .25 .08
❑ 305 Jose Oquendo .15 .05
❑ 306 Terry Pendleton .25 .08
❑ 307 Pat Perry .15 .05
❑ 308 Ozzie Smith 1.00 .40
❑ 309 Ray Soff .15 .05
❑ 310 John Tudor .25 .08
❑ 311 Andy Van Slyke UER .40 .15
❑ 312 Todd Worrell .15 .05
❑ 313 Dann Bilardello .15 .05
❑ 314 Hubie Brooks .15 .05
❑ 315 Tim Burke .15 .05
❑ 316 Andre Dawson .25 .08
❑ 317 Mike Fitzgerald .15 .05
❑ 318 Tom Foley .15 .05
❑ 319 Andres Galarraga .25 .08
❑ 320 Joe Hesketh .15 .05
❑ 321 Wallace Johnson .15 .05
❑ 322 Wayne Krenchicki .15 .05
❑ 323 Vance Law .15 .05
❑ 324 Dennis Martinez .25 .08
❑ 325 Bob McClure .15 .05
❑ 326 Andy McGaffigan .15 .05
❑ 327 Al Newman RC .15 .05
❑ 328 Tim Raines .25 .08
❑ 329 Jeff Reardon .25 .08
❑ 330 Luis Rivera RC .25 .08
❑ 331 Bob Sebra .15 .05
❑ 332 Bryn Smith .15 .05
❑ 333 Jay Tibbs .15 .05
❑ 334 Tim Wallach .15 .05
❑ 335 Mitch Webster .15 .05
❑ 336 Jim Wohlford .15 .05
❑ 337 Floyd Youmans .15 .05
❑ 338 Chris Bosio RC .50 .20
❑ 339 Glenn Braggs RC .25 .08
❑ 340 Rick Cerone .15 .05
❑ 341 Mark Clear .15 .05
❑ 342 Bryan Clutterbuck .15 .05
❑ 343 Cecil Cooper .25 .08
❑ 344 Rob Deer .15 .05
❑ 345 Jim Gantner .15 .05
❑ 346 Ted Higuera .15 .05
❑ 347 John Henry Johnson .15 .05
❑ 348 Tim Leary .15 .05
❑ 349 Rick Manning .15 .05
❑ 350 Paul Molitor .25 .08
❑ 351 Charlie Moore .15 .05
❑ 352 Juan Nieves .15 .05
❑ 353 Ben Oglivie .25 .08
❑ 354 Dan Plesac .15 .05
❑ 355 Ernest Riles .15 .05
❑ 356 Billy Joe Robidoux .15 .05
❑ 357 Bill Schroeder .15 .05
❑ 358 Dale Sveum .15 .05
❑ 359 Gorman Thomas .25 .08
❑ 360 Bill Wegman .15 .05
❑ 361 Robin Yount 1.00 .40
❑ 362 Steve Balboni .15 .05
❑ 363 Scott Bankhead .15 .05
❑ 364 Buddy Biancalana .15 .05
❑ 365 Bud Black .15 .05
❑ 366 George Brett 1.50 .60
❑ 367 Steve Farr .15 .05
❑ 368 Mark Gubicza .15 .05
❑ 369 Bo Jackson RC 8.00 3.00
❑ 370 Danny Jackson .15 .05
❑ 371 Mike Kingery RC .25 .08
❑ 372 Rudy Law .15 .05
❑ 373 Charlie Leibrandt .15 .05
❑ 374 Dennis Leonard .15 .05
❑ 375 Hal McRae .25 .08
❑ 376 Jorge Orta .15 .05
❑ 377 Jamie Quirk .15 .05
❑ 378 Dan Quisenberry .15 .05
❑ 379 Bret Saberhagen .25 .08
❑ 380 Angel Salazar .15 .05
❑ 381 Lonnie Smith .15 .05
❑ 382 Jim Sundberg .25 .08
❑ 383 Frank White .25 .08
❑ 384 Willie Wilson .25 .08
❑ 385 Joaquin Andujar .25 .08
❑ 386 Doug Bair .15 .05
❑ 387 Dusty Baker .25 .08
❑ 388 Bruce Bochte .15 .05
❑ 389 Jose Canseco 1.50 .60
❑ 390 Chris Codiroli .15 .05
❑ 391 Mike Davis .15 .05
❑ 392 Alfredo Griffin .15 .05
❑ 393 Moose Haas .15 .05
❑ 394 Donnie Hill .15 .05
❑ 395 Jay Howell .15 .05
❑ 396 Dave Kingman .25 .08
❑ 397 Carney Lansford .25 .08
❑ 398 Dave Leiper .15 .05
❑ 399 Bill Mooneyham .15 .05
❑ 400 Dwayne Murphy .15 .05
❑ 401 Steve Ontiveros .15 .05
❑ 402 Tony Phillips .15 .05
❑ 403 Eric Plunk .15 .05
❑ 404 Jose Rijo .25 .08
❑ 405 Terry Steinbach RC 1.25 .50
❑ 406 Dave Stewart .25 .08
❑ 407 Mickey Tettleton .15 .05
❑ 408 Dave Von Ohlen .15 .05
❑ 409 Jerry Willard .15 .05
❑ 410 Curt Young .15 .05
❑ 411 Bruce Bochy .15 .05
❑ 412 Dave Dravecky .15 .05
❑ 413 Tim Flannery .15 .05
❑ 414 Steve Garvey .25 .08
❑ 415 Rich Gossage .25 .08
❑ 416 Tony Gwynn 1.00 .40
❑ 417 Andy Hawkins .15 .05
❑ 418 LaMarr Hoyt .15 .05
❑ 419 Terry Kennedy .15 .05
❑ 420 John Kruk RC 2.00 .75
❑ 421 Dave LaPoint .15 .05
❑ 422 Craig Lefferts .15 .05
❑ 423 Carmelo Martinez .15 .05
❑ 424 Lance McCullers .15 .05
❑ 425 Kevin McReynolds .15 .05
❑ 426 Graig Nettles .25 .08
❑ 427 Bip Roberts RC .50 .20
❑ 428 Jerry Royster .15 .05
❑ 429 Benito Santiago .25 .08
❑ 430 Eric Show .15 .05
❑ 431 Bob Stoddard .15 .05
❑ 432 Garry Templeton .25 .08
❑ 433 Gene Walter .15 .05
❑ 434 Ed Whitson .15 .05
❑ 435 Marvell Wynne .15 .05
❑ 436 Dave Anderson .15 .05
❑ 437 Greg Brock .15 .05
❑ 438 Enos Cabell .15 .05
❑ 439 Mariano Duncan .15 .05
❑ 440 Pedro Guerrero .25 .08
❑ 441 Orel Hershiser .40 .15
❑ 442 Rick Honeycutt .15 .05
❑ 443 Ken Howell .15 .05
❑ 444 Ken Landreaux .15 .05
❑ 445 Bill Madlock .25 .08
❑ 446 Mike Marshall .15 .05
❑ 447 Len Matuszek .15 .05
❑ 448 Tom Niedenfuer .15 .05
❑ 449 Alejandro Pena .15 .05
❑ 450 Dennis Powell .15 .05
❑ 451 Jerry Reuss .15 .05
❑ 452 Bill Russell .25 .08
❑ 453 Steve Sax .15 .05
❑ 454 Mike Scioscia .25 .08
❑ 455 Franklin Stubbs .15 .05
❑ 456 Alex Trevino .15 .05
❑ 457 Fernando Valenzuela .25 .08
❑ 458 Ed VandeBerg .15 .05
❑ 459 Bob Welch .25 .08
❑ 460 Reggie Williams .15 .05
❑ 461 Don Aase .15 .05
❑ 462 Juan Beniquez .15 .05
❑ 463 Mike Boddicker .15 .05
❑ 464 Juan Bonilla .15 .05
❑ 465 Rich Bordi .15 .05
❑ 466 Storm Davis .15 .05
❑ 467 Rick Dempsey .15 .05
❑ 468 Ken Dixon .15 .05
❑ 469 Jim Dwyer .15 .05
❑ 470 Mike Flanagan .15 .05
❑ 471 Jackie Gutierrez .15 .05
❑ 472 Brad Havens .15 .05
❑ 473 Lee Lacy .15 .05
❑ 474 Fred Lynn .25 .08
❑ 475 Scott McGregor .15 .05
❑ 476 Eddie Murray .60 .25
❑ 477 Tom O'Malley .15 .05
❑ 478 Cal Ripken 2.50 1.00
❑ 479 Larry Sheets .15 .05
❑ 480 John Shelby .15 .05
❑ 481 Nate Snell .15 .05
❑ 482 Jim Traber .15 .05
❑ 483 Mike Young .15 .05
❑ 484 Neil Allen .15 .05
❑ 485 Harold Baines .25 .08
❑ 486 Floyd Bannister .15 .05
❑ 487 Daryl Boston .15 .05
❑ 488 Ivan Calderon .15 .05
❑ 489 John Cangelosi .15 .05
❑ 490 Steve Carlton .25 .08
❑ 491 Joe Cowley .15 .05
❑ 492 Julio Cruz .15 .05
❑ 493 Bill Dawley .15 .05
❑ 494 Jose DeLeon .15 .05
❑ 495 Richard Dotson .15 .05
❑ 496 Carlton Fisk .40 .15
❑ 497 Ozzie Guillen .40 .15
❑ 498 Jerry Hairston .15 .05
❑ 499 Ron Hassey .15 .05
❑ 500 Tim Hulett .15 .05
❑ 501 Bob James .15 .05
❑ 502 Steve Lyons .15 .05
❑ 503 Joel McKeon .15 .05
❑ 504 Gene Nelson .15 .05
❑ 505 Dave Schmidt .15 .05
❑ 506 Ray Searage .15 .05
❑ 507 Bobby Thigpen RC .50 .20
❑ 508 Greg Walker .15 .05
❑ 509 Jim Acker .15 .05
❑ 510 Doyle Alexander .15 .05
❑ 511 Paul Assenmacher .50 .20
❑ 512 Bruce Benedict .15 .05
❑ 513 Chris Chambliss .25 .08
❑ 514 Jeff Dedmon .15 .05
❑ 515 Gene Garber .15 .05
❑ 516 Ken Griffey .25 .08
❑ 517 Terry Harper .15 .05
❑ 518 Bob Horner .25 .08
❑ 519 Glenn Hubbard .15 .05
❑ 520 Rick Mahler .15 .05
❑ 521 Omar Moreno .15 .05
❑ 522 Dale Murphy .40 .15
❑ 523 Ken Oberkfell .15 .05
❑ 524 Ed Olwine .15 .05
❑ 525 David Palmer .15 .05
❑ 526 Rafael Ramirez .15 .05
❑ 527 Billy Sample .15 .05
❑ 528 Ted Simmons .25 .08

❑ 529 Zane Smith .15 .05
❑ 530 Bruce Sutter .25 .08
❑ 531 Andres Thomas .15 .05
❑ 532 Ozzie Virgil .15 .05
❑ 533 Allan Anderson RC .15 .05
❑ 534 Keith Atherton .15 .05
❑ 535 Billy Beane .25 .08
❑ 536 Bert Blyleven .25 .08
❑ 537 Tom Brunansky .15 .05
❑ 538 Randy Bush .15 .05
❑ 539 George Frazier .15 .05
❑ 540 Gary Gaetti .25 .08
❑ 541 Greg Gagne .15 .05
❑ 542 Mickey Hatcher .15 .05
❑ 543 Neal Heaton .15 .05
❑ 544 Kent Hrbek .25 .08
❑ 545 Roy Lee Jackson .15 .05
❑ 546 Tim Laudner .15 .05
❑ 547 Steve Lombardozzi .15 .05
❑ 548 Mark Portugal RC * .50 .20
❑ 549 Kirby Puckett 1.00 .40
❑ 550 Jeff Reed .15 .05
❑ 551 Mark Salas .15 .05
❑ 552 Roy Smalley .15 .05
❑ 553 Mike Smithson .15 .05
❑ 554 Frank Viola .25 .08
❑ 555 Thad Bosley .15 .05
❑ 556 Ron Cey .25 .08
❑ 557 Jody Davis .15 .05
❑ 558 Ron Davis .15 .05
❑ 559 Bob Dernier .15 .05
❑ 560 Frank DiPino .15 .05
❑ 561 Shawon Dunston UER
(Wrong birth year
listed on c .15 .05
❑ 562 Leon Durham .15 .05
❑ 563 Dennis Eckersley .40 .15
❑ 564 Terry Francona .25 .08
❑ 565 Dave Gumpert .15 .05
❑ 566 Guy Hoffman .15 .05
❑ 567 Ed Lynch .15 .05
❑ 568 Gary Matthews .25 .08
❑ 569 Keith Moreland .15 .05
❑ 570 Jamie Moyer RC 2.00 .75
❑ 571 Jerry Mumphrey .15 .05
❑ 572 Ryne Sandberg 1.25 .50
❑ 573 Scott Sanderson .15 .05
❑ 574 Lee Smith .25 .08
❑ 575 Chris Speier .15 .05
❑ 576 Rick Sutcliffe .25 .08
❑ 577 Manny Trillo .15 .05
❑ 578 Steve Trout .15 .05
❑ 579 Karl Best .15 .05
❑ 580 Scott Bradley .15 .05
❑ 581 Phil Bradley .15 .05
❑ 582 Mickey Brantley .15 .05
❑ 583 Mike G. Brown P .15 .05
❑ 584 Alvin Davis .15 .05
❑ 585 Lee Guetterman .15 .05
❑ 586 Mark Huismann .15 .05
❑ 587 Bob Kearney .15 .05
❑ 588 Pete Ladd .15 .05
❑ 589 Mark Langston .15 .05
❑ 590 Mike Moore .15 .05
❑ 591 Mike Morgan .15 .05
❑ 592 John Moses .15 .05
❑ 593 Ken Phelps .15 .05
❑ 594 Jim Presley .15 .05
❑ 595 Rey Quinones UER
(Quinonez on front) .15 .05
❑ 596 Harold Reynolds .25 .08
❑ 597 Bill Swift .15 .05
❑ 598 Danny Tartabull .15 .05
❑ 599 Steve Yeager .25 .08
❑ 600 Matt Young .15 .05
❑ 601 Bill Almon .15 .05
❑ 602 Rafael Belliard RC .50 .20
❑ 603 Mike Bielecki .15 .05
❑ 604 Barry Bonds RC 30.00 12.50
❑ 605 Bobby Bonilla RC 1.25 .50
❑ 606 Sid Bream .15 .05
❑ 607 Mike C. Brown .15 .05
❑ 608 Pat Clements .15 .05
❑ 609 Mike Diaz .15 .05
❑ 610 Cecilio Guante .15 .05
❑ 611 Barry Jones .15 .05
❑ 612 Bob Kipper .15 .05
❑ 613 Larry McWilliams .15 .05
❑ 614 Jim Morrison .15 .05
❑ 615 Joe Orsulak .15 .05
❑ 616 Junior Ortiz .15 .05
❑ 617 Tony Pena .15 .05
❑ 618 Johnny Ray .15 .05
❑ 619 Rick Reuschel .25 .08
❑ 620 R.J. Reynolds .15 .05
❑ 621 Rick Rhoden .15 .05
❑ 622 Don Robinson .15 .05
❑ 623 Bob Walk .15 .05
❑ 624 Jim Winn .15 .05
❑ 625 J.Canseco/P.Incaviglia .75 .30
❑ 626 300 Game Winners
Don Sutton
Phil Niekro .25 .08
❑ 627 AL Firemen
Dave Righetti
Don Aase .15 .05
❑ 628 J.Canseco/W.Joyner .75 .30
❑ 629 Magic Mets .40 .15
❑ 630 NL Best Righties
Mike Scott
Mike Krukow .15 .05
❑ 631 Sensational Southpaws
Fernando Valenzuela
John F .15 .05
❑ 632 Count'Em
Bob Horner .15 .05
❑ 633 J.Canseco/Rice/Puckett .75 .30
❑ 634 R.Clemens/G.Carter .60 .25
❑ 635 Steve Carlton 4000 .25 .08
❑ 636 Eddie Murray/G.Davis .60 .25
❑ 637 W.Boggs/K.Hernandez .25 .08
❑ 638 D.Mattingly/Strawberry 1.00 .40
❑ 639 R.Sandberg/D.Parker .60 .25
❑ 640 R.Clemens/D.Gooden .60 .25
❑ 641 AL West Stoppers
Mike Witt
Charlie Hough .15 .05
❑ 642 Doubles and Triples
Juan Samuel
Tim Raines .25 .08
❑ 643 Outfielders with Punch
Harold Baines
Jesse Barfi .25 .08
❑ 644 G.Swindell/D.Clark RC .50 .20
❑ 645 R.Karkovice/R.Morman RC .50 .20
❑ 646 D.White/W.Fraser RC 1.25 .50
❑ 647 M.Stanley/J.Browne RC .50 .20
❑ 648 D.Magadan/P.Lombardi RC .50 .20
❑ 649 J.Gonzalez/R.Bryant RC .25 .08
❑ 650 J.Jones/R.Asadoor RC .25 .08
❑ 651 T.Jones/M.Freeman RC .25 .08
❑ 652 K.Seitzer/J.Stefero RC .50 .20
❑ 653 R.Nelson/S.Fireovid RC .25 .08
❑ 654 CL: Mets/Red Sox
Astros/Angels .15 .05
❑ 655 CL: Yankees/Rangers
Tigers/Phillies .15 .05
❑ 656 CL: Reds/Blue Jays
Indians/Giants
ERR (230/231 w) .15 .05
❑ 657 CL: Cardinals/Expos
Brewers/Royals .15 .05
❑ 658 CL: A's/Padres
Dodgers/Orioles .15 .05
❑ 659 CL: White Sox/Braves
Twins/Cubs .15 .05
❑ 660 CL: Mariners/Pirates
Special Cards
ER (580/581 w) .15 .05

1987 Fleer Update

❑ COMP.FACT.SET (132) 15.00 6.00
❑ 1 Scott Bankhead .10 .02
❑ 2 Eric Bell .15 .05
❑ 3 Juan Beniquez .10 .02
❑ 4 Juan Berenguer .10 .02
❑ 5 Mike Birkbeck .15 .05
❑ 6 Randy Bockus .10 .02
❑ 7 Rod Booker .10 .02
❑ 8 Thad Bosley .10 .02
❑ 9 Greg Brock .10 .02
❑ 10 Bob Brower .10 .02

❑ 11 Chris Brown .10 .02
❑ 12 Jerry Browne .15 .05
❑ 13 Ralph Bryant .10 .02
❑ 14 DeWayne Buice .10 .02
❑ 15 Ellis Burks XRC .75 .30
❑ 16 Casey Candaele .10 .02
❑ 17 Steve Carlton .15 .05
❑ 18 Juan Castillo .15 .05
❑ 19 Chuck Crim .10 .02
❑ 20 Mark Davidson .10 .02
❑ 21 Mark Davis .10 .02
❑ 22 Storm Davis .10 .02
❑ 23 Bill Dawley .10 .02
❑ 24 Andre Dawson .15 .05
❑ 25 Brian Dayett .10 .02
❑ 26 Rick Dempsey .10 .02
❑ 27 Ken Dowell .10 .02
❑ 28 Dave Dravecky .10 .02
❑ 29 Mike Dunne .10 .02
❑ 30 Dennis Eckersley .25 .08
❑ 31 Cecil Fielder .15 .05
❑ 32 Brian Fisher .10 .02
❑ 33 Willie Fraser .15 .05
❑ 34 Ken Gerhart .10 .02
❑ 35 Jim Gott .10 .02
❑ 36 Dan Gladden .10 .02
❑ 37 Mike Greenwell XRC .30 .10
❑ 38 Cecilio Guante .10 .02
❑ 39 Albert Hall .10 .02
❑ 40 Atlee Hammaker .10 .02
❑ 41 Mickey Hatcher .10 .02
❑ 42 Mike Heath .10 .02
❑ 43 Neal Heaton .10 .02
❑ 44 Mike Henneman XRC .30 .10
❑ 45 Guy Hoffman .10 .02
❑ 46 Charles Hudson .10 .02
❑ 47 Chuck Jackson .10 .02
❑ 48 Mike Jackson XRC .30 .10
❑ 49 Reggie Jackson .25 .08
❑ 50 Chris James .10 .02
❑ 51 Dion James .10 .02
❑ 52 Stan Javier .10 .02
❑ 53 Stan Jefferson .10 .02
❑ 54 Jimmy Jones .15 .05
❑ 55 Tracy Jones .10 .02
❑ 56 Terry Kennedy .10 .02
❑ 57 Mike Kingery .15 .05
❑ 58 Ray Knight .15 .05
❑ 59 Gene Larkin XRC .30 .10
❑ 60 Mike LaValliere .30 .10
❑ 61 Jack Lazorko .10 .02
❑ 62 Terry Leach .10 .02
❑ 63 Rick Leach .10 .02
❑ 64 Craig Lefferts .10 .02
❑ 65 Jim Lindeman .15 .05
❑ 66 Bill Long .10 .02
❑ 67 Mike Loynd XRC .15 .05
❑ 68 Greg Maddux XRC 8.00 3.00
❑ 69 Bill Madlock .15 .05
❑ 70 Dave Magadan .30 .10
❑ 71 Joe Magrane XRC .15 .05
❑ 72 Fred Manrique .10 .02
❑ 73 Mike Mason .10 .02
❑ 74 Lloyd McClendon XRC .30 .10
❑ 75 Fred McGriff 1.00 .40
❑ 76 Mark McGwire 5.00 2.00
❑ 77 Mark McLemore .15 .05
❑ 78 Kevin McReynolds .10 .02

❑ 79 Dave Meads	.10	.02
❑ 80 Greg Minton	.10	.02
❑ 81 John Mitchell XRC	.15	.05
❑ 82 Kevin Mitchell	.25	.08
❑ 83 John Morris	.10	.02
❑ 84 Jeff Musselman	.10	.02
❑ 85 Randy Myers XRC	.75	.30
❑ 86 Gene Nelson	.10	.02
❑ 87 Joe Niekro	.10	.02
❑ 88 Tom Nieto	.10	.02
❑ 89 Reid Nichols	.10	.02
❑ 90 Matt Nokes XRC	.30	.10
❑ 91 Dickie Noles	.10	.02
❑ 92 Edwin Nunez	.10	.02
❑ 93 Jose Nunez XRC	.10	.02
❑ 94 Paul O'Neill	.40	.15
❑ 95 Jim Paciorek	.10	.02
❑ 96 Lance Parrish	.15	.05
❑ 97 Bill Pecota XRC	.15	.05
❑ 98 Tony Pena	.10	.02
❑ 99 Luis Polonia XRC	.30	.10
❑ 100 Randy Ready	.10	.02
❑ 101 Jeff Reardon	.15	.05
❑ 102 Gary Redus	.10	.02
❑ 103 Rick Rhoden	.10	.02
❑ 104 Wally Ritchie	.10	.02
❑ 105 Jeff M. Robinson UER (Wrong Jeff's stats on back	.10	.02
❑ 106 Mark Salas	.10	.02
❑ 107 Dave Schmidt	.10	.02
❑ 108 Kevin Seitzer UER	.30	.10
❑ 109 John Shelby	.10	.02
❑ 110 John Smiley XRC	.30	.10
❑ 111 Lary Sorensen	.10	.02
❑ 112 Chris Speier	.10	.02
❑ 113 Randy St.Claire	.10	.02
❑ 114 Jim Sundberg	.15	.05
❑ 115 B.J. Surhoff XRC	.75	.30
❑ 116 Greg Swindell	.30	.10
❑ 117 Danny Tartabull	.10	.02
❑ 118 Dorn Taylor	.10	.02
❑ 119 Lee Tunnell	.10	.02
❑ 120 Ed VandeBerg	.10	.02
❑ 121 Andy Van Slyke	.25	.08
❑ 122 Gary Ward	.10	.02
❑ 123 Devon White	.75	.30
❑ 124 Alan Wiggins	.10	.02
❑ 125 Bill Wilkinson	.10	.02
❑ 126 Jim Winn	.10	.02
❑ 127 Frank Williams	.10	.02
❑ 128 Ken Williams	.10	.02
❑ 129 Matt Williams XRC	1.50	.60
❑ 130 Herm Winningham	.10	.02
❑ 131 Matt Young	.10	.02
❑ 132 Checklist 1-132	.10	.02

1988 Fleer

❑ COMPLETE SET (660)	15.00	6.00
❑ COMP.RETAIL SET (660)	15.00	6.00
❑ COMP.HOBBY SET (672)	15.00	6.00
❑ 1 Keith Atherton	.10	.02
❑ 2 Don Baylor	.15	.05
❑ 3 Juan Berenguer	.10	.02
❑ 4 Bert Blyleven	.15	.05
❑ 5 Tom Brunansky	.10	.02
❑ 6 Randy Bush	.10	.02
❑ 7 Steve Carlton	.15	.05
❑ 8 Mark Davidson	.10	.02
❑ 9 George Frazier	.10	.02
❑ 10 Gary Gaetti	.15	.05
❑ 11 Greg Gagne	.10	.02
❑ 12 Dan Gladden	.10	.02
❑ 13 Kent Hrbek	.15	.05
❑ 14 Gene Larkin RC*	.40	.15
❑ 15 Tim Laudner	.10	.02
❑ 16 Steve Lombardozzi	.10	.02
❑ 17 Al Newman	.10	.02
❑ 18 Joe Niekro	.10	.02
❑ 19 Kirby Puckett	.30	.10
❑ 20 Jeff Reardon	.15	.05
❑ 21A Dan Schatzeder ERR (Misspelled Schatzader on car)	.15	.05
❑ 21B Dan Schatzeder COR	.10	.02
❑ 22 Roy Smalley	.10	.02
❑ 23 Mike Smithson	.10	.02
❑ 24 Les Straker	.10	.02
❑ 25 Frank Viola	.15	.05
❑ 26 Jack Clark	.15	.05
❑ 27 Vince Coleman	.10	.02
❑ 28 Danny Cox	.10	.02
❑ 29 Bill Dawley	.10	.02
❑ 30 Ken Dayley	.10	.02
❑ 31 Doug DeCinces	.10	.02
❑ 32 Curt Ford	.10	.02
❑ 33 Bob Forsch	.10	.02
❑ 34 David Green	.10	.02
❑ 35 Tom Herr	.10	.02
❑ 36 Ricky Horton	.10	.02
❑ 37 Lance Johnson RC	.40	.15
❑ 38 Steve Lake	.10	.02
❑ 39 Jim Lindeman	.10	.02
❑ 40 Joe Magrane RC*	.40	.15
❑ 41 Greg Mathews	.10	.02
❑ 42 Willie McGee	.15	.05
❑ 43 John Morris	.10	.02
❑ 44 Jose Oquendo	.10	.02
❑ 45 Tony Pena	.10	.02
❑ 46 Terry Pendleton	.15	.05
❑ 47 Ozzie Smith	.50	.20
❑ 48 John Tudor	.15	.05
❑ 49 Lee Tunnell	.10	.02
❑ 50 Todd Worrell	.10	.02
❑ 51 Doyle Alexander	.10	.02
❑ 52 Dave Bergman	.10	.02
❑ 53 Tom Brookens	.10	.02
❑ 54 Darrell Evans	.15	.05
❑ 55 Kirk Gibson	.30	.10
❑ 56 Mike Heath	.10	.02
❑ 57 Mike Henneman RC*	.40	.15
❑ 58 Willie Hernandez	.10	.02
❑ 59 Larry Herndon	.10	.02
❑ 60 Eric King	.10	.02
❑ 61 Chet Lemon	.15	.05
❑ 62 Scott Lusader	.10	.02
❑ 63 Bill Madlock	.15	.05
❑ 64 Jack Morris	.15	.05
❑ 65 Jim Morrison	.10	.02
❑ 66 Matt Nokes RC*	.40	.15
❑ 67 Dan Petry	.10	.02
❑ 68A Jeff M. Robinson ERR (Stats for Jeff D. Robinson	.20	.07
❑ 68B Jeff M. Robinson COR (Born 12-14-61)	.10	.02
❑ 69 Pat Sheridan	.10	.02
❑ 70 Nate Snell	.10	.02
❑ 71 Frank Tanana	.15	.05
❑ 72 Walt Terrell	.10	.02
❑ 73 Mark Thurmond	.10	.02
❑ 74 Alan Trammell	.15	.05
❑ 75 Lou Whitaker	.15	.05
❑ 76 Mike Aldrete	.10	.02
❑ 77 Bob Brenly	.10	.02
❑ 78 Will Clark	.30	.10
❑ 79 Chili Davis	.15	.05
❑ 80 Kelly Downs	.10	.02
❑ 81 Dave Dravecky	.10	.02
❑ 82 Scott Garrelts	.10	.02
❑ 83 Atlee Hammaker	.10	.02
❑ 84 Dave Henderson	.10	.02
❑ 85 Mike Krukow	.10	.02
❑ 86 Mike LaCoss	.10	.02
❑ 87 Craig Lefferts	.10	.02
❑ 88 Jeff Leonard	.10	.02
❑ 89 Candy Maldonado	.10	.02
❑ 90 Eddie Milner	.10	.02
❑ 91 Bob Melvin	.10	.02
❑ 92 Kevin Mitchell	.15	.05
❑ 93 Jon Perlman	.10	.02
❑ 94 Rick Reuschel	.15	.05
❑ 95 Don Robinson	.10	.02
❑ 96 Chris Speier	.10	.02
❑ 97 Harry Spilman	.10	.02
❑ 98 Robby Thompson	.10	.02
❑ 99 Jose Uribe	.10	.02
❑ 100 Mark Wasinger	.10	.02
❑ 101 Matt Williams RC	1.50	.60
❑ 102 Jesse Barfield	.15	.05
❑ 103 George Bell	.15	.05
❑ 104 Juan Beniquez	.10	.02
❑ 105 John Cerutti	.10	.02
❑ 106 Jim Clancy	.10	.02
❑ 107 Rob Ducey	.10	.02
❑ 108 Mark Eichhorn	.10	.02
❑ 109 Tony Fernandez	.10	.02
❑ 110 Cecil Fielder	.15	.05
❑ 111 Kelly Gruber	.10	.02
❑ 112 Tom Henke	.10	.02
❑ 113A Garth Iorg ERR (Misspelled Iorq on card front)	.20	.07
❑ 113B Garth Iorg COR	.10	.02
❑ 114 Jimmy Key	.15	.05
❑ 115 Rick Leach	.10	.02
❑ 116 Manny Lee	.10	.02
❑ 117 Nelson Liriano	.10	.02
❑ 118 Fred McGriff	.30	.10
❑ 119 Lloyd Moseby	.10	.02
❑ 120 Rance Mulliniks	.10	.02
❑ 121 Jeff Musselman	.10	.02
❑ 122 Jose Nunez	.10	.02
❑ 123 Dave Stieb	.15	.05
❑ 124 Willie Upshaw	.10	.02
❑ 125 Duane Ward	.10	.02
❑ 126 Ernie Whitt	.10	.02
❑ 127 Rick Aguilera	.10	.02
❑ 128 Wally Backman	.10	.02
❑ 129 Mark Carreon RC	.15	.05
❑ 130 Gary Carter	.15	.05
❑ 131 David Cone	.15	.05
❑ 132 Ron Darling	.15	.05
❑ 133 Len Dykstra	.15	.05
❑ 134 Sid Fernandez	.10	.02
❑ 135 Dwight Gooden	.15	.05
❑ 136 Keith Hernandez	.15	.05
❑ 137 Gregg Jefferies RC	.40	.15
❑ 138 Howard Johnson	.15	.05
❑ 139 Terry Leach	.10	.02
❑ 140 Barry Lyons	.10	.02
❑ 141 Dave Magadan	.10	.02
❑ 142 Roger McDowell	.10	.02
❑ 143 Kevin McReynolds	.10	.02
❑ 144 Keith Miller RC	.40	.15
❑ 145 John Mitchell RC	.15	.05
❑ 146 Randy Myers	.15	.05
❑ 147 Bob Ojeda	.10	.02
❑ 148 Jesse Orosco	.10	.02
❑ 149 Rafael Santana	.10	.02
❑ 150 Doug Sisk	.10	.02
❑ 151 Darryl Strawberry	.15	.05
❑ 152 Tim Teufel	.10	.02
❑ 153 Gene Walter	.10	.02
❑ 154 Mookie Wilson	.15	.05
❑ 155 Jay Aldrich	.10	.02
❑ 156 Chris Bosio	.10	.02
❑ 157 Glenn Braggs	.10	.02
❑ 158 Greg Brock	.10	.02
❑ 159 Juan Castillo	.10	.02
❑ 160 Mark Clear	.10	.02
❑ 161 Cecil Cooper	.15	.05
❑ 162 Chuck Crim	.10	.02
❑ 163 Rob Deer	.10	.02
❑ 164 Mike Felder	.10	.02
❑ 165 Jim Gantner	.10	.02
❑ 166 Ted Higuera	.10	.02
❑ 167 Steve Kiefer	.10	.02
❑ 168 Rick Manning	.10	.02
❑ 169 Paul Molitor	.15	.05

❑ 170	Juan Nieves	.10	.02
❑ 171	Dan Plesac	.10	.02
❑ 172	Earnest Riles	.10	.02
❑ 173	Bill Schroeder	.10	.02
❑ 174	Steve Stanicek	.10	.02
❑ 175	B.J. Surhoff	.15	.05
❑ 176	Dale Sveum	.10	.02
❑ 177	Bill Wegman	.10	.02
❑ 178	Robin Yount	.50	.20
❑ 179	Hubie Brooks	.10	.02
❑ 180	Tim Burke	.10	.02
❑ 181	Casey Candaele	.10	.02
❑ 182	Mike Fitzgerald	.10	.02
❑ 183	Tom Foley	.10	.02
❑ 184	Andres Galarraga	.15	.05
❑ 185	Neal Heaton	.10	.02
❑ 186	Wallace Johnson	.10	.02
❑ 187	Vance Law	.10	.02
❑ 188	Dennis Martinez	.15	.05
❑ 189	Bob McClure	.10	.02
❑ 190	Andy McGaffigan	.10	.02
❑ 191	Reid Nichols	.10	.02
❑ 192	Pascual Perez	.10	.02
❑ 193	Tim Raines	.15	.05
❑ 194	Jeff Reed	.10	.02
❑ 195	Bob Sebra	.10	.02
❑ 196	Bryn Smith	.10	.02
❑ 197	Randy St.Claire	.10	.02
❑ 198	Tim Wallach	.10	.02
❑ 199	Mitch Webster	.10	.02
❑ 200	Herm Winningham	.10	.02
❑ 201	Floyd Youmans	.10	.02
❑ 202	Brad Arnsberg	.10	.02
❑ 203	Rick Cerone	.10	.02
❑ 204	Pat Clements	.10	.02
❑ 205	Henry Cotto	.10	.02
❑ 206	Mike Easler	.10	.02
❑ 207	Ron Guidry	.15	.05
❑ 208	Bill Gullickson	.10	.02
❑ 209	Rickey Henderson	.30	.10
❑ 210	Charles Hudson	.10	.02
❑ 211	Tommy John	.15	.05
❑ 212	Roberto Kelly RC	.40	.15
❑ 213	Ron Kittle	.10	.02
❑ 214	Don Mattingly	1.00	.40
❑ 215	Bobby Meacham	.10	.02
❑ 216	Mike Pagliarulo	.10	.02
❑ 217	Dan Pasqua	.10	.02
❑ 218	Willie Randolph	.15	.05
❑ 219	Rick Rhoden	.10	.02
❑ 220	Dave Righetti	.15	.05
❑ 221	Jerry Royster	.10	.02
❑ 222	Tim Stoddard	.10	.02
❑ 223	Wayne Tolleson	.10	.02
❑ 224	Gary Ward	.10	.02
❑ 225	Claudell Washington	.10	.02
❑ 226	Dave Winfield	.15	.05
❑ 227	Buddy Bell	.15	.05
❑ 228	Tom Browning	.10	.02
❑ 229	Dave Concepcion	.15	.05
❑ 230	Kal Daniels	.10	.02
❑ 231	Eric Davis	.15	.05
❑ 232	Bo Diaz	.10	.02
❑ 233	Nick Esasky (Has a dollar sign before '87 SB tot	.10	.02
❑ 234	John Franco	.15	.05
❑ 235	Guy Hoffman	.10	.02
❑ 236	Tom Hume	.10	.02
❑ 237	Tracy Jones	.10	.02
❑ 238	Bill Landrum	.10	.02
❑ 239	Barry Larkin	.20	.07
❑ 240	Terry McGriff	.10	.02
❑ 241	Rob Murphy	.10	.02
❑ 242	Ron Oester	.10	.02
❑ 243	Dave Parker	.15	.05
❑ 244	Pat Perry	.10	.02
❑ 245	Ted Power	.10	.02
❑ 246	Dennis Rasmussen	.10	.02
❑ 247	Ron Robinson	.10	.02
❑ 248	Kurt Stillwell	.10	.02
❑ 249	Jeff Treadway RC	.40	.15
❑ 250	Frank Williams	.10	.02
❑ 251	Steve Balboni	.10	.02
❑ 252	Bud Black	.10	.02
❑ 253	Thad Bosley	.10	.02
❑ 254	George Brett	.75	.30
❑ 255	John Davis	.10	.02
❑ 256	Steve Farr	.10	.02
❑ 257	Gene Garber	.10	.02
❑ 258	Jerry Don Gleaton	.10	.02
❑ 259	Mark Gubicza	.10	.02
❑ 260	Bo Jackson	.30	.10
❑ 261	Danny Jackson	.10	.02
❑ 262	Ross Jones	.10	.02
❑ 263	Charlie Leibrandt	.10	.02
❑ 264	Bill Pecota RC*	.15	.05
❑ 265	Melido Perez RC	.40	.15
❑ 266	Jamie Quirk	.10	.02
❑ 267	Dan Quisenberry	.10	.02
❑ 268	Bret Saberhagen	.15	.05
❑ 269	Angel Salazar	.10	.02
❑ 270	Kevin Seitzer UER (Wrong birth year)	.15	.05
❑ 271	Danny Tartabull	.10	.02
❑ 272	Gary Thurman	.10	.02
❑ 273	Frank White	.15	.05
❑ 274	Willie Wilson	.15	.05
❑ 275	Tony Bernazard	.10	.02
❑ 276	Jose Canseco	.75	.30
❑ 277	Mike Davis	.10	.02
❑ 278	Storm Davis	.10	.02
❑ 279	Dennis Eckersley	.20	.07
❑ 280	Alfredo Griffin	.10	.02
❑ 281	Rick Honeycutt	.10	.02
❑ 282	Jay Howell	.10	.02
❑ 283	Reggie Jackson	.20	.07
❑ 284	Dennis Lamp	.10	.02
❑ 285	Carney Lansford	.15	.05
❑ 286	Mark McGwire	2.50	1.00
❑ 287	Dwayne Murphy	.10	.02
❑ 288	Gene Nelson	.10	.02
❑ 289	Steve Ontiveros	.10	.02
❑ 290	Tony Phillips	.10	.02
❑ 291	Eric Plunk	.10	.02
❑ 292	Luis Polonia RC*	.40	.15
❑ 293	Rick Rodriguez	.10	.02
❑ 294	Terry Steinbach	.15	.05
❑ 295	Dave Stewart	.15	.05
❑ 296	Curt Young	.10	.02
❑ 297	Luis Aguayo	.10	.02
❑ 298	Steve Bedrosian	.10	.02
❑ 299	Jeff Calhoun	.10	.02
❑ 300	Don Carman	.10	.02
❑ 301	Todd Frohwirth	.10	.02
❑ 302	Greg Gross	.10	.02
❑ 303	Kevin Gross	.10	.02
❑ 304	Von Hayes	.10	.02
❑ 305	Keith Hughes	.10	.02
❑ 306	Mike Jackson RC*	.40	.15
❑ 307	Chris James	.10	.02
❑ 308	Steve Jeltz	.10	.02
❑ 309	Mike Maddux	.10	.02
❑ 310	Lance Parrish	.15	.05
❑ 311	Shane Rawley	.10	.02
❑ 312	Wally Ritchie	.10	.02
❑ 313	Bruce Ruffin	.10	.02
❑ 314	Juan Samuel	.10	.02
❑ 315	Mike Schmidt	.75	.30
❑ 316	Rick Schu	.10	.02
❑ 317	Jeff Stone	.10	.02
❑ 318	Kent Tekulve	.10	.02
❑ 319	Milt Thompson	.10	.02
❑ 320	Glenn Wilson	.10	.02
❑ 321	Rafael Belliard	.10	.02
❑ 322	Barry Bonds	3.00	1.25
❑ 323	Bobby Bonilla	.15	.05
❑ 324	Sid Bream	.10	.02
❑ 325	John Cangelosi	.10	.02
❑ 326	Mike Diaz	.10	.02
❑ 327	Doug Drabek	.10	.02
❑ 328	Mike Dunne	.10	.02
❑ 329	Brian Fisher	.10	.02
❑ 330	Brett Gideon	.10	.02
❑ 331	Terry Harper	.10	.02
❑ 332	Bob Kipper	.10	.02
❑ 333	Mike LaValliere	.10	.02
❑ 334	Jose Lind RC	.40	.15
❑ 335	Junior Ortiz	.10	.02
❑ 336	Vicente Palacios	.10	.02
❑ 337	Bob Patterson	.10	.02
❑ 338	Al Pedrique	.10	.02
❑ 339	R.J. Reynolds	.10	.02
❑ 340	John Smiley RC*	.40	.15
❑ 341	Andy Van Slyke UER (Wrong batting and throwing l)	.20	.07
❑ 342	Bob Walk	.10	.02
❑ 343	Marty Barrett	.10	.02
❑ 344	Todd Benzinger RC*	.40	.15
❑ 345	Wade Boggs	.20	.07
❑ 346	Tom Bolton	.10	.02
❑ 347	Oil Can Boyd	.10	.02
❑ 348	Ellis Burks RC	.50	.20
❑ 349	Roger Clemens	1.50	.60
❑ 350	Steve Crawford	.10	.02
❑ 351	Dwight Evans	.20	.07
❑ 352	Wes Gardner	.10	.02
❑ 353	Rich Gedman	.10	.02
❑ 354	Mike Greenwell	.10	.02
❑ 355	Sam Horn RC	.15	.05
❑ 356	Bruce Hurst	.10	.02
❑ 357	John Marzano	.10	.02
❑ 358	Al Nipper	.10	.02
❑ 359	Spike Owen	.10	.02
❑ 360	Jody Reed RC	.40	.15
❑ 361	Jim Rice	.15	.05
❑ 362	Ed Romero	.10	.02
❑ 363	Kevin Romine	.10	.02
❑ 364	Joe Sambito	.10	.02
❑ 365	Calvin Schiraldi	.10	.02
❑ 366	Jeff Sellers	.10	.02
❑ 367	Bob Stanley	.10	.02
❑ 368	Scott Bankhead	.10	.02
❑ 369	Phil Bradley	.10	.02
❑ 370	Scott Bradley	.10	.02
❑ 371	Mickey Brantley	.10	.02
❑ 372	Mike Campbell	.10	.02
❑ 373	Alvin Davis	.10	.02
❑ 374	Lee Guetterman	.10	.02
❑ 375	Dave Hengel	.10	.02
❑ 376	Mike Kingery	.10	.02
❑ 377	Mark Langston	.10	.02
❑ 378	Edgar Martinez RC	5.00	2.00
❑ 379	Mike Moore	.10	.02
❑ 380	Mike Morgan	.10	.02
❑ 381	John Moses	.10	.02
❑ 382	Donell Nixon	.10	.02
❑ 383	Edwin Nunez	.10	.02
❑ 384	Ken Phelps	.10	.02
❑ 385	Jim Presley	.10	.02
❑ 386	Rey Quinones	.10	.02
❑ 387	Jerry Reed	.10	.02
❑ 388	Harold Reynolds	.15	.05
❑ 389	Dave Valle	.10	.02
❑ 390	Bill Wilkinson	.10	.02
❑ 391	Harold Baines	.15	.05
❑ 392	Floyd Bannister	.10	.02
❑ 393	Daryl Boston	.10	.02
❑ 394	Ivan Calderon	.10	.02
❑ 395	Jose DeLeon	.10	.02
❑ 396	Richard Dotson	.10	.02
❑ 397	Carlton Fisk	.20	.07
❑ 398	Ozzie Guillen	.15	.05
❑ 399	Ron Hassey	.10	.02
❑ 400	Donnie Hill	.10	.02
❑ 401	Bob James	.10	.02
❑ 402	Dave LaPoint	.10	.02
❑ 403	Bill Lindsey	.10	.02
❑ 404	Bill Long	.10	.02
❑ 405	Steve Lyons	.10	.02
❑ 406	Fred Manrique	.10	.02
❑ 407	Jack McDowell RC	.50	.20
❑ 408	Gary Redus	.10	.02
❑ 409	Ray Searage	.10	.02
❑ 410	Bobby Thigpen	.10	.02
❑ 411	Greg Walker	.10	.02
❑ 412	Ken Williams	.10	.02
❑ 413	Jim Winn	.10	.02
❑ 414	Jody Davis	.10	.02
❑ 415	Andre Dawson	.15	.05
❑ 416	Brian Dayett	.10	.02
❑ 417	Bob Dernier	.10	.02
❑ 418	Frank DiPino	.10	.02
❑ 419	Shawon Dunston	.10	.02
❑ 420	Leon Durham	.10	.02
❑ 421	Les Lancaster	.10	.02
❑ 422	Ed Lynch	.10	.02

Card	Player		
❑ 423	Greg Maddux	1.50	.60
❑ 424	Dave Martinez	.10	.02
❑ 425A	Keith Moreland ERR	1.50	.60
❑ 425B	Keith Moreland COR (Bat on shoulder)	.15	.05
❑ 426	Jamie Moyer	.15	.05
❑ 427	Jerry Mumphrey	.10	.02
❑ 428	Paul Noce	.10	.02
❑ 429	Rafael Palmeiro	.60	.25
❑ 430	Wade Rowdon	.10	.02
❑ 431	Ryne Sandberg	.60	.25
❑ 432	Scott Sanderson	.10	.02
❑ 433	Lee Smith	.15	.05
❑ 434	Jim Sundberg	.15	.05
❑ 435	Rick Sutcliffe	.15	.05
❑ 436	Manny Trillo	.10	.02
❑ 437	Juan Agosto	.10	.02
❑ 438	Larry Andersen	.10	.02
❑ 439	Alan Ashby	.10	.02
❑ 440	Kevin Bass	.10	.02
❑ 441	Ken Caminiti RC	3.00	1.25
❑ 442	Rocky Childress	.10	.02
❑ 443	Jose Cruz	.15	.05
❑ 444	Danny Darwin	.10	.02
❑ 445	Glenn Davis	.10	.02
❑ 446	Jim Deshaies	.10	.02
❑ 447	Bill Doran	.10	.02
❑ 448	Ty Gainey	.10	.02
❑ 449	Billy Hatcher	.10	.02
❑ 450	Jeff Heathcock	.10	.02
❑ 451	Bob Knepper	.10	.02
❑ 452	Rob Mallicoat	.10	.02
❑ 453	Dave Meads	.10	.02
❑ 454	Craig Reynolds	.10	.02
❑ 455	Nolan Ryan	1.50	.60
❑ 456	Mike Scott	.15	.05
❑ 457	Dave Smith	.10	.02
❑ 458	Denny Walling	.10	.02
❑ 459	Robbie Wine	.10	.02
❑ 460	Gerald Young	.10	.02
❑ 461	Bob Brower	.10	.02
❑ 462A	Jerry Browne ERR	1.50	.60
❑ 462B	Jerry Browne COR (Black player)	.15	.05
❑ 463	Steve Buechele	.10	.02
❑ 464	Edwin Correa	.10	.02
❑ 465	Cecil Espy	.10	.02
❑ 466	Scott Fletcher	.10	.02
❑ 467	Jose Guzman	.10	.02
❑ 468	Greg Harris	.10	.02
❑ 469	Charlie Hough	.15	.05
❑ 470	Pete Incaviglia	.10	.02
❑ 471	Paul Kilgus	.10	.02
❑ 472	Mike Loynd	.10	.02
❑ 473	Oddibe McDowell	.10	.02
❑ 474	Dale Mohorcic	.10	.02
❑ 475	Pete O'Brien	.10	.02
❑ 476	Larry Parrish	.10	.02
❑ 477	Geno Petralli	.10	.02
❑ 478	Jeff Russell	.10	.02
❑ 479	Ruben Sierra	.15	.05
❑ 480	Mike Stanley	.10	.02
❑ 481	Curtis Wilkerson	.10	.02
❑ 482	Mitch Williams	.10	.02
❑ 483	Bobby Witt	.10	.02
❑ 484	Tony Armas	.15	.05
❑ 485	Bob Boone	.15	.05
❑ 486	Bill Buckner	.15	.05
❑ 487	DeWayne Buice	.10	.02
❑ 488	Brian Downing	.15	.05
❑ 489	Chuck Finley	.15	.05
❑ 490	Willie Fraser UER (Wrong bio stats, for George H)	.10	.02
❑ 491	Jack Howell	.10	.02
❑ 492	Ruppert Jones	.10	.02
❑ 493	Wally Joyner	.15	.05
❑ 494	Jack Lazorko	.10	.02
❑ 495	Gary Lucas	.10	.02
❑ 496	Kirk McCaskill	.10	.02
❑ 497	Mark McLemore	.10	.02
❑ 498	Darrell Miller	.10	.02
❑ 499	Greg Minton	.10	.02
❑ 500	Donnie Moore	.10	.02
❑ 501	Gus Polidor	.10	.02
❑ 502	Johnny Ray	.10	.02
❑ 503	Mark Ryal	.10	.02
❑ 504	Dick Schofield	.10	.02
❑ 505	Don Sutton	.15	.05
❑ 506	Devon White	.15	.05
❑ 507	Mike Witt	.10	.02
❑ 508	Dave Anderson	.10	.02
❑ 509	Tim Belcher	.10	.02
❑ 510	Ralph Bryant	.10	.02
❑ 511	Tim Crews RC	.40	.15
❑ 512	Mike Devereaux RC	.40	.15
❑ 513	Mariano Duncan	.10	.02
❑ 514	Pedro Guerrero	.15	.05
❑ 515	Jeff Hamilton	.10	.02
❑ 516	Mickey Hatcher	.10	.02
❑ 517	Brad Havens	.10	.02
❑ 518	Orel Hershiser	.15	.05
❑ 519	Shawn Hillegas	.10	.02
❑ 520	Ken Howell	.10	.02
❑ 521	Tim Leary	.10	.02
❑ 522	Mike Marshall	.10	.02
❑ 523	Steve Sax	.10	.02
❑ 524	Mike Scioscia	.15	.05
❑ 525	Mike Sharperson	.10	.02
❑ 526	John Shelby	.10	.02
❑ 527	Franklin Stubbs	.10	.02
❑ 528	Fernando Valenzuela	.15	.05
❑ 529	Bob Welch	.15	.05
❑ 530	Matt Young	.10	.02
❑ 531	Jim Acker	.10	.02
❑ 532	Paul Assenmacher	.10	.02
❑ 533	Jeff Blauser RC	.40	.15
❑ 534	Joe Boever	.10	.02
❑ 535	Martin Clary	.10	.02
❑ 536	Kevin Coffman	.10	.02
❑ 537	Jeff Dedmon	.10	.02
❑ 538	Ron Gant RC	.50	.20
❑ 539	Tom Glavine RC	4.00	1.50
❑ 540	Ken Griffey	.15	.05
❑ 541	Albert Hall	.10	.02
❑ 542	Glenn Hubbard	.10	.02
❑ 543	Dion James	.10	.02
❑ 544	Dale Murphy	.20	.07
❑ 545	Ken Oberkfell	.10	.02
❑ 546	David Palmer	.10	.02
❑ 547	Gerald Perry	.10	.02
❑ 548	Charlie Puleo	.10	.02
❑ 549	Ted Simmons	.15	.05
❑ 550	Zane Smith	.10	.02
❑ 551	Andres Thomas	.10	.02
❑ 552	Ozzie Virgil	.10	.02
❑ 553	Don Aase	.10	.02
❑ 554	Jeff Ballard	.10	.02
❑ 555	Eric Bell	.10	.02
❑ 556	Mike Boddicker	.10	.02
❑ 557	Ken Dixon	.10	.02
❑ 558	Jim Dwyer	.10	.02
❑ 559	Ken Gerhart	.10	.02
❑ 560	Rene Gonzales RC	.15	.05
❑ 561	Mike Griffin	.10	.02
❑ 562	John Habyan UER (Misspelled Hayban on both sides	.10	.02
❑ 563	Terry Kennedy	.10	.02
❑ 564	Ray Knight	.15	.05
❑ 565	Lee Lacy	.10	.02
❑ 566	Fred Lynn	.15	.05
❑ 567	Eddie Murray	.30	.10
❑ 568	Tom Niedenfuer	.10	.02
❑ 569	Bill Ripken RC*	.40	.15
❑ 570	Cal Ripken	1.25	.50
❑ 571	Dave Schmidt	.10	.02
❑ 572	Larry Sheets	.10	.02
❑ 573	Pete Stanicek	.10	.02
❑ 574	Mark Williamson	.10	.02
❑ 575	Mike Young	.10	.02
❑ 576	Shawn Abner	.10	.02
❑ 577	Greg Booker	.10	.02
❑ 578	Chris Brown	.10	.02
❑ 579	Keith Comstock	.10	.02
❑ 580	Joey Cora RC	.40	.15
❑ 581	Mark Davis	.10	.02
❑ 582	Tim Flannery (With surfboard)	.20	.07
❑ 583	Goose Gossage	.15	.05
❑ 584	Mark Grant	.10	.02
❑ 585	Tony Gwynn	.50	.20
❑ 586	Andy Hawkins	.10	.02
❑ 587	Stan Jefferson	.10	.02
❑ 588	Jimmy Jones	.10	.02
❑ 589	John Kruk	.15	.05
❑ 590	Shane Mack	.10	.02
❑ 591	Carmelo Martinez	.10	.02
❑ 592	Lance McCullers UER (6'11" tall)	.10	.02
❑ 593	Eric Nolte	.10	.02
❑ 594	Randy Ready	.10	.02
❑ 595	Luis Salazar	.10	.02
❑ 596	Benito Santiago	.15	.05
❑ 597	Eric Show	.10	.02
❑ 598	Garry Templeton	.15	.05
❑ 599	Ed Whitson	.10	.02
❑ 600	Scott Bailes	.10	.02
❑ 601	Chris Bando	.10	.02
❑ 602	Jay Bell RC	.50	.20
❑ 603	Brett Butler	.15	.05
❑ 604	Tom Candiotti	.10	.02
❑ 605	Joe Carter	.15	.05
❑ 606	Carmen Castillo	.10	.02
❑ 607	Brian Dorsett	.10	.02
❑ 608	John Farrell RC	.15	.05
❑ 609	Julio Franco	.15	.05
❑ 610	Mel Hall	.10	.02
❑ 611	Tommy Hinzo	.10	.02
❑ 612	Brook Jacoby	.10	.02
❑ 613	Doug Jones RC	.40	.15
❑ 614	Ken Schrom	.10	.02
❑ 615	Cory Snyder	.10	.02
❑ 616	Sammy Stewart	.10	.02
❑ 617	Greg Swindell	.10	.02
❑ 618	Pat Tabler	.10	.02
❑ 619	Ed VandeBerg	.10	.02
❑ 620	Eddie Williams RC	.15	.05
❑ 621	Rich Yett	.10	.02
❑ 622	Slugging Sophomores Wally Joyner Cory Snyder	.15	.05
❑ 623	Dominican Dynamite George Bell Pedro Guerrero	.10	.02
❑ 624	M.McGwire/J.Canseco	1.50	.60
❑ 625	Classic Relief Dave Righetti Dan Plesac	.10	.02
❑ 626	All Star Righties Bret Saberhagen Mike Witt Jac	.15	.05
❑ 627	Game Closers John Franco Steve Bedrosian	.10	.02
❑ 628	O.Smith/R.Sandberg	.30	.10
❑ 629	Mark McGwire HL	1.25	.50
❑ 630	Greenwell/Burks/Benz	.30	.10
❑ 631	Tony Gwynn/T.Raines	.20	.07
❑ 632	Pitching Magic Mike Scott Orel Hershiser	.15	.05
❑ 633	M.McGwire/P.Tabler	1.25	.50
❑ 634	Tony Gwynn/V.Coleman	.20	.07
❑ 635	C.Ripken/Trammell/Fern	.50	.20
❑ 636	Mike Schmidt/G.Carter	.30	.10
❑ 637	D.Strawberry/E.Davis	.15	.05
❑ 638	M.Nokes/K.Puckett	.20	.07
❑ 639	NL All-Stars Keith Hernandez Dale Murphy	.15	.05
❑ 640	Ripken Brothers	.75	.30
❑ 641	Mark Grace RC	3.00	1.25
❑ 642	D.Berryhill/J.Montgomery RC	.40	.15
❑ 643	F.Fermin/J.Reid RC	.15	.05
❑ 644	G.Myers/G.Tabor RC	.40	.15
❑ 645	J.Meyer/J.Eppard RC	.15	.05
❑ 646	A.Peterson RC/R.Velarde RC	.40	.15
❑ 647	P.Smith/C.Gwynn RC	.40	.15
❑ 648	T.Newell/G.Jelks RC	.15	.05
❑ 649	M.Diaz/C.Parker RC	.15	.05
❑ 650	J.Savage/T.Simmons RC	.15	.05
❑ 651	John Burkett RC	.40	.15
❑ 652	Walt Weiss RC	.50	.20
❑ 653	Jeff King RC	.40	.15
❑ 654	CL: Twins/Cards Tigers/Giants UER		

Card		
(90 Bob Melvin	.10	.02
❑ 655 CL: Blue Jays/Mets Brewers/Expos UER (Mets liste	.10	.02
❑ 656 CL: Yankees/Reds Royals/A's	.10	.02
❑ 657 CL: Phillies/Pirates Red Sox/Mariners	.10	.02
❑ 658 CL: White Sox/Cubs Astros/Rangers	.10	.02
❑ 659 CL: Angels/Dodgers Braves/Orioles	.10	.02
❑ 660 CL: Padres/Indians Rookies/Specials	.10	.02

1988 Fleer Update

Card		
❑ COMP.FACT.SET (132)	10.00	4.00
❑ 1 Jose Bautista XRC	.25	.08
❑ 2 Joe Orsulak	.10	.02
❑ 3 Doug Sisk	.10	.02
❑ 4 Craig Worthington	.10	.02
❑ 5 Mike Boddicker	.10	.02
❑ 6 Rick Cerone	.10	.02
❑ 7 Larry Parrish	.10	.02
❑ 8 Lee Smith	.20	.07
❑ 9 Mike Smithson	.10	.02
❑ 10 John Trautwein	.10	.02
❑ 11 Sherman Corbett	.10	.02
❑ 12 Chili Davis	.20	.07
❑ 13 Jim Eppard	.10	.02
❑ 14 Bryan Harvey XRC	.50	.20
❑ 15 John Davis	.10	.02
❑ 16 Dave Gallagher	.10	.02
❑ 17 Ricky Horton	.10	.02
❑ 18 Dan Pasqua	.10	.02
❑ 19 Melido Perez	.10	.02
❑ 20 Jose Segura	.10	.02
❑ 21 Andy Allanson	.10	.02
❑ 22 Jon Perlman	.10	.02
❑ 23 Domingo Ramos	.10	.02
❑ 24 Rick Rodriguez	.10	.02
❑ 25 Willie Upshaw	.10	.02
❑ 26 Paul Gibson	.10	.02
❑ 27 Don Heinkel	.10	.02
❑ 28 Ray Knight	.20	.07
❑ 29 Gary Pettis	.10	.02
❑ 30 Luis Salazar	.10	.02
❑ 31 Mike Macfarlane XRC	.50	.20
❑ 32 Jeff Montgomery	.50	.20
❑ 33 Ted Power	.10	.02
❑ 34 Israel Sanchez	.10	.02
❑ 35 Kurt Stillwell	.10	.02
❑ 36 Pat Tabler	.10	.02
❑ 37 Don August	.10	.02
❑ 38 Darryl Hamilton XRC	.50	.20
❑ 39 Jeff Leonard	.10	.02
❑ 40 Joey Meyer	.10	.02
❑ 41 Allan Anderson	.10	.02
❑ 42 Brian Harper	.10	.02
❑ 43 Tom Herr	.10	.02
❑ 44 Charlie Lea	.10	.02
❑ 45 John Moses (Listed as Hohn on checklist card)	.10	.02
❑ 46 John Candelaria	.10	.02
❑ 47 Jack Clark	.20	.07
❑ 48 Richard Dotson	.10	.02
❑ 49 Al Leiter XRC	1.00	.40
❑ 50 Rafael Santana	.10	.02
❑ 51 Don Slaught	.10	.02
❑ 52 Todd Burns	.10	.02
❑ 53 Dave Henderson	.10	.02
❑ 54 Doug Jennings	.10	.02
❑ 55 Dave Parker	.20	.07
❑ 56 Walt Weiss	.75	.30
❑ 57 Bob Welch	.20	.07
❑ 58 Henry Cotto	.10	.02
❑ 59 Mario Diaz UER (Listed as Marion on card front)	.10	.02
❑ 60 Mike Jackson	.20	.07
❑ 61 Bill Swift	.10	.02
❑ 62 Jose Cecena	.10	.02
❑ 63 Ray Hayward	.10	.02
❑ 64 Jim Steels UER (Listed as Jim Steele on card bac)	.10	.02
❑ 65 Pat Borders XRC	.50	.20
❑ 66 Sil Campusano	.10	.02
❑ 67 Mike Flanagan	.10	.02
❑ 68 Todd Stottlemyre XRC	.50	.20
❑ 69 David Wells XRC	1.50	.60
❑ 70 Jose Alvarez XRC	.25	.08
❑ 71 Paul Runge	.10	.02
❑ 72 Cesar Jimenez (Card was intended for German Jimi)	.10	.02
❑ 73 Pete Smith	.10	.02
❑ 74 John Smoltz XRC	4.00	1.50
❑ 75 Damon Berryhill	.25	.08
❑ 76 Goose Gossage	.20	.07
❑ 77 Mark Grace	2.00	.75
❑ 78 Darrin Jackson	.25	.08
❑ 79 Vance Law	.10	.02
❑ 80 Jeff Pico	.10	.02
❑ 81 Gary Varsho	.10	.02
❑ 82 Tim Birtsas	.10	.02
❑ 83 Rob Dibble XRC	.75	.30
❑ 84 Danny Jackson	.10	.02
❑ 85 Paul O'Neill	.30	.10
❑ 86 Jose Rijo	.20	.07
❑ 87 Chris Sabo XRC	.75	.30
❑ 88 John Fishel	.10	.02
❑ 89 Craig Biggio XRC	4.00	1.50
❑ 90 Terry Puhl	.10	.02
❑ 91 Rafael Ramirez	.10	.02
❑ 92 Louie Meadows	.10	.02
❑ 93 Kirk Gibson	.50	.20
❑ 94 Alfredo Griffin	.10	.02
❑ 95 Jay Howell	.10	.02
❑ 96 Jesse Orosco	.10	.02
❑ 97 Alejandro Pena	.10	.02
❑ 98 Tracy Woodson XRC*	.25	.08
❑ 99 John Dopson	.10	.02
❑ 100 Brian Holman XRC	.25	.08
❑ 101 Rex Hudler	.10	.02
❑ 102 Jeff Parrett	.10	.02
❑ 103 Nelson Santovenia	.10	.02
❑ 104 Kevin Elster	.10	.02
❑ 105 Jeff Innis	.10	.02
❑ 106 Mackey Sasser XRC*	.50	.20
❑ 107 Phil Bradley	.10	.02
❑ 108 Danny Clay	.10	.02
❑ 109 Greg Harris	.10	.02
❑ 110 Ricky Jordan XRC	.50	.20
❑ 111 David Palmer	.10	.02
❑ 112 Jim Gott	.10	.02
❑ 113 Tommy Gregg UER (Photo actually Randy Milligan)	.10	.02
❑ 114 Barry Jones	.10	.02
❑ 115 Randy Milligan XRC*	.25	.08
❑ 116 Luis Alicea XRC	.50	.20
❑ 117 Tom Brunansky	.10	.02
❑ 118 John Costello	.10	.02
❑ 119 Jose DeLeon	.10	.02
❑ 120 Bob Horner	.20	.07
❑ 121 Scott Terry	.10	.02
❑ 122 Roberto Alomar XRC	2.00	.75
❑ 123 Dave Leiper	.10	.02
❑ 124 Keith Moreland	.10	.02
❑ 125 Mark Parent	.10	.02
❑ 126 Dennis Rasmussen	.10	.02
❑ 127 Randy Bockus	.10	.02
❑ 128 Brett Butler	.20	.07
❑ 129 Donell Nixon	.10	.02
❑ 130 Earnest Riles	.10	.02
❑ 131 Roger Samuels	.10	.02
❑ 132 Checklist U1-U132	.10	.02

1989 Fleer

Card		
❑ COMPLETE SET (660)	15.00	6.00
❑ COMP.FACT.SET (672)	15.00	6.00
❑ 1 Don Baylor	.10	.02
❑ 2 Lance Blankenship RC	.10	.02
❑ 3 Todd Burns UER	.05	.01
❑ 4 Greg Cadaret UER	.05	.01
❑ 5 Jose Canseco	.25	.08
❑ 6 Storm Davis	.05	.01
❑ 7 Dennis Eckersley	.15	.05
❑ 8 Mike Gallego	.05	.01
❑ 9 Ron Hassey	.05	.01
❑ 10 Dave Henderson	.05	.01
❑ 11 Rick Honeycutt	.05	.01
❑ 12 Glenn Hubbard	.05	.01
❑ 13 Stan Javier	.05	.01
❑ 14 Doug Jennings	.05	.01
❑ 15 Felix Jose RC	.10	.02
❑ 16 Carney Lansford	.10	.02
❑ 17 Mark McGwire	1.00	.40
❑ 18 Gene Nelson	.05	.01
❑ 19 Dave Parker	.10	.02
❑ 20 Eric Plunk	.05	.01
❑ 21 Luis Polonia	.05	.01
❑ 22 Terry Steinbach	.10	.02
❑ 23 Dave Stewart	.10	.02
❑ 24 Walt Weiss	.05	.01
❑ 25 Bob Welch	.10	.02
❑ 26 Curt Young	.05	.01
❑ 27 Rick Aguilera	.05	.01
❑ 28 Wally Backman	.05	.01
❑ 29 Mark Carreon UER	.05	.01
❑ 30 Gary Carter	.10	.02
❑ 31 David Cone	.10	.02
❑ 32 Ron Darling	.10	.02
❑ 33 Len Dykstra	.10	.02
❑ 34 Kevin Elster	.05	.01
❑ 35 Sid Fernandez	.05	.01
❑ 36 Dwight Gooden	.10	.02
❑ 37 Keith Hernandez	.10	.02
❑ 38 Gregg Jefferies	.05	.01
❑ 39 Howard Johnson	.10	.02
❑ 40 Terry Leach	.05	.01
❑ 41 Dave Magadan UER	.05	.01
❑ 42 Bob McClure	.05	.01
❑ 43 Roger McDowell UER	.05	.01
❑ 44 Kevin McReynolds	.05	.01
❑ 45 Keith A. Miller	.05	.01
❑ 46 Randy Myers	.10	.02
❑ 47 Bob Ojeda	.05	.01
❑ 48 Mackey Sasser	.05	.01
❑ 49 Darryl Strawberry	.10	.02
❑ 50 Tim Teufel	.05	.01
❑ 51 Dave West RC	.10	.02
❑ 52 Mookie Wilson	.10	.02
❑ 53 Dave Anderson	.05	.01
❑ 54 Tim Belcher	.05	.01
❑ 55 Mike Davis	.05	.01
❑ 56 Mike Devereaux	.05	.01
❑ 57 Kirk Gibson	.10	.02
❑ 58 Alfredo Griffin	.05	.01
❑ 59 Chris Gwynn	.05	.01

❑ 60 Jeff Hamilton .05 .01
❑ 61A Danny Heep ERR .25 .08
❑ 61B Danny Heep COR .05 .01
❑ 62 Orel Hershiser .10 .02
❑ 63 Brian Holton .05 .01
❑ 64 Jay Howell .05 .01
❑ 65 Tim Leary .05 .01
❑ 66 Mike Marshall .05 .01
❑ 67 Ramon Martinez RC .25 .08
❑ 68 Jesse Orosco .05 .01
❑ 69 Alejandro Pena .05 .01
❑ 70 Steve Sax .05 .01
❑ 71 Mike Scioscia .10 .02
❑ 72 Mike Sharperson .05 .01
❑ 73 John Shelby .05 .01
❑ 74 Franklin Stubbs .05 .01
❑ 75 John Tudor .10 .02
❑ 76 Fernando Valenzuela .10 .02
❑ 77 Tracy Woodson .05 .01
❑ 78 Marty Barrett .05 .01
❑ 79 Todd Benzinger .05 .01
❑ 80 Mike Boddicker UER .05 .01
❑ 81 Wade Boggs .15 .05
❑ 82 Oil Can Boyd .05 .01
❑ 83 Ellis Burks .10 .02
❑ 84 Rick Cerone .05 .01
❑ 85 Roger Clemens 1.00 .40
❑ 86 Steve Curry .05 .01
❑ 87 Dwight Evans .15 .05
❑ 88 Wes Gardner .05 .01
❑ 89 Rich Gedman .05 .01
❑ 90 Mike Greenwell .05 .01
❑ 91 Bruce Hurst .05 .01
❑ 92 Dennis Lamp .05 .01
❑ 93 Spike Owen .05 .01
❑ 94 Larry Parrish UER .05 .01
❑ 95 Carlos Quintana RC .10 .02
❑ 96 Jody Reed .05 .01
❑ 97 Jim Rice .10 .02
❑ 98A Kevin Romine ERR .25 .08
❑ 98B Kevin Romine COR .05 .01
❑ 99 Lee Smith .10 .02
❑ 100 Mike Smithson .05 .01
❑ 101 Bob Stanley .05 .01
❑ 102 Allan Anderson .05 .01
❑ 103 Keith Atherton .05 .01
❑ 104 Juan Berenguer .05 .01
❑ 105 Bert Blyleven .10 .02
❑ 106 Eric Bullock UER .05 .01
❑ 107 Randy Bush .05 .01
❑ 108 John Christensen .05 .01
❑ 109 Mark Davidson .05 .01
❑ 110 Gary Gaetti .10 .02
❑ 111 Grog Gagne .05 .01
❑ 112 Dan Gladden .05 .01
❑ 113 German Gonzalez .05 .01
❑ 114 Brian Harper .05 .01
❑ 115 Tom Herr .05 .01
❑ 116 Kent Hrbek .10 .02
❑ 117 Gene Larkin .05 .01
❑ 118 Tim Laudner .05 .01
❑ 119 Charlie Lea .05 .01
❑ 120 Steve Lombardozzi .05 .01
❑ 121A John Moses ERR .25 .08
❑ 121B John Moses COR .05 .01
❑ 122 Al Newman .05 .01
❑ 123 Mark Portugal .05 .01
❑ 124 Kirby Puckett .25 .08
❑ 125 Jeff Reardon .10 .02
❑ 126 Fred Toliver .05 .01
❑ 127 Frank Viola .10 .02
❑ 128 Doyle Alexander .05 .01
❑ 129 Dave Bergman .05 .01
❑ 130A Tom Brookens ERR .75 .30
❑ 130B Tom Brookens COR .05 .01
❑ 131 Paul Gibson .05 .01
❑ 132A Mike Heath ERR .75 .30
❑ 132B Mike Heath COR .05 .01
❑ 133 Don Heinkel .05 .01
❑ 134 Mike Henneman .05 .01
❑ 135 Guillermo Hernandez .05 .01
❑ 136 Eric King .05 .01
❑ 137 Chet Lemon .10 .02
❑ 138 Fred Lynn UER .10 .02
❑ 139 Jack Morris .10 .02
❑ 140 Matt Nokes .05 .01
❑ 141 Gary Pettis .05 .01
❑ 142 Ted Power .05 .01
❑ 143 Jeff M. Robinson .05 .01
❑ 144 Luis Salazar .05 .01
❑ 145 Steve Searcy .05 .01
❑ 146 Pat Sheridan .05 .01
❑ 147 Frank Tanana .10 .02
❑ 148 Alan Trammell .10 .02
❑ 149 Walt Terrell .05 .01
❑ 150 Jim Walewander .05 .01
❑ 151 Lou Whitaker .10 .02
❑ 152 Tim Birtsas .05 .01
❑ 153 Tom Browning .05 .01
❑ 154 Keith Brown .05 .01
❑ 155 Norm Charlton RC .25 .08
❑ 156 Dave Concepcion .10 .02
❑ 157 Kal Daniels .05 .01
❑ 158 Eric Davis .10 .02
❑ 159 Bo Diaz .05 .01
❑ 160 Rob Dibble RC .40 .15
❑ 161 Nick Esasky .05 .01
❑ 162 John Franco .10 .02
❑ 163 Danny Jackson .05 .01
❑ 164 Barry Larkin .15 .05
❑ 165 Rob Murphy .05 .01
❑ 166 Paul O'Neill .15 .05
❑ 167 Jeff Reed .05 .01
❑ 168 Jose Rijo .10 .02
❑ 169 Ron Robinson .05 .01
❑ 170 Chris Sabo RC .40 .15
❑ 171 Candy Sierra .05 .01
❑ 172 Van Snider .05 .01
❑ 173A J.Treadway ERR Target 25.00 10.00
❑ 173B Jeff Treadway No Target .05 .01
❑ 174 Frank Williams UER .05 .01
❑ 175 Herm Winningham .05 .01
❑ 176 Jim Adduci .05 .01
❑ 177 Don August .05 .01
❑ 178 Mike Birkbeck .05 .01
❑ 179 Chris Bosio .05 .01
❑ 180 Glenn Braggs .05 .01
❑ 181 Greg Brock .05 .01
❑ 182 Mark Clear .05 .01
❑ 183 Chuck Crim .05 .01
❑ 184 Rob Deer .05 .01
❑ 185 Tom Filer .05 .01
❑ 186 Jim Gantner .05 .01
❑ 187 Darryl Hamilton RC .25 .08
❑ 188 Ted Higuera .05 .01
❑ 189 Odell Jones .05 .01
❑ 190 Jeffrey Leonard .05 .01
❑ 191 Joey Meyer .05 .01
❑ 192 Paul Mirabella .05 .01
❑ 193 Paul Molitor .10 .02
❑ 194 Charlie O'Brien .05 .01
❑ 195 Dan Plesac .05 .01
❑ 196 Gary Sheffield RC 1.50 .60
❑ 197 B.J. Surhoff .10 .02
❑ 198 Dale Sveum .05 .01
❑ 199 Bill Wegman .05 .01
❑ 200 Robin Yount .40 .15
❑ 201 Rafael Belliard .05 .01
❑ 202 Barry Bonds 1.50 .60
❑ 203 Bobby Bonilla .10 .02
❑ 204 Sid Bream .05 .01
❑ 205 Benny Distefano .05 .01
❑ 206 Doug Drabek .05 .01
❑ 207 Mike Dunne .05 .01
❑ 208 Felix Fermin .05 .01
❑ 209 Brian Fisher .05 .01
❑ 210 Jim Gott .05 .01
❑ 211 Bob Kipper .05 .01
❑ 212 Dave LaPoint .05 .01
❑ 213 Mike LaValliere .05 .01
❑ 214 Jose Lind .05 .01
❑ 215 Junior Ortiz .05 .01
❑ 216 Vicente Palacios .05 .01
❑ 217 Tom Prince .05 .01
❑ 218 Gary Redus .05 .01
❑ 219 R.J. Reynolds .05 .01
❑ 220 Jeff D. Robinson .05 .01
❑ 221 John Smiley .05 .01
❑ 222 Andy Van Slyke .15 .05
❑ 223 Bob Walk .05 .01
❑ 224 Glenn Wilson .05 .01
❑ 225 Jesse Barfield .10 .02
❑ 226 George Bell .10 .02
❑ 227 Pat Borders RC .25 .08
❑ 228 John Cerutti .05 .01
❑ 229 Jim Clancy .05 .01
❑ 230 Mark Eichhorn .05 .01
❑ 231 Tony Fernandez .05 .01
❑ 232 Cecil Fielder .10 .02
❑ 233 Mike Flanagan .05 .01
❑ 234 Kelly Gruber .05 .01
❑ 235 Tom Henke .05 .01
❑ 236 Jimmy Key .10 .02
❑ 237 Rick Leach .05 .01
❑ 238 Manny Lee UER .05 .01
❑ 239 Nelson Liriano .05 .01
❑ 240 Fred McGriff .15 .05
❑ 241 Lloyd Moseby .05 .01
❑ 242 Rance Mulliniks .05 .01
❑ 243 Jeff Musselman .05 .01
❑ 244 Dave Stieb .10 .02
❑ 245 Todd Stottlemyre .05 .01
❑ 246 Duane Ward .05 .01
❑ 247 David Wells .10 .02
❑ 248 Ernie Whitt UER .05 .01
❑ 249 Luis Aguayo .05 .01
❑ 250A Neil Allen ERR .75 .30
❑ 250B Neil Allen COR .05 .01
❑ 251 John Candelaria .05 .01
❑ 252 Jack Clark .10 .02
❑ 253 Richard Dotson .05 .01
❑ 254 Rickey Henderson .25 .08
❑ 255 Tommy John .10 .02
❑ 256 Roberto Kelly .05 .01
❑ 257 Al Leiter .25 .08
❑ 258 Don Mattingly .60 .25
❑ 259 Dale Mohorcic .05 .01
❑ 260 Hal Morris RC .25 .08
❑ 261 Scott Nielsen .05 .01
❑ 262 Mike Pagliarulo UER .05 .01
❑ 263 Hipolito Pena .05 .01
❑ 264 Ken Phelps .05 .01
❑ 265 Willie Randolph .10 .02
❑ 266 Rick Rhoden .05 .01
❑ 267 Dave Righetti .10 .02
❑ 268 Rafael Santana .05 .01
❑ 269 Steve Shields .05 .01
❑ 270 Joel Skinner .05 .01
❑ 271 Don Slaught .05 .01
❑ 272 Claudell Washington .05 .01
❑ 273 Gary Ward .05 .01
❑ 274 Dave Winfield .10 .02
❑ 275 Luis Aquino .05 .01
❑ 276 Floyd Bannister .05 .01
❑ 277 George Brett .60 .25
❑ 278 Bill Buckner .10 .02
❑ 279 Nick Capra .05 .01
❑ 280 Jose DeJesus .05 .01
❑ 281 Steve Farr .05 .01
❑ 282 Jerry Don Gleaton .05 .01
❑ 283 Mark Gubicza .05 .01
❑ 284 Tom Gordon RC .50 .20
❑ 285 Bo Jackson .25 .08
❑ 286 Charlie Leibrandt .05 .01
❑ 287 Mike Macfarlane RC .25 .08
❑ 288 Jeff Montgomery .05 .01
❑ 289 Bill Pecota UER .05 .01
❑ 290 Jamie Quirk .05 .01
❑ 291 Bret Saberhagen .10 .02
❑ 292 Kevin Seitzer .05 .01
❑ 293 Kurt Stillwell .05 .01
❑ 294 Pat Tabler .05 .01
❑ 295 Danny Tartabull .05 .01
❑ 296 Gary Thurman .05 .01
❑ 297 Frank White .10 .02
❑ 298 Willie Wilson .10 .02
❑ 299 Roberto Alomar .25 .08
❑ 300 Sandy Alomar Jr. RC .40 .15
❑ 301 Chris Brown .05 .01
❑ 302 Mike Brumley UER .05 .01
❑ 303 Mark Davis .05 .01
❑ 304 Mark Grant .05 .01
❑ 305 Tony Gwynn .30 .10
❑ 306 Greg W.Harris RC .10 .02
❑ 307 Andy Hawkins .05 .01
❑ 308 Jimmy Jones .05 .01
❑ 309 John Kruk .10 .02
❑ 310 Dave Leiper .05 .01

Card	Player	Price	Price
❑ 311	Carmelo Martinez	.05	.01
❑ 312	Lance McCullers	.05	.01
❑ 313	Keith Moreland	.05	.01
❑ 314	Dennis Rasmussen	.05	.01
❑ 315	Randy Ready UER	.05	.01
❑ 316	Benito Santiago	.10	.02
❑ 317	Eric Show	.05	.01
❑ 318	Todd Simmons	.05	.01
❑ 319	Garry Templeton	.10	.02
❑ 320	Dickie Thon	.05	.01
❑ 321	Ed Whitson	.05	.01
❑ 322	Marvell Wynne	.05	.01
❑ 323	Mike Aldrete	.05	.01
❑ 324	Brett Butler	.10	.02
❑ 325	Will Clark	.15	.05
❑ 326	Kelly Downs UER	.05	.01
❑ 327	Dave Dravecky	.05	.01
❑ 328	Scott Garrelts	.05	.01
❑ 329	Atlee Hammaker	.05	.01
❑ 330	Charlie Hayes RC	.25	.08
❑ 331	Mike Krukow	.05	.01
❑ 332	Craig Lefferts	.05	.01
❑ 333	Candy Maldonado	.05	.01
❑ 334	Kirt Manwaring UER	.05	.01
❑ 335	Bob Melvin	.05	.01
❑ 336	Kevin Mitchell	.10	.02
❑ 337	Donell Nixon	.05	.01
❑ 338	Tony Perezchica	.05	.01
❑ 339	Joe Price	.05	.01
❑ 340	Rick Reuschel	.10	.02
❑ 341	Earnest Riles	.05	.01
❑ 342	Don Robinson	.05	.01
❑ 343	Chris Speier	.05	.01
❑ 344	Robby Thompson UER	.05	.01
❑ 345	Jose Uribe	.05	.01
❑ 346	Matt Williams	.25	.08
❑ 347	Trevor Wilson RC	.10	.02
❑ 348	Juan Agosto	.05	.01
❑ 349	Larry Andersen	.05	.01
❑ 350A	Alan Ashby ERR	2.00	.75
❑ 350B	Alan Ashby COR	.05	.01
❑ 351	Kevin Bass	.05	.01
❑ 352	Buddy Bell	.10	.02
❑ 353	Craig Biggio RC	1.50	.60
❑ 354	Danny Darwin	.05	.01
❑ 355	Glenn Davis	.05	.01
❑ 356	Jim Deshaies	.05	.01
❑ 357	Bill Doran	.05	.01
❑ 358	John Fishel	.05	.01
❑ 359	Billy Hatcher	.05	.01
❑ 360	Bob Knepper	.05	.01
❑ 361	Louie Meadows UER	.05	.01
❑ 362	Dave Meads	.05	.01
❑ 363	Jim Pankovits	.05	.01
❑ 364	Terry Puhl	.05	.01
❑ 365	Rafael Ramirez	.05	.01
❑ 366	Craig Reynolds	.05	.01
❑ 367	Mike Scott	.10	.02
❑ 368	Nolan Ryan	1.00	.40
❑ 369	Dave Smith	.05	.01
❑ 370	Gerald Young	.05	.01
❑ 371	Hubie Brooks	.05	.01
❑ 372	Tim Burke	.05	.01
❑ 373	John Dopson	.05	.01
❑ 374	Mike R. Fitzgerald	.05	.01
❑ 375	Tom Foley	.05	.01
❑ 376	Andres Galarraga UER	.10	.02
❑ 377	Neal Heaton	.05	.01
❑ 378	Joe Hesketh	.05	.01
❑ 379	Brian Holman RC	.10	.02
❑ 380	Rex Hudler	.05	.01
❑ 381	Randy Johnson RC	2.50	1.00
❑ 381B	R.Johnson Marlboro ERR	25.00	10.00
❑ 382	Wallace Johnson	.05	.01
❑ 383	Tracy Jones	.05	.01
❑ 384	Dave Martinez	.05	.01
❑ 385	Dennis Martinez	.10	.02
❑ 386	Andy McGaffigan	.05	.01
❑ 387	Otis Nixon	.05	.01
❑ 388	Johnny Paredes	.05	.01
❑ 389	Jeff Parrett	.05	.01
❑ 390	Pascual Perez	.05	.01
❑ 391	Tim Raines	.10	.02
❑ 392	Luis Rivera	.05	.01
❑ 393	Nelson Santovenia	.05	.01
❑ 394	Bryn Smith	.05	.01
❑ 395	Tim Wallach	.05	.01
❑ 396	Andy Allanson UER	.05	.01
❑ 397	Rod Allen	.05	.01
❑ 398	Scott Bailes	.05	.01
❑ 399	Tom Candiotti	.05	.01
❑ 400	Joe Carter	.10	.02
❑ 401	Carmen Castillo UER	.05	.01
❑ 402	Dave Clark UER#	.05	.01
❑ 403	John Farrell UER	.05	.01
❑ 404	Julio Franco	.10	.02
❑ 405	Don Gordon	.05	.01
❑ 406	Mel Hall	.05	.01
❑ 407	Brad Havens	.05	.01
❑ 408	Brook Jacoby	.05	.01
❑ 409	Doug Jones	.05	.01
❑ 410	Jeff Kaiser	.05	.01
❑ 411	Luis Medina	.05	.01
❑ 412	Cory Snyder	.05	.01
❑ 413	Greg Swindell	.05	.01
❑ 414	Ron Tingley UER	.05	.01
❑ 415	Willie Upshaw	.05	.01
❑ 416	Ron Washington	.05	.01
❑ 417	Rich Yett	.05	.01
❑ 418	Damon Berryhill	.05	.01
❑ 419	Mike Bielecki	.05	.01
❑ 420	Doug Dascenzo	.05	.01
❑ 421	Jody Davis UER	.05	.01
❑ 422	Andre Dawson	.10	.02
❑ 423	Frank DiPino	.05	.01
❑ 424	Shawon Dunston	.05	.01
❑ 425	Rich Gossage	.10	.02
❑ 426	Mark Grace	.25	.08
❑ 427	Mike Harkey RC	.10	.02
❑ 428	Darrin Jackson	.10	.02
❑ 429	Les Lancaster	.05	.01
❑ 430	Vance Law	.05	.01
❑ 431	Greg Maddux	.50	.20
❑ 432	Jamie Moyer	.10	.02
❑ 433	Al Nipper	.05	.01
❑ 434	Rafael Palmeiro	.25	.08
❑ 435	Pat Perry	.05	.01
❑ 436	Jeff Pico	.05	.01
❑ 437	Ryne Sandberg	.40	.15
❑ 438	Calvin Schiraldi	.05	.01
❑ 439	Rick Sutcliffe	.10	.02
❑ 440A	Manny Trillo ERR	2.00	.75
❑ 440B	Manny Trillo COR	.05	.01
❑ 441	Gary Varsho UER	.05	.01
❑ 442	Mitch Webster	.05	.01
❑ 443	Luis Alicea RC	.25	.08
❑ 444	Tom Brunansky	.05	.01
❑ 445	Vince Coleman UER	.05	.01
❑ 446	John Costello UER	.05	.01
❑ 447	Danny Cox	.05	.01
❑ 448	Ken Dayley	.05	.01
❑ 449	Jose DeLeon	.05	.01
❑ 450	Curt Ford	.05	.01
❑ 451	Pedro Guerrero	.10	.02
❑ 452	Bob Horner	.10	.02
❑ 453	Tim Jones	.05	.01
❑ 454	Steve Lake	.05	.01
❑ 455	Joe Magrane UER	.05	.01
❑ 456	Greg Mathews	.05	.01
❑ 457	Willie McGee	.10	.02
❑ 458	Larry McWilliams	.05	.01
❑ 459	Jose Oquendo	.05	.01
❑ 460	Tony Pena	.05	.01
❑ 461	Terry Pendleton	.10	.02
❑ 462	Steve Peters UER	.05	.01
❑ 463	Ozzie Smith	.40	.15
❑ 464	Scott Terry	.05	.01
❑ 465	Denny Walling	.05	.01
❑ 466	Todd Worrell	.05	.01
❑ 467	Tony Armas UER	.10	.02
❑ 468	Dante Bichette RC	.40	.15
❑ 469	Bob Boone	.10	.02
❑ 470	Terry Clark	.05	.01
❑ 471	Stu Cliburn	.05	.01
❑ 472	Mike Cook UER	.05	.01
❑ 473	Sherman Corbett	.05	.01
❑ 474	Chili Davis	.10	.02
❑ 475	Brian Downing	.10	.02
❑ 476	Jim Eppard	.05	.01
❑ 477	Chuck Finley	.10	.02
❑ 478	Willie Fraser	.05	.01
❑ 479	Bryan Harvey UER RC	.25	.08
❑ 480	Jack Howell	.05	.01
❑ 481	Wally Joyner UER	.10	.02
❑ 482	Jack Lazorko	.05	.01
❑ 483	Kirk McCaskill	.05	.01
❑ 484	Mark McLemore	.05	.01
❑ 485	Greg Minton	.05	.01
❑ 486	Dan Petry	.05	.01
❑ 487	Johnny Ray	.05	.01
❑ 488	Dick Schofield	.05	.01
❑ 489	Devon White	.10	.02
❑ 490	Mike Witt	.05	.01
❑ 491	Harold Baines	.10	.02
❑ 492	Daryl Boston	.05	.01
❑ 493	Ivan Calderon UER	.05	.01
❑ 494	Mike Diaz	.05	.01
❑ 495	Carlton Fisk	.15	.05
❑ 496	Dave Gallagher	.05	.01
❑ 497	Ozzie Guillen	.10	.02
❑ 498	Shawn Hillegas	.05	.01
❑ 499	Lance Johnson	.05	.01
❑ 500	Barry Jones	.05	.01
❑ 501	Bill Long	.05	.01
❑ 502	Steve Lyons	.05	.01
❑ 503	Fred Manrique	.05	.01
❑ 504	Jack McDowell	.10	.02
❑ 505	Donn Pall	.05	.01
❑ 506	Kelly Paris	.05	.01
❑ 507	Dan Pasqua	.05	.01
❑ 508	Ken Patterson	.05	.01
❑ 509	Melido Perez	.05	.01
❑ 510	Jerry Reuss	.05	.01
❑ 511	Mark Salas	.05	.01
❑ 512	Bobby Thigpen UER	.05	.01
❑ 513	Mike Woodard	.05	.01
❑ 514	Bob Brower	.05	.01
❑ 515	Steve Buechele	.05	.01
❑ 516	Jose Cecena	.05	.01
❑ 517	Cecil Espy	.05	.01
❑ 518	Scott Fletcher	.05	.01
❑ 519	Cecilio Guante	.05	.01
❑ 520	Jose Guzman	.05	.01
❑ 521	Ray Hayward	.05	.01
❑ 522	Charlie Hough	.10	.02
❑ 523	Pete Incaviglia	.05	.01
❑ 524	Mike Jeffcoat	.05	.01
❑ 525	Paul Kilgus	.05	.01
❑ 526	Chad Kreuter RC	.25	.08
❑ 527	Jeff Kunkel	.05	.01
❑ 528	Oddibe McDowell	.05	.01
❑ 529	Pete O'Brien	.05	.01
❑ 530	Geno Petralli	.05	.01
❑ 531	Jeff Russell	.05	.01
❑ 532	Ruben Sierra	.10	.02
❑ 533	Mike Stanley	.05	.01
❑ 534A	Ed VandeBerg ERR	2.00	.75
❑ 534B	Ed VandeBerg COR	.05	.01
❑ 535	Curtis Wilkerson ERR	.05	.01
❑ 536	Mitch Williams	.05	.01
❑ 537	Bobby Witt UER	.05	.01
❑ 538	Steve Balboni	.05	.01
❑ 539	Scott Bankhead	.05	.01
❑ 540	Scott Bradley	.05	.01
❑ 541	Mickey Brantley	.05	.01
❑ 542	Jay Buhner	.10	.02
❑ 543	Mike Campbell	.05	.01
❑ 544	Darnell Coles	.05	.01
❑ 545	Henry Cotto	.05	.01
❑ 546	Alvin Davis	.05	.01
❑ 547	Mario Diaz	.05	.01
❑ 548	Ken Griffey Jr. RC	8.00	3.00
❑ 549	Erik Hanson RC	.25	.08
❑ 550	Mike Jackson UER	.05	.01
❑ 551	Mark Langston	.05	.01
❑ 552	Edgar Martinez	.25	.08
❑ 553	Bill McGuire	.05	.01
❑ 554	Mike Moore	.05	.01
❑ 555	Jim Presley	.05	.01
❑ 556	Rey Quinones	.05	.01
❑ 557	Jerry Reed	.05	.01
❑ 558	Harold Reynolds	.10	.02
❑ 559	Mike Schooler	.05	.01
❑ 560	Bill Swift	.05	.01
❑ 561	Dave Valle	.05	.01
❑ 562	Steve Bedrosian	.05	.01
❑ 563	Phil Bradley	.05	.01
❑ 564	Don Carman	.05	.01

❑ 565 Bob Dernier .05 .01
❑ 566 Marvin Freeman .05 .01
❑ 567 Todd Frohwirth .05 .01
❑ 568 Greg Gross .05 .01
❑ 569 Kevin Gross .05 .01
❑ 570 Greg A. Harris .05 .01
❑ 571 Von Hayes .05 .01
❑ 572 Chris James .05 .01
❑ 573 Steve Jeltz .05 .01
❑ 574 Ron Jones UER .10 .02
❑ 575 Ricky Jordan RC .25 .08
❑ 576 Mike Maddux .05 .01
❑ 577 David Palmer .05 .01
❑ 578 Lance Parrish .10 .02
❑ 579 Shane Rawley .05 .01
❑ 580 Bruce Ruffin .05 .01
❑ 581 Juan Samuel .05 .01
❑ 582 Mike Schmidt .50 .20
❑ 583 Kent Tekulve .05 .01
❑ 584 Milt Thompson UER .05 .01
❑ 585 Jose Alvarez RC .10 .02
❑ 586 Paul Assenmacher .05 .01
❑ 587 Bruce Benedict .05 .01
❑ 588 Jeff Blauser .05 .01
❑ 589 Terry Blocker .05 .01
❑ 590 Ron Gant .10 .02
❑ 591 Tom Glavine .25 .08
❑ 592 Tommy Gregg .05 .01
❑ 593 Albert Hall .05 .01
❑ 594 Dion James .05 .01
❑ 595 Rick Mahler .05 .01
❑ 596 Dale Murphy .15 .05
❑ 597 Gerald Perry .05 .01
❑ 598 Charlie Puleo .05 .01
❑ 599 Ted Simmons .10 .02
❑ 600 Pete Smith .05 .01
❑ 601 Zane Smith .05 .01
❑ 602 John Smoltz RC 1.50 .60
❑ 603 Bruce Sutter .10 .02
❑ 604 Andres Thomas .05 .01
❑ 605 Ozzie Virgil .05 .01
❑ 606 Brady Anderson RC .40 .15
❑ 607 Jeff Ballard .05 .01
❑ 608 Jose Bautista RC .10 .02
❑ 609 Ken Gerhart .05 .01
❑ 610 Terry Kennedy .05 .01
❑ 611 Eddie Murray .25 .08
❑ 612 Carl Nichols UER .05 .01
❑ 613 Tom Niedenfuer .05 .01
❑ 614 Joe Orsulak .05 .01
❑ 615 Oswald Peraza UER .05 .01
❑ 616A Bill Ripken Rick Face 15.00 6.00
❑ 616B Bill Ripken Whiteout 120.00 60.00
❑ 616C Bill Ripken White Scribble 25.00 10.00
❑ 616D Bill Ripken Black Scribble 15.00 6.00
❑ 616E Bill Ripken Black Box 5.00 2.00
❑ 617 Cal Ripken .75 .30
❑ 618 Dave Schmidt .05 .01
❑ 619 Rick Schu .05 .01
❑ 620 Larry Sheets .05 .01
❑ 621 Doug Sisk .05 .01
❑ 622 Pete Stanicek .05 .01
❑ 623 Mickey Tettleton .05 .01
❑ 624 Jay Tibbs .05 .01
❑ 625 Jim Traber .05 .01
❑ 626 Mark Williamson .05 .01
❑ 627 Craig Worthington .05 .01
❑ 628 Jose Canseco 40/40 .25 .08
❑ 629 Tom Browning Perfect .05 .01
❑ 630 R.Alomar/S.Alomar .25 .08
❑ 631 W.Clark/R.Palmeiro .15 .05
❑ 632 D.Strawberry/W.Clark .10 .02
❑ 633 W.Boggs/C.Lansford .10 .02
❑ 634 McGwire/Cans/Stein .75 .30
❑ 635 M.Davis/D.Gooden .05 .01
❑ 636 D.Jackson/D.Cone UER .05 .01
❑ 637 C.Sabo/B.Bonilla UER .10 .02
❑ 638 A.Galarraga/G.Perry UER .05 .01
❑ 639 K.Puckett/E.Davis .15 .05
❑ 640 S.Wilson/C.Drew .05 .01
❑ 641 K.Brown/K.Reimer .25 .08
❑ 642 B.Pounders RC/J.Clark .10 .02
❑ 643 M.Capel/D.Hall .05 .01
❑ 644 J.Girardi RC/R.Roomes .40 .15
❑ 645 L.Harris RC/M.Brown .25 .08
❑ 646 L.De Los Santos/J.Campbell .05 .01
❑ 647 R.Kramer/M.Garcia .05 .01
❑ 648 T.Lovullo RC/R.Palacios .10 .02
❑ 649 J.Corsi/B.Milacki .05 .01
❑ 650 G.Hall/M.Rochford .05 .01
❑ 651 T.Taylor/V.Lovelace RC .10 .02
❑ 652 K.Hill RC/D.Cook .25 .08
❑ 653 S.Service/S.Turner .05 .01
❑ 654 CL: Oakland/Mets
Dodgers/Red Sox
(10 Henderson;#) .05 .01
❑ 655A CL: Twins/Tigers ERR
Reds/Brewers
(179 Boslo and) .05 .01
❑ 655B CL: Twins/Tigers COR
Reds/Brewers
(179 Boslo but) .05 .01
❑ 656 CL: Pirates/Blue Jays
Yankees/Royals
(225 Jess B) .05 .01
❑ 657 CL: Padres/Giants
Astros/Expos
(367/368 wrong) .05 .01
❑ 658 CL: Indians/Cubs
Cardinals/Angels
(449 Deleon) .05 .01
❑ 659 CL: White Sox/Rangers
Mariners/Phillies .05 .01
❑ 660 CL: Braves/Orioles
Specials/Checklists
(632 hyph) .05 .01

1989 Fleer Update

❑ COMP.FACT.SET (132) 5.00 2.00
❑ 1 Phil Bradley .05 .01
❑ 2 Mike Devereaux .05 .01
❑ 3 Steve Finley RC .75 .30
❑ 4 Kevin Hickey .05 .01
❑ 5 Brian Holton .05 .01
❑ 6 Bob Milacki .05 .01
❑ 7 Randy Milligan .05 .01
❑ 8 John Dopson .05 .01
❑ 9 Nick Esasky .05 .01
❑ 10 Rob Murphy .05 .01
❑ 11 Jim Abbott RC 1.00 .40
❑ 12 Bert Blyleven .10 .02
❑ 13 Jeff Manto RC .10 .02
❑ 14 Bob McClure .05 .01
❑ 15 Lance Parrish .10 .02
❑ 16 Lee Stevens RC .25 .08
❑ 17 Claudell Washington .05 .01
❑ 18 Mark Davis RC .25 .08
❑ 19 Eric King .05 .01
❑ 20 Ron Kittle .05 .01
❑ 21 Matt Merullo .05 .01
❑ 22 Steve Rosenberg .05 .01
❑ 23 Robin Ventura RC .75 .30
❑ 24 Keith Atherton .05 .01
❑ 25 Albert Belle RC 1.00 .40
❑ 26 Jerry Browne .05 .01
❑ 27 Felix Fermin .05 .01
❑ 28 Brad Komminsk .05 .01
❑ 29 Pete O'Brien .05 .01
❑ 30 Mike Brumley .05 .01
❑ 31 Tracy Jones .05 .01
❑ 32 Mike Schwabe .05 .01
❑ 33 Gary Ward .05 .01
❑ 34 Frank Williams .05 .01
❑ 35 Kevin Appier RC .50 .20
❑ 36 Bob Boone .10 .02
❑ 37 Luis DeLosSantos .05 .01
❑ 38 Jim Eisenreich .05 .01
❑ 39 Jaime Navarro RC .10 .02
❑ 40 Billy Spiers RC .25 .08
❑ 41 Greg Vaughn RC .40 .15
❑ 42 Randy Veres .05 .01
❑ 43 Wally Backman .05 .01
❑ 44 Shane Rawley .05 .01
❑ 45 Steve Balboni .05 .01
❑ 46 Jesse Barfield .10 .02
❑ 47 Alvaro Espinoza .05 .01
❑ 48 Bob Geren RC .05 .01
❑ 49 Mel Hall .05 .01
❑ 50 Andy Hawkins .05 .01
❑ 51 Hensley Meulens RC .10 .02
❑ 52 Steve Sax .05 .01
❑ 53 Deion Sanders RC 1.50 .60
❑ 54 Rickey Henderson .25 .08
❑ 55 Mike Moore .05 .01
❑ 56 Tony Phillips .05 .01
❑ 57 Greg Briley .10 .02
❑ 58 Gene Harris RC .10 .02
❑ 59 Randy Johnson 2.50 1.00
❑ 60 Jeffrey Leonard .05 .01
❑ 61 Dennis Powell .05 .01
❑ 62 Omar Vizquel RC 1.00 .40
❑ 63 Kevin Brown .25 .08
❑ 64 Julio Franco .10 .02
❑ 65 Jamie Moyer .10 .02
❑ 66 Rafael Palmeiro .25 .08
❑ 67 Nolan Ryan 1.50 .60
❑ 68 Francisco Cabrera RC .10 .02
❑ 69 Junior Felix RC .10 .02
❑ 70 Al Leiter .25 .08
❑ 71 Alex Sanchez RC .05 .01
❑ 72 Geronimo Berroa .05 .01
❑ 73 Derek Lilliquist RC .10 .02
❑ 74 Lonnie Smith .05 .01
❑ 75 Jeff Treadway .05 .01
❑ 76 Paul Kilgus .05 .01
❑ 77 Lloyd McClendon .05 .01
❑ 78 Scott Sanderson .05 .01
❑ 79 Dwight Smith RC .25 .08
❑ 80 Jerome Walton RC .25 .08
❑ 81 Mitch Williams .05 .01
❑ 82 Steve Wilson .10 .02
❑ 83 Todd Benzinger .05 .01
❑ 84 Ken Griffey Sr. .10 .02
❑ 85 Rick Mahler .05 .01
❑ 86 Rolando Roomes .05 .01
❑ 87 Scott Scudder RC .10 .02
❑ 88 Jim Clancy .05 .01
❑ 89 Rick Rhoden .05 .01
❑ 90 Dan Schatzeder .05 .01
❑ 91 Mike Morgan .05 .01
❑ 92 Eddie Murray .25 .08
❑ 93 Willie Randolph .10 .02
❑ 94 Ray Searage .05 .01
❑ 95 Mike Aldrete .05 .01
❑ 96 Kevin Gross .05 .01
❑ 97 Mark Langston .05 .01
❑ 98 Spike Owen .05 .01
❑ 99 Zane Smith .05 .01
❑ 100 Don Aase .05 .01
❑ 101 Barry Lyons .05 .01
❑ 102 Juan Samuel .05 .01
❑ 103 Wally Whitehurst RC .10 .02
❑ 104 Dennis Cook .05 .01
❑ 105 Len Dykstra .10 .02
❑ 106 Charlie Hayes .25 .08
❑ 107 Tommy Herr .05 .01
❑ 108 Ken Howell .05 .01
❑ 109 John Kruk .10 .02
❑ 110 Roger McDowell .05 .01
❑ 111 Terry Mulholland .05 .01
❑ 112 Jeff Parrett .05 .01
❑ 113 Neal Heaton .05 .01
❑ 114 Jeff King .05 .01
❑ 115 Randy Kramer .05 .01
❑ 116 Bill Landrum .05 .01
❑ 117 Cris Carpenter RC * .10 .02
❑ 118 Frank DiPino .05 .01
❑ 119 Ken Hill .25 .08
❑ 120 Dan Quisenberry .05 .01
❑ 121 Milt Thompson .05 .01

❑ 122 Todd Zeile RC .40 .15
❑ 123 Jack Clark .10 .02
❑ 124 Bruce Hurst .05 .01
❑ 125 Mark Parent .05 .01
❑ 126 Bip Roberts .05 .01
❑ 127 Jeff Brantley UER RC .25 .08
❑ 128 Terry Kennedy .05 .01
❑ 129 Mike LaCoss .05 .01
❑ 130 Greg Litton .05 .01
❑ 131 Mike Schmidt SPEC .75 .30
❑ 132 Checklist 1-132 .05 .01

1990 Fleer

❑ COMPLETE SET (660) 15.00 6.00
❑ COMP.RETAIL SET (660) 15.00 6.00
❑ COMP.HOBBY SET (672) 15.00 6.00
❑ 1 Lance Blankenship .05 .01
❑ 2 Todd Burns .05 .01
❑ 3 Jose Canseco .15 .05
❑ 4 Jim Corsi .05 .01
❑ 5 Storm Davis .05 .01
❑ 6 Dennis Eckersley .10 .02
❑ 7 Mike Gallego .05 .01
❑ 8 Ron Hassey .05 .01
❑ 9 Dave Henderson .05 .01
❑ 10 Rickey Henderson .25 .08
❑ 11 Rick Honeycutt .05 .01
❑ 12 Stan Javier .05 .01
❑ 13 Felix Jose .05 .01
❑ 14 Carney Lansford .10 .02
❑ 15 Mark McGwire 1.00 .40
❑ 16 Mike Moore .05 .01
❑ 17 Gene Nelson .05 .01
❑ 18 Dave Parker .10 .02
❑ 19 Tony Phillips .05 .01
❑ 20 Terry Steinbach .05 .01
❑ 21 Dave Stewart .10 .02
❑ 22 Walt Weiss .05 .01
❑ 23 Bob Welch .05 .01
❑ 24 Curt Young .05 .01
❑ 25 Paul Assenmacher .05 .01
❑ 26 Damon Berryhill .05 .01
❑ 27 Mike Bielecki .05 .01
❑ 28 Kevin Blankenship .05 .01
❑ 29 Andre Dawson .10 .02
❑ 30 Shawon Dunston .05 .01
❑ 31 Joe Girardi .15 .05
❑ 32 Mark Grace .15 .05
❑ 33 Mike Harkey .05 .01
❑ 34 Paul Kilgus .05 .01
❑ 35 Les Lancaster .05 .01
❑ 36 Vance Law .05 .01
❑ 37 Greg Maddux .40 .15
❑ 38 Lloyd McClendon .05 .01
❑ 39 Jeff Pico .05 .01
❑ 40 Ryne Sandberg .40 .15
❑ 41 Scott Sanderson .05 .01
❑ 42 Dwight Smith .05 .01
❑ 43 Rick Sutcliffe .10 .02
❑ 44 Jerome Walton .05 .01
❑ 45 Mitch Webster .05 .01
❑ 46 Curt Wilkerson .05 .01
❑ 47 Dean Wilkins RC .05 .01
❑ 48 Mitch Williams .05 .01
❑ 49 Steve Wilson .05 .01
❑ 50 Steve Bedrosian .05 .01
❑ 51 Mike Benjamin RC .10 .02
❑ 52 Jeff Brantley .05 .01
❑ 53 Brett Butler .10 .02
❑ 54 Will Clark UER .10 .02
❑ 55 Kelly Downs .05 .01
❑ 56 Scott Garrelts .05 .01
❑ 57 Atlee Hammaker .05 .01
❑ 58 Terry Kennedy .05 .01
❑ 59 Mike LaCoss .05 .01
❑ 60 Craig Lefferts .05 .01
❑ 61 Greg Litton .05 .01
❑ 62 Candy Maldonado .05 .01
❑ 63 Kirt Manwaring UER (No '88 Phoenix stats as note) .05 .01
❑ 64 Randy McCament RC .05 .01
❑ 65 Kevin Mitchell .05 .01
❑ 66 Donell Nixon .05 .01
❑ 67 Ken Oberkfell .05 .01
❑ 68 Rick Reuschel .05 .01
❑ 69 Ernest Riles .05 .01
❑ 70 Don Robinson .05 .01
❑ 71 Pat Sheridan .05 .01
❑ 72 Chris Speier .05 .01
❑ 73 Robby Thompson .05 .01
❑ 74 Jose Uribe .05 .01
❑ 75 Matt Williams .10 .02
❑ 76 George Bell .05 .01
❑ 77 Pat Borders .05 .01
❑ 78 John Cerutti .05 .01
❑ 79 Junior Felix .05 .01
❑ 80 Tony Fernandez .05 .01
❑ 81 Mike Flanagan .05 .01
❑ 82 Mauro Gozzo RC .05 .01
❑ 83 Kelly Gruber .05 .01
❑ 84 Tom Henke .05 .01
❑ 85 Jimmy Key .10 .02
❑ 86 Manny Lee .05 .01
❑ 87 Nelson Liriano UER (Should say 'led the IL' ins) .05 .01
❑ 88 Lee Mazzilli .05 .01
❑ 89 Fred McGriff .25 .08
❑ 90 Lloyd Moseby .05 .01
❑ 91 Rance Mulliniks .05 .01
❑ 92 Alex Sanchez .05 .01
❑ 93 Dave Stieb .10 .02
❑ 94 Todd Stottlemyre .10 .02
❑ 95 Duane Ward UER (Double line of '87 Syracuse stat) .05 .01
❑ 96 David Wells .10 .02
❑ 97 Ernie Whitt .05 .01
❑ 98 Frank Wills .05 .01
❑ 99 Mookie Wilson .10 .02
❑ 100 Kevin Appier .10 .02
❑ 101 Luis Aquino .05 .01
❑ 102 Bob Boone .10 .02
❑ 103 George Brett .60 .25
❑ 104 Jose DeJesus .05 .01
❑ 105 Luis De Los Santos .05 .01
❑ 106 Jim Eisenreich .05 .01
❑ 107 Steve Farr .05 .01
❑ 108 Tom Gordon .10 .02
❑ 109 Mark Gubicza .05 .01
❑ 110 Bo Jackson .25 .08
❑ 111 Terry Leach .05 .01
❑ 112 Charlie Leibrandt .05 .01
❑ 113 Rick Luecken RC .05 .01
❑ 114 Mike Macfarlane .05 .01
❑ 115 Jeff Montgomery .10 .02
❑ 116 Bret Saberhagen .10 .02
❑ 117 Kevin Seitzer .05 .01
❑ 118 Kurt Stillwell .05 .01
❑ 119 Pat Tabler .05 .01
❑ 120 Danny Tartabull .05 .01
❑ 121 Gary Thurman .05 .01
❑ 122 Frank White .10 .02
❑ 123 Willie Wilson .05 .01
❑ 124 Matt Winters RC .05 .01
❑ 125 Jim Abbott .15 .05
❑ 126 Tony Armas .05 .01
❑ 127 Dante Bichette .10 .02
❑ 128 Bert Blyleven .10 .02
❑ 129 Chili Davis .10 .02
❑ 130 Brian Downing .05 .01
❑ 131 Mike Fetters RC .25 .08
❑ 132 Chuck Finley .10 .02
❑ 133 Willie Fraser .05 .01
❑ 134 Bryan Harvey .05 .01
❑ 135 Jack Howell .05 .01
❑ 136 Wally Joyner .10 .02
❑ 137 Jeff Manto .05 .01
❑ 138 Kirk McCaskill .05 .01
❑ 139 Bob McClure .05 .01
❑ 140 Greg Minton .05 .01
❑ 141 Lance Parrish .05 .01
❑ 142 Dan Petry .05 .01
❑ 143 Johnny Ray .05 .01
❑ 144 Dick Schofield .05 .01
❑ 145 Lee Stevens .10 .02
❑ 146 Claudell Washington .05 .01
❑ 147 Devon White .10 .02
❑ 148 Mike Witt .05 .01
❑ 149 Roberto Alomar .15 .05
❑ 150 Sandy Alomar Jr. .10 .02
❑ 151 Andy Benes .10 .02
❑ 152 Jack Clark .10 .02
❑ 153 Pat Clements .05 .01
❑ 154 Joey Cora .10 .02
❑ 155 Mark Davis .05 .01
❑ 156 Mark Grant .05 .01
❑ 157 Tony Gwynn .30 .10
❑ 158 Greg W. Harris .05 .01
❑ 159 Bruce Hurst .05 .01
❑ 160 Darrin Jackson .05 .01
❑ 161 Chris James .05 .01
❑ 162 Carmelo Martinez .05 .01
❑ 163 Mike Pagliarulo .05 .01
❑ 164 Mark Parent .05 .01
❑ 165 Dennis Rasmussen .05 .01
❑ 166 Bip Roberts .05 .01
❑ 167 Benito Santiago .10 .02
❑ 168 Calvin Schiraldi .05 .01
❑ 169 Eric Show .05 .01
❑ 170 Garry Templeton .05 .01
❑ 171 Ed Whitson .05 .01
❑ 172 Brady Anderson .10 .02
❑ 173 Jeff Ballard .05 .01
❑ 174 Phil Bradley .05 .01
❑ 175 Mike Devereaux .05 .01
❑ 176 Steve Finley .10 .02
❑ 177 Pete Harnisch .05 .01
❑ 178 Kevin Hickey .05 .01
❑ 179 Brian Holton .05 .01
❑ 180 Ben McDonald RC .25 .08
❑ 181 Bob Melvin .05 .01
❑ 182 Bob Milacki .05 .01
❑ 183 Randy Milligan UER (Double line of '87 stats) .05 .01
❑ 184 Gregg Olson .10 .02
❑ 185 Joe Orsulak .05 .01
❑ 186 Bill Ripken .05 .01
❑ 187 Cal Ripken .75 .30
❑ 188 Dave Schmidt .05 .01
❑ 189 Larry Sheets .05 .01
❑ 190 Mickey Tettleton .05 .01
❑ 191 Mark Thurmond .05 .01
❑ 192 Jay Tibbs .05 .01
❑ 193 Jim Traber .05 .01
❑ 194 Mark Williamson .05 .01
❑ 195 Craig Worthington .05 .01
❑ 196 Don Aase .05 .01
❑ 197 Blaine Beatty RC .05 .01
❑ 198 Mark Carroon .05 .01
❑ 199 Gary Carter .10 .02
❑ 200 David Cone .10 .02
❑ 201 Ron Darling .05 .01
❑ 202 Kevin Elster .05 .01
❑ 203 Sid Fernandez .05 .01
❑ 204 Dwight Gooden .10 .02
❑ 205 Keith Hernandez .10 .02
❑ 206 Jeff Innis RC .05 .01
❑ 207 Gregg Jefferies .10 .02
❑ 208 Howard Johnson .05 .01
❑ 209 Barry Lyons UER (Double line of '87 stats) .05 .01
❑ 210 Dave Magadan .05 .01
❑ 211 Kevin McReynolds .05 .01
❑ 212 Jeff Musselman .05 .01
❑ 213 Randy Myers .10 .02
❑ 214 Bob Ojeda .05 .01

❑ 215 Juan Samuel .05 .01
❑ 216 Mackey Sasser .05 .01
❑ 217 Darryl Strawberry .10 .02
❑ 218 Tim Teufel .05 .01
❑ 219 Frank Viola .05 .01
❑ 220 Juan Agosto .05 .01
❑ 221 Larry Andersen .05 .01
❑ 222 Eric Anthony RC .10 .02
❑ 223 Kevin Bass .05 .01
❑ 224 Craig Biggio .25 .08
❑ 225 Ken Caminiti .10 .02
❑ 226 Jim Clancy .05 .01
❑ 227 Danny Darwin .05 .01
❑ 228 Glenn Davis .05 .01
❑ 229 Jim Deshaies .05 .01
❑ 230 Bill Doran .05 .01
❑ 231 Bob Forsch .05 .01
❑ 232 Brian Meyer .05 .01
❑ 233 Terry Puhl .05 .01
❑ 234 Rafael Ramirez .05 .01
❑ 235 Rick Rhoden .05 .01
❑ 236 Dan Schatzeder .05 .01
❑ 237 Mike Scott .05 .01
❑ 238 Dave Smith .05 .01
❑ 239 Alex Trevino .05 .01
❑ 240 Glenn Wilson .05 .01
❑ 241 Gerald Young .05 .01
❑ 242 Tom Brunansky .05 .01
❑ 243 Cris Carpenter .05 .01
❑ 244 Alex Cole RC .10 .02
❑ 245 Vince Coleman .05 .01
❑ 246 John Costello .05 .01
❑ 247 Ken Dayley .05 .01
❑ 248 Jose DeLeon .05 .01
❑ 249 Frank DiPino .05 .01
❑ 250 Pedro Guerrero .05 .01
❑ 251 Ken Hill .10 .02
❑ 252 Joe Magrane .05 .01
❑ 253 Willie McGee UER (No decimal point before 353) .10 .02
❑ 254 John Morris .05 .01
❑ 255 Jose Oquendo .05 .01
❑ 256 Tony Pena .05 .01
❑ 257 Terry Pendleton .10 .02
❑ 258 Ted Power .05 .01
❑ 259 Dan Quisenberry .05 .01
❑ 260 Ozzie Smith .40 .15
❑ 261 Scott Terry .05 .01
❑ 262 Milt Thompson .05 .01
❑ 263 Denny Walling .05 .01
❑ 264 Todd Worrell .05 .01
❑ 265 Todd Zeile .10 .02
❑ 266 Marty Barrett .05 .01
❑ 267 Mike Boddicker .05 .01
❑ 268 Wade Boggs .15 .05
❑ 269 Ellis Burks .15 .05
❑ 270 Rick Cerone .05 .01
❑ 271 Roger Clemens 1.00 .40
❑ 272 John Dopson .05 .01
❑ 273 Nick Esasky .05 .01
❑ 274 Dwight Evans .15 .05
❑ 275 Wes Gardner .05 .01
❑ 276 Rich Gedman .05 .01
❑ 277 Mike Greenwell .05 .01
❑ 278 Danny Heep .05 .01
❑ 279 Eric Hetzel .05 .01
❑ 280 Dennis Lamp .05 .01
❑ 281 Rob Murphy UER ('89 stats say Reds, should say R .05 .01
❑ 282 Joe Price .05 .01
❑ 283 Carlos Quintana .05 .01
❑ 284 Jody Reed .05 .01
❑ 285 Luis Rivera .05 .01
❑ 286 Kevin Romine .05 .01
❑ 287 Lee Smith .10 .02
❑ 288 Mike Smithson .05 .01
❑ 289 Bob Stanley .05 .01
❑ 290 Harold Baines .10 .02
❑ 291 Kevin Brown .10 .02
❑ 292 Steve Buechele .05 .01
❑ 293 Scott Coolbaugh RC .05 .01
❑ 294 Jack Daugherty RC .05 .01
❑ 295 Cecil Espy .05 .01
❑ 296 Julio Franco .10 .02
❑ 297 Juan Gonzalez RC 1.00 .40
❑ 298 Cecilio Guante .05 .01
❑ 299 Drew Hall .05 .01
❑ 300 Charlie Hough .10 .02
❑ 301 Pete Incaviglia .05 .01
❑ 302 Mike Jeffcoat .05 .01
❑ 303 Chad Kreuter .05 .01
❑ 304 Jeff Kunkel .05 .01
❑ 305 Rick Leach .05 .01
❑ 306 Fred Manrique .05 .01
❑ 307 Jamie Moyer .10 .02
❑ 308 Rafael Palmeiro .15 .05
❑ 309 Geno Petralli .05 .01
❑ 310 Kevin Reimer .05 .01
❑ 311 Kenny Rogers .10 .02
❑ 312 Jeff Russell .05 .01
❑ 313 Nolan Ryan 1.00 .40
❑ 314 Ruben Sierra .10 .02
❑ 315 Bobby Witt .05 .01
❑ 316 Chris Bosio .05 .01
❑ 317 Glenn Braggs UER (Stats say 111 K's, but bio say .05 .01
❑ 318 Greg Brock .05 .01
❑ 319 Chuck Crim .05 .01
❑ 320 Rob Deer .05 .01
❑ 321 Mike Felder .05 .01
❑ 322 Tom Filer .05 .01
❑ 323 Tony Fossas RC .05 .01
❑ 324 Jim Gantner .05 .01
❑ 325 Darryl Hamilton .05 .01
❑ 326 Teddy Higuera .05 .01
❑ 327 Mark Knudson .05 .01
❑ 328 Bill Krueger UER ('86 stats missing) .05 .01
❑ 329 Tim McIntosh RC .10 .02
❑ 330 Paul Molitor .10 .02
❑ 331 Jaime Navarro .05 .01
❑ 332 Charlie O'Brien .05 .01
❑ 333 Jeff Peterek RC .05 .01
❑ 334 Dan Plesac .05 .01
❑ 335 Jerry Reuss .05 .01
❑ 336 Gary Sheffield .25 .08
❑ 337 Bill Spiers .05 .01
❑ 338 B.J. Surhoff .10 .02
❑ 339 Greg Vaughn .05 .01
❑ 340 Robin Yount .40 .15
❑ 341 Hubie Brooks .05 .01
❑ 342 Tim Burke .05 .01
❑ 343 Mike Fitzgerald .05 .01
❑ 344 Tom Foley .05 .01
❑ 345 Andres Galarraga .10 .02
❑ 346 Damaso Garcia .05 .01
❑ 347 Marquis Grissom RC .40 .15
❑ 348 Kevin Gross .05 .01
❑ 349 Joe Hesketh .05 .01
❑ 350 Jeff Huson RC .05 .01
❑ 351 Wallace Johnson .05 .01
❑ 352 Mark Langston .05 .01
❑ 353A Dave Martinez Yellow 2.00 .75
❑ 353B Dave Martinez Red .05 .01
❑ 354 Dennis Martinez UER ('87 ERA is 616, should be 6 .10 .02
❑ 355 Andy McGaffigan .05 .01
❑ 356 Otis Nixon .05 .01
❑ 357 Spike Owen .05 .01
❑ 358 Pascual Perez .05 .01
❑ 359 Tim Raines .10 .02
❑ 360 Nelson Santovenia .05 .01
❑ 361 Bryn Smith .05 .01
❑ 362 Zane Smith .05 .01
❑ 363 Larry Walker RC 1.00 .40
❑ 364 Tim Wallach .05 .01
❑ 365 Rick Aguilera .10 .02
❑ 366 Allan Anderson .05 .01
❑ 367 Wally Backman .05 .01
❑ 368 Doug Baker .05 .01
❑ 369 Juan Berenguer .05 .01
❑ 370 Randy Bush .05 .01
❑ 371 Carmelo Castillo .05 .01
❑ 372 Mike Dyer RC .05 .01
❑ 373 Gary Gaetti .10 .02
❑ 374 Greg Gagne .05 .01
❑ 375 Dan Gladden .05 .01
❑ 376 German Gonzalez UER (Bio says 31 saves in '88, b) .05 .01
❑ 377 Brian Harper .05 .01
❑ 378 Kent Hrbek .10 .02
❑ 379 Gene Larkin .05 .01
❑ 380 Tim Laudner UER (No decimal point before '85 BA) .05 .01
❑ 381 John Moses .05 .01
❑ 382 Al Newman .05 .01
❑ 383 Kirby Puckett .25 .08
❑ 384 Shane Rawley .05 .01
❑ 385 Jeff Reardon .10 .02
❑ 386 Roy Smith .05 .01
❑ 387 Gary Wayne .05 .01
❑ 388 Dave West .05 .01
❑ 389 Tim Belcher .05 .01
❑ 390 Tim Crews UER (Stats say 163 IP for '83, but bio) .05 .01
❑ 391 Mike Davis .05 .01
❑ 392 Rick Dempsey .05 .01
❑ 393 Kirk Gibson .10 .02
❑ 394 Jose Gonzalez .05 .01
❑ 395 Alfredo Griffin .05 .01
❑ 396 Jeff Hamilton .05 .01
❑ 397 Lenny Harris .05 .01
❑ 398 Mickey Hatcher .05 .01
❑ 399 Orel Hershiser .10 .02
❑ 400 Jay Howell .05 .01
❑ 401 Mike Marshall .05 .01
❑ 402 Ramon Martinez .05 .01
❑ 403 Mike Morgan .05 .01
❑ 404 Eddie Murray .25 .08
❑ 405 Alejandro Pena .05 .01
❑ 406 Willie Randolph .10 .02
❑ 407 Mike Scioscia .05 .01
❑ 408 Ray Searage .05 .01
❑ 409 Fernando Valenzuela .10 .02
❑ 410 Jose Vizcaino RC .25 .08
❑ 411 John Wetteland .25 .08
❑ 412 Jack Armstrong .05 .01
❑ 413 Todd Benzinger UER (Bio says .323 at Pawtucket,) .05 .01
❑ 414 Tim Birtsas .05 .01
❑ 415 Tom Browning .05 .01
❑ 416 Norm Charlton .05 .01
❑ 417 Eric Davis .10 .02
❑ 418 Rob Dibble .10 .02
❑ 419 John Franco .10 .02
❑ 420 Ken Griffey Sr. .10 .02
❑ 421 Chris Hammond RC .10 .02
❑ 422 Danny Jackson .05 .01
❑ 423 Barry Larkin .15 .05
❑ 424 Tim Leary .05 .01
❑ 425 Rick Mahler .05 .01
❑ 426 Joe Oliver .05 .01
❑ 427 Paul O'Neill .15 .05
❑ 428 Luis Quinones UER ('86-'88 stats are omitted fro) .05 .01
❑ 429 Jeff Reed .05 .01
❑ 430 Jose Rijo .05 .01
❑ 431 Ron Robinson .05 .01
❑ 432 Rolando Roomes .05 .01
❑ 433 Chris Sabo .05 .01
❑ 434 Scott Scudder .05 .01
❑ 435 Herm Winningham .05 .01
❑ 436 Steve Balboni .05 .01
❑ 437 Jesse Barfield .05 .01
❑ 438 Mike Blowers RC .10 .02
❑ 439 Tom Brookens .05 .01
❑ 440 Greg Cadaret .05 .01
❑ 441 Alvaro Espinoza UER (Career games say 218, shoul) .05 .01
❑ 442 Bob Geren .05 .01
❑ 443 Lee Guetterman .05 .01
❑ 444 Mel Hall .05 .01
❑ 445 Andy Hawkins .05 .01
❑ 446 Roberto Kelly .05 .01
❑ 447 Don Mattingly .60 .25
❑ 448 Lance McCullers .05 .01
❑ 449 Hensley Meulens .05 .01
❑ 450 Dale Mohorcic .05 .01

❑ 451 Clay Parker .05 .01
❑ 452 Eric Plunk .05 .01
❑ 453 Dave Righetti .05 .01
❑ 454 Deion Sanders .25 .08
❑ 455 Steve Sax .05 .01
❑ 456 Don Slaught .05 .01
❑ 457 Walt Terrell .05 .01
❑ 458 Dave Winfield .10 .02
❑ 459 Jay Bell .10 .02
❑ 460 Rafael Belliard .05 .01
❑ 461 Barry Bonds 1.00 .40
❑ 462 Bobby Bonilla .10 .02
❑ 463 Sid Bream .05 .01
❑ 464 Benny Distefano .05 .01
❑ 465 Doug Drabek .05 .01
❑ 466 Jim Gott .05 .01
❑ 467 Billy Hatcher UER (.1 hits for Cubs in 1984) .05 .01
❑ 468 Neal Heaton .05 .01
❑ 469 Jeff King .05 .01
❑ 470 Bob Kipper .05 .01
❑ 471 Randy Kramer .05 .01
❑ 472 Bill Landrum .05 .01
❑ 473 Mike LaValliere .05 .01
❑ 474 Jose Lind .05 .01
❑ 475 Junior Ortiz .05 .01
❑ 476 Gary Redus .05 .01
❑ 477 Rick Reed RC .25 .08
❑ 478 R.J. Reynolds .05 .01
❑ 479 Jeff D. Robinson .05 .01
❑ 480 John Smiley .05 .01
❑ 481 Andy Van Slyke .15 .05
❑ 482 Bob Walk .05 .01
❑ 483 Andy Allanson .05 .01
❑ 484 Scott Bailes .05 .01
❑ 485 Albert Belle .25 .08
❑ 486 Bud Black .05 .01
❑ 487 Jerry Browne .05 .01
❑ 488 Tom Candiotti .05 .01
❑ 489 Joe Carter .10 .02
❑ 490 Dave Clark (No '84 stats) .05 .01
❑ 491 John Farrell .05 .01
❑ 492 Felix Fermin .05 .01
❑ 493 Brook Jacoby .05 .01
❑ 494 Dion James .05 .01
❑ 495 Doug Jones .05 .01
❑ 496 Brad Komminsk .05 .01
❑ 497 Rod Nichols .05 .01
❑ 498 Pete O'Brien .05 .01
❑ 499 Steve Olin RC .10 .02
❑ 500 Jesse Orosco .05 .01
❑ 501 Joel Skinner .05 .01
❑ 502 Cory Snyder .05 .01
❑ 503 Greg Swindell .05 .01
❑ 504 Rich Yett .05 .01
❑ 505 Scott Bankhead .05 .01
❑ 506 Scott Bradley .05 .01
❑ 507 Greg Briley UER (28 SB's in bio, but 27 in stats .05 .01
❑ 508 Jay Buhner .10 .02
❑ 509 Darnell Coles .05 .01
❑ 510 Keith Comstock .05 .01
❑ 511 Henry Cotto .05 .01
❑ 512 Alvin Davis .05 .01
❑ 513 Ken Griffey Jr. .75 .30
❑ 514 Erik Hanson .05 .01
❑ 515 Gene Harris .05 .01
❑ 516 Brian Holman .05 .01
❑ 517 Mike Jackson .05 .01
❑ 518 Randy Johnson .50 .20
❑ 519 Jeffrey Leonard .05 .01
❑ 520 Edgar Martinez .15 .05
❑ 521 Dennis Powell .05 .01
❑ 522 Jim Presley .05 .01
❑ 523 Jerry Reed .05 .01
❑ 524 Harold Reynolds .10 .02
❑ 525 Mike Schooler .05 .01
❑ 526 Bill Swift .05 .01
❑ 527 Dave Valle .05 .01
❑ 528 Omar Vizquel .25 .08
❑ 529 Ivan Calderon .05 .01
❑ 530 Carlton Fisk UER .15 .05
❑ 531 Scott Fletcher .05 .01
❑ 532 Dave Gallagher .05 .01
❑ 533 Ozzie Guillen .10 .02
❑ 534 Greg Hibbard RC .10 .02
❑ 535 Shawn Hillegas .05 .01
❑ 536 Lance Johnson .05 .01
❑ 537 Eric King .05 .01
❑ 538 Ron Kittle .05 .01
❑ 539 Steve Lyons .05 .01
❑ 540 Carlos Martinez .05 .01
❑ 541 Tom McCarthy .05 .01
❑ 542 Matt Merullo (Had 5 ML runs scored entering '90,) .05 .01
❑ 543 Donn Pall UER (Stats say pro career began in '85) .05 .01
❑ 544 Dan Pasqua .05 .01
❑ 545 Ken Patterson .05 .01
❑ 546 Melido Perez .05 .01
❑ 547 Steve Rosenberg .05 .01
❑ 548 Sammy Sosa RC 2.50 1.00
❑ 549 Bobby Thigpen .05 .01
❑ 550 Robin Ventura .25 .08
❑ 551 Greg Walker .05 .01
❑ 552 Don Carman .05 .01
❑ 553 Pat Combs (6 walks for Phillies in '89 in stats,) .05 .01
❑ 554 Dennis Cook .05 .01
❑ 555 Darren Daulton .10 .02
❑ 556 Len Dykstra .10 .02
❑ 557 Curt Ford .05 .01
❑ 558 Charlie Hayes .05 .01
❑ 559 Von Hayes .05 .01
❑ 560 Tommy Herr .05 .01
❑ 561 Ken Howell .05 .01
❑ 562 Steve Jeltz .05 .01
❑ 563 Ron Jones .05 .01
❑ 564 Ricky Jordan UER (Duplicate line of statistics o) .05 .01
❑ 565 John Kruk .10 .02
❑ 566 Steve Lake .05 .01
❑ 567 Roger McDowell .05 .01
❑ 568 Terry Mulholland UER ('Did You Know' refers t) .05 .01
❑ 569 Dwayne Murphy .05 .01
❑ 570 Jeff Parrett .05 .01
❑ 571 Randy Ready .05 .01
❑ 572 Bruce Ruffin .05 .01
❑ 573 Dickie Thon .05 .01
❑ 574 Jose Alvarez UER ('78 and '79 stats are reversed) .05 .01
❑ 575 Geronimo Berroa .05 .01
❑ 576 Jeff Blauser .05 .01
❑ 577 Joe Boever .05 .01
❑ 578 Marty Clary UER (No comma between city and state) .05 .01
❑ 579 Jody Davis .05 .01
❑ 580 Mark Eichhorn .05 .01
❑ 581 Darrell Evans .10 .02
❑ 582 Ron Gant .10 .02
❑ 583 Tom Glavine .15 .05
❑ 584 Tommy Greene RC .10 .02
❑ 585 Tommy Gregg .05 .01
❑ 586 David Justice RC .50 .20
❑ 587 Mark Lemke .05 .01
❑ 588 Derek Lilliquist .05 .01
❑ 589 Oddibe McDowell .05 .01
❑ 590 Kent Mercker RC .05 .01
❑ 591 Dale Murphy .15 .05
❑ 592 Gerald Perry .05 .01
❑ 593 Lonnie Smith .05 .01
❑ 594 Pete Smith .05 .01
❑ 595 John Smoltz .25 .08
❑ 596 Mike Stanton UER RC .25 .08
❑ 597 Andres Thomas .05 .01
❑ 598 Jeff Treadway .05 .01
❑ 599 Doyle Alexander .05 .01
❑ 600 Dave Bergman .05 .01
❑ 601 Brian DuBois RC .05 .01
❑ 602 Paul Gibson .05 .01
❑ 603 Mike Heath .05 .01
❑ 604 Mike Henneman .05 .01
❑ 605 Guillermo Hernandez .05 .01
❑ 606 Shawn Holman RC .05 .01
❑ 607 Tracy Jones .05 .01
❑ 608 Chet Lemon .05 .01
❑ 609 Fred Lynn .05 .01
❑ 610 Jack Morris .10 .02
❑ 611 Matt Nokes .05 .01
❑ 612 Gary Pettis .05 .01
❑ 613 Kevin Ritz RC .05 .01
❑ 614 Jeff M. Robinson ('88 stats are not in line) .05 .01
❑ 615 Steve Searcy .05 .01
❑ 616 Frank Tanana .05 .01
❑ 617 Alan Trammell .10 .02
❑ 618 Gary Ward .05 .01
❑ 619 Lou Whitaker .10 .02
❑ 620 Frank Williams .05 .01
❑ 621A George Brett '80 ERR 2.00 .75
❑ 621B George Brett '80 .30 .10
❑ 622 Fern.Valenzuela '81 .05 .01
❑ 623 Dale Murphy '82 .15 .05
❑ 624A Cal Ripkin '83 ERR 5.00 2.00
❑ 624B Cal Ripken '83 COR .40 .15
❑ 625 Ryne Sandberg '84 .25 .08
❑ 626 Don Mattingly '85 .20 .07
❑ 627 Roger Clemens '86 .50 .20
❑ 628 George Bell '87 .05 .01
❑ 629 Jose Canseco '88 UER .10 .02
❑ 630A Will Clark '89 ERR 32 1.00 .40
❑ 630B Will Clark '89 COR 321 .15 .05
❑ 631 M.Davis/M.Williams .05 .01
❑ 632 W.Boggs/M.Greenwell .10 .02
❑ 633 M.Gubicza/J.Russell .05 .01
❑ 634 C.Ripken/T.Fernandez .25 .08
❑ 635 K.Puckett/Bo Jackson .15 .05
❑ 636 N.Ryan/M.Scott .40 .15
❑ 637 W.Clark/K.Mitchell .10 .02
❑ 638 M.McGwire/D.Mattingly .30 .10
❑ 639 R.Sandberg/H.Johnson .25 .08
❑ 640 R.Seanez RC/C.Charland RC .10 .02
❑ 641 G.Canale RC/K.Maas RC .25 .08
❑ 642 Kelly Mann RC/D.Hansen RC .25 .08
❑ 643 G.Smith RC/S.Tate RC .10 .02
❑ 644 T.Drees RC/D.Howitt RC .10 .02
❑ 645 M.Roesler RC/D.May RC .10 .02
❑ 646 S.Hemond RC/M.Gardner RC .10 .02
❑ 647 John Orton RC/S.Leius RC .10 .02
❑ 648 R.Monteleone RC/D.Williams RC .10 .02
❑ 649 M.Huff RC/S.Frey RC .10 .02
❑ 650 C.McElroy RC/M.Alou RC .75 .30
❑ 651 B.Rose RC/M.Hartley RC .25 .08
❑ 652 M.Kinzer RC/W.Edwards RC .10 .02
❑ 653 D.DeShields RC/J.Grimsley RC .25 .08
❑ 654 CL: A's/Cubs Giants/Blue Jays .05 .01
❑ 655 CL: Royals/Angels Padres/Orioles .05 .01
❑ 656 CL: Mets/Astros Cards/Red Sox .05 .01
❑ 657 CL: Rangers/Brewers Expos/Twins .05 .01
❑ 658 CL: Dodgers/Reds Yankees/Pirates .05 .01
❑ 659 CL: Indians/Mariners White Sox/Phillies .05 .01
❑ 660A CL: Braves/Tigers Specials/Checklists (Checklist) .05 .01
❑ 660B CL: Braves/Tigers Specials/Checklists (Checklist .05 .01

1991 Fleer

❑ COMPLETE SET (720) 8.00 3.00
❑ COMP.RETAIL SET (732) 10.00 4.00
❑ COMP.HOBBY SET (732) 10.00 4.00
❑ 1 Troy Afenir RC .05 .01
❑ 2 Harold Baines .10 .02
❑ 3 Lance Blankenship .05 .01
❑ 4 Todd Burns .05 .01
❑ 5 Jose Canseco .15 .05

❑ 6 Dennis Eckersley .10 .02
❑ 7 Mike Gallego .05 .01
❑ 8 Ron Hassey .05 .01
❑ 9 Dave Henderson .05 .01
❑ 10 Rickey Henderson .25 .08
❑ 11 Rick Honeycutt .05 .01
❑ 12 Doug Jennings .05 .01
❑ 13 Joe Klink .05 .01
❑ 14 Carney Lansford .10 .02
❑ 15 Darren Lewis .05 .01
❑ 16 Willie McGee UER .10 .02
❑ 17 Mark McGwire UER .75 .30
❑ 18 Mike Moore .05 .01
❑ 19 Gene Nelson .05 .01
❑ 20 Dave Otto .05 .01
❑ 21 Jamie Quirk .05 .01
❑ 22 Willie Randolph .10 .02
❑ 23 Scott Sanderson .05 .01
❑ 24 Terry Steinbach .05 .01
❑ 25 Dave Stewart .10 .02
❑ 26 Walt Weiss .05 .01
❑ 27 Bob Welch .05 .01
❑ 28 Curt Young .05 .01
❑ 29 Wally Backman .05 .01
❑ 30 Stan Belinda UER .05 .01
❑ 31 Jay Bell .10 .02
❑ 32 Rafael Belliard .05 .01
❑ 33 Barry Bonds 1.00 .40
❑ 34 Bobby Bonilla .10 .02
❑ 35 Sid Bream .05 .01
❑ 36 Doug Drabek .05 .01
❑ 37 Carlos Garcia RC .10 .02
❑ 38 Neal Heaton .05 .01
❑ 39 Jeff King .05 .01
❑ 40 Bob Kipper .05 .01
❑ 41 Bill Landrum .05 .01
❑ 42 Mike LaValliere .05 .01
❑ 43 Jose Lind .05 .01
❑ 44 Carmelo Martinez .05 .01
❑ 45 Bob Patterson .05 .01
❑ 46 Ted Power .05 .01
❑ 47 Gary Redus .05 .01
❑ 48 R.J. Reynolds .05 .01
❑ 49 Don Slaught .05 .01
❑ 50 John Smiley .05 .01
❑ 51 Zane Smith .05 .01
❑ 52 Randy Tomlin RC .10 .02
❑ 53 Andy Van Slyke .15 .05
❑ 54 Bob Walk .05 .01
❑ 55 Jack Armstrong .05 .01
❑ 56 Todd Benzinger .05 .01
❑ 57 Glenn Braggs .05 .01
❑ 58 Keith Brown .05 .01
❑ 59 Tom Browning .05 .01
❑ 60 Norm Charlton .05 .01
❑ 61 Eric Davis .10 .02
❑ 62 Rob Dibble .10 .02
❑ 63 Bill Doran .05 .01
❑ 64 Mariano Duncan .05 .01
❑ 65 Chris Hammond .05 .01
❑ 66 Billy Hatcher .05 .01
❑ 67 Danny Jackson .05 .01
❑ 68 Barry Larkin .15 .05
❑ 69 Tim Layana UER .05 .01
❑ 70 Terry Lee RC .05 .01
❑ 71 Rick Mahler .05 .01
❑ 72 Hal Morris .05 .01
❑ 73 Randy Myers .05 .01
❑ 74 Ron Oester .05 .01
❑ 75 Joe Oliver .05 .01
❑ 76 Paul O'Neill .15 .05
❑ 77 Luis Quinones .05 .01
❑ 78 Jeff Reed .05 .01
❑ 79 Jose Rijo .05 .01
❑ 80 Chris Sabo .05 .01
❑ 81 Scott Scudder .05 .01
❑ 82 Herm Winningham .05 .01
❑ 83 Larry Andersen .05 .01
❑ 84 Marty Barrett .05 .01
❑ 85 Mike Boddicker .05 .01
❑ 86 Wade Boggs .15 .05
❑ 87 Tom Bolton .05 .01
❑ 88 Tom Brunansky .05 .01
❑ 89 Ellis Burks .10 .02
❑ 90 Roger Clemens .75 .30
❑ 91 Scott Cooper .05 .01
❑ 92 John Dopson .05 .01
❑ 93 Dwight Evans .15 .05
❑ 94 Wes Gardner .05 .01
❑ 95 Jeff Gray .05 .01
❑ 96 Mike Greenwell .05 .01
❑ 97 Greg A. Harris .05 .01
❑ 98 Daryl Irvine RC .05 .01
❑ 99 Dana Kiecker .05 .01
❑ 100 Randy Kutcher .05 .01
❑ 101 Dennis Lamp .05 .01
❑ 102 Mike Marshall .05 .01
❑ 103 John Marzano .05 .01
❑ 104 Rob Murphy .05 .01
❑ 105 Tim Naehring .05 .01
❑ 106 Tony Pena .05 .01
❑ 107 Phil Plantier RC .25 .08
❑ 108 Carlos Quintana .05 .01
❑ 109 Jeff Reardon .10 .02
❑ 110 Jerry Reed .05 .01
❑ 111 Jody Reed .05 .01
❑ 112 Luis Rivera UER .05 .01
❑ 113 Kevin Romine .05 .01
❑ 114 Phil Bradley .05 .01
❑ 115 Ivan Calderon .05 .01
❑ 116 Wayne Edwards .05 .01
❑ 117 Alex Fernandez .05 .01
❑ 118 Carlton Fisk .15 .05
❑ 119 Scott Fletcher .05 .01
❑ 120 Craig Grebeck .05 .01
❑ 121 Ozzie Guillen .10 .02
❑ 122 Greg Hibbard .05 .01
❑ 123 Lance Johnson UER .05 .01
❑ 124 Barry Jones .05 .01
❑ 125 Ron Karkovice .05 .01
❑ 126 Eric King .05 .01
❑ 127 Steve Lyons .05 .01
❑ 128 Carlos Martinez .05 .01
❑ 129 Jack McDowell UER .05 .01
❑ 130 Donn Pall .05 .01
❑ 131 Dan Pasqua .05 .01
❑ 132 Ken Patterson .05 .01
❑ 133 Melido Perez .05 .01
❑ 134 Adam Peterson .05 .01
❑ 135 Scott Radinsky .05 .01
❑ 136 Sammy Sosa .25 .08
❑ 137 Bobby Thigpen .05 .01
❑ 138 Frank Thomas .25 .08
❑ 139 Robin Ventura .10 .02
❑ 140 Daryl Boston .05 .01
❑ 141 Chuck Carr .05 .01
❑ 142 Mark Carreon .05 .01
❑ 143 David Cone .10 .02
❑ 144 Ron Darling .05 .01
❑ 145 Kevin Elster .05 .01
❑ 146 Sid Fernandez .05 .01
❑ 147 John Franco .10 .02
❑ 148 Dwight Gooden .10 .02
❑ 149 Tom Herr .05 .01
❑ 150 Todd Hundley .05 .01
❑ 151 Gregg Jefferies .05 .01
❑ 152 Howard Johnson .05 .01
❑ 153 Dave Magadan .05 .01
❑ 154 Kevin McReynolds .05 .01
❑ 155 Keith Miller UER
(Text says Rochester in
'87, st) .05 .01
❑ 156 Bob Ojeda .05 .01
❑ 157 Tom O'Malley .05 .01
❑ 158 Alejandro Pena .05 .01
❑ 159 Darren Reed .05 .01
❑ 160 Mackey Sasser .05 .01
❑ 161 Darryl Strawberry .10 .02
❑ 162 Tim Teufel .05 .01
❑ 163 Kelvin Torve .05 .01
❑ 164 Julio Valera .05 .01
❑ 165 Frank Viola .10 .02
❑ 166 Wally Whitehurst .05 .01
❑ 167 Jim Acker .05 .01
❑ 168 Derek Bell .10 .02
❑ 169 George Bell .05 .01
❑ 170 Willie Blair .05 .01
❑ 171 Pat Borders .05 .01
❑ 172 John Cerutti .05 .01
❑ 173 Junior Felix .05 .01
❑ 174 Tony Fernandez .05 .01
❑ 175 Kelly Gruber UER
(Born in Houston,
should be Bel) .05 .01
❑ 176 Tom Henke .05 .01
❑ 177 Glenallen Hill .05 .01
❑ 178 Jimmy Key .10 .02
❑ 179 Manny Lee .05 .01
❑ 180 Fred McGriff .15 .05
❑ 181 Rance Mulliniks .05 .01
❑ 182 Greg Myers .05 .01
❑ 183 John Olerud .10 .02
❑ 184 Luis Sojo .05 .01
❑ 185 Dave Stieb .05 .01
❑ 186 Todd Stottlemyre .05 .01
❑ 187 Duane Ward .05 .01
❑ 188 David Wells .10 .02
❑ 189 Mark Whiten .05 .01
❑ 190 Ken Williams .05 .01
❑ 191 Frank Wills .05 .01
❑ 192 Mookie Wilson .10 .02
❑ 193 Don Aase .05 .01
❑ 194 Tim Belcher UER
(Born Sparta, Ohio,
should say M) .05 .01
❑ 195 Hubie Brooks .05 .01
❑ 196 Dennis Cook .05 .01
❑ 197 Tim Crews .05 .01
❑ 198 Kal Daniels .05 .01
❑ 199 Kirk Gibson .10 .02
❑ 200 Jim Gott .05 .01
❑ 201 Alfredo Griffin .05 .01
❑ 202 Chris Gwynn .05 .01
❑ 203 Dave Hansen .05 .01
❑ 204 Lenny Harris .05 .01
❑ 205 Mike Hartley .05 .01
❑ 206 Mickey Hatcher .05 .01
❑ 207 Carlos Hernandez .05 .01
❑ 208 Orel Hershiser .10 .02
❑ 209 Jay Howell UER
(No 1982 Yankee stats) .05 .01
❑ 210 Mike Huff .05 .01
❑ 211 Stan Javier .05 .01
❑ 212 Ramon Martinez .05 .01
❑ 213 Mike Morgan .05 .01
❑ 214 Eddie Murray .25 .08
❑ 215 Jim Neidlinger RC .05 .01
❑ 216 Jose Offerman .05 .01
❑ 217 Jim Poole .05 .01
❑ 218 Juan Samuel .05 .01
❑ 219 Mike Scioscia .05 .01
❑ 220 Ray Searage .05 .01
❑ 221 Mike Sharperson .05 .01
❑ 222 Fernando Valenzuela .10 .02
❑ 223 Jose Vizcaino .05 .01
❑ 224 Mike Aldrete .05 .01
❑ 225 Scott Anderson RC .05 .01
❑ 226 Dennis Boyd .05 .01
❑ 227 Tim Burke .05 .01
❑ 228 Delino DeShields .10 .02
❑ 229 Mike Fitzgerald .05 .01
❑ 230 Tom Foley .05 .01
❑ 231 Steve Frey .05 .01
❑ 232 Andres Galarraga .10 .02
❑ 233 Mark Gardner .05 .01
❑ 234 Marquis Grissom .10 .02
❑ 235 Kevin Gross
(No date given for
first Expos win) .05 .01
❑ 236 Drew Hall .05 .01

Card		
❑ 237 Dave Martinez	.05	.01
❑ 238 Dennis Martinez	.10	.02
❑ 239 Dale Mohorcic	.05	.01
❑ 240 Chris Nabholz	.05	.01
❑ 241 Otis Nixon	.05	.01
❑ 242 Junior Noboa	.05	.01
❑ 243 Spike Owen	.05	.01
❑ 244 Tim Raines	.10	.02
❑ 245 Mel Rojas UER (Stats show 3.60 ERA, bio says 3.1)	.05	.01
❑ 246 Scott Ruskin	.05	.01
❑ 247 Bill Sampen	.05	.01
❑ 248 Nelson Santovenia	.05	.01
❑ 249 Dave Schmidt	.05	.01
❑ 250 Larry Walker	.25	.08
❑ 251 Tim Wallach	.05	.01
❑ 252 Dave Anderson	.05	.01
❑ 253 Kevin Bass	.05	.01
❑ 254 Steve Bedrosian	.05	.01
❑ 255 Jeff Brantley	.05	.01
❑ 256 John Burkett	.05	.01
❑ 257 Brett Butler	.10	.02
❑ 258 Gary Carter	.10	.02
❑ 259 Will Clark	.15	.05
❑ 260 Steve Decker RC	.10	.02
❑ 261 Kelly Downs	.05	.01
❑ 262 Scott Garrelts	.05	.01
❑ 263 Terry Kennedy	.05	.01
❑ 264 Mike LaCoss	.05	.01
❑ 265 Mark Leonard RC	.05	.01
❑ 266 Greg Litton	.05	.01
❑ 267 Kevin Mitchell	.05	.01
❑ 268 Randy O'Neal	.05	.01
❑ 269 Rick Parker	.05	.01
❑ 270 Rick Reuschel	.05	.01
❑ 271 Ernest Riles	.05	.01
❑ 272 Don Robinson	.05	.01
❑ 273 Robby Thompson	.05	.01
❑ 274 Mark Thurmond	.05	.01
❑ 275 Jose Uribe	.05	.01
❑ 276 Matt Williams	.10	.02
❑ 277 Trevor Wilson	.05	.01
❑ 278 Gerald Alexander RC	.05	.01
❑ 279 Brad Arnsberg	.05	.01
❑ 280 Kevin Belcher RC	.05	.01
❑ 281 Joe Bitker RC	.05	.01
❑ 282 Kevin Brown	.10	.02
❑ 283 Steve Buechele	.05	.01
❑ 284 Jack Daugherty	.05	.01
❑ 285 Julio Franco	.10	.02
❑ 286 Juan Gonzalez	.25	.08
❑ 287 Bill Haselman RC	.05	.01
❑ 288 Charlie Hough	.10	.02
❑ 289 Jeff Huson	.05	.01
❑ 290 Pete Incaviglia	.05	.01
❑ 291 Mike Jeffcoat	.05	.01
❑ 292 Jeff Kunkel	.05	.01
❑ 293 Gary Mielke	.05	.01
❑ 294 Jamie Moyer	.10	.02
❑ 295 Rafael Palmeiro	.15	.05
❑ 296 Geno Petralli	.05	.01
❑ 297 Gary Pettis	.05	.01
❑ 298 Kevin Reimer	.05	.01
❑ 299 Kenny Rogers	.10	.02
❑ 300 Jeff Russell	.05	.01
❑ 301 John Russell	.05	.01
❑ 302 Nolan Ryan	1.00	.40
❑ 303 Ruben Sierra	.10	.02
❑ 304 Bobby Witt	.05	.01
❑ 305 Jim Abbott	.15	.05
❑ 306 Kent Anderson	.05	.01
❑ 307 Dante Bichette	.10	.02
❑ 308 Bert Blyleven	.10	.02
❑ 309 Chili Davis	.10	.02
❑ 310 Brian Downing	.05	.01
❑ 311 Mark Eichhorn	.05	.01
❑ 312 Mike Fetters	.05	.01
❑ 313 Chuck Finley	.10	.02
❑ 314 Willie Fraser	.05	.01
❑ 315 Bryan Harvey	.05	.01
❑ 316 Donnie Hill	.05	.01
❑ 317 Wally Joyner	.10	.02
❑ 318 Mark Langston	.05	.01
❑ 319 Kirk McCaskill	.05	.01
❑ 320 John Orton	.05	.01
❑ 321 Lance Parrish	.10	.02
❑ 322 Luis Polonia UER (1984 Madfison, should be Madis)	.05	.01
❑ 323 Johnny Ray	.05	.01
❑ 324 Bobby Rose	.05	.01
❑ 325 Dick Schofield	.05	.01
❑ 326 Rick Schu	.05	.01
❑ 327 Lee Stevens	.05	.01
❑ 328 Devon White	.10	.02
❑ 329 Dave Winfield	.10	.02
❑ 330 Cliff Young	.05	.01
❑ 331 Dave Bergman	.05	.01
❑ 332 Phil Clark RC	.10	.02
❑ 333 Darnell Coles	.05	.01
❑ 334 Milt Cuyler	.05	.01
❑ 335 Cecil Fielder	.10	.02
❑ 336 Travis Fryman	.10	.02
❑ 337 Paul Gibson	.05	.01
❑ 338 Jerry Don Gleaton	.05	.01
❑ 339 Mike Heath	.05	.01
❑ 340 Mike Henneman	.05	.01
❑ 341 Chet Lemon	.05	.01
❑ 342 Lance McCullers	.05	.01
❑ 343 Jack Morris	.10	.02
❑ 344 Lloyd Moseby	.05	.01
❑ 345 Edwin Nunez	.05	.01
❑ 346 Clay Parker	.05	.01
❑ 347 Dan Petry	.05	.01
❑ 348 Tony Phillips	.05	.01
❑ 349 Jeff M. Robinson	.05	.01
❑ 350 Mark Salas	.05	.01
❑ 351 Mike Schwabe	.05	.01
❑ 352 Larry Sheets	.05	.01
❑ 353 John Shelby	.05	.01
❑ 354 Frank Tanana	.05	.01
❑ 355 Alan Trammell	.10	.02
❑ 356 Gary Ward	.05	.01
❑ 357 Lou Whitaker	.10	.02
❑ 358 Beau Allred	.05	.01
❑ 359 Sandy Alomar Jr.	.05	.01
❑ 360 Carlos Baerga	.05	.01
❑ 361 Kevin Bearse	.05	.01
❑ 362 Tom Brookens	.05	.01
❑ 363 Jerry Browne UER (No dot over i in first text li)	.05	.01
❑ 364 Tom Candiotti	.05	.01
❑ 365 Alex Cole	.05	.01
❑ 366 John Farrell UER (Born in Neptune, should be Mon)	.05	.01
❑ 367 Felix Fermin	.05	.01
❑ 368 Keith Hernandez	.10	.02
❑ 369 Brook Jacoby	.05	.01
❑ 370 Chris James	.05	.01
❑ 371 Dion James	.05	.01
❑ 372 Doug Jones	.05	.01
❑ 373 Candy Maldonado	.05	.01
❑ 374 Steve Olin	.05	.01
❑ 375 Jesse Orosco	.05	.01
❑ 376 Rudy Seanez	.05	.01
❑ 377 Joel Skinner	.05	.01
❑ 378 Cory Snyder	.05	.01
❑ 379 Greg Swindell	.05	.01
❑ 380 Sergio Valdez	.05	.01
❑ 381 Mike Walker	.05	.01
❑ 382 Colby Ward RC	.05	.01
❑ 383 Turner Ward RC	.25	.08
❑ 384 Mitch Webster	.05	.01
❑ 385 Kevin Wickander	.05	.01
❑ 386 Darrel Akerfelds	.05	.01
❑ 387 Joe Boever	.05	.01
❑ 388 Rod Booker	.05	.01
❑ 389 Sil Campusano	.05	.01
❑ 390 Don Carman	.05	.01
❑ 391 Wes Chamberlain RC	.25	.08
❑ 392 Pat Combs	.05	.01
❑ 393 Darren Daulton	.10	.02
❑ 394 Jose DeJesus	.05	.01
❑ 395A Len Dykstra	.10	.02
❑ 395B Len Dykstra	.10	.02
❑ 396 Jason Grimsley	.05	.01
❑ 397 Charlie Hayes	.05	.01
❑ 398 Von Hayes	.05	.01
❑ 399 Dave Hollins UER	.05	.01
❑ 400 Ken Howell	.05	.01
❑ 401 Ricky Jordan	.05	.01
❑ 402 John Kruk	.10	.02
❑ 403 Steve Lake	.05	.01
❑ 404 Chuck Malone	.05	.01
❑ 405 Roger McDowell UER (Says Phillies is saves, shou)	.05	.01
❑ 406 Chuck McElroy	.05	.01
❑ 407 Mickey Morandini	.05	.01
❑ 408 Terry Mulholland	.05	.01
❑ 409 Dale Murphy	.15	.05
❑ 410A Randy Ready ERR (No Brewers stats listed for 198)	.05	.01
❑ 410B Randy Ready COR	.05	.01
❑ 411 Bruce Ruffin	.05	.01
❑ 412 Dickie Thon	.05	.01
❑ 413 Paul Assenmacher	.05	.01
❑ 414 Damon Berryhill	.05	.01
❑ 415 Mike Bielecki	.05	.01
❑ 416 Shawn Boskie	.05	.01
❑ 417 Dave Clark	.05	.01
❑ 418 Doug Dascenzo	.05	.01
❑ 419A Andre Dawson ERR	.10	.02
❑ 419B Andre Dawson COR	.10	.02
❑ 420 Shawon Dunston	.05	.01
❑ 421 Joe Girardi	.05	.01
❑ 422 Mark Grace	.15	.05
❑ 423 Mike Harkey	.05	.01
❑ 424 Les Lancaster	.05	.01
❑ 425 Bill Long	.05	.01
❑ 426 Greg Maddux	.40	.15
❑ 427 Derrick May	.05	.01
❑ 428 Jeff Pico	.05	.01
❑ 429 Domingo Ramos	.05	.01
❑ 430 Luis Salazar	.05	.01
❑ 431 Ryne Sandberg	.40	.15
❑ 432 Dwight Smith	.05	.01
❑ 433 Greg Smith	.05	.01
❑ 434 Rick Sutcliffe	.10	.02
❑ 435 Gary Varsho	.05	.01
❑ 436 Hector Villanueva	.05	.01
❑ 437 Jerome Walton	.05	.01
❑ 438 Curtis Wilkerson	.05	.01
❑ 439 Mitch Williams	.05	.01
❑ 440 Steve Wilson	.05	.01
❑ 441 Marvell Wynne	.05	.01
❑ 442 Scott Bankhead	.05	.01
❑ 443 Scott Bradley	.05	.01
❑ 444 Greg Briley	.05	.01
❑ 445 Mike Brumley UER	.05	.01
❑ 446 Jay Buhner	.10	.02
❑ 447 Dave Burba RC	.25	.08
❑ 448 Henry Cotto	.05	.01
❑ 449 Alvin Davis	.05	.01
❑ 450 Ken Griffey Jr.	.50	.20
❑ 450A Ken Griffey Jr. ERR	1.00	.40
❑ 451 Erik Hanson	.05	.01
❑ 452 Gene Harris UER (63 career runs, should be 73)	.05	.01
❑ 453 Brian Holman	.05	.01
❑ 454 Mike Jackson	.05	.01
❑ 455 Randy Johnson	.30	.10
❑ 456 Jeffrey Leonard	.05	.01
❑ 457 Edgar Martinez	.15	.05
❑ 458 Tino Martinez	.25	.08
❑ 459 Pete O'Brien UER (1987 BA .266, should be .286)	.05	.01
❑ 460 Harold Reynolds	.10	.02
❑ 461 Mike Schooler	.05	.01
❑ 462 Bill Swift	.05	.01
❑ 463 David Valle	.05	.01
❑ 464 Omar Vizquel	.15	.05
❑ 465 Matt Young	.05	.01
❑ 466 Brady Anderson	.10	.02
❑ 467 Jeff Ballard UER (Missing top of right parenthes)	.05	.01
❑ 468 Juan Bell	.05	.01
❑ 469A Mike Devereaux (First line of text ends with six)	.10	.02
❑ 469B Mike Devereaux		

Card		
(First line of text ends with run)	.10	.02
❑ 470 Steve Finley	.10	.02
❑ 471 Dave Gallagher	.05	.01
❑ 472 Leo Gomez	.05	.01
❑ 473 Rene Gonzales	.05	.01
❑ 474 Pete Harnisch	.05	.01
❑ 475 Kevin Hickey	.05	.01
❑ 476 Chris Hoiles	.05	.01
❑ 477 Sam Horn	.05	.01
❑ 478 Tim Hulett (Photo shows National Leaguer sliding)	.05	.01
❑ 479 Dave Johnson	.05	.01
❑ 480 Ron Kittle UER (Edmonton misspelled as Edmundton)	.05	.01
❑ 481 Ben McDonald	.05	.01
❑ 482 Bob Melvin	.05	.01
❑ 483 Bob Milacki	.05	.01
❑ 484 Randy Milligan	.05	.01
❑ 485 John Mitchell	.05	.01
❑ 486 Gregg Olson	.05	.01
❑ 487 Joe Orsulak	.05	.01
❑ 488 Joe Price	.05	.01
❑ 489 Bill Ripken	.05	.01
❑ 490 Cal Ripken	.75	.30
❑ 491 Curt Schilling	.25	.08
❑ 492 David Segui	.05	.01
❑ 493 Anthony Telford RC	.05	.01
❑ 494 Mickey Tettleton	.05	.01
❑ 495 Mark Williamson	.05	.01
❑ 496 Craig Worthington	.05	.01
❑ 497 Juan Agosto	.05	.01
❑ 498 Eric Anthony	.05	.01
❑ 499 Craig Biggio	.15	.05
❑ 500 Ken Caminiti UER	.10	.02
❑ 501 Casey Candaele	.05	.01
❑ 502 Andujar Cedeno	.05	.01
❑ 503 Danny Darwin	.05	.01
❑ 504 Mark Davidson	.05	.01
❑ 505 Glenn Davis	.05	.01
❑ 506 Jim Deshaies	.05	.01
❑ 507 Luis Gonzalez RC	.50	.20
❑ 508 Bill Gullickson	.05	.01
❑ 509 Xavier Hernandez	.05	.01
❑ 510 Brian Meyer	.05	.01
❑ 511 Ken Oberkfell	.05	.01
❑ 512 Mark Portugal	.05	.01
❑ 513 Rafael Ramirez	.05	.01
❑ 514 Karl Rhodes	.05	.01
❑ 515 Mike Scott	.05	.01
❑ 516 Mike Simms RC	.05	.01
❑ 517 Dave Smith	.05	.01
❑ 518 Franklin Stubbs	.05	.01
❑ 519 Glenn Wilson	.05	.01
❑ 520 Eric Yelding UER (Text has 63 steals, stats have)	.05	.01
❑ 521 Gerald Young	.05	.01
❑ 522 Shawn Abner	.05	.01
❑ 523 Roberto Alomar	.15	.05
❑ 524 Andy Benes	.05	.01
❑ 525 Joe Carter	.10	.02
❑ 526 Jack Clark	.10	.02
❑ 527 Joey Cora	.05	.01
❑ 528 Paul Faries RC	.05	.01
❑ 529 Tony Gwynn	.30	.10
❑ 530 Atlee Hammaker	.05	.01
❑ 531 Greg W. Harris	.05	.01
❑ 532 Thomas Howard	.05	.01
❑ 533 Bruce Hurst	.05	.01
❑ 534 Craig Lefferts	.05	.01
❑ 535 Derek Lilliquist	.05	.01
❑ 536 Fred Lynn	.05	.01
❑ 537 Mike Pagliarulo	.05	.01
❑ 538 Mark Parent	.05	.01
❑ 539 Dennis Rasmussen	.05	.01
❑ 540 Bip Roberts	.05	.01
❑ 541 Richard Rodriguez RC	.05	.01
❑ 542 Benito Santiago	.10	.02
❑ 543 Calvin Schiraldi	.05	.01
❑ 544 Eric Show	.05	.01
❑ 545 Phil Stephenson	.05	.01
❑ 546 Garry Templeton UER (Born 3/24/57, should be 3/2)	.05	.01
❑ 547 Ed Whitson	.05	.01
❑ 548 Eddie Williams	.05	.01
❑ 549 Kevin Appier	.10	.02
❑ 550 Luis Aquino	.05	.01
❑ 551 Bob Boone	.10	.02
❑ 552 George Brett	.60	.25
❑ 553 Jeff Conine RC	.40	.15
❑ 554 Steve Crawford	.05	.01
❑ 555 Mark Davis	.05	.01
❑ 556 Storm Davis	.05	.01
❑ 557 Jim Eisenreich	.05	.01
❑ 558 Steve Farr	.05	.01
❑ 559 Tom Gordon	.05	.01
❑ 560 Mark Gubicza	.05	.01
❑ 561 Bo Jackson	.25	.08
❑ 562 Mike Macfarlane	.05	.01
❑ 563 Brian McRae RC	.25	.08
❑ 564 Jeff Montgomery	.05	.01
❑ 565 Bill Pecota	.05	.01
❑ 566 Gerald Perry	.05	.01
❑ 567 Bret Saberhagen	.10	.02
❑ 568 Jeff Schulz RC	.05	.01
❑ 569 Kevin Seitzer	.05	.01
❑ 570 Terry Shumpert	.05	.01
❑ 571 Kurt Stillwell	.05	.01
❑ 572 Danny Tartabull	.05	.01
❑ 573 Gary Thurman	.05	.01
❑ 574 Frank White	.10	.02
❑ 575 Willie Wilson	.05	.01
❑ 576 Chris Bosio	.05	.01
❑ 577 Greg Brock	.05	.01
❑ 578 George Canale	.05	.01
❑ 579 Chuck Crim	.05	.01
❑ 580 Rob Deer	.05	.01
❑ 581 Edgar Diaz	.05	.01
❑ 582 Tom Edens RC	.05	.01
❑ 583 Mike Felder	.05	.01
❑ 584 Jim Gantner	.05	.01
❑ 585 Darryl Hamilton	.05	.01
❑ 586 Ted Higuera	.05	.01
❑ 587 Mark Knudson	.05	.01
❑ 588 Bill Krueger	.05	.01
❑ 589 Tim McIntosh	.05	.01
❑ 590 Paul Mirabella	.05	.01
❑ 591 Paul Molitor	.10	.02
❑ 592 Jaime Navarro	.05	.01
❑ 593 Dave Parker	.10	.02
❑ 594 Dan Plesac	.05	.01
❑ 595 Ron Robinson	.05	.01
❑ 596 Gary Sheffield	.10	.02
❑ 597 Bill Spiers	.05	.01
❑ 598 B.J. Surhoff	.10	.02
❑ 599 Greg Vaughn	.05	.01
❑ 600 Randy Veres	.05	.01
❑ 601 Robin Yount	.40	.15
❑ 602 Rick Aguilera	.10	.02
❑ 603 Allan Anderson	.05	.01
❑ 604 Juan Berenguer	.05	.01
❑ 605 Randy Bush	.05	.01
❑ 606 Carmelo Castillo	.05	.01
❑ 607 Tim Drummond	.05	.01
❑ 608 Scott Erickson	.05	.01
❑ 609 Gary Gaetti	.10	.02
❑ 610 Greg Gagne	.05	.01
❑ 611 Dan Gladden	.05	.01
❑ 612 Mark Guthrie	.05	.01
❑ 613 Brian Harper	.05	.01
❑ 614 Kent Hrbek	.10	.02
❑ 615 Gene Larkin	.05	.01
❑ 616 Terry Leach	.05	.01
❑ 617 Nelson Liriano	.05	.01
❑ 618 Shane Mack	.05	.01
❑ 619 John Moses	.05	.01
❑ 620 Pedro Munoz RC	.10	.02
❑ 621 Al Newman	.05	.01
❑ 622 Junior Ortiz	.05	.01
❑ 623 Kirby Puckett	.25	.08
❑ 624 Roy Smith	.05	.01
❑ 625 Kevin Tapani	.05	.01
❑ 626 Gary Wayne	.05	.01
❑ 627 David West	.05	.01
❑ 628 Cris Carpenter	.05	.01
❑ 629 Vince Coleman	.05	.01
❑ 630 Ken Dayley	.05	.01
❑ 631A Jose DeLeon ERR	.05	.01
❑ 631B Jose DeLeon COR	.05	.01
❑ 632 Frank DiPino	.05	.01
❑ 633 Bernard Gilkey	.05	.01
❑ 634A Pedro Guerrero ERR	.10	.02
❑ 634B Pedro Guerrero COR	.10	.02
❑ 635 Ken Hill	.05	.01
❑ 636 Felix Jose	.05	.01
❑ 637 Ray Lankford	.10	.02
❑ 638 Joe Magrane	.05	.01
❑ 639 Tom Niedenfuer	.05	.01
❑ 640 Jose Oquendo	.05	.01
❑ 641 Tom Pagnozzi	.05	.01
❑ 642 Terry Pendleton	.10	.02
❑ 643 Mike Perez RC	.10	.02
❑ 644 Bryn Smith	.05	.01
❑ 645 Lee Smith	.10	.02
❑ 646 Ozzie Smith	.40	.15
❑ 647 Scott Terry	.05	.01
❑ 648 Bob Tewksbury	.05	.01
❑ 649 Milt Thompson	.05	.01
❑ 650 John Tudor	.05	.01
❑ 651 Denny Walling	.05	.01
❑ 652 Craig Wilson RC	.05	.01
❑ 653 Todd Worrell	.05	.01
❑ 654 Todd Zeile	.05	.01
❑ 655 Oscar Azocar	.05	.01
❑ 656 Steve Balboni UER (Born 1/5/57, should be 1/16)	.05	.01
❑ 657 Jesse Barfield	.05	.01
❑ 658 Greg Cadaret	.05	.01
❑ 659 Chuck Cary	.05	.01
❑ 660 Rick Cerone	.05	.01
❑ 661 Dave Eiland	.05	.01
❑ 662 Alvaro Espinoza	.05	.01
❑ 663 Bob Geren	.05	.01
❑ 664 Lee Guetterman	.05	.01
❑ 665 Mel Hall	.05	.01
❑ 666 Andy Hawkins	.05	.01
❑ 667 Jimmy Jones	.05	.01
❑ 668 Roberto Kelly	.05	.01
❑ 669 Dave LaPoint UER (No '81 Brewers stats, totals a)	.05	.01
❑ 670 Tim Leary	.05	.01
❑ 671 Jim Leyritz	.05	.01
❑ 672 Kevin Maas	.05	.01
❑ 673 Don Mattingly	.60	.25
❑ 674 Matt Nokes	.05	.01
❑ 675 Pascual Perez	.05	.01
❑ 676 Eric Plunk	.05	.01
❑ 677 Dave Righetti	.10	.02
❑ 678 Jeff D. Robinson	.05	.01
❑ 679 Steve Sax	.05	.01
❑ 680 Mike Witt	.05	.01
❑ 681 Steve Avery UER	.05	.01
❑ 682 Mike Bell RC	.05	.01
❑ 683 Jeff Blauser	.05	.01
❑ 684 Francisco Cabrera UER (Born 10/16, should say 10)	.05	.01
❑ 685 Tony Castillo	.05	.01
❑ 686 Marty Clary UER (Shown pitching righty, but bio)	.05	.01
❑ 687 Nick Esasky	.05	.01
❑ 688 Ron Gant	.10	.02
❑ 689 Tom Glavine	.15	.05
❑ 690 Mark Grant	.05	.01
❑ 691 Tommy Gregg	.05	.01
❑ 692 Dwayne Henry	.05	.01
❑ 693 David Justice	.10	.02
❑ 694 Jimmy Kremers	.05	.01
❑ 695 Charlie Leibrandt	.05	.01
❑ 696 Mark Lemke	.05	.01
❑ 697 Oddibe McDowell	.05	.01
❑ 698 Greg Olson	.05	.01
❑ 699 Jeff Parrett	.05	.01
❑ 700 Jim Presley	.05	.01
❑ 701 Victor Rosario RC	.05	.01
❑ 702 Lonnie Smith	.05	.01
❑ 703 Pete Smith	.05	.01
❑ 704 John Smoltz	.15	.05
❑ 705 Mike Stanton	.05	.01
❑ 706 Andres Thomas	.05	.01
❑ 707 Jeff Treadway	.05	.01

Card	Mint	NRMT
❑ 708 Jim Vatcher RC	.05	.01
❑ 709 R.Sandberg/C.Fielder	.25	.08
❑ 710 K.Griffey Jr./B.Bonds	1.00	.40
❑ 711 B.Bonilla/B.Larkin	.10	.02
❑ 712 Top Game Savers Bobby Thigpen John Franco	.05	.01
❑ 713 A.Dawson/R.Sandberg UER	.25	.08
❑ 714 CL:A's/Pirates Reds/Red Sox	.05	.01
❑ 715 CL:White Sox/Mets Blue Jays/Dodgers	.05	.01
❑ 716 CL:Expos/Giants Rangers/Angels	.05	.01
❑ 717 CL:Tigers/Indians Phillies/Cubs	.05	.01
❑ 718 CL:Mariners/Orioles Astros/Padres	.05	.01
❑ 719 CL:Royals/Brewers Twins/Cardinals	.05	.01
❑ 720 CL:Yankees/Braves Superstars/Specials	.05	.01

1992 Fleer

Card	Mint	NRMT
❑ COMPLETE SET (720)	10.00	4.00
❑ COMP.HOBBY SET (732)	20.00	8.00
❑ COMP.RETAIL SET (732)	20.00	8.00
❑ 1 Brady Anderson	.10	.02
❑ 2 Jose Bautista	.10	.02
❑ 3 Juan Bell	.10	.02
❑ 4 Glenn Davis	.10	.02
❑ 5 Mike Devereaux	.10	.02
❑ 6 Dwight Evans	.15	.05
❑ 7 Mike Flanagan	.10	.02
❑ 8 Leo Gomez	.10	.02
❑ 9 Chris Hoiles	.10	.02
❑ 10 Sam Horn	.10	.02
❑ 11 Tim Hulett	.10	.02
❑ 12 Dave Johnson	.10	.02
❑ 13 Chito Martinez	.10	.02
❑ 14 Ben McDonald	.10	.02
❑ 15 Bob Melvin	.10	.02
❑ 16 Luis Mercedes	.10	.02
❑ 17 Jose Mesa	.10	.02
❑ 18 Bob Milacki	.10	.02
❑ 19 Randy Milligan	.10	.02
❑ 20 Mike Mussina	.25	.08
❑ 21 Gregg Olson	.10	.02
❑ 22 Joe Orsulak	.10	.02
❑ 23 Jim Poole	.10	.02
❑ 24 Arthur Rhodes	.10	.02
❑ 25 Billy Ripken	.10	.02
❑ 26 Cal Ripken	.75	.30
❑ 27 David Segui	.10	.02
❑ 28 Roy Smith	.10	.02
❑ 29 Anthony Telford	.10	.02
❑ 30 Mark Williamson	.10	.02
❑ 31 Craig Worthington	.10	.02
❑ 32 Wade Boggs	.15	.05
❑ 33 Tom Bolton	.10	.02
❑ 34 Tom Brunansky	.10	.02
❑ 35 Ellis Burks	.10	.02
❑ 36 Jack Clark	.10	.02
❑ 37 Roger Clemens	.50	.20
❑ 38 Danny Darwin	.10	.02
❑ 39 Mike Greenwell	.10	.02
❑ 40 Joe Hesketh	.10	.02
❑ 41 Daryl Irvine	.10	.02
❑ 42 Dennis Lamp	.10	.02
❑ 43 Tony Pena	.10	.02
❑ 44 Phil Plantier	.10	.02
❑ 45 Carlos Quintana	.10	.02
❑ 46 Jeff Reardon	.10	.02
❑ 47 Jody Reed	.10	.02
❑ 48 Luis Rivera	.10	.02
❑ 49 Mo Vaughn	.10	.02
❑ 50 Jim Abbott	.15	.05
❑ 51 Kyle Abbott	.10	.02
❑ 52 Ruben Amaro	.10	.02
❑ 53 Scott Bailes	.10	.02
❑ 54 Chris Beasley	.10	.02
❑ 55 Mark Eichhorn	.10	.02
❑ 56 Mike Fetters	.10	.02
❑ 57 Chuck Finley	.10	.02
❑ 58 Gary Gaetti	.10	.02
❑ 59 Dave Gallagher	.10	.02
❑ 60 Donnie Hill	.10	.02
❑ 61 Bryan Harvey UER (Lee Smith led the Majors with	.10	.02
❑ 62 Wally Joyner	.10	.02
❑ 63 Mark Langston	.10	.02
❑ 64 Kirk McCaskill	.10	.02
❑ 65 John Orton	.10	.02
❑ 66 Lance Parrish	.10	.02
❑ 67 Luis Polonia	.10	.02
❑ 68 Bobby Rose	.10	.02
❑ 69 Dick Schofield	.10	.02
❑ 70 Luis Sojo	.10	.02
❑ 71 Lee Stevens	.10	.02
❑ 72 Dave Winfield	.10	.02
❑ 73 Cliff Young	.10	.02
❑ 74 Wilson Alvarez	.10	.02
❑ 75 Esteban Beltre	.10	.02
❑ 76 Joey Cora	.10	.02
❑ 77 Brian Drahman	.10	.02
❑ 78 Alex Fernandez	.10	.02
❑ 79 Carlton Fisk	.15	.05
❑ 80 Scott Fletcher	.10	.02
❑ 81 Craig Grebeck	.10	.02
❑ 82 Ozzie Guillen	.10	.02
❑ 83 Greg Hibbard	.10	.02
❑ 84 Charlie Hough	.10	.02
❑ 85 Mike Huff	.10	.02
❑ 86 Bo Jackson	.25	.08
❑ 87 Lance Johnson	.10	.02
❑ 88 Ron Karkovice	.10	.02
❑ 89 Jack McDowell	.10	.02
❑ 90 Matt Merullo	.10	.02
❑ 91 Warren Newson	.10	.02
❑ 92 Donn Pall UER (Called Dunn on card back)	.10	.02
❑ 93 Dan Pasqua	.10	.02
❑ 94 Ken Patterson	.10	.02
❑ 95 Melido Perez	.10	.02
❑ 96 Scott Radinsky	.10	.02
❑ 97 Tim Raines	.10	.02
❑ 98 Sammy Sosa	.25	.08
❑ 99 Bobby Thigpen	.10	.02
❑ 100 Frank Thomas	.25	.08
❑ 101 Robin Ventura	.10	.02
❑ 102 Mike Aldrete	.10	.02
❑ 103 Sandy Alomar Jr.	.10	.02
❑ 104 Carlos Baerga	.10	.02
❑ 105 Albert Belle	.10	.02
❑ 106 Willie Blair	.10	.02
❑ 107 Jerry Browne	.10	.02
❑ 108 Alex Cole	.10	.02
❑ 109 Felix Fermin	.10	.02
❑ 110 Glenallen Hill	.10	.02
❑ 111 Shawn Hillegas	.10	.02
❑ 112 Chris James	.10	.02
❑ 113 Reggie Jefferson	.10	.02
❑ 114 Doug Jones	.10	.02
❑ 115 Eric King	.10	.02
❑ 116 Mark Lewis	.10	.02
❑ 117 Carlos Martinez	.10	.02
❑ 118 Charles Nagy UER (Throws right, but card says le	.10	.02
❑ 119 Rod Nichols	.10	.02
❑ 120 Steve Olin	.10	.02
❑ 121 Jesse Orosco	.10	.02
❑ 122 Rudy Seanez	.10	.02
❑ 123 Joel Skinner	.10	.02
❑ 124 Greg Swindell	.10	.02
❑ 125 Jim Thome	.25	.08
❑ 126 Mark Whiten	.10	.02
❑ 127 Scott Aldred	.10	.02
❑ 128 Andy Allanson	.10	.02
❑ 129 John Cerutti	.10	.02
❑ 130 Milt Cuyler	.10	.02
❑ 131 Mike Dalton	.10	.02
❑ 132 Rob Deer	.10	.02
❑ 133 Cecil Fielder	.10	.02
❑ 134 Travis Fryman	.10	.02
❑ 135 Dan Gakeler	.10	.02
❑ 136 Paul Gibson	.10	.02
❑ 137 Bill Gullickson	.10	.02
❑ 138 Mike Henneman	.10	.02
❑ 139 Pete Incaviglia	.10	.02
❑ 140 Mark Leiter	.10	.02
❑ 141 Scott Livingstone	.10	.02
❑ 142 Lloyd Moseby	.10	.02
❑ 143 Tony Phillips	.10	.02
❑ 144 Mark Salas	.10	.02
❑ 145 Frank Tanana	.10	.02
❑ 146 Walt Terrell	.10	.02
❑ 147 Mickey Tettleton	.10	.02
❑ 148 Alan Trammell	.10	.02
❑ 149 Lou Whitaker	.10	.02
❑ 150 Kevin Appier	.10	.02
❑ 151 Luis Aquino	.10	.02
❑ 152 Todd Benzinger	.10	.02
❑ 153 Mike Boddicker	.10	.02
❑ 154 George Brett	.60	.25
❑ 155 Storm Davis	.10	.02
❑ 156 Jim Eisenreich	.10	.02
❑ 157 Kirk Gibson	.10	.02
❑ 158 Tom Gordon	.10	.02
❑ 159 Mark Gubicza	.10	.02
❑ 160 David Howard	.10	.02
❑ 161 Mike Macfarlane	.10	.02
❑ 162 Brent Mayne	.10	.02
❑ 163 Brian McRae	.10	.02
❑ 164 Jeff Montgomery	.10	.02
❑ 165 Bill Pecota	.10	.02
❑ 166 Harvey Pulliam	.10	.02
❑ 167 Bret Saberhagen	.10	.02
❑ 168 Kevin Seitzer	.10	.02
❑ 169 Terry Shumpert	.10	.02
❑ 170 Kurt Stillwell	.10	.02
❑ 171 Danny Tartabull	.10	.02
❑ 172 Gary Thurman	.10	.02
❑ 173 Dante Bichette	.10	.02
❑ 174 Kevin D. Brown	.10	.02
❑ 175 Chuck Crim	.10	.02
❑ 176 Jim Gantner	.10	.02
❑ 177 Darryl Hamilton	.10	.02
❑ 178 Ted Higuera	.10	.02
❑ 179 Darren Holmes	.10	.02
❑ 180 Mark Lee	.10	.02
❑ 181 Julio Machado	.10	.02
❑ 182 Paul Molitor	.10	.02
❑ 183 Jaime Navarro	.10	.02
❑ 184 Edwin Nunez	.10	.02
❑ 185 Dan Plesac	.10	.02
❑ 186 Willie Randolph	.10	.02
❑ 187 Ron Robinson	.10	.02
❑ 188 Gary Sheffield	.10	.02
❑ 189 Bill Spiers	.10	.02
❑ 190 B.J. Surhoff	.10	.02
❑ 191 Dale Sveum	.10	.02
❑ 192 Greg Vaughn	.10	.02
❑ 193 Bill Wegman	.10	.02
❑ 194 Robin Yount	.40	.15
❑ 195 Rick Aguilera	.10	.02
❑ 196 Allan Anderson	.10	.02
❑ 197 Steve Bedrosian	.10	.02
❑ 198 Randy Bush	.10	.02
❑ 199 Larry Casian	.10	.02
❑ 200 Chili Davis	.10	.02
❑ 201 Scott Erickson	.10	.02
❑ 202 Greg Gagne	.10	.02
❑ 203 Dan Gladden	.10	.02
❑ 204 Brian Harper	.10	.02
❑ 205 Kent Hrbek	.10	.02
❑ 206 Chuck Knoblauch UER	.10	.02
❑ 207 Gene Larkin	.10	.02

	Player		
❑ 208	Terry Leach	.10	.02
❑ 209	Scott Leius	.10	.02
❑ 210	Shane Mack	.10	.02
❑ 211	Jack Morris	.10	.02
❑ 212	Pedro Munoz	.10	.02
❑ 213	Denny Neagle	.10	.02
❑ 214	Al Newman	.10	.02
❑ 215	Junior Ortiz	.10	.02
❑ 216	Mike Pagliarulo	.10	.02
❑ 217	Kirby Puckett	.25	.08
❑ 218	Paul Sorrento	.10	.02
❑ 219	Kevin Tapani	.10	.02
❑ 220	Lenny Webster	.10	.02
❑ 221	Jesse Barfield	.10	.02
❑ 222	Greg Cadaret	.10	.02
❑ 223	Dave Eiland	.10	.02
❑ 224	Alvaro Espinoza	.10	.02
❑ 225	Steve Farr	.10	.02
❑ 226	Bob Geren	.10	.02
❑ 227	Lee Guetterman	.10	.02
❑ 228	John Habyan	.10	.02
❑ 229	Mel Hall	.10	.02
❑ 230	Steve Howe	.10	.02
❑ 231	Mike Humphreys	.10	.02
❑ 232	Scott Kamieniecki	.10	.02
❑ 233	Pat Kelly	.10	.02
❑ 234	Roberto Kelly	.10	.02
❑ 235	Tim Leary	.10	.02
❑ 236	Kevin Maas	.10	.02
❑ 237	Don Mattingly	.60	.25
❑ 238	Hensley Meulens	.10	.02
❑ 239	Matt Nokes	.10	.02
❑ 240	Pascual Perez	.10	.02
❑ 241	Eric Plunk	.10	.02
❑ 242	John Ramos	.10	.02
❑ 243	Scott Sanderson	.10	.02
❑ 244	Steve Sax	.10	.02
❑ 245	Wade Taylor	.10	.02
❑ 246	Randy Velarde	.10	.02
❑ 247	Bernie Williams	.15	.05
❑ 248	Troy Afenir	.10	.02
❑ 249	Harold Baines	.10	.02
❑ 250	Lance Blankenship	.10	.02
❑ 251	Mike Bordick	.10	.02
❑ 252	Jose Canseco	.15	.05
❑ 253	Steve Chitren	.10	.02
❑ 254	Ron Darling	.10	.02
❑ 255	Dennis Eckersley	.10	.02
❑ 256	Mike Gallego	.10	.02
❑ 257	Dave Henderson	.10	.02
❑ 258	Rickey Henderson	.25	.08
❑ 259	Rick Honeycutt	.10	.02
❑ 260	Brook Jacoby	.10	.02
❑ 261	Carney Lansford	.10	.02
❑ 262	Mark McGwire	.60	.25
❑ 263	Mike Moore	.10	.02
❑ 264	Gene Nelson	.10	.02
❑ 265	Jamie Quirk	.10	.02
❑ 266	Joe Slusarski	.10	.02
❑ 267	Terry Steinbach	.10	.02
❑ 268	Dave Stewart	.10	.02
❑ 269	Todd Van Poppel	.10	.02
❑ 270	Walt Weiss	.10	.02
❑ 271	Bob Welch	.10	.02
❑ 272	Curt Young	.10	.02
❑ 273	Scott Bradley	.10	.02
❑ 274	Greg Briley	.10	.02
❑ 275	Jay Buhner	.10	.02
❑ 276	Henry Cotto	.10	.02
❑ 277	Alvin Davis	.10	.02
❑ 278	Rich DeLucia	.10	.02
❑ 279	Ken Griffey Jr.	.40	.15
❑ 280	Erik Hanson	.10	.02
❑ 281	Brian Holman	.10	.02
❑ 282	Mike Jackson	.10	.02
❑ 283	Randy Johnson	.25	.08
❑ 284	Tracy Jones	.10	.02
❑ 285	Bill Krueger	.10	.02
❑ 286	Edgar Martinez	.15	.05
❑ 287	Tino Martinez	.15	.05
❑ 288	Rob Murphy	.10	.02
❑ 289	Pete O'Brien	.10	.02
❑ 290	Alonzo Powell	.10	.02
❑ 291	Harold Reynolds	.10	.02
❑ 292	Mike Schooler	.10	.02
❑ 293	Russ Swan	.10	.02
❑ 294	Bill Swift	.10	.02
❑ 295	Dave Valle	.10	.02
❑ 296	Omar Vizquel	.15	.05
❑ 297	Gerald Alexander	.10	.02
❑ 298	Brad Arnsberg	.10	.02
❑ 299	Kevin Brown	.10	.02
❑ 300	Jack Daugherty	.10	.02
❑ 301	Mario Diaz	.10	.02
❑ 302	Brian Downing	.10	.02
❑ 303	Julio Franco	.10	.02
❑ 304	Juan Gonzalez	.15	.05
❑ 305	Rich Gossage	.10	.02
❑ 306	Jose Guzman	.10	.02
❑ 307	Jose Hernandez RC	.25	.08
❑ 308	Jeff Huson	.10	.02
❑ 309	Mike Jeffcoat	.10	.02
❑ 310	Terry Mathews	.10	.02
❑ 311	Rafael Palmeiro	.15	.05
❑ 312	Dean Palmer	.10	.02
❑ 313	Geno Petralli	.10	.02
❑ 314	Gary Pettis	.10	.02
❑ 315	Kevin Reimer	.10	.02
❑ 316	Ivan Rodriguez	.25	.08
❑ 317	Kenny Rogers	.10	.02
❑ 318	Wayne Rosenthal	.10	.02
❑ 319	Jeff Russell	.10	.02
❑ 320	Nolan Ryan	1.00	.40
❑ 321	Ruben Sierra	.10	.02
❑ 322	Jim Acker	.10	.02
❑ 323	Roberto Alomar	.15	.05
❑ 324	Derek Bell	.10	.02
❑ 325	Pat Borders	.10	.02
❑ 326	Tom Candiotti	.10	.02
❑ 327	Joe Carter	.10	.02
❑ 328	Rob Ducey	.10	.02
❑ 329	Kelly Gruber	.10	.02
❑ 330	Juan Guzman	.10	.02
❑ 331	Tom Henke	.10	.02
❑ 332	Jimmy Key	.10	.02
❑ 333	Manny Lee	.10	.02
❑ 334	Al Leiter	.10	.02
❑ 335	Bob MacDonald	.10	.02
❑ 336	Candy Maldonado	.10	.02
❑ 337	Rance Mulliniks	.10	.02
❑ 338	Greg Myers	.10	.02
❑ 339	John Olerud UER	.10	.02
❑ 340	Ed Sprague	.10	.02
❑ 341	Dave Stieb	.10	.02
❑ 342	Todd Stottlemyre	.10	.02
❑ 343	Mike Timlin	.10	.02
❑ 344	Duane Ward	.10	.02
❑ 345	David Wells	.10	.02
❑ 346	Devon White	.10	.02
❑ 347	Mookie Wilson	.10	.02
❑ 348	Eddie Zosky	.10	.02
❑ 349	Steve Avery	.10	.02
❑ 350	Mike Bell	.10	.02
❑ 351	Rafael Belliard	.10	.02
❑ 352	Juan Berenguer	.10	.02
❑ 353	Jeff Blauser	.10	.02
❑ 354	Sid Bream	.10	.02
❑ 355	Francisco Cabrera	.10	.02
❑ 356	Marvin Freeman	.10	.02
❑ 357	Ron Gant	.10	.02
❑ 358	Tom Glavine	.15	.05
❑ 359	Brian Hunter	.10	.02
❑ 360	David Justice	.10	.02
❑ 361	Charlie Leibrandt	.10	.02
❑ 362	Mark Lemke	.10	.02
❑ 363	Kent Mercker	.10	.02
❑ 364	Keith Mitchell	.10	.02
❑ 365	Greg Olson	.10	.02
❑ 366	Terry Pendleton	.10	.02
❑ 367	Armando Reynoso RC	.25	.08
❑ 368	Deion Sanders	.15	.05
❑ 369	Lonnie Smith	.10	.02
❑ 370	Pete Smith	.10	.02
❑ 371	John Smoltz	.15	.05
❑ 372	Mike Stanton	.10	.02
❑ 373	Jeff Treadway	.10	.02
❑ 374	Mark Wohlers	.10	.02
❑ 375	Paul Assenmacher	.10	.02
❑ 376	George Bell	.10	.02
❑ 377	Shawn Boskie	.10	.02
❑ 378	Frank Castillo	.10	.02
❑ 379	Andre Dawson	.10	.02
❑ 380	Shawon Dunston	.10	.02
❑ 381	Mark Grace	.15	.05
❑ 382	Mike Harkey	.10	.02
❑ 383	Danny Jackson	.10	.02
❑ 384	Les Lancaster	.10	.02
❑ 385	Ced Landrum	.10	.02
❑ 386	Greg Maddux	.40	.15
❑ 387	Derrick May	.10	.02
❑ 388	Chuck McElroy	.10	.02
❑ 389	Ryne Sandberg	.40	.15
❑ 390	Heathcliff Slocumb	.10	.02
❑ 391	Dave Smith	.10	.02
❑ 392	Dwight Smith	.10	.02
❑ 393	Rick Sutcliffe	.10	.02
❑ 394	Hector Villanueva	.10	.02
❑ 395	Chico Walker	.10	.02
❑ 396	Jerome Walton	.10	.02
❑ 397	Rick Wilkins	.10	.02
❑ 398	Jack Armstrong	.10	.02
❑ 399	Freddie Benavides	.10	.02
❑ 400	Glenn Braggs	.10	.02
❑ 401	Tom Browning	.10	.02
❑ 402	Norm Charlton	.10	.02
❑ 403	Eric Davis	.10	.02
❑ 404	Rob Dibble	.10	.02
❑ 405	Bill Doran	.10	.02
❑ 406	Mariano Duncan	.10	.02
❑ 407	Kip Gross	.10	.02
❑ 408	Chris Hammond	.10	.02
❑ 409	Billy Hatcher	.10	.02
❑ 410	Chris Jones	.10	.02
❑ 411	Barry Larkin	.15	.05
❑ 412	Hal Morris	.10	.02
❑ 413	Randy Myers	.10	.02
❑ 414	Joe Oliver	.10	.02
❑ 415	Paul O'Neill	.15	.05
❑ 416	Ted Power	.10	.02
❑ 417	Luis Quinones	.10	.02
❑ 418	Jeff Reed	.10	.02
❑ 419	Jose Rijo	.10	.02
❑ 420	Chris Sabo	.10	.02
❑ 421	Reggie Sanders	.10	.02
❑ 422	Scott Scudder	.10	.02
❑ 423	Glenn Sutko	.10	.02
❑ 424	Eric Anthony	.10	.02
❑ 425	Jeff Bagwell	.25	.08
❑ 426	Craig Biggio	.15	.05
❑ 427	Ken Caminiti	.10	.02
❑ 428	Casey Candaele	.10	.02
❑ 429	Mike Capel	.10	.02
❑ 430	Andujar Cedeno	.10	.02
❑ 431	Jim Corsi	.10	.02
❑ 432	Mark Davidson	.10	.02
❑ 433	Steve Finley	.10	.02
❑ 434	Luis Gonzalez	.10	.02
❑ 435	Pete Harnisch	.10	.02
❑ 436	Dwayne Henry	.10	.02
❑ 437	Xavier Hernandez	.10	.02
❑ 438	Jimmy Jones	.10	.02
❑ 439	Darryl Kile	.10	.02
❑ 440	Rob Mallicoat	.10	.02
❑ 441	Andy Mota	.10	.02
❑ 442	Al Osuna	.10	.02
❑ 443	Mark Portugal	.10	.02
❑ 444	Scott Servais	.10	.02
❑ 445	Mike Simms	.10	.02
❑ 446	Gerald Young	.10	.02
❑ 447	Tim Belcher	.10	.02
❑ 448	Brett Butler	.10	.02
❑ 449	John Candelaria	.10	.02
❑ 450	Gary Carter	.10	.02
❑ 451	Dennis Cook	.10	.02
❑ 452	Tim Crews	.10	.02
❑ 453	Kal Daniels	.10	.02
❑ 454	Jim Gott	.10	.02
❑ 455	Alfredo Griffin	.10	.02
❑ 456	Kevin Gross	.10	.02
❑ 457	Chris Gwynn	.10	.02
❑ 458	Lenny Harris	.10	.02
❑ 459	Orel Hershiser	.10	.02
❑ 460	Jay Howell	.10	.02
❑ 461	Stan Javier	.10	.02
❑ 462	Eric Karros	.10	.02
❑ 463	Ramon Martinez UER (Card says bats right, should)	.10	.02

❑ 464 Roger McDowell UER (Wins add up to 54, totals ha) .10 .02
❑ 465 Mike Morgan .10 .02
❑ 466 Eddie Murray .25 .08
❑ 467 Jose Offerman .10 .02
❑ 468 Bob Ojeda .10 .02
❑ 469 Juan Samuel .10 .02
❑ 470 Mike Scioscia .10 .02
❑ 471 Darryl Strawberry .10 .02
❑ 472 Bret Barberie .10 .02
❑ 473 Brian Barnes .10 .02
❑ 474 Eric Bullock .10 .02
❑ 475 Ivan Calderon .10 .02
❑ 476 Delino DeShields .10 .02
❑ 477 Jeff Fassero .10 .02
❑ 478 Mike Fitzgerald .10 .02
❑ 479 Steve Frey .10 .02
❑ 480 Andres Galarraga .10 .02
❑ 481 Mark Gardner .10 .02
❑ 482 Marquis Grissom .10 .02
❑ 483 Chris Haney .10 .02
❑ 484 Barry Jones .10 .02
❑ 485 Dave Martinez .10 .02
❑ 486 Dennis Martinez .10 .02
❑ 487 Chris Nabholz .10 .02
❑ 488 Spike Owen .10 .02
❑ 489 Gilberto Reyes .10 .02
❑ 490 Mel Rojas .10 .02
❑ 491 Scott Ruskin .10 .02
❑ 492 Bill Sampen .10 .02
❑ 493 Larry Walker .15 .05
❑ 494 Tim Wallach .10 .02
❑ 495 Daryl Boston .10 .02
❑ 496 Hubie Brooks .10 .02
❑ 497 Tim Burke .10 .02
❑ 498 Mark Carreon .10 .02
❑ 499 Tony Castillo .10 .02
❑ 500 Vince Coleman .10 .02
❑ 501 David Cone .10 .02
❑ 502 Kevin Elster .10 .02
❑ 503 Sid Fernandez .10 .02
❑ 504 John Franco .10 .02
❑ 505 Dwight Gooden .10 .02
❑ 506 Todd Hundley .10 .02
❑ 507 Jeff Innis .10 .02
❑ 508 Gregg Jefferies .10 .02
❑ 509 Howard Johnson .10 .02
❑ 510 Dave Magadan .10 .02
❑ 511 Terry McDaniel .10 .02
❑ 512 Kevin McReynolds .10 .02
❑ 513 Keith Miller .10 .02
❑ 514 Charlie O'Brien .10 .02
❑ 515 Mackey Sasser .10 .02
❑ 516 Pete Schourek .10 .02
❑ 517 Julio Valera .10 .02
❑ 518 Frank Viola .10 .02
❑ 519 Wally Whitehurst .10 .02
❑ 520 Anthony Young .10 .02
❑ 521 Andy Ashby .10 .02
❑ 522 Kim Batiste .10 .02
❑ 523 Joe Boever .10 .02
❑ 524 Wes Chamberlain .10 .02
❑ 525 Pat Combs .10 .02
❑ 526 Danny Cox .10 .02
❑ 527 Darren Daulton .10 .02
❑ 528 Jose DeJesus .10 .02
❑ 529 Len Dykstra .10 .02
❑ 530 Darrin Fletcher .10 .02
❑ 531 Tommy Greene .10 .02
❑ 532 Jason Grimsley .10 .02
❑ 533 Charlie Hayes .10 .02
❑ 534 Von Hayes .10 .02
❑ 535 Dave Hollins .10 .02
❑ 536 Ricky Jordan .10 .02
❑ 537 John Kruk .10 .02
❑ 538 Jim Lindeman .10 .02
❑ 539 Mickey Morandini .10 .02
❑ 540 Terry Mulholland .10 .02
❑ 541 Dale Murphy .15 .05
❑ 542 Randy Ready .10 .02
❑ 543 Wally Ritchie UER (Letters in data are cut off o) .10 .02
❑ 544 Bruce Ruffin .10 .02
❑ 545 Steve Searcy .10 .02
❑ 546 Dickie Thon .10 .02
❑ 547 Mitch Williams .10 .02
❑ 548 Stan Belinda .10 .02
❑ 549 Jay Bell .10 .02
❑ 550 Barry Bonds 1.00 .40
❑ 551 Bobby Bonilla .10 .02
❑ 552 Steve Buechele .10 .02
❑ 553 Doug Drabek .10 .02
❑ 554 Neal Heaton .10 .02
❑ 555 Jeff King .10 .02
❑ 556 Bob Kipper .10 .02
❑ 557 Bill Landrum .10 .02
❑ 558 Mike LaValliere .10 .02
❑ 559 Jose Lind .10 .02
❑ 560 Lloyd McClendon .10 .02
❑ 561 Orlando Merced .10 .02
❑ 562 Bob Patterson .10 .02
❑ 563 Joe Redfield .10 .02
❑ 564 Gary Redus .10 .02
❑ 565 Rosario Rodriguez .10 .02
❑ 566 Don Slaught .10 .02
❑ 567 John Smiley .10 .02
❑ 568 Zane Smith .10 .02
❑ 569 Randy Tomlin .10 .02
❑ 570 Andy Van Slyke .15 .05
❑ 571 Gary Varsho .10 .02
❑ 572 Bob Walk .10 .02
❑ 573 John Wehner UER (Actually played for Carolina in) .10 .02
❑ 574 Juan Agosto .10 .02
❑ 575 Cris Carpenter .10 .02
❑ 576 Jose DeLeon .10 .02
❑ 577 Rich Gedman .10 .02
❑ 578 Bernard Gilkey .10 .02
❑ 579 Pedro Guerrero .10 .02
❑ 580 Ken Hill .10 .02
❑ 581 Rex Hudler .10 .02
❑ 582 Felix Jose .10 .02
❑ 583 Ray Lankford .10 .02
❑ 584 Omar Olivares .10 .02
❑ 585 Jose Oquendo .10 .02
❑ 586 Tom Pagnozzi .10 .02
❑ 587 Geronimo Pena .10 .02
❑ 588 Mike Perez .10 .02
❑ 589 Gerald Perry .10 .02
❑ 590 Bryn Smith .10 .02
❑ 591 Lee Smith .10 .02
❑ 592 Ozzie Smith .40 .15
❑ 593 Scott Terry .10 .02
❑ 594 Bob Tewksbury .10 .02
❑ 595 Milt Thompson .10 .02
❑ 596 Todd Zeile .10 .02
❑ 597 Larry Andersen .10 .02
❑ 598 Oscar Azocar .10 .02
❑ 599 Andy Benes .10 .02
❑ 600 Ricky Bones .10 .02
❑ 601 Jerald Clark .10 .02
❑ 602 Pat Clements .10 .02
❑ 603 Paul Faries .10 .02
❑ 604 Tony Fernandez .10 .02
❑ 605 Tony Gwynn .30 .10
❑ 606 Greg W. Harris .10 .02
❑ 607 Thomas Howard .10 .02
❑ 608 Bruce Hurst .10 .02
❑ 609 Darrin Jackson .10 .02
❑ 610 Tom Lampkin .10 .02
❑ 611 Craig Lefferts .10 .02
❑ 612 Jim Lewis RC .10 .02
❑ 613 Mike Maddux .10 .02
❑ 614 Fred McGriff .15 .05
❑ 615 Jose Melendez .10 .02
❑ 616 Jose Mota .10 .02
❑ 617 Dennis Rasmussen .10 .02
❑ 618 Bip Roberts .10 .02
❑ 619 Rich Rodriguez .10 .02
❑ 620 Benito Santiago .10 .02
❑ 621 Craig Shipley .10 .02
❑ 622 Tim Teufel .10 .02
❑ 623 Kevin Ward .10 .02
❑ 624 Ed Whitson .10 .02
❑ 625 Dave Anderson .10 .02
❑ 626 Kevin Bass .10 .02
❑ 627 Rod Beck RC .40 .15
❑ 628 Bud Black .10 .02
❑ 629 Jeff Brantley .10 .02
❑ 630 John Burkett .10 .02
❑ 631 Will Clark .15 .05
❑ 632 Royce Clayton .10 .02
❑ 633 Steve Decker .10 .02
❑ 634 Kelly Downs .10 .02
❑ 635 Mike Felder .10 .02
❑ 636 Scott Garrelts .10 .02
❑ 637 Eric Gunderson .10 .02
❑ 638 Bryan Hickerson RC .10 .02
❑ 639 Darren Lewis .10 .02
❑ 640 Greg Litton .10 .02
❑ 641 Kirt Manwaring .10 .02
❑ 642 Paul McClellan .10 .02
❑ 643 Willie McGee .10 .02
❑ 644 Kevin Mitchell .10 .02
❑ 645 Francisco Oliveras .10 .02
❑ 646 Mike Remlinger .10 .02
❑ 647 Dave Righetti .10 .02
❑ 648 Robby Thompson .10 .02
❑ 649 Jose Uribe .10 .02
❑ 650 Matt Williams .10 .02
❑ 651 Trevor Wilson .10 .02
❑ 652 Tom Goodwin MLP UER .10 .02
❑ 653 Terry Bross MLP .10 .02
❑ 654 Mike Christopher MLP .10 .02
❑ 655 Kenny Lofton .15 .05
❑ 656 Chris Cron MLP .10 .02
❑ 657 Willie Banks MLP .10 .02
❑ 658 Pat Rice MLP .10 .02
❑ 659A Rob Mauer ERR .75 .30
❑ 659B Rob Maurer MLP COR .10 .02
❑ 660 Don Harris MLP .10 .02
❑ 661 Henry Rodriguez MLP .10 .02
❑ 662 Cliff Brantley MLP .10 .02
❑ 663 Mike Linskey MLP UER .10 .02
❑ 664 Gary DiSarcina MLP .10 .02
❑ 665 Gil Heredia RC .25 .08
❑ 666 Vinny Castilla RC 1.00 .40
❑ 667 Paul Abbott MLP .10 .02
❑ 668 Monty Fariss MLP UER (Called Paul on back) .10 .02
❑ 669 Jarvis Brown MLP .10 .02
❑ 670 Wayne Kirby RC .10 .02
❑ 671 Scott Brosius RC .40 .15
❑ 672 Bob Hamelin .10 .02
❑ 673 Joel Johnston MLP .10 .02
❑ 674 Tim Spehr MLP .10 .02
❑ 675A Jeff Gardner ERR P .75 .30
❑ 675B Jeff Gardner MLP COR .10 .02
❑ 676 Rico Rossy MLP .10 .02
❑ 677 Roberto Hernandez MLP .10 .02
❑ 678 Ted Wood MLP .10 .02
❑ 679 Cal Eldred .10 .02
❑ 680 Sean Berry MLP .10 .02
❑ 681 Rickey Henderson RS .15 .05
❑ 682 Nolan Ryan RS .50 .20
❑ 683 Dennis Martinez RS .10 .02
❑ 684 Wilson Alvarez RS .10 .02
❑ 685 Joe Carter RS .10 .02
❑ 686 Dave Winfield RS .10 .02
❑ 687 David Cone RS .10 .02
❑ 688 Jose Canseco LL UER .10 .02
❑ 689 Howard Johnson LL .10 .02
❑ 690 Julio Franco LL .10 .02
❑ 691 Terry Pendleton LL .10 .02
❑ 692 Cecil Fielder LL .10 .02
❑ 693 Scott Erickson LL .10 .02
❑ 694 Tom Glavine LL .10 .02
❑ 695 Dennis Martinez LL .10 .02
❑ 696 Bryan Harvey LL .10 .02
❑ 697 Lee Smith LL .10 .02
❑ 698 Roberto/Sandy Alomar .10 .02
❑ 699 B.Bonilla/W.Clark .10 .02
❑ 700 Wohlers/Mercker/Pena .10 .02
❑ 701 B.Jackson/F.Thomas .15 .05
❑ 702 P.Molitor/Butler .10 .02
❑ 703 C.Ripken/J.Carter .40 .15
❑ 704 B.Larkin/K.Puckett .15 .05
❑ 705 M.Vaughn/C.Fielder .10 .02
❑ 706 R.Martinez/O.Guillen .10 .02
❑ 707 H.Baines/W.Boggs .10 .02
❑ 708 Robin Yount PV .25 .08
❑ 709 Ken Griffey Jr. PV .25 .08
❑ 710 Nolan Ryan PV .50 .20
❑ 711 Cal Ripken PV .40 .15
❑ 712 Frank Thomas PV .15 .05

❑ 713 David Justice PV .10 .02
❑ 714 Checklist 1-101 .10 .02
❑ 715 Checklist 102-194 .10 .02
❑ 716 Checklist 195-296 .10 .02
❑ 717 Checklist 297-397 .10 .02
❑ 718 Checklist 398-494 .10 .02
❑ 719 Checklist 495-596 .10 .02
❑ 720A Checklist 597-720 ERR (659 Rob Mauer) .10 .02
❑ 720B Checklist 597-720 COR (659 Rob Maurer) .10 .02

1992 Fleer Update

❑ COMP.FACT.SET (136) 60.00 30.00
❑ COMPLETE SET (132) 60.00 30.00
❑ 1 Todd Frohwirth .50 .20
❑ 2 Alan Mills .50 .20
❑ 3 Rick Sutcliffe 1.00 .40
❑ 4 John Valentin RC 1.50 .60
❑ 5 Frank Viola 1.00 .40
❑ 6 Bob Zupcic RC .50 .20
❑ 7 Mike Butcher .50 .20
❑ 8 Chad Curtis RC 1.50 .60
❑ 9 Damion Easley RC 1.50 .60
❑ 10 Tim Salmon 1.50 .60
❑ 11 Julio Valera .50 .20
❑ 12 George Bell .50 .20
❑ 13 Roberto Hernandez .50 .20
❑ 14 Shawn Jeter RC .50 .20
❑ 15 Thomas Howard .50 .20
❑ 16 Jesse Levis .50 .20
❑ 17 Kenny Lofton 1.50 .60
❑ 18 Paul Sorrento .50 .20
❑ 19 Rico Brogna .50 .20
❑ 20 John Doherty RC .50 .20
❑ 21 Dan Gladden .50 .20
❑ 22 Buddy Groom RC .50 .20
❑ 23 Shawn Hare RC .50 .20
❑ 24 John Kiely .50 .20
❑ 25 Kurt Knudsen .50 .20
❑ 26 Gregg Jefferies .50 .20
❑ 27 Wally Joyner 1.00 .40
❑ 28 Kevin Koslofski .50 .20
❑ 29 Kevin McReynolds .50 .20
❑ 30 Rusty Meacham .50 .20
❑ 31 Keith Miller .50 .20
❑ 32 Hipolito Pichardo RC .50 .20
❑ 33 Jim Austin .50 .20
❑ 34 Scott Fletcher .50 .20
❑ 35 John Jaha RC 1.50 .60
❑ 36 Pat Listach RC 1.50 .60
❑ 37 Dave Nilsson .50 .20
❑ 38 Kevin Seitzer .50 .20
❑ 39 Tom Edens .50 .20
❑ 40 Pat Mahomes RC 1.50 .60
❑ 41 John Smiley .50 .20
❑ 42 Charlie Hayes .50 .20
❑ 43 Sam Militello .50 .20
❑ 44 Andy Stankiewicz .50 .20
❑ 45 Danny Tartabull .50 .20
❑ 46 Bob Wickman 2.50 1.00
❑ 47 Jerry Browne .50 .20
❑ 48 Kevin Campbell .50 .20
❑ 49 Vince Horsman .50 .20
❑ 50 Troy Neel RC .50 .20
❑ 51 Ruben Sierra 1.00 .40
❑ 52 Bruce Walton .50 .20
❑ 53 Willie Wilson .50 .20
❑ 54 Bret Boone 1.50 .60
❑ 55 Dave Fleming .50 .20
❑ 56 Kevin Mitchell .50 .20
❑ 57 Jeff Nelson RC 2.50 1.00
❑ 58 Shane Turner .50 .20
❑ 59 Jose Canseco 1.50 .60
❑ 60 Jeff Frye RC .50 .20
❑ 61 Danny Leon .50 .20
❑ 62 Roger Pavlik RC .50 .20
❑ 63 David Cone 1.00 .40
❑ 64 Pat Hentgen .50 .20
❑ 65 Randy Knorr .50 .20
❑ 66 Jack Morris 1.00 .40
❑ 67 Dave Winfield 1.00 .40
❑ 68 David Nied RC .50 .20
❑ 69 Otis Nixon .50 .20
❑ 70 Alejandro Pena .50 .20
❑ 71 Jeff Reardon 1.00 .40
❑ 72 Alex Arias RC .50 .20
❑ 73 Jim Bullinger .50 .20
❑ 74 Mike Morgan .50 .20
❑ 75 Rey Sanchez RC 1.50 .60
❑ 76 Bob Scanlan .50 .20
❑ 77 Sammy Sosa Cubs 4.00 1.50
❑ 78 Scott Bankhead .50 .20
❑ 79 Tim Belcher .50 .20
❑ 80 Steve Foster .50 .20
❑ 81 Willie Greene .50 .20
❑ 82 Bip Roberts .50 .20
❑ 83 Scott Ruskin .50 .20
❑ 84 Greg Swindell .50 .20
❑ 85 Juan Guerrero .50 .20
❑ 86 Butch Henry .50 .20
❑ 87 Doug Jones .50 .20
❑ 88 Brian Williams RC .50 .20
❑ 89 Tom Candiotti .50 .20
❑ 90 Eric Davis 1.00 .40
❑ 91 Carlos Hernandez .50 .20
❑ 92 Mike Piazza RC 40.00 20.00
❑ 93 Mike Sharperson .50 .20
❑ 94 Eric Young RC 1.50 .60
❑ 95 Moises Alou 1.00 .40
❑ 96 Greg Colbrunn .50 .20
❑ 97 Wil Cordero .50 .20
❑ 98 Ken Hill .50 .20
❑ 99 John Vander Wal RC 1.50 .60
❑ 100 John Wetteland 1.00 .40
❑ 101 Bobby Bonilla 1.00 .40
❑ 102 Eric Hillman RC .50 .20
❑ 103 Pat Howell .50 .20
❑ 104 Jeff Kent RC 15.00 6.00
❑ 105 Dick Schofield .50 .20
❑ 106 Ryan Thompson RC .50 .20
❑ 107 Chico Walker .50 .20
❑ 108 Juan Bell .50 .20
❑ 109 Mariano Duncan .50 .20
❑ 110 Jeff Grotewold .50 .20
❑ 111 Ben Rivera .50 .20
❑ 112 Curt Schilling 1.50 .60
❑ 113 Victor Cole .50 .20
❑ 114 Al Martin RC 1.50 .60
❑ 115 Roger Mason .50 .20
❑ 116 Blas Minor .50 .20
❑ 117 Tim Wakefield RC 10.00 4.00
❑ 118 Mark Clark RC .50 .20
❑ 119 Rheal Cormier .50 .20
❑ 120 Donovan Osborne .50 .20
❑ 121 Todd Worrell .50 .20
❑ 122 Jeremy Hernandez RC .50 .20
❑ 123 Randy Myers .50 .20
❑ 124 Frank Seminara RC .50 .20
❑ 125 Gary Sheffield 1.00 .40
❑ 126 Dan Walters .50 .20
❑ 127 Steve Hosey .50 .20
❑ 128 Mike Jackson .50 .20
❑ 129 Jim Pena .50 .20
❑ 130 Cory Snyder .50 .20
❑ 131 Bill Swift .50 .20
❑ 132 Checklist U1-U132 .50 .20

1993 Fleer

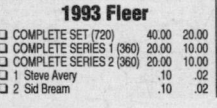

❑ COMPLETE SET (720) 40.00 20.00
❑ COMPLETE SERIES 1 (360) 20.00 10.00
❑ COMPLETE SERIES 2 (360) 20.00 10.00
❑ 1 Steve Avery .10 .02
❑ 2 Sid Bream .10 .02

❑ 3 Ron Gant .20 .07
❑ 4 Tom Glavine .30 .10
❑ 5 Brian Hunter .10 .02
❑ 6 Ryan Klesko .20 .07
❑ 7 Charlie Leibrandt .10 .02
❑ 8 Kent Mercker .10 .02
❑ 9 David Nied .10 .02
❑ 10 Otis Nixon .10 .02
❑ 11 Greg Olson .10 .02
❑ 12 Terry Pendleton .20 .07
❑ 13 Deion Sanders .30 .10
❑ 14 John Smoltz .30 .10
❑ 15 Mike Stanton .10 .02
❑ 16 Mark Wohlers .10 .02
❑ 17 Paul Assenmacher .10 .02
❑ 18 Steve Buechele .10 .02
❑ 19 Shawon Dunston .10 .02
❑ 20 Mark Grace .30 .10
❑ 21 Derrick May .10 .02
❑ 22 Chuck McElroy .10 .02
❑ 23 Mike Morgan .10 .02
❑ 24 Rey Sanchez .10 .02
❑ 25 Ryne Sandberg .75 .30
❑ 26 Bob Scanlan .10 .02
❑ 27 Sammy Sosa .50 .20
❑ 28 Rick Wilkins .10 .02
❑ 29 Bobby Ayala RC .10 .02
❑ 30 Tim Belcher .10 .02
❑ 31 Jeff Branson .10 .02
❑ 32 Norm Charlton .10 .02
❑ 33 Steve Foster .10 .02
❑ 34 Willie Greene .10 .02
❑ 35 Chris Hammond .10 .02
❑ 36 Milt Hill .10 .02
❑ 37 Hal Morris .10 .02
❑ 38 Joe Oliver .10 .02
❑ 39 Paul O'Neill .30 .10
❑ 40 Tim Pugh RC .10 .02
❑ 41 Jose Rijo .10 .02
❑ 42 Bip Roberts .10 .02
❑ 43 Chris Sabo .10 .02
❑ 44 Reggie Sanders .20 .07
❑ 45 Eric Anthony .10 .02
❑ 46 Jeff Bagwell .30 .10
❑ 47 Craig Biggio .30 .10
❑ 48 Joe Boever .10 .02
❑ 49 Casey Candaele .10 .02
❑ 50 Steve Finley .20 .07
❑ 51 Luis Gonzalez .20 .07
❑ 52 Pete Harnisch .10 .02
❑ 53 Xavier Hernandez .10 .02
❑ 54 Doug Jones .10 .02
❑ 55 Eddie Taubensee .10 .02
❑ 56 Brian Williams .10 .02
❑ 57 Pedro Astacio .10 .02
❑ 58 Todd Benzinger .10 .02
❑ 59 Brett Butler .20 .07
❑ 60 Tom Candiotti .10 .02
❑ 61 Lenny Harris .10 .02
❑ 62 Carlos Hernandez .10 .02
❑ 63 Orel Hershiser .20 .07
❑ 64 Eric Karros .20 .07
❑ 65 Ramon Martinez .10 .02
❑ 66 Jose Offerman .10 .02
❑ 67 Mike Scioscia .10 .02
❑ 68 Mike Sharperson .10 .02
❑ 69 Eric Young .10 .02
❑ 70 Moises Alou .20 .07

Card	Player		
❑ 71	Ivan Calderon	.10	.02
❑ 72	Archi Cianfrocco	.10	.02
❑ 73	Wil Cordero	.10	.02
❑ 74	Delino DeShields	.10	.02
❑ 75	Mark Gardner	.10	.02
❑ 76	Ken Hill	.10	.02
❑ 77	Tim Laker RC	.10	.02
❑ 78	Chris Nabholz	.10	.02
❑ 79	Mel Rojas	.10	.02
❑ 80	John Vander Wal UER (Misspelled Vander Wall in I)	.10	.02
❑ 81	Larry Walker	.20	.07
❑ 82	Tim Wallach	.10	.02
❑ 83	John Wetteland	.20	.07
❑ 84	Bobby Bonilla	.20	.07
❑ 85	Daryl Boston	.10	.02
❑ 86	Sid Fernandez	.10	.02
❑ 87	Eric Hillman	.10	.02
❑ 88	Todd Hundley	.10	.02
❑ 89	Howard Johnson	.10	.02
❑ 90	Jeff Kent	.50	.20
❑ 91	Eddie Murray	.50	.20
❑ 92	Bill Pecota	.10	.02
❑ 93	Bret Saberhagen	.20	.07
❑ 94	Dick Schofield	.10	.02
❑ 95	Pete Schourek	.10	.02
❑ 96	Anthony Young	.10	.02
❑ 97	Ruben Amaro	.10	.02
❑ 98	Juan Bell	.10	.02
❑ 99	Wes Chamberlain	.10	.02
❑ 100	Darren Daulton	.20	.07
❑ 101	Mariano Duncan	.10	.02
❑ 102	Mike Hartley	.10	.02
❑ 103	Ricky Jordan	.10	.02
❑ 104	John Kruk	.20	.07
❑ 105	Mickey Morandini	.10	.02
❑ 106	Terry Mulholland	.10	.02
❑ 107	Ben Rivera	.10	.02
❑ 108	Curt Schilling	.20	.07
❑ 109	Keith Shepherd RC	.10	.02
❑ 110	Stan Belinda	.10	.02
❑ 111	Jay Bell	.20	.07
❑ 112	Barry Bonds	1.50	.60
❑ 113	Jeff King	.10	.02
❑ 114	Mike LaValliere	.10	.02
❑ 115	Jose Lind	.10	.02
❑ 116	Roger Mason	.10	.02
❑ 117	Orlando Merced	.10	.02
❑ 118	Bob Patterson	.10	.02
❑ 119	Don Slaught	.10	.02
❑ 120	Zane Smith	.10	.02
❑ 121	Randy Tomlin	.10	.02
❑ 122	Andy Van Slyke	.30	.10
❑ 123	Tim Wakefield	.50	.20
❑ 124	Rheal Cormier	.10	.02
❑ 125	Bernard Gilkey	.10	.02
❑ 126	Felix Jose	.10	.02
❑ 127	Ray Lankford	.20	.07
❑ 128	Bob McClure	.10	.02
❑ 129	Donovan Osborne	.10	.02
❑ 130	Tom Pagnozzi	.10	.02
❑ 131	Geronimo Pena	.10	.02
❑ 132	Mike Perez	.10	.02
❑ 133	Lee Smith	.20	.07
❑ 134	Bob Tewksbury	.10	.02
❑ 135	Todd Worrell	.10	.02
❑ 136	Todd Zeile	.10	.02
❑ 137	Jerald Clark	.10	.02
❑ 138	Tony Gwynn	.60	.25
❑ 139	Greg W. Harris	.10	.02
❑ 140	Jeremy Hernandez	.10	.02
❑ 141	Darrin Jackson	.10	.02
❑ 142	Mike Maddux	.10	.02
❑ 143	Fred McGriff	.30	.10
❑ 144	Jose Melendez	.10	.02
❑ 145	Rich Rodriguez	.10	.02
❑ 146	Frank Seminara	.10	.02
❑ 147	Gary Sheffield	.20	.07
❑ 148	Kurt Stillwell	.10	.02
❑ 149	Dan Walters	.10	.02
❑ 150	Rod Beck	.10	.02
❑ 151	Bud Black	.10	.02
❑ 152	Jeff Brantley	.10	.02
❑ 153	John Burkett	.10	.02
❑ 154	Will Clark	.30	.10
❑ 155	Royce Clayton	.10	.02
❑ 156	Mike Jackson	.10	.02
❑ 157	Darren Lewis	.10	.02
❑ 158	Kirt Manwaring	.10	.02
❑ 159	Willie McGee	.20	.07
❑ 160	Cory Snyder	.10	.02
❑ 161	Bill Swift	.10	.02
❑ 162	Trevor Wilson	.10	.02
❑ 163	Brady Anderson	.20	.07
❑ 164	Glenn Davis	.10	.02
❑ 165	Mike Devereaux	.10	.02
❑ 166	Todd Frohwirth	.10	.02
❑ 167	Leo Gomez	.10	.02
❑ 168	Chris Hoiles	.10	.02
❑ 169	Ben McDonald	.10	.02
❑ 170	Randy Milligan	.10	.02
❑ 171	Alan Mills	.10	.02
❑ 172	Mike Mussina	.30	.10
❑ 173	Gregg Olson	.10	.02
❑ 174	Arthur Rhodes	.10	.02
❑ 175	David Segui	.10	.02
❑ 176	Ellis Burks	.20	.07
❑ 177	Roger Clemens	1.00	.40
❑ 178	Scott Cooper	.10	.02
❑ 179	Danny Darwin	.10	.02
❑ 180	Tony Fossas	.10	.02
❑ 181	Paul Quantrill	.10	.02
❑ 182	Jody Reed	.10	.02
❑ 183	John Valentin	.10	.02
❑ 184	Mo Vaughn	.20	.07
❑ 185	Frank Viola	.20	.07
❑ 186	Bob Zupcic	.10	.02
❑ 187	Jim Abbott	.30	.10
❑ 188	Gary DiSarcina	.10	.02
❑ 189	Damion Easley	.10	.02
❑ 190	Junior Felix	.10	.02
❑ 191	Chuck Finley	.20	.07
❑ 192	Joe Grahe	.10	.02
❑ 193	Bryan Harvey	.10	.02
❑ 194	Mark Langston	.10	.02
❑ 195	John Orton	.10	.02
❑ 196	Luis Polonia	.10	.02
❑ 197	Tim Salmon	.30	.10
❑ 198	Luis Sojo	.10	.02
❑ 199	Wilson Alvarez	.10	.02
❑ 200	George Bell	.10	.02
❑ 201	Alex Fernandez	.10	.02
❑ 202	Craig Grebeck	.10	.02
❑ 203	Ozzie Guillen	.20	.07
❑ 204	Lance Johnson	.10	.02
❑ 205	Ron Karkovice	.10	.02
❑ 206	Kirk McCaskill	.10	.02
❑ 207	Jack McDowell	.10	.02
❑ 208	Scott Radinsky	.10	.02
❑ 209	Tim Raines	.20	.07
❑ 210	Frank Thomas	.50	.20
❑ 211	Robin Ventura	.20	.07
❑ 212	Sandy Alomar Jr.	.10	.02
❑ 213	Carlos Baerga	.10	.02
❑ 214	Dennis Cook	.10	.02
❑ 215	Thomas Howard	.10	.02
❑ 216	Mark Lewis	.10	.02
❑ 217	Derek Lilliquist	.10	.02
❑ 218	Kenny Lofton	.20	.07
❑ 219	Charles Nagy	.10	.02
❑ 220	Steve Olin	.10	.02
❑ 221	Paul Sorrento	.10	.02
❑ 222	Jim Thome	.30	.10
❑ 223	Mark Whiten	.10	.02
❑ 224	Milt Cuyler	.10	.02
❑ 225	Rob Deer	.10	.02
❑ 226	John Doherty	.10	.02
❑ 227	Cecil Fielder	.20	.07
❑ 228	Travis Fryman	.20	.07
❑ 229	Mike Henneman	.10	.02
❑ 230	John Kiely UER (Card has batting stats of Pat Ke)	.10	.02
❑ 231	Kurt Knudsen	.10	.02
❑ 232	Scott Livingstone	.10	.02
❑ 233	Tony Phillips	.10	.02
❑ 234	Mickey Tettleton	.10	.02
❑ 235	Kevin Appier	.20	.07
❑ 236	George Brett	1.25	.50
❑ 237	Tom Gordon	.10	.02
❑ 238	Gregg Jefferies	.10	.02
❑ 239	Wally Joyner	.20	.07
❑ 240	Kevin Koslofski	.10	.02
❑ 241	Mike Macfarlane	.10	.02
❑ 242	Brian McRae	.10	.02
❑ 243	Rusty Meacham	.10	.02
❑ 244	Keith Miller	.10	.02
❑ 245	Jeff Montgomery	.10	.02
❑ 246	Hipolito Pichardo	.10	.02
❑ 247	Ricky Bones	.10	.02
❑ 248	Cal Eldred	.10	.02
❑ 249	Mike Fetters	.10	.02
❑ 250	Darryl Hamilton	.10	.02
❑ 251	Doug Henry	.10	.02
❑ 252	John Jaha	.10	.02
❑ 253	Pat Listach	.10	.02
❑ 254	Paul Molitor	.20	.07
❑ 255	Jaime Navarro	.10	.02
❑ 256	Kevin Seitzer	.10	.02
❑ 257	B.J. Surhoff	.20	.07
❑ 258	Greg Vaughn	.10	.02
❑ 259	Bill Wegman	.10	.02
❑ 260	Robin Yount	.75	.30
❑ 261	Rick Aguilera	.10	.02
❑ 262	Chili Davis	.20	.07
❑ 263	Scott Erickson	.10	.02
❑ 264	Greg Gagne	.10	.02
❑ 265	Mark Guthrie	.10	.02
❑ 266	Brian Harper	.10	.02
❑ 267	Kent Hrbek	.20	.07
❑ 268	Terry Jorgensen	.10	.02
❑ 269	Gene Larkin	.10	.02
❑ 270	Scott Leius	.10	.02
❑ 271	Pat Mahomes	.10	.02
❑ 272	Pedro Munoz	.10	.02
❑ 273	Kirby Puckett	.50	.20
❑ 274	Kevin Tapani	.10	.02
❑ 275	Carl Willis	.10	.02
❑ 276	Steve Farr	.10	.02
❑ 277	John Habyan	.10	.02
❑ 278	Mel Hall	.10	.02
❑ 279	Charlie Hayes	.10	.02
❑ 280	Pat Kelly	.10	.02
❑ 281	Don Mattingly	1.25	.50
❑ 282	Sam Militello	.10	.02
❑ 283	Matt Nokes	.10	.02
❑ 284	Melido Perez	.10	.02
❑ 285	Andy Stankiewicz	.10	.02
❑ 286	Danny Tartabull	.10	.02
❑ 287	Randy Velarde	.10	.02
❑ 288	Bob Wickman	.10	.02
❑ 289	Bernie Williams	.30	.10
❑ 290	Lance Blankenship	.10	.02
❑ 291	Mike Bordick	.10	.02
❑ 292	Jerry Browne	.10	.02
❑ 293	Dennis Eckersley	.20	.07
❑ 294	Rickey Henderson	.50	.20
❑ 295	Vince Horsman	.10	.02
❑ 296	Mark McGwire	1.25	.50
❑ 297	Jeff Parrett	.10	.02
❑ 298	Ruben Sierra	.20	.07
❑ 299	Terry Steinbach	.10	.02
❑ 300	Walt Weiss	.10	.02
❑ 301	Bob Welch	.10	.02
❑ 302	Willie Wilson	.10	.02
❑ 303	Bobby Witt	.10	.02
❑ 304	Bret Boone	.20	.07
❑ 305	Jay Buhner	.20	.07
❑ 306	Dave Fleming	.10	.02
❑ 307	Ken Griffey Jr.	.75	.30
❑ 308	Erik Hanson	.10	.02
❑ 309	Edgar Martinez	.30	.10
❑ 310	Tino Martinez	.30	.10
❑ 311	Jeff Nelson	.10	.02
❑ 312	Dennis Powell	.10	.02
❑ 313	Mike Schooler	.10	.02
❑ 314	Russ Swan	.10	.02
❑ 315	Dave Valle	.10	.02
❑ 316	Omar Vizquel	.30	.10
❑ 317	Kevin Brown	.20	.07
❑ 318	Todd Burns	.10	.02
❑ 319	Jose Canseco	.30	.10
❑ 320	Julio Franco	.20	.07
❑ 321	Jeff Frye	.10	.02
❑ 322	Juan Gonzalez	.20	.07
❑ 323	Jose Guzman	.10	.02
❑ 324	Jeff Huson	.10	.02

❑	325	Dean Palmer	.20	.07
❑	326	Kevin Reimer	.10	.02
❑	327	Ivan Rodriguez	.30	.10
❑	328	Kenny Rogers	.20	.07
❑	329	Dan Smith	.10	.02
❑	330	Roberto Alomar	.30	.10
❑	331	Derek Bell	.10	.02
❑	332	Pat Borders	.10	.02
❑	333	Joe Carter	.20	.07
❑	334	Kelly Gruber	.10	.02
❑	335	Tom Henke	.10	.02
❑	336	Jimmy Key	.20	.07
❑	337	Manuel Lee	.10	.02
❑	338	Candy Maldonado	.10	.02
❑	339	John Olerud	.20	.07
❑	340	Todd Stottlemyre	.10	.02
❑	341	Duane Ward	.10	.02
❑	342	Devon White	.20	.07
❑	343	Dave Winfield	.20	.07
❑	344	Edgar Martinez LL	.20	.07
❑	345	Cecil Fielder LL	.10	.02
❑	346	Kenny Lofton LL	.10	.02
❑	347	Jack Morris LL	.10	.02
❑	348	Roger Clemens LL	.50	.20
❑	349	Fred McGriff RT	.20	.07
❑	350	Barry Bonds RT	.75	.30
❑	351	Gary Sheffield RT	.10	.02
❑	352	Darren Daulton RT	.10	.02
❑	353	Dave Hollins RT	.10	.02
❑	354	P.Martinez/R.Martinez	.50	.20
❑	355	K.Puckett/I.Rodriguez	.30	.10
❑	356	Sandberg/Sheffield	.50	.20
❑	357	R.Alomar/Knoblauch/Baerg	.20	.07
❑	358	Checklist 1-120	.10	.02
❑	359	Checklist 121-240	.10	.02
❑	360	Checklist 241-360	.10	.02
❑	361	Rafael Belliard	.10	.02
❑	362	Damon Berryhill	.10	.02
❑	363	Mike Bielecki	.10	.02
❑	364	Jeff Blauser	.10	.02
❑	365	Francisco Cabrera	.10	.02
❑	366	Marvin Freeman	.10	.02
❑	367	David Justice	.20	.07
❑	368	Mark Lemke	.10	.02
❑	369	Alejandro Pena	.10	.02
❑	370	Jeff Reardon	.20	.07
❑	371	Lonnie Smith	.10	.02
❑	372	Pete Smith	.10	.02
❑	373	Shawn Boskie	.10	.02
❑	374	Jim Bullinger	.10	.02
❑	375	Frank Castillo	.10	.02
❑	376	Doug Dascenzo	.10	.02
❑	377	Andre Dawson	.20	.07
❑	378	Mike Harkey	.10	.02
❑	379	Greg Hibbard	.10	.02
❑	380	Greg Maddux	.75	.30
❑	381	Ken Patterson	.10	.02
❑	382	Jeff D. Robinson	.10	.02
❑	383	Luis Salazar	.10	.02
❑	384	Dwight Smith	.10	.02
❑	385	Jose Vizcaino	.10	.02
❑	386	Scott Bankhead	.10	.02
❑	387	Tom Browning	.10	.02
❑	388	Darnell Coles	.10	.02
❑	389	Rob Dibble	.20	.07
❑	390	Bill Doran	.10	.02
❑	391	Dwayne Henry	.10	.02
❑	392	Cesar Hernandez	.10	.02
❑	393	Roberto Kelly	.10	.02
❑	394	Barry Larkin	.30	.10
❑	395	Dave Martinez	.10	.02
❑	396	Kevin Mitchell	.10	.02
❑	397	Jeff Reed	.10	.02
❑	398	Scott Ruskin	.10	.02
❑	399	Greg Swindell	.10	.02
❑	400	Dan Wilson	.20	.07
❑	401	Andy Ashby	.10	.02
❑	402	Freddie Benavides	.10	.02
❑	403	Dante Bichette	.20	.07
❑	404	Willie Blair	.10	.02
❑	405	Denis Boucher	.10	.02
❑	406	Vinny Castilla	.50	.20
❑	407	Braulio Castillo	.10	.02
❑	408	Alex Cole	.10	.02
❑	409	Andres Galarraga	.20	.07
❑	410	Joe Girardi	.10	.02
❑	411	Butch Henry	.10	.02
❑	412	Darren Holmes	.10	.02
❑	413	Calvin Jones	.10	.02
❑	414	Steve Reed RC	.10	.02
❑	415	Kevin Ritz	.10	.02
❑	416	Jim Tatum RC	.10	.02
❑	417	Jack Armstrong	.10	.02
❑	418	Bret Barberie	.10	.02
❑	419	Ryan Bowen	.10	.02
❑	420	Cris Carpenter	.10	.02
❑	421	Chuck Carr	.10	.02
❑	422	Scott Chiamparino	.10	.02
❑	423	Jeff Conine	.20	.07
❑	424	Jim Corsi	.10	.02
❑	425	Steve Decker	.10	.02
❑	426	Chris Donnels	.10	.02
❑	427	Monty Fariss	.10	.02
❑	428	Bob Natal	.10	.02
❑	429	Pat Rapp	.10	.02
❑	430	Dave Weathers	.10	.02
❑	431	Nigel Wilson	.10	.02
❑	432	Ken Caminiti	.20	.07
❑	433	Andujar Cedeno	.10	.02
❑	434	Tom Edens	.10	.02
❑	435	Juan Guerrero	.10	.02
❑	436	Pete Incaviglia	.10	.02
❑	437	Jimmy Jones	.10	.02
❑	438	Darryl Kile	.20	.07
❑	439	Rob Murphy	.10	.02
❑	440	Al Osuna	.10	.02
❑	441	Mark Portugal	.10	.02
❑	442	Scott Servais	.10	.02
❑	443	John Candelaria	.10	.02
❑	444	Tim Crews	.10	.02
❑	445	Eric Davis	.20	.07
❑	446	Tom Goodwin	.10	.02
❑	447	Jim Gott	.10	.02
❑	448	Kevin Gross	.10	.02
❑	449	Dave Hansen	.10	.02
❑	450	Jay Howell	.10	.02
❑	451	Roger McDowell	.10	.02
❑	452	Bob Ojeda	.10	.02
❑	453	Henry Rodriguez	.10	.02
❑	454	Darryl Strawberry	.20	.07
❑	455	Mitch Webster	.10	.02
❑	456	Steve Wilson	.10	.02
❑	457	Brian Barnes	.10	.02
❑	458	Sean Berry	.10	.02
❑	459	Jeff Fassero	.10	.02
❑	460	Darrin Fletcher	.10	.02
❑	461	Marquis Grissom	.20	.07
❑	462	Dennis Martinez	.20	.07
❑	463	Spike Owen	.10	.02
❑	464	Matt Stairs	.10	.02
❑	465	Sergio Valdez	.10	.02
❑	466	Kevin Bass	.10	.02
❑	467	Vince Coleman	.10	.02
❑	468	Mark Dewey	.10	.02
❑	469	Kevin Elster	.10	.02
❑	470	Tony Fernandez	.10	.02
❑	471	John Franco	.20	.07
❑	472	Dave Gallagher	.10	.02
❑	473	Paul Gibson	.10	.02
❑	474	Dwight Gooden	.20	.07
❑	475	Lee Guetterman	.10	.02
❑	476	Jeff Innis	.10	.02
❑	477	Dave Magadan	.10	.02
❑	478	Charlie O'Brien	.10	.02
❑	479	Willie Randolph	.20	.07
❑	480	Mackey Sasser	.10	.02
❑	481	Ryan Thompson	.10	.02
❑	482	Chico Walker	.10	.02
❑	483	Kyle Abbott	.10	.02
❑	484	Bob Ayrault	.10	.02
❑	485	Kim Batiste	.10	.02
❑	486	Cliff Brantley	.10	.02
❑	487	Jose DeLeon	.10	.02
❑	488	Len Dykstra	.20	.07
❑	489	Tommy Greene	.10	.02
❑	490	Jeff Grotewold	.10	.02
❑	491	Dave Hollins	.10	.02
❑	492	Danny Jackson	.10	.02
❑	493	Stan Javier	.10	.02
❑	494	Tom Marsh	.10	.02
❑	495	Greg Mathews	.10	.02
❑	496	Dale Murphy	.30	.10
❑	497	Todd Pratt RC	.20	.07
❑	498	Mitch Williams	.10	.02
❑	499	Danny Cox	.10	.02
❑	500	Doug Drabek	.10	.02
❑	501	Carlos Garcia	.10	.02
❑	502	Lloyd McClendon	.10	.02
❑	503	Denny Neagle	.20	.07
❑	504	Gary Redus	.10	.02
❑	505	Bob Walk	.10	.02
❑	506	John Wehner	.10	.02
❑	507	Luis Alicea	.10	.02
❑	508	Mark Clark	.10	.02
❑	509	Pedro Guerrero	.20	.07
❑	510	Rex Hudler	.10	.02
❑	511	Brian Jordan	.20	.07
❑	512	Omar Olivares	.10	.02
❑	513	Jose Oquendo	.10	.02
❑	514	Gerald Perry	.10	.02
❑	515	Bryn Smith	.10	.02
❑	516	Craig Wilson	.10	.02
❑	517	Tracy Woodson	.10	.02
❑	518	Larry Andersen	.10	.02
❑	519	Andy Benes	.10	.02
❑	520	Jim Deshaies	.10	.02
❑	521	Bruce Hurst	.10	.02
❑	522	Randy Myers	.10	.02
❑	523	Benito Santiago	.20	.07
❑	524	Tim Scott	.10	.02
❑	525	Tim Teufel	.10	.02
❑	526	Mike Benjamin	.10	.02
❑	527	Dave Burba	.10	.02
❑	528	Craig Colbert	.10	.02
❑	529	Mike Felder	.10	.02
❑	530	Bryan Hickerson	.10	.02
❑	531	Chris James	.10	.02
❑	532	Mark Leonard	.10	.02
❑	533	Greg Litton	.10	.02
❑	534	Francisco Oliveras	.10	.02
❑	535	John Patterson	.10	.02
❑	536	Jim Pena	.10	.02
❑	537	Dave Righetti	.20	.07
❑	538	Robby Thompson	.10	.02
❑	539	Jose Uribe	.10	.02
❑	540	Matt Williams	.20	.07
❑	541	Storm Davis	.10	.02
❑	542	Sam Horn	.10	.02
❑	543	Tim Hulett	.10	.02
❑	544	Craig Lefferts	.10	.02
❑	545	Chito Martinez	.10	.02
❑	546	Mark McLemore	.10	.02
❑	547	Luis Mercedes	.10	.02
❑	548	Bob Milacki	.10	.02
❑	549	Joe Orsulak	.10	.02
❑	550	Billy Ripken	.10	.02
❑	551	Cal Ripken	1.50	.60
❑	552	Rick Sutcliffe	.20	.07
❑	553	Jeff Tackett	.10	.02
❑	554	Wade Boggs	.30	.10
❑	555	Tom Brunansky	.10	.02
❑	556	Jack Clark	.20	.07
❑	557	John Dopson	.10	.02
❑	558	Mike Gardiner	.10	.02
❑	559	Mike Greenwell	.10	.02
❑	560	Greg A. Harris	.10	.02
❑	561	Billy Hatcher	.10	.02
❑	562	Joe Hesketh	.10	.02
❑	563	Tony Pena	.10	.02
❑	564	Phil Plantier	.10	.02
❑	565	Luis Rivera	.10	.02
❑	566	Herm Winningham	.10	.02
❑	567	Matt Young	.10	.02
❑	568	Bert Blyleven	.20	.07
❑	569	Mike Butcher	.10	.02
❑	570	Chuck Crim	.10	.02
❑	571	Chad Curtis	.10	.02
❑	572	Tim Fortugno	.10	.02
❑	573	Steve Frey	.10	.02
❑	574	Gary Gaetti	.20	.07
❑	575	Scott Lewis	.10	.02
❑	576	Lee Stevens	.10	.02
❑	577	Ron Tingley	.10	.02
❑	578	Julio Valera	.10	.02
❑	579	Shawn Abner	.10	.02
❑	580	Joey Cora	.10	.02
❑	581	Chris Cron	.10	.02
❑	582	Carlton Fisk	.30	.10

❑ 583	Roberto Hernandez	.10	.02
❑ 584	Charlie Hough	.20	.07
❑ 585	Terry Leach	.10	.02
❑ 586	Donn Pall	.10	.02
❑ 587	Dan Pasqua	.10	.02
❑ 588	Steve Sax	.10	.02
❑ 589	Bobby Thigpen	.10	.02
❑ 590	Albert Belle	.20	.07
❑ 591	Felix Fermin	.10	.02
❑ 592	Glenallen Hill	.10	.02
❑ 593	Brook Jacoby	.10	.02
❑ 594	Reggie Jefferson	.10	.02
❑ 595	Carlos Martinez	.10	.02
❑ 596	Jose Mesa	.10	.02
❑ 597	Rod Nichols	.10	.02
❑ 598	Junior Ortiz	.10	.02
❑ 599	Eric Plunk	.10	.02
❑ 600	Ted Power	.10	.02
❑ 601	Scott Scudder	.10	.02
❑ 602	Kevin Wickander	.10	.02
❑ 603	Skeeter Barnes	.10	.02
❑ 604	Mark Carreon	.10	.02
❑ 605	Dan Gladden	.10	.02
❑ 606	Bill Gullickson	.10	.02
❑ 607	Chad Kreuter	.10	.02
❑ 608	Mark Leiter	.10	.02
❑ 609	Mike Munoz	.10	.02
❑ 610	Rich Rowland	.10	.02
❑ 611	Frank Tanana	.10	.02
❑ 612	Walt Terrell	.10	.02
❑ 613	Alan Trammell	.20	.07
❑ 614	Lou Whitaker	.20	.07
❑ 615	Luis Aquino	.10	.02
❑ 616	Mike Boddicker	.10	.02
❑ 617	Jim Eisenreich	.10	.02
❑ 618	Mark Gubicza	.10	.02
❑ 619	David Howard	.10	.02
❑ 620	Mike Magnante	.10	.02
❑ 621	Brent Mayne	.10	.02
❑ 622	Kevin McReynolds	.10	.02
❑ 623	Eddie Pierce RC	.10	.02
❑ 624	Bill Sampen	.10	.02
❑ 625	Steve Shifflett	.10	.02
❑ 626	Gary Thurman	.10	.02
❑ 627	Curt Wilkerson	.10	.02
❑ 628	Chris Bosio	.10	.02
❑ 629	Scott Fletcher	.10	.02
❑ 630	Jim Gantner	.10	.02
❑ 631	Dave Nilsson	.10	.02
❑ 632	Jesse Orosco	.10	.02
❑ 633	Dan Plesac	.10	.02
❑ 634	Ron Robinson	.10	.02
❑ 635	Bill Spiers	.10	.02
❑ 636	Franklin Stubbs	.10	.02
❑ 637	Willie Banks	.10	.02
❑ 638	Randy Bush	.10	.02
❑ 639	Chuck Knoblauch	.20	.07
❑ 640	Shane Mack	.10	.02
❑ 641	Mike Pagliarulo	.10	.02
❑ 642	Jeff Reboulet	.10	.02
❑ 643	John Smiley	.10	.02
❑ 644	Mike Trombley	.10	.02
❑ 645	Gary Wayne	.10	.02
❑ 646	Lenny Webster	.10	.02
❑ 647	Tim Burke	.10	.02
❑ 648	Mike Gallego	.10	.02
❑ 649	Dion James	.10	.02
❑ 650	Jeff Johnson	.10	.02
❑ 651	Scott Kamieniecki	.10	.02
❑ 652	Kevin Maas	.10	.02
❑ 653	Rich Monteleone	.10	.02
❑ 654	Jerry Nielsen	.10	.02
❑ 655	Scott Sanderson	.10	.02
❑ 656	Mike Stanley	.10	.02
❑ 657	Gerald Williams	.10	.02
❑ 658	Curt Young	.10	.02
❑ 659	Harold Baines	.20	.07
❑ 660	Kevin Campbell	.10	.02
❑ 661	Ron Darling	.10	.02
❑ 662	Kelly Downs	.10	.02
❑ 663	Eric Fox	.10	.02
❑ 664	Dave Henderson	.10	.02
❑ 665	Rick Honeycutt	.10	.02
❑ 666	Mike Moore	.10	.02
❑ 667	Jamie Quirk	.10	.02
❑ 668	Jeff Russell	.10	.02
❑ 669	Dave Stewart	.20	.07
❑ 670	Greg Briley	.10	.02
❑ 671	Dave Cochrane	.10	.02
❑ 672	Henry Cotto	.10	.02
❑ 673	Rich DeLucia	.10	.02
❑ 674	Brian Fisher	.10	.02
❑ 675	Mark Grant	.10	.02
❑ 676	Randy Johnson	.50	.20
❑ 677	Tim Leary	.10	.02
❑ 678	Pete O'Brien	.10	.02
❑ 679	Lance Parrish	.20	.07
❑ 680	Harold Reynolds	.20	.07
❑ 681	Shane Turner	.10	.02
❑ 682	Jack Daugherty	.10	.02
❑ 683	David Hulse RC	.10	.02
❑ 684	Terry Mathews	.10	.02
❑ 685	Al Newman	.10	.02
❑ 686	Edwin Nunez	.10	.02
❑ 687	Rafael Palmeiro	.30	.10
❑ 688	Roger Pavlik	.10	.02
❑ 689	Geno Petralli	.10	.02
❑ 690	Nolan Ryan	2.00	.75
❑ 691	David Cone	.20	.07
❑ 692	Alfredo Griffin	.10	.02
❑ 693	Juan Guzman	.10	.02
❑ 694	Pat Hentgen	.10	.02
❑ 695	Randy Knorr	.10	.02
❑ 696	Bob MacDonald	.10	.02
❑ 697	Jack Morris	.20	.07
❑ 698	Ed Sprague	.10	.02
❑ 699	Dave Stieb	.10	.02
❑ 700	Pat Tabler	.10	.02
❑ 701	Mike Timlin	.10	.02
❑ 702	David Wells	.20	.07
❑ 703	Eddie Zosky	.10	.02
❑ 704	Gary Sheffield LL	.10	.02
❑ 705	Darren Daulton LL	.10	.02
❑ 706	Marquis Grissom LL	.10	.02
❑ 707	Greg Maddux LL	.50	.20
❑ 708	Bill Swift LL	.10	.02
❑ 709	Juan Gonzalez RT	.10	.02
❑ 710	Mark McGwire RT	.60	.25
❑ 711	Cecil Fielder RT	.10	.02
❑ 712	Albert Belle RT	.20	.07
❑ 713	Joe Carter RT	.10	.02
❑ 714	F.Thomas/C.Fielder	.30	.10
❑ 715	L.Walker/D.Daulton SS	.20	.07
❑ 716	E.Martinez/R.Ventura SS	.20	.07
❑ 717	R.Clemens/D.Eckersley	.50	.20
❑ 718	Checklist 361-480	.10	.02
❑ 719	Checklist 481-600	.10	.02
❑ 720	Checklist 601-720	.10	.02

1993 Fleer Final Edition

❑	COMP.FACT.SET (310)	10.00	4.00
❑	COMPLETE SET (300)	8.00	3.00
❑ 1	Steve Bedrosian	.10	.02
❑ 2	Jay Howell	.10	.02
❑ 3	Greg Maddux	.75	.30
❑ 4	Greg McMichael RC	.15	.05
❑ 5	Tony Tarasco RC	.15	.05
❑ 6	Jose Bautista	.10	.02
❑ 7	Jose Guzman	.10	.02
❑ 8	Greg Hibbard	.10	.02
❑ 9	Candy Maldonado	.10	.02
❑ 10	Randy Myers	.10	.02
❑ 11	Matt Walbeck RC	.40	.15
❑ 12	Turk Wendell	.10	.02
❑ 13	Willie Wilson	.10	.02
❑ 14	Greg Cadaret	.10	.02
❑ 15	Roberto Kelly	.10	.02
❑ 16	Randy Milligan	.10	.02
❑ 17	Kevin Mitchell	.10	.02
❑ 18	Jeff Reardon	.20	.07
❑ 19	John Roper	.10	.02
❑ 20	John Smiley	.10	.02
❑ 21	Andy Ashby	.10	.02
❑ 22	Dante Bichette	.20	.07
❑ 23	Willie Blair	.10	.02
❑ 24	Pedro Castellano	.10	.02
❑ 25	Vinny Castilla	.50	.20
❑ 26	Jerald Clark	.10	.02
❑ 27	Alex Cole	.10	.02
❑ 28	Scott Fredrickson RC	.15	.05
❑ 29	Jay Gainer RC	.15	.05
❑ 30	Andres Galarraga	.20	.07
❑ 31	Joe Girardi	.10	.02
❑ 32	Ryan Hawblitzel	.10	.02
❑ 33	Charlie Hayes	.10	.02
❑ 34	Darren Holmes	.10	.02
❑ 35	Chris Jones	.10	.02
❑ 36	David Nied	.10	.02
❑ 37	Jayhawk Owens RC	.15	.05
❑ 38	Lance Painter RC	.40	.15
❑ 39	Jeff Parrett	.10	.02
❑ 40	Steve Reed	.10	.02
❑ 41	Armando Reynoso	.10	.02
❑ 42	Bruce Ruffin	.10	.02
❑ 43	Danny Sheaffer RC	.15	.05
❑ 44	Keith Shepherd	.10	.02
❑ 45	Jim Tatum	.10	.02
❑ 46	Gary Wayne	.10	.02
❑ 47	Eric Young	.10	.02
❑ 48	Luis Aquino	.10	.02
❑ 49	Alex Arias	.10	.02
❑ 50	Jack Armstrong	.10	.02
❑ 51	Bret Barberie	.10	.02
❑ 52	Geronimo Berroa	.10	.02
❑ 53	Ryan Bowen	.10	.02
❑ 54	Greg Briley	.10	.02
❑ 55	Cris Carpenter	.10	.02
❑ 56	Chuck Carr	.10	.02
❑ 57	Jeff Conine	.20	.07
❑ 58	Jim Corsi	.10	.02
❑ 59	Orestes Destrade	.10	.02
❑ 60	Junior Felix	.10	.02
❑ 61	Chris Hammond	.10	.02
❑ 62	Bryan Harvey	.10	.02
❑ 63	Charlie Hough	.20	.07
❑ 64	Joe Klink	.10	.02
❑ 65	Richie Lewis RC	.15	.05
❑ 66	Mitch Lyden RC	.15	.05
❑ 67	Bob Natal	.10	.02
❑ 68	Scott Pose RC	.15	.05
❑ 69	Rich Renteria	.10	.02
❑ 70	Benito Santiago	.20	.07
❑ 71	Gary Sheffield	.20	.07
❑ 72	Matt Turner RC	.15	.05
❑ 73	Walt Weiss	.10	.02
❑ 74	Darrell Whitmore RC	.15	.05
❑ 75	Nigel Wilson	.10	.02
❑ 76	Kevin Bass	.10	.02
❑ 77	Doug Drabek	.10	.02
❑ 78	Tom Edens	.10	.02
❑ 79	Chris James	.10	.02
❑ 80	Greg Swindell	.10	.02
❑ 81	Omar Daal RC	.15	.05
❑ 82	Raul Mondesi	.20	.07
❑ 83	Jody Reed	.10	.02
❑ 84	Cory Snyder	.10	.02
❑ 85	Rick Trlicek	.10	.02
❑ 86	Tim Wallach	.10	.02
❑ 87	Todd Worrell	.10	.02
❑ 88	Tavo Alvarez	.10	.02
❑ 89	Frank Bolick	.10	.02
❑ 90	Kent Bottenfield	.10	.02
❑ 91	Greg Colbrunn	.10	.02
❑ 92	Cliff Floyd	.20	.07
❑ 93	Lou Frazier RC	.15	.05
❑ 94	Mike Gardiner	.10	.02
❑ 95	Mike Lansing RC	.40	.15
❑ 96	Bill Risley	.10	.02
❑ 97	Jeff Shaw	.10	.02
❑ 98	Kevin Baez	.10	.02

❑ 99 Tim Bogar RC .15 .05
❑ 100 Jeromy Burnitz .20 .07
❑ 101 Mike Draper .10 .02
❑ 102 Darrin Jackson .10 .02
❑ 103 Mike Maddux .10 .02
❑ 104 Joe Orsulak .10 .02
❑ 105 Doug Saunders RC .15 .05
❑ 106 Frank Tanana .10 .02
❑ 107 Dave Telgheder RC .15 .05
❑ 108 Larry Andersen .10 .02
❑ 109 Jim Eisenreich .10 .02
❑ 110 Pete Incaviglia .10 .02
❑ 111 Danny Jackson .10 .02
❑ 112 David West .10 .02
❑ 113 Al Martin .10 .02
❑ 114 Blas Minor .10 .02
❑ 115 Dennis Moeller .10 .02
❑ 116 William Pennyfeather .10 .02
❑ 117 Rich Robertson RC .15 .05
❑ 118 Ben Shelton .10 .02
❑ 119 Lonnie Smith .10 .02
❑ 120 Freddie Toliver .10 .02
❑ 121 Paul Wagner .10 .02
❑ 122 Kevin Young .20 .07
❑ 123 Rene Arocha RC .40 .15
❑ 124 Gregg Jefferies .10 .02
❑ 125 Paul Kilgus .10 .02
❑ 126 Les Lancaster .10 .02
❑ 127 Joe Magrane .10 .02
❑ 128 Rob Murphy .10 .02
❑ 129 Erik Pappas .10 .02
❑ 130 Stan Royer .10 .02
❑ 131 Ozzie Smith .75 .30
❑ 132 Tom Urbani RC .15 .05
❑ 133 Mark Whiten .10 .02
❑ 134 Derek Bell .10 .02
❑ 135 Doug Brocail .10 .02
❑ 136 Phil Clark .10 .02
❑ 137 Mark Ettles RC .15 .05
❑ 138 Jeff Gardner .10 .02
❑ 139 Pat Gomez RC .15 .05
❑ 140 Ricky Gutierrez .10 .02
❑ 141 Gene Harris .10 .02
❑ 142 Kevin Higgins .10 .02
❑ 143 Trevor Hoffman .50 .20
❑ 144 Phil Plantier .10 .02
❑ 145 Kerry Taylor RC .15 .05
❑ 146 Guillermo Velasquez .10 .02
❑ 147 Wally Whitehurst .10 .02
❑ 148 Tim Worrell RC .40 .15
❑ 149 Todd Benzinger .10 .02
❑ 150 Barry Bonds 1.50 .60
❑ 151 Greg Brummett RC .15 .05
❑ 152 Mark Carreon .10 .02
❑ 153 Dave Martinez .10 .02
❑ 154 Jeff Reed .10 .02
❑ 155 Kevin Rogers .10 .02
❑ 156 Harold Baines .20 .07
❑ 157 Damon Buford .10 .02
❑ 158 Paul Carey RC .15 .05
❑ 159 Jeffrey Hammonds .10 .02
❑ 160 Jamie Moyer .20 .07
❑ 161 Sherman Obando RC .15 .05
❑ 162 John O'Donoghue RC .15 .05
❑ 163 Brad Pennington .10 .02
❑ 164 Jim Poole .10 .02
❑ 165 Harold Reynolds .20 .07
❑ 166 Fernando Valenzuela .20 .07
❑ 167 Jack Voigt RC .15 .05
❑ 168 Mark Williamson .10 .02
❑ 169 Scott Bankhead .10 .02
❑ 170 Greg Blosser .10 .02
❑ 171 Jim Byrd RC .15 .05
❑ 172 Ivan Calderon .10 .02
❑ 173 Andre Dawson .20 .07
❑ 174 Scott Fletcher .10 .02
❑ 175 Jose Melendez .10 .02
❑ 176 Carlos Quintana .10 .02
❑ 177 Jeff Russell .10 .02
❑ 178 Aaron Sele .10 .02
❑ 179 Rod Correia RC .15 .05
❑ 180 Chili Davis .20 .07
❑ 181 Jim Edmonds RC 3.00 1.25
❑ 182 Rene Gonzales .10 .02
❑ 183 Hilly Hathaway RC .15 .05
❑ 184 Torey Lovullo .10 .02
❑ 185 Greg Myers .10 .02
❑ 186 Gene Nelson .10 .02
❑ 187 Troy Percival .30 .10
❑ 188 Scott Sanderson .10 .02
❑ 189 Darryl Scott RC .15 .05
❑ 190 J.T.Snow RC .60 .25
❑ 191 Russ Springer .10 .02
❑ 192 Jason Bere .10 .02
❑ 193 Rodney Bolton .10 .02
❑ 194 Ellis Burks .20 .07
❑ 195 Bo Jackson .50 .20
❑ 196 Mike LaValliere .10 .02
❑ 197 Scott Ruffcorn .10 .02
❑ 198 Jeff Schwarz .10 .02
❑ 199 Jerry DiPoto .10 .02
❑ 200 Alvaro Espinoza .10 .02
❑ 201 Wayne Kirby .10 .02
❑ 202 Tom Kramer RC .15 .05
❑ 203 Jesse Levis .10 .02
❑ 204 Manny Ramirez .75 .30
❑ 205 Jeff Treadway .10 .02
❑ 206 Bill Wertz RC .15 .05
❑ 207 Cliff Young .10 .02
❑ 208 Matt Young .10 .02
❑ 209 Kirk Gibson .20 .07
❑ 210 Greg Gohr .10 .02
❑ 211 Bill Krueger .10 .02
❑ 212 Bob MacDonald .10 .02
❑ 213 Mike Moore .10 .02
❑ 214 David Wells .20 .07
❑ 215 Billy Brewer .10 .02
❑ 216 David Cone .20 .07
❑ 217 Greg Gagne .10 .02
❑ 218 Mark Gardner .10 .02
❑ 219 Chris Haney .10 .02
❑ 220 Phil Hiatt .10 .02
❑ 221 Jose Lind .10 .02
❑ 222 Juan Bell .10 .02
❑ 223 Tom Brunansky .10 .02
❑ 224 Mike Ignasiak .10 .02
❑ 225 Joe Kmak .10 .02
❑ 226 Tom Lampkin .10 .02
❑ 227 Graeme Lloyd RC .40 .15
❑ 228 Carlos Maldonado .10 .02
❑ 229 Matt Mieske .10 .02
❑ 230 Angel Miranda .10 .02
❑ 231 Troy O'Leary RC .40 .15
❑ 232 Kevin Reimer .10 .02
❑ 233 Larry Casian .10 .02
❑ 234 Jim Deshaies .10 .02
❑ 235 Eddie Guardado RC .60 .25
❑ 236 Chip Hale .10 .02
❑ 237 Mike Maksudian RC .15 .05
❑ 238 David McCarty .10 .02
❑ 239 Pat Meares RC .40 .15
❑ 240 George Tsamis RC .15 .05
❑ 241 Dave Winfield .20 .07
❑ 242 Jim Abbott .30 .10
❑ 243 Wade Boggs .30 .10
❑ 244 Andy Cook RC .15 .05
❑ 245 Russ Davis RC .15 .05
❑ 246 Mike Humphreys .10 .02
❑ 247 Jimmy Key .20 .07
❑ 248 Jim Leyritz .10 .02
❑ 249 Bobby Munoz .10 .02
❑ 250 Paul O'Neill .30 .10
❑ 251 Spike Owen .10 .02
❑ 252 Dave Silvestri .10 .02
❑ 253 Marcos Armas RC .15 .05
❑ 254 Brent Gates .10 .02
❑ 255 Rich Gossage .20 .07
❑ 256 Scott Lydy RC .15 .05
❑ 257 Henry Mercedes .10 .02
❑ 258 Mike Mohler RC .40 .15
❑ 259 Troy Neel .10 .02
❑ 260 Edwin Nunez .10 .02
❑ 261 Craig Paquette .10 .02
❑ 262 Kevin Seitzer .10 .02
❑ 263 Rich Amaral .10 .02
❑ 264 Mike Blowers .10 .02
❑ 265 Chris Bosio .10 .02
❑ 266 Norm Charlton .10 .02
❑ 267 Jim Converse RC .15 .05
❑ 268 John Cummings RC .15 .05
❑ 269 Mike Felder .10 .02
❑ 270 Mike Hampton .20 .07
❑ 271 Bill Haselman .10 .02
❑ 272 Dwayne Henry .10 .02
❑ 273 Greg Litton .10 .02
❑ 274 Mackey Sasser .10 .02
❑ 275 Lee Tinsley .10 .02
❑ 276 David Wainhouse .10 .02
❑ 277 Jeff Bronkey .10 .02
❑ 278 Benji Gil .10 .02
❑ 279 Tom Henke .10 .02
❑ 280 Charlie Leibrandt .10 .02
❑ 281 Robb Nen .20 .07
❑ 282 Bill Ripken .10 .02
❑ 283 Jon Shave RC .15 .05
❑ 284 Doug Strange .10 .02
❑ 285 Matt Whiteside RC .15 .05
❑ 286 Scott Brow RC .15 .05
❑ 287 Willie Canate RC .15 .05
❑ 288 Tony Castillo .10 .02
❑ 289 Domingo Cedeno RC .15 .05
❑ 290 Darnell Coles .10 .02
❑ 291 Danny Cox .10 .02
❑ 292 Mark Eichhorn .10 .02
❑ 293 Tony Fernandez .10 .02
❑ 294 Al Leiter .20 .07
❑ 295 Paul Molitor .20 .07
❑ 296 Dave Stewart .20 .07
❑ 297 Woody Williams RC .60 .25
❑ 298 Checklist F1-F100 .10 .02
❑ 299 Checklist F101-F200 .10 .02
❑ 300 Checklist F201-F300 .10 .02

1994 Fleer

❑ COMPLETE SET (720) 50.00 25.00
❑ 1 Brady Anderson .30 .10
❑ 2 Harold Baines .30 .10
❑ 3 Mike Devereaux .15 .05
❑ 4 Todd Frohwirth .15 .05
❑ 5 Jeffrey Hammonds .15 .05
❑ 6 Chris Hoiles .15 .05
❑ 7 Tim Hulett .15 .05
❑ 8 Ben McDonald .15 .05
❑ 9 Mark McLemore .15 .05
❑ 10 Alan Mills .15 .05
❑ 11 Jamie Moyer .30 .10
❑ 12 Mike Mussina .50 .20
❑ 13 Gregg Olson .15 .05
❑ 14 Mike Pagliarulo .15 .05
❑ 15 Brad Pennington .15 .05
❑ 16 Jim Poole .15 .05
❑ 17 Harold Reynolds .30 .10
❑ 18 Arthur Rhodes .15 .05
❑ 19 Cal Ripken 2.50 1.00
❑ 20 David Segui .15 .05
❑ 21 Rick Sutcliffe .30 .10
❑ 22 Fernando Valenzuela .30 .10
❑ 23 Jack Voigt .15 .05
❑ 24 Mark Williamson .15 .05
❑ 25 Scott Bankhead .15 .05
❑ 26 Roger Clemens 1.50 .60
❑ 27 Scott Cooper .15 .05
❑ 28 Danny Darwin .15 .05
❑ 29 Andre Dawson .30 .10
❑ 30 Rob Deer .15 .05
❑ 31 John Dopson .15 .05
❑ 32 Scott Fletcher .15 .05
❑ 33 Mike Greenwell .15 .05
❑ 34 Greg A. Harris .15 .05
❑ 35 Billy Hatcher .15 .05

❑ 36	Bob Melvin	.15	.05
❑ 37	Tony Pena	.15	.05
❑ 38	Paul Quantrill	.15	.05
❑ 39	Carlos Quintana	.15	.05
❑ 40	Ernest Riles	.15	.05
❑ 41	Jeff Russell	.15	.05
❑ 42	Ken Ryan	.15	.05
❑ 43	Aaron Sele	.15	.05
❑ 44	John Valentin	.15	.05
❑ 45	Mo Vaughn	.30	.10
❑ 46	Frank Viola	.30	.10
❑ 47	Bob Zupcic	.15	.05
❑ 48	Mike Butcher	.15	.05
❑ 49	Rod Correia	.15	.05
❑ 50	Chad Curtis	.15	.05
❑ 51	Chili Davis	.30	.10
❑ 52	Gary DiSarcina	.15	.05
❑ 53	Damion Easley	.15	.05
❑ 54	Jim Edmonds	.75	.30
❑ 55	Chuck Finley	.30	.10
❑ 56	Steve Frey	.15	.05
❑ 57	Rene Gonzales	.15	.05
❑ 58	Joe Grahe	.15	.05
❑ 59	Hilly Hathaway	.15	.05
❑ 60	Stan Javier	.15	.05
❑ 61	Mark Langston	.15	.05
❑ 62	Phil Leftwich RC	.15	.05
❑ 63	Torey Lovullo	.15	.05
❑ 64	Joe Magrane	.15	.05
❑ 65	Greg Myers	.15	.05
❑ 66	Ken Patterson	.15	.05
❑ 67	Eduardo Perez	.15	.05
❑ 68	Luis Polonia	.15	.05
❑ 69	Tim Salmon	.50	.20
❑ 70	J.T.Snow	.30	.10
❑ 71	Ron Tingley	.15	.05
❑ 72	Julio Valera	.15	.05
❑ 73	Wilson Alvarez	.15	.05
❑ 74	Tim Belcher	.15	.05
❑ 75	George Bell	.15	.05
❑ 76	Jason Bere	.15	.05
❑ 77	Rod Bolton	.15	.05
❑ 78	Ellis Burks	.30	.10
❑ 79	Joey Cora	.15	.05
❑ 80	Alex Fernandez	.15	.05
❑ 81	Craig Grebeck	.15	.05
❑ 82	Ozzie Guillen	.30	.10
❑ 83	Roberto Hernandez	.15	.05
❑ 84	Bo Jackson	.75	.30
❑ 85	Lance Johnson	.15	.05
❑ 86	Ron Karkovice	.15	.05
❑ 87	Mike LaValliere	.15	.05
❑ 88	Kirk McCaskill	.15	.05
❑ 89	Jack McDowell	.15	.05
❑ 90	Warren Newson	.15	.05
❑ 91	Dan Pasqua	.15	.05
❑ 92	Scott Radinsky	.15	.05
❑ 93	Tim Raines	.30	.10
❑ 94	Steve Sax	.15	.05
❑ 95	Jeff Schwarz	.15	.05
❑ 96	Frank Thomas	.75	.30
❑ 97	Robin Ventura	.30	.10
❑ 98	Sandy Alomar Jr.	.15	.05
❑ 99	Carlos Baerga	.15	.05
❑ 100	Albert Belle	.30	.10
❑ 101	Mark Clark	.15	.05
❑ 102	Jerry DiPoto	.15	.05
❑ 103	Alvaro Espinoza	.15	.05
❑ 104	Felix Fermin	.15	.05
❑ 105	Jeremy Hernandez	.15	.05
❑ 106	Reggie Jefferson	.15	.05
❑ 107	Wayne Kirby	.15	.05
❑ 108	Tom Kramer	.15	.05
❑ 109	Mark Lewis	.15	.05
❑ 110	Derek Lilliquist	.15	.05
❑ 111	Kenny Lofton	.30	.10
❑ 112	Candy Maldonado	.15	.05
❑ 113	Jose Mesa	.15	.05
❑ 114	Jeff Mutis	.15	.05
❑ 115	Charles Nagy	.15	.05
❑ 116	Bob Ojeda	.15	.05
❑ 117	Junior Ortiz	.15	.05
❑ 118	Eric Plunk	.15	.05
❑ 119	Manny Ramirez	.75	.30
❑ 120	Paul Sorrento	.15	.05
❑ 121	Jim Thome	.50	.20
❑ 122	Jeff Treadway	.15	.05
❑ 123	Bill Wertz	.15	.05
❑ 124	Skeeter Barnes	.15	.05
❑ 125	Milt Cuyler	.15	.05
❑ 126	Eric Davis	.30	.10
❑ 127	John Doherty	.15	.05
❑ 128	Cecil Fielder	.30	.10
❑ 129	Travis Fryman	.30	.10
❑ 130	Kirk Gibson	.30	.10
❑ 131	Dan Gladden	.15	.05
❑ 132	Greg Gohr	.15	.05
❑ 133	Chris Gomez	.15	.05
❑ 134	Bill Gullickson	.15	.05
❑ 135	Mike Henneman	.15	.05
❑ 136	Kurt Knudsen	.15	.05
❑ 137	Chad Kreuter	.15	.05
❑ 138	Bill Krueger	.15	.05
❑ 139	Scott Livingstone	.15	.05
❑ 140	Bob MacDonald	.15	.05
❑ 141	Mike Moore	.15	.05
❑ 142	Tony Phillips	.15	.05
❑ 143	Mickey Tettleton	.15	.05
❑ 144	Alan Trammell	.30	.10
❑ 145	David Wells	.30	.10
❑ 146	Lou Whitaker	.30	.10
❑ 147	Kevin Appier	.30	.10
❑ 148	Stan Belinda	.15	.05
❑ 149	George Brett	2.00	.75
❑ 150	Billy Brewer	.15	.05
❑ 151	Hubie Brooks	.15	.05
❑ 152	David Cone	.30	.10
❑ 153	Gary Gaetti	.30	.10
❑ 154	Greg Gagne	.15	.05
❑ 155	Tom Gordon	.15	.05
❑ 156	Mark Gubicza	.15	.05
❑ 157	Chris Gwynn	.15	.05
❑ 158	John Habyan	.15	.05
❑ 159	Chris Haney	.15	.05
❑ 160	Phil Hiatt	.15	.05
❑ 161	Felix Jose	.15	.05
❑ 162	Wally Joyner	.30	.10
❑ 163	Jose Lind	.15	.05
❑ 164	Mike Macfarlane	.15	.05
❑ 165	Mike Magnante	.15	.05
❑ 166	Brent Mayne	.15	.05
❑ 167	Brian McRae	.15	.05
❑ 168	Kevin McReynolds	.15	.05
❑ 169	Keith Miller	.15	.05
❑ 170	Jeff Montgomery	.15	.05
❑ 171	Hipolito Pichardo	.15	.05
❑ 172	Rico Rossy	.15	.05
❑ 173	Juan Bell	.15	.05
❑ 174	Ricky Bones	.15	.05
❑ 175	Cal Eldred	.15	.05
❑ 176	Mike Fetters	.15	.05
❑ 177	Darryl Hamilton	.15	.05
❑ 178	Doug Henry	.15	.05
❑ 179	Mike Ignasiak	.15	.05
❑ 180	John Jaha	.15	.05
❑ 181	Pat Listach	.15	.05
❑ 182	Graeme Lloyd	.15	.05
❑ 183	Matt Mieske	.15	.05
❑ 184	Angel Miranda	.15	.05
❑ 185	Jaime Navarro	.15	.05
❑ 186	Dave Nilsson	.15	.05
❑ 187	Troy O'Leary	.15	.05
❑ 188	Jesse Orosco	.15	.05
❑ 189	Kevin Reimer	.15	.05
❑ 190	Kevin Seitzer	.15	.05
❑ 191	Bill Spiers	.15	.05
❑ 192	B.J. Surhoff	.30	.10
❑ 193	Dickie Thon	.15	.05
❑ 194	Jose Valentin	.15	.05
❑ 195	Greg Vaughn	.15	.05
❑ 196	Bill Wegman	.15	.05
❑ 197	Robin Yount	1.25	.50
❑ 198	Rick Aguilera	.15	.05
❑ 199	Willie Banks	.15	.05
❑ 200	Bernardo Brito	.15	.05
❑ 201	Larry Casian	.15	.05
❑ 202	Scott Erickson	.15	.05
❑ 203	Eddie Guardado	.30	.10
❑ 204	Mark Guthrie	.15	.05
❑ 205	Chip Hale	.15	.05
❑ 206	Brian Harper	.15	.05
❑ 207	Mike Hartley	.15	.05
❑ 208	Kent Hrbek	.30	.10
❑ 209	Terry Jorgensen	.15	.05
❑ 210	Chuck Knoblauch	.30	.10
❑ 211	Gene Larkin	.15	.05
❑ 212	Shane Mack	.15	.05
❑ 213	David McCarty	.15	.05
❑ 214	Pat Meares	.15	.05
❑ 215	Pedro Munoz	.15	.05
❑ 216	Derek Parks	.15	.05
❑ 217	Kirby Puckett	.75	.30
❑ 218	Jeff Reboulet	.15	.05
❑ 219	Kevin Tapani	.15	.05
❑ 220	Mike Trombley	.15	.05
❑ 221	George Tsamis	.15	.05
❑ 222	Carl Willis	.15	.05
❑ 223	Dave Winfield	.30	.10
❑ 224	Jim Abbott	.50	.20
❑ 225	Paul Assenmacher	.15	.05
❑ 226	Wade Boggs	.50	.20
❑ 227	Russ Davis	.15	.05
❑ 228	Steve Farr	.15	.05
❑ 229	Mike Gallego	.15	.05
❑ 230	Paul Gibson	.15	.05
❑ 231	Steve Howe	.15	.05
❑ 232	Dion James	.15	.05
❑ 233	Domingo Jean	.15	.05
❑ 234	Scott Kamieniecki	.15	.05
❑ 235	Pat Kelly	.15	.05
❑ 236	Jimmy Key	.30	.10
❑ 237	Jim Leyritz	.15	.05
❑ 238	Kevin Maas	.15	.05
❑ 239	Don Mattingly	2.00	.75
❑ 240	Rich Monteleone	.15	.05
❑ 241	Bobby Munoz	.15	.05
❑ 242	Matt Nokes	.15	.05
❑ 243	Paul O'Neill	.50	.20
❑ 244	Spike Owen	.15	.05
❑ 245	Melido Perez	.15	.05
❑ 246	Lee Smith	.30	.10
❑ 247	Mike Stanley	.15	.05
❑ 248	Danny Tartabull	.15	.05
❑ 249	Randy Velarde	.15	.05
❑ 250	Bob Wickman	.15	.05
❑ 251	Bernie Williams	.50	.20
❑ 252	Mike Aldrete	.15	.05
❑ 253	Marcos Armas	.15	.05
❑ 254	Lance Blankenship	.15	.05
❑ 255	Mike Bordick	.15	.05
❑ 256	Scott Brosius	.30	.10
❑ 257	Jerry Browne	.15	.05
❑ 258	Ron Darling	.15	.05
❑ 259	Kelly Downs	.15	.05
❑ 260	Dennis Eckersley	.30	.10
❑ 261	Brent Gates	.15	.05
❑ 262	Rich Gossage	.30	.10
❑ 263	Scott Hemond	.15	.05
❑ 264	Dave Henderson	.15	.05
❑ 265	Rick Honeycutt	.15	.05
❑ 266	Vince Horsman	.15	.05
❑ 267	Scott Lydy	.15	.05
❑ 268	Mark McGwire	2.00	.75
❑ 269	Mike Mohler	.15	.05
❑ 270	Troy Neel	.15	.05
❑ 271	Edwin Nunez	.15	.05
❑ 272	Craig Paquette	.15	.05
❑ 273	Ruben Sierra	.30	.10
❑ 274	Terry Steinbach	.15	.05
❑ 275	Todd Van Poppel	.15	.05
❑ 276	Bob Welch	.15	.05
❑ 277	Bobby Witt	.15	.05
❑ 278	Rich Amaral	.15	.05
❑ 279	Mike Blowers	.15	.05
❑ 280	Bret Boone UER	.30	.10
❑ 281	Chris Bosio	.15	.05
❑ 282	Jay Buhner	.30	.10
❑ 283	Norm Charlton	.15	.05
❑ 284	Mike Felder	.15	.05
❑ 285	Dave Fleming	.15	.05
❑ 286	Ken Griffey Jr.	1.25	.50
❑ 287	Erik Hanson	.15	.05
❑ 288	Bill Haselman	.15	.05
❑ 289	Brad Holman RC	.15	.05
❑ 290	Randy Johnson	.75	.30
❑ 291	Tim Leary	.15	.05
❑ 292	Greg Litton	.15	.05
❑ 293	Dave Magadan	.15	.05

❑	294	Edgar Martinez	.50	.20
❑	295	Tino Martinez	.50	.20
❑	296	Jeff Nelson	.15	.05
❑	297	Erik Plantenberg RC	.15	.05
❑	298	Mackey Sasser	.15	.05
❑	299	Brian Turang RC	.15	.05
❑	300	Dave Valle	.15	.05
❑	301	Omar Vizquel	.50	.20
❑	302	Brian Bohanon	.15	.05
❑	303	Kevin Brown	.30	.10
❑	304	Jose Canseco	.50	.20
❑	305	Mario Diaz	.15	.05
❑	306	Julio Franco	.30	.10
❑	307	Juan Gonzalez	.30	.10
❑	308	Tom Henke	.15	.05
❑	309	David Hulse	.15	.05
❑	310	Manuel Lee	.15	.05
❑	311	Craig Lefferts	.15	.05
❑	312	Charlie Leibrandt	.15	.05
❑	313	Rafael Palmeiro	.50	.20
❑	314	Dean Palmer	.30	.10
❑	315	Roger Pavlik	.15	.05
❑	316	Dan Peltier	.15	.05
❑	317	Gene Petralli	.15	.05
❑	318	Gary Redus	.15	.05
❑	319	Ivan Rodriguez	.50	.20
❑	320	Kenny Rogers	.30	.10
❑	321	Nolan Ryan	3.00	1.25
❑	322	Doug Strange	.15	.05
❑	323	Matt Whiteside	.15	.05
❑	324	Roberto Alomar	.50	.20
❑	325	Pat Borders	.15	.05
❑	326	Joe Carter	.30	.10
❑	327	Tony Castillo	.15	.05
❑	328	Darnell Coles	.15	.05
❑	329	Danny Cox	.15	.05
❑	330	Mark Eichhorn	.15	.05
❑	331	Tony Fernandez	.15	.05
❑	332	Alfredo Griffin	.15	.05
❑	333	Juan Guzman	.15	.05
❑	334	Rickey Henderson	.75	.30
❑	335	Pat Hentgen	.15	.05
❑	336	Randy Knorr	.15	.05
❑	337	Al Leiter	.30	.10
❑	338	Paul Molitor	.30	.10
❑	339	Jack Morris	.30	.10
❑	340	John Olerud	.30	.10
❑	341	Dick Schofield	.15	.05
❑	342	Ed Sprague	.15	.05
❑	343	Dave Stewart	.30	.10
❑	344	Todd Stottlemyre	.15	.05
❑	345	Mike Timlin	.15	.05
❑	346	Duane Ward	.15	.05
❑	347	Turner Ward	.15	.05
❑	348	Devon White	.30	.10
❑	349	Woody Williams	.30	.10
❑	350	Steve Avery	.15	.05
❑	351	Steve Bedrosian	.15	.05
❑	352	Rafael Belliard	.15	.05
❑	353	Damon Berryhill	.15	.05
❑	354	Jeff Blauser	.15	.05
❑	355	Sid Bream	.15	.05
❑	356	Francisco Cabrera	.15	.05
❑	357	Marvin Freeman	.15	.05
❑	358	Ron Gant	.30	.10
❑	359	Tom Glavine	.50	.20
❑	360	Jay Howell	.15	.05
❑	361	David Justice	.30	.10
❑	362	Ryan Klesko	.30	.10
❑	363	Mark Lemke	.15	.05
❑	364	Javier Lopez	.30	.10
❑	365	Greg Maddux	1.25	.50
❑	366	Fred McGriff	.50	.20
❑	367	Greg McMichael	.15	.05
❑	368	Kent Mercker	.15	.05
❑	369	Otis Nixon	.15	.05
❑	370	Greg Olson	.15	.05
❑	371	Bill Pecota	.15	.05
❑	372	Terry Pendleton	.30	.10
❑	373	Deion Sanders	.50	.20
❑	374	Pete Smith	.15	.05
❑	375	John Smoltz	.50	.20
❑	376	Mike Stanton	.15	.05
❑	377	Tony Tarasco	.15	.05
❑	378	Mark Wohlers	.15	.05
❑	379	Jose Bautista	.15	.05
❑	380	Shawn Boskie	.15	.05
❑	381	Steve Buechele	.15	.05
❑	382	Frank Castillo	.15	.05
❑	383	Mark Grace	.50	.20
❑	384	Jose Guzman	.15	.05
❑	385	Mike Harkey	.15	.05
❑	386	Greg Hibbard	.15	.05
❑	387	Glenallen Hill	.15	.05
❑	388	Steve Lake	.15	.05
❑	389	Derrick May	.15	.05
❑	390	Chuck McElroy	.15	.05
❑	391	Mike Morgan	.15	.05
❑	392	Randy Myers	.15	.05
❑	393	Dan Plesac	.15	.05
❑	394	Kevin Roberson	.15	.05
❑	395	Rey Sanchez	.15	.05
❑	396	Ryne Sandberg	1.25	.50
❑	397	Bob Scanlan	.15	.05
❑	398	Dwight Smith	.15	.05
❑	399	Sammy Sosa	.75	.30
❑	400	Jose Vizcaino	.15	.05
❑	401	Rick Wilkins	.15	.05
❑	402	Willie Wilson	.15	.05
❑	403	Eric Yelding	.15	.05
❑	404	Bobby Ayala	.15	.05
❑	405	Jeff Branson	.15	.05
❑	406	Tom Browning	.15	.05
❑	407	Jacob Brumfield	.15	.05
❑	408	Tim Costo	.15	.05
❑	409	Rob Dibble	.30	.10
❑	410	Willie Greene	.15	.05
❑	411	Thomas Howard	.15	.05
❑	412	Roberto Kelly	.15	.05
❑	413	Bill Landrum	.15	.05
❑	414	Barry Larkin	.50	.20
❑	415	Larry Luebbers RC	.15	.05
❑	416	Kevin Mitchell	.15	.05
❑	417	Hal Morris	.15	.05
❑	418	Joe Oliver	.15	.05
❑	419	Tim Pugh	.15	.05
❑	420	Jeff Reardon	.30	.10
❑	421	Jose Rijo	.15	.05
❑	422	Bip Roberts	.15	.05
❑	423	John Roper	.15	.05
❑	424	Johnny Ruffin	.15	.05
❑	425	Chris Sabo	.15	.05
❑	426	Juan Samuel	.15	.05
❑	427	Reggie Sanders	.30	.10
❑	428	Scott Service	.15	.05
❑	429	John Smiley	.15	.05
❑	430	Jerry Spradlin RC	.15	.05
❑	431	Kevin Wickander	.15	.05
❑	432	Freddie Benavides	.15	.05
❑	433	Dante Bichette	.30	.10
❑	434	Willie Blair	.15	.05
❑	435	Daryl Boston	.15	.05
❑	436	Kent Bottenfield	.15	.05
❑	437	Vinny Castilla	.30	.10
❑	438	Jerald Clark	.15	.05
❑	439	Alex Cole	.15	.05
❑	440	Andres Galarraga	.30	.10
❑	441	Joe Girardi	.15	.05
❑	442	Greg W. Harris	.15	.05
❑	443	Charlie Hayes	.15	.05
❑	444	Darren Holmes	.15	.05
❑	445	Chris Jones	.15	.05
❑	446	Roberto Mejia	.15	.05
❑	447	David Nied	.15	.05
❑	448	Jayhawk Owens	.15	.05
❑	449	Jeff Parrett	.15	.05
❑	450	Steve Reed	.15	.05
❑	451	Armando Reynoso	.15	.05
❑	452	Bruce Ruffin	.15	.05
❑	453	Mo Sanford	.15	.05
❑	454	Danny Sheaffer	.15	.05
❑	455	Jim Tatum	.15	.05
❑	456	Gary Wayne	.15	.05
❑	457	Eric Young	.15	.05
❑	458	Luis Aquino	.15	.05
❑	459	Alex Arias	.15	.05
❑	460	Jack Armstrong	.15	.05
❑	461	Bret Barberie	.15	.05
❑	462	Ryan Bowen	.15	.05
❑	463	Chuck Carr	.15	.05
❑	464	Jeff Conine	.30	.10
❑	465	Henry Cotto	.15	.05
❑	466	Orestes Destrade	.15	.05
❑	467	Chris Hammond	.15	.05
❑	468	Bryan Harvey	.15	.05
❑	469	Charlie Hough	.30	.10
❑	470	Joe Klink	.15	.05
❑	471	Richie Lewis	.15	.05
❑	472	Bob Natal	.15	.05
❑	473	Pat Rapp	.15	.05
❑	474	Rich Renteria	.15	.05
❑	475	Rich Rodriguez	.15	.05
❑	476	Benito Santiago	.30	.10
❑	477	Gary Sheffield	.30	.10
❑	478	Matt Turner	.15	.05
❑	479	David Weathers	.15	.05
❑	480	Walt Weiss	.15	.05
❑	481	Darrell Whitmore	.15	.05
❑	482	Eric Anthony	.15	.05
❑	483	Jeff Bagwell	.50	.20
❑	484	Kevin Bass	.15	.05
❑	485	Craig Biggio	.50	.20
❑	486	Ken Caminiti	.30	.10
❑	487	Andujar Cedeno	.15	.05
❑	488	Chris Donnels	.15	.05
❑	489	Doug Drabek	.15	.05
❑	490	Steve Finley	.30	.10
❑	491	Luis Gonzalez	.30	.10
❑	492	Pete Harnisch	.15	.05
❑	493	Xavier Hernandez	.15	.05
❑	494	Doug Jones	.15	.05
❑	495	Todd Jones	.15	.05
❑	496	Darryl Kile	.30	.10
❑	497	Al Osuna	.15	.05
❑	498	Mark Portugal	.15	.05
❑	499	Scott Servais	.15	.05
❑	500	Greg Swindell	.15	.05
❑	501	Eddie Taubensee	.15	.05
❑	502	Jose Uribe	.15	.05
❑	503	Brian Williams	.15	.05
❑	504	Billy Ashley	.15	.05
❑	505	Pedro Astacio	.15	.05
❑	506	Brett Butler	.30	.10
❑	507	Tom Candiotti	.15	.05
❑	508	Omar Daal	.15	.05
❑	509	Jim Gott	.15	.05
❑	510	Kevin Gross	.15	.05
❑	511	Dave Hansen	.15	.05
❑	512	Carlos Hernandez	.15	.05
❑	513	Orel Hershiser	.30	.10
❑	514	Eric Karros	.30	.10
❑	515	Pedro Martinez	.75	.30
❑	516	Ramon Martinez	.15	.05
❑	517	Roger McDowell	.15	.05
❑	518	Raul Mondesi	.30	.10
❑	519	Jose Offerman	.15	.05
❑	520	Mike Piazza	1.50	.60
❑	521	Jody Reed	.15	.05
❑	522	Henry Rodriguez	.15	.05
❑	523	Mike Sharperson	.15	.05
❑	524	Cory Snyder	.15	.05
❑	525	Darryl Strawberry	.30	.10
❑	526	Rick Trlicek	.15	.05
❑	527	Tim Wallach	.15	.05
❑	528	Mitch Webster	.15	.05
❑	529	Steve Wilson	.15	.05
❑	530	Todd Worrell	.15	.05
❑	531	Moises Alou	.30	.10
❑	532	Brian Barnes	.15	.05
❑	533	Sean Berry	.15	.05
❑	534	Greg Colbrunn	.15	.05
❑	535	Delino DeShields	.15	.05
❑	536	Jeff Fassero	.15	.05
❑	537	Darrin Fletcher	.15	.05
❑	538	Cliff Floyd	.30	.10
❑	539	Lou Frazier	.15	.05

❑	540 Marquis Grissom	.30	.10
❑	541 Butch Henry	.15	.05
❑	542 Ken Hill	.15	.05
❑	543 Mike Lansing	.15	.05
❑	544 Brian Looney RC	.15	.05
❑	545 Dennis Martinez	.30	.10
❑	546 Chris Nabholz	.15	.05
❑	547 Randy Ready	.15	.05
❑	548 Mel Rojas	.15	.05
❑	549 Kirk Rueter	.15	.05
❑	550 Tim Scott	.15	.05
❑	551 Jeff Shaw	.15	.05
❑	552 Tim Spehr	.15	.05
❑	553 John Vander Wal	.15	.05
❑	554 Larry Walker	.30	.10
❑	555 John Wetteland	.30	.10
❑	556 Rondell White	.30	.10
❑	557 Tim Bogar	.15	.05
❑	558 Bobby Bonilla	.30	.10
❑	559 Jeromy Burnitz	.30	.10
❑	560 Sid Fernandez	.15	.05
❑	561 John Franco	.30	.10
❑	562 Dave Gallagher	.15	.05
❑	563 Dwight Gooden	.30	.10
❑	564 Eric Hillman	.15	.05
❑	565 Todd Hundley	.15	.05
❑	566 Jeff Innis	.15	.05
❑	567 Darrin Jackson	.15	.05
❑	568 Howard Johnson	.15	.05
❑	569 Bobby Jones	.15	.05
❑	570 Jeff Kent	.50	.20
❑	571 Mike Maddux	.15	.05
❑	572 Jeff McKnight	.15	.05
❑	573 Eddie Murray	.75	.30
❑	574 Charlie O'Brien	.15	.05
❑	575 Joe Orsulak	.15	.05
❑	576 Bret Saberhagen	.30	.10
❑	577 Pete Schourek	.15	.05
❑	578 Dave Telgheder	.15	.05
❑	579 Ryan Thompson	.15	.05
❑	580 Anthony Young	.15	.05
❑	581 Ruben Amaro	.15	.05
❑	582 Larry Andersen	.15	.05
❑	583 Kim Batiste	.15	.05
❑	584 Wes Chamberlain	.15	.05
❑	585 Darren Daulton	.30	.10
❑	586 Mariano Duncan	.15	.05
❑	587 Lenny Dykstra	.30	.10
❑	588 Jim Eisenreich	.15	.05
❑	589 Tommy Greene	.15	.05
❑	590 Dave Hollins	.15	.05
❑	591 Pete Incaviglia	.15	.05
❑	592 Danny Jackson	.15	.05
❑	593 Ricky Jordan	.15	.05
❑	594 John Kruk	.30	.10
❑	595 Roger Mason	.15	.05
❑	596 Mickey Morandini	.15	.05
❑	597 Terry Mulholland	.15	.05
❑	598 Todd Pratt	.15	.05
❑	599 Ben Rivera	.15	.05
❑	600 Curt Schilling	.30	.10
❑	601 Kevin Stocker	.15	.05
❑	602 Milt Thompson	.15	.05
❑	603 David West	.15	.05
❑	604 Mitch Williams	.15	.05
❑	605 Jay Bell	.30	.10
❑	606 Dave Clark	.15	.05
❑	607 Steve Cooke	.15	.05
❑	608 Tom Foley	.15	.05
❑	609 Carlos Garcia	.15	.05
❑	610 Joel Johnston	.15	.05
❑	611 Jeff King	.15	.05
❑	612 Al Martin	.15	.05
❑	613 Lloyd McClendon	.15	.05
❑	614 Orlando Merced	.15	.05
❑	615 Blas Minor	.15	.05
❑	616 Denny Neagle	.30	.10
❑	617 Mark Petkovsek RC	.15	.05
❑	618 Tom Prince	.15	.05
❑	619 Don Slaught	.15	.05
❑	620 Zane Smith	.15	.05
❑	621 Randy Tomlin	.15	.05
❑	622 Andy Van Slyke	.50	.20
❑	623 Paul Wagner	.15	.05
❑	624 Tim Wakefield	.50	.20
❑	625 Bob Walk	.15	.05
❑	626 Kevin Young	.15	.05
❑	627 Luis Alicea	.15	.05
❑	628 Rene Arocha	.15	.05
❑	629 Rod Brewer	.15	.05
❑	630 Rheal Cormier	.15	.05
❑	631 Bernard Gilkey	.15	.05
❑	632 Lee Guetterman	.15	.05
❑	633 Gregg Jefferies	.15	.05
❑	634 Brian Jordan	.30	.10
❑	635 Les Lancaster	.15	.05
❑	636 Ray Lankford	.30	.10
❑	637 Rob Murphy	.15	.05
❑	638 Omar Olivares	.15	.05
❑	639 Jose Oquendo	.15	.05
❑	640 Donovan Osborne	.15	.05
❑	641 Tom Pagnozzi	.15	.05
❑	642 Erik Pappas	.15	.05
❑	643 Geronimo Pena	.15	.05
❑	644 Mike Perez	.15	.05
❑	645 Gerald Perry	.15	.05
❑	646 Ozzie Smith	1.25	.50
❑	647 Bob Tewksbury	.15	.05
❑	648 Allen Watson	.15	.05
❑	649 Mark Whiten	.15	.05
❑	650 Tracy Woodson	.15	.05
❑	651 Todd Zeile	.15	.05
❑	652 Andy Ashby	.15	.05
❑	653 Brad Ausmus	.50	.20
❑	654 Billy Bean	.15	.05
❑	655 Derek Bell	.15	.05
❑	656 Andy Benes	.15	.05
❑	657 Doug Brocail	.15	.05
❑	658 Jarvis Brown	.15	.05
❑	659 Archi Cianfrocco	.15	.05
❑	660 Phil Clark	.15	.05
❑	661 Mark Davis	.15	.05
❑	662 Jeff Gardner	.15	.05
❑	663 Pat Gomez	.15	.05
❑	664 Ricky Gutierrez	.15	.05
❑	665 Tony Gwynn	1.00	.40
❑	666 Gene Harris	.15	.05
❑	667 Kevin Higgins	.15	.05
❑	668 Trevor Hoffman	.50	.20
❑	669 Pedro A.Martinez RC	.15	.05
❑	670 Tim Mauser	.15	.05
❑	671 Melvin Nieves	.15	.05
❑	672 Phil Plantier	.15	.05
❑	673 Frank Seminara	.15	.05
❑	674 Craig Shipley	.15	.05
❑	675 Kerry Taylor	.15	.05
❑	676 Tim Teufel	.15	.05
❑	677 Guillermo Velasquez	.15	.05
❑	678 Wally Whitehurst	.15	.05
❑	679 Tim Worrell	.15	.05
❑	680 Rod Beck	.15	.05
❑	681 Mike Benjamin	.15	.05
❑	682 Todd Benzinger	.15	.05
❑	683 Bud Black	.15	.05
❑	684 Barry Bonds	2.00	.75
❑	685 Jeff Brantley	.15	.05
❑	686 Dave Burba	.15	.05
❑	687 John Burkett	.15	.05
❑	688 Mark Carreon	.15	.05
❑	689 Will Clark	.50	.20
❑	690 Royce Clayton	.15	.05
❑	691 Bryan Hickerson	.15	.05
❑	692 Mike Jackson	.15	.05
❑	693 Darren Lewis	.15	.05
❑	694 Kirt Manwaring	.15	.05
❑	695 Dave Martinez	.15	.05
❑	696 Willie McGee	.30	.10
❑	697 John Patterson	.15	.05
❑	698 Jeff Reed	.15	.05
❑	699 Kevin Rogers	.15	.05
❑	700 Scott Sanderson	.15	.05
❑	701 Steve Scarsone	.15	.05
❑	702 Billy Swift	.15	.05
❑	703 Robby Thompson	.15	.05
❑	704 Matt Williams	.30	.10
❑	705 Trevor Wilson	.15	.05
❑	706 McGriff/Gant/Justice	.30	.10
❑	707 J.Olerud/P.Molitor	.30	.10
❑	708 M.Mussina/J.McDowell	.30	.10
❑	709 L.Whitaker/A.Trammell	.30	.10
❑	710 R.Palmeiro/J.Gonzalez	.30	.10
❑	711 B.Butler/T.Gwynn	.50	.20
❑	712 K.Puckett/C.Knoblauch	.50	.20
❑	713 M.Piazza/E.Karros	.75	.30
❑	714 Checklist 1	.15	.05
❑	715 Checklist 2	.15	.05
❑	716 Checklist 3	.15	.05
❑	717 Checklist 4	.15	.05
❑	718 Checklist 5	.15	.05
❑	719 Checklist 6	.15	.05
❑	720 Checklist 7	.15	.05
❑	P69 Tim Salmon Promo	1.00	.40

1994 Fleer Update

❑	COMP.FACT.SET (210)	50.00	25.00
❑	1 Mark Eichhorn	.25	.08
❑	2 Sid Fernandez	.25	.08
❑	3 Leo Gomez	.25	.08
❑	4 Mike Oquist	.25	.08
❑	5 Rafael Palmeiro	.75	.30
❑	6 Chris Sabo	.25	.08
❑	7 Dwight Smith	.25	.08
❑	8 Lee Smith	.50	.20
❑	9 Damon Berryhill	.25	.08
❑	10 Wes Chamberlain	.25	.08
❑	11 Gar Finnvold	.25	.08
❑	12 Chris Howard	.25	.08
❑	13 Tim Naehring	.25	.08
❑	14 Otis Nixon	.25	.08
❑	15 Brian Anderson RC	.50	.20
❑	16 Jorge Fabregas	.25	.08
❑	17 Rex Hudler	.25	.08
❑	18 Bo Jackson	1.25	.50
❑	19 Mark Leiter	.25	.08
❑	20 Spike Owen	.25	.08
❑	21 Harold Reynolds	.50	.20
❑	22 Chris Turner	.25	.08
❑	23 Dennis Cook	.25	.08
❑	24 Jose DeLeon	.25	.08
❑	25 Julio Franco	.50	.20
❑	26 Joe Hall	.25	.08
❑	27 Darrin Jackson	.25	.08
❑	28 Dane Johnson	.25	.08
❑	29 Norberto Martin	.25	.08
❑	30 Scott Sanderson	.25	.08
❑	31 Jason Grimsley	.25	.08
❑	32 Dennis Martinez	.50	.20
❑	33 Jack Morris	.50	.20
❑	34 Eddie Murray	1.25	.50
❑	35 Chad Ogea	.25	.08
❑	36 Tony Pena	.25	.08
❑	37 Paul Shuey	.25	.08
❑	38 Omar Vizquel	.75	.30
❑	39 Danny Bautista	.25	.08
❑	40 Tim Belcher	.25	.08
❑	41 Joe Boever	.25	.08
❑	42 Storm Davis	.25	.08
❑	43 Junior Felix	.25	.08
❑	44 Mike Gardiner	.25	.08
❑	45 Buddy Groom	.25	.08
❑	46 Juan Samuel	.25	.08
❑	47 Vince Coleman	.25	.08
❑	48 Bob Hamelin	.25	.08
❑	49 Dave Henderson	.25	.08
❑	50 Rusty Meacham	.25	.08
❑	51 Terry Shumpert	.25	.08
❑	52 Jeff Bronkey	.25	.08
❑	53 Alex Diaz	.25	.08
❑	54 Brian Harper	.25	.08
❑	55 Jose Mercedes	.25	.08

❑	56	Jody Reed	.25	.08
❑	57	Bob Scanlan	.25	.08
❑	58	Turner Ward	.25	.08
❑	59	Rich Becker	.25	.08
❑	60	Alex Cole	.25	.08
❑	61	Denny Hocking	.25	.08
❑	62	Scott Leius	.25	.08
❑	63	Pat Mahomes	.25	.08
❑	64	Carlos Pulido	.25	.08
❑	65	Dave Stevens	.25	.08
❑	66	Matt Walbeck	.25	.08
❑	67	Xavier Hernandez	.25	.08
❑	68	Sterling Hitchcock	.25	.08
❑	69	Terry Mulholland	.25	.08
❑	70	Luis Polonia	.25	.08
❑	71	Gerald Williams	.25	.08
❑	72	Mark Acre RC	.25	.08
❑	73	Geronimo Berroa	.25	.08
❑	74	Rickey Henderson	1.25	.50
❑	75	Stan Javier	.25	.08
❑	76	Steve Karsay	.25	.08
❑	77	Carlos Reyes	.25	.08
❑	78	Bill Taylor RC	.50	.20
❑	79	Eric Anthony	.25	.08
❑	80	Bobby Ayala	.25	.08
❑	81	Tim Davis	.25	.08
❑	82	Felix Fermin	.25	.08
❑	83	Reggie Jefferson	.25	.08
❑	84	Keith Mitchell	.25	.08
❑	85	Bill Risley	.25	.08
❑	86	Alex Rodriguez RC !	40.00	15.00
❑	87	Roger Salkeld	.25	.08
❑	88	Dan Wilson	.25	.08
❑	89	Cris Carpenter	.25	.08
❑	90	Will Clark	.75	.30
❑	91	Jeff Frye	.25	.08
❑	92	Rick Helling	.25	.08
❑	93	Chris James	.25	.08
❑	94	Oddibe McDowell	.25	.08
❑	95	Billy Ripken	.25	.08
❑	96	Carlos Delgado	.75	.30
❑	97	Alex Gonzalez	.25	.08
❑	98	Shawn Green	1.25	.50
❑	99	Darren Hall	.25	.08
❑	100	Mike Huff	.25	.08
❑	101	Mike Kelly	.25	.08
❑	102	Roberto Kelly	.25	.08
❑	103	Charlie O'Brien	.25	.08
❑	104	Jose Oliva	.25	.08
❑	105	Gregg Olson	.25	.08
❑	106	Willie Banks	.25	.08
❑	107	Jim Bullinger	.25	.08
❑	108	Chuck Crim	.25	.08
❑	109	Shawon Dunston	.25	.08
❑	110	Karl Rhodes	.25	.08
❑	111	Steve Trachsel	.25	.08
❑	112	Anthony Young	.25	.08
❑	113	Eddie Zambrano	.25	.08
❑	114	Bret Boone	.50	.20
❑	115	Jeff Brantley	.25	.08
❑	116	Hector Carrasco	.25	.08
❑	117	Tony Fernandez	.25	.08
❑	118	Tim Fortugno	.25	.08
❑	119	Erik Hanson	.25	.08
❑	120	Chuck McElroy	.25	.08
❑	121	Deion Sanders	.75	.30
❑	122	Ellis Burks	.50	.20
❑	123	Marvin Freeman	.25	.08
❑	124	Mike Harkey	.25	.08
❑	125	Howard Johnson	.25	.08
❑	126	Mike Kingery	.25	.08
❑	127	Nelson Liriano	.25	.08
❑	128	Marcus Moore	.25	.08
❑	129	Mike Munoz	.25	.08
❑	130	Kevin Ritz	.25	.08
❑	131	Walt Weiss	.25	.08
❑	132	Kurt Abbott RC	.25	.08
❑	133	Jerry Browne	.25	.08
❑	134	Greg Colbrunn	.25	.08
❑	135	Jeremy Hernandez	.25	.08
❑	136	Dave Magadan	.25	.08
❑	137	Kurt Miller	.25	.08
❑	138	Robb Nen	.50	.20
❑	139	Jesus Tavarez RC	.25	.08
❑	140	Sid Bream	.25	.08
❑	141	Tom Edens	.25	.08

❑	142	Tony Eusebio	.25	.08
❑	143	John Hudek RC	.25	.08
❑	144	Brian L.Hunter	.25	.08
❑	145	Orlando Miller	.25	.08
❑	146	James Mouton	.25	.08
❑	147	Shane Reynolds	.25	.08
❑	148	Rafael Bournigal	.25	.08
❑	149	Delino DeShields	.25	.08
❑	150	Garey Ingram RC	.25	.08
❑	151	Chan Ho Park RC	.75	.30
❑	152	Wil Cordero	.25	.08
❑	153	Pedro Martinez	1.25	.50
❑	154	Randy Milligan	.25	.08
❑	155	Lenny Webster	.25	.08
❑	156	Rico Brogna	.25	.08
❑	157	Josias Manzanillo	.25	.08
❑	158	Kevin McReynolds	.25	.08
❑	159	Mike Remlinger	.25	.08
❑	160	David Segui	.25	.08
❑	161	Pete Smith	.25	.08
❑	162	Kelly Stinnett RC	.50	.20
❑	163	Jose Vizcaino	.25	.08
❑	164	Billy Hatcher	.25	.08
❑	165	Doug Jones	.25	.08
❑	166	Mike Lieberthal	.50	.20
❑	167	Tony Longmire	.25	.08
❑	168	Bobby Munoz	.25	.08
❑	169	Paul Quantrill	.25	.08
❑	170	Heathcliff Slocumb	.25	.08
❑	171	Fernando Valenzuela	.50	.20
❑	172	Mark Dewey	.25	.08
❑	173	Brian R. Hunter	.25	.08
❑	174	Jon Lieber	.50	.20
❑	175	Ravelo Manzanillo	.25	.08
❑	176	Dan Miceli	.25	.08
❑	177	Rick White	.25	.08
❑	178	Bryan Eversgerd	.25	.08
❑	179	John Habyan	.25	.08
❑	180	Terry McGriff	.25	.08
❑	181	Vicente Palacios	.25	.08
❑	182	Rich Rodriguez	.25	.08
❑	183	Rick Sutcliffe	.50	.20
❑	184	Donnie Elliott	.25	.08
❑	185	Joey Hamilton	.25	.08
❑	186	Tim Hyers RC	.25	.08
❑	187	Luis Lopez	.25	.08
❑	188	Ray McDavid	.25	.08
❑	189	Bip Roberts	.25	.08
❑	190	Scott Sanders	.25	.08
❑	191	Eddie Williams	.25	.08
❑	192	Steve Frey	.25	.08
❑	193	Pat Gomez	.25	.08
❑	194	Rich Monteleone	.25	.08
❑	195	Mark Portugal	.25	.08
❑	196	Darryl Strawberry	.50	.20
❑	197	Salomon Torres	.25	.08
❑	198	W.VanLandingham RC	.25	.08
❑	199	Checklist	.25	.08
❑	200	Checklist	.25	.08

1995 Fleer

❑		COMPLETE SET (600)	50.00	20.00
❑	1	Brady Anderson	.30	.10
❑	2	Harold Baines	.30	.10
❑	3	Damon Buford	.15	.05
❑	4	Mike Devereaux	.15	.05
❑	5	Mark Eichhorn	.15	.05
❑	6	Sid Fernandez	.15	.05
❑	7	Leo Gomez	.15	.05
❑	8	Jeffrey Hammonds	.15	.05
❑	9	Chris Hoiles	.15	.05
❑	10	Rick Krivda	.15	.05
❑	11	Ben McDonald	.15	.05
❑	12	Mark McLemore	.15	.05
❑	13	Alan Mills	.15	.05
❑	14	Jamie Moyer	.30	.10
❑	15	Mike Mussina	.50	.20
❑	16	Mike Oquist	.15	.05
❑	17	Rafael Palmeiro	.50	.20
❑	18	Arthur Rhodes	.15	.05
❑	19	Cal Ripken	2.50	1.00
❑	20	Chris Sabo	.15	.05
❑	21	Lee Smith	.30	.10
❑	22	Jack Voigt	.15	.05
❑	23	Damon Berryhill	.15	.05
❑	24	Tom Brunansky	.15	.05
❑	25	Wes Chamberlain	.15	.05
❑	26	Roger Clemens	1.50	.60
❑	27	Scott Cooper	.15	.05
❑	28	Andre Dawson	.30	.10
❑	29	Gar Finnvold	.15	.05
❑	30	Tony Fossas	.15	.05
❑	31	Mike Greenwell	.15	.05
❑	32	Joe Hesketh	.15	.05
❑	33	Chris Howard	.15	.05
❑	34	Chris Nabholz	.15	.05
❑	35	Tim Naehring	.15	.05
❑	36	Otis Nixon	.15	.05
❑	37	Carlos Rodriguez	.15	.05
❑	38	Rich Rowland	.15	.05
❑	39	Ken Ryan	.15	.05
❑	40	Aaron Sele	.15	.05
❑	41	John Valentin	.15	.05
❑	42	Mo Vaughn	.30	.10
❑	43	Frank Viola	.30	.10
❑	44	Danny Bautista	.15	.05
❑	45	Joe Boever	.15	.05
❑	46	Milt Cuyler	.15	.05
❑	47	Storm Davis	.15	.05
❑	48	John Doherty	.15	.05
❑	49	Junior Felix	.15	.05
❑	50	Cecil Fielder	.30	.10
❑	51	Travis Fryman	.30	.10
❑	52	Mike Gardiner	.15	.05
❑	53	Kirk Gibson	.30	.10
❑	54	Chris Gomez	.15	.05
❑	55	Buddy Groom	.15	.05
❑	56	Mike Henneman	.15	.05
❑	57	Chad Kreuter	.15	.05
❑	58	Mike Moore	.15	.05
❑	59	Tony Phillips	.15	.05
❑	60	Juan Samuel	.15	.05
❑	61	Mickey Tettleton	.15	.05
❑	62	Alan Trammell	.30	.10
❑	63	David Wells	.30	.10
❑	64	Lou Whitaker	.30	.10
❑	65	Jim Abbott	.50	.20
❑	66	Joe Ausanio	.15	.05
❑	67	Wade Boggs	.50	.20
❑	68	Mike Gallego	.15	.05
❑	69	Xavier Hernandez	.15	.05
❑	70	Sterling Hitchcock	.15	.05
❑	71	Steve Howe	.15	.05
❑	72	Scott Kamieniecki	.15	.05
❑	73	Pat Kelly	.15	.05
❑	74	Jimmy Key	.30	.10
❑	75	Jim Leyritz	.15	.05
❑	76	Don Mattingly	2.00	.75
❑	77	Terry Mulholland	.15	.05
❑	78	Paul O'Neill	.50	.20
❑	79	Melido Perez	.15	.05
❑	80	Luis Polonia	.15	.05
❑	81	Mike Stanley	.15	.05
❑	82	Danny Tartabull	.15	.05
❑	83	Randy Velarde	.15	.05
❑	84	Bob Wickman	.15	.05
❑	85	Bernie Williams	.50	.20
❑	86	Gerald Williams	.15	.05
❑	87	Roberto Alomar	.50	.20
❑	88	Pat Borders	.15	.05
❑	89	Joe Carter	.30	.10
❑	90	Tony Castillo	.15	.05
❑	91	Brad Cornett RC	.15	.05
❑	92	Carlos Delgado	.30	.10

❑	93	Alex Gonzalez	.15	.05
❑	94	Shawn Green	.30	.10
❑	95	Juan Guzman	.15	.05
❑	96	Darren Hall	.15	.05
❑	97	Pat Hentgen	.15	.05
❑	98	Mike Huff	.15	.05
❑	99	Randy Knorr	.15	.05
❑	100	Al Leiter	.30	.10
❑	101	Paul Molitor	.30	.10
❑	102	John Olerud	.30	.10
❑	103	Dick Schofield	.15	.05
❑	104	Ed Sprague	.15	.05
❑	105	Dave Stewart	.30	.10
❑	106	Todd Stottlemyre	.15	.05
❑	107	Devon White	.30	.10
❑	108	Woody Williams	.15	.05
❑	109	Wilson Alvarez	.15	.05
❑	110	Paul Assenmacher	.15	.05
❑	111	Jason Bere	.15	.05
❑	112	Dennis Cook	.15	.05
❑	113	Joey Cora	.15	.05
❑	114	Jose DeLeon	.15	.05
❑	115	Alex Fernandez	.15	.05
❑	116	Julio Franco	.30	.10
❑	117	Craig Grebeck	.15	.05
❑	118	Ozzie Guillen	.30	.10
❑	119	Roberto Hernandez	.15	.05
❑	120	Darrin Jackson	.15	.05
❑	121	Lance Johnson	.15	.05
❑	122	Ron Karkovice	.15	.05
❑	123	Mike LaValliere	.15	.05
❑	124	Norberto Martin	.15	.05
❑	125	Kirk McCaskill	.15	.05
❑	126	Jack McDowell	.15	.05
❑	127	Tim Raines	.30	.10
❑	128	Frank Thomas	.75	.30
❑	129	Robin Ventura	.30	.10
❑	130	Sandy Alomar Jr.	.15	.05
❑	131	Carlos Baerga	.15	.05
❑	132	Albert Belle	.30	.10
❑	133	Mark Clark	.15	.05
❑	134	Alvaro Espinoza	.15	.05
❑	135	Jason Grimsley	.15	.05
❑	136	Wayne Kirby	.15	.05
❑	137	Kenny Lofton	.30	.10
❑	138	Albie Lopez	.15	.05
❑	139	Dennis Martinez	.30	.10
❑	140	Jose Mesa	.15	.05
❑	141	Eddie Murray	.75	.30
❑	142	Charles Nagy	.15	.05
❑	143	Tony Pena	.15	.05
❑	144	Eric Plunk	.15	.05
❑	145	Manny Ramirez	.50	.20
❑	146	Jeff Russell	.15	.05
❑	147	Paul Shuey	.15	.05
❑	148	Paul Sorrento	.15	.05
❑	149	Jim Thome	.50	.20
❑	150	Omar Vizquel	.50	.20
❑	151	Dave Winfield	.30	.10
❑	152	Kevin Appier	.30	.10
❑	153	Billy Brewer	.15	.05
❑	154	Vince Coleman	.15	.05
❑	155	David Cone	.30	.10
❑	156	Gary Gaetti	.30	.10
❑	157	Greg Gagne	.15	.05
❑	158	Tom Gordon	.15	.05
❑	159	Mark Gubicza	.15	.05
❑	160	Bob Hamelin	.15	.05
❑	161	Dave Henderson	.15	.05
❑	162	Felix Jose	.15	.05
❑	163	Wally Joyner	.30	.10
❑	164	Jose Lind	.15	.05
❑	165	Mike Macfarlane	.15	.05
❑	166	Mike Magnante	.15	.05
❑	167	Brent Mayne	.15	.05
❑	168	Brian McRae	.15	.05
❑	169	Rusty Meacham	.15	.05
❑	170	Jeff Montgomery	.15	.05
❑	171	Hipolito Pichardo	.15	.05
❑	172	Terry Shumpert	.15	.05
❑	173	Michael Tucker	.15	.05
❑	174	Ricky Bones	.15	.05
❑	175	Jeff Cirillo	.15	.05
❑	176	Alex Diaz	.15	.05
❑	177	Cal Eldred	.15	.05
❑	178	Mike Fetters	.15	.05
❑	179	Darryl Hamilton	.15	.05
❑	180	Brian Harper	.15	.05
❑	181	John Jaha	.15	.05
❑	182	Pat Listach	.15	.05
❑	183	Graeme Lloyd	.15	.05
❑	184	Jose Mercedes	.15	.05
❑	185	Matt Mieske	.15	.05
❑	186	Dave Nilsson	.15	.05
❑	187	Jody Reed	.15	.05
❑	188	Bob Scanlan	.15	.05
❑	189	Kevin Seitzer	.15	.05
❑	190	Bill Spiers	.15	.05
❑	191	B.J. Surhoff	.30	.10
❑	192	Jose Valentin	.15	.05
❑	193	Greg Vaughn	.15	.05
❑	194	Turner Ward	.15	.05
❑	195	Bill Wegman	.15	.05
❑	196	Rick Aguilera	.15	.05
❑	197	Rich Becker	.15	.05
❑	198	Alex Cole	.15	.05
❑	199	Marty Cordova	.15	.05
❑	200	Steve Dunn	.15	.05
❑	201	Scott Erickson	.15	.05
❑	202	Mark Guthrie	.15	.05
❑	203	Chip Hale	.15	.05
❑	204	LaTroy Hawkins	.15	.05
❑	205	Denny Hocking	.15	.05
❑	206	Chuck Knoblauch	.30	.10
❑	207	Scott Leius	.15	.05
❑	208	Shane Mack	.15	.05
❑	209	Pat Mahomes	.15	.05
❑	210	Pat Meares	.15	.05
❑	211	Pedro Munoz	.15	.05
❑	212	Kirby Puckett	.75	.30
❑	213	Jeff Reboulet	.15	.05
❑	214	Dave Stevens	.15	.05
❑	215	Kevin Tapani	.15	.05
❑	216	Matt Walbeck	.15	.05
❑	217	Carl Willis	.15	.05
❑	218	Brian Anderson	.15	.05
❑	219	Chad Curtis	.15	.05
❑	220	Chili Davis	.30	.10
❑	221	Gary DiSarcina	.15	.05
❑	222	Damion Easley	.15	.05
❑	223	Jim Edmonds	.50	.20
❑	224	Chuck Finley	.30	.10
❑	225	Joe Grahe	.15	.05
❑	226	Rex Hudler	.15	.05
❑	227	Bo Jackson	.75	.30
❑	228	Mark Langston	.15	.05
❑	229	Phil Leftwich	.15	.05
❑	230	Mark Leiter	.15	.05
❑	231	Spike Owen	.15	.05
❑	232	Bob Patterson	.15	.05
❑	233	Troy Percival	.30	.10
❑	234	Eduardo Perez	.15	.05
❑	235	Tim Salmon	.50	.20
❑	236	J.T. Snow	.30	.10
❑	237	Chris Turner	.15	.05
❑	238	Mark Acre	.15	.05
❑	239	Geronimo Berroa	.15	.05
❑	240	Mike Bordick	.15	.05
❑	241	John Briscoe	.15	.05
❑	242	Scott Brosius	.30	.10
❑	243	Ron Darling	.15	.05
❑	244	Dennis Eckersley	.30	.10
❑	245	Brent Gates	.15	.05
❑	246	Rickey Henderson	.75	.30
❑	247	Stan Javier	.15	.05
❑	248	Steve Karsay	.15	.05
❑	249	Mark McGwire	2.00	.75
❑	250	Troy Neel	.15	.05
❑	251	Steve Ontiveros	.15	.05
❑	252	Carlos Reyes	.15	.05
❑	253	Ruben Sierra	.30	.10
❑	254	Terry Steinbach	.15	.05
❑	255	Bill Taylor	.15	.05
❑	256	Todd Van Poppel	.15	.05
❑	257	Bobby Witt	.15	.05
❑	258	Rich Amaral	.15	.05
❑	259	Eric Anthony	.15	.05
❑	260	Bobby Ayala	.15	.05
❑	261	Mike Blowers	.15	.05
❑	262	Chris Bosio	.15	.05
❑	263	Jay Buhner	.30	.10
❑	264	John Cummings	.15	.05
❑	265	Tim Davis	.15	.05
❑	266	Felix Fermin	.15	.05
❑	267	Dave Fleming	.15	.05
❑	268	Goose Gossage	.30	.10
❑	269	Ken Griffey Jr.	1.25	.50
❑	270	Reggie Jefferson	.15	.05
❑	271	Randy Johnson	.75	.30
❑	272	Edgar Martinez	.50	.20
❑	273	Tino Martinez	.50	.20
❑	274	Greg Pirkl	.15	.05
❑	275	Bill Risley	.15	.05
❑	276	Roger Salkeld	.15	.05
❑	277	Luis Sojo	.15	.05
❑	278	Mac Suzuki	.15	.05
❑	279	Dan Wilson	.15	.05
❑	280	Kevin Brown	.30	.10
❑	281	Jose Canseco	.50	.20
❑	282	Cris Carpenter	.15	.05
❑	283	Will Clark	.50	.20
❑	284	Jeff Frye	.15	.05
❑	285	Juan Gonzalez	.30	.10
❑	286	Rick Helling	.15	.05
❑	287	Tom Henke	.15	.05
❑	288	David Hulse	.15	.05
❑	289	Chris James	.15	.05
❑	290	Manuel Lee	.15	.05
❑	291	Oddibe McDowell	.15	.05
❑	292	Dean Palmer	.30	.10
❑	293	Roger Pavlik	.15	.05
❑	294	Bill Ripken	.15	.05
❑	295	Ivan Rodriguez	.50	.20
❑	296	Kenny Rogers	.30	.10
❑	297	Doug Strange	.15	.05
❑	298	Matt Whiteside	.15	.05
❑	299	Steve Avery	.15	.05
❑	300	Steve Bedrosian	.15	.05
❑	301	Rafael Belliard	.15	.05
❑	302	Jeff Blauser	.15	.05
❑	303	Dave Gallagher	.15	.05
❑	304	Tom Glavine	.50	.20
❑	305	David Justice	.30	.10
❑	306	Mike Kelly	.15	.05
❑	307	Roberto Kelly	.15	.05
❑	308	Ryan Klesko	.30	.10
❑	309	Mark Lemke	.15	.05
❑	310	Javier Lopez	.30	.10
❑	311	Greg Maddux	1.25	.50
❑	312	Fred McGriff	.50	.20
❑	313	Greg McMichael	.15	.05
❑	314	Kent Mercker	.15	.05
❑	315	Charlie O'Brien	.15	.05
❑	316	Jose Oliva	.15	.05
❑	317	Terry Pendleton	.30	.10
❑	318	John Smoltz	.50	.20
❑	319	Mike Stanton	.15	.05
❑	320	Tony Tarasco	.15	.05
❑	321	Terrell Wade	.15	.05
❑	322	Mark Wohlers	.15	.05
❑	323	Kurt Abbott	.15	.05
❑	324	Luis Aquino	.15	.05
❑	325	Bret Barberie	.15	.05
❑	326	Ryan Bowen	.15	.05
❑	327	Jerry Browne	.15	.05
❑	328	Chuck Carr	.15	.05
❑	329	Matias Carrillo	.15	.05
❑	330	Greg Colbrunn	.15	.05
❑	331	Jeff Conine	.30	.10
❑	332	Mark Gardner	.15	.05
❑	333	Chris Hammond	.15	.05
❑	334	Bryan Harvey	.15	.05
❑	335	Richie Lewis	.15	.05
❑	336	Dave Magadan	.15	.05
❑	337	Terry Mathews	.15	.05
❑	338	Robb Nen	.30	.10
❑	339	Yorkis Perez	.15	.05
❑	340	Pat Rapp	.15	.05
❑	341	Benito Santiago	.30	.10
❑	342	Gary Sheffield	.30	.10
❑	343	Dave Weathers	.15	.05
❑	344	Moises Alou	.30	.10
❑	345	Sean Berry	.15	.05
❑	346	Wil Cordero	.15	.05
❑	347	Joey Eischen	.15	.05
❑	348	Jeff Fassero	.15	.05
❑	349	Darrin Fletcher	.15	.05
❑	350	Cliff Floyd	.30	.10

❑	351 Marquis Grissom	.30	.10
❑	352 Butch Henry	.15	.05
❑	353 Gil Heredia	.15	.05
❑	354 Ken Hill	.15	.05
❑	355 Mike Lansing	.15	.05
❑	356 Pedro Martinez	.50	.20
❑	357 Mel Rojas	.15	.05
❑	358 Kirk Rueter	.15	.05
❑	359 Tim Scott	.15	.05
❑	360 Jeff Shaw	.15	.05
❑	361 Larry Walker	.30	.10
❑	362 Lenny Webster	.15	.05
❑	363 John Wetteland	.30	.10
❑	364 Rondell White	.30	.10
❑	365 Bobby Bonilla	.30	.10
❑	366 Rico Brogna	.15	.05
❑	367 Jeromy Burnitz	.30	.10
❑	368 John Franco	.30	.10
❑	369 Dwight Gooden	.30	.10
❑	370 Todd Hundley	.15	.05
❑	371 Jason Jacome	.15	.05
❑	372 Bobby Jones	.15	.05
❑	373 Jeff Kent	.30	.10
❑	374 Jim Lindeman	.15	.05
❑	375 Josias Manzanillo	.15	.05
❑	376 Roger Mason	.15	.05
❑	377 Kevin McReynolds	.15	.05
❑	378 Joe Orsulak	.15	.05
❑	379 Bill Pulsipher	.15	.05
❑	380 Bret Saberhagen	.30	.10
❑	381 David Segui	.15	.05
❑	382 Pete Smith	.15	.05
❑	383 Kelly Stinnett	.15	.05
❑	384 Ryan Thompson	.15	.05
❑	385 Jose Vizcaino	.15	.05
❑	386 Toby Borland	.15	.05
❑	387 Ricky Bottalico	.15	.05
❑	388 Darren Daulton	.30	.10
❑	389 Mariano Duncan	.15	.05
❑	390 Lenny Dykstra	.30	.10
❑	391 Jim Eisenreich	.15	.05
❑	392 Tommy Greene	.15	.05
❑	393 Dave Hollins	.15	.05
❑	394 Pete Incaviglia	.15	.05
❑	395 Danny Jackson	.15	.05
❑	396 Doug Jones	.15	.05
❑	397 Ricky Jordan	.15	.05
❑	398 John Kruk	.30	.10
❑	399 Mike Lieberthal	.30	.10
❑	400 Tony Longmire	.15	.05
❑	401 Mickey Morandini	.15	.05
❑	402 Bobby Munoz	.15	.05
❑	403 Curt Schilling	.30	.10
❑	404 Heathcliff Slocumb	.15	.05
❑	405 Kevin Stocker	.15	.05
❑	406 Fernando Valenzuela	.30	.10
❑	407 David West	.15	.05
❑	408 Willie Banks	.15	.05
❑	409 Jose Bautista	.15	.05
❑	410 Steve Buechele	.15	.05
❑	411 Jim Bullinger	.15	.05
❑	412 Chuck Crim	.15	.05
❑	413 Shawon Dunston	.15	.05
❑	414 Kevin Foster	.15	.05
❑	415 Mark Grace	.50	.20
❑	416 Jose Hernandez	.15	.05
❑	417 Glenallen Hill	.15	.05
❑	418 Brooks Kieschnick	.15	.05
❑	419 Derrick May	.15	.05
❑	420 Randy Myers	.15	.05
❑	421 Dan Plesac	.15	.05
❑	422 Karl Rhodes	.15	.05
❑	423 Rey Sanchez	.15	.05
❑	424 Sammy Sosa	.75	.30
❑	425 Steve Trachsel	.15	.05
❑	426 Rick Wilkins	.15	.05
❑	427 Anthony Young	.15	.05
❑	428 Eddie Zambrano	.15	.05
❑	429 Bret Boone	.30	.10
❑	430 Jeff Branson	.15	.05
❑	431 Jeff Brantley	.15	.05
❑	432 Hector Carrasco	.15	.05
❑	433 Brian Dorsett	.15	.05
❑	434 Tony Fernandez	.15	.05
❑	435 Tim Fortugno	.15	.05
❑	436 Erik Hanson	.15	.05
❑	437 Thomas Howard	.15	.05
❑	438 Kevin Jarvis	.15	.05
❑	439 Barry Larkin	.50	.20
❑	440 Chuck McElroy	.15	.05
❑	441 Kevin Mitchell	.15	.05
❑	442 Hal Morris	.15	.05
❑	443 Jose Rijo	.15	.05
❑	444 John Roper	.15	.05
❑	445 Johnny Ruffin	.15	.05
❑	446 Deion Sanders	.50	.20
❑	447 Reggie Sanders	.30	.10
❑	448 Pete Schourek	.15	.05
❑	449 John Smiley	.15	.05
❑	450 Eddie Taubensee	.15	.05
❑	451 Jeff Bagwell	.50	.20
❑	452 Kevin Bass	.15	.05
❑	453 Craig Biggio	.50	.20
❑	454 Ken Caminiti	.30	.10
❑	455 Andujar Cedeno	.15	.05
❑	456 Doug Drabek	.15	.05
❑	457 Tony Eusebio	.15	.05
❑	458 Mike Felder	.15	.05
❑	459 Steve Finley	.30	.10
❑	460 Luis Gonzalez	.30	.10
❑	461 Mike Hampton	.30	.10
❑	462 Pete Harnisch	.15	.05
❑	463 John Hudek	.15	.05
❑	464 Todd Jones	.15	.05
❑	465 Darryl Kile	.30	.10
❑	466 James Mouton	.15	.05
❑	467 Shane Reynolds	.15	.05
❑	468 Scott Servais	.15	.05
❑	469 Greg Swindell	.15	.05
❑	470 Dave Veres RC	.40	.15
❑	471 Brian Williams	.15	.05
❑	472 Jay Bell	.30	.10
❑	473 Jacob Brumfield	.15	.05
❑	474 Dave Clark	.15	.05
❑	475 Steve Cooke	.15	.05
❑	476 Midre Cummings	.15	.05
❑	477 Mark Dewey	.15	.05
❑	478 Tom Foley	.15	.05
❑	479 Carlos Garcia	.15	.05
❑	480 Jeff King	.15	.05
❑	481 Jon Lieber	.15	.05
❑	482 Ravelo Manzanillo	.15	.05
❑	483 Al Martin	.15	.05
❑	484 Orlando Merced	.15	.05
❑	485 Danny Miceli	.15	.05
❑	486 Denny Neagle	.30	.10
❑	487 Lance Parrish	.30	.10
❑	488 Don Slaught	.15	.05
❑	489 Zane Smith	.15	.05
❑	490 Andy Van Slyke	.50	.20
❑	491 Paul Wagner	.15	.05
❑	492 Rick White	.15	.05
❑	493 Luis Alicea	.15	.05
❑	494 Rene Arocha	.15	.05
❑	495 Rheal Cormier	.15	.05
❑	496 Bryan Eversgerd	.15	.05
❑	497 Bernard Gilkey	.15	.05
❑	498 John Habyan	.15	.05
❑	499 Gregg Jefferies	.15	.05
❑	500 Brian Jordan	.30	.10
❑	501 Ray Lankford	.30	.10
❑	502 John Mabry	.15	.05
❑	503 Terry McGriff	.15	.05
❑	504 Tom Pagnozzi	.15	.05
❑	505 Vicente Palacios	.15	.05
❑	506 Geronimo Pena	.15	.05
❑	507 Gerald Perry	.15	.05
❑	508 Rich Rodriguez	.15	.05
❑	509 Ozzie Smith	1.25	.50
❑	510 Bob Tewksbury	.15	.05
❑	511 Allen Watson	.15	.05
❑	512 Mark Whiten	.15	.05
❑	513 Todd Zeile	.15	.05
❑	514 Dante Bichette	.30	.10
❑	515 Willie Blair	.15	.05
❑	516 Ellis Burks	.30	.10
❑	517 Marvin Freeman	.15	.05
❑	518 Andres Galarraga	.30	.10
❑	519 Joe Girardi	.15	.05
❑	520 Greg W. Harris	.15	.05
❑	521 Charlie Hayes	.15	.05
❑	522 Mike Kingery	.15	.05
❑	523 Nelson Liriano	.15	.05
❑	524 Mike Munoz	.15	.05
❑	525 David Nied	.15	.05
❑	526 Steve Reed	.15	.05
❑	527 Kevin Ritz	.15	.05
❑	528 Bruce Ruffin	.15	.05
❑	529 John Vander Wal	.15	.05
❑	530 Walt Weiss	.15	.05
❑	531 Eric Young	.15	.05
❑	532 Billy Ashley	.15	.05
❑	533 Pedro Astacio	.15	.05
❑	534 Rafael Bournigal	.15	.05
❑	535 Brett Butler	.30	.10
❑	536 Tom Candiotti	.15	.05
❑	537 Omar Daal	.15	.05
❑	538 Delino DeShields	.15	.05
❑	539 Darren Dreifort	.15	.05
❑	540 Kevin Gross	.15	.05
❑	541 Orel Hershiser	.30	.10
❑	542 Garey Ingram	.15	.05
❑	543 Eric Karros	.30	.10
❑	544 Ramon Martinez	.15	.05
❑	545 Raul Mondesi	.30	.10
❑	546 Chan Ho Park	.30	.10
❑	547 Mike Piazza	1.25	.50
❑	548 Henry Rodriguez	.15	.05
❑	549 Rudy Seanez	.15	.05
❑	550 Ismael Valdes	.15	.05
❑	551 Tim Wallach	.15	.05
❑	552 Todd Worrell	.15	.05
❑	553 Andy Ashby	.15	.05
❑	554 Brad Ausmus	.30	.10
❑	555 Derek Bell	.15	.05
❑	556 Andy Benes	.15	.05
❑	557 Phil Clark	.15	.05
❑	558 Donnie Elliott	.15	.05
❑	559 Ricky Gutierrez	.15	.05
❑	560 Tony Gwynn	1.00	.40
❑	561 Joey Hamilton	.15	.05
❑	562 Trevor Hoffman	.30	.10
❑	563 Luis Lopez	.15	.05
❑	564 Pedro A. Martinez	.15	.05
❑	565 Tim Mauser	.15	.05
❑	566 Phil Plantier	.15	.05
❑	567 Bip Roberts	.15	.05
❑	568 Scott Sanders	.15	.05
❑	569 Craig Shipley	.15	.05
❑	570 Jeff Tabaka	.15	.05
❑	571 Eddie Williams	.15	.05
❑	572 Rod Beck	.15	.05
❑	573 Mike Benjamin	.15	.05
❑	574 Barry Bonds	2.00	.75
❑	575 Dave Burba	.15	.05
❑	576 John Burkett	.15	.05
❑	577 Mark Carreon	.15	.05
❑	578 Royce Clayton	.15	.05
❑	579 Steve Frey	.15	.05
❑	580 Bryan Hickerson	.15	.05
❑	581 Mike Jackson	.15	.05
❑	582 Darren Lewis	.15	.05
❑	583 Kirt Manwaring	.15	.05
❑	584 Rich Monteleone	.15	.05
❑	585 John Patterson	.15	.05
❑	586 J.R. Phillips	.15	.05
❑	587 Mark Portugal	.15	.05
❑	588 Joe Rosselli	.15	.05
❑	589 Darryl Strawberry	.30	.10
❑	590 Bill Swift	.15	.05
❑	591 Robby Thompson	.15	.05
❑	592 William VanLandingham	.15	.05
❑	593 Matt Williams	.30	.10
❑	594 Checklist	.15	.05
❑	595 Checklist	.15	.05
❑	596 Checklist	.15	.05
❑	597 Checklist	.15	.05
❑	598 Checklist	.15	.05
❑	599 Checklist	.15	.05
❑	600 Checklist	.15	.05

1996 Fleer

❑	COMPLETE SET (600)	80.00	40.00
❑	1 Manny Alexander	.30	.10
❑	2 Brady Anderson	.30	.10
❑	3 Harold Baines	.30	.10
❑	4 Armando Benitez	.30	.10
❑	5 Bobby Bonilla	.30	.10

❑ 6 Kevin Brown .30 .10
❑ 7 Scott Erickson .30 .10
❑ 8 Curtis Goodwin .30 .10
❑ 9 Jeffrey Hammonds .30 .10
❑ 10 Jimmy Haynes .30 .10
❑ 11 Chris Hoiles .30 .10
❑ 12 Doug Jones .30 .10
❑ 13 Rick Krivda .30 .10
❑ 14 Jeff Manto .30 .10
❑ 15 Ben McDonald .30 .10
❑ 16 Jamie Moyer .30 .10
❑ 17 Mike Mussina .50 .20
❑ 18 Jesse Orosco .30 .10
❑ 19 Rafael Palmeiro .50 .20
❑ 20 Cal Ripken 2.50 1.00
❑ 21 Rick Aguilera .30 .10
❑ 22 Luis Alicea .30 .10
❑ 23 Stan Belinda .30 .10
❑ 24 Jose Canseco .50 .20
❑ 25 Roger Clemens 1.50 .60
❑ 26 Vaughn Eshelman .30 .10
❑ 27 Mike Greenwell .30 .10
❑ 28 Erik Hanson .30 .10
❑ 29 Dwayne Hosey .30 .10
❑ 30 Mike Macfarlane UER .30 .10
❑ 31 Tim Naehring .30 .10
❑ 32 Troy O'Leary .30 .10
❑ 33 Aaron Sele .30 .10
❑ 34 Zane Smith .30 .10
❑ 35 Jeff Suppan .30 .10
❑ 36 Lee Tinsley .30 .10
❑ 37 John Valentin .30 .10
❑ 38 Mo Vaughn .30 .10
❑ 39 Tim Wakefield .30 .10
❑ 40 Jim Abbott .50 .20
❑ 41 Brian Anderson .30 .10
❑ 42 Garret Anderson .30 .10
❑ 43 Chili Davis .30 .10
❑ 44 Gary DiSarcina .30 .10
❑ 45 Damion Easley .30 .10
❑ 46 Jim Edmonds .30 .10
❑ 47 Chuck Finley .30 .10
❑ 48 Todd Greene .30 .10
❑ 49 Mike Harkey .30 .10
❑ 50 Mike James .30 .10
❑ 51 Mark Langston .30 .10
❑ 52 Greg Myers .30 .10
❑ 53 Orlando Palmeiro .30 .10
❑ 54 Bob Patterson .30 .10
❑ 55 Troy Percival .30 .10
❑ 56 Tony Phillips .30 .10
❑ 57 Tim Salmon .50 .20
❑ 58 Lee Smith .30 .10
❑ 59 J.T. Snow .30 .10
❑ 60 Randy Velarde .30 .10
❑ 61 Wilson Alvarez .30 .10
❑ 62 Luis Andujar .30 .10
❑ 63 Jason Bere .30 .10
❑ 64 Ray Durham .30 .10
❑ 65 Alex Fernandez .30 .10
❑ 66 Ozzie Guillen .30 .10
❑ 67 Roberto Hernandez .30 .10
❑ 68 Lance Johnson .30 .10
❑ 69 Matt Karchner .30 .10
❑ 70 Ron Karkovice .30 .10
❑ 71 Norberto Martin .30 .10
❑ 72 Dave Martinez .30 .10
❑ 73 Kirk McCaskill .30 .10
❑ 74 Lyle Mouton .30 .10
❑ 75 Tim Raines .30 .10
❑ 76 Mike Sirotka RC .30 .10
❑ 77 Frank Thomas .75 .30
❑ 78 Larry Thomas .30 .10
❑ 79 Robin Ventura .30 .10
❑ 80 Sandy Alomar Jr. .30 .10
❑ 81 Paul Assenmacher .30 .10
❑ 82 Carlos Baerga .30 .10
❑ 83 Albert Belle .30 .10
❑ 84 Mark Clark .30 .10
❑ 85 Alan Embree .30 .10
❑ 86 Alvaro Espinoza .30 .10
❑ 87 Orel Hershiser .30 .10
❑ 88 Ken Hill .30 .10
❑ 89 Kenny Lofton .30 .10
❑ 90 Dennis Martinez .30 .10
❑ 91 Jose Mesa .30 .10
❑ 92 Eddie Murray .75 .30
❑ 93 Charles Nagy .30 .10
❑ 94 Chad Ogea .30 .10
❑ 95 Tony Pena .30 .10
❑ 96 Herb Perry .30 .10
❑ 97 Eric Plunk .30 .10
❑ 98 Jim Poole .30 .10
❑ 99 Manny Ramirez .50 .20
❑ 100 Paul Sorrento .30 .10
❑ 101 Julian Tavarez .30 .10
❑ 102 Jim Thome .50 .20
❑ 103 Omar Vizquel .50 .20
❑ 104 Dave Winfield .30 .10
❑ 105 Danny Bautista .30 .10
❑ 106 Joe Boever .30 .10
❑ 107 Chad Curtis .30 .10
❑ 108 John Doherty .30 .10
❑ 109 Cecil Fielder .30 .10
❑ 110 John Flaherty .30 .10
❑ 111 Travis Fryman .30 .10
❑ 112 Chris Gomez .30 .10
❑ 113 Bob Higginson .30 .10
❑ 114 Mark Lewis .30 .10
❑ 115 Jose Lima .30 .10
❑ 116 Felipe Lira .30 .10
❑ 117 Brian Maxcy .30 .10
❑ 118 C.J. Nitkowski .30 .10
❑ 119 Phil Plantier .30 .10
❑ 120 Clint Sodowsky .30 .10
❑ 121 Alan Trammell .30 .10
❑ 122 Lou Whitaker .30 .10
❑ 123 Kevin Appier .30 .10
❑ 124 Johnny Damon .50 .20
❑ 125 Gary Gaetti .30 .10
❑ 126 Tom Goodwin .30 .10
❑ 127 Tom Gordon .30 .10
❑ 128 Mark Gubicza .30 .10
❑ 129 Bob Hamelin .30 .10
❑ 130 David Howard .30 .10
❑ 131 Jason Jacome .30 .10
❑ 132 Wally Joyner .30 .10
❑ 133 Keith Lockhart .30 .10
❑ 134 Brent Mayne .30 .10
❑ 135 Jeff Montgomery .30 .10
❑ 136 Jon Nunnally .30 .10
❑ 137 Juan Samuel .30 .10
❑ 138 Mike Sweeney RC 1.00 .40
❑ 139 Michael Tucker .30 .10
❑ 140 Joe Vitiello .30 .10
❑ 141 Ricky Bones .30 .10
❑ 142 Chuck Carr .30 .10
❑ 143 Jeff Cirillo .30 .10
❑ 144 Mike Fetters .30 .10
❑ 145 Darryl Hamilton .30 .10
❑ 146 David Hulse .30 .10
❑ 147 John Jaha .30 .10
❑ 148 Scott Karl .30 .10
❑ 149 Mark Kiefer .30 .10
❑ 150 Pat Listach .30 .10
❑ 151 Mark Loretta .30 .10
❑ 152 Mike Matheny .30 .10
❑ 153 Matt Mieske .30 .10
❑ 154 Dave Nilsson .30 .10
❑ 155 Joe Oliver .30 .10
❑ 156 Al Reyes .30 .10
❑ 157 Kevin Seitzer .30 .10
❑ 158 Steve Sparks .30 .10
❑ 159 B.J. Surhoff .30 .10
❑ 160 Jose Valentin .30 .10
❑ 161 Greg Vaughn .30 .10
❑ 162 Fernando Vina .30 .10
❑ 163 Rich Becker .30 .10
❑ 164 Ron Coomer .30 .10
❑ 165 Marty Cordova .30 .10
❑ 166 Chuck Knoblauch .30 .10
❑ 167 Matt Lawton RC .50 .20
❑ 168 Pat Meares .30 .10
❑ 169 Paul Molitor .30 .10
❑ 170 Pedro Munoz .30 .10
❑ 171 Jose Parra .30 .10
❑ 172 Kirby Puckett .75 .30
❑ 173 Brad Radke .30 .10
❑ 174 Jeff Reboulet .30 .10
❑ 175 Rich Robertson .30 .10
❑ 176 Frank Rodriguez .30 .10
❑ 177 Scott Stahoviak .30 .10
❑ 178 Dave Stevens .30 .10
❑ 179 Matt Walbeck .30 .10
❑ 180 Wade Boggs .50 .20
❑ 181 David Cone .30 .10
❑ 182 Tony Fernandez .30 .10
❑ 183 Joe Girardi .30 .10
❑ 184 Derek Jeter 2.00 .75
❑ 185 Scott Kamieniecki .30 .10
❑ 186 Pat Kelly .30 .10
❑ 187 Jim Leyritz .30 .10
❑ 188 Tino Martinez .50 .20
❑ 189 Don Mattingly 2.00 .75
❑ 190 Jack McDowell .30 .10
❑ 191 Jeff Nelson .30 .10
❑ 192 Paul O'Neill .50 .20
❑ 193 Melido Perez .30 .10
❑ 194 Andy Pettitte .50 .20
❑ 195 Mariano Rivera .75 .30
❑ 196 Ruben Sierra .30 .10
❑ 197 Mike Stanley .30 .10
❑ 198 Darryl Strawberry .30 .10
❑ 199 John Wetteland .30 .10
❑ 200 Bob Wickman .30 .10
❑ 201 Bernie Williams .50 .20
❑ 202 Mark Acre .30 .10
❑ 203 Geronimo Berroa .30 .10
❑ 204 Mike Bordick .30 .10
❑ 205 Scott Brosius .30 .10
❑ 206 Dennis Eckersley .30 .10
❑ 207 Brent Gates .30 .10
❑ 208 Jason Giambi .30 .10
❑ 209 Rickey Henderson .75 .30
❑ 210 Jose Herrera .30 .10
❑ 211 Stan Javier .30 .10
❑ 212 Doug Johns .30 .10
❑ 213 Mark McGwire 2.00 .75
❑ 214 Steve Ontiveros .30 .10
❑ 215 Craig Paquette .30 .10
❑ 216 Ariel Prieto .30 .10
❑ 217 Carlos Reyes .30 .10
❑ 218 Terry Steinbach .30 .10
❑ 219 Todd Stottlemyre .30 .10
❑ 220 Danny Tartabull .30 .10
❑ 221 Todd Van Poppel .30 .10
❑ 222 John Wasdin .30 .10
❑ 223 George Williams .30 .10
❑ 224 Steve Wojciechowski .30 .10
❑ 225 Rich Amaral .30 .10
❑ 226 Bobby Ayala .30 .10
❑ 227 Tim Belcher .30 .10
❑ 228 Andy Benes .30 .10
❑ 229 Chris Bosio .30 .10
❑ 230 Darren Bragg .30 .10
❑ 231 Jay Buhner .30 .10
❑ 232 Norm Charlton .30 .10
❑ 233 Vince Coleman .30 .10
❑ 234 Joey Cora .30 .10
❑ 235 Russ Davis .30 .10
❑ 236 Alex Diaz .30 .10
❑ 237 Felix Fermin .30 .10
❑ 238 Ken Griffey Jr. 1.25 .50
❑ 239 Sterling Hitchcock .30 .10
❑ 240 Randy Johnson .75 .30
❑ 241 Edgar Martinez .50 .20
❑ 242 Bill Risley .30 .10
❑ 243 Alex Rodriguez 1.50 .60
❑ 244 Luis Sojo .30 .10
❑ 245 Dan Wilson .30 .10

❑	246	Bob Wolcott	.30	.10
❑	247	Will Clark	.50	.20
❑	248	Jeff Frye	.30	.10
❑	249	Benji Gil	.30	.10
❑	250	Juan Gonzalez	.30	.10
❑	251	Rusty Greer	.30	.10
❑	252	Kevin Gross	.30	.10
❑	253	Roger McDowell	.30	.10
❑	254	Mark McLemore	.30	.10
❑	255	Otis Nixon	.30	.10
❑	256	Luis Ortiz	.30	.10
❑	257	Mike Pagliarulo	.30	.10
❑	258	Dean Palmer	.30	.10
❑	259	Roger Pavlik	.30	.10
❑	260	Ivan Rodriguez	.50	.20
❑	261	Kenny Rogers	.30	.10
❑	262	Jeff Russell	.30	.10
❑	263	Mickey Tettleton	.30	.10
❑	264	Bob Tewksbury	.30	.10
❑	265	Dave Valle	.30	.10
❑	266	Matt Whiteside	.30	.10
❑	267	Roberto Alomar	.50	.20
❑	268	Joe Carter	.30	.10
❑	269	Tony Castillo	.30	.10
❑	270	Domingo Cedeno	.30	.10
❑	271	Tim Crabtree UER	.30	.10
❑	272	Carlos Delgado	.30	.10
❑	273	Alex Gonzalez	.30	.10
❑	274	Shawn Green	.30	.10
❑	275	Juan Guzman	.30	.10
❑	276	Pat Hentgen	.30	.10
❑	277	Al Leiter	.30	.10
❑	278	Sandy Martinez	.30	.10
❑	279	Paul Menhart	.30	.10
❑	280	John Olerud	.30	.10
❑	281	Paul Quantrill	.30	.10
❑	282	Ken Robinson	.30	.10
❑	283	Ed Sprague	.30	.10
❑	284	Mike Timlin	.30	.10
❑	285	Steve Avery	.30	.10
❑	286	Rafael Belliard	.30	.10
❑	287	Jeff Blauser	.30	.10
❑	288	Pedro Borbon	.30	.10
❑	289	Brad Clontz	.30	.10
❑	290	Mike Devereaux	.30	.10
❑	291	Tom Glavine	.50	.20
❑	292	Marquis Grissom	.30	.10
❑	293	Chipper Jones	.75	.30
❑	294	David Justice	.30	.10
❑	295	Mike Kelly	.30	.10
❑	296	Ryan Klesko	.30	.10
❑	297	Mark Lemke	.30	.10
❑	298	Javier Lopez	.30	.10
❑	299	Greg Maddux	1.25	.50
❑	300	Fred McGriff	.50	.20
❑	301	Greg McMichael	.30	.10
❑	302	Kent Mercker	.30	.10
❑	303	Mike Mordecai	.30	.10
❑	304	Charlie O'Brien	.30	.10
❑	305	Eduardo Perez	.30	.10
❑	306	Luis Polonia	.30	.10
❑	307	Jason Schmidt	.50	.20
❑	308	John Smoltz	.50	.20
❑	309	Terrell Wade	.30	.10
❑	310	Mark Wohlers	.30	.10
❑	311	Scott Bullett	.30	.10
❑	312	Jim Bullinger	.30	.10
❑	313	Larry Casian	.30	.10
❑	314	Frank Castillo	.30	.10
❑	315	Shawon Dunston	.30	.10
❑	316	Kevin Foster	.30	.10
❑	317	Matt Franco	.30	.10
❑	318	Luis Gonzalez	.30	.10
❑	319	Mark Grace	.50	.20
❑	320	Jose Hernandez	.30	.10
❑	321	Mike Hubbard	.30	.10
❑	322	Brian McRae	.30	.10
❑	323	Randy Myers	.30	.10
❑	324	Jaime Navarro	.30	.10
❑	325	Mark Parent	.30	.10
❑	326	Mike Perez	.30	.10
❑	327	Rey Sanchez	.30	.10
❑	328	Ryne Sandberg	1.25	.50
❑	329	Scott Servais	.30	.10
❑	330	Sammy Sosa	.75	.30
❑	331	Ozzie Timmons	.30	.10
❑	332	Steve Trachsel	.30	.10
❑	333	Todd Zeile	.30	.10
❑	334	Bret Boone	.30	.10
❑	335	Jeff Branson	.30	.10
❑	336	Jeff Brantley	.30	.10
❑	337	Dave Burba	.30	.10
❑	338	Hector Carrasco	.30	.10
❑	339	Mariano Duncan	.30	.10
❑	340	Ron Gant	.30	.10
❑	341	Lenny Harris	.30	.10
❑	342	Xavier Hernandez	.30	.10
❑	343	Thomas Howard	.30	.10
❑	344	Mike Jackson	.30	.10
❑	345	Barry Larkin	.50	.20
❑	346	Darren Lewis	.30	.10
❑	347	Hal Morris	.30	.10
❑	348	Eric Owens	.30	.10
❑	349	Mark Portugal	.30	.10
❑	350	Jose Rijo	.30	.10
❑	351	Reggie Sanders	.30	.10
❑	352	Benito Santiago	.30	.10
❑	353	Pete Schourek	.30	.10
❑	354	John Smiley	.30	.10
❑	355	Eddie Taubensee	.30	.10
❑	356	Jerome Walton	.30	.10
❑	357	David Wells	.30	.10
❑	358	Roger Bailey	.30	.10
❑	359	Jason Bates	.30	.10
❑	360	Dante Bichette	.30	.10
❑	361	Ellis Burks	.30	.10
❑	362	Vinny Castilla	.30	.10
❑	363	Andres Galarraga	.30	.10
❑	364	Darren Holmes	.30	.10
❑	365	Mike Kingery	.30	.10
❑	366	Curt Leskanic	.30	.10
❑	367	Quinton McCracken	.30	.10
❑	368	Mike Munoz	.30	.10
❑	369	David Nied	.30	.10
❑	370	Steve Reed	.30	.10
❑	371	Bryan Rekar	.30	.10
❑	372	Kevin Ritz	.30	.10
❑	373	Bruce Ruffin	.30	.10
❑	374	Bret Saberhagen	.30	.10
❑	375	Bill Swift	.30	.10
❑	376	John Vander Wal	.30	.10
❑	377	Larry Walker	.30	.10
❑	378	Walt Weiss	.30	.10
❑	379	Eric Young	.30	.10
❑	380	Kurt Abbott	.30	.10
❑	381	Alex Arias	.30	.10
❑	382	Jerry Browne	.30	.10
❑	383	John Burkett	.30	.10
❑	384	Greg Colbrunn	.30	.10
❑	385	Jeff Conine	.30	.10
❑	386	Andre Dawson	.30	.10
❑	387	Chris Hammond	.30	.10
❑	388	Charles Johnson	.30	.10
❑	389	Terry Mathews	.30	.10
❑	390	Robb Nen	.30	.10
❑	391	Joe Orsulak	.30	.10
❑	392	Terry Pendleton	.30	.10
❑	393	Pat Rapp	.30	.10
❑	394	Gary Sheffield	.30	.10
❑	395	Jesus Tavarez	.30	.10
❑	396	Marc Valdes	.30	.10
❑	397	Quilvio Veras	.30	.10
❑	398	Randy Veres	.30	.10
❑	399	Devon White	.30	.10
❑	400	Jeff Bagwell	.50	.20
❑	401	Derek Bell	.30	.10
❑	402	Craig Biggio	.50	.20
❑	403	John Cangelosi	.30	.10
❑	404	Jim Dougherty	.30	.10
❑	405	Doug Drabek	.30	.10
❑	406	Tony Eusebio	.30	.10
❑	407	Ricky Gutierrez	.30	.10
❑	408	Mike Hampton	.30	.10
❑	409	Dean Hartgraves	.30	.10
❑	410	John Hudek	.30	.10
❑	411	Brian Hunter	.30	.10
❑	412	Todd Jones	.30	.10
❑	413	Darryl Kile	.30	.10
❑	414	Dave Magadan	.30	.10
❑	415	Derrick May	.30	.10
❑	416	Orlando Miller	.30	.10
❑	417	James Mouton	.30	.10
❑	418	Shane Reynolds	.30	.10
❑	419	Greg Swindell	.30	.10
❑	420	Jeff Tabaka	.30	.10
❑	421	Dave Veres	.30	.10
❑	422	Billy Wagner	.30	.10
❑	423	Donne Wall	.30	.10
❑	424	Rick Wilkins	.30	.10
❑	425	Billy Ashley	.30	.10
❑	426	Mike Blowers	.30	.10
❑	427	Brett Butler	.30	.10
❑	428	Tom Candiotti	.30	.10
❑	429	Juan Castro	.30	.10
❑	430	John Cummings	.30	.10
❑	431	Delino DeShields	.30	.10
❑	432	Joey Eischen	.30	.10
❑	433	Chad Fonville	.30	.10
❑	434	Greg Gagne	.30	.10
❑	435	Dave Hansen	.30	.10
❑	436	Carlos Hernandez	.30	.10
❑	437	Todd Hollandsworth	.30	.10
❑	438	Eric Karros	.30	.10
❑	439	Roberto Kelly	.30	.10
❑	440	Ramon Martinez	.30	.10
❑	441	Raul Mondesi	.30	.10
❑	442	Hideo Nomo	.75	.30
❑	443	Antonio Osuna	.30	.10
❑	444	Chan Ho Park	.30	.10
❑	445	Mike Piazza	1.25	.50
❑	446	Felix Rodriguez	.30	.10
❑	447	Kevin Tapani	.30	.10
❑	448	Ismael Valdes	.30	.10
❑	449	Todd Worrell	.30	.10
❑	450	Moises Alou	.30	.10
❑	451	Shane Andrews	.30	.10
❑	452	Yamil Benitez	.30	.10
❑	453	Sean Berry	.30	.10
❑	454	Wil Cordero	.30	.10
❑	455	Jeff Fassero	.30	.10
❑	456	Darrin Fletcher	.30	.10
❑	457	Cliff Floyd	.30	.10
❑	458	Mark Grudzielanek	.30	.10
❑	459	Gil Heredia	.30	.10
❑	460	Tim Laker	.30	.10
❑	461	Mike Lansing	.30	.10
❑	462	Pedro Martinez	.50	.20
❑	463	Carlos Perez	.30	.10
❑	464	Curtis Pride	.30	.10
❑	465	Mel Rojas	.30	.10
❑	466	Kirk Rueter	.30	.10
❑	467	F.P. Santangelo	.30	.10
❑	468	Tim Scott	.30	.10
❑	469	David Segui	.30	.10
❑	470	Tony Tarasco	.30	.10
❑	471	Rondell White	.30	.10
❑	472	Edgardo Alfonzo	.30	.10
❑	473	Tim Bogar	.30	.10
❑	474	Rico Brogna	.30	.10
❑	475	Damon Buford	.30	.10
❑	476	Paul Byrd	.30	.10
❑	477	Carl Everett	.30	.10
❑	478	John Franco	.30	.10
❑	479	Todd Hundley	.30	.10
❑	480	Butch Huskey	.30	.10
❑	481	Jason Isringhausen	.30	.10
❑	482	Bobby Jones	.30	.10
❑	483	Chris Jones	.30	.10
❑	484	Jeff Kent	.30	.10
❑	485	Dave Mlicki	.30	.10
❑	486	Robert Person	.30	.10
❑	487	Bill Pulsipher	.30	.10
❑	488	Kelly Stinnett	.30	.10
❑	489	Ryan Thompson	.30	.10
❑	490	Jose Vizcaino	.30	.10
❑	491	Howard Battle	.30	.10
❑	492	Toby Borland	.30	.10
❑	493	Ricky Bottalico	.30	.10
❑	494	Darren Daulton	.30	.10
❑	495	Lenny Dykstra	.30	.10
❑	496	Jim Eisenreich	.30	.10
❑	497	Sid Fernandez	.30	.10
❑	498	Tyler Green	.30	.10
❑	499	Charlie Hayes	.30	.10
❑	500	Gregg Jefferies	.30	.10
❑	501	Kevin Jordan	.30	.10
❑	502	Tony Longmire	.30	.10
❑	503	Tom Marsh	.30	.10

❑ 504 Michael Mimbs .30 .10
❑ 505 Mickey Morandini .30 .10
❑ 506 Gene Schall .30 .10
❑ 507 Curt Schilling .30 .10
❑ 508 Heathcliff Slocumb .30 .10
❑ 509 Kevin Stocker .30 .10
❑ 510 Andy Van Slyke .50 .20
❑ 511 Lenny Webster .30 .10
❑ 512 Mark Whiten .30 .10
❑ 513 Mike Williams .30 .10
❑ 514 Jay Bell .30 .10
❑ 515 Jacob Brumfield .30 .10
❑ 516 Jason Christiansen .30 .10
❑ 517 Dave Clark .30 .10
❑ 518 Midre Cummings .30 .10
❑ 519 Angelo Encarnacion .30 .10
❑ 520 John Ericks .30 .10
❑ 521 Carlos Garcia .30 .10
❑ 522 Mark Johnson .30 .10
❑ 523 Jeff King .30 .10
❑ 524 Nelson Liriano .30 .10
❑ 525 Esteban Loaiza .30 .10
❑ 526 Al Martin .30 .10
❑ 527 Orlando Merced .30 .10
❑ 528 Dan Miceli .30 .10
❑ 529 Ramon Morel .30 .10
❑ 530 Denny Neagle .30 .10
❑ 531 Steve Parris .30 .10
❑ 532 Dan Plesac .30 .10
❑ 533 Don Slaught .30 .10
❑ 534 Paul Wagner .30 .10
❑ 535 John Wehner .30 .10
❑ 536 Kevin Young .30 .10
❑ 537 Allen Battle .30 .10
❑ 538 David Bell .30 .10
❑ 539 Alan Benes .30 .10
❑ 540 Scott Cooper .30 .10
❑ 541 Tripp Cromer .30 .10
❑ 542 Tony Fossas .30 .10
❑ 543 Bernard Gilkey .30 .10
❑ 544 Tom Henke .30 .10
❑ 545 Brian Jordan .30 .10
❑ 546 Ray Lankford .30 .10
❑ 547 John Mabry .30 .10
❑ 548 T.J. Mathews .30 .10
❑ 549 Mike Morgan .30 .10
❑ 550 Jose Oliva .30 .10
❑ 551 Jose Oquendo .30 .10
❑ 552 Donovan Osborne .30 .10
❑ 553 Tom Pagnozzi .30 .10
❑ 554 Mark Petkovsek .30 .10
❑ 555 Danny Sheaffer .30 .10
❑ 556 Ozzie Smith 1.25 .50
❑ 557 Mark Sweeney .30 .10
❑ 558 Allen Watson .30 .10
❑ 559 Andy Ashby .30 .10
❑ 560 Brad Ausmus .30 .10
❑ 561 Willie Blair .30 .10
❑ 562 Ken Caminiti .30 .10
❑ 563 Andujar Cedeno .30 .10
❑ 564 Glenn Dishman .30 .10
❑ 565 Steve Finley .30 .10
❑ 566 Bryce Florie .30 .10
❑ 567 Tony Gwynn 1.00 .40
❑ 568 Joey Hamilton .30 .10
❑ 569 Dustin Hermanson UER .30 .10
❑ 570 Trevor Hoffman .30 .10
❑ 571 Brian Johnson .30 .10
❑ 572 Marc Kroon .30 .10
❑ 573 Scott Livingstone .30 .10
❑ 574 Marc Newfield .30 .10
❑ 575 Melvin Nieves .30 .10
❑ 576 Jody Reed .30 .10
❑ 577 Bip Roberts .30 .10
❑ 578 Scott Sanders .30 .10
❑ 579 Fernando Valenzuela .30 .10
❑ 580 Eddie Williams .30 .10
❑ 581 Rod Beck .30 .10
❑ 582 Marvin Benard RC .30 .10
❑ 583 Barry Bonds 2.00 .75
❑ 584 Jamie Brewington RC .30 .10
❑ 585 Mark Carreon .30 .10
❑ 586 Royce Clayton .30 .10
❑ 587 Shawn Estes .30 .10
❑ 588 Glenallen Hill .30 .10
❑ 589 Mark Leiter .30 .10
❑ 590 Kirt Manwaring .30 .10
❑ 591 David McCarty .30 .10
❑ 592 Terry Mulholland .30 .10
❑ 593 John Patterson .30 .10
❑ 594 J.R. Phillips .30 .10
❑ 595 Deion Sanders .50 .20
❑ 596 Steve Scarsone .30 .10
❑ 597 Robby Thompson .30 .10
❑ 598 Sergio Valdez .30 .10
❑ 599 William Van Landingham .30 .10
❑ 600 Matt Williams .30 .10
❑ P20 Cal Ripken Promo 3.00 1.25

1997 Fleer

❑ COMPLETE SET (761) 140.00 70.00
❑ COMPLETE SERIES 1 (500) 60.00 30.00
❑ COMPLETE SERIES 2 (261) 80.00 40.00
❑ COMMON CARD (1-750) .30 .10
❑ COMMON CARD (751-761) .50 .20
❑ 1 Roberto Alomar .50 .20
❑ 2 Brady Anderson .30 .10
❑ 3 Bobby Bonilla .30 .10
❑ 4 Rocky Coppinger .30 .10
❑ 5 Cesar Devarez .30 .10
❑ 6 Scott Erickson .30 .10
❑ 7 Jeffrey Hammonds .30 .10
❑ 8 Chris Hoiles .30 .10
❑ 9 Eddie Murray .75 .30
❑ 10 Mike Mussina .50 .20
❑ 11 Randy Myers .30 .10
❑ 12 Rafael Palmeiro .50 .20
❑ 13 Cal Ripken 2.50 1.00
❑ 14 B.J. Surhoff .30 .10
❑ 15 David Wells .30 .10
❑ 16 Todd Zeile .30 .10
❑ 17 Darren Bragg .30 .10
❑ 18 Jose Canseco .50 .20
❑ 19 Roger Clemens 1.50 .60
❑ 20 Wil Cordero .30 .10
❑ 21 Jeff Frye .30 .10
❑ 22 Nomar Garciaparra 1.25 .50
❑ 23 Tom Gordon .30 .10
❑ 24 Mike Greenwell .30 .10
❑ 25 Reggie Jefferson .30 .10
❑ 26 Jose Malave .30 .10
❑ 27 Tim Naehring .30 .10
❑ 28 Troy O'Leary .30 .10
❑ 29 Heathcliff Slocumb .30 .10
❑ 30 Mike Stanley .30 .10
❑ 31 John Valentin .30 .10
❑ 32 Mo Vaughn .30 .10
❑ 33 Tim Wakefield .30 .10
❑ 34 Garret Anderson .30 .10
❑ 35 George Arias .30 .10
❑ 36 Shawn Boskie .30 .10
❑ 37 Chili Davis .30 .10
❑ 38 Jason Dickson .30 .10
❑ 39 Gary DiSarcina .30 .10
❑ 40 Jim Edmonds .30 .10
❑ 41 Darin Erstad .30 .10
❑ 42 Jorge Fabregas .30 .10
❑ 43 Chuck Finley .30 .10
❑ 44 Todd Greene .30 .10
❑ 45 Mike Holtz .30 .10
❑ 46 Rex Hudler .30 .10
❑ 47 Mike James .30 .10
❑ 48 Mark Langston .30 .10
❑ 49 Troy Percival .30 .10
❑ 50 Tim Salmon .50 .20
❑ 51 Jeff Schmidt .30 .10
❑ 52 J.T. Snow .30 .10
❑ 53 Randy Velarde .30 .10
❑ 54 Wilson Alvarez .30 .10
❑ 55 Harold Baines .30 .10
❑ 56 James Baldwin .30 .10
❑ 57 Jason Bere .30 .10
❑ 58 Mike Cameron .30 .10
❑ 59 Ray Durham .30 .10
❑ 60 Alex Fernandez .30 .10
❑ 61 Ozzie Guillen .30 .10
❑ 62 Roberto Hernandez .30 .10
❑ 63 Ron Karkovice .30 .10
❑ 64 Darren Lewis .30 .10
❑ 65 Dave Martinez .30 .10
❑ 66 Lyle Mouton .30 .10
❑ 67 Greg Norton .30 .10
❑ 68 Tony Phillips .30 .10
❑ 69 Chris Snopek .30 .10
❑ 70 Kevin Tapani .30 .10
❑ 71 Danny Tartabull .30 .10
❑ 72 Frank Thomas .75 .30
❑ 73 Robin Ventura .30 .10
❑ 74 Sandy Alomar Jr. .30 .10
❑ 75 Albert Belle .30 .10
❑ 76 Mark Carreon .30 .10
❑ 77 Julio Franco .30 .10
❑ 78 Brian Giles RC 1.50 .60
❑ 79 Orel Hershiser .30 .10
❑ 80 Kenny Lofton .30 .10
❑ 81 Dennis Martinez .30 .10
❑ 82 Jack McDowell .30 .10
❑ 83 Jose Mesa .30 .10
❑ 84 Charles Nagy .30 .10
❑ 85 Chad Ogea .30 .10
❑ 86 Eric Plunk .30 .10
❑ 87 Manny Ramirez .50 .20
❑ 88 Kevin Seitzer .30 .10
❑ 89 Julian Tavarez .30 .10
❑ 90 Jim Thome .50 .20
❑ 91 Jose Vizcaino .30 .10
❑ 92 Omar Vizquel .50 .20
❑ 93 Brad Ausmus .30 .10
❑ 94 Kimera Bartee .30 .10
❑ 95 Raul Casanova .30 .10
❑ 96 Tony Clark .30 .10
❑ 97 John Cummings .30 .10
❑ 98 Travis Fryman .30 .10
❑ 99 Bob Higginson .30 .10
❑ 100 Mark Lewis .30 .10
❑ 101 Felipe Lira .30 .10
❑ 102 Phil Nevin .30 .10
❑ 103 Melvin Nieves .30 .10
❑ 104 Curtis Pride .30 .10
❑ 105 A.J. Sager .30 .10
❑ 106 Ruben Sierra .30 .10
❑ 107 Justin Thompson .30 .10
❑ 108 Alan Trammell .30 .10
❑ 109 Kevin Appier .30 .10
❑ 110 Tim Belcher .30 .10
❑ 111 Jaime Bluma .30 .10
❑ 112 Johnny Damon .50 .20
❑ 113 Tom Goodwin .30 .10
❑ 114 Chris Haney .30 .10
❑ 115 Keith Lockhart .30 .10
❑ 116 Mike Macfarlane .30 .10
❑ 117 Jeff Montgomery .30 .10
❑ 118 Jose Offerman .30 .10
❑ 119 Craig Paquette .30 .10
❑ 120 Joe Randa .30 .10
❑ 121 Bip Roberts .30 .10
❑ 122 Jose Rosado .30 .10
❑ 123 Mike Sweeney .30 .10
❑ 124 Michael Tucker .30 .10
❑ 125 Jeromy Burnitz .30 .10
❑ 126 Jeff Cirillo .30 .10
❑ 127 Jeff D'Amico .30 .10
❑ 128 Mike Fetters .30 .10
❑ 129 John Jaha .30 .10
❑ 130 Scott Karl .30 .10
❑ 131 Jesse Levis .30 .10
❑ 132 Mark Loretta .30 .10
❑ 133 Mike Matheny .30 .10
❑ 134 Ben McDonald .30 .10

❑ 135 Matt Mieske .30 .10
❑ 136 Marc Newfield .30 .10
❑ 137 Dave Nilsson .30 .10
❑ 138 Jose Valentin .30 .10
❑ 139 Fernando Vina .30 .10
❑ 140 Bob Wickman .30 .10
❑ 141 Gerald Williams .30 .10
❑ 142 Rick Aguilera .30 .10
❑ 143 Rich Becker .30 .10
❑ 144 Ron Coomer .30 .10
❑ 145 Marty Cordova .30 .10
❑ 146 Roberto Kelly .30 .10
❑ 147 Chuck Knoblauch .30 .10
❑ 148 Matt Lawton .30 .10
❑ 149 Pat Meares .30 .10
❑ 150 Travis Miller .30 .10
❑ 151 Paul Molitor .30 .10
❑ 152 Greg Myers .30 .10
❑ 153 Dan Naulty .30 .10
❑ 154 Kirby Puckett .75 .30
❑ 155 Brad Radke .30 .10
❑ 156 Frank Rodriguez .30 .10
❑ 157 Scott Stahoviak .30 .10
❑ 158 Dave Stevens .30 .10
❑ 159 Matt Walbeck .30 .10
❑ 160 Todd Walker .30 .10
❑ 161 Wade Boggs .50 .20
❑ 162 David Cone .30 .10
❑ 163 Mariano Duncan .30 .10
❑ 164 Cecil Fielder .30 .10
❑ 165 Joe Girardi .30 .10
❑ 166 Dwight Gooden .30 .10
❑ 167 Charlie Hayes .30 .10
❑ 168 Derek Jeter 2.00 .75
❑ 169 Jimmy Key .30 .10
❑ 170 Jim Leyritz .30 .10
❑ 171 Tino Martinez .50 .20
❑ 172 Ramiro Mendoza RC .30 .10
❑ 173 Jeff Nelson .30 .10
❑ 174 Paul O'Neill .50 .20
❑ 175 Andy Pettitte .50 .20
❑ 176 Mariano Rivera .75 .30
❑ 177 Ruben Rivera .30 .10
❑ 178 Kenny Rogers .30 .10
❑ 179 Darryl Strawberry .30 .10
❑ 180 John Wetteland .30 .10
❑ 181 Bernie Williams .50 .20
❑ 182 Willie Adams .30 .10
❑ 183 Tony Batista .30 .10
❑ 184 Geronimo Berroa .30 .10
❑ 185 Mike Bordick .30 .10
❑ 186 Scott Brosius .30 .10
❑ 187 Bobby Chouinard .30 .10
❑ 188 Jim Corsi .30 .10
❑ 189 Brent Gates .30 .10
❑ 190 Jason Giambi .30 .10
❑ 191 Jose Herrera .30 .10
❑ 192 Damon Mashore .30 .10
❑ 193 Mark McGwire 2.00 .75
❑ 194 Mike Mohler .30 .10
❑ 195 Scott Spiezio .30 .10
❑ 196 Terry Steinbach .30 .10
❑ 197 Bill Taylor .30 .10
❑ 198 John Wasdin .30 .10
❑ 199 Steve Wojciechowski .30 .10
❑ 200 Ernie Young .30 .10
❑ 201 Rich Amaral .30 .10
❑ 202 Jay Buhner .30 .10
❑ 203 Norm Charlton .30 .10
❑ 204 Joey Cora .30 .10
❑ 205 Russ Davis .30 .10
❑ 206 Ken Griffey Jr. 1.25 .50
❑ 207 Sterling Hitchcock .30 .10
❑ 208 Brian Hunter .30 .10
❑ 209 Raul Ibanez .30 .10
❑ 210 Randy Johnson .75 .30
❑ 211 Edgar Martinez .50 .20
❑ 212 Jamie Moyer .30 .10
❑ 213 Alex Rodriguez 1.25 .50
❑ 214 Paul Sorrento .30 .10
❑ 215 Matt Wagner .30 .10
❑ 216 Bob Wells .30 .10
❑ 217 Dan Wilson .30 .10
❑ 218 Damon Buford .30 .10
❑ 219 Will Clark .50 .20
❑ 220 Kevin Elster .30 .10
❑ 221 Juan Gonzalez .30 .10
❑ 222 Rusty Greer .30 .10
❑ 223 Kevin Gross .30 .10
❑ 224 Darryl Hamilton .30 .10
❑ 225 Mike Henneman .30 .10
❑ 226 Ken Hill .30 .10
❑ 227 Mark McLemore .30 .10
❑ 228 Darren Oliver .30 .10
❑ 229 Dean Palmer .30 .10
❑ 230 Roger Pavlik .30 .10
❑ 231 Ivan Rodriguez .50 .20
❑ 232 Mickey Tettleton .30 .10
❑ 233 Bobby Witt .30 .10
❑ 234 Jacob Brumfield .30 .10
❑ 235 Joe Carter .30 .10
❑ 236 Tim Crabtree .30 .10
❑ 237 Carlos Delgado .30 .10
❑ 238 Huck Flener .30 .10
❑ 239 Alex Gonzalez .30 .10
❑ 240 Shawn Green .30 .10
❑ 241 Juan Guzman .30 .10
❑ 242 Pat Hentgen .30 .10
❑ 243 Marty Janzen .30 .10
❑ 244 Sandy Martinez .30 .10
❑ 245 Otis Nixon .30 .10
❑ 246 Charlie O'Brien .30 .10
❑ 247 John Olerud .30 .10
❑ 248 Robert Perez .30 .10
❑ 249 Ed Sprague .30 .10
❑ 250 Mike Timlin .30 .10
❑ 251 Steve Avery .30 .10
❑ 252 Jeff Blauser .30 .10
❑ 253 Brad Clontz .30 .10
❑ 254 Jermaine Dye .30 .10
❑ 255 Tom Glavine .50 .20
❑ 256 Marquis Grissom .30 .10
❑ 257 Andruw Jones .50 .20
❑ 258 Chipper Jones .75 .30
❑ 259 David Justice .30 .10
❑ 260 Ryan Klesko .30 .10
❑ 261 Mark Lemke .30 .10
❑ 262 Javier Lopez .30 .10
❑ 263 Greg Maddux 1.25 .50
❑ 264 Fred McGriff .50 .20
❑ 265 Greg McMichael .30 .10
❑ 266 Denny Neagle .30 .10
❑ 267 Terry Pendleton .30 .10
❑ 268 Eddie Perez .30 .10
❑ 269 John Smoltz .50 .20
❑ 270 Terrell Wade .30 .10
❑ 271 Mark Wohlers .30 .10
❑ 272 Terry Adams .30 .10
❑ 273 Brant Brown .30 .10
❑ 274 Leo Gomez .30 .10
❑ 275 Luis Gonzalez .30 .10
❑ 276 Mark Grace .50 .20
❑ 277 Tyler Houston .30 .10
❑ 278 Robin Jennings .30 .10
❑ 279 Brooks Kieschnick .30 .10
❑ 280 Brian McRae .30 .10
❑ 281 Jaime Navarro .30 .10
❑ 282 Ryne Sandberg 1.25 .50
❑ 283 Scott Servais .30 .10
❑ 284 Sammy Sosa .75 .30
❑ 285 Dave Swartzbaugh .30 .10
❑ 286 Amaury Telemaco .30 .10
❑ 287 Steve Trachsel .30 .10
❑ 288 Pedro Valdes .30 .10
❑ 289 Turk Wendell .30 .10
❑ 290 Bret Boone .30 .10
❑ 291 Jeff Branson .30 .10
❑ 292 Jeff Brantley .30 .10
❑ 293 Eric Davis .30 .10
❑ 294 Willie Greene .30 .10
❑ 295 Thomas Howard .30 .10
❑ 296 Barry Larkin .50 .20
❑ 297 Kevin Mitchell .30 .10
❑ 298 Hal Morris .30 .10
❑ 299 Chad Mottola .30 .10
❑ 300 Joe Oliver .30 .10
❑ 301 Mark Portugal .30 .10
❑ 302 Roger Salkeld .30 .10
❑ 303 Reggie Sanders .30 .10
❑ 304 Pete Schourek .30 .10
❑ 305 John Smiley .30 .10
❑ 306 Eddie Taubensee .30 .10
❑ 307 Dante Bichette .30 .10
❑ 308 Ellis Burks .30 .10
❑ 309 Vinny Castilla .30 .10
❑ 310 Andres Galarraga .30 .10
❑ 311 Curt Leskanic .30 .10
❑ 312 Quinton McCracken .30 .10
❑ 313 Neifi Perez .30 .10
❑ 314 Jeff Reed .30 .10
❑ 315 Steve Reed .30 .10
❑ 316 Armando Reynoso .30 .10
❑ 317 Kevin Ritz .30 .10
❑ 318 Bruce Ruffin .30 .10
❑ 319 Larry Walker .30 .10
❑ 320 Walt Weiss .30 .10
❑ 321 Jamey Wright .30 .10
❑ 322 Eric Young .30 .10
❑ 323 Kurt Abbott .30 .10
❑ 324 Alex Arias .30 .10
❑ 325 Kevin Brown .30 .10
❑ 326 Luis Castillo .30 .10
❑ 327 Greg Colbrunn .30 .10
❑ 328 Jeff Conine .30 .10
❑ 329 Andre Dawson .30 .10
❑ 330 Charles Johnson .30 .10
❑ 331 Al Leiter .30 .10
❑ 332 Ralph Milliard .30 .10
❑ 333 Robb Nen .30 .10
❑ 334 Pat Rapp .30 .10
❑ 335 Edgar Renteria .30 .10
❑ 336 Gary Sheffield .30 .10
❑ 337 Devon White .30 .10
❑ 338 Bob Abreu .50 .20
❑ 339 Jeff Bagwell .50 .20
❑ 340 Derek Bell .30 .10
❑ 341 Sean Berry .30 .10
❑ 342 Craig Biggio .50 .20
❑ 343 Doug Drabek .30 .10
❑ 344 Tony Eusebio .30 .10
❑ 345 Ricky Gutierrez .30 .10
❑ 346 Mike Hampton .30 .10
❑ 347 Brian Hunter .30 .10
❑ 348 Todd Jones .30 .10
❑ 349 Darryl Kile .30 .10
❑ 350 Derrick May .30 .10
❑ 351 Orlando Miller .30 .10
❑ 352 James Mouton .30 .10
❑ 353 Shane Reynolds .30 .10
❑ 354 Billy Wagner .30 .10
❑ 355 Donne Wall .30 .10
❑ 356 Mike Blowers .30 .10
❑ 357 Brett Butler .30 .10
❑ 358 Roger Cedeno .30 .10
❑ 359 Chad Curtis .30 .10
❑ 360 Delino DeShields .30 .10
❑ 361 Greg Gagne .30 .10
❑ 362 Karim Garcia .30 .10
❑ 363 Wilton Guerrero .30 .10
❑ 364 Todd Hollandsworth .30 .10
❑ 365 Eric Karros .30 .10
❑ 366 Ramon Martinez .30 .10
❑ 367 Raul Mondesi .30 .10
❑ 368 Hideo Nomo .75 .30
❑ 369 Antonio Osuna .30 .10
❑ 370 Chan Ho Park .30 .10
❑ 371 Mike Piazza 1.25 .50
❑ 372 Ismael Valdes .30 .10
❑ 373 Todd Worrell .30 .10
❑ 374 Moises Alou .30 .10
❑ 375 Shane Andrews .30 .10
❑ 376 Yamil Benitez .30 .10
❑ 377 Jeff Fassero .30 .10
❑ 378 Darrin Fletcher .30 .10
❑ 379 Cliff Floyd .30 .10
❑ 380 Mark Grudzielanek .30 .10
❑ 381 Mike Lansing .30 .10
❑ 382 Barry Manuel .30 .10
❑ 383 Pedro Martinez .50 .20
❑ 384 Henry Rodriguez .30 .10
❑ 385 Mel Rojas .30 .10
❑ 386 F.P. Santangelo .30 .10
❑ 387 David Segui .30 .10
❑ 388 Ugueth Urbina .30 .10
❑ 389 Rondell White .30 .10
❑ 390 Edgardo Alfonzo .30 .10
❑ 391 Carlos Baerga .30 .10
❑ 392 Mark Clark .30 .10

	#	Player		
❑	393	Alvaro Espinoza	.30	.10
❑	394	John Franco	.30	.10
❑	395	Bernard Gilkey	.30	.10
❑	396	Pete Harnisch	.30	.10
❑	397	Todd Hundley	.30	.10
❑	398	Butch Huskey	.30	.10
❑	399	Jason Isringhausen	.30	.10
❑	400	Lance Johnson	.30	.10
❑	401	Bobby Jones	.30	.10
❑	402	Alex Ochoa	.30	.10
❑	403	Rey Ordonez	.30	.10
❑	404	Robert Person	.30	.10
❑	405	Paul Wilson	.30	.10
❑	406	Matt Beech	.30	.10
❑	407	Ron Blazier	.30	.10
❑	408	Ricky Bottalico	.30	.10
❑	409	Lenny Dykstra	.30	.10
❑	410	Jim Eisenreich	.30	.10
❑	411	Bobby Estalella	.30	.10
❑	412	Mike Grace	.30	.10
❑	413	Gregg Jefferies	.30	.10
❑	414	Mike Lieberthal	.30	.10
❑	415	Wendell Magee	.30	.10
❑	416	Mickey Morandini	.30	.10
❑	417	Ricky Otero	.30	.10
❑	418	Scott Rolen	.50	.20
❑	419	Ken Ryan	.30	.10
❑	420	Benito Santiago	.30	.10
❑	421	Curt Schilling	.30	.10
❑	422	Kevin Sefcik	.30	.10
❑	423	Jermaine Allensworth	.30	.10
❑	424	Trey Beamon	.30	.10
❑	425	Jay Bell	.30	.10
❑	426	Francisco Cordova	.30	.10
❑	427	Carlos Garcia	.30	.10
❑	428	Mark Johnson	.30	.10
❑	429	Jason Kendall	.30	.10
❑	430	Jeff King	.30	.10
❑	431	Jon Lieber	.30	.10
❑	432	Al Martin	.30	.10
❑	433	Orlando Merced	.30	.10
❑	434	Ramon Morel	.30	.10
❑	435	Matt Ruebel	.30	.10
❑	436	Jason Schmidt	.30	.10
❑	437	Marc Wilkins	.30	.10
❑	438	Alan Benes	.30	.10
❑	439	Andy Benes	.30	.10
❑	440	Royce Clayton	.30	.10
❑	441	Dennis Eckersley	.30	.10
❑	442	Gary Gaetti	.30	.10
❑	443	Ron Gant	.30	.10
❑	444	Aaron Holbert	.30	.10
❑	445	Brian Jordan	.30	.10
❑	446	Ray Lankford	.30	.10
❑	447	John Mabry	.30	.10
❑	448	T.J. Mathews	.30	.10
❑	449	Willie McGee	.30	.10
❑	450	Donovan Osborne	.30	.10
❑	451	Tom Pagnozzi	.30	.10
❑	452	Ozzie Smith	1.25	.50
❑	453	Todd Stottlemyre	.30	.10
❑	454	Mark Sweeney	.30	.10
❑	455	Dmitri Young	.30	.10
❑	456	Andy Ashby	.30	.10
❑	457	Ken Caminiti	.30	.10
❑	458	Archi Cianfrocco	.30	.10
❑	459	Steve Finley	.30	.10
❑	460	John Flaherty	.30	.10
❑	461	Chris Gomez	.30	.10
❑	462	Tony Gwynn	1.00	.40
❑	463	Joey Hamilton	.30	.10
❑	464	Rickey Henderson	.75	.30
❑	465	Trevor Hoffman	.30	.10
❑	466	Brian Johnson	.30	.10
❑	467	Wally Joyner	.30	.10
❑	468	Jody Reed	.30	.10
❑	469	Scott Sanders	.30	.10
❑	470	Bob Tewksbury	.30	.10
❑	471	Fernando Valenzuela	.30	.10
❑	472	Greg Vaughn	.30	.10
❑	473	Tim Worrell	.30	.10
❑	474	Rich Aurilia	.30	.10
❑	475	Rod Beck	.30	.10
❑	476	Marvin Benard	.30	.10
❑	477	Barry Bonds	2.00	.75
❑	478	Jay Canizaro	.30	.10
❑	479	Shawon Dunston	.30	.10
❑	480	Shawn Estes	.30	.10
❑	481	Mark Gardner	.30	.10
❑	482	Glenallen Hill	.30	.10
❑	483	Stan Javier	.30	.10
❑	484	Marcus Jensen	.30	.10
❑	485	Bill Mueller RC	1.25	.50
❑	486	Wm. VanLandingham	.30	.10
❑	487	Allen Watson	.30	.10
❑	488	Rick Wilkins	.30	.10
❑	489	Matt Williams	.30	.10
❑	490	Desi Wilson	.30	.10
❑	491	Albert Belle CL	.30	.10
❑	492	Ken Griffey Jr. CL	.75	.30
❑	493	Andruw Jones CL	.30	.10
❑	494	Chipper Jones CL	.50	.20
❑	495	Mark McGwire CL	1.00	.40
❑	496	Paul Molitor CL	.30	.10
❑	497	Mike Piazza CL	.75	.30
❑	498	Cal Ripken CL	1.25	.50
❑	499	Alex Rodriguez CL	.75	.30
❑	500	Frank Thomas CL	.50	.20
❑	501	Kenny Lofton	.30	.10
❑	502	Carlos Perez	.30	.10
❑	503	Tim Raines	.30	.10
❑	504	Danny Patterson	.30	.10
❑	505	Derrick May	.30	.10
❑	506	Dave Hollins	.30	.10
❑	507	Felipe Crespo	.30	.10
❑	508	Brian Banks	.30	.10
❑	509	Jeff Kent	.30	.10
❑	510	Bubba Trammell RC	.40	.15
❑	511	Robert Person	.30	.10
❑	512	David Arias-Ortiz RC	70.00	40.00
❑	513	Ryan Jones	.30	.10
❑	514	David Justice	.30	.10
❑	515	Will Cunnane	.30	.10
❑	516	Russ Johnson	.30	.10
❑	517	John Burkett	.30	.10
❑	518	Robinson Checo RC	.30	.10
❑	519	Ricardo Rincon RC	.30	.10
❑	520	Woody Williams	.30	.10
❑	521	Rick Helling	.30	.10
❑	522	Jorge Posada	.50	.20
❑	523	Kevin Orie	.30	.10
❑	524	Fernando Tatis RC	.30	.10
❑	525	Jermaine Dye	.30	.10
❑	526	Brian Hunter	.30	.10
❑	527	Greg McMichael	.30	.10
❑	528	Matt Wagner	.30	.10
❑	529	Richie Sexson	.30	.10
❑	530	Scott Ruffcorn	.30	.10
❑	531	Luis Gonzalez	.30	.10
❑	532	Mike Johnson RC	.30	.10
❑	533	Mark Petkovsek	.30	.10
❑	534	Doug Drabek	.30	.10
❑	535	Jose Canseco	.50	.20
❑	536	Bobby Bonilla	.30	.10
❑	537	J.T. Snow	.30	.10
❑	538	Shawon Dunston	.30	.10
❑	539	John Ericks	.30	.10
❑	540	Terry Steinbach	.30	.10
❑	541	Jay Bell	.30	.10
❑	542	Joe Borowski RC	.40	.15
❑	543	David Wells	.30	.10
❑	544	Justin Towle RC	.30	.10
❑	545	Mike Blowers	.30	.10
❑	546	Shannon Stewart	.30	.10
❑	547	Rudy Pemberton	.30	.10
❑	548	Bill Swift	.30	.10
❑	549	Osvaldo Fernandez	.30	.10
❑	550	Eddie Murray	.75	.30
❑	551	Don Wengert	.30	.10
❑	552	Brad Ausmus	.30	.10
❑	553	Carlos Garcia	.30	.10
❑	554	Jose Guillen	.30	.10
❑	555	Rheal Cormier	.30	.10
❑	556	Doug Brocail	.30	.10
❑	557	Rex Hudler	.30	.10
❑	558	Armando Benitez	.30	.10
❑	559	Eli Marrero	.30	.10
❑	560	Ricky Ledee RC	.40	.15
❑	561	Bartolo Colon	.30	.10
❑	562	Quilvio Veras	.30	.10
❑	563	Alex Fernandez	.30	.10
❑	564	Darren Dreifort	.30	.10
❑	565	Benji Gil	.30	.10
❑	566	Kent Mercker	.30	.10
❑	567	Glendon Rusch	.30	.10
❑	568	Ramon Tatis RC	.30	.10
❑	569	Roger Clemens	1.50	.60
❑	570	Mark Lewis	.30	.10
❑	571	Emil Brown RC	.30	.10
❑	572	Jaime Navarro	.30	.10
❑	573	Sherman Obando	.30	.10
❑	574	John Wasdin	.30	.10
❑	575	Calvin Maduro	.30	.10
❑	576	Todd Jones	.30	.10
❑	577	Orlando Merced	.30	.10
❑	578	Cal Eldred	.30	.10
❑	579	Mark Gubicza	.30	.10
❑	580	Michael Tucker	.30	.10
❑	581	Tony Saunders RC	.30	.10
❑	582	Garvin Alston	.30	.10
❑	583	Joe Roa	.30	.10
❑	584	Brady Raggio RC	.30	.10
❑	585	Jimmy Key	.30	.10
❑	586	Marc Sagmoen RC	.30	.10
❑	587	Jim Bullinger	.30	.10
❑	588	Yorkis Perez	.30	.10
❑	589	Jose Cruz Jr. RC	.40	.15
❑	590	Mike Stanton	.30	.10
❑	591	Deivi Cruz RC	.40	.15
❑	592	Steve Karsay	.30	.10
❑	593	Mike Trombley	.30	.10
❑	594	Doug Glanville	.30	.10
❑	595	Scott Sanders	.30	.10
❑	596	Thomas Howard	.30	.10
❑	597	T.J. Staton RC	.30	.10
❑	598	Garrett Stephenson	.30	.10
❑	599	Rico Brogna	.30	.10
❑	600	Albert Belle	.30	.10
❑	601	Jose Vizcaino	.30	.10
❑	602	Chili Davis	.30	.10
❑	603	Shane Mack	.30	.10
❑	604	Jim Eisenreich	.30	.10
❑	605	Todd Zeile	.30	.10
❑	606	Brian Boehringer RC	.30	.10
❑	607	Paul Shuey	.30	.10
❑	608	Kevin Tapani	.30	.10
❑	609	John Wetteland	.30	.10
❑	610	Jim Leyritz	.30	.10
❑	611	Ray Montgomery RC	.30	.10
❑	612	Doug Bochtler	.30	.10
❑	613	Wady Almonte RC	.30	.10
❑	614	Danny Tartabull	.30	.10
❑	615	Orlando Miller	.30	.10
❑	616	Bobby Ayala	.30	.10
❑	617	Tony Graffanino	.30	.10
❑	618	Marc Valdes	.30	.10
❑	619	Ron Villone	.30	.10
❑	620	Derrek Lee	.50	.20
❑	621	Greg Colbrunn	.30	.10
❑	622	Felix Heredia RC	.40	.15
❑	623	Carl Everett	.30	.10
❑	624	Mark Thompson	.30	.10
❑	625	Jeff Granger	.30	.10
❑	626	Damian Jackson	.30	.10
❑	627	Mark Leiter	.30	.10
❑	628	Chris Holt	.30	.10
❑	629	Dario Veras RC	.30	.10
❑	630	Dave Burba	.30	.10
❑	631	Darryl Hamilton	.30	.10
❑	632	Mark Acre	.30	.10
❑	633	Fernando Hernandez RC	.30	.10
❑	634	Terry Mulholland	.30	.10
❑	635	Dustin Hermanson	.30	.10
❑	636	Delino DeShields	.30	.10
❑	637	Steve Avery	.30	.10
❑	638	Tony Womack RC	.40	.15
❑	639	Mark Whiten	.30	.10
❑	640	Marquis Grissom	.30	.10
❑	641	Xavier Hernandez	.30	.10
❑	642	Eric Davis	.30	.10
❑	643	Bob Tewksbury	.30	.10
❑	644	Dante Powell	.30	.10
❑	645	Carlos Castillo RC	.30	.10
❑	646	Chris Widger	.30	.10
❑	647	Moises Alou	.30	.10
❑	648	Pat Listach	.30	.10
❑	649	Edgar Ramos RC	.30	.10
❑	650	Deion Sanders	.50	.20

❑	651	John Olerud	.30	.10
❑	652	Todd Dunwoody	.30	.10
❑	653	Randall Simon RC	.40	.15
❑	654	Dan Carlson	.30	.10
❑	655	Matt Williams	.30	.10
❑	656	Jeff King	.30	.10
❑	657	Luis Alicea	.30	.10
❑	658	Brian Moehler RC	.40	.15
❑	659	Ariel Prieto	.30	.10
❑	660	Kevin Elster	.30	.10
❑	661	Mark Hutton	.30	.10
❑	662	Aaron Sele	.30	.10
❑	663	Graeme Lloyd	.30	.10
❑	664	John Burke	.30	.10
❑	665	Mel Rojas	.30	.10
❑	666	Sid Fernandez	.30	.10
❑	667	Pedro Astacio	.30	.10
❑	668	Jeff Abbott	.30	.10
❑	669	Darren Daulton	.30	.10
❑	670	Mike Bordick	.30	.10
❑	671	Sterling Hitchcock	.30	.10
❑	672	Damion Easley	.30	.10
❑	673	Armando Reynoso	.30	.10
❑	674	Pat Cline	.30	.10
❑	675	Orlando Cabrera RC	.75	.30
❑	676	Alan Embree	.30	.10
❑	677	Brian Bevil	.30	.10
❑	678	David Weathers	.30	.10
❑	679	Cliff Floyd	.30	.10
❑	680	Joe Randa	.30	.10
❑	681	Bill Haselman	.30	.10
❑	682	Jeff Fassero	.30	.10
❑	683	Matt Morris	.30	.10
❑	684	Mark Portugal	.30	.10
❑	685	Lee Smith	.30	.10
❑	686	Pokey Reese	.30	.10
❑	687	Benito Santiago	.30	.10
❑	688	Brian Johnson	.30	.10
❑	689	Brent Brede RC	.30	.10
❑	690	Shigetoshi Hasegawa RC	.50	.20
❑	691	Julio Santana	.30	.10
❑	692	Steve Kline	.30	.10
❑	693	Julian Tavarez	.30	.10
❑	694	John Hudek	.30	.10
❑	695	Manny Alexander	.30	.10
❑	696	Roberto Alomar ENC	.30	.10
❑	697	Jeff Bagwell ENC	.30	.10
❑	698	Barry Bonds ENC	1.00	.40
❑	699	Ken Caminiti ENC	.30	.10
❑	700	Juan Gonzalez ENC	.30	.10
❑	701	Ken Griffey Jr. ENC	.75	.30
❑	702	Tony Gwynn ENC	.50	.20
❑	703	Derek Jeter ENC	1.00	.40
❑	704	Andruw Jones ENC	.50	.20
❑	705	Chipper Jones ENC	.50	.20
❑	706	Barry Larkin ENC	.30	.10
❑	707	Greg Maddux ENC	.75	.30
❑	708	Mark McGwire ENC	1.00	.40
❑	709	Paul Molitor ENC	.30	.10
❑	710	Hideo Nomo ENC	.30	.10
❑	711	Andy Pettitte ENC	.30	.10
❑	712	Mike Piazza ENC	.75	.30
❑	713	Manny Ramirez ENC	.50	.20
❑	714	Cal Ripken ENC	1.25	.50
❑	715	Alex Rodriguez ENC	.75	.30
❑	716	Ryne Sandberg ENC	.75	.30
❑	717	John Smoltz ENC	.30	.10
❑	718	Frank Thomas ENC	.50	.20
❑	719	Mo Vaughn ENC	.30	.10
❑	720	Bernie Williams ENC	.30	.10
❑	721	Tim Salmon CL	.30	.10
❑	722	Greg Maddux CL	.75	.30
❑	723	Cal Ripken CL	1.25	.50
❑	724	Mo Vaughn CL	.30	.10
❑	725	Ryne Sandberg CL	.75	.30
❑	726	Frank Thomas CL	.50	.20
❑	727	Barry Larkin CL	.30	.10
❑	728	Manny Ramirez CL	.30	.10
❑	729	Andres Galarraga CL	.30	.10
❑	730	Tony Clark CL	.30	.10
❑	731	Gary Sheffield CL	.30	.10
❑	732	Jeff Bagwell CL	.30	.10
❑	733	Kevin Appier CL	.30	.10
❑	734	Mike Piazza CL	.75	.30
❑	735	Jeff Cirillo CL	.30	.10
❑	736	Paul Molitor CL	.30	.10
❑	737	Henry Rodriguez CL	.30	.10
❑	738	Todd Hundley CL	.30	.10
❑	739	Derek Jeter CL	1.00	.40
❑	740	Mark McGwire CL	1.00	.40
❑	741	Curt Schilling CL	.30	.10
❑	742	Jason Kendall CL	.30	.10
❑	743	Tony Gwynn CL	.50	.20
❑	744	Barry Bonds CL	1.00	.40
❑	745	Ken Griffey Jr. CL	.75	.30
❑	746	Brian Jordan CL	.30	.10
❑	747	Juan Gonzalez CL	.30	.10
❑	748	Joe Carter CL	.30	.10
❑	749	Arizona Diamondbacks CL	.30	.10
❑	750	Tampa Bay Devil Rays CL	.30	.10
❑	751	Hideki Irabu RC	.75	.30
❑	752	Jeremi Gonzalez RC	.50	.20
❑	753	Mario Valdez RC	.50	.20
❑	754	Aaron Boone	.75	.30
❑	755	Brett Tomko	.50	.20
❑	756	Jaret Wright RC	.75	.30
❑	757	Ryan McGuire	.50	.20
❑	758	Jason McDonald	.50	.20
❑	759	Adrian Brown RC	.50	.20
❑	760	Keith Foulke RC	2.00	.75
❑	761	Bonus Checklist (751-761)	.50	.20
❑	P489	Matt Williams Promo	1.00	.40
❑	NNO	A.Jones Circa AU/200	25.00	10.00

2002 Fleer

❑		COMPLETE SET (540)	80.00	30.00
❑		COMMON CARD (1-540)	.25	.08
❑		COMMON CARD (492-531)	.50	.20
❑	1	Darin Erstad FP	.25	.08
❑	2	Randy Johnson FP	.60	.25
❑	3	Chipper Jones FP	.60	.25
❑	4	Jay Gibbons FP	.25	.08
❑	5	Nomar Garciaparra FP	1.00	.40
❑	6	Sammy Sosa FP	.60	.25
❑	7	Frank Thomas FP	.60	.25
❑	8	Ken Griffey Jr. FP	1.00	.40
❑	9	Jim Thome FP	.40	.15
❑	10	Todd Helton FP	.40	.15
❑	11	Jeff Weaver FP	.25	.08
❑	12	Cliff Floyd FP	.25	.08
❑	13	Jeff Bagwell FP	.40	.15
❑	14	Mike Sweeney FP	.25	.08
❑	15	Adrian Beltre FP	.25	.08
❑	16	Richie Sexson FP	.25	.08
❑	17	Brad Radke FP	.25	.08
❑	18	Vladimir Guerrero FP	.60	.25
❑	19	Mike Piazza FP	1.00	.40
❑	20	Derek Jeter FP	1.25	.50
❑	21	Eric Chavez FP	.25	.08
❑	22	Pat Burrell FP	.25	.08
❑	23	Brian Giles FP	.25	.08
❑	24	Trevor Hoffman FP	.25	.08
❑	25	Barry Bonds FP	1.00	.40
❑	26	Ichiro Suzuki FP	1.00	.40
❑	27	Albert Pujols FP	1.00	.40
❑	28	Ben Grieve FP	.25	.08
❑	29	Alex Rodriguez FP	1.00	.40
❑	30	Carlos Delgado FP	.25	.08
❑	31	Miguel Tejada	.40	.15
❑	32	Todd Hollandsworth	.25	.08
❑	33	Marlon Anderson	.25	.08
❑	34	Kerry Robinson	.25	.08
❑	35	Chris Richard	.25	.08
❑	36	Jamey Wright	.25	.08
❑	37	Ray Lankford	.40	.15
❑	38	Mike Bordick	.40	.15
❑	39	Danny Graves	.25	.08
❑	40	A.J. Pierzynski	.40	.15
❑	41	Shannon Stewart	.40	.15
❑	42	Tony Armas Jr.	.25	.08
❑	43	Brad Ausmus	.40	.15
❑	44	Alfonso Soriano	.40	.15
❑	45	Junior Spivey	.25	.08
❑	46	Brent Mayne	.25	.08
❑	47	Jim Thome	.60	.25
❑	48	Dan Wilson	.25	.08
❑	49	Geoff Jenkins	.25	.08
❑	50	Kris Benson	.25	.08
❑	51	Rafael Furcal	.40	.15
❑	52	Wiki Gonzalez	.25	.08
❑	53	Jeff Kent	.40	.15
❑	54	Curt Schilling	.40	.15
❑	55	Ken Harvey	.25	.08
❑	56	Roosevelt Brown	.25	.08
❑	57	David Segui	.25	.08
❑	58	Mario Valdez	.25	.08
❑	59	Adam Dunn	.40	.15
❑	60	Bob Howry	.25	.08
❑	61	Michael Barrett	.25	.08
❑	62	Garret Anderson	.40	.15
❑	63	Kelvim Escobar	.25	.08
❑	64	Ben Grieve	.25	.08
❑	65	Randy Johnson	1.00	.40
❑	66	Jose Offerman	.25	.08
❑	67	Jason Kendall	.40	.15
❑	68	Joel Pineiro	.25	.08
❑	69	Alex Escobar	.25	.08
❑	70	Chris George	.25	.08
❑	71	Bobby Higginson	.40	.15
❑	72	Nomar Garciaparra	1.50	.60
❑	73	Pat Burrell	.40	.15
❑	74	Lee Stevens	.25	.08
❑	75	Felipe Lopez	.25	.08
❑	76	Al Leiter	.40	.15
❑	77	Jim Edmonds	.40	.15
❑	78	Al Levine	.25	.08
❑	79	Raul Mondesi	.40	.15
❑	80	Jose Valentin	.25	.08
❑	81	Matt Clement	.40	.15
❑	82	Richard Hidalgo	.25	.08
❑	83	Jamie Moyer	.40	.15
❑	84	Brian Schneider	.25	.08
❑	85	John Franco	.40	.15
❑	86	Brian Buchanan	.25	.08
❑	87	Roy Oswalt	.40	.15
❑	88	Johnny Estrada	.25	.08
❑	89	Marcus Giles	.40	.15
❑	90	Carlos Valderrama	.25	.08
❑	91	Mark Mulder	.40	.15
❑	92	Mark Grace	.60	.25
❑	93	Andy Ashby	.25	.08
❑	94	Woody Williams	.25	.08
❑	95	Ben Petrick	.25	.08
❑	96	Roy Halladay	.40	.15
❑	97	Fred McGriff	.60	.25
❑	98	Shawn Green	.40	.15
❑	99	Todd Hundley	.25	.08
❑	100	Carlos Febles	.25	.08
❑	101	Jason Marquis	.25	.08
❑	102	Mike Redmond	.25	.08
❑	103	Shane Halter	.25	.08
❑	104	Trot Nixon	.40	.15
❑	105	Jeremy Giambi	.25	.08
❑	106	Carlos Delgado	.40	.15
❑	107	Richie Sexson	.40	.15
❑	108	Russ Ortiz	.25	.08
❑	109	David Ortiz	1.00	.40
❑	110	Curtis Leskanic	.25	.08
❑	111	Jay Payton	.25	.08
❑	112	Travis Phelps	.25	.08
❑	113	J.T. Snow	.40	.15
❑	114	Edgar Renteria	.40	.15
❑	115	Freddy Garcia	.40	.15
❑	116	Cliff Floyd	.40	.15
❑	117	Charles Nagy	.25	.08
❑	118	Tony Batista	.25	.08
❑	119	Rafael Palmeiro	.60	.25
❑	120	Darren Dreifort	.25	.08
❑	121	Warren Morris	.25	.08
❑	122	Augie Ojeda	.25	.08

❑ 123 Rusty Greer .40 .15
❑ 124 Esteban Yan .25 .08
❑ 125 Corey Patterson .25 .08
❑ 126 Matt Ginter .25 .08
❑ 127 Matt Lawton .25 .08
❑ 128 Miguel Batista .25 .08
❑ 129 Randy Winn .25 .08
❑ 130 Eric Milton .25 .08
❑ 131 Jack Wilson .25 .08
❑ 132 Sean Casey .40 .15
❑ 133 Mike Sweeney .40 .15
❑ 134 Jason Tyner .25 .08
❑ 135 Carlos Hernandez .25 .08
❑ 136 Shea Hillenbrand .40 .15
❑ 137 Shawn Wooten .25 .08
❑ 138 Peter Bergeron .25 .08
❑ 139 Travis Lee .25 .08
❑ 140 Craig Wilson .25 .08
❑ 141 Carlos Guillen .40 .15
❑ 142 Chipper Jones 1.00 .40
❑ 143 Gabe Kapler .40 .15
❑ 144 Raul Ibanez .25 .08
❑ 145 Eric Chavez .40 .15
❑ 146 D'Angelo Jimenez .25 .08
❑ 147 Chad Hermansen .25 .08
❑ 148 Joe Kennedy .25 .08
❑ 149 Mariano Rivera 1.00 .40
❑ 150 Jeff Bagwell .60 .25
❑ 151 Joe McEwing .25 .08
❑ 152 Ronnie Belliard .25 .08
❑ 153 Desi Relaford .25 .08
❑ 154 Vinny Castilla .40 .15
❑ 155 Tim Hudson .40 .15
❑ 156 Wilton Guerrero .25 .08
❑ 157 Raul Casanova .25 .08
❑ 158 Edgardo Alfonzo .25 .08
❑ 159 Derrek Lee .60 .25
❑ 160 Phil Nevin .40 .15
❑ 161 Roger Clemens 2.00 .75
❑ 162 Jason LaRue .25 .08
❑ 163 Brian Lawrence .25 .08
❑ 164 Adrian Beltre .40 .15
❑ 165 Troy Glaus .40 .15
❑ 166 Jeff Weaver .25 .08
❑ 167 B.J. Surhoff .40 .15
❑ 168 Eric Byrnes .25 .08
❑ 169 Mike Sirotka .25 .08
❑ 170 Bill Haselman .25 .08
❑ 171 Javier Vazquez .40 .15
❑ 172 Sidney Ponson .25 .08
❑ 173 Adam Everett .25 .08
❑ 174 Bubba Trammell .25 .08
❑ 175 Robb Nen .40 .15
❑ 176 Barry Larkin .60 .25
❑ 177 Tony Graffanino .25 .08
❑ 178 Rich Garces .25 .08
❑ 179 Juan Uribe .25 .08
❑ 180 Tom Glavine .60 .25
❑ 181 Eric Karros .40 .15
❑ 182 Michael Cuddyer .25 .08
❑ 183 Wade Miller .25 .08
❑ 184 Matt Williams .40 .15
❑ 185 Matt Morris .40 .15
❑ 186 Rickey Henderson 1.00 .40
❑ 187 Trevor Hoffman .40 .15
❑ 188 Wilson Betemit .25 .08
❑ 189 Steve Karsay .25 .08
❑ 190 Frank Catalanotto .25 .08
❑ 191 Jason Schmidt .40 .15
❑ 192 Roger Cedeno .25 .08
❑ 193 Magglio Ordonez .40 .15
❑ 194 Pat Hentgen .25 .08
❑ 195 Mike Lieberthal .40 .15
❑ 196 Andy Pettitte .60 .25
❑ 197 Jay Gibbons .25 .08
❑ 198 Rolando Arrojo .25 .08
❑ 199 Joe Mays .25 .08
❑ 200 Aubrey Huff .40 .15
❑ 201 Nelson Figueroa .25 .08
❑ 202 Paul Konerko .40 .15
❑ 203 Ken Griffey Jr. 1.50 .60
❑ 204 Brandon Duckworth .25 .08
❑ 205 Sammy Sosa 1.00 .40
❑ 206 Carl Everett .40 .15
❑ 207 Scott Rolen .60 .25
❑ 208 Orlando Hernandez .40 .15
❑ 209 Todd Helton .60 .25
❑ 210 Preston Wilson .40 .15
❑ 211 Gil Meche .25 .08
❑ 212 Bill Mueller .40 .15
❑ 213 Craig Biggio .60 .25
❑ 214 Dean Palmer .40 .15
❑ 215 Randy Wolf .25 .08
❑ 216 Jeff Suppan .25 .08
❑ 217 Jimmy Rollins .40 .15
❑ 218 Alexis Gomez .25 .08
❑ 219 Ellis Burks .40 .15
❑ 220 Ramon E. Martinez .25 .08
❑ 221 Ramiro Mendoza .25 .08
❑ 222 Einar Diaz .25 .08
❑ 223 Brent Abernathy .25 .08
❑ 224 Darin Erstad .40 .15
❑ 225 Reggie Taylor .25 .08
❑ 226 Jason Jennings .25 .08
❑ 227 Ray Durham .40 .15
❑ 228 John Parrish .25 .08
❑ 229 Kevin Young .25 .08
❑ 230 Xavier Nady .25 .08
❑ 231 Juan Cruz .25 .08
❑ 232 Greg Norton .25 .08
❑ 233 Barry Bonds 2.50 1.00
❑ 234 Kip Wells .25 .08
❑ 235 Paul LoDuca .40 .15
❑ 236 Javy Lopez .40 .15
❑ 237 Luis Castillo .25 .08
❑ 238 Tom Gordon .25 .08
❑ 239 Mike Mordecai .25 .08
❑ 240 Damian Rolls .25 .08
❑ 241 Julio Lugo .25 .08
❑ 242 Ichiro Suzuki 2.00 .75
❑ 243 Tony Womack .25 .08
❑ 244 Matt Anderson .25 .08
❑ 245 Carlos Lee .40 .15
❑ 246 Alex Rodriguez 1.50 .60
❑ 247 Bernie Williams .60 .25
❑ 248 Scott Sullivan .25 .08
❑ 249 Mike Hampton .40 .15
❑ 250 Orlando Cabrera .40 .15
❑ 251 Benito Santiago .40 .15
❑ 252 Steve Finley .40 .15
❑ 253 Dave Williams .25 .08
❑ 254 Adam Kennedy .25 .08
❑ 255 Omar Vizquel .60 .25
❑ 256 Garrett Stephenson .25 .08
❑ 257 Fernando Tatis .25 .08
❑ 258 Mike Piazza 1.50 .60
❑ 259 Scott Spiezio .25 .08
❑ 260 Jacque Jones .40 .15
❑ 261 Russell Branyan .25 .08
❑ 262 Mark McLemore .25 .08
❑ 263 Mitch Meluskey .25 .08
❑ 264 Marlon Byrd .25 .08
❑ 265 Kyle Farnsworth .25 .08
❑ 266 Billy Sylvester .25 .08
❑ 267 C.C. Sabathia .40 .15
❑ 268 Mark Buehrle .40 .15
❑ 269 Geoff Blum .25 .08
❑ 270 Bret Prinz .25 .08
❑ 271 Placido Polanco .25 .08
❑ 272 John Olerud .40 .15
❑ 273 Pedro Martinez .60 .25
❑ 274 Doug Mientkiewicz .40 .15
❑ 275 Jason Bere .25 .08
❑ 276 Bud Smith .25 .08
❑ 277 Terrence Long .25 .08
❑ 278 Troy Percival .40 .15
❑ 279 Derek Jeter 2.50 1.00
❑ 280 Eric Owens .25 .08
❑ 281 Jay Bell .40 .15
❑ 282 Mike Cameron .25 .08
❑ 283 Joe Randa .40 .15
❑ 284 Brian Roberts .40 .15
❑ 285 Ryan Klesko .40 .15
❑ 286 Ryan Dempster .25 .08
❑ 287 Cristian Guzman .25 .08
❑ 288 Tim Salmon .60 .25
❑ 289 Mark Johnson .25 .08
❑ 290 Brian Giles .40 .15
❑ 291 Jon Lieber .25 .08
❑ 292 Fernando Vina .25 .08
❑ 293 Mike Mussina .60 .25
❑ 294 Juan Pierre .40 .15
❑ 295 Carlos Beltran .40 .15
❑ 296 Vladimir Guerrero 1.00 .40
❑ 297 Orlando Merced .25 .08
❑ 298 Jose Hernandez .25 .08
❑ 299 Mike Lamb .25 .08
❑ 300 David Eckstein .40 .15
❑ 301 Mark Loretta .25 .08
❑ 302 Greg Vaughn .25 .08
❑ 303 Jose Vidro .25 .08
❑ 304 Jose Ortiz .25 .08
❑ 305 Mark Grudzielanek .25 .08
❑ 306 Rob Bell .25 .08
❑ 307 Elmer Dessens .25 .08
❑ 308 Tomas Perez .25 .08
❑ 309 Jerry Hairston Jr. .25 .08
❑ 310 Mike Stanton .25 .08
❑ 311 Todd Walker .25 .08
❑ 312 Jason Varitek 1.00 .40
❑ 313 Masato Yoshii .25 .08
❑ 314 Ben Sheets .40 .15
❑ 315 Roberto Hernandez .25 .08
❑ 316 Eli Marrero .25 .08
❑ 317 Josh Beckett .40 .15
❑ 318 Robert Fick .25 .08
❑ 319 Aramis Ramirez .40 .15
❑ 320 Bartolo Colon .40 .15
❑ 321 Kenny Kelly .25 .08
❑ 322 Luis Gonzalez .40 .15
❑ 323 John Smoltz .60 .25
❑ 324 Homer Bush .25 .08
❑ 325 Kevin Millwood .40 .15
❑ 326 Manny Ramirez .60 .25
❑ 327 Armando Benitez .25 .08
❑ 328 Luis Alicea .25 .08
❑ 329 Mark Kotsay .40 .15
❑ 330 Felix Rodriguez .25 .08
❑ 331 Eddie Taubensee .25 .08
❑ 332 John Burkett .25 .08
❑ 333 Ramon Ortiz .25 .08
❑ 334 Daryle Ward .25 .08
❑ 335 Jarrod Washburn .25 .08
❑ 336 Benji Gil .25 .08
❑ 337 Mike Lowell .40 .15
❑ 338 Larry Walker .40 .15
❑ 339 Andruw Jones .60 .25
❑ 340 Scott Elarton .25 .08
❑ 341 Tony McKnight .25 .08
❑ 342 Frank Thomas 1.00 .40
❑ 343 Kevin Brown .40 .15
❑ 344 Jermaine Dye .40 .15
❑ 345 Luis Rivas .25 .08
❑ 346 Jeff Conine .40 .15
❑ 347 Bobby Kielty .25 .08
❑ 348 Jeffrey Hammonds .25 .08
❑ 349 Keith Foulke .40 .15
❑ 350 Dave Martinez .25 .08
❑ 351 Adam Eaton .25 .08
❑ 352 Brandon Inge .25 .08
❑ 353 Tyler Houston .25 .08
❑ 354 Bobby Abreu .40 .15
❑ 355 Ivan Rodriguez .60 .25
❑ 356 Doug Glanville .25 .08
❑ 357 Jorge Julio .25 .08
❑ 358 Kerry Wood .40 .15
❑ 359 Eric Munson .25 .08
❑ 360 Joe Crede .40 .15
❑ 361 Denny Neagle .25 .08
❑ 362 Vance Wilson .25 .08
❑ 363 Neifi Perez .25 .08
❑ 364 Darryl Kile .40 .15
❑ 365 Jose Macias .25 .08
❑ 366 Michael Coleman .25 .08
❑ 367 Erubiel Durazo .25 .08
❑ 368 Darrin Fletcher .25 .08
❑ 369 Matt White .25 .08
❑ 370 Marvin Benard .25 .08
❑ 371 Brad Penny .25 .08
❑ 372 Chuck Finley .40 .15
❑ 373 Delino DeShields .25 .08
❑ 374 Adrian Brown .25 .08
❑ 375 Corey Koskie .25 .08
❑ 376 Kazuhiro Sasaki .40 .15
❑ 377 Brent Butler .25 .08
❑ 378 Paul Wilson .25 .08
❑ 379 Scott Williamson .25 .08
❑ 380 Mike Young 1.00 .40

❑ 381	Toby Hall	.25	.08
❑ 382	Shane Reynolds	.25	.08
❑ 383	Tom Goodwin	.25	.08
❑ 384	Seth Etherton	.25	.08
❑ 385	Billy Wagner	.40	.15
❑ 386	Josh Phelps	.25	.08
❑ 387	Kyle Lohse	.25	.08
❑ 388	Jeremy Fikac	.25	.08
❑ 389	Jorge Posada	.60	.25
❑ 390	Bret Boone	.40	.15
❑ 391	Angel Berroa	.25	.08
❑ 392	Matt Mantei	.25	.08
❑ 393	Alex Gonzalez	.25	.08
❑ 394	Scott Strickland	.25	.08
❑ 395	Charles Johnson	.40	.15
❑ 396	Ramon Hernandez	.25	.08
❑ 397	Damian Jackson	.25	.08
❑ 398	Albert Pujols	2.00	.75
❑ 399	Gary Bennett	.25	.08
❑ 400	Edgar Martinez	.60	.25
❑ 401	Carl Pavano	.40	.15
❑ 402	Chris Gomez	.25	.08
❑ 403	Jaret Wright	.25	.08
❑ 404	Lance Berkman	.40	.15
❑ 405	Robert Person	.25	.08
❑ 406	Brook Fordyce	.25	.08
❑ 407	Adam Pettyjohn	.25	.08
❑ 408	Chris Carpenter	.40	.15
❑ 409	Rey Ordonez	.25	.08
❑ 410	Eric Gagne	.40	.15
❑ 411	Damion Easley	.25	.08
❑ 412	A.J. Burnett	.40	.15
❑ 413	Aaron Boone	.40	.15
❑ 414	J.D. Drew	.40	.15
❑ 415	Kelly Stinnett	.25	.08
❑ 416	Mark Quinn	.25	.08
❑ 417	Brad Radke	.40	.15
❑ 418	Jose Cruz Jr.	.25	.08
❑ 419	Greg Maddux	1.50	.60
❑ 420	Steve Cox	.25	.08
❑ 421	Torii Hunter	.40	.15
❑ 422	Sandy Alomar Jr.	.25	.08
❑ 423	Barry Zito	.40	.15
❑ 424	Bill Hall	.40	.15
❑ 425	Marquis Grissom	.40	.15
❑ 426	Rich Aurilia	.25	.08
❑ 427	Royce Clayton	.25	.08
❑ 428	Travis Fryman	.40	.15
❑ 429	Pablo Ozuna	.25	.08
❑ 430	David Dellucci	.25	.08
❑ 431	Vernon Wells	.40	.15
❑ 432	Gregg Zaun CP	.25	.08
❑ 433	Alex Gonzalez CP	.25	.08
❑ 434	Hideo Nomo CP	1.00	.40
❑ 435	Jeromy Burnitz CP	.40	.15
❑ 436	Gary Sheffield CP	.40	.15
❑ 437	Tino Martinez CP	.60	.25
❑ 438	Tsuyoshi Shinjo CP	.40	.15
❑ 439	Chan Ho Park CP	.40	.15
❑ 440	Tony Clark CP	.25	.08
❑ 441	Brad Fullmer CP	.25	.08
❑ 442	Jason Giambi CP	.25	.08
❑ 443	Billy Koch CP	.25	.08
❑ 444	Mo Vaughn CP	.40	.15
❑ 445	Alex Ochoa CP	.25	.08
❑ 446	Darren Lewis CP	.25	.08
❑ 447	John Rocker CP	.40	.15
❑ 448	Scott Hatteberg CP	.25	.08
❑ 449	Brady Anderson CP	.40	.15
❑ 450	Chuck Knoblauch CP	.40	.15
❑ 451	Pokey Reese CP	.25	.08
❑ 452	Brian Jordan CP	.40	.15
❑ 453	Albie Lopez CP	.25	.08
❑ 454	David Bell CP	.25	.08
❑ 455	Juan Gonzalez CP	.40	.15
❑ 456	Terry Adams CP	.25	.08
❑ 457	Kenny Lofton CP	.40	.15
❑ 458	Shawn Estes CP	.25	.08
❑ 459	Josh Fogg CP	.25	.08
❑ 460	Dmitri Young CP	.40	.15
❑ 461	Johnny Damon Sox CP	.60	.25
❑ 462	Chris Singleton CP	.25	.08
❑ 463	Ricky Ledee CP	.25	.08
❑ 464	Dustin Hermanson CP	.25	.08
❑ 465	Aaron Sele CP	.25	.08
❑ 466	Chris Stynes CP	.25	.08
❑ 467	Matt Stairs CP	.25	.08
❑ 468	Kevin Appier CP	.40	.15
❑ 469	Omar Daal CP	.25	.08
❑ 470	Moises Alou CP	.40	.15
❑ 471	Juan Encarnacion CP	.25	.08
❑ 472	Robin Ventura CP	.40	.15
❑ 473	Eric Hinske CP	.25	.08
❑ 474	Rondell White CP	.40	.15
❑ 475	Carlos Pena CP	.25	.08
❑ 476	Craig Paquette CP	.25	.08
❑ 477	Marty Cordova CP	.25	.08
❑ 478	Brett Tomko CP	.25	.08
❑ 479	Reggie Sanders CP	.25	.08
❑ 480	Roberto Alomar CP	.60	.25
❑ 481	Jeff Cirillo CP	.25	.08
❑ 482	Todd Zeile CP	.40	.15
❑ 483	John Vander Wal CP	.25	.08
❑ 484	Rick Helling CP	.25	.08
❑ 485	Jeff D'Amico CP	.25	.08
❑ 486	David Justice CP	.40	.15
❑ 487	Jason Isringhausen CP	.40	.15
❑ 488	Shigetoshi Hasegawa CP	.40	.15
❑ 489	Eric Young CP	.25	.08
❑ 490	David Wells CP	.40	.15
❑ 491	Ruben Sierra CP	.25	.08
❑ 492	Aaron Cook FF RC	.75	.30
❑ 493	Takahito Nomura FF RC	.75	.30
❑ 494	Austin Kearns FF	.50	.20
❑ 495	Kazuhisa Ishii FF RC	1.25	.50
❑ 496	Mark Teixeira FF	2.00	.75
❑ 497	Rene Reyes FF RC	.75	.30
❑ 498	Tim Spooneybarger FF	.50	.20
❑ 499	Ben Broussard FF	.50	.20
❑ 500	Eric Cyr FF	.50	.20
❑ 501	Anastacio Martinez FF RC	.75	.30
❑ 502	Morgan Ensberg FF	.75	.30
❑ 503	Steve Kent FF RC	.75	.30
❑ 504	Franklin Nunez FF RC	.75	.30
❑ 505	Adam Walker FF RC	.75	.30
❑ 506	Anderson Machado FF RC	.75	.30
❑ 507	Ryan Drese FF	.50	.20
❑ 508	Luis Ugueto FF RC	.75	.30
❑ 509	Jorge Nunez FF RC	.75	.30
❑ 510	Colby Lewis FF	.50	.20
❑ 511	Ron Calloway FF RC	.75	.30
❑ 512	Hansel Izquierdo FF RC	.75	.30
❑ 513	Jason Lane FF	.75	.30
❑ 514	Rafael Soriano FF	.50	.20
❑ 515	Jackson Melian FF	.50	.20
❑ 516	Edwin Almonte FF RC	.75	.30
❑ 517	Satoru Komiyama FF RC	.75	.30
❑ 518	Corey Thurman FF RC	.75	.30
❑ 519	Jorge De La Rosa FF RC	.75	.30
❑ 520	Victor Martinez FF	2.00	.75
❑ 521	Dewon Brazelton FF	.50	.20
❑ 522	Marlon Byrd FF	.50	.20
❑ 523	Jae Seo FF	.50	.20
❑ 524	Orlando Hudson FF	.50	.20
❑ 525	Sean Burroughs FF	.50	.20
❑ 526	Ryan Langerhans FF	.75	.30
❑ 527	David Kelton FF	.50	.20
❑ 528	So Taguchi FF RC	1.25	.50
❑ 529	Tyler Walker FF	.50	.20
❑ 530	Hank Blalock FF	1.25	.50
❑ 531	Mark Prior FF	1.25	.50
❑ 532	Yankee Stadium CL	.40	.15
❑ 533	Fenway Park CL	.40	.15
❑ 534	Wrigley Field CL	.40	.15
❑ 535	Dodger Stadium CL	.40	.15
❑ 536	Camden Yards CL	.40	.15
❑ 537	PacBell Park CL	.25	.08
❑ 538	Jacobs Field CL	.25	.08
❑ 539	SAFECO Field CL	.25	.08
❑ 540	Miller Field CL	.25	.08
❑ P279	Derek Jeter Promo		

2006 Fleer

❑	Alay Soler RC		
❑	COMP.FACT.SET (430)	50.00	20.00
❑	COMPLETE SET (400)	40.00	15.00
❑	COMMON CARD (1-400)	.40	.15
❑	COMMON ROOKIE	.50	.20
❑	COMMON ROOKIE (401-430)	.60	.25
❑	401-430 AVAIL. IN FLEER FACT.SET		
❑ 1	Adam Kennedy	.40	.15
❑ 2	Bartolo Colon	.40	.15
❑ 3	Bengie Molina	.40	.15
❑ 4	Chone Figgins	.40	.15
❑ 5	Dallas McPherson	.40	.15
❑ 6	Darin Erstad	.40	.15
❑ 7	Francisco Rodriguez	.40	.15
❑ 8	Garret Anderson	.40	.15
❑ 9	Jarrod Washburn	.40	.15
❑ 10	John Lackey	.40	.15
❑ 11	Orlando Cabrera	.40	.15
❑ 12	Ryan Theriot RC	.50	.20
❑ 13	Steve Finley	.40	.15
❑ 14	Vladimir Guerrero	1.00	.40
❑ 15	Adam Everett	.40	.15
❑ 16	Andy Pettitte	.40	.15
❑ 17	Charlton Jimerson (RC)	.50	.20
❑ 18	Brad Lidge	.40	.15
❑ 19	Chris Burke	.40	.15
❑ 20	Craig Biggio	.60	.25
❑ 21	Jason Lane	.40	.15
❑ 22	Jeff Bagwell	.60	.25
❑ 23	Lance Berkman	.40	.15
❑ 24	Morgan Ensberg	.40	.15
❑ 25	Roger Clemens	2.00	.75
❑ 26	Roy Oswalt	.40	.15
❑ 27	Willy Taveras	.40	.15
❑ 28	Barry Zito	.40	.15
❑ 29	Bobby Crosby	.40	.15
❑ 30	Bobby Kielty	.40	.15
❑ 31	Dan Johnson	.40	.15
❑ 32	Danny Haren	.40	.15
❑ 33	Eric Chavez	.40	.15
❑ 34	Huston Street	.40	.15
❑ 35	Jason Kendall	.40	.15
❑ 36	Jay Payton	.40	.15
❑ 37	Joe Blanton	.40	.15
❑ 38	Mark Kotsay	.40	.15
❑ 39	Nick Swisher	.40	.15
❑ 40	Rich Harden	.40	.15
❑ 41	Ron Flores RC	.50	.20
❑ 42	Alex Rios	.40	.15
❑ 43	John-Ford Griffin (RC)	.50	.20
❑ 44	Dave Bush	.40	.15
❑ 45	Eric Hinske	.40	.15
❑ 46	Frank Catalanotto	.40	.15
❑ 47	Gustavo Chacin	.40	.15
❑ 48	Josh Towers	.40	.15
❑ 49	Miguel Batista	.40	.15
❑ 50	Orlando Hudson	.40	.15
❑ 51	Roy Halladay	.40	.15
❑ 52	Shea Hillenbrand	.40	.15
❑ 53	Shaun Marcum (RC)	.50	.20
❑ 54	Vernon Wells	.40	.15
❑ 55	Adam LaRoche	.40	.15
❑ 56	Andruw Jones	.60	.25
❑ 57	Chipper Jones	1.00	.40
❑ 58	Anthony Lerew (RC)	.50	.20
❑ 59	Jeff Francoeur	1.00	.40
❑ 60	John Smoltz	.60	.25
❑ 61	Johnny Estrada	.40	.15
❑ 62	Julio Franco	.40	.15
❑ 63	Joey Devine RC	.50	.20
❑ 64	Marcus Giles	.40	.15
❑ 65	Mike Hampton	.40	.15
❑ 66	Rafael Furcal	.40	.15
❑ 67	Chuck James (RC)	.75	.30
❑ 68	Tim Hudson	.40	.15
❑ 69	Ben Sheets	.40	.15
❑ 70	Bill Hall	.40	.15

❑ 71 Brady Clark .40 .15
❑ 72 Carlos Lee .40 .15
❑ 73 Chris Capuano .40 .15
❑ 74 Nelson Cruz (RC) .50 .20
❑ 75 Derrick Turnbow .40 .15
❑ 76 Doug Davis .40 .15
❑ 77 Geoff Jenkins .40 .15
❑ 78 J.J. Hardy .40 .15
❑ 79 Lyle Overbay .40 .15
❑ 80 Prince Fielder 1.50 .60
❑ 81 Rickie Weeks .40 .15
❑ 82 Albert Pujols 2.00 .75
❑ 83 Chris Carpenter .40 .15
❑ 84 David Eckstein .40 .15
❑ 85 Jason Isringhausen .40 .15
❑ 86 Tyler Johnson (RC) .50 .20
❑ 87 Adam Wainwright (RC) .50 .20
❑ 88 Jim Edmonds .60 .25
❑ 89 Chris Duncan (RC) .50 .20
❑ 90 Mark Grudzielanek .40 .15
❑ 91 Mark Mulder .40 .15
❑ 92 Matt Morris .40 .15
❑ 93 Reggie Sanders .40 .15
❑ 94 Scott Rolen .60 .25
❑ 95 Yadier Molina .40 .15
❑ 96 Aramis Ramirez .40 .15
❑ 97 Carlos Zambrano .40 .15
❑ 98 Corey Patterson .40 .15
❑ 99 Derrek Lee .40 .15
❑ 100 Glendon Rusch .40 .15
❑ 101 Greg Maddux 1.50 .60
❑ 102 Jeromy Burnitz .40 .15
❑ 103 Kerry Wood .40 .15
❑ 104 Mark Prior .60 .25
❑ 105 Michael Barrett .40 .15
❑ 106 Geovany Soto (RC) .50 .20
❑ 107 Nomar Garciaparra 1.00 .40
❑ 108 Ryan Dempster .40 .15
❑ 109 Todd Walker .40 .15
❑ 110 Alex S. Gonzalez .40 .15
❑ 111 Aubrey Huff .40 .15
❑ 112 Victor Diaz .40 .15
❑ 113 Carl Crawford .40 .15
❑ 114 Danys Baez .40 .15
❑ 115 Joey Gathright .40 .15
❑ 116 Jonny Gomes .40 .15
❑ 117 Jorge Cantu .40 .15
❑ 118 Julio Lugo .40 .15
❑ 119 Rocco Baldelli .40 .15
❑ 120 Scott Kazmir .60 .25
❑ 121 Toby Hall .40 .15
❑ 122 Tim Corcoran RC .50 .20
❑ 123 Alex Cintron .40 .15
❑ 124 Brandon Webb .40 .15
❑ 125 Chad Tracy .40 .15
❑ 126 Dustin Nippert (RC) .50 .20
❑ 127 Claudio Vargas .40 .15
❑ 128 Craig Counsell .40 .15
❑ 129 Javier Vazquez .40 .15
❑ 130 Jose Valverde .40 .15
❑ 131 Luis Gonzalez .40 .15
❑ 132 Royce Clayton .40 .15
❑ 133 Russ Ortiz .40 .15
❑ 134 Shawn Green .40 .15
❑ 135 Tony Clark .40 .15
❑ 136 Troy Glaus .40 .15
❑ 137 Brad Penny .40 .15
❑ 138 Cesar Izturis .40 .15
❑ 139 Derek Lowe .40 .15
❑ 140 Eric Gagne .40 .15
❑ 141 Hee Seop Choi .40 .15
❑ 142 J.D. Drew .40 .15
❑ 143 Jason Phillips .40 .15
❑ 144 Jayson Werth .40 .15
❑ 145 Jeff Kent .40 .15
❑ 146 Jeff Weaver .40 .15
❑ 147 Milton Bradley .40 .15
❑ 148 Odalis Perez .40 .15
❑ 149 Hong-Chih Kuo (RC) 1.25 .50
❑ 150 Brian Myrow RC .50 .20
❑ 151 Armando Benitez .40 .15
❑ 152 Edgardo Alfonzo .40 .15
❑ 153 J.T. Snow .40 .15
❑ 154 Jason Schmidt .40 .15
❑ 155 Lance Niekro .40 .15
❑ 156 Doug Clark (RC) .50 .20
❑ 157 Dan Ortmeier (RC) .50 .20
❑ 158 Moises Alou .40 .15
❑ 159 Noah Lowry .40 .15
❑ 160 Omar Vizquel .60 .25
❑ 161 Pedro Feliz .40 .15
❑ 162 Randy Winn .40 .15
❑ 163 Jeremy Accardo RC .50 .20
❑ 164 Aaron Boone .40 .15
❑ 165 Ryan Garko (RC) .50 .20
❑ 166 C.C. Sabathia .40 .15
❑ 167 Casey Blake .40 .15
❑ 168 Cliff Lee .40 .15
❑ 169 Coco Crisp .40 .15
❑ 170 Grady Sizemore .60 .25
❑ 171 Jake Westbrook .40 .15
❑ 172 Jhonny Peralta .40 .15
❑ 173 Kevin Millwood .40 .15
❑ 174 Scott Elarton .40 .15
❑ 175 Travis Hafner .40 .15
❑ 176 Victor Martinez .40 .15
❑ 177 Adrian Beltre .40 .15
❑ 178 Eddie Guardado .40 .15
❑ 179 Felix Hernandez .60 .25
❑ 180 Gil Meche .40 .15
❑ 181 Ichiro Suzuki 1.50 .60
❑ 182 Jamie Moyer .40 .15
❑ 183 Jeremy Reed .40 .15
❑ 184 Jaime Bubela (RC) .40 .15
❑ 185 Raul Ibanez .40 .15
❑ 186 Richie Sexson .40 .15
❑ 187 Ryan Franklin .40 .15
❑ 188 Jeff Harris RC .40 .15
❑ 189 A.J. Burnett .40 .15
❑ 190 Josh Wilson (RC) .50 .20
❑ 191 Josh Johnson (RC) .75 .30
❑ 192 Carlos Delgado .40 .15
❑ 193 Dontrelle Willis .40 .15
❑ 194 Bernie Castro (RC) .50 .20
❑ 195 Josh Beckett .40 .15
❑ 196 Juan Encarnacion .40 .15
❑ 197 Juan Pierre .40 .15
❑ 198 Robert Andino RC .50 .20
❑ 199 Miguel Cabrera .60 .25
❑ 200 Ryan Jorgensen RC .50 .20
❑ 201 Paul Lo Duca .40 .15
❑ 202 Todd Jones .40 .15
❑ 203 Braden Looper .40 .15
❑ 204 Carlos Beltran .40 .15
❑ 205 Cliff Floyd .40 .15
❑ 206 David Wright 1.50 .60
❑ 207 Doug Mientkiewicz .40 .15
❑ 208 Jae Seo .40 .15
❑ 209 Jose Reyes .40 .15
❑ 210 Anderson Hernandez (RC) .50 .20
❑ 211 Miguel Cairo .40 .15
❑ 212 Mike Cameron .40 .15
❑ 213 Mike Piazza 1.00 .40
❑ 214 Pedro Martinez .60 .25
❑ 215 Tom Glavine .60 .25
❑ 216 Tim Hamulack (RC) .40 .15
❑ 217 Brad Wilkerson .40 .15
❑ 218 Darrell Rasner (RC) .40 .15
❑ 219 Chad Cordero .40 .15
❑ 220 Cristian Guzman .40 .15
❑ 221 Jason Bergmann RC .50 .20
❑ 222 John Patterson .40 .15
❑ 223 Jose Guillen .40 .15
❑ 224 Jose Vidro .40 .15
❑ 225 Livan Hernandez .40 .15
❑ 226 Nick Johnson .40 .15
❑ 227 Preston Wilson .40 .15
❑ 228 Ryan Zimmerman (RC) 3.00 1.25
❑ 229 Vinny Castilla .40 .15
❑ 230 B.J. Ryan .40 .15
❑ 231 B.J. Surhoff .40 .15
❑ 232 Brian Roberts .40 .15
❑ 233 Walter Young (RC) .50 .20
❑ 234 Daniel Cabrera .40 .15
❑ 235 Erik Bedard .40 .15
❑ 236 Javy Lopez .40 .15
❑ 237 Jay Gibbons .40 .15
❑ 238 Luis Matos .40 .15
❑ 239 Melvin Mora .40 .15
❑ 240 Miguel Tejada .40 .15
❑ 241 Rafael Palmeiro .60 .25
❑ 242 Alejandro Freire RC .40 .15
❑ 243 Sammy Sosa 1.00 .40
❑ 244 Adam Eaton .40 .15
❑ 245 Brian Giles .40 .15
❑ 246 Brian Lawrence .40 .15
❑ 247 Dave Roberts .40 .15
❑ 248 Jake Peavy .40 .15
❑ 249 Khalil Greene .60 .25
❑ 250 Mark Loretta .40 .15
❑ 251 Ramon Hernandez .40 .15
❑ 252 Ryan Klesko .40 .15
❑ 253 Trevor Hoffman .40 .15
❑ 254 Woody Williams .40 .15
❑ 255 Craig Breslow RC .50 .20
❑ 256 Billy Wagner .40 .15
❑ 257 Bobby Abreu .40 .15
❑ 258 Brett Myers .40 .15
❑ 259 Chase Utley 1.00 .40
❑ 260 David Bell .40 .15
❑ 261 Jim Thome .60 .25
❑ 262 Jimmy Rollins .40 .15
❑ 263 Jon Lieber .40 .15
❑ 264 Danny Sandoval RC .50 .20
❑ 265 Mike Lieberthal .40 .15
❑ 266 Pat Burrell .40 .15
❑ 267 Randy Wolf .40 .15
❑ 268 Ryan Howard 1.50 .60
❑ 269 J.J. Furmaniak (RC) .50 .20
❑ 270 Ronny Paulino (RC) .50 .20
❑ 271 Craig Wilson .40 .15
❑ 272 Bryan Bullington (RC) .50 .20
❑ 273 Jack Wilson .40 .15
❑ 274 Jason Bay .40 .15
❑ 275 Matt Capps (RC) .50 .20
❑ 276 Oliver Perez .40 .15
❑ 277 Rob Mackowiak .40 .15
❑ 278 Tom Gorzelanny (RC) .50 .20
❑ 279 Zach Duke .40 .15
❑ 280 Alfonso Soriano .40 .15
❑ 281 Chris R. Young .40 .15
❑ 282 David Dellucci .40 .15
❑ 283 Francisco Cordero .40 .15
❑ 284 Jason Botts (RC) UER .50 .20
❑ 285 Hank Blalock .40 .15
❑ 286 Josh Rupe (RC) .50 .20
❑ 287 Kevin Mench .40 .15
❑ 288 Laynce Nix .40 .15
❑ 289 Mark Teixeira .60 .25
❑ 290 Michael Young .40 .15
❑ 291 Richard Hidalgo .40 .15
❑ 292 Scott Feldman RC .50 .20
❑ 293 Bill Mueller .40 .15
❑ 294 Hanley Ramirez (RC) 1.25 .50
❑ 295 Curt Schilling .60 .25
❑ 296 David Ortiz 1.00 .40
❑ 297 Alejandro Machado (RC) .50 .20
❑ 298 Edgar Renteria .40 .15
❑ 299 Jason Varitek 1.00 .40
❑ 300 Johnny Damon .60 .25
❑ 301 Keith Foulke .40 .15
❑ 302 Manny Ramirez .60 .25
❑ 303 Matt Clement .40 .15
❑ 304 Craig Hansen RC 2.00 .75
❑ 305 Tim Wakefield .40 .15
❑ 306 Trot Nixon .40 .15
❑ 307 Aaron Harang .40 .15
❑ 308 Adam Dunn .40 .15
❑ 309 Austin Kearns .40 .15
❑ 310 Brandon Claussen .40 .15
❑ 311 Chris Booker (RC) .50 .20
❑ 312 Edwin Encarnacion .40 .15
❑ 313 Chris Denorfia (RC) .50 .20
❑ 314 Felipe Lopez .40 .15
❑ 315 Miguel Perez (RC) .50 .20
❑ 316 Ken Griffey Jr. 1.50 .60
❑ 317 Ryan Freel .40 .15
❑ 318 Sean Casey .40 .15
❑ 319 Wily Mo Pena .40 .15
❑ 320 Mike Esposito (RC) .50 .20
❑ 321 Aaron Miles .40 .15
❑ 322 Brad Hawpe .40 .15
❑ 323 Brian Fuentes .40 .15
❑ 324 Clint Barmes .40 .15
❑ 325 Cory Sullivan .40 .15
❑ 326 Garrett Atkins .40 .15
❑ 327 J.D. Closser .40 .15
❑ 328 Jeff Francis .40 .15

❑ 329 Luis Gonzalez	.40	.15
❑ 330 Matt Holliday	.40	.15
❑ 331 Todd Helton	.60	.25
❑ 332 Angel Berroa	.40	.15
❑ 333 David DeJesus	.40	.15
❑ 334 Emil Brown	.40	.15
❑ 335 Jeremy Affeldt	.40	.15
❑ 336 Chris Demaria RC	.50	.20
❑ 337 Mark Teahen	.40	.15
❑ 338 Matt Stairs	.40	.15
❑ 339 Steve Stemle RC	.50	.20
❑ 340 Mike Sweeney	.40	.15
❑ 341 Runelvys Hernandez	.40	.15
❑ 342 Jonah Bayliss RC	.50	.20
❑ 343 Zack Greinke	.40	.15
❑ 344 Brandon Inge	.40	.15
❑ 345 Carlos Guillen	.40	.15
❑ 346 Carlos Pena	.40	.15
❑ 347 Chris Shelton	.40	.15
❑ 348 Craig Monroe	.40	.15
❑ 349 Dmitri Young	.40	.15
❑ 350 Ivan Rodriguez	.60	.25
❑ 351 Jeremy Bonderman	.40	.15
❑ 352 Magglio Ordonez	.40	.15
❑ 353 Mark Woodyard (RC)	.50	.20
❑ 354 Omar Infante	.40	.15
❑ 355 Placido Polanco	.40	.15
❑ 356 Rondell White	.40	.15
❑ 357 Brad Radke	.40	.15
❑ 358 Carlos Silva	.40	.15
❑ 359 Jacque Jones	.40	.15
❑ 360 Joe Mauer	.60	.25
❑ 361 Chris Heintz RC	.50	.20
❑ 362 Joe Nathan	.40	.15
❑ 363 Johan Santana	.60	.25
❑ 364 Justin Morneau	.40	.15
❑ 365 Francisco Liriano (RC)	2.50	1.00
❑ 366 Travis Bowyer (RC)	.50	.20
❑ 367 Michael Cuddyer	.40	.15
❑ 368 Scott Baker	.40	.15
❑ 369 Shannon Stewart	.40	.15
❑ 370 Torii Hunter	.40	.15
❑ 371 A.J. Pierzynski	.40	.15
❑ 372 Aaron Rowand	.40	.15
❑ 373 Carl Everett	.40	.15
❑ 374 Dustin Hermanson	.40	.15
❑ 375 Frank Thomas	1.00	.40
❑ 376 Freddy Garcia	.40	.15
❑ 377 Jermaine Dye	.40	.15
❑ 378 Joe Crede	.40	.15
❑ 379 Jon Garland	.40	.15
❑ 380 Jose Contreras	.40	.15
❑ 381 Juan Uribe	.40	.15
❑ 382 Mark Buehrle	.40	.15
❑ 383 Orlando Hernandez	.40	.15
❑ 384 Paul Konerko	.40	.15
❑ 385 Scott Podsednik	.40	.15
❑ 386 Tadahito Iguchi	.40	.15
❑ 387 Alex Rodriguez	1.50	.60
❑ 388 Bernie Williams	.60	.25
❑ 389 Chien-Ming Wang	1.50	.60
❑ 390 Derek Jeter	2.50	1.00
❑ 391 Gary Sheffield	.40	.15
❑ 392 Hideki Matsui	1.50	.60
❑ 393 Jason Giambi	.40	.15
❑ 394 Jorge Posada	.60	.25
❑ 395 Mike Vento (RC)	.50	.20
❑ 396 Mariano Rivera	1.00	.40
❑ 397 Mike Mussina	.60	.25
❑ 398 Randy Johnson	1.00	.40
❑ 399 Robinson Cano	.60	.25
❑ 400 Tino Martinez	.40	.15
❑ 401 Alay Soler RC	.60	.25
❑ 402 Boof Bonser (RC)	.60	.25
❑ 403 Cole Hamels (RC)	1.50	.60
❑ 404 Ian Kinsler (RC)	1.00	.40
❑ 405 Jason Kubel (RC)	.60	.25
❑ 406 Joel Zumaya (RC)	1.50	.60
❑ 407 Jonathan Papelbon (RC)	3.00	1.25
❑ 408 Jered Weaver (RC)	3.00	1.25
❑ 409 Kendry Morales (RC)	1.50	.60
❑ 410 Lastings Milledge (RC)	1.00	.40
❑ 411 Matt Kemp (RC)	1.00	.40
❑ 412 Taylor Buchholz (RC)	1.00	.40
❑ 413 Andre Ethier (RC)	2.50	1.00
❑ 414 Dan Uggla (RC)	1.50	.60
❑ 415 Jeremy Sowers (RC)	.60	.25
❑ 416 Chad Billingsley (RC)	1.00	.40
❑ 417 Josh Barfield (RC)	.60	.25
❑ 418 Matt Cain (RC)	1.00	.40
❑ 419 Fausto Carmona (RC)	.60	.25
❑ 420 Josh Willingham (RC)	.60	.25
❑ 421 Jeremy Hermida (RC)	1.00	.40
❑ 422 Conor Jackson (RC)	1.00	.40
❑ 423 Dave Gassner (RC)	.60	.25
❑ 424 Brian Bannister (RC)	.60	.25
❑ 425 Fernando Nieve (RC)	.60	.25
❑ 426 Justin Verlander (RC)	2.50	1.00
❑ 427 Scott Olsen (RC)	.60	.25
❑ 428 Takashi Saito RC	.60	.25
❑ 429 Willie Eyre (RC)	.60	.25
❑ 430 Travis Ishikawa (RC)	.60	.25

2001 Fleer Showcase

❑ COMP.SET w/o SP's (100)	30.00	12.50
❑ COMMON CARD (1-100)	.50	.20
❑ COMMON CARD (101-115)	5.00	2.00
❑ COMMON CARD (116-125)	8.00	3.00
❑ COMMON CARD (126 -160)	5.00	2.00
❑ 1 Tony Gwynn	1.50	.60
❑ 2 Barry Larkin	.75	.30
❑ 3 Chan Ho Park	.50	.20
❑ 4 Darin Erstad	.50	.20
❑ 5 Rafael Furcal	.50	.20
❑ 6 Roger Cedeno	.50	.20
❑ 7 Timo Perez	.50	.20
❑ 8 Rick Ankiel	.50	.20
❑ 9 Pokey Reese	.50	.20
❑ 10 Jeromy Burnitz	.50	.20
❑ 11 Phil Nevin	.50	.20
❑ 12 Matt Williams	.50	.20
❑ 13 Mike Hampton	.50	.20
❑ 14 Fernando Tatis	.50	.20
❑ 15 Kazuhiro Sasaki	.50	.20
❑ 16 Jim Thome	.75	.30
❑ 17 Geoff Jenkins	.50	.20
❑ 18 Jeff Kent	.50	.20
❑ 19 Tom Glavine	.75	.30
❑ 20 Dean Palmer	.50	.20
❑ 21 Todd Zeile	.50	.20
❑ 22 Edgar Renteria	.50	.20
❑ 23 Andruw Jones	.75	.30
❑ 24 Juan Encarnacion	.50	.20
❑ 25 Robin Ventura	.50	.20
❑ 26 J.D. Drew	.50	.20
❑ 27 Ray Durham	.50	.20
❑ 28 Richard Hidalgo	.50	.20
❑ 29 Eric Chavez	.50	.20
❑ 30 Rafael Palmeiro	.75	.30
❑ 31 Steve Finley	.50	.20
❑ 32 Jeff Weaver	.50	.20
❑ 33 Al Leiter	.50	.20
❑ 34 Jim Edmonds	.50	.20
❑ 35 Garret Anderson	.50	.20
❑ 36 Larry Walker	.50	.20
❑ 37 Jose Vidro	.50	.20
❑ 38 Mike Cameron	.50	.20
❑ 39 Brady Anderson	.50	.20
❑ 40 Mike Lowell	.50	.20
❑ 41 Bernie Williams	.75	.30
❑ 42 Gary Sheffield	.50	.20
❑ 43 John Smoltz	.75	.30
❑ 44 Mike Mussina	.75	.30
❑ 45 Greg Vaughn	.50	.20
❑ 46 Juan Gonzalez	.50	.20
❑ 47 Matt Lawton	.50	.20
❑ 48 Robb Nen	.50	.20
❑ 49 Brad Radke	.50	.20
❑ 50 Edgar Martinez	.75	.30
❑ 51 Mike Bordick	.50	.20
❑ 52 Shawn Green	.50	.20
❑ 53 Carl Everett	.50	.20
❑ 54 Adrian Beltre	.50	.20
❑ 55 Kerry Wood	.50	.20
❑ 56 Kevin Brown	.50	.20
❑ 57 Brian Giles	.50	.20
❑ 58 Greg Maddux	2.00	.75
❑ 59 Preston Wilson	.50	.20
❑ 60 Orlando Hernandez	.50	.20
❑ 61 Ben Grieve	.50	.20
❑ 62 Jermaine Dye	.50	.20
❑ 63 Travis Lee	.50	.20
❑ 64 Jose Cruz Jr.	.50	.20
❑ 65 Rondell White	.50	.20
❑ 66 Carlos Beltran	.50	.20
❑ 67 Scott Rolen	.75	.30
❑ 68 Brad Fullmer	.50	.20
❑ 69 David Wells	.50	.20
❑ 70 Mike Sweeney	.50	.20
❑ 71 Barry Zito	.75	.30
❑ 72 Tony Batista	.50	.20
❑ 73 Curt Schilling	.50	.20
❑ 74 Jeff Cirillo	.50	.20
❑ 75 Edgardo Alfonzo	.50	.20
❑ 76 John Olerud	.50	.20
❑ 77 Carlos Lee	.50	.20
❑ 78 Moises Alou	.50	.20
❑ 79 Tim Hudson	.50	.20
❑ 80 Andres Galarraga	.50	.20
❑ 81 Roberto Alomar	.75	.30
❑ 82 Richie Sexson	.50	.20
❑ 83 Trevor Hoffman	.50	.20
❑ 84 Omar Vizquel	.75	.30
❑ 85 Jacque Jones	.50	.20
❑ 86 J.T. Snow	.50	.20
❑ 87 Sean Casey	.50	.20
❑ 88 Craig Biggio	.75	.30
❑ 89 Mariano Rivera	1.25	.50
❑ 90 Rusty Greer	.50	.20
❑ 91 Barry Bonds	3.00	1.25
❑ 92 Pedro Martinez	.75	.30
❑ 93 Cal Ripken	4.00	1.50
❑ 94 Pat Burrell	.50	.20
❑ 95 Chipper Jones	1.25	.50
❑ 96 Magglio Ordonez	.50	.20
❑ 97 Jeff Bagwell	.75	.30
❑ 98 Randy Johnson	1.25	.50
❑ 99 Frank Thomas	1.25	.50
❑ 100 Jason Kendall	.50	.20
❑ 101 Nomar Garciaparra AC	12.00	5.00
❑ 102 Mark McGwire AC	20.00	8.00
❑ 103 Troy Glaus AC	5.00	2.00
❑ 104 Ivan Rodriguez AC	5.00	2.00
❑ 105 Manny Ramirez Sox AC	5.00	2.00
❑ 106 Derek Jeter AC	20.00	8.00
❑ 107 Alex Rodriguez AC	12.00	5.00
❑ 108 Ken Griffey Jr. AC	12.00	5.00
❑ 109 Todd Helton AC	5.00	2.00
❑ 110 Sammy Sosa AC	8.00	3.00
❑ 111 Vladimir Guerrero AC	8.00	3.00
❑ 112 Mike Piazza AC	12.00	5.00
❑ 113 Roger Clemens AC	15.00	6.00
❑ 114 Jason Giambi AC	5.00	2.00
❑ 115 Carlos Delgado AC	5.00	2.00
❑ 116 Ichiro Suzuki AC RC	125.00	75.00
❑ 117 Morgan Ensberg AC RC	12.00	5.00
❑ 118 Carlos Valderrama AC RC	8.00	3.00
❑ 119 Erick Almonte AC RC	8.00	3.00
❑ 120 Tsuyoshi Shinjo AC RC	12.00	5.00
❑ 121 Albert Pujols AC RC	250.00	150.00
❑ 122 Wilson Betemit AC RC	12.00	5.00
❑ 123 Adrian Hernandez AC RC	8.00	3.00
❑ 124 Jackson Melian AC RC	8.00	3.00
❑ 125 Drew Henson AC RC	12.00	5.00
❑ 126 Paul Phillips RS RC	5.00	2.00
❑ 127 Esix Snead RS RC	5.00	2.00
❑ 128 Ryan Freel RS RC	5.00	2.00
❑ 129 Junior Spivey RS RC	8.00	3.00
❑ 130 Elpidio Guzman RS RC	5.00	2.00
❑ 131 Juan Diaz RS RC	5.00	2.00

❑ 132 Andres Torres RS RC 5.00 2.00
❑ 133 Jay Gibbons RS RC 8.00 3.00
❑ 134 Bill Ortega RS RC 5.00 2.00
❑ 135 Alexis Gomez RS RC 5.00 2.00
❑ 136 Wilkin Ruan RS RC 5.00 2.00
❑ 137 Henry Mateo RS RC 5.00 2.00
❑ 138 Juan Uribe RS RC 8.00 3.00
❑ 139 Johnny Estrada RS RC 8.00 3.00
❑ 140 Jaisen Randolph RS RC 5.00 2.00
❑ 141 Eric Hinske RS RC 8.00 3.00
❑ 142 Jack Wilson RS RC 8.00 3.00
❑ 143 Cody Ransom RS RC 5.00 2.00
❑ 144 Nate Frese RS RC 5.00 2.00
❑ 145 John Grabow RS RC 5.00 2.00
❑ 146 Christian Parker RS RC 5.00 2.00
❑ 147 Brian Lawrence RS RC 5.00 2.00
❑ 148 Brandon Duckworth RS RC 5.00 2.00
❑ 149 Winston Abreu RS RC 5.00 2.00
❑ 150 Horacio Ramirez RS RC 8.00 3.00
❑ 151 Nick Maness RS RC 5.00 2.00
❑ 152 Blaine Neal RS RC 5.00 2.00
❑ 153 Billy Sylvester RS RC 5.00 2.00
❑ 154 David Elder RS RC 5.00 2.00
❑ 155 Bert Snow RS RC 5.00 2.00
❑ 156 Claudio Vargas RS RC 5.00 2.00
❑ 157 Martin Vargas RS RC 5.00 2.00
❑ 158 Grant Balfour RS RC 5.00 2.00
❑ 159 Randy Keisler RS 5.00 2.00
❑ 160 Zach Day RS RC 5.00 2.00
❑ P1 Tony Gwynn Promo 2.00 .75
❑ MM3 Derek Jeter MM/2000 12.00 5.00
❑ NNO Derek Jeter MM AU/100 120.0060.00

2003 Fleer Showcase

❑ COMP.LO SET w/o SP's (105) 25.00 10.00
❑ COMMON CARD (1-95) .50 .20
❑ COMMON CARD (96-105) 1.00 .40
❑ COMMON CARD (106-135) 3.00 1.25
❑ 106-135 ODDS 1:3 HOBBY, 1:12 RETAIL
❑ 106-115 DIST IN JERSEY & RETAIL PACKS
❑ 116-125 DIST IN LEATHER & RETAIL PACKS
❑ 126-135 DIST IN LUMBER & RETAIL PACKS
❑ COMMON CARD (136-145) 4.00 1.50
❑ 1 David Eckstein .50 .20
❑ 2 Curt Schilling .50 .20
❑ 3 Jay Gibbons .50 .20
❑ 4 Kerry Wood .50 .20
❑ 5 Jeff Bagwell .75 .30
❑ 6 Hideo Nomo 1.25 .50
❑ 7 Tim Hudson .50 .20
❑ 8 J.D. Drew .50 .20
❑ 9 Josh Phelps .50 .20
❑ 10 Bartolo Colon .50 .20
❑ 11 Bobby Abreu .50 .20
❑ 12 Matt Morris .50 .20
❑ 13 Kazuhiro Sasaki .50 .20
❑ 14 Sean Burroughs .50 .20
❑ 15 Vicente Padilla .50 .20
❑ 16 Jorge Posada .75 .30
❑ 17 Torii Hunter .50 .20
❑ 18 Richie Sexson .50 .20
❑ 19 Lance Berkman .50 .20
❑ 20 Todd Helton .75 .30
❑ 21 Paul Konerko .50 .20
❑ 22 Pedro Martinez .75 .30
❑ 23 Rodrigo Lopez .50 .20
❑ 24 Gary Sheffield .50 .20
❑ 25 Darin Erstad .50 .20
❑ 26 Nomar Garciaparra 2.00 .75
❑ 27 Adam Dunn .50 .20
❑ 28 Jason Giambi .50 .20
❑ 29 Miguel Tejada .50 .20
❑ 30 Chipper Jones 1.25 .50
❑ 31 Alex Rodriguez 2.00 .75
❑ 32 Barry Bonds 3.00 1.25
❑ 33 Roger Clemens 2.50 1.00
❑ 34 Sammy Sosa 1.25 .50
❑ 35 Randy Johnson 1.25 .50
❑ 36 Tim Salmon .75 .30
❑ 37 Shea Hillenbrand .50 .20
❑ 38 Larry Walker .50 .20
❑ 39 A.J. Burnett .50 .20
❑ 40 Shawn Green .50 .20
❑ 41 Cristian Guzman .50 .20
❑ 42 Bernie Williams .75 .30
❑ 43 Mark Mulder .50 .20
❑ 44 Brian Giles .50 .20
❑ 45 Bret Boone .50 .20
❑ 46 Juan Gonzalez .50 .20
❑ 47 Roy Halladay .50 .20
❑ 48 Wade Miller .50 .20
❑ 49 Jeff Kent .50 .20
❑ 50 Carlos Delgado .50 .20
❑ 51 Mike Lowell .50 .20
❑ 52 Jim Edmonds .50 .20
❑ 53 Ivan Rodriguez .75 .30
❑ 54 Aubrey Huff .50 .20
❑ 55 Ryan Klesko .50 .20
❑ 56 Paul Lo Duca .50 .20
❑ 57 Roy Oswalt .50 .20
❑ 58 Omar Vizquel .75 .30
❑ 59 Manny Ramirez .75 .30
❑ 60 Andruw Jones .75 .30
❑ 61 Troy Glaus .50 .20
❑ 62 Ichiro Suzuki 2.50 1.00
❑ 63 Albert Pujols 2.50 1.00
❑ 64 Derek Jeter 3.00 1.25
❑ 65 Mark Prior .75 .30
❑ 66 Ken Griffey Jr. 2.00 .75
❑ 67 Vladimir Guerrero 1.25 .50
❑ 68 Mike Piazza 2.00 .75
❑ 69 Alfonso Soriano .50 .20
❑ 70 Greg Maddux 2.00 .75
❑ 71 Adam Kennedy .50 .20
❑ 72 Junior Spivey .50 .20
❑ 73 Tom Glavine .75 .30
❑ 74 Derek Lowe .50 .20
❑ 75 Magglio Ordonez .50 .20
❑ 76 Jim Thome .75 .30
❑ 77 Robert Fick .50 .20
❑ 78 Josh Beckett .50 .20
❑ 79 Mike Sweeney .50 .20
❑ 80 Kazuhisa Ishii .50 .20
❑ 81 Roberto Alomar .75 .30
❑ 82 Barry Zito .50 .20
❑ 83 Pat Burrell .50 .20
❑ 84 Scott Rolen .75 .30
❑ 85 John Olerud .50 .20
❑ 86 Eric Hinske .50 .20
❑ 87 Rafael Palmeiro .75 .30
❑ 88 Edgar Martinez .75 .30
❑ 89 Eric Chavez .50 .20
❑ 90 Jose Vidro .50 .20
❑ 91 Craig Biggio .75 .30
❑ 92 Rich Aurilia .50 .20
❑ 93 Austin Kearns .50 .20
❑ 94 Luis Gonzalez .50 .20
❑ 95 Garret Anderson .50 .20
❑ 96 Yogi Berra 2.00 .75
❑ 97 Al Kaline 2.00 .75
❑ 98 Robin Yount 2.00 .75
❑ 99 Reggie Jackson 1.50 .60
❑ 100 Harmon Killebrew 2.00 .75
❑ 101 Eddie Mathews 2.00 .75
❑ 102 Willie McCovey 1.00 .40
❑ 103 Nolan Ryan 4.00 1.50
❑ 104 Mike Schmidt 2.50 1.00
❑ 105 Tom Seaver 1.50 .60
❑ 106 Francisco Rodriguez ST 3.00 1.25
❑ 107 Carl Crawford ST 3.00 1.25
❑ 108 Ben Howard ST 3.00 1.25
❑ 109 Hank Blalock ST 3.00 1.25
❑ 110 Hee Seop Choi ST 3.00 1.25
❑ 111 Kirk Saarloos ST 3.00 1.25
❑ 112 Lew Ford ST RC 5.00 2.00
❑ 113 Andy Van Hekken ST 3.00 1.25
❑ 114 Drew Henson ST 3.00 1.25
❑ 115 Marlon Byrd ST 3.00 1.25
❑ 116 Jayson Werth ST 3.00 1.25
❑ 117 Willie Bloomquist ST 3.00 1.25
❑ 118 Joe Borchard ST 3.00 1.25
❑ 119 Mark Teixeira ST 5.00 2.00
❑ 120 Bobby Hill ST 3.00 1.25
❑ 121 Jason Lane ST 3.00 1.25
❑ 122 Omar Infante ST 3.00 1.25
❑ 123 Victor Martinez ST 5.00 2.00
❑ 124 Jorge Padilla ST 3.00 1.25
❑ 125 John Lackey ST 3.00 1.25
❑ 126 Anderson Machado ST 3.00 1.25
❑ 127 Rodrigo Rosario ST 3.00 1.25
❑ 128 Freddy Sanchez ST 3.00 1.25
❑ 129 Tony Alvarez ST 3.00 1.25
❑ 130 Matt Thornton ST 3.00 1.25
❑ 131 Joe Thurston ST 3.00 1.25
❑ 132 Brett Myers ST 3.00 1.25
❑ 133 Nook Logan ST RC 5.00 2.00
❑ 134 Chris Snelling ST 3.00 1.25
❑ 135 Termel Sledge ST RC 3.00 1.25
❑ 136 Chien-Ming Wang ST RC 30.00 12.50
❑ 137 Rickie Weeks ST RC 8.00 3.00
❑ 138 Brandon Webb ST RC 6.00 2.50
❑ 139 Hideki Matsui ST RC 15.00 6.00
❑ 140 Michael Hessman ST RC 4.00 1.50
❑ 141 Ryan Wagner ST RC 4.00 1.50
❑ 142 Bo Hart ST RC 4.00 1.50
❑ 143 Edwin Jackson ST RC 5.00 2.00
❑ 144 Jose Contreras ST RC 5.00 2.00
❑ 145 Delmon Young ST RC 15.00 6.00

2005 Fleer Showcase

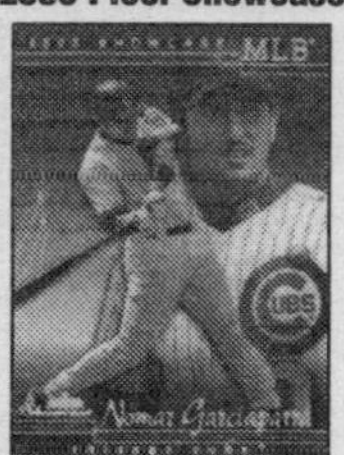

❑ COMP.SET w/o SP's (100) 40.00 15.00
❑ COMMON CARD (1-100) .75 .30
❑ COMP.ST SUBSET (10) 25.00 10.00
❑ COMMON CARD (101-110) 2.00 .75
❑ 101-110 ODDS 1:5 HOBBY, 1:12 RETAIL
❑ COMMON CARD (111-135) 3.00 1.25
❑ 111-135 ODDDS 1:20 HOBBY, 1:48 RETAIL
❑ 1 Albert Pujols 4.00 1.50
❑ 2 Rocco Baldelli .75 .30
❑ 3 Bernie Williams 1.25 .50
❑ 4 Shawn Green .75 .30
❑ 5 Garret Anderson .75 .30
❑ 6 Paul Konerko .75 .30
❑ 7 Mike Sweeney .75 .30
❑ 8 Jim Thome 1.25 .50
❑ 9 Mark Teixeira 1.25 .50
❑ 10 Mark Prior 1.25 .50
❑ 11 Angel Berroa .75 .30
❑ 12 Barry Zito .75 .30
❑ 13 Carlos Delgado .75 .30
❑ 14 Troy Glaus .75 .30
❑ 15 Travis Hafner .75 .30
❑ 16 Lyle Overbay .75 .30
❑ 17 David Ortiz 1.25 .50
❑ 18 Ivan Rodriguez 1.25 .50
❑ 19 Jack Wilson .75 .30
❑ 20 Jason Schmidt .75 .30
❑ 21 Mike Piazza 2.00 .75
❑ 22 David Eckstein .75 .30
❑ 23 Ben Sheets .75 .30
❑ 24 Randy Johnson 2.00 .75
❑ 25 Jacque Jones .75 .30

❑ 26 Jody Gerut .75 .30
❑ 27 Kris Benson .75 .30
❑ 28 Luis Gonzalez .75 .30
❑ 29 Victor Martinez .75 .30
❑ 30 Torii Hunter .75 .30
❑ 31 Gary Sheffield .75 .30
❑ 32 Miguel Tejada .75 .30
❑ 33 Dontrelle Willis .75 .30
❑ 34 Bret Boone .75 .30
❑ 35 Kaz Matsui .75 .30
❑ 36 Shea Hillenbrand .75 .30
❑ 37 Wily Mo Pena .75 .30
❑ 38 Johan Santana 2.00 .75
❑ 39 Derek Jeter 4.00 1.50
❑ 40 Chipper Jones 2.00 .75
❑ 41 Sean Casey .75 .30
❑ 42 Corey Koskie .75 .30
❑ 43 Alex Rodriguez 3.00 1.25
❑ 44 Andruw Jones 1.25 .50
❑ 45 Austin Kearns .75 .30
❑ 46 Jose Vidro .75 .30
❑ 47 Adam Dunn .75 .30
❑ 48 Adrian Beltre .75 .30
❑ 49 Bobby Abreu .75 .30
❑ 50 Michael Young .75 .30
❑ 51 Freddy Garcia .75 .30
❑ 52 Eric Gagne .75 .30
❑ 53 Chase Utley 1.25 .50
❑ 54 Alfonso Soriano .75 .30
❑ 55 Nick Johnson .75 .30
❑ 56 Johnny Estrada .75 .30
❑ 57 Jeff Bagwell 1.25 .50
❑ 58 Randy Winn .75 .30
❑ 59 Roy Halladay .75 .30
❑ 60 J.D. Drew .75 .30
❑ 61 Craig Biggio 1.25 .50
❑ 62 Scott Rolen 1.25 .50
❑ 63 Nomar Garciaparra 2.00 .75
❑ 64 Matt Holliday .75 .30
❑ 65 Billy Wagner .75 .30
❑ 66 Carl Crawford .75 .30
❑ 67 Pedro Martinez 1.25 .50
❑ 68 Jeremy Bonderman .75 .30
❑ 69 Jason Bay .75 .30
❑ 70 A.J. Pierzynski .75 .30
❑ 71 Vladimir Guerrero 2.00 .75
❑ 72 Rickie Weeks .75 .30
❑ 73 Mark Loretta .75 .30
❑ 74 Todd Helton 1.25 .50
❑ 75 Manny Ramirez 1.25 .50
❑ 76 Carlos Guillen .75 .30
❑ 77 Khalil Greene 1.25 .50
❑ 78 Javy Lopez .75 .30
❑ 79 Josh Beckett .75 .30
❑ 80 Ichiro Suzuki 4.00 1.50
❑ 81 Magglio Ordonez .75 .30
❑ 82 Ken Harvey .75 .30
❑ 83 Mark Mulder .75 .30
❑ 84 Hank Blalock .75 .30
❑ 85 Richard Hidalgo .75 .30
❑ 86 Curt Schilling 1.25 .50
❑ 87 Jeromy Burnitz .75 .30
❑ 88 Craig Wilson .75 .30
❑ 89 Aubrey Huff .75 .30
❑ 90 Kerry Wood .75 .30
❑ 91 Andy Pettitte 1.25 .50
❑ 92 Tim Hudson .75 .30
❑ 93 Jim Edmonds .75 .30
❑ 94 Melvin Mora .75 .30
❑ 95 Miguel Cabrera .75 .30
❑ 96 Trevor Hoffman .75 .30
❑ 97 J.T. Snow .75 .30
❑ 98 Sammy Sosa 2.00 .75
❑ 99 Roger Clemens 3.00 1.25
❑ 100 Eric Chavez .75 .30
❑ 101 B.J. Upton ST 3.00 1.25
❑ 102 Gavin Floyd ST 2.00 .75
❑ 103 Casey Kotchman ST 2.00 .75
❑ 104 David Wright ST 10.00 4.00
❑ 105 Dioner Navarro ST 2.00 .75
❑ 106 Scott Kazmir ST 5.00 2.00
❑ 107 Andres Blanco ST 2.00 .75
❑ 108 Joey Gathright ST 2.00 .75
❑ 109 Jon Knott ST 2.00 .75
❑ 110 Charlton Jimerson ST 2.00 .75
❑ 111 Larry Doby SH 3.00 1.25
❑ 112 Reggie Jackson SH 5.00 2.00
❑ 113 Enos Slaughter SH 3.00 1.25
❑ 114 Bill Skowron SH 3.00 1.25
❑ 115 Duke Snider SH 5.00 2.00
❑ 116 Harmon Killebrew SH 8.00 3.00
❑ 117 Willie McCovey SH 5.00 2.00
❑ 118 Rollie Fingers SH 3.00 1.25
❑ 119 Preacher Roe SH 3.00 1.25
❑ 120 Carlton Fisk SH 5.00 2.00
❑ 121 Andre Dawson SH 3.00 1.25
❑ 122 Orlando Cepeda SH 3.00 1.25
❑ 123 Bucky Dent SH 3.00 1.25
❑ 124 Cal Ripken SH 20.00 8.00
❑ 125 Nolan Ryan SH 15.00 6.00
❑ 126 Tony Perez SH 3.00 1.25
❑ 127 Mike Schmidt SH 12.00 5.00
❑ 128 Johnny Bench SH 8.00 3.00
❑ 129 Sparky Anderson SH 3.00 1.25
❑ 130 Ted Williams SH 12.00 5.00
❑ 131 Al Kaline SH 8.00 3.00
❑ 132 Carl Yastrzemski SH 10.00 4.00
❑ 133 Eddie Murray SH 8.00 3.00
❑ 134 Roberto Clemente SH 15.00 6.00
❑ 135 Yogi Berra SH 8.00 3.00

1998 Fleer Tradition Update

❑ COMP.FACT.SET (100) 15.00 6.00
❑ U1 Mark McGwire HL 1.25 .50
❑ U2 Sammy Sosa HL .30 .10
❑ U3 Roger Clemens HL 1.00 .40
❑ U4 Barry Bonds HL 1.50 .60
❑ U5 Kerry Wood HL .25 .08
❑ U6 Paul Molitor HL .20 .07
❑ U7 Ken Griffey Jr. HL .75 .30
❑ U8 Cal Ripken HL 1.50 .60
❑ U9 David Wells HL .20 .07
❑ U10 Alex Rodriguez HL .75 .30
❑ U11 Angel Pena RC .40 .15
❑ U12 Bruce Chen .20 .07
❑ U13 Craig Wilson .20 .07
❑ U14 Orlando Hernandez RC 2.00 .75
❑ U15 Aramis Ramirez .20 .07
❑ U16 Aaron Boone .20 .07
❑ U17 Bob Henley .20 .07
❑ U18 Juan Guzman .20 .07
❑ U19 Darryl Hamilton .20 .07
❑ U20 Jay Payton .20 .07
❑ U21 Jeremy Powell .20 .07
❑ U22 Ben Davis .20 .07
❑ U23 Preston Wilson .20 .07
❑ U24 Jim Parque RC .60 .25
❑ U25 Odalis Perez RC 1.50 .60
❑ U26 Ronnie Belliard .20 .07
❑ U27 Royce Clayton .20 .07
❑ U28 George Lombard .20 .07
❑ U29 Tony Phillips .20 .07
❑ U30 Fernando Seguignol RC .40 .15
❑ U31 Armando Rios RC .60 .25
❑ U32 Jerry Hairston Jr. RC .60 .25
❑ U33 Justin Baughman RC .40 .15
❑ U34 Seth Greisinger .20 .07
❑ U35 Alex Gonzalez .20 .07
❑ U36 Michael Barrett .20 .07
❑ U37 Carlos Beltran 1.00 .40
❑ U38 Ellis Burks .20 .07
❑ U39 Jose Jimenez RC 1.00 .40
❑ U40 Carlos Guillen .20 .07
❑ U41 Marlon Anderson .20 .07
❑ U42 Scott Elarton .20 .07
❑ U43 Glenallen Hill .20 .07
❑ U44 Shane Monahan .20 .07
❑ U45 Dennis Martinez .20 .07
❑ U46 Carlos Febles RC .60 .25
❑ U47 Carlos Perez .20 .07
❑ U48 Wilton Guerrero .20 .07
❑ U49 Randy Johnson .50 .20
❑ U50 Brian Simmons RC .40 .15
❑ U51 Carlton Loewer .20 .07
❑ U52 Mark DeRosa RC 1.00 .40
❑ U53 Tim Young RC .40 .15
❑ U54 Gary Gaetti .20 .07
❑ U55 Eric Chavez .20 .07
❑ U56 Carl Pavano .20 .07
❑ U57 Mike Stanley .20 .07
❑ U58 Todd Stottlemyre .20 .07
❑ U59 Gabe Kapler RC 1.00 .40
❑ U60 Mike Jerzembeck RC .40 .15
❑ U61 Mitch Meluskey RC .60 .25
❑ U62 Bill Pulsipher .20 .07
❑ U63 Derrick Gibson .20 .07
❑ U64 John Rocker RC 1.00 .40
❑ U65 Calvin Pickering .20 .07
❑ U66 Blake Stein .20 .07
❑ U67 Fernando Tatis .20 .07
❑ U68 Gabe Alvarez .20 .07
❑ U69 Jeffrey Hammonds .20 .07
❑ U70 Adrian Beltre .20 .07
❑ U71 Ryan Bradley RC .40 .15
❑ U72 Edgard Clemente .20 .07
❑ U73 Rick Croushore RC .40 .15
❑ U74 Matt Clement .20 .07
❑ U75 Dermal Brown .20 .07
❑ U76 Paul Bako .20 .07
❑ U77 Placido Polanco RC 1.00 .40
❑ U78 Jay Tessmer .20 .07
❑ U79 Jarrod Washburn .20 .07
❑ U80 Kevin Witt .20 .07
❑ U81 Mike Metcalfe .20 .07
❑ U82 Daryle Ward .20 .07
❑ U83 Benj Sampson RC .40 .15
❑ U84 Mike Kinkade RC .40 .15
❑ U85 Randy Winn .20 .07
❑ U86 Jeff Shaw .20 .07
❑ U87 Troy Glaus RC 3.00 1.25
❑ U88 Hideo Nomo .50 .20
❑ U89 Mark Grudzielanek .20 .07
❑ U90 Mike Frank RC .40 .15
❑ U91 Bobby Howry RC .40 .15
❑ U92 Ryan Minor RC .40 .15
❑ U93 Corey Koskie RC 1.00 .40
❑ U94 Matt Anderson RC .40 .15
❑ U95 Joe Carter .20 .07
❑ U96 Paul Konerko .20 .07
❑ U97 Sidney Ponson .20 .07
❑ U98 Jeremy Giambi RC .60 .25
❑ U99 Jeff Kubenka RC .40 .15
❑ U100 J.D. Drew RC 2.00 .75

1999 Fleer Tradition Update

❑ COMP.FACT.SET (150) 25.00 10.00
❑ U1 Rick Ankiel RC .75 .30
❑ U2 Peter Bergeron RC .25 .08
❑ U3 Pat Burrell RC 2.00 .75
❑ U4 Eric Munson RC .40 .15

❑ U5 Alfonso Soriano RC 5.00 2.00
❑ U6 Tim Hudson RC 2.00 .75
❑ U7 Erubiel Durazo RC .40 .15
❑ U8 Chad Hermansen .20 .07
❑ U9 Jeff Zimmerman RC .25 .08
❑ U10 Jesus Pena RC .25 .08
❑ U11 Ramon Hernandez .25 .08
❑ U12 Trent Durrington RC .25 .08
❑ U13 Tony Armas Jr. .20 .07
❑ U14 Mike Fyhrie RC .25 .08
❑ U15 Danny Kolb RC .75 .30
❑ U16 Mike Porzio RC .25 .08
❑ U17 Will Brunson RC .25 .08
❑ U18 Mike Duvall RC .25 .08
❑ U19 Doug Mientkiewicz RC .75 .30
❑ U20 Gabe Molina RC .25 .08
❑ U21 Luis Vizcaino RC .25 .08
❑ U22 Robinson Cancel RC .25 .08
❑ U23 Brett Laxton RC .25 .08
❑ U24 Joe McEwing RC .25 .08
❑ U25 Justin Speier RC .25 .08
❑ U26 Kip Wells RC .40 .15
❑ U27 Armando Almanza RC .25 .08
❑ U28 Joe Davenport RC .25 .08
❑ U29 Yamid Haad RC .25 .08
❑ U30 John Halama .20 .07
❑ U31 Adam Kennedy .20 .07
❑ U32 Micah Bowie RC .25 .08
❑ U33 Gookie Dawkins RC .40 .15
❑ U34 Ryan Rupe RC .25 .08
❑ U35 B.J. Ryan RC 2.00 .75
❑ U36 Chance Sanford RC .25 .08
❑ U37 Anthony Shumaker RC .25 .08
❑ U38 Ryan Glynn RC .25 .08
❑ U39 Roosevelt Brown RC .25 .08
❑ U40 Ben Molina RC .75 .30
❑ U41 Scott Williamson .20 .07
❑ U42 Eric Gagne RC 5.00 2.00
❑ U43 John McDonald RC .25 .08
❑ U44 Scott Sauerbeck RC .25 .08
❑ U45 Mike Venafro RC .25 .08
❑ U46 Edwards Guzman RC .25 .08
❑ U47 Richard Barker RC .25 .08
❑ U48 Braden Looper .20 .07
❑ U49 Chad Meyers RC .25 .08
❑ U50 Scott Strickland RC .25 .08
❑ U51 Billy Koch .20 .07
❑ U52 David Newhan RC .40 .15
❑ U53 David Riske RC .25 .08
❑ U54 Jose Santiago RC .25 .08
❑ U55 Miguel Del Toro RC .25 .08
❑ U56 Orber Moreno RC .25 .08
❑ U57 Dave Roberts RC .75 .30
❑ U58 Tim Byrdak RC .25 .08
❑ U59 David Lee RC .25 .08
❑ U60 Guillermo Mota RC .25 .08
❑ U61 Wilton Veras RC .25 .08
❑ U62 Joe Mays RC .40 .15
❑ U63 Jose Fernandez RC .25 .08
❑ U64 Ray King RC .25 .08
❑ U65 Chris Petersen RC .25 .08
❑ U66 Vernon Wells .20 .07
❑ U67 Ruben Mateo .20 .07
❑ U68 Ben Petrick .20 .07
❑ U69 Chris Tremie RC .25 .08
❑ U70 Lance Berkman .20 .07
❑ U71 Dan Smith RC .25 .08
❑ U72 Carlos Eduardo Hernandez RC .40 .15
❑ U73 Chad Harville RC .25 .08
❑ U74 Damaso Marte RC .25 .08
❑ U75 Aaron Myette RC .25 .08
❑ U76 Willis Roberts RC .25 .08
❑ U77 Erik Sabel RC .25 .08
❑ U78 Hector Almonte RC .25 .08
❑ U79 Kris Benson .20 .07
❑ U80 Pat Daneker RC .25 .08
❑ U81 Freddy Garcia RC 1.00 .40
❑ U82 Byung-Hyun Kim RC 1.00 .40
❑ U83 Wily Pena RC 3.00 1.25
❑ U84 Dan Wheeler RC .40 .15
❑ U85 Tim Harikkala RC .25 .08
❑ U86 Derrin Ebert RC .25 .08
❑ U87 Horacio Estrada RC .25 .08
❑ U88 Liu Rodriguez RC .25 .08
❑ U89 Jordan Zimmerman RC .25 .08
❑ U90 A.J. Burnett RC 1.00 .40
❑ U91 Doug Davis RC 1.00 .40
❑ U92 Rob Ramsay RC .25 .08
❑ U93 Clay Bellinger RC .25 .08
❑ U94 Charlie Greene RC .25 .08
❑ U95 Bo Porter RC .25 .08
❑ U96 Jorge Toca RC .40 .15
❑ U97 Casey Blake RC 1.25 .50
❑ U98 Amaury Garcia RC .25 .08
❑ U99 Jose Molina RC .40 .15
❑ U100 Melvin Mora RC 3.00 1.25
❑ U101 Joe Nathan RC 1.25 .50
❑ U102 Juan Pena RC .25 .08
❑ U103 Dave Borkowski RC .25 .08
❑ U104 Eddie Gaillard RC .25 .08
❑ U105 Glen Barker RC .25 .08
❑ U106 Brett Hinchliffe RC .25 .08
❑ U107 Carlos Lee .20 .07
❑ U108 Rob Ryan RC .25 .08
❑ U109 Jeff Weaver RC .75 .30
❑ U110 Ed Yarnall .20 .07
❑ U111 Nelson Cruz RC .25 .08
❑ U112 Cleatus Davidson RC .25 .08
❑ U113 Tim Kubinski RC .25 .08
❑ U114 Sean Spencer RC .25 .08
❑ U115 Joe Winkelsas RC .25 .08
❑ U116 Mike Colangelo RC .25 .08
❑ U117 Tom Davey RC .25 .08
❑ U118 Warren Morris .20 .07
❑ U119 Dan Murray RC .25 .08
❑ U120 Jose Nieves RC .25 .08
❑ U121 Mark Quinn RC .25 .08
❑ U122 Josh Beckett RC 10.00 4.00
❑ U123 Chad Allen RC .25 .08
❑ U124 Mike Figga .25 .08
❑ U125 Beiker Graterol RC .25 .08
❑ U126 Aaron Scheffer RC .25 .08
❑ U127 Wiki Gonzalez RC .40 .15
❑ U128 Ramon E.Martinez RC .25 .08
❑ U129 Matt Riley RC .40 .15
❑ U130 Chris Woodward RC .25 .08
❑ U131 Albert Belle .20 .07
❑ U132 Roger Cedeno .20 .07
❑ U133 Roger Clemens 1.00 .40
❑ U134 Brian Giles .20 .07
❑ U135 Rickey Henderson .50 .20
❑ U136 Randy Johnson .50 .20
❑ U137 Brian Jordan .20 .07
❑ U138 Paul Konerko .20 .07
❑ U139 Hideo Nomo .50 .20
❑ U140 Kenny Rogers .20 .07
❑ U141 Wade Boggs HL .30 .10
❑ U142 Jose Canseco HL .20 .07
❑ U143 Roger Clemens HL 1.00 .40
❑ U144 David Cone HL .20 .07
❑ U145 Tony Gwynn HL .60 .25
❑ U146 Mark McGwire HL 1.25 .50
❑ U147 Cal Ripken HL 1.50 .60
❑ U148 Alex Rodriguez HL .75 .30
❑ U149 Fernando Tatis HL .20 .07
❑ U150 Robin Ventura HL .20 .07

2000 Fleer Tradition

❑ COMPLETE SET (450) 50.00 20.00
❑ 1 AL Home Run LL .75 .30
❑ 2 NL Home Run LL .75 .30
❑ 3 AL RBI LL .30 .10
❑ 4 NL RBI LL .75 .30
❑ 5 AL Avg LL .75 .30
❑ 6 NL Avg LL .30 .10
❑ 7 AL Wins LL .30 .10
❑ 8 NL Wins LL .30 .10
❑ 9 AL ERA LL .30 .10
❑ 10 NL ERA LL .50 .20
❑ 11 Matt Mantei .30 .10
❑ 12 John Rocker .30 .10
❑ 13 Kyle Farnsworth .30 .10
❑ 14 Juan Guzman .30 .10
❑ 15 Manny Ramirez .50 .20
❑ 16 M.Riley/C.Pickering .30 .10
❑ 17 Tony Clark .30 .10
❑ 18 Brian Meadows .30 .10
❑ 19 Orber Moreno .30 .10
❑ 20 Eric Karros .30 .10
❑ 21 Steve Woodard .30 .10
❑ 22 Scott Brosius .30 .10
❑ 23 Gary Bennett .30 .10
❑ 24 J.Wood/D.Borkowski .30 .10
❑ 25 Joe McEwing .30 .10
❑ 26 Juan Gonzalez .30 .10
❑ 27 Roy Halladay .30 .10
❑ 28 Trevor Hoffman .30 .10
❑ 29 Arizona Diamondbacks .30 .10
❑ 30 Domingo Guzman RC .30 .10
❑ 31 Bret Boone .30 .10
❑ 32 Nomar Garciaparra 1.25 .50
❑ 33 Bo Porter .30 .10
❑ 34 Eddie Taubensee .30 .10
❑ 35 Pedro Astacio .30 .10
❑ 36 Derek Bell .30 .10
❑ 37 Jacque Jones .30 .10
❑ 38 Ricky Ledee .30 .10
❑ 39 Jeff Kent .30 .10
❑ 40 Matt Williams .30 .10
❑ 41 A.Soriano/D.Jimenez .75 .30
❑ 42 B.J. Surhoff .30 .10
❑ 43 Denny Neagle .30 .10
❑ 44 Omar Vizquel .50 .20
❑ 45 Jeff Bagwell .50 .20
❑ 46 Mark Grudzielanek .30 .10
❑ 47 LaTroy Hawkins .30 .10
❑ 48 Orlando Hernandez .30 .10
❑ 49 Checklist/K.Griffey Jr. .75 .30
❑ 50 Fernando Tatis .30 .10
❑ 51 Quilvio Veras .30 .10
❑ 52 Wayne Gomes .30 .10
❑ 53 Rick Helling .30 .10
❑ 54 Shannon Stewart .30 .10
❑ 55 D.Brown/M.Quinn .30 .10
❑ 56 Randy Johnson .75 .30
❑ 57 Greg Maddux 1.25 .50
❑ 58 Mike Cameron .30 .10
❑ 59 Matt Anderson .30 .10
❑ 60 Milwaukee Brewers .30 .10
❑ 61 Derrek Lee .50 .20
❑ 62 Mike Sweeney .30 .10
❑ 63 Fernando Vina .30 .10
❑ 64 Orlando Cabrera .30 .10
❑ 65 Doug Glanville .30 .10
❑ 66 Stan Spencer .30 .10
❑ 67 Ray Lankford .30 .10
❑ 68 Kelly Dransfeldt .30 .10
❑ 69 Alex Gonzalez .30 .10
❑ 70 R.Branyan/D.Peoples .30 .10
❑ 71 Jim Edmonds .30 .10
❑ 72 Brady Anderson .30 .10
❑ 73 Mike Stanley .30 .10
❑ 74 Travis Fryman .30 .10
❑ 75 Carlos Febles .30 .10
❑ 76 Bobby Higginson .30 .10
❑ 77 Carlos Perez .30 .10
❑ 78 S.Cox/A.Sanchez .30 .10
❑ 79 Dustin Hermanson .30 .10
❑ 80 Kenny Rogers .30 .10
❑ 81 Miguel Tejada .30 .10
❑ 82 Ben Davis .30 .10
❑ 83 Reggie Sanders .30 .10
❑ 84 Eric Davis .30 .10
❑ 85 J.D. Drew .30 .10
❑ 86 Ryan Rupe .30 .10
❑ 87 Bobby Smith .30 .10
❑ 88 Jose Cruz Jr. .30 .10
❑ 89 Carlos Delgado .30 .10
❑ 90 Toronto Blue Jays .30 .10
❑ 91 D.Stark RC/G.Meche .30 .10

	No.	Card		
❑	92	Randy Velarde	.30	.10
❑	93	Aaron Boone	.30	.10
❑	94	Javy Lopez	.30	.10
❑	95	Johnny Damon	.50	.20
❑	96	Jon Lieber	.30	.10
❑	97	Montreal Expos	.30	.10
❑	98	Mark Kotsay	.30	.10
❑	99	Luis Gonzalez	.30	.10
❑	100	Larry Walker	.30	.10
❑	101	Adrian Beltre	.30	.10
❑	102	Alex Ochoa	.30	.10
❑	103	Michael Barrett	.30	.10
❑	104	Tampa Bay Devil Rays	.30	.10
❑	105	Rey Ordonez	.30	.10
❑	106	Derek Jeter	1.50	.60
❑	107	Mike Lieberthal	.30	.10
❑	108	Ellis Burks	.30	.10
❑	109	Steve Finley	.30	.10
❑	110	Ryan Klesko	.30	.10
❑	111	Steve Avery	.30	.10
❑	112	Dave Veres	.30	.10
❑	113	Cliff Floyd	.30	.10
❑	114	Shane Reynolds	.30	.10
❑	115	Kevin Brown	.50	.20
❑	116	Dave Nilsson	.30	.10
❑	117	Mike Trombley	.30	.10
❑	118	Todd Walker	.30	.10
❑	119	John Olerud	.30	.10
❑	120	Chuck Knoblauch	.30	.10
❑	121	Checklist/N.Garciaparra	.75	.30
❑	122	Trot Nixon	.30	.10
❑	123	Erubiel Durazo	.30	.10
❑	124	Edwards Guzman	.30	.10
❑	125	Curt Schilling	.30	.10
❑	126	Brian Jordan	.30	.10
❑	127	Cleveland Indians	.30	.10
❑	128	Benito Santiago	.30	.10
❑	129	Frank Thomas	.75	.30
❑	130	Neifi Perez	.30	.10
❑	131	Alex Fernandez	.30	.10
❑	132	Jose Lima	.30	.10
❑	133	J.Toca/M.Mora	.30	.10
❑	134	Scott Karl	.30	.10
❑	135	Brad Radke	.30	.10
❑	136	Paul O'Neill	.50	.20
❑	137	Kris Benson	.30	.10
❑	138	Colorado Rockies	.30	.10
❑	139	Jason Phillips	.30	.10
❑	140	Robb Nen	.30	.10
❑	141	Ken Hill	.30	.10
❑	142	Charles Johnson	.30	.10
❑	143	Paul Konerko	.30	.10
❑	144	Dmitri Young	.30	.10
❑	145	Justin Thompson	.30	.10
❑	146	Mark Loretta	.30	.10
❑	147	Edgardo Alfonzo	.30	.10
❑	148	Armando Benitez	.30	.10
❑	149	Octavio Dotel	.30	.10
❑	150	Wade Boggs	.50	.20
❑	151	Ramon Hernandez	.30	.10
❑	152	Freddy Garcia	.30	.10
❑	153	Edgar Martinez	.50	.20
❑	154	Ivan Rodriguez	.50	.20
❑	155	Kansas City Royals	.30	.10
❑	156	C.Davidson/C.Guzman	.30	.10
❑	157	Andy Benes	.30	.10
❑	158	Todd Dunwoody	.30	.10
❑	159	Pedro Martinez	.50	.20
❑	160	Mike Caruso	.30	.10
❑	161	Mike Sirotka	.30	.10
❑	162	Houston Astros	.30	.10
❑	163	Darryl Kile	.30	.10
❑	164	Chipper Jones	.75	.30
❑	165	Carl Everett	.30	.10
❑	166	Geoff Jenkins	.30	.10
❑	167	Dan Perkins	.30	.10
❑	168	Andy Pettitte	.50	.20
❑	169	Francisco Cordova	.30	.10
❑	170	Jay Buhner	.30	.10
❑	171	Jay Bell	.30	.10
❑	172	Andruw Jones	.50	.20
❑	173	Bobby Howry	.30	.10
❑	174	Chris Singleton	.30	.10
❑	175	Todd Helton	.50	.20
❑	176	A.J. Burnett	.30	.10
❑	177	Marquis Grissom	.30	.10
❑	178	Eric Milton	.30	.10
❑	179	Los Angeles Dodgers	.30	.10
❑	180	Kevin Appier	.30	.10
❑	181	Brian Giles	.30	.10
❑	182	Tom Davey	.30	.10
❑	183	Mo Vaughn	.30	.10
❑	184	Jose Hernandez	.30	.10
❑	185	Jim Parque	.30	.10
❑	186	Derrick Gibson	.30	.10
❑	187	Bruce Aven	.30	.10
❑	188	Jeff Cirillo	.30	.10
❑	189	Doug Mientkiewicz	.30	.10
❑	190	Eric Chavez	.30	.10
❑	191	Al Martin	.30	.10
❑	192	Tom Glavine	.50	.20
❑	193	Butch Huskey	.30	.10
❑	194	Ray Durham	.30	.10
❑	195	Greg Vaughn	.30	.10
❑	196	Vinny Castilla	.30	.10
❑	197	Ken Caminiti	.30	.10
❑	198	Joe Mays	.30	.10
❑	199	Chicago White Sox	.30	.10
❑	200	Mariano Rivera	.75	.30
❑	201	Checklist/M.McGwire	1.00	.40
❑	202	Pat Meares	.30	.10
❑	203	Andres Galarraga	.30	.10
❑	204	Tom Gordon	.30	.10
❑	205	Henry Rodriguez	.30	.10
❑	206	Brett Tomko	.30	.10
❑	207	Dante Bichette	.30	.10
❑	208	Craig Biggio	.50	.20
❑	209	Matt Lawton	.30	.10
❑	210	Tino Martinez	.50	.20
❑	211	A.Myette/J.Paul	.30	.10
❑	212	Warren Morris	.30	.10
❑	213	San Diego Padres	.30	.10
❑	214	Ramon E. Martinez	.30	.10
❑	215	Troy Percival	.30	.10
❑	216	Jason Johnson	.30	.10
❑	217	Carlos Lee	.30	.10
❑	218	Scott Williamson	.30	.10
❑	219	Jeff Weaver	.30	.10
❑	220	Ronnie Belliard	.30	.10
❑	221	Jason Giambi	.30	.10
❑	222	Ken Griffey Jr.	1.25	.50
❑	223	John Halama	.30	.10
❑	224	Brett Hinchliffe	.30	.10
❑	225	Wilson Alvarez	.30	.10
❑	226	Rolando Arrojo	.30	.10
❑	227	Ruben Mateo	.30	.10
❑	228	Rafael Palmeiro	.50	.20
❑	229	David Wells	.30	.10
❑	230	Eric Gagne	.75	.30
❑	231	Tim Salmon	.50	.20
❑	232	Mike Mussina	.50	.20
❑	233	Magglio Ordonez	.30	.10
❑	234	Ron Villone	.30	.10
❑	235	Antonio Alfonseca	.30	.10
❑	236	Jeromy Burnitz	.30	.10
❑	237	Ben Grieve	.30	.10
❑	238	Giomar Guevara	.30	.10
❑	239	Garret Anderson	.30	.10
❑	240	John Smoltz	.50	.20
❑	241	Mark Grace	.50	.20
❑	242	C.Liniak/J.Molina	.30	.10
❑	243	Damion Easley	.30	.10
❑	244	Jeff Montgomery	.30	.10
❑	245	Kenny Lofton	.30	.10
❑	246	Masato Yoshii	.30	.10
❑	247	Philadelphia Phillies	.30	.10
❑	248	Raul Mondesi	.30	.10
❑	249	Marlon Anderson	.30	.10
❑	250	Shawn Green	.30	.10
❑	251	Sterling Hitchcock	.30	.10
❑	252	R.Wolf/A.Shumaker	.30	.10
❑	253	Jeff Fassero	.30	.10
❑	254	Eli Marrero	.30	.10
❑	255	Cincinnati Reds	.30	.10
❑	256	Rick Ankiel	.30	.10
❑	257	Darin Erstad	.30	.10
❑	258	Albert Belle	.30	.10
❑	259	Bartolo Colon	.30	.10
❑	260	Bret Saberhagen	.30	.10
❑	261	Carlos Beltran	.30	.10
❑	262	Glenallen Hill	.30	.10
❑	263	Gregg Jefferies	.30	.10
❑	264	Matt Clement	.30	.10
❑	265	Miguel Del Toro	.30	.10
❑	266	R.Cancel/K.Barker	.30	.10
❑	267	San Francisco Giants	.30	.10
❑	268	Kent Bottenfield	.30	.10
❑	269	Fred McGriff	.50	.20
❑	270	Chris Carpenter	.30	.10
❑	271	Atlanta Braves	.30	.10
❑	272	Tomo Ohka RC	.40	.15
❑	273	Will Clark	.50	.20
❑	274	Troy O'Leary	.30	.10
❑	275	Checklist/S.Sosa	.50	.20
❑	276	Travis Lee	.30	.10
❑	277	Sean Casey	.30	.10
❑	278	Ron Gant	.30	.10
❑	279	Roger Clemens	1.50	.60
❑	280	Phil Nevin	.30	.10
❑	281	Mike Piazza	1.25	.50
❑	282	Mike Lowell	.30	.10
❑	283	Kevin Millwood	.30	.10
❑	284	Joe Randa	.30	.10
❑	285	Jeff Shaw	.30	.10
❑	286	Jason Varitek	.75	.30
❑	287	Harold Baines	.30	.10
❑	288	Gabe Kapler	.30	.10
❑	289	Chuck Finley	.30	.10
❑	290	Carl Pavano	.30	.10
❑	291	Brad Ausmus	.30	.10
❑	292	Brad Fullmer	.30	.10
❑	293	Boston Red Sox	.30	.10
❑	294	Bob Wickman	.30	.10
❑	295	Billy Wagner	.30	.10
❑	296	Shawn Estes	.30	.10
❑	297	Gary Sheffield	.30	.10
❑	298	Fernando Seguignol	.30	.10
❑	299	Omar Olivares	.30	.10
❑	300	Baltimore Orioles	.30	.10
❑	301	Matt Stairs	.30	.10
❑	302	Andy Ashby	.30	.10
❑	303	Todd Greene	.30	.10
❑	304	Jesse Garcia	.30	.10
❑	305	Kerry Wood	.30	.10
❑	306	Roberto Alomar	.50	.20
❑	307	New York Mets	.30	.10
❑	308	Dean Palmer	.30	.10
❑	309	Mike Hampton	.30	.10
❑	310	Devon White	.30	.10
❑	311	Mike Garcia RC	.30	.10
❑	312	Tim Hudson	.30	.10
❑	313	John Franco	.30	.10
❑	314	Jason Schmidt	.30	.10
❑	315	J.T. Snow	.30	.10
❑	316	Ed Sprague	.30	.10
❑	317	Chris Widger	.30	.10
❑	318	Luther Hackman RC	.30	.10
❑	319	Jose Mesa	.30	.10
❑	320	Jose Canseco	.50	.20
❑	321	John Wetteland	.30	.10
❑	322	Minnesota Twins	.30	.10
❑	323	Jeff DaVanon RC	.40	.15
❑	324	Tony Womack	.30	.10
❑	325	Rod Beck	.30	.10
❑	326	Mickey Morandini	.30	.10
❑	327	Pokey Reese	.30	.10
❑	328	Jaret Wright	.30	.10
❑	329	Glen Barker	.30	.10
❑	330	Darren Dreifort	.30	.10
❑	331	Torii Hunter	.30	.10
❑	332	T.Armas/P.Bergeron	.30	.10
❑	333	Hideki Irabu	.30	.10
❑	334	Desi Relaford	.30	.10
❑	335	Barry Bonds	2.00	.75
❑	336	Gary DiSarcina	.30	.10
❑	337	Gerald Williams	.30	.10
❑	338	John Valentin	.30	.10
❑	339	David Justice	.30	.10
❑	340	Juan Encarnacion	.30	.10
❑	341	Jeremy Giambi	.30	.10
❑	342	Chan Ho Park	.30	.10
❑	343	Vladimir Guerrero	.75	.30
❑	344	Robin Ventura	.50	.20
❑	345	Bob Abreu	.30	.10
❑	346	Tony Gwynn	1.00	.40
❑	347	Jose Jimenez	.30	.10
❑	348	Royce Clayton	.30	.10
❑	349	Kelvim Escobar	.30	.10

❑ 350	Chicago Cubs	.30	.10
❑ 351	T.Dawkins/J.LaRue	.30	.10
❑ 352	Barry Larkin	.50	.20
❑ 353	Cal Ripken	2.50	1.00
❑ 354	Checklist/A.Rodriguez	.75	.30
❑ 355	Todd Stottlemyre	.30	.10
❑ 356	Terry Adams	.30	.10
❑ 357	Pittsburgh Pirates	.30	.10
❑ 358	Jim Thome	.50	.20
❑ 359	C.Lee/D.Davis	.30	.10
❑ 360	Moises Alou	.30	.10
❑ 361	Todd Hollandsworth	.30	.10
❑ 362	Marty Cordova	.30	.10
❑ 363	David Cone	.30	.10
❑ 364	J.Nathan/W.Delgado	.30	.10
❑ 365	Paul Byrd	.30	.10
❑ 366	Edgar Renteria	.30	.10
❑ 367	Rusty Greer	.30	.10
❑ 368	David Segui	.30	.10
❑ 369	New York Yankees	.50	.20
❑ 370	D.Ward/C.Hernandez	.30	.10
❑ 371	Troy Glaus	.30	.10
❑ 372	Delion DeShields	.30	.10
❑ 373	Jose Offerman	.30	.10
❑ 374	Sammy Sosa	.75	.30
❑ 375	Sandy Alomar Jr.	.30	.10
❑ 376	Masao Kida	.30	.10
❑ 377	Richard Hidalgo	.30	.10
❑ 378	Ismael Valdes	.30	.10
❑ 379	Ugueth Urbina	.30	.10
❑ 380	Darryl Hamilton	.30	.10
❑ 381	John Jaha	.30	.10
❑ 382	St. Louis Cardinals	.30	.10
❑ 383	Scott Sauerbeck	.30	.10
❑ 384	Russ Ortiz	.30	.10
❑ 385	Jamie Moyer	.30	.10
❑ 386	Dave Martinez	.30	.10
❑ 387	Todd Zeile	.30	.10
❑ 388	Anaheim Angels	.30	.10
❑ 389	R.Ryan/N.Bierbrodt	.30	.10
❑ 390	Rickey Henderson	.75	.30
❑ 391	Alex Rodriguez	1.25	.50
❑ 392	Texas Rangers	.30	.10
❑ 393	Roberto Hernandez	.30	.10
❑ 394	Tony Batista	.30	.10
❑ 395	Oakland Athletics	.30	.10
❑ 396	Dave Cortes RC	.30	.10
❑ 397	Gregg Olson	.30	.10
❑ 398	Sidney Ponson	.30	.10
❑ 399	Micah Bowie	.30	.10
❑ 400	Mark McGwire	2.00	.75
❑ 401	Florida Marlins	.30	.10
❑ 402	Chad Allen	.30	.10
❑ 403	C.Blake/V.Wells	.30	.10
❑ 404	Pete Harnisch	.30	.10
❑ 405	Preston Wilson	.30	.10
❑ 406	Richie Sexson	.30	.10
❑ 407	Rico Brogna	.30	.10
❑ 408	Todd Hundley	.30	.10
❑ 409	Wally Joyner	.30	.10
❑ 410	Tom Goodwin	.30	.10
❑ 411	Joey Hamilton	.30	.10
❑ 412	Detroit Tigers	.30	.10
❑ 413	Michael Tejera RC	.30	.10
❑ 414	Alex Gonzalez	.30	.10
❑ 415	Jermaine Dye	.30	.10
❑ 416	Jose Rosada	.30	.10
❑ 417	Wilton Guerrero	.30	.10
❑ 418	Rondell White	.30	.10
❑ 419	Al Leiter	.30	.10
❑ 420	Bernie Williams	.50	.20
❑ 421	A.J. Hinch	.30	.10
❑ 422	Pat Burrell	.30	.10
❑ 423	Scott Rolen	.50	.20
❑ 424	Jason Kendall	.30	.10
❑ 425	Kevin Young	.30	.10
❑ 426	Eric Owens	.30	.10
❑ 427	Checklist/D.Jeter	.75	.30
❑ 428	Livan Hernandez	.30	.10
❑ 429	Russ Davis	.30	.10
❑ 430	Dan Wilson	.30	.10
❑ 431	Quinton McCracken	.30	.10
❑ 432	Homer Bush	.30	.10
❑ 433	Seattle Mariners	.30	.10
❑ 434	C.Harville/L.Vizcaino	.30	.10
❑ 435	Carlos Beltran AW	.30	.10
❑ 436	Scott Williamson AW	.30	.10
❑ 437	Pedro Martinez AW	.50	.20
❑ 438	Randy Johnson AW	.50	.20
❑ 439	Ivan Rodriguez AW	.30	.10
❑ 440	Chipper Jones AW	.50	.20
❑ 441	Bernie Williams DIV	.30	.10
❑ 442	Pedro Martinez DIV	.50	.20
❑ 443	Derek Jeter DIV	1.00	.40
❑ 444	Brian Jordan DIV	.30	.10
❑ 445	Todd Pratt DIV	.30	.10
❑ 446	Kevin Millwood DIV	.30	.10
❑ 447	Orlando Hernandez WS	.30	.10
❑ 448	Derek Jeter WS	1.00	.40
❑ 449	Chad Curtis WS	.30	.10
❑ 450	Roger Clemens WS	.75	.30
❑ P353	Cal Ripken Promo	3.00	1.25

2000 Fleer Tradition Update

❑	COMP.FACT.SET (149)	20.00	8.00
❑ 1	Ken Griffey Jr. SH	.75	.30
❑ 2	Cal Ripken SH	1.00	.40
❑ 3	Randy Velarde SH	.30	.10
❑ 4	Fred McGriff SH	.30	.10
❑ 5	Derek Jeter SH	.75	.30
❑ 6	Tom Glavine SH	.30	.10
❑ 7	Brent Mayne SH	.30	.10
❑ 8	Alex Ochoa SH	.30	.10
❑ 9	Scott Sheldon SH	.30	.10
❑ 10	Randy Johnson SH	.50	.20
❑ 11	Daniel Garibay RC	.30	.10
❑ 12	Brad Fullmer	.30	.10
❑ 13	Kazuhiro Sasaki RC	.60	.25
❑ 14	Andy Tracy RC	.30	.10
❑ 15	Bret Boone	.30	.10
❑ 16	Chad Durbin RC	.40	.15
❑ 17	Mark Buehrle RC	3.00	1.25
❑ 18	Julio Zuleta RC	.30	.10
❑ 19	Jeremy Giambi	.30	.10
❑ 20	Gene Stechschulte RC	.30	.10
❑ 21	L.Pote/B.Molina	.30	.10
❑ 22	Darrell Einertson RC	.30	.10
❑ 23	Ken Griffey Jr.	1.25	.50
❑ 24	J.Sparks RC/D.Wheeler	.30	.10
❑ 25	Aaron Fultz RC	.30	.10
❑ 26	Derek Bell	.30	.10
❑ 27	R.Bell/D.Cromer	.30	.10
❑ 28	Robert Fick	.30	.10
❑ 29	Darryl Kile	.30	.10
❑ 30	C.Andrews/J.Bale RC	.30	.10
❑ 31	Dave Veres	.30	.10
❑ 32	Hector Mercado RC	.30	.10
❑ 33	Willie Morales RC	.30	.10
❑ 34	K.Wunsch/K.Wells	.30	.10
❑ 35	Hideki Irabu	.30	.10
❑ 36	Sean DePaula RC	.30	.10
❑ 37	D.Wise/C.Woodward	.30	.10
❑ 38	Curt Schilling	.30	.10
❑ 39	Mark Johnson	.30	.10
❑ 40	Mike Cameron	.30	.10
❑ 41	S.Sheldon/T.Evans	.30	.10
❑ 42	Brett Tomko	.30	.10
❑ 43	Johan Santana RC	15.00	6.00
❑ 44	Andy Benes	.30	.10
❑ 45	M.LeCroy/M.Redman	.30	.10
❑ 46	Ryan Klesko	.30	.10
❑ 47	Andy Ashby	.30	.10
❑ 48	Octavio Dotel	.30	.10
❑ 49	Eric Byrnes RC	.40	.15
❑ 50	Does Not Exist		
❑ 51	Kenny Rogers	.30	.10
❑ 52	Ben Weber RC	.30	.10
❑ 53	M.Blank/S.Strickland	.30	.10
❑ 54	Tom Goodwin	.30	.10
❑ 55	Jim Edmonds Cards	.30	.10
❑ 56	Derrick Turnbow RC	1.50	.60
❑ 57	Mark Mulder	.30	.10
❑ 58	T.Brock/R.Quevedo	.30	.10
❑ 59	Danny Young RC	.30	.10
❑ 60	Fernando Vina	.30	.10
❑ 61	Justin Brunette RC	.30	.10
❑ 62	Jimmy Anderson	.30	.10
❑ 63	Reggie Sanders	.30	.10
❑ 64	Adam Kennedy	.30	.10
❑ 65	J.Garcia/B.Ryan	.30	.10
❑ 66	Al Martin	.30	.10
❑ 67	Kevin Walker RC	.30	.10
❑ 68	Brad Penny	.30	.10
❑ 69	B.J. Surhoff	.30	.10
❑ 70	G.Blum/T.Coquillette RC	.30	.10
❑ 71	Jose Jimenez	.30	.10
❑ 72	Chuck Finley	.30	.10
❑ 73	V.De Los Santos/E.Stull	.30	.10
❑ 74	Terry Adams	.30	.10
❑ 75	Rafael Furcal	.30	.10
❑ 76	J.Roskos/M.Darr	.30	.10
❑ 77	Quilvio Veras	.30	.10
❑ 78	A.Almanza/N.Rolison	.30	.10
❑ 79	Greg Vaughn	.30	.10
❑ 80	Keith McDonald RC	.30	.10
❑ 81	Eric Cammack RC	.30	.10
❑ 82	H.Estrada/R.King	.30	.10
❑ 83	Kory DeHaan	.30	.10
❑ 84	Kevin Hodges RC	.30	.10
❑ 85	Mike Lamb RC	.60	.25
❑ 86	Shawn Green	.30	.10
❑ 87	D.Reichert/J.Rakers	.30	.10
❑ 88	Adam Piatt	.30	.10
❑ 89	Mike Garcia	.30	.10
❑ 90	Rodrigo Lopez RC	.60	.25
❑ 91	John Olerud	.30	.10
❑ 92	B.Zito RC/T.Long	4.00	1.50
❑ 93	Jimmy Rollins	.30	.10
❑ 94	Denny Neagle	.30	.10
❑ 95	Rickey Henderson	.75	.30
❑ 96	A.Eaton/B.Carlyle	.30	.10
❑ 97	Brian O'Connor RC	.30	.10
❑ 98	Andy Thompson RC	.30	.10
❑ 99	Jason Boyd RC	.30	.10
❑ 100	J.Pineiro RC/C.Guillen	1.00	.40
❑ 101	Raul Gonzalez RC	.30	.10
❑ 102	Brandon Kolb RC	.30	.10
❑ 103	J.Maxwell/M.Lincoln	.30	.10
❑ 104	Luis Matos RC	.40	.15
❑ 105	Morgan Burkhart RC	.30	.10
❑ 106	I.Villegas/S.Sisco RC	.30	.10
❑ 107	David Justice Yankees	.30	.10
❑ 108	Pablo Ozuna	.30	.10
❑ 109	Jose Canseco Yankees	.50	.20
❑ 110	A.Cora/S.Gilbert	.30	.10
❑ 111	Will Clark Cardinals	.50	.20
❑ 112	K.Luuloa/E.Weaver	.30	.10
❑ 113	Bruce Chen	.30	.10
❑ 114	Adam Hyzdu	.30	.10
❑ 115	S.Forster/Y.Lara RC	.30	.10
❑ 116	A.McDill RC/J.Macias	.30	.10
❑ 117	Kevin Nicholson	.30	.10
❑ 118	I.Alcantara/T.Young	.30	.10
❑ 119	Juan Alvarez RC	.30	.10
❑ 120	J.Lugo/M.Meluskey	.30	.10
❑ 121	B.J. Waszgis RC	.30	.10
❑ 122	J.D'Amico RC/B.Laxton	.30	.10
❑ 123	Ricky Ledee	.30	.10
❑ 124	M.DeRosa/J.Marquis	.30	.10
❑ 125	Alex Cabrera RC	.40	.15
❑ 126	A.Ojeda RC/G.Matthews Jr.	.30	.10
❑ 127	Richie Sexson	.30	.10
❑ 128	S.Perez/H.Ramirez RC	.30	.10
❑ 129	Rondell White	.30	.10
❑ 130	Craig House RC	.30	.10
❑ 131	K.Beirne/J.Garland	.30	.10
❑ 132	Wayne Franklin RC	.30	.10
❑ 133	Henry Rodriguez	.30	.10
❑ 134	J.Payton/J.Mann	.30	.10

No.	Card		
135	Ron Gant	.30	.10
136	P.Crawford/S.Lee RC	.30	.10
137	Kent Bottenfield	.30	.10
138	Rocky Biddle RC	.30	.10
139	Travis Lee	.30	.10
140	Ryan Vogelsong RC	.30	.10
141	J.Conti/G.Guzman RC	.30	.10
142	M.Watson RC/T.Drew	.30	.10
143	J.Parrish/C.Richard RC	.30	.10
144	J.Cardona/B.Villafuerte RC	.30	.10
145	T.Redman/S.Sparks RC	.60	.25
146	B.Schneider/M.Skrmetta RC	.30	.10
147	Pasqual Coco RC	.30	.10
148	L.Barcelo RC/J.Crede	1.00	.40
149	Jace Brewer RC	.30	.10
150	T.De La Rosa RC/M.Bradley	.40	.15
MP1	Mickey Mantle Pants	200.00	125.00

2001 Fleer Tradition

No.	Card		
	COMP.FACT.SET (485)	100.00	50.00
	COMPLETE SET (450)	50.00	20.00
	COMMON CARD (1-450)	.30	.10
	COMMON CARD (451-485)	.50	.20
1	Andres Galarraga	.30	.10
2	Armando Rios	.30	.10
3	Julio Lugo	.30	.10
4	Darryl Hamilton	.30	.10
5	Dave Veres	.30	.10
6	Edgardo Alfonzo	.30	.10
7	Brook Fordyce	.30	.10
8	Eric Karros	.30	.10
9	Neifi Perez	.30	.10
10	Jim Edmonds	.30	.10
11	Barry Larkin	.50	.20
12	Trot Nixon	.30	.10
13	Andy Pettitte	.50	.20
14	Jose Guillen	.30	.10
15	David Wells	.30	.10
16	Magglio Ordonez	.30	.10
17	David Segui	.30	.10
17A	David Segui ERR (Card has no number on the back)	.30	.10
18	Juan Encarnacion	.30	.10
19	Robert Person	.30	.10
20	Quilvio Veras	.30	.10
21	Mo Vaughn	.30	.10
22	B.J. Surhoff	.30	.10
23	Ken Caminiti	.30	.10
24	Frank Catalanotto	.30	.10
25	Luis Gonzalez	.30	.10
26	Pete Harnisch	.30	.10
27	Alex Gonzalez	.30	.10
28	Mark Quinn	.30	.10
29	Luis Castillo	.30	.10
30	Rick Helling	.30	.10
31	Barry Bonds	2.00	.75
32	Warren Morris	.30	.10
33	Aaron Boone	.30	.10
34	Ricky Gutierrez	.30	.10
35	Preston Wilson	.30	.10
36	Erubiel Durazo	.30	.10
37	Jermaine Dye	.30	.10
38	John Rocker	.30	.10
39	Mark Grudzielanek	.30	.10
40	Pedro Martinez	.50	.20
41	Phil Nevin	.30	.10
42	Luis Matos	.30	.10
43	Orlando Hernandez	.30	.10
44	Steve Cox	.30	.10
45	James Baldwin	.30	.10
46	Rafael Furcal	.30	.10
47	Todd Zeile	.30	.10
48	Elmer Dessens	.30	.10
49	Russell Branyan	.30	.10
50	Juan Gonzalez	.30	.10
51	Mac Suzuki	.30	.10
52	Adam Kennedy	.30	.10
53	Randy Velarde	.30	.10
54	David Bell	.30	.10
55	Royce Clayton	.30	.10
56	Greg Colbrunn	.30	.10
57	Rey Ordonez	.30	.10
58	Kevin Millwood	.30	.10
59	Fernando Vina	.30	.10
60	Eddie Taubensee	.30	.10
61	Enrique Wilson	.30	.10
62	Jay Bell	.30	.10
63	Brian Moehler	.30	.10
64	Brad Fullmer	.30	.10
65	Ben Petrick	.30	.10
66	Orlando Cabrera	.30	.10
67	Shane Reynolds	.30	.10
68	Mitch Meluskey	.30	.10
69	Jeff Shaw	.30	.10
70	Chipper Jones	.75	.30
71	Tomo Ohka	.30	.10
72	Ruben Rivera	.30	.10
73	Mike Sirotka	.30	.10
74	Scott Rolen	.50	.20
75	Glendon Rusch	.30	.10
76	Miguel Tejada	.30	.10
77	Brady Anderson	.30	.10
78	Bartolo Colon	.30	.10
79	Ron Coomer	.30	.10
80	Gary DiSarcina	.30	.10
81	Geoff Jenkins	.30	.10
82	Billy Koch	.30	.10
83	Mike Lamb	.30	.10
84	Alex Rodriguez	1.25	.50
85	Denny Neagle	.30	.10
86	Michael Tucker	.30	.10
87	Edgar Renteria	.30	.10
88	Brian Anderson	.30	.10
89	Glenallen Hill	.30	.10
90	Aramis Ramirez	.30	.10
91	Rondell White	.30	.10
92	Tony Womack	.30	.10
93	Jeffrey Hammonds	.30	.10
94	Freddy Garcia	.30	.10
95	Bill Mueller	.30	.10
96	Mike Lieberthal	.30	.10
97	Michael Barrett	.30	.10
98	Derrek Lee	.50	.20
99	Bill Spiers	.30	.10
100	Derek Lowe	.30	.10
101	Javy Lopez	.30	.10
102	Adrian Beltre	.30	.10
103	Jim Parque	.30	.10
104	Marquis Grissom	.30	.10
105	Eric Chavez	.30	.10
106	Todd Jones	.30	.10
107	Eric Owens	.30	.10
108	Roger Clemens	1.50	.60
109	Denny Hocking	.30	.10
110	Roberto Hernandez	.30	.10
111	Albert Belle	.30	.10
112	Troy Glaus	.30	.10
113	Ivan Rodriguez	.50	.20
114	Carlos Guillen	.30	.10
115	Chuck Finley	.30	.10
116	Dmitri Young	.30	.10
117	Paul Konerko	.30	.10
118	Damon Buford	.30	.10
119	Fernando Tatis	.30	.10
120	Larry Walker	.30	.10
121	Jason Kendall	.30	.10
122	Matt Williams	.30	.10
123	Henry Rodriguez	.30	.10
124	Placido Polanco	.30	.10
125	Bobby Estalella	.30	.10
126	Pat Burrell	.30	.10
127	Mark Loretta	.30	.10
128	Moises Alou	.30	.10
129	Tino Martinez	.50	.20
130	Milton Bradley	.30	.10
131	Todd Hundley	.30	.10
132	Keith Foulke	.30	.10
133	Robert Fick	.30	.10
134	Cristian Guzman	.30	.10
135	Rusty Greer	.30	.10
136	John Olerud	.30	.10
137	Mariano Rivera	.75	.30
138	Jeromy Burnitz	.30	.10
139	Dave Burba	.30	.10
140	Ken Griffey Jr.	1.25	.50
141	Tony Gwynn	1.00	.40
142	Carlos Delgado	.30	.10
143	Edgar Martinez	.50	.20
144	Ramon Hernandez	.30	.10
145	Pedro Astacio	.30	.10
146	Ray Lankford	.30	.10
147	Mike Mussina	.50	.20
148	Ray Durham	.30	.10
149	Lee Stevens	.30	.10
150	Jay Canizaro	.30	.10
151	Adrian Brown	.30	.10
152	Mike Piazza	1.25	.50
153	Cliff Floyd	.30	.10
154	Jose Vidro	.30	.10
155	Jason Giambi	.30	.10
156	Andruw Jones	.50	.20
157	Robin Ventura	.30	.10
158	Gary Sheffield	.30	.10
159	Jeff D'Amico	.30	.10
160	Chuck Knoblauch	.30	.10
161	Roger Cedeno	.30	.10
162	Jim Thome	.50	.20
163	Peter Bergeron	.30	.10
164	Kerry Wood	.30	.10
165	Gabe Kapler	.30	.10
166	Corey Koskie	.30	.10
167	Doug Glanville	.30	.10
168	Brent Mayne	.30	.10
169	Scott Spiezio	.30	.10
170	Steve Karsay	.30	.10
171	Al Martin	.30	.10
172	Fred McGriff	.50	.20
173	Gabe White	.30	.10
174	Alex Gonzalez	.30	.10
175	Mike Darr	.30	.10
176	Bengie Molina	.30	.10
177	Ben Grieve	.30	.10
178	Marlon Anderson	.30	.10
179	Brian Giles	.30	.10
180	Jose Valentin	.30	.10
181	Brian Jordan	.30	.10
182	Randy Johnson	.75	.30
183	Ricky Ledee	.30	.10
184	Russ Ortiz	.30	.10
185	Mike Lowell	.30	.10
186	Curtis Leskanic	.30	.10
187	Bob Abreu	.30	.10
188	Derek Jeter	2.00	.75
189	Lance Berkman	.30	.10
190	Roberto Alomar	.50	.20
191	Darin Erstad	.30	.10
192	Richie Sexson	.30	.10
193	Alex Ochoa	.30	.10
194	Carlos Febles	.30	.10
195	David Ortiz	.75	.30
196	Shawn Green	.30	.10
197	Mike Sweeney	.30	.10
198	Vladimir Guerrero	.75	.30
199	Jose Jimenez	.30	.10
200	Travis Lee	.30	.10
201	Rickey Henderson	.75	.30
202	Bob Wickman	.30	.10
203	Miguel Cairo	.30	.10
204	Steve Finley	.30	.10
205	Tony Batista	.30	.10
206	Jamey Wright	.30	.10
207	Terrence Long	.30	.10
208	Trevor Hoffman	.30	.10
209	John VanderWal	.30	.10
210	Greg Maddux	1.25	.50
211	Tim Salmon	.50	.20
212	Herbert Perry	.30	.10
213	Marvin Benard	.30	.10
214	Jose Offerman	.30	.10
215	Jay Payton	.30	.10

	No.	Player	Hi	Lo
❑	216	Jon Lieber	.30	.10
❑	217	Mark Kotsay	.30	.10
❑	218	Scott Brosius	.30	.10
❑	219	Scott Williamson	.30	.10
❑	220	Omar Vizquel	.50	.20
❑	221	Mike Hampton	.30	.10
❑	222	Richard Hidalgo	.30	.10
❑	223	Rey Sanchez	.30	.10
❑	224	Matt Lawton	.30	.10
❑	225	Bruce Chen	.30	.10
❑	226	Ryan Klesko	.30	.10
❑	227	Garret Anderson	.30	.10
❑	228	Kevin Brown	.30	.10
❑	229	Mike Cameron	.30	.10
❑	230	Tony Clark	.30	.10
❑	231	Curt Schilling	.30	.10
❑	232	Vinny Castilla	.30	.10
❑	233	Carl Pavano	.30	.10
❑	234	Eric Davis	.30	.10
❑	235	Darrin Fletcher	.30	.10
❑	236	Matt Stairs	.30	.10
❑	237	Octavio Dotel	.30	.10
❑	238	Mark Grace	.50	.20
❑	239	John Smoltz	.50	.20
❑	240	Matt Clement	.30	.10
❑	241	Ellis Burks	.30	.10
❑	242	Charles Johnson	.30	.10
❑	243	Jeff Bagwell	.50	.20
❑	244	Derek Bell	.30	.10
❑	245	Nomar Garciaparra	1.25	.50
❑	246	Jorge Posada	.50	.20
❑	247	Ryan Dempster	.30	.10
❑	248	J.T. Snow	.30	.10
❑	249	Eric Young	.30	.10
❑	250	Daryle Ward	.30	.10
❑	251	Joe Randa	.30	.10
❑	252	Travis Fryman	.30	.10
❑	253	Mike Williams	.30	.10
❑	254	Jacque Jones	.30	.10
❑	255	Scott Elarton	.30	.10
❑	256	Mark McGwire	2.00	.75
❑	257	Jay Buhner	.30	.10
❑	258	Randy Wolf	.30	.10
❑	259	Sammy Sosa	.75	.30
❑	260	Chan Ho Park	.30	.10
❑	261	Damion Easley	.30	.10
❑	262	Rick Ankiel	.30	.10
❑	263	Frank Thomas	.75	.30
❑	264	Kris Benson	.30	.10
❑	265	Luis Alicea	.30	.10
❑	266	Jeromy Burnitz	.30	.10
❑	267	Geoff Blum	.30	.10
❑	268	Joe Girardi	.30	.10
❑	269	Livan Hernandez	.30	.10
❑	270	Jeff Conine	.30	.10
❑	271	Danny Graves	.30	.10
❑	272	Craig Biggio	.50	.20
❑	273	Jose Canseco	.50	.20
❑	274	Tom Glavine	.50	.20
❑	275	Ruben Mateo	.30	.10
❑	276	Jeff Kent	.30	.10
❑	277	Kevin Young	.30	.10
❑	278	A.J. Burnett	.30	.10
❑	279	Dante Bichette	.30	.10
❑	280	Sandy Alomar Jr.	.30	.10
❑	281	John Wetteland	.30	.10
❑	282	Torii Hunter	.30	.10
❑	283	Jarrod Washburn	.30	.10
❑	284	Rich Aurilia	.30	.10
❑	285	Jeff Cirillo	.30	.10
❑	286	Fernando Seguignol	.30	.10
❑	287	Darren Dreifort	.30	.10
❑	288	Deivi Cruz	.30	.10
❑	289	Pokey Reese	.30	.10
❑	290	Garrett Stephenson	.30	.10
❑	291	Bret Boone	.30	.10
❑	292	Tim Hudson	.30	.10
❑	293	John Flaherty	.30	.10
❑	294	Shannon Stewart	.30	.10
❑	295	Shawn Estes	.30	.10
❑	296	Wilton Guerrero	.30	.10
❑	297	Delino DeShields	.30	.10
❑	298	David Justice	.30	.10
❑	299	Harold Baines	.30	.10
❑	300	Al Leiter	.30	.10
❑	301	Wil Cordero	.30	.10
❑	302	Antonio Alfonseca	.30	.10
❑	303	Sean Casey	.30	.10
❑	304	Carlos Beltran	.30	.10
❑	305	Brad Radke	.30	.10
❑	306	Jason Varitek	.75	.30
❑	307	Shigetoshi Hasegawa	.30	.10
❑	308	Todd Stottlemyre	.30	.10
❑	309	Raul Mondesi	.30	.10
❑	310	Mike Bordick	.30	.10
❑	311	Darryl Kile	.30	.10
❑	312	Dean Palmer	.30	.10
❑	313	Johnny Damon	.50	.20
❑	314	Todd Helton	.50	.20
❑	315	Chad Hermansen	.30	.10
❑	316	Kevin Appier	.30	.10
❑	317	Greg Vaughn	.30	.10
❑	318	Robb Nen	.30	.10
❑	319	Jose Cruz Jr.	.30	.10
❑	320	Ron Belliard	.30	.10
❑	321	Bernie Williams	.50	.20
❑	322	Melvin Mora	.30	.10
❑	323	Kenny Lofton	.30	.10
❑	324	Armando Benitez	.30	.10
❑	325	Carlos Lee	.30	.10
❑	326	Damian Jackson	.30	.10
❑	327	Eric Milton	.30	.10
❑	328	J.D. Drew	.30	.10
❑	329	Byung-Hyun Kim	.30	.10
❑	330	Chris Stynes	.30	.10
❑	331	Kazuhiro Sasaki	.30	.10
❑	332	Troy O'Leary	.30	.10
❑	333	Pat Hentgen	.30	.10
❑	334	Brad Ausmus	.30	.10
❑	335	Todd Walker	.30	.10
❑	336	Jason Isringhausen	.30	.10
❑	337	Gerald Williams	.30	.10
❑	338	Aaron Sele	.30	.10
❑	339	Paul O'Neill	.50	.20
❑	340	Cal Ripken	2.50	1.00
❑	341	Manny Ramirez	.50	.20
❑	342	Will Clark	.50	.20
❑	343	Mark Redman	.30	.10
❑	344	Bubba Trammell	.30	.10
❑	345	Troy Percival	.30	.10
❑	346	Chris Singleton	.30	.10
❑	347	Rafael Palmeiro	.50	.20
❑	348	Carl Everett	.30	.10
❑	349	Andy Benes	.30	.10
❑	350	Bobby Higginson	.30	.10
❑	351	Alex Cabrera	.30	.10
❑	352	Barry Zito	.50	.20
❑	353	Jace Brewer	.30	.10
❑	354	Paxton Crawford	.30	.10
❑	355	Oswaldo Mairena	.30	.10
❑	356	Joe Crede	.75	.30
❑	357	A.J. Pierzynski	.30	.10
❑	358	Daniel Garibay	.30	.10
❑	359	Jason Tyner	.30	.10
❑	360	Nate Rolison	.30	.10
❑	361	Scott Downs	.30	.10
❑	362	Keith Ginter	.30	.10
❑	363	Juan Pierre	.30	.10
❑	364	Adam Bernero	.30	.10
❑	365	Chris Richard	.30	.10
❑	366	Joey Nation	.30	.10
❑	367	Aubrey Huff	.30	.10
❑	368	Adam Eaton	.30	.10
❑	369	Jose Ortiz	.30	.10
❑	370	Eric Munson	.30	.10
❑	371	Matt Kinney	.30	.10
❑	372	Eric Byrnes	.30	.10
❑	373	Keith McDonald	.30	.10
❑	374	Matt Wise	.30	.10
❑	375	Timo Perez	.30	.10
❑	376	Julio Zuleta	.30	.10
❑	377	Jimmy Rollins	.30	.10
❑	378	Xavier Nady	.30	.10
❑	379	Ryan Kohlmeier	.30	.10
❑	380	Corey Patterson	.30	.10
❑	381	Todd Helton LL	.30	.10
❑	382	Moises Alou LL	.30	.10
❑	383	Vladimir Guerrero LL	.50	.20
❑	384	Luis Castillo LL	.30	.10
❑	385	Jeffrey Hammonds LL	.30	.10
❑	386	Nomar Garciaparra LL	.75	.30
❑	387	Carlos Delgado LL	.30	.10
❑	388	Darin Erstad LL	.30	.10
❑	389	Manny Ramirez LL	.30	.10
❑	390	Mike Sweeney LL	.30	.10
❑	391	Sammy Sosa LL	.50	.20
❑	392	Barry Bonds LL	1.00	.40
❑	393	Jeff Bagwell LL	.30	.10
❑	394	Richard Hidalgo LL	.30	.10
❑	395	Vladimir Guerrero LL	.50	.20
❑	396	Troy Glaus LL	.30	.10
❑	397	Frank Thomas LL	.50	.20
❑	398	Carlos Delgado LL	.30	.10
❑	399	David Justice LL	.30	.10
❑	400	Jason Giambi LL	.30	.10
❑	401	Randy Johnson LL	.50	.20
❑	402	Kevin Brown LL	.30	.10
❑	403	Greg Maddux LL	.75	.30
❑	404	Al Leiter LL	.30	.10
❑	405	Mike Hampton LL	.30	.10
❑	406	Pedro Martinez LL	.50	.20
❑	407	Roger Clemens LL	.75	.30
❑	408	Mike Sirotka LL	.30	.10
❑	409	Mike Mussina LL	.30	.10
❑	410	Bartolo Colon LL	.30	.10
❑	411	Subway Series WS	.50	.20
❑	412	Jose Vizcaino WS	.50	.20
❑	413	Jose Vizcaino WS	.50	.20
❑	414	Roger Clemens WS	.75	.30
❑	415	Benitez/Alfonzo/Perez WS	.30	.10
❑	416	Al Leiter WS	.50	.20
❑	417	Luis Sojo WS	.50	.20
❑	418	Yankees 3-Peat WS	.75	.30
❑	419	Derek Jeter WS	1.00	.40
❑	420	Toast of the Town WS	.50	.20
❑	421	Atlanta Braves CL	.30	.10
❑	422	New York Mets CL	.75	.30
❑	423	Florida Marlins CL	.30	.10
❑	424	Philadelphia Phillies CL	.30	.10
❑	425	Montreal Expos CL	.30	.10
❑	426	St. Louis Cardinals CL	.30	.10
❑	427	Cincinnati Reds CL	.30	.10
❑	428	Chicago Cubs CL	.50	.20
❑	429	Milwaukee Brewers CL	.30	.10
❑	430	Houston Astros CL	.30	.10
❑	431	Pittsburgh Pirates CL	.50	.20
❑	432	San Francisco Giants CL	.30	.10
❑	433	Arizona Diamondbacks CL	.30	.10
❑	434	Los Angeles Dodgers CL UER	.30	.10
❑	435	Colorado Rockies CL UER	.30	.10
❑	436	San Diego Padres CL	.30	.10
❑	437	New York Yankees CL	.75	.30
❑	438	Boston Red Sox CL	.50	.20
❑	439	Baltimore Orioles CL	.30	.10
❑	440	Toronto Blue Jays CL	.30	.10
❑	441	Tampa Bay Devil Rays CL	.30	.10
❑	442	Chicago White Sox CL	.50	.20
❑	443	Cleveland Indians CL	.30	.10
❑	444	Detoit Tigers CL	.30	.10
❑	445	Kansas City Royals CL	.30	.10
❑	446	Minnesota Twins CL	.30	.10
❑	447	Seattle Mariners CL	.30	.10
❑	448	Oakland Athletics CL	.30	.10
❑	449	Anaheim Angels CL	.30	.10
❑	450	Texas Rangers CL	.30	.10
❑	451	Albert Pujols RC	70.00	40.00
❑	452	Ichiro Suzuki RC	15.00	6.00
❑	453	Tsuyoshi Shinjo RC	.75	.30
❑	454	Johnny Estrada RC	.75	.30
❑	455	Elpidio Guzman RC	.50	.20
❑	456	Adrian Hernandez RC	.50	.20
❑	457	Rafael Soriano RC	.50	.20
❑	458	Drew Henson RC	.75	.30
❑	459	Juan Uribe RC	.75	.30
❑	460	Matt White RC	.50	.20
❑	461	Endy Chavez RC	.50	.20
❑	462	Bud Smith RC	.50	.20
❑	463	Morgan Ensberg RC	2.50	1.00
❑	464	Jay Gibbons RC	.75	.30
❑	465	Jackson Melian RC	.50	.20
❑	466	Junior Spivey RC	.75	.30
❑	467	Juan Cruz RC	.50	.20
❑	468	Wilson Betemit RC	2.50	1.00
❑	469	Alexis Gomez RC	.50	.20
❑	470	Mark Teixeira RC	10.00	4.00
❑	471	Erick Almonte RC	.50	.20
❑	472	Travis Hafner RC	8.00	3.00
❑	473	Carlos Valderrama RC	.50	.20

❑ 474 Brandon Duckworth RC .50 .20
❑ 475 Ryan Freel RC 1.50 .60
❑ 476 Wilkin Ruan RC .50 .20
❑ 477 Andres Torres RC .50 .20
❑ 478 Josh Towers RC .75 .30
❑ 479 Kyle Lohse RC .75 .30
❑ 480 Jason Michaels RC .50 .20
❑ 481 Alfonso Soriano .75 .30
❑ 482 C.C. Sabathia .50 .20
❑ 483 Roy Oswalt 1.25 .50
❑ 484 Ben Sheets .75 .30
❑ 485 Adam Dunn .75 .30
❑ NNO Uncut Sheet EXCH/100 2.00 .75

2003 Fleer Tradition Update

❑ COMP.SET w/o SP's (285) 40.00 15.00
❑ COMMON CARD (1-285) .30 .10
❑ COMMON CARD (286-299) 1.00 .40
❑ COMMON RC (286-299) 1.00 .40
❑ 286-299 STATED ODDS 1:4 HOB/RET
❑ COMMON CARD (300-398) 1.00 .40
❑ COMMON RC (300-398) 1.00 .40
❑ 300-398 ISSUED IN MINI-BOXES
❑ ONE MINI-BOX PER UPDATE BOX
❑ 25 CARDS PER MINI-BOX
❑ 1 Aaron Boone .30 .10
❑ 2 Carl Everett .30 .10
❑ 3 Eduardo Perez .30 .10
❑ 4 Jason Michaels .30 .10
❑ 5 Karim Garcia .30 .10
❑ 6 Rainer Olmedo .30 .10
❑ 7 Scott Williamson .30 .10
❑ 8 Adam Kennedy .30 .10
❑ 9 Carl Pavano .30 .10
❑ 10 Eli Marrero .30 .10
❑ 11 Jason Simontacchi .30 .10
❑ 12 Keith Foulke .30 .10
❑ 13 Preston Wilson .30 .10
❑ 14 Scott Hatteberg .30 .10
❑ 15 Adam Dunn .30 .10
❑ 16 Carlos Baerga .30 .10
❑ 17 Elmer Dessens .30 .10
❑ 18 Javier Vazquez .30 .10
❑ 19 Kenny Rogers .30 .10
❑ 20 Quinton McCracken .30 .10
❑ 21 Shane Reynolds .30 .10
❑ 22 Adam Eaton .30 .10
❑ 23 Carlos Zambrano .30 .10
❑ 24 Enrique Wilson .30 .10
❑ 25 Jeff DaVanon .30 .10
❑ 26 Kenny Lofton .30 .10
❑ 27 Ramon Castro .30 .10
❑ 28 Shannon Stewart .30 .10
❑ 29 Al Martin .30 .10
❑ 30 Carlos Guillen .30 .10
❑ 31 Eric Karros .30 .10
❑ 32 Tim Worrell .30 .10
❑ 33 Kevin Millwood .30 .10
❑ 34 Randall Simon .30 .10
❑ 35 Shawn Chacon .30 .10
❑ 36 Alex Rodriguez 1.25 .50
❑ 37 Casey Blake .30 .10
❑ 38 Eric Munson .30 .10
❑ 39 Jeff Kent .30 .10
❑ 40 Kris Benson .30 .10
❑ 41 Randy Winn .30 .10
❑ 42 Shea Hillenbrand .30 .10
❑ 43 Alfonso Soriano .30 .10
❑ 44 Chris George .30 .10
❑ 45 Eric Bruntlett .30 .10
❑ 46 Jeromy Burnitz .30 .10
❑ 47 Kyle Farnsworth .30 .10
❑ 48 Torii Hunter .30 .10
❑ 49 Sidney Ponson .30 .10
❑ 50 Andres Galarraga .30 .10
❑ 51 Chris Singleton .30 .10
❑ 52 Eric Gagne .30 .10
❑ 53 Jesse Foppert .30 .10
❑ 54 Lance Carter .30 .10
❑ 55 Ray Durham .30 .10
❑ 56 Tanyon Sturtze .30 .10
❑ 57 Andy Ashby .30 .10
❑ 58 Cliff Floyd .30 .10
❑ 59 Eric Young .30 .10
❑ 60 Jhonny Peralta 1.25 .50
❑ 61 Livan Hernandez .30 .10
❑ 62 Reggie Sanders .30 .10
❑ 63 Tim Spooneybarger .30 .10
❑ 64 Angel Berroa .30 .10
❑ 65 Coco Crisp .50 .20
❑ 66 Eric Hinske .30 .10
❑ 67 Jim Edmonds .30 .10
❑ 68 Luis Matos .30 .10
❑ 69 Rickey Henderson .75 .30
❑ 70 Todd Walker .30 .10
❑ 71 Antonio Alfonseca .30 .10
❑ 72 Corey Koskie .30 .10
❑ 73 Erubiel Durazo .30 .10
❑ 74 Jim Thome .50 .20
❑ 75 Lyle Overbay .30 .10
❑ 76 Robert Fick .30 .10
❑ 77 Todd Hollandsworth .30 .10
❑ 78 Aramis Ramirez .30 .10
❑ 79 Cristian Guzman .30 .10
❑ 80 Esteban Loaiza .30 .10
❑ 81 Jody Gerut .30 .10
❑ 82 Mark Grudzielanek .30 .10
❑ 83 Roberto Alomar .50 .20
❑ 84 Todd Hundley .30 .10
❑ 85 Mike Hampton .30 .10
❑ 86 Curt Schilling .30 .10
❑ 87 Francisco Rodriguez .30 .10
❑ 88 John Lackey .30 .10
❑ 89 Mark Redman .30 .10
❑ 90 Robin Ventura .30 .10
❑ 91 Todd Zeile .30 .10
❑ 92 B.J. Surhoff .30 .10
❑ 93 Raul Mondesi .30 .10
❑ 94 Frank Catalanotto .30 .10
❑ 95 John Smoltz .50 .20
❑ 96 Mark Ellis .30 .10
❑ 97 Rocco Baldelli .30 .10
❑ 98 Todd Pratt .30 .10
❑ 99 Barry Bonds 2.00 .75
❑ 100 Danny Graves .30 .10
❑ 101 Fred McGriff .50 .20
❑ 102 John Burkett .30 .10
❑ 103 Marquis Grissom .30 .10
❑ 104 Rocky Biddle .30 .10
❑ 105 Tom Glavine .50 .20
❑ 106 Bartolo Colon .30 .10
❑ 107 Darren Bragg .30 .10
❑ 108 Gabe Kapler .30 .10
❑ 109 John Franco .30 .10
❑ 110 Matt Mantei .30 .10
❑ 111 Rod Beck .30 .10
❑ 112 Tomo Ohka .30 .10
❑ 113 Ben Petrick .30 .10
❑ 114 Darren Dreifort .30 .10
❑ 115 Garret Anderson .30 .10
❑ 116 John Vander Wal .30 .10
❑ 117 Melvin Mora .30 .10
❑ 118 Rodrigo Lopez .30 .10
❑ 119 Raul Ibanez .30 .10
❑ 120 Benito Santiago .30 .10
❑ 121 David Ortiz Sox .75 .30
❑ 122 Gary Bennett .30 .10
❑ 123 Jon Garland .30 .10
❑ 124 Michael Young .50 .20
❑ 125 Rodrigo Rosario .30 .10
❑ 126 Travis Lee .30 .10
❑ 127 Bill Mueller .30 .10
❑ 128 Derek Lowe .30 .10
❑ 129 Gil Meche .30 .10
❑ 130 Jose Guillen .30 .10
❑ 131 Miguel Cabrera .75 .30
❑ 132 Ron Calloway .30 .10
❑ 133 Troy Percival .30 .10
❑ 134 Billy Koch .30 .10
❑ 135 Dmitri Young .30 .10
❑ 136 Glendon Rusch .30 .10
❑ 137 Jose Jimenez .30 .10
❑ 138 Miguel Tejada .30 .10
❑ 139 John Thomson .30 .10
❑ 140 Troy O'Leary .30 .10
❑ 141 Bobby Kielty .30 .10
❑ 142 Dontrelle Willis .75 .30
❑ 143 Greg Myers .30 .10
❑ 144 Jose Vizcaino .30 .10
❑ 145 Mike MacDougal .30 .10
❑ 146 Ronnie Belliard .30 .10
❑ 147 Tyler Houston .30 .10
❑ 148 Brady Clark .30 .10
❑ 149 Edgardo Alfonzo .30 .10
❑ 150 Guillermo Mota .30 .10
❑ 151 Jose Lima .30 .10
❑ 152 Mike Williams .30 .10
❑ 153 Roy Oswalt .30 .10
❑ 154 Scott Podsednik 5.00 2.00
❑ 155 Brandon Lyon .30 .10
❑ 156 Henry Mateo .30 .10
❑ 157 Jose Macias .30 .10
❑ 158 Mike Bordick .30 .10
❑ 159 Royce Clayton .30 .10
❑ 160 Vance Wilson .30 .10
❑ 161 Brent Abernathy .30 .10
❑ 162 Horacio Ramirez .30 .10
❑ 163 Jose Reyes .30 .10
❑ 164 Nick Punto .30 .10
❑ 165 Ruben Sierra .30 .10
❑ 166 Victor Zambrano .30 .10
❑ 167 Brett Tomko .30 .10
❑ 168 Ivan Rodriguez .50 .20
❑ 169 Jose Mesa .30 .10
❑ 170 Octavio Dotel .30 .10
❑ 171 Russ Ortiz .30 .10
❑ 172 Vladimir Guerrero .75 .30
❑ 173 Brian Lawrence .30 .10
❑ 174 Jae Weong Seo .30 .10
❑ 175 Jose Cruz Jr. .30 .10
❑ 176 Pat Burrell .30 .10
❑ 177 Russell Branyan .30 .10
❑ 178 Warren Morris .30 .10
❑ 179 Brian Boehringer .30 .10
❑ 180 Jason Johnson .30 .10
❑ 181 Josh Phelps .30 .10
❑ 182 Paul Konerko .30 .10
❑ 183 Ryan Franklin .30 .10
❑ 184 Wes Helms .30 .10
❑ 185 Brooks Kieschnick .30 .10
❑ 186 Jason Davis .30 .10
❑ 187 Juan Pierre .30 .10
❑ 188 Paul Wilson .30 .10
❑ 189 Sammy Sosa .75 .30
❑ 190 Wil Cordero .30 .10
❑ 191 Byung-Hyun Kim .30 .10
❑ 192 Juan Encarnacion .30 .10
❑ 193 Placido Polanco .30 .10
❑ 194 Sandy Alomar Jr. .30 .10
❑ 195 Julio Lugo .30 .10
❑ 196 Junior Spivey .30 .10
❑ 197 Woody Williams .30 .10
❑ 198 Xavier Nady .30 .10
❑ 199 Mark Loretta .30 .10
❑ 200 Deivi Cruz .30 .10
❑ 201 Jorge Posada AS .30 .10
❑ 202 Carlos Delgado AS .30 .10
❑ 203 Alfonso Soriano AS .30 .10
❑ 204 Alex Rodriguez AS .75 .30
❑ 205 Troy Glaus AS .30 .10
❑ 206 Garret Anderson AS .30 .10
❑ 207 Hideki Matsui AS 2.00 .75
❑ 208 Ichiro Suzuki AS .75 .30
❑ 209 Esteban Loaiza AS .30 .10
❑ 210 Manny Ramirez AS .50 .20
❑ 211 Roger Clemens AS .75 .30
❑ 212 Roy Halladay AS .30 .10
❑ 213 Jason Giambi AS .30 .10
❑ 214 Edgar Martinez AS .30 .10

❑	215	Bret Boone AS	.30	.10
❑	216	Hank Blalock AS	.30	.10
❑	217	Nomar Garciaparra AS	.75	.30
❑	218	Vernon Wells AS	.30	.10
❑	219	Melvin Mora AS	.30	.10
❑	220	Magglio Ordonez AS	.30	.10
❑	221	Mike Sweeney AS	.30	.10
❑	222	Barry Zito AS	.30	.10
❑	223	Carl Everett AS	.30	.10
❑	224	Shigetoshi Hasegawa AS	.30	.10
❑	225	Jamie Moyer AS	.30	.10
❑	226	Mark Mulder AS	.30	.10
❑	227	Eddie Guardado AS	.30	.10
❑	228	Ramon Hernandez AS	.30	.10
❑	229	Keith Foulke AS	.30	.10
❑	230	Javy Lopez AS	.30	.10
❑	231	Todd Helton AS	.30	.10
❑	232	Marcus Giles AS	.30	.10
❑	233	Edgar Renteria AS	.30	.10
❑	234	Scott Rolen AS	.30	.10
❑	235	Barry Bonds AS	1.00	.40
❑	236	Albert Pujols AS	.75	.30
❑	237	Gary Sheffield AS	.30	.10
❑	238	Jim Edmonds AS	.30	.10
❑	239	Jason Schmidt AS	.30	.10
❑	240	Mark Prior AS	.30	.10
❑	241	Dontrelle Willis AS	.50	.20
❑	242	Kerry Wood AS	.30	.10
❑	243	Kevin Brown AS	.30	.10
❑	244	Woody Williams AS	.30	.10
❑	245	Paul Lo Duca AS	.30	.10
❑	246	Richie Sexson AS	.30	.10
❑	247	Jose Vidro AS	.30	.10
❑	248	Luis Castillo AS	.30	.10
❑	249	Aaron Boone AS	.30	.10
❑	250	Mike Lowell AS	.30	.10
❑	251	Rafael Furcal AS	.30	.10
❑	252	Andruw Jones AS	.30	.10
❑	253	Preston Wilson AS	.30	.10
❑	254	John Smoltz AS	.30	.10
❑	255	Eric Gagne AS	.30	.10
❑	256	Randy Wolf AS	.30	.10
❑	257	Billy Wagner AS	.30	.10
❑	258	Luis Gonzalez AS	.30	.10
❑	259	Russ Ortiz AS	.30	.10
❑	260	J.Thome/P.Martinez IL	.50	.20
❑	261	A.Soriano/J.Bagwell IL	.50	.20
❑	262	D.Willis/R.Baldelli IL	.50	.20
❑	263	C.Delgado/V.Guerrero IL	.50	.20
❑	264	S.Sosa/M.Ordonez IL	.75	.30
❑	265	J.Giambi/A.Dunn IL	.30	.10
❑	266	M.Sweeney/A.Pujols IL	.75	.30
❑	267	B.Bonds/T.Hunter IL	1.00	.40
❑	268	I.Suzuki/A.Jones IL	.75	.30
❑	269	C.Jones/H.Blalock IL	.50	.20
❑	270	M.Prior/V.Wells IL	.30	.10
❑	271	N.Garciaparra/S.Rolen IL	.75	.30
❑	272	A.Rodriguez/L.Berkman IL	.75	.30
❑	273	R.Clemens/K.Wood IL	.75	.30
❑	274	D.Jeter/J.Reyes IL	1.00	.40
❑	275	G.Maddux/B.Zito IL	.75	.30
❑	276	Carlos Delgado TT	.30	.10
❑	277	J.D. Drew TT	.30	.10
❑	278	Barry Bonds TT	1.00	.40
❑	279	Albert Pujols TT	.75	.30
❑	280	Jim Thome TT	.30	.10
❑	281	Sammy Sosa TT	.50	.20
❑	282	Alfonso Soriano TT	.30	.10
❑	283	Hideki Matsui TT	2.00	.75
❑	284	Mike Piazza TT	.75	.30
❑	285	Vladimir Guerrero TT	.50	.20
❑	286	Rich Harden ROO	1.50	.60
❑	287	Chin-Hui Tsao ROO	1.00	.40
❑	288	Edwin Jackson ROO RC	1.50	.60
❑	289	Chien-Ming Wang ROO RC	10.00	4.00
❑	290	Josh Willingham ROO RC	2.50	1.00
❑	291	Matt Kata ROO RC	1.00	.40
❑	292	Jose Contreras ROO RC	2.00	.75
❑	293	Chris Bootcheck ROO	1.00	.40
❑	294	Javier A. Lopez ROO RC	1.00	.40
❑	295	Delmon Young ROO RC	8.00	3.00
❑	296	Pedro Liriano ROO	1.00	.40
❑	297	Noah Lowry ROO	1.50	.60
❑	298	Khalil Greene ROO	2.50	1.00
❑	299	Rob Bowen ROO	1.00	.40
❑	300	Bo Hart ROO RC	1.00	.40
❑	301	Beau Kemp ROO RC	1.00	.40
❑	302	Gerald Laird ROO	1.00	.40
❑	303	Miguel Ojeda ROO RC	1.00	.40
❑	304	Todd Wellemeyer ROO RC	1.00	.40
❑	305	Ryan Wagner ROO RC	1.00	.40
❑	306	Jeff Duncan ROO RC	1.00	.40
❑	307	Wilfredo Ledezma ROO RC	1.00	.40
❑	308	Wes Obermueller ROO	1.00	.40
❑	309	Bernie Castro ROO RC	1.00	.40
❑	310	Tim Olson ROO RC	1.00	.40
❑	311	Colin Porter ROO RC	1.00	.40
❑	312	Francisco Cruceta ROO RC	1.00	.40
❑	313	Guillermo Quiroz ROO RC	1.00	.40
❑	314	Brian Stokes ROO RC	1.00	.40
❑	315	Robby Hammock ROO RC	1.00	.40
❑	316	Lew Ford ROO RC	1.50	.60
❑	317	Todd Linden ROO	1.00	.40
❑	318	Mike Gallo ROO RC	1.00	.40
❑	319	Francisco Rosario ROO RC	1.00	.40
❑	320	Rosman Garcia ROO RC	1.00	.40
❑	321	Felix Sanchez ROO RC	1.00	.40
❑	322	Chad Gaudin ROO RC	1.00	.40
❑	323	Phil Seibel ROO RC	1.00	.40
❑	324	Jason Gilfillan ROO RC	1.00	.40
❑	325	Termel Sledge ROO RC	1.00	.40
❑	326	Alfredo Gonzalez ROO RC	1.00	.40
❑	327	Josh Stewart ROO RC	1.00	.40
❑	328	Jeremy Griffiths ROO RC	1.00	.40
❑	329	Cory Stewart ROO RC	1.00	.40
❑	330	Josh Hall ROO RC	1.00	.40
❑	331	Arnie Munoz ROO RC	1.00	.40
❑	332	Garrett Atkins ROO	1.00	.40
❑	333	Neal Cotts ROO	1.00	.40
❑	334	Dan Haren ROO RC	2.00	.75
❑	335	Shane Victorino ROO RC	2.00	.75
❑	336	David Sanders ROO RC	1.00	.40
❑	337	Oscar Villarreal ROO RC	1.00	.40
❑	338	Michael Hessman ROO RC	1.00	.40
❑	339	Andrew Brown ROO RC	1.50	.60
❑	340	Kevin Hooper ROO	1.00	.40
❑	341	Prentice Redman ROO RC	1.00	.40
❑	342	Brandon Webb ROO RC	5.00	2.00
❑	343	Jimmy Gobble ROO	1.00	.40
❑	344	Pete LaForest ROO RC	1.00	.40
❑	345	Chris Waters ROO RC	1.00	.40
❑	346	Hideki Matsui ROO RC	8.00	3.00
❑	347	Chris Capuano ROO RC	2.00	.75
❑	348	Jon Leicester ROO RC	1.00	.40
❑	349	Mike Nicolas ROO RC	1.00	.40
❑	350	Nook Logan ROO RC	1.50	.60
❑	351	Craig Brazell ROO RC	1.00	.40
❑	352	Aaron Looper ROO RC	1.00	.40
❑	353	D.J. Carrasco ROO RC	1.00	.40
❑	354	Clint Barmes ROO RC	2.00	.75
❑	355	Doug Waechter ROO RC	1.50	.60
❑	356	Julio Manon ROO RC	1.00	.40
❑	357	Jeremy Bonderman ROO RC	6.00	2.50
❑	358	Diegomar Markwell ROO RC	1.00	.40
❑	359	Dave Matranga ROO RC	1.00	.40
❑	360	Luis Ayala ROO RC	1.00	.40
❑	361	Jason Stanford ROO	1.00	.40
❑	362	Roger Deago ROO RC	1.00	.40
❑	363	Geoff Geary ROO RC	1.00	.40
❑	364	Edgar Gonzalez ROO RC	1.00	.40
❑	365	Michel Hernandez ROO RC	1.00	.40
❑	366	Aquilino Lopez ROO RC	1.00	.40
❑	367	David Manning ROO	1.00	.40
❑	368	Carlos Mendez ROO RC	1.00	.40
❑	369	Matt Miller ROO RC	1.00	.40
❑	370	Michael Nakamura ROO RC	1.00	.40
❑	371	Mike Neu ROO RC	1.00	.40
❑	372	Ramon Nivar ROO RC	1.00	.40
❑	373	Kevin Ohme ROO RC	1.00	.40
❑	374	Alex Prieto ROO RC	1.00	.40
❑	375	Stephen Randolph ROO RC	1.00	.40
❑	376	Brian Sweeney ROO RC	1.00	.40
❑	377	Matt Diaz ROO RC	2.00	.75
❑	378	Mike Gonzalez ROO	1.00	.40
❑	379	Daniel Cabrera ROO RC	2.00	.75
❑	380	Fernando Cabrera ROO RC	1.00	.40
❑	381	David DeJesus ROO RC	2.00	.75
❑	382	Mike Ryan ROO RC	1.00	.40
❑	383	Rick Roberts ROO RC	1.00	.40
❑	384	Seung Song ROO	1.00	.40
❑	385	Rickie Weeks ROO RC	5.00	2.00
❑	386	Humberto Quintero ROO RC	1.00	.40
❑	387	Alexis Rios ROO	1.00	.40
❑	388	Aaron Miles ROO RC	1.50	.60
❑	389	Tom Gregorio ROO RC	1.00	.40
❑	390	Anthony Ferrari ROO RC	1.00	.40
❑	391	Kevin Correia ROO RC	1.00	.40
❑	392	Rafael Betancourt ROO RC	1.50	.60
❑	393	Rett Johnson ROO RC	1.00	.40
❑	394	Richard Fischer ROO RC	1.00	.40
❑	395	Greg Aquino ROO RC	1.00	.40
❑	396	Daniel Garcia ROO RC	1.00	.40
❑	397	Sergio Mitre ROO RC	1.50	.60
❑	398	Edwin Almonte ROO	1.00	.40

2004 Fleer Tradition

❑		COMPLETE SET (500)	150.00	75.00
❑		COMP.SET w/o SP's (400)	40.00	15.00
❑		COMMON CARD (1-400)	.30	.10
❑		COMMON CARD (401-470)	1.00	.40
❑		COMMON CARD (471-500)	1.00	.40
❑		401-445 STATED ODDS 1:2		
❑		446-461 STATED ODDS 1:6		
❑		462-470 STATED ODDS 1:9		
❑		471-500 STATED ODDS 1:3		
❑	1	Juan Pierre WS	.30	.10
❑	2	Josh Beckett WS	.30	.10
❑	3	Ivan Rodriguez WS	.50	.20
❑	4	Miguel Cabrera WS	.50	.20
❑	5	Dontrelle Willis WS	.50	.20
❑	6	Derek Jeter WS	1.50	.60
❑	7	Jason Giambi WS	.30	.10
❑	8	Bernie Williams WS	.50	.20
❑	9	Alfonso Soriano WS	.30	.10
❑	10	Hideki Matsui WS	1.25	.50
❑	11	Anderson/Ortiz/Lackey TL	.30	.10
❑	12	Gonzalez/Webb/Schilling TL	.30	.10
❑	13	Lopez/Sheffield/Ortiz TL	.30	.10
❑	14	Batista/Gibb/Ponson/John TL	.30	.10
❑	15	Manny/Nomar/Lowe/Pedro TL	.50	.20
❑	16	Sosa/Prior/Wood TL	.50	.20
❑	17	Thomas/Lee/Loaiza TL	.50	.20
❑	18	Dunn/Casey/Reit/Wilson TL	.30	.10
❑	19	Gerut/Sabathia TL	.30	.10
❑	20	Wilson/Oliver/Jennings TL	.30	.10
❑	21	Young/Maroth/Bonderman TL	.30	.10
❑	22	Lowell/Willis/Beckett TL	.50	.20
❑	23	Bagwell/Robertson/Miller TL	.30	.10
❑	24	Beltran/May TL	.30	.10
❑	25	Beltre/Green/Nomo/Brown TL	.30	.10
❑	26	Sexson/Sheets TL	.30	.10
❑	27	Hunter/Radke/Santana TL	.50	.20
❑	28	Vlad/Cabrera/Livan/Vazq TL	.50	.20
❑	29	Floyd/Wigg/Trach/Leiter TL	.30	.10
❑	30	Giambi/Pettitte/Mussina TL	.50	.20
❑	31	Chavez/Tejada/Hudson TL	.30	.10
❑	32	Thome/Wolf TL	.30	.10
❑	33	Sanders/Fogg/Wells TL	.30	.10
❑	34	Klesko/Loretta/Peavy TL	.30	.10
❑	35	Cruz Jr./Alfonzo/Schmidt TL	.30	.10
❑	36	Boone/Moyer/Pineiro TL	.30	.10
❑	37	Pujols/Williams TL	.75	.30
❑	38	Huff/Zambrano TL	.30	.10
❑	39	A.Rodriguez/Thomson TL	.75	.30
❑	40	Delgado/Halladay TL	.30	.10
❑	41	Greg Maddux	1.25	.50
❑	42	Ben Grieve	.30	.10
❑	43	Darin Erstad	.30	.10
❑	44	Ruben Sierra	.30	.10
❑	45	Byung-Hyung Kim	.30	.10

❑	46	Freddy Garcia	.30	.10
❑	47	Richard Hidalgo	.30	.10
❑	48	Tike Redman	.30	.10
❑	49	Kevin Millwood	.30	.10
❑	50	Marquis Grissom	.30	.10
❑	51	Jae Weong Seo	.30	.10
❑	52	Wil Cordero	.30	.10
❑	53	LaTroy Hawkins	.30	.10
❑	54	Jolbert Cabrera	.30	.10
❑	55	Kevin Appier	.30	.10
❑	56	John Lackey	.30	.10
❑	57	Garret Anderson	.30	.10
❑	58	R.A. Dickey	.30	.10
❑	59	David Segui	.30	.10
❑	60	Erubiel Durazo	.30	.10
❑	61	Bobby Abreu	.30	.10
❑	62	Travis Hafner	.30	.10
❑	63	Victor Zambrano	.30	.10
❑	64	Randy Johnson	.75	.30
❑	65	Bernie Williams	.50	.20
❑	66	J.T. Snow	.30	.10
❑	67	Sammy Sosa	.75	.30
❑	68	Al Leiter	.30	.10
❑	69	Jason Jennings	.30	.10
❑	70	Matt Morris	.30	.10
❑	71	Mike Hampton	.30	.10
❑	72	Juan Encarnacion	.30	.10
❑	73	Alex Gonzalez	.30	.10
❑	74	Bartolo Colon	.30	.10
❑	75	Brett Myers	.30	.10
❑	76	Michael Young	.30	.10
❑	77	Ichiro Suzuki	1.50	.60
❑	78	Jason Johnson	.30	.10
❑	79	Brad Ausmus	.30	.10
❑	80	Ted Lilly	.30	.10
❑	81	Ken Griffey Jr.	1.25	.50
❑	82	Chone Figgins	.30	.10
❑	83	Edgar Martinez	.50	.20
❑	84	Adam Eaton	.30	.10
❑	85	Ken Harvey	.30	.10
❑	86	Francisco Rodriguez	.30	.10
❑	87	Bill Mueller	.30	.10
❑	88	Mike Maroth	.30	.10
❑	89	Charles Johnson	.30	.10
❑	90	Jhonny Peralta	.30	.10
❑	91	Kip Wells	.30	.10
❑	92	Cesar Izturis	.30	.10
❑	93	Matt Clement	.30	.10
❑	94	Lyle Overbay	.30	.10
❑	95	Kirk Rueter	.30	.10
❑	96	Cristian Guzman	.30	.10
❑	97	Garrett Stephenson	.30	.10
❑	98	Lance Berkman	.30	.10
❑	99	Brett Tomko	.30	.10
❑	100	Chris Stynes	.30	.10
❑	101	Nate Cornejo	.30	.10
❑	102	Aaron Rowand	.30	.10
❑	103	Javier Vazquez	.30	.10
❑	104	Jason Kendall	.30	.10
❑	105	Mark Redman	.30	.10
❑	106	Benito Santiago	.30	.10
❑	107	C.C. Sabathia	.30	.10
❑	108	David Wells	.30	.10
❑	109	Mark Ellis	.30	.10
❑	110	Casey Blake	.30	.10
❑	111	Sean Burroughs	.30	.10
❑	112	Carlos Beltran	.30	.10
❑	113	Ramon Hernandez	.30	.10
❑	114	Eric Hinske	.30	.10
❑	115	Luis Gonzalez	.30	.10
❑	116	Jarrod Washburn	.30	.10
❑	117	Ronnie Belliard	.30	.10
❑	118	Troy Percival	.30	.10
❑	119	Jose Valentin	.30	.10
❑	120	Chase Utley	.50	.20
❑	121	Odalis Perez	.30	.10
❑	122	Steve Finley	.30	.10
❑	123	Bret Boone	.30	.10
❑	124	Jeff Conine	.30	.10
❑	125	Josh Fogg	.30	.10
❑	126	Neifi Perez	.30	.10
❑	127	Ben Sheets	.30	.10
❑	128	Randy Winn	.30	.10
❑	129	Matt Stairs	.30	.10
❑	130	Carlos Delgado	.30	.10
❑	131	Morgan Ensberg	.30	.10
❑	132	Vinny Castilla	.30	.10
❑	133	Matt Mantei	.30	.10
❑	134	Alex Rodriguez	1.25	.50
❑	135	Matthew LeCroy	.30	.10
❑	136	Woody Williams	.30	.10
❑	137	Frank Catalanotto	.30	.10
❑	138	Rondell White	.30	.10
❑	139	Scott Rolen	.50	.20
❑	140	Cliff Floyd	.30	.10
❑	141	Chipper Jones	.75	.30
❑	142	Robin Ventura	.30	.10
❑	143	Mariano Rivera	.75	.30
❑	144	Brady Clark	.30	.10
❑	145	Ramon Ortiz	.30	.10
❑	146	Omar Infante	.30	.10
❑	147	Mike Matheny	.30	.10
❑	148	Pedro Martinez	.50	.20
❑	149	Carlos Baerga	.30	.10
❑	150	Shannon Stewart	.30	.10
❑	151	Travis Lee	.30	.10
❑	152	Eric Byrnes	.30	.10
❑	153	Rafael Furcal	.30	.10
❑	154	B.J. Surhoff	.30	.10
❑	155	Zach Day	.30	.10
❑	156	Marlon Anderson	.30	.10
❑	157	Mark Hendrickson	.30	.10
❑	158	Mike Mussina	.50	.20
❑	159	Randall Simon	.30	.10
❑	160	Jeff DaVanon	.30	.10
❑	161	Joel Pineiro	.30	.10
❑	162	Vernon Wells	.30	.10
❑	163	Adam Kennedy	.30	.10
❑	164	Trot Nixon	.30	.10
❑	165	Rodrigo Lopez	.30	.10
❑	166	Curt Schilling	.30	.10
❑	167	Horacio Ramirez	.30	.10
❑	168	Jason Marquis	.30	.10
❑	169	Magglio Ordonez	.30	.10
❑	170	Scott Schoeneweis	.30	.10
❑	171	Andruw Jones	.50	.20
❑	172	Tino Martinez	.50	.20
❑	173	Moises Alou	.30	.10
❑	174	Kelvim Escobar	.30	.10
❑	175	Xavier Nady	.30	.10
❑	176	Ramon Martinez	.30	.10
❑	177	Pat Hentgen	.30	.10
❑	178	Austin Kearns	.30	.10
❑	179	D'Angelo Jimenez	.30	.10
❑	180	Deivi Cruz	.30	.10
❑	181	John Smoltz	.50	.20
❑	182	Toby Hall	.30	.10
❑	183	Mark Buehrle	.30	.10
❑	184	Howie Clark	.30	.10
❑	185	David Ortiz	.75	.30
❑	186	Raul Mondesi	.30	.10
❑	187	Milton Bradley	.30	.10
❑	188	Jorge Julio	.30	.10
❑	189	Victor Martinez	.30	.10
❑	190	Gabe Kapler	.30	.10
❑	191	Julio Franco	.30	.10
❑	192	Ryan Freel	.30	.10
❑	193	Brad Fullmer	.30	.10
❑	194	Joe Borowski	.30	.10
❑	195	Darren Oliver	.30	.10
❑	196	Jason Varitek	.75	.30
❑	197	Greg Myers	.30	.10
❑	198	Eric Munson	.30	.10
❑	199	Tim Wakefield	.30	.10
❑	200	Kyle Farnsworth	.30	.10
❑	201	Johnny Vander Wal	.30	.10
❑	202	Alex Escobar	.30	.10
❑	203	Sean Casey	.30	.10
❑	204	John Thomson	.30	.10
❑	205	Carlos Zambrano	.30	.10
❑	206	Kenny Lofton	.30	.10
❑	207	Marcus Giles	.30	.10
❑	208	Wade Miller	.30	.10
❑	209	Geoff Blum	.30	.10
❑	210	Jason LaRue	.30	.10
❑	211	Omar Vizquel	.50	.20
❑	212	Carlos Pena	.30	.10
❑	213	Adam Dunn	.30	.10
❑	214	Oscar Villarreal	.30	.10
❑	215	Paul Konerko	.30	.10
❑	216	Hideo Nomo	.75	.30
❑	217	Mike Sweeney	.30	.10
❑	218	Coco Crisp	.30	.10
❑	219	Shawn Chacon	.30	.10
❑	220	Brook Fordyce	.30	.10
❑	221	Josh Beckett	.30	.10
❑	222	Paul Wilson	.30	.10
❑	223	Josh Towers	.30	.10
❑	224	Geoff Jenkins	.30	.10
❑	225	Shawn Green	.30	.10
❑	226	Derrek Lee	.50	.20
❑	227	Karim Garcia	.30	.10
❑	228	Preston Wilson	.30	.10
❑	229	Dane Sardinha	.30	.10
❑	230	Aramis Ramirez	.30	.10
❑	231	Doug Mientkiewicz	.30	.10
❑	232	Jay Gibbons	.30	.10
❑	233	Adam Everett	.30	.10
❑	234	Brooks Kieschnick	.30	.10
❑	235	Dmitri Young	.30	.10
❑	236	Brad Penny	.30	.10
❑	237	Todd Zeile	.30	.10
❑	238	Eric Gagne	.30	.10
❑	239	Esteban Loaiza	.30	.10
❑	240	Billy Wagner	.30	.10
❑	241	Nomar Garciaparra	1.25	.50
❑	242	Desi Relaford	.30	.10
❑	243	Luis Rivas	.30	.10
❑	244	Andy Pettitte	.50	.20
❑	245	Ty Wigginton	.30	.10
❑	246	Edgar Gonzalez	.30	.10
❑	247	Brian Anderson	.30	.10
❑	248	Richie Sexson	.30	.10
❑	249	Russell Branyan	.30	.10
❑	250	Jose Guillen	.30	.10
❑	251	Chin-Hui Tsao	.30	.10
❑	252	Jose Hernandez	.30	.10
❑	253	Kevin Brown	.30	.10
❑	254	Pete LaForest	.30	.10
❑	255	Adrian Beltre	.30	.10
❑	256	Jacque Jones	.30	.10
❑	257	Jimmy Rollins	.30	.10
❑	258	Brandon Phillips	.30	.10
❑	259	Derek Jeter	1.50	.60
❑	260	Carl Everett	.30	.10
❑	261	Wes Helms	.30	.10
❑	262	Kyle Lohse	.30	.10
❑	263	Jason Phillips	.30	.10
❑	264	Jake Peavy	.30	.10
❑	265	Orlando Hernandez	.30	.10
❑	266	Keith Foulke	.30	.10
❑	267	Brad Wilkerson	.30	.10
❑	268	Corey Koskie	.30	.10
❑	269	Josh Hall	.30	.10
❑	270	Bobby Higginson	.30	.10
❑	271	Andres Galarraga	.30	.10
❑	272	Alfonso Soriano	.30	.10
❑	273	Carlos Rivera	.30	.10
❑	274	Steve Trachsel	.30	.10
❑	275	David Bell	.30	.10
❑	276	Endy Chavez	.30	.10
❑	277	Jay Payton	.30	.10
❑	278	Mark Mulder	.30	.10
❑	279	Terrence Long	.30	.10
❑	280	A.J. Burnett	.30	.10
❑	281	Pokey Reese	.30	.10
❑	282	Phil Nevin	.30	.10
❑	283	Jose Contreras	.30	.10
❑	284	Jim Thome	.50	.20
❑	285	Pat Burrell	.30	.10
❑	286	Luis Castillo	.30	.10
❑	287	Juan Uribe	.30	.10
❑	288	Raul Ibanez	.30	.10
❑	289	Sidney Ponson	.30	.10
❑	290	Scott Hatteberg	.30	.10
❑	291	Jack Wilson	.30	.10
❑	292	Reggie Sanders	.30	.10
❑	293	Brian Giles	.30	.10
❑	294	Craig Biggio	.50	.20
❑	295	Kazuhisa Ishii	.30	.10
❑	296	Jim Edmonds	.30	.10
❑	297	Trevor Hoffman	.30	.10
❑	298	Ray Durham	.30	.10
❑	299	Mike Lieberthal	.30	.10
❑	300	Tim Worrell	.30	.10
❑	301	Chris George	.30	.10
❑	302	Jamie Moyer	.30	.10
❑	303	Mike Cameron	.30	.10

❑ 304 Matt Kinney .30 .10
❑ 305 Aubrey Huff .30 .10
❑ 306 Brian Lawrence .30 .10
❑ 307 Carlos Guillen .30 .10
❑ 308 J.D. Drew .30 .10
❑ 309 Paul Lo Duca .30 .10
❑ 310 Tim Salmon .50 .20
❑ 311 Jason Schmidt .30 .10
❑ 312 A.J. Pierzynski .30 .10
❑ 313 Lance Carter .30 .10
❑ 314 Julio Lugo .30 .10
❑ 315 Johan Santana .75 .30
❑ 316 Laynce Nix .30 .10
❑ 317 John Olerud .30 .10
❑ 318 Robb Quinlan .30 .10
❑ 319 Scott Spiezio .30 .10
❑ 320 Tony Clark .30 .10
❑ 321 Jose Vidro .30 .10
❑ 322 Shea Hillenbrand .30 .10
❑ 323 Doug Glanville .30 .10
❑ 324 Orlando Palmeiro .30 .10
❑ 325 Juan Gonzalez .30 .10
❑ 326 Jason Giambi .30 .10
❑ 327 Junior Spivey .30 .10
❑ 328 Tom Glavine .50 .20
❑ 329 Reed Johnson .30 .10
❑ 330 David Eckstein .30 .10
❑ 331 Damian Jackson .30 .10
❑ 332 Orlando Hudson .30 .10
❑ 333 Barry Zito .30 .10
❑ 334 Robert Fick .30 .10
❑ 335 Aaron Boone .30 .10
❑ 336 Rafael Palmeiro .50 .20
❑ 337 Bobby Kielty .30 .10
❑ 338 Tony Batista .30 .10
❑ 339 Ryan Dempster .30 .10
❑ 340 Derek Lowe .30 .10
❑ 341 Alex Cintron .30 .10
❑ 342 Jermaine Dye .30 .10
❑ 343 John Burkett .30 .10
❑ 344 Javy Lopez .30 .10
❑ 345 Eric Karros .30 .10
❑ 346 Corey Patterson .30 .10
❑ 347 Josh Phelps .30 .10
❑ 348 Ryan Klesko .30 .10
❑ 349 Craig Wilson .30 .10
❑ 350 Brian Roberts .30 .10
❑ 351 Roberto Alomar .50 .20
❑ 352 Frank Thomas .75 .30
❑ 353 Gary Sheffield .30 .10
❑ 354 Alex Gonzalez .30 .10
❑ 355 Jose Cruz Jr. .30 .10
❑ 356 Jerome Williams .30 .10
❑ 357 Mark Kotsay .30 .10
❑ 358 Chris Reitsma .30 .10
❑ 359 Carlos Lee .30 .10
❑ 360 Todd Helton .50 .20
❑ 361 Gil Meche .30 .10
❑ 362 Ryan Franklin .30 .10
❑ 363 Josh Bard .30 .10
❑ 364 Juan Pierre .30 .10
❑ 365 Barry Larkin .50 .20
❑ 366 Edgar Renteria .30 .10
❑ 367 Alex Sanchez .30 .10
❑ 368 Jeff Bagwell .50 .20
❑ 369 Ben Broussard .30 .10
❑ 370 Chan-Ho Park .30 .10
❑ 371 Darrell May .30 .10
❑ 372 Roy Oswalt .30 .10
❑ 373 Craig Monroe .30 .10
❑ 374 Fred McGriff .50 .20
❑ 375 Bengie Molina .30 .10
❑ 376 Aaron Guiel .30 .10
❑ 377 Jeriome Robertson .30 .10
❑ 378 Kenny Rogers .30 .10
❑ 379 Colby Lewis .30 .10
❑ 380 Jeromy Burnitz .30 .10
❑ 381 Orlando Cabrera .30 .10
❑ 382 Joe Randa .30 .10
❑ 383 Miguel Batista .30 .10
❑ 384 Brad Radke .30 .10
❑ 385 Jeremy Giambi .30 .10
❑ 386 Vladimir Guerrero .75 .30
❑ 387 Melvin Mora .30 .10
❑ 388 Royce Clayton .30 .10
❑ 389 Danny Garcia .30 .10
❑ 390 Manny Ramirez .50 .20
❑ 391 Dave McCarty .30 .10
❑ 392 Mark Grudzielanek .30 .10
❑ 393 Mike Piazza 1.25 .50
❑ 394 Jorge Posada .50 .20
❑ 395 Tim Hudson .30 .10
❑ 396 Placido Polanco .30 .10
❑ 397 Mark Loretta .30 .10
❑ 398 Jesse Foppert .30 .10
❑ 399 Albert Pujols 1.50 .60
❑ 400 Jeremi Gonzalez .30 .10
❑ 401 Paul Bako SP 1.00 .40
❑ 402 Luis Matos SP 1.00 .40
❑ 403 Johnny Damon SP 1.50 .60
❑ 404 Kerry Wood SP 1.00 .40
❑ 405 Joe Crede SP 1.00 .40
❑ 406 Jason Davis SP 1.00 .40
❑ 407 Larry Walker SP 1.00 .40
❑ 408 Ivan Rodriguez SP 1.50 .60
❑ 409 Nick Johnson SP 1.00 .40
❑ 410 Jose Lima SP 1.00 .40
❑ 411 Brian Jordan SP 1.00 .40
❑ 412 Eddie Guardado SP 1.00 .40
❑ 413 Ron Calloway SP 1.00 .40
❑ 414 Aaron Heilman SP 1.00 .40
❑ 415 Eric Chavez SP 1.00 .40
❑ 416 Randy Wolf SP 1.00 .40
❑ 417 Jason Bay SP 1.00 .40
❑ 418 Edgardo Alfonzo SP 1.00 .40
❑ 419 Kazuhiro Sasaki SP 1.00 .40
❑ 420 Eduardo Perez SP 1.00 .40
❑ 421 Carl Crawford SP 1.00 .40
❑ 422 Troy Glaus SP 1.00 .40
❑ 423 Joaquin Benoit SP 1.00 .40
❑ 424 Russ Ortiz SP 1.00 .40
❑ 425 Larry Bigbie SP 1.00 .40
❑ 426 Todd Walker SP 1.00 .40
❑ 427 Kris Benson SP 1.00 .40
❑ 428 Sandy Alomar Jr. SP 1.00 .40
❑ 429 Jody Gerut SP 1.00 .40
❑ 430 Rene Reyes SP 1.00 .40
❑ 431 Mike Lowell SP 1.00 .40
❑ 432 Jeff Kent SP 1.00 .40
❑ 433 Mike MacDougal SP 1.00 .40
❑ 434 Dave Roberts SP 1.00 .40
❑ 435 Torii Hunter SP 1.00 .40
❑ 436 Tomo Ohka SP 1.00 .40
❑ 437 Jeremy Griffiths SP 1.00 .40
❑ 438 Miguel Tejada SP 1.00 .40
❑ 439 Vicente Padilla SP 1.00 .40
❑ 440 Bobby Hill SP 1.00 .40
❑ 441 Rich Aurilia SP 1.00 .40
❑ 442 Shigetoshi Hasegawa SP 1.00 .40
❑ 443 So Taguchi SP 1.00 .40
❑ 444 Damian Rolls SP 1.00 .40
❑ 445 Roy Halladay SP 1.00 .40
❑ 446 Rocco Baldelli SO SP 1.00 .40
❑ 447 Dontrelle Willis SO SP 1.50 .60
❑ 448 Mark Prior SO SP 1.50 .60
❑ 449 Jason Lane SO SP 1.00 .40
❑ 450 Angel Berroa SO SP 1.00 .40
❑ 451 Jose Reyes SO SP 1.00 .40
❑ 452 Ryan Wagner SO SP 1.00 .40
❑ 453 Marlon Byrd SO SP 1.00 .40
❑ 454 Hee Seop Choi SO SP 1.00 .40
❑ 455 Brandon Webb SO SP 1.00 .40
❑ 456 Bo Hart SO SP 1.00 .40
❑ 457 Hank Blalock SO SP 1.00 .40
❑ 458 Mark Teixeira SO SP 1.50 .60
❑ 459 Hideki Matsui SO SP 4.00 1.50
❑ 460 Scott Podsednik SO SP 1.00 .40
❑ 461 Miguel Cabrera SO SP 1.50 .60
❑ 462 Josh Beckett AW SP 1.00 .40
❑ 463 Mariano Rivera AW SP 2.50 1.00
❑ 464 Ivan Rodriguez AW SP 1.50 .60
❑ 465 Alex Rodriguez AW SP 4.00 1.50
❑ 466 Albert Pujols AW SP 5.00 2.00
❑ 467 Roy Halladay AW SP 1.00 .40
❑ 468 Eric Gagne AW SP 1.00 .40
❑ 469 Angel Berroa AW SP 1.00 .40
❑ 470 Dontrelle Willis AW SP 1.50 .60
❑ 471 Boot/Gregorio/Fischer SP 1.00 .40
❑ 472 Kata/Olson/Hammock SP 1.00 .40
❑ 473 Hessman/Waters/Aquino SP 1.00 .40
❑ 474 Mendez/Cabrera/Guthrie SP 1.00 .40
❑ 475 Almonte/Seibel/Sanchez SP 1.00 .40
❑ 476 Wellemeyer/Leicester/Mitre SP 1.00 .40
❑ 477 Stewart/Cotts/Miles SP 1.00 .40
❑ 478 Sledge/Hall/Claussen SP 1.00 .40
❑ 479 Cruceta/Stanford/Betan SP 1.00 .40
❑ 480 Lopez/Atkins/Barmes SP 1.50 .60
❑ 481 Ledez/Logan/Bonderman SP 1.50 .60
❑ 482 Willingham/Hoop/Roberts SP 1.00 .40
❑ 483 Porter/Gallo/Matranga SP 1.00 .40
❑ 484 DeJesus/Gilfillan/Gobble SP 1.00 .40
❑ 485 Hill/Gonzalez/Brown SP 1.00 .40
❑ 486 Weeks/Liriano/Oberm SP 1.50 .60
❑ 487 Prieto/Ryan/Ford SP 1.00 .40
❑ 488 Manon/Ayala/Song SP 1.00 .40
❑ 489 Duncan/Redman/Brazell SP 1.50 .60
❑ 490 Wang/M.Hern/M.Gonz SP 5.00 2.00
❑ 491 Harden/Neu/Geary SP 1.50 .60
❑ 492 Markwell/Gaudin/Sanders SP 1.00 .40
❑ 493 Kemp/Nakamura/Carrasco SP 1.00 .40
❑ 494 Greene/Ojeda/Castro SP 2.50 1.00
❑ 495 Lowry/Linden/Correia SP 1.50 .60
❑ 496 Looper/Sweeney/R.John SP 1.00 .40
❑ 497 J.Gall RC/Haren/Ohme SP 2.50 1.00
❑ 498 Young/Waechter/Diaz SP 2.50 1.00
❑ 499 Laird/Garcia/Nivar SP 1.00 .40
❑ 500 Rios/Quiroz/Rosario SP 1.50 .60

2005 Fleer Tradition

❑ COMPLETE SET (350) 150.00 75.00
❑ COMP.SET w/o SP's (300) 40.00 15.00
❑ COMMON CARD (1-300) .30 .10
❑ COMMON CARD (301-330) 5.00 2.00
❑ COMMON CARD (331-350) 1.00 .40
❑ 301-350 STATED ODDS 1:2 H, 1:4 R
❑ 1 Johan/Schil/Westbrook SL .50 .20
❑ 2 Sheets/Peavy/Randy SL .50 .20
❑ 3 Johan/Colon/Schilling SL .30 .10
❑ 4 Pavanvo/Oswalt/Clemens SL .75 .30
❑ 5 Johan/Pedro/Schilling SL .30 .10
❑ 6 Schmidt/Randy/Sheets SL .50 .20
❑ 7 Mora/Guerrero/Ichiro SL .75 .30
❑ 8 Beltre/Helton/Loretta SL .30 .10
❑ 9 Manny/Konerko/Ortiz SL .50 .20
❑ 10 Pujols/Beltre/Dunn SL .75 .30
❑ 11 Ortiz/Manny/Tejada SL .50 .20
❑ 12 Pujols/Castilla/Rolen SL .50 .20
❑ 13 Jason Bay .30 .10
❑ 14 Greg Maddux 1.25 .50
❑ 15 Melvin Mora .30 .10
❑ 16 Matt Stairs .30 .10
❑ 17 Scott Podsednik .30 .10
❑ 18 Bartolo Colon .30 .10
❑ 19 Roger Clemens 1.25 .50
❑ 20 Eric Hinske .30 .10
❑ 21 Johnny Estrada .30 .10
❑ 22 Brett Tomko .30 .10
❑ 23 John Buck .30 .10
❑ 24 Nomar Garciaparra .75 .30
❑ 25 Milton Bradley .30 .10
❑ 26 Craig Biggio .50 .20
❑ 27 Kyle Denney .30 .10
❑ 28 Brad Penny .30 .10
❑ 29 Todd Helton .50 .20
❑ 30 Luis Gonzalez .30 .10
❑ 31 Bill Hall .30 .10
❑ 32 Ruben Sierra .30 .10
❑ 33 Zack Greinke .30 .10
❑ 34 Sandy Alomar Jr. .30 .10
❑ 35 Jason Giambi .30 .10

❑ 36 Ben Sheets .30 .10
❑ 37 Edgardo Alfonzo .30 .10
❑ 38 Kenny Rogers .30 .10
❑ 39 Coco Crisp .30 .10
❑ 40 Randy Choate .30 .10
❑ 41 Braden Looper .30 .10
❑ 42 Adam Dunn .30 .10
❑ 43 Adam Eaton .30 .10
❑ 44 Luis Castillo .30 .10
❑ 45 Casey Fossum .30 .10
❑ 46 Mike Piazza .75 .30
❑ 47 Juan Pierre .30 .10
❑ 48 Doug Davis .30 .10
❑ 49 Manny Ramirez .50 .20
❑ 50 Travis Hafner .30 .10
❑ 51 Jack Wilson .30 .10
❑ 52 Mike Maroth .30 .10
❑ 53 Ken Harvey .30 .10
❑ 54 Brooks Kieschnick .30 .10
❑ 55 Brad Fullmer .30 .10
❑ 56 Octavio Dotel .30 .10
❑ 57 Mike Matheny .30 .10
❑ 58 Andruw Jones .50 .20
❑ 59 Alfonso Soriano .30 .10
❑ 60 Royce Clayton .30 .10
❑ 61 Jon Garland .30 .10
❑ 62 John Mabry .30 .10
❑ 63 Rafael Palmeiro .50 .20
❑ 64 Garett Atkins .30 .10
❑ 65 Brian Meadows .30 .10
❑ 66 Tony Armas Jr. .30 .10
❑ 67 Toby Hall .30 .10
❑ 68 Carlos Baerga .30 .10
❑ 69 Barry Larkin .50 .20
❑ 70 Jody Gerut .30 .10
❑ 71 Brent Mayne .30 .10
❑ 72 Shigetoshi Hasegawa .30 .10
❑ 73 Jose Cruz Jr. .30 .10
❑ 74 Dan Wilson .30 .10
❑ 75 Sidney Ponson .30 .10
❑ 76 Jason Jennings .30 .10
❑ 77 A.J. Burnett .30 .10
❑ 78 Tony Batista .30 .10
❑ 79 Kris Benson .30 .10
❑ 80 Sean Burroughs .30 .10
❑ 81 Eric Young .30 .10
❑ 82 Casey Kotchman .30 .10
❑ 83 Derrek Lee .50 .20
❑ 84 Mariano Rivera .75 .30
❑ 85 Julio Franco .30 .10
❑ 86 Corey Patterson .30 .10
❑ 87 Carlos Beltran .30 .10
❑ 88 Trevor Hoffman .30 .10
❑ 89 Danny Garcia .30 .10
❑ 90 Marcos Scutaro .30 .10
❑ 91 Marquis Grissom .30 .10
❑ 92 Aubrey Huff .30 .10
❑ 93 Tony Womack .30 .10
❑ 94 Placido Polanco .30 .10
❑ 95 Bengie Molina .30 .10
❑ 96 Roger Cedeno .30 .10
❑ 97 Geoff Jenkins .30 .10
❑ 98 Kip Wells .30 .10
❑ 99 Derek Jeter 1.50 .60
❑ 100 Omar Infante .30 .10
❑ 101 Phil Nevin .30 .10
❑ 102 Edgar Renteria .30 .10
❑ 103 B.J. Surhoff .30 .10
❑ 104 David DeJesus .30 .10
❑ 105 Raul Ibanez .30 .10
❑ 106 Hank Blalock .30 .10
❑ 107 Shawn Estes .30 .10
❑ 108 Wily Mo Pena .30 .10
❑ 109 Shawn Green .30 .10
❑ 110 David Wright 2.00 .75
❑ 111 Kenny Lofton .30 .10
❑ 112 Matt Clement .30 .10
❑ 113 Cesar Izturis .30 .10
❑ 114 John Lackey .30 .10
❑ 115 Torii Hunter .30 .10
❑ 116 Charles Johnson .30 .10
❑ 117 Ray Durham .30 .10
❑ 118 Luke Hudson .30 .10
❑ 119 Jeremy Bonderman .30 .10
❑ 120 Sean Casey .30 .10
❑ 121 Johnny Damon .50 .20
❑ 122 Eric Milton .30 .10
❑ 123 Shea Hillenbrand .30 .10
❑ 124 Johan Santana .75 .30
❑ 125 Jim Edmonds .30 .10
❑ 126 Javier Vazquez .30 .10
❑ 127 Jon Adkins .30 .10
❑ 128 Mike Lowell .30 .10
❑ 129 Khalil Greene .50 .20
❑ 130 Quinton McCracken .30 .10
❑ 131 Edgar Martinez .50 .20
❑ 132 Matt Lawton .30 .10
❑ 133 Jeff Weaver .30 .10
❑ 134 Marlon Byrd .30 .10
❑ 135 John Smoltz .50 .20
❑ 136 Grady Sizemore .50 .20
❑ 137 Brian Roberts .30 .10
❑ 138 Dee Brown .30 .10
❑ 139 Joel Pineiro .30 .10
❑ 140 David Dellucci .30 .10
❑ 141 Bobby Higginson .30 .10
❑ 142 Ryan Madson .30 .10
❑ 143 Scott Hatteberg .30 .10
❑ 144 Greg Zaun .30 .10
❑ 145 Brian Jordan .30 .10
❑ 146 Jason Isringhausen .30 .10
❑ 147 Vinnie Chulk .30 .10
❑ 148 Al Leiter .30 .10
❑ 149 Pedro Martinez .50 .20
❑ 150 Carlos Guillen .30 .10
❑ 151 Randy Wolf .30 .10
❑ 152 Vernon Wells .30 .10
❑ 153 Barry Zito .30 .10
❑ 154 Pedro Feliz .30 .10
❑ 155 Omar Vizquel .50 .20
❑ 156 Chone Figgins .30 .10
❑ 157 David Ortiz .50 .20
❑ 158 Sunny Kim .30 .10
❑ 159 Adam Kennedy .30 .10
❑ 160 Carlos Lee .30 .10
❑ 161 Rick Ankiel .30 .10
❑ 162 Roy Oswalt .30 .10
❑ 163 Armando Benitez .30 .10
❑ 164 Erubiel Durazo .30 .10
❑ 165 Adam Hyzdu .30 .10
❑ 166 Esteban Yan .30 .10
❑ 167 Victor Santos .30 .10
❑ 168 Kevin Millwood .30 .10
❑ 169 Andy Pettitte .50 .20
❑ 170 Mike Cameron .30 .10
❑ 171 Scott Rolen .50 .20
❑ 172 Trot Nixon .30 .10
❑ 173 Eric Munson .30 .10
❑ 174 Roy Halladay .30 .10
❑ 175 Juan Encarnacion .30 .10
❑ 176 Eric Chavez .30 .10
❑ 177 Termel Sledge .30 .10
❑ 178 Jason Schmidt .30 .10
❑ 179 Endy Chavez .30 .10
❑ 180 Carlos Zambrano .30 .10
❑ 181 Carlos Delgado .30 .10
❑ 182 Dewon Brazelton .30 .10
❑ 183 J.D. Drew .30 .10
❑ 184 Orlando Cabrera .30 .10
❑ 185 Craig Wilson .30 .10
❑ 186 Chin-Hui Tsao .30 .10
❑ 187 Jolbert Cabrera .30 .10
❑ 188 Rod Barajas .30 .10
❑ 189 Craig Monroe .30 .10
❑ 190 Dave Berg .30 .10
❑ 191 Carlos Silva .30 .10
❑ 192 Eric Gagne .30 .10
❑ 193 Marcus Giles .30 .10
❑ 194 Nick Johnson .30 .10
❑ 195 Kelvim Escobar .30 .10
❑ 196 Wade Miller .30 .10
❑ 197 David Bell .30 .10
❑ 198 Rondell White .30 .10
❑ 199 Brian Giles .30 .10
❑ 200 Jeromy Burnitz .30 .10
❑ 201 Carl Pavano .30 .10
❑ 202 Alex Rios .30 .10
❑ 203 Ryan Freel .30 .10
❑ 204 R.A. Dickey .30 .10
❑ 205 Miguel Cairo .30 .10
❑ 206 Kerry Wood .30 .10
❑ 207 C.C. Sabathia .30 .10
❑ 208 Jaime Cerda .30 .10
❑ 209 Jerome Williams .30 .10
❑ 210 Ryan Wagner .30 .10
❑ 211 Javy Lopez .30 .10
❑ 212 Tike Redman .30 .10
❑ 213 Richie Sexson .30 .10
❑ 214 Shannon Stewart .30 .10
❑ 215 Ben Davis .30 .10
❑ 216 Jeff Bagwell .50 .20
❑ 217 David Wells .30 .10
❑ 218 Justin Leone .30 .10
❑ 219 Brad Radke .30 .10
❑ 220 Ramon Santiago .30 .10
❑ 221 Richard Hidalgo .30 .10
❑ 222 Aaron Miles .30 .10
❑ 223 Mark Loretta .30 .10
❑ 224 Aaron Boone .30 .10
❑ 225 Steve Trachsel .30 .10
❑ 226 Geoff Blum .30 .10
❑ 227 Shingo Takatsu .30 .10
❑ 228 Kevin Youkilis .30 .10
❑ 229 Laynce Nix .30 .10
❑ 230 Daniel Cabrera .30 .10
❑ 231 Kyle Lohse .30 .10
❑ 232 Todd Pratt .30 .10
❑ 233 Reed Johnson .30 .10
❑ 234 Lance Berkman .30 .10
❑ 235 Hideki Matsui 1.25 .50
❑ 236 Randy Winn .30 .10
❑ 237 Joe Randa .30 .10
❑ 238 Bob Howry .30 .10
❑ 239 Jason LaRue .30 .10
❑ 240 Jose Valentin .30 .10
❑ 241 Livan Hernandez .30 .10
❑ 242 Jamie Moyer .30 .10
❑ 243 Garret Anderson .30 .10
❑ 244 Brad Ausmus .30 .10
❑ 245 Russell Branyan .30 .10
❑ 246 Paul Wilson .30 .10
❑ 247 Tim Wakefield .30 .10
❑ 248 Roberto Alomar .50 .20
❑ 249 Kazuhisa Ishii .30 .10
❑ 250 Tino Martinez .50 .20
❑ 251 Tomo Ohka .30 .10
❑ 252 Mark Redman .30 .10
❑ 253 Paul Byrd .30 .10
❑ 254 Greg Aquino .30 .10
❑ 255 Adrian Beltre .30 .10
❑ 256 Ricky Ledee .30 .10
❑ 257 Josh Fogg .30 .10
❑ 258 Derek Lowe .30 .10
❑ 259 Lew Ford .30 .10
❑ 260 Bobby Crosby .30 .10
❑ 261 Jim Thome .50 .20
❑ 262 Jaret Wright .30 .10
❑ 263 Chin-Feng Chen .30 .10
❑ 264 Troy Glaus .30 .10
❑ 265 Jorge Sosa .30 .10
❑ 266 Mike Lamb .30 .10
❑ 267 Russ Ortiz .30 .10
❑ 268 Reggie Sanders .30 .10
❑ 269 Orlando Hudson .30 .10
❑ 270 Rodrigo Lopez .30 .10
❑ 271 Jose Vidro .30 .10
❑ 272 Akinori Otsuka .30 .10
❑ 273 Victor Martinez .30 .10
❑ 274 Carl Crawford .30 .10
❑ 275 Roberto Novoa .30 .10
❑ 276 Brian Lawrence .30 .10
❑ 277 Angel Berroa .30 .10
❑ 278 Josh Beckett .30 .10
❑ 279 Lyle Overbay .30 .10
❑ 280 Dustin Hermanson .30 .10
❑ 281 Jeff Conine .30 .10
❑ 282 Mark Prior .50 .20
❑ 283 Kevin Brown .30 .10
❑ 284 Magglio Ordonez .30 .10
❑ 285 Dontrelle Willis .30 .10
❑ 286 Dallas McPherson .30 .10
❑ 287 Rafael Furcal .30 .10
❑ 288 Ty Wigginton .30 .10
❑ 289 Moises Alou .30 .10
❑ 290 A.J. Pierzynski .30 .10
❑ 291 Todd Walker .30 .10
❑ 292 Hideo Nomo .75 .30
❑ 293 Larry Walker .50 .20

❑ 294 Choo Freeman .30 .10
❑ 295 Eduardo Perez .30 .10
❑ 296 Miguel Tejada .30 .10
❑ 297 Corey Koskie .30 .10
❑ 298 Jermaine Dye .30 .10
❑ 299 John Riedling .30 .10
❑ 300 John Olerud .30 .10
❑ 301 Bittner/Woods/Jenks TP 5.00 2.00
❑ 302 Kroeger/Daigle/Medders TP 5.00 2.00
❑ 303 K.Johnson/Thom/Meyer TP 5.00 2.00
❑ 304 E.Rod/Hannam/Maine TP 5.00 2.00
❑ 305 A.Mart/Gamble/Dinardo TP 5.00 2.00
❑ 306 Cedeno/Vasquez/Pinto TP 5.00 2.00
❑ 307 Munoz/Wing/Diaz TP 5.00 2.00
❑ 308 Bergolla/Olmedo/E.Enc TP 5.00 2.00
❑ 309 Gomez/Ochoa/Tadano TP 5.00 2.00
❑ 310 Miller/Baker/Holliday TP 5.00 2.00
❑ 311 Larris/Grander/Raburn TP 5.00 2.00
❑ 312 Wilson/Kensing/Cave TP 5.00 2.00
❑ 313 H.Gim/Taveras/Buch TP 5.00 2.00
❑ 314 Gotay/Bass/Blanco TP 5.00 2.00
❑ 315 Hanrahan/Aybar/Braz TP 5.00 2.00
❑ 316 Krynzel/Hendr/Hart TP 5.00 2.00
❑ 317 Miller/Kubel/Durbin TP 5.00 2.00
❑ 318 Izturis/Cordero/Watson TP 5.00 2.00
❑ 319 Diaz/Baldiris/Lydon TP 5.00 2.00
❑ 320 Sierra/Navarro/Henn TP 5.00 2.00
❑ 321 Swish/Blant/D.Johnson TP 5.00 2.00
❑ 322 Howard/Floyd/Bucktrot TP 5.00 2.00
❑ 323 Doumit/Burnett/Bradley TP 5.00 2.00
❑ 324 Germ/Tucker/Guzman TP 5.00 2.00
❑ 325 Aardsma/Knoedler/Simon TP 5.002.00
❑ 326 Lopez/Rivera/Baek TP 5.00 2.00
❑ 327 Molina/Rust/Wainwright TP 5.00 2.00
❑ 328 Cantu/Kazmir/Upton TP 5.00 2.00
❑ 329 Gonzalez/Nivar/Bourg TP 5.00 2.00
❑ 330 Adams/McGow/Chacin TP 5.00 2.00
❑ 331 Alfonso Soriano AW 1.00 .40
❑ 332 Albert Pujols AW 3.00 1.25
❑ 333 David Ortiz AW 1.50 .60
❑ 334 Manny Ramirez AW 1.50 .60
❑ 335 Jason Bay AW 1.00 .40
❑ 336 Bobby Crosby AW 1.00 .40
❑ 337 Roger Clemens AW 2.50 1.00
❑ 338 Johan Santana AW 1.50 .60
❑ 339 Jim Thome AW 1.50 .60
❑ 340 Vladimir Guerrero AW 1.50 .60
❑ 341 David Ortiz PS 1.50 .60
❑ 342 Alex Rodriguez PS 2.50 1.00
❑ 343 Albert Pujols PS 3.00 1.25
❑ 344 Carlos Beltran PS 1.00 .40
❑ 345 Johnny Damon PS 1.50 .60
❑ 346 Scott Rolen PS 1.50 .60
❑ 347 Larry Walker PS 1.50 .60
❑ 348 Curt Schilling PS 1.50 .60
❑ 349 Pedro Martinez PS 1.50 .60
❑ 350 David Ortiz PS 1.50 .60

2006 Fleer Tradition

❑ COMPLETE SET (200) 30.00 12.50
❑ COMMON CARD (1-200) .30 .12
❑ COMMON RC (1-200) .50 .20
❑ OVERALL PLATE ODDS 1:288 HOBBY
❑ PLATE PRINT RUN 1 SET PER COLOR
❑ BLACK-CYAN-MAGENTA-YELLOW ISSUED
❑ NO PLATE PRICING DUE TO SCARCITY
❑ EXQUISITE EXCH ODDS 1:864 HOBBY
❑ EXQUISITE EXCH DEADLINE 07/27/07

❑ 1 Andruw Jones .50 .20
❑ 2 Chipper Jones .75 .30
❑ 3 John Smoltz .50 .20
❑ 4 Tim Hudson .30 .12
❑ 5 Joey Devine RC .50 .20
❑ 6 Chuck James (RC) .75 .30
❑ 7 Alay Soler RC .50 .20
❑ 8 Conor Jackson (RC) .75 .30
❑ 9 Luis Gonzalez .30 .12
❑ 10 Brandon Webb .30 .12
❑ 11 Chad Tracy .30 .12
❑ 12 Orlando Hudson .30 .12
❑ 13 Shawn Green .30 .12
❑ 14 Vladimir Guerrero .75 .30
❑ 15 Bartolo Colon .30 .12
❑ 16 Chone Figgins .30 .12
❑ 17 Garret Anderson .30 .12
❑ 18 Francisco Rodriguez .30 .12
❑ 19 Casey Kotchman .30 .12
❑ 20 Lance Berkman .30 .12
❑ 21 Craig Biggio .50 .20
❑ 22 Andy Pettitte .30 .12
❑ 23 Morgan Ensberg .30 .12
❑ 24 Brad Lidge .30 .12
❑ 25 Jered Weaver (RC) 2.50 1.00
❑ 26 Roy Oswalt .30 .12
❑ 27 Eric Chavez .30 .12
❑ 28 Rich Harden .30 .12
❑ 29 Cole Hamels (RC) 1.25 .50
❑ 30 Huston Street .30 .12
❑ 31 Bobby Crosby .30 .12
❑ 32 Nick Swisher .30 .12
❑ 33 Vernon Wells .30 .12
❑ 34 Roy Halladay .30 .12
❑ 35 A.J. Burnett .30 .12
❑ 36 Troy Glaus .30 .12
❑ 37 B.J. Ryan .30 .12
❑ 38 Bengie Molina .30 .12
❑ 39 Alex Rios .30 .12
❑ 40 Prince Fielder (RC) 2.00 .75
❑ 41 Jose Capellan (RC) .50 .20
❑ 42 Rickie Weeks .30 .12
❑ 43 Ben Sheets .30 .12
❑ 44 Carlos Lee .30 .12
❑ 45 J.J. Hardy .30 .12
❑ 46 Albert Pujols 1.50 .60
❑ 47 Skip Schumaker (RC) .50 .20
❑ 48 Adam Wainwright (RC) .50 .20
❑ 49 Jim Edmonds .50 .20
❑ 50 Scott Rolen .50 .20
❑ 51 Chris Carpenter .30 .12
❑ 52 David Eckstein .30 .12
❑ 53 Derrek Lee .30 .12
❑ 54 Jon Lester RC 4.00 1.50
❑ 55 Mark Prior .50 .20
❑ 56 Aramis Ramirez .30 .12
❑ 57 Juan Pierre .30 .12
❑ 58 Greg Maddux 1.25 .50
❑ 59 Michael Barrett .30 .12
❑ 60 Carl Crawford .30 .12
❑ 61 Scott Kazmir .50 .20
❑ 62 Jorge Cantu .30 .12
❑ 63 Jonny Gomes .30 .12
❑ 64 Julio Lugo .30 .12
❑ 65 Aubrey Huff .30 .12
❑ 66 Jeff Kent .30 .12
❑ 67 Nomar Garciaparra .75 .30
❑ 68 Rafael Furcal .30 .12
❑ 69 Tim Hamulack (RC) .50 .20
❑ 70 Chad Billingsley (RC) .75 .30
❑ 71 Hong-Chih Kuo (RC) 1.25 .50
❑ 72 J.D. Drew .30 .12
❑ 73 Moises Alou .30 .12
❑ 74 Randy Winn .30 .12
❑ 75 Jason Schmidt .30 .12
❑ 76 Jeremy Accardo RC .50 .20
❑ 77 Matt Cain (RC) .75 .30
❑ 78 Joel Zumaya (RC) 1.25 .50
❑ 79 Travis Hafner .30 .12
❑ 80 Victor Martinez .30 .12
❑ 81 Grady Sizemore .50 .20
❑ 82 C.C. Sabathia .30 .12
❑ 83 Jhonny Peralta .30 .12
❑ 84 Jason Michaels .30 .12
❑ 85 Jeremy Sowers (RC) .50 .20
❑ 86 Ichiro Suzuki 1.25 .50

❑ 87 Richie Sexson .30 .12
❑ 88 Adrian Beltre .30 .12
❑ 89 Felix Hernandez .50 .20
❑ 90 Kenji Johjima RC 2.50 1.00
❑ 91 Jeff Harris RC .50 .20
❑ 92 Taylor Buchholz (RC) .75 .30
❑ 93 Miguel Cabrera .50 .20
❑ 94 Dontrelle Willis .30 .12
❑ 95 Jeremy Hermida (RC) .75 .30
❑ 96 Mike Jacobs (RC) .50 .20
❑ 97 Josh Johnson (RC) .75 .30
❑ 98 Hanley Ramirez (RC) 1.25 .50
❑ 99 Josh Willingham (RC) .50 .20
❑ 100 Dan Uggla (RC) 1.25 .50
❑ 101 David Wright 1.25 .50
❑ 102 Jose Reyes .30 .12
❑ 103 Pedro Martinez .50 .20
❑ 104 Carlos Beltran .30 .12
❑ 105 Carlos Delgado .30 .12
❑ 106 Billy Wagner .30 .12
❑ 107 Lastings Milledge (RC) .75 .30
❑ 108 Alfonso Soriano .30 .12
❑ 109 Jose Vidro .30 .12
❑ 110 Livan Hernandez .30 .12
❑ 111 Matt Kemp (RC) .75 .30
❑ 112 Brandon Watson (RC) .50 .20
❑ 113 Ryan Zimmerman (RC) 3.00 1.25
❑ 114 Miguel Tejada .30 .12
❑ 115 Ramon Hernandez .30 .12
❑ 116 Brian Roberts .30 .12
❑ 117 Melvin Mora .30 .12
❑ 118 Erik Bedard .30 .12
❑ 119 Jay Gibbons .30 .12
❑ 120 Aaron Rakers (RC) .50 .20
❑ 121 Jake Peavy .30 .12
❑ 122 Brian Giles .30 .12
❑ 123 Khalil Greene .50 .20
❑ 124 Trevor Hoffman .30 .12
❑ 125 Josh Barfield (RC) .50 .20
❑ 126 Ben Johnson (RC) .50 .20
❑ 127 Ryan Howard 1.25 .50
❑ 128 Bobby Abreu .30 .12
❑ 129 Chase Utley .75 .30
❑ 130 Pat Burrell .30 .12
❑ 131 Jimmy Rollins .30 .12
❑ 132 Brett Myers .30 .12
❑ 133 Mike Thompson RC .50 .20
❑ 134 Jason Bay .30 .12
❑ 135 Oliver Perez .30 .12
❑ 136 Matt Capps (RC) .50 .20
❑ 137 Paul Maholm (RC) .50 .20
❑ 138 Nate McLouth (RC) .50 .20
❑ 139 John Van Benschoten (RC) .50 .20
❑ 140 Mark Teixeira .50 .20
❑ 141 Michael Young .30 .12
❑ 142 Hank Blalock .30 .12
❑ 143 Kevin Millwood .30 .12
❑ 144 Laynce Nix .30 .12
❑ 145 Francisco Cordero .30 .12
❑ 146 Ian Kinsler (RC) .75 .30
❑ 147 David Ortiz .75 .30
❑ 148 Manny Ramirez .50 .20
❑ 149 Jason Varitek .75 .30
❑ 150 Curt Schilling .50 .20
❑ 151 Josh Beckett .30 .12
❑ 152 Coco Crisp .30 .12
❑ 153 Jonathan Papelbon (RC) 2.50 1.00
❑ 154 Ken Griffey Jr. 1.25 .50
❑ 155 Adam Dunn .30 .12
❑ 156 Felipe Lopez .30 .12
❑ 157 Bronson Arroyo .30 .12
❑ 158 Ryan Freel .30 .12
❑ 159 Chris Denorfia (RC) .50 .20
❑ 160 Todd Helton .50 .20
❑ 161 Garrett Atkins .30 .12
❑ 162 Matt Holliday .30 .12
❑ 163 Clint Barmes .30 .12
❑ 164 Kendry Morales (RC) 1.25 .50
❑ 165 Ryan Shealy (RC) .50 .20
❑ 166 Josh Wilson (RC) .50 .20
❑ 167 Reggie Sanders .30 .12
❑ 168 Angel Berroa .30 .12
❑ 169 Mike Sweeney .30 .12
❑ 170 Mark Grudzielanek .30 .12
❑ 171 Jeremy Affeldt .30 .12
❑ 172 Steve Stemle RC .50 .20

❑ 173 Justin Verlander (RC) 2.00 .75
❑ 174 Ivan Rodriguez .50 .20
❑ 175 Chris Shelton .30 .12
❑ 176 Jeremy Bonderman .30 .12
❑ 177 Magglio Ordonez .30 .12
❑ 178 Carlos Guillen .30 .12
❑ 179 Placido Polanco .30 .12
❑ 180 Johan Santana .50 .20
❑ 181 Torii Hunter .30 .12
❑ 182 Joe Nathan .30 .12
❑ 183 Joe Mauer .50 .20
❑ 184 Dave Gassner (RC) .50 .20
❑ 185 Jason Kubel (RC) .50 .20
❑ 186 Francisco Liriano (RC) 2.50 1.00
❑ 187 Jim Thome .50 .20
❑ 188 Paul Konerko .30 .12
❑ 189 Scott Podsednik .30 .12
❑ 190 Tadahito Iguchi .30 .12
❑ 191 A.J. Pierzynski .30 .12
❑ 192 Jose Contreras .30 .12
❑ 193 Brian Anderson (RC) .50 .20
❑ 194 Hideki Matsui .75 .30
❑ 195 Wil Nieves (RC) .50 .20
❑ 196 Alex Rodriguez 1.25 .50
❑ 197 Gary Sheffield .30 .12
❑ 198 Randy Johnson .75 .30
❑ 199 Johnny Damon .50 .20
❑ 200 Derek Jeter 2.00 .75
❑ NNO Exquisite Redemption 200.00 125.00

1933 Goudey

❑ COMPLETE SET (239) 40000.00 25000.00
❑ COMMON CARD (1-52) 75.00 45.00
❑ COMMON (41/43/53-240) 60.00 35.00
❑ WRAPPER (1-CENT, BAT.) 100.00 75.00
❑ WRAPPER (1-CENT, AD) 175.00 150.00
❑ 1 Benny Bengough RC 1500.00 900.00
❑ 2 Dazzy Vance RC 200.00 125.00
❑ 3 Hugh Critz BAT RC 75.00 40.00
❑ 4 Heinie Schuble RC 75.00 45.00
❑ 5 Babe Herman RC 75.00 40.00
❑ 6 Jimmy Dykes RC 75.00 40.00
❑ 7 Ted Lyons RC 150.00 90.00
❑ 8 Roy Johnson RC 75.00 45.00
❑ 9 Dave Harris RC 75.00 45.00
❑ 10 Glenn Myatt RC 75.00 45.00
❑ 11 Billy Rogell RC 75.00 45.00
❑ 12 George Pipgras RC 75.00 45.00
❑ 13 Fresco Thompson RC 75.00 45.00
❑ 14 Henry Johnson RC 75.00 45.00
❑ 15 Victor Sorrell RC 75.00 45.00
❑ 16 George Blaeholder RC 75.00 45.00
❑ 17 Watson Clark RC 75.00 45.00
❑ 18 Muddy Ruel RC 75.00 45.00
❑ 19 Bill Dickey RC 350.00 200.00
❑ 20 Bill Terry THROW RC 250.00 150.00
❑ 21 Phil Collins RC 75.00 45.00
❑ 22 Pie Traynor RC 250.00 150.00
❑ 23 Kiki Cuyler RC 200.00 125.00
❑ 24 Horace Ford RC 75.00 45.00
❑ 25 Paul Waner RC 200.00 125.00
❑ 26 Bill Cissell RC 75.00 45.00
❑ 27 George Connally RC 75.00 45.00
❑ 28 Dick Bartell RC 75.00 40.00
❑ 29 Jimmie Foxx RC 600.00 350.00
❑ 30 Frank Hogan RC 75.00 45.00
❑ 31 Tony Lazzeri RC 400.00 250.00
❑ 32 Bud Clancy RC 75.00 40.00
❑ 33 Ralph Kress RC 75.00 45.00
❑ 34 Bob O'Farrell RC 75.00 45.00
❑ 35 Al Simmons RC 350.00 200.00
❑ 36 Tommy Thevenow RC 75.00 45.00
❑ 37 Jimmy Wilson RC 75.00 45.00
❑ 38 Fred Brickell RC 75.00 45.00
❑ 39 Mark Koenig RC 75.00 40.00
❑ 40 Taylor Douthit RC 75.00 45.00
❑ 41 Gus Mancuso CATCH 60.00 35.00
❑ 42 Eddie Collins RC 150.00 90.00
❑ 43 Lew Fonseca RC 60.00 35.00
❑ 44 Jim Bottomley RC 150.00 90.00
❑ 45 Larry Benton RC 75.00 45.00
❑ 46 Ethan Allen RC 75.00 40.00
❑ 47 Heinie Manush BAT RC 175.00 100.00
❑ 48 Marty McManus RC 75.00 45.00
❑ 49 Frankie Frisch RC 300.00 175.00
❑ 50 Ed Brandt RC 75.00 45.00
❑ 51 Charlie Grimm RC 75.00 40.00
❑ 52 Andy Cohen RC 75.00 45.00
❑ 53 Babe Ruth RC 6000.00 3500.00
❑ 54 Ray Kremer RC 60.00 35.00
❑ 55 Pat Malone RC 60.00 35.00
❑ 56 Red Ruffing RC 175.00 100.00
❑ 57 Earl Clark RC 60.00 35.00
❑ 58 Lefty O'Doul RC 125.00 75.00
❑ 59 Bing Miller RC 60.00 35.00
❑ 60 Waite Hoyt RC 125.00 75.00
❑ 61 Max Bishop RC 60.00 35.00
❑ 62 Pepper Martin RC 125.00 75.00
❑ 63 Joe Cronin BAT RC 150.00 90.00
❑ 64 Burleigh Grimes RC 250.00 150.00
❑ 65 Milt Gaston RC 60.00 35.00
❑ 66 George Grantham RC 60.00 35.00
❑ 67 Guy Bush RC 60.00 35.00
❑ 68 Horace Lisenbee RC 60.00 35.00
❑ 69 Randy Moore RC 60.00 35.00
❑ 70 Floyd (Pete) Scott RC 60.00 35.00
❑ 71 Robert J. Burke RC 60.00 35.00
❑ 72 Owen Carroll RC 60.00 35.00
❑ 73 Jesse Haines RC 125.00 75.00
❑ 74 Eppa Rixey RC 150.00 90.00
❑ 75 Willie Kamm RC 60.00 35.00
❑ 76 Mickey Cochrane RC 500.00 300.00
❑ 77 Adam Comorosky RC 60.00 35.00
❑ 78 Jack Quinn RC 60.00 35.00
❑ 79 Red Faber RC 125.00 75.00
❑ 80 Clyde Manion RC 60.00 35.00
❑ 81 Sam Jones RC 60.00 35.00
❑ 82 Dib Williams RC 60.00 35.00
❑ 83 Pete Jablonowski RC 60.00 35.00
❑ 84 Glenn Spencer RC 60.00 35.00
❑ 85 Heinie Sand RC 60.00 35.00
❑ 86 Phil Todt RC 60.00 35.00
❑ 87 Frank O'Rourke RC 60.00 35.00
❑ 88 Russell Rollings RC 60.00 35.00
❑ 89 Tris Speaker RET 300.00 175.00
❑ 90 Jess Petty RC 60.00 35.00
❑ 91 Tom Zachary RC 60.00 35.00
❑ 92 Lou Gehrig RC 2500.00 1500.00
❑ 93 John Welch RC 60.00 35.00
❑ 94 Bill Walker RC 60.00 35.00
❑ 95 Alvin Crowder RC 60.00 35.00
❑ 96 Willis Hudlin RC 60.00 35.00
❑ 97 Joe Morrissey RC 60.00 35.00
❑ 98 Wally Berger RC 75.00 45.00
❑ 99 Tony Cuccinello RC 75.00 45.00
❑ 100 George Uhle RC 60.00 35.00
❑ 101 Richard Coffman RC 60.00 35.00
❑ 102 Travis Jackson RC 150.00 90.00
❑ 103 Earle Combs RC 125.00 75.00
❑ 104 Fred Marberry RC 60.00 35.00
❑ 105 Bernie Friberg RC 60.00 35.00
❑ 106 Napoleon Lajoie SP 25000.00 15000.00
❑ 107 Heinie Manush RC 125.00 75.00
❑ 108 Joe Kuhel RC 60.00 35.00
❑ 109 Joe Cronin RC 300.00 175.00
❑ 110 Goose Goslin RC 250.00 150.00
❑ 111 Monte Weaver RC 60.00 35.00
❑ 112 Fred Schulte RC 60.00 35.00
❑ 113 Oswald Bluege POR RC 60.00 35.00
❑ 114 Luke Sewell FIELD RC 75.00 45.00
❑ 115 Cliff Heathcote RC 60.00 35.00
❑ 116 Eddie Morgan RC 60.00 35.00
❑ 117 Rabbit Maranville RC 125.00 75.00
❑ 118 Val Picinich RC 60.00 35.00
❑ 119 Rogers Hornsby Field RC 600.00 350.00
❑ 120 Carl Reynolds RC 60.00 35.00
❑ 121 Walter Stewart RC 60.00 35.00
❑ 122 Alvin Crowder RC 60.00 35.00
❑ 123 Jack Russell RC 60.00 35.00
❑ 124 Earl Whitehill RC 60.00 35.00
❑ 125 Bill Terry RC 250.00 150.00
❑ 126 Joe Moore BAT RC 60.00 35.00
❑ 127 Mel Ott RC 400.00 250.00
❑ 128 Chuck Klein RC 175.00 100.00
❑ 129 Hal Schumacher PIT RC 60.00 35.00
❑ 130 Fred Fitzsimmons POR RC 60.00 35.00
❑ 131 Fred Frankhouse RC 60.00 35.00
❑ 132 Jim Elliott RC 60.00 35.00
❑ 133 Fred Lindstrom RC 125.00 75.00
❑ 134 Sam Rice RC 200.00 125.00
❑ 135 Woody English RC 60.00 35.00
❑ 136 Flint Rhem RC 60.00 35.00
❑ 137 Red Lucas RC 60.00 35.00
❑ 138 Herb Pennock RC 175.00 100.00
❑ 139 Ben Cantwell RC 60.00 35.00
❑ 140 Bump Hadley RC 60.00 35.00
❑ 141 Ray Benge RC 60.00 35.00
❑ 142 Paul Richards RC 75.00 45.00
❑ 143 Glenn Wright RC 60.00 35.00
❑ 144 Babe Ruth Bat DP RC 4000.00 2500.00
❑ 145 Rube Walberg RC 60.00 35.00
❑ 146 Walter Stewart PIT RC 60.00 35.00
❑ 147 Leo Durocher RC 200.00 125.00
❑ 148 Eddie Farrell RC 60.00 35.00
❑ 149 Babe Ruth RC 5000.00 3000.00
❑ 150 Ray Kolp RC 60.00 35.00
❑ 151 Jake Flowers RC 60.00 35.00
❑ 152 Zack Taylor RC 60.00 35.00
❑ 153 Buddy Myer RC 60.00 35.00
❑ 154 Jimmie Foxx RC 600.00 350.00
❑ 155 Joe Judge RC 60.00 35.00
❑ 156 Danny MacFayden RC 60.00 35.00
❑ 157 Sam Byrd RC 60.00 35.00
❑ 158 Moe Berg RC 400.00 250.00
❑ 159 Oswald Bluege FIELD RC 60.00 35.00
❑ 160 Lou Gehrig RC 3000.00 1800.00
❑ 161 Al Spohrer RC 60.00 35.00
❑ 162 Leo Mangum RC 60.00 35.00
❑ 163 Luke Sewell POR RC 75.00 45.00
❑ 164 Lloyd Waner RC 250.00 150.00
❑ 165 Joe Sewell RC 125.00 75.00
❑ 166 Sam West RC 60.00 35.00
❑ 167 Jack Russell RC 60.00 35.00
❑ 168 Goose Goslin RC 200.00 125.00
❑ 169 Al Thomas RC 60.00 35.00
❑ 170 Harry McCurdy RC 60.00 35.00
❑ 171 Charlie Jamieson RC 60.00 35.00
❑ 172 Billy Hargrave RC 60.00 35.00
❑ 173 Roscoe Holm RC 60.00 35.00
❑ 174 Warren (Curly) Ogden RC 60.00 35.00
❑ 175 Dan Howley MG RC 60.00 35.00
❑ 176 John Ogden RC 60.00 35.00
❑ 177 Walter French RC 60.00 35.00
❑ 178 Jackie Warner RC 60.00 35.00
❑ 179 Fred Leach RC 60.00 35.00
❑ 180 Eddie Moore RC 60.00 35.00
❑ 181 Babe Ruth RC 4000.00 2500.00
❑ 182 Andy High RC 60.00 35.00
❑ 183 Rube Walberg RC 60.00 35.00
❑ 184 Charley Berry RC 60.00 35.00
❑ 185 Bob Smith RC 60.00 35.00
❑ 186 John Schulte RC 60.00 35.00
❑ 187 Heinie Manush RC 150.00 90.00
❑ 188 Rogers Hornsby RC 600.00 350.00
❑ 189 Joe Cronin RC 200.00 125.00
❑ 190 Fred Schulte RC 60.00 35.00
❑ 191 Ben Chapman RC 75.00 45.00
❑ 192 Walter Brown RC 60.00 35.00
❑ 193 Lynford Lary RC 60.00 35.00
❑ 194 Earl Averill RC 200.00 125.00
❑ 195 Evar Swanson RC 60.00 35.00
❑ 196 Leroy Mahaffey RC 60.00 35.00
❑ 197 Rick Ferrell RC 125.00 75.00
❑ 198 Jack Burns RC 60.00 35.00
❑ 199 Tom Bridges RC 60.00 35.00
❑ 200 Bill Hallahan RC 60.00 35.00
❑ 201 Ernie Orsatti RC 60.00 35.00
❑ 202 Gabby Hartnett RC 250.00 150.00
❑ 203 Lon Warneke RC 60.00 35.00
❑ 204 Riggs Stephenson RC 60.00 35.00
❑ 205 Heinie Meine RC 60.00 35.00
❑ 206 Gus Suhr RC 60.00 35.00

❑ 207 Mel Ott Bat RC	400.00	250.00
❑ 208 Bernie James RC	60.00	35.00
❑ 209 Adolfo Luque RC	75.00	45.00
❑ 210 Spud Davis RC	60.00	35.00
❑ 211 Hack Wilson RC	400.00	250.00
❑ 212 Billy Urbanski RC	60.00	35.00
❑ 213 Earl Adams RC	60.00	35.00
❑ 214 John Kerr RC	60.00	35.00
❑ 215 Russ Van Atta RC	60.00	35.00
❑ 216 Lefty Gomez RC	300.00	175.00
❑ 217 Frank Crosetti RC	150.00	90.00
❑ 218 Wes Ferrell RC	75.00	45.00
❑ 219 Mule Haas UER RC	60.00	35.00
❑ 220 Lefty Grove RC	500.00	300.00
❑ 221 Dale Alexander RC	60.00	35.00
❑ 222 Charley Gehringer RC	400.00	250.00
❑ 223 Dizzy Dean RC	800.00	500.00
❑ 224 Frank Demaree RC	60.00	35.00
❑ 225 Bill Jurges RC	60.00	35.00
❑ 226 Charley Root RC	60.00	35.00
❑ 227 Billy Herman RC	150.00	90.00
❑ 228 Tony Piet RC	60.00	35.00
❑ 229 Arky Vaughan RC	150.00	90.00
❑ 230 Carl Hubbell PIT RC	400.00	250.00
❑ 231 Joe Moore FIELD RC	60.00	35.00
❑ 232 Lefty O'Doul RC	125.00	75.00
❑ 233 Johnny Vergez RC	60.00	35.00
❑ 234 Carl Hubbell RC	400.00	250.00
❑ 235 Fred Fitzsimmons PIT RC	60.00	35.00
❑ 236 George Davis RC	60.00	35.00
❑ 237 Gus Mancuso FIELD RC	60.00	35.00
❑ 238 Hugh Critz FIELD RC	60.00	35.00
❑ 239 Leroy Parmelee RC	60.00	35.00
❑ 240 Hal Schumacher RC	125.00	75.00

1934 Goudey

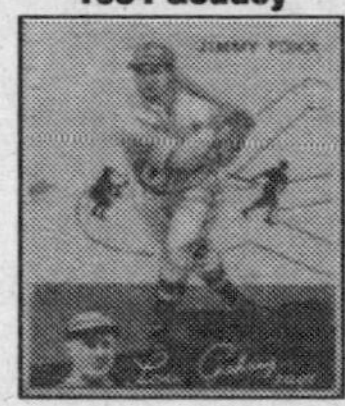

❑ COMPLETE SET (96)	16000.00	9000.00
❑ COMMON CARD (1-48)	50.00	30.00
❑ COMMON CARD (49-72)	75.00	40.00
❑ COMMON CARD (73-96)	175.00	100.00
❑ WRAPPER (1-CENT, WHT.)	100.00	75.00
❑ WRAPPER (1-CENT, CLR.)	100.00	75.00
❑ 1 Jimmie Foxx	750.00	450.00
❑ 2 Mickey Cochrane	175.00	100.00
❑ 3 Charlie Grimm	60.00	35.00
❑ 4 Woody English	50.00	30.00
❑ 5 Ed Brandt	50.00	30.00
❑ 6 Dizzy Dean	700.00	400.00
❑ 7 Leo Durocher	175.00	100.00
❑ 8 Tony Piet	50.00	30.00
❑ 9 Ben Chapman	60.00	35.00
❑ 10 Chuck Klein	150.00	90.00
❑ 11 Paul Waner	150.00	90.00
❑ 12 Carl Hubbell	175.00	100.00
❑ 13 Frankie Frisch	175.00	100.00
❑ 14 Willie Kamm	50.00	30.00
❑ 15 Alvin Crowder	50.00	30.00
❑ 16 Joe Kuhel	50.00	30.00
❑ 17 Hugh Critz	50.00	30.00
❑ 18 Heinie Manush	125.00	75.00
❑ 19 Lefty Grove	300.00	175.00
❑ 20 Frank Hogan	50.00	30.00
❑ 21 Bill Terry	200.00	125.00
❑ 22 Arky Vaughan	125.00	75.00
❑ 23 Charley Gehringer	200.00	125.00
❑ 24 Ray Benge	50.00	30.00
❑ 25 Roger Cramer RC	60.00	35.00
❑ 26 Gerald Walker RC	50.00	30.00
❑ 27 Luke Appling RC	150.00	90.00
❑ 28 Ed Coleman RC	50.00	30.00
❑ 29 Larry French RC	50.00	30.00
❑ 30 Julius Solters RC	50.00	30.00
❑ 31 Buck Jordan RC	50.00	30.00
❑ 32 Blondy Ryan RC	50.00	30.00
❑ 33 Don Hurst RC	50.00	30.00
❑ 34 Chick Hafey RC	125.00	75.00
❑ 35 Ernie Lombardi RC	150.00	90.00
❑ 36 Walter Betts RC	50.00	30.00
❑ 37 Lou Gehrig	3000.00	2000.00
❑ 38 Oral Hildebrand RC	50.00	30.00
❑ 39 Fred Walker RC	50.00	30.00
❑ 40 John Stone	50.00	30.00
❑ 41 George Earnshaw RC	50.00	30.00
❑ 42 John Allen RC	50.00	30.00
❑ 43 Dick Porter RC	50.00	30.00
❑ 44 Tom Bridges	60.00	35.00
❑ 45 Oscar Melillo RC	50.00	30.00
❑ 46 Joe Stripp RC	50.00	30.00
❑ 47 John Frederick RC	50.00	30.00
❑ 48 Tex Carleton RC	50.00	30.00
❑ 49 Sam Leslie RC	75.00	40.00
❑ 50 Walter Beck RC	75.00	40.00
❑ 51 Rip Collins RC	75.00	40.00
❑ 52 Herman Bell RC	75.00	40.00
❑ 53 George Watkins RC	75.00	40.00
❑ 54 Wesley Schulmerich RC	75.00	40.00
❑ 55 Ed Holley RC	75.00	40.00
❑ 56 Mark Koenig	100.00	60.00
❑ 57 Bill Swift RC	75.00	40.00
❑ 58 Earl Grace RC	75.00	40.00
❑ 59 Joe Mowry RC	75.00	40.00
❑ 60 Lynn Nelson RC	75.00	40.00
❑ 61 Lou Gehrig	3000.00	2000.00
❑ 62 Hank Greenberg RC	700.00	400.00
❑ 63 Minter Hayes RC	75.00	40.00
❑ 64 Frank Grube RC	75.00	40.00
❑ 65 Cliff Bolton RC	75.00	40.00
❑ 66 Mel Harder RC	100.00	60.00
❑ 67 Bob Weiland RC	75.00	40.00
❑ 68 Bob Johnson RC	100.00	60.00
❑ 69 John Marcum RC	75.00	40.00
❑ 70 Pete Fox RC	75.00	40.00
❑ 71 Lyle Tinning RC	75.00	40.00
❑ 72 Arndt Jorgens RC	75.00	40.00
❑ 73 Ed Wells RC	175.00	100.00
❑ 74 Bob Boken RC	175.00	100.00
❑ 75 Bill Werber RC	175.00	100.00
❑ 76 Hal Trosky RC	200.00	125.00
❑ 77 Joe Vosmik RC	175.00	100.00
❑ 78 Pinky Higgins RC	200.00	125.00
❑ 79 Eddie Durham RC	175.00	100.00
❑ 80 Marty McManus CK	175.00	100.00
❑ 81 Bob Brown CK RC	175.00	100.00
❑ 82 Bill Hallahan CK	175.00	100.00
❑ 83 Jim Mooney CK RC	175.00	100.00
❑ 84 Paul Derringer CK RC	225.00	125.00
❑ 85 Adam Comorosky CK	175.00	100.00
❑ 86 Lloyd Johnson CK RC	175.00	100.00
❑ 87 George Darrow CK RC	175.00	100.00
❑ 88 Homer Peel CK RC	175.00	100.00
❑ 89 Linus Frey CK RC	175.00	100.00
❑ 90 KiKi Cuyler CK	350.00	200.00
❑ 91 Dolph Camilli CK RC	200.00	125.00
❑ 92 Steve Larkin RC	175.00	100.00
❑ 93 Fred Ostermueller RC	175.00	100.00
❑ 94 Red Rolfe RC	200.00	125.00
❑ 95 Myril Hoag RC	175.00	100.00
❑ 96 James DeShong RC	500.00	300.00

2004 Greats of the Game

❑ COMPLETE SERIES 1 (80)	40.00	15.00
❑ COMPLETE SERIES 2 (65)	25.00	10.00
❑ 1 Lou Gehrig	3.00	1.25
❑ 2 Ty Cobb	2.50	1.00
❑ 3 Dizzy Dean	2.00	.75
❑ 4 Jimmie Foxx	2.00	.75
❑ 5 Hank Greenberg	2.00	.75
❑ 6 Babe Ruth	5.00	2.00
❑ 7 Honus Wagner	2.00	.75
❑ 8 Mickey Cochrane	.75	.30
❑ 9 Pepper Martin	.75	.30
❑ 10 Charlie Gehringer	.75	.30
❑ 11 Carl Hubbell	1.25	.50
❑ 12 Bill Terry	.75	.30
❑ 13 Mel Ott	2.00	.75
❑ 14 Bill Dickey	1.25	.50
❑ 15 Ted Williams	4.00	1.50

❑ 16 Roger Maris Yanks	2.00	.75
❑ 17 Thurman Munson	2.00	.75
❑ 18 Phil Rizzuto	1.25	.50
❑ 19 Stan Musial	3.00	1.25
❑ 20 Duke Snider Brooklyn	1.25	.50
❑ 21 Reggie Jackson Yanks	1.25	.50
❑ 22 Don Mattingly	4.00	1.50
❑ 23 Vida Blue	.75	.30
❑ 24 Harmon Killebrew	2.00	.75
❑ 25 Lou Brock	1.25	.50
❑ 26 Al Kaline	2.00	.75
❑ 27 Dave Parker	.75	.30
❑ 28 Nolan Ryan Astros	5.00	2.00
❑ 29 Jim Rice	.75	.30
❑ 30 Paul Molitor Brewers	.75	.30
❑ 31 Dwight Evans	1.25	.50
❑ 32 Brooks Robinson	1.25	.50
❑ 33 Jose Canseco	1.25	.50
❑ 34 Alan Trammell	.75	.30
❑ 35 Johnny Bench	2.00	.75
❑ 36 Carlton Fisk R.Sox	1.25	.50
❑ 37 Jim Palmer	.75	.30
❑ 38 George Brett	4.00	1.50
❑ 39 Mike Schmidt	4.00	1.50
❑ 40 Tony Perez	.75	.30
❑ 41 Paul Blair	.50	.20
❑ 42 Fred Lynn	.75	.30
❑ 43 Carl Yastrzemski	3.00	1.25
❑ 44 Steve Carlton Phils	.75	.30
❑ 45 Dennis Eckersley	1.25	.50
❑ 46 Tom Seaver Mets	1.25	.50
❑ 47 Juan Marichal	.75	.30
❑ 48 Tony Gwynn	2.50	1.00
❑ 49 Moose Skowron	.75	.30
❑ 50 Bob Gibson	1.25	.50
❑ 51 Luis Tiant	.75	.30
❑ 52 Eddie Murray O's	2.00	.75
❑ 53 Frank Robinson Reds	.75	.30
❑ 54 Rocky Colavito	1.25	.50
❑ 55 Bobby Shantz	.50	.20
❑ 56 Ernie Banks	2.00	.75
❑ 57 Rod Carew Angels	1.25	.50
❑ 58 Gorman Thomas	.75	.30
❑ 59 Bernie Carbo	.50	.20
❑ 60 Joe Rudi	.50	.20
❑ 61 Graig Nettles	.75	.30
❑ 62 Ron Guidry	.75	.30
❑ 63 Whitey Ford	1.25	.50
❑ 64 George Kell	.75	.30
❑ 65 Cal Ripken	6.00	2.50
❑ 66 Willie McCovey	1.25	.50
❑ 67 Bo Jackson	2.00	.75
❑ 68 Kirby Puckett	2.00	.75
❑ 69 Ted Kluszewski	1.25	.50
❑ 70 Johnny Podres	.75	.30
❑ 71 Davey Lopes	.75	.30
❑ 72 Chris Short	.50	.20
❑ 73 Jeff Torborg	.50	.20
❑ 74 Bill Freehan	.75	.30
❑ 75 Frank Tanana	.75	.30
❑ 76 Jack Morris	.75	.30
❑ 77 Rick Dempsey	.50	.20
❑ 78 Yogi Berra	2.00	.75
❑ 79 Tim McCarver	.75	.30
❑ 80 Rusty Staub	.75	.30
❑ 81 Tony Lazzeri	.75	.30
❑ 82 Al Rosen	.75	.30
❑ 83 Willie McGee	.75	.30

	Card		
❑	84 Preacher Roe	.75	.30
❑	85 Dave Kingman	.75	.30
❑	86 Luis Aparicio	.75	.30
❑	87 John Kruk	1.25	.50
❑	88 Bing Miller	.50	.20
❑	89 Joe Charboneau	.50	.20
❑	90 Mark Fidrych	.75	.30
❑	91 Catfish Hunter	1.25	.50
❑	92 Nap Lajoie	1.25	.50
❑	93 Eddie Murray Indians	2.00	.75
❑	94 Johnny Pesky	.50	.20
❑	95 Tom Seaver Reds	1.25	.50
❑	96 Frank Robinson O's	.75	.30
❑	97 Enos Slaughter	.75	.30
❑	98 Cecil Travis	.50	.20
❑	99 Robin Yount	2.00	.75
❑	100 Don Zimmer	.75	.30
❑	101 Babe Herman	.50	.20
❑	102 Ron Santo	1.25	.50
❑	103 Willie Stargell	1.25	.50
❑	104 Paul Molitor Jays	.75	.30
❑	105 Jimmy Piersall	.75	.30
❑	106 Johnny Sain	.75	.30
❑	107 Joe Pepitone	.75	.30
❑	108 Ryne Sandberg	4.00	1.50
❑	109 Jim Thorpe	3.00	1.25
❑	110 Steve Garvey	.75	.30
❑	111 Ray Knight	.50	.20
❑	112 Fernando Valenzuela	.75	.30
❑	113 Will Clark	1.25	.50
❑	114 Tony Kubek	1.25	.50
❑	115 Jim Bouton	.75	.30
❑	116 Jerry Koosman	.75	.30
❑	117 Steve Carlton Cards	.75	.30
❑	118 Richie Ashburn	1.25	.50
❑	119 Roberto Clemente	5.00	2.00
❑	120 Paul O'Neill	1.25	.50
❑	121 Reggie Jackson Angels	1.25	.50
❑	122 Andre Dawson	.75	.30
❑	123 Hoyt Wilhelm	.75	.30
❑	124 Dale Murphy	1.25	.50
❑	125 Dwight Gooden	.75	.30
❑	126 Roger Maris Cards	2.00	.75
❑	127 Bill Mazeroski	1.25	.50
❑	128 Don Newcombe	.75	.30
❑	129 Robin Roberts	.75	.30
❑	130 Duke Snider LA	1.25	.50
❑	131 Eddie Mathews	2.00	.75
❑	132 Wade Boggs	1.25	.50
❑	133 Rollie Fingers	.75	.30
❑	134 Frankie Frisch	.75	.30
❑	135 Billy Williams	.75	.30
❑	136 Rod Carew Twins	1.25	.50
❑	137 Dom DiMaggio	.75	.30
❑	138 Orel Hershiser	.75	.30
❑	139 Gary Carter	.75	.30
❑	140 Keith Hernandez	.75	.30
❑	141 Bob Lemon	.75	.30
❑	142 Nolan Ryan Angels	5.00	2.00
❑	143 Ozzie Smith	3.00	1.25
❑	144 Rick Sutcliffe	.75	.30
❑	145 Carlton Fisk W.Sox	1.25	.50

2006 Greats of the Game

	Card		
❑	COMPLETE SET (100)	50.00	20.00
❑	COMMON CARD (1-100)	.75	.30
❑	ONE PLATE PER FOIL PLATE PACK		
❑	PLATE PACKS ISSUED TO DEALERS		
❑	PLATE PRINT RUN 1 SET PER COLOR		
❑	BLACK-CYAN-MAGENTA-YELLOW ISSUED		
❑	NO PLATE PRICING DUE TO SCARCITY		
❑	1 Al Kaline	2.00	.75
❑	2 Alan Trammell	.75	.30
❑	3 Andre Dawson	.75	.30
❑	4 Barry Larkin	1.25	.50
❑	5 Bill Buckner	.75	.30
❑	6 Bill Freehan	.75	.30
❑	7 Bill Madlock	.75	.30
❑	8 Bill Mazeroski	1.25	.50
❑	9 Billy Williams	.75	.30
❑	10 Bo Jackson	2.00	.75
❑	11 Bob Feller	.75	.30
❑	12 Bob Gibson	1.25	.50
❑	13 Bobby Doerr	.75	.30
❑	14 Bobby Murcer	.75	.30
❑	15 Boog Powell	.75	.30
❑	16 Brooks Robinson	1.25	.50
❑	17 Bruce Sutter	.75	.30
❑	18 Bucky Dent	.75	.30
❑	19 Cal Ripken	8.00	3.00
❑	20 Rico Petrocelli	.75	.30
❑	21 Carlton Fisk	1.25	.50
❑	22 Chris Chambliss	.75	.30
❑	23 Dave Concepcion	.75	.30
❑	24 Dave Parker	.75	.30
❑	25 Dave Winfield	.75	.30
❑	26 David Cone	.75	.30
❑	27 Denny McLain	.75	.30
❑	28 Don Mattingly	4.00	1.50
❑	29 Don Newcombe	.75	.30
❑	30 Don Sutton	.75	.30
❑	31 Dusty Baker	.75	.30
❑	32 Dwight Evans	.75	.30
❑	33 Eric Davis	.75	.30
❑	34 Ernie Banks	2.00	.75
❑	35 Fergie Jenkins	.75	.30
❑	36 Frank Robinson	.75	.30
❑	37 Fred Lynn	.75	.30
❑	38 Fred McGriff	1.25	.50
❑	39 Andre Thornton	.75	.30
❑	40 Garry Maddox	.75	.30
❑	41 Gary Matthews	.75	.30
❑	42 Gaylord Perry	.75	.30
❑	43 George Foster	.75	.30
❑	44 George Kell	.75	.30
❑	45 Graig Nettles	.75	.30
❑	46 Greg Luzinski	.75	.30
❑	47 Harmon Killebrew	2.00	.75
❑	48 Jack Clark	.75	.30
❑	49 Jack Morris	.75	.30
❑	50 Jim Palmer	.75	.30
❑	51 Jim Rice	.75	.30
❑	52 Joe Morgan	.75	.30
❑	53 John Kruk	.75	.30
❑	54 Johnny Bench	2.00	.75
❑	55 Jose Canseco	1.25	.50
❑	56 Kirby Puckett	2.00	.75
❑	57 Kirk Gibson	.75	.30
❑	58 Lee Mazzilli	.75	.30
❑	59 Lou Brock	1.25	.50
❑	60 Lou Piniella	.75	.30
❑	61 Luis Aparicio	.75	.30
❑	62 Luis Tiant	.75	.30
❑	63 Mark Fidrych	.75	.30
❑	64 Mark Grace	1.25	.50
❑	65 Maury Wills	.75	.30
❑	66 Mike Schmidt	3.00	1.25
❑	67 Nolan Ryan	5.00	2.00
❑	68 Ozzie Smith	3.00	1.25
❑	69 Paul Molitor	.75	.30
❑	70 Paul O'Neill	1.25	.50
❑	71 Phil Niekro	.75	.30
❑	72 Ralph Kiner	1.25	.50
❑	73 Randy Hundley	.75	.30
❑	74 Red Schoendienst	.75	.30
❑	75 Reggie Jackson	1.25	.50
❑	76 Robin Yount	2.00	.75
❑	77 Rod Carew	1.25	.50
❑	78 Rollie Fingers	.75	.30
❑	79 Ron Cey	.75	.30
❑	80 Ron Guidry	.75	.30
❑	81 Ron Santo	1.25	.50
❑	82 Rusty Staub	.75	.30
❑	83 Ryne Sandberg	4.00	1.50
❑	84 Sparky Lyle	.75	.30
❑	85 Stan Musial	3.00	1.25
❑	86 Steve Carlton	.75	.30
❑	87 Steve Garvey	.75	.30
❑	88 Steve Sax	.75	.30
❑	89 Tommy Herr	.75	.30
❑	90 Tim McCarver	.75	.30
❑	91 Tim Raines	.75	.30
❑	92 Tom Seaver	1.25	.50
❑	93 Tony Gwynn	2.50	1.00
❑	94 Tony Perez	.75	.30
❑	95 Wade Boggs	1.25	.50
❑	96 Whitey Ford	1.25	.50
❑	97 Will Clark	1.25	.50
❑	98 Willie Horton	.75	.30
❑	99 Willie McCovey	1.25	.50
❑	100 Yogi Berra	2.00	.75

1949 Leaf

	Card		
❑	COMPLETE SET (98)	30000.00	20000.00
❑	COMMON CARD (1-168)	25.00	15.00
❑	COMMON SP's	300.00	200.00
❑	WRAPPER (1-CENT)	160.00	120.00
❑	1 Joe DiMaggio	3000.00	1800.00
❑	3 Babe Ruth	2500.00	1500.00
❑	4 Stan Musial	1000.00	600.00
❑	5 Virgil Trucks SP RC	400.00	250.00
❑	8 S.Paige SP RC	12000.00	7000.00
❑	10 Dizzy Trout	40.00	25.00
❑	11 Phil Rizzuto	350.00	200.00
❑	13 Cass Michaels SP RC	300.00	200.00
❑	14 Billy Johnson	40.00	25.00
❑	17 Frank Overmire RC	25.00	15.00
❑	19 Johnny Wyrostek SP	300.00	200.00
❑	20 Hank Sauer SP	400.00	250.00
❑	22 Al Evans RC	25.00	15.00
❑	26 Sam Chapman	40.00	25.00
❑	27 Mickey Harris RC	25.00	15.00
❑	28 Jim Hegan RC	40.00	25.00
❑	29 Elmer Valo RC	40.00	25.00
❑	30 Billy Goodman SP RC	400.00	250.00
❑	31 Lou Brissie RC	25.00	15.00
❑	32 Warren Spahn	350.00	200.00
❑	33 Peanuts Lowrey SP RC	300.00	200.00
❑	36 Al Zarilla SP	300.00	200.00
❑	38 Ted Kluszewski RC	200.00	125.00
❑	39 Ewell Blackwell	60.00	35.00
❑	42 Kent Peterson RC	25.00	15.00
❑	43 Ed Stevens SP RC	300.00	200.00
❑	45 Ken Keltner SP RC	300.00	200.00
❑	46 Johnny Mize	100.00	60.00
❑	47 George Vico RC	25.00	15.00
❑	48 Johnny Schmitz SP RC	300.00	200.00
❑	49 Del Ennis RC	60.00	35.00
❑	50 Dick Wakefield RC	25.00	15.00
❑	51 Alvin Dark SP RC	500.00	300.00
❑	53 Johnny VanderMeer	100.00	60.00
❑	54 Bobby Adams SP RC	300.00	200.00
❑	55 Tommy Henrich SP	500.00	300.00
❑	56 Larry Jansen	40.00	25.00
❑	57 Bob McCall RC	25.00	15.00
❑	59 Luke Appling	100.00	60.00
❑	61 Jake Early RC	25.00	15.00
❑	62 Eddie Joost SP	300.00	200.00
❑	63 Barney McCosky SP	300.00	200.00
❑	65 Bob Elliott UER	100.00	60.00
❑	66 Orval Grove SP RC	300.00	200.00
❑	68 Eddie Miller SP	300.00	200.00
❑	70 Honus Wagner	350.00	200.00

❏ 72 Hank Edwards RC	25.00	15.00
❏ 73 Pat Seerey RC	25.00	15.00
❏ 75 Dom DiMaggio SP	600.00	350.00
❏ 76 Ted Williams	1200.00	700.00
❏ 77 Roy Smalley RC	25.00	15.00
❏ 78 Hoot Evers SP RC	300.00	200.00
❏ 79 Jackie Robinson RC	1500.00	900.00
❏ 81 Whitey Kurowski SP RC	300.00	200.00
❏ 82 Johnny Lindell	40.00	25.00
❏ 83 Bobby Doerr	100.00	60.00
❏ 84 Sid Hudson	25.00	15.00
❏ 85 Dave Philley SP RC	400.00	250.00
❏ 86 Ralph Weigel RC	25.00	15.00
❏ 88 Frank Gustine SP RC	300.00	200.00
❏ 91 Ralph Kiner	200.00	125.00
❏ 93 Bob Feller SP	2000.00	1400.00
❏ 95 Snuffy Stirnweiss	40.00	25.00
❏ 97 Marty Marion	60.00	35.00
❏ 98 Hal Newhouser SP RC	600.00	350.00
❏ 102A G.Hermansk ERR	250.00	150.00
❏ 102B Gene Hermanski COR RC	40.00	25.00
❏ 104 Eddie Stewart SP RC	300.00	200.00
❏ 106 Lou Boudreau MG RC	100.00	60.00
❏ 108 Matt Batts SP RC	300.00	200.00
❏ 111 Jerry Priddy RC	25.00	15.00
❏ 113 Dutch Leonard SP	300.00	200.00
❏ 117 Joe Gordon RC	40.00	25.00
❏ 120 George Kell SP RC	600.00	350.00
❏ 121 Johnny Pesky SP RC	400.00	250.00
❏ 123 Cliff Fannin SP RC	300.00	200.00
❏ 125 Andy Pafko RC	25.00	15.00
❏ 127 Enos Slaughter SP	800.00	500.00
❏ 128 Buddy Rosar	25.00	15.00
❏ 129 Kirby Higbe SP	300.00	200.00
❏ 131 Sid Gordon SP	300.00	200.00
❏ 133 Tommy Holmes SP RC	500.00	300.00
❏ 136A C.Aberson Full Slv RC	25.00	15.00
❏ 136B C.Aberson Short Slv	250.00	150.00
❏ 137 Harry Walker SP RC	400.00	250.00
❏ 138 Larry Doby SP RC	700.00	400.00
❏ 139 Johnny Hopp RC	25.00	15.00
❏ 142 D.Murtaugh SP RC	400.00	250.00
❏ 143 Dick Sisler SP RC	300.00	200.00
❏ 144 Bob Dillinger SP RC	300.00	200.00
❏ 146 Pete Reiser SP	500.00	300.00
❏ 149 Hank Majeski SP RC	300.00	200.00
❏ 153 Floyd Baker SP RC	300.00	200.00
❏ 158 H.Brecheen SP RC	400.00	250.00
❏ 159 Mizell Platt RC	25.00	15.00
❏ 160 Bob Scheffing SP RC	300.00	200.00
❏ 161 V.Stephens SP RC	400.00	250.00
❏ 163 F.Hutchinson SP RC	400.00	250.00
❏ 165 Dale Mitchell SP RC	400.00	250.00
❏ 168 Phil Cavarretta SP RC	500.00	300.00
❏ NNO Album		

1990 Leaf

❏ COMPLETE SET (528)	80.00	40.00
❏ COMPLETE SERIES 1 (264)	50.00	25.00
❏ COMPLETE SERIES 2 (264)	30.00	15.00
❏ COMP. BERRA PUZZLE	1.00	.40
❏ 1 Introductory Card	.40	.15
❏ 2 Mike Henneman	.40	.15
❏ 3 Steve Bedrosian	.40	.15
❏ 4 Mike Scott	.40	.15
❏ 5 Allan Anderson	.40	.15
❏ 6 Rick Sutcliffe	.60	.25
❏ 7 Gregg Olson	.60	.25
❏ 8 Kevin Elster	.40	.15
❏ 9 Pete O'Brien	.40	.15
❏ 10 Carlton Fisk	1.00	.40
❏ 11 Joe Magrane	.40	.15
❏ 12 Roger Clemens	4.00	1.50
❏ 13 Tom Glavine	1.00	.40
❏ 14 Tom Gordon	.60	.25
❏ 15 Todd Benzinger	.40	.15
❏ 16 Hubie Brooks	.40	.15
❏ 17 Roberto Kelly	.40	.15
❏ 18 Barry Larkin	1.00	.40
❏ 19 Mike Boddicker	.40	.15
❏ 20 Roger McDowell	.40	.15
❏ 21 Nolan Ryan	5.00	2.00
❏ 22 John Farrell	.40	.15
❏ 23 Bruce Hurst	.40	.15
❏ 24 Wally Joyner	.60	.25
❏ 25 Greg Maddux	5.00	2.00
❏ 26 Chris Bosio	.40	.15
❏ 27 John Cerutti	.40	.15
❏ 28 Tim Burke	.40	.15
❏ 29 Dennis Eckersley	.60	.25
❏ 30 Glenn Davis	.40	.15
❏ 31 Jim Abbott	1.00	.40
❏ 32 Mike LaValliere	.40	.15
❏ 33 Andres Thomas	.40	.15
❏ 34 Lou Whitaker	.60	.25
❏ 35 Alvin Davis	.40	.15
❏ 36 Melido Perez	.40	.15
❏ 37 Craig Biggio	1.50	.60
❏ 38 Rick Aguilera	.60	.25
❏ 39 Pete Harnisch	.40	.15
❏ 40 David Cone	.60	.25
❏ 41 Scott Garrelts	.40	.15
❏ 42 Jay Howell	.40	.15
❏ 43 Eric King	.40	.15
❏ 44 Pedro Guerrero	.40	.15
❏ 45 Mike Bielecki	.40	.15
❏ 46 Bob Boone	.60	.25
❏ 47 Kevin Brown	.60	.25
❏ 48 Jerry Browne	.40	.15
❏ 49 Mike Scioscia	.40	.15
❏ 50 Chuck Cary	.40	.15
❏ 51 Wade Boggs	1.00	.40
❏ 52 Von Hayes	.40	.15
❏ 53 Tony Fernandez	.40	.15
❏ 54 Dennis Martinez	.60	.25
❏ 55 Tom Candiotti	.40	.15
❏ 56 Andy Benes	.60	.25
❏ 57 Rob Dibble	.60	.25
❏ 58 Chuck Crim	.40	.15
❏ 59 John Smoltz	1.50	.60
❏ 60 Mike Heath	.40	.15
❏ 61 Kevin Gross	.40	.15
❏ 62 Mark McGwire	4.00	1.50
❏ 63 Bert Blyleven	.60	.25
❏ 64 Bob Walk	.40	.15
❏ 65 Mickey Tettleton	.40	.15
❏ 66 Sid Fernandez	.40	.15
❏ 67 Terry Kennedy	.40	.15
❏ 68 Fernando Valenzuela	.60	.25
❏ 69 Don Mattingly	4.00	1.50
❏ 70 Paul O'Neill	1.00	.40
❏ 71 Robin Yount	2.50	1.00
❏ 72 Bret Saberhagen	.60	.25
❏ 73 Geno Petralli	.40	.15
❏ 74 Brook Jacoby	.40	.15
❏ 75 Roberto Alomar	1.00	.40
❏ 76 Devon White	.60	.25
❏ 77 Jose Lind	.40	.15
❏ 78 Pat Combs	.40	.15
❏ 79 Dave Stieb	.60	.25
❏ 80 Tim Wallach	.40	.15
❏ 81 Dave Stewart	.60	.25
❏ 82 Eric Anthony RC	.40	.15
❏ 83 Randy Bush	.40	.15
❏ 84 Rickey Henderson CL	.60	.25
❏ 85 Jaime Navarro	.40	.15
❏ 86 Tommy Gregg	.40	.15
❏ 87 Frank Tanana	.40	.15
❏ 88 Omar Vizquel	1.50	.60
❏ 89 Ivan Calderon	.40	.15
❏ 90 Vince Coleman	.40	.15
❏ 91 Barry Bonds	5.00	2.00
❏ 92 Randy Milligan	.40	.15
❏ 93 Frank Viola	.40	.15
❏ 94 Matt Williams	.60	.25
❏ 95 Alfredo Griffin	.40	.15
❏ 96 Steve Sax	.40	.15
❏ 97 Gary Gaetti	.60	.25
❏ 98 Ryne Sandberg	3.00	1.25
❏ 99 Danny Tartabull	.40	.15
❏ 100 Rafael Palmeiro	1.00	.40
❏ 101 Jesse Orosco	.40	.15
❏ 102 Garry Templeton	.40	.15
❏ 103 Frank DiPino	.40	.15
❏ 104 Tony Pena	.40	.15
❏ 105 Dickie Thon	.40	.15
❏ 106 Kelly Gruber	.40	.15
❏ 107 Marquis Grissom RC	2.00	.75
❏ 108 Jose Canseco	1.00	.40
❏ 109 Mike Blowers RC	.40	.15
❏ 110 Tom Browning	.40	.15
❏ 111 Greg Vaughn	.40	.15
❏ 112 Oddibe McDowell	.40	.15
❏ 113 Gary Ward	.40	.15
❏ 114 Jay Buhner	.60	.25
❏ 115 Eric Show	.40	.15
❏ 116 Bryan Harvey	.40	.15
❏ 117 Andy Van Slyke	1.00	.40
❏ 118 Jeff Ballard	.40	.15
❏ 119 Barry Lyons	.40	.15
❏ 120 Kevin Mitchell	.40	.15
❏ 121 Mike Gallego	.40	.15
❏ 122 Dave Smith	.40	.15
❏ 123 Kirby Puckett	1.50	.60
❏ 124 Jerome Walton	.40	.15
❏ 125 Bo Jackson	1.50	.60
❏ 126 Harold Baines	.60	.25
❏ 127 Scott Bankhead	.40	.15
❏ 128 Ozzie Guillen	.60	.25
❏ 129 Jose Oquendo UER (League misspelled as Legue)	.40	.15
❏ 130 John Dopson	.40	.15
❏ 131 Charlie Hayes	.40	.15
❏ 132 Fred McGriff	1.50	.60
❏ 133 Chet Lemon	.40	.15
❏ 134 Gary Carter	.60	.25
❏ 135 Rafael Ramirez	.40	.15
❏ 136 Shane Mack	.40	.15
❏ 137 Mark Grace	1.00	.40
❏ 138 Phil Bradley	.40	.15
❏ 139 Dwight Gooden	.60	.25
❏ 140 Harold Reynolds	.60	.25
❏ 141 Scott Fletcher	.40	.15
❏ 142 Ozzie Smith	2.50	1.00
❏ 143 Mike Greenwell	.40	.15
❏ 144 Pete Smith	.40	.15
❏ 145 Mark Gubicza	.40	.15
❏ 146 Chris Sabo	.40	.15
❏ 147 Ramon Martinez	.40	.15
❏ 148 Tim Leary	.40	.15
❏ 149 Randy Myers	.60	.25
❏ 150 Jody Reed	.40	.15
❏ 151 Bruce Ruffin	.40	.15
❏ 152 Jeff Russell	.40	.15
❏ 153 Doug Jones	.40	.15
❏ 154 Tony Gwynn	2.00	.75
❏ 155 Mark Langston	.40	.15
❏ 156 Mitch Williams	.40	.15
❏ 157 Gary Sheffield	1.50	.60
❏ 158 Tom Henke	.40	.15
❏ 159 Oil Can Boyd	.40	.15
❏ 160 Rickey Henderson	1.50	.60
❏ 161 Bill Doran	.40	.15
❏ 162 Chuck Finley	.60	.25
❏ 163 Jeff King	.40	.15
❏ 164 Nick Esasky	.40	.15
❏ 165 Cecil Fielder	.60	.25
❏ 166 Dave Valle	.40	.15
❏ 167 Robin Ventura	1.50	.60
❏ 168 Jim Deshaies	.40	.15
❏ 169 Juan Berenguer	.40	.15
❏ 170 Craig Worthington	.40	.15
❏ 171 Gregg Jefferies	.60	.25
❏ 172 Will Clark	1.00	.40
❏ 173 Kirk Gibson	.60	.25
❏ 174 Checklist 89-176 (Carlton Fisk)	.60	.25
❏ 175 Bobby Thigpen	.40	.15
❏ 176 John Tudor	.40	.15

❑	177	Andre Dawson	.60	.25
❑	178	George Brett	4.00	1.50
❑	179	Steve Buechele	.40	.15
❑	180	Albert Belle	1.50	.60
❑	181	Eddie Murray	1.50	.60
❑	182	Bob Geren	.40	.15
❑	183	Rob Murphy	.40	.15
❑	184	Tom Herr	.40	.15
❑	185	George Bell	.40	.15
❑	186	Spike Owen	.40	.15
❑	187	Cory Snyder	.40	.15
❑	188	Fred Lynn	.40	.15
❑	189	Eric Davis	.60	.25
❑	190	Dave Parker	.60	.25
❑	191	Jeff Blauser	.40	.15
❑	192	Matt Nokes	.40	.15
❑	193	Delino DeShields RC	1.00	.40
❑	194	Scott Sanderson	.40	.15
❑	195	Lance Parrish	.40	.15
❑	196	Bobby Bonilla	.60	.25
❑	197	Cal Ripken	5.00	2.00
❑	198	Kevin McReynolds	.40	.15
❑	199	Robby Thompson	.40	.15
❑	200	Tim Belcher	.40	.15
❑	201	Jesse Barfield	.40	.15
❑	202	Mariano Duncan	.40	.15
❑	203	Bill Spiers	.40	.15
❑	204	Frank White	.60	.25
❑	205	Julio Franco	.60	.25
❑	206	Greg Swindell	.40	.15
❑	207	Benito Santiago	.60	.25
❑	208	Johnny Ray	.40	.15
❑	209	Gary Redus	.40	.15
❑	210	Jeff Parrett	.40	.15
❑	211	Jimmy Key	.60	.25
❑	212	Tim Raines	.60	.25
❑	213	Carney Lansford	.60	.25
❑	214	Gerald Young	.40	.15
❑	215	Gene Larkin	.40	.15
❑	216	Dan Plesac	.40	.15
❑	217	Lonnie Smith	.40	.15
❑	218	Alan Trammell	.60	.25
❑	219	Jeffrey Leonard	.40	.15
❑	220	Sammy Sosa RC	20.00	8.00
❑	221	Todd Zeile	.60	.25
❑	222	Bill Landrum	.40	.15
❑	223	Mike Devereaux	.40	.15
❑	224	Mike Marshall	.40	.15
❑	225	Jose Uribe	.40	.15
❑	226	Juan Samuel	.40	.15
❑	227	Mel Hall	.40	.15
❑	228	Kent Hrbek	.60	.25
❑	229	Shawon Dunston	.40	.15
❑	230	Kevin Seitzer	.40	.15
❑	231	Pete Incaviglia	.40	.15
❑	232	Sandy Alomar Jr.	.60	.25
❑	233	Bip Roberts	.40	.15
❑	234	Scott Terry	.40	.15
❑	235	Dwight Evans	1.00	.40
❑	236	Ricky Jordan	.40	.15
❑	237	John Olerud RC	3.00	1.25
❑	238	Zane Smith	.40	.15
❑	239	Walt Weiss	.40	.15
❑	240	Alvaro Espinoza	.40	.15
❑	241	Billy Hatcher	.40	.15
❑	242	Paul Molitor	.60	.25
❑	243	Dale Murphy	1.00	.40
❑	244	Dave Bergman	.40	.15
❑	245	Ken Griffey Jr.	5.00	2.00
❑	246	Ed Whitson	.40	.15
❑	247	Kirk McCaskill	.40	.15
❑	248	Jay Bell	.60	.25
❑	249	Ben McDonald RC	1.00	.40
❑	250	Darryl Strawberry	.60	.25
❑	251	Brett Butler	.60	.25
❑	252	Terry Steinbach	.40	.15
❑	253	Ken Caminiti	.60	.25
❑	254	Dan Gladden	.40	.15
❑	255	Dwight Smith	.40	.15
❑	256	Kurt Stillwell	.40	.15
❑	257	Ruben Sierra	.60	.25
❑	258	Mike Schooler	.40	.15
❑	259	Lance Johnson	.40	.15
❑	260	Terry Pendleton	.60	.25
❑	261	Ellis Burks	1.00	.40
❑	262	Len Dykstra	.60	.25
❑	263	Mookie Wilson	.60	.25
❑	264	Nolan Ryan CL UER	1.50	.60
❑	265	Nolan Ryan SPEC	2.50	1.00
❑	266	Brian DuBois RC	.40	.15
❑	267	Don Robinson	.40	.15
❑	268	Glenn Wilson	.40	.15
❑	269	Kevin Tapani RC	1.00	.40
❑	270	Marvell Wynne	.40	.15
❑	271	Bill Ripken	.40	.15
❑	272	Howard Johnson	.40	.15
❑	273	Brian Holman	.40	.15
❑	274	Dan Pasqua	.40	.15
❑	275	Ken Dayley	.40	.15
❑	276	Jeff Reardon	.60	.25
❑	277	Jim Presley	.40	.15
❑	278	Jim Eisenreich	.40	.15
❑	279	Danny Jackson	.40	.15
❑	280	Orel Hershiser	.60	.25
❑	281	Andy Hawkins	.40	.15
❑	282	Jose Rijo	.40	.15
❑	283	Luis Rivera	.40	.15
❑	284	John Kruk	.60	.25
❑	285	Jeff Huson RC	.40	.15
❑	286	Joel Skinner	.40	.15
❑	287	Jack Clark	.60	.25
❑	288	Chili Davis	.60	.25
❑	289	Joe Girardi	1.00	.40
❑	290	B.J. Surhoff	.60	.25
❑	291	Luis Sojo RC	.40	.15
❑	292	Tom Foley	.40	.15
❑	293	Mike Moore	.40	.15
❑	294	Ken Oberkfell	.40	.15
❑	295	Luis Polonia	.40	.15
❑	296	Doug Drabek	.40	.15
❑	297	David Justice RC	3.00	1.25
❑	298	Paul Gibson	.40	.15
❑	299	Edgar Martinez	1.00	.40
❑	300	Frank Thomas RC	20.00	8.00
❑	301	Eric Yelding RC	.40	.15
❑	302	Greg Gagne	.40	.15
❑	303	Brad Komminsk	.40	.15
❑	304	Ron Darling	.40	.15
❑	305	Kevin Bass	.40	.15
❑	306	Jeff Hamilton	.40	.15
❑	307	Ron Karkovice	.40	.15
❑	308	M.Thompson UER Lankford	1.00	.40
❑	309	Mike Harkey	.40	.15
❑	310	Mel Stottlemyre Jr.	.40	.15
❑	311	Kenny Rogers	.60	.25
❑	312	Mitch Webster	.40	.15
❑	313	Kal Daniels	.40	.15
❑	314	Matt Nokes	.40	.15
❑	315	Dennis Lamp	.40	.15
❑	316	Ken Howell	.40	.15
❑	317	Glenallen Hill	.40	.15
❑	318	Dave Martinez	.40	.15
❑	319	Chris James	.40	.15
❑	320	Mike Pagliarulo	.40	.15
❑	321	Hal Morris	.40	.15
❑	322	Rob Deer	.40	.15
❑	323	Greg Olson (C) RC	.40	.15
❑	324	Tony Phillips	.40	.15
❑	325	Larry Walker RC	8.00	3.00
❑	326	Ron Hassey	.40	.15
❑	327	Jack Howell	.40	.15
❑	328	John Smiley	.40	.15
❑	329	Steve Finley	.60	.25
❑	330	Dave Magadan	.40	.15
❑	331	Greg Litton	.40	.15
❑	332	Mickey Hatcher	.40	.15
❑	333	Lee Guetterman	.40	.15
❑	334	Norm Charlton	.40	.15
❑	335	Edgar Diaz RC	.40	.15
❑	336	Willie Wilson	.40	.15
❑	337	Bobby Witt	.40	.15
❑	338	Candy Maldonado	.40	.15
❑	339	Craig Lefferts	.40	.15
❑	340	Dante Bichette	.60	.25
❑	341	Wally Backman	.40	.15
❑	342	Dennis Cook	.40	.15
❑	343	Pat Borders	.40	.15
❑	344	Wallace Johnson	.40	.15
❑	345	Willie Randolph	.60	.25
❑	346	Danny Darwin	.40	.15
❑	347	Al Newman	.40	.15
❑	348	Mark Knudson	.40	.15
❑	349	Joe Boever	.40	.15
❑	350	Larry Sheets	.40	.15
❑	351	Mike Jackson	.40	.15
❑	352	Wayne Edwards RC	.40	.15
❑	353	Bernard Gilkey RC	1.00	.40
❑	354	Don Slaught	.40	.15
❑	355	Joe Orsulak	.40	.15
❑	356	John Franco	.60	.25
❑	357	Jeff Brantley	.40	.15
❑	358	Mike Morgan	.40	.15
❑	359	Deion Sanders	1.50	.60
❑	360	Terry Leach	.40	.15
❑	361	Les Lancaster	.40	.15
❑	362	Storm Davis	.40	.15
❑	363	Scott Coolbaugh RC	.40	.15
❑	364	Checklist 265-352 (Ozzie Smith)	1.00	.40
❑	365	Cecilio Guante	.40	.15
❑	366	Joey Cora	.60	.25
❑	367	Willie McGee	.60	.25
❑	368	Jerry Reed	.40	.15
❑	369	Darren Daulton	.60	.25
❑	370	Manny Lee	.40	.15
❑	371	Mark Gardner RC	.40	.15
❑	372	Rick Honeycutt	.40	.15
❑	373	Steve Balboni	.40	.15
❑	374	Jack Armstrong	.40	.15
❑	375	Charlie O'Brien	.40	.15
❑	376	Ron Gant	.60	.25
❑	377	Lloyd Moseby	.40	.15
❑	378	Gene Harris	.40	.15
❑	379	Joe Carter	.60	.25
❑	380	Scott Bailes	.40	.15
❑	381	R.J. Reynolds	.40	.15
❑	382	Bob Melvin	.40	.15
❑	383	Tim Teufel	.40	.15
❑	384	John Burkett	.40	.15
❑	385	Felix Jose	.40	.15
❑	386	Larry Andersen	.40	.15
❑	387	David West	.40	.15
❑	388	Luis Salazar	.40	.15
❑	389	Mike Macfarlane	.40	.15
❑	390	Charlie Hough	.60	.25
❑	391	Greg Briley	.40	.15
❑	392	Donn Pall	.40	.15
❑	393	Bryn Smith	.40	.15
❑	394	Carlos Quintana	.40	.15
❑	395	Steve Lake	.40	.15
❑	396	Mark Whiten RC	1.00	.40
❑	397	Edwin Nunez	.40	.15
❑	398	Rick Parker RC	.40	.15
❑	399	Mark Portugal	.40	.15
❑	400	Roy Smith	.40	.15
❑	401	Hector Villanueva RC	.40	.15
❑	402	Bob Milacki	.40	.15
❑	403	Alejandro Pena	.40	.15
❑	404	Scott Bradley	.40	.15
❑	405	Ron Kittle	.40	.15
❑	406	Bob Tewksbury	.40	.15
❑	407	Wes Gardner	.40	.15
❑	408	Ernie Whitt	.40	.15
❑	409	Terry Shumpert RC	.40	.15
❑	410	Tim Layana RC	.40	.15
❑	411	Chris Gwynn	.40	.15
❑	412	Jeff D. Robinson	.40	.15
❑	413	Scott Scudder	.40	.15
❑	414	Kevin Romine	.40	.15
❑	415	Jose DeJesus	.40	.15
❑	416	Mike Jeffcoat	.40	.15
❑	417	Rudy Seanez RC	.40	.15
❑	418	Mike Dunne	.40	.15
❑	419	Dick Schofield	.40	.15
❑	420	Steve Wilson	.40	.15
❑	421	Bill Krueger	.40	.15
❑	422	Junior Felix	.40	.15
❑	423	Drew Hall	.40	.15
❑	424	Curt Young	.40	.15
❑	425	Franklin Stubbs	.40	.15
❑	426	Dave Winfield	.60	.25
❑	427	Rick Reed RC	1.00	.40
❑	428	Charlie Leibrandt	.40	.15
❑	429	Jeff M. Robinson	.40	.15
❑	430	Erik Hanson	.40	.15
❑	431	Barry Jones	.40	.15
❑	432	Alex Trevino	.40	.15
❑	433	John Moses	.40	.15

❑ 434 Dave Wayne Johnson RC	.40	.15
❑ 435 Mackey Sasser	.40	.15
❑ 436 Rick Leach	.40	.15
❑ 437 Lenny Harris	.40	.15
❑ 438 Carlos Martinez	.40	.15
❑ 439 Rex Hudler	.40	.15
❑ 440 Domingo Ramos	.40	.15
❑ 441 Gerald Perry	.40	.15
❑ 442 Jeff Russell	.40	.15
❑ 443 Carlos Baerga RC	1.00	.40
❑ 444 Will Clark CL	.60	.25
❑ 445 Stan Javier	.40	.15
❑ 446 Kevin Maas RC	1.00	.40
❑ 447 Tom Brunansky	.40	.15
❑ 448 Carmelo Martinez	.40	.15
❑ 449 Willie Blair RC	.40	.15
❑ 450 Andres Galarraga	.60	.25
❑ 451 Bud Black	.40	.15
❑ 452 Greg W. Harris	.40	.15
❑ 453 Joe Oliver	.40	.15
❑ 454 Greg Brock	.40	.15
❑ 455 Jeff Treadway	.40	.15
❑ 456 Lance McCullers	.40	.15
❑ 457 Dave Schmidt	.40	.15
❑ 458 Todd Burns	.40	.15
❑ 459 Max Venable	.40	.15
❑ 460 Neal Heaton	.40	.15
❑ 461 Mark Williamson	.40	.15
❑ 462 Keith Miller	.40	.15
❑ 463 Mike LaCoss	.40	.15
❑ 464 Jose Offerman RC	1.00	.40
❑ 465 Jim Leyritz RC	2.00	.75
❑ 466 Glenn Braggs	.40	.15
❑ 467 Ron Robinson	.40	.15
❑ 468 Mark Davis	.40	.15
❑ 469 Gary Pettis	.40	.15
❑ 470 Keith Hernandez	.60	.25
❑ 471 Dennis Rasmussen	.40	.15
❑ 472 Mark Eichhorn	.40	.15
❑ 473 Ted Power	.40	.15
❑ 474 Terry Mulholland	.40	.15
❑ 475 Todd Stottlemyre	.60	.25
❑ 476 Jerry Goff RC	.40	.15
❑ 477 Gene Nelson	.40	.15
❑ 478 Rich Gedman	.40	.15
❑ 479 Brian Harper	.40	.15
❑ 480 Mike Felder	.40	.15
❑ 481 Steve Avery	.40	.15
❑ 482 Jack Morris	.60	.25
❑ 483 Randy Johnson	3.00	1.25
❑ 484 Scott Radinsky RC	.40	.15
❑ 485 Jose DeLeon	.40	.15
❑ 486 Stan Belinda RC	.40	.15
❑ 487 Brian Holton	.40	.15
❑ 488 Mark Carreon	.40	.15
❑ 489 Trevor Wilson	.40	.15
❑ 490 Mike Sharperson	.40	.15
❑ 491 Alan Mills RC	.40	.15
❑ 492 John Candelaria	.40	.15
❑ 493 Paul Assenmacher	.40	.15
❑ 494 Steve Crawford	.40	.15
❑ 495 Brad Arnsberg	.40	.15
❑ 496 Sergio Valdez RC	.40	.15
❑ 497 Mark Parent	.40	.15
❑ 498 Tom Pagnozzi	.40	.15
❑ 499 Greg A. Harris	.40	.15
❑ 500 Randy Ready	.40	.15
❑ 501 Duane Ward	.40	.15
❑ 502 Nelson Santovenia	.40	.15
❑ 503 Joe Klink RC	.40	.15
❑ 504 Eric Plunk	.40	.15
❑ 505 Jeff Reed	.40	.15
❑ 506 Ted Higuera	.40	.15
❑ 507 Joe Hesketh	.40	.15
❑ 508 Dan Petry	.40	.15
❑ 509 Matt Young	.40	.15
❑ 510 Jerald Clark	.40	.15
❑ 511 John Orton RC	.40	.15
❑ 512 Scott Ruskin RC	.40	.15
❑ 513 Chris Hoiles RC	1.00	.40
❑ 514 Daryl Boston	.40	.15
❑ 515 Francisco Oliveras	.40	.15
❑ 516 Ozzie Canseco	.40	.15
❑ 517 Xavier Hernandez RC	.40	.15
❑ 518 Fred Manrique	.40	.15
❑ 519 Shawn Boskie RC	.40	.15
❑ 520 Jeff Montgomery	.60	.25
❑ 521 Jack Daugherty RC	.40	.15
❑ 522 Keith Comstock	.40	.15
❑ 523 Greg Hibbard RC	.40	.15
❑ 524 Lee Smith	.60	.25
❑ 525 Dana Kiecker RC	.40	.15
❑ 526 Darrel Akerfelds	.40	.15
❑ 527 Greg Myers	.40	.15
❑ 528 Ryne Sandberg CL	1.50	.60

1993 Leaf

❑ COMPLETE SET (550)	35.00	14.00
❑ COMPLETE SERIES 1 (220)	15.00	6.00
❑ COMPLETE SERIES 2 (220)	15.00	6.00
❑ COMPLETE UPDATE (110)	5.00	2.00
❑ COMMON RC	.15	.05
❑ 1 Ben McDonald	.15	.05
❑ 2 Sid Fernandez	.15	.05
❑ 3 Juan Guzman	.15	.05
❑ 4 Curt Schilling	.30	.10
❑ 5 Ivan Rodriguez	.50	.20
❑ 6 Don Slaught	.15	.05
❑ 7 Terry Steinbach	.15	.05
❑ 8 Todd Zeile	.15	.05
❑ 9 Andy Stankiewicz	.15	.05
❑ 10 Tim Teufel	.15	.05
❑ 11 Marvin Freeman	.15	.05
❑ 12 Jim Austin	.15	.05
❑ 13 Bob Scanlan	.15	.05
❑ 14 Rusty Meacham	.15	.05
❑ 15 Casey Candaele	.15	.05
❑ 16 Travis Fryman	.30	.10
❑ 17 Jose Offerman	.15	.05
❑ 18 Albert Belle	.30	.10
❑ 19 John Vander Wal	.15	.05
❑ 20 Dan Pasqua	.15	.05
❑ 21 Frank Viola	.30	.10
❑ 22 Terry Mulholland	.15	.05
❑ 23 Gregg Olson	.15	.05
❑ 24 Randy Tomlin	.15	.05
❑ 25 Todd Stottlemyre	.15	.05
❑ 26 Jose Oquendo	.15	.05
❑ 27 Julio Franco	.30	.10
❑ 28 Tony Gwynn	1.00	.40
❑ 29 Ruben Sierra	.30	.10
❑ 30 Robby Thompson	.15	.05
❑ 31 Jim Bullinger	.15	.05
❑ 32 Rick Aguilera	.15	.05
❑ 33 Scott Servais	.15	.05
❑ 34 Cal Eldred	.15	.05
❑ 35 Mike Piazza	3.00	1.25
❑ 36 Brent Mayne	.15	.05
❑ 37 Wil Cordero	.15	.05
❑ 38 Milt Cuyler	.15	.05
❑ 39 Howard Johnson	.15	.05
❑ 40 Kenny Lofton	.30	.10
❑ 41 Alex Fernandez	.15	.05
❑ 42 Denny Neagle	.30	.10
❑ 43 Tony Pena	.15	.05
❑ 44 Bob Tewksbury	.15	.05
❑ 45 Glenn Davis	.15	.05
❑ 46 Fred McGriff	.50	.20
❑ 47 John Olerud	.30	.10
❑ 48 Steve Hosey	.15	.05
❑ 49 Rafael Palmeiro	.50	.20
❑ 50 David Justice	.30	.10
❑ 51 Pete Harnisch	.15	.05
❑ 52 Sam Militello	.15	.05
❑ 53 Orel Hershiser	.30	.10
❑ 54 Pat Mahomes	.15	.05
❑ 55 Greg Colbrunn	.15	.05
❑ 56 Greg Vaughn	.15	.05
❑ 57 Vince Coleman	.15	.05
❑ 58 Brian McRae	.15	.05
❑ 59 Len Dykstra	.30	.10
❑ 60 Dan Gladden	.15	.05
❑ 61 Ted Power	.15	.05
❑ 62 Donovan Osborne	.15	.05
❑ 63 Ron Karkovice	.15	.05
❑ 64 Frank Seminara	.15	.05
❑ 65 Bob Zupcic	.15	.05
❑ 66 Kirt Manwaring	.15	.05
❑ 67 Mike Devereaux	.15	.05
❑ 68 Mark Lemke	.15	.05
❑ 69 Devon White	.30	.10
❑ 70 Sammy Sosa	.75	.30
❑ 71 Pedro Astacio	.15	.05
❑ 72 Dennis Eckersley	.30	.10
❑ 73 Chris Nabholz	.15	.05
❑ 74 Melido Perez	.15	.05
❑ 75 Todd Hundley	.15	.05
❑ 76 Kent Hrbek	.30	.10
❑ 77 Mickey Morandini	.15	.05
❑ 78 Tim McIntosh	.15	.05
❑ 79 Andy Van Slyke	.50	.20
❑ 80 Kevin McReynolds	.15	.05
❑ 81 Mike Henneman	.15	.05
❑ 82 Greg W. Harris	.15	.05
❑ 83 Sandy Alomar Jr.	.15	.05
❑ 84 Mike Jackson	.15	.05
❑ 85 Ozzie Guillen	.30	.10
❑ 86 Jeff Blauser	.15	.05
❑ 87 John Valentin	.15	.05
❑ 88 Rey Sanchez	.15	.05
❑ 89 Rick Sutcliffe	.30	.10
❑ 90 Luis Gonzalez	.30	.10
❑ 91 Jeff Fassero	.15	.05
❑ 92 Kenny Rogers	.30	.10
❑ 93 Bret Saberhagen	.30	.10
❑ 94 Bob Welch	.15	.05
❑ 95 Darren Daulton	.30	.10
❑ 96 Mike Gallego	.15	.05
❑ 97 Orlando Merced	.15	.05
❑ 98 Chuck Knoblauch	.30	.10
❑ 99 Bernard Gilkey	.15	.05
❑ 100 Billy Ashley	.15	.05
❑ 101 Kevin Appier	.30	.10
❑ 102 Jeff Brantley	.15	.05
❑ 103 Bill Gullickson	.15	.05
❑ 104 John Smoltz	.50	.20
❑ 105 Paul Sorrento	.15	.05
❑ 106 Steve Buechele	.15	.05
❑ 107 Steve Sax	.15	.05
❑ 108 Andujar Cedeno	.15	.05
❑ 109 Billy Hatcher	.15	.05
❑ 110 Checklist	.15	.05
❑ 111 Alan Mills	.15	.05
❑ 112 John Franco	.30	.10
❑ 113 Jack Morris	.30	.10
❑ 114 Mitch Williams	.15	.05
❑ 115 Nolan Ryan	3.00	1.25
❑ 116 Jay Bell	.30	.10
❑ 117 Mike Bordick	.15	.05
❑ 118 Geronimo Pena	.15	.05
❑ 119 Danny Tartabull	.15	.05
❑ 120 Checklist	.15	.05
❑ 121 Steve Avery	.15	.05
❑ 122 Ricky Bones	.15	.05
❑ 123 Mike Morgan	.15	.05
❑ 124 Jeff Montgomery	.15	.05
❑ 125 Jeff Bagwell	.50	.20
❑ 126 Tony Phillips	.15	.05
❑ 127 Lenny Harris	.15	.05
❑ 128 Glenallen Hill	.15	.05
❑ 129 Marquis Grissom	.30	.10
❑ 130 Gerald Williams UER (Bernie Williams picture and)	.15	.05
❑ 131 Greg A. Harris	.15	.05
❑ 132 Tommy Greene	.15	.05
❑ 133 Chris Hoiles	.15	.05
❑ 134 Bob Walk	.15	.05
❑ 135 Duane Ward	.15	.05
❑ 136 Tom Pagnozzi	.15	.05

❑ 137 Jeff Huson	.15	.05
❑ 138 Kurt Stillwell	.15	.05
❑ 139 Dave Henderson	.15	.05
❑ 140 Darrin Jackson	.15	.05
❑ 141 Frank Castillo	.15	.05
❑ 142 Scott Erickson	.15	.05
❑ 143 Darryl Kile	.30	.10
❑ 144 Bill Wegman	.15	.05
❑ 145 Steve Wilson	.15	.05
❑ 146 George Brett	2.00	.75
❑ 147 Moises Alou	.30	.10
❑ 148 Lou Whitaker	.30	.10
❑ 149 Chico Walker	.15	.05
❑ 150 Jerry Browne	.15	.05
❑ 151 Kirk McCaskill	.15	.05
❑ 152 Zane Smith	.15	.05
❑ 153 Matt Young	.15	.05
❑ 154 Lee Smith	.30	.10
❑ 155 Leo Gomez	.15	.05
❑ 156 Dan Walters	.15	.05
❑ 157 Pat Borders	.15	.05
❑ 158 Matt Williams	.30	.10
❑ 159 Dean Palmer	.30	.10
❑ 160 John Patterson	.15	.05
❑ 161 Doug Jones	.15	.05
❑ 162 John Habyan	.15	.05
❑ 163 Pedro Martinez	1.50	.60
❑ 164 Carl Willis	.15	.05
❑ 165 Darrin Fletcher	.15	.05
❑ 166 B.J. Surhoff	.30	.10
❑ 167 Eddie Murray	.75	.30
❑ 168 Keith Miller	.15	.05
❑ 169 Ricky Jordan	.15	.05
❑ 170 Juan Gonzalez	.30	.10
❑ 171 Charles Nagy	.15	.05
❑ 172 Mark Clark	.15	.05
❑ 173 Bobby Thigpen	.15	.05
❑ 174 Tim Scott	.15	.05
❑ 175 Scott Cooper	.15	.05
❑ 176 Royce Clayton	.15	.05
❑ 177 Brady Anderson	.30	.10
❑ 178 Sid Bream	.15	.05
❑ 179 Derek Bell	.15	.05
❑ 180 Otis Nixon	.15	.05
❑ 181 Kevin Gross	.15	.05
❑ 182 Ron Darling	.15	.05
❑ 183 John Wetteland	.30	.10
❑ 184 Mike Stanley	.15	.05
❑ 185 Jeff Kent	.75	.30
❑ 186 Brian Harper	.15	.05
❑ 187 Mariano Duncan	.15	.05
❑ 188 Robin Yount	1.25	.50
❑ 189 Al Martin	.15	.05
❑ 190 Eddie Zosky	.15	.05
❑ 191 Mike Munoz	.15	.05
❑ 192 Andy Benes	.15	.05
❑ 193 Dennis Cook	.15	.05
❑ 194 Bill Swift	.15	.05
❑ 195 Frank Thomas	.75	.30
❑ 195A Frank Thomas (Franklin visible on batting glove)	1.25	.50
❑ 196 Damon Berryhill	.15	.05
❑ 197 Mike Greenwell	.15	.05
❑ 198 Mark Grace	.50	.20
❑ 199 Darryl Hamilton	.15	.05
❑ 200 Derrick May	.15	.05
❑ 201 Ken Hill	.15	.05
❑ 202 Kevin Brown	.30	.10
❑ 203 Dwight Gooden	.30	.10
❑ 204 Bobby Witt	.15	.05
❑ 205 Juan Bell	.15	.05
❑ 206 Kevin Maas	.15	.05
❑ 207 Jeff King	.15	.05
❑ 208 Scott Leius	.15	.05
❑ 209 Rheal Cormier	.15	.05
❑ 210 Darryl Strawberry	.30	.10
❑ 211 Tom Gordon	.15	.05
❑ 212 Bud Black	.15	.05
❑ 213 Mickey Tettleton	.15	.05
❑ 214 Pete Smith	.15	.05
❑ 215 Felix Fermin	.15	.05
❑ 216 Rick Wilkins	.15	.05
❑ 217 George Bell	.15	.05
❑ 218 Eric Anthony	.15	.05
❑ 219 Pedro Munoz	.15	.05
❑ 220 Checklist	.15	.05
❑ 221 Lance Blankenship	.15	.05
❑ 222 Deion Sanders	.50	.20
❑ 223 Craig Biggio	.50	.20
❑ 224 Ryne Sandberg	1.25	.50
❑ 225 Ron Gant	.30	.10
❑ 226 Tom Brunansky	.15	.05
❑ 227 Chad Curtis	.15	.05
❑ 228 Joe Carter	.30	.10
❑ 229 Brian Jordan	.30	.10
❑ 230 Brett Butler	.30	.10
❑ 231 Frank Bolick	.15	.05
❑ 232 Rod Beck	.15	.05
❑ 233 Carlos Baerga	.15	.05
❑ 234 Eric Karros	.30	.10
❑ 235 Jack Armstrong	.15	.05
❑ 236 Bobby Bonilla	.30	.10
❑ 237 Don Mattingly	2.00	.75
❑ 238 Jeff Gardner	.15	.05
❑ 239 Dave Hollins	.15	.05
❑ 240 Steve Cooke	.15	.05
❑ 241 Jose Canseco	.50	.20
❑ 242 Ivan Calderon	.15	.05
❑ 243 Tim Belcher	.15	.05
❑ 244 Freddie Benavides	.15	.05
❑ 245 Roberto Alomar	.50	.20
❑ 246 Rob Deer	.15	.05
❑ 247 Will Clark	.50	.20
❑ 248 Mike Felder	.15	.05
❑ 249 Harold Baines	.30	.10
❑ 250 David Cone	.30	.10
❑ 251 Mark Guthrie	.15	.05
❑ 252 Ellis Burks	.30	.10
❑ 253 Jim Abbott	.50	.20
❑ 254 Chili Davis	.30	.10
❑ 255 Chris Bosio	.15	.05
❑ 256 Bret Barberie	.15	.05
❑ 257 Hal Morris	.15	.05
❑ 258 Dante Bichette	.30	.10
❑ 259 Storm Davis	.15	.05
❑ 260 Gary DiSarcina	.15	.05
❑ 261 Ken Caminiti	.30	.10
❑ 262 Paul Molitor	.30	.10
❑ 263 Joe Oliver	.15	.05
❑ 264 Pat Listach	.15	.05
❑ 265 Gregg Jefferies	.15	.05
❑ 266 Jose Guzman	.15	.05
❑ 267 Eric Davis	.30	.10
❑ 268 Delino DeShields	.15	.05
❑ 269 Barry Bonds	2.00	.75
❑ 270 Mike Bielecki	.15	.05
❑ 271 Jay Buhner	.30	.10
❑ 272 Scott Pose RC	.15	.05
❑ 273 Tony Fernandez	.15	.05
❑ 274 Chito Martinez	.15	.05
❑ 275 Phil Plantier	.15	.05
❑ 276 Pete Incaviglia	.15	.05
❑ 277 Carlos Garcia	.15	.05
❑ 278 Tom Henke	.15	.05
❑ 279 Roger Clemens	1.50	.60
❑ 280 Rob Dibble	.30	.10
❑ 281 Daryl Boston	.15	.05
❑ 282 Greg Gagne	.15	.05
❑ 283 Cecil Fielder	.30	.10
❑ 284 Carlton Fisk	.50	.20
❑ 285 Wade Boggs	.50	.20
❑ 286 Damion Easley	.15	.05
❑ 287 Norm Charlton	.15	.05
❑ 288 Jeff Conine	.30	.10
❑ 289 Roberto Kelly	.15	.05
❑ 290 Jerald Clark	.15	.05
❑ 291 Rickey Henderson	.75	.30
❑ 292 Chuck Finley	.30	.10
❑ 293 Doug Drabek	.15	.05
❑ 294 Dave Stewart	.30	.10
❑ 295 Tom Glavine	.50	.20
❑ 296 Jaime Navarro	.15	.05
❑ 297 Ray Lankford	.30	.10
❑ 298 Greg Hibbard	.15	.05
❑ 299 Jody Reed	.15	.05
❑ 300 Dennis Martinez	.30	.10
❑ 301 Dave Martinez	.15	.05
❑ 302 Reggie Jefferson	.15	.05
❑ 303 John Cummings RC	.15	.05
❑ 304 Orestes Destrade	.15	.05
❑ 305 Mike Maddux	.15	.05
❑ 306 David Segui	.15	.05
❑ 307 Gary Sheffield	.30	.10
❑ 308 Danny Jackson	.15	.05
❑ 309 Craig Lefferts	.15	.05
❑ 310 Andre Dawson	.30	.10
❑ 311 Barry Larkin	.50	.20
❑ 312 Alex Cole	.15	.05
❑ 313 Mark Gardner	.15	.05
❑ 314 Kirk Gibson	.30	.10
❑ 315 Shane Mack	.15	.05
❑ 316 Bo Jackson	.75	.30
❑ 317 Jimmy Key	.30	.10
❑ 318 Greg Myers	.15	.05
❑ 319 Ken Griffey Jr.	1.25	.50
❑ 320 Monty Fariss	.15	.05
❑ 321 Kevin Mitchell	.15	.05
❑ 322 Andres Galarraga	.30	.10
❑ 323 Mark McGwire	2.00	.75
❑ 324 Mark Langston	.15	.05
❑ 325 Steve Finley	.30	.10
❑ 326 Greg Maddux	1.25	.50
❑ 327 Dave Nilsson	.15	.05
❑ 328 Ozzie Smith	1.25	.50
❑ 329 Candy Maldonado	.15	.05
❑ 330 Checklist	.15	.05
❑ 331 Tim Pugh RC	.15	.05
❑ 332 Joe Girardi	.15	.05
❑ 333 Junior Felix	.15	.05
❑ 334 Greg Swindell	.15	.05
❑ 335 Ramon Martinez	.15	.05
❑ 336 Sean Berry	.15	.05
❑ 337 Joe Orsulak	.15	.05
❑ 338 Wes Chamberlain	.15	.05
❑ 339 Stan Belinda	.15	.05
❑ 340 Checklist UER (306 Luis Mercedes)	.15	.05
❑ 341 Bruce Hurst	.15	.05
❑ 342 John Burkett	.15	.05
❑ 343 Mike Mussina	.50	.20
❑ 344 Scott Fletcher	.15	.05
❑ 345 Rene Gonzales	.15	.05
❑ 346 Roberto Hernandez	.15	.05
❑ 347 Carlos Martinez	.15	.05
❑ 348 Bill Krueger	.15	.05
❑ 349 Felix Jose	.15	.05
❑ 350 John Jaha	.15	.05
❑ 351 Willie Banks	.15	.05
❑ 352 Matt Nokes	.15	.05
❑ 353 Kevin Seitzer	.15	.05
❑ 354 Erik Hanson	.15	.05
❑ 355 David Hulse RC	.15	.05
❑ 356 Domingo Martinez RC	.15	.05
❑ 357 Greg Olson	.15	.05
❑ 358 Randy Myers	.15	.05
❑ 359 Tom Browning	.15	.05
❑ 360 Charlie Hayes	.15	.05
❑ 361 Bryan Harvey	.15	.05
❑ 362 Eddie Taubensee	.15	.05
❑ 363 Tim Wallach	.15	.05
❑ 364 Mel Rojas	.15	.05
❑ 365 Frank Tanana	.15	.05
❑ 366 John Kruk	.30	.10
❑ 367 Tim Laker RC	.15	.05
❑ 368 Rich Rodriguez	.15	.05
❑ 369 Darren Lewis	.15	.05
❑ 370 Harold Reynolds	.30	.10
❑ 371 Jose Melendez	.15	.05
❑ 372 Joe Grahe	.15	.05
❑ 373 Lance Johnson	.15	.05
❑ 374 Jose Mesa	.15	.05
❑ 375 Scott Livingstone	.15	.05
❑ 376 Wally Joyner	.30	.10
❑ 377 Kevin Reimer	.15	.05
❑ 378 Kirby Puckett	.75	.30
❑ 379 Paul O'Neill	.50	.20
❑ 380 Randy Johnson	.75	.30
❑ 381 Manuel Lee	.15	.05
❑ 382 Dick Schofield	.15	.05
❑ 383 Darren Holmes	.15	.05
❑ 384 Charlie Hough	.30	.10
❑ 385 John Orton	.15	.05
❑ 386 Edgar Martinez	.50	.20
❑ 387 Terry Pendleton	.30	.10
❑ 388 Dan Plesac	.15	.05
❑ 389 Jeff Reardon	.30	.10
❑ 390 David Nied	.15	.05
❑ 391 Dave Magadan	.15	.05

❑	392	Larry Walker	.30	.10
❑	393	Ben Rivera	.15	.05
❑	394	Lonnie Smith	.15	.05
❑	395	Craig Shipley	.15	.05
❑	396	Willie McGee	.30	.10
❑	397	Arthur Rhodes	.15	.05
❑	398	Mike Stanton	.15	.05
❑	399	Luis Polonia	.15	.05
❑	400	Jack McDowell	.15	.05
❑	401	Mike Moore	.15	.05
❑	402	Jose Lind	.15	.05
❑	403	Bill Spiers	.15	.05
❑	404	Kevin Tapani	.15	.05
❑	405	Spike Owen	.15	.05
❑	406	Tino Martinez	.50	.20
❑	407	Charlie Leibrandt	.15	.05
❑	408	Ed Sprague	.15	.05
❑	409	Bryn Smith	.15	.05
❑	410	Benito Santiago	.30	.10
❑	411	Jose Rijo	.15	.05
❑	412	Pete O'Brien	.15	.05
❑	413	Willie Wilson	.15	.05
❑	414	Bip Roberts	.15	.05
❑	415	Eric Young	.15	.05
❑	416	Walt Weiss	.15	.05
❑	417	Milt Thompson	.15	.05
❑	418	Chris Sabo	.15	.05
❑	419	Scott Sanderson	.15	.05
❑	420	Tim Raines	.30	.10
❑	421	Alan Trammell	.30	.10
❑	422	Mike Macfarlane	.15	.05
❑	423	Dave Winfield	.30	.10
❑	424	Bob Wickman	.15	.05
❑	425	David Valle	.15	.05
❑	426	Gary Redus	.15	.05
❑	427	Turner Ward	.15	.05
❑	428	Reggie Sanders	.30	.10
❑	429	Todd Worrell	.15	.05
❑	430	Julio Valera	.15	.05
❑	431	Cal Ripken	2.50	1.00
❑	432	Mo Vaughn	.30	.10
❑	433	John Smiley	.15	.05
❑	434	Omar Vizquel	.50	.20
❑	435	Billy Ripken	.15	.05
❑	436	Cory Snyder	.15	.05
❑	437	Carlos Quintana	.15	.05
❑	438	Omar Olivares	.15	.05
❑	439	Robin Ventura	.30	.10
❑	440	Checklist	.15	.05
❑	441	Kevin Higgins	.15	.05
❑	442	Carlos Hernandez	.15	.05
❑	443	Dan Peltier	.15	.05
❑	444	Derek Lilliquist	.15	.05
❑	445	Tim Salmon	.50	.20
❑	446	Sherman Obando RC	.15	.05
❑	447	Pat Kelly	.15	.05
❑	448	Todd Van Poppel	.15	.05
❑	449	Mark Whiten	.15	.05
❑	450	Checklist	.15	.05
❑	451	Pat Meares RC	.40	.15
❑	452	Tony Tarasco RC	.15	.05
❑	453	Chris Gwynn	.15	.05
❑	454	Armando Reynoso	.15	.05
❑	455	Danny Darwin	.15	.05
❑	456	Willie Greene	.15	.05
❑	457	Mike Blowers	.15	.05
❑	458	Kevin Roberson RC	.15	.05
❑	459	Graeme Lloyd RC	.40	.15
❑	460	David West	.15	.05
❑	461	Joey Cora	.15	.05
❑	462	Alex Arias	.15	.05
❑	463	Chad Kreuter	.15	.05
❑	464	Mike Lansing RC	.40	.15
❑	465	Mike Timlin	.15	.05
❑	466	Paul Wagner	.15	.05
❑	467	Mark Portugal	.15	.05
❑	468	Jim Leyritz	.15	.05
❑	469	Ryan Klesko	.30	.10
❑	470	Mario Diaz	.15	.05
❑	471	Guillermo Velasquez	.15	.05
❑	472	Fernando Valenzuela	.30	.10
❑	473	Raul Mondesi	.30	.10
❑	474	Mike Pagliarulo	.15	.05
❑	475	Chris Hammond	.15	.05
❑	476	Torey Lovullo	.15	.05
❑	477	Trevor Wilson	.15	.05
❑	478	Marcos Armas RC	.15	.05
❑	479	Dave Gallagher	.15	.05
❑	480	Jeff Treadway	.15	.05
❑	481	Jeff Branson	.15	.05
❑	482	Dickie Thon	.15	.05
❑	483	Eduardo Perez	.15	.05
❑	484	David Wells	.30	.10
❑	485	Brian Williams	.15	.05
❑	486	Domingo Cedeno RC	.15	.05
❑	487	Tom Candiotti	.15	.05
❑	488	Steve Frey	.15	.05
❑	489	Greg McMichael RC	.15	.05
❑	490	Marc Newfield	.15	.05
❑	491	Larry Andersen	.15	.05
❑	492	Damon Buford	.15	.05
❑	493	Ricky Gutierrez	.15	.05
❑	494	Jeff Russell	.15	.05
❑	495	Vinny Castilla	.75	.30
❑	496	Wilson Alvarez	.15	.05
❑	497	Scott Bullett	.15	.05
❑	498	Larry Casian	.15	.05
❑	499	Jose Vizcaino	.15	.05
❑	500	J.T.Snow RC	.60	.25
❑	501	Bryan Hickerson	.15	.05
❑	502	Jeremy Hernandez	.15	.05
❑	503	Jeromy Burnitz	.30	.10
❑	504	Steve Farr	.15	.05
❑	505	Jayhawk Owens RC	.15	.05
❑	506	Craig Paquette	.15	.05
❑	507	Jim Eisenreich	.15	.05
❑	508	Matt Whiteside RC	.15	.05
❑	509	Luis Aquino	.15	.05
❑	510	Mike LaValliere	.15	.05
❑	511	Jim Gott	.15	.05
❑	512	Mark McLemore	.15	.05
❑	513	Randy Milligan	.15	.05
❑	514	Gary Gaetti	.30	.10
❑	515	Lou Frazier RC	.15	.05
❑	516	Rich Amaral	.15	.05
❑	517	Gene Harris	.15	.05
❑	518	Aaron Sele	.15	.05
❑	519	Mark Wohlers	.15	.05
❑	520	Scott Kamieniecki	.15	.05
❑	521	Kent Mercker	.15	.05
❑	522	Jim Deshaies	.15	.05
❑	523	Kevin Stocker	.15	.05
❑	524	Jason Bere	.15	.05
❑	525	Tim Bogar RC	.15	.05
❑	526	Brad Pennington	.15	.05
❑	527	Curt Leskanic RC	.40	.15
❑	528	Wayne Kirby	.15	.05
❑	529	Tim Costo	.15	.05
❑	530	Doug Henry	.15	.05
❑	531	Trevor Hoffman	.75	.30
❑	532	Kelly Gruber	.15	.05
❑	533	Mike Harkey	.15	.05
❑	534	John Doherty	.15	.05
❑	535	Erik Pappas	.15	.05
❑	536	Brent Gates	.15	.05
❑	537	Roger McDowell	.15	.05
❑	538	Chris Haney	.15	.05
❑	539	Blas Minor	.15	.05
❑	540	Pat Hentgen	.15	.05
❑	541	Chuck Carr	.15	.05
❑	542	Doug Strange	.15	.05
❑	543	Xavier Hernandez	.15	.05
❑	544	Paul Quantrill	.15	.05
❑	545	Anthony Young	.15	.05
❑	546	Bret Boone	.30	.10
❑	547	Dwight Smith	.15	.05
❑	548	Bobby Munoz	.15	.05
❑	549	Russ Springer	.15	.05
❑	550	Roger Pavlik	.15	.05
❑	DW	Dave Winfield 3000 Hits	1.00	.40
❑	FT	Frank Thomas AU/3500	50.00	20.00

2003 Leaf

❑		COMP.LO SET (320)	40.00	15.00
❑		COMP.UPDATE SET (9)	8.00	3.00
❑		COMMON CARD (1-270)	.30	.10
❑		COMMON CARD (271-320)	.40	.15
❑		COMMON CARD (321-329)	.50	.20
❑	1	Brad Fullmer	.30	.10
❑	2	Darin Erstad	.30	.10
❑	3	David Eckstein	.30	.10
❑	4	Garret Anderson	.30	.10

❑	5	Jarrod Washburn	.30	.10
❑	6	Kevin Appier	.30	.10
❑	7	Tim Salmon	.50	.20
❑	8	Troy Glaus	.30	.10
❑	9	Troy Percival	.30	.10
❑	10	Buddy Groom	.30	.10
❑	11	Jay Gibbons	.30	.10
❑	12	Jeff Conine	.30	.10
❑	13	Marty Cordova	.30	.10
❑	14	Melvin Mora	.30	.10
❑	15	Rodrigo Lopez	.30	.10
❑	16	Tony Batista	.30	.10
❑	17	Jorge Julio	.30	.10
❑	18	Cliff Floyd	.30	.10
❑	19	Derek Lowe	.30	.10
❑	20	Jason Varitek	.75	.30
❑	21	Johnny Damon	.50	.20
❑	22	Manny Ramirez	.50	.20
❑	23	Nomar Garciaparra	1.25	.50
❑	24	Pedro Martinez	.50	.20
❑	25	Rickey Henderson	.75	.30
❑	26	Shea Hillenbrand	.30	.10
❑	27	Trot Nixon	.30	.10
❑	28	Carlos Lee	.30	.10
❑	29	Frank Thomas	.75	.30
❑	30	Jose Valentin	.30	.10
❑	31	Magglio Ordonez	.30	.10
❑	32	Mark Buehrle	.30	.10
❑	33	Paul Konerko	.30	.10
❑	34	C.C. Sabathia	.30	.10
❑	35	Danys Baez	.30	.10
❑	36	Ellis Burks	.30	.10
❑	37	Jim Thome	.50	.20
❑	38	Omar Vizquel	.50	.20
❑	39	Ricky Gutierrez	.30	.10
❑	40	Travis Fryman	.30	.10
❑	41A	Bobby Higginson	.30	.10
❑	41B	Carlos Pena	.30	.10
❑	43	Juan Acevedo	.30	.10
❑	44	Mark Redman	.30	.10
❑	45	Randall Simon	.30	.10
❑	46	Robert Fick	.30	.10
❑	47	Steve Sparks	.30	.10
❑	48	Carlos Beltran	.30	.10
❑	49	Joe Randa	.30	.10
❑	50	Michael Tucker	.30	.10
❑	51	Mike Sweeney	.30	.10
❑	52	Paul Byrd	.30	.10
❑	53	Raul Ibanez	.30	.10
❑	54	Runelvys Hernandez	.30	.10
❑	55	A.J. Pierzynski	.30	.10
❑	56	Brad Radke	.30	.10
❑	57	Corey Koskie	.30	.10
❑	58	Cristian Guzman	.30	.10
❑	59	David Ortiz	.75	.30
❑	60	Doug Mientkiewicz	.30	.10
❑	61	Dustan Mohr	.30	.10
❑	62	Eddie Guardado	.30	.10
❑	63	Jacque Jones	.30	.10
❑	64	Torii Hunter	.30	.10
❑	65	Alfonso Soriano	.30	.10
❑	66	Andy Pettitte	.50	.20
❑	67	Bernie Williams	.50	.20
❑	68	David Wells	.30	.10
❑	69	Derek Jeter	2.00	.75
❑	70	Jason Giambi	.30	.10
❑	71	Jeff Weaver	.30	.10
❑	72	Jorge Posada	.50	.20

❑ 73	Mike Mussina	.50	.20
❑ 74	Nick Johnson	.30	.10
❑ 75	Raul Mondesi	.30	.10
❑ 76	Robin Ventura	.30	.10
❑ 77	Roger Clemens	1.50	.60
❑ 78	Barry Zito	.30	.10
❑ 79	Billy Koch	.30	.10
❑ 80	David Justice	.30	.10
❑ 81	Eric Chavez	.30	.10
❑ 82	Jermaine Dye	.30	.10
❑ 83	Mark Mulder	.30	.10
❑ 84	Miguel Tejada	.30	.10
❑ 85	Ray Durham	.30	.10
❑ 86	Scott Hatteberg	.30	.10
❑ 87	Ted Lilly	.30	.10
❑ 88	Tim Hudson	.30	.10
❑ 89	Bret Boone	.30	.10
❑ 90	Carlos Guillen	.30	.10
❑ 91	Chris Snelling	.30	.10
❑ 92	Dan Wilson	.30	.10
❑ 93	Edgar Martinez	.50	.20
❑ 94	Freddy Garcia	.30	.10
❑ 95	Ichiro Suzuki	1.50	.60
❑ 96	Jamie Moyer	.30	.10
❑ 97	Joel Pineiro	.30	.10
❑ 98	John Olerud	.30	.10
❑ 99	Mark McLemore	.30	.10
❑ 100	Mike Cameron	.30	.10
❑ 101	Kazuhiro Sasaki	.30	.10
❑ 102	Aubrey Huff	.30	.10
❑ 103	Ben Grieve	.30	.10
❑ 104	Joe Kennedy	.30	.10
❑ 105	Paul Wilson	.30	.10
❑ 106	Randy Winn	.30	.10
❑ 107	Steve Cox	.30	.10
❑ 108	Alex Rodriguez	1.25	.50
❑ 109	Chan Ho Park	.30	.10
❑ 110	Hank Blalock	.30	.10
❑ 111	Herbert Perry	.30	.10
❑ 112	Ivan Rodriguez	.50	.20
❑ 113	Juan Gonzalez	.30	.10
❑ 114	Kenny Rogers	.30	.10
❑ 115	Kevin Mench	.30	.10
❑ 116	Rafael Palmeiro	.50	.20
❑ 117	Carlos Delgado	.30	.10
❑ 118	Eric Hinske	.30	.10
❑ 119	Jose Cruz	.30	.10
❑ 120	Josh Phelps	.30	.10
❑ 121	Roy Halladay	.30	.10
❑ 122	Shannon Stewart	.30	.10
❑ 123	Vernon Wells	.30	.10
❑ 124	Curt Schilling	.30	.10
❑ 125	Junior Spivey	.30	.10
❑ 126	Luis Gonzalez	.30	.10
❑ 127	Mark Grace	.50	.20
❑ 128	Randy Johnson	.75	.30
❑ 129	Steve Finley	.30	.10
❑ 130	Tony Womack	.30	.10
❑ 131	Andruw Jones	.50	.20
❑ 132	Chipper Jones	.75	.30
❑ 133	Gary Sheffield	.30	.10
❑ 134	Greg Maddux	1.25	.50
❑ 135	John Smoltz	.50	.20
❑ 136	Kevin Millwood	.30	.10
❑ 137	Rafael Furcal	.30	.10
❑ 138	Tom Glavine	.50	.20
❑ 139	Alex Gonzalez	.30	.10
❑ 140	Corey Patterson	.30	.10
❑ 141	Fred McGriff	.50	.20
❑ 142	Jon Lieber	.30	.10
❑ 143	Kerry Wood	.30	.10
❑ 144	Mark Prior	.50	.20
❑ 145	Matt Clement	.30	.10
❑ 146	Moises Alou	.30	.10
❑ 147	Sammy Sosa	.75	.30
❑ 148	Aaron Boone	.30	.10
❑ 149	Adam Dunn	.30	.10
❑ 150	Austin Kearns	.30	.10
❑ 151	Barry Larkin	.50	.20
❑ 152	Danny Graves	.30	.10
❑ 153	Elmer Dessens	.30	.10
❑ 154	Ken Griffey Jr.	1.25	.50
❑ 155	Sean Casey	.30	.10
❑ 156	Todd Walker	.30	.10
❑ 157	Gabe Kapler	.30	.10
❑ 158	Jason Jennings	.30	.10
❑ 159	Jay Payton	.30	.10
❑ 160	Larry Walker	.30	.10
❑ 161	Mike Hampton	.30	.10
❑ 162	Todd Helton	.50	.20
❑ 163	Todd Zeile	.30	.10
❑ 164	A.J. Burnett	.30	.10
❑ 165	Derrek Lee	.50	.20
❑ 166	Josh Beckett	.30	.10
❑ 167	Juan Encarnacion	.30	.10
❑ 168	Luis Castillo	.30	.10
❑ 169	Mike Lowell	.30	.10
❑ 170	Preston Wilson	.30	.10
❑ 171	Billy Wagner	.30	.10
❑ 172	Craig Biggio	.50	.20
❑ 173	Daryle Ward	.30	.10
❑ 174	Jeff Bagwell	.50	.20
❑ 175	Lance Berkman	.30	.10
❑ 176	Octavio Dotel	.30	.10
❑ 177	Richard Hidalgo	.30	.10
❑ 178	Roy Oswalt	.30	.10
❑ 179	Adrian Beltre	.30	.10
❑ 180	Eric Gagne	.30	.10
❑ 181	Eric Karros	.30	.10
❑ 182	Hideo Nomo	.75	.30
❑ 183	Kazuhisa Ishii	.30	.10
❑ 184	Kevin Brown	.30	.10
❑ 185	Mark Grudzielanek	.30	.10
❑ 186	Odalis Perez	.30	.10
❑ 187	Paul Lo Duca	.30	.10
❑ 188	Shawn Green	.30	.10
❑ 189	Alex Sanchez	.30	.10
❑ 190	Ben Sheets	.30	.10
❑ 191	Jeffrey Hammonds	.30	.10
❑ 192	Jose Hernandez	.30	.10
❑ 193	Takahito Nomura	.30	.10
❑ 194	Richie Sexson	.30	.10
❑ 195	Andres Galarraga	.30	.10
❑ 196	Bartolo Colon	.30	.10
❑ 197	Brad Wilkerson	.30	.10
❑ 198	Javier Vazquez	.30	.10
❑ 199	Jose Vidro	.30	.10
❑ 200	Michael Barrett	.30	.10
❑ 201	Tomo Ohka	.30	.10
❑ 202	Vladimir Guerrero	.75	.30
❑ 203	Al Leiter	.30	.10
❑ 204	Armando Benitez	.30	.10
❑ 205	Edgardo Alfonzo	.30	.10
❑ 206	Mike Piazza	1.25	.50
❑ 207	Mo Vaughn	.30	.10
❑ 208	Pedro Astacio	.30	.10
❑ 209	Roberto Alomar	.50	.20
❑ 210	Roger Cedeno	.30	.10
❑ 211	Timo Perez	.30	.10
❑ 212	Bobby Abreu	.30	.10
❑ 213	Jimmy Rollins	.30	.10
❑ 214	Mike Lieberthal	.30	.10
❑ 215	Pat Burrell	.30	.10
❑ 216	Randy Wolf	.30	.10
❑ 217	Travis Lee	.30	.10
❑ 218	Vicente Padilla	.30	.10
❑ 219	Aramis Ramirez	.30	.10
❑ 220	Brian Giles	.30	.10
❑ 221	Craig Wilson	.30	.10
❑ 222	Jason Kendall	.30	.10
❑ 223	Josh Fogg	.30	.10
❑ 224	Kevin Young	.30	.10
❑ 225	Kip Wells	.30	.10
❑ 226	Mike Williams	.30	.10
❑ 227	Brett Tomko	.30	.10
❑ 228	Brian Lawrence	.30	.10
❑ 229	Mark Kotsay	.30	.10
❑ 230	Oliver Perez	.30	.10
❑ 231	Phil Nevin	.30	.10
❑ 232	Ryan Klesko	.30	.10
❑ 233	Sean Burroughs	.30	.10
❑ 234	Trevor Hoffman	.30	.10
❑ 235	Barry Bonds	2.00	.75
❑ 236	Benito Santiago	.30	.10
❑ 237	Jeff Kent	.30	.10
❑ 238	Kirk Rueter	.30	.10
❑ 239	Livan Hernandez	.30	.10
❑ 240	Kenny Lofton	.30	.10
❑ 241	Rich Aurilia	.30	.10
❑ 242	Russ Ortiz	.30	.10
❑ 243	Albert Pujols	1.50	.60
❑ 244	Edgar Renteria	.30	.10
❑ 245	J.D. Drew	.30	.10
❑ 246	Jason Isringhausen	.30	.10
❑ 247	Jim Edmonds	.30	.10
❑ 248	Matt Morris	.30	.10
❑ 249	Tino Martinez	.50	.20
❑ 250	Scott Rolen	.50	.20
❑ 251	Curt Schilling PT	.30	.10
❑ 252	Ivan Rodriguez PT	.30	.10
❑ 253	Mike Piazza PT	.75	.30
❑ 254	Sammy Sosa PT	.50	.20
❑ 255	Matt Williams PT	.30	.10
❑ 256	Frank Thomas PT	.50	.20
❑ 257	Barry Bonds PT	1.00	.40
❑ 258	Roger Clemens PT	.75	.30
❑ 259	Rickey Henderson PT	.75	.30
❑ 260	Ken Griffey Jr. PT	.75	.30
❑ 261	Greg Maddux PT	.75	.30
❑ 262	Randy Johnson PT	.50	.20
❑ 263	Jeff Bagwell PT	.30	.10
❑ 264	Roberto Alomar PT	.30	.10
❑ 265	Tom Glavine PT	.30	.10
❑ 266	Juan Gonzalez PT	.30	.10
❑ 267	Mark Grace PT	.30	.10
❑ 268	Mike Mussina PT	.30	.10
❑ 269	Ryan Klesko PT	.30	.10
❑ 270	Fred McGriff PT	.30	.10
❑ 271	Joe Borchard ROO	.40	.15
❑ 272	Chris Snelling ROO	.40	.15
❑ 273	Brian Tallet ROO	.40	.15
❑ 274	Cliff Lee ROO	.40	.15
❑ 275	Freddy Sanchez ROO	.40	.15
❑ 276	Chone Figgins ROO	.40	.15
❑ 277	Kevin Cash ROO	.40	.15
❑ 278	Josh Bard ROO	.40	.15
❑ 279	Jeriome Robertson ROO	.40	.15
❑ 280	Jeremy Hill ROO	.40	.15
❑ 281	Shane Nance ROO	.40	.15
❑ 282	Jeff Baker ROO	.40	.15
❑ 283	Trey Hodges ROO	.40	.15
❑ 284	Eric Eckenstahler ROO	.40	.15
❑ 285	Jim Rushford ROO	.40	.15
❑ 286	Carlos Rivera ROO	.40	.15
❑ 287	Josh Bonifay ROO	.40	.15
❑ 288	Garrett Atkins ROO	.40	.15
❑ 289	Nic Jackson ROO	.40	.15
❑ 290	Corwin Malone ROO	.40	.15
❑ 291	Jimmy Gobble ROO	.40	.15
❑ 292	Josh Wilson ROO	.40	.15
❑ 293	Clint Barmes ROO RC	1.00	.40
❑ 294	Jon Adkins ROO	.40	.15
❑ 295	Tim Kalita ROO	.40	.15
❑ 296	Nelson Castro ROO	.40	.15
❑ 297	Colin Young ROO	.40	.15
❑ 298	Adrian Burnside ROO	.40	.15
❑ 299	Luis Martinez ROO	.40	.15
❑ 300	Termel Sledge ROO RC	.40	.15
❑ 301	Todd Donovan ROO	.40	.15
❑ 302	Jeremy Ward ROO	.40	.15
❑ 303	Wilson Valdez ROO	.40	.15
❑ 304	Jose Contreras ROO RC	.75	.30
❑ 305	Marshall McDougall ROO	.40	.15
❑ 306	Mitch Wylie ROO	.40	.15
❑ 307	Ron Calloway ROO	.40	.15
❑ 308	Jose Valverde ROO	.40	.15
❑ 309	Jason Davis ROO	.40	.15
❑ 310	Scotty Layfield ROO	.40	.15
❑ 311	Matt Thornton ROO	.40	.15
❑ 312	Adam Walker ROO	.40	.15
❑ 313	Gustavo Chacin ROO	.40	.15
❑ 314	Ron Chiavacci ROO	.40	.15
❑ 315	Wilbert Nieves ROO	.40	.15
❑ 316	Cliff Bartosh ROO	.40	.15
❑ 317	Miko Gonzalez ROO	.40	.15
❑ 318	Jeremy Guthrie ROO	.40	.15
❑ 319	Eric Junge ROO	.40	.15
❑ 320	Ben Kozlowski ROO	.40	.15
❑ 321	Hideki Matsui ROO RC	2.00	.75
❑ 322	Ramon Nivar ROO RC	.50	.20
❑ 323	Adam Loewen ROO RC	.50	.20
❑ 324	Brandon Webb ROO RC	2.00	.75
❑ 325	Chien-Ming Wang ROO RC	4.00	1.50
❑ 326	Delmon Young ROO RC	3.00	1.25
❑ 327	Ryan Wagner ROO RC	.50	.20
❑ 328	Dan Haren ROO RC	.50	.20
❑ 329	Rickie Weeks ROO RC	1.50	.60

2005 Leaf

Card		
❑ COMPLETE SET (300)	150.00	75.00
❑ COMP.SETw/o SP's (200)	25.00	10.00
❑ COMMON CARD (1-200)	.30	.10
❑ COMMON CARD (201-250)	2.00	.75
❑ 201-250 STATED ODDS 1:3		
❑ COMMON CARD (251-300)	1.50	.60
❑ 251-270 STATED ODDS 1:6		
❑ 271-300 STATED ODDS 1:4		
❑ 1 Bartolo Colon	.30	.10
❑ 2 Casey Kotchman	.30	.10
❑ 3 Chone Figgins	.30	.10
❑ 4 Darin Erstad	.30	.10
❑ 5 Francisco Rodriguez	.30	.10
❑ 6 Garret Anderson	.30	.10
❑ 7 Jarrod Washburn	.30	.10
❑ 8 Troy Glaus	.30	.10
❑ 9 Vladimir Guerrero	.75	.30
❑ 10 Brandon Webb	.30	.10
❑ 11 Casey Fossum	.30	.10
❑ 12 Luis Gonzalez	.30	.10
❑ 13 Randy Johnson	.75	.30
❑ 14 Richie Sexson	.30	.10
❑ 15 Andruw Jones	.50	.20
❑ 16 Chipper Jones	.75	.30
❑ 17 J.D. Drew	.30	.10
❑ 18 John Smoltz	.50	.20
❑ 19 Johnny Estrada	.30	.10
❑ 20 Marcus Giles	.30	.10
❑ 21 Rafael Furcal	.30	.10
❑ 22 Russ Ortiz	.30	.10
❑ 23 Javy Lopez	.30	.10
❑ 24 Jay Gibbons	.30	.10
❑ 25 Melvin Mora	.30	.10
❑ 26 Miguel Tejada	.30	.10
❑ 27 Rafael Palmeiro	.50	.20
❑ 28 Sidney Ponson	.30	.10
❑ 29 Bill Mueller	.30	.10
❑ 30 Curt Schilling	.50	.20
❑ 31 David Ortiz	1.00	.40
❑ 32 Doug Mientkiewicz	.30	.10
❑ 33 Jason Varitek	.75	.30
❑ 34 Johnny Damon	.50	.20
❑ 35 Manny Ramirez	.50	.20
❑ 36 Pedro Martinez	.50	.20
❑ 37 Trot Nixon	.30	.10
❑ 38 Aramis Ramirez	.30	.10
❑ 39 Corey Patterson	.30	.10
❑ 40 Derrek Lee	.50	.20
❑ 41 Greg Maddux	1.25	.50
❑ 42 Kerry Wood	.30	.10
❑ 43 Mark Prior	.50	.20
❑ 44 Moises Alou	.30	.10
❑ 45 Nomar Garciaparra	.75	.30
❑ 46 Sammy Sosa	.75	.30
❑ 47 Carlos Lee	.30	.10
❑ 48 Kip Wells	.30	.10
❑ 49 Magglio Ordonez	.30	.10
❑ 50 Mark Buehrle	.30	.10
❑ 51 Paul Konerko	.30	.10
❑ 52 Roberto Alomar	.50	.20
❑ 53 Adam Dunn	.30	.10
❑ 54 Austin Kearns	.30	.10
❑ 55 Barry Larkin	.50	.20
❑ 56 Danny Graves	.30	.10
❑ 57 Ken Griffey Jr.	1.25	.50
❑ 58 Sean Casey	.30	.10
❑ 59 C.C. Sabathia	.30	.10
❑ 60 Cliff Lee	.30	.10
❑ 61 Jody Gerut	.30	.10
❑ 62 Omar Vizquel	.30	.10
❑ 63 Travis Hafner	.30	.10
❑ 64 Victor Martinez	.30	.10
❑ 65 Charles Johnson	.30	.10
❑ 66 Jason Jennings	.30	.10
❑ 67 Jeromy Burnitz	.30	.10
❑ 68 Preston Wilson	.30	.10
❑ 69 Todd Helton	.50	.20
❑ 70 Bobby Higginson	.30	.10
❑ 71 Dmitri Young	.30	.10
❑ 72 Eric Munson	.30	.10
❑ 73 Ivan Rodriguez	.50	.20
❑ 74 Jeremy Bonderman	.30	.10
❑ 75 Rondell White	.30	.10
❑ 76 A.J. Burnett	.30	.10
❑ 77 Carl Pavano	.30	.10
❑ 78 Dontrelle Willis	.30	.10
❑ 79 Hee Seop Choi	.30	.10
❑ 80 Josh Beckett	.30	.10
❑ 81 Juan Pierre	.30	.10
❑ 82 Miguel Cabrera	.50	.20
❑ 83 Mike Lowell	.30	.10
❑ 84 Paul Lo Duca	.30	.10
❑ 85 Andy Pettitte	.50	.20
❑ 86 Carlos Beltran	.30	.10
❑ 87 Craig Biggio	.50	.20
❑ 88 Jeff Bagwell	.50	.20
❑ 89 Jeff Kent	.30	.10
❑ 90 Lance Berkman	.30	.10
❑ 91 Roger Clemens	1.25	.50
❑ 92 Roy Oswalt	.30	.10
❑ 93 Andres Blanco	.30	.10
❑ 94 Jeremy Affeldt	.30	.10
❑ 95 Juan Gonzalez	.30	.10
❑ 96 Ken Harvey	.30	.10
❑ 97 Mike Sweeney	.30	.10
❑ 98 Zack Greinke	.30	.10
❑ 99 Adrian Beltre	.30	.10
❑ 100 Brad Penny	.30	.10
❑ 101 Eric Gagne	.30	.10
❑ 102 Kazuhisa Ishii	.30	.10
❑ 103 Milton Bradley	.30	.10
❑ 104 Shawn Green	.30	.10
❑ 105 Steve Finley	.30	.10
❑ 106 Ben Sheets	.30	.10
❑ 107 Bill Hall	.30	.10
❑ 108 Danny Kolb	.30	.10
❑ 109 Geoff Jenkins	.30	.10
❑ 110 Junior Spivey	.30	.10
❑ 111 Lyle Overbay	.30	.10
❑ 112 Scott Podsednik	.30	.10
❑ 113 A.J. Pierzynski	.30	.10
❑ 114 Brad Radke	.30	.10
❑ 115 Corey Koskie	.30	.10
❑ 116 Jacque Jones	.30	.10
❑ 117 Joe Mauer	.75	.30
❑ 118 Joe Nathan	.30	.10
❑ 119 Shannon Stewart	.30	.10
❑ 120 Torii Hunter	.30	.10
❑ 121 Brad Wilkerson	.30	.10
❑ 122 Jeff Fassero	.30	.10
❑ 123 Jose Vidro	.30	.10
❑ 124 Livan Hernandez	.30	.10
❑ 125 Nick Johnson	.30	.10
❑ 126 Al Leiter	.30	.10
❑ 127 Jose Reyes	.30	.10
❑ 128 Kazuo Matsui	.30	.10
❑ 129 Mike Cameron	.30	.10
❑ 130 Mike Piazza	.75	.30
❑ 131 Richard Hidalgo	.30	.10
❑ 132 Tom Glavine	.50	.20
❑ 133 Alex Rodriguez	1.25	.50
❑ 134 Bernie Williams	.50	.20
❑ 135 Derek Jeter	1.50	.60
❑ 136 Gary Sheffield	.30	.10
❑ 137 Jason Giambi	.30	.10
❑ 138 Javier Vazquez	.30	.10
❑ 139 Jorge Posada	.50	.20
❑ 140 Kevin Brown	.30	.10
❑ 141 Mariano Rivera	.75	.30
❑ 142 Mike Mussina	.50	.20
❑ 143 Barry Zito	.30	.10
❑ 144 Bobby Crosby	.30	.10
❑ 145 Eric Chavez	.30	.10
❑ 146 Erubiel Durazo	.30	.10
❑ 147 Jermaine Dye	.30	.10
❑ 148 Mark Mulder	.30	.10
❑ 149 Tim Hudson	.30	.10
❑ 150 Bobby Abreu	.30	.10
❑ 151 Eric Milton	.30	.10
❑ 152 Jim Thome	.50	.20
❑ 153 Kevin Millwood	.30	.10
❑ 154 Mike Lieberthal	.30	.10
❑ 155 Pat Burrell	.30	.10
❑ 156 Randy Wolf	.30	.10
❑ 157 Craig Wilson	.30	.10
❑ 158 Jack Wilson	.30	.10
❑ 159 Jason Bay	.30	.10
❑ 160 Jason Kendall	.30	.10
❑ 161 Kris Benson	.30	.10
❑ 162 Brian Giles	.30	.10
❑ 163 Jake Peavy	.30	.10
❑ 164 Jay Payton	.30	.10
❑ 165 Khalil Greene	.50	.20
❑ 166 Mark Loretta	.30	.10
❑ 167 Ryan Klesko	.30	.10
❑ 168 Sean Burroughs	.30	.10
❑ 169 David Aardsma	.30	.10
❑ 170 Edgardo Alfonzo	.30	.10
❑ 171 Jason Schmidt	.30	.10
❑ 172 Merkin Valdez	.30	.10
❑ 173 Ray Durham	.30	.10
❑ 174 Bret Boone	.30	.10
❑ 175 Dan Wilson	.30	.10
❑ 176 Ichiro Suzuki	1.50	.60
❑ 177 Jamie Moyer	.30	.10
❑ 178 Rich Aurilia	.30	.10
❑ 179 Albert Pujols	1.50	.60
❑ 180 Edgar Renteria	.30	.10
❑ 181 Jason Isringhausen	.30	.10
❑ 182 Jeff Suppan	.30	.10
❑ 183 Jim Edmonds	.30	.10
❑ 184 Scott Rolen	.50	.20
❑ 185 Woody Williams	.30	.10
❑ 186 Aubrey Huff	.30	.10
❑ 187 Carl Crawford	.30	.10
❑ 188 Dewon Brazelton	.30	.10
❑ 189 Jose Cruz Jr.	.30	.10
❑ 190 Rocco Baldelli	.30	.10
❑ 191 Alfonso Soriano	.30	.10
❑ 192 Hank Blalock	.30	.10
❑ 193 Kenny Rogers	.30	.10
❑ 194 Laynce Nix	.30	.10
❑ 195 Mark Teixeira	.50	.20
❑ 196 Michael Young	.30	.10
❑ 197 Alexis Rios	.30	.10
❑ 198 Carlos Delgado	.30	.10
❑ 199 Roy Halladay	.30	.10
❑ 200 Vernon Wells	.30	.10
❑ 201 Josh Kroeger PROS	2.00	.75
❑ 202 Angel Guzman PROS	2.00	.75
❑ 203 Brad Halsey PROS	2.00	.75
❑ 204 Bucky Jacobsen PROS	2.00	.75
❑ 205 Carlos Hines PROS	2.00	.75
❑ 206 Carlos Vasquez PROS	2.00	.75
❑ 207 Billy Traber PROS	2.00	.75
❑ 208 Bubba Crosby PROS	2.00	.75
❑ 209 Chris Oxspring PROS	2.00	.75
❑ 210 Chris Shelton PROS	3.00	1.25
❑ 211 Colby Miller PROS	2.00	.75
❑ 212 Dave Crouthers PROS	2.00	.75
❑ 213 Dennis Sarfate PROS	2.00	.75
❑ 214 Don Kelly PROS	2.00	.75
❑ 215 Edwardo Sierra PROS	2.00	.75
❑ 216 Edwin Moreno PROS	2.00	.75
❑ 217 Fernando Nieve PROS	2.00	.75
❑ 218 Freddy Guzman PROS	2.00	.75
❑ 219 Greg Dobbs PROS	2.00	.75
❑ 220 Hector Gimenez PROS	2.00	.75
❑ 221 Andy Green PROS	2.00	.75
❑ 222 Jason Bartlett PROS	2.00	.75
❑ 223 Jerry Gil PROS	2.00	.75
❑ 224 Jesse Crain PROS	3.00	1.25
❑ 225 Joey Gathright PROS	2.00	.75
❑ 226 John Gall PROS	2.00	.75
❑ 227 Jorge Sequea PROS	2.00	.75
❑ 228 Jorge Vasquez PROS	2.00	.75
❑ 229 Josh Labandeira PROS	2.00	.75
❑ 230 Justin Leone PROS	2.00	.75

❑ 231	Lance Cormier PROS	2.00	.75
❑ 232	Lincoln Holdzkom PROS	2.00	.75
❑ 233	Miguel Olivo PROS	2.00	.75
❑ 234	Mike Rouse PROS	2.00	.75
❑ 235	Onil Joseph PROS	2.00	.75
❑ 236	Phil Stockman PROS	2.00	.75
❑ 237	Ramon Ramirez PROS	2.00	.75
❑ 238	Robb Quinlan PROS	2.00	.75
❑ 239	Roberto Novoa PROS	2.00	.75
❑ 240	Ronald Belisario PROS	2.00	.75
❑ 241	Ronny Cedeno PROS	3.00	1.25
❑ 242	Ruddy Yan PROS	2.00	.75
❑ 243	Ryan Meaux PROS	2.00	.75
❑ 244	Ryan Wing PROS	2.00	.75
❑ 245	Scott Proctor PROS	2.00	.75
❑ 246	Sean Henn PROS	2.00	.75
❑ 247	Tim Bausher PROS	2.00	.75
❑ 248	Tim Bittner PROS	2.00	.75
❑ 249	William Bergolla PROS	2.00	.75
❑ 250	Yadier Molina PROS	3.00	1.25
❑ 251	Bernie Williams PTT	2.00	.75
❑ 252	Craig Biggio PTT	2.00	.75
❑ 253	Chipper Jones PTT	2.00	.75
❑ 254	Greg Maddux PTT	3.00	1.25
❑ 255	Sammy Sosa PTT	2.00	.75
❑ 256	Mike Mussina PTT	2.00	.75
❑ 257	Tim Salmon PTT	2.00	.75
❑ 258	Barry Larkin PTT	2.00	.75
❑ 259	Randy Johnson PTT	2.00	.75
❑ 260	Jeff Bagwell PTT	2.00	.75
❑ 261	Roberto Alomar PTT	2.00	.75
❑ 262	Tom Glavine PTT	2.00	.75
❑ 263	Roger Clemens PTT	3.00	1.25
❑ 264	Alex Rodriguez PTT	3.00	1.25
❑ 265	Ivan Rodriguez PTT	2.00	.75
❑ 266	Pedro Martinez PTT	2.00	.75
❑ 267	Ken Griffey Jr. PTT	3.00	1.25
❑ 268	Jim Thome PTT	2.00	.75
❑ 269	Frank Thomas PTT	2.00	.75
❑ 270	Mike Piazza PTT	2.00	.75
❑ 271	Garret Anderson TC	1.50	.60
❑ 272	Luis Gonzalez TC	1.50	.60
❑ 273	John Smoltz TC	2.00	.75
❑ 274	Rafael Palmeiro TC	2.00	.75
❑ 275	Curt Schilling TC	2.00	.75
❑ 276	Mark Prior TC	2.00	.75
❑ 277	Magglio Ordonez TC	1.50	.60
❑ 278	Adam Dunn TC	1.50	.60
❑ 279	Travis Hafner TC	1.50	.60
❑ 280	Jeromy Burnitz TC	1.50	.60
❑ 281	Carlos Guillen TC	1.50	.60
❑ 282	Dontrelle Willis TC	1.50	.60
❑ 283	Carlos Beltran TC	1.50	.60
❑ 284	Zack Greinke TC	1.50	.60
❑ 285	Adrian Beltre TC	1.50	.60
❑ 286	Ben Sheets TC	1.50	.60
❑ 287	Johan Santana TC	2.00	.75
❑ 288	Livan Hernandez TC	1.50	.60
❑ 289	Kazuo Matsui TC	1.50	.60
❑ 290	Derek Jeter TC	4.00	1.50
❑ 291	Tim Hudson TC	1.50	.60
❑ 292	Eric Milton TC	1.50	.60
❑ 293	Jason Kendall TC	1.50	.60
❑ 294	Jake Peavy TC	1.50	.60
❑ 295	Ray Durham TC	1.50	.60
❑ 296	Ichiro Suzuki TC	4.00	1.50
❑ 297	Scott Rolen TC	2.00	.75
❑ 298	Carl Crawford TC	1.50	.60
❑ 299	Hank Blalock TC	1.50	.60
❑ 300	Roy Halladay TC	1.50	.60

1998 Leaf Rookies and Stars

❑	COMPLETE SET (339)	250.00	125.00
❑	COMP.SET w/o SP's (200)	25.00	10.00
❑	COMMON (1-130/231-300)	.30	.10
❑	COMMON CARD (131-190)	1.00	.40
❑	COMMON CARD (191-230)	2.00	.75
❑	COMMON RC (191-230)	2.00	.75
❑	COMMON CARD (301-339)	2.50	1.00
❑	COMMON RC (301-339)	2.50	1.00
❑ 1	Andy Pettitte	.50	.20
❑ 2	Roberto Alomar	.50	.20
❑ 3	Randy Johnson	.75	.30
❑ 4	Manny Ramirez	.50	.20
❑ 5	Paul Molitor	.30	.10
❑ 6	Mike Mussina	.50	.20
❑ 7	Jim Thome	.50	.20
❑ 8	Tino Martinez	.50	.20
❑ 9	Gary Sheffield	.30	.10
❑ 10	Chuck Knoblauch	.30	.10
❑ 11	Bernie Williams	.50	.20
❑ 12	Tim Salmon	.50	.20
❑ 13	Sammy Sosa	.75	.30
❑ 14	Wade Boggs	.50	.20
❑ 15	Andres Galarraga	.30	.10
❑ 16	Pedro Martinez	.50	.20
❑ 17	David Justice	.30	.10
❑ 18	Chan Ho Park	.30	.10
❑ 19	Jay Buhner	.30	.10
❑ 20	Ryan Klesko	.30	.10
❑ 21	Barry Larkin	.50	.20
❑ 22	Will Clark	.50	.20
❑ 23	Raul Mondesi	.30	.10
❑ 24	Rickey Henderson	.75	.30
❑ 25	Jim Edmonds	.30	.10
❑ 26	Ken Griffey Jr.	1.25	.50
❑ 27	Frank Thomas	.75	.30
❑ 28	Cal Ripken	2.50	1.00
❑ 29	Alex Rodriguez	1.25	.50
❑ 30	Mike Piazza	1.25	.50
❑ 31	Greg Maddux	1.25	.50
❑ 32	Chipper Jones	.75	.30
❑ 33	Tony Gwynn	1.00	.40
❑ 34	Derek Jeter	2.00	.75
❑ 35	Jeff Bagwell	.50	.20
❑ 36	Juan Gonzalez	.30	.10
❑ 37	Nomar Garciaparra	1.25	.50
❑ 38	Andruw Jones	.50	.20
❑ 39	Hideo Nomo	.75	.30
❑ 40	Roger Clemens	1.50	.60
❑ 41	Mark McGwire	2.00	.75
❑ 42	Scott Rolen	.50	.20
❑ 43	Vladimir Guerrero	.75	.30
❑ 44	Barry Bonds	2.00	.75
❑ 45	Darin Erstad	.30	.10
❑ 46	Albert Belle	.30	.10
❑ 47	Kenny Lofton	.30	.10
❑ 48	Mo Vaughn	.30	.10
❑ 49	Ivan Rodriguez	.50	.20
❑ 50	Jose Cruz Jr.	.30	.10
❑ 51	Tony Clark	.30	.10
❑ 52	Larry Walker	.30	.10
❑ 53	Mark Grace	.50	.20
❑ 54	Edgar Martinez	.50	.20
❑ 55	Fred McGriff	.50	.20
❑ 56	Rafael Palmeiro	.50	.20
❑ 57	Matt Williams	.30	.10
❑ 58	Craig Biggio	.50	.20
❑ 59	Ken Caminiti	.30	.10
❑ 60	Jose Canseco	.50	.20
❑ 61	Brady Anderson	.30	.10
❑ 62	Moises Alou	.30	.10
❑ 63	Justin Thompson	.30	.10
❑ 64	John Smoltz	.50	.20
❑ 65	Carlos Delgado	.30	.10
❑ 66	J.T. Snow	.30	.10
❑ 67	Jason Giambi	.30	.10
❑ 68	Garret Anderson	.30	.10
❑ 69	Rondell White	.30	.10
❑ 70	Eric Karros	.30	.10
❑ 71	Javier Lopez	.30	.10
❑ 72	Pat Hentgen	.30	.10
❑ 73	Dante Bichette	.30	.10
❑ 74	Charles Johnson	.30	.10
❑ 75	Tom Glavine	.50	.20
❑ 76	Rusty Greer	.30	.10
❑ 77	Travis Fryman	.30	.10
❑ 78	Todd Hundley	.30	.10
❑ 79	Ray Lankford	.30	.10
❑ 80	Denny Neagle	.30	.10
❑ 81	Henry Rodriguez	.30	.10
❑ 82	Sandy Alomar Jr.	.30	.10
❑ 83	Robin Ventura	.30	.10
❑ 84	John Olerud	.30	.10
❑ 85	Omar Vizquel	.50	.20
❑ 86	Darren Dreifort	.30	.10
❑ 87	Kevin Brown	.30	.10
❑ 88	Curt Schilling	.30	.10
❑ 89	Francisco Cordova	.30	.10
❑ 90	Brad Radke	.30	.10
❑ 91	David Cone	.30	.10
❑ 92	Paul O'Neill	.50	.20
❑ 93	Vinny Castilla	.30	.10
❑ 94	Marquis Grissom	.30	.10
❑ 95	Brian L.Hunter	.30	.10
❑ 96	Kevin Appier	.30	.10
❑ 97	Bobby Bonilla	.30	.10
❑ 98	Eric Young	.30	.10
❑ 99	Jason Kendall	.30	.10
❑ 100	Shawn Green	.30	.10
❑ 101	Edgardo Alfonzo	.30	.10
❑ 102	Alan Benes	.30	.10
❑ 103	Bobby Higginson	.30	.10
❑ 104	Todd Greene	.30	.10
❑ 105	Jose Guillen	.30	.10
❑ 106	Neifi Perez	.30	.10
❑ 107	Edgar Renteria	.30	.10
❑ 108	Chris Stynes	.30	.10
❑ 109	Todd Walker	.30	.10
❑ 110	Brian Jordan	.30	.10
❑ 111	Joe Carter	.30	.10
❑ 112	Ellis Burks	.30	.10
❑ 113	Brett Tomko	.30	.10
❑ 114	Mike Cameron	.30	.10
❑ 115	Shannon Stewart	.30	.10
❑ 116	Kevin Orie	.30	.10
❑ 117	Brian Giles	.30	.10
❑ 118	Hideki Irabu	.30	.10
❑ 119	Delino DeShields	.30	.10
❑ 120	David Segui	.30	.10
❑ 121	Dustin Hermanson	.30	.10
❑ 122	Kevin Young	.30	.10
❑ 123	Jay Bell	.30	.10
❑ 124	Doug Glanville	.30	.10
❑ 125	John Roskos RC	.30	.10
❑ 126	Damon Hollins	.30	.10
❑ 127	Matt Stairs	.30	.10
❑ 128	Cliff Floyd	.30	.10
❑ 129	Derek Bell	.30	.10
❑ 130	Darryl Strawberry	.30	.10
❑ 131	Ken Griffey Jr. PT SP	4.00	1.50
❑ 132	Tim Salmon PT SP	1.50	.60
❑ 133	Manny Ramirez PT SP	1.50	.60
❑ 134	Paul Konerko PT SP	1.00	.40
❑ 135	Frank Thomas PT SP	2.50	1.00
❑ 136	Todd Helton PT SP	1.50	.60
❑ 137	Larry Walker PT SP	1.00	.40
❑ 138	Mo Vaughn PT SP	1.00	.40
❑ 139	Travis Lee PT SP	1.00	.40
❑ 140	Ivan Rodriguez PT SP	1.50	.60
❑ 141	Ben Grieve PT SP	1.00	.40
❑ 142	Brad Fullmer PT SP	1.00	.40
❑ 143	Alex Rodriguez PT SP	4.00	1.50
❑ 144	Mike Piazza PT SP	4.00	1.50
❑ 145	Greg Maddux PT SP	4.00	1.50
❑ 146	Chipper Jones PT SP	2.50	1.00
❑ 147	Kenny Lofton PT SP	1.00	.40
❑ 148	Albert Belle PT SP	1.00	.40
❑ 149	Barry Bonds PT SP	6.00	2.50
❑ 150	Vladimir Guerrero PT SP	2.50	1.00
❑ 151	Tony Gwynn PT SP	3.00	1.25
❑ 152	Derek Jeter PT SP	6.00	2.50
❑ 153	Jeff Bagwell PT SP	1.50	.60
❑ 154	Juan Gonzalez PT SP	1.00	.40
❑ 155	N.Garciaparra PT SP	4.00	1.50
❑ 156	Andruw Jones PT SP	1.50	.60
❑ 157	Hideo Nomo PT SP	2.50	1.00
❑ 158	Roger Clemens PT SP	5.00	2.00

❑ 159 Mark McGwire PT SP 6.00 2.50
❑ 160 Scott Rolen PT SP 1.50 .60
❑ 161 Travis Lee TLU SP 1.00 .40
❑ 162 Ben Grieve TLU SP 1.00 .40
❑ 163 Jose Guillen TLU SP 1.00 .40
❑ 164 Mike Piazza TLU SP 4.00 1.50
❑ 165 Kevin Appier TLU SP 1.00 .40
❑ 166 Marquis Grissom TLU SP 1.00 .40
❑ 167 Rusty Greer TLU SP 1.00 .40
❑ 168 Ken Caminiti TLU SP 1.00 .40
❑ 169 Craig Biggio TLU SP 1.50 .60
❑ 170 Ken Griffey Jr. TLU SP 4.00 1.50
❑ 171 Larry Walker TLU SP 1.00 .40
❑ 172 Barry Larkin TLU SP 1.50 .60
❑ 173 A.Galarraga TLU SP 1.00 .40
❑ 174 Wade Boggs TLU SP 1.50 .60
❑ 175 Sammy Sosa TLU SP 2.50 1.00
❑ 176 Todd Dunwoody TLU SP 1.00 .40
❑ 177 Jim Thome TLU SP 1.50 .60
❑ 178 Paul Molitor TLU SP 1.00 .40
❑ 179 Tony Clark TLU SP 1.00 .40
❑ 180 Jose Cruz Jr. TLU SP 1.00 .40
❑ 181 Darin Erstad TLU SP 1.00 .40
❑ 182 Barry Bonds TLU SP 6.00 2.50
❑ 183 Vlad.Guerrero TLU SP 2.50 1.00
❑ 184 Scott Rolen TLU SP 1.50 .60
❑ 185 Mark McGwire TLU SP 6.00 2.50
❑ 186 N.Garciaparra TLU SP 4.00 1.50
❑ 187 Gary Sheffield TLU SP 1.00 .40
❑ 188 Cal Ripken TLU SP 8.00 3.00
❑ 189 Frank Thomas TLU SP 2.50 1.00
❑ 190 Andy Pettitte TLU SP 1.50 .60
❑ 191 Paul Konerko SP 2.00 .75
❑ 192 Todd Helton SP 3.00 1.25
❑ 193 Mark Kotsay SP 2.00 .75
❑ 194 Brad Fullmer SP 2.00 .75
❑ 195 Kevin Millwood SP RC 8.00 3.00
❑ 196 David Ortiz SP 12.00 5.00
❑ 197 Kerry Wood SP 2.50 1.00
❑ 198 Miguel Tejada SP 5.00 2.00
❑ 199 Fernando Tatis SP 2.00 .75
❑ 200 Jaret Wright SP 2.00 .75
❑ 201 Ben Grieve SP 2.00 .75
❑ 202 Travis Lee SP 2.00 .75
❑ 203 Wes Helms SP 2.00 .75
❑ 204 Geoff Jenkins SP 10.00 4.00
❑ 205 Russell Branyan SP 2.00 .75
❑ 206 Esteban Yan SP RC 3.00 1.25
❑ 207 Ben Ford SP RC 2.00 .75
❑ 208 Rich Butler SP RC 2.00 .75
❑ 209 Ryan Jackson SP RC 2.00 .75
❑ 210 A.J. Hinch SP 2.00 .75
❑ 211 Magglio Ordonez SP RC 25.00 10.00
❑ 212 Dave Dellucci SP RC 5.00 2.00
❑ 213 Billy McMillon SP 2.00 .75
❑ 214 Mike Lowell SP RC 10.00 4.00
❑ 215 Todd Erdos SP RC 2.00 .75
❑ 216 Carlos Mendoza SP RC 2.00 .75
❑ 217 Frank Catalanotto SP RC 5.00 2.00
❑ 218 Julio Ramirez SP RC 3.00 1.25
❑ 219 John Halama SP RC 3.00 1.25
❑ 220 Wilson Delgado SP 2.00 .75
❑ 221 Mike Judd SP RC 3.00 1.25
❑ 222 Rolando Arrojo SP RC 3.00 1.25
❑ 223 Jason LaRue SP RC 3.00 1.25
❑ 224 Manny Aybar SP RC 3.00 1.25
❑ 225 Jorge Velandia SP 2.00 .75
❑ 226 Mike Kinkade SP RC 3.00 1.25
❑ 227 Carlos Lee SP RC 20.00 8.00
❑ 228 Bobby Hughes SP 2.00 .75
❑ 229 Ryan Christenson SP RC 2.00 .75
❑ 230 Masato Yoshii SP RC 3.00 1.25
❑ 231 Richard Hidalgo .30 .10
❑ 232 Rafael Medina .30 .10
❑ 233 Damian Jackson .30 .10
❑ 234 Derek Lowe .30 .10
❑ 235 Mario Valdez .30 .10
❑ 236 Eli Marrero .30 .10
❑ 237 Juan Encarnacion .30 .10
❑ 238 Livan Hernandez .30 .10
❑ 239 Bruce Chen .30 .10
❑ 240 Eric Milton .30 .10
❑ 241 Jason Varitek .75 .30
❑ 242 Scott Elarton .30 .10
❑ 243 Manuel Barrios RC .30 .10
❑ 244 Mike Caruso .30 .10
❑ 245 Tom Evans .30 .10
❑ 246 Pat Cline .30 .10
❑ 247 Matt Clement .30 .10
❑ 248 Karim Garcia .30 .10
❑ 249 Richie Sexson .30 .10
❑ 250 Sidney Ponson .30 .10
❑ 251 Randall Simon .30 .10
❑ 252 Tony Saunders .30 .10
❑ 253 Javier Valentin .30 .10
❑ 254 Danny Clyburn .30 .10
❑ 255 Michael Coleman .30 .10
❑ 256 Hanley Frias RC .30 .10
❑ 257 Miguel Cairo .30 .10
❑ 258 Rob Stanifer RC .30 .10
❑ 259 Lou Collier .30 .10
❑ 260 Abraham Nunez .30 .10
❑ 261 Ricky Ledee .30 .10
❑ 262 Carl Pavano .30 .10
❑ 263 Derrek Lee .50 .20
❑ 264 Jeff Abbott .30 .10
❑ 265 Bob Abreu .30 .10
❑ 266 Bartolo Colon .30 .10
❑ 267 Mike Drumright .30 .10
❑ 268 Daryle Ward .30 .10
❑ 269 Gabe Alvarez .30 .10
❑ 270 Josh Booty .30 .10
❑ 271 Damian Moss .30 .10
❑ 272 Brian Rose .30 .10
❑ 273 Jarrod Washburn .30 .10
❑ 274 Bobby Estalella .30 .10
❑ 275 Enrique Wilson .30 .10
❑ 276 Derrick Gibson .30 .10
❑ 277 Ken Cloude .30 .10
❑ 278 Kevin Witt .30 .10
❑ 279 Donnie Sadler .30 .10
❑ 280 Sean Casey .30 .10
❑ 281 Jacob Cruz .30 .10
❑ 282 Ron Wright .30 .10
❑ 283 Jeremi Gonzalez .30 .10
❑ 284 Desi Relaford .30 .10
❑ 285 Bobby Smith .30 .10
❑ 286 Javier Vazquez .30 .10
❑ 287 Steve Woodard .30 .10
❑ 288 Greg Norton .30 .10
❑ 289 Cliff Politte .30 .10
❑ 290 Felix Heredia .30 .10
❑ 291 Braden Looper .30 .10
❑ 292 Felix Martinez .30 .10
❑ 293 Brian Meadows .30 .10
❑ 294 Edwin Diaz .30 .10
❑ 295 Pat Watkins .30 .10
❑ 296 Marc Pisciotta RC .30 .10
❑ 297 Rick Gorecki .30 .10
❑ 298 DaRond Stovall .30 .10
❑ 299 Andy Larkin .30 .10
❑ 300 Felix Rodriguez .30 .10
❑ 301 Blake Stein SP 2.50 1.00
❑ 302 John Rocker SP RC 6.00 2.50
❑ 303 Justin Baughman SP RC 2.50 1.00
❑ 304 Jesus Sanchez SP RC 4.00 1.50
❑ 305 Randy Winn SP 2.50 1.00
❑ 306 Lou Merloni SP 2.50 1.00
❑ 307 Jim Parque SP RC 4.00 1.50
❑ 308 Dennis Reyes SP 2.50 1.00
❑ 309 Orlando Hernandez SP RC 10.00 4.00
❑ 310 Jason Johnson SP 2.50 1.00
❑ 311 Torii Hunter SP 2.50 1.00
❑ 312 Mike Piazza Marlins SP 10.00 4.00
❑ 313 Mike Frank SP RC 2.50 1.00
❑ 314 Troy Glaus SP RC 80.00 40.00
❑ 315 Jin Ho Cho SP RC 4.00 1.50
❑ 316 Ruben Mateo SP RC 2.50 1.00
❑ 317 Ryan Minor SP RC 4.00 1.50
❑ 318 Aramis Ramirez SP 2.50 1.00
❑ 319 Adrian Beltre SP 2.50 1.00
❑ 320 Matt Anderson SP RC 2.50 1.00
❑ 321 Gabe Kapler SP RC 6.00 2.50
❑ 322 Jeremy Giambi SP RC 4.00 1.50
❑ 323 Carlos Beltran SP 8.00 3.00
❑ 324 Dermal Brown SP 2.50 1.00
❑ 325 Ben Davis SP 2.50 1.00
❑ 326 Eric Chavez SP 2.50 1.00
❑ 327 Bobby Howry SP RC 2.50 1.00
❑ 328 Roy Halladay SP 2.50 1.00
❑ 329 George Lombard SP 2.50 1.00
❑ 330 Michael Barrett SP 2.50 1.00
❑ 331 Fernando Seguignol SP RC 2.50 1.00
❑ 332 J.D. Drew SP RC 20.00 8.00
❑ 333 Odalis Perez SP RC 10.00 4.00
❑ 334 Alex Cora SP RC 4.00 1.50
❑ 335 Placido Polanco SP RC 5.00 2.00
❑ 336 Armando Rios SP RC 4.00 1.50
❑ 337 Sammy Sosa HR SP 6.00 2.50
❑ 338 Mark McGwire HR SP 15.00 6.00
❑ 339 S.Sosa/M.McGwire CL SP 10.00 4.00

2001 Leaf Rookies and Stars

❑ COMP.SET w/o SP'S (100) 20.00 8.00
❑ COMMON CARD (1-100) .30 .10
❑ COMMON CARD (101-200) 3.00 1.25
❑ COMMON CARD (201-300) 5.00 2.00
❑ 1 Alex Rodriguez 1.25 .50
❑ 2 Derek Jeter 2.00 .75
❑ 3 Aramis Ramirez .30 .10
❑ 4 Cliff Floyd .30 .10
❑ 5 Nomar Garciaparra 1.25 .50
❑ 6 Craig Biggio .50 .20
❑ 7 Ivan Rodriguez .50 .20
❑ 8 Cal Ripken 2.50 1.00
❑ 9 Fred McGriff .50 .20
❑ 10 Chipper Jones .75 .30
❑ 11 Roberto Alomar .50 .20
❑ 12 Moises Alou .30 .10
❑ 13 Freddy Garcia .30 .10
❑ 14 Bobby Abreu .30 .10
❑ 15 Shawn Green .30 .10
❑ 16 Jason Giambi .30 .10
❑ 17 Todd Helton .50 .20
❑ 18 Robert Fick .30 .10
❑ 19 Tony Gwynn 1.00 .40
❑ 20 Luis Gonzalez .30 .10
❑ 21 Sean Casey .30 .10
❑ 22 Roger Clemens 1.50 .60
❑ 23 Brian Giles .30 .10
❑ 24 Manny Ramirez Sox .50 .20
❑ 25 Barry Bonds 2.00 .75
❑ 26 Richard Hidalgo .30 .10
❑ 27 Vladimir Guerrero .75 .30
❑ 28 Kevin Brown .30 .10
❑ 29 Mike Sweeney .30 .10
❑ 30 Ken Griffey Jr. 1.25 .50
❑ 31 Mike Piazza 1.25 .50
❑ 32 Richie Sexson .30 .10
❑ 33 Matt Morris .30 .10
❑ 34 Jorge Posada .50 .20
❑ 35 Eric Chavez .30 .10
❑ 36 Mark Buehrle .50 .20
❑ 37 Jeff Bagwell .50 .20
❑ 38 Curt Schilling .30 .10
❑ 39 Bartolo Colon .30 .10
❑ 40 Mark Quinn .30 .10
❑ 41 Tony Clark .30 .10
❑ 42 Brad Radke .30 .10
❑ 43 Gary Sheffield .30 .10
❑ 44 Doug Mientkiewicz .30 .10
❑ 45 Pedro Martinez .50 .20
❑ 46 Carlos Lee .30 .10
❑ 47 Troy Glaus .30 .10
❑ 48 Preston Wilson .30 .10
❑ 49 Phil Nevin .30 .10
❑ 50 Chan Ho Park .30 .10
❑ 51 Randy Johnson .75 .30
❑ 52 Jermaine Dye .30 .10

❑ 53 Terrence Long .30 .10
❑ 54 Joe Mays .30 .10
❑ 55 Scott Rolen .50 .20
❑ 56 Miguel Tejada .30 .10
❑ 57 Jim Thome .50 .20
❑ 58 Jose Vidro .30 .10
❑ 59 Gabe Kapler .30 .10
❑ 60 Darin Erstad .30 .10
❑ 61 Jim Edmonds .30 .10
❑ 62 Jarrod Washburn .30 .10
❑ 63 Tom Glavine .50 .20
❑ 64 Adrian Beltre .30 .10
❑ 65 Sammy Sosa .75 .30
❑ 66 Juan Gonzalez .30 .10
❑ 67 Rafael Furcal .30 .10
❑ 68 Mike Mussina .50 .20
❑ 69 Mark McGwire 2.00 .75
❑ 70 Ryan Klesko .30 .10
❑ 71 Raul Mondesi .30 .10
❑ 72 Trot Nixon .30 .10
❑ 73 Barry Larkin .50 .20
❑ 74 Rafael Palmeiro .50 .20
❑ 75 Mark Mulder .30 .10
❑ 76 Carlos Delgado .30 .10
❑ 77 Mike Hampton .30 .10
❑ 78 Carl Everett .30 .10
❑ 79 Paul Konerko .30 .10
❑ 80 Larry Walker .30 .10
❑ 81 Kerry Wood .30 .10
❑ 82 Frank Thomas .75 .30
❑ 83 Andruw Jones .50 .20
❑ 84 Eric Milton .30 .10
❑ 85 Ben Grieve .30 .10
❑ 86 Carlos Beltran .30 .10
❑ 87 Tim Hudson .30 .10
❑ 88 Hideo Nomo .75 .30
❑ 89 Greg Maddux 1.25 .50
❑ 90 Edgar Martinez .50 .20
❑ 91 Lance Berkman .30 .10
❑ 92 Pat Burrell .30 .10
❑ 93 Jeff Kent .30 .10
❑ 94 Magglio Ordonez .30 .10
❑ 95 Cristian Guzman .30 .10
❑ 96 Jose Canseco .50 .20
❑ 97 J.D. Drew .30 .10
❑ 98 Bernie Williams .50 .20
❑ 99 Kazuhiro Sasaki .30 .10
❑ 100 Rickey Henderson .75 .30
❑ 101 Wilson Guzman RC 3.00 1.25
❑ 102 Nick Neugebauer 3.00 1.25
❑ 103 Lance Davis RC 3.00 1.25
❑ 104 Felipe Lopez 3.00 1.25
❑ 105 Toby Hall 3.00 1.25
❑ 106 Jack Cust 3.00 1.25
❑ 107 Jason Karnuth RC 3.00 1.25
❑ 108 Bart Miadich RC 3.00 1.25
❑ 109 Brian Roberts RC 8.00 3.00
❑ 110 Brandon Larson RC 3.00 1.25
❑ 111 Sean Douglass RC 3.00 1.25
❑ 112 Joe Crede 5.00 2.00
❑ 113 Tim Redding 3.00 1.25
❑ 114 Adam Johnson 3.00 1.25
❑ 115 Marcus Giles 3.00 1.25
❑ 116 Jose Ortiz 3.00 1.25
❑ 117 Jose Mieses RC 3.00 1.25
❑ 118 Nick Maness RC 3.00 1.25
❑ 119 Les Walrond RC 3.00 1.25
❑ 120 Travis Phelps RC 3.00 1.25
❑ 121 Troy Mattes RC 3.00 1.25
❑ 122 Carlos Garcia RC 3.00 1.25
❑ 123 Bill Ortega RC 3.00 1.25
❑ 124 Gene Altman RC 3.00 1.25
❑ 125 Nate Frese RC 3.00 1.25
❑ 126 Alfonso Soriano 5.00 2.00
❑ 127 Jose Nunez RC 3.00 1.25
❑ 128 Bob File RC 3.00 1.25
❑ 129 Dan Wright 3.00 1.25
❑ 130 Nick Johnson 3.00 1.25
❑ 131 Brent Abernathy 3.00 1.25
❑ 132 Steve Green RC 3.00 1.25
❑ 133 Billy Sylvester RC 3.00 1.25
❑ 134 Scott MacRae RC 3.00 1.25
❑ 135 Kris Keller RC 3.00 1.25
❑ 136 Scott Stewart RC 3.00 1.25
❑ 137 Henry Mateo RC 3.00 1.25
❑ 138 Timo Perez 3.00 1.25
❑ 139 Nate Teut RC 3.00 1.25
❑ 140 Jason Michaels RC 3.00 1.25
❑ 141 Junior Spivey RC 5.00 2.00
❑ 142 Carlos Pena 3.00 1.25
❑ 143 Wilmy Caceres RC 3.00 1.25
❑ 144 David Lundquist 3.00 1.25
❑ 145 Jack Wilson RC 5.00 2.00
❑ 146 Jeremy Fikac RC 3.00 1.25
❑ 147 Alex Escobar 3.00 1.25
❑ 148 Abraham Nunez 3.00 1.25
❑ 149 Xavier Nady 3.00 1.25
❑ 150 Michael Cuddyer 3.00 1.25
❑ 151 Greg Miller RC 3.00 1.25
❑ 152 Eric Munson 3.00 1.25
❑ 153 Aubrey Huff 3.00 1.25
❑ 154 Tim Christman RC 3.00 1.25
❑ 155 Erick Almonte RC 3.00 1.25
❑ 156 Mike Penney RC 3.00 1.25
❑ 157 Delvin James RC 3.00 1.25
❑ 158 Ben Sheets 5.00 2.00
❑ 159 Jason Hart 3.00 1.25
❑ 160 Jose Acevedo RC 3.00 1.25
❑ 161 Will Ohman RC 3.00 1.25
❑ 162 Erik Hiljus RC 3.00 1.25
❑ 163 Juan Moreno RC 3.00 1.25
❑ 164 Mike Koplove RC 3.00 1.25
❑ 165 Pedro Santana RC 3.00 1.25
❑ 166 Jimmy Rollins 3.00 1.25
❑ 167 Matt White RC 3.00 1.25
❑ 168 Cesar Crespo RC 3.00 1.25
❑ 169 Carlos Hernandez 3.00 1.25
❑ 170 Chris George 3.00 1.25
❑ 171 Brad Voyles RC 3.00 1.25
❑ 172 Luis Pineda RC 3.00 1.25
❑ 173 Carlos Zambrano 5.00 2.00
❑ 174 Nate Cornejo 3.00 1.25
❑ 175 Jason Smith RC 3.00 1.25
❑ 176 Craig Monroe RC 8.00 3.00
❑ 177 Cody Ransom RC 3.00 1.25
❑ 178 John Grabow RC 3.00 1.25
❑ 179 Pedro Feliz 3.00 1.25
❑ 180 Jeremy Owens RC 3.00 1.25
❑ 181 Kurt Ainsworth 3.00 1.25
❑ 182 Luis Lopez 3.00 1.25
❑ 183 Stubby Clapp RC 3.00 1.25
❑ 184 Ryan Freel RC 8.00 3.00
❑ 185 Duaner Sanchez RC 3.00 1.25
❑ 186 Jason Jennings 3.00 1.25
❑ 187 Kyle Lohse RC 5.00 2.00
❑ 188 Jerrod Riggan RC 3.00 1.25
❑ 189 Joe Beimel RC 3.00 1.25
❑ 190 Nick Punto RC 3.00 1.25
❑ 191 Willie Harris RC 3.00 1.25
❑ 192 Ryan Jensen RC 3.00 1.25
❑ 193 Adam Pettyjohn RC 3.00 1.25
❑ 194 Donaldo Mendez RC 3.00 1.25
❑ 195 Bret Prinz RC 3.00 1.25
❑ 196 Paul Phillips RC 3.00 1.25
❑ 197 Brian Lawrence RC 3.00 1.25
❑ 198 Cesar Izturis 3.00 1.25
❑ 199 Blaine Neal RC 3.00 1.25
❑ 200 Josh Fogg RC 5.00 2.00
❑ 201 Josh Towers RC 8.00 3.00
❑ 202 Tim Spooneybarger RC 5.00 2.00
❑ 203 Michael Rivera RC 5.00 2.00
❑ 204 Juan Cruz RC 5.00 2.00
❑ 205 Albert Pujols RC 200.00 125.00
❑ 206 Josh Beckett 8.00 3.00
❑ 207 Roy Oswalt 8.00 3.00
❑ 208 Elpidio Guzman RC 5.00 2.00
❑ 209 Horacio Ramirez RC 8.00 3.00
❑ 210 Corey Patterson 5.00 2.00
❑ 211 Geronimo Gil RC 5.00 2.00
❑ 212 Jay Gibbons RC 8.00 3.00
❑ 213 Orlando Woodards RC 5.00 2.00
❑ 214 David Espinosa 5.00 2.00
❑ 215 Angel Berroa RC 8.00 3.00
❑ 216 Brandon Duckworth RC 5.00 2.00
❑ 217 Brian Reith RC 5.00 2.00
❑ 218 David Brous RC 5.00 2.00
❑ 219 Bud Smith RC 5.00 2.00
❑ 220 Ramon Vazquez RC 5.00 2.00
❑ 221 Mark Teixeira RC 30.00 12.50
❑ 222 Justin Atchley RC 5.00 2.00
❑ 223 Tony Cogan RC 5.00 2.00
❑ 224 Grant Balfour RC 5.00 2.00
❑ 225 Ricardo Rodriguez RC 5.00 2.00
❑ 226 Brian Rogers RC 5.00 2.00
❑ 227 Adam Dunn 8.00 3.00
❑ 228 Wilson Betemit RC 8.00 3.00
❑ 229 Juan Diaz RC 5.00 2.00
❑ 230 Jackson Melian RC 5.00 2.00
❑ 231 Claudio Vargas RC 5.00 2.00
❑ 232 Wilkin Ruan RC 5.00 2.00
❑ 233 Justin Duchscherer RC 5.00 2.00
❑ 234 Kevin Olsen RC 5.00 2.00
❑ 235 Tony Fiore RC 5.00 2.00
❑ 236 Jeremy Affeldt RC 5.00 2.00
❑ 237 Mike Maroth RC 5.00 2.00
❑ 238 C.C. Sabathia 5.00 2.00
❑ 239 Cory Aldridge RC 5.00 2.00
❑ 240 Zach Day RC 5.00 2.00
❑ 241 Brett Jodie RC 5.00 2.00
❑ 242 Winston Abreu RC 5.00 2.00
❑ 243 Travis Hafner RC 25.00 10.00
❑ 244 Joe Kennedy RC 8.00 3.00
❑ 245 Rick Bauer RC 5.00 2.00
❑ 246 Mike Young 8.00 3.00
❑ 247 Ken Vining RC 5.00 2.00
❑ 248 Doug Nickle RC 5.00 2.00
❑ 249 Pablo Ozuna 5.00 2.00
❑ 250 Dustan Mohr RC 5.00 2.00
❑ 251 Ichiro Suzuki RC 50.00 20.00
❑ 252 Ryan Drese RC 8.00 3.00
❑ 253 Morgan Ensberg RC 8.00 3.00
❑ 254 George Perez RC 5.00 2.00
❑ 255 Roy Smith RC 5.00 2.00
❑ 256 Juan Uribe RC 8.00 3.00
❑ 257 Dewon Brazelton RC 5.00 2.00
❑ 258 Endy Chavez RC 5.00 2.00
❑ 259 Kris Foster RC 5.00 2.00
❑ 260 Eric Knott RC 5.00 2.00
❑ 261 Corky Miller RC 5.00 2.00
❑ 262 Larry Bigbie 5.00 2.00
❑ 263 Andres Torres RC 5.00 2.00
❑ 264 Adrian Hernandez RC 5.00 2.00
❑ 265 Johnny Estrada RC 8.00 3.00
❑ 266 David Williams RC 5.00 2.00
❑ 267 Steve Lomasney 5.00 2.00
❑ 268 Victor Zambrano RC 8.00 3.00
❑ 269 Keith Ginter 5.00 2.00
❑ 270 Casey Fossum RC 5.00 2.00
❑ 271 Josue Perez RC 5.00 2.00
❑ 272 Josh Phelps 5.00 2.00
❑ 273 Mark Prior RC 25.00 10.00
❑ 274 Brandon Berger RC 5.00 2.00
❑ 275 Scott Podsednik RC 12.00 5.00
❑ 276 Jorge Julio RC 5.00 2.00
❑ 277 Esix Snead RC 5.00 2.00
❑ 278 Brandon Knight RC 5.00 2.00
❑ 279 Saul Rivera RC 5.00 2.00
❑ 280 Benito Baez RC 5.00 2.00
❑ 281 Rob MacKowiak RC 8.00 3.00
❑ 282 Eric Hinske RC 8.00 3.00
❑ 283 Juan Rivera 5.00 2.00
❑ 284 Kevin Joseph RC 5.00 2.00
❑ 285 Juan A. Pena RC 5.00 2.00
❑ 286 Brandon Lyon RC 5.00 2.00
❑ 287 Adam Everett 5.00 2.00
❑ 288 Eric Valent 5.00 2.00
❑ 289 Ken Harvey 5.00 2.00
❑ 290 Bert Snow RC 5.00 2.00
❑ 291 Wily Mo Pena 5.00 2.00
❑ 292 Rafael Soriano RC 5.00 2.00
❑ 293 Carlos Valderrama RC 5.00 2.00
❑ 294 Christian Parker RC 5.00 2.00
❑ 295 Tsuyoshi Shinjo RC 8.00 3.00
❑ 296 Martin Vargas RC 5.00 2.00
❑ 297 Luke Hudson RC 5.00 2.00
❑ 298 Dee Brown 5.00 2.00
❑ 299 Alexis Gomez RC 5.00 2.00
❑ 300 Angel Santos RC 5.00 2.00

1939 Play Ball

❑ COMPLETE SET (161) 10000.00 6000.00
❑ COMMON CARD (1-115) 20.00 12.00
❑ COMMON CARD (116-162) 75.00 40.00
❑ WRAPPER (1-CENT) 200.00 150.00
❑ 1 Jake Powell RC 60.00 30.00
❑ 2 Lee Grissom RC 20.00 12.00
❑ 3 Red Ruffing 75.00 40.00
❑ 4 Eldon Auker RC 20.00 12.00

❑	5 Luke Sewell	25.00	15.00
❑	6 Leo Durocher	100.00	60.00
❑	7 Bobby Doerr RC	75.00	40.00
❑	8 Henry Pippen RC	20.00	12.00
❑	9 James Tobin RC	20.00	12.00
❑	10 James DeShong	20.00	12.00
❑	11 Johnny Rizzo RC	20.00	12.00
❑	12 Hershel Martin RC	20.00	12.00
❑	13 Luke Hamlin RC	20.00	12.00
❑	14 Jim Tabor RC	20.00	12.00
❑	15 Paul Derringer	30.00	18.00
❑	16 John Peacock RC	20.00	12.00
❑	17 Emerson Dickman RC	20.00	12.00
❑	18 Harry Danning RC	20.00	12.00
❑	19 Paul Dean RC	40.00	25.00
❑	20 Joe Heving RC	20.00	12.00
❑	21 Dutch Leonard RC	30.00	18.00
❑	22 Bucky Walters RC	30.00	18.00
❑	23 Burgess Whitehead RC	20.00	12.00
❑	24 Richard Coffman	20.00	12.00
❑	25 George Selkirk RC	40.00	25.00
❑	26 Joe DiMaggio RC	1400.00	900.00
❑	27 Fred Ostermueller	20.00	12.00
❑	28 Sylvester Johnson RC	20.00	12.00
❑	29 John(Jack) Wilson RC	20.00	12.00
❑	30 Bill Dickey	125.00	75.00
❑	31 Sam West	20.00	12.00
❑	32 Bob Seeds RC	20.00	12.00
❑	33 Del Young RC	20.00	12.00
❑	34 Frank Demaree	20.00	12.00
❑	35 Bill Jurges	20.00	12.00
❑	36 Frank McCormick RC	20.00	12.00
❑	37 Virgil Davis	20.00	12.00
❑	38 Billy Myers RC	20.00	12.00
❑	39 Rick Ferrell	75.00	40.00
❑	40 James Bagby Jr. RC	20.00	12.00
❑	41 Lon Warneke	25.00	15.00
❑	42 Arndt Jorgens	20.00	12.00
❑	43 Melo Almada RC	25.00	15.00
❑	44 Don Heffner RC	20.00	12.00
❑	45 Merrill May RC	20.00	12.00
❑	46 Morris Arnovich RC	20.00	12.00
❑	47 Buddy Lewis RC	20.00	12.00
❑	48 Lefty Gomez	125.00	75.00
❑	49 Eddie Miller RC	20.00	12.00
❑	50 Charley Gehringer	125.00	75.00
❑	51 Mel Ott	125.00	75.00
❑	52 Tommy Henrich RC	40.00	25.00
❑	53 Carl Hubbell	125.00	75.00
❑	54 Harry Gumpert RC	20.00	12.00
❑	55 Arky Vaughan	75.00	40.00
❑	56 Hank Greenberg	200.00	125.00
❑	57 Buddy Hassett RC	20.00	12.00
❑	58 Lou Chiozza RC	20.00	12.00
❑	59 Ken Chase RC	20.00	12.00
❑	60 Schoolboy Rowe RC	40.00	25.00
❑	61 Tony Cuccinello	25.00	15.00
❑	62 Tom Carey RC	20.00	12.00
❑	63 Emmett Mueller RC	20.00	12.00
❑	64 Wally Moses RC	25.00	15.00
❑	65 Harry Craft RC	25.00	15.00
❑	66 Jimmy Ripple RC	20.00	12.00
❑	67 Ed Joost RC	25.00	15.00
❑	68 Fred Sington RC	20.00	12.00
❑	69 Elbie Fletcher RC	20.00	12.00
❑	70 Fred Frankhouse	20.00	12.00
❑	71 Monte Pearson RC	30.00	18.00
❑	72 Debs Garms RC	20.00	12.00
❑	73 Hal Schumacher	25.00	15.00
❑	74 Cookie Lavagetto RC	25.00	15.00
❑	75 Stan Bordagaray RC	20.00	12.00
❑	76 Goody Rosen RC	20.00	12.00
❑	77 Lew Riggs RC	20.00	12.00
❑	78 Julius Solters	20.00	12.00
❑	79 Jo Jo Moore	20.00	12.00
❑	80 Pete Fox	20.00	12.00
❑	81 Babe Dahlgren RC	30.00	18.00
❑	82 Chuck Klein	100.00	60.00
❑	83 Gus Suhr	20.00	12.00
❑	84 Skeeter Newsom RC	20.00	12.00
❑	85 Johnny Cooney RC	20.00	12.00
❑	86 Dolph Camilli	25.00	15.00
❑	87 Milburn Shoffner RC	20.00	12.00
❑	88 Charlie Keller RC	40.00	25.00
❑	89 Lloyd Waner	75.00	40.00
❑	90 Robert Klinger RC	20.00	12.00
❑	91 John Knott RC	20.00	12.00
❑	92 Ted Williams RC	1500.00	900.00
❑	93 Charles Gelbert RC	20.00	12.00
❑	94 Heinie Manush	75.00	40.00
❑	95 Whit Wyatt RC	25.00	15.00
❑	96 Babe Phelps RC	20.00	12.00
❑	97 Bob Johnson	30.00	18.00
❑	98 Pinky Whitney RC	20.00	12.00
❑	99 Wally Berger	30.00	18.00
❑	100 Buddy Myer	25.00	15.00
❑	101 Roger Cramer	25.00	15.00
❑	102 Lem (Pep) Young RC	20.00	12.00
❑	103 Moe Berg	125.00	75.00
❑	104 Tom Bridges	25.00	15.00
❑	105 Rabbit McNair RC	20.00	12.00
❑	106 Dolly Stark UMP	30.00	18.00
❑	107 Joe Vosmik	20.00	12.00
❑	108 Frank Hayes	20.00	12.00
❑	109 Myril Hoag	20.00	12.00
❑	110 Fred Fitzsimmons	25.00	15.00
❑	111 Van Lingle Mungo RC	30.00	18.00
❑	112 Paul Waner	100.00	60.00
❑	113 Al Schacht	30.00	18.00
❑	114 Cecil Travis RC	25.00	15.00
❑	115 Ralph Kress	20.00	12.00
❑	116 Gene Desautels RC	75.00	40.00
❑	117 Wayne Ambler RC	75.00	40.00
❑	118 Lynn Nelson	75.00	40.00
❑	119 Will Hershberger RC	100.00	50.00
❑	120 Rabbit Warstler RC	75.00	40.00
❑	121 Bill Posedel RC	75.00	40.00
❑	122 George McQuinn RC	75.00	40.00
❑	123 Ray T. Davis RC	75.00	40.00
❑	124 Walter Brown	75.00	40.00
❑	125 Cliff Melton RC	75.00	40.00
❑	126 Not issued		
❑	127 Gil Brack RC	75.00	40.00
❑	128 Joe Bowman RC	75.00	40.00
❑	129 Bill Swift	75.00	40.00
❑	130 Bill Brubaker RC	75.00	40.00
❑	131 Mort Cooper RC	100.00	50.00
❑	132 Jim Brown RC	75.00	40.00
❑	133 Lynn Myers RC	75.00	40.00
❑	134 Tot Presnell RC	75.00	40.00
❑	135 Mickey Owen RC	100.00	50.00
❑	136 Roy Bell RC	75.00	40.00
❑	137 Pete Appleton	75.00	40.00
❑	138 George Case RC	100.00	50.00
❑	139 Vito Tamulis RC	75.00	40.00
❑	140 Ray Hayworth RC	75.00	40.00
❑	141 Pete Coscarart RC	75.00	40.00
❑	142 Ira Hutchinson RC	75.00	40.00
❑	143 Earl Averill	175.00	100.00
❑	144 Zeke Bonura RC	100.00	50.00
❑	145 Hugh Mulcahy RC	75.00	40.00
❑	146 Tom Sunkel RC	75.00	40.00
❑	147 George Coffman RC	75.00	40.00
❑	148 Bill Trotter RC	75.00	40.00
❑	149 Max West RC	75.00	40.00
❑	150 James Walkup RC	75.00	40.00
❑	151 Hugh Casey RC	100.00	50.00
❑	152 Roy Weatherly RC	75.00	40.00
❑	153 Dizzy Trout RC	100.00	50.00
❑	154 Johnny Hudson RC	75.00	40.00
❑	155 Jimmy Outlaw RC	75.00	40.00
❑	156 Ray Berres RC	75.00	40.00
❑	157 Don Padgett RC	75.00	40.00
❑	158 Bud Thomas RC	75.00	40.00
❑	159 Red Evans RC	75.00	40.00
❑	160 Gene Moore RC	75.00	40.00
❑	161 Lonnie Frey	75.00	40.00
❑	162 Whitey Moore RC	100.00	50.00

1940 Play Ball

❑	COMPLETE SET (240)	15000.00	10000.00
❑	COMMON CARD (1-120)	20.00	12.00
❑	COMMON CARD (121-180)	20.00	12.00
❑	COMMON CARD (181-240)	70.00	35.00
❑	WRAP.(1-CENT, DIFF. COL.)	800.00	700.00
❑	1 Joe DiMaggio	2500.00	1500.00
❑	2 Art Jorgens	25.00	15.00
❑	3 Babe Dahlgren	25.00	15.00
❑	4 Tommy Henrich		
❑	5 Monte Pearson	25.00	15.00
❑	6 Lefty Gomez	150.00	90.00
❑	7 Bill Dickey	175.00	100.00
❑	8 George Selkirk	25.00	15.00
❑	9 Charlie Keller		
❑	10 Red Ruffing	90.00	50.00
❑	11 Jake Powell	25.00	15.00
❑	12 Johnny Schulte	20.00	12.00
❑	13 Jack Knott	20.00	12.00
❑	14 Rabbit McNair	20.00	12.00
❑	15 George Case	25.00	15.00
❑	16 Cecil Travis	25.00	15.00
❑	17 Buddy Myer	25.00	15.00
❑	18 Charlie Gelbert	20.00	12.00
❑	19 Ken Chase	20.00	12.00
❑	20 Buddy Lewis	20.00	12.00
❑	21 Rick Ferrell	80.00	45.00
❑	22 Sammy West	20.00	12.00
❑	23 Dutch Leonard	25.00	15.00
❑	24 Frank Hayes	20.00	12.00
❑	25 Bob Johnson	25.00	15.00
❑	26 Wally Moses	25.00	15.00
❑	27 Ted Williams	1200.00	800.00
❑	28 Gene Desautels	20.00	12.00
❑	29 Doc Cramer	25.00	15.00
❑	30 Moe Berg	150.00	90.00
❑	31 Jack Wilson	20.00	12.00
❑	32 Jim Bagby	20.00	12.00
❑	33 Fritz Ostermueller	20.00	12.00
❑	34 John Peacock	20.00	12.00
❑	35 Joe Heving	20.00	12.00
❑	36 Jim Tabor	20.00	12.00
❑	37 Emerson Dickman	20.00	12.00
❑	38 Bobby Doerr	90.00	50.00
❑	39 Tom Carey	20.00	12.00
❑	40 Hank Greenberg	200.00	100.00
❑	41 Charley Gehringer	150.00	90.00
❑	42 Bud Thomas	20.00	12.00
❑	43 Pete Fox	20.00	12.00
❑	44 Dizzy Trout	25.00	15.00
❑	45 Red Kress	20.00	12.00
❑	46 Earl Averill	90.00	50.00
❑	47 Oscar Vitt RC	20.00	12.00
❑	48 Luke Sewell	25.00	15.00
❑	49 Stormy Weatherly	20.00	12.00
❑	50 Hal Trosky	25.00	15.00
❑	51 Don Heffner	20.00	12.00
❑	52 Myril Hoag	20.00	12.00
❑	53 George McQuinn	25.00	15.00
❑	54 Bill Trotter	20.00	12.00
❑	55 Slick Coffman	20.00	12.00
❑	56 Eddie Miller RC	25.00	15.00
❑	57 Max West	20.00	12.00
❑	58 Bill Posedel	20.00	12.00
❑	59 Rabbit Warstler	20.00	12.00

❑ 60	John Cooney	20.00	12.00
❑ 61	Tony Cuccinello	25.00	15.00
❑ 62	Buddy Hassett	20.00	12.00
❑ 63	Pete Coscarart	20.00	12.00
❑ 64	Van Lingle Mungo	25.00	15.00
❑ 65	Fred Fitzsimmons	25.00	15.00
❑ 66	Babe Phelps	20.00	12.00
❑ 67	Whit Wyatt	25.00	15.00
❑ 68	Dolph Camilli	25.00	15.00
❑ 69	Cookie Lavagetto	25.00	15.00
❑ 70	Luke Hamlin (Hot Potato)	20.00	12.00
❑ 71	Mel Almada	20.00	12.00
❑ 72	Chuck Dressen RC	25.00	15.00
❑ 73	Bucky Walters	25.00	15.00
❑ 74	Paul(Duke) Derringer	25.00	15.00
❑ 75	Frank (Buck) McCormick	25.00	15.00
❑ 76	Lonny Frey	20.00	12.00
❑ 77	Willard Hershberger	25.00	15.00
❑ 78	Lew Riggs	20.00	12.00
❑ 79	Harry Craft	25.00	15.00
❑ 80	Billy Myers	20.00	12.00
❑ 81	Wally Berger	25.00	15.00
❑ 82	Hank Gowdy CO	25.00	15.00
❑ 83	Cliff Melton	20.00	12.00
❑ 84	Jo Jo Moore	20.00	12.00
❑ 85	Hal Schumacher	25.00	15.00
❑ 86	Harry Gumbert	20.00	12.00
❑ 87	Carl Hubbell	125.00	75.00
❑ 88	Mel Ott	175.00	100.00
❑ 89	Bill Jurges	20.00	12.00
❑ 90	Frank Demaree	20.00	12.00
❑ 91	Bob Seeds	20.00	12.00
❑ 92	Whitey Whitehead	20.00	12.00
❑ 93	Harry Danning	20.00	12.00
❑ 94	Gus Suhr	20.00	12.00
❑ 95	Hugh Mulcahy	20.00	12.00
❑ 96	Heinie Mueller	20.00	12.00
❑ 97	Morry Arnovich	20.00	12.00
❑ 98	Pinky May	20.00	12.00
❑ 99	Syl Johnson	20.00	12.00
❑ 100	Hersh Martin	20.00	12.00
❑ 101	Del Young	20.00	12.00
❑ 102	Chuck Klein	100.00	60.00
❑ 103	Elbie Fletcher	20.00	12.00
❑ 104	Paul Waner	90.00	50.00
❑ 105	Lloyd Waner	80.00	45.00
❑ 106	Pep Young	20.00	12.00
❑ 107	Arky Vaughan	80.00	45.00
❑ 108	Johnny Rizzo	20.00	12.00
❑ 109	Don Padgett	20.00	12.00
❑ 110	Tom Sunkel	20.00	12.00
❑ 111	Mickey Owen	25.00	15.00
❑ 112	Jimmy Brown	20.00	12.00
❑ 113	Mort Cooper	25.00	15.00
❑ 114	Lon Warneke	25.00	15.00
❑ 115	Mike Gonzalez CO	25.00	15.00
❑ 116	Al Schacht	25.00	15.00
❑ 117	Dolly Stark UMP	25.00	15.00
❑ 118	Waite Hoyt	90.00	50.00
❑ 119	Grover C. Alexander	175.00	100.00
❑ 120	Walter Johnson	200.00	100.00
❑ 121	Atley Donald RC	25.00	15.00
❑ 122	Sandy Sundra RC	25.00	15.00
❑ 123	Hildy Hildebrand	25.00	15.00
❑ 124	Earle Combs	100.00	60.00
❑ 125	Art Fletcher RC	25.00	15.00
❑ 126	Jake Solters	20.00	12.00
❑ 127	Muddy Ruel	20.00	12.00
❑ 128	Pete Appleton	20.00	12.00
❑ 129	Bucky Harris MG RC	80.00	45.00
❑ 130	Clyde Milan RC	25.00	15.00
❑ 131	Zeke Bonura	25.00	15.00
❑ 132	Connie Mack MG RC	150.00	75.00
❑ 133	Jimmie Foxx	200.00	100.00
❑ 134	Joe Cronin	100.00	60.00
❑ 135	Line Drive Nelson	20.00	12.00
❑ 136	Cotton Pippen	20.00	12.00
❑ 137	Bing Miller	20.00	12.00
❑ 138	Beau Bell	20.00	12.00
❑ 139	Elden Auker	20.00	12.00
❑ 140	Dick Coffman	20.00	12.00
❑ 141	Casey Stengel MG RC	175.00	100.00
❑ 142	George Kelly RC	90.00	50.00
❑ 143	Gene Moore	20.00	12.00
❑ 144	Joe Vosmik	20.00	12.00
❑ 145	Vito Tamulis	20.00	12.00
❑ 146	Tot Pressnell	20.00	12.00
❑ 147	Johnny Hudson	20.00	12.00
❑ 148	Hugh Casey	25.00	15.00
❑ 149	Pinky Shoffner	20.00	12.00
❑ 150	Whitey Moore	20.00	12.00
❑ 151	Edwin Joost	25.00	15.00
❑ 152	Jimmy Wilson	20.00	12.00
❑ 153	Bill McKechnie MG RC	80.00	45.00
❑ 154	Jumbo Brown	20.00	12.00
❑ 155	Ray Hayworth	20.00	12.00
❑ 156	Daffy Dean		
❑ 157	Lou Chiozza	20.00	12.00
❑ 158	Travis Jackson	90.00	50.00
❑ 159	Pancho Snyder RC	20.00	12.00
❑ 160	Hans Lobert CO	20.00	12.00
❑ 161	Debs Garms	20.00	12.00
❑ 162	Joe Bowman	20.00	12.00
❑ 163	Spud Davis	20.00	12.00
❑ 164	Ray Berres	20.00	12.00
❑ 165	Bob Klinger	20.00	12.00
❑ 166	Bill Brubaker	20.00	12.00
❑ 167	Frankie Frisch MG	90.00	50.00
❑ 168	Honus Wagner CO	200.00	100.00
❑ 169	Gabby Street	20.00	12.00
❑ 170	Tris Speaker	175.00	100.00
❑ 171	Harry Heilmann	80.00	45.00
❑ 172	Chief Bender	80.00	45.00
❑ 173	Napoleon Lajoie	175.00	100.00
❑ 174	Johnny Evers	90.00	50.00
❑ 175	Christy Mathewson	250.00	150.00
❑ 176	Heinie Manush	90.00	50.00
❑ 177	Frank Baker	100.00	60.00
❑ 178	Max Carey	90.00	50.00
❑ 179	George Sisler	125.00	75.00
❑ 180	Mickey Cochrane	150.00	90.00
❑ 181	Spud Chandler RC	80.00	45.00
❑ 182	Knick Knickerbocker RC	70.00	35.00
❑ 183	Marvin Breuer RC	70.00	35.00
❑ 184	Mule Haas	70.00	35.00
❑ 185	Joe Kuhel	70.00	35.00
❑ 186	Taft Wright RC	70.00	35.00
❑ 187	Jimmy Dykes MG	80.00	45.00
❑ 188	Joe Krakauskas RC	70.00	35.00
❑ 189	Jim Bloodworth RC	70.00	35.00
❑ 190	Charley Berry	70.00	35.00
❑ 191	John Babich RC	70.00	35.00
❑ 192	Dick Siebert RC	70.00	35.00
❑ 193	Chubby Dean RC	70.00	35.00
❑ 194	Sam Chapman RC	70.00	35.00
❑ 195	Dee Miles RC	70.00	35.00
❑ 196	Red (Nonny) Nonnenkamp RC	70.00	35.00
❑ 197	Lou Finney RC	70.00	35.00
❑ 198	Denny Galehouse RC	70.00	35.00
❑ 199	Pinky Higgins	70.00	35.00
❑ 200	Soup Campbell RC	70.00	35.00
❑ 201	Barney McCosky RC	70.00	35.00
❑ 202	Al Milnar RC	70.00	35.00
❑ 203	Bad News Hale RC	70.00	35.00
❑ 204	Harry Eisenstat RC	70.00	35.00
❑ 205	Rollie Hemsley RC	70.00	35.00
❑ 206	Chet Laabs RC	70.00	35.00
❑ 207	Gus Mancuso	70.00	35.00
❑ 208	Lee Gamble RC	70.00	35.00
❑ 209	Hy Vandenberg RC	70.00	35.00
❑ 210	Bill Lohrman RC	70.00	35.00
❑ 211	Pop Joiner RC	70.00	35.00
❑ 212	Babe Young RC	70.00	35.00
❑ 213	John Rucker RC	70.00	35.00
❑ 214	Ken O'Dea RC	70.00	35.00
❑ 215	Johnnie McCarthy RC	70.00	35.00
❑ 216	Joe Marty RC	70.00	35.00
❑ 217	Walter Beck	70.00	35.00
❑ 218	Wally Millies RC	70.00	35.00
❑ 219	Russ Bauers RC	70.00	35.00
❑ 220	Mace Brown RC	70.00	35.00
❑ 221	Lee Handley RC	70.00	35.00
❑ 222	Max Butcher RC	70.00	35.00
❑ 223	Hughie Jennings	150.00	90.00
❑ 224	Pie Traynor	175.00	100.00
❑ 225	Joe Jackson	2500.00	1500.00
❑ 226	Harry Hooper	150.00	90.00
❑ 227	Jesse Haines	150.00	90.00
❑ 228	Charlie Grimm	80.00	45.00
❑ 229	Buck Herzog	70.00	35.00
❑ 230	Red Faber	175.00	100.00
❑ 231	Dolf Luque	100.00	60.00
❑ 232	Goose Goslin	150.00	90.00
❑ 233	George Earnshaw	80.00	45.00
❑ 234	Frank Chance	150.00	90.00
❑ 235	John McGraw	175.00	100.00
❑ 236	Jim Bottomley	150.00	90.00
❑ 237	Willie Keeler	175.00	100.00
❑ 238	Tony Lazzeri	175.00	100.00
❑ 239	George Uhle	70.00	35.00
❑ 240	Bill Atwood RC	100.00	60.00

1941 Play Ball

❑	COMPLETE SET (72)	10000.00	6000.00
❑	COMMON CARD (1-48)	40.00	20.00
❑	COMMON CARD (49-72)	60.00	30.00
❑	WRAPPER (1-CENT)	800.00	700.00
❑ 1	Eddie Miller	125.00	75.00
❑ 2	Max West	40.00	20.00
❑ 3	Bucky Walters	45.00	25.00
❑ 4	Paul Derringer	50.00	30.00
❑ 5	Frank (Buck) McCormick	45.00	25.00
❑ 6	Carl Hubbell	175.00	100.00
❑ 7	Harry Danning	40.00	20.00
❑ 8	Mel Ott	225.00	125.00
❑ 9	Pinky May	40.00	20.00
❑ 10	Arky Vaughan	100.00	60.00
❑ 11	Debs Garms	40.00	20.00
❑ 12	Jimmy Brown	40.00	20.00
❑ 13	Jimmie Foxx	300.00	175.00
❑ 14	Ted Williams	1500.00	900.00
❑ 15	Joe Cronin	125.00	75.00
❑ 16	Hal Trosky	45.00	25.00
❑ 17	Roy Weatherly	40.00	20.00
❑ 18	Hank Greenberg	300.00	175.00
❑ 19	Charley Gehringer	200.00	125.00
❑ 20	Red Ruffing	125.00	75.00
❑ 21	Charlie Keller	60.00	35.00
❑ 22	Bob Johnson	50.00	30.00
❑ 23	George McQuinn	40.00	20.00
❑ 24	Dutch Leonard	45.00	25.00
❑ 25	Gene Moore	40.00	20.00
❑ 26	Harry Gumpert	40.00	20.00
❑ 27	Babe Young	40.00	20.00
❑ 28	Joe Marty	40.00	20.00
❑ 29	Jack Wilson	40.00	20.00
❑ 30	Lou Finney	40.00	20.00
❑ 31	Joe Kuhel	40.00	20.00
❑ 32	Taft Wright	40.00	20.00
❑ 33	Al Milnar	40.00	20.00
❑ 34	Rollie Hemsley	40.00	20.00
❑ 35	Pinky Higgins	45.00	25.00
❑ 36	Barney McCosky	40.00	20.00
❑ 37	Bruce Campbell RC	40.00	20.00
❑ 38	Atley Donald	50.00	30.00
❑ 39	Tommy Henrich	60.00	35.00
❑ 40	John Babich	40.00	20.00
❑ 41	Frank (Blimp) Hayes	40.00	20.00
❑ 42	Wally Moses	45.00	25.00
❑ 43	Al Brancato RC	40.00	20.00
❑ 44	Sam Chapman	40.00	20.00
❑ 45	Eldon Auker	40.00	20.00
❑ 46	Sid Hudson RC	40.00	20.00
❑ 47	Buddy Lewis	40.00	20.00
❑ 48	Cecil Travis	45.00	25.00
❑ 49	Babe Dahlgren	65.00	35.00
❑ 50	Johnny Cooney	60.00	30.00
❑ 51	Dolph Camilli	65.00	35.00
❑ 52	Kirby Higbe RC	60.00	30.00
❑ 53	Luke Hamlin	60.00	30.00

❑ 54 Pee Wee Reese RC	600.00	350.00
❑ 55 Whit Wyatt	65.00	35.00
❑ 56 Johnny VanderMeer RC	100.00	60.00
❑ 57 Moe Arnovich	60.00	30.00
❑ 58 Frank Demaree	60.00	30.00
❑ 59 Bill Jurges	60.00	30.00
❑ 60 Chuck Klein	150.00	90.00
❑ 61 Vince DiMaggio RC	225.00	125.00
❑ 62 Elbie Fletcher	60.00	30.00
❑ 63 Dom DiMaggio RC	250.00	150.00
❑ 64 Bobby Doerr	175.00	100.00
❑ 65 Tommy Bridges	65.00	35.00
❑ 66 Harland Clift RC	60.00	30.00
❑ 67 Walt Judnich RC	60.00	30.00
❑ 68 John Knott	60.00	30.00
❑ 69 George Case	65.00	35.00
❑ 70 Bill Dickey	400.00	250.00
❑ 71 Joe DiMaggio	2500.00	1500.00
❑ 72 Lefty Gomez	475.00	275.00

1988 Score

❑ COMPLETE SET (660)	10.00	5.00
❑ COMP.FACT.SET (660)	15.00	7.50
❑ 1 Don Mattingly	.60	.25
❑ 2 Wade Boggs	.15	.05
❑ 3 Tim Raines	.10	.02
❑ 4 Andre Dawson	.10	.02
❑ 5 Mark McGwire	1.50	.60
❑ 6 Kevin Seitzer	.05	.01
❑ 7 Wally Joyner	.10	.02
❑ 8 Jesse Barfield	.10	.02
❑ 9 Pedro Guerrero	.10	.02
❑ 10 Eric Davis	.10	.02
❑ 11 George Brett	.50	.20
❑ 12 Ozzie Smith	.30	.10
❑ 13 Rickey Henderson	.20	.07
❑ 14 Jim Rice	.10	.02
❑ 15 Matt Nokes RC*	.25	.08
❑ 16 Mike Schmidt	.50	.20
❑ 17 Dave Parker	.10	.02
❑ 18 Eddie Murray	.20	.07
❑ 19 Andres Galarraga	.10	.02
❑ 20 Tony Fernandez	.05	.01
❑ 21 Kevin McReynolds	.05	.01
❑ 22 B.J. Surhoff	.10	.02
❑ 23 Pat Tabler	.05	.01
❑ 24 Kirby Puckett	.20	.07
❑ 25 Benito Santiago	.10	.02
❑ 26 Ryne Sandberg	.40	.15
❑ 27 Kelly Downs	.05	.01
❑ 28 Jose Cruz	.10	.02
❑ 29 Pete O'Brien	.05	.01
❑ 30 Mark Langston	.05	.01
❑ 31 Lee Smith	.10	.02
❑ 32 Juan Samuel	.05	.01
❑ 33 Kevin Bass	.05	.01
❑ 34 R.J. Reynolds	.05	.01
❑ 35 Steve Sax	.05	.01
❑ 36 John Kruk	.10	.02
❑ 37 Alan Trammell	.10	.02
❑ 38 Chris Bosio	.05	.01
❑ 39 Brook Jacoby	.05	.01
❑ 40 Willie McGee UER (Excited misspelled as excitd)	.10	.02
❑ 41 Dave Magadan	.05	.01
❑ 42 Fred Lynn	.10	.02
❑ 43 Kent Hrbek	.10	.02
❑ 44 Brian Downing	.10	.02
❑ 45 Jose Canseco	.50	.20
❑ 46 Jim Presley	.05	.01
❑ 47 Mike Stanley	.05	.01
❑ 48 Tony Pena	.05	.01
❑ 49 David Cone	.10	.02
❑ 50 Rick Sutcliffe	.10	.02
❑ 51 Doug Drabek	.05	.01
❑ 52 Bill Doran	.05	.01
❑ 53 Mike Scioscia	.10	.02
❑ 54 Candy Maldonado	.05	.01
❑ 55 Dave Winfield	.10	.02
❑ 56 Lou Whitaker	.10	.02
❑ 57 Tom Henke	.05	.01
❑ 58 Ken Gerhart	.05	.01
❑ 59 Glenn Braggs	.05	.01
❑ 60 Julio Franco	.10	.02
❑ 61 Charlie Leibrandt	.05	.01
❑ 62 Gary Gaetti	.10	.02
❑ 63 Bob Boone	.10	.02
❑ 64 Luis Polonia RC*	.25	.08
❑ 65 Dwight Evans	.15	.05
❑ 66 Phil Bradley	.05	.01
❑ 67 Mike Boddicker	.05	.01
❑ 68 Vince Coleman	.05	.01
❑ 69 Howard Johnson	.10	.02
❑ 70 Tim Wallach	.05	.01
❑ 71 Keith Moreland	.05	.01
❑ 72 Barry Larkin	.15	.05
❑ 73 Alan Ashby	.05	.01
❑ 74 Rick Rhoden	.05	.01
❑ 75 Darrell Evans	.10	.02
❑ 76 Dave Stieb	.10	.02
❑ 77 Dan Plesac	.05	.01
❑ 78 Will Clark	.20	.07
❑ 79 Frank White	.10	.02
❑ 80 Joe Carter	.10	.02
❑ 81 Mike Witt	.05	.01
❑ 82 Terry Steinbach	.10	.02
❑ 83 Alvin Davis	.05	.01
❑ 84 Tommy Herr	.10	.02
❑ 85 Vance Law	.05	.01
❑ 86 Kal Daniels	.05	.01
❑ 87 Rick Honeycutt UER (Wrong years for stats on bac)	.05	.01
❑ 88 Alfredo Griffin	.05	.01
❑ 89 Bret Saberhagen	.10	.02
❑ 90 Bert Blyleven	.10	.02
❑ 91 Jeff Reardon	.10	.02
❑ 92 Cory Snyder	.05	.01
❑ 93A Greg Walker ERR	2.00	.75
❑ 93B Greg Walker COR (93 of 660)	.05	.01
❑ 94 Joe Magrane RC*	.25	.08
❑ 95 Rob Deer	.05	.01
❑ 96 Ray Knight	.10	.02
❑ 97 Casey Candaele	.05	.01
❑ 98 John Cerutti	.05	.01
❑ 99 Buddy Bell	.10	.02
❑ 100 Jack Clark	.10	.02
❑ 101 Eric Bell	.05	.01
❑ 102 Willie Wilson	.10	.02
❑ 103 Dave Schmidt	.05	.01
❑ 104 Dennis Eckersley UER	.15	.05
❑ 105 Don Sutton	.10	.02
❑ 106 Danny Tartabull	.05	.01
❑ 107 Fred McGriff	.20	.07
❑ 108 Les Straker	.05	.01
❑ 109 Lloyd Moseby	.05	.01
❑ 110 Roger Clemens	1.00	.40
❑ 111 Glenn Hubbard	.05	.01
❑ 112 Ken Williams	.05	.01
❑ 113 Ruben Sierra	.10	.02
❑ 114 Stan Jefferson	.05	.01
❑ 115 Milt Thompson	.05	.01
❑ 116 Bobby Bonilla	.10	.02
❑ 117 Wayne Tolleson	.05	.01
❑ 118 Matt Williams RC	.75	.30
❑ 119 Chet Lemon	.10	.02
❑ 120 Dale Sveum	.05	.01
❑ 121 Dennis Boyd	.05	.01
❑ 122 Brett Butler	.10	.02
❑ 123 Terry Kennedy	.05	.01
❑ 124 Jack Howell	.05	.01
❑ 125 Curt Young	.05	.01
❑ 126A Dave Valle ERR (Misspelled Dale on card front)	.10	.02
❑ 126B Dave Valle COR	.05	.01
❑ 127 Curt Wilkerson	.05	.01
❑ 128 Tim Teufel	.05	.01
❑ 129 Ozzie Virgil	.05	.01
❑ 130 Brian Fisher	.05	.01
❑ 131 Lance Parrish	.10	.02
❑ 132 Tom Browning	.05	.01
❑ 133A Larry Andersen ERR (Misspelled Anderson on card)	.10	.02
❑ 133B Larry Andersen COR	.05	.01
❑ 134A Bob Brenly ERR (Misspelled Brenley on card front)	.10	.02
❑ 134B Bob Brenly COR	.05	.01
❑ 135 Mike Marshall	.05	.01
❑ 136 Gerald Perry	.05	.01
❑ 137 Bobby Meacham	.05	.01
❑ 138 Larry Herndon	.05	.01
❑ 139 Fred Manrique	.05	.01
❑ 140 Charlie Hough	.10	.02
❑ 141 Ron Darling	.10	.02
❑ 142 Herm Winningham	.05	.01
❑ 143 Mike Diaz	.05	.01
❑ 144 Mike Jackson RC*	.25	.08
❑ 145 Denny Walling	.05	.01
❑ 146 Robby Thompson	.05	.01
❑ 147 Franklin Stubbs	.05	.01
❑ 148 Albert Hall	.05	.01
❑ 149 Bobby Witt	.05	.01
❑ 150 Lance McCullers	.05	.01
❑ 151 Scott Bradley	.05	.01
❑ 152 Mark McLemore	.05	.01
❑ 153 Tim Laudner	.05	.01
❑ 154 Greg Swindell	.05	.01
❑ 155 Marty Barrett	.05	.01
❑ 156 Mike Heath	.05	.01
❑ 157 Gary Ward	.05	.01
❑ 158A Lee Mazzilli ERR (Misspelled Mazilli on card fro)	.10	.02
❑ 158B Lee Mazzilli COR	.10	.02
❑ 159 Tom Foley	.05	.01
❑ 160 Robin Yount	.30	.10
❑ 161 Steve Bedrosian	.05	.01
❑ 162 Bob Walk	.05	.01
❑ 163 Nick Esasky	.05	.01
❑ 164 Ken Caminiti RC	2.00	.75
❑ 165 Jose Uribe	.05	.01
❑ 166 Dave Anderson	.05	.01
❑ 167 Ed Whitson	.05	.01
❑ 168 Ernie Whitt	.05	.01
❑ 169 Cecil Cooper	.10	.02
❑ 170 Mike Pagliarulo	.05	.01
❑ 171 Pat Sheridan	.05	.01
❑ 172 Chris Bando	.05	.01
❑ 173 Lee Lacy	.05	.01
❑ 174 Steve Lombardozzi	.05	.01
❑ 175 Mike Greenwell	.05	.01
❑ 176 Greg Minton	.05	.01
❑ 177 Moose Haas	.05	.01
❑ 178 Mike Kingery	.05	.01
❑ 179 Greg A. Harris	.05	.01
❑ 180 Bo Jackson	.20	.07
❑ 181 Carmelo Martinez	.05	.01
❑ 182 Alex Trevino	.05	.01
❑ 183 Ron Oester	.05	.01
❑ 184 Danny Darwin	.05	.01
❑ 185 Mike Krukow	.05	.01
❑ 186 Rafael Palmeiro	.40	.15
❑ 187 Tim Burke	.05	.01
❑ 188 Roger McDowell	.05	.01
❑ 189 Garry Templeton	.10	.02
❑ 190 Terry Pendleton	.10	.02
❑ 191 Larry Parrish	.05	.01
❑ 192 Rey Quinones	.05	.01
❑ 193 Joaquin Andujar	.10	.02
❑ 194 Tom Brunansky	.05	.01
❑ 195 Donnie Moore	.05	.01
❑ 196 Dan Pasqua	.05	.01
❑ 197 Jim Gantner	.05	.01
❑ 198 Mark Eichhorn	.05	.01
❑ 199 John Grubb	.05	.01

Card	Price 1	Price 2
❑ 200 Bill Ripken RC*	.25	.08
❑ 201 Sam Horn RC	.10	.02
❑ 202 Todd Worrell	.05	.01
❑ 203 Terry Leach	.05	.01
❑ 204 Garth Iorg	.05	.01
❑ 205 Brian Dayett	.05	.01
❑ 206 Bo Diaz	.05	.01
❑ 207 Craig Reynolds	.05	.01
❑ 208 Brian Holton	.05	.01
❑ 209 Marvell Wynne UER (Misspelled Marvelle on card f)	.05	.01
❑ 210 Dave Concepcion	.10	.02
❑ 211 Mike Davis	.05	.01
❑ 212 Devon White	.10	.02
❑ 213 Mickey Brantley	.05	.01
❑ 214 Greg Gagne	.05	.01
❑ 215 Oddibe McDowell	.05	.01
❑ 216 Jimmy Key	.10	.02
❑ 217 Dave Bergman	.05	.01
❑ 218 Calvin Schiraldi	.05	.01
❑ 219 Larry Sheets	.05	.01
❑ 220 Mike Easler	.05	.01
❑ 221 Kurt Stillwell	.05	.01
❑ 222 Chuck Jackson	.05	.01
❑ 223 Dave Martinez	.05	.01
❑ 224 Tim Leary	.05	.01
❑ 225 Steve Garvey	.10	.02
❑ 226 Greg Mathews	.05	.01
❑ 227 Doug Sisk	.05	.01
❑ 228 Dave Henderson (Wearing Red Sox uniform; Red Sox)	.05	.01
❑ 229 Jimmy Dwyer	.05	.01
❑ 230 Larry Owen	.05	.01
❑ 231 Andre Thornton	.05	.01
❑ 232 Mark Salas	.05	.01
❑ 233 Tom Brookens	.05	.01
❑ 234 Greg Brock	.05	.01
❑ 235 Rance Mulliniks	.05	.01
❑ 236 Bob Brower	.05	.01
❑ 237 Joe Niekro	.05	.01
❑ 238 Scott Bankhead	.05	.01
❑ 239 Doug DeCinces	.05	.01
❑ 240 Tommy John	.10	.02
❑ 241 Rich Gedman	.05	.01
❑ 242 Ted Power	.05	.01
❑ 243 Dave Meads	.05	.01
❑ 244 Jim Sundberg	.10	.02
❑ 245 Ken Oberkfell	.05	.01
❑ 246 Jimmy Jones	.05	.01
❑ 247 Ken Landreaux	.05	.01
❑ 248 Jose Oquendo	.05	.01
❑ 249 John Mitchell RC	.10	.02
❑ 250 Don Baylor	.10	.02
❑ 251 Scott Fletcher	.05	.01
❑ 252 Al Newman	.05	.01
❑ 253 Carney Lansford	.10	.02
❑ 254 Johnny Ray	.05	.01
❑ 255 Gary Pettis	.05	.01
❑ 256 Ken Phelps	.05	.01
❑ 257 Rick Leach	.05	.01
❑ 258 Tim Stoddard	.05	.01
❑ 259 Ed Romero	.05	.01
❑ 260 Sid Bream	.05	.01
❑ 261A Tom Niedenfuer ERR (Misspelled Neidenfuer on car)	.10	.02
❑ 261B Tom Niedenfuer COR	.05	.01
❑ 262 Rick Dempsey	.05	.01
❑ 263 Lonnie Smith	.05	.01
❑ 264 Bob Forsch	.05	.01
❑ 265 Barry Bonds	2.00	.75
❑ 266 Willie Randolph	.10	.02
❑ 267 Mike Ramsey	.05	.01
❑ 268 Don Slaught	.05	.01
❑ 269 Mickey Tettleton	.05	.01
❑ 270 Jerry Reuss	.05	.01
❑ 271 Marc Sullivan	.05	.01
❑ 272 Jim Morrison	.05	.01
❑ 273 Steve Balboni	.05	.01
❑ 274 Dick Schofield	.05	.01
❑ 275 John Tudor	.10	.02
❑ 276 Gene Larkin RC*	.25	.08
❑ 277 Harold Reynolds	.10	.02
❑ 278 Jerry Browne	.05	.01
❑ 279 Willie Upshaw	.05	.01
❑ 280 Ted Higuera	.05	.01
❑ 281 Terry McGriff	.05	.01
❑ 282 Terry Puhl	.05	.01
❑ 283 Mark Wasinger	.05	.01
❑ 284 Luis Salazar	.05	.01
❑ 285 Ted Simmons	.10	.02
❑ 286 John Shelby	.05	.01
❑ 287 John Smiley RC*	.25	.08
❑ 288 Curt Ford	.05	.01
❑ 289 Steve Crawford	.05	.01
❑ 290 Dan Quisenberry	.05	.01
❑ 291 Alan Wiggins	.05	.01
❑ 292 Randy Bush	.05	.01
❑ 293 John Candelaria	.05	.01
❑ 294 Tony Phillips	.05	.01
❑ 295 Mike Morgan	.05	.01
❑ 296 Bill Wegman	.05	.01
❑ 297A Terry Francona ERR (Misspelled Franconia on card)	.10	.02
❑ 297B Terry Francona COR	.10	.02
❑ 298 Mickey Hatcher	.05	.01
❑ 299 Andres Thomas	.05	.01
❑ 300 Bob Stanley	.05	.01
❑ 301 Al Pedrique	.05	.01
❑ 302 Jim Lindeman	.05	.01
❑ 303 Wally Backman	.05	.01
❑ 304 Paul O'Neill	.15	.05
❑ 305 Hubie Brooks	.05	.01
❑ 306 Steve Buechele	.05	.01
❑ 307 Bobby Thigpen	.05	.01
❑ 308 George Hendrick	.10	.02
❑ 309 John Moses	.05	.01
❑ 310 Ron Guidry	.10	.02
❑ 311 Bill Schroeder	.05	.01
❑ 312 Jose Nunez	.05	.01
❑ 313 Bud Black	.05	.01
❑ 314 Joe Sambito	.05	.01
❑ 315 Scott McGregor	.05	.01
❑ 316 Rafael Santana	.05	.01
❑ 317 Frank Williams	.05	.01
❑ 318 Mike Fitzgerald	.05	.01
❑ 319 Rick Mahler	.05	.01
❑ 320 Jim Gott	.05	.01
❑ 321 Mariano Duncan	.05	.01
❑ 322 Jose Guzman	.05	.01
❑ 323 Lee Guetterman	.05	.01
❑ 324 Dan Gladden	.05	.01
❑ 325 Gary Carter	.10	.02
❑ 326 Tracy Jones	.05	.01
❑ 327 Floyd Youmans	.05	.01
❑ 328 Bill Dawley	.05	.01
❑ 329 Paul Noce	.05	.01
❑ 330 Angel Salazar	.05	.01
❑ 331 Goose Gossage	.10	.02
❑ 332 George Frazier	.05	.01
❑ 333 Ruppert Jones	.05	.01
❑ 334 Billy Joe Robidoux	.05	.01
❑ 335 Mike Scott	.10	.02
❑ 336 Randy Myers	.10	.02
❑ 337 Bob Sebra	.05	.01
❑ 338 Eric Show	.05	.01
❑ 339 Mitch Williams	.05	.01
❑ 340 Paul Molitor	.10	.02
❑ 341 Gus Polidor	.05	.01
❑ 342 Steve Trout	.05	.01
❑ 343 Jerry Don Gleaton	.05	.01
❑ 344 Bob Knepper	.05	.01
❑ 345 Mitch Webster	.05	.01
❑ 346 John Morris	.05	.01
❑ 347 Andy Hawkins	.05	.01
❑ 348 Dave Leiper	.05	.01
❑ 349 Ernest Riles	.05	.01
❑ 350 Dwight Gooden	.10	.02
❑ 351 Dave Righetti	.10	.02
❑ 352 Pat Dodson	.05	.01
❑ 353 John Habyan	.05	.01
❑ 354 Jim Deshaies	.05	.01
❑ 355 Butch Wynegar	.05	.01
❑ 356 Bryn Smith	.05	.01
❑ 357 Matt Young	.05	.01
❑ 358 Tom Pagnozzi RC	.10	.02
❑ 359 Floyd Rayford	.05	.01
❑ 360 Darryl Strawberry	.10	.02
❑ 361 Sal Butera	.05	.01
❑ 362 Domingo Ramos	.05	.01
❑ 363 Chris Brown	.05	.01
❑ 364 Jose Gonzalez	.05	.01
❑ 365 Dave Smith	.05	.01
❑ 366 Andy McGaffigan	.05	.01
❑ 367 Stan Javier	.05	.01
❑ 368 Henry Cotto	.05	.01
❑ 369 Mike Birkbeck	.05	.01
❑ 370 Len Dykstra	.10	.02
❑ 371 Dave Collins	.05	.01
❑ 372 Spike Owen	.05	.01
❑ 373 Geno Petralli	.05	.01
❑ 374 Ron Karkovice	.05	.01
❑ 375 Shane Rawley	.05	.01
❑ 376 DeWayne Buice	.05	.01
❑ 377 Bill Pecota RC*	.10	.02
❑ 378 Leon Durham	.05	.01
❑ 379 Ed Olwine	.05	.01
❑ 380 Bruce Hurst	.05	.01
❑ 381 Bob McClure	.05	.01
❑ 382 Mark Thurmond	.05	.01
❑ 383 Buddy Biancalana	.05	.01
❑ 384 Tim Conroy	.05	.01
❑ 385 Tony Gwynn	.30	.10
❑ 386 Greg Gross	.05	.01
❑ 387 Barry Lyons	.05	.01
❑ 388 Mike Felder	.05	.01
❑ 389 Pat Clements	.05	.01
❑ 390 Ken Griffey	.10	.02
❑ 391 Mark Davis	.05	.01
❑ 392 Jose Rijo	.10	.02
❑ 393 Mike Young	.05	.01
❑ 394 Willie Fraser	.05	.01
❑ 395 Dion James	.05	.01
❑ 396 Steve Shields	.05	.01
❑ 397 Randy St.Claire	.05	.01
❑ 398 Danny Jackson	.05	.01
❑ 399 Cecil Fielder	.10	.02
❑ 400 Keith Hernandez	.10	.02
❑ 401 Don Carman	.05	.01
❑ 402 Chuck Crim	.05	.01
❑ 403 Rob Woodward	.05	.01
❑ 404 Junior Ortiz	.05	.01
❑ 405 Glenn Wilson	.05	.01
❑ 406 Ken Howell	.05	.01
❑ 407 Jeff Kunkel	.05	.01
❑ 408 Jeff Reed	.05	.01
❑ 409 Chris James	.05	.01
❑ 410 Zane Smith	.05	.01
❑ 411 Ken Dixon	.05	.01
❑ 412 Ricky Horton	.05	.01
❑ 413 Frank DiPino	.05	.01
❑ 414 Shane Mack	.05	.01
❑ 415 Danny Cox	.05	.01
❑ 416 Andy Van Slyke	.15	.05
❑ 417 Danny Heep	.05	.01
❑ 418 John Cangelosi	.05	.01
❑ 419A John Christensen ERR (Christiansen on card front)	.10	.02
❑ 419B John Christensen COR	.05	.01
❑ 420 Joey Cora RC	.25	.08
❑ 421 Mike LaValliere	.05	.01
❑ 422 Kelly Gruber	.05	.01
❑ 423 Bruce Benedict	.05	.01
❑ 424 Len Matuszek	.05	.01
❑ 425 Kent Tekulve	.05	.01
❑ 426 Rafael Ramirez	.05	.01
❑ 427 Mike Flanagan	.05	.01
❑ 428 Mike Gallego	.05	.01
❑ 429 Juan Castillo	.05	.01
❑ 430 Neal Heaton	.05	.01
❑ 431 Phil Garner	.10	.02
❑ 432 Mike Dunne	.05	.01
❑ 433 Wallace Johnson	.05	.01
❑ 434 Jack O'Connor	.05	.01
❑ 435 Steve Jeltz	.05	.01
❑ 436 Donell Nixon	.05	.01
❑ 437 Jack Lazorko	.05	.01
❑ 438 Keith Comstock	.05	.01
❑ 439 Jeff D. Robinson	.05	.01
❑ 440 Graig Nettles	.10	.02
❑ 441 Mel Hall	.05	.01
❑ 442 Gerald Young	.05	.01
❑ 443 Gary Redus	.05	.01
❑ 444 Charlie Moore	.05	.01

❑ 445 Bill Madlock .10 .02
❑ 446 Mark Clear .05 .01
❑ 447 Greg Booker .05 .01
❑ 448 Rick Schu .05 .01
❑ 449 Ron Kittle .05 .01
❑ 450 Dale Murphy .15 .05
❑ 451 Bob Dernier .05 .01
❑ 452 Dale Mohorcic .05 .01
❑ 453 Rafael Belliard .05 .01
❑ 454 Charlie Puleo .05 .01
❑ 455 Dwayne Murphy .05 .01
❑ 456 Jim Eisenreich .05 .01
❑ 457 David Palmer .05 .01
❑ 458 Dave Stewart .10 .02
❑ 459 Pascual Perez .05 .01
❑ 460 Glenn Davis .05 .01
❑ 461 Dan Petry .05 .01
❑ 462 Jim Winn .05 .01
❑ 463 Darrell Miller .05 .01
❑ 464 Mike Moore .05 .01
❑ 465 Mike LaCoss .05 .01
❑ 466 Steve Farr .05 .01
❑ 467 Jerry Mumphrey .05 .01
❑ 468 Kevin Gross .05 .01
❑ 469 Bruce Bochy .05 .01
❑ 470 Orel Hershiser .10 .02
❑ 471 Eric King .05 .01
❑ 472 Ellis Burks RC .40 .15
❑ 473 Darren Daulton .10 .02
❑ 474 Mookie Wilson .10 .02
❑ 475 Frank Viola .10 .02
❑ 476 Ron Robinson .05 .01
❑ 477 Bob Melvin .05 .01
❑ 478 Jeff Musselman .05 .01
❑ 479 Charlie Kerfeld .05 .01
❑ 480 Richard Dotson .05 .01
❑ 481 Kevin Mitchell .10 .02
❑ 482 Gary Roenicke .05 .01
❑ 483 Tim Flannery .05 .01
❑ 484 Rich Yett .05 .01
❑ 485 Pete Incaviglia .05 .01
❑ 486 Rick Cerone .05 .01
❑ 487 Tony Armas .10 .02
❑ 488 Jerry Reed .05 .01
❑ 489 Dave Lopes .10 .02
❑ 490 Frank Tanana .10 .02
❑ 491 Mike Loynd .05 .01
❑ 492 Bruce Ruffin .05 .01
❑ 493 Chris Speier .05 .01
❑ 494 Tom Hume .05 .01
❑ 495 Jesse Orosco .05 .01
❑ 496 Robbie Wine UER (Misspelled Robby on card front) .05 .01
❑ 497 Jeff Montgomery RC .25 .08
❑ 498 Jeff Dedmon .05 .01
❑ 499 Luis Aguayo .05 .01
❑ 500 Reggie Jackson A's .15 .05
❑ 501 Reggie Jackson O's .15 .05
❑ 502 Reggie Jackson Yankees .15 .05
❑ 503 Reggie Jackson Angels .15 .05
❑ 504 Reggie Jackson A's .15 .05
❑ 505 Billy Hatcher .05 .01
❑ 506 Ed Lynch .05 .01
❑ 507 Willie Hernandez .05 .01
❑ 508 Jose DeLeon .05 .01
❑ 509 Joel Youngblood .05 .01
❑ 510 Bob Welch .10 .02
❑ 511 Steve Ontiveros .05 .01
❑ 512 Randy Ready .05 .01
❑ 513 Juan Nieves .05 .01
❑ 514 Jeff Russell .05 .01
❑ 515 Von Hayes .05 .01
❑ 516 Mark Gubicza .05 .01
❑ 517 Ken Dayley .05 .01
❑ 518 Don Aase .05 .01
❑ 519 Rick Reuschel .10 .02
❑ 520 Mike Henneman RC* .25 .08
❑ 521 Rick Aguilera .05 .01
❑ 522 Jay Howell .05 .01
❑ 523 Ed Correa .05 .01
❑ 524 Manny Trillo .05 .01
❑ 525 Kirk Gibson .20 .07
❑ 526 Wally Ritchie .05 .01
❑ 527 Al Nipper .05 .01
❑ 528 Atlee Hammaker .05 .01
❑ 529 Shawon Dunston .05 .01
❑ 530 Jim Clancy .05 .01
❑ 531 Tom Paciorek .05 .01
❑ 532 Joel Skinner .05 .01
❑ 533 Scott Garrelts .05 .01
❑ 534 Tom O'Malley .05 .01
❑ 535 John Franco .10 .02
❑ 536 Paul Kilgus .05 .01
❑ 537 Darrell Porter .05 .01
❑ 538 Walt Terrell .05 .01
❑ 539 Bill Long .05 .01
❑ 540 George Bell .10 .02
❑ 541 Jeff Sellers .05 .01
❑ 542 Joe Boever .05 .01
❑ 543 Steve Howe .05 .01
❑ 544 Scott Sanderson .05 .01
❑ 545 Jack Morris .10 .02
❑ 546 Todd Benzinger RC* .25 .08
❑ 547 Steve Henderson .05 .01
❑ 548 Eddie Milner .05 .01
❑ 549 Jeff M. Robinson .05 .01
❑ 550 Cal Ripken .75 .30
❑ 551 Jody Davis .05 .01
❑ 552 Kirk McCaskill .05 .01
❑ 553 Craig Lefferts .05 .01
❑ 554 Darnell Coles .05 .01
❑ 555 Phil Niekro .10 .02
❑ 556 Mike Aldrete .05 .01
❑ 557 Pat Perry .05 .01
❑ 558 Juan Agosto .05 .01
❑ 559 Rob Murphy .05 .01
❑ 560 Dennis Rasmussen .05 .01
❑ 561 Manny Lee .05 .01
❑ 562 Jeff Blauser RC .25 .08
❑ 563 Bob Ojeda .05 .01
❑ 564 Dave Dravecky .05 .01
❑ 565 Gene Garber .05 .01
❑ 566 Ron Roenicke .05 .01
❑ 567 Tommy Hinzo .05 .01
❑ 568 Eric Nolte .05 .01
❑ 569 Ed Hearn .05 .01
❑ 570 Mark Davidson .05 .01
❑ 571 Jim Walewander .05 .01
❑ 572 Donnie Hill UER (84 Stolen Base total listed as) .05 .01
❑ 573 Jamie Moyer .10 .02
❑ 574 Ken Schrom .05 .01
❑ 575 Nolan Ryan 1.00 .40
❑ 576 Jim Acker .05 .01
❑ 577 Jamie Quirk .05 .01
❑ 578 Jay Aldrich .05 .01
❑ 579 Claudell Washington .05 .01
❑ 580 Jeff Leonard .05 .01
❑ 581 Carmen Castillo .05 .01
❑ 582 Daryl Boston .05 .01
❑ 583 Jeff DeWillis .05 .01
❑ 584 John Marzano .05 .01
❑ 585 Bill Gullickson .05 .01
❑ 586 Andy Allanson .05 .01
❑ 587 Lee Tunnell UER (1987 stat line reads .4.84 ERA) .05 .01
❑ 588 Gene Nelson .05 .01
❑ 589 Dave LaPoint .05 .01
❑ 590 Harold Baines .10 .02
❑ 591 Bill Buckner .10 .02
❑ 592 Carlton Fisk .15 .05
❑ 593 Rick Manning .05 .01
❑ 594 Doug Jones RC .25 .08
❑ 595 Tom Candiotti .05 .01
❑ 596 Steve Lake .05 .01
❑ 597 Jose Lind RC .25 .08
❑ 598 Ross Jones .05 .01
❑ 599 Gary Matthews .10 .02
❑ 600 Fernando Valenzuela .10 .02
❑ 601 Dennis Martinez .10 .02
❑ 602 Les Lancaster .05 .01
❑ 603 Ozzie Guillen .10 .02
❑ 604 Tony Bernazard .05 .01
❑ 605 Chili Davis .10 .02
❑ 606 Roy Smalley .05 .01
❑ 607 Ivan Calderon .05 .01
❑ 608 Jay Tibbs .05 .01
❑ 609 Guy Hoffman .05 .01
❑ 610 Doyle Alexander .05 .01
❑ 611 Mike Bielecki .05 .01
❑ 612 Shawn Hillegas .05 .01
❑ 613 Keith Atherton .05 .01
❑ 614 Eric Plunk .05 .01
❑ 615 Sid Fernandez .05 .01
❑ 616 Dennis Lamp .05 .01
❑ 617 Dave Engle .05 .01
❑ 618 Harry Spilman .05 .01
❑ 619 Don Robinson .05 .01
❑ 620 John Farrell RC .10 .02
❑ 621 Nelson Liriano .05 .01
❑ 622 Floyd Bannister .05 .01
❑ 623 Randy Milligan RC .10 .02
❑ 624 Kevin Elster .05 .01
❑ 625 Jody Reed RC .25 .08
❑ 626 Shawn Abner .05 .01
❑ 627 Kirt Manwaring RC .25 .08
❑ 628 Pete Stanicek .05 .01
❑ 629 Rob Ducey .05 .01
❑ 630 Steve Kiefer .05 .01
❑ 631 Gary Thurman .05 .01
❑ 632 Darrel Akerfelds .05 .01
❑ 633 Dave Clark .05 .01
❑ 634 Roberto Kelly RC .25 .08
❑ 635 Keith Hughes .05 .01
❑ 636 John Davis .05 .01
❑ 637 Mike Devereaux RC .25 .08
❑ 638 Tom Glavine RC 2.50 1.00
❑ 639 Keith Miller RC .25 .08
❑ 640 Chris Gwynn UER RC .25 .08
❑ 641 Tim Crews RC .25 .08
❑ 642 Mackey Sasser RC .25 .08
❑ 643 Vicente Palacios .05 .01
❑ 644 Kevin Romine .05 .01
❑ 645 Gregg Jefferies RC .25 .08
❑ 646 Jeff Treadway RC .25 .08
❑ 647 Ron Gant RC .40 .15
❑ 648 M.McGwire/M.Nokes .75 .30
❑ 649 Eric Davis and Tim Raines (Speed and Power) .10 .02
❑ 650 Don Mattingly/J.Clark .30 .10
❑ 651 C.Ripken/Trammell/Fern .25 .08
❑ 652 Vince Coleman HL (100 Stolen Bases) .05 .01
❑ 653 Kirby Puckett HL .15 .05
❑ 654 Benito Santiago HL .05 .01
❑ 655 Juan Nieves HL (No Hitter) .05 .01
❑ 656 Steve Bedrosian HL (Saves Record) .05 .01
❑ 657 Mike Schmidt HL .20 .07
❑ 658 Don Mattingly HL .30 .10
❑ 659 Mark McGwire HL .75 .30
❑ 660 Paul Molitor HL .05 .01

1988 Score Rookie/Traded

❑ COMP.FACT.SET (110) 40.00 15.00
❑ 1T Jack Clark .75 .30
❑ 2T Danny Jackson .25 .08
❑ 3T Brett Butler .75 .30
❑ 4T Kurt Stillwell .25 .08
❑ 5T Tom Brunansky .25 .08
❑ 6T Dennis Lamp .25 .08
❑ 7T Jose DeLeon .25 .08
❑ 8T Tom Herr .25 .08
❑ 9T Keith Moreland .25 .08

❑ 10T	Kirk Gibson	2.00	.75
❑ 11T	Bud Black	.25	.08
❑ 12T	Rafael Ramirez	.25	.08
❑ 13T	Luis Salazar	.25	.08
❑ 14T	Goose Gossage	.75	.30
❑ 15T	Bob Welch	.75	.30
❑ 16T	Vance Law	.25	.08
❑ 17T	Ray Knight	.75	.30
❑ 18T	Dan Quisenberry	.25	.08
❑ 19T	Don Slaught	.25	.08
❑ 20T	Lee Smith	.75	.30
❑ 21T	Rick Cerone	.25	.08
❑ 22T	Pat Tabler	.25	.08
❑ 23T	Larry McWilliams	.25	.08
❑ 24T	Ricky Horton	.25	.08
❑ 25T	Graig Nettles	.75	.30
❑ 26T	Dan Petry	.25	.08
❑ 27T	Jose Rijo	.75	.30
❑ 28T	Chili Davis	.75	.30
❑ 29T	Dickie Thon	.25	.08
❑ 30T	Mackey Sasser	.25	.08
❑ 31T	Mickey Tettleton	.25	.08
❑ 32T	Rick Dempsey	.25	.08
❑ 33T	Ron Hassey	.25	.08
❑ 34T	Phil Bradley	.25	.08
❑ 35T	Jay Howell	.25	.08
❑ 36T	Bill Buckner	.75	.30
❑ 37T	Alfredo Griffin	.25	.08
❑ 38T	Gary Pettis	.25	.08
❑ 39T	Calvin Schiraldi	.25	.08
❑ 40T	John Candelaria	.25	.08
❑ 41T	Joe Orsulak	.25	.08
❑ 42T	Willie Upshaw	.25	.08
❑ 43T	Herm Winningham	.25	.08
❑ 44T	Ron Kittle	.25	.08
❑ 45T	Bob Dernier	.25	.08
❑ 46T	Steve Balboni	.25	.08
❑ 47T	Steve Shields	.25	.08
❑ 48T	Henry Cotto	.25	.08
❑ 49T	Dave Henderson	.25	.08
❑ 50T	Dave Parker	.75	.30
❑ 51T	Mike Young	.25	.08
❑ 52T	Mark Salas	.25	.08
❑ 53T	Mike Davis	.25	.08
❑ 54T	Rafael Santana	.25	.08
❑ 55T	Don Baylor	.75	.30
❑ 56T	Dan Pasqua	.25	.08
❑ 57T	Ernest Riles	.25	.08
❑ 58T	Glenn Hubbard	.25	.08
❑ 59T	Mike Smithson	.25	.08
❑ 60T	Richard Dotson	.25	.08
❑ 61T	Jerry Reuss	.25	.08
❑ 62T	Mike Jackson	.75	.30
❑ 63T	Floyd Bannister	.25	.08
❑ 64T	Jesse Orosco	.25	.08
❑ 65T	Larry Parrish	.25	.08
❑ 66T	Jeff Bittiger	.25	.08
❑ 67T	Ray Hayward	.25	.08
❑ 68T	Ricky Jordan XRC	.75	.30
❑ 69T	Tommy Gregg	.25	.08
❑ 70T	Brady Anderson XRC	1.25	.50
❑ 71T	Jeff Montgomery	.75	.30
❑ 72T	Darryl Hamilton XRC	.75	.30
❑ 73T	Cecil Espy	.25	.08
❑ 74T	Greg Briley XRC	.25	.08
❑ 75T	Joey Meyer	.25	.08
❑ 76T	Mike Macfarlane XRC	.75	.30
❑ 77T	Oswald Peraza	.25	.08
❑ 78T	Jack Armstrong XRC	.25	.08
❑ 79T	Don Heinkel	.25	.08
❑ 80T	Mark Grace XRC	8.00	3.00
❑ 81T	Steve Curry	.25	.08
❑ 82T	Damon Berryhill XRC*	.75	.30
❑ 83T	Steve Ellsworth	.25	.08
❑ 84T	Pete Smith XRC*	.25	.08
❑ 85T	Jack McDowell XRC	1.25	.50
❑ 86T	Rob Dibble XRC	1.25	.50
❑ 87T	Bryan Harvey XRC	.75	.30
❑ 88T	John Dopson	.25	.08
❑ 89T	Dave Gallagher	.25	.08
❑ 90T	Todd Stottlemyre XRC	.75	.30
❑ 91T	Mike Schooler	.25	.08
❑ 92T	Don Gordon	.25	.08
❑ 93T	Sil Campusano	.25	.08
❑ 94T	Jeff Pico	.25	.08
❑ 95T	Jay Buhner XRC	2.00	.75
❑ 96T	Nelson Santovenia	.25	.08
❑ 97T	Al Leiter XRC	3.00	1.25
❑ 98T	Luis Alicea XRC	.75	.30
❑ 99T	Pat Borders XRC	.75	.30
❑ 100T	Chris Sabo XRC	1.25	.50
❑ 101T	Tim Belcher	.25	.08
❑ 102T	Walt Weiss XRC*	1.25	.50
❑ 103T	Craig Biggio XRC	15.00	6.00
❑ 104T	Don August	.25	.08
❑ 105T	Roberto Alomar XRC	10.00	4.00
❑ 106T	Todd Burns	.25	.08
❑ 107T	John Costello	.25	.08
❑ 108T	Melido Perez XRC*	.75	.30
❑ 109T	Darrin Jackson XRC*	.25	.08
❑ 110T	Orestes Destrade XRC	.25	.08

1989 Score Rookie/Traded

❑ COMP.FACT.SET (110)		15.00	6.00
❑ 1T	Rafael Palmeiro	.25	.08
❑ 2T	Nolan Ryan	1.50	.60
❑ 3T	Jack Clark	.10	.02
❑ 4T	Dave LaPoint	.05	.01
❑ 5T	Mike Moore	.05	.01
❑ 6T	Pete O'Brien	.05	.01
❑ 7T	Jeffrey Leonard	.05	.01
❑ 8T	Rob Murphy	.05	.01
❑ 9T	Tom Herr	.05	.01
❑ 10T	Claudell Washington	.05	.01
❑ 11T	Mike Pagliarulo	.05	.01
❑ 12T	Steve Lake	.05	.01
❑ 13T	Spike Owen	.05	.01
❑ 14T	Andy Hawkins	.05	.01
❑ 15T	Todd Benzinger	.05	.01
❑ 16T	Mookie Wilson	.10	.02
❑ 17T	Bert Blyleven	.10	.02
❑ 18T	Jeff Treadway	.05	.01
❑ 19T	Bruce Hurst	.05	.01
❑ 20T	Steve Sax	.05	.01
❑ 21T	Juan Samuel	.05	.01
❑ 22T	Jesse Barfield	.10	.02
❑ 23T	Carmen Castillo	.05	.01
❑ 24T	Terry Leach	.05	.01
❑ 25T	Mark Langston	.05	.01
❑ 26T	Eric King	.05	.01
❑ 27T	Steve Balboni	.05	.01
❑ 28T	Len Dykstra	.10	.02
❑ 29T	Keith Moreland	.05	.01
❑ 30T	Terry Kennedy	.05	.01
❑ 31T	Eddie Murray	.25	.08
❑ 32T	Mitch Williams	.05	.01
❑ 33T	Jeff Parrett	.05	.01
❑ 34T	Wally Backman	.05	.01
❑ 35T	Julio Franco	.10	.02
❑ 36T	Lance Parrish	.10	.02
❑ 37T	Nick Esasky	.05	.01
❑ 38T	Luis Polonia	.05	.01
❑ 39T	Kevin Gross	.05	.01
❑ 40T	John Dopson	.05	.01
❑ 41T	Willie Randolph	.10	.02
❑ 42T	Jim Clancy	.05	.01
❑ 43T	Tracy Jones	.05	.01
❑ 44T	Phil Bradley	.05	.01
❑ 45T	Milt Thompson	.05	.01
❑ 46T	Chris James	.05	.01
❑ 47T	Scott Fletcher	.05	.01
❑ 48T	Kal Daniels	.05	.01
❑ 49T	Steve Bedrosian	.05	.01
❑ 50T	Rickey Henderson	.25	.08
❑ 51T	Dion James	.05	.01
❑ 52T	Tim Leary	.05	.01
❑ 53T	Roger McDowell	.05	.01
❑ 54T	Mel Hall	.05	.01
❑ 55T	Dickie Thon	.05	.01
❑ 56T	Zane Smith	.05	.01
❑ 57T	Danny Heep	.05	.01
❑ 58T	Bob McClure	.05	.01
❑ 59T	Brian Holton	.05	.01
❑ 60T	Randy Ready	.05	.01
❑ 61T	Bob Melvin	.05	.01
❑ 62T	Harold Baines	.10	.02
❑ 63T	Lance McCullers	.05	.01
❑ 64T	Jody Davis	.05	.01
❑ 65T	Darrell Evans	.10	.02
❑ 66T	Joel Youngblood	.05	.01
❑ 67T	Frank Viola	.10	.02
❑ 68T	Mike Aldrete	.05	.01
❑ 69T	Greg Cadaret	.05	.01
❑ 70T	John Kruk	.10	.02
❑ 71T	Pat Sheridan	.05	.01
❑ 72T	Oddibe McDowell	.05	.01
❑ 73T	Tom Brookens	.05	.01
❑ 74T	Bob Boone	.10	.02
❑ 75T	Walt Terrell	.05	.01
❑ 76T	Joel Skinner	.05	.01
❑ 77T	Randy Johnson	2.00	.75
❑ 78T	Felix Fermin	.05	.01
❑ 79T	Rick Mahler	.05	.01
❑ 80T	Richard Dotson	.05	.01
❑ 81T	Cris Carpenter RC *	.10	.02
❑ 82T	Billy Spiers RC	.25	.08
❑ 83T	Junior Felix RC	.10	.02
❑ 84T	Joe Girardi RC	.40	.15
❑ 85T	Jerome Walton RC	.25	.08
❑ 86T	Greg Litton	.05	.01
❑ 87T	Greg W.Harris RC	.10	.02
❑ 88T	Jim Abbott RC	1.00	.40
❑ 89T	Kevin Brown	.25	.08
❑ 90T	John Wetteland RC	.40	.15
❑ 91T	Gary Wayne	.05	.01
❑ 92T	Rich Monteleone	.05	.01
❑ 93T	Bob Geren RC	.05	.01
❑ 94T	Clay Parker	.05	.01
❑ 95T	Steve Finley RC	.75	.30
❑ 96T	Gregg Olson RC	.25	.08
❑ 97T	Ken Patterson	.05	.01
❑ 98T	Ken Hill RC	.25	.08
❑ 99T	Scott Scudder RC	.10	.02
❑ 100T	Ken Griffey Jr. RC	8.00	3.00
❑ 101T	Jeff Brantley RC	.25	.08
❑ 102T	Donn Pall	.05	.01
❑ 103T	Carlos Martinez RC	.10	.02
❑ 104T	Joe Oliver RC	.25	.08
❑ 105T	Omar Vizquel RC	1.00	.40
❑ 106T	Albert Belle RC	1.00	.40
❑ 107T	Kenny Rogers RC	2.00	.75
❑ 108T	Mark Carreon	.05	.01
❑ 109T	Rolando Roomes	.05	.01
❑ 110T	Pete Harnisch RC	.25	.08

1990 Score

❑ COMPLETE SET (704)		15.00	6.00
❑ COMP.RETAIL SET (704)		15.00	6.00
❑ COMP.HOBBY SET (714)		15.00	6.00
❑ 1	Don Mattingly	.60	.25
❑ 2	Cal Ripken	.75	.30

❑ 3 Dwight Evans	.15	.05
❑ 4 Barry Bonds	1.00	.40
❑ 5 Kevin McReynolds	.05	.01
❑ 6 Ozzie Guillen	.10	.02
❑ 7 Terry Kennedy	.05	.01
❑ 8 Bryan Harvey	.05	.01
❑ 9 Alan Trammell	.10	.02
❑ 10 Cory Snyder	.05	.01
❑ 11 Jody Reed	.05	.01
❑ 12 Roberto Alomar	.15	.05
❑ 13 Pedro Guerrero	.05	.01
❑ 14 Gary Redus	.05	.01
❑ 15 Marty Barrett	.05	.01
❑ 16 Ricky Jordan	.05	.01
❑ 17 Joe Magrane	.05	.01
❑ 18 Sid Fernandez	.05	.01
❑ 19 Richard Dotson	.05	.01
❑ 20 Jack Clark	.10	.02
❑ 21 Bob Walk	.05	.01
❑ 22 Ron Karkovice	.05	.01
❑ 23 Lenny Harris	.05	.01
❑ 24 Phil Bradley	.05	.01
❑ 25 Andres Galarraga	.10	.02
❑ 26 Brian Downing	.05	.01
❑ 27 Dave Martinez	.05	.01
❑ 28 Eric King	.05	.01
❑ 29 Barry Lyons	.05	.01
❑ 30 Dave Schmidt	.05	.01
❑ 31 Mike Boddicker	.05	.01
❑ 32 Tom Foley	.05	.01
❑ 33 Brady Anderson	.10	.02
❑ 34 Jim Presley	.05	.01
❑ 35 Lance Parrish	.05	.01
❑ 36 Von Hayes	.05	.01
❑ 37 Lee Smith	.10	.02
❑ 38 Herm Winningham	.05	.01
❑ 39 Alejandro Pena	.05	.01
❑ 40 Mike Scott	.05	.01
❑ 41 Joe Orsulak	.05	.01
❑ 42 Rafael Ramirez	.05	.01
❑ 43 Gerald Young	.05	.01
❑ 44 Dick Schofield	.05	.01
❑ 45 Dave Smith	.05	.01
❑ 46 Dave Magadan	.05	.01
❑ 47 Dennis Martinez	.10	.02
❑ 48 Greg Minton	.05	.01
❑ 49 Milt Thompson	.05	.01
❑ 50 Orel Hershiser	.10	.02
❑ 51 Bip Roberts	.05	.01
❑ 52 Jerry Browne	.05	.01
❑ 53 Bob Ojeda	.05	.01
❑ 54 Fernando Valenzuela	.10	.02
❑ 55 Matt Nokes	.05	.01
❑ 56 Brook Jacoby	.05	.01
❑ 57 Frank Tanana	.05	.01
❑ 58 Scott Fletcher	.05	.01
❑ 59 Ron Oester	.05	.01
❑ 60 Bob Boone	.10	.02
❑ 61 Dan Gladden	.05	.01
❑ 62 Darnell Coles	.05	.01
❑ 63 Gregg Olson	.10	.02
❑ 64 Todd Burns	.05	.01
❑ 65 Todd Benzinger	.05	.01
❑ 66 Dale Murphy	.15	.05
❑ 67 Mike Flanagan	.05	.01
❑ 68 Jose Oquendo	.05	.01
❑ 69 Cecil Espy	.05	.01
❑ 70 Chris Sabo	.05	.01
❑ 71 Shane Rawley	.05	.01
❑ 72 Tom Brunansky	.05	.01
❑ 73 Vance Law	.05	.01
❑ 74 B.J. Surhoff	.10	.02
❑ 75 Lou Whitaker	.10	.02
❑ 76 Ken Caminiti UER	.10	.02
❑ 77 Nelson Liriano	.05	.01
❑ 78 Tommy Gregg	.05	.01
❑ 79 Don Slaught	.05	.01
❑ 80 Eddie Murray	.25	.08
❑ 81 Joe Boever	.05	.01
❑ 82 Charlie Leibrandt	.05	.01
❑ 83 Jose Lind	.05	.01
❑ 84 Tony Phillips	.05	.01
❑ 85 Mitch Webster	.05	.01
❑ 86 Dan Plesac	.05	.01
❑ 87 Rick Mahler	.05	.01
❑ 88 Steve Lyons	.05	.01
❑ 89 Tony Fernandez	.05	.01
❑ 90 Ryne Sandberg	.40	.15
❑ 91 Nick Esasky	.05	.01
❑ 92 Luis Salazar	.05	.01
❑ 93 Pete Incaviglia	.05	.01
❑ 94 Ivan Calderon	.05	.01
❑ 95 Jeff Treadway	.05	.01
❑ 96 Kurt Stillwell	.05	.01
❑ 97 Gary Sheffield	.25	.08
❑ 98 Jeffrey Leonard	.05	.01
❑ 99 Andres Thomas	.05	.01
❑ 100 Roberto Kelly	.05	.01
❑ 101 Alvaro Espinoza	.05	.01
❑ 102 Greg Gagne	.05	.01
❑ 103 John Farrell	.05	.01
❑ 104 Willie Wilson	.05	.01
❑ 105 Glenn Braggs	.05	.01
❑ 106 Chet Lemon	.05	.01
❑ 107A Jamie Moyer ERR	.10	.02
❑ 107B Jamie Moyer COR	.50	.20
❑ 108 Chuck Crim	.05	.01
❑ 109 Dave Valle	.05	.01
❑ 110 Walt Weiss	.05	.01
❑ 111 Larry Sheets	.05	.01
❑ 112 Don Robinson	.05	.01
❑ 113 Danny Heep	.05	.01
❑ 114 Carmelo Martinez	.05	.01
❑ 115 Dave Gallagher	.05	.01
❑ 116 Mike LaValliere	.05	.01
❑ 117 Bob McClure	.05	.01
❑ 118 Rene Gonzales	.05	.01
❑ 119 Mark Parent	.05	.01
❑ 120 Wally Joyner	.10	.02
❑ 121 Mark Gubicza	.05	.01
❑ 122 Tony Pena	.05	.01
❑ 123 Carmelo Castillo	.05	.01
❑ 124 Howard Johnson	.05	.01
❑ 125 Steve Sax	.05	.01
❑ 126 Tim Belcher	.05	.01
❑ 127 Tim Burke	.05	.01
❑ 128 Al Newman	.05	.01
❑ 129 Dennis Rasmussen	.05	.01
❑ 130 Doug Jones	.05	.01
❑ 131 Fred Lynn	.05	.01
❑ 132 Jeff Hamilton	.05	.01
❑ 133 German Gonzalez	.05	.01
❑ 134 John Morris	.05	.01
❑ 135 Dave Parker	.10	.02
❑ 136 Gary Pettis	.05	.01
❑ 137 Dennis Boyd	.05	.01
❑ 138 Candy Maldonado	.05	.01
❑ 139 Rick Cerone	.05	.01
❑ 140 George Brett	.60	.25
❑ 141 Dave Clark	.05	.01
❑ 142 Dickie Thon	.05	.01
❑ 143 Junior Ortiz	.05	.01
❑ 144 Don August	.05	.01
❑ 145 Gary Gaetti	.10	.02
❑ 146 Kirt Manwaring	.05	.01
❑ 147 Jeff Reed	.05	.01
❑ 148 Jose Alvarez	.05	.01
❑ 149 Mike Schooler	.05	.01
❑ 150 Mark Grace	.15	.05
❑ 151 Geronimo Berroa	.05	.01
❑ 152 Barry Jones	.05	.01
❑ 153 Geno Petralli	.05	.01
❑ 154 Jim Deshaies	.05	.01
❑ 155 Barry Larkin	.15	.05
❑ 156 Alfredo Griffin	.05	.01
❑ 157 Tom Henke	.05	.01
❑ 158 Mike Jeffcoat	.05	.01
❑ 159 Bob Welch	.05	.01
❑ 160 Julio Franco	.10	.02
❑ 161 Henry Cotto	.05	.01
❑ 162 Terry Steinbach	.05	.01
❑ 163 Damon Berryhill	.05	.01
❑ 164 Tim Crews	.05	.01
❑ 165 Tom Browning	.05	.01
❑ 166 Fred Manrique	.05	.01
❑ 167 Harold Reynolds	.10	.02
❑ 168A Ron Hassey ERR (27 on back)	.05	.01
❑ 168B Ron Hassey COR	.50	.20
❑ 169 Shawon Dunston	.05	.01
❑ 170 Bobby Bonilla	.10	.02
❑ 171 Tommy Herr	.05	.01
❑ 172 Mike Heath	.05	.01
❑ 173 Rich Gedman	.05	.01
❑ 174 Bill Ripken	.05	.01
❑ 175 Pete O'Brien	.05	.01
❑ 176A Lloyd McClendon ERR (Uniform number on back list)	.05	.01
❑ 176B Lloyd McClendon COR (Uniform number on back list)	.50	.20
❑ 177 Brian Holton	.05	.01
❑ 178 Jeff Blauser	.05	.01
❑ 179 Jim Eisenreich	.05	.01
❑ 180 Bert Blyleven	.10	.02
❑ 181 Rob Murphy	.05	.01
❑ 182 Bill Doran	.05	.01
❑ 183 Curt Ford	.05	.01
❑ 184 Mike Henneman	.05	.01
❑ 185 Eric Davis	.10	.02
❑ 186 Lance McCullers	.05	.01
❑ 187 Steve Davis RC	.05	.01
❑ 188 Bill Wegman	.05	.01
❑ 189 Brian Harper	.05	.01
❑ 190 Mike Moore	.05	.01
❑ 191 Dale Mohorcic	.05	.01
❑ 192 Tim Wallach	.05	.01
❑ 193 Keith Hernandez	.10	.02
❑ 194 Dave Righetti	.05	.01
❑ 195A Bret Saberhagen ERR (Joke)	.10	.02
❑ 195B Bret Saberhagen COR (Joker)	.50	.20
❑ 196 Paul Kilgus	.05	.01
❑ 197 Bud Black	.05	.01
❑ 198 Juan Samuel	.05	.01
❑ 199 Kevin Seitzer	.05	.01
❑ 200 Darryl Strawberry	.10	.02
❑ 201 Dave Stieb	.10	.02
❑ 202 Charlie Hough	.10	.02
❑ 203 Jack Morris	.10	.02
❑ 204 Rance Mulliniks	.05	.01
❑ 205 Alvin Davis	.05	.01
❑ 206 Jack Howell	.05	.01
❑ 207 Ken Patterson	.05	.01
❑ 208 Terry Pendleton	.10	.02
❑ 209 Craig Lefferts	.05	.01
❑ 210 Kevin Brown UER (First mention of '89 Rangers sh)	.10	.02
❑ 211 Dan Petry	.05	.01
❑ 212 Dave Leiper	.05	.01
❑ 213 Daryl Boston	.05	.01
❑ 214 Kevin Hickey	.05	.01
❑ 215 Mike Krukow	.05	.01
❑ 216 Terry Francona	.10	.02
❑ 217 Kirk McCaskill	.05	.01
❑ 218 Scott Bailes	.05	.01
❑ 219 Bob Forsch	.05	.01
❑ 220A Mike Aldrete ERR (25 on back)	.05	.01
❑ 220B Mike Aldrete COR (24 on back)	.50	.20
❑ 221 Steve Buechele	.05	.01
❑ 222 Jesse Barfield	.05	.01
❑ 223 Juan Berenguer	.05	.01
❑ 224 Andy McGaffigan	.05	.01
❑ 225 Pete Smith	.05	.01
❑ 226 Mike Witt	.05	.01
❑ 227 Jay Howell	.05	.01
❑ 228 Scott Bradley	.05	.01
❑ 229 Jerome Walton	.05	.01
❑ 230 Greg Swindell	.05	.01
❑ 231 Atlee Hammaker	.05	.01
❑ 232A Mike Devereaux ERR (RF on front)	.05	.01
❑ 232B Mike Devereaux COR	.50	.20
❑ 233 Ken Hill	.10	.02
❑ 234 Craig Worthington	.05	.01
❑ 235 Scott Terry	.05	.01
❑ 236 Brett Butler	.10	.02
❑ 237 Doyle Alexander	.05	.01
❑ 238 Dave Anderson	.05	.01
❑ 239 Bob Milacki	.05	.01
❑ 240 Dwight Smith	.05	.01
❑ 241 Otis Nixon	.05	.01
❑ 242 Pat Tabler	.05	.01

❑ 243 Derek Lilliquist .05 .01
❑ 244 Danny Tartabull .05 .01
❑ 245 Wade Boggs .15 .05
❑ 246 Scott Garrelts (Should say Relief Pitcher on fro) .05 .01
❑ 247 Spike Owen .05 .01
❑ 248 Norm Charlton .05 .01
❑ 249 Gerald Perry .05 .01
❑ 250 Nolan Ryan 1.00 .40
❑ 251 Kevin Gross .05 .01
❑ 252 Randy Milligan .05 .01
❑ 253 Mike LaCoss .05 .01
❑ 254 Dave Bergman .05 .01
❑ 255 Tony Gwynn .30 .10
❑ 256 Felix Fermin .05 .01
❑ 257 Greg W. Harris .05 .01
❑ 258 Junior Felix .05 .01
❑ 259 Mark Davis .05 .01
❑ 260 Vince Coleman .05 .01
❑ 261 Paul Gibson .05 .01
❑ 262 Mitch Williams .05 .01
❑ 263 Jeff Russell .05 .01
❑ 264 Omar Vizquel .25 .08
❑ 265 Andre Dawson .10 .02
❑ 266 Storm Davis .05 .01
❑ 267 Guillermo Hernandez .05 .01
❑ 268 Mike Felder .05 .01
❑ 269 Tom Candiotti .05 .01
❑ 270 Bruce Hurst .05 .01
❑ 271 Fred McGriff .25 .08
❑ 272 Glenn Davis .05 .01
❑ 273 John Franco .10 .02
❑ 274 Rich Yett .05 .01
❑ 275 Craig Biggio .25 .08
❑ 276 Gene Larkin .05 .01
❑ 277 Rob Dibble .10 .02
❑ 278 Randy Bush .05 .01
❑ 279 Kevin Bass .05 .01
❑ 280A Bo Jackson ERR Watham .25 .08
❑ 280B Bo Jackson COR Wathan .75 .30
❑ 281 Wally Backman .05 .01
❑ 282 Larry Andersen .05 .01
❑ 283 Chris Bosio .05 .01
❑ 284 Juan Agosto .05 .01
❑ 285 Ozzie Smith .40 .15
❑ 286 George Bell .05 .01
❑ 287 Rex Hudler .05 .01
❑ 288 Pat Borders .05 .01
❑ 289 Danny Jackson .05 .01
❑ 290 Carlton Fisk .15 .05
❑ 291 Tracy Jones .05 .01
❑ 292 Allan Anderson .05 .01
❑ 293 Johnny Ray .05 .01
❑ 294 Lee Guetterman .05 .01
❑ 295 Paul O'Neill .15 .05
❑ 296 Carney Lansford .10 .02
❑ 297 Tom Brookens .05 .01
❑ 298 Claudell Washington .05 .01
❑ 299 Hubie Brooks .05 .01
❑ 300 Will Clark .15 .05
❑ 301 Kenny Rogers .10 .02
❑ 302 Darrell Evans .10 .02
❑ 303 Greg Briley .05 .01
❑ 304 Donn Pall .05 .01
❑ 305 Teddy Higuera .05 .01
❑ 306 Dan Pasqua .05 .01
❑ 307 Dave Winfield .10 .02
❑ 308 Dennis Powell .05 .01
❑ 309 Jose DeLeon .05 .01
❑ 310 Roger Clemens 1.00 .40
❑ 311 Melido Perez .05 .01
❑ 312 Devon White .10 .02
❑ 313 Dwight Gooden .10 .02
❑ 314 Carlos Martinez .05 .01
❑ 315 Dennis Eckersley .10 .02
❑ 316 Clay Parker UER (Height 6'11") .05 .01
❑ 317 Rick Honeycutt .05 .01
❑ 318 Tim Laudner .05 .01
❑ 319 Joe Carter .10 .02
❑ 320 Robin Yount .40 .15
❑ 321 Felix Jose .05 .01
❑ 322 Mickey Tettleton .05 .01
❑ 323 Mike Gallego .05 .01
❑ 324 Edgar Martinez .15 .05
❑ 325 Dave Henderson .05 .01
❑ 326 Chili Davis .10 .02
❑ 327 Steve Balboni .05 .01
❑ 328 Jody Davis .05 .01
❑ 329 Shawn Hillegas .05 .01
❑ 330 Jim Abbott .15 .05
❑ 331 John Dopson .05 .01
❑ 332 Mark Williamson .05 .01
❑ 333 Jeff D. Robinson .05 .01
❑ 334 John Smiley .05 .01
❑ 335 Bobby Thigpen .05 .01
❑ 336 Garry Templeton .05 .01
❑ 337 Marvell Wynne .05 .01
❑ 338A Ken Griffey Sr. ERR (Uniform number on back list) .10 .02
❑ 338B Ken Griffey Sr. COR .50 .20
❑ 339 Steve Finley .10 .02
❑ 340 Ellis Burks .15 .05
❑ 341 Frank Williams .05 .01
❑ 342 Mike Morgan .05 .01
❑ 343 Kevin Mitchell .05 .01
❑ 344 Joel Youngblood .05 .01
❑ 345 Mike Greenwell .05 .01
❑ 346 Glenn Wilson .05 .01
❑ 347 John Costello .05 .01
❑ 348 Wes Gardner .05 .01
❑ 349 Jeff Ballard .05 .01
❑ 350 Mark Thurmond UER (ERA is 192, should be 1.92) .05 .01
❑ 351 Randy Myers .10 .02
❑ 352 Shawn Abner .05 .01
❑ 353 Jesse Orosco .05 .01
❑ 354 Greg Walker .05 .01
❑ 355 Pete Harnisch .05 .01
❑ 356 Steve Farr .05 .01
❑ 357 Dave LaPoint .05 .01
❑ 358 Willie Fraser .05 .01
❑ 359 Mickey Hatcher .05 .01
❑ 360 Rickey Henderson .25 .08
❑ 361 Mike Fitzgerald .05 .01
❑ 362 Bill Schroeder .05 .01
❑ 363 Mark Carreon .05 .01
❑ 364 Ron Jones .05 .01
❑ 365 Jeff Montgomery .10 .02
❑ 366 Bill Krueger .05 .01
❑ 367 John Cangelosi .05 .01
❑ 368 Jose Gonzalez .05 .01
❑ 369 Greg Hibbard RC .10 .02
❑ 370 John Smoltz .25 .08
❑ 371 Jeff Brantley .05 .01
❑ 372 Frank White .10 .02
❑ 373 Ed Whitson .05 .01
❑ 374 Willie McGee .10 .02
❑ 375 Jose Canseco .15 .05
❑ 376 Randy Ready .05 .01
❑ 377 Don Aase .05 .01
❑ 378 Tony Armas .05 .01
❑ 379 Steve Bedrosian .05 .01
❑ 380 Chuck Finley .10 .02
❑ 381 Kent Hrbek .10 .02
❑ 382 Jim Gantner .05 .01
❑ 383 Mel Hall .05 .01
❑ 384 Mike Marshall .05 .01
❑ 385 Mark McGwire 1.00 .40
❑ 386 Wayne Tolleson .05 .01
❑ 387 Brian Holman .05 .01
❑ 388 John Wetteland .25 .08
❑ 389 Darren Daulton .10 .02
❑ 390 Rob Deer .05 .01
❑ 391 John Moses .05 .01
❑ 392 Todd Worrell .05 .01
❑ 393 Chuck Cary .05 .01
❑ 394 Stan Javier .05 .01
❑ 395 Willie Randolph .10 .02
❑ 396 Bill Buckner .05 .01
❑ 397 Robby Thompson .05 .01
❑ 398 Mike Scioscia .05 .01
❑ 399 Lonnie Smith .05 .01
❑ 400 Kirby Puckett .25 .08
❑ 401 Mark Langston .05 .01
❑ 402 Danny Darwin .05 .01
❑ 403 Greg Maddux .40 .15
❑ 404 Lloyd Moseby .05 .01
❑ 405 Rafael Palmeiro .15 .05
❑ 406 Chad Kreuter .05 .01
❑ 407 Jimmy Key .10 .02
❑ 408 Tim Birtsas .05 .01
❑ 409 Tim Raines .10 .02
❑ 410 Dave Stewart .10 .02
❑ 411 Eric Yelding RC .05 .01
❑ 412 Kent Anderson .05 .01
❑ 413 Les Lancaster .05 .01
❑ 414 Rick Dempsey .05 .01
❑ 415 Randy Johnson .50 .20
❑ 416 Gary Carter .10 .02
❑ 417 Rolando Roomes .05 .01
❑ 418 Dan Schatzeder .05 .01
❑ 419 Bryn Smith .05 .01
❑ 420 Ruben Sierra .10 .02
❑ 421 Steve Jeltz .05 .01
❑ 422 Ken Oberkfell .05 .01
❑ 423 Sid Bream .05 .01
❑ 424 Jim Clancy .05 .01
❑ 425 Kelly Gruber .05 .01
❑ 426 Rick Leach .05 .01
❑ 427 Len Dykstra .10 .02
❑ 428 Jeff Pico .05 .01
❑ 429 John Cerutti .05 .01
❑ 430 David Cone .10 .02
❑ 431 Jeff Kunkel .05 .01
❑ 432 Luis Aquino .05 .01
❑ 433 Ernie Whitt .05 .01
❑ 434 Bo Diaz .05 .01
❑ 435 Steve Lake .05 .01
❑ 436 Pat Perry .05 .01
❑ 437 Mike Davis .05 .01
❑ 438 Cecilio Guante .05 .01
❑ 439 Duane Ward .05 .01
❑ 440 Andy Van Slyke .15 .05
❑ 441 Gene Nelson .05 .01
❑ 442 Luis Polonia .05 .01
❑ 443 Kevin Elster .05 .01
❑ 444 Keith Moreland .05 .01
❑ 445 Roger McDowell .05 .01
❑ 446 Ron Darling .05 .01
❑ 447 Ernest Riles .05 .01
❑ 448 Mookie Wilson .10 .02
❑ 449A Billy Spiers ERR (No birth year) .05 .01
❑ 449B Billy Spiers COR (Born in 1966) .50 .20
❑ 450 Rick Sutcliffe .10 .02
❑ 451 Nelson Santovenia .05 .01
❑ 452 Andy Allanson .05 .01
❑ 453 Bob Melvin .05 .01
❑ 454 Benito Santiago .10 .02
❑ 455 Jose Uribe .05 .01
❑ 456 Bill Landrum .05 .01
❑ 457 Bobby Witt .05 .01
❑ 458 Kevin Romine .05 .01
❑ 459 Lee Mazzilli .05 .01
❑ 460 Paul Molitor .10 .02
❑ 461 Ramon Martinez .05 .01
❑ 462 Frank DiPino .05 .01
❑ 463 Walt Terrell .05 .01
❑ 464 Bob Geren .05 .01
❑ 465 Rick Reuschel .05 .01
❑ 466 Mark Grant .05 .01
❑ 467 John Kruk .10 .02
❑ 468 Gregg Jefferies .10 .02
❑ 469 R.J. Reynolds .05 .01
❑ 470 Harold Baines .10 .02
❑ 471 Dennis Lamp .05 .01
❑ 472 Tom Gordon .10 .02
❑ 473 Terry Puhl .05 .01
❑ 474 Curt Wilkerson .05 .01
❑ 475 Dan Quisenberry .05 .01
❑ 476 Oddibe McDowell .05 .01
❑ 477A Zane Smith ERR .05 .01
❑ 477B Zane Smith COR .50 .20
❑ 478 Franklin Stubbs .05 .01
❑ 479 Wallace Johnson .05 .01
❑ 480 Jay Tibbs .05 .01
❑ 481 Tom Glavine .15 .05
❑ 482 Manny Lee .05 .01
❑ 483 Joe Hesketh UER (Says Rookiess on back& should s) .05 .01
❑ 484 Mike Bielecki .05 .01
❑ 485 Greg Brock .05 .01

❑ 486 Pascual Perez .05 .01
❑ 487 Kirk Gibson .10 .02
❑ 488 Scott Sanderson .05 .01
❑ 489 Domingo Ramos .05 .01
❑ 490 Kal Daniels .05 .01
❑ 491A David Wells ERR .10 .02
❑ 491B David Wells COR .50 .20
❑ 492 Jerry Reed .05 .01
❑ 493 Eric Show .05 .01
❑ 494 Mike Pagliarulo .05 .01
❑ 495 Ron Robinson .05 .01
❑ 496 Brad Komminsk .05 .01
❑ 497 Greg Litton .05 .01
❑ 498 Chris James .05 .01
❑ 499 Luis Quinones .05 .01
❑ 500 Frank Viola .05 .01
❑ 501 Tim Teufel UER (Twins '85& the s is lower case&) .05 .01
❑ 502 Terry Leach .05 .01
❑ 503 Matt Williams .10 .02
❑ 504 Tim Leary .05 .01
❑ 505 Doug Drabek .05 .01
❑ 506 Mariano Duncan .05 .01
❑ 507 Charlie Hayes .05 .01
❑ 508 Albert Belle .25 .08
❑ 509 Pat Sheridan .05 .01
❑ 510 Mackey Sasser .05 .01
❑ 511 Jose Rijo .05 .01
❑ 512 Mike Smithson .05 .01
❑ 513 Gary Ward .05 .01
❑ 514 Dion James .05 .01
❑ 515 Jim Gott .05 .01
❑ 516 Drew Hall .05 .01
❑ 517 Doug Bair .05 .01
❑ 518 Scott Scudder .05 .01
❑ 519 Rick Aguilera .10 .02
❑ 520 Rafael Belliard .05 .01
❑ 521 Jay Buhner .10 .02
❑ 522 Jeff Reardon .10 .02
❑ 523 Steve Rosenberg .05 .01
❑ 524 Randy Velarde .05 .01
❑ 525 Jeff Musselman .05 .01
❑ 526 Bill Long .05 .01
❑ 527 Gary Wayne .05 .01
❑ 528 Dave Wayne Johnson RC .05 .01
❑ 529 Ron Kittle .05 .01
❑ 530 Erik Hanson UER (5th line on back says seson& sh) .05 .01
❑ 531 Steve Wilson .05 .01
❑ 532 Joey Meyer .05 .01
❑ 533 Curt Young .05 .01
❑ 534 Kelly Downs .05 .01
❑ 535 Joe Girardi .15 .05
❑ 536 Lance Blankenship .05 .01
❑ 537 Greg Mathews .05 .01
❑ 538 Donell Nixon .05 .01
❑ 539 Mark Knudson .05 .01
❑ 540 Jeff Wetherby RC .05 .01
❑ 541 Darrin Jackson .05 .01
❑ 542 Terry Mulholland .05 .01
❑ 543 Eric Hetzel .05 .01
❑ 544 Rick Reed RC .25 .08
❑ 545 Dennis Cook .05 .01
❑ 546 Mike Jackson .05 .01
❑ 547 Brian Fisher .05 .01
❑ 548 Gene Harris .05 .01
❑ 549 Jeff King .05 .01
❑ 550 Dave Dravecky .25 .08
❑ 551 Randy Kutcher .05 .01
❑ 552 Mark Portugal .05 .01
❑ 553 Jim Corsi .05 .01
❑ 554 Todd Stottlemyre .10 .02
❑ 555 Scott Bankhead .05 .01
❑ 556 Ken Dayley .05 .01
❑ 557 Rick Wrona .05 .01
❑ 558 Sammy Sosa RC 2.50 1.00
❑ 559 Keith Miller .05 .01
❑ 560 Ken Griffey Jr. .75 .30
❑ 561A R.Sandberg HL ERR 3B 8.00 3.00
❑ 561B R.Sandberg HL COR .25 .08
❑ 562 Billy Hatcher .05 .01
❑ 563 Jay Bell .10 .02
❑ 564 Jack Daugherty RC .05 .01
❑ 565 Rich Monteleone .05 .01
❑ 566 Bo Jackson AS-MVP .10 .02
❑ 567 Tony Fossas RC .05 .01
❑ 568 Roy Smith .05 .01
❑ 569 Jaime Navarro .05 .01
❑ 570 Lance Johnson .05 .01
❑ 571 Mike Dyer RC .05 .01
❑ 572 Kevin Ritz RC .05 .01
❑ 573 Dave West .05 .01
❑ 574 Gary Mielke RC .05 .01
❑ 575 Scott Lusader .05 .01
❑ 576 Joe Oliver .05 .01
❑ 577 Sandy Alomar Jr. .10 .02
❑ 578 Andy Benes UER .10 .02
❑ 579 Tim Jones .05 .01
❑ 580 Randy McCament RC .05 .01
❑ 581 Curt Schilling 1.00 .40
❑ 582 John Orton RC .10 .02
❑ 583A Milt Cuyler ERR RC .10 .02
❑ 583B Milt Cuyler COR .50 .20
❑ 584 Eric Anthony RC .10 .02
❑ 585 Greg Vaughn .05 .01
❑ 586 Deion Sanders .25 .08
❑ 587 Jose DeJesus .05 .01
❑ 588 Chip Hale RC .05 .01
❑ 589 John Olerud RC .50 .20
❑ 590 Steve Olin RC .25 .08
❑ 591 Marquis Grissom RC .40 .15
❑ 592 Moises Alou RC .75 .30
❑ 593 Mark Lemke .05 .01
❑ 594 Dean Palmer RC .25 .08
❑ 595 Robin Ventura .25 .08
❑ 596 Tino Martinez .50 .20
❑ 597 Mike Huff RC .05 .01
❑ 598 Scott Hemond RC .10 .02
❑ 599 Wally Whitehurst .05 .01
❑ 600 Todd Zeile .10 .02
❑ 601 Glenallen Hill .05 .01
❑ 602 Hal Morris .05 .01
❑ 603 Juan Bell .05 .01
❑ 604 Bobby Rose .05 .01
❑ 605 Matt Merullo .05 .01
❑ 606 Kevin Maas RC .25 .08
❑ 607 Randy Nosek RC .05 .01
❑ 608A Billy Bates RC .05 .01
❑ 608B Billy Bates (Text has no mention of triples) .05 .01
❑ 609 Mike Stanton RC .25 .08
❑ 610 Mauro Gozzo RC .05 .01
❑ 611 Charles Nagy .05 .01
❑ 612 Scott Coolbaugh RC .05 .01
❑ 613 Jose Vizcaino RC .25 .08
❑ 614 Greg Smith RC .05 .01
❑ 615 Jeff Huson RC .10 .02
❑ 616 Mickey Weston RC .05 .01
❑ 617 John Pawlowski .05 .01
❑ 618A Joe Skalski ERR (27 on back) .05 .01
❑ 618B Joe Skalski COR .50 .20
❑ 619 Bernie Williams RC 1.50 .60
❑ 620 Shawn Holman RC .05 .01
❑ 621 Gary Eave RC .05 .01
❑ 622 Darrin Fletcher UER RC .10 .02
❑ 623 Pat Combs .05 .01
❑ 624 Mike Blowers RC .10 .02
❑ 625 Kevin Appier .10 .02
❑ 626 Pat Austin .05 .01
❑ 627 Kelly Mann RC .05 .01
❑ 628 Matt Kinzer RC .05 .01
❑ 629 Chris Hammond RC .10 .02
❑ 630 Dean Wilkins RC .05 .01
❑ 631 Larry Walker RC 1.00 .40
❑ 632 Blaine Beatty RC .05 .01
❑ 633A Tommy Barrett ERR .05 .01
❑ 633B Tommy Barrett COR .50 .20
❑ 634 Stan Belinda RC .10 .02
❑ 635 Mike (Texas) Smith RC .05 .01
❑ 636 Hensley Meulens .05 .01
❑ 637 Juan Gonzalez RC 1.00 .40
❑ 638 Lenny Webster RC .10 .02
❑ 639 Mark Gardner RC .10 .02
❑ 640 Tommy Greene RC .10 .02
❑ 641 Mike Hartley RC .05 .01
❑ 642 Phil Stephenson .05 .01
❑ 643 Kevin Mmahat RC .05 .01
❑ 644 Ed Whited RC .05 .01
❑ 645 Delino DeShields RC .25 .08
❑ 646 Kevin Blankenship .05 .01
❑ 647 Paul Sorrento RC .25 .08
❑ 648 Mike Roesler RC .05 .01
❑ 649 Jason Grimsley RC .10 .02
❑ 650 David Justice RC .50 .20
❑ 651 Scott Cooper RC .10 .02
❑ 652 Dave Eiland .05 .01
❑ 653 Mike Munoz RC .05 .01
❑ 654 Jeff Fischer RC .05 .01
❑ 655 Terry Jorgensen RC .05 .01
❑ 656 George Canale RC .05 .01
❑ 657 Brian DuBois UER RC .05 .01
❑ 658 Carlos Quintana .05 .01
❑ 659 Luis de los Santos .05 .01
❑ 660 Jerald Clark .05 .01
❑ 661 Donald Harris RC .05 .01
❑ 662 Paul Coleman RC .10 .02
❑ 663 Frank Thomas RC 2.00 .75
❑ 664 Brent Mayne RC .25 .08
❑ 665 Eddie Zosky RC .10 .02
❑ 666 Steve Hosey RC .10 .02
❑ 667 Scott Bryant RC .10 .02
❑ 668 Tom Goodwin RC .25 .08
❑ 669 Cal Eldred RC .25 .08
❑ 670 Earl Cunningham RC .10 .02
❑ 671 Alan Zinter RC .10 .02
❑ 672 Chuck Knoblauch RC .40 .15
❑ 673 Kyle Abbott RC .05 .01
❑ 674 Roger Salkeld RC .05 .01
❑ 675 Mo Vaughn RC .50 .20
❑ 676 Keith (Kiki) Jones RC .05 .01
❑ 677 Tyler Houston RC .25 .08
❑ 678 Jeff Jackson RC .10 .02
❑ 679 Greg Gohr RC .10 .02
❑ 680 Ben McDonald RC .25 .08
❑ 681 Greg Blosser RC .10 .02
❑ 682 Willie Greene RC .25 .08
❑ 683A Wade Boggs DT ERR .10 .02
❑ 683B Wade Boggs DT COR .50 .20
❑ 684 Will Clark DT .10 .02
❑ 685 Tony Gwynn DT .15 .05
❑ 686 Rickey Henderson DT .15 .05
❑ 687 Bo Jackson DT .10 .02
❑ 688 Mark Langston DT .05 .01
❑ 689 Barry Larkin DT .10 .02
❑ 690 Kirby Puckett DT .15 .05
❑ 691 Ryne Sandberg DT .25 .08
❑ 692 Mike Scott DT .05 .01
❑ 693A Terry Steinbach DT ERR (cathers) .05 .01
❑ 693B Terry Steinbach DT COR (catchers) .05 .01
❑ 694 Bobby Thigpen DT .05 .01
❑ 695 Mitch Williams DT .05 .01
❑ 696 Nolan Ryan HL .40 .15
❑ 697 Bo Jackson FB/BB .50 .20
❑ 698 Rickey Henderson ALCS .15 .05
❑ 699 Will Clark NLCS .10 .02
❑ 700 WS Games 1/2 (Dave Stewart Mike Moore) .10 .02
❑ 701 Candlestick/Earthquake .25 .08
❑ 702 WS Game 3 .15 .05
❑ 703 WS Game 4/Wrap-up (A's Sweep Battle of the Bay) .05 .01
❑ 704 Wade Boggs HL .10 .02

1991 Score

❑ COMPLETE SET (893) 20.00 8.00
❑ COMP.FACT.SET (900) 25.00 10.00
❑ 1 Jose Canseco .15 .05
❑ 2 Ken Griffey Jr. .50 .20
❑ 3 Ryne Sandberg .40 .15
❑ 4 Nolan Ryan 1.00 .40
❑ 5 Bo Jackson .25 .08
❑ 6 Bret Saberhagen UER (In bio& missed misspelled a) .05 .01
❑ 7 Will Clark .15 .05
❑ 8 Ellis Burks .10 .02
❑ 9 Joe Carter .10 .02
❑ 10 Rickey Henderson .25 .08
❑ 11 Ozzie Guillen .10 .02
❑ 12 Wade Boggs .15 .05

❑ 13 Jerome Walton .05 .01
❑ 14 John Franco .10 .02
❑ 15 Ricky Jordan UER
(League misspelled
as legue) .05 .01
❑ 16 Wally Backman .05 .01
❑ 17 Rob Dibble .10 .02
❑ 18 Glenn Braggs .05 .01
❑ 19 Cory Snyder .05 .01
❑ 20 Kal Daniels .05 .01
❑ 21 Mark Langston .05 .01
❑ 22 Kevin Gross .05 .01
❑ 23 Don Mattingly .60 .25
❑ 24 Dave Righetti .10 .02
❑ 25 Roberto Alomar .15 .05
❑ 26 Robby Thompson .05 .01
❑ 27 Jack McDowell .05 .01
❑ 28 Bip Roberts UER
(Bio reads playd) .05 .01
❑ 29 Jay Howell .05 .01
❑ 30 Dave Stieb UER
(17 wins in bio&
18 in stats) .05 .01
❑ 31 Johnny Ray .05 .01
❑ 32 Steve Sax .05 .01
❑ 33 Terry Mulholland .05 .01
❑ 34 Lee Guetterman .05 .01
❑ 35 Tim Raines .10 .02
❑ 36 Scott Fletcher .05 .01
❑ 37 Lance Parrish .10 .02
❑ 38 Tony Phillips UER
(Born 4/15&
should be 4/25) .05 .01
❑ 39 Todd Stottlemyre .05 .01
❑ 40 Alan Trammell .10 .02
❑ 41 Todd Burns .05 .01
❑ 42 Mookie Wilson .10 .02
❑ 43 Chris Bosio .05 .01
❑ 44 Jeffrey Leonard .05 .01
❑ 45 Doug Jones .05 .01
❑ 46 Mike Scott UER .05 .01
❑ 47 Andy Hawkins .05 .01
❑ 48 Harold Reynolds .10 .02
❑ 49 Paul Molitor .10 .02
❑ 50 John Farrell .05 .01
❑ 51 Danny Darwin .05 .01
❑ 52 Jeff Blauser .05 .01
❑ 53 John Tudor UER
(41 wins in '81) .05 .01
❑ 54 Milt Thompson .05 .01
❑ 55 David Justice .10 .02
❑ 56 Greg Olson .05 .01
❑ 57 Willie Blair .05 .01
❑ 58 Rick Parker .05 .01
❑ 59 Shawn Boskie .05 .01
❑ 60 Kevin Tapani .05 .01
❑ 61 Dave Hollins .05 .01
❑ 62 Scott Radinsky .05 .01
❑ 63 Francisco Cabrera .05 .01
❑ 64 Tim Layana .05 .01
❑ 65 Jim Leyritz .05 .01
❑ 66 Wayne Edwards .05 .01
❑ 67 Lee Stevens .05 .01
❑ 68 Bill Sampen UER
(Fourth line& long
is spelled al) .05 .01
❑ 69 Craig Grebeck UER
(Born in Cerritos&
not Johnsto) .05 .01
❑ 70 John Burkett .05 .01
❑ 71 Hector Villanueva .05 .01
❑ 72 Oscar Azocar .05 .01
❑ 73 Alan Mills .05 .01
❑ 74 Carlos Baerga .05 .01
❑ 75 Charles Nagy .05 .01
❑ 76 Tim Drummond .05 .01
❑ 77 Dana Kiecker .05 .01
❑ 78 Tom Edens RC .05 .01
❑ 79 Kent Mercker .05 .01
❑ 80 Steve Avery .05 .01
❑ 81 Lee Smith .10 .02
❑ 82 Dave Martinez .05 .01
❑ 83 Dave Winfield .10 .02
❑ 84 Bill Spiers .05 .01
❑ 85 Dan Pasqua .05 .01
❑ 86 Randy Milligan .05 .01
❑ 87 Tracy Jones .05 .01
❑ 88 Greg Myers .05 .01
❑ 89 Keith Hernandez .10 .02
❑ 90 Todd Benzinger .05 .01
❑ 91 Mike Jackson .05 .01
❑ 92 Mike Stanley .05 .01
❑ 93 Candy Maldonado .05 .01
❑ 94 John Kruk UER .10 .02
❑ 95 Cal Ripken .75 .30
❑ 96 Willie Fraser .05 .01
❑ 97 Mike Felder .05 .01
❑ 98 Bill Landrum .05 .01
❑ 99 Chuck Crim .05 .01
❑ 100 Chuck Finley .10 .02
❑ 101 Kirt Manwaring .05 .01
❑ 102 Jaime Navarro .05 .01
❑ 103 Dickie Thon .05 .01
❑ 104 Brian Downing .05 .01
❑ 105 Jim Abbott .15 .05
❑ 106 Tom Brookens .05 .01
❑ 107 Darryl Hamilton UER
(Bio info is for
Jeff Hamilt) .05 .01
❑ 108 Bryan Harvey .05 .01
❑ 109 Greg A. Harris UER
(Shown pitching lefty&
bio sa) .05 .01
❑ 110 Greg Swindell .05 .01
❑ 111 Juan Berenguer .05 .01
❑ 112 Mike Heath .05 .01
❑ 113 Scott Bradley .05 .01
❑ 114 Jack Morris .10 .02
❑ 115 Barry Jones .05 .01
❑ 116 Kevin Romine .05 .01
❑ 117 Garry Templeton .05 .01
❑ 118 Scott Sanderson .05 .01
❑ 119 Roberto Kelly .05 .01
❑ 120 George Brett .60 .25
❑ 121 Oddibe McDowell .05 .01
❑ 122 Jim Acker .05 .01
❑ 123 Bill Swift UER
(Born 12/27/61,
should be 10/27) .05 .01
❑ 124 Eric King .05 .01
❑ 125 Jay Buhner .10 .02
❑ 126 Matt Young .05 .01
❑ 127 Alvaro Espinoza .05 .01
❑ 128 Greg Hibbard .05 .01
❑ 129 Jeff M. Robinson .05 .01
❑ 130 Mike Greenwell .05 .01
❑ 131 Dion James .05 .01
❑ 132 Donn Pall UER
(1988 ERA in stats 0.00) .05 .01
❑ 133 Lloyd Moseby .05 .01
❑ 134 Randy Velarde .05 .01
❑ 135 Allan Anderson .05 .01
❑ 136 Mark Davis .05 .01
❑ 137 Eric Davis .10 .02
❑ 138 Phil Stephenson .05 .01
❑ 139 Felix Fermin .05 .01
❑ 140 Pedro Guerrero .10 .02
❑ 141 Charlie Hough .10 .02
❑ 142 Mike Henneman .05 .01
❑ 143 Jeff Montgomery .05 .01
❑ 144 Lenny Harris .05 .01
❑ 145 Bruce Hurst .05 .01
❑ 146 Eric Anthony .05 .01
❑ 147 Paul Assenmacher .05 .01
❑ 148 Jesse Barfield .05 .01
❑ 149 Carlos Quintana .05 .01
❑ 150 Dave Stewart .10 .02
❑ 151 Roy Smith .05 .01
❑ 152 Paul Gibson .05 .01
❑ 153 Mickey Hatcher .05 .01
❑ 154 Jim Eisenreich .05 .01
❑ 155 Kenny Rogers .10 .02
❑ 156 Dave Schmidt .05 .01
❑ 157 Lance Johnson .05 .01
❑ 158 Dave West .05 .01
❑ 159 Steve Balboni .05 .01
❑ 160 Jeff Brantley .05 .01
❑ 161 Craig Biggio .15 .05
❑ 162 Brook Jacoby .05 .01
❑ 163 Dan Gladden .05 .01
❑ 164 Jeff Reardon UER .10 .02
❑ 165 Mark Carreon .05 .01
❑ 166 Mel Hall .05 .01
❑ 167 Gary Mielke .05 .01
❑ 168 Cecil Fielder .10 .02
❑ 169 Darrin Jackson .05 .01
❑ 170 Rick Aguilera .10 .02
❑ 171 Walt Weiss .05 .01
❑ 172 Steve Farr .05 .01
❑ 173 Jody Reed .05 .01
❑ 174 Mike Jeffcoat .05 .01
❑ 175 Mark Grace .15 .05
❑ 176 Larry Sheets .05 .01
❑ 177 Bill Gullickson .05 .01
❑ 178 Chris Gwynn .05 .01
❑ 179 Melido Perez .05 .01
❑ 180 Sid Fernandez UER
(779 runs in 1990) .05 .01
❑ 181 Tim Burke .05 .01
❑ 182 Gary Pettis .05 .01
❑ 183 Rob Murphy .05 .01
❑ 184 Craig Lefferts .05 .01
❑ 185 Howard Johnson .05 .01
❑ 186 Ken Caminiti .10 .02
❑ 187 Tim Belcher .05 .01
❑ 188 Greg Cadaret .05 .01
❑ 189 Matt Williams .10 .02
❑ 190 Dave Magadan .05 .01
❑ 191 Geno Petralli .05 .01
❑ 192 Jeff D. Robinson .05 .01
❑ 193 Jim Deshaies .05 .01
❑ 194 Willie Randolph .10 .02
❑ 195 George Bell .05 .01
❑ 196 Hubie Brooks .05 .01
❑ 197 Tom Gordon .05 .01
❑ 198 Mike Fitzgerald .05 .01
❑ 199 Mike Pagliarulo .05 .01
❑ 200 Kirby Puckett .25 .08
❑ 201 Shawon Dunston .05 .01
❑ 202 Dennis Boyd .05 .01
❑ 203 Junior Felix UER
(Text has him in NL) .05 .01
❑ 204 Alejandro Pena .05 .01
❑ 205 Pete Smith .05 .01
❑ 206 Tom Glavine .15 .05
❑ 207 Luis Salazar .05 .01
❑ 208 John Smoltz .15 .05
❑ 209 Doug Dascenzo .05 .01
❑ 210 Tim Wallach .05 .01
❑ 211 Greg Gagne .05 .01
❑ 212 Mark Gubicza .05 .01
❑ 213 Mark Parent .05 .01
❑ 214 Ken Oberkfell .05 .01
❑ 215 Gary Carter .10 .02
❑ 216 Rafael Palmeiro .15 .05
❑ 217 Tom Niedenfuer .05 .01
❑ 218 Dave LaPoint .05 .01
❑ 219 Jeff Treadway .05 .01
❑ 220 Mitch Williams UER
('89 ERA shown as 2.76&
shoul) .05 .01
❑ 221 Jose DeLeon .05 .01
❑ 222 Mike LaValliere .05 .01
❑ 223 Darrel Akerfelds .05 .01
❑ 224A Kent Anderson ERR
(First line& flachy
should rea) .10 .02
❑ 224B Kent Anderson COR
(Corrected in
factory sets) .10 .02

❑ 225 Dwight Evans .15 .05
❑ 226 Gary Redus .05 .01
❑ 227 Paul O'Neill .15 .05
❑ 228 Marty Barrett .05 .01
❑ 229 Tom Browning .05 .01
❑ 230 Terry Pendleton .10 .02
❑ 231 Jack Armstrong .05 .01
❑ 232 Mike Boddicker .05 .01
❑ 233 Neal Heaton .05 .01
❑ 234 Marquis Grissom .10 .02
❑ 235 Bert Blyleven .10 .02
❑ 236 Curt Young .05 .01
❑ 237 Don Carman .05 .01
❑ 238 Charlie Hayes .05 .01
❑ 239 Mark Knudson .05 .01
❑ 240 Todd Zeile .05 .01
❑ 241 Larry Walker .25 .08
❑ 242 Jerald Clark .05 .01
❑ 243 Jeff Ballard .05 .01
❑ 244 Jeff King .05 .01
❑ 245 Tom Brunansky .05 .01
❑ 246 Darren Daulton .10 .02
❑ 247 Scott Terry .05 .01
❑ 248 Rob Deer .05 .01
❑ 249 Brady Anderson UER .10 .02
❑ 250 Len Dykstra .10 .02
❑ 251 Greg W. Harris .05 .01
❑ 252 Mike Hartley .05 .01
❑ 253 Joey Cora .05 .01
❑ 254 Ivan Calderon .05 .01
❑ 255 Ted Power .05 .01
❑ 256 Sammy Sosa .25 .08
❑ 257 Steve Buechele .05 .01
❑ 258 Mike Devereaux UER
(No comma between
city and st .05 .01
❑ 259 Brad Komminsk UER
(Last text line&
Ba should be .05 .01
❑ 260 Ted Higuera .05 .01
❑ 261 Shawn Abner .05 .01
❑ 262 Dave Valle .05 .01
❑ 263 Jeff Huson .05 .01
❑ 264 Edgar Martinez .15 .05
❑ 265 Carlton Fisk .15 .05
❑ 266 Steve Finley .10 .02
❑ 267 John Wetteland .10 .02
❑ 268 Kevin Appier .10 .02
❑ 269 Steve Lyons .05 .01
❑ 270 Mickey Tettleton .05 .01
❑ 271 Luis Rivera .05 .01
❑ 272 Steve Jeltz .05 .01
❑ 273 R.J. Reynolds .05 .01
❑ 274 Carlos Martinez .05 .01
❑ 275 Dan Plesac .05 .01
❑ 276 Mike Morgan UER
(Total IP shown as
1149.1& shoul .05 .01
❑ 277 Jeff Russell .05 .01
❑ 278 Pete Incaviglia .05 .01
❑ 279 Kevin Seitzer UER
(Bio has 200 hits twice
and .3 .05 .01
❑ 280 Bobby Thigpen .05 .01
❑ 281 Stan Javier UER
(Born 1/9,
should say 9/1) .05 .01
❑ 282 Henry Cotto .05 .01
❑ 283 Gary Wayne .05 .01
❑ 284 Shane Mack .05 .01
❑ 285 Brian Holman .05 .01
❑ 286 Gerald Perry .05 .01
❑ 287 Steve Crawford .05 .01
❑ 288 Nelson Liriano .05 .01
❑ 289 Don Aase .05 .01
❑ 290 Randy Johnson .30 .10
❑ 291 Harold Baines .10 .02
❑ 292 Kent Hrbek .10 .02
❑ 293A Les Lancaster ERR
(No comma between
Dallas and T .05 .01
❑ 293B Les Lancaster COR
(Corrected in
factory sets) .05 .01
❑ 294 Jeff Musselman .05 .01
❑ 295 Kurt Stillwell .05 .01
❑ 296 Stan Belinda .05 .01
❑ 297 Lou Whitaker .10 .02
❑ 298 Glenn Wilson .05 .01
❑ 299 Omar Vizquel UER .15 .05
❑ 300 Ramon Martinez .05 .01
❑ 301 Dwight Smith .05 .01
❑ 302 Tim Crews .05 .01
❑ 303 Lance Blankenship .05 .01
❑ 304 Sid Bream .05 .01
❑ 305 Rafael Ramirez .05 .01
❑ 306 Steve Wilson .05 .01
❑ 307 Mackey Sasser .05 .01
❑ 308 Franklin Stubbs .05 .01
❑ 309 Jack Daugherty UER
(Born 6/3/60,
should say July .05 .01
❑ 310 Eddie Murray .25 .08
❑ 311 Bob Welch .05 .01
❑ 312 Brian Harper .05 .01
❑ 313 Lance McCullers .05 .01
❑ 314 Dave Smith .05 .01
❑ 315 Bobby Bonilla .10 .02
❑ 316 Jerry Don Gleaton .05 .01
❑ 317 Greg Maddux .40 .15
❑ 318 Keith Miller .05 .01
❑ 319 Mark Portugal .05 .01
❑ 320 Robin Ventura .10 .02
❑ 321 Bob Ojeda .05 .01
❑ 322 Mike Harkey .05 .01
❑ 323 Jay Bell .10 .02
❑ 324 Mark McGwire .75 .30
❑ 325 Gary Gaetti .10 .02
❑ 326 Jeff Pico .05 .01
❑ 327 Kevin McReynolds .05 .01
❑ 328 Frank Tanana .05 .01
❑ 329 Eric Yelding UER
(Listed as 6'3"
should be 5'11 .05 .01
❑ 330 Barry Bonds 1.00 .40
❑ 331 Brian McRae RC .25 .08
❑ 332 Pedro Munoz RC .10 .02
❑ 333 Daryl Irvine RC .05 .01
❑ 334 Chris Hoiles .05 .01
❑ 335 Thomas Howard .05 .01
❑ 336 Jeff Schulz RC .05 .01
❑ 337 Jeff Manto .05 .01
❑ 338 Beau Allred .05 .01
❑ 339 Mike Bordick RC .40 .15
❑ 340 Todd Hundley .05 .01
❑ 341 Jim Vatcher UER RC .05 .01
❑ 342 Luis Sojo .05 .01
❑ 343 Jose Offerman UER .05 .01
❑ 344 Pete Coachman RC .05 .01
❑ 345 Mike Benjamin .05 .01
❑ 346 Ozzie Canseco .05 .01
❑ 347 Tim McIntosh .05 .01
❑ 348 Phil Plantier RC .10 .02
❑ 349 Terry Shumpert .05 .01
❑ 350 Darren Lewis FSC .05 .01
❑ 351 David Walsh RC .05 .01
❑ 352A Scott Chiamparino
ERR (Bats left&
should be righ .10 .02
❑ 352B Scott Chiamparino
COR (corrected in
factory sets .10 .02
❑ 353 Julio Valera
UER (Progressed mis
spelled as pro .05 .01
❑ 354 Anthony Telford RC .05 .01
❑ 355 Kevin Wickander .05 .01
❑ 356 Tim Naehring .05 .01
❑ 357 Jim Poole .05 .01
❑ 358 Mark Whiten FSC UER .05 .01
❑ 359 Terry Wells RC .05 .01
❑ 360 Rafael Valdez .05 .01
❑ 361 Mel Stottlemyre Jr. .05 .01
❑ 362 David Segui .05 .01
❑ 363 Paul Abbott RC .05 .01
❑ 364 Steve Howard .05 .01
❑ 365 Karl Rhodes .05 .01
❑ 366 Rafael Novoa RC .05 .01
❑ 367 Joe Grahe RC .05 .01
❑ 368 Darren Reed .05 .01
❑ 369 Jeff McKnight .05 .01
❑ 370 Scott Leius .05 .01
❑ 371 Mark Dewey RC .05 .01
❑ 372 Mark Lee UER RC .10 .02
❑ 373 Rosario Rodriguez UER RC .05 .01
❑ 374 Chuck McElroy .05 .01
❑ 375 Mike Bell RC .05 .01
❑ 376 Mickey Morandini .05 .01
❑ 377 Bill Haselman RC .05 .01
❑ 378 Dave Pavlas RC .05 .01
❑ 379 Derrick May .05 .01
❑ 380 Jeromy Burnitz RC .40 .15
❑ 381 Donald Peters RC .05 .01
❑ 382 Alex Fernandez .05 .01
❑ 383 Mike Mussina RC 2.00 .75
❑ 384 Dan Smith RC .10 .02
❑ 385 Lance Dickson RC .10 .02
❑ 386 Carl Everett RC .50 .20
❑ 387 Tom Nevers RC .10 .02
❑ 388 Adam Hyzdu RC .25 .08
❑ 389 Todd Van Poppel RC .25 .08
❑ 390 Rondell White RC .40 .15
❑ 391 Marc Newfield RC .10 .02
❑ 392 Julio Franco AS .05 .01
❑ 393 Wade Boggs AS .10 .02
❑ 394 Ozzie Guillen AS .05 .01
❑ 395 Cecil Fielder AS .05 .01
❑ 396 Ken Griffey Jr. AS .25 .08
❑ 397 Rickey Henderson AS .15 .05
❑ 398 Jose Canseco AS .10 .02
❑ 399 Roger Clemens AS .40 .15
❑ 400 Sandy Alomar Jr. AS .05 .01
❑ 401 Bobby Thigpen AS .05 .01
❑ 402 Bobby Bonilla MB .05 .01
❑ 403 Eric Davis MB .05 .01
❑ 404 Fred McGriff MB .10 .02
❑ 405 Glenn Davis MB .05 .01
❑ 406 Kevin Mitchell MB .05 .01
❑ 407 Rob Dibble KM .05 .01
❑ 408 Ramon Martinez KM .05 .01
❑ 409 David Cone KM .05 .01
❑ 410 Bobby Witt KM .05 .01
❑ 411 Mark Langston KM .05 .01
❑ 412 Bo Jackson RIF .10 .02
❑ 413 Shawon Dunston RIF
UER (In the baseball&
should .05 .01
❑ 414 Jesse Barfield RIF .05 .01
❑ 415 Ken Caminiti RIF .05 .01
❑ 416 Benito Santiago RIF .05 .01
❑ 417 Nolan Ryan HL .50 .20
❑ 418 Bobby Thigpen HL UER
(Back refers to Hal
McRae J .05 .01
❑ 419 Ramon Martinez HL .05 .01
❑ 420 Bo Jackson HL .10 .02
❑ 421 Carlton Fisk HL .10 .02
❑ 422 Jimmy Key .10 .02
❑ 423 Junior Noboa .05 .01
❑ 424 Al Newman .05 .01
❑ 425 Pat Borders .05 .01
❑ 426 Von Hayes .05 .01
❑ 427 Tim Teufel .05 .01
❑ 428 Eric Plunk UER
(Text says Eric's had&
no apostro .05 .01
❑ 429 John Moses .05 .01
❑ 430 Mike Witt .05 .01
❑ 431 Otis Nixon .05 .01
❑ 432 Tony Fernandez .05 .01
❑ 433 Rance Mulliniks .05 .01
❑ 434 Dan Petry .05 .01
❑ 435 Bob Geren .05 .01
❑ 436 Steve Frey .05 .01
❑ 437 Jamie Moyer .10 .02
❑ 438 Junior Ortiz .05 .01
❑ 439 Tom O'Malley .05 .01
❑ 440 Pat Combs .05 .01
❑ 441 Jose Canseco DT .15 .05
❑ 442 Alfredo Griffin .05 .01
❑ 443 Andres Galarraga .10 .02
❑ 444 Bryn Smith .05 .01
❑ 445 Andre Dawson .10 .02
❑ 446 Juan Samuel .05 .01
❑ 447 Mike Aldrete .05 .01
❑ 448 Ron Gant .10 .02
❑ 449 Fernando Valenzuela .10 .02
❑ 450 Vince Coleman UER

(Should say topped majors in s) .05 .01
❑ 451 Kevin Mitchell .05 .01
❑ 452 Spike Owen .05 .01
❑ 453 Mike Bielecki .05 .01
❑ 454 Dennis Martinez .10 .02
❑ 455 Brett Butler .10 .02
❑ 456 Ron Darling .05 .01
❑ 457 Dennis Rasmussen .05 .01
❑ 458 Ken Howell .05 .01
❑ 459 Steve Bedrosian .05 .01
❑ 460 Frank Viola .10 .02
❑ 461 Jose Lind .05 .01
❑ 462 Chris Sabo .05 .01
❑ 463 Dante Bichette .10 .02
❑ 464 Rick Mahler .05 .01
❑ 465 John Smiley .05 .01
❑ 466 Devon White .10 .02
❑ 467 John Orton .05 .01
❑ 468 Mike Stanton .05 .01
❑ 469 Billy Hatcher .05 .01
❑ 470 Wally Joyner .10 .02
❑ 471 Gene Larkin .05 .01
❑ 472 Doug Drabek .05 .01
❑ 473 Gary Sheffield .10 .02
❑ 474 David Wells .10 .02
❑ 475 Andy Van Slyke .15 .05
❑ 476 Mike Gallego .05 .01
❑ 477 B.J. Surhoff .10 .02
❑ 478 Gene Nelson .05 .01
❑ 479 Mariano Duncan .05 .01
❑ 480 Fred McGriff .15 .05
❑ 481 Jerry Browne .05 .01
❑ 482 Alvin Davis .05 .01
❑ 483 Bill Wegman .05 .01
❑ 484 Dave Parker .10 .02
❑ 485 Dennis Eckersley .10 .02
❑ 486 Erik Hanson UER (Basketball misspelled as baseke) .05 .01
❑ 487 Bill Ripken .05 .01
❑ 488 Tom Candiotti .05 .01
❑ 489 Mike Schooler .05 .01
❑ 490 Gregg Olson .05 .01
❑ 491 Chris James .05 .01
❑ 492 Pete Harnisch .05 .01
❑ 493 Julio Franco .10 .02
❑ 494 Greg Briley .05 .01
❑ 495 Ruben Sierra .10 .02
❑ 496 Steve Olin .05 .01
❑ 497 Mike Fetters .05 .01
❑ 498 Mark Williamson .05 .01
❑ 499 Bob Tewksbury .05 .01
❑ 500 Tony Gwynn .30 .10
❑ 501 Randy Myers .05 .01
❑ 502 Keith Comstock .05 .01
❑ 503 Craig Worthington UER (DeCinces misspelled DiCin) .05 .01
❑ 504 Mark Eichhorn UER (Stats incomplete& doesn't hav) .05 .01
❑ 505 Barry Larkin .15 .05
❑ 506 Dave Johnson .05 .01
❑ 507 Bobby Witt .05 .01
❑ 508 Joe Orsulak .05 .01
❑ 509 Pete O'Brien .05 .01
❑ 510 Brad Arnsberg .05 .01
❑ 511 Storm Davis .05 .01
❑ 512 Bob Milacki .05 .01
❑ 513 Bill Pecota .05 .01
❑ 514 Glenallen Hill .05 .01
❑ 515 Danny Tartabull .05 .01
❑ 516 Mike Moore .05 .01
❑ 517 Ron Robinson UER (577 K's in 1990) .05 .01
❑ 518 Mark Gardner .05 .01
❑ 519 Rick Wrona .05 .01
❑ 520 Mike Scioscia .05 .01
❑ 521 Frank Wills .05 .01
❑ 522 Greg Brock .05 .01
❑ 523 Jack Clark .10 .02
❑ 524 Bruce Ruffin .05 .01
❑ 525 Robin Yount .40 .15
❑ 526 Tom Foley .05 .01
❑ 527 Pat Perry .05 .01
❑ 528 Greg Vaughn .05 .01
❑ 529 Wally Whitehurst .05 .01
❑ 530 Norm Charlton .05 .01
❑ 531 Marvell Wynne .05 .01
❑ 532 Jim Gantner .05 .01
❑ 533 Greg Litton .05 .01
❑ 534 Manny Lee .05 .01
❑ 535 Scott Bailes .05 .01
❑ 536 Charlie Leibrandt .05 .01
❑ 537 Roger McDowell .05 .01
❑ 538 Andy Benes .05 .01
❑ 539 Rick Honeycutt .05 .01
❑ 540 Dwight Gooden .10 .02
❑ 541 Scott Garrelts .05 .01
❑ 542 Dave Clark .05 .01
❑ 543 Lonnie Smith .05 .01
❑ 544 Rick Reuschel .05 .01
❑ 545 Delino DeShields .10 .02
❑ 546 Mike Sharperson .05 .01
❑ 547 Mike Kingery .05 .01
❑ 548 Terry Kennedy .05 .01
❑ 549 David Cone .10 .02
❑ 550 Orel Hershiser .10 .02
❑ 551 Matt Nokes .05 .01
❑ 552 Eddie Williams .05 .01
❑ 553 Frank DiPino .05 .01
❑ 554 Fred Lynn .05 .01
❑ 555 Alex Cole .05 .01
❑ 556 Terry Leach .05 .01
❑ 557 Chet Lemon .05 .01
❑ 558 Paul Mirabella .05 .01
❑ 559 Bill Long .05 .01
❑ 560 Phil Bradley .05 .01
❑ 561 Duane Ward .05 .01
❑ 562 Dave Bergman .05 .01
❑ 563 Eric Show .05 .01
❑ 564 Xavier Hernandez .05 .01
❑ 565 Jeff Parrett .05 .01
❑ 566 Chuck Cary .05 .01
❑ 567 Ken Hill .05 .01
❑ 568 Bob Welch Hand (Complement should be compliment) .05 .01
❑ 569 John Mitchell .05 .01
❑ 570 Travis Fryman .10 .02
❑ 571 Derek Lilliquist .05 .01
❑ 572 Steve Lake .05 .01
❑ 573 John Barfield .05 .01
❑ 574 Randy Bush .05 .01
❑ 575 Joe Magrane .05 .01
❑ 576 Eddie Diaz .05 .01
❑ 577 Casey Candaele .05 .01
❑ 578 Jesse Orosco .05 .01
❑ 579 Tom Henke .05 .01
❑ 580 Rick Cerone UER (Actually his third go-round wit) .05 .01
❑ 581 Drew Hall .05 .01
❑ 582 Tony Castillo .05 .01
❑ 583 Jimmy Jones .05 .01
❑ 584 Rick Reed .05 .01
❑ 585 Joe Girardi .05 .01
❑ 586 Jeff Gray RC .05 .01
❑ 587 Luis Polonia .05 .01
❑ 588 Joe Klink .05 .01
❑ 589 Rex Hudler .05 .01
❑ 590 Kirk McCaskill .05 .01
❑ 591 Juan Agosto .05 .01
❑ 592 Wes Gardner .05 .01
❑ 593 Rich Rodriguez RC .05 .01
❑ 594 Mitch Webster .05 .01
❑ 595 Kelly Gruber .05 .01
❑ 596 Dale Mohorcic .05 .01
❑ 597 Willie McGee .10 .02
❑ 598 Bill Krueger .05 .01
❑ 599 Bob Walk UER (Cards says he's 33& but actually h) .05 .01
❑ 600 Kevin Maas .05 .01
❑ 601 Danny Jackson .05 .01
❑ 602 Craig McMurtry UER (Anonymously misspelled anoni) .05 .01
❑ 603 Curtis Wilkerson .05 .01
❑ 604 Adam Peterson .05 .01
❑ 605 Sam Horn .05 .01
❑ 606 Tommy Gregg .05 .01
❑ 607 Ken Dayley .05 .01
❑ 608 Carmelo Castillo .05 .01
❑ 609 John Shelby .05 .01
❑ 610 Don Slaught .05 .01
❑ 611 Calvin Schiraldi .05 .01
❑ 612 Dennis Lamp .05 .01
❑ 613 Andres Thomas .05 .01
❑ 614 Jose Gonzalez .05 .01
❑ 615 Randy Ready .05 .01
❑ 616 Kevin Bass .05 .01
❑ 617 Mike Marshall .05 .01
❑ 618 Daryl Boston .05 .01
❑ 619 Andy McGaffigan .05 .01
❑ 620 Joe Oliver .05 .01
❑ 621 Jim Gott .05 .01
❑ 622 Jose Oquendo .05 .01
❑ 623 Jose DeJesus .05 .01
❑ 624 Mike Brumley .05 .01
❑ 625 John Olerud .10 .02
❑ 626 Ernest Riles .05 .01
❑ 627 Gene Harris .05 .01
❑ 628 Jose Uribe .05 .01
❑ 629 Darnell Coles .05 .01
❑ 630 Carney Lansford .10 .02
❑ 631 Tim Leary .05 .01
❑ 632 Tim Hulett .05 .01
❑ 633 Kevin Elster .05 .01
❑ 634 Tony Fossas .05 .01
❑ 635 Francisco Oliveras .05 .01
❑ 636 Bob Patterson .05 .01
❑ 637 Gary Ward .05 .01
❑ 638 Rene Gonzales .05 .01
❑ 639 Don Robinson .05 .01
❑ 640 Darryl Strawberry .10 .02
❑ 641 Dave Anderson .05 .01
❑ 642 Scott Scudder .05 .01
❑ 643 Reggie Harris UER (Hepatitis misspelled as hepit) .05 .01
❑ 644 Dave Henderson .05 .01
❑ 645 Ben McDonald .05 .01
❑ 646 Bob Kipper .05 .01
❑ 647 Hal Morris UER (It's should be its) .05 .01
❑ 648 Tim Birtsas .05 .01
❑ 649 Steve Searcy .05 .01
❑ 650 Dale Murphy .15 .05
❑ 651 Ron Oester .05 .01
❑ 652 Mike LaCoss .05 .01
❑ 653 Ron Jones .05 .01
❑ 654 Kelly Downs .05 .01
❑ 655 Roger Clemens .75 .30
❑ 656 Herm Winningham .05 .01
❑ 657 Trevor Wilson .05 .01
❑ 658 Jose Rijo .05 .01
❑ 659 Dann Bilardello UER (Bio has 13 games& 1 hit& an) .05 .01
❑ 660 Gregg Jefferies .05 .01
❑ 661 Doug Drabek AS UER (Through is mis-spelled thou) .05 .01
❑ 662 Randy Myers AS .05 .01
❑ 663 Benny Santiago AS .05 .01
❑ 664 Will Clark AS .10 .02
❑ 665 Ryne Sandberg AS .25 .08
❑ 666 Barry Larkin AS UER (Line 13& coolly misspelled) .10 .02
❑ 667 Matt Williams AS .05 .01
❑ 668 Barry Bonds AS .50 .20
❑ 669 Eric Davis AS .05 .01
❑ 670 Bobby Bonilla AS .05 .01
❑ 671 Chipper Jones RC 4.00 1.50
❑ 672 Eric Christopherson RC .10 .02
❑ 673 Robbie Beckett RC .10 .02
❑ 674 Shane Andrews RC .25 .08
❑ 675 Steve Karsay RC .25 .08
❑ 676 Aaron Holbert RC .10 .02
❑ 677 Donovan Osborne RC .10 .02
❑ 678 Todd Ritchie RC .25 .08
❑ 679 Ronnie Walden RC .10 .02
❑ 680 Tim Costo RC .10 .02
❑ 681 Dan Wilson RC .25 .08
❑ 682 Kurt Miller RC .10 .02

❑ 683 Mike Lieberthal RC .40 .15
❑ 684 Roger Clemens KM .40 .15
❑ 685 Dwight Gooden KM .05 .01
❑ 686 Nolan Ryan KM .50 .20
❑ 687 Frank Viola KM .05 .01
❑ 688 Erik Hanson KM .05 .01
❑ 689 Matt Williams MB .05 .01
❑ 690 Jose Canseco MB .10 .02
❑ 691 Darryl Strawberry MB .05 .01
❑ 692 Bo Jackson MB .10 .02
❑ 693 Cecil Fielder MB .05 .01
❑ 694 Sandy Alomar Jr. RF .05 .01
❑ 695 Cory Snyder RF .05 .01
❑ 696 Eric Davis RF .05 .01
❑ 697 Ken Griffey Jr. RF .25 .08
❑ 698 Andy Van Slyke RF UER .10 .02
❑ 699 Langston/Witt NH
(Mark Langston
Mike Witt) .05 .01
❑ 700 Randy Johnson NH .15 .05
❑ 701 Nolan Ryan NH .50 .20
❑ 702 Dave Stewart NH .05 .01
❑ 703 Fernando Valenzuela NH .05 .01
❑ 704 Andy Hawkins NH .05 .01
❑ 705 Melido Perez NH .05 .01
❑ 706 Terry Mulholland NH .05 .01
❑ 707 Dave Stieb NH .05 .01
❑ 708 Brian Barnes RC .05 .01
❑ 709 Bernard Gilkey .05 .01
❑ 710 Steve Decker RC .05 .01
❑ 711 Paul Faries RC .05 .01
❑ 712 Paul Marak RC .05 .01
❑ 713 Wes Chamberlain RC .10 .02
❑ 714 Kevin Belcher RC .05 .01
❑ 715 Dan Boone UER
(IP adds up to 101,
but card has 1) .05 .01
❑ 716 Steve Adkins RC .05 .01
❑ 717 Geronimo Pena .05 .01
❑ 718 Howard Farmer .05 .01
❑ 719 Mark Leonard RC .05 .01
❑ 720 Tom Lampkin .05 .01
❑ 721 Mike Gardiner RC .05 .01
❑ 722 Jeff Conine RC .40 .15
❑ 723 Efrain Valdez RC .05 .01
❑ 724 Chuck Malone .05 .01
❑ 725 Leo Gomez .05 .01
❑ 726 Paul McClellan RC .05 .01
❑ 727 Mark Leiter RC .10 .02
❑ 728 Rich DeLucia UER RC .05 .01
❑ 729 Mel Rojas .05 .01
❑ 730 Hector Wagner RC .05 .01
❑ 731 Ray Lankford .10 .02
❑ 732 Turner Ward RC .10 .02
❑ 733 Gerald Alexander RC .05 .01
❑ 734 Scott Anderson RC .05 .01
❑ 735 Tony Perezchica .05 .01
❑ 736 Jimmy Kremers .05 .01
❑ 737 American Flag/Peace .25 .08
❑ 738 Mike York RC .05 .01
❑ 739 Mike Rochford .05 .01
❑ 740 Scott Aldred .05 .01
❑ 741 Rico Brogna .05 .01
❑ 742 Dave Burba RC .25 .08
❑ 743 Ray Stephens RC .05 .01
❑ 744 Eric Gunderson .05 .01
❑ 745 Troy Afenir RC .05 .01
❑ 746 Jeff Shaw .05 .01
❑ 747 Orlando Merced RC .10 .02
❑ 748 Omar Olivares UER RC .10 .02
❑ 749 Jerry Kutzler .05 .01
❑ 750 Mo Vaughn .10 .02
❑ 751 Matt Stark RC .05 .01
❑ 752 Randy Hennis RC .05 .01
❑ 753 Andujar Cedeno .05 .01
❑ 754 Kelvin Torve .05 .01
❑ 755 Joe Kraemer .05 .01
❑ 756 Phil Clark RC .10 .02
❑ 757 Ed Vosberg RC .05 .01
❑ 758 Mike Perez RC .10 .02
❑ 759 Scott Lewis RC .05 .01
❑ 760 Steve Chitren RC .05 .01
❑ 761 Ray Young RC .05 .01
❑ 762 Andres Santana .05 .01
❑ 763 Rodney McCray RC .05 .01
❑ 764 Sean Berry UER RC .10 .02
❑ 765 Brent Mayne .05 .01
❑ 766 Mike Simms RC .05 .01
❑ 767 Glenn Sutko RC .05 .01
❑ 768 Gary DiSarcina .05 .01
❑ 769 George Brett HL .25 .08
❑ 770 Cecil Fielder HL .05 .01
❑ 771 Jim Presley .05 .01
❑ 772 John Dopson .05 .01
❑ 773 Bo Jackson Breaker .10 .02
❑ 774 Brent Knackert UER
(Born in 1954& shown
throwing) .05 .01
❑ 775 Bill Doran UER
(Reds in NL East) .05 .01
❑ 776 Dick Schofield .05 .01
❑ 777 Nelson Santovenia .05 .01
❑ 778 Mark Guthrie .05 .01
❑ 779 Mark Lemke .05 .01
❑ 780 Terry Steinbach .05 .01
❑ 781 Tom Bolton .05 .01
❑ 782 Randy Tomlin RC .10 .02
❑ 783 Jeff Kunkel .05 .01
❑ 784 Felix Jose .05 .01
❑ 785 Rick Sutcliffe .10 .02
❑ 786 John Cerutti .05 .01
❑ 787 Jose Vizcaino UER .05 .01
❑ 788 Curt Schilling .25 .08
❑ 789 Ed Whitson .05 .01
❑ 790 Tony Pena .05 .01
❑ 791 John Candelaria .05 .01
❑ 792 Carmelo Martinez .05 .01
❑ 793 Sandy Alomar Jr. UER .05 .01
❑ 794 Jim Neidlinger RC .05 .01
❑ 795 Barry Larkin WS
and Chris Sabo .10 .02
❑ 796 Paul Sorrento .05 .01
❑ 797 Tom Pagnozzi .05 .01
❑ 798 Tino Martinez .25 .08
❑ 799 Scott Ruskin UER
(Text says first three
seasons) .05 .01
❑ 800 Kirk Gibson .10 .02
❑ 801 Walt Terrell .05 .01
❑ 802 John Russell .05 .01
❑ 803 Chili Davis .10 .02
❑ 804 Chris Nabholz .05 .01
❑ 805 Juan Gonzalez .25 .08
❑ 806 Ron Hassey .05 .01
❑ 807 Todd Worrell .05 .01
❑ 808 Tommy Greene .05 .01
❑ 809 Joel Skinner UER
(Joel& not Bob& was
drafted in) .05 .01
❑ 810 Benito Santiago .10 .02
❑ 811 Pat Tabler UER
(Line 3& always
misspelled alway) .05 .01
❑ 812 Scott Erickson UER RC .05 .01
❑ 813 Moises Alou .10 .02
❑ 814 Dale Sveum .05 .01
❑ 815 Ryne Sandberg MANYR .25 .08
❑ 816 Rick Dempsey .05 .01
❑ 817 Scott Bankhead .05 .01
❑ 818 Jason Grimsley .05 .01
❑ 819 Doug Jennings .05 .01
❑ 820 Tom Herr .05 .01
❑ 821 Rob Ducey .05 .01
❑ 822 Luis Quinones .05 .01
❑ 823 Greg Minton .05 .01
❑ 824 Mark Grant .05 .01
❑ 825 Ozzie Smith .40 .15
❑ 826 Dave Eiland .05 .01
❑ 827 Danny Heep .05 .01
❑ 828 Hensley Meulens .05 .01
❑ 829 Charlie O'Brien .05 .01
❑ 830 Glenn Davis .05 .01
❑ 831 John Marzano UER
(International mis-
spelled Int) .05 .01
❑ 832 Steve Ontiveros .05 .01
❑ 833 Ron Karkovice .05 .01
❑ 834 Jerry Goff .05 .01
❑ 835 Ken Griffey Sr. .10 .02
❑ 836 Kevin Reimer .05 .01
❑ 837 Randy Kutcher UER
(Infectious mis-
spelled infec) .05 .01
❑ 838 Mike Blowers .05 .01
❑ 839 Mike Macfarlane .05 .01
❑ 840 Frank Thomas .25 .08
❑ 841 K.Griffey Jr./K.Griffey Sr. .40 .15
❑ 842 Jack Howell .05 .01
❑ 843 Goose Gozzo .05 .01
❑ 844 Gerald Young .05 .01
❑ 845 Zane Smith .05 .01
❑ 846 Kevin Brown .10 .02
❑ 847 Sil Campusano .05 .01
❑ 848 Larry Andersen .05 .01
❑ 849 Cal Ripken FRAN .40 .15
❑ 850 Roger Clemens FRAN .40 .15
❑ 851 Sandy Alomar Jr. FRAN .05 .01
❑ 852 Alan Trammell FRAN .10 .02
❑ 853 George Brett FRAN .25 .08
❑ 854 Robin Yount FRAN .25 .08
❑ 855 Kirby Puckett FRAN .15 .05
❑ 856 Don Mattingly FRAN .30 .10
❑ 857 Rickey Henderson FRAN .15 .05
❑ 858 Ken Griffey Jr. FRAN .25 .08
❑ 859 Ruben Sierra FRAN .05 .01
❑ 860 John Olerud FRAN .05 .01
❑ 861 David Justice FRAN .05 .01
❑ 862 Ryne Sandberg FRAN .25 .08
❑ 863 Eric Davis FRAN .05 .01
❑ 864 Darryl Strawberry FRAN .05 .01
❑ 865 Tim Wallach FRAN .05 .01
❑ 866 Dwight Gooden FRAN .05 .01
❑ 867 Len Dykstra FRAN .05 .01
❑ 868 Barry Bonds FRAN .50 .20
❑ 869 Todd Zeile FRAN .05 .01
❑ 870 Benito Santiago FRAN .05 .01
❑ 871 Will Clark FRAN .10 .02
❑ 872 Craig Biggio FRAN .10 .02
❑ 873 Wally Joyner FRAN .05 .01
❑ 874 Frank Thomas FRAN .15 .05
❑ 875 Rickey Henderson MVP .15 .05
❑ 876 Barry Bonds MVP .50 .20
❑ 877 Bob Welch CY .05 .01
❑ 878 Doug Drabek CY .05 .01
❑ 879 Sandy Alomar Jr. ROY .05 .01
❑ 880 David Justice ROY .05 .01
❑ 881 Damon Berryhill .05 .01
❑ 882 Frank Viola DT .05 .01
❑ 883 Dave Stewart DT .05 .01
❑ 884 Doug Jones DT .05 .01
❑ 885 Randy Myers DT .05 .01
❑ 886 Will Clark DT .10 .02
❑ 887 Roberto Alomar DT .10 .02
❑ 888 Barry Larkin DT .10 .02
❑ 889 Wade Boggs DT .15 .05
❑ 890 Rickey Henderson DT .25 .08
❑ 891 Kirby Puckett DT .15 .05
❑ 892 Ken Griffey Jr. DT .50 .20
❑ 893 Benny Santiago DT .10 .02

1992 Score

❑ COMPLETE SET (893) 15.00 6.00
❑ COMP.FACT.SET (910) 20.00 8.00
❑ COMPLETE SERIES 1 (442) 8.00 3.00
❑ COMPLETE SERIES 2 (451) 8.00 3.00
❑ 1 Ken Griffey Jr. .40 .15
❑ 2 Nolan Ryan 1.00 .40
❑ 3 Will Clark .15 .05
❑ 4 David Justice .10 .02
❑ 5 Dave Henderson .05 .01

❑	6 Bret Saberhagen	.10	.02
❑	7 Fred McGriff	.15	.05
❑	8 Erik Hanson	.05	.01
❑	9 Darryl Strawberry	.10	.02
❑	10 Dwight Goodon	.10	.02
❑	11 Juan Gonzalez	.15	.05
❑	12 Mark Langston	.05	.01
❑	13 Lonnie Smith	.05	.01
❑	14 Jeff Montgomery	.05	.01
❑	15 Roberto Alomar	.15	.05
❑	16 Delino DeShields	.05	.01
❑	17 Steve Bedrosian	.05	.01
❑	18 Terry Pendleton	.10	.02
❑	19 Mark Carreon	.05	.01
❑	20 Mark McGwire	.60	.25
❑	21 Roger Clemens	.50	.20
❑	22 Chuck Crim	.05	.01
❑	23 Don Mattingly	.60	.25
❑	24 Dickie Thon	.05	.01
❑	25 Ron Gant	.10	.02
❑	26 Milt Cuyler	.05	.01
❑	27 Mike Macfarlane	.05	.01
❑	28 Dan Gladden	.05	.01
❑	29 Melido Perez	.05	.01
❑	30 Willie Randolph	.10	.02
❑	31 Albert Belle	.10	.02
❑	32 Dave Winfield	.10	.02
❑	33 Jimmy Jones	.05	.01
❑	34 Kevin Gross	.05	.01
❑	35 Andres Galarraga	.10	.02
❑	36 Mike Devereaux	.05	.01
❑	37 Chris Bosio	.05	.01
❑	38 Mike LaValliere	.05	.01
❑	39 Gary Gaetti	.10	.02
❑	40 Felix Jose	.05	.01
❑	41 Alvaro Espinoza	.05	.01
❑	42 Rick Aguilera	.10	.02
❑	43 Mike Gallego	.05	.01
❑	44 Eric Davis	.10	.02
❑	45 George Bell	.05	.01
❑	46 Tom Brunansky	.05	.01
❑	47 Steve Farr	.05	.01
❑	48 Duane Ward	.05	.01
❑	49 David Wells	.10	.02
❑	50 Cecil Fielder	.10	.02
❑	51 Walt Weiss	.05	.01
❑	52 Todd Zeile	.05	.01
❑	53 Doug Jones	.05	.01
❑	54 Bob Walk	.05	.01
❑	55 Rafael Palmeiro	.15	.05
❑	56 Rob Deer	.05	.01
❑	57 Paul O'Neill	.15	.05
❑	58 Jeff Reardon	.10	.02
❑	59 Randy Ready	.05	.01
❑	60 Scott Erickson	.05	.01
❑	61 Paul Molitor	.10	.02
❑	62 Jack McDowell	.05	.01
❑	63 Jim Acker	.05	.01
❑	64 Jay Buhner	.10	.02
❑	65 Travis Fryman	.10	.02
❑	66 Marquis Grissom	.10	.02
❑	67 Mike Harkey	.05	.01
❑	68 Luis Polonia	.05	.01
❑	69 Ken Caminiti	.10	.02
❑	70 Chris Sabo	.05	.01
❑	71 Gregg Olson	.05	.01
❑	72 Carlton Fisk	.15	.05
❑	73 Juan Samuel	.05	.01
❑	74 Todd Stottlemyre	.05	.01
❑	75 Andre Dawson	.10	.02
❑	76 Alvin Davis	.05	.01
❑	77 Bill Doran	.05	.01
❑	78 B.J. Surhoff	.10	.02
❑	79 Kirk McCaskill	.05	.01
❑	80 Dale Murphy	.15	.05
❑	81 Jose DeLeon	.05	.01
❑	82 Alex Fernandez	.05	.01
❑	83 Ivan Calderon	.05	.01
❑	84 Brent Mayne	.05	.01
❑	85 Jody Reed	.05	.01
❑	86 Randy Tomlin	.05	.01
❑	87 Randy Milligan	.05	.01
❑	88 Pascual Perez	.05	.01
❑	89 Hensley Meulens	.05	.01
❑	90 Joe Carter	.10	.02
❑	91 Mike Moore	.05	.01
❑	92 Ozzie Guillen	.10	.02
❑	93 Shawn Hillegas	.05	.01
❑	94 Chili Davis	.10	.02
❑	95 Vince Coleman	.05	.01
❑	96 Jimmy Key	.10	.02
❑	97 Billy Ripken	.05	.01
❑	98 Dave Smith	.05	.01
❑	99 Tom Bolton	.05	.01
❑	100 Barry Larkin	.15	.05
❑	101 Kenny Rogers	.10	.02
❑	102 Mike Boddicker	.05	.01
❑	103 Kevin Elster	.05	.01
❑	104 Ken Hill	.05	.01
❑	105 Charlie Leibrandt	.05	.01
❑	106 Pat Combs	.05	.01
❑	107 Hubie Brooks	.05	.01
❑	108 Julio Franco	.10	.02
❑	109 Vicente Palacios	.05	.01
❑	110 Kal Daniels	.05	.01
❑	111 Bruce Hurst	.05	.01
❑	112 Willie McGee	.10	.02
❑	113 Ted Power	.05	.01
❑	114 Milt Thompson	.05	.01
❑	115 Doug Drabek	.05	.01
❑	116 Rafael Belliard	.05	.01
❑	117 Scott Garrelts	.05	.01
❑	118 Terry Mulholland	.05	.01
❑	119 Jay Howell	.05	.01
❑	120 Danny Jackson	.05	.01
❑	121 Scott Ruskin	.05	.01
❑	122 Robin Ventura	.10	.02
❑	123 Bip Roberts	.05	.01
❑	124 Jeff Russell	.05	.01
❑	125 Hal Morris	.05	.01
❑	126 Teddy Higuera	.05	.01
❑	127 Luis Sojo	.05	.01
❑	128 Carlos Baerga	.05	.01
❑	129 Jeff Ballard	.05	.01
❑	130 Tom Gordon	.05	.01
❑	131 Sid Bream	.05	.01
❑	132 Rance Mulliniks	.05	.01
❑	133 Andy Benes	.05	.01
❑	134 Mickey Tettleton	.05	.01
❑	135 Rich DeLucia	.05	.01
❑	136 Tom Pagnozzi	.05	.01
❑	137 Harold Baines	.10	.02
❑	138 Danny Darwin	.05	.01
❑	139 Kevin Bass	.05	.01
❑	140 Chris Nabholz	.05	.01
❑	141 Pete O'Brien	.05	.01
❑	142 Jeff Treadway	.05	.01
❑	143 Mickey Morandini	.05	.01
❑	144 Eric King	.05	.01
❑	145 Danny Tartabull	.05	.01
❑	146 Lance Johnson	.05	.01
❑	147 Casey Candaele	.05	.01
❑	148 Felix Fermin	.05	.01
❑	149 Rich Rodriguez	.05	.01
❑	150 Dwight Evans	.15	.05
❑	151 Joe Klink	.05	.01
❑	152 Kevin Reimer	.05	.01
❑	153 Orlando Merced	.05	.01
❑	154 Mel Hall	.05	.01
❑	155 Randy Myers	.05	.01
❑	156 Greg A. Harris	.05	.01
❑	157 Jeff Brantley	.05	.01
❑	158 Jim Eisenreich	.05	.01
❑	159 Luis Rivera	.05	.01
❑	160 Cris Carpenter	.05	.01
❑	161 Bruce Ruffin	.05	.01
❑	162 Omar Vizquel	.15	.05
❑	163 Gerald Alexander	.05	.01
❑	164 Mark Guthrie	.05	.01
❑	165 Scott Lewis	.05	.01
❑	166 Bill Sampen	.05	.01
❑	167 Dave Anderson	.05	.01
❑	168 Kevin McReynolds	.05	.01
❑	169 Jose Vizcaino	.05	.01
❑	170 Bob Geren	.05	.01
❑	171 Mike Morgan	.05	.01
❑	172 Jim Gott	.05	.01
❑	173 Mike Pagliarulo	.05	.01
❑	174 Mike Jeffcoat	.05	.01
❑	175 Craig Lefferts	.05	.01
❑	176 Steve Finley	.10	.02
❑	177 Wally Backman	.05	.01
❑	178 Kent Mercker	.05	.01
❑	179 John Cerutti	.05	.01
❑	180 Jay Bell	.10	.02
❑	181 Dale Sveum	.05	.01
❑	182 Greg Gagne	.05	.01
❑	183 Donnie Hill	.05	.01
❑	184 Rex Hudler	.05	.01
❑	185 Pat Kelly	.05	.01
❑	186 Jeff D. Robinson	.05	.01
❑	187 Jeff Gray	.05	.01
❑	188 Jerry Willard	.05	.01
❑	189 Carlos Quintana	.05	.01
❑	190 Dennis Eckersley	.10	.02
❑	191 Kelly Downs	.05	.01
❑	192 Gregg Jefferies	.05	.01
❑	193 Darrin Fletcher	.05	.01
❑	194 Mike Jackson	.05	.01
❑	195 Eddie Murray	.25	.08
❑	196 Bill Landrum	.05	.01
❑	197 Eric Yelding	.05	.01
❑	198 Devon White	.10	.02
❑	199 Larry Walker	.15	.05
❑	200 Ryne Sandberg	.40	.15
❑	201 Dave Magadan	.05	.01
❑	202 Steve Chitren	.05	.01
❑	203 Scott Fletcher	.05	.01
❑	204 Dwayne Henry	.05	.01
❑	205 Scott Coolbaugh	.05	.01
❑	206 Tracy Jones	.05	.01
❑	207 Von Hayes	.05	.01
❑	208 Bob Melvin	.05	.01
❑	209 Scott Scudder	.05	.01
❑	210 Luis Gonzalez	.10	.02
❑	211 Scott Sanderson	.05	.01
❑	212 Chris Donnels	.05	.01
❑	213 Heathcliff Slocumb	.05	.01
❑	214 Mike Timlin	.05	.01
❑	215 Brian Harper	.05	.01
❑	216 Juan Berenguer UER (Decimal point missing in IP)	.05	.01
❑	217 Mike Henneman	.05	.01
❑	218 Bill Spiers	.05	.01
❑	219 Scott Terry	.05	.01
❑	220 Frank Viola	.10	.02
❑	221 Mark Eichhorn	.05	.01
❑	222 Ernest Riles	.05	.01
❑	223 Ray Lankford	.10	.02
❑	224 Pete Harnisch	.05	.01
❑	225 Bobby Bonilla	.10	.02
❑	226 Mike Scioscia	.05	.01
❑	227 Joel Skinner	.05	.01
❑	228 Brian Holman	.05	.01
❑	229 Gilberto Reyes	.05	.01
❑	230 Matt Williams	.10	.02
❑	231 Jaime Navarro	.05	.01
❑	232 Jose Rijo	.05	.01
❑	233 Atlee Hammaker	.05	.01
❑	234 Tim Teufel	.05	.01
❑	235 John Kruk	.10	.02
❑	236 Kurt Stillwell	.05	.01
❑	237 Dan Pasqua	.05	.01
❑	238 Tim Crews	.05	.01
❑	239 Dave Gallagher	.05	.01
❑	240 Leo Gomez	.05	.01
❑	241 Steve Avery	.05	.01
❑	242 Bill Gullickson	.05	.01
❑	243 Mark Portugal	.05	.01
❑	244 Lee Guetterman	.05	.01
❑	245 Benito Santiago	.10	.02
❑	246 Jim Gantner	.05	.01
❑	247 Robby Thompson	.05	.01
❑	248 Terry Shumpert	.05	.01
❑	249 Mike Bell	.05	.01
❑	250 Harold Reynolds	.10	.02
❑	251 Mike Felder	.05	.01
❑	252 Bill Pecota	.05	.01
❑	253 Bill Krueger	.05	.01
❑	254 Alfredo Griffin	.05	.01
❑	255 Lou Whitaker	.10	.02
❑	256 Roy Smith	.05	.01
❑	257 Jerald Clark	.05	.01
❑	258 Sammy Sosa	.25	.08
❑	259 Tim Naehring	.05	.01
❑	260 Dave Righetti	.10	.02
❑	261 Paul Gibson	.05	.01

❑ 262 Chris James .05 .01
❑ 263 Larry Andersen .05 .01
❑ 264 Storm Davis .05 .01
❑ 265 Jose Lind .05 .01
❑ 266 Greg Hibbard .05 .01
❑ 267 Norm Charlton .05 .01
❑ 268 Paul Kilgus .05 .01
❑ 269 Greg Maddux .40 .15
❑ 270 Ellis Burks .10 .02
❑ 271 Frank Tanana .05 .01
❑ 272 Gene Larkin .05 .01
❑ 273 Ron Hassey .05 .01
❑ 274 Jeff M. Robinson .05 .01
❑ 275 Steve Howe .05 .01
❑ 276 Daryl Boston .05 .01
❑ 277 Mark Lee .05 .01
❑ 278 Jose Segura .05 .01
❑ 279 Lance Blankenship .05 .01
❑ 280 Don Slaught .05 .01
❑ 281 Russ Swan .05 .01
❑ 282 Bob Tewksbury .05 .01
❑ 283 Geno Petralli .05 .01
❑ 284 Shane Mack .05 .01
❑ 285 Bob Scanlan .05 .01
❑ 286 Tim Leary .05 .01
❑ 287 John Smoltz .15 .05
❑ 288 Pat Borders .05 .01
❑ 289 Mark Davidson .05 .01
❑ 290 Sam Horn .05 .01
❑ 291 Lenny Harris .05 .01
❑ 292 Franklin Stubbs .05 .01
❑ 293 Thomas Howard .05 .01
❑ 294 Steve Lyons .05 .01
❑ 295 Francisco Oliveras .05 .01
❑ 296 Terry Leach .05 .01
❑ 297 Barry Jones .05 .01
❑ 298 Lance Parrish .10 .02
❑ 299 Wally Whitehurst .05 .01
❑ 300 Bob Welch .05 .01
❑ 301 Charlie Hayes .05 .01
❑ 302 Charlie Hough .10 .02
❑ 303 Gary Redus .05 .01
❑ 304 Scott Bradley .05 .01
❑ 305 Jose Oquendo .05 .01
❑ 306 Pete Incaviglia .05 .01
❑ 307 Marvin Freeman .05 .01
❑ 308 Gary Pettis .05 .01
❑ 309 Joe Slusarski .05 .01
❑ 310 Kevin Seitzer .05 .01
❑ 311 Jeff Reed .05 .01
❑ 312 Pat Tabler .05 .01
❑ 313 Mike Maddux .05 .01
❑ 314 Bob Milacki .05 .01
❑ 315 Eric Anthony .05 .01
❑ 316 Dante Bichette .10 .02
❑ 317 Steve Decker .05 .01
❑ 318 Jack Clark .10 .02
❑ 319 Doug Dascenzo .05 .01
❑ 320 Scott Leius .05 .01
❑ 321 Jim Lindeman .05 .01
❑ 322 Bryan Harvey .05 .01
❑ 323 Spike Owen .05 .01
❑ 324 Roberto Kelly .05 .01
❑ 325 Stan Belinda .05 .01
❑ 326 Joey Cora .05 .01
❑ 327 Jeff Innis .05 .01
❑ 328 Willie Wilson .05 .01
❑ 329 Juan Agosto .05 .01
❑ 330 Charles Nagy .05 .01
❑ 331 Scott Bailes .05 .01
❑ 332 Pete Schourek .05 .01
❑ 333 Mike Flanagan .05 .01
❑ 334 Omar Olivares .05 .01
❑ 335 Dennis Lamp .05 .01
❑ 336 Tommy Greene .05 .01
❑ 337 Randy Velarde .05 .01
❑ 338 Tom Lampkin .05 .01
❑ 339 John Russell .05 .01
❑ 340 Bob Kipper .05 .01
❑ 341 Todd Burns .05 .01
❑ 342 Ron Jones .05 .01
❑ 343 Dave Valle .05 .01
❑ 344 Mike Heath .05 .01
❑ 345 John Olerud .10 .02
❑ 346 Gerald Young .05 .01
❑ 347 Ken Patterson .05 .01
❑ 348 Les Lancaster .05 .01
❑ 349 Steve Crawford .05 .01
❑ 350 John Candelaria .05 .01
❑ 351 Mike Aldrete .05 .01
❑ 352 Mariano Duncan .05 .01
❑ 353 Julio Machado .05 .01
❑ 354 Ken Williams .05 .01
❑ 355 Walt Terrell .05 .01
❑ 356 Mitch Williams .05 .01
❑ 357 Al Newman .05 .01
❑ 358 Bud Black .05 .01
❑ 359 Joe Hesketh .05 .01
❑ 360 Paul Assenmacher .05 .01
❑ 361 Bo Jackson .25 .08
❑ 362 Jeff Blauser .05 .01
❑ 363 Mike Brumley .05 .01
❑ 364 Jim Deshaies .05 .01
❑ 365 Brady Anderson .10 .02
❑ 366 Chuck McElroy .05 .01
❑ 367 Matt Merullo .05 .01
❑ 368 Tim Belcher .05 .01
❑ 369 Luis Aquino .05 .01
❑ 370 Joe Oliver .05 .01
❑ 371 Greg Swindell .05 .01
❑ 372 Lee Stevens .05 .01
❑ 373 Mark Knudson .05 .01
❑ 374 Bill Wegman .05 .01
❑ 375 Jerry Don Gleaton .05 .01
❑ 376 Pedro Guerrero .10 .02
❑ 377 Randy Bush .05 .01
❑ 378 Greg W. Harris .05 .01
❑ 379 Eric Plunk .05 .01
❑ 380 Jose DeJesus .05 .01
❑ 381 Bobby Witt .05 .01
❑ 382 Curtis Wilkerson .05 .01
❑ 383 Gene Nelson .05 .01
❑ 384 Wes Chamberlain .05 .01
❑ 385 Tom Henke .05 .01
❑ 386 Mark Lemke .05 .01
❑ 387 Greg Briley .05 .01
❑ 388 Rafael Ramirez .05 .01
❑ 389 Tony Fossas .05 .01
❑ 390 Henry Cotto .05 .01
❑ 391 Tim Hulett .05 .01
❑ 392 Dean Palmer .10 .02
❑ 393 Glenn Braggs .05 .01
❑ 394 Mark Salas .05 .01
❑ 395 Rusty Meacham .05 .01
❑ 396 Andy Ashby .05 .01
❑ 397 Jose Melendez .05 .01
❑ 398 Warren Newson .05 .01
❑ 399 Frank Castillo .05 .01
❑ 400 Chito Martinez .05 .01
❑ 401 Bernie Williams .15 .05
❑ 402 Derek Bell .10 .02
❑ 403 Javier Ortiz .05 .01
❑ 404 Tim Sherrill .05 .01
❑ 405 Rob MacDonald .05 .01
❑ 406 Phil Plantier .05 .01
❑ 407 Troy Afenir .05 .01
❑ 408 Gino Minutelli .05 .01
❑ 409 Reggie Jefferson .05 .01
❑ 410 Mike Remlinger .05 .01
❑ 411 Carlos Rodriguez .05 .01
❑ 412 Joe Redfield .05 .01
❑ 413 Alonzo Powell .05 .01
❑ 414 Scott Livingstone UER (Travis Fryman& not Woody&) .05 .01
❑ 415 Scott Kamieniecki .05 .01
❑ 416 Tim Spehr .05 .01
❑ 417 Brian Hunter .05 .01
❑ 418 Ced Landrum .05 .01
❑ 419 Bret Barberie .05 .01
❑ 420 Kevin Morton .05 .01
❑ 421 Doug Henry RC .10 .02
❑ 422 Doug Piatt .05 .01
❑ 423 Pat Rice .05 .01
❑ 424 Juan Guzman .05 .01
❑ 425 Nolan Ryan SPEC .50 .20
❑ 426 Tommy Greene NH .05 .01
❑ 427 Bob Milacki and Mike Flanagan NH (Mark Williamso) .05 .01
❑ 428 Wilson Alvarez NH .05 .01
❑ 429 Otis Nixon HL .05 .01
❑ 430 Rickey Henderson HL .15 .05
❑ 431 Cecil Fielder AS .05 .01
❑ 432 Julio Franco AS .05 .01
❑ 433 Cal Ripken AS .40 .15
❑ 434 Wade Boggs AS .10 .02
❑ 435 Joe Carter AS .05 .01
❑ 436 Ken Griffey Jr. AS .25 .08
❑ 437 Ruben Sierra AS .05 .01
❑ 438 Scott Erickson AS .05 .01
❑ 439 Tom Henke AS .05 .01
❑ 440 Terry Steinbach AS .05 .01
❑ 441 Rickey Henderson DT .25 .08
❑ 442 Ryne Sandberg DT .40 .15
❑ 443 Otis Nixon .05 .01
❑ 444 Scott Radinsky .05 .01
❑ 445 Mark Grace .15 .05
❑ 446 Tony Pena .05 .01
❑ 447 Billy Hatcher .05 .01
❑ 448 Glenallen Hill .05 .01
❑ 449 Chris Gwynn .05 .01
❑ 450 Tom Glavine .15 .05
❑ 451 John Habyan .05 .01
❑ 452 Al Osuna .05 .01
❑ 453 Tony Phillips .05 .01
❑ 454 Greg Cadaret .05 .01
❑ 455 Rob Dibble .10 .02
❑ 456 Rick Honeycutt .05 .01
❑ 457 Jerome Walton .05 .01
❑ 458 Mookie Wilson .10 .02
❑ 459 Mark Gubicza .05 .01
❑ 460 Craig Biggio .15 .05
❑ 461 Dave Cochrane .05 .01
❑ 462 Keith Miller .05 .01
❑ 463 Alex Cole .05 .01
❑ 464 Pete Smith .05 .01
❑ 465 Brett Butler .10 .02
❑ 466 Jeff Huson .05 .01
❑ 467 Steve Lake .05 .01
❑ 468 Lloyd Moseby .05 .01
❑ 469 Tim McIntosh .05 .01
❑ 470 Dennis Martinez .10 .02
❑ 471 Greg Myers .05 .01
❑ 472 Mackey Sasser .05 .01
❑ 473 Junior Ortiz .05 .01
❑ 474 Greg Olson .05 .01
❑ 475 Steve Sax .05 .01
❑ 476 Ricky Jordan .05 .01
❑ 477 Max Venable .05 .01
❑ 478 Brian McRae .05 .01
❑ 479 Doug Simons .05 .01
❑ 480 Rickey Henderson .25 .08
❑ 481 Gary Varsho .05 .01
❑ 482 Carl Willis .05 .01
❑ 483 Rick Wilkins .05 .01
❑ 484 Donn Pall .05 .01
❑ 485 Edgar Martinez .15 .05
❑ 486 Tom Foley .05 .01
❑ 487 Mark Williamson .05 .01
❑ 488 Jack Armstrong .05 .01
❑ 489 Gary Carter .10 .02
❑ 490 Ruben Sierra .10 .02
❑ 491 Gerald Perry .05 .01
❑ 492 Rob Murphy .05 .01
❑ 493 Zane Smith .05 .01
❑ 494 Darryl Kile .10 .02
❑ 495 Kelly Gruber .05 .01
❑ 496 Jerry Browne .05 .01
❑ 497 Darryl Hamilton .05 .01
❑ 498 Mike Stanton .05 .01
❑ 499 Mark Leonard .05 .01
❑ 500 Jose Canseco .15 .05
❑ 501 Dave Martinez .05 .01
❑ 502 Jose Guzman .05 .01
❑ 503 Terry Kennedy .05 .01
❑ 504 Ed Sprague .05 .01
❑ 505 Frank Thomas .25 .08
❑ 506 Darren Daulton .10 .02
❑ 507 Kevin Tapani .05 .01
❑ 508 Luis Salazar .05 .01
❑ 509 Paul Faries .05 .01
❑ 510 Sandy Alomar Jr. .05 .01
❑ 511 Jeff King .05 .01
❑ 512 Gary Thurman .05 .01
❑ 513 Chris Hammond .05 .01
❑ 514 Pedro Munoz .05 .01
❑ 515 Alan Trammell .10 .02

Card		
❑ 516 Geronimo Pena	.05	.01
❑ 517 Rodney McCray UER (Stole 6 bases in 1990& not 5;)	.05	.01
❑ 518 Manny Lee	.05	.01
❑ 519 Junior Felix	.05	.01
❑ 520 Kirk Gibson	.10	.02
❑ 521 Darrin Jackson	.05	.01
❑ 522 John Burkett	.05	.01
❑ 523 Jeff Johnson	.05	.01
❑ 524 Jim Corsi	.05	.01
❑ 525 Robin Yount	.40	.15
❑ 526 Jamie Quirk	.05	.01
❑ 527 Bob Ojeda	.05	.01
❑ 528 Mark Lewis	.05	.01
❑ 529 Bryn Smith	.05	.01
❑ 530 Kent Hrbek	.10	.02
❑ 531 Dennis Boyd	.05	.01
❑ 532 Ron Karkovice	.05	.01
❑ 533 Don August	.05	.01
❑ 534 Todd Frohwirth	.05	.01
❑ 535 Wally Joyner	.10	.02
❑ 536 Dennis Rasmussen	.05	.01
❑ 537 Andy Allanson	.05	.01
❑ 538 Rich Gossage	.10	.02
❑ 539 John Marzano	.05	.01
❑ 540 Cal Ripken	.75	.30
❑ 541 Bill Swift UER (Brewers logo on front)	.05	.01
❑ 542 Kevin Appier	.10	.02
❑ 543 Dave Bergman	.05	.01
❑ 544 Bernard Gilkey	.05	.01
❑ 545 Mike Greenwell	.05	.01
❑ 546 Jose Uribe	.05	.01
❑ 547 Jesse Orosco	.05	.01
❑ 548 Bob Patterson	.05	.01
❑ 549 Mike Stanley	.05	.01
❑ 550 Howard Johnson	.05	.01
❑ 551 Joe Orsulak	.05	.01
❑ 552 Dick Schofield	.05	.01
❑ 553 Dave Hollins	.05	.01
❑ 554 David Segui	.05	.01
❑ 555 Barry Bonds	1.00	.40
❑ 556 Mo Vaughn	.10	.02
❑ 557 Craig Wilson	.05	.01
❑ 558 Bobby Rose	.05	.01
❑ 559 Rod Nichols	.05	.01
❑ 560 Len Dykstra	.10	.02
❑ 561 Craig Grebeck	.05	.01
❑ 562 Darren Lewis	.05	.01
❑ 563 Todd Benzinger	.05	.01
❑ 564 Ed Whitson	.05	.01
❑ 565 Jesse Barfield	.05	.01
❑ 566 Lloyd McClendon	.05	.01
❑ 567 Dan Plesac	.05	.01
❑ 568 Danny Cox	.05	.01
❑ 569 Skeeter Barnes	.05	.01
❑ 570 Bobby Thigpen	.05	.01
❑ 571 Deion Sanders	.15	.05
❑ 572 Chuck Knoblauch	.10	.02
❑ 573 Matt Nokes	.05	.01
❑ 574 Herm Winningham	.05	.01
❑ 575 Tom Candiotti	.05	.01
❑ 576 Jeff Bagwell	.25	.08
❑ 577 Brook Jacoby	.05	.01
❑ 578 Chico Walker	.05	.01
❑ 579 Brian Downing	.05	.01
❑ 580 Dave Stewart	.10	.02
❑ 581 Francisco Cabrera	.05	.01
❑ 582 Rene Gonzales	.05	.01
❑ 583 Stan Javier	.05	.01
❑ 584 Randy Johnson	.25	.08
❑ 585 Chuck Finley	.10	.02
❑ 586 Mark Gardner	.05	.01
❑ 587 Mark Whiten	.05	.01
❑ 588 Garry Templeton	.05	.01
❑ 589 Gary Sheffield	.10	.02
❑ 590 Ozzie Smith	.40	.15
❑ 591 Candy Maldonado	.05	.01
❑ 592 Mike Sharperson	.05	.01
❑ 593 Carlos Martinez	.05	.01
❑ 594 Scott Bankhead	.05	.01
❑ 595 Tim Wallach	.05	.01
❑ 596 Tino Martinez	.15	.05
❑ 597 Roger McDowell	.05	.01
❑ 598 Cory Snyder	.05	.01
❑ 599 Andujar Cedeno	.05	.01
❑ 600 Kirby Puckett	.25	.08
❑ 601 Rick Parker	.05	.01
❑ 602 Todd Hundley	.05	.01
❑ 603 Greg Litton	.05	.01
❑ 604 Dave Johnson	.05	.01
❑ 605 John Franco	.10	.02
❑ 606 Mike Fetters	.05	.01
❑ 607 Luis Alicea	.05	.01
❑ 608 Trevor Wilson	.05	.01
❑ 609 Rob Ducey	.05	.01
❑ 610 Ramon Martinez	.05	.01
❑ 611 Dave Burba	.05	.01
❑ 612 Dwight Smith	.05	.01
❑ 613 Kevin Maas	.05	.01
❑ 614 John Costello	.05	.01
❑ 615 Glenn Davis	.05	.01
❑ 616 Shawn Abner	.05	.01
❑ 617 Scott Hemond	.05	.01
❑ 618 Tom Prince	.05	.01
❑ 619 Wally Ritchie	.05	.01
❑ 620 Jim Abbott	.15	.05
❑ 621 Charlie O'Brien	.05	.01
❑ 622 Jack Daugherty	.05	.01
❑ 623 Tommy Gregg	.05	.01
❑ 624 Jeff Shaw	.05	.01
❑ 625 Tony Gwynn	.30	.10
❑ 626 Mark Leiter	.05	.01
❑ 627 Jim Clancy	.05	.01
❑ 628 Tim Layana	.05	.01
❑ 629 Jeff Schaefer	.05	.01
❑ 630 Lee Smith	.10	.02
❑ 631 Wade Taylor	.05	.01
❑ 632 Mike Simms	.05	.01
❑ 633 Terry Steinbach	.05	.01
❑ 634 Shawon Dunston	.05	.01
❑ 635 Tim Raines	.10	.02
❑ 636 Kirt Manwaring	.05	.01
❑ 637 Warren Cromartie	.05	.01
❑ 638 Luis Quinones	.05	.01
❑ 639 Greg Vaughn	.05	.01
❑ 640 Kevin Mitchell	.05	.01
❑ 641 Chris Hoiles	.05	.01
❑ 642 Tom Browning	.05	.01
❑ 643 Mitch Webster	.05	.01
❑ 644 Steve Olin	.05	.01
❑ 645 Tony Fernandez	.05	.01
❑ 646 Juan Bell	.05	.01
❑ 647 Joe Boever	.05	.01
❑ 648 Carney Lansford	.10	.02
❑ 649 Mike Benjamin	.05	.01
❑ 650 George Brett	.60	.25
❑ 651 Tim Burke	.05	.01
❑ 652 Jack Morris	.10	.02
❑ 653 Orel Hershiser	.10	.02
❑ 654 Mike Schooler	.05	.01
❑ 655 Andy Van Slyke	.15	.05
❑ 656 Dave Stieb	.05	.01
❑ 657 Dave Clark	.05	.01
❑ 658 Ben McDonald	.05	.01
❑ 659 John Smiley	.05	.01
❑ 660 Wade Boggs	.15	.05
❑ 661 Eric Bullock	.05	.01
❑ 662 Eric Show	.05	.01
❑ 663 Lenny Webster	.05	.01
❑ 664 Mike Huff	.05	.01
❑ 665 Rick Sutcliffe	.10	.02
❑ 666 Jeff Manto	.05	.01
❑ 667 Mike Fitzgerald	.05	.01
❑ 668 Matt Young	.05	.01
❑ 669 Dave West	.05	.01
❑ 670 Mike Hartley	.05	.01
❑ 671 Curt Schilling	.15	.05
❑ 672 Brian Bohanon	.05	.01
❑ 673 Cecil Espy	.05	.01
❑ 674 Joe Grahe	.05	.01
❑ 675 Sid Fernandez	.05	.01
❑ 676 Edwin Nunez	.05	.01
❑ 677 Hector Villanueva	.05	.01
❑ 678 Sean Berry	.05	.01
❑ 679 Dave Eiland	.05	.01
❑ 680 David Cone	.10	.02
❑ 681 Mike Bordick	.05	.01
❑ 682 Tony Castillo	.05	.01
❑ 683 John Barfield	.05	.01
❑ 684 Jeff Hamilton	.05	.01
❑ 685 Ken Dayley	.05	.01
❑ 686 Carmelo Martinez	.05	.01
❑ 687 Mike Capel	.05	.01
❑ 688 Scott Chiamparino	.05	.01
❑ 689 Rich Gedman	.05	.01
❑ 690 Rich Monteleone	.05	.01
❑ 691 Alejandro Pena	.05	.01
❑ 692 Oscar Azocar	.05	.01
❑ 693 Jim Poole	.05	.01
❑ 694 Mike Gardiner	.05	.01
❑ 695 Steve Buechele	.05	.01
❑ 696 Rudy Seanez	.05	.01
❑ 697 Paul Abbott	.05	.01
❑ 698 Steve Searcy	.05	.01
❑ 699 Jose Offerman	.05	.01
❑ 700 Ivan Rodriguez	.25	.08
❑ 701 Joe Girardi	.05	.01
❑ 702 Tony Perezchica	.05	.01
❑ 703 Paul McClellan	.05	.01
❑ 704 David Howard	.05	.01
❑ 705 Dan Petry	.05	.01
❑ 706 Jack Howell	.05	.01
❑ 707 Jose Mesa	.05	.01
❑ 708 Randy St. Claire	.05	.01
❑ 709 Kevin Brown	.10	.02
❑ 710 Ron Darling	.05	.01
❑ 711 Jason Grimsley	.05	.01
❑ 712 John Orton	.05	.01
❑ 713 Shawn Boskie	.05	.01
❑ 714 Pat Clements	.05	.01
❑ 715 Brian Barnes	.05	.01
❑ 716 Luis Lopez	.05	.01
❑ 717 Bob McClure	.05	.01
❑ 718 Mark Davis	.05	.01
❑ 719 Dann Bilardello	.05	.01
❑ 720 Tom Edens	.05	.01
❑ 721 Willie Fraser	.05	.01
❑ 722 Curt Young	.05	.01
❑ 723 Neal Heaton	.05	.01
❑ 724 Craig Worthington	.05	.01
❑ 725 Mel Rojas	.05	.01
❑ 726 Daryl Irvine	.05	.01
❑ 727 Roger Mason	.05	.01
❑ 728 Kirk Dressendorfer	.05	.01
❑ 729 Scott Aldred	.05	.01
❑ 730 Willie Blair	.05	.01
❑ 731 Allan Anderson	.05	.01
❑ 732 Dana Kiecker	.05	.01
❑ 733 Jose Gonzalez	.05	.01
❑ 734 Brian Drahman	.05	.01
❑ 735 Brad Komminsk	.05	.01
❑ 736 Arthur Rhodes	.05	.01
❑ 737 Terry Mathews	.05	.01
❑ 738 Jeff Fassero	.05	.01
❑ 739 Mike Magnante RC	.10	.02
❑ 740 Kip Gross	.05	.01
❑ 741 Jim Hunter	.05	.01
❑ 742 Jose Mota	.05	.01
❑ 743 Joe Bitker	.05	.01
❑ 744 Tim Mauser	.05	.01
❑ 745 Ramon Garcia	.05	.01
❑ 746 Rod Beck RC	.25	.08
❑ 747 Jim Austin RC	.05	.01
❑ 748 Keith Mitchell	.05	.01
❑ 749 Wayne Rosenthal	.05	.01
❑ 750 Bryan Hickerson RC	.10	.02
❑ 751 Bruce Egloff	.05	.01
❑ 752 John Wehner	.05	.01
❑ 753 Darren Holmes	.05	.01
❑ 754 Dave Hansen	.05	.01
❑ 755 Mike Mussina	.25	.08
❑ 756 Anthony Young	.05	.01
❑ 757 Ron Tingley	.05	.01
❑ 758 Ricky Bones	.05	.01
❑ 759 Mark Wohlers	.05	.01
❑ 760 Wilson Alvarez	.05	.01
❑ 761 Harvey Pulliam	.05	.01
❑ 762 Ryan Bowen	.05	.01
❑ 763 Terry Bross	.05	.01
❑ 764 Joel Johnston	.05	.01
❑ 765 Terry McDaniel	.05	.01
❑ 766 Esteban Beltre	.05	.01
❑ 767 Rob Maurer	.05	.01
❑ 768 Ted Wood	.05	.01
❑ 769 Mo Sanford	.05	.01
❑ 770 Jeff Carter	.05	.01

❑ 771 Gil Heredia RC .25 .08
❑ 772 Monty Fariss .05 .01
❑ 773 Will Clark AS .10 .02
❑ 774 Ryne Sandberg AS .25 .08
❑ 775 Barry Larkin AS .10 .02
❑ 776 Howard Johnson AS .05 .01
❑ 777 Barry Bonds AS .50 .20
❑ 778 Brett Butler AS .05 .01
❑ 779 Tony Gwynn AS .15 .05
❑ 780 Ramon Martinez AS .05 .01
❑ 781 Lee Smith AS .05 .01
❑ 782 Mike Scioscia AS .05 .01
❑ 783 Dennis Martinez HL UER .05 .01
❑ 784 Dennis Martinez NH .05 .01
❑ 785 Mark Gardner NH .05 .01
❑ 786 Bret Saberhagen NH .05 .01
❑ 787 Kent Mercker NH
Mark Wohlers
Alejandro Pena .05 .01
❑ 788 Cal Ripken MVP .40 .15
❑ 789 Terry Pendleton MVP .05 .01
❑ 790 Roger Clemens CY .25 .08
❑ 791 Tom Glavine CY .10 .02
❑ 792 Chuck Knoblauch ROY .05 .01
❑ 793 Jeff Bagwell ROY .15 .05
❑ 794 Cal Ripken MOY .40 .15
❑ 795 David Cone HL .05 .01
❑ 796 Kirby Puckett HL .15 .05
❑ 797 Steve Avery HL .05 .01
❑ 798 Jack Morris HL .05 .01
❑ 799 Allen Watson RC .10 .02
❑ 800 Manny Ramirez RC 4.00 1.50
❑ 801 Cliff Floyd RC .75 .30
❑ 802 Al Shirley RC .10 .02
❑ 803 Brian Barber RC .10 .02
❑ 804 Jon Farrell RC .10 .02
❑ 805 Brent Gates RC .10 .02
❑ 806 Scott Ruffcorn RC .10 .02
❑ 807 Tyrone Hill RC .10 .02
❑ 808 Benji Gil RC .25 .08
❑ 809 Aaron Sele RC .25 .08
❑ 810 Tyler Green RC .10 .02
❑ 811 Chris Jones .05 .01
❑ 812 Steve Wilson .05 .01
❑ 813 Freddie Benavides .05 .01
❑ 814 Don Wakamatsu .05 .01
❑ 815 Mike Humphreys .05 .01
❑ 816 Scott Servais .05 .01
❑ 817 Rico Rossy .05 .01
❑ 818 John Ramos .05 .01
❑ 819 Rob Mallicoat .05 .01
❑ 820 Milt Hill .05 .01
❑ 821 Carlos Garcia .05 .01
❑ 822 Stan Royer .05 .01
❑ 823 Jeff Plympton .05 .01
❑ 824 Braulio Castillo .05 .01
❑ 825 David Haas .05 .01
❑ 826 Luis Mercedes .05 .01
❑ 827 Eric Karros .10 .02
❑ 828 Shawn Hare RC .10 .02
❑ 829 Reggie Sanders .10 .02
❑ 830 Tom Goodwin .05 .01
❑ 831 Dan Gakeler .05 .01
❑ 832 Stacy Jones .05 .01
❑ 833 Kim Batiste .05 .01
❑ 834 Cal Eldred .05 .01
❑ 835 Chris George .05 .01
❑ 836 Wayne Housie .05 .01
❑ 837 Mike Ignasiak .05 .01
❑ 838 Josias Manzanillo RC .10 .02
❑ 839 Jim Olander .05 .01
❑ 840 Gary Cooper .05 .01
❑ 841 Royce Clayton .05 .01
❑ 842 Hector Fajardo RC .10 .02
❑ 843 Blaine Beatty .05 .01
❑ 844 Jorge Pedre .05 .01
❑ 845 Kenny Lofton .15 .05
❑ 846 Scott Brosius RC .50 .20
❑ 847 Chris Cron .05 .01
❑ 848 Denis Boucher .05 .01
❑ 849 Kyle Abbott .05 .01
❑ 850 Bob Zupcic RC .10 .02
❑ 851 Rheal Cormier .05 .01
❑ 852 Jimmy Lewis RC .05 .01
❑ 853 Anthony Telford .05 .01
❑ 854 Cliff Brantley .05 .01
❑ 855 Kevin Campbell .05 .01
❑ 856 Craig Shipley .05 .01
❑ 857 Chuck Carr .05 .01
❑ 858 Tony Eusebio .10 .02
❑ 859 Jim Thome .25 .08
❑ 860 Vinny Castilla RC 1.00 .40
❑ 861 Dann Howitt .05 .01
❑ 862 Kevin Ward .05 .01
❑ 863 Steve Wapnick .05 .01
❑ 864 Rod Brewer RC .10 .02
❑ 865 Todd Van Poppel .05 .01
❑ 866 Jose Hernandez RC .25 .08
❑ 867 Amalio Carreno .05 .01
❑ 868 Calvin Jones .05 .01
❑ 869 Jeff Gardner .05 .01
❑ 870 Jarvis Brown .05 .01
❑ 871 Eddie Taubensee RC .25 .08
❑ 872 Andy Mota .05 .01
❑ 873 Chris Haney .05 .01
❑ 874 Roberto Hernandez .05 .01
❑ 875 Laddie Renfroe .05 .01
❑ 876 Scott Cooper .05 .01
❑ 877 Armando Reynoso RC .25 .08
❑ 878 Ty Cobb MEMO .25 .08
❑ 879 Babe Ruth MEMO .50 .20
❑ 880 Honus Wagner MEMO .25 .08
❑ 881 Lou Gehrig MEMO .40 .15
❑ 882 Satchel Paige MEMO .25 .08
❑ 883 Will Clark DT .10 .02
❑ 884 Cal Ripken DT 2.00 .75
❑ 885 Wade Boggs DT .10 .02
❑ 886 Kirby Puckett DT .15 .05
❑ 887 Tony Gwynn DT .15 .05
❑ 888 Craig Biggio DT .10 .02
❑ 889 Scott Erickson DT .05 .01
❑ 890 Tom Glavine DT .10 .02
❑ 891 Rob Dibble DT .10 .02
❑ 892 Mitch Williams DT .05 .01
❑ 893 Frank Thomas DT .15 .05
❑ X672 C.Knob 90S AU/3000 25.00 10.00

1992 Score Rookie/Traded

❑ COMP.FACT.SET (110) 8.00 3.00
❑ 1T Gary Sheffield .30 .10
❑ 2T Kevin Seitzer .20 .07
❑ 3T Danny Tartabull .20 .07
❑ 4T Steve Sax .20 .07
❑ 5T Bobby Bonilla .30 .10
❑ 6T Frank Viola .30 .10
❑ 7T Dave Winfield .30 .10
❑ 8T Rick Sutcliffe .30 .10
❑ 9T Jose Canseco .50 .20
❑ 10T Greg Swindell .20 .07
❑ 11T Eddie Murray .75 .30
❑ 12T Randy Myers .20 .07
❑ 13T Wally Joyner .30 .10
❑ 14T Kenny Lofton .50 .20
❑ 15T Jack Morris .30 .10
❑ 16T Charlie Hayes .20 .07
❑ 17T Pete Incaviglia .20 .07
❑ 18T Kevin Mitchell .20 .07
❑ 19T Kurt Stillwell .20 .07
❑ 20T Bret Saberhagen .30 .10
❑ 21T Steve Buechele .20 .07
❑ 22T John Smiley .20 .07
❑ 23T Sammy Sosa Cubs .75 .30
❑ 24T George Bell .20 .07
❑ 25T Curt Schilling .50 .20
❑ 26T Dick Schofield .20 .07
❑ 27T David Cone .30 .10
❑ 28T Dan Gladden .20 .07
❑ 29T Kirk McCaskill .20 .07
❑ 30T Mike Gallego .20 .07
❑ 31T Kevin McReynolds .20 .07
❑ 32T Bill Swift .20 .07
❑ 33T Dave Martinez .20 .07
❑ 34T Storm Davis .20 .07
❑ 35T Willie Randolph .30 .10
❑ 36T Melido Perez .20 .07
❑ 37T Mark Carreon .20 .07
❑ 38T Doug Jones .20 .07
❑ 39T Gregg Jefferies .20 .07
❑ 40T Mike Jackson .20 .07
❑ 41T Dickie Thon .20 .07
❑ 42T Eric King .20 .07
❑ 43T Herm Winningham .20 .07
❑ 44T Derek Lilliquist .20 .07
❑ 45T Dave Anderson .20 .07
❑ 46T Jeff Reardon .30 .10
❑ 47T Scott Bankhead .20 .07
❑ 48T Cory Snyder .20 .07
❑ 49T Al Newman .20 .07
❑ 50T Keith Miller .20 .07
❑ 51T Dave Burba .20 .07
❑ 52T Bill Pecota .20 .07
❑ 53T Chuck Crim .20 .07
❑ 54T Mariano Duncan .20 .07
❑ 55T Dave Gallagher .20 .07
❑ 56T Chris Gwynn .20 .07
❑ 57T Scott Ruskin .20 .07
❑ 58T Jack Armstrong .20 .07
❑ 59T Gary Carter .30 .10
❑ 60T Andres Galarraga .30 .10
❑ 61T Ken Hill .20 .07
❑ 62T Eric Davis .30 .10
❑ 63T Ruben Sierra .30 .10
❑ 64T Darrin Fletcher .20 .07
❑ 65T Tim Belcher .20 .07
❑ 66T Mike Morgan .20 .07
❑ 67T Scott Scudder .20 .07
❑ 68T Tom Candiotti .20 .07
❑ 69T Hubie Brooks .20 .07
❑ 70T Kal Daniels .20 .07
❑ 71T Bruce Ruffin .20 .07
❑ 72T Billy Hatcher .20 .07
❑ 73T Bob Melvin .20 .07
❑ 74T Lee Guetterman .20 .07
❑ 75T Rene Gonzales .20 .07
❑ 76T Kevin Bass .20 .07
❑ 77T Tom Bolton .20 .07
❑ 78T John Wetteland .30 .10
❑ 79T Bip Roberts .20 .07
❑ 80T Pat Listach RC .40 .15
❑ 81T John Doherty RC .20 .07
❑ 82T Sam Militello .20 .07
❑ 83T Brian Jordan RC .60 .25
❑ 84T Jeff Kent RC 3.00 1.25
❑ 85T Dave Fleming .20 .07
❑ 86T Jeff Tackett .20 .07
❑ 87T Chad Curtis RC .40 .15
❑ 88T Eric Fox RC .20 .07
❑ 89T Denny Neagle .30 .10
❑ 90T Donovan Osborne .20 .07
❑ 91T Carlos Hernandez .20 .07
❑ 92T Tim Wakefield RC 3.00 1.20
❑ 93T Tim Salmon .50 .20
❑ 94T Dave Nilsson .20 .07
❑ 95T Mike Perez .20 .07
❑ 96T Pat Hentgen .20 .07
❑ 97T Frank Seminara RC .20 .07
❑ 98T Ruben Amaro .20 .07
❑ 99T Archi Cianfrocco RC .20 .07
❑ 100T Andy Stankiewicz .20 .07
❑ 101T Jim Bullinger .20 .07
❑ 102T Pat Mahomes RC .40 .15
❑ 103T Hipolito Pichardo RC .20 .07
❑ 104T Bret Boone .50 .20
❑ 105T John Vander Wal .20 .07
❑ 106T Vince Horsman .20 .07
❑ 107T Jim Austin .20 .07
❑ 108T Brian Williams RC .20 .07
❑ 109T Dan Walters .20 .07
❑ 110T Wil Cordero .20 .07

1993 Score

❑	COMPLETE SET (660)	40.00	15.00
❑	1 Ken Griffey Jr.	.75	.30
❑	2 Gary Sheffield	.20	.07
❑	3 Frank Thomas	.50	.20
❑	4 Ryne Sandberg	.75	.30
❑	5 Larry Walker	.20	.07
❑	6 Cal Ripken	1.50	.60
❑	7 Roger Clemens	1.00	.40
❑	8 Bobby Bonilla	.20	.07
❑	9 Carlos Baerga	.10	.02
❑	10 Darren Daulton	.20	.07
❑	11 Travis Fryman	.20	.07
❑	12 Andy Van Slyke	.30	.10
❑	13 Jose Canseco	.30	.10
❑	14 Roberto Alomar	.30	.10
❑	15 Tom Glavine	.30	.10
❑	16 Barry Larkin	.30	.10
❑	17 Gregg Jefferies	.10	.02
❑	18 Craig Biggio	.30	.10
❑	19 Shane Mack	.10	.02
❑	20 Brett Butler	.20	.07
❑	21 Dennis Eckersley	.20	.07
❑	22 Will Clark	.30	.10
❑	23 Don Mattingly	1.25	.50
❑	24 Tony Gwynn	.60	.25
❑	25 Ivan Rodriguez	.30	.10
❑	26 Shawon Dunston	.10	.02
❑	27 Mike Mussina	.30	.10
❑	28 Marquis Grissom	.20	.07
❑	29 Charles Nagy	.10	.02
❑	30 Len Dykstra	.20	.07
❑	31 Cecil Fielder	.20	.07
❑	32 Jay Bell	.20	.07
❑	33 B.J. Surhoff	.20	.07
❑	34 Bob Tewksbury	.10	.02
❑	35 Danny Tartabull	.10	.02
❑	36 Terry Pendleton	.20	.07
❑	37 Jack Morris	.20	.07
❑	38 Hal Morris	.10	.02
❑	39 Luis Polonia	.10	.02
❑	40 Ken Caminiti	.20	.07
❑	41 Robin Ventura	.20	.07
❑	42 Darryl Strawberry	.20	.07
❑	43 Wally Joyner	.20	.07
❑	44 Fred McGriff	.30	.10
❑	45 Kevin Tapani	.10	.02
❑	46 Matt Williams	.20	.07
❑	47 Robin Yount	.75	.30
❑	48 Ken Hill	.10	.02
❑	49 Edgar Martinez	.30	.10
❑	50 Mark Grace	.30	.10
❑	51 Juan Gonzalez	.20	.07
❑	52 Curt Schilling	.20	.07
❑	53 Dwight Gooden	.20	.07
❑	54 Chris Hoiles	.10	.02
❑	55 Frank Viola	.20	.07
❑	56 Ray Lankford	.20	.07
❑	57 George Brett	1.25	.50
❑	58 Kenny Lofton	.20	.07
❑	59 Nolan Ryan	2.00	.75
❑	60 Mickey Tettleton	.10	.02
❑	61 John Smoltz	.30	.10
❑	62 Howard Johnson	.10	.02
❑	63 Eric Karros	.20	.07
❑	64 Rick Aguilera	.10	.02
❑	65 Steve Finley	.20	.07
❑	66 Mark Langston	.10	.02
❑	67 Bill Swift	.10	.02
❑	68 John Olerud	.20	.07
❑	69 Kevin McReynolds	.10	.02
❑	70 Jack McDowell	.10	.02
❑	71 Rickey Henderson	.50	.20
❑	72 Brian Harper	.10	.02
❑	73 Mike Morgan	.10	.02
❑	74 Rafael Palmeiro	.30	.10
❑	75 Dennis Martinez	.20	.07
❑	76 Tino Martinez	.30	.10
❑	77 Eddie Murray	.50	.20
❑	78 Ellis Burks	.20	.07
❑	79 John Kruk	.20	.07
❑	80 Gregg Olson	.10	.02
❑	81 Bernard Gilkey	.10	.02
❑	82 Milt Cuyler	.10	.02
❑	83 Mike LaValliere	.10	.02
❑	84 Albert Belle	.20	.07
❑	85 Bip Roberts	.10	.02
❑	86 Melido Perez	.10	.02
❑	87 Otis Nixon	.10	.02
❑	88 Bill Spiers	.10	.02
❑	89 Jeff Bagwell	.30	.10
❑	90 Orel Hershiser	.20	.07
❑	91 Andy Benes	.10	.02
❑	92 Devon White	.20	.07
❑	93 Willie McGee	.20	.07
❑	94 Ozzie Guillen	.20	.07
❑	95 Ivan Calderon	.10	.02
❑	96 Keith Miller	.10	.02
❑	97 Steve Buechele	.10	.02
❑	98 Kent Hrbek	.20	.07
❑	99 Dave Hollins	.10	.02
❑	100 Mike Bordick	.10	.02
❑	101 Randy Tomlin	.10	.02
❑	102 Omar Vizquel	.30	.10
❑	103 Lee Smith	.20	.07
❑	104 Leo Gomez	.10	.02
❑	105 Jose Rijo	.10	.02
❑	106 Mark Whiten	.10	.02
❑	107 David Justice	.20	.07
❑	108 Eddie Taubensee	.10	.02
❑	109 Lance Johnson	.10	.02
❑	110 Felix Jose	.10	.02
❑	111 Mike Harkey	.10	.02
❑	112 Randy Milligan	.10	.02
❑	113 Anthony Young	.10	.02
❑	114 Rico Brogna	.10	.02
❑	115 Bret Saberhagen	.20	.07
❑	116 Sandy Alomar Jr.	.10	.02
❑	117 Terry Mulholland	.10	.02
❑	118 Darryl Hamilton	.10	.02
❑	119 Todd Zeile	.10	.02
❑	120 Bernie Williams	.30	.10
❑	121 Zane Smith	.10	.02
❑	122 Derek Bell	.10	.02
❑	123 Deion Sanders	.30	.10
❑	124 Luis Sojo	.10	.02
❑	125 Joe Oliver	.10	.02
❑	126 Craig Grebeck	.10	.02
❑	127 Andujar Cedeno	.10	.02
❑	128 Brian McRae	.10	.02
❑	129 Jose Offerman	.10	.02
❑	130 Pedro Munoz	.10	.02
❑	131 Bud Black	.10	.02
❑	132 Mo Vaughn	.20	.07
❑	133 Bruce Hurst	.10	.02
❑	134 Dave Henderson	.10	.02
❑	135 Tom Pagnozzi	.10	.02
❑	136 Erik Hanson	.10	.02
❑	137 Orlando Merced	.10	.02
❑	138 Dean Palmer	.20	.07
❑	139 John Franco	.20	.07
❑	140 Brady Anderson	.20	.07
❑	141 Ricky Jordan	.10	.02
❑	142 Jeff Blauser	.10	.02
❑	143 Sammy Sosa	.50	.20
❑	144 Bob Walk	.10	.02
❑	145 Delino DeShields	.10	.02
❑	146 Kevin Brown	.20	.07
❑	147 Mark Lemke	.10	.02
❑	148 Chuck Knoblauch	.20	.07
❑	149 Chris Sabo	.10	.02
❑	150 Bobby Witt	.10	.02
❑	151 Luis Gonzalez	.20	.07
❑	152 Ron Karkovice	.10	.02
❑	153 Jeff Brantley	.10	.02
❑	154 Kevin Appier	.20	.07
❑	155 Darrin Jackson	.10	.02
❑	156 Kelly Gruber	.10	.02
❑	157 Royce Clayton	.10	.02
❑	158 Chuck Finley	.20	.07
❑	159 Jeff King	.10	.02
❑	160 Greg Vaughn	.10	.02
❑	161 Geronimo Pena	.10	.02
❑	162 Steve Farr	.10	.02
❑	163 Jose Oquendo	.10	.02
❑	164 Mark Lewis	.10	.02
❑	165 John Wetteland	.20	.07
❑	166 Mike Henneman	.10	.02
❑	167 Todd Hundley	.10	.02
❑	168 Wes Chamberlain	.10	.02
❑	169 Steve Avery	.10	.02
❑	170 Mike Devereaux	.10	.02
❑	171 Reggie Sanders	.20	.07
❑	172 Jay Buhner	.20	.07
❑	173 Eric Anthony	.10	.02
❑	174 John Burkett	.10	.02
❑	175 Tom Candiotti	.10	.02
❑	176 Phil Plantier	.10	.02
❑	177 Doug Henry	.10	.02
❑	178 Scott Leius	.10	.02
❑	179 Kirt Manwaring	.10	.02
❑	180 Jeff Parrett	.10	.02
❑	181 Don Slaught	.10	.02
❑	182 Scott Radinsky	.10	.02
❑	183 Luis Alicea	.10	.02
❑	184 Tom Gordon	.10	.02
❑	185 Rick Wilkins	.10	.02
❑	186 Todd Stottlemyre	.10	.02
❑	187 Moises Alou	.20	.07
❑	188 Joe Grahe	.10	.02
❑	189 Jeff Kent	.50	.20
❑	190 Bill Wegman	.10	.02
❑	191 Kim Batiste	.10	.02
❑	192 Matt Nokes	.10	.02
❑	193 Mark Wohlers	.10	.02
❑	194 Paul Sorrento	.10	.02
❑	195 Chris Hammond	.10	.02
❑	196 Scott Livingstone	.10	.02
❑	197 Doug Jones	.10	.02
❑	198 Scott Cooper	.10	.02
❑	199 Ramon Martinez	.10	.02
❑	200 Dave Valle	.10	.02
❑	201 Mariano Duncan	.10	.02
❑	202 Ben McDonald	.10	.02
❑	203 Darren Lewis	.10	.02
❑	204 Kenny Rogers	.20	.07
❑	205 Manuel Lee	.10	.02
❑	206 Scott Erickson	.10	.02
❑	207 Dan Gladden	.10	.02
❑	208 Bob Welch	.10	.02
❑	209 Greg Olson	.10	.02
❑	210 Dan Pasqua	.10	.02
❑	211 Tim Wallach	.10	.02
❑	212 Jeff Montgomery	.10	.02
❑	213 Derrick May	.10	.02
❑	214 Ed Sprague	.10	.02
❑	215 David Haas	.10	.02
❑	216 Darrin Fletcher	.10	.02
❑	217 Brian Jordan	.20	.07
❑	218 Jaime Navarro	.10	.02
❑	219 Randy Velarde	.10	.02
❑	220 Ron Gant	.20	.07
❑	221 Paul Quantrill	.10	.02
❑	222 Damion Easley	.10	.02
❑	223 Charlie Hough	.20	.07
❑	224 Brad Brink	.10	.02
❑	225 Barry Manuel	.10	.02
❑	226 Kevin Koslofski	.10	.02
❑	227 Ryan Thompson	.10	.02
❑	228 Mike Munoz	.10	.02
❑	229 Dan Wilson	.20	.07
❑	230 Peter Hoy	.10	.02
❑	231 Pedro Astacio	.10	.02
❑	232 Matt Stairs	.10	.02
❑	233 Jeff Reboulet	.10	.02
❑	234 Manny Alexander	.10	.02
❑	235 Willie Banks	.10	.02
❑	236 John Jaha	.10	.02
❑	237 Scooter Tucker	.10	.02

❑	238	Russ Springer	.10	.02
❑	239	Paul Miller	.10	.02
❑	240	Dan Peltier	.10	.02
❑	241	Ozzie Canseco	.10	.02
❑	242	Ben Rivera	.10	.02
❑	243	John Valentin	.10	.02
❑	244	Henry Rodriguez	.10	.02
❑	245	Derek Parks	.10	.02
❑	246	Carlos Garcia	.10	.02
❑	247	Tim Pugh RC	.10	.02
❑	248	Melvin Nieves	.10	.02
❑	249	Rich Amaral	.10	.02
❑	250	Willie Greene	.10	.02
❑	251	Tim Scott	.10	.02
❑	252	Dave Silvestri	.10	.02
❑	253	Rob Mallicoat	.10	.02
❑	254	Donald Harris	.10	.02
❑	255	Craig Colbert	.10	.02
❑	256	Jose Guzman	.10	.02
❑	257	Domingo Martinez RC	.10	.02
❑	258	William Suero	.10	.02
❑	259	Juan Guerrero	.10	.02
❑	260	J.T.Snow RC	.50	.20
❑	261	Tony Pena	.10	.02
❑	262	Tim Fortugno	.10	.02
❑	263	Tom Marsh	.10	.02
❑	264	Kurt Knudsen	.10	.02
❑	265	Tim Costo	.10	.02
❑	266	Steve Shifflett	.10	.02
❑	267	Billy Ashley	.10	.02
❑	268	Jerry Nielsen	.10	.02
❑	269	Pete Young	.10	.02
❑	270	Johnny Guzman	.10	.02
❑	271	Greg Colbrunn	.10	.02
❑	272	Jeff Nelson	.10	.02
❑	273	Kevin Young	.20	.07
❑	274	Jeff Frye	.10	.02
❑	275	J.T. Bruett	.10	.02
❑	276	Todd Pratt RC	.25	.08
❑	277	Mike Butcher	.10	.02
❑	278	John Flaherty	.10	.02
❑	279	John Patterson	.10	.02
❑	280	Eric Hillman	.10	.02
❑	281	Bien Figueroa	.10	.02
❑	282	Shane Reynolds	.10	.02
❑	283	Rich Rowland	.10	.02
❑	284	Steve Foster	.10	.02
❑	285	Dave Mlicki	.10	.02
❑	286	Mike Piazza	3.00	1.25
❑	287	Mike Trombley	.10	.02
❑	288	Jim Pena	.10	.02
❑	289	Bob Ayrault	.10	.02
❑	290	Henry Mercedes	.10	.02
❑	291	Bob Wickman	.10	.02
❑	292	Jacob Brumfield	.10	.02
❑	293	David Hulse RC	.10	.02
❑	294	Ryan Klesko	.20	.07
❑	295	Doug Linton	.10	.02
❑	296	Steve Cooke	.10	.02
❑	297	Eddie Zosky	.10	.02
❑	298	Gerald Williams	.10	.02
❑	299	Jonathan Hurst	.10	.02
❑	300	Larry Carter RC	.10	.02
❑	301	William Pennyfeather	.10	.02
❑	302	Cesar Hernandez	.10	.02
❑	303	Steve Hosey	.10	.02
❑	304	Blas Minor	.10	.02
❑	305	Jeff Grotewald	.10	.02
❑	306	Bernardo Brito	.10	.02
❑	307	Rafael Bournigal	.10	.02
❑	308	Jeff Branson	.10	.02
❑	309	Tom Quinlan RC	.10	.02
❑	310	Pat Gomez RC	.10	.02
❑	311	Sterling Hitchcock RC	.25	.08
❑	312	Kent Bottenfield	.10	.02
❑	313	Alan Trammell	.20	.07
❑	314	Cris Colon	.10	.02
❑	315	Paul Wagner	.10	.02
❑	316	Matt Maysey	.10	.02
❑	317	Mike Stanton	.10	.02
❑	318	Rick Trlicek	.10	.02
❑	319	Kevin Rogers	.10	.02
❑	320	Mark Clark	.10	.02
❑	321	Pedro Martinez	1.00	.40
❑	322	Al Martin	.10	.02
❑	323	Mike Macfarlane	.10	.02
❑	324	Rey Sanchez	.10	.02
❑	325	Roger Pavlik	.10	.02
❑	326	Troy Neel	.10	.02
❑	327	Kerry Woodson	.10	.02
❑	328	Wayne Kirby	.10	.02
❑	329	Ken Ryan RC	.25	.08
❑	330	Jesse Levis	.10	.02
❑	331	Jim Austin	.10	.02
❑	332	Dan Walters	.10	.02
❑	333	Brian Williams	.10	.02
❑	334	Wil Cordero	.10	.02
❑	335	Bret Boone	.20	.07
❑	336	Hipolito Pichardo	.10	.02
❑	337	Pat Mahomes	.10	.02
❑	338	Andy Stankiewicz	.10	.02
❑	339	Jim Bullinger	.10	.02
❑	340	Archi Cianfrocco	.10	.02
❑	341	Ruben Amaro	.10	.02
❑	342	Frank Seminara	.10	.02
❑	343	Pat Hentgen	.10	.02
❑	344	Dave Nilsson	.10	.02
❑	345	Mike Perez	.10	.02
❑	346	Tim Salmon	.30	.10
❑	347	Tim Wakefield	.50	.20
❑	348	Carlos Hernandez	.10	.02
❑	349	Donovan Osborne	.10	.02
❑	350	Denny Neagle	.20	.07
❑	351	Sam Militello	.10	.02
❑	352	Eric Fox	.10	.02
❑	353	John Doherty	.10	.02
❑	354	Chad Curtis	.10	.02
❑	355	Jeff Tackett	.10	.02
❑	356	Dave Fleming	.10	.02
❑	357	Pat Listach	.10	.02
❑	358	Kevin Wickander	.10	.02
❑	359	John Vander Wal	.10	.02
❑	360	Arthur Rhodes	.10	.02
❑	361	Bob Scanlan	.10	.02
❑	362	Bob Zupcic	.10	.02
❑	363	Mel Rojas	.10	.02
❑	364	Jim Thome	.30	.10
❑	365	Bill Pecota	.10	.02
❑	366	Mark Carreon	.10	.02
❑	367	Mitch Williams	.10	.02
❑	368	Cal Eldred	.10	.02
❑	369	Stan Belinda	.10	.02
❑	370	Pat Kelly	.10	.02
❑	371	Rheal Cormier	.10	.02
❑	372	Juan Guzman	.10	.02
❑	373	Damon Berryhill	.10	.02
❑	374	Gary DiSarcina	.10	.02
❑	375	Norm Charlton	.10	.02
❑	376	Roberto Hernandez	.10	.02
❑	377	Scott Kamieniecki	.10	.02
❑	378	Rusty Meacham	.10	.02
❑	379	Kurt Stillwell	.10	.02
❑	380	Lloyd McClendon	.10	.02
❑	381	Mark Leonard	.10	.02
❑	382	Jerry Browne	.10	.02
❑	383	Glenn Davis	.10	.02
❑	384	Randy Johnson	.50	.20
❑	385	Mike Greenwell	.10	.02
❑	386	Scott Chiamparino	.10	.02
❑	387	George Bell	.10	.02
❑	388	Steve Olin	.10	.02
❑	389	Chuck McElroy	.10	.02
❑	390	Mark Gardner	.10	.02
❑	391	Rod Beck	.10	.02
❑	392	Dennis Rasmussen	.10	.02
❑	393	Charlie Leibrandt	.10	.02
❑	394	Julio Franco	.20	.07
❑	395	Pete Harnisch	.10	.02
❑	396	Sid Bream	.10	.02
❑	397	Milt Thompson	.10	.02
❑	398	Glenallen Hill	.10	.02
❑	399	Chico Walker	.10	.02
❑	400	Alex Cole	.10	.02
❑	401	Trevor Wilson	.10	.02
❑	402	Jeff Conine	.20	.07
❑	403	Kyle Abbott	.10	.02
❑	404	Tom Browning	.10	.02
❑	405	Jerald Clark	.10	.02
❑	406	Vince Horsman	.10	.02
❑	407	Kevin Mitchell	.10	.02
❑	408	Pete Smith	.10	.02
❑	409	Jeff Innis	.10	.02
❑	410	Mike Timlin	.10	.02
❑	411	Charlie Hayes	.10	.02
❑	412	Alex Fernandez	.10	.02
❑	413	Jeff Russell	.10	.02
❑	414	Jody Reed	.10	.02
❑	415	Mickey Morandini	.10	.02
❑	416	Darnell Coles	.10	.02
❑	417	Xavier Hernandez	.10	.02
❑	418	Steve Sax	.10	.02
❑	419	Joe Girardi	.10	.02
❑	420	Mike Fetters	.10	.02
❑	421	Danny Jackson	.10	.02
❑	422	Jim Gott	.10	.02
❑	423	Tim Belcher	.10	.02
❑	424	Jose Mesa	.10	.02
❑	425	Junior Felix	.10	.02
❑	426	Thomas Howard	.10	.02
❑	427	Julio Valera	.10	.02
❑	428	Dante Bichette	.20	.07
❑	429	Mike Sharperson	.10	.02
❑	430	Darryl Kile	.20	.07
❑	431	Lonnie Smith	.10	.02
❑	432	Monty Fariss	.10	.02
❑	433	Reggie Jefferson	.10	.02
❑	434	Bob McClure	.10	.02
❑	435	Craig Lefferts	.10	.02
❑	436	Duane Ward	.10	.02
❑	437	Shawn Abner	.10	.02
❑	438	Roberto Kelly	.10	.02
❑	439	Paul O'Neill	.30	.10
❑	440	Alan Mills	.10	.02
❑	441	Roger Mason	.10	.02
❑	442	Gary Pettis	.10	.02
❑	443	Steve Lake	.10	.02
❑	444	Gene Larkin	.10	.02
❑	445	Larry Andersen	.10	.02
❑	446	Doug Dascenzo	.10	.02
❑	447	Daryl Boston	.10	.02
❑	448	John Candelaria	.10	.02
❑	449	Storm Davis	.10	.02
❑	450	Tom Edens	.10	.02
❑	451	Mike Maddux	.10	.02
❑	452	Tim Naehring	.10	.02
❑	453	John Orton	.10	.02
❑	454	Joey Cora	.10	.02
❑	455	Chuck Crim	.10	.02
❑	456	Dan Plesac	.10	.02
❑	457	Mike Bielecki	.10	.02
❑	458	Terry Jorgensen	.10	.02
❑	459	John Habyan	.10	.02
❑	460	Pete O'Brien	.10	.02
❑	461	Jeff Treadway	.10	.02
❑	462	Frank Castillo	.10	.02
❑	463	Jimmy Jones	.10	.02
❑	464	Tommy Greene	.10	.02
❑	465	Tracy Woodson	.10	.02
❑	466	Rich Rodriguez	.10	.02
❑	467	Joe Hesketh	.10	.02
❑	468	Greg Myers	.10	.02
❑	469	Kirk McCaskill	.10	.02
❑	470	Ricky Bones	.10	.02
❑	471	Lenny Webster	.10	.02
❑	472	Francisco Cabrera	.10	.02
❑	473	Turner Ward	.10	.02
❑	474	Dwayne Henry	.10	.02
❑	475	Al Osuna	.10	.02
❑	476	Craig Wilson	.10	.02
❑	477	Chris Nabholz	.10	.02
❑	478	Rafael Belliard	.10	.02
❑	479	Terry Leach	.10	.02
❑	480	Tim Teufel	.10	.02
❑	481	Dennis Eckersley AW	.20	.07
❑	482	Barry Bonds MVP	.75	.30
❑	483	Dennis Eckersley AW	.20	.07
❑	484	Greg Maddux CY	.50	.20
❑	485	Pat Listach AW	.10	.02
❑	486	Eric Karros AW	.10	.02
❑	487	Jamie Arnold RC	.10	.02
❑	488	B.J.Wallace	.10	.02
❑	489	Derek Jeter RC	10.00	4.00
❑	490	Jason Kendall RC	1.00	.40
❑	491	Rick Helling	.10	.02
❑	492	Derek Wallace RC	.10	.02
❑	493	Sean Lowe RC	.10	.02
❑	494	Shannon Stewart RC	.75	.30
❑	495	Benji Grigsby RC	.10	.02

❑	496	Todd Steverson RC	.10	.02
❑	497	Dan Serafini RC	.10	.02
❑	498	Michael Tucker	.10	.02
❑	499	Chris Roberts	.10	.02
❑	500	Pete Janicki RC	.10	.02
❑	501	Jeff Schmidt RC	.10	.02
❑	502	Edgar Martinez AS	.20	.07
❑	503	Omar Vizquel AS	.20	.07
❑	504	Ken Griffey Jr. AS	.50	.20
❑	505	Kirby Puckett AS	.30	.10
❑	506	Joe Carter AS	.10	.02
❑	507	Ivan Rodriguez AS	.20	.07
❑	508	Jack Morris AS	.10	.02
❑	509	Dennis Eckersley AS	.20	.07
❑	510	Frank Thomas AS	.30	.10
❑	511	Roberto Alomar AS	.20	.07
❑	512	Mickey Morandini AS	.10	.02
❑	513	Dennis Eckersley HL	.20	.07
❑	514	Jeff Reardon HL	.10	.02
❑	515	Danny Tartabull HL	.10	.02
❑	516	Bip Roberts HL	.10	.02
❑	517	George Brett HL	.60	.25
❑	518	Robin Yount HL	.50	.20
❑	519	Kevin Gross HL	.10	.02
❑	520	Ed Sprague WS	.10	.02
❑	521	Dave Winfield WS	.10	.02
❑	522	Ozzie Smith AS	.50	.20
❑	523	Barry Bonds AS	.75	.30
❑	524	Andy Van Slyke AS	.20	.07
❑	525	Tony Gwynn AS	.30	.10
❑	526	Darren Daulton AS	.10	.02
❑	527	Greg Maddux AS	.50	.20
❑	528	Fred McGriff AS	.30	.10
❑	529	Lee Smith AS	.10	.02
❑	530	Ryne Sandberg AS	.50	.20
❑	531	Gary Sheffield AS	.10	.02
❑	532	Ozzie Smith DT	.50	.20
❑	533	Kirby Puckett DT	.30	.10
❑	534	Gary Sheffield DT	.10	.02
❑	535	Andy Van Slyke DT	.20	.07
❑	536	Ken Griffey Jr. DT	.50	.20
❑	537	Ivan Rodriguez DT	.20	.07
❑	538	Charles Nagy DT	.10	.02
❑	539	Tom Glavine DT	.20	.07
❑	540	Dennis Eckersley DT	.20	.07
❑	541	Frank Thomas DT	.30	.10
❑	542	Roberto Alomar DT	.20	.07
❑	543	Sean Berry	.10	.02
❑	544	Mike Schooler	.10	.02
❑	545	Chuck Carr	.10	.02
❑	546	Lenny Harris	.10	.02
❑	547	Gary Scott	.10	.02
❑	548	Derek Lilliquist	.10	.02
❑	549	Brian Hunter	.10	.02
❑	550	Kirby Puckett MOY	.30	.10
❑	551	Jim Eisenreich	.10	.02
❑	552	Andre Dawson	.20	.07
❑	553	David Nied	.10	.02
❑	554	Spike Owen	.10	.02
❑	555	Greg Gagne	.10	.02
❑	556	Sid Fernandez	.10	.02
❑	557	Mark McGwire	1.25	.50
❑	558	Bryan Harvey	.10	.02
❑	559	Harold Reynolds	.20	.07
❑	560	Barry Bonds	1.50	.60
❑	561	Eric Wedge RC	.25	.08
❑	562	Ozzie Smith	.75	.30
❑	563	Rick Sutcliffe	.20	.07
❑	564	Jeff Reardon	.20	.07
❑	565	Alex Arias	.10	.02
❑	566	Greg Swindell	.10	.02
❑	567	Brook Jacoby	.10	.02
❑	568	Pete Incaviglia	.10	.02
❑	569	Butch Henry	.10	.02
❑	570	Eric Davis	.20	.07
❑	571	Kevin Seitzer	.10	.02
❑	572	Tony Fernandez	.10	.02
❑	573	Steve Reed RC	.10	.02
❑	574	Cory Snyder	.10	.02
❑	575	Joe Carter	.20	.07
❑	576	Greg Maddux	.75	.30
❑	577	Bert Blyleven UER (Should say 3701 career strike)	.20	.07
❑	578	Kevin Bass	.10	.02
❑	579	Carlton Fisk	.30	.10
❑	580	Doug Drabek	.10	.02
❑	581	Mark Gubicza	.10	.02
❑	582	Bobby Thigpen	.10	.02
❑	583	Chili Davis	.20	.07
❑	584	Scott Bankhead	.10	.02
❑	585	Harold Baines	.20	.07
❑	586	Eric Young	.10	.02
❑	587	Lance Parrish	.20	.07
❑	588	Juan Bell	.10	.02
❑	589	Bob Ojeda	.10	.02
❑	590	Joe Orsulak	.10	.02
❑	591	Benito Santiago	.20	.07
❑	592	Wade Boggs	.30	.10
❑	593	Robby Thompson	.10	.02
❑	594	Eric Plunk	.10	.02
❑	595	Hensley Meulens	.10	.02
❑	596	Lou Whitaker	.20	.07
❑	597	Dale Murphy	.30	.10
❑	598	Paul Molitor	.20	.07
❑	599	Greg W. Harris	.10	.02
❑	600	Darren Holmes	.10	.02
❑	601	Dave Martinez	.10	.02
❑	602	Tom Henke	.10	.02
❑	603	Mike Benjamin	.10	.02
❑	604	Rene Gonzales	.10	.02
❑	605	Roger McDowell	.10	.02
❑	606	Kirby Puckett	.50	.20
❑	607	Randy Myers	.10	.02
❑	608	Ruben Sierra	.20	.07
❑	609	Wilson Alvarez	.10	.02
❑	610	David Segui	.10	.02
❑	611	Juan Samuel	.10	.02
❑	612	Tom Brunansky	.10	.02
❑	613	Willie Randolph	.20	.07
❑	614	Tony Phillips	.10	.02
❑	615	Candy Maldonado	.10	.02
❑	616	Chris Bosio	.10	.02
❑	617	Bret Barberie	.10	.02
❑	618	Scott Sanderson	.10	.02
❑	619	Ron Darling	.10	.02
❑	620	Dave Winfield	.20	.07
❑	621	Mike Felder	.10	.02
❑	622	Greg Hibbard	.10	.02
❑	623	Mike Scioscia	.10	.02
❑	624	John Smiley	.10	.02
❑	625	Alejandro Pena	.10	.02
❑	626	Terry Steinbach	.10	.02
❑	627	Freddie Benavides	.10	.02
❑	628	Kevin Reimer	.10	.02
❑	629	Braulio Castillo	.10	.02
❑	630	Dave Stieb	.10	.02
❑	631	Dave Magadan	.10	.02
❑	632	Scott Fletcher	.10	.02
❑	633	Cris Carpenter	.10	.02
❑	634	Kevin Maas	.10	.02
❑	635	Todd Worrell	.10	.02
❑	636	Rob Deer	.10	.02
❑	637	Dwight Smith	.10	.02
❑	638	Chito Martinez	.10	.02
❑	639	Jimmy Key	.20	.07
❑	640	Greg A. Harris	.10	.02
❑	641	Mike Moore	.10	.02
❑	642	Pat Borders	.10	.02
❑	643	Bill Gullickson	.10	.02
❑	644	Gary Gaetti	.20	.07
❑	645	David Howard	.10	.02
❑	646	Jim Abbott	.30	.10
❑	647	Willie Wilson	.10	.02
❑	648	David Wells	.20	.07
❑	649	Andres Galarraga	.20	.07
❑	650	Vince Coleman	.10	.02
❑	651	Rob Dibble	.20	.07
❑	652	Frank Tanana	.10	.02
❑	653	Steve Decker	.10	.02
❑	654	David Cone	.20	.07
❑	655	Jack Armstrong	.10	.02
❑	656	Dave Stewart	.20	.07
❑	657	Billy Hatcher	.10	.02
❑	658	Tim Raines	.20	.07
❑	659	Walt Weiss	.10	.02
❑	660	Jose Lind	.10	.02

1994 Score

❑	COMPLETE SET (660)	24.00	10.00
❑	COMPLETE SERIES 1 (330)	12.00	5.00
❑	COMPLETE SERIES 2 (330)	12.00	5.00

❑	1	Barry Bonds	1.50	.60
❑	2	John Olerud	.20	.07
❑	3	Ken Griffey Jr.	.75	.30
❑	4	Jeff Bagwell	.30	.10
❑	5	John Burkett	.10	.02
❑	6	Jack McDowell	.10	.02
❑	7	Albert Belle	.20	.07
❑	8	Andres Galarraga	.20	.07
❑	9	Mike Mussina	.30	.10
❑	10	Will Clark	.30	.10
❑	11	Travis Fryman	.20	.07
❑	12	Tony Gwynn	.60	.25
❑	13	Robin Yount	.75	.30
❑	14	Dave Magadan	.10	.02
❑	15	Paul O'Neill	.30	.10
❑	16	Ray Lankford	.20	.07
❑	17	Damion Easley	.10	.02
❑	18	Andy Van Slyke	.30	.10
❑	19	Brian McRae	.10	.02
❑	20	Ryne Sandberg	.75	.30
❑	21	Kirby Puckett	.50	.20
❑	22	Dwight Gooden	.20	.07
❑	23	Don Mattingly	1.25	.50
❑	24	Kevin Mitchell	.10	.02
❑	25	Roger Clemens	1.00	.40
❑	26	Eric Karros	.20	.07
❑	27	Juan Gonzalez	.20	.07
❑	28	John Kruk	.20	.07
❑	29	Gregg Jefferies	.10	.02
❑	30	Tom Glavine	.30	.10
❑	31	Ivan Rodriguez	.30	.10
❑	32	Jay Bell	.20	.07
❑	33	Randy Johnson	.50	.20
❑	34	Darren Daulton	.20	.07
❑	35	Rickey Henderson	.50	.20
❑	36	Eddie Murray	.50	.20
❑	37	Brian Harper	.10	.02
❑	38	Delino DeShields	.10	.02
❑	39	Jose Lind	.10	.02
❑	40	Benito Santiago	.20	.07
❑	41	Frank Thomas	.50	.20
❑	42	Mark Grace	.30	.10
❑	43	Roberto Alomar	.30	.10
❑	44	Andy Benes	.10	.02
❑	45	Luis Polonia	.10	.02
❑	46	Brett Butler	.20	.07
❑	47	Terry Steinbach	.10	.02
❑	48	Craig Biggio	.30	.10
❑	49	Greg Vaughn	.10	.02
❑	50	Charlie Hayes	.10	.02
❑	51	Mickey Tettleton	.10	.02
❑	52	Jose Rijo	.10	.02
❑	53	Carlos Baerga	.10	.02
❑	54	Jeff Blauser	.10	.02
❑	55	Leo Gomez	.10	.02
❑	56	Bob Tewksbury	.10	.02
❑	57	Mo Vaughn	.20	.07
❑	58	Orlando Merced	.10	.02
❑	59	Tino Martinez	.30	.10
❑	60	Lenny Dykstra	.20	.07
❑	61	Jose Canseco	.30	.10
❑	62	Tony Fernandez	.10	.02
❑	63	Donovan Osborne	.10	.02
❑	64	Ken Hill	.10	.02
❑	65	Kent Hrbek	.20	.07
❑	66	Bryan Harvey	.10	.02
❑	67	Wally Joyner	.20	.07
❑	68	Derrick May	.10	.02

❑	69 Lance Johnson	.10	.02
❑	70 Willie McGee	.20	.07
❑	71 Mark Langston	.10	.02
❑	72 Terry Pendleton	.20	.07
❑	73 Joe Carter	.20	.07
❑	74 Barry Larkin	.30	.10
❑	75 Jimmy Key	.20	.07
❑	76 Joe Girardi	.10	.02
❑	77 B.J. Surhoff	.20	.07
❑	78 Pete Harnisch	.10	.02
❑	79 Lou Whitaker UER	.20	.07
❑	80 Cory Snyder	.10	.02
❑	81 Kenny Lofton	.20	.07
❑	82 Fred McGriff	.30	.10
❑	83 Mike Greenwell	.10	.02
❑	84 Mike Perez	.10	.02
❑	85 Cal Ripken	1.50	.60
❑	86 Don Slaught	.10	.02
❑	87 Omar Vizquel	.30	.10
❑	88 Curt Schilling	.20	.07
❑	89 Chuck Knoblauch	.20	.07
❑	90 Moises Alou	.20	.07
❑	91 Greg Gagne	.10	.02
❑	92 Bret Saberhagen	.20	.07
❑	93 Ozzie Guillen	.20	.07
❑	94 Matt Williams	.20	.07
❑	95 Chad Curtis	.10	.02
❑	96 Mike Harkey	.10	.02
❑	97 Devon White	.20	.07
❑	98 Walt Weiss	.10	.02
❑	99 Kevin Brown	.20	.07
❑	100 Gary Sheffield	.20	.07
❑	101 Wade Boggs	.30	.10
❑	102 Orel Hershiser	.20	.07
❑	103 Tony Phillips	.10	.02
❑	104 Andujar Cedeno	.10	.02
❑	105 Bill Spiers	.10	.02
❑	106 Otis Nixon	.10	.02
❑	107 Felix Fermin	:10	.02
❑	108 Bip Roberts	.10	.02
❑	109 Dennis Eckersley	.20	.07
❑	110 Dante Bichette	.20	.07
❑	111 Ben McDonald	.10	.02
❑	112 Jim Poole	.10	.02
❑	113 John Dopson	.10	.02
❑	114 Rob Dibble	.20	.07
❑	115 Jeff Treadway	.10	.02
❑	116 Ricky Jordan	.10	.02
❑	117 Mike Henneman	.10	.02
❑	118 Willie Blair	.10	.02
❑	119 Doug Henry	.10	.02
❑	120 Gerald Perry	.10	.02
❑	121 Greg Myers	.10	.02
❑	122 John Franco	.20	.07
❑	123 Roger Mason	.10	.02
❑	124 Chris Hammond	.10	.02
❑	125 Hubie Brooks	.10	.02
❑	126 Kent Mercker	.10	.02
❑	127 Jim Abbott	.30	.10
❑	128 Kevin Bass	.10	.02
❑	129 Rick Aguilera	.10	.02
❑	130 Mitch Webster	.10	.02
❑	131 Eric Plunk	.10	.02
❑	132 Mark Carreon	.10	.02
❑	133 Dave Stewart	.20	.07
❑	134 Willie Wilson	.10	.02
❑	135 Dave Fleming	.10	.02
❑	136 Jeff Tackett	.10	.02
❑	137 Geno Petralli	.10	.02
❑	138 Gene Harris	.10	.02
❑	139 Scott Bankhead	.10	.02
❑	140 Trevor Wilson	.10	.02
❑	141 Alvaro Espinoza	.10	.02
❑	142 Ryan Bowen	.10	.02
❑	143 Mike Moore	.10	.02
❑	144 Bill Pecota	.10	.02
❑	145 Jaime Navarro	.10	.02
❑	146 Jack Daugherty	.10	.02
❑	147 Bob Wickman	.10	.02
❑	148 Chris Jones	.10	.02
❑	149 Todd Stottlemyre	.10	.02
❑	150 Brian Williams	.10	.02
❑	151 Chuck Finley	.20	.07
❑	152 Lenny Harris	.10	.02
❑	153 Alex Fernandez	.10	.02
❑	154 Candy Maldonado	.10	.02

❑	155 Jeff Montgomery	.10	.02
❑	156 David West	.10	.02
❑	157 Mark Williamson	.10	.02
❑	158 Milt Thompson	.10	.02
❑	159 Ron Darling	.10	.02
❑	160 Stan Belinda	.10	.02
❑	161 Henry Cotto	.10	.02
❑	162 Mel Rojas	.10	.02
❑	163 Doug Strange	.10	.02
❑	164 Rene Arocha	.10	.02
❑	165 Tim Hulett	.10	.02
❑	166 Steve Avery	.10	.02
❑	167 Jim Thome	.30	.10
❑	168 Tom Browning	.10	.02
❑	169 Mario Diaz	.10	.02
❑	170 Steve Reed	.10	.02
❑	171 Scott Livingstone	.10	.02
❑	172 Chris Donnels	.10	.02
❑	173 John Jaha	.10	.02
❑	174 Carlos Hernandez	.10	.02
❑	175 Dion James	.10	.02
❑	176 Bud Black	.10	.02
❑	177 Tony Castillo	.10	.02
❑	178 Jose Guzman	.10	.02
❑	179 Torey Lovullo	.10	.02
❑	180 John Vander Wal	.10	.02
❑	181 Mike LaValliere	.10	.02
❑	182 Sid Fernandez	.10	.02
❑	183 Brent Mayne	.10	.02
❑	184 Terry Mulholland	.10	.02
❑	185 Willie Banks	.10	.02
❑	186 Steve Cooke	.10	.02
❑	187 Brent Gates	.10	.02
❑	188 Erik Pappas	.10	.02
❑	189 Bill Haselman	.10	.02
❑	190 Fernando Valenzuela	.20	.07
❑	191 Gary Redus	.10	.02
❑	192 Danny Darwin	.10	.02
❑	193 Mark Portugal	.10	.02
❑	194 Derek Lilliquist	.10	.02
❑	195 Charlie O'Brien	.10	.02
❑	196 Matt Nokes	.10	.02
❑	197 Danny Sheaffer	.10	.02
❑	198 Bill Gullickson	.10	.02
❑	199 Alex Arias	.10	.02
❑	200 Mike Fetters	.10	.02
❑	201 Brian Jordan	.20	.07
❑	202 Joe Grahe	.10	.02
❑	203 Tom Candiotti	.10	.02
❑	204 Jeremy Hernandez	.10	.02
❑	205 Mike Stanton	.10	.02
❑	206 David Howard	.10	.02
❑	207 Darren Holmes	.10	.02
❑	208 Rick Honeycutt	.10	.02
❑	209 Danny Jackson	.10	.02
❑	210 Rich Amaral	.10	.02
❑	211 Blas Minor	.10	.02
❑	212 Kenny Rogers	.20	.07
❑	213 Jim Leyritz	.10	.02
❑	214 Mike Morgan	.10	.02
❑	215 Dan Gladden	.10	.02
❑	216 Randy Velarde	.10	.02
❑	217 Mitch Williams	.10	.02
❑	218 Hipolito Pichardo	.10	.02
❑	219 Dave Burba	.10	.02
❑	220 Wilson Alvarez	.10	.02
❑	221 Bob Zupcic	.10	.02
❑	222 Francisco Cabrera	.10	.02
❑	223 Julio Valera	.10	.02
❑	224 Paul Assenmacher	.10	.02
❑	225 Jeff Branson	.10	.02
❑	226 Todd Frohwirth	.10	.02
❑	227 Armando Reynoso	.10	.02
❑	228 Rich Rowland	.10	.02
❑	229 Freddie Benavides	.10	.02
❑	230 Wayne Kirby	.10	.02
❑	231 Darryl Kile	.20	.07
❑	232 Skeeter Barnes	.10	.02
❑	233 Ramon Martinez	.10	.02
❑	234 Tom Gordon	.10	.02
❑	235 Dave Gallagher	.10	.02
❑	236 Ricky Bones	.10	.02
❑	237 Larry Andersen	.10	.02
❑	238 Pat Meares	.10	.02
❑	239 Zane Smith	.10	.02
❑	240 Tim Leary	.10	.02

❑	241 Phil Clark	.10	.02
❑	242 Danny Cox	.10	.02
❑	243 Mike Jackson	.10	.02
❑	244 Mike Gallego	.10	.02
❑	245 Lee Smith	.20	.07
❑	246 Todd Jones	.10	.02
❑	247 Steve Bedrosian	.10	.02
❑	248 Troy Neel	.10	.02
❑	249 Jose Bautista	.10	.02
❑	250 Steve Frey	.10	.02
❑	251 Jeff Reardon	.20	.07
❑	252 Stan Javier	.10	.02
❑	253 Mo Sanford	.10	.02
❑	254 Steve Sax	.10	.02
❑	255 Luis Aquino	.10	.02
❑	256 Domingo Jean	.10	.02
❑	257 Scott Servais	.10	.02
❑	258 Brad Pennington	.10	.02
❑	259 Dave Hansen	.10	.02
❑	260 Rich Gossage	.20	.07
❑	261 Jeff Fassero	.10	.02
❑	262 Junior Ortiz	.10	.02
❑	263 Anthony Young	.10	.02
❑	264 Chris Bosio	.10	.02
❑	265 Ruben Amaro	.10	.02
❑	266 Mark Eichhorn	.10	.02
❑	267 Dave Clark	.10	.02
❑	268 Gary Thurman	.10	.02
❑	269 Les Lancaster	.10	.02
❑	270 Jamie Moyer	.20	.07
❑	271 Ricky Gutierrez	.10	.02
❑	272 Greg A. Harris	.10	.02
❑	273 Mike Benjamin	.10	.02
❑	274 Gene Nelson	.10	.02
❑	275 Damon Berryhill	.10	.02
❑	276 Scott Radinsky	.10	.02
❑	277 Mike Aldrete	.10	.02
❑	278 Jerry DiPoto	.10	.02
❑	279 Chris Haney	.10	.02
❑	280 Richie Lewis	.10	.02
❑	281 Jarvis Brown	.10	.02
❑	282 Juan Bell	.10	.02
❑	283 Joe Klink	.10	.02
❑	284 Graeme Lloyd	.10	.02
❑	285 Casey Candaele	.10	.02
❑	286 Bob MacDonald	.10	.02
❑	287 Mike Sharperson	.10	.02
❑	288 Gene Larkin	.10	.02
❑	289 Brian Barnes	.10	.02
❑	290 David McCarty	.10	.02
❑	291 Jeff Innis	.10	.02
❑	292 Bob Patterson	.10	.02
❑	293 Ben Rivera	.10	.02
❑	294 John Habyan	.10	.02
❑	295 Rich Rodriguez	.10	.02
❑	296 Edwin Nunez	.10	.02
❑	297 Rod Brewer	.10	.02
❑	298 Mike Timlin	.10	.02
❑	299 Jesse Orosco	.10	.02
❑	300 Gary Gaetti	.20	.07
❑	301 Todd Benzinger	.10	.02
❑	302 Jeff Nelson	.10	.02
❑	303 Rafael Belliard	.10	.02
❑	304 Matt Whiteside	.10	.02
❑	305 Vinny Castilla	.20	.07
❑	306 Matt Turner	.10	.02
❑	307 Eduardo Perez	.10	.02
❑	308 Joel Johnston	.10	.02
❑	309 Chris Gomez	.10	.02
❑	310 Pat Rapp	.10	.02
❑	311 Jim Tatum	.10	.02
❑	312 Kirk Rueter	.10	.02
❑	313 John Flaherty	.10	.02
❑	314 Tom Kramer	.10	.02
❑	315 Mark Whiten	.10	.02
❑	316 Chris Bosio	.10	.02
❑	317 Baltimore Orioles CL	.10	.02
❑	318 Boston Red Sox CL UER (Viola listed as 316; shoul)	.10	.02
❑	319 California Angels CL	.10	.02
❑	320 Chicago White Sox CL	.10	.02
❑	321 Cleveland Indians CL	.10	.02
❑	322 Detroit Tigers CL	.10	.02
❑	323 Kansas City Royals CL	.10	.02
❑	324 Milwaukee Brewers CL	.10	.02
❑	325 Minnesota Twins CL	.10	.02

❑ 326 New York Yankees CL .10 .02
❑ 327 Oakland Athletics CL .10 .02
❑ 328 Seattle Mariners CL .10 .02
❑ 329 Texas Rangers CL .10 .02
❑ 330 Toronto Blue Jays CL .10 .02
❑ 331 Frank Viola .20 .07
❑ 332 Ron Gant .20 .07
❑ 333 Charles Nagy .10 .02
❑ 334 Roberto Kelly .10 .02
❑ 335 Brady Anderson .20 .07
❑ 336 Alex Cole .10 .02
❑ 337 Alan Trammell .20 .07
❑ 338 Derek Bell .10 .02
❑ 339 Bernie Williams .30 .10
❑ 340 Jose Offerman .10 .02
❑ 341 Bill Wegman .10 .02
❑ 342 Ken Caminiti .20 .07
❑ 343 Pat Borders .10 .02
❑ 344 Kirt Manwaring .10 .02
❑ 345 Chili Davis .20 .07
❑ 346 Steve Buechele .10 .02
❑ 347 Robin Ventura .20 .07
❑ 348 Teddy Higuera .10 .02
❑ 349 Jerry Browne .10 .02
❑ 350 Scott Kamieniecki .10 .02
❑ 351 Kevin Tapani .10 .02
❑ 352 Marquis Grissom .20 .07
❑ 353 Jay Buhner .20 .07
❑ 354 Dave Hollins .10 .02
❑ 355 Dan Wilson .10 .02
❑ 356 Bob Walk .10 .02
❑ 357 Chris Hoiles .10 .02
❑ 358 Todd Zeile .10 .02
❑ 359 Kevin Appier .20 .07
❑ 360 Chris Sabo .10 .02
❑ 361 David Segui .10 .02
❑ 362 Jerald Clark .10 .02
❑ 363 Tony Pena .10 .02
❑ 364 Steve Finley .20 .07
❑ 365 Roger Pavlik .10 .02
❑ 366 John Smoltz .30 .10
❑ 367 Scott Fletcher .10 .02
❑ 368 Jody Reed .10 .02
❑ 369 David Wells .20 .07
❑ 370 Jose Vizcaino .10 .02
❑ 371 Pat Listach .10 .02
❑ 372 Orestes Destrade .10 .02
❑ 373 Danny Tartabull .10 .02
❑ 374 Greg W. Harris .10 .02
❑ 375 Juan Guzman .10 .02
❑ 376 Larry Walker .20 .07
❑ 377 Gary DiSarcina .10 .02
❑ 378 Bobby Bonilla .20 .07
❑ 379 Tim Raines .20 .07
❑ 380 Tommy Greene .10 .02
❑ 381 Chris Gwynn .10 .02
❑ 382 Jeff King .10 .02
❑ 383 Shane Mack .10 .02
❑ 384 Ozzie Smith .75 .30
❑ 385 Eddie Zambrano RC .10 .02
❑ 386 Mike Devereaux .10 .02
❑ 387 Erik Hanson .10 .02
❑ 388 Scott Cooper .10 .02
❑ 389 Dean Palmer .20 .07
❑ 390 John Wetteland .20 .07
❑ 391 Reggie Jefferson .10 .02
❑ 392 Mark Lemke .10 .02
❑ 393 Cecil Fielder .20 .07
❑ 394 Reggie Sanders .20 .07
❑ 395 Darryl Hamilton .10 .02
❑ 396 Daryl Boston .10 .02
❑ 397 Pat Kelly .10 .02
❑ 398 Joe Orsulak .10 .02
❑ 399 Ed Sprague .10 .02
❑ 400 Eric Anthony .10 .02
❑ 401 Scott Sanderson .10 .02
❑ 402 Jim Gott .10 .02
❑ 403 Ron Karkovice .10 .02
❑ 404 Phil Plantier .10 .02
❑ 405 David Cone .20 .07
❑ 406 Robby Thompson .10 .02
❑ 407 Dave Winfield .20 .07
❑ 408 Dwight Smith .10 .02
❑ 409 Ruben Sierra .20 .07
❑ 410 Jack Armstrong .10 .02
❑ 411 Mike Felder .10 .02
❑ 412 Wil Cordero .10 .02
❑ 413 Julio Franco .20 .07
❑ 414 Howard Johnson .10 .02
❑ 415 Mark McLemore .10 .02
❑ 416 Pete Incaviglia .10 .02
❑ 417 John Valentin .10 .02
❑ 418 Tim Wakefield .30 .10
❑ 419 Jose Mesa .10 .02
❑ 420 Bernard Gilkey .10 .02
❑ 421 Kirk Gibson .20 .07
❑ 422 David Justice .20 .07
❑ 423 Tom Brunansky .10 .02
❑ 424 John Smiley .10 .02
❑ 425 Kevin Maas .10 .02
❑ 426 Doug Drabek .10 .02
❑ 427 Paul Molitor .20 .07
❑ 428 Darryl Strawberry .20 .07
❑ 429 Tim Naehring .10 .02
❑ 430 Bill Swift .10 .02
❑ 431 Ellis Burks .20 .07
❑ 432 Greg Hibbard .10 .02
❑ 433 Felix Jose .10 .02
❑ 434 Bret Barberie .10 .02
❑ 435 Pedro Munoz .10 .02
❑ 436 Darrin Fletcher .10 .02
❑ 437 Bobby Witt .10 .02
❑ 438 Wes Chamberlain .10 .02
❑ 439 Mackey Sasser .10 .02
❑ 440 Mark Whiten .10 .02
❑ 441 Harold Reynolds .20 .07
❑ 442 Greg Olson .10 .02
❑ 443 Billy Hatcher .10 .02
❑ 444 Joe Oliver .10 .02
❑ 445 Sandy Alomar Jr. .10 .02
❑ 446 Tim Wallach .10 .02
❑ 447 Karl Rhodes .10 .02
❑ 448 Royce Clayton .10 .02
❑ 449 Cal Eldred .10 .02
❑ 450 Rick Wilkins .10 .02
❑ 451 Mike Stanley .10 .02
❑ 452 Charlie Hough .20 .07
❑ 453 Jack Morris .20 .07
❑ 454 Jon Ratliff RC .10 .02
❑ 455 Rene Gonzales .10 .02
❑ 456 Eddie Taubensee .10 .02
❑ 457 Roberto Hernandez .10 .02
❑ 458 Todd Hundley .10 .02
❑ 459 Mike Macfarlane .10 .02
❑ 460 Mickey Morandini .10 .02
❑ 461 Scott Erickson .10 .02
❑ 462 Lonnie Smith .10 .02
❑ 463 Dave Henderson .10 .02
❑ 464 Ryan Klesko .20 .07
❑ 465 Edgar Martinez .30 .10
❑ 466 Tom Pagnozzi .10 .02
❑ 467 Charlie Leibrandt .10 .02
❑ 468 Brian Anderson RC .25 .08
❑ 469 Harold Baines .20 .07
❑ 470 Tim Belcher .10 .02
❑ 471 Andre Dawson .20 .07
❑ 472 Eric Young .10 .02
❑ 473 Paul Sorrento .10 .02
❑ 474 Luis Gonzalez .20 .07
❑ 475 Rob Deer .10 .02
❑ 476 Mike Piazza 1.00 .40
❑ 477 Kevin Reimer .10 .02
❑ 478 Jeff Gardner .10 .02
❑ 479 Melido Perez .10 .02
❑ 480 Darren Lewis .10 .02
❑ 481 Duane Ward .10 .02
❑ 482 Rey Sanchez .10 .02
❑ 483 Mark Lewis .10 .02
❑ 484 Jeff Conine .20 .07
❑ 485 Joey Cora .10 .02
❑ 486 Trot Nixon RC 1.00 .40
❑ 487 Kevin McReynolds .10 .02
❑ 488 Mike Lansing .10 .02
❑ 489 Mike Pagliarulo .10 .02
❑ 490 Mariano Duncan .10 .02
❑ 491 Mike Bordick .10 .02
❑ 492 Kevin Young .10 .02
❑ 493 Dave Valle .10 .02
❑ 494 Wayne Gomes RC .10 .02
❑ 495 Rafael Palmeiro .30 .10
❑ 496 Deion Sanders .30 .10
❑ 497 Rick Sutcliffe .20 .07
❑ 498 Randy Milligan .10 .02
❑ 499 Carlos Quintana .10 .02
❑ 500 Chris Turner .10 .02
❑ 501 Thomas Howard .10 .02
❑ 502 Greg Swindell .10 .02
❑ 503 Chad Kreuter .10 .02
❑ 504 Eric Davis .20 .07
❑ 505 Dickie Thon .10 .02
❑ 506 Matt Drews RC .10 .02
❑ 507 Spike Owen .10 .02
❑ 508 Rod Beck .10 .02
❑ 509 Pat Hentgen .10 .02
❑ 510 Sammy Sosa .50 .20
❑ 511 J.T. Snow .20 .07
❑ 512 Chuck Carr .10 .02
❑ 513 Bo Jackson .50 .20
❑ 514 Dennis Martinez .20 .07
❑ 515 Phil Hiatt .10 .02
❑ 516 Jeff Kent .30 .10
❑ 517 Brooks Kieschnick RC .10 .02
❑ 518 Kirk Presley RC .10 .02
❑ 519 Kevin Seitzer .10 .02
❑ 520 Carlos Garcia .10 .02
❑ 521 Mike Blowers .10 .02
❑ 522 Luis Alicea .10 .02
❑ 523 David Hulse .10 .02
❑ 524 Greg Maddux .75 .30
❑ 525 Gregg Olson .10 .02
❑ 526 Hal Morris .10 .02
❑ 527 Daron Kirkreit .10 .02
❑ 528 David Nied .10 .02
❑ 529 Jeff Russell .10 .02
❑ 530 Kevin Gross .10 .02
❑ 531 John Doherty .10 .02
❑ 532 Matt Brunson RC .10 .02
❑ 533 Dave Nilsson .10 .02
❑ 534 Randy Myers .10 .02
❑ 535 Steve Farr .10 .02
❑ 536 Billy Wagner RC 1.25 .50
❑ 537 Darnell Coles .10 .02
❑ 538 Frank Tanana .10 .02
❑ 539 Tim Salmon .30 .10
❑ 540 Kim Batiste .10 .02
❑ 541 George Bell .10 .02
❑ 542 Tom Henke .10 .02
❑ 543 Sam Horn .10 .02
❑ 544 Doug Jones .10 .02
❑ 545 Scott Leius .10 .02
❑ 546 Al Martin .10 .02
❑ 547 Bob Welch .10 .02
❑ 548 Scott Christman RC .10 .02
❑ 549 Norm Charlton .10 .02
❑ 550 Mark McGwire 1.25 .50
❑ 551 Greg McMichael .10 .02
❑ 552 Tim Costo .10 .02
❑ 553 Rodney Bolton .10 .02
❑ 554 Pedro Martinez .50 .20
❑ 555 Marc Valdes .10 .02
❑ 556 Darrell Whitmore .10 .02
❑ 557 Tim Bogar .10 .02
❑ 558 Steve Karsay .10 .02
❑ 559 Danny Bautista .10 .02
❑ 560 Jeffrey Hammonds .10 .02
❑ 561 Aaron Sele .10 .02
❑ 562 Russ Springer .10 .02
❑ 563 Jason Bere .10 .02
❑ 564 Billy Brewer .10 .02
❑ 565 Sterling Hitchcock .10 .02
❑ 566 Bobby Munoz .10 .02
❑ 567 Craig Paquette .10 .02
❑ 568 Bret Boone .20 .07
❑ 569 Dan Peltier .10 .02
❑ 570 Jeromy Burnitz .20 .07
❑ 571 John Wasdin RC .10 .02
❑ 572 Chipper Jones .50 .20
❑ 573 Jamey Wright RC .10 .02
❑ 574 Jeff Granger .10 .02
❑ 575 Jay Powell RC .10 .02
❑ 576 Ryan Thompson .10 .02
❑ 577 Lou Frazier .10 .02
❑ 578 Paul Wagner .10 .02
❑ 579 Brad Ausmus .30 .10
❑ 580 Jack Voigt .10 .02
❑ 581 Kevin Rogers .10 .02
❑ 582 Damon Buford .10 .02
❑ 583 Paul Quantrill .10 .02

❑	584 Marc Newfield	.10	.02
❑	585 Derrek Lee RC	2.00	.75
❑	586 Shane Reynolds	.10	.02
❑	587 Cliff Floyd	.20	.07
❑	588 Jeff Schwarz	.10	.02
❑	589 Ross Powell RC	.10	.02
❑	590 Gerald Williams	.10	.02
❑	591 Mike Trombley	.10	.02
❑	592 Ken Ryan	.10	.02
❑	593 John O'Donoghue	.10	.02
❑	594 Rod Correia	.10	.02
❑	595 Darrell Sherman	.10	.02
❑	596 Steve Scarsone	.10	.02
❑	597 Sherman Obando	.10	.02
❑	598 Kurt Abbott RC	.10	.02
❑	599 Dave Telgheder	.10	.02
❑	600 Rick Trlicek	.10	.02
❑	601 Carl Everett	.20	.07
❑	602 Luis Ortiz	.10	.02
❑	603 Larry Luebbers	.10	.02
❑	604 Kevin Roberson	.10	.02
❑	605 Butch Huskey	.10	.02
❑	606 Benji Gil	.10	.02
❑	607 Todd Van Poppel	.10	.02
❑	608 Mark Hutton	.10	.02
❑	609 Chip Hale	.10	.02
❑	610 Matt Maysey	.10	.02
❑	611 Scott Ruffcorn	.10	.02
❑	612 Hilly Hathaway	.10	.02
❑	613 Allen Watson	.10	.02
❑	614 Carlos Delgado	.30	.10
❑	615 Roberto Mejia	.10	.02
❑	616 Turk Wendell	.10	.02
❑	617 Tony Tarasco	.10	.02
❑	618 Raul Mondesi	.20	.07
❑	619 Kevin Stocker	.10	.02
❑	620 Javier Lopez	.20	.07
❑	621 Keith Kessinger	.10	.02
❑	622 Bob Hamelin	.10	.02
❑	623 John Roper	.10	.02
❑	624 Lenny Dykstra WS	.10	.02
❑	625 Joe Carter WS	.10	.02
❑	626 Jim Abbott HL	.20	.07
❑	627 Lee Smith HL	.10	.02
❑	628 Ken Griffey Jr. HL	.50	.20
❑	629 Dave Winfield HL	.10	.02
❑	630 Darryl Kile HL	.10	.02
❑	631 Frank Thomas MVP	.30	.10
❑	632 Barry Bonds MVP	.75	.30
❑	633 Jack McDowell AL CY	.10	.02
❑	634 Greg Maddux CY	.50	.20
❑	635 Tim Salmon ROY	.20	.07
❑	636 Mike Piazza ROY	.50	.20
❑	637 Brian Turang RC	.10	.02
❑	638 Rondell White	.20	.07
❑	639 Nigel Wilson	.10	.02
❑	640 Torii Hunter RC	1.00	.40
❑	641 Salomon Torres	.10	.02
❑	642 Kevin Higgins	.10	.02
❑	643 Eric Wedge	.10	.02
❑	644 Roger Salkeld	.10	.02
❑	645 Manny Ramirez	.50	.20
❑	646 Jeff McNeely	.10	.02
❑	647 Checklist Atlanta Braves	.10	.02
❑	648 Checklist Chicago Cubs	.10	.02
❑	649 Checklist Cincinnati Reds	.10	.02
❑	650 Checklist Colorado Rockies	.10	.02
❑	651 Checklist Florida Marlins	.10	.02
❑	652 Checklist Houston Astros	.10	.02
❑	653 Checklist Los Angeles Dodgers	.10	.02
❑	654 Checklist Montreal Expos	.10	.02
❑	655 Checklist New York Mets	.10	.02
❑	656 Checklist Philadelphia Phillies	.10	.02
❑	657 Checklist Pittsburgh Pirates	.10	.02
❑	658 Checklist St. Louis Cardinals	.10	.02
❑	659 Checklist San Diego Padres	.10	.02
❑	660 Checklist San Francisco Giants	.10	.02

1994 Score Rookie/Traded

❑	COMPLETE SET (165)	15.00	6.00
❑	ACTUAL CARD REDEEMED IN 1995		
❑	RT1 Will Clark	.50	.20
❑	RT2 Lee Smith	.30	.10
❑	RT3 Bo Jackson	.75	.30
❑	RT4 Ellis Burks	.30	.10
❑	RT5 Eddie Murray	.75	.30
❑	RT6 Delino DeShields	.15	.05
❑	RT7 Erik Hanson	.15	.05
❑	RT8 Rafael Palmeiro	.50	.20
❑	RT9 Luis Polonia	.15	.05
❑	RT10 Omar Vizquel	.50	.20
❑	RT11 Kurt Abbott	.15	.05
❑	RT12 Vince Coleman	.15	.05
❑	RT13 Rickey Henderson	.75	.30
❑	RT14 Terry Mulholland	.15	.05
❑	RT15 Greg Hibbard	.15	.05
❑	RT16 Walt Weiss	.15	.05
❑	RT17 Chris Sabo	.15	.05
❑	RT18 Dave Henderson	.15	.05
❑	RT19 Rick Sutcliffe	.30	.10
❑	RT20 Harold Reynolds	.30	.10
❑	RT21 Jack Morris	.30	.10
❑	RT22 Dan Wilson	.15	.05
❑	RT23 Dave Magadan	.15	.05
❑	RT24 Dennis Martinez	.30	.10
❑	RT25 Wes Chamberlain	.15	.05
❑	RT26 Otis Nixon	.15	.05
❑	RT27 Eric Anthony	.15	.05
❑	RT28 Randy Milligan	.15	.05
❑	RT29 Julio Franco	.30	.10
❑	RT30 Kevin McReynolds	.15	.05
❑	RT31 Anthony Young	.15	.05
❑	RT32 Brian Harper	.15	.05
❑	RT33 Gene Harris	.15	.05
❑	RT34 Eddie Taubensee	.15	.05
❑	RT35 David Segui	.15	.05
❑	RT36 Stan Javier	.15	.05
❑	RT37 Felix Fermin	.15	.05
❑	RT38 Darrin Jackson	.15	.05
❑	RT39 Tony Fernandez	.15	.05
❑	RT40 Jose Vizcaino	.15	.05
❑	RT41 Willie Banks	.15	.05
❑	RT42 Brian Hunter	.15	.05
❑	RT43 Reggie Jefferson	.15	.05
❑	RT44 Junior Felix	.15	.05
❑	RT45 Jack Armstrong	.15	.05
❑	RT46 Bip Roberts	.15	.05
❑	RT47 Jerry Browne	.15	.05
❑	RT48 Marvin Freeman	.15	.05
❑	RT49 Jody Reed	.15	.05
❑	RT50 Alex Cole	.15	.05
❑	RT51 Sid Fernandez	.15	.05
❑	RT52 Pete Smith	.15	.05
❑	RT53 Xavier Hernandez	.15	.05
❑	RT54 Scott Sanderson	.15	.05
❑	RT55 Turner Ward	.15	.05
❑	RT56 Rex Hudler	.15	.05
❑	RT57 Deion Sanders	.50	.20
❑	RT58 Sid Bream	.15	.05
❑	RT59 Tony Pena	.15	.05
❑	RT60 Bret Boone	.30	.10
❑	RT61 Bobby Ayala	.15	.05
❑	RT62 Pedro Martinez	.75	.30
❑	RT63 Howard Johnson	.15	.05
❑	RT64 Mark Portugal	.15	.05
❑	RT65 Roberto Kelly	.15	.05
❑	RT66 Spike Owen	.15	.05
❑	RT67 Jeff Treadway	.15	.05
❑	RT68 Mike Harkey	.15	.05
❑	RT69 Doug Jones	.15	.05
❑	RT70 Steve Farr	.15	.05
❑	RT71 Billy Taylor RC	.15	.05
❑	RT72 Manny Ramirez	.75	.30
❑	RT73 Bob Hamelin	.15	.05
❑	RT74 Steve Karsay	.15	.05
❑	RT75 Ryan Klesko	.30	.10
❑	RT76 Cliff Floyd	.30	.10
❑	RT77 Jeffrey Hammonds	.15	.05
❑	RT78 Javier Lopez	.30	.10
❑	RT79 Roger Salkeld	.15	.05
❑	RT80 Hector Carrasco	.15	.05
❑	RT81 Gerald Williams	.15	.05
❑	RT82 Raul Mondesi	.30	.10
❑	RT83 Sterling Hitchcock	.15	.05
❑	RT84 Danny Bautista	.15	.05
❑	RT85 Chris Turner	.15	.05
❑	RT86 Shane Reynolds	.15	.05
❑	RT87 Rondell White	.30	.10
❑	RT88 Salomon Torres	.15	.05
❑	RT89 Turk Wendell	.15	.05
❑	RT90 Tony Tarasco	.15	.05
❑	RT91 Shawn Green	.75	.30
❑	RT92 Greg Colbrunn	.15	.05
❑	RT93 Eddie Zambrano	.15	.05
❑	RT94 Rich Becker	.15	.05
❑	RT95 Chris Gomez	.15	.05
❑	RT96 John Patterson	.15	.05
❑	RT97 Derek Parks	.15	.05
❑	RT98 Rich Rowland	.15	.05
❑	RT99 James Mouton	.15	.05
❑	RT100 Tim Hyers RC	.15	.05
❑	RT101 Jose Valentin	.15	.05
❑	RT102 Carlos Delgado	.50	.20
❑	RT103 Robert Eenhoorn	.15	.05
❑	RT104 John Hudek RC	.15	.05
❑	RT105 Domingo Cedeno	.15	.05
❑	RT106 Denny Hocking	.15	.05
❑	RT107 Greg Pirkl	.15	.05
❑	RT108 Mark Smith	.15	.05
❑	RT109 Paul Shuey	.15	.05
❑	RT110 Jorge Fabregas	.15	.05
❑	RT111 Rikkert Faneyte RC	.15	.05
❑	RT112 Rob Butler	.15	.05
❑	RT113 Darren Oliver RC	.30	.10
❑	RT114 Troy O'Leary	.15	.05
❑	RT115 Scott Brow	.15	.05
❑	RT116 Tony Eusebio	.15	.05
❑	RT117 Carlos Reyes	.15	.05
❑	RT118 J.R. Phillips	.15	.05
❑	RT119 Alex Diaz	.15	.05
❑	RT120 Charles Johnson	.30	.10
❑	RT121 Nate Minchey	.15	.05
❑	RT122 Scott Sanders	.15	.05
❑	RT123 Daryl Boston	.15	.05
❑	RT124 Joey Hamilton	.15	.05
❑	RT125 Brian Anderson	.30	.10
❑	RT126 Dan Miceli	.15	.05
❑	RT127 Tom Brunansky	.15	.05
❑	RT128 Dave Staton	.15	.05
❑	RT129 Mike Oquist	.15	.05
❑	RT130 John Mabry RC	.30	.10
❑	RT131 Norberto Martin	.15	.05
❑	RT132 Hector Fajardo	.15	.05
❑	RT133 Mark Hutton	.15	.05
❑	RT134 Fernando Vina	.15	.05
❑	RT135 Lee Tinsley	.15	.05
❑	RT136 Chan Ho Park RC	.50	.20
❑	RT137 Paul Spoljaric	.15	.05
❑	RT138 Matias Carrillo	.15	.05
❑	RT139 Mark Kiefer	.15	.05
❑	RT140 Stan Royer	.15	.05
❑	RT141 Bryan Eversgerd	.15	.05
❑	RT142 Brian L. Hunter	.15	.05
❑	RT143 Joe Hall	.15	.05
❑	RT144 Johnny Ruffin	.15	.05

Card	Player	Price	Price
❑ RT145	Alex Gonzalez	.15	.05
❑ RT146	Keith Lockhart RC	.30	.10
❑ RT147	Tom Marsh	.15	.05
❑ RT148	Tony Longmire	.15	.05
❑ RT149	Keith Mitchell	.15	.05
❑ RT150	Melvin Nieves	.15	.05
❑ RT151	Kelly Stinnett RC	.15	.05
❑ RT152	Miguel Jimenez	.15	.05
❑ RT153	Jeff Juden	.15	.05
❑ RT154	Matt Walbeck	.15	.05
❑ RT155	Marc Newfield	.15	.05
❑ RT156	Matt Mieske	.15	.05
❑ RT157	Marcus Moore	.15	.05
❑ RT158	Jose Lima RC SP	5.00	2.00
❑ RT159	Mike Kelly	.15	.05
❑ RT160	Jim Edmonds	.75	.30
❑ RT161	Steve Trachsel	.15	.05
❑ RT162	Greg Blosser	.15	.05
❑ RT163	Mark Acre RC	.15	.05
❑ RT164	AL Checklist	.15	.05
❑ RT165	NL Checklist	.15	.05
❑ HC1	Alex Rodriguez CU	400.00	300.00
❑ NNO	September Call-Up Trade EXP	2.00	.75

1993 SP

Card	Player	Price	Price
❑	COMPLETE SET (290)	80.00	40.00
❑	COMMON CARD (1-270)	.50	.20
❑	FOIL PROSPECTS (271-290)	1.00	.40
❑ 1	Roberto Alomar AS	1.25	.50
❑ 2	Wade Boggs AS	1.25	.50
❑ 3	Joe Carter AS	.50	.20
❑ 4	Ken Griffey Jr. AS	3.00	1.25
❑ 5	Mark Langston AS	.50	.20
❑ 6	John Olerud AS	.75	.30
❑ 7	Kirby Puckett AS	2.00	.75
❑ 8	Cal Ripken AS	6.00	2.50
❑ 9	Ivan Rodriguez AS	1.25	.50
❑ 10	Barry Bonds AS	5.00	2.00
❑ 11	Darren Daulton AS	.75	.30
❑ 12	Marquis Grissom AS	.75	.30
❑ 13	David Justice AS	.75	.30
❑ 14	John Kruk AS	.75	.30
❑ 15	Barry Larkin AS	1.25	.50
❑ 16	Terry Mulholland AS	.50	.20
❑ 17	Ryne Sandberg AS	3.00	1.25
❑ 18	Gary Sheffield AS	.75	.30
❑ 19	Chad Curtis	.50	.20
❑ 20	Chili Davis	.75	.30
❑ 21	Gary DiSarcina	.50	.20
❑ 22	Damion Easley	.50	.20
❑ 23	Chuck Finley	.75	.30
❑ 24	Luis Polonia	.50	.20
❑ 25	Tim Salmon	1.25	.50
❑ 26	J.T.Snow RC	1.25	.50
❑ 27	Russ Springer	.50	.20
❑ 28	Jeff Bagwell	1.25	.50
❑ 29	Craig Biggio	1.25	.50
❑ 30	Ken Caminiti	.75	.30
❑ 31	Andujar Cedeno	.50	.20
❑ 32	Doug Drabek	.50	.20
❑ 33	Steve Finley	.75	.30
❑ 34	Luis Gonzalez	.75	.30
❑ 35	Pete Harnisch	.50	.20
❑ 36	Darryl Kile	.75	.30
❑ 37	Mike Bordick	.50	.20
❑ 38	Dennis Eckersley	.75	.30
❑ 39	Brent Gates	.50	.20
❑ 40	Rickey Henderson	2.00	.75
❑ 41	Mark McGwire	5.00	2.00
❑ 42	Craig Paquette	.50	.20
❑ 43	Ruben Sierra	.75	.30
❑ 44	Terry Steinbach	.50	.20
❑ 45	Todd Van Poppel	.50	.20
❑ 46	Pat Borders	.50	.20
❑ 47	Tony Fernandez	.50	.20
❑ 48	Juan Guzman	.50	.20
❑ 49	Pat Hentgen	.50	.20
❑ 50	Paul Molitor	.75	.30
❑ 51	Jack Morris	.75	.30
❑ 52	Ed Sprague	.50	.20
❑ 53	Duane Ward	.50	.20
❑ 54	Devon White	.75	.30
❑ 55	Steve Avery	.50	.20
❑ 56	Jeff Blauser	.50	.20
❑ 57	Ron Gant	.75	.30
❑ 58	Tom Glavine	1.25	.50
❑ 59	Greg Maddux	3.00	1.25
❑ 60	Fred McGriff	1.25	.50
❑ 61	Terry Pendleton	.75	.30
❑ 62	Deion Sanders	1.25	.50
❑ 63	John Smoltz	1.25	.50
❑ 64	Cal Eldred	.50	.20
❑ 65	Darryl Hamilton	.50	.20
❑ 66	John Jaha	.50	.20
❑ 67	Pat Listach	.50	.20
❑ 68	Jaime Navarro	.50	.20
❑ 69	Kevin Reimer	.50	.20
❑ 70	B.J. Surhoff	.75	.30
❑ 71	Greg Vaughn	.50	.20
❑ 72	Robin Yount	3.00	1.25
❑ 73	Rene Arocha RC	.75	.30
❑ 74	Bernard Gilkey	.50	.20
❑ 75	Gregg Jefferies	.50	.20
❑ 76	Ray Lankford	.75	.30
❑ 77	Tom Pagnozzi	.50	.20
❑ 78	Lee Smith	.75	.30
❑ 79	Ozzie Smith	3.00	1.25
❑ 80	Bob Tewksbury	.50	.20
❑ 81	Mark Whiten	.50	.20
❑ 82	Steve Buechele	.50	.20
❑ 83	Mark Grace	1.25	.50
❑ 84	Jose Guzman	.50	.20
❑ 85	Derrick May	.50	.20
❑ 86	Mike Morgan	.50	.20
❑ 87	Randy Myers	.50	.20
❑ 88	Kevin Roberson RC	.50	.20
❑ 89	Sammy Sosa	2.00	.75
❑ 90	Rick Wilkins	.50	.20
❑ 91	Brett Butler	.75	.30
❑ 92	Eric Davis	.75	.30
❑ 93	Orel Hershiser	.75	.30
❑ 94	Eric Karros	.75	.30
❑ 95	Ramon Martinez	.50	.20
❑ 96	Raul Mondesi	.75	.30
❑ 97	Jose Offerman	.50	.20
❑ 98	Mike Piazza	5.00	2.00
❑ 99	Darryl Strawberry	.75	.30
❑ 100	Moises Alou	.75	.30
❑ 101	Wil Cordero	.50	.20
❑ 102	Delino DeShields	.50	.20
❑ 103	Darrin Fletcher	.50	.20
❑ 104	Ken Hill	.50	.20
❑ 105	Mike Lansing RC	.75	.30
❑ 106	Dennis Martinez	.75	.30
❑ 107	Larry Walker	.75	.30
❑ 108	John Wetteland	.75	.30
❑ 109	Rod Beck	.50	.20
❑ 110	John Burkett	.50	.20
❑ 111	Will Clark	1.25	.50
❑ 112	Royce Clayton	.50	.20
❑ 113	Darren Lewis	.50	.20
❑ 114	Willie McGee	.75	.30
❑ 115	Bill Swift	.50	.20
❑ 116	Robby Thompson	.50	.20
❑ 117	Matt Williams	.75	.30
❑ 118	Sandy Alomar Jr.	.50	.20
❑ 119	Carlos Baerga	.50	.20
❑ 120	Albert Belle	.75	.30
❑ 121	Reggie Jefferson	.50	.20
❑ 122	Wayne Kirby	.50	.20
❑ 123	Kenny Lofton	.75	.30
❑ 124	Carlos Martinez	.50	.20
❑ 125	Charles Nagy	.50	.20
❑ 126	Paul Sorrento	.50	.20
❑ 127	Rich Amaral	.50	.20
❑ 128	Jay Buhner	.75	.30
❑ 129	Norm Charlton	.50	.20
❑ 130	Dave Fleming	.50	.20
❑ 131	Erik Hanson	.50	.20
❑ 132	Randy Johnson	2.00	.75
❑ 133	Edgar Martinez	1.25	.50
❑ 134	Tino Martinez	1.25	.50
❑ 135	Omar Vizquel	1.25	.50
❑ 136	Bret Barberie	.50	.20
❑ 137	Chuck Carr	.50	.20
❑ 138	Jeff Conine	.75	.30
❑ 139	Orestes Destrade	.50	.20
❑ 140	Chris Hammond	.50	.20
❑ 141	Bryan Harvey	.50	.20
❑ 142	Benito Santiago	.75	.30
❑ 143	Walt Weiss	.50	.20
❑ 144	Darrell Whitmore RC	.50	.20
❑ 145	Tim Bogar RC	.50	.20
❑ 146	Bobby Bonilla	.75	.30
❑ 147	Jeromy Burnitz	.75	.30
❑ 148	Vince Coleman	.50	.20
❑ 149	Dwight Gooden	.75	.30
❑ 150	Todd Hundley	.50	.20
❑ 151	Howard Johnson	.50	.20
❑ 152	Eddie Murray	2.00	.75
❑ 153	Bret Saberhagen	.75	.30
❑ 154	Brady Anderson	.75	.30
❑ 155	Mike Devereaux	.50	.20
❑ 156	Jeffrey Hammonds	.50	.20
❑ 157	Chris Hoiles	.50	.20
❑ 158	Ben McDonald	.50	.20
❑ 159	Mark McLemore	.50	.20
❑ 160	Mike Mussina	1.25	.50
❑ 161	Gregg Olson	.50	.20
❑ 162	David Segui	.50	.20
❑ 163	Derek Bell	.50	.20
❑ 164	Andy Benes	.50	.20
❑ 165	Archi Cianfrocco	.50	.20
❑ 166	Ricky Gutierrez	.50	.20
❑ 167	Tony Gwynn	2.50	1.00
❑ 168	Gene Harris	.50	.20
❑ 169	Trevor Hoffman	2.00	.75
❑ 170	Ray McDavid RC	.50	.20
❑ 171	Phil Plantier	.50	.20
❑ 172	Mariano Duncan	.50	.20
❑ 173	Len Dykstra	.75	.30
❑ 174	Tommy Greene	.50	.20
❑ 175	Dave Hollins	.50	.20
❑ 176	Pete Incaviglia	.50	.20
❑ 177	Mickey Morandini	.50	.20
❑ 178	Curt Schilling	.75	.30
❑ 179	Kevin Stocker	.50	.20
❑ 180	Mitch Williams	.50	.20
❑ 181	Stan Belinda	.50	.20
❑ 182	Jay Bell	.75	.30
❑ 183	Steve Cooke	.50	.20
❑ 184	Carlos Garcia	.50	.20
❑ 185	Jeff King	.50	.20
❑ 186	Orlando Merced	.50	.20
❑ 187	Don Slaught	.50	.20
❑ 188	Andy Van Slyke	1.25	.50
❑ 189	Kevin Young	.75	.30
❑ 190	Kevin Brown	.75	.30
❑ 191	Jose Canseco	1.25	.50
❑ 192	Julio Franco	.75	.30
❑ 193	Benji Gil	.50	.20
❑ 194	Juan Gonzalez	.75	.30
❑ 195	Tom Henke	.50	.20
❑ 196	Rafael Palmeiro	1.25	.50
❑ 197	Dean Palmer	.75	.30
❑ 198	Nolan Ryan	8.00	3.00
❑ 199	Roger Clemens	4.00	1.50
❑ 200	Scott Cooper	.50	.20
❑ 201	Andre Dawson	.75	.30
❑ 202	Mike Greenwell	.50	.20
❑ 203	Carlos Quintana	.50	.20
❑ 204	Jeff Russell	.50	.20
❑ 205	Aaron Sele	.50	.20
❑ 206	Mo Vaughn	.75	.30
❑ 207	Frank Viola	.75	.30
❑ 208	Rob Dibble	.75	.30
❑ 209	Roberto Kelly	.50	.20
❑ 210	Kevin Mitchell	.50	.20
❑ 211	Hal Morris	.50	.20
❑ 212	Joe Oliver	.50	.20

❑ 213 Jose Rijo .50 .20
❑ 214 Bip Roberts .50 .20
❑ 215 Chris Sabo .50 .20
❑ 216 Reggie Sanders .75 .30
❑ 217 Dante Bichette .75 .30
❑ 218 Jerald Clark .50 .20
❑ 219 Alex Cole .50 .20
❑ 220 Andres Galarraga .75 .30
❑ 221 Joe Girardi .50 .20
❑ 222 Charlie Hayes .50 .20
❑ 223 Roberto Mejia RC .50 .20
❑ 224 Armando Reynoso .50 .20
❑ 225 Eric Young .50 .20
❑ 226 Kevin Appier .75 .30
❑ 227 George Brett 5.00 2.00
❑ 228 David Cone .75 .30
❑ 229 Phil Hiatt .50 .20
❑ 230 Felix Jose .50 .20
❑ 231 Wally Joyner .75 .30
❑ 232 Mike Macfarlane .50 .20
❑ 233 Brian McRae .50 .20
❑ 234 Jeff Montgomery .50 .20
❑ 235 Rob Deer .50 .20
❑ 236 Cecil Fielder .75 .30
❑ 237 Travis Fryman .75 .30
❑ 238 Mike Henneman .50 .20
❑ 239 Tony Phillips .50 .20
❑ 240 Mickey Tettleton .50 .20
❑ 241 Alan Trammell .75 .30
❑ 242 David Wells .75 .30
❑ 243 Lou Whitaker .75 .30
❑ 244 Rick Aguilera .50 .20
❑ 245 Scott Erickson .50 .20
❑ 246 Brian Harper .50 .20
❑ 247 Kent Hrbek .75 .30
❑ 248 Chuck Knoblauch .75 .30
❑ 249 Shane Mack .50 .20
❑ 250 David McCarty .50 .20
❑ 251 Pedro Munoz .50 .20
❑ 252 Dave Winfield .75 .30
❑ 253 Alex Fernandez .50 .20
❑ 254 Ozzie Guillen .75 .30
❑ 255 Bo Jackson 2.00 .75
❑ 256 Lance Johnson .50 .20
❑ 257 Ron Karkovice .50 .20
❑ 258 Jack McDowell .50 .20
❑ 259 Tim Raines .75 .30
❑ 260 Frank Thomas 2.00 .75
❑ 261 Robin Ventura .75 .30
❑ 262 Jim Abbott 1.25 .50
❑ 263 Steve Farr .50 .20
❑ 264 Jimmy Key .75 .30
❑ 265 Don Mattingly 5.00 2.00
❑ 266 Paul O'Neill 1.25 .50
❑ 267 Mike Stanley .50 .20
❑ 268 Danny Tartabull .50 .20
❑ 269 Bob Wickman .50 .20
❑ 270 Bernie Williams 1.25 .50
❑ 271 Jason Bere FOIL 1.00 .40
❑ 272 Roger Cedeno FOIL RC 1.50 .60
❑ 273 Johnny Damon FOIL RC 12.00 5.00
❑ 274 Russ Davis FOIL RC 1.50 .60
❑ 275 Carlos Delgado FOIL 4.00 1.50
❑ 276 Carl Everett FOIL 1.50 .60
❑ 277 Cliff Floyd FOIL .75 .30
❑ 278 Alex Gonzalez FOIL 1.00 .40
❑ 279 Derek Jeter FOIL RC ! 60.00 30.00
❑ 280 Chipper Jones FOIL 4.00 1.50
❑ 281 Javier Lopez FOIL 1.25 .50
❑ 282 Chad Mottola FOIL RC 1.00 .40
❑ 283 Marc Newfield FOIL 1.00 .40
❑ 284 Eduardo Perez FOIL 1.00 .40
❑ 285 Manny Ramirez FOIL 5.00 2.00
❑ 286 Todd Steverson FOIL RC 1.00 .40
❑ 287 Michael Tucker FOIL 1.00 .40
❑ 288 Allen Watson FOIL 1.00 .40
❑ 289 Rondell White FOIL 1.50 .60
❑ 290 Dmitri Young FOIL 1.50 .60

1994 SP

❑ COMPLETE SET (200) 120.00 60.00
❑ COMMON CARD (21-200) .20 .07
❑ COMMON FOIL (1-20) .50 .20
❑ 1 Mike Bell FOIL RC .50 .20
❑ 2 D.J. Boston FOIL RC .50 .20
❑ 3 Johnny Damon FOIL 2.00 .75
❑ 4 Brad Fullmer FOIL RC 1.00 .40
❑ 5 Joey Hamilton FOIL .50 .20
❑ 6 Todd Hollandsworth FOIL .50 .20
❑ 7 Brian L.Hunter FOIL .50 .20
❑ 8 LaTroy Hawkins FOIL RC 1.00 .40
❑ 9 Brooks Kieschnick FOIL RC .50 .20
❑ 10 Derrek Lee FOIL RC 12.00 5.00
❑ 11 Trot Nixon FOIL RC 4.00 1.50
❑ 12 Alex Ochoa FOIL .50 .20
❑ 13 Chan Ho Park FOIL RC 2.00 .75
❑ 14 Kirk Presley FOIL RC .50 .20
❑ 15 Alex Rodriguez FOIL RC 80.00 40.00
❑ 16 Jose Silva FOIL RC .50 .20
❑ 17 Terrell Wade FOIL RC .50 .20
❑ 18 Billy Wagner FOIL RC 4.00 1.50
❑ 19 Glenn Williams FOIL RC .50 .20
❑ 20 Preston Wilson FOIL 1.00 .40
❑ 21 Brian Anderson RC .40 .15
❑ 22 Chad Curtis .20 .07
❑ 23 Chili Davis .40 .15
❑ 24 Bo Jackson 1.00 .40
❑ 25 Mark Langston .20 .07
❑ 26 Tim Salmon .60 .25
❑ 27 Jeff Bagwell .60 .25
❑ 28 Craig Biggio .60 .25
❑ 29 Ken Caminiti .40 .15
❑ 30 Doug Drabek .20 .07
❑ 31 John Hudek RC .20 .07
❑ 32 Greg Swindell .20 .07
❑ 33 Brent Gates .20 .07
❑ 34 Rickey Henderson 1.00 .40
❑ 35 Steve Karsay .20 .07
❑ 36 Mark McGwire 2.50 1.00
❑ 37 Ruben Sierra .40 .15
❑ 38 Terry Steinbach .20 .07
❑ 39 Roberto Alomar .60 .25
❑ 40 Joe Carter .40 .15
❑ 41 Carlos Delgado .60 .25
❑ 42 Alex Gonzalez .20 .07
❑ 43 Juan Guzman .20 .07
❑ 44 Paul Molitor .40 .15
❑ 45 John Olerud .40 .15
❑ 46 Devon White .40 .15
❑ 47 Steve Avery .20 .07
❑ 48 Jeff Blauser .20 .07
❑ 49 Tom Glavine .60 .25
❑ 50 David Justice .40 .15
❑ 51 Roberto Kelly .20 .07
❑ 52 Ryan Klesko .40 .15
❑ 53 Javier Lopez .40 .15
❑ 54 Greg Maddux 1.50 .60
❑ 55 Fred McGriff .60 .25
❑ 56 Ricky Bones .20 .07
❑ 57 Cal Eldred .20 .07
❑ 58 Brian Harper .20 .07
❑ 59 Pat Listach .20 .07
❑ 60 B.J. Surhoff .40 .15
❑ 61 Greg Vaughn .20 .07
❑ 62 Bernard Gilkey .20 .07
❑ 63 Gregg Jefferies .20 .07
❑ 64 Ray Lankford .40 .15
❑ 65 Ozzie Smith 1.50 .60
❑ 66 Bob Tewksbury .20 .07
❑ 67 Mark Whiten .20 .07
❑ 68 Todd Zeile .20 .07
❑ 69 Mark Grace .60 .25
❑ 70 Randy Myers .20 .07
❑ 71 Ryne Sandberg 1.50 .60
❑ 72 Sammy Sosa 1.00 .40
❑ 73 Steve Trachsel .20 .07
❑ 74 Rick Wilkins .20 .07
❑ 75 Brett Butler .40 .15
❑ 76 Delino DeShields .20 .07
❑ 77 Orel Hershiser .40 .15
❑ 78 Eric Karros .40 .15
❑ 79 Raul Mondesi .40 .15
❑ 80 Mike Piazza 2.00 .75
❑ 81 Tim Wallach .20 .07
❑ 82 Moises Alou .40 .15
❑ 83 Cliff Floyd .40 .15
❑ 84 Marquis Grissom .40 .15
❑ 85 Pedro Martinez 1.00 .40
❑ 86 Larry Walker .40 .15
❑ 87 John Wetteland .40 .15
❑ 88 Rondell White .40 .15
❑ 89 Rod Beck .20 .07
❑ 90 Barry Bonds 2.50 1.00
❑ 91 John Burkett .20 .07
❑ 92 Royce Clayton .20 .07
❑ 93 Billy Swift .20 .07
❑ 94 Robby Thompson .20 .07
❑ 95 Matt Williams .40 .15
❑ 96 Carlos Baerga .20 .07
❑ 97 Albert Belle .40 .15
❑ 98 Kenny Lofton .40 .15
❑ 99 Dennis Martinez .40 .15
❑ 100 Eddie Murray 1.00 .40
❑ 101 Manny Ramirez 1.00 .40
❑ 102 Eric Anthony .20 .07
❑ 103 Chris Bosio .20 .07
❑ 104 Jay Buhner .40 .15
❑ 105 Ken Griffey Jr. 1.50 .60
❑ 106 Randy Johnson 1.00 .40
❑ 107 Edgar Martinez .60 .25
❑ 108 Chuck Carr .20 .07
❑ 109 Jeff Conine .40 .15
❑ 110 Carl Everett .40 .15
❑ 111 Chris Hammond .20 .07
❑ 112 Bryan Harvey .20 .07
❑ 113 Charles Johnson .40 .15
❑ 114 Gary Sheffield .40 .15
❑ 115 Bobby Bonilla .40 .15
❑ 116 Dwight Gooden .40 .15
❑ 117 Todd Hundley .20 .07
❑ 118 Bobby Jones .20 .07
❑ 119 Jeff Kent .60 .25
❑ 120 Bret Saberhagen .40 .15
❑ 121 Jeffrey Hammonds .20 .07
❑ 122 Chris Hoiles .20 .07
❑ 123 Ben McDonald .20 .07
❑ 124 Mike Mussina .60 .25
❑ 125 Rafael Palmeiro .60 .25
❑ 126 Cal Ripken 3.00 1.25
❑ 127 Lee Smith .40 .15
❑ 128 Derek Bell .20 .07
❑ 129 Andy Benes .20 .07
❑ 130 Tony Gwynn 1.25 .50
❑ 131 Trevor Hoffman .60 .25
❑ 132 Phil Plantier .20 .07
❑ 133 Bip Roberts .20 .07
❑ 134 Darren Daulton .40 .15
❑ 135 Lenny Dykstra .40 .15
❑ 136 Dave Hollins .20 .07
❑ 137 Danny Jackson .20 .07
❑ 138 John Kruk .40 .15
❑ 139 Kevin Stocker .20 .07
❑ 140 Jay Bell .40 .15
❑ 141 Carlos Garcia .20 .07
❑ 142 Jeff King .20 .07
❑ 143 Orlando Merced .20 .07
❑ 144 Andy Van Slyke .60 .25
❑ 145 Rick White .20 .07
❑ 146 Jose Canseco .60 .25
❑ 147 Will Clark .60 .25
❑ 148 Juan Gonzalez .40 .15
❑ 149 Rick Helling .20 .07
❑ 150 Dean Palmer .40 .15
❑ 151 Ivan Rodriguez .60 .25
❑ 152 Roger Clemens 2.00 .75
❑ 153 Scott Cooper .20 .07
❑ 154 Andre Dawson .40 .15
❑ 155 Mike Greenwell .20 .07
❑ 156 Aaron Sele .20 .07
❑ 157 Mo Vaughn .40 .15

❑ 158	Bret Boone	.40	.15
❑ 159	Barry Larkin	.60	.25
❑ 160	Kevin Mitchell	.20	.07
❑ 161	Jose Rijo	.20	.07
❑ 162	Deion Sanders	.60	.25
❑ 163	Reggie Sanders	.40	.15
❑ 164	Dante Bichette	.40	.15
❑ 165	Ellis Burks	.40	.15
❑ 166	Andres Galarraga	.40	.15
❑ 167	Charlie Hayes	.20	.07
❑ 168	David Nied	.20	.07
❑ 169	Walt Weiss	.20	.07
❑ 170	Kevin Appier	.40	.15
❑ 171	David Cone	.40	.15
❑ 172	Jeff Granger	.20	.07
❑ 173	Felix Jose	.20	.07
❑ 174	Wally Joyner	.40	.15
❑ 175	Brian McRae	.20	.07
❑ 176	Cecil Fielder	.40	.15
❑ 177	Travis Fryman	.40	.15
❑ 178	Mike Henneman	.20	.07
❑ 179	Tony Phillips	.20	.07
❑ 180	Mickey Tettleton	.20	.07
❑ 181	Alan Trammell	.40	.15
❑ 182	Rick Aguilera	.20	.07
❑ 183	Rich Becker	.20	.07
❑ 184	Scott Erickson	.20	.07
❑ 185	Chuck Knoblauch	.40	.15
❑ 186	Kirby Puckett	1.00	.40
❑ 187	Dave Winfield	.40	.15
❑ 188	Wilson Alvarez	.20	.07
❑ 189	Jason Bere	.20	.07
❑ 190	Alex Fernandez	.20	.07
❑ 191	Julio Franco	.40	.15
❑ 192	Jack McDowell	.20	.07
❑ 193	Frank Thomas	1.00	.40
❑ 194	Robin Ventura	.40	.15
❑ 195	Jim Abbott	.60	.25
❑ 196	Wade Boggs	.60	.25
❑ 197	Jimmy Key	.40	.15
❑ 198	Don Mattingly	2.50	1.00
❑ 199	Paul O'Neill	.60	.25
❑ 200	Danny Tartabull	.20	.07
❑ P24	Ken Griffey Jr. Promo	2.00	.75

2000 SP Authentic

❑	COMP.BASIC w/o SP's (90)	25.00	10.00
❑	COMP.UPDATE w/o SP'S (30)	10.00	4.00
❑	COMMON CARD (1-90)	.40	.15
❑	COMMON SUP (91-105)	3.00	1.25
❑	COMMON FW (106-135)	5.00	2.00
❑	COMMON FW (136-164)	5.00	2.00
❑	COMMON CARD (166-195)	.60	.25
❑ 1	Mo Vaughn	.40	.15
❑ 2	Troy Glaus	.40	.15
❑ 3	Jason Giambi	.40	.15
❑ 4	Tim Hudson	.40	.15
❑ 5	Eric Chavez	.40	.15
❑ 6	Shannon Stewart	.40	.15
❑ 7	Raul Mondesi	.40	.15
❑ 8	Carlos Delgado	.40	.15
❑ 9	Jose Canseco	.60	.25
❑ 10	Vinny Castilla	.40	.15
❑ 11	Greg Vaughn	.40	.15
❑ 12	Manny Ramirez	.60	.25
❑ 13	Roberto Alomar	.60	.25
❑ 14	Jim Thome	.60	.25
❑ 15	Richie Sexson	.40	.15
❑ 16	Alex Rodriguez	1.50	.60
❑ 17	Freddy Garcia	.40	.15
❑ 18	John Olerud	.40	.15
❑ 19	Albert Belle	.40	.15
❑ 20	Cal Ripken	3.00	1.25
❑ 21	Mike Mussina	.60	.25
❑ 22	Ivan Rodriguez	.60	.25
❑ 23	Gabe Kapler	.40	.15
❑ 24	Rafael Palmeiro	.60	.25
❑ 25	Nomar Garciaparra	1.50	.60
❑ 26	Pedro Martinez	.60	.25
❑ 27	Carl Everett	.40	.15
❑ 28	Carlos Beltran	.40	.15
❑ 29	Jermaine Dye	.40	.15
❑ 30	Juan Gonzalez	.40	.15
❑ 31	Dean Palmer	.40	.15
❑ 32	Corey Koskie	.40	.15
❑ 33	Jacque Jones	.40	.15
❑ 34	Frank Thomas	1.00	.40
❑ 35	Paul Konerko	.40	.15
❑ 36	Magglio Ordonez	.40	.15
❑ 37	Bernie Williams	.60	.25
❑ 38	Derek Jeter	2.50	1.00
❑ 39	Roger Clemens	2.00	.75
❑ 40	Mariano Rivera	1.00	.40
❑ 41	Jeff Bagwell	.60	.25
❑ 42	Craig Biggio	.60	.25
❑ 43	Jose Lima	.40	.15
❑ 44	Moises Alou	.40	.15
❑ 45	Chipper Jones	1.00	.40
❑ 46	Greg Maddux	1.50	.60
❑ 47	Andruw Jones	.60	.25
❑ 48	Andres Galarraga	.40	.15
❑ 49	Jeromy Burnitz	.40	.15
❑ 50	Geoff Jenkins	.40	.15
❑ 51	Mark McGwire	2.50	1.00
❑ 52	Fernando Tatis	.40	.15
❑ 53	J.D. Drew	.40	.15
❑ 54	Sammy Sosa	1.00	.40
❑ 55	Kerry Wood	.40	.15
❑ 56	Mark Grace	.60	.25
❑ 57	Matt Williams	.40	.15
❑ 58	Randy Johnson	1.00	.40
❑ 59	Erubiel Durazo	.40	.15
❑ 60	Gary Sheffield	.40	.15
❑ 61	Kevin Brown	.60	.25
❑ 62	Shawn Green	.40	.15
❑ 63	Vladimir Guerrero	1.00	.40
❑ 64	Michael Barrett	.40	.15
❑ 65	Barry Bonds	2.50	1.00
❑ 66	Jeff Kent	.40	.15
❑ 67	Russ Ortiz	.40	.15
❑ 68	Preston Wilson	.40	.15
❑ 69	Mike Lowell	.40	.15
❑ 70	Mike Piazza	1.50	.60
❑ 71	Mike Hampton	.40	.15
❑ 72	Robin Ventura	.40	.15
❑ 73	Edgardo Alfonzo	.40	.15
❑ 74	Tony Gwynn	1.25	.50
❑ 75	Ryan Klesko	.40	.15
❑ 76	Trevor Hoffman	.40	.15
❑ 77	Scott Rolen	.60	.25
❑ 78	Bob Abreu	.40	.15
❑ 79	Mike Lieberthal	.40	.15
❑ 80	Curt Schilling	.40	.15
❑ 81	Jason Kendall	.40	.15
❑ 82	Brian Giles	.40	.15
❑ 83	Kris Benson	.40	.15
❑ 84	Ken Griffey Jr.	1.50	.60
❑ 85	Sean Casey	.40	.15
❑ 86	Pokey Reese	.40	.15
❑ 87	Barry Larkin	.60	.25
❑ 88	Larry Walker	.40	.15
❑ 89	Todd Helton	.60	.25
❑ 90	Jeff Cirillo	.40	.15
❑ 91	Ken Griffey Jr. SUP	8.00	3.00
❑ 92	Mark McGwire SUP	12.00	5.00
❑ 93	Chipper Jones SUP	5.00	2.00
❑ 94	Derek Jeter SUP	12.00	5.00
❑ 95	Shawn Green SUP	3.00	1.25
❑ 96	Pedro Martinez SUP	3.00	1.25
❑ 97	Mike Piazza SUP	8.00	3.00
❑ 98	Alex Rodriguez SUP	8.00	3.00
❑ 99	Jeff Bagwell SUP	3.00	1.25
❑ 100	Cal Ripken SUP	15.00	6.00
❑ 101	Sammy Sosa SUP	5.00	2.00
❑ 102	Barry Bonds SUP	12.00	5.00
❑ 103	Jose Canseco SUP	3.00	1.25
❑ 104	Nomar Garciaparra SUP	8.00	3.00
❑ 105	Ivan Rodriguez SUP	3.00	1.25
❑ 106	Rick Ankiel FW	5.00	2.00
❑ 107	Pat Burrell FW	3.00	1.25
❑ 108	Vernon Wells FW	5.00	2.00
❑ 109	Nick Johnson FW	5.00	2.00
❑ 110	Kip Wells FW	5.00	2.00
❑ 111	Matt Riley FW	5.00	2.00
❑ 112	Alfonso Soriano FW	8.00	3.00
❑ 113	Josh Beckett FW	8.00	3.00
❑ 114	Danys Baez FW RC	5.00	2.00
❑ 115	Travis Dawkins FW	5.00	2.00
❑ 116	Eric Gagne FW	8.00	3.00
❑ 117	Mike Lamb FW RC	8.00	3.00
❑ 118	Eric Munson FW	5.00	2.00
❑ 119	Wilfredo Rodriguez FW RC	5.00	2.00
❑ 120	Kazuhiro Sasaki FW RC	8.00	3.00
❑ 121	Chad Hutchinson FW	5.00	2.00
❑ 122	Peter Bergeron FW	5.00	2.00
❑ 123	Wascar Serrano FW RC	5.00	2.00
❑ 124	Tony Armas Jr. FW	5.00	2.00
❑ 125	Ramon Ortiz FW	5.00	2.00
❑ 126	Adam Kennedy FW	5.00	2.00
❑ 127	Joe Crede FW	10.00	4.00
❑ 128	Roosevelt Brown FW	5.00	2.00
❑ 129	Mark Mulder FW	5.00	2.00
❑ 130	Brad Penny FW	5.00	2.00
❑ 131	Terrence Long FW	5.00	2.00
❑ 132	Ruben Mateo FW	5.00	2.00
❑ 133	Wily Mo Pena FW	5.00	2.00
❑ 134	Rafael Furcal FW	5.00	2.00
❑ 135	Mario Encarnacion FW	5.00	2.00
❑ 136	Barry Zito FW RC	20.00	8.00
❑ 137	Aaron McNeal FW RC	5.00	2.00
❑ 138	Timo Perez FW RC	5.00	2.00
❑ 139	Sun Woo Kim FW RC	5.00	2.00
❑ 140	Xavier Nady FW RC	10.00	4.00
❑ 141	Matt Wheatland FW RC	5.00	2.00
❑ 142	Brent Abernathy FW RC	5.00	2.00
❑ 143	Cory Vance FW RC	5.00	2.00
❑ 144	Scott Heard FW RC	5.00	2.00
❑ 145	Mike Meyers FW RC	5.00	2.00
❑ 146	Ben Diggins FW RC	5.00	2.00
❑ 147	Luis Matos FW RC	5.00	2.00
❑ 148	Ben Sheets FW RC	12.00	5.00
❑ 149	Kurt Ainsworth FW RC	5.00	2.00
❑ 150	Dave Krynzel FW RC	5.00	2.00
❑ 151	Alex Cabrera FW RC	5.00	2.00
❑ 152	Mike Tonis FW RC	5.00	2.00
❑ 153	Dane Sardinha FW RC	5.00	2.00
❑ 154	Keith Ginter FW RC	5.00	2.00
❑ 155	David Espinosa FW RC	5.00	2.00
❑ 156	Joe Torres FW RC	5.00	2.00
❑ 157	Daylan Holt FW RC	5.00	2.00
❑ 158	Koyie Hill FW RC	5.00	2.00
❑ 159	Brad Wilkerson FW RC	8.00	3.00
❑ 160	Juan Pierre FW RC	8.00	3.00
❑ 161	Matt Ginter FW RC	5.00	2.00
❑ 162	Dane Artman FW RC	5.00	2.00
❑ 163	Jon Rauch FW RC	5.00	2.00
❑ 164	Sean Burnett FW RC	5.00	2.00
❑ 165	Does Not Exist		
❑ 166	Darin Erstad	.60	.25
❑ 167	Ben Grieve	.60	.25
❑ 168	David Wells	.60	.25
❑ 169	Fred McGriff	1.00	.40
❑ 170	Bob Wickman	.60	.25
❑ 171	Al Martin	.60	.25
❑ 172	Melvin Mora	.60	.25
❑ 173	Ricky Ledee	.60	.25
❑ 174	Dante Bichette	.60	.25
❑ 175	Mike Sweeney	.60	.25
❑ 176	Bobby Higginson	.60	.25
❑ 177	Matt Lawton	.60	.25
❑ 178	Charles Johnson	.60	.25
❑ 179	David Justice	.60	.25
❑ 180	Richard Hidalgo	.60	.25
❑ 181	B.J. Surhoff	.60	.25
❑ 182	Richie Sexson	.60	.25
❑ 183	Jim Edmonds	.60	.25
❑ 184	Rondell White	.60	.25
❑ 185	Curt Schilling	.60	.25
❑ 186	Tom Goodwin	.60	.25
❑ 187	Jose Vidro	.60	.25

❑ 188	Ellis Burks	.60	.25
❑ 189	Henry Rodriguez	.60	.25
❑ 190	Mike Bordick	.60	.25
❑ 191	Eric Owens	.60	.25
❑ 192	Travis Lee	.60	.25
❑ 193	Kevin Young	.60	.25
❑ 194	Aaron Boone	.60	.25
❑ 195	Todd Hollandsworth	.60	.25
❑ SPA	Ken Griffey Jr. Sample	2.00	.75

2001 SP Authentic

❑	COMP.BASIC w/o SP's (90)	25.00	10.00
❑	COMP.UPDATE w/o SP's (30)	10.00	4.00
❑	COMMON CARD (1-90)	.40	.15
❑	COMMON FW (91-135)	8.00	3.00
❑	COMMON SS (136-180)	5.00	2.00
❑	COMMON CARD (181-210)	.60	.25
❑	COMMON CARD (211-240)	6.00	2.50
❑ 1	Troy Glaus	.40	.15
❑ 2	Darin Erstad	.40	.15
❑ 3	Jason Giambi	.40	.15
❑ 4	Tim Hudson	.40	.15
❑ 5	Eric Chavez	.40	.15
❑ 6	Miguel Tejada	.40	.15
❑ 7	Jose Ortiz	.40	.15
❑ 8	Carlos Delgado	.40	.15
❑ 9	Tony Batista	.40	.15
❑ 10	Raul Mondesi	.40	.15
❑ 11	Aubrey Huff	.40	.15
❑ 12	Greg Vaughn	.40	.15
❑ 13	Roberto Alomar	.60	.25
❑ 14	Juan Gonzalez	.40	.15
❑ 15	Jim Thome	.60	.25
❑ 16	Omar Vizquel	.60	.25
❑ 17	Edgar Martinez	.60	.25
❑ 18	Freddy Garcia	.40	.15
❑ 19	Cal Ripken	3.00	1.25
❑ 20	Ivan Rodriguez	.60	.25
❑ 21	Rafael Palmeiro	.60	.25
❑ 22	Alex Rodriguez	1.50	.60
❑ 23	Manny Ramirez Sox	.60	.25
❑ 24	Pedro Martinez	.60	.25
❑ 25	Nomar Garciaparra	1.50	.60
❑ 26	Mike Sweeney	.40	.15
❑ 27	Jermaine Dye	.40	.15
❑ 28	Bobby Higginson	.40	.15
❑ 29	Dean Palmer	.40	.15
❑ 30	Matt Lawton	.40	.15
❑ 31	Eric Milton	.40	.15
❑ 32	Frank Thomas	1.00	.40
❑ 33	Maggio Ordonez	.40	.15
❑ 34	David Wells	.40	.15
❑ 35	Paul Konerko	.40	.15
❑ 36	Derek Jeter	2.50	1.00
❑ 37	Bernie Williams	.60	.25
❑ 38	Roger Clemens	2.00	.75
❑ 39	Mike Mussina	.60	.25
❑ 40	Jorge Posada	.60	.25
❑ 41	Jeff Bagwell	.60	.25
❑ 42	Richard Hidalgo	.40	.15
❑ 43	Craig Biggio	.60	.25
❑ 44	Greg Maddux	1.50	.60
❑ 45	Chipper Jones	1.00	.40
❑ 46	Andruw Jones	.60	.25
❑ 47	Rafael Furcal	.40	.15
❑ 48	Tom Glavine	.60	.25
❑ 49	Jeromy Burnitz	.40	.15
❑ 50	Jeffrey Hammonds	.40	.15
❑ 51	Mark McGwire	2.50	1.00
❑ 52	Jim Edmonds	.40	.15
❑ 53	Rick Ankiel	.40	.15
❑ 54	J.D. Drew	.40	.15
❑ 55	Sammy Sosa	1.00	.40
❑ 56	Corey Patterson	.40	.15
❑ 57	Kerry Wood	.40	.15
❑ 58	Randy Johnson	1.00	.40
❑ 59	Luis Gonzalez	.40	.15
❑ 60	Curt Schilling	.40	.15
❑ 61	Gary Sheffield	.40	.15
❑ 62	Shawn Green	.40	.15
❑ 63	Kevin Brown	.40	.15
❑ 64	Vladimir Guerrero	1.00	.40
❑ 65	Jose Vidro	.40	.15
❑ 66	Barry Bonds	2.50	1.00
❑ 67	Jeff Kent	.40	.15
❑ 68	Livan Hernandez	.40	.15
❑ 69	Preston Wilson	.40	.15
❑ 70	Charles Johnson	.40	.15
❑ 71	Ryan Dempster	.40	.15
❑ 72	Mike Piazza	1.50	.60
❑ 73	Al Leiter	.40	.15
❑ 74	Edgardo Alfonzo	.40	.15
❑ 75	Robin Ventura	.40	.15
❑ 76	Tony Gwynn	1.25	.50
❑ 77	Phil Nevin	.40	.15
❑ 78	Trevor Hoffman	.40	.15
❑ 79	Scott Rolen	.60	.25
❑ 80	Pat Burrell	.40	.15
❑ 81	Bob Abreu	.40	.15
❑ 82	Jason Kendall	.40	.15
❑ 83	Brian Giles	.40	.15
❑ 84	Kris Benson	.40	.15
❑ 85	Ken Griffey Jr.	1.50	.60
❑ 86	Barry Larkin	.60	.25
❑ 87	Sean Casey	.40	.15
❑ 88	Todd Helton	.60	.25
❑ 89	Mike Hampton	.40	.15
❑ 90	Larry Walker	.40	.15
❑ 91	Ichiro Suzuki FW RC	150.00	90.00
❑ 92	Wilson Betemit FW RC	15.00	6.00
❑ 93	Adrian Hernandez FW RC	8.00	3.00
❑ 94	Juan Uribe FW RC	10.00	4.00
❑ 95	Travis Hafner FW RC	60.00	30.00
❑ 96	Morgan Ensberg FW RC	15.00	6.00
❑ 97	Sean Douglass FW RC	8.00	3.00
❑ 98	Juan Diaz FW RC	8.00	3.00
❑ 99	Erick Almonte FW RC	8.00	3.00
❑ 100	Ryan Freel FW RC	8.00	3.00
❑ 101	Elpidio Guzman FW RC	8.00	3.00
❑ 102	Christian Parker FW RC	8.00	3.00
❑ 103	Josh Fogg FW RC	8.00	3.00
❑ 104	Bert Snow FW RC	8.00	3.00
❑ 105	Horacio Ramirez FW RC	10.00	4.00
❑ 106	Ricardo Rodriguez FW RC	8.00	3.00
❑ 107	Tyler Walker FW RC	8.00	3.00
❑ 108	Jose Mieses FW RC	8.00	3.00
❑ 109	Billy Sylvester FW RC	8.00	3.00
❑ 110	Martin Vargas FW RC	8.00	3.00
❑ 111	Andres Torres FW RC	8.00	3.00
❑ 112	Greg Miller FW RC	8.00	3.00
❑ 113	Alexis Gomez FW RC	8.00	3.00
❑ 114	Grant Balfour FW RC	8.00	3.00
❑ 115	Henry Mateo FW RC	8.00	3.00
❑ 116	Esix Snead FW RC	8.00	3.00
❑ 117	Jackson Melian FW RC	8.00	3.00
❑ 118	Nate Teut FW RC	8.00	3.00
❑ 119	Tsuyoshi Shinjo FW RC	10.00	4.00
❑ 120	Carlos Valderrama FW RC	8.00	3.00
❑ 121	Johnny Estrada FW RC	10.00	4.00
❑ 122	Jason Michaels FW RC	8.00	3.00
❑ 123	William Ortega FW RC	8.00	3.00
❑ 124	Jason Smith FW RC	8.00	3.00
❑ 125	Brian Lawrence FW RC	8.00	3.00
❑ 126	Albert Pujols FW RC	600.00	450.00
❑ 127	Wilkin Ruan FW RC	8.00	3.00
❑ 128	Josh Towers FW RC	10.00	4.00
❑ 129	Kris Keller FW RC	8.00	3.00
❑ 130	Nick Maness FW RC	8.00	3.00
❑ 131	Jack Wilson FW RC	10.00	4.00
❑ 132	Brandon Duckworth FW RC	8.00	3.00
❑ 133	Mike Penney FW RC	8.00	3.00
❑ 134	Jay Gibbons FW RC	10.00	4.00
❑ 135	Cesar Crespo FW RC	8.00	3.00
❑ 136	Ken Griffey Jr. SS	10.00	4.00
❑ 137	Mark McGwire SS	15.00	6.00
❑ 138	Derek Jeter SS	15.00	6.00
❑ 139	Alex Rodriguez SS	10.00	4.00
❑ 140	Sammy Sosa SS	6.00	2.50
❑ 141	Carlos Delgado SS	5.00	2.00
❑ 142	Cal Ripken SS	20.00	8.00
❑ 143	Pedro Martinez SS	5.00	2.00
❑ 144	Frank Thomas SS	6.00	2.50
❑ 145	Juan Gonzalez SS	5.00	2.00
❑ 146	Troy Glaus SS	5.00	2.00
❑ 147	Jason Giambi SS	5.00	2.00
❑ 148	Ivan Rodriguez SS	5.00	2.00
❑ 149	Chipper Jones SS	6.00	2.50
❑ 150	Vladimir Guerrero SS	6.00	2.50
❑ 151	Mike Piazza SS	10.00	4.00
❑ 152	Jeff Bagwell SS	5.00	2.00
❑ 153	Randy Johnson SS	6.00	2.50
❑ 154	Todd Helton SS	5.00	2.00
❑ 155	Gary Sheffield SS	5.00	2.00
❑ 156	Tony Gwynn SS	8.00	3.00
❑ 157	Barry Bonds SS	15.00	6.00
❑ 158	Nomar Garciaparra SS	10.00	4.00
❑ 159	Bernie Williams SS	5.00	2.00
❑ 160	Greg Vaughn SS	5.00	2.00
❑ 161	David Wells SS	5.00	2.00
❑ 162	Roberto Alomar SS	5.00	2.00
❑ 163	Jermaine Dye SS	5.00	2.00
❑ 164	Rafael Palmeiro SS	5.00	2.00
❑ 165	Andruw Jones SS	5.00	2.00
❑ 166	Preston Wilson SS	5.00	2.00
❑ 167	Edgardo Alfonzo SS	5.00	2.00
❑ 168	Pat Burrell SS	5.00	2.00
❑ 169	Jim Edmonds SS	5.00	2.00
❑ 170	Mike Hampton SS	5.00	2.00
❑ 171	Jeff Kent SS	5.00	2.00
❑ 172	Kevin Brown SS	5.00	2.00
❑ 173	Manny Ramirez Sox SS	5.00	2.00
❑ 174	Maggio Ordonez SS	5.00	2.00
❑ 175	Roger Clemens SS	12.00	5.00
❑ 176	Jim Thome SS	5.00	2.00
❑ 177	Barry Zito SS	5.00	2.00
❑ 178	Brian Giles SS	5.00	2.00
❑ 179	Rick Ankiel SS	5.00	2.00
❑ 180	Corey Patterson SS	5.00	2.00
❑ 181	Garret Anderson	.60	.25
❑ 182	Jermaine Dye	.60	.25
❑ 183	Shannon Stewart	.60	.25
❑ 184	Ben Grieve	.60	.25
❑ 185	Ellis Burks	.60	.25
❑ 186	John Olerud	.60	.25
❑ 187	Tony Batista	.60	.25
❑ 188	Ruben Sierra	.60	.25
❑ 189	Carl Everett	.60	.25
❑ 190	Neifi Perez	.60	.25
❑ 191	Tony Clark	.60	.25
❑ 192	Doug Mientkiewicz	.60	.25
❑ 193	Carlos Lee	.60	.25
❑ 194	Jorge Posada	1.00	.40
❑ 195	Lance Berkman	5.00	2.00
❑ 196	Ken Caminiti	.60	.25
❑ 197	Ben Sheets	1.00	.40
❑ 198	Matt Morris	.60	.25
❑ 199	Fred McGriff	1.00	.40
❑ 200	Mark Grace	1.00	.40
❑ 201	Paul LoDuca	.60	.25
❑ 202	Tony Armas Jr.	.60	.25
❑ 203	Andres Galarraga	.60	.25
❑ 204	Cliff Floyd	.60	.25
❑ 205	Matt Lawton	.60	.25
❑ 206	Ryan Klesko	.60	.25
❑ 207	Jimmy Rollins	.60	.25
❑ 208	Aramis Ramirez	.60	.25
❑ 209	Aaron Boone	.60	.25
❑ 210	Jose Ortiz	.60	.25
❑ 211	Mark Prior FW RC	40.00	15.00
❑ 212	Mark Teixeira FW RC	80.00	40.00
❑ 213	Bud Smith FW RC	6.00	2.50
❑ 214	Wilmy Caceres FW RC	6.00	2.50
❑ 215	Dave Williams FW RC	6.00	2.50
❑ 216	Delvin James FW RC	6.00	2.50
❑ 217	Endy Chavez FW RC	6.00	2.50
❑ 218	Doug Nickle FW RC	6.00	2.50
❑ 219	Bret Prinz FW RC	6.00	2.50
❑ 220	Troy Mattes FW RC	6.00	2.50
❑ 221	Duaner Sanchez FW RC	6.00	2.50
❑ 222	Dewon Brazelton FW RC	6.00	2.50

❑ 223 Brian Bowles FW RC	6.00	2.50
❑ 224 Donaldo Mendez FW RC	6.00	2.50
❑ 225 Jorge Julio FW RC	6.00	2.50
❑ 226 Matt White FW RC	6.00	2.50
❑ 227 Casey Fossum FW RC	6.00	2.50
❑ 228 Mike Rivera FW RC	6.00	2.50
❑ 229 Joe Kennedy FW RC	8.00	3.00
❑ 230 Kyle Lohse FW RC	8.00	3.00
❑ 231 Juan Cruz FW RC	6.00	2.50
❑ 232 Jeremy Affeldt FW RC	6.00	2.50
❑ 233 Brandon Lyon FW RC	6.00	2.50
❑ 234 Brian Roberts FW RC	20.00	8.00
❑ 235 Willie Harris FW RC	6.00	2.50
❑ 236 Pedro Santana FW RC	6.00	2.50
❑ 237 Rafael Soriano FW RC	6.00	2.50
❑ 238 Steve Green FW RC	6.00	2.50
❑ 239 Junior Spivey FW RC	8.00	3.00
❑ 240 Rob Mackowiak FW RC	8.00	3.00
❑ NNO Ken Griffey Jr. Promo	2.00	.75

2002 SP Authentic

❑ COMP.LOW w/o SP's (90)	15.00	6.00
❑ COMP.UPDATE w/o SP's (30)	10.00	4.00
❑ COMMON CARD (1-90)	.40	.15
❑ COMMON (91-135/201-230)	5.00	2.00
❑ COMMON CARD (136-170)	10.00	4.00
❑ COMMON CARD (171-200)	.60	.25
❑ 1 Troy Glaus	.40	.15
❑ 2 Darin Erstad	.40	.15
❑ 3 Barry Zito	.40	.15
❑ 4 Eric Chavez	.40	.15
❑ 5 Tim Hudson	.40	.15
❑ 6 Miguel Tejada	.40	.15
❑ 7 Carlos Delgado	.40	.15
❑ 8 Shannon Stewart	.40	.15
❑ 9 Ben Grieve	.40	.15
❑ 10 Jim Thome	.60	.25
❑ 11 C.C. Sabathia	.40	.15
❑ 12 Ichiro Suzuki	2.00	.75
❑ 13 Freddy Garcia	.40	.15
❑ 14 Edgar Martinez	.60	.25
❑ 15 Bret Boone	.40	.15
❑ 16 Jeff Conine	.40	.15
❑ 17 Alex Rodriguez	1.50	.60
❑ 18 Juan Gonzalez	.40	.15
❑ 19 Ivan Rodriguez	.60	.25
❑ 20 Rafael Palmeiro	.60	.25
❑ 21 Hank Blalock	.60	.25
❑ 22 Pedro Martinez	.60	.25
❑ 23 Manny Ramirez	.60	.25
❑ 24 Nomar Garciaparra	1.50	.60
❑ 25 Carlos Beltran	.40	.15
❑ 26 Mike Sweeney	.40	.15
❑ 27 Randall Simon	.40	.15
❑ 28 Dmitri Young	.40	.15
❑ 29 Bobby Higginson	.40	.15
❑ 30 Corey Koskie	.40	.15
❑ 31 Eric Milton	.40	.15
❑ 32 Torii Hunter	.40	.15
❑ 33 Joe Mays	.40	.15
❑ 34 Frank Thomas	1.00	.40
❑ 35 Mark Buehrle	.40	.15
❑ 36 Magglio Ordonez	.40	.15
❑ 37 Kenny Lofton	.40	.15
❑ 38 Roger Clemens	2.00	.75
❑ 39 Derek Jeter	2.50	1.00
❑ 40 Jason Giambi	.40	.15
❑ 41 Bernie Williams	.60	.25
❑ 42 Alfonso Soriano	.40	.15
❑ 43 Lance Berkman	.40	.15
❑ 44 Roy Oswalt	.40	.15
❑ 45 Jeff Bagwell	.60	.25
❑ 46 Craig Biggio	.60	.25
❑ 47 Chipper Jones	1.00	.40
❑ 48 Greg Maddux	1.50	.60
❑ 49 Gary Sheffield	.40	.15
❑ 50 Andruw Jones	.60	.25
❑ 51 Ben Sheets	.40	.15
❑ 52 Richie Sexson	.40	.15
❑ 53 Albert Pujols	2.00	.75
❑ 54 Matt Morris	.40	.15
❑ 55 J.D. Drew	.40	.15
❑ 56 Sammy Sosa	1.00	.40
❑ 57 Kerry Wood	.40	.15
❑ 58 Corey Patterson	.40	.15
❑ 59 Mark Prior	.60	.25
❑ 60 Randy Johnson	1.00	.40
❑ 61 Luis Gonzalez	.40	.15
❑ 62 Curt Schilling	.40	.15
❑ 63 Shawn Green	.40	.15
❑ 64 Kevin Brown	.40	.15
❑ 65 Hideo Nomo	1.00	.40
❑ 66 Vladimir Guerrero	1.00	.40
❑ 67 Jose Vidro	.40	.15
❑ 68 Barry Bonds	2.50	1.00
❑ 69 Jeff Kent	.40	.15
❑ 70 Rich Aurilia	.40	.15
❑ 71 Preston Wilson	.40	.15
❑ 72 Josh Beckett	.40	.15
❑ 73 Mike Lowell	.40	.15
❑ 74 Roberto Alomar	.60	.25
❑ 75 Mo Vaughn	.40	.15
❑ 76 Jeromy Burnitz	.40	.15
❑ 77 Mike Piazza	1.50	.60
❑ 78 Sean Burroughs	.40	.15
❑ 79 Phil Nevin	.40	.15
❑ 80 Bobby Abreu	.40	.15
❑ 81 Pat Burrell	.40	.15
❑ 82 Scott Rolen	.60	.25
❑ 83 Jason Kendall	.40	.15
❑ 84 Brian Giles	.40	.15
❑ 85 Ken Griffey Jr.	1.50	.60
❑ 86 Adam Dunn	.40	.15
❑ 87 Sean Casey	.40	.15
❑ 88 Todd Helton	.60	.25
❑ 89 Larry Walker	.40	.15
❑ 90 Mike Hampton	.40	.15
❑ 91 Brandon Puffer FW RC	5.00	2.00
❑ 92 Tom Shearn FW RC	5.00	2.00
❑ 93 Chris Baker FW RC	5.00	2.00
❑ 94 Gustavo Chacin FW RC	8.00	3.00
❑ 95 Joe Orloski FW RC	5.00	2.00
❑ 96 Mike Smith FW RC	5.00	2.00
❑ 97 John Ennis FW RC	5.00	2.00
❑ 98 John Foster FW RC	5.00	2.00
❑ 99 Kevin Gryboski FW RC	5.00	2.00
❑ 100 Brian Mallette FW RC	5.00	2.00
❑ 101 Takahito Nomura FW RC	5.00	2.00
❑ 102 So Taguchi FW RC	8.00	3.00
❑ 103 Jeremy Lambert FW RC	5.00	2.00
❑ 104 Jason Simontacchi FW RC	5.00	2.00
❑ 105 Jorge Sosa FW RC	8.00	3.00
❑ 106 Brandon Backe FW RC	8.00	3.00
❑ 107 P.J. Bevis FW RC	5.00	2.00
❑ 108 Jeremy Ward FW RC	5.00	2.00
❑ 109 Doug Devore FW RC	5.00	2.00
❑ 110 Ron Chiavacci FW	5.00	2.00
❑ 111 Ron Calloway FW RC	5.00	2.00
❑ 112 Nelson Castro FW RC	5.00	2.00
❑ 113 Deivis Santos FW	5.00	2.00
❑ 114 Earl Snyder FW RC	5.00	2.00
❑ 115 Julio Mateo FW RC	5.00	2.00
❑ 116 J.J. Putz FW RC	5.00	2.00
❑ 117 Allan Simpson FW RC	5.00	2.00
❑ 118 Satoru Komiyama FW RC	5.00	2.00
❑ 119 Adam Walker FW RC	5.00	2.00
❑ 120 Oliver Perez FW RC	8.00	3.00
❑ 121 Cliff Bartosh FW RC	5.00	2.00
❑ 122 Todd Donovan FW RC	5.00	2.00
❑ 123 Elio Serrano FW RC	5.00	2.00
❑ 124 Pete Zamora FW RC	5.00	2.00
❑ 125 Mike Gonzalez FW RC	5.00	2.00
❑ 126 Travis Hughes FW RC	5.00	2.00
❑ 127 Jorge De La Rosa FW RC	5.00	2.00
❑ 128 Anastacio Martinez FW RC	5.00	2.00
❑ 129 Colin Young FW RC	5.00	2.00
❑ 130 Nate Field FW RC	5.00	2.00
❑ 131 Tim Kalita FW RC	5.00	2.00
❑ 132 Julius Matos FW RC	5.00	2.00
❑ 133 Terry Pearson FW RC	5.00	2.00
❑ 134 Kyle Kane FW RC	5.00	2.00
❑ 135 Mitch Wylie FW RC	5.00	2.00
❑ 136 Rodrigo Rosario AU RC	10.00	4.00
❑ 137 Franklyn German AU RC	10.00	4.00
❑ 138 Reed Johnson AU RC	15.00	6.00
❑ 139 Luis Martinez AU RC	10.00	4.00
❑ 140 Michael Crudale AU RC	10.00	4.00
❑ 141 Francis Beltran AU RC	10.00	4.00
❑ 142 Steve Kent AU RC	10.00	4.00
❑ 143 Felix Escalona AU RC	10.00	4.00
❑ 144 Jose Valverde AU RC	10.00	4.00
❑ 145 Victor Alvarez AU RC	10.00	4.00
❑ 146 Kazuhisa Ishii AU/249 RC	40.00	15.00
❑ 147 Jorge Nunez AU RC	10.00	4.00
❑ 148 Eric Good AU RC	10.00	4.00
❑ 149 Luis Ugueto AU RC	10.00	4.00
❑ 150 Matt Thornton AU RC	10.00	4.00
❑ 151 Wilson Valdez AU RC	10.00	4.00
❑ 152 Han Izquierdo AU/249 RC	40.00	15.00
❑ 153 Jaime Cerda AU RC	10.00	4.00
❑ 154 Mark Corey AU RC	10.00	4.00
❑ 155 Tyler Yates AU RC	10.00	4.00
❑ 156 Steve Bechler AU RC	10.00	4.00
❑ 157 Ben Howard AU/249 RC	40.00	15.00
❑ 158 Anderson Machado AU RC	10.00	4.00
❑ 159 Jorge Padilla AU RC	10.00	4.00
❑ 160 Eric Junge AU RC	10.00	4.00
❑ 161 Adrian Burnside AU RC	10.00	4.00
❑ 162 Josh Hancock AU RC	10.00	4.00
❑ 163 Chris Booker AU RC	10.00	4.00
❑ 164 Cam Esslinger AU RC	10.00	4.00
❑ 165 Rene Reyes AU RC	10.00	4.00
❑ 166 Aaron Cook AU RC	10.00	4.00
❑ 167 Juan Brito AU RC	10.00	4.00
❑ 168 Miguel Ascencio AU RC	10.00	4.00
❑ 169 Kevin Frederick AU RC	10.00	4.00
❑ 170 Edwin Almonte AU RC	10.00	4.00
❑ 171 Erubiel Durazo	.60	.25
❑ 172 Junior Spivey	.60	.25
❑ 173 Geronimo Gil	.60	.25
❑ 174 Cliff Floyd	.60	.25
❑ 175 Brandon Larson	.60	.25
❑ 176 Aaron Boone	.60	.25
❑ 177 Shawn Estes	.60	.25
❑ 178 Austin Kearns	.60	.25
❑ 179 Joe Borchard	.60	.25
❑ 180 Russell Branyan	.60	.25
❑ 181 Jay Payton	.60	.25
❑ 182 Andres Torres	.60	.25
❑ 183 Andy Van Hekken	.60	.25
❑ 184 Alex Sanchez	.60	.25
❑ 185 Endy Chavez	.60	.25
❑ 186 Bartolo Colon	.60	.25
❑ 187 Raul Mondesi	.60	.25
❑ 188 Robin Ventura	.60	.25
❑ 189 Mike Mussina	1.00	.40
❑ 190 Jorge Posada	1.00	.40
❑ 191 Ted Lilly	.60	.25
❑ 192 Ray Durham	.60	.25
❑ 193 Brett Myers	.60	.25
❑ 194 Marlon Byrd	.60	.25
❑ 195 Vicente Padilla	.60	.25
❑ 196 Josh Fogg	.60	.25
❑ 197 Kenny Lofton	.60	.25
❑ 198 Scott Rolen	1.00	.40
❑ 199 Jason Lane	.60	.25
❑ 200 Josh Phelps	.60	.25
❑ 201 Travis Driskill FW RC	5.00	2.00
❑ 202 Howie Clark FW RC	5.00	2.00
❑ 203 Mike Mahoney FW	5.00	2.00
❑ 204 Brian Tallet FW RC	5.00	2.00
❑ 205 Kirk Saarloos FW RC	5.00	2.00
❑ 206 Barry Wesson FW RC	5.00	2.00
❑ 207 Aaron Guiel FW RC	5.00	2.00
❑ 208 Shawn Sedlacek FW RC	5.00	2.00
❑ 209 Jose Diaz FW RC	5.00	2.00
❑ 210 Jorge Nunez FW	5.00	2.00
❑ 211 Danny Mota FW RC	5.00	2.00
❑ 212 David Ross FW RC	8.00	3.00
❑ 213 Jayson Durocher FW RC	5.00	2.00

❑ 214 Shane Nance FW RC 5.00 2.00
❑ 215 Wil Nieves FW RC 5.00 2.00
❑ 216 Freddy Sanchez FW RC 10.00 4.00
❑ 217 Alex Pelaez FW RC 5.00 2.00
❑ 218 Jamey Carroll FW RC 8.00 3.00
❑ 219 J.J. Trujillo FW RC 5.00 2.00
❑ 220 Kevin Pickford FW RC 5.00 2.00
❑ 221 Clay Condrey FW RC 5.00 2.00
❑ 222 Chris Snelling FW RC 6.00 2.50
❑ 223 Cliff Lee FW RC 8.00 3.00
❑ 224 Jeremy Hill FW RC 5.00 2.00
❑ 225 Jose Rodriguez FW RC 5.00 2.00
❑ 226 Lance Carter FW RC 5.00 2.00
❑ 227 Ken Huckaby FW RC 5.00 2.00
❑ 228 Scott Wiggins FW RC 5.00 2.00
❑ 229 Corey Thurman FW RC 5.00 2.00
❑ 230 Kevin Cash FW RC 5.00 2.00
❑ RJ-D Joe DiMaggio AU Poster 200.00 125.00

2003 SP Authentic

❑ COMP.LO SET w/o SP's (90) 15.00 6.00
❑ COMMON CARD (1-90) .40 .15
❑ COMMON CARD (91-123) 3.00 1.25
❑ COMMON CARD (124-150) 3.00 1.25
❑ COMMON CARD (151-180) 5.00 2.00
❑ COMMON CARD (181-189) 15.00 6.00
❑ 91-189 RANDOM INSERTS IN PACKS
❑ COMMON CARD (190-239) 5.00 2.00
❑ 190-239 RANDOM IN 03 UD FINITE PACKS
❑ 190-239 PRINT RUN 699 SERIAL #'d SETS
❑ 1 Darin Erstad .40 .15
❑ 2 Garret Anderson .40 .15
❑ 3 Troy Glaus .40 .15
❑ 4 Eric Chavez .40 .15
❑ 5 Barry Zito .40 .15
❑ 6 Miguel Tejada .40 .15
❑ 7 Eric Hinske .40 .15
❑ 8 Carlos Delgado .40 .15
❑ 9 Josh Phelps .40 .15
❑ 10 Ben Grieve .40 .15
❑ 11 Carl Crawford .40 .15
❑ 12 Omar Vizquel .60 .25
❑ 13 Matt Lawton .40 .15
❑ 14 C.C. Sabathia .40 .15
❑ 15 Ichiro Suzuki 2.00 .75
❑ 16 John Olerud .40 .15
❑ 17 Freddy Garcia .40 .15
❑ 18 Jay Gibbons .40 .15
❑ 19 Tony Batista .40 .15
❑ 20 Melvin Mora .40 .15
❑ 21 Alex Rodriguez 1.50 .60
❑ 22 Rafael Palmeiro .60 .25
❑ 23 Hank Blalock .40 .15
❑ 24 Nomar Garciaparra 1.50 .60
❑ 25 Pedro Martinez .60 .25
❑ 26 Johnny Damon .60 .25
❑ 27 Mike Sweeney .40 .15
❑ 28 Carlos Febles .40 .15
❑ 29 Carlos Beltran .40 .15
❑ 30 Carlos Pena .40 .15
❑ 31 Eric Munson .40 .15
❑ 32 Bobby Higginson .40 .15
❑ 33 Torii Hunter .40 .15
❑ 34 Doug Mientkiewicz .40 .15
❑ 35 Jacque Jones .40 .15
❑ 36 Paul Konerko .40 .15
❑ 37 Bartolo Colon .40 .15
❑ 38 Maggio Ordonez .40 .15
❑ 39 Derek Jeter 2.50 1.00
❑ 40 Bernie Williams .60 .25
❑ 41 Jason Giambi .40 .15
❑ 42 Alfonso Soriano .40 .15
❑ 43 Roger Clemens 2.00 .75
❑ 44 Jeff Bagwell .60 .25
❑ 45 Jeff Kent .40 .15
❑ 46 Lance Berkman .40 .15
❑ 47 Chipper Jones 1.00 .40
❑ 48 Andruw Jones .60 .25
❑ 49 Gary Sheffield .40 .15
❑ 50 Ben Sheets .40 .15
❑ 51 Richie Sexson .40 .15
❑ 52 Geoff Jenkins .40 .15
❑ 53 Jim Edmonds .40 .15
❑ 54 Albert Pujols 2.00 .75
❑ 55 Scott Rolen .60 .25
❑ 56 Sammy Sosa 1.00 .40
❑ 57 Kerry Wood .40 .15
❑ 58 Eric Karros .40 .15
❑ 59 Luis Gonzalez .40 .15
❑ 60 Randy Johnson 1.00 .40
❑ 61 Curt Schilling .40 .15
❑ 62 Fred McGriff .60 .25
❑ 63 Shawn Green .40 .15
❑ 64 Paul Lo Duca .40 .15
❑ 65 Vladimir Guerrero 1.00 .40
❑ 66 Jose Vidro .40 .15
❑ 67 Barry Bonds 2.50 1.00
❑ 68 Rich Aurilia .40 .15
❑ 69 Edgardo Alfonzo .40 .15
❑ 70 Ivan Rodriguez .60 .25
❑ 71 Mike Lowell .40 .15
❑ 72 Derrek Lee .60 .25
❑ 73 Tom Glavine .60 .25
❑ 74 Mike Piazza 1.50 .60
❑ 75 Roberto Alomar .60 .25
❑ 76 Ryan Klesko .40 .15
❑ 77 Phil Nevin .40 .15
❑ 78 Mark Kotsay .40 .15
❑ 79 Jim Thome .60 .25
❑ 80 Pat Burrell .40 .15
❑ 81 Bobby Abreu .40 .15
❑ 82 Jason Kendall .40 .15
❑ 83 Brian Giles .40 .15
❑ 84 Aramis Ramirez .40 .15
❑ 85 Austin Kearns .40 .15
❑ 86 Ken Griffey Jr. 1.50 .60
❑ 87 Adam Dunn .40 .15
❑ 88 Larry Walker .40 .15
❑ 89 Todd Helton .60 .25
❑ 90 Preston Wilson .40 .15
❑ 91 Derek Jeter RA 8.00 3.00
❑ 92 Johnny Damon RA 3.00 1.25
❑ 93 Chipper Jones RA 3.00 1.25
❑ 94 Manny Ramirez RA 3.00 1.25
❑ 95 Trot Nixon RA 3.00 1.25
❑ 96 Alex Rodriguez RA 5.00 2.00
❑ 97 Chan Ho Park RA 3.00 1.25
❑ 98 Brad Fullmer RA 3.00 1.25
❑ 99 Billy Wagner RA 3.00 1.25
❑ 100 Hideo Nomo RA 3.00 1.25
❑ 101 Freddy Garcia RA 3.00 1.25
❑ 102 Darin Erstad RA 3.00 1.25
❑ 103 Jose Cruz Jr. RA 3.00 1.25
❑ 104 Nomar Garciaparra RA 5.00 2.00
❑ 105 Magglio Ordonez RA 3.00 1.25
❑ 106 Kerry Wood RA 3.00 1.25
❑ 107 Troy Glaus RA 3.00 1.25
❑ 108 J.D. Drew RA 3.00 1.25
❑ 109 Alfonso Soriano RA 3.00 1.25
❑ 110 Danys Baez RA 3.00 1.25
❑ 111 Kazuhiro Sasaki RA 3.00 1.25
❑ 112 Barry Zito RA 3.00 1.25
❑ 113 Brent Abernathy RA 3.00 1.25
❑ 114 Ben Diggins RA 3.00 1.25
❑ 115 Ben Sheets RA 3.00 1.25
❑ 116 Brad Wilkerson RA 3.00 1.25
❑ 117 Juan Pierre RA 3.00 1.25
❑ 118 Jon Rauch RA 3.00 1.25
❑ 119 Ichiro Suzuki RA 6.00 2.50
❑ 120 Albert Pujols RA 6.00 2.50
❑ 121 Mark Prior RA 3.00 1.25
❑ 122 Mark Teixeira RA 3.00 1.25
❑ 123 Kazuhisa Ishii RA 3.00 1.25
❑ 124 Troy Glaus B93 3.00 1.25
❑ 125 Randy Johnson B93 3.00 1.25
❑ 126 Curt Schilling B93 3.00 1.25
❑ 127 Chipper Jones B93 3.00 1.25
❑ 128 Greg Maddux B93 5.00 2.00
❑ 129 Nomar Garciaparra B93 5.00 2.00
❑ 130 Pedro Martinez B93 3.00 1.25
❑ 131 Sammy Sosa B93 3.00 1.25
❑ 132 Mark Prior B93 3.00 1.25
❑ 133 Ken Griffey Jr. B93 5.00 2.00
❑ 134 Adam Dunn B93 3.00 1.25
❑ 135 Jeff Bagwell B93 3.00 1.25
❑ 136 Vladimir Guerrero B93 3.00 1.25
❑ 137 Mike Piazza B93 5.00 2.00
❑ 138 Tom Glavine B93 3.00 1.25
❑ 139 Derek Jeter B93 8.00 3.00
❑ 140 Roger Clemens B93 6.00 2.50
❑ 141 Jason Giambi B93 3.00 1.25
❑ 142 Alfonso Soriano B93 3.00 1.25
❑ 143 Miguel Tejada B93 3.00 1.25
❑ 144 Barry Zito B93 3.00 1.25
❑ 145 Jim Thome B93 3.00 1.25
❑ 146 Barry Bonds B93 8.00 3.00
❑ 147 Ichiro Suzuki B93 6.00 2.50
❑ 148 Albert Pujols B93 6.00 2.50
❑ 149 Alex Rodriguez B93 5.00 2.00
❑ 150 Carlos Delgado B93 3.00 1.25
❑ 151 Rich Fischer FW RC 5.00 2.00
❑ 152 Brandon Webb FW RC 12.00 5.00
❑ 153 Rob Hammock FW RC 5.00 2.00
❑ 154 Matt Kata FW RC 5.00 2.00
❑ 155 Tim Olson FW RC 5.00 2.00
❑ 156 Oscar Villarreal FW RC 5.00 2.00
❑ 157 Michael Hessman FW RC 5.00 2.00
❑ 158 Daniel Cabrera FW RC 8.00 3.00
❑ 159 Jon Leicester FW RC 5.00 2.00
❑ 160 Todd Wellemeyer FW RC 5.00 2.00
❑ 161 Felix Sanchez FW RC 5.00 2.00
❑ 162 David Sanders FW RC 5.00 2.00
❑ 163 Josh Stewart FW RC 5.00 2.00
❑ 164 Arnie Munoz FW RC 5.00 2.00
❑ 165 Ryan Cameron FW RC 5.00 2.00
❑ 166 Clint Barmes FW RC 5.00 2.00
❑ 167 Josh Willingham FW RC 10.00 4.00
❑ 169 Willie Eyre FW RC 5.00 2.00
❑ 170 Brent Hoard FW RC 5.00 2.00
❑ 171 Terrmel Sledge FW RC 5.00 2.00
❑ 172 Phil Seibel FW RC 5.00 2.00
❑ 173 Craig Brazell FW RC 5.00 2.00
❑ 174 Jeff Duncan FW RC 5.00 2.00
❑ 176 Bernie Castro FW RC 5.00 2.00
❑ 177 Mike Nicolas FW RC 5.00 2.00
❑ 178 Rett Johnson FW RC 5.00 2.00
❑ 179 Bobby Madritsch FW RC 5.00 2.00
❑ 180 Chris Capuano FW RC 25.00 10.00
❑ 181 Hid Matsui FW AU RC 300.00 175.00
❑ 182 Jose Contreras FW AU RC 30.0012.50
❑ 183 Lew Ford FW AU RC 25.00 10.00
❑ 184 Jeremy Griffiths FW AU RC 15.00 6.00
❑ 185 G.Quiroz FW AU RC 15.00 6.00
❑ 186 Alej Machado FW AU RC 15.00 6.00
❑ 187 Fran Cruceta FW AU RC 15.00 6.00
❑ 188 Prentice Redman FW AU RC 15.006.00
❑ 189 Shane Bazzell FW AU RC 15.00 6.00
❑ 190 Aaron Looper FW RC 5.00 2.00
❑ 191 Alex Prieto FW RC 5.00 2.00
❑ 192 Alfredo Gonzalez FW RC 5.00 2.00
❑ 193 Andrew Brown FW RC 8.00 3.00
❑ 194 Anthony Ferrari FW RC 5.00 2.00
❑ 195 Aquilino Lopez FW RC 5.00 2.00
❑ 196 Beau Kemp FW RC 5.00 2.00
❑ 197 Bo Hart FW RC 5.00 2.00
❑ 198 Chad Gaudin FW RC 5.00 2.00
❑ 199 Colin Porter FW RC 5.00 2.00
❑ 200 D.J. Carrasco FW RC 5.00 2.00
❑ 201 Dan Haren FW RC 8.00 3.00
❑ 202 Danny Garcia FW RC 5.00 2.00
❑ 203 Jon Switzer FW 5.00 2.00
❑ 204 Edwin Jackson FW RC 8.00 3.00
❑ 205 Fernando Cabrera FW RC 5.00 2.00
❑ 206 Garrett Atkins FW 5.00 2.00
❑ 207 Gerald Laird FW 5.00 2.00
❑ 208 Greg Jones FW RC 5.00 2.00
❑ 209 Ian Ferguson FW RC 5.00 2.00
❑ 210 Jason Roach FW RC 5.00 2.00
❑ 211 Jason Shiell FW RC 5.00 2.00
❑ 212 Jeremy Bonderman FW RC 25.00 10.00

❑ 213 Jeremy Wedel FW RC 5.00 2.00
❑ 214 Jhonny Peralta FW 8.00 3.00
❑ 215 Delmon Young FW RC 50.00 25.00
❑ 216 Jorge DePaula FW 5.00 2.00
❑ 217 Josh Hall FW RC 5.00 2.00
❑ 218 Julio Manon FW RC 5.00 2.00
❑ 219 Kevin Correia FW RC 5.00 2.00
❑ 220 Kevin Ohme FW RC 5.00 2.00
❑ 221 Kevin Tolar FW RC 5.00 2.00
❑ 222 Luis Ayala FW RC 5.00 2.00
❑ 223 Luis De Los Santos FW 5.00 2.00
❑ 224 Chad Cordero FW RC 10.00 4.00
❑ 225 Mark Malaska FW RC 5.00 2.00
❑ 226 Khalil Greene FW 8.00 3.00
❑ 227 Michael Nakamura FW RC 5.00 2.00
❑ 228 Michel Hernandez FW RC 5.00 2.00
❑ 229 Miguel Ojeda FW RC 5.00 2.00
❑ 230 Mike Neu FW RC 5.00 2.00
❑ 231 Nate Bland FW RC 5.00 2.00
❑ 232 Pete LaForest FW RC 5.00 2.00
❑ 233 Rickie Weeks FW RC 20.00 8.00
❑ 234 Rosman Garcia FW RC 5.00 2.00
❑ 235 Ryan Wagner FW RC 5.00 2.00
❑ 236 Lance Niekro FW 5.00 2.00
❑ 237 Tom Gregorio FW RC 5.00 2.00
❑ 238 Tommy Phelps FW 5.00 2.00
❑ 239 Wilfredo Ledezma FW RC 5.00 2.00

2004 SP Authentic

❑ COMP.SET w/o SP's (90) 15.00 6.00
❑ COMMON CARD (1-90) .40 .15
❑ COMMON (91-132/178-191) 5.00 2.00
❑ 91-132/178-191 OVERALL FW ODDS 1:24
❑ 91-132/178-179/181-191 PRINT 704 #'d SETS
❑ 91-132/178-179/181-191 #'d FROM 296-999
❑ CARD 180 PRINT RUN 999 #'d COPIES
❑ CARD 180 #'d FROM 1-999
❑ COMMON CARD (133-177) 3.00 1.25
❑ 133-177 STATED ODDS 1:24
❑ 133-177 PRINT RUN 999 SERIAL #'d SETS
❑ 1 Bret Boone .40 .15
❑ 2 Gary Sheffield .40 .15
❑ 3 Rafael Palmeiro .60 .25
❑ 4 Jorge Posada .60 .25
❑ 5 Derek Jeter 2.00 .75
❑ 6 Garret Anderson .40 .15
❑ 7 Bartolo Colon .40 .15
❑ 8 Kevin Brown .40 .15
❑ 9 Shea Hillenbrand .40 .15
❑ 10 Ryan Klesko .40 .15
❑ 11 Bobby Abreu .40 .15
❑ 12 Scott Rolen .60 .25
❑ 13 Alfonso Soriano .40 .15
❑ 14 Jason Giambi .40 .15
❑ 15 Tom Glavine .60 .25
❑ 16 Hideo Nomo 1.00 .40
❑ 17 Johan Santana 1.00 .40
❑ 18 Sammy Sosa 1.00 .40
❑ 19 Rickie Weeks .40 .15
❑ 20 Barry Zito .40 .15
❑ 21 Kerry Wood .40 .15
❑ 22 Austin Kearns .40 .15
❑ 23 Shawn Green .40 .15
❑ 24 Miguel Cabrera .60 .25
❑ 25 Richard Hidalgo .40 .15
❑ 26 Andruw Jones .60 .25
❑ 27 Randy Wolf .40 .15
❑ 28 David Ortiz 1.00 .40
❑ 29 Roy Oswalt .40 .15
❑ 30 Vernon Wells .40 .15
❑ 31 Ben Sheets .40 .15
❑ 32 Mike Lowell .40 .15
❑ 33 Todd Helton .60 .25
❑ 34 Jacque Jones .40 .15
❑ 35 Mike Sweeney .40 .15
❑ 36 Hank Blalock .40 .15
❑ 37 Jason Schmidt .40 .15
❑ 38 Jeff Kent .40 .15
❑ 39 Josh Beckett .40 .15
❑ 40 Manny Ramirez .60 .25
❑ 41 Torii Hunter .40 .15
❑ 42 Brian Giles .40 .15
❑ 43 Javier Vazquez .40 .15
❑ 44 Jim Edmonds .40 .15
❑ 45 Dmitri Young .40 .15
❑ 46 Preston Wilson .40 .15
❑ 47 Jeff Bagwell .60 .25
❑ 48 Pedro Martinez .60 .25
❑ 49 Eric Chavez .40 .15
❑ 50 Ken Griffey Jr. 1.50 .60
❑ 51 Shannon Stewart .40 .15
❑ 52 Rafael Furcal .40 .15
❑ 53 Brandon Webb .40 .15
❑ 54 Juan Pierre .40 .15
❑ 55 Roger Clemens 2.00 .75
❑ 56 Geoff Jenkins .40 .15
❑ 57 Lance Berkman .40 .15
❑ 58 Albert Pujols 2.00 .75
❑ 59 Frank Thomas 1.00 .40
❑ 60 Edgar Martinez .60 .25
❑ 61 Tim Hudson .40 .15
❑ 62 Eric Gagne .40 .15
❑ 63 Richie Sexson .40 .15
❑ 64 Corey Patterson .40 .15
❑ 65 Nomar Garciaparra 1.50 .60
❑ 66 Hideki Matsui 1.50 .60
❑ 67 Mark Teixeira .60 .25
❑ 68 Troy Glaus .40 .15
❑ 69 Carlos Lee .40 .15
❑ 70 Mike Mussina .60 .25
❑ 71 Magglio Ordonez .40 .15
❑ 72 Roy Halladay .40 .15
❑ 73 Ichiro Suzuki 2.00 .75
❑ 74 Randy Johnson 1.00 .40
❑ 75 Luis Gonzalez .40 .15
❑ 76 Mark Prior .60 .25
❑ 77 Carlos Beltran .40 .15
❑ 78 Ivan Rodriguez .60 .25
❑ 79 Alex Rodriguez 1.50 .60
❑ 80 Dontrelle Willis .60 .25
❑ 81 Mike Piazza 1.50 .60
❑ 82 Curt Schilling .60 .25
❑ 83 Vladimir Guerrero 1.00 .40
❑ 84 Greg Maddux 1.50 .60
❑ 85 Jim Thome .60 .25
❑ 86 Miguel Tejada .40 .15
❑ 87 Carlos Delgado .40 .15
❑ 88 Jose Reyes .40 .15
❑ 89 Matt Morris .40 .15
❑ 90 Mark Mulder .40 .15
❑ 91 Angel Chavez FW RC 5.00 2.00
❑ 92 Brandon Medders FW RC 5.00 2.00
❑ 93 Carlos Vasquez FW RC 5.00 2.00
❑ 94 Chris Aguila FW RC 5.00 2.00
❑ 95 Colby Miller FW RC 5.00 2.00
❑ 96 Dave Crouthers FW RC 5.00 2.00
❑ 97 Dennis Sarfate FW RC 5.00 2.00
❑ 98 Donnie Kelly FW RC 5.00 2.00
❑ 99 Merkin Valdez FW RC 5.00 2.00
❑ 100 Eddy Rodriguez FW RC 5.00 2.00
❑ 101 Edwin Moreno FW RC 5.00 2.00
❑ 102 Enemencio Pacheco FW RC 5.00 2.00
❑ 103 Roberto Novoa FW RC 5.00 2.00
❑ 104 Greg Dobbs FW RC 5.00 2.00
❑ 105 Hector Gimenez FW RC 5.00 2.00
❑ 106 Ian Snell FW RC 8.00 3.00
❑ 107 Jake Woods FW RC 5.00 2.00
❑ 108 Jamie Brown FW RC 5.00 2.00
❑ 109 Jason Frasor FW RC 5.00 2.00
❑ 110 Jerome Gamble FW RC 5.00 2.00
❑ 111 Jerry Gil FW RC 5.00 2.00
❑ 112 Jesse Harper FW RC 5.00 2.00
❑ 113 Jorge Vasquez FW RC 5.00 2.00
❑ 114 Jose Capellan FW RC 5.00 2.00
❑ 115 Josh Labandeira FW RC 5.00 2.00
❑ 116 Justin Hampson FW RC 5.00 2.00
❑ 117 Justin Huisman FW RC 5.00 2.00
❑ 118 Justin Leone FW RC 5.00 2.00
❑ 119 Lincoln Holdzkom FW RC 5.00 2.00
❑ 120 Lino Urdaneta FW RC 5.00 2.00
❑ 121 Mike Gosling FW RC 5.00 2.00
❑ 122 Mike Johnston FW RC 5.00 2.00
❑ 123 Mike Rouse FW RC 5.00 2.00
❑ 124 Scott Proctor FW RC 5.00 2.00
❑ 125 Roman Colon FW RC 5.00 2.00
❑ 126 Ronny Cedeno FW RC 8.00 3.00
❑ 127 Ryan Meaux FW RC 5.00 2.00
❑ 128 Scott Dohmann FW RC 5.00 2.00
❑ 129 Sean Henn FW RC 5.00 2.00
❑ 130 Tim Bausher FW RC 5.00 2.00
❑ 131 Tim Bittner FW RC 5.00 2.00
❑ 132 William Bergolla FW RC 5.00 2.00
❑ 133 Rick Ferrell ASM 3.00 1.25
❑ 134 Joe DiMaggio ASM 5.00 2.00
❑ 135 Bob Feller ASM 3.00 1.25
❑ 136 Ted Williams ASM 8.00 3.00
❑ 137 Stan Musial ASM 5.00 2.00
❑ 138 Larry Doby ASM 3.00 1.25
❑ 139 Red Schoendienst ASM 3.00 1.25
❑ 140 Enos Slaughter ASM 3.00 1.25
❑ 141 Stan Musial ASM 5.00 2.00
❑ 142 Mickey Mantle ASM 10.00 4.00
❑ 143 Ted Williams ASM 8.00 3.00
❑ 144 Mickey Mantle ASM 10.00 4.00
❑ 145 Stan Musial ASM 5.00 2.00
❑ 146 Tom Seaver ASM 4.00 1.50
❑ 147 Willie McCovey ASM 4.00 1.50
❑ 148 Bob Gibson ASM 4.00 1.50
❑ 149 Frank Robinson ASM 3.00 1.25
❑ 150 Joe Morgan ASM 3.00 1.25
❑ 151 Billy Williams ASM 3.00 1.25
❑ 152 Catfish Hunter ASM 4.00 1.50
❑ 153 Joe Morgan ASM 3.00 1.25
❑ 154 Joe Morgan ASM 3.00 1.25
❑ 155 Mike Schmidt ASM 8.00 3.00
❑ 156 Tommy Lasorda ASM 3.00 1.25
❑ 157 Robin Yount ASM 4.00 1.50
❑ 158 Nolan Ryan ASM 10.00 4.00
❑ 159 John Franco ASM 3.00 1.25
❑ 160 Nolan Ryan ASM 10.00 4.00
❑ 161 Ken Griffey Jr. ASM 5.00 2.00
❑ 162 Cal Ripken ASM 10.00 4.00
❑ 163 Ken Griffey Jr. ASM 5.00 2.00
❑ 164 Gary Sheffield ASM 3.00 1.25
❑ 165 Fred McGriff ASM 4.00 1.50
❑ 166 Hideo Nomo ASM 4.00 1.50
❑ 167 Mike Piazza ASM 5.00 2.00
❑ 168 Sandy Alomar Jr. ASM 3.00 1.25
❑ 169 Roberto Alomar ASM 4.00 1.50
❑ 170 Ted Williams ASM 8.00 3.00
❑ 171 Pedro Martinez ASM 4.00 1.50
❑ 172 Derek Jeter ASM 6.00 2.50
❑ 173 Cal Ripken ASM 10.00 4.00
❑ 174 Torii Hunter ASM 3.00 1.25
❑ 175 Alfonso Soriano ASM 3.00 1.25
❑ 176 Hank Blalock ASM 3.00 1.25
❑ 177 Ichiro Suzuki ASM 6.00 2.50
❑ 178 Orlando Rodriguez FW RC 5.00 2.00
❑ 179 Ramon Ramirez FW RC 5.00 2.00
❑ 180 Kazuo Matsui FW RC 5.00 2.00
❑ 181 Kevin Cave FW RC 5.00 2.00
❑ 182 John Gall FW RC 5.00 2.00
❑ 183 Freddy Guzman FW RC 5.00 2.00
❑ 184 Chris Oxspring FW RC 5.00 2.00
❑ 185 Rusty Tucker FW RC 5.00 2.00
❑ 186 Jorge Sequea FW RC 5.00 2.00
❑ 187 Carlos Hines FW RC 5.00 2.00
❑ 188 Michael Vento FW RC 5.00 2.00
❑ 189 Ryan Wing FW RC 5.00 2.00
❑ 190 Jeff Bennett FW RC 5.00 2.00
❑ 191 Luis A. Gonzalez FW RC 5.00 2.00

2005 SP Authentic

❑ COMP.BASIC SET (100) 25.00 10.00
❑ COMMON CARD (1-100) .40 .15
❑ COMMON RETIRED 1-100 .40 .15
❑ 1-100 ISSUED IN 05 SP COLLECTION PACKS
❑ COMMON AUTO (101-186) 10.00 4.00
❑ 101-186 ODDS APPX 1:8 '05 UD UPDATE
❑ 101-186 PRINT RUN 185 SERIAL #'d SETS

❑ 105, 115, 118-119, 142, 154 DO NOT EXIST
❑ 161, 180, 183, 186 DO NOT EXIST
❑ 1 A.J. Burnett .40 .15
❑ 2 Aaron Rowand .40 .15
❑ 3 Adam Dunn .40 .15
❑ 4 Adrian Beltre .40 .15
❑ 5 Adrian Gonzalez .40 .15
❑ 6 Akinori Otsuka .40 .15
❑ 7 Albert Pujols 2.00 .75
❑ 8 Andre Dawson .40 .15
❑ 9 Andruw Jones .60 .25
❑ 10 Aramis Ramirez .40 .15
❑ 11 Barry Larkin .60 .25
❑ 12 Ben Sheets .40 .15
❑ 13 Bo Jackson 1.00 .40
❑ 14 Bobby Abreu .40 .15
❑ 15 Bobby Crosby .40 .15
❑ 16 Bronson Arroyo .40 .15
❑ 17 Cal Ripken 3.00 1.25
❑ 18 Carl Crawford .40 .15
❑ 19 Carlos Zambrano .40 .15
❑ 20 Casey Kotchman .40 .15
❑ 21 Cesar Izturis .40 .15
❑ 22 Chone Figgins .40 .15
❑ 23 Corey Patterson .40 .15
❑ 24 Craig Biggio .60 .25
❑ 25 Dale Murphy .60 .25
❑ 26 Dallas McPherson .40 .15
❑ 27 Danny Haren .40 .15
❑ 28 Darryl Strawberry .40 .15
❑ 29 David Ortiz .60 .25
❑ 30 David Wright 1.50 .60
❑ 31 Derek Jeter 2.00 .75
❑ 32 Derrek Lee .60 .25
❑ 33 Don Mattingly 2.00 .75
❑ 34 Dwight Gooden .40 .15
❑ 35 Edgar Renteria .40 .15
❑ 36 Eric Chavez .40 .15
❑ 37 Eric Gagne .40 .15
❑ 38 Gary Sheffield .40 .15
❑ 39 Gavin Floyd .40 .15
❑ 40 Pedro Martinez .60 .25
❑ 41 Greg Maddux 1.50 .60
❑ 42 Hank Blalock .40 .15
❑ 43 Huston Street .60 .25
❑ 44 J.D. Drew .40 .15
❑ 45 Jake Peavy .40 .15
❑ 46 Jake Westbrook .40 .15
❑ 47 Jason Bay .40 .15
❑ 48 Austin Kearns .40 .15
❑ 49 Jeremy Reed .40 .15
❑ 50 Jim Rice .40 .15
❑ 51 Jimmy Rollins .40 .15
❑ 52 Joe Blanton .40 .15
❑ 53 Joe Mauer 1.00 .40
❑ 54 Johan Santana 1.00 .40
❑ 55 John Smoltz .60 .25
❑ 56 Johnny Estrada .40 .15
❑ 57 Jose Reyes .40 .15
❑ 58 Ken Griffey Jr. 1.50 .60
❑ 59 Kerry Wood .40 .15
❑ 60 Khalil Greene .60 .25
❑ 61 Marcus Giles .40 .15
❑ 62 Melvin Mora .40 .15
❑ 63 Mark Grace .60 .25
❑ 64 Mark Mulder .40 .15
❑ 65 Mark Prior .60 .25
❑ 66 Mark Teixeria .60 .25
❑ 67 Matt Clement .40 .15
❑ 68 Michael Young .40 .15
❑ 69 Miguel Cabrera .60 .25
❑ 70 Miguel Tejada .40 .15
❑ 71 Mike Piazza 1.00 .40
❑ 72 Mike Schmidt 2.00 .75
❑ 73 Nolan Ryan 2.50 1.00
❑ 74 Oliver Perez .40 .15
❑ 75 Nick Johnson .40 .15
❑ 76 Paul Molitor .40 .15
❑ 77 Rafael Palmeiro .60 .25
❑ 78 Randy Johnson 1.00 .40
❑ 79 Reggie Jackson .60 .25
❑ 80 Rich Harden .40 .15
❑ 81 Rickie Weeks .40 .15
❑ 82 Robin Yount 1.00 .40
❑ 83 Roger Clemens 1.50 .60
❑ 84 Roy Oswalt .40 .15
❑ 85 Ryan Howard 2.50 1.00
❑ 86 Ryne Sandberg 2.00 .75
❑ 87 Scott Kazmir .40 .15
❑ 88 Scott Rolen .60 .25
❑ 89 Sean Burroughs .40 .15
❑ 90 Sean Casey .40 .15
❑ 91 Shingo Takatsu .40 .15
❑ 92 Tim Hudson .40 .15
❑ 93 Tony Gwynn 1.25 .50
❑ 94 Torii Hunter .40 .15
❑ 95 Travis Hafner .40 .15
❑ 96 Victor Martinez .40 .15
❑ 97 Vladimir Guerrero 1.00 .40
❑ 98 Wade Boggs .60 .25
❑ 99 Will Clark .60 .25
❑ 100 Yadier Molina .40 .15
❑ 101 Adam Shabala AU RC 10.00 4.00
❑ 102 Ambiorix Burgos AU RC 10.00 4.00
❑ 103 Ambiorix Concepcion AU RC 10.00 4.00
❑ 104 Anibal Sanchez AU RC 80.00 40.00
❑ 106 Brandon McCarthy AU RC 40.0015.00
❑ 107 Brian Burres AU RC 10.00 4.00
❑ 108 Carlos Ruiz AU RC 25.00 10.00
❑ 109 Casey Rogowski AU RC 15.00 6.00
❑ 110 Chad Orvella AU RC 10.00 4.00
❑ 111 Chris Resop AU RC 15.00 6.00
❑ 112 Chris Roberson AU RC 10.00 4.00
❑ 113 Chris Seddon AU RC 10.00 4.00
❑ 114 Colter Bean AU RC 15.00 6.00
❑ 116 Dave Gassner AU RC 10.00 4.00
❑ 117 Brian Anderson AU RC 40.00 15.00
❑ 120 Devon Lowery AU RC 10.00 4.00
❑ 121 Enrique Gonzalez AU RC 15.00 6.00
❑ 122 Eude Brito AU RC 10.00 4.00
❑ 123 Francisco Butto AU RC 10.00 4.00
❑ 124 Franquelis Osoria AU RC 10.00 4.00
❑ 125 Garrett Jones AU RC 10.00 4.00
❑ 126 Geovany Soto AU RC 10.00 4.00
❑ 127 Hayden Penn AU RC 25.00 10.00
❑ 128 Ismael Ramirez AU RC 10.00 4.00
❑ 129 Jared Gothreaux AU RC 10.00 4.00
❑ 130 Jason Hammel AU RC 10.00 4.00
❑ 131 Jeff Miller AU RC 10.00 4.00
❑ 132 Jeff Niemann AU RC 25.00 10.00
❑ 133 Joel Peralta AU RC 10.00 4.00
❑ 134 John Hattig AU RC 10.00 4.00
❑ 135 Jorge Campillo AU RC 10.00 4.00
❑ 136 Juan Morillo AU RC 10.00 4.00
❑ 137 Justin Verlander AU RC 200.00125.00
❑ 138 Ryan Garko AU RC 50.00 25.00
❑ 139 Keiichi Yabu AU RC 15.00 6.00
❑ 140 Kendry Morales AU RC 100.00 50.00
❑ 141 Luis Hernandez AU RC 10.00 4.00
❑ 143 Luis O.Rodriguez AU RC 10.00 4.00
❑ 144 Luke Scott AU RC 60.00 30.00
❑ 145 Marcos Carvajal AU RC 10.00 4.00
❑ 146 Mark Woodyard AU RC 10.00 4.00
❑ 147 Matt A.Smith AU RC 10.00 4.00
❑ 148 Matthew Lindstrom AU RC 10.00 4.00
❑ 149 Miguel Negron AU RC 15.00 6.00
❑ 150 Mike Morse AU RC 15.00 6.00
❑ 151 Nate McLouth AU RC 15.00 6.00
❑ 152 Nelson Cruz AU RC 50.00 25.00
❑ 153 Nick Masset AU RC 10.00 4.00
❑ 155 Paulino Reynoso AU RC 10.00 4.00
❑ 156 Pedro Lopez AU RC 10.00 4.00
❑ 157 Pete Orr AU RC 10.00 4.00
❑ 158 Philip Humber AU RC 25.00 10.00
❑ 159 Prince Fielder AU RC 175.00 100.00
❑ 160 Randy Messenger AU RC 10.00 4.00
❑ 162 Raul Tablado AU RC 10.00 4.00
❑ 163 Ronny Paulino AU RC 25.00 10.00
❑ 164 Russ Rohlicek AU RC 10.00 4.00
❑ 165 Russell Martin AU RC 50.00 25.00
❑ 166 Scott Baker AU RC 15.00 6.00
❑ 167 Scott Munter AU RC 10.00 4.00
❑ 168 Sean Thompson AU RC 10.00 4.00
❑ 169 Sean Tracey AU RC 10.00 4.00
❑ 170 Shane Costa AU RC 10.00 4.00
❑ 171 Stephen Drew AU RC 150.00 90.00
❑ 172 Steve Schmoll AU RC 10.00 4.00
❑ 173 Tadahito Iguchi AU RC 80.00 40.00
❑ 174 Tony Giarratano AU RC 10.00 4.00
❑ 175 Tony Pena AU RC 10.00 4.00
❑ 176 Travis Bowyer AU RC 10.00 4.00
❑ 177 Ubaldo Jimenez AU RC 15.00 6.00
❑ 178 Wladimir Balentien AU RC 25.00 10.00
❑ 179 Yorman Bazardo AU RC 10.00 4.00
❑ 181 Ryan Zimmerman AU RC 225.00 150.00
❑ 182 Chris Denorfia AU RC 25.00 10.00
❑ 184 Jermaine Van Buren AU 10.00 4.00
❑ 185 Mark McLemore AU RC 10.00 4.00

2004 SP Legendary Cuts

❑ COMPLETE SET (126) 40.00 15.00
❑ 1 Al Kaline 1.50 .60
❑ 2 Al Lopez .60 .25
❑ 3 Alan Trammell .60 .25
❑ 4 Andre Dawson .60 .25
❑ 5 Babe Ruth 5.00 2.00
❑ 6 Bert Campaneris .40 .15
❑ 7 Bill Mazeroski 1.00 .40
❑ 8 Bill Russell .40 .15
❑ 9 Billy Williams .60 .25
❑ 10 Bob Feller 1.00 .40
❑ 11 Bob Gibson 1.00 .40
❑ 12 Bob Lemon .60 .25
❑ 13 Bobby Doerr .60 .25
❑ 14 Brooks Robinson 1.00 .40
❑ 15 Cal Ripken 5.00 2.00
❑ 16 Carl Yastrzemski 2.50 1.00
❑ 17 Carlton Fisk 1.00 .40
❑ 18 Catfish Hunter .60 .25
❑ 19 Dale Murphy 1.00 .40
❑ 20 Darryl Strawberry .60 .25
❑ 21 Dave Concepcion .60 .25
❑ 22 Dave Winfield .60 .25
❑ 23 Dennis Eckersley .60 .25
❑ 24 Denny McLain .60 .25
❑ 25 Don Drysdale 1.00 .40
❑ 26 Don Larsen .60 .25
❑ 27 Don Mattingly 3.00 1.25
❑ 28 Don Sutton .60 .25
❑ 29 Duke Snider 1.00 .40
❑ 30 Dusty Baker .60 .25
❑ 31 Dwight Gooden .60 .25
❑ 32 Earl Weaver .40 .15
❑ 33 Early Wynn .60 .25
❑ 34 Eddie Mathews 1.50 .60
❑ 35 Eddie Murray 1.50 .60
❑ 36 Enos Slaughter .60 .25
❑ 37 Ernie Banks 1.50 .60
❑ 38 Fergie Jenkins .60 .25
❑ 39 Frank Robinson .60 .25
❑ 40 Fred Lynn .40 .15
❑ 41 Gary Carter .60 .25

❑ 42	Gaylord Perry	.60	.25
❑ 43	George Brett	3.00	1.25
❑ 44	George Foster	.40	.15
❑ 45	George Kell	.60	.25
❑ 46	Greg Luzinski	.60	.25
❑ 47	Hal Newhouser	.60	.25
❑ 48	Hank Greenberg	1.50	.60
❑ 49	Harmon Killebrew	1.50	.60
❑ 50	Honus Wagner	1.50	.60
❑ 51	Hoyt Wilhelm	.60	.25
❑ 52	Jackie Robinson	1.50	.60
❑ 53	Jim Bunning	1.00	.40
❑ 54	Jim Palmer	.60	.25
❑ 55	Jimmie Foxx	1.50	.60
❑ 56	Joe Carter	.60	.25
❑ 57	Joe DiMaggio	2.50	1.00
❑ 58	Joe Morgan	.60	.25
❑ 59	Joe Torre	1.00	.40
❑ 60	Johnny Bench	1.50	.60
❑ 61	Johnny Podres	.60	.25
❑ 62	Johnny Roseboro	.40	.15
❑ 63	Johnny Sain	.60	.25
❑ 64	Juan Marichal	.60	.25
❑ 65	Keith Hernandez	.60	.25
❑ 66	Kirby Puckett	1.50	.60
❑ 67	Kirk Gibson	.60	.25
❑ 68	Will Clark	1.00	.40
❑ 69	Jim Rice	.60	.25
❑ 70	Larry Doby	.60	.25
❑ 71	Lou Boudreau	.60	.25
❑ 72	Lou Brock	1.00	.40
❑ 73	Lou Gehrig	2.50	1.00
❑ 74	Lou Piniella	.60	.25
❑ 75	Luis Aparicio	.60	.25
❑ 76	Mark Grace	1.00	.40
❑ 77	Mel Ott	1.50	.60
❑ 78	Mickey Lolich	.60	.25
❑ 79	Mickey Mantle	8.00	3.00
❑ 80	Mike Greenwell	.40	.15
❑ 81	Mike Schmidt	3.00	1.25
❑ 82	Monte Irvin	.60	.25
❑ 83	Nellie Fox	1.00	.40
❑ 84	Nolan Ryan	4.00	1.50
❑ 85	Orlando Cepeda	.60	.25
❑ 86	Ozzie Smith	2.50	1.00
❑ 87	Paul Molitor	.60	.25
❑ 88	Pee Wee Reese	1.00	.40
❑ 89	Phil Niekro	.60	.25
❑ 90	Phil Rizzuto	1.00	.40
❑ 91	Ralph Kiner	1.00	.40
❑ 92	Red Rolfe	.40	.15
❑ 93	Red Schoendienst	.60	.25
❑ 94	Reggie Smith	.40	.15
❑ 95	Rich Gossage	.60	.25
❑ 96	Richie Ashburn	1.00	.40
❑ 97	Rick Ferrell	.60	.25
❑ 98	Elston Howard	.60	.25
❑ 99	Roberto Clemente	4.00	1.50
❑ 100	Robin Roberts	.60	.25
❑ 101	Robin Yount	1.50	.60
❑ 102	Roger Maris	1.50	.60
❑ 103	Rollie Fingers	.60	.25
❑ 104	Ron Santo	1.00	.40
❑ 105	Roy Campanella	1.50	.60
❑ 106	Ryne Sandberg	3.00	1.25
❑ 107	Sparky Anderson	.60	.25
❑ 108	Sparky Lyle	.40	.15
❑ 109	Stan Musial	2.50	1.00
❑ 110	Steve Carlton	.60	.25
❑ 111	Steve Garvey	.60	.25
❑ 112	Ted Williams	3.00	1.25
❑ 113	Thurman Munson	1.50	.60
❑ 114	Tom Seaver	1.00	.40
❑ 115	Tommy Henrich	.60	.25
❑ 116	Tommy Lasorda	.60	.25
❑ 117	Tony Gwynn	2.00	.75
❑ 118	Tony Perez	.60	.25
❑ 119	Ty Cobb	2.00	.75
❑ 120	Wade Boggs	1.00	.40
❑ 121	Warren Spahn	1.00	.40
❑ 122	Whitey Ford	1.00	.40
❑ 123	Willie McCovey	1.00	.40
❑ 124	Willie Randolph	.60	.25
❑ 125	Willie Stargell	1.00	.40
❑ 126	Yogi Berra	1.50	.60

2005 SP Legendary Cuts

❑	COMPLETE SET (90)	25.00	10.00
❑	COMMON CARD (1-90)	.40	.15
❑ 1	Al Kaline	1.50	.60
❑ 2	Babe Ruth	5.00	2.00
❑ 3	Bill Mazeroski	1.00	.40
❑ 4	Billy Williams	.60	.25
❑ 5	Bob Feller	1.00	.40
❑ 6	Bob Gibson	1.00	.40
❑ 7	Bob Lemon	.60	.25
❑ 8	Bobby Doerr	.60	.25
❑ 9	Brooks Robinson	1.00	.40
❑ 10	Carl Yastrzemski	2.50	1.00
❑ 11	Carlton Fisk	1.00	.40
❑ 12	Casey Stengel	1.00	.40
❑ 13	Catfish Hunter	.60	.25
❑ 14	Christy Mathewson	1.50	.60
❑ 15	Cy Young	1.50	.60
❑ 16	Dennis Eckersley	.60	.25
❑ 17	Dizzy Dean	1.00	.40
❑ 18	Don Drysdale	1.00	.40
❑ 19	Don Sutton	.60	.25
❑ 20	Duke Snider	1.00	.40
❑ 21	Early Wynn	.60	.25
❑ 22	Eddie Mathews	1.50	.60
❑ 23	Eddie Murray	1.50	.60
❑ 24	Enos Slaughter	.60	.25
❑ 25	Ernie Banks	1.50	.60
❑ 26	Fergie Jenkins	.60	.25
❑ 27	Frank Robinson	.60	.25
❑ 28	Gary Carter	.60	.25
❑ 29	Gaylord Perry	.60	.25
❑ 30	Reggie Jackson	1.00	.40
❑ 31	George Kell	.60	.25
❑ 32	George Sisler	.60	.25
❑ 33	Hal Newhouser	.60	.25
❑ 34	Harmon Killebrew	1.50	.60
❑ 35	Honus Wagner	1.50	.60
❑ 36	Jackie Robinson	1.50	.60
❑ 37	Jim Bunning	1.00	.40
❑ 38	Jim Palmer	.60	.25
❑ 39	Jimmie Foxx	1.50	.60
❑ 40	Joe DiMaggio	2.50	1.00
❑ 41	Joe Morgan	.60	.25
❑ 42	Johnny Bench	1.50	.60
❑ 43	Johnny Mize	.60	.25
❑ 44	Juan Marichal	.60	.25
❑ 45	Kirby Puckett	1.50	.60
❑ 46	Larry Doby	.60	.25
❑ 47	Lefty Grove	1.00	.40
❑ 48	Lou Boudreau	.60	.25
❑ 49	Lou Brock	1.00	.40
❑ 50	Lou Gehrig	2.50	1.00
❑ 51	Luis Aparicio	.60	.25
❑ 52	Mel Ott	1.50	.60
❑ 53	Mickey Cochrane	.60	.25
❑ 54	Mickey Mantle	8.00	3.00
❑ 55	Mike Schmidt	3.00	1.25
❑ 56	Monte Irvin	.60	.25
❑ 57	Nolan Ryan	4.00	1.50
❑ 58	Orlando Cepeda	.60	.25
❑ 59	Ozzie Smith	2.50	1.00
❑ 60	Paul Molitor	.60	.25
❑ 61	Pee Wee Reese	1.00	.40
❑ 62	Phil Niekro	.60	.25
❑ 63	Phil Rizzuto	1.00	.40
❑ 64	Ralph Kiner	1.00	.40
❑ 65	Red Schoendienst	.60	.25
❑ 66	Richie Ashburn	1.00	.40
❑ 67	Rick Ferrell	.60	.25
❑ 68	Robin Roberts	.60	.25
❑ 69	Robin Yount	1.50	.60
❑ 70	Rod Carew	1.00	.40
❑ 71	Rogers Hornsby	1.00	.40
❑ 72	Rollie Fingers	.60	.25
❑ 73	Roy Campanella	1.50	.60
❑ 74	Ryne Sandberg	3.00	1.25
❑ 75	Satchel Paige	1.50	.60
❑ 76	Stan Musial	2.50	1.00
❑ 77	Steve Carlton	.60	.25
❑ 78	Ted Williams	3.00	1.25
❑ 79	Thurman Munson	1.50	.60
❑ 80	Tom Seaver	1.00	.40
❑ 81	Tony Gwynn	2.00	.75
❑ 82	Tony Perez	.60	.25
❑ 83	Ty Cobb	2.00	.75
❑ 84	Wade Boggs	1.00	.40
❑ 85	Walter Johnson	1.50	.60
❑ 86	Warren Spahn	1.00	.40
❑ 87	Whitey Ford	1.00	.40
❑ 88	Willie McCovey	1.00	.40
❑ 89	Willie Stargell	1.00	.40
❑ 90	Yogi Berra	1.50	.60

2006 SP Legendary Cuts

❑	COMP.SET w/o SP's (100)	25.00	10.00
❑	COMMON CARD (1-100)	.60	.25
❑	COMMON CARD (101-200)	5.00	2.00
❑	101-200: ONE BASIC OR BRONZE PER BOX		
❑	101-200 PRINT RUN 550 SERIAL #'d SETS		
❑	EXQUISITE EXCH ODDS 1:60		
❑	EXQUISITE EXCH DEADLINE 07/27/07		
❑ 1	Juan Marichal	.60	.25
❑ 2	Monte Irvin	.60	.25
❑ 3	Will Clark	1.00	.40
❑ 4	Willie McCovey	1.00	.40
❑ 5	Eddie Gaedel	.60	.25
❑ 6	Ken Williams	.60	.25
❑ 7	Earl Battey	.60	.25
❑ 8	Rick Ferrell	.60	.25
❑ 9	Bob Gibson	1.00	.40
❑ 10	Elmer Flick	.60	.25
❑ 11	Joe Medwick	.60	.25
❑ 12	Lou Brock	1.00	.40
❑ 13	Ozzie Smith	2.50	1.00
❑ 14	Red Schoendienst	.60	.25
❑ 15	Stan Musial	2.50	1.00
❑ 16	Tony Oliva	.60	.25
❑ 17	Phil Niekro	.60	.25
❑ 18	Boog Powell	.60	.25
❑ 19	Brooks Robinson	1.00	.40
❑ 20	Cal Ripken	6.00	2.50
❑ 21	Eddie Murray	1.50	.60
❑ 22	Frank Robinson	.60	.25
❑ 23	Jim Palmer	.60	.25
❑ 24	Jocko Conlon	.60	.25
❑ 25	Carlton Fisk	1.00	.40
❑ 26	Dwight Evans	.60	.25
❑ 27	Fred Lynn	.60	.25
❑ 28	Jim Rice	.60	.25
❑ 29	Ted Williams	4.00	1.50
❑ 30	Wade Boggs	1.00	.40
❑ 31	Hugh Duffy	.60	.25
❑ 32	Kid Nichols	.60	.25
❑ 33	Johnny Vander Meer	.60	.25

❑ 34	Dolph Camilli	.60	.25
❑ 35	Carl Yastrzemski	2.50	1.00
❑ 36	Chick Hafey	.60	.25
❑ 37	Kirby Higbe	.60	.25
❑ 38	Pee Wee Reese	1.00	.40
❑ 39	Pete Reiser	.60	.25
❑ 40	Don Sutton	.60	.25
❑ 41	Rod Carew	1.00	.40
❑ 42	Andre Dawson	.60	.25
❑ 43	Billy Herman	.60	.25
❑ 44	Billy Williams	.60	.25
❑ 45	Charley Root	.60	.25
❑ 46	Hack Wilson	1.00	.40
❑ 47	Ernie Banks	1.50	.60
❑ 48	Fergie Jenkins	.60	.25
❑ 49	Gabby Hartnett	.60	.25
❑ 50	Ken Hubbs	.60	.25
❑ 51	Kiki Cuyler	.60	.25
❑ 52	Mark Grace	1.00	.40
❑ 53	Ryne Sandberg	3.00	1.25
❑ 54	Harold Newhouser	.60	.25
❑ 55	Charlie Robertson	.60	.25
❑ 56	Harold Baines	.60	.25
❑ 57	Luis Aparicio	.60	.25
❑ 58	Luke Appling	.60	.25
❑ 59	Nellie Fox	1.00	.40
❑ 60	Ray Schalk	.60	.25
❑ 61	Red Faber	.60	.25
❑ 62	Sloppy Thurston	.60	.25
❑ 63	Freddie Lindstrom	.60	.25
❑ 64	Vern Kennedy	.60	.25
❑ 65	Barry Larkin	1.00	.40
❑ 66	Bucky Walters	.60	.25
❑ 67	Dolf Luque	.60	.25
❑ 68	Al Campanis	.60	.25
❑ 69	Ernie Lombardi	.60	.25
❑ 70	George Foster	.60	.25
❑ 71	Joe Morgan	.60	.25
❑ 72	Johnny Bench	1.50	.60
❑ 73	Ken Griffey Sr.	.60	.25
❑ 74	Ted Kluszewski	1.00	.40
❑ 75	Tony Perez	.60	.25
❑ 76	Wally Post	.60	.25
❑ 77	Bob Feller	.60	.25
❑ 78	Bob Lemon	.60	.25
❑ 79	Earl Averill	.60	.25
❑ 80	Joe Sewell	.60	.25
❑ 81	Johnny Hodapp	.60	.25
❑ 82	Larry Doby	.60	.25
❑ 83	Lou Boudreau	.60	.25
❑ 84	Rocky Colavito	1.00	.40
❑ 85	Stan Coveleski	.60	.25
❑ 86	Nap Lajoie	1.00	.40
❑ 87	Al Kaline	1.50	.60
❑ 88	Alan Trammell	.60	.25
❑ 89	Charlie Gehringer	.60	.25
❑ 90	Denny McLain	.60	.25
❑ 91	Hank Greenberg	1.50	.60
❑ 92	Jack Morris	.60	.25
❑ 93	Mark Fidrych	.60	.25
❑ 94	Ray Boone	.60	.25
❑ 95	Rudy York	.60	.25
❑ 96	Buck Leonard	.60	.25
❑ 97	Bo Jackson	1.50	.60
❑ 98	Zoilo Versalles	.60	.25
❑ 99	John Kruk	.60	.25
❑ 100	Don Drysdale	1.00	.40
❑ 101	Cecil Cooper	5.00	2.00
❑ 102	Vic Wertz	5.00	2.00
❑ 103	Kirk Gibson	5.00	2.00
❑ 104	Maury Wills	5.00	2.00
❑ 105	Steve Garvey	5.00	2.00
❑ 106	Warren Spahn	8.00	3.00
❑ 107	Paul Molitor	5.00	2.00
❑ 108	Robin Yount	8.00	3.00
❑ 109	Rollie Fingers	5.00	2.00
❑ 110	Bob Allison	5.00	2.00
❑ 111	Kirby Puckett	8.00	3.00
❑ 112	Tim Raines	5.00	2.00
❑ 113	George Pipgras	5.00	2.00
❑ 114	Eddie Grant	5.00	2.00
❑ 115	Hoyt Wilhelm	5.00	2.00
❑ 116	Sal Maglie	5.00	2.00
❑ 117	Ron Santo	8.00	3.00
❑ 118	Wally Joyner	5.00	2.00
❑ 119	Tom Seaver	8.00	3.00
❑ 120	Tommie Agee	5.00	2.00
❑ 121	Harmon Killebrew	8.00	3.00
❑ 122	Bill Dickey	5.00	2.00
❑ 123	Early Wynn	5.00	2.00
❑ 124	Bobby Murcer	8.00	3.00
❑ 125	Bucky Dent	5.00	2.00
❑ 126	Dave Winfield	5.00	2.00
❑ 127	Don Larsen	5.00	2.00
❑ 128	Don Mattingly	10.00	4.00
❑ 129	Earle Combs	5.00	2.00
❑ 130	Ed Lopat	5.00	2.00
❑ 131	Elston Howard	5.00	2.00
❑ 132	Everett Scott	5.00	2.00
❑ 133	Goose Gossage	5.00	2.00
❑ 134	Graig Nettles	5.00	2.00
❑ 135	Joe DiMaggio	10.00	4.00
❑ 136	Lou Piniella	5.00	2.00
❑ 137	Bill Skowron	5.00	2.00
❑ 138	Phil Rizzuto	8.00	3:00
❑ 139	Red Ruffing	5.00	2.00
❑ 140	Reggie Jackson	8.00	3.00
❑ 141	Roger Maris	8.00	3.00
❑ 142	Ron Guidry	5.00	2.00
❑ 143	Tiny Bonham	5.00	2.00
❑ 144	Bruce Sutter	5.00	2.00
❑ 145	Tony Lazzeri	5.00	2.00
❑ 146	Waite Hoyt	5.00	2.00
❑ 147	Whitey Ford	8.00	3.00
❑ 148	Steve Sax	5.00	2.00
❑ 149	Yogi Berra	8.00	3.00
❑ 150	Enos Slaughter	5.00	2.00
❑ 151	Catfish Hunter	5.00	2.00
❑ 152	Dennis Eckersley	5.00	2.00
❑ 153	Jose Canseco	8.00	3.00
❑ 154	Al Rosen	5.00	2.00
❑ 155	Al Simmons	5.00	2.00
❑ 156	Chief Bender	5.00	2.00
❑ 157	Cy Williams	5.00	2.00
❑ 158	Mike Schmidt	10.00	4.00
❑ 159	Richie Ashburn	8.00	3.00
❑ 160	Robin Roberts	5.00	2.00
❑ 161	Steve Carlton	5.00	2.00
❑ 162	Judy Johnson	5.00	2.00
❑ 163	Al Oliver	5.00	2.00
❑ 164	Bill Mazeroski	8.00	3.00
❑ 165	Dave Parker	5.00	2.00
❑ 166	Max Carey	5.00	2.00
❑ 167	Pie Traynor	5.00	2.00
❑ 168	Ralph Kiner	5.00	2.00
❑ 169	Roberto Clemente	15.00	6.00
❑ 170	Willie Stargell	5.00	2.00
❑ 171	Gaylord Perry	5.00	2.00
❑ 172	Tony Gwynn	8.00	3.00
❑ 173	Nolan Ryan	10.00	4.00
❑ 174	Joe Carter	5.00	2.00
❑ 175	Frank Howard	5.00	2.00
❑ 176	George Kell	5.00	2.00
❑ 177	Heinie Manush	5.00	2.00
❑ 178	Sam Rice	5.00	2.00
❑ 179	Babe Ruth	15.00	6.00
❑ 180	Casey Stengel	8.00	3.00
❑ 181	Christy Mathewson	8.00	3.00
❑ 182	Cy Young	8.00	3.00
❑ 183	Dizzy Dean	8.00	3.00
❑ 184	Eddie Mathews	8.00	3.00
❑ 185	George Sisler	5.00	2.00
❑ 186	Honus Wagner	8.00	3.00
❑ 187	Jackie Robinson	8.00	3.00
❑ 188	Jimmie Foxx	8.00	3.00
❑ 189	Johnny Mize	5.00	2.00
❑ 190	Lefty Gomez	5.00	2.00
❑ 191	Lou Gehrig	10.00	4.00
❑ 192	Mel Ott	8.00	3.00
❑ 193	Mickey Cochrane	5.00	2.00
❑ 194	Rogers Hornsby	8.00	3.00
❑ 195	Roy Campanella	8.00	3.00
❑ 196	Satchel Paige	8.00	3.00
❑ 197	Thurman Munson	8.00	3.00
❑ 198	Ty Cobb	10.00	4.00
❑ 199	Walter Johnson	8.00	3.00
❑ 200	Lefty Grove	5.00	2.00
❑ NNO	Exquisite Redemption	200.00	125.00

2004 SP Prospects

❑	COMP.ROOKIES SET (198)	50.00	20.00
❑	COMMON CARD (1-90)	1.00	.40
❑	1-90 APPX. 2X TOUGHER THAN 91-290		
❑	COMMON CARD (91-190	1.00	.40
❑	91-190 ODDS TWO PER PACK		
❑	COMMON CARD (191-290)	1.00	.40
❑	191-290 APPX.TWO PER PACK		
❑	OVERALL AU ODDS 1:5		
❑	AU PRINT RUNS B/WN 400-600 PER		
❑	233/237/345/438-443/445 DO NOT EXIST		
❑ 1	Roger Clemens	5.00	2.00
❑ 2	Melvin Mora	1.00	.40
❑ 3	Dontrelle Willis	1.50	.60
❑ 4	Jose Vidro	1.00	.40
❑ 5	Oliver Perez	1.00	.40
❑ 6	Carlos Zambrano	1.00	.40
❑ 7	Chipper Jones	2.50	1.00
❑ 8	Greg Maddux	4.00	1.50
❑ 9	Curt Schilling	1.50	.60
❑ 10	Jose Reyes	1.00	.40
❑ 11	David Ortiz	2.50	1.00
❑ 12	Mike Piazza	4.00	1.50
❑ 13	Jason Schmidt	1.00	.40
❑ 14	Randy Johnson	2.50	1.00
❑ 15	Magglio Ordonez	1.00	.40
❑ 16	Mike Mussina	1.50	.60
❑ 17	Jake Peavy	1.00	.40
❑ 18	Jim Edmonds	1.00	.40
❑ 19	Ken Griffey Jr.	4.00	1.50
❑ 20	Jason Giambi	1.00	.40
❑ 21	Mike Sweeney	1.00	.40
❑ 22	Carlos Lee	1.00	.40
❑ 23	Craig Wilson	1.00	.40
❑ 24	Pedro Martinez	1.50	.60
❑ 25	Bobby Abreu	1.00	.40
❑ 26	Mike Lowell	1.00	.40
❑ 27	Miguel Cabrera	1.50	.60
❑ 28	Hank Blalock	1.00	.40
❑ 29	Frank Thomas	2.50	1.00
❑ 30	Manny Ramirez	1.50	.60
❑ 31	Mark Mulder	1.00	.40
❑ 32	Scott Podsednik	1.00	.40
❑ 33	Albert Pujols	5.00	2.00
❑ 34	Preston Wilson	1.00	.40
❑ 35	Todd Helton	1.50	.60
❑ 36	Victor Martinez	1.00	.40
❑ 37	Kerry Wood	1.00	.40
❑ 38	Carlos Beltran	1.00	.40
❑ 39	Vernon Wells	1.00	.40
❑ 40	Sammy Sosa	2.50	1.00
❑ 41	Pat Burrell	1.00	.40
❑ 42	Tim Hudson	1.00	.40
❑ 43	Eric Gagne	1.00	.40
❑ 44	Jim Thome	1.50	.60
❑ 45	Vladimir Guerrero	2.50	1.00
❑ 46	Travis Hafner	1.00	.40
❑ 47	Rickie Weeks	1.00	.40
❑ 48	Miguel Tejada	1.00	.40
❑ 49	Ivan Rodriguez	1.50	.60
❑ 50	J.D. Drew	1.00	.40
❑ 51	Ben Sheets	1.00	.40
❑ 52	Garret Anderson	1.00	.40
❑ 53	Aubrey Huff	1.00	.40
❑ 54	Nomar Garciaparra	4.00	1.50
❑ 55	Luis Gonzalez	1.00	.40
❑ 56	Lance Berkman	1.00	.40

- ❑ 57 Ichiro Suzuki 5.00 2.00
- ❑ 58 Torii Hunter 1.00 .40
- ❑ 59 Adam Dunn 1.00 .40
- ❑ 60 Mark Teixeira 1.50 .60
- ❑ 61 Bret Boone 1.00 .40
- ❑ 62 Roy Oswalt 1.00 .40
- ❑ 63 Joe Mauer 1.25 .50
- ❑ 64 Scott Rolen 1.50 .60
- ❑ 65 Hideki Matsui 4.00 1.50
- ❑ 66 Richie Sexson 1.00 .40
- ❑ 67 Jeff Kent 1.00 .40
- ❑ 68 Barry Zito 1.00 .40
- ❑ 69 C.C. Sabathia 1.00 .40
- ❑ 70 Carlos Delgado 1.00 .40
- ❑ 71 Gary Sheffield 1.00 .40
- ❑ 72 Shawn Green 1.00 .40
- ❑ 73 Jason Bay 1.00 .40
- ❑ 74 Andruw Jones 1.50 .60
- ❑ 75 Jeff Bagwell 1.50 .60
- ❑ 76 Rafael Palmeiro 1.50 .60
- ❑ 77 Alex Rodriguez 4.00 1.50
- ❑ 78 Adrian Beltre 1.00 .40
- ❑ 79 Troy Glaus 1.00 .40
- ❑ 80 Tom Glavine 1.50 .60
- ❑ 81 Paul Konerko 1.00 .40
- ❑ 82 Alfonso Soriano 1.00 .40
- ❑ 83 Roy Halladay 1.00 .40
- ❑ 84 Derek Jeter 5.00 2.00
- ❑ 85 Josh Beckett 1.00 .40
- ❑ 86 Delmon Young 1.50 .60
- ❑ 87 Brian Giles 1.00 .40
- ❑ 88 Eric Chavez 1.00 .40
- ❑ 89 Lyle Overbay 1.00 .40
- ❑ 90 Mark Prior 1.50 .60
- ❑ 91 Shawn Camp RC 1.00 .40
- ❑ 92 Travis Smith 1.00 .40
- ❑ 93 Juan Padilla RC 1.00 .40
- ❑ 94 Brad Halsey RC 1.50 .60
- ❑ 95 Scott Kazmir RC 6.00 2.50
- ❑ 96 Sam Narron RC 1.00 .40
- ❑ 97 Frank Francisco RC 1.00 .40
- ❑ 98 Mike Johnston RC 1.00 .40
- ❑ 99 Sam McConnell RC 1.00 .40
- ❑ 100 Josh Labandeira RC 1.00 .40
- ❑ 101 Kazuhito Tadano RC 1.50 .60
- ❑ 102 Hector Gimenez RC 1.00 .40
- ❑ 103 David Aardsma RC 1.50 .60
- ❑ 104 Charles Thomas RC 1.00 .40
- ❑ 105 Ian Snell RC 2.00 .75
- ❑ 106 Jeff Keppinger RC 1.00 .40
- ❑ 107 Michael Vento RC 1.50 .60
- ❑ 108 Jerry Gil RC 1.00 .40
- ❑ 109 Marty McLeary RC 1.00 .40
- ❑ 110 Donnie Kelly RC 1.00 .40
- ❑ 111 Roman Colon RC 1.00 .40
- ❑ 112 Travis Blackley RC 1.00 .40
- ❑ 113 Edwardo Sierra RC 1.50 .60
- ❑ 114 Chris Shelton RC 2.00 .75
- ❑ 115 Bartolome Fortunato RC 1.00 .40
- ❑ 116 Brandon Medders RC 1.00 .40
- ❑ 117 Merkin Valdez RC 1.50 .60
- ❑ 118 Carlos Vasquez RC 1.50 .60
- ❑ 119 Shingo Takatsu RC 1.50 .60
- ❑ 120 Aarom Baldiris RC 1.50 .60
- ❑ 121 Chris Aguila RC 1.00 .40
- ❑ 122 Jimmy Serrano RC 1.00 .40
- ❑ 123 Mike Gosling RC 1.00 .40
- ❑ 124 Brian Dallimore RC 1.00 .40
- ❑ 125 Ronald Belisario RC 1.00 .40
- ❑ 126 George Sherrill RC 1.00 .40
- ❑ 127 Fernando Nieve RC 1.50 .60
- ❑ 128 Abe Alvarez RC 1.50 .60
- ❑ 129 Jeff Bennett RC 1.00 .40
- ❑ 130 Ryan Meaux RC 1.00 .40
- ❑ 131 Edwin Moreno RC 1.50 .60
- ❑ 132 Jesse Crain RC 1.50 .60
- ❑ 133 Scott Dohmann RC 1.00 .40
- ❑ 134 Ronny Cedeno RC 2.00 .75
- ❑ 135 Orlando Rodriguez RC 1.00 .40
- ❑ 136 Michael Wuertz RC 1.50 .60
- ❑ 137 Justin Hampson RC 1.00 .40
- ❑ 138 Matt Treanor RC 1.00 .40
- ❑ 139 Andy Green RC 1.00 .40
- ❑ 140 Yadier Molina RC 2.50 1.00
- ❑ 141 Joe Nelson RC 1.00 .40
- ❑ 142 Justin Lehr RC 1.00 .40
- ❑ 143 Ryan Wing RC 1.00 .40
- ❑ 144 Kevin Cave RC 1.00 .40
- ❑ 145 Evan Rust RC 1.00 .40
- ❑ 146 Mike Rouse RC 1.00 .40
- ❑ 147 Lance Cormier RC 1.00 .40
- ❑ 148 Eduardo Villacis RC 1.00 .40
- ❑ 149 Justin Knoedler RC 1.00 .40
- ❑ 150 Freddy Guzman RC 1.00 .40
- ❑ 151 Casey Daigle RC 1.00 .40
- ❑ 152 Joey Gathright RC 2.00 .75
- ❑ 153 Tim Bittner RC 1.00 .40
- ❑ 154 Scott Atchison RC 1.00 .40
- ❑ 155 Ivan Ochoa RC 1.00 .40
- ❑ 156 Lincoln Holdzkom RC 1.00 .40
- ❑ 157 Onil Joseph RC 1.00 .40
- ❑ 158 Jason Bartlett RC 1.50 .60
- ❑ 159 Jon Knott RC 1.00 .40
- ❑ 160 Jake Woods RC 1.00 .40
- ❑ 161 Jerome Gamble RC 1.00 .40
- ❑ 162 Sean Henn RC 1.00 .40
- ❑ 163 Kazuo Matsui RC 1.50 .60
- ❑ 164 Roberto Novoa RC 1.50 .60
- ❑ 165 Eddy Rodriguez RC 1.50 .60
- ❑ 166 Ramon Ramirez RC 1.00 .40
- ❑ 167 Enemencio Pacheco RC 1.00 .40
- ❑ 168 Chad Bentz RC 1.00 .40
- ❑ 169 Chris Oxspring RC 1.00 .40
- ❑ 170 Justin Leone RC 1.50 .60
- ❑ 171 Joe Horgan RC 1.00 .40
- ❑ 172 Jose Capellan RC 1.50 .60
- ❑ 173 Greg Dobbs RC 1.00 .40
- ❑ 174 Jason Frasor RC 1.00 .40
- ❑ 175 Shawn Hill RC 1.00 .40
- ❑ 176 Carlos Hines RC 1.00 .40
- ❑ 177 John Gall RC 1.50 .60
- ❑ 178 Steve Andrade RC 1.00 .40
- ❑ 179 Scott Proctor RC 1.50 .60
- ❑ 180 Rusty Tucker RC 1.50 .60
- ❑ 181 Dave Crouthers RC 1.00 .40
- ❑ 182 Franklyn Gracesqui RC 1.00 .40
- ❑ 183 Justin Germano RC 1.00 .40
- ❑ 184 Alfredo Simon RC 1.00 .40
- ❑ 185 Jorge Sequea RC 1.00 .40
- ❑ 186 Nick Regilio RC 1.00 .40
- ❑ 187 Justin Huisman RC 1.00 .40
- ❑ 188 Akinori Otsuka RC 1.00 .40
- ❑ 189 Luis Gonzalez RC 1.00 .40
- ❑ 190 Renyel Pinto RC 1.50 .60
- ❑ 191 Joshua Leblanc RC 1.50 .60
- ❑ 192 Devin Ivany RC 2.00 .75
- ❑ 193 Chad Blackwell RC 1.50 .60
- ❑ 194 Brandon Burgess RC 1.50 .60
- ❑ 195 Cory Patton RC 1.50 .60
- ❑ 196 Daniel Batz RC 1.50 .60
- ❑ 197 Adam Russell RC 1.50 .60
- ❑ 198 Jarrett Hoffpauir RC 2.00 .75
- ❑ 199 Patrick Bryant RC 1.50 .60
- ❑ 200 Sean Gamble RC 2.00 .75
- ❑ 201 Jermaine Brock RC 2.00 .75
- ❑ 202 Ben Zobrist RC 2.00 .75
- ❑ 203 Clay Meredith RC 2.00 .75
- ❑ 204 Derek Tharpe RC 1.50 .60
- ❑ 205 Bradley McCann RC 2.50 1.00
- ❑ 206 Justin Hedrick RC 1.50 .60
- ❑ 207 Clint Sammons RC 2.00 .75
- ❑ 208 Richard Steik RC 1.50 .60
- ❑ 209 Fernando Perez RC 2.00 .75
- ❑ 210 Mark Jecmen RC 1.50 .60
- ❑ 211 Benjamin Harrison RC 1.50 .60
- ❑ 212 Jason Quarles RC 1.50 .60
- ❑ 213 William Layman RC 1.50 .60
- ❑ 214 Koley Kolberg RC 1.50 .60
- ❑ 215 Randy Dicken RC 1.00 .40
- ❑ 216 Barry Richmond RC 1.50 .60
- ❑ 217 Timothy Murphey RC 1.50 .60
- ❑ 218 John Hardy RC 1.50 .60
- ❑ 219 Sebastien Boucher RC 2.00 .75
- ❑ 220 Andrew Alvarado RC 1.50 .60
- ❑ 221 Patrick Perry RC 2.00 .75
- ❑ 222 Jarod McAuliff RC 1.50 .60
- ❑ 223 Jared Gaston RC 1.50 .60
- ❑ 224 William Thompson RC 1.50 .60
- ❑ 225 Lucas French RC 1.50 .60
- ❑ 226 Brandon Parillo RC 2.00 .75
- ❑ 227 Gregory Goetz RC 1.50 .60
- ❑ 228 David Haehnel RC 2.00 .75
- ❑ 229 James Miller RC 1.50 .60
- ❑ 230 Mark Roberts RC 1.50 .60
- ❑ 231 Eric Ridener RC 1.50 .60
- ❑ 232 Freddy Sandoval RC 1.50 .60
- ❑ 234 Carlos Medero-Stullz RC 1.50 .60
- ❑ 235 Matthew Shepherd RC 1.50 .60
- ❑ 236 Thomas Hubbard RC 1.50 .60
- ❑ 238 Kyle Bono RC 2.00 .75
- ❑ 239 Craig Moldrem RC 1.00 .40
- ❑ 240 Brandon Timm RC 2.00 .75
- ❑ 241 Mike Carp RC 2.50 1.00
- ❑ 242 Joseph Muro RC 1.50 .60
- ❑ 243 Derek Decarlo RC 1.50 .60
- ❑ 244 Christopher Niesel RC 2.00 .75
- ❑ 245 Trevor Lawhorn RC 2.00 .75
- ❑ 246 Joey Howell RC 2.00 .75
- ❑ 247 Dustin Hahn RC 1.50 .60
- ❑ 248 James Fasano RC 2.00 .75
- ❑ 249 Hainley Statia RC 2.00 .75
- ❑ 250 Brandon Conway RC 1.50 .60
- ❑ 251 Christopher McConnell RC 2.50 1.00
- ❑ 252 Austin Shappi RC 2.00 .75
- ❑ 253 Joseph Metropoulos RC 2.00 .75
- ❑ 254 David Nicholson RC 2.00 .75
- ❑ 255 Ryan McCarthy RC 2.00 .75
- ❑ 256 Michael Parisi RC 1.50 .60
- ❑ 257 Andrew Macfarlane RC 1.50 .60
- ❑ 258 Jeffrey Dominguez RC 2.00 .75
- ❑ 259 Troy Patton RC 5.00 2.00
- ❑ 260 Ryan Norwood RC 2.50 1.00
- ❑ 261 Chad Boyd RC 1.50 .60
- ❑ 262 Grant Plumley RC 1.50 .60
- ❑ 263 Jeffrey Katz RC 2.00 .75
- ❑ 264 Cory Middleton RC 1.50 .60
- ❑ 265 Andrew Moffitt RC 1.00 .40
- ❑ 266 Jarrett Grube RC 1.50 .60
- ❑ 267 Derek Hankins RC 1.50 .60
- ❑ 268 Douglas Reinhardt RC 1.50 .60
- ❑ 269 Duron Legrande RC 1.50 .60
- ❑ 270 Steven Jackson RC 1.50 .60
- ❑ 271 Brian Hall RC 2.00 .75
- ❑ 272 Cory Wade RC 2.00 .75
- ❑ 273 John Grogan RC 1.50 .60
- ❑ 274 Robert Asanovich RC 2.00 .75
- ❑ 275 Kevin Hart RC 2.00 .75
- ❑ 276 Matthew Guillory RC 1.50 .60
- ❑ 277 Clifton Remole RC 1.50 .60
- ❑ 278 David Trahan RC 1.50 .60
- ❑ 279 Kristian Bell RC 1.00 .40
- ❑ 280 Christopher Westervelt RC 1.50 .60
- ❑ 281 Garry Bakker RC 1.50 .60
- ❑ 282 Jonathan Ash RC 2.00 .75
- ❑ 283 Ryan Phillips RC 1.50 .60
- ❑ 284 Wesley Letson RC 1.50 .60
- ❑ 285 Jeffrey Landing RC 1.50 .60
- ❑ 286 Mark Worrell RC 1.50 .60
- ❑ 287 Sean Gallagher RC 5.00 2.00
- ❑ 288 Nicholas Blasi RC 1.50 .60
- ❑ 289 Kevin Frandsen RC 3.00 1.25
- ❑ 290 Richard Mercado RC 1.50 .60
- ❑ 291 Matt Bush AU 400/RC 30.00 15.00
- ❑ 292 Mark Rogers AU 400/RC 25.00 10.00
- ❑ 293 Homer Bailey AU 400/RC 80.00 50.00
- ❑ 294 Chris Nelson AU 400/RC 50.00 30.00
- ❑ 295 T.Diamond AU 400/RC 40.00 20.00
- ❑ 296 Neil Walker AU 400/RC 40.00 20.00
- ❑ 297 Bill Bray AU 400/RC 10.00 4.00
- ❑ 298 David Purcey AU 400/RC 15.00 6.00
- ❑ 299 Scott Elbert AU 400/RC 50.00 20.00
- ❑ 300 Josh Fields AU 400/RC 60.00 35.00
- ❑ 301 Chris Lambert AU 400/RC 25.00 10.00
- ❑ 302 Trevor Plouffe AU 400/RC 30.00 15.00
- ❑ 303 Greg Golson AU 400/RC 25.00 10.00
- ❑ 304 Philip Hughes AU 400/RC 175.00 100.00
- ❑ 305 Kyle Waldrop AU 400/RC 25.00 10.00
- ❑ 306 Richie Robnett AU 350/RC 30.00 15.00
- ❑ 307 T.Tankersley AU 400/RC 15.00 6.00
- ❑ 308 Blake Dewitt AU 400/RC 40.00 20.00
- ❑ 309 Eric Hurley AU 400/RC 30.00 15.00
- ❑ 310 J.Howell AU 400/RC EX * 15.00 6.00
- ❑ 311 Zachary Jackson AU 400/RC 15.00 6.00
- ❑ 312 Justin Orenduff AU 400/RC 15.00 6.00
- ❑ 313 Tyler Lumsden AU 400/RC 15.00 6.00
- ❑ 314 Matthew Fox AU 600/RC 8.00 3.00
- ❑ 315 Danny Putnam AU 450/RC 15.00 6.00
- ❑ 316 Jon Poterson AU 400/RC 15.00 6.00

❑	317 Gio Gonzalez AU 400/RC	30.00	15.00
❑	318 Jay Rainville AU 475/RC	25.00	10.00
❑	319 Huston Street AU 400/RC	40.00	20.00
❑	320 Jeff Marquez AU 400/RC	15.00	6.00
❑	321 Eric Beattie AU 500/RC	15.00	6.00
❑	322 Reid Brignac AU 325/RC	125.00	75.00
❑	323 Y.Gallardo AU 400/RC	60.00	35.00
❑	324 Justin Hoyman AU 400/RC	15.00	6.00
❑	325 B.J. Szymanski AU 400/RC	20.00	8.00
❑	326 Seth Smith AU 600/RC	25.00	10.00
❑	327 Karl Herren AU 600/RC	15.00	6.00
❑	328 Brian Bixler AU 600/RC	8.00	3.00
❑	329 Wesley Whisler AU 600/RC	8.00	3.00
❑	330 E.San Pedro AU 400/RC	15.00	6.00
❑	331 Billy Buckner AU 400/RC	15.00	6.00
❑	332 Jon Zeringue AU 400/RC	25.00	10.00
❑	333 Curtis Thigpen AU 400/RC	15.00	6.00
❑	334 Blake Johnson AU 400/RC	15.00	6.00
❑	335 Donald Lucy AU 400/RC	10.00	4.00
❑	336 Michael Ferris AU 600/RC	12.00	5.00
❑	337 A.Swarzak AU 600/RC	25.00	10.00
❑	338 Jason Jaramillo AU 400/RC	20.00	8.00
❑	339 Hunter Pence AU 600/RC	90.00	60.00
❑	340 Dustin Pedroia AU 400/RC	50.00	25.00
❑	341 Grant Johnson AU 400/RC	15.00	6.00
❑	342 Kurt Suzuki AU 400/RC	30.00	15.00
❑	343 Jason Vargas AU 600/RC	25.00	10.00
❑	344 Raymond Liotta AU 400/RC	30.00	15.00
❑	346 Eric Campbell AU 400/RC	70.00	40.00
❑	347 Jeffrey Frazier AU 400/RC	15.00	6.00
❑	348 G.Hernandez AU 400/RC	25.00	10.00
❑	349 Wade Davis AU 600/RC	30.00	15.00
❑	350 J.Wahpepah AU 400/RC	10.00	4.00
❑	351 Scott Lewis AU 400/RC	15.00	6.00
❑	352 Jeff Fiorentino AU 400/RC	20.00	8.00
❑	353 S.Register AU 600/RC	8.00	3.00
❑	354 Michael Schlact AU 400/RC	10.00	4.00
❑	355 Eddie Prasch AU 400/RC	15.00	6.00
❑	356 Adam Lind AU 400/RC	70.00	40.00
❑	357 Ian Desmond AU 400/RC	25.00	10.00
❑	358 Josh Johnson AU 575/RC	12.00	5.00
❑	359 Garrett Mock AU 600/RC	8.00	3.00
❑	360 Danny Hill AU 600/RC	8.00	3.00
❑	361 Cory Dunlap AU 600/RC	25.00	10.00
❑	362 Grant Hansen AU 600/RC	8.00	3.00
❑	363 Eric Haberer AU 400/RC	10.00	4.00
❑	364 E.Morlan AU 400/RC	15.00	6.00
❑	365 James Happ AU 600/RC	15.00	6.00
❑	366 M.Tuiasosopo AU 600/RC	50.00	20.00
❑	367 Jordan Parraz AU 400/RC	15.00	6.00
❑	368 Andrew Dobies AU 400/RC	15.00	6.00
❑	369 Mark Reed AU 400/RC	25.00	10.00
❑	370 Jason Windsor AU 400/RC	20.00	8.00
❑	371 Gregory Burns AU 600/RC	15.00	6.00
❑	372 Christian Garcia AU 600/RC	15.00	6.00
❑	373 John Bowker AU 575/RC	25.00	10.00
❑	374 J.C. Holt AU 550/RC	12.00	5.00
❑	375 Daryl Jones AU 400/RC	25.00	10.00
❑	376 Collin Mahoney AU 400/RC	15.00	6.00
❑	377 A.Hathaway AU 400/RC	15.00	6.00
❑	378 Matthew Spring AU 400/RC	10.00	4.00
❑	379 Joshua Baker AU 400/RC	10.00	4.00
❑	380 Charles Lofgren AU 400/RC	30.00	15.00
❑	381 Raf Gonzalez AU 400/RC	10.00	4.00
❑	382 Brad Bergesen AU 575/RC	8.00	3.00
❑	383 Brandon Boggs AU 400/RC	15.00	6.00
❑	384 J.Bauserman AU 400/RC	10.00	4.00
❑	385 Collin Balester AU 500/RC	25.00	10.00
❑	386 James Moore AU 400/RC	10.00	4.00
❑	387 Robert Janssen AU 400/RC	25.00	10.00
❑	388 Luis Guerra AU 400/RC	15.00	6.00
❑	389 Lucas Harrell AU 550/RC	15.00	6.00
❑	390 Donnie Smith AU 500/RC	12.00	5.00
❑	391 Mark Robinson AU 525/RC	12.00	5.00
❑	392 Louis Marson AU 550/RC	15.00	6.00
❑	393 Rob Johnson AU 600/RC	12.00	5.00
❑	394 L.Santangelo AU 600/RC	12.00	5.00
❑	395 T.Hottovy AU 400/RC	15.00	6.00
❑	396 Ryan Webb AU 400/RC	15.00	6.00
❑	397 Jamar Walton AU 400/RC	15.00	6.00
❑	398 Jason Jones AU 400/RC	25.00	10.00
❑	399 Clay Timpner AU 600/RC	12.00	5.00
❑	400 James Parr AU 400/RC	15.00	6.00
❑	401 Sean Kazmar AU 400/RC	10.00	4.00
❑	402 Andrew Kown AU 400/RC	15.00	6.00
❑	403 Jacob McGee AU 600/RC	25.00	10.00
❑	404 Michael Butia AU 600/RC	8.00	3.00
❑	405 Paul Janish AU 500/RC	15.00	6.00
❑	406 Matthew Macri AU 400/RC	25.00	10.00
❑	407 Mike Nickeas AU 500/RC	12.00	5.00
❑	408 Kyle Bloom AU 550/RC	10.00	4.00
❑	409 Luis Rivera AU 500/RC	12.00	5.00
❑	410 William Bunn AU 600/RC	25.00	10.00
❑	411 Enrique Barrera AU 400/RC	25.00	10.00
❑	412 R.Klosterman AU 400/RC	10.00	4.00
❑	413 John Raglani AU 515/RC	20.00	8.00
❑	414 Brandon Allen AU 500/RC	20.00	8.00
❑	415 A.Baldwin AU 600/RC	8.00	3.00
❑	416 Mark Lowe AU 400/RC	40.00	20.00
❑	417 Mitch Einertson AU 400/RC	15.00	6.00
❑	418 Ryan Schroyer AU 600/RC	12.00	5.00
❑	419 Bradley Davis AU 400/RC	10.00	4.00
❑	420 Jesse Hoover AU 500/RC	12.00	5.00
❑	421 G.Broshuis AU 400/RC	20.00	8.00
❑	422 Peter Pope AU 400/RC	20.00	8.00
❑	423 Brent Dlugach AU 400/RC	15.00	6.00
❑	424 Ryan Coultas AU 400/RC	15.00	6.00
❑	425 Ryan Royster AU 400/RC	20.00	8.00
❑	426 S.Chapman AU 400/RC	15.00	6.00
❑	427 B.Chamberlin AU 400/RC	15.00	6.00
❑	428 J.Koshansky AU 550/RC	60.00	35.00
❑	429 William Susdorf AU 400/RC	10.00	4.00
❑	430 A.J. Johnson AU 400/RC	20.00	8.00
❑	431 Jeremy Sowers AU 400/RC	50.00	30.00
❑	432 Justin Pekarek AU 400/RC	15.00	6.00
❑	433 Brett Smith AU 400/RC	15.00	6.00
❑	434 Matt Durkin AU 400/RC	15.00	6.00
❑	435 Daniel Barone AU 400/RC	10.00	4.00
❑	436 Scott Hyde AU 400/RC	15.00	6.00
❑	437 T.Everidge AU 400/RC	20.00	8.00
❑	444 Mark Trumbo AU 400/RC	30.00	15.00
❑	446 Eric Patterson AU 400/RC	25.00	10.00
❑	447 Michael Rozier AU 400/RC	15.00	6.00

1996 SPx

❑	COMPLETE SET (60)	50.00	20.00
❑	1 Greg Maddux	3.00	1.25
❑	2 Chipper Jones	2.00	.75
❑	3 Fred McGriff	1.25	.50
❑	4 Tom Glavine	1.25	.50
❑	5 Cal Ripken	6.00	2.50
❑	6 Roberto Alomar	1.25	.50
❑	7 Rafael Palmeiro	1.25	.50
❑	8 Jose Canseco	1.25	.50
❑	9 Roger Clemens	4.00	1.50
❑	10 Mo Vaughn	.75	.30
❑	11 Jim Edmonds	.75	.30
❑	12 Tim Salmon	1.25	.50
❑	13 Sammy Sosa	2.00	.75
❑	14 Ryne Sandberg	3.00	1.25
❑	15 Mark Grace	1.25	.50
❑	16 Frank Thomas	2.00	.75
❑	17 Barry Larkin	1.25	.50
❑	18 Kenny Lofton	.75	.30
❑	19 Albert Belle	.75	.30
❑	20 Eddie Murray	2.00	.75
❑	21 Manny Ramirez	1.25	.50
❑	22 Dante Bichette	.75	.30
❑	23 Larry Walker	.75	.30
❑	24 Vinny Castilla	.75	.30
❑	25 Andres Galarraga	.75	.30
❑	26 Cecil Fielder	.75	.30
❑	27 Gary Sheffield	.75	.30
❑	28 Craig Biggio	1.25	.50
❑	29 Jeff Bagwell	1.25	.50
❑	30 Derek Bell	.75	.30
❑	31 Johnny Damon	1.25	.50
❑	32 Eric Karros	.75	.30
❑	33 Mike Piazza	3.00	1.25
❑	34 Raul Mondesi	.75	.30
❑	35 Hideo Nomo	2.00	.75
❑	36 Kirby Puckett	2.00	.75
❑	37 Paul Molitor	.75	.30
❑	38 Marty Cordova	.75	.30
❑	39 Rondell White	.75	.30
❑	40 Jason Isringhausen	.75	.30
❑	41 Paul Wilson	.75	.30
❑	42 Rey Ordonez	.75	.30
❑	43 Derek Jeter	5.00	2.00
❑	44 Wade Boggs	1.25	.50
❑	45 Mark McGwire	5.00	2.00
❑	46 Jason Kendall	.75	.30
❑	47 Ron Gant	.75	.30
❑	48 Ozzie Smith	3.00	1.25
❑	49 Tony Gwynn	2.50	1.00
❑	50 Ken Caminiti	.75	.30
❑	51 Barry Bonds	5.00	2.00
❑	52 Matt Williams	.75	.30
❑	53 Osvaldo Fernandez	.75	.30
❑	54 Jay Buhner	.75	.30
❑	55 Ken Griffey Jr.	3.00	1.25
❑	56 Randy Johnson	2.00	.75
❑	57 Alex Rodriguez	4.00	1.50
❑	58 Juan Gonzalez	.75	.30
❑	59 Joe Carter	.75	.30
❑	60 Carlos Delgado	.75	.30
❑	KG1 Ken Griffey Jr. Comm.	5.00	2.00
❑	MP1 Mike Piazza Trib.	5.00	2.00
❑	KGA1 Ken Griffey Jr. Auto.	150.00	75.00
❑	MPA1 Mike Piazza Auto.	200.00	125.00

1998 SPx Finite

❑	COMP.YM SER.1 (30)	40.00	15.00
❑	COMMON YM (1-30)	1.50	.60
❑	COMP.PE SER.1 (20)	120.00	50.00
❑	COMMON PE (31-50)	2.50	1.00
❑	COMP.BASIC SER.1 (90)	80.00	30.00
❑	COMMON CARD (51-140)	1.00	.40
❑	COMP.SF SER.1 (30)	100.00	40.00
❑	COMMON SF (141-170)	1.25	.50
❑	COMP.HG SER.1 (10)	150.00	60.00
❑	COMMON HG (171-180)	4.00	1.50
❑	COMP.YM SER.2 (30)	60.00	25.00
❑	COMMON YM (181-210)	1.50	.60
❑	COMP.PP SER.2 (30)	80.00	30.00
❑	COMMON PP (211-240)	1.25	.50
❑	COMP.BASIC SER.2 (90)	50.00	20.00
❑	COMMON CARD (241-330)	1.00	.40
❑	COMP.TW SER.2 (20)	30.00	12.50
❑	COMMON TW (331-350)	2.50	1.00
❑	COMP.CG SER.2 (10)	150.00	60.00
❑	COMMON CG (351-360)	4.00	1.50
❑	1 Nomar Garciaparra YM	6.00	2.50
❑	2 Miguel Tejada YM	4.00	1.50
❑	3 Mike Cameron YM	1.50	.60
❑	4 Ken Cloude YM	1.50	.60
❑	5 Jaret Wright YM	1.50	.60
❑	6 Mark Kotsay YM	1.50	.60
❑	7 Craig Counsell YM	1.50	.60
❑	8 Jose Guillen YM	1.50	.60
❑	9 Neifi Perez YM	1.50	.60
❑	10 Jose Cruz Jr. YM	1.50	.60

❑	11	Brett Tomko YM	1.50	.60
❑	12	Matt Morris YM	1.50	.60
❑	13	Justin Thompson YM	1.50	.60
❑	14	Jeremi Gonzalez YM	1.50	.60
❑	15	Scott Rolen YM	2.50	1.00
❑	16	Vladimir Guerrero YM	4.00	1.50
❑	17	Brad Fullmer YM	1.50	.60
❑	18	Brian Giles YM	1.50	.60
❑	19	Todd Dunwoody YM	1.50	.60
❑	20	Ben Grieve YM	1.50	.60
❑	21	Juan Encarnacion YM	1.50	.60
❑	22	Aaron Boone YM	1.50	.60
❑	23	Richie Sexson YM	1.50	.60
❑	24	Richard Hidalgo YM	1.50	.60
❑	25	Andruw Jones YM	2.50	1.00
❑	26	Todd Helton YM	2.50	1.00
❑	27	Paul Konerko YM	1.50	.60
❑	28	Dante Powell YM	1.50	.60
❑	29	Eli Marrero YM	1.50	.60
❑	30	Derek Jeter YM	10.00	4.00
❑	31	Mike Piazza PE	10.00	4.00
❑	32	Tony Clark PE	2.50	1.00
❑	33	Larry Walker PE	2.50	1.00
❑	34	Jim Thome PE	4.00	1.50
❑	35	Juan Gonzalez PE	5.00	2.00
❑	36	Jeff Bagwell PE	4.00	1.50
❑	37	Jay Buhner PE	2.50	1.00
❑	38	Tim Salmon PE	4.00	1.50
❑	39	Albert Belle PE	2.50	1.00
❑	40	Mark McGwire PE	15.00	6.00
❑	41	Sammy Sosa PE	6.00	2.50
❑	42	Mo Vaughn PE	2.50	1.00
❑	43	Manny Ramirez PE	4.00	1.50
❑	44	Tino Martinez PE	4.00	1.50
❑	45	Frank Thomas PE	6.00	2.50
❑	46	Nomar Garciaparra PE	10.00	4.00
❑	47	Alex Rodriguez PE	10.00	4.00
❑	48	Chipper Jones PE	6.00	2.50
❑	49	Barry Bonds PE	15.00	6.00
❑	50	Ken Griffey Jr. PE	10.00	4.00
❑	51	Jason Dickson	1.00	.40
❑	52	Jim Edmonds	1.00	.40
❑	53	Darin Erstad	1.00	.40
❑	54	Tim Salmon	1.50	.60
❑	55	Chipper Jones	2.50	1.00
❑	56	Ryan Klesko	1.00	.40
❑	57	Tom Glavine	1.50	.60
❑	58	Denny Neagle	1.00	.40
❑	59	John Smoltz	1.50	.60
❑	60	Javy Lopez	1.00	.40
❑	61	Roberto Alomar	1.50	.60
❑	62	Rafael Palmeiro	1.50	.60
❑	63	Mike Mussina	1.50	.60
❑	64	Cal Ripken	8.00	3.00
❑	65	Mo Vaughn	1.00	.40
❑	66	Tim Naehring	1.00	.40
❑	67	John Valentin	1.00	.40
❑	68	Mark Grace	1.50	.60
❑	69	Kevin Orie	1.00	.40
❑	70	Sammy Sosa	2.50	1.00
❑	71	Albert Belle	1.00	.40
❑	72	Frank Thomas	2.50	1.00
❑	73	Robin Ventura	1.00	.40
❑	74	David Justice	1.00	.40
❑	75	Kenny Lofton	1.00	.40
❑	76	Omar Vizquel	1.50	.60
❑	77	Manny Ramirez	1.50	.60
❑	78	Jim Thome	1.50	.60
❑	79	Dante Bichette	1.00	.40
❑	80	Larry Walker	1.00	.40
❑	81	Vinny Castilla	1.00	.40
❑	82	Ellis Burks	1.00	.40
❑	83	Bobby Higginson	1.00	.40
❑	84	Brian Hunter	1.00	.40
❑	85	Tony Clark	1.00	.40
❑	86	Mike Hampton	1.00	.40
❑	87	Jeff Bagwell	1.50	.60
❑	88	Craig Biggio	1.50	.60
❑	89	Derek Bell	1.00	.40
❑	90	Mike Piazza	4.00	1.50
❑	91	Ramon Martinez	1.00	.40
❑	92	Raul Mondesi	1.00	.40
❑	93	Hideo Nomo	2.50	1.00
❑	94	Eric Karros	1.00	.40
❑	95	Paul Molitor	1.00	.40
❑	96	Marty Cordova	1.00	.40
❑	97	Brad Radke	1.00	.40
❑	98	Mark Grudzielanek	1.00	.40
❑	99	Carlos Perez	1.00	.40
❑	100	Rondell White	1.00	.40
❑	101	Todd Hundley	1.00	.40
❑	102	Edgardo Alfonzo	1.00	.40
❑	103	John Franco	1.00	.40
❑	104	John Olerud	1.00	.40
❑	105	Tino Martinez	1.50	.60
❑	106	David Cone	1.00	.40
❑	107	Paul O'Neill	1.50	.60
❑	108	Andy Pettitte	1.50	.60
❑	109	Bernie Williams	1.50	.60
❑	110	Rickey Henderson	4.00	1.50
❑	111	Jason Giambi	1.00	.40
❑	112	Matt Stairs	1.00	.40
❑	113	Gregg Jefferies	1.00	.40
❑	114	Rico Brogna	1.00	.40
❑	115	Curt Schilling	1.00	.40
❑	116	Jason Schmidt	1.00	.40
❑	117	Jose Guillen	1.00	.40
❑	118	Kevin Young	1.00	.40
❑	119	Ray Lankford	1.00	.40
❑	120	Mark McGwire	6.00	2.50
❑	121	Delino DeShields	1.00	.40
❑	122	Ken Caminiti	1.00	.40
❑	123	Tony Gwynn	3.00	1.25
❑	124	Trevor Hoffman	1.00	.40
❑	125	Barry Bonds	6.00	2.50
❑	126	Jeff Kent	1.00	.40
❑	127	Shawn Estes	1.00	.40
❑	128	J.T. Snow	1.00	.40
❑	129	Jay Buhner	1.00	.40
❑	130	Ken Griffey Jr.	4.00	1.50
❑	131	Dan Wilson	1.00	.40
❑	132	Edgar Martinez	1.50	.60
❑	133	Alex Rodriguez	4.00	1.50
❑	134	Rusty Greer	1.00	.40
❑	135	Juan Gonzalez	1.00	.40
❑	136	Fernando Tatis	1.00	.40
❑	137	Ivan Rodriguez	1.50	.60
❑	138	Carlos Delgado	1.00	.40
❑	139	Pat Hentgen	1.00	.40
❑	140	Roger Clemens	5.00	2.00
❑	141	Chipper Jones SF	3.00	1.25
❑	142	Greg Maddux SF	5.00	2.00
❑	143	Rafael Palmeiro SF	2.00	.75
❑	144	Mike Mussina SF	2.00	.75
❑	145	Cal Ripken SF	10.00	4.00
❑	146	Nomar Garciaparra SF	5.00	2.00
❑	147	Mo Vaughn SF	1.25	.50
❑	148	Sammy Sosa SF	3.00	1.25
❑	149	Albert Belle SF	1.25	.50
❑	150	Frank Thomas SF	3.00	1.25
❑	151	Jim Thome SF	2.00	.75
❑	152	Kenny Lofton SF	1.25	.50
❑	153	Manny Ramirez SF	2.00	.75
❑	154	Larry Walker SF	1.25	.50
❑	155	Jeff Bagwell SF	2.00	.75
❑	156	Craig Biggio SF	2.00	.75
❑	157	Mike Piazza SF	5.00	2.00
❑	158	Paul Molitor SF	1.25	.50
❑	159	Derek Jeter SF	8.00	3.00
❑	160	Tino Martinez SF	2.00	.75
❑	161	Curt Schilling SF	1.25	.50
❑	162	Mark McGwire SF	8.00	3.00
❑	163	Tony Gwynn SF	4.00	1.50
❑	164	Barry Bonds SF	8.00	3.00
❑	165	Ken Griffey Jr. SF	5.00	2.00
❑	166	Randy Johnson SF	3.00	1.25
❑	167	Alex Rodriguez SF	5.00	2.00
❑	168	Juan Gonzalez SF	1.25	.50
❑	169	Ivan Rodriguez SF	2.00	.75
❑	170	Roger Clemens SF	6.00	2.50
❑	171	Greg Maddux HG	15.00	6.00
❑	172	Cal Ripken HG	30.00	12.50
❑	173	Frank Thomas HG	10.00	4.00
❑	174	Jeff Bagwell HG	6.00	2.50
❑	175	Mike Piazza HG	15.00	6.00
❑	176	Mark McGwire HG	25.00	10.00
❑	177	Barry Bonds HG	25.00	10.00
❑	178	Ken Griffey Jr. HG	15.00	6.00
❑	179	Alex Rodriguez HG	15.00	6.00
❑	180	Roger Clemens HG	20.00	8.00
❑	181	Mike Caruso YM	1.50	.60
❑	182	David Ortiz YM	5.00	2.00
❑	183	Gabe Alvarez YM	1.50	.60
❑	184	Gary Matthews Jr. YM RC	2.50	1.00
❑	185	Kerry Wood YM	2.00	.75
❑	186	Carl Pavano YM	1.50	.60
❑	187	Alex Gonzalez YM	1.50	.60
❑	188	Masato Yoshii YM RC	1.50	.60
❑	189	Larry Sutton YM	1.50	.60
❑	190	Russell Branyan YM	1.50	.60
❑	191	Bruce Chen YM	1.50	.60
❑	192	Rolando Arrojo YM RC	1.50	.60
❑	193	Ryan Christenson YM RC	1.50	.60
❑	194	Cliff Politte YM	1.50	.60
❑	195	A.J. Hinch YM	1.50	.60
❑	196	Kevin Witt YM	1.50	.60
❑	197	Daryle Ward YM	1.50	.60
❑	198	Corey Koskie YM RC	2.50	1.00
❑	199	Mike Lowell YM RC	8.00	3.00
❑	200	Travis Lee YM	1.50	.60
❑	201	Kevin Millwood YM RC	5.00	2.00
❑	202	Robert Smith YM	1.50	.60
❑	203	Magglio Ordonez YM RC	12.00	5.00
❑	204	Eric Milton YM	1.50	.60
❑	205	Geoff Jenkins YM	1.50	.60
❑	206	Rich Butler YM RC	1.50	.60
❑	207	Mike Kinkade YM RC	1.50	.60
❑	208	Braden Looper YM	1.50	.60
❑	209	Matt Clement YM	1.50	.60
❑	210	Derrek Lee YM	2.50	1.00
❑	211	Randy Johnson PP	3.00	1.25
❑	212	John Smoltz PP	2.00	.75
❑	213	Roger Clemens PP	6.00	2.50
❑	214	Curt Schilling PP	1.25	.50
❑	215	Pedro Martinez PP	2.00	.75
❑	216	Vinny Castilla PP	1.25	.50
❑	217	Jose Cruz Jr. PP	1.25	.50
❑	218	Jim Thome PP	2.00	.75
❑	219	Alex Rodriguez PP	5.00	2.00
❑	220	Frank Thomas PP	3.00	1.25
❑	221	Tim Salmon PP	2.00	.75
❑	222	Larry Walker PP	1.25	.50
❑	223	Albert Belle PP	1.25	.50
❑	224	Manny Ramirez PP	2.00	.75
❑	225	Mark McGwire PP	8.00	3.00
❑	226	Mo Vaughn PP	1.25	.50
❑	227	Andres Galarraga PP	1.25	.50
❑	228	Scott Rolen PP	2.00	.75
❑	229	Travis Lee PP	1.25	.50
❑	230	Mike Piazza PP	5.00	2.00
❑	231	Nomar Garciaparra PP	5.00	2.00
❑	232	Andruw Jones PP	2.00	.75
❑	233	Barry Bonds PP	8.00	3.00
❑	234	Jeff Bagwell PP	2.00	.75
❑	235	Juan Gonzalez PP	1.25	.50
❑	236	Tino Martinez PP	2.00	.75
❑	237	Vladimir Guerrero PP	3.00	1.25
❑	238	Rafael Palmeiro PP	2.00	.75
❑	239	Russell Branyan PP	1.25	.50
❑	240	Ken Griffey Jr. PP	5.00	2.00
❑	241	Cecil Fielder	1.00	.40
❑	242	Chuck Finley	1.00	.40
❑	243	Jay Bell	1.00	.40
❑	244	Andy Benes	1.00	.40
❑	245	Matt Williams	1.00	.40
❑	246	Brian Anderson	1.00	.40
❑	247	Dave Dellucci RC	1.50	.60
❑	248	Andres Galarraga	1.00	.40
❑	249	Andruw Jones	1.50	.60
❑	250	Greg Maddux	4.00	1.50
❑	251	Brady Anderson	1.00	.40
❑	252	Joe Carter	1.00	.40
❑	253	Eric Davis	1.00	.40
❑	254	Pedro Martinez	1.50	.60
❑	255	Nomar Garciaparra	4.00	1.50
❑	256	Dennis Eckersley	1.00	.40
❑	257	Henry Rodriguez	1.00	.40
❑	258	Jeff Blauser	1.00	.40
❑	259	Jaime Navarro	1.00	.40
❑	260	Ray Durham	1.00	.40
❑	261	Chris Stynes	1.00	.40
❑	262	Willie Greene	1.00	.40
❑	263	Reggie Sanders	1.00	.40
❑	264	Bret Boone	1.00	.40
❑	265	Barry Larkin	1.50	.60
❑	266	Travis Fryman	1.00	.40
❑	267	Charles Nagy	1.00	.40
❑	268	Sandy Alomar Jr.	1.00	.40

❑ 269	Darryl Kile	1.00	.40
❑ 270	Mike Lansing	1.00	.40
❑ 271	Pedro Astacio	1.00	.40
❑ 272	Damion Easley	1.00	.40
❑ 273	Joe Randa	1.00	.40
❑ 274	Luis Gonzalez	1.00	.40
❑ 275	Mike Piazza	4.00	1.50
❑ 276	Todd Zeile	1.00	.40
❑ 277	Edgar Renteria	1.00	.40
❑ 278	Livan Hernandez	1.00	.40
❑ 279	Cliff Floyd	1.00	.40
❑ 280	Moises Alou	1.00	.40
❑ 281	Billy Wagner	1.00	.40
❑ 282	Jeff King	1.00	.40
❑ 283	Hal Morris	1.00	.40
❑ 284	Johnny Damon	1.50	.60
❑ 285	Dean Palmer	1.00	.40
❑ 286	Tim Belcher	1.00	.40
❑ 287	Eric Young	1.00	.40
❑ 288	Bobby Bonilla	1.00	.40
❑ 289	Gary Sheffield	1.00	.40
❑ 290	Chan Ho Park	1.00	.40
❑ 291	Charles Johnson	1.00	.40
❑ 292	Jeff Cirillo	1.00	.40
❑ 293	Jeromy Burnitz	1.00	.40
❑ 294	Jose Valentin	1.00	.40
❑ 295	Marquis Grissom	1.00	.40
❑ 296	Todd Walker	1.00	.40
❑ 297	Terry Steinbach	1.00	.40
❑ 298	Rick Aguilera	1.00	.40
❑ 299	Vladimir Guerrero	2.50	1.00
❑ 300	Rey Ordonez	1.00	.40
❑ 301	Butch Huskey	1.00	.40
❑ 302	Bernard Gilkey	1.00	.40
❑ 303	Mariano Rivera	2.50	1.00
❑ 304	Chuck Knoblauch	1.00	.40
❑ 305	Derek Jeter	6.00	2.50
❑ 306	Ricky Bottalico	1.00	.40
❑ 307	Bob Abreu	1.00	.40
❑ 308	Scott Rolen	1.50	.60
❑ 309	Al Martin	1.00	.40
❑ 310	Jason Kendall	1.00	.40
❑ 311	Brian Jordan	1.00	.40
❑ 312	Ron Gant	1.00	.40
❑ 313	Todd Stottlemyre	1.00	.40
❑ 314	Greg Vaughn	1.00	.40
❑ 315	Kevin Brown	1.50	.60
❑ 316	Wally Joyner	1.00	.40
❑ 317	Robb Nen	1.00	.40
❑ 318	Orel Hershiser	1.00	.40
❑ 319	Russ Davis	1.00	.40
❑ 320	Randy Johnson	2.50	1.00
❑ 321	Quinton McCracken	1.00	.40
❑ 322	Tony Saunders	1.00	.40
❑ 323	Wilson Alvarez	1.00	.40
❑ 324	Wade Boggs	1.50	.60
❑ 325	Fred McGriff	1.50	.60
❑ 326	Lee Stevens	1.00	.40
❑ 327	John Wetteland	1.00	.40
❑ 328	Jose Canseco	1.50	.60
❑ 329	Randy Myers	1.00	.40
❑ 330	Jose Cruz Jr.	1.00	.40
❑ 331	Matt Williams TW	2.50	1.00
❑ 332	Andres Galarraga TW	2.50	1.00
❑ 333	Walt Weiss TW	2.50	1.00
❑ 334	Joe Carter TW	2.50	1.00
❑ 335	Pedro Martinez TW	4.00	1.50
❑ 336	Henry Rodriguez TW	2.50	1.00
❑ 337	Travis Fryman TW	2.50	1.00
❑ 338	Darryl Kile TW	2.50	1.00
❑ 339	Mike Lansing TW	2.50	1.00
❑ 340	Mike Piazza TW	10.00	4.00
❑ 341	Moises Alou TW	2.50	1.00
❑ 342	Charles Johnson TW	2.50	1.00
❑ 343	Chuck Knoblauch TW	2.50	1.00
❑ 344	Rickey Henderson TW	6.00	2.50
❑ 345	Kevin Brown TW	4.00	1.50
❑ 346	Orel Hershiser TW	2.50	1.00
❑ 347	Wade Boggs TW	4.00	1.50
❑ 348	Fred McGriff TW	4.00	1.50
❑ 349	Jose Canseco TW	4.00	1.50
❑ 350	Gary Sheffield TW	2.50	1.00
❑ 351	Travis Lee CG	4.00	1.50
❑ 352	Nomar Garciaparra CG	15.00	6.00
❑ 353	Frank Thomas CG	10.00	4.00
❑ 354	Cal Ripken CG	30.00	12.50
❑ 355	Mark McGwire CG	25.00	10.00
❑ 356	Mike Piazza CG	15.00	6.00
❑ 357	Alex Rodriguez CG	15.00	6.00
❑ 358	Barry Bonds CG	25.00	10.00
❑ 359	Tony Gwynn CG	12.00	5.00
❑ 360	Ken Griffey Jr. CG	15.00	6.00

1999 SPx

❑	COMP.SET w/o SP's (80)	25.00	10.00
❑	COMMON MCGWIRE (1-10)	1.50	.60
❑	COMMON CARD (11-80)	.50	.20
❑	COMMON SP (81-120)	10.00	4.00
❑ 1	Mark McGwire 61	3.00	1.25
❑ 2	Mark McGwire 62	3.00	1.25
❑ 3	Mark McGwire 63	1.50	.60
❑ 4	Mark McGwire 64	1.50	.60
❑ 5	Mark McGwire 65	1.50	.60
❑ 6	Mark McGwire 66	1.50	.60
❑ 7	Mark McGwire 67	1.50	.60
❑ 8	Mark McGwire 68	1.50	.60
❑ 9	Mark McGwire 69	1.50	.60
❑ 10	Mark McGwire 70	4.00	1.50
❑ 11	Mo Vaughn	.50	.20
❑ 12	Darin Erstad	.50	.20
❑ 13	Travis Lee	.50	.20
❑ 14	Randy Johnson	1.25	.50
❑ 15	Matt Williams	.50	.20
❑ 16	Chipper Jones	1.25	.50
❑ 17	Greg Maddux	2.00	.75
❑ 18	Andruw Jones	.75	.30
❑ 19	Andres Galarraga	.50	.20
❑ 20	Cal Ripken	4.00	1.50
❑ 21	Albert Belle	.50	.20
❑ 22	Mike Mussina	.75	.30
❑ 23	Nomar Garciaparra	2.00	.75
❑ 24	Pedro Martinez	.75	.30
❑ 25	John Valentin	.50	.20
❑ 26	Kerry Wood	.50	.20
❑ 27	Sammy Sosa	1.25	.50
❑ 28	Mark Grace	.75	.30
❑ 29	Frank Thomas	1.25	.50
❑ 30	Mike Caruso	.50	.20
❑ 31	Barry Larkin	.75	.30
❑ 32	Sean Casey	.50	.20
❑ 33	Jim Thome	.75	.30
❑ 34	Kenny Lofton	.50	.20
❑ 35	Manny Ramirez	.75	.30
❑ 36	Larry Walker	.50	.20
❑ 37	Todd Helton	.75	.30
❑ 38	Vinny Castilla	.50	.20
❑ 39	Tony Clark	.50	.20
❑ 40	Derrek Lee	.75	.30
❑ 41	Mark Kotsay	.50	.20
❑ 42	Jeff Bagwell	.75	.30
❑ 43	Craig Biggio	.75	.30
❑ 44	Moises Alou	.50	.20
❑ 45	Larry Sutton	.50	.20
❑ 46	Johnny Damon	.75	.30
❑ 47	Gary Sheffield	.50	.20
❑ 48	Raul Mondesi	.50	.20
❑ 49	Jeromy Burnitz	.50	.20
❑ 50	Todd Walker	.50	.20
❑ 51	David Ortiz	1.25	.50
❑ 52	Vladimir Guerrero	1.25	.50
❑ 53	Rondell White	.50	.20
❑ 54	Mike Piazza	2.00	.75
❑ 55	Derek Jeter	3.00	1.25
❑ 56	Tino Martinez	.75	.30
❑ 57	Roger Clemens	2.50	1.00
❑ 58	Ben Grieve	.50	.20
❑ 59	A.J. Hinch	.50	.20
❑ 60	Scott Rolen	.75	.30
❑ 61	Doug Glanville	.50	.20
❑ 62	Aramis Ramirez	.50	.20
❑ 63	Jose Guillen	.50	.20
❑ 64	Tony Gwynn	1.50	.60
❑ 65	Greg Vaughn	.50	.20
❑ 66	Ruben Rivera	.50	.20
❑ 67	Barry Bonds	3.00	1.25
❑ 68	J.T. Snow	.50	.20
❑ 69	Alex Rodriguez	2.00	.75
❑ 70	Ken Griffey Jr.	2.00	.75
❑ 71	Jay Buhner	.50	.20
❑ 72	Mark McGwire	3.00	1.25
❑ 73	Fernando Tatis	.50	.20
❑ 74	Quinton McCracken	.50	.20
❑ 75	Wade Boggs	.75	.30
❑ 76	Ivan Rodriguez	.75	.30
❑ 77	Juan Gonzalez	.50	.20
❑ 78	Rafael Palmeiro	.75	.30
❑ 79	Jose Cruz Jr.	.50	.20
❑ 80	Carlos Delgado	.50	.20
❑ 81	Troy Glaus SP	15.00	6.00
❑ 82	Vladimir Nunez SP	10.00	4.00
❑ 83	George Lombard SP	10.00	4.00
❑ 84	Bruce Chen SP	10.00	4.00
❑ 85	Ryan Minor SP	10.00	4.00
❑ 86	Calvin Pickering SP	10.00	4.00
❑ 87	Jin Ho Cho SP	10.00	4.00
❑ 88	Russ Branyan SP	10.00	4.00
❑ 89	Derrick Gibson SP	10.00	4.00
❑ 90	Gabe Kapler SP AU	15.00	6.00
❑ 91	Matt Anderson SP	10.00	4.00
❑ 92	Robert Fick SP	10.00	4.00
❑ 93	Juan Encarnacion SP	10.00	4.00
❑ 94	Preston Wilson SP	10.00	4.00
❑ 95	Alex Gonzalez SP	10.00	4.00
❑ 96	Carlos Beltran SP	15.00	6.00
❑ 97	Jeremy Giambi SP	10.00	4.00
❑ 98	Dee Brown SP	10.00	4.00
❑ 99	Adrian Beltre SP	10.00	4.00
❑ 100	Alex Cora SP	10.00	4.00
❑ 101	Angel Pena SP	10.00	4.00
❑ 102	Geoff Jenkins SP	10.00	4.00
❑ 103	Ronnie Belliard SP	10.00	4.00
❑ 104	Corey Koskie SP	10.00	4.00
❑ 105	A.J. Pierzynski SP	10.00	4.00
❑ 106	Michael Barrett SP	10.00	4.00
❑ 107	Fernando Seguignol SP	10.00	4.00
❑ 108	Mike Kinkade SP	10.00	4.00
❑ 109	Mike Lowell SP	10.00	4.00
❑ 110	Ricky Ledee SP	10.00	4.00
❑ 111	Eric Chavez SP	10.00	4.00
❑ 112	Abraham Nunez SP	10.00	4.00
❑ 113	Matt Clement SP	10.00	4.00
❑ 114	Ben Davis SP	10.00	4.00
❑ 115	Mike Darr SP	10.00	4.00
❑ 116	Ramon E.Martinez SP RC	10.00	4.00
❑ 117	Carlos Guillen SP	10.00	4.00
❑ 118	Shane Monahan SP	10.00	4.00
❑ 119	J.D. Drew SP AU	15.00	6.00
❑ 120	Kevin Witt SP	10.00	4.00
❑ 24EAST	Ken Griffey Jr. Sample	2.00	.75

2000 SPx

❑ COMP.BASIC w/o SP's (90) 25.00 10.00
❑ COMP.UPDATE w/o SP's (30) 10.00 4.00
❑ COMMON CARD (1-90) .50 .20
❑ COMMON AU/1500 (91-120) 10.00 4.00
❑ COMMON (121-135/182-196) 8.00 3.00
❑ COMMON CARD (136-151) 10.00 4.00
❑ COMMON CARD (152-181) .75 .30
❑ 1 Troy Glaus .50 .20
❑ 2 Mo Vaughn .50 .20
❑ 3 Ramon Ortiz .50 .20
❑ 4 Jeff Bagwell .75 .30
❑ 5 Moises Alou .50 .20
❑ 6 Craig Biggio .75 .30
❑ 7 Jose Lima .50 .20
❑ 8 Jason Giambi .50 .20
❑ 9 John Jaha .50 .20
❑ 10 Matt Stairs .50 .20
❑ 11 Chipper Jones 1.25 .50
❑ 12 Greg Maddux 2.00 .75
❑ 13 Andres Galarraga .50 .20
❑ 14 Andruw Jones .75 .30
❑ 15 Jeromy Burnitz .50 .20
❑ 16 Ron Belliard .50 .20
❑ 17 Carlos Delgado .50 .20
❑ 18 David Wells .50 .20
❑ 19 Tony Batista .50 .20
❑ 20 Shannon Stewart .50 .20
❑ 21 Sammy Sosa 1.25 .50
❑ 22 Mark Grace .75 .30
❑ 23 Henry Rodriguez .50 .20
❑ 24 Mark McGwire 3.00 1.25
❑ 25 J.D. Drew .50 .20
❑ 26 Luis Gonzalez .50 .20
❑ 27 Randy Johnson 1.25 .50
❑ 28 Matt Williams .50 .20
❑ 29 Steve Finley .50 .20
❑ 30 Shawn Green .50 .20
❑ 31 Kevin Brown .75 .30
❑ 32 Gary Sheffield .50 .20
❑ 33 Jose Canseco .75 .30
❑ 34 Greg Vaughn .50 .20
❑ 35 Vladimir Guerrero 1.25 .50
❑ 36 Michael Barrett .50 .20
❑ 37 Russ Ortiz .50 .20
❑ 38 Barry Bonds 3.00 1.25
❑ 39 Jeff Kent .50 .20
❑ 40 Richie Sexson .50 .20
❑ 41 Manny Ramirez .75 .30
❑ 42 Jim Thome .75 .30
❑ 43 Roberto Alomar .75 .30
❑ 44 Edgar Martinez .75 .30
❑ 45 Alex Rodriguez 2.00 .75
❑ 46 John Olerud .50 .20
❑ 47 Alex Gonzalez .50 .20
❑ 48 Cliff Floyd .50 .20
❑ 49 Mike Piazza 2.00 .75
❑ 50 Al Leiter .50 .20
❑ 51 Robin Ventura .75 .30
❑ 52 Edgardo Alfonzo .50 .20
❑ 53 Albert Belle .50 .20
❑ 54 Cal Ripken 4.00 1.50
❑ 55 B.J. Surhoff .50 .20
❑ 56 Tony Gwynn 1.50 .60
❑ 57 Trevor Hoffman .50 .20
❑ 58 Brian Giles .50 .20
❑ 59 Jason Kendall .50 .20
❑ 60 Kris Benson .50 .20
❑ 61 Bob Abreu .50 .20
❑ 62 Scott Rolen .75 .30
❑ 63 Curt Schilling .50 .20
❑ 64 Mike Lieberthal .50 .20
❑ 65 Sean Casey .50 .20
❑ 66 Dante Bichette .50 .20
❑ 67 Ken Griffey Jr. 2.00 .75
❑ 68 Pokey Reese .50 .20
❑ 69 Mike Sweeney .50 .20
❑ 70 Carlos Febles .50 .20
❑ 71 Ivan Rodriguez .75 .30
❑ 72 Ruben Mateo .50 .20
❑ 73 Rafael Palmeiro .75 .30
❑ 74 Larry Walker .50 .20
❑ 75 Todd Helton .75 .30
❑ 76 Nomar Garciaparra 2.00 .75
❑ 77 Pedro Martinez .75 .30
❑ 78 Troy O'Leary .50 .20
❑ 79 Jacque Jones .50 .20
❑ 80 Corey Koskie .50 .20
❑ 81 Juan Gonzalez .50 .20
❑ 82 Dean Palmer .50 .20
❑ 83 Juan Encarnacion .50 .20
❑ 84 Frank Thomas 1.25 .50
❑ 85 Magglio Ordonez .50 .20
❑ 86 Paul Konerko .50 .20
❑ 87 Bernie Williams .75 .30
❑ 88 Derek Jeter 3.00 1.25
❑ 89 Roger Clemens 2.50 1.00
❑ 90 Orlando Hernandez .50 .20
❑ 91 Vernon Wells AU/1500 25.00 10.00
❑ 92 Rick Ankiel AU/1500 10.00 4.00
❑ 93 Eric Chavez AU/1500 25.00 10.00
❑ 94 Alfonso Soriano AU/1500 60.00 30.00
❑ 95 Eric Gagne AU/1500 60.00 30.00
❑ 96 Rob Bell AU/1500 10.00 4.00
❑ 97 Matt Riley AU/1500 10.00 4.00
❑ 98 Josh Beckett AU/1500 80.00 40.00
❑ 99 Ben Petrick AU/1500 10.00 4.00
❑ 100 Rob Ramsay AU/1500 10.00 4.00
❑ 101 Scott Williamson AU/1500 10.00 4.00
❑ 102 Doug Davis AU/1500 15.00 6.00
❑ 103 Eric Munson AU/1500 10.00 4.00
❑ 104 Pat Burrell AU/500 80.00 40.00
❑ 105 Jim Morris AU/1500 25.00 10.00
❑ 106 Gabe Kapler AU/500 40.00 15.00
❑ 107 Lance Berkman/1000 8.00 3.00
❑ 108 Erubiel Durazo AU/1500 10.00 4.00
❑ 109 Tim Hudson AU/1500 40.00 15.00
❑ 110 Ben Davis AU/1500 10.00 4.00
❑ 111 Nick Johnson AU/1500 15.00 6.00
❑ 112 Octavio Dotel AU/1500 10.00 4.00
❑ 113 Jerry Hairston/1000 8.00 3.00
❑ 114 Ruben Mateo/1000 8.00 3.00
❑ 115 Chris Singleton/1000 8.00 3.00
❑ 116 Bruce Chen AU/1500 10.00 4.00
❑ 117 Derrick Gibson/1000 8.00 3.00
❑ 118 Carlos Beltran AU/500 125.00 75.00
❑ 119 Freddy Garcia AU/1500 15.00 6.00
❑ 120 Preston Wilson AU/1500 15.00 6.00
❑ 121 Brad Wilkerson/1600 RC 10.00 4.00
❑ 122 Roy Oswalt/1600 RC 150.00 100.00
❑ 123 Wascar Serrano/1600 RC 8.00 3.00
❑ 124 Sean Burnett/1600 RC 8.00 3.00
❑ 125 Alex Cabrera/1600 RC 8.00 3.00
❑ 126 Timo Perez/1600 RC 8.00 3.00
❑ 127 Juan Pierre/1600 RC 10.00 4.00
❑ 128 Daylan Holt/1600 RC 8.00 3.00
❑ 129 Tomokazu Ohka/1600 RC 8.00 3.00
❑ 130 Kazuhiro Sasaki/1600 RC 10.00 4.00
❑ 131 Kurt Ainsworth/1600 RC 8.00 3.00
❑ 132 Brent Abernathy/1600 RC 8.00 3.00
❑ 133 Danys Baez/1600 RC 8.00 3.00
❑ 134 Brad Cresse/1600 RC 8.00 3.00
❑ 135 Ryan Franklin/1600 RC 8.00 3.00
❑ 136 Mike Lamb AU/1500 RC 15.00 6.00
❑ 137 David Espinosa AU/1500 RC 10.00 4.00
❑ 138 Matt Wheatland AU/1500 RC 10.00 4.00
❑ 139 Xavier Nady AU/1500 RC 40.00 15.00
❑ 140 Scott Heard AU/1500 RC 10.00 4.00
❑ 141 P.Coco AU/1500 UER54 RC 10.004.00
❑ 142 Justin Miller AU/1500 RC 10.00 4.00
❑ 143 Dave Krynzel AU/1500 RC 10.00 4.00
❑ 144 Dane Sardinha AU/1500 RC 10.004.00
❑ 145 Ben Sheets AU/1500 RC 50.00 20.00
❑ 146 Leo Estrella AU/1500 RC 10.00 4.00
❑ 147 Ben Diggins AU/1500 RC 10.00 4.00
❑ 148 Barry Zito AU/1500 RC 80.00 40.00
❑ 149 Joe Torres AU/1500 RC 10.00 4.00
❑ 150 Mike Meyers AU/1500 RC 10.00 4.00
❑ 151 Kris Wilson AU/1500 RC 10.00 4.00
❑ 152 Darin Erstad .75 .30
❑ 153 Richard Hidalgo .75 .30
❑ 154 Eric Chavez .75 .30
❑ 155 B.J. Surhoff .75 .30
❑ 156 Richie Sexson .75 .30
❑ 157 Raul Mondesi .75 .30
❑ 158 Rondell White .75 .30
❑ 159 Jim Edmonds .75 .30
❑ 160 Curt Schilling .75 .30
❑ 161 Tom Goodwin .75 .30
❑ 162 Fred McGriff 1.25 .50
❑ 163 Jose Vidro .75 .30
❑ 164 Ellis Burks .75 .30
❑ 165 David Segui .75 .30
❑ 166 Aaron Sele .75 .30
❑ 167 Henry Rodriguez .75 .30
❑ 168 Mike Bordick .75 .30
❑ 169 Mike Mussina 1.25 .50
❑ 170 Ryan Klesko .75 .30
❑ 171 Kevin Young .75 .30
❑ 172 Travis Lee .75 .30
❑ 173 Aaron Boone .75 .30
❑ 174 Jermaine Dye .75 .30
❑ 175 Ricky Ledee .75 .30
❑ 176 Jeffrey Hammonds .75 .30
❑ 177 Carl Everett .75 .30
❑ 178 Matt Lawton .75 .30
❑ 179 Bobby Higginson .75 .30
❑ 180 Charles Johnson .75 .30
❑ 181 David Justice .75 .30
❑ 182 Joey Nation/1600 RC 8.00 3.00
❑ 183 Rico Washington/1600 RC 8.00 3.00
❑ 184 Luis Matos/1600 RC 8.00 3.00
❑ 185 Chris Wakeland/1600 RC 8.00 3.00
❑ 186 Sun Woo Kim/1600 RC 8.00 3.00
❑ 187 Keith Ginter/1600 RC 8.00 3.00
❑ 188 Geraldo Guzman/1600 RC 8.00 3.00
❑ 189 Jay Spurgeon/1600 RC 8.00 3.00
❑ 190 Jace Brewer/1600 RC 8.00 3.00
❑ 191 Juan Guzman/1600 RC 8.00 3.00
❑ 192 Ross Gload/1600 RC 8.00 3.00
❑ 193 Paxton Crawford/1600 RC 8.00 3.00
❑ 194 Ryan Kohlmeier/1600 RC 8.00 3.00
❑ 195 Julio Zuleta/1600 RC 8.00 3.00
❑ 196 Matt Ginter/1600 RC 8.00 3.00

2001 SPx

❑ COMP.BASIC w/o SP's (90) 25.00 10.00
❑ COMP.UPDATE w/o SP's (30) 10.00 4.00
❑ COMMON CARD (1-90) .50 .20
❑ COMMON YS (91-120) 5.00 2.00
❑ COMMON JSY (121-135) 8.00 3.00
❑ COMMON JSY AU (136-150) 15.00 6.00
❑ COMMON CARD (151-180) .75 .30
❑ COMMON CARD (181-205) 5.00 2.00
❑ 1 Darin Erstad .50 .20
❑ 2 Troy Glaus .50 .20
❑ 3 Mo Vaughn .50 .20
❑ 4 Johnny Damon .75 .30
❑ 5 Jason Giambi .50 .20
❑ 6 Tim Hudson .50 .20
❑ 7 Miguel Tejada .50 .20
❑ 8 Carlos Delgado .50 .20
❑ 9 Raul Mondesi .50 .20
❑ 10 Tony Batista .50 .20
❑ 11 Ben Grieve .50 .20
❑ 12 Greg Vaughn .50 .20
❑ 13 Juan Gonzalez .50 .20
❑ 14 Jim Thome .75 .30
❑ 15 Roberto Alomar .75 .30
❑ 16 John Olerud .50 .20
❑ 17 Edgar Martinez .75 .30
❑ 18 Albert Belle .50 .20
❑ 19 Cal Ripken 4.00 1.50
❑ 20 Ivan Rodriguez .75 .30
❑ 21 Rafael Palmeiro .75 .30
❑ 22 Alex Rodriguez 2.00 .75
❑ 23 Nomar Garciaparra 2.00 .75
❑ 24 Pedro Martinez .75 .30
❑ 25 Manny Ramirez Sox .75 .30
❑ 26 Jermaine Dye .50 .20
❑ 27 Mark Quinn .50 .20

❑ 28 Carlos Beltran .50 .20
❑ 29 Tony Clark .50 .20
❑ 30 Bobby Higginson .50 .20
❑ 31 Eric Milton .50 .20
❑ 32 Matt Lawton .50 .20
❑ 33 Frank Thomas 1.25 .50
❑ 34 Magglio Ordonez .50 .20
❑ 35 Ray Durham .50 .20
❑ 36 David Wells .50 .20
❑ 37 Derek Jeter 3.00 1.25
❑ 38 Bernie Williams .75 .30
❑ 39 Roger Clemens 2.50 1.00
❑ 40 David Justice .50 .20
❑ 41 Jeff Bagwell .75 .30
❑ 42 Richard Hidalgo .50 .20
❑ 43 Moises Alou .50 .20
❑ 44 Chipper Jones 1.25 .50
❑ 45 Andruw Jones .75 .30
❑ 46 Greg Maddux 2.00 .75
❑ 47 Rafael Furcal .50 .20
❑ 48 Jeromy Burnitz .50 .20
❑ 49 Geoff Jenkins .50 .20
❑ 50 Mark McGwire 3.00 1.25
❑ 51 Jim Edmonds .50 .20
❑ 52 Rick Ankiel .50 .20
❑ 53 Edgar Renteria .50 .20
❑ 54 Sammy Sosa 1.25 .50
❑ 55 Kerry Wood .50 .20
❑ 56 Rondell White .50 .20
❑ 57 Randy Johnson 1.25 .50
❑ 58 Steve Finley .50 .20
❑ 59 Matt Williams .50 .20
❑ 60 Luis Gonzalez .50 .20
❑ 61 Kevin Brown .50 .20
❑ 62 Gary Sheffield .50 .20
❑ 63 Shawn Green .50 .20
❑ 64 Vladimir Guerrero 1.25 .50
❑ 65 Jose Vidro .50 .20
❑ 66 Barry Bonds 3.00 1.25
❑ 67 Jeff Kent .50 .20
❑ 68 Livan Hernandez .50 .20
❑ 69 Preston Wilson .50 .20
❑ 70 Charles Johnson .50 .20
❑ 71 Cliff Floyd .50 .20
❑ 72 Mike Piazza 2.00 .75
❑ 73 Edgardo Alfonzo .50 .20
❑ 74 Jay Payton .50 .20
❑ 75 Robin Ventura .50 .20
❑ 76 Tony Gwynn 1.50 .60
❑ 77 Phil Nevin .50 .20
❑ 78 Ryan Klesko .50 .20
❑ 79 Scott Rolen .75 .30
❑ 80 Pat Burrell .50 .20
❑ 81 Bob Abreu .50 .20
❑ 82 Brian Giles .50 .20
❑ 83 Kris Benson .50 .20
❑ 84 Jason Kendall .50 .20
❑ 85 Ken Griffey Jr. 2.00 .75
❑ 86 Barry Larkin .75 .30
❑ 87 Sean Casey .50 .20
❑ 88 Todd Helton .75 .30
❑ 89 Larry Walker .50 .20
❑ 90 Mike Hampton .50 .20
❑ 91 Billy Sylvester YS RC 5.00 2.00
❑ 92 Josh Towers YS RC 8.00 3.00
❑ 93 Zach Day YS RC 5.00 2.00
❑ 94 Martin Vargas YS RC 5.00 2.00
❑ 95 Adam Pettyjohn YS RC 5.00 2.00
❑ 96 Andres Torres YS RC 5.00 2.00
❑ 97 Kris Keller YS RC 5.00 2.00
❑ 98 Blaine Neal YS RC 5.00 2.00
❑ 99 Kyle Kessel YS RC 5.00 2.00
❑ 100 Greg Miller YS RC 5.00 2.00
❑ 101 Shawn Sonnier YS 5.00 2.00
❑ 102 Alexis Gomez YS RC 5.00 2.00
❑ 103 Grant Balfour YS RC 5.00 2.00
❑ 104 Henry Mateo YS RC 5.00 2.00
❑ 105 Wilken Ruan YS RC 5.00 2.00
❑ 106 Nick Maness YS RC 5.00 2.00
❑ 107 Jason Michaels YS RC 5.00 2.00
❑ 108 Esix Snead YS RC 5.00 2.00
❑ 109 William Ortega YS RC 5.00 2.00
❑ 110 David Elder YS RC 5.00 2.00
❑ 111 Jackson Melian YS RC 5.00 2.00
❑ 112 Nate Teut YS RC 5.00 2.00
❑ 113 Jason Smith YS RC 5.00 2.00
❑ 114 Mike Penney YS RC 5.00 2.00
❑ 115 Jose Mieses YS RC 5.00 2.00
❑ 116 Juan Pena YS 5.00 2.00
❑ 117 Brian Lawrence YS RC 5.00 2.00
❑ 118 Jeremy Owens YS RC 5.00 2.00
❑ 119 Carlos Valderrama YS RC 5.00 2.00
❑ 120 Rafael Soriano YS RC 5.00 2.00
❑ 121 Horacio Ramirez JSY RC 10.00 4.00
❑ 122 Ricardo Rodriguez JSY RC 8.00 3.00
❑ 123 Juan Diaz JSY RC 8.00 3.00
❑ 124 Donnie Bridges JSY 8.00 3.00
❑ 125 Tyler Walker JSY RC 8.00 3.00
❑ 126 Erick Almonte JSY RC 8.00 3.00
❑ 127 Jesus Colome JSY 8.00 3.00
❑ 128 Ryan Freel JSY RC 10.00 4.00
❑ 129 Elpidio Guzman JSY RC 8.00 3.00
❑ 130 Jack Cust JSY 8.00 3.00
❑ 131 Eric Hinske JSY RC 10.00 4.00
❑ 132 Josh Fogg JSY RC 8.00 3.00
❑ 133 Juan Uribe JSY RC 10.00 4.00
❑ 134 Bert Snow JSY RC 8.00 3.00
❑ 135 Pedro Feliz JSY 8.00 3.00
❑ 136 Wilson Betemit JSY AU RC 40.00 15.00
❑ 137 Sean Douglass JSY AU RC 15.00 6.00
❑ 138 Dernell Stenson JSY AU 15.00 6.00
❑ 139 Brandon Inge JSY AU 15.00 6.00
❑ 140 Mor.Ensberg JSY AU RC 40.00 15.00
❑ 141 Brian Cole JSY AU 15.00 6.00
❑ 142 A.Hernandez JSY AU RC 15.00 6.00
❑ 143 B.Duckworth JSY AU RC 15.00 6.00
❑ 144 Jack Wilson JSY AU RC 25.00 10.00
❑ 145 Travis Hafner JSY AU RC 125.00 75.00
❑ 146 Carlos Pena JSY AU 15.00 6.00
❑ 147 Corey Patterson JSY AU 15.00 6.00
❑ 148 Xavier Nady JSY AU 25.00 10.00
❑ 149 Jason Hart JSY AU 15.00 6.00
❑ 150 I.Suzuki JSY AU RC 800.00 500.00
❑ 151 Garret Anderson .75 .30
❑ 152 Jermaine Dye .75 .30
❑ 153 Shannon Stewart .75 .30
❑ 154 Toby Hall .75 .30
❑ 155 C.C. Sabathia .75 .30
❑ 156 Bret Boone .75 .30
❑ 157 Tony Batista .75 .30
❑ 158 Gabe Kapler .75 .30
❑ 159 Carl Everett .75 .30
❑ 160 Mike Sweeney .75 .30
❑ 161 Dean Palmer .75 .30
❑ 162 Doug Mientkiewicz .75 .30
❑ 163 Carlos Lee .75 .30
❑ 164 Mike Mussina 1.25 .50
❑ 165 Lance Berkman .75 .30
❑ 166 Ken Caminiti .75 .30
❑ 167 Ben Sheets 1.25 .50
❑ 168 Matt Morris .75 .30
❑ 169 Fred McGriff 1.25 .50
❑ 170 Curt Schilling .75 .30
❑ 171 Paul LoDuca .75 .30
❑ 172 Javier Vazquez .75 .30
❑ 173 Rich Aurilia .75 .30
❑ 174 A.J. Burnett .75 .30
❑ 175 Al Leiter .75 .30
❑ 176 Mark Kotsay .75 .30
❑ 177 Jimmy Rollins .75 .30
❑ 178 Aramis Ramirez .75 .30
❑ 179 Aaron Boone .75 .30
❑ 180 Jeff Cirillo .75 .30
❑ 181 Johnny Estrada YS RC 8.00 3.00
❑ 182 Dave Williams YS RC 5.00 2.00
❑ 183 Donaldo Mendez YS RC 5.00 2.00
❑ 184 Junior Spivey YS RC 8.00 3.00
❑ 185 Jay Gibbons YS RC 8.00 3.00
❑ 186 Kyle Lohse YS RC 8.00 3.00
❑ 187 Willie Harris YS RC 5.00 2.00
❑ 188 Juan Cruz YS RC 5.00 2.00
❑ 189 Joe Kennedy YS RC 8.00 3.00
❑ 190 Duaner Sanchez YS RC 5.00 2.00
❑ 191 Jorge Julio YS RC 5.00 2.00
❑ 192 Cesar Crespo YS RC 5.00 2.00
❑ 193 Casey Fossum YS RC 5.00 2.00
❑ 194 Brian Roberts YS RC 15.00 6.00
❑ 195 Troy Mattes YS RC 5.00 2.00
❑ 196 Rob Mackowiak YS RC 8.00 3.00
❑ 197 Tsuyoshi Shinjo YS RC 8.00 3.00
❑ 198 Nick Punto YS RC 5.00 2.00
❑ 199 Wilmy Caceres YS RC 5.00 2.00
❑ 200 Jeremy Affeldt YS RC 5.00 2.00
❑ 201 Bret Prinz YS RC 5.00 2.00
❑ 202 Delvin James YS RC 5.00 2.00
❑ 203 Luis Pineda YS RC 5.00 2.00
❑ 204 Matt White YS RC 5.00 2.00
❑ 205 Brandon Knight YS RC 5.00 2.00
❑ 206 Albert Pujols YS AU RC 1200.00 800.00
❑ 207 Mark Teixeira YS AU RC 150.00 90.00
❑ 208 Mark Prior YS AU RC 60.00 30.00
❑ 209 Dewon Brazelton YS AU RC 15.00 6.00
❑ 210 Bud Smith YS AU RC 15.00 6.00

2002 SPx

❑ COMP.LOW w/o SP's (90) 25.00 10.00
❑ COMP.UPDATE w/o SP's (30) 10.00 4.00
❑ COMMON CARD (1-90) .50 .20
❑ COMMON CARD (91-120) 8.00 3.00
❑ COMMON CARD (121-150) 15.00 6.00
❑ COMMON CARD (151-190) 8.00 3.00
❑ COMMON CARD (191-220) .75 .30
❑ COMMON CARD (221-250) 10.00 4.00
❑ 1 Troy Glaus .50 .20
❑ 2 Darin Erstad .50 .20
❑ 3 David Justice .50 .20
❑ 4 Tim Hudson .50 .20
❑ 5 Miguel Tejada .50 .20
❑ 6 Barry Zito .50 .20
❑ 7 Carlos Delgado .50 .20
❑ 8 Shannon Stewart .50 .20
❑ 9 Greg Vaughn .50 .20
❑ 10 Toby Hall .50 .20
❑ 11 Jim Thome .75 .30
❑ 12 C.C. Sabathia .50 .20
❑ 13 Ichiro Suzuki 2.50 1.00
❑ 14 Edgar Martinez .75 .30
❑ 15 Freddy Garcia .50 .20
❑ 16 Mike Cameron .50 .20
❑ 17 Jeff Conine .50 .20
❑ 18 Tony Batista .50 .20
❑ 19 Alex Rodriguez 2.00 .75
❑ 20 Rafael Palmeiro .75 .30
❑ 21 Ivan Rodriguez .75 .30
❑ 22 Carl Everett .50 .20
❑ 23 Pedro Martinez .75 .30
❑ 24 Manny Ramirez .75 .30
❑ 25 Nomar Garciaparra 2.00 .75
❑ 26 Johnny Damon Sox .75 .30
❑ 27 Mike Sweeney .50 .20
❑ 28 Carlos Beltran .50 .20
❑ 29 Dmitri Young .50 .20
❑ 30 Joe Mays .50 .20
❑ 31 Doug Mientkiewicz .50 .20
❑ 32 Cristian Guzman .50 .20
❑ 33 Corey Koskie .50 .20
❑ 34 Frank Thomas 1.25 .50
❑ 35 Magglio Ordonez .50 .20
❑ 36 Mark Buehrle .50 .20
❑ 37 Bernie Williams .75 .30
❑ 38 Roger Clemens 2.50 1.00
❑ 39 Derek Jeter 3.00 1.25
❑ 40 Jason Giambi .50 .20
❑ 41 Mike Mussina .75 .30
❑ 42 Lance Berkman .50 .20
❑ 43 Jeff Bagwell .75 .30
❑ 44 Roy Oswalt .50 .20
❑ 45 Greg Maddux 2.00 .75
❑ 46 Chipper Jones 1.25 .50
❑ 47 Andruw Jones .75 .30

❑ 48 Gary Sheffield .50 .20
❑ 49 Geoff Jenkins .50 .20
❑ 50 Richie Sexson .50 .20
❑ 51 Ben Sheets .50 .20
❑ 52 Albert Pujols 2.50 1.00
❑ 53 J.D. Drew .50 .20
❑ 54 Jim Edmonds .50 .20
❑ 55 Sammy Sosa 1.25 .50
❑ 56 Moises Alou .50 .20
❑ 57 Kerry Wood .50 .20
❑ 58 Jon Lieber .50 .20
❑ 59 Fred McGriff .75 .30
❑ 60 Randy Johnson 1.25 .50
❑ 61 Luis Gonzalez .50 .20
❑ 62 Curt Schilling .50 .20
❑ 63 Kevin Brown .50 .20
❑ 64 Hideo Nomo 1.25 .50
❑ 65 Shawn Green .50 .20
❑ 66 Vladimir Guerrero 1.25 .50
❑ 67 Jose Vidro .50 .20
❑ 68 Barry Bonds 3.00 1.25
❑ 69 Jeff Kent .50 .20
❑ 70 Rich Aurilia .50 .20
❑ 71 Cliff Floyd .50 .20
❑ 72 Josh Beckett .50 .20
❑ 73 Preston Wilson .50 .20
❑ 74 Mike Piazza 2.00 .75
❑ 75 Mo Vaughn .50 .20
❑ 76 Jeromy Burnitz .50 .20
❑ 77 Roberto Alomar .75 .30
❑ 78 Phil Nevin .50 .20
❑ 79 Ryan Klesko .50 .20
❑ 80 Scott Rolen .75 .30
❑ 81 Bobby Abreu .50 .20
❑ 82 Jimmy Rollins .50 .20
❑ 83 Brian Giles .50 .20
❑ 84 Aramis Ramirez .50 .20
❑ 85 Ken Griffey Jr. 2.00 .75
❑ 86 Sean Casey .50 .20
❑ 87 Barry Larkin .75 .30
❑ 88 Mike Hampton .50 .20
❑ 89 Larry Walker .50 .20
❑ 90 Todd Helton .75 .30
❑ 91A Ron Calloway YS RC 8.00 3.00
❑ 91P Ron Calloway YS RC 8.00 3.00
❑ 92A Joe Orloski YS RC 8.00 3.00
❑ 92P Joe Orloski YS RC 8.00 3.00
❑ 93A Anderson Machado YS RC 8.00 3.00
❑ 93P Anderson Machado YS RC 8.00 3.00
❑ 94A Eric Good YS RC 8.00 3.00
❑ 94P Eric Good YS RC 8.00 3.00
❑ 95A Reed Johnson YS RC 10.00 4.00
❑ 95P Reed Johnson YS RC 10.00 4.00
❑ 96A Brendan Donnelly YS RC 8.00 3.00
❑ 96P Brendan Donnelly YS RC 8.00 3.00
❑ 97A Chris Baker YS RC 8.00 3.00
❑ 97P Chris Baker YS RC 8.00 3.00
❑ 98A Wilson Valdez YS RC 8.00 3.00
❑ 98P Wilson Valdez YS RC 8.00 3.00
❑ 99A Scotty Layfield YS RC 8.00 3.00
❑ 99P Scotty Layfield YS RC 8.00 3.00
❑ 100A P.J. Bevis YS RC 8.00 3.00
❑ 100P P.J. Bevis YS RC 8.00 3.00
❑ 101A Edwin Almonte YS RC 8.00 3.00
❑ 101P Edwin Almonte YS RC 8.00 3.00
❑ 102A Francis Beltran YS RC 8.00 3.00
❑ 102P Francis Beltran YS RC 8.00 3.00
❑ 103A Val Pascucci YS 8.00 3.00
❑ 103P Val Pascucci YS 8.00 3.00
❑ 104A Nelson Castro YS RC 8.00 3.00
❑ 104P Nelson Castro YS RC 8.00 3.00
❑ 105A Michael Crudale YS RC 8.00 3.00
❑ 105P Michael Crudale YS RC 8.00 3.00
❑ 106A Colin Young YS RC 8.00 3.00
❑ 106P Colin Young YS RC 8.00 3.00
❑ 107A Todd Donovan YS RC 8.00 3.00
❑ 107P Todd Donovan YS RC 8.00 3.00
❑ 108A Felix Escalona YS RC 8.00 3.00
❑ 108P Felix Escalona YS RC 8.00 3.00
❑ 109A Brandon Backe YS RC 10.00 4.00
❑ 109P Brandon Backe YS RC 10.00 4.00
❑ 110A Corey Thurman YS RC 8.00 3.00
❑ 110P Corey Thurman YS RC 8.00 3.00
❑ 111A Kyle Kane YS RC 8.00 3.00
❑ 111P Kyle Kane YS RC 8.00 3.00
❑ 112A Allan Simpson YS RC 8.00 3.00
❑ 112P Allan Simpson YS RC 8.00 3.00
❑ 113A Jose Valverde YS RC 8.00 3.00
❑ 113P Jose Valverde YS RC 8.00 3.00
❑ 114A Chris Booker YS RC 8.00 3.00
❑ 114P Chris Booker YS RC 8.00 3.00
❑ 115A Brandon Puffer YS RC 8.00 3.00
❑ 115P Brandon Puffer YS RC 8.00 3.00
❑ 116A John Foster YS RC 8.00 3.00
❑ 116P John Foster YS RC 8.00 3.00
❑ 117A Cliff Bartosh YS RC 8.00 3.00
❑ 117P Cliff Bartosh YS RC 8.00 3.00
❑ 118A Gustavo Chacin YS RC 10.00 4.00
❑ 118P Gustavo Chacin YS RC 10.00 4.00
❑ 119A Steve Kent YS RC 8.00 3.00
❑ 119P Steve Kent YS RC 8.00 3.00
❑ 120A Nate Field YS RC 8.00 3.00
❑ 120P Nate Field YS RC 8.00 3.00
❑ 121 Victor Alvarez AU RC 10.00 4.00
❑ 122 Steve Bechler AU RC 10.00 4.00
❑ 123 Adrian Burnside AU RC 10.00 4.00
❑ 124 Marlon Byrd AU 15.00 6.00
❑ 125 Jaime Cerda AU RC 10.00 4.00
❑ 126 Brandon Claussen AU 15.00 6.00
❑ 127 Mark Corey AU RC 10.00 4.00
❑ 128 Doug Devore AU RC 10.00 4.00
❑ 129 Kazuhisa Ishii AU SP RC 60.00 30.00
❑ 130 John Ennis AU RC 10.00 4.00
❑ 131 Kevin Frederick AU RC 10.00 4.00
❑ 132 Josh Hancock AU RC 10.00 4.00
❑ 133 Ben Howard AU RC 10.00 4.00
❑ 134 Orlando Hudson AU 15.00 6.00
❑ 135 Hansel Izquierdo AU RC 10.00 4.00
❑ 136 Eric Junge AU RC 10.00 4.00
❑ 137 Austin Kearns AU 15.00 6.00
❑ 138 Victor Martinez AU 25.00 10.00
❑ 139 Luis Martinez AU RC 10.00 4.00
❑ 140 Danny Mota AU RC 10.00 4.00
❑ 141 Jorge Padilla AU RC 10.00 4.00
❑ 142 Andy Pratt AU RC 10.00 4.00
❑ 143 Rene Reyes AU RC 10.00 4.00
❑ 144 Rodrigo Rosario AU RC 10.00 4.00
❑ 145 Tom Shearn AU RC 10.00 4.00
❑ 146 So Taguchi AU SP RC 25.00 10.00
❑ 147 Dennis Tankersley AU 15.00 6.00
❑ 148 Matt Thornton AU RC 10.00 4.00
❑ 149 Jeremy Ward AU RC 10.00 4.00
❑ 150 Mitch Wylie AU RC 10.00 4.00
❑ 151 Pedro Martinez JSY/800 10.00 4.00
❑ 152 Cal Ripken JSY/800 25.00 10.00
❑ 153 Roger Clemens JSY/800 15.00 6.00
❑ 154 Bernie Williams JSY/800 10.00 4.00
❑ 155 Jason Giambi JSY/700 8.00 3.00
❑ 156 Robin Ventura JSY/800 8.00 3.00
❑ 157 Carlos Delgado JSY/800 8.00 3.00
❑ 158 Frank Thomas JSY/800 10.00 4.00
❑ 159 Magglio Ordonez JSY/800 8.00 3.00
❑ 160 Jim Thome JSY/800 10.00 4.00
❑ 161 Darin Erstad JSY/800 8.00 3.00
❑ 162 Tim Salmon JSY/800 10.00 4.00
❑ 163 Tim Hudson JSY/800 8.00 3.00
❑ 164 Barry Zito JSY/800 8.00 3.00
❑ 165 Ichiro Suzuki JSY/800 25.00 10.00
❑ 166 Edgar Martinez JSY/800 10.00 4.00
❑ 167 Alex Rodriguez JSY/800 15.00 6.00
❑ 168 Ivan Rodriguez JSY/800 10.00 4.00
❑ 169 Juan Gonzalez JSY/800 8.00 3.00
❑ 170 Greg Maddux JSY/800 15.00 6.00
❑ 171 Chipper Jones JSY/800 10.00 4.00
❑ 172 Andruw Jones JSY/800 10.00 4.00
❑ 173 Tom Glavine JSY/800 10.00 4.00
❑ 174 Mike Piazza JSY/800 15.00 4.00
❑ 175 Roberto Alomar JSY/800 10.00 4.00
❑ 176 Scott Rolen JSY/800 10.00 4.00
❑ 177 Sammy Sosa JSY/800 10.00 4.00
❑ 178 Moises Alou JSY/800 8.00 3.00
❑ 179 Ken Griffey Jr. JSY/700 20.00 8.00
❑ 180 Jeff Bagwell JSY/800 10.00 4.00
❑ 181 Jim Edmonds JSY/800 8.00 3.00
❑ 182 J.D. Drew JSY/800 8.00 3.00
❑ 183 Brian Giles JSY/800 8.00 3.00
❑ 184 Randy Johnson JSY/800 10.00 4.00
❑ 185 Curt Schilling JSY/800 8.00 3.00
❑ 186 Luis Gonzalez JSY/800 8.00 3.00
❑ 187 Todd Helton JSY/800 10.00 4.00
❑ 188 Shawn Green JSY/800 8.00 3.00
❑ 189 David Wells JSY/800 8.00 3.00
❑ 190 Jeff Kent JSY/800 8.00 3.00
❑ 191 Tom Glavine 1.25 .50
❑ 192 Cliff Floyd .75 .30
❑ 193 Mark Prior 1.25 .50
❑ 194 Corey Patterson .75 .30
❑ 195 Paul Konerko .75 .30
❑ 196 Adam Dunn .75 .30
❑ 197 Joe Borchard .75 .30
❑ 198 Carlos Pena .75 .30
❑ 199 Juan Encarnacion .75 .30
❑ 200 Luis Castillo .75 .30
❑ 201 Torii Hunter .75 .30
❑ 202 Hee Seop Choi .75 .30
❑ 203 Bartolo Colon .75 .30
❑ 204 Raul Mondesi .75 .30
❑ 205 Jeff Weaver .75 .30
❑ 206 Eric Munson .75 .30
❑ 207 Alfonso Soriano .75 .30
❑ 208 Ray Durham .75 .30
❑ 209 Eric Chavez .75 .30
❑ 210 Brett Myers .75 .30
❑ 211 Jeremy Giambi .75 .30
❑ 212 Vicente Padilla .75 .30
❑ 213 Felipe Lopez .75 .30
❑ 214 Sean Burroughs .75 .30
❑ 215 Kenny Lofton .75 .30
❑ 216 Scott Rolen 1.25 .50
❑ 217 Carl Crawford .75 .30
❑ 218 Juan Gonzalez .75 .30
❑ 219 Orlando Hudson .75 .30
❑ 220 Eric Hinske .75 .30
❑ 221 Adam Walker AU RC 10.00 4.00
❑ 222 Aaron Cook AU RC 10.00 4.00
❑ 223 Cam Esslinger AU RC 10.00 4.00
❑ 224 Kirk Saarloos AU RC 10.00 4.00
❑ 225 Jose Diaz AU RC 10.00 4.00
❑ 226 David Ross AU RC 25.00 10.00
❑ 227 Jayson Durocher AU RC 10.00 4.00
❑ 228 Brian Mallette AU RC 10.00 4.00
❑ 229 Aaron Guiel AU RC 10.00 4.00
❑ 230 Jorge Nunez AU RC 10.00 4.00
❑ 231 Satoru Komiyama AU RC 25.00 10.00
❑ 232 Tyler Yates AU RC 10.00 4.00
❑ 233 Pete Zamora AU RC 10.00 4.00
❑ 234 Mike Gonzalez AU RC 10.00 4.00
❑ 235 Oliver Perez AU RC 25.00 10.00
❑ 236 Julius Matos AU RC 10.00 4.00
❑ 237 Andy Shibilo AU RC 10.00 4.00
❑ 238 Jason Simontacchi AU RC 10.00 4.00
❑ 239 Ron Chiavacci AU 10.00 4.00
❑ 240 Deivis Santos AU 10.00 4.00
❑ 241 Travis Driskill AU RC 10.00 4.00
❑ 242 Jorge De La Rosa AU RC 10.00 4.00
❑ 243 Anastacio Martinez AU RC 10.00 4.00
❑ 244 Earl Snyder AU RC 10.00 4.00
❑ 245 Freddy Sanchez AU RC 30.00 15.00
❑ 246 Miguel Asencio AU RC 10.00 4.00
❑ 247 Juan Brito AU RC 10.00 4.00
❑ 248 Franklyn German AU RC 10.00 4.00
❑ 249 Chris Snelling AU RC 15.00 6.00
❑ 250 Ken Huckaby AU RC 10.00 4.00

2003 SPx

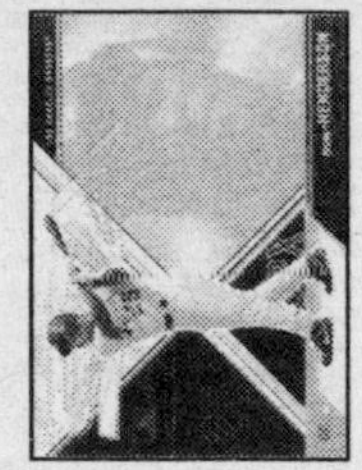

❑ COMP.LO SET w/o SP's (100) 25.00 10.00
❑ COMP.LO SET w/ SP's (125) 100.00 50.00
❑ COMMON CARD (1-125) .50 .20
❑ COMMON SP (1-125) 4.00 1.50
❑ COMMON CARD (126-160) 8.00 3.00

- ❑ COMMON CARD (161-178) 15.00 6.00
- ❑ 163-178 PRINT RUN 1224 SERIAL #'d SETS
- ❑ 126-178 RANDOM INSERTS IN SPx PACKS
- ❑ COMMON CARD (179-193) 15.00 6.00
- ❑ COMMON CARD (381-387) 15.00 6.00
- ❑ 1 Darin Erstad .50 .20
- ❑ 2 Garret Anderson .50 .20
- ❑ 3 Tim Salmon .75 .30
- ❑ 4 Troy Glaus SP 4.00 1.50
- ❑ 5 Luis Gonzalez .50 .20
- ❑ 6 Randy Johnson 1.25 .50
- ❑ 7 Curt Schilling .50 .20
- ❑ 8 Lyle Overbay .50 .20
- ❑ 9 Andruw Jones SP 4.00 1.50
- ❑ 10 Gary Sheffield .50 .20
- ❑ 11 Rafael Furcal .50 .20
- ❑ 12 Greg Maddux 2.00 .75
- ❑ 13 Chipper Jones SP 5.00 2.00
- ❑ 14 Tony Batista .50 .20
- ❑ 15 Rodrigo Lopez .50 .20
- ❑ 16 Jay Gibbons .50 .20
- ❑ 17 Byung-Hyun Kim .50 .20
- ❑ 18 Johnny Damon .75 .30
- ❑ 19 Derek Lowe .50 .20
- ❑ 20 Nomar Garciaparra SP 8.00 3.00
- ❑ 21 Pedro Martinez .75 .30
- ❑ 22 Manny Ramirez SP 4.00 1.50
- ❑ 23 Mark Prior .75 .30
- ❑ 24 Kerry Wood .50 .20
- ❑ 25 Corey Patterson .50 .20
- ❑ 26 Sammy Sosa SP 5.00 2.00
- ❑ 27 Moises Alou .50 .20
- ❑ 28 Magglio Ordonez .50 .20
- ❑ 29 Frank Thomas 1.25 .50
- ❑ 30 Paul Konerko .50 .20
- ❑ 31 Bartolo Colon .50 .20
- ❑ 32 Adam Dunn .50 .20
- ❑ 33 Austin Kearns .50 .20
- ❑ 34 Aaron Boone .50 .20
- ❑ 35 Ken Griffey Jr. SP 8.00 3.00
- ❑ 36 Omar Vizquel .75 .30
- ❑ 37 C.C. Sabathia .50 .20
- ❑ 38 Jason Davis .50 .20
- ❑ 39 Travis Hafner .50 .20
- ❑ 40 Brandon Phillips .50 .20
- ❑ 41 Larry Walker .50 .20
- ❑ 42 Preston Wilson .50 .20
- ❑ 43 Jay Payton .50 .20
- ❑ 44 Todd Helton .75 .30
- ❑ 45 Carlos Pena .50 .20
- ❑ 46 Eric Munson .50 .20
- ❑ 47 Ivan Rodriguez .75 .30
- ❑ 48 Josh Beckett .50 .20
- ❑ 49 Alex Gonzalez .50 .20
- ❑ 50 Roy Oswalt .50 .20
- ❑ 51 Craig Biggio .75 .30
- ❑ 52 Jeff Bagwell .75 .30
- ❑ 53 Dontrelle Willis SP 5.00 2.00
- ❑ 54 Mike Sweeney .50 .20
- ❑ 55 Carlos Beltran .50 .20
- ❑ 56 Brent Mayne .50 .20
- ❑ 57 Hideo Nomo 1.25 .50
- ❑ 58 Rickey Henderson 1.25 .50
- ❑ 59 Adrian Beltre .50 .20
- ❑ 60 Miguel Cabrera SP 5.00 2.00
- ❑ 61 Kazuhisa Ishii .50 .20
- ❑ 62 Ben Sheets .50 .20
- ❑ 63 Richie Sexson .50 .20
- ❑ 64 Torii Hunter SP 4.00 1.50
- ❑ 65 Jacque Jones .50 .20
- ❑ 66 Joe Mays .50 .20
- ❑ 67 Corey Koskie .50 .20
- ❑ 68 A.J. Pierzynski .50 .20
- ❑ 69 Jose Vidro .50 .20
- ❑ 70 Vladimir Guerrero SP 5.00 2.00
- ❑ 71 Tom Glavine .75 .30
- ❑ 72 Jose Reyes SP 4.00 1.50
- ❑ 73 Aaron Heilman .50 .20
- ❑ 74 Mike Piazza 2.00 .75
- ❑ 75 Jorge Posada .75 .30
- ❑ 76 Mike Mussina .75 .30
- ❑ 77 Robin Ventura .50 .20
- ❑ 78 Mariano Rivera 1.25 .50
- ❑ 79 Roger Clemens SP 10.00 4.00
- ❑ 80 Jason Giambi .50 .20
- ❑ 81 Bernie Williams .75 .30
- ❑ 82 Alfonso Soriano SP 4.00 1.50
- ❑ 83 Derek Jeter SP 12.00 5.00
- ❑ 84 Miguel Tejada SP 4.00 1.50
- ❑ 85 Eric Chavez .50 .20
- ❑ 86 Tim Hudson .50 .20
- ❑ 87 Barry Zito .50 .20
- ❑ 88 Mark Mulder .50 .20
- ❑ 89 Erubiel Durazo .50 .20
- ❑ 90 Pat Burrell .50 .20
- ❑ 91 Jim Thome SP 4.00 1.50
- ❑ 92 Bobby Abreu .50 .20
- ❑ 93 Brian Giles .50 .20
- ❑ 94 Reggie Sanders SP 4.00 1.50
- ❑ 95 Kenny Lofton .50 .20
- ❑ 96 Ryan Klesko .50 .20
- ❑ 97 Sean Burroughs .50 .20
- ❑ 98 Edgardo Alfonzo .50 .20
- ❑ 99 Rich Aurilia .50 .20
- ❑ 100 Jose Cruz Jr. .50 .20
- ❑ 101 Barry Bonds SP 12.00 5.00
- ❑ 102 Mike Cameron .50 .20
- ❑ 103 Kazuhiro Sasaki .50 .20
- ❑ 104 Bret Boone .50 .20
- ❑ 105 Ichiro Suzuki SP 10.00 4.00
- ❑ 106 J.D. Drew .50 .20
- ❑ 107 Jim Edmonds .50 .20
- ❑ 108 Scott Rolen SP 4.00 1.50
- ❑ 109 Matt Morris .50 .20
- ❑ 110 Tino Martinez .75 .30
- ❑ 111 Albert Pujols SP 10.00 4.00
- ❑ 112 Damian Rolls .50 .20
- ❑ 113 Carl Crawford .50 .20
- ❑ 114 Rocco Baldelli SP 4.00 1.50
- ❑ 115 Hank Blalock .50 .20
- ❑ 116 Alex Rodriguez SP 8.00 3.00
- ❑ 117 Kevin Mench .50 .20
- ❑ 118 Rafael Palmeiro .75 .30
- ❑ 119 Mark Teixeira .75 .30
- ❑ 120 Shannon Stewart .50 .20
- ❑ 121 Vernon Wells .50 .20
- ❑ 122 Josh Phelps .50 .20
- ❑ 123 Eric Hinske .50 .20
- ❑ 124 Orlando Hudson .50 .20
- ❑ 125 Carlos Delgado SP 4.00 1.50
- ❑ 126 Jason Roach ROO RC 8.00 3.00
- ❑ 127 Dan Haren ROO RC 10.00 4.00
- ❑ 128 Luis Ayala ROO RC 8.00 3.00
- ❑ 129 Bo Hart ROO RC 8.00 3.00
- ❑ 130 Wilfredo Ledezma ROO RC 8.00 3.00
- ❑ 131 Rick Roberts ROO RC 8.00 3.00
- ❑ 132 Miguel Ojeda ROO RC 8.00 3.00
- ❑ 133 Aquilino Lopez ROO RC 8.00 3.00
- ❑ 134 Roger Deago ROO RC 8.00 3.00
- ❑ 135 Arnie Munoz ROO RC 8.00 3.00
- ❑ 136 Brent Hoard ROO RC 8.00 3.00
- ❑ 137 Termel Sledge ROO RC 8.00 3.00
- ❑ 138 Ryan Cameron ROO RC 8.00 3.00
- ❑ 139 Prentice Redman ROO RC 8.00 3.00
- ❑ 140 Clint Barmes ROO RC 6.00 2.50
- ❑ 141 Jeremy Griffiths ROO RC 8.00 3.00
- ❑ 142 Jon Leicester ROO RC 8.00 3.00
- ❑ 143 Brandon Webb ROO RC 15.00 6.00
- ❑ 144 Todd Wellemeyer ROO RC 8.00 3.00
- ❑ 145 Felix Sanchez ROO RC 8.00 3.00
- ❑ 146 Anthony Ferrari ROO RC 8.00 3.00
- ❑ 147 Ian Ferguson ROO RC 8.00 3.00
- ❑ 148 Michael Nakamura ROO RC 8.00 3.00
- ❑ 149 Lew Ford ROO RC 10.00 4.00
- ❑ 150 Nate Bland ROO RC 8.00 3.00
- ❑ 151 David Matranga ROO RC 8.00 3.00
- ❑ 152 Edgar Gonzalez ROO RC 8.00 3.00
- ❑ 153 Carlos Mendez ROO RC 8.00 3.00
- ❑ 154 Jason Gilfillan ROO RC 8.00 3.00
- ❑ 155 Mike Neu ROO RC 8.00 3.00
- ❑ 156 Jason Shiell ROO RC 8.00 3.00
- ❑ 157 Jeff Duncan ROO RC 8.00 3.00
- ❑ 158 Oscar Villarreal ROO RC 8.00 3.00
- ❑ 159 Diegomar Markwell ROO RC 8.00 3.00
- ❑ 160 Joe Valentine ROO RC 8.00 3.00
- ❑ 161 Hideki Matsui AU JSY RC 400.00 275.00
- ❑ 162 Jose Contreras AU RC 40.00 20.00
- ❑ 163 Willie Eyre AU JSY RC 15.00 6.00
- ❑ 164 Matt Bruback AU JSY RC 15.00 6.00
- ❑ 165 Rett Johnson AU JSY RC 15.00 6.00
- ❑ 166 Jeremy Griffiths AU JSY 15.00 6.00
- ❑ 167 Fran Cruceta AU JSY RC 15.00 6.00
- ❑ 168 Fern Cabrera AU JSY RC 15.00 6.00
- ❑ 169 Jhonny Peralta AU JSY 25.00 10.00
- ❑ 170 Shane Bazzell AU JSY RC 15.00 6.00
- ❑ 171 Bob Madritsch AU JSY RC 25.00 10.00
- ❑ 172 Phil Seibel AU JSY RC 15.00 6.00
- ❑ 173 J.Willingham AU JSY RC 50.00 25.00
- ❑ 174 Rob Hammock AU JSY RC 15.00 6.00
- ❑ 175 A.Machado AU JSY RC 15.00 6.00
- ❑ 176 David Sanders AU JSY RC 15.00 6.00
- ❑ 177 Matt Kata AU JSY RC 15.00 6.00
- ❑ 178 Heath Bell AU JSY RC 15.00 6.00
- ❑ 179 Chad Gaudin ROO RC 15.00 6.00
- ❑ 180 Chris Capuano ROO RC 25.00 10.00
- ❑ 181 Danny Garcia ROO RC 15.00 6.00
- ❑ 182 Delmon Young ROO 80.00 50.00
- ❑ 183 Edwin Jackson ROO RC 20.00 8.00
- ❑ 184 Greg Jones ROO RC 15.00 6.00
- ❑ 185 Jeremy Bonderman ROO RC 50.00 20.00
- ❑ 186 Jorge DePaula ROO 15.00 6.00
- ❑ 187 Khalil Greene ROO 20.00 8.00
- ❑ 188 Chad Cordero ROO RC 25.00 10.00
- ❑ 189 Miguel Cabrera ROO 20.00 8.00
- ❑ 190 Rich Harden ROO 20.00 8.00
- ❑ 191 Rickie Weeks ROO 40.00 15.00
- ❑ 192 Rosman Garcia ROO RC 15.00 6.00
- ❑ 193 Tom Gregorio ROO RC 15.00 6.00
- ❑ 381 Andrew Brown AU JSY RC 15.00 6.00
- ❑ 382 Delm Young AU JSY RC 450.00 350.00
- ❑ 383 Colin Porter AU JSY RC 15.00 6.00
- ❑ 385 Rick. Weeks AU JSY RC 175.00 100.00
- ❑ 386 David Matranga AU JSY RC 15.00 6.00
- ❑ 387 Bo Hart AU JSY 15.00 6.00

2004 SPx

- ❑ COMP.SET w/o SP's (100) 25.00 10.00
- ❑ COMMON CARD (1-100) .50 .20
- ❑ COMMON CARD (101-110) 8.00 3.00
- ❑ 101-110 STATED ODDS 1:18
- ❑ COMMON CARD (111-145) 5.00 2.00
- ❑ 111-145 PRINT RUN 1599 SERIAL #'d SETS
- ❑ COMMON CARD (146-154) 8.00 3.00
- ❑ 146-154 PRINT RUN 499 SERIAL #'d SETS
- ❑ COMMON CARD (155-160) 8.00 3.00
- ❑ 155-160 PRINT RUN 299 SERIAL #'d SETS
- ❑ 111-160 ODDS W/SPECTRUM 1:9
- ❑ 161-202 ODDS W/SPECTRUM 1:18
- ❑ 161-202 PRINT RUN 799 SERIAL #'d SETS
- ❑ EXCHANGE DEADLINE 12/03/07
- ❑ MASTER PLATE ODDS 1:2500
- ❑ MASTER PLATE PRINT RUN 1 #'d SET
- ❑ NO PLATE PRICING DUE TO SCARCITY
- ❑ 1 Alfonso Soriano .50 .20
- ❑ 2 Todd Helton .75 .30
- ❑ 3 Andruw Jones .75 .30
- ❑ 4 Eric Gagne .50 .20
- ❑ 5 Craig Wilson .50 .20
- ❑ 6 Brian Giles .50 .20
- ❑ 7 Miguel Tejada .50 .20
- ❑ 8 Kevin Brown .50 .20
- ❑ 9 Shawn Green .50 .20
- ❑ 10 Ben Sheets .50 .20
- ❑ 11 John Smoltz .75 .30
- ❑ 12 Tim Hudson .50 .20
- ❑ 13 Jason Schmidt .50 .20
- ❑ 14 Paul Konerko .50 .20
- ❑ 15 Randy Johnson 1.25 .50
- ❑ 16 Roy Oswalt .50 .20
- ❑ 17 Mike Lowell .50 .20

❑ 18 Carlos Lee .50 .20
❑ 19 Sean Burroughs .50 .20
❑ 20 Edgar Renteria .50 .20
❑ 21 Michael Young .50 .20
❑ 22 Jose Vidro .50 .20
❑ 23 Scott Rolen .75 .30
❑ 24 Rafael Furcal .50 .20
❑ 25 Tom Glavine .75 .30
❑ 26 Scott Podsednik .50 .20
❑ 27 Gary Sheffield .50 .20
❑ 28 Eric Chavez .50 .20
❑ 29 Mark Prior .75 .30
❑ 30 Chipper Jones 1.25 .50
❑ 31 Frank Thomas 1.25 .50
❑ 32 Victor Martinez .50 .20
❑ 33 Jake Peavy .50 .20
❑ 34 Carlos Beltran .50 .20
❑ 35 Roy Halladay .50 .20
❑ 36 Mark Teixeira .75 .30
❑ 37 Jacque Jones .50 .20
❑ 38 Mike Sweeney .50 .20
❑ 39 Troy Glaus .50 .20
❑ 40 Pat Burrell .50 .20
❑ 41 Ichiro Suzuki 2.50 1.00
❑ 42 Vladimir Guerrero 1.25 .50
❑ 43 Bobby Abreu .50 .20
❑ 44 Jim Edmonds .50 .20
❑ 45 Garret Anderson .50 .20
❑ 46 J.D. Drew .50 .20
❑ 47 C.C. Sabathia .50 .20
❑ 48 Joe Mauer 1.25 .50
❑ 49 Phil Nevin .50 .20
❑ 50 Hank Blalock .50 .20
❑ 51 Carlos Zambrano .50 .20
❑ 52 Mike Piazza 2.00 .75
❑ 53 Manny Ramirez .75 .30
❑ 54 Lance Berkman .50 .20
❑ 55 Delmon Young .75 .30
❑ 56 Nomar Garciaparra 2.00 .75
❑ 57 Alex Rodriguez 2.00 .75
❑ 58 Rickie Weeks .50 .20
❑ 59 Adrian Beltre .50 .20
❑ 60 Albert Pujols 2.50 1.00
❑ 61 Richie Sexson .50 .20
❑ 62 Maggio Ordonez .50 .20
❑ 63 Derrek Lee .75 .30
❑ 64 Sammy Sosa 1.25 .50
❑ 65 Jason Giambi .50 .20
❑ 66 Curt Schilling .75 .30
❑ 67 Jorge Posada .75 .30
❑ 68 Rafael Palmeiro .75 .30
❑ 69 Jeff Kent .50 .20
❑ 70 Jose Reyes .50 .20
❑ 71 David Ortiz 1.25 .50
❑ 72 Aubrey Huff .50 .20
❑ 73 Jim Thome .75 .30
❑ 74 Andy Pettitte .75 .30
❑ 75 Barry Zito .50 .20
❑ 76 Carlos Delgado .50 .20
❑ 77 Hideki Matsui 2.00 .75
❑ 78 Sean Casey .50 .20
❑ 79 Luis Gonzalez .50 .20
❑ 80 Marcus Giles .50 .20
❑ 81 Preston Wilson .50 .20
❑ 82 Javy Lopez .50 .20
❑ 83 Mark Mulder .50 .20
❑ 84 Derek Jeter 2.50 1.00
❑ 85 Miguel Cabrera .75 .30
❑ 86 Vernon Wells .50 .20
❑ 87 Roger Clemens 2.50 1.00
❑ 88 Lyle Overbay .50 .20
❑ 89 Bret Boone .50 .20
❑ 90 Melvin Mora .50 .20
❑ 91 Greg Maddux 2.00 .75
❑ 92 Kerry Wood .50 .20
❑ 93 Ivan Rodriguez .75 .30
❑ 94 Pedro Martinez .75 .30
❑ 95 Jeff Bagwell .75 .30
❑ 96 Torii Hunter .50 .20
❑ 97 Ken Griffey Jr. 2.00 .75
❑ 98 Mike Mussina .75 .30
❑ 99 Oliver Perez .50 .20
❑ 100 Josh Beckett .50 .20
❑ 101 Bob Gibson LGD 8.00 3.00
❑ 102 Cal Ripken LGD 15.00 6.00
❑ 103 Ted Williams LGD 8.00 3.00
❑ 104 Nolan Ryan LGD 10.00 4.00
❑ 105 Mickey Mantle LGD 15.00 6.00
❑ 106 Ernie Banks LGD 8.00 3.00
❑ 107 Joe DiMaggio LGD 8.00 3.00
❑ 108 Stan Musial LGD 8.00 3.00
❑ 109 Tom Seaver LGD 8.00 3.00
❑ 110 Mike Schmidt LGD 10.00 4.00
❑ 111 Jerry Gil T1 RC 5.00 2.00
❑ 112 Dioner Navarro T1 RC 8.00 3.00
❑ 113 Bartolome Fortunato T1 RC 5.00 2.00
❑ 114 Carlos Hines T1 RC 5.00 2.00
❑ 115 Franklyn Gracesqui T1 RC 5.00 2.00
❑ 116 Aarom Baldiris T1 RC 8.00 3.00
❑ 117 Casey Daigle T1 RC 5.00 2.00
❑ 118 Joey Gathright T1 RC 8.00 3.00
❑ 119 William Bergolla T1 RC 5.00 2.00
❑ 120 Jeff Bennett T1 RC 5.00 2.00
❑ 121 Lincoln Holdzkom T1 RC 5.00 2.00
❑ 122 Jorge Vasquez T1 RC 5.00 2.00
❑ 123 Donnie Kelly T1 RC 5.00 2.00
❑ 124 Yadier Molina T1 RC 8.00 3.00
❑ 125 Ryan Wing T1 RC 5.00 2.00
❑ 126 Justin Germano T1 RC 5.00 2.00
❑ 127 Freddy Guzman T1 RC 5.00 2.00
❑ 128 Onil Joseph T1 RC 5.00 2.00
❑ 129 Roman Colon T1 RC 5.00 2.00
❑ 130 Roberto Novoa T1 RC 8.00 3.00
❑ 131 Renyel Pinto T1 RC 8.00 3.00
❑ 132 Evan Rust T1 RC 5.00 2.00
❑ 133 Orlando Rodriguez T1 RC 5.00 2.00
❑ 134 Edwardo Sierra T1 RC 8.00 3.00
❑ 135 Mike Rose T1 RC 5.00 2.00
❑ 136 Phil Stockman T1 RC 5.00 2.00
❑ 137 Greg Dobbs T1 RC 5.00 2.00
❑ 138 Brad Halsey T1 RC 8.00 3.00
❑ 139 David Aardsma T1 RC 8.00 3.00
❑ 140 Joe Hietpas T1 RC 5.00 2.00
❑ 141 Josh Labandeira T1 RC 5.00 2.00
❑ 142 Mariano Gomez T1 RC 5.00 2.00
❑ 143 Jeff Bajenaru T1 RC 5.00 2.00
❑ 144 Travis Blackley T1 RC 5.00 2.00
❑ 145 Abe Alvarez T1 RC 8.00 3.00
❑ 146 Ramon Ramirez T2 RC 8.00 3.00
❑ 147 Edwin Moreno T2 RC 10.00 4.00
❑ 148 Ronny Cedeno T2 RC 10.00 4.00
❑ 149 Hector Gimenez T2 RC 8.00 3.00
❑ 150 Carlos Vasquez T2 RC 10.00 4.00
❑ 151 Jesse Crain T2 RC 15.00 6.00
❑ 152 Logan Kensing T2 RC 8.00 3.00
❑ 153 Sean Henn T2 RC 8.00 3.00
❑ 154 Rusty Tucker T2 RC 10.00 4.00
❑ 155 Justin Lehr T3 RC 8.00 3.00
❑ 156 Ian Snell T3 RC 10.00 4.00
❑ 157 Merkin Valdez T3 RC 8.00 3.00
❑ 158 Scott Proctor T3 RC 10.00 4.00
❑ 159 Jose Capellan T3 RC 10.00 4.00
❑ 160 Kazuo Matsui T3 RC 8.00 3.00
❑ 161 Chris Oxspring AU JSY RC 15.00 6.00
❑ 162 Jimmy Serrano AU JSY RC 15.00 6.00
❑ 163 Jeff Keppinger AU JSY RC 15.00 6.00
❑ 164 B.Medders AU JSY RC 15.00 6.00
❑ 165 Brian Dallimore AU JSY RC 15.00 6.00
❑ 166 Chad Bentz AU JSY RC 15.00 6.00
❑ 167 Chris Aguila AU JSY RC 15.00 6.00
❑ 168 Chris Saenz AU JSY RC 15.00 6.00
❑ 169 Frank Francisco AU JSY RC 15.00 6.00
❑ 170 Colby Miller AU JSY RC 15.00 6.00
❑ 171 D.Crouth AU JSY RC EXCH 15.00 6.00
❑ 172 Charles Thomas AU JSY RC 15.00 6.00
❑ 173 Dennis Sarfate AU JSY RC 15.00 6.00
❑ 174 Lance Cormier AU JSY RC 15.00 6.00
❑ 175 Joe Horgan AU JSY RC 15.00 6.00
❑ 176 Fernando Nieve AU JSY RC 15.00 6.00
❑ 177 Jake Woods AU JSY RC 15.00 6.00
❑ 178 Matt Treanor AU JSY RC 15.00 6.00
❑ 179 Jerome Gamble AU JSY RC 15.00 6.00
❑ 180 John Gall AU JSY RC 25.00 10.00
❑ 181 Jorge Sequea AU JSY RC 15.00 6.00
❑ 182 Justin Hampson AU JSY RC 15.00 6.00
❑ 183 Justin Huisman AU JSY RC 15.00 6.00
❑ 184 Justin Knoedler AU JSY RC 15.00 6.00
❑ 185 Justin Leone AU JSY RC 25.00 10.00
❑ 186 Scott Atchison AU JSY RC 15.00 6.00
❑ 187 Jon Knott AU JSY RC 15.00 6.00
❑ 188 Kevin Cave AU JSY RC 15.00 6.00
❑ 189 Jason Frasor AU JSY RC 15.00 6.00
❑ 190 George Sherrill AU JSY RC 15.00 6.00
❑ 191 Mike Gosling AU JSY RC 15.00 6.00
❑ 192 Mike Johnston AU JSY RC 15.00 6.00
❑ 193 Mike Rouse AU JSY RC 15.00 6.00
❑ 194 Nick Regilio AU JSY RC 15.00 6.00
❑ 195 Ryan Meaux AU JSY RC 15.00 6.00
❑ 196 Scott Dohmann AU JSY RC 15.00 6.00
❑ 197 Shawn Camp AU JSY RC 15.00 6.00
❑ 198 Shawn Hill AU JSY RC 15.00 6.00
❑ 199 Shingo Takatsu AU JSY RC 15.00 6.00
❑ 200 Tim Bausher AU JSY RC 15.00 6.00
❑ 201 Tim Bittner AU JSY RC 15.00 6.00
❑ 202 Scott Kazmir AU JSY RC 50.00 20.00

2005 SPx

❑ COMP.BASIC SET (100) 25.00 10.00
❑ COMMON CARD (1-100) .40 .15
❑ COMMON RC (1-100) .40 .15
❑ 1-100 ISSUED IN 05 SP COLLECTION PACKS
❑ COMMON AUTO (101-180) 10.00 4.00
❑ 101-180 ODDS APPX 1:8 '05 UD UPDATE
❑ 101-180 PRINT RUN 185 SERIAL #'d SETS
❑ 105, 117, 139, 149, 155, 172 DO NOT EXIST
❑ 175, 178, 180 DO NOT EXIST
❑ 1 Aaron Harang .40 .15
❑ 2 Aaron Rowand .40 .15
❑ 3 Aaron Miles .40 .15
❑ 4 Adrian Gonzalez .40 .15
❑ 5 Alex Rios .40 .15
❑ 6 Angel Berroa .40 .15
❑ 7 B.J. Upton .40 .15
❑ 8 Brandon Claussen .40 .15
❑ 9 Andy Marte .40 .15
❑ 10 Brandon Webb .40 .15
❑ 11 Bronson Arroyo .40 .15
❑ 12 Casey Kotchman .40 .15
❑ 13 Cesar Izturis .40 .15
❑ 14 Chad Cordero .40 .15
❑ 15 Chad Tracy .40 .15
❑ 16 Charles Thomas .40 .15
❑ 17 Chase Utley .60 .25
❑ 18 Chone Figgins .40 .15
❑ 19 Chris Burke .40 .15
❑ 20 Cliff Lee .40 .15
❑ 21 Clint Barmes .40 .15
❑ 22 Coco Crisp .40 .15
❑ 23 Bill Hall .40 .15
❑ 24 Dallas McPherson .40 .15
❑ 25 Brad Halsey .40 .15
❑ 26 Daniel Cabrera .40 .15
❑ 27 Danny Haren .40 .15
❑ 28 Dave Bush .40 .15
❑ 29 David DeJesus .40 .15
❑ 30 D.J. Houlton RC .60 .25
❑ 31 Derek Jeter 2.00 .75
❑ 32 Dewon Brazelton .40 .15
❑ 33 Edwin Jackson .40 .15
❑ 34 Brad Hawpe .40 .15
❑ 35 Brandon Inge .40 .15
❑ 36 Brett Myers .40 .15
❑ 37 Garrett Atkins .40 .15
❑ 38 Gavin Floyd .40 .15
❑ 39 Grady Sizemore .60 .25
❑ 40 Guillermo Mota .40 .15
❑ 41 Carlos Guillen .40 .15
❑ 42 Gustavo Chacin .40 .15
❑ 43 Huston Street .60 .25
❑ 44 Chris Duffy .40 .15

❑ 45 J.D. Closser .40 .15
❑ 46 J.J. Hardy .40 .15
❑ 47 Jason Bartlett .40 .15
❑ 48 Jason DuBois .40 .15
❑ 49 Chris Shelton .60 .25
❑ 50 Jason Lane .40 .15
❑ 51 Jayson Werth .40 .15
❑ 52 Jeff Baker .40 .15
❑ 53 Jeff Francis .40 .15
❑ 54 Jeremy Bonderman .40 .15
❑ 55 Jeremy Reed .40 .15
❑ 56 Jerome Williams .40 .15
❑ 57 Jesse Crain .40 .15
❑ 58 Chris Young .40 .15
❑ 59 Jhonny Peralta .40 .15
❑ 60 Joe Blanton .40 .15
❑ 61 Joe Crede .40 .15
❑ 62 Joel Pineiro .40 .15
❑ 63 Joey Gathright .40 .15
❑ 64 John Buck .40 .15
❑ 65 Jonny Gomes .40 .15
❑ 66 Jorge Cantu .40 .15
❑ 67 Dan Johnson .40 .15
❑ 68 Jose Valverde .40 .15
❑ 69 Ervin Santana .40 .15
❑ 70 Justin Morneau .40 .15
❑ 71 Keiichi Yabu RC .60 .25
❑ 72 Ken Griffey Jr. 1.50 .60
❑ 73 Jason Repko .40 .15
❑ 74 Kevin Youkilis .40 .15
❑ 75 Koyie Hill .40 .15
❑ 76 Laynce Nix .40 .15
❑ 77 Luke Scott RC 2.00 .75
❑ 78 Juan Rivera .40 .15
❑ 79 Justin Duchscherer .40 .15
❑ 80 Mark Teahen .40 .15
❑ 81 Lance Niekro .40 .15
❑ 82 Michael Cuddyer .40 .15
❑ 83 Nick Swisher .40 .15
❑ 84 Noah Lowry .40 .15
❑ 85 Matt Holliday .40 .15
❑ 86 Reed Johnson .40 .15
❑ 87 Rich Harden .40 .15
❑ 88 Robb Quinlan .40 .15
❑ 89 Nick Johnson .40 .15
❑ 90 Ryan Howard 2.50 1.00
❑ 91 Nook Logan .40 .15
❑ 92 Steve Schmoll RC .60 .25
❑ 93 Tadahito Iguchi RC 4.00 1.50
❑ 94 Willy Taveras .40 .15
❑ 95 Wily Mo Pena .40 .15
❑ 96 Xavier Nady .40 .15
❑ 97 Yadier Molina .40 .15
❑ 98 Yhency Brazoban .40 .15
❑ 99 Ryan Freel .40 .15
❑ 100 Zack Greinke .40 .15
❑ 101 Adam Shabala AU RC 10.00 4.00
❑ 102 Ambiorix Burgos AU RC 10.00 4.00
❑ 103 Ambiorix Concepcion AU RC 10.00 4.00
❑ 104 Anibal Sanchez AU RC 60.00 30.00
❑ 106 Brandon McCarthy AU RC 30.0012.50
❑ 107 Brian Burres AU RC 10.00 4.00
❑ 108 Carlos Ruiz AU RC 15.00 6.00
❑ 109 Casey Rogowski AU RC 15.00 6.00
❑ 110 Chad Orvella AU RC 10.00 4.00
❑ 111 Chris Resop AU RC 15.00 6.00
❑ 112 Chris Roberson AU RC 10.00 4.00
❑ 113 Chris Seddon AU RC 10.00 4.00
❑ 114 Colter Bean AU RC 15.00 6.00
❑ 115 Dave Gassner AU RC 10.00 4.00
❑ 116 Brian Anderson AU RC 40.00 15.00
❑ 118 Devon Lowery AU RC 10.00 4.00
❑ 119 Enrique Gonzalez AU RC 15.00 6.00
❑ 120 Eude Brito AU RC 10.00 4.00
❑ 121 Francisco Butto AU RC 10.00 4.00
❑ 122 Franquelis Osoria AU RC 10.00 4.00
❑ 123 Garrett Jones AU RC 10.00 4.00
❑ 124 Geovany Soto AU RC 10.00 4.00
❑ 125 Hayden Penn AU RC 20.00 8.00
❑ 126 Ismael Ramirez AU RC 10.00 4.00
❑ 127 Jared Gothreaux AU RC 10.00 4.00
❑ 128 Jason Hammel AU RC 10.00 4.00
❑ 129 Jeff Miller AU RC 10.00 4.00
❑ 130 Jeff Niemann AU RC 20.00 8.00
❑ 131 Joel Peralta AU RC 10.00 4.00
❑ 132 John Hattig AU RC 10.00 4.00
❑ 133 Jorge Campillo AU RC 10.00 4.00
❑ 134 Juan Morillo AU RC 10.00 4.00
❑ 135 Justin Verlander AU RC 150.00 90.00
❑ 136 Ryan Garko AU RC 40.00 15.00
❑ 137 Kendry Morales AU RC 80.00 40.00
❑ 138 Luis Hernandez AU RC 10.00 4.00
❑ 140 Luis O.Rodriguez AU RC 10.00 4.00
❑ 141 Mark Woodyard AU RC 10.00 4.00
❑ 142 Matt A.Smith AU RC 10.00 4.00
❑ 143 Matthew Lindstrom AU RC 10.00 4.00
❑ 144 Miguel Negron AU RC 15.00 6.00
❑ 145 Mike Morse AU RC 15.00 6.00
❑ 146 Nate McLouth AU RC 15.00 6.00
❑ 147 Nelson Cruz AU RC 40.00 15.00
❑ 148 Nick Masset AU RC 10.00 4.00
❑ 150 Paulino Reynoso AU RC 10.00 4.00
❑ 151 Pedro Lopez AU RC 10.00 4.00
❑ 152 Philip Humber AU RC 25.00 10.00
❑ 153 Prince Fielder AU RC 125.00 75.00
❑ 154 Randy Messenger AU RC 10.00 4.00
❑ 156 Raul Tablado AU RC 10.00 4.00
❑ 157 Ronny Paulino AU RC 15.00 6.00
❑ 158 Russ Rohlicek AU RC 10.00 4.00
❑ 159 Russell Martin AU RC 40.00 15.00
❑ 160 Scott Baker AU RC 15.00 6.00
❑ 161 Scott Munter AU RC 10.00 4.00
❑ 162 Sean Thompson AU RC 10.00 4.00
❑ 163 Sean Tracey AU RC 10.00 4.00
❑ 164 Shane Costa AU RC 10.00 4.00
❑ 165 Stephen Drew AU RC 125.00 75.00
❑ 166 Tony Giarratano AU RC 10.00 4.00
❑ 167 Tony Pena AU RC 10.00 4.00
❑ 168 Travis Bowyer AU RC 10.00 4.00
❑ 169 Ubaldo Jimenez AU RC 15.00 6.00
❑ 170 Wladimir Balentien AU RC 20.00 8.00
❑ 171 Yorman Bazardo AU RC 10.00 4.00
❑ 173 Ryan Zimmerman AU RC 150.0090.00
❑ 174 Chris Denorfia AU RC 15.00 6.00
❑ 176 Jermaine Van Buren AU 10.00 4.00
❑ 177 Mark McLemore AU RC 10.00 4.00
❑ 179 Ryan Speier AU RC 10.00 4.00

2006 SPx

❑ COMP.BASIC SET (100) 25.00 10.00
❑ COMMON CARD (1-100) .40 .15
❑ COMMON AU p/r 659-999 10.00 4.00
❑ AU UNLISTED p/r 659-999 20.00 8.00
❑ COMMON AU p/r 350-500 10.00 4.00
❑ OVERALL 101-161 AU ODDS 1:9
❑ 101-161 AU EXCH DEADLINE 09/07/08
❑ 101-161 AU PRINT RUN B/WN 190-999 PER
❑ 101-161 PRINTING PLATE ODDS 1:224
❑ 101-161 PLATES PRINT RUN 1 SET PER CLR
❑ 101-161 PLATES FEATURE AUTOS
❑ BLACK-CYAN-MAGENTA-YELLOW ISSUED
❑ NO PLATE PRICING DUE TO SCARCITY
❑ EXQUISITE EXCH ODDS 1:36
❑ EXQUISITE EXCH DEADLINE 07/27/07
❑ 1 Luis Gonzalez .40 .15
❑ 2 Chad Tracy .40 .15
❑ 3 Brandon Webb .40 .15
❑ 4 Andruw Jones .60 .25
❑ 5 Chipper Jones 1.00 .40
❑ 6 John Smoltz .60 .25
❑ 7 Tim Hudson .40 .15
❑ 8 Miguel Tejada .40 .15
❑ 9 Brian Roberts .40 .15
❑ 10 Ramon Hernandez .40 .15
❑ 11 Curt Schilling .60 .25
❑ 12 David Ortiz 1.00 .40
❑ 13 Manny Ramirez .60 .25
❑ 14 Jason Varitek 1.00 .40
❑ 15 Josh Beckett .40 .15
❑ 16 Greg Maddux 1.50 .60
❑ 17 Derrek Lee .40 .15
❑ 18 Mark Prior .60 .25
❑ 19 Aramis Ramirez .40 .15
❑ 20 Jim Thome .60 .25
❑ 21 Paul Konerko .40 .15
❑ 22 Scott Podsednik .40 .15
❑ 23 Jose Contreras .40 .15
❑ 24 Ken Griffey Jr. 1.50 .60
❑ 25 Adam Dunn .40 .15
❑ 26 Felipe Lopez .40 .15
❑ 27 Travis Hafner .40 .15
❑ 28 Victor Martinez .40 .15
❑ 29 Grady Sizemore .60 .25
❑ 30 Jhonny Peralta .40 .15
❑ 31 Todd Helton .60 .25
❑ 32 Garrett Atkins .40 .15
❑ 33 Clint Barmes .40 .15
❑ 34 Ivan Rodriguez .60 .25
❑ 35 Chris Shelton .40 .15
❑ 36 Jeremy Bonderman .40 .15
❑ 37 Miguel Cabrera .60 .25
❑ 38 Dontrelle Willis .40 .15
❑ 39 Lance Berkman .40 .15
❑ 40 Morgan Ensberg .40 .15
❑ 41 Roy Oswalt .40 .15
❑ 42 Reggie Sanders .40 .15
❑ 43 Mike Sweeney .40 .15
❑ 44 Vladimir Guerrero 1.00 .40
❑ 45 Bartolo Colon .40 .15
❑ 46 Chone Figgins .40 .15
❑ 47 Nomar Garciaparra 1.00 .40
❑ 48 Jeff Kent .40 .15
❑ 49 J.D. Drew .40 .15
❑ 50 Carlos Lee .40 .15
❑ 51 Ben Sheets .40 .15
❑ 52 Rickie Weeks .40 .15
❑ 53 Johan Santana .60 .25
❑ 54 Torii Hunter .40 .15
❑ 55 Joe Mauer .60 .25
❑ 56 Pedro Martinez .60 .25
❑ 57 David Wright 1.50 .60
❑ 58 Carlos Beltran .40 .15
❑ 59 Carlos Delgado .40 .15
❑ 60 Jose Reyes .40 .15
❑ 61 Derek Jeter 2.50 1.00
❑ 62 Alex Rodriguez 1.50 .60
❑ 63 Randy Johnson 1.00 .40
❑ 64 Hideki Matsui 1.00 .40
❑ 65 Gary Sheffield .40 .15
❑ 66 Rich Harden .40 .15
❑ 67 Eric Chavez .40 .15
❑ 68 Huston Street .40 .15
❑ 69 Bobby Crosby .40 .15
❑ 70 Bobby Abreu .40 .15
❑ 71 Ryan Howard 1.50 .60
❑ 72 Chase Utley 1.00 .40
❑ 73 Pat Burrell .40 .15
❑ 74 Jason Bay .40 .15
❑ 75 Sean Casey .40 .15
❑ 76 Mike Piazza 1.00 .40
❑ 77 Jake Peavy .40 .15
❑ 78 Brian Giles .40 .15
❑ 79 Milton Bradley .40 .15
❑ 80 Omar Vizquel .60 .25
❑ 81 Jason Schmidt .40 .15
❑ 82 Ichiro Suzuki 1.50 .60
❑ 83 Felix Hernandez .60 .25
❑ 84 Richie Sexson .40 .15
❑ 85 Albert Pujols 2.00 .75
❑ 86 Chris Carpenter .40 .15
❑ 87 Scott Rolen .60 .25
❑ 88 Jim Edmonds .60 .25
❑ 89 Carl Crawford .40 .15
❑ 90 Jonny Gomes .40 .15
❑ 91 Scott Kazmir .60 .25
❑ 92 Mark Teixeira .60 .25
❑ 93 Michael Young .40 .15
❑ 94 Phil Nevin .40 .15
❑ 95 Vernon Wells .40 .15
❑ 96 Roy Halladay .40 .15

❑ 97 Troy Glaus .40 .15
❑ 98 Alfonso Soriano .40 .15
❑ 99 Nick Johnson .40 .15
❑ 100 Jose Vidro .40 .15
❑ 101 Conor Jackson AU/999 (RC) 15.00 6.00
❑ 102 J.Weaver AU/299 (RC) EXCH 50.00 20.00
❑ 103 Macay McBride AU/999 (RC) 10.00 4.00
❑ 104 Aaron Rakers AU/499 (RC) 10.00 4.00
❑ 105 J.Papelbon AU/499 (RC) 50.00 20.00
❑ 106 J.Bergmann AU/999 RC 10.00 4.00
❑ 107 S.Drew AU/350 (RC) 50.00 20.00
❑ 108 Chris Denorfia AU/999 (RC) 10.00 4.00
❑ 109 Kelly Shoppach AU/999 (RC) 10.00 4.00
❑ 110 Ryan Shealy AU/999 (RC) 10.00 4.00
❑ 111 Josh Wilson AU/999 (RC) 10.00 4.00
❑ 112 Brian Anderson AU/999 (RC) 10.00 4.00
❑ 113 J.Verlander AU/749 (RC) 40.00 15.00
❑ 114 J.Hermida AU/999 (RC) 15.00 6.00
❑ 115 Mike Jacobs AU/999 (RC) 10.00 4.00
❑ 116 Josh Johnson AU/999 (RC) 15.00 6.00
❑ 117 Hanley Ramirez AU/659 (RC) 20.00 8.00
❑ 118 Chris Resop AU/999 (RC) 10.00 4.00
❑ 119 J.Willingham AU/999 (RC) 10.00 4.00
❑ 120 Cole Hamels AU/499 (RC) 40.00 15.00
❑ 121 Matt Cain AU/999 (RC) 20.00 8.00
❑ 122 Steve Stemle AU/999 RC 10.00 4.00
❑ 123 Tim Hamulack AU/999 (RC) 10.00 4.00
❑ 124 Choo Freeman AU/999 (RC) 10.00 4.00
❑ 125 H.Kuo AU/999 (RC) 50.00 20.00
❑ 126 Cody Ross AU/999 (RC) 10.00 4.00
❑ 127 Jose Capellan AU/999 (RC) 10.00 4.00
❑ 128 Prince Fielder AU/190 (RC) 50.00 20.00
❑ 129 David Gassner AU/999 (RC) 10.00 4.00
❑ 130 Jason Kubel AU/999 (RC) 10.00 4.00
❑ 131 F.Liriano AU/299 (RC) 60.00 30.00
❑ 132 A.Hernandez AU/999 (RC) 10.00 4.00
❑ 133 Joey Devine AU/499 RC 10.00 4.00
❑ 134 Chris Booker AU/999 (RC) 10.00 4.00
❑ 135 Matt Capps AU/999 (RC) 10.00 4.00
❑ 136 Paul Maholm AU/999 (RC) 10.00 4.00
❑ 137 Nate McLouth AU/999 (RC) 10.00 4.00
❑ 138 J.Van Benschoten AU/999 (RC) 10.00 4.00
❑ 139 Jeff Harris AU/999 RC 10.00 4.00
❑ 140 Ben Johnson AU/999 (RC) 10.00 4.00
❑ 141 Wil Nieves AU/999 (RC) 10.00 4.00
❑ 142 G.Quiroz AU/999 (RC) 10.00 4.00
❑ 143 Josh Rupe AU/500 (RC) 10.00 4.00
❑ 144 Skip Schumaker AU/999 (RC) 10.00 4.00
❑ 145 Jack Taschner AU/999 (RC) 10.00 4.00
❑ 146 A.Wainwright AU/999 (RC) 15.00 6.00
❑ 147 Alay Soler AU/499 RC 25.00 10.00
❑ 148 Kendry Morales AU/999 (RC) 15.00 6.00
❑ 149 Ian Kinsler AU/999 (RC) 15.00 6.00
❑ 150 Jason Hammel AU/999 (RC) 10.00 4.00
❑ 151 C.Billingsley AU/499 (RC) 25.00 10.00
❑ 152 Boof Bonser AU/999 (RC) 15.00 6.00
❑ 153 Peter Moylan AU/999 RC 10.00 4.00
❑ 154 Chris Britton AU/999 RC 10.00 4.00
❑ 155 Takashi Saito AU/999 RC 50.00 20.00
❑ 156 Scott Dunn AU/999 (RC) 10.00 4.00
❑ 157 J.Zumaya AU/299 (RC) EXCH 30.00 12.50
❑ 158 Dan Uggla AU/999 (RC) 30.00 12.50
❑ 159 Taylor Buchholz AU/999 (RC) 10.00 4.00
❑ 160 M.Cabrera AU/499 (RC) EXCH 40.00 15.00
❑ NNO Exquisite Redemption 200.00 125.00

2001 Sweet Spot

❑ COMP.BASIC w/o SP's (60) 20.00 8.00
❑ COMP.UPDATE w/o SP's (30) 10.00 4.00
❑ COMMON CARD (1-60) .40 .15
❑ COMMON CARD (61-90) 10.00 4.00
❑ COMMON CARD (91-120) .60 .25
❑ COMMON CARD (121-150) 5.00 2.00
❑ 1 Troy Glaus .40 .15
❑ 2 Darin Erstad .40 .15
❑ 3 Jason Giambi .40 .15
❑ 4 Tim Hudson .40 .15
❑ 5 Ben Grieve .40 .15
❑ 6 Carlos Delgado .40 .15
❑ 7 David Wells .40 .15
❑ 8 Greg Vaughn .40 .15
❑ 9 Roberto Alomar .60 .25
❑ 10 Jim Thome .60 .25
❑ 11 John Olerud .40 .15
❑ 12 Edgar Martinez .60 .25
❑ 13 Cal Ripken 3.00 1.25
❑ 14 Albert Belle .40 .15
❑ 15 Ivan Rodriguez .60 .25
❑ 16 Alex Rodriguez Rangers 3.00 1.25
❑ 17 Pedro Martinez .60 .25
❑ 18 Nomar Garciaparra 1.50 .60
❑ 19 Manny Ramirez .60 .25
❑ 20 Jermaine Dye .40 .15
❑ 21 Juan Gonzalez .40 .15
❑ 22 Dean Palmer .40 .15
❑ 23 Matt Lawton .40 .15
❑ 24 Eric Milton .40 .15
❑ 25 Frank Thomas 1.00 .40
❑ 26 Magglio Ordonez .40 .15
❑ 27 Derek Jeter 2.50 1.00
❑ 28 Bernie Williams .60 .25
❑ 29 Roger Clemens 2.00 .75
❑ 30 Jeff Bagwell .60 .25
❑ 31 Richard Hidalgo .40 .15
❑ 32 Chipper Jones 1.00 .40
❑ 33 Greg Maddux 1.50 .60
❑ 34 Richie Sexson .40 .15
❑ 35 Jeromy Burnitz .40 .15
❑ 36 Mark McGwire 2.50 1.00
❑ 37 Jim Edmonds .40 .15
❑ 38 Sammy Sosa 1.00 .40
❑ 39 Randy Johnson 1.00 .40
❑ 40 Steve Finley .40 .15
❑ 41 Gary Sheffield .40 .15
❑ 42 Shawn Green .40 .15
❑ 43 Vladimir Guerrero 1.00 .40
❑ 44 Jose Vidro .40 .15
❑ 45 Barry Bonds 2.50 1.00
❑ 46 Jeff Kent .40 .15
❑ 47 Preston Wilson .40 .15
❑ 48 Luis Castillo .40 .15
❑ 49 Mike Piazza 1.50 .60
❑ 50 Edgardo Alfonzo .40 .15
❑ 51 Tony Gwynn 1.25 .50
❑ 52 Ryan Klesko .40 .15
❑ 53 Scott Rolen .60 .25
❑ 54 Bob Abreu .40 .15
❑ 55 Jason Kendall .40 .15
❑ 56 Brian Giles .40 .15
❑ 57 Ken Griffey Jr. 1.50 .60
❑ 58 Barry Larkin .60 .25
❑ 59 Todd Helton .60 .25
❑ 60 Mike Hampton UER .40 .15
❑ 61 Corey Patterson SB 10.00 4.00
❑ 62 Ichiro Suzuki SB RC 200.00 125.00
❑ 63 Jason Grilli SB 10.00 4.00
❑ 64 Brian Cole SB 10.00 4.00
❑ 65 Juan Pierre SB 10.00 4.00
❑ 66 Matt Ginter SB 10.00 4.00
❑ 67 Jimmy Rollins SB 10.00 4.00
❑ 68 Jason Smith SB RC 10.00 4.00
❑ 69 Israel Alcantara SB 10.00 4.00
❑ 70 Adam Pettyjohn SB RC 10.00 4.00
❑ 71 Luke Prokopec SB 10.00 4.00
❑ 72 Barry Zito SB 12.00 5.00
❑ 73 Keith Ginter SB 10.00 4.00
❑ 74 Sun Woo Kim SB 10.00 4.00
❑ 75 Ross Gload SB 10.00 4.00
❑ 76 Matt Wise SB 10.00 4.00
❑ 77 Aubrey Huff SB 10.00 4.00
❑ 78 Ryan Franklin SB 10.00 4.00
❑ 79 Brandon Inge SB 10.00 4.00
❑ 80 Wes Helms SB 10.00 4.00
❑ 81 Junior Spivey SB RC 12.00 5.00
❑ 82 Ryan Vogelsong SB 10.00 4.00
❑ 83 John Parrish SB 10.00 4.00
❑ 84 Joe Crede SB 12.00 5.00
❑ 85 Damian Rolls SB 10.00 4.00
❑ 86 Esix Snead SB RC 10.00 4.00
❑ 87 Rocky Biddle SB 10.00 4.00
❑ 88 Brady Clark SB 10.00 4.00
❑ 89 Timo Perez SB 10.00 4.00
❑ 90 Jay Spurgeon SB 10.00 4.00
❑ 91 Garret Anderson .60 .25
❑ 92 Jermaine Dye .60 .25
❑ 93 Shannon Stewart .60 .25
❑ 94 Ben Grieve .60 .25
❑ 95 Juan Gonzalez .60 .25
❑ 96 Brett Boone .60 .25
❑ 97 Tony Batista .60 .25
❑ 98 Rafael Palmeiro 1.00 .40
❑ 99 Carl Everett .60 .25
❑ 100 Mike Sweeney .60 .25
❑ 101 Tony Clark .60 .25
❑ 102 Doug Mientkiewicz .60 .25
❑ 103 Jose Canseco 1.00 .40
❑ 104 Mike Mussina 1.00 .40
❑ 105 Lance Berkman .60 .25
❑ 106 Andruw Jones 1.00 .40
❑ 107 Geoff Jenkins .60 .25
❑ 108 Matt Morris .60 .25
❑ 109 Fred McGriff 1.00 .40
❑ 110 Luis Gonzalez .60 .25
❑ 111 Kevin Brown .60 .25
❑ 112 Tony Armas Jr. .60 .25
❑ 113 John Vander Wal .60 .25
❑ 114 Cliff Floyd .60 .25
❑ 115 Matt Lawton .60 .25
❑ 116 Phil Nevin .60 .25
❑ 117 Pat Burrell .60 .25
❑ 118 Aramis Ramirez .60 .25
❑ 119 Sean Casey .60 .25
❑ 120 Larry Walker .60 .25
❑ 121 Albert Pujols SB RC 250.00 150.00
❑ 122 Johnny Estrada SB RC 5.00 2.00
❑ 123 Wilson Betemit SB RC 8.00 3.00
❑ 124 Adrian Hernandez SB RC 5.00 2.00
❑ 125 Morgan Ensberg SB RC 8.00 3.00
❑ 126 Horacio Ramirez SB RC 5.00 2.00
❑ 127 Josh Towers SB RC 5.00 2.00
❑ 128 Juan Uribe SB RC 5.00 2.00
❑ 129 Wilken Ruan SB RC 5.00 2.00
❑ 130 Andres Torres SB RC 5.00 2.00
❑ 131 Brian Lawrence SB RC 5.00 2.00
❑ 132 Ryan Freel SB RC 5.00 2.00
❑ 133 Brandon Duckworth SB RC 5.00 2.00
❑ 134 Juan Diaz SB RC 5.00 2.00
❑ 135 Rafael Soriano SB RC 5.00 2.00
❑ 136 Ricardo Rodriguez SB RC 5.00 2.00
❑ 137 Bud Smith SB RC 5.00 2.00
❑ 138 Mark Teixeira SB RC 30.00 12.50
❑ 139 Mark Prior SB RC 15.00 6.00
❑ 140 Jackson Melian SB RC 5.00 2.00
❑ 141 Dewon Brazelton SB RC 5.00 2.00
❑ 142 Greg Miller SB RC 5.00 2.00
❑ 143 Billy Sylvester SB RC 5.00 2.00
❑ 144 Elpidio Guzman SB RC 5.00 2.00
❑ 145 Jack Wilson SB RC 5.00 2.00
❑ 146 Jose Mieses SB RC 5.00 2.00
❑ 147 Brandon Lyon SB RC 5.00 2.00
❑ 148 Tsuyoshi Shinjo SB RC 5.00 2.00
❑ 149 Juan Cruz SB RC 5.00 2.00
❑ 150 Jay Gibbons SB RC 5.00 2.00

2002 Sweet Spot

❑ COMP.SET w/o SP's (90) 20.00 8.00
❑ COMMON CARD (1-90) .40 .15
❑ COMMON CARD (91-130) 4.00 1.50
❑ COMMON TIER 1 AU (131-145) 15.00 6.00
❑ COMMON TIER 2 AU (131-145) 25.00 10.00
❑ COMMON CARD (146-175) 10.00 4.00
❑ MCGWIRE AU EXCH.RANDOM IN PACKS
❑ 1 Troy Glaus .40 .15
❑ 2 Darin Erstad .40 .15
❑ 3 Tim Hudson .40 .15
❑ 4 Eric Chavez .40 .15
❑ 5 Barry Zito .40 .15
❑ 6 Miguel Tejada .40 .15
❑ 7 Carlos Delgado .40 .15

No.	Card		
❑ 8	Eric Hinske	.40	.15
❑ 9	Ben Grieve	.40	.15
❑ 10	Jim Thome	.60	.25
❑ 11	C.C. Sabathia	.40	.15
❑ 12	Omar Vizquel	.60	.25
❑ 13	Ichiro Suzuki	2.00	.75
❑ 14	Edgar Martinez	.60	.25
❑ 15	Bret Boone	.40	.15
❑ 16	Freddy Garcia	.40	.15
❑ 17	Tony Batista	.40	.15
❑ 18	Geronimo Gil	.40	.15
❑ 19	Alex Rodriguez	1.50	.60
❑ 20	Rafael Palmeiro	.60	.25
❑ 21	Ivan Rodriguez	.60	.25
❑ 22	Hank Blalock	.60	.25
❑ 23	Juan Gonzalez	.40	.15
❑ 24	Nomar Garciaparra	1.50	.60
❑ 25	Pedro Martinez	.60	.25
❑ 26	Manny Ramirez	.60	.25
❑ 27	Mike Sweeney	.40	.15
❑ 28	Carlos Beltran	.40	.15
❑ 29	Dmitri Young	.40	.15
❑ 30	Torii Hunter	.40	.15
❑ 31	Eric Milton	.40	.15
❑ 32	Corey Koskie	.40	.15
❑ 33	Frank Thomas	1.00	.40
❑ 34	Mark Buehrle	.40	.15
❑ 35	Magglio Ordonez	.40	.15
❑ 36	Roger Clemens	2.00	.75
❑ 37	Derek Jeter	2.50	1.00
❑ 38	Jason Giambi	.40	.15
❑ 39	Alfonso Soriano	.40	.15
❑ 40	Bernie Williams	.60	.25
❑ 41	Jeff Bagwell	.60	.25
❑ 42	Roy Oswalt	.40	.15
❑ 43	Lance Berkman	.40	.15
❑ 44	Greg Maddux	1.50	.60
❑ 45	Chipper Jones	1.00	.40
❑ 46	Gary Sheffield	.40	.15
❑ 47	Andruw Jones	.60	.25
❑ 48	Richie Sexson	.40	.15
❑ 49	Ben Sheets	.40	.15
❑ 50	Albert Pujols	2.00	.75
❑ 51	Matt Morris	.40	.15
❑ 52	J.D. Drew	.40	.15
❑ 53	Sammy Sosa	1.00	.40
❑ 54	Kerry Wood	.40	.15
❑ 55	Mark Prior	.60	25.00
❑ 56	Moises Alou	.40	.15
❑ 57	Corey Patterson	.40	.15
❑ 58	Randy Johnson	1.00	.40
❑ 59	Luis Gonzalez	.40	.15
❑ 60	Curt Schilling	.40	.15
❑ 61	Shawn Green	.40	.15
❑ 62	Kevin Brown	.40	.15
❑ 63	Paul Lo Duca	.40	.15
❑ 64	Adrian Beltre	.40	.15
❑ 65	Vladimir Guerrero	1.00	.40
❑ 66	Jose Vidro	.40	.15
❑ 67	Javier Vazquez	.40	.15
❑ 68	Barry Bonds	2.50	1.00
❑ 69	Jeff Kent	.40	.15
❑ 70	Rich Aurilia	.40	.15
❑ 71	Mike Lowell	.40	.15
❑ 72	Josh Beckett	.40	.15
❑ 73	Brad Penny	.40	.15
❑ 74	Roberto Alomar	.60	.25
❑ 75	Mike Piazza	1.50	.60
❑ 76	Jeromy Burnitz	.40	.15
❑ 77	Mo Vaughn	.40	.15
❑ 78	Phil Nevin	.40	.15
❑ 79	Sean Burroughs	.40	.15
❑ 80	Jeremy Giambi	.40	.15
❑ 81	Bobby Abreu	.40	.15
❑ 82	Jimmy Rollins	.40	.15
❑ 83	Pat Burrell	.40	.15
❑ 84	Brian Giles	.40	.15
❑ 85	Aramis Ramirez	.40	.15
❑ 86	Ken Griffey Jr.	1.50	.60
❑ 87	Adam Dunn	.40	.15
❑ 88	Austin Kearns	.40	.15
❑ 89	Todd Helton	.60	.25
❑ 90	Larry Walker	.40	.15
❑ 91	Earl Snyder SB RC	4.00	1.50
❑ 92	Jorge Padilla SB RC	4.00	1.50
❑ 93	Felix Escalona SB RC	4.00	1.50
❑ 94	John Foster SB RC	4.00	1.50
❑ 95	Brandon Puffer SB RC	4.00	1.50
❑ 96	Steve Bechler SB RC	4.00	1.50
❑ 97	Hansel Izquierdo SB RC	4.00	1.50
❑ 98	Chris Baker SB RC	4.00	1.50
❑ 99	Jeremy Ward SB RC	4.00	1.50
❑ 100	Kevin Frederick SB RC	4.00	1.50
❑ 101	Josh Hancock SB RC	4.00	1.50
❑ 102	Allan Simpson SB RC	4.00	1.50
❑ 103	Mitch Wylie SB RC	4.00	1.50
❑ 104	Mark Corey SB RC	4.00	1.50
❑ 105	Victor Alvarez SB RC	4.00	1.50
❑ 106	Todd Donovan SB RC	4.00	1.50
❑ 107	Nelson Castro SB RC	4.00	1.50
❑ 108	Chris Booker SB RC	4.00	1.50
❑ 109	Corey Thurman SB RC	4.00	1.50
❑ 110	Kirk Saarloos SB RC	4.00	1.50
❑ 111	Michael Crudale SB RC	4.00	1.50
❑ 112	Jason Simontacchi SB RC	4.00	1.50
❑ 113	Ron Calloway SB RC	4.00	1.50
❑ 114	Brandon Backe SB RC	5.00	2.00
❑ 115	Tom Shearn SB RC	4.00	1.50
❑ 116	Oliver Perez SB RC	5.00	2.00
❑ 117	Kyle Kane SB RC	4.00	1.50
❑ 118	Francis Beltran SB RC	4.00	1.50
❑ 119	So Taguchi SB RC	5.00	2.00
❑ 120	Doug Devore SB RC	4.00	1.50
❑ 121	Juan Brito SB RC	4.00	1.50
❑ 122	Cliff Bartosh SB RC	4.00	1.50
❑ 123	Eric Junge SB RC	4.00	1.50
❑ 124	Joe Orloski SB RC	4.00	1.50
❑ 125	Scotty Layfield SB RC	4.00	1.50
❑ 126	Jorge Sosa SB RC	5.00	2.00
❑ 127	Satoru Komiyama SB RC	4.00	1.50
❑ 128	Edwin Almonte SB RC	4.00	1.50
❑ 129	Takahito Nomura SB RC	4.00	1.50
❑ 130	John Ennis SB RC	4.00	1.50
❑ 131	Kazuhisa Ishii T2 AU RC	80.00	40.00
❑ 132	Ben Howard T2 AU RC	25.00	10.00
❑ 133	Aaron Cook T1 AU RC	15.00	6.00
❑ 134	Andy Machado T1 AU RC	15.00	6.00
❑ 135	Luis Ugueto T1 AU RC	15.00	6.00
❑ 136	Tyler Yates T1 AU RC	15.00	6.00
❑ 137	Rodrigo Rosario T1 AU RC	15.00	6.00
❑ 138	Jaime Cerda T1 AU RC	15.00	6.00
❑ 139	Luis Martinez T1 AU RC	15.00	6.00
❑ 140	Rene Reyes T1 AU RC	15.00	6.00
❑ 141	Eric Good T1 AU RC	15.00	6.00
❑ 142	Matt Thornton T2 AU RC	25.00	10.00
❑ 143	Steve Kent T1 AU RC	15.00	6.00
❑ 144	Jose Valverde T1 AU RC	15.00	6.00
❑ 145	Adrian Burnside T1 AU RC	15.00	6.00
❑ 146	Barry Bonds GF	25.00	10.00
❑ 147	Ken Griffey Jr. GF	15.00	6.00
❑ 148	Alex Rodriguez GF	15.00	6.00
❑ 149	Jason Giambi GF	4.00	1.50
❑ 150	Chipper Jones GF	10.00	4.00
❑ 151	Nomar Garciaparra GF	15.00	6.00
❑ 152	Mike Piazza GF	15.00	6.00
❑ 153	Sammy Sosa GF	10.00	4.00
❑ 154	Derek Jeter GF	25.00	10.00
❑ 155	Jeff Bagwell GF	10.00	4.00
❑ 156	Albert Pujols GF	15.00	6.00
❑ 157	Ichiro Suzuki GF	15.00	6.00
❑ 158	Randy Johnson GF	10.00	4.00
❑ 159	Frank Thomas GF	10.00	4.00
❑ 160	Greg Maddux GF	15.00	6.00
❑ 161	Jim Thome GF	10.00	4.00
❑ 162	Scott Rolen GF	10.00	4.00
❑ 163	Shawn Green GF	10.00	4.00
❑ 164	Vladimir Guerrero GF	10.00	4.00
❑ 165	Troy Glaus GF	10.00	4.00
❑ 166	Carlos Delgado GF	10.00	4.00
❑ 167	Luis Gonzalez GF	10.00	4.00
❑ 168	Roger Clemens GF	20.00	8.00
❑ 169	Todd Helton GF	10.00	4.00
❑ 170	Eric Chavez GF	10.00	4.00
❑ 171	Rafael Palmeiro GF	10.00	4.00
❑ 172	Pedro Martinez GF	10.00	4.00
❑ 173	Lance Berkman GF	10.00	4.00
❑ 174	Josh Beckett GF	10.00	4.00
❑ 175	Sean Burroughs GF	10.00	4.00
❑ MM	Mark McGwire AU EXCH/100		

2003 Sweet Spot

No.	Card		
❑	COMP.SET w/o SP's (100)	20.00	8.00
❑	COMP.SET w/SP's (130)	120.00	60.00
❑	COMMON CARD (1-130)	.50	.20
❑	COMMON SP (1-130)	3.00	1.25
❑	COMMON CARD (131-190)	3.00	1.25
❑	131-190 PRINT RUN 2003 SERIAL #'d SETS		
❑	COMMON P1 (191-232)	4.00	1.50
❑	P1 191-232 PRINT RUN 500 SERIAL #'d SETS		
❑	COMMON P2-P3 (191-232)	3.00	1.25
❑	P2 191-232 PRINT RUN 1200 SERIAL #'d SETS		
❑	P3 191-232 PRINT RUN 1430 SERIAL #'d SETS		
❑ 1	Darin Erstad	.50	.20
❑ 2	Garret Anderson	.50	.20
❑ 3	Tim Salmon	.75	.30
❑ 4	Troy Glaus	.50	.20
❑ 5	Luis Gonzalez	.50	.20
❑ 6	Randy Johnson	1.25	.50
❑ 7	Curt Schilling	.50	.20
❑ 8	Lyle Overbay	.50	.20
❑ 9	Andruw Jones SP	4.00	1.50
❑ 10	Gary Sheffield SP	3.00	1.25
❑ 11	Rafael Furcal SP	3.00	1.25
❑ 12	Greg Maddux SP	6.00	2.50
❑ 13	Chipper Jones SP	4.00	1.50
❑ 14	Tony Batista	.50	.20
❑ 15	Rodrigo Lopez	.50	.20
❑ 16	Jay Gibbons	.50	.20
❑ 17	Jason Johnson	.50	.20
❑ 18	Byung-Hyun Kim SP	3.00	1.25
❑ 19	Johnny Damon SP	4.00	1.50
❑ 20	Derek Lowe SP	3.00	1.25
❑ 21	Nomar Garciaparra SP	6.00	2.50
❑ 22	Pedro Martinez SP	4.00	1.50
❑ 23	Manny Ramirez SP	4.00	1.50
❑ 24	Mark Prior	.75	.30
❑ 25	Kerry Wood	.50	.20
❑ 26	Corey Patterson	.50	.20
❑ 27	Sammy Sosa	1.25	.50
❑ 28	Moises Alou	.50	.20
❑ 29	Magglio Ordonez	.50	.20
❑ 30	Frank Thomas	1.25	.50
❑ 31	Paul Konerko	.50	.20
❑ 32	Roberto Alomar	.75	.30
❑ 33	Adam Dunn	.50	.20
❑ 34	Austin Kearns	.50	.20
❑ 35	Ryan Wagner RC	.50	.20
❑ 36	Ken Griffey Jr.	2.00	.75
❑ 37	Sean Casey	.50	.20
❑ 38	Omar Vizquel	.75	.30
❑ 39	C.C. Sabathia	.50	.20
❑ 40	Jason Davis	.50	.20
❑ 41	Travis Hafner	.50	.20

❑ 42 Brandon Phillips .50 .20
❑ 43 Larry Walker .50 .20
❑ 44 Preston Wilson .50 .20
❑ 45 Jay Payton .50 .20
❑ 46 Todd Helton .75 .30
❑ 47 Carlos Pena .50 .20
❑ 48 Eric Munson .50 .20
❑ 49 Ivan Rodriguez .75 .30
❑ 50 Josh Beckett .50 .20
❑ 51 Alex Gonzalez .50 .20
❑ 52 Roy Oswalt .50 .20
❑ 53 Craig Biggio .75 .30
❑ 54 Jeff Bagwell .75 .30
❑ 55 Lance Berkman .50 .20
❑ 56 Mike Sweeney .50 .20
❑ 57 Carlos Beltran .50 .20
❑ 58 Brent Mayne .50 .20
❑ 59 Mike MacDougal .50 .20
❑ 60 Hideo Nomo 1.25 .50
❑ 61 Dave Roberts .50 .20
❑ 62 Adrian Beltre .50 .20
❑ 63 Shawn Green .50 .20
❑ 64 Kazuhisa Ishii .50 .20
❑ 65 Rickey Henderson 1.25 .50
❑ 66 Richie Sexson .50 .20
❑ 67 Torii Hunter .50 .20
❑ 68 Jacque Jones .50 .20
❑ 69 Joe Mays .50 .20
❑ 70 Corey Koskie .50 .20
❑ 71 A.J. Pierzynski .50 .20
❑ 72 Jose Vidro .50 .20
❑ 73 Vladimir Guerrero 1.25 .50
❑ 74 Tom Glavine .75 .30
❑ 75 Mike Piazza 2.00 .75
❑ 76 Jose Reyes .50 .20
❑ 77 Jae Weong Seo .50 .20
❑ 78 Jorge Posada SP 4.00 1.50
❑ 79 Mike Mussina SP 4.00 1.50
❑ 80 Robin Ventura SP 3.00 1.25
❑ 81 Mariano Rivera SP 4.00 1.50
❑ 82 Roger Clemens SP 8.00 3.00
❑ 83 Jason Giambi SP 3.00 1.25
❑ 84 Bernie Williams SP 4.00 1.50
❑ 85 Alfonso Soriano SP 3.00 1.25
❑ 86 Derek Jeter 3.00 1.25
❑ 87 Miguel Tejada .50 .20
❑ 88 Eric Chavez .50 .20
❑ 89 Tim Hudson .50 .20
❑ 90 Barry Zito .50 .20
❑ 91 Mark Mulder .50 .20
❑ 92 Erubiel Durazo .50 .20
❑ 93 Pat Burrell .50 .20
❑ 94 Jim Thome .75 .30
❑ 95 Bobby Abreu .50 .20
❑ 96 Brian Giles .50 .20
❑ 97 Reggie Sanders .50 .20
❑ 98 Jose Hernandez .50 .20
❑ 99 Ryan Klesko .50 .20
❑ 100 Sean Burroughs .50 .20
❑ 101 Edgardo Alfonzo SP 3.00 1.25
❑ 102 Rich Aurilia SP 3.00 1.25
❑ 103 Jose Cruz Jr. SP 3.00 1.25
❑ 104 Barry Bonds SP 10.00 4.00
❑ 105 Andres Galarraga SP 3.00 1.25
❑ 106 Mike Cameron .50 .20
❑ 107 Kazuhiro Sasaki .50 .20
❑ 108 Bret Boone .50 .20
❑ 109 Ichiro Suzuki 2.50 1.00
❑ 110 John Olerud .50 .20
❑ 111 J.D. Drew SP 3.00 1.25
❑ 112 Jim Edmonds SP 3.00 1.25
❑ 113 Scott Rolen SP 4.00 1.50
❑ 114 Matt Morris SP 3.00 1.25
❑ 115 Tino Martinez SP 4.00 1.50
❑ 116 Albert Pujols SP 8.00 3.00
❑ 117 Jared Sandberg .50 .20
❑ 118 Carl Crawford .50 .20
❑ 119 Rafael Palmeiro .75 .30
❑ 120 Hank Blalock .50 .20
❑ 121 Alex Rodriguez SP 6.00 2.50
❑ 122 Kevin Mench .50 .20
❑ 123 Juan Gonzalez .50 .20
❑ 124 Mark Teixeira .75 .30
❑ 125 Shannon Stewart .50 .20
❑ 126 Vernon Wells .50 .20
❑ 127 Josh Phelps .50 .20
❑ 128 Eric Hinske .50 .20
❑ 129 Orlando Hudson .50 .20
❑ 130 Carlos Delgado .50 .20
❑ 131 Jason Shiell SB RC 3.00 1.25
❑ 132 Kevin Tolar SB RC 3.00 1.25
❑ 133 Nathan Bland SB RC 3.00 1.25
❑ 134 Brent Hoard SB RC 3.00 1.25
❑ 135 Jon Pridie SB RC 3.00 1.25
❑ 136 Mike Ryan SB RC 3.00 1.25
❑ 137 Francisco Rosario SB RC 3.00 1.25
❑ 138 Runelvys Hernandez SB 3.00 1.25
❑ 139 Guillermo Quiroz SB RC 3.00 1.25
❑ 140 Chin-Hui Tsao SB 3.00 1.25
❑ 141 Rett Johnson SB RC 3.00 1.25
❑ 142 Colin Porter SB RC 3.00 1.25
❑ 143 Jose Castillo SB 3.00 1.25
❑ 144 Chris Waters SB RC 3.00 1.25
❑ 145 Jeremy Guthrie SB 3.00 1.25
❑ 146 Pedro Liriano SB 3.00 1.25
❑ 147 Joe Borowski SB 3.00 1.25
❑ 148 Felix Sanchez SB RC 3.00 1.25
❑ 149 Todd Wellemeyer SB RC 3.00 1.25
❑ 150 Gerald Laird SB 3.00 1.25
❑ 151 Brandon Webb SB RC 8.00 3.00
❑ 152 Tommy Whiteman SB 3.00 1.25
❑ 153 Carlos Rivera SB 3.00 1.25
❑ 154 Rick Roberts SB RC 3.00 1.25
❑ 155 Termel Sledge SB RC 3.00 1.25
❑ 156 Jeff Duncan SB RC 3.00 1.25
❑ 157 Craig Brazell SB RC 3.00 1.25
❑ 158 Bernie Castro SB RC 3.00 1.25
❑ 159 Cory Stewart SB RC 3.00 1.25
❑ 160 Brandon Villafuerte SB 3.00 1.25
❑ 161 Tommy Phelps SB 3.00 1.25
❑ 162 Josh Hall SB RC 3.00 1.25
❑ 163 Ryan Cameron SB RC 3.00 1.25
❑ 164 Garret Atkins SB 3.00 1.25
❑ 165 Brian Stokes SB RC 3.00 1.25
❑ 166 Rafael Betancourt SB RC 4.00 1.50
❑ 167 Jaime Cerda SB 3.00 1.25
❑ 168 D.J. Carrasco SB RC 3.00 1.25
❑ 169 Ian Ferguson SB RC 3.00 1.25
❑ 170 Jorge Cordova SB RC 3.00 1.25
❑ 171 Eric Munson SB 3.00 1.25
❑ 172 Nook Logan SB RC 4.00 1.50
❑ 173 Jeremy Bonderman SB RC 12.00 5.00
❑ 174 Kyle Snyder SB 3.00 1.25
❑ 175 Rich Harden SB 4.00 1.50
❑ 176 Kevin Ohme SB RC 3.00 1.25
❑ 177 Roger Deago SB RC 3.00 1.25
❑ 178 Marlon Byrd SB 3.00 1.25
❑ 179 Dontrelle Willis SB 4.00 1.50
❑ 180 Bobby Hill SB 3.00 1.25
❑ 181 Jesse Foppert SB 3.00 1.25
❑ 182 Andrew Good SB 3.00 1.25
❑ 183 Chase Utley SB 4.00 1.50
❑ 184 Bo Hart SB RC 3.00 1.25
❑ 185 Dan Haren SB RC 4.00 1.50
❑ 186 Tim Olson SB RC 3.00 1.25
❑ 187 Joe Thurston SB 3.00 1.25
❑ 188 Jason Anderson SB 3.00 1.25
❑ 189 Jason Gilfillan SB RC 3.00 1.25
❑ 190 Rickie Weeks SB RC 8.00 3.00
❑ 191 Hideki Matsui SB P1 RC 25.00 10.00
❑ 192 Jose Contreras SB P3 RC 4.00 1.50
❑ 193 Willie Eyre SB P3 RC 3.00 1.25
❑ 194 Matt Bruback SB P3 RC 3.00 1.25
❑ 195 Heath Bell SB P3 RC 3.00 1.25
❑ 196 Lew Ford SB P3 RC 4.00 1.50
❑ 197 Jeremy Griffiths SB P3 RC 3.00 1.25
❑ 198 Oscar Villarreal SB P1 RC 4.00 1.50
❑ 199 Francisco Cruceta SB P3 RC 3.00 1.25
❑ 200 Fern Cabrera SB P3 RC 3.00 1.25
❑ 201 Jhonny Peralta SB P3 4.00 1.50
❑ 202 Shane Bazzell SB P3 RC 3.00 1.25
❑ 203 Bobby Madritsch SB P1 RC 4.00 1.50
❑ 204 Phil Seibel SB P3 RC 3.00 1.25
❑ 205 Josh Willingham SB P3 RC 5.00 2.00
❑ 206 Rob Hammock SB P1 RC 4.00 1.50
❑ 207 Alejandro Machado SB P3 RC 3.00 1.25
❑ 208 David Sanders SB P3 RC 3.00 1.25
❑ 209 Mike Neu SB P1 RC 4.00 1.50
❑ 210 Andrew Brown SB P3 RC 4.00 1.50
❑ 211 Nate Robertson SB P3 RC 5.00 2.00
❑ 212 Miguel Ojeda SB P3 RC 3.00 1.25
❑ 213 Beau Kemp SB P3 RC 3.00 1.25
❑ 214 Aaron Looper SB P3 RC 3.00 1.25
❑ 215 Alfredo Gonzalez SB P3 RC 3.00 1.25
❑ 216 Rich Fischer SB P1 RC 4.00 1.50
❑ 218 Jeremy Wedel SB P3 RC 3.00 1.25
❑ 219 Prentice Redman SB P3 RC 3.00 1.25
❑ 220 Michel Hernandez SB P3 RC 3.00 1.25
❑ 221 Rocco Baldelli SB P1 4.00 1.50
❑ 222 Luis Ayala SB P3 RC 3.00 1.25
❑ 223 Arnaldo Munoz SB P3 RC 3.00 1.25
❑ 224 Wilfredo Ledezma SB P3 RC 3.00 1.25
❑ 225 Chris Capuano SB P3 RC 4.00 1.50
❑ 226 Aquilino Lopez SB P3 RC 3.00 1.25
❑ 227 Joe Valentine SB P1 RC 4.00 1.50
❑ 228 Matt Kata SB P2 RC 3.00 1.25
❑ 229 Diegomar Markwell SB P2 RC 3.00 1.25
❑ 230 Clint Barmes SB P2 RC 3.00 1.25
❑ 231 Mike Nicolas SB P1 RC 4.00 1.50
❑ 232 Jon Leicester SB P2 RC 3.00 1.25

2004 Sweet Spot

❑ COMP.SET w/o SP's (90) 20.00 8.00
❑ COMMON CARD (1-90) .50 .20
❑ COMMON (91-170/261-262) 4.00 1.50
❑ 91-170/261-262 STATED ODDS 1:12
❑ 91-170/261-262 PRINT RUN 799 #'d SETS
❑ COMMON CARD (171-230) 4.00 1.50
❑ 171-230 PRINT RUN 399 SERIAL #'d SETS
❑ COMMON CARD (231-250) 4.00 1.50
❑ 231-250 PRINT RUN 299 SERIAL #'d SETS
❑ COMMON CARD (251-260) 6.00 2.50
❑ 251-260 PRINT RUN 199 SERIAL #'d SETS
❑ 171-260/Ltd 10/W99 OVERALL ODDS 1:12
❑ OVERALL PLATES ODDS 1:360 HOBBY
❑ PLATES PRINT RUN 1 SET PER COLOR
❑ BLACK-CYAN-MAGENTA-YELLOW ISSUED
❑ NO PLATES PRICING DUE TO SACRCITY
❑ 1 Albert Pujols 2.50 1.00
❑ 2 Alex Rodriguez 2.00 .75
❑ 3 Alfonso Soriano .50 .20
❑ 4 Andruw Jones .75 .30
❑ 5 Andy Pettitte .75 .30
❑ 6 Aubrey Huff .50 .20
❑ 7 Austin Kearns .50 .20
❑ 8 Barry Zito .50 .20
❑ 9 Bobby Abreu .50 .20
❑ 10 Brandon Webb .50 .20
❑ 11 Bret Boone .50 .20
❑ 12 Brian Giles .50 .20
❑ 13 C.C. Sabathia .50 .20
❑ 14 Carlos Beltran .50 .20
❑ 15 Carlos Delgado .50 .20
❑ 16 Chipper Jones 1.25 .50
❑ 17 Cliff Floyd .50 .20
❑ 18 Curt Schilling .75 .30
❑ 19 Delmon Young .75 .30
❑ 20 Derek Jeter 2.50 1.00
❑ 21 Dontrelle Willis .75 .30
❑ 22 Edgar Martinez .75 .30
❑ 23 Edgar Renteria .50 .20
❑ 24 Eric Chavez .50 .20
❑ 25 Eric Gagne .50 .20
❑ 26 Frank Thomas 1.25 .50
❑ 27 Garret Anderson .50 .20
❑ 28 Gary Sheffield .50 .20
❑ 29 Geoff Jenkins .50 .20
❑ 30 Greg Maddux 2.00 .75
❑ 31 Hank Blalock .50 .20
❑ 32 Hideo Nomo 1.25 .50

❑ 33 Ichiro Suzuki 2.50 1.00
❑ 34 Ivan Rodriguez .75 .30
❑ 35 Jacque Jones .50 .20
❑ 36 Jason Giambi .50 .20
❑ 37 Jason Schmidt .50 .20
❑ 38 Javier Vazquez .50 .20
❑ 39 Javy Lopez .50 .20
❑ 40 Jeff Bagwell .75 .30
❑ 41 Jim Edmonds .50 .20
❑ 42 Jim Thome .75 .30
❑ 43 Joe Mauer 1.25 .50
❑ 44 John Smoltz .50 .20
❑ 45 Jose Cruz Jr. .50 .20
❑ 46 Jose Reyes .50 .20
❑ 47 Jose Vidro .50 .20
❑ 48 Josh Beckett .50 .20
❑ 49 Ken Griffey Jr. 2.00 .75
❑ 50 Kerry Wood .50 .20
❑ 51 Kevin Brown .50 .20
❑ 52 Larry Walker .50 .20
❑ 53 Magglio Ordonez .50 .20
❑ 54 Manny Ramirez .75 .30
❑ 55 Mark Mulder .50 .20
❑ 56 Mark Prior .75 .30
❑ 57 Mark Teixeira .75 .30
❑ 58 Miguel Cabrera .75 .30
❑ 59 Miguel Tejada .50 .20
❑ 60 Mike Lowell .50 .20
❑ 61 Mike Mussina .75 .30
❑ 62 Mike Piazza 2.00 .75
❑ 63 Nomar Garciaparra 2.00 .75
❑ 64 Orlando Cabrera .50 .20
❑ 65 Pat Burrell .50 .20
❑ 66 Pedro Martinez .75 .30
❑ 67 Phil Nevin .50 .20
❑ 68 Preston Wilson .50 .20
❑ 69 Rafael Furcal .50 .20
❑ 70 Rafael Palmeiro .75 .30
❑ 71 Randy Johnson 1.25 .50
❑ 72 Craig Wilson .50 .20
❑ 73 Rich Harden .50 .20
❑ 74 Richie Sexson .50 .20
❑ 75 Rickie Weeks .50 .20
❑ 76 Rocco Baldelli .50 .20
❑ 77 Roger Clemens 2.50 1.00
❑ 78 Roy Halladay .50 .20
❑ 79 Roy Oswalt .50 .20
❑ 80 Ryan Klesko .50 .20
❑ 81 Sammy Sosa 1.25 .50
❑ 82 Scott Podsednik .50 .20
❑ 83 Scott Rolen .75 .30
❑ 84 Shawn Green .50 .20
❑ 85 Tim Hudson .50 .20
❑ 86 Todd Helton .75 .30
❑ 87 Torii Hunter .50 .20
❑ 88 Troy Glaus .50 .20
❑ 89 Vernon Wells .50 .20
❑ 90 Vladimir Guerrero 1.25 .50
❑ 91 Aarom Baldiris SB RC 5.00 2.00
❑ 92 Akinori Otsuka SB RC 4.00 1.50
❑ 93 Andres Blanco SB RC 4.00 1.50
❑ 94 Angel Chavez SB RC 4.00 1.50
❑ 95 Brian Dallimore SB RC 4.00 1.50
❑ 96 Carlos Hines SB RC 4.00 1.50
❑ 97 Carlos Vasquez SB RC 5.00 2.00
❑ 98 Casey Daigle SB RC 4.00 1.50
❑ 99 Chad Bentz SB RC 4.00 1.50
❑ 100 Chris Aguila SB RC 4.00 1.50
❑ 101 Chris Oxspring SB RC 4.00 1.50
❑ 102 Chris Saenz SB RC 4.00 1.50
❑ 103 Chris Shelton SB RC 5.00 2.00
❑ 104 Colby Miller SB RC 4.00 1.50
❑ 105 Dave Crouthers SB RC 4.00 1.50
❑ 106 David Aardsma SB RC 5.00 2.00
❑ 107 Dennis Sarfate SB RC 4.00 1.50
❑ 108 Donnie Kelly SB RC 4.00 1.50
❑ 109 Eddy Rodriguez SB RC 5.00 2.00
❑ 110 Eduardo Villacis SB RC 4.00 1.50
❑ 111 Edwin Moreno SB RC 5.00 2.00
❑ 112 Enemencio Pacheco SB RC 4.00 1.50
❑ 113 Fernando Nieve SB RC 5.00 2.00
❑ 114 Franklyn Gracesqui SB RC 4.00 1.50
❑ 115 Freddy Guzman SB RC 4.00 1.50
❑ 116 Greg Dobbs SB RC 4.00 1.50
❑ 117 Hector Gimenez SB RC 4.00 1.50
❑ 118 Ian Snell SB RC 5.00 2.00
❑ 119 Ivan Ochoa SB RC 4.00 1.50
❑ 120 Jake Woods SB RC 4.00 1.50
❑ 121 Jamie Brown SB RC 4.00 1.50
❑ 122 Jason Bartlett SB RC 5.00 2.00
❑ 123 Jason Frasor SB RC 4.00 1.50
❑ 124 Jeff Bennett SB RC 4.00 1.50
❑ 125 Jerome Gamble SB RC 4.00 1.50
❑ 126 Jerry Gil SB RC 4.00 1.50
❑ 127 Brandon Medders SB RC 4.00 1.50
❑ 128 Ryan Meaux SB RC 4.00 1.50
❑ 129 John Gall SB RC 5.00 2.00
❑ 130 Jorge Sequea SB RC 4.00 1.50
❑ 131 Jorge Vasquez SB RC 4.00 1.50
❑ 132 Jose Capellan SB RC 5.00 2.00
❑ 133 Josh Labandeira SB RC 4.00 1.50
❑ 134 Justin Germano SB RC 4.00 1.50
❑ 135 Justin Hampson SB RC 4.00 1.50
❑ 136 Justin Huisman SB RC 4.00 1.50
❑ 137 Justin Knoedler SB RC 4.00 1.50
❑ 138 Justin Leone SB RC 5.00 2.00
❑ 139 Kazuhito Tadano SB RC 5.00 2.00
❑ 140 Kazuo Matsui SB RC 5.00 2.00
❑ 141 Kevin Cave SB RC 4.00 1.50
❑ 142 Lincoln Holdzkom SB RC 4.00 1.50
❑ 143 Lino Urdaneta SB RC 4.00 1.50
❑ 144 Luis A. Gonzalez SB RC 4.00 1.50
❑ 145 Mariano Gomez SB RC 4.00 1.50
❑ 146 Merkin Valdez SB RC 5.00 2.00
❑ 147 Michael Vento SB RC 5.00 2.00
❑ 148 Michael Wuertz SB RC 5.00 2.00
❑ 149 Mike Gosling SB RC 4.00 1.50
❑ 150 Mike Johnston SB RC 4.00 1.50
❑ 151 Mike Rouse SB RC 4.00 1.50
❑ 152 Nick Regilio SB RC 4.00 1.50
❑ 153 Onil Joseph SB RC 4.00 1.50
❑ 154 Orlando Rodriguez SB RC 4.00 1.50
❑ 155 Ramon Ramirez SB RC 4.00 1.50
❑ 156 Renyel Pinto SB RC 5.00 2.00
❑ 157 Roberto Novoa SB RC 5.00 2.00
❑ 158 Roman Colon SB RC 4.00 1.50
❑ 159 Ronald Belisario SB RC 4.00 1.50
❑ 160 Ronny Cedeno SB RC 5.00 2.00
❑ 161 Rusty Tucker SB RC 5.00 2.00
❑ 162 Ryan Wing SB RC 4.00 1.50
❑ 163 Scott Dohmann SB RC 4.00 1.50
❑ 164 Scott Proctor SB RC 5.00 2.00
❑ 165 Sean Henn SB RC 4.00 1.50
❑ 166 Shawn Camp SB RC 4.00 1.50
❑ 167 Shawn Hill SB RC 4.00 1.50
❑ 168 Shingo Takatsu SB RC 5.00 2.00
❑ 169 Tim Hamulack SB RC 4.00 1.50
❑ 170 William Bergolla SB RC 4.00 1.50
❑ 171 Adam Dunn SF 4.00 1.50
❑ 172 Albert Pujols SF 10.00 4.00
❑ 173 Alex Rodriguez SF 8.00 3.00
❑ 174 Alfonso Soriano SF 4.00 1.50
❑ 175 Andruw Jones SF 5.00 2.00
❑ 176 Bret Boone SF 4.00 1.50
❑ 177 Brian Giles SF 4.00 1.50
❑ 178 Carlos Delgado SF 4.00 1.50
❑ 179 Derrek Lee SF 5.00 2.00
❑ 180 Eric Chavez SF 4.00 1.50
❑ 181 Frank Thomas SF 5.00 2.00
❑ 182 Garret Anderson SF 4.00 1.50
❑ 183 Gary Sheffield SF 4.00 1.50
❑ 184 Hank Blalock SF 4.00 1.50
❑ 185 Jason Giambi SF 4.00 1.50
❑ 186 Javy Lopez SF 4.00 1.50
❑ 187 Jeff Bagwell SF 5.00 2.00
❑ 188 Jim Edmonds SF 4.00 1.50
❑ 189 Jim Thome SF 5.00 2.00
❑ 190 Ken Griffey Jr. SF 8.00 3.00
❑ 191 Lance Berkman SF 4.00 1.50
❑ 192 Magglio Ordonez SF 4.00 1.50
❑ 193 Manny Ramirez SF 5.00 2.00
❑ 194 Mike Lowell SF 4.00 1.50
❑ 195 Mike Piazza SF 8.00 3.00
❑ 196 Preston Wilson SF 4.00 1.50
❑ 197 Rafael Palmeiro SF 5.00 2.00
❑ 198 Richie Sexson SF 4.00 1.50
❑ 199 Sammy Sosa SF 5.00 2.00
❑ 200 Scott Rolen SF 5.00 2.00
❑ 201 Shawn Green SF 4.00 1.50
❑ 202 Todd Helton SF 5.00 2.00
❑ 203 Troy Glaus SF 4.00 1.50
❑ 204 Vernon Wells SF 4.00 1.50
❑ 205 Vladimir Guerrero SF 5.00 2.00
❑ 206 G.Anderson/V.Guerrero SL 5.00 2.00
❑ 207 L.Gonzalez/R.Sexson SL 4.00 1.50
❑ 208 A.Jones/C.Jones SL 5.00 2.00
❑ 209 J.Lopez/M.Tejada SL 4.00 1.50
❑ 210 M.Ramirez/D.Ortiz SL 5.00 2.00
❑ 211 D.Lee/S.Sosa SL 5.00 2.00
❑ 212 F.Thomas/M.Ordonez SL 5.00 2.00
❑ 213 A.Kearns/K.Griffey Jr. SL 8.00 3.00
❑ 214 P.Wilson/T.Helton SL 5.00 2.00
❑ 215 D.Young/I.Rodriguez SL 5.00 2.00
❑ 216 M.Cabrera/M.Lowell SL 5.00 2.00
❑ 217 J.Bagwell/L.Berkman SL 5.00 2.00
❑ 218 L.Overbay/G.Jenkins SL 4.00 1.50
❑ 219 A.Beltre/S.Green SL 4.00 1.50
❑ 220 J.Jones/T.Hunter SL 4.00 1.50
❑ 221 J.Vidro/N.Johnson SL 4.00 1.50
❑ 222 K.Matsui/M.Piazza SL 8.00 3.00
❑ 223 A.Rodriguez/J.Giambi SL 8.00 3.00
❑ 224 E.Chavez/J.Dye SL 4.00 1.50
❑ 225 J.Thome/P.Burrell SL 5.00 2.00
❑ 226 B.Giles/P.Nevin SL 4.00 1.50
❑ 227 B.Boone/I.Suzuki SL 10.00 4.00
❑ 228 A.Pujols/S.Rolen SL 10.00 4.00
❑ 229 H.Blalock/M.Teixeira SL 5.00 2.00
❑ 230 C.Delgado/V.Wells SL 4.00 1.50
❑ 231 Albert Pujols PD 10.00 4.00
❑ 232 Alex Rodriguez PD 8.00 3.00
❑ 233 Chipper Jones PD 5.00 2.00
❑ 234 Craig Biggio PD 5.00 2.00
❑ 235 Curt Schilling PD 5.00 2.00
❑ 236 Derek Jeter PD 10.00 4.00
❑ 237 Ivan Rodriguez PD 5.00 2.00
❑ 238 Jeff Bagwell PD 5.00 2.00
❑ 239 Jim Edmonds PD 4.00 1.50
❑ 240 Jim Thome PD 5.00 2.00
❑ 241 Josh Beckett PD 4.00 1.50
❑ 242 Kerry Wood PD 4.00 1.50
❑ 243 Kevin Brown PD 4.00 1.50
❑ 244 Mark Prior PD 5.00 2.00
❑ 245 Miguel Tejada PD 4.00 1.50
❑ 246 Mike Mussina PD 5.00 2.00
❑ 247 Nomar Garciaparra PD 8.00 3.00
❑ 248 Pedro Martinez PD 5.00 2.00
❑ 249 Randy Johnson PD 5.00 2.00
❑ 250 Roger Clemens PD 10.00 4.00
❑ 251 A.Rodriguez/D.Jeter DD 15.00 6.00
❑ 252 A.Soriano/H.Blalock DD 6.00 2.50
❑ 253 B.Abreu/P.Burrell DD 6.00 2.50
❑ 254 E.Renteria/S.Rolen DD 8.00 3.00
❑ 255 G.Anderson/V.Guerrero DD 8.00 3.00
❑ 256 J.Bagwell/J.Kent DD 8.00 3.00
❑ 257 J.Reyes/K.Matsui DD 8.00 3.00
❑ 258 K.Greene/S.Burroughs DD 8.00 3.00
❑ 259 M.Giles/R.Furcal DD 6.00 2.50
❑ 260 M.Ramirez/J.Damon DD 8.00 3.00
❑ 261 Tim Bausher SB RC 4.00 1.50
❑ 262 Tim Bittner SB RC 4.00 1.50

2005 Sweet Spot

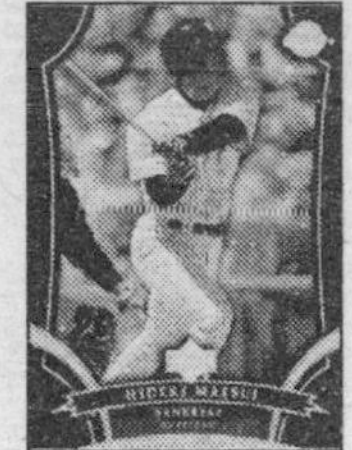

❑ COMP.BASIC SET (90) 20.00 8.00
❑ COMP.UPDATE SET (84) 25.00 10.00
❑ COMMON CARD (1-90) .50 .20
❑ COMMON CARD (91-174) 1.00 .40
❑ 91-174 ONE PER '05 UD UPDATE PACK
❑ 1 Magglio Ordonez .50 .20
❑ 2 Craig Biggio .75 .30
❑ 3 Hank Blalock .50 .20

❑ 4 Nomar Garciaparra	1.25	.50
❑ 5 Ken Griffey Jr.	2.00	.75
❑ 6 Khalil Greene	.75	.30
❑ 7 Andruw Jones	.75	.30
❑ 8 Ichiro Suzuki	2.50	1.00
❑ 9 Philip Humber RC	1.25	.50
❑ 10 Vladimir Guerrero	1.25	.50
❑ 11 Carlos Delgado	.50	.20
❑ 12 Jeff Niemann RC	1.25	.50
❑ 13 Chipper Jones	1.25	.50
❑ 14 Jose Vidro	.50	.20
❑ 15 Miguel Cabrera	.75	.30
❑ 16 Albert Pujols	2.50	1.00
❑ 17 Tadahito Iguchi RC	2.00	.75
❑ 18 Norihiro Nakamura RC	1.50	.60
❑ 19 Jeff Bagwell	.75	.30
❑ 20 Troy Glaus	.50	.20
❑ 21 Scott Rolen	.75	.30
❑ 22 Derek Lowe	.50	.20
❑ 23 Mark Prior	.75	.30
❑ 24 Bobby Abreu	.50	.20
❑ 25 David Wright	2.00	.75
❑ 26 Barry Zito	.50	.20
❑ 27 Livan Hernandez	.50	.20
❑ 28 Mark Teixeira	.75	.30
❑ 29 Manny Ramirez	.75	.30
❑ 30 Paul Konerko	.50	.20
❑ 31 Victor Martinez	.50	.20
❑ 32 Greg Maddux	2.00	.75
❑ 33 Jim Thome	.75	.30
❑ 34 Miguel Tejada	.50	.20
❑ 35 Ivan Rodriguez	.75	.30
❑ 36 Carlos Beltran	.50	.20
❑ 37 Steve Finley	.50	.20
❑ 38 Torii Hunter	.50	.20
❑ 39 Bobby Crosby	.50	.20
❑ 40 Jorge Posada	.75	.30
❑ 41 Ben Sheets	.50	.20
❑ 42 Mike Piazza	1.25	.50
❑ 43 Luis Gonzalez	.50	.20
❑ 44 Joe Mauer	1.25	.50
❑ 45 Shawn Green	.50	.20
❑ 46 Eric Gagne	.50	.20
❑ 47 Kerry Wood	.50	.20
❑ 48 Derek Jeter	3.00	1.25
❑ 49 Josh Beckett	.50	.20
❑ 50 Alex Rodriguez	2.00	.75
❑ 51 Aubrey Huff	.50	.20
❑ 52 Eric Chavez	.50	.20
❑ 53 Sammy Sosa	1.25	.50
❑ 54 Roger Clemens	2.00	.75
❑ 55 Mike Mussina	.75	.30
❑ 56 Mike Sweeney	.50	.20
❑ 57 Oliver Perez	.50	.20
❑ 58 Tim Hudson	.50	.20
❑ 59 Justin Verlander RC	4.00	1.50
❑ 60 Johan Santana	1.25	.50
❑ 61 Hideki Matsui	2.00	.75
❑ 62 Mark Mulder	.50	.20
❑ 63 Jake Peavy	.50	.20
❑ 64 Adam Dunn	.50	.20
❑ 65 Dallas McPherson	.50	.20
❑ 66 Jeff Kent	.50	.20
❑ 67 Pedro Martinez	.75	.30
❑ 68 J.D. Drew	.50	.20
❑ 69 Frank Thomas	1.25	.50
❑ 70 Kazuo Matsui	.50	.20
❑ 71 Travis Hafner	.50	.20
❑ 72 John Smoltz	.75	.30
❑ 73 Jason Schmidt	.50	.20
❑ 74 Carlos Lee	.50	.20
❑ 75 Todd Helton	.75	.30
❑ 76 David Ortiz	1.25	.50
❑ 77 Roy Oswalt	.50	.20
❑ 78 Brian Giles	.50	.20
❑ 79 Gary Sheffield	.50	.20
❑ 80 Jason Bay	.50	.20
❑ 81 Alfonso Soriano	.50	.20
❑ 82 Randy Johnson	1.25	.50
❑ 83 Tom Glavine	.75	.30
❑ 84 Richie Sexson	.50	.20
❑ 85 Curt Schilling	.75	.30
❑ 86 Adrian Beltre	.50	.20
❑ 87 Jim Edmonds	.50	.20
❑ 88 Roy Halladay	.50	.20
❑ 89 Johnny Damon	.75	.30
❑ 90 Lance Berkman	.50	.20
❑ 91 Adam Shabala SB RC	1.00	.40
❑ 92 Ambiorix Burgos SB RC	1.00	.40
❑ 93 Ambiorix Concepcion SB RC	1.00	.40
❑ 94 Anibal Sanchez SB RC	3.00	1.25
❑ 95 Bill McCarthy SB RC	1.00	.40
❑ 96 Brandon McCarthy SB RC	1.50	.60
❑ 97 Brian Burres SB RC	1.00	.40
❑ 98 Carlos Ruiz SB RC	1.00	.40
❑ 99 Casey Rogowski SB RC	1.25	.50
❑ 100 Chad Orvella SB RC	1.00	.40
❑ 101 Chris Resop SB RC	1.00	.40
❑ 102 Chris Roberson SB RC	1.00	.40
❑ 103 Chris Seddon SB RC	1.00	.40
❑ 104 Colter Bean SB RC	1.00	.40
❑ 105 Dae-Sung Koo SB RC	1.00	.40
❑ 106 Ryan Zimmerman SB RC	8.00	3.00
❑ 107 Dave Gassner SB RC	1.00	.40
❑ 108 Brian Anderson SB RC	1.50	.60
❑ 109 D.J. Houlton SB RC	1.00	.40
❑ 110 Derek Wathan SB RC	1.00	.40
❑ 111 Devon Lowery SB RC	1.00	.40
❑ 112 Enrique Gonzalez SB RC	1.00	.40
❑ 113 Chris Denorfia SB RC	1.25	.50
❑ 114 Eude Brito SB RC	1.00	.40
❑ 115 Francisco Butto SB RC	1.00	.40
❑ 116 Franquelis Osoria SB RC	1.00	.40
❑ 117 Garrett Jones SB RC	1.00	.40
❑ 118 Geovany Soto SB RC	1.00	.40
❑ 119 Hayden Penn SB RC	1.25	.50
❑ 120 Ismael Ramirez SB RC	1.00	.40
❑ 121 Jared Gothreaux SB RC	1.00	.40
❑ 122 Jason Hammel SB RC	1.00	.40
❑ 123 Dana Eveland SB RC	1.00	.40
❑ 124 Jeff Miller SB RC	1.00	.40
❑ 125 Jermaine Van Buren SB	1.00	.40
❑ 126 Joel Peralta SB RC	1.00	.40
❑ 127 John Hattig SB RC	1.00	.40
❑ 128 Jorge Campillo SB RC	1.00	.40
❑ 129 Juan Morillo SB RC	1.00	.40
❑ 130 Ryan Garko SB RC	2.00	.75
❑ 131 Keiichi Yabu SB RC	1.00	.40
❑ 132 Kendry Morales SB RC	2.50	1.00
❑ 133 Luis Hernandez SB RC	1.00	.40
❑ 134 Mark McLemore SB RC	1.00	.40
❑ 135 Luis Pena SB RC	1.00	.40
❑ 136 Luis O.Rodriguez SB RC	1.00	.40
❑ 137 Luke Scott SB RC	2.00	.75
❑ 138 Marcos Carvajal SB RC	1.00	.40
❑ 139 Mark Woodyard SB RC	1.00	.40
❑ 140 Matt A.Smith SB RC	1.00	.40
❑ 141 Matthew Lindstrom SB RC	1.00	.40
❑ 142 Miguel Negron SB RC	1.25	.50
❑ 143 Mike Morse SB RC	1.00	.40
❑ 144 Nate McLouth SB RC	1.25	.50
❑ 145 Nelson Cruz SB RC	2.00	.75
❑ 146 Nick Masset SB RC	1.00	.40
❑ 147 Ryan Spilborghs SB RC	1.25	.50
❑ 148 Oscar Robles SB RC	1.00	.40
❑ 149 Paulino Reynoso SB RC	1.00	.40
❑ 150 Pedro Lopez SB RC	1.00	.40
❑ 151 Pete Orr SB RC	1.00	.40
❑ 152 Prince Fielder SB RC	4.00	1.50
❑ 153 Randy Messenger SB RC	1.00	.40
❑ 154 Randy Williams SB RC	1.00	.40
❑ 155 Raul Tablado SB RC	1.00	.40
❑ 156 Ronny Paulino SB RC	1.25	.50
❑ 157 Russ Rohlicek SB RC	1.00	.40
❑ 158 Russell Martin SB RC	2.00	.75
❑ 159 Scott Baker SB RC	1.25	.50
❑ 160 Scott Munter SB RC	1.00	.40
❑ 161 Sean Thompson SB RC	1.00	.40
❑ 162 Sean Tracey SB RC	1.00	.40
❑ 163 Shane Costa SB RC	1.00	.40
❑ 164 Stephen Drew SB RC	5.00	2.00
❑ 165 Steve Schmoll SB RC	1.00	.40
❑ 166 Ryan Speier SB RC	1.00	.40
❑ 167 Tadahito Iguchi SB	2.00	.75
❑ 168 Tony Giarratano SB RC	1.00	.40
❑ 169 Tony Pena SB RC	1.00	.40
❑ 170 Travis Bowyer SB RC	1.00	.40
❑ 171 Ubaldo Jimenez SB RC	1.00	.40
❑ 172 Wladimir Balentien SB RC	1.25	.50
❑ 173 Yorman Bazardo SB RC	1.00	.40
❑ 174 Yuniesky Betancourt SB RC	2.00	.75

2006 Sweet Spot

❑ COMP.SET w/o AU's (100)	25.00	10.00
❑ COMMON CARD (1-100)	.50	.20
❑ OVERALL AU ODDS 1:12		
❑ AU PRINT RUNS B/WN 45-275 PER		
❑ EXCHANGE DEADLINE 05/25/08		
❑ ASTERISK = PARTIAL EXCHANGE		
❑ 1 Bartolo Colon	.50	.20
❑ 2 Garret Anderson	.50	.20
❑ 3 Francisco Rodriguez	.50	.20
❑ 4 Dallas McPherson	.50	.20
❑ 5 Andy Pettitte	.50	.20
❑ 6 Lance Berkman	.50	.20
❑ 7 Willy Taveras	.50	.20
❑ 8 Bobby Crosby	.50	.20
❑ 9 Dan Haren	.50	.20
❑ 10 Nick Swisher	.50	.20
❑ 11 Vernon Wells	.50	.20
❑ 12 Orlando Hudson	.50	.20
❑ 13 Roy Halladay	.50	.20
❑ 14 Andruw Jones	.75	.30
❑ 15 Chipper Jones	1.25	.50
❑ 16 Jeff Francoeur	1.25	.50
❑ 17 John Smoltz	.75	.30
❑ 18 Carlos Lee	.50	.20
❑ 19 Rickie Weeks	.50	.20
❑ 20 Bill Hall	.50	.20
❑ 21 Jim Edmonds	.75	.30
❑ 22 David Eckstein	.50	.20
❑ 23 Mark Mulder	.50	.20
❑ 24 Aramis Ramirez	.50	.20
❑ 25 Greg Maddux	2.00	.75
❑ 26 Nomar Garciaparra	1.25	.50
❑ 27 Carlos Zambrano	.50	.20
❑ 28 Scott Kazmir	.75	.30
❑ 29 Jorge Cantu	.50	.20
❑ 30 Carl Crawford	.50	.20
❑ 31 Luis Gonzalez	.50	.20
❑ 32 Troy Glaus	.50	.20
❑ 33 Shawn Green	.50	.20
❑ 34 Jeff Kent	.50	.20
❑ 35 Milton Bradley	.50	.20
❑ 36 Cesar Izturis	.50	.20
❑ 37 Omar Vizquel	.75	.30
❑ 38 Moises Alou	.50	.20
❑ 39 Randy Winn	.50	.20
❑ 40 Jason Schmidt	.50	.20
❑ 41 Coco Crisp	.50	.20
❑ 42 C.C. Sabathia	.50	.20
❑ 43 Cliff Lee	.50	.20
❑ 44 Ichiro Suzuki	2.00	.75
❑ 45 Richie Sexson	.50	.20
❑ 46 Jeremy Reed	.50	.20
❑ 47 Carlos Delgado	.50	.20
❑ 48 Miguel Cabrera	.75	.30
❑ 49 Luis Castillo	.50	.20
❑ 50 Carlos Beltran	.50	.20
❑ 51 Tom Glavine	.75	.30
❑ 52 David Wright	2.00	.75
❑ 53 Cliff Floyd	.50	.20
❑ 54 Chad Cordero	.50	.20
❑ 55 Jose Vidro	.50	.20
❑ 56 Jose Guillen	.50	.20
❑ 57 Nick Johnson	.50	.20
❑ 58 Miguel Tejada	.50	.20
❑ 59 Melvin Mora	.50	.20
❑ 60 Javy Lopez	.50	.20
❑ 61 Khalil Greene	.75	.30

❑ 62 Brian Giles .50 .20
❑ 63 Trevor Hoffman .50 .20
❑ 64 Bobby Abreu .50 .20
❑ 65 Jimmy Rollins .50 .20
❑ 66 Pat Burrell .50 .20
❑ 67 Billy Wagner .50 .20
❑ 68 Jack Wilson .50 .20
❑ 69 Zach Duke .50 .20
❑ 70 Craig Wilson .50 .20
❑ 71 Mark Teixeira .75 .30
❑ 72 Hank Blalock .50 .20
❑ 73 David Dellucci .50 .20
❑ 74 Manny Ramirez .75 .30
❑ 75 Johnny Damon .75 .30
❑ 76 Jason Varitek 1.25 .50
❑ 77 Trot Nixon .50 .20
❑ 78 Adam Dunn .50 .20
❑ 79 Felipe Lopez .50 .20
❑ 80 Brandon Claussen .50 .20
❑ 81 Sean Casey .50 .20
❑ 82 Todd Helton .75 .30
❑ 83 Clint Barmes .50 .20
❑ 84 Matt Holliday .50 .20
❑ 85 Mike Sweeney .50 .20
❑ 86 Zack Greinke .50 .20
❑ 87 David DeJesus .50 .20
❑ 88 Ivan Rodriguez .75 .30
❑ 89 Jeremy Bonderman .50 .20
❑ 90 Magglio Ordonez .50 .20
❑ 91 Torii Hunter .50 .20
❑ 92 Joe Nathan .50 .20
❑ 93 Michael Cuddyer .50 .20
❑ 94 Paul Konerko .50 .20
❑ 95 Jermaine Dye .50 .20
❑ 96 Jon Garland .50 .20
❑ 97 Alex Rodriguez 2.00 .75
❑ 98 Hideki Matsui 1.25 .50
❑ 99 Jason Giambi .50 .20
❑ 100 Mariano Rivera 1.25 .50
❑ 101 Adrian Beltre AU/99 40.00 15.00
❑ 102 Matt Cain AU/275 (RC) 40.00 15.00
❑ 103 Craig Biggio AU/99 60.00 30.00
❑ 104 Eric Chavez AU/99 30.00 12.50
❑ 105 J.D. Drew AU/99 30.00 12.50
❑ 106 Eric Gagne AU/99 50.00 20.00
❑ 107 Tim Hudson AU/99 40.00 15.00
❑ 108 Tom Glavine AU/275 50.00 20.00
❑ 109 David Ortiz AU/99 80.00 40.00
❑ 110 Scott Rolen AU/275 40.00 15.00
❑ 111 Johan Santana AU/99 50.00 20.00
❑ 112 Curt Schilling AU/96 80.00 40.00
❑ 113 John Smoltz AU/99 60.00 30.00
❑ 114 Alfonso Soriano AU/99 60.00 30.00
❑ 115 Kerry Wood AU/99 30.00 12.50
❑ 116 Edwin Jackson AU/99 20.00 8.00
❑ 117 Felix Hernandez AU/125 50.00 20.00
❑ 118 Prince Fielder AU/99 (RC) 80.00 40.00
❑ 119 Vladimir Guerrero AU/86 60.00 30.00
❑ 120 Roger Clemens AU/99 150.00 75.00
❑ 121 Albert Pujols AU/45 300.00 175.00
❑ 122 Chris Carpenter AU/99 50.00 20.00
❑ 123 Derrek Lee AU/99 40.00 15.00
❑ 124 Dontrelle Willis AU/99 30.00 12.50
❑ 125 Roy Oswalt AU/99 40.00 15.00
❑ 126 Ryan Garko AU/275 (RC) 25.00 10.00
❑ 127 Tadahito Iguchi AU/275 50.00 20.00
❑ 128 Mark Loretta AU/275 25.00 10.00
❑ 129 Joe Mauer AU/275 50.00 20.00
❑ 130 Victor Martinez AU/275 25.00 10.00
❑ 131 Wily Mo Pena AU/275 25.00 10.00
❑ 132 Oliver Perez AU/274 15.00 6.00
❑ 133 C.Patterson AU/275 EXCH 25.00 10.00
❑ 134 Ben Sheets AU/275 25.00 10.00
❑ 135 Michael Young AU/275 25.00 10.00
❑ 136 Jonny Gomes AU/275 15.00 6.00
❑ 137 Derek Jeter AU/99 200.00 125.00
❑ 138 K.Griffey Jr. AU/275 EXCH * 80.00 40.00
❑ 139 R.Zimmerman AU/275 (RC) 60.00 30.00
❑ 140 Scott Baker AU/275 (RC) 15.00 6.00
❑ 141 Huston Street AU/275 25.00 10.00
❑ 142 Jason Bay AU/275 EXCH 25.00 10.00
❑ 143 Ryan Howard AU/275 80.00 40.00
❑ 145 Travis Hafner AU/275 25.00 10.00
❑ 146 Brian Myrow AU/275 RC 15.00 6.00
❑ 147 Scott Podsednik AU/275 25.00 10.00
❑ 148 Brian Roberts AU/275 25.00 10.00
❑ 149 Grady Sizemore AU/135 40.00 15.00
❑ 150 Chris Demaria AU/275 RC 15.00 6.00
❑ 151 Jonah Bayliss AU/275 RC 15.00 6.00
❑ 152 Geovany Soto AU/275 (RC) 15.00 6.00
❑ 153 Lyle Overbay AU/275 15.00 6.00
❑ 154 Joey Devine AU/275 RC 15.00 6.00
❑ 155 A.Freire AU/275 RC 15.00 6.00
❑ 156 Conor Jackson AU/275 (RC) 25.00 10.00
❑ 157 Danny Sandoval AU/275 RC 15.00 6.00
❑ 158 Chase Utley AU/275 50.00 20.00
❑ 159 Jeff Harris AU/275 RC 15.00 6.00
❑ 160 Ron Flores AU/275 RC 15.00 6.00
❑ 161 Scott Feldman AU/275 RC 15.00 6.00
❑ 162 Yadier Molina AU/275 25.00 10.00
❑ 163 Tim Corcoran AU/275 RC 15.00 6.00
❑ 164 Craig Hansen AU/275 RC 40.00 15.00
❑ 165 Jason Bergmann AU/275 RC 15.00 6.00
❑ 166 Craig Breslow AU/275 RC 15.00 6.00
❑ 167 Jhonny Peralta AU/275 15.00 6.00
❑ 168 J.Hermida AU/275 (RC) 25.00 10.00
❑ 169 Scott Kazmir AU/275 25.00 10.00
❑ 170 Bobby Crosby AU/99 30.00 12.50
❑ 171 Rich Harden AU/275 15.00 6.00
❑ 172 Casey Kotchman AU/275 15.00 6.00
❑ 173 Tim Hamulack AU/275 (RC) 15.00 6.00
❑ 174 Justin Morneau AU/275 25.00 10.00
❑ 175 Jake Peavy AU/275 25.00 10.00
❑ 176 Y.Betancourt AU/275 25.00 10.00
❑ 177 Jeremy Accardo AU/275 RC 15.00 6.00
❑ 178 Jorge Cantu AU/200 25.00 10.00
❑ 179 Marlon Byrd AU/275 15.00 6.00
❑ 180 R.Jorgensen AU/275 RC 15.00 6.00
❑ 181 C.Denorfia AU/275 (RC) 15.00 6.00
❑ 182 Steve Stemle AU/275 RC 15.00 6.00
❑ 183 Robert Andino AU/275 RC 15.00 6.00
❑ 184 Chris Heintz AU/275 RC 15.00 6.00

2003 Sweet Spot Classics

❑ COMP.SET w/o SP's (89) 40.00 15.00
❑ COMMON (1-74/76-90) .75 .30
❑ COMMON CARD (91-120) 8.00 3.00
❑ COMMON CARD (121-150) 5.00 2.00
❑ 1 Al Hrabosky .75 .30
❑ 2 Al Lopez .75 .30
❑ 3 Andre Dawson .75 .30
❑ 4 Bill Buckner .75 .30
❑ 5 Billy Williams .75 .30
❑ 6 Bob Feller .75 .30
❑ 7 Bob Lemon .75 .30
❑ 8 Bobby Doerr .75 .30
❑ 9 Cecil Cooper .75 .30
❑ 10 Cal Ripken 6.00 2.50
❑ 11 Carlton Fisk 1.25 .50
❑ 12 Catfish Hunter 1.25 .50
❑ 13 Chris Chambliss .75 .30
❑ 14 Dale Murphy 1.25 .50
❑ 15 Gaylord Perry .75 .30
❑ 16 Dave Kingman .75 .30
❑ 17 Dave Parker .75 .30
❑ 18 Dave Stewart .75 .30
❑ 19 David Cone .75 .30
❑ 20 Dennis Eckersley .75 .30
❑ 21 Don Baylor .75 .30
❑ 22 Don Sutton .75 .30
❑ 23 Duke Snider 1.25 .50
❑ 24 Dwight Evans 1.25 .50
❑ 25 Dwight Gooden .75 .30
❑ 26 Earl Weaver MG .75 .30
❑ 27 Early Wynn .75 .30
❑ 28 Eddie Mathews 2.00 .75
❑ 29 Enos Slaughter .75 .30
❑ 30 Ernie Banks 2.00 .75
❑ 31 Fred Lynn .75 .30
❑ 32 Fred Stanley .75 .30
❑ 33 Gary Carter .75 .30
❑ 34 George Foster .75 .30
❑ 35 Hal Newhouser .75 .30
❑ 36 George Kell .75 .30
❑ 37 Harmon Killebrew 2.00 .75
❑ 38 Hoyt Wilhelm .75 .30
❑ 39 Jack Morris .75 .30
❑ 40 Jim Bunning .75 .30
❑ 41 Jim Gilliam .75 .30
❑ 42 Jim Leyritz .75 .30
❑ 43 Jimmy Key .75 .30
❑ 44 Joe Carter .75 .30
❑ 45 Joe Morgan .75 .30
❑ 46 John Montefusco .75 .30
❑ 47 Johnny Bench 2.00 .75
❑ 48 Johnny Podres .75 .30
❑ 49 Jose Canseco 1.25 .50
❑ 50 Juan Marichal .75 .30
❑ 51 Keith Hernandez .75 .30
❑ 52 Ken Griffey Sr. .75 .30
❑ 53 Kirby Puckett 2.00 .75
❑ 54 Kirk Gibson .75 .30
❑ 55 Larry Doby .75 .30
❑ 56 Lee May .75 .30
❑ 57 Lee Mazzilli .75 .30
❑ 58 Lou Boudreau .75 .30
❑ 59 Mark McGwire 5.00 2.00
❑ 60 Maury Wills .75 .30
❑ 61 Mike Pagliarulo .75 .30
❑ 62 Monte Irvin .75 .30
❑ 63 Nolan Ryan 5.00 2.00
❑ 64 Orlando Cepeda .75 .30
❑ 65 Ozzie Smith 3.00 1.25
❑ 66 Paul O'Neill 1.25 .50
❑ 67 Pee Wee Reese 1.25 .50
❑ 68 Phil Niekro .75 .30
❑ 69 Ralph Kiner .75 .30
❑ 70 Red Schoendienst .75 .30
❑ 71 Richie Ashburn 1.25 .50
❑ 72 Rick Ferrell .75 .30
❑ 73 Robin Roberts .75 .30
❑ 74 Robin Yount 2.00 .75
❑ 75 Hideki Matsui/1999 XRC 15.00 6.00
❑ 75B Rod Carew ERR
❑ 76 Rollie Fingers .75 .30
❑ 77 Ron Cey .75 .30
❑ 78 Tom Seaver 1.25 .50
❑ 79 Sparky Anderson MG .75 .30
❑ 80 Stan Musial 3.00 1.25
❑ 81 Steve Garvey .75 .30
❑ 82 Ted Williams 4.00 1.50
❑ 83 Tommy Lasorda .75 .30
❑ 84 Tony Gwynn 2.50 1.00
❑ 85 Tony Perez .75 .30
❑ 86 Vida Blue .75 .30
❑ 87 Warren Spahn 1.25 .50
❑ 88 Bob Gibson 1.25 .50
❑ 89 Willie McCovey .75 .30
❑ 90 Willie Stargell 1.25 .50
❑ 91 Ted Williams TB 8.00 3.00
❑ 92 Ted Williams TB 8.00 3.00
❑ 93 Ted Williams TB 8.00 3.00
❑ 94 Ted Williams TB 8.00 3.00
❑ 95 Ted Williams TB 8.00 3.00
❑ 96 Ted Williams TB 8.00 3.00
❑ 97 Ted Williams TB 8.00 3.00
❑ 98 Ted Williams TB 8.00 3.00
❑ 99 Ted Williams TB 8.00 3.00
❑ 100 Ted Williams TB 8.00 3.00
❑ 101 Ted Williams TB 8.00 3.00
❑ 102 Ted Williams TB 8.00 3.00
❑ 103 Ted Williams TB 8.00 3.00
❑ 104 Ted Williams TB 8.00 3.00
❑ 105 Ted Williams TB 8.00 3.00
❑ 106 Ted Williams TB 8.00 3.00
❑ 106B Ted Williams TB 8.00 3.00
❑ 107 Ted Williams TB 8.00 3.00
❑ 108 Ted Williams TB 8.00 3.00
❑ 109 Ted Williams TB 8.00 3.00
❑ 110 Ted Williams TB 8.00 3.00

❑ 111	Ted Williams TB	8.00	3.00
❑ 112	Ted Williams TB	8.00	3.00
❑ 113	Ted Williams TB	8.00	3.00
❑ 114	Ted Williams TB	8.00	3.00
❑ 115	Ted Williams TB	8.00	3.00
❑ 117	Ted Williams TB	8.00	3.00
❑ 118	Ted Williams TB	8.00	3.00
❑ 119	Ted Williams TB	8.00	3.00
❑ 120	Ted Williams TB	8.00	3.00
❑ 121	Babe Ruth YH	15.00	6.00
❑ 122	Bucky Dent YH	5.00	2.00
❑ 123	Casey Stengel YH	5.00	2.00
❑ 124	Dave Righetti YH	5.00	2.00
❑ 125	Dave Winfield YH	5.00	2.00
❑ 126	Dick Tidrow YH	5.00	2.00
❑ 127	Dock Ellis YH	5.00	2.00
❑ 128	Don Mattingly YH	12.00	5.00
❑ 129	Hank Bauer YH	5.00	2.00
❑ 130	Jim Bouton YH	5.00	2.00
❑ 131	Jim Kaat YH	5.00	2.00
❑ 132	Joe DiMaggio YH	10.00	4.00
❑ 133	Joe Torre YH	5.00	2.00
❑ 134	Lou Piniella YH	5.00	2.00
❑ 135	Mel Stottlemyre YH	5.00	2.00
❑ 136	Mickey Mantle YH	20.00	8.00
❑ 137	Mickey Rivers YH	5.00	2.00
❑ 138	Phil Rizzuto YH	5.00	2.00
❑ 139	Ralph Branca YH	5.00	2.00
❑ 140	Ralph Houk YH	5.00	2.00
❑ 141	Roger Maris YH	8.00	3.00
❑ 142	Ron Guidry YH	5.00	2.00
❑ 143	Ruben Amaro Sr. YH	5.00	2.00
❑ 144	Sparky Lyle YH	5.00	2.00
❑ 145	Thurman Munson YH	8.00	3.00
❑ 146	Tommy Henrich YH	5.00	2.00
❑ 147	Tommy John YH	5.00	2.00
❑ 148	Tony Kubek YH	5.00	2.00
❑ 149	Whitey Ford YH	5.00	2.00
❑ 150	Yogi Berra YH	8.00	3.00

2005 Sweet Spot Classic

❑	COMPLETE SET (100)	40.00	15.00
❑ 1	Al Kaline	2.00	.75
❑ 2	Al Rosen	.75	.30
❑ 3	Babe Ruth	6.00	2.50
❑ 4	Bill Mazeroski	1.25	.50
❑ 5	Billy Williams	.75	.30
❑ 6	Bob Feller	1.25	.50
❑ 7	Bob Gibson	1.25	.50
❑ 8	Bobby Doerr	.75	.30
❑ 9	Brooks Robinson	1.25	.50
❑ 10	Cal Ripken	6.00	2.50
❑ 11	Carl Yastrzemski	3.00	1.25
❑ 12	Carlton Fisk	1.25	.50
❑ 13	Casey Stengel	1.25	.50
❑ 14	Christy Mathewson	2.00	.75
❑ 15	Cy Young	2.00	.75
❑ 16	Dale Murphy	1.25	.50
❑ 17	Dave Winfield	.75	.30
❑ 18	Dennis Eckersley	.75	.30
❑ 19	Dizzy Dean	1.25	.50
❑ 20	Don Drysdale	1.25	.50
❑ 21	Don Mattingly	4.00	1.50
❑ 22	Don Newcombe	.75	.30
❑ 23	Don Sutton	.75	.30
❑ 24	Duke Snider	1.25	.50
❑ 25	Dwight Evans	1.25	.50
❑ 26	Eddie Mathews	2.00	.75
❑ 27	Eddie Murray	2.00	.75
❑ 28	Enos Slaughter	.75	.30
❑ 29	Ernie Banks	2.00	.75
❑ 30	Frank Howard	.75	.30
❑ 31	Frank Robinson	.75	.30
❑ 32	Gary Carter	.75	.30
❑ 33	Gaylord Perry	.75	.30
❑ 34	George Brett	4.00	1.50
❑ 35	George Kell	.75	.30
❑ 36	George Sisler	.75	.30
❑ 37	Larry Doby	.75	.30
❑ 38	Harmon Killebrew	2.00	.75
❑ 39	Honus Wagner	2.00	.75
❑ 40	Jackie Robinson	2.00	.75
❑ 41	Jim Bunning	.75	.30
❑ 42	Jim Palmer	.75	.30
❑ 43	Jim Rice	.75	.30
❑ 44	Jimmie Foxx	2.00	.75
❑ 45	Joe DiMaggio	4.00	1.50
❑ 46	Joe Morgan	.75	.30
❑ 47	Johnny Bench	2.00	.75
❑ 48	Johnny Mize	.75	.30
❑ 49	Johnny Podres	.75	.30
❑ 50	Juan Marichal	.75	.30
❑ 51	Keith Hernandez	.75	.30
❑ 52	Kirby Puckett	2.00	.75
❑ 53	Lefty Grove	.75	.30
❑ 54	Lou Brock	1.25	.50
❑ 55	Lou Gehrig	4.00	1.50
❑ 56	Luis Aparicio	.75	.30
❑ 57	Fergie Jenkins	.75	.30
❑ 58	Maury Wills	.75	.30
❑ 59	Mel Ott	2.00	.75
❑ 60	Mickey Cochrane	.75	.30
❑ 61	Mickey Mantle	8.00	3.00
❑ 62	Mike Schmidt	4.00	1.50
❑ 63	Monte Irvin	.75	.30
❑ 64	Nolan Ryan	5.00	2.00
❑ 65	Orlando Cepeda	.75	.30
❑ 66	Ozzie Smith	3.00	1.25
❑ 67	Paul Molitor	.75	.30
❑ 68	Pee Wee Reese	1.25	.50
❑ 69	Phil Niekro	.75	.30
❑ 70	Phil Rizzuto	1.25	.50
❑ 71	Ralph Kiner	1.25	.50
❑ 72	Richie Ashburn	1.25	.50
❑ 73	Roberto Clemente	5.00	2.00
❑ 74	Robin Roberts	.75	.30
❑ 75	Robin Yount	2.00	.75
❑ 76	Rocky Colavito	1.25	.50
❑ 77	Rod Carew	1.25	.50
❑ 78	Rogers Hornsby	2.00	.75
❑ 79	Rollie Fingers	.75	.30
❑ 80	Roy Campanella	2.00	.75
❑ 81	Bob Lemon	.75	.30
❑ 82	Red Schoendienst	.75	.30
❑ 83	Satchel Paige	2.00	.75
❑ 84	Stan Musial	3.00	1.25
❑ 85	Steve Carlton	.75	.30
❑ 86	Ted Williams	4.00	1.50
❑ 87	Thurman Munson	2.00	.75
❑ 88	Tom Seaver	1.25	.50
❑ 89	Tony Gwynn	2.50	1.00
❑ 90	Tony Perez	1.25	.50
❑ 91	Ty Cobb	3.00	1.25
❑ 92	Wade Boggs	1.25	.50
❑ 93	Walter Johnson	2.00	.75
❑ 94	Warren Spahn	1.25	.50
❑ 95	Whitey Ford	1.25	.50
❑ 96	Will Clark	1.25	.50
❑ 97	Catfish Hunter	1.25	.50
❑ 98	Willie McCovey	1.25	.50
❑ 99	Willie Stargell	1.25	.50
❑ 100	Yogi Berra	2.00	.75

1911 T205

❑	COMPLETE SET (218)	35000.00	20000.00
❑	COMMON MAJOR (1-186)	150.00	90.00
❑	COM. MINOR (187-198)	300.00	150.00
❑ 1	Ed Abbaticchio	150.00	90.00
❑ 2	Red Ames	150.00	90.00
❑ 3	Jimmy Archer	150.00	90.00
❑ 4	Jimmy Austin	150.00	90.00
❑ 5	Bill Bailey	150.00	90.00
❑ 6	Frank Baker	500.00	300.00
❑ 7	Neal Ball	150.00	90.00

❑ 8A	Cy Barger Full B	150.00	90.00
❑ 8B	Cy Barger Part B	400.00	250.00
❑ 9	Jack Barry	150.00	90.00
❑ 10	Johnny Bates	150.00	90.00
❑ 11	Fred Beck	150.00	90.00
❑ 12	Beals Becker	150.00	90.00
❑ 13	George Bell	150.00	90.00
❑ 14	Chief Bender	250.00	150.00
❑ 15	Bill Bergen	150.00	90.00
❑ 16	Bob Bescher	150.00	90.00
❑ 17	Joe Birmingham	150.00	90.00
❑ 18	Russ Blackburne	150.00	90.00
❑ 19	Kitty Bransfield	150.00	90.00
❑ 20A	R.Bresnahan Closed	250.00	150.00
❑ 20B	R.Bresnahan Open	500.00	300.00
❑ 21	Al Bridwell	150.00	90.00
❑ 22	Mordecai Brown	500.00	300.00
❑ 23	Bobby Byrne	150.00	90.00
❑ 24	Howie Camnitz	150.00	90.00
❑ 25	Bill Carrigan	150.00	90.00
❑ 26	Frank Chance	400.00	250.00
❑ 27A	Hal Chase Last Name	400.00	250.00
❑ 27B	Hal Chase Full Name	200.00	120.00
❑ 28	Eddie Cicotte	250.00	150.00
❑ 29	Fred Clarke	500.00	300.00
❑ 30	Ty Cobb	6000.00	3500.00
❑ 31A	E.Collins Mouth Closed	400.00	250.00
❑ 31B	E.Collins Mouth Open	600.00	350.00
❑ 32	Frank Corridon	150.00	90.00
❑ 33A	Otis Crandall (Otis)	150.00	90.00
❑ 33B	Otis Crandall (Olis)	150.00	90.00
❑ 34	Lou Criger	150.00	90.00
❑ 35	Bill Dahlen	200.00	120.00
❑ 36	Jake Daubert	200.00	120.00
❑ 37	Jim Delahanty	150.00	90.00
❑ 38	Art Devlin	150.00	90.00
❑ 39	Josh Devore	150.00	90.00
❑ 40	Walt Dickson	150.00	90.00
❑ 41	Jiggs Donohue	200.00	120.00
❑ 42	Red Dooin	150.00	90.00
❑ 43	Mickey Doolan	150.00	90.00
❑ 44A	Patsy Dougherty White	200.00	120.00
❑ 44B	Patsy Dougherty Red	150.00	90.00
❑ 45	Tom Downey	150.00	90.00
❑ 46	Larry Doyle	150.00	90.00
❑ 47	Hugh Duffy	400.00	250.00
❑ 48	Jimmy Dygert	150.00	90.00
❑ 49	Dick Egan	150.00	90.00
❑ 50	Kid Elberfeld	150.00	90.00
❑ 51	Clyde Engle	150.00	90.00
❑ 52	Steve Evans	150.00	90.00
❑ 53	Johnny Evers	250.00	150.00
❑ 54	Bob Ewing	150.00	90.00
❑ 55	George Ferguson	150.00	90.00
❑ 56	Ray Fisher	200.00	120.00
❑ 57	Art Fletcher	150.00	90.00
❑ 58	John Flynn	150.00	90.00
❑ 59A	Russ Ford Dark Cap	150.00	90.00
❑ 59B	Russ Ford Light Cap	200.00	120.00
❑ 60	Bill Foxen	150.00	90.00
❑ 61	Art Fromme	150.00	90.00
❑ 62	Earl Gardner	150.00	90.00
❑ 63	Harry Gaspar	150.00	90.00
❑ 64	George Gibson	150.00	90.00
❑ 65	Wilbur Good	150.00	90.00
❑ 66A	P.Graham Rustlers	150.00	90.00
❑ 66B	P.Graham Cubs	500.00	300.00
❑ 67	Eddie Grant	200.00	120.00

- ❑ 68A Dolly Gray w/Stats 150.00 90.00
- ❑ 68B Dolly Gray w/o Stats 500.00 300.00
- ❑ 69 Clark Griffith 400.00 250.00
- ❑ 70 Bob Groom 150.00 90.00
- ❑ 71A Bob Harmon Both Ears 150.00 90.00
- ❑ 71B Bob Harmon Left Ear 400.00 250.00
- ❑ 72 Topsy Hartsel 150.00 90.00
- ❑ 73 Arnold Hauser 150.00 90.00
- ❑ 74 Charlie Hemphill 150.00 90.00
- ❑ 75 Buck Herzog 150.00 90.00
- ❑ 76A D.Hoblitzell No Stats 12000.00 7000.00
- ❑ 76B D.Hoblitzell w/o CIN 150.00 90.00
- ❑ 76C D.Hoblitzell w/CIN 200.00 120.00
- ❑ 76D D.Hoblitzell (Hoblitzel) 150.00 90.00
- ❑ 77 Danny Hoffman 150.00 90.00
- ❑ 78 Miller Huggins 500.00 300.00
- ❑ 79 John Hummell 150.00 90.00
- ❑ 80 Fred Jacklitsch 150.00 90.00
- ❑ 81 Hughie Jennings 400.00 250.00
- ❑ 82 Walter Johnson 2500.00 1500.00
- ❑ 83 Davy Jones 150.00 90.00
- ❑ 84 Tom Jones 150.00 90.00
- ❑ 85 Addie Joss 1000.00 600.00
- ❑ 86 Ed Karger 200.00 120.00
- ❑ 87 Ed Killian 150.00 90.00
- ❑ 88 Red Kleinow 200.00 120.00
- ❑ 89 John Kling 150.00 90.00
- ❑ 90 John Knight 150.00 90.00
- ❑ 91 Ed Konetchy 150.00 90.00
- ❑ 92 Harry Krause 150.00 90.00
- ❑ 93 Rube Kroh 150.00 90.00
- ❑ 94 Frank Lang 150.00 90.00
- ❑ 95 Frank LaPorte 150.00 90.00
- ❑ 96A Arlie Latham (W.A.) 150.00 90.00
- ❑ 96B Arlie Latham (A.) 150.00 90.00
- ❑ 97 Tommy Leach 150.00 90.00
- ❑ 98 Sam Leever 150.00 90.00
- ❑ 99A Lefty Leifield (A.) 150.00 90.00
- ❑ 99B Lefty Leifield (A.P.) 150.00 90.00
- ❑ 100 Ed Lennox 150.00 90.00
- ❑ 101 Paddy Livingston 150.00 90.00
- ❑ 102 Hans Lobert 150.00 90.00
- ❑ 103 Bris Lord 150.00 90.00
- ❑ 104 Harry Lord 150.00 90.00
- ❑ 105 John Lush 150.00 90.00
- ❑ 106 Nick Maddox 150.00 90.00
- ❑ 107 Sherry Magee 150.00 90.00
- ❑ 108 Rube Marquard 500.00 300.00
- ❑ 109 Christy Mathewson 2500.00 1500.00
- ❑ 110 Al Mattern 150.00 90.00
- ❑ 111 George McBride 150.00 90.00
- ❑ 112 Amby McConnell 150.00 90.00
- ❑ 113 Pryor McElveen 150.00 90.00
- ❑ 114 John McGraw MG 500.00 300.00
- ❑ 115 Harry McIntire 150.00 90.00
- ❑ 116 Matty McIntyre 150.00 90.00
- ❑ 117 Larry McLean 150.00 90.00
- ❑ 118 Fred Merkle 150.00 90.00
- ❑ 119 Chief Meyers 150.00 90.00
- ❑ 120 Clyde Milan 150.00 90.00
- ❑ 121 Dots Miller 150.00 90.00
- ❑ 122 Mike Mitchell 150.00 90.00
- ❑ 123A Pat Moran Extra Stat 400.00 250.00
- ❑ 123B Pat Moran 150.00 90.00
- ❑ 124 George Moriarity 150.00 90.00
- ❑ 125 George Mullin 150.00 90.00
- ❑ 126 Danny Murphy 150.00 90.00
- ❑ 127 Red Murray 150.00 90.00
- ❑ 128 Tom Needham 150.00 90.00
- ❑ 129 Rebel Oakes 150.00 90.00
- ❑ 130 Rube Oldring 150.00 90.00
- ❑ 131 Charley O'Leary 150.00 90.00
- ❑ 132 Fred Olmstead 150.00 90.00
- ❑ 133 Orval Overall 150.00 90.00
- ❑ 134 Freddy Parent 150.00 90.00
- ❑ 135 Dode Paskert 150.00 90.00
- ❑ 136 Fred Payne 150.00 90.00
- ❑ 137 Barney Pelty 150.00 90.00
- ❑ 138 Jack Pfiester 150.00 90.00
- ❑ 139 Ed Phelps 150.00 90.00
- ❑ 140 Decon Phillippe 150.00 90.00
- ❑ 141 Jack Quinn 150.00 90.00
- ❑ 142 Bugs Raymond 200.00 120.00
- ❑ 143 Ed Reulbach 150.00 90.00
- ❑ 144 Lewis Richie 150.00 90.00
- ❑ 145 Jack Rowan 200.00 120.00
- ❑ 146 Nap Rucker 150.00 90.00
- ❑ 147 Doc Scanlan 200.00 120.00
- ❑ 148 Germany Schaefer 150.00 90.00
- ❑ 149 Admiral Schlei 150.00 90.00
- ❑ 150 Boss Schmidt 150.00 90.00
- ❑ 151 Wildfire Schulte 150.00 90.00
- ❑ 152 Jim Scott 150.00 90.00
- ❑ 153 Bayard Sharpe 150.00 90.00
- ❑ 154A David Shean Rustlers 150.00 90.00
- ❑ 154B David Shean Cubs 500.00 300.00
- ❑ 155 Jimmy Sheckard 150.00 90.00
- ❑ 156 Hack Simmons 150.00 90.00
- ❑ 157 Tony Smith 150.00 90.00
- ❑ 158 Fred Snodgrass 150.00 90.00
- ❑ 159 Tris Speaker 1200.00 700.00
- ❑ 160 Jake Stahl 150.00 90.00
- ❑ 161 Oscar Stanage 150.00 90.00
- ❑ 162 Harry Steinfeldt 150.00 90.00
- ❑ 163 George Stone 150.00 90.00
- ❑ 164 George Stovall 150.00 90.00
- ❑ 165 Gabby Street 150.00 90.00
- ❑ 166 George Suggs 200.00 120.00
- ❑ 167 Ed Summers 150.00 90.00
- ❑ 168 Jeff Sweeney 200.00 120.00
- ❑ 169 Lee Tannehill 150.00 90.00
- ❑ 170 Ira Thomas 150.00 90.00
- ❑ 171 Joe Tinker 800.00 500.00
- ❑ 172 John Titus 150.00 90.00
- ❑ 173 Terry Turner 400.00 250.00
- ❑ 174 Hippo Vaughn 200.00 120.00
- ❑ 175 Heinie Wagner 200.00 120.00
- ❑ 176A B.Wallace w/cap 250.00 150.00
- ❑ 176B B.Wallace w/o Cap 1 600.00 350.00
- ❑ 176C B.Wallace w/o Cap 2 400.00 250.00
- ❑ 177 Ed Walsh 600.00 350.00
- ❑ 178 Zach Wheat 400.00 250.00
- ❑ 179 Doc White 150.00 90.00
- ❑ 180 Kirby White 200.00 120.00
- ❑ 181 Kaiser Wilhelm 200.00 120.00
- ❑ 182 Ed Willett 150.00 90.00
- ❑ 183A H.Wiltse Both Ears 150.00 90.00
- ❑ 183B H.Wiltse Right Ear 400.00 250.00
- ❑ 184 Owen Wilson 150.00 90.00
- ❑ 185 Harry Wolter 150.00 90.00
- ❑ 186 Cy Young 2500.00 1500.00
- ❑ 187 Doc Adkins 250.00 150.00
- ❑ 188 Jack Dunn 250.00 150.00
- ❑ 189 George Merritt 250.00 150.00
- ❑ 190 Charles Hanford 250.00 150.00
- ❑ 191 Hick Cady 250.00 150.00
- ❑ 192 James Frick 250.00 150.00
- ❑ 193 Wyatt Lee 250.00 150.00
- ❑ 194 Lewis McAllister 250.00 150.00
- ❑ 195 John Nee 250.00 150.00
- ❑ 196 Jimmy Collins 600.00 350.00
- ❑ 197 James Phelan 250.00 150.00
- ❑ 198 Emil Batch 250.00 150.00

1909 T206

- ❑ COMPLETE SET (520) 55000.00 30000.00
- ❑ COMMON MAJOR (1-389) 100.00 50.00
- ❑ COMMON MINOR (390-475) 100.00 50.00
- ❑ COM. SO. LEA. (476-523) 250.00 125.00
- ❑ 1 Ed Abbaticchio Follow Through 120.00 60.00
- ❑ 2 Ed Abbaticchio Waiting 150.00 75.00
- ❑ 3 Bill Abstein 120.00 60.00
- ❑ 4 Whitey Alperman 150.00 75.00
- ❑ 5 Red Ames Portrait 150.00 75.00
- ❑ 6 Red Ames Hands over Head 120.00 60.00
- ❑ 7 Red Ames Hands over Chest 150.00 75.00
- ❑ 8 Frank Arellanes 120.00 60.00
- ❑ 9 Jake Atz 120.00 60.00
- ❑ 10 Frank Baker 800.00 400.00
- ❑ 11 Neal Ball New York 150.00 75.00
- ❑ 12 Neal Ball Cleveland 120.00 60.00
- ❑ 13 Jap Barbeau 120.00 60.00
- ❑ 14 Jack Barry 120.00 60.00
- ❑ 15 Johnny Bates 150.00 75.00
- ❑ 16 Ginger Beaumont 150.00 75.00
- ❑ 17 Fred Beck 120.00 60.00
- ❑ 18 Beals Becker 120.00 60.00
- ❑ 19 George Bell Pitching 120.00 60.00
- ❑ 20 George Bell Hands over Head 150.00 75.00
- ❑ 21 Chief Bender Portrait 1000.00 500.00
- ❑ 22 Chief Bender w/Trees 1000.00 500.00
- ❑ 23 Chief Bender w/o Trees 800.00 400.00
- ❑ 24 Bill Bergen Catching 120.00 60.00
- ❑ 25 Bill Bergen Batting 150.00 75.00
- ❑ 26 Heinie Berger 120.00 60.00
- ❑ 27 Bob Bescher Fly Ball 120.00 60.00
- ❑ 28 Bob Bescher Portrait 120.00 60.00
- ❑ 29 Joe Birmingham 150.00 75.00
- ❑ 30 Jack Bliss 120.00 60.00
- ❑ 31 Frank Bowerman 150.00 75.00
- ❑ 32 Bill Bradley Portrait 150.00 75.00
- ❑ 33 Bill Bradley Batting 120.00 60.00
- ❑ 34 Kitty Bransfield 150.00 75.00
- ❑ 35 Roger Bresnahan Portrait 600.00 300.00
- ❑ 36 Roger Bresnahan Batting 600.00 300.00
- ❑ 37 Al Bridwell Portrait 150.00 75.00
- ❑ 38 Al Bridwell Sweater 120.00 60.00
- ❑ 39 George Brown Chicago 250.00 125.00
- ❑ 40 George Brown Wash 800.00 400.00
- ❑ 41 Mord.Brown Portrait 1000.00 500.00
- ❑ 42 Mord.Brown Chi Shirt 1000.00 500.00
- ❑ 43 Mord.Brown Cubs Shirt 1000.00 500.00
- ❑ 44 Al Burch Fielding 120.00 60.00
- ❑ 45 Al Burch Batting 250.00 125.00
- ❑ 46 Bill Burns 120.00 60.00
- ❑ 47 Donie Bush 150.00 75.00
- ❑ 48 Bobby Byrne 120.00 60.00
- ❑ 49 Howie Camnitz Arms Folded 150.00 75.00
- ❑ 50 Howie Camnitz Hands over Head 120.00 60.00
- ❑ 51 Howie Camnitz Throwing 120.00 60.00
- ❑ 52 Billy Campbell 120.00 60.00
- ❑ 53 Bill Carrigan 120.00 60.00
- ❑ 54 F.Chance Cubs Shirt 1000.00 500.00
- ❑ 55 F.Chance Chi Shirt 1000.00 500.00
- ❑ 56 Frank Chance Batting 800.00 400.00
- ❑ 57 Chappy Charles 120.00 60.00
- ❑ 58 Hal Chase Blue Portrait 250.00 125.00
- ❑ 59 Hal Chase Pink Portrait 400.00 200.00
- ❑ 60 Hal Chase Holding Cup 250.00 125.00
- ❑ 61 H.Chase Throw Drk Cap 250.00 125.00
- ❑ 62 H.Chase Throw Wht Cap 300.00 150.00
- ❑ 63 Jack Chesbro 500.00 250.00
- ❑ 64 Eddie Cicotte 400.00 200.00
- ❑ 65 Fred Clarke Portrait 400.00 200.00
- ❑ 66 Fred Clarke w/Bat 400.00 200.00
- ❑ 67 Nig Clarke 150.00 75.00
- ❑ 68 T.Cobb Red Portrait 3000.00 1500.00
- ❑ 69 T.Cobb Green Portrait 4000.00 2500.00
- ❑ 70 T.Cobb Bat on Shldr 3000.00 1500.00
- ❑ 71 T.Cobb Bat off Shldr 3000.00 1500.00
- ❑ 72 Eddie Collins 800.00 400.00
- ❑ 73 Wid Conroy Fielding 150.00 75.00
- ❑ 74 Wid Conroy Bat on Shldr 120.00 60.00
- ❑ 75 Harry Covaleski 150.00 75.00
- ❑ 76 Doc Crandall w/o Cap 120.00 60.00
- ❑ 77 Doc Crandall w/Cap 120.00 60.00
- ❑ 78 S.Crawford Batting 1000.00 500.00
- ❑ 79 S.Crawford Throwing 1000.00 500.00
- ❑ 80 Birdie Cree 120.00 60.00
- ❑ 81 Lou Criger 150.00 75.00
- ❑ 82 Dode Criss 150.00 75.00
- ❑ 83 Bill Dahlen Boston 250.00 125.00
- ❑ 84 Bill Dahlen Brooklyn 400.00 200.00
- ❑ 85 George Davis 400.00 200.00
- ❑ 86 Harry Davis (Davis) 120.00 60.00
- ❑ 87 Harry Davis (H.Davis) 150.00 75.00
- ❑ 88 Jim Delehanty 150.00 75.00
- ❑ 89 Ray Demmitt Stl 6000.00 3000.00
- ❑ 90 Ray Demmitt NY 150.00 75.00

❑ 91 Art Devlin 150.00 75.00
❑ 92 Josh Devore 120.00 60.00
❑ 93 Bill Dineen 120.00 60.00
❑ 94 Mike Donlin Fielding 250.00 125.00
❑ 95 Mike Donlin Sitting 250.00 125.00
❑ 96 Mike Donlin Batting 150.00 75.00
❑ 97 Jiggs Donohue 150.00 75.00
❑ 98 Bill Donovan Portrait 150.00 75.00
❑ 99 Bill Donovan Throwing 120.00 60.00
❑ 100 Red Dooin 150.00 75.00
❑ 101 Mickey Doolan Fielding 120.00 60.00
❑ 102 Mickey Doolan Batting 120.00 60.00
❑ 103 Mickey Doolan (Doolin) 150.00 75.00
❑ 104 Patsy Dougherty Portrait 150.00 75.00
❑ 105 Patsy Dougherty Fielding 120.0060.00
❑ 106 Tom Downey Batting 120.00 60.00
❑ 107 Tom Downey Fielding 120.00 60.00
❑ 108A Joe Doyle 250.00 125.00
❑ 108B Joe Doyle Nat'l 8000.00 4000.00
❑ 109 Larry Doyle Sweater 150.00 75.00
❑ 110 Larry Doyle Throwing 250.00 125.00
❑ 111 Larry Doyle Bat on Shldr 150.00 75.00
❑ 112 Jean Dubuc 120.00 60.00
❑ 113 Hugh Duffy 800.00 400.00
❑ 114 Joe Dunn 120.00 60.00
❑ 115 Bull Durham 150.00 75.00
❑ 116 Jimmy Dygert 120.00 60.00
❑ 117 Ted Easterly 120.00 60.00
❑ 118 Dick Egan 120.00 60.00
❑ 119 Kid Elberfeld Fielding 120.00 60.00
❑ 120 Kid Elberfeld Wash Port 1500.00 750.00
❑ 121 Kid Elberfeld NY Port 150.00 75.00
❑ 122 Clyde Engle 120.00 60.00
❑ 123 Steve Evans 120.00 60.00
❑ 124 J.Evers Portrait 1200.00 600.00
❑ 125 J.Evers Cubs Shirt 1000.00 500.00
❑ 126 J.Evers Chi Shirt 1000.00 500.00
❑ 127 Bob Ewing 150.00 75.00
❑ 128 George Ferguson 120.00 60.00
❑ 129 Hobe Ferris 150.00 75.00
❑ 130 Lou Fiene Portrait 120.00 60.00
❑ 131 Lou Fiene Throwing 120.00 60.00
❑ 132 Art Fletcher 120.00 60.00
❑ 133 Elmer Flick 600.00 300.00
❑ 134 Russ Ford 120.00 60.00
❑ 135 John Frill 120.00 60.00
❑ 136 Art Fromme 120.00 60.00
❑ 137 Chick Gandil 500.00 250.00
❑ 138 Bob Ganley 150.00 75.00
❑ 139 Harry Gasper 120.00 60.00
❑ 140 Rube Geyer 120.00 60.00
❑ 141 George Gibson 150.00 75.00
❑ 142 Billy Gilbert 150.00 75.00
❑ 143 Wilbur Goode 150.00 75.00
❑ 144 Bill Graham 120.00 60.00
❑ 145 Peaches Graham 120.00 60.00
❑ 146 Dolly Gray 150.00 75.00
❑ 147 Clark Griffith Portrait 500.00 250.00
❑ 148 Clark Griffith Batting 500.00 250.00
❑ 149 Bob Groom 120.00 60.00
❑ 150 Ed Hahn 150.00 75.00
❑ 151 Topsy Hartsel 120.00 60.00
❑ 152 Charlie Hemphill 150.00 75.00
❑ 153 Buck Herzog New York 150.00 75.00
❑ 154 Buck Herzog Boston 120.00 60.00
❑ 155 Bill Hinchman 150.00 75.00
❑ 156 Doc Hoblitzell 120.00 60.00
❑ 157 Danny Hoffman 120.00 60.00
❑ 158 Solly Hofman 120.00 60.00
❑ 159 Del Howard 120.00 60.00
❑ 160 Harry Howell Portrait 120.00 60.00
❑ 161 Harry Howell Hand on Hip 120.0060.00
❑ 162 M.Huggins Portrait 800.00 400.00
❑ 163 M.Huggins Mouth 800.00 400.00
❑ 164 Rudy Hulswitt 120.00 60.00
❑ 165 John Hummel 120.00 60.00
❑ 166 George Hunter 120.00 60.00
❑ 167 Frank Isbell 150.00 75.00
❑ 168 Fred Jacklitsch 150.00 75.00
❑ 169 H.Jennings Port 800.00 400.00
❑ 170 H.Jennings One 800.00 400.00
❑ 171 H.Jennings Both 800.00 400.00
❑ 172 Walter Johnson Port 2000.001000.00
❑ 173 Walter Johnson Hands 2000.00
1000.00
❑ 174 Davy Jones 120.00 60.00

❑ 175 Fielder Jones Portrait 150.00 75.00
❑ 176 Fielder Jones Hands on Hips 150.00 75.00
❑ 177 Tom Jones 150.00 75.00
❑ 178 Tim Jordan Portrait 150.00 75.00
❑ 179 Tim Jordan Batting 120.00 60.00
❑ 180 Addie Joss Portrait 1200.00 600.00
❑ 181 Addie Joss Pitching 1000.00 500.00
❑ 182 Ed Karger 150.00 75.00
❑ 183 Willie Keeler Portrait 1200.00 600.00
❑ 184 Willie Keeler Batting 1000.00 500.00
❑ 185 Ed Killian Portrait 150.00 75.00
❑ 186 Ed Killian Pitching 120.00 60.00
❑ 187 Red Kleinow Batting 150.00 75.00
❑ 188 Red Kleinow Catch NY 120.00 60.00
❑ 189 Red Kleinow Catch Bos 1500.00750.00
❑ 190 Johnny Kling 150.00 75.00
❑ 191 Otto Knabe 120.00 60.00
❑ 192 John Knight Portrait 120.00 60.00
❑ 193 John Knight Batting 120.00 60.00
❑ 194 Ed Konetchy Awaiting Ball 120.00 60.00
❑ 195 Ed Konetchy Glove over Head 150.00 75.00
❑ 196 Harry Krause Portrait 120.00 60.00
❑ 197 Harry Krause Pitching 120.00 60.00
❑ 198 Rube Kroh 120.00 60.00
❑ 199 Nap Lajoie Portrait 1500.00 750.00
❑ 200 Nap Lajoie Batting 1200.00 600.00
❑ 201 Nap Lajoie Throwing 1200.00 600.00
❑ 202 Joe Lake NY 150.00 75.00
❑ 203 Joe Lake Stl Hands over Head 120.00 60.00
❑ 204 Joe Lake Stl Throwing 120.00 60.00
❑ 205 Frank LaPorte 120.00 30.00
❑ 206 Arlie Latham 150.00 75.00
❑ 207 Tommy Leach Portrait 150.00 75.00
❑ 208 Tommy Leach Fielding 120.00 60.00
❑ 209 Lefty Leifield Batting 120.00 60.00
❑ 210 Lefty Hands behind Head 150.00 75.00
❑ 211 Ed Lennox 120.00 60.00
❑ 212 Glenn Liebhardt 150.00 75.00
❑ 213 Vive Lindaman 250.00 125.00
❑ 214 Paddy Livingstone 120.00 60.00
❑ 215 Hans Lobert 150.00 75.00
❑ 216 Harry Lord 120.00 60.00
❑ 217 Harry Lumley 150.00 75.00
❑ 218 Carl Lundgren 600.00 300.00
❑ 219 Nick Maddox. 120.00 60.00
❑ 220 Sherry Magee Portrait 250.00 125.00
❑ 221 Sherry Magee Batting 120.00 60.00
❑ 222 Sherry Magie Port ERR 20000.00 10000.00
❑ 223 Rube Manning Batting 150.00 75.00
❑ 224 Rube Manning
Hands over Head 120.00 60.00
❑ 225 R.Marquard Portrait 1000.00 500.00
❑ 226 R.Marquard Pitching 800.00 400.00
❑ 227 R.Marquard Standing 800.00 400.00
❑ 228 Doc Marshall 120.00 60.00
❑ 229 C.Mathewson Portrait 2500.001250.00
❑ 230 C.Mathewson Wht Cap 2000.00 1000.00
❑ 231 C.Mathewson Drk Cap 2000.00 1000.00
❑ 232 Al Mattern 120.00 60.00
❑ 233 Jack McAleese 120.00 60.00
❑ 234 George McBride 120.00 60.00
❑ 235 Moose McCormick 120.00 60.00
❑ 236 Pryor McElveen 120.00 60.00
❑ 237 J.McGraw w/o Cap 1000.00 500.00
❑ 238 J.McGraw w/Cap 1000.00 500.00
❑ 239 J.McGraw Finger 1000.00 500.00
❑ 240 J.McGraw Glove-Hip 1000.00 500.00
❑ 241 Harry McIntire Brooklyn 150.00 75.00
❑ 242 Harry McIntire Brooklyn-Chi 120.00 60.00
❑ 243 Matty McIntyre 120.00 60.00
❑ 244 Larry McLean 120.00 60.00
❑ 245 George McQuillan Throwing 150.00 75.00
❑ 246 George McQuillan Batting 120.0060.00
❑ 247 Fred Merkle Portrait 250.00 125.00
❑ 248 Fred Merkle Throwing 250.00 125.00
❑ 249 Chief Meyers 120.00 60.00
❑ 250 Chief Meyers Fielding 120.00 60.00
❑ 251 Chief Meyers Batting 150.00 75.00
❑ 252 Clyde Milan 120.00 60.00
❑ 253 Dots Miller 120.00 60.00
❑ 254 Mike Mitchell 120.00 60.00
❑ 255 Pat Moran 120.00 60.00
❑ 256 George Moriarty 120.00 60.00
❑ 257 Mike Mowrey 120.00 60.00
❑ 258 George Mullen 120.00 60.00
❑ 259 George Mullin Throwing 150.00 75.00

❑ 260 George Mullin Batting 120.00 60.00
❑ 261 Danny Murphy Throwing 150.00 75.00
❑ 262 Danny Murphy Bat on Shoulder 120.00 60.00
❑ 263 Red Murray Sweater 120.00 60.00
❑ 264 Red Murray Bat on shoulder 120.00 60.00
❑ 265 Tom Needham 120.00 60.00
❑ 266 Simon Nicholls 150.00 75.00
❑ 267 Simon Nichols 120.00 60.00
❑ 268 Harry Niles 150.00 75.00
❑ 269 Rebel Oakes 120.00 60.00
❑ 270 Bill O'Hara NY 120.00 60.00
❑ 271 Bill O'Hara Stl 6000.003000.00
❑ 272 Rube Oldring Fielding 150.00 75.00
❑ 273 Rube Oldring Bat on Shoulder 150.00 75.00
❑ 274 Charley O'Leary Portrait 150.00 75.00
❑ 275 Charley O'Leary
Hands on Knees 120.00 60.00
❑ 276 Orval Overall Portrait 150.00 75.00
❑ 277 Orval Overall Follow Through 120.00 60.00
❑ 278 Orval Overall Hiding Ball 120.00 60.00
❑ 279 Frank Owen 150.00 75.00
❑ 280 Freddy Parent 150.00 75.00
❑ 281 Dode Paskert 120.00 60.00
❑ 282 Jim Pastorius 150.00 75.00
❑ 283 Harry Pattee 300.00 150.00
❑ 284 Fred Payne 120.00 60.00
❑ 285 Barney Pelty Horizontal 250.00 125.00
❑ 286 Barney Pelty Vertical 120.00 60.00
❑ 287 George Perring 120.00 60.00
❑ 288 Jeff Pfeffer 120.00 60.00
❑ 289 Jack Pfeister Sitting 120.00 60.00
❑ 290 Jack Pfeister Pitching 120.00 60.00
❑ 291 Ed Phelps 120.00 60.00
❑ 292 Deacon Phillippe 250.00 125.00
❑ 293 Eddie Plank 40000.00 20000.00
❑ 294 Jack Powell 150.00 75.00
❑ 295 Mike Powers 250.00 125.00
❑ 296 Billy Purtell 120.00 60.00
❑ 297 Jack Quinn 120.00 60.00
❑ 298 Bugs Raymond 150.00 75.00
❑ 299 Ed Reulbach Pitching 250.00 125.00
❑ 300 Ed Reulbach Hands at Side 250.00 125.00
❑ 301 Bob Rhoades Hand in Air 120.00 60.00
❑ 302 Bob Rhoades Ready to Pitch 120.00 60.00
❑ 303 Charlie Rhodes 120.00 60.00
❑ 304 Claude Ritchey 150.00 75.00
❑ 305 Claude Rossman 120.00 60.00
❑ 306 Nap Rucker Portrait 250.00 125.00
❑ 307 Nap Rucker Pitching 150.00 75.00
❑ 308 Germany Schaefer Wash 150.00 75.00
❑ 309 Germany Schaefer Det 150.00 75.00
❑ 310 Admiral Schlei Sweater 120.00 60.00
❑ 311 Admiral Schlei Batting 120.00 60.00
❑ 312 Admiral Schlei Fielding 150.00 75.00
❑ 313 Boss Schmidt Portrait 120.00 60.00
❑ 314 Boss Schmidt Throwing 150.00 75.00
❑ 315 Frank Schulte Back Turned 120.00 60.00
❑ 316 Frank Schulte Front Pose 150.0075.00
❑ 317 Jim Scott 120.00 60.00
❑ 318 Cy Seymour Portrait 120.00 60.00
❑ 319 Cy Seymour Throwing 120.00 60.00
❑ 320 Cy Seymour Batting 150.00 75.00
❑ 321 Al Shaw 150.00 75.00
❑ 322 Jimmy Sheckard Throwing 120.00 60.00
❑ 323 Jimmy Sheckard Side View 150.00 75.00
❑ 324 Bill Shipke 150.00 75.00
❑ 325 Frank Smith Listed-Smith 120.0060.00
❑ 326 Frank Smith Chi-Bos 800.00 400.00
❑ 327 Frank Smith Listed-F.Smith 150.00 75.00
❑ 328 Happy Smith 120.00 60.00
❑ 329 F.Snodgrass Bat 150.00 75.00
❑ 329A F.Snodgrass Bat UER 4000.00 2500.00
❑ 330 F.Snodgrass Catching 150.00 75.00
❑ 331 Bob Spade 150.00 75.00
❑ 332 Tris Speaker 1500.00 750.00
❑ 333 Tubby Spencer 150.00 75.00
❑ 334 Jake Stahl Fly Ball 150.00 75.00
❑ 335 Jake Stahl Arms Down 150.00 75.00
❑ 336 Oscar Stanage 120.00 60.00
❑ 337 Charlie Starr 120.00 60.00
❑ 338 Harry Steinfeldt Portrait 250.00 125.00
❑ 339 Harry Steinfeldt Batting 150.00 75.00
❑ 340 Jim Stephens 120.00 60.00
❑ 341 George Stone 150.00 75.00
❑ 342 George Stovall Portrait 150.00 75.00
❑ 343 George Stovall Batting 120.00 60.00

❑ 344 Gabby Street Portrait 150.00 75.00
❑ 345 Gabby Street Catching 120.00 60.00
❑ 346 Billy Sullivan 150.00 75.00
❑ 347 Ed Summers 120.00 60.00
❑ 348 Jeff Sweeney 120.00 60.00
❑ 349 Bill Sweeney 120.00 60.00
❑ 350 Jesse Tannehill 120.00 60.00
❑ 351 Lee Tan- Listed-L.Tannehill 150.00 75.00
❑ 352 Lee Tan- Listed-Tannehill 120.00 60.00
❑ 353 Fred Tenney 150.00 75.00
❑ 354 Ira Thomas 120.00 60.00
❑ 355 J.Tinker Bat off Shldr 1200.00 600.00
❑ 356 J.Tinker Bat on Shldr 1200.00 600.00
❑ 357 J.Tinker Portrait 1500.00 750.00
❑ 358 J.Tinker Hand-Knee 1200.00 600.00
❑ 359 John Titus 120.00 60.00
❑ 360 Terry Turner 150.00 75.00
❑ 361 Bob Unglaub 120.00 60.00
❑ 362 R.Waddell Portrait 1200.00 600.00
❑ 363 R.Waddell Pitching 1000.00 500.00
❑ 364 Heinie Wagner Left Shldr 250.00 125.00
❑ 365 Heinie Wagner Right Shldr 150.00 75.00
❑ 366 Honus Wagner 600000.00 300000.00
❑ 367 Bobby Wallace 800.00 400.00
❑ 368 Ed Walsh 1200.00 600.00
❑ 369 Jack Warhop 120.00 60.00
❑ 370 Jake Weimer 150.00 75.00
❑ 371 Zach Wheat 800.00 400.00
❑ 372 Doc White Portrait 150.00 75.00
❑ 373 Doc White Pitching 120.00 60.00
❑ 374 Kaiser Wilhelm Batting 120.00 60.00
❑ 375 Kaiser Wilhelm Hands to Chest 150.00 75.00
❑ 376 Ed Willett Batting 120.00 60.00
❑ 377 Ed Willett Pitching 120.00 60.00
❑ 378 Jimmy Williams 150.00 75.00
❑ 379 Vic Willis Pitt 500.00 250.00
❑ 380 Vic Willis Stl Pitch 400.00 200.00
❑ 381 Vic Willis Stl Bat 400.00 200.00
❑ 382 Chief Wilson 120.00 60.00
❑ 383 Hooks Wiltse Portrait 150.00 75.00
❑ 384 Hooks Wiltse Sweater 120.00 60.00
❑ 385 Hooks Wiltse Pirching 120.00 60.00
❑ 386 Cy Young Portrait 2500.00 1250.00
❑ 387 Cy Young Pitch Front 2000.00 1000.00
❑ 388 Cy Young Pitch Side 2000.00 1000.00
❑ 389 Heinie Zimmerman: 120.00 60.00
❑ 390 Fred Abbott 100.00 50.00
❑ 391 Merle (Doc) Adkins 100.00 50.00
❑ 392 John Anderson 100.00 50.00
❑ 393 Herman Armbruster 100.00 50.00
❑ 394 Harry Arndt 100.00 50.00
❑ 395 Cy Barger 120.00 60.00
❑ 396 John Barry 100.00 50.00
❑ 397 Emil H. Batch 100.00 50.00
❑ 398 Jake Beckley 500.00 250.00
❑ 399 Lena Blackburne 150.00 75.00
❑ 400 David Brain 100.00 50.00
❑ 401 Roy Brashear 100.00 50.00
❑ 402 Fred Burchell 100.00 50.00
❑ 403 Jimmy Burke 100.00 50.00
❑ 404 John Butler 100.00 50.00
❑ 405 Charles Carr 100.00 50.00
❑ 406 Doc Casey 100.00 50.00
❑ 407 Peter Cassidy 100.00 50.00
❑ 408 Wm. Chappelle 120.00 60.00
❑ 409 Wm. Clancy 100.00 50.00
❑ 410 Joshua Clarke 100.00 50.00
❑ 411 William Clymer 100.00 50.00
❑ 412 Jimmy Collins 800.00 400.00
❑ 413 Bunk Congalton 100.00 50.00
❑ 414 Gavvy Cravath 250.00 125.00
❑ 415 Monte Cross 120.00 60.00
❑ 416 Paul Davidson 100.00 50.00
❑ 417 Frank Delehanty 150.00 75.00
❑ 418 Rube Dessau 100.00 50.00
❑ 419 Gus Dorner 100.00 50.00
❑ 420 Jerome Downs 100.00 50.00
❑ 421 Jack Dunn 150.00 75.00
❑ 422 James Flanagan 100.00 50.00
❑ 423 James Freeman 100.00 50.00
❑ 424 John Ganzel 100.00 50.00
❑ 425 Myron Grimshaw 100.00 50.00
❑ 426 Robert Hall 100.00 50.00
❑ 427 William Hallman 120.00 60.00
❑ 428 John Hannifan 100.00 50.00
❑ 429 Jack Hayden 100.00 50.00
❑ 430 Harry Hinchman 100.00 50.00
❑ 431 Harry C. Hoffman 100.00 50.00
❑ 432 James B. Jackson 120.00 60.00
❑ 433 Joe Kelley 500.00 250.00
❑ 434 Rube Kissinger 120.00 60.00
❑ 435 Otto Krueger 100.00 50.00
❑ 436 William Lattimore 100.00 50.00
❑ 437 James Lavender 100.00 50.00
❑ 438 Carl Lundgren 100.00 50.00
❑ 439 Wm. Malarkey 120.00 60.00
❑ 440 Wm. Maloney 100.00 50.00
❑ 441 Dennis McGann 100.00 50.00
❑ 442 James McGinley 100.00 50.00
❑ 443 Joe McGinnity 500.00 250.00
❑ 444 Ulysses McGlynn 100.00 50.00
❑ 445 George Merritt 100.00 50.00
❑ 446 Wm. Milligan 100.00 50.00
❑ 447 Fred Mitchell. 100.00 50.00
❑ 448 Dan Moeller 100.00 50.00
❑ 449 Joseph H. Moran 100.00 50.00
❑ 450 Wm. Nattress 100.00 50.00
❑ 451 Frank Oberlin 100.00 50.00
❑ 452 Peter O'Brien 100.00 50.00
❑ 453 Wm. O'Neil 100.00 50.00
❑ 454 James Phelan 100.00 50.00
❑ 455 Oliver Pickering 100.00 50.00
❑ 456 Philip Poland 100.00 50.00
❑ 457 Ambrose Puttman 100.00 50.00
❑ 458 Lee Quillen 100.00 50.00
❑ 459 Newton Randall 100.00 50.00
❑ 460 Louis Ritter 100.00 50.00
❑ 461 Dick Rudolph 100.00 50.00
❑ 462 George Schirm 100.00 50.00
❑ 463 Larry Schlafly 100.00 50.00
❑ 464 Ossie Schreckengost 120.00 60.00
❑ 465 William Shannon 100.00 50.00
❑ 466 Bayard Sharpe 100.00 50.00
❑ 466A Bayard Shappe UER 1000.00 500.00
❑ 467 Royal Shaw 100.00 50.00
❑ 468 James Slagle 100.00 50.00
❑ 469 George Henry Smith 100.00 50.00
❑ 470 Samuel Strang 100.00 50.00
❑ 471 Luther Taylor 250.00 125.00
❑ 472 John Thielman 100.00 50.00
❑ 473 John F. White 100.00 50.00
❑ 474 William Wright 100.00 50.00
❑ 475 Irving M. Young 120.00 60.00
❑ 476 Jack Bastian 250.00 125.00
❑ 477 Harry Bay 250.00 125.00
❑ 478 Wm. Bernhard 250.00 125.00
❑ 479 Ted Breitenstein 250.00 125.00
❑ 480 George Carey 250.00 125.00
❑ 481 Cad Coles 250.00 125.00
❑ 482 Wm. Cranston 250.00 125.00
❑ 483 Roy Ellam 250.00 125.00
❑ 484 Edward Foster 250.00 125.00
❑ 485 Charles Fritz 250.00 125.00
❑ 486 Ed Greminger 250.00 125.00
❑ 487 Guiheen 250.00 '125.00
❑ 488 William F. Hart 250.00 125.00
❑ 489 James Henry Hart 250.00 125.00
❑ 490 J.R. Helm 250.00 125.00
❑ 491 Gordon Hickman 250.00 125.00
❑ 492 Buck Hooker 250.00 125.00
❑ 493 Ernie Howard 250.00 125.00
❑ 494 A.O. Jordan 250.00 125.00
❑ 495 J.F. Kiernan 250.00 125.00
❑ 496 Frank King 250.00 125.00
❑ 497 James LaFitte 250.00 125.00
❑ 498 Harry Lentz 250.00 125.00
❑ 499 Perry Lipe 250.00 125.00
❑ 500 George Manion 250.00 125.00
❑ 501 McCauley 250.00 125.00
❑ 502 Charles B. Miller 250.00 125.00
❑ 503 Carlton Molesworth 250.00 125.00
❑ 504 Dominic Mullaney 250.00 125.00
❑ 505 Albert Orth 250.00 125.00
❑ 506 William Otey 250.00 125.00
❑ 507 George Paige 250.00 125.00
❑ 508 Hub Perdue 300.00 150.00
❑ 509 Archie Persons 250.00 125.00
❑ 510 Edward Reagan 250.00 125.00
❑ 511 R.H. Revelle 250.00 125.00
❑ 512 Isaac Rockenfeld 250.00 125.00
❑ 513 Ray Ryan 250.00 125.00
❑ 514 Charles Seitz 250.00 125.00
❑ 515 Frank Shaughnessy 300.00 150.00
❑ 516 Carlos Smith 250.00 125.00
❑ 517 Sid Smith 250.00 125.00
❑ 518 M.R.(Dolly) Stark 300.00 150.00
❑ 519 Tony Thebo 250.00 125.00
❑ 520 Woodie Thornton 250.00 125.00
❑ 521 Juan Violat 250.00 125.00
❑ 522 James Westlake 250.00 125.00
❑ 523 Foley White 250.00 125.00

1952 Topps

❑ COMP.MASTER SET (487) 80000.00 40000.00
❑ COMPLETE SET (407) 65000.00 40000.00
❑ COMMON CARD (1-80) 60.00 35.00
❑ COMMON CARD (81-250) 40.00 20.00
❑ COMMON CARD (251-310) 50.00 30.00
❑ COMMON CARD (311-407) 250.00 150.00
❑ WRAPPER (1-CENT) 250.00 200.00
❑ WRAPPER (5-CENT) 100.00 75.00
❑ 1 Andy Pafko 5000.00 3000.00
❑ 1A Andy Pafko Black 3000.00 1800.00
❑ 2 Pete Runnels RC 250.00 150.00
❑ 2A Pete Runnels Black 250.00 150.00
❑ 3 Hank Thompson 70.00 40.00
❑ 3A Hank Thompson Black 70.00 40.00
❑ 4 Don Lenhardt 60.00 35.00
❑ 4A Don Lenhardt Black 60.00 35.00
❑ 5 Larry Jansen 70.00 40.00
❑ 5A Larry Jansen Black 70.00 40.00
❑ 6 Grady Hatton 60.00 35.00
❑ 6A Grady Hatton Black 60.00 35.00
❑ 7 Wayne Terwilliger 60.00 35.00
❑ 7A Wayne Terwilliger Black 60.00 35.00
❑ 8 Fred Marsh RC 60.00 35.00
❑ 8A Fred Marsh Black 60.00 35.00
❑ 9 Robert Hogue RC 60.00 35.00
❑ 9A Robert Hogue Black 60.00 35.00
❑ 10 Al Rosen 70.00 40.00
❑ 10A Al Rosen Black 70.00 40.00
❑ 11 Phil Rizzuto 400.00 250.00
❑ 11A Phil Rizzuto Black 350.00 200.00
❑ 12 Monty Basgall RC 60.00 35.00
❑ 12A Monty Basgall Black 60.00 35.00
❑ 13 Johnny Wyrostek 60.00 35.00
❑ 13A Johnny Wyrostek Black 60.00 35.00
❑ 14 Bob Elliott 70.00 40.00
❑ 14A Bob Elliott Black 70.00 40.00
❑ 15 Johnny Pesky 70.00 40.00
❑ 15A Johnny Pesky Black 70.00 40.00
❑ 16 Gene Hermanski 60.00 35.00
❑ 16A Gene Hermanski Black 60.00 35.00
❑ 17 Jim Hegan 70.00 40.00
❑ 17A Jim Hegan Black 70.00 40.00
❑ 18 Merrill Combs RC 60.00 35.00
❑ 18A Merrill Combs Black 60.00 35.00
❑ 19 Johnny Bucha RC 60.00 35.00
❑ 19A Johnny Bucha Black 60.00 35.00
❑ 20 Billy Loes SP RC 150.00 90.00
❑ 20A Billy Loes Black 150.00 90.00
❑ 21 Ferris Fain 70.00 40.00
❑ 21A Ferris Fain Black 70.00 40.00
❑ 22 Dom DiMaggio 125.00 75.00
❑ 22A Dom DiMaggio Black 100.00 60.00
❑ 23 Billy Goodman 70.00 40.00
❑ 23A Billy Goodman Black 70.00 40.00
❑ 24 Luke Easter 80.00 50.00
❑ 24A Luke Easter Black 80.00 50.00
❑ 25 Johnny Groth 60.00 35.00

❑ 25A Johnny Groth Black	60.00	35.00
❑ 26 Monte Irvin	150.00	90.00
❑ 26A Monte Irvin Black	150.00	90.00
❑ 27 Sam Jethroe	70.00	40.00
❑ 27A Sam Jethroe Black	70.00	40.00
❑ 28 Jerry Priddy	60.00	35.00
❑ 28A Jerry Priddy Black	60.00	35.00
❑ 29 Ted Kluszewski	125.00	75.00
❑ 29A Ted Kluszewski Black	125.00	75.00
❑ 30 Mel Parnell	70.00	40.00
❑ 30A Mel Parnell Black	70.00	40.00
❑ 31 Gus Zernial Baseballs	80.00	50.00
❑ 31A Gus Zernial Black	80.00	50.00
❑ 32 Eddie Robinson	60.00	35.00
❑ 32A Eddie Robinson Black	60.00	35.00
❑ 33 Warren Spahn	300.00	175.00
❑ 33A Warren Spahn Black	300.00	175.00
❑ 34 Elmer Valo	60.00	35.00
❑ 34A Elmer Valo Black	60.00	35.00
❑ 35 Hank Sauer	70.00	40.00
❑ 35A Hank Sauer Black	70.00	40.00
❑ 36 Gil Hodges	300.00	175.00
❑ 36A Gil Hodges Black	300.00	175.00
❑ 37 Duke Snider	500.00	300.00
❑ 37A Duke Snider Black	500.00	300.00
❑ 38 Wally Westlake	60.00	35.00
❑ 38A Wally Westlake Black	60.00	35.00
❑ 39 Dizzy Trout	70.00	40.00
❑ 39A Dizzy Trout Black	70.00	40.00
❑ 40 Irv Noren	70.00	40.00
❑ 40A Irv Noren Black	70.00	40.00
❑ 41 Bob Wellman RC	60.00	35.00
❑ 41A Bob Wellman Black	60.00	35.00
❑ 42 Lou Kretlow RC	60.00	35.00
❑ 42A Lou Kretlow Black	60.00	35.00
❑ 43 Ray Scarborough	60.00	35.00
❑ 43A Ray Scarborough Black	60.00	35.00
❑ 44 Con Dempsey RC	60.00	35.00
❑ 44A Con Dempsey Black	60.00	35.00
❑ 45 Eddie Joost	60.00	35.00
❑ 45A Eddie Joost Black	60.00	35.00
❑ 46 Gordon Goldsberry RC	60.00	35.00
❑ 46A Gordon Goldsberry Black	60.00	35.00
❑ 47 Willie Jones	70.00	40.00
❑ 47A Willie Jones Black	70.00	40.00
❑ 48A Joe Page ERR BLA	400.00	250.00
❑ 48B Joe Page COR BLA	125.00	75.00
❑ 48C Joe Page COR Red	125.00	75.00
❑ 49A John Sain ERR BLA	400.00	250.00
❑ 49B John Sain COR BLA	125.00	75.00
❑ 49C Joe Page COR Red	125.00	75.00
❑ 50 Marv Rickert RC	60.00	35.00
❑ 50A Marv Rickert Black	60.00	35.00
❑ 51 Jim Russell	60.00	35.00
❑ 51A Jim Russell Black	60.00	35.00
❑ 52 Don Mueller	70.00	40.00
❑ 52A Don Mueller Black	70.00	40.00
❑ 53 Chris Van Cuyk RC	60.00	35.00
❑ 53A Chris Van Cuyk Black	60.00	35.00
❑ 54 Leo Kiely RC	60.00	35.00
❑ 54A Leo Kiely Black	60.00	35.00
❑ 55 Ray Boone	80.00	50.00
❑ 55A Ray Boone Black	80.00	50.00
❑ 56 Tommy Glaviano	60.00	35.00
❑ 56A Tommy Glaviano Black	60.00	35.00
❑ 57 Ed Lopat	100.00	60.00
❑ 57A Ed Lopat Black	100.00	60.00
❑ 58 Bob Mahoney RC	60.00	35.00
❑ 58A Bob Mahoney Black	60.00	35.00
❑ 59 Robin Roberts	175.00	100.00
❑ 59A Robin Roberts Black	175.00	100.00
❑ 60 Sid Hudson	60.00	35.00
❑ 60A Sid Hudson Black	60.00	35.00
❑ 61 Tookie Gilbert	60.00	35.00
❑ 61A Tookie Gilbert Black	60.00	35.00
❑ 62 Chuck Stobbs RC	60.00	35.00
❑ 62A Chuck Stobbs Black	60.00	35.00
❑ 63 Howie Pollet	60.00	35.00
❑ 63A Howie Pollet Black	60.00	35.00
❑ 64 Roy Sievers	70.00	40.00
❑ 64A Roy Sievers Black	70.00	40.00
❑ 65 Enos Slaughter	175.00	100.00
❑ 65A Enos Slaughter Black	175.00	100.00
❑ 66 Preacher Roe	100.00	60.00
❑ 66A Preacher Roe Black	100.00	60.00
❑ 67 Allie Reynolds	125.00	75.00
❑ 67A Allie Reynolds Black	125.00	75.00
❑ 68 Cliff Chambers	60.00	35.00
❑ 68A Cliff Chambers Black	60.00	35.00
❑ 69 Virgil Stallcup	60.00	35.00
❑ 69A Virgil Stallcup Black	60.00	35.00
❑ 70 Al Zarilla	60.00	35.00
❑ 70A Al Zarilla Black	60.00	35.00
❑ 71 Tom Upton RC	60.00	35.00
❑ 71A Tom Upton Black	60.00	35.00
❑ 72 Karl Olson RC	60.00	35.00
❑ 72A Karl Olson Black	60.00	35.00
❑ 73 Bill Werle	60.00	35.00
❑ 73A Bill Werle Black	60.00	35.00
❑ 74 Andy Hansen RC	60.00	35.00
❑ 74A Andy Hansen Black	60.00	35.00
❑ 75 Wes Westrum	70.00	40.00
❑ 75A Wes Westrum Black	70.00	40.00
❑ 76 Eddie Stanky	70.00	40.00
❑ 76A Eddie Stanky Black	70.00	40.00
❑ 77 Bob Kennedy	70.00	40.00
❑ 77A Bob Kennedy Black	70.00	40.00
❑ 78 Ellis Kinder	60.00	35.00
❑ 78A Ellis Kinder Black	60.00	35.00
❑ 79 Gerry Staley	60.00	35.00
❑ 79A Gerry Staley Black	60.00	35.00
❑ 80 Herman Wehmeier	80.00	50.00
❑ 80A Herman Wehmeier Black	80.00	50.00
❑ 81 Vern Law	80.00	50.00
❑ 82 Duane Pillette	40.00	20.00
❑ 83 Billy Johnson	40.00	20.00
❑ 84 Vern Stephens	50.00	30.00
❑ 85 Bob Kuzava	50.00	30.00
❑ 86 Ted Gray	40.00	20.00
❑ 87 Dale Coogan	40.00	20.00
❑ 88 Bob Feller	250.00	150.00
❑ 89 Johnny Lipon	40.00	20.00
❑ 90 Mickey Grasso	40.00	20.00
❑ 91 Red Schoendienst	150.00	90.00
❑ 92 Dale Mitchell	50.00	30.00
❑ 93 Al Sima RC	40.00	20.00
❑ 94 Sam Mele	40.00	20.00
❑ 95 Ken Holcombe	40.00	20.00
❑ 96 Willard Marshall	40.00	20.00
❑ 97 Earl Torgeson	40.00	20.00
❑ 98 Billy Pierce	50.00	30.00
❑ 99 Gene Woodling	60.00	35.00
❑ 100 Del Rice	40.00	20.00
❑ 101 Max Lanier	40.00	20.00
❑ 102 Bill Kennedy	40.00	20.00
❑ 103 Cliff Mapes	40.00	20.00
❑ 104 Don Kolloway	40.00	20.00
❑ 105 Johnny Pramesa	40.00	20.00
❑ 106 Mickey Vernon	60.00	35.00
❑ 107 Connie Ryan	40.00	20.00
❑ 108 Jim Konstanty	60.00	35.00
❑ 109 Ted Wilks	40.00	20.00
❑ 110 Dutch Leonard	40.00	20.00
❑ 111 Peanuts Lowrey	40.00	20.00
❑ 112 Hank Majeski	40.00	20.00
❑ 113 Dick Sisler	50.00	30.00
❑ 114 Willard Ramsdell	40.00	20.00
❑ 115 George Munger	40.00	20.00
❑ 116 Carl Scheib	40.00	20.00
❑ 117 Sherm Lollar	50.00	30.00
❑ 118 Ken Raffensberger	40.00	20.00
❑ 119 Mickey McDermott	40.00	20.00
❑ 120 Bob Chakales RC	40.00	20.00
❑ 121 Gus Niarhos	40.00	20.00
❑ 122 Jackie Jensen	80.00	50.00
❑ 123 Eddie Yost	50.00	30.00
❑ 124 Monte Kennedy	40.00	20.00
❑ 125 Bill Rigney	40.00	20.00
❑ 126 Fred Hutchinson	50.00	30.00
❑ 127 Paul Minner RC	40.00	20.00
❑ 128 Don Bollweg RC	40.00	20.00
❑ 129 Johnny Mize	150.00	90.00
❑ 130 Sheldon Jones	40.00	20.00
❑ 131 Morrie Martin RC	40.00	20.00
❑ 132 Clyde Kluttz RC	40.00	20.00
❑ 133 Al Widmar	40.00	20.00
❑ 134 Joe Tipton	40.00	20.00
❑ 135 Dixie Howell	40.00	20.00
❑ 136 Johnny Schmitz	40.00	20.00
❑ 137 Roy McMillan RC	50.00	30.00
❑ 138 Bill MacDonald	40.00	20.00
❑ 139 Ken Wood	40.00	20.00
❑ 140 Johnny Antonelli	60.00	35.00
❑ 141 Clint Hartung	40.00	20.00
❑ 142 Harry Perkowski RC	40.00	20.00
❑ 143 Les Moss	40.00	20.00
❑ 144 Ed Blake RC	40.00	20.00
❑ 145 Joe Haynes	40.00	20.00
❑ 146 Frank House RC	40.00	20.00
❑ 147 Bob Young RC	40.00	20.00
❑ 148 Johnny Klippstein	40.00	20.00
❑ 149 Dick Kryhoski	40.00	20.00
❑ 150 Ted Beard	40.00	20.00
❑ 151 Wally Post RC	50.00	30.00
❑ 152 Al Evans	40.00	20.00
❑ 153 Bob Rush	40.00	20.00
❑ 154 Joe Muir RC	40.00	20.00
❑ 155 Frank Overmire	40.00	20.00
❑ 156 Frank Hiller RC	40.00	20.00
❑ 157 Bob Usher	40.00	20.00
❑ 158 Eddie Waitkus	40.00	20.00
❑ 159 Saul Rogovin RC	40.00	20.00
❑ 160 Owen Friend	40.00	20.00
❑ 161 Bud Byerly RC	40.00	20.00
❑ 162 Del Crandall	50.00	30.00
❑ 163 Stan Rojek	40.00	20.00
❑ 164 Walt Dubiel	40.00	20.00
❑ 165 Eddie Kazak	40.00	20.00
❑ 166 Paul LaPalme RC	40.00	20.00
❑ 167 Bill Howerton	40.00	20.00
❑ 168 Charlie Silvera RC	60.00	35.00
❑ 169 Howie Judson	40.00	20.00
❑ 170 Gus Bell	50.00	30.00
❑ 171 Ed Erautt RC	40.00	20.00
❑ 172 Eddie Miksis	40.00	20.00
❑ 173 Roy Smalley	40.00	20.00
❑ 174 Clarence Marshall RC	60.00	35.00
❑ 175 Billy Martin RC	500.00	300.00
❑ 176 Hank Edwards	40.00	20.00
❑ 177 Bill Wight	40.00	20.00
❑ 178 Cass Michaels	40.00	20.00
❑ 179 Frank Smith RC	40.00	20.00
❑ 180 Charlie Maxwell RC	50.00	30.00
❑ 181 Bob Swift	40.00	20.00
❑ 182 Billy Hitchcock	40.00	20.00
❑ 183 Erv Dusak	40.00	20.00
❑ 184 Bob Ramazzotti	40.00	20.00
❑ 185 Bill Nicholson	50.00	30.00
❑ 186 Walt Masterson	40.00	20.00
❑ 187 Bob Miller	40.00	20.00
❑ 188 Clarence Podbielan RC	40.00	20.00
❑ 189 Pete Reiser	60.00	35.00
❑ 190 Don Johnson RC	40.00	20.00
❑ 191 Yogi Berra	800.00	500.00
❑ 192 Myron Ginsberg RC	40.00	20.00
❑ 193 Harry Simpson RC	50.00	30.00
❑ 194 Joe Hatton	40.00	20.00
❑ 195 Minnie Minoso RC	150.00	90.00
❑ 196 Solly Hemus RC	60.00	35.00
❑ 197 George Strickland RC	40.00	20.00
❑ 198 Phil Haugstad RC	40.00	20.00
❑ 199 George Zuverink RC	40.00	20.00
❑ 200 Ralph Houk RC	80.00	50.00
❑ 201 Alex Kellner	40.00	20.00
❑ 202 Joe Collins RC	60.00	35.00
❑ 203 Curt Simmons	60.00	35.00
❑ 204 Ron Northey	40.00	20.00
❑ 205 Clyde King	60.00	35.00
❑ 206 Joe Ostrowski RC	40.00	20.00
❑ 207 Mickey Harris	40.00	20.00
❑ 208 Marlin Stuart RC	40.00	20.00
❑ 209 Howie Fox	40.00	20.00
❑ 210 Dick Fowler	40.00	20.00
❑ 211 Ray Coleman	40.00	20.00
❑ 212 Ned Garver	40.00	20.00
❑ 213 Nippy Jones	40.00	20.00
❑ 214 Johnny Hopp	50.00	30.00
❑ 215 Hank Bauer	100.00	60.00
❑ 216 Richie Ashburn	250.00	150.00
❑ 217 Snuffy Stirnweiss	50.00	30.00
❑ 218 Clyde McCullough	40.00	20.00
❑ 219 Bobby Shantz	60.00	35.00
❑ 220 Joe Presko RC	40.00	20.00
❑ 221 Granny Hamner	40.00	20.00
❑ 222 Hoot Evers	40.00	20.00
❑ 223 Del Ennis	50.00	30.00
❑ 224 Bruce Edwards	40.00	20.00
❑ 225 Frank Baumholtz	40.00	20.00

❑ 226 Dave Philley 40.00 20.00
❑ 227 Joe Garagiola 80.00 50.00
❑ 228 Al Brazle 40.00 20.00
❑ 229 Gene Bearden UER 40.00 20.00
❑ 230 Matt Batts 40.00 20.00
❑ 231 Sam Zoldak 40.00 20.00
❑ 232 Billy Cox 50.00 30.00
❑ 233 Bob Friend RC 80.00 50.00
❑ 234 Steve Souchock RC 40.00 20.00
❑ 235 Walt Dropo 40.00 20.00
❑ 236 Ed Fitzgerald 40.00 20.00
❑ 237 Jerry Coleman 60.00 35.00
❑ 238 Art Houtteman 40.00 20.00
❑ 239 Rocky Bridges RC 50.00 30.00
❑ 240 Jack Phillips RC 40.00 20.00
❑ 241 Tommy Byrne 40.00 20.00
❑ 242 Tom Poholsky RC 40.00 20.00
❑ 243 Larry Doby 80.00 50.00
❑ 244 Vic Wertz 40.00 20.00
❑ 245 Sherry Robertson 40.00 20.00
❑ 246 George Kell 80.00 50.00
❑ 247 Randy Gumpert 40.00 20.00
❑ 248 Frank Shea 40.00 20.00
❑ 249 Bobby Adams 40.00 20.00
❑ 250 Carl Erskine 100.00 60.00
❑ 251 Chico Carrasquel 50.00 30.00
❑ 252 Vern Bickford 50.00 30.00
❑ 253 John Berardino 100.00 60.00
❑ 254 Joe Dobson 50.00 30.00
❑ 255 Clyde Vollmer 50.00 30.00
❑ 256 Pete Suder 50.00 30.00
❑ 257 Bobby Avila 60.00 35.00
❑ 258 Steve Gromek 60.00 35.00
❑ 259 Bob Addis RC 50.00 30.00
❑ 260 Pete Castiglione 50.00 30.00
❑ 261 Willie Mays 3000.00 2000.00
❑ 262 Virgil Trucks 60.00 35.00
❑ 263 Harry Brecheen 60.00 35.00
❑ 264 Roy Hartsfield 50.00 30.00
❑ 265 Chuck Diering 50.00 30.00
❑ 266 Murry Dickson 50.00 30.00
❑ 267 Sid Gordon 60.00 35.00
❑ 268 Bob Lemon 150.00 90.00
❑ 269 Willard Nixon 50.00 30.00
❑ 270 Lou Brissie 50.00 30.00
❑ 271 Jim Delsing 60.00 35.00
❑ 272 Mike Garcia 80.00 50.00
❑ 273 Erv Palica 50.00 30.00
❑ 274 Ralph Branca 125.00 75.00
❑ 275 Pat Mullin 50.00 30.00
❑ 276 Jim Wilson RC 50.00 30.00
❑ 277 Early Wynn 175.00 100.00
❑ 278 Allie Clark 50.00 30.00
❑ 279 Eddie Stewart 50.00 30.00
❑ 280 Cloyd Boyer 80.00 50.00
❑ 281 Tommy Brown SP 80.00 50.00
❑ 282 Birdie Tebbetts SP 80.00 50.00
❑ 283 Phil Masi SP 60.00 35.00
❑ 284 Hank Arft SP 60.00 35.00
❑ 285 Cliff Fannin SP 60.00 35.00
❑ 286 Joe DeMaestri SP RC 60.00 35.00
❑ 287 Steve Bilko SP 60.00 35.00
❑ 288 Chet Nichols SP RC 80.00 50.00
❑ 289 Tommy Holmes MG 100.00 60.00
❑ 290 Joe Astroth SP 60.00 35.00
❑ 291 Gil Coan SP 60.00 35.00
❑ 292 Floyd Baker SP 60.00 35.00
❑ 293 Sibby Sisti SP 60.00 35.00
❑ 294 Walker Cooper SP 60.00 35.00
❑ 295 Phil Cavarretta 80.00 50.00
❑ 296 Red Rolfe MG 60.00 35.00
❑ 297 Andy Seminick SP 60.00 35.00
❑ 298 Bob Ross SP RC 60.00 35.00
❑ 299 Ray Murray SP RC 80.00 50.00
❑ 300 Barney McCosky SP 80.00 50.00
❑ 301 Bob Porterfield 50.00 30.00
❑ 302 Max Surkont RC 50.00 30.00
❑ 303 Harry Dorish 50.00 30.00
❑ 304 Sam Dente 50.00 30.00
❑ 305 Paul Richards MG 60.00 35.00
❑ 306 Lou Sleater RC 50.00 30.00
❑ 307 Frank Campos RC 50.00 30.00
❑ 307A Frank Campos Star
❑ 308 Luis Aloma 50.00 30.00
❑ 309 Jim Busby 60.00 35.00
❑ 310 George Metkovich 100.00 60.00
❑ 311 Mickey Mantle DP 20000.00 12000.00
❑ 311A Mickey Mantle Stitch
❑ 312 Jackie Robinson DP 2000.00 1200.00
❑ 312A Jackie Robinson Stitch
❑ 313 Bobby Thomson DP 350.00 200.00
❑ 313A Bobby Thomson Stitch
❑ 314 Roy Campanella 2500.00 1500.00
❑ 315 Leo Durocher MG 600.00 350.00
❑ 316 Dave Williams RC 300.00 175.00
❑ 317 Conrado Marrero 300.00 175.00
❑ 318 Harold Gregg RC 300.00 175.00
❑ 319 Rube Walker RC 250.00 150.00
❑ 320 John Rutherford RC 300.00 175.00
❑ 321 Joe Black RC 350.00 200.00
❑ 322 Randy Jackson RC 300.00 175.00
❑ 323 Bubba Church 250.00 150.00
❑ 324 Warren Hacker 250.00 150.00
❑ 325 Bill Serena 300.00 175.00
❑ 326 George Shuba RC 400.00 250.00
❑ 327 Al Wilson RC 250.00 150.00
❑ 328 Bob Borkowski RC 300.00 175.00
❑ 329 Ike Delock RC 300.00 175.00
❑ 330 Turk Lown RC 300.00 175.00
❑ 331 Tom Morgan RC 300.00 175.00
❑ 332 Tony Bartirome RC 300.00 175.00
❑ 333 Pee Wee Reese 1800.00 1000.00
❑ 334 Wilmer Mizell RC 300.00 175.00
❑ 335 Ted Lepcio RC 250.00 150.00
❑ 336 Dave Koslo 250.00 150.00
❑ 337 Jim Hearn 300.00 175.00
❑ 338 Sal Yvars RC 300.00 175.00
❑ 339 Russ Meyer 300.00 175.00
❑ 340 Bob Hooper 300.00 175.00
❑ 341 Hal Jeffcoat 300.00 175.00
❑ 342 Clem Labine RC 400.00 250.00
❑ 343 Dick Gernert RC 250.00 150.00
❑ 344 Ewell Blackwell 300.00 175.00
❑ 345 Sammy White RC 250.00 150.00
❑ 346 George Spencer RC 250.00 150.00
❑ 347 Joe Adcock 400.00 250.00
❑ 348 Robert Kelly RC 250.00 150.00
❑ 349 Bob Cain 300.00 175.00
❑ 350 Cal Abrams 300.00 175.00
❑ 351 Alvin Dark 300.00 175.00
❑ 352 Karl Drews 300.00 175.00
❑ 353 Bobby Del Greco RC 300.00 175.00
❑ 354 Fred Hatfield RC 300.00 175.00
❑ 355 Bobby Morgan 300.00 175.00
❑ 356 Toby Atwell RC 300.00 175.00
❑ 357 Smoky Burgess 300.00 175.00
❑ 358 John Kucab RC 300.00 175.00
❑ 359 Dee Fondy RC 250.00 150.00
❑ 360 George Crowe RC 300.00 175.00
❑ 361 Bill Posedel CO 250.00 150.00
❑ 362 Ken Heintzelman 300.00 175.00
❑ 363 Dick Rozek RC 300.00 175.00
❑ 364 Clyde Sukeforth CO RC 300.00 175.00
❑ 365 Cookie Lavagetto CO 400.00 250.00
❑ 366 Dave Madison RC 250.00 150.00
❑ 367 Ben Thorpe RC 300.00 175.00
❑ 368 Ed Wright RC 300.00 175.00
❑ 369 Dick Groat RC 400.00 250.00
❑ 370 Billy Hoeft RC 300.00 175.00
❑ 371 Bobby Hofman 250.00 150.00
❑ 372 Gil McDougald RC 500.00 300.00
❑ 373 Jim Turner CO RC 400.00 250.00
❑ 374 Al Benton RC 250.00 150.00
❑ 375 John Merson RC 250.00 150.00
❑ 376 Faye Throneberry RC 250.00 150.00
❑ 377 Chuck Dressen MG 400.00 250.00
❑ 378 Leroy Fusselman RC 300.00 175.00
❑ 379 Joe Rossi RC 250.00 150.00
❑ 380 Clem Koshorek RC 250.00 150.00
❑ 381 Milton Stock CO RC 300.00 175.00
❑ 382 Sam Jones RC 350.00 200.00
❑ 383 Del Wilber RC 250.00 150.00
❑ 384 Frank Crosetti CO 500.00 300.00
❑ 385 Herman Franks CO RC 250.00 150.00
❑ 386 Ed Yuhas RC 300.00 175.00
❑ 387 Billy Meyer MG 250.00 150.00
❑ 388 Bob Chipman 250.00 150.00
❑ 389 Ben Wade RC 300.00 175.00
❑ 390 Rocky Nelson RC 300.00 175.00
❑ 391 Ben Chapman CO UER 250.00 150.00
❑ 392 Hoyt Wilhelm RC 800.00 500.00
❑ 393 Ebba St.Claire RC 300.00 175.00
❑ 394 Billy Herman CO 600.00 350.00
❑ 395 Jake Pitler CO 300.00 175.00
❑ 396 Dick Williams RC 500.00 300.00
❑ 397 Forrest Main RC 250.00 150.00
❑ 398 Hal Rice 250.00 150.00
❑ 399 Jim Fridley RC 250.00 150.00
❑ 400 Bill Dickey CO 1000.00 600.00
❑ 401 Bob Schultz RC 300.00 175.00
❑ 402 Earl Harrist RC 300.00 175.00
❑ 403 Bill Miller RC 300.00 175.00
❑ 404 Dick Brodowski RC 300.00 175.00
❑ 405 Eddie Pellagrini 300.00 175.00
❑ 406 Joe Nuxhall RC 400.00 250.00
❑ 407 Eddie Mathews RC 10000.00 6000.00

1953 Topps

❑ COMPLETE SET (274) 15000.00 9000.00
❑ COMMON CARD (1-165) 30.00 15.00
❑ COMMON CARD (166-220) 25.00 12.50
❑ COMMON DP (1-220) 15.00 7.50
❑ COMMON CARD (221-280) 100.00 50.00
❑ NOT ISSUED (253/261/267)
❑ NOT ISSUED (268/271/275)
❑ WRAP.(1-CENT, DATED) 200.00 150.00
❑ WRAP.(1-CENT,NO DATE) 300.00 250.00
❑ WRAP.(5-CENT, DATED) 400.00 300.00
❑ WRAP.(5-CENT,NO DATE) 350.00 275.00
❑ 1 Jackie Robinson DP 800.00 500.00
❑ 2 Luke Easter DP 20.00 10.00
❑ 3 George Crowe 40.00 25.00
❑ 4 Ben Wade 30.00 15.00
❑ 5 Joe Dobson 30.00 15.00
❑ 6 Sam Jones 40.00 25.00
❑ 7 Bob Borkowski DP 15.00 7.50
❑ 8 Clem Koshorek DP 15.00 7.50
❑ 9 Joe Collins 60.00 35.00
❑ 10 Smoky Burgess SP 80.00 50.00
❑ 11 Sal Yvars 30.00 15.00
❑ 12 Howie Judson DP 15.00 7.50
❑ 13 Conrado Marrero DP 15.00 7.50
❑ 14 Clem Labine DP 20.00 10.00
❑ 15 Bobo Newsom DP RC 20.00 10.00
❑ 16 Peanuts Lowrey DP 15.00 7.50
❑ 17 Billy Hitchcock 30.00 15.00
❑ 18 Ted Lepcio DP 15.00 7.50
❑ 19 Mel Parnell DP 20.00 10.00
❑ 20 Hank Thompson 40.00 25.00
❑ 21 Billy Johnson 30.00 15.00
❑ 22 Howie Fox 30.00 15.00
❑ 23 Toby Atwell DP 15.00 7.50
❑ 24 Ferris Fain 40.00 25.00
❑ 25 Ray Boone 40.00 25.00
❑ 26 Dale Mitchell DP 20.00 10.00
❑ 27 Roy Campanella DP 300.00 175.00
❑ 28 Eddie Pellagrini 30.00 15.00
❑ 29 Hal Jeffcoat 30.00 15.00
❑ 30 Willard Nixon 30.00 15.00
❑ 31 Ewell Blackwell 60.00 35.00
❑ 32 Clyde Vollmer 30.00 15.00
❑ 33 Bob Kennedy DP 15.00 7.50
❑ 34 George Shuba 40.00 25.00
❑ 35 Irv Noren DP 15.00 7.50
❑ 36 Johnny Groth DP 15.00 7.50
❑ 37 Eddie Mathews DP 250.00 150.00
❑ 38 Jim Hearn DP 15.00 7.50
❑ 39 Eddie Miksis 30.00 15.00
❑ 40 John Lipon 30.00 15.00
❑ 41 Enos Slaughter 80.00 50.00

❑	42 Gus Zernial DP	20.00	10.00
❑	43 Gil McDougald	60.00	35.00
❑	44 Ellis Kinder SP	60.00	35.00
❑	45 Grady Hatton DP	15.00	7.50
❑	46 Johnny Klippstein DP	15.00	7.50
❑	47 Bubba Church DP	15.00	7.50
❑	48 Bob Del Greco DP	15.00	7.50
❑	49 Faye Throneberry DP	15.00	7.50
❑	50 Chuck Dressen DP	20.00	10.00
❑	51 Frank Campos DP	15.00	7.50
❑	52 Ted Gray DP	15.00	7.50
❑	53 Sherm Lollar DP	20.00	10.00
❑	54 Bob Feller DP	150.00	90.00
❑	55 Maurice McDermott DP	15.00	7.50
❑	56 Gerry Staley DP	15.00	7.50
❑	57 Carl Scheib	30.00	15.00
❑	58 George Metkovich	30.00	15.00
❑	59 Karl Drews DP	15.00	7.50
❑	60 Cloyd Boyer DP	15.00	7.50
❑	61 Early Wynn SP	125.00	75.00
❑	62 Monte Irvin DP	40.00	25.00
❑	63 Gus Niarhos DP	15.00	7.50
❑	64 Dave Philley	30.00	15.00
❑	65 Earl Harrist	30.00	15.00
❑	66 Minnie Minoso	60.00	35.00
❑	67 Roy Sievers DP	20.00	10.00
❑	68 Del Rice	30.00	15.00
❑	69 Dick Brodowski	30.00	15.00
❑	70 Ed Yuhas	30.00	15.00
❑	71 Tony Bartirome	30.00	15.00
❑	72 Fred Hutchinson SP	60.00	35.00
❑	73 Eddie Robinson	30.00	15.00
❑	74 Joe Rossi	30.00	15.00
❑	75 Mike Garcia	40.00	25.00
❑	76 Pee Wee Reese	175.00	100.00
❑	77 Johnny Mize DP	80.00	50.00
❑	78 Red Schoendienst	80.00	50.00
❑	79 Johnny Wyrostek	30.00	15.00
❑	80 Jim Hegan	40.00	25.00
❑	81 Joe Black SP	80.00	50.00
❑	82 Mickey Mantle	3500.00	2500.00
❑	83 Howie Pollet	30.00	15.00
❑	84 Bob Hooper DP	15.00	7.50
❑	85 Bobby Morgan DP	15.00	7.50
❑	86 Billy Martin	125.00	75.00
❑	87 Ed Lopat	60.00	35.00
❑	88 Willie Jones DP	15.00	7.50
❑	89 Chuck Stobbs DP	15.00	7.50
❑	90 Hank Edwards DP	15.00	7.50
❑	91 Ebba St.Claire DP	15.00	7.50
❑	92 Paul Minner DP	15.00	7.50
❑	93 Hal Rice DP	15.00	7.50
❑	94 Bill Kennedy DP	15.00	7.50
❑	95 Willard Marshall DP	15.00	7.50
❑	96 Virgil Trucks	40.00	25.00
❑	97 Don Kolloway DP	15.00	7.50
❑	98 Cal Abrams DP	15.00	7.50
❑	99 Dave Madison	30.00	15.00
❑	100 Bill Miller	30.00	15.00
❑	101 Ted Wilks	30.00	15.00
❑	102 Connie Ryan DP	15.00	7.50
❑	103 Joe Astroth DP	15.00	7.50
❑	104 Yogi Berra	400.00	250.00
❑	105 Joe Nuxhall DP	20.00	10.00
❑	106 Johnny Antonelli	40.00	25.00
❑	107 Danny O'Connell DP	15.00	7.50
❑	108 Bob Porterfield DP	15.00	7.50
❑	109 Alvin Dark	60.00	35.00
❑	110 Herman Wehmeier DP	15.00	7.50
❑	111 Hank Sauer DP	15.00	7.50
❑	112 Ned Garver DP	15.00	7.50
❑	113 Jerry Priddy	30.00	15.00
❑	114 Phil Rizzuto	250.00	150.00
❑	115 George Spencer	30.00	15.00
❑	116 Frank Smith DP	15.00	7.50
❑	117 Sid Gordon DP	15.00	7.50
❑	118 Gus Bell DP	20.00	10.00
❑	119 Johnny Sain SP	60.00	35.00
❑	120 Davey Williams	40.00	25.00
❑	121 Walt Dropo	40.00	25.00
❑	122 Elmer Valo	30.00	15.00
❑	123 Tommy Byrne DP	15.00	7.50
❑	124 Sibby Sisti DP	15.00	7.50
❑	125 Dick Williams DP	20.00	10.00
❑	126 Bill Connelly DP RC	15.00	7.50
❑	127 Clint Courtney DP RC	15.00	7.50
❑	128 Wilmer Mizell DP	20.00	10.00
❑	129 Keith Thomas RC	30.00	15.00
❑	130 Turk Lown DP	15.00	7.50
❑	131 Harry Byrd DP RC	15.00	7.50
❑	132 Tom Morgan	30.00	15.00
❑	133 Gil Coan	30.00	15.00
❑	134 Rube Walker	40.00	25.00
❑	135 Al Rosen DP	20.00	10.00
❑	136 Ken Heintzelman DP	15.00	7.50
❑	137 John Rutherford DP	15.00	7.50
❑	138 George Kell	80.00	50.00
❑	139 Sammy White	30.00	15.00
❑	140 Tommy Glaviano	30.00	15.00
❑	141 Allie Reynolds DP	15.00	7.50
❑	142 Vic Wertz	40.00	25.00
❑	143 Billy Pierce	60.00	35.00
❑	144 Bob Schultz DP	15.00	7.50
❑	145 Harry Dorish DP	15.00	7.50
❑	146 Granny Hamner	30.00	15.00
❑	147 Warren Spahn	175.00	100.00
❑	148 Mickey Grasso	30.00	15.00
❑	149 Dom DiMaggio DP	15.00	7.50
❑	150 Harry Simpson DP	15.00	7.50
❑	151 Hoyt Wilhelm	100.00	60.00
❑	152 Bob Adams DP	15.00	7.50
❑	153 Andy Seminick DP	15.00	7.50
❑	154 Dick Groat	40.00	25.00
❑	155 Dutch Leonard	30.00	15.00
❑	156 Jim Rivera DP RC	20.00	10.00
❑	157 Bob Addis DP	15.00	7.50
❑	158 Johnny Logan RC	40.00	25.00
❑	159 Wayne Terwilliger DP	15.00	7.50
❑	160 Bob Young	30.00	15.00
❑	161 Vern Bickford DP	15.00	7.50
❑	162 Ted Kluszewski	60.00	35.00
❑	163 Fred Hatfield DP	15.00	7.50
❑	164 Frank Shea DP	15.00	7.50
❑	165 Billy Hoeft	30.00	15.00
❑	166 Billy Hunter RC	25.00	12.50
❑	167 Art Schult RC	25.00	12.50
❑	168 Willard Schmidt RC	25.00	12.50
❑	169 Dizzy Trout	30.00	15.00
❑	170 Bill Werle	25.00	12.50
❑	171 Bill Glynn RC	25.00	12.50
❑	172 Rip Repulski RC	25.00	12.50
❑	173 Preston Ward	25.00	12.50
❑	174 Billy Loes	30.00	15.00
❑	175 Ron Kline RC	25.00	12.50
❑	176 Don Hoak RC	40.00	25.00
❑	177 Jim Dyck RC	25.00	12.50
❑	178 Jim Waugh RC	25.00	12.50
❑	179 Gene Hermanski	25.00	12.50
❑	180 Virgil Stallcup	25.00	12.50
❑	181 Al Zarilla	25.00	12.50
❑	182 Bobby Hofman	25.00	12.50
❑	183 Stu Miller RC	40.00	25.00
❑	184 Hal Brown RC	25.00	12.50
❑	185 Jim Pendleton RC	25.00	12.50
❑	186 Charlie Bishop RC	25.00	12.50
❑	187 Jim Fridley	25.00	12.50
❑	188 Andy Carey RC	40.00	25.00
❑	189 Ray Jablonski RC	25.00	12.50
❑	190 Dixie Walker CO	30.00	15.00
❑	191 Ralph Kiner	80.00	50.00
❑	192 Wally Westlake	25.00	12.50
❑	193 Mike Clark RC	25.00	12.50
❑	194 Eddie Kazak	25.00	12.50
❑	195 Ed McGhee RC	25.00	12.50
❑	196 Bob Keegan RC	25.00	12.50
❑	197 Del Crandall	40.00	25.00
❑	198 Forrest Main	25.00	12.50
❑	199 Marion Fricano RC	25.00	12.50
❑	200 Gordon Goldsberry	25.00	12.50
❑	201 Paul LaPalme	25.00	12.50
❑	202 Carl Sawatski RC	25.00	12.50
❑	203 Cliff Fannin	25.00	12.50
❑	204 Dick Bokelman RC	25.00	12.50
❑	205 Vern Benson RC	25.00	12.50
❑	206 Ed Bailey RC	30.00	15.00
❑	207 Whitey Ford	300.00	175.00
❑	208 Jim Wilson	25.00	12.50
❑	209 Jim Greengrass RC	25.00	12.50
❑	210 Bob Cerv RC	40.00	25.00
❑	211 J.W. Porter RC	25.00	12.50
❑	212 Jack Dittmer RC	25.00	12.50
❑	213 Ray Scarborough	25.00	12.50
❑	214 Bill Bruton RC	40.00	25.00
❑	215 Gene Conley RC	30.00	15.00
❑	216 Jim Hughes RC	25.00	12.50
❑	217 Murray Wall RC	25.00	12.50
❑	218 Les Fusselman	25.00	12.50
❑	219 Pete Runnels UER (Photo actually Don Johnson)	30.00	15.00
❑	220 Satchel Paige UER	600.00	350.00
❑	221 Bob Milliken RC	100.00	50.00
❑	222 Vic Janowicz DP RC	50.00	25.00
❑	223 Johnny O'Brien DP RC	50.00	25.00
❑	224 Lou Sleater DP	50.00	25.00
❑	225 Bobby Shantz	125.00	75.00
❑	226 Ed Erautt	100.00	50.00
❑	227 Morrie Martin	100.00	50.00
❑	228 Hal Newhouser	150.00	90.00
❑	229 Rocky Krsnich RC	100.00	50.00
❑	230 Johnny Lindell DP	50.00	25.00
❑	231 Solly Hemus DP	50.00	25.00
❑	232 Dick Kokos	100.00	50.00
❑	233 Al Aber RC	100.00	50.00
❑	234 Ray Murray DP	50.00	25.00
❑	235 John Hetki DP RC	50.00	25.00
❑	236 Harry Perkowski DP	50.00	25.00
❑	237 Bud Podbielan DP	50.00	25.00
❑	238 Cal Hogue DP RC	50.00	25.00
❑	239 Jim Delsing	100.00	50.00
❑	240 Fred Marsh	100.00	50.00
❑	241 Al Sima DP	50.00	25.00
❑	242 Charlie Silvera	125.00	75.00
❑	243 Carlos Bernier DP RC	50.00	25.00
❑	244 Willie Mays	2500.00	1500.00
❑	245 Bill Norman CO	100.00	50.00
❑	246 Roy Face RC DP RC	80.00	50.00
❑	247 Mike Sandlock DP RC	50.00	25.00
❑	248 Gene Stephens DP RC	50.00	25.00
❑	249 Eddie O'Brien RC	100.00	50.00
❑	250 Bob Wilson RC	100.00	50.00
❑	251 Sid Hudson	100.00	50.00
❑	252 Hank Foiles RC	100.00	50.00
❑	253 Does not exist		
❑	254 Preacher Roe DP	80.00	50.00
❑	255 Dixie Howell	100.00	50.00
❑	256 Les Peden RC	100.00	50.00
❑	257 Bob Boyd RC	100.00	50.00
❑	258 Jim Gilliam RC	400.00	250.00
❑	259 Roy McMillan DP	50.00	25.00
❑	260 Sam Calderone RC	100.00	50.00
❑	261 Does not exist		
❑	262 Bob Oldis RC	100.00	50.00
❑	263 Johnny Podres RC	300.00	175.00
❑	264 Gene Woodling DP	60.00	30.00
❑	265 Jackie Jensen	125.00	75.00
❑	266 Bob Cain	100.00	50.00
❑	267 Does not exist		
❑	268 Does not exist		
❑	269 Duane Pillette	100.00	50.00
❑	270 Vern Stephens	125.00	75.00
❑	271 Does not exist		
❑	272 Bill Antonello RC	100.00	50.00
❑	273 Harvey Haddix RC	150.00	90.00
❑	274 John Riddle CO	100.00	50.00
❑	275 Does not exist		
❑	276 Ken Raffensberger	100.00	50.00
❑	277 Don Lund RC	100.00	50.00
❑	278 Willie Miranda RC	100.00	50.00
❑	279 Joe Coleman DP	50.00	25.00
❑	280 Milt Bolling RC	350.00	200.00

1954 Topps

❑	COMPLETE SET (250)	8000.00	5000.00
❑	COMMON (1-50/76-250)	15.00	7.50
❑	COMMON CARD (51-75)	25.00	12.50
❑	WRAP.(1-CENT, DATED)	200.00	150.00
❑	WRAP.(1-CENT, UNDAT)	150.00	100.00
❑	WRAP.(5-CENT, DATED)	300.00	250.00
❑	WRAP.(5-CENT, UNDAT)	250.00	200.00
❑	1 Ted Williams	800.00	500.00
❑	2 Gus Zernial	25.00	12.50
❑	3 Monte Irvin	50.00	25.00
❑	4 Hank Sauer	25.00	12.50
❑	5 Ed Lopat	25.00	12.50
❑	6 Pete Runnels	25.00	12.50
❑	7 Ted Kluszewski	50.00	25.00
❑	8 Bob Young	15.00	7.50

❑ 9 Harvey Haddix 25.00 12.50
❑ 10 Jackie Robinson 400.00 250.00
❑ 11 Paul Leslie Smith RC 15.00 7.50
❑ 12 Del Crandall 25.00 12.50
❑ 13 Billy Martin 100.00 60.00
❑ 14 Preacher Roe UER 25.00 12.50
❑ 15 Al Rosen 25.00 12.50
❑ 16 Vic Janowicz 25.00 12.50
❑ 17 Phil Rizzuto 125.00 75.00
❑ 18 Walt Dropo 25.00 12.50
❑ 19 Johnny Lipon 15.00 7.50
❑ 20 Warren Spahn 125.00 75.00
❑ 21 Bobby Shantz 25.00 12.50
❑ 22 Jim Greengrass 15.00 7.50
❑ 23 Luke Easter 25.00 12.50
❑ 24 Granny Hamner 15.00 7.50
❑ 25 Harvey Kuenn RC 40.00 20.00
❑ 26 Ray Jablonski 15.00 7.50
❑ 27 Ferris Fain 25.00 12.50
❑ 28 Paul Minner 15.00 7.50
❑ 29 Jim Hegan 25.00 12.50
❑ 30 Eddie Mathews 100.00 60.00
❑ 31 Johnny Klippstein 15.00 7.50
❑ 32 Duke Snider 200.00 125.00
❑ 33 Johnny Schmitz 15.00 7.50
❑ 34 Jim Rivera 15.00 7.50
❑ 35 Jim Gilliam 50.00 25.00
❑ 36 Hoyt Wilhelm 50.00 25.00
❑ 37 Whitey Ford 200.00 125.00
❑ 38 Eddie Stanky MG 25.00 12.50
❑ 39 Sherm Lollar 25.00 12.50
❑ 40 Mel Parnell 25.00 12.50
❑ 41 Willie Jones 15.00 7.50
❑ 42 Don Mueller 25.00 12.50
❑ 43 Dick Groat 25.00 12.50
❑ 44 Ned Garver 15.00 7.50
❑ 45 Richie Ashburn 80.00 50.00
❑ 46 Ken Raffensberger 15.00 7.50
❑ 47 Ellis Kinder 15.00 7.50
❑ 48 Billy Hunter 25.00 12.50
❑ 49 Ray Murray 15.00 7.50
❑ 50 Yogi Berra 300.00 175.00
❑ 51 Johnny Lindell 25.00 12.50
❑ 52 Vic Power RC 30.00 15.00
❑ 53 Jack Dittmer 25.00 12.50
❑ 54 Vern Stephens 30.00 15.00
❑ 55 Phil Cavarretta MG 30.00 15.00
❑ 56 Willie Miranda 25.00 12.50
❑ 57 Luis Aloma 25.00 12.50
❑ 58 Bob Wilson 25.00 12.50
❑ 59 Gene Conley 30.00 15.00
❑ 60 Frank Baumholtz 25.00 12.50
❑ 61 Bob Cain 25.00 12.50
❑ 62 Eddie Robinson 25.00 12.50
❑ 63 Johnny Pesky 30.00 15.00
❑ 64 Hank Thompson 25.00 12.50
❑ 65 Bob Swift CO 25.00 12.50
❑ 66 Ted Lepcio 25.00 12.50
❑ 67 Jim Willis RC 25.00 12.50
❑ 68 Sam Calderone 25.00 12.50
❑ 69 Bud Podbielan 25.00 12.50
❑ 70 Larry Doby 60.00 30.00
❑ 71 Frank Smith 25.00 12.50
❑ 72 Preston Ward 25.00 12.50
❑ 73 Wayne Terwilliger 25.00 12.50
❑ 74 Bill Taylor RC 25.00 12.50
❑ 75 Fred Haney MG RC 25.00 12.50
❑ 76 Bob Scheffing CO 15.00 7.50
❑ 77 Ray Boone 25.00 12.50
❑ 78 Ted Kazanski RC 15.00 7.50
❑ 79 Andy Pafko 25.00 12.50
❑ 80 Jackie Jensen 25.00 12.50
❑ 81 Dave Hoskins RC 15.00 7.50
❑ 82 Milt Bolling 15.00 7.50
❑ 83 Joe Collins 25.00 12.50
❑ 84 Dick Cole RC 15.00 7.50
❑ 85 Bob Turley RC 40.00 20.00
❑ 86 Billy Herman CO 25.00 12.50
❑ 87 Roy Face 25.00 12.50
❑ 88 Matt Batts 15.00 7.50
❑ 89 Howie Pollet 15.00 7.50
❑ 90 Willie Mays 800.00 500.00
❑ 91 Bob Oldis 15.00 7.50
❑ 92 Wally Westlake 15.00 7.50
❑ 93 Sid Hudson 15.00 7.50
❑ 94 Ernie Banks RC 1250.00 750.00
❑ 95 Hal Rice 15.00 7.50
❑ 96 Charlie Silvera 25.00 12.50
❑ 97 Jerald Hal Lane RC 15.00 7.50
❑ 98 Joe Black 40.00 20.00
❑ 99 Bobby Hofman 15.00 7.50
❑ 100 Bob Keegan 15.00 7.50
❑ 101 Gene Woodling 25.00 12.50
❑ 102 Gil Hodges 80.00 50.00
❑ 103 Jim Lemon RC 15.00 7.50
❑ 104 Mike Sandlock 15.00 7.50
❑ 105 Andy Carey 25.00 12.50
❑ 106 Dick Kokos 15.00 7.50
❑ 107 Duane Pillette 15.00 7.50
❑ 108 Thornton Kipper RC 15.00 7.50
❑ 109 Bill Bruton 25.00 12.50
❑ 110 Harry Dorish 15.00 7.50
❑ 111 Jim Delsing 15.00 7.50
❑ 112 Bill Renna RC 15.00 7.50
❑ 113 Bob Boyd 15.00 7.50
❑ 114 Dean Stone RC 15.00 7.50
❑ 115 Rip Repulski 15.00 7.50
❑ 116 Steve Bilko 15.00 7.50
❑ 117 Solly Hemus 15.00 7.50
❑ 118 Carl Scheib 15.00 7.50
❑ 119 Johnny Antonelli 25.00 12.50
❑ 120 Roy McMillan 25.00 12.50
❑ 121 Clem Labine 25.00 12.50
❑ 122 Johnny Logan 25.00 12.50
❑ 123 Bobby Adams 15.00 7.50
❑ 124 Marion Fricano 15.00 7.50
❑ 125 Harry Perkowski 15.00 7.50
❑ 126 Ben Wade 15.00 7.50
❑ 127 Steve O'Neill MG 15.00 7.50
❑ 128 Hank Aaron RC 1800.00 1000.00
❑ 129 Forrest Jacobs RC 15.00 7.50
❑ 130 Hank Bauer 25.00 12.50
❑ 131 Reno Bertoia RC 25.00 12.50
❑ 132 Tommy Lasorda RC 250.00 150.00
❑ 133 Del Baker CO 15.00 7.50
❑ 134 Cal Hogue 15.00 7.50
❑ 135 Joe Presko 15.00 7.50
❑ 136 Connie Ryan 15.00 7.50
❑ 137 Wally Moon RC 40.00 20.00
❑ 138 Bob Borkowski 15.00 7.50
❑ 139 J.O'Brien/E.O'Brien 50.00 25.00
❑ 140 Tom Wright 15.00 7.50
❑ 141 Joey Jay RC 25.00 12.50
❑ 142 Tom Poholsky 15.00 7.50
❑ 143 Rollie Hemsley CO 15.00 7.50
❑ 144 Bill Werle 15.00 7.50
❑ 145 Elmer Valo 15.00 7.50
❑ 146 Don Johnson 15.00 7.50
❑ 147 Johnny Riddle CO 15.00 7.50
❑ 148 Bob Trice RC 15.00 7.50
❑ 149 Al Robertson 15.00 7.50
❑ 150 Dick Kryhoski 15.00 7.50
❑ 151 Alex Grammas RC 15.00 7.50
❑ 152 Michael Blyzka RC 15.00 7.50
❑ 153 Al Walker 25.00 12.50
❑ 154 Mike Fornieles RC 15.00 7.50
❑ 155 Bob Kennedy 25.00 12.50
❑ 156 Joe Coleman 25.00 12.50
❑ 157 Don Lenhardt 25.00 12.50
❑ 158 Peanuts Lowrey 15.00 7.50
❑ 159 Dave Philley 15.00 7.50
❑ 160 Ralph Kress CO 15.00 7.50
❑ 161 John Hetki 15.00 7.50
❑ 162 Herman Wehmeier 15.00 7.50
❑ 163 Frank House 15.00 7.50
❑ 164 Stu Miller 25.00 12.50
❑ 165 Jim Pendleton 15.00 7.50
❑ 166 Johnny Podres 40.00 20.00
❑ 167 Don Lund 15.00 7.50
❑ 168 Morrie Martin 25.00 12.50
❑ 169 Jim Hughes 40.00 20.00
❑ 170 Dusty Rhodes RC 25.00 12.50
❑ 171 Leo Kiely 15.00 7.50
❑ 172 Harold Brown RC 15.00 7.50
❑ 173 Jack Harshman RC 15.00 7.50
❑ 174 Tom Qualters RC 15.00 7.50
❑ 175 Frank Leja RC 25.00 12.50
❑ 176 Robert Keely CO 15.00 7.50
❑ 177 Bob Milliken 15.00 7.50
❑ 178 Bill Glynn UER 15.00 7.50
❑ 179 Gair Allie RC 15.00 7.50
❑ 180 Wes Westrum 25.00 12.50
❑ 181 Mel Roach RC 15.00 7.50
❑ 182 Chuck Harmon RC 15.00 7.50
❑ 183 Earle Combs CO 25.00 12.50
❑ 184 Ed Bailey 15.00 7.50
❑ 185 Chuck Stobbs 15.00 7.50
❑ 186 Karl Olson 15.00 7.50
❑ 187 Heinie Manush CO 25.00 12.50
❑ 188 Dave Jolly RC 15.00 7.50
❑ 189 Bob Ross 15.00 7.50
❑ 190 Ray Herbert RC 15.00 7.50
❑ 191 Dick Schofield RC 25.00 12.50
❑ 192 Ellis Deal CO 15.00 7.50
❑ 193 Johnny Hopp CO 25.00 12.50
❑ 194 Bill Sarni RC 15.00 7.50
❑ 195 Billy Consolo RC 15.00 7.50
❑ 196 Stan Jok RC 15.00 7.50
❑ 197 Lynwood Rowe CO 25.00 12.50
❑ 198 Carl Sawatski 15.00 7.50
❑ 199 Glenn (Rocky) Nelson 15.00 7.50
❑ 200 Larry Jansen 25.00 12.50
❑ 201 Al Kaline RC 700.00 400.00
❑ 202 Bob Purkey RC 25.00 12.50
❑ 203 Harry Brecheen CO 25.00 12.50
❑ 204 Angel Scull RC 15.00 7.50
❑ 205 Johnny Sain 40.00 20.00
❑ 206 Ray Crone RC 15.00 7.50
❑ 207 Tom Oliver CO RC 15.00 7.50
❑ 208 Grady Hatton 15.00 7.50
❑ 209 Chuck Thompson RC 15.00 7.50
❑ 210 Bob Buhl RC 25.00 12.50
❑ 211 Don Hoak 25.00 12.50
❑ 212 Bob Micelotta RC 15.00 7.50
❑ 213 Johnny Fitzpatrick CO RC 15.00 7.50
❑ 214 Arnie Portocarrero RC 15.00 7.50
❑ 215 Ed McGhee 25.00 12.50
❑ 216 Al Sima 15.00 7.50
❑ 217 Paul Schreiber CO RC 15.00 7.50
❑ 218 Fred Marsh 15.00 7.50
❑ 219 Chuck Kress RC 15.00 7.50
❑ 220 Ruben Gomez RC 25.00 12.50
❑ 221 Dick Brodowski 15.00 7.50
❑ 222 Bill Wilson RC 15.00 7.50
❑ 223 Joe Haynes CO 15.00 7.50
❑ 224 Dick Weik RC 15.00 7.50
❑ 225 Don Liddle RC 15.00 7.50
❑ 226 Jehosie Heard RC 25.00 12.50
❑ 227 Buster Mills CO RC 15.00 7.50
❑ 228 Gene Hermanski 15.00 7.50
❑ 229 Bob Talbot RC 15.00 7.50
❑ 230 Bob Kuzava 25.00 12.50
❑ 231 Roy Smalley 15.00 7.50
❑ 232 Lou Limmer RC 15.00 7.50
❑ 233 Augie Galan CO 15.00 7.50
❑ 234 Jerry Lynch RC 15.00 7.50
❑ 235 Vern Law 25.00 12.50
❑ 236 Paul Penson RC 15.00 7.50
❑ 237 Mike Ryba CO RC 15.00 7.50
❑ 238 Al Aber 15.00 7.50
❑ 239 Bill Skowron RC 100.00 60.00
❑ 240 Sam Mele 25.00 12.50
❑ 241 Robert Miller RC 15.00 7.50
❑ 242 Curt Roberts RC 15.00 7.50
❑ 243 Ray Blades CO RC 15.00 7.50
❑ 244 Leroy Wheat RC 15.00 7.50
❑ 245 Roy Sievers 25.00 12.50
❑ 246 Howie Fox 15.00 7.50
❑ 247 Ed Mayo CO 15.00 7.50
❑ 248 Al Smith RC 25.00 12.50

- ❑ 249 Wilmer Mizell 25.00 12.50
- ❑ 250 Ted Williams 800.00 500.00

1955 Topps

- ❑ COMPLETE SET (206) 8000.00 5000.00
- ❑ COMMON CARD (1-150) 12.00 6.00
- ❑ COMMON CARD (151-160) 20.00 10.00
- ❑ COMMON CARD (161-210) 30.00 15.00
- ❑ NOT ISSUED (175/186/203/209)
- ❑ WRAP.(1-CENT, DATED) 150.00 100.00
- ❑ WRAP.(1-CENT, UNDAT) 50.00 40.00
- ❑ WRAP.(5-CENT, DATED) 150.00 100.00
- ❑ WRAP.(5-CENT, UNDAT) 100.00 75.00
- ❑ 1 Dusty Rhodes 125.00 75.00
- ❑ 2 Ted Williams 600.00 350.00
- ❑ 3 Art Fowler RC 15.00 7.50
- ❑ 4 Al Kaline 150.00 90.00
- ❑ 5 Jim Gilliam 40.00 20.00
- ❑ 6 Stan Hack MG RC 25.00 12.50
- ❑ 7 Jim Hegan 15.00 7.50
- ❑ 8 Harold Smith RC 12.00 6.00
- ❑ 9 Robert Miller 12.00 6.00
- ❑ 10 Bob Keegan 12.00 6.00
- ❑ 11 Ferris Fain 15.00 7.50
- ❑ 12 Vernon (Jake) Thies RC 12.00 6.00
- ❑ 13 Fred Marsh 12.00 6.00
- ❑ 14 Jim Finigan RC 12.00 6.00
- ❑ 15 Jim Pendleton 12.00 6.00
- ❑ 16 Roy Sievers 15.00 7.50
- ❑ 17 Bobby Hofman 12.00 6.00
- ❑ 18 Russ Kemmerer RC 12.00 6.00
- ❑ 19 Billy Herman CO 15.00 7.50
- ❑ 20 Andy Carey 15.00 7.50
- ❑ 21 Alex Grammas 12.00 6.00
- ❑ 22 Bill Skowron 40.00 20.00
- ❑ 23 Jack Parks RC 12.00 6.00
- ❑ 24 Hal Newhouser 40.00 20.00
- ❑ 25 Johnny Podres 25.00 12.50
- ❑ 26 Dick Groat 15.00 7.50
- ❑ 27 Billy Gardner RC 15.00 7.50
- ❑ 28 Ernie Banks 200.00 125.00
- ❑ 29 Herman Wehmeier 12.00 6.00
- ❑ 30 Vic Power 15.00 7.50
- ❑ 31 Warren Spahn 100.00 60.00
- ❑ 32 Warren McGhee RC 12.00 6.00
- ❑ 33 Tom Qualters 12.00 6.00
- ❑ 34 Wayne Terwilliger 12.00 6.00
- ❑ 35 Dave Jolly 12.00 6.00
- ❑ 36 Leo Kiely 12.00 6.00
- ❑ 37 Joe Cunningham RC 15.00 7.50
- ❑ 38 Bob Turley 15.00 7.50
- ❑ 39 Bill Glynn 12.00 6.00
- ❑ 40 Don Hoak 15.00 7.50
- ❑ 41 Chuck Stobbs 12.00 6.00
- ❑ 42 John (Windy) McCall RC 12.00 6.00
- ❑ 43 Harvey Haddix 15.00 7.50
- ❑ 44 Harold Valentine RC 12.00 6.00
- ❑ 45 Hank Sauer 15.00 7.50
- ❑ 46 Ted Kazanski 12.00 6.00
- ❑ 47 Hank Aaron 400.00 250.00
- ❑ 48 Bob Kennedy 15.00 7.50
- ❑ 49 J.W. Porter 12.00 6.00
- ❑ 50 Jackie Robinson 500.00 300.00
- ❑ 51 Jim Hughes 15.00 7.50
- ❑ 52 Bill Tremel RC 12.00 6.00
- ❑ 53 Bill Taylor 12.00 6.00
- ❑ 54 Lou Limmer 12.00 6.00
- ❑ 55 Rip Repulski 12.00 6.00
- ❑ 56 Ray Jablonski 12.00 6.00
- ❑ 57 Billy O'Dell RC 12.00 6.00
- ❑ 58 Jim Rivera 12.00 0.00
- ❑ 59 Gair Allie 12.00 6.00
- ❑ 60 Dean Stone 12.00 6.00
- ❑ 61 Forrest Jacobs 12.00 6.00
- ❑ 62 Thornton Kipper 12.00 6.00
- ❑ 63 Joe Collins 15.00 7.50
- ❑ 64 Gus Triandos RC 15.00 7.50
- ❑ 65 Ray Boone 15.00 7.50
- ❑ 66 Ron Jackson RC 12.00 6.00
- ❑ 67 Wally Moon 15.00 7.50
- ❑ 68 Jim Davis RC 12.00 6.00
- ❑ 69 Ed Bailey 15.00 7.50
- ❑ 70 Al Rosen 15.00 7.50
- ❑ 71 Ruben Gomez 12.00 6.00
- ❑ 72 Karl Olson 12.00 6.00
- ❑ 73 Jack Shepard RC 12.00 6.00
- ❑ 74 Bob Borkowski 12.00 6.00
- ❑ 75 Sandy Amoros RC 40.00 20.00
- ❑ 76 Howie Pollet 12.00 6.00
- ❑ 77 Arnie Portocarrero 12.00 6.00
- ❑ 78 Gordon Jones RC 12.00 6.00
- ❑ 79 Clyde (Danny) Schell RC 12.00 6.00
- ❑ 80 Bob Grim RC 15.00 7.50
- ❑ 81 Gene Conley 15.00 7.50
- ❑ 82 Chuck Harmon 12.00 6.00
- ❑ 83 Tom Brewer RC 12.00 6.00
- ❑ 84 Camilo Pascual RC 15.00 7.50
- ❑ 85 Don Mossi RC 25.00 12.50
- ❑ 86 Bill Wilson 12.00 6.00
- ❑ 87 Frank House 12.00 6.00
- ❑ 88 Bob Skinner RC 15.00 7.50
- ❑ 89 Joe Frazier RC 15.00 7.50
- ❑ 90 Karl Spooner RC 15.00 7.50
- ❑ 91 Milt Bolling 12.00 6.00
- ❑ 92 Don Zimmer RC 25.00 12.50
- ❑ 93 Steve Bilko 12.00 6.00
- ❑ 94 Reno Bertoia 12.00 6.00
- ❑ 95 Preston Ward 12.00 6.00
- ❑ 96 Chuck Bishop 12.00 6.00
- ❑ 97 Carlos Paula RC 12.00 6.00
- ❑ 98 John Riddle CO 12.00 6.00
- ❑ 99 Frank Leja 12.00 6.00
- ❑ 100 Monte Irvin 40.00 20.00
- ❑ 101 Johnny Gray RC 12.00 6.00
- ❑ 102 Wally Westlake 12.00 6.00
- ❑ 103 Chuck White RC 12.00 6.00
- ❑ 104 Jack Harshman 12.00 6.00
- ❑ 105 Chuck Diering 12.00 6.00
- ❑ 106 Frank Sullivan RC 12.00 6.00
- ❑ 107 Curt Roberts 12.00 6.00
- ❑ 108 Rube Walker 15.00 7.50
- ❑ 109 Ed Lopat 15.00 7.50
- ❑ 110 Gus Zernial 15.00 7.50
- ❑ 111 Bob Milliken 15.00 7.50
- ❑ 112 Nelson King RC 12.00 6.00
- ❑ 113 Harry Brecheen CO 15.00 7.50
- ❑ 114 Louis Ortiz RC 12.00 6.00
- ❑ 115 Ellis Kinder 12.00 6.00
- ❑ 116 Tom Hurd RC 12.00 6.00
- ❑ 117 Mel Roach 12.00 6.00
- ❑ 118 Bob Purkey 12.00 6.00
- ❑ 119 Bob Lennon RC 12.00 6.00
- ❑ 120 Ted Kluszewski 80.00 50.00
- ❑ 121 Bill Renna 12.00 6.00
- ❑ 122 Carl Sawatski 12.00 6.00
- ❑ 123 Sandy Koufax RC 1200.00 700.00
- ❑ 124 Harmon Killebrew RC 250.00 150.00
- ❑ 125 Ken Boyer RC 80.00 50.00
- ❑ 126 Dick Hall RC 12.00 6.00
- ❑ 127 Dale Long RC 15.00 7.50
- ❑ 128 Ted Lepcio 12.00 6.00
- ❑ 129 Elvin Tappe 15.00 7.50
- ❑ 130 Mayo Smith MG RC 12.00 6.00
- ❑ 131 Grady Hatton 12.00 6.00
- ❑ 132 Bob Trice 12.00 6.00
- ❑ 133 Dave Hoskins 12.00 6.00
- ❑ 134 Joey Jay 15.00 7.50
- ❑ 135 Johnny O'Brien 15.00 7.50
- ❑ 136 Veston (Bunky) Stewart RC 12.00 6.00
- ❑ 137 Harry Elliott RC 12.00 6.00
- ❑ 138 Ray Herbert 12.00 6.00
- ❑ 139 Steve Kraly RC 12.00 6.00
- ❑ 140 Mel Parnell 15.00 7.50
- ❑ 141 Tom Wright 12.00 6.00
- ❑ 142 Jerry Lynch 15.00 7.50
- ❑ 143 John Schofield 15.00 7.50
- ❑ 144 Joe Amalfitano RC 12.00 6.00
- ❑ 145 Elmer Valo 12.00 6.00
- ❑ 146 Dick Donovan RC 12.00 6.00
- ❑ 147 Hugh Pepper RC 12.00 6.00
- ❑ 148 Hector Brown 12.00 6.00
- ❑ 149 Ray Crone 12.00 6.00
- ❑ 150 Mike Higgins MG 12.00 6.00
- ❑ 151 Ralph Kress CO 20.00 10.00
- ❑ 152 Harry Agganis RC 100.00 60.00
- ❑ 153 Bud Podbielan 25.00 12.50
- ❑ 154 Willie Miranda 20.00 10.00
- ❑ 155 Eddie Mathews 200.00 125.00
- ❑ 156 Joe Black 50.00 30.00
- ❑ 157 Robert Miller 20.00 10.00
- ❑ 158 Tommy Carroll RC 25.00 12.50
- ❑ 159 Johnny Schmitz 20.00 10.00
- ❑ 160 Ray Narleski RC 20.00 10.00
- ❑ 161 Chuck Tanner RC 40.00 20.00
- ❑ 162 Joe Coleman 30.00 15.00
- ❑ 163 Faye Throneberry 30.00 15.00
- ❑ 164 Roberto Clemente RC 2000.00 1200.00
- ❑ 165 Don Johnson 30.00 15.00
- ❑ 166 Hank Bauer 80.00 50.00
- ❑ 167 Tom Casagrande RC 30.00 15.00
- ❑ 168 Duane Pillette 30.00 15.00
- ❑ 169 Bob Oldis 40.00 20.00
- ❑ 170 Jim Pearce DP RC 15.00 7.50
- ❑ 171 Dick Brodowski 30.00 15.00
- ❑ 172 Frank Baumholtz DP 15.00 7.50
- ❑ 173 Bob Kline RC 30.00 15.00
- ❑ 174 Rudy Minarcin RC 30.00 15.00
- ❑ 175 Does not exist
- ❑ 176 Norm Zauchin RC 30.00 15.00
- ❑ 177 Al Robertson 30.00 15.00
- ❑ 178 Bobby Adams 30.00 15.00
- ❑ 179 Jim Bolger RC 30.00 15.00
- ❑ 180 Clem Labine 60.00 30.00
- ❑ 181 Roy McMillan 40.00 20.00
- ❑ 182 Humberto Robinson RC 30.00 15.00
- ❑ 183 Anthony Jacobs RC 30.00 15.00
- ❑ 184 Harry Perkowski DP 15.00 7.50
- ❑ 185 Don Ferrarese RC 30.00 15.00
- ❑ 186 Does not exist
- ❑ 187 Gil Hodges 175.00 100.00
- ❑ 188 Charlie Silvera DP 15.00 7.50
- ❑ 189 Phil Rizzuto 175.00 100.00
- ❑ 190 Gene Woodling 40.00 20.00
- ❑ 191 Eddie Stanky MG 40.00 20.00
- ❑ 192 Jim Delsing 40.00 20.00
- ❑ 193 Johnny Sain 60.00 30.00
- ❑ 194 Willie Mays 600.00 350.00
- ❑ 195 Ed Roebuck RC 60.00 30.00
- ❑ 196 Gale Wade RC 30.00 15.00
- ❑ 197 Al Smith 60.00 30.00
- ❑ 198 Yogi Berra 300.00 175.00
- ❑ 199 Bert Hamric RC 40.00 20.00
- ❑ 200 Jackie Jensen 60.00 30.00
- ❑ 201 Sherman Lollar 40.00 20.00
- ❑ 202 Jim Owens RC 30.00 15.00
- ❑ 203 Does not exist
- ❑ 204 Frank Smith 30.00 15.00
- ❑ 205 Gene Freese RC 40.00 20.00
- ❑ 206 Pete Daley RC 30.00 15.00
- ❑ 207 Billy Consolo 30.00 15.00
- ❑ 208 Ray Moore RC 40.00 20.00
- ❑ 209 Does not exist
- ❑ 210 Duke Snider 600.00 350.00

1956 Topps

- ❑ COMPLETE SET (340) 8000.00 5000.00
- ❑ COMMON CARD (1-100) 10.00 5.00
- ❑ COMMON CARD (101-180) 12.00 6.00
- ❑ COMMON CARD (261-340) 12.00 6.00
- ❑ COMMON CARD (181-260) 15.00 7.50
- ❑ WRAP.(1-CENT) 250.00 200.00
- ❑ WRAP.(1-CENT, REPEAT) 100.00 75.00
- ❑ WRAPPER (5-CENT) 200.00 150.00
- ❑ 1 Will Harridge PRES 125.00 75.00
- ❑ 2 Warren Giles PRES DP 50.00 30.00
- ❑ 3 Elmer Valo 15.00 7.50
- ❑ 4 Carlos Paula 15.00 7.50
- ❑ 5 Ted Williams 500.00 300.00
- ❑ 6 Ray Boone 25.00 15.00
- ❑ 7 Ron Negray RC 10.00 5.00

❑ 8 Walter Alston MG RC 40.00 25.00
❑ 9 Ruben Gomez DP 10.00 5.00
❑ 10 Warren Spahn 120.00 70.00
❑ 11A Chicago Cubs TC Center 30.00 15.00
❑ 11B Chicago Cubs TC D'55 80.00 50.00
❑ 11C Chicago Cubs TC Left 30.00 15.00
❑ 12 Andy Carey 15.00 7.50
❑ 13 Roy Face 15.00 7.50
❑ 14 Ken Boyer DP 15.00 7.50
❑ 15 Ernie Banks DP 100.00 60.00
❑ 16 Hector Lopez RC 15.00 7.50
❑ 17 Gene Conley 15.00 7.50
❑ 18 Dick Donovan 10.00 5.00
❑ 19 Chuck Diering DP 10.00 5.00
❑ 20 Al Kaline 125.00 75.00
❑ 21 Joe Collins DP 15.00 7.50
❑ 22 Jim Finigan 10.00 5.00
❑ 23 Fred Marsh 10.00 5.00
❑ 24 Dick Groat 15.00 7.50
❑ 25 Ted Kluszewski 80.00 50.00
❑ 25A Ted Kluszewski GB
❑ 26 Grady Hatton 10.00 5.00
❑ 27 Nelson Burbrink DP RC 10.00 5.00
❑ 28 Bobby Hofman 10.00 5.00
❑ 29 Jack Harshman 10.00 5.00
❑ 30 Jackie Robinson DP 250.00 150.00
❑ 31 Hank Aaron UER DP 350.00 200.00
❑ 32 Frank House 10.00 5.00
❑ 33 Roberto Clemente 400.00 250.00
❑ 34 Tom Brewer DP 10.00 5.00
❑ 35 Al Rosen 15.00 7.50
❑ 36 Rudy Minarcin 15.00 7.50
❑ 37 Alex Grammas 10.00 5.00
❑ 38 Bob Kennedy 15.00 7.50
❑ 39 Don Mossi 15.00 7.50
❑ 40 Bob Turley 15.00 7.50
❑ 41 Hank Sauer 15.00 7.50
❑ 42 Sandy Amoros 25.00 15.00
❑ 43 Ray Moore 10.00 5.00
❑ 44 Windy McCall 10.00 5.00
❑ 45 Gus Zernial 15.00 7.50
❑ 46 Gene Freese DP 10.00 5.00
❑ 47 Art Fowler 10.00 5.00
❑ 48 Jim Hegan 15.00 7.50
❑ 49 Pedro Ramos RC 10.00 5.00
❑ 50 Dusty Rhodes DP 15.00 7.50
❑ 51 Ernie Oravetz RC 10.00 5.00
❑ 52 Bob Grim DP 15.00 7.50
❑ 53 Arnie Portocarrero 10.00 5.00
❑ 54 Bob Keegan 10.00 5.00
❑ 55 Wally Moon 15.00 7.50
❑ 56 Dale Long 15.00 7.50
❑ 57 Duke Maas RC 10.00 5.00
❑ 58 Ed Roebuck 25.00 15.00
❑ 59 Jose Santiago RC 10.00 5.00
❑ 60 Mayo Smith MG DP 10.00 5.00
❑ 61 Bill Skowron 25.00 15.00
❑ 62 Hal Smith 15.00 7.50
❑ 63 Roger Craig RC 40.00 25.00
❑ 64 Luis Arroyo RC 10.00 5.00
❑ 65 Johnny O'Brien 15.00 7.50
❑ 66 Bob Speake DP RC 10.00 5.00
❑ 67 Vic Power 15.00 7.50
❑ 68 Chuck Stobbs 10.00 5.00
❑ 69 Chuck Tanner 15.00 7.50
❑ 70 Jim Rivera 10.00 5.00
❑ 71 Frank Sullivan 10.00 5.00
❑ 72A Philadelphia Phil TC Center 30.00 15.00
❑ 72B Philadelphia Phillies TC D'55 80.00 50.00
❑ 72C Philadelphia Phillies TC Left DP 30.00 15.00
❑ 73 Wayne Terwilliger 10.00 5.00
❑ 74 Jim King RC 10.00 5.00
❑ 75 Roy Sievers DP 15.00 7.50
❑ 76 Ray Crone 10.00 5.00
❑ 77 Harvey Haddix 15.00 7.50
❑ 78 Herman Wehmeier 10.00 5.00
❑ 79 Sandy Koufax 350.00 200.00
❑ 80 Gus Triandos DP 10.00 5.00
❑ 81 Wally Westlake 10.00 5.00
❑ 82 Bill Renna DP 10.00 5.00
❑ 83 Karl Spooner 15.00 7.50
❑ 84 Babe Birrer RC 10.00 5.00
❑ 85A Cleveland Indians TC Center 30.00 15.00
❑ 85B Cleveland Indians TC D'55 80.0050.00
❑ 85C Cleveland Indians TC Left 30.00 15.00
❑ 86 Ray Jablonski DP 10.00 5.00
❑ 87 Dean Stone 10.00 5.00
❑ 88 Johnny Kucks RC 15.00 7.50
❑ 89 Norm Zauchin 10.00 5.00
❑ 90A Cincinnati Redlegs TC Center 30.00 15.00
❑ 90B Cincinnati Reds TC D'55 80.00 50.00
❑ 90C Cincinnati Reds TC Left 30.00 15.00
❑ 91 Gail Harris RC 10.00 5.00
❑ 92 Bob (Red) Wilson 10.00 5.00
❑ 93 George Susce 10.00 5.00
❑ 94 Ron Kline 10.00 5.00
❑ 95A Milwaukee Braves TC Center 40.00 20.00
❑ 95B Milwaukee Braves TC D'55 80.00 50.00
❑ 95C Milwaukee Braves TC Left 40.00 20.00
❑ 96 Bill Tremel 10.00 5.00
❑ 97 Jerry Lynch 15.00 7.50
❑ 98 Camilo Pascual 15.00 7.50
❑ 99 Don Zimmer 25.00 15.00
❑ 100A Baltimore Orioles TC Center 40.00 20.00
❑ 100B Baltimore Orioles TC D'55 80.0050.00
❑ 100C Baltimore Orioles TC Left 40.0020.00
❑ 101 Roy Campanella 150.00 90.00
❑ 102 Jim Davis 12.00 6.00
❑ 103 Willie Miranda 12.00 6.00
❑ 104 Bob Lennon 12.00 6.00
❑ 105 Al Smith 12.00 6.00
❑ 106 Joe Astroth 12.00 6.00
❑ 107 Eddie Mathews 100.00 60.00
❑ 108 Laurin Pepper 12.00 6.00
❑ 109 Enos Slaughter 40.00 25.00
❑ 110 Yogi Berra 175.00 100.00
❑ 111 Boston Red Sox TC 40.00 20.00
❑ 112 Dee Fondy 12.00 6.00
❑ 113 Phil Rizzuto 150.00 90.00
❑ 114 Jim Owens 15.00 7.50
❑ 115 Jackie Jensen 15.00 7.50
❑ 116 Eddie O'Brien 12.00 6.00
❑ 117 Virgil Trucks 15.00 7.50
❑ 118 Nellie Fox 80.00 50.00
❑ 119 Larry Jackson RC 15.00 7.50
❑ 120 Richie Ashburn 60.00 35.00
❑ 121 Pittsburgh Pirates TC 40.00 20.00
❑ 122 Willard Nixon 12.00 6.00
❑ 123 Roy McMillan 15.00 7.50
❑ 124 Don Kaiser 12.00 6.00
❑ 125 Minnie Minoso 40.00 25.00
❑ 126 Jim Brady RC 12.00 6.00
❑ 127 Willie Jones 15.00 7.50
❑ 128 Eddie Yost 15.00 7.50
❑ 129 Jake Martin RC 12.00 6.00
❑ 130 Willie Mays 300.00 175.00
❑ 131 Bob Roselli RC 12.00 6.00
❑ 132 Bobby Avila 12.00 6.00
❑ 133 Ray Narleski 12.00 6.00
❑ 134 St. Louis Cardinals TC 40.00 20.00
❑ 135 Mickey Mantle 1500.00 900.00
❑ 136 Johnny Logan 15.00 7.50
❑ 137 Al Silvera RC 12.00 6.00
❑ 138 Johnny Antonelli 15.00 7.50
❑ 139 Tommy Carroll 15.00 7.50
❑ 140 Herb Score RC 60.00 35.00
❑ 141 Joe Frazier 12.00 6.00
❑ 142 Gene Baker 12.00 6.00
❑ 143 Jim Piersall 15.00 7.50
❑ 144 Leroy Powell RC 12.00 6.00
❑ 145 Gil Hodges 60.00 35.00
❑ 146 Washington Nationals TC 40.00 20.00
❑ 147 Earl Torgeson 12.00 6.00
❑ 148 Alvin Dark 15.00 7.50
❑ 149 Dixie Howell 12.00 6.00
❑ 150 Duke Snider 125.00 75.00
❑ 151 Spook Jacobs 15.00 7.50
❑ 152 Billy Hoeft 15.00 7.50
❑ 153 Frank Thomas 15.00 7.50
❑ 154 Dave Pope 12.00 6.00
❑ 155 Harvey Kuenn 15.00 7.50
❑ 156 Wes Westrum 15.00 7.50
❑ 157 Dick Brodowski 12.00 6.00
❑ 158 Wally Post 15.00 7.50
❑ 159 Clint Courtney 12.00 6.00
❑ 160 Billy Pierce 15.00 7.50
❑ 161 Joe DeMaestri 12.00 6.00
❑ 162 Dave (Gus) Bell 15.00 7.50
❑ 163 Gene Woodling 15.00 7.50
❑ 164 Harmon Killebrew 100.00 60.00
❑ 165 Red Schoendienst 40.00 25.00
❑ 166 Brooklyn Dodgers TC 200.00 125.00
❑ 167 Harry Dorish 12.00 6.00
❑ 168 Sammy White 12.00 6.00
❑ 169 Bob Nelson RC 12.00 6.00
❑ 170 Bill Virdon 15.00 7.50
❑ 171 Jim Wilson 12.00 6.00
❑ 172 Frank Torre RC 15.00 7.50
❑ 173 Johnny Podres 25.00 15.00
❑ 174 Glen Gorbous RC 12.00 6.00
❑ 175 Del Crandall 15.00 7.50
❑ 176 Alex Kellner 12.00 6.00
❑ 177 Hank Bauer 25.00 15.00
❑ 178 Joe Black 15.00 7.50
❑ 179 Harry Chiti 12.00 6.00
❑ 180 Robin Roberts 50.00 30.00
❑ 181 Billy Martin 125.00 75.00
❑ 182 Paul Minner 15.00 7.50
❑ 183 Stan Lopata 20.00 10.00
❑ 184 Don Bessent RC 20.00 10.00
❑ 185 Bill Bruton 20.00 10.00
❑ 186 Ron Jackson 15.00 7.50
❑ 187 Early Wynn 50.00 30.00
❑ 188 Chicago White Sox TC 50.00 30.00
❑ 189 Ned Garver 15.00 7.50
❑ 190 Carl Furillo 30.00 18.00
❑ 191 Frank Lary 20.00 10.00
❑ 192 Smoky Burgess 20.00 10.00
❑ 193 Wilmer Mizell 20.00 10.00
❑ 194 Monte Irvin 30.00 18.00
❑ 195 George Kell 30.00 18.00
❑ 196 Tom Poholsky 15.00 7.50
❑ 197 Granny Hamner 15.00 7.50
❑ 198 Ed Fitzgerald 15.00 7.50
❑ 199 Hank Thompson 20.00 10.00
❑ 200 Bob Feller 125.00 75.00
❑ 201 Rip Repulski 15.00 7.50
❑ 202 Jim Hearn 15.00 7.50
❑ 203 Bill Tuttle 15.00 7.50
❑ 204 Art Swanson RC 15.00 7.50
❑ 205 Whitey Lockman 20.00 10.00
❑ 206 Erv Palica 15.00 7.50
❑ 207 Jim Small RC 15.00 7.50
❑ 208 Elston Howard 60.00 35.00
❑ 209 Max Surkont 15.00 7.50
❑ 210 Mike Garcia 20.00 10.00
❑ 211 Murry Dickson 15.00 7.50
❑ 212 Johnny Temple 15.00 7.50
❑ 213 Detroit Tigers TC 60.00 35.00
❑ 214 Bob Rush 15.00 7.50
❑ 215 Tommy Byrne 20.00 10.00
❑ 216 Jerry Schoonmaker RC 15.00 7.50
❑ 217 Billy Klaus 15.00 7.50
❑ 218 Joe Nuxhall UER 20.00 10.00
❑ 219 Lew Burdette 20.00 10.00
❑ 220 Del Ennis 20.00 10.00
❑ 221 Bob Friend 20.00 10.00
❑ 222 Dave Philley 15.00 7.50
❑ 223 Randy Jackson 15.00 7.50
❑ 224 Bud Podbielan 15.00 7.50
❑ 225 Gil McDougald 50.00 30.00
❑ 226 New York Giants TC 80.00 50.00
❑ 227 Russ Meyer 15.00 7.50
❑ 228 Mickey Vernon 20.00 10.00
❑ 229 Harry Brecheen CO 20.00 10.00
❑ 230 Chico Carrasquel 15.00 7.50
❑ 231 Bob Hale RC 15.00 7.50
❑ 232 Toby Atwell 15.00 7.50
❑ 233 Carl Erskine 30.00 18.00
❑ 234 Pete Runnels 15.00 7.50

- ❑ 235 Don Newcombe 50.00 30.00
- ❑ 236 Kansas City Athletics TC 40.00 20.00
- ❑ 237 Jose Valdivielso RC 15.00 7.50
- ❑ 238 Walt Dropo 20.00 10.00
- ❑ 239 Harry Simpson 15.00 7.50
- ❑ 240 Whitey Ford 125.00 75.00
- ❑ 241 Don Mueller UER 20.00 10.00
- ❑ 242 Hershell Freeman 15.00 7.50
- ❑ 243 Sherm Lollar 20.00 10.00
- ❑ 244 Bob Buhl 30.00 18.00
- ❑ 245 Billy Goodman 20.00 10.00
- ❑ 246 Tom Gorman 15.00 7.50
- ❑ 247 Bill Sarni 15.00 7.50
- ❑ 248 Bob Porterfield 15.00 7.50
- ❑ 249 Johnny Klippstein 15.00 7.50
- ❑ 250 Larry Doby 30.00 18.00
- ❑ 251 New York Yankees TC UER 250.00 150.00
- ❑ 252 Vern Law 20.00 10.00
- ❑ 253 Irv Noren 30.00 18.00
- ❑ 254 George Crowe 15.00 7.50
- ❑ 255 Bob Lemon 50.00 30.00
- ❑ 256 Tom Hurd 15.00 7.50
- ❑ 257 Bobby Thomson 30.00 18.00
- ❑ 258 Art Ditmar 15.00 7.50
- ❑ 259 Sam Jones 20.00 10.00
- ❑ 260 Pee Wee Reese 150.00 90.00
- ❑ 261 Bobby Shantz 15.00 7.50
- ❑ 262 Howie Pollet 12.00 6.00
- ❑ 263 Bob Miller 12.00 6.00
- ❑ 264 Ray Monzant RC 12.00 6.00
- ❑ 265 Sandy Consuegra 12.00 6.00
- ❑ 266 Don Ferrarese 12.00 6.00
- ❑ 267 Bob Nieman 12.00 6.00
- ❑ 268 Dale Mitchell 15.00 7.50
- ❑ 269 Jack Meyer RC 12.00 6.00
- ❑ 270 Billy Loes 15.00 7.50
- ❑ 271 Foster Castleman RC 12.00 6.00
- ❑ 272 Danny O'Connell 12.00 6.00
- ❑ 273 Walker Cooper 12.00 6.00
- ❑ 274 Frank Baumholtz 12.00 6.00
- ❑ 275 Jim Greengrass 12.00 6.00
- ❑ 276 George Zuverink 12.00 6.00
- ❑ 277 Daryl Spencer 12.00 6.00
- ❑ 278 Chet Nichols 12.00 6.00
- ❑ 279 Johnny Groth 12.00 6.00
- ❑ 280 Jim Gilliam 40.00 25.00
- ❑ 281 Art Houtteman 12.00 6.00
- ❑ 282 Warren Hacker 12.00 6.00
- ❑ 283 Hal R.Smith RC 15.00 7.50
- ❑ 284 Ike Delock 12.00 6.00
- ❑ 285 Eddie Miksis 12.00 6.00
- ❑ 286 Bill Wight 12.00 6.00
- ❑ 287 Bobby Adams 12.00 6.00
- ❑ 288 Bob Cerv 40.00 25.00
- ❑ 289 Hal Jeffcoat 12.00 6.00
- ❑ 290 Curt Simmons 15.00 7.50
- ❑ 291 Frank Kellert RC 12.00 6.00
- ❑ 292 Luis Aparicio RC 150.00 90.00
- ❑ 293 Stu Miller 25.00 15.00
- ❑ 294 Ernie Johnson 15.00 7.50
- ❑ 295 Clem Labine 15.00 7.50
- ❑ 296 Andy Seminick 12.00 6.00
- ❑ 297 Bob Skinner 15.00 7.50
- ❑ 298 Johnny Schmitz 12.00 6.00
- ❑ 299 Charlie Neal 40.00 25.00
- ❑ 300 Vic Wertz 15.00 7.50
- ❑ 301 Marv Grissom 12.00 6.00
- ❑ 302 Eddie Robinson 12.00 6.00
- ❑ 303 Jim Dyck 12.00 6.00
- ❑ 304 Frank Malzone 15.00 7.50
- ❑ 305 Brooks Lawrence 12.00 6.00
- ❑ 306 Curt Roberts 12.00 6.00
- ❑ 307 Hoyt Wilhelm 40.00 25.00
- ❑ 308 Chuck Harmon 12.00 6.00
- ❑ 309 Don Blasingame RC 15.00 7.50
- ❑ 310 Steve Gromek 12.00 6.00
- ❑ 311 Hal Naragon 12.00 6.00
- ❑ 312 Andy Pafko 15.00 7.50
- ❑ 313 Gene Stephens 12.00 6.00
- ❑ 314 Hobie Landrith 12.00 6.00
- ❑ 315 Milt Bolling 12.00 6.00
- ❑ 316 Jerry Coleman 15.00 7.50
- ❑ 317 Al Aber 12.00 6.00
- ❑ 318 Fred Hatfield 12.00 6.00
- ❑ 319 Jack Crimian RC 12.00 6.00
- ❑ 320 Joe Adcock 15.00 7.50
- ❑ 321 Jim Konstanty 15.00 7.50
- ❑ 322 Karl Olson 12.00 6.00
- ❑ 323 Willard Schmidt 12.00 6.00
- ❑ 324 Rocky Bridges 15.00 7.50
- ❑ 325 Don Liddle 12.00 6.00
- ❑ 326 Connie Johnson RC 12.00 6.00
- ❑ 327 Bob Wiesler RC 12.00 6.00
- ❑ 328 Preston Ward 12.00 6.00
- ❑ 329 Lou Berberet RC 12.00 6.00
- ❑ 330 Jim Busby 15.00 7.50
- ❑ 331 Dick Hall 12.00 6.00
- ❑ 332 Don Larsen 60.00 35.00
- ❑ 333 Rube Walker 12.00 6.00
- ❑ 334 Bob Miller 15.00 7.50
- ❑ 335 Don Hoak 15.00 7.50
- ❑ 336 Ellis Kinder 12.00 6.00
- ❑ 337 Bobby Morgan 12.00 6.00
- ❑ 338 Jim Delsing 12.00 6.00
- ❑ 339 Rance Pless RC 12.00 6.00
- ❑ 340 Mickey McDermott 60.00 35.00
- ❑ NNO Checklist 1/3 300.00 175.00
- ❑ NNO Checklist 2/4 300.00 175.00

1957 Topps

- ❑ COMPLETE SET (407) 10000.00 7000.00
- ❑ COMMON CARD (1-88) 10.00 5.00
- ❑ COMMON CARD (89-176) 8.00 4.00
- ❑ COMMON CARD (177-264) 8.00 4.00
- ❑ COMMON CARD (265-352) 20.00 10.00
- ❑ COMMON CARD (353-407) 8.00 4.00
- ❑ COMMON DP (265-352) 12.00 6.00
- ❑ WRAPPER (1-CENT) 300.00 250.00
- ❑ WRAPPER (5-CENT) 200.00 150.00
- ❑ 1 Ted Williams 600.00 350.00
- ❑ 2 Yogi Berra 200.00 125.00
- ❑ 3 Dale Long 20.00 10.00
- ❑ 4 Johnny Logan 20.00 10.00
- ❑ 5 Sal Maglie 20.00 10.00
- ❑ 6 Hector Lopez 15.00 7.50
- ❑ 7 Luis Aparicio 30.00 15.00
- ❑ 8 Don Mossi 15.00 7.50
- ❑ 9 Johnny Temple 15.00 7.50
- ❑ 10 Willie Mays 400.00 250.00
- ❑ 11 George Zuverink 10.00 5.00
- ❑ 12 Dick Groat 20.00 10.00
- ❑ 13 Wally Burnette RC 10.00 5.00
- ❑ 14 Bob Nieman 10.00 5.00
- ❑ 15 Robin Roberts 30.00 15.00
- ❑ 16 Walt Moryn 10.00 5.00
- ❑ 17 Billy Gardner 10.00 5.00
- ❑ 18 Don Drysdale RC 250.00 150.00
- ❑ 19 Bob Wilson 10.00 5.00
- ❑ 20 Hank Aaron UER 300.00 175.00
- ❑ 21 Frank Sullivan 10.00 5.00
- ❑ 22 Jerry Snyder UER 10.00 5.00
- ❑ 23 Sherm Lollar 15.00 7.50
- ❑ 24 Bill Mazeroski RC 80.00 50.00
- ❑ 25 Whitey Ford 150.00 90.00
- ❑ 26 Bob Boyd 10.00 5.00
- ❑ 27 Ted Kazanski 10.00 5.00
- ❑ 28 Gene Conley 15.00 7.50
- ❑ 29 Whitey Herzog RC 30.00 15.00
- ❑ 30 Pee Wee Reese 80.00 50.00
- ❑ 31 Ron Northey 10.00 5.00
- ❑ 32 Hershell Freeman 10.00 5.00
- ❑ 33 Jim Small 10.00 5.00
- ❑ 34 Tom Sturdivant RC 15.00 7.50
- ❑ 35 Frank Robinson RC 300.00 175.00
- ❑ 36 Bob Grim 10.00 5.00
- ❑ 37 Frank Torre 15.00 7.50
- ❑ 38 Nellie Fox 50.00 30.00
- ❑ 39 Al Worthington RC 10.00 5.00
- ❑ 40 Early Wynn 30.00 15.00
- ❑ 41 Hal W. Smith 10.00 5.00
- ❑ 42 Dee Fondy 10.00 5.00
- ❑ 43 Connie Johnson 10.00 5.00
- ❑ 44 Joe DeMaestri 10.00 5.00
- ❑ 45 Carl Furillo 30.00 15.00
- ❑ 46 Robert J. Miller 10.00 5.00
- ❑ 47 Don Blasingame 10.00 5.00
- ❑ 48 Bill Bruton 15.00 7.50
- ❑ 49 Daryl Spencer 10.00 5.00
- ❑ 50 Herb Score 30.00 15.00
- ❑ 51 Clint Courtney 10.00 5.00
- ❑ 52 Lee Walls 10.00 5.00
- ❑ 53 Clem Labine 20.00 10.00
- ❑ 54 Elmer Valo 10.00 5.00
- ❑ 55 Ernie Banks 125.00 75.00
- ❑ 56 Dave Sisler RC 10.00 5.00
- ❑ 57 Jim Lemon 15.00 7.50
- ❑ 58 Ruben Gomez 10.00 5.00
- ❑ 59 Dick Williams 15.00 7.50
- ❑ 60 Billy Hoeft 15.00 7.50
- ❑ 61 Dusty Rhodes 15.00 7.50
- ❑ 62 Billy Martin 60.00 35.00
- ❑ 63 Ike Delock 10.00 5.00
- ❑ 64 Pete Runnels 15.00 7.50
- ❑ 65 Wally Moon 15.00 7.50
- ❑ 66 Brooks Lawrence 10.00 5.00
- ❑ 67 Chico Carrasquel 10.00 5.00
- ❑ 68 Ray Crone 10.00 5.00
- ❑ 69 Roy McMillan 15.00 7.50
- ❑ 70 Richie Ashburn 50.00 30.00
- ❑ 71 Murry Dickson 10.00 5.00
- ❑ 72 Bill Tuttle 10.00 5.00
- ❑ 73 George Crowe 10.00 5.00
- ❑ 74 Vito Valentinetti RC 10.00 5.00
- ❑ 75 Jimmy Piersall 15.00 7.50
- ❑ 76 Roberto Clemente 300.00 175.00
- ❑ 77 Paul Foytack RC 10.00 5.00
- ❑ 78 Vic Wertz 15.00 7.50
- ❑ 79 Lindy McDaniel RC 15.00 7.50
- ❑ 80 Gil Hodges 50.00 30.00
- ❑ 81 Herman Wehmeier 10.00 5.00
- ❑ 82 Elston Howard 30.00 15.00
- ❑ 83 Lou Skizas RC 10.00 5.00
- ❑ 84 Moe Drabowsky RC 15.00 7.50
- ❑ 85 Larry Doby 30.00 15.00
- ❑ 86 Bill Sarni 10.00 5.00
- ❑ 87 Tom Gorman 10.00 5.00
- ❑ 88 Harvey Kuenn 15.00 7.50
- ❑ 89 Roy Sievers 15.00 7.50
- ❑ 90 Warren Spahn 80.00 50.00
- ❑ 91 Mack Burk RC 8.00 4.00
- ❑ 92 Mickey Vernon 15.00 7.50
- ❑ 93 Hal Jeffcoat 8.00 4.00
- ❑ 94 Bobby Del Greco 8.00 4.00
- ❑ 95 Mickey Mantle 1000.00 600.00
- ❑ 96 Hank Aguirre RC 8.00 4.00
- ❑ 97 New York Yankees TC 100.00 60.00
- ❑ 98 Alvin Dark 15.00 7.50
- ❑ 99 Bob Keegan 8.00 4.00
- ❑ 100 W.Giles/W.Harridge 15.00 7.50
- ❑ 101 Chuck Stobbs 8.00 4.00
- ❑ 102 Ray Boone 15.00 7.50
- ❑ 103 Joe Nuxhall 15.00 7.50
- ❑ 104 Hank Foiles 8.00 4.00
- ❑ 105 Johnny Antonelli 15.00 7.50
- ❑ 106 Ray Moore 8.00 4.00
- ❑ 107 Jim Rivera 8.00 4.00
- ❑ 108 Tommy Byrne 15.00 7.50
- ❑ 109 Hank Thompson 8.00 4.00
- ❑ 110 Bill Virdon 15.00 7.50
- ❑ 111 Hal R. Smith 8.00 4.00
- ❑ 112 Tom Brewer 8.00 4.00
- ❑ 113 Wilmer Mizell 15.00 7.50
- ❑ 114 Milwaukee Braves TC 20.00 10.00
- ❑ 115 Jim Gilliam 15.00 7.50
- ❑ 116 Mike Fornieles 8.00 4.00
- ❑ 117 Joe Adcock 20.00 10.00
- ❑ 118 Bob Porterfield 8.00 4.00
- ❑ 119 Stan Lopata 8.00 4.00
- ❑ 120 Bob Lemon 30.00 15.00
- ❑ 121 Clete Boyer RC 30.00 15.00

	No.	Card		
❑	122	Ken Boyer	20.00	10.00
❑	123	Steve Ridzik	8.00	4.00
❑	124	Dave Philley	8.00	4.00
❑	125	Al Kaline	100.00	60.00
❑	126	Bob Wiesler	8.00	4.00
❑	127	Bob Buhl	15.00	7.50
❑	128	Ed Bailey	15.00	7.50
❑	129	Saul Rogovin	8.00	4.00
❑	130	Don Newcombe	20.00	10.00
❑	131	Milt Bolling	8.00	4.00
❑	132	Art Ditmar	15.00	7.50
❑	133	Del Crandall	15.00	7.50
❑	134	Don Kaiser	8.00	4.00
❑	135	Bill Skowron	20.00	10.00
❑	136	Jim Hegan	15.00	7.50
❑	137	Bob Rush	8.00	4.00
❑	138	Minnie Minoso	20.00	10.00
❑	139	Lou Kretlow	8.00	4.00
❑	140	Frank Thomas	15.00	7.50
❑	141	Al Aber	8.00	4.00
❑	142	Charley Thompson	8.00	4.00
❑	143	Andy Pafko	15.00	7.50
❑	144	Ray Narleski	8.00	4.00
❑	145	Al Smith	8.00	4.00
❑	146	Don Ferrarese	8.00	4.00
❑	147	Al Walker	8.00	4.00
❑	148	Don Mueller	15.00	7.50
❑	149	Bob Kennedy	15.00	7.50
❑	150	Bob Friend	15.00	7.50
❑	151	Willie Miranda	8.00	4.00
❑	152	Jack Harshman	8.00	4.00
❑	153	Karl Olson	8.00	4.00
❑	154	Red Schoendienst	30.00	15.00
❑	155	Jim Brosnan	15.00	7.50
❑	156	Gus Triandos	15.00	7.50
❑	157	Wally Post	15.00	7.50
❑	158	Curt Simmons	15.00	7.50
❑	159	Solly Drake RC	8.00	4.00
❑	160	Billy Pierce	15.00	7.50
❑	161	Pittsburgh Pirates TC	15.00	7.50
❑	162	Jack Meyer	8.00	4.00
❑	163	Sammy White	8.00	4.00
❑	164	Tommy Carroll	8.00	4.00
❑	165	Ted Kluszewski	100.00	60.00
❑	166	Roy Face	15.00	7.50
❑	167	Vic Power	15.00	7.50
❑	168	Frank Lary	15.00	7.50
❑	169	Herb Plews RC	8.00	4.00
❑	170	Duke Snider	125.00	75.00
❑	171	Boston Red Sox TC	15.00	7.50
❑	172	Gene Woodling	15.00	7.50
❑	173	Roger Craig	15.00	7.50
❑	174	Willie Jones	8.00	4.00
❑	175	Don Larsen	30.00	15.00
❑	176A	Gene Bakep ERR	350.00	200.00
❑	176B	Gene Baker COR	15.00	7.50
❑	177	Eddie Yost	15.00	7.50
❑	178	Don Bessent	8.00	4.00
❑	179	Ernie Oravetz	8.00	4.00
❑	180	Gus Bell	15.00	7.50
❑	181	Dick Donovan	8.00	4.00
❑	182	Hobie Landrith	8.00	4.00
❑	183	Chicago Cubs TC	15.00	7.50
❑	184	Tito Francona RC	8.00	4.00
❑	185	Johnny Kucks	15.00	7.50
❑	186	Jim King	15.00	7.50
❑	187	Virgil Trucks	15.00	7.50
❑	188	Felix Mantilla RC	15.00	7.50
❑	189	Willard Nixon	8.00	4.00
❑	190	Randy Jackson	8.00	4.00
❑	191	Joe Margoneri RC	8.00	4.00
❑	192	Jerry Coleman	15.00	7.50
❑	193	Del Rice	8.00	4.00
❑	194	Hal Brown	8.00	4.00
❑	195	Bobby Avila	8.00	4.00
❑	196	Larry Jackson	15.00	7.50
❑	197	Hank Sauer	15.00	7.50
❑	198	Detroit Tigers TC	15.00	7.50
❑	199	Vern Law	15.00	7.50
❑	200	Gil McDougald	15.00	7.50
❑	201	Sandy Amoros	15.00	7.50
❑	202	Dick Gernert	8.00	4.00
❑	203	Hoyt Wilhelm	30.00	15.00
❑	204	Kansas City Athletics TC	15.00	7.50
❑	205	Charlie Maxwell	15.00	7.50
❑	206	Willard Schmidt	8.00	4.00
❑	207	Gordon (Billy) Hunter	8.00	4.00
❑	208	Lew Burdette	15.00	7.50
❑	209	Bob Skinner	15.00	7.50
❑	210	Roy Campanella	150.00	90.00
❑	211	Camilo Pascual	15.00	7.50
❑	212	Rocky Colavito RC	125.00	75.00
❑	213	Les Moss	8.00	4.00
❑	214	Philadelphia Phillies TC	15.00	7.50
❑	215	Enos Slaughter	30.00	15.00
❑	216	Marv Grissom	8.00	4.00
❑	217	Gene Stephens	8.00	4.00
❑	218	Ray Jablonski	8.00	4.00
❑	219	Tom Acker RC	8.00	4.00
❑	220	Jackie Jensen	20.00	10.00
❑	221	Dixie Howell	8.00	4.00
❑	222	Alex Grammas	8.00	4.00
❑	223	Frank House	8.00	4.00
❑	224	Marv Blaylock	8.00	4.00
❑	225	Harry Simpson	8.00	4.00
❑	226	Preston Ward	8.00	4.00
❑	227	Gerry Staley	8.00	4.00
❑	228	Smoky Burgess UER	15.00	7.50
❑	229	George Susce	8.00	4.00
❑	230	George Kell	30.00	15.00
❑	231	Solly Hemus	8.00	4.00
❑	232	Whitey Lockman	15.00	7.50
❑	233	Art Fowler	8.00	4.00
❑	234	Dick Cole	8.00	4.00
❑	235	Tom Poholsky	8.00	4.00
❑	236	Joe Ginsberg	8.00	4.00
❑	237	Foster Castleman	8.00	4.00
❑	238	Eddie Robinson	8.00	4.00
❑	239	Tom Morgan	8.00	4.00
❑	240	Hank Bauer	15.00	7.50
❑	241	Joe Lonnett RC	8.00	4.00
❑	242	Charlie Neal	15.00	7.50
❑	243	St. Louis Cardinals TC	15.00	7.50
❑	244	Billy Loes	15.00	7.50
❑	245	Rip Repulski	8.00	4.00
❑	246	Jose Valdivielso	8.00	4.00
❑	247	Turk Lown	8.00	4.00
❑	248	Jim Finigan	8.00	4.00
❑	249	Dave Pope	8.00	4.00
❑	250	Eddie Mathews	50.00	30.00
❑	251	Baltimore Orioles TC	15.00	7.50
❑	252	Carl Erskine	15.00	7.50
❑	253	Gus Zernial	15.00	7.50
❑	254	Ron Negray	8.00	4.00
❑	255	Charlie Silvera	15.00	7.50
❑	256	Ron Kline	8.00	4.00
❑	257	Walt Dropo	8.00	4.00
❑	258	Steve Gromek	8.00	4.00
❑	259	Eddie O'Brien	8.00	4.00
❑	260	Del Ennis	15.00	7.50
❑	261	Bob Chakales	8.00	4.00
❑	262	Bobby Thomson	15.00	7.50
❑	263	George Strickland	8.00	4.00
❑	264	Bob Turley	15.00	7.50
❑	265	Harvey Haddix DP	12.00	6.00
❑	266	Ken Kuhn DP RC	12.00	6.00
❑	267	Danny Kravitz RC	20.00	10.00
❑	268	Jack Collum	20.00	10.00
❑	269	Bob Cerv	30.00	15.00
❑	270	Washington Senators TC	60.00	35.00
❑	271	Danny O'Connell DP	12.00	6.00
❑	272	Bobby Shantz	30.00	15.00
❑	273	Jim Davis	20.00	10.00
❑	274	Don Hoak	15.00	7.50
❑	275	Cleveland Indians TC UER	60.00	35.00
❑	276	Jim Pyburn RC	20.00	10.00
❑	277	Johnny Podres DP	40.00	20.00
❑	278	Fred Hatfield DP	12.00	6.00
❑	279	Bob Thurman RC	20.00	10.00
❑	280	Alex Kellner	20.00	10.00
❑	281	Gail Harris	20.00	10.00
❑	282	Jack Dittmer DP	12.00	6.00
❑	283	Wes Covington DP RC	12.00	6.00
❑	284	Don Zimmer	40.00	20.00
❑	285	Ned Garver	20.00	10.00
❑	286	Bobby Richardson RC	125.00	75.00
❑	287	Sam Jones	20.00	10.00
❑	288	Ted Lepcio	20.00	10.00
❑	289	Jim Bolger DP	12.00	6.00
❑	290	Andy Carey DP	40.00	20.00
❑	291	Windy McCall	20.00	10.00
❑	292	Billy Klaus	20.00	10.00
❑	293	Ted Abernathy RC	20.00	10.00
❑	294	Rocky Bridges DP	12.00	6.00
❑	295	Joe Collins DP	40.00	20.00
❑	296	Johnny Klippstein	20.00	10.00
❑	297	Jack Crimian	20.00	10.00
❑	298	Irv Noren DP	12.00	6.00
❑	299	Chuck Harmon	20.00	10.00
❑	300	Mike Garcia	30.00	15.00
❑	301	Sammy Esposito DP RC	20.00	10.00
❑	302	Sandy Koufax DP	350.00	200.00
❑	303	Billy Goodman	30.00	15.00
❑	304	Joe Cunningham	30.00	15.00
❑	305	Chico Fernandez	20.00	10.00
❑	306	Darrell Johnson DP RC	12.00	6.00
❑	307	Jack D. Phillips DP	12.00	6.00
❑	308	Dick Hall	20.00	10.00
❑	309	Jim Busby DP	12.00	6.00
❑	310	Max Surkont DP	12.00	6.00
❑	311	Al Pilarcik DP RC	12.00	6.00
❑	312	Tony Kubek DP RC	100.00	60.00
❑	313	Mel Parnell	15.00	7.50
❑	314	Ed Bouchee DP RC	12.00	6.00
❑	315	Lou Berberet DP	12.00	6.00
❑	316	Billy O'Dell	20.00	10.00
❑	317	New York Giants TC	80.00	50.00
❑	318	Mickey McDermott	20.00	10.00
❑	319	Gino Cimoli RC	20.00	10.00
❑	320	Neil Chrisley RC	20.00	10.00
❑	321	John (Red) Murff RC	20.00	10.00
❑	322	Cincinnati Reds TC	80.00	50.00
❑	323	Wes Westrum	30.00	15.00
❑	324	Brooklyn Dodgers TC	150.00	90.00
❑	325	Frank Bolling	20.00	10.00
❑	326	Pedro Ramos	20.00	10.00
❑	327	Jim Pendleton	20.00	10.00
❑	328	Brooks Robinson RC	400.00	250.00
❑	329	Chicago White Sox TC	60.00	35.00
❑	330	Jim Wilson	20.00	10.00
❑	331	Ray Katt	20.00	10.00
❑	332	Bob Bowman RC	20.00	10.00
❑	333	Ernie Johnson	20.00	10.00
❑	334	Jerry Schoonmaker	20.00	10.00
❑	335	Granny Hamner	20.00	10.00
❑	336	Haywood Sullivan RC	40.00	20.00
❑	337	Rene Valdes RC	20.00	10.00
❑	338	Jim Bunning RC	150.00	90.00
❑	339	Bob Speake	20.00	10.00
❑	340	Bill Wight	20.00	10.00
❑	341	Don Gross RC	20.00	10.00
❑	342	Gene Mauch	30.00	15.00
❑	343	Taylor Phillips RC	15.00	7.50
❑	344	Paul LaPalme	20.00	10.00
❑	345	Paul Smith	20.00	10.00
❑	346	Dick Littlefield	20.00	10.00
❑	347	Hal Naragon	20.00	10.00
❑	348	Jim Hearn	20.00	10.00
❑	349	Nellie King	20.00	10.00
❑	350	Eddie Miksis	20.00	10.00
❑	351	Dave Hillman RC	20.00	10.00
❑	352	Ellis Kinder	20.00	10.00
❑	353	Cal Neeman RC	8.00	4.00
❑	354	Rip Coleman RC	8.00	4.00
❑	355	Frank Malzone	15.00	7.50
❑	356	Faye Throneberry	8.00	4.00
❑	357	Earl Torgeson	8.00	4.00
❑	358	Jerry Lynch	15.00	7.50
❑	359	Tom Cheney RC	8.00	4.00
❑	360	Johnny Groth	8.00	4.00
❑	361	Curt Barclay RC	8.00	4.00
❑	362	Roman Mejias RC	15.00	7.50
❑	363	Eddie Kasko RC	8.00	4.00
❑	364	Cal McLish RC	15.00	7.50
❑	365	Ozzie Virgil RC	8.00	4.00
❑	366	Ken Lehman	8.00	4.00
❑	367	Ed Fitzgerald	8.00	4.00
❑	368	Bob Purkey	8.00	4.00
❑	369	Milt Graff RC	8.00	4.00
❑	370	Warren Hacker	8.00	4.00
❑	371	Bob Lennon	8.00	4.00
❑	372	Norm Zauchin	8.00	4.00
❑	373	Pete Whisenant RC	8.00	4.00
❑	374	Don Cardwell RC	8.00	4.00
❑	375	Jim Landis RC	15.00	7.50
❑	376	Don Elston RC	8.00	4.00
❑	377	Andre Rodgers RC	8.00	4.00
❑	378	Elmer Singleton	8.00	4.00

❑ 379 Don Lee RC	8.00	4.00
❑ 380 Walker Cooper	8.00	4.00
❑ 381 Dean Stone	8.00	4.00
❑ 382 Jim Brideweser	8.00	4.00
❑ 383 Juan Pizarro RC	8.00	4.00
❑ 384 Bobby G. Smith RC	8.00	4.00
❑ 385 Art Houtteman	8.00	4.00
❑ 386 Lyle Luttrell RC	8.00	4.00
❑ 387 Jack Sanford RC	15.00	7.50
❑ 388 Pete Daley	8.00	4.00
❑ 389 Dave Jolly	8.00	4.00
❑ 390 Reno Bertoia	8.00	4.00
❑ 391 Ralph Terry RC	15.00	7.50
❑ 392 Chuck Tanner	15.00	7.50
❑ 393 Raul Sanchez RC	8.00	4.00
❑ 394 Luis Arroyo	15.00	7.50
❑ 395 Bubba Phillips	8.00	4.00
❑ 396 Casey Wise RC	8.00	4.00
❑ 397 Roy Smalley	8.00	4.00
❑ 398 Al Cicotte RC	15.00	7.50
❑ 399 Billy Consolo	8.00	4.00
❑ 400 Fur/Hodges/Campy/Snider	250.00	150.00
❑ 401 Earl Battey RC	15.00	7.50
❑ 402 Jim Pisoni RC	8.00	4.00
❑ 403 Dick Hyde RC	8.00	4.00
❑ 404 Harry Anderson RC	8.00	4.00
❑ 405 Duke Maas	8.00	4.00
❑ 406 Bob Hale	8.00	4.00
❑ 407 Y.Berra/M.Mantle	600.00	350.00
❑ CC1 Contest May 4	100.00	60.00
❑ CC2 Contest May 25	100.00	60.00
❑ CC3 Contest June 22	125.00	75.00
❑ CC4 Contest July 19	125.00	75.00
❑ NNO Checklist 1/2 Bazooka	250.00	150.00
❑ NNO Checklist 1/2 Blony	250.00	150.00
❑ NNO Checklist 2/3 Bazooka	400.00	250.00
❑ NNO Checklist 2/3 Blony	400.00	250.00
❑ NNO Checklist 3/4 Bazooka	800.00	500.00
❑ NNO Checklist 3/4 Blony	600.00	350.00
❑ NNO Checklist 4/5 Bazooka	1000.00	600.00
❑ NNO Checklist 4/5 Blony	800.00	500.00
❑ NNO Lucky Penny Card	100.00	60.00

1958 Topps

❑ COMP. MASTER SET (534)	12000.00	8000.00
❑ COMPLETE SET (494)	6000.00	4000.00
❑ COMMON CARD (1-110)	12.00	6.00
❑ COMMON CARD (111-495)	8.00	4.00
❑ WRAPPER (1-CENT)	100.00	75.00
❑ WRAPPER (5-CENT)	125.00	100.00
❑ 1 Ted Williams	600.00	350.00
❑ 2A Bob Lemon	30.00	15.00
❑ 2B Bob Lemon YT	60.00	35.00
❑ 3 Alex Kellner	12.00	6.00
❑ 4 Hank Foiles	12.00	6.00
❑ 5 Willie Mays	300.00	175.00
❑ 6 George Zuverink	12.00	6.00
❑ 7 Dale Long	15.00	7.50
❑ 8A Eddie Kasko	12.00	6.00
❑ 8B Eddie Kasko YN	40.00	20.00
❑ 9 Hank Bauer	20.00	10.00
❑ 10 Lew Burdette	20.00	10.00
❑ 11A Jim Rivera	12.00	6.00
❑ 11B Jim Rivera YT	40.00	20.00
❑ 12 George Crowe	12.00	6.00
❑ 13A Billy Hoeft	12.00	6.00
❑ 13B Billy Hoeft YN	40.00	20.00
❑ 14 Rip Repulski	12.00	6.00
❑ 15 Jim Lemon	15.00	7.50
❑ 16 Charlie Neal	15.00	7.50
❑ 17 Felix Mantilla	12.00	6.00
❑ 18 Frank Sullivan	12.00	6.00
❑ 19 San Francisco Giants TC	40.00	20.00
❑ 20A Gil McDougald	20.00	10.00
❑ 20B Gil McDougald YN	60.00	35.00
❑ 21 Curt Barclay	12.00	6.00
❑ 22 Hal Naragon	12.00	6.00
❑ 23A Bill Tuttle	12.00	6.00
❑ 23B Bill Tuttle YN	40.00	20.00
❑ 24A Hobie Landrith	12.00	6.00
❑ 24B Hobie Landrith YN	40.00	20.00
❑ 25 Don Drysdale	100.00	60.00
❑ 26 Ron Jackson	12.00	6.00
❑ 27 Bud Freeman	12.00	6.00
❑ 28 Jim Busby	12.00	6.00
❑ 29 Ted Lepcio	12.00	6.00
❑ 30A Hank Aaron	200.00	125.00
❑ 30B Hank Aaron YN	600.00	350.00
❑ 31 Tex Clevenger RC	12.00	6.00
❑ 32A J.W. Porter	12.00	6.00
❑ 32B J.W. Porter YN	40.00	20.00
❑ 33A Cal Neeman	12.00	6.00
❑ 33B Cal Neeman YT	40.00	20.00
❑ 34 Bob Thurman	12.00	6.00
❑ 35A Don Mossi	15.00	7.50
❑ 35B Don Mossi YT	40.00	20.00
❑ 36 Ted Kazanski	12.00	6.00
❑ 37 Mike McCormick UER RC	15.00	7.50
❑ 38 Dick Gernert	12.00	6.00
❑ 39 Bob Martyn RC	12.00	6.00
❑ 40 George Kell	30.00	15.00
❑ 41 Dave Hillman	12.00	6.00
❑ 42 John Roseboro RC	30.00	15.00
❑ 43 Sal Maglie	15.00	7.50
❑ 44 Washington Senators TC	20.00	10.00
❑ 45 Dick Groat	15.00	7.50
❑ 46A Lou Sleater	12.00	6.00
❑ 46B Lou Sleater YN	40.00	20.00
❑ 47 Roger Maris RC	500.00	300.00
❑ 48 Chuck Harmon	12.00	6.00
❑ 49 Smoky Burgess	15.00	7.50
❑ 50A Billy Pierce	15.00	7.50
❑ 50B Billy Pierce YT	40.00	20.00
❑ 51 Del Rice	12.00	6.00
❑ 52A Roberto Clemente	300.00	175.00
❑ 52B Roberto Clemente YT	500.00	300.00
❑ 53A Morrie Martin	12.00	6.00
❑ 53B Morrie Martin YN	40.00	20.00
❑ 54 Norm Siebern RC	20.00	10.00
❑ 55 Chico Carrasquel	12.00	6.00
❑ 56 Bill Fischer RC	12.00	6.00
❑ 57A Tim Thompson	12.00	6.00
❑ 57B Tim Thompson YN	40.00	20.00
❑ 58A Art Schult	12.00	6.00
❑ 58B Art Schult YT	40.00	20.00
❑ 59 Dave Sisler	12.00	6.00
❑ 60A Del Ennis	15.00	7.50
❑ 60B Del Ennis YN	40.00	20.00
❑ 61A Darrell Johnson	12.00	6.00
❑ 61B Darrell Johnson YN	40.00	20.00
❑ 62 Joe DeMaestri	12.00	6.00
❑ 63 Joe Nuxhall	15.00	7.50
❑ 64 Joe Lonnett	12.00	6.00
❑ 65A Von McDaniel RC	12.00	6.00
❑ 65B Von McDaniel YN	40.00	20.00
❑ 66 Lee Walls	12.00	6.00
❑ 67 Joe Ginsberg	12.00	6.00
❑ 68 Daryl Spencer	12.00	6.00
❑ 69 Wally Burnette	12.00	6.00
❑ 70A Al Kaline	100.00	60.00
❑ 70B Al Kaline YN	250.00	150.00
❑ 71 Los Angeles Dodgers TC	60.00	35.00
❑ 72 Bud Byerly UER	12.00	6.00
❑ 73 Pete Daley	12.00	6.00
❑ 74 Roy Face	15.00	7.50
❑ 75 Gus Bell	15.00	7.50
❑ 76A Dick Farrell RC	12.00	6.00
❑ 76B Dick Farrell YT	40.00	20.00
❑ 77A Don Zimmer	15.00	7.50
❑ 77B Don Zimmer YT	40.00	20.00
❑ 78A Ernie Johnson	15.00	7.50
❑ 78B Ernie Johnson YN	40.00	20.00
❑ 79A Dick Williams	15.00	7.50
❑ 79B Dick Williams YT	40.00	20.00
❑ 80 Dick Drott RC	12.00	6.00
❑ 81A Steve Boros RC	12.00	6.00
❑ 81B Steve Boros YT	40.00	20.00
❑ 82 Ron Kline	12.00	6.00
❑ 83 Bob Hazle RC	12.00	6.00
❑ 84 Billy O'Dell	12.00	6.00
❑ 85A Luis Aparicio	30.00	15.00
❑ 85B Luis Aparicio YT	80.00	50.00
❑ 86 Valmy Thomas RC	12.00	6.00
❑ 87 Johnny Kucks	12.00	6.00
❑ 88 Duke Snider	80.00	50.00
❑ 89 Billy Klaus	12.00	6.00
❑ 90 Robin Roberts	30.00	15.00
❑ 91 Chuck Tanner	15.00	7.50
❑ 92A Clint Courtney	12.00	6.00
❑ 92B Clint Courtney YN	40.00	20.00
❑ 93 Sandy Amoros	15.00	7.50
❑ 94 Bob Skinner	15.00	7.50
❑ 95 Frank Bolling	12.00	6.00
❑ 96 Joe Durham RC	12.00	6.00
❑ 97A Larry Jackson	12.00	6.00
❑ 97B Larry Jackson YN	40.00	20.00
❑ 98A Billy Hunter	12.00	6.00
❑ 98B Billy Hunter YN	40.00	20.00
❑ 99 Bobby Adams	12.00	6.00
❑ 100A Early Wynn	30.00	15.00
❑ 100B Early Wynn YT	80.00	50.00
❑ 101A Bobby Richardson	30.00	15.00
❑ 101B B.Richardson YN	60.00	35.00
❑ 102 George Strickland	12.00	6.00
❑ 103 Jerry Lynch	15.00	7.50
❑ 104 Jim Pendleton	12.00	6.00
❑ 105 Billy Gardner	12.00	6.00
❑ 106 Dick Schofield	15.00	7.50
❑ 107 Ossie Virgil	12.00	6.00
❑ 108A Jim Landis	12.00	6.00
❑ 108B Jim Landis YT	40.00	20.00
❑ 109 Herb Plews	12.00	6.00
❑ 110 Johnny Logan	15.00	7.50
❑ 111 Stu Miller	10.00	5.00
❑ 112 Gus Zernial	10.00	5.00
❑ 113 Jerry Walker RC	8.00	4.00
❑ 114 Irv Noren	10.00	5.00
❑ 115 Jim Bunning	30.00	15.00
❑ 116 Dave Philley	8.00	4.00
❑ 117 Frank Torre	10.00	5.00
❑ 118 Harvey Haddix	10.00	5.00
❑ 119 Harry Chiti	8.00	4.00
❑ 120 Johnny Podres	10.00	5.00
❑ 121 Eddie Miksis	8.00	4.00
❑ 122 Walt Moryn	8.00	4.00
❑ 123 Dick Tomanek RC	8.00	4.00
❑ 124 Bobby Usher	8.00	4.00
❑ 125 Alvin Dark	10.00	5.00
❑ 126 Stan Palys RC	8.00	4.00
❑ 127 Tom Sturdivant	10.00	5.00
❑ 128 Willie Kirkland RC	8.00	4.00
❑ 129 Jim Derrington RC	8.00	4.00
❑ 130 Jackie Jensen	10.00	5.00
❑ 131 Bob Henrich RC	8.00	4.00
❑ 132 Vern Law	10.00	5.00
❑ 133 Russ Nixon RC	8.00	4.00
❑ 134 Philadelphia Phillies TC	15.00	7.50
❑ 135 Mike (Moe)Drabowsky	10.00	5.00
❑ 136 Jim Finigan	8.00	4.00
❑ 137 Russ Kemmerer	8.00	4.00
❑ 138 Earl Torgeson	8.00	4.00
❑ 139 George Brunet RC	8.00	4.00
❑ 140 Wes Covington	10.00	5.00
❑ 141 Ken Lehman	8.00	4.00
❑ 142 Enos Slaughter	25.00	12.50
❑ 143 Billy Muffett RC	8.00	4.00
❑ 144 Bobby Morgan	8.00	4.00
❑ 145 Never issued		
❑ 146 Dick Gray RC	8.00	4.00
❑ 147 Don McMahon RC	8.00	4.00
❑ 148 Billy Consolo	8.00	4.00
❑ 149 Tom Acker	8.00	4.00
❑ 150 Mickey Mantle	1000.00	600.00
❑ 151 Buddy Pritchard RC	8.00	4.00
❑ 152 Johnny Antonelli	10.00	5.00
❑ 153 Les Moss	8.00	4.00
❑ 154 Harry Byrd	8.00	4.00
❑ 155 Hector Lopez	10.00	5.00
❑ 156 Dick Hyde	8.00	4.00
❑ 157 Dee Fondy	8.00	4.00

❑ 158 Cleveland Indians TC 15.00 7.50
❑ 159 Taylor Phillips 8.00 4.00
❑ 160 Don Hoak 10.00 5.00
❑ 161 Don Larsen 15.00 7.50
❑ 162 Gil Hodges 40.00 20.00
❑ 163 Jim Wilson 8.00 4.00
❑ 164 Bob Taylor RC 8.00 4.00
❑ 165 Bob Nieman 8.00 4.00
❑ 166 Danny O'Connell 8.00 4.00
❑ 167 Frank Baumann RC 8.00 4.00
❑ 168 Joe Cunningham 8.00 4.00
❑ 169 Ralph Terry 10.00 5.00
❑ 170 Vic Wertz 10.00 5.00
❑ 171 Harry Anderson 8.00 4.00
❑ 172 Don Gross 8.00 4.00
❑ 173 Eddie Yost 8.00 4.00
❑ 174 Kansas City Athletics TC 15.00 7.50
❑ 175 Marv Throneberry RC 15.00 7.50
❑ 176 Bob Buhl 10.00 5.00
❑ 177 Al Smith 8.00 4.00
❑ 178 Ted Kluszewski 25.00 12.50
❑ 179 Willie Miranda 8.00 4.00
❑ 180 Lindy McDaniel 10.00 5.00
❑ 181 Willie Jones 8.00 4.00
❑ 182 Joe Caffie RC 8.00 4.00
❑ 183 Dave Jolly 8.00 4.00
❑ 184 Elvin Tappe 8.00 4.00
❑ 185 Ray Boone 10.00 5.00
❑ 186 Jack Meyer 8.00 4.00
❑ 187 Sandy Koufax 250.00 150.00
❑ 188 Milt Bolling UER 8.00 4.00
❑ 189 George Susce 8.00 4.00
❑ 190 Red Schoendienst 25.00 12.50
❑ 191 Art Ceccarelli RC 8.00 4.00
❑ 192 Milt Graff 8.00 4.00
❑ 193 Jerry Lumpe RC 8.00 4.00
❑ 194 Roger Craig 10.00 5.00
❑ 195 Whitey Lockman 10.00 5.00
❑ 196 Mike Garcia 10.00 5.00
❑ 197 Haywood Sullivan 10.00 5.00
❑ 198 Bill Virdon 10.00 5.00
❑ 199 Don Blasingame 8.00 4.00
❑ 200 Bob Keegan 8.00 4.00
❑ 201 Jim Bolger 8.00 4.00
❑ 202 Woody Held RC 8.00 4.00
❑ 203 Al Walker 8.00 4.00
❑ 204 Leo Kiely 8.00 4.00
❑ 205 Johnny Temple 10.00 5.00
❑ 206 Bob Shaw RC 8.00 4.00
❑ 207 Solly Hemus 8.00 4.00
❑ 208 Cal McLish 8.00 4.00
❑ 209 Bob Anderson RC 8.00 4.00
❑ 210 Wally Moon 10.00 5.00
❑ 211 Pete Burnside RC 8.00 4.00
❑ 212 Bubba Phillips 8.00 4.00
❑ 213 Red Wilson 8.00 4.00
❑ 214 Willard Schmidt 8.00 4.00
❑ 215 Jim Gilliam 15.00 7.50
❑ 216 St. Louis Cardinals TC 15.00 7.50
❑ 217 Jack Harshman 8.00 4.00
❑ 218 Dick Rand RC 8.00 4.00
❑ 219 Camilo Pascual 10.00 5.00
❑ 220 Tom Brewer 8.00 4.00
❑ 221 Jerry Kindall RC 8.00 4.00
❑ 222 Bud Daley RC 8.00 4.00
❑ 223 Andy Pafko 10.00 5.00
❑ 224 Bob Grim 10.00 5.00
❑ 225 Billy Goodman 10.00 5.00
❑ 226 Bob Smith RC 8.00 4.00
❑ 227 Gene Stephens 8.00 4.00
❑ 228 Duke Maas 8.00 4.00
❑ 229 Frank Zupo RC 8.00 4.00
❑ 230 Richie Ashburn 40.00 20.00
❑ 231 Lloyd Merritt RC 8.00 4.00
❑ 232 Reno Bertoia 8.00 4.00
❑ 233 Mickey Vernon 10.00 5.00
❑ 234 Carl Sawatski 8.00 4.00
❑ 235 Tom Gorman 8.00 4.00
❑ 236 Ed Fitzgerald 8.00 4.00
❑ 237 Bill Wight 8.00 4.00
❑ 238 Bill Mazeroski 30.00 15.00
❑ 239 Chuck Stobbs 8.00 4.00
❑ 240 Bill Skowron 25.00 12.50
❑ 241 Dick Littlefield 8.00 4.00
❑ 242 Johnny Klippstein 8.00 4.00
❑ 243 Larry Raines RC 8.00 4.00
❑ 244 Don Demeter RC 8.00 4.00
❑ 245 Frank Lary 10.00 5.00
❑ 246 New York Yankees TC 100.00 60.00
❑ 247 Casey Wise 8.00 4.00
❑ 248 Herman Wehmeier 8.00 4.00
❑ 249 Ray Moore 8.00 4.00
❑ 250 Roy Sievers 10.00 5.00
❑ 251 Warren Hacker 8.00 4.00
❑ 252 Bob Trowbridge RC 8.00 4.00
❑ 253 Don Mueller 10.00 5.00
❑ 254 Alex Grammas 8.00 4.00
❑ 255 Bob Turley 10.00 5.00
❑ 256 Chicago White Sox TC 15.00 7.50
❑ 257 Hal Smith 8.00 4.00
❑ 258 Carl Erskine 15.00 7.50
❑ 259 Al Pilarcik 8.00 4.00
❑ 260 Frank Malzone 10.00 5.00
❑ 261 Turk Lown 8.00 4.00
❑ 262 Johnny Groth 8.00 4.00
❑ 263 Eddie Bressoud RC 10.00 5.00
❑ 264 Jack Sanford 10.00 5.00
❑ 265 Pete Runnels 10.00 5.00
❑ 266 Connie Johnson 8.00 4.00
❑ 267 Sherm Lollar 10.00 5.00
❑ 268 Granny Hamner 8.00 4.00
❑ 269 Paul Smith 8.00 4.00
❑ 270 Warren Spahn 60.00 35.00
❑ 271 Billy Martin 40.00 20.00
❑ 272 Ray Crone 8.00 4.00
❑ 273 Hal Smith 8.00 4.00
❑ 274 Rocky Bridges 8.00 4.00
❑ 275 Elston Howard 15.00 7.50
❑ 276 Bobby Avila 8.00 4.00
❑ 277 Virgil Trucks 10.00 5.00
❑ 278 Mack Burk 8.00 4.00
❑ 279 Bob Boyd 8.00 4.00
❑ 280 Jim Piersall 10.00 5.00
❑ 281 Sammy Taylor RC 8.00 4.00
❑ 282 Paul Foytack 8.00 4.00
❑ 283 Ray Shearer RC 8.00 4.00
❑ 284 Ray Katt 8.00 4.00
❑ 285 Frank Robinson 100.00 60.00
❑ 286 Gino Cimoli 8.00 4.00
❑ 287 Sam Jones 10.00 5.00
❑ 288 Harmon Killebrew 100.00 60.00
❑ 289 B.Shantz/L.Burdette 10.00 5.00
❑ 290 Dick Donovan 8.00 4.00
❑ 291 Don Landrum RC 8.00 4.00
❑ 292 Ned Garver 8.00 4.00
❑ 293 Gene Freese 8.00 4.00
❑ 294 Hal Jeffcoat 8.00 4.00
❑ 295 Minnie Minoso 25.00 12.50
❑ 296 Ryne Duren RC 15.00 7.50
❑ 297 Don Buddin RC 8.00 4.00
❑ 298 Jim Hearn 8.00 4.00
❑ 299 Harry Simpson 8.00 4.00
❑ 300 W.Harridge/W.Giles 15.00 7.50
❑ 301 Randy Jackson 8.00 4.00
❑ 302 Mike Baxes RC 8.00 4.00
❑ 303 Neil Chrisley 8.00 4.00
❑ 304 H.Kuenn/A.Kaline 25.00 12.50
❑ 305 Clem Labine 10.00 5.00
❑ 306 Whammy Douglas RC 8.00 4.00
❑ 307 Brooks Robinson 100.00 60.00
❑ 308 Paul Giel 10.00 5.00
❑ 309 Gail Harris 8.00 4.00
❑ 310 Ernie Banks 100.00 60.00
❑ 311 Bob Purkey 8.00 4.00
❑ 312 Boston Red Sox TC 15.00 7.50
❑ 313 Bob Rush 8.00 4.00
❑ 314 D.Snider/W.Alston 50.00 30.00
❑ 315 Bob Friend 10.00 5.00
❑ 316 Tito Francona 10.00 5.00
❑ 317 Albie Pearson RC 10.00 5.00
❑ 318 Frank House 8.00 4.00
❑ 319 Lou Skizas 8.00 4.00
❑ 320 Whitey Ford 60.00 35.00
❑ 321 T.Kluszewski/T.Williams 100.00 60.00
❑ 322 Harding Peterson RC 10.00 5.00
❑ 323 Elmer Valo 8.00 4.00
❑ 324 Hoyt Wilhelm 25.00 12.50
❑ 325 Joe Adcock 10.00 5.00
❑ 326 Bob Miller 8.00 4.00
❑ 327 Chicago Cubs TC 15.00 7.50
❑ 328 Ike Delock 8.00 4.00
❑ 329 Bob Cerv 10.00 5.00
❑ 330 Ed Bailey 10.00 5.00
❑ 331 Pedro Ramos 8.00 4.00
❑ 332 Jim King 8.00 4.00
❑ 333 Andy Carey 10.00 5.00
❑ 334 B.Friend/B.Pierce 10.00 5.00
❑ 335 Ruben Gomez 8.00 4.00
❑ 336 Bert Hamric 8.00 4.00
❑ 337 Hank Aguirre 8.00 4.00
❑ 338 Walt Dropo 10.00 5.00
❑ 339 Fred Hatfield 8.00 4.00
❑ 340 Don Newcombe 15.00 7.50
❑ 341 Pittsburgh Pirates TC 15.00 7.50
❑ 342 Jim Brosnan 10.00 5.00
❑ 343 Orlando Cepeda RC 100.00 60.00
❑ 344 Bob Porterfield 8.00 4.00
❑ 345 Jim Hegan 10.00 5.00
❑ 346 Steve Bilko 8.00 4.00
❑ 347 Don Rudolph RC 8.00 4.00
❑ 348 Chico Fernandez 8.00 4.00
❑ 349 Murry Dickson 8.00 4.00
❑ 350 Ken Boyer 25.00 12.50
❑ 351 Cran/Math/Aaron/Adcock 40.00 20.00
❑ 352 Herb Score 15.00 7.50
❑ 353 Stan Lopata 8.00 4.00
❑ 354 Art Ditmar 10.00 5.00
❑ 355 Bill Bruton 10.00 5.00
❑ 356 Bob Malkmus RC 8.00 4.00
❑ 357 Danny McDevitt RC 8.00 4.00
❑ 358 Gene Baker 8.00 4.00
❑ 359 Billy Loes 10.00 5.00
❑ 360 Roy McMillan 10.00 5.00
❑ 361 Mike Fornieles 8.00 4.00
❑ 362 Ray Jablonski 8.00 4.00
❑ 363 Don Elston 8.00 4.00
❑ 364 Earl Battey 8.00 4.00
❑ 365 Tom Morgan 8.00 4.00
❑ 366 Gene Green RC 8.00 4.00
❑ 367 Jack Urban RC 8.00 4.00
❑ 368 Rocky Colavito 50.00 30.00
❑ 369 Ralph Lumenti RC 8.00 4.00
❑ 370 Yogi Berra 100.00 60.00
❑ 371 Marty Keough RC 8.00 4.00
❑ 372 Don Cardwell 8.00 4.00
❑ 373 Joe Pignatano RC 8.00 4.00
❑ 374 Brooks Lawrence 8.00 4.00
❑ 375 Pee Wee Reese 80.00 50.00
❑ 376 Charley Rabe RC 8.00 4.00
❑ 377A Milwaukee Braves TC Alpha 15.00 7.50
❑ 377B Milwaukee Braves TC Num 100.00 60.00
❑ 378 Hank Sauer 10.00 5.00
❑ 379 Ray Herbert 8.00 4.00
❑ 380 Charlie Maxwell 10.00 5.00
❑ 381 Hal Brown 8.00 4.00
❑ 382 Al Cicotte 8.00 4.00
❑ 383 Lou Berberet 8.00 4.00
❑ 384 John Goryl RC 8.00 4.00
❑ 385 Wilmer Mizell 10.00 5.00
❑ 386 Bailey/Tebbets/F.Rob 15.00 7.50
❑ 387 Wally Post 10.00 5.00
❑ 388 Billy Moran RC 8.00 4.00
❑ 389 Bill Taylor 8.00 4.00
❑ 390 Del Crandall 10.00 5.00
❑ 391 Dave Melton RC 8.00 4.00
❑ 392 Bennie Daniels RC 8.00 4.00
❑ 393 Tony Kubek 30.00 15.00
❑ 394 Jim Grant RC 8.00 4.00
❑ 395 Willard Nixon 8.00 4.00
❑ 396 Dutch Dotterer RC 8.00 4.00
❑ 397A Detroit Tigers TC Alpha 15.00 7.50
❑ 397B Detroit Tigers TC Num 100.00 60.00
❑ 398 Gene Woodling 10.00 5.00
❑ 399 Marv Grissom 8.00 4.00
❑ 400 Nellie Fox 40.00 20.00
❑ 401 Don Bessent 8.00 4.00
❑ 402 Bobby Gene Smith 8.00 4.00
❑ 403 Steve Korcheck RC 8.00 4.00
❑ 404 Curt Simmons 10.00 5.00
❑ 405 Ken Aspromonte RC 8.00 4.00
❑ 406 Vic Power 10.00 5.00
❑ 407 Carlton Willey RC 10.00 5.00
❑ 408A Baltimore Orioles TC Alpha 15.00 7.50
❑ 408B Baltimore Orioles TC Num 100.00 60.00
❑ 409 Frank Thomas 10.00 5.00
❑ 410 Murray Wall 8.00 4.00
❑ 411 Tony Taylor RC 10.00 5.00
❑ 412 Gerry Staley 8.00 4.00

❑ 413 Jim Davenport RC 8.00 4.00
❑ 414 Sammy White 8.00 4.00
❑ 415 Bob Bowman 8.00 4.00
❑ 416 Foster Castleman 8.00 4.00
❑ 417 Carl Furillo 15.00 7.50
❑ 418 M.Mantle/H.Aaron 400.00 250.00
❑ 419 Bobby Shantz 10.00 5.00
❑ 420 Vada Pinson RC 40.00 20.00
❑ 421 Dixie Howell 8.00 4.00
❑ 422 Norm Zauchin 8.00 4.00
❑ 423 Phil Clark RC 8.00 4.00
❑ 424 Larry Doby 25.00 12.50
❑ 425 Sammy Esposito 8.00 4.00
❑ 426 Johnny O'Brien 10.00 5.00
❑ 427 Al Worthington 8.00 4.00
❑ 428A Cincinnati Reds TC Alpha 15.00 7.50
❑ 428B Cincinnati Reds TC Num 100.00 60.00
❑ 429 Gus Triandos 10.00 5.00
❑ 430 Bobby Thomson 10.00 5.00
❑ 431 Gene Conley 10.00 5.00
❑ 432 John Powers RC 8.00 4.00
❑ 433A Pancho Herrer ERR 600.00 350.00
❑ 433B Pancho Herrera COR RC 10.00 5.00
❑ 434 Harvey Kuenn 10.00 5.00
❑ 435 Ed Roebuck 10.00 5.00
❑ 436 W.Mays/D.Snider 100.00 60.00
❑ 437 Bob Speake 8.00 4.00
❑ 438 Whitey Herzog 10.00 5.00
❑ 439 Ray Narleski 8.00 4.00
❑ 440 Eddie Mathews 80.00 50.00
❑ 441 Jim Marshall RC 10.00 5.00
❑ 442 Phil Paine RC 8.00 4.00
❑ 443 Billy Harrell SP RC 20.00 10.00
❑ 444 Danny Kravitz 8.00 4.00
❑ 445 Bob Smith RC 8.00 4.00
❑ 446 Carroll Hardy SP RC 20.00 10.00
❑ 447 Ray Monzant 8.00 4.00
❑ 448 Charley Lau RC 10.00 5.00
❑ 449 Gene Fodge RC 8.00 4.00
❑ 450 Preston Ward SP 20.00 10.00
❑ 451 Joe Taylor RC 8.00 4.00
❑ 452 Roman Mejias 8.00 4.00
❑ 453 Tom Qualters 8.00 4.00
❑ 454 Harry Hanebrink RC 8.00 4.00
❑ 455 Hal Griggs RC 8.00 4.00
❑ 456 Dick Brown RC 8.00 4.00
❑ 457 Milt Pappas RC 10.00 5.00
❑ 458 Julio Becquer RC 8.00 4.00
❑ 459 Ron Blackburn RC 8.00 4.00
❑ 460 Chuck Essegian RC 8.00 4.00
❑ 461 Ed Mayer RC 8.00 4.00
❑ 462 Gary Geiger SP RC 20.00 10.00
❑ 463 Vito Valentinetti 8.00 4.00
❑ 464 Curt Flood RC 30.00 15.00
❑ 465 Arnie Portocarrero 8.00 4.00
❑ 466 Pete Whisenant 8.00 4.00
❑ 467 Glen Hobbie RC 8.00 4.00
❑ 468 Bob Schmidt RC 8.00 4.00
❑ 469 Don Ferrarese 8.00 4.00
❑ 470 R.C. Stevens RC 8.00 4.00
❑ 471 Lenny Green RC 8.00 4.00
❑ 472 Joey Jay 10.00 5.00
❑ 473 Bill Renna 8.00 4.00
❑ 474 Roman Semproch RC 8.00 4.00
❑ 475 F.Haney/C.Stengel AS 25.00 12.50
❑ 476 Stan Musial AS TP 50.00 30.00
❑ 477 Bill Skowron AS 10.00 5.00
❑ 478 Johnny Temple AS UER 8.00 4.00
❑ 479 Nellie Fox AS 15.00 7.50
❑ 480 Eddie Mathews AS 30.00 15.00
❑ 481 Frank Malzone AS 8.00 4.00
❑ 482 Ernie Banks AS 40.00 20.00
❑ 483 Luis Aparicio AS 15.00 7.50
❑ 484 Frank Robinson AS 40.00 20.00
❑ 485 Ted Williams AS 150.00 90.00
❑ 486 Willie Mays AS 60.00 35.00
❑ 487 Mickey Mantle AS TP 200.00 125.00
❑ 488 Hank Aaron AS 60.00 35.00
❑ 489 Jackie Jensen AS 10.00 5.00
❑ 490 Ed Bailey AS 8.00 4.00
❑ 491 Sherm Lollar AS 8.00 4.00
❑ 492 Bob Friend AS 8.00 4.00
❑ 493 Bob Turley AS 10.00 5.00
❑ 494 Warren Spahn AS 25.00 12.50
❑ 495 Herb Score AS 15.00 7.50
❑ NNO Contest Cards 40.00 20.00

1959 Topps

❑ COMPLETE SET (572) 5000.00 3000.00
❑ COMMON CARD (1-110) 6.00 3.00
❑ COMMON CARD (111-506) 4.00 2.00
❑ COMMON CARD (507-572) 15.00 7.50
❑ WRAPPER (1-CENT) 125.00 100.00
❑ WRAPPER (5-CENT) 100.00 75.00
❑ 1 Ford Frick COMM 60.00 35.00
❑ 2 Eddie Yost 8.00 4.00
❑ 3 Don McMahon 8.00 4.00
❑ 4 Albie Pearson 8.00 4.00
❑ 5 Dick Donovan 8.00 4.00
❑ 6 Alex Grammas 6.00 3.00
❑ 7 Al Pilarcik 6.00 3.00
❑ 8 Philadelphia Phillies CL 80.00 50.00
❑ 9 Paul Giel 8.00 4.00
❑ 10 Mickey Mantle 1000.00 600.00
❑ 11 Billy Hunter 8.00 4.00
❑ 12 Vern Law 8.00 4.00
❑ 13 Dick Gernert 6.00 3.00
❑ 14 Pete Whisenant 6.00 3.00
❑ 15 Dick Drott 6.00 3.00
❑ 16 Joe Pignatano 6.00 3.00
❑ 17 Thomas/Murtaugh/Klusz 8.00 4.00
❑ 18 Jack Urban 6.00 3.00
❑ 19 Eddie Bressoud 6.00 3.00
❑ 20 Duke Snider 60.00 35.00
❑ 21 Connie Johnson 6.00 3.00
❑ 22 Al Smith 8.00 4.00
❑ 23 Murry Dickson 8.00 4.00
❑ 24 Red Wilson 6.00 3.00
❑ 25 Don Hoak 8.00 4.00
❑ 26 Chuck Stobbs 6.00 3.00
❑ 27 Andy Pafko 8.00 4.00
❑ 28 Al Worthington 6.00 3.00
❑ 29 Jim Bolger 6.00 3.00
❑ 30 Nellie Fox 30.00 15.00
❑ 31 Ken Lehman 6.00 3.00
❑ 32 Don Buddin 6.00 3.00
❑ 33 Ed Fitzgerald 6.00 3.00
❑ 34 Al Kaline/C.Maxwell 20.00 10.00
❑ 35 Ted Kluszewski 12.00 6.00
❑ 36 Hank Aguirre 6.00 3.00
❑ 37 Gene Green 6.00 3.00
❑ 38 Morrie Martin 6.00 3.00
❑ 39 Ed Bouchee 6.00 3.00
❑ 40A Warren Spahn ERR 80.00 50.00
❑ 40B Warren Spahn ERR 100.00 60.00
❑ 40C Warren Spahn COR 60.00 35.00
❑ 41 Bob Martyn 6.00 3.00
❑ 42 Murray Wall 6.00 3.00
❑ 43 Steve Bilko 6.00 3.00
❑ 44 Vito Valentinetti 6.00 3.00
❑ 45 Andy Carey 8.00 4.00
❑ 46 Bill R. Henry 6.00 3.00
❑ 47 Jim Finigan 6.00 3.00
❑ 48 Baltimore Orioles CL 25.00 12.50
❑ 49 Bill Hall RC 6.00 3.00
❑ 50 Willie Mays 175.00 100.00
❑ 51 Rip Coleman 6.00 3.00
❑ 52 Coot Veal RC 6.00 3.00
❑ 53 Stan Williams RC 8.00 4.00
❑ 54 Mel Roach 6.00 3.00
❑ 55 Tom Brewer 6.00 3.00
❑ 56 Carl Sawatski 6.00 3.00
❑ 57 Al Cicotte 6.00 3.00
❑ 58 Eddie Miksis 6.00 3.00
❑ 59 Irv Noren 8.00 4.00
❑ 60 Bob Turley 8.00 4.00
❑ 61 Dick Brown 6.00 3.00
❑ 62 Tony Taylor 8.00 4.00
❑ 63 Jim Hearn 6.00 3.00
❑ 64 Joe DeMaestri 6.00 3.00
❑ 65 Frank Torre 8.00 4.00
❑ 66 Joe Ginsberg 6.00 3.00
❑ 67 Brooks Lawrence 6.00 3.00
❑ 68 Dick Schofield 8.00 4.00
❑ 69 San Francisco Giants CL 25.00 12.50
❑ 70 Harvey Kuenn 8.00 4.00
❑ 71 Don Bessent 6.00 3.00
❑ 72 Bill Renna 6.00 3.00
❑ 73 Ron Jackson 8.00 4.00
❑ 74 Lemon/Lavagetto/Sievers 8.00 4.00
❑ 75 Sam Jones 8.00 4.00
❑ 76 Bobby Richardson 20.00 10.00
❑ 77 John Goryl 6.00 3.00
❑ 78 Pedro Ramos 6.00 3.00
❑ 79 Harry Chiti 6.00 3.00
❑ 80 Minnie Minoso 12.00 6.00
❑ 81 Hal Jeffcoat 6.00 3.00
❑ 82 Bob Boyd 6.00 3.00
❑ 83 Bob Smith 6.00 3.00
❑ 84 Reno Bertoia 6.00 3.00
❑ 85 Harry Anderson 6.00 3.00
❑ 86 Bob Keegan 8.00 4.00
❑ 87 Danny O'Connell 6.00 3.00
❑ 88 Herb Score 12.00 6.00
❑ 89 Billy Gardner 6.00 3.00
❑ 90 Bill Skowron 12.00 6.00
❑ 91 Herb Moford RC 6.00 3.00
❑ 92 Dave Philley 6.00 3.00
❑ 93 Julio Becquer 6.00 3.00
❑ 94 Chicago White Sox CL 40.00 20.00
❑ 95 Carl Willey 6.00 3.00
❑ 96 Lou Berberet 6.00 3.00
❑ 97 Jerry Lynch 8.00 4.00
❑ 98 Arnie Portocarrero 6.00 3.00
❑ 99 Ted Kazanski 6.00 3.00
❑ 100 Bob Cerv 8.00 4.00
❑ 101 Alex Kellner 6.00 3.00
❑ 102 Felipe Alou RC 30.00 15.00
❑ 103 Billy Goodman 8.00 4.00
❑ 104 Del Rice 8.00 4.00
❑ 105 Lee Walls 6.00 3.00
❑ 106 Hal Woodeshick RC 6.00 3.00
❑ 107 Norm Larker RC 8.00 4.00
❑ 108 Zack Monroe RC 8.00 4.00
❑ 109 Bob Schmidt 6.00 3.00
❑ 110 George Witt RC 8.00 4.00
❑ 111 Cincinnati Redlegs CL 15.00 7.50
❑ 112 Billy Consolo 4.00 2.00
❑ 113 Taylor Phillips 4.00 2.00
❑ 114 Earl Battey 8.00 4.00
❑ 115 Mickey Vernon 8.00 4.00
❑ 116 Bob Allison RS RC 12.00 6.00
❑ 117 John Blanchard RS RC 12.00 6.00
❑ 118 John Buzhardt RS RC 5.00 2.50
❑ 119 Johnny Callison RS RC 12.00 6.00
❑ 120 Chuck Coles RS RC 5.00 2.50
❑ 121 Bob Conley RS RC 5.00 2.50
❑ 122 Bennie Daniels RS 5.00 2.50
❑ 123 Don Dillard RS RC 5.00 2.50
❑ 124 Dan Dobbek RS RC 5.00 2.50
❑ 125 Ron Fairly RS RC 12.00 6.00
❑ 126 Eddie Haas RS RC 5.00 2.50
❑ 127 Kent Hadley RS RC 5.00 2.50
❑ 128 Bob Hartman RS RC 5.00 2.50
❑ 129 Frank Herrera RS 5.00 2.50
❑ 130 Lou Jackson RS RC 5.00 2.50
❑ 131 Deron Johnson RS RC 12.00 6.00
❑ 132 Don Lee RS 5.00 2.50
❑ 133 Bob Lillis RS RC 5.00 2.50
❑ 134 Jim McDaniel RS RC 5.00 2.50
❑ 135 Gene Oliver RS RC 5.00 2.50
❑ 136 Jim O'Toole RS RC 5.00 2.50
❑ 137 Dick Ricketts RS RC 5.00 2.50
❑ 138 John Romano RS RC 5.00 2.50
❑ 139 Ed Sadowski RS RC 5.00 2.50
❑ 140 Charlie Secrest RS RC 5.00 2.50
❑ 141 Joe Shipley RS RC 5.00 2.50
❑ 142 Dick Stigman RS RC 5.00 2.50
❑ 143 Willie Tasby RS RC 5.00 2.50
❑ 144 Jerry Walker RS 5.00 2.50

❑ 145 Dom Zanni RS RC 5.00 2.50
❑ 146 Jerry Zimmerman RS RC 5.00 2.50
❑ 147 Long/Banks/Moryn 30.00 15.00
❑ 148 Mike McCormick 8.00 4.00
❑ 149 Jim Bunning 20.00 10.00
❑ 150 Stan Musial 120.00 60.00
❑ 151 Bob Malkmus 4.00 2.00
❑ 152 Johnny Klippstein 4.00 2.00
❑ 153 Jim Marshall 4.00 2.00
❑ 154 Ray Herbert 4.00 2.00
❑ 155 Enos Slaughter 20.00 10.00
❑ 156 B.Pierce/R.Roberts 12.00 6.00
❑ 157 Felix Mantilla 4.00 2.00
❑ 158 Walt Dropo 4.00 2.00
❑ 159 Bob Shaw 8.00 4.00
❑ 160 Dick Groat 8.00 4.00
❑ 161 Frank Baumann 4.00 2.00
❑ 162 Bobby G. Smith 4.00 2.00
❑ 163 Sandy Koufax 150.00 90.00
❑ 164 Johnny Groth 4.00 2.00
❑ 165 Bill Bruton 4.00 2.00
❑ 166 Minoso/Colavito/Doby 30.00 15.00
❑ 167 Duke Maas 4.00 2.00
❑ 168 Carroll Hardy 4.00 2.00
❑ 169 Ted Abernathy 4.00 2.00
❑ 170 Gene Woodling 8.00 4.00
❑ 171 Willard Schmidt 4.00 2.00
❑ 172 Kansas City Athletics CL 15.00 7.50
❑ 173 Bill Monbouquette RC 8.00 4.00
❑ 174 Jim Pendleton 4.00 2.00
❑ 175 Dick Farrell 8.00 4.00
❑ 176 Preston Ward 4.00 2.00
❑ 177 John Briggs RC 4.00 2.00
❑ 178 Ruben Amaro RC 12.00 6.00
❑ 179 Don Rudolph 4.00 2.00
❑ 180 Yogi Berra 80.00 50.00
❑ 181 Bob Porterfield 4.00 2.00
❑ 182 Milt Graff 4.00 2.00
❑ 183 Stu Miller 8.00 4.00
❑ 184 Harvey Haddix 8.00 4.00
❑ 185 Jim Busby 4.00 2.00
❑ 186 Mudcat Grant 8.00 4.00
❑ 187 Bubba Phillips 8.00 4.00
❑ 188 Juan Pizarro 4.00 2.00
❑ 189 Neil Chrisley 4.00 2.00
❑ 190 Bill Virdon 8.00 4.00
❑ 191 Russ Kemmerer 4.00 2.00
❑ 192 Charlie Beamon RC 4.00 2.00
❑ 193 Sammy Taylor 4.00 2.00
❑ 194 Jim Brosnan 8.00 4.00
❑ 195 Rip Repulski 4.00 2.00
❑ 196 Billy Moran 4.00 2.00
❑ 197 Ray Semproch 4.00 2.00
❑ 198 Jim Davenport 8.00 4.00
❑ 199 Leo Kiely 4.00 2.00
❑ 200 W.Giles NL PRES 8.00 4.00
❑ 201 Tom Acker 4.00 2.00
❑ 202 Roger Maris 125.00 75.00
❑ 203 Ossie Virgil 4.00 2.00
❑ 204 Casey Wise 4.00 2.00
❑ 205 Don Larsen 8.00 4.00
❑ 206 Carl Furillo 12.00 6.00
❑ 207 George Strickland 4.00 2.00
❑ 208 Willie Jones 4.00 2.00
❑ 209 Lenny Green 4.00 2.00
❑ 210 Ed Bailey 4.00 2.00
❑ 211 Bob Blaylock RC 4.00 2.00
❑ 212 H.Aaron/E.Mathews 80.00 50.00
❑ 213 Jim Rivera 8.00 4.00
❑ 214 Marcelino Solis RC 4.00 2.00
❑ 215 Jim Lemon 8.00 4.00
❑ 216 Andre Rodgers 4.00 2.00
❑ 217 Carl Erskine 12.00 6.00
❑ 218 Roman Mejias 4.00 2.00
❑ 219 George Zuverink 4.00 2.00
❑ 220 Frank Malzone 8.00 4.00
❑ 221 Bob Bowman 4.00 2.00
❑ 222 Bobby Shantz 8.00 4.00
❑ 223 St. Louis Cardinals CL 15.00 7.50
❑ 224 Claude Osteen RC 8.00 4.00
❑ 225 Johnny Logan 8.00 4.00
❑ 226 Art Ceccarelli 4.00 2.00
❑ 227 Hal W. Smith 4.00 2.00
❑ 228 Don Gross 4.00 2.00
❑ 229 Vic Power 8.00 4.00
❑ 230 Bill Fischer 4.00 2.00
❑ 231 Ellis Burton RC 4.00 2.00
❑ 232 Eddie Kasko 4.00 2.00
❑ 233 Paul Foytack 4.00 2.00
❑ 234 Chuck Tanner 8.00 4.00
❑ 235 Valmy Thomas 4.00 2.00
❑ 236 Ted Bowsfield RC 4.00 2.00
❑ 237 McDougald/Turley/B.Rich 12.00 6.00
❑ 238 Gene Baker 4.00 2.00
❑ 239 Bob Trowbridge 4.00 2.00
❑ 240 Hank Bauer 12.00 6.00
❑ 241 Billy Muffett 4.00 2.00
❑ 242 Ron Samford RC 4.00 2.00
❑ 243 Marv Grissom 4.00 2.00
❑ 244 Ted Gray 4.00 2.00
❑ 245 Ned Garver 4.00 2.00
❑ 246 J.W. Porter 4.00 2.00
❑ 247 Don Ferrarese 4.00 2.00
❑ 248 Boston Red Sox CL 15.00 7.50
❑ 249 Bobby Adams 4.00 2.00
❑ 250 Billy O'Dell 4.00 2.00
❑ 251 Clete Boyer 12.00 6.00
❑ 252 Ray Boone 8.00 4.00
❑ 253 Seth Morehead RC 4.00 2.00
❑ 254 Zeke Bella RC 4.00 2.00
❑ 255 Del Ennis 8.00 4.00
❑ 256 Jerry Davie RC 4.00 2.00
❑ 257 Leon Wagner RC 8.00 4.00
❑ 258 Fred Kipp RC 4.00 2.00
❑ 259 Jim Pisoni 4.00 2.00
❑ 260 Early Wynn UER 20.00 10.00
❑ 261 Gene Stephens 4.00 2.00
❑ 262 Podres/Labine/Drysdale 12.00 6.00
❑ 263 Bud Daley 4.00 2.00
❑ 264 Chico Carrasquel 4.00 2.00
❑ 265 Ron Kline 4.00 2.00
❑ 266 Woody Held 4.00 2.00
❑ 267 John Romonosky RC 4.00 2.00
❑ 268 Tito Francona 8.00 4.00
❑ 269 Jack Meyer 4.00 2.00
❑ 270 Gil Hodges 30.00 15.00
❑ 271 Orlando Pena RC 4.00 2.00
❑ 272 Jerry Lumpe 4.00 2.00
❑ 273 Joey Jay 8.00 4.00
❑ 274 Jerry Kindall 8.00 4.00
❑ 275 Jack Sanford 8.00 4.00
❑ 276 Pete Daley 4.00 2.00
❑ 277 Turk Lown 8.00 4.00
❑ 278 Chuck Essegian 4.00 2.00
❑ 279 Ernie Johnson 4.00 2.00
❑ 280 Frank Bolling 4.00 2.00
❑ 281 Walt Craddock RC 4.00 2.00
❑ 282 R.C. Stevens 4.00 2.00
❑ 283 Russ Heman RC 4.00 2.00
❑ 284 Steve Korcheck 4.00 2.00
❑ 285 Joe Cunningham 4.00 2.00
❑ 286 Dean Stone 4.00 2.00
❑ 287 Don Zimmer 12.00 6.00
❑ 288 Dutch Dotterer 4.00 2.00
❑ 289 Johnny Kucks 8.00 4.00
❑ 290 Wes Covington 4.00 2.00
❑ 291 P.Ramos/C.Pascual 4.00 2.00
❑ 292 Dick Williams 8.00 4.00
❑ 293 Ray Moore 4.00 2.00
❑ 294 Hank Foiles 4.00 2.00
❑ 295 Billy Martin 30.00 15.00
❑ 296 Ernie Broglio RC 4.00 2.00
❑ 297 Jackie Brandt RC 4.00 2.00
❑ 298 Tex Clevenger 4.00 2.00
❑ 299 Billy Klaus 4.00 2.00
❑ 300 Richie Ashburn 30.00 15.00
❑ 301 Earl Averill Jr. RC 4.00 2.00
❑ 302 Don Mossi 8.00 4.00
❑ 303 Marty Keough 4.00 2.00
❑ 304 Chicago Cubs CL 15.00 7.50
❑ 305 Curt Raydon RC 4.00 2.00
❑ 306 Jim Gilliam 8.00 4.00
❑ 307 Curt Barclay 4.00 2.00
❑ 308 Norm Siebern 4.00 2.00
❑ 309 Sal Maglie 8.00 4.00
❑ 310 Luis Aparicio 20.00 10.00
❑ 311 Norm Zauchin 4.00 2.00
❑ 312 Don Newcombe 8.00 4.00
❑ 313 Frank House 4.00 2.00
❑ 314 Don Cardwell 4.00 2.00
❑ 315 Joe Adcock 8.00 4.00
❑ 316A Ralph Lumenti UER 4.00 2.00
❑ 316B Ralph Lumenti UER 80.00 50.00
❑ 317 R.Ashburn/W.Mays 80.00 50.00
❑ 318 Rocky Bridges 4.00 2.00
❑ 319 Dave Hillman 4.00 2.00
❑ 320 Bob Skinner 8.00 4.00
❑ 321A Bob Giallombardo RC 8.00 4.00
❑ 321B Bob Giallombardo ERR 80.00 50.00
❑ 322A Harry Hanebrink TR 8.00 4.00
❑ 322B H.Hanebrink ERR 80.00 50.00
❑ 323 Frank Sullivan 4.00 2.00
❑ 324 Don Demeter 4.00 2.00
❑ 325 Ken Boyer 12.00 6.00
❑ 326 Marv Throneberry 8.00 4.00
❑ 327 Gary Bell RC 4.00 2.00
❑ 328 Lou Skizas 4.00 2.00
❑ 329 Detroit Tigers CL 15.00 7.50
❑ 330 Gus Triandos 8.00 4.00
❑ 331 Steve Boros 4.00 2.00
❑ 332 Ray Monzant 4.00 2.00
❑ 333 Harry Simpson 4.00 2.00
❑ 334 Glen Hobbie 4.00 2.00
❑ 335 Johnny Temple 8.00 4.00
❑ 336A Billy Loes TR 8.00 4.00
❑ 336B Billy Loes ERR 80.00 50.00
❑ 337 George Crowe 4.00 2.00
❑ 338 Sparky Anderson RC 60.00 35.00
❑ 339 Roy Face 8.00 4.00
❑ 340 Roy Sievers 8.00 4.00
❑ 341 Tom Qualters 4.00 2.00
❑ 342 Ray Jablonski 4.00 2.00
❑ 343 Billy Hoeft 4.00 2.00
❑ 344 Russ Nixon 4.00 2.00
❑ 345 Gil McDougald 12.00 6.00
❑ 346 D.Sisler/T.Brewer 4.00 2.00
❑ 347 Bob Buhl 4.00 2.00
❑ 348 Ted Lepcio 4.00 2.00
❑ 349 Hoyt Wilhelm 20.00 10.00
❑ 350 Ernie Banks 80.00 50.00
❑ 351 Earl Torgeson 4.00 2.00
❑ 352 Robin Roberts 20.00 10.00
❑ 353 Curt Flood 8.00 4.00
❑ 354 Pete Burnside 4.00 2.00
❑ 355 Jimmy Piersall 8.00 4.00
❑ 356 Bob Mabe RC 4.00 2.00
❑ 357 Dick Stuart RC 8.00 4.00
❑ 358 Ralph Terry 8.00 4.00
❑ 359 Bill White RC 20.00 10.00
❑ 360 Al Kaline 60.00 35.00
❑ 361 Willard Nixon 4.00 2.00
❑ 362A Dolan Nichols RC 4.00 2.00
❑ 362B Dolan Nichols ERR 80.00 50.00
❑ 363 Bobby Avila 4.00 2.00
❑ 364 Danny McDevitt 4.00 2.00
❑ 365 Gus Bell 8.00 4.00
❑ 366 Humberto Robinson 4.00 2.00
❑ 367 Cal Neeman 4.00 2.00
❑ 368 Don Mueller 8.00 4.00
❑ 369 Dick Tomanek 4.00 2.00
❑ 370 Pete Runnels 8.00 4.00
❑ 371 Dick Brodowski 4.00 2.00
❑ 372 Jim Hegan 8.00 4.00
❑ 373 Herb Plews 4.00 2.00
❑ 374 Art Ditmar 8.00 4.00
❑ 375 Bob Nieman 4.00 2.00
❑ 376 Hal Naragon 4.00 2.00
❑ 377 John Antonelli 8.00 4.00
❑ 378 Gail Harris 4.00 2.00
❑ 379 Bob Miller 4.00 2.00
❑ 380 Hank Aaron 150.00 90.00
❑ 381 Mike Baxes 4.00 2.00
❑ 382 Curt Simmons 8.00 4.00
❑ 383 D.Larsen/C.Stengel 12.00 6.00
❑ 384 Dave Sisler 4.00 2.00
❑ 385 Sherm Lollar 8.00 4.00
❑ 386 Jim Delsing 4.00 2.00
❑ 387 Don Drysdale 50.00 30.00
❑ 388 Bob Will RC 4.00 2.00
❑ 389 Joe Nuxhall 8.00 4.00
❑ 390 Orlando Cepeda 20.00 10.00
❑ 391 Milt Pappas 8.00 4.00
❑ 392 Whitey Herzog 8.00 4.00
❑ 393 Frank Lary 8.00 4.00
❑ 394 Randy Jackson 4.00 2.00
❑ 395 Elston Howard 12.00 6.00
❑ 396 Bob Rush 4.00 2.00
❑ 397 Washington Senators CL 15.00 7.50

❑	398	Wally Post	8.00	4.00
❑	399	Larry Jackson	4.00	2.00
❑	400	Jackie Jensen	8.00	4.00
❑	401	Ron Blackburn	4.00	2.00
❑	402	Hector Lopez	8.00	4.00
❑	403	Clem Labine	8.00	4.00
❑	404	Hank Sauer	8.00	4.00
❑	405	Roy McMillan	8.00	4.00
❑	406	Solly Drake	4.00	2.00
❑	407	Moe Drabowsky	8.00	4.00
❑	408	N.Fox/L.Aparicio	40.00	20.00
❑	409	Gus Zernial	8.00	4.00
❑	410	Billy Pierce	8.00	4.00
❑	411	Whitey Lockman	8.00	4.00
❑	412	Stan Lopata	4.00	2.00
❑	413	Camilo Pascual UER	8.00	4.00
❑	414	Dale Long	8.00	4.00
❑	415	Bill Mazeroski	12.00	6.00
❑	416	Haywood Sullivan	8.00	4.00
❑	417	Virgil Trucks	8.00	4.00
❑	418	Gino Cimoli	4.00	2.00
❑	419	Milwaukee Braves CL	15.00	7.50
❑	420	Rocky Colavito	30.00	15.00
❑	421	Herman Wehmeier	4.00	2.00
❑	422	Hobie Landrith	4.00	2.00
❑	423	Bob Grim	8.00	4.00
❑	424	Ken Aspromonte	4.00	2.00
❑	425	Del Crandall	8.00	4.00
❑	426	Gerry Staley	8.00	4.00
❑	427	Charlie Neal	8.00	4.00
❑	428	Kline/Friend/Law/Face	4.00	2.00
❑	429	Bobby Thomson	8.00	4.00
❑	430	Whitey Ford	60.00	35.00
❑	431	Whammy Douglas	4.00	2.00
❑	432	Smoky Burgess	8.00	4.00
❑	433	Billy Harrell	4.00	2.00
❑	434	Hal Griggs	4.00	2.00
❑	435	Frank Robinson	50.00	30.00
❑	436	Granny Hamner	4.00	2.00
❑	437	Ike Delock	4.00	2.00
❑	438	Sammy Esposito	4.00	2.00
❑	439	Brooks Robinson	50.00	30.00
❑	440	Lew Burdette UER	8.00	4.00
❑	441	John Roseboro	8.00	4.00
❑	442	Ray Narleski	4.00	2.00
❑	443	Daryl Spencer	4.00	2.00
❑	444	Ron Hansen RC	8.00	4.00
❑	445	Cal McLish	4.00	2.00
❑	446	Rocky Nelson	4.00	2.00
❑	447	Bob Anderson	4.00	2.00
❑	448	Vada Pinson UER	12.00	6.00
❑	449	Tom Gorman	4.00	2.00
❑	450	Eddie Mathews	40.00	20.00
❑	451	Jimmy Constable RC	4.00	2.00
❑	452	Chico Fernandez	4.00	2.00
❑	453	Les Moss	4.00	2.00
❑	454	Phil Clark	4.00	2.00
❑	455	Larry Doby	12.00	6.00
❑	456	Jerry Casale RC	4.00	2.00
❑	457	Los Angeles Dodgers CL	30.00	15.00
❑	458	Gordon Jones	4.00	2.00
❑	459	Bill Tuttle	4.00	2.00
❑	460	Bob Friend	8.00	4.00
❑	461	Mickey Mantle BT	125.00	75.00
❑	462	Rocky Colavito BT	12.00	6.00
❑	463	Al Kaline BT	30.00	15.00
❑	464	Willie Mays BT	40.00	20.00
❑	465	Roy Sievers BT	8.00	4.00
❑	466	Billy Pierce BT	8.00	4.00
❑	467	Hank Aaron BT	40.00	20.00
❑	468	Duke Snider BT	20.00	10.00
❑	469	Ernie Banks BT	20.00	10.00
❑	470	Stan Musial BT	30.00	15.00
❑	471	Tom Sturdivant	4.00	2.00
❑	472	Gene Freese	4.00	2.00
❑	473	Mike Fornieles	4.00	2.00
❑	474	Moe Thacker RC	4.00	2.00
❑	475	Jack Harshman	4.00	2.00
❑	476	Cleveland Indians CL	15.00	7.50
❑	477	Barry Latman RC	4.00	2.00
❑	478	Roberto Clemente	175.00	100.00
❑	479	Lindy McDaniel	8.00	4.00
❑	480	Red Schoendienst	12.00	6.00
❑	481	Charlie Maxwell	8.00	4.00
❑	482	Russ Meyer	4.00	2.00
❑	483	Clint Courtney	4.00	2.00
❑	484	Willie Kirkland	4.00	2.00
❑	485	Ryne Duren	8.00	4.00
❑	486	Sammy White	4.00	2.00
❑	487	Hal Brown	4.00	2.00
❑	488	Walt Moryn	4.00	2.00
❑	489	John Powers	4.00	2.00
❑	490	Frank Thomas	8.00	4.00
❑	491	Don Blasingame	4.00	2.00
❑	492	Gene Conley	8.00	4.00
❑	493	Jim Landis	8.00	4.00
❑	494	Don Pavletich RC	4.00	2.00
❑	495	Johnny Podres	12.00	6.00
❑	496	Wayne Terwilliger UER	4.00	2.00
❑	497	Hal R. Smith	4.00	2.00
❑	498	Dick Hyde	4.00	2.00
❑	499	Johnny O'Brien	8.00	4.00
❑	500	Vic Wertz	8.00	4.00
❑	501	Bob Tiefenauer RC	4.00	2.00
❑	502	Alvin Dark	8.00	4.00
❑	503	Jim Owens	4.00	2.00
❑	504	Ossie Alvarez RC	4.00	2.00
❑	505	Tony Kubek	12.00	6.00
❑	506	Bob Purkey	4.00	2.00
❑	507	Bob Hale	15.00	7.50
❑	508	Art Fowler	15.00	7.50
❑	509	Norm Cash RC	80.00	50.00
❑	510	New York Yankees CL	125.00	75.00
❑	511	George Susce	15.00	7.50
❑	512	George Altman RC	15.00	7.50
❑	513	Tommy Carroll	15.00	7.50
❑	514	Bob Gibson RC	300.00	175.00
❑	515	Harmon Killebrew	125.00	75.00
❑	516	Mike Garcia	20.00	10.00
❑	517	Joe Koppe RC	15.00	7.50
❑	518	Mike Cuellar UER RC	30.00	18.00
❑	519	Runnels/Gernert/Malzone	20.00	10.00
❑	520	Don Elston	15.00	7.50
❑	521	Gary Geiger	15.00	7.50
❑	522	Gene Snyder RC	15.00	7.50
❑	523	Harry Bright RC	15.00	7.50
❑	524	Larry Osborne RC	15.00	7.50
❑	525	Jim Coates RC	20.00	10.00
❑	526	Bob Speake	15.00	7.50
❑	527	Solly Hemus	15.00	7.50
❑	528	Pittsburgh Pirates CL	80.00	50.00
❑	529	George Bamberger RC	20.00	10.00
❑	530	Wally Moon	20.00	10.00
❑	531	Ray Webster RC	15.00	7.50
❑	532	Mark Freeman RC	15.00	7.50
❑	533	Darrell Johnson	20.00	10.00
❑	534	Faye Throneberry	15.00	7.50
❑	535	Ruben Gomez	15.00	7.50
❑	536	Danny Kravitz	15.00	7.50
❑	537	Rudolph Arias RC	15.00	7.50
❑	538	Chick King	15.00	7.50
❑	539	Gary Blaylock RC	15.00	7.50
❑	540	Willie Miranda	15.00	7.50
❑	541	Bob Thurman	15.00	7.50
❑	542	Jim Perry RC	30.00	18.00
❑	543	Skinner/Virdon/Clemente	125.00	75.00
❑	544	Lee Tate RC	15.00	7.50
❑	545	Tom Morgan	15.00	7.50
❑	546	Al Schroll	15.00	7.50
❑	547	Jim Baxes RC	15.00	7.50
❑	548	Elmer Singleton	15.00	7.50
❑	549	Howie Nunn RC	15.00	7.50
❑	550	R.Campanella Courage	150.00	90.00
❑	551	Fred Haney AS MG	15.00	7.50
❑	552	Casey Stengel AS	30.00	18.00
❑	553	Orlando Cepeda AS	30.00	18.00
❑	554	Bill Skowron AS	20.00	10.00
❑	555	Bill Mazeroski AS	30.00	18.00
❑	556	Nellie Fox AS	40.00	20.00
❑	557	Ken Boyer AS	30.00	18.00
❑	558	Frank Malzone AS	15.00	7.50
❑	559	Ernie Banks AS	60.00	35.00
❑	560	Luis Aparicio AS	40.00	25.00
❑	561	Hank Aaron AS	125.00	75.00
❑	562	Al Kaline AS	60.00	35.00
❑	563	Willie Mays AS	125.00	75.00
❑	564	Mickey Mantle AS	300.00	175.00
❑	565	Wes Covington AS	20.00	10.00
❑	566	Roy Sievers AS	15.00	7.50
❑	567	Del Crandall AS	15.00	7.50
❑	568	Gus Triandos AS	15.00	7.50
❑	569	Bob Friend AS	15.00	7.50
❑	570	Bob Turley AS	15.00	7.50
❑	571	Warren Spahn AS	50.00	30.00
❑	572	Billy Pierce AS	40.00	25.00

1960 Topps

❑		COMPLETE SET (572)	5000.00	3000.00
❑		COMMON CARD (1-440)	4.00	2.00
❑		COMMON CARD (441-506)	8.00	4.00
❑		COMMON CARD (507-572)	15.00	7.50
❑		WRAPPER (1-CENT)	900.00	750.00
❑		WRAP. (1-CENT REPEAT)	500.00	400.00
❑		WRAPPER (5-CENT)	40.00	30.00
❑	1	Early Wynn	40.00	20.00
❑	2	Roman Mejias	4.00	2.00
❑	3	Joe Adcock	6.00	3.00
❑	4	Bob Purkey	4.00	2.00
❑	5	Wally Moon	6.00	3.00
❑	6	Lou Berberet	4.00	2.00
❑	7	W.Mays/B.Rigney	25.00	12.50
❑	8	Bud Daley	4.00	2.00
❑	9	Faye Throneberry	4.00	2.00
❑	10	Ernie Banks	50.00	30.00
❑	11	Norm Siebern	4.00	2.00
❑	12	Milt Pappas	6.00	3.00
❑	13	Wally Post	6.00	3.00
❑	14	Jim Grant	6.00	3.00
❑	15	Pete Runnels	6.00	3.00
❑	16	Ernie Broglio	6.00	3.00
❑	17	Johnny Callison	6.00	3.00
❑	18	Los Angeles Dodgers CL	50.00	30.00
❑	19	Felix Mantilla	4.00	2.00
❑	20	Roy Face	6.00	3.00
❑	21	Dutch Dotterer	4.00	2.00
❑	22	Rocky Bridges	4.00	2.00
❑	23	Eddie Fisher RC	4.00	2.00
❑	24	Dick Gray	4.00	2.00
❑	25	Roy Sievers	6.00	3.00
❑	26	Wayne Terwilliger	4.00	2.00
❑	27	Dick Drott	4.00	2.00
❑	28	Brooks Robinson	50.00	30.00
❑	29	Clem Labine	6.00	3.00
❑	30	Tito Francona	4.00	2.00
❑	31	Sammy Esposito	4.00	2.00
❑	32	J.O'Toole/V.Pinson	4.00	2.00
❑	33	Tom Morgan	4.00	2.00
❑	34	Sparky Anderson	15.00	7.50
❑	35	Whitey Ford	50.00	30.00
❑	36	Russ Nixon	4.00	2.00
❑	37	Bill Bruton	4.00	2.00
❑	38	Jerry Casale	4.00	2.00
❑	39	Earl Averill Jr.	4.00	2.00
❑	40	Joe Cunningham	4.00	2.00
❑	41	Barry Latman	4.00	2.00
❑	42	Hobie Landrith	4.00	2.00
❑	43	Washington Senators CL	10.00	5.00
❑	44	Bobby Locke RC	4.00	2.00
❑	45	Roy McMillan	6.00	3.00
❑	46	Jack Fisher RC	4.00	2.00
❑	47	Don Zimmer	6.00	3.00
❑	48	Hal W. Smith	4.00	2.00
❑	49	Curt Raydon	4.00	2.00
❑	50	Al Kaline	50.00	30.00
❑	51	Jim Coates	6.00	3.00
❑	52	Dave Philley	4.00	2.00
❑	53	Jackie Brandt	4.00	2.00
❑	54	Mike Fornieles	4.00	2.00
❑	55	Bill Mazeroski	15.00	7.50
❑	56	Steve Korcheck	4.00	2.00

❑ 57 T.Lown/G.Staley	4.00	2.00
❑ 58 Gino Cimoli	4.00	2.00
❑ 59 Juan Pizarro	4.00	2.00
❑ 60 Gus Triandos	6.00	3.00
❑ 61 Eddie Kasko	4.00	2.00
❑ 62 Roger Craig	6.00	3.00
❑ 63 George Strickland	4.00	2.00
❑ 64 Jack Meyer	4.00	2.00
❑ 65 Elston Howard	6.00	3.00
❑ 66 Bob Trowbridge	4.00	2.00
❑ 67 Jose Pagan RC	4.00	2.00
❑ 68 Dave Hillman	4.00	2.00
❑ 69 Billy Goodman	6.00	3.00
❑ 70 Lew Burdette UER	6.00	3.00
❑ 71 Marty Keough	4.00	2.00
❑ 72 Detroit Tigers CL	25.00	12.50
❑ 73 Bob Gibson	50.00	30.00
❑ 74 Walt Moryn	4.00	2.00
❑ 75 Vic Power	6.00	3.00
❑ 76 Bill Fischer	4.00	2.00
❑ 77 Hank Foiles	4.00	2.00
❑ 78 Bob Grim	4.00	2.00
❑ 79 Walt Dropo	4.00	2.00
❑ 80 Johnny Antonelli	6.00	3.00
❑ 81 Russ Snyder RC	4.00	2.00
❑ 82 Ruben Gomez	4.00	2.00
❑ 83 Tony Kubek	15.00	7.50
❑ 84 Hal R. Smith	4.00	2.00
❑ 85 Frank Lary	6.00	3.00
❑ 86 Dick Gernert	4.00	2.00
❑ 87 John Romonosky	4.00	2.00
❑ 88 John Roseboro	6.00	3.00
❑ 89 Hal Brown	4.00	2.00
❑ 90 Bobby Avila	4.00	2.00
❑ 91 Bennie Daniels	4.00	2.00
❑ 92 Whitey Herzog	6.00	3.00
❑ 93 Art Schult	4.00	2.00
❑ 94 Leo Kiely	4.00	2.00
❑ 95 Frank Thomas	6.00	3.00
❑ 96 Ralph Terry	6.00	3.00
❑ 97 Ted Lepcio	4.00	2.00
❑ 98 Gordon Jones	4.00	2.00
❑ 99 Lenny Green	4.00	2.00
❑ 100 Nellie Fox	20.00	10.00
❑ 101 Bob Miller RC	4.00	2.00
❑ 102 Kent Hadley	4.00	2.00
❑ 103 Dick Farrell	6.00	3.00
❑ 104 Dick Schofield	6.00	3.00
❑ 105 Larry Sherry RC	6.00	3.00
❑ 106 Billy Gardner	4.00	2.00
❑ 107 Carlton Willey	4.00	2.00
❑ 108 Pete Daley	4.00	2.00
❑ 109 Clete Boyer	15.00	7.50
❑ 110 Cal McLish	4.00	2.00
❑ 111 Vic Wertz	6.00	3.00
❑ 112 Jack Harshman	4.00	2.00
❑ 113 Bob Skinner	4.00	2.00
❑ 114 Ken Aspromonte	4.00	2.00
❑ 115 R.Face/H.Wilhelm	6.00	3.00
❑ 116 Jim Rivera	4.00	2.00
❑ 117 Tom Borland RS	4.00	2.00
❑ 118 Bob Bruce RS RC	4.00	2.00
❑ 119 Chico Cardenas RS RC	6.00	3.00
❑ 120 Duke Carmel RS RC	4.00	2.00
❑ 121 Camilo Carreon RS RC	4.00	2.00
❑ 122 Don Dillard RS	4.00	2.00
❑ 123 Dan Dobbek RS	4.00	2.00
❑ 124 Jim Donohue RS RC	4.00	2.00
❑ 125 Dick Ellsworth RS RC	6.00	3.00
❑ 126 Chuck Estrada RS RC	4.00	2.00
❑ 127 Ron Hansen RS	6.00	3.00
❑ 128 Bill Harris RS RC	4.00	2.00
❑ 129 Bob Hartman RS	4.00	2.00
❑ 130 Frank Herrera RS	4.00	2.00
❑ 131 Ed Hobaugh RS RC	4.00	2.00
❑ 132 Frank Howard RS RC	25.00	12.50
❑ 133 Julian Javier RS RC	6.00	3.00
❑ 134 Deron Johnson RS	6.00	3.00
❑ 135 Ken Johnson RS RC	4.00	2.00
❑ 136 Jim Kaat RS RC	40.00	20.00
❑ 137 Lou Klimchock RS RC	4.00	2.00
❑ 138 Art Mahaffey RS RC	6.00	3.00
❑ 139 Carl Mathias RS RC	4.00	2.00
❑ 140 Julio Navarro RS RC	4.00	2.00
❑ 141 Jim Proctor RS RC	4.00	2.00
❑ 142 Bill Short RS RC	4.00	2.00
❑ 143 Al Spangler RS RC	4.00	2.00
❑ 144 Al Stieglitz RS RC	4.00	2.00
❑ 145 Jim Umbricht RS RC	4.00	2.00
❑ 146 Ted Wieand RS RC	4.00	2.00
❑ 147 Bob Will RS	4.00	2.00
❑ 148 C.Yastrzemski RS RC	200.00	125.00
❑ 149 Bob Nieman	4.00	2.00
❑ 150 Billy Pierce	6.00	3.00
❑ 151 San Francisco Giants CL	10.00	5.00
❑ 152 Gail Harris	4.00	2.00
❑ 153 Bobby Thomson	6.00	3.00
❑ 154 Jim Davenport	6.00	3.00
❑ 155 Charlie Neal	6.00	3.00
❑ 156 Art Ceccarelli	4.00	2.00
❑ 157 Rocky Nelson	6.00	3.00
❑ 158 Wes Covington	6.00	3.00
❑ 159 Jim Piersall	6.00	3.00
❑ 160 M.Mantle/K.Boyer	125.00	75.00
❑ 161 Ray Narleski	4.00	2.00
❑ 162 Sammy Taylor	4.00	2.00
❑ 163 Hector Lopez	6.00	3.00
❑ 164 Cincinnati Reds CL	10.00	5.00
❑ 165 Jack Sanford	6.00	3.00
❑ 166 Chuck Essegian	4.00	2.00
❑ 167 Valmy Thomas	4.00	2.00
❑ 168 Alex Grammas	4.00	2.00
❑ 169 Jake Striker RC	4.00	2.00
❑ 170 Del Crandall	6.00	3.00
❑ 171 Johnny Groth	4.00	2.00
❑ 172 Willie Kirkland	4.00	2.00
❑ 173 Billy Martin	20.00	10.00
❑ 174 Cleveland Indians CL	10.00	5.00
❑ 175 Pedro Ramos	4.00	2.00
❑ 176 Vada Pinson	6.00	3.00
❑ 177 Johnny Kucks	4.00	2.00
❑ 178 Woody Held	4.00	2.00
❑ 179 Rip Coleman	4.00	2.00
❑ 180 Harry Simpson	4.00	2.00
❑ 181 Billy Loes	6.00	3.00
❑ 182 Glen Hobbie	4.00	2.00
❑ 183 Eli Grba RC	4.00	2.00
❑ 184 Gary Geiger	4.00	2.00
❑ 185 Jim Owens	4.00	2.00
❑ 186 Dave Sisler	4.00	2.00
❑ 187 Jay Hook RC	4.00	2.00
❑ 188 Dick Williams	6.00	3.00
❑ 189 Don McMahon	4.00	2.00
❑ 190 Gene Woodling	6.00	3.00
❑ 191 Johnny Klippstein	4.00	2.00
❑ 192 Danny O'Connell	4.00	2.00
❑ 193 Dick Hyde	4.00	2.00
❑ 194 Bobby Gene Smith	4.00	2.00
❑ 195 Lindy McDaniel	6.00	3.00
❑ 196 Andy Carey	6.00	3.00
❑ 197 Ron Kline	4.00	2.00
❑ 198 Jerry Lynch	6.00	3.00
❑ 199 Dick Donovan	6.00	3.00
❑ 200 Willie Mays	125.00	75.00
❑ 201 Larry Osborne	4.00	2.00
❑ 202 Fred Kipp	4.00	2.00
❑ 203 Sammy White	4.00	2.00
❑ 204 Ryne Duren	6.00	3.00
❑ 205 Johnny Logan	6.00	3.00
❑ 206 Claude Osteen	6.00	3.00
❑ 207 Bob Boyd	4.00	2.00
❑ 208 Chicago White Sox CL	10.00	5.00
❑ 209 Ron Blackburn	4.00	2.00
❑ 210 Harmon Killebrew	40.00	20.00
❑ 211 Taylor Phillips	4.00	2.00
❑ 212 Walter Alston MG	10.00	5.00
❑ 213 Chuck Dressen MG	6.00	3.00
❑ 214 Jimmy Dykes MG	6.00	3.00
❑ 215 Bob Elliott MG	6.00	3.00
❑ 216 Joe Gordon MG	6.00	3.00
❑ 217 Charlie Grimm MG	6.00	3.00
❑ 218 Solly Hemus MG	4.00	2.00
❑ 219 Fred Hutchinson MG	6.00	3.00
❑ 220 Billy Jurges MG	4.00	2.00
❑ 221 Cookie Lavagetto MG	4.00	2.00
❑ 222 Al Lopez MG	10.00	5.00
❑ 223 Danny Murtaugh MG	6.00	3.00
❑ 224 Paul Richards MG	6.00	3.00
❑ 225 Bill Rigney MG	4.00	2.00
❑ 226 Eddie Sawyer MG	4.00	2.00
❑ 227 Casey Stengel MG	15.00	7.50
❑ 228 Ernie Johnson	6.00	3.00
❑ 229 Joe M. Morgan RC	4.00	2.00
❑ 230 Burdette/Spahn/Buhl	10.00	5.00
❑ 231 Hal Naragon	4.00	2.00
❑ 232 Jim Busby	4.00	2.00
❑ 233 Don Elston	4.00	2.00
❑ 234 Don Demeter	4.00	2.00
❑ 235 Gus Bell	6.00	3.00
❑ 236 Dick Ricketts	4.00	2.00
❑ 237 Elmer Valo	4.00	2.00
❑ 238 Danny Kravitz	4.00	2.00
❑ 239 Joe Shipley	4.00	2.00
❑ 240 Luis Aparicio	15.00	7.50
❑ 241 Albie Pearson	6.00	3.00
❑ 242 St. Louis Cardinals CL	10.00	5.00
❑ 243 Bubba Phillips	4.00	2.00
❑ 244 Hal Griggs	4.00	2.00
❑ 245 Eddie Yost	6.00	3.00
❑ 246 Lee Maye RC	6.00	3.00
❑ 247 Gil McDougald	10.00	5.00
❑ 248 Del Rice	4.00	2.00
❑ 249 Earl Wilson RC	6.00	3.00
❑ 250 Stan Musial	100.00	60.00
❑ 251 Bob Malkmus	4.00	2.00
❑ 252 Ray Herbert	4.00	2.00
❑ 253 Eddie Bressoud	4.00	2.00
❑ 254 Arnie Portocarrero	4.00	2.00
❑ 255 Jim Gilliam	6.00	3.00
❑ 256 Dick Brown	4.00	2.00
❑ 257 Gordy Coleman RC	4.00	2.00
❑ 258 Dick Groat	6.00	3.00
❑ 259 George Altman	4.00	2.00
❑ 260 R.Colavito/T.Francona	15.00	7.50
❑ 261 Pete Burnside	4.00	2.00
❑ 262 Hank Bauer	6.00	3.00
❑ 263 Darrell Johnson	4.00	2.00
❑ 264 Robin Roberts	15.00	7.50
❑ 265 Rip Repulski	4.00	2.00
❑ 266 Joey Jay	6.00	3.00
❑ 267 Jim Marshall	4.00	2.00
❑ 268 Al Worthington	4.00	2.00
❑ 269 Gene Green	4.00	2.00
❑ 270 Bob Turley	6.00	3.00
❑ 271 Julio Becquer	4.00	2.00
❑ 272 Fred Green RC	6.00	3.00
❑ 273 Neil Chrisley	4.00	2.00
❑ 274 Tom Acker	4.00	2.00
❑ 275 Curt Flood	6.00	3.00
❑ 276 Ken McBride RC	4.00	2.00
❑ 277 Harry Bright	4.00	2.00
❑ 278 Stan Williams	6.00	3.00
❑ 279 Chuck Tanner	6.00	3.00
❑ 280 Frank Sullivan	4.00	2.00
❑ 281 Ray Boone	6.00	3.00
❑ 282 Joe Nuxhall	6.00	3.00
❑ 283 Johnny Blanchard	6.00	3.00
❑ 284 Don Gross	4.00	2.00
❑ 285 Harry Anderson	4.00	2.00
❑ 286 Ray Semproch	4.00	2.00
❑ 287 Felipe Alou	6.00	3.00
❑ 288 Bob Mabe	4.00	2.00
❑ 289 Willie Jones	4.00	2.00
❑ 290 Jerry Lumpe	4.00	2.00
❑ 291 Bob Keegan	4.00	2.00
❑ 292 J.Pignatano/J.Roseboro	6.00	3.00
❑ 293 Gene Conley	6.00	3.00
❑ 294 Tony Taylor	6.00	3.00
❑ 295 Gil Hodges	25.00	12.50
❑ 296 Nelson Chittum RC	4.00	2.00
❑ 297 Reno Bertoia	4.00	2.00
❑ 298 George Witt	4.00	2.00
❑ 299 Earl Torgeson	4.00	2.00
❑ 300 Hank Aaron	125.00	75.00
❑ 301 Jerry Davie	4.00	2.00
❑ 302 Philadelphia Phillies CL	10.00	5.00
❑ 303 Billy O'Dell	4.00	2.00
❑ 304 Joe Ginsberg	4.00	2.00
❑ 305 Richie Ashburn	20.00	10.00
❑ 306 Frank Baumann	4.00	2.00
❑ 307 Gene Oliver	4.00	2.00
❑ 308 Dick Hall	4.00	2.00
❑ 309 Bob Hale	4.00	2.00
❑ 310 Frank Malzone	6.00	3.00
❑ 311 Raul Sanchez	4.00	2.00
❑ 312 Charley Lau	6.00	3.00
❑ 313 Turk Lown	4.00	2.00
❑ 314 Chico Fernandez	4.00	2.00

	No.	Card		
❑	315	Bobby Shantz	10.00	5.00
❑	316	W.McCovey ASR RC	125.00	75.00
❑	317	Pumpsie Green ASR RC	6.00	3.00
❑	318	Jim Baxes ASR	6.00	3.00
❑	319	Joe Koppe ASR	6.00	3.00
❑	320	Bob Allison ASR	6.00	3.00
❑	321	Ron Fairly ASR	6.00	3.00
❑	322	Willie Tasby ASR	6.00	3.00
❑	323	John Romano ASR	6.00	3.00
❑	324	Jim Perry ASR	6.00	3.00
❑	325	Jim O'Toole ASR	6.00	3.00
❑	326	Roberto Clemente	175.00	100.00
❑	327	Ray Sadecki RC	4.00	2.00
❑	328	Earl Battey	4.00	2.00
❑	329	Zack Monroe	4.00	2.00
❑	330	Harvey Kuenn	6.00	3.00
❑	331	Henry Mason RC	4.00	2.00
❑	332	New York Yankees CL	80.00	50.00
❑	333	Danny McDevitt	4.00	2.00
❑	334	Ted Abernathy	4.00	2.00
❑	335	Red Schoendienst	15.00	7.50
❑	336	Ike Delock	4.00	2.00
❑	337	Cal Neeman	4.00	2.00
❑	338	Ray Monzant	4.00	2.00
❑	339	Harry Chiti	4.00	2.00
❑	340	Harvey Haddix	6.00	3.00
❑	341	Carroll Hardy	4.00	2.00
❑	342	Casey Wise	4.00	2.00
❑	343	Sandy Koufax	125.00	75.00
❑	344	Clint Courtney	4.00	2.00
❑	345	Don Newcombe	6.00	3.00
❑	346	J.C. Martin UER RC	6.00	3.00
❑	347	Ed Bouchee	4.00	2.00
❑	348	Barry Shetrone RC	4.00	2.00
❑	349	Moe Drabowsky	6.00	3.00
❑	350	Mickey Mantle	600.00	350.00
❑	351	Don Nottebart RC	4.00	2.00
❑	352	Bell/F.Robinson/Lynch	10.00	5.00
❑	353	Don Larsen	6.00	3.00
❑	354	Bob Lillis	4.00	2.00
❑	355	Bill White	6.00	3.00
❑	356	Joe Amalfitano	4.00	2.00
❑	357	Al Schroll	4.00	2.00
❑	358	Joe DeMaestri	4.00	2.00
❑	359	Buddy Gilbert RC	4.00	2.00
❑	360	Herb Score	6.00	3.00
❑	361	Bob Oldis	6.00	3.00
❑	362	Russ Kemmerer	4.00	2.00
❑	363	Gene Stephens	4.00	2.00
❑	364	Paul Foytack	4.00	2.00
❑	365	Minnie Minoso	10.00	5.00
❑	366	Dallas Green RC	10.00	5.00
❑	367	Bill Tuttle	4.00	2.00
❑	368	Daryl Spencer	4.00	2.00
❑	369	Billy Hoeft	4.00	2.00
❑	370	Bill Skowron	10.00	5.00
❑	371	Bud Byerly	4.00	2.00
❑	372	Frank House	4.00	2.00
❑	373	Don Hoak	6.00	3.00
❑	374	Bob Buhl	6.00	3.00
❑	375	Dale Long	10.00	5.00
❑	376	John Briggs	4.00	2.00
❑	377	Roger Maris	100.00	60.00
❑	378	Stu Miller	6.00	3.00
❑	379	Red Wilson	4.00	2.00
❑	380	Bob Shaw	4.00	2.00
❑	381	Milwaukee Braves CL	10.00	5.00
❑	382	Ted Bowsfield	4.00	2.00
❑	383	Leon Wagner	4.00	2.00
❑	384	Don Cardwell	4.00	2.00
❑	385	Charlie Neal WS1	8.00	4.00
❑	386	Charlie Neal WS2	8.00	4.00
❑	387	Carl Furillo WS3	8.00	4.00
❑	388	Gil Hodges WS4	10.00	5.00
❑	389	L.Aparicio WS5 w/M.Wills	10.00	5.00
❑	390	Scrambling After Ball WS6	8.00	4.00
❑	391	Champs Celebrate WS	8.00	4.00
❑	392	Tex Clevenger	4.00	2.00
❑	393	Smoky Burgess	6.00	3.00
❑	394	Norm Larker	6.00	3.00
❑	395	Hoyt Wilhelm	15.00	7.50
❑	396	Steve Bilko	4.00	2.00
❑	397	Don Blasingame	4.00	2.00
❑	398	Mike Cuellar	6.00	3.00
❑	399	Pappas/Fisher/Walker	6.00	3.00
❑	400	Rocky Colavito	20.00	10.00
❑	401	Bob Duliba RC	4.00	2.00
❑	402	Dick Stuart	15.00	7.50
❑	403	Ed Sadowski	4.00	2.00
❑	404	Bob Rush	4.00	2.00
❑	405	Bobby Richardson	15.00	7.50
❑	406	Billy Klaus	4.00	2.00
❑	407	Gary Peters UER RC	6.00	3.00
❑	408	Carl Furillo	10.00	5.00
❑	409	Ron Samford	4.00	2.00
❑	410	Sam Jones	6.00	3.00
❑	411	Ed Bailey	4.00	2.00
❑	412	Bob Anderson	4.00	2.00
❑	413	Kansas City Athletics CL	10.00	5.00
❑	414	Don Williams RC	4.00	2.00
❑	415	Bob Cerv	4.00	2.00
❑	416	Humberto Robinson	4.00	2.00
❑	417	Chuck Cottier RC	4.00	2.00
❑	418	Don Mossi	6.00	3.00
❑	419	George Crowe	4.00	2.00
❑	420	Eddie Mathews	40.00	20.00
❑	421	Duke Maas	4.00	2.00
❑	422	John Powers	4.00	2.00
❑	423	Ed Fitzgerald	4.00	2.00
❑	424	Pete Whisenant	4.00	2.00
❑	425	Johnny Podres	6.00	3.00
❑	426	Ron Jackson	4.00	2.00
❑	427	Al Grunwald RC	4.00	2.00
❑	428	Al Smith	4.00	2.00
❑	429	Nellie Fox/H.Kuenn	10.00	5.00
❑	430	Art Ditmar	4.00	2.00
❑	431	Andre Rodgers	4.00	2.00
❑	432	Chuck Stobbs	4.00	2.00
❑	433	Irv Noren	4.00	2.00
❑	434	Brooks Lawrence	6.00	3.00
❑	435	Gene Freese	4.00	2.00
❑	436	Marv Throneberry	6.00	3.00
❑	437	Bob Friend	6.00	3.00
❑	438	Jim Coker RC	4.00	2.00
❑	439	Tom Brewer	4.00	2.00
❑	440	Jim Lemon	6.00	3.00
❑	441	Gary Bell	10.00	5.00
❑	442	Joe Pignatano	8.00	4.00
❑	443	Charlie Maxwell	8.00	4.00
❑	444	Jerry Kindall	8.00	4.00
❑	445	Warren Spahn	50.00	30.00
❑	446	Ellis Burton	8.00	4.00
❑	447	Ray Moore	8.00	4.00
❑	448	Jim Gentile RC	15.00	7.50
❑	449	Jim Brosnan	8.00	4.00
❑	450	Orlando Cepeda	25.00	12.50
❑	451	Curt Simmons	8.00	4.00
❑	452	Ray Webster	8.00	4.00
❑	453	Vern Law	25.00	12.50
❑	454	Hal Woodeshick	8.00	4.00
❑	455	Baltimore Coaches	8.00	4.00
❑	456	Red Sox Coaches	10.00	5.00
❑	457	Cubs Coaches	8.00	4.00
❑	458	White Sox Coaches	8.00	4.00
❑	459	Reds Coaches	8.00	4.00
❑	460	Indians Coaches	15.00	7.50
❑	461	Tigers Coaches	10.00	5.00
❑	462	Athletics Coaches	8.00	4.00
❑	463	Dodgers Coaches	8.00	4.00
❑	464	Braves Coaches	8.00	4.00
❑	465	Yankees Coaches	25.00	12.50
❑	466	Phillies Coaches	8.00	4.00
❑	467	Pirates Coaches	8.00	4.00
❑	468	Cardinals Coaches	8.00	4.00
❑	469	Giants Coaches	8.00	4.00
❑	470	Senators Coaches	8.00	4.00
❑	471	Ned Garver	8.00	4.00
❑	472	Alvin Dark	8.00	4.00
❑	473	Al Cicotte	8.00	4.00
❑	474	Haywood Sullivan	8.00	4.00
❑	475	Don Drysdale	40.00	20.00
❑	476	Lou Johnson RC	8.00	4.00
❑	477	Don Ferrarese	8.00	4.00
❑	478	Frank Torre	8.00	4.00
❑	479	Georges Maranda RC	8.00	4.00
❑	480	Yogi Berra	80.00	50.00
❑	481	Wes Stock RC	8.00	4.00
❑	482	Frank Bolling	8.00	4.00
❑	483	Camilo Pascual	8.00	4.00
❑	484	Pittsburgh Pirates CL	40.00	20.00
❑	485	Ken Boyer	15.00	7.50
❑	486	Bobby Del Greco	8.00	4.00
❑	487	Tom Sturdivant	8.00	4.00
❑	488	Norm Cash	25.00	12.50
❑	489	Steve Ridzik	8.00	4.00
❑	490	Frank Robinson	50.00	30.00
❑	491	Mel Roach	8.00	4.00
❑	492	Larry Jackson	8.00	4.00
❑	493	Duke Snider	50.00	30.00
❑	494	Baltimore Orioles CL	25.00	12.50
❑	495	Sherm Lollar	8.00	4.00
❑	496	Bill Virdon	10.00	5.00
❑	497	John Tsitouris	8.00	4.00
❑	498	Al Pilarcik	8.00	4.00
❑	499	Johnny James RC	10.00	5.00
❑	500	Johnny Temple	8.00	4.00
❑	501	Bob Schmidt	8.00	4.00
❑	502	Jim Bunning	25.00	12.50
❑	503	Don Lee	8.00	4.00
❑	504	Seth Morehead	8.00	4.00
❑	505	Ted Kluszewski	25.00	12.50
❑	506	Lee Walls	8.00	4.00
❑	507	Dick Stigman	15.00	7.50
❑	508	Billy Consolo	15.00	7.50
❑	509	Tommy Davis RC	25.00	12.50
❑	510	Gerry Staley	15.00	7.50
❑	511	Ken Walters RC	15.00	7.50
❑	512	Joe Gibbon RC	15.00	7.50
❑	513	Chicago Cubs CL	30.00	15.00
❑	514	Steve Barber RC	15.00	7.50
❑	515	Stan Lopata	15.00	7.50
❑	516	Marty Kutyna RC	15.00	7.50
❑	517	Charlie James RC	25.00	12.50
❑	518	Tony Gonzalez RC	15.00	7.50
❑	519	Ed Roebuck	15.00	7.50
❑	520	Don Buddin	15.00	7.50
❑	521	Mike Lee RC	15.00	7.50
❑	522	Ken Hunt RC	30.00	15.00
❑	523	Clay Dalrymple RC	15.00	7.50
❑	524	Bill Henry	15.00	7.50
❑	525	Marv Breeding RC	15.00	7.50
❑	526	Paul Giel	25.00	12.50
❑	527	Jose Valdivielso	25.00	12.50
❑	528	Ben Johnson RC	15.00	7.50
❑	529	Norm Sherry RC	20.00	10.00
❑	530	Mike McCormick	15.00	7.50
❑	531	Sandy Amoros	20.00	10.00
❑	532	Mike Garcia	20.00	10.00
❑	533	Lu Clinton RC	15.00	7.50
❑	534	Ken MacKenzie RC	15.00	7.50
❑	535	Whitey Lockman	15.00	7.50
❑	536	Wynn Hawkins RC	15.00	7.50
❑	537	Boston Red Sox CL	30.00	15.00
❑	538	Frank Barnes RC	15.00	7.50
❑	539	Gene Baker	15.00	7.50
❑	540	Jerry Walker	15.00	7.50
❑	541	Tony Curry RC	15.00	7.50
❑	542	Ken Hamlin RC	15.00	7.50
❑	543	Elio Chacon RC	15.00	7.50
❑	544	Bill Monbouquette	20.00	10.00
❑	545	Carl Sawatski	15.00	7.50
❑	546	Hank Aguirre	15.00	7.50
❑	547	Bob Aspromonte RC	20.00	10.00
❑	548	Don Mincher RC	15.00	7.50
❑	549	John Buzhardt	15.00	7.50
❑	550	Jim Landis	15.00	7.50
❑	551	Ed Rakow RC	15.00	7.50
❑	552	Walt Bond RC	15.00	7.50
❑	553	Bill Skowron AS	20.00	10.00
❑	554	Willie McCovey AS	40.00	20.00
❑	555	Nellie Fox AS	30.00	15.00
❑	556	Charlie Neal AS	15.00	7.50
❑	557	Frank Malzone AS	15.00	7.50
❑	558	Eddie Mathews AS	40.00	20.00
❑	559	Luis Aparicio AS	30.00	15.00
❑	560	Ernie Banks AS	60.00	35.00
❑	561	Al Kaline AS	60.00	35.00
❑	562	Joe Cunningham AS	15.00	7.50
❑	563	Mickey Mantle AS	250.00	150.00
❑	564	Willie Mays AS	100.00	60.00
❑	565	Roger Maris AS	100.00	60.00
❑	566	Hank Aaron AS	100.00	60.00
❑	567	Sherm Lollar AS	15.00	7.50
❑	568	Del Crandall AS	15.00	7.50
❑	569	Camilo Pascual AS	15.00	7.50
❑	570	Don Drysdale AS	40.00	20.00
❑	571	Billy Pierce AS	15.00	7.50
❑	572	Johnny Antonelli AS	30.00	15.00

❑ 58A Gino Cimoli Cards
❑ NNO Iron-on team transfer 5.00 2.00
❑ 102A Kent Hadley A's

1961 Topps

❑ COMPLETE SET (587) 7000.00 4500.00
❑ COMMON CARD (1-370) 3.00 1.50
❑ COMMON CARD (371-446) 4.00 2.00
❑ COMMON CARD (447-522) 8.00 4.00
❑ COMMON CARD (523-589) 30.00 15.00
❑ NOT ISSUED (587/588)
❑ WRAPPER (1-CENT) 200.00 150.00
❑ WRAP.(1-CENT, REPEAT) 100.00 75.00
❑ WRAPPER (5-CENT) 40.00 30.00
❑ 1 Dick Groat 30.00 15.00
❑ 2 Roger Maris 250.00 150.00
❑ 3 John Buzhardt 3.00 1.50
❑ 4 Lenny Green 3.00 1.50
❑ 5 John Romano 3.00 1.50
❑ 6 Ed Roebuck 3.00 1.50
❑ 7 Chicago White Sox TC 8.00 4.00
❑ 8 Dick Williams 6.00 3.00
❑ 9 Bob Purkey 3.00 1.50
❑ 10 Brooks Robinson 50.00 30.00
❑ 11 Curt Simmons 6.00 3.00
❑ 12 Moe Thacker 3.00 1.50
❑ 13 Chuck Cottier 3.00 1.50
❑ 14 Don Mossi 6.00 3.00
❑ 15 Willie Kirkland 3.00 1.50
❑ 16 Billy Muffett 3.00 1.50
❑ 17 Checklist 1 10.00 5.00
❑ 18 Jim Grant 6.00 3.00
❑ 19 Clete Boyer 8.00 4.00
❑ 20 Robin Roberts 15.00 7.50
❑ 21 Zoilo Versalles UER RC 8.00 4.00
❑ 22 Clem Labine 6.00 3.00
❑ 23 Don Demeter 3.00 1.50
❑ 24 Ken Johnson 6.00 3.00
❑ 25 Pinson/Bell/F.Robinson 8.00 4.00
❑ 26 Wes Stock 3.00 1.50
❑ 27 Jerry Kindall 3.00 1.50
❑ 28 Hector Lopez 6.00 3.00
❑ 29 Don Nottebart 3.00 1.50
❑ 30 Nellie Fox 15.00 7.50
❑ 31 Bob Schmidt 3.00 1.50
❑ 32 Ray Sadecki 3.00 1.50
❑ 33 Gary Geiger 3.00 1.50
❑ 34 Wynn Hawkins 3.00 1.50
❑ 35 Ron Santo RC 40.00 20.00
❑ 36 Jack Kralick RC 3.00 1.50
❑ 37 Charley Maxwell 6.00 3.00
❑ 38 Bob Lillis 3.00 1.50
❑ 39 Leo Posada RC 3.00 1.50
❑ 40 Bob Turley 6.00 3.00
❑ 41 Groat/Mays/Clemente LL 40.00 20.00
❑ 42 Runnels/Minoso/Skow LL 8.00 4.00
❑ 43 Banks/Aaron/Mathews LL 30.00 15.00
❑ 44 Mante/Maris/Colavito LL 80.00 50.00
❑ 45 McCormick/Drysdale LL 8.00 4.00
❑ 46 Baumann/Bunning/Dit LL 8.00 4.00
❑ 47 Broglio/Spahn/Burdette LL 8.00 4.00
❑ 48 Estrada/Perry/Daley LL 8.00 4.00
❑ 49 Drysdale/Koufax LL 20.00 10.00
❑ 50 Bunning/Ramos/Wynn LL 8.00 4.00
❑ 51 Detroit Tigers TC 8.00 4.00
❑ 52 George Crowe 3.00 1.50
❑ 53 Russ Nixon 3.00 1.50
❑ 54 Earl Francis RC 3.00 1.50
❑ 55 Jim Davenport 6.00 3.00
❑ 56 Russ Kemmerer 3.00 1.50
❑ 57 Marv Throneberry 6.00 3.00
❑ 58 Joe Schaffernoth RC 3.00 1.50
❑ 59 Jim Woods 3.00 1.50
❑ 60 Woody Held 3.00 1.50
❑ 61 Ron Piche RC 3.00 1.50
❑ 62 Al Pilarcik 3.00 1.50
❑ 63 Jim Kaat 8.00 4.00
❑ 64 Alex Grammas 3.00 1.50
❑ 65 Ted Kluszewski 8.00 4.00
❑ 66 Bill Henry 3.00 1.50
❑ 67 Ossie Virgil 3.00 1.50
❑ 68 Deron Johnson 6.00 3.00
❑ 69 Earl Wilson 6.00 3.00
❑ 70 Bill Virdon 6.00 3.00
❑ 71 Jerry Adair 3.00 1.50
❑ 72 Stu Miller 6.00 3.00
❑ 73 Al Spangler 3.00 1.50
❑ 74 Joe Pignatano 3.00 1.50
❑ 75 L.McDaniel/L.Jackson 6.00 3.00
❑ 76 Harry Anderson 3.00 1.50
❑ 77 Dick Stigman 3.00 1.50
❑ 78 Lee Walls 6.00 3.00
❑ 79 Joe Ginsberg 3.00 1.50
❑ 80 Harmon Killebrew 20.00 10.00
❑ 81 Tracy Stallard RC 3.00 1.50
❑ 82 Joe Christopher RC 3.00 1.50
❑ 83 Bob Bruce 3.00 1.50
❑ 84 Lee Maye 3.00 1.50
❑ 85 Jerry Walker 3.00 1.50
❑ 86 Los Angeles Dodgers TC 8.00 4.00
❑ 87 Joe Amalfitano 3.00 1.50
❑ 88 Richie Ashburn 15.00 7.50
❑ 89 Billy Martin 15.00 7.50
❑ 90 Gerry Staley 3.00 1.50
❑ 91 Walt Moryn 3.00 1.50
❑ 92 Hal Naragon 3.00 1.50
❑ 93 Tony Gonzalez 3.00 1.50
❑ 94 Johnny Kucks 3.00 1.50
❑ 95 Norm Cash 8.00 4.00
❑ 96 Billy O'Dell 3.00 1.50
❑ 97 Jerry Lynch 6.00 3.00
❑ 98A Checklist 2 Red 10.00 5.00
❑ 98B Checklist 2 Yellow B/W 10.00 5.00
❑ 98C Checklist 2 Yellow W/B 10.00 5.00
❑ 99 Don Buddin UER 3.00 1.50
❑ 100 Harvey Haddix 6.00 3.00
❑ 101 Bubba Phillips 3.00 1.50
❑ 102 Gene Stephens 3.00 1.50
❑ 103 Ruben Amaro 3.00 1.50
❑ 104 John Blanchard 8.00 4.00
❑ 105 Carl Willey 3.00 1.50
❑ 106 Whitey Herzog 3.00 1.50
❑ 107 Seth Morehead 3.00 1.50
❑ 108 Dan Dobbek 3.00 1.50
❑ 109 Johnny Podres 8.00 4.00
❑ 110 Vada Pinson 8.00 4.00
❑ 111 Jack Meyer 3.00 1.50
❑ 112 Chico Fernandez 3.00 1.50
❑ 113 Mike Fornieles 3.00 1.50
❑ 114 Hobie Landrith 3.00 1.50
❑ 115 Johnny Antonelli 6.00 3.00
❑ 116 Joe DeMaestri 3.00 1.50
❑ 117 Dale Long 6.00 3.00
❑ 118 Chris Cannizzaro RC 3.00 1.50
❑ 119 Siebern/Bauer/Lumpe 6.00 3.00
❑ 120 Eddie Mathews 30.00 15.00
❑ 121 Eli Grba 6.00 3.00
❑ 122 Chicago Cubs TC 8.00 4.00
❑ 123 Billy Gardner 3.00 1.50
❑ 124 J.C. Martin 3.00 1.50
❑ 125 Steve Barber 3.00 1.50
❑ 126 Dick Stuart 6.00 3.00
❑ 127 Ron Kline 3.00 1.50
❑ 128 Rip Repulski 3.00 1.50
❑ 129 Ed Hobaugh 3.00 1.50
❑ 130 Norm Larker 3.00 1.50
❑ 131 Paul Richards MG 6.00 3.00
❑ 132 Al Lopez MG 8.00 4.00
❑ 133 Ralph Houk MG 6.00 3.00
❑ 134 Mickey Vernon MG 6.00 3.00
❑ 135 Fred Hutchinson MG 6.00 3.00
❑ 136 Walter Alston MG 8.00 4.00
❑ 137 Chuck Dressen MG 6.00 3.00
❑ 138 Danny Murtaugh MG 6.00 3.00
❑ 139 Solly Hemus MG 6.00 3.00
❑ 140 Gus Triandos 6.00 3.00
❑ 141 Billy Williams RC 60.00 35.00
❑ 142 Luis Arroyo 6.00 3.00
❑ 143 Russ Snyder 3.00 1.50
❑ 144 Jim Coker 3.00 1.50
❑ 145 Bob Buhl 6.00 3.00
❑ 146 Marty Keough 3.00 1.50
❑ 147 Ed Rakow 3.00 1.50
❑ 148 Julian Javier 6.00 3.00
❑ 149 Bob Oldis 3.00 1.50
❑ 150 Willie Mays 100.00 60.00
❑ 151 Jim Donohue 3.00 1.50
❑ 152 Earl Torgeson 3.00 1.50
❑ 153 Don Lee 3.00 1.50
❑ 154 Bobby Del Greco 3.00 1.50
❑ 155 Johnny Temple 6.00 3.00
❑ 156 Ken Hunt 6.00 3.00
❑ 157 Cal McLish 3.00 1.50
❑ 158 Pete Daley 3.00 1.50
❑ 159 Baltimore Orioles TC 8.00 4.00
❑ 160 Whitey Ford UER 50.00 30.00
❑ 161 Sherman Jones UER RC 3.00 1.50
❑ 162 Jay Hook 3.00 1.50
❑ 163 Ed Sadowski 3.00 1.50
❑ 164 Felix Mantilla 3.00 1.50
❑ 165 Gino Cimoli 3.00 1.50
❑ 166 Danny Kravitz 3.00 1.50
❑ 167 San Francisco Giants TC 8.00 4.00
❑ 168 Tommy Davis 8.00 4.00
❑ 169 Don Elston 3.00 1.50
❑ 170 Al Smith 3.00 1.50
❑ 171 Paul Foytack 3.00 1.50
❑ 172 Don Dillard 3.00 1.50
❑ 173 Malzone/Wertz/Jensen 6.00 3.00
❑ 174 Ray Semproch 3.00 1.50
❑ 175 Gene Freese 3.00 1.50
❑ 176 Ken Aspromonte 3.00 1.50
❑ 177 Don Larsen 6.00 3.00
❑ 178 Bob Nieman 3.00 1.50
❑ 179 Joe Koppe 3.00 1.50
❑ 180 Bobby Richardson 12.00 6.00
❑ 181 Fred Green 3.00 1.50
❑ 182 Dave Nicholson RC 3.00 1.50
❑ 183 Andre Rodgers 3.00 1.50
❑ 184 Steve Bilko 6.00 3.00
❑ 185 Herb Score 6.00 3.00
❑ 186 Elmer Valo 6.00 3.00
❑ 187 Billy Klaus 3.00 1.50
❑ 188 Jim Marshall 3.00 1.50
❑ 189A Checklist 3 Copyright 263 10.00 5.00
❑ 189B Checklist 3 Copyright 264 10.00 5.00
❑ 190 Stan Williams 6.00 3.00
❑ 191 Mike de la Hoz RC 3.00 1.50
❑ 192 Dick Brown 3.00 1.50
❑ 193 Gene Conley 6.00 3.00
❑ 194 Gordy Coleman 6.00 3.00
❑ 195 Jerry Casale 3.00 1.50
❑ 196 Ed Bouchee 3.00 1.50
❑ 197 Dick Hall 3.00 1.50
❑ 198 Carl Sawatski 3.00 1.50
❑ 199 Bob Boyd 3.00 1.50
❑ 200 Warren Spahn 40.00 20.00
❑ 201 Pete Whisenant 3.00 1.50
❑ 202 Al Neiger RC 3.00 1.50
❑ 203 Eddie Bressoud 3.00 1.50
❑ 204 Bob Skinner 6.00 3.00
❑ 205 Billy Pierce 6.00 3.00
❑ 206 Gene Green 3.00 1.50
❑ 207 S.Koufax/J.Podres 30.00 15.00
❑ 208 Larry Osborne 3.00 1.50
❑ 209 Ken McBride 3.00 1.50
❑ 210 Pete Runnels 6.00 3.00
❑ 211 Bob Gibson 40.00 20.00
❑ 212 Haywood Sullivan 6.00 3.00
❑ 213 Bill Stafford RC 3.00 1.50
❑ 214 Danny Murphy RC 6.00 3.00
❑ 215 Gus Bell 6.00 3.00
❑ 216 Ted Bowsfield 3.00 1.50
❑ 217 Mel Roach 3.00 1.50
❑ 218 Hal Brown 3.00 1.50
❑ 219 Gene Mauch MG 6.00 3.00
❑ 220 Alvin Dark MG 6.00 3.00
❑ 221 Mike Higgins MG 3.00 1.50
❑ 222 Jimmy Dykes MG 6.00 3.00
❑ 223 Bob Scheffing MG 3.00 1.50

No.	Card		
224	Joe Gordon MG	6.00	3.00
225	Bill Rigney MG	6.00	3.00
226	Cookie Lavagetto MG	6.00	3.00
227	Juan Pizarro	3.00	1.50
228	New York Yankees TC	60.00	35.00
229	Rudy Hernandez RC	3.00	1.50
230	Don Hoak	6.00	3.00
231	Dick Drott	3.00	1.50
232	Bill White	6.00	3.00
233	Joey Jay	6.00	3.00
234	Ted Lepcio	3.00	1.50
235	Camilo Pascual	6.00	3.00
236	Don Gile RC	3.00	1.50
237	Billy Loes	6.00	3.00
238	Jim Gilliam	6.00	3.00
239	Dave Sisler	3.00	1.50
240	Ron Hansen	3.00	1.50
241	Al Cicotte	3.00	1.50
242	Hal Smith	3.00	1.50
243	Frank Lary	6.00	3.00
244	Chico Cardenas	6.00	3.00
245	Joe Adcock	6.00	3.00
246	Bob Davis RC	3.00	1.50
247	Billy Goodman	6.00	3.00
248	Ed Keegan RC	3.00	1.50
249	Cincinnati Reds TC	8.00	4.00
250	V.Law/R.Face	6.00	3.00
251	Bill Bruton	3.00	1.50
252	Bill Short	3.00	1.50
253	Sammy Taylor	3.00	1.50
254	Ted Sadowski RC	6.00	3.00
255	Vic Power	6.00	3.00
256	Billy Hoeft	3.00	1.50
257	Carroll Hardy	3.00	1.50
258	Jack Sanford	6.00	3.00
259	John Schaive RC	3.00	1.50
260	Don Drysdale	30.00	15.00
261	Charlie Lau	6.00	3.00
262	Tony Curry	3.00	1.50
263	Ken Hamlin	3.00	1.50
264	Glen Hobbie	3.00	1.50
265	Tony Kubek	12.00	6.00
266	Lindy McDaniel	6.00	3.00
267	Norm Siebern	3.00	1.50
268	Ike Delock	3.00	1.50
269	Harry Chiti	3.00	1.50
270	Bob Friend	6.00	3.00
271	Jim Landis	3.00	1.50
272	Tom Morgan	3.00	1.50
273A	Checklist 4 Copyright 336	15.00	7.50
273B	Checklist 4 Copyright 339	10.00	5.00
274	Gary Bell	3.00	1.50
275	Gene Woodling	6.00	3.00
276	Ray Rippelmeyer RC	3.00	1.50
277	Hank Foiles	3.00	1.50
278	Don McMahon	3.00	1.50
279	Jose Pagan	3.00	1.50
280	Frank Howard	8.00	4.00
281	Frank Sullivan	3.00	1.50
282	Faye Throneberry	3.00	1.50
283	Bob Anderson	3.00	1.50
284	Dick Gernert	3.00	1.50
285	Sherm Lollar	6.00	3.00
286	George Witt	3.00	1.50
287	Carl Yastrzemski	50.00	30.00
288	Albie Pearson	6.00	3.00
289	Ray Moore	3.00	1.50
290	Stan Musial	100.00	60.00
291	Tex Clevenger	3.00	1.50
292	Jim Baumer RC	3.00	1.50
293	Tom Sturdivant	3.00	1.50
294	Don Blasingame	3.00	1.50
295	Milt Pappas	6.00	3.00
296	Wes Covington	6.00	3.00
297	Kansas City Athletics TC	8.00	4.00
298	Jim Golden RC	3.00	1.50
299	Clay Dalrymple	3.00	1.50
300	Mickey Mantle	600.00	350.00
301	Chet Nichols	3.00	1.50
302	Al Heist RC	3.00	1.50
303	Gary Peters	6.00	3.00
304	Rocky Nelson	3.00	1.50
305	Mike McCormick	6.00	3.00
306	Bill Virdon WS1	10.00	5.00
307	Mickey Mantle WS2	80.00	50.00
308	Bobby Richardson WS3	12.00	6.00
309	Gino Cimoli WS4	10.00	5.00
310	Roy Face WS5	10.00	5.00
311	Whitey Ford WS6	15.00	7.50
312	Bill Mazeroski WS7	20.00	10.00
313	Pirates Celebrate WS	15.00	7.50
314	Bob Miller	3.00	1.50
315	Earl Battey	6.00	3.00
316	Bobby Gene Smith	3.00	1.50
317	Jim Brewer RC	3.00	1.50
318	Danny O'Connell	3.00	1.50
319	Valmy Thomas	3.00	1.50
320	Lou Burdette	6.00	3.00
321	Marv Breeding	3.00	1.50
322	Bill Kunkel RC	6.00	3.00
323	Sammy Esposito	3.00	1.50
324	Hank Aguirre	3.00	1.50
325	Wally Moon	6.00	3.00
326	Dave Hillman	3.00	1.50
327	Matty Alou RC	12.00	6.00
328	Jim O'Toole	6.00	3.00
329	Julio Becquer	3.00	1.50
330	Rocky Colavito	20.00	10.00
331	Ned Garver	3.00	1.50
332	Dutch Dotterer UER	3.00	1.50
333	Fritz Brickell	3.00	1.50
334	Walt Bond	3.00	1.50
335	Frank Bolling	3.00	1.50
336	Don Mincher	6.00	3.00
337	Wynn/Lopez/Score	8.00	4.00
338	Don Landrum	3.00	1.50
339	Gene Baker	3.00	1.50
340	Vic Wertz	6.00	3.00
341	Jim Owens	3.00	1.50
342	Clint Courtney	3.00	1.50
343	Earl Robinson RC	3.00	1.50
344	Sandy Koufax	100.00	60.00
345	Jimmy Piersall	8.00	4.00
346	Howie Nunn	3.00	1.50
347	St. Louis Cardinals TC	8.00	4.00
348	Steve Boros	3.00	1.50
349	Danny McDevitt	3.00	1.50
350	Ernie Banks	40.00	20.00
351	Jim King	3.00	1.50
352	Bob Shaw	3.00	1.50
353	Howie Bedell RC	3.00	1.50
354	Billy Harrell	6.00	3.00
355	Bob Allison	8.00	4.00
356	Ryne Duren	3.00	1.50
357	Daryl Spencer	3.00	1.50
358	Earl Averill Jr.	6.00	3.00
359	Dallas Green	3.00	1.50
360	Frank Robinson	40.00	20.00
361A	Checklist 5 No Ad on Back	15.00	7.50
361B	Checklist 5 Ad on Back	15.00	7.50
362	Frank Funk RC	3.00	1.50
363	John Roseboro	6.00	3.00
364	Moe Drabowsky	6.00	3.00
365	Jerry Lumpe	3.00	1.50
366	Eddie Fisher	3.00	1.50
367	Jim Rivera	3.00	1.50
368	Bennie Daniels	3.00	1.50
369	Dave Philley	3.00	1.50
370	Roy Face	6.00	3.00
371	Bill Skowron SP	50.00	30.00
372	Bob Hendley RC	4.00	2.00
373	Boston Red Sox TC	8.00	4.00
374	Paul Giel	4.00	2.00
375	Ken Boyer	12.00	6.00
376	Mike Roarke RC	6.00	3.00
377	Ruben Gomez	4.00	2.00
378	Wally Post	6.00	3.00
379	Bobby Shantz	4.00	2.00
380	Minnie Minoso	8.00	4.00
381	Dave Wickersham RC	4.00	2.00
382	Frank Thomas	6.00	3.00
383	McCormick/Sanford/O'Dell	6.00	3.00
384	Chuck Essegian	4.00	2.00
385	Jim Perry	6.00	3.00
386	Joe Hicks	4.00	2.00
387	Duke Maas	4.00	2.00
388	Roberto Clemente	125.00	75.00
389	Ralph Terry	6.00	3.00
390	Del Crandall	8.00	4.00
391	Winston Brown RC	4.00	2.00
392	Reno Bertoia	4.00	2.00
393	D.Cardwell/G.Hobbie	4.00	2.00
394	Ken Walters	4.00	2.00
395	Chuck Estrada	6.00	3.00
396	Bob Aspromonte	4.00	2.00
397	Hal Woodeshick	4.00	2.00
398	Hank Bauer	6.00	3.00
399	Cliff Cook RC	4.00	2.00
400	Vern Law	6.00	3.00
401	Babe Ruth 60th HR	60.00	35.00
402	Don Larsen Perfect SP	25.00	12.50
403	26 Inning Tie/Oeschger/Cadore	8.00	4.00
404	Rogers Hornsby .424	12.00	6.00
405	Lou Gehrig Streak	80.00	50.00
406	Mickey Mantle 565 HR	100.00	60.00
407	Jack Chesbro Wins 41	8.00	4.00
408	Christy Mathewson K's SP	20.00	10.00
409	Walter Johnson Shutout	12.00	6.00
410	Harvey Haddix 12 Perfect	8.00	4.00
411	Tony Taylor	6.00	3.00
412	Larry Sherry	6.00	3.00
413	Eddie Yost	6.00	3.00
414	Dick Donovan	6.00	3.00
415	Hank Aaron	125.00	75.00
416	Dick Howser RC	8.00	4.00
417	Juan Marichal SP RC	100.00	60.00
418	Ed Bailey	6.00	3.00
419	Tom Borland	4.00	2.00
420	Ernie Broglio	6.00	3.00
421	Ty Cline SP RC	20.00	10.00
422	Bud Daley	4.00	2.00
423	Charlie Neal SP	20.00	10.00
424	Turk Lown	4.00	2.00
425	Yogi Berra	80.00	50.00
426	Milwaukee Braves TC UER	12.00	6.00
427	Dick Ellsworth	6.00	3.00
428	Ray Barker SP RC	20.00	10.00
429	Al Kaline	50.00	30.00
430	Bill Mazeroski SP	50.00	30.00
431	Chuck Stobbs	4.00	2.00
432	Coot Veal	6.00	3.00
433	Art Mahaffey	4.00	2.00
434	Tom Brewer	4.00	2.00
435	Orlando Cepeda UER	12.00	6.00
436	Jim Maloney SP RC	20.00	10.00
437A	Checklist 6 440 Louis	15.00	7.50
437B	Checklist 6 440 Luis	15.00	7.50
438	Curt Flood	8.00	4.00
439	Phil Regan RC	6.00	3.00
440	Luis Aparicio	12.00	6.00
441	Dick Bertell RC	4.00	2.00
442	Gordon Jones	4.00	2.00
443	Duke Snider	50.00	30.00
444	Joe Nuxhall	6.00	3.00
445	Frank Malzone	6.00	3.00
446	Bob Taylor	4.00	2.00
447	Harry Bright	8.00	4.00
448	Del Rice	15.00	7.50
449	Bob Bolin RC	8.00	4.00
450	Jim Lemon	8.00	4.00
451	Spencer/White/Broglio	8.00	4.00
452	Bob Allen RC	8.00	4.00
453	Dick Schofield	8.00	4.00
454	Pumpsie Green	8.00	4.00
455	Early Wynn	15.00	7.50
456	Hal Bevan	8.00	4.00
457	Johnny James	8.00	4.00
458	Willie Tasby	8.00	4.00
459	Terry Fox RC	10.00	5.00
460	Gil Hodges	25.00	12.50
461	Smoky Burgess	15.00	7.50
462	Lou Klimchock	8.00	4.00
463	Jack Fisher See 426	8.00	4.00
464	Lee Thomas RC	10.00	5.00
465	Roy McMillan	15.00	7.50
466	Ron Moeller RC	8.00	4.00
467	Cleveland Indians TC	12.00	6.00
468	John Callison	10.00	5.00
469	Ralph Lumenti	8.00	4.00
470	Roy Sievers	10.00	5.00
471	Phil Rizzuto MVP	25.00	12.50
472	Yogi Berra MVP SP	50.00	30.00
473	Bob Shantz MVP	8.00	4.00
474	Al Rosen MVP	10.00	5.00
475	Mickey Mantle MVP	200.00	125.00
476	Jackie Jensen MVP	10.00	5.00
477	Nellie Fox MVP	15.00	7.50
478	Roger Maris MVP	60.00	35.00

❑ 479 Jim Konstanty MVP 8.00 4.00
❑ 480 Roy Campanella MVP 40.00 20.00
❑ 481 Hank Sauer MVP 8.00 4.00
❑ 482 Willie Mays MVP 50.00 30.00
❑ 483 Don Newcombe MVP 10.00 5.00
❑ 484 Hank Aaron MVP 50.00 30.00
❑ 485 Ernie Banks MVP 40.00 20.00
❑ 486 Dick Groat MVP 10.00 5.00
❑ 487 Gene Oliver 8.00 4.00
❑ 488 Joe McClain RC 10.00 5.00
❑ 489 Walt Dropo 8.00 4.00
❑ 490 Jim Bunning 25.00 12.50
❑ 491 Philadelphia Phillies TC 12.00 6.00
❑ 492 Ron Fairly 10.00 5.00
❑ 493 Don Zimmer UER 10.00 5.00
❑ 494 Tom Cheney 15.00 7.50
❑ 495 Elston Howard 10.00 5.00
❑ 496 Ken MacKenzie 8.00 4.00
❑ 497 Willie Jones 8.00 4.00
❑ 498 Ray Herbert 8.00 4.00
❑ 499 Chuck Schilling RC 8.00 4.00
❑ 500 Harvey Kuenn 10.00 5.00
❑ 501 John DeMerit RC 8.00 4.00
❑ 502 Choo Choo Coleman RC 10.00 5.00
❑ 503 Tito Francona 8.00 4.00
❑ 504 Billy Consolo 8.00 4.00
❑ 505 Red Schoendienst 15.00 7.50
❑ 506 Willie Davis RC 15.00 7.50
❑ 507 Pete Burnside 8.00 4.00
❑ 508 Rocky Bridges 8.00 4.00
❑ 509 Camilo Carreon 8.00 4.00
❑ 510 Art Ditmar 8.00 4.00
❑ 511 Joe M. Morgan 8.00 4.00
❑ 512 Bob Will 8.00 4.00
❑ 513 Jim Brosnan 8.00 4.00
❑ 514 Jake Wood RC 8.00 4.00
❑ 515 Jackie Brandt 8.00 4.00
❑ 516 Checklist 7 15.00 7.50
❑ 517 Willie McCovey 40.00 20.00
❑ 518 Andy Carey 8.00 4.00
❑ 519 Jim Pagliaroni RC 8.00 4.00
❑ 520 Joe Cunningham 8.00 4.00
❑ 521 N.Sherry/L.Sherry 8.00 4.00
❑ 522 Dick Farrell UER 15.00 7.50
❑ 523 Joe Gibbon 30.00 15.00
❑ 524 Johnny Logan 30.00 15.00
❑ 525 Ron Perranoski RC 60.00 35.00
❑ 526 R.C. Stevens 30.00 15.00
❑ 527 Gene Leek RC 30.00 15.00
❑ 528 Pedro Ramos 30.00 15.00
❑ 529 Bob Roselli 30.00 15.00
❑ 530 Bob Malkmus 30.00 15.00
❑ 531 Jim Coates 50.00 25.00
❑ 532 Bob Hale 30.00 15.00
❑ 533 Jack Curtis RC 30.00 15.00
❑ 534 Eddie Kasko 40.00 20.00
❑ 535 Larry Jackson 30.00 15.00
❑ 536 Bill Tuttle 30.00 15.00
❑ 537 Bobby Locke 30.00 15.00
❑ 538 Chuck Hiller RC 30.00 15.00
❑ 539 Johnny Klippstein 30.00 15.00
❑ 540 Jackie Jensen 40.00 20.00
❑ 541 Rollie Sheldon RC 50.00 25.00
❑ 542 Minnesota Twins TC 60.00 35.00
❑ 543 Roger Craig 40.00 20.00
❑ 544 George Thomas RC 50.00 25.00
❑ 545 Hoyt Wilhelm 60.00 35.00
❑ 546 Marty Kutyna 30.00 15.00
❑ 547 Leon Wagner 30.00 15.00
❑ 548 Ted Wills 30.00 15.00
❑ 549 Hal R. Smith 30.00 15.00
❑ 550 Frank Baumann 30.00 15.00
❑ 551 George Altman 40.00 20.00
❑ 552 Jim Archer RC 30.00 15.00
❑ 553 Bill Fischer 30.00 15.00
❑ 554 Pittsburgh Pirates TC 80.00 50.00
❑ 555 Sam Jones 30.00 15.00
❑ 556 Ken R. Hunt RC 30.00 15.00
❑ 557 Jose Valdivielso 30.00 15.00
❑ 558 Don Ferrarese 30.00 15.00
❑ 559 Jim Gentile 60.00 35.00
❑ 560 Barry Latman 40.00 20.00
❑ 561 Charley James 30.00 15.00
❑ 562 Bill Monbouquette 30.00 15.00
❑ 563 Bob Cerv 60.00 35.00
❑ 564 Don Cardwell 30.00 15.00
❑ 565 Felipe Alou 50.00 25.00
❑ 566 Paul Richards AS MG 30.00 15.00
❑ 567 Danny Murtaugh AS MG 30.00 15.00
❑ 568 Bill Skowron AS 50.00 25.00
❑ 569 Frank Herrera AS 40.00 20.00
❑ 570 Nellie Fox AS 60.00 35.00
❑ 571 Bill Mazeroski AS 60.00 35.00
❑ 572 Brooks Robinson AS 80.00 50.00
❑ 573 Ken Boyer AS 50.00 25.00
❑ 574 Luis Aparicio AS 60.00 35.00
❑ 575 Ernie Banks AS 80.00 50.00
❑ 576 Roger Maris AS 175.00 100.00
❑ 577 Hank Aaron AS 150.00 90.00
❑ 578 Mickey Mantle AS 500.00 300.00
❑ 579 Willie Mays AS 150.00 90.00
❑ 580 Al Kaline AS 80.00 50.00
❑ 581 Frank Robinson AS 80.00 50.00
❑ 582 Earl Battey AS 30.00 15.00
❑ 583 Del Crandall AS 30.00 15.00
❑ 584 Jim Perry AS 30.00 15.00
❑ 585 Bob Friend AS 30.00 15.00
❑ 586 Whitey Ford AS 100.00 60.00
❑ 589 Warren Spahn AS 100.00 60.00

1962 Topps

❑ COMP. MASTER SET (689) 7000.00 6000.00
❑ COMPLETE SET (598) 6000.00 4500.00
❑ COMMON CARD (1-370) 5.00 2.50
❑ COMMON CARD (371-446) 6.00 3.00
❑ COMMON CARD (447-522) 12.00 6.00
❑ COMMON CARD (523-598) 20.00 10.00
❑ WRAPPER (1-CENT) 100.00 75.00
❑ WRAPPER (5-CENT) 30.00 20.00
❑ 1 Roger Maris 500.00 300.00
❑ 2 Jim Brosnan 5.00 2.50
❑ 3 Pete Runnels 5.00 2.50
❑ 4 John DeMerit 8.00 4.00
❑ 5 Sandy Koufax UER 150.00 90.00
❑ 6 Marv Breeding 5.00 2.50
❑ 7 Frank Thomas 10.00 5.00
❑ 8 Ray Herbert 5.00 2.50
❑ 9 Jim Davenport 8.00 4.00
❑ 10 Roberto Clemente 200.00 125.00
❑ 11 Tom Morgan 5.00 2.50
❑ 12 Harry Craft MG 8.00 4.00
❑ 13 Dick Howser 8.00 4.00
❑ 14 Bill White 8.00 4.00
❑ 15 Dick Donovan 5.00 2.50
❑ 16 Darrell Johnson 5.00 2.50
❑ 17 Johnny Callison 8.00 4.00
❑ 18 M.Mantle/W.Mays 175.00 100.00
❑ 19 Ray Washburn RC 5.00 2.50
❑ 20 Rocky Colavito 15.00 7.50
❑ 21 Jim Kaat 8.00 4.00
❑ 22A Checklist 1 ERR 12.00 6.00
❑ 22B Checklist 1 COR 12.00 6.00
❑ 23 Norm Larker 5.00 2.50
❑ 24 Detroit Tigers TC 10.00 5.00
❑ 25 Ernie Banks 50.00 30.00
❑ 26 Chris Cannizzaro 8.00 4.00
❑ 27 Chuck Cottier 5.00 2.50
❑ 28 Minnie Minoso 10.00 5.00
❑ 29 Casey Stengel MG 20.00 10.00
❑ 30 Eddie Mathews 40.00 20.00
❑ 31 Tom Tresh RC 15.00 7.50
❑ 32 John Roseboro 8.00 4.00
❑ 33 Don Larsen 8.00 4.00
❑ 34 Johnny Temple 8.00 4.00
❑ 35 Don Schwall RC 10.00 5.00
❑ 36 Don Leppert RC 5.00 2.50
❑ 37 Latman/Stigman/Perry 5.00 2.50
❑ 38 Gene Stephens 5.00 2.50
❑ 39 Joe Koppe 5.00 2.50
❑ 40 Orlando Cepeda 15.00 7.50
❑ 41 Cliff Cook 5.00 2.50
❑ 42 Jim King 5.00 2.50
❑ 43 Los Angeles Dodgers TC 10.00 5.00
❑ 44 Don Taussig RC 5.00 2.50
❑ 45 Brooks Robinson 50.00 30.00
❑ 46 Jack Baldschun RC 5.00 2.50
❑ 47 Bob Will 5.00 2.50
❑ 48 Ralph Terry 8.00 4.00
❑ 49 Hal Jones RC 5.00 2.50
❑ 50 Stan Musial 100.00 60.00
❑ 51 Cash/Kaline/Howard LL 8.00 4.00
❑ 52 Clemente/Pins/Boyer LL 20.00 10.00
❑ 53 Maris/Mantle/Kill LL 100.00 60.00
❑ 54 Cepeda/Mays/F.Rob LL 20.00 10.00
❑ 55 Donovan/Staff/Mossi LL 8.00 4.00
❑ 56 Spahn/O'Toole/Simm LL 8.00 4.00
❑ 57 Ford/Lary/Bunning LL 8.00 4.00
❑ 58 Spahn/Jay/O'Toole LL 8.00 4.00
❑ 59 Pascual/Ford/Bunning LL 8.00 4.00
❑ 60 Koufax/Will/Drysdale LL 20.00 10.00
❑ 61 St. Louis Cardinals TC 10.00 5.00
❑ 62 Steve Boros 5.00 2.50
❑ 63 Tony Cloninger RC 8.00 4.00
❑ 64 Russ Snyder 5.00 2.50
❑ 65 Bobby Richardson 10.00 5.00
❑ 66 Cuno Barragan RC 5.00 2.50
❑ 67 Harvey Haddix 8.00 4.00
❑ 68 Ken Hunt 5.00 2.50
❑ 69 Phil Ortega RC 5.00 2.50
❑ 70 Harmon Killebrew 25.00 12.50
❑ 71 Dick LeMay RC 5.00 2.50
❑ 72 Boros/Scheffing/Wood 5.00 2.50
❑ 73 Nellie Fox 20.00 10.00
❑ 74 Bob Lillis 8.00 4.00
❑ 75 Milt Pappas 8.00 4.00
❑ 76 Howie Bedell 5.00 2.50
❑ 77 Tony Taylor 8.00 4.00
❑ 78 Gene Green 5.00 2.50
❑ 79 Ed Hobaugh 5.00 2.50
❑ 80 Vada Pinson 8.00 4.00
❑ 81 Jim Pagliaroni 5.00 2.50
❑ 82 Deron Johnson 8.00 4.00
❑ 83 Larry Jackson 5.00 2.50
❑ 84 Lenny Green 5.00 2.50
❑ 85 Gil Hodges 20.00 10.00
❑ 86 Donn Clendenon RC 8.00 4.00
❑ 87 Mike Roarke 5.00 2.50
❑ 88 Ralph Houk MG 8.00 4.00
❑ 89 Barney Schultz RC 5.00 2.50
❑ 90 Jimmy Piersall 8.00 4.00
❑ 91 J.C. Martin 5.00 2.50
❑ 92 Sam Jones 5.00 2.50
❑ 93 John Blanchard 8.00 4.00
❑ 94 Jay Hook 8.00 4.00
❑ 95 Don Hoak 8.00 4.00
❑ 96 Eli Grba 5.00 2.50
❑ 97 Tito Francona 5.00 2.50
❑ 98 Checklist 2 12.00 6.00
❑ 99 Boog Powell RC 30.00 15.00
❑ 100 Warren Spahn 40.00 20.00
❑ 101 Carroll Hardy 5.00 2.50
❑ 102 Al Schroll 5.00 2.50
❑ 103 Don Blasingame 5.00 2.50
❑ 104 Ted Savage RC 5.00 2.50
❑ 105 Don Mossi 8.00 4.00
❑ 106 Carl Sawatski 5.00 2.50
❑ 107 Mike McCormick 8.00 4.00
❑ 108 Willie Davis 8.00 4.00
❑ 109 Bob Shaw 5.00 2.50
❑ 110 Bill Skowron 8.00 4.00
❑ 110A Bill Skowron Green Tint 8.00 4.00
❑ 111 Dallas Green 8.00 4.00
❑ 111A Dallas Green Green Tint 8.00 4.00
❑ 112 Hank Foiles 5.00 2.50
❑ 112A Hank Foiles Green Tint 5.00 2.50
❑ 113 Chicago White Sox TC 10.00 5.00
❑ 113A Chicago White Sox TC Green Tint 10.00 5.00
❑ 114 Howie Koplitz RC 5.00 2.50
❑ 114A Howie Koplitz Green Tint 5.00 2.50
❑ 115 Bob Skinner 8.00 4.00

❑ 115A Bob Skinner Green Tint 8.00 4.00
❑ 116 Herb Score 8.00 4.00
❑ 116A Herb Score Green Tint 8.00 4.00
❑ 117 Gary Geiger 8.00 4.00
❑ 117A Gary Geiger Green Tint 8.00 4.00
❑ 118 Julian Javier 8.00 4.00
❑ 118A Julian Javier Green Tint 8.00 4.00
❑ 119 Danny Murphy 5.00 2.50
❑ 119A Danny Murphy Green Tint 5.00 2.50
❑ 120 Bob Purkey 5.00 2.50
❑ 120A Bob Purkey Green Tint 5.00 2.50
❑ 121 Billy Hitchcock MG 5.00 2.50
❑ 121A Billy Hitchcock Green Tint 5.00 2.50
❑ 122 Norm Bass RC 5.00 2.50
❑ 122A Norm Bass Green Tint 5.00 2.50
❑ 123 Mike de la Hoz 5.00 2.50
❑ 123A Mike de la Hoz Green Tint 5.00 2.50
❑ 124 Bill Pleis RC 5.00 2.50
❑ 124A Bill Pleis Green Tint 5.00 2.50
❑ 125 Gene Woodling 8.00 4.00
❑ 125A Gene Woodling Green Tint 8.00 4.00
❑ 126 Al Cicotte 5.00 2.50
❑ 126A Al Cicotte Green Tint 5.00 2.50
❑ 127 Siebern/Bauer/Lumpe 5.00 2.50
❑ 127A Siebern/Bauer/Lumpe Green Tint 5.00 2.50
❑ 128 Art Fowler 5.00 2.50
❑ 128A Art Fowler Green Tint 5.00 2.50
❑ 129A Lee Walls Facing Right 5.00 2.50
❑ 129B Lee Walls Facing Left 30.00 15.00
❑ 130 Frank Bolling 5.00 2.50
❑ 130A Frank Bolling Green Tint 5.00 2.50
❑ 131 Pete Richert RC 5.00 2.50
❑ 131A Pete Richert Green Tint 5.00 2.50
❑ 132A Los Angeles Angels TC w/o Photo 10.00 5.00
❑ 132B Los Angeles Angels TC w/Photo 30.00 15.00
❑ 133 Felipe Alou 8.00 4.00
❑ 133A Felipe Alou Green Tint 8.00 4.00
❑ 134A Billy Hoeft 5.00 2.50
❑ 134B Billy Hoeft Green Tint 30.00 15.00
❑ 135 Babe Ruth Boy 20.00 10.00
❑ 135A Babe Ruth Boy Green 20.00 10.00
❑ 136 B.Ruth/J.Ruppert 20.00 10.00
❑ 136A B.Ruth/J.Ruppert Green 20.00 10.00
❑ 137 B.Ruth/M.Huggins 20.00 10.00
❑ 137A B.Ruth/M.Huggins Green 20.00 10.00
❑ 138 Babe Ruth Slugger 20.00 10.00
❑ 138A Babe Ruth Slugger Green 20.00 10.00
❑ 139A Babe Ruth Story 30.00 15.00
❑ 139B Hal Reniff Portrait 15.00 7.50
❑ 139C Hal Reniff Pitching 60.00 35.00
❑ 140 B.Ruth/L.Gehrig 60.00 35.00
❑ 140A B.Ruth/L.Gehrig Green 60.00 35.00
❑ 141 Babe Ruth Twilight 20.00 10.00
❑ 141A Babe Ruth Twilight Green 20.00 10.00
❑ 142 Babe Ruth Coaching 20.00 10.00
❑ 142A Babe Ruth Coaching Green 20.00 10.00
❑ 143 Babe Ruth Sports Hero 20.00 10.00
❑ 143A Babe Ruth Sports Hero Green 20.00 10.00
❑ 144 Babe Ruth Farewell Speech 20.00 10.00
❑ 144A B.Ruth Farewell Speech Green 20.00 10.00
❑ 145 Barry Latman 5.00 2.50
❑ 145A Barry Latman Green Tint 5.00 2.50
❑ 146 Don Demeter 5.00 2.50
❑ 146A Don Demeter Green Tint 5.00 2.50
❑ 147A Bill Kunkel Portrait 5.00 2.50
❑ 147B Bill Kunkel Pitching 30.00 15.00
❑ 148 Wally Post 5.00 2.50
❑ 148A Wally Post Green Tint 5.00 2.50
❑ 149 Bob Duliba 5.00 2.50
❑ 149A Bob Duliba Green Tint 5.00 2.50
❑ 150 Al Kaline 50.00 30.00
❑ 150A Al Kaline Green Tint 50.00 30.00
❑ 151 Johnny Klippstein 5.00 2.50
❑ 151A Johnny Klippstei Green Tint 5.00 2.50
❑ 152 Mickey Vernon MG 8.00 4.00
❑ 152A Mickey Vernon MG Green Tint 8.00 4.00
❑ 153 Pumpsie Green 6.00 3.00
❑ 153A Pumpsie Green Green Tint 6.00 3.00
❑ 154 Lee Thomas 6.00 3.00
❑ 154A Lee Thomas Green Tint 6.00 3.00
❑ 155 Stu Miller 6.00 3.00
❑ 155A Stu Miller Green Tint 6.00 3.00
❑ 156 Merritt Ranew RC 5.00 2.50
❑ 156A Merritt Ranew Green Tint 5.00 2.50
❑ 157 Wes Covington 8.00 4.00
❑ 157A Wes Covington Green Tint 8.00 4.00
❑ 158 Milwaukee Braves TC 10.00 5.00
❑ 158A Milwaukee Braves TC Green Tint 15.00 7.50
❑ 159 Hal Reniff RC 8.00 4.00
❑ 160 Dick Stuart 8.00 4.00
❑ 160A Dick Stuart Green Tint 8.00 4.00
❑ 161 Frank Baumann 5.00 2.50
❑ 161A Frank Baumann Green Tint 5.00 2.50
❑ 162 Sammy Drake RC 5.00 2.50
❑ 162A Sammy Drake Green Tint 5.00 2.50
❑ 163 B.Gardner/C.Boyer 8.00 4.00
❑ 163A B.Gardner/C.Boyer Green Tint 8.00 4.00
❑ 164 Hal Naragon 5.00 2.50
❑ 164A Hal Naragon Green Tint 5.00 2.50
❑ 165 Jackie Brandt 5.00 2.50
❑ 165A Jackie Brandt Green Tint 5.00 2.50
❑ 166 Don Lee 5.00 2.50
❑ 166A Don Lee Green Tint 5.00 2.50
❑ 167 Tim McCarver RC 30.00 15.00
❑ 167A Tim McCarver Green Tint 30.00 15.00
❑ 168 Leo Posada 5.00 2.50
❑ 168A Leo Posada Green Tint 5.00 2.50
❑ 169 Bob Cerv 10.00 5.00
❑ 169A Bob Cerv Green Tint 10.00 5.00
❑ 170 Ron Santo 15.00 7.50
❑ 170A Ron Santo Green Tint 15.00 7.50
❑ 171 Dave Sisler 5.00 2.50
❑ 171A Dave Sisler Green Tint 5.00 2.50
❑ 172 Fred Hutchinson MG 8.00 4.00
❑ 172A Fred Hutchinson MG Green Tint 8.00 4.00
❑ 173 Chico Fernandez 5.00 2.50
❑ 173A Chico Fernandez Green Tint 5.00 2.50
❑ 174A Carl Willey w/o Cap 5.00 2.50
❑ 174B Carl Willey w/Cap 30.00 15.00
❑ 175 Frank Howard 10.00 5.00
❑ 175A Frank Howard Green Tint 10.00 5.00
❑ 176A Eddie Yost Portrait 5.00 2.50
❑ 176B Eddie Yost Batting 30.00 15.00
❑ 177 Bobby Shantz 8.00 4.00
❑ 177A Bobby Shantz Green Tint 8.00 4.00
❑ 178 Camilo Carreon 5.00 2.50
❑ 178A Camilo Carreon Green Tint 5.00 2.50
❑ 179 Tom Sturdivant 5.00 2.50
❑ 179A Tom Sturdivant Green Tint 5.00 2.50
❑ 180 Bob Allison 10.00 5.00
❑ 180A Bob Allison Green Tint 10.00 5.00
❑ 181 Paul Brown RC 5.00 2.50
❑ 181A Paul Brown Green Tint 5.00 2.50
❑ 182 Bob Nieman 5.00 2.50
❑ 182A Bob Nieman Green Tint 5.00 2.50
❑ 183 Roger Craig 8.00 4.00
❑ 183A Roger Craig Green Tint 8.00 4.00
❑ 184 Haywood Sullivan 8.00 4.00
❑ 184A Haywood Sullivan Green Tint 8.00 4.00
❑ 185 Roland Sheldon 10.00 5.00
❑ 185A Roland Sheldon Green Tint 10.00 5.00
❑ 186 Mack Jones RC 5.00 2.50
❑ 186A Mack Jones Green Tint 5.00 2.50
❑ 187 Gene Conley 5.00 2.50
❑ 187A Gene Conley Green Tint 5.00 2.50
❑ 188 Chuck Hiller 5.00 2.50
❑ 188A Chuck Hiller Green Tint 5.00 2.50
❑ 189 Dick Hall 5.00 2.50
❑ 189A Dick Hall Green Tint 5.00 2.50
❑ 190A Wally Moon Portrait 8.00 4.00
❑ 190B Wally Moon Batting 30.00 15.00
❑ 191 Jim Brewer 5.00 2.50
❑ 191A Jim Brewer Green Tint 5.00 2.50
❑ 192A Checklist 3 w/o Comma 12.00 6.00
❑ 192B Checklist 3 w/Comma 15.00 7.50
❑ 193 Eddie Kasko 5.00 2.50
❑ 193A Eddie Kasko Green Tint 5.00 2.50
❑ 194 Dean Chance RC 8.00 4.00
❑ 194A Dean Chance Green Tint 8.00 4.00
❑ 195 Joe Cunningham 5.00 2.50
❑ 195A Joe Cunningham Green Tint 5.00 2.50
❑ 196 Terry Fox 5.00 2.50
❑ 196A Terry Fox Green Tint 5.00 2.50
❑ 197 Daryl Spencer 5.00 2.50
❑ 198 Johnny Keane MG 5.00 2.50
❑ 199 Gaylord Perry RC 80.00 50.00
❑ 200 Mickey Mantle 600.00 350.00
❑ 201 Ike Delock 5.00 2.50
❑ 202 Carl Warwick RC 5.00 2.50
❑ 203 Jack Fisher 5.00 2.50
❑ 204 Johnny Weekly RC 5.00 2.50
❑ 205 Gene Freese 5.00 2.50
❑ 206 Washington Senators TC 10.00 5.00
❑ 207 Pete Burnside 5.00 2.50
❑ 208 Billy Martin 20.00 10.00
❑ 209 Jim Fregosi RC 15.00 7.50
❑ 210 Roy Face 8.00 4.00
❑ 211 F.Bolling/R.McMillan 5.00 2.50
❑ 212 Jim Owens 5.00 2.50
❑ 213 Richie Ashburn 20.00 10.00
❑ 214 Dom Zanni 5.00 2.50
❑ 215 Woody Held 5.00 2.50
❑ 216 Ron Kline 5.00 2.50
❑ 217 Walter Alston MG 10.00 5.00
❑ 218 Joe Torre RC 40.00 20.00
❑ 219 Al Downing RC 8.00 4.00
❑ 220 Roy Sievers 8.00 4.00
❑ 221 Bill Short 5.00 2.50
❑ 222 Jerry Zimmerman 5.00 2.50
❑ 223 Alex Grammas 5.00 2.50
❑ 224 Don Rudolph 5.00 2.50
❑ 225 Frank Malzone 8.00 4.00
❑ 226 San Francisco Giants TC 10.00 5.00
❑ 227 Bob Tiefenauer 5.00 2.50
❑ 228 Dale Long 10.00 5.00
❑ 229 Jesus McFarlane RC 5.00 2.50
❑ 230 Camilo Pascual 8.00 4.00
❑ 231 Ernie Bowman RC 5.00 2.50
❑ 232 Yanks Win Opener WS1 10.00 5.00
❑ 233 Joey Jay WS2 10.00 5.00
❑ 234 Roger Maris WS3 25.00 12.50
❑ 235 Whitey Ford WS4 15.00 7.50
❑ 236 Yanks Crush Reds WS5 10.00 5.00
❑ 237 Yanks Celebrate WS 10.00 5.00
❑ 238 Norm Sherry 5.00 2.50
❑ 239 Cecil Butler RC 5.00 2.50
❑ 240 George Altman 5.00 2.50
❑ 241 Johnny Kucks 5.00 2.50
❑ 242 Mel McGaha MG RC 5.00 2.50
❑ 243 Robin Roberts 15.00 7.50
❑ 244 Don Gile 5.00 2.50
❑ 245 Ron Hansen 5.00 2.50
❑ 246 Art Ditmar 5.00 2.50
❑ 247 Joe Pignatano 5.00 2.50
❑ 248 Bob Aspromonte 8.00 4.00
❑ 249 Ed Keegan 5.00 2.50
❑ 250 Norm Cash 10.00 5.00
❑ 251 New York Yankees TC 50.00 30.00
❑ 252 Earl Francis 5.00 2.50
❑ 253 Harry Chiti CO 5.00 2.50
❑ 254 Gordon Windhorn RC 5.00 2.50
❑ 255 Juan Pizarro 5.00 2.50
❑ 256 Elio Chacon 8.00 4.00
❑ 257 Jack Spring RC 5.00 2.50
❑ 258 Marty Keough 5.00 2.50
❑ 259 Lou Klimchock 5.00 2.50
❑ 260 Billy Pierce 8.00 4.00
❑ 261 George Alusik RC 5.00 2.50
❑ 262 Bob Schmidt 5.00 2.50
❑ 263 Purkey/Turner/Jay 5.00 2.50
❑ 264 Dick Ellsworth 8.00 4.00
❑ 265 Joe Adcock 8.00 4.00
❑ 266 John Anderson RC 5.00 2.50
❑ 267 Dan Dobbek 5.00 2.50
❑ 268 Ken McBride 5.00 2.50
❑ 269 Bob Oldis 5.00 2.50
❑ 270 Dick Groat 8.00 4.00
❑ 271 Ray Rippelmeyer 5.00 2.50
❑ 272 Earl Robinson 5.00 2.50
❑ 273 Gary Bell 5.00 2.50
❑ 274 Sammy Taylor 5.00 2.50
❑ 275 Norm Siebern 5.00 2.50
❑ 276 Hal Kolstad RC 5.00 2.50
❑ 277 Checklist 4 15.00 7.50
❑ 278 Ken Johnson 8.00 4.00
❑ 279 Hobie Landrith UER 8.00 4.00
❑ 280 Johnny Podres 8.00 4.00
❑ 281 Jake Gibbs RC 10.00 5.00
❑ 282 Dave Hillman 5.00 2.50
❑ 283 Charlie Smith RC 5.00 2.50
❑ 284 Ruben Amaro 5.00 2.50
❑ 285 Curt Simmons 8.00 4.00

❑ 286	Al Lopez MG	10.00	5.00
❑ 287	George Witt	5.00	2.50
❑ 288	Billy Williams	30.00	15.00
❑ 289	Mike Krsnich RC	5.00	2.50
❑ 290	Jim Gentile	8.00	4.00
❑ 291	Hal Stowe RC	5.00	2.50
❑ 292	Jerry Kindall	5.00	2.50
❑ 293	Bob Miller	8.00	4.00
❑ 294	Philadelphia Phillies TC	10.00	5.00
❑ 295	Vern Law	8.00	4.00
❑ 296	Ken Hamlin	5.00	2.50
❑ 297	Ron Perranoski	8.00	4.00
❑ 298	Bill Tuttle	5.00	2.50
❑ 299	Don Wert RC	5.00	2.50
❑ 300	Willie Mays	250.00	150.00
❑ 301	Galen Cisco RC	5.00	2.50
❑ 302	Johnny Edwards RC	5.00	2.50
❑ 303	Frank Torre	8.00	4.00
❑ 304	Dick Farrell	8.00	4.00
❑ 305	Jerry Lumpe	5.00	2.50
❑ 306	L.McDaniel/L.Jackson	5.00	2.50
❑ 307	Jim Grant	8.00	4.00
❑ 308	Neil Chrisley	8.00	4.00
❑ 309	Moe Morhardt RC	5.00	2.50
❑ 310	Whitey Ford	50.00	30.00
❑ 311	Tony Kubek IA	8.00	4.00
❑ 312	Warren Spahn IA	15.00	7.50
❑ 313	Roger Maris IA	80.00	50.00
❑ 314	Rocky Colavito IA	8.00	4.00
❑ 315	Whitey Ford IA	15.00	7.50
❑ 316	Harmon Killebrew IA	15.00	7.50
❑ 317	Stan Musial IA	20.00	10.00
❑ 318	Mickey Mantle IA	150.00	90.00
❑ 319	Mike McCormick IA	5.00	2.50
❑ 320	Hank Aaron	150.00	90.00
❑ 321	Lee Stange RC	5.00	2.50
❑ 322	Alvin Dark MG	8.00	4.00
❑ 323	Don Landrum	5.00	2.50
❑ 324	Joe McClain	5.00	2.50
❑ 325	Luis Aparicio	15.00	7.50
❑ 326	Tom Parsons RC	5.00	2.50
❑ 327	Ozzie Virgil	5.00	2.50
❑ 328	Ken Walters	5.00	2.50
❑ 329	Bob Bolin	5.00	2.50
❑ 330	John Romano	5.00	2.50
❑ 331	Moe Drabowsky	8.00	4.00
❑ 332	Don Buddin	5.00	2.50
❑ 333	Frank Cipriani RC	5.00	2.50
❑ 334	Boston Red Sox TC	10.00	5.00
❑ 335	Bill Bruton	5.00	2.50
❑ 336	Billy Muffett	5.00	2.50
❑ 337	Jim Marshall	8.00	4.00
❑ 338	Billy Gardner	5.00	2.50
❑ 339	Jose Valdivielso	5.00	2.50
❑ 340	Don Drysdale	50.00	30.00
❑ 341	Mike Hershberger RC	5.00	2.50
❑ 342	Ed Rakow	5.00	2.50
❑ 343	Albie Pearson	8.00	4.00
❑ 344	Ed Bauta RC	5.00	2.50
❑ 345	Chuck Schilling	5.00	2.50
❑ 346	Jack Kralick	5.00	2.50
❑ 347	Chuck Hinton RC	5.00	2.50
❑ 348	Larry Burright RC	8.00	4.00
❑ 349	Paul Foytack	5.00	2.50
❑ 350	Frank Robinson	50.00	30.00
❑ 351	J.Torre/D.Crandall	8.00	4.00
❑ 352	Frank Sullivan	5.00	2.50
❑ 353	Bill Mazeroski	15.00	7.50
❑ 354	Roman Mejias	8.00	4.00
❑ 355	Steve Barber	5.00	2.50
❑ 356	Tom Haller RC	5.00	2.50
❑ 357	Jerry Walker	5.00	2.50
❑ 358	Tommy Davis	8.00	4.00
❑ 359	Bobby Locke	5.00	2.50
❑ 360	Yogi Berra	80.00	50.00
❑ 361	Bob Hendley	5.00	2.50
❑ 362	Ty Cline	5.00	2.50
❑ 363	Bob Roselli	5.00	2.50
❑ 364	Ken Hunt	5.00	2.50
❑ 365	Charlie Neal	8.00	4.00
❑ 366	Phil Regan	8.00	4.00
❑ 367	Checklist 5	15.00	7.50
❑ 368	Bob Tillman RC	5.00	2.50
❑ 369	Ted Bowsfield	5.00	2.50
❑ 370	Ken Boyer	10.00	5.00
❑ 371	Earl Battey	6.00	3.00
❑ 372	Jack Curtis	6.00	3.00
❑ 373	Al Heist	6.00	3.00
❑ 374	Gene Mauch MG	10.00	5.00
❑ 375	Ron Fairly	10.00	5.00
❑ 376	Bud Daley	8.00	4.00
❑ 377	John Orsino RC	6.00	3.00
❑ 378	Bennie Daniels	6.00	3.00
❑ 379	Chuck Essegian	6.00	3.00
❑ 380	Lew Burdette	10.00	5.00
❑ 381	Chico Cardenas	10.00	5.00
❑ 382	Dick Williams	8.00	4.00
❑ 383	Ray Sadecki	6.00	3.00
❑ 384	Kansas City Athletics TC	10.00	5.00
❑ 385	Early Wynn	15.00	7.50
❑ 386	Don Mincher	8.00	4.00
❑ 387	Lou Brock RC	125.00	75.00
❑ 388	Ryne Duren	8.00	4.00
❑ 389	Smoky Burgess	10.00	5.00
❑ 390	Orlando Cepeda AS	10.00	5.00
❑ 391	Bill Mazeroski AS	10.00	5.00
❑ 392	Ken Boyer AS UER	8.00	4.00
❑ 393	Roy McMillan AS	6.00	3.00
❑ 394	Hank Aaron AS	50.00	30.00
❑ 395	Willie Mays AS	50.00	30.00
❑ 396	Frank Robinson AS	15.00	7.50
❑ 397	John Roseboro AS	6.00	3.00
❑ 398	Don Drysdale AS	15.00	7.50
❑ 399	Warren Spahn AS	15.00	7.50
❑ 400	Elston Howard	10.00	5.00
❑ 401	O.Cepeda/R.Maris	60.00	35.00
❑ 402	Gino Cimoli	6.00	3.00
❑ 403	Chet Nichols	6.00	3.00
❑ 404	Tim Harkness RC	8.00	4.00
❑ 405	Jim Perry	8.00	4.00
❑ 406	Bob Taylor	6.00	3.00
❑ 407	Hank Aguirre	6.00	3.00
❑ 408	Gus Bell	8.00	4.00
❑ 409	Pittsburgh Pirates TC	10.00	5.00
❑ 410	Al Smith	6.00	3.00
❑ 411	Danny O'Connell	6.00	3.00
❑ 412	Charlie James	6.00	3.00
❑ 413	Matty Alou	10.00	5.00
❑ 414	Joe Gaines RC	6.00	3.00
❑ 415	Bill Virdon	10.00	5.00
❑ 416	Bob Scheffing MG	6.00	3.00
❑ 417	Joe Azcue RC	6.00	3.00
❑ 418	Andy Carey	6.00	3.00
❑ 419	Bob Bruce	8.00	4.00
❑ 420	Gus Triandos	8.00	4.00
❑ 421	Ken MacKenzie	8.00	4.00
❑ 422	Steve Bilko	6.00	3.00
❑ 423	R.Face/H.Wilhelm	10.00	5.00
❑ 424	Al McBean RC	6.00	3.00
❑ 425	Carl Yastrzemski	125.00	75.00
❑ 426	Bob Farley RC	6.00	3.00
❑ 427	Jake Wood	6.00	3.00
❑ 428	Joe Hicks	6.00	3.00
❑ 429	Billy O'Dell	6.00	3.00
❑ 430	Tony Kubek	15.00	7.50
❑ 431	Bob (Buck) Rodgers RC	8.00	4.00
❑ 432	Jim Pendleton	6.00	3.00
❑ 433	Jim Archer	6.00	3.00
❑ 434	Clay Dalrymple	6.00	3.00
❑ 435	Larry Sherry	8.00	4.00
❑ 436	Felix Mantilla	8.00	4.00
❑ 437	Ray Moore	6.00	3.00
❑ 438	Dick Brown	6.00	3.00
❑ 439	Jerry Buchek RC	6.00	3.00
❑ 440	Joey Jay	6.00	3.00
❑ 441	Checklist 6	15.00	7.50
❑ 442	Wes Stock	6.00	3.00
❑ 443	Del Crandall	8.00	4.00
❑ 444	Ted Wills	6.00	3.00
❑ 445	Vic Power	8.00	4.00
❑ 446	Don Elston	6.00	3.00
❑ 447	Willie Kirkland	12.00	6.00
❑ 448	Joe Gibbon	12.00	6.00
❑ 449	Jerry Adair	12.00	6.00
❑ 450	Jim O'Toole	15.00	7.50
❑ 451	Jose Tartabull RC	15.00	7.50
❑ 452	Earl Averill Jr.	12.00	6.00
❑ 453	Cal McLish	12.00	6.00
❑ 454	Floyd Robinson RC	12.00	6.00
❑ 455	Luis Arroyo	15.00	7.50
❑ 456	Joe Amalfitano	15.00	7.50
❑ 457	Lou Clinton	12.00	6.00
❑ 458A	Bob Buhl Emblem	15.00	7.50
❑ 458B	Bob Buhl No Emblem	50.00	30.00
❑ 459	Ed Bailey	12.00	6.00
❑ 460	Jim Bunning	20.00	10.00
❑ 461	Ken Hubbs RC	30.00	15.00
❑ 462A	Willie Tasby Emblem	12.00	6.00
❑ 462B	Willie Tasby No Emblem	50.00	30.00
❑ 463	Hank Bauer MG	15.00	7.50
❑ 464	Al Jackson RC	12.00	6.00
❑ 465	Cincinnati Reds TC	20.00	10.00
❑ 466	Norm Cash AS	15.00	7.50
❑ 467	Chuck Schilling AS	12.00	6.00
❑ 468	Brooks Robinson AS	25.00	12.50
❑ 469	Luis Aparicio AS	15.00	7.50
❑ 470	Al Kaline AS	25.00	12.50
❑ 471	Mickey Mantle AS	200.00	125.00
❑ 472	Rocky Colavito AS	15.00	7.50
❑ 473	Elston Howard AS	15.00	7.50
❑ 474	Frank Lary AS	12.00	6.00
❑ 475	Whitey Ford AS	20.00	10.00
❑ 476	Baltimore Orioles TC	20.00	10.00
❑ 477	Andre Rodgers	12.00	6.00
❑ 478	Don Zimmer	20.00	10.00
❑ 479	Joel Horlen RC	12.00	6.00
❑ 480	Harvey Kuenn	15.00	7.50
❑ 481	Vic Wertz	15.00	7.50
❑ 482	Sam Mele MG	12.00	6.00
❑ 483	Don McMahon	12.00	6.00
❑ 484	Dick Schofield	12.00	6.00
❑ 485	Pedro Ramos	12.00	6.00
❑ 486	Jim Gilliam	15.00	7.50
❑ 487	Jerry Lynch	12.00	6.00
❑ 488	Hal Brown	12.00	6.00
❑ 489	Julio Gotay RC	12.00	6.00
❑ 490	Clete Boyer UER	15.00	7.50
❑ 491	Leon Wagner	12.00	6.00
❑ 492	Hal W. Smith	15.00	7.50
❑ 493	Danny McDevitt	12.00	6.00
❑ 494	Sammy White	12.00	6.00
❑ 495	Don Cardwell	12.00	6.00
❑ 496	Wayne Causey RC	12.00	6.00
❑ 497	Ed Bouchee	15.00	7.50
❑ 498	Jim Donohue	12.00	6.00
❑ 499	Zoilo Versalles	15.00	7.50
❑ 500	Duke Snider	60.00	35.00
❑ 501	Claude Osteen	15.00	7.50
❑ 502	Hector Lopez	15.00	7.50
❑ 503	Danny Murtaugh MG	15.00	7.50
❑ 504	Eddie Bressoud	12.00	6.00
❑ 505	Juan Marichal	40.00	20.00
❑ 506	Charlie Maxwell	15.00	7.50
❑ 507	Ernie Broglio	15.00	7.50
❑ 508	Gordy Coleman	15.00	7.50
❑ 509	Dave Giusti RC	15.00	7.50
❑ 510	Jim Lemon	12.00	6.00
❑ 511	Bubba Phillips	12.00	6.00
❑ 512	Mike Fornieles	12.00	6.00
❑ 513	Whitey Herzog	15.00	7.50
❑ 514	Sherm Lollar	15.00	7.50
❑ 515	Stan Williams	15.00	7.50
❑ 516A	Checklist 7 White	15.00	7.50
❑ 516B	Checklist 7 Yellow	15.00	7.50
❑ 517	Dave Wickersham	12.00	6.00
❑ 518	Lee Maye	12.00	6.00
❑ 519	Bob Johnson RC	12.00	6.00
❑ 520	Bob Friend	15.00	7.50
❑ 521	Jacke Davis UER RC	12.00	6.00
❑ 522	Lindy McDaniel	15.00	7.50
❑ 523	Russ Nixon SP	30.00	18.00
❑ 524	Howie Nunn SP	30.00	18.00
❑ 525	George Thomas	20.00	10.00
❑ 526	Hal Woodeshick SP	30.00	18.00
❑ 527	Dick McAuliffe RC	30.00	18.00
❑ 528	Turk Lown	20.00	10.00
❑ 529	John Schaive SP	30.00	18.00
❑ 530	Bob Gibson SP	125.00	75.00
❑ 531	Bobby G. Smith	20.00	10.00
❑ 532	Dick Stigman	20.00	10.00
❑ 533	Charley Lau SP	30.00	18.00
❑ 534	Tony Gonzalez SP	30.00	18.00
❑ 535	Ed Roebuck	20.00	10.00
❑ 536	Dick Gernert	20.00	10.00
❑ 537	Cleveland Indians TC	50.00	30.00
❑ 538	Jack Sanford	20.00	10.00
❑ 539	Billy Moran	20.00	10.00
❑ 540	Jim Landis SP	30.00	18.00

❑ 541 Don Nottebart SP 30.00 18.00
❑ 542 Dave Philley 20.00 10.00
❑ 543 Bob Allen SP 30.00 18.00
❑ 544 Willie McCovey SP 125.00 75.00
❑ 545 Hoyt Wilhelm SP 50.00 30.00
❑ 546 Moe Thacker SP 30.00 18.00
❑ 547 Don Ferrarese 20.00 10.00
❑ 548 Bobby Del Greco 20.00 10.00
❑ 549 Bill Rigney MG SP 30.00 18.00
❑ 550 Art Mahaffey SP 30.00 18.00
❑ 551 Harry Bright 20.00 10.00
❑ 552 Chicago Cubs TC SP 50.00 30.00
❑ 553 Jim Coates 30.00 18.00
❑ 554 Bubba Morton SP RC 30.00 18.00
❑ 555 John Buzhardt SP 30.00 18.00
❑ 556 Al Spangler 20.00 10.00
❑ 557 Bob Anderson SP 30.00 18.00
❑ 558 John Goryl 20.00 10.00
❑ 559 Mike Higgins MG 20.00 10.00
❑ 560 Chuck Estrada SP 30.00 18.00
❑ 561 Gene Oliver SP 30.00 18.00
❑ 562 Bill Henry 20.00 10.00
❑ 563 Ken Aspromonte 20.00 10.00
❑ 564 Bob Grim 20.00 10.00
❑ 565 Jose Pagan 20.00 10.00
❑ 566 Marty Kutyna SP 30.00 18.00
❑ 567 Tracy Stallard SP 30.00 18.00
❑ 568 Jim Golden 20.00 10.00
❑ 569 Ed Sadowski SP 30.00 18.00
❑ 570 Bill Stafford SP 30.00 18.00
❑ 571 Billy Klaus SP 30.00 18.00
❑ 572 Bob G.Miller SP 30.00 18.00
❑ 573 Johnny Logan 20.00 10.00
❑ 574 Dean Stone 20.00 10.00
❑ 575 Red Schoendienst SP 50.00 30.00
❑ 576 Russ Kemmerer SP 30.00 18.00
❑ 577 Dave Nicholson SP 30.00 18.00
❑ 578 Jim Duffalo RC 20.00 10.00
❑ 579 Jim Schaffer SP RC 30.00 18.00
❑ 580 Bill Monbouquette 20.00 10.00
❑ 581 Mel Roach 20.00 10.00
❑ 582 Ron Piche 20.00 10.00
❑ 583 Larry Osborne 20.00 10.00
❑ 584 Minnesota Twins TC SP 60.00 35.00
❑ 585 Glen Hobbie SP 30.00 18.00
❑ 586 Sammy Esposito SP 30.00 18.00
❑ 587 Frank Funk SP 30.00 18.00
❑ 588 Birdie Tebbetts MG 20.00 10.00
❑ 589 Bob Turley 30.00 18.00
❑ 590 Curt Flood 30.00 18.00
❑ 591 Sam McDowell SP RC 80.00 50.00
❑ 592 Jim Bouton SP RC 80.00 50.00
❑ 593 Rookie Pitchers SP 50.00 30.00
❑ 594 Bob Uecker SP RC 80.00 50.00
❑ 595 Rookie Infielders SP 50.00 30.00
❑ 596 Joe Pepitone SP RC 80.00 50.00
❑ 597 Rookie Infielders SP 50.00 30.00
❑ 598 Rookie Outfielders SP 80.00 50.00

1963 Topps

❑ COMPLETE SET (576) 5000.00 3400.00
❑ COMMON CARD (1-196) 4.00 2.00
❑ COMMON CARD (197-283) 5.00 2.50
❑ COMMON CARD (284-370) 5.00 2.50
❑ COMMON CARD (371-446) 5.00 2.50
❑ COMMON CARD (447-522) 25.00 12.50
❑ COMMON CARD (523-576) 15.00 7.50
❑ WRAPPER (1-CENT) 40.00 30.00
❑ WRAPPER (5-CENT) 30.00 20.00
❑ 1 F.Rob/Musial/Aaron LL 40.00 20.00
❑ 2 Runnels/Mantle/Rob LL 50.00 30.00
❑ 3 Mays/Aaron/Rob/Cep/Banks LL 40.00 20.00
❑ 4 Kill/Cash/Colav/Maris LL 20.00 10.00
❑ 5 Koufax/Gibson/Drysdale LL 25.00 12.50
❑ 6 Aguirre/Roberts/Ford LL 10.00 5.00
❑ 7 Drysdale/Sanf/Purk LL 10.00 5.00
❑ 8 Terry/Donovan/Bunning LL 8.00 4.00
❑ 9 Drysdale/Koufax/Gibson LL 30.00 15.00
❑ 10 Pascual/Bunning/Kaat LL 8.00 4.00
❑ 11 Lee Walls 4.00 2.00
❑ 12 Steve Barber 4.00 2.00
❑ 13 Philadelphia Phillies TC 8.00 4.00
❑ 14 Pedro Ramos 4.00 2.00
❑ 15 Ken Hubbs UER NPO 10.00 5.00
❑ 16 Al Smith 4.00 2.00
❑ 17 Ryne Duren 8.00 4.00
❑ 18 Burg/Stu/Clemente/Skin 80.00 50.00
❑ 19 Pete Burnside 4.00 2.00
❑ 20 Tony Kubek 10.00 5.00
❑ 21 Marty Keough 4.00 2.00
❑ 22 Curt Simmons 8.00 4.00
❑ 23 Ed Lopat MG 8.00 4.00
❑ 24 Bob Bruce 4.00 2.00
❑ 25 Al Kaline 50.00 30.00
❑ 26 Ray Moore 4.00 2.00
❑ 27 Choo Choo Coleman 8.00 4.00
❑ 28 Mike Fornieles 4.00 2.00
❑ 29A Rookie Stars 1962 10.00 5.00
❑ 29B Rookie Stars 1963 4.00 2.00
❑ 30 Harvey Kuenn 8.00 4.00
❑ 31 Cal Koonce RC 4.00 2.00
❑ 32 Tony Gonzalez 4.00 2.00
❑ 33 Bo Belinsky 8.00 4.00
❑ 34 Dick Schofield 4.00 2.00
❑ 35 John Buzhardt 4.00 2.00
❑ 36 Jerry Kindall 4.00 2.00
❑ 37 Jerry Lynch 4.00 2.00
❑ 38 Bud Daley 8.00 4.00
❑ 39 Los Angeles Angels TC 8.00 4.00
❑ 40 Vic Power 8.00 4.00
❑ 41 Charley Lau 8.00 4.00
❑ 42 Stan Williams 8.00 4.00
❑ 43 C.Stengel/G.Woodling 8.00 4.00
❑ 44 Terry Fox 4.00 2.00
❑ 45 Bob Aspromonte 4.00 2.00
❑ 46 Tommie Aaron RC 8.00 4.00
❑ 47 Don Lock RC 4.00 2.00
❑ 48 Birdie Tebbetts MG 8.00 4.00
❑ 49 Dal Maxvill RC 8.00 4.00
❑ 50 Billy Pierce 8.00 4.00
❑ 51 George Alusik 4.00 2.00
❑ 52 Chuck Schilling 4.00 2.00
❑ 53 Joe Moeller RC 8.00 4.00
❑ 54A Dave DeBusschere 62 15.00 7.50
❑ 54B Dave DeBusschere 63 RC 8.00 4.00
❑ 55 Bill Virdon 8.00 4.00
❑ 56 Dennis Bennett RC 4.00 2.00
❑ 57 Billy Moran 4.00 2.00
❑ 58 Bob Will 4.00 2.00
❑ 59 Craig Anderson 4.00 2.00
❑ 60 Elston Howard 8.00 4.00
❑ 61 Ernie Bowman 4.00 2.00
❑ 62 Bob Hendley 4.00 2.00
❑ 63 Cincinnati Reds TC 8.00 4.00
❑ 64 Dick McAuliffe 8.00 4.00
❑ 65 Jackie Brandt 4.00 2.00
❑ 66 Mike Joyce RC 4.00 2.00
❑ 67 Ed Charles 4.00 2.00
❑ 68 G.Hodges/D.Snider 25.00 12.50
❑ 69 Bud Zipfel RC 4.00 2.00
❑ 70 Jim O'Toole 8.00 4.00
❑ 71 Bobby Wine RC 8.00 4.00
❑ 72 Johnny Romano 4.00 2.00
❑ 73 Bobby Bragan MG RC 8.00 4.00
❑ 74 Denny Lemaster RC 4.00 2.00
❑ 75 Bob Allison 8.00 4.00
❑ 76 Earl Wilson 8.00 4.00
❑ 77 Al Spangler 4.00 2.00
❑ 78 Marv Throneberry 8.00 4.00
❑ 79 Checklist 1 12.00 6.00
❑ 80 Jim Gilliam 8.00 4.00
❑ 81 Jim Schaffer 4.00 2.00
❑ 82 Ed Rakow 4.00 2.00
❑ 83 Charley James 4.00 2.00
❑ 84 Ron Kline 4.00 2.00
❑ 85 Tom Haller 8.00 4.00
❑ 86 Charley Maxwell 8.00 4.00
❑ 87 Bob Veale 8.00 4.00
❑ 88 Ron Hansen 4.00 2.00
❑ 89 Dick Stigman 4.00 2.00
❑ 90 Gordy Coleman 8.00 4.00
❑ 91 Dallas Green 8.00 4.00
❑ 92 Hector Lopez 8.00 4.00
❑ 93 Galen Cisco 4.00 2.00
❑ 94 Bob Schmidt 4.00 2.00
❑ 95 Larry Jackson 4.00 2.00
❑ 96 Lou Clinton 4.00 2.00
❑ 97 Bob Duliba 4.00 2.00
❑ 98 George Thomas 4.00 2.00
❑ 99 Jim Umbricht 4.00 2.00
❑ 100 Joe Cunningham 4.00 2.00
❑ 101 Joe Gibbon 4.00 2.00
❑ 102A Checklist 2 Red/Yellow 12.00 6.00
❑ 102B Checklist 2 White/Red 12.00 6.00
❑ 103 Chuck Essegian 4.00 2.00
❑ 104 Lew Krausse RC 4.00 2.00
❑ 105 Ron Fairly 8.00 4.00
❑ 106 Bobby Bolin 4.00 2.00
❑ 107 Jim Hickman 8.00 4.00
❑ 108 Hoyt Wilhelm 10.00 5.00
❑ 109 Lee Maye 4.00 2.00
❑ 110 Rich Rollins 8.00 4.00
❑ 111 Al Jackson 4.00 2.00
❑ 112 Dick Brown 4.00 2.00
❑ 113 Don Landrum UER 4.00 2.00
❑ 114 Dan Osinski RC 4.00 2.00
❑ 115 Carl Yastrzemski 40.00 20.00
❑ 116 Jim Brosnan 8.00 4.00
❑ 117 Jacke Davis 4.00 2.00
❑ 118 Sherm Lollar 4.00 2.00
❑ 119 Bob Lillis 4.00 2.00
❑ 120 Roger Maris 80.00 50.00
❑ 121 Jim Hannan RC 4.00 2.00
❑ 122 Julio Gotay 4.00 2.00
❑ 123 Frank Howard 8.00 4.00
❑ 124 Dick Howser 8.00 4.00
❑ 125 Robin Roberts 15.00 7.50
❑ 126 Bob Uecker 15.00 7.50
❑ 127 Bill Tuttle 4.00 2.00
❑ 128 Matty Alou 8.00 4.00
❑ 129 Gary Bell 4.00 2.00
❑ 130 Dick Groat 8.00 4.00
❑ 131 Washington Senators TC 8.00 4.00
❑ 132 Jack Hamilton 4.00 2.00
❑ 133 Gene Freese 4.00 2.00
❑ 134 Bob Scheffing MG 4.00 2.00
❑ 135 Richie Ashburn 20.00 10.00
❑ 136 Ike Delock 4.00 2.00
❑ 137 Mack Jones 4.00 2.00
❑ 138 W.Mays/S.Musial 80.00 50.00
❑ 139 Earl Averill Jr. 4.00 2.00
❑ 140 Frank Lary 8.00 4.00
❑ 141 Manny Mota RC 8.00 4.00
❑ 142 Whitey Ford WS1 10.00 5.00
❑ 143 Jack Sanford WS2 8.00 4.00
❑ 144 Roger Maris WS3 15.00 7.50
❑ 145 Chuck Hiller WS4 8.00 4.00
❑ 146 Tom Tresh WS5 8.00 4.00
❑ 147 Billy Pierce WS6 8.00 4.00
❑ 148 Ralph Terry WS7 8.00 4.00
❑ 149 Marv Breeding 4.00 2.00
❑ 150 Johnny Podres 8.00 4.00
❑ 151 Pittsburgh Pirates TC 8.00 4.00
❑ 152 Ron Nischwitz 4.00 2.00
❑ 153 Hal Smith 4.00 2.00
❑ 154 Walter Alston MG 8.00 4.00
❑ 155 Bill Stafford 4.00 2.00
❑ 156 Roy McMillan 8.00 4.00
❑ 157 Diego Segui RC 8.00 4.00
❑ 158 Tommy Harper RC 8.00 4.00
❑ 159 Jim Pagliaroni 4.00 2.00
❑ 160 Juan Pizarro 4.00 2.00
❑ 161 Frank Torre 8.00 4.00
❑ 162 Minnesota Twins TC 8.00 4.00
❑ 163 Don Larsen 8.00 4.00
❑ 164 Bubba Morton 4.00 2.00
❑ 165 Jim Kaat 8.00 4.00
❑ 166 Johnny Keane MG 4.00 2.00
❑ 167 Jim Fregosi 8.00 4.00
❑ 168 Russ Nixon 4.00 2.00

❑ 169 Gaylord Perry 25.00 12.50
❑ 170 Joe Adcock 8.00 4.00
❑ 171 Steve Hamilton RC 4.00 2.00
❑ 172 Gene Oliver 4.00 2.00
❑ 173 Tresh/Mantle/Richardson 150.00 90.00
❑ 174 Larry Burright 4.00 2.00
❑ 175 Bob Buhl 8.00 4.00
❑ 176 Jim King 4.00 2.00
❑ 177 Bubba Phillips 4.00 2.00
❑ 178 Johnny Edwards 4.00 2.00
❑ 179 Ron Piche 4.00 2.00
❑ 180 Bill Skowron 8.00 4.00
❑ 181 Sammy Esposito 4.00 2.00
❑ 182 Albie Pearson 8.00 4.00
❑ 183 Joe Pepitone 8.00 4.00
❑ 184 Vern Law 8.00 4.00
❑ 185 Chuck Hiller 4.00 2.00
❑ 186 Jerry Zimmerman 4.00 2.00
❑ 187 Willie Kirkland 4.00 2.00
❑ 188 Eddie Bressoud 4.00 2.00
❑ 189 Dave Giusti 8.00 4.00
❑ 190 Minnie Minoso 8.00 4.00
❑ 191 Checklist 3 12.00 6.00
❑ 192 Clay Dalrymple 4.00 2.00
❑ 193 Andre Rodgers 4.00 2.00
❑ 194 Joe Nuxhall 8.00 4.00
❑ 195 Manny Jimenez 4.00 2.00
❑ 196 Doug Camilli 4.00 2.00
❑ 197 Roger Craig 8.00 4.00
❑ 198 Lenny Green 5.00 2.50
❑ 199 Joe Amalfitano 5.00 2.50
❑ 200 Mickey Mantle 600.00 350.00
❑ 201 Cecil Butler 5.00 2.50
❑ 202 Boston Red Sox TC 8.00 4.00
❑ 203 Chico Cardenas 8.00 4.00
❑ 204 Don Nottebart 5.00 2.50
❑ 205 Luis Aparicio 15.00 7.50
❑ 206 Ray Washburn 5.00 2.50
❑ 207 Ken Hunt 5.00 2.50
❑ 208 Rookie Stars 5.00 2.50
❑ 209 Hobie Landrith 5.00 2.50
❑ 210 Sandy Koufax 150.00 90.00
❑ 211 Fred Whitfield RC 5.00 2.50
❑ 212 Glen Hobbie 5.00 2.50
❑ 213 Billy Hitchcock MG 5.00 2.50
❑ 214 Orlando Pena 5.00 2.50
❑ 215 Bob Skinner 8.00 4.00
❑ 216 Gene Conley 8.00 4.00
❑ 217 Joe Christopher 5.00 2.50
❑ 218 Lary/Mossi/Bunning 8.00 4.00
❑ 219 Chuck Cottier 5.00 2.50
❑ 220 Camilo Pascual 8.00 4.00
❑ 221 Cookie Rojas RC 8.00 4.00
❑ 222 Chicago Cubs TC 8.00 4.00
❑ 223 Eddie Fisher 5.00 2.50
❑ 224 Mike Roarke 5.00 2.50
❑ 225 Joey Jay 5.00 2.50
❑ 226 Julian Javier 8.00 4.00
❑ 227 Jim Grant 8.00 4.00
❑ 228 Tony Oliva RC 50.00 30.00
❑ 229 Willie Davis 8.00 4.00
❑ 230 Pete Runnels 8.00 4.00
❑ 231 Eli Grba UER 5.00 2.50
❑ 232 Frank Malzone 8.00 4.00
❑ 233 Casey Stengel MG 20.00 10.00
❑ 234 Dave Nicholson 5.00 2.50
❑ 235 Billy O'Dell 5.00 2.50
❑ 236 Bill Bryan RC 5.00 2.50
❑ 237 Jim Coates 8.00 4.00
❑ 238 Lou Johnson 5.00 2.50
❑ 239 Harvey Haddix 8.00 4.00
❑ 240 Rocky Colavito 15.00 7.50
❑ 241 Billy Smith RC 5.00 2.50
❑ 242 E.Banks/H.Aaron 60.00 35.00
❑ 243 Don Leppert 5.00 2.50
❑ 244 John Tsitouris 5.00 2.50
❑ 245 Gil Hodges 20.00 10.00
❑ 246 Lee Stange 5.00 2.50
❑ 247 New York Yankees TC 50.00 30.00
❑ 248 Tito Francona 5.00 2.50
❑ 249 Leo Burke RC 5.00 2.50
❑ 250 Stan Musial 100.00 60.00
❑ 251 Jack Lamabe 5.00 2.50
❑ 252 Ron Santo 10.00 5.00
❑ 253 Rookie Stars 5.00 2.50
❑ 254 Mike Hershberger 5.00 2.50
❑ 255 Bob Shaw 5.00 2.50
❑ 256 Jerry Lumpe 5.00 2.50
❑ 257 Hank Aguirre 5.00 2.50
❑ 258 Alvin Dark MG 8.00 4.00
❑ 259 Johnny Logan 8.00 4.00
❑ 260 Jim Gentile 8.00 4.00
❑ 261 Bob Miller 5.00 2.50
❑ 262 Ellis Burton 5.00 2.50
❑ 263 Dave Stenhouse 5.00 2.50
❑ 264 Phil Linz 5.00 2.50
❑ 265 Vada Pinson 8.00 4.00
❑ 266 Bob Allen 5.00 2.50
❑ 267 Carl Sawatski 5.00 2.50
❑ 268 Don Demeter 5.00 2.50
❑ 269 Don Mincher 5.00 2.50
❑ 270 Felipe Alou 8.00 4.00
❑ 271 Dean Stone 5.00 2.50
❑ 272 Danny Murphy 5.00 2.50
❑ 273 Sammy Taylor 5.00 2.50
❑ 274 Checklist 4 12.00 6.00
❑ 275 Eddie Mathews 30.00 15.00
❑ 276 Barry Shetrone 5.00 2.50
❑ 277 Dick Farrell 5.00 2.50
❑ 278 Chico Fernandez 5.00 2.50
❑ 279 Wally Moon 8.00 4.00
❑ 280 Bob (Buck) Rodgers 5.00 2.50
❑ 281 Tom Sturdivant 5.00 2.50
❑ 282 Bobby Del Greco 5.00 2.50
❑ 283 Roy Sievers 8.00 4.00
❑ 284 Dave Sisler 5.00 2.50
❑ 285 Dick Stuart 8.00 4.00
❑ 286 Stu Miller 8.00 4.00
❑ 287 Dick Bertell 5.00 2.50
❑ 288 Chicago White Sox TC 10.00 5.00
❑ 289 Hal Brown 5.00 2.50
❑ 290 Bill White 8.00 4.00
❑ 291 Don Rudolph 5.00 2.50
❑ 292 Pumpsie Green 8.00 4.00
❑ 293 Bill Pleis 5.00 2.50
❑ 294 Bill Rigney MG 5.00 2.50
❑ 295 Ed Roebuck 5.00 2.50
❑ 296 Doc Edwards 5.00 2.50
❑ 297 Jim Golden 5.00 2.50
❑ 298 Don Dillard 5.00 2.50
❑ 299 Rookie Stars 8.00 4.00
❑ 300 Willie Mays 150.00 90.00
❑ 301 Bill Fischer 5.00 2.50
❑ 302 Whitey Herzog 8.00 4.00
❑ 303 Earl Francis 5.00 2.50
❑ 304 Harry Bright 5.00 2.50
❑ 305 Don Hoak 5.00 2.50
❑ 306 E.Battey/E.Howard 10.00 5.00
❑ 307 Chet Nichols 5.00 2.50
❑ 308 Camilo Carreon 5.00 2.50
❑ 309 Jim Brewer 5.00 2.50
❑ 310 Tommy Davis 8.00 4.00
❑ 311 Joe McClain 5.00 2.50
❑ 312 Houston Colts TC 25.00 12.50
❑ 313 Ernie Broglio 5.00 2.50
❑ 314 John Goryl 5.00 2.50
❑ 315 Ralph Terry 8.00 4.00
❑ 316 Norm Sherry 8.00 4.00
❑ 317 Sam McDowell 8.00 4.00
❑ 318 Gene Mauch MG 8.00 4.00
❑ 319 Joe Gaines 5.00 2.50
❑ 320 Warren Spahn 60.00 35.00
❑ 321 Gino Cimoli 5.00 2.50
❑ 322 Bob Turley 8.00 4.00
❑ 323 Bill Mazeroski 15.00 7.50
❑ 324 Vic Davalillo RC 8.00 4.00
❑ 325 Jack Sanford 5.00 2.50
❑ 326 Hank Foiles 5.00 2.50
❑ 327 Paul Foytack 5.00 2.50
❑ 328 Dick Williams 8.00 4.00
❑ 329 Lindy McDaniel 8.00 4.00
❑ 330 Chuck Hinton 5.00 2.50
❑ 331 Stafford/Pierce 8.00 4.00
❑ 332 Joel Horlen 8.00 4.00
❑ 333 Carl Warwick 5.00 2.50
❑ 334 Wynn Hawkins 5.00 2.50
❑ 335 Leon Wagner 5.00 2.50
❑ 336 Ed Bauta 5.00 2.50
❑ 337 Los Angeles Dodgers TC 25.00 12.50
❑ 338 Russ Kemmerer 5.00 2.50
❑ 339 Ted Bowsfield 5.00 2.50
❑ 340 Yogi Berra P/CO 100.00 60.00
❑ 341 Jack Baldschun 5.00 2.50
❑ 342 Gene Woodling 8.00 4.00
❑ 343 Johnny Pesky MG 8.00 4.00
❑ 344 Don Schwall 5.00 2.50
❑ 345 Brooks Robinson 60.00 35.00
❑ 346 Billy Hoeft 5.00 2.50
❑ 347 Joe Torre 15.00 7.50
❑ 348 Vic Wertz 8.00 4.00
❑ 349 Zoilo Versalles 8.00 4.00
❑ 350 Bob Purkey 5.00 2.50
❑ 351 Al Luplow 5.00 2.50
❑ 352 Ken Johnson 5.00 2.50
❑ 353 Billy Williams 30.00 15.00
❑ 354 Dom Zanni 5.00 2.50
❑ 355 Dean Chance 8.00 4.00
❑ 356 John Schaive 5.00 2.50
❑ 357 George Altman 5.00 2.50
❑ 358 Milt Pappas 8.00 4.00
❑ 359 Haywood Sullivan 8.00 4.00
❑ 360 Don Drysdale 60.00 35.00
❑ 361 Clete Boyer 10.00 5.00
❑ 362 Checklist 5 12.00 6.00
❑ 363 Dick Radatz 8.00 4.00
❑ 364 Howie Goss 5.00 2.50
❑ 365 Jim Bunning 20.00 10.00
❑ 366 Tony Taylor 8.00 4.00
❑ 367 Tony Cloninger 5.00 2.50
❑ 368 Ed Bailey 5.00 2.50
❑ 369 Jim Lemon 5.00 2.50
❑ 370 Dick Donovan 5.00 2.50
❑ 371 Rod Kanehl 8.00 4.00
❑ 372 Don Lee 5.00 2.50
❑ 373 Jim Campbell RC 5.00 2.50
❑ 374 Claude Osteen 8.00 4.00
❑ 375 Ken Boyer 15.00 7.50
❑ 376 John Wyatt RC 5.00 2.50
❑ 377 Baltimore Orioles TC 10.00 5.00
❑ 378 Bill Henry 5.00 2.50
❑ 379 Bob Anderson 5.00 2.50
❑ 380 Ernie Banks UER 100.00 60.00
❑ 381 Frank Baumann 5.00 2.50
❑ 382 Ralph Houk MG 10.00 5.00
❑ 383 Pete Richert 5.00 2.50
❑ 384 Bob Tillman 5.00 2.50
❑ 385 Art Mahaffey 5.00 2.50
❑ 386 Rookie Stars 5.00 2.50
❑ 387 Al McBean 5.00 2.50
❑ 388 Jim Davenport 8.00 4.00
❑ 389 Frank Sullivan 5.00 2.50
❑ 390 Hank Aaron 175.00 100.00
❑ 391 Bill Dailey RC 5.00 2.50
❑ 392 Romano/Francona 5.00 2.50
❑ 393 Ken MacKenzie 8.00 4.00
❑ 394 Tim McCarver 15.00 7.50
❑ 395 Don McMahon 5.00 2.50
❑ 396 Joe Koppe 5.00 2.50
❑ 397 Kansas City Athletics TC 10.00 5.00
❑ 398 Boog Powell 25.00 12.50
❑ 399 Dick Ellsworth 5.00 2.50
❑ 400 Frank Robinson 60.00 35.00
❑ 401 Jim Bouton 15.00 7.50
❑ 402 Mickey Vernon MG 8.00 4.00
❑ 403 Ron Perranoski 8.00 4.00
❑ 404 Bob Oldis 5.00 2.50
❑ 405 Floyd Robinson 5.00 2.50
❑ 406 Howie Koplitz 5.00 2.50
❑ 407 Rookie Stars 8.00 4.00
❑ 408 Billy Gardner 5.00 2.50
❑ 409 Roy Face 8.00 4.00
❑ 410 Earl Battey 5.00 2.50
❑ 411 Jim Constable 5.00 2.50
❑ 412 Podres/Drysdale/Koufax 50.00 30.00
❑ 413 Jerry Walker 5.00 2.50
❑ 414 Ty Cline 5.00 2.50
❑ 415 Bob Gibson 60.00 35.00
❑ 416 Alex Grammas 5.00 2.50
❑ 417 San Francisco Giants TC 10.00 5.00
❑ 418 John Orsino 5.00 2.50
❑ 419 Tracy Stallard 5.00 2.50
❑ 420 Bobby Richardson 15.00 7.50
❑ 421 Tom Morgan 5.00 2.50
❑ 422 Fred Hutchinson MG 8.00 4.00
❑ 423 Ed Hobaugh 5.00 2.50
❑ 424 Charlie Smith 5.00 2.50
❑ 425 Smoky Burgess 8.00 4.00
❑ 426 Barry Latman 5.00 2.50

- ❑ 427 Bernie Allen 5.00 2.50
- ❑ 428 Carl Boles RC 5.00 2.50
- ❑ 429 Lew Burdette 8.00 4.00
- ❑ 430 Norm Siebern 5.00 2.50
- ❑ 431A Checklist 6 White/Red 12.00 6.00
- ❑ 431B Checklist 6 Black/Orange 30.00 15.00
- ❑ 432 Roman Mejias 5.00 2.50
- ❑ 433 Denis Menke 5.00 2.50
- ❑ 434 John Callison 8.00 4.00
- ❑ 435 Woody Held 5.00 2.50
- ❑ 436 Tim Harkness 8.00 4.00
- ❑ 437 Bill Bruton 5.00 2.50
- ❑ 438 Wes Stock 5.00 2.50
- ❑ 439 Don Zimmer 8.00 4.00
- ❑ 440 Juan Marichal 30.00 15.00
- ❑ 441 Lee Thomas 8.00 4.00
- ❑ 442 J.C. Hartman RC 5.00 2.50
- ❑ 443 Jimmy Piersall 8.00 4.00
- ❑ 444 Jim Maloney 8.00 4.00
- ❑ 445 Norm Cash 10.00 5.00
- ❑ 446 Whitey Ford 60.00 35.00
- ❑ 447 Felix Mantilla 25.00 12.50
- ❑ 448 Jack Kralick 25.00 12.50
- ❑ 449 Jose Tartabull 25.00 12.50
- ❑ 450 Bob Friend 30.00 15.00
- ❑ 451 Cleveland Indians TC 40.00 20.00
- ❑ 452 Barney Schultz 25.00 12.50
- ❑ 453 Jake Wood 25.00 12.50
- ❑ 454A Art Fowler White 25.00 12.50
- ❑ 454B Art Fowler Orange 30.00 15.00
- ❑ 455 Ruben Amaro 25.00 12.50
- ❑ 456 Jim Coker 25.00 12.50
- ❑ 457 Tex Clevenger 25.00 12.50
- ❑ 458 Al Lopez MG 30.00 15.00
- ❑ 459 Dick LeMay 25.00 12.50
- ❑ 460 Del Crandall 30.00 15.00
- ❑ 461 Norm Bass 25.00 12.50
- ❑ 462 Wally Post 25.00 12.50
- ❑ 463 Joe Schaffernoth 25.00 12.50
- ❑ 464 Ken Aspromonte 25.00 12.50
- ❑ 465 Chuck Estrada 25.00 12.50
- ❑ 466 Bill Freehan SP RC 60.00 35.00
- ❑ 467 Phil Ortega 25.00 12.50
- ❑ 468 Carroll Hardy 30.00 15.00
- ❑ 469 Jay Hook 30.00 15.00
- ❑ 470 Tom Tresh SP 60.00 35.00
- ❑ 471 Ken Retzer 25.00 12.50
- ❑ 472 Lou Brock 80.00 50.00
- ❑ 473 New York Mets TC 100.00 60.00
- ❑ 474 Jack Fisher 25.00 12.50
- ❑ 475 Gus Triandos 30.00 15.00
- ❑ 476 Frank Funk 25.00 12.50
- ❑ 477 Donn Clendenon 30.00 15.00
- ❑ 478 Paul Brown 25.00 12.50
- ❑ 479 Ed Brinkman RC 25.00 12.50
- ❑ 480 Bill Monbouquette 25.00 12.50
- ❑ 481 Bob Taylor 25.00 12.50
- ❑ 482 Felix Torres 25.00 12.50
- ❑ 483 Jim Owens UER 25.00 12.50
- ❑ 484 Dale Long SP 30.00 15.00
- ❑ 485 Jim Landis 25.00 12.50
- ❑ 486 Ray Sadecki 25.00 12.50
- ❑ 487 John Roseboro 30.00 15.00
- ❑ 488 Jerry Adair 25.00 12.50
- ❑ 489 Paul Toth RC 25.00 12.50
- ❑ 490 Willie McCovey 100.00 60.00
- ❑ 491 Harry Craft MG 25.00 12.50
- ❑ 492 Dave Wickersham 25.00 12.50
- ❑ 493 Walt Bond 25.00 12.50
- ❑ 494 Phil Regan 25.00 12.50
- ❑ 495 Frank Thomas SP 30.00 15.00
- ❑ 496 Rookie Stars 30.00 15.00
- ❑ 497 Bennie Daniels 25.00 12.50
- ❑ 498 Eddie Kasko 25.00 12.50
- ❑ 499 J.C. Martin 25.00 12.50
- ❑ 500 Harmon Killebrew SP 150.00 90.00
- ❑ 501 Joe Azcue 25.00 12.50
- ❑ 502 Daryl Spencer 25.00 12.50
- ❑ 503 Milwaukee Braves TC 40.00 20.00
- ❑ 504 Bob Johnson 25.00 12.50
- ❑ 505 Curt Flood 40.00 20.00
- ❑ 506 Gene Green 25.00 12.50
- ❑ 507 Roland Sheldon 30.00 15.00
- ❑ 508 Ted Savage 25.00 12.50
- ❑ 509A Checklist 7 Centered 30.00 15.00
- ❑ 509B Checklist 7 Right 30.00 15.00
- ❑ 510 Ken McBride 25.00 12.50
- ❑ 511 Charlie Neal 30.00 15.00
- ❑ 512 Cal McLish 25.00 12.50
- ❑ 513 Gary Geiger 25.00 12.50
- ❑ 514 Larry Osborne 25.00 12.50
- ❑ 515 Don Elston 25.00 12.50
- ❑ 516 Purnell Goldy RC 25.00 12.50
- ❑ 517 Hal Woodeshick 25.00 12.50
- ❑ 518 Don Blasingame 25.00 12.50
- ❑ 519 Claude Raymond RC 25.00 12.50
- ❑ 520 Orlando Cepeda 40.00 20.00
- ❑ 521 Dan Pfister 25.00 12.50
- ❑ 522 Rookie Stars 30.00 15.00
- ❑ 523 Bill Kunkel 15.00 7.50
- ❑ 524 St. Louis Cardinals TC 30.00 15.00
- ❑ 525 Nellie Fox 50.00 30.00
- ❑ 526 Dick Hall 15.00 7.50
- ❑ 527 Ed Sadowski 15.00 7.50
- ❑ 528 Carl Willey 15.00 7.50
- ❑ 529 Wes Covington 15.00 7.50
- ❑ 530 Don Mossi 20.00 10.00
- ❑ 531 Sam Mele MG 15.00 7.50
- ❑ 532 Steve Boros 15.00 7.50
- ❑ 533 Bobby Shantz 20.00 10.00
- ❑ 534 Ken Walters 15.00 7.50
- ❑ 535 Jim Perry 20.00 10.00
- ❑ 536 Norm Larker 15.00 7.50
- ❑ 537 Pete Rose RC 1000.00 600.00
- ❑ 538 George Brunet 15.00 7.50
- ❑ 539 Wayne Causey 15.00 7.50
- ❑ 540 Roberto Clemente 250.00 150.00
- ❑ 541 Ron Moeller 15.00 7.50
- ❑ 542 Lou Klimchock 15.00 7.50
- ❑ 543 Russ Snyder 15.00 7.50
- ❑ 544 Rusty Staub RC 50.00 30.00
- ❑ 545 Jose Pagan 15.00 7.50
- ❑ 546 Hal Reniff 20.00 10.00
- ❑ 547 Gus Bell 15.00 7.50
- ❑ 548 Tom Satriano RC 15.00 7.50
- ❑ 549 Rookie Stars 15.00 7.50
- ❑ 550 Duke Snider 80.00 50.00
- ❑ 551 Billy Klaus 15.00 7.50
- ❑ 552 Detroit Tigers TC 50.00 30.00
- ❑ 553 Willie Stargell RC 125.00 75.00
- ❑ 554 Hank Fischer RC 15.00 7.50
- ❑ 555 John Blanchard 20.00 10.00
- ❑ 556 Al Worthington 15.00 7.50
- ❑ 557 Cuno Barragan 15.00 7.50
- ❑ 558 Ron Hunt RC 20.00 10.00
- ❑ 559 Danny Murtaugh MG 15.00 7.50
- ❑ 560 Ray Herbert 15.00 7.50
- ❑ 561 Mike De La Hoz 15.00 7.50
- ❑ 562 Dave McNally RC 30.00 15.00
- ❑ 563 Mike McCormick 15.00 7.50
- ❑ 564 George Banks RC 15.00 7.50
- ❑ 565 Larry Sherry 15.00 7.50
- ❑ 566 Cliff Cook 15.00 7.50
- ❑ 567 Jim Duffalo 15.00 7.50
- ❑ 568 Bob Sadowski 15.00 7.50
- ❑ 569 Luis Arroyo 20.00 10.00
- ❑ 570 Frank Bolling 15.00 7.50
- ❑ 571 Johnny Klippstein 15.00 7.50
- ❑ 572 Jack Spring 15.00 7.50
- ❑ 573 Coot Veal 15.00 7.50
- ❑ 574 Hal Kolstad 15.00 7.50
- ❑ 575 Don Cardwell 15.00 7.50
- ❑ 576 Johnny Temple 30.00 15.00

1964 Topps

- ❑ COMPLETE SET (587) 3500.00 2500.00
- ❑ COMMON CARD (1-196) 3.00 1.50
- ❑ COMMON CARD (197-370) 4.00 2.00
- ❑ COMMON CARD (371-522) 8.00 4.00
- ❑ COMMON CARD (523-587) 15.00 7.50
- ❑ WRAPPER (1-CENT) 100.00 75.00
- ❑ WRAP.(1-CENT, REPEAT) 125.00 100.00
- ❑ WRAPPER (5-CENT) 30.00 20.00
- ❑ WRAPPER (5-CENT, COIN) 40.00 30.00
- ❑ 1 Koufax/Ellis/Friend LL 30.00 15.00
- ❑ 2 Peters/Pizarro/Pascual LL 8.00 4.00
- ❑ 3 Koufax/Marichal/Spahn LL 20.00 10.00
- ❑ 4 Ford/Pascual/Bouton LL 8.00 4.00
- ❑ 5 Koufax/Malon/Drysdale LL 15.00 7.50
- ❑ 6 Pascual/Bunning/Stigman LL 8.00 4.00
- ❑ 7 Clemente/Groat/Aaron LL 20.00 10.00
- ❑ 8 Yaz/Kaline/Rollins LL 15.00 7.50

BRAVES

ED MATHEWS 3b-of

- ❑ 9 Aaron/McCov/Mays/Cep LL 30.00 15.00
- ❑ 10 Killebrew/Stuart/Allison LL 8.00 4.00
- ❑ 11 Aaron/Boyer/White LL 15.00 7.50
- ❑ 12 Stuart/Kaline/Killebrew LL 8.00 4.00
- ❑ 13 Hoyt Wilhelm 12.00 6.00
- ❑ 14 D.Nen RC/N.Willhite RC 3.00 1.50
- ❑ 15 Zoilo Versalles 6.00 3.00
- ❑ 16 John Boozer 3.00 1.50
- ❑ 17 Willie Kirkland 3.00 1.50
- ❑ 18 Billy O'Dell 3.00 1.50
- ❑ 19 Don Wert 3.00 1.50
- ❑ 20 Bob Friend 6.00 3.00
- ❑ 21 Yogi Berra MG 40.00 20.00
- ❑ 22 Jerry Adair 3.00 1.50
- ❑ 23 Chris Zachary RC 3.00 1.50
- ❑ 24 Carl Sawatski 3.00 1.50
- ❑ 25 Bill Monbouquette 3.00 1.50
- ❑ 26 Gino Cimoli 3.00 1.50
- ❑ 27 New York Mets TC 8.00 4.00
- ❑ 28 Claude Osteen 6.00 3.00
- ❑ 29 Lou Brock 40.00 20.00
- ❑ 30 Ron Perranoski 6.00 3.00
- ❑ 31 Dave Nicholson 3.00 1.50
- ❑ 32 Dean Chance 6.00 3.00
- ❑ 33 S.Ellis/M.Queen 6.00 3.00
- ❑ 34 Jim Perry 6.00 3.00
- ❑ 35 Eddie Mathews 20.00 10.00
- ❑ 36 Hal Reniff 3.00 1.50
- ❑ 37 Smoky Burgess 6.00 3.00
- ❑ 38 Jim Wynn RC 8.00 4.00
- ❑ 39 Hank Aguirre 3.00 1.50
- ❑ 40 Dick Groat 6.00 3.00
- ❑ 41 W.McCovey/L.Wagner 8.00 4.00
- ❑ 42 Moe Drabowsky 6.00 3.00
- ❑ 43 Roy Sievers 6.00 3.00
- ❑ 44 Duke Carmel 3.00 1.50
- ❑ 45 Milt Pappas 6.00 3.00
- ❑ 46 Ed Brinkman 3.00 1.50
- ❑ 47 J.Alou RC/R.Herbel 6.00 3.00
- ❑ 48 Bob Perry RC 3.00 1.50
- ❑ 49 Bill Henry 3.00 1.50
- ❑ 50 Mickey Mantle 500.00 300.00
- ❑ 51 Pete Richert 3.00 1.50
- ❑ 52 Chuck Hinton 3.00 1.50
- ❑ 53 Denis Menke 3.00 1.50
- ❑ 54 Sam Mele MG 3.00 1.50
- ❑ 55 Ernie Banks 40.00 20.00
- ❑ 56 Hal Brown 3.00 1.50
- ❑ 57 Tim Harkness 6.00 3.00
- ❑ 58 Don Demeter 6.00 3.00
- ❑ 59 Ernie Broglio 3.00 1.50
- ❑ 60 Frank Malzone 6.00 3.00
- ❑ 61 B.Rodgers/E.Sadowski 6.00 3.00
- ❑ 62 Ted Savage 3.00 1.50
- ❑ 63 John Orsino 3.00 1.50
- ❑ 64 Ted Abernathy 3.00 1.50
- ❑ 65 Felipe Alou 6.00 3.00
- ❑ 66 Eddie Fisher 3.00 1.50
- ❑ 67 Detroit Tigers TC 6.00 3.00
- ❑ 68 Willie Davis 6.00 3.00
- ❑ 69 Clete Boyer 6.00 3.00
- ❑ 70 Joe Torre 8.00 4.00
- ❑ 71 Jack Spring 3.00 1.50
- ❑ 72 Chico Cardenas 6.00 3.00
- ❑ 73 Jimmie Hall RC 8.00 4.00
- ❑ 74 B.Priddy RC/T.Butters 3.00 1.50
- ❑ 75 Wayne Causey 3.00 1.50
- ❑ 76 Checklist 1 10.00 5.00
- ❑ 77 Jerry Walker 3.00 1.50

No.	Card		
❑ 78	Merritt Ranew	3.00	1.50
❑ 79	Bob Heffner RC	3.00	1.50
❑ 80	Vada Pinson	8.00	4.00
❑ 81	N.Fox/H.Killebrew	12.00	6.00
❑ 82	Jim Davenport	6.00	3.00
❑ 83	Gus Triandos	6.00	3.00
❑ 84	Carl Willey	3.00	1.50
❑ 85	Pete Ward	3.00	1.50
❑ 86	Al Downing	6.00	3.00
❑ 87	St. Louis Cardinals TC	6.00	3.00
❑ 88	John Roseboro	6.00	3.00
❑ 89	Boog Powell	6.00	3.00
❑ 90	Earl Battey	3.00	1.50
❑ 91	Bob Bailey	6.00	3.00
❑ 92	Steve Ridzik	3.00	1.50
❑ 93	Gary Geiger	3.00	1.50
❑ 94	J.Britton RC/L.Maxie RC	3.00	1.50
❑ 95	George Altman	3.00	1.50
❑ 96	Bob Buhl	6.00	3.00
❑ 97	Jim Fregosi	6.00	3.00
❑ 98	Bill Bruton	3.00	1.50
❑ 99	Al Stanek RC	3.00	1.50
❑ 100	Elston Howard	6.00	3.00
❑ 101	Walt Alston MG	8.00	4.00
❑ 102	Checklist 2	10.00	5.00
❑ 103	Curt Flood	6.00	3.00
❑ 104	Art Mahaffey	6.00	3.00
❑ 105	Woody Held	3.00	1.50
❑ 106	Joe Nuxhall	6.00	3.00
❑ 107	B.Howard RC/F.Kruetzer RC	3.00	1.50
❑ 108	John Wyatt	3.00	1.50
❑ 109	Rusty Staub	6.00	3.00
❑ 110	Albie Pearson	6.00	3.00
❑ 111	Don Elston	3.00	1.50
❑ 112	Bob Tillman	3.00	1.50
❑ 113	Grover Powell RC	6.00	3.00
❑ 114	Don Lock	3.00	1.50
❑ 115	Frank Bolling	3.00	1.50
❑ 116	J.Ward RC/T.Oliva	12.00	6.00
❑ 117	Earl Francis	3.00	1.50
❑ 118	John Blanchard	6.00	3.00
❑ 119	Gary Kolb RC	3.00	1.50
❑ 120	Don Drysdale	20.00	10.00
❑ 121	Pete Runnels	6.00	3.00
❑ 122	Don McMahon	3.00	1.50
❑ 123	Jose Pagan	3.00	1.50
❑ 124	Orlando Pena	3.00	1.50
❑ 125	Pete Rose UER	250.00	150.00
❑ 126	Russ Snyder	3.00	1.50
❑ 127	A.Gatewood RC/D.Simpson	3.00	1.50
❑ 128	Mickey Lolich RC	20.00	10.00
❑ 129	Amado Samuel	3.00	1.50
❑ 130	Gary Peters	6.00	3.00
❑ 131	Steve Boros	3.00	1.50
❑ 132	Milwaukee Braves TC	6.00	3.00
❑ 133	Jim Grant	6.00	3.00
❑ 134	Don Zimmer	6.00	3.00
❑ 135	Johnny Callison	6.00	3.00
❑ 136	Sandy Koufax WS1	20.00	10.00
❑ 137	Willie Davis WS2	8.00	4.00
❑ 138	Ron Fairly WS3	8.00	4.00
❑ 139	Frank Howard WS4	8.00	4.00
❑ 140	Dodgers Celebrate WS	8.00	4.00
❑ 141	Danny Murtaugh MG	6.00	3.00
❑ 142	John Bateman	3.00	1.50
❑ 143	Bubba Phillips	3.00	1.50
❑ 144	Al Worthington	3.00	1.50
❑ 145	Norm Siebern	3.00	1.50
❑ 146	T.John RC/B.Chance RC	30.00	15.00
❑ 147	Ray Sadecki	3.00	1.50
❑ 148	J.C. Martin	3.00	1.50
❑ 149	Paul Foytack	3.00	1.50
❑ 150	Willie Mays	125.00	75.00
❑ 151	Kansas City Athletics TC	6.00	3.00
❑ 152	Denny Lemaster	3.00	1.50
❑ 153	Dick Williams	6.00	3.00
❑ 154	Dick Tracewski RC	6.00	3.00
❑ 155	Duke Snider	30.00	15.00
❑ 156	Bill Dailey	3.00	1.50
❑ 157	Gene Mauch MG	6.00	3.00
❑ 158	Ken Johnson	3.00	1.50
❑ 159	Charlie Dees RC	3.00	1.50
❑ 160	Ken Boyer	6.00	3.00
❑ 161	Dave McNally	6.00	3.00
❑ 162	D.Sisler/V.Pinson	6.00	3.00
❑ 163	Donn Clendenon	6.00	3.00
❑ 164	Bud Daley	3.00	1.50
❑ 165	Jerry Lumpe	3.00	1.50
❑ 166	Marty Keough	3.00	1.50
❑ 167	M.Brumley RC/L.Piniella RC	30.00	15.00
❑ 168	Al Weis	3.00	1.50
❑ 169	Del Crandall	6.00	3.00
❑ 170	Dick Radatz	6.00	3.00
❑ 171	Ty Cline	3.00	1.50
❑ 172	Cleveland Indians TC	6.00	3.00
❑ 173	Ryne Duren	6.00	3.00
❑ 174	Doc Edwards	3.00	1.50
❑ 175	Billy Williams	12.00	6.00
❑ 176	Tracy Stallard	3.00	1.50
❑ 177	Harmon Killebrew	20.00	10.00
❑ 178	Hank Bauer MG	6.00	3.00
❑ 179	Carl Warwick	3.00	1.50
❑ 180	Tommy Davis	6.00	3.00
❑ 181	Dave Wickersham	3.00	1.50
❑ 182	C.Yastrzemski/C.Schilling	15.00	7.50
❑ 183	Ron Taylor	3.00	1.50
❑ 184	Al Luplow	3.00	1.50
❑ 185	Jim O'Toole	6.00	3.00
❑ 186	Roman Mejias	3.00	1.50
❑ 187	Ed Roebuck	3.00	1.50
❑ 188	Checklist 3	10.00	5.00
❑ 189	Bob Hendley	3.00	1.50
❑ 190	Bobby Richardson	8.00	4.00
❑ 191	Clay Dalrymple	6.00	3.00
❑ 192	J.Boccabella RC/B.Cowan RC	3.00	1.50
❑ 193	Jerry Lynch	3.00	1.50
❑ 194	John Goryl	3.00	1.50
❑ 195	Floyd Robinson	3.00	1.50
❑ 196	Jim Gentile	3.00	1.50
❑ 197	Frank Lary	6.00	3.00
❑ 198	Len Gabrielson	4.00	2.00
❑ 199	Joe Azcue	4.00	2.00
❑ 200	Sandy Koufax	120.00	70.00
❑ 201	S.Bowens RC/W.Bunker RC	6.00	3.00
❑ 202	Galen Cisco	6.00	3.00
❑ 203	John Kennedy RC	6.00	3.00
❑ 204	Matty Alou	6.00	3.00
❑ 205	Nellie Fox	12.00	6.00
❑ 206	Steve Hamilton	6.00	3.00
❑ 207	Fred Hutchinson MG	6.00	3.00
❑ 208	Wes Covington	6.00	3.00
❑ 209	Bob Allen	4.00	2.00
❑ 210	Carl Yastrzemski	40.00	20.00
❑ 211	Jim Coker	4.00	2.00
❑ 212	Pete Lovrich	4.00	2.00
❑ 213	Los Angeles Angels TC	6.00	3.00
❑ 214	Ken McMullen	6.00	3.00
❑ 215	Ray Herbert	4.00	2.00
❑ 216	Mike de la Hoz	4.00	2.00
❑ 217	Jim King	4.00	2.00
❑ 218	Hank Fischer	4.00	2.00
❑ 219	A.Downing/J.Bouton	6.00	3.00
❑ 220	Dick Ellsworth	6.00	3.00
❑ 221	Bob Saverine	4.00	2.00
❑ 222	Billy Pierce	6.00	3.00
❑ 223	George Banks	4.00	2.00
❑ 224	Tommie Sisk	4.00	2.00
❑ 225	Roger Maris	60.00	35.00
❑ 226	J.Grote RC/L.Yellen RC	6.00	3.00
❑ 227	Barry Latman	4.00	2.00
❑ 228	Felix Mantilla	4.00	2.00
❑ 229	Charley Lau	6.00	3.00
❑ 230	Brooks Robinson	40.00	20.00
❑ 231	Dick Calmus RC	4.00	2.00
❑ 232	Al Lopez MG	8.00	4.00
❑ 233	Hal Smith	4.00	2.00
❑ 234	Gary Bell	4.00	2.00
❑ 235	Ron Hunt	4.00	2.00
❑ 236	Bill Faul	4.00	2.00
❑ 237	Chicago Cubs TC	6.00	3.00
❑ 238	Roy McMillan	6.00	3.00
❑ 239	Herm Starrette RC	4.00	2.00
❑ 240	Bill White	6.00	3.00
❑ 241	Jim Owens	4.00	2.00
❑ 242	Harvey Kuenn	6.00	3.00
❑ 243	R.Allen RC/J.Hernstein	30.00	15.00
❑ 244	Tony LaRussa RC	30.00	15.00
❑ 245	Dick Stigman	4.00	2.00
❑ 246	Manny Mota	6.00	3.00
❑ 247	Dave DeBusschere	6.00	3.00
❑ 248	Johnny Pesky MG	6.00	3.00
❑ 249	Doug Camilli	4.00	2.00
❑ 250	Al Kaline	40.00	20.00
❑ 251	Choo Choo Coleman	6.00	3.00
❑ 252	Ken Aspromonte	4.00	2.00
❑ 253	Wally Post	6.00	3.00
❑ 254	Don Hoak	6.00	3.00
❑ 255	Lee Thomas	6.00	3.00
❑ 256	Johnny Weekly	4.00	2.00
❑ 257	San Francisco Giants TC	6.00	3.00
❑ 258	Garry Roggenburk	4.00	2.00
❑ 259	Harry Bright	4.00	2.00
❑ 260	Frank Robinson	40.00	20.00
❑ 261	Jim Hannan	4.00	2.00
❑ 262	M.Shannon RC/H.Fanok	8.00	4.00
❑ 263	Chuck Estrada	4.00	2.00
❑ 264	Jim Landis	4.00	2.00
❑ 265	Jim Bunning	12.00	6.00
❑ 266	Gene Freese	4.00	2.00
❑ 267	Wilbur Wood RC	6.00	3.00
❑ 268	D.Murtaugh/B.Virdon	6.00	3.00
❑ 269	Ellis Burton	4.00	2.00
❑ 270	Rich Rollins	6.00	3.00
❑ 271	Bob Sadowski	4.00	2.00
❑ 272	Jake Wood	4.00	2.00
❑ 273	Mel Nelson	4.00	2.00
❑ 274	Checklist 4	10.00	5.00
❑ 275	John Tsitouris	4.00	2.00
❑ 276	Jose Tartabull	6.00	3.00
❑ 277	Ken Retzer	4.00	2.00
❑ 278	Bobby Shantz	6.00	3.00
❑ 279	Joe Koppe	4.00	2.00
❑ 280	Juan Marichal	15.00	7.50
❑ 281	J.,Gibbs/T.Metclaf RC	6.00	3.00
❑ 282	Bob Bruce	4.00	2.00
❑ 283	Tom McCraw RC	4.00	2.00
❑ 284	Dick Schofield	4.00	2.00
❑ 285	Robin Roberts	15.00	7.50
❑ 286	Don Landrum	4.00	2.00
❑ 287	T.Conig.RC/B.Spans.RC	50.00	30.00
❑ 288	Al Moran	4.00	2.00
❑ 289	Frank Funk	4.00	2.00
❑ 290	Bob Allison	6.00	3.00
❑ 291	Phil Ortega	4.00	2.00
❑ 292	Mike Roarke	4.00	2.00
❑ 293	Philadelphia Phillies TC	6.00	3.00
❑ 294	Ken L. Hunt	4.00	2.00
❑ 295	Roger Craig	6.00	3.00
❑ 296	Ed Kirkpatrick	4.00	2.00
❑ 297	Ken MacKenzie	4.00	2.00
❑ 298	Harry Craft MG	4.00	2.00
❑ 299	Bill Stafford	4.00	2.00
❑ 300	Hank Aaron	100.00	60.00
❑ 301	Larry Brown RC	4.00	2.00
❑ 302	Dan Pfister	4.00	2.00
❑ 303	Jim Campbell	4.00	2.00
❑ 304	Bob Johnson	4.00	2.00
❑ 305	Jack Lamabe	4.00	2.00
❑ 306	Willie Mays/O.Cepeda	40.00	20.00
❑ 307	Joe Gibbon	4.00	2.00
❑ 308	Gene Stephens	4.00	2.00
❑ 309	Paul Toth	4.00	2.00
❑ 310	Jim Gilliam	6.00	3.00
❑ 311	Tom W. Brown RC	6.00	3.00
❑ 312	F.Fisher RC/F.Gladding RC	4.00	2.00
❑ 313	Chuck Hiller	4.00	2.00
❑ 314	Jerry Buchek	4.00	2.00
❑ 315	Bo Belinsky	6.00	3.00
❑ 316	Gene Oliver	4.00	2.00
❑ 317	Al Smith	4.00	2.00
❑ 318	Minnesota Twins TC	6.00	3.00
❑ 319	Paul Brown	4.00	2.00
❑ 320	Rocky Colavito	12.00	6.00
❑ 321	Bob Lillis	4.00	2.00
❑ 322	George Brunet	4.00	2.00
❑ 323	John Buzhardt	4.00	2.00
❑ 324	Casey Stengel MG	15.00	7.50
❑ 325	Hector Lopez	6.00	3.00
❑ 326	Ron Brand RC	4.00	2.00
❑ 327	Don Blasingame	4.00	2.00
❑ 328	Bob Shaw	4.00	2.00
❑ 329	Russ Nixon	4.00	2.00
❑ 330	Tommy Harper	6.00	3.00
❑ 331	Maris/Cash/Mantle/Kaline	150.00	90.00
❑ 332	Ray Washburn	4.00	2.00
❑ 333	Billy Moran	4.00	2.00
❑ 334	Lew Krausse	4.00	2.00
❑ 335	Don Mossi	6.00	3.00

❑ 336 Andre Rodgers 4.00 2.00
❑ 337 A.Ferrara RC/J.Torborg RC 6.00 3.00
❑ 338 Jack Kralick 4.00 2.00
❑ 339 Walt Bond 4.00 2.00
❑ 340 Joe Cunningham 4.00 2.00
❑ 341 Jim Roland 4.00 2.00
❑ 342 Willie Stargell 30.00 15.00
❑ 343 Washington Senators TC 6.00 3.00
❑ 344 Phil Linz 6.00 3.00
❑ 345 Frank Thomas 8.00 4.00
❑ 346 Joey Jay 4.00 2.00
❑ 347 Bobby Wine 6.00 3.00
❑ 348 Ed Lopat MG 6.00 3.00
❑ 349 Art Fowler 4.00 2.00
❑ 350 Willie McCovey 25.00 12.50
❑ 351 Dan Schneider 4.00 2.00
❑ 352 Eddie Bressoud 4.00 2.00
❑ 353 Wally Moon 6.00 3.00
❑ 354 Dave Giusti 4.00 2.00
❑ 355 Vic Power 6.00 3.00
❑ 356 B.McCool RC/C.Ruiz 6.00 3.00
❑ 357 Charley James 4.00 2.00
❑ 358 Ron Kline 4.00 2.00
❑ 359 Jim Schaffer 4.00 2.00
❑ 360 Joe Pepitone 12.00 6.00
❑ 361 Jay Hook 4.00 2.00
❑ 362 Checklist 5 10.00 5.00
❑ 363 Dick McAuliffe 6.00 3.00
❑ 364 Joe Gaines 4.00 2.00
❑ 365 Cal McLish 6.00 3.00
❑ 366 Nelson Mathews 4.00 2.00
❑ 367 Fred Whitfield 4.00 2.00
❑ 368 F.Ackley RC/D.Buford RC 6.00 3.00
❑ 369 Jerry Zimmerman 4.00 2.00
❑ 370 Hal Woodeshick 4.00 2.00
❑ 371 Frank Howard 8.00 4.00
❑ 372 Howie Koplitz 8.00 4.00
❑ 373 Pittsburgh Pirates TC 12.00 6.00
❑ 374 Bobby Bolin 8.00 4.00
❑ 375 Ron Santo 10.00 5.00
❑ 376 Dave Morehead 8.00 4.00
❑ 377 Bob Skinner 8.00 4.00
❑ 378 W.Woodward RC/J.Smith 10.00 5.00
❑ 379 Tony Gonzalez 8.00 4.00
❑ 380 Whitey Ford 40.00 20.00
❑ 381 Bob Taylor 8.00 4.00
❑ 382 Wes Stock 8.00 4.00
❑ 383 Bill Rigney MG 8.00 4.00
❑ 384 Ron Hansen 8.00 4.00
❑ 385 Curt Simmons 10.00 5.00
❑ 386 Lenny Green 8.00 4.00
❑ 387 Terry Fox 8.00 4.00
❑ 388 J.O'Donoghue RC/G.Williams 10.00 5.00
❑ 389 Jim Umbricht 10.00 5.00
❑ 390 Orlando Cepeda 25.00 12.50
❑ 391 Sam McDowell 10.00 5.00
❑ 392 Jim Pagliaroni 8.00 4.00
❑ 393 C.Stengel/E.Kranepool 15.00 7.50
❑ 394 Bob Miller 8.00 4.00
❑ 395 Tom Tresh 10.00 5.00
❑ 396 Dennis Bennett 8.00 4.00
❑ 397 Chuck Cottier 8.00 4.00
❑ 398 B.Haas/D.Smith 10.00 5.00
❑ 399 Jackie Brandt 8.00 4.00
❑ 400 Warren Spahn 40.00 20.00
❑ 401 Charlie Maxwell 8.00 4.00
❑ 402 Tom Sturdivant 8.00 4.00
❑ 403 Cincinnati Reds TC 12.00 6.00
❑ 404 Tony Martinez 8.00 4.00
❑ 405 Ken McBride 8.00 4.00
❑ 406 Al Spangler 8.00 4.00
❑ 407 Bill Freehan 10.00 5.00
❑ 408 J.Stewart RC/F.Burdette RC 8.00 4.00
❑ 409 Bill Fischer 8.00 4.00
❑ 410 Dick Stuart 10.00 5.00
❑ 411 Lee Walls 8.00 4.00
❑ 412 Ray Culp 10.00 5.00
❑ 413 Johnny Keane MG 8.00 4.00
❑ 414 Jack Sanford 8.00 4.00
❑ 415 Tony Kubek 15.00 7.50
❑ 416 Lee Maye 8.00 4.00
❑ 417 Don Cardwell 8.00 4.00
❑ 418 D.Knowles RC/B.Narum RC 10.00 5.00
❑ 419 Ken Harrelson RC 15.00 7.50
❑ 420 Jim Maloney 10.00 5.00
❑ 421 Camilo Carreon 8.00 4.00
❑ 422 Jack Fisher 8.00 4.00
❑ 423 H.Aaron/W.Mays 125.00 75.00
❑ 424 Dick Bertell 8.00 4.00
❑ 425 Norm Cash 10.00 5.00
❑ 426 Bob Rodgers 8.00 4.00
❑ 427 Don Rudolph 8.00 4.00
❑ 428 A.Skeen RC/P.Smith RC 8.00 4.00
❑ 429 Tim McCarver 10.00 5.00
❑ 430 Juan Pizarro 8.00 4.00
❑ 431 George Alusik 8.00 4.00
❑ 432 Ruben Amaro 10.00 5.00
❑ 433 New York Yankees TC 40.00 20.00
❑ 434 Don Nottebart 8.00 4.00
❑ 435 Vic Davalillo 8.00 4.00
❑ 436 Charlie Neal 10.00 5.00
❑ 437 Ed Bailey 8.00 4.00
❑ 438 Checklist 6 15.00 7.50
❑ 439 Harvey Haddix 10.00 5.00
❑ 440 Roberto Clemente UER 250.00 150.00
❑ 441 Bob Duliba 8.00 4.00
❑ 442 Pumpsie Green 10.00 5.00
❑ 443 Chuck Dressen MG 10.00 5.00
❑ 444 Larry Jackson 8.00 4.00
❑ 445 Bill Skowron 10.00 5.00
❑ 446 Julian Javier 15.00 7.50
❑ 447 Ted Bowsfield 8.00 4.00
❑ 448 Cookie Rojas 10.00 5.00
❑ 449 Deron Johnson 10.00 5.00
❑ 450 Steve Barber 8.00 4.00
❑ 451 Joe Amalfitano 8.00 4.00
❑ 452 G.Garrido RC/J.Hart RC 10.00 5.00
❑ 453 Frank Baumann 8.00 4.00
❑ 454 Tommie Aaron 10.00 5.00
❑ 455 Bernie Allen 8.00 4.00
❑ 456 W.Parker RC/J.Werhas RC 10.00 5.00
❑ 457 Jesse Gonder 8.00 4.00
❑ 458 Ralph Terry 10.00 5.00
❑ 459 P.Charton RC/D.Jones RC 8.00 4.00
❑ 460 Bob Gibson 40.00 20.00
❑ 461 George Thomas 8.00 4.00
❑ 462 Birdie Tebbetts MG 8.00 4.00
❑ 463 Don Leppert 8.00 4.00
❑ 464 Dallas Green 15.00 7.50
❑ 465 Mike Hershberger 8.00 4.00
❑ 466 D.Green RC/A.Monteagudo RC 10.00 5.00
❑ 467 Bob Aspromonte 8.00 4.00
❑ 468 Gaylord Perry 40.00 20.00
❑ 469 F.Norman RC/S.Slaughter RC 10.00 5.00
❑ 470 Jim Bouton 10.00 5.00
❑ 471 Gates Brown RC 10.00 5.00
❑ 472 Vern Law 10.00 5.00
❑ 473 Baltimore Orioles TC 12.00 6.00
❑ 474 Larry Sherry 10.00 5.00
❑ 475 Ed Charles 8.00 4.00
❑ 476 R.Carty RC/D.Kelley RC 15.00 7.50
❑ 477 Mike Joyce 8.00 4.00
❑ 478 Dick Howser 10.00 5.00
❑ 479 D.Bakenhaster RC/J.Lewis RC 8.00 4.00
❑ 480 Bob Purkey 8.00 4.00
❑ 481 Chuck Schilling 8.00 4.00
❑ 482 J.Briggs RC/D.Cater RC 10.00 5.00
❑ 483 Fred Valentine RC 8.00 4.00
❑ 484 Bill Pleis 8.00 4.00
❑ 485 Tom Haller 8.00 4.00
❑ 486 Bob Kennedy MG 8.00 4.00
❑ 487 Mike McCormick 10.00 5.00
❑ 488 P.Mikkelsen RC/B.Meyer RC 15.00 7.50
❑ 489 Julio Navarro 8.00 4.00
❑ 490 Ron Fairly 10.00 5.00
❑ 491 Ed Rakow 8.00 4.00
❑ 492 J.Beauchamp RC/M.White RC 8.00 4.00
❑ 493 Don Lee 8.00 4.00
❑ 494 Al Jackson 8.00 4.00
❑ 495 Bill Virdon 10.00 5.00
❑ 496 Chicago White Sox TC 12.00 6.00
❑ 497 Jeoff Long RC 8.00 4.00
❑ 498 Dave Stenhouse 8.00 4.00
❑ 499 C.Slamon RC/G.Seyfried RC 8.00 4.00
❑ 500 Camilo Pascual 10.00 5.00
❑ 501 Bob Veale 10.00 5.00
❑ 502 B.Knoop RC/B.Lee RC 8.00 4.00
❑ 503 Earl Wilson 8.00 4.00
❑ 504 Claude Raymond 8.00 4.00
❑ 505 Stan Williams 8.00 4.00
❑ 506 Bobby Bragan MG 8.00 4.00
❑ 507 Johnny Edwards 8.00 4.00
❑ 508 Diego Segui 8.00 4.00
❑ 509 G.Alley RC/O.McFarlane RC 10.00 5.00
❑ 510 Lindy McDaniel 10.00 5.00
❑ 511 Lou Jackson 10.00 5.00
❑ 512 W.Horton RC/J.Sparma RC 15.00 7.50
❑ 513 Don Larsen 10.00 5.00
❑ 514 Jim Hickman 10.00 5.00
❑ 515 Johnny Romano 8.00 4.00
❑ 516 J.Arrigo RC/D.Siebler RC 8.00 4.00
❑ 517A Checklist 7 ERR 25.00 12.50
❑ 517B Checklist 7 COR 15.00 7.50
❑ 518 Carl Bouldin 8.00 4.00
❑ 519 Charlie Smith 8.00 4.00
❑ 520 Jack Baldschun 10.00 5.00
❑ 521 Tom Satriano 8.00 4.00
❑ 522 Bob Tiefenauer 8.00 4.00
❑ 523 Lou Burdette UER 20.00 10.00
❑ 524 J.Dickson RC/B.Klaus RC 15.00 7.50
❑ 525 Al McBean 15.00 7.50
❑ 526 Lou Clinton 15.00 7.50
❑ 527 Larry Bearnarth 15.00 7.50
❑ 528 D.Duncan RC/T.Reynolds RC 20.00 10.00
❑ 529 Alvin Dark MG 20.00 10.00
❑ 530 Leon Wagner 15.00 7.50
❑ 531 Los Angeles Dodgers TC 25.00 12.50
❑ 532 B.Bloomfield RC/J.Nossek RC 15.00 7.50
❑ 533 Johnny Klippstein 15.00 7.50
❑ 534 Gus Bell 15.00 7.50
❑ 535 Phil Regan 15.00 7.50
❑ 536 L.Elliot/J.Stephenson RC 15.00 7.50
❑ 537 Dan Osinski 15.00 7.50
❑ 538 Minnie Minoso 20.00 10.00
❑ 539 Roy Face 20.00 10.00
❑ 540 Luis Aparicio 40.00 20.00
❑ 541 P.Roof/P.Niekro RC 80.00 50.00
❑ 542 Don Mincher 15.00 7.50
❑ 543 Bob Uecker 40.00 20.00
❑ 544 S.Hertz RC/J.Hoerner RC 15.00 7.50
❑ 545 Max Alvis 15.00 7.50
❑ 546 Joe Christopher 15.00 7.50
❑ 547 Gil Hodges MG 30.00 15.00
❑ 548 W.Schurr RC/P.Speckenbach RC 20.00 10.00
❑ 549 Joe Moeller 15.00 7.50
❑ 550 Ken Hubbs MEM 40.00 20.00
❑ 551 Billy Hoeft 15.00 7.50
❑ 552 T.Kelley RC/S.Siebert RC 15.00 7.50
❑ 553 Jim Brewer 15.00 7.50
❑ 554 Hank Foiles 15.00 7.50
❑ 555 Lee Stange 15.00 7.50
❑ 556 S.Dillon RC/R.Locke RC 15.00 7.50
❑ 557 Leo Burke 15.00 7.50
❑ 558 Don Schwall 15.00 7.50
❑ 559 Dick Phillips 15.00 7.50
❑ 560 Dick Farrell 15.00 7.50
❑ 561 D.Bennett RC/R.Wise RC 20.00 10.00
❑ 562 Pedro Ramos 15.00 7.50
❑ 563 Dal Maxvill 20.00 10.00
❑ 564 J.McCabe RC/J.McNertney RC 20.00 10.00
❑ 565 Stu Miller 15.00 7.50
❑ 566 Ed Kranepool 20.00 10.00
❑ 567 Jim Kaat 20.00 10.00
❑ 568 P.Gagliano RC/C.Peterson RC 15.00 7.50
❑ 569 Fred Newman 15.00 7.50
❑ 570 Bill Mazeroski 40.00 20.00
❑ 571 Gene Conley 15.00 7.50
❑ 572 D.Gray RC/D.Egan 15.00 7.50
❑ 573 Jim Duffalo 15.00 7.50
❑ 574 Manny Jimenez 15.00 7.50
❑ 575 Tony Cloninger 15.00 7.50
❑ 576 J.Hinsley RC/B.Wakefield RC 15.00 7.50
❑ 577 Gordy Coleman 15.00 7.50
❑ 578 Glen Hobbie 15.00 7.50
❑ 579 Boston Red Sox TC 25.00 12.50
❑ 580 Johnny Podres 20.00 10.00
❑ 581 P.Gonzalez/A.Moore RC 20.00 10.00
❑ 582 Rod Kanehl 20.00 10.00
❑ 583 Tito Francona 15.00 7.50
❑ 584 Joel Horlen 15.00 7.50
❑ 585 Tony Taylor 20.00 10.00
❑ 586 Jimmy Piersall 20.00 10.00
❑ 587 Bennie Daniels 20.00 10.00

1965 Topps

❑ COMPLETE SET (598) 4000.00 2500.00
❑ COMMON CARD (1-196) 2.00 1.00
❑ COMMON CARD (197-283) 2.50 1.25

❑ COMMON CARD (284-370) 4.00 2.00
❑ COMMON CARD (371-598) 8.00 4.00
❑ WRAPPER (1-CENT) 125.00 100.00
❑ WRAPPER (5-CENT) 100.00 75.00
❑ 1 Oliva/Howard/Brooks LL 20.00 10.00
❑ 2 Clemente/Aaron/Carty LL 25.00 12.50
❑ 3 Killebrew/Mantle/Powell LL 50.00 30.00
❑ 4 Mays/B.Will/Cepeda LL 15.00 7.50
❑ 5 Brooks/Kill/Mantle LL 40.00 20.00
❑ 6 Boyer/Mays Santo LL 12.00 6.00
❑ 7 D.Chance/J.Horlen LL 5.00 2.50
❑ 8 S.Koufax/D.Drysdale LL 20.00 10.00
❑ 9 Chance/Peters/Wick LL 5.00 2.50
❑ 10 Jackson/Sad/Marichal LL 5.00 2.50
❑ 11 Downing/Chance/Pascual LL 5.00 2.50
❑ 12 Veale/Drysdale/Gibson LL 10.00 5.00
❑ 13 Pedro Ramos 4.00 2.00
❑ 14 Len Gabrielson 2.00 1.00
❑ 15 Robin Roberts 10.00 5.00
❑ 16 Joe Morgan RC DP 60.00 35.00
❑ 17 Johnny Romano 2.00 1.00
❑ 18 Bill McCool 2.00 1.00
❑ 19 Gates Brown 4.00 2.00
❑ 20 Jim Bunning 10.00 5.00
❑ 21 Don Blasingame 2.00 1.00
❑ 22 Charlie Smith 2.00 1.00
❑ 23 Bob Tiefenauer 2.00 1.00
❑ 24 Minnesota Twins TC 6.00 3.00
❑ 25 Al McBean 2.00 1.00
❑ 26 Bobby Knoop 2.00 1.00
❑ 27 Dick Bertell 2.00 1.00
❑ 28 Barney Schultz 2.00 1.00
❑ 29 Felix Mantilla 2.00 1.00
❑ 30 Jim Bouton 6.00 3.00
❑ 31 Mike White 2.00 1.00
❑ 32 Herman Franks MG 2.00 1.00
❑ 33 Jackie Brandt 2.00 1.00
❑ 34 Cal Koonce 2.00 1.00
❑ 35 Ed Charles 2.00 1.00
❑ 36 Bobby Wine 2.00 1.00
❑ 37 Fred Gladding 2.00 1.00
❑ 38 Jim King 2.00 1.00
❑ 39 Gerry Arrigo 2.00 1.00
❑ 40 Frank Howard 6.00 3.00
❑ 41 B.Howard/M.Staehle RC 2.00 1.00
❑ 42 Earl Wilson 4.00 2.00
❑ 43 Mike Shannon 4.00 2.00
❑ 44 Wade Blasingame RC 2.00 1.00
❑ 45 Roy McMillan 4.00 2.00
❑ 46 Bob Lee 2.00 1.00
❑ 47 Tommy Harper 4.00 2.00
❑ 48 Claude Raymond 4.00 2.00
❑ 49 C.Blefary RC/J.Miller 4.00 2.00
❑ 50 Juan Marichal 10.00 5.00
❑ 51 Bill Bryan 2.00 1.00
❑ 52 Ed Roebuck 2.00 1.00
❑ 53 Dick McAuliffe 4.00 2.00
❑ 54 Joe Gibbon 2.00 1.00
❑ 55 Tony Conigliaro 15.00 7.50
❑ 56 Ron Kline 2.00 1.00
❑ 57 St. Louis Cardinals TC 6.00 3.00
❑ 58 Fred Talbot RC 2.00 1.00
❑ 59 Nate Oliver 2.00 1.00
❑ 60 Jim O'Toole 4.00 2.00
❑ 61 Chris Cannizzaro 2.00 1.00
❑ 62 Jim Kaat UER DP 6.00 3.00
❑ 63 Ty Cline 2.00 1.00
❑ 64 Lou Burdette 4.00 2.00
❑ 65 Tony Kubek 10.00 5.00
❑ 66 Bill Rigney MG 2.00 1.00
❑ 67 Harvey Haddix 4.00 2.00
❑ 68 Del Crandall 4.00 2.00
❑ 69 Bill Virdon 4.00 2.00
❑ 70 Bill Skowron 6.00 3.00
❑ 71 John O'Donoghue 2.00 1.00
❑ 72 Tony Gonzalez 2.00 1.00
❑ 73 Dennis Ribant RC 2.00 1.00
❑ 74 R.Petrocelli RC/J.Steph RC 10.00 5.00
❑ 75 Deron Johnson 4.00 2.00
❑ 76 Sam McDowell 6.00 3.00
❑ 77 Doug Camilli 2.00 1.00
❑ 78 Dal Maxvill 2.00 1.00
❑ 79A Checklist 1 Cannizzaro 10.00 5.00
❑ 79B Checklist 1 C.Cannizzaro 10.00 5.00
❑ 80 Turk Farrell 2.00 1.00
❑ 81 Don Buford 4.00 2.00
❑ 82 S.Alomar RC/J.Braun RC 6.00 3.00
❑ 83 George Thomas 2.00 1.00
❑ 84 Ron Herbel 2.00 1.00
❑ 85 Willie Smith RC 2.00 1.00
❑ 86 Buster Narum 2.00 1.00
❑ 87 Nelson Mathews 2.00 1.00
❑ 88 Jack Lamabe 2.00 1.00
❑ 89 Mike Hershberger 2.00 1.00
❑ 90 Rich Rollins 4.00 2.00
❑ 91 Chicago Cubs TC 6.00 3.00
❑ 92 Dick Howser 4.00 2.00
❑ 93 Jack Fisher 2.00 1.00
❑ 94 Charlie Lau 4.00 2.00
❑ 95 Bill Mazeroski DP 6.00 3.00
❑ 96 Sonny Siebert 4.00 2.00
❑ 97 Pedro Gonzalez 2.00 1.00
❑ 98 Bob Miller 2.00 1.00
❑ 99 Gil Hodges MG 6.00 3.00
❑ 100 Ken Boyer 10.00 5.00
❑ 101 Fred Newman 2.00 1.00
❑ 102 Steve Boros 2.00 1.00
❑ 103 Harvey Kuenn 4.00 2.00
❑ 104 Checklist 2 10.00 5.00
❑ 105 Chico Salmon 2.00 1.00
❑ 106 Gene Oliver 2.00 1.00
❑ 107 P.Corrales RC/C.Shockley RC 4.00 2.00
❑ 108 Don Mincher 2.00 1.00
❑ 109 Walt Bond 2.00 1.00
❑ 110 Ron Santo 6.00 3.00
❑ 111 Lee Thomas 4.00 2.00
❑ 112 Derrell Griffith RC 2.00 1.00
❑ 113 Steve Barber 2.00 1.00
❑ 114 Jim Hickman 4.00 2.00
❑ 115 Bobby Richardson 10.00 5.00
❑ 116 D.Dowling RC/B.Tolan RC 4.00 2.00
❑ 117 Wes Stock 2.00 1.00
❑ 118 Hal Lanier RC 4.00 2.00
❑ 119 John Kennedy 2.00 1.00
❑ 120 Frank Robinson 40.00 20.00
❑ 121 Gene Alley 4.00 2.00
❑ 122 Bill Pleis 2.00 1.00
❑ 123 Frank Thomas 4.00 2.00
❑ 124 Tom Satriano 2.00 1.00
❑ 125 Juan Pizarro 2.00 1.00
❑ 126 Los Angeles Dodgers TC 6.00 3.00
❑ 127 Frank Lary 2.00 1.00
❑ 128 Vic Davalillo 2.00 1.00
❑ 129 Bennie Daniels 2.00 1.00
❑ 130 Al Kaline 40.00 20.00
❑ 131 Johnny Keane MG 2.00 1.00
❑ 132 Cards Take Opener WS1 10.00 5.00
❑ 133 Mel Stottlemyre WS2 6.00 3.00
❑ 134 Mickey Mantle WS3 80.00 50.00
❑ 135 Ken Boyer WS4 10.00 5.00
❑ 136 Tim McCarver WS5 6.00 3.00
❑ 137 Jim Bouton WS6 6.00 3.00
❑ 138 Bob Gibson WS7 12.00 6.00
❑ 139 Cards Celebrate WS 6.00 3.00
❑ 140 Dean Chance 4.00 2.00
❑ 141 Charlie James 2.00 1.00
❑ 142 Bill Monbouquette 2.00 1.00
❑ 143 J.Gelnar RC/J.May RC 2.00 1.00
❑ 144 Ed Kranepool 4.00 2.00
❑ 145 Luis Tiant RC 10.00 5.00
❑ 146 Ron Hansen 2.00 1.00
❑ 147 Dennis Bennett 2.00 1.00
❑ 148 Willie Kirkland 2.00 1.00
❑ 149 Wayne Schurr 2.00 1.00
❑ 150 Brooks Robinson 40.00 20.00
❑ 151 Kansas City Athletics TC 6.00 3.00
❑ 152 Phil Ortega 2.00 1.00
❑ 153 Norm Cash 6.00 3.00
❑ 154 Bob Humphreys RC 2.00 1.00
❑ 155 Roger Maris 60.00 35.00
❑ 156 Bob Sadowski 2.00 1.00
❑ 157 Zoilo Versalles 4.00 2.00
❑ 158 Dick Sisler 2.00 1.00
❑ 159 Jim Duffalo 2.00 1.00
❑ 160 Roberto Clemente UER 175.00 100.00
❑ 161 Frank Baumann 2.00 1.00
❑ 162 Russ Nixon 2.00 1.00
❑ 163 Johnny Briggs 2.00 1.00
❑ 164 Al Spangler 2.00 1.00
❑ 165 Dick Ellsworth 2.00 1.00
❑ 166 G.Culver RC/T.Agee RC 4.00 2.00
❑ 167 Bill Wakefield 2.00 1.00
❑ 168 Dick Green 2.00 1.00
❑ 169 Dave Vineyard RC 2.00 1.00
❑ 170 Hank Aaron 150.00 90.00
❑ 171 Jim Roland 2.00 1.00
❑ 172 Jimmy Piersall 6.00 3.00
❑ 173 Detroit Tigers TC 6.00 3.00
❑ 174 Joey Jay 2.00 1.00
❑ 175 Bob Aspromonte 2.00 1.00
❑ 176 Willie McCovey 20.00 10.00
❑ 177 Pete Mikkelsen 2.00 1.00
❑ 178 Dalton Jones 2.00 1.00
❑ 179 Hal Woodeshick 2.00 1.00
❑ 180 Bob Allison 4.00 2.00
❑ 181 D.Loun RC/J.McCabe 2.00 1.00
❑ 182 Mike de la Hoz 2.00 1.00
❑ 183 Dave Nicholson 2.00 1.00
❑ 184 John Boozer 2.00 1.00
❑ 185 Max Alvis 2.00 1.00
❑ 186 Billy Cowan 2.00 1.00
❑ 187 Casey Stengel MG 15.00 7.50
❑ 188 Sam Bowens 2.00 1.00
❑ 189 Checklist 3 10.00 5.00
❑ 190 Bill White 6.00 3.00
❑ 191 Phil Regan 4.00 2.00
❑ 192 Jim Coker 2.00 1.00
❑ 193 Gaylord Perry 15.00 7.50
❑ 194 B.Kelso RC/R.Reichardt RC 2.00 1.00
❑ 195 Bob Veale 4.00 2.00
❑ 196 Ron Fairly 4.00 2.00
❑ 197 Diego Segui 2.50 1.25
❑ 198 Smoky Burgess 4.00 2.00
❑ 199 Bob Heffner 2.50 1.25
❑ 200 Joe Torre 6.00 3.00
❑ 201 S.Valdespino RC/C.Tovar RC 4.00 2.00
❑ 202 Leo Burke 2.50 1.25
❑ 203 Dallas Green 4.00 2.00
❑ 204 Russ Snyder 2.50 1.25
❑ 205 Warren Spahn 30.00 15.00
❑ 206 Willie Horton 4.00 2.00
❑ 207 Pete Rose 175.00 100.00
❑ 208 Tommy John 6.00 3.00
❑ 209 Pittsburgh Pirates TC 6.00 3.00
❑ 210 Jim Fregosi 4.00 2.00
❑ 211 Steve Ridzik 2.50 1.25
❑ 212 Ron Brand 2.50 1.25
❑ 213 Jim Davenport 2.50 1.25
❑ 214 Bob Purkey 2.50 1.25
❑ 215 Pete Ward 2.50 1.25
❑ 216 Al Worthington 2.50 1.25
❑ 217 Walter Alston MG 6.00 3.00
❑ 218 Dick Schofield 2.50 1.25
❑ 219 Bob Meyer 2.50 1.25
❑ 220 Billy Williams 10.00 5.00
❑ 221 John Tsitouris 2.50 1.25
❑ 222 Bob Tillman 2.50 1.25
❑ 223 Dan Osinski 2.50 1.25
❑ 224 Bob Chance 2.50 1.25
❑ 225 Bo Belinsky 4.00 2.00
❑ 226 E.Jimenez RC/J.Gibbs 6.00 3.00
❑ 227 Bobby Klaus 2.50 1.25
❑ 228 Jack Sanford 2.50 1.25
❑ 229 Lou Clinton 2.50 1.25
❑ 230 Ray Sadecki 2.50 1.25
❑ 231 Jerry Adair 2.50 1.25
❑ 232 Steve Blass RC 4.00 2.00
❑ 233 Don Zimmer 4.00 2.00
❑ 234 Chicago White Sox TC 6.00 3.00
❑ 235 Chuck Hinton 2.50 1.25

	No.	Card	Price 1	Price 2
❑	236	Denny McLain RC	25.00	12.50
❑	237	Bernie Allen	2.50	1.25
❑	238	Joe Moeller	2.50	1.25
❑	239	Doc Edwards	2.50	1.25
❑	240	Bob Bruce	2.50	1.25
❑	241	Mack Jones	2.50	1.25
❑	242	George Brunet	2.50	1.25
❑	243	T.Davidson RC/T.Helms RC	4.00	2.00
❑	244	Lindy McDaniel	4.00	2.00
❑	245	Joe Pepitone	6.00	3.00
❑	246	Tom Butters	4.00	2.00
❑	247	Wally Moon	4.00	2.00
❑	248	Gus Triandos	4.00	2.00
❑	249	Dave McNally	4.00	2.00
❑	250	Willie Mays	150.00	90.00
❑	251	Billy Herman MG	4.00	2.00
❑	252	Pete Richert	2.50	1.25
❑	253	Danny Cater	2.50	1.25
❑	254	Roland Sheldon	2.50	1.25
❑	255	Camilo Pascual	4.00	2.00
❑	256	Tito Francona	2.50	1.25
❑	257	Jim Wynn	4.00	2.00
❑	258	Larry Bearnarth	2.50	1.25
❑	259	J.Northrup RC/R.Oyler RC	6.00	3.00
❑	260	Don Drysdale	20.00	10.00
❑	261	Duke Carmel	2.50	1.25
❑	262	Bud Daley	2.50	1.25
❑	263	Marty Keough	2.50	1.25
❑	264	Bob Buhl	4.00	2.00
❑	265	Jim Pagliaroni	2.50	1.25
❑	266	Bert Campaneris RC	10.00	5.00
❑	267	Washington Senators TC	6.00	3.00
❑	268	Ken McBride	2.50	1.25
❑	269	Frank Bolling	2.50	1.25
❑	270	Milt Pappas	4.00	2.00
❑	271	Don Wert	4.00	2.00
❑	272	Chuck Schilling	2.50	1.25
❑	273	Checklist 4	10.00	5.00
❑	274	Lum Harris MG RC	2.50	1.25
❑	275	Dick Groat	6.00	3.00
❑	276	Hoyt Wilhelm	10.00	5.00
❑	277	Johnny Lewis	2.50	1.25
❑	278	Ken Retzer	2.50	1.25
❑	279	Dick Tracewski	2.50	1.25
❑	280	Dick Stuart	4.00	2.00
❑	281	Bill Stafford	2.50	1.25
❑	282	D.Est RC/M.Murakami RC	40.00	20.00
❑	283	Fred Whitfield	2.50	1.25
❑	284	Nick Willhite	4.00	2.00
❑	285	Ron Hunt	4.00	2.00
❑	286	J.Dickson/A.Monteagudo	4.00	2.00
❑	287	Gary Kolb	4.00	2.00
❑	288	Jack Hamilton	4.00	2.00
❑	289	Gordy Coleman	6.00	3.00
❑	290	Wally Bunker	6.00	3.00
❑	291	Jerry Lynch	4.00	2.00
❑	292	Larry Yellen	4.00	2.00
❑	293	Los Angeles Angels TC	6.00	3.00
❑	294	Tim McCarver	10.00	5.00
❑	295	Dick Radatz	6.00	3.00
❑	296	Tony Taylor	6.00	3.00
❑	297	Dave DeBusschere	10.00	5.00
❑	298	Jim Stewart	4.00	2.00
❑	299	Jerry Zimmerman	4.00	2.00
❑	300	Sandy Koufax	100.00	60.00
❑	301	Birdie Tebbetts MG	6.00	3.00
❑	302	Al Stanek	4.00	2.00
❑	303	John Orsino	4.00	2.00
❑	304	Dave Stenhouse	4.00	2.00
❑	305	Rico Carty	6.00	3.00
❑	306	Bubba Phillips	4.00	2.00
❑	307	Barry Latman	4.00	2.00
❑	308	C.Jones RC/T.Parsons	6.00	3.00
❑	309	Steve Hamilton	6.00	3.00
❑	310	Johnny Callison	6.00	3.00
❑	311	Orlando Pena	4.00	2.00
❑	312	Joe Nuxhall	4.00	2.00
❑	313	Jim Schaffer	4.00	2.00
❑	314	Sterling Slaughter	4.00	2.00
❑	315	Frank Malzone	6.00	3.00
❑	316	Cincinnati Reds TC	6.00	3.00
❑	317	Don McMahon	4.00	2.00
❑	318	Matty Alou	6.00	3.00
❑	319	Ken McMullen	4.00	2.00
❑	320	Bob Gibson	50.00	30.00
❑	321	Rusty Staub	10.00	5.00
❑	322	Rick Wise	6.00	3.00
❑	323	Hank Bauer MG	6.00	3.00
❑	324	Bobby Locke	4.00	2.00
❑	325	Donn Clendenon	6.00	3.00
❑	326	Dwight Siebler	4.00	2.00
❑	327	Denis Menke	4.00	2.00
❑	328	Eddie Fisher	4.00	2.00
❑	329	Hawk Taylor RC	4.00	2.00
❑	330	Whitey Ford	40.00	20.00
❑	331	A.Ferrara/J.Purdin RC	6.00	3.00
❑	332	Ted Abernathy	4.00	2.00
❑	333	Tom Reynolds	4.00	2.00
❑	334	Vic Roznovsky RC	4.00	2.00
❑	335	Mickey Lolich	6.00	3.00
❑	336	Woody Held	4.00	2.00
❑	337	Mike Cuellar	6.00	3.00
❑	338	Philadelphia Phillies TC	6.00	3.00
❑	339	Ryne Duren	6.00	3.00
❑	340	Tony Oliva	20.00	10.00
❑	341	Bob Bolin	4.00	2.00
❑	342	Bob Rodgers	6.00	3.00
❑	343	Mike McCormick	6.00	3.00
❑	344	Wes Parker	6.00	3.00
❑	345	Floyd Robinson	4.00	2.00
❑	346	Bobby Bragan MG	4.00	2.00
❑	347	Roy Face	6.00	3.00
❑	348	George Banks	4.00	2.00
❑	349	Larry Miller RC	4.00	2.00
❑	350	Mickey Mantle	600.00	350.00
❑	351	Jim Perry	6.00	3.00
❑	352	Alex Johnson RC	6.00	3.00
❑	353	Jerry Lumpe	4.00	2.00
❑	354	B.Ott RC/J.Warner RC	4.00	2.00
❑	355	Vada Pinson	10.00	5.00
❑	356	Bill Spanswick	4.00	2.00
❑	357	Carl Warwick	4.00	2.00
❑	358	Albie Pearson	6.00	3.00
❑	359	Ken Johnson	4.00	2.00
❑	360	Orlando Cepeda	15.00	7.50
❑	361	Checklist 5	12.00	6.00
❑	362	Don Schwall	4.00	2.00
❑	363	Bob Johnson	4.00	2.00
❑	364	Galen Cisco	4.00	2.00
❑	365	Jim Gentile	6.00	3.00
❑	366	Dan Schneider	4.00	2.00
❑	367	Leon Wagner	4.00	2.00
❑	368	K.Berry RC/J.Gibson RC	6.00	3.00
❑	369	Phil Linz	6.00	3.00
❑	370	Tommy Davis	6.00	3.00
❑	371	Frank Kreutzer	8.00	4.00
❑	372	Clay Dalrymple	8.00	4.00
❑	373	Curt Simmons	8.00	4.00
❑	374	J.Cardenal RC/D.Simpson	8.00	4.00
❑	375	Dave Wickersham	8.00	4.00
❑	376	Jim Landis	8.00	4.00
❑	377	Willie Stargell	25.00	12.50
❑	378	Chuck Estrada	8.00	4.00
❑	379	San Francisco Giants TC	8.00	4.00
❑	380	Rocky Colavito	25.00	12.50
❑	381	Al Jackson	8.00	4.00
❑	382	J.C. Martin	8.00	4.00
❑	383	Felipe Alou	15.00	7.50
❑	384	Johnny Klippstein	8.00	4.00
❑	385	Carl Yastrzemski	60.00	35.00
❑	386	P.Jaeckel RC/F.Norman	8.00	4.00
❑	387	Johnny Podres	15.00	7.50
❑	388	John Blanchard	15.00	7.50
❑	389	Don Larsen	15.00	7.50
❑	390	Bill Freehan	15.00	7.50
❑	391	Mel McGaha MG	8.00	4.00
❑	392	Bob Friend	15.00	7.50
❑	393	Ed Kirkpatrick	8.00	4.00
❑	394	Jim Hannan	8.00	4.00
❑	395	Jim Ray Hart	8.00	4.00
❑	396	Frank Bertaina RC	8.00	4.00
❑	397	Jerry Buchek	8.00	4.00
❑	398	D.Neville RC/A.Shamsky RC	15.00	7.50
❑	399	Ray Herbert	8.00	4.00
❑	400	Harmon Killebrew	50.00	30.00
❑	401	Carl Willey	8.00	4.00
❑	402	Joe Amalfitano	8.00	4.00
❑	403	Boston Red Sox TC	8.00	4.00
❑	404	Stan Williams	8.00	4.00
❑	405	John Roseboro	20.00	10.00
❑	406	Ralph Terry	15.00	7.50
❑	407	Lee Maye	8.00	4.00
❑	408	Larry Sherry	8.00	4.00
❑	409	J.Beauchamp RC/L.Dierker RC	15.00	7.50
❑	410	Luis Aparicio	25.00	12.50
❑	411	Roger Craig	15.00	7.50
❑	412	Bob Bailey	8.00	4.00
❑	413	Hal Reniff	8.00	4.00
❑	414	Al Lopez MG	15.00	7.50
❑	415	Curt Flood	15.00	7.50
❑	416	Jim Brewer	8.00	4.00
❑	417	Ed Brinkman	8.00	4.00
❑	418	Johnny Edwards	8.00	4.00
❑	419	Ruben Amaro	8.00	4.00
❑	420	Larry Jackson	8.00	4.00
❑	421	G.Dotter RC/J.Ward	8.00	4.00
❑	422	Aubrey Gatewood	8.00	4.00
❑	423	Jesse Gonder	8.00	4.00
❑	424	Gary Bell	8.00	4.00
❑	425	Wayne Causey	8.00	4.00
❑	426	Milwaukee Braves TC	8.00	4.00
❑	427	Bob Saverine	8.00	4.00
❑	428	Bob Shaw	8.00	4.00
❑	429	Don Demeter	8.00	4.00
❑	430	Gary Peters	8.00	4.00
❑	431	N.Briles RC/W.Spiezio RC	15.00	7.50
❑	432	Jim Grant	15.00	7.50
❑	433	John Bateman	8.00	4.00
❑	434	Dave Morehead	8.00	4.00
❑	435	Willie Davis	15.00	7.50
❑	436	Don Elston	8.00	4.00
❑	437	Chico Cardenas	15.00	7.50
❑	438	Harry Walker MG	8.00	4.00
❑	439	Moe Drabowsky	15.00	7.50
❑	440	Tom Tresh	15.00	7.50
❑	441	Denny Lemaster	8.00	4.00
❑	442	Vic Power	8.00	4.00
❑	443	Checklist 6	12.00	6.00
❑	444	Bob Hendley	8.00	4.00
❑	445	Don Lock	8.00	4.00
❑	446	Art Mahaffey	8.00	4.00
❑	447	Julian Javier	15.00	7.50
❑	448	Lee Stange	8.00	4.00
❑	449	J.Hinsley/G.Kroll RC	15.00	7.50
❑	450	Elston Howard	15.00	7.50
❑	451	Jim Owens	8.00	4.00
❑	452	Gary Geiger	8.00	4.00
❑	453	W.Crawford RC/J.Werhas	15.00	7.50
❑	454	Ed Rakow	8.00	4.00
❑	455	Norm Siebern	8.00	4.00
❑	456	Bill Henry	8.00	4.00
❑	457	Bob Kennedy MG	15.00	7.50
❑	458	John Buzhardt	8.00	4.00
❑	459	Frank Kostro	8.00	4.00
❑	460	Richie Allen	40.00	20.00
❑	461	C.Carroll RC/P.Niekro	50.00	30.00
❑	462	Lew Krausse UER	8.00	4.00
❑	463	Manny Mota	15.00	7.50
❑	464	Ron Piche	8.00	4.00
❑	465	Tom Haller	15.00	7.50
❑	466	P.Craig RC/D.Nen	8.00	4.00
❑	467	Ray Washburn	8.00	4.00
❑	468	Larry Brown	8.00	4.00
❑	469	Don Nottebart	8.00	4.00
❑	470	Yogi Berra P/CO	50.00	30.00
❑	471	Billy Hoeft	8.00	4.00
❑	472	Don Pavletich	8.00	4.00
❑	473	P.Blair RC/D.Johnson RC	15.00	7.50
❑	474	Cookie Rojas	15.00	7.50
❑	475	Clete Boyer	15.00	7.50
❑	476	Billy O'Dell	8.00	4.00
❑	477	Steve Carlton RC	175.00	100.00
❑	478	Wilbur Wood	15.00	7.50
❑	479	Ken Harrelson	15.00	7.50
❑	480	Joel Horlen	8.00	4.00
❑	481	Cleveland Indians TC	10.00	6.00
❑	482	Bob Priddy	8.00	4.00
❑	483	George Smith RC	8.00	4.00
❑	484	Ron Perranoski	20.00	10.00
❑	485	Nellie Fox	25.00	12.50
❑	486	T.Egan/P.Rogan RC	8.00	4.00
❑	487	Woody Woodward	15.00	7.50
❑	488	Ted Wills	8.00	4.00
❑	489	Gene Mauch MG	15.00	7.50
❑	490	Earl Battey	8.00	4.00
❑	491	Tracy Stallard	8.00	4.00
❑	492	Gene Freese	8.00	4.00
❑	493	B.Roman RC/B.Brubaker RC	8.00	4.00

❑ 494 Jay Ritchie RC	8.00	4.00
❑ 495 Joe Christopher	8.00	4.00
❑ 496 Joe Cunningham	8.00	4.00
❑ 497 K.Henderson RC/J.Hiatt RC	15.00	7.50
❑ 498 Gene Stephens	8.00	4.00
❑ 499 Stu Miller	15.00	7.50
❑ 500 Eddie Mathews	40.00	20.00
❑ 501 R.Gagliano RC/J.Rittwage RC	8.00	4.00
❑ 502 Don Cardwell	8.00	4.00
❑ 503 Phil Gagliano	8.00	4.00
❑ 504 Jerry Grote	15.00	7.50
❑ 505 Ray Culp	8.00	4.00
❑ 506 Sam Mele MG	8.00	4.00
❑ 507 Sammy Ellis	8.00	4.00
❑ 508 Checklist 7	12.00	6.00
❑ 509 B.Guindon RC/G.Vezendy RC	8.00	4.00
❑ 510 Ernie Banks	80.00	50.00
❑ 511 Ron Locke	8.00	4.00
❑ 512 Cap Peterson	8.00	4.00
❑ 513 New York Yankees TC	40.00	20.00
❑ 514 Joe Azcue	8.00	4.00
❑ 515 Vern Law	15.00	7.50
❑ 516 Al Weis	8.00	4.00
❑ 517 P.Schaal RC/J.Warner	15.00	7.50
❑ 518 Ken Rowe	8.00	4.00
❑ 519 Bob Uecker UER	30.00	15.00
❑ 520 Tony Cloninger	8.00	4.00
❑ 521 D.Bennett/M.Stevens RC	8.00	4.00
❑ 522 Hank Aguirre	8.00	4.00
❑ 523 Mike Brumley SP	12.00	6.00
❑ 524 Dave Giusti SP	12.00	6.00
❑ 525 Eddie Bressoud	8.00	4.00
❑ 526 J.Odom/J.Hunter SP RC	80.00	50.00
❑ 527 Jeff Torborg SP	12.00	6.00
❑ 528 George Altman	8.00	4.00
❑ 529 Jerry Fosnow SP RC	12.00	6.00
❑ 530 Jim Maloney	15.00	7.50
❑ 531 Chuck Hiller	8.00	4.00
❑ 532 Hector Lopez	15.00	7.50
❑ 533 R.Swob/T.McGraw SP RC	25.00	12.50
❑ 534 John Herrnstein	8.00	4.00
❑ 535 Jack Kralick SP	12.00	6.00
❑ 536 Andre Rodgers SP	12.00	6.00
❑ 537 Lopez/Roof/May RC	8.00	4.00
❑ 538 Chuck Dressen MG SP	12.00	6.00
❑ 539 Herm Starrette	8.00	4.00
❑ 540 Lou Brock SP	50.00	30.00
❑ 541 G.Bollo RC/B.Locker RC	8.00	4.00
❑ 542 Lou Klimchock	8.00	4.00
❑ 543 Ed Connolly SP RC	12.00	6.00
❑ 544 Howie Reed RC	8.00	4.00
❑ 545 Jesus Alou SP	15.00	7.50
❑ 546 Davis/Hed/Bark/Weav RC	8.00	4.00
❑ 547 Jake Wood SP	12.00	6.00
❑ 548 Dick Stigman	8.00	4.00
❑ 549 R.Pena RC/G.Beckert RC	20.00	10.00
❑ 550 Mel Stottlemyre SP RC	30.00	15.00
❑ 551 New York Mets TC SP	30.00	15.00
❑ 552 Julio Gotay	8.00	4.00
❑ 553 Coombs/Ratliff/McClure RC	8.00	4.00
❑ 554 Chico Ruiz SP	12.00	6.00
❑ 555 Jack Baldschun SP	12.00	6.00
❑ 556 R.Schoendienst SP	25.00	12.50
❑ 557 Jose Santiago	8.00	4.00
❑ 558 Tommie Sisk	8.00	4.00
❑ 559 Ed Bailey SP	12.00	6.00
❑ 560 Boog Powell SP	25.00	12.50
❑ 561 Dab/Kek/Valle/Lefebvre RC	15.00	7.50
❑ 562 Billy Moran	8.00	4.00
❑ 563 Julio Navarro	8.00	4.00
❑ 564 Mel Nelson	8.00	4.00
❑ 565 Ernie Broglio SP	12.00	6.00
❑ 566 Blanco/Moschitto/Lopez RC	12.00	6.00
❑ 567 Tommie Aaron	8.00	4.00
❑ 568 Ron Taylor SP	12.00	6.00
❑ 569 Gino Cimoli SP	12.00	6.00
❑ 570 Claude Osteen SP	15.00	7.50
❑ 571 Ossie Virgil SP	12.00	6.00
❑ 572 Baltimore Orioles TC SP	25.00	12.50
❑ 573 Jim Lonborg SP RC	25.00	12.50
❑ 574 Roy Sievers	15.00	7.50
❑ 575 Jose Pagan	8.00	4.00
❑ 576 Terry Fox SP	12.00	6.00
❑ 577 Knowles/Busch/Schein RC	12.00	6.00
❑ 578 Camilo Carreon SP	12.00	6.00
❑ 579 Dick Smith SP	12.00	6.00
❑ 580 Jimmie Hall SP	12.00	6.00
❑ 581 Tony Perez SP RC	80.00	50.00
❑ 582 Bob Schmidt SP	12.00	6.00
❑ 583 Wes Covington SP	12.00	6.00
❑ 584 Harry Bright	15.00	7.50
❑ 585 Hank Fischer	8.00	4.00
❑ 586 Tom McCraw SP	12.00	6.00
❑ 587 Joe Sparma	8.00	4.00
❑ 588 Lenny Green	8.00	4.00
❑ 589 F.Linzy RC/B.Schroder RC	12.00	6.00
❑ 590 John Wyatt	8.00	4.00
❑ 591 Bob Skinner SP	12.00	6.00
❑ 592 Frank Bork SP RC	12.00	6.00
❑ 593 J.Sullivan RC/J.Moore RC SP	12.00	6.00
❑ 594 Joe Gaines	8.00	4.00
❑ 595 Don Lee	8.00	4.00
❑ 596 Don Landrum SP	12.00	6.00
❑ 597 Nossek/Sevcik/Reese RC	8.00	4.00
❑ 598 Al Downing SP	25.00	12.50

1966 Topps

❑ COMPLETE SET (598)	4000.00	2500.00
❑ COMMON CARD (1-109)	1.50	.75
❑ COMMON CARD (110-283)	2.00	1.00
❑ COMMON CARD (284-370)	3.00	1.50
❑ COMMON CARD (371-446)	5.00	2.50
❑ COMMON CARD (447-522)	10.00	5.00
❑ COMMON CARD (523-598)	15.00	7.50
❑ COMMON SP (523-598)	30.00	15.00
❑ WRAPPER (5-CENT)	25.00	20.00
❑ 1 Willie Mays	250.00	150.00
❑ 2 Ted Abernathy	1.50	.75
❑ 3 Sam Mele MG	1.50	.75
❑ 4 Ray Culp	1.50	.75
❑ 5 Jim Fregosi	2.00	1.00
❑ 6 Chuck Schilling	1.50	.75
❑ 7 Tracy Stallard	1.50	.75
❑ 8 Floyd Robinson	1.50	.75
❑ 9 Clete Boyer	2.00	1.00
❑ 10 Tony Cloninger	1.50	.75
❑ 11 B.Alyea RC/P.Craig	1.50	.75
❑ 12 John Tsitouris	1.50	.75
❑ 13 Lou Johnson	2.00	1.00
❑ 14 Norm Siebern	1.50	.75
❑ 15 Vern Law	2.00	1.00
❑ 16 Larry Brown	1.50	.75
❑ 17 John Stephenson	1.50	.75
❑ 18 Roland Sheldon	1.50	.75
❑ 19 San Francisco Giants TC	5.00	2.50
❑ 20 Willie Horton	2.00	1.00
❑ 21 Don Nottebart	1.50	.75
❑ 22 Joe Nossek	1.50	.75
❑ 23 Jack Sanford	1.50	.75
❑ 24 Don Kessinger RC	4.00	2.00
❑ 25 Pete Ward	1.50	.75
❑ 26 Ray Sadecki	1.50	.75
❑ 27 D.Knowles/A.Etchebarren RC	1.50	.75
❑ 28 Phil Niekro	20.00	10.00
❑ 29 Mike Brumley	1.50	.75
❑ 30 Pete Rose UER DP	100.00	60.00
❑ 31 Jack Cullen	2.00	1.00
❑ 32 Adolfo Phillips RC	1.50	.75
❑ 33 Jim Pagliaroni	1.50	.75
❑ 34 Checklist 1	8.00	4.00
❑ 35 Ron Swoboda	4.00	2.00
❑ 36 Jim Hunter UER DP	20.00	10.00
❑ 37 Billy Herman MG	2.00	1.00
❑ 38 Ron Nischwitz	1.50	.75

❑ 39 Ken Henderson	1.50	.75
❑ 40 Jim Grant	1.50	.75
❑ 41 Don LeJohn RC	1.50	.75
❑ 42 Aubrey Gatewood	1.50	.75
❑ 43A D.Landrum Dark Button	2.00	1.00
❑ 43B D.Landrum Airbrush Button	20.00	10.00
❑ 43C D.Landrum No Button	2.00	1.00
❑ 44 B.Davis/T.Kelley	1.50	.75
❑ 45 Jim Gentile	2.00	1.00
❑ 46 Howie Koplitz	1.50	.75
❑ 47 J.C. Martin	1.50	.75
❑ 48 Paul Blair	2.00	1.00
❑ 49 Woody Woodward	2.00	1.00
❑ 50 Mickey Mantle DP	350.00	200.00
❑ 51 Gordon Richardson RC	1.50	.75
❑ 52 W.Covington/J.Callison	4.00	2.00
❑ 53 Bob Duliba	1.50	.75
❑ 54 Jose Pagan	1.50	.75
❑ 55 Ken Harrelson	2.00	1.00
❑ 56 Sandy Valdespino	1.50	.75
❑ 57 Jim Lefebvre	2.00	1.00
❑ 58 Dave Wickersham	1.50	.75
❑ 59 Cincinnati Reds TC	5.00	2.50
❑ 60 Curt Flood	4.00	2.00
❑ 61 Bob Bolin	1.50	.75
❑ 62A Merritt Ranew Sold Line	2.00	1.00
❑ 62B Merritt Ranew NTR	30.00	15.00
❑ 63 Jim Stewart	1.50	.75
❑ 64 Bob Bruce	1.50	.75
❑ 65 Leon Wagner	1.50	.75
❑ 66 Al Weis	1.50	.75
❑ 67 C.Jones/D.Selma RC	4.00	2.00
❑ 68 Hal Reniff	1.50	.75
❑ 69 Ken Hamlin	1.50	.75
❑ 70 Carl Yastrzemski	30.00	15.00
❑ 71 Frank Carpin RC	1.50	.75
❑ 72 Tony Perez	25.00	12.50
❑ 73 Jerry Zimmerman	1.50	.75
❑ 74 Don Mossi	2.00	1.00
❑ 75 Tommy Davis	2.00	1.00
❑ 76 Red Schoendienst MG	4.00	2.00
❑ 77 John Orsino	1.50	.75
❑ 78 Frank Linzy	1.50	.75
❑ 79 Joe Pepitone	4.00	2.00
❑ 80 Richie Allen	6.00	3.00
❑ 81 Ray Oyler	1.50	.75
❑ 82 Bob Hendley	1.50	.75
❑ 83 Albie Pearson	2.00	1.00
❑ 84 J.Beauchamp/D.Kelley	1.50	.75
❑ 85 Eddie Fisher	1.50	.75
❑ 86 John Bateman	1.50	.75
❑ 87 Dan Napoleon	1.50	.75
❑ 88 Fred Whitfield	1.50	.75
❑ 89 Ted Davidson	1.50	.75
❑ 90 Luis Aparicio DP	8.00	4.00
❑ 91A Bob Uecker TR	10.00	5.00
❑ 91B Bob Uecker NTR	40.00	20.00
❑ 92 New York Yankees TC	15.00	7.50
❑ 93 Jim Lonborg DP	2.00	1.00
❑ 94 Matty Alou	2.00	1.00
❑ 95 Pete Richert	1.50	.75
❑ 96 Felipe Alou	4.00	2.00
❑ 97 Jim Merritt RC	1.50	.75
❑ 98 Don Demeter	1.50	.75
❑ 99 W.Stargell/D.Clendenon	6.00	3.00
❑ 100 Sandy Koufax DP	100.00	60.00
❑ 101A Checklist 2 Spahn ERR	15.00	7.50
❑ 101B Cheklist 2 Henry COR	10.00	5.00
❑ 102 Ed Kirkpatrick	1.50	.75
❑ 103A Dick Groat TR	2.00	1.00
❑ 103B Dick Groat NTR	40.00	20.00
❑ 104A Alex Johnson TR	2.00	1.00
❑ 104B Alex Johnson NTR	30.00	15.00
❑ 105 Milt Pappas	2.00	1.00
❑ 106 Rusty Staub	4.00	2.00
❑ 107 L.Stahl RC/R.Tompkins RC	1.50	.75
❑ 108 Bobby Klaus	1.50	.75
❑ 109 Ralph Terry	2.00	1.00
❑ 110 Ernie Banks	30.00	15.00
❑ 111 Gary Peters	2.00	1.00
❑ 112 Manny Mota	4.00	2.00
❑ 113 Hank Aguirre	2.00	1.00
❑ 114 Jim Gosger	2.00	1.00
❑ 115 Bill Henry	2.00	1.00
❑ 116 Walter Alston MG	6.00	3.00
❑ 117 Jake Gibbs	2.00	1.00

❑	118	Mike McCormick	2.00	1.00
❑	119	Art Shamsky	2.00	1.00
❑	120	Harmon Killebrew	15.00	7.50
❑	121	Ray Herbert	2.00	1.00
❑	122	Joe Gaines	2.00	1.00
❑	123	F.Bork/J.May	2.00	1.00
❑	124	Tug McGraw	4.00	2.00
❑	125	Lou Brock	20.00	10.00
❑	126	Jim Palmer UER RC	100.00	60.00
❑	127	Ken Berry	2.00	1.00
❑	128	Jim Landis	2.00	1.00
❑	129	Jack Kralick	2.00	1.00
❑	130	Joe Torre	6.00	3.00
❑	131	California Angels TC	5.00	2.50
❑	132	Orlando Cepeda	8.00	4.00
❑	133	Don McMahon	2.00	1.00
❑	134	Wes Parker	4.00	2.00
❑	135	Dave Morehead	2.00	1.00
❑	136	Woody Held	2.00	1.00
❑	137	Pat Corrales	2.00	1.00
❑	138	Roger Repoz RC	2.00	1.00
❑	139	B.Browne RC/D.Young RC	2.00	1.00
❑	140	Jim Maloney	4.00	2.00
❑	141	Tom McCraw	2.00	1.00
❑	142	Don Dennis RC	2.00	1.00
❑	143	Jose Tartabull	4.00	2.00
❑	144	Don Schwall	2.00	1.00
❑	145	Bill Freehan	4.00	2.00
❑	146	George Altman	2.00	1.00
❑	147	Lum Harris MG	2.00	1.00
❑	148	Bob Johnson	2.00	1.00
❑	149	Dick Nen	2.00	1.00
❑	150	Rocky Colavito	8.00	4.00
❑	151	Gary Wagner RC	2.00	1.00
❑	152	Frank Malzone	4.00	2.00
❑	153	Rico Carty	4.00	2.00
❑	154	Chuck Hiller	2.00	1.00
❑	155	Marcelino Lopez	2.00	1.00
❑	156	D.Schofield/H.Lanier	2.00	1.00
❑	157	Rene Lachemann	2.00	1.00
❑	158	Jim Brewer	2.00	1.00
❑	159	Chico Ruiz	2.00	1.00
❑	160	Whitey Ford	30.00	15.00
❑	161	Jerry Lumpe	2.00	1.00
❑	162	Lee Maye	2.00	1.00
❑	163	Tito Francona	2.00	1.00
❑	164	T.Agee/M.Staehle	4.00	2.00
❑	165	Don Lock	2.00	1.00
❑	166	Chris Krug RC	2.00	1.00
❑	167	Boog Powell	6.00	3.00
❑	168	Dan Osinski	2.00	1.00
❑	169	Duke Sims RC	2.00	1.00
❑	170	Cookie Rojas	4.00	2.00
❑	171	Nick Willhite	2.00	1.00
❑	172	New York Mets TC	5.00	2.50
❑	173	Al Spangler	2.00	1.00
❑	174	Ron Taylor	2.00	1.00
❑	175	Bert Campaneris	4.00	2.00
❑	176	Jim Davenport	2.00	1.00
❑	177	Hector Lopez	2.00	1.00
❑	178	Bob Tillman	2.00	1.00
❑	179	D.Aust RC/B.Tolan	4.00	2.00
❑	180	Vada Pinson	4.00	2.00
❑	181	Al Worthington	2.00	1.00
❑	182	Jerry Lynch	2.00	1.00
❑	183A	Checklist 3 Large Print	8.00	4.00
❑	183B	Checklist 3 Small Print	8.00	4.00
❑	184	Denis Menke	2.00	1.00
❑	185	Bob Buhl	4.00	2.00
❑	186	Ruben Amaro	2.00	1.00
❑	187	Chuck Dressen MG	4.00	2.00
❑	188	Al Luplow	2.00	1.00
❑	189	John Roseboro	4.00	2.00
❑	190	Jimmie Hall	2.00	1.00
❑	191	Darrell Sutherland RC	2.00	1.00
❑	192	Vic Power	4.00	2.00
❑	193	Dave McNally	4.00	2.00
❑	194	Washington Senators TC	5.00	2.50
❑	195	Joe Morgan	15.00	7.50
❑	196	Don Pavletich	2.00	1.00
❑	197	Sonny Siebert	2.00	1.00
❑	198	Mickey Stanley RC	6.00	3.00
❑	199	Skowron/Romano/Robinson	4.00	2.00
❑	200	Eddie Mathews	15.00	7.50
❑	201	Jim Dickson	2.00	1.00
❑	202	Clay Dalrymple	2.00	1.00
❑	203	Jose Santiago	2.00	1.00
❑	204	Chicago Cubs TC	5.00	2.50
❑	205	Tom Tresh	4.00	2.00
❑	206	Al Jackson	2.00	1.00
❑	207	Frank Quilici RC	2.00	1.00
❑	208	Bob Miller	2.00	1.00
❑	209	F.Fisher/J.Hiller RC	4.00	2.00
❑	210	Bill Mazeroski	8.00	4.00
❑	211	Frank Kreutzer	2.00	1.00
❑	212	Ed Kranepool	4.00	2.00
❑	213	Fred Newman	2.00	1.00
❑	214	Tommy Harper	4.00	2.00
❑	215	Clemente/Aaron/Mays LL	50.00	30.00
❑	216	Oliva/Yaz/Davalillo LL	5.00	2.50
❑	217	Mays/McCovey/B.Will LL	20.00	10.00
❑	218	Conigliaro/Cash/Horton LL	5.00	2.50
❑	219	Johnson/F.Rob/Mays LL	12.00	6.00
❑	220	Colavito/Horton/Oliva LL	5.00	2.50
❑	221	Koufax/Marichal/Law LL	12.00	6.00
❑	222	McDowell/Fisher/Siebert LL	5.00	2.50
❑	223	Koufax/Clon/Drysdale LL	12.00	6.00
❑	224	Grant/Stottlemyre/Kaat LL	5.00	2.50
❑	225	Koufax/Veale/Gibson LL	12.00	6.00
❑	226	McDowell/Lolich/McLain LL	5.00	2.50
❑	227	Russ Nixon	2.00	1.00
❑	228	Larry Dierker	4.00	2.00
❑	229	Hank Bauer MG	4.00	2.00
❑	230	Johnny Callison	4.00	2.00
❑	231	Floyd Weaver	2.00	1.00
❑	232	Glenn Beckert	4.00	2.00
❑	233	Dom Zanni	2.00	1.00
❑	234	R.Beck RC/R.White RC	8.00	4.00
❑	235	Don Cardwell	2.00	1.00
❑	236	Mike Hershberger	2.00	1.00
❑	237	Billy O'Dell	2.00	1.00
❑	238	Los Angeles Dodgers TC	5.00	2.50
❑	239	Orlando Pena	2.00	1.00
❑	240	Earl Battey	2.00	1.00
❑	241	Dennis Ribant	2.00	1.00
❑	242	Jesus Alou	2.00	1.00
❑	243	Nelson Briles	4.00	2.00
❑	244	C.Harrison RC//S.Jackson	2.00	1.00
❑	245	John Buzhardt	2.00	1.00
❑	246	Ed Bailey	2.00	1.00
❑	247	Carl Warwick	2.00	1.00
❑	248	Pete Mikkelsen	2.00	1.00
❑	249	Bill Rigney MG	2.00	1.00
❑	250	Sammy Ellis	2.00	1.00
❑	251	Ed Brinkman	2.00	1.00
❑	252	Denny Lemaster	2.00	1.00
❑	253	Don Wert	2.00	1.00
❑	254	Fergie Jenkins RC	60.00	35.00
❑	255	Willie Stargell	20.00	10.00
❑	256	Lew Krausse	2.00	1.00
❑	257	Jeff Torborg	4.00	2.00
❑	258	Dave Giusti	2.00	1.00
❑	259	Boston Red Sox TC	5.00	2.50
❑	260	Bob Shaw	2.00	1.00
❑	261	Ron Hansen	2.00	1.00
❑	262	Jack Hamilton	2.00	1.00
❑	263	Tom Egan	2.00	1.00
❑	264	A.Kosco RC/T.Uhlaender RC	2.00	1.00
❑	265	Stu Miller	4.00	2.00
❑	266	Pedro Gonzalez UER	2.00	1.00
❑	267	Joe Sparma	2.00	1.00
❑	268	John Blanchard	2.00	1.00
❑	269	Don Heffner MG	2.00	1.00
❑	270	Claude Osteen	4.00	2.00
❑	271	Hal Lanier	2.00	1.00
❑	272	Jack Baldschun	2.00	1.00
❑	273	B.Aspromonte/R.Staub	4.00	2.00
❑	274	Buster Narum	2.00	1.00
❑	275	Tim McCarver	4.00	2.00
❑	276	Jim Bouton	4.00	2.00
❑	277	George Thomas	2.00	1.00
❑	278	Cal Koonce	2.00	1.00
❑	279A	Checklist 4 Black Cap	8.00	4.00
❑	279B	Checklist 4 Red Cap	8.00	4.00
❑	280	Bobby Knoop	2.00	1.00
❑	281	Bruce Howard	2.00	1.00
❑	282	Johnny Lewis	2.00	1.00
❑	283	Jim Perry	4.00	2.00
❑	284	Bobby Wine	3.00	1.50
❑	285	Luis Tiant	5.00	2.50
❑	286	Gary Geiger	3.00	1.50
❑	287	Jack Aker RC	3.00	1.50
❑	288	D.Sutton RC/B.Singer RC	60.00	35.00
❑	289	Larry Sherry	3.00	1.50
❑	290	Ron Santo	5.00	2.50
❑	291	Moe Drabowsky	5.00	2.50
❑	202	Jim Coker	3.00	1.50
❑	293	Mike Shannon	5.00	2.50
❑	294	Steve Ridzik	3.00	1.50
❑	295	Jim Ray Hart	5.00	2.50
❑	296	Johnny Keane MG	5.00	2.50
❑	297	Jim Owens	3.00	1.50
❑	298	Rico Petrocelli	5.00	2.50
❑	299	Lou Burdette	5.00	2.50
❑	300	Roberto Clemente	150.00	90.00
❑	301	Greg Bollo	3.00	1.50
❑	302	Ernie Bowman	3.00	1.50
❑	303	Cleveland Indians TC	5.00	2.50
❑	304	John Herrnstein	3.00	1.50
❑	305	Camilo Pascual	5.00	2.50
❑	306	Ty Cline	3.00	1.50
❑	307	Clay Carroll	5.00	2.50
❑	308	Tom Haller	5.00	2.50
❑	309	Diego Segui	3.00	1.50
❑	310	Frank Robinson	40.00	20.00
❑	311	T.Helms/D.Simpson	5.00	2.50
❑	312	Bob Saverine	3.00	1.50
❑	313	Chris Zachary	3.00	1.50
❑	314	Hector Valle	3.00	1.50
❑	315	Norm Cash	5.00	2.50
❑	316	Jack Fisher	3.00	1.50
❑	317	Dalton Jones	3.00	1.50
❑	318	Harry Walker MG	3.00	1.50
❑	319	Gene Freese	3.00	1.50
❑	320	Bob Gibson	25.00	12.50
❑	321	Rick Reichardt	3.00	1.50
❑	322	Bill Faul	3.00	1.50
❑	323	Ray Barker	3.00	1.50
❑	324	John Boozer	3.00	1.50
❑	325	Vic Davalillo	3.00	1.50
❑	326	Atlanta Braves TC	5.00	2.50
❑	327	Bernie Allen	3.00	1.50
❑	328	Jerry Grote	5.00	2.50
❑	329	Pete Charton	3.00	1.50
❑	330	Ron Fairly	5.00	2.50
❑	331	Ron Herbel	3.00	1.50
❑	332	Bill Bryan	3.00	1.50
❑	333	J.Coleman RC/J.French RC	3.00	1.50
❑	334	Marty Keough	3.00	1.50
❑	335	Juan Pizarro	3.00	1.50
❑	336	Gene Alley	5.00	2.50
❑	337	Fred Gladding	3.00	1.50
❑	338	Dal Maxvill	3.00	1.50
❑	339	Del Crandall	5.00	2.50
❑	340	Dean Chance	5.00	2.50
❑	341	Wes Westrum MG	5.00	2.50
❑	342	Bob Humphreys	3.00	1.50
❑	343	Joe Christopher	3.00	1.50
❑	344	Steve Blass	5.00	2.50
❑	345	Bob Allison	5.00	2.50
❑	346	Mike de la Hoz	3.00	1.50
❑	347	Phil Regan	5.00	2.50
❑	348	Baltimore Orioles TC	8.00	4.00
❑	349	Cap Peterson	3.00	1.50
❑	350	Mel Stottlemyre	8.00	4.00
❑	351	Fred Valentine	3.00	1.50
❑	352	Bob Aspromonte	3.00	1.50
❑	353	Al McBean	3.00	1.50
❑	354	Smoky Burgess	5.00	2.50
❑	355	Wade Blasingame	3.00	1.50
❑	356	O.Johnson RC/K.Sanders RC	3.00	1.50
❑	357	Gerry Arrigo	3.00	1.50
❑	358	Charlie Smith	3.00	1.50
❑	359	Johnny Briggs	3.00	1.50
❑	360	Ron Hunt	3.00	1.50
❑	361	Tom Satriano	3.00	1.50
❑	362	Gates Brown	5.00	2.50
❑	363	Checklist 5	10.00	5.00
❑	364	Nate Oliver	3.00	1.50
❑	365	Roger Maris UER	50.00	30.00
❑	366	Wayne Causey	3.00	1.50
❑	367	Mel Nelson	3.00	1.50
❑	368	Charlie Lau	5.00	2.50
❑	369	Jim King	3.00	1.50
❑	370	Chico Cardenas	3.00	1.50
❑	371	Lee Stange	5.00	2.50
❑	372	Harvey Kuenn	8.00	4.00
❑	373	J.Hiatt/D.Estelle	8.00	4.00

❑ 374 Bob Locker 5.00 2.50
❑ 375 Donn Clendenon 8.00 4.00
❑ 376 Paul Schaal 5.00 2.50
❑ 377 Turk Farrell 5.00 2.50
❑ 378 Dick Tracewski 5.00 2.50
❑ 379 St. Louis Cardinals TC 10.00 5.00
❑ 380 Tony Conigliaro 10.00 5.00
❑ 381 Hank Fischer 5.00 2.50
❑ 382 Phil Roof 5.00 2.50
❑ 383 Jackie Brandt 5.00 2.50
❑ 384 Al Downing 8.00 4.00
❑ 385 Ken Boyer 10.00 5.00
❑ 386 Gil Hodges MG 8.00 4.00
❑ 387 Howie Reed 5.00 2.50
❑ 388 Don Mincher 5.00 2.50
❑ 389 Jim O'Toole 8.00 4.00
❑ 390 Brooks Robinson 50.00 30.00
❑ 391 Chuck Hinton 5.00 2.50
❑ 392 B.Hands RC/R.Hundley RC 8.00 4.00
❑ 393 George Brunet 5.00 2.50
❑ 394 Ron Brand 5.00 2.50
❑ 395 Len Gabrielson 5.00 2.50
❑ 396 Jerry Stephenson 5.00 2.50
❑ 397 Bill White 8.00 4.00
❑ 398 Danny Cater 5.00 2.50
❑ 399 Ray Washburn 5.00 2.50
❑ 400 Zoilo Versalles 8.00 4.00
❑ 401 Ken McMullen 5.00 2.50
❑ 402 Jim Hickman 5.00 2.50
❑ 403 Fred Talbot 5.00 2.50
❑ 404 Pittsburgh Pirates TC 10.00 5.00
❑ 405 Elston Howard 8.00 4.00
❑ 406 Joey Jay 5.00 2.50
❑ 407 John Kennedy 5.00 2.50
❑ 408 Lee Thomas 8.00 4.00
❑ 409 Billy Hoeft 5.00 2.50
❑ 410 Al Kaline 40.00 20.00
❑ 411 Gene Mauch MG 5.00 2.50
❑ 412 Sam Bowens 5.00 2.50
❑ 413 Johnny Romano 5.00 2.50
❑ 414 Dan Coombs 5.00 2.50
❑ 415 Max Alvis 5.00 2.50
❑ 416 Phil Ortega 5.00 2.50
❑ 417 J.McGlothlin RC/E.Sukla RC 5.00 2.50
❑ 418 Phil Gagliano 5.00 2.50
❑ 419 Mike Ryan 5.00 2.50
❑ 420 Juan Marichal 15.00 7.50
❑ 421 Roy McMillan 8.00 4.00
❑ 422 Ed Charles 5.00 2.50
❑ 423 Ernie Broglio 5.00 2.50
❑ 424 L.May RC/D.Osteen RC 10.00 5.00
❑ 425 Bob Veale 8.00 4.00
❑ 426 Chicago White Sox TC 10.00 5.00
❑ 427 John Miller 5.00 2.50
❑ 428 Sandy Alomar 5.00 2.50
❑ 429 Bill Monbouquette 5.00 2.50
❑ 430 Don Drysdale 20.00 10.00
❑ 431 Walt Bond 5.00 2.50
❑ 432 Bob Heffner 5.00 2.50
❑ 433 Alvin Dark MG 8.00 4.00
❑ 434 Willie Kirkland 5.00 2.50
❑ 435 Jim Bunning 15.00 7.50
❑ 436 Julian Javier 8.00 4.00
❑ 437 Al Stanek 5.00 2.50
❑ 438 Willie Smith 5.00 2.50
❑ 439 Pedro Ramos 5.00 2.50
❑ 440 Deron Johnson 8.00 4.00
❑ 441 Tommie Sisk 5.00 2.50
❑ 442 E.Barnowski RC/E.Watt RC 5.00 2.50
❑ 443 Bill Wakefield 3.00 1.50
❑ 444 Checklist 6 10.00 5.00
❑ 445 Jim Kaat 10.00 5.00
❑ 446 Mack Jones 5.00 2.50
❑ 447 D.Ellsw UER Hubbs 15.00 7.50
❑ 448 Eddie Stanky MG 10.00 5.00
❑ 449 Joe Moeller 10.00 5.00
❑ 450 Tony Oliva 15.00 7.50
❑ 451 Barry Latman 10.00 5.00
❑ 452 Joe Azcue 10.00 5.00
❑ 453 Ron Kline 10.00 5.00
❑ 454 Jerry Buchek 10.00 5.00
❑ 455 Mickey Lolich 15.00 7.50
❑ 456 D.Brandon RC/J.Foy RC 10.00 5.00
❑ 457 Joe Gibbon 10.00 5.00
❑ 458 Manny Jiminez 10.00 5.00
❑ 459 Bill McCool 10.00 5.00
❑ 460 Curt Blefary 10.00 5.00
❑ 461 Roy Face 15.00 7.50
❑ 462 Bob Rodgers 10.00 5.00
❑ 463 Philadelphia Phillies TC 15.00 7.50
❑ 464 Larry Bearnarth 10.00 5.00
❑ 465 Don Buford 10.00 5.00
❑ 466 Ken Johnson 10.00 5.00
❑ 467 Vic Roznovsky 10.00 5.00
❑ 468 Johnny Podres 15.00 7.50
❑ 469 B.Murcer RC/D.Womack RC 30.00 15.00
❑ 470 Sam McDowell 15.00 7.50
❑ 471 Bob Skinner 10.00 5.00
❑ 472 Terry Fox 10.00 5.00
❑ 473 Rich Rollins 10.00 5.00
❑ 474 Dick Schofield 10.00 5.00
❑ 475 Dick Radatz 10.00 5.00
❑ 476 Bobby Bragan MG 10.00 5.00
❑ 477 Steve Barber 10.00 5.00
❑ 478 Tony Gonzalez 10.00 5.00
❑ 479 Jim Hannan 10.00 5.00
❑ 480 Dick Stuart 10.00 5.00
❑ 481 Bob Lee 10.00 5.00
❑ 482 J.Boccabella/D.Dowling 10.00 5.00
❑ 483 Joe Nuxhall 10.00 5.00
❑ 484 Wes Covington 10.00 5.00
❑ 485 Bob Bailey 10.00 5.00
❑ 486 Tommy John 15.00 7.50
❑ 487 Al Ferrara 10.00 5.00
❑ 488 George Banks 10.00 5.00
❑ 489 Curt Simmons 10.00 5.00
❑ 490 Bobby Richardson 25.00 12.50
❑ 491 Dennis Bennett 10.00 5.00
❑ 492 Kansas City Athletics TC 15.00 7.50
❑ 493 Johnny Klippstein 10.00 5.00
❑ 494 Gordy Coleman 10.00 5.00
❑ 495 Dick McAuliffe 15.00 7.50
❑ 496 Lindy McDaniel 10.00 5.00
❑ 497 Chris Cannizzaro 10.00 5.00
❑ 498 L.Walker RC/W.Fryman RC 10.00 5.00
❑ 499 Wally Bunker 10.00 5.00
❑ 500 Hank Aaron 125.00 75.00
❑ 501 John O'Donoghue 10.00 5.00
❑ 502 Lenny Green UER 10.00 5.00
❑ 503 Steve Hamilton 15.00 7.50
❑ 504 Grady Hatton MG 10.00 5.00
❑ 505 Jose Cardenal 10.00 5.00
❑ 506 Bo Belinsky 15.00 7.50
❑ 507 Johnny Edwards 10.00 5.00
❑ 508 Steve Hargan RC 15.00 7.50
❑ 509 Jake Wood 10.00 5.00
❑ 510 Hoyt Wilhelm 25.00 12.50
❑ 511 B.Barton RC/T.Fuentes RC 10.00 5.00
❑ 512 Dick Stigman 10.00 5.00
❑ 513 Camilo Carreon 10.00 5.00
❑ 514 Hal Woodeshick 10.00 5.00
❑ 515 Frank Howard 15.00 7.50
❑ 516 Eddie Bressoud 10.00 5.00
❑ 517A Checklist 7 White Sox 15.00 7.50
❑ 517B Checklist 7 W.Sox 15.00 7.50
❑ 518 H.Hippauf RC/A.Umbach RC 10.00 5.00
❑ 519 Bob Friend 15.00 7.50
❑ 520 Jim Wynn 15.00 7.50
❑ 521 John Wyatt 10.00 5.00
❑ 522 Phil Linz 10.00 5.00
❑ 523 Bob Sadowski 10.00 5.00
❑ 524 O.Brown RC/D.Mason RC SP 30.00 15.00
❑ 525 Gary Bell SP 30.00 15.00
❑ 526 Minnesota Twins TC SP 100.00 60.00
❑ 527 Julio Navarro 15.00 7.50
❑ 528 Jesse Gonder SP 30.00 15.00
❑ 529 Elia/Higgins/Voss RC 15.00 7.50
❑ 530 Robin Roberts 50.00 30.00
❑ 531 Joe Cunningham 15.00 7.50
❑ 532 A.Monteagudo SP 30.00 15.00
❑ 533 Jerry Adair SP 30.00 15.00
❑ 534 D.Eilers RC/R.Gardner RC 15.00 7.50
❑ 535 Willie Davis SP 40.00 20.00
❑ 536 Dick Egan 15.00 7.50
❑ 537 Herman Franks MG 15.00 7.50
❑ 538 Bob Allen SP 30.00 15.00
❑ 539 B.Heath RC/C.Sembera RC 25.00 12.50
❑ 540 Denny McLain SP 60.00 35.00
❑ 541 Gene Oliver SP 30.00 15.00
❑ 542 George Smith 15.00 7.50
❑ 543 Roger Craig SP 30.00 15.00
❑ 544 Hoerner/Kernek/Williams RC SP 30.00 15.00
❑ 545 Dick Green SP 30.00 15.00
❑ 546 Dwight Siebler 25.00 12.50
❑ 547 Horace Clarke SP RC 40.00 20.00
❑ 548 Gary Kroll SP 30.00 15.00
❑ 549 A.Closter RC/C.Cox RC 15.00 7.50
❑ 550 Willie McCovey SP 100.00 60.00
❑ 551 Bob Purkey SP 30.00 15.00
❑ 552 B.Tebbetts MG SP 30.00 15.00
❑ 553 P.Garrett RC/J.Warner 15.00 7.50
❑ 554 Jim Northrup SP 30.00 15.00
❑ 555 Ron Perranoski SP 30.00 15.00
❑ 556 Mel Queen SP 30.00 15.00
❑ 557 Felix Mantilla SP 30.00 15.00
❑ 558 Grilli/Magrini/Scott RC 20.00 10.00
❑ 559 Roberto Pena SP 30.00 15.00
❑ 560 Joel Horlen 15.00 7.50
❑ 561 Choo Choo Coleman SP 30.00 15.00
❑ 562 Russ Snyder 25.00 12.50
❑ 563 P.Cimino RC/C.Tovar RC 15.00 7.50
❑ 564 Bob Chance SP 30.00 15.00
❑ 565 Jimmy Piersall SP 40.00 20.00
❑ 566 Mike Cuellar SP 30.00 15.00
❑ 567 Dick Howser SP 40.00 20.00
❑ 568 P.Lindblad RC/R.Stone RC 15.00 7.50
❑ 569 Orlando McFarlane SP 30.00 15.00
❑ 570 Art Mahaffey SP 30.00 15.00
❑ 571 Dave Roberts SP 30.00 15.00
❑ 572 Bob Priddy 15.00 7.50
❑ 573 Derrell Griffith 15.00 7.50
❑ 574 B.Hepler RC/B.Murphy RC 15.00 7.50
❑ 575 Earl Wilson 15.00 7.50
❑ 576 Dave Nicholson SP 30.00 15.00
❑ 577 Jack Lamabe SP 30.00 15.00
❑ 578 Chi Chi Olivo SP RC 30.00 15.00
❑ 579 Bertaina/Brabender/Johnson RC 20.00 10.00
❑ 580 Billy Williams SP 60.00 35.00
❑ 581 Tony Martinez 15.00 7.50
❑ 582 Garry Roggenburk 15.00 7.50
❑ 583 Detroit Tigers TC SP 125.00 75.00
❑ 584 F.Fernandez RC/F.Peterson RC 15.00 7.50
❑ 585 Tony Taylor 25.00 12.50
❑ 586 Claude Raymond SP 30.00 15.00
❑ 587 Dick Bertell 15.00 7.50
❑ 588 C.Dobson RC/K.Suarez RC 15.00 7.50
❑ 589 Lou Klimchock SP 30.00 15.00
❑ 590 Bill Skowron SP 40.00 20.00
❑ 591 B.Shirley RC/G.Jackson RC SP 40.00 20.00
❑ 592 Andre Rodgers 15.00 7.50
❑ 593 Doug Camilli SP 30.00 15.00
❑ 594 Chico Salmon 15.00 7.50
❑ 595 Larry Jackson 15.00 7.50
❑ 596 N.Colbert RC/G.Sims RC SP 30.00 15.00
❑ 597 John Sullivan 15.00 7.50
❑ 598 Gaylord Perry SP 175.00 100.00

1967 Topps

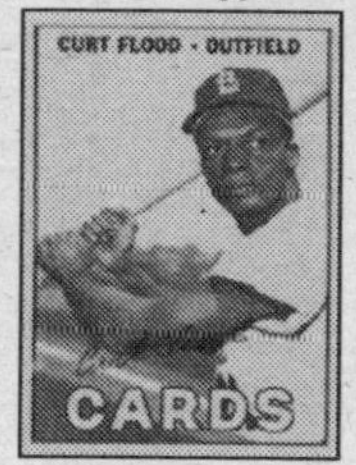

❑ COMPLETE SET (609) 5000.00 3000.00
❑ COMMON CARD (1-109) 1.50 .75
❑ COMMON CARD (110-283) 2.00 1.00
❑ COMMON CARD (284-370) 2.50 1.25
❑ COMMON CARD (371-457) 4.00 2.00
❑ COMMON CARD (458-533) 6.00 3.00
❑ COMMON CARD (534-609) 15.00 7.50
❑ COMMON DP (534-609) 8.00 4.00
❑ WRAPPER (5-CENT) 25.00 20.00
❑ 1 Robinson/Bauer/Robinson DP 25.00 12.50
❑ 2 Jack Hamilton 1.50 .75
❑ 3 Duke Sims 1.50 .75

❑ 4 Hal Lanier	1.50	.75
❑ 5 Whitey Ford UER	20.00	10.00
❑ 6 Dick Simpson	1.50	.75
❑ 7 Don McMahon	1.50	.75
❑ 8 Chuck Harrison	1.50	.75
❑ 9 Ron Hansen	1.50	.75
❑ 10 Matty Alou	4.00	2.00
❑ 11 Barry Moore RC	1.50	.75
❑ 12 J.Campanis RC/B.Singer	4.00	2.00
❑ 13 Joe Sparma	1.50	.75
❑ 14 Phil Linz	4.00	2.00
❑ 15 Earl Battey	1.50	.75
❑ 16 Bill Hands	1.50	.75
❑ 17 Jim Gosger	1.50	.75
❑ 18 Gene Oliver	1.50	.75
❑ 19 Jim McGlothlin	1.50	.75
❑ 20 Orlando Cepeda	8.00	4.00
❑ 21 Dave Bristol MG RC	1.50	.75
❑ 22 Gene Brabender	1.50	.75
❑ 23 Larry Elliot	1.50	.75
❑ 24 Bob Allen	1.50	.75
❑ 25 Elston Howard	4.00	2.00
❑ 26A Bob Priddy NTR	30.00	15.00
❑ 26B Bob Priddy TR	4.00	2.00
❑ 27 Bob Saverine	1.50	.75
❑ 28 Barry Latman	1.50	.75
❑ 29 Tom McCraw	1.50	.75
❑ 30 Al Kaline DP	20.00	10.00
❑ 31 Jim Brewer	1.50	.75
❑ 32 Bob Bailey	4.00	2.00
❑ 33 S.Bando RC/R.Schwartz RC	6.00	3.00
❑ 34 Pete Cimino	1.50	.75
❑ 35 Rico Carty	4.00	2.00
❑ 36 Bob Tillman	1.50	.75
❑ 37 Rick Wise	4.00	2.00
❑ 38 Bob Johnson	1.50	.75
❑ 39 Curt Simmons	4.00	2.00
❑ 40 Rick Reichardt	1.50	.75
❑ 41 Joe Hoerner	1.50	.75
❑ 42 New York Mets TC	10.00	5.00
❑ 43 Chico Salmon	1.50	.75
❑ 44 Joe Nuxhall	4.00	2.00
❑ 45 Roger Maris	50.00	30.00
❑ 45A R.Maris Yanks/Blank Back	1000.00	600.00
❑ 46 Lindy McDaniel	4.00	2.00
❑ 47 Ken McMullen	1.50	.75
❑ 48 Bill Freehan	4.00	2.00
❑ 49 Roy Face	4.00	2.00
❑ 50 Tony Oliva	6.00	3.00
❑ 51 D.Adlesh RC/W.Bales RC	1.50	.75
❑ 52 Dennis Higgins	1.50	.75
❑ 53 Clay Dalrymple	1.50	.75
❑ 54 Dick Green	1.50	.75
❑ 55 Don Drysdale	15.00	7.50
❑ 56 Jose Tartabull	4.00	2.00
❑ 57 Pat Jarvis RC	4.00	2.00
❑ 58A Paul Schaal Green Bat	20.00	10.00
❑ 58B P.Schaal Normal Bat	1.50	.75
❑ 59 Ralph Terry	4.00	2.00
❑ 60 Luis Aparicio	8.00	4.00
❑ 61 Gordy Coleman	1.50	.75
❑ 62 Frank Robinson CL1	8.00	4.00
❑ 63 L.Brock/C.Flood	8.00	4.00
❑ 64 Fred Valentine	1.50	.75
❑ 65 Tom Haller	4.00	2.00
❑ 66 Manny Mota	4.00	2.00
❑ 67 Ken Berry	1.50	.75
❑ 68 Bob Buhl	4.00	2.00
❑ 69 Vic Davalillo	1.50	.75
❑ 70 Ron Santo	6.00	3.00
❑ 71 Camilo Pascual	4.00	2.00
❑ 72 G.Korince ERR RC/T.Matchick RC	1.50	.75
❑ 73 Rusty Staub	6.00	3.00
❑ 74 Wes Stock	1.50	.75
❑ 75 George Scott	4.00	2.00
❑ 76 Jim Barbieri RC	1.50	.75
❑ 77 Dooley Womack	4.00	2.00
❑ 78 Pat Corrales	1.50	.75
❑ 79 Bubba Morton	1.50	.75
❑ 80 Jim Maloney	4.00	2.00
❑ 81 Eddie Stanky MG	4.00	2.00
❑ 82 Steve Barber	1.50	.75
❑ 83 Ollie Brown	1.50	.75
❑ 84 Tommie Sisk	1.50	.75
❑ 85 Johnny Callison	4.00	2.00
❑ 86A Mike McCormick NTR	30.00	15.00
❑ 86B Mike McCormick TR	4.00	2.00
❑ 87 George Altman	1.50	.75
❑ 88 Mickey Lolich	4.00	2.00
❑ 89 Felix Millan RC	4.00	2.00
❑ 90 Jim Nash RC	1.50	.75
❑ 91 Johnny Lewis	1.50	.75
❑ 92 Ray Washburn	1.50	.75
❑ 93 S.Bahnsen RC/B.Murcer	4.00	2.00
❑ 94 Ron Fairly	4.00	2.00
❑ 95 Sonny Siebert	1.50	.75
❑ 96 Art Shamsky	1.50	.75
❑ 97 Mike Cuellar	4.00	2.00
❑ 98 Rich Rollins	1.50	.75
❑ 99 Lee Stange	1.50	.75
❑ 100 Frank Robinson DP	15.00	7.50
❑ 101 Ken Johnson	1.50	.75
❑ 102 Philadelphia Phillies TC	4.00	2.00
❑ 103 Mickey Mantle CL2 DP	20.00	10.00
❑ 104 Minnie Rojas RC	1.50	.75
❑ 105 Ken Boyer	6.00	3.00
❑ 106 Randy Hundley	4.00	2.00
❑ 107 Joel Horlen	1.50	.75
❑ 108 Alex Johnson	4.00	2.00
❑ 109 R.Colavito/L.Wagner	6.00	3.00
❑ 110 Jack Aker	4.00	2.00
❑ 111 John Kennedy	2.00	1.00
❑ 112 Dave Wickersham	2.00	1.00
❑ 113 Dave Nicholson	2.00	1.00
❑ 114 Jack Baldschun	2.00	1.00
❑ 115 Paul Casanova RC	2.00	1.00
❑ 116 Herman Franks MG	2.00	1.00
❑ 117 Darrell Brandon	2.00	1.00
❑ 118 Bernie Allen	2.00	1.00
❑ 119 Wade Blasingame	2.00	1.00
❑ 120 Floyd Robinson	2.00	1.00
❑ 121 Eddie Bressoud	2.00	1.00
❑ 122 George Brunet	2.00	1.00
❑ 123 J.Price RC/L.Walker	4.00	2.00
❑ 124 Jim Stewart	2.00	1.00
❑ 125 Moe Drabowsky	4.00	2.00
❑ 126 Tony Taylor	2.00	1.00
❑ 127 John O'Donoghue	2.00	1.00
❑ 128 Ed Spiezio RC	2.00	1.00
❑ 129 Phil Roof	2.00	1.00
❑ 130 Phil Regan	4.00	2.00
❑ 131 New York Yankees TC	10.00	5.00
❑ 132 Ozzie Virgil	2.00	1.00
❑ 133 Ron Kline	2.00	1.00
❑ 134 Gates Brown	6.00	3.00
❑ 135 Deron Johnson	4.00	2.00
❑ 136 Carroll Sembera	2.00	1.00
❑ 137 R.Clark RC/J.Ollum	2.00	1.00
❑ 138 Dick Kelley	2.00	1.00
❑ 139 Dalton Jones	4.00	2.00
❑ 140 Willie Stargell	20.00	10.00
❑ 141 John Miller	2.00	1.00
❑ 142 Jackie Brandt	2.00	1.00
❑ 143 P.Ward/D.Buford	2.00	1.00
❑ 144 Bill Hepler	2.00	1.00
❑ 145 Larry Brown	2.00	1.00
❑ 146 Steve Carlton	50.00	30.00
❑ 147 Tom Egan	2.00	1.00
❑ 148 Adolfo Phillips	2.00	1.00
❑ 149 Joe Moeller	2.00	1.00
❑ 150 Mickey Mantle	350.00	200.00
❑ 151 Moe Drabowsky WS1	5.00	2.50
❑ 152 Jim Palmer WS2	8.00	4.00
❑ 153 Paul Blair WS3	5.00	2.50
❑ 154 Robinson/McNally WS4	5.00	2.50
❑ 155 Orioles Celebrate WS	5.00	2.50
❑ 156 Ron Herbel	2.00	1.00
❑ 157 Danny Cater	2.00	1.00
❑ 158 Jimmie Coker	2.00	1.00
❑ 159 Bruce Howard	2.00	1.00
❑ 160 Willie Davis	4.00	2.00
❑ 161 Dick Williams MG	4.00	2.00
❑ 162 Billy O'Dell	2.00	1.00
❑ 163 Vic Roznovsky	2.00	1.00
❑ 164 Dwight Siebler UER	2.00	1.00
❑ 165 Cleon Jones	4.00	2.00
❑ 166 Eddie Mathews	15.00	7.50
❑ 167 J.Coleman RC/T.Cullen RC	2.00	1.00
❑ 168 Ray Culp	2.00	1.00
❑ 169 Horace Clarke	4.00	2.00
❑ 170 Dick McAuliffe	4.00	2.00
❑ 171 Cal Koonce	2.00	1.00
❑ 172 Bill Heath	2.00	1.00
❑ 173 St. Louis Cardinals TC	4.00	2.00
❑ 174 Dick Radatz	4.00	2.00
❑ 175 Bobby Knoop	2.00	1.00
❑ 176 Sammy Ellis	2.00	1.00
❑ 177 Tito Fuentes	1.50	.75
❑ 178 John Buzhardt	2.00	1.00
❑ 179 C.Vaughan RC/C.Epshaw RC	4.002.00	
❑ 180 Curt Blefary	2.00	1.00
❑ 181 Terry Fox	2.00	1.00
❑ 182 Ed Charles	2.00	1.00
❑ 183 Jim Pagliaroni	2.00	1.00
❑ 184 George Thomas	2.00	1.00
❑ 185 Ken Holtzman RC	4.00	2.00
❑ 186 E.Kranepool/R.Swoboda	4.00	2.00
❑ 187 Pedro Ramos	2.00	1.00
❑ 188 Ken Harrelson	4.00	2.00
❑ 189 Chuck Hinton	2.00	1.00
❑ 190 Turk Farrell	2.00	1.00
❑ 191A W.Mays CL3 214 Tom	10.00	5.00
❑ 191B W.Mays CL3 214 Dick	12.00	6.00
❑ 192 Fred Gladding	2.00	1.00
❑ 193 Jose Cardenal	4.00	2.00
❑ 194 Bob Allison	4.00	2.00
❑ 195 Al Jackson	2.00	1.00
❑ 196 Johnny Romano	2.00	1.00
❑ 197 Ron Perranoski	4.00	2.00
❑ 198 Chuck Hiller	2.00	1.00
❑ 199 Billy Hitchcock MG	2.00	1.00
❑ 200 Willie Mays UER	100.00	60.00
❑ 201 Hal Reniff	4.00	2.00
❑ 202 Johnny Edwards	2.00	1.00
❑ 203 Al McBean	2.00	1.00
❑ 204 M.Epstein RC/T.Phoebus RC	6.003.00	
❑ 205 Dick Groat	4.00	2.00
❑ 206 Dennis Bennett	2.00	1.00
❑ 207 John Orsino	2.00	1.00
❑ 208 Jack Lamabe	2.00	1.00
❑ 209 Joe Nossek	2.00	1.00
❑ 210 Bob Gibson	20.00	10.00
❑ 211 Minnesota Twins TC	4.00	2.00
❑ 212 Chris Zachary	2.00	1.00
❑ 213 Jay Johnstone RC	4.00	2.00
❑ 214 Dick Kelley	2.00	1.00
❑ 215 Ernie Banks	20.00	10.00
❑ 216 A.Kaline/N.Cash	8.00	4.00
❑ 217 Rob Gardner	2.00	1.00
❑ 218 Wes Parker	4.00	2.00
❑ 219 Clay Carroll	4.00	2.00
❑ 220 Jim Ray Hart	4.00	2.00
❑ 221 Woody Fryman	4.00	2.00
❑ 222 D.Osteen/L.May	4.00	2.00
❑ 223 Mike Ryan	4.00	2.00
❑ 224 Walt Bond	2.00	1.00
❑ 225 Mel Stottlemyre	6.00	3.00
❑ 226 Julian Javier	4.00	2.00
❑ 227 Paul Lindblad	2.00	1.00
❑ 228 Gil Hodges MG	6.00	3.00
❑ 229 Larry Jackson	2.00	1.00
❑ 230 Boog Powell	6.00	3.00
❑ 231 John Bateman	2.00	1.00
❑ 232 Don Buford	2.00	1.00
❑ 233 Peters/Horlen/Hargan LL	4.00	2.00
❑ 234 Koufax/Cuellar/Marichal LL	15.00	7.50
❑ 235 Kaat/McLain/Wilson LL	6.00	3.00
❑ 236 Koufax/Mari/Gibs/Perry LL	25.00	12.50
❑ 237 McDowell/Kaat/Wilson LL	6.00	3.00
❑ 238 Koufax/Bunning/Veale LL	12.00	6.00
❑ 239 F.Rob/Oliva/Kaline LL	10.00	5.00
❑ 240 Alou/Alou/Carty LL	6.00	3.00
❑ 241 F.Rob/Killebrew/Powell LL	10.00	5.00
❑ 242 Aaron/Clemente/Allen LL	25.00	12.50
❑ 243 F.Rob/Killebrew/Powell LL	10.00	5.00
❑ 244 Aaron/Allen/Mays LL	20.00	10.00
❑ 245 Curt Flood	6.00	3.00
❑ 246 Jim Perry	4.00	2.00
❑ 247 Jerry Lumpe	2.00	1.00
❑ 248 Gene Mauch MG	4.00	2.00
❑ 249 Nick Willhite	2.00	1.00
❑ 250 Hank Aaron UER	80.00	50.00
❑ 251 Woody Held	2.00	1.00
❑ 252 Bob Bolin	2.00	1.00
❑ 253 B.Davis/G.Gil RC	2.00	1.00
❑ 254 Milt Pappas	4.00	2.00
❑ 255 Frank Howard	4.00	2.00
❑ 256 Bob Hendley	2.00	1.00

❑ 257 Charlie Smith 2.00 1.00
❑ 258 Lee Maye 2.00 1.00
❑ 259 Don Dennis 2.00 1.00
❑ 260 Jim Lefebvre 4.00 2.00
❑ 261 John Wyatt 2.00 1.00
❑ 262 Kansas City Athletics TC 4.00 2.00
❑ 263 Hank Aguirre 2.00 1.00
❑ 264 Ron Swoboda 4.00 2.00
❑ 265 Lou Burdette 4.00 2.00
❑ 266 W.Stargell/D.Clendenon 4.00 2.00
❑ 267 Don Schwall 2.00 1.00
❑ 268 Johnny Briggs 2.00 1.00
❑ 269 Don Nottebart 2.00 1.00
❑ 270 Zoilo Versalles 2.00 1.00
❑ 271 Eddie Watt 2.00 1.00
❑ 272 B.Connors RC/D.Dowling 4.00 2.00
❑ 273 Dick Lines RC 2.00 1.00
❑ 274 Bob Aspromonte 2.00 1.00
❑ 275 Fred Whitfield 2.00 1.00
❑ 276 Bruce Brubaker 2.00 1.00
❑ 277 Steve Whitaker RC 6.00 3.00
❑ 278 Jim Kaat CL4 8.00 4.00
❑ 279 Frank Linzy 2.00 1.00
❑ 280 Tony Conigliaro 8.00 4.00
❑ 281 Bob Rodgers 2.00 1.00
❑ 282 John Odom 2.00 1.00
❑ 283 Gene Alley 4.00 2.00
❑ 284 Johnny Podres 4.00 2.00
❑ 285 Lou Brock 20.00 10.00
❑ 286 Wayne Causey 2.50 1.25
❑ 287 G.Goosen RC/B.Shirley 2.50 1.25
❑ 288 Denny Lemaster 2.50 1.25
❑ 289 Tom Tresh 5.00 2.50
❑ 290 Bill White 5.00 2.50
❑ 291 Jim Hannan 2.50 1.25
❑ 292 Don Pavletich 2.50 1.25
❑ 293 Ed Kirkpatrick 2.50 1.25
❑ 294 Walter Alston MG 8.00 4.00
❑ 295 Sam McDowell 5.00 2.50
❑ 296 Glenn Beckert 5.00 2.50
❑ 297 Dave Morehead 5.00 2.50
❑ 298 Ron Davis RC 2.50 1.25
❑ 299 Norm Siebern 2.50 1.25
❑ 300 Jim Kaat 5.00 2.50
❑ 301 Jesse Gonder 2.50 1.25
❑ 302 Baltimore Orioles TC 8.00 4.00
❑ 303 Gil Blanco 2.50 1.25
❑ 304 Phil Gagliano 2.50 1.25
❑ 305 Earl Wilson 5.00 2.50
❑ 306 Bud Harrelson RC 5.00 2.50
❑ 307 Jim Beauchamp 2.50 1.25
❑ 308 Al Downing 5.00 2.50
❑ 309 J.Callison/R.Allen 5.00 2.50
❑ 310 Gary Peters 2.50 1.25
❑ 311 Ed Brinkman 2.50 1.25
❑ 312 Don Mincher 2.50 1.25
❑ 313 Bob Lee 2.50 1.25
❑ 314 M.Andrews RC/R.Smith RC 8.00 4.00
❑ 315 Billy Williams 15.00 7.50
❑ 316 Jack Kralick 2.50 1.25
❑ 317 Cesar Tovar 2.50 1.25
❑ 318 Dave Giusti 2.50 1.25
❑ 319 Paul Blair 5.00 2.50
❑ 320 Gaylord Perry 15.00 7.50
❑ 321 Mayo Smith MG 2.50 1.25
❑ 322 Jose Pagan 2.50 1.25
❑ 323 Mike Hershberger 2.50 1.25
❑ 324 Hal Woodeshick 2.50 1.25
❑ 325 Chico Cardenas 5.00 2.50
❑ 326 Bob Uecker 10.00 5.00
❑ 327 California Angels TC 8.00 4.00
❑ 328 Clete Boyer UER 5.00 2.50
❑ 329 Charlie Lau 5.00 2.50
❑ 330 Claude Osteen 5.00 2.50
❑ 331 Joe Foy 5.00 2.50
❑ 332 Jesus Alou 2.50 1.25
❑ 333 Fergie Jenkins 20.00 10.00
❑ 334 H.Killebrew/B.Allison 10.00 5.00
❑ 335 Bob Veale 5.00 2.50
❑ 336 Joe Azcue 2.50 1.25
❑ 337 Joe Morgan 15.00 7.50
❑ 338 Bob Locker 2.50 1.25
❑ 339 Chico Ruiz 2.50 1.25
❑ 340 Joe Pepitone 8.00 4.00
❑ 341 D.Dietz RC/B.Sorrell 2.50 1.25
❑ 342 Hank Fischer 2.50 1.25
❑ 343 Tom Satriano 2.50 1.25
❑ 344 Ossie Chavarria RC 2.50 1.25
❑ 345 Stu Miller 5.00 2.50
❑ 346 Jim Hickman 2.50 1.25
❑ 347 Grady Hatton MG 2.50 1.25
❑ 348 Tug McGraw 5.00 2.50
❑ 349 Bob Chance 2.50 1.25
❑ 350 Joe Torre 8.00 4.00
❑ 351 Vern Law 5.00 2.50
❑ 352 Ray Oyler 2.50 1.25
❑ 353 Bill McCool 2.50 1.25
❑ 354 Chicago Cubs TC 8.00 4.00
❑ 355 Carl Yastrzemski 60.00 35.00
❑ 356 Larry Jaster RC 2.50 1.25
❑ 357 Bill Skowron 5.00 2.50
❑ 358 Ruben Amaro 2.50 1.25
❑ 359 Dick Ellsworth 2.50 1.25
❑ 360 Leon Wagner 2.50 1.25
❑ 361 Roberto Clemente CL5 15.00 7.50
❑ 362 Darold Knowles 2.50 1.25
❑ 363 Davey Johnson 5.00 2.50
❑ 364 Claude Raymond 2.50 1.25
❑ 365 John Roseboro 5.00 2.50
❑ 366 Andy Kosco 2.50 1.25
❑ 367 B.Kelso/D.Wallace RC 2.50 1.25
❑ 368 Jack Hiatt 2.50 1.25
❑ 369 Jim Hunter 15.00 7.50
❑ 370 Tommy Davis 5.00 2.50
❑ 371 Jim Lonborg 8.00 4.00
❑ 372 Mike de la Hoz 4.00 2.00
❑ 373 D.Josephson RC/F.Klages RC DP 4.00 2.00
❑ 374A Mel Queen ERR 20.00 10.00
❑ 374B Mel Queen COR DP 4.00 2.00
❑ 375 Jake Gibbs 8.00 4.00
❑ 376 Don Lock DP 4.00 2.00
❑ 377 Luis Tiant 8.00 4.00
❑ 378 Detroit Tigers TC UER 8.00 4.00
❑ 379 Jerry May DP 4.00 2.00
❑ 380 Dean Chance DP 4.00 2.00
❑ 381 Dick Schofield DP 4.00 2.00
❑ 382 Dave McNally 8.00 4.00
❑ 383 Ken Henderson DP 4.00 2.00
❑ 384 J.Cosman RC/D.Hughes RC 4.00 2.00
❑ 385 Jim Fregosi 8.00 4.00
❑ 386 Dick Selma DP 4.00 2.00
❑ 387 Cap Peterson DP 4.00 2.00
❑ 388 Arnold Earley DP 4.00 2.00
❑ 389 Alvin Dark MG DP 8.00 4.00
❑ 390 Jim Wynn DP 8.00 4.00
❑ 391 Wilbur Wood DP 8.00 4.00
❑ 392 Tommy Harper DP 8.00 4.00
❑ 393 Jim Bouton DP 8.00 4.00
❑ 394 Jake Wood DP 4.00 2.00
❑ 395 Chris Short RC 8.00 4.00
❑ 396 D.Menke/T.Cloninger 4.00 2.00
❑ 397 Willie Smith DP 4.00 2.00
❑ 398 Jeff Torborg 8.00 4.00
❑ 399 Al Worthington DP 4.00 2.00
❑ 400 Roberto Clemente DP 120.00 70.00
❑ 401 Jim Coates 4.00 2.00
❑ 402A G.Jackson/B.Wilson Stat Line 20.00 10.00
❑ 402B G.Jackson/B.Wilson RC DP 8.00 4.00
❑ 403 Dick Nen 4.00 2.00
❑ 404 Nelson Briles 8.00 4.00
❑ 405 Russ Snyder 4.00 2.00
❑ 406 Lee Elia DP 4.00 2.00
❑ 407 Cincinnati Reds TC 8.00 4.00
❑ 408 Jim Northrup DP 8.00 4.00
❑ 409 Ray Sadecki 4.00 2.00
❑ 410 Lou Johnson DP 4.00 2.00
❑ 411 Dick Howser DP 4.00 2.00
❑ 412 N.Miller RC/D.Rader RC 8.00 4.00
❑ 413 Jerry Grote 4.00 2.00
❑ 414 Casey Cox 4.00 2.00
❑ 415 Sonny Jackson 4.00 2.00
❑ 416 Roger Repoz 4.00 2.00
❑ 417A Bob Bruce ERR 30.00 15.00
❑ 417B Bob Bruce COR DP 4.00 2.00
❑ 418 Sam Mele MG 4.00 2.00
❑ 419 Don Kessinger DP 8.00 4.00
❑ 420 Denny McLain 12.00 6.00
❑ 421 Dal Maxvill DP 4.00 2.00
❑ 422 Hoyt Wilhelm 15.00 7.50
❑ 423 W.Mays/W.McCovey DP 25.00 12.50
❑ 424 Pedro Gonzalez 4.00 2.00
❑ 425 Pete Mikkelsen 4.00 2.00
❑ 426 Lou Clinton 4.00 2.00
❑ 427A Ruben Gomez ERR 20.00 10.00
❑ 427B Ruben Gomez COR DP 4.00 2.00
❑ 428 T.Hutton RC/G.Michael RC DP 8.00 4.00
❑ 429 Garry Roggenburk DP 4.00 2.00
❑ 430 Pete Rose 100.00 60.00
❑ 431 Ted Uhlaender 4.00 2.00
❑ 432 Jimmie Hall DP 4.00 2.00
❑ 433 Al Luplow DP 4.00 2.00
❑ 434 Eddie Fisher DP 4.00 2.00
❑ 435 Mack Jones DP 4.00 2.00
❑ 436 Pete Ward 4.00 2.00
❑ 437 Washington Senators TC 8.00 4.00
❑ 438 Chuck Dobson 4.00 2.00
❑ 439 Byron Browne 4.00 2.00
❑ 440 Steve Hargan 4.00 2.00
❑ 441 Jim Davenport 4.00 2.00
❑ 442 B.Robinson RC/J.Verbanic RC DP 8.00 4.00
❑ 443 Tito Francona DP 4.00 2.00
❑ 444 George Smith 4.00 2.00
❑ 445 Don Sutton 25.00 12.50
❑ 446 Russ Nixon DP 4.00 2.00
❑ 447A Bo Belinsky ERR DP 4.00 2.00
❑ 447B Bo Belinsky COR 8.00 4.00
❑ 448 Harry Walker MG DP 4.00 2.00
❑ 449 Orlando Pena 4.00 2.00
❑ 450 Richie Allen 8.00 4.00
❑ 451 Fred Newman DP 4.00 2.00
❑ 452 Ed Kranepool 8.00 4.00
❑ 453 Aurelio Monteagudo DP 4.00 2.00
❑ 454A J.Marichal CL6 No Ear DP 12.00 6.00
❑ 454B Juan Marichal CL6 w/Ear DP 12.00 6.00
❑ 455 Tommie Agee 8.00 4.00
❑ 456 Phil Niekro 15.00 7.50
❑ 457 Andy Etchebarren DP 8.00 4.00
❑ 458 Lee Thomas 6.00 3.00
❑ 459 D.Bosman RC/P.Craig 6.00 3.00
❑ 460 Harmon Killebrew 60.00 35.00
❑ 461 Bob Miller 12.00 6.00
❑ 462 Bob Barton 6.00 3.00
❑ 463 S.McDowell/S.Siebert 12.00 6.00
❑ 464 Dan Coombs 6.00 3.00
❑ 465 Willie Horton 12.00 6.00
❑ 466 Bobby Wine 6.00 3.00
❑ 467 Jim O'Toole 6.00 3.00
❑ 468 Ralph Houk MG 6.00 3.00
❑ 469 Len Gabrielson 6.00 3.00
❑ 470 Bob Shaw 6.00 3.00
❑ 471 Rene Lachemann 6.00 3.00
❑ 472 J.Gelnar/G.Spriggs RC 6.00 3.00
❑ 473 Jose Santiago 6.00 3.00
❑ 474 Bob Tolan 6.00 3.00
❑ 475 Jim Palmer 80.00 50.00
❑ 476 Tony Perez SP 60.00 35.00
❑ 477 Atlanta Braves TC 15.00 7.50
❑ 478 Bob Humphreys 6.00 3.00
❑ 479 Gary Bell 6.00 3.00
❑ 480 Willie McCovey 40.00 20.00
❑ 481 Leo Durocher MG 20.00 10.00
❑ 482 Bill Monbouquette 6.00 3.00
❑ 483 Jim Landis 6.00 3.00
❑ 484 Jerry Adair 6.00 3.00
❑ 485 Tim McCarver 25.00 12.50
❑ 486 R.Reese RC/B.Whitby RC 6.00 3.00
❑ 487 Tommie Reynolds 6.00 3.00
❑ 488 Gerry Arrigo 6.00 3.00
❑ 489 Doug Clemens RC 6.00 3.00
❑ 490 Tony Cloninger 6.00 3.00
❑ 491 Sam Bowens 6.00 3.00
❑ 492 Pittsburgh Pirates TC 15.00 7.50
❑ 493 Phil Ortega 6.00 3.00
❑ 494 Bill Rigney MG 6.00 3.00
❑ 495 Fritz Peterson 6.00 3.00
❑ 496 Orlando McFarlane 6.00 3.00
❑ 497 Ron Campbell RC 6.00 3.00
❑ 498 Larry Dierker 12.00 6.00
❑ 499 G.Culver/J.Vidal RC 6.00 3.00
❑ 500 Juan Marichal 25.00 12.50
❑ 501 Jerry Zimmerman 6.00 3.00
❑ 502 Derrell Griffith 6.00 3.00
❑ 503 Los Angeles Dodgers TC 20.00 10.00
❑ 504 Orlando Martinez RC 6.00 3.00
❑ 505 Tommy Helms 12.00 6.00
❑ 506 Smoky Burgess 6.00 3.00
❑ 507 E.Barnowski/L.Haney RC 6.00 3.00
❑ 508 Dick Hall 6.00 3.00

❑ 509 Jim King 6.00 3.00
❑ 510 Bill Mazeroski 25.00 12.50
❑ 511 Don Wert 6.00 3.00
❑ 512 Red Schoendienst MG 25.00 12.50
❑ 513 Marcelino Lopez 6.00 3.00
❑ 514 John Werhas 6.00 3.00
❑ 515 Bert Campaneris 12.00 6.00
❑ 516 San Francisco Giants TC 15.00 7.50
❑ 517 Fred Talbot 12.00 6.00
❑ 518 Denis Menke 6.00 3.00
❑ 519 Ted Davidson 6.00 3.00
❑ 520 Max Alvis 6.00 3.00
❑ 521 B.Powell/C.Blefary 12.00 6.00
❑ 522 John Stephenson 6.00 3.00
❑ 523 Jim Merritt 6.00 3.00
❑ 524 Felix Mantilla 6.00 3.00
❑ 525 Ron Hunt 6.00 3.00
❑ 526 P.Dobson RC/G.Korince RC 6.00 3.00
❑ 527 Dennis Ribant 6.00 3.00
❑ 528 Rico Petrocelli 20.00 10.00
❑ 529 Gary Wagner 6.00 3.00
❑ 530 Felipe Alou 12.00 6.00
❑ 531 B.Robinson CL7 DP 15.00 7.50
❑ 532 Jim Hicks RC 6.00 3.00
❑ 533 Jack Fisher 6.00 3.00
❑ 534 Hank Bauer MG DP 8.00 4.00
❑ 535 Donn Clendenon 25.00 12.50
❑ 536 J.Niekro RC/P.Popovich RC 50.00 30.00
❑ 537 Chuck Estrada DP 8.00 4.00
❑ 538 J.C. Martin 15.00 7.50
❑ 539 Dick Egan DP 8.00 4.00
❑ 540 Norm Cash 50.00 30.00
❑ 541 Joe Gibbon 15.00 7.50
❑ 542 R.Monday RC/T.Pierce RC DP 15.00 7.50
❑ 543 Dan Schneider 15.00 7.50
❑ 544 Cleveland Indians TC 30.00 15.00
❑ 545 Jim Grant 25.00 12.50
❑ 546 Woody Woodward 25.00 12.50
❑ 547 R.Gibson RC/B.Rohr RC DP 8.00 4.00
❑ 548 Tony Gonzalez DP 8.00 4.00
❑ 549 Jack Sanford 15.00 7.50
❑ 550 Vada Pinson DP 10.00 5.00
❑ 551 Doug Camilli DP 8.00 4.00
❑ 552 Ted Savage 25.00 12.50
❑ 553 M.Hegan RC/T.Tillotson 40.00 20.00
❑ 554 Andre Rodgers DP 8.00 4.00
❑ 555 Don Cardwell 25.00 12.50
❑ 556 Al Weis DP 8.00 4.00
❑ 557 Al Ferrara 25.00 12.50
❑ 558 M.Belanger RC/B.Dillman RC 50.00 30.00
❑ 559 Dick Tracewski DP 8.00 4.00
❑ 560 Jim Bunning 60.00 35.00
❑ 561 Sandy Alomar 40.00 20.00
❑ 562 Steve Blass DP 8.00 4.00
❑ 563 Joe Adcock MG 40.00 20.00
❑ 564 A.Harris RC/A.Pointer RC DP 8.00 4.00
❑ 565 Lew Krausse 25.00 12.50
❑ 566 Gary Geiger DP 8.00 4.00
❑ 567 Steve Hamilton 40.00 20.00
❑ 568 John Sullivan 40.00 20.00
❑ 569 Rod Carew RC DP 300.00 175.00
❑ 570 Maury Wills 80.00 50.00
❑ 571 Larry Sherry 25.00 12.50
❑ 572 Don Demeter 25.00 12.50
❑ 573 Chicago White Sox TC 30.00 15.00
❑ 574 Jerry Buchek 25.00 12.50
❑ 575 Dave Boswell RC 15.00 7.50
❑ 576 R.Hernandez RC/N.Gigon RC 40.00 20.00
❑ 577 Bill Short 15.00 7.50
❑ 578 John Boccabella 15.00 7.50
❑ 579 Bill Henry 15.00 7.50
❑ 580 Rocky Colavito 150.00 90.00
❑ 581 Tom Seaver RC 600.00 350.00
❑ 582 Jim Owens DP 8.00 4.00
❑ 583 Ray Barker 40.00 20.00
❑ 584 Jimmy Piersall 40.00 20.00
❑ 585 Wally Bunker 25.00 12.50
❑ 586 Manny Jimenez 15.00 7.50
❑ 587 D.Shaw RC/G.Sutherland RC 40.00 20.00
❑ 588 Johnny Klippstein DP 8.00 4.00
❑ 589 Dave Ricketts DP 8.00 4.00
❑ 590 Pete Richert 15.00 7.50
❑ 591 Ty Cline 25.00 12.50
❑ 592 J.Shellenback RC/R.Willis RC 25.00 12.50
❑ 593 Wes Westrum MG 50.00 30.00
❑ 594 Dan Osinski 40.00 20.00
❑ 595 Cookie Rojas 25.00 12.50
❑ 596 Galen Cisco DP 8.00 4.00
❑ 597 Ted Abernathy 15.00 7.50
❑ 598 W.Williams RC/E.Stroud RC 25.00 12.50
❑ 599 Bob Duliba DP 8.00 4.00
❑ 600 Brooks Robinson 250.00 150.00
❑ 601 Bill Bryan DP 8.00 4.00
❑ 602 Juan Pizarro 40.00 20.00
❑ 603 T.Talton RC/R.Webster RC 25.00 12.50
❑ 604 Boston Red Sox TC 125.00 75.00
❑ 605 Mike Shannon 50.00 30.00
❑ 606 Ron Taylor 25.00 12.50
❑ 607 Mickey Stanley 50.00 30.00
❑ 608 R.Nye RC/J.Upham RC DP 8.00 4.00
❑ 609 Tommy John 80.00 50.00

1968 Topps

❑ COMPLETE SET (598) 3000.00 1800.00
❑ COMMON CARD (1-457) 2.00 .75
❑ COMMON CARD (458-598) 4.00 1.50
❑ WRAPPER (5-CENT) 25.00 20.00
❑ 1 Clemente/Gonz/Alou LL 30.00 15.00
❑ 2 Yaz/F.Rob/Kaline LL 15.00 7.50
❑ 3 Cep/Clemente/Aaron LL 20.00 10.00
❑ 4 Yaz/Killebrew/F.Rob LL 15.00 7.50
❑ 5 Aaron/Santo/McCovey LL 8.00 4.00
❑ 6 Yaz/Killebrew/Howard LL 8.00 4.00
❑ 7 Niekro/Bunning/Short LL 4.00 1.50
❑ 8 Horlen/Peters/Siebert LL 4.00 1.50
❑ 9 McCor/Jenkins/Bunning LL 4.00 1.50
❑ 10A Lonb/Wils/Chance LL ERR 4.00 1.50
❑ 10B Lonb/Wils/Chance LL COR 4.00 1.50
❑ 11 Bunning/Jenkins/Perry LL 6.00 3.00
❑ 12 Lonborg/McDow/Chance LL 4.00 1.50
❑ 13 Chuck Hartenstein RC 2.00 .75
❑ 14 Jerry McNertney 2.00 .75
❑ 15 Ron Hunt 2.00 .75
❑ 16 L.Piniella/R.Scheinblum 6.00 3.00
❑ 17 Dick Hall 2.00 .75
❑ 18 Mike Hershberger 2.00 .75
❑ 19 Juan Pizarro 2.00 .75
❑ 20 Brooks Robinson 25.00 12.50
❑ 21 Ron Davis 2.00 .75
❑ 22 Pat Dobson 4.00 1.50
❑ 23 Chico Cardenas 4.00 1.50
❑ 24 Bobby Locke 2.00 .75
❑ 25 Julian Javier 4.00 1.50
❑ 26 Darrell Brandon 2.00 .75
❑ 27 Gil Hodges MG 8.00 4.00
❑ 28 Ted Uhlaender 2.00 .75
❑ 29 Joe Verbanic 2.00 .75
❑ 30 Joe Torre 6.00 3.00
❑ 31 Ed Stroud 2.00 .75
❑ 32 Joe Gibbon 2.00 .75
❑ 33 Pete Ward 2.00 .75
❑ 34 Al Ferrara 2.00 .75
❑ 35 Steve Hargan 2.00 .75
❑ 36 B.Moose RC/B.Robertson RC 4.00 1.50
❑ 37 Billy Williams 8.00 4.00
❑ 38 Tony Pierce 2.00 .75
❑ 39 Cookie Rojas 2.00 .75
❑ 40 Denny McLain 8.00 4.00
❑ 41 Julio Gotay 2.00 .75
❑ 42 Larry Haney 2.00 .75
❑ 43 Gary Bell 2.00 .75
❑ 44 Frank Kostro 2.00 .75
❑ 45 Tom Seaver DP 50.00 30.00
❑ 46 Dave Ricketts 2.00 .75
❑ 47 Ralph Houk MG 4.00 1.50
❑ 48 Ted Davidson 2.00 .75
❑ 49A E.Brinkman White 2.00 .75
❑ 49B E.Brinkman Yellow Tm 50.00 30.00
❑ 50 Willie Mays 60.00 35.00
❑ 51 Bob Locker 2.00 .75
❑ 52 Hawk Taylor 2.00 .75
❑ 53 Gene Alley 4.00 1.50
❑ 54 Stan Williams 2.00 .75
❑ 55 Felipe Alou 4.00 1.50
❑ 56 D.Leonhard RC/D.May RC 2.00 .75
❑ 57 Dan Schneider 2.00 .75
❑ 58 Eddie Mathews 15.00 7.50
❑ 59 Don Lock 2.00 .75
❑ 60 Ken Holtzman 4.00 1.50
❑ 61 Reggie Smith 4.00 1.50
❑ 62 Chuck Dobson 2.00 .75
❑ 63 Dick Kenworthy RC 2.00 .75
❑ 64 Jim Merritt 2.00 .75
❑ 65 John Roseboro 4.00 1.50
❑ 66A Casey Cox White 2.00 .75
❑ 66B C.Cox Yellow Tm 100.00 60.00
❑ 67 Checklist 1/Kaat 6.00 3.00
❑ 68 Ron Willis 2.00 .75
❑ 69 Tom Tresh 4.00 1.50
❑ 70 Bob Veale 4.00 1.50
❑ 71 Vern Fuller RC 2.00 .75
❑ 72 Tommy John 6.00 3.00
❑ 73 Jim Ray Hart 4.00 1.50
❑ 74 Milt Pappas 4.00 1.50
❑ 75 Don Mincher 2.00 .75
❑ 76 J.Britton/R.Reed RC 4.00 1.50
❑ 77 Don Wilson RC 4.00 1.50
❑ 78 Jim Northrup 6.00 3.00
❑ 79 Ted Kubiak RC 2.00 .75
❑ 80 Rod Carew 50.00 30.00
❑ 81 Larry Jackson 2.00 .75
❑ 82 Sam Bowens 2.00 .75
❑ 83 John Stephenson 2.00 .75
❑ 84 Bob Tolan 2.00 .75
❑ 85 Gaylord Perry 8.00 4.00
❑ 86 Willie Stargell 8.00 4.00
❑ 87 Dick Williams MG 4.00 1.50
❑ 88 Phil Regan 4.00 1.50
❑ 89 Jake Gibbs 4.00 1.50
❑ 90 Vada Pinson 4.00 1.50
❑ 91 Jim Ollom RC 2.00 .75
❑ 92 Ed Kranepool 4.00 1.50
❑ 93 Tony Cloninger 2.00 .75
❑ 94 Lee Maye 2.00 .75
❑ 95 Bob Aspromonte 2.00 .75
❑ 96 F.Coggins RC/D.Nold 2.00 .75
❑ 97 Tom Phoebus 2.00 .75
❑ 98 Gary Sutherland 2.00 .75
❑ 99 Rocky Colavito 8.00 4.00
❑ 100 Bob Gibson 25.00 12.50
❑ 101 Glenn Beckert 4.00 1.50
❑ 102 Jose Cardenal 4.00 1.50
❑ 103 Don Sutton 8.00 4.00
❑ 104 Dick Dietz 2.00 .75
❑ 105 Al Downing 4.00 1.50
❑ 106 Dalton Jones 2.00 .75
❑ 107A Checklist 2/Marichal Wide 6.00 3.00
❑ 107B Checklist 2/J.Marichal Fine 6.00 3.00
❑ 108 Don Pavletich 2.00 .75
❑ 109 Bert Campaneris 4.00 1.50
❑ 110 Hank Aaron 60.00 35.00
❑ 111 Rich Reese 2.00 .75
❑ 112 Woody Fryman 2.00 .75
❑ 113 T.Matchick/D.Patterson RC 4.00 1.50
❑ 114 Ron Swoboda 4.00 1.50
❑ 115 Sam McDowell 4.00 1.50
❑ 116 Ken McMullen 2.00 .75
❑ 117 Larry Jaster 2.00 .75
❑ 118 Mark Belanger 4.00 1.50
❑ 119 Ted Savage 2.00 .75
❑ 120 Mel Stottlemyre 4.00 1.50
❑ 121 Jimmie Hall 2.00 .75
❑ 122 Gene Mauch MG 4.00 1.50
❑ 123 Jose Santiago 2.00 .75
❑ 124 Nate Oliver 2.00 .75
❑ 125 Joel Horlen 2.00 .75
❑ 126 Bobby Etheridge RC 2.00 .75
❑ 127 Paul Lindblad 2.00 .75
❑ 128 T.Dukes RC/A.Harris 2.00 .75
❑ 129 Mickey Stanley 6.00 3.00

❑ 130 Tony Perez 8.00 4.00
❑ 131 Frank Bertaina 2.00 .75
❑ 132 Bud Harrelson 4.00 1.50
❑ 133 Fred Whitfield 2.00 .75
❑ 134 Pat Jarvis 2.00 .75
❑ 135 Paul Blair 4.00 1.50
❑ 136 Randy Hundley 4.00 1.50
❑ 137 Minnesota Twins TC 4.00 1.50
❑ 138 Ruben Amaro 2.00 .75
❑ 139 Chris Short 2.00 .75
❑ 140 Tony Conigliaro 8.00 4.00
❑ 141 Dal Maxvill 2.00 .75
❑ 142 B.Bradford RC/B.Voss 2.00 .75
❑ 143 Pete Cimino 2.00 .75
❑ 144 Joe Morgan 12.00 6.00
❑ 145 Don Drysdale 12.00 6.00
❑ 146 Sal Bando 4.00 1.50
❑ 147 Frank Linzy 2.00 .75
❑ 148 Dave Bristol MG 2.00 .75
❑ 149 Bob Saverine 2.00 .75
❑ 150 Roberto Clemente 80.00 50.00
❑ 151 Lou Brock WS1 10.00 5.00
❑ 152 Carl Yastrzemski WS2 10.00 5.00
❑ 153 Nelson Briles WS3 5.00 2.00
❑ 154 Bob Gibson WS4 10.00 5.00
❑ 155 Jim Lonborg WS5 5.00 2.00
❑ 156 Rico Petrocelli WS6 5.00 2.00
❑ 157 St. Louis Wins It WS7 5.00 2.00
❑ 158 Cardinals Celebrate WS 5.00 2.00
❑ 159 Don Kessinger 4.00 1.50
❑ 160 Earl Wilson 4.00 1.50
❑ 161 Norm Miller 2.00 .75
❑ 162 H.Gilson RC/M.Torrez RC 4.00 1.50
❑ 163 Gene Brabender 2.00 .75
❑ 164 Ramon Webster 2.00 .75
❑ 165 Tony Oliva 6.00 3.00
❑ 166 Claude Raymond 2.00 .75
❑ 167 Elston Howard 6.00 3.00
❑ 168 Los Angeles Dodgers TC 4.00 1.50
❑ 169 Bob Bolin 2.00 .75
❑ 170 Jim Fregosi 4.00 1.50
❑ 171 Don Nottebart 2.00 .75
❑ 172 Walt Williams 2.00 .75
❑ 173 John Boozer 2.00 .75
❑ 174 Bob Tillman 2.00 .75
❑ 175 Maury Wills 6.00 3.00
❑ 176 Bob Allen 2.00 .75
❑ 177 N.Ryan RC/J.Koosman RC 500.00 300.00
❑ 178 Don Wert 4.00 1.50
❑ 179 Bill Stoneman RC 2.00 .75
❑ 180 Curt Flood 6.00 3.00
❑ 181 Jerry Zimmerman 2.00 .75
❑ 182 Dave Giusti 2.00 .75
❑ 183 Bob Kennedy MG 4.00 1.50
❑ 184 Lou Johnson 2.00 .75
❑ 185 Tom Haller 2.00 .75
❑ 186 Eddie Watt 2.00 .75
❑ 187 Sonny Jackson 2.00 .75
❑ 188 Cap Peterson 2.00 .75
❑ 189 Bill Landis RC 2.00 .75
❑ 190 Bill White 4.00 1.50
❑ 191 Dan Frisella RC 2.00 .75
❑ 192A Checklist 3/Yaz Ball 8.00 4.00
❑ 192B Checklist 3/Yaz Game 8.00 4.00
❑ 193 Jack Hamilton 2.00 .75
❑ 194 Don Buford 2.00 .75
❑ 195 Joe Pepitone 4.00 1.50
❑ 196 Gary Nolan RC 4.00 1.50
❑ 197 Larry Brown 2.00 .75
❑ 198 Roy Face 4.00 1.50
❑ 199 R.Rodriguez RC/D.Osteen 2.00 .75
❑ 200 Orlando Cepeda 8.00 4.00
❑ 201 Mike Marshall RC 4.00 1.50
❑ 202 Adolfo Phillips 2.00 .75
❑ 203 Dick Kelley 2.00 .75
❑ 204 Andy Etchebarren 2.00 .75
❑ 205 Juan Marichal 8.00 4.00
❑ 206 Cal Ermer MG RC 2.00 .75
❑ 207 Carroll Sembera 2.00 .75
❑ 208 Willie Davis 4.00 1.50
❑ 209 Tim Cullen 2.00 .75
❑ 210 Gary Peters 2.00 .75
❑ 211 J.C. Martin 2.00 .75
❑ 212 Dave Morehead 2.00 .75
❑ 213 Chico Ruiz 2.00 .75
❑ 214 S.Bahnsen/F.Fernandez 4.00 1.50
❑ 215 Jim Bunning 8.00 4.00
❑ 216 Bubba Morton 2.00 .75
❑ 217 Dick Farrell 2.00 .75
❑ 218 Ken Suarez 2.00 .75
❑ 219 Rob Gardner 2.00 .75
❑ 220 Harmon Killebrew 15.00 7.50
❑ 221 Atlanta Braves TC 4.00 1.50
❑ 222 Jim Hardin RC 2.00 .75
❑ 223 Ollie Brown 2.00 .75
❑ 224 Jack Aker 2.00 .75
❑ 225 Richie Allen 6.00 3.00
❑ 226 Jimmie Price 2.00 .75
❑ 227 Joe Hoerner 2.00 .75
❑ 228 J.Billingham RC/J.Fairey RC 4.00 1.50
❑ 229 Fred Klages 2.00 .75
❑ 230 Pete Rose 60.00 35.00
❑ 231 Dave Baldwin RC 2.00 .75
❑ 232 Denis Menke 2.00 .75
❑ 233 George Scott 4.00 1.50
❑ 234 Bill Monbouquette 2.00 .75
❑ 235 Ron Santo 8.00 4.00
❑ 236 Tug McGraw 6.00 3.00
❑ 237 Alvin Dark MG 4.00 1.50
❑ 238 Tom Satriano 2.00 .75
❑ 239 Bill Henry 2.00 .75
❑ 240 Al Kaline 40.00 20.00
❑ 241 Felix Millan 2.00 .75
❑ 242 Moe Drabowsky 4.00 1.50
❑ 243 Rich Rollins 2.00 .75
❑ 244 John Donaldson RC 2.00 .75
❑ 245 Tony Gonzalez 2.00 .75
❑ 246 Fritz Peterson 4.00 1.50
❑ 247 Johnny Bench RC 125.00 75.00
❑ 248 Fred Valentine 2.00 .75
❑ 249 Bill Singer 2.00 .75
❑ 250 Carl Yastrzemski 30.00 15.00
❑ 251 Manny Sanguillen RC 6.00 3.00
❑ 252 California Angels TC 4.00 1.50
❑ 253 Dick Hughes 2.00 .75
❑ 254 Cleon Jones 4.00 1.50
❑ 255 Dean Chance 4.00 1.50
❑ 256 Norm Cash 6.00 3.00
❑ 257 Phil Niekro 8.00 4.00
❑ 258 J.Arcia RC/B.Schlesinger 2.00 .75
❑ 259 Ken Boyer 6.00 3.00
❑ 260 Jim Wynn 4.00 1.50
❑ 261 Dave Duncan 4.00 1.50
❑ 262 Rick Wise 4.00 1.50
❑ 263 Horace Clarke 4.00 1.50
❑ 264 Ted Abernathy 2.00 .75
❑ 265 Tommy Davis 4.00 1.50
❑ 266 Paul Popovich 2.00 .75
❑ 267 Herman Franks MG 2.00 .75
❑ 268 Bob Humphreys 2.00 .75
❑ 269 Bob Tiefenauer 2.00 .75
❑ 270 Matty Alou 4.00 1.50
❑ 271 Bobby Knoop 2.00 .75
❑ 272 Ray Culp 2.00 .75
❑ 273 Dave Johnson 4.00 1.50
❑ 274 Mike Cuellar 4.00 1.50
❑ 275 Tim McCarver 6.00 3.00
❑ 276 Jim Roland 2.00 .75
❑ 277 Jerry Buchek 2.00 .75
❑ 278 Checklist 4/Cepeda 6.00 3.00
❑ 279 Bill Hands 2.00 .75
❑ 280 Mickey Mantle 350.00 200.00
❑ 281 Jim Campanis 2.00 .75
❑ 282 Rick Monday 4.00 1.50
❑ 283 Mel Queen 2.00 .75
❑ 284 Johnny Briggs 2.00 .75
❑ 285 Dick McAuliffe 6.00 3.00
❑ 286 Cecil Upshaw 2.00 .75
❑ 287 M.Abarbanel RC/C.Carlos RC 2.00 .75
❑ 288 Dave Wickersham 2.00 .75
❑ 289 Woody Held 2.00 .75
❑ 290 Willie McCovey 12.00 6.00
❑ 291 Dick Lines 2.00 .75
❑ 292 Art Shamsky 2.00 .75
❑ 293 Bruce Howard 2.00 .75
❑ 294 Red Schoendienst MG 6.00 3.00
❑ 295 Sonny Siebert 2.00 .75
❑ 296 Byron Browne 2.00 .75
❑ 297 Russ Gibson 2.00 .75
❑ 298 Jim Brewer 2.00 .75
❑ 299 Gene Michael 4.00 1.50
❑ 300 Rusty Staub 4.00 1.50
❑ 301 G.Mitterwald RC/R.Renick RC 2.00 .75
❑ 302 Gerry Arrigo 2.00 .75
❑ 303 Dick Green 4.00 1.50
❑ 304 Sandy Valdespino 2.00 .75
❑ 305 Minnie Rojas 2.00 .75
❑ 306 Mike Ryan 2.00 .75
❑ 307 John Hiller 4.00 1.50
❑ 308 Pittsburgh Pirates TC 4.00 1.50
❑ 309 Ken Henderson 2.00 .75
❑ 310 Luis Aparicio 8.00 4.00
❑ 311 Jack Lamabe 2.00 .75
❑ 312 Curt Blefary 2.00 .75
❑ 313 Al Weis 2.00 .75
❑ 314 B.Rohr/G.Spriggs 2.00 .75
❑ 315 Zoilo Versalles 2.00 .75
❑ 316 Steve Barber 2.00 .75
❑ 317 Ron Brand 2.00 .75
❑ 318 Chico Salmon 2.00 .75
❑ 319 George Culver 2.00 .75
❑ 320 Frank Howard 4.00 1.50
❑ 321 Leo Durocher MG 6.00 3.00
❑ 322 Dave Boswell 2.00 .75
❑ 323 Deron Johnson 4.00 1.50
❑ 324 Jim Nash 2.00 .75
❑ 325 Manny Mota 4.00 1.50
❑ 326 Dennis Ribant 2.00 .75
❑ 327 Tony Taylor 4.00 1.50
❑ 328 C.Vinson RC/J.Weaver RC 2.00 .75
❑ 329 Duane Josephson 2.00 .75
❑ 330 Roger Maris 50.00 30.00
❑ 331 Dan Osinski 2.00 .75
❑ 332 Doug Rader 4.00 1.50
❑ 333 Ron Herbel 2.00 .75
❑ 334 Baltimore Orioles TC 4.00 1.50
❑ 335 Bob Allison 4.00 1.50
❑ 336 John Purdin 2.00 .75
❑ 337 Bill Robinson 4.00 1.50
❑ 338 Bob Johnson 2.00 .75
❑ 339 Rich Nye 2.00 .75
❑ 340 Max Alvis 2.00 .75
❑ 341 Jim Lemon MG 2.00 .75
❑ 342 Ken Johnson 2.00 .75
❑ 343 Jim Gosger 2.00 .75
❑ 344 Donn Clendenon 4.00 1.50
❑ 345 Bob Hendley 2.00 .75
❑ 346 Jerry Adair 2.00 .75
❑ 347 George Brunet 2.00 .75
❑ 348 L.Colton RC/D.Thoenen RC 2.00 .75
❑ 349 Ed Spiezio 4.00 1.50
❑ 350 Hoyt Wilhelm 8.00 4.00
❑ 351 Bob Barton 2.00 .75
❑ 352 Jackie Hernandez RC 2.00 .75
❑ 353 Mack Jones 2.00 .75
❑ 354 Pete Richert 2.00 .75
❑ 355 Ernie Banks 25.00 12.50
❑ 356A Checklist 5/Holtzman Center 6.00 3.00
❑ 356B Checklist 5/Holtzman Right 6.00 3.00
❑ 357 Len Gabrielson 2.00 .75
❑ 358 Mike Epstein 2.00 .75
❑ 359 Joe Moeller 2.00 .75
❑ 360 Willie Horton 6.00 3.00
❑ 361 Harmon Killebrew AS 8.00 4.00
❑ 362 Orlando Cepeda AS 6.00 3.00
❑ 363 Rod Carew AS 8.00 4.00
❑ 364 Joe Morgan AS 8.00 4.00
❑ 365 Brooks Robinson AS 8.00 4.00
❑ 366 Ron Santo AS 6.00 3.00
❑ 367 Jim Fregosi AS 4.00 1.50
❑ 368 Gene Alley AS 4.00 1.50
❑ 369 Carl Yastrzemski AS 10.00 5.00
❑ 370 Hank Aaron AS 20.00 10.00
❑ 371 Tony Oliva AS 6.00 3.00
❑ 372 Lou Brock AS 8.00 4.00
❑ 373 Frank Robinson AS 8.00 4.00
❑ 374 Roberto Clemente AS 30.00 15.00
❑ 375 Bill Freehan AS 4.00 1.50
❑ 376 Tim McCarver AS 4.00 1.50
❑ 377 Joel Horlen AS 4.00 1.50
❑ 378 Bob Gibson AS 8.00 4.00
❑ 379 Gary Peters AS 4.00 1.50
❑ 380 Ken Holtzman AS 4.00 1.50
❑ 381 Boog Powell 4.00 1.50
❑ 382 Ramon Hernandez 2.00 .75
❑ 383 Steve Whitaker 2.00 .75
❑ 384 B.Henry/H.McRae RC 6.00 3.00
❑ 385 Jim Hunter 10.00 5.00

❑ 386 Greg Goossen 2.00 .75
❑ 387 Joe Foy 2.00 .75
❑ 388 Ray Washburn 2.00 .75
❑ 389 Jay Johnstone 4.00 1.50
❑ 390 Bill Mazeroski 8.00 4.00
❑ 391 Bob Priddy 2.00 .75
❑ 392 Grady Hatton MG 2.00 .75
❑ 393 Jim Perry 4.00 1.50
❑ 394 Tommie Aaron 6.00 3.00
❑ 395 Camilo Pascual 4.00 1.50
❑ 396 Bobby Wine 2.00 .75
❑ 397 Vic Davalillo 2.00 .75
❑ 398 Jim Grant 2.00 .75
❑ 399 Ray Oyler 4.00 1.50
❑ 400A Mike McCormick YT 4.00 1.50
❑ 400B M.McCormick White Tm 150.00 90.00
❑ 401 Mets Team 4.00 1.50
❑ 402 Mike Hegan 4.00 1.50
❑ 403 John Buzhardt 2.00 .75
❑ 404 Floyd Robinson 2.00 .75
❑ 405 Tommy Helms 4.00 1.50
❑ 406 Dick Ellsworth 2.00 .75
❑ 407 Gary Kolb 2.00 .75
❑ 408 Steve Carlton 30.00 15.00
❑ 409 F.Peters RC/R.Stone 2.00 .75
❑ 410 Ferguson Jenkins 10.00 5.00
❑ 411 Ron Hansen 2.00 .75
❑ 412 Clay Carroll 4.00 1.50
❑ 413 Tom McCraw 2.00 .75
❑ 414 Mickey Lolich 8.00 4.00
❑ 415 Johnny Callison 4.00 1.50
❑ 416 Bill Rigney MG 2.00 .75
❑ 417 Willie Crawford 2.00 .75
❑ 418 Eddie Fisher 2.00 .75
❑ 419 Jack Hiatt 2.00 .75
❑ 420 Cesar Tovar 2.00 .75
❑ 421 Ron Taylor 2.00 .75
❑ 422 Rene Lachemann 2.00 .75
❑ 423 Fred Gladding 2.00 .75
❑ 424 Chicago White Sox TC 4.00 1.50
❑ 425 Jim Maloney 4.00 1.50
❑ 426 Hank Allen 2.00 .75
❑ 427 Dick Calmus 2.00 .75
❑ 428 Vic Roznovsky 2.00 .75
❑ 429 Tommie Sisk 2.00 .75
❑ 430 Rico Petrocelli 4.00 1.50
❑ 431 Dooley Womack 2.00 .75
❑ 432 B.Davis/J.Vidal 2.00 .75
❑ 433 Bob Rodgers 2.00 .75
❑ 434 Ricardo Joseph RC 2.00 .75
❑ 435 Ron Perranoski 4.00 1.50
❑ 436 Hal Lanier 2.00 .75
❑ 437 Don Cardwell 2.00 .75
❑ 438 Lee Thomas 4.00 1.50
❑ 439 Lum Harris MG 2.00 .75
❑ 440 Claude Osteen 4.00 1.50
❑ 441 Alex Johnson 4.00 1.50
❑ 442 Dick Bosman 2.00 .75
❑ 443 Joe Azcue 2.00 .75
❑ 444 Jack Fisher 2.00 .75
❑ 445 Mike Shannon 4.00 1.50
❑ 446 Ron Kline 2.00 .75
❑ 447 G.Korince/F.Lasher RC 4.00 1.50
❑ 448 Gary Wagner 2.00 .75
❑ 449 Gene Oliver 2.00 .75
❑ 450 Jim Kaat 6.00 3.00
❑ 451 Al Spangler 2.00 .75
❑ 452 Jesus Alou 2.00 .75
❑ 453 Sammy Ellis 2.00 .75
❑ 454A Checklist 6/F.Rob Complete 8.00 4.00
❑ 454B Checklist 6/F.Rob Partial 8.00 4.00
❑ 455 Rico Carty 4.00 1.50
❑ 456 John O'Donoghue 2.00 .75
❑ 457 Jim Lefebvre 4.00 1.50
❑ 458 Lew Krausse 6.00 3.00
❑ 459 Dick Simpson 4.00 1.50
❑ 460 Jim Lonborg 6.00 3.00
❑ 461 Chuck Hiller 4.00 1.50
❑ 462 Barry Moore 4.00 1.50
❑ 463 Jim Schaffer 4.00 1.50
❑ 464 Don McMahon 4.00 1.50
❑ 465 Tommie Agee 10.00 5.00
❑ 466 Bill Dillman 4.00 1.50
❑ 467 Dick Howser 10.00 5.00
❑ 468 Larry Sherry 4.00 1.50
❑ 469 Ty Cline 4.00 1.50
❑ 470 Bill Freehan 10.00 5.00
❑ 471 Orlando Pena 4.00 1.50
❑ 472 Walter Alston MG 6.00 3.00
❑ 473 Al Worthington 4.00 1.50
❑ 474 Paul Schaal 4.00 1.50
❑ 475 Joe Niekro 6.00 3.00
❑ 476 Woody Woodward 4.00 1.50
❑ 477 Philadelphia Phillies TC 8.00 4.00
❑ 478 Dave McNally 6.00 3.00
❑ 479 Phil Gagliano 6.00 3.00
❑ 480 Oliva/Chico/Clemente 80.00 50.00
❑ 481 John Wyatt 4.00 1.50
❑ 482 Jose Pagan 4.00 1.50
❑ 483 Darold Knowles 4.00 1.50
❑ 484 Phil Roof 4.00 1.50
❑ 485 Ken Berry 6.00 3.00
❑ 486 Cal Koonce 4.00 1.50
❑ 487 Lee May 10.00 5.00
❑ 488 Dick Tracewski 6.00 3.00
❑ 489 Wally Bunker 4.00 1.50
❑ 490 Kill/Mays/Mantle 150.00 90.00
❑ 491 Denny Lemaster 4.00 1.50
❑ 492 Jeff Torborg 6.00 3.00
❑ 493 Jim McGlothlin 4.00 1.50
❑ 494 Ray Sadecki 4.00 1.50
❑ 495 Leon Wagner 4.00 1.50
❑ 496 Steve Hamilton 6.00 3.00
❑ 497 St. Louis Cardinals TC 8.00 4.00
❑ 498 Bill Bryan 6.00 3.00
❑ 499 Steve Blass 6.00 3.00
❑ 500 Frank Robinson 30.00 15.00
❑ 501 John Odom 6.00 3.00
❑ 502 Mike Andrews 4.00 1.50
❑ 503 Al Jackson 6.00 3.00
❑ 504 Russ Snyder 4.00 1.50
❑ 505 Joe Sparma 10.00 5.00
❑ 506 Clarence Jones RC 4.00 1.50
❑ 507 Wade Blasingame 4.00 1.50
❑ 508 Duke Sims 4.00 1.50
❑ 509 Dennis Higgins 4.00 1.50
❑ 510 Ron Fairly 10.00 5.00
❑ 511 Bill Kelso 4.00 1.50
❑ 512 Grant Jackson 4.00 1.50
❑ 513 Hank Bauer MG 6.00 3.00
❑ 514 Al McBean 4.00 1.50
❑ 515 Russ Nixon 4.00 1.50
❑ 516 Pete Mikkelsen 4.00 1.50
❑ 517 Diego Segui 6.00 3.00
❑ 518A Checklist 7/Boyer ERR 12.00 6.00
❑ 518B Checklist 7/Boyer COR 12.00 6.00
❑ 519 Jerry Stephenson 4.00 1.50
❑ 520 Lou Brock 25.00 12.50
❑ 521 Don Shaw 4.00 1.50
❑ 522 Wayne Causey 4.00 1.50
❑ 523 John Tsitouris 4.00 1.50
❑ 524 Andy Kosco 6.00 3.00
❑ 525 Jim Davenport 4.00 1.50
❑ 526 Bill Denehy 4.00 1.50
❑ 527 Tito Francona 4.00 1.50
❑ 528 Detroit Tigers TC 60.00 35.00
❑ 529 Bruce Von Hoff RC 4.00 1.50
❑ 530 B.Robinson/F.Robinson 40.00 20.00
❑ 531 Chuck Hinton 4.00 1.50
❑ 532 Luis Tiant 6.00 3.00
❑ 533 Wes Parker 6.00 3.00
❑ 534 Bob Miller 6.00 3.00
❑ 535 Danny Cater 6.00 3.00
❑ 536 Bill Short 4.00 1.50
❑ 537 Norm Siebern 6.00 3.00
❑ 538 Manny Jimenez 6.00 3.00
❑ 539 J.Ray RC/M.Ferraro RC 4.00 1.50
❑ 540 Nelson Briles 6.00 3.00
❑ 541 Sandy Alomar 6.00 3.00
❑ 542 John Boccabella 4.00 1.50
❑ 543 Bob Lee 4.00 1.50
❑ 544 Mayo Smith MG 12.00 6.00
❑ 545 Lindy McDaniel 6.00 3.00
❑ 546 Roy White 6.00 3.00
❑ 547 Dan Coombs 4.00 1.50
❑ 548 Bernie Allen 4.00 1.50
❑ 549 C.Motton RC/R.Nelson RC 4.00 1.50
❑ 550 Clete Boyer 6.00 3.00
❑ 551 Darrell Sutherland 4.00 1.50
❑ 552 Ed Kirkpatrick 4.00 1.50
❑ 553 Hank Aguirre 4.00 1.50
❑ 554 Oakland Athletics TC 10.00 5.00
❑ 555 Jose Tartabull 6.00 3.00
❑ 556 Dick Selma 4.00 1.50
❑ 557 Frank Quilici 6.00 3.00
❑ 558 Johnny Edwards 4.00 1.50
❑ 559 C.Taylor RC/L.Walker 4.00 1.50
❑ 560 Paul Casanova 4.00 1.50
❑ 561 Lee Elia 4.00 1.50
❑ 562 Jim Bouton 6.00 3.00
❑ 563 Ed Charles 4.00 1.50
❑ 564 Eddie Stanky MG 6.00 3.00
❑ 565 Larry Dierker 6.00 3.00
❑ 566 Ken Harrelson 6.00 3.00
❑ 567 Clay Dalrymple 4.00 1.50
❑ 568 Willie Smith 4.00 1.50
❑ 569 I.Murrell RC/L.Rohr RC 4.00 1.50
❑ 570 Rick Reichardt 4.00 1.50
❑ 571 Tony LaRussa 12.00 6.00
❑ 572 Don Bosch RC 4.00 1.50
❑ 573 Joe Coleman 4.00 1.50
❑ 574 Cincinnati Reds TC 10.00 5.00
❑ 575 Jim Palmer 40.00 20.00
❑ 576 Dave Adlesh 4.00 1.50
❑ 577 Fred Talbot 4.00 1.50
❑ 578 Orlando Martinez 4.00 1.50
❑ 579 L.Hisle RC/M.Lum RC 10.00 5.00
❑ 580 Bob Bailey 4.00 1.50
❑ 581 Garry Roggenburk 4.00 1.50
❑ 582 Jerry Grote 10.00 5.00
❑ 583 Gates Brown 10.00 5.00
❑ 584 Larry Shepard MG RC 4.00 1.50
❑ 585 Wilbur Wood 6.00 3.00
❑ 586 Jim Pagliaroni 6.00 3.00
❑ 587 Roger Repoz 4.00 1.50
❑ 588 Dick Schofield 4.00 1.50
❑ 589 R.Clark/M.Ogier RC 4.00 1.50
❑ 590 Tommy Harper 6.00 3.00
❑ 591 Dick Nen 4.00 1.50
❑ 592 John Bateman 4.00 1.50
❑ 593 Lee Stange 4.00 1.50
❑ 594 Phil Linz 6.00 3.00
❑ 595 Phil Ortega 4.00 1.50
❑ 596 Charlie Smith 4.00 1.50
❑ 597 Bill McCool 4.00 1.50
❑ 598 Jerry May 6.00 3.00

1969 Topps

❑ COMP. MASTER SET (695) 5000.00 2500.00
❑ COMPLETE SET (664) 2800.00 1700.00
❑ COMMON (1-218/328-512) 1.50 .60
❑ COMMON CARD (219-327) 2.50 1.00
❑ COMMON CARD (513-588) 2.00 .75
❑ COMMON CARD (589-664) 3.00 1.25
❑ WRAPPER (5-CENT) 20.00 15.00
❑ 1 Yaz/Cater/Oliva LL 15.00 7.50
❑ 2 Rose/Alou/Alou LL 8.00 4.00
❑ 3 Harrelson/Howard/North LL 4.00 1.50
❑ 4 McCovey/Santo/B.Will LL 6.00 3.00
❑ 5 Howard/Horton/Harrelson LL 4.00 1.50
❑ 6 McCovey/Allen/Banks LL 6.00 3.00
❑ 7 Tiant/McDow/McNally LL 4.00 1.50
❑ 8 Gibson/Bolin/Veale LL 6.00 3.00
❑ 9 McLain/McNal/Tiant/Stott LL 4.00 1.50
❑ 10 Marichal/Gibson/Jenkins LL 8.00 4.00
❑ 11 McDowell/McLain/Tiant LL 4.00 1.50
❑ 12 Gibson/Jenkins/Singer LL 4.00 1.50
❑ 13 Mickey Stanley 2.50 1.00
❑ 14 Al McBean 1.50 .60
❑ 15 Boog Powell 4.00 1.50

❑ 16 C.Gutierrez RC/R.Robertson RC 1.50 .60
❑ 17 Mike Marshall 2.50 1.00
❑ 18 Dick Schofield 1.50 .60
❑ 19 Ken Suarez 1.50 .60
❑ 20 Ernie Banks 20.00 10.00
❑ 21 Jose Santiago 1.50 .60
❑ 22 Jesus Alou 2.50 1.00
❑ 23 Lew Krausse 1.50 .60
❑ 24 Walt Alston MG 4.00 1.50
❑ 25 Roy White 2.50 1.00
❑ 26 Clay Carroll 2.50 1.00
❑ 27 Bernie Allen 1.50 .60
❑ 28 Mike Ryan 1.50 .60
❑ 29 Dave Morehead 1.50 .60
❑ 30 Bob Allison 2.50 1.00
❑ 31 G.Gentry RC/A.Otis RC 2.50 1.00
❑ 32 Sammy Ellis 1.50 .60
❑ 33 Wayne Causey 1.50 .60
❑ 34 Gary Peters 1.50 .60
❑ 35 Joe Morgan 10.00 5.00
❑ 36 Luke Walker 1.50 .60
❑ 37 Curt Motton 1.50 .60
❑ 38 Zoilo Versalles 2.50 1.00
❑ 39 Dick Hughes 1.50 .60
❑ 40 Mayo Smith MG 1.50 .60
❑ 41 Bob Barton 1.50 .60
❑ 42 Tommy Harper 2.50 1.00
❑ 43 Joe Niekro 2.50 1.00
❑ 44 Danny Cater 1.50 .60
❑ 45 Maury Wills 2.50 1.00
❑ 46 Fritz Peterson 2.50 1.00
❑ 47A P.Popovich Thick Airbrush 2.50 1.00
❑ 47B P.Popovich Light Airbrush 2.50 1.00
❑ 47C P.Popovich C on Helmet 25.00 12.50
❑ 48 Brant Alyea 1.50 .60
❑ 49A S.Jones/E.Rodriguez ERR 25.00 12.50
❑ 49B S.Jones RC/E.Rodriguez RC 1.50 .60
❑ 50 Roberto Clemente UER 60.00 35.00
❑ 51 Woody Fryman 2.50 1.00
❑ 52 Mike Andrews 1.50 .60
❑ 53 Sonny Jackson 1.50 .60
❑ 54 Cisco Carlos 1.50 .60
❑ 55 Jerry Grote 2.50 1.00
❑ 56 Rich Reese 1.50 .60
❑ 57 Checklist 1/McLain 6.00 3.00
❑ 58 Fred Gladding 1.50 .60
❑ 59 Jay Johnstone 2.50 1.00
❑ 60 Nelson Briles 2.50 1.00
❑ 61 Jimmie Hall 1.50 .60
❑ 62 Chico Salmon 1.50 .60
❑ 63 Jim Hickman 2.50 1.00
❑ 64 Bill Monbouquette 1.50 .60
❑ 65 Willie Davis 2.50 1.00
❑ 66 M.Adamson RC/M.Rettenmund RC 1.50 .60
❑ 67 Bill Stoneman 2.50 1.00
❑ 68 Dave Duncan 2.50 1.00
❑ 69 Steve Hamilton 2.50 1.00
❑ 70 Tommy Helms 2.50 1.00
❑ 71 Steve Whitaker 2.50 1.00
❑ 72 Ron Taylor 1.50 .60
❑ 73 Johnny Briggs 1.50 .60
❑ 74 Preston Gomez MG 2.50 1.00
❑ 75 Luis Aparicio 6.00 3.00
❑ 76 Norm Miller 1.50 .60
❑ 77A R.Perranoski No LA 2.50 1.00
❑ 77B R.Perranoski LA Cap 25.00 12.50
❑ 78 Tom Satriano 1.50 .60
❑ 79 Milt Pappas 2.50 1.00
❑ 80 Norm Cash 2.50 1.00
❑ 81 Mel Queen 1.50 .60
❑ 82 R.Hebner RC/A.Oliver RC 8.00 4.00
❑ 83 Mike Ferraro 2.50 1.00
❑ 84 Bob Humphreys 1.50 .60
❑ 85 Lou Brock 20.00 10.00
❑ 86 Pete Richert 1.50 .60
❑ 87 Horace Clarke 2.50 1.00
❑ 88 Rich Nye 1.50 .60
❑ 89 Russ Gibson 1.50 .60
❑ 90 Jerry Koosman 2.50 1.00
❑ 91 Alvin Dark MG 2.50 1.00
❑ 92 Jack Billingham 2.50 1.00
❑ 93 Joe Foy 2.50 1.00
❑ 94 Hank Aguirre 1.50 .60
❑ 95 Johnny Bench 50.00 30.00
❑ 96 Denny Lemaster 1.50 .60
❑ 97 Buddy Bradford 1.50 .60
❑ 98 Dave Giusti 1.50 .60
❑ 99A D.Morris RC/G.Nettles RC 15.00 7.50
❑ 99B D.Morris/G.Nettles ERR 15.00 7.50
❑ 100 Hank Aaron 50.00 30.00
❑ 101 Daryl Patterson 1.50 .60
❑ 102 Jim Davenport 1.50 .60
❑ 103 Roger Repoz 1.50 .60
❑ 104 Steve Blass 1.50 .60
❑ 105 Rick Monday 2.50 1.00
❑ 106 Jim Hannan 1.50 .60
❑ 107A Checklist 2/Gibson ERR 6.00 3.00
❑ 107B Checklist 2/Gibson COR 8.00 4.00
❑ 108 Tony Taylor 2.50 1.00
❑ 109 Jim Lonborg 2.50 1.00
❑ 110 Mike Shannon 2.50 1.00
❑ 111 John Morris RC 1.50 .60
❑ 112 J.C. Martin 2.50 1.00
❑ 113 Dave May 1.50 .60
❑ 114 A.Closter/J.Cumberland RC 2.50 1.00
❑ 115 Bill Hands 1.50 .60
❑ 116 Chuck Harrison 1.50 .60
❑ 117 Jim Fairey 2.50 1.00
❑ 118 Stan Williams 1.50 .60
❑ 119 Doug Rader 2.50 1.00
❑ 120 Pete Rose 50.00 30.00
❑ 121 Joe Grzenda RC 1.50 .60
❑ 122 Ron Fairly 2.50 1.00
❑ 123 Wilbur Wood 2.50 1.00
❑ 124 Hank Bauer MG 2.50 1.00
❑ 125 Ray Sadecki 1.50 .60
❑ 126 Dick Tracewski 1.50 .60
❑ 127 Kevin Collins 2.50 1.00
❑ 128 Tommie Aaron 2.50 1.00
❑ 129 Bill McCool 1.50 .60
❑ 130 Carl Yastrzemski 20.00 10.00
❑ 131 Chris Cannizzaro 1.50 .60
❑ 132 Dave Baldwin 1.50 .60
❑ 133 Johnny Callison 2.50 1.00
❑ 134 Jim Weaver 1.50 .60
❑ 135 Tommy Davis 2.50 1.00
❑ 136 S.Huntz RC/M.Torrez 1.50 .60
❑ 137 Wally Bunker 1.50 .60
❑ 138 John Bateman 1.50 .60
❑ 139 Andy Kosco 1.50 .60
❑ 140 Jim Lefebvre 2.50 1.00
❑ 141 Bill Dillman 1.50 .60
❑ 142 Woody Woodward 1.50 .60
❑ 143 Joe Nossek 1.50 .60
❑ 144 Bob Hendley 2.50 1.00
❑ 145 Max Alvis 1.50 .60
❑ 146 Jim Perry 2.50 1.00
❑ 147 Leo Durocher MG 4.00 1.50
❑ 148 Lee Stange 1.50 .60
❑ 149 Ollie Brown 2.50 1.00
❑ 150 Denny McLain 4.00 1.50
❑ 151A C.Dalrymple Portrait 1.50 .60
❑ 151B C.Dalrymple Catch 15.00 7.50
❑ 152 Tommie Sisk 1.50 .60
❑ 153 Ed Brinkman 1.50 .60
❑ 154 Jim Britton 1.50 .60
❑ 155 Pete Ward 1.50 .60
❑ 156 H.Gilson/L.McFadden RC 1.50 .60
❑ 157 Bob Rodgers 2.50 1.00
❑ 158 Joe Gibbon 1.50 .60
❑ 159 Jerry Adair 1.50 .60
❑ 160 Vada Pinson 2.50 1.00
❑ 161 John Purdin 1.50 .60
❑ 162 Bob Gibson WS1 8.00 4.00
❑ 163 Willie Horton WS2 6.00 3.00
❑ 164 T.McCarv w/Maris WS3 12.00 6.00
❑ 165 Lou Brock WS4 8.00 4.00
❑ 166 Al Kaline WS5 8.00 4.00
❑ 167 Jim Northrup WS6 6.00 3.00
❑ 168 M.Lolich/B.Gibson WS7 8.00 4.00
❑ 169 Tigers Celebrate WS 6.00 3.00
❑ 170 Frank Howard 2.50 1.00
❑ 171 Glenn Beckert 2.50 1.00
❑ 172 Jerry Stephenson 1.50 .60
❑ 173 B.Christian RC/G.Nyman RC 1.50 .60
❑ 174 Grant Jackson 1.50 .60
❑ 175 Jim Bunning 6.00 3.00
❑ 176 Joe Azcue 1.50 .60
❑ 177 Ron Reed 1.50 .60
❑ 178 Ray Oyler 2.50 1.00
❑ 179 Don Pavletich 1.50 .60
❑ 180 Willie Horton 2.50 1.00
❑ 181 Mel Nelson 1.50 .60
❑ 182 Bill Rigney MG 1.50 .60
❑ 183 Don Shaw 2.50 1.00
❑ 184 Roberto Pena 1.50 .60
❑ 185 Tom Phoebus 1.50 .60
❑ 186 Johnny Edwards 1.50 .60
❑ 187 Leon Wagner 1.50 .60
❑ 188 Rick Wise 2.50 1.00
❑ 189 J.Lahoud RC/J.Thibodeau RC 1.50 .60
❑ 190 Willie Mays 80.00 50.00
❑ 191 Lindy McDaniel 2.50 1.00
❑ 192 Jose Pagan 1.50 .60
❑ 193 Don Cardwell 2.50 1.00
❑ 194 Ted Uhlaender 1.50 .60
❑ 195 John Odom 1.50 .60
❑ 196 Lum Harris MG 1.50 .60
❑ 197 Dick Selma 1.50 .60
❑ 198 Willie Smith 1.50 .60
❑ 199 Jim French 1.50 .60
❑ 200 Bob Gibson 12.00 6.00
❑ 201 Russ Snyder 1.50 .60
❑ 202 Don Wilson 2.50 1.00
❑ 203 Dave Johnson 2.50 1.00
❑ 204 Jack Hiatt 1.50 .60
❑ 205 Rick Reichardt 1.50 .60
❑ 206 L.Hisle/B.Lersch RC 2.50 1.00
❑ 207 Roy Face 2.50 1.00
❑ 208A D.Clendenon Houston 2.50 1.00
❑ 208B D.Clendenon Expos 15.00 7.50
❑ 209 Larry Haney UER 1.50 .60
❑ 210 Felix Millan 1.50 .60
❑ 211 Galen Cisco 1.50 .60
❑ 212 Tom Tresh 2.50 1.00
❑ 213 Gerry Arrigo 1.50 .60
❑ 214 Checklist 3 6.00 3.00
❑ 215 Rico Petrocelli 2.50 1.00
❑ 216 Don Sutton DP 6.00 3.00
❑ 217 John Donaldson 1.50 .60
❑ 218 John Roseboro 2.50 1.00
❑ 219 Fred Patek RC 4.00 1.50
❑ 220 Sam McDowell 4.00 1.50
❑ 221 Art Shamsky 4.00 1.50
❑ 222 Duane Josephson 2.50 1.00
❑ 223 Tom Dukes 4.00 1.50
❑ 224 B.Harrelson RC/S.Kealey RC 2.50 1.00
❑ 225 Don Kessinger 4.00 1.50
❑ 226 Bruce Howard 2.50 1.00
❑ 227 Frank Johnson RC 2.50 1.00
❑ 228 Dave Leonhard 2.50 1.00
❑ 229 Don Lock 2.50 1.00
❑ 230 Rusty Staub UER 4.00 1.50
❑ 231 Pat Dobson 4.00 1.50
❑ 232 Dave Ricketts 2.50 1.00
❑ 233 Steve Barber 4.00 1.50
❑ 234 Dave Bristol MG 2.50 1.00
❑ 235 Jim Hunter 10.00 5.00
❑ 236 Manny Mota 4.00 1.50
❑ 237 Bobby Cox RC 10.00 5.00
❑ 238 Ken Johnson 2.50 1.00
❑ 239 Bob Taylor 4.00 1.50
❑ 240 Ken Harrelson 4.00 1.50
❑ 241 Jim Brewer 2.50 1.00
❑ 242 Frank Kostro 2.50 1.00
❑ 243 Ron Kline 2.50 1.00
❑ 244 R.Fosse RC/G.Woodson RC 4.00 1.50
❑ 245 Ed Charles 4.00 1.50
❑ 246 Joe Coleman 2.50 1.00
❑ 247 Gene Oliver 2.50 1.00
❑ 248 Bob Priddy 2.50 1.00
❑ 249 Ed Spiezio 4.00 1.50
❑ 250 Frank Robinson 20.00 10.00
❑ 251 Ron Herbel 2.50 1.00
❑ 252 Chuck Cottier 2.50 1.00
❑ 253 Jerry Johnson RC 2.50 1.00
❑ 254 Joe Schultz MG RC 4.00 1.50
❑ 255 Steve Carlton 30.00 15.00
❑ 256 Gates Brown 4.00 1.50
❑ 257 Jim Ray 2.50 1.00
❑ 258 Jackie Hernandez 4.00 1.50
❑ 259 Bill Short 2.50 1.00
❑ 260 Reggie Jackson RC 300.00 175.00
❑ 261 Bob Johnson 2.50 1.00
❑ 262 Mike Kekich 4.00 1.50
❑ 263 Jerry May 2.50 1.00
❑ 264 Bill Landis 2.50 1.00
❑ 265 Chico Cardenas 4.00 1.50

- ❑ 266 T.Hutton/A.Foster RC 4.00 1.50
- ❑ 267 Vicente Romo RC 2.50 1.00
- ❑ 268 Al Spangler 2.50 1.00
- ❑ 269 Al Weis 4.00 1.50
- ❑ 270 Mickey Lolich 4.00 1.50
- ❑ 271 Larry Stahl 4.00 1.50
- ❑ 272 Ed Stroud 2.50 1.00
- ❑ 273 Ron Willis 2.50 1.00
- ❑ 274 Clyde King MG 2.50 1.00
- ❑ 275 Vic Davalillo 2.50 1.00
- ❑ 276 Gary Wagner 2.50 1.00
- ❑ 277 Elrod Hendricks RC 2.50 1.00
- ❑ 278 Gary Geiger UER 2.50 1.00
- ❑ 279 Roger Nelson 4.00 1.50
- ❑ 280 Alex Johnson 4.00 1.50
- ❑ 281 Ted Kubiak 2.50 1.00
- ❑ 282 Pat Jarvis 2.50 1.00
- ❑ 283 Sandy Alomar 4.00 1.50
- ❑ 284 J.Robertson RC/M.Wegener RC 4.00 1.50
- ❑ 285 Don Mincher 4.00 1.50
- ❑ 286 Dock Ellis RC 4.00 1.50
- ❑ 287 Jose Tartabull 4.00 1.50
- ❑ 288 Ken Holtzman 4.00 1.50
- ❑ 289 Bart Shirley 2.50 1.00
- ❑ 290 Jim Kaat 4.00 1.50
- ❑ 291 Vern Fuller 2.50 1.00
- ❑ 292 Al Downing 4.00 1.50
- ❑ 293 Dick Dietz 2.50 1.00
- ❑ 294 Jim Lemon MG 2.50 1.00
- ❑ 295 Tony Perez 12.00 6.00
- ❑ 296 Andy Messersmith RC 4.00 1.50
- ❑ 297 Deron Johnson 2.50 1.00
- ❑ 298 Dave Nicholson 4.00 1.50
- ❑ 299 Mark Belanger 4.00 1.50
- ❑ 300 Felipe Alou 4.00 1.50
- ❑ 301 Darrell Brandon 4.00 1.50
- ❑ 302 Jim Pagliaroni 2.50 1.00
- ❑ 303 Cal Koonce 4.00 1.50
- ❑ 304 B.Davis/C.Gaston RC 6.00 3.00
- ❑ 305 Dick McAuliffe 4.00 1.50
- ❑ 306 Jim Grant 4.00 1.50
- ❑ 307 Gary Kolb 2.50 1.00
- ❑ 308 Wade Blasingame 2.50 1.00
- ❑ 309 Walt Williams 2.50 1.00
- ❑ 310 Tom Haller 2.50 1.00
- ❑ 311 Sparky Lyle RC 10.00 5.00
- ❑ 312 Lee Elia 2.50 1.00
- ❑ 313 Bill Robinson 4.00 1.50
- ❑ 314 Checklist 4/Drysdale 6.00 3.00
- ❑ 315 Eddie Fisher 2.50 1.00
- ❑ 316 Hal Lanier 2.50 1.00
- ❑ 317 Bruce Look RC 2.50 1.00
- ❑ 318 Jack Fisher 2.50 1.00
- ❑ 319 Ken McMullen UER 2.50 1.00
- ❑ 320 Dal Maxvill 2.50 1.00
- ❑ 321 Jim McAndrew RC 4.00 1.50
- ❑ 322 Jose Vidal 4.00 1.50
- ❑ 323 Larry Miller 2.50 1.00
- ❑ 324 L.Cain RC/D.Campbell RC 4.00 1.50
- ❑ 325 Jose Cardenal 4.00 1.50
- ❑ 326 Gary Sutherland 4.00 1.50
- ❑ 327 Willie Crawford 2.50 1.00
- ❑ 328 Joel Horlen 1.50 .60
- ❑ 329 Rick Joseph 1.50 .60
- ❑ 330 Tony Conigliaro 4.00 1.50
- ❑ 331 G.Garrido/T.House RC 2.50 1.00
- ❑ 332 Fred Talbot 1.50 .60
- ❑ 333 Ivan Murrell 1.50 .60
- ❑ 334 Phil Roof 1.50 .60
- ❑ 335 Bill Mazeroski 6.00 3.00
- ❑ 336 Jim Roland 1.50 .60
- ❑ 337 Marty Martinez RC 1.50 .60
- ❑ 338 Del Unser RC 1.50 .60
- ❑ 339 S.Mingori RC/J.Pena RC 1.50 .60
- ❑ 340 Dave McNally 2.50 1.00
- ❑ 341 Dave Adlesh 1.50 .60
- ❑ 342 Bubba Morton 1.50 .60
- ❑ 343 Dan Frisella 1.50 .60
- ❑ 344 Tom Matchick 1.50 .60
- ❑ 345 Frank Linzy 1.50 .60
- ❑ 346 Wayne Comer RC 1.50 .60
- ❑ 347 Randy Hundley 2.50 1.00
- ❑ 348 Steve Hargan 1.50 .60
- ❑ 349 Dick Williams MG 2.50 1.00
- ❑ 350 Richie Allen 4.00 1.50
- ❑ 351 Carroll Sembera 1.50 .60
- ❑ 352 Paul Schaal 2.50 1.00
- ❑ 353 Jeff Torborg 2.50 1.00
- ❑ 354 Nate Oliver 1.50 .60
- ❑ 355 Phil Niekro 6.00 3.00
- ❑ 356 Frank Quilici 1.50 .60
- ❑ 357 Carl Taylor 1.50 .60
- ❑ 358 G.Lauzerique RC/R.Rodriguez 1.50 .60
- ❑ 359 Dick Kelley 1.50 .60
- ❑ 360 Jim Wynn 2.50 1.00
- ❑ 361 Gary Holman RC 1.50 .60
- ❑ 362 Jim Maloney 2.50 1.00
- ❑ 363 Russ Nixon 1.50 .60
- ❑ 364 Tommie Agee 4.00 1.50
- ❑ 365 Jim Fregosi 2.50 1.00
- ❑ 366 Bo Belinsky 2.50 1.00
- ❑ 367 Lou Johnson 2.50 1.00
- ❑ 368 Vic Roznovsky 1.50 .60
- ❑ 369 Bob Skinner MG 2.50 1.00
- ❑ 370 Juan Marichal 8.00 4.00
- ❑ 371 Sal Bando 2.50 1.00
- ❑ 372 Adolfo Phillips 1.50 .60
- ❑ 373 Fred Lasher 1.50 .60
- ❑ 374 Bob Tillman 1.50 .60
- ❑ 375 Harmon Killebrew 15.00 7.50
- ❑ 376 M.Fiore RC/J.Rooker RC 1.50 .60
- ❑ 377 Gary Bell 2.50 1.00
- ❑ 378 Jose Herrera RC 1.50 .60
- ❑ 379 Ken Boyer 2.50 1.00
- ❑ 380 Stan Bahnsen 2.50 1.00
- ❑ 381 Ed Kranepool 2.50 1.00
- ❑ 382 Pat Corrales 2.50 1.00
- ❑ 383 Casey Cox 1.50 .60
- ❑ 384 Larry Shepard MG 1.50 .60
- ❑ 385 Orlando Cepeda 6.00 3.00
- ❑ 386 Jim McGlothlin 1.50 .60
- ❑ 387 Bobby Klaus 1.50 .60
- ❑ 388 Tom McCraw 1.50 .60
- ❑ 389 Dan Coombs 1.50 .60
- ❑ 390 Bill Freehan 2.50 1.00
- ❑ 391 Ray Culp 1.50 .60
- ❑ 392 Bob Burda RC 1.50 .60
- ❑ 393 Gene Brabender 2.50 1.00
- ❑ 394 L.Piniella/M.Staehle 6.00 3.00
- ❑ 395 Chris Short 1.50 .60
- ❑ 396 Jim Campanis 1.50 .60
- ❑ 397 Chuck Dobson 1.50 .60
- ❑ 398 Tito Francona 1.50 .60
- ❑ 399 Bob Bailey 2.50 1.00
- ❑ 400 Don Drysdale 15.00 7.50
- ❑ 401 Jake Gibbs 2.50 1.00
- ❑ 402 Ken Boswell RC 2.50 1.00
- ❑ 403 Bob Miller 1.50 .60
- ❑ 404 V.LaRose RC/G.Ross RC 2.50 1.00
- ❑ 405 Lee May 2.50 1.00
- ❑ 406 Phil Ortega 1.50 .60
- ❑ 407 Tom Egan 1.50 .60
- ❑ 408 Nate Colbert 1.50 .60
- ❑ 409 Bob Moose 1.50 .60
- ❑ 410 Al Kaline 25.00 12.50
- ❑ 411 Larry Dierker 2.50 1.00
- ❑ 412 Checklist 5/Mantle DP 15.00 7.50
- ❑ 413 Roland Sheldon 2.50 1.00
- ❑ 414 Duke Sims 1.50 .60
- ❑ 415 Ray Washburn 1.50 .60
- ❑ 416 Willie McCovey AS 8.00 4.00
- ❑ 417 Ken Harrelson AS 3.00 1.25
- ❑ 418 Tommy Helms AS 3.00 1.25
- ❑ 419 Rod Carew AS 10.00 5.00
- ❑ 420 Ron Santo AS 4.00 1.50
- ❑ 421 Brooks Robinson AS 8.00 4.00
- ❑ 422 Don Kessinger AS 3.00 1.25
- ❑ 423 Bert Campaneris AS 4.00 1.50
- ❑ 424 Pete Rose AS 15.00 7.50
- ❑ 425 Carl Yastrzemski AS 10.00 5.00
- ❑ 426 Curt Flood AS 4.00 1.50
- ❑ 427 Tony Oliva AS 4.00 1.50
- ❑ 428 Lou Brock AS 6.00 3.00
- ❑ 429 Willie Horton AS 3.00 1.25
- ❑ 430 Johnny Bench AS 10.00 5.00
- ❑ 431 Bill Freehan AS 4.00 1.50
- ❑ 432 Bob Gibson AS 6.00 3.00
- ❑ 433 Denny McLain AS 3.00 1.25
- ❑ 434 Jerry Koosman AS 3.00 1.25
- ❑ 435 Sam McDowell AS 2.50 1.00
- ❑ 436 Gene Alley 2.50 1.00
- ❑ 437 Luis Alcaraz RC 1.50 .60
- ❑ 438 Gary Waslewski RC 1.50 .60
- ❑ 439 E.Herrmann RC/D.Lazar RC 1.50 .60
- ❑ 440A Willie McCovey 15.00 7.50
- ❑ 440B Willie McCovey WL 100.00 60.00
- ❑ 441A Dennis Higgins 1.50 .60
- ❑ 441B Dennis Higgins WL
- ❑ 442 Ty Cline 1.50 .60
- ❑ 443 Don Wert 1.50 .60
- ❑ 444A Joe Moeller 1.50 .60
- ❑ 444B Joe Moeller WL
- ❑ 445 Bobby Knoop 1.50 .60
- ❑ 446 Claude Raymond 1.50 .60
- ❑ 447A Ralph Houk MG 2.50 1.00
- ❑ 447B Ralph Houk MG WL
- ❑ 448 Bob Tolan 2.50 1.00
- ❑ 449 Paul Lindblad 1.50 .60
- ❑ 450 Billy Williams 8.00 4.00
- ❑ 451A Rich Rollins 2.50 1.00
- ❑ 451B Rich Rollins WL
- ❑ 452A Al Ferrara 1.50 .60
- ❑ 452B Al Ferrara WL
- ❑ 453 Mike Cuellar 2.50 1.00
- ❑ 454A L.Colton/D.Money RC 2.50 1.00
- ❑ 454B L.Colton/D.Money WL
- ❑ 455 Sonny Siebert 1.50 .60
- ❑ 456 Bud Harrelson 2.50 1.00
- ❑ 457 Dalton Jones 1.50 .60
- ❑ 458 Curt Blefary 1.50 .60
- ❑ 459 Dave Boswell 1.50 .60
- ❑ 460 Joe Torre 4.00 1.50
- ❑ 461A Mike Epstein 1.50 .60
- ❑ 461B Mike Epstein WL
- ❑ 462 R.Schoendienst MG 2.50 1.00
- ❑ 463 Dennis Ribant 1.50 .60
- ❑ 464A Dave Marshall RC 1.50 .60
- ❑ 464B Dave Marshall WL
- ❑ 465 Tommy John 4.00 1.50
- ❑ 466 John Boccabella 2.50 1.00
- ❑ 467 Tommie Reynolds 1.50 .60
- ❑ 468A B.Dal Canton RC/B.Robertson 1.50 .60
- ❑ 468B B.Dal Canton/B.Robertson WL
- ❑ 469 Chico Ruiz 1.50 .60
- ❑ 470A Mel Stottlemyre 2.50 1.00
- ❑ 470B Mel Stottlemyre WL 30.00 15.00
- ❑ 471A Ted Savage 1.50 .60
- ❑ 471B Ted Savage WL
- ❑ 472 Jim Price 1.50 .60
- ❑ 473A Jose Arcia 1.50 .60
- ❑ 473B Jose Arcia WL
- ❑ 474 Tom Murphy RC 1.50 .60
- ❑ 475 Tim McCarver 4.00 1.50
- ❑ 476A K.Brett RC/G.Moses 2.50 1.00
- ❑ 476B K.Brett/G.Moses WL 30.00 15.00
- ❑ 477 Jeff James RC 1.50 .60
- ❑ 478 Don Buford 1.50 .60
- ❑ 479 Richie Scheinblum 1.50 .60
- ❑ 480 Tom Seaver 80.00 50.00
- ❑ 481 Bill Melton RC 2.50 1.00
- ❑ 482A Jim Gosger 1.50 .60
- ❑ 482B Jim Gosger WL
- ❑ 483 Ted Abernathy 1.50 .60
- ❑ 484 Joe Gordon MG 2.50 1.00
- ❑ 485A Gaylord Perry 10.00 5.00
- ❑ 485B Gaylord Perry WL 80.00 50.00
- ❑ 486A Paul Casanova 1.50 .60
- ❑ 486B Paul Casanova WL
- ❑ 487 Denis Menke 1.50 .60
- ❑ 488 Joe Sparma 1.50 .60
- ❑ 489 Clete Boyer 2.50 1.00
- ❑ 490 Matty Alou 2.50 1.00
- ❑ 491A J.Crider RC/G.Mitterwald 1.50 .60
- ❑ 491B J.Crider/G.Mitterwald WL
- ❑ 492 Tony Cloninger 1.50 .60
- ❑ 493A Wes Parker 2.50 1.00
- ❑ 493B Wes Parker WL
- ❑ 494 Ken Berry 1.50 .60
- ❑ 495 Bert Campaneris 2.50 1.00
- ❑ 496 Larry Jaster 1.50 .60
- ❑ 497 Julian Javier 2.50 1.00
- ❑ 498 Juan Pizarro 2.50 1.00
- ❑ 499 D.Bryant RC/S.Shea RC 1.50 .60
- ❑ 500A Mickey Mantle UER 350.00 200.00
- ❑ 500B Mickey Mantle UER WL 2000.00 1200.00
- ❑ 501A Tony Gonzalez 2.50 1.00
- ❑ 501B Tony Gonzalez WL
- ❑ 502 Minnie Rojas 1.50 .60

- ❑ 503 Larry Brown 1.50 .60
- ❑ 504 Checklist 6/B.Robinson 8.00 4.00
- ❑ 505A Bobby Bolin 1.50 .60
- ❑ 505B Bobby Bolin WL
- ❑ 506 Paul Blair 2.50 1.00
- ❑ 507 Cookie Rojas 2.50 1.00
- ❑ 508 Moe Drabowsky 2.50 1.00
- ❑ 509 Manny Sanguillen 2.50 1.00
- ❑ 510 Rod Carew 40.00 20.00
- ❑ 511A Diego Segui 2.50 1.00
- ❑ 511B Diego Segui WL
- ❑ 512 Cleon Jones 2.50 1.00
- ❑ 513 Camilo Pascual 3.00 1.25
- ❑ 514 Mike Lum 2.00 .75
- ❑ 515 Dick Green 2.00 .75
- ❑ 516 Earl Weaver MG RC 20.00 10.00
- ❑ 517 Mike McCormick 3.00 1.25
- ❑ 518 Fred Whitfield 2.00 .75
- ❑ 519 J.Kenney RC/L.Boehmer RC 2.00 .75
- ❑ 520 Bob Veale 3.00 1.25
- ❑ 521 George Thomas 2.00 .75
- ❑ 522 Joe Hoerner 2.00 .75
- ❑ 523 Bob Chance 2.00 .75
- ❑ 524 J.Laboy RC/F.Wicker RC 3.00 1.25
- ❑ 525 Earl Wilson 3.00 1.25
- ❑ 526 Hector Torres RC 2.00 .75
- ❑ 527 Al Lopez MG 5.00 2.00
- ❑ 528 Claude Osteen 3.00 1.25
- ❑ 529 Ed Kirkpatrick 3.00 1.25
- ❑ 530 Cesar Tovar 2.00 .75
- ❑ 531 Dick Farrell 2.00 .75
- ❑ 532 Phoeb/Hard/McNally/Cuellar 3.00 1.25
- ❑ 533 Nolan Ryan 200.00 125.00
- ❑ 534 Jerry McNertney 3.00 1.25
- ❑ 535 Phil Regan 3.00 1.25
- ❑ 536 D.Breeden RC/D.Roberts RC 2.00 .75
- ❑ 537 Mike Paul RC 2.00 .75
- ❑ 538 Charlie Smith 2.00 .75
- ❑ 539 T.Williams/M.Epstein 12.00 6.00
- ❑ 540 Curt Flood 3.00 1.25
- ❑ 541 Joe Verbanic 2.00 .75
- ❑ 542 Bob Aspromonte 2.00 .75
- ❑ 543 Fred Newman 2.00 .75
- ❑ 544 M.Kilkenny RC/R.Woods RC 2.00 .75
- ❑ 545 Willie Stargell 12.00 6.00
- ❑ 546 Jim Nash 2.00 .75
- ❑ 547 Billy Martin MG 5.00 2.00
- ❑ 548 Bob Locker 2.00 .75
- ❑ 549 Ron Brand 2.00 .75
- ❑ 550 Brooks Robinson 30.00 15.00
- ❑ 551 Wayne Granger RC 2.00 .75
- ❑ 552 T.Sizemore RC/B.Sudakis RC 3.00 1.25
- ❑ 553 Ron Davis 2.00 .75
- ❑ 554 Frank Bertaina 2.00 .75
- ❑ 555 Jim Ray Hart 3.00 1.25
- ❑ 556 Bando/Campaneris/Cater 3.00 1.25
- ❑ 557 Frank Fernandez 2.00 .75
- ❑ 558 Tom Burgmeier RC 3.00 1.25
- ❑ 559 J.Hague RC/J.Hicks 2.00 .75
- ❑ 560 Luis Tiant 3.00 1.25
- ❑ 561 Ron Clark 2.00 .75
- ❑ 562 Bob Watson RC 8.00 4.00
- ❑ 563 Marty Pattin RC 3.00 1.25
- ❑ 564 Gil Hodges MG 10.00 5.00
- ❑ 565 Hoyt Wilhelm 8.00 4.00
- ❑ 566 Ron Hansen 2.00 .75
- ❑ 567 E.Jimenez/J.Shellenback 2.00 .75
- ❑ 568 Cecil Upshaw 2.00 .75
- ❑ 569 Billy Harris 1.50 .60
- ❑ 570 Ron Santo 8.00 4.00
- ❑ 571 Cap Peterson 2.00 .75
- ❑ 572 W.McCovey/J.Marichal 15.00 7.50
- ❑ 573 Jim Palmer 30.00 15.00
- ❑ 574 George Scott 3.00 1.25
- ❑ 575 Bill Singer 3.00 1.25
- ❑ 576 R.Stone/B.Wilson 2.00 .75
- ❑ 577 Mike Hegan 3.00 1.25
- ❑ 578 Don Bosch 2.00 .75
- ❑ 579 Dave Nelson RC 2.00 .75
- ❑ 580 Jim Northrup 3.00 1.25
- ❑ 581 Gary Nolan 3.00 1.25
- ❑ 582A Checklist 7/Oliva White 6.00 3.00
- ❑ 582B Checklist 7/Oliva Red 8.00 4.00
- ❑ 583 Clyde Wright RC 2.00 .75
- ❑ 584 Don Mason 2.00 .75
- ❑ 585 Ron Swoboda 3.00 1.25
- ❑ 586 Tim Cullen 2.00 .75
- ❑ 587 Joe Rudi RC 8.00 4.00
- ❑ 588 Bill White 3.00 1.25
- ❑ 589 Joe Pepitone 5.00 2.00
- ❑ 590 Rico Carty 5.00 2.00
- ❑ 591 Mike Hedlund 3.00 1.25
- ❑ 592 R.Robles RC/A.Santorini RC 5.00 2.00
- ❑ 593 Don Nottebart 3.00 1.25
- ❑ 594 Dooley Womack 3.00 1.25
- ❑ 595 Lee Maye 3.00 1.25
- ❑ 596 Chuck Hartenstein 3.00 1.25
- ❑ 597 Rollie Fingers RC 40.00 20.00
- ❑ 598 Ruben Amaro 3.00 1.25
- ❑ 599 John Boozer 3.00 1.25
- ❑ 600 Tony Oliva 8.00 4.00
- ❑ 601 Tug McGraw SP 8.00 4.00
- ❑ 602 Distaso/Young/Qualls RC 5.00 2.00
- ❑ 603 Joe Keough RC 3.00 1.25
- ❑ 604 Bobby Etheridge 3.00 1.25
- ❑ 605 Dick Ellsworth 3.00 1.25
- ❑ 606 Gene Mauch MG 5.00 2.00
- ❑ 607 Dick Bosman 3.00 1.25
- ❑ 608 Dick Simpson 3.00 1.25
- ❑ 609 Phil Gagliano 3.00 1.25
- ❑ 610 Jim Hardin 3.00 1.25
- ❑ 611 Didier/Hriniak/Niebauer RC 5.00 2.00
- ❑ 612 Jack Aker 5.00 2.00
- ❑ 613 Jim Beauchamp 3.00 1.25
- ❑ 614 T.Griffin RC/S.Guinn RC 3.00 1.25
- ❑ 615 Len Gabrielson 3.00 1.25
- ❑ 616 Don McMahon 3.00 1.25
- ❑ 617 Jesse Gonder 3.00 1.25
- ❑ 618 Ramon Webster 3.00 1.25
- ❑ 619 Butler/Kelly/Rios RC 5.00 2.00
- ❑ 620 Dean Chance 5.00 2.00
- ❑ 621 Bill Voss 3.00 1.25
- ❑ 622 Dan Osinski 3.00 1.25
- ❑ 623 Hank Allen 3.00 1.25
- ❑ 624 Chaney/Dyer/Harmon RC 5.00 2.00
- ❑ 625 Mack Jones UER 5.00 2.00
- ❑ 626 Gene Michael 5.00 2.00
- ❑ 627 George Stone RC 3.00 1.25
- ❑ 628 Conigliaro/O'Brien/Wenz RC 5.00 2.00
- ❑ 629 Jack Hamilton 3.00 1.25
- ❑ 630 Bobby Bonds RC 30.00 15.00
- ❑ 631 John Kennedy 5.00 2.00
- ❑ 632 Jon Warden RC 3.00 1.25
- ❑ 633 Harry Walker MG 3.00 1.25
- ❑ 634 Andy Etchebarren 3.00 1.25
- ❑ 635 George Culver 3.00 1.25
- ❑ 636 Woody Held 3.00 1.25
- ❑ 637 DaVanon/Reberger/Kirby RC 5.00 2.00
- ❑ 638 Ed Sprague RC 3.00 1.25
- ❑ 639 Barry Moore 3.00 1.25
- ❑ 640 Ferguson Jenkins 20.00 10.00
- ❑ 641 Darwin/Miller/Dean RC 5.00 2.00
- ❑ 642 John Hiller 3.00 1.25
- ❑ 643 Billy Cowan 3.00 1.25
- ❑ 644 Chuck Hinton 3.00 1.25
- ❑ 645 George Brunet 3.00 1.25
- ❑ 646 D.McGinn RC/C.Morton RC 5.00 2.00
- ❑ 647 Dave Wickersham 3.00 1.25
- ❑ 648 Bobby Wine 5.00 2.00
- ❑ 649 Al Jackson 3.00 1.25
- ❑ 650 Ted Williams MG 20.00 10.00
- ❑ 651 Gus Gil 5.00 2.00
- ❑ 652 Eddie Watt 3.00 1.25
- ❑ 653 Aurelio Rodriguez UER RC 5.00 2.00
- ❑ 654 May/Secrist/Morales RC 5.00 2.00
- ❑ 655 Mike Hershberger 3.00 1.25
- ❑ 656 Dan Schneider 3.00 1.25
- ❑ 657 Bobby Murcer 8.00 4.00
- ❑ 658 Hall/Burbach/Miles RC 3.00 1.25
- ❑ 659 Johnny Podres 5.00 2.00
- ❑ 660 Reggie Smith 5.00 2.00
- ❑ 661 Jim Merritt 3.00 1.25
- ❑ 662 Drago/Spriggs/Oliver RC 5.00 2.00
- ❑ 663 Dick Radatz 5.00 2.00
- ❑ 664 Ron Hunt 5.00 2.00

1970 Topps

- ❑ COMPLETE SET (720) 2000.00 1200.00
- ❑ COMMON CARD (1-132) .75 .30
- ❑ COMMON CARD (133-372) 1.00 .40
- ❑ COMMON CARD (373-459) 1.50 .60
- ❑ COMMON CARD (460-546) 2.00 .75
- ❑ COMMON CARD (547-633) 4.00 1.50
- ❑ COMMON CARD (634-720) 10.00 5.00
- ❑ WRAPPER (10-CENT) 20.00 15.00
- ❑ 1 New York Mets TC 30.00 15.00
- ❑ 2 Diego Segui 1.00 .40
- ❑ 3 Darrel Chaney .75 .30
- ❑ 4 Tom Egan .75 .30
- ❑ 5 Wes Parker 1.00 .40
- ❑ 6 Grant Jackson .75 .30
- ❑ 7 G.Boyd RC/R.Nagelson RC .75 .30
- ❑ 8 Jose Martinez RC .75 .30
- ❑ 9 Checklist 1 12.00 6.00
- ❑ 10 Carl Yastrzemski 20.00 10.00
- ❑ 11 Nate Colbert .75 .30
- ❑ 12 John Hiller .75 .30
- ❑ 13 Jack Hiatt .75 .30
- ❑ 14 Hank Allen .75 .30
- ❑ 15 Larry Dierker .75 .30
- ❑ 16 Charlie Metro MG RC .75 .30
- ❑ 17 Hoyt Wilhelm 4.00 1.50
- ❑ 18 Carlos May 1.00 .40
- ❑ 19 John Boccabella .75 .30
- ❑ 20 Dave McNally 1.00 .40
- ❑ 21 V.Blue RC/G.Tenace RC 4.00 1.50
- ❑ 22 Ray Washburn .75 .30
- ❑ 23 Bill Robinson 1.00 .40
- ❑ 24 Dick Selma .75 .30
- ❑ 25 Cesar Tovar .75 .30
- ❑ 26 Tug McGraw 2.00 .75
- ❑ 27 Chuck Hinton .75 .30
- ❑ 28 Billy Wilson .75 .30
- ❑ 29 Sandy Alomar 1.00 .40
- ❑ 30 Matty Alou 1.00 .40
- ❑ 31 Marty Pattin 1.00 .40
- ❑ 32 Harry Walker MG .75 .30
- ❑ 33 Don Wert .75 .30
- ❑ 34 Willie Crawford .75 .30
- ❑ 35 Joel Horlen .75 .30
- ❑ 36 D.Breeden/B.Carbo RC 1.00 .40
- ❑ 37 Dick Drago .75 .30
- ❑ 38 Mack Jones .75 .30
- ❑ 39 Mike Nagy RC .75 .30
- ❑ 40 Richie Allen 2.00 .75
- ❑ 41 George Lauzerique .75 .30
- ❑ 42 Tito Fuentes .75 .30
- ❑ 43 Jack Aker .75 .30
- ❑ 44 Roberto Pena .75 .30
- ❑ 45 Dave Johnson 1.00 .40
- ❑ 46 Ken Rudolph RC .75 .30
- ❑ 47 Bob Miller .75 .30
- ❑ 48 Gil Garrido .75 .30
- ❑ 49 Tim Cullen .75 .30
- ❑ 50 Tommie Agee 1.00 .40
- ❑ 51 Bob Christian .75 .30
- ❑ 52 Bruce Dal Canton .75 .30
- ❑ 53 John Kennedy .75 .30
- ❑ 54 Jeff Torborg 1.00 .40
- ❑ 55 John Odom .75 .30
- ❑ 56 J.Lis RC/S.Reid RC .75 .30
- ❑ 57 Pat Kelly .75 .30
- ❑ 58 Dave Marshall .75 .30
- ❑ 59 Dick Ellsworth .75 .30
- ❑ 60 Jim Wynn 1.00 .40
- ❑ 61 Rose/Clemente/Jones LL 12.00 6.00
- ❑ 62 Carew/Smith/Oliva LL 2.00 .75
- ❑ 63 McCovey/Santo/Perez LL 2.00 .75
- ❑ 64 Kill/Powell/Jackson LL 4.00 1.50

- ❑ 65 McCovey/Aaron/May LL 4.00 1.50
- ❑ 66 Kill/Howard/Jackson LL 4.00 1.50
- ❑ 67 Marichal/Carlton/Gibson LL 4.00 1.50
- ❑ 68 Bosman/Palmer/Cuellar LL 1.00 .40
- ❑ 69 Seav/Niek/Jenk/Marl LL 4.00 1.50
- ❑ 70 McLain/Cuellar/Boswell LL 1.00 .40
- ❑ 71 Jenkins/Gibson/Singer LL 2.00 .75
- ❑ 72 McDowell/Lolich/Mess LL 1.00 .40
- ❑ 73 Wayne Granger .75 .30
- ❑ 74 G.Washburn RC/W.Wolf .75 .30
- ❑ 75 Jim Kaat 1.00 .40
- ❑ 76 Carl Taylor .75 .30
- ❑ 77 Frank Linzy .75 .30
- ❑ 78 Joe Lahoud .75 .30
- ❑ 79 Clay Kirby .75 .30
- ❑ 80 Don Kessinger 1.00 .40
- ❑ 81 Dave May .75 .30
- ❑ 82 Frank Fernandez .75 .30
- ❑ 83 Don Cardwell .75 .30
- ❑ 84 Paul Casanova .75 .30
- ❑ 85 Max Alvis .75 .30
- ❑ 86 Lum Harris MG .75 .30
- ❑ 87 Steve Renko RC .75 .30
- ❑ 88 M.Fuentes RC/D.Baney RC 1.00 .40
- ❑ 89 Juan Rios .75 .30
- ❑ 90 Tim McCarver 1.00 .40
- ❑ 91 Rich Morales .75 .30
- ❑ 92 George Culver .75 .30
- ❑ 93 Rick Renick .75 .30
- ❑ 94 Freddie Patek 1.00 .40
- ❑ 95 Earl Wilson 1.00 .40
- ❑ 96 L.Lee RC/J.Reuss RC 1.00 .40
- ❑ 97 Joe Moeller .75 .30
- ❑ 98 Gates Brown 1.00 .40
- ❑ 99 Bobby Pfeil RC .75 .30
- ❑ 100 Mel Stottlemyre 1.00 .40
- ❑ 101 Bobby Floyd .75 .30
- ❑ 102 Joe Rudi 1.00 .40
- ❑ 103 Frank Reberger .75 .30
- ❑ 104 Gerry Moses .75 .30
- ❑ 105 Tony Gonzalez .75 .30
- ❑ 106 Darold Knowles .75 .30
- ❑ 107 Bobby Etheridge .75 .30
- ❑ 108 Tom Burgmeier .75 .30
- ❑ 109 G.Jestadt RC/C.Morton .75 .30
- ❑ 110 Bob Moose .75 .30
- ❑ 111 Mike Hegan 1.00 .40
- ❑ 112 Dave Nelson .75 .30
- ❑ 113 Jim Ray .75 .30
- ❑ 114 Gene Michael 1.00 .40
- ❑ 115 Alex Johnson 1.00 .40
- ❑ 116 Sparky Lyle 1.00 .40
- ❑ 117 Don Young .75 .30
- ❑ 118 George Mitterwald .75 .30
- ❑ 119 Chuck Taylor RC .75 .30
- ❑ 120 Sal Bando 1.00 .40
- ❑ 121 F.Beene RC/T.Crowley RC .75 .30
- ❑ 122 George Stone .75 .30
- ❑ 123 Don Gutteridge MG RC .75 .30
- ❑ 124 Larry Jaster .75 .30
- ❑ 125 Deron Johnson .75 .30
- ❑ 126 Marty Martinez .75 .30
- ❑ 127 Joe Coleman .75 .30
- ❑ 128A Checklist 2 R Perranoski 6.00 3.00
- ❑ 128B Checklist 2 R. Perranoski 6.00 3.00
- ❑ 129 Jimmie Price .75 .30
- ❑ 130 Ollie Brown .75 .30
- ❑ 131 R.Lamb RC/B.Stinson RC .75 .30
- ❑ 132 Jim McGlothlin .75 .30
- ❑ 133 Clay Carroll 1.00 .40
- ❑ 134 Danny Walton RC 1.00 .40
- ❑ 135 Dick Dietz 1.00 .40
- ❑ 136 Steve Hargan 1.00 .40
- ❑ 137 Art Shamsky 1.00 .40
- ❑ 138 Joe Foy 1.00 .40
- ❑ 139 Rich Nye 1.00 .40
- ❑ 140 Reggie Jackson 50.00 30.00
- ❑ 141 D.Cash RC/J.Jeter RC 1.50 .60
- ❑ 142 Fritz Peterson 1.00 .40
- ❑ 143 Phil Gagliano 1.00 .40
- ❑ 144 Ray Culp 1.00 .40
- ❑ 145 Rico Carty 1.50 .60
- ❑ 146 Danny Murphy 1.00 .40
- ❑ 147 Angel Hermoso RC 1.00 .40
- ❑ 148 Earl Weaver MG 3.00 1.25
- ❑ 149 Billy Champion RC 1.00 .40
- ❑ 150 Harmon Killebrew 8.00 4.00
- ❑ 151 Dave Roberts 1.00 .40
- ❑ 152 Ike Brown RC 1.00 .40
- ❑ 153 Gary Gentry 1.00 .40
- ❑ 154 J.Miles/J.Dukes RC 1.00 .40
- ❑ 155 Denis Menke 1.00 .40
- ❑ 156 Eddie Fisher 1.00 .40
- ❑ 157 Manny Mota 1.50 .60
- ❑ 158 Jerry McNertney 1.50 .60
- ❑ 159 Tommy Helms 1.50 .60
- ❑ 160 Phil Niekro 5.00 2.00
- ❑ 161 Richie Scheinblum 1.00 .40
- ❑ 162 Jerry Johnson 1.00 .40
- ❑ 163 Syd O'Brien 1.00 .40
- ❑ 164 Ty Cline 1.00 .40
- ❑ 165 Ed Kirkpatrick 1.00 .40
- ❑ 166 Al Oliver 3.00 1.25
- ❑ 167 Bill Burbach 1.00 .40
- ❑ 168 Dave Watkins RC 1.00 .40
- ❑ 169 Tom Hall 1.00 .40
- ❑ 170 Billy Williams 5.00 2.00
- ❑ 171 Jim Nash 1.00 .40
- ❑ 172 G.Hill RC/R.Garr RC 1.50 .60
- ❑ 173 Jim Hicks 1.00 .40
- ❑ 174 Ted Sizemore 1.50 .60
- ❑ 175 Dick Bosman 1.00 .40
- ❑ 176 Jim Ray Hart 1.50 .60
- ❑ 177 Jim Northrup 1.50 .60
- ❑ 178 Denny Lemaster 1.00 .40
- ❑ 179 Ivan Murrell 1.00 .40
- ❑ 180 Tommy John 1.50 .60
- ❑ 181 Sparky Anderson MG 5.00 2.00
- ❑ 182 Dick Hall 1.00 .40
- ❑ 183 Jerry Grote 1.50 .60
- ❑ 184 Ray Fosse 1.00 .40
- ❑ 185 Don Mincher 1.50 .60
- ❑ 186 Rick Joseph 1.00 .40
- ❑ 187 Mike Hedlund 1.00 .40
- ❑ 188 Manny Sanguillen 1.50 .60
- ❑ 189 Thurman Munson RC 100.00 60.00
- ❑ 190 Joe Torre 3.00 1.25
- ❑ 191 Vicente Romo 1.00 .40
- ❑ 192 Jim Qualls 1.00 .40
- ❑ 193 Mike Wegener 1.00 .40
- ❑ 194 Chuck Manuel RC 1.00 .40
- ❑ 195 Tom Seaver NLCS1 15.00 7.50
- ❑ 196 Ken Boswell NLCS2 2.00 .75
- ❑ 197 Nolan Ryan NLCS3 30.00 15.00
- ❑ 198 Mets Celebrate/w/Ryan 15.00 7.50
- ❑ 199 Mike Cuellar ALCS1 2.00 .75
- ❑ 200 Boog Powell ALCS2 3.00 1.25
- ❑ 201 B.Powell/A.Etch ALCS3 2.00 .75
- ❑ 202 Orioles Celebrate ALCS 2.00 .75
- ❑ 203 Rudy May 1.00 .40
- ❑ 204 Len Gabrielson 1.00 .40
- ❑ 205 Bert Campaneris 1.50 .60
- ❑ 206 Clete Boyer 1.50 .60
- ❑ 207 N.McRae RC/B.Reed RC 1.00 .40
- ❑ 208 Fred Gladding 1.00 .40
- ❑ 209 Ken Suarez 1.00 .40
- ❑ 210 Juan Marichal 5.00 2.00
- ❑ 211 Ted Williams MG UER 15.00 7.50
- ❑ 212 Al Santorini 1.00 .40
- ❑ 213 Andy Etchebarren 1.00 .40
- ❑ 214 Ken Boswell 1.00 .40
- ❑ 215 Reggie Smith 1.50 .60
- ❑ 216 Chuck Hartenstein 1.00 .40
- ❑ 217 Ron Hansen 1.00 .40
- ❑ 218 Ron Stone 1.00 .40
- ❑ 219 Jerry Kenney 1.00 .40
- ❑ 220 Steve Carlton 15.00 7.50
- ❑ 221 Ron Brand 1.00 .40
- ❑ 222 Jim Rooker 1.00 .40
- ❑ 223 Nate Oliver 1.00 .40
- ❑ 224 Steve Barber 1.50 .60
- ❑ 225 Lee May 1.50 .60
- ❑ 226 Ron Perranoski 1.00 .40
- ❑ 227 J.Mayberry RC/B.Watkins RC 1.50 .60
- ❑ 228 Aurelio Rodriguez 1.00 .40
- ❑ 229 Rich Robertson 1.00 .40
- ❑ 230 Brooks Robinson 15.00 7.50
- ❑ 231 Luis Tiant 1.50 .60
- ❑ 232 Bob Didier 1.00 .40
- ❑ 233 Lew Krausse 1.00 .40
- ❑ 234 Tommy Dean 1.00 .40
- ❑ 235 Mike Epstein 1.00 .40
- ❑ 236 Bob Veale 1.00 .40
- ❑ 237 Russ Gibson 1.00 .40
- ❑ 238 Jose Laboy 1.00 .40
- ❑ 239 Ken Berry 1.00 .40
- ❑ 240 Ferguson Jenkins 5.00 2.00
- ❑ 241 A.Fitzmorris RC/S.Northey RC 1.00 .40
- ❑ 242 Walt Alston MG 3.00 1.25
- ❑ 243 Joe Sparma 1.00 .40
- ❑ 244A Checklist 3 Red Bat 6.00 3.00
- ❑ 244B Checklist 3 Brown Bat 6.00 3.00
- ❑ 245 Leo Cardenas 1.00 .40
- ❑ 246 Jim McAndrew 1.00 .40
- ❑ 247 Lou Klimchock 1.00 .40
- ❑ 248 Jesus Alou 1.00 .40
- ❑ 249 Bob Locker 1.00 .40
- ❑ 250 Willie McCovey UER 10.00 5.00
- ❑ 251 Dick Schofield 1.00 .40
- ❑ 252 Lowell Palmer RC 1.00 .40
- ❑ 253 Ron Woods 1.00 .40
- ❑ 254 Camilo Pascual 1.00 .40
- ❑ 255 Jim Spencer RC 1.00 .40
- ❑ 256 Vic Davalillo 1.00 .40
- ❑ 257 Dennis Higgins 1.00 .40
- ❑ 258 Paul Popovich 1.00 .40
- ❑ 259 Tommie Reynolds 1.00 .40
- ❑ 260 Claude Osteen 1.00 .40
- ❑ 261 Curt Motton 1.00 .40
- ❑ 262 J.Morales RC/J.Williams RC 1.00 .40
- ❑ 263 Duane Josephson 1.00 .40
- ❑ 264 Rich Hebner 1.00 .40
- ❑ 265 Randy Hundley 1.00 .40
- ❑ 266 Wally Bunker 1.00 .40
- ❑ 267 H.Hill RC/P.Ratliff 1.00 .40
- ❑ 268 Claude Raymond 1.00 .40
- ❑ 269 Cesar Gutierrez 1.00 .40
- ❑ 270 Chris Short 1.00 .40
- ❑ 271 Greg Goossen 1.50 .60
- ❑ 272 Hector Torres 1.00 .40
- ❑ 273 Ralph Houk MG 1.50 .60
- ❑ 274 Gerry Arrigo 1.00 .40
- ❑ 275 Duke Sims 1.00 .40
- ❑ 276 Ron Hunt 1.00 .40
- ❑ 277 Paul Doyle RC 1.00 .40
- ❑ 278 Tommie Aaron 1.00 .40
- ❑ 279 Bill Lee RC 1.50 .60
- ❑ 280 Donn Clendenon 1.50 .60
- ❑ 281 Casey Cox 1.00 .40
- ❑ 282 Steve Huntz 1.00 .40
- ❑ 283 Angel Bravo RC 1.00 .40
- ❑ 284 Jack Baldschun 1.00 .40
- ❑ 285 Paul Blair 1.50 .60
- ❑ 286 J.Jenkins RC/B.Buckner RC 5.00 2.00
- ❑ 287 Fred Talbot 1.00 .40
- ❑ 288 Larry Hisle 1.50 .60
- ❑ 289 Gene Brabender 1.00 .40
- ❑ 290 Rod Carew 15.00 7.50
- ❑ 291 Leo Durocher MG 3.00 1.25
- ❑ 292 Eddie Leon RC 1.00 .40
- ❑ 293 Bob Bailey 1.50 .60
- ❑ 294 Jose Azcue 1.00 .40
- ❑ 295 Cecil Upshaw 1.00 .40
- ❑ 296 Woody Woodward 1.00 .40
- ❑ 297 Curt Blefary 1.00 .40
- ❑ 298 Ken Henderson 1.00 .40
- ❑ 299 Buddy Bradford 1.00 .40
- ❑ 300 Tom Seaver 30.00 15.00
- ❑ 301 Chico Salmon 1.00 .40
- ❑ 302 Jeff James 1.00 .40
- ❑ 303 Brant Alyea 1.00 .40
- ❑ 304 Bill Russell RC 5.00 2.00
- ❑ 305 Don Buford WS1 4.00 1.50
- ❑ 306 Donn Clendenon WS2 4.00 1.50
- ❑ 307 Tommie Agee WS3 4.00 1.50
- ❑ 308 J.C. Martin WS4 4.00 1.50
- ❑ 309 Jerry Koosman WS5 4.00 1.50
- ❑ 310 Mets Celebrate WS 5.00 2.00
- ❑ 311 Dick Green 1.00 .40
- ❑ 312 Mike Torrez 1.00 .40
- ❑ 313 Mayo Smith MG 1.00 .40
- ❑ 314 Bill McCool 1.00 .40
- ❑ 315 Luis Aparicio 5.00 2.00
- ❑ 316 Skip Guinn 1.00 .40
- ❑ 317 B.Conigliaro/L.Alvarado RC 1.50 .60
- ❑ 318 Willie Smith 1.00 .40
- ❑ 319 Clay Dalrymple 1.00 .40
- ❑ 320 Jim Maloney 1.50 .60

321	Lou Piniella	1.50	.60
322	Luke Walker	1.00	.40
323	Wayne Comer	1.00	.40
324	Tony Taylor	1.50	.60
325	Dave Boswell	1.00	.40
326	Bill Voss	1.00	.40
327	Hal King RC	1.00	.40
328	George Brunet	1.00	.40
329	Chris Cannizzaro	1.00	.40
330	Lou Brock	10.00	5.00
331	Chuck Dobson	1.00	.40
332	Bobby Wine	1.00	.40
333	Bobby Murcer	1.50	.60
334	Phil Regan	1.00	.40
335	Bill Freehan	1.50	.60
336	Del Unser	1.00	.40
337	Mike McCormick	1.50	.60
338	Paul Schaal	1.00	.40
339	Johnny Edwards	1.00	.40
340	Tony Conigliaro	3.00	1.25
341	Bill Sudakis	1.00	.40
342	Wilbur Wood	1.50	.60
343A	Checklist 4 Red Bat	6.00	3.00
343B	Checklist 4 Brown Bat	6.00	3.00
344	Marcelino Lopez	1.00	.40
345	Al Ferrara	1.00	.40
346	Red Schoendienst MG	1.50	.60
347	Russ Snyder	1.00	.40
348	M.Jorgensen RC/J.Hudson RC	1.50	.60
349	Steve Hamilton	1.00	.40
350	Roberto Clemente	60.00	35.00
351	Tom Murphy	1.00	.40
352	Bob Barton	1.00	.40
353	Stan Williams	1.00	.40
354	Amos Otis	1.50	.60
355	Doug Rader	1.00	.40
356	Fred Lasher	1.00	.40
357	Bob Burda	1.00	.40
358	Pedro Borbon RC	1.50	.60
359	Phil Roof	1.00	.40
360	Curt Flood	1.50	.60
361	Ray Jarvis	1.00	.40
362	Joe Hague	1.00	.40
363	Tom Shopay RC	1.00	.40
364	Dan McGinn	1.00	.40
365	Zoilo Versalles	1.00	.40
366	Barry Moore	1.00	.40
367	Mike Lum	1.00	.40
368	Ed Herrmann	1.00	.40
369	Alan Foster	1.00	.40
370	Tommy Harper	1.50	.60
371	Rod Gaspar RC	1.00	.40
372	Dave Giusti	1.00	.40
373	Roy White	2.00	.75
374	Tommie Sisk	1.50	.60
375	Johnny Callison	2.00	.75
376	Lefty Phillips MG RC	1.50	.60
377	Bill Butler	1.50	.60
378	Jim Davenport	1.50	.60
379	Tom Tischinski RC	1.50	.60
380	Tony Perez	6.00	3.00
381	B.Brooks RC/M.Olivo RC	1.50	.60
382	Jack DiLauro RC	1.50	.60
383	Mickey Stanley	2.00	.75
384	Gary Neibauer	1.50	.60
385	George Scott	2.00	.75
386	Bill Dillman	1.50	.60
387	Baltimore Orioles TC	3.00	1.25
388	Byron Browne	1.50	.60
389	Jim Shellenback	1.50	.60
390	Willie Davis	2.00	.75
391	Larry Brown	1.50	.60
392	Walt Hriniak	2.00	.75
393	John Gelnar	1.50	.60
394	Gil Hodges MG	4.00	1.50
395	Walt Williams	1.50	.60
396	Steve Blass	2.00	.75
397	Roger Repoz	1.50	.60
398	Bill Stoneman	1.50	.60
399	New York Yankees TC	3.00	1.25
400	Denny McLain	4.00	1.50
401	J.Harrell RC/B.Williams RC	1.50	.60
402	Ellie Rodriguez	1.50	.60
403	Jim Bunning	6.00	3.00
404	Rich Reese	1.50	.60
405	Bill Hands	1.50	.60
406	Mike Andrews	1.50	.60
407	Bob Watson	2.00	.75
408	Paul Lindblad	1.50	.60
409	Bob Tolan	1.50	.60
410	Boog Powell	4.00	1.50
411	Los Angeles Dodgers TC	3.00	1.25
412	Larry Burchart	1.50	.60
413	Sonny Jackson	1.50	.60
414	Paul Edmondson RC	1.50	.60
415	Julian Javier	2.00	.75
416	Joe Verbanic	1.50	.60
417	John Bateman	1.50	.60
418	John Donaldson	1.50	.60
419	Ron Taylor	1.50	.60
420	Ken McMullen	2.00	.75
421	Pat Dobson	2.00	.75
422	Kansas City Royals TC	3.00	1.25
423	Jerry May	1.50	.60
424	Mike Kilkenny	1.50	.60
425	Bobby Bonds	6.00	3.00
426	Bill Rigney MG	1.50	.60
427	Fred Norman	1.50	.60
428	Don Buford	1.50	.60
429	R.Bobb RC/J.Cosman	1.50	.60
430	Andy Messersmith	2.00	.75
431	Ron Swoboda	2.00	.75
432A	Checklist 5 Yellow Ltr	6.00	3.00
432B	Checklist 5 White Ltr	6.00	3.00
433	Ron Bryant RC	1.50	.60
434	Felipe Alou	2.00	.75
435	Nelson Briles	2.00	.75
436	Philadelphia Phillies TC	3.00	1.25
437	Danny Cater	1.50	.60
438	Pat Jarvis	1.50	.60
439	Lee Maye	1.50	.60
440	Bill Mazeroski	6.00	3.00
441	John O'Donoghue	1.50	.60
442	Gene Mauch MG	2.00	.75
443	Al Jackson	1.50	.60
444	B.Farmer RC/J.Matias RC	1.50	.60
445	Vada Pinson	2.00	.75
446	Billy Grabarkewitz RC	1.50	.60
447	Lee Stange	1.50	.60
448	Houston Astros TC	3.00	1.25
449	Jim Palmer	12.00	6.00
450	Willie McCovey AS	6.00	3.00
451	Boog Powell AS	4.00	1.50
452	Felix Millan AS	2.00	.75
453	Rod Carew AS	6.00	3.00
454	Ron Santo AS	4.00	1.50
455	Brooks Robinson AS	6.00	3.00
456	Don Kessinger AS	2.00	.75
457	Rico Petrocelli AS	4.00	1.50
458	Pete Rose AS	15.00	7.50
459	Reggie Jackson AS	12.00	6.00
460	Matty Alou AS	3.00	1.25
461	Carl Yastrzemski AS	10.00	5.00
462	Hank Aaron AS	15.00	7.50
463	Frank Robinson AS	8.00	4.00
464	Johnny Bench AS	15.00	7.50
465	Bill Freehan AS	3.00	1.25
466	Juan Marichal AS	5.00	2.00
467	Denny McLain AS	3.00	1.25
468	Jerry Koosman AS	3.00	1.25
469	Sam McDowell AS	3.00	1.25
470	Willie Stargell	10.00	5.00
471	Chris Zachary	2.00	.75
472	Atlanta Braves TC	4.00	1.50
473	Don Bryant	2.00	.75
474	Dick Kelley	2.00	.75
475	Dick McAuliffe	3.00	1.25
476	Don Shaw	2.00	.75
477	A.Severinsen RC/R.Freed RC	2.00	.75
478	Bobby Heise RC	2.00	.75
479	Dick Woodson RC	2.00	.75
480	Glenn Beckert	3.00	1.25
481	Jose Tartabull	2.00	.75
482	Tom Hilgendorf RC	2.00	.75
483	Gail Hopkins RC	2.00	.75
484	Gary Nolan	3.00	1.25
485	Jay Johnstone	3.00	1.25
486	Terry Harmon	2.00	.75
487	Cisco Carlos	2.00	.75
488	J.C. Martin	2.00	.75
489	Eddie Kasko MG	2.00	.75
490	Bill Singer	3.00	1.25
491	Graig Nettles	5.00	2.00
492	K.Lampard RC/S.Spinks RC	2.00	.75
493	Lindy McDaniel	3.00	1.25
494	Larry Stahl	2.00	.75
495	Dave Morehead	2.00	.75
496	Steve Whitaker	2.00	.75
497	Eddie Watt	2.00	.75
498	Al Weis	2.00	.75
499	Skip Lockwood	3.00	1.25
500	Hank Aaron	50.00	30.00
501	Chicago White Sox TC	4.00	1.50
502	Rollie Fingers	10.00	5.00
503	Dal Maxvill	2.00	.75
504	Don Pavletich	2.00	.75
505	Ken Holtzman	3.00	1.25
506	Ed Stroud	2.00	.75
507	Pat Corrales	2.00	.75
508	Joe Niekro	3.00	1.25
509	Montreal Expos TC	4.00	1.50
510	Tony Oliva	5.00	2.00
511	Joe Hoerner	2.00	.75
512	Billy Harris	2.00	.75
513	Preston Gomez MG	2.00	.75
514	Steve Hovley RC	2.00	.75
515	Don Wilson	3.00	1.25
516	J.Ellis RC/J.Lyttle RC	2.00	.75
517	Joe Gibbon	2.00	.75
518	Bill Melton	2.00	.75
519	Don McMahon	2.00	.75
520	Willie Horton	3.00	1.25
521	Cal Koonce	2.00	.75
522	California Angels TC	4.00	1.50
523	Jose Pena	2.00	.75
524	Alvin Dark MG	3.00	1.25
525	Jerry Adair	2.00	.75
526	Ron Herbel	2.00	.75
527	Don Bosch	2.00	.75
528	Elrod Hendricks	2.00	.75
529	Bob Aspromonte	2.00	.75
530	Bob Gibson	15.00	7.50
531	Ron Clark	2.00	.75
532	Danny Murtaugh MG	3.00	1.25
533	Buzz Stephen RC	2.00	.75
534	Minnesota Twins TC	4.00	1.50
535	Andy Kosco	2.00	.75
536	Mike Kekich	2.00	.75
537	Joe Morgan	10.00	5.00
538	Bob Humphreys	2.00	.75
539	D.Doyle RC/L.Bowa RC	8.00	4.00
540	Gary Peters	2.00	.75
541	Bill Heath	2.00	.75
542	Checklist 6	6.00	3.00
543	Clyde Wright	2.00	.75
544	Cincinnati Reds TC	4.00	1.50
545	Ken Harrelson	3.00	1.25
546	Ron Reed	2.00	.75
547	Rick Monday	6.00	3.00
548	Howie Reed	4.00	1.50
549	St. Louis Cardinals TC	6.00	3.00
550	Frank Howard	6.00	3.00
551	Dock Ellis	6.00	3.00
552	O'Riley/Paepke/Rico RC	4.00	1.50
553	Jim Lefebvre	6.00	3.00
554	Tom Timmermann RC	4.00	1.50
555	Orlando Cepeda	12.00	6.00
556	Dave Bristol MG	6.00	3.00
557	Ed Kranepool	6.00	3.00
558	Vern Fuller	4.00	1.50
559	Tommy Davis	6.00	3.00
560	Gaylord Perry	12.00	6.00
561	Tom McCraw	4.00	1.50
562	Ted Abernathy	4.00	1.50
563	Boston Red Sox TC	6.00	3.00
564	Johnny Briggs	4.00	1.50
565	Jim Hunter	12.00	6.00
566	Gene Alley	6.00	3.00
567	Bob Oliver	4.00	1.50
568	Stan Bahnsen	6.00	3.00
569	Cookie Rojas	6.00	3.00
570	Jim Fregosi	6.00	3.00
571	Jim Brewer	4.00	1.50
572	Frank Quilici	4.00	1.50
573	Corkins/Robles/Slocum RC	4.00	1.50
574	Bobby Bolin	6.00	3.00
575	Cleon Jones	6.00	3.00
576	Milt Pappas	6.00	3.00

❑ 577 Bernie Allen 4.00 1.50
❑ 578 Tom Griffin 4.00 1.50
❑ 579 Detroit Tigers TC 6.00 3.00
❑ 580 Pete Rose 60.00 35.00
❑ 581 Tom Satriano 4.00 1.50
❑ 582 Mike Paul 4.00 1.50
❑ 583 Hal Lanier 4.00 1.50
❑ 584 Al Downing 6.00 3.00
❑ 585 Rusty Staub 8.00 4.00
❑ 586 Rickey Clark RC 4.00 1.50
❑ 587 Jose Arcia 4.00 1.50
❑ 588A Checklist 7 Adolfo 8.00 4.00
❑ 588B Checklist 7 Adolpho 6.00 3.00
❑ 589 Joe Keough 4.00 1.50
❑ 590 Mike Cuellar 6.00 3.00
❑ 591 Mike Ryan UER 4.00 1.50
❑ 592 Daryl Patterson 4.00 1.50
❑ 593 Chicago Cubs TC 8.00 4.00
❑ 594 Jake Gibbs 4.00 1.50
❑ 595 Maury Wills 8.00 4.00
❑ 596 Mike Hershberger 6.00 3.00
❑ 597 Sonny Siebert 4.00 1.50
❑ 598 Joe Pepitone 6.00 3.00
❑ 599 Stelmaszek/Martin/Such RC 4.00 1.50
❑ 600 Willie Mays 80.00 50.00
❑ 601 Pete Richert 4.00 1.50
❑ 602 Ted Savage 4.00 1.50
❑ 603 Ray Oyler 4.00 1.50
❑ 604 Cito Gaston 6.00 3.00
❑ 605 Rick Wise 6.00 3.00
❑ 606 Chico Ruiz 4.00 1.50
❑ 607 Gary Waslewski 4.00 1.50
❑ 608 Pittsburgh Pirates TC 6.00 3.00
❑ 609 Buck Martinez RC 6.00 3.00
❑ 610 Jerry Koosman 8.00 4.00
❑ 611 Norm Cash 6.00 3.00
❑ 612 Jim Hickman 6.00 3.00
❑ 613 Dave Baldwin 6.00 3.00
❑ 614 Mike Shannon 6.00 3.00
❑ 615 Mark Belanger 6.00 3.00
❑ 616 Jim Merritt 4.00 1.50
❑ 617 Jim French 4.00 1.50
❑ 618 Billy Wynne RC 4.00 1.50
❑ 619 Norm Miller 4.00 1.50
❑ 620 Jim Perry 6.00 3.00
❑ 621 McQueen/Evans/Kester RC 12.00 6.00
❑ 622 Don Sutton 12.00 6.00
❑ 623 Horace Clarke 6.00 3.00
❑ 624 Clyde King MG 4.00 1.50
❑ 625 Dean Chance 4.00 1.50
❑ 626 Dave Ricketts 4.00 1.50
❑ 627 Gary Wagner 4.00 1.50
❑ 628 Wayne Garrett RC 4.00 1.50
❑ 629 Merv Rettenmund 4.00 1.50
❑ 630 Ernie Banks 50.00 30.00
❑ 631 Oakland Athletics TC 6.00 3.00
❑ 632 Gary Sutherland 4.00 1.50
❑ 633 Roger Nelson 4.00 1.50
❑ 634 Bud Harrelson 15.00 7.50
❑ 635 Bob Allison 15.00 7.50
❑ 636 Jim Stewart 10.00 5.00
❑ 637 Cleveland Indians TC 12.00 6.00
❑ 638 Frank Bertaina 10.00 5.00
❑ 639 Dave Campbell 15.00 7.50
❑ 640 Al Kaline 50.00 30.00
❑ 641 Al McBean 10.00 5.00
❑ 642 Garrett/Lund/Tatum RC 10.00 5.00
❑ 643 Jose Pagan 10.00 5.00
❑ 644 Gerry Nyman 10.00 5.00
❑ 645 Don Money 15.00 7.50
❑ 646 Jim Britton 10.00 5.00
❑ 647 Tom Matchick 10.00 5.00
❑ 648 Larry Haney 10.00 5.00
❑ 649 Jimmie Hall 10.00 5.00
❑ 650 Sam McDowell 15.00 7.50
❑ 651 Jim Gosger 10.00 5.00
❑ 652 Rich Rollins 15.00 7.50
❑ 653 Moe Drabowsky 10.00 5.00
❑ 654 Gamble/Day/Mangual RC 15.00 7.50
❑ 655 John Roseboro 15.00 7.50
❑ 656 Jim Hardin 10.00 5.00
❑ 657 San Diego Padres TC 12.00 6.00
❑ 658 Ken Tatum RC 10.00 5.00
❑ 659 Pete Ward 10.00 5.00
❑ 660 Johnny Bench 80.00 50.00
❑ 661 Jerry Robertson 10.00 5.00
❑ 662 Frank Lucchesi MG RC 10.00 5.00
❑ 663 Tito Francona 10.00 5.00
❑ 664 Bob Robertson 10.00 5.00
❑ 665 Jim Lonborg 15.00 7.50
❑ 666 Adolpho Phillips 10.00 5.00
❑ 667 Bob Meyer 15.00 7.50
❑ 668 Bob Tillman 10.00 5.00
❑ 669 Johnson/Lazar/Scott RC 10.00 5.00
❑ 670 Ron Santo 15.00 7.50
❑ 671 Jim Campanis 10.00 5.00
❑ 672 Leon McFadden 10.00 5.00
❑ 673 Ted Uhlaender 10.00 5.00
❑ 674 Dave Leonhard 10.00 5.00
❑ 675 Jose Cardenal 15.00 7.50
❑ 676 Washington Senators TC 12.00 6.00
❑ 677 Woodie Fryman 10.00 5.00
❑ 678 Dave Duncan 15.00 7.50
❑ 679 Ray Sadecki 10.00 5.00
❑ 680 Rico Petrocelli 15.00 7.50
❑ 681 Bob Garibaldi RC 10.00 5.00
❑ 682 Dalton Jones 10.00 5.00
❑ 683 Geishart/McRae/Simpson RC 15.00 7.50
❑ 684 Jack Fisher 10.00 5.00
❑ 685 Tom Haller 10.00 5.00
❑ 686 Jackie Hernandez 10.00 5.00
❑ 687 Bob Priddy 10.00 5.00
❑ 688 Ted Kubiak 15.00 7.50
❑ 689 Frank Tepedino RC 15.00 7.50
❑ 690 Ron Fairly 15.00 7.50
❑ 691 Joe Grzenda 10.00 5.00
❑ 692 Duffy Dyer 10.00 5.00
❑ 693 Bob Johnson 10.00 5.00
❑ 694 Gary Ross 10.00 5.00
❑ 695 Bobby Knoop 10.00 5.00
❑ 696 San Francisco Giants TC 12.00 6.00
❑ 697 Jim Hannan 10.00 5.00
❑ 698 Tom Tresh 15.00 7.50
❑ 699 Hank Aguirre 10.00 5.00
❑ 700 Frank Robinson 50.00 30.00
❑ 701 Jack Billingham 10.00 5.00
❑ 702 Johnson/Klimkowski/Zepp RC 10.00 5.00
❑ 703 Lou Marone RC 10.00 5.00
❑ 704 Frank Baker RC 10.00 5.00
❑ 705 Tony Cloninger UER 10.00 5.00
❑ 706 John McNamara MG RC 10.00 5.00
❑ 707 Kevin Collins 10.00 5.00
❑ 708 Jose Santiago 10.00 5.00
❑ 709 Mike Fiore 10.00 5.00
❑ 710 Felix Millan 10.00 5.00
❑ 711 Ed Brinkman 10.00 5.00
❑ 712 Nolan Ryan 200.00 125.00
❑ 713 Seattle Pilots TC 25.00 12.50
❑ 714 Al Spangler 10.00 5.00
❑ 715 Mickey Lolich 15.00 7.50
❑ 716 Campisi/Cleveland/Guzman RC 15.00 7.50
❑ 717 Tom Phoebus 10.00 5.00
❑ 718 Ed Spiezio 10.00 5.00
❑ 719 Jim Roland 10.00 5.00
❑ 720 Rick Reichardt 15.00 7.50

1971 Topps

❑ COMPLETE SET (752) 2500.00 1500.00
❑ COMMON CARD (1-393) 1.50 .60
❑ COMMON CARD (394-523) 2.50 1.00
❑ COMMON CARD (524-643) 4.00 1.50
❑ COMMON CARD (644-752) 8.00 4.00
❑ COMMON SP (644-752) 12.00 6.00
❑ WRAPPER (10-CENT) 15.00 10.00

❑ 1 Baltimore Orioles TC 20.00 10.00
❑ 2 Dock Ellis 1.50 .60
❑ 3 Dick McAuliffe 2.00 .75
❑ 4 Vic Davalillo 1.50 .60
❑ 5 Thurman Munson 120.00 70.00
❑ 6 Ed Spiezio 1.50 .60
❑ 7 Jim Holt RC 1.50 .60
❑ 8 Mike McQueen 1.50 .60
❑ 9 George Scott 2.00 .75
❑ 10 Claude Osteen 2.00 .75
❑ 11 Elliott Maddox RC 1.50 .60
❑ 12 Johnny Callison 2.00 .75
❑ 13 C.Brinkman RC/D.Moloney RC 1.50 .60
❑ 14 Dave Concepcion RC 15.00 7.50
❑ 15 Andy Messersmith 2.00 .75
❑ 16 Ken Singleton RC 4.00 1.50
❑ 17 Billy Sorrell 1.50 .60
❑ 18 Norm Miller 1.50 .60
❑ 19 Skip Pitlock RC 1.50 .60
❑ 20 Reggie Jackson 50.00 30.00
❑ 21 Dan McGinn 1.50 .60
❑ 22 Phil Roof 1.50 .60
❑ 23 Oscar Gamble 1.50 .60
❑ 24 Rich Hand RC 1.50 .60
❑ 25 Cito Gaston 2.00 .75
❑ 26 Bert Blyleven RC 20.00 10.00
❑ 27 F.Cambria RC/G.Clines RC 1.50 .60
❑ 28 Ron Klimkowski 1.50 .60
❑ 29 Don Buford 1.50 .60
❑ 30 Phil Niekro 6.00 3.00
❑ 31 Eddie Kasko MG 1.50 .60
❑ 32 Jerry DaVanon 1.50 .60
❑ 33 Del Unser 1.50 .60
❑ 34 Sandy Vance RC 1.50 .60
❑ 35 Lou Piniella 2.00 .75
❑ 36 Dean Chance 2.00 .75
❑ 37 Rich McKinney RC 1.50 .60
❑ 38 Jim Colborn RC 1.50 .60
❑ 39 L.LaGrow RC/G.Lamont RC 2.00 .75
❑ 40 Lee May 2.00 .75
❑ 41 Rick Austin RC 1.50 .60
❑ 42 Boots Day 1.50 .60
❑ 43 Steve Kealey 1.50 .60
❑ 44 Johnny Edwards 1.50 .60
❑ 45 Jim Hunter 6.00 3.00
❑ 46 Dave Campbell 2.00 .75
❑ 47 Johnny Jeter 1.50 .60
❑ 48 Dave Baldwin 1.50 .60
❑ 49 Don Money 1.50 .60
❑ 50 Willie McCovey 10.00 5.00
❑ 51 Steve Kline RC 1.50 .60
❑ 52 O.Brown RC/E.Williams RC 1.50 .60
❑ 53 Paul Blair 2.00 .75
❑ 54 Checklist 1 10.00 5.00
❑ 55 Steve Carlton 20.00 10.00
❑ 56 Duane Josephson 1.50 .60
❑ 57 Von Joshua RC 1.50 .60
❑ 58 Bill Lee 2.00 .75
❑ 59 Gene Mauch MG 2.00 .75
❑ 60 Dick Bosman 1.50 .60
❑ 61 Johnson/Yaz/Oliva LL 4.00 1.50
❑ 62 Carty/Torre/Sang LL 2.00 .75
❑ 63 Howard/Conig/Powell LL 4.00 1.50
❑ 64 Bench/Perez/B.Will LL 6.00 3.00
❑ 65 Howard/Killebrew/Yaz LL 4.00 1.50
❑ 66 Bench/B.Will/Perez LL 6.00 3.00
❑ 67 Segui/Palmer/Wright LL 4.00 1.50
❑ 68 Seaver/Simp/Walk LL 4.00 1.50
❑ 69 Cuellar/McNally/Perry LL 2.00 .75
❑ 70 Gibson/Perry/Jenkins LL 6.00 3.00
❑ 71 McDowell/Lolich/John LL 2.00 .75
❑ 72 Seaver/Gibson/Jenkins LL 6.00 3.00
❑ 73 George Brunet 1.50 .60
❑ 74 P.Hamm RC/J.Nettles RC 1.50 .60
❑ 75 Gary Nolan 2.00 .75
❑ 76 Ted Savage 1.50 .60
❑ 77 Mike Compton RC 1.50 .60
❑ 78 Jim Spencer 1.50 .60
❑ 79 Wade Blasingame 1.50 .60
❑ 80 Bill Melton 1.50 .60
❑ 81 Felix Millan 1.50 .60
❑ 82 Casey Cox 1.50 .60
❑ 83 T.Foli RC/R.Bobb 2.00 .75
❑ 84 Marcel Lachemann RC 1.50 .60
❑ 85 Billy Grabarkewitz 1.50 .60
❑ 86 Mike Kilkenny 1.50 .60

❑ 87 Jack Heidemann RC 1.50 .60
❑ 88 Hal King 1.50 .60
❑ 89 Ken Brett 1.50 .60
❑ 90 Joe Pepitone 2.00 .75
❑ 91 Bob Lemon MG 2.00 .75
❑ 92 Fred Wenz 1.50 .60
❑ 93 N.McRae/D.Riddleberger 1.50 .60
❑ 94 Don Hahn RC 1.50 .60
❑ 95 Luis Tiant 2.00 .75
❑ 96 Joe Hague 1.50 .60
❑ 97 Floyd Wicker 1.50 .60
❑ 98 Joe Decker RC 1.50 .60
❑ 99 Mark Belanger 2.00 .75
❑ 100 Pete Rose 80.00 50.00
❑ 101 Les Cain 1.50 .60
❑ 102 K.Forsch RC/L.Howard RC 2.00 .75
❑ 103 Rich Severson RC 1.50 .60
❑ 104 Dan Frisella 1.50 .60
❑ 105 Tony Conigliaro 2.00 .75
❑ 106 Tom Dukes 1.50 .60
❑ 107 Roy Foster RC 1.50 .60
❑ 108 John Cumberland 1.50 .60
❑ 109 Steve Hovley 1.50 .60
❑ 110 Bill Mazeroski 6.00 3.00
❑ 111 L.Colson RC/B.Mitchell RC 1.50 .60
❑ 112 Manny Mota 2.00 .75
❑ 113 Jerry Crider 1.50 .60
❑ 114 Billy Conigliaro 2.00 .75
❑ 115 Donn Clendenon 2.00 .75
❑ 116 Ken Sanders 1.50 .60
❑ 117 Ted Simmons RC 8.00 4.00
❑ 118 Cookie Rojas 2.00 .75
❑ 119 Frank Lucchesi MG 1.50 .60
❑ 120 Willie Horton 2.00 .75
❑ 121 J.Dunegan/R.Skidmore RC 1.50 .60
❑ 122 Eddie Watt 1.50 .60
❑ 123A Checklist 2 Right 10.00 5.00
❑ 123B Checklist 2 Centered 10.00 5.00
❑ 124 Don Gullett RC 2.00 .75
❑ 125 Ray Fosse 1.50 .60
❑ 126 Danny Coombs 1.50 .60
❑ 127 Danny Thompson RC 2.00 .75
❑ 128 Frank Johnson 1.50 .60
❑ 129 Aurelio Monteagudo 1.50 .60
❑ 130 Denis Menke 1.50 .60
❑ 131 Curt Blefary 1.50 .60
❑ 132 Jose Laboy 1.50 .60
❑ 133 Mickey Lolich 2.00 .75
❑ 134 Jose Arcia 1.50 .60
❑ 135 Rick Monday 2.00 .75
❑ 136 Duffy Dyer 1.50 .60
❑ 137 Marcelino Lopez 1.50 .60
❑ 138 J.Lis/W.Montanez RC 2.00 .75
❑ 139 Paul Casanova 1.50 .60
❑ 140 Gaylord Perry 6.00 3.00
❑ 141 Frank Quilici 1.50 .60
❑ 142 Mack Jones 1.50 .60
❑ 143 Steve Blass 2.00 .75
❑ 144 Jackie Hernandez 1.50 .60
❑ 145 Bill Singer 2.00 .75
❑ 146 Ralph Houk MG 2.00 .75
❑ 147 Bob Priddy 1.50 .60
❑ 148 John Mayberry 2.00 .75
❑ 149 Mike Hershberger 1.50 .60
❑ 150 Sam McDowell 2.00 .75
❑ 151 Tommy Davis 2.00 .75
❑ 152 L.Allen RC/W.Llenas RC 1.50 .60
❑ 153 Gary Ross 1.50 .60
❑ 154 Cesar Gutierrez 1.50 .60
❑ 155 Ken Henderson 1.50 .60
❑ 156 Bart Johnson 1.50 .60
❑ 157 Bob Bailey 2.00 .75
❑ 158 Jerry Reuss 2.00 .75
❑ 159 Jarvis Tatum 1.50 .60
❑ 160 Tom Seaver 30.00 15.00
❑ 161 Coin Checklist 10.00 5.00
❑ 162 Jack Billingham 1.50 .60
❑ 163 Buck Martinez 2.00 .75
❑ 164 F.Duffy RC/M.Wilcox RC 2.00 .75
❑ 165 Cesar Tovar 1.50 .60
❑ 166 Joe Hoerner 1.50 .60
❑ 167 Tom Grieve RC 2.00 .75
❑ 168 Bruce Dal Canton 1.50 .60
❑ 169 Ed Herrmann 1.50 .60
❑ 170 Mike Cuellar 2.00 .75
❑ 171 Bobby Wine 1.50 .60
❑ 172 Duke Sims 1.50 .60
❑ 173 Gil Garrido 1.50 .60
❑ 174 Dave LaRoche RC 1.50 .60
❑ 175 Jim Hickman 1.50 .60
❑ 176 B.Montgomery RC/D.Griffin RC 2.00 .75
❑ 177 Hal McRae 2.00 .75
❑ 178 Dave Duncan 2.00 .75
❑ 179 Mike Corkins 1.50 .60
❑ 180 Al Kaline UER 20.00 10.00
❑ 181 Hal Lanier 1.50 .60
❑ 182 Al Downing 2.00 .75
❑ 183 Gil Hodges MG 4.00 1.50
❑ 184 Stan Bahnsen 1.50 .60
❑ 185 Julian Javier 1.50 .60
❑ 186 Bob Spence RC 1.50 .60
❑ 187 Ted Abernathy 1.50 .60
❑ 188 B.Valentine RC/M.Strahler RC 6.00 3.00
❑ 189 George Mitterwald 1.50 .60
❑ 190 Bob Tolan 1.50 .60
❑ 191 Mike Andrews 1.50 .60
❑ 192 Billy Wilson 1.50 .60
❑ 193 Bob Grich RC 4.00 1.50
❑ 194 Mike Lum 1.50 .60
❑ 195 Boog Powell ALCS 2.00 .75
❑ 196 Dave McNally ALCS 2.00 .75
❑ 197 Jim Palmer ALCS 4.00 1.50
❑ 198 Orioles Celebrate ALCS 2.00 .75
❑ 199 Ty Cline NLCS 2.00 .75
❑ 200 Bobby Tolan NLCS 2.00 .75
❑ 201 Ty Cline NLCS 2.00 .75
❑ 202 Reds Celebrate NLCS 2.00 .75
❑ 203 Larry Gura RC 2.00 .75
❑ 204 B.Smith RC/G.Kopacz RC 1.50 .60
❑ 205 Gerry Moses 1.50 .60
❑ 206 Checklist 3 10.00 5.00
❑ 207 Alan Foster 1.50 .60
❑ 208 Billy Martin MG 4.00 1.50
❑ 209 Steve Renko 1.50 .60
❑ 210 Rod Carew 15.00 7.50
❑ 211 Phil Hennigan RC 1.50 .60
❑ 212 Rich Hebner 2.00 .75
❑ 213 Frank Baker RC 1.50 .60
❑ 214 Al Ferrara 1.50 .60
❑ 215 Diego Segui 1.50 .60
❑ 216 R.Cleveland/L.Melendez RC 1.50 .60
❑ 217 Ed Stroud 1.50 .60
❑ 218 Tony Cloninger 1.50 .60
❑ 219 Elrod Hendricks 1.50 .60
❑ 220 Ron Santo 4.00 1.50
❑ 221 Dave Morehead 1.50 .60
❑ 222 Bob Watson 2.00 .75
❑ 223 Cecil Upshaw 1.50 .60
❑ 224 Alan Gallagher RC 1.50 .60
❑ 225 Gary Peters 1.50 .60
❑ 226 Bill Russell 2.00 .75
❑ 227 Floyd Weaver 1.50 .60
❑ 228 Wayne Garrett 1.50 .60
❑ 229 Jim Hannan 1.50 .60
❑ 230 Willie Stargell 15.00 7.50
❑ 231 V.Colbert RC/J.Lowenstein RC 2.00 .75
❑ 232 John Strohmayer RC 1.50 .60
❑ 233 Larry Bowa 2.00 .75
❑ 234 Jim Lyttle 1.50 .60
❑ 235 Nate Colbert 1.50 .60
❑ 236 Bob Humphreys 1.50 .60
❑ 237 Cesar Cedeno RC 2.00 .75
❑ 238 Chuck Dobson 1.50 .60
❑ 239 Red Schoendienst MG 2.00 .75
❑ 240 Clyde Wright 1.50 .60
❑ 241 Dave Nelson 1.50 .60
❑ 242 Jim Ray 1.50 .60
❑ 243 Carlos May 1.50 .60
❑ 244 Bob Tillman 1.50 .60
❑ 245 Jim Kaat 2.00 .75
❑ 246 Tony Taylor 1.50 .60
❑ 247 J.Cram RC/P.Splittorff RC 2.00 .75
❑ 248 Hoyt Wilhelm 6.00 3.00
❑ 249 Chico Salmon 1.50 .60
❑ 250 Johnny Bench 50.00 30.00
❑ 251 Frank Reberger 1.50 .60
❑ 252 Eddie Leon 1.50 .60
❑ 253 Bill Sudakis 1.50 .60
❑ 254 Cal Koonce 1.50 .60
❑ 255 Bob Robertson 2.00 .75
❑ 256 Tony Gonzalez 1.50 .60
❑ 257 Nelson Briles 2.00 .75
❑ 258 Dick Green 1.50 .60
❑ 259 Dave Marshall 1.50 .60
❑ 260 Tommy Harper 2.00 .75
❑ 261 Darold Knowles 1.50 .60
❑ 262 J.Williams/D.Robinson RC 1.50 .60
❑ 263 John Ellis 1.50 .60
❑ 264 Joe Morgan 8.00 4.00
❑ 265 Jim Northrup 2.00 .75
❑ 266 Bill Stoneman 1.50 .60
❑ 267 Rich Morales 1.50 .60
❑ 268 Philadelphia Phillies TC 4.00 1.50
❑ 269 Gail Hopkins 1.50 .60
❑ 270 Rico Carty 2.00 .75
❑ 271 Bill Zepp 1.50 .60
❑ 272 Tommy Helms 2.00 .75
❑ 273 Pete Richert 1.50 .60
❑ 274 Ron Slocum 1.50 .60
❑ 275 Vada Pinson 2.00 .75
❑ 276 M.Davison RC/G.Foster RC 8.00 4.00
❑ 277 Gary Waslewski 1.50 .60
❑ 278 Jerry Grote 2.00 .75
❑ 279 Lefty Phillips MG 1.50 .60
❑ 280 Ferguson Jenkins 6.00 3.00
❑ 281 Danny Walton 1.50 .60
❑ 282 Jose Pagan 1.50 .60
❑ 283 Dick Such 1.50 .60
❑ 284 Jim Gosger 1.50 .60
❑ 285 Sal Bando 2.00 .75
❑ 286 Jerry McNertney 1.50 .60
❑ 287 Mike Fiore 1.50 .60
❑ 288 Joe Moeller 1.50 .60
❑ 289 Chicago White Sox TC 4.00 1.50
❑ 290 Tony Oliva 4.00 1.50
❑ 291 George Culver 1.50 .60
❑ 292 Jay Johnstone 2.00 .75
❑ 293 Pat Corrales 2.00 .75
❑ 294 Steve Dunning RC 1.50 .60
❑ 295 Bobby Bonds 4.00 1.50
❑ 296 Tom Timmermann 1.50 .60
❑ 297 Johnny Briggs 1.50 .60
❑ 298 Jim Nelson RC 1.50 .60
❑ 299 Ed Kirkpatrick 1.50 .60
❑ 300 Brooks Robinson 20.00 10.00
❑ 301 Earl Wilson 1.50 .60
❑ 302 Phil Gagliano 1.50 .60
❑ 303 Lindy McDaniel 2.00 .75
❑ 304 Ron Brand 1.50 .60
❑ 305 Reggie Smith 2.00 .75
❑ 306 Jim Nash 1.50 .60
❑ 307 Don Wert 1.50 .60
❑ 308 St. Louis Cardinals TC 4.00 1.50
❑ 309 Dick Ellsworth 1.50 .60
❑ 310 Tommie Agee 2.00 .75
❑ 311 Lee Stange 1.50 .60
❑ 312 Harry Walker MG 1.50 .60
❑ 313 Tom Hall 1.50 .60
❑ 314 Jeff Torborg 2.00 .75
❑ 315 Ron Fairly 2.00 .75
❑ 316 Fred Scherman RC 1.50 .60
❑ 317 J.Driscoll RC/A.Mangual 1.50 .60
❑ 318 Rudy May 1.50 .60
❑ 319 Ty Cline 1.50 .60
❑ 320 Dave McNally 2.00 .75
❑ 321 Tom Matchick 1.50 .60
❑ 322 Jim Beauchamp 1.50 .60
❑ 323 Billy Champion 1.50 .60
❑ 324 Graig Nettles 2.00 .75
❑ 325 Juan Marichal 8.00 4.00
❑ 326 Richie Scheinblum 1.50 .60
❑ 327 Boog Powell WS 2.00 .75
❑ 328 Don Buford WS 2.00 .75
❑ 329 Frank Robinson WS 4.00 1.50
❑ 330 Reds Stay Alive WS 2.00 .75
❑ 331 Brooks Robinson WS 6.00 3.00
❑ 332 Orioles Celebrate WS 2.00 .75
❑ 333 Clay Kirby 1.50 .60
❑ 334 Roberto Pena 1.50 .60
❑ 335 Jerry Koosman 2.00 .75
❑ 336 Detroit Tigers TC 4.00 1.50
❑ 337 Jesus Alou 1.50 .60
❑ 338 Gene Tenace 2.00 .75
❑ 339 Wayne Simpson 1.50 .60
❑ 340 Rico Petrocelli 2.00 .75
❑ 341 Steve Garvey RC 40.00 20.00
❑ 342 Frank Tepedino 2.00 .75
❑ 343 E.Acosta RC/M.May RC 2.00 .75

❑ 344 Ellie Rodriguez 1.50 .60
❑ 345 Joel Horlen 1.50 .60
❑ 346 Lum Harris MG 1.50 .60
❑ 347 Ted Uhlaender 1.50 .60
❑ 348 Fred Norman 1.50 .60
❑ 349 Rich Reese 1.50 .60
❑ 350 Billy Williams 6.00 3.00
❑ 351 Jim Shellenback 1.50 .60
❑ 352 Denny Doyle 1.50 .60
❑ 353 Carl Taylor 1.50 .60
❑ 354 Don McMahon 1.50 .60
❑ 355 Bud Harrelson w/Ryan 4.00 1.50
❑ 356 Bob Locker 1.50 .60
❑ 357 Cincinnati Reds TC 4.00 1.50
❑ 358 Danny Cater 1.50 .60
❑ 359 Ron Reed 1.50 .60
❑ 360 Jim Fregosi 2.00 .75
❑ 361 Don Sutton 6.00 3.00
❑ 362 M.Adamson/R.Freed 1.50 .60
❑ 363 Mike Nagy 1.50 .60
❑ 364 Tommy Dean 1.50 .60
❑ 365 Bob Johnson 1.50 .60
❑ 366 Ron Stone 1.50 .60
❑ 367 Dalton Jones 1.50 .60
❑ 368 Bob Veale 2.00 .75
❑ 369 Checklist 4 10.00 5.00
❑ 370 Joe Torre 4.00 1.50
❑ 371 Jack Hiatt 1.50 .60
❑ 372 Lew Krausse 1.50 .60
❑ 373 Tom McCraw 1.50 .60
❑ 374 Clete Boyer 2.00 .75
❑ 375 Steve Hargan 1.50 .60
❑ 376 C.Mashore RC/E.McAnally RC 1.50 .60
❑ 377 Greg Garrett 1.50 .60
❑ 378 Tito Fuentes 1.50 .60
❑ 379 Wayne Granger 1.50 .60
❑ 380 Ted Williams MG 12.00 6.00
❑ 381 Fred Gladding 1.50 .60
❑ 382 Jake Gibbs 1.50 .60
❑ 383 Rod Gaspar 1.50 .60
❑ 384 Rollie Fingers 6.00 3.00
❑ 385 Maury Wills 4.00 1.50
❑ 386 Boston Red Sox TC 2.00 .75
❑ 387 Ron Herbel 1.50 .60
❑ 388 Al Oliver 4.00 1.50
❑ 389 Ed Brinkman 1.50 .60
❑ 390 Glenn Beckert 2.00 .75
❑ 391 S.Brye RC/C.Nash RC 2.00 .75
❑ 392 Grant Jackson 1.50 .60
❑ 393 Merv Rettenmund 2.00 .75
❑ 394 Clay Carroll 2.50 1.00
❑ 395 Roy White 4.00 1.50
❑ 396 Dick Schofield 2.50 1.00
❑ 397 Alvin Dark MG 4.00 1.50
❑ 398 Howie Reed 2.50 1.00
❑ 399 Jim French 2.50 1.00
❑ 400 Hank Aaron 60.00 35.00
❑ 401 Tom Murphy 2.50 1.00
❑ 402 Los Angeles Dodgers TC 6.00 3.00
❑ 403 Joe Coleman 2.50 1.00
❑ 404 B.Harris RC/R.Metzger RC 2.50 1.00
❑ 405 Leo Cardenas 2.50 1.00
❑ 406 Ray Sadecki 2.50 1.00
❑ 407 Joe Rudi 4.00 1.50
❑ 408 Rafael Robles 2.50 1.00
❑ 409 Don Pavletich 2.50 1.00
❑ 410 Ken Holtzman 4.00 1.50
❑ 411 George Spriggs 2.50 1.00
❑ 412 Jerry Johnson 2.50 1.00
❑ 413 Pat Kelly 2.50 1.00
❑ 414 Woodie Fryman 2.50 1.00
❑ 415 Mike Hegan 2.50 1.00
❑ 416 Gene Alley 2.50 1.00
❑ 417 Dick Hall 2.50 1.00
❑ 418 Adolfo Phillips 2.50 1.00
❑ 419 Ron Hansen 2.50 1.00
❑ 420 Jim Merritt 2.50 1.00
❑ 421 John Stephenson 2.50 1.00
❑ 422 Frank Bertaina 2.50 1.00
❑ 423 D.Saunders/T.Marting RC 2.50 1.00
❑ 424 Roberto Rodriquez 2.50 1.00
❑ 425 Doug Rader 4.00 1.50
❑ 426 Chris Cannizzaro 2.50 1.00
❑ 427 Bernie Allen 2.50 1.00
❑ 428 Jim McAndrew 2.50 1.00
❑ 429 Chuck Hinton 2.50 1.00
❑ 430 Wes Parker 4.00 1.50
❑ 431 Tom Burgmeier 2.50 1.00
❑ 432 Bob Didier 2.50 1.00
❑ 433 Skip Lockwood 2.50 1.00
❑ 434 Gary Sutherland 2.50 1.00
❑ 435 Jose Cardenal 4.00 1.50
❑ 436 Wilbur Wood 4.00 1.50
❑ 437 Danny Murtaugh MG 4.00 1.50
❑ 438 Mike McCormick 4.00 1.50
❑ 439 G.Luzinski RC/S.Reid 6.00 3.00
❑ 440 Bert Campaneris 4.00 1.50
❑ 441 Milt Pappas 4.00 1.50
❑ 442 California Angels TC 4.00 1.50
❑ 443 Rich Robertson 2.50 1.00
❑ 444 Jimmie Price 2.50 1.00
❑ 445 Art Shamsky 2.50 1.00
❑ 446 Bobby Bolin 2.50 1.00
❑ 447 Cesar Geronimo RC 4.00 1.50
❑ 448 Dave Roberts 2.50 1.00
❑ 449 Brant Alyea 2.50 1.00
❑ 450 Bob Gibson 15.00 7.50
❑ 451 Joe Keough 2.50 1.00
❑ 452 John Boccabella 2.50 1.00
❑ 453 Terry Crowley 2.50 1.00
❑ 454 Mike Paul 2.50 1.00
❑ 455 Don Kessinger 4.00 1.50
❑ 456 Bob Meyer 2.50 1.00
❑ 457 Willie Smith 2.50 1.00
❑ 458 R.Lolich RC/D.Lemonds RC 2.50 1.00
❑ 459 Jim Lefebvre 2.50 1.00
❑ 460 Fritz Peterson 2.50 1.00
❑ 461 Jim Ray Hart 2.50 1.00
❑ 462 Washington Senators TC 6.00 3.00
❑ 463 Tom Kelley 2.50 1.00
❑ 464 Aurelio Rodriguez 2.50 1.00
❑ 465 Tim McCarver 6.00 3.00
❑ 466 Ken Berry 2.50 1.00
❑ 467 Al Santorini 2.50 1.00
❑ 468 Frank Fernandez 2.50 1.00
❑ 469 Bob Aspromonte 2.50 1.00
❑ 470 Bob Oliver 2.50 1.00
❑ 471 Tom Griffin 2.50 1.00
❑ 472 Ken Rudolph 2.50 1.00
❑ 473 Gary Wagner 2.50 1.00
❑ 474 Jim Fairey 2.50 1.00
❑ 475 Ron Perranoski 2.50 1.00
❑ 476 Dal Maxvill 2.50 1.00
❑ 477 Earl Weaver MG 6.00 3.00
❑ 478 Bernie Carbo 2.50 1.00
❑ 479 Dennis Higgins 2.50 1.00
❑ 480 Manny Sanguillen 4.00 1.50
❑ 481 Daryl Patterson 2.50 1.00
❑ 482 San Diego Padres TC 6.00 3.00
❑ 483 Gene Michael 2.50 1.00
❑ 484 Don Wilson 2.50 1.00
❑ 485 Ken McMullen 2.50 1.00
❑ 486 Steve Huntz 2.50 1.00
❑ 487 Paul Schaal 2.50 1.00
❑ 488 Jerry Stephenson 2.50 1.00
❑ 489 Luis Alvarado 2.50 1.00
❑ 490 Deron Johnson 2.50 1.00
❑ 491 Jim Hardin 2.50 1.00
❑ 492 Ken Boswell 2.50 1.00
❑ 493 Dave May 2.50 1.00
❑ 494 R.Garr/R.Kester 4.00 1.50
❑ 495 Felipe Alou 4.00 1.50
❑ 496 Woody Woodward 2.50 1.00
❑ 497 Horacio Pina RC 2.50 1.00
❑ 498 John Kennedy 2.50 1.00
❑ 499 Checklist 5 10.00 5.00
❑ 500 Jim Perry 4.00 1.50
❑ 501 Andy Etchebarren 2.50 1.00
❑ 502 Chicago Cubs TC 6.00 3.00
❑ 503 Gates Brown 4.00 1.50
❑ 504 Ken Wright RC 2.50 1.00
❑ 505 Ollie Brown 2.50 1.00
❑ 506 Bobby Knoop 2.50 1.00
❑ 507 George Stone 2.50 1.00
❑ 508 Roger Repoz 2.50 1.00
❑ 509 Jim Grant 2.50 1.00
❑ 510 Ken Harrelson 4.00 1.50
❑ 511 Chris Short w/Rose 4.00 1.50
❑ 512 D.Mills RC/M.Garman RC 2.50 1.00
❑ 513 Nolan Ryan 150.00 90.00
❑ 514 Ron Woods 2.50 1.00
❑ 515 Carl Morton 2.50 1.00
❑ 516 Ted Kubiak 2.50 1.00
❑ 517 Charlie Fox MG RC 2.50 1.00
❑ 518 Joe Grzenda 2.50 1.00
❑ 519 Willie Crawford 2.50 1.00
❑ 520 Tommy John 6.00 3.00
❑ 521 Leron Lee 2.50 1.00
❑ 522 Minnesota Twins TC 6.00 3.00
❑ 523 John Odom 2.50 1.00
❑ 524 Mickey Stanley 6.00 3.00
❑ 525 Ernie Banks 50.00 30.00
❑ 526 Ray Jarvis 4.00 1.50
❑ 527 Cleon Jones 6.00 3.00
❑ 528 Wally Bunker 4.00 1.50
❑ 529 Hernandez/Bucker/Perez RC 6.00 3.00
❑ 530 Carl Yastrzemski 30.00 15.00
❑ 531 Mike Torrez 4.00 1.50
❑ 532 Bill Rigney MG 4.00 1.50
❑ 533 Mike Ryan 4.00 1.50
❑ 534 Luke Walker 4.00 1.50
❑ 535 Curt Flood 6.00 3.00
❑ 536 Claude Raymond 4.00 1.50
❑ 537 Tom Egan 4.00 1.50
❑ 538 Angel Bravo 4.00 1.50
❑ 539 Larry Brown 4.00 1.50
❑ 540 Larry Dierker 6.00 3.00
❑ 541 Bob Burda 4.00 1.50
❑ 542 Bob Miller 4.00 1.50
❑ 543 New York Yankees TC 10.00 5.00
❑ 544 Vida Blue 6.00 3.00
❑ 545 Dick Dietz 4.00 1.50
❑ 546 John Matias 4.00 1.50
❑ 547 Pat Dobson 6.00 3.00
❑ 548 Don Mason 4.00 1.50
❑ 549 Jim Brewer 6.00 3.00
❑ 550 Harmon Killebrew 25.00 12.50
❑ 551 Frank Linzy 4.00 1.50
❑ 552 Buddy Bradford 4.00 1.50
❑ 553 Kevin Collins 4.00 1.50
❑ 554 Lowell Palmer 4.00 1.50
❑ 555 Walt Williams 4.00 1.50
❑ 556 Jim McGlothlin 4.00 1.50
❑ 557 Tom Satriano 4.00 1.50
❑ 558 Hector Torres 4.00 1.50
❑ 559 Cox/Gogolewsk/Jones RC 4.00 1.50
❑ 560 Rusty Staub 6.00 3.00
❑ 561 Syd O'Brien 4.00 1.50
❑ 562 Dave Giusti 4.00 1.50
❑ 563 San Francisco Giants TC 8.00 4.00
❑ 564 Al Fitzmorris 4.00 1.50
❑ 565 Jim Wynn 6.00 3.00
❑ 566 Tim Cullen 4.00 1.50
❑ 567 Walt Alston MG 8.00 4.00
❑ 568 Sal Campisi 4.00 1.50
❑ 569 Ivan Murrell 4.00 1.50
❑ 570 Jim Palmer 30.00 15.00
❑ 571 Ted Sizemore 4.00 1.50
❑ 572 Jerry Kenney 4.00 1.50
❑ 573 Ed Kranepool 6.00 3.00
❑ 574 Jim Bunning 8.00 4.00
❑ 575 Bill Freehan 6.00 3.00
❑ 576 Garrett/Davis/Jestadt RC 4.00 1.50
❑ 577 Jim Lonborg 6.00 3.00
❑ 578 Ron Hunt 4.00 1.50
❑ 579 Marty Pattin 4.00 1.50
❑ 580 Tony Perez 20.00 10.00
❑ 581 Roger Nelson 4.00 1.50
❑ 582 Dave Cash 6.00 3.00
❑ 583 Ron Cook RC 4.00 1.50
❑ 584 Cleveland Indians TC 8.00 4.00
❑ 585 Willie Davis 6.00 3.00
❑ 586 Dick Woodson 4.00 1.50
❑ 587 Sonny Jackson 4.00 1.50
❑ 588 Tom Bradley RC 4.00 1.50
❑ 589 Bob Barton 4.00 1.50
❑ 590 Alex Johnson 6.00 3.00
❑ 591 Jackie Brown RC 4.00 1.50
❑ 592 Randy Hundley 6.00 3.00
❑ 593 Jack Aker 4.00 1.50
❑ 594 Chlupsa/Stinson/Hrabosky RC 6.00 3.00
❑ 595 Dave Johnson 6.00 3.00
❑ 596 Mike Jorgensen 4.00 1.50
❑ 597 Ken Suarez 4.00 1.50
❑ 598 Rick Wise 6.00 3.00
❑ 599 Norm Cash 6.00 3.00
❑ 600 Willie Mays 100.00 60.00
❑ 601 Ken Tatum 4.00 1.50

❑ 602 Marty Martinez 4.00 1.50
❑ 603 Pittsburgh Pirates TC 8.00 4.00
❑ 604 John Gelnar 4.00 1.50
❑ 605 Orlando Cepeda 8.00 4.00
❑ 606 Chuck Taylor 4.00 1.50
❑ 607 Paul Ratliff 4.00 1.50
❑ 608 Mike Wegener 4.00 1.50
❑ 609 Leo Durocher MG 8.00 4.00
❑ 610 Amos Otis 6.00 3.00
❑ 611 Tom Phoebus 4.00 1.50
❑ 612 Camilli/Ford/Mingori RC 4.00 1.50
❑ 613 Pedro Borbon 4.00 1.50
❑ 614 Billy Cowan 4.00 1.50
❑ 615 Mel Stottlemyre 6.00 3.00
❑ 616 Larry Hisle 6.00 3.00
❑ 617 Clay Dalrymple 4.00 1.50
❑ 618 Tug McGraw 6.00 3.00
❑ 619A Checklist 6 ERR w/o Copy 10.00 5.00
❑ 619B Checklist 6 COR w/Copy 6.00 3.00
❑ 620 Frank Howard 6.00 3.00
❑ 621 Ron Bryant 4.00 1.50
❑ 622 Joe Lahoud 4.00 1.50
❑ 623 Pat Jarvis 4.00 1.50
❑ 624 Oakland Athletics TC 8.00 4.00
❑ 625 Lou Brock 30.00 15.00
❑ 626 Freddie Patek 6.00 3.00
❑ 627 Steve Hamilton 4.00 1.50
❑ 628 John Bateman 4.00 1.50
❑ 629 John Hiller 6.00 3.00
❑ 630 Roberto Clemente 150.00 90.00
❑ 631 Eddie Fisher 4.00 1.50
❑ 632 Darrel Chaney 4.00 1.50
❑ 633 Brooks/Koegel/Northey RC 4.00 1.50
❑ 634 Phil Regan 4.00 1.50
❑ 635 Bobby Murcer 6.00 3.00
❑ 636 Denny Lemaster 4.00 1.50
❑ 637 Dave Bristol MG 4.00 1.50
❑ 638 Stan Williams 4.00 1.50
❑ 639 Tom Haller 4.00 1.50
❑ 640 Frank Robinson 40.00 20.00
❑ 641 New York Mets TC 15.00 7.50
❑ 642 Jim Roland 4.00 1.50
❑ 643 Rick Reichardt 4.00 1.50
❑ 644 Jim Stewart SP 12.00 6.00
❑ 645 Jim Maloney SP 15.00 7.50
❑ 646 Bobby Floyd SP 12.00 6.00
❑ 647 Juan Pizarro 8.00 4.00
❑ 648 Folkers/Martinez/Matlack RC 25.00 12.50
❑ 649 Sparky Lyle SP 15.00 7.50
❑ 650 Richie Allen SP 30.00 15.00
❑ 651 Jerry Robertson SP 12.00 6.00
❑ 652 Atlanta Braves TC 12.00 6.00
❑ 653 Russ Snyder SP 12.00 6.00
❑ 654 Don Shaw SP 12.00 6.00
❑ 655 Mike Epstein SP 12.00 6.00
❑ 656 Gerry Nyman SP 12.00 6.00
❑ 657 Jose Azcue 8.00 4.00
❑ 658 Paul Lindblad SP 12.00 6.00
❑ 659 Byron Browne SP 12.00 6.00
❑ 660 Ray Culp 8.00 4.00
❑ 661 Chuck Tanner MG SP 15.00 7.50
❑ 662 Mike Hedlund SP 12.00 6.00
❑ 663 Marv Staehle 8.00 4.00
❑ 664 Reynolds/Reynolds/Reynolds RC 12.00 6.00
❑ 665 Ron Swoboda SP 15.00 7.50
❑ 666 Gene Brabender SP 12.00 6.00
❑ 667 Pete Ward 8.00 4.00
❑ 668 Gary Neibauer 8.00 4.00
❑ 669 Ike Brown SP 12.00 6.00
❑ 670 Bill Hands 8.00 4.00
❑ 671 Bill Voss SP 12.00 6.00
❑ 672 Ed Crosby SP RC 12.00 6.00
❑ 673 Gerry Janeski SP RC 12.00 6.00
❑ 674 Montreal Expos TC 12.00 6.00
❑ 675 Dave Boswell 8.00 4.00
❑ 676 Tommie Reynolds 8.00 4.00
❑ 677 Jack DiLauro SP 12.00 6.00
❑ 678 George Thomas 8.00 4.00
❑ 679 Don O'Riley 8.00 4.00
❑ 680 Don Mincher SP 12.00 6.00
❑ 681 Bill Butler 8.00 4.00
❑ 682 Terry Harmon 8.00 4.00
❑ 683 Bill Burbach SP 12.00 6.00
❑ 684 Curt Motton 8.00 4.00
❑ 685 Moe Drabowsky 8.00 4.00
❑ 686 Chico Ruiz SP 12.00 6.00
❑ 687 Ron Taylor SP 12.00 6.00
❑ 688 S.Anderson MG SP 30.00 15.00
❑ 689 Frank Baker 8.00 4.00
❑ 690 Bob Moose 8.00 4.00
❑ 691 Bobby Heise 8.00 4.00
❑ 692 Haydel/Moret/Twitchell RC 12.00 6.00
❑ 693 Jose Pena SP 12.00 6.00
❑ 694 Rick Renick SP 12.00 6.00
❑ 695 Joe Niekro 12.00 6.00
❑ 696 Jerry Morales 8.00 4.00
❑ 697 Rickey Clark SP 12.00 6.00
❑ 698 Milwaukee Brewers TC SP 20.00 10.00
❑ 699 Jim Britton 8.00 4.00
❑ 700 Boog Powell SP 25.00 12.50
❑ 701 Bob Garibaldi 8.00 4.00
❑ 702 Milt Ramirez RC 8.00 4.00
❑ 703 Mike Kekich 8.00 4.00
❑ 704 J.C. Martin SP 12.00 6.00
❑ 705 Dick Selma SP 12.00 6.00
❑ 706 Joe Foy SP 12.00 6.00
❑ 707 Fred Lasher 8.00 4.00
❑ 708 Russ Nagelson SP 12.00 6.00
❑ 709 Baker/Baylor/Pac SP RC 80.00 50.00
❑ 710 Sonny Siebert 8.00 4.00
❑ 711 Larry Stahl SP 12.00 6.00
❑ 712 Jose Martinez 8.00 4.00
❑ 713 Mike Marshall SP 15.00 7.50
❑ 714 Dick Williams MG SP 15.00 7.50
❑ 715 Horace Clarke SP 15.00 7.50
❑ 716 Dave Leonhard 8.00 4.00
❑ 717 Tommie Aaron SP 12.00 6.00
❑ 718 Billy Wynne 8.00 4.00
❑ 719 Jerry May SP 12.00 6.00
❑ 720 Matty Alou 12.00 6.00
❑ 721 John Morris 8.00 4.00
❑ 722 Houston Astros TC SP 20.00 10.00
❑ 723 Vicente Romo SP 12.00 6.00
❑ 724 Tom Tischinski SP 12.00 6.00
❑ 725 Gary Gentry SP 12.00 6.00
❑ 726 Paul Popovich 8.00 4.00
❑ 727 Ray Lamb SP 12.00 6.00
❑ 728 Redmond/Lampard/Williams RC 8.00 4.00
❑ 729 Dick Billings RC 8.00 4.00
❑ 730 Jim Rooker 8.00 4.00
❑ 731 Jim Qualls SP 12.00 6.00
❑ 732 Bob Reed 8.00 4.00
❑ 733 Lee Maye SP 12.00 6.00
❑ 734 Rob Gardner SP 12.00 6.00
❑ 735 Mike Shannon SP 15.00 7.50
❑ 736 Mel Queen SP 12.00 6.00
❑ 737 Preston Gomez MG SP 12.00 6.00
❑ 738 Russ Gibson SP 12.00 6.00
❑ 739 Barry Lersch SP 12.00 6.00
❑ 740 Luis Aparicio SP 30.00 15.00
❑ 741 Skip Guinn 8.00 4.00
❑ 742 Kansas City Royals TC 12.00 6.00
❑ 743 John O'Donoghue SP 12.00 6.00
❑ 744 Chuck Manuel SP 12.00 6.00
❑ 745 Sandy Alomar SP 12.00 6.00
❑ 746 Andy Kosco 8.00 4.00
❑ 747 Severinsen/Spinks/Moore RC 8.00 4.00
❑ 748 John Purdin SP 12.00 6.00
❑ 749 Ken Szotkiewicz RC 8.00 4.00
❑ 750 Denny McLain SP 25.00 12.50
❑ 751 Al Weis SP 15.00 7.50
❑ 752 Dick Drago 12.00 6.00

1972 Topps

CARDINALS
BOB GIBSON

❑ COMPLETE SET (787) 1500.00 1000.00
❑ COMMON CARD (1-132) .60 .25
❑ COMMON CARD (133-263) 1.00 .40
❑ COMMON CARD (264-394) 1.25 .50
❑ COMMON CARD (395-525) 1.50 .60
❑ COMMON CARD (526-656) 4.00 1.50
❑ COMMON CARD (657-787) 12.00 6.00
❑ WRAPPER (10-CENT) 15.00 10.00
❑ 1 Pittsburgh Pirates TC 8.00 4.00
❑ 2 Ray Culp .60 .25
❑ 3 Bob Tolan .60 .25
❑ 4 Checklist 1-132 6.00 3.00
❑ 5 John Bateman .60 .25
❑ 6 Fred Scherman .60 .25
❑ 7 Enzo Hernandez .60 .25
❑ 8 Ron Swoboda 1.25 .50
❑ 9 Stan Williams .60 .25
❑ 10 Amos Otis 1.25 .50
❑ 11 Bobby Valentine 1.25 .50
❑ 12 Jose Cardenal .60 .25
❑ 13 Joe Grzenda .60 .25
❑ 14 Koegel/Anderson/Twitchell RC .60 .25
❑ 15 Walt Williams .60 .25
❑ 16 Mike Jorgensen .60 .25
❑ 17 Dave Duncan 1.25 .50
❑ 18A Juan Pizarro Yellow .60 .25
❑ 18B Juan Pizarro Green 5.00 2.00
❑ 19 Billy Cowan .60 .25
❑ 20 Don Wilson .60 .25
❑ 21 Atlanta Braves TC 1.50 .60
❑ 22 Rob Gardner .60 .25
❑ 23 Ted Kubiak .60 .25
❑ 24 Ted Ford .60 .25
❑ 25 Bill Singer .60 .25
❑ 26 Andy Etchebarren .60 .25
❑ 27 Bob Johnson .60 .25
❑ 28 Gebhard/Brye Haydel RC .60 .25
❑ 29A Bill Bonham Yellow RC .60 .25
❑ 29B Bill Bonham Green 5.00 2.00
❑ 30 Rico Petrocelli 1.25 .50
❑ 31 Cleon Jones 1.25 .50
❑ 32 Cleon Jones IA .60 .25
❑ 33 Billy Martin MG 4.00 1.50
❑ 34 Billy Martin IA 2.50 1.00
❑ 35 Jerry Johnson .60 .25
❑ 36 Jerry Johnson IA .60 .25
❑ 37 Carl Yastrzemski 10.00 5.00
❑ 38 Carl Yastrzemski IA 8.00 4.00
❑ 39 Bob Barton .60 .25
❑ 40 Bob Barton IA .60 .25
❑ 41 Tommy Davis 1.25 .50
❑ 42 Tommy Davis IA .60 .25
❑ 43 Rick Wise 1.25 .50
❑ 44 Rick Wise IA .60 .25
❑ 45A Glenn Beckert Yellow 1.25 .50
❑ 45B Glenn Beckert Green 5.00 2.00
❑ 46 Glenn Beckert IA .60 .25
❑ 47 John Ellis .60 .25
❑ 48 John Ellis IA .60 .25
❑ 49 Willie Mays 40.00 20.00
❑ 50 Willie Mays IA 20.00 10.00
❑ 51 Harmon Killebrew 8.00 4.00
❑ 52 Harmon Killebrew IA 4.00 1.50
❑ 53 Bud Harrelson 1.25 .50
❑ 54 Bud Harrelson IA .60 .25
❑ 55 Clyde Wright .60 .25
❑ 56 Rich Chiles RC .60 .25
❑ 57 Bob Oliver .60 .25
❑ 58 Ernie McAnally .60 .25
❑ 59 Fred Stanley RC .60 .25
❑ 60 Manny Sanguillen 1.25 .50
❑ 61 Hooten/Hisler/Stephenson RC 1.25 .50
❑ 62 Angel Mangual .60 .25
❑ 63 Duke Sims .60 .25
❑ 64 Pete Broberg RC .60 .25
❑ 65 Cesar Cedeno 1.25 .50
❑ 66 Ray Corbin RC .60 .25
❑ 67 Red Schoendienst MG 2.50 1.00
❑ 68 Jim York RC .60 .25
❑ 69 Roger Freed .60 .25
❑ 70 Mike Cuellar 1.25 .50
❑ 71 California Angels TC 1.50 .60
❑ 72 Bruce Kison RC .60 .25
❑ 73 Steve Huntz .60 .25
❑ 74 Cecil Upshaw .60 .25
❑ 75 Bert Campaneris 1.25 .50

❑ 76 Don Carrithers RC .60 .25
❑ 77 Ron Theobald RC .60 .25
❑ 78 Steve Arlin RC .60 .25
❑ 79 C.Fisk RC/C.Cooper RC 50.00 30.00
❑ 80 Tony Perez 4.00 1.50
❑ 81 Mike Hedlund .60 .25
❑ 82 Ron Woods .60 .25
❑ 83 Dalton Jones .60 .25
❑ 84 Vince Colbert .60 .25
❑ 85 Torre/Garr/Beckert LL 2.50 1.00
❑ 86 Oliva/Murcer/Rett LL 2.50 1.00
❑ 87 Torre/Stargell/Aaron LL 4.00 1.50
❑ 88 Kill/F.Rob/Smith LL 4.00 1.50
❑ 89 Stargell/Aaron/May LL 2.50 1.00
❑ 90 Melton/Cash/Jackson LL 2.50 1.00
❑ 91 Seaver/Roberts/Wilson LL 2.50 1.00
❑ 92 Blue/Wood/Palmer LL 2.50 1.00
❑ 93 Jenkins/Carlton/Seaver LL 4.00 1.50
❑ 94 Lolich/Blue/Wood LL 2.50 1.00
❑ 95 Seaver/Jenkins/Stone LL 4.00 1.50
❑ 96 Lolich/Blue/Coleman LL 2.50 1.00
❑ 97 Tom Kelley .60 .25
❑ 98 Chuck Tanner MG 1.25 .50
❑ 99 Ross Grimsley RC .60 .25
❑ 100 Frank Robinson 8.00 4.00
❑ 101 Grief/Richard/Busse RC 2.50 1.00
❑ 102 Lloyd Allen .60 .25
❑ 103 Checklist 133-263 6.00 3.00
❑ 104 Toby Harrah RC 1.25 .50
❑ 105 Gary Gentry .60 .25
❑ 106 Milwaukee Brewers TC 1.50 .60
❑ 107 Jose Cruz RC 1.25 .50
❑ 108 Gary Waslewski .60 .25
❑ 109 Jerry May .60 .25
❑ 110 Ron Hunt .60 .25
❑ 111 Jim Grant .60 .25
❑ 112 Greg Luzinski 1.25 .50
❑ 113 Rogelio Moret .60 .25
❑ 114 Bill Buckner 1.25 .50
❑ 115 Jim Fregosi 1.25 .50
❑ 116 Ed Farmer RC .60 .25
❑ 117A Cleo James Yellow RC .60 .25
❑ 117B Cleo James Green 5.00 2.00
❑ 118 Skip Lockwood .60 .25
❑ 119 Marty Perez .60 .25
❑ 120 Bill Freehan 1.25 .50
❑ 121 Ed Sprague .60 .25
❑ 122 Larry Biittner RC .60 .25
❑ 123 Ed Acosta .60 .25
❑ 124 Closter/Torres/Hambright RC .60 .25
❑ 125 Dave Cash 1.25 .50
❑ 126 Bart Johnson .60 .25
❑ 127 Duffy Dyer .60 .25
❑ 128 Eddie Watt .60 .25
❑ 129 Charlie Fox MG .60 .25
❑ 130 Bob Gibson 8.00 4.00
❑ 131 Jim Nettles .60 .25
❑ 132 Joe Morgan 6.00 3.00
❑ 133 Joe Keough 1.00 .40
❑ 134 Carl Morton 1.00 .40
❑ 135 Vada Pinson 2.00 .75
❑ 136 Darrel Chaney 1.00 .40
❑ 137 Dick Williams MG 2.00 .75
❑ 138 Mike Kekich 1.00 .40
❑ 139 Tim McCarver 2.00 .75
❑ 140 Pat Dobson 2.00 .75
❑ 141 Capra/Stanton/Matlack RC 2.00 .75
❑ 142 Chris Chambliss RC 4.00 1.50
❑ 143 Garry Jestadt 1.00 .40
❑ 144 Marty Pattin 1.00 .40
❑ 145 Don Kessinger 2.00 .75
❑ 146 Steve Kealey 1.00 .40
❑ 147 Dave Kingman RC 6.00 3.00
❑ 148 Dick Billings 1.00 .40
❑ 149 Gary Neibauer 1.00 .40
❑ 150 Norm Cash 2.00 .75
❑ 151 Jim Brewer 1.00 .40
❑ 152 Gene Clines 1.00 .40
❑ 153 Rick Auerbach RC 1.00 .40
❑ 154 Ted Simmons 4.00 1.50
❑ 155 Larry Dierker 1.00 .40
❑ 156 Minnesota Twins TC 2.00 .75
❑ 157 Don Gullett 1.00 .40
❑ 158 Jerry Kenney 1.00 .40
❑ 159 John Boccabella 1.00 .40
❑ 160 Andy Messersmith 2.00 .75
❑ 161 Brock Davis 1.00 .40
❑ 162 Bell/Porter/Reynolds RC 2.00 .75
❑ 163 Tug McGraw 4.00 1.50
❑ 164 Tug McGraw IA 2.00 .75
❑ 165 Chris Speier RC 2.00 .75
❑ 166 Chris Speier IA 1.00 .40
❑ 167 Deron Johnson 1.00 .40
❑ 168 Deron Johnson IA 1.00 .40
❑ 169 Vida Blue 4.00 1.50
❑ 170 Vida Blue IA 2.00 .75
❑ 171 Darrell Evans 4.00 1.50
❑ 172 Darrell Evans IA 2.00 .75
❑ 173 Clay Kirby 1.00 .40
❑ 174 Clay Kirby IA 1.00 .40
❑ 175 Tom Haller 1.00 .40
❑ 176 Tom Haller IA 1.00 .40
❑ 177 Paul Schaal 1.00 .40
❑ 178 Paul Schaal IA 1.00 .40
❑ 179 Dock Ellis 1.00 .40
❑ 180 Dock Ellis IA 1.00 .40
❑ 181 Ed Kranepool 2.00 .75
❑ 182 Ed Kranepool IA 1.00 .40
❑ 183 Bill Melton 1.00 .40
❑ 184 Bill Melton IA 1.00 .40
❑ 185 Ron Bryant 1.00 .40
❑ 186 Ron Bryant IA 1.00 .40
❑ 187 Gates Brown 1.00 .40
❑ 188 Frank Lucchesi MG 1.00 .40
❑ 189 Gene Tenace 2.00 .75
❑ 190 Dave Giusti 1.00 .40
❑ 191 Jeff Burroughs RC 4.00 1.50
❑ 192 Chicago Cubs TC 2.00 .75
❑ 193 Kurt Bevacqua RC 1.00 .40
❑ 194 Fred Norman 1.00 .40
❑ 195 Orlando Cepeda 6.00 3.00
❑ 196 Mel Queen 1.00 .40
❑ 197 Johnny Briggs 1.00 .40
❑ 198 Hough/O'Brien/Strahler RC 6.00 3.00
❑ 199 Mike Fiore 1.00 .40
❑ 200 Lou Brock 8.00 4.00
❑ 201 Phil Roof 1.00 .40
❑ 202 Scipio Spinks 1.00 .40
❑ 203 Ron Blomberg RC 1.00 .40
❑ 204 Tommy Helms 1.00 .40
❑ 205 Dick Drago 1.00 .40
❑ 206 Dal Maxvill 1.00 .40
❑ 207 Tom Egan 1.00 .40
❑ 208 Milt Pappas 2.00 .75
❑ 209 Joe Rudi 2.00 .75
❑ 210 Denny McLain 2.00 .75
❑ 211 Gary Sutherland 1.00 .40
❑ 212 Grant Jackson 1.00 .40
❑ 213 Parker/Kusnyer/Silverio RC 1.00 .40
❑ 214 Mike McQueen 1.00 .40
❑ 215 Alex Johnson 2.00 .75
❑ 216 Joe Niekro 2.00 .75
❑ 217 Roger Metzger 1.00 .40
❑ 218 Eddie Kasko MG 1.00 .40
❑ 219 Rennie Stennett RC 2.00 .75
❑ 220 Jim Perry 2.00 .75
❑ 221 NL Playoffs Bucs 2.00 .75
❑ 222 AL Playoffs B.Robinson 4.00 1.50
❑ 223 Dave McNally WS 2.00 .75
❑ 224 D.Johnson/M.Belanger WS 2.00 .75
❑ 225 Manny Sanguillen WS 2.00 .75
❑ 226 Roberto Clemente WS 8.00 4.00
❑ 227 Nellie Briles WS 2.00 .75
❑ 228 F.Robinson/M.Sanguillen WS 2.00 .75
❑ 229 Steve Blass WS 2.00 .75
❑ 230 Pirates Celebrate WS 2.00 .75
❑ 231 Casey Cox 1.00 .40
❑ 232 Arnold/Barr/Rader RC 1.00 .40
❑ 233 Jay Johnstone 2.00 .75
❑ 234 Ron Taylor 1.00 .40
❑ 235 Merv Rettenmund 1.00 .40
❑ 236 Jim McGlothlin 1.00 .40
❑ 237 New York Yankees TC 2.00 .75
❑ 238 Leron Lee 1.00 .40
❑ 239 Tom Timmermann 1.00 .40
❑ 240 Richie Allen 2.00 .75
❑ 241 Rollie Fingers 6.00 3.00
❑ 242 Don Mincher 1.00 .40
❑ 243 Frank Linzy 1.00 .40
❑ 244 Steve Braun RC 1.00 .40
❑ 245 Tommie Agee 2.00 .75
❑ 246 Tom Burgmeier 1.00 .40
❑ 247 Milt May 1.00 .40
❑ 248 Tom Bradley 1.00 .40
❑ 249 Harry Walker MG 1.00 .40
❑ 250 Boog Powell 2.00 .75
❑ 251 Checklist 264-394 6.00 3.00
❑ 252 Ken Reynolds 1.00 .40
❑ 253 Sandy Alomar 2.00 .75
❑ 254 Boots Day 1.00 .40
❑ 255 Jim Lonborg 2.00 .75
❑ 256 George Foster 2.00 .75
❑ 257 Foor/Hosley/Jata RC 1.00 .40
❑ 258 Randy Hundley 1.00 .40
❑ 259 Sparky Lyle 2.00 .75
❑ 260 Ralph Garr 2.00 .75
❑ 261 Steve Mingori 1.00 .40
❑ 262 San Diego Padres TC 2.00 .75
❑ 263 Felipe Alou 2.00 .75
❑ 264 Tommy John 2.00 .75
❑ 265 Wes Parker 2.00 .75
❑ 266 Bobby Bolin 1.25 .50
❑ 267 Dave Concepcion 4.00 1.50
❑ 268 D.Anderson RC/C.Floethe RC 1.25 .50
❑ 269 Don Hahn 1.25 .50
❑ 270 Jim Palmer 8.00 4.00
❑ 271 Ken Rudolph 1.25 .50
❑ 272 Mickey Rivers RC 2.00 .75
❑ 273 Bobby Floyd 1.25 .50
❑ 274 Al Severinsen 1.25 .50
❑ 275 Cesar Tovar 1.25 .50
❑ 276 Gene Mauch MG 2.00 .75
❑ 277 Elliott Maddox 1.25 .50
❑ 278 Dennis Higgins 1.25 .50
❑ 279 Larry Brown 1.25 .50
❑ 280 Willie McCovey 6.00 3.00
❑ 281 Bill Parsons RC 1.25 .50
❑ 282 Houston Astros TC 2.00 .75
❑ 283 Darrell Brandon 1.25 .50
❑ 284 Ike Brown 1.25 .50
❑ 285 Gaylord Perry 6.00 3.00
❑ 286 Gene Alley 1.25 .50
❑ 287 Jim Hardin 1.25 .50
❑ 288 Johnny Jeter 1.25 .50
❑ 289 Syd O'Brien 1.25 .50
❑ 290 Sonny Siebert 1.25 .50
❑ 291 Hal McRae 2.00 .75
❑ 292 Hal McRae IA 1.25 .50
❑ 293 Dan Frisella 1.25 .50
❑ 294 Dan Frisella IA 1.25 .50
❑ 295 Dick Dietz 1.25 .50
❑ 296 Dick Dietz IA 1.25 .50
❑ 297 Claude Osteen 2.00 .75
❑ 298 Claude Osteen IA 1.25 .50
❑ 299 Hank Aaron 40.00 20.00
❑ 300 Hank Aaron IA 20.00 10.00
❑ 301 George Mitterwald 1.25 .50
❑ 302 George Mitterwald IA 1.25 .50
❑ 303 Joe Pepitone 2.00 .75
❑ 304 Joe Pepitone IA 1.25 .50
❑ 305 Ken Boswell 1.25 .50
❑ 306 Ken Boswell IA 1.25 .50
❑ 307 Steve Renko 1.25 .50
❑ 308 Steve Renko IA 1.25 .50
❑ 309 Roberto Clemente 50.00 30.00
❑ 310 Roberto Clemente IA 25.00 12.50
❑ 311 Clay Carroll 1.25 .50
❑ 312 Clay Carroll IA 1.25 .50
❑ 313 Luis Aparicio 6.00 3.00
❑ 314 Luis Aparicio IA 2.00 .75
❑ 315 Paul Splittorff 1.25 .50
❑ 316 Bibby/Roque/Guzman RC 2.00 .75
❑ 317 Rich Hand 1.25 .50
❑ 318 Sonny Jackson 1.25 .50
❑ 319 Aurelio Rodriguez 1.25 .50
❑ 320 Steve Blass 2.00 .75
❑ 321 Joe Lahoud 1.25 .50
❑ 322 Jose Pena 1.25 .50
❑ 323 Earl Weaver MG 4.00 1.50
❑ 324 Mike Ryan 1.25 .50
❑ 325 Mel Stottlemyre 2.00 .75
❑ 326 Pat Kelly 1.25 .50
❑ 327 Steve Stone RC 2.00 .75
❑ 328 Boston Red Sox TC 2.00 .75
❑ 329 Roy Foster 1.25 .50
❑ 330 Jim Hunter 6.00 3.00
❑ 331 Stan Swanson RC 1.25 .50
❑ 332 Buck Martinez 1.25 .50

❑ 333 Steve Barber 1.25 .50
❑ 334 Fahey/Mason Ragland RC 1.25 .50
❑ 335 Bill Hands 1.25 .50
❑ 336 Marty Martinez 1.25 .50
❑ 337 Mike Kilkenny 1.25 .50
❑ 338 Bob Grich 2.00 .75
❑ 339 Ron Cook 1.25 .50
❑ 340 Roy White 2.00 .75
❑ 341 Joe Torre KP 1.25 .50
❑ 342 Wilbur Wood KP 1.25 .50
❑ 343 Willie Stargell KP 2.00 .75
❑ 344 Dave McNally KP 1.25 .50
❑ 345 Rick Wise KP 1.25 .50
❑ 346 Jim Fregosi KP 1.25 .50
❑ 347 Tom Seaver KP 4.00 1.50
❑ 348 Sal Bando KP 1.25 .50
❑ 349 Al Fitzmorris 1.25 .50
❑ 350 Frank Howard 2.00 .75
❑ 351 House/Kester/Britton 2.00 .75
❑ 352 Dave LaRoche 1.25 .50
❑ 353 Art Shamsky 1.25 .50
❑ 354 Tom Murphy 1.25 .50
❑ 355 Bob Watson 2.00 .75
❑ 356 Gerry Moses 1.25 .50
❑ 357 Woody Fryman 1.25 .50
❑ 358 Sparky Anderson MG 4.00 1.50
❑ 359 Don Pavletich 1.25 .50
❑ 360 Dave Roberts 1.25 .50
❑ 361 Mike Andrews 1.25 .50
❑ 362 New York Mets TC 2.00 .75
❑ 363 Ron Klimkowski 1.25 .50
❑ 364 Johnny Callison 2.00 .75
❑ 365 Dick Bosman 2.00 .75
❑ 366 Jimmy Rosario RC 1.25 .50
❑ 367 Ron Perranoski 1.25 .50
❑ 368 Danny Thompson 1.25 .50
❑ 369 Jim Lefebvre 2.00 .75
❑ 370 Don Buford 1.25 .50
❑ 371 Denny Lemaster 1.25 .50
❑ 372 L.Clemons RC/M.Montgomery RC 1.25 .50
❑ 373 John Mayberry 2.00 .75
❑ 374 Jack Heidemann 1.25 .50
❑ 375 Reggie Cleveland 1.25 .50
❑ 376 Andy Kosco 1.25 .50
❑ 377 Terry Harmon 1.25 .50
❑ 378 Checklist 395-525 6.00 3.00
❑ 379 Ken Berry 1.25 .50
❑ 380 Earl Williams 1.25 .50
❑ 381 Chicago White Sox TC 2.00 .75
❑ 382 Joe Gibbon 1.25 .50
❑ 383 Brant Alyea 1.25 .50
❑ 384 Dave Campbell 2.00 .75
❑ 385 Mickey Stanley 2.00 .75
❑ 386 Jim Colborn 1.25 .50
❑ 387 Horace Clarke 2.00 .75
❑ 388 Charlie Williams RC 1.25 .50
❑ 389 Bill Rigney MG 1.25 .50
❑ 390 Willie Davis 2.00 .75
❑ 391 Ken Sanders 1.25 .50
❑ 392 F.Cambria/R.Zisk RC 2.00 .75
❑ 393 Curt Motton 1.25 .50
❑ 394 Ken Forsch 2.00 .75
❑ 395 Matty Alou 2.00 .75
❑ 396 Paul Lindblad 1.50 .60
❑ 397 Philadelphia Phillies TC 2.00 .75
❑ 398 Larry Hisle 2.00 .75
❑ 399 Milt Wilcox 2.00 .75
❑ 400 Tony Oliva 4.00 1.50
❑ 401 Jim Nash 1.50 .60
❑ 402 Bobby Heise 1.50 .60
❑ 403 John Cumberland 1.50 .60
❑ 404 Jeff Torborg 2.00 .75
❑ 405 Ron Fairly 2.00 .75
❑ 406 George Hendrick RC 2.00 .75
❑ 407 Chuck Taylor 1.50 .60
❑ 408 Jim Northrup 2.00 .75
❑ 409 Frank Baker 1.50 .60
❑ 410 Ferguson Jenkins 6.00 3.00
❑ 411 Bob Montgomery 1.50 .60
❑ 412 Dick Kelley 1.50 .60
❑ 413 D.Eddy RC/D.Lemonds 1.50 .60
❑ 414 Bob Miller 1.50 .60
❑ 415 Cookie Rojas 2.00 .75
❑ 416 Johnny Edwards 1.50 .60
❑ 417 Tom Hall 1.50 .60
❑ 418 Tom Shopay 1.50 .60
❑ 419 Jim Spencer 1.50 .60
❑ 420 Steve Carlton 20.00 10.00
❑ 421 Ellie Rodriguez 1.50 .60
❑ 422 Ray Lamb 1.50 .60
❑ 423 Oscar Gamble 2.00 .75
❑ 424 Bill Gogolewski 1.50 .60
❑ 425 Ken Singleton 2.00 .75
❑ 426 Ken Singleton IA 1.50 .60
❑ 427 Tito Fuentes 1.50 .60
❑ 428 Tito Fuentes IA 1.50 .60
❑ 429 Bob Robertson 1.50 .60
❑ 430 Bob Robertson IA 1.50 .60
❑ 431 Cito Gaston 2.00 .75
❑ 432 Cito Gaston IA 2.00 .75
❑ 433 Johnny Bench 25.00 12.50
❑ 434 Johnny Bench IA 15.00 7.50
❑ 435 Reggie Jackson 30.00 15.00
❑ 436 Reggie Jackson IA 12.00 6.00
❑ 437 Maury Wills 2.00 .75
❑ 438 Maury Wills IA 2.00 .75
❑ 439 Billy Williams 6.00 3.00
❑ 440 Billy Williams IA 4.00 1.50
❑ 441 Thurman Munson 15.00 7.50
❑ 442 Thurman Munson IA 8.00 4.00
❑ 443 Ken Henderson 1.50 .60
❑ 444 Ken Henderson IA 1.50 .60
❑ 445 Tom Seaver 30.00 15.00
❑ 446 Tom Seaver IA 15.00 7.50
❑ 447 Willie Stargell 8.00 4.00
❑ 448 Willie Stargell IA 4.00 1.50
❑ 449 Bob Lemon MG 2.00 .75
❑ 450 Mickey Lolich 2.00 .75
❑ 451 Tony LaRussa 4.00 1.50
❑ 452 Ed Herrmann 1.50 .60
❑ 453 Barry Lersch 1.50 .60
❑ 454 Oakland Athletics TC 2.00 .75
❑ 455 Tommy Harper 2.00 .75
❑ 456 Mark Belanger 2.00 .75
❑ 457 Fast/Thomas/Ivie RC 1.50 .60
❑ 458 Aurelio Monteagudo 1.50 .60
❑ 459 Rick Renick 1.50 .60
❑ 460 Al Downing 1.50 .60
❑ 461 Tim Cullen 1.50 .60
❑ 462 Rickey Clark 1.50 .60
❑ 463 Bernie Carbo 1.50 .60
❑ 464 Jim Roland 1.50 .60
❑ 465 Gil Hodges MG 4.00 1.50
❑ 466 Norm Miller 1.50 .60
❑ 467 Steve Kline 1.50 .60
❑ 468 Richie Scheinblum 1.50 .60
❑ 469 Ron Herbel 1.50 .60
❑ 470 Ray Fosse 1.50 .60
❑ 471 Luke Walker 1.50 .60
❑ 472 Phil Gagliano 1.50 .60
❑ 473 Dan McGinn 1.50 .60
❑ 474 Baylor/Harrison/Oates RC 15.00 7.50
❑ 475 Gary Nolan 2.00 .75
❑ 476 Lee Richard RC 1.50 .60
❑ 477 Tom Phoebus 1.50 .60
❑ 478 Checklist 526-656 6.00 3.00
❑ 479 Don Shaw 1.50 .60
❑ 480 Lee May 2.00 .75
❑ 481 Billy Conigliaro 2.00 .75
❑ 482 Joe Hoerner 1.50 .60
❑ 483 Ken Suarez 1.50 .60
❑ 484 Lum Harris MG 1.50 .60
❑ 485 Phil Regan 2.00 .75
❑ 486 John Lowenstein 1.50 .60
❑ 487 Detroit Tigers TC 2.00 .75
❑ 488 Mike Nagy 1.50 .60
❑ 489 T.Humphrey RC/K.Lampard 1.50 .60
❑ 490 Dave McNally 2.00 .75
❑ 491 Lou Piniella KP 2.00 .75
❑ 492 Mel Stottlemyre KP 2.00 .75
❑ 493 Bob Bailey KP 2.00 .75
❑ 494 Willie Horton KP 2.00 .75
❑ 495 Bill Melton KP 2.00 .75
❑ 496 Bud Harrelson KP 2.00 .75
❑ 497 Jim Perry KP 2.00 .75
❑ 498 Brooks Robinson KP 4.00 1.50
❑ 499 Vicente Romo 1.50 .60
❑ 500 Joe Torre 4.00 1.50
❑ 501 Pete Hamm 1.50 .60
❑ 502 Jackie Hernandez 1.50 .60
❑ 503 Gary Peters 1.50 .60
❑ 504 Ed Spiezio 1.50 .60
❑ 505 Mike Marshall 2.00 .75
❑ 506 Ley/Moyer/Tidrow RC 1.50 .60
❑ 507 Fred Gladding 1.50 .60
❑ 508 Elrod Hendricks 1.50 .60
❑ 509 Don McMahon 1.50 .60
❑ 510 Ted Williams MG 12.00 6.00
❑ 511 Tony Taylor 2.00 .75
❑ 512 Paul Popovich 1.50 .60
❑ 513 Lindy McDaniel 2.00 .75
❑ 514 Ted Sizemore 1.50 .60
❑ 515 Bert Blyleven 4.00 1.50
❑ 516 Oscar Brown 1.50 .60
❑ 517 Ken Brett 1.50 .60
❑ 518 Wayne Garrett 1.50 .60
❑ 519 Ted Abernathy 1.50 .60
❑ 520 Larry Bowa 2.00 .75
❑ 521 Alan Foster 1.50 .60
❑ 522 Los Angeles Dodgers TC 2.00 .75
❑ 523 Chuck Dobson 1.50 .60
❑ 524 E.Armbrister RC/M.Behney RC 1.50 .60
❑ 525 Carlos May 2.00 .75
❑ 526 Bob Bailey 6.00 3.00
❑ 527 Dave Leonhard 4.00 1.50
❑ 528 Ron Stone 4.00 1.50
❑ 529 Dave Nelson 6.00 3.00
❑ 530 Don Sutton 12.00 6.00
❑ 531 Freddie Patek 6.00 3.00
❑ 532 Fred Kendall RC 4.00 1.50
❑ 533 Ralph Houk MG 6.00 3.00
❑ 534 Jim Hickman 6.00 3.00
❑ 535 Ed Brinkman 4.00 1.50
❑ 536 Doug Rader 6.00 3.00
❑ 537 Bob Locker 4.00 1.50
❑ 538 Charlie Sands RC 4.00 1.50
❑ 539 Terry Forster RC 6.00 3.00
❑ 540 Felix Millan 4.00 1.50
❑ 541 Roger Repoz 4.00 1.50
❑ 542 Jack Billingham 4.00 1.50
❑ 543 Duane Josephson 4.00 1.50
❑ 544 Ted Martinez 4.00 1.50
❑ 545 Wayne Granger 4.00 1.50
❑ 546 Joe Hague 4.00 1.50
❑ 547 Cleveland Indians TC 8.00 4.00
❑ 548 Frank Reberger 4.00 1.50
❑ 549 Dave May 4.00 1.50
❑ 550 Brooks Robinson 25.00 12.50
❑ 551 Ollie Brown 4.00 1.50
❑ 552 Ollie Brown IA 4.00 1.50
❑ 553 Wilbur Wood 6.00 3.00
❑ 554 Wilbur Wood IA 4.00 1.50
❑ 555 Ron Santo 8.00 4.00
❑ 556 Ron Santo IA 6.00 3.00
❑ 557 John Odom 4.00 1.50
❑ 558 John Odom IA 4.00 1.50
❑ 559 Pete Rose 50.00 30.00
❑ 560 Pete Rose IA 25.00 12.50
❑ 561 Leo Cardenas 4.00 1.50
❑ 562 Leo Cardenas IA 4.00 1.50
❑ 563 Ray Sadecki 4.00 1.50
❑ 564 Ray Sadecki IA 4.00 1.50
❑ 565 Reggie Smith 6.00 3.00
❑ 566 Reggie Smith IA 4.00 1.50
❑ 567 Juan Marichal 12.00 6.00
❑ 568 Juan Marichal IA 6.00 3.00
❑ 569 Ed Kirkpatrick 4.00 1.50
❑ 570 Ed Kirkpatrick IA 4.00 1.50
❑ 571 Nate Colbert 4.00 1.50
❑ 572 Nate Colbert IA 4.00 1.50
❑ 573 Fritz Peterson 4.00 1.50
❑ 574 Fritz Peterson IA 4.00 1.50
❑ 575 Al Oliver 8.00 4.00
❑ 576 Leo Durocher MG 6.00 3.00
❑ 577 Mike Paul 6.00 3.00
❑ 578 Billy Grabarkewitz 4.00 1.50
❑ 579 Doyle Alexander RC 6.00 3.00
❑ 580 Lou Piniella 6.00 3.00
❑ 581 Wade Blasingame 4.00 1.50
❑ 582 Montreal Expos TC 8.00 4.00
❑ 583 Darold Knowles 4.00 1.50
❑ 584 Jerry McNertney 4.00 1.50
❑ 585 George Scott 6.00 3.00
❑ 586 Denis Menke 4.00 1.50
❑ 587 Billy Wilson 4.00 1.50
❑ 588 Jim Holt 4.00 1.50
❑ 589 Hal Lanier 4.00 1.50
❑ 590 Graig Nettles 8.00 4.00

❑ 591	Paul Casanova	4.00	1.50
❑ 592	Lew Krausse	4.00	1.50
❑ 593	Rich Morales	4.00	1.50
❑ 594	Jim Beauchamp	4.00	1.50
❑ 595	Nolan Ryan	100.00	60.00
❑ 596	Manny Mota	6.00	3.00
❑ 597	Jim Magnuson RC	4.00	1.50
❑ 598	Hal King	6.00	3.00
❑ 599	Billy Champion	4.00	1.50
❑ 600	Al Kaline	25.00	12.50
❑ 601	George Stone	4.00	1.50
❑ 602	Dave Bristol MG	4.00	1.50
❑ 603	Jim Ray	4.00	1.50
❑ 604A	Checklist 657-787 Right Copy	12.00	6.00
❑ 604B	Checklist 657-787 Left Copy	12.00	6.00
❑ 605	Nelson Briles	6.00	3.00
❑ 606	Luis Melendez	4.00	1.50
❑ 607	Frank Duffy	4.00	1.50
❑ 608	Mike Corkins	4.00	1.50
❑ 609	Tom Grieve	6.00	3.00
❑ 610	Bill Stoneman	6.00	3.00
❑ 611	Rich Reese	4.00	1.50
❑ 612	Joe Decker	4.00	1.50
❑ 613	Mike Ferraro	4.00	1.50
❑ 614	Ted Uhlaender	4.00	1.50
❑ 615	Steve Hargan	4.00	1.50
❑ 616	Joe Ferguson RC	6.00	3.00
❑ 617	Kansas City Royals TC	8.00	4.00
❑ 618	Rich Robertson	4.00	1.50
❑ 619	Rich McKinney	4.00	1.50
❑ 620	Phil Niekro	12.00	6.00
❑ 621	Commish Award	8.00	4.00
❑ 622	MVP Award	8.00	4.00
❑ 623	Cy Young Award	8.00	4.00
❑ 624	Minor Lg POY Award	8.00	4.00
❑ 625	Rookie of the Year	8.00	4.00
❑ 626	Babe Ruth Award	8.00	4.00
❑ 627	Moe Drabowsky	4.00	1.50
❑ 628	Terry Crowley	4.00	1.50
❑ 629	Paul Doyle	4.00	1.50
❑ 630	Rich Hebner	6.00	3.00
❑ 631	John Strohmayer	4.00	1.50
❑ 632	Mike Hegan	4.00	1.50
❑ 633	Jack Hiatt	4.00	1.50
❑ 634	Dick Woodson	4.00	1.50
❑ 635	Don Money	6.00	3.00
❑ 636	Bill Lee	6.00	3.00
❑ 637	Preston Gomez MG	4.00	1.50
❑ 638	Ken Wright	4.00	1.50
❑ 639	J.C. Martin	4.00	1.50
❑ 640	Joe Coleman	4.00	1.50
❑ 641	Mike Lum	4.00	1.50
❑ 642	Dennis Riddleberger RC	4.00	1.50
❑ 643	Russ Gibson	4.00	1.50
❑ 644	Bernie Allen	4.00	1.50
❑ 645	Jim Maloney	6.00	3.00
❑ 646	Chico Salmon	4.00	1.50
❑ 647	Bob Moose	4.00	1.50
❑ 648	Jim Lyttle	4.00	1.50
❑ 649	Pete Richert	4.00	1.50
❑ 650	Sal Bando	6.00	3.00
❑ 651	Cincinnati Reds TC	8.00	4.00
❑ 652	Marcelino Lopez	4.00	1.50
❑ 653	Jim Fairey	4.00	1.50
❑ 654	Horacio Pina	6.00	3.00
❑ 655	Jerry Grote	4.00	1.50
❑ 656	Rudy May	4.00	1.50
❑ 657	Bobby Wine	12.00	6.00
❑ 658	Steve Dunning	12.00	6.00
❑ 659	Bob Aspromonte	12.00	6.00
❑ 660	Paul Blair	15.00	7.50
❑ 661	Bill Virdon MG	12.00	6.00
❑ 662	Stan Bahnsen	12.00	6.00
❑ 663	Fran Healy RC	15.00	7.50
❑ 664	Bobby Knoop	12.00	6.00
❑ 665	Chris Short	12.00	6.00
❑ 666	Hector Torres	12.00	6.00
❑ 667	Ray Newman RC	12.00	6.00
❑ 668	Texas Rangers TC	30.00	15.00
❑ 669	Willie Crawford	12.00	6.00
❑ 670	Ken Holtzman	15.00	7.50
❑ 671	Donn Clendenon	15.00	7.50
❑ 672	Archie Reynolds	12.00	6.00
❑ 673	Dave Marshall	12.00	6.00
❑ 674	John Kennedy	12.00	6.00
❑ 675	Pat Jarvis	12.00	6.00
❑ 676	Danny Cater	12.00	6.00
❑ 677	Ivan Murrell	12.00	6.00
❑ 678	Steve Luebber RC	12.00	6.00
❑ 679	B.Fenwick RC/B.Stinson	12.00	6.00
❑ 680	Dave Johnson	15.00	7.50
❑ 681	Bobby Pfeil	12.00	6.00
❑ 682	Mike McCormick	15.00	7.50
❑ 683	Steve Hovley	12.00	6.00
❑ 684	Hal Breeden RC	12.00	6.00
❑ 685	Joel Horlen	12.00	6.00
❑ 686	Steve Garvey	40.00	20.00
❑ 687	Del Unser	12.00	6.00
❑ 688	St. Louis Cardinals TC	20.00	10.00
❑ 689	Eddie Fisher	12.00	6.00
❑ 690	Willie Montanez	15.00	7.50
❑ 691	Curt Blefary	12.00	6.00
❑ 692	Curt Blefary IA	12.00	6.00
❑ 693	Alan Gallagher	12.00	6.00
❑ 694	Alan Gallagher IA	12.00	6.00
❑ 695	Rod Carew	50.00	30.00
❑ 696	Rod Carew IA	30.00	15.00
❑ 697	Jerry Koosman	15.00	7.50
❑ 698	Jerry Koosman IA	15.00	7.50
❑ 699	Bobby Murcer	15.00	7.50
❑ 700	Bobby Murcer IA	15.00	7.50
❑ 701	Jose Pagan	12.00	6.00
❑ 702	Jose Pagan IA	12.00	6.00
❑ 703	Doug Griffin	12.00	6.00
❑ 704	Doug Griffin IA	12.00	6.00
❑ 705	Pat Corrales	15.00	7.50
❑ 706	Pat Corrales IA	12.00	6.00
❑ 707	Tim Foli	12.00	6.00
❑ 708	Tim Foli IA	12.00	6.00
❑ 709	Jim Kaat	15.00	7.50
❑ 710	Jim Kaat IA	15.00	7.50
❑ 711	Bobby Bonds	20.00	10.00
❑ 712	Bobby Bonds IA	15.00	7.50
❑ 713	Gene Michael	20.00	10.00
❑ 714	Gene Michael IA	15.00	7.50
❑ 715	Mike Epstein	12.00	6.00
❑ 716	Jesus Alou	12.00	6.00
❑ 717	Bruce Dal Canton	12.00	6.00
❑ 718	Del Rice MG	12.00	6.00
❑ 719	Cesar Geronimo	12.00	6.00
❑ 720	Sam McDowell	15.00	7.50
❑ 721	Eddie Leon	12.00	6.00
❑ 722	Bill Sudakis	12.00	6.00
❑ 723	Al Santorini	12.00	6.00
❑ 724	Curtis/Hinton/Scott RC	12.00	6.00
❑ 725	Dick McAuliffe	15.00	7.50
❑ 726	Dick Selma	12.00	6.00
❑ 727	Jose Laboy	12.00	6.00
❑ 728	Gail Hopkins	12.00	6.00
❑ 729	Bob Veale	15.00	7.50
❑ 730	Rick Monday	15.00	7.50
❑ 731	Baltimore Orioles TC	20.00	10.00
❑ 732	George Culver	12.00	6.00
❑ 733	Jim Ray Hart	15.00	7.50
❑ 734	Bob Burda	12.00	6.00
❑ 735	Diego Segui	12.00	6.00
❑ 736	Bill Russell	15.00	7.50
❑ 737	Len Randle RC	15.00	7.50
❑ 738	Jim Merritt	12.00	6.00
❑ 739	Don Mason	12.00	6.00
❑ 740	Rico Carty	15.00	7.50
❑ 741	Hutton/Milner/Miller RC	15.00	7.50
❑ 742	Jim Rooker	12.00	6.00
❑ 743	Cesar Gutierrez	12.00	6.00
❑ 744	Jim Slaton RC	12.00	6.00
❑ 745	Julian Javier	15.00	7.50
❑ 746	Lowell Palmer	12.00	6.00
❑ 747	Jim Stewart	12.00	6.00
❑ 748	Phil Hennigan	12.00	6.00
❑ 749	Walt Alston MG	20.00	10.00
❑ 750	Willie Horton	15.00	7.50
❑ 751	Steve Carlton TR	40.00	20.00
❑ 752	Joe Morgan TR	40.00	20.00
❑ 753	Denny McLain TR	20.00	10.00
❑ 754	Frank Robinson TR	40.00	20.00
❑ 755	Jim Fregosi TR	15.00	7.50
❑ 756	Rick Wise TR	15.00	7.50
❑ 757	Jose Cardenal TR	15.00	7.50
❑ 758	Gil Garrido	12.00	6.00
❑ 759	Chris Cannizzaro	12.00	6.00
❑ 760	Bill Mazeroski	25.00	12.50
❑ 761	Oglivie/Cey/Williams RC	25.00	12.50
❑ 762	Wayne Simpson	12.00	6.00
❑ 763	Ron Hansen	12.00	6.00
❑ 764	Dusty Baker	20.00	10.00
❑ 765	Ken McMullen	12.00	6.00
❑ 766	Steve Hamilton	12.00	6.00
❑ 767	Tom McCraw	15.00	7.50
❑ 768	Denny Doyle	12.00	6.00
❑ 769	Jack Aker	12.00	6.00
❑ 770	Jim Wynn	15.00	7.50
❑ 771	San Francisco Giants TC	20.00	10.00
❑ 772	Ken Tatum	12.00	6.00
❑ 773	Ron Brand	12.00	6.00
❑ 774	Luis Alvarado	12.00	6.00
❑ 775	Jerry Reuss	15.00	7.50
❑ 776	Bill Voss	12.00	6.00
❑ 777	Hoyt Wilhelm	25.00	12.50
❑ 778	Albury/Dempsey/Strickland RC	20.00	10.00
❑ 779	Tony Cloninger	12.00	6.00
❑ 780	Dick Green	12.00	6.00
❑ 781	Jim McAndrew	12.00	6.00
❑ 782	Larry Stahl	12.00	6.00
❑ 783	Les Cain	12.00	6.00
❑ 784	Ken Aspromonte	12.00	6.00
❑ 785	Vic Davalillo	12.00	6.00
❑ 786	Chuck Brinkman	12.00	6.00
❑ 787	Ron Reed	15.00	7.50

1973 Topps

❑	COMPLETE SET (660)	700.00	400.00
❑	COMMON CARD (1-264)	.50	.20
❑	COMMON CARD (265-396)	.75	.30
❑	COMMON CARD (397-528)	1.25	.50
❑	COMMON CARD (529-660)	3.00	1.25
❑	WRAPPER (10-CENT, BAT)	15.00	10.00
❑	WRAPPER (10-CENT)	15.00	10.00
❑ 1	Ruth/Aaron/Mays HR	40.00	20.00
❑ 2	Rich Hebner	1.50	.60
❑ 3	Jim Lonborg	1.50	.60
❑ 4	John Milner	.50	.20
❑ 5	Ed Brinkman	.50	.20
❑ 6	Mac Scarce RC	.50	.20
❑ 7	Texas Rangers TC	2.00	.75
❑ 8	Tom Hall	.50	.20
❑ 9	Johnny Oates	1.50	.60
❑ 10	Don Sutton	4.00	1.50
❑ 11	Chris Chambliss UER	1.50	.60
❑ 12A	Don Zimmer MG w/o Ear	3.00	1.25
❑ 12B	Don Zimmer MG w/Ear	.75	.30
❑ 13	George Hendrick	1.50	.60
❑ 14	Sonny Siebert	.50	.20
❑ 15	Ralph Garr	1.50	.60
❑ 16	Steve Braun	.50	.20
❑ 17	Fred Gladding	.50	.20
❑ 18	Leroy Stanton	.50	.20
❑ 19	Tim Foli	.50	.20
❑ 20	Stan Bahnsen	.50	.20
❑ 21	Randy Hundley	1.50	.60
❑ 22	Ted Abernathy	.50	.20
❑ 23	Dave Kingman	1.50	.60
❑ 24	Al Santorini	.50	.20
❑ 25	Roy White	1.50	.60
❑ 26	Pittsburgh Pirates TC	2.00	.75
❑ 27	Bill Gogolewski	.50	.20
❑ 28	Hal McRae	1.50	.60
❑ 29	Tony Taylor	1.50	.60
❑ 30	Tug McGraw	1.50	.60
❑ 31	Buddy Bell RC	2.50	1.00
❑ 32	Fred Norman	.50	.20

❑ 33 Jim Breazeale RC .50 .20
❑ 34 Pat Dobson .50 .20
❑ 35 Willie Davis 1.50 .60
❑ 36 Steve Barber .50 .20
❑ 37 Bill Robinson 1.50 .60
❑ 38 Mike Epstein .50 .20
❑ 39 Dave Roberts .50 .20
❑ 40 Reggie Smith 1.50 .60
❑ 41 Tom Walker RC .50 .20
❑ 42 Mike Andrews .50 .20
❑ 43 Randy Moffitt RC .50 .20
❑ 44 Rick Monday 1.50 .60
❑ 45 Ellie Rodriguez UER .50 .20
❑ 46 Lindy McDaniel 1.50 .60
❑ 47 Luis Melendez .50 .20
❑ 48 Paul Splittorff .50 .20
❑ 49A Frank Quilici MG Solid 3.00 1.25
❑ 49B Frank Quilici MG Natural .75 .30
❑ 50 Roberto Clemente 40.00 20.00
❑ 51 Chuck Seelbach RC .50 .20
❑ 52 Denis Menke .50 .20
❑ 53 Steve Dunning .50 .20
❑ 54 Checklist 1-132 3.00 1.25
❑ 55 Jon Matlack 1.50 .60
❑ 56 Merv Rettenmund .50 .20
❑ 57 Derrel Thomas .50 .20
❑ 58 Mike Paul .50 .20
❑ 59 Steve Yeager RC 1.50 .60
❑ 60 Ken Holtzman 1.50 .60
❑ 61 B.Williams/R.Carew LL 2.50 1.00
❑ 62 J.Bench/D.Allen LL 2.50 1.00
❑ 63 J.Bench/D.Allen LL 2.50 1.00
❑ 64 L.Brock/Campaneris LL 1.50 .60
❑ 65 S.Carlton/L.Tiant LL 1.50 .60
❑ 66 Carlton/Perry/Wood LL 1.50 .60
❑ 67 S.Carlton/N.Ryan LL 25.00 12.50
❑ 68 C.Carroll/S.Lyle LL 1.50 .60
❑ 69 Phil Gagliano .50 .20
❑ 70 Milt Pappas 1.50 .60
❑ 71 Johnny Briggs .50 .20
❑ 72 Ron Reed .50 .20
❑ 73 Ed Herrmann .50 .20
❑ 74 Billy Champion .50 .20
❑ 75 Vada Pinson 1.50 .60
❑ 76 Doug Rader .50 .20
❑ 77 Mike Torrez 1.50 .60
❑ 78 Richie Scheinblum .50 .20
❑ 79 Jim Willoughby RC .50 .20
❑ 80 Tony Oliva UER 2.50 1.00
❑ 81A W.Lockman MG w/Banks Solid 1.50 .60
❑ 81B W.Lockman MG w/Banks Natural 1.50 .60
❑ 82 Fritz Peterson .50 .20
❑ 83 Leron Lee .50 .20
❑ 84 Rollie Fingers 4.00 1.50
❑ 85 Ted Simmons 1.50 .60
❑ 86 Tom McCraw .50 .20
❑ 87 Ken Boswell .50 .20
❑ 88 Mickey Stanley 1.50 .60
❑ 89 Jack Billingham .50 .20
❑ 90 Brooks Robinson 8.00 4.00
❑ 91 Los Angeles Dodgers TC 2.00 .75
❑ 92 Jerry Bell .50 .20
❑ 93 Jesus Alou .50 .20
❑ 94 Dick Billings .50 .20
❑ 95 Steve Blass 1.50 .60
❑ 96 Doug Griffin .50 .20
❑ 97 Willie Montanez 1.50 .60
❑ 98 Dick Woodson .50 .20
❑ 99 Carl Taylor .50 .20
❑ 100 Hank Aaron 40.00 20.00
❑ 101 Ken Henderson .50 .20
❑ 102 Rudy May .50 .20
❑ 103 Celerino Sanchez RC .50 .20
❑ 104 Reggie Cleveland .50 .20
❑ 105 Carlos May .50 .20
❑ 106 Terry Humphrey .50 .20
❑ 107 Phil Hennigan .50 .20
❑ 108 Bill Russell 1.50 .60
❑ 109 Doyle Alexander 1.50 .60
❑ 110 Bob Watson 1.50 .60
❑ 111 Dave Nelson .50 .20
❑ 112 Gary Ross .50 .20
❑ 113 Jerry Grote 1.50 .60
❑ 114 Lynn McGlothen RC .50 .20
❑ 115 Ron Santo 1.50 .60
❑ 116A Ralph Houk MG Solid 3.00 1.25
❑ 116B Ralph Houk MG Natural .75 .30
❑ 117 Ramon Hernandez .50 .20
❑ 118 John Mayberry 1.50 .60
❑ 119 Larry Bowa 1.50 .60
❑ 120 Joe Coleman .50 .20
❑ 121 Dave Rader .50 .20
❑ 122 Jim Strickland .50 .20
❑ 123 Sandy Alomar 1.50 .60
❑ 124 Jim Hardin .50 .20
❑ 125 Ron Fairly 1.50 .60
❑ 126 Jim Brewer .50 .20
❑ 127 Milwaukee Brewers TC 2.00 .75
❑ 128 Ted Sizemore .50 .20
❑ 129 Terry Forster 1.50 .60
❑ 130 Pete Rose 30.00 15.00
❑ 131A Eddie Kasko MG w/oEar 3.00 1.25
❑ 131B Eddie Kasko MG w/Ear 1.50 .60
❑ 132 Matty Alou 1.50 .60
❑ 133 Dave Roberts RC .50 .20
❑ 134 Milt Wilcox .50 .20
❑ 135 Lee May UER 1.50 .60
❑ 136A Earl Weaver MG Orange 1.50 .60
❑ 136B Earl Weaver MG Pale 3.00 1.25
❑ 137 Jim Beauchamp .50 .20
❑ 138 Horacio Pina .50 .20
❑ 139 Carmen Fanzone RC .50 .20
❑ 140 Lou Piniella 2.50 1.00
❑ 141 Bruce Kison .50 .20
❑ 142 Thurman Munson 8.00 4.00
❑ 143 John Curtis .50 .20
❑ 144 Marty Perez .50 .20
❑ 145 Bobby Bonds 2.50 1.00
❑ 146 Woodie Fryman .50 .20
❑ 147 Mike Anderson .50 .20
❑ 148 Dave Goltz RC .50 .20
❑ 149 Ron Hunt .50 .20
❑ 150 Wilbur Wood 1.50 .60
❑ 151 Wes Parker 1.50 .60
❑ 152 Dave May .50 .20
❑ 153 Al Hrabosky 1.50 .60
❑ 154 Jeff Torborg 1.50 .60
❑ 155 Sal Bando 1.50 .60
❑ 156 Cesar Geronimo .50 .20
❑ 157 Denny Riddleberger .50 .20
❑ 158 Houston Astros TC 2.00 .75
❑ 159 Cito Gaston 1.50 .60
❑ 160 Jim Palmer 6.00 3.00
❑ 161 Ted Martinez .50 .20
❑ 162 Pete Broberg .50 .20
❑ 163 Vic Davalillo .50 .20
❑ 164 Monty Montgomery .50 .20
❑ 165 Luis Aparicio 4.00 1.50
❑ 166 Terry Harmon .50 .20
❑ 167 Steve Stone 1.50 .60
❑ 168 Jim Northrup 1.50 .60
❑ 169 Ron Schueler RC 1.50 .60
❑ 170 Harmon Killebrew 5.00 2.00
❑ 171 Bernie Carbo .50 .20
❑ 172 Steve Kline .50 .20
❑ 173 Hal Breeden .50 .20
❑ 174 Goose Gossage RC 6.00 3.00
❑ 175 Frank Robinson 6.00 3.00
❑ 176 Chuck Taylor .50 .20
❑ 177 Bill Plummer RC .50 .20
❑ 178 Don Rose RC .50 .20
❑ 179A Dick Williams w/Ear 4.00 1.50
❑ 179B Dick Williams w/o Ear 1.50 .60
❑ 180 Ferguson Jenkins 4.00 1.50
❑ 181 Jack Brohamer RC .50 .20
❑ 182 Mike Caldwell RC 1.50 .60
❑ 183 Don Buford .50 .20
❑ 184 Jerry Koosman 1.50 .60
❑ 185 Jim Wynn 1.50 .60
❑ 186 Bill Fahey .50 .20
❑ 187 Luke Walker .50 .20
❑ 188 Cookie Rojas 1.50 .60
❑ 189 Greg Luzinski 2.50 1.00
❑ 190 Bob Gibson 8.00 4.00
❑ 191 Detroit Tigers TC 2.50 1.00
❑ 192 Pat Jarvis .50 .20
❑ 193 Carlton Fisk 10.00 5.00
❑ 194 Jorge Orta RC .50 .20
❑ 195 Clay Carroll .50 .20
❑ 196 Ken McMullen .50 .20
❑ 197 Ed Goodson RC .50 .20
❑ 198 Horace Clarke .50 .20
❑ 199 Bert Blyleven 2.50 1.00
❑ 200 Billy Williams 4.00 1.50
❑ 201 George Hendrick ALCS 1.50 .60
❑ 202 George Foster NLCS 1.50 .60
❑ 203 Gene Tenace WS 1.50 .60
❑ 204 A's Two Straight WS 1.50 .60
❑ 205 Tony Perez WS 2.50 1.00
❑ 206 Gene Tenace WS 1.50 .60
❑ 207 Blue Moon Odom WS 1.50 .60
❑ 208 Johnny Bench WS 5.00 2.00
❑ 209 Bert Campaneris WS 1.50 .60
❑ 210 A's Win WS .50 .20
❑ 211 Balor Moore .50 .20
❑ 212 Joe Lahoud .50 .20
❑ 213 Steve Garvey 5.00 2.00
❑ 214 Dave Hamilton RC .50 .20
❑ 215 Dusty Baker 2.50 1.00
❑ 216 Toby Harrah 1.50 .60
❑ 217 Don Wilson .50 .20
❑ 218 Aurelio Rodriguez .50 .20
❑ 219 St. Louis Cardinals TC 2.50 1.00
❑ 220 Nolan Ryan 50.00 30.00
❑ 221 Fred Kendall .50 .20
❑ 222 Rob Gardner .50 .20
❑ 223 Bud Harrelson 1.50 .60
❑ 224 Bill Lee 1.50 .60
❑ 225 Al Oliver 1.50 .60
❑ 226 Ray Fosse .50 .20
❑ 227 Wayne Twitchell .50 .20
❑ 228 Bobby Darwin .50 .20
❑ 229 Roric Harrison .50 .20
❑ 230 Joe Morgan 6.00 3.00
❑ 231 Bill Parsons .50 .20
❑ 232 Ken Singleton 1.50 .60
❑ 233 Ed Kirkpatrick .50 .20
❑ 234 Bill North RC .50 .20
❑ 235 Jim Hunter 4.00 1.50
❑ 236 Tito Fuentes .50 .20
❑ 237A Eddie Mathews MG w/Ear 1.50 .60
❑ 237B Eddie Mathews MG w/o Ear 3.00 1.25
❑ 238 Tony Muser RC .50 .20
❑ 239 Pete Richert .50 .20
❑ 240 Bobby Murcer 1.50 .60
❑ 241 Dwain Anderson .50 .20
❑ 242 George Culver .50 .20
❑ 243 California Angels TC 2.50 1.00
❑ 244 Ed Acosta .50 .20
❑ 245 Carl Yastrzemski 10.00 5.00
❑ 246 Ken Sanders .50 .20
❑ 247 Del Unser .50 .20
❑ 248 Jerry Johnson .50 .20
❑ 249 Larry Biittner .50 .20
❑ 250 Manny Sanguillen 1.50 .60
❑ 251 Roger Nelson .50 .20
❑ 252A Charlie Fox MG Orange 4.00 1.50
❑ 252B Charlie Fox MG Pale 1.50 .60
❑ 253 Mark Belanger 1.50 .60
❑ 254 Bill Stoneman .50 .20
❑ 255 Reggie Jackson 15.00 7.50
❑ 256 Chris Zachary .50 .20
❑ 257A Yogi Berra MG Orange 3.00 1.25
❑ 257B Yogi Berra MG Pale 5.00 2.00
❑ 258 Tommy John 1.50 .60
❑ 259 Jim Holt .50 .20
❑ 260 Gary Nolan 1.50 .60
❑ 261 Pat Kelly .50 .20
❑ 262 Jack Aker .50 .20
❑ 263 George Scott 1.50 .60
❑ 264 Checklist 133-264 3.00 1.25
❑ 265 Gene Michael 1.50 .60
❑ 266 Mike Lum .75 .30
❑ 267 Lloyd Allen .75 .30
❑ 268 Jerry Morales .75 .30
❑ 269 Tim McCarver 1.50 .60
❑ 270 Luis Tiant 1.50 .60
❑ 271 Tom Hutton .75 .30
❑ 272 Ed Farmer .75 .30
❑ 273 Chris Speier .75 .30
❑ 274 Darold Knowles .75 .30
❑ 275 Tony Perez 4.00 1.50
❑ 276 Joe Lovitto RC .75 .30
❑ 277 Bob Miller .75 .30
❑ 278 Baltimore Orioles TC 1.50 .60
❑ 279 Mike Strahler .75 .30
❑ 280 Al Kaline 8.00 4.00
❑ 281 Mike Jorgensen .75 .30

No.	Card	Price	Price
282	Steve Hovley	.75	.30
283	Ray Sadecki	.75	.30
284	Glenn Borgmann RC	.75	.30
285	Don Kessinger	1.50	.60
286	Frank Linzy	.75	.30
287	Eddie Leon	.75	.30
288	Gary Gentry	.75	.30
289	Bob Oliver	.75	.30
290	Cesar Cedeno	1.50	.60
291	Rogelio Moret	.75	.30
292	Jose Cruz	1.50	.60
293	Bernie Allen	.75	.30
294	Steve Arlin	.75	.30
295	Bert Campaneris	1.50	.60
296	Sparky Anderson MG	2.50	1.00
297	Walt Williams	.75	.30
298	Ron Bryant	.75	.30
299	Ted Ford	.75	.30
300	Steve Carlton	10.00	5.00
301	Billy Grabarkewitz	.75	.30
302	Terry Crowley	.75	.30
303	Nelson Briles	.75	.30
304	Duke Sims	.75	.30
305	Willie Mays	40.00	20.00
306	Tom Burgmeier	.75	.30
307	Boots Day	.75	.30
308	Skip Lockwood	.75	.30
309	Paul Popovich	.75	.30
310	Dick Allen	1.50	.60
311	Joe Decker	.75	.30
312	Oscar Brown	.75	.30
313	Jim Ray	.75	.30
314	Ron Swoboda	1.50	.60
315	John Odom	.75	.30
316	San Diego Padres TC	1.50	.60
317	Danny Cater	.75	.30
318	Jim McGlothlin	.75	.30
319	Jim Spencer	.75	.30
320	Lou Brock	8.00	4.00
321	Rich Hinton	.75	.30
322	Garry Maddox RC	1.50	.60
323	Billy Martin MG	1.50	.60
324	Al Downing	.75	.30
325	Boog Powell	1.50	.60
326	Darrell Brandon	.75	.30
327	John Lowenstein	.75	.30
328	Bill Bonham	.75	.30
329	Ed Kranepool	1.50	.60
330	Rod Carew	8.00	4.00
331	Carl Morton	.75	.30
332	John Felske RC	.75	.30
333	Gene Clines	.75	.30
334	Freddie Patek	.75	.30
335	Bob Tolan	.75	.30
336	Tom Bradley	.75	.30
337	Dave Duncan	1.50	.60
338	Checklist 265-396	3.00	1.25
339	Dick Tidrow	.75	.30
340	Nate Colbert	.75	.30
341	Jim Palmer KP	2.50	1.00
342	Sam McDowell KP	.75	.30
343	Bobby Murcer KP	.75	.30
344	Jim Hunter KP	2.50	1.00
345	Chris Speier KP	.75	.30
346	Gaylord Perry KP	1.50	.60
347	Kansas City Royals TC	1.50	.60
348	Rennie Stennett	.75	.30
349	Dick McAuliffe	.75	.30
350	Tom Seaver	12.00	6.00
351	Jimmy Stewart	.75	.30
352	Don Stanhouse RC	.75	.30
353	Steve Brye	.75	.30
354	Billy Parker	.75	.30
355	Mike Marshall	1.50	.60
356	Chuck Tanner MG	4.00	1.50
357	Ross Grimsley	.75	.30
358	Jim Nettles	.75	.30
359	Cecil Upshaw	.75	.30
360	Joe Rudi UER	1.50	.60
361	Fran Healy	.75	.30
362	Eddie Watt	.75	.30
363	Jackie Hernandez	.75	.30
364	Rick Wise	.75	.30
365	Rico Petrocelli	1.50	.60
366	Brock Davis	.75	.30
367	Burt Hooton	1.50	.60
368	Bill Buckner	1.50	.60
369	Lerrin LaGrow	.75	.30
370	Willie Stargell	5.00	2.00
371	Mike Kekich	.75	.30
372	Oscar Gamble	.75	.30
373	Clyde Wright	.75	.30
374	Darrell Evans	1.50	.60
375	Larry Dierker	1.50	.60
376	Frank Duffy	.75	.30
377	Gene Mauch MG	4.00	1.50
378	Len Randle	.75	.30
379	Cy Acosta RC	.75	.30
380	Johnny Bench	12.00	6.00
381	Vicente Romo	.75	.30
382	Mike Hegan	.75	.30
383	Diego Segui	.75	.30
384	Don Baylor	4.00	1.50
385	Jim Perry	1.50	.60
386	Don Money	.75	.30
387	Jim Barr	.75	.30
388	Ben Oglivie	1.50	.60
389	New York Mets TC	4.00	1.50
390	Mickey Lolich	1.50	.60
391	Lee Lacy RC	1.50	.60
392	Dick Drago	.75	.30
393	Jose Cardenal	.75	.30
394	Sparky Lyle	1.50	.60
395	Roger Metzger	.75	.30
396	Grant Jackson	.75	.30
397	Dave Cash	1.25	.50
398	Rich Hand	1.25	.50
399	George Foster	2.00	.75
400	Gaylord Perry	5.00	2.00
401	Clyde Mashore	1.25	.50
402	Jack Hiatt	1.25	.50
403	Sonny Jackson	1.25	.50
404	Chuck Brinkman	1.25	.50
405	Cesar Tovar	1.25	.50
406	Paul Lindblad	1.25	.50
407	Felix Millan	1.25	.50
408	Jim Colborn	1.25	.50
409	Ivan Murrell	1.25	.50
410	Willie McCovey	6.00	3.00
411	Ray Corbin	1.25	.50
412	Manny Mota	2.00	.75
413	Tom Timmermann	1.25	.50
414	Ken Rudolph	1.25	.50
415	Marty Pattin	1.25	.50
416	Paul Schaal	1.25	.50
417	Scipio Spinks	1.25	.50
418	Bob Grich	2.00	.75
419	Casey Cox	1.25	.50
420	Tommie Agee	1.25	.50
421A	B.Winkles MG RC Orange	1.50	.60
421B	Bobby Winkles MG Pale	3.00	1.25
422	Bob Robertson	1.25	.50
423	Johnny Jeter	1.25	.50
424	Denny Doyle	1.25	.50
425	Alex Johnson	1.25	.50
426	Dave LaRoche	1.25	.50
427	Rick Auerbach	1.25	.50
428	Wayne Simpson	1.25	.50
429	Jim Fairey	1.25	.50
430	Vida Blue	2.00	.75
431	Gerry Moses	1.25	.50
432	Dan Frisella	1.25	.50
433	Willie Horton	2.00	.75
434	San Francisco Giants TC	3.00	1.25
435	Rico Carty	2.00	.75
436	Jim McAndrew	1.25	.50
437	John Kennedy	1.25	.50
438	Enzo Hernandez	1.25	.50
439	Eddie Fisher	1.25	.50
440	Glenn Beckert	1.25	.50
441	Gail Hopkins	1.25	.50
442	Dick Dietz	1.25	.50
443	Danny Thompson	1.25	.50
444	Ken Brett	1.25	.50
445	Ken Berry	1.25	.50
446	Jerry Reuss	2.00	.75
447	Joe Hague	1.25	.50
448	John Hiller	1.25	.50
449A	K.Aspro MG w/Spahn Point	4.00	1.50
449B	K.Aspro MG w/Spahn Round	4.00	1.50
450	Joe Torre	3.00	1.25
451	John Vukovich RC	1.25	.50
452	Paul Casanova	1.25	.50
453	Checklist 397-528	3.00	1.25
454	Tom Haller	1.25	.50
455	Bill Melton	1.25	.50
456	Dick Green	1.25	.50
457	John Strohmayer	1.25	.50
458	Jim Mason	1.25	.50
459	Jimmy Howarth RC	1.25	.50
460	Bill Freehan	2.00	.75
461	Mike Corkins	1.25	.50
462	Ron Blomberg	1.25	.50
463	Ken Tatum	1.25	.50
464	Chicago Cubs TC	3.00	1.25
465	Dave Giusti	1.25	.50
466	Jose Arcia	1.25	.50
467	Mike Ryan	1.25	.50
468	Tom Griffin	1.25	.50
469	Dan Monzon RC	1.25	.50
470	Mike Cuellar	2.00	.75
471	Ty Cobb LDR	10.00	5.00
472	Lou Gehrig LDR	15.00	7.50
473	Hank Aaron LDR	10.00	5.00
474	Babe Ruth LDR	20.00	10.00
475	Ty Cobb LDR	8.00	4.00
476	Walter Johnson LDR	3.00	1.25
477	Cy Young LDR	3.00	1.25
478	Walter Johnson LDR	3.00	1.25
479	Hal Lanier	1.25	.50
480	Juan Marichal	5.00	2.00
481	Chicago White Sox TC	3.00	1.25
482	Rick Reuschel RC	3.00	1.25
483	Dal Maxvill	1.25	.50
484	Ernie McAnally	1.25	.50
485	Norm Cash	2.00	.75
486A	D.Ozark MG RC Orange	1.50	.60
486B	Danny Ozark MG Pale	3.00	1.25
487	Bruce Dal Canton	1.25	.50
488	Dave Campbell	2.00	.75
489	Jeff Burroughs	2.00	.75
490	Claude Osteen	2.00	.75
491	Bob Montgomery	1.25	.50
492	Pedro Borbon	1.25	.50
493	Duffy Dyer	1.25	.50
494	Rich Morales	1.25	.50
495	Tommy Helms	1.25	.50
496	Ray Lamb	1.25	.50
497A	R.Schoen MG Orange	2.00	.75
497B	R.Schoen MG Pale	3.00	1.25
498	Graig Nettles	3.00	1.25
499	Bob Moose	1.25	.50
500	Oakland Athletics TC	3.00	1.25
501	Larry Gura	1.25	.50
502	Bobby Valentine	3.00	1.25
503	Phil Niekro	5.00	2.00
504	Earl Williams	1.25	.50
505	Bob Bailey	1.25	.50
506	Bart Johnson	1.25	.50
507	Darrel Chaney	1.25	.50
508	Gates Brown	1.25	.50
509	Jim Nash	1.25	.50
510	Amos Otis	2.00	.75
511	Sam McDowell	2.00	.75
512	Dalton Jones	1.25	.50
513	Dave Marshall	1.25	.50
514	Jerry Kenney	1.25	.50
515	Andy Messersmith	2.00	.75
516	Danny Walton	1.25	.50
517A	Bill Virdon MG w/o Ear	1.50	.60
517B	Bill Virdon MG w/Ear	3.00	1.25
518	Bob Veale	1.25	.50
519	Johnny Edwards	1.25	.50
520	Mel Stottlemyre	2.00	.75
521	Atlanta Braves TC	3.00	1.25
522	Leo Cardenas	1.25	.50
523	Wayne Granger	1.25	.50
524	Gene Tenace	2.00	.75
525	Jim Fregosi	2.00	.75
526	Ollie Brown	1.25	.50
527	Dan McGinn	1.25	.50
528	Paul Blair	1.25	.50
529	Milt May	3.00	1.25
530	Jim Kaat	5.00	2.00
531	Ron Woods	3.00	1.25
532	Steve Mingori	3.00	1.25
533	Larry Stahl	3.00	1.25
534	Dave Lemonds	3.00	1.25

❑ 535 Johnny Callison 5.00 2.00
❑ 536 Philadelphia Phillies TC 6.00 3.00
❑ 537 Bill Slayback RC 3.00 1.25
❑ 538 Jim Ray Hart 5.00 2.00
❑ 539 Tom Murphy 3.00 1.25
❑ 540 Cleon Jones 5.00 2.00
❑ 541 Bob Bolin 3.00 1.25
❑ 542 Pat Corrales 5.00 2.00
❑ 543 Alan Foster 3.00 1.25
❑ 544 Von Joshua 3.00 1.25
❑ 545 Orlando Cepeda 8.00 4.00
❑ 546 Jim York 3.00 1.25
❑ 547 Bobby Heise 3.00 1.25
❑ 548 Don Durham RC 3.00 1.25
❑ 549 Whitey Herzog MG 5.00 2.00
❑ 550 Dave Johnson 5.00 2.00
❑ 551 Mike Kilkenny 3.00 1.25
❑ 552 J.C. Martin 3.00 1.25
❑ 553 Mickey Scott 3.00 1.25
❑ 554 Dave Concepcion 5.00 2.00
❑ 555 Bill Hands 3.00 1.25
❑ 556 New York Yankees TC 8.00 4.00
❑ 557 Bernie Williams 3.00 1.25
❑ 558 Jerry May 3.00 1.25
❑ 559 Barry Lersch 3.00 1.25
❑ 560 Frank Howard 5.00 2.00
❑ 561 Jim Geddes RC 3.00 1.25
❑ 562 Wayne Garrett 3.00 1.25
❑ 563 Larry Haney 3.00 1.25
❑ 564 Mike Thompson RC 3.00 1.25
❑ 565 Jim Hickman 3.00 1.25
❑ 566 Lew Krausse 3.00 1.25
❑ 567 Bob Fenwick 3.00 1.25
❑ 568 Ray Newman 3.00 1.25
❑ 569 Walt Alston MG 8.00 4.00
❑ 570 Bill Singer 5.00 2.00
❑ 571 Rusty Torres 3.00 1.25
❑ 572 Gary Sutherland 3.00 1.25
❑ 573 Fred Beene 3.00 1.25
❑ 574 Bob Didier 3.00 1.25
❑ 575 Dock Ellis 3.00 1.25
❑ 576 Montreal Expos TC 6.00 3.00
❑ 577 Eric Soderholm RC 3.00 1.25
❑ 578 Ken Wright 3.00 1.25
❑ 579 Tom Grieve 5.00 2.00
❑ 580 Joe Pepitone 5.00 2.00
❑ 581 Steve Kealey 3.00 1.25
❑ 582 Darrell Porter 5.00 2.00
❑ 583 Bill Grief 3.00 1.25
❑ 584 Chris Arnold 3.00 1.25
❑ 585 Joe Niekro 5.00 2.00
❑ 586 Bill Sudakis 3.00 1.25
❑ 587 Rich McKinney 3.00 1.25
❑ 588 Checklist 529-660 20.00 10.00
❑ 589 Ken Forsch 3.00 1.25
❑ 590 Deron Johnson 3.00 1.25
❑ 591 Mike Hedlund 3.00 1.25
❑ 592 John Boccabella 3.00 1.25
❑ 593 Jack McKeon MG RC 4.00 1.50
❑ 594 Vic Harris RC 3.00 1.25
❑ 595 Don Gullett 5.00 2.00
❑ 596 Boston Red Sox TC 6.00 3.00
❑ 597 Mickey Rivers 5.00 2.00
❑ 598 Phil Roof 3.00 1.25
❑ 599 Ed Crosby 3.00 1.25
❑ 600 Dave McNally 5.00 2.00
❑ 601 Robles/Pena/Stelmaszek RC 5.00 2.00
❑ 602 Behney/Garcia/Rau RC 5.00 2.00
❑ 603 Hughes/McNulty/Reitz RC 5.00 2.00
❑ 604 Jefferson/O'Toole/Stampe RC 5.00 2.00
❑ 605 Cabell/Bourque/Marquez RC 5.00 2.00
❑ 606 Matthews/Pac/Roque RC 5.00 2.00
❑ 607 Frias/Busse/Guerrero RC 5.00 2.00
❑ 608 Busby/Colpaert/Medich RC 5.00 2.00
❑ 609 Blanks/Garcia/Lopes RC 5.00 2.00
❑ 610 Freeman/Hough/Webb RC 5.00 2.00
❑ 611 Coggins/Wohlford/Zisk RC 5.00 2.00
❑ 612 Lawson/Reynolds/Strom RC 5.00 2.00
❑ 613 Boone/Jutze/Ivie RC 15.00 7.50
❑ 614 Bumbry/Evans/Spikes RC 20.00 10.00
❑ 615 Mike Schmidt RC 150.00 90.00
❑ 616 Angelini/Blateric/Garman RC 5.00 2.00
❑ 617 Rich Chiles 3.00 1.25
❑ 618 Andy Etchebarren 3.00 1.25
❑ 619 Billy Wilson 3.00 1.25
❑ 620 Tommy Harper 5.00 2.00
❑ 621 Joe Ferguson 5.00 2.00
❑ 622 Larry Hisle 5.00 2.00
❑ 623 Steve Renko 3.00 1.25
❑ 624 Leo Durocher MG 5.00 2.00
❑ 625 Angel Mangual 3.00 1.25
❑ 626 Bob Barton 3.00 1.25
❑ 627 Luis Alvarado 3.00 1.25
❑ 628 Jim Slaton 3.00 1.25
❑ 629 Cleveland Indians TC 6.00 3.00
❑ 630 Denny McLain 8.00 4.00
❑ 631 Tom Matchick 3.00 1.25
❑ 632 Dick Selma 3.00 1.25
❑ 633 Ike Brown 3.00 1.25
❑ 634 Alan Closter 3.00 1.25
❑ 635 Gene Alley 5.00 2.00
❑ 636 Rickey Clark 3.00 1.25
❑ 637 Norm Miller 3.00 1.25
❑ 638 Ken Reynolds 3.00 1.25
❑ 639 Willie Crawford 3.00 1.25
❑ 640 Dick Bosman 3.00 1.25
❑ 641 Cincinnati Reds TC 6.00 3.00
❑ 642 Jose Laboy 3.00 1.25
❑ 643 Al Fitzmorris 3.00 1.25
❑ 644 Jack Heidemann 3.00 1.25
❑ 645 Bob Locker 3.00 1.25
❑ 646 Del Crandall MG 4.00 1.50
❑ 647 George Stone 3.00 1.25
❑ 648 Tom Egan 3.00 1.25
❑ 649 Rich Folkers 3.00 1.25
❑ 650 Felipe Alou 5.00 2.00
❑ 651 Don Carrithers 3.00 1.25
❑ 652 Ted Kubiak 3.00 1.25
❑ 653 Joe Hoerner 3.00 1.25
❑ 654 Minnesota Twins TC 6.00 3.00
❑ 655 Clay Kirby 3.00 1.25
❑ 656 John Ellis 3.00 1.25
❑ 657 Bob Johnson 3.00 1.25
❑ 658 Elliott Maddox 3.00 1.25
❑ 659 Jose Pagan 3.00 1.25
❑ 660 Fred Scherman 5.00 2.00

1974 Topps

❑ COMPLETE SET (660) 400.00 250.00
❑ COMP.FACT.SET (660) 600.00 350.00
❑ WRAPPERS (10-CENTS) 10.00 5.00
❑ 1 Hank Aaron 715 50.00 25.00
❑ 2 Aaron Special 54-57 8.00 4.00
❑ 3 Aaron Special 58-61 8.00 4.00
❑ 4 Aaron Special 62-65 8.00 4.00
❑ 5 Aaron Special 66-69 8.00 4.00
❑ 6 Aaron Special 70-73 8.00 4.00
❑ 7 Jim Hunter 4.00 1.50
❑ 8 George Theodore RC .50 .20
❑ 9 Mickey Lolich 1.00 .40
❑ 10 Johnny Bench 15.00 6.00
❑ 11 Jim Bibby .50 .20
❑ 12 Dave May .50 .20
❑ 13 Tom Hilgendorf .50 .20
❑ 14 Paul Popovich .50 .20
❑ 15 Joe Torre 2.00 .75
❑ 16 Baltimore Orioles TC 1.00 .40
❑ 17 Doug Bird RC .50 .20
❑ 18 Gary Thomasson RC .50 .20
❑ 19 Gerry Moses .50 .20
❑ 20 Nolan Ryan 40.00 20.00
❑ 21 Bob Gallagher RC .50 .20
❑ 22 Cy Acosta .50 .20
❑ 23 Craig Robinson RC .50 .20
❑ 24 John Hiller 1.00 .40
❑ 25 Ken Singleton 1.00 .40
❑ 26 Bill Campbell RC .50 .20
❑ 27 George Scott 1.00 .40
❑ 28 Manny Sanguillen 1.00 .40
❑ 29 Phil Niekro 3.00 1.25
❑ 30 Bobby Bonds 2.00 .75
❑ 31 Preston Gomez MG 1.00 .40
❑ 32A Johnny Grubb SD RC 1.00 .40
❑ 32B Johnny Grubb WASH 4.00 1.50
❑ 33 Don Newhauser RC .50 .20
❑ 34 Andy Kosco .50 .20
❑ 35 Gaylord Perry 3.00 1.25
❑ 36 St. Louis Cardinals TC 1.00 .40
❑ 37 Dave Sells RC .50 .20
❑ 38 Don Kessinger 1.00 .40
❑ 39 Ken Suarez .50 .20
❑ 40 Jim Palmer 8.00 3.00
❑ 41 Bobby Floyd .50 .20
❑ 42 Claude Osteen 1.00 .40
❑ 43 Jim Wynn 1.00 .40
❑ 44 Mel Stottlemyre 1.00 .40
❑ 45 Dave Johnson 1.00 .40
❑ 46 Pat Kelly .50 .20
❑ 47 Dick Ruthven RC .50 .20
❑ 48 Dick Sharon RC .50 .20
❑ 49 Steve Renko .50 .20
❑ 50 Rod Carew 8.00 3.00
❑ 51 Bobby Heise .50 .20
❑ 52 Al Oliver 1.00 .40
❑ 53A Fred Kendall SD 1.00 .40
❑ 53B Fred Kendall WASH 4.00 1.50
❑ 54 Elias Sosa RC .50 .20
❑ 55 Frank Robinson 8.00 3.00
❑ 56 New York Mets TC 1.00 .40
❑ 57 Darold Knowles .50 .20
❑ 58 Charlie Spikes .50 .20
❑ 59 Ross Grimsley .50 .20
❑ 60 Lou Brock 6.00 2.50
❑ 61 Luis Aparicio 3.00 1.25
❑ 62 Bob Locker .50 .20
❑ 63 Bill Sudakis .50 .20
❑ 64 Doug Rau .50 .20
❑ 65 Amos Otis 1.00 .40
❑ 66 Sparky Lyle 1.00 .40
❑ 67 Tommy Helms .50 .20
❑ 68 Grant Jackson .50 .20
❑ 69 Del Unser .50 .20
❑ 70 Dick Allen 2.00 .75
❑ 71 Dan Frisella .50 .20
❑ 72 Aurelio Rodriguez .50 .20
❑ 73 Mike Marshall 2.00 .75
❑ 74 Minnesota Twins TC 1.00 .40
❑ 75 Jim Colborn .50 .20
❑ 76 Mickey Rivers 1.00 .40
❑ 77A Rich Troedson SD 1.00 .40
❑ 77B Rich Troedson WASH 4.00 1.50
❑ 78 Charlie Fox MG 1.00 .40
❑ 79 Gene Tenace 1.00 .40
❑ 80 Tom Seaver 12.00 5.00
❑ 81 Frank Duffy .50 .20
❑ 82 Dave Giusti .50 .20
❑ 83 Orlando Cepeda 3.00 1.25
❑ 84 Rick Wise .50 .20
❑ 85 Joe Morgan 8.00 3.00
❑ 86 Joe Ferguson 1.00 .40
❑ 87 Fergie Jenkins 3.00 1.25
❑ 88 Freddie Patek 1.00 .40
❑ 89 Jackie Brown .50 .20
❑ 90 Bobby Murcer 1.00 .40
❑ 91 Ken Forsch .50 .20
❑ 92 Paul Blair 1.00 .40
❑ 93 Rod Gilbreath RC .50 .20
❑ 94 Detroit Tigers TC 1.00 .40
❑ 95 Steve Carlton 8.00 3.00
❑ 96 Jerry Hairston RC .50 .20
❑ 97 Bob Bailey .50 .20
❑ 98 Bert Blyleven 2.00 .75
❑ 99 Del Crandall MG 1.00 .40
❑ 100 Willie Stargell 6.00 2.50
❑ 101 Bobby Valentine 1.00 .40
❑ 102A Bill Greif SD 1.00 .40
❑ 102B Bill Greif WASH 4.00 1.50
❑ 103 Sal Bando 1.00 .40
❑ 104 Ron Bryant .50 .20
❑ 105 Carlton Fisk 12.00 5.00

106	Harry Parker RC	.50	.20
107	Alex Johnson	.50	.20
108	Al Hrabosky	1.00	.40
109	Bob Grich	1.00	.40
110	Billy Williams	3.00	1.25
111	Clay Carroll	.50	.20
112	Davey Lopes	2.00	.75
113	Dick Drago	.50	.20
114	California Angels TC	1.00	.40
115	Willie Horton	1.00	.40
116	Jerry Reuss	1.00	.40
117	Ron Blomberg	.50	.20
118	Bill Lee	1.00	.40
119	Danny Ozark MG	1.00	.40
120	Wilbur Wood	.50	.20
121	Larry Lintz RC	.50	.20
122	Jim Holt	.50	.20
123	Nelson Briles	1.00	.40
124	Bobby Coluccio RC	.50	.20
125A	Nate Colbert SD	1.00	.40
125B	Nate Colbert WASH	4.00	1.50
126	Checklist 1-132	3.00	1.25
127	Tom Paciorek	1.00	.40
128	John Ellis	.50	.20
129	Chris Speier	.50	.20
130	Reggie Jackson	15.00	6.00
131	Bob Boone	2.00	.75
132	Felix Millan	.50	.20
133	David Clyde RC	1.00	.40
134	Denis Menke	.50	.20
135	Roy White	1.00	.40
136	Rick Reuschel	1.00	.40
137	Al Bumbry	1.00	.40
138	Eddie Brinkman	.50	.20
139	Aurelio Monteagudo	.50	.20
140	Darrell Evans	2.00	.75
141	Pat Bourque	.50	.20
142	Pedro Garcia	.50	.20
143	Dick Woodson	.50	.20
144	Walter Alston MG	3.00	1.25
145	Dock Ellis	.50	.20
146	Ron Fairly	1.00	.40
147	Bart Johnson	.50	.20
148A	Dave Hilton SD	1.00	.40
148B	Dave Hilton WASH	4.00	1.50
149	Mac Scarce	.50	.20
150	John Mayberry	1.00	.40
151	Diego Segui	.50	.20
152	Oscar Gamble	1.00	.40
153	Jon Matlack	1.00	.40
154	Houston Astros TC	1.00	.40
155	Bert Campaneris	1.00	.40
156	Randy Moffitt	.50	.20
157	Vic Harris	.50	.20
158	Jack Billingham	.50	.20
159	Jim Ray Hart	.50	.20
160	Brooks Robinson	8.00	3.00
161	Ray Burris UER RC	1.00	.40
162	Bill Freehan	1.00	.40
163	Ken Berry	.50	.20
164	Tom House	.50	.20
165	Willie Davis	1.00	.40
166	Jack McKeon MG	1.00	.40
167	Luis Tiant	2.00	.75
168	Danny Thompson	.50	.20
169	Steve Rogers RC	2.00	.75
170	Bill Melton	.50	.20
171	Eduardo Rodriguez RC	.50	.20
172	Gene Clines	.50	.20
173A	Randy Jones SD RC	2.00	.75
173B	Randy Jones WASH	5.00	2.00
174	Bill Robinson	1.00	.40
175	Reggie Cleveland	.50	.20
176	John Lowenstein	.50	.20
177	Dave Roberts	.50	.20
178	Garry Maddox	1.00	.40
179	Yogi Berra MG	5.00	2.00
180	Ken Holtzman	1.00	.40
181	Cesar Geronimo	.50	.20
182	Lindy McDaniel	1.00	.40
183	Johnny Oates	1.00	.40
184	Texas Rangers TC	1.00	.40
185	Jose Cardenal	.50	.20
186	Fred Scherman	.50	.20
187	Don Baylor	2.00	.75
188	Rudy Meoli RC	.50	.20
189	Jim Brewer	.50	.20
190	Tony Oliva	2.00	.75
191	Al Fitzmorris	.50	.20
192	Mario Guerrero	.50	.20
193	Tom Walker	.50	.20
194	Darrell Porter	1.00	.40
195	Carlos May	.50	.20
196	Jim Fregosi	1.00	.40
197A	Vicente Romo SD	1.00	.40
197B	Vicente Romo WASH	4.00	1.50
198	Dave Cash	.50	.20
199	Mike Kekich	.50	.20
200	Cesar Cedeno	1.00	.40
201	R.Carew/P.Rose LL	6.00	2.50
202	R.Jackson/W.Stargell LL	5.00	2.00
203	R.Jackson/W.Stargell LL	5.00	2.00
204	T.Harper/L.Brock LL	2.00	.75
205	W.Wood/R.Bryant LL	1.00	.40
206	J.Palmer/T.Seaver LL	5.00	2.00
207	N.Ryan/T.Seaver LL	12.00	5.00
208	J.Hiller/M.Marshall LL	1.00	.40
209	Ted Sizemore	.50	.20
210	Bill Singer	.50	.20
211	Chicago Cubs TC	1.00	.40
212	Rollie Fingers	3.00	1.25
213	Dave Rader	.50	.20
214	Billy Grabarkewitz	.50	.20
215	Al Kaline UER	10.00	4.00
216	Ray Sadecki	.50	.20
217	Tim Foli	.50	.20
218	Johnny Briggs	.50	.20
219	Doug Griffin	.50	.20
220	Don Sutton	3.00	1.25
221	Chuck Tanner MG	1.00	.40
222	Ramon Hernandez	.50	.20
223	Jeff Burroughs	2.00	.75
224	Roger Metzger	.50	.20
225	Paul Splittorff	.50	.20
226A	San Diego Padres TC SD	2.00	.75
226B	San Diego Padres TC WASH	8.00	3.00
227	Mike Lum	.50	.20
228	Ted Kubiak	.50	.20
229	Fritz Peterson	.50	.20
230	Tony Perez	4.00	1.50
231	Dick Tidrow	.50	.20
232	Steve Brye	.50	.20
233	Jim Barr	.50	.20
234	John Milner	.50	.20
235	Dave McNally	1.00	.40
236	Red Schoendienst MG	3.00	1.25
237	Ken Brett	.50	.20
238	F.Healy w/Munson	.50	.20
239	Bill Russell	1.00	.40
240	Joe Coleman	.50	.20
241A	Glenn Bookort SD	1.00	.40
241B	Glenn Beckert WASH	4.00	1.50
242	Bill Gogolewski	.50	.20
243	Bob Oliver	.50	.20
244	Carl Morton	.50	.20
245	Cleon Jones	.50	.20
246	Oakland Athletics TC	2.00	.75
247	Rick Miller	.50	.20
248	Tom Hall	.50	.20
249	George Mitterwald	.50	.20
250A	Willie McCovey SD	8.00	3.00
250B	Willie McCovey WASH	25.00	10.00
251	Graig Nettles	2.00	.75
252	Dave Parker RC	10.00	4.00
253	John Boccabella	.50	.20
254	Stan Bahnsen	.50	.20
255	Larry Bowa	1.00	.40
256	Tom Griffin	.50	.20
257	Buddy Bell	2.00	.75
258	Jerry Morales	.50	.20
259	Bob Reynolds	.50	.20
260	Ted Simmons	2.00	.75
261	Jerry Bell	.50	.20
262	Ed Kirkpatrick	.50	.20
263	Checklist 133-264	3.00	1.25
264	Joe Rudi	1.00	.40
265	Tug McGraw	2.00	.75
266	Jim Northrup	1.00	.40
267	Andy Messersmith	1.00	.40
268	Tom Grieve	1.00	.40
269	Bob Johnson	.50	.20
270	Ron Santo	2.00	.75
271	Bill Hands	.50	.20
272	Paul Casanova	.50	.20
273	Checklist 265-396	3.00	1.25
274	Fred Beene	.50	.20
275	Ron Hunt	.50	.20
276	Bobby Winkles MG	1.00	.40
277	Gary Nolan	1.00	.40
278	Cookie Rojas	1.00	.40
279	Jim Crawford RC	.50	.20
280	Carl Yastrzemski	12.00	5.00
281	San Francisco Giants TC	1.00	.40
282	Doyle Alexander	1.00	.40
283	Mike Schmidt	20.00	8.00
284	Dave Duncan	1.00	.40
285	Reggie Smith	1.00	.40
286	Tony Muser	.50	.20
287	Clay Kirby	.50	.20
288	Gorman Thomas RC	2.00	.75
289	Rick Auerbach	.50	.20
290	Vida Blue	1.00	.40
291	Don Hahn	.50	.20
292	Chuck Seelbach	.50	.20
293	Milt May	.50	.20
294	Steve Foucault RC	.50	.20
295	Rick Monday	1.00	.40
296	Ray Corbin	.50	.20
297	Hal Breeden	.50	.20
298	Roric Harrison	.50	.20
299	Gene Michael	.50	.20
300	Pete Rose	25.00	10.00
301	Bob Montgomery	.50	.20
302	Rudy May	.50	.20
303	George Hendrick	1.00	.40
304	Don Wilson	.50	.20
305	Tito Fuentes	.50	.20
306	Earl Weaver MG	3.00	1.25
307	Luis Melendez	.50	.20
308	Bruce Dal Canton	.50	.20
309A	Dave Roberts SD	1.00	.40
309B	Dave Roberts WASH	6.00	2.50
310	Terry Forster	1.00	.40
311	Jerry Grote	1.00	.40
312	Deron Johnson	.50	.20
313	Barry Lersch	.50	.20
314	Milwaukee Brewers TC	1.00	.40
315	Ron Cey	2.00	.75
316	Jim Perry	1.00	.40
317	Richie Zisk	1.00	.40
318	Jim Merritt	.50	.20
319	Randy Hundley	.50	.20
320	Dusty Baker	2.00	.75
321	Steve Braun	.50	.20
322	Ernie McAnally	.50	.20
323	Richie Scheinblum	.50	.20
324	Steve Kline	.50	.20
325	Tommy Harper	1.00	.40
326	Sparky Anderson MG	3.00	1.25
327	Tom Timmermann	.50	.20
328	Skip Jutze	.50	.20
329	Mark Belanger	1.00	.40
330	Juan Marichal	5.00	2.00
331	C.Fisk/J.Bench AS	5.00	2.00
332	D.Allen/H.Aaron AS	8.00	3.00
333	R.Carew/J.Morgan AS	4.00	1.50
334	B.Robinson/R.Santo AS	2.00	.75
335	B.Campaneris/C.Speier AS	1.00	.40
336	B.Murcer/P.Rose AS	5.00	2.00
337	A.Otis/C.Cedeno AS	1.00	.40
338	R.Jackson/B.Williams AS	5.00	2.00
339	J.Hunter/R.Wise AS	3.00	1.25
340	Thurman Munson	8.00	3.00
341	Dan Driessen RC	1.00	.40
342	Jim Lonborg	1.00	.40
343	Kansas City Royals TC	1.00	.40
344	Mike Caldwell	.50	.20
345	Bill North	.50	.20
346	Ron Reed	.50	.20
347	Sandy Alomar	1.00	.40
348	Pete Richert	.50	.20
349	John Vukovich	.50	.20
350	Bob Gibson	8.00	3.00
351	Dwight Evans	3.00	1.25
352	Bill Stoneman	.50	.20
353	Rich Coggins	.50	.20
354	Whitey Lockman MG	1.00	.40
355	Dave Nelson	.50	.20

❑ 356 Jerry Koosman 1.00 .40
❑ 357 Buddy Bradford .50 .20
❑ 358 Dal Maxvill .50 .20
❑ 359 Brent Strom .50 .20
❑ 360 Greg Luzinski 2.00 .75
❑ 361 Don Carrithers .50 .20
❑ 362 Hal King .50 .20
❑ 363 New York Yankees TC 2.00 .75
❑ 364A Cito Gaston SD 2.00 .75
❑ 364B Cito Gaston WASH 8.00 3.00
❑ 365 Steve Busby 1.00 .40
❑ 366 Larry Hisle 1.00 .40
❑ 367 Norm Cash 2.00 .75
❑ 368 Manny Mota 1.00 .40
❑ 369 Paul Lindblad .50 .20
❑ 370 Bob Watson 1.00 .40
❑ 371 Jim Slaton .50 .20
❑ 372 Ken Reitz .50 .20
❑ 373 John Curtis .50 .20
❑ 374 Marty Perez .50 .20
❑ 375 Earl Williams .50 .20
❑ 376 Jorge Orta .50 .20
❑ 377 Ron Woods .50 .20
❑ 378 Burt Hooton 1.00 .40
❑ 379 Billy Martin MG 2.00 .75
❑ 380 Bud Harrelson 1.00 .40
❑ 381 Charlie Sands .50 .20
❑ 382 Bob Moose .50 .20
❑ 383 Philadelphia Phillies TC 1.00 .40
❑ 384 Chris Chambliss 1.00 .40
❑ 385 Don Gullett 1.00 .40
❑ 386 Gary Matthews 2.00 .75
❑ 387A Rich Morales SD 1.00 .40
❑ 387B Rich Morales WASH 6.00 2.50
❑ 388 Phil Roof .50 .20
❑ 389 Gates Brown .50 .20
❑ 390 Lou Piniella 2.00 .75
❑ 391 Billy Champion .50 .20
❑ 392 Dick Green .50 .20
❑ 393 Orlando Pena .50 .20
❑ 394 Ken Henderson .50 .20
❑ 395 Doug Rader .50 .20
❑ 396 Tommy Davis 1.00 .40
❑ 397 George Stone .50 .20
❑ 398 Duke Sims .50 .20
❑ 399 Mike Paul .50 .20
❑ 400 Harmon Killebrew 6.00 2.50
❑ 401 Elliott Maddox .50 .20
❑ 402 Jim Rooker .50 .20
❑ 403 Darrell Johnson MG 1.00 .40
❑ 404 Jim Howarth .50 .20
❑ 405 Ellie Rodriguez .50 .20
❑ 406 Steve Arlin .50 .20
❑ 407 Jim Wohlford .50 .20
❑ 408 Charlie Hough 1.00 .40
❑ 409 Ike Brown .50 .20
❑ 410 Pedro Borbon .50 .20
❑ 411 Frank Baker .50 .20
❑ 412 Chuck Taylor .50 .20
❑ 413 Don Money 1.00 .40
❑ 414 Checklist 397-528 3.00 1.25
❑ 415 Gary Gentry .50 .20
❑ 416 Chicago White Sox TC 1.00 .40
❑ 417 Rich Folkers .50 .20
❑ 418 Walt Williams .50 .20
❑ 419 Wayne Twitchell .50 .20
❑ 420 Ray Fosse .50 .20
❑ 421 Dan Fife RC .50 .20
❑ 422 Gonzalo Marquez .50 .20
❑ 423 Fred Stanley .50 .20
❑ 424 Jim Beauchamp .50 .20
❑ 425 Pete Broberg .50 .20
❑ 426 Rennie Stennett .50 .20
❑ 427 Bobby Bolin .50 .20
❑ 428 Gary Sutherland .50 .20
❑ 429 Dick Lange RC .50 .20
❑ 430 Matty Alou 1.00 .40
❑ 431 Gene Garber RC 1.00 .40
❑ 432 Chris Arnold .50 .20
❑ 433 Lerrin LaGrow .50 .20
❑ 434 Ken McMullen .50 .20
❑ 435 Dave Concepcion 2.00 .75
❑ 436 Don Hood RC .50 .20
❑ 437 Jim Lyttle .50 .20
❑ 438 Ed Herrmann .50 .20
❑ 439 Norm Miller .50 .20
❑ 440 Jim Kaat 2.00 .75
❑ 441 Tom Ragland .50 .20
❑ 442 Alan Foster .50 .20
❑ 443 Tom Hutton .50 .20
❑ 444 Vic Davalillo .50 .20
❑ 445 George Medich .50 .20
❑ 446 Len Randle .50 .20
❑ 447 Frank Quilici MG 1.00 .40
❑ 448 Ron Hodges RC .50 .20
❑ 449 Tom McCraw .50 .20
❑ 450 Rich Hebner 1.00 .40
❑ 451 Tommy John 2.00 .75
❑ 452 Gene Hiser .50 .20
❑ 453 Balor Moore .50 .20
❑ 454 Kurt Bevacqua .50 .20
❑ 455 Tom Bradley .50 .20
❑ 456 Dave Winfield RC 50.00 25.00
❑ 457 Chuck Goggin RC .50 .20
❑ 458 Jim Ray .50 .20
❑ 459 Cincinnati Reds TC 2.00 .75
❑ 460 Boog Powell 2.00 .75
❑ 461 John Odom .50 .20
❑ 462 Luis Alvarado .50 .20
❑ 463 Pat Dobson .50 .20
❑ 464 Jose Cruz 2.00 .75
❑ 465 Dick Bosman .50 .20
❑ 466 Dick Billings .50 .20
❑ 467 Winston Llenas .50 .20
❑ 468 Pepe Frias .50 .20
❑ 469 Joe Decker .50 .20
❑ 470 Reggie Jackson ALCS 5.00 2.00
❑ 471 Jon Matlack NLCS 1.00 .40
❑ 472 Darold Knowles WS1 1.00 .40
❑ 473 Willie Mays WS 8.00 3.00
❑ 474 Bert Campaneris WS3 1.00 .40
❑ 475 Rusty Staub WS4 1.00 .40
❑ 476 Cleon Jones WS5 1.00 .40
❑ 477 Reggie Jackson WS 5.00 2.00
❑ 478 Bert Campaneris WS7 1.00 .40
❑ 479 A's Celebrate WS 1.00 .40
❑ 480 Willie Crawford .50 .20
❑ 481 Jerry Terrell RC .50 .20
❑ 482 Bob Didier .50 .20
❑ 483 Atlanta Braves TC 1.00 .40
❑ 484 Carmen Fanzone .50 .20
❑ 485 Felipe Alou 2.00 .75
❑ 486 Steve Stone 1.00 .40
❑ 487 Ted Martinez .50 .20
❑ 488 Andy Etchebarren .50 .20
❑ 489 Danny Murtaugh MG 1.00 .40
❑ 490 Vada Pinson 2.00 .75
❑ 491 Roger Nelson .50 .20
❑ 492 Mike Rogodzinski RC .50 .20
❑ 493 Joe Hoerner .50 .20
❑ 494 Ed Goodson .50 .20
❑ 495 Dick McAuliffe 1.00 .40
❑ 496 Tom Murphy .50 .20
❑ 497 Bobby Mitchell .50 .20
❑ 498 Pat Corrales .50 .20
❑ 499 Rusty Torres .50 .20
❑ 500 Lee May 1.00 .40
❑ 501 Eddie Leon .50 .20
❑ 502 Dave LaRoche .50 .20
❑ 503 Eric Soderholm .50 .20
❑ 504 Joe Niekro 1.00 .40
❑ 505 Bill Buckner 1.00 .40
❑ 506 Ed Farmer .50 .20
❑ 507 Larry Stahl .50 .20
❑ 508 Montreal Expos TC 1.00 .40
❑ 509 Jesse Jefferson .50 .20
❑ 510 Wayne Garrett .50 .20
❑ 511 Toby Harrah 1.00 .40
❑ 512 Joe Lahoud .50 .20
❑ 513 Jim Campanis .50 .20
❑ 514 Paul Schaal .50 .20
❑ 515 Willie Montanez .50 .20
❑ 516 Horacio Pina .50 .20
❑ 517 Mike Hegan .50 .20
❑ 518 Derrel Thomas .50 .20
❑ 519 Bill Sharp RC .50 .20
❑ 520 Tim McCarver 2.00 .75
❑ 521 Ken Aspromonte MG 1.00 .40
❑ 522 J.R. Richard 2.00 .75
❑ 523 Cecil Cooper 2.00 .75
❑ 524 Bill Plummer .50 .20
❑ 525 Clyde Wright .50 .20
❑ 526 Frank Tepedino 1.00 .40
❑ 527 Bobby Darwin .50 .20
❑ 528 Bill Bonham .50 .20
❑ 529 Horace Clarke 1.00 .40
❑ 530 Mickey Stanley 1.00 .40
❑ 531 Gene Mauch MG 1.00 .40
❑ 532 Skip Lockwood .50 .20
❑ 533 Mike Phillips RC .50 .20
❑ 534 Eddie Watt .50 .20
❑ 535 Bob Tolan .50 .20
❑ 536 Duffy Dyer .50 .20
❑ 537 Steve Mingori .50 .20
❑ 538 Cesar Tovar .50 .20
❑ 539 Lloyd Allen .50 .20
❑ 540 Bob Robertson .50 .20
❑ 541 Cleveland Indians TC 1.00 .40
❑ 542 Goose Gossage 2.00 .75
❑ 543 Danny Cater .50 .20
❑ 544 Ron Schueler .50 .20
❑ 545 Billy Conigliaro 1.00 .40
❑ 546 Mike Corkins .50 .20
❑ 547 Glenn Borgmann .50 .20
❑ 548 Sonny Siebert .50 .20
❑ 549 Mike Jorgensen .50 .20
❑ 550 Sam McDowell 1.00 .40
❑ 551 Von Joshua .50 .20
❑ 552 Denny Doyle .50 .20
❑ 553 Jim Willoughby .50 .20
❑ 554 Tim Johnson RC .50 .20
❑ 555 Woodie Fryman .50 .20
❑ 556 Dave Campbell 1.00 .40
❑ 557 Jim McGlothlin .50 .20
❑ 558 Bill Fahey .50 .20
❑ 559 Darrel Chaney .50 .20
❑ 560 Mike Cuellar 1.00 .40
❑ 561 Ed Kranepool 1.00 .40
❑ 562 Jack Aker .50 .20
❑ 563 Hal McRae 1.00 .40
❑ 564 Mike Ryan .50 .20
❑ 565 Milt Wilcox .50 .20
❑ 566 Jackie Hernandez .50 .20
❑ 567 Boston Red Sox TC 1.00 .40
❑ 568 Mike Torrez 1.00 .40
❑ 569 Rick Dempsey 1.00 .40
❑ 570 Ralph Garr 1.00 .40
❑ 571 Rich Hand .50 .20
❑ 572 Enzo Hernandez .50 .20
❑ 573 Mike Adams RC .50 .20
❑ 574 Bill Parsons .50 .20
❑ 575 Steve Garvey 3.00 1.25
❑ 576 Scipio Spinks .50 .20
❑ 577 Mike Sadek RC .50 .20
❑ 578 Ralph Houk MG 1.00 .40
❑ 579 Cecil Upshaw .50 .20
❑ 580 Jim Spencer .50 .20
❑ 581 Fred Norman .50 .20
❑ 582 Bucky Dent RC 5.00 2.00
❑ 583 Marty Pattin .50 .20
❑ 584 Ken Rudolph .50 .20
❑ 585 Merv Rettenmund .50 .20
❑ 586 Jack Brohamer .50 .20
❑ 587 Larry Christenson RC .50 .20
❑ 588 Hal Lanier .50 .20
❑ 589 Boots Day .50 .20
❑ 590 Roger Moret .50 .20
❑ 591 Sonny Jackson .50 .20
❑ 592 Ed Bane RC .50 .20
❑ 593 Steve Yeager 1.00 .40
❑ 594 Leroy Stanton .50 .20
❑ 595 Steve Blass 1.00 .40
❑ 596 Gar/Hold/Lit/Pole RC .50 .20
❑ 597 Chalk/Gam/Mac/Trillo RC 1.00 .40
❑ 598 Ken Griffey RC 12.00 5.00
❑ 599A Dior/Freis/Ric/Shan Wash 2.00 .75
❑ 599B Dior/Freis/Ric/Shan Lg 3.00 1.25
❑ 599C Dior/Freis/Ric/Shan Sm 6.00 2.50
❑ 600 Cash/Cox/Madlock/Sand RC 5.00 2.00
❑ 601 Arm/Bladt/Downing/McBride RC 3.00 1.25
❑ 602 Abb/Henn/Swan/Voss RC 1.00 .40
❑ 603 Foote/Lund/Moore/Robles RC 1.00 .40
❑ 604 Hugh/Knox/Thornton/White RC 5.00 2.00
❑ 605 Alb/Frail/Kob/Tanana RC 4.00 1.50
❑ 606 Fuller/Howard/Smith/Velez RC 1.00 .40
❑ 607 Fost/Hein/Ros/Taveras RC 1.00 .40
❑ 608A Apod/Ban/D'Acq/Wall ERR 2.00 .75
❑ 608B Apod/Ban/D'Acq/Wall RC 1.00 .40

- ❑ 609 Rico Petrocelli 1.00 .40
- ❑ 610 Dave Kingman 2.00 .75
- ❑ 611 Rich Stelmaszek .50 .20
- ❑ 612 Luke Walker .50 .20
- ❑ 613 Dan Monzon .50 .20
- ❑ 614 Adrian Devine RC .50 .20
- ❑ 615 Johnny Jeter UER .50 .20
- ❑ 616 Larry Gura .50 .20
- ❑ 617 Ted Ford .50 .20
- ❑ 618 Jim Mason .50 .20
- ❑ 619 Mike Anderson .50 .20
- ❑ 620 Al Downing .50 .20
- ❑ 621 Bernie Carbo .50 .20
- ❑ 622 Phil Gagliano .50 .20
- ❑ 623 Celerino Sanchez .50 .20
- ❑ 624 Bob Miller .50 .20
- ❑ 625 Ollie Brown .50 .20
- ❑ 626 Pittsburgh Pirates TC 1.00 .40
- ❑ 627 Carl Taylor .50 .20
- ❑ 628 Ivan Murrell .50 .20
- ❑ 629 Rusty Staub 2.00 .75
- ❑ 630 Tommie Agee 1.00 .40
- ❑ 631 Steve Barber .50 .20
- ❑ 632 George Culver .50 .20
- ❑ 633 Dave Hamilton .50 .20
- ❑ 634 Eddie Mathews MG 3.00 1.25
- ❑ 635 Johnny Edwards .50 .20
- ❑ 636 Dave Goltz .50 .20
- ❑ 637 Checklist 529-660 3.00 1.25
- ❑ 638 Ken Sanders .50 .20
- ❑ 639 Joe Lovitto .50 .20
- ❑ 640 Milt Pappas 1.00 .40
- ❑ 641 Chuck Brinkman .50 .20
- ❑ 642 Terry Harmon .50 .20
- ❑ 643 Los Angeles Dodgers TC 1.00 .40
- ❑ 644 Wayne Granger .50 .20
- ❑ 645 Ken Boswell .50 .20
- ❑ 646 George Foster 2.00 .75
- ❑ 647 Juan Beniquez RC .50 .20
- ❑ 648 Terry Crowley .50 .20
- ❑ 649 Fernando Gonzalez RC .50 .20
- ❑ 650 Mike Epstein .50 .20
- ❑ 651 Leron Lee .50 .20
- ❑ 652 Gail Hopkins .50 .20
- ❑ 653 Bob Stinson .50 .20
- ❑ 654A Jesus Alou NPOF 4.00 1.50
- ❑ 654B Jesus Alou COR 1.00 .40
- ❑ 655 Mike Tyson RC .50 .20
- ❑ 656 Adrian Garrett .50 .20
- ❑ 657 Jim Shellenback .50 .20
- ❑ 658 Lee Lacy .50 .20
- ❑ 659 Joe Lis .50 .20
- ❑ 660 Larry Dierker 2.00 .75

1975 Topps

- ❑ COMPLETE SET (660) 500.00 300.00
- ❑ WRAPPER (15-CENT) 8.00 4.00
- ❑ 1 Hank Aaron HL 30.00 12.50
- ❑ 2 Lou Brock HL 3.00 1.25
- ❑ 3 Bob Gibson HL 3.00 1.25
- ❑ 4 Al Kaline HL 6.00 2.50
- ❑ 5 Nolan Ryan HL 15.00 6.00
- ❑ 6 Mike Marshall HL 1.00 .40
- ❑ 7 Ryan/Busby/Bosman HL 8.00 3.00
- ❑ 8 Rogelio Moret .50 .20
- ❑ 9 Frank Tepedino 1.00 .40
- ❑ 10 Willie Davis 1.00 .40
- ❑ 11 Bill Melton .50 .20
- ❑ 12 David Clyde .50 .20
- ❑ 13 Gene Locklear RC 1.00 .40
- ❑ 14 Milt Wilcox .50 .20
- ❑ 15 Jose Cardenal 1.00 .40
- ❑ 16 Frank Tanana 2.00 .75
- ❑ 17 Dave Concepcion 2.00 .75
- ❑ 18 Detroit Tigers CL/Houk 2.00 .75
- ❑ 19 Jerry Koosman 1.00 .40
- ❑ 20 Thurman Munson 8.00 3.00
- ❑ 21 Rollie Fingers 3.00 1.25
- ❑ 22 Dave Cash .50 .20
- ❑ 23 Bill Russell 1.00 .40
- ❑ 24 Al Fitzmorris .50 .20
- ❑ 25 Lee May 1.00 .40
- ❑ 26 Dave McNally 1.00 .40
- ❑ 27 Ken Reitz .50 .20
- ❑ 28 Tom Murphy .50 .20
- ❑ 29 Dave Parker 3.00 1.25
- ❑ 30 Bert Blyleven 2.00 .75
- ❑ 31 Dave Rader .50 .20
- ❑ 32 Reggie Cleveland .50 .20
- ❑ 33 Dusty Baker 2.00 .75
- ❑ 34 Steve Renko .50 .20
- ❑ 35 Ron Santo 1.00 .40
- ❑ 36 Joe Lovitto .50 .20
- ❑ 37 Dave Freisleben .50 .20
- ❑ 38 Buddy Bell 2.00 .75
- ❑ 39 Andre Thornton 1.00 .40
- ❑ 40 Bill Singer .50 .20
- ❑ 41 Cesar Geronimo 1.00 .40
- ❑ 42 Joe Coleman .50 .20
- ❑ 43 Cleon Jones 1.00 .40
- ❑ 44 Pat Dobson .50 .20
- ❑ 45 Joe Rudi 1.00 .40
- ❑ 46 Philadelphia Phillies CL/Ozark 2.00 .75
- ❑ 47 Tommy John 2.00 .75
- ❑ 48 Freddie Patek 1.00 .40
- ❑ 49 Larry Dierker 1.00 .40
- ❑ 50 Brooks Robinson 8.00 3.00
- ❑ 51 Bob Forsch RC 1.00 .40
- ❑ 52 Darrell Porter 1.00 .40
- ❑ 53 Dave Giusti .50 .20
- ❑ 54 Eric Soderholm .50 .20
- ❑ 55 Bobby Bonds 2.00 .75
- ❑ 56 Rick Wise 1.00 .40
- ❑ 57 Dave Johnson 1.00 .40
- ❑ 58 Chuck Taylor .50 .20
- ❑ 59 Ken Henderson .50 .20
- ❑ 60 Fergie Jenkins 3.00 1.25
- ❑ 61 Dave Winfield 15.00 6.00
- ❑ 62 Fritz Peterson .50 .20
- ❑ 63 Steve Swisher RC .50 .20
- ❑ 64 Dave Chalk .50 .20
- ❑ 65 Don Gullett 1.00 .40
- ❑ 66 Willie Horton 1.00 .40
- ❑ 67 Tug McGraw 1.00 .40
- ❑ 68 Ron Blomberg .50 .20
- ❑ 69 John Odom .50 .20
- ❑ 70 Mike Schmidt 20.00 8.00
- ❑ 71 Charlie Hough 1.00 .40
- ❑ 72 Kansas City Royals CL/McKeon 2.00 .75
- ❑ 73 J.R. Richard 1.00 .40
- ❑ 74 Mark Belanger 1.00 .40
- ❑ 75 Ted Simmons 2.00 .75
- ❑ 76 Ed Sprague .50 .20
- ❑ 77 Richie Zisk 1.00 .40
- ❑ 78 Ray Corbin .50 .20
- ❑ 79 Gary Matthews 1.00 .40
- ❑ 80 Carlton Fisk 8.00 3.00
- ❑ 81 Ron Reed .50 .20
- ❑ 82 Pat Kelly .50 .20
- ❑ 83 Jim Merritt .50 .20
- ❑ 84 Enzo Hernandez .50 .20
- ❑ 85 Bill Bonham .50 .20
- ❑ 86 Joe Lis .50 .20
- ❑ 87 George Foster 2.00 .75
- ❑ 88 Tom Egan .50 .20
- ❑ 89 Jim Ray .50 .20
- ❑ 90 Rusty Staub 2.00 .75
- ❑ 91 Dick Green .50 .20
- ❑ 92 Cecil Upshaw .50 .20
- ❑ 93 Davey Lopes 2.00 .75
- ❑ 94 Jim Lonborg 1.00 .40
- ❑ 95 John Mayberry 1.00 .40
- ❑ 96 Mike Cosgrove RC .50 .20
- ❑ 97 Earl Williams .50 .20
- ❑ 98 Rich Folkers .50 .20
- ❑ 99 Mike Hegan .50 .20
- ❑ 100 Willie Stargell 4.00 1.50
- ❑ 101 Montreal Expos CL/Mauch 2.00 .75
- ❑ 102 Joe Decker .50 .20
- ❑ 103 Rick Miller .50 .20
- ❑ 104 Bill Madlock 2.00 .75
- ❑ 105 Buzz Capra .50 .20
- ❑ 106 Mike Hargrove UER RC 3.00 1.25
- ❑ 107 Jim Barr .50 .20
- ❑ 108 Tom Hall .50 .20
- ❑ 109 George Hendrick 1.00 .40
- ❑ 110 Wilbur Wood .50 .20
- ❑ 111 Wayne Garrett .50 .20
- ❑ 112 Larry Hardy RC .50 .20
- ❑ 113 Elliott Maddox .50 .20
- ❑ 114 Dick Lange .50 .20
- ❑ 115 Joe Ferguson .50 .20
- ❑ 116 Lerrin LaGrow .50 .20
- ❑ 117 Baltimore Orioles CL/Weaver 3.00 1.25
- ❑ 118 Mike Anderson .50 .20
- ❑ 119 Tommy Helms .50 .20
- ❑ 120 Steve Busby UER 1.00 .40
- ❑ 121 Bill North .50 .20
- ❑ 122 Al Hrabosky 1.00 .40
- ❑ 123 Johnny Briggs .50 .20
- ❑ 124 Jerry Reuss 1.00 .40
- ❑ 125 Ken Singleton 1.00 .40
- ❑ 126 Checklist 1-132 3.00 1.25
- ❑ 127 Glenn Borgmann .50 .20
- ❑ 128 Bill Lee 1.00 .40
- ❑ 129 Rick Monday 1.00 .40
- ❑ 130 Phil Niekro 3.00 1.25
- ❑ 131 Toby Harrah 1.00 .40
- ❑ 132 Randy Moffitt .50 .20
- ❑ 133 Dan Driessen 1.00 .40
- ❑ 134 Ron Hodges .50 .20
- ❑ 135 Charlie Spikes .50 .20
- ❑ 136 Jim Mason .50 .20
- ❑ 137 Terry Forster 1.00 .40
- ❑ 138 Del Unser .50 .20
- ❑ 139 Horacio Pina .50 .20
- ❑ 140 Steve Garvey 3.00 1.25
- ❑ 141 Mickey Stanley 1.00 .40
- ❑ 142 Bob Reynolds .50 .20
- ❑ 143 Cliff Johnson RC 1.00 .40
- ❑ 144 Jim Wohlford .50 .20
- ❑ 145 Ken Holtzman 1.00 .40
- ❑ 146 San Diego Padres CL/McNamara 2.00 .75
- ❑ 147 Pedro Garcia .50 .20
- ❑ 148 Jim Rooker .50 .20
- ❑ 149 Tim Foli .50 .20
- ❑ 150 Bob Gibson 6.00 2.50
- ❑ 151 Steve Brye .50 .20
- ❑ 152 Mario Guerrero .50 .20
- ❑ 153 Rick Reuschel 1.00 .40
- ❑ 154 Mike Lum .50 .20
- ❑ 155 Jim Bibby .50 .20
- ❑ 156 Dave Kingman 2.00 .75
- ❑ 157 Pedro Borbon 1.00 .40
- ❑ 158 Jerry Grote .50 .20
- ❑ 159 Steve Arlin .50 .20
- ❑ 160 Graig Nettles 2.00 .75
- ❑ 161 Stan Bahnsen .50 .20
- ❑ 162 Willie Montanez .50 .20
- ❑ 163 Jim Brewer .50 .20
- ❑ 164 Mickey Rivers 1.00 .40
- ❑ 165 Doug Rader 1.00 .40
- ❑ 166 Woodie Fryman .50 .20
- ❑ 167 Rich Coggins .50 .20
- ❑ 168 Bill Greif .50 .20
- ❑ 169 Cookie Rojas .50 .20
- ❑ 170 Bert Campaneris 1.00 .40
- ❑ 171 Ed Kirkpatrick .50 .20
- ❑ 172 Boston Red Sox CL/Johnson 3.00 1.25
- ❑ 173 Steve Rogers 1.00 .40
- ❑ 174 Bake McBride 1.00 .40
- ❑ 175 Don Money 1.00 .40
- ❑ 176 Burt Hooton 1.00 .40
- ❑ 177 Vic Correll RC .50 .20
- ❑ 178 Cesar Tovar .50 .20
- ❑ 179 Tom Bradley .50 .20
- ❑ 180 Joe Morgan 6.00 2.50
- ❑ 181 Fred Beene .50 .20
- ❑ 182 Don Hahn .50 .20
- ❑ 183 Mel Stottlemyre 1.00 .40

No.	Card		
❑ 184	Jorge Orta	.50	.20
❑ 185	Steve Carlton	8.00	3.00
❑ 186	Willie Crawford	.50	.20
❑ 187	Denny Doyle	.50	.20
❑ 188	Tom Griffin	.50	.20
❑ 189	Y.Berra/Campanella MVP	4.00	1.50
❑ 190	B.Shantz/H.Sauer MVP	2.00	.75
❑ 191	Al Rosen/Campanella MVP	2.00	.75
❑ 192	Y.Berra/W.Mays MVP	4.00	1.50
❑ 193	Y.Berra/Campanella MVP	3.00	1.25
❑ 194	M.Mantle/D.Newcombe MVP	10.00	4.00
❑ 195	M.Mantle/H.Aaron MVP	12.00	5.00
❑ 196	J.Jensen/E.Banks MVP	3.00	1.25
❑ 197	N.Fox/E.Banks MVP	2.00	.75
❑ 198	R.Maris/D.Groat MVP	2.00	.75
❑ 199	R.Maris/F.Robinson MVP	3.00	1.25
❑ 200	M.Mantle/M.Wills MVP	10.00	4.00
❑ 201	E.Howard/S.Koufax MVP	2.00	.75
❑ 202	B.Robinson/K.Boyer MVP	1.00	.40
❑ 203	Z.Versailes/W.Mays MVP	2.00	.75
❑ 204	F.Robinson/B.Clemente MVP	6.00	2.50
❑ 205	C.Yastrzemski/O.Cepeda MVP	2.00	.75
❑ 206	D.McLain/B.Gibson MVP	2.00	.75
❑ 207	H.Killebrew/W.McCovey MVP	1.00	.40
❑ 208	B.Powell/J.Bench MVP	2.00	.75
❑ 209	V.Blue/J.Torre MVP	2.00	.75
❑ 210	R.Allen/J.Bench MVP	2.00	.75
❑ 211	R.Jackson/P.Rose MVP	5.00	2.00
❑ 212	J.Burroughs/S.Garvey MVP	2.00	.75
❑ 213	Oscar Gamble	1.00	.40
❑ 214	Harry Parker	.50	.20
❑ 215	Bobby Valentine	1.00	.40
❑ 216	San Francisco Giants CL/Westrum	2.00	.75
❑ 217	Lou Piniella	2.00	.75
❑ 218	Jerry Johnson	.50	.20
❑ 219	Ed Herrmann	.50	.20
❑ 220	Don Sutton	3.00	1.25
❑ 221	Aurelio Rodriguez	.50	.20
❑ 222	Dan Spillner RC	.50	.20
❑ 223	Robin Yount RC	50.00	25.00
❑ 224	Ramon Hernandez	.50	.20
❑ 225	Bob Grich	1.00	.40
❑ 226	Bill Campbell	.50	.20
❑ 227	Bob Watson	1.00	.40
❑ 228	George Brett RC	80.00	40.00
❑ 229	Barry Foote	.50	.20
❑ 230	Jim Hunter	4.00	1.50
❑ 231	Mike Tyson	.50	.20
❑ 232	Diego Segui	.50	.20
❑ 233	Billy Grabarkewitz	.50	.20
❑ 234	Tom Grieve	1.00	.40
❑ 235	Jack Billingham	1.00	.40
❑ 236	California Angels CL/Williams	2.00	.75
❑ 237	Carl Morton	1.00	.40
❑ 238	Dave Duncan	1.00	.40
❑ 239	George Stone	.50	.20
❑ 240	Garry Maddox	1.00	.40
❑ 241	Dick Tidrow	.50	.20
❑ 242	Jay Johnstone	1.00	.40
❑ 243	Jim Kaat	2.00	.75
❑ 244	Bill Buckner	1.00	.40
❑ 245	Mickey Lolich	2.00	.75
❑ 246	St. Louis Cardinals CL/Schoen	2.00	.75
❑ 247	Enos Cabell	.50	.20
❑ 248	Randy Jones	2.00	.75
❑ 240	Danny Thompson	.50	.20
❑ 250	Ken Brett	.50	.20
❑ 251	Fran Healy	.50	.20
❑ 252	Fred Scherman	.50	.20
❑ 253	Jesus Alou	.50	.20
❑ 254	Mike Torrez	1.00	.40
❑ 255	Dwight Evans	2.00	.75
❑ 256	Billy Champion	.50	.20
❑ 257	Checklist: 133-264	3.00	1.25
❑ 258	Dave LaRoche	.50	.20
❑ 259	Len Randle	.50	.20
❑ 260	Johnny Bench	15.00	6.00
❑ 261	Andy Hassler RC	.50	.20
❑ 262	Rowland Office RC	.50	.20
❑ 263	Jim Perry	1.00	.40
❑ 264	John Milner	.50	.20
❑ 265	Ron Bryant	.50	.20
❑ 266	Sandy Alomar	1.00	.40
❑ 267	Dick Ruthven	.50	.20
❑ 268	Hal McRae	1.00	.40
❑ 269	Doug Rau	.50	.20
❑ 270	Ron Fairly	1.00	.40
❑ 271	Gerry Moses	.50	.20
❑ 272	Lynn McGlothen	.50	.20
❑ 273	Steve Braun	.50	.20
❑ 274	Vicente Romo	.50	.20
❑ 275	Paul Blair	1.00	.40
❑ 276	Chicago White Sox CL/Tanner	2.00	.75
❑ 277	Frank Taveras	.50	.20
❑ 278	Paul Lindblad	.50	.20
❑ 279	Milt May	.50	.20
❑ 280	Carl Yastrzemski	12.00	5.00
❑ 281	Jim Slaton	.50	.20
❑ 282	Jerry Morales	.50	.20
❑ 283	Steve Foucault	.50	.20
❑ 284	Ken Griffey Sr.	4.00	1.50
❑ 285	Ellie Rodriguez	.50	.20
❑ 286	Mike Jorgensen	.50	.20
❑ 287	Roric Harrison	.50	.20
❑ 288	Bruce Ellingsen RC	.50	.20
❑ 289	Ken Rudolph	.50	.20
❑ 290	Jon Matlack	.50	.20
❑ 291	Bill Sudakis	.50	.20
❑ 292	Ron Schueler	.50	.20
❑ 293	Dick Sharon	.50	.20
❑ 294	Geoff Zahn RC	.50	.20
❑ 295	Vada Pinson	2.00	.75
❑ 296	Alan Foster	.50	.20
❑ 297	Craig Kusick RC	.50	.20
❑ 298	Johnny Grubb	.50	.20
❑ 299	Bucky Dent	2.00	.75
❑ 300	Reggie Jackson	15.00	6.00
❑ 301	Dave Roberts	.50	.20
❑ 302	Rick Burleson RC	1.00	.40
❑ 303	Grant Jackson	.50	.20
❑ 304	Pittsburgh Pirates CL/Murtaugh	2.00	.75
❑ 305	Jim Colborn	.50	.20
❑ 306	R.Carew/R.Garr LL	2.00	.75
❑ 307	D.Allen/M.Schmidt LL	4.00	1.50
❑ 308	J.Burroughs/J.Bench LL	2.00	.75
❑ 309	B.North/L.Brock LL	2.00	.75
❑ 310	Hunter/Jenk/Mess/Niek LL	2.00	.75
❑ 311	J.Hunter/B.Capra LL	2.00	.75
❑ 312	N.Ryan/S.Carlton LL	12.00	5.00
❑ 313	T.Forster/M.Marshall LL	1.00	.40
❑ 314	Buck Martinez	.50	.20
❑ 315	Don Kessinger	1.00	.40
❑ 316	Jackie Brown	.50	.20
❑ 317	Joe Lahoud	.50	.20
❑ 318	Ernie McAnally	.50	.20
❑ 319	Johnny Oates	1.00	.40
❑ 320	Pete Rose	30.00	12.50
❑ 321	Rudy May	.50	.20
❑ 322	Ed Goodson	.50	.20
❑ 323	Fred Holdsworth	.50	.20
❑ 324	Ed Kranepool	1.00	.40
❑ 325	Tony Oliva	2.00	.75
❑ 326	Wayne Twitchell	.50	.20
❑ 327	Jerry Hairston	.50	.20
❑ 328	Sonny Siebert	.50	.20
❑ 329	Ted Kubiak	.50	.20
❑ 330	Mike Marshall	1.00	.40
❑ 331	Cleveland Indians CL/Robinson	2.00	.75
❑ 332	Fred Kendall	.50	.20
❑ 333	Dick Drago	.50	.20
❑ 334	Greg Gross RC	.50	.20
❑ 335	Jim Palmer	6.00	2.50
❑ 336	Rennie Stennett	.50	.20
❑ 337	Kevin Kobel	.50	.20
❑ 338	Rich Stelmaszek	.50	.20
❑ 339	Jim Fregosi	1.00	.40
❑ 340	Paul Splittorff	.50	.20
❑ 341	Hal Breeden	.50	.20
❑ 342	Leroy Stanton	.50	.20
❑ 343	Danny Frisella	.50	.20
❑ 344	Ben Oglivie	1.00	.40
❑ 345	Clay Carroll	1.00	.40
❑ 346	Bobby Darwin	.50	.20
❑ 347	Mike Caldwell	.50	.20
❑ 348	Tony Muser	.50	.20
❑ 349	Ray Sadecki	.50	.20
❑ 350	Bobby Murcer	1.00	.40
❑ 351	Bob Boone	2.00	.75
❑ 352	Darold Knowles	.50	.20
❑ 353	Luis Melendez	.50	.20
❑ 354	Dick Bosman	.50	.20
❑ 355	Chris Cannizzaro	.50	.20
❑ 356	Rico Petrocelli	1.00	.40
❑ 357	Ken Forsch UER	.50	.20
❑ 358	Al Bumbry	1.00	.40
❑ 359	Paul Popovich	.50	.20
❑ 360	George Scott	1.00	.40
❑ 361	Los Angeles Dodgers CL/Alston	2.00	.75
❑ 362	Steve Hargan	.50	.20
❑ 363	Carmen Fanzone	.50	.20
❑ 364	Doug Bird	.50	.20
❑ 365	Bob Bailey	.50	.20
❑ 366	Ken Sanders	.50	.20
❑ 367	Craig Robinson	.50	.20
❑ 368	Vic Albury	.50	.20
❑ 369	Merv Rettenmund	.50	.20
❑ 370	Tom Seaver	12.00	5.00
❑ 371	Gates Brown	.50	.20
❑ 372	John D'Acquisto	.50	.20
❑ 373	Bill Sharp	.50	.20
❑ 374	Eddie Watt	.50	.20
❑ 375	Roy White	1.00	.40
❑ 376	Steve Yeager	1.00	.40
❑ 377	Tom Hilgendorf	.50	.20
❑ 378	Derrel Thomas	.50	.20
❑ 379	Bernie Carbo	.50	.20
❑ 380	Sal Bando	1.00	.40
❑ 381	John Curtis	.50	.20
❑ 382	Don Baylor	2.00	.75
❑ 383	Jim York	.50	.20
❑ 384	Milwaukee Brewers CL/Crandall	2.00	.75
❑ 385	Dock Ellis	.50	.20
❑ 386	Checklist: 265-396 UER	3.00	1.25
❑ 387	Jim Spencer	.50	.20
❑ 388	Steve Stone	1.00	.40
❑ 389	Tony Solaita RC	.50	.20
❑ 390	Ron Cey	2.00	.75
❑ 391	Don DeMola RC	.50	.20
❑ 392	Bruce Bochte RC	1.00	.40
❑ 393	Gary Gentry	.50	.20
❑ 394	Larvell Blanks	.50	.20
❑ 395	Bud Harrelson	1.00	.40
❑ 396	Fred Norman	1.00	.40
❑ 397	Bill Freehan	1.00	.40
❑ 398	Elias Sosa	.50	.20
❑ 399	Terry Harmon	.50	.20
❑ 400	Dick Allen	2.00	.75
❑ 401	Mike Wallace	.50	.20
❑ 402	Bob Tolan	.50	.20
❑ 403	Tom Buskey RC	.50	.20
❑ 404	Ted Sizemore	.50	.20
❑ 405	John Montague RC	.50	.20
❑ 406	Bob Gallagher	.50	.20
❑ 407	Herb Washington RC	2.00	.75
❑ 408	Clyde Wright UER	.50	.20
❑ 409	Bob Robertson	.50	.20
❑ 410	Mike Cuellar UER	1.00	.40
❑ 411	George Mitterwald	.50	.20
❑ 412	Bill Hands	.50	.20
❑ 413	Marty Pattin	.50	.20
❑ 414	Manny Mota	1.00	.40
❑ 415	John Hiller	1.00	.40
❑ 416	Larry Lintz	.50	.20
❑ 417	Skip Lockwood	.50	.20
❑ 418	Leo Foster	.50	.20
❑ 419	Dave Goltz	.50	.20
❑ 420	Larry Bowa	2.00	.75
❑ 421	New York Mets CL/Berra	3.00	1.25
❑ 422	Brian Downing	1.00	.40
❑ 423	Clay Kirby	.50	.20
❑ 424	John Lowenstein	.50	.20
❑ 425	Tito Fuentes	.50	.20
❑ 426	George Medich	.50	.20
❑ 427	Clarence Gaston	1.00	.40
❑ 428	Dave Hamilton	.50	.20
❑ 429	Jim Dwyer RC	.50	.20
❑ 430	Luis Tiant	2.00	.75
❑ 431	Rod Gilbreath	.50	.20
❑ 432	Ken Berry	.50	.20
❑ 433	Larry Demery RC	.50	.20
❑ 434	Bob Locker	.50	.20
❑ 435	Dave Nelson	.50	.20
❑ 436	Ken Frailing	.50	.20
❑ 437	Al Cowens RC	1.00	.40
❑ 438	Don Carrithers	.50	.20
❑ 439	Ed Brinkman	.50	.20
❑ 440	Andy Messersmith	1.00	.40
❑ 441	Bobby Heise	.50	.20

❑ 442 Maximino Leon RC .50 .20
❑ 443 Minnesota Twins CL/Quilici 2.00 .75
❑ 444 Gene Garber 1.00 .40
❑ 445 Felix Millan .50 .20
❑ 446 Bart Johnson .50 .20
❑ 447 Terry Crowley .50 .20
❑ 448 Frank Duffy .50 .20
❑ 449 Charlie Williams .50 .20
❑ 450 Willie McCovey 6.00 2.50
❑ 451 Rick Dempsey 1.00 .40
❑ 452 Angel Mangual .50 .20
❑ 453 Claude Osteen 1.00 .40
❑ 454 Doug Griffin .50 .20
❑ 455 Don Wilson .50 .20
❑ 456 Bob Coluccio .50 .20
❑ 457 Mario Mendoza RC .50 .20
❑ 458 Ross Grimsley .50 .20
❑ 459 1974 AL Championships 1.00 .40
❑ 460 1974 NL Championships 2.00 .75
❑ 461 Reggie Jackson WS1 5.00 2.00
❑ 462 W.Alston/J.Ferguson WS2 1.00 .40
❑ 463 Rollie Fingers WS3 2.00 .75
❑ 464 A's Batter WS4 1.00 .40
❑ 465 Joe Rudi WS5 1.00 .40
❑ 466 A's Do it Again WS 2.00 .75
❑ 467 Ed Halicki RC .50 .20
❑ 468 Bobby Mitchell .50 .20
❑ 469 Tom Dettore RC .50 .20
❑ 470 Jeff Burroughs 1.00 .40
❑ 471 Bob Stinson .50 .20
❑ 472 Bruce Dal Canton .50 .20
❑ 473 Ken McMullen .50 .20
❑ 474 Luke Walker .50 .20
❑ 475 Darrell Evans 1.00 .40
❑ 476 Ed Figueroa RC .50 .20
❑ 477 Tom Hutton .50 .20
❑ 478 Tom Burgmeier .50 .20
❑ 479 Ken Boswell .50 .20
❑ 480 Carlos May .50 .20
❑ 481 Will McEnaney RC 1.00 .40
❑ 482 Tom McCraw .50 .20
❑ 483 Steve Ontiveros .50 .20
❑ 484 Glenn Beckert 1.00 .40
❑ 485 Sparky Lyle 1.00 .40
❑ 486 Ray Fosse .50 .20
❑ 487 Houston Astros CL/Gomez 2.00 .75
❑ 488 Bill Travers RC .50 .20
❑ 489 Cecil Cooper 2.00 .75
❑ 490 Reggie Smith 1.00 .40
❑ 491 Doyle Alexander 1.00 .40
❑ 492 Rich Hebner 1.00 .40
❑ 493 Don Stanhouse .50 .20
❑ 494 Pete LaCock RC .50 .20
❑ 495 Nelson Briles 1.00 .40
❑ 496 Pepe Frias .50 .20
❑ 497 Jim Nettles .50 .20
❑ 498 Al Downing .50 .20
❑ 499 Marty Perez .50 .20
❑ 500 Nolan Ryan 50.00 25.00
❑ 501 Bill Robinson 1.00 .40
❑ 502 Pat Bourque .50 .20
❑ 503 Fred Stanley .50 .20
❑ 504 Buddy Bradford .50 .20
❑ 505 Chris Speier .50 .20
❑ 506 Leron Lee .50 .20
❑ 507 Tom Carroll RC .50 .20
❑ 508 Bob Hansen RC .50 .20
❑ 509 Dave Hilton .50 .20
❑ 510 Vida Blue 1.00 .40
❑ 511 Texas Rangers CL/Martin 2.00 .75
❑ 512 Larry Milbourne RC .50 .20
❑ 513 Dick Pole .50 .20
❑ 514 Jose Cruz 2.00 .75
❑ 515 Manny Sanguillen 1.00 .40
❑ 516 Don Hood .50 .20
❑ 517 Checklist: 397-528 3.00 1.25
❑ 518 Leo Cardenas .50 .20
❑ 519 Jim Todd RC .50 .20
❑ 520 Amos Otis 1.00 .40
❑ 521 Dennis Blair RC .50 .20
❑ 522 Gary Sutherland .50 .20
❑ 523 Tom Paciorek 1.00 .40
❑ 524 John Doherty RC .50 .20
❑ 525 Tom House .50 .20
❑ 526 Larry Hisle 1.00 .40
❑ 527 Mac Scarce .50 .20
❑ 528 Eddie Leon .50 .20
❑ 529 Gary Thomasson .50 .20
❑ 530 Gaylord Perry 3.00 1.25
❑ 531 Cincinnati Reds CL/Anderson 5.00 2.00
❑ 532 Gorman Thomas 1.00 .40
❑ 533 Rudy Meoli .50 .20
❑ 534 Alex Johnson .50 .20
❑ 535 Gene Tenace 1.00 .40
❑ 536 Bob Moose .50 .20
❑ 537 Tommy Harper 1.00 .40
❑ 538 Duffy Dyer .50 .20
❑ 539 Jesse Jefferson .50 .20
❑ 540 Lou Brock 6.00 2.50
❑ 541 Roger Metzger .50 .20
❑ 542 Pete Broberg .50 .20
❑ 543 Larry Biittner .50 .20
❑ 544 Steve Mingori .50 .20
❑ 545 Billy Williams 3.00 1.25
❑ 546 John Knox .50 .20
❑ 547 Von Joshua .50 .20
❑ 548 Charlie Sands .50 .20
❑ 549 Bill Butler .50 .20
❑ 550 Ralph Garr 1.00 .40
❑ 551 Larry Christenson .50 .20
❑ 552 Jack Brohamer .50 .20
❑ 553 John Boccabella .50 .20
❑ 554 Goose Gossage 2.00 .75
❑ 555 Al Oliver 1.00 .40
❑ 556 Tim Johnson .50 .20
❑ 557 Larry Gura .50 .20
❑ 558 Dave Roberts .50 .20
❑ 559 Bob Montgomery .50 .20
❑ 560 Tony Perez 4.00 1.50
❑ 561 Oakland Athletics CL/Dark 2.00 .75
❑ 562 Gary Nolan 1.00 .40
❑ 563 Wilbur Howard .50 .20
❑ 564 Tommy Davis 1.00 .40
❑ 565 Joe Torre 2.00 .75
❑ 566 Ray Burris .50 .20
❑ 567 Jim Sundberg RC 2.00 .75
❑ 568 Dale Murray RC .50 .20
❑ 569 Frank White 1.00 .40
❑ 570 Jim Wynn 1.00 .40
❑ 571 Dave Lemanczyk RC .50 .20
❑ 572 Roger Nelson .50 .20
❑ 573 Orlando Pena .50 .20
❑ 574 Tony Taylor .50 .20
❑ 575 Gene Clines .50 .20
❑ 576 Phil Roof .50 .20
❑ 577 John Morris .50 .20
❑ 578 Dave Tomlin RC .50 .20
❑ 579 Skip Pitlock .50 .20
❑ 580 Frank Robinson 6.00 2.50
❑ 581 Darrel Chaney .50 .20
❑ 582 Eduardo Rodriguez .50 .20
❑ 583 Andy Etchebarren .50 .20
❑ 584 Mike Garman .50 .20
❑ 585 Chris Chambliss 1.00 .40
❑ 586 Tim McCarver 2.00 .75
❑ 587 Chris Ward RC .50 .20
❑ 588 Rick Auerbach .50 .20
❑ 589 Atlanta Braves CL/King 2.00 .75
❑ 590 Cesar Cedeno 1.00 .40
❑ 591 Glenn Abbott .50 .20
❑ 592 Balor Moore .50 .20
❑ 593 Gene Lamont .50 .20
❑ 594 Jim Fuller .50 .20
❑ 595 Joe Niekro 1.00 .40
❑ 596 Ollie Brown .50 .20
❑ 597 Winston Llenas .50 .20
❑ 598 Bruce Kison .50 .20
❑ 599 Nate Colbert .50 .20
❑ 600 Rod Carew 8.00 3.00
❑ 601 Juan Beniquez .50 .20
❑ 602 John Vukovich .50 .20
❑ 603 Lew Krausse .50 .20
❑ 604 Oscar Zamora RC .50 .20
❑ 605 John Ellis .50 .20
❑ 606 Bruce Miller RC .50 .20
❑ 607 Jim Holt .50 .20
❑ 608 Gene Michael .50 .20
❑ 609 Elrod Hendricks .50 .20
❑ 610 Ron Hunt .50 .20
❑ 611 New York Yankees CL/Virdon 2.00 .75
❑ 612 Terry Hughes .50 .20
❑ 613 Bill Parsons .50 .20
❑ 614 Kuc/Mill/Ruhle/Sieb RC 1.00 .40
❑ 615 Darcy/Leonard/Und/Webb RC 2.00 .75
❑ 616 Jim Rice RC 15.00 6.00
❑ 617 Cubb/DeCinces/Sand/Trillo RC 2.00 .75
❑ 618 East/John/McGregor/Rhoden RC 1.00 .40
❑ 619 Ayala/Nyman/Smith Turner RC 1.00 .40
❑ 620 Gary Carter RC 15.00 6.00
❑ 621 Denny/Eastwick/Kern/Vein RC 2.00 .75
❑ 622 Fred Lynn RC 8.00 3.00
❑ 623 K.Hern RC/P.Garner RC 10.00 4.00
❑ 624 Kon/Lavelle/Otten/Sol RC 1.00 .40
❑ 625 Boog Powell 2.00 .75
❑ 626 Larry Haney UER .50 .20
❑ 627 Tom Walker .50 .20
❑ 628 Ron LeFlore RC 1.00 .40
❑ 629 Joe Hoerner .50 .20
❑ 630 Greg Luzinski 2.00 .75
❑ 631 Lee Lacy .50 .20
❑ 632 Morris Nettles RC .50 .20
❑ 633 Paul Casanova .50 .20
❑ 634 Cy Acosta .50 .20
❑ 635 Chuck Dobson .50 .20
❑ 636 Charlie Moore .50 .20
❑ 637 Ted Martinez .50 .20
❑ 638 Chicago Cubs CL/Marshall 2.00 .75
❑ 639 Steve Kline .50 .20
❑ 640 Harmon Killebrew 6.00 2.50
❑ 641 Jim Northrup 1.00 .40
❑ 642 Mike Phillips .50 .20
❑ 643 Brent Strom .50 .20
❑ 644 Bill Fahey .50 .20
❑ 645 Danny Cater .50 .20
❑ 646 Checklist: 529-660 3.00 1.25
❑ 647 Claudell Washington RC 2.00 .75
❑ 648 Dave Pagan RC .50 .20
❑ 649 Jack Heidemann .50 .20
❑ 650 Dave May .50 .20
❑ 651 John Morlan RC .50 .20
❑ 652 Lindy McDaniel 1.00 .40
❑ 653 Lee Richard UER .50 .20
❑ 654 Jerry Terrell .50 .20
❑ 655 Rico Carty 1.00 .40
❑ 656 Bill Plummer .50 .20
❑ 657 Bob Oliver .50 .20
❑ 658 Vic Harris .50 .20
❑ 659 Bob Apodaca .50 .20
❑ 660 Hank Aaron 30.00 12.50

1976 Topps

❑ COMPLETE SET (660) 250.00 150.00
❑ 1 Hank Aaron RB 15.00 6.00
❑ 2 Bobby Bonds RB 1.50 .60
❑ 3 Mickey Lolich RB .75 .30
❑ 4 Dave Lopes RB .75 .30
❑ 5 Tom Seaver RB 5.00 2.00
❑ 6 Rennie Stennett RB .75 .30
❑ 7 Jim Umbarger RC .40 .15
❑ 8 Tito Fuentes .40 .15
❑ 9 Paul Lindblad .40 .15
❑ 10 Lou Brock 5.00 2.00
❑ 11 Jim Hughes .40 .15
❑ 12 Richie Zisk .75 .30
❑ 13 John Wockenfuss RC .40 .15
❑ 14 Gene Garber .75 .30
❑ 15 George Scott .75 .30
❑ 16 Bob Apodaca .40 .15
❑ 17 New York Yankees CL/Martin 1.50 .60
❑ 18 Dale Murray .40 .15

❑ 19	George Brett	30.00	12.50
❑ 20	Bob Watson	.75	.30
❑ 21	Dave LaRoche	.40	.15
❑ 22	Bill Russell	.75	.30
❑ 23	Brian Downing	.40	.15
❑ 24	Cesar Geronimo	.75	.30
❑ 25	Mike Torrez	.75	.30
❑ 26	Andre Thornton	.75	.30
❑ 27	Ed Figueroa	.40	.15
❑ 28	Dusty Baker	1.50	.60
❑ 29	Rick Burleson	.75	.30
❑ 30	John Montefusco RC	.75	.30
❑ 31	Len Randle	.40	.15
❑ 32	Danny Frisella	.40	.15
❑ 33	Bill North	.40	.15
❑ 34	Mike Garman	.40	.15
❑ 35	Tony Oliva	1.50	.60
❑ 36	Frank Taveras	.40	.15
❑ 37	John Hiller	.75	.30
❑ 38	Garry Maddox	.75	.30
❑ 39	Pete Broberg	.40	.15
❑ 40	Dave Kingman	1.50	.60
❑ 41	Tippy Martinez RC	.75	.30
❑ 42	Barry Foote	.40	.15
❑ 43	Paul Splittorff	.40	.15
❑ 44	Doug Rader	.75	.30
❑ 45	Boog Powell	1.50	.60
❑ 46	Los Angeles Dodgers CL/Alston	1.50	.60
❑ 47	Jesse Jefferson	.40	.15
❑ 48	Dave Concepcion	1.50	.60
❑ 49	Dave Duncan	.75	.30
❑ 50	Fred Lynn	1.50	.60
❑ 51	Ray Burris	.40	.15
❑ 52	Dave Chalk	.40	.15
❑ 53	Mike Beard RC	.40	.15
❑ 54	Dave Rader	.40	.15
❑ 55	Gaylord Perry	2.50	1.00
❑ 56	Bob Tolan	.40	.15
❑ 57	Phil Garner	.75	.30
❑ 58	Ron Reed	.40	.15
❑ 59	Larry Hisle	.75	.30
❑ 60	Jerry Reuss	.75	.30
❑ 61	Ron LeFlore	.75	.30
❑ 62	Johnny Oates	.75	.30
❑ 63	Bobby Darwin	.40	.15
❑ 64	Jerry Koosman	.75	.30
❑ 65	Chris Chambliss	.75	.30
❑ 66	Gus/Buddy Bell FS	.75	.30
❑ 67	Bob/Ray Boone FS	.75	.30
❑ 68	Joe/Joe Jr. Coleman FS	.40	.15
❑ 69	Jim/Mike Hegan FS	.40	.15
❑ 70	Roy/Roy Jr. Smalley FS	.75	.30
❑ 71	Steve Rogers	.75	.30
❑ 72	Hal McRae	.75	.30
❑ 73	Baltimore Orioles CL/Weaver	1.50	.60
❑ 74	Oscar Gamble	.75	.30
❑ 75	Larry Dierker	.75	.30
❑ 76	Willie Crawford	.40	.15
❑ 77	Pedro Borbon	.75	.30
❑ 78	Cecil Cooper	.75	.30
❑ 79	Jerry Morales	.40	.15
❑ 80	Jim Kaat	1.50	.60
❑ 81	Darrell Evans	.75	.30
❑ 82	Von Joshua	.40	.15
❑ 83	Jim Spencer	.40	.15
❑ 84	Brent Strom	.40	.15
❑ 85	Mickey Rivers	.75	.30
❑ 86	Mike Tyson	.40	.15
❑ 87	Tom Burgmeier	.40	.15
❑ 88	Duffy Dyer	.40	.15
❑ 89	Vern Ruhle	.40	.15
❑ 90	Sal Bando	.75	.30
❑ 91	Tom Hutton	.40	.15
❑ 92	Eduardo Rodriguez	.40	.15
❑ 93	Mike Phillips	.40	.15
❑ 94	Jim Dwyer	.40	.15
❑ 95	Brooks Robinson	6.00	2.50
❑ 96	Doug Bird	.40	.15
❑ 97	Wilbur Howard	.40	.15
❑ 98	Dennis Eckersley RC	30.00	12.50
❑ 99	Lee Lacy	.40	.15
❑ 100	Jim Hunter	3.00	1.25
❑ 101	Pete LaCock	.40	.15
❑ 102	Jim Willoughby	.40	.15
❑ 103	Biff Pocoroba RC	.40	.15
❑ 104	Cincinnati Reds CL/Anderson	2.50	1.00
❑ 105	Gary Lavelle	.40	.15
❑ 106	Tom Grieve	.75	.30
❑ 107	Dave Roberts	.40	.15
❑ 108	Don Kirkwood RC	.40	.15
❑ 109	Larry Lintz	.40	.15
❑ 110	Carlos May	.40	.15
❑ 111	Danny Thompson	.40	.15
❑ 112	Kent Tekulve RC	1.50	.60
❑ 113	Gary Sutherland	.40	.15
❑ 114	Jay Johnstone	.75	.30
❑ 115	Ken Holtzman	.75	.30
❑ 116	Charlie Moore	.40	.15
❑ 117	Mike Jorgensen	.40	.15
❑ 118	Boston Red Sox CL/Johnson	1.50	.60
❑ 119	Checklist 1-132	1.50	.60
❑ 120	Rusty Staub	.75	.30
❑ 121	Tony Solaita	.40	.15
❑ 122	Mike Cosgrove	.40	.15
❑ 123	Walt Williams	.40	.15
❑ 124	Doug Rau	.40	.15
❑ 125	Don Baylor	1.50	.60
❑ 126	Tom Dettore	.40	.15
❑ 127	Larvell Blanks	.40	.15
❑ 128	Ken Griffey Sr.	2.50	1.00
❑ 129	Andy Etchebarren	.40	.15
❑ 130	Luis Tiant	1.50	.60
❑ 131	Bill Stein RC	.40	.15
❑ 132	Don Hood	.40	.15
❑ 133	Gary Matthews	.75	.30
❑ 134	Mike Ivie	.40	.15
❑ 135	Bake McBride	.75	.30
❑ 136	Dave Goltz	.40	.15
❑ 137	Bill Robinson	.75	.30
❑ 138	Lerrin LaGrow	.40	.15
❑ 139	Gorman Thomas	.75	.30
❑ 140	Vida Blue	.75	.30
❑ 141	Larry Parrish RC	1.50	.60
❑ 142	Dick Drago	.40	.15
❑ 143	Jerry Grote	.40	.15
❑ 144	Al Fitzmorris	.40	.15
❑ 145	Larry Bowa	.75	.30
❑ 146	George Medich	.40	.15
❑ 147	Houston Astros CL/Virdon	1.50	.60
❑ 148	Stan Thomas RC	.40	.15
❑ 149	Tommy Davis	.75	.30
❑ 150	Steve Garvey	2.50	1.00
❑ 151	Bill Bonham	.40	.15
❑ 152	Leroy Stanton	.40	.15
❑ 153	Buzz Capra	.40	.15
❑ 154	Bucky Dent	.75	.30
❑ 155	Jack Billingham	.75	.30
❑ 156	Rico Carty	.75	.30
❑ 157	Mike Caldwell	.40	.15
❑ 158	Ken Reitz	.40	.15
❑ 159	Jerry Terrell	.40	.15
❑ 160	Dave Winfield	10.00	4.00
❑ 161	Bruce Kison	.40	.15
❑ 162	Jack Pierce RC	.40	.15
❑ 163	Jim Slaton	.40	.15
❑ 164	Pepe Mangual	.40	.15
❑ 165	Gene Tenace	.75	.30
❑ 166	Skip Lockwood	.40	.15
❑ 167	Freddie Patek	.75	.30
❑ 168	Tom Hilgendorf	.40	.15
❑ 169	Graig Nettles	1.50	.60
❑ 170	Rick Wise	.40	.15
❑ 171	Greg Gross	.40	.15
❑ 172	Texas Rangers CL/Lucchesi	1.50	.60
❑ 173	Steve Swisher	.40	.15
❑ 174	Charlie Hough	.75	.30
❑ 175	Ken Singleton	.75	.30
❑ 176	Dick Lange	.40	.15
❑ 177	Marty Perez	.40	.15
❑ 178	Tom Buskey	.40	.15
❑ 179	George Foster	1.50	.60
❑ 180	Goose Gossage	1.50	.60
❑ 181	Willie Montanez	.40	.15
❑ 182	Harry Rasmussen	.40	.15
❑ 183	Steve Braun	.40	.15
❑ 184	Bill Greif	.40	.15
❑ 185	Dave Parker	1.50	.60
❑ 186	Tom Walker	.40	.15
❑ 187	Pedro Garcia	.40	.15
❑ 188	Fred Scherman	.40	.15
❑ 189	Claudell Washington	.75	.30
❑ 190	Jon Matlack	.40	.15
❑ 191	Madlock/Simm/Mang LL	.75	.30
❑ 192	Carew/Lynn/Munson LL	2.50	1.00
❑ 193	Schmidt/King/Luz LL	3.00	1.25
❑ 194	Reggie/Scott/Mayb LL	3.00	1.25
❑ 195	Luz/Bench/Perez LL	1.50	.60
❑ 196	Scott/Mayb/Lynn LL	.75	.30
❑ 197	Lopes/Morgan/Brock LL	1.50	.60
❑ 198	Rivers/Wash/Otis LL	.75	.30
❑ 199	Seaver/Jones/Mess LL	2.50	1.00
❑ 200	Hunter/Palmer/Blue LL	1.50	.60
❑ 201	Jones/Mess/Seaver LL	1.50	.60
❑ 202	Palmer/Hunter/Eck LL	3.00	1.25
❑ 203	Seaver/Mont/Mess LL	2.50	1.00
❑ 204	Tanana/Blyleven/Perry LL	.75	.30
❑ 205	A.Hrabosky/G.Gossage LL	.75	.30
❑ 206	Manny Trillo	.40	.15
❑ 207	Andy Hassler	.40	.15
❑ 208	Mike Lum	.40	.15
❑ 209	Alan Ashby RC	.40	.15
❑ 210	Lee May	.75	.30
❑ 211	Clay Carroll	.75	.30
❑ 212	Pat Kelly	.40	.15
❑ 213	Dave Heaverlo RC	.40	.15
❑ 214	Eric Soderholm	.40	.15
❑ 215	Reggie Smith	.75	.30
❑ 216	Montreal Expos CL/Kuehl	1.50	.60
❑ 217	Dave Freisleben	.40	.15
❑ 218	John Knox	.40	.15
❑ 219	Tom Murphy	.40	.15
❑ 220	Manny Sanguillen	.75	.30
❑ 221	Jim Todd	.40	.15
❑ 222	Wayne Garrett	.40	.15
❑ 223	Ollie Brown	.40	.15
❑ 224	Jim York	.40	.15
❑ 225	Roy White	.75	.30
❑ 226	Jim Sundberg	.75	.30
❑ 227	Oscar Zamora	.40	.15
❑ 228	John Hale RC	.40	.15
❑ 229	Jerry Remy RC	.40	.15
❑ 230	Carl Yastrzemski	10.00	4.00
❑ 231	Tom House	.40	.15
❑ 232	Frank Duffy	.40	.15
❑ 233	Grant Jackson	.40	.15
❑ 234	Mike Sadek	.40	.15
❑ 235	Bert Blyleven	1.50	.60
❑ 236	Kansas City Royals CL/Herzog	1.50	.60
❑ 237	Dave Hamilton	.40	.15
❑ 238	Larry Biittner	.40	.15
❑ 239	John Curtis	.40	.15
❑ 240	Pete Rose	25.00	10.00
❑ 241	Hector Torres	.40	.15
❑ 242	Dan Meyer	.40	.15
❑ 243	Jim Rooker	.40	.15
❑ 244	Bill Sharp	.40	.15
❑ 245	Felix Millan	.40	.15
❑ 246	Cesar Tovar	.40	.15
❑ 247	Terry Harmon	.40	.15
❑ 248	Dick Tidrow	.40	.15
❑ 249	Cliff Johnson	.75	.30
❑ 250	Fergie Jenkins	2.50	1.00
❑ 251	Rick Monday	.75	.30
❑ 252	Tim Nordbrook RC	.40	.15
❑ 253	Bill Buckner	.75	.30
❑ 254	Rudy Meoli	.40	.15
❑ 255	Fritz Peterson	.40	.15
❑ 256	Rowland Office	.40	.15
❑ 257	Ross Grimsley	.40	.15
❑ 258	Nyls Nyman	.40	.15
❑ 259	Darrel Chaney	.40	.15
❑ 260	Steve Busby	.40	.15
❑ 261	Gary Thomasson	.40	.15
❑ 262	Checklist 133-264	1.50	.60
❑ 263	Lyman Bostock RC	1.50	.60
❑ 264	Steve Renko	.40	.15
❑ 265	Willie Davis	.75	.30
❑ 266	Alan Foster	.40	.15
❑ 267	Aurelio Rodriguez	.40	.15
❑ 268	Del Unser	.40	.15
❑ 269	Rick Austin	.40	.15
❑ 270	Willie Stargell	3.00	1.25
❑ 271	Jim Lonborg	.75	.30
❑ 272	Rick Dempsey	.75	.30
❑ 273	Joe Niekro	.75	.30
❑ 274	Tommy Harper	.75	.30
❑ 275	Rick Manning RC	.40	.15
❑ 276	Mickey Scott	.40	.15

❑ 277 Chicago Cubs CL/Marshall 1.50 .60
❑ 278 Bernie Carbo .40 .15
❑ 279 Roy Howell RC .40 .15
❑ 280 Burt Hooton .75 .30
❑ 281 Dave May .40 .15
❑ 282 Dan Osborn RC .40 .15
❑ 283 Merv Rettenmund .40 .15
❑ 284 Steve Ontiveros .40 .15
❑ 285 Mike Cuellar .75 .30
❑ 286 Jim Wohlford .40 .15
❑ 287 Pete Mackanin .40 .15
❑ 288 Bill Campbell .40 .15
❑ 289 Enzo Hernandez .40 .15
❑ 290 Ted Simmons .75 .30
❑ 291 Ken Sanders .40 .15
❑ 292 Leon Roberts .40 .15
❑ 293 Bill Castro RC .40 .15
❑ 294 Ed Kirkpatrick .40 .15
❑ 295 Dave Cash .40 .15
❑ 296 Pat Dobson .40 .15
❑ 297 Roger Metzger .40 .15
❑ 298 Dick Bosman .40 .15
❑ 299 Champ Summers RC .40 .15
❑ 300 Johnny Bench 12.00 5.00
❑ 301 Jackie Brown .40 .15
❑ 302 Rick Miller .40 .15
❑ 303 Steve Foucault .40 .15
❑ 304 California Angels CL/Williams 1.50 .60
❑ 305 Andy Messersmith .75 .30
❑ 306 Rod Gilbreath .40 .15
❑ 307 Al Bumbry .75 .30
❑ 308 Jim Barr .40 .15
❑ 309 Bill Melton .40 .15
❑ 310 Randy Jones .75 .30
❑ 311 Cookie Rojas .40 .15
❑ 312 Don Carrithers .40 .15
❑ 313 Dan Ford RC .40 .15
❑ 314 Ed Kranepool .40 .15
❑ 315 Al Hrabosky .75 .30
❑ 316 Robin Yount 15.00 6.00
❑ 317 John Candelaria RC 1.50 .60
❑ 318 Bob Boone 1.50 .60
❑ 319 Larry Gura .40 .15
❑ 320 Willie Horton .75 .30
❑ 321 Jose Cruz 1.50 .60
❑ 322 Glenn Abbott .40 .15
❑ 323 Rob Sperring RC .40 .15
❑ 324 Jim Bibby .40 .15
❑ 325 Tony Perez 3.00 1.25
❑ 326 Dick Pole .40 .15
❑ 327 Dave Moates RC .40 .15
❑ 328 Carl Morton .40 .15
❑ 329 Joe Ferguson .40 .15
❑ 330 Nolan Ryan 25.00 10.00
❑ 331 San Diego Padres CL/McNamara 1.50 .60
❑ 332 Charlie Williams .40 .15
❑ 333 Bob Coluccio .40 .15
❑ 334 Dennis Leonard .75 .30
❑ 335 Bob Grich .75 .30
❑ 336 Vic Albury .40 .15
❑ 337 Bud Harrelson .75 .30
❑ 338 Bob Bailey .40 .15
❑ 339 John Denny .75 .30
❑ 340 Jim Rice 4.00 1.50
❑ 341 Lou Gehrig ATG 12.00 5.00
❑ 342 Rogers Hornsby ATG 3.00 1.25
❑ 343 Pie Traynor ATG 1.50 .60
❑ 344 Honus Wagner ATG 5.00 2.00
❑ 345 Babe Ruth ATG 15.00 6.00
❑ 346 Ty Cobb ATG 12.00 5.00
❑ 347 Ted Williams ATG 12.00 5.00
❑ 348 Mickey Cochrane ATG 1.50 .60
❑ 349 Walter Johnson ATG 5.00 2.00
❑ 350 Lefty Grove ATG 1.50 .60
❑ 351 Randy Hundley .75 .30
❑ 352 Dave Giusti .40 .15
❑ 353 Sixto Lezcano RC .75 .30
❑ 354 Ron Blomberg .40 .15
❑ 355 Steve Carlton 6.00 2.50
❑ 356 Ted Martinez .40 .15
❑ 357 Ken Forsch .40 .15
❑ 358 Buddy Bell .75 .30
❑ 359 Rick Reuschel .75 .30
❑ 360 Jeff Burroughs .75 .30
❑ 361 Detroit Tigers CL/Houk 1.50 .60
❑ 362 Will McEnaney .75 .30
❑ 363 Dave Collins RC .75 .30
❑ 364 Elias Sosa .40 .15
❑ 365 Carlton Fisk 6.00 2.50
❑ 366 Bobby Valentine .75 .30
❑ 367 Bruce Miller .40 .15
❑ 368 Wilbur Wood .40 .15
❑ 369 Frank White .75 .30
❑ 370 Ron Cey .75 .30
❑ 371 Elrod Hendricks .40 .15
❑ 372 Rick Baldwin RC .40 .15
❑ 373 Johnny Briggs .40 .15
❑ 374 Dan Warthen RC .40 .15
❑ 375 Ron Fairly .75 .30
❑ 376 Rich Hebner .75 .30
❑ 377 Mike Hegan .40 .15
❑ 378 Steve Stone .75 .30
❑ 379 Ken Boswell .40 .15
❑ 380 Bobby Bonds 1.50 .60
❑ 381 Denny Doyle .40 .15
❑ 382 Matt Alexander RC .40 .15
❑ 383 John Ellis .40 .15
❑ 384 Philadelphia Phillies CL/Ozark 1.50 .60
❑ 385 Mickey Lolich .75 .30
❑ 386 Ed Goodson .40 .15
❑ 387 Mike Miley RC .40 .15
❑ 388 Stan Perzanowski RC .40 .15
❑ 389 Glenn Adams RC .40 .15
❑ 390 Don Gullett .75 .30
❑ 391 Jerry Hairston .40 .15
❑ 392 Checklist 265-396 1.50 .60
❑ 393 Paul Mitchell RC .40 .15
❑ 394 Fran Healy .40 .15
❑ 395 Jim Wynn .75 .30
❑ 396 Bill Lee .40 .15
❑ 397 Tim Foli .40 .15
❑ 398 Dave Tomlin .40 .15
❑ 399 Luis Melendez .40 .15
❑ 400 Rod Carew 6.00 2.50
❑ 401 Ken Brett .40 .15
❑ 402 Don Money .75 .30
❑ 403 Geoff Zahn .40 .15
❑ 404 Enos Cabell .40 .15
❑ 405 Rollie Fingers 2.50 1.00
❑ 406 Ed Herrmann .40 .15
❑ 407 Tom Underwood .40 .15
❑ 408 Charlie Spikes .40 .15
❑ 409 Dave Lemanczyk .40 .15
❑ 410 Ralph Garr .75 .30
❑ 411 Bill Singer .40 .15
❑ 412 Toby Harrah .75 .30
❑ 413 Pete Varney RC .40 .15
❑ 414 Wayne Garland .40 .15
❑ 415 Vada Pinson 1.50 .60
❑ 416 Tommy John 1.50 .60
❑ 417 Gene Clines .40 .15
❑ 418 Jose Morales RC .40 .15
❑ 419 Reggie Cleveland .40 .15
❑ 420 Joe Morgan 5.00 2.00
❑ 421 Oakland Athletics CL 1.50 .60
❑ 422 Johnny Grubb .40 .15
❑ 423 Ed Halicki .40 .15
❑ 424 Phil Roof .40 .15
❑ 425 Rennie Stennett .40 .15
❑ 426 Bob Forsch .40 .15
❑ 427 Kurt Bevacqua .40 .15
❑ 428 Jim Crawford .40 .15
❑ 429 Fred Stanley .40 .15
❑ 430 Jose Cardenal .75 .30
❑ 431 Dick Ruthven .40 .15
❑ 432 Tom Veryzer .40 .15
❑ 433 Rick Waits RC .40 .15
❑ 434 Morris Nettles .40 .15
❑ 435 Phil Niekro 2.50 1.00
❑ 436 Bill Fahey .40 .15
❑ 437 Terry Forster .40 .15
❑ 438 Doug DeCinces .75 .30
❑ 439 Rick Rhoden .75 .30
❑ 440 John Mayberry .75 .30
❑ 441 Gary Carter 4.00 1.50
❑ 442 Hank Webb .40 .15
❑ 443 San Francisco Giants CL 1.50 .60
❑ 444 Gary Nolan .75 .30
❑ 445 Rico Petrocelli .75 .30
❑ 446 Larry Haney .40 .15
❑ 447 Gene Locklear .75 .30
❑ 448 Tom Johnson .40 .15
❑ 449 Bob Robertson .40 .15
❑ 450 Jim Palmer 5.00 2.00
❑ 451 Buddy Bradford .40 .15
❑ 452 Tom Hausman RC .40 .15
❑ 453 Lou Piniella 1.50 .60
❑ 454 Tom Griffin .40 .15
❑ 455 Dick Allen 1.50 .60
❑ 456 Joe Coleman .40 .15
❑ 457 Ed Crosby .40 .15
❑ 458 Earl Williams .40 .15
❑ 459 Jim Brewer .40 .15
❑ 460 Cesar Cedeno .75 .30
❑ 461 NL/AL Champs .75 .30
❑ 462 1975 WS/Reds Champs .75 .30
❑ 463 Steve Hargan .40 .15
❑ 464 Ken Henderson .40 .15
❑ 465 Mike Marshall .75 .30
❑ 466 Bob Stinson .40 .15
❑ 467 Woodie Fryman .40 .15
❑ 468 Jesus Alou .40 .15
❑ 469 Rawly Eastwick .75 .30
❑ 470 Bobby Murcer .75 .30
❑ 471 Jim Burton .40 .15
❑ 472 Bob Davis RC .40 .15
❑ 473 Paul Blair .75 .30
❑ 474 Ray Corbin .40 .15
❑ 475 Joe Rudi .75 .30
❑ 476 Bob Moose .40 .15
❑ 477 Cleveland Indians CL/Robinson 1.50 .60
❑ 478 Lynn McGlothen .40 .15
❑ 479 Bobby Mitchell .40 .15
❑ 480 Mike Schmidt 15.00 6.00
❑ 481 Rudy May .40 .15
❑ 482 Tim Hosley .40 .15
❑ 483 Mickey Stanley .40 .15
❑ 484 Eric Raich RC .40 .15
❑ 485 Mike Hargrove .75 .30
❑ 486 Bruce Dal Canton .40 .15
❑ 487 Leron Lee .40 .15
❑ 488 Claude Osteen .75 .30
❑ 489 Skip Jutze .40 .15
❑ 490 Frank Tanana .75 .30
❑ 491 Terry Crowley .40 .15
❑ 492 Marty Pattin .40 .15
❑ 493 Derrel Thomas .40 .15
❑ 494 Craig Swan .75 .30
❑ 495 Nate Colbert .40 .15
❑ 496 Juan Beniquez .40 .15
❑ 497 Joe McIntosh RC .40 .15
❑ 498 Glenn Borgmann .40 .15
❑ 499 Mario Guerrero .40 .15
❑ 500 Reggie Jackson 12.00 5.00
❑ 501 Billy Champion .40 .15
❑ 502 Tim McCarver 1.50 .60
❑ 503 Elliott Maddox .40 .15
❑ 504 Pittsburgh Pirates CL/Murtaugh 1.50 .60
❑ 505 Mark Belanger .75 .30
❑ 506 George Mitterwald .40 .15
❑ 507 Ray Bare RC .40 .15
❑ 508 Duane Kuiper RC .40 .15
❑ 509 Bill Hands .40 .15
❑ 510 Amos Otis .75 .30
❑ 511 Jamie Easterley .40 .15
❑ 512 Ellie Rodriguez .40 .15
❑ 513 Bart Johnson .40 .15
❑ 514 Dan Driessen .75 .30
❑ 515 Steve Yeager .75 .30
❑ 516 Wayne Granger .40 .15
❑ 517 John Milner .40 .15
❑ 518 Doug Flynn RC .40 .15
❑ 519 Steve Brye .40 .15
❑ 520 Willie McCovey 5.00 2.00
❑ 521 Jim Colborn .40 .15
❑ 522 Ted Sizemore .40 .15
❑ 523 Bob Montgomery .40 .15
❑ 524 Pete Falcone RC .40 .15
❑ 525 Billy Williams 2.50 1.00
❑ 526 Checklist 397-528 1.50 .60
❑ 527 Mike Anderson .40 .15
❑ 528 Dock Ellis .40 .15
❑ 529 Deron Johnson .40 .15
❑ 530 Don Sutton 2.50 1.00
❑ 531 New York Mets CL/Frazier 1.50 .60
❑ 532 Milt May .40 .15
❑ 533 Lee Richard .40 .15
❑ 534 Stan Bahnsen .40 .15

❑	535	Dave Nelson	.40	.15
❑	536	Mike Thompson	.40	.15
❑	537	Tony Muser	.40	.15
❑	538	Pat Darcy	.40	.15
❑	539	John Balaz RC	.40	.15
❑	540	Bill Freehan	.75	.30
❑	541	Steve Mingori	.40	.15
❑	542	Keith Hernandez	.75	.30
❑	543	Wayne Twitchell	.40	.15
❑	544	Pepe Frias	.40	.15
❑	545	Sparky Lyle	.75	.30
❑	546	Dave Rosello	.40	.15
❑	547	Roric Harrison	.40	.15
❑	548	Manny Mota	.75	.30
❑	549	Randy Tate RC	.40	.15
❑	550	Hank Aaron	25.00	10.00
❑	551	Jerry DaVanon	.40	.15
❑	552	Terry Humphrey	.40	.15
❑	553	Randy Moffitt	.40	.15
❑	554	Ray Fosse	.40	.15
❑	555	Dyar Miller	.40	.15
❑	556	Minnesota Twins CL/Mauch	1.50	.60
❑	557	Dan Spillner	.40	.15
❑	558	Clarence Gaston	.75	.30
❑	559	Clyde Wright	.40	.15
❑	560	Jorge Orta	.40	.15
❑	561	Tom Carroll	.40	.15
❑	562	Adrian Garrett	.40	.15
❑	563	Larry Demery	.40	.15
❑	564	Kurt Bevacqua GUM	1.50	.60
❑	565	Tug McGraw	.75	.30
❑	566	Ken McMullen	.40	.15
❑	567	George Stone	.40	.15
❑	568	Rob Andrews RC	.40	.15
❑	569	Nelson Briles	.75	.30
❑	570	George Hendrick	.75	.30
❑	571	Don DeMola	.40	.15
❑	572	Rich Coggins	.40	.15
❑	573	Bill Travers	.40	.15
❑	574	Don Kessinger	.75	.30
❑	575	Dwight Evans	1.50	.60
❑	576	Maximino Leon	.40	.15
❑	577	Marc Hill	.40	.15
❑	578	Ted Kubiak	.40	.15
❑	579	Clay Kirby	.40	.15
❑	580	Bert Campaneris	.75	.30
❑	581	St. Louis Cardinals CL/Schoendienst	1.50	.60
❑	582	Mike Kekich	.40	.15
❑	583	Tommy Helms	.40	.15
❑	584	Stan Wall RC	.40	.15
❑	585	Joe Torre	1.50	.60
❑	586	Ron Schueler	.40	.15
❑	587	Leo Cardenas	.40	.15
❑	588	Kevin Kobel	.40	.15
❑	589	Alc/Flanagan/Pac/Torr RC	1.50	.60
❑	590	Cruz/Lemon/Valen/Whit RC	.75	.30
❑	591	Grilli/Mitch/Sosa/Throop RC	.75	.30
❑	592	Randolph/McK/Roy/Sta RC	5.00	2.00
❑	593	And/Crosby/Litell/Metzger RC	.75	.30
❑	594	Mer/Ott/Still/White RC	.75	.30
❑	595	DeFil/Lerch/Monge/Barr RC	.75	.30
❑	596	Rey/John/LeMas/Manuel RC	.75	.30
❑	597	Aase/Kucek/LaCorte/Pazik RC	.75	.30
❑	598	Cruz/Quirk/Turner/Wallis RC	.75	.30
❑	599	Dres/Guidry/McCl/Zach RC	8.00	3.00
❑	600	Tom Seaver	10.00	4.00
❑	601	Ken Rudolph	.40	.15
❑	602	Doug Konieczny	.40	.15
❑	603	Jim Holt	.40	.15
❑	604	Joe Lovitto	.40	.15
❑	605	Al Downing	.40	.15
❑	606	Milwaukee Brewers CL/Grammas	1.50	.60
❑	607	Rich Hinton	.40	.15
❑	608	Vic Correll	.40	.15
❑	609	Fred Norman	.40	.15
❑	610	Greg Luzinski	1.50	.60
❑	611	Rich Folkers	.40	.15
❑	612	Joe Lahoud	.40	.15
❑	613	Tim Johnson	.40	.15
❑	614	Fernando Arroyo RC	.40	.15
❑	615	Mike Cubbage	.40	.15
❑	616	Buck Martinez	.40	.15
❑	617	Darold Knowles	.40	.15
❑	618	Jack Brohamer	.40	.15
❑	619	Bill Butler	.40	.15
❑	620	Al Oliver	.75	.30
❑	621	Tom Hall	.40	.15
❑	622	Rick Auerbach	.40	.15
❑	623	Bob Allietta RC	.40	.15
❑	624	Tony Taylor	.40	.15
❑	625	J.R. Richard	.75	.30
❑	626	Bob Sheldon	.40	.15
❑	627	Bill Plummer	.40	.15
❑	628	John D'Acquisto	.40	.15
❑	629	Sandy Alomar	.75	.30
❑	630	Chris Speier	.40	.15
❑	631	Atlanta Braves CL/Bristol	1.50	.60
❑	632	Rogelio Moret	.40	.15
❑	633	John Stearns RC	.75	.30
❑	634	Larry Christenson	.40	.15
❑	635	Jim Fregosi	.75	.30
❑	636	Joe Decker	.40	.15
❑	637	Bruce Bochte	.40	.15
❑	638	Doyle Alexander	.75	.30
❑	639	Fred Kendall	.40	.15
❑	640	Bill Madlock	1.50	.60
❑	641	Tom Paciorek	.75	.30
❑	642	Dennis Blair	.40	.15
❑	643	Checklist 529-660	1.50	.60
❑	644	Tom Bradley	.40	.15
❑	645	Darrell Porter	.75	.30
❑	646	John Lowenstein	.40	.15
❑	647	Ramon Hernandez	.40	.15
❑	648	Al Cowens	.75	.30
❑	649	Dave Roberts	.40	.15
❑	650	Thurman Munson	6.00	2.50
❑	651	John Odom	.40	.15
❑	652	Ed Armbrister	.40	.15
❑	653	Mike Norris RC	.75	.30
❑	654	Doug Griffin	.40	.15
❑	655	Mike Vail RC	.40	.15
❑	656	Chicago White Sox CL/Tanner	1.50	.60
❑	657	Roy Smalley RC	.75	.30
❑	658	Jerry Johnson	.40	.15
❑	659	Ben Oglivie	.75	.30
❑	660	Davey Lopes	1.50	.60

1977 Topps

❑		COMPLETE SET (660)	225.00	125.00
❑	1	G.Brett/B.Madlock LL	8.00	3.00
❑	2	G.Nettles/M.Schmidt LL	2.50	1.00
❑	3	L.May/G.Foster LL	1.50	.60
❑	4	B.North/D.Lopes LL	.75	.30
❑	5	J.Palmer/R.Jones LL	1.50	.60
❑	6	N.Ryan/T.Seaver LL	15.00	6.00
❑	7	M.Fidrych/J.Denny LL	.75	.30
❑	8	B.Campbell/R.Eastwick LL	.75	.30
❑	9	Doug Rader	.30	.10
❑	10	Reggie Jackson	10.00	4.00
❑	11	Rob Dressler	.30	.10
❑	12	Larry Haney	.30	.10
❑	13	Luis Gomez RC	.30	.10
❑	14	Tommy Smith	.30	.10
❑	15	Don Gullett	.75	.30
❑	16	Bob Jones RC	.30	.10
❑	17	Steve Stone	.75	.30
❑	18	Cleveland Indians CL/Robinson	1.50	.60
❑	19	John D'Acquisto	.30	.10
❑	20	Graig Nettles	1.50	.60
❑	21	Ken Forsch	.30	.10
❑	22	Bill Freehan	.75	.30
❑	23	Dan Driessen	.30	.10
❑	24	Carl Morton	.30	.10
❑	25	Dwight Evans	1.50	.60
❑	26	Ray Sadecki	.30	.10
❑	27	Bill Buckner	.75	.30
❑	28	Woodie Fryman	.30	.10
❑	29	Bucky Dent	.75	.30
❑	30	Greg Luzinski	1.50	.60
❑	31	Jim Todd	.30	.10
❑	32	Checklist 1-132	1.50	.60
❑	33	Wayne Garland	.30	.10
❑	34	California Angels CL/Sherry	1.50	.60
❑	35	Rennie Stennett	.30	.10
❑	36	John Ellis	.30	.10
❑	37	Steve Hargan	.30	.10
❑	38	Craig Kusick	.30	.10
❑	39	Tom Griffin	.30	.10
❑	40	Bobby Murcer	.75	.30
❑	41	Jim Kern	.30	.10
❑	42	Jose Cruz	.75	.30
❑	43	Ray Bare	.30	.10
❑	44	Bud Harrelson	.75	.30
❑	45	Rawly Eastwick	.30	.10
❑	46	Buck Martinez	.30	.10
❑	47	Lynn McGlothen	.30	.10
❑	48	Tom Paciorek	.75	.30
❑	49	Grant Jackson	.30	.10
❑	50	Ron Cey	.75	.30
❑	51	Milwaukee Brewers CL/Grammas	1.50	.60
❑	52	Ellis Valentine	.30	.10
❑	53	Paul Mitchell	.30	.10
❑	54	Sandy Alomar	.75	.30
❑	55	Jeff Burroughs	.75	.30
❑	56	Rudy May	.30	.10
❑	57	Marc Hill	.30	.10
❑	58	Chet Lemon	.75	.30
❑	59	Larry Christenson	.30	.10
❑	60	Jim Rice	2.50	1.00
❑	61	Manny Sanguillen	.75	.30
❑	62	Eric Raich	.30	.10
❑	63	Tito Fuentes	.30	.10
❑	64	Larry Biittner	.30	.10
❑	65	Skip Lockwood	.30	.10
❑	66	Roy Smalley	.75	.30
❑	67	Joaquin Andujar RC	.75	.30
❑	68	Bruce Bochte	.30	.10
❑	69	Jim Crawford	.30	.10
❑	70	Johnny Bench	10.00	4.00
❑	71	Dock Ellis	.30	.10
❑	72	Mike Anderson	.30	.10
❑	73	Charlie Williams	.30	.10
❑	74	Oakland Athletics CL/McKeon	1.50	.60
❑	75	Dennis Leonard	.75	.30
❑	76	Tim Foli	.30	.10
❑	77	Dyar Miller	.30	.10
❑	78	Bob Davis	.30	.10
❑	79	Don Money	.75	.30
❑	80	Andy Messersmith	.75	.30
❑	81	Juan Beniquez	.30	.10
❑	82	Jim Rooker	.30	.10
❑	83	Kevin Bell RC	.30	.10
❑	84	Ollie Brown	.30	.10
❑	85	Duane Kuiper	.30	.10
❑	86	Pat Zachry	.30	.10
❑	87	Glenn Borgmann	.30	.10
❑	88	Stan Wall	.30	.10
❑	89	Butch Hobson RC	.75	.30
❑	90	Cesar Cedeno	.75	.30
❑	91	John Verhoeven RC	.30	.10
❑	92	Dave Rosello	.30	.10
❑	93	Tom Poquette	.30	.10
❑	94	Craig Swan	.30	.10
❑	95	Keith Hernandez	.75	.30
❑	96	Lou Piniella	.75	.30
❑	97	Dave Heaverlo	.30	.10
❑	98	Milt May	.30	.10
❑	99	Tom Hausman	.30	.10
❑	100	Joe Morgan	4.00	1.50
❑	101	Dick Bosman	.30	.10
❑	102	Jose Morales	.30	.10
❑	103	Mike Bacsik RC	.30	.10
❑	104	Omar Moreno RC	.75	.30
❑	105	Steve Yeager	.75	.30
❑	106	Mike Flanagan	.75	.30
❑	107	Bill Melton	.30	.10
❑	108	Alan Foster	.30	.10
❑	109	Jorge Orta	.30	.10
❑	110	Steve Carlton	5.00	2.00
❑	111	Rico Petrocelli	.75	.30

	No.	Card		
❑	112	Bill Greif	.30	.10
❑	113	Toronto Blue Jays CL/Hartsfield	1.50	.60
❑	114	Bruce Dal Canton	.30	.10
❑	115	Rick Manning	.30	.10
❑	116	Joe Niekro	.75	.30
❑	117	Frank White	.75	.30
❑	118	Rick Jones RC	.30	.10
❑	119	John Stearns	.30	.10
❑	120	Rod Carew	5.00	2.00
❑	121	Gary Nolan	.30	.10
❑	122	Ben Oglivie	.75	.30
❑	123	Fred Stanley	.30	.10
❑	124	George Mitterwald	.30	.10
❑	125	Bill Travers	.30	.10
❑	126	Rod Gilbreath	.30	.10
❑	127	Ron Fairly	.75	.30
❑	128	Tommy John	1.50	.60
❑	129	Mike Sadek	.30	.10
❑	130	Al Oliver	.75	.30
❑	131	Orlando Ramirez RC	.30	.10
❑	132	Chip Lang RC	.30	.10
❑	133	Ralph Garr	.75	.30
❑	134	San Diego Padres CL/McNamara	1.50	.60
❑	135	Mark Belanger	.75	.30
❑	136	Jerry Mumphrey RC	.75	.30
❑	137	Jeff Terpko RC	.30	.10
❑	138	Bob Stinson	.30	.10
❑	139	Fred Norman	.30	.10
❑	140	Mike Schmidt	12.00	5.00
❑	141	Mark Littell	.30	.10
❑	142	Steve Dillard RC	.30	.10
❑	143	Ed Herrmann	.30	.10
❑	144	Bruce Sutter RC	15.00	6.00
❑	145	Tom Veryzer	.30	.10
❑	146	Dusty Baker	1.50	.60
❑	147	Jackie Brown	.30	.10
❑	148	Fran Healy	.30	.10
❑	149	Mike Cubbage	.30	.10
❑	150	Tom Seaver	8.00	3.00
❑	151	Johnny LeMaster	.30	.10
❑	152	Gaylord Perry	2.50	1.00
❑	153	Ron Jackson RC	.30	.10
❑	154	Dave Giusti	.30	.10
❑	155	Joe Rudi	.75	.30
❑	156	Pete Mackanin	.30	.10
❑	157	Ken Brett	.30	.10
❑	158	Ted Kubiak	.30	.10
❑	159	Bernie Carbo	.30	.10
❑	160	Will McEnaney	.30	.10
❑	161	Garry Templeton RC	1.50	.60
❑	162	Mike Cuellar	.75	.30
❑	163	Dave Hilton	.30	.10
❑	164	Tug McGraw	.75	.30
❑	165	Jim Wynn	.75	.30
❑	166	Bill Campbell	.30	.10
❑	167	Rich Hebner	.75	.30
❑	168	Charlie Spikes	.30	.10
❑	169	Darold Knowles	.30	.10
❑	170	Thurman Munson	5.00	2.00
❑	171	Ken Sanders	.30	.10
❑	172	John Milner	.30	.10
❑	173	Chuck Scrivener RC	.30	.10
❑	174	Nelson Briles	.75	.30
❑	175	Butch Wynegar RC	.75	.30
❑	176	Bob Robertson	.30	.10
❑	177	Bart Johnson	.30	.10
❑	178	Bombo Rivera RC	.30	.10
❑	179	Paul Hartzell RC	.30	.10
❑	180	Dave Lopes	.75	.30
❑	181	Ken McMullen	.30	.10
❑	182	Dan Spillner	.30	.10
❑	183	St.Louis Cardinals CL/V.Rapp	1.50	.60
❑	184	Bo McLaughlin RC	.30	.10
❑	185	Sixto Lezcano	.30	.10
❑	186	Doug Flynn	.30	.10
❑	187	Dick Pole	.30	.10
❑	188	Bob Tolan	.30	.10
❑	189	Rick Dempsey	.75	.30
❑	190	Ray Burris	.30	.10
❑	191	Doug Griffin	.30	.10
❑	192	Clarence Gaston	.75	.30
❑	193	Larry Gura	.30	.10
❑	194	Gary Matthews	.75	.30
❑	195	Ed Figueroa	.30	.10
❑	196	Len Randle	.30	.10
❑	197	Ed Ott	.30	.10
❑	198	Wilbur Wood	.30	.10
❑	199	Pepe Frias	.30	.10
❑	200	Frank Tanana	.75	.30
❑	201	Ed Kranepool	.30	.10
❑	202	Tom Johnson	.30	.10
❑	203	Ed Armbrister	.30	.10
❑	204	Jeff Newman RC	.30	.10
❑	205	Pete Falcone	.30	.10
❑	206	Boog Powell	1.50	.60
❑	207	Glenn Abbott	.30	.10
❑	208	Checklist 133-264	1.50	.60
❑	209	Rob Andrews	.30	.10
❑	210	Fred Lynn	.75	.30
❑	211	San Francisco Giants CL/Altobelli	1.50	.60
❑	212	Jim Mason	.30	.10
❑	213	Maximino Leon	.30	.10
❑	214	Darrell Porter	.75	.30
❑	215	Butch Metzger	.30	.10
❑	216	Doug DeCinces	.75	.30
❑	217	Tom Underwood	.30	.10
❑	218	John Wathan RC	.75	.30
❑	219	Joe Coleman	.30	.10
❑	220	Chris Chambliss	.75	.30
❑	221	Bob Bailey	.30	.10
❑	222	Francisco Barrios RC	.30	.10
❑	223	Earl Williams	.30	.10
❑	224	Rusty Torres	.30	.10
❑	225	Bob Apodaca	.30	.10
❑	226	Leroy Stanton	.75	.30
❑	227	Joe Sambito RC	.30	.10
❑	228	Minnesota Twins CL/Mauch	1.50	.60
❑	229	Don Kessinger	.75	.30
❑	230	Vida Blue	.75	.30
❑	231	George Brett RB	8.00	3.00
❑	232	Minnie Minoso RB	.75	.30
❑	233	Jose Morales RB	.30	.10
❑	234	Nolan Ryan RB	15.00	6.00
❑	235	Cecil Cooper	.75	.30
❑	236	Tom Buskey	.30	.10
❑	237	Gene Clines	.30	.10
❑	238	Tippy Martinez	.30	.10
❑	239	Bill Plummer	.30	.10
❑	240	Ron LeFlore	.75	.30
❑	241	Dave Tomlin	.30	.10
❑	242	Ken Henderson	.30	.10
❑	243	Ron Reed	.30	.10
❑	244	John Mayberry	.75	.30
❑	245	Rick Rhoden	.75	.30
❑	246	Mike Vail	.30	.10
❑	247	Chris Knapp RC	.30	.10
❑	248	Wilbur Howard	.30	.10
❑	249	Pete Redfern RC	.30	.10
❑	250	Bill Madlock	.75	.30
❑	251	Tony Muser	.30	.10
❑	252	Dale Murray	.30	.10
❑	253	John Hale	.30	.10
❑	254	Doyle Alexander	.30	.10
❑	255	George Scott	.75	.30
❑	256	Joe Hoerner	.30	.10
❑	257	Mike Miley	.30	.10
❑	258	Luis Tiant	.75	.30
❑	259	New York Mets CL/Frazier	1.50	.60
❑	260	J.R. Richard	.75	.30
❑	261	Phil Garner	.75	.30
❑	262	Al Cowens	.75	.30
❑	263	Mike Marshall	.75	.30
❑	264	Tom Hutton	.30	.10
❑	265	Mark Fidrych RC	3.00	1.25
❑	266	Derrel Thomas	.30	.10
❑	267	Ray Fosse	.30	.10
❑	268	Rick Sawyer RC	.30	.10
❑	269	Joe Lis	.30	.10
❑	270	Dave Parker	1.50	.60
❑	271	Terry Forster	.30	.10
❑	272	Lee Lacy	.30	.10
❑	273	Eric Soderholm	.30	.10
❑	274	Don Stanhouse	.30	.10
❑	275	Mike Hargrove	.75	.30
❑	276	Chris Chambliss ALCS	1.50	.60
❑	277	Pete Rose NLCS	5.00	2.00
❑	278	Danny Frisella	.30	.10
❑	279	Joe Wallis	.30	.10
❑	280	Jim Hunter	2.50	1.00
❑	281	Roy Staiger	.30	.10
❑	282	Sid Monge	.30	.10
❑	283	Jerry DaVanon	.30	.10
❑	284	Mike Norris	.30	.10
❑	285	Brooks Robinson	5.00	2.00
❑	286	Johnny Grubb	.30	.10
❑	287	Cincinnati Reds CL/Anderson	1.50	.60
❑	288	Bob Montgomery	.30	.10
❑	289	Gene Garber	.75	.30
❑	290	Amos Otis	.75	.30
❑	291	Jason Thompson RC	.75	.30
❑	292	Rogelio Moret	.30	.10
❑	293	Jack Brohamer	.30	.10
❑	294	George Medich	.30	.10
❑	295	Gary Carter	2.50	1.00
❑	296	Don Hood	.30	.10
❑	297	Ken Reitz	.30	.10
❑	298	Charlie Hough	.75	.30
❑	299	Otto Velez	.75	.30
❑	300	Jerry Koosman	.75	.30
❑	301	Toby Harrah	.75	.30
❑	302	Mike Garman	.30	.10
❑	303	Gene Tenace	.75	.30
❑	304	Jim Hughes	.30	.10
❑	305	Mickey Rivers	.75	.30
❑	306	Rick Waits	.30	.10
❑	307	Gary Sutherland	.30	.10
❑	308	Gene Pentz RC	.30	.10
❑	309	Boston Red Sox CL/Zimmer	1.50	.60
❑	310	Larry Bowa	.75	.30
❑	311	Vern Ruhle	.30	.10
❑	312	Rob Belloir RC	.30	.10
❑	313	Paul Blair	.75	.30
❑	314	Steve Mingori	.30	.10
❑	315	Dave Chalk	.30	.10
❑	316	Steve Rogers	.30	.10
❑	317	Kurt Bevacqua	.30	.10
❑	318	Duffy Dyer	.30	.10
❑	319	Goose Gossage	1.50	.60
❑	320	Ken Griffey Sr.	1.50	.60
❑	321	Dave Goltz	.30	.10
❑	322	Bill Russell	.75	.30
❑	323	Larry Lintz	.30	.10
❑	324	John Curtis	.30	.10
❑	325	Mike Ivie	.30	.10
❑	326	Jesse Jefferson	.30	.10
❑	327	Houston Astros CL/Virdon	1.50	.60
❑	328	Tommy Boggs RC	.30	.10
❑	329	Ron Hodges	.30	.10
❑	330	George Hendrick	.75	.30
❑	331	Jim Colborn	.30	.10
❑	332	Elliott Maddox	.30	.10
❑	333	Paul Reuschel RC	.30	.10
❑	334	Bill Stein	.30	.10
❑	335	Bill Robinson	.75	.30
❑	336	Denny Doyle	.30	.10
❑	337	Ron Schueler	.30	.10
❑	338	Dave Duncan	.75	.30
❑	339	Adrian Devine	.30	.10
❑	340	Hal McRae	.75	.30
❑	341	Joe Kerrigan RC	.30	.10
❑	342	Jerry Remy	.30	.10
❑	343	Ed Halicki	.30	.10
❑	344	Brian Downing	.75	.30
❑	345	Reggie Smith	.75	.30
❑	346	Bill Singer	.30	.10
❑	347	George Foster	1.50	.60
❑	348	Brent Strom	.30	.10
❑	349	Jim Holt	.30	.10
❑	350	Larry Dierker	.75	.30
❑	351	Jim Sundberg	.75	.30
❑	352	Mike Phillips	.30	.10
❑	353	Stan Thomas	.30	.10
❑	354	Pittsburgh Pirates CL/Tanner	1.50	.60
❑	355	Lou Brock	4.00	1.50
❑	356	Checklist 265-396	1.50	.60
❑	357	Tim McCarver	1.50	.60
❑	358	Tom House	.30	.10
❑	359	Willie Randolph	1.50	.60
❑	360	Rick Monday	.75	.30
❑	361	Eduardo Rodriguez	.30	.10
❑	362	Tommy Davis	.75	.30
❑	363	Dave Roberts	.30	.10
❑	364	Vic Correll	.30	.10
❑	365	Mike Torrez	.75	.30
❑	366	Ted Sizemore	.30	.10
❑	367	Dave Hamilton	.30	.10
❑	368	Mike Jorgensen	.30	.10
❑	369	Terry Humphrey	.30	.10

❑	370	John Montefusco	.30	.10
❑	371	Kansas City Royals CL/Herzog	1.50	.60
❑	372	Rich Folkers	.30	.10
❑	373	Bert Campaneris	.75	.30
❑	374	Kent Tekulve	.75	.30
❑	375	Larry Hisle	.75	.30
❑	376	Nino Espinosa RC	.30	.10
❑	377	Dave McKay	.30	.10
❑	378	Jim Umbarger	.30	.10
❑	379	Larry Cox RC	.30	.10
❑	380	Lee May	.75	.30
❑	381	Bob Forsch	.30	.10
❑	382	Charlie Moore	.30	.10
❑	383	Stan Bahnsen	.30	.10
❑	384	Darrel Chaney	.30	.10
❑	385	Dave LaRoche	.30	.10
❑	386	Manny Mota	.75	.30
❑	387	New York Yankees CL/Martin	2.50	1.00
❑	388	Terry Harmon	.30	.10
❑	389	Ken Kravec RC	.30	.10
❑	390	Dave Winfield	6.00	2.50
❑	391	Dan Warthen	.30	.10
❑	392	Phil Roof	.30	.10
❑	393	John Lowenstein	.30	.10
❑	394	Bill Laxton RC	.30	.10
❑	395	Manny Trillo	.30	.10
❑	396	Tom Murphy	.30	.10
❑	397	Larry Herndon RC	.75	.30
❑	398	Tom Burgmeier	.30	.10
❑	399	Bruce Boisclair RC	.30	.10
❑	400	Steve Garvey	2.50	1.00
❑	401	Mickey Scott	.30	.10
❑	402	Tommy Helms	.30	.10
❑	403	Tom Grieve	.75	.30
❑	404	Eric Rasmussen RC	.30	.10
❑	405	Claudell Washington	.75	.30
❑	406	Tim Johnson	.30	.10
❑	407	Dave Freisleben	.30	.10
❑	408	Cesar Tovar	.30	.10
❑	409	Pete Broberg	.30	.10
❑	410	Willie Montanez	.30	.10
❑	411	J.Morgan/J.Bench WS	2.50	1.00
❑	412	Johnny Bench WS	2.50	1.00
❑	413	Cincy Wins WS	.75	.30
❑	414	Tommy Harper	.75	.30
❑	415	Jay Johnstone	.75	.30
❑	416	Chuck Hartenstein	.30	.10
❑	417	Wayne Garrett	.30	.10
❑	418	Chicago White Sox CL/Lemon	1.50	.60
❑	419	Steve Swisher	.30	.10
❑	420	Rusty Staub	1.50	.60
❑	421	Doug Rau	.30	.10
❑	422	Freddie Patek	.75	.30
❑	423	Gary Lavelle	.30	.10
❑	424	Steve Brye	.30	.10
❑	425	Joe Torre	1.50	.60
❑	426	Dick Drago	.30	.10
❑	427	Dave Rader	.30	.10
❑	428	Texas Rangers CL/Lucchesi	1.50	.60
❑	429	Ken Boswell	.30	.10
❑	430	Fergie Jenkins	2.50	1.00
❑	431	Dave Collins UER	.75	.30
❑	432	Buzz Capra	.30	.10
❑	433	Nate Colbert TBC	.30	.10
❑	434	Carl Yastrzemski TBC	1.50	.60
❑	435	Maury Wills TBC	.75	.30
❑	436	Bob Keegan TBC	.30	.10
❑	437	Ralph Kiner TBC	1.50	.60
❑	438	Marty Perez	.30	.10
❑	439	Gorman Thomas	.75	.30
❑	440	Jon Matlack	.30	.10
❑	441	Larvell Blanks	.30	.10
❑	442	Atlanta Braves CL/Bristol	1.50	.60
❑	443	Lamar Johnson	.30	.10
❑	444	Wayne Twitchell	.30	.10
❑	445	Ken Singleton	.75	.30
❑	446	Bill Bonham	.30	.10
❑	447	Jerry Turner	.30	.10
❑	448	Ellie Rodriguez	.30	.10
❑	449	Al Fitzmorris	.30	.10
❑	450	Pete Rose	20.00	8.00
❑	451	Checklist 397-528	1.50	.60
❑	452	Mike Caldwell	.30	.10
❑	453	Pedro Garcia	.30	.10
❑	454	Andy Etchebarren	.30	.10
❑	455	Rick Wise	.30	.10
❑	456	Leon Roberts	.30	.10
❑	457	Steve Luebber	.30	.10
❑	458	Leo Foster	.30	.10
❑	459	Steve Foucault	.30	.10
❑	460	Willie Stargell	2.50	1.00
❑	461	Dick Tidrow	.30	.10
❑	462	Don Baylor	1.50	.60
❑	463	Jamie Quirk	.30	.10
❑	464	Randy Moffitt	.30	.10
❑	465	Rico Carty	.75	.30
❑	466	Fred Holdsworth	.30	.10
❑	467	Philadelphia Phillies CL/Ozark	1.50	.60
❑	468	Ramon Hernandez	.30	.10
❑	469	Pat Kelly	.30	.10
❑	470	Ted Simmons	.75	.30
❑	471	Del Unser	.30	.10
❑	472	Aase/McCl/Patt/Wehr RC	.30	.10
❑	473	Andre Dawson RC	20.00	8.00
❑	474	Bailor/Gar/Reyn/Tav RC	.75	.30
❑	475	Batt/Camp/McGr/Sarm RC	.75	.30
❑	476	Dale Murphy RC	15.00	6.00
❑	477	Ault/Dauer/Gonz/Mank RC	.75	.30
❑	478	Gid/Hoot/John/Lemong RC	.75	.30
❑	479	Assel/Gross/Mej/Woods RC	.75	.30
❑	480	Carl Yastrzemski	8.00	3.00
❑	481	Roger Metzger	.30	.10
❑	482	Tony Solaita	.30	.10
❑	483	Richie Zisk	.30	.10
❑	484	Burt Hooton	.75	.30
❑	485	Roy White	.75	.30
❑	486	Ed Bane	.30	.10
❑	487	And/Glynn/Hend/Terl RC	.75	.30
❑	488	Clark/Jon/Mazzilli/Tho RC	3.00	1.25
❑	489	Barker/Ler/Mint/Overy RC	.75	.30
❑	490	Almon/Klutts/McM/Wag RC	.75	.30
❑	491	Dup/Martinez/Mitch/Sykes RC	3.00	1.25
❑	492	Armas/Kemp/Lop/Woods RC	.75	.30
❑	493	Krukow/Ott/Wheel/Will RC	.75	.30
❑	494	Bern/Cha/Gantner/Wills RC	1.50	.60
❑	495	Al Hrabosky	.75	.30
❑	496	Gary Thomasson	.30	.10
❑	497	Clay Carroll	.30	.10
❑	498	Sal Bando	.75	.30
❑	499	Pablo Torrealba	.30	.10
❑	500	Dave Kingman	1.50	.60
❑	501	Jim Bibby	.30	.10
❑	502	Randy Hundley	.30	.10
❑	503	Bill Lee	.30	.10
❑	504	Los Angeles Dodgers CL/Lasorda	1.50	.60
❑	505	Oscar Gamble	.75	.30
❑	506	Steve Grilli	.30	.10
❑	507	Mike Hegan	.30	.10
❑	508	Dave Pagan	.30	.10
❑	509	Cookie Rojas	.75	.30
❑	510	John Candelaria	.30	.10
❑	511	Bill Fahey	.30	.10
❑	512	Jack Billingham	.30	.10
❑	513	Jerry Terrell	.30	.10
❑	514	Cliff Johnson	.30	.10
❑	515	Chris Speier	.30	.10
❑	516	Bake McBride	.75	.30
❑	517	Pete Vuckovich RC	.75	.30
❑	518	Chicago Cubs CL/Franks	1.50	.60
❑	519	Don Kirkwood	.30	.10
❑	520	Garry Maddox	.30	.10
❑	521	Bob Grich	.75	.30
❑	522	Enzo Hernandez	.30	.10
❑	523	Rollie Fingers	2.50	1.00
❑	524	Rowland Office	.30	.10
❑	525	Dennis Eckersley	5.00	2.50
❑	526	Larry Parrish	.75	.30
❑	527	Dan Meyer	.75	.30
❑	528	Bill Castro	.30	.10
❑	529	Jim Essian RC	.30	.10
❑	530	Rick Reuschel	.75	.30
❑	531	Lyman Bostock	.75	.30
❑	532	Jim Willoughby	.30	.10
❑	533	Mickey Stanley	.30	.10
❑	534	Paul Splittorff	.30	.10
❑	535	Cesar Geronimo	.30	.10
❑	536	Vic Albury	.30	.10
❑	537	Dave Roberts	.30	.10
❑	538	Frank Taveras	.30	.10
❑	539	Mike Wallace	.30	.10
❑	540	Bob Watson	.75	.30
❑	541	John Denny	.75	.30
❑	542	Frank Duffy	.30	.10
❑	543	Ron Blomberg	.30	.10
❑	544	Gary Ross	.30	.10
❑	545	Bob Boone	.75	.30
❑	546	Baltimore Orioles CL/Weaver	1.50	.60
❑	547	Willie McCovey	4.00	1.50
❑	548	Joel Youngblood RC	.30	.10
❑	549	Jerry Royster	.30	.10
❑	550	Randy Jones	.30	.10
❑	551	Bill North	.30	.10
❑	552	Pepe Mangual	.30	.10
❑	553	Jack Heidemann	.30	.10
❑	554	Bruce Kimm RC	.30	.10
❑	555	Dan Ford	.30	.10
❑	556	Doug Bird	.30	.10
❑	557	Jerry White	.30	.10
❑	558	Elias Sosa	.30	.10
❑	559	Alan Bannister RC	.30	.10
❑	560	Dave Concepcion	1.50	.60
❑	561	Pete LaCock	.30	.10
❑	562	Checklist 529-660	1.50	.60
❑	563	Bruce Kison	.30	.10
❑	564	Alan Ashby	.30	.10
❑	565	Mickey Lolich	.75	.30
❑	566	Rick Miller	.30	.10
❑	567	Enos Cabell	.30	.10
❑	568	Carlos May	.30	.10
❑	569	Jim Lonborg	.75	.30
❑	570	Bobby Bonds	1.50	.60
❑	571	Darrell Evans	.75	.30
❑	572	Ross Grimsley	.30	.10
❑	573	Joe Ferguson	.30	.10
❑	574	Aurelio Rodriguez	.30	.10
❑	575	Dick Ruthven	.30	.10
❑	576	Fred Kendall	.30	.10
❑	577	Jerry Augustine RC	.30	.10
❑	578	Bob Randall RC	.30	.10
❑	579	Don Carrithers	.30	.10
❑	580	George Brett	15.00	6.00
❑	581	Pedro Borbon	.30	.10
❑	582	Ed Kirkpatrick	.30	.10
❑	583	Paul Lindblad	.30	.10
❑	584	Ed Goodson	.30	.10
❑	585	Rick Burleson	.75	.30
❑	586	Steve Renko	.30	.10
❑	587	Rick Baldwin	.30	.10
❑	588	Dave Moates	.30	.10
❑	589	Mike Cosgrove	.30	.10
❑	590	Buddy Bell	.75	.30
❑	591	Chris Arnold	.30	.10
❑	592	Dan Briggs RC	.30	.10
❑	593	Dennis Blair	.30	.10
❑	594	Biff Pocoroba	.30	.10
❑	595	John Hiller	.30	.10
❑	596	Jerry Martin RC	.30	.10
❑	597	Seattle Mariners CL/Johnson	1.50	.60
❑	598	Sparky Lyle	.75	.30
❑	599	Mike Tyson	.30	.10
❑	600	Jim Palmer	4.00	1.50
❑	601	Mike Lum	.30	.10
❑	602	Andy Hassler	.30	.10
❑	603	Willie Davis	.75	.30
❑	604	Jim Slaton	.30	.10
❑	605	Felix Millan	.30	.10
❑	606	Steve Braun	.30	.10
❑	607	Larry Demery	.30	.10
❑	608	Roy Howell	.30	.10
❑	609	Jim Barr	.30	.10
❑	610	Jose Cardenal	.75	.30
❑	611	Dave Lemanczyk	.30	.10
❑	612	Barry Foote	.30	.10
❑	613	Reggie Cleveland	.30	.10
❑	614	Greg Gross	.30	.10
❑	615	Phil Niekro	2.50	1.00
❑	616	Tommy Sandt RC	.30	.10
❑	617	Bobby Darwin	.30	.10
❑	618	Pat Dobson	.30	.10
❑	619	Johnny Oates	.75	.30
❑	620	Don Sutton	2.50	1.00
❑	621	Detroit Tigers CL/Houk	1.50	.60
❑	622	Jim Wohlford	.30	.10
❑	623	Jack Kucek	.30	.10
❑	624	Hector Cruz	.30	.10
❑	625	Ken Holtzman	.75	.30
❑	626	Al Bumbry	.75	.30
❑	627	Bob Myrick RC	.30	.10

❑ 628 Mario Guerrero .30 .10
❑ 629 Bobby Valentine .75 .30
❑ 630 Bert Blyleven 1.50 .60
❑ 631 Brett Brothers 6.00 2.50
❑ 632 Forsch Brothers .75 .30
❑ 633 May Brothers .75 .30
❑ 634 Reuschel Brothers UER .75 .30
❑ 635 Robin Yount 8.00 3.00
❑ 636 Santo Alcala .30 .10
❑ 637 Alex Johnson .30 .10
❑ 638 Jim Kaat 1.50 .60
❑ 639 Jerry Morales .30 .10
❑ 640 Carlton Fisk 5.00 2.00
❑ 641 Dan Larson RC .30 .10
❑ 642 Willie Crawford .30 .10
❑ 643 Mike Pazik .30 .10
❑ 644 Matt Alexander .30 .10
❑ 645 Jerry Reuss .75 .30
❑ 646 Andres Mora RC .30 .10
❑ 647 Montreal Expos CL/Williams 1.50 .60
❑ 648 Jim Spencer .30 .10
❑ 649 Dave Cash .30 .10
❑ 650 Nolan Ryan 30.00 12.50
❑ 651 Von Joshua .30 .10
❑ 652 Tom Walker .30 .10
❑ 653 Diego Segui .75 .30
❑ 654 Ron Pruitt RC .30 .10
❑ 655 Tony Perez 2.50 1.00
❑ 656 Ron Guidry 1.50 .60
❑ 657 Mick Kelleher RC .30 .10
❑ 658 Marty Pattin .30 .10
❑ 659 Merv Rettenmund .30 .10
❑ 660 Willie Horton 1.50 .60

1978 Topps

❑ COMPLETE SET (726) 200.00 125.00
❑ COMMON CARD (1-726) .25 .08
❑ COMMON CARD DP .15 .05
❑ 1 Lou Brock RB 3.00 1.25
❑ 2 Sparky Lyle RB .60 .25
❑ 3 Willie McCovey RB 2.50 1.00
❑ 4 Brooks Robinson RB 1.25 .50
❑ 5 Pete Rose RB 8.00 3.00
❑ 6 Nolan Ryan RB 15.00 6.00
❑ 7 Reggie Jackson RB 4.00 1.50
❑ 8 Mike Sadek .25 .08
❑ 9 Doug DeCinces .60 .25
❑ 10 Phil Niekro 2.50 1.00
❑ 11 Rick Manning .25 .08
❑ 12 Don Aase .25 .08
❑ 13 Art Howe RC .60 .25
❑ 14 Lerrin LaGrow .25 .08
❑ 15 Tony Perez DP 1.25 .50
❑ 16 Roy White .60 .25
❑ 17 Mike Krukow .25 .08
❑ 18 Bob Grich .60 .25
❑ 19 Darrell Porter .60 .25
❑ 20 Pete Rose DP 12.00 5.00
❑ 21 Steve Kemp .25 .08
❑ 22 Charlie Hough .60 .25
❑ 23 Bump Wills .25 .08
❑ 24 Don Money DP .15 .05
❑ 25 Jon Matlack .25 .08
❑ 26 Rich Hebner .60 .25
❑ 27 Geoff Zahn .25 .08
❑ 28 Ed Ott .25 .08
❑ 29 Bob Lacey RC .25 .08
❑ 30 George Hendrick .60 .25
❑ 31 Glenn Abbott .25 .08
❑ 32 Garry Templeton .60 .25
❑ 33 Dave Lemanczyk .25 .08
❑ 34 Willie McCovey 3.00 1.25
❑ 35 Sparky Lyle .60 .25
❑ 36 Eddie Murray RC 50.00 20.00
❑ 37 Rick Waits .25 .08
❑ 38 Willie Montanez .25 .08
❑ 39 Floyd Bannister RC .25 .08
❑ 40 Carl Yastrzemski 6.00 2.50
❑ 41 Burt Hooton .60 .25
❑ 42 Jorge Orta .25 .08
❑ 43 Bill Atkinson RC .25 .08
❑ 44 Toby Harrah .60 .25
❑ 45 Mark Fidrych 2.50 1.00
❑ 46 Al Cowens .60 .25
❑ 47 Jack Billingham .25 .08
❑ 48 Don Baylor 1.25 .50
❑ 49 Ed Kranepool .60 .25
❑ 50 Rick Reuschel .60 .25
❑ 51 Charlie Moore DP .15 .05
❑ 52 Jim Lonborg .60 .25
❑ 53 Phil Garner DP .25 .08
❑ 54 Tom Johnson .25 .08
❑ 55 Mitchell Page RC .25 .08
❑ 56 Randy Jones .25 .08
❑ 57 Dan Meyer .25 .08
❑ 58 Bob Forsch .25 .08
❑ 59 Otto Velez .25 .08
❑ 60 Thurman Munson 4.00 1.50
❑ 61 Larvell Blanks .25 .08
❑ 62 Jim Barr .25 .08
❑ 63 Don Zimmer MG .60 .25
❑ 64 Gene Pentz .25 .08
❑ 65 Ken Singleton .60 .25
❑ 66 Chicago White Sox CL 1.25 .50
❑ 67 Claudell Washington .60 .25
❑ 68 Steve Foucault DP .15 .05
❑ 69 Mike Vail .25 .08
❑ 70 Goose Gossage 1.25 .50
❑ 71 Terry Humphrey .25 .08
❑ 72 Andre Dawson 4.00 1.50
❑ 73 Andy Hassler .25 .08
❑ 74 Checklist 1-121 1.25 .50
❑ 75 Dick Ruthven .25 .08
❑ 76 Steve Ontiveros .25 .08
❑ 77 Ed Kirkpatrick .25 .08
❑ 78 Pablo Torrealba .25 .08
❑ 79 Darrell Johnson MG DP .15 .05
❑ 80 Ken Griffey Sr. 1.25 .50
❑ 81 Pete Redfern .25 .08
❑ 82 San Francisco Giants CL 1.25 .50
❑ 83 Bob Montgomery .25 .08
❑ 84 Kent Tekulve .60 .25
❑ 85 Ron Fairly .60 .25
❑ 86 Dave Tomlin .25 .08
❑ 87 John Lowenstein .25 .08
❑ 88 Mike Phillips .25 .08
❑ 89 Ken Clay RC .25 .08
❑ 90 Larry Bowa 1.25 .50
❑ 91 Oscar Zamora .25 .08
❑ 92 Adrian Devine .25 .08
❑ 93 Bobby Cox DP .15 .05
❑ 94 Chuck Scrivener .25 .08
❑ 95 Jamie Quirk .25 .08
❑ 96 Baltimore Orioles CL 1.25 .50
❑ 97 Stan Bahnsen .25 .08
❑ 98 Jim Essian .60 .25
❑ 99 Willie Hernandez RC 1.25 .50
❑ 100 George Brett 15.00 6.00
❑ 101 Sid Monge .25 .08
❑ 102 Matt Alexander .25 .08
❑ 103 Tom Murphy .25 .08
❑ 104 Lee Lacy .25 .08
❑ 105 Reggie Cleveland .25 .08
❑ 106 Bill Plummer .25 .08
❑ 107 Ed Halicki .25 .08
❑ 108 Von Joshua .25 .08
❑ 109 Joe Torre MG .60 .25
❑ 110 Richie Zisk .25 .08
❑ 111 Mike Tyson .25 .08
❑ 112 Houston Astros CL 1.25 .50
❑ 113 Don Carrithers .25 .08
❑ 114 Paul Blair .60 .25
❑ 115 Gary Nolan .25 .08
❑ 116 Tucker Ashford RC .25 .08
❑ 117 John Montague .25 .08
❑ 118 Terry Harmon .25 .08
❑ 119 Dennis Martinez 2.50 1.00
❑ 120 Gary Carter 2.50 1.00
❑ 121 Alvis Woods .25 .08
❑ 122 Dennis Eckersley 3.00 1.25
❑ 123 Manny Trillo .25 .08
❑ 124 Dave Rozema RC .25 .08
❑ 125 George Scott .60 .25
❑ 126 Paul Moskau RC .25 .08
❑ 127 Chet Lemon .60 .25
❑ 128 Bill Russell .60 .25
❑ 129 Jim Colborn .25 .08
❑ 130 Jeff Burroughs .60 .25
❑ 131 Bert Blyleven 1.25 .50
❑ 132 Enos Cabell .25 .08
❑ 133 Jerry Augustine .25 .08
❑ 134 Steve Henderson RC .25 .08
❑ 135 Ron Guidry DP 1.25 .50
❑ 136 Ted Sizemore .25 .08
❑ 137 Craig Kusick .25 .08
❑ 138 Larry Demery .25 .08
❑ 139 Wayne Gross .25 .08
❑ 140 Rollie Fingers 2.50 1.00
❑ 141 Ruppert Jones .25 .08
❑ 142 John Montefusco .25 .08
❑ 143 Keith Hernandez .60 .25
❑ 144 Jesse Jefferson .25 .08
❑ 145 Rick Monday .60 .25
❑ 146 Doyle Alexander .60 .25
❑ 147 Lee Mazzilli .25 .08
❑ 148 Andre Thornton .60 .25
❑ 149 Dale Murray .25 .08
❑ 150 Bobby Bonds 1.25 .50
❑ 151 Milt Wilcox .25 .08
❑ 152 Ivan DeJesus RC .25 .08
❑ 153 Steve Stone .60 .25
❑ 154 Cecil Cooper DP .25 .08
❑ 155 Butch Hobson .25 .08
❑ 156 Andy Messersmith .60 .25
❑ 157 Pete LaCock DP .15 .05
❑ 158 Joaquin Andujar .60 .25
❑ 159 Lou Piniella .60 .25
❑ 160 Jim Palmer 3.00 1.25
❑ 161 Bob Boone 1.25 .50
❑ 162 Paul Thormodsgard RC .25 .08
❑ 163 Bill North .25 .08
❑ 164 Bob Owchinko RC .25 .08
❑ 165 Rennie Stennett .25 .08
❑ 166 Carlos Lopez .25 .08
❑ 167 Tim Foli .25 .08
❑ 168 Reggie Smith .60 .25
❑ 169 Jerry Johnson .25 .08
❑ 170 Lou Brock 3.00 1.25
❑ 171 Pat Zachry .25 .08
❑ 172 Mike Hargrove .60 .25
❑ 173 Robin Yount UER 5.00 2.00
❑ 174 Wayne Garland .25 .08
❑ 175 Jerry Morales .25 .08
❑ 176 Milt May .25 .08
❑ 177 Gene Garber DP .25 .08
❑ 178 Dave Chalk .25 .08
❑ 179 Dick Tidrow .25 .08
❑ 180 Dave Concepcion 1.25 .50
❑ 181 Ken Forsch .25 .08
❑ 182 Jim Spencer .25 .08
❑ 183 Doug Bird .25 .08
❑ 184 Checklist 122-242 1.25 .50
❑ 185 Ellis Valentine .25 .08
❑ 186 Bob Stanley DP RC .15 .05
❑ 187 Jerry Royster DP .15 .05
❑ 188 Al Bumbry .60 .25
❑ 189 Tom Lasorda MG DP 2.50 1.00
❑ 190 John Candelaria .60 .25
❑ 191 Rodney Scott RC .25 .08
❑ 192 San Diego Padres CL 1.25 .50
❑ 193 Rich Chiles .25 .08
❑ 194 Derrel Thomas .25 .08
❑ 195 Larry Dierker .60 .25
❑ 196 Bob Bailor .25 .08
❑ 197 Nino Espinosa .25 .08
❑ 198 Ron Pruitt .25 .08
❑ 199 Craig Reynolds .25 .08
❑ 200 Reggie Jackson 8.00 3.00
❑ 201 D.Parker/R.Carew LL 1.25 .50
❑ 202 G.Foster/J.Rice LL DP .60 .25

❑ 203 G.Foster/L.Hisle LL .60 .25
❑ 204 F.Taveras/F.Patek LL DP .25 .08
❑ 205 Carlton/Gol/Leon/Palm LL 2.50 1.00
❑ 206 P.Niekro/N.Ryan LL DP 6.00 2.50
❑ 207 J.Cand/F.Tanana LL DP .60 .25
❑ 208 R.Fingers/B.Campbell LL 1.25 .50
❑ 209 Dock Ellis .25 .08
❑ 210 Jose Cardenal .25 .08
❑ 211 Earl Weaver MG DP 1.25 .50
❑ 212 Mike Caldwell .25 .08
❑ 213 Alan Bannister .25 .08
❑ 214 California Angels CL 1.25 .50
❑ 215 Darrell Evans .60 .25
❑ 216 Mike Paxton RC .25 .08
❑ 217 Rod Gilbreath .25 .08
❑ 218 Marty Pattin .25 .08
❑ 219 Mike Cubbage .25 .08
❑ 220 Pedro Borbon .25 .08
❑ 221 Chris Speier .25 .08
❑ 222 Jerry Martin .25 .08
❑ 223 Bruce Kison .25 .08
❑ 224 Jerry Tabb RC .25 .08
❑ 225 Don Gullett DP .25 .08
❑ 226 Joe Ferguson .25 .08
❑ 227 Al Fitzmorris .25 .08
❑ 228 Manny Mota DP .25 .08
❑ 229 Leo Foster .25 .08
❑ 230 Al Hrabosky .60 .25
❑ 231 Wayne Nordhagen RC .25 .08
❑ 232 Mickey Stanley .25 .08
❑ 233 Dick Pole .25 .08
❑ 234 Herman Franks MG .25 .08
❑ 235 Tim McCarver .60 .25
❑ 236 Terry Whitfield .25 .08
❑ 237 Rich Dauer .25 .08
❑ 238 Juan Beniquez .25 .08
❑ 239 Dyar Miller .25 .08
❑ 240 Gene Tenace .60 .25
❑ 241 Pete Vuckovich .60 .25
❑ 242 Barry Bonnell DP RC .15 .05
❑ 243 Bob McClure .25 .08
❑ 244 Montreal Expos CL DP .60 .25
❑ 245 Rick Burleson .60 .25
❑ 246 Dan Driessen .25 .08
❑ 247 Larry Christenson .25 .08
❑ 248 Frank White DP .60 .25
❑ 249 Dave Goltz DP .15 .05
❑ 250 Graig Nettles DP .60 .25
❑ 251 Don Kirkwood .25 .08
❑ 252 Steve Swisher DP .15 .05
❑ 253 Jim Kern .25 .08
❑ 254 Dave Collins .60 .25
❑ 255 Jerry Reuss .60 .25
❑ 256 Joe Altobelli MG RC .25 .08
❑ 257 Hector Cruz .25 .08
❑ 258 John Hiller .25 .08
❑ 259 Los Angeles Dodgers CL 1.25 .50
❑ 260 Bert Campaneris .60 .25
❑ 261 Tim Hosley .25 .08
❑ 262 Rudy May .25 .08
❑ 263 Danny Walton .25 .08
❑ 264 Jamie Easterly .25 .08
❑ 265 Sal Bando DP .60 .25
❑ 266 Bob Shirley RC .25 .08
❑ 267 Doug Ault .25 .08
❑ 268 Gil Flores RC .25 .08
❑ 269 Wayne Twitchell .25 .08
❑ 270 Carlton Fisk 4.00 1.50
❑ 271 Randy Lerch DP .15 .05
❑ 272 Royle Stillman .25 .08
❑ 273 Fred Norman .25 .08
❑ 274 Freddie Patek .60 .25
❑ 275 Dan Ford .25 .08
❑ 276 Bill Bonham DP .15 .05
❑ 277 Bruce Boisclair .25 .08
❑ 278 Enrique Romo RC .25 .08
❑ 279 Bill Virdon MG .25 .08
❑ 280 Buddy Bell .60 .25
❑ 281 Eric Rasmussen DP .15 .05
❑ 282 New York Yankees CL 2.50 1.00
❑ 283 Omar Moreno .25 .08
❑ 284 Randy Moffitt .25 .08
❑ 285 Steve Yeager DP .60 .25
❑ 286 Ben Oglivie .60 .25
❑ 287 Kiko Garcia .25 .08
❑ 288 Dave Hamilton .25 .08
❑ 289 Checklist 243-363 1.25 .50
❑ 290 Willie Horton .60 .25
❑ 291 Gary Ross .25 .08
❑ 292 Gene Richards .25 .08
❑ 293 Mike Willis .25 .08
❑ 294 Larry Parrish .60 .25
❑ 295 Bill Lee .25 .08
❑ 296 Biff Pocoroba .25 .08
❑ 297 Warren Brusstar DP RC .15 .05
❑ 298 Tony Armas .60 .25
❑ 299 Whitey Herzog MG .60 .25
❑ 300 Joe Morgan 3.00 1.25
❑ 301 Buddy Schultz RC .25 .08
❑ 302 Chicago Cubs CL 1.25 .50
❑ 303 Sam Hinds RC .25 .08
❑ 304 John Milner .25 .08
❑ 305 Rico Carty .60 .25
❑ 306 Joe Niekro .60 .25
❑ 307 Glenn Borgmann .25 .08
❑ 308 Jim Rooker .25 .08
❑ 309 Cliff Johnson .25 .08
❑ 310 Don Sutton 2.50 1.00
❑ 311 Jose Baez DP RC .15 .05
❑ 312 Greg Minton .25 .08
❑ 313 Andy Etchebarren .25 .08
❑ 314 Paul Lindblad .25 .08
❑ 315 Mark Belanger .60 .25
❑ 316 Henry Cruz DP .15 .05
❑ 317 Dave Johnson .25 .08
❑ 318 Tom Griffin .25 .08
❑ 319 Alan Ashby .25 .08
❑ 320 Fred Lynn .60 .25
❑ 321 Santo Alcala .25 .08
❑ 322 Tom Paciorek .60 .25
❑ 323 Jim Fregosi DP .25 .08
❑ 324 Vern Rapp MG RC .25 .08
❑ 325 Bruce Sutter 3.00 1.25
❑ 326 Mike Lum DP .15 .05
❑ 327 Rick Langford DP RC .15 .05
❑ 328 Milwaukee Brewers CL 1.25 .50
❑ 329 John Verhoeven .25 .08
❑ 330 Bob Watson .60 .25
❑ 331 Mark Littell .25 .08
❑ 332 Duane Kuiper .25 .08
❑ 333 Jim Todd .25 .08
❑ 334 John Stearns .25 .08
❑ 335 Bucky Dent .60 .25
❑ 336 Steve Busby .25 .08
❑ 337 Tom Grieve .60 .25
❑ 338 Dave Heaverlo .25 .08
❑ 339 Mario Guerrero .25 .08
❑ 340 Bake McBride .60 .25
❑ 341 Mike Flanagan .60 .25
❑ 342 Aurelio Rodriguez .25 .08
❑ 343 John Wathan DP .15 .05
❑ 344 Sam Ewing RC .25 .08
❑ 345 Luis Tiant .60 .25
❑ 346 Larry Biittner .25 .08
❑ 347 Terry Forster .25 .08
❑ 348 Del Unser .25 .08
❑ 349 Rick Camp DP .15 .05
❑ 350 Steve Garvey 2.50 1.00
❑ 351 Jeff Torborg .60 .25
❑ 352 Tony Scott RC .25 .08
❑ 353 Doug Bair RC .25 .08
❑ 354 Cesar Geronimo .25 .08
❑ 355 Bill Travers .25 .08
❑ 356 New York Mets CL 1.25 .50
❑ 357 Tom Poquette .25 .08
❑ 358 Mark Lemongello .25 .08
❑ 359 Marc Hill .25 .08
❑ 360 Mike Schmidt 10.00 4.00
❑ 361 Chris Knapp .25 .08
❑ 362 Dave May .25 .08
❑ 363 Bob Randall .25 .08
❑ 364 Jerry Turner .25 .08
❑ 365 Ed Figueroa .25 .08
❑ 366 Larry Milbourne DP .15 .05
❑ 367 Rick Dempsey .60 .25
❑ 368 Balor Moore .25 .08
❑ 369 Tim Nordbrook .25 .08
❑ 370 Rusty Staub 1.25 .50
❑ 371 Ray Burris .25 .08
❑ 372 Brian Asselstine .25 .08
❑ 373 Jim Willoughby .25 .08
❑ 374 Jose Morales .25 .08
❑ 375 Tommy John 1.25 .50
❑ 376 Jim Wohlford .25 .08
❑ 377 Manny Sarmiento .25 .08
❑ 378 Bobby Winkles MG .25 .08
❑ 379 Skip Lockwood .25 .08
❑ 380 Ted Simmons .60 .25
❑ 381 Philadelphia Phillies CL 1.25 .50
❑ 382 Joe Lahoud .25 .08
❑ 383 Mario Mendoza .25 .08
❑ 384 Jack Clark 1.25 .50
❑ 385 Tito Fuentes .25 .08
❑ 386 Bob Gorinski RC .25 .08
❑ 387 Ken Holtzman .60 .25
❑ 388 Bill Fahey DP .15 .05
❑ 389 Julio Gonzalez RC .25 .08
❑ 390 Oscar Gamble .60 .25
❑ 391 Larry Haney .25 .08
❑ 392 Billy Almon .25 .08
❑ 393 Tippy Martinez .60 .25
❑ 394 Roy Howell DP .15 .05
❑ 395 Jim Hughes .25 .08
❑ 396 Bob Stinson DP .15 .05
❑ 397 Greg Gross .25 .08
❑ 398 Don Hood .25 .08
❑ 399 Pete Mackanin .25 .08
❑ 400 Nolan Ryan 25.00 10.00
❑ 401 Sparky Anderson MG .60 .25
❑ 402 Dave Campbell .25 .08
❑ 403 Bud Harrelson .60 .25
❑ 404 Detroit Tigers CL 1.25 .50
❑ 405 Rawly Eastwick .25 .08
❑ 406 Mike Jorgensen .25 .08
❑ 407 Odell Jones RC .25 .08
❑ 408 Joe Zdeb RC .25 .08
❑ 409 Ron Schueler .25 .08
❑ 410 Bill Madlock .60 .25
❑ 411 Mickey Rivers ALCS .60 .25
❑ 412 Davey Lopes NLCS .60 .25
❑ 413 Reggie Jackson WS 4.00 1.50
❑ 414 Darold Knowles DP .15 .05
❑ 415 Ray Fosse .25 .08
❑ 416 Jack Brohamer .25 .08
❑ 417 Mike Garman DP .15 .05
❑ 418 Tony Muser .25 .08
❑ 419 Jerry Garvin RC .25 .08
❑ 420 Greg Luzinski 1.25 .50
❑ 421 Junior Moore RC .25 .08
❑ 422 Steve Braun .25 .08
❑ 423 Dave Rosello .25 .08
❑ 424 Boston Red Sox CL 1.25 .50
❑ 425 Steve Rogers DP .25 .08
❑ 426 Fred Kendall .25 .08
❑ 427 Mario Soto RC .60 .25
❑ 428 Joel Youngblood .25 .08
❑ 429 Mike Barlow RC .25 .08
❑ 430 Al Oliver .60 .25
❑ 431 Butch Metzger .25 .08
❑ 432 Terry Bulling RC .25 .08
❑ 433 Fernando Gonzalez .25 .08
❑ 434 Mike Norris .25 .08
❑ 435 Checklist 364-484 1.25 .50
❑ 436 Vic Harris DP .15 .05
❑ 437 Bo McLaughlin .25 .08
❑ 438 John Ellis .25 .08
❑ 439 Ken Kravec .25 .08
❑ 440 Dave Lopes .60 .25
❑ 441 Larry Gura .25 .08
❑ 442 Elliott Maddox .25 .08
❑ 443 Darrel Chaney .25 .08
❑ 444 Roy Hartsfield MG .25 .08
❑ 445 Mike Ivie .25 .08
❑ 446 Tug McGraw .60 .25
❑ 447 Leroy Stanton .25 .08
❑ 448 Bill Castro .25 .08
❑ 449 Tim Blackwell DP RC .15 .05
❑ 450 Tom Seaver 6.00 2.50
❑ 451 Minnesota Twins CL 1.25 .50
❑ 452 Jerry Mumphrey .25 .08
❑ 453 Doug Flynn .25 .08
❑ 454 Dave LaRoche .25 .08
❑ 455 Bill Robinson .60 .25
❑ 456 Vern Ruhle .25 .08
❑ 457 Bob Bailey .25 .08
❑ 458 Jeff Newman .25 .08
❑ 459 Charlie Spikes .25 .08
❑ 460 Jim Hunter 2.50 1.00

❑ 461 Rob Andrews DP .15 .05
❑ 462 Rogelio Moret .25 .08
❑ 463 Kevin Bell .25 .08
❑ 464 Jerry Grote .25 .08
❑ 465 Hal McRae .60 .25
❑ 466 Dennis Blair .25 .08
❑ 467 Alvin Dark MG .60 .25
❑ 468 Warren Cromartie RC .60 .25
❑ 469 Rick Cerone .60 .25
❑ 470 J.R. Richard .60 .25
❑ 471 Roy Smalley .60 .25
❑ 472 Ron Reed .25 .08
❑ 473 Bill Buckner .60 .25
❑ 474 Jim Slaton .25 .08
❑ 475 Gary Matthews .60 .25
❑ 476 Bill Stein .25 .08
❑ 477 Doug Capilla RC .25 .08
❑ 478 Jerry Remy .25 .08
❑ 479 St. Louis Cardinals CL 1.25 .50
❑ 480 Ron LeFlore .60 .25
❑ 481 Jackson Todd RC .25 .08
❑ 482 Rick Miller .25 .08
❑ 483 Ken Macha RC .25 .08
❑ 484 Jim Norris RC .25 .08
❑ 485 Chris Chambliss .60 .25
❑ 486 John Curtis .25 .08
❑ 487 Jim Tyrone .25 .08
❑ 488 Dan Spillner .25 .08
❑ 489 Rudy Meoli .25 .08
❑ 490 Amos Otis .60 .25
❑ 491 Scott McGregor .60 .25
❑ 492 Jim Sundberg .60 .25
❑ 493 Steve Renko .25 .08
❑ 494 Chuck Tanner MG .60 .25
❑ 495 Dave Cash .25 .08
❑ 496 Jim Clancy DP RC .15 .05
❑ 497 Glenn Adams .25 .08
❑ 498 Joe Sambito .25 .08
❑ 499 Seattle Mariners CL 1.25 .50
❑ 500 George Foster 1.25 .50
❑ 501 Dave Roberts .25 .08
❑ 502 Pat Rockett RC .25 .08
❑ 503 Ike Hampton RC .25 .08
❑ 504 Roger Freed .25 .08
❑ 505 Felix Millan .25 .08
❑ 506 Ron Blomberg .25 .08
❑ 507 Willie Crawford .25 .08
❑ 508 Johnny Oates .60 .25
❑ 509 Brent Strom .25 .08
❑ 510 Willie Stargell 2.50 1.00
❑ 511 Frank Duffy .25 .08
❑ 512 Larry Herndon .25 .08
❑ 513 Barry Foote .25 .08
❑ 514 Rob Sperring .25 .08
❑ 515 Tim Corcoran RC .25 .08
❑ 516 Gary Beare RC .25 .08
❑ 517 Andres Mora .25 .08
❑ 518 Tommy Boggs DP .15 .05
❑ 519 Brian Downing .60 .25
❑ 520 Larry Hisle .25 .08
❑ 521 Steve Staggs RC .25 .08
❑ 522 Dick Williams MG .60 .25
❑ 523 Donnie Moore RC .25 .08
❑ 524 Bernie Carbo .25 .08
❑ 525 Jerry Terrell .25 .08
❑ 526 Cincinnati Reds CL 1.25 .50
❑ 527 Vic Correll .25 .08
❑ 528 Rob Picciolo RC .25 .08
❑ 529 Paul Hartzell .25 .08
❑ 530 Dave Winfield 4.00 1.50
❑ 531 Tom Underwood .25 .08
❑ 532 Skip Jutze .25 .08
❑ 533 Sandy Alomar .60 .25
❑ 534 Wilbur Howard .25 .08
❑ 535 Checklist 485-605 1.25 .50
❑ 536 Roric Harrison .25 .08
❑ 537 Bruce Bochte .25 .08
❑ 538 Johnny LeMaster .25 .08
❑ 539 Vic Davalillo DP .15 .05
❑ 540 Steve Carlton 4.00 1.50
❑ 541 Larry Cox .25 .08
❑ 542 Tim Johnson .25 .08
❑ 543 Larry Harlow DP RC .15 .05
❑ 544 Len Randle DP .15 .05
❑ 545 Bill Campbell .25 .08
❑ 546 Ted Martinez .25 .08
❑ 547 John Scott .25 .08
❑ 548 Billy Hunter MG DP .15 .05
❑ 549 Joe Kerrigan .25 .08
❑ 550 John Mayberry .60 .25
❑ 551 Atlanta Braves CL 1.25 .50
❑ 552 Francisco Barrios .25 .08
❑ 553 Terry Puhl RC .60 .25
❑ 554 Joe Coleman .25 .08
❑ 555 Butch Wynegar .25 .08
❑ 556 Ed Armbrister .25 .08
❑ 557 Tony Solaita .25 .08
❑ 558 Paul Mitchell .25 .08
❑ 559 Phil Mankowski .25 .08
❑ 560 Dave Parker 1.25 .50
❑ 561 Charlie Williams .25 .08
❑ 562 Glenn Burke RC .25 .08
❑ 563 Dave Rader .25 .08
❑ 564 Mick Kelleher .25 .08
❑ 565 Jerry Koosman .60 .25
❑ 566 Merv Rettenmund .25 .08
❑ 567 Dick Drago .25 .08
❑ 568 Tom Hutton .25 .08
❑ 569 Lary Sorensen RC .25 .08
❑ 570 Dave Kingman 1.25 .50
❑ 571 Buck Martinez .25 .08
❑ 572 Rick Wise .25 .08
❑ 573 Luis Gomez .25 .08
❑ 574 Bob Lemon MG 1.25 .50
❑ 575 Pat Dobson .25 .08
❑ 576 Sam Mejias .25 .08
❑ 577 Oakland Athletics CL 1.25 .50
❑ 578 Buzz Capra .25 .08
❑ 579 Rance Mulliniks RC .25 .08
❑ 580 Rod Carew 4.00 1.50
❑ 581 Lynn McGlothen .25 .08
❑ 582 Fran Healy .25 .08
❑ 583 George Medich .25 .08
❑ 584 John Hale .25 .08
❑ 585 Woodie Fryman DP .15 .05
❑ 586 Ed Goodson .25 .08
❑ 587 John Urrea RC .25 .08
❑ 588 Jim Mason .25 .08
❑ 589 Bob Knepper RC .25 .08
❑ 590 Bobby Murcer .60 .25
❑ 591 George Zeber RC .25 .08
❑ 592 Bob Apodaca .25 .08
❑ 593 Dave Skaggs RC .25 .08
❑ 594 Dave Freisleben .25 .08
❑ 595 Sixto Lezcano .25 .08
❑ 596 Gary Wheelock .25 .08
❑ 597 Steve Dillard .25 .08
❑ 598 Eddie Solomon .25 .08
❑ 599 Gary Woods .25 .08
❑ 600 Frank Tanana .60 .25
❑ 601 Gene Mauch MG .60 .25
❑ 602 Eric Soderholm .25 .08
❑ 603 Will McEnaney .25 .08
❑ 604 Earl Williams .25 .08
❑ 605 Rick Rhoden .60 .25
❑ 606 Pittsburgh Pirates CL 1.25 .50
❑ 607 Fernando Arroyo .25 .08
❑ 608 Johnny Grubb .25 .08
❑ 609 John Denny .25 .08
❑ 610 Garry Maddox .60 .25
❑ 611 Pat Scanlon RC .25 .08
❑ 612 Ken Henderson .25 .08
❑ 613 Marty Perez .25 .08
❑ 614 Joe Wallis .25 .08
❑ 615 Clay Carroll .25 .08
❑ 616 Pat Kelly .25 .08
❑ 617 Joe Nolan RC .25 .08
❑ 618 Tommy Helms .25 .08
❑ 619 Thad Bosley DP RC .15 .05
❑ 620 Willie Randolph 1.25 .50
❑ 621 Craig Swan DP .15 .05
❑ 622 Champ Summers .25 .08
❑ 623 Eduardo Rodriguez .25 .08
❑ 624 Gary Alexander DP .15 .05
❑ 625 Jose Cruz .60 .25
❑ 626 Toronto Blue Jays CL DP 1.25 .50
❑ 627 David Johnson .25 .08
❑ 628 Ralph Garr .60 .25
❑ 629 Don Stanhouse .25 .08
❑ 630 Ron Cey 1.25 .50
❑ 631 Danny Ozark MG .25 .08
❑ 632 Rowland Office .25 .08
❑ 633 Tom Veryzer .25 .08
❑ 634 Len Barker .25 .08
❑ 635 Joe Rudi .60 .25
❑ 636 Jim Bibby .25 .08
❑ 637 Duffy Dyer .25 .08
❑ 638 Paul Splittorff .25 .08
❑ 639 Gene Clines .25 .08
❑ 640 Lee May DP .25 .08
❑ 641 Doug Rau .25 .08
❑ 642 Denny Doyle .25 .08
❑ 643 Tom House .25 .08
❑ 644 Jim Dwyer .25 .08
❑ 645 Mike Torrez .60 .25
❑ 646 Rick Auerbach DP .15 .05
❑ 647 Steve Dunning .25 .08
❑ 648 Gary Thomasson .25 .08
❑ 649 Moose Haas RC .25 .08
❑ 650 Cesar Cedeno .60 .25
❑ 651 Doug Rader .25 .08
❑ 652 Checklist 606-726 1.25 .50
❑ 653 Ron Hodges DP .15 .05
❑ 654 Pepe Frias .25 .08
❑ 655 Lyman Bostock .60 .25
❑ 656 Dave Garcia MG RC .25 .08
❑ 657 Bombo Rivera .25 .08
❑ 658 Manny Sanguillen .60 .25
❑ 659 Texas Rangers CL 1.25 .50
❑ 660 Jason Thompson .60 .25
❑ 661 Grant Jackson .25 .08
❑ 662 Paul Dade RC .25 .08
❑ 663 Paul Reuschel .25 .08
❑ 664 Fred Stanley .25 .08
❑ 665 Dennis Leonard .60 .25
❑ 666 Billy Smith RC .25 .08
❑ 667 Jeff Byrd RC .25 .08
❑ 668 Dusty Baker 1.25 .50
❑ 669 Pete Falcone .25 .08
❑ 670 Jim Rice 1.25 .50
❑ 671 Gary Lavelle .25 .08
❑ 672 Don Kessinger .60 .25
❑ 673 Steve Brye .25 .08
❑ 674 Ray Knight RC 2.50 1.00
❑ 675 Jay Johnstone .60 .25
❑ 676 Bob Myrick .25 .08
❑ 677 Ed Herrmann .25 .08
❑ 678 Tom Burgmeier .25 .08
❑ 679 Wayne Garrett .25 .08
❑ 680 Vida Blue .60 .25
❑ 681 Rob Belloir .25 .08
❑ 682 Ken Brett .25 .08
❑ 683 Mike Champion .25 .08
❑ 684 Ralph Houk MG .60 .25
❑ 685 Frank Taveras .25 .08
❑ 686 Gaylord Perry 2.50 1.00
❑ 687 Julio Cruz RC .25 .08
❑ 688 George Mitterwald .25 .08
❑ 689 Cleveland Indians CL 1.25 .50
❑ 690 Mickey Rivers .60 .25
❑ 691 Ross Grimsley .25 .08
❑ 692 Ken Reitz .25 .08
❑ 693 Lamar Johnson .25 .08
❑ 694 Elias Sosa .25 .08
❑ 695 Dwight Evans 1.25 .50
❑ 696 Steve Mingori .25 .08
❑ 697 Roger Metzger .25 .08
❑ 698 Juan Bernhardt .25 .08
❑ 699 Jackie Brown .25 .08
❑ 700 Johnny Bench 8.00 3.00
❑ 701 Hume/Land/McC/Tay RC .60 .25
❑ 702 Nah/Pas/Sweet/Wer RC .60 .25
❑ 703 Jack Morris DP RC 5.00 2.00
❑ 704 Lou Whitaker RC 8.00 3.00
❑ 705 Berg/Milone/Hurdle/Nor RC 1.25 .50
❑ 706 Cage/Cox/Put/Rev RC .60 .25
❑ 707 P.Molitor RC/A.Trammell RC 50.00 20.00
❑ 708 Diaz/Murphy/Parrish/Whitt RC 4.00 1.50
❑ 709 Burke/Keough/Rau/Schat RC .60 .25
❑ 710 Alston/Bos/Easler/Smith RC 1.25 .50
❑ 711 Camp/Lamp/Mit/Tho DP RC .25 .08
❑ 712 Bobby Valentine .60 .25
❑ 713 Bob Davis .25 .08
❑ 714 Mike Anderson .25 .08
❑ 715 Jim Kaat 1.25 .50
❑ 716 Clarence Gaston .60 .25
❑ 717 Nelson Briles .25 .08
❑ 718 Ron Jackson .25 .08

❑ 719 Randy Elliott RC .25 .08
❑ 720 Fergie Jenkins 2.50 1.00
❑ 721 Billy Martin MG 1.25 .50
❑ 722 Pete Broberg .25 .08
❑ 723 John Wockenfuss .25 .08
❑ 724 Kansas City Royals CL 1.25 .50
❑ 725 Kurt Bevacqua .25 .08
❑ 726 Wilbur Wood 1.25 .50

1979 Topps

❑ COMPLETE SET (726) 175.00 100.00
❑ COMMON CARD (1-726) .25 .08
❑ COMMON CARD DP .15 .05
❑ 1 R.Carew/D.Parker LL 2.50 1.00
❑ 2 J.Rice/G.Foster LL 1.50 .60
❑ 3 J.Rice/G.Foster LL 1.50 .60
❑ 4 R.LeFlore/O.Moreno LL .75 .30
❑ 5 R.Guidry/G.Perry LL .75 .30
❑ 6 N.Ryan/J.Richard LL 5.00 2.00
❑ 7 R.Guidry/C.Swan LL .75 .30
❑ 8 R.Gossage/R.Fingers LL 1.50 .60
❑ 9 Dave Campbell .25 .08
❑ 10 Lee May .75 .30
❑ 11 Marc Hill .25 .08
❑ 12 Dick Drago .25 .08
❑ 13 Paul Dade .25 .08
❑ 14 Rafael Landestoy RC .25 .08
❑ 15 Ross Grimsley .25 .08
❑ 16 Fred Stanley .25 .08
❑ 17 Donnie Moore .25 .08
❑ 18 Tony Solaita .25 .08
❑ 19 Larry Gura DP .15 .05
❑ 20 Joe Morgan DP 2.50 1.00
❑ 21 Kevin Kobel .25 .08
❑ 22 Mike Jorgensen .25 .08
❑ 23 Terry Forster .25 .08
❑ 24 Paul Molitor 10.00 4.00
❑ 25 Steve Carlton 3.00 1.25
❑ 26 Jamie Quirk .25 .08
❑ 27 Dave Goltz .25 .08
❑ 28 Steve Brye .25 .08
❑ 29 Rick Langford .25 .08
❑ 30 Dave Winfield 4.00 1.50
❑ 31 Tom House DP .15 .05
❑ 32 Jerry Mumphrey .25 .08
❑ 33 Dave Rozema .25 .08
❑ 34 Rob Andrews .25 .08
❑ 35 Ed Figueroa .25 .08
❑ 36 Alan Ashby .25 .08
❑ 37 Joe Kerrigan DP .15 .05
❑ 38 Bernie Carbo .25 .08
❑ 39 Dale Murphy 3.00 1.25
❑ 40 Dennis Eckersley 2.50 1.00
❑ 41 Minnesota Twins CL/Mauch 1.50 .60
❑ 42 Ron Blomberg .25 .08
❑ 43 Wayne Twitchell .25 .08
❑ 44 Kurt Bevacqua .25 .08
❑ 45 Al Hrabosky .75 .30
❑ 46 Ron Hodges .25 .08
❑ 47 Fred Norman .25 .08
❑ 48 Merv Rettenmund .25 .08
❑ 49 Vern Ruhle .25 .08
❑ 50 Steve Garvey DP 1.50 .60
❑ 51 Ray Fosse DP .15 .05
❑ 52 Randy Lerch .25 .08
❑ 53 Mick Kelleher .25 .08
❑ 54 Dell Alston DP .15 .05
❑ 55 Willie Stargell 2.50 1.00
❑ 56 John Hale .25 .08
❑ 57 Eric Rasmussen .25 .08
❑ 58 Bob Randall DP .15 .05
❑ 59 John Denny DP .25 .08
❑ 60 Mickey Rivers .75 .30
❑ 61 Bo Diaz .25 .08
❑ 62 Randy Moffitt .25 .08
❑ 63 Jack Brohamer .25 .08
❑ 64 Tom Underwood .25 .08
❑ 65 Mark Belanger .75 .30
❑ 66 Detroit Tigers CL/Moss 1.50 .60
❑ 67 Jim Mason DP .15 .05
❑ 68 Joe Niekro DP .25 .08
❑ 69 Elliott Maddox .25 .08
❑ 70 John Candelaria .75 .30
❑ 71 Brian Downing .75 .30
❑ 72 Steve Mingori .25 .08
❑ 73 Ken Henderson .25 .08
❑ 74 Shane Rawley RC .25 .08
❑ 75 Steve Yeager .75 .30
❑ 76 Warren Cromartie .75 .30
❑ 77 Dan Briggs DP .15 .05
❑ 78 Elias Sosa .25 .08
❑ 79 Ted Cox .25 .08
❑ 80 Jason Thompson .75 .30
❑ 81 Roger Erickson RC .25 .08
❑ 82 New York Mets CL/Torre 1.50 .60
❑ 83 Fred Kendall .25 .08
❑ 84 Greg Minton .25 .08
❑ 85 Gary Matthews .75 .30
❑ 86 Rodney Scott .25 .08
❑ 87 Pete Falcone .25 .08
❑ 88 Bob Molinaro RC .25 .08
❑ 89 Dick Tidrow .25 .08
❑ 90 Bob Boone 1.50 .60
❑ 91 Terry Crowley .25 .08
❑ 92 Jim Bibby .25 .08
❑ 93 Phil Mankowski .25 .08
❑ 94 Len Barker .25 .08
❑ 95 Robin Yount 5.00 2.00
❑ 96 Cleveland Indians CL/Torborg 1.50 .60
❑ 97 Sam Mejias .25 .08
❑ 98 Ray Burris .25 .08
❑ 99 John Wathan .75 .30
❑ 100 Tom Seaver DP 4.00 1.50
❑ 101 Roy Howell .25 .08
❑ 102 Mike Anderson .25 .08
❑ 103 Jim Todd .25 .08
❑ 104 Johnny Oates DP .25 .08
❑ 105 Rick Camp DP .15 .05
❑ 106 Frank Duffy .25 .08
❑ 107 Jesus Alou DP .15 .05
❑ 108 Eduardo Rodriguez .25 .08
❑ 109 Joel Youngblood .25 .08
❑ 110 Vida Blue .75 .30
❑ 111 Roger Freed .25 .08
❑ 112 Philadelphia Phillies CL/Ozark 1.50 .60
❑ 113 Pete Redfern .25 .08
❑ 114 Cliff Johnson .25 .08
❑ 115 Nolan Ryan 20.00 8.00
❑ 116 Ozzie Smith RC 60.00 30.00
❑ 117 Grant Jackson .25 .08
❑ 118 Bud Harrelson .75 .30
❑ 119 Don Stanhouse .25 .08
❑ 120 Jim Sundberg .75 .30
❑ 121 Checklist 1-121 DP .75 .30
❑ 122 Mike Paxton .25 .08
❑ 123 Lou Whitaker 2.50 1.00
❑ 124 Dan Schatzeder .25 .08
❑ 125 Rick Burleson .25 .08
❑ 126 Doug Bair .25 .08
❑ 127 Thad Bosley .25 .08
❑ 128 Ted Martinez .25 .08
❑ 129 Marty Pattin DP .15 .05
❑ 130 Bob Watson DP .25 .08
❑ 131 Jim Clancy .25 .08
❑ 132 Rowland Office .25 .08
❑ 133 Bill Castro .25 .08
❑ 134 Alan Bannister .25 .08
❑ 135 Bobby Murcer .75 .30
❑ 136 Jim Kaat .75 .30
❑ 137 Larry Wolfe DP RC .15 .05
❑ 138 Mark Lee RC .25 .08
❑ 139 Luis Pujols RC .25 .08
❑ 140 Don Gullett .75 .30
❑ 141 Tom Paciorek .75 .30
❑ 142 Charlie Williams .25 .08
❑ 143 Tony Scott .25 .08
❑ 144 Sandy Alomar .25 .08
❑ 145 Rick Rhoden .25 .08
❑ 146 Duane Kuiper .25 .08
❑ 147 Dave Hamilton .25 .08
❑ 148 Bruce Boisclair .25 .08
❑ 149 Manny Sarmiento .25 .08
❑ 150 Wayne Cage .25 .08
❑ 151 John Hiller .25 .08
❑ 152 Rick Cerone .25 .08
❑ 153 Dennis Lamp .25 .08
❑ 154 Jim Gantner DP .25 .08
❑ 155 Dwight Evans 1.50 .60
❑ 156 Buddy Solomon RC .25 .08
❑ 157 U.L. Washington UER .25 .08
❑ 158 Joe Sambito .25 .08
❑ 159 Roy White .75 .30
❑ 160 Mike Flanagan 1.50 .60
❑ 161 Barry Foote .25 .08
❑ 162 Tom Johnson .25 .08
❑ 163 Glenn Burke .25 .08
❑ 164 Mickey Lolich .75 .30
❑ 165 Frank Taveras .25 .08
❑ 166 Leon Roberts .25 .08
❑ 167 Roger Metzger DP .15 .05
❑ 168 Dave Freisleben .25 .08
❑ 169 Bill Nahorodny .25 .08
❑ 170 Don Sutton 2.50 1.00
❑ 171 Gene Clines .25 .08
❑ 172 Mike Bruhert RC .25 .08
❑ 173 John Lowenstein .25 .08
❑ 174 Rick Auerbach .25 .08
❑ 175 George Hendrick 1.50 .60
❑ 176 Aurelio Rodriguez .25 .08
❑ 177 Ron Reed .25 .08
❑ 178 Alvis Woods .25 .08
❑ 179 Jim Beattie DP RC .15 .05
❑ 180 Larry Hisle .25 .08
❑ 181 Mike Garman .25 .08
❑ 182 Tim Johnson .25 .08
❑ 183 Paul Splittorff .25 .08
❑ 184 Darrel Chaney .25 .08
❑ 185 Mike Torrez .75 .30
❑ 186 Eric Soderholm .25 .08
❑ 187 Mark Lemongello .25 .08
❑ 188 Pat Kelly .25 .08
❑ 189 Ed Whitson RC .25 .08
❑ 190 Ron Cey .75 .30
❑ 191 Mike Norris .25 .08
❑ 192 St. Louis Cardinals CL/Boyer 1.50 .60
❑ 193 Glenn Adams .25 .08
❑ 194 Randy Jones .25 .08
❑ 195 Bill Madlock .75 .30
❑ 196 Steve Kemp DP .25 .08
❑ 197 Bob Apodaca .25 .08
❑ 198 Johnny Grubb .25 .08
❑ 199 Larry Milbourne .25 .08
❑ 200 Johnny Bench DP 5.00 2.00
❑ 201 Mike Edwards RB .25 .08
❑ 202 Ron Guidry RB .75 .30
❑ 203 J.R. Richard RB .25 .08
❑ 204 Pete Rose RB 5.00 2.00
❑ 205 John Stearns RB .25 .08
❑ 206 Sammy Stewart RB .25 .08
❑ 207 Dave Lemanczyk .25 .08
❑ 208 Clarence Gaston .25 .08
❑ 209 Reggie Cleveland .25 .08
❑ 210 Larry Bowa .75 .30
❑ 211 Dennis Martinez 2.50 1.00
❑ 212 Carney Lansford RC 1.50 .60
❑ 213 Bill Travers .25 .08
❑ 214 Boston Red Sox CL/Zimmer 1.50 .60
❑ 215 Willie McCovey 2.50 1.00
❑ 216 Wilbur Wood .25 .08
❑ 217 Steve Dillard .25 .08
❑ 218 Dennis Leonard .75 .30
❑ 219 Roy Smalley .75 .30
❑ 220 Cesar Geronimo .25 .08
❑ 221 Jesse Jefferson .25 .08
❑ 222 Bob Beall RC .25 .08
❑ 223 Kent Tekulve .75 .30
❑ 224 Dave Revering .25 .08
❑ 225 Goose Gossage 1.50 .60
❑ 226 Ron Pruitt .25 .08
❑ 227 Steve Stone .75 .30

❑ 228 Vic Davalillo .25 .08
❑ 229 Doug Flynn .25 .08
❑ 230 Bob Forsch .25 .08
❑ 231 John Wockenfuss .25 .08
❑ 232 Jimmy Sexton RC .25 .08
❑ 233 Paul Mitchell .25 .08
❑ 234 Toby Harrah .75 .30
❑ 235 Steve Rogers .25 .08
❑ 236 Jim Dwyer .25 .08
❑ 237 Billy Smith .25 .08
❑ 238 Balor Moore .25 .08
❑ 239 Willie Horton .75 .30
❑ 240 Rick Reuschel .75 .30
❑ 241 Checklist 122-242 DP .75 .30
❑ 242 Pablo Torrealba .25 .08
❑ 243 Buck Martinez DP .15 .05
❑ 244 Pittsburgh Pirates CL/Tanner 1.50 .60
❑ 245 Jeff Burroughs .75 .30
❑ 246 Darrell Jackson RC .25 .08
❑ 247 Tucker Ashford DP .15 .05
❑ 248 Pete LaCock .25 .08
❑ 249 Paul Thormodsgard .25 .08
❑ 250 Willie Randolph .75 .30
❑ 251 Jack Morris 2.50 1.00
❑ 252 Bob Stinson .25 .08
❑ 253 Rick Wise .25 .08
❑ 254 Luis Gomez .25 .08
❑ 255 Tommy John 1.50 .60
❑ 256 Mike Sadek .25 .08
❑ 257 Adrian Devine .25 .08
❑ 258 Mike Phillips .25 .08
❑ 259 Cincinnati Reds CL/Anderson 1.50 .60
❑ 260 Richie Zisk .25 .08
❑ 261 Mario Guerrero .25 .08
❑ 262 Nelson Briles .25 .08
❑ 263 Oscar Gamble .75 .30
❑ 264 Don Robinson RC .25 .08
❑ 265 Don Money .25 .08
❑ 266 Jim Willoughby .25 .08
❑ 267 Joe Rudi .75 .30
❑ 268 Julio Gonzalez .25 .08
❑ 269 Woodie Fryman .25 .08
❑ 270 Butch Hobson .75 .30
❑ 271 Rawly Eastwick .25 .08
❑ 272 Tim Corcoran .25 .08
❑ 273 Jerry Terrell .25 .08
❑ 274 Willie Norwood .25 .08
❑ 275 Junior Moore .25 .08
❑ 276 Jim Colborn .25 .08
❑ 277 Tom Grieve .75 .30
❑ 278 Andy Messersmith .75 .30
❑ 279 Jerry Grote DP .15 .05
❑ 280 Andre Thornton .75 .30
❑ 281 Vic Correll DP .15 .05
❑ 282 Toronto Blue Jays CL/Hartsfield .75 .30
❑ 283 Ken Kravec .25 .08
❑ 284 Johnnie LeMaster .25 .08
❑ 285 Bobby Bonds 1.50 .60
❑ 286 Duffy Dyer .25 .08
❑ 287 Andres Mora .25 .08
❑ 288 Milt Wilcox .25 .08
❑ 289 Jose Cruz 1.50 .60
❑ 290 Dave Lopes .75 .30
❑ 291 Tom Griffin .25 .08
❑ 292 Don Reynolds RC .25 .08
❑ 293 Jerry Garvin .25 .08
❑ 294 Pepe Frias .25 .08
❑ 295 Mitchell Page .25 .08
❑ 296 Preston Hanna RC .25 .08
❑ 297 Ted Sizemore .25 .08
❑ 298 Rich Gale RC .25 .08
❑ 299 Steve Ontiveros .25 .08
❑ 300 Rod Carew 3.00 1.25
❑ 301 Tom Hume .25 .08
❑ 302 Atlanta Braves CL/Cox 1.50 .60
❑ 303 Lary Sorensen DP .15 .05
❑ 304 Steve Swisher .25 .08
❑ 305 Willie Montanez .25 .08
❑ 306 Floyd Bannister .25 .08
❑ 307 Larvell Blanks .25 .08
❑ 308 Bert Blyleven 1.50 .60
❑ 309 Ralph Garr .75 .30
❑ 310 Thurman Munson 3.00 1.25
❑ 311 Gary Lavelle .25 .08
❑ 312 Bob Robertson .25 .08
❑ 313 Dyar Miller .25 .08
❑ 314 Larry Harlow .25 .08
❑ 315 Jon Matlack .25 .08
❑ 316 Milt May .25 .08
❑ 317 Jose Cardenal .75 .30
❑ 318 Bob Welch RC 2.50 1.00
❑ 319 Wayne Garrett .25 .08
❑ 320 Carl Yastrzemski 5.00 2.00
❑ 321 Gaylord Perry 2.50 1.00
❑ 322 Danny Goodwin RC .25 .08
❑ 323 Lynn McGlothen .25 .08
❑ 324 Mike Tyson .25 .08
❑ 325 Cecil Cooper .75 .30
❑ 326 Pedro Borbon .25 .08
❑ 327 Art Howe DP .25 .08
❑ 328 Oakland Athletics CL/McKeon 1.50 .60
❑ 329 Joe Coleman .25 .08
❑ 330 George Brett 10.00 4.00
❑ 331 Mickey Mahler .25 .08
❑ 332 Gary Alexander .25 .08
❑ 333 Chet Lemon .75 .30
❑ 334 Craig Swan .25 .08
❑ 335 Chris Chambliss .75 .30
❑ 336 Bobby Thompson RC .25 .08
❑ 337 John Montague .25 .08
❑ 338 Vic Harris .25 .08
❑ 339 Ron Jackson .25 .08
❑ 340 Jim Palmer 2.50 1.00
❑ 341 Willie Upshaw RC .75 .30
❑ 342 Dave Roberts .25 .08
❑ 343 Ed Glynn .25 .08
❑ 344 Jerry Royster .25 .08
❑ 345 Tug McGraw .75 .30
❑ 346 Bill Buckner .75 .30
❑ 347 Doug Rau .25 .08
❑ 348 Andre Dawson 3.00 1.25
❑ 349 Jim Wright RC .25 .08
❑ 350 Garry Templeton .75 .30
❑ 351 Wayne Nordhagen DP .15 .05
❑ 352 Steve Renko .25 .08
❑ 353 Checklist 243-363 1.50 .60
❑ 354 Bill Bonham .25 .08
❑ 355 Lee Mazzilli .25 .08
❑ 356 San Francisco Giants CL/Altobelli 1.50 .60
❑ 357 Jerry Augustine .25 .08
❑ 358 Alan Trammell 3.00 1.25
❑ 359 Dan Spillner DP .15 .05
❑ 360 Amos Otis .75 .30
❑ 361 Tom Dixon RC .25 .08
❑ 362 Mike Cubbage .25 .08
❑ 363 Craig Skok RC .25 .08
❑ 364 Gene Richards .25 .08
❑ 365 Sparky Lyle .75 .30
❑ 366 Juan Bernhardt .25 .08
❑ 367 Dave Skaggs .25 .08
❑ 368 Don Aase .25 .08
❑ 369A Bump Wills ERR 3.00 1.25
❑ 369B Bump Wills COR 3.00 1.25
❑ 370 Dave Kingman 1.50 .60
❑ 371 Jeff Holly RC .25 .08
❑ 372 Lamar Johnson .25 .08
❑ 373 Lance Rautzhan .25 .08
❑ 374 Ed Herrmann .25 .08
❑ 375 Bill Campbell .25 .08
❑ 376 Gorman Thomas .75 .30
❑ 377 Paul Moskau .25 .08
❑ 378 Rob Picciolo DP .15 .05
❑ 379 Dale Murray .25 .08
❑ 380 John Mayberry .75 .30
❑ 381 Houston Astros CL/Virdon 1.50 .60
❑ 382 Jerry Martin .25 .08
❑ 383 Phil Garner .75 .30
❑ 384 Tommy Boggs .25 .08
❑ 385 Dan Ford .25 .08
❑ 386 Francisco Barrios .25 .08
❑ 387 Gary Thomasson .25 .08
❑ 388 Jack Billingham .25 .08
❑ 389 Joe Zdeb .25 .08
❑ 390 Rollie Fingers 2.50 1.00
❑ 391 Al Oliver .75 .30
❑ 392 Doug Ault .25 .08
❑ 393 Scott McGregor .75 .30
❑ 394 Randy Stein RC .25 .08
❑ 395 Dave Cash .25 .08
❑ 396 Bill Plummer .25 .08
❑ 397 Sergio Ferrer RC .25 .08
❑ 398 Ivan DeJesus .25 .08
❑ 399 David Clyde .25 .08
❑ 400 Jim Rice 1.50 .60
❑ 401 Ray Knight .75 .30
❑ 402 Paul Hartzell .25 .08
❑ 403 Tim Foli .25 .08
❑ 404 Chicago White Sox CL/Kessinger 1.50 .60
❑ 405 Butch Wynegar DP .15 .05
❑ 406 Joe Wallis DP .15 .05
❑ 407 Pete Vuckovich .75 .30
❑ 408 Charlie Moore DP .15 .05
❑ 409 Willie Wilson RC 1.50 .60
❑ 410 Darrell Evans 1.50 .60
❑ 411 G.Sisler/T.Cobb ATL 2.50 1.00
❑ 412 H.Wilson/H.Aaron ATL 2.50 1.00
❑ 413 R.Maris/H.Aaron ATL 4.00 1.50
❑ 414 R.Hornsby/T.Cobb ATL 2.50 1.00
❑ 415 L.Brock/L.Brock ATL 1.50 .60
❑ 416 J.Chesbro/C.Young ATL .75 .30
❑ 417 N.Ryan/W.Johnson ATL DP 5.00 2.00
❑ 418 D.Leonard/W.Johnson ATL DP .25 .08
❑ 419 Dick Ruthven .25 .08
❑ 420 Ken Griffey Sr. .75 .30
❑ 421 Doug DeCinces .75 .30
❑ 422 Ruppert Jones .25 .08
❑ 423 Bob Montgomery .25 .08
❑ 424 California Angels CL/Fregosi 1.50 .60
❑ 425 Rick Manning .25 .08
❑ 426 Chris Speier .25 .08
❑ 427 Andy Replogle RC .25 .08
❑ 428 Bobby Valentine .75 .30
❑ 429 John Urrea DP .15 .05
❑ 430 Dave Parker .75 .30
❑ 431 Glenn Borgmann .25 .08
❑ 432 Dave Heaverlo .25 .08
❑ 433 Larry Biittner .25 .08
❑ 434 Ken Clay .25 .08
❑ 435 Gene Tenace .75 .30
❑ 436 Hector Cruz .25 .08
❑ 437 Rick Williams RC .25 .08
❑ 438 Horace Speed RC .25 .08
❑ 439 Frank White .75 .30
❑ 440 Rusty Staub 1.50 .60
❑ 441 Lee Lacy .25 .08
❑ 442 Doyle Alexander .25 .08
❑ 443 Bruce Bochte .25 .08
❑ 444 Aurelio Lopez RC .25 .08
❑ 445 Steve Henderson .25 .08
❑ 446 Jim Lonborg .75 .30
❑ 447 Manny Sanguillen .75 .30
❑ 448 Moose Haas .25 .08
❑ 449 Bombo Rivera .25 .08
❑ 450 Dave Concepcion 1.50 .60
❑ 451 Kansas City Royals CL/Herzog 1.50 .60
❑ 452 Jerry Morales .25 .08
❑ 453 Chris Knapp .25 .08
❑ 454 Len Randle .25 .08
❑ 455 Bill Lee DP .15 .05
❑ 456 Chuck Baker RC .25 .08
❑ 457 Bruce Sutter 2.50 1.00
❑ 458 Jim Essian .25 .08
❑ 459 Sid Monge .25 .08
❑ 460 Graig Nettles 1.50 .60
❑ 461 Jim Barr DP .15 .05
❑ 462 Otto Velez .25 .08
❑ 463 Steve Comer RC .25 .08
❑ 464 Joe Nolan .25 .08
❑ 465 Reggie Smith .75 .30
❑ 466 Mark Littell .25 .08
❑ 467 Don Kessinger DP .25 .08
❑ 468 Stan Bahnsen DP .15 .05
❑ 469 Lance Parrish 1.50 .60
❑ 470 Garry Maddox DP .25 .08
❑ 471 Joaquin Andujar .75 .30
❑ 472 Craig Kusick .25 .08
❑ 473 Dave Roberts .25 .08
❑ 474 Dick Davis RC .25 .08
❑ 475 Dan Driessen .25 .08
❑ 476 Tom Poquette .25 .08
❑ 477 Bob Grich .75 .30
❑ 478 Juan Beniquez .25 .08
❑ 479 San Diego Padres CL/Craig 1.50 .60
❑ 480 Fred Lynn .75 .30
❑ 481 Skip Lockwood .25 .08
❑ 482 Craig Reynolds .25 .08
❑ 483 Checklist 364-484 DP .75 .30
❑ 484 Rick Waits .25 .08

❑ 485 Bucky Dent .75 .30
❑ 486 Bob Knepper .25 .08
❑ 487 Miguel Dilone .25 .08
❑ 488 Bob Owchinko .25 .08
❑ 489 Larry Cox UER .25 .08
❑ 490 Al Cowens .75 .30
❑ 491 Tippy Martinez .25 .08
❑ 492 Bob Bailor .25 .08
❑ 493 Larry Christenson .25 .08
❑ 494 Jerry White .25 .08
❑ 495 Tony Perez 2.50 1.00
❑ 496 Barry Bonnell DP .15 .05
❑ 497 Glenn Abbott .25 .08
❑ 498 Rich Chiles .25 .08
❑ 499 Texas Rangers CL/Corrrales 1.50 .60
❑ 500 Ron Guidry .75 .30
❑ 501 Junior Kennedy RC .25 .08
❑ 502 Steve Braun .25 .08
❑ 503 Terry Humphrey .25 .08
❑ 504 Larry McWilliams RC .25 .08
❑ 505 Ed Kranepool .25 .08
❑ 506 John D'Acquisto .25 .08
❑ 507 Tony Armas .75 .30
❑ 508 Charlie Hough .75 .30
❑ 509 Mario Mendoza UER .25 .08
❑ 510 Ted Simmons 1.50 .60
❑ 511 Paul Reuschel DP .15 .05
❑ 512 Jack Clark .75 .30
❑ 513 Dave Johnson .75 .30
❑ 514 Mike Proly RC .25 .08
❑ 515 Enos Cabell .25 .08
❑ 516 Champ Summers DP .15 .05
❑ 517 Al Bumbry .75 .30
❑ 518 Jim Umbarger .25 .08
❑ 519 Ben Oglivie .75 .30
❑ 520 Gary Carter 1.50 .60
❑ 521 Sam Ewing .25 .08
❑ 522 Ken Holtzman .75 .30
❑ 523 John Milner .25 .08
❑ 524 Tom Burgmeier .25 .08
❑ 525 Freddie Patek .25 .08
❑ 526 Los Angeles Dodgers CL/Lasorda 1.50 .60
❑ 527 Lerrin LaGrow .25 .08
❑ 528 Wayne Gross DP .15 .05
❑ 529 Brian Asselstine .25 .08
❑ 530 Frank Tanana .75 .30
❑ 531 Fernando Gonzalez .25 .08
❑ 532 Buddy Schultz .25 .08
❑ 533 Leroy Stanton .25 .08
❑ 534 Ken Forsch .25 .08
❑ 535 Ellis Valentine .25 .08
❑ 536 Jerry Reuss .75 .30
❑ 537 Tom Veryzer .25 .08
❑ 538 Mike Ivie DP .15 .05
❑ 539 John Ellis .25 .08
❑ 540 Greg Luzinski .75 .30
❑ 541 Jim Slaton .25 .08
❑ 542 Rick Bosetti .25 .08
❑ 543 Kiko Garcia .25 .08
❑ 544 Fergie Jenkins 2.50 1.00
❑ 545 John Stearns .25 .08
❑ 546 Bill Russell .75 .30
❑ 547 Clint Hurdle .25 .08
❑ 548 Enrique Romo .25 .08
❑ 549 Bob Bailey .25 .08
❑ 550 Sal Bando .75 .30
❑ 551 Chicago Cubs CL/Franks 1.50 .60
❑ 552 Jose Morales .25 .08
❑ 553 Denny Walling .25 .08
❑ 554 Matt Keough .25 .08
❑ 555 Biff Pocoroba .25 .08
❑ 556 Mike Lum .25 .08
❑ 557 Ken Brett .25 .08
❑ 558 Jay Johnstone .75 .30
❑ 559 Greg Pryor RC .25 .08
❑ 560 John Montefusco .25 .08
❑ 561 Ed Ott .25 .08
❑ 562 Dusty Baker 1.50 .60
❑ 563 Roy Thomas .25 .08
❑ 564 Jerry Turner .25 .08
❑ 565 Rico Carty .75 .30
❑ 566 Nino Espinosa .25 .08
❑ 567 Richie Hebner .75 .30
❑ 568 Carlos Lopez .25 .08
❑ 569 Bob Sykes .25 .08
❑ 570 Cesar Cedeno .75 .30
❑ 571 Darrell Porter .75 .30
❑ 572 Rod Gilbreath .25 .08
❑ 573 Jim Kern .25 .08
❑ 574 Claudell Washington .75 .30
❑ 575 Luis Tiant .75 .30
❑ 576 Mike Parrott RC .25 .08
❑ 577 Milwaukee Brewers CL/Bamberger 1.50 .60
❑ 578 Pete Broberg .25 .08
❑ 579 Greg Gross .25 .08
❑ 580 Ron Fairly .75 .30
❑ 581 Darold Knowles .25 .08
❑ 582 Paul Blair .75 .30
❑ 583 Julio Cruz .25 .08
❑ 584 Jim Rooker .25 .08
❑ 585 Hal McRae 1.50 .60
❑ 586 Bob Horner RC 1.50 .60
❑ 587 Ken Reitz .25 .08
❑ 588 Tom Murphy .25 .08
❑ 589 Terry Whitfield .25 .08
❑ 590 J.R. Richard .75 .30
❑ 591 Mike Hargrove .75 .30
❑ 592 Mike Krukow .25 .08
❑ 593 Rick Dempsey .75 .30
❑ 594 Bob Shirley .25 .08
❑ 595 Phil Niekro 2.50 1.00
❑ 596 Jim Wohlford .25 .08
❑ 597 Bob Stanley .25 .08
❑ 598 Mark Wagner .25 .08
❑ 599 Jim Spencer .25 .08
❑ 600 George Foster .75 .30
❑ 601 Dave LaRoche .25 .08
❑ 602 Checklist 485-605 1.50 .60
❑ 603 Rudy May .25 .08
❑ 604 Jeff Newman .25 .08
❑ 605 Rick Monday DP .25 .08
❑ 606 Montreal Expos CL/Williams 1.50 .60
❑ 607 Omar Moreno .25 .08
❑ 608 Dave McKay .25 .08
❑ 609 Silvio Martinez RC .25 .08
❑ 610 Mike Schmidt 8.00 3.00
❑ 611 Jim Norris .25 .08
❑ 612 Rick Honeycutt RC .75 .30
❑ 613 Mike Edwards RC .25 .08
❑ 614 Willie Hernandez .75 .30
❑ 615 Ken Singleton .75 .30
❑ 616 Billy Almon .25 .08
❑ 617 Terry Puhl .25 .08
❑ 618 Jerry Remy .25 .08
❑ 619 Ken Landreaux RC .75 .30
❑ 620 Bert Campaneris .75 .30
❑ 621 Pat Zachry .25 .08
❑ 622 Dave Collins .75 .30
❑ 623 Bob McClure .25 .08
❑ 624 Larry Herndon .25 .08
❑ 625 Mark Fidrych 2.50 1.00
❑ 626 New York Yankees CL/Lemon 1.50 .60
❑ 627 Gary Serum RC .25 .08
❑ 628 Del Unser .25 .08
❑ 629 Gene Garber .75 .30
❑ 630 Bake McBride .75 .30
❑ 631 Jorge Orta .25 .08
❑ 632 Don Kirkwood .25 .08
❑ 633 Rob Wilfong DP RC .15 .05
❑ 634 Paul Lindblad .25 .08
❑ 635 Don Baylor 1.50 .60
❑ 636 Wayne Garland .25 .08
❑ 637 Bill Robinson .75 .30
❑ 638 Al Fitzmorris .25 .08
❑ 639 Manny Trillo .25 .08
❑ 640 Eddie Murray 12.00 5.00
❑ 641 Bobby Castillo RC .25 .08
❑ 642 Wilbur Howard DP .15 .05
❑ 643 Tom Hausman .25 .08
❑ 644 Manny Mota .75 .30
❑ 645 George Scott DP .25 .08
❑ 646 Rick Sweet .25 .08
❑ 647 Bob Lacey .25 .08
❑ 648 Lou Piniella .75 .30
❑ 649 John Curtis .25 .08
❑ 650 Pete Rose 12.00 5.00
❑ 651 Mike Caldwell .25 .08
❑ 652 Stan Papi RC .25 .08
❑ 653 Warren Brusstar DP .15 .05
❑ 654 Rick Miller .25 .08
❑ 655 Jerry Koosman .75 .30
❑ 656 Hosken Powell RC .25 .08
❑ 657 George Medich .25 .08
❑ 658 Taylor Duncan RC .25 .08
❑ 659 Seattle Mariners CL/Johnson 1.50 .60
❑ 660 Ron LeFlore DP .25 .08
❑ 661 Bruce Kison .25 .08
❑ 662 Kevin Bell .25 .08
❑ 663 Mike Vail .25 .08
❑ 664 Doug Bird .25 .08
❑ 665 Lou Brock 2.50 1.00
❑ 666 Rich Dauer .25 .08
❑ 667 Don Hood .25 .08
❑ 668 Bill North .25 .08
❑ 669 Checklist 606-726 1.50 .60
❑ 670 Jim Hunter DP 1.50 .60
❑ 671 Joe Ferguson DP .15 .05
❑ 672 Ed Halicki .25 .08
❑ 673 Tom Hutton .25 .08
❑ 674 Dave Tomlin .25 .08
❑ 675 Tim McCarver 1.50 .60
❑ 676 Johnny Sutton RC .25 .08
❑ 677 Larry Parrish .75 .30
❑ 678 Geoff Zahn .25 .08
❑ 679 Derrel Thomas .25 .08
❑ 680 Carlton Fisk 3.00 1.25
❑ 681 John Henry Johnson RC .25 .08
❑ 682 Dave Chalk .25 .08
❑ 683 Dan Meyer DP .15 .05
❑ 684 Jamie Easterly DP .15 .05
❑ 685 Sixto Lezcano .25 .08
❑ 686 Ron Schueler DP .15 .05
❑ 687 Rennie Stennett .25 .08
❑ 688 Mike Willis .25 .08
❑ 689 Baltimore Orioles CL/Weaver 1.50 .60
❑ 690 Buddy Bell DP .25 .08
❑ 691 Dock Ellis DP .15 .05
❑ 692 Mickey Stanley .25 .08
❑ 693 Dave Rader .25 .08
❑ 694 Burt Hooton .75 .30
❑ 695 Keith Hernandez .75 .30
❑ 696 Andy Hassler .25 .08
❑ 697 Dave Bergman .25 .08
❑ 698 Bill Stein .25 .08
❑ 699 Hal Dues RC .25 .08
❑ 700 Reggie Jackson DP 5.00 2.00
❑ 701 Corey/Flinn/Stewart RC .75 .30
❑ 702 Finch/Hancock/Ripley RC .75 .30
❑ 703 Anderson/Frost/Slater RC .75 .30
❑ 704 Baumgarten/Colbern/Squires RC .75 .30
❑ 705 Griffin/Norrid/Oliver RC 1.50 .60
❑ 706 Stegman/Tobik/Young RC .75 .30
❑ 707 Bass/Gaudet/McGilberry RC 1.50 .60
❑ 708 Bass/Romero/Yost RC 1.50 .60
❑ 709 Perlozzo/Sofield/Stanfield RC .75 .30
❑ 710 Doyle/Heath/Rajisch RC .75 .30
❑ 711 Murphy/Robinson/Wirth RC 1.50 .60
❑ 712 Anderson/Biercevicz/McLaughlin RC .75 .30
❑ 713 Darwin/Putnam/Sample RC 1.50 .60
❑ 714 Cruz/Kelly/Whitt RC .75 .30
❑ 715 Benedict/Hubbard/Whisenton RC 1.50 .60
❑ 716 Geisel/Pagel/Thompson RC .75 .30
❑ 717 LaCoss/Oester/Spilman RC .75 .30
❑ 718 Bochy/Fischlin/Pisker RC .75 .30
❑ 719 Guerrero/Law/Simpson RC 1.50 .60
❑ 720 Fry/Pirtle/Sanderson RC 1.50 .60
❑ 721 Berenguer/Bernard/Norman RC .75 .30
❑ 722 Morrison/Smith/Wright RC 1.50 .60
❑ 723 Berra/Cotes/Wiltbank RC .75 .30
❑ 724 Bruno/Frazier/Kennedy RC 1.50 .60
❑ 725 Beswick/Mura/Perkins RC .75 .30
❑ 726 Johnston/Strain/Tamargo RC .75 .30

1980 Topps

❑ COMPLETE SET (726) 120.00 70.00
❑ COMMON CARD (1-726) .25 .08
❑ COMMON DP .25 .08
❑ 1 L.Brock/C.Yastrzemski HL 2.50 1.00
❑ 2 Willie McCovey HL .75 .30
❑ 3 Manny Mota HL .25 .08
❑ 4 Pete Rose HL 3.00 1.25
❑ 5 Garry Templeton HL .25 .08
❑ 6 Del Unser HL .25 .08
❑ 7 Mike Lum .25 .08
❑ 8 Craig Swan .25 .08
❑ 9 Steve Braun .25 .08
❑ 10 Dennis Martinez .75 .30
❑ 11 Jimmy Sexton .25 .08

❑ 12 John Curtis DP .25 .08
❑ 13 Ron Pruitt .25 .08
❑ 14 Dave Cash .75 .30
❑ 15 Bill Campbell .25 .08
❑ 16 Jerry Narron RC .25 .08
❑ 17 Bruce Sutter 1.50 .60
❑ 18 Ron Jackson .25 .08
❑ 19 Balor Moore .25 .08
❑ 20 Dan Ford .25 .08
❑ 21 Manny Sarmiento .25 .08
❑ 22 Pat Putnam .25 .08
❑ 23 Derrel Thomas .25 .08
❑ 24 Jim Slaton .25 .08
❑ 25 Lee Mazzilli .75 .30
❑ 26 Marty Pattin .25 .08
❑ 27 Del Unser .25 .08
❑ 28 Bruce Kison .25 .08
❑ 29 Mark Wagner .25 .08
❑ 30 Vida Blue .75 .30
❑ 31 Jay Johnstone .25 .08
❑ 32 Julio Cruz DP .25 .08
❑ 33 Tony Scott .25 .08
❑ 34 Jeff Newman DP .25 .08
❑ 35 Luis Tiant .75 .30
❑ 36 Rusty Torres .25 .08
❑ 37 Kiko Garcia .25 .08
❑ 38 Dan Spillner DP .25 .08
❑ 39 Rowland Office .25 .08
❑ 40 Carlton Fisk 2.50 1.00
❑ 41 Texas Rangers CL/Corrrales .75 .30
❑ 42 David Palmer RC .25 .08
❑ 43 Bombo Rivera .25 .08
❑ 44 Bill Fahey .25 .08
❑ 45 Frank White .75 .30
❑ 46 Rico Carty .75 .30
❑ 47 Bill Bonham DP .25 .08
❑ 48 Rick Miller .25 .08
❑ 49 Mario Guerrero .25 .08
❑ 50 J.R. Richard .75 .30
❑ 51 Joe Ferguson DP .25 .08
❑ 52 Warren Brusstar .25 .08
❑ 53 Ben Oglivie .75 .30
❑ 54 Dennis Lamp .25 .08
❑ 55 Bill Madlock .75 .30
❑ 56 Bobby Valentine .75 .30
❑ 57 Pete Vuckovich .25 .08
❑ 58 Doug Flynn .25 .08
❑ 59 Eddy Putman RC .25 .08
❑ 60 Bucky Dent .75 .30
❑ 61 Gary Serum .25 .08
❑ 62 Mike Ivie .25 .08
❑ 63 Bob Stanley .25 .08
❑ 64 Joe Nolan .25 .08
❑ 65 Al Bumbry .75 .30
❑ 66 Kansas City Royals CL/Frey .75 .30
❑ 67 Doyle Alexander .25 .08
❑ 68 Larry Harlow .25 .08
❑ 69 Rick Williams .25 .08
❑ 70 Gary Carter 1.50 .60
❑ 71 John Milner DP .25 .08
❑ 72 Fred Howard DP RC .25 .08
❑ 73 Dave Collins .25 .08
❑ 74 Sid Monge .25 .08
❑ 75 Bill Russell .75 .30
❑ 76 John Stearns .25 .08
❑ 77 Dave Stieb RC 1.50 .60
❑ 78 Ruppert Jones .25 .08
❑ 79 Bob Owchinko .25 .08
❑ 80 Ron LeFlore .75 .30
❑ 81 Ted Sizemore .25 .08
❑ 82 Houston Astros CL/Virdon .75 .30
❑ 83 Steve Trout RC .25 .08
❑ 84 Gary Lavelle .25 .08
❑ 85 Ted Simmons .75 .30
❑ 86 Dave Hamilton .25 .08
❑ 87 Pepe Frias .25 .08
❑ 88 Ken Landreaux .25 .08
❑ 89 Don Hood .25 .08
❑ 90 Manny Trillo .75 .30
❑ 91 Rick Dempsey .75 .30
❑ 92 Rick Rhoden .25 .08
❑ 93 Dave Roberts DP .25 .08
❑ 94 Neil Allen RC .25 .08
❑ 95 Cecil Cooper .75 .30
❑ 96 Oakland Athletics CL/Marshall .75 .30
❑ 97 Bill Lee .75 .30
❑ 98 Jerry Terrell .25 .08
❑ 99 Victor Cruz .25 .08
❑ 100 Johnny Bench 3.00 1.25
❑ 101 Aurelio Lopez .25 .08
❑ 102 Rich Dauer .25 .08
❑ 103 Bill Caudill RC .25 .08
❑ 104 Manny Mota .75 .30
❑ 105 Frank Tanana .75 .30
❑ 106 Jeff Leonard RC 1.50 .60
❑ 107 Francisco Barrios .25 .08
❑ 108 Bob Horner .75 .30
❑ 109 Bill Travers .25 .08
❑ 110 Fred Lynn DP .50 .20
❑ 111 Bob Knepper .25 .08
❑ 112 Chicago White Sox CL/LaRussa .75 .30
❑ 113 Geoff Zahn .25 .08
❑ 114 Juan Beniquez .25 .08
❑ 115 Sparky Lyle .75 .30
❑ 116 Larry Cox .25 .08
❑ 117 Dock Ellis .75 .30
❑ 118 Phil Garner .75 .30
❑ 119 Sammy Stewart .25 .08
❑ 120 Greg Luzinski .75 .30
❑ 121 Checklist 1-121 .75 .30
❑ 122 Dave Rosello DP .25 .08
❑ 123 Lynn Jones RC .25 .08
❑ 124 Dave Lemanczyk .25 .08
❑ 125 Tony Perez .75 .30
❑ 126 Dave Tomlin .25 .08
❑ 127 Gary Thomasson .25 .08
❑ 128 Tom Burgmeier .25 .08
❑ 129 Craig Reynolds .25 .08
❑ 130 Amos Otis .75 .30
❑ 131 Paul Mitchell .25 .08
❑ 132 Biff Pocoroba .25 .08
❑ 133 Jerry Turner .25 .08
❑ 134 Matt Keough .25 .08
❑ 135 Bill Buckner .75 .30
❑ 136 Dick Ruthven .25 .08
❑ 137 John Castino RC .25 .08
❑ 138 Ross Baumgarten .25 .08
❑ 139 Dane Iorg RC .25 .08
❑ 140 Rich Gossage .75 .30
❑ 141 Gary Alexander .25 .08
❑ 142 Phil Huffman RC .25 .08
❑ 143 Bruce Bochte DP .25 .08
❑ 144 Steve Comer .25 .08
❑ 145 Darrell Evans .75 .30
❑ 146 Bob Welch .75 .30
❑ 147 Terry Puhl .25 .08
❑ 148 Manny Sanguillen .75 .30
❑ 149 Tom Hume .25 .08
❑ 150 Jason Thompson .25 .08
❑ 151 Tom Hausman DP .25 .08
❑ 152 John Fulgham RC .25 .08
❑ 153 Tim Blackwell .25 .08
❑ 154 Lary Sorensen .25 .08
❑ 155 Jerry Remy .25 .08
❑ 156 Tony Brizzolara RC .25 .08
❑ 157 Willie Wilson DP .50 .20
❑ 158 Rob Picciolo DP .25 .08
❑ 159 Ken Clay .25 .08
❑ 160 Eddie Murray 5.00 2.00
❑ 161 Larry Christenson .25 .08
❑ 162 Bob Randall .25 .08
❑ 163 Steve Swisher .25 .08
❑ 164 Greg Pryor .25 .08
❑ 165 Omar Moreno .25 .08
❑ 166 Glenn Abbott .25 .08
❑ 167 Jack Clark .75 .30
❑ 168 Rick Waits .25 .08
❑ 169 Luis Gomez .25 .08
❑ 170 Burt Hooton .75 .30
❑ 171 Fernando Gonzalez .25 .08
❑ 172 Ron Hodges .25 .08
❑ 173 John Henry Johnson .25 .08
❑ 174 Ray Knight .75 .30
❑ 175 Rick Reuschel .75 .30
❑ 176 Champ Summers .25 .08
❑ 177 Dave Heaverlo .25 .08
❑ 178 Tim McCarver .75 .30
❑ 179 Ron Davis RC .25 .08
❑ 180 Warren Cromartie .25 .08
❑ 181 Moose Haas .25 .08
❑ 182 Ken Reitz .25 .08
❑ 183 Jim Anderson DP .25 .08
❑ 184 Steve Renko DP .25 .08
❑ 185 Hal McRae .75 .30
❑ 186 Junior Moore .25 .08
❑ 187 Alan Ashby .25 .08
❑ 188 Terry Crowley .25 .08
❑ 189 Kevin Kobel .25 .08
❑ 190 Buddy Bell .75 .30
❑ 191 Ted Martinez .25 .08
❑ 192 Atlanta Braves CL/Cox .75 .30
❑ 193 Dave Goltz .25 .08
❑ 194 Mike Easler .25 .08
❑ 195 John Montefusco .75 .30
❑ 196 Lance Parrish .75 .30
❑ 197 Byron McLaughlin .25 .08
❑ 198 Dell Alston DP .25 .08
❑ 199 Mike LaCoss .25 .08
❑ 200 Jim Rice .75 .30
❑ 201 K.Hernandez/F.Lynn LL .75 .30
❑ 202 D.Kingman/G.Thomas LL 1.50 .60
❑ 203 D.Winfield/D.Baylor LL 1.50 .60
❑ 204 O.Moreno/W.Wilson LL .75 .30
❑ 205 Niekro/Niekro/Flan LL .75 .30
❑ 206 J.Richard/N.Ryan LL 5.00 2.00
❑ 207 J.Richard/R.Guidry LL .75 .30
❑ 208 Wayne Cage .25 .08
❑ 209 Von Joshua .25 .08
❑ 210 Steve Carlton 1.50 .60
❑ 211 Dave Skaggs DP .25 .08
❑ 212 Dave Roberts .25 .08
❑ 213 Mike Jorgensen DP .25 .08
❑ 214 California Angels CL/Fregosi .75 .30
❑ 215 Sixto Lezcano .25 .08
❑ 216 Phil Mankowski .25 .08
❑ 217 Ed Halicki .25 .08
❑ 218 Jose Morales .25 .08
❑ 219 Steve Mingori .25 .08
❑ 220 Dave Concepcion .75 .30
❑ 221 Joe Cannon RC .25 .08
❑ 222 Ron Hassey RC .25 .08
❑ 223 Bob Sykes .25 .08
❑ 224 Willie Montanez .25 .08
❑ 225 Lou Piniella .75 .30
❑ 226 Bill Stein .25 .08
❑ 227 Len Barker .75 .30
❑ 228 Johnny Oates .75 .30
❑ 229 Jim Bibby .25 .08
❑ 230 Dave Winfield 1.50 .60
❑ 231 Steve McCatty .25 .08
❑ 232 Alan Trammell 1.50 .60
❑ 233 LaRue Washington RC .25 .08
❑ 234 Vern Ruhle .25 .08
❑ 235 Andre Dawson 1.50 .60
❑ 236 Marc Hill .25 .08
❑ 237 Scott McGregor .75 .30
❑ 238 Rob Wilfong .25 .08
❑ 239 Don Aase .25 .08
❑ 240 Dave Kingman .75 .30
❑ 241 Checklist 122-242 .75 .30
❑ 242 Lamar Johnson .25 .08
❑ 243 Jerry Augustine .25 .08
❑ 244 St. Louis Cardinals CL/Boyer .75 .30
❑ 245 Phil Niekro .75 .30
❑ 246 Tim Foli DP .25 .08
❑ 247 Frank Riccelli .25 .08
❑ 248 Jamie Quirk .25 .08
❑ 249 Jim Clancy .25 .08
❑ 250 Jim Kaat .75 .30
❑ 251 Kip Young .25 .08

❑ 252 Ted Cox .25 .08
❑ 253 John Montague .25 .08
❑ 254 Paul Dade DP .25 .08
❑ 255 Dusty Baker DP .50 .20
❑ 256 Roger Erickson .25 .08
❑ 257 Larry Herndon .25 .08
❑ 258 Paul Moskau .25 .08
❑ 259 New York Mets CL/Torre 1.50 .60
❑ 260 Al Oliver .75 .30
❑ 261 Dave Chalk .25 .08
❑ 262 Benny Ayala .25 .08
❑ 263 Dave LaRoche DP .25 .08
❑ 264 Bill Robinson .25 .08
❑ 265 Robin Yount 3.00 1.25
❑ 266 Bernie Carbo .25 .08
❑ 267 Dan Schatzeder .25 .08
❑ 268 Rafael Landestoy .25 .08
❑ 269 Dave Tobik .25 .08
❑ 270 Mike Schmidt DP 3.00 1.25
❑ 271 Dick Drago DP .25 .08
❑ 272 Ralph Garr .75 .30
❑ 273 Eduardo Rodriguez .25 .08
❑ 274 Dale Murphy 2.50 1.00
❑ 275 Jerry Koosman .75 .30
❑ 276 Tom Veryzer .25 .08
❑ 277 Rick Bosetti .25 .08
❑ 278 Jim Spencer .25 .08
❑ 279 Rob Andrews .25 .08
❑ 280 Gaylord Perry .75 .30
❑ 281 Paul Blair .75 .30
❑ 282 Seattle Mariners CL/Johnson .75 .30
❑ 283 John Ellis .25 .08
❑ 284 Larry Murray DP RC .25 .08
❑ 285 Don Baylor .75 .30
❑ 286 Darold Knowles DP .25 .08
❑ 287 John Lowenstein .25 .08
❑ 288 Dave Rozema .25 .08
❑ 289 Bruce Bochy .25 .08
❑ 290 Steve Garvey 1.50 .60
❑ 291 Randy Scarberry RC .25 .08
❑ 292 Dale Berra .25 .08
❑ 293 Elias Sosa .25 .08
❑ 294 Charlie Spikes .25 .08
❑ 295 Larry Gura .25 .08
❑ 296 Dave Rader .25 .08
❑ 297 Tim Johnson .25 .08
❑ 298 Ken Holtzman .75 .30
❑ 299 Steve Henderson .25 .08
❑ 300 Ron Guidry .75 .30
❑ 301 Mike Edwards .25 .08
❑ 302 Los Angeles Dodgers CL/Lasorda 1.50 .60
❑ 303 Bill Castro .25 .08
❑ 304 Butch Wynegar .25 .08
❑ 305 Randy Jones .75 .30
❑ 306 Denny Walling .25 .08
❑ 307 Rick Honeycutt .25 .08
❑ 308 Mike Hargrove .75 .30
❑ 309 Larry McWilliams .25 .08
❑ 310 Dave Parker .75 .30
❑ 311 Roger Metzger .25 .08
❑ 312 Mike Barlow .25 .08
❑ 313 Johnny Grubb .25 .08
❑ 314 Tim Stoddard RC .25 .08
❑ 315 Steve Kemp .75 .30
❑ 316 Bob Lacey .25 .08
❑ 317 Mike Anderson DP .25 .08
❑ 318 Jerry Reuss .75 .30
❑ 319 Chris Speier .25 .08
❑ 320 Dennis Eckersley 1.50 .60
❑ 321 Keith Hernandez .75 .30
❑ 322 Claudell Washington .25 .08
❑ 323 Mick Kelleher .25 .08
❑ 324 Tom Underwood .25 .08
❑ 325 Dan Driessen .25 .08
❑ 326 Bo McLaughlin .25 .08
❑ 327 Ray Fosse DP .50 .20
❑ 328 Minnesota Twins CL/Mauch .75 .30
❑ 329 Bert Roberge RC .25 .08
❑ 330 Al Cowens .75 .30
❑ 331 Richie Hebner .25 .08
❑ 332 Enrique Romo .25 .08
❑ 333 Jim Norris DP .25 .08
❑ 334 Jim Beattie .25 .08
❑ 335 Willie McCovey 1.50 .60
❑ 336 George Medich .25 .08
❑ 337 Carney Lansford .75 .30
❑ 338 John Wockenfuss .25 .08
❑ 339 John D'Acquisto .25 .08
❑ 340 Ken Singleton .75 .30
❑ 341 Jim Essian .25 .08
❑ 342 Odell Jones .25 .08
❑ 343 Mike Vail .25 .08
❑ 344 Randy Lerch .25 .08
❑ 345 Larry Parrish .75 .30
❑ 346 Buddy Solomon .25 .08
❑ 347 Harry Chappas RC .25 .08
❑ 348 Checklist 243-363 .75 .30
❑ 349 Jack Brohamer .25 .08
❑ 350 George Hendrick .75 .30
❑ 351 Bob Davis .25 .08
❑ 352 Dan Briggs .25 .08
❑ 353 Andy Hassler .25 .08
❑ 354 Rick Auerbach .25 .08
❑ 355 Gary Matthews .75 .30
❑ 356 San Diego Padres CL/Coleman .75 .30
❑ 357 Bob McClure .25 .08
❑ 358 Lou Whitaker .75 .30
❑ 359 Randy Moffitt .25 .08
❑ 360 Darrell Porter DP .50 .20
❑ 361 Wayne Garland .25 .08
❑ 362 Danny Goodwin .25 .08
❑ 363 Wayne Gross .25 .08
❑ 364 Ray Burris .25 .08
❑ 365 Bobby Murcer .75 .30
❑ 366 Rob Dressler .25 .08
❑ 367 Billy Smith .25 .08
❑ 368 Willie Aikens RC .25 .08
❑ 369 Jim Kern .25 .08
❑ 370 Cesar Cedeno .75 .30
❑ 371 Jack Morris .75 .30
❑ 372 Joel Youngblood .25 .08
❑ 373 Dan Petry DP RC .75 .30
❑ 374 Jim Gantner .75 .30
❑ 375 Ross Grimsley .25 .08
❑ 376 Gary Allenson RC .25 .08
❑ 377 Junior Kennedy .25 .08
❑ 378 Jerry Mumphrey .25 .08
❑ 379 Kevin Bell .25 .08
❑ 380 Garry Maddox .75 .30
❑ 381 Chicago Cubs CL/Gomez .75 .30
❑ 382 Dave Freisleben .25 .08
❑ 383 Ed Ott .25 .08
❑ 384 Joey McLaughlin RC .25 .08
❑ 385 Enos Cabell .25 .08
❑ 386 Darrell Jackson .25 .08
❑ 387A F.Stanley Yellow 2.00 .75
❑ 387B F.Stanley Red Name .25 .08
❑ 388 Mike Paxton .25 .08
❑ 389 Pete LaCock .25 .08
❑ 390 Fergie Jenkins .75 .30
❑ 391 Tony Armas DP .50 .20
❑ 392 Milt Wilcox .25 .08
❑ 393 Ozzie Smith 10.00 4.00
❑ 394 Reggie Cleveland .25 .08
❑ 395 Ellis Valentine .25 .08
❑ 396 Dan Meyer .25 .08
❑ 397 Roy Thomas DP .25 .08
❑ 398 Barry Foote .25 .08
❑ 399 Mike Proly DP .25 .08
❑ 400 George Foster .75 .30
❑ 401 Pete Falcone .25 .08
❑ 402 Merv Rettenmund .25 .08
❑ 403 Pete Redfern DP .25 .08
❑ 404 Baltimore Orioles CL/Weaver .75 .30
❑ 405 Dwight Evans 1.50 .60
❑ 406 Paul Molitor 4.00 1.50
❑ 407 Tony Solaita .25 .08
❑ 408 Bill North .25 .08
❑ 409 Paul Splittorff .25 .08
❑ 410 Bobby Bonds .75 .30
❑ 411 Frank LaCorte .25 .08
❑ 412 Thad Bosley .25 .08
❑ 413 Allen Ripley .25 .08
❑ 414 George Scott .75 .30
❑ 415 Bill Atkinson .25 .08
❑ 416 Tom Brookens RC .25 .08
❑ 417 Craig Chamberlain DP RC .25 .08
❑ 418 Roger Freed DP .25 .08
❑ 419 Vic Correll .25 .08
❑ 420 Butch Hobson .25 .08
❑ 421 Doug Bird .25 .08
❑ 422 Larry Milbourne .25 .08
❑ 423 Dave Frost .25 .08
❑ 424 New York Yankees CL/Howser .75 .30
❑ 424A New York Yankees CL/Martin
❑ 425 Mark Belanger .75 .30
❑ 426 Grant Jackson .25 .08
❑ 427 Tom Hutton DP .25 .08
❑ 428 Pat Zachry .25 .08
❑ 429 Duane Kuiper .25 .08
❑ 430 Larry Hisle DP .25 .08
❑ 431 Mike Krukow .25 .08
❑ 432 Willie Norwood .25 .08
❑ 433 Rich Gale .25 .08
❑ 434 Johnnie LeMaster .25 .08
❑ 435 Don Gullett .75 .30
❑ 436 Billy Almon .25 .08
❑ 437 Joe Niekro .75 .30
❑ 438 Dave Revering .25 .08
❑ 439 Mike Phillips .25 .08
❑ 440 Don Sutton .75 .30
❑ 441 Eric Soderholm .25 .08
❑ 442 Jorge Orta .25 .08
❑ 443 Mike Parrott .25 .08
❑ 444 Alvis Woods .25 .08
❑ 445 Mark Fidrych .75 .30
❑ 446 Duffy Dyer .25 .08
❑ 447 Nino Espinosa .25 .08
❑ 448 Jim Wohlford .25 .08
❑ 449 Doug Bair .25 .08
❑ 450 George Brett 8.00 3.00
❑ 451 Cleveland Indians CL/Garcia .75 .30
❑ 452 Steve Dillard .25 .08
❑ 453 Mike Bacsik .25 .08
❑ 454 Tom Donohue RC .25 .08
❑ 455 Mike Torrez .75 .30
❑ 456 Frank Taveras .25 .08
❑ 457 Bert Blyleven .75 .30
❑ 458 Billy Sample .25 .08
❑ 459 Mickey Lolich DP .50 .20
❑ 460 Willie Randolph .75 .30
❑ 461 Dwayne Murphy .25 .08
❑ 462 Mike Sadek DP .25 .08
❑ 463 Jerry Royster .25 .08
❑ 464 John Denny .75 .30
❑ 465 Rick Monday .75 .30
❑ 466 Mike Squires .25 .08
❑ 467 Jesse Jefferson .25 .08
❑ 468 Aurelio Rodriguez .25 .08
❑ 469 Randy Niemann DP RC .25 .08
❑ 470 Bob Boone .75 .30
❑ 471 Hosken Powell DP .25 .08
❑ 472 Willie Hernandez .75 .30
❑ 473 Bump Wills .25 .08
❑ 474 Steve Busby .25 .08
❑ 475 Cesar Geronimo .75 .30
❑ 476 Bob Shirley .25 .08
❑ 477 Buck Martinez .25 .08
❑ 478 Gil Flores .25 .08
❑ 479 Montreal Expos CL/Williams .75 .30
❑ 480 Bob Watson .75 .30
❑ 481 Tom Paciorek .75 .30
❑ 482 Rickey Henderson RC 50.00 20.00
❑ 483 Bo Diaz .25 .08
❑ 484 Checklist 364-484 .75 .30
❑ 485 Mickey Rivers .75 .30
❑ 486 Mike Tyson DP .25 .08
❑ 487 Wayne Nordhagen .25 .08
❑ 488 Roy Howell .25 .08
❑ 489 Preston Hanna DP .25 .08
❑ 490 Lee May .75 .30
❑ 491 Steve Mura DP .25 .08
❑ 492 Todd Cruz RC .25 .08
❑ 493 Jerry Martin .25 .08
❑ 494 Craig Minetto RC .25 .08
❑ 495 Bake McBride .75 .30
❑ 496 Silvio Martinez .25 .08
❑ 497 Jim Mason .25 .08
❑ 498 Danny Darwin .25 .08
❑ 499 San Francisco Giants CL/Bristol .75 .30
❑ 500 Tom Seaver 3.00 1.25
❑ 501 Rennie Stennett .25 .08
❑ 502 Rich Wortham DP RC .25 .08
❑ 503 Mike Cubbage .25 .08
❑ 504 Gene Garber .25 .08
❑ 505 Bert Campaneris .75 .30
❑ 506 Tom Buskey .25 .08
❑ 507 Leon Roberts .25 .08

❑ 508 U.L. Washington .25 .08
❑ 509 Ed Glynn .25 .08
❑ 510 Ron Cey .75 .30
❑ 511 Eric Wilkins RC .25 .08
❑ 512 Jose Cardenal .25 .08
❑ 513 Tom Dixon DP .25 .08
❑ 514 Steve Ontiveros .25 .08
❑ 515 Mike Caldwell UER .25 .08
❑ 516 Hector Cruz .25 .08
❑ 517 Don Stanhouse .25 .08
❑ 518 Nelson Norman RC .25 .08
❑ 519 Steve Nicosia RC .25 .08
❑ 520 Steve Rogers .75 .30
❑ 521 Ken Brett .25 .08
❑ 522 Jim Morrison .25 .08
❑ 523 Ken Henderson .25 .08
❑ 524 Jim Wright DP .25 .08
❑ 525 Clint Hurdle .25 .08
❑ 526 Philadelphia Phillies CL/Green .75 .30
❑ 527 Doug Rau DP .25 .08
❑ 528 Adrian Devine .25 .08
❑ 529 Jim Barr .25 .08
❑ 530 Jim Sundberg DP .50 .20
❑ 531 Eric Rasmussen .25 .08
❑ 532 Willie Horton .75 .30
❑ 533 Checklist 485-605 .75 .30
❑ 534 Andre Thornton .75 .30
❑ 535 Bob Forsch .25 .08
❑ 536 Lee Lacy .25 .08
❑ 537 Alex Trevino RC .25 .08
❑ 538 Joe Strain .25 .08
❑ 539 Rudy May .25 .08
❑ 540 Pete Rose 8.00 3.00
❑ 541 Miguel Dilone .25 .08
❑ 542 Joe Coleman .25 .08
❑ 543 Pat Kelly .25 .08
❑ 544 Rick Sutcliffe RC 1.50 .60
❑ 545 Jeff Burroughs .75 .30
❑ 546 Rick Langford .25 .08
❑ 547 John Wathan .25 .08
❑ 548 Dave Rajsich .25 .08
❑ 549 Larry Wolfe .25 .08
❑ 550 Ken Griffey Sr. .75 .30
❑ 551 Pittsburgh Pirates CL/Tanner .75 .30
❑ 552 Bill Nahorodny .25 .08
❑ 553 Dick Davis .25 .08
❑ 554 Art Howe .75 .30
❑ 555 Ed Figueroa .25 .08
❑ 556 Joe Rudi .75 .30
❑ 557 Mark Lee .25 .08
❑ 558 Alfredo Griffin .25 .08
❑ 559 Dale Murray .25 .08
❑ 560 Dave Lopes .75 .30
❑ 561 Eddie Whitson .25 .08
❑ 562 Joe Wallis .25 .08
❑ 563 Will McEnaney .25 .08
❑ 564 Rick Manning .25 .08
❑ 565 Dennis Leonard .25 .08
❑ 566 Bud Harrelson .75 .30
❑ 567 Skip Lockwood .25 .08
❑ 568 Gary Roenicke RC .25 .08
❑ 569 Terry Kennedy .25 .08
❑ 570 Roy Smalley .75 .30
❑ 571 Joe Sambito .25 .08
❑ 572 Jerry Morales DP .25 .08
❑ 573 Kent Tekulve .75 .30
❑ 574 Scot Thompson .25 .08
❑ 575 Ken Kravec .25 .08
❑ 576 Jim Dwyer .25 .08
❑ 577 Toronto Blue Jays CL/Matlick .75 .30
❑ 578 Scott Sanderson .25 .08
❑ 579 Charlie Moore .25 .08
❑ 580 Nolan Ryan 15.00 6.00
❑ 581 Bob Bailor .25 .08
❑ 582 Brian Doyle .25 .08
❑ 583 Bob Stinson .25 .08
❑ 584 Kurt Bevacqua .25 .08
❑ 585 Al Hrabosky .75 .30
❑ 586 Mitchell Page .25 .08
❑ 587 Garry Templeton .75 .30
❑ 588 Greg Minton .25 .08
❑ 589 Chet Lemon .75 .30
❑ 590 Jim Palmer 1.50 .60
❑ 591 Rick Cerone .25 .08
❑ 592 Jon Matlack .75 .30
❑ 593 Jesus Alou .25 .08
❑ 594 Dick Tidrow .25 .08
❑ 595 Don Money .25 .08
❑ 596 Rick Matula RC .25 .08
❑ 597 Tom Poquette .25 .08
❑ 598 Fred Kendall DP .25 .08
❑ 599 Mike Norris .25 .08
❑ 600 Reggie Jackson 3.00 1.25
❑ 601 Buddy Schultz .25 .08
❑ 602 Brian Downing .75 .30
❑ 603 Jack Billingham DP .25 .08
❑ 604 Glenn Adams .25 .08
❑ 605 Terry Forster .75 .30
❑ 606 Cincinnati Reds CL/McNamara .75 .30
❑ 607 Woodie Fryman .25 .08
❑ 608 Alan Bannister .25 .08
❑ 609 Ron Reed .25 .08
❑ 610 Willie Stargell 1.50 .60
❑ 611 Jerry Garvin DP .25 .08
❑ 612 Cliff Johnson .25 .08
❑ 613 Randy Stein .25 .08
❑ 614 John Hiller .25 .08
❑ 615 Doug DeCinces .75 .30
❑ 616 Gene Richards .25 .08
❑ 617 Joaquin Andujar .75 .30
❑ 618 Bob Montgomery DP .25 .08
❑ 619 Sergio Ferrer .25 .08
❑ 620 Richie Zisk .75 .30
❑ 621 Bob Grich .75 .30
❑ 622 Mario Soto .75 .30
❑ 623 Gorman Thomas .75 .30
❑ 624 Lerrin LaGrow .25 .08
❑ 625 Chris Chambliss .75 .30
❑ 626 Detroit Tigers CL/Anderson .75 .30
❑ 627 Pedro Borbon .25 .08
❑ 628 Doug Capilla .25 .08
❑ 629 Jim Todd .25 .08
❑ 630 Larry Bowa .75 .30
❑ 631 Mark Littell .25 .08
❑ 632 Barry Bonnell .25 .08
❑ 633 Bob Apodaca .25 .08
❑ 634 Glenn Borgmann DP .25 .08
❑ 635 John Candelaria .75 .30
❑ 636 Toby Harrah .75 .30
❑ 637 Joe Simpson .25 .08
❑ 638 Mark Clear RC .25 .08
❑ 639 Larry Biittner .25 .08
❑ 640 Mike Flanagan .75 .30
❑ 641 Ed Kranepool .75 .30
❑ 642 Ken Forsch DP .25 .08
❑ 643 John Mayberry .75 .30
❑ 644 Charlie Hough .75 .30
❑ 645 Rick Burleson .75 .30
❑ 646 Checklist 606-726 .75 .30
❑ 647 Milt May .25 .08
❑ 648 Roy White .75 .30
❑ 649 Tom Griffin .25 .08
❑ 650 Joe Morgan 1.50 .60
❑ 651 Rollie Fingers .75 .30
❑ 652 Mario Mendoza .25 .08
❑ 653 Stan Bahnsen .25 .08
❑ 654 Bruce Boisclair DP .25 .08
❑ 655 Tug McGraw .75 .30
❑ 656 Larvell Blanks .25 .08
❑ 657 Dave Edwards RC .25 .08
❑ 658 Chris Knapp .25 .08
❑ 659 Milwaukee Brewers CL/Bamberger .75 .30
❑ 660 Rusty Staub .75 .30
❑ 661 Corey/Ford/Krenchiki RC .25 .08
❑ 662 Finch/O'Berry/Rainey RC .25 .08
❑ 663 Botting/Clark/Thon RC .75 .30
❑ 664 Colbern/Hoffman/Robinson RC .25 .08
❑ 665 Andersen/Cuellar/Wihtol RC .25 .08
❑ 666 Chris/Greene/Robbins RC .25 .08
❑ 667 Mart/Pasch/Quisenberry RC .75 .30
❑ 668 Boitano/Mueller/Sakata RC .25 .08
❑ 669 Graham/Sofield/Ward RC .75 .30
❑ 670 Brown/Gulden/Jones RC .25 .08
❑ 671 Bryant/Kingman/Morgan RC .75 .30
❑ 672 Beamon/Craig/Vasquez RC .25 .08
❑ 673 Allard/Gleaton/Mahlberg RC .25 .08
❑ 674 Edge/Kelly/Wilborn RC .25 .08
❑ 675 Benedict/Bradford/Miller RC .25 .08
❑ 676 Geisel/Macko/Pagel RC .25 .08
❑ 677 DeFreites/Pastore/Spilman RC .25 .08
❑ 678 Baldwin/Knicely/Ladd RC .25 .08
❑ 679 Beckwith/Hatcher/Patterson RC .75 .30
❑ 680 Bernazard/Miller/Tamargo RC .25 .08
❑ 681 Norman/Orosco/Scott RC 1.50 .60
❑ 682 Aviles/Noles/Saucier RC .25 .08
❑ 683 Boyland/Lois/Saferight RC .25 .08
❑ 684 Frazier/Herr/O'Brien RC .75 .30
❑ 685 Flannery/Greer/Wilhelm RC .25 .08
❑ 686 Johnston/Littlejohn/Nastu RC .25 .08
❑ 687 Mike Heath DP .25 .08
❑ 688 Steve Stone .75 .30
❑ 689 Boston Red Sox CL/Zimmer .75 .30
❑ 690 Tommy John .75 .30
❑ 691 Ivan DeJesus .25 .08
❑ 692 Rawly Eastwick DP .50 .20
❑ 693 Craig Kusick .25 .08
❑ 694 Jim Rooker .25 .08
❑ 695 Reggie Smith .75 .30
❑ 696 Julio Gonzalez .25 .08
❑ 697 David Clyde .25 .08
❑ 698 Oscar Gamble .75 .30
❑ 699 Floyd Bannister .25 .08
❑ 700 Rod Carew DP .75 .30
❑ 701 Ken Oberkfell RC .25 .08
❑ 702 Ed Farmer .25 .08
❑ 703 Otto Velez .25 .08
❑ 704 Gene Tenace .75 .30
❑ 705 Freddie Patek .75 .30
❑ 706 Tippy Martinez .25 .08
❑ 707 Elliott Maddox .25 .08
❑ 708 Bob Tolan .25 .08
❑ 709 Pat Underwood RC .25 .08
❑ 710 Graig Nettles .75 .30
❑ 711 Bob Galasso RC .25 .08
❑ 712 Rodney Scott .25 .08
❑ 713 Terry Whitfield .25 .08
❑ 714 Fred Norman .25 .08
❑ 715 Sal Bando .75 .30
❑ 716 Lynn McGlothen .25 .08
❑ 717 Mickey Klutts DP .25 .08
❑ 718 Greg Gross .25 .08
❑ 719 Don Robinson .75 .30
❑ 720 Carl Yastrzemski DP 2.00 .75
❑ 721 Paul Hartzell .25 .08
❑ 722 Jose Cruz .75 .30
❑ 723 Shane Rawley .25 .08
❑ 724 Jerry White .25 .08
❑ 725 Rick Wise .25 .08
❑ 726 Steve Yeager .75 .30

1981 Topps

❑ COMPLETE SET (726) 50.00 20.00
❑ COMMON CARD (1-726) .15 .05
❑ COMMON CARD DP .15 .05
❑ 1 G.Brett/B.Buckner LL 3.00 1.25
❑ 2 Reggie/Ogliv/Schmidt LL 1.50 .60
❑ 3 C.Cooper/M.Schmidt LL 1.50 .60
❑ 4 R.Henderson/LeFlore LL 3.00 1.25
❑ 5 S.Stone/S.Carlton LL .40 .15
❑ 6 Len Barker/S.Carlton LL .40 .15
❑ 7 R.May/D.Sutton LL .40 .15
❑ 8 Quis/Fingers/Hume LL .40 .15
❑ 9 Pete LaCock DP .15 .05
❑ 10 Mike Flanagan .15 .05
❑ 11 Jim Wohlford DP .15 .05
❑ 12 Mark Clear .15 .05
❑ 13 Joe Charboneau RC 1.50 .60
❑ 14 John Tudor RC 1.50 .60
❑ 15 Larry Parrish .15 .05
❑ 16 Ron Davis .15 .05

❑ 17 Cliff Johnson .15 .05
❑ 18 Glenn Adams .15 .05
❑ 19 Jim Clancy .15 .05
❑ 20 Jeff Burroughs .40 .15
❑ 21 Ron Oester .15 .05
❑ 22 Danny Darwin .15 .05
❑ 23 Alex Trevino .15 .05
❑ 24 Don Stanhouse .15 .05
❑ 25 Sixto Lezcano .15 .05
❑ 26 U.L. Washington .15 .05
❑ 27 Champ Summers DP .15 .05
❑ 28 Enrique Romo .15 .05
❑ 29 Gene Tenace .40 .15
❑ 30 Jack Clark .40 .15
❑ 31 Checklist 1-121 DP .25 .08
❑ 32 Ken Oberkfell .15 .05
❑ 33 Rick Honeycutt .15 .05
❑ 34 Aurelio Rodriguez .15 .05
❑ 35 Mitchell Page .15 .05
❑ 36 Ed Farmer .15 .05
❑ 37 Gary Roenicke .15 .05
❑ 38 Win Remmerswaal RC .15 .05
❑ 39 Tom Veryzer .15 .05
❑ 40 Tug McGraw .40 .15
❑ 41 Babcock/Butcher/Gleaton RC .25 .08
❑ 42 Jerry White DP .15 .05
❑ 43 Jose Morales .15 .05
❑ 44 Larry McWilliams .15 .05
❑ 45 Enos Cabell .15 .05
❑ 46 Rick Bosetti .15 .05
❑ 47 Ken Brett .15 .05
❑ 48 Dave Skaggs .15 .05
❑ 49 Bob Shirley .15 .05
❑ 50 Dave Lopes .40 .15
❑ 51 Bill Robinson DP .15 .05
❑ 52 Hector Cruz .15 .05
❑ 53 Kevin Saucier .15 .05
❑ 54 Ivan DeJesus .15 .05
❑ 55 Mike Norris .15 .05
❑ 56 Buck Martinez .15 .05
❑ 57 Dave Roberts .15 .05
❑ 58 Joel Youngblood .15 .05
❑ 59 Dan Petry .15 .05
❑ 60 Willie Randolph .40 .15
❑ 61 Butch Wynegar .15 .05
❑ 62 Joe Pettini RC .15 .05
❑ 63 Steve Renko DP .15 .05
❑ 64 Brian Asselstine .15 .05
❑ 65 Scott McGregor .15 .05
❑ 66 Castillo/Ireland/M.Jones RC .25 .08
❑ 67 Ken Kravec .15 .05
❑ 68 Matt Alexander DP .15 .05
❑ 69 Ed Halicki .15 .05
❑ 70 Al Oliver DP .25 .08
❑ 71 Hal Dues .15 .05
❑ 72 Barry Evans DP RC .15 .05
❑ 73 Doug Bair .15 .05
❑ 74 Mike Hargrove .15 .05
❑ 75 Reggie Smith .40 .15
❑ 76 Mario Mendoza .15 .05
❑ 77 Mike Barlow .15 .05
❑ 78 Steve Dillard .15 .05
❑ 79 Bruce Robbins .15 .05
❑ 80 Rusty Staub .40 .15
❑ 81 Dave Stapleton RC .15 .05
❑ 82 Heep/Knicely/Sprowl RC .25 .08
❑ 83 Mike Proly .15 .05
❑ 84 Johnnie LoMaster .15 .05
❑ 85 Mike Caldwell .15 .05
❑ 86 Wayne Gross .15 .05
❑ 87 Rick Camp .15 .05
❑ 88 Joe Lefebvre RC .15 .05
❑ 89 Darrell Jackson .15 .05
❑ 90 Bake McBride .40 .15
❑ 91 Tim Stoddard DP .15 .05
❑ 92 Mike Easler .15 .05
❑ 93 Ed Glynn DP .15 .05
❑ 94 Harry Spilman DP .15 .05
❑ 95 Jim Sundberg .40 .15
❑ 96 Beard/Camacho/Dempsey RC .25 .08
❑ 97 Chris Speier .15 .05
❑ 98 Clint Hurdle .15 .05
❑ 99 Eric Wilkins .15 .05
❑ 100 Rod Carew .75 .30
❑ 101 Benny Ayala .15 .05
❑ 102 Dave Tobik .15 .05
❑ 103 Jerry Martin .15 .05
❑ 104 Terry Forster .40 .15
❑ 105 Jose Cruz .40 .15
❑ 106 Don Money .15 .05
❑ 107 Rich Wortham .15 .05
❑ 108 Bruce Benedict .15 .05
❑ 109 Mike Scott .40 .15
❑ 110 Carl Yastrzemski 2.50 1.00
❑ 111 Greg Minton .15 .05
❑ 112 Kuntz/Mullins/Sutherland RC .25 .08
❑ 113 Mike Phillips .15 .05
❑ 114 Tom Underwood .15 .05
❑ 115 Roy Smalley .40 .15
❑ 116 Joe Simpson .15 .05
❑ 117 Pete Falcone .15 .05
❑ 118 Kurt Bevacqua .15 .05
❑ 119 Tippy Martinez .15 .05
❑ 120 Larry Bowa .40 .15
❑ 121 Larry Harlow .15 .05
❑ 122 John Denny .15 .05
❑ 123 Al Cowens .15 .05
❑ 124 Jerry Garvin .15 .05
❑ 125 Andre Dawson .75 .30
❑ 126 Charlie Leibrandt RC .75 .30
❑ 127 Rudy Law .15 .05
❑ 128 Gary Allenson DP .15 .05
❑ 129 Art Howe .15 .05
❑ 130 Larry Gura .15 .05
❑ 131 Keith Moreland RC .15 .05
❑ 132 Tommy Boggs .15 .05
❑ 133 Jeff Cox RC .15 .05
❑ 134 Steve Mura .15 .05
❑ 135 Gorman Thomas .40 .15
❑ 136 Doug Capilla .15 .05
❑ 137 Hosken Powell .15 .05
❑ 138 Rich Dotson DP RC .15 .05
❑ 139 Oscar Gamble .15 .05
❑ 140 Bob Forsch .15 .05
❑ 141 Miguel Dilone .15 .05
❑ 142 Jackson Todd .15 .05
❑ 143 Dan Meyer .15 .05
❑ 144 Allen Ripley .15 .05
❑ 145 Mickey Rivers .15 .05
❑ 146 Bobby Castillo .15 .05
❑ 147 Dale Berra .15 .05
❑ 148 Randy Niemann .15 .05
❑ 149 Joe Nolan RC .15 .05
❑ 150 Mark Fidrych .40 .15
❑ 151 Claudell Washington .15 .05
❑ 152 John Urrea .15 .05
❑ 153 Tom Poquette .15 .05
❑ 154 Rick Langford .15 .05
❑ 155 Chris Chambliss .40 .15
❑ 156 Bob McClure .15 .05
❑ 157 John Wathan .15 .05
❑ 158 Fergie Jenkins .40 .15
❑ 159 Brian Doyle .15 .05
❑ 160 Garry Maddox .15 .05
❑ 161 Dan Graham .15 .05
❑ 162 Doug Corbett RC .15 .05
❑ 163 Bill Almon RC .15 .05
❑ 164 LaMarr Hoyt RC .75 .30
❑ 165 Tony Scott .15 .05
❑ 166 Floyd Bannister .15 .05
❑ 167 Terry Whitfield .15 .05
❑ 168 Don Robinson DP .15 .05
❑ 169 John Mayberry .15 .05
❑ 170 Ross Grimsley .15 .05
❑ 171 Gene Richards .15 .05
❑ 172 Gary Woods .15 .05
❑ 173 Bump Wills .15 .05
❑ 174 Doug Rau .15 .05
❑ 175 Dave Collins .15 .05
❑ 176 Mike Krukow RC .15 .05
❑ 177 Rick Peters RC .15 .05
❑ 178 Jim Essian DP .15 .05
❑ 179 Rudy May .15 .05
❑ 180 Pete Rose 5.00 2.00
❑ 181 Elias Sosa .15 .05
❑ 182 Bob Grich .40 .15
❑ 183 Dick Davis DP .15 .05
❑ 184 Jim Dwyer .15 .05
❑ 185 Dennis Leonard .15 .05
❑ 186 Wayne Nordhagen .15 .05
❑ 187 Mike Parrott .15 .05
❑ 188 Doug DeCinces .15 .05
❑ 189 Craig Swan .15 .05
❑ 190 Cesar Cedeno .40 .15
❑ 191 Rick Sutcliffe .40 .15
❑ 192 Harper/Miller/Ramirez RC .25 .08
❑ 193 Pete Vuckovich .15 .05
❑ 194 Rod Scurry RC .15 .05
❑ 195 Rich Murray RC .15 .05
❑ 196 Duffy Dyer .15 .05
❑ 197 Jim Kern .15 .05
❑ 198 Jerry Dybzinski RC .15 .05
❑ 199 Chuck Rainey .15 .05
❑ 200 George Foster .40 .15
❑ 201 Johnny Bench RB .75 .30
❑ 202 Steve Carlton RB .40 .15
❑ 203 Bill Gullickson RB .15 .05
❑ 204 R.LeFlore/R.Scott RB .40 .15
❑ 205 Pete Rose RB 1.50 .60
❑ 206 Mike Schmidt RB 1.50 .60
❑ 207 Ozzie Smith RB 2.00 .75
❑ 208 Willie Wilson RB .15 .05
❑ 209 Dickie Thon DP .15 .05
❑ 210 Jim Palmer .75 .30
❑ 211 Derrel Thomas .15 .05
❑ 212 Steve Nicosia .15 .05
❑ 213 Al Holland RC .15 .05
❑ 214 Botting/Dorsey/J.Harris RC .25 .08
❑ 215 Larry Hisle .15 .05
❑ 216 John Henry Johnson .15 .05
❑ 217 Rich Hebner .15 .05
❑ 218 Paul Splittorff .15 .05
❑ 219 Ken Landreaux .15 .05
❑ 220 Tom Seaver 1.50 .60
❑ 221 Bob Davis .15 .05
❑ 222 Jorge Orta .15 .05
❑ 223 Roy Lee Jackson RC .15 .05
❑ 224 Pat Zachry .15 .05
❑ 225 Ruppert Jones .15 .05
❑ 226 Manny Sanguillen DP .25 .08
❑ 227 Fred Martinez RC .15 .05
❑ 228 Tom Paciorek .15 .05
❑ 229 Rollie Fingers .40 .15
❑ 230 George Hendrick .40 .15
❑ 231 Joe Beckwith .15 .05
❑ 232 Mickey Klutts .15 .05
❑ 233 Skip Lockwood .15 .05
❑ 234 Lou Whitaker .75 .30
❑ 235 Scott Sanderson .15 .05
❑ 236 Mike Ivie .15 .05
❑ 237 Charlie Moore .15 .05
❑ 238 Willie Hernandez .15 .05
❑ 239 Rick Miller DP .15 .05
❑ 240 Nolan Ryan 8.00 3.00
❑ 241 Checklist 122-242 DP .25 .08
❑ 242 Chet Lemon .40 .15
❑ 243 Sal Butera RC .15 .05
❑ 244 Landrum/Olmsted/Rincon RC .25 .08
❑ 245 Ed Figueroa .15 .05
❑ 246 Ed Ott DP .15 .05
❑ 247 Glenn Hubbard DP .15 .05
❑ 248 Joey McLaughlin .15 .05
❑ 249 Larry Cox .15 .05
❑ 250 Ron Guidry .40 .15
❑ 251 Tom Brookens .15 .05
❑ 252 Victor Cruz .15 .05
❑ 253 Dave Bergman .15 .05
❑ 254 Ozzie Smith 5.00 2.00
❑ 255 Mark Littell .15 .05
❑ 256 Bombo Rivera .15 .05
❑ 257 Rennie Stennett .15 .05
❑ 258 Joe Price RC .15 .05
❑ 259 M.Wilson/H.Brooks RC 5.00 2.00
❑ 260 Ron Cey .40 .15
❑ 261 Rickey Henderson 10.00 4.00
❑ 262 Sammy Stewart .15 .05
❑ 263 Brian Downing .40 .15
❑ 264 Jim Norris .15 .05
❑ 265 John Candelaria .40 .15
❑ 266 Tom Herr .15 .05
❑ 267 Stan Bahnsen .15 .05
❑ 268 Jerry Royster .15 .05
❑ 269 Ken Forsch .15 .05
❑ 270 Greg Luzinski .40 .15
❑ 271 Bill Castro .15 .05
❑ 272 Bruce Kimm .15 .05
❑ 273 Stan Papi .15 .05
❑ 274 Craig Chamberlain .15 .05

❑ 275	Dwight Evans	.75	.30
❑ 276	Dan Spillner	.15	.05
❑ 277	Alfredo Griffin	.15	.05
❑ 278	Rick Sofield	.15	.05
❑ 279	Bob Knopper	.15	.05
❑ 280	Ken Griffey	.40	.15
❑ 281	Fred Stanley	.15	.05
❑ 282	Anderson/Biercevicz/Craig RC	.25	.08
❑ 283	Billy Sample	.15	.05
❑ 284	Brian Kingman	.15	.05
❑ 285	Jerry Turner	.15	.05
❑ 286	Dave Frost	.15	.05
❑ 287	Lenn Sakata	.15	.05
❑ 288	Bob Clark	.15	.05
❑ 289	Mickey Hatcher	.15	.05
❑ 290	Bob Boone DP	.25	.08
❑ 291	Aurelio Lopez	.15	.05
❑ 292	Mike Squires	.15	.05
❑ 293	Charlie Lea RC	.15	.05
❑ 294	Mike Tyson DP	.15	.05
❑ 295	Hal McRae	.40	.15
❑ 296	Bill Nahorodny DP	.15	.05
❑ 297	Bob Bailor	.15	.05
❑ 298	Buddy Solomon	.15	.05
❑ 299	Elliott Maddox	.15	.05
❑ 300	Paul Molitor	1.50	.60
❑ 301	Matt Keough	.15	.05
❑ 302	F.Valenzuela/M.Scioscia RC	8.00	3.00
❑ 303	Johnny Oates	.40	.15
❑ 304	John Castino	.15	.05
❑ 305	Ken Clay	.15	.05
❑ 306	Juan Beniquez DP	.15	.05
❑ 307	Gene Garber	.15	.05
❑ 308	Rick Manning	.15	.05
❑ 309	Luis Salazar RC	.75	.30
❑ 310	Vida Blue DP	.25	.08
❑ 311	Freddie Patek	.15	.05
❑ 312	Rick Rhoden	.15	.05
❑ 313	Luis Pujols	.15	.05
❑ 314	Rich Dauer	.15	.05
❑ 315	Kirk Gibson RC	8.00	3.00
❑ 316	Craig Minetto	.15	.05
❑ 317	Lonnie Smith	.40	.15
❑ 318	Steve Yeager	.40	.15
❑ 319	Rowland Office	.15	.05
❑ 320	Tom Burgmeier	.15	.05
❑ 321	Leon Durham RC	.75	.30
❑ 322	Neil Allen	.15	.05
❑ 323	Jim Morrison DP	.15	.05
❑ 324	Mike Willis	.15	.05
❑ 325	Ray Knight	.40	.15
❑ 326	Biff Pocoroba	.15	.05
❑ 327	Moose Haas	.15	.05
❑ 328	Engle/Johnston/G.Ward	.25	.08
❑ 329	Joaquin Andujar	.40	.15
❑ 330	Frank White	.40	.15
❑ 331	Dennis Lamp	.15	.05
❑ 332	Lee Lacy DP	.15	.05
❑ 333	Sid Monge	.15	.05
❑ 334	Dane Iorg	.15	.05
❑ 335	Rick Cerone	.15	.05
❑ 336	Eddie Whitson	.15	.05
❑ 337	Lynn Jones	.15	.05
❑ 338	Checklist 243-363	.40	.15
❑ 339	John Ellis	.15	.05
❑ 340	Bruce Kison	.15	.05
❑ 341	Dwayne Murphy	.15	.05
❑ 342	Eric Rasmussen DP	.15	.05
❑ 343	Frank Taveras	.15	.05
❑ 344	Byron McLaughlin	.15	.05
❑ 345	Warren Cromartie	.15	.05
❑ 346	Larry Christenson DP	.15	.05
❑ 347	Harold Baines RC	3.00	1.25
❑ 348	Bob Sykes	.15	.05
❑ 349	Glenn Hoffman RC	.15	.05
❑ 350	J.R. Richard	.40	.15
❑ 351	Otto Velez	.15	.05
❑ 352	Dick Tidrow DP	.15	.05
❑ 353	Terry Kennedy	.15	.05
❑ 354	Mario Soto	.40	.15
❑ 355	Bob Horner	.40	.15
❑ 356	Stablein/Stimac/Tellmann RC	.25	.08
❑ 357	Jim Slaton	.15	.05
❑ 358	Mark Wagner	.15	.05
❑ 359	Tom Hausman	.15	.05
❑ 360	Willie Wilson	.40	.15
❑ 361	Joe Strain	.15	.05
❑ 362	Bo Diaz	.15	.05
❑ 363	Geoff Zahn	.15	.05
❑ 364	Mike Davis RC	.25	.08
❑ 365	Graig Nettles DP	.25	.08
❑ 366	Mike Ramsey RC	.25	.08
❑ 367	Dennis Martinez	.40	.15
❑ 368	Leon Roberts	.15	.05
❑ 369	Frank Tanana	.40	.15
❑ 370	Dave Winfield	.75	.30
❑ 371	Charlie Hough	.40	.15
❑ 372	Jay Johnstone	.15	.05
❑ 373	Pat Underwood	.15	.05
❑ 374	Tommy Hutton	.15	.05
❑ 375	Dave Concepcion	.40	.15
❑ 376	Ron Reed	.15	.05
❑ 377	Jerry Morales	.15	.05
❑ 378	Dave Rader	.15	.05
❑ 379	Lary Sorensen	.15	.05
❑ 380	Willie Stargell	.75	.30
❑ 381	Lezcano/Macko/Martz RC	.25	.08
❑ 382	Paul Mirabella RC	.15	.05
❑ 383	Eric Soderholm DP	.15	.05
❑ 384	Mike Sadek	.15	.05
❑ 385	Joe Sambito	.15	.05
❑ 386	Dave Edwards	.15	.05
❑ 387	Phil Niekro	.40	.15
❑ 388	Andre Thornton	.40	.15
❑ 389	Marty Pattin	.15	.05
❑ 390	Cesar Geronimo	.15	.05
❑ 391	Dave Lemanczyk DP	.15	.05
❑ 392	Lance Parrish	.40	.15
❑ 393	Broderick Perkins	.15	.05
❑ 394	Woodie Fryman	.15	.05
❑ 395	Scot Thompson	.15	.05
❑ 396	Bill Campbell	.15	.05
❑ 397	Julio Cruz	.15	.05
❑ 398	Ross Baumgarten	.15	.05
❑ 399	Boddicker/Corey/Rayford RC	.75	.30
❑ 400	Reggie Jackson	1.50	.60
❑ 401	George Brett ALCS	2.50	1.00
❑ 402	NL Champs	.75	.30
❑ 403	Larry Bowa WS	.75	.30
❑ 404	Tug McGraw WS	.75	.30
❑ 405	Nino Espinosa	.15	.05
❑ 406	Dickie Noles	.15	.05
❑ 407	Ernie Whitt	.15	.05
❑ 408	Fernando Arroyo	.15	.05
❑ 409	Larry Herndon	.15	.05
❑ 410	Bert Campaneris	.40	.15
❑ 411	Terry Puhl	.15	.05
❑ 412	Britt Burns RC	.15	.05
❑ 413	Tony Bernazard	.15	.05
❑ 414	John Pacella DP RC	.15	.05
❑ 415	Ben Oglivie	.40	.15
❑ 416	Gary Alexander	.15	.05
❑ 417	Dan Schatzeder	.15	.05
❑ 418	Bobby Brown	.15	.05
❑ 419	Tom Hume	.15	.05
❑ 420	Keith Hernandez	.40	.15
❑ 421	Bob Stanley	.15	.05
❑ 422	Dan Ford	.15	.05
❑ 423	Shane Rawley	.15	.05
❑ 424	Lollar/Robinson/Werth RC	.25	.08
❑ 425	Al Bumbry	.15	.05
❑ 426	Warren Brusstar	.15	.05
❑ 427	John D'Acquisto	.15	.05
❑ 428	John Stearns	.15	.05
❑ 429	Mick Kelleher	.15	.05
❑ 430	Jim Bibby	.15	.05
❑ 431	Dave Roberts	.15	.05
❑ 432	Len Barker	.40	.15
❑ 433	Rance Mulliniks	.15	.05
❑ 434	Roger Erickson	.15	.05
❑ 435	Jim Spencer	.15	.05
❑ 436	Gary Lucas RC	.15	.05
❑ 437	Mike Heath DP	.15	.05
❑ 438	John Montefusco	.15	.05
❑ 439	Denny Walling	.15	.05
❑ 440	Jerry Reuss	.15	.05
❑ 441	Ken Reitz	.15	.05
❑ 442	Ron Pruitt	.15	.05
❑ 443	Jim Beattie DP	.15	.05
❑ 444	Garth Iorg	.15	.05
❑ 445	Ellis Valentine	.15	.05
❑ 446	Checklist 364-484	.40	.15
❑ 447	Junior Kennedy DP	.15	.05
❑ 448	Tim Corcoran	.15	.05
❑ 449	Paul Mitchell	.15	.05
❑ 450	Dave Kingman DP	.25	.08
❑ 451	Bando/Brennan/Wihtol RC	.25	.08
❑ 452	Renie Martin	.15	.05
❑ 453	Rob Wilfong DP	.15	.05
❑ 454	Andy Hassler	.15	.05
❑ 455	Rick Burleson	.15	.05
❑ 456	Jeff Reardon RC	1.50	.60
❑ 457	Mike Lum	.15	.05
❑ 458	Randy Jones	.40	.15
❑ 459	Greg Gross	.15	.05
❑ 460	Rich Gossage	.40	.15
❑ 461	Dave McKay RC	.15	.05
❑ 462	Jack Brohamer	.15	.05
❑ 463	Milt May	.15	.05
❑ 464	Adrian Devine	.15	.05
❑ 465	Bill Russell	.40	.15
❑ 466	Bob Molinaro	.15	.05
❑ 467	Dave Stieb	.40	.15
❑ 468	John Wockenfuss	.15	.05
❑ 469	Jeff Leonard	.40	.15
❑ 470	Manny Trillo	.15	.05
❑ 471	Mike Vail	.15	.05
❑ 472	Dyar Miller DP	.15	.05
❑ 473	Jose Cardenal	.15	.05
❑ 474	Mike LaCoss	.15	.05
❑ 475	Buddy Bell	.40	.15
❑ 476	Jerry Koosman	.40	.15
❑ 477	Luis Gomez	.15	.05
❑ 478	Juan Eichelberger RC	.15	.05
❑ 479	Tim Raines RC	4.00	1.50
❑ 480	Carlton Fisk	.75	.30
❑ 481	Bob Lacey DP	.15	.05
❑ 482	Jim Gantner	.15	.05
❑ 483	Mike Griffin RC	.25	.08
❑ 484	Max Venable DP RC	.15	.05
❑ 485	Garry Templeton	.40	.15
❑ 486	Marc Hill	.15	.05
❑ 487	Dewey Robinson	.15	.05
❑ 488	Damaso Garcia RC	.15	.05
❑ 489	John Littlefield RC	.15	.05
❑ 490	Eddie Murray	2.50	1.00
❑ 491	Gordy Pladson RC	.15	.05
❑ 492	Barry Foote	.15	.05
❑ 493	Dan Quisenberry	.15	.05
❑ 494	Bob Walk RC	.75	.30
❑ 495	Dusty Baker	.40	.15
❑ 496	Paul Dade	.15	.05
❑ 497	Fred Norman	.15	.05
❑ 498	Pat Putnam	.15	.05
❑ 499	Frank Pastore	.15	.05
❑ 500	Jim Rice	.40	.15
❑ 501	Tim Foli DP	.15	.05
❑ 502	Bourjos/Hargesheimer/Rowland RC	.25	.08
❑ 503	Steve McCatty	.15	.05
❑ 504	Dale Murphy	.75	.30
❑ 505	Jason Thompson	.15	.05
❑ 506	Phil Huffman	.15	.05
❑ 507	Jamie Quirk	.15	.05
❑ 508	Rob Dressler	.15	.05
❑ 509	Pete Mackanin	.15	.05
❑ 510	Lee Mazzilli	.40	.15
❑ 511	Wayne Garland	.15	.05
❑ 512	Gary Thomasson	.15	.05
❑ 513	Frank LaCorte	.15	.05
❑ 514	George Riley RC	.15	.05
❑ 515	Robin Yount	2.50	1.00
❑ 516	Doug Bird	.15	.05
❑ 517	Richie Zisk	.15	.05
❑ 518	Grant Jackson	.15	.05
❑ 519	John Tamargo DP	.15	.05
❑ 520	Steve Stone	.15	.05
❑ 521	Sam Mejias	.15	.05
❑ 522	Mike Colbern	.15	.05
❑ 523	John Fulgham	.15	.05
❑ 524	Willie Aikens	.15	.05
❑ 525	Mike Torrez	.15	.05
❑ 526	Bystrom/Loviglio/Wright RC	.25	.08
❑ 527	Danny Goodwin	.15	.05
❑ 528	Gary Matthews	.40	.15
❑ 529	Dave LaRoche	.15	.05
❑ 530	Steve Garvey	.75	.30
❑ 531	John Curtis	.15	.05
❑ 532	Bill Stein	.15	.05

Card		
❑ 533 Jesus Figueroa RC	.15	.05
❑ 534 Dave Smith RC	.75	.30
❑ 535 Omar Moreno	.15	.05
❑ 536 Bob Owchinko DP	.15	.05
❑ 537 Ron Hodges	.15	.05
❑ 538 Tom Griffin	.15	.05
❑ 539 Rodney Scott	.15	.05
❑ 540 Mike Schmidt DP	2.00	.75
❑ 541 Steve Swisher	.15	.05
❑ 542 Larry Bradford DP	.15	.05
❑ 543 Terry Crowley	.15	.05
❑ 544 Rich Gale	.15	.05
❑ 545 Johnny Grubb	.15	.05
❑ 546 Paul Moskau	.15	.05
❑ 547 Mario Guerrero	.15	.05
❑ 548 Dave Goltz	.15	.05
❑ 549 Jerry Remy	.15	.05
❑ 550 Tommy John	.40	.15
❑ 551 Law/Pena/Perez RC	.75	.30
❑ 552 Steve Trout	.15	.05
❑ 553 Tim Blackwell	.15	.05
❑ 554 Bert Blyleven	.40	.15
❑ 555 Cecil Cooper	.40	.15
❑ 556 Jerry Mumphrey	.15	.05
❑ 557 Chris Knapp	.15	.05
❑ 558 Barry Bonnell	.15	.05
❑ 559 Willie Montanez	.15	.05
❑ 560 Joe Morgan	.75	.30
❑ 561 Dennis Littlejohn	.15	.05
❑ 562 Checklist 485-605	.40	.15
❑ 563 Jim Kaat	.40	.15
❑ 564 Ron Hassey DP	.15	.05
❑ 565 Burt Hooton	.15	.05
❑ 566 Del Unser	.15	.05
❑ 567 Mark Bomback RC	.15	.05
❑ 568 Dave Revering	.15	.05
❑ 569 Al Williams DP RC	.15	.05
❑ 570 Ken Singleton	.40	.15
❑ 571 Todd Cruz	.15	.05
❑ 572 Jack Morris	.75	.30
❑ 573 Phil Garner	.40	.15
❑ 574 Bill Caudill	.15	.05
❑ 575 Tony Perez	.75	.30
❑ 576 Reggie Cleveland	.15	.05
❑ 577 Leal/Milner/Schrom RC	.25	.08
❑ 578 Bill Gullickson RC	.75	.30
❑ 579 Tim Flannery	.15	.05
❑ 580 Don Baylor	.40	.15
❑ 581 Roy Howell	.15	.05
❑ 582 Gaylord Perry	.40	.15
❑ 583 Larry Milbourne	.15	.05
❑ 584 Randy Lerch	.15	.05
❑ 585 Amos Otis	.40	.15
❑ 586 Silvio Martinez	.15	.05
❑ 587 Jeff Newman	.15	.05
❑ 588 Gary Lavelle	.15	.05
❑ 589 Lamar Johnson	.15	.05
❑ 590 Bruce Sutter	.75	.30
❑ 591 John Lowenstein	.15	.05
❑ 592 Steve Comer	.15	.05
❑ 593 Steve Kemp	.15	.05
❑ 594 Preston Hanna DP	.15	.05
❑ 595 Butch Hobson	.15	.05
❑ 596 Jerry Augustine	.15	.05
❑ 597 Rafael Landestoy	.15	.05
❑ 598 George Vukovich DP RC	.15	.05
❑ 599 Dennis Kinney RC	.15	.05
❑ 600 Johnny Bench	1.50	.60
❑ 601 Don Aase	.15	.05
❑ 602 Bobby Murcer	.40	.15
❑ 603 John Verhoeven	.15	.05
❑ 604 Rob Picciolo	.15	.05
❑ 605 Don Sutton	.40	.15
❑ 606 Berenyi/Combe/Householder DP RC	.25	.08
❑ 607 David Palmer	.15	.05
❑ 608 Greg Pryor	.15	.05
❑ 609 Lynn McGlothen	.15	.05
❑ 610 Darrell Porter	.15	.05
❑ 611 Rick Matula DP	.15	.05
❑ 612 Duane Kuiper	.15	.05
❑ 613 Jim Anderson	.15	.05
❑ 614 Dave Rozema	.15	.05
❑ 615 Rick Dempsey	.15	.05
❑ 616 Rick Wise	.15	.05
❑ 617 Craig Reynolds	.15	.05
❑ 618 John Milner	.15	.05
❑ 619 Steve Henderson	.15	.05
❑ 620 Dennis Eckersley	.75	.30
❑ 621 Tom Donohue	.15	.05
❑ 622 Randy Moffitt	.15	.05
❑ 623 Sal Bando	.40	.15
❑ 624 Bob Welch	.40	.15
❑ 625 Bill Buckner	.40	.15
❑ 626 Steffen/Ujdur/Weaver RC	.25	.08
❑ 627 Luis Tiant	.40	.15
❑ 628 Vic Correll	.15	.05
❑ 629 Tony Armas	.40	.15
❑ 630 Steve Carlton	.75	.30
❑ 631 Ron Jackson	.15	.05
❑ 632 Alan Bannister	.15	.05
❑ 633 Bill Lee	.40	.15
❑ 634 Doug Flynn	.15	.05
❑ 635 Bobby Bonds	.40	.15
❑ 636 Al Hrabosky	.40	.15
❑ 637 Jerry Narron	.15	.05
❑ 638 Checklist 606-726	.40	.15
❑ 639 Carney Lansford	.40	.15
❑ 640 Dave Parker	.40	.15
❑ 641 Mark Belanger	.15	.05
❑ 642 Vern Ruhle	.15	.05
❑ 643 Lloyd Moseby RC	.75	.30
❑ 644 Ramon Aviles DP	.15	.05
❑ 645 Rick Reuschel	.40	.15
❑ 646 Marvis Foley RC	.15	.05
❑ 647 Dick Drago	.15	.05
❑ 648 Darrell Evans	.40	.15
❑ 649 Manny Sarmiento	.15	.05
❑ 650 Bucky Dent	.40	.15
❑ 651 Pedro Guerrero	.40	.15
❑ 652 John Montague	.15	.05
❑ 653 Bill Fahey	.15	.05
❑ 654 Ray Burris	.15	.05
❑ 655 Dan Driessen	.15	.05
❑ 656 Jon Matlack	.15	.05
❑ 657 Mike Cubbage DP	.15	.05
❑ 658 Milt Wilcox	.15	.05
❑ 659 Flinn/Romero/Yost	.75	.30
❑ 660 Gary Carter	.75	.30
❑ 661 Orioles Team CL Earl Weaver MG	.40	.15
❑ 662 Red Sox Team CL Ralph Houk MG	.40	.15
❑ 663 Angels Team CL Jim Fregosi MG	.40	.15
❑ 664 White Sox Team/Mgr. Tony LaRussa (Checklist back	.40	.15
❑ 665 Indians Team CL Dave Garcia MG	.40	.15
❑ 666 Tigers Team/Mgr. Sparky Anderson (Checklist back	.40	.15
❑ 667 Royals Team CL Jim Frey MG	.40	.15
❑ 668 Brewers Team CL Bob Rodgers MG	.40	.15
❑ 669 Twins Team CL. John Goryl MG	.40	.15
❑ 670 Yankees Team CL Gene Michael MG	.40	.15
❑ 671 A's Team CL Billy Martin MG	.75	.30
❑ 672 Mariners Team CL Maury Wills MG	.40	.15
❑ 673 Rangers Team CL Don Zimmer MG	.40	.15
❑ 674 Blue Jays Team/Mgr. Bobby Mattick (Checklist bac	.40	.15
❑ 675 Braves Team CL Bobby Cox MG	.40	.15
❑ 676 Cubs Team CL Joe Amalfitano MG	.40	.15
❑ 677 Reds Team CL John McNamara MG	.40	.15
❑ 678 Astros Team CL Bill Virdon MG	.40	.15
❑ 679 Dodgers Team CL Tom Lasorda MG	.75	.30
❑ 680 Expos Team CL Dick Williams MG	.40	.15
❑ 681 Mets Team CL Joe Torre MG	.75	.30

Card		
❑ 682 Phillies Team CL Dallas Green MG	.40	.15
❑ 683 Pirates Team CL Chuck Tanner MG	.40	.15
❑ 684 Cardinals Team/Mgr. Whitey Herzog (Checklist bac	.40	.15
❑ 685 Padres Team CL Frank Howard MG	.40	.15
❑ 686 Giants Team CL Dave Bristol MG	.40	.15
❑ 687 Jeff Jones RC	.15	.05
❑ 688 Kiko Garcia	.15	.05
❑ 689 Bruce Hurst RC	.75	.30
❑ 690 Bob Watson	.15	.05
❑ 691 Dick Ruthven	.15	.05
❑ 692 Lenny Randle	.15	.05
❑ 693 Steve Howe RC	.25	.08
❑ 694 Bud Harrelson DP	.25	.08
❑ 695 Kent Tekulve	.15	.05
❑ 696 Alan Ashby	.15	.05
❑ 697 Rick Waits	.15	.05
❑ 698 Mike Jorgensen	.15	.05
❑ 699 Glenn Abbott	.15	.05
❑ 700 George Brett	4.00	1.50
❑ 701 Joe Rudi	.40	.15
❑ 702 George Medich	.15	.05
❑ 703 Alvis Woods	.15	.05
❑ 704 Bill Travers DP	.15	.05
❑ 705 Ted Simmons	.40	.15
❑ 706 Dave Ford RC	.15	.05
❑ 707 Dave Cash	.15	.05
❑ 708 Doyle Alexander	.15	.05
❑ 709 Alan Trammell DP	.50	.20
❑ 710 Ron LeFlore DP	.25	.08
❑ 711 Joe Ferguson	.15	.05
❑ 712 Bill Bonham	.15	.05
❑ 713 Bill North	.15	.05
❑ 714 Pete Redfern	.15	.05
❑ 715 Bill Madlock	.40	.15
❑ 716 Glenn Borgmann	.15	.05
❑ 717 Jim Barr DP	.15	.05
❑ 718 Larry Biittner	.15	.05
❑ 719 Sparky Lyle	.40	.15
❑ 720 Fred Lynn	.40	.15
❑ 721 Toby Harrah	.40	.15
❑ 722 Joe Niekro	.15	.05
❑ 723 Bruce Bochte	.15	.05
❑ 724 Lou Piniella	.40	.15
❑ 725 Steve Rogers	.40	.15
❑ 726 Rick Monday	.40	.15

1981 Topps Traded

Card		
❑ COMP.FACT.SET (132)	25.00	10.00
❑ 727 Danny Ainge XRC	5.00	2.00
❑ 728 Doyle Alexander	.25	.08
❑ 729 Gary Alexander	.25	.08
❑ 730 Bill Almon	.25	.08
❑ 731 Joaquin Andujar	1.00	.40
❑ 732 Bob Bailor	.25	.08
❑ 733 Juan Beniquez	.25	.08
❑ 734 Dave Bergman	.25	.08
❑ 735 Tony Bernazard	.25	.08
❑ 736 Larry Biittner	.25	.08
❑ 737 Doug Bird	.25	.08
❑ 738 Bert Blyleven	1.00	.40
❑ 739 Mark Bomback	.25	.08

❑ 740 Bobby Bonds 1.00 .40
❑ 741 Rick Bosetti .25 .08
❑ 742 Hubie Brooks 2.00 .75
❑ 743 Rick Burleson .25 .08
❑ 744 Ray Burris .25 .08
❑ 745 Jeff Burroughs 1.00 .40
❑ 746 Enos Cabell .25 .08
❑ 747 Ken Clay .25 .08
❑ 748 Mark Clear .25 .08
❑ 749 Larry Cox .25 .08
❑ 750 Hector Cruz .25 .08
❑ 751 Victor Cruz .25 .08
❑ 752 Mike Cubbage .25 .08
❑ 753 Dick Davis .25 .08
❑ 754 Brian Doyle .25 .08
❑ 755 Dick Drago .25 .08
❑ 756 Leon Durham 1.00 .40
❑ 757 Jim Dwyer .25 .08
❑ 758 Dave Edwards .25 .08
❑ 759 Jim Essian .25 .08
❑ 760 Bill Fahey .25 .08
❑ 761 Rollie Fingers 1.00 .40
❑ 762 Carlton Fisk 2.00 .75
❑ 763 Barry Foote .25 .08
❑ 764 Ken Forsch .25 .08
❑ 765 Kiko Garcia .25 .08
❑ 766 Cesar Geronimo .25 .08
❑ 767 Gary Gray XRC .25 .08
❑ 768 Mickey Hatcher .25 .08
❑ 769 Steve Henderson .25 .08
❑ 770 Marc Hill .25 .08
❑ 771 Butch Hobson .25 .08
❑ 772 Rick Honeycutt .25 .08
❑ 773 Roy Howell .25 .08
❑ 774 Mike Ivie .25 .08
❑ 775 Roy Lee Jackson .25 .08
❑ 776 Cliff Johnson .25 .08
❑ 777 Randy Jones 1.00 .40
❑ 778 Ruppert Jones .25 .08
❑ 779 Mick Kelleher .25 .08
❑ 780 Terry Kennedy .25 .08
❑ 781 Dave Kingman 1.00 .40
❑ 782 Bob Knepper .25 .08
❑ 783 Ken Kravec .25 .08
❑ 784 Bob Lacey .25 .08
❑ 785 Dennis Lamp .25 .08
❑ 786 Rafael Landestoy .25 .08
❑ 787 Ken Landreaux .25 .08
❑ 788 Carney Lansford 1.00 .40
❑ 789 Dave LaRoche .25 .08
❑ 790 Joe Lefebvre .25 .08
❑ 791 Ron LeFlore 1.00 .40
❑ 792 Randy Lerch .25 .08
❑ 793 Sixto Lezcano .25 .08
❑ 794 John Littlefield .25 .08
❑ 795 Mike Lum .25 .08
❑ 796 Greg Luzinski 1.00 .40
❑ 797 Fred Lynn 1.00 .40
❑ 798 Jerry Martin .25 .08
❑ 799 Buck Martinez .25 .08
❑ 800 Gary Matthews 1.00 .40
❑ 801 Mario Mendoza .25 .08
❑ 802 Larry Milbourne .25 .08
❑ 803 Rick Miller .25 .08
❑ 804 John Montefusco .25 .08
❑ 805 Jerry Morales .25 .08
❑ 806 Jose Morales .25 .08
❑ 807 Joe Morgan 2.00 .75
❑ 808 Jerry Mumphrey .25 .08
❑ 809 Gene Nelson XRC .25 .08
❑ 810 Ed Ott .25 .08
❑ 811 Bob Owchinko .25 .08
❑ 812 Gaylord Perry 1.00 .40
❑ 813 Mike Phillips .25 .08
❑ 814 Darrell Porter .25 .08
❑ 815 Mike Proly .25 .08
❑ 816 Tim Raines 5.00 2.00
❑ 817 Lenny Randle .25 .08
❑ 818 Doug Rau .25 .08
❑ 819 Jeff Reardon 2.00 .75
❑ 820 Ken Reitz .25 .08
❑ 821 Steve Renko .25 .08
❑ 822 Rick Reuschel 1.00 .40
❑ 823 Dave Revering .25 .08
❑ 824 Dave Roberts .25 .08
❑ 825 Leon Roberts .25 .08
❑ 826 Joe Rudi 1.00 .40
❑ 827 Kevin Saucier .25 .08
❑ 828 Tony Scott .25 .08
❑ 829 Bob Shirley .25 .08
❑ 830 Ted Simmons 1.00 .40
❑ 831 Lary Sorensen .25 .08
❑ 832 Jim Spencer .25 .08
❑ 833 Harry Spilman .25 .08
❑ 834 Fred Stanley .25 .08
❑ 835 Rusty Staub 1.00 .40
❑ 836 Bill Stein .25 .08
❑ 837 Joe Strain .25 .08
❑ 838 Bruce Sutter 2.00 .75
❑ 839 Don Sutton 1.00 .40
❑ 840 Steve Swisher .25 .08
❑ 841 Frank Tanana 1.00 .40
❑ 842 Gene Tenace 1.00 .40
❑ 843 Jason Thompson .25 .08
❑ 844 Dickie Thon .25 .08
❑ 845 Bill Travers .25 .08
❑ 846 Tom Underwood .25 .08
❑ 847 John Urrea .25 .08
❑ 848 Mike Vail .25 .08
❑ 849 Ellis Valentine .25 .08
❑ 850 Fernando Valenzuela 10.00 4.00
❑ 851 Pete Vuckovich .25 .08
❑ 852 Mark Wagner .25 .08
❑ 853 Bob Walk 1.00 .40
❑ 854 Claudell Washington .25 .08
❑ 855 Dave Winfield 2.00 .75
❑ 856 Geoff Zahn .25 .08
❑ 857 Richie Zisk .25 .08
❑ 858 Checklist 727-858 .25 .08

1982 Topps

❑ COMPLETE SET (792) 80.00 40.00
❑ 1 Steve Carlton HL .30 .10
❑ 2 Ron Davis HL
Fans 8 straight
in relief .15 .05
❑ 3 Tim Raines HL .30 .10
❑ 4 Pete Rose HL .60 .25
❑ 5 Nolan Ryan HL 3.00 1.25
❑ 6 Fernando Valenzuela HL
8 shutouts as rookie .60 .25
❑ 7 Scott Sanderson .15 .05
❑ 8 Rich Dauer .15 .05
❑ 9 Ron Guidry .30 .10
❑ 10 Ron Guidry SA .15 .05
❑ 11 Gary Alexander .15 .05
❑ 12 Moose Haas .15 .05
❑ 13 Lamar Johnson .15 .05
❑ 14 Steve Howe .15 .05
❑ 15 Ellis Valentine .15 .05
❑ 16 Steve Comer .15 .05
❑ 17 Darrell Evans .30 .10
❑ 18 Fernando Arroyo .15 .05
❑ 19 Ernie Whitt .15 .05
❑ 20 Garry Maddox .15 .05
❑ 21 Cal Ripken RC 50.00 20.00
❑ 22 Jim Beattie .15 .05
❑ 23 Willie Hernandez .15 .05
❑ 24 Dave Frost .15 .05
❑ 25 Jerry Remy .15 .05
❑ 26 Jorge Orta .15 .05
❑ 27 Tom Herr .15 .05
❑ 28 John Urrea .15 .05
❑ 29 Dwayne Murphy .15 .05
❑ 30 Tom Seaver 1.25 .50
❑ 31 Tom Seaver SA .30 .10
❑ 32 Gene Garber .15 .05
❑ 33 Jerry Morales .15 .05
❑ 34 Joe Sambito .15 .05
❑ 35 Willie Aikens .15 .05
❑ 36 Rangers TL
BA: Al Oliver
Pitching: Doc Medich .60 .25
❑ 37 Dan Graham .15 .05
❑ 38 Charlie Lea .15 .05
❑ 39 Lou Whitaker .30 .10
❑ 40 Dave Parker .30 .10
❑ 41 Dave Parker SA .15 .05
❑ 42 Rick Sofield .15 .05
❑ 43 Mike Cubbage .15 .05
❑ 44 Britt Burns .15 .05
❑ 45 Rick Cerone .15 .05
❑ 46 Jerry Augustine .15 .05
❑ 47 Jeff Leonard .15 .05
❑ 48 Bobby Castillo .15 .05
❑ 49 Alvis Woods .15 .05
❑ 50 Buddy Bell .30 .10
❑ 51 Howell/Lezcano/Waller RC .75 .30
❑ 52 Larry Andersen .15 .05
❑ 53 Greg Gross .15 .05
❑ 54 Ron Hassey .15 .05
❑ 55 Rick Burleson .15 .05
❑ 56 Mark Littell .15 .05
❑ 57 Craig Reynolds .15 .05
❑ 58 John D'Acquisto .15 .05
❑ 59 Rich Gedman .75 .30
❑ 60 Tony Armas .30 .10
❑ 61 Tommy Boggs .15 .05
❑ 62 Mike Tyson .15 .05
❑ 63 Mario Soto .30 .10
❑ 64 Lynn Jones .15 .05
❑ 65 Terry Kennedy .15 .05
❑ 66 Astros TL/Nolan Ryan 2.00 .75
❑ 67 Rich Gale .15 .05
❑ 68 Roy Howell .15 .05
❑ 69 Al Williams .15 .05
❑ 70 Tim Raines .60 .25
❑ 71 Roy Lee Jackson .15 .05
❑ 72 Rick Auerbach .15 .05
❑ 73 Buddy Solomon .15 .05
❑ 74 Bob Clark .15 .05
❑ 75 Tommy John .30 .10
❑ 76 Greg Pryor .15 .05
❑ 77 Miguel Dilone .15 .05
❑ 78 George Medich .15 .05
❑ 79 Bob Bailor .15 .05
❑ 80 Jim Palmer .30 .10
❑ 81 Jim Palmer SA .15 .05
❑ 82 Bob Welch .30 .10
❑ 83 Balboni/McGaf/Rob RC .75 .30
❑ 84 Rennie Stennett .15 .05
❑ 85 Lynn McGlothen .15 .05
❑ 86 Dane Iorg .15 .05
❑ 87 Matt Keough .15 .05
❑ 88 Biff Pocoroba .15 .05
❑ 89 Steve Henderson .15 .05
❑ 90 Nolan Ryan 6.00 2.50
❑ 91 Carney Lansford .30 .10
❑ 92 Brad Havens .15 .05
❑ 93 Larry Hisle .15 .05
❑ 94 Andy Hassler .15 .05
❑ 95 Ozzie Smith 2.50 1.00
❑ 96 Royals TL/George Brett 1.25 .50
❑ 97 Paul Moskau .15 .05
❑ 98 Terry Bulling .15 .05
❑ 99 Barry Bonnell .15 .05
❑ 100 Mike Schmidt 3.00 1.25
❑ 101 Mike Schmidt SA 1.25 .50
❑ 102 Dan Briggs .15 .05
❑ 103 Bob Lacey .15 .05
❑ 104 Rance Mulliniks .15 .05
❑ 105 Kirk Gibson 1.25 .50
❑ 106 Enrique Romo .15 .05
❑ 107 Wayne Krenchicki .15 .05
❑ 108 Bob Sykes .15 .05
❑ 109 Dave Revering .15 .05
❑ 110 Carlton Fisk .60 .25
❑ 111 Carlton Fisk SA .30 .10
❑ 112 Billy Sample .15 .05
❑ 113 Steve McCatty .15 .05

❑ 114 Ken Landreaux .15 .05
❑ 115 Gaylord Perry .30 .10
❑ 116 Jim Wohlford .15 .05
❑ 117 Rawly Eastwick .30 .10
❑ 118 Francona/Mills/Smith RC 5.00 2.00
❑ 119 Joe Pittman .15 .05
❑ 120 Gary Lucas .15 .05
❑ 121 Ed Lynch .15 .05
❑ 122 Jamie Easterly UER
(Photo actually
Reggie Clevel .15 .05
❑ 123 Danny Goodwin .15 .05
❑ 124 Reid Nichols .15 .05
❑ 125 Danny Ainge .30 .10
❑ 126 Braves TL
BA: Claudell Washington
Pitching: Rick .60 .25
❑ 127 Lonnie Smith .15 .05
❑ 128 Frank Pastore .15 .05
❑ 129 Checklist 1-132 .30 .10
❑ 130 Julio Cruz .15 .05
❑ 131 Stan Bahnsen .15 .05
❑ 132 Lee May .15 .05
❑ 133 Pat Underwood .15 .05
❑ 134 Dan Ford .15 .05
❑ 135 Andy Rincon .15 .05
❑ 136 Lenn Sakata .15 .05
❑ 137 George Cappuzzello .15 .05
❑ 138 Tony Pena .30 .10
❑ 139 Jeff Jones .15 .05
❑ 140 Ron LeFlore .30 .10
❑ 141 Bando/Brennan/Hayes RC .75 .30
❑ 142 Dave LaRoche .15 .05
❑ 143 Mookie Wilson .30 .10
❑ 144 Fred Breining .15 .05
❑ 145 Bob Horner .30 .10
❑ 146 Mike Griffin .15 .05
❑ 147 Denny Walling .15 .05
❑ 148 Mickey Klutts .15 .05
❑ 149 Pat Putnam .15 .05
❑ 150 Ted Simmons .30 .10
❑ 151 Dave Edwards .15 .05
❑ 152 Ramon Aviles .15 .05
❑ 153 Roger Erickson .15 .05
❑ 154 Dennis Werth .15 .05
❑ 155 Otto Velez .15 .05
❑ 156 A's TL/Rickey Henderson 1.25 .50
❑ 157 Steve Crawford .15 .05
❑ 158 Brian Downing .30 .10
❑ 159 Larry Biittner .15 .05
❑ 160 Luis Tiant .30 .10
❑ 161 Bill Madlock
Carney Lansford LL .30 .10
❑ 162 Schmidt/Armas/Murray LL 1.25 .50
❑ 163 Mike Schmidt/E.Murray LL 1.25 .50
❑ 164 T.Raines/R.Henderson LL 1.25 .50
❑ 165 Seav/Martinez/Morris LL .30 .10
❑ 166 Strikeout Leaders
Fernando Valenzuela
Len Barker .30 .10
❑ 167 N.Ryan/S.McCatty LL 2.00 .75
❑ 168 B.Sutter/R.Fingers LL .30 .10
❑ 169 Charlie Leibrandt .15 .05
❑ 170 Jim Bibby .15 .05
❑ 171 Brenly/Davis/Tufts RC 1.50 .60
❑ 172 Bill Gullickson .15 .05
❑ 173 Jamie Quirk .15 .05
❑ 174 Dave Ford .15 .05
❑ 175 Jerry Mumphrey .15 .05
❑ 176 Dewey Robinson .15 .05
❑ 177 John Ellis .15 .05
❑ 178 Dyar Miller .15 .05
❑ 179 Steve Garvey .30 .10
❑ 180 Steve Garvey SA .15 .05
❑ 181 Silvio Martinez .15 .05
❑ 182 Larry Herndon .15 .05
❑ 183 Mike Proly .15 .05
❑ 184 Mick Kelleher .15 .05
❑ 185 Phil Niekro .30 .10
❑ 186 Cardinals TL
BA: Keith Hernandez
Pitching: Bob F .30 .10
❑ 187 Jeff Newman .15 .05
❑ 188 Randy Martz .15 .05
❑ 189 Glenn Hoffman .15 .05
❑ 190 J.R. Richard .30 .10
❑ 191 Tim Wallach RC 1.50 .60
❑ 192 Broderick Perkins .15 .05
❑ 193 Darrell Jackson .15 .05
❑ 194 Mike Vail .15 .05
❑ 195 Paul Molitor .30 .10
❑ 196 Willie Upshaw .75 .30
❑ 197 Shane Rawley .15 .05
❑ 198 Chris Speier .15 .05
❑ 199 Don Aase .15 .05
❑ 200 George Brett 3.00 1.25
❑ 201 George Brett SA 1.50 .60
❑ 202 Rick Manning .15 .05
❑ 203 Barfield/Miln/Wells RC 1.50 .60
❑ 204 Gary Roenicke .15 .05
❑ 205 Neil Allen .15 .05
❑ 206 Tony Bernazard .15 .05
❑ 207 Rod Scurry .15 .05
❑ 208 Bobby Murcer .30 .10
❑ 209 Gary Lavelle .15 .05
❑ 210 Keith Hernandez .30 .10
❑ 211 Dan Petry .15 .05
❑ 212 Mario Mendoza .15 .05
❑ 213 Dave Stewart RC 2.50 1.00
❑ 214 Brian Asselstine .15 .05
❑ 215 Mike Krukow .15 .05
❑ 216 White Sox TL
BA: Chet Lemon
Pitching: Dennis Lam .60 .25
❑ 217 Bo McLaughlin .15 .05
❑ 218 Dave Roberts .15 .05
❑ 219 John Curtis .15 .05
❑ 220 Manny Trillo .15 .05
❑ 221 Jim Slaton .15 .05
❑ 222 Butch Wynegar .15 .05
❑ 223 Lloyd Moseby .15 .05
❑ 224 Bruce Bochte .15 .05
❑ 225 Mike Torrez .15 .05
❑ 226 Checklist 133-264 .60 .25
❑ 227 Ray Burris .15 .05
❑ 228 Sam Mejias .15 .05
❑ 229 Geoff Zahn .15 .05
❑ 230 Willie Wilson .30 .10
❑ 231 Davis/Dernier/Virgil RC .75 .30
❑ 232 Terry Crowley .15 .05
❑ 233 Duane Kuiper .15 .05
❑ 234 Ron Hodges .15 .05
❑ 235 Mike Easler .15 .05
❑ 236 John Martin RC .25 .08
❑ 237 Rusty Kuntz .15 .05
❑ 238 Kevin Saucier .15 .05
❑ 239 Jon Matlack .15 .05
❑ 240 Bucky Dent .30 .10
❑ 241 Bucky Dent SA .15 .05
❑ 242 Milt May .15 .05
❑ 243 Bob Owchinko .15 .05
❑ 244 Rufino Linares .15 .05
❑ 245 Ken Reitz .15 .05
❑ 246 New York Mets TL
BA: Hubie Brooks
Pitching: Mike .60 .25
❑ 247 Pedro Guerrero .30 .10
❑ 248 Frank LaCorte .15 .05
❑ 249 Tim Flannery .15 .05
❑ 250 Tug McGraw .30 .10
❑ 251 Fred Lynn .30 .10
❑ 252 Fred Lynn SA .15 .05
❑ 253 Chuck Baker .15 .05
❑ 254 George Bell RC 1.50 .60
❑ 255 Tony Perez .60 .25
❑ 256 Tony Perez SA .30 .10
❑ 257 Larry Harlow .15 .05
❑ 258 Bo Diaz .15 .05
❑ 259 Rodney Scott .15 .05
❑ 260 Bruce Sutter .60 .25
❑ 261 Bailey/Castilio/Rucker RC .15 .05
❑ 262 Doug Bair .15 .05
❑ 263 Victor Cruz .15 .05
❑ 264 Dan Quisenberry .15 .05
❑ 265 Al Bumbry .15 .05
❑ 266 Rick Leach .15 .05
❑ 267 Kurt Bevacqua .15 .05
❑ 268 Rickey Keeton .15 .05
❑ 269 Jim Essian .15 .05
❑ 270 Rusty Staub .30 .10
❑ 271 Larry Bradford .15 .05
❑ 272 Bump Wills .15 .05
❑ 273 Doug Bird .15 .05
❑ 274 Bob Ojeda RC .75 .30
❑ 275 Bob Watson .15 .05
❑ 276 Angels TL/Rod Carew .60 .25
❑ 277 Terry Puhl .15 .05
❑ 278 John Littlefield .15 .05
❑ 279 Bill Russell .30 .10
❑ 280 Ben Oglivie .30 .10
❑ 281 John Verhoeven .15 .05
❑ 282 Ken Macha .15 .05
❑ 283 Brian Allard .15 .05
❑ 284 Bob Grich .30 .10
❑ 285 Sparky Lyle .30 .10
❑ 286 Bill Fahey .15 .05
❑ 287 Alan Bannister .15 .05
❑ 288 Garry Templeton .30 .10
❑ 289 Bob Stanley .15 .05
❑ 290 Ken Singleton .30 .10
❑ 291 Law/Long/Ray RC .30 .10
❑ 292 David Palmer .15 .05
❑ 293 Rob Picciolo .15 .05
❑ 294 Mike LaCoss .15 .05
❑ 295 Jason Thompson .15 .05
❑ 296 Bob Walk .15 .05
❑ 297 Clint Hurdle .15 .05
❑ 298 Danny Darwin .15 .05
❑ 299 Steve Trout .15 .05
❑ 300 Reggie Jackson .60 .25
❑ 301 Reggie Jackson SA .30 .10
❑ 302 Doug Flynn .15 .05
❑ 303 Bill Caudill .15 .05
❑ 304 Johnnie LeMaster .15 .05
❑ 305 Don Sutton .30 .10
❑ 306 Don Sutton SA .15 .05
❑ 307 Randy Bass .75 .30
❑ 308 Charlie Moore .15 .05
❑ 309 Pete Redfern .15 .05
❑ 310 Mike Hargrove .15 .05
❑ 311 Dusty Baker
Burt Hooton TL .30 .10
❑ 312 Lenny Randle .15 .05
❑ 313 John Harris .15 .05
❑ 314 Buck Martinez .15 .05
❑ 315 Burt Hooton .15 .05
❑ 316 Steve Braun .15 .05
❑ 317 Dick Ruthven .15 .05
❑ 318 Mike Heath .15 .05
❑ 319 Dave Rozema .15 .05
❑ 320 Chris Chambliss .30 .10
❑ 321 Chris Chambliss SA .15 .05
❑ 322 Garry Hancock .15 .05
❑ 323 Bill Lee .30 .10
❑ 324 Steve Dillard .15 .05
❑ 325 Jose Cruz .30 .10
❑ 326 Pete Falcone .15 .05
❑ 327 Joe Nolan .15 .05
❑ 328 Ed Farmer .15 .05
❑ 329 U.L. Washington .15 .05
❑ 330 Rick Wise .15 .05
❑ 331 Benny Ayala .15 .05
❑ 332 Don Robinson .15 .05
❑ 333 DiPino/Edwards/Porter RC .15 .05
❑ 334 Aurelio Rodriguez .15 .05
❑ 335 Jim Sundberg .30 .10
❑ 336 Mariners TL
BA: Tom Paciorek
Pitching: Glenn Abb .60 .25
❑ 337 Pete Rose AS .60 .25
❑ 338 Dave Lopes AS .15 .05
❑ 339 Mike Schmidt AS 1.25 .50
❑ 340 Dave Concepcion AS .15 .05
❑ 341 Andre Dawson AS .15 .05
❑ 342A George Foster AS
(With autograph) .30 .10
❑ 342B G.Foster AS ERR NO AU 1.25 .50
❑ 343 Dave Parker AS .15 .05
❑ 344 Gary Carter AS .15 .05
❑ 345 Fernando Valenzuela AS .60 .25
❑ 346 Tom Seaver AS .30 .10
❑ 346B Tom Seaver AS COR .30 .10
❑ 347 Bruce Sutter AS .30 .10
❑ 348 Derrel Thomas .15 .05
❑ 349 George Frazier .15 .05
❑ 350 Thad Bosley .15 .05
❑ 351 Brown/Comb/House RC .15 .05
❑ 352 Dick Davis .15 .05

❑ 353 Jack O'Connor .15 .05
❑ 354 Roberto Ramos .15 .05
❑ 355 Dwight Evans .60 .25
❑ 356 Denny Lewallyn .15 .05
❑ 357 Butch Hobson .15 .05
❑ 358 Mike Parrott .15 .05
❑ 359 Jim Dwyer .15 .05
❑ 360 Len Barker .15 .05
❑ 361 Rafael Landestoy .15 .05
❑ 362 Jim Wright UER
(Wrong Jim Wright
pictured) .15 .05
❑ 363 Bob Molinaro .15 .05
❑ 364 Doyle Alexander .15 .05
❑ 365 Bill Madlock .30 .10
❑ 366 Padres TL
BA: Luis Salazar
Pitching: Juan
Eiche .60 .25
❑ 367 Jim Kaat .30 .10
❑ 368 Alex Trevino .15 .05
❑ 369 Champ Summers .15 .05
❑ 370 Mike Norris .15 .05
❑ 371 Jerry Don Gleaton .15 .05
❑ 372 Luis Gomez .15 .05
❑ 373 Gene Nelson .15 .05
❑ 374 Tim Blackwell .15 .05
❑ 375 Dusty Baker .30 .10
❑ 376 Chris Welsh .15 .05
❑ 377 Kiko Garcia .15 .05
❑ 378 Mike Caldwell .15 .05
❑ 379 Rob Wilfong .15 .05
❑ 380 Dave Stieb .30 .10
❑ 381 Bruce Hurst
Dave Schmidt RC
Julio Valdez RC .15 .05
❑ 382 Joe Simpson .15 .05
❑ 383A Pascual Perez ERR NPO 40.00 15.00
❑ 383B Pascual Perez COR .30 .10
❑ 384 Keith Moreland .15 .05
❑ 385 Ken Forsch .15 .05
❑ 386 Jerry White .15 .05
❑ 387 Tom Veryzer .15 .05
❑ 388 Joe Rudi .30 .10
❑ 389 George Vukovich .15 .05
❑ 390 Eddie Murray 1.25 .50
❑ 391 Dave Tobik .15 .05
❑ 392 Rick Bosetti .15 .05
❑ 393 Al Hrabosky .15 .05
❑ 394 Checklist 265-396 .60 .25
❑ 395 Omar Moreno .15 .05
❑ 396 Twins TL
BA: John Castino
Pitching: Fernando
Ar .60 .25
❑ 397 Ken Brett .15 .05
❑ 398 Mike Squires .15 .05
❑ 399 Pat Zachry .15 .05
❑ 400 Johnny Bench 1.25 .50
❑ 401 Johnny Bench SA .60 .25
❑ 402 Bill Stein .15 .05
❑ 403 Jim Tracy .30 .10
❑ 404 Dickie Thon .15 .05
❑ 405 Rick Reuschel .30 .10
❑ 406 Al Holland .15 .05
❑ 407 Danny Boone .15 .05
❑ 408 Ed Romero .15 .05
❑ 409 Don Cooper .15 .05
❑ 410 Ron Cey .30 .10
❑ 411 Ron Cey SA .15 .05
❑ 412 Luis Leal .15 .05
❑ 413 Dan Meyer .15 .05
❑ 414 Elias Sosa .15 .05
❑ 415 Don Baylor .30 .10
❑ 416 Marty Bystrom .15 .05
❑ 417 Pat Kelly .15 .05
❑ 418 Butcher/John/Schmidt RC .15 .05
❑ 419 Steve Stone .15 .05
❑ 420 George Hendrick .30 .10
❑ 421 Mark Clear .15 .05
❑ 422 Cliff Johnson .15 .05
❑ 423 Stan Papi .15 .05
❑ 424 Bruce Benedict .15 .05
❑ 425 John Candelaria .15 .05
❑ 426 Orioles TL/Eddie Murray .60 .25
❑ 427 Ron Oester .15 .05
❑ 428 LaMarr Hoyt .15 .05
❑ 429 John Wathan .15 .05
❑ 430 Vida Blue .30 .10
❑ 431 Vida Blue SA .15 .05
❑ 432 Mike Scott .30 .10
❑ 433 Alan Ashby .15 .05
❑ 434 Joe Lefebvre .15 .05
❑ 435 Robin Yount 2.00 .75
❑ 436 Joe Strain .15 .05
❑ 437 Juan Berenguer .15 .05
❑ 438 Pete Mackanin .15 .05
❑ 439 Dave Righetti RC 2.50 1.00
❑ 440 Jeff Burroughs .15 .05
❑ 441 Heep/Smith/Sprowl RC .15 .05
❑ 442 Bruce Kison .15 .05
❑ 443 Mark Wagner .15 .05
❑ 444 Terry Forster .30 .10
❑ 445 Larry Parrish .15 .05
❑ 446 Wayne Garland .15 .05
❑ 447 Darrell Porter .15 .05
❑ 448 Darrell Porter SA .15 .05
❑ 449 Luis Aguayo .15 .05
❑ 450 Jack Morris .30 .10
❑ 451 Ed Miller .15 .05
❑ 452 Lee Smith RC 3.00 1.25
❑ 453 Art Howe .15 .05
❑ 454 Rick Langford .15 .05
❑ 455 Tom Burgmeier .15 .05
❑ 456 Chicago Cubs TL
BA: Bill Buckner
Pitching: Randy .30 .10
❑ 457 Tim Stoddard .15 .05
❑ 458 Willie Montanez .15 .05
❑ 459 Bruce Berenyi .15 .05
❑ 460 Jack Clark .30 .10
❑ 461 Rich Dotson .15 .05
❑ 462 Dave Chalk .15 .05
❑ 463 Jim Kern .15 .05
❑ 464 Juan Bonilla RC .25 .08
❑ 465 Lee Mazzilli .30 .10
❑ 466 Randy Lerch .15 .05
❑ 467 Mickey Hatcher .15 .05
❑ 468 Floyd Bannister .15 .05
❑ 469 Ed Ott .15 .05
❑ 470 John Mayberry .15 .05
❑ 471 Hammaker/Jones/Motley RC .15 .05
❑ 472 Oscar Gamble .15 .05
❑ 473 Mike Stanton .15 .05
❑ 474 Ken Oberkfell .15 .05
❑ 475 Alan Trammell .30 .10
❑ 476 Brian Kingman .15 .05
❑ 477 Steve Yeager .30 .10
❑ 478 Ray Searage .15 .05
❑ 479 Rowland Office .15 .05
❑ 480 Steve Carlton .60 .25
❑ 481 Steve Carlton SA .30 .10
❑ 482 Glenn Hubbard .15 .05
❑ 483 Gary Woods .15 .05
❑ 484 Ivan DeJesus .15 .05
❑ 485 Kent Tekulve .15 .05
❑ 486 Yankees TL
BA: Jerry Mumphrey
Pitching: Tommy Jo .30 .10
❑ 487 Bob McClure .15 .05
❑ 488 Ron Jackson .15 .05
❑ 489 Rick Dempsey .15 .05
❑ 490 Dennis Eckersley .60 .25
❑ 491 Checklist 397-528 .60 .25
❑ 492 Joe Price .15 .05
❑ 493 Chet Lemon .30 .10
❑ 494 Hubie Brooks .15 .05
❑ 495 Dennis Leonard .15 .05
❑ 496 Johnny Grubb .15 .05
❑ 497 Jim Anderson .15 .05
❑ 498 Dave Bergman .15 .05
❑ 499 Paul Mirabella .15 .05
❑ 500 Rod Carew .60 .25
❑ 501 Rod Carew SA .30 .10
❑ 502 Brett Butler RC 1.50 .60
❑ 503 Julio Gonzalez .15 .05
❑ 504 Rick Peters .15 .05
❑ 505 Graig Nettles .30 .10
❑ 506 Graig Nettles SA .15 .05
❑ 507 Terry Harper .15 .05
❑ 508 Jody Davis .15 .05
❑ 509 Harry Spilman .15 .05
❑ 510 Fernando Valenzuela 1.25 .50
❑ 511 Ruppert Jones .15 .05
❑ 512 Jerry Dybzinski .15 .05
❑ 513 Rick Rhoden .15 .05
❑ 514 Joe Ferguson .15 .05
❑ 515 Larry Bowa .30 .10
❑ 516 Larry Bowa SA .15 .05
❑ 517 Mark Brouhard .15 .05
❑ 518 Garth Iorg .15 .05
❑ 519 Glenn Adams .15 .05
❑ 520 Mike Flanagan .15 .05
❑ 521 Bill Almon .15 .05
❑ 522 Chuck Rainey .15 .05
❑ 523 Gary Gray .15 .05
❑ 524 Tom Hausman .15 .05
❑ 525 Ray Knight .30 .10
❑ 526 Expos TL
BA: Warren Cromartie
Pitching: Bill Gul .60 .25
❑ 527 John Henry Johnson .15 .05
❑ 528 Matt Alexander .15 .05
❑ 529 Allen Ripley .15 .05
❑ 530 Dickie Noles .15 .05
❑ 531 Bordi/Budaska/Moore RC .15 .05
❑ 532 Toby Harrah .30 .10
❑ 533 Joaquin Andujar .30 .10
❑ 534 Dave McKay .15 .05
❑ 535 Lance Parrish .30 .10
❑ 536 Rafael Ramirez .15 .05
❑ 537 Doug Capilla .15 .05
❑ 538 Lou Piniella .30 .10
❑ 539 Vern Ruhle .15 .05
❑ 540 Andre Dawson .30 .10
❑ 541 Barry Evans .15 .05
❑ 542 Ned Yost .15 .05
❑ 543 Bill Robinson .15 .05
❑ 544 Larry Christenson .15 .05
❑ 545 Reggie Smith .30 .10
❑ 546 Reggie Smith SA .15 .05
❑ 547 Rod Carew AS .30 .10
❑ 548 Willie Randolph AS .15 .05
❑ 549 George Brett AS 1.50 .60
❑ 550 Bucky Dent AS .15 .05
❑ 551 Reggie Jackson AS .30 .10
❑ 552 Ken Singleton AS .15 .05
❑ 553 Dave Winfield AS .15 .05
❑ 554 Carlton Fisk AS .30 .10
❑ 555 Scott McGregor AS .15 .05
❑ 556 Jack Morris AS .15 .05
❑ 557 Rich Gossage AS .15 .05
❑ 558 John Tudor .30 .10
❑ 559 Indians TL
BA: Mike Hargrove
Pitching: Bert Blyl .30 .10
❑ 560 Doug Corbett .15 .05
❑ 561 Brum/DeLeon/Hoof RC .15 .05
❑ 562 Mike O'Berry .15 .05
❑ 563 Ross Baumgarten .15 .05
❑ 564 Doug DeCinces .15 .05
❑ 565 Jackson Todd .15 .05
❑ 566 Mike Jorgensen .15 .05
❑ 567 Bob Babcock .15 .05
❑ 568 Joe Pettini .15 .05
❑ 569 Willie Randolph .30 .10
❑ 570 Willie Randolph SA .15 .05
❑ 571 Glenn Abbott .15 .05
❑ 572 Juan Beniquez .15 .05
❑ 573 Rick Waits .15 .05
❑ 574 Mike Ramsey .15 .05
❑ 575 Al Cowens .15 .05
❑ 576 Giants TL
BA: Milt May
Pitching: Vida Blue
(Che .60 .25
❑ 577 Rick Monday .30 .10
❑ 578 Shooty Babitt .15 .05
❑ 579 Rick Mahler .15 .05
❑ 580 Bobby Bonds .30 .10
❑ 581 Ron Reed .15 .05
❑ 582 Luis Pujols .15 .05
❑ 583 Tippy Martinez .15 .05
❑ 584 Hosken Powell .15 .05
❑ 585 Rollie Fingers .30 .10
❑ 586 Rollie Fingers SA .15 .05
❑ 587 Tim Lollar .15 .05
❑ 588 Dale Berra .15 .05

❑ 589 Dave Stapleton .15 .05
❑ 590 Al Oliver .30 .10
❑ 591 Al Oliver SA .15 .05
❑ 592 Craig Swan .15 .05
❑ 593 Billy Smith .15 .05
❑ 594 Renie Martin .15 .05
❑ 595 Dave Collins .15 .05
❑ 596 Damaso Garcia .15 .05
❑ 597 Wayne Nordhagen .15 .05
❑ 598 Bob Galasso .15 .05
❑ 599 Lovig/Patt/Suth RC .15 .05
❑ 600 Dave Winfield .30 .10
❑ 601 Sid Monge .15 .05
❑ 602 Freddie Patek .15 .05
❑ 603 Rich Hebner .15 .05
❑ 604 Orlando Sanchez .15 .05
❑ 605 Steve Rogers .30 .10
❑ 606 Blue Jays TL
BA: John Mayberry
Pitching: Dave St .30 .10
❑ 607 Leon Durham .15 .05
❑ 608 Jerry Royster .15 .05
❑ 609 Rick Sutcliffe .30 .10
❑ 610 Rickey Henderson 4.00 1.50
❑ 611 Joe Niekro .15 .05
❑ 612 Gary Ward .15 .05
❑ 613 Jim Gantner .15 .05
❑ 614 Juan Eichelberger .15 .05
❑ 615 Bob Boone .30 .10
❑ 616 Bob Boone SA .15 .05
❑ 617 Scott McGregor .15 .05
❑ 618 Tim Foli .15 .05
❑ 619 Bill Campbell .15 .05
❑ 620 Ken Griffey .30 .10
❑ 621 Ken Griffey SA .15 .05
❑ 622 Dennis Lamp .15 .05
❑ 623 Gardenhire/Leach/Leary RC .75 .30
❑ 624 Fergie Jenkins .30 .10
❑ 625 Hal McRae .30 .10
❑ 626 Randy Jones .15 .05
❑ 627 Enos Cabell .15 .05
❑ 628 Bill Travers .15 .05
❑ 629 John Wockenfuss .15 .05
❑ 630 Joe Charboneau .30 .10
❑ 631 Gene Tenace .30 .10
❑ 632 Bryan Clark RC .25 .08
❑ 633 Mitchell Page .15 .05
❑ 634 Checklist 529-660 .60 .25
❑ 635 Ron Davis .15 .05
❑ 636 Phillies TL/Rose/Carlton 1.25 .50
❑ 637 Rick Camp .15 .05
❑ 638 John Milner .15 .05
❑ 639 Ken Kravec .15 .05
❑ 640 Cesar Cedeno .30 .10
❑ 641 Steve Mura .15 .05
❑ 642 Mike Scioscia .30 .10
❑ 643 Pete Vuckovich .15 .05
❑ 644 John Castino .15 .05
❑ 645 Frank White .30 .10
❑ 646 Frank White SA .15 .05
❑ 647 Warren Brusstar .15 .05
❑ 648 Jose Morales .15 .05
❑ 649 Ken Clay .15 .05
❑ 650 Carl Yastrzemski 2.00 .75
❑ 651 Carl Yastrzemski SA 1.25 .50
❑ 652 Steve Nicosia .15 .05
❑ 653 Brunansky/Sanch/Scon RC 1.50 .60
❑ 654 Jim Morrison .15 .05
❑ 655 Joel Youngblood .15 .05
❑ 656 Eddie Whitson .15 .05
❑ 657 Tom Poquette .15 .05
❑ 658 Tito Landrum .15 .05
❑ 659 Fred Martinez .15 .05
❑ 660 Dave Concepcion .30 .10
❑ 661 Dave Concepcion SA .15 .05
❑ 662 Luis Salazar .15 .05
❑ 663 Hector Cruz .15 .05
❑ 664 Dan Spillner .15 .05
❑ 665 Jim Clancy .15 .05
❑ 666 Tigers TL
BA: Steve Kemp
Pitching: Dan Petry C .60 .25
❑ 667 Jeff Reardon .30 .10
❑ 668 Dale Murphy .60 .25
❑ 669 Larry Milbourne .15 .05
❑ 670 Steve Kemp .15 .05
❑ 671 Mike Davis .15 .05
❑ 672 Bob Knepper .15 .05
❑ 673 Keith Drumwright .15 .05
❑ 674 Dave Goltz .15 .05
❑ 675 Cecil Cooper .30 .10
❑ 676 Sal Butera .15 .05
❑ 677 Alfredo Griffin .15 .05
❑ 678 Tom Paciorek .15 .05
❑ 679 Sammy Stewart .15 .05
❑ 680 Gary Matthews .30 .10
❑ 681 Marshall/Roen/Sax RC 1.50 .60
❑ 682 Jesse Jefferson .15 .05
❑ 683 Phil Garner .30 .10
❑ 684 Harold Baines .30 .10
❑ 685 Bert Blyleven .30 .10
❑ 686 Gary Allenson .15 .05
❑ 687 Greg Minton .15 .05
❑ 688 Leon Roberts .15 .05
❑ 689 Lary Sorensen .15 .05
❑ 690 Dave Kingman .30 .10
❑ 691 Dan Schatzeder .15 .05
❑ 692 Wayne Gross .15 .05
❑ 693 Cesar Geronimo .15 .05
❑ 694 Dave Wehrmeister .15 .05
❑ 695 Warren Cromartie .15 .05
❑ 696 Pirates TL
BA: Bill Madlock
Pitching: Eddie Solo .60 .25
❑ 697 John Montefusco .15 .05
❑ 698 Tony Scott .15 .05
❑ 699 Dick Tidrow .15 .05
❑ 700 George Foster .30 .10
❑ 701 George Foster SA .15 .05
❑ 702 Steve Renko .15 .05
❑ 703 Brewers TL
BA: Cecil Cooper
Pitching: Pete Vucko .60 .25
❑ 704 Mickey Rivers .15 .05
❑ 705 Mickey Rivers SA .15 .05
❑ 706 Barry Foote .15 .05
❑ 707 Mark Bomback .15 .05
❑ 708 Gene Richards .15 .05
❑ 709 Don Money .15 .05
❑ 710 Jerry Reuss .15 .05
❑ 711 Edler/Henderson/Walton RC .75 .30
❑ 712 Dennis Martinez .30 .10
❑ 713 Del Unser .15 .05
❑ 714 Jerry Koosman .30 .10
❑ 715 Willie Stargell .60 .25
❑ 716 Willie Stargell SA .30 .10
❑ 717 Rick Miller .15 .05
❑ 718 Charlie Hough .30 .10
❑ 719 Jerry Narron .15 .05
❑ 720 Greg Luzinski .30 .10
❑ 721 Greg Luzinski SA .15 .05
❑ 722 Jerry Martin .15 .05
❑ 723 Junior Kennedy .15 .05
❑ 724 Dave Rosello .15 .05
❑ 725 Amos Otis .30 .10
❑ 726 Amos Otis SA .15 .05
❑ 727 Sixto Lezcano .15 .05
❑ 728 Aurelio Lopez .15 .05
❑ 729 Jim Spencer .15 .05
❑ 730 Gary Carter .30 .10
❑ 731 Armstrong/Gwosdz/Kuhaulua RC .15 .05
❑ 732 Mike Lum .15 .05
❑ 733 Larry McWilliams .15 .05
❑ 734 Mike Ivie .15 .05
❑ 735 Rudy May .15 .05
❑ 736 Jerry Turner .15 .05
❑ 737 Reggie Cleveland .15 .05
❑ 738 Dave Engle .15 .05
❑ 739 Joey McLaughlin .15 .05
❑ 740 Dave Lopes .30 .10
❑ 741 Dave Lopes SA .15 .05
❑ 742 Dick Drago .15 .05
❑ 743 John Stearns .15 .05
❑ 744 Mike Witt .75 .30
❑ 745 Bake McBride .30 .10
❑ 746 Andre Thornton .15 .05
❑ 747 John Lowenstein .15 .05
❑ 748 Marc Hill .15 .05
❑ 749 Bob Shirley .15 .05
❑ 750 Jim Rice .30 .10
❑ 751 Rick Honeycutt .15 .05
❑ 752 Lee Lacy .15 .05
❑ 753 Tom Brookens .15 .05
❑ 754 Joe Morgan .30 .10
❑ 755 Joe Morgan SA .15 .05
❑ 756 Reds TL/Griffey/Seaver .30 .10
❑ 757 Tom Underwood .15 .05
❑ 758 Claudell Washington .15 .05
❑ 759 Paul Splittorff .15 .05
❑ 760 Bill Buckner .30 .10
❑ 761 Dave Smith .15 .05
❑ 762 Mike Phillips .15 .05
❑ 763 Tom Hume .15 .05
❑ 764 Steve Swisher .15 .05
❑ 765 Gorman Thomas .30 .10
❑ 766 Faedo/Hrbek/Laudner RC 1.50 .60
❑ 767 Roy Smalley .15 .05
❑ 768 Jerry Garvin .15 .05
❑ 769 Richie Zisk .15 .05
❑ 770 Rich Gossage .30 .10
❑ 771 Rich Gossage SA .15 .05
❑ 772 Bert Campaneris .30 .10
❑ 773 John Denny .15 .05
❑ 774 Jay Johnstone .15 .05
❑ 775 Bob Forsch .15 .05
❑ 776 Mark Belanger .15 .05
❑ 777 Tom Griffin .15 .05
❑ 778 Kevin Hickey RC .25 .08
❑ 779 Grant Jackson .15 .05
❑ 780 Pete Rose 4.00 1.50
❑ 781 Pete Rose SA 1.25 .50
❑ 782 Frank Taveras .15 .05
❑ 783 Greg Harris RC .25 .08
❑ 784 Milt Wilcox .15 .05
❑ 785 Dan Driessen .15 .05
❑ 786 Red Sox TL
BA: Carney Lansford
Pitching: Mike To .60 .25
❑ 787 Fred Stanley .15 .05
❑ 788 Woodie Fryman .15 .05
❑ 789 Checklist 661-792 .60 .25
❑ 790 Larry Gura .15 .05
❑ 791 Bobby Brown .15 .05
❑ 792 Frank Tanana .30 .10

1982 Topps Traded

❑ COMP.FACT.SET (132) 175.00 100.00
❑ 1T Doyle Alexander .50 .20
❑ 2T Jesse Barfield 3.00 1.25
❑ 3T Ross Baumgarten .50 .20
❑ 4T Steve Bedrosian 1.50 .60
❑ 5T Mark Belanger .50 .20
❑ 6T Kurt Bevacqua .50 .20
❑ 7T Tim Blackwell .50 .20
❑ 8T Vida Blue 1.00 .40
❑ 9T Bob Boone 1.00 .40
❑ 10T Larry Bowa 1.00 .40
❑ 11T Dan Briggs .50 .20
❑ 12T Bobby Brown .50 .20
❑ 13T Tom Brunansky 3.00 1.25
❑ 14T Jeff Burroughs .50 .20
❑ 15T Enos Cabell .50 .20
❑ 16T Bill Campbell .50 .20
❑ 17T Bobby Castillo .50 .20
❑ 18T Bill Caudill .50 .20
❑ 19T Cesar Cedeno 1.00 .40
❑ 20T Dave Collins .50 .20
❑ 21T Doug Corbett .50 .20
❑ 22T Al Cowens .50 .20
❑ 23T Chili Davis 3.00 1.25

❑ 24T	Dick Davis	.50	.20
❑ 25T	Ron Davis	.50	.20
❑ 26T	Doug DeCinces	.50	.20
❑ 27T	Ivan DeJesus	.50	.20
❑ 28T	Bob Dernier	.50	.20
❑ 29T	Bo Diaz	.50	.20
❑ 30T	Roger Erickson	.50	.20
❑ 31T	Jim Essian	.50	.20
❑ 32T	Ed Farmer	.50	.20
❑ 33T	Doug Flynn	.50	.20
❑ 34T	Tim Foli	.50	.20
❑ 35T	Dan Ford	.50	.20
❑ 36T	George Foster	1.00	.40
❑ 37T	Dave Frost	.50	.20
❑ 38T	Rich Gale	.50	.20
❑ 39T	Ron Gardenhire	1.50	.60
❑ 40T	Ken Griffey	1.00	.40
❑ 41T	Greg Harris	.50	.20
❑ 42T	Von Hayes	1.50	.60
❑ 43T	Larry Herndon	.50	.20
❑ 44T	Kent Hrbek	3.00	1.25
❑ 45T	Mike Ivie	.50	.20
❑ 46T	Grant Jackson	.50	.20
❑ 47T	Reggie Jackson	2.00	.75
❑ 48T	Ron Jackson	.50	.20
❑ 49T	Fergie Jenkins	1.00	.40
❑ 50T	Lamar Johnson	.50	.20
❑ 51T	Randy Johnson	.50	.20
❑ 52T	Jay Johnstone	.50	.20
❑ 53T	Mick Kelleher	.50	.20
❑ 54T	Steve Kemp	.50	.20
❑ 55T	Junior Kennedy	.50	.20
❑ 56T	Jim Kern	.50	.20
❑ 57T	Ray Knight	1.00	.40
❑ 58T	Wayne Krenchicki	.50	.20
❑ 59T	Mike Krukow	.50	.20
❑ 60T	Duane Kuiper	.50	.20
❑ 61T	Mike LaCoss	.50	.20
❑ 62T	Chet Lemon	1.00	.40
❑ 63T	Sixto Lezcano	.50	.20
❑ 64T	Dave Lopes	1.00	.40
❑ 65T	Jerry Martin	.50	.20
❑ 66T	Renie Martin	.50	.20
❑ 67T	John Mayberry	.50	.20
❑ 68T	Lee Mazzilli	1.00	.40
❑ 69T	Bake McBride	1.00	.40
❑ 70T	Dan Meyer	.50	.20
❑ 71T	Larry Milbourne	.50	.20
❑ 72T	Eddie Milner	.50	.20
❑ 73T	Sid Monge	.50	.20
❑ 74T	John Montefusco	.50	.20
❑ 75T	Jose Morales	.50	.20
❑ 76T	Keith Moreland	.50	.20
❑ 77T	Jim Morrison	.50	.20
❑ 78T	Rance Mulliniks	.50	.20
❑ 79T	Steve Mura	.50	.20
❑ 80T	Gene Nelson	.50	.20
❑ 81T	Joe Nolan	.50	.20
❑ 82T	Dickie Noles	.50	.20
❑ 83T	Al Oliver	1.00	.40
❑ 84T	Jorge Orta	.50	.20
❑ 85T	Tom Paciorek	.50	.20
❑ 86T	Larry Parrish	.50	.20
❑ 87T	Jack Perconte	.50	.20
❑ 88T	Gaylord Perry	1.00	.40
❑ 89T	Rob Picciolo	.50	.20
❑ 90T	Joe Pittman	.50	.20
❑ 91T	Hosken Powell	.50	.20
❑ 92T	Mike Proly	.50	.20
❑ 93T	Greg Pryor	.50	.20
❑ 94T	Charlie Puleo	.50	.20
❑ 95T	Shane Rawley	.50	.20
❑ 96T	Johnny Ray	1.50	.60
❑ 97T	Dave Revering	.50	.20
❑ 98T	Cal Ripken	150.00	75.00
❑ 99T	Allen Ripley	.50	.20
❑ 100T	Bill Robinson	.50	.20
❑ 101T	Aurelio Rodriguez	.50	.20
❑ 102T	Joe Rudi	1.00	.40
❑ 103T	Steve Sax	3.00	1.25
❑ 104T	Dan Schatzeder	.50	.20
❑ 105T	Bob Shirley	.50	.20
❑ 106T	Eric Show XRC	1.50	.60
❑ 107T	Roy Smalley	.50	.20
❑ 108T	Lonnie Smith	.50	.20
❑ 109T	Ozzie Smith	15.00	6.00
❑ 110T	Reggie Smith	1.00	.40
❑ 111T	Lary Sorensen	.50	.20
❑ 112T	Elias Sosa	.50	.20
❑ 113T	Mike Stanton	.50	.20
❑ 114T	Steve Stroughter	.50	.20
❑ 115T	Champ Summers	.50	.20
❑ 116T	Rick Sutcliffe	1.00	.40
❑ 117T	Frank Tanana	1.00	.40
❑ 118T	Frank Taveras	.50	.20
❑ 119T	Garry Templeton	1.00	.40
❑ 120T	Alex Trevino	.50	.20
❑ 121T	Jerry Turner	.50	.20
❑ 122T	Ed VandeBerg	.50	.20
❑ 123T	Tom Veryzer	.50	.20
❑ 124T	Ron Washington	.50	.20
❑ 125T	Bob Watson	.50	.20
❑ 126T	Dennis Werth	.50	.20
❑ 127T	Eddie Whitson	.50	.20
❑ 128T	Rob Wilfong	.50	.20
❑ 129T	Bump Wills	.50	.20
❑ 130T	Gary Woods	.50	.20
❑ 131T	Butch Wynegar	.50	.20
❑ 132T	Checklist: 1-132	.50	.20

1983 Topps

❑	COMPLETE SET (792)	80.00	40.00
❑ 1	Tony Armas RB	.30	.10
❑ 2	Rickey Henderson RB	1.25	.50
❑ 3	Greg Minton RB	.15	.05
❑ 4	Lance Parrish RB	.15	.05
❑ 5	Manny Trillo RB	.15	.05
❑ 6	John Wathan RB	.15	.05
❑ 7	Gene Richards	.15	.05
❑ 8	Steve Balboni	.15	.05
❑ 9	Joey McLaughlin	.15	.05
❑ 10	Gorman Thomas	.30	.10
❑ 11	Billy Gardner MG	.15	.05
❑ 12	Paul Mirabella	.15	.05
❑ 13	Larry Herndon	.15	.05
❑ 14	Frank LaCorte	.15	.05
❑ 15	Ron Cey	.30	.10
❑ 16	George Vukovich	.15	.05
❑ 17	Kent Tekulve	.15	.05
❑ 18	Kent Tekulve SV	.15	.05
❑ 19	Oscar Gamble	.15	.05
❑ 20	Carlton Fisk	.60	.25
❑ 21	Orioles TL/Murray/Palmer	.60	.25
❑ 22	Randy Martz	.15	.05
❑ 23	Mike Heath	.15	.05
❑ 24	Steve Mura	.15	.05
❑ 25	Hal McRae	.30	.10
❑ 26	Jerry Royster	.15	.05
❑ 27	Doug Corbett	.15	.05
❑ 28	Bruce Bochte	.15	.05
❑ 29	Randy Jones	.15	.05
❑ 30	Jim Rice	.30	.10
❑ 31	Bill Gullickson	.15	.05
❑ 32	Dave Bergman	.15	.05
❑ 33	Jack O'Connor	.15	.05
❑ 34	Paul Householder	.15	.05
❑ 35	Rollie Fingers	.30	.10
❑ 36	Rollie Fingers SV	.15	.05
❑ 37	Darrell Johnson MG	.15	.05
❑ 38	Tim Flannery	.15	.05
❑ 39	Terry Puhl	.15	.05
❑ 40	Fernando Valenzuela	.30	.10
❑ 41	Jerry Turner	.15	.05
❑ 42	Dale Murray	.15	.05
❑ 43	Bob Dernier	.15	.05
❑ 44	Don Robinson	.15	.05
❑ 45	John Mayberry	.15	.05
❑ 46	Richard Dotson	.15	.05
❑ 47	Dave McKay	.15	.05
❑ 48	Lary Sorensen	.15	.05
❑ 49	Willie McGee RC	2.50	1.00
❑ 50	Bob Horner UER	.30	.10
❑ 51	Cubs TL/F.Jenkins	.15	.05
❑ 52	Onix Concepcion	.15	.05
❑ 53	Mike Witt	.15	.05
❑ 54	Jim Maler	.15	.05
❑ 55	Mookie Wilson	.30	.10
❑ 56	Chuck Rainey	.15	.05
❑ 57	Tim Blackwell	.15	.05
❑ 58	Al Holland	.15	.05
❑ 59	Benny Ayala	.15	.05
❑ 60	Johnny Bench	1.25	.50
❑ 61	Johnny Bench SV	.60	.25
❑ 62	Bob McClure	.15	.05
❑ 63	Rick Monday	.30	.10
❑ 64	Bill Stein	.15	.05
❑ 65	Jack Morris	.30	.10
❑ 66	Bob Lillis MG	.15	.05
❑ 67	Sal Butera	.15	.05
❑ 68	Eric Show RC	.75	.30
❑ 69	Lee Lacy	.15	.05
❑ 70	Steve Carlton	.60	.25
❑ 71	Steve Carlton SV	.30	.10
❑ 72	Tom Paciorek	.15	.05
❑ 73	Allen Ripley	.15	.05
❑ 74	Julio Gonzalez	.15	.05
❑ 75	Amos Otis	.30	.10
❑ 76	Rick Mahler	.15	.05
❑ 77	Hosken Powell	.15	.05
❑ 78	Bill Caudill	.15	.05
❑ 79	Mick Kelleher	.15	.05
❑ 80	George Foster	.30	.10
❑ 81	J.Mumphrey/D.Righetti TL	.30	.10
❑ 82	Bruce Hurst	.15	.05
❑ 83	Ryne Sandberg RC	15.00	6.00
❑ 84	Milt May	.15	.05
❑ 85	Ken Singleton	.30	.10
❑ 86	Tom Hume	.15	.05
❑ 87	Joe Rudi	.30	.10
❑ 88	Jim Gantner	.15	.05
❑ 89	Leon Roberts	.15	.05
❑ 90	Jerry Reuss	.15	.05
❑ 91	Larry Milbourne	.15	.05
❑ 92	Mike LaCoss	.15	.05
❑ 93	John Castino	.15	.05
❑ 94	Dave Edwards	.15	.05
❑ 95	Alan Trammell	.30	.10
❑ 96	Dick Howser MG	.15	.05
❑ 97	Ross Baumgarten	.15	.05
❑ 98	Vance Law	.15	.05
❑ 99	Dickie Noles	.15	.05
❑ 100	Pete Rose	4.00	1.50
❑ 101	Pete Rose SV	1.25	.50
❑ 102	Dave Beard	.15	.05
❑ 103	Darrell Porter	.15	.05
❑ 104	Bob Walk	.15	.05
❑ 105	Don Baylor	.30	.10
❑ 106	Gene Nelson	.15	.05
❑ 107	Mike Jorgensen	.15	.05
❑ 108	Glenn Hoffman	.15	.05
❑ 109	Luis Leal	.15	.05
❑ 110	Ken Griffey	.30	.10
❑ 111	Montreal Expos TL BA: Al Oliver ERA: Steve Roger	.30	.10
❑ 112	Bob Shirley	.15	.05
❑ 113	Ron Roenicke	.15	.05
❑ 114	Jim Slaton	.15	.05
❑ 115	Chili Davis	.30	.10
❑ 116	Dave Schmidt	.15	.05
❑ 117	Alan Knicely	.15	.05
❑ 118	Chris Welsh	.15	.05
❑ 119	Tom Brookens	.15	.05
❑ 120	Len Barker	.15	.05
❑ 121	Mickey Hatcher	.15	.05
❑ 122	Jimmy Smith	.15	.05
❑ 123	George Frazier	.15	.05
❑ 124	Marc Hill	.15	.05
❑ 125	Leon Durham	.15	.05
❑ 126	Joe Torre MG	.30	.10

❑ 127 Preston Hanna .15 .05
❑ 128 Mike Ramsey .15 .05
❑ 129 Checklist: 1-132 .30 .10
❑ 130 Dave Stieb .30 .10
❑ 131 Ed Ott .15 .05
❑ 132 Todd Cruz .15 .05
❑ 133 Jim Barr .15 .05
❑ 134 Hubie Brooks .15 .05
❑ 135 Dwight Evans .60 .25
❑ 136 Willie Aikens .15 .05
❑ 137 Woodie Fryman .15 .05
❑ 138 Rick Dempsey .15 .05
❑ 139 Bruce Berenyi .15 .05
❑ 140 Willie Randolph .30 .10
❑ 141 Indians TL
BA: Toby Harrah
ERA: Rick Sutcliffe .30 .10
❑ 142 Mike Caldwell .15 .05
❑ 143 Joe Pettini .15 .05
❑ 144 Mark Wagner .15 .05
❑ 145 Don Sutton .30 .10
❑ 146 Don Sutton SV .15 .05
❑ 147 Rick Leach .15 .05
❑ 148 Dave Roberts .15 .05
❑ 149 Johnny Ray .15 .05
❑ 150 Bruce Sutter .60 .25
❑ 151 Bruce Sutter SV .30 .10
❑ 152 Jay Johnstone .15 .05
❑ 153 Jerry Koosman .30 .10
❑ 154 Johnnie LeMaster .15 .05
❑ 155 Dan Quisenberry .15 .05
❑ 156 Billy Martin MG .60 .25
❑ 157 Steve Bedrosian .15 .05
❑ 158 Rob Wilfong .15 .05
❑ 159 Mike Stanton .15 .05
❑ 160 Dave Kingman .30 .10
❑ 161 Dave Kingman SV .15 .05
❑ 162 Mark Clear .15 .05
❑ 163 Cal Ripken 10.00 4.00
❑ 164 David Palmer .15 .05
❑ 165 Dan Driessen .15 .05
❑ 166 John Pacella .15 .05
❑ 167 Mark Brouhard .15 .05
❑ 168 Juan Eichelberger .15 .05
❑ 169 Doug Flynn .15 .05
❑ 170 Steve Howe .15 .05
❑ 171 Giants TL/Joe Morgan .30 .10
❑ 172 Vern Ruhle .15 .05
❑ 173 Jim Morrison .15 .05
❑ 174 Jerry Ujdur .15 .05
❑ 175 Bo Diaz .15 .05
❑ 176 Dave Righetti .30 .10
❑ 177 Harold Baines .30 .10
❑ 178 Luis Tiant .30 .10
❑ 179 Luis Tiant SV .15 .05
❑ 180 Rickey Henderson 2.50 1.00
❑ 181 Terry Felton .15 .05
❑ 182 Mike Fischlin .15 .05
❑ 183 Ed VandeBerg .15 .05
❑ 184 Bob Clark .15 .05
❑ 185 Tim Lollar .15 .05
❑ 186 Whitey Herzog MG .30 .10
❑ 187 Terry Leach .15 .05
❑ 188 Rick Miller .15 .05
❑ 189 Dan Schatzeder .15 .05
❑ 190 Cecil Cooper .30 .10
❑ 191 Joe Price .15 .05
❑ 192 Floyd Rayford .15 .05
❑ 193 Harry Spilman .15 .05
❑ 194 Cesar Geronimo .15 .05
❑ 195 Bob Stoddard .15 .05
❑ 196 Bill Fahey .15 .05
❑ 197 Jim Eisenreich RC .75 .30
❑ 198 Kiko Garcia .15 .05
❑ 199 Marty Bystrom .15 .05
❑ 200 Rod Carew .60 .25
❑ 201 Rod Carew SV .30 .10
❑ 202 Blue Jays TL
BA: Damaso Garcia
ERA: Dave Stieb .30 .10
❑ 203 Mike Morgan .15 .05
❑ 204 Junior Kennedy .15 .05
❑ 205 Dave Parker .30 .10
❑ 206 Ken Oberkfell .15 .05
❑ 207 Rick Camp .15 .05
❑ 208 Dan Meyer .15 .05
❑ 209 Mike Moore RC .75 .30
❑ 210 Jack Clark .30 .10
❑ 211 John Denny .15 .05
❑ 212 John Stearns .15 .05
❑ 213 Tom Burgmeier .15 .05
❑ 214 Jerry White .15 .05
❑ 215 Mario Soto .30 .10
❑ 216 Tony LaRussa MG .30 .10
❑ 217 Tim Stoddard .15 .05
❑ 218 Roy Howell .15 .05
❑ 219 Mike Armstrong .15 .05
❑ 220 Dusty Baker .30 .10
❑ 221 Joe Niekro .15 .05
❑ 222 Damaso Garcia .15 .05
❑ 223 John Montefusco .15 .05
❑ 224 Mickey Rivers .15 .05
❑ 225 Enos Cabell .15 .05
❑ 226 Enrique Romo .15 .05
❑ 227 Chris Bando .15 .05
❑ 228 Joaquin Andujar .30 .10
❑ 229 Phillies TL/S.Carlton .15 .05
❑ 230 Fergie Jenkins .30 .10
❑ 231 Fergie Jenkins SV .15 .05
❑ 232 Tom Brunansky .30 .10
❑ 233 Wayne Gross .15 .05
❑ 234 Larry Andersen .15 .05
❑ 235 Claudell Washington .15 .05
❑ 236 Steve Renko .15 .05
❑ 237 Dan Norman .15 .05
❑ 238 Bud Black RC .75 .30
❑ 239 Dave Stapleton .15 .05
❑ 240 Rich Gossage .30 .10
❑ 241 Rich Gossage SV .15 .05
❑ 242 Joe Nolan .15 .05
❑ 243 Duane Walker .15 .05
❑ 244 Dwight Bernard .15 .05
❑ 245 Steve Sax .30 .10
❑ 246 George Bamberger MG .15 .05
❑ 247 Dave Smith .15 .05
❑ 248 Bake McBride .30 .10
❑ 249 Checklist: 133-264 .30 .10
❑ 250 Bill Buckner .30 .10
❑ 251 Alan Wiggins .15 .05
❑ 252 Luis Aguayo .15 .05
❑ 253 Larry McWilliams .15 .05
❑ 254 Rick Cerone .15 .05
❑ 255 Gene Garber .15 .05
❑ 256 Gene Garber SV .15 .05
❑ 257 Jesse Barfield .30 .10
❑ 258 Manny Castillo .15 .05
❑ 259 Jeff Jones .15 .05
❑ 260 Steve Kemp .15 .05
❑ 261 Tigers TL
BA: Larry Herndon
ERA: Dan Petry
(Che .30 .10
❑ 262 Ron Jackson .15 .05
❑ 263 Renie Martin .15 .05
❑ 264 Jamie Quirk .15 .05
❑ 265 Joel Youngblood .15 .05
❑ 266 Paul Boris .15 .05
❑ 267 Terry Francona .30 .10
❑ 268 Storm Davis RC .75 .30
❑ 269 Ron Oester .15 .05
❑ 270 Dennis Eckersley .60 .25
❑ 271 Ed Romero .15 .05
❑ 272 Frank Tanana .30 .10
❑ 273 Mark Belanger .15 .05
❑ 274 Terry Kennedy .15 .05
❑ 275 Ray Knight .30 .10
❑ 276 Gene Mauch MG .15 .05
❑ 277 Rance Mulliniks .15 .05
❑ 278 Kevin Hickey .15 .05
❑ 279 Greg Gross .15 .05
❑ 280 Bert Blyleven .30 .10
❑ 281 Andre Robertson .15 .05
❑ 282 R.Smith w/Sandberg 1.25 .50
❑ 283 Reggie Smith SV .15 .05
❑ 284 Jeff Lahti .15 .05
❑ 285 Lance Parrish .30 .10
❑ 286 Rick Langford .15 .05
❑ 287 Bobby Brown .15 .05
❑ 288 Joe Cowley .15 .05
❑ 289 Jerry Dybzinski .15 .05
❑ 290 Jeff Reardon .30 .10
❑ 291 Bill Madlock
John Candelaria TL .30 .10
❑ 292 Craig Swan .15 .05
❑ 293 Glenn Gulliver .15 .05
❑ 294 Dave Engle .15 .05
❑ 295 Jerry Remy .15 .05
❑ 296 Greg Harris .15 .05
❑ 297 Ned Yost .15 .05
❑ 298 Floyd Chiffer .15 .05
❑ 299 George Wright RC .75 .30
❑ 300 Mike Schmidt 3.00 1.25
❑ 301 Mike Schmidt SV 1.25 .50
❑ 302 Ernie Whitt .15 .05
❑ 303 Miguel Dilone .15 .05
❑ 304 Dave Rucker .15 .05
❑ 305 Larry Bowa .30 .10
❑ 306 Tom Lasorda MG .60 .25
❑ 307 Lou Piniella .30 .10
❑ 308 Jesus Vega .15 .05
❑ 309 Jeff Leonard .15 .05
❑ 310 Greg Luzinski .30 .10
❑ 311 Glenn Brummer .15 .05
❑ 312 Brian Kingman .15 .05
❑ 313 Gary Gray .15 .05
❑ 314 Ken Dayley .15 .05
❑ 315 Rick Burleson .15 .05
❑ 316 Paul Splittorff .15 .05
❑ 317 Gary Rajsich .15 .05
❑ 318 John Tudor .30 .10
❑ 319 Lenn Sakata .15 .05
❑ 320 Steve Rogers .30 .10
❑ 321 Brewers TL/Robin Yount 1.25 .50
❑ 322 Dave Van Gorder .15 .05
❑ 323 Luis DeLeon .15 .05
❑ 324 Mike Marshall .15 .05
❑ 325 Von Hayes .15 .05
❑ 326 Garth Iorg .15 .05
❑ 327 Bobby Castillo .15 .05
❑ 328 Craig Reynolds .15 .05
❑ 329 Randy Niemann .15 .05
❑ 330 Buddy Bell .30 .10
❑ 331 Mike Krukow .15 .05
❑ 332 Glenn Wilson .75 .30
❑ 333 Dave LaRoche .15 .05
❑ 334 Dave LaRoche SV .15 .05
❑ 335 Steve Henderson .15 .05
❑ 336 Rene Lachemann MG .15 .05
❑ 337 Tito Landrum .15 .05
❑ 338 Bob Owchinko .15 .05
❑ 339 Terry Harper .15 .05
❑ 340 Larry Gura .15 .05
❑ 341 Doug DeCinces .15 .05
❑ 342 Atlee Hammaker .15 .05
❑ 343 Bob Bailor .15 .05
❑ 344 Roger LaFrancois .15 .05
❑ 345 Jim Clancy .15 .05
❑ 346 Joe Pittman .15 .05
❑ 347 Sammy Stewart .15 .05
❑ 348 Alan Bannister .15 .05
❑ 349 Checklist: 265-396 .30 .10
❑ 350 Robin Yount 2.00 .75
❑ 351 Reds TL
BA: Cesar Cedeno
ERA: Mario Soto
(Check .30 .10
❑ 352 Mike Scioscia .30 .10
❑ 353 Steve Comer .15 .05
❑ 354 Randy Johnson .15 .05
❑ 355 Jim Bibby .15 .05
❑ 356 Gary Woods .15 .05
❑ 357 Len Matuszek .15 .05
❑ 358 Jerry Garvin .15 .05
❑ 359 Dave Collins .15 .05
❑ 360 Nolan Ryan 6.00 2.50
❑ 361 Nolan Ryan SV 3.00 1.25
❑ 362 Bill Almon .15 .05
❑ 363 John Stuper .15 .05
❑ 364 Brett Butler .30 .10
❑ 365 Dave Lopes .30 .10
❑ 366 Dick Williams MG .15 .05
❑ 367 Bud Anderson .15 .05
❑ 368 Richie Zisk .15 .05
❑ 369 Jesse Orosco .15 .05
❑ 370 Gary Carter .30 .10
❑ 371 Mike Richardt .15 .05
❑ 372 Terry Crowley .15 .05
❑ 373 Kevin Saucier .15 .05

❑ 374 Wayne Krenchicki .15 .05
❑ 375 Pete Vuckovich .15 .05
❑ 376 Ken Landreaux .15 .05
❑ 377 Lee May .15 .05
❑ 378 Lee May SV .15 .05
❑ 379 Guy Sularz .15 .05
❑ 380 Ron Davis .15 .05
❑ 381 Red Sox TL
BA: Jim Rice
ERA: Bob Stanley
(Check) .30 .10
❑ 382 Bob Knepper .15 .05
❑ 383 Ozzie Virgil .15 .05
❑ 384 Dave Dravecky RC 1.50 .60
❑ 385 Mike Easler .15 .05
❑ 386 Rod Carew AS .30 .10
❑ 387 Bob Grich AS .15 .05
❑ 388 George Brett AS 1.50 .60
❑ 389 Robin Yount AS 1.25 .50
❑ 390 Reggie Jackson AS .30 .10
❑ 391 Rickey Henderson AS 1.25 .50
❑ 392 Fred Lynn AS .15 .05
❑ 393 Carlton Fisk AS .30 .10
❑ 394 Pete Vuckovich AS .15 .05
❑ 395 Larry Gura AS .15 .05
❑ 396 Dan Quisenberry AS .15 .05
❑ 397 Pete Rose AS .60 .25
❑ 398 Manny Trillo AS .15 .05
❑ 399 Mike Schmidt AS 1.25 .50
❑ 400 Dave Concepcion AS .15 .05
❑ 401 Dale Murphy AS .30 .10
❑ 402 Andre Dawson AS .15 .05
❑ 403 Tim Raines AS .15 .05
❑ 404 Gary Carter AS .15 .05
❑ 405 Steve Rogers AS .15 .05
❑ 406 Steve Carlton AS .30 .10
❑ 407 Bruce Sutter AS .30 .10
❑ 408 Rudy May .15 .05
❑ 409 Marvis Foley .15 .05
❑ 410 Phil Niekro .30 .10
❑ 411 Phil Niekro SV .15 .05
❑ 412 Rangers TL
BA: Buddy Bell
ERA: Charlie Hough C .30 .10
❑ 413 Matt Keough .15 .05
❑ 414 Julio Cruz .15 .05
❑ 415 Bob Forsch .15 .05
❑ 416 Joe Ferguson .15 .05
❑ 417 Tom Hausman .15 .05
❑ 418 Greg Pryor .15 .05
❑ 419 Steve Crawford .15 .05
❑ 420 Al Oliver .30 .10
❑ 421 Al Oliver SV .15 .05
❑ 422 George Cappuzzello .15 .05
❑ 423 Tom Lawless .15 .05
❑ 424 Jerry Augustine .15 .05
❑ 425 Pedro Guerrero .30 .10
❑ 426 Earl Weaver MG .30 .10
❑ 427 Roy Lee Jackson .15 .05
❑ 428 Champ Summers .15 .05
❑ 429 Eddie Whitson .15 .05
❑ 430 Kirk Gibson .30 .10
❑ 431 Gary Gaetti RC 1.50 .60
❑ 432 Porfirio Altamirano .15 .05
❑ 433 Dale Berra .15 .05
❑ 434 Dennis Lamp .15 .05
❑ 435 Tony Armas .30 .10
❑ 436 Bill Campbell .15 .05
❑ 437 Rick Sweet .15 .05
❑ 438 Dave LaPoint .15 .05
❑ 439 Rafael Ramirez .15 .05
❑ 440 Ron Guidry .30 .10
❑ 441 Astros TL
BA: Ray Knight
ERA: Joe Niekro
(Check) .30 .10
❑ 442 Brian Downing .30 .10
❑ 443 Don Hood .15 .05
❑ 444 Wally Backman .15 .05
❑ 445 Mike Flanagan .15 .05
❑ 446 Reid Nichols .15 .05
❑ 447 Bryn Smith .15 .05
❑ 448 Darrell Evans .30 .10
❑ 449 Eddie Milner .15 .05
❑ 450 Ted Simmons .30 .10
❑ 451 Ted Simmons SV .15 .05
❑ 452 Lloyd Moseby .15 .05
❑ 453 Lamar Johnson .15 .05
❑ 454 Bob Welch .30 .10
❑ 455 Sixto Lezcano .15 .05
❑ 456 Lee Elia MG .15 .05
❑ 457 Milt Wilcox .15 .05
❑ 458 Ron Washington .15 .05
❑ 459 Ed Farmer .15 .05
❑ 460 Roy Smalley .15 .05
❑ 461 Steve Trout .15 .05
❑ 462 Steve Nicosia .15 .05
❑ 463 Gaylord Perry .30 .10
❑ 464 Gaylord Perry SV .15 .05
❑ 465 Lonnie Smith .15 .05
❑ 466 Tom Underwood .15 .05
❑ 467 Rufino Linares .15 .05
❑ 468 Dave Goltz .15 .05
❑ 469 Ron Gardenhire .15 .05
❑ 470 Greg Minton .15 .05
❑ 471 Kansas City Royals TL
BA: Willie Wilson
ERA: Vid .30 .10
❑ 472 Gary Allenson .15 .05
❑ 473 John Lowenstein .15 .05
❑ 474 Ray Burris .15 .05
❑ 475 Cesar Cedeno .30 .10
❑ 476 Rob Picciolo .15 .05
❑ 477 Tom Niedenfuer .15 .05
❑ 478 Phil Garner .30 .10
❑ 479 Charlie Hough .30 .10
❑ 480 Toby Harrah .30 .10
❑ 481 Scot Thompson .15 .05
❑ 482 Tony Gwynn RC 25.00 10.00
❑ 483 Lynn Jones .15 .05
❑ 484 Dick Ruthven .15 .05
❑ 485 Omar Moreno .15 .05
❑ 486 Clyde King MG .15 .05
❑ 487 Jerry Hairston .15 .05
❑ 488 Alfredo Griffin .15 .05
❑ 489 Tom Herr .15 .05
❑ 490 Jim Palmer .30 .10
❑ 491 Jim Palmer SV .15 .05
❑ 492 Paul Serna .15 .05
❑ 493 Steve McCatty .15 .05
❑ 494 Bob Brenly .15 .05
❑ 495 Warren Cromartie .15 .05
❑ 496 Tom Veryzer .15 .05
❑ 497 Rick Sutcliffe .30 .10
❑ 498 Wade Boggs RC 15.00 6.00
❑ 499 Jeff Little .15 .05
❑ 500 Reggie Jackson .60 .25
❑ 501 Reggie Jackson SV .30 .10
❑ 502 Braves TL/Murphy/Niekro .60 .25
❑ 503 Moose Haas .15 .05
❑ 504 Don Werner .15 .05
❑ 505 Garry Templeton .30 .10
❑ 506 Jim Gott RC .75 .30
❑ 507 Tony Scott .15 .05
❑ 508 Tom Filer .15 .05
❑ 509 Lou Whitaker .30 .10
❑ 510 Tug McGraw .30 .10
❑ 511 Tug McGraw SV .15 .05
❑ 512 Doyle Alexander .15 .05
❑ 513 Fred Stanley .15 .05
❑ 514 Rudy Law .15 .05
❑ 515 Gene Tenace .30 .10
❑ 516 Bill Virdon MG .15 .05
❑ 517 Gary Ward .15 .05
❑ 518 Bill Laskey .15 .05
❑ 519 Terry Bulling .15 .05
❑ 520 Fred Lynn .30 .10
❑ 521 Bruce Benedict .15 .05
❑ 522 Pat Zachry .15 .05
❑ 523 Carney Lansford .30 .10
❑ 524 Tom Brennan .15 .05
❑ 525 Frank White .30 .10
❑ 526 Checklist: 397-528 .30 .10
❑ 527 Larry Biittner .15 .05
❑ 528 Jamie Easterly .15 .05
❑ 529 Tim Laudner .15 .05
❑ 530 Eddie Murray 1.25 .50
❑ 531 A's TL/Rickey Henderson 1.25 .50
❑ 532 Dave Stewart .30 .10
❑ 533 Luis Salazar .15 .05
❑ 534 John Butcher .15 .05
❑ 535 Manny Trillo .15 .05
❑ 536 John Wockenfuss .15 .05
❑ 537 Rod Scurry .15 .05
❑ 538 Danny Heep .15 .05
❑ 539 Roger Erickson .15 .05
❑ 540 Ozzie Smith 2.00 .75
❑ 541 Britt Burns .15 .05
❑ 542 Jody Davis .15 .05
❑ 543 Alan Fowlkes .15 .05
❑ 544 Larry Whisenton .15 .05
❑ 545 Floyd Bannister .15 .05
❑ 546 Dave Garcia MG .15 .05
❑ 547 Geoff Zahn .15 .05
❑ 548 Brian Giles .15 .05
❑ 549 Charlie Puleo .15 .05
❑ 550 Carl Yastrzemski 2.00 .75
❑ 551 Carl Yastrzemski SV 1.25 .50
❑ 552 Tim Wallach .30 .10
❑ 553 Dennis Martinez .30 .10
❑ 554 Mike Vail .15 .05
❑ 555 Steve Yeager .30 .10
❑ 556 Willie Upshaw .15 .05
❑ 557 Rick Honeycutt .15 .05
❑ 558 Dickie Thon .15 .05
❑ 559 Pete Redfern .15 .05
❑ 560 Ron LeFlore .30 .10
❑ 561 Cardinals TL
BA: Lonnie Smith
ERA: Joaquin Anduj .30 .10
❑ 562 Dave Rozema .15 .05
❑ 563 Juan Bonilla .15 .05
❑ 564 Sid Monge .15 .05
❑ 565 Bucky Dent .30 .10
❑ 566 Manny Sarmiento .15 .05
❑ 567 Joe Simpson .15 .05
❑ 568 Willie Hernandez .15 .05
❑ 569 Jack Perconte .15 .05
❑ 570 Vida Blue .30 .10
❑ 571 Mickey Klutts .15 .05
❑ 572 Bob Watson .15 .05
❑ 573 Andy Hassler .15 .05
❑ 574 Glenn Adams .15 .05
❑ 575 Neil Allen .15 .05
❑ 576 Frank Robinson MG .60 .25
❑ 577 Luis Aponte .15 .05
❑ 578 David Green RC .75 .30
❑ 579 Rich Dauer .15 .05
❑ 580 Tom Seaver 1.25 .50
❑ 581 Tom Seaver SV .30 .10
❑ 582 Marshall Edwards .15 .05
❑ 583 Terry Forster .30 .10
❑ 584 Dave Hostetler .15 .05
❑ 585 Jose Cruz .30 .10
❑ 586 Frank Viola RC 2.50 1.00
❑ 587 Ivan DeJesus .15 .05
❑ 588 Pat Underwood .15 .05
❑ 589 Alvis Woods .15 .05
❑ 590 Tony Pena .15 .05
❑ 591 White Sox TL
BA: Greg Luzinski
ERA: LaMarr Hoyt# .30 .10
❑ 592 Shane Rawley .15 .05
❑ 593 Broderick Perkins .15 .05
❑ 594 Eric Rasmussen .15 .05
❑ 595 Tim Raines .30 .10
❑ 596 Randy Johnson .15 .05
❑ 597 Mike Proly .15 .05
❑ 598 Dwayne Murphy .15 .05
❑ 599 Don Aase .15 .05
❑ 600 George Brett 3.00 1.25
❑ 601 Ed Lynch .15 .05
❑ 602 Rich Gedman .15 .05
❑ 603 Joe Morgan .30 .10
❑ 604 Joe Morgan SV .15 .05
❑ 605 Gary Roenicke .15 .05
❑ 606 Bobby Cox MG .30 .10
❑ 607 Charlie Leibrandt .15 .05
❑ 608 Don Money .15 .05
❑ 609 Danny Darwin .15 .05
❑ 610 Steve Garvey .30 .10
❑ 611 Bert Roberge .15 .05
❑ 612 Steve Swisher .15 .05
❑ 613 Mike Ivie .15 .05
❑ 614 Ed Glynn .15 .05
❑ 615 Garry Maddox .15 .05
❑ 616 Bill Nahorodny .15 .05
❑ 617 Butch Wynegar .15 .05

❑ 618 LaMarr Hoyt	.15	.05
❑ 619 Keith Moreland	.15	.05
❑ 620 Mike Norris	.15	.05
❑ 621 New York Mets TL		
BA: Mookie Wilson		
ERA: Craig Sw	.30	.10
❑ 622 Dave Edler	.15	.05
❑ 623 Luis Sanchez	.15	.05
❑ 624 Glenn Hubbard	.15	.05
❑ 625 Ken Forsch	.15	.05
❑ 626 Jerry Martin	.15	.05
❑ 627 Doug Bair	.15	.05
❑ 628 Julio Valdez	.15	.05
❑ 629 Charlie Lea	.15	.05
❑ 630 Paul Molitor	.30	.10
❑ 631 Tippy Martinez	.15	.05
❑ 632 Alex Trevino	.15	.05
❑ 633 Vicente Romo	.15	.05
❑ 634 Max Venable	.15	.05
❑ 635 Graig Nettles	.30	.10
❑ 636 Graig Nettles SV	.15	.05
❑ 637 Pat Corrales MG	.15	.05
❑ 638 Dan Petry	.15	.05
❑ 639 Art Howe	.15	.05
❑ 640 Andre Thornton	.15	.05
❑ 641 Billy Sample	.15	.05
❑ 642 Checklist: 529-660	.30	.10
❑ 643 Bump Wills	.15	.05
❑ 644 Joe Lefebvre	.15	.05
❑ 645 Bill Madlock	.30	.10
❑ 646 Jim Essian	.15	.05
❑ 647 Bobby Mitchell	.15	.05
❑ 648 Jeff Burroughs	.15	.05
❑ 649 Tommy Boggs	.15	.05
❑ 650 George Hendrick	.30	.10
❑ 651 Angels TL/Rod Carew	.30	.10
❑ 652 Butch Hobson	.15	.05
❑ 653 Ellis Valentine	.15	.05
❑ 654 Bob Ojeda	.15	.05
❑ 655 Al Bumbry	.15	.05
❑ 656 Dave Frost	.15	.05
❑ 657 Mike Gates	.15	.05
❑ 658 Frank Pastore	.15	.05
❑ 659 Charlie Moore	.15	.05
❑ 660 Mike Hargrove	.15	.05
❑ 661 Bill Russell	.30	.10
❑ 662 Joe Sambito	.15	.05
❑ 663 Tom O'Malley	.15	.05
❑ 664 Bob Molinaro	.15	.05
❑ 665 Jim Sundberg	.30	.10
❑ 666 Sparky Anderson MG	.30	.10
❑ 667 Dick Davis	.15	.05
❑ 668 Larry Christenson	.15	.05
❑ 669 Mike Squires	.15	.05
❑ 670 Jerry Mumphrey	.15	.05
❑ 671 Lenny Faedo	.15	.05
❑ 672 Jim Kaat	.30	.10
❑ 673 Jim Kaat SV	.15	.05
❑ 674 Kurt Bevacqua	.15	.05
❑ 675 Jim Beattie	.15	.05
❑ 676 Biff Pocoroba	.15	.05
❑ 677 Dave Revering	.15	.05
❑ 678 Juan Beniquez	.15	.05
❑ 679 Mike Scott	.30	.10
❑ 680 Andre Dawson	.30	.10
❑ 681 Dodgers Leaders		
BA: Pedro Guerrero		
ERA: Fernando	.30	.10
❑ 682 Bob Stanley	.15	.05
❑ 683 Dan Ford	.15	.05
❑ 684 Rafael Landestoy	.15	.05
❑ 685 Lee Mazzilli	.30	.10
❑ 686 Randy Lerch	.15	.05
❑ 687 U.L. Washington	.15	.05
❑ 688 Jim Wohlford	.15	.05
❑ 689 Ron Hassey	.15	.05
❑ 690 Kent Hrbek	.30	.10
❑ 691 Dave Tobik	.15	.05
❑ 692 Denny Walling	.15	.05
❑ 693 Sparky Lyle	.30	.10
❑ 694 Sparky Lyle SV	.15	.05
❑ 695 Ruppert Jones	.15	.05
❑ 696 Chuck Tanner MG	.15	.05
❑ 697 Barry Foote	.15	.05
❑ 698 Tony Bernazard	.15	.05
❑ 699 Lee Smith	.60	.25
❑ 700 Keith Hernandez	.30	.10
❑ 701 Willie Wilson		
Al Oliver LL	.30	.10
❑ 702 Reggie/Thomas/Kingman LL	.30	.10
❑ 703 RBI Leaders		
AL: Hal McRae		
NL: Dale Murphy		
NL: A	.60	.25
❑ 704 R.Henderson/T.Raines LL	1.25	.50
❑ 705 L.Hoyt/S.Carlton LL	.30	.10
❑ 706 F.Bannister/Carlton LL	.30	.10
❑ 707 Rick Sutcliffe		
Steve Rogers LL	.30	.10
❑ 708 Leading Firemen		
AL: Dan Quisenberry		
NL: Bruce Su	.30	.10
❑ 709 Jimmy Sexton	.15	.05
❑ 710 Willie Wilson	.30	.10
❑ 711 Mariners TL		
BA: Bruce Bochte		
ERA: Jim Beattie	.30	.10
❑ 712 Bruce Kison	.15	.05
❑ 713 Ron Hodges	.15	.05
❑ 714 Wayne Nordhagen	.15	.05
❑ 715 Tony Perez	.60	.25
❑ 716 Tony Perez SV	.30	.10
❑ 717 Scott Sanderson	.15	.05
❑ 718 Jim Dwyer	.15	.05
❑ 719 Rich Gale	.15	.05
❑ 720 Dave Concepcion	.30	.10
❑ 721 John Martin	.15	.05
❑ 722 Jorge Orta	.15	.05
❑ 723 Randy Moffitt	.15	.05
❑ 724 Johnny Grubb	.15	.05
❑ 725 Dan Spillner	.15	.05
❑ 726 Harvey Kuenn MG	.15	.05
❑ 727 Chet Lemon	.30	.10
❑ 728 Ron Reed	.15	.05
❑ 729 Jerry Morales	.15	.05
❑ 730 Jason Thompson	.15	.05
❑ 731 Al Williams	.15	.05
❑ 732 Dave Henderson	.15	.05
❑ 733 Buck Martinez	.15	.05
❑ 734 Steve Braun	.15	.05
❑ 735 Tommy John	.30	.10
❑ 736 Tommy John SV	.15	.05
❑ 737 Mitchell Page	.15	.05
❑ 738 Tim Foli	.15	.05
❑ 739 Rick Ownbey	.15	.05
❑ 740 Rusty Staub	.30	.10
❑ 741 Rusty Staub SV	.15	.05
❑ 742 Padres TL		
BA: Terry Kennedy		
ERA: Tim Lollar		
(Ch)	.30	.10
❑ 743 Mike Torrez	.15	.05
❑ 744 Brad Mills	.15	.05
❑ 745 Scott McGregor	.15	.05
❑ 746 John Wathan	.15	.05
❑ 747 Fred Breining	.15	.05
❑ 748 Derrel Thomas	.15	.05
❑ 749 Jon Matlack	.15	.05
❑ 750 Ben Oglivie	.30	.10
❑ 751 Brad Havens	.15	.05
❑ 752 Luis Pujols	.15	.05
❑ 753 Elias Sosa	.15	.05
❑ 754 Bill Robinson	.15	.05
❑ 755 John Candelaria	.15	.05
❑ 766 Russ Nixon MG	.15	.05
❑ 757 Rick Manning	.15	.05
❑ 758 Aurelio Rodriguez	.15	.05
❑ 759 Doug Bird	.15	.05
❑ 760 Dale Murphy	.60	.25
❑ 761 Gary Lucas	.15	.05
❑ 762 Cliff Johnson	.15	.05
❑ 763 Al Cowens	.15	.05
❑ 764 Pete Falcone	.15	.05
❑ 765 Bob Boone	.30	.10
❑ 766 Barry Bonnell	.15	.05
❑ 767 Duane Kuiper	.15	.05
❑ 768 Chris Speier	.15	.05
❑ 769 Checklist: 661-792	.30	.10
❑ 770 Dave Winfield	.30	.10
❑ 771 Twins TL		
BA: Kent Hrbek		
ERA: Bobby Castillo		
(Ch)	.30	.10
❑ 772 Jim Kern	.15	.05
❑ 773 Larry Hisle	.15	.05
❑ 774 Alan Ashby	.15	.05
❑ 775 Burt Hooton	.15	.05
❑ 776 Larry Parrish	.15	.05
❑ 777 John Curtis	.15	.05
❑ 778 Rich Hebner	.15	.05
❑ 779 Rick Waits	.15	.05
❑ 780 Gary Matthews	.30	.10
❑ 781 Rick Rhoden	.15	.05
❑ 782 Bobby Murcer	.30	.10
❑ 783 Bobby Murcer SV	.15	.05
❑ 784 Jeff Newman	.15	.05
❑ 785 Dennis Leonard	.15	.05
❑ 786 Ralph Houk MG	.15	.05
❑ 787 Dick Tidrow	.15	.05
❑ 788 Dane Iorg	.15	.05
❑ 789 Bryan Clark	.15	.05
❑ 790 Bob Grich	.30	.10
❑ 791 Gary Lavelle	.15	.05
❑ 792 Chris Chambliss	.30	.10
❑ XX Game Insert Card	.10	.05

1983 Topps Traded

❑ COMP.FACT.SET (132)	40.00	15.00
❑ 1T Neil Allen	.25	.08
❑ 2T Bill Almon	.25	.08
❑ 3T Joe Altobelli MG	.25	.08
❑ 4T Tony Armas	1.00	.40
❑ 5T Doug Bair	.25	.08
❑ 6T Steve Baker	.25	.08
❑ 7T Floyd Bannister	.25	.08
❑ 8T Don Baylor	1.00	.40
❑ 9T Tony Bernazard	.25	.08
❑ 10T Larry Biittner	.25	.08
❑ 11T Dann Bilardello	.25	.08
❑ 12T Doug Bird	.25	.08
❑ 13T Steve Boros MG	.25	.08
❑ 14T Greg Brock	.25	.08
❑ 15T Mike C. Brown	.25	.08
❑ 16T Tom Burgmeier	.25	.08
❑ 17T Randy Bush	.25	.08
❑ 18T Bert Campaneris	1.00	.40
❑ 19T Ron Cey	1.00	.40
❑ 20T Chris Codiroli	.25	.08
❑ 21T Dave Collins	.25	.08
❑ 22T Terry Crowley	.25	.08
❑ 23T Julio Cruz	.25	.08
❑ 24T Mike Davis	.25	.08
❑ 25T Frank DiPino	.25	.08
❑ 26T Bill Doran XRC	1.00	.40
❑ 27T Jerry Dybzinski	.25	.08
❑ 28T Jamie Easterly	.25	.08
❑ 29T Juan Eichelberger	.25	.08
❑ 30T Jim Essian	.25	.08
❑ 31T Pete Falcone	.25	.08
❑ 32T Mike Ferraro MG	.25	.08
❑ 33T Terry Forster	1.00	.40
❑ 34T Julio Franco XRC	8.00	3.00
❑ 35T Rich Gale	.25	.08
❑ 36T Kiko Garcia	.25	.08
❑ 37T Steve Garvey	1.00	.40
❑ 38T Johnny Grubb	.25	.08
❑ 39T Mel Hall XRC	1.00	.40
❑ 40T Von Hayes	.25	.08
❑ 41T Danny Heep	.25	.08

❑ 42T Steve Henderson .25 .08
❑ 43T Keith Hernandez 1.00 .40
❑ 44T Leo Hernandez .25 .08
❑ 45T Willie Hernandez .25 .08
❑ 46T Al Holland .25 .08
❑ 47T Frank Howard MG 1.00 .40
❑ 48T Bobby Johnson .25 .08
❑ 49T Cliff Johnson .25 .08
❑ 50T Odell Jones .25 .08
❑ 51T Mike Jorgensen .25 .08
❑ 52T Bob Kearney .25 .08
❑ 53T Steve Kemp .25 .08
❑ 54T Matt Keough .25 .08
❑ 55T Ron Kittle XRC 2.00 .75
❑ 56T Mickey Klutts .25 .08
❑ 57T Alan Knicely .25 .08
❑ 58T Mike Krukow .25 .08
❑ 59T Rafael Landestoy .25 .08
❑ 60T Carney Lansford 1.00 .40
❑ 61T Joe Lefebvre .25 .08
❑ 62T Bryan Little .25 .08
❑ 63T Aurelio Lopez .25 .08
❑ 64T Mike Madden .25 .08
❑ 65T Rick Manning .25 .08
❑ 66T Billy Martin MG 2.00 .75
❑ 67T Lee Mazzilli 1.00 .40
❑ 68T Andy McGaffigan .25 .08
❑ 69T Craig McMurtry .25 .08
❑ 70T John McNamara MG .25 .08
❑ 71T Orlando Mercado .25 .08
❑ 72T Larry Milbourne .25 .08
❑ 73T Randy Moffitt .25 .08
❑ 74T Sid Monge .25 .08
❑ 75T Jose Morales .25 .08
❑ 76T Omar Moreno .25 .08
❑ 77T Joe Morgan 1.00 .40
❑ 78T Mike Morgan .25 .08
❑ 79T Dale Murray .25 .08
❑ 80T Jeff Newman .25 .08
❑ 81T Pete O'Brien XRC 1.00 .40
❑ 82T Jorge Orta .25 .08
❑ 83T Alejandro Pena XRC 2.00 .75
❑ 84T Pascual Perez .25 .08
❑ 85T Tony Perez 2.00 .75
❑ 86T Broderick Perkins .25 .08
❑ 87T Tony Phillips XRC 2.00 .75
❑ 88T Charlie Puleo .25 .08
❑ 89T Pat Putnam .25 .08
❑ 90T Jamie Quirk .25 .08
❑ 91T Doug Rader MG .25 .08
❑ 92T Chuck Rainey .25 .08
❑ 93T Bobby Ramos .25 .08
❑ 94T Gary Redus XRC 1.00 .40
❑ 95T Steve Renko .25 .08
❑ 96T Leon Roberts .25 .08
❑ 97T Aurelio Rodriguez .25 .08
❑ 98T Dick Ruthven .25 .08
❑ 99T Daryl Sconiers .25 .08
❑ 100T Mike Scott 1.00 .40
❑ 101T Tom Seaver 2.00 .75
❑ 102T John Shelby .25 .08
❑ 103T Bob Shirley .25 .08
❑ 104T Joe Simpson .25 .08
❑ 105T Doug Sisk .25 .08
❑ 106T Mike Smithson .25 .08
❑ 107T Elias Sosa .25 .08
❑ 108T Darryl Strawberry XRC 20.00 8.00
❑ 109T Tom Tellmann .25 .08
❑ 110T Gene Tenace 1.00 .40
❑ 111T Gorman Thomas 1.00 .40
❑ 112T Dick Tidrow .25 .08
❑ 113T Dave Tobik .25 .08
❑ 114T Wayne Tolleson .25 .08
❑ 115T Mike Torrez .25 .08
❑ 116T Manny Trillo .25 .08
❑ 117T Steve Trout .25 .08
❑ 118T Lee Tunnell .25 .08
❑ 119T Mike Vail .25 .08
❑ 120T Ellis Valentine .25 .08
❑ 121T Tom Veryzer .25 .08
❑ 122T George Vukovich .25 .08
❑ 123T Rick Waits .25 .08
❑ 124T Greg Walker 1.00 .40
❑ 125T Chris Welsh .25 .08
❑ 126T Len Whitehouse .25 .08
❑ 127T Eddie Whitson .25 .08
❑ 128T Jim Wohlford .25 .08
❑ 129T Matt Young XRC 1.00 .40
❑ 130T Joel Youngblood .25 .08
❑ 131T Pat Zachry .25 .08
❑ 132T Checklist 1T-132T .25 .08

1984 Topps

❑ COMPLETE SET (792) 50.00 20.00
❑ 1 Steve Carlton HL .25 .08
❑ 2 Rickey Henderson HL .60 .25
❑ 3 Dan Quisenberry HL Sets save record .15 .05
❑ 4 N.Ryan/Carlton/Perry HL 1.00 .40
❑ 5 Dave Righetti& Bob Forsch& and Mike Warren HL .25 .08
❑ 6 J.Bench/G.Perry/C.Yaz HL .40 .15
❑ 7 Gary Lucas .15 .05
❑ 8 Don Mattingly RC 15.00 6.00
❑ 9 Jim Gott .15 .05
❑ 10 Robin Yount 1.00 .40
❑ 11 Minnesota Twins TL Kent Hrbek Ken Schrom (Check) .25 .08
❑ 12 Billy Sample .15 .05
❑ 13 Scott Holman .15 .05
❑ 14 Tom Brookens .25 .08
❑ 15 Burt Hooton .15 .05
❑ 16 Omar Moreno .15 .05
❑ 17 John Denny .15 .05
❑ 18 Dale Berra .15 .05
❑ 19 Ray Fontenot .15 .05
❑ 20 Greg Luzinski .25 .08
❑ 21 Joe Altobelli MG .15 .05
❑ 22 Bryan Clark .15 .05
❑ 23 Keith Moreland .15 .05
❑ 24 John Martin .15 .05
❑ 25 Glenn Hubbard .15 .05
❑ 26 Bud Black .15 .05
❑ 27 Daryl Sconiers .15 .05
❑ 28 Frank Viola .40 .15
❑ 29 Danny Heep .15 .05
❑ 30 Wade Boggs 1.50 .60
❑ 31 Andy McGaffigan .15 .05
❑ 32 Bobby Ramos .15 .05
❑ 33 Tom Burgmeier .15 .05
❑ 34 Eddie Milner .15 .05
❑ 35 Don Sutton .25 .08
❑ 36 Denny Walling .15 .05
❑ 37 Texas Rangers TL Buddy Bell Rick Honeycutt (Che) .25 .08
❑ 38 Luis DeLeon .15 .05
❑ 39 Garth Iorg .15 .05
❑ 40 Dusty Baker .25 .08
❑ 41 Tony Bernazard .15 .05
❑ 42 Johnny Grubb .15 .05
❑ 43 Ron Reed .15 .05
❑ 44 Jim Morrison .15 .05
❑ 45 Jerry Mumphrey .15 .05
❑ 46 Ray Smith .15 .05
❑ 47 Rudy Law .15 .05
❑ 48 Julio Franco .25 .08
❑ 49 John Stuper .15 .05
❑ 50 Chris Chambliss .25 .08
❑ 51 Jim Frey MG .15 .05
❑ 52 Paul Splittorff .15 .05
❑ 53 Juan Beniquez .15 .05
❑ 54 Jesse Orosco .15 .05
❑ 55 Dave Concepcion .25 .08
❑ 56 Gary Allenson .15 .05
❑ 57 Dan Schatzeder .15 .05
❑ 58 Max Venable .15 .05
❑ 59 Sammy Stewart .15 .05
❑ 60 Paul Molitor .25 .08
❑ 61 Chris Codiroli .15 .05
❑ 62 Dave Hostetler .15 .05
❑ 63 Ed VandeBerg .15 .05
❑ 64 Mike Scioscia .25 .08
❑ 65 Kirk Gibson .60 .25
❑ 66 Astros TL/Nolan Ryan 1.00 .40
❑ 67 Gary Ward .15 .05
❑ 68 Luis Salazar .15 .05
❑ 69 Rod Scurry .15 .05
❑ 70 Gary Matthews .25 .08
❑ 71 Leo Hernandez .15 .05
❑ 72 Mike Squires .15 .05
❑ 73 Jody Davis .15 .05
❑ 74 Jerry Martin .15 .05
❑ 75 Bob Forsch .15 .05
❑ 76 Alfredo Griffin .15 .05
❑ 77 Brett Butler .25 .08
❑ 78 Mike Torrez .15 .05
❑ 79 Rob Wilfong .15 .05
❑ 80 Steve Rogers .25 .08
❑ 81 Billy Martin MG .40 .15
❑ 82 Doug Bird .15 .05
❑ 83 Richie Zisk .15 .05
❑ 84 Lenny Faedo .15 .05
❑ 85 Atlee Hammaker .15 .05
❑ 86 John Shelby .15 .05
❑ 87 Frank Pastore .15 .05
❑ 88 Rob Picciolo .15 .05
❑ 89 Mike Smithson .15 .05
❑ 90 Pedro Guerrero .25 .08
❑ 91 Dan Spillner .15 .05
❑ 92 Lloyd Moseby .15 .05
❑ 93 Bob Knepper .15 .05
❑ 94 Mario Ramirez .15 .05
❑ 95 Aurelio Lopez .25 .08
❑ 96 Kansas City Royals TL Hal McRae Larry Gura (Che) .25 .08
❑ 97 LaMarr Hoyt .15 .05
❑ 98 Steve Nicosia .15 .05
❑ 99 Craig Lefferts RC .15 .05
❑ 100 Reggie Jackson .40 .15
❑ 101 Porfirio Altamirano .15 .05
❑ 102 Ken Oberkfell .15 .05
❑ 103 Dwayne Murphy .15 .05
❑ 104 Ken Dayley .15 .05
❑ 105 Tony Armas .25 .08
❑ 106 Tim Stoddard .15 .05
❑ 107 Ned Yost .15 .05
❑ 108 Randy Moffitt .15 .05
❑ 109 Brad Wellman .15 .05
❑ 110 Ron Guidry .25 .08
❑ 111 Bill Virdon MG .15 .05
❑ 112 Tom Niedenfuer .15 .05
❑ 113 Kelly Paris .15 .05
❑ 114 Checklist 1-132 .25 .08
❑ 115 Andre Thornton .15 .05
❑ 116 George Bjorkman .15 .05
❑ 117 Tom Veryzer .15 .05
❑ 118 Charlie Hough .25 .08
❑ 119 John Wockenfuss .15 .05
❑ 120 Keith Hernandez .25 .08
❑ 121 Pat Sheridan .15 .05
❑ 122 Cecilio Guante .15 .05
❑ 123 Butch Wynegar .15 .05
❑ 124 Damaso Garcia .15 .05
❑ 125 Britt Burns .15 .05
❑ 126 Braves TL/Dale Murphy .40 .15
❑ 127 Mike Madden .15 .05
❑ 128 Rick Manning .15 .05
❑ 129 Bill Laskey .15 .05
❑ 130 Ozzie Smith 1.00 .40
❑ 131 W.Boggs/B.Madlock LL .60 .25
❑ 132 Mike Schmidt/J.Rice LL .60 .25
❑ 133 D.Murphy/Coop/Rice LL .40 .15

❑ 134 T.Raines/R.Henderson LL .60 .25
❑ 135 John Denny
LaMarr Hoyt LL .60 .25
❑ 136 S.Carlton/J.Morris LL .25 .08
❑ 137 A.Hammaker/R.Honeycutt LL .25 .08
❑ 138 Al Holland
Dan Quisenberry LL .25 .08
❑ 139 Bert Campaneris .25 .08
❑ 140 Storm Davis .15 .05
❑ 141 Pat Corrales MG .15 .05
❑ 142 Rich Gale .15 .05
❑ 143 Jose Morales .15 .05
❑ 144 Brian Harper RC .40 .15
❑ 145 Gary Lavelle .15 .05
❑ 146 Ed Romero .15 .05
❑ 147 Dan Petry .25 .08
❑ 148 Joe Lefebvre .15 .05
❑ 149 Jon Matlack .15 .05
❑ 150 Dale Murphy .40 .15
❑ 151 Steve Trout .15 .05
❑ 152 Glenn Brummer .15 .05
❑ 153 Dick Tidrow .15 .05
❑ 154 Dave Henderson .25 .08
❑ 155 Frank White .25 .08
❑ 156 A's TL/Rickey Henderson .60 .25
❑ 157 Gary Gaetti .40 .15
❑ 158 John Curtis .15 .05
❑ 159 Darryl Cias .15 .05
❑ 160 Mario Soto .25 .08
❑ 161 Junior Ortiz .15 .05
❑ 162 Bob Ojeda .15 .05
❑ 163 Lorenzo Gray .15 .05
❑ 164 Scott Sanderson .15 .05
❑ 165 Ken Singleton .25 .08
❑ 166 Jamie Nelson .15 .05
❑ 167 Marshall Edwards .15 .05
❑ 168 Juan Bonilla .15 .05
❑ 169 Larry Parrish .15 .05
❑ 170 Jerry Reuss .15 .05
❑ 171 Frank Robinson MG .40 .15
❑ 172 Frank DiPino .15 .05
❑ 173 Marvell Wynne .40 .15
❑ 174 Juan Berenguer .15 .05
❑ 175 Graig Nettles .25 .08
❑ 176 Lee Smith .25 .08
❑ 177 Jerry Hairston .15 .05
❑ 178 Bill Krueger RC .15 .05
❑ 179 Buck Martinez .15 .05
❑ 180 Manny Trillo .15 .05
❑ 181 Roy Thomas .15 .05
❑ 182 Darryl Strawberry RC 3.00 1.25
❑ 183 Al Williams .15 .05
❑ 184 Mike O'Berry .15 .05
❑ 185 Sixto Lezcano .15 .05
❑ 186 Cardinal TL
Lonnie Smith
John Stuper
(Checklist .25 .08
❑ 187 Luis Aponte .15 .05
❑ 188 Bryan Little .15 .05
❑ 189 Tim Conroy .15 .05
❑ 190 Ben Oglivie .25 .08
❑ 191 Mike Boddicker .15 .05
❑ 192 Nick Esasky .15 .05
❑ 193 Darrell Brown .15 .05
❑ 194 Domingo Ramos .15 .05
❑ 195 Jack Morris .25 .08
❑ 196 Don Slaught .25 .08
❑ 197 Garry Hancock .15 .05
❑ 198 Bill Doran RC* .40 .15
❑ 199 Willie Hernandez .15 .05
❑ 200 Andre Dawson .25 .08
❑ 201 Bruce Kison .15 .05
❑ 202 Bobby Cox MG .25 .08
❑ 203 Matt Keough .15 .05
❑ 204 Bobby Meacham .15 .05
❑ 205 Greg Minton .15 .05
❑ 206 Andy Van Slyke RC 1.50 .60
❑ 207 Donnie Moore .15 .05
❑ 208 Jose Oquendo RC .40 .15
❑ 209 Manny Sarmiento .15 .05
❑ 210 Joe Morgan .25 .08
❑ 211 Rick Sweet .15 .05
❑ 212 Broderick Perkins .15 .05
❑ 213 Bruce Hurst .15 .05
❑ 214 Paul Householder .15 .05
❑ 215 Tippy Martinez .15 .05
❑ 216 White Sox TL/C.Fisk .25 .08
❑ 217 Alan Ashby .15 .05
❑ 218 Rick Waits .15 .05
❑ 219 Joe Simpson .15 .05
❑ 220 Fernando Valenzuela .25 .08
❑ 221 Cliff Johnson .15 .05
❑ 222 Rick Honeycutt .15 .05
❑ 223 Wayne Krenchicki .15 .05
❑ 224 Sid Monge .15 .05
❑ 225 Lee Mazzilli .25 .08
❑ 226 Juan Eichelberger .15 .05
❑ 227 Steve Braun .15 .05
❑ 228 John Rabb .15 .05
❑ 229 Paul Owens MG .15 .05
❑ 230 Rickey Henderson 1.00 .40
❑ 231 Gary Woods .15 .05
❑ 232 Tim Wallach .15 .05
❑ 233 Checklist 133-264 .25 .08
❑ 234 Rafael Ramirez .15 .05
❑ 235 Matt Young RC .40 .15
❑ 236 Ellis Valentine .15 .05
❑ 237 John Castino .15 .05
❑ 238 Reid Nichols .15 .05
❑ 239 Jay Howell .15 .05
❑ 240 Eddie Murray .60 .25
❑ 241 Bill Almon .15 .05
❑ 242 Alex Trevino .15 .05
❑ 243 Pete Ladd .15 .05
❑ 244 Candy Maldonado .15 .05
❑ 245 Rick Sutcliffe .25 .08
❑ 246 Mets TL/Tom Seaver .25 .08
❑ 247 Onix Concepcion .15 .05
❑ 248 Bill Dawley .15 .05
❑ 249 Jay Johnstone .15 .05
❑ 250 Bill Madlock .25 .08
❑ 251 Tony Gwynn 2.50 1.00
❑ 252 Larry Christenson .15 .05
❑ 253 Jim Wohlford .15 .05
❑ 254 Shane Rawley .15 .05
❑ 255 Bruce Benedict .15 .05
❑ 256 Dave Geisel .15 .05
❑ 257 Julio Cruz .15 .05
❑ 258 Luis Sanchez .15 .05
❑ 259 Sparky Anderson MG .25 .08
❑ 260 Scott McGregor .15 .05
❑ 261 Bobby Brown .15 .05
❑ 262 Tom Candiotti RC .75 .30
❑ 263 Jack Fimple .15 .05
❑ 264 Doug Frobel RC .15 .05
❑ 265 Donnie Hill .15 .05
❑ 266 Steve Lubratich .15 .05
❑ 267 Carmelo Martinez .15 .05
❑ 268 Jack O'Connor .15 .05
❑ 269 Aurelio Rodriguez .15 .05
❑ 270 Jeff Russell RC .40 .15
❑ 271 Moose Haas .15 .05
❑ 272 Rick Dempsey .15 .05
❑ 273 Charlie Puleo .15 .05
❑ 274 Rick Monday .25 .08
❑ 275 Len Matuszek .15 .05
❑ 276 Angels TL/Rod Carew .25 .08
❑ 277 Eddie Whitson .15 .05
❑ 278 George Bell .25 .08
❑ 279 Ivan DeJesus .15 .05
❑ 280 Floyd Bannister .15 .05
❑ 281 Larry Milbourne .15 .05
❑ 282 Jim Barr .15 .05
❑ 283 Larry Biittner .15 .05
❑ 284 Howard Bailey .15 .05
❑ 285 Darrell Porter .15 .05
❑ 286 Lary Sorensen .15 .05
❑ 287 Warren Cromartie .15 .05
❑ 288 Jim Beattie .15 .05
❑ 289 Randy Johnson .15 .05
❑ 290 Dave Dravecky .15 .05
❑ 291 Chuck Tanner MG .15 .05
❑ 292 Tony Scott .15 .05
❑ 293 Ed Lynch .15 .05
❑ 294 U.L. Washington .15 .05
❑ 295 Mike Flanagan .15 .05
❑ 296 Jeff Newman .15 .05
❑ 297 Bruce Berenyi .15 .05
❑ 298 Jim Gantner .15 .05
❑ 299 John Butcher .15 .05
❑ 300 Pete Rose 2.00 .75
❑ 301 Frank LaCorte .15 .05
❑ 302 Barry Bonnell .15 .05
❑ 303 Marty Castillo .15 .05
❑ 304 Warren Brusstar .15 .05
❑ 305 Roy Smalley .15 .05
❑ 306 Dodgers TL
Pedro Guerrero
Bob Welch
(Checklist) .25 .08
❑ 307 Bobby Mitchell .15 .05
❑ 308 Ron Hassey .15 .05
❑ 309 Tony Phillips RC .75 .30
❑ 310 Willie McGee .25 .08
❑ 311 Jerry Koosman .25 .08
❑ 312 Jorge Orta .15 .05
❑ 313 Mike Jorgensen .15 .05
❑ 314 Orlando Mercado .15 .05
❑ 315 Bob Grich .25 .08
❑ 316 Mark Bradley .15 .05
❑ 317 Greg Pryor .15 .05
❑ 318 Bill Gullickson .15 .05
❑ 319 Al Bumbry .15 .05
❑ 320 Bob Stanley .15 .05
❑ 321 Harvey Kuenn MG .15 .05
❑ 322 Ken Schrom .15 .05
❑ 323 Alan Knicely .15 .05
❑ 324 Alejandro Pena RC* .75 .30
❑ 325 Darrell Evans .25 .08
❑ 326 Bob Kearney .15 .05
❑ 327 Ruppert Jones .15 .05
❑ 328 Vern Ruhle .15 .05
❑ 329 Pat Tabler .15 .05
❑ 330 John Candelaria .15 .05
❑ 331 Bucky Dent .25 .08
❑ 332 Kevin Gross RC .40 .15
❑ 333 Larry Herndon .25 .08
❑ 334 Chuck Rainey .15 .05
❑ 335 Don Baylor .25 .08
❑ 336 Seattle Mariners TL
Pat Putnam
Matt Young
(Chec) .25 .08
❑ 337 Kevin Hagen .15 .05
❑ 338 Mike Warren .15 .05
❑ 339 Roy Lee Jackson .15 .05
❑ 340 Hal McRae .25 .08
❑ 341 Dave Tobik .15 .05
❑ 342 Tim Foli .15 .05
❑ 343 Mark Davis .15 .05
❑ 344 Rick Miller .15 .05
❑ 345 Kent Hrbek .25 .08
❑ 346 Kurt Bevacqua .15 .05
❑ 347 Allan Ramirez .15 .05
❑ 348 Toby Harrah .25 .08
❑ 349 Bob L. Gibson RC .15 .05
❑ 350 George Foster .25 .08
❑ 351 Russ Nixon MG .15 .05
❑ 352 Dave Stewart .25 .08
❑ 353 Jim Anderson .15 .05
❑ 354 Jeff Burroughs .15 .05
❑ 355 Jason Thompson .15 .05
❑ 356 Glenn Abbott .15 .05
❑ 357 Ron Cey .25 .08
❑ 358 Bob Dernier .15 .05
❑ 359 Jim Acker .15 .05
❑ 360 Willie Randolph .25 .08
❑ 361 Dave Smith .15 .05
❑ 362 David Green .15 .05
❑ 363 Tim Laudner .15 .05
❑ 364 Scott Fletcher .15 .05
❑ 365 Steve Bedrosian .15 .05
❑ 366 Padres TL
Terry Kennedy
Dave Dravecky
(Checklis) .25 .08
❑ 367 Jamie Easterly .15 .05
❑ 368 Hubie Brooks .15 .05
❑ 369 Steve McCatty .15 .05
❑ 370 Tim Raines .25 .08
❑ 371 Dave Gumpert .15 .05
❑ 372 Gary Roenicke .15 .05
❑ 373 Bill Scherrer .15 .05
❑ 374 Don Money .15 .05
❑ 375 Dennis Leonard .15 .05
❑ 376 Dave Anderson RC .15 .05
❑ 377 Danny Darwin .15 .05

Card		
❑ 378 Bob Brenly	.15	.05
❑ 379 Checklist 265-396	.25	.08
❑ 380 Steve Garvey	.25	.08
❑ 381 Ralph Houk MG	.15	.05
❑ 382 Chris Nyman	.15	.05
❑ 383 Terry Puhl	.15	.05
❑ 384 Lee Tunnell	.15	.05
❑ 385 Tony Perez	.40	.15
❑ 386 George Hendrick AS	.15	.05
❑ 387 Johnny Ray AS	.15	.05
❑ 388 Mike Schmidt AS	.60	.25
❑ 389 Ozzie Smith AS	.60	.25
❑ 390 Tim Raines AS	.15	.05
❑ 391 Dale Murphy AS	.25	.08
❑ 392 Andre Dawson AS	.15	.05
❑ 393 Gary Carter AS	.15	.05
❑ 394 Steve Rogers AS	.15	.05
❑ 395 Steve Carlton AS	.25	.08
❑ 396 Jesse Orosco AS	.15	.05
❑ 397 Eddie Murray AS	.40	.15
❑ 398 Lou Whitaker AS	.15	.05
❑ 399 George Brett AS	.60	.25
❑ 400 Cal Ripken AS	2.00	.75
❑ 401 Jim Rice AS	.15	.05
❑ 402 Dave Winfield AS	.15	.05
❑ 403 Lloyd Moseby AS	.15	.05
❑ 404 Ted Simmons AS	.15	.05
❑ 405 LaMarr Hoyt AS	.15	.05
❑ 406 Ron Guidry AS	.15	.05
❑ 407 Dan Quisenberry AS	.15	.05
❑ 408 Lou Piniella	.25	.08
❑ 409 Juan Agosto	.15	.05
❑ 410 Claudell Washington	.15	.05
❑ 411 Houston Jimenez	.15	.05
❑ 412 Doug Rader MG	.15	.05
❑ 413 Spike Owen RC	.40	.15
❑ 414 Mitchell Page	.15	.05
❑ 415 Tommy John	.25	.08
❑ 416 Dane Iorg	.15	.05
❑ 417 Mike Armstrong	.15	.05
❑ 418 Ron Hodges	.15	.05
❑ 419 John Henry Johnson	.15	.05
❑ 420 Cecil Cooper	.25	.08
❑ 421 Charlie Lea	.15	.05
❑ 422 Jose Cruz	.25	.08
❑ 423 Mike Morgan	.15	.05
❑ 424 Dann Bilardello	.15	.05
❑ 425 Steve Howe	.15	.05
❑ 426 Orioles TL/Cal Ripken	1.50	.60
❑ 427 Rick Leach	.15	.05
❑ 428 Fred Breining	.15	.05
❑ 429 Randy Bush	.15	.05
❑ 430 Rusty Staub	.25	.08
❑ 431 Chris Bando	.15	.05
❑ 432 Charles Hudson	.15	.05
❑ 433 Rich Hebner	.15	.05
❑ 434 Harold Baines	.25	.08
❑ 435 Neil Allen	.15	.05
❑ 436 Rick Peters	.15	.05
❑ 437 Mike Proly	.15	.05
❑ 438 Biff Pocoroba	.15	.05
❑ 439 Bob Stoddard	.15	.05
❑ 440 Steve Kemp	.15	.05
❑ 441 Bob Lillis MG	.15	.05
❑ 442 Byron McLaughlin	.15	.05
❑ 443 Benny Ayala	.15	.05
❑ 444 Steve Renko	.15	.05
❑ 445 Jerry Remy	.15	.05
❑ 446 Luis Pujols	.15	.05
❑ 447 Tom Brunansky	.15	.05
❑ 448 Ben Hayes	.15	.05
❑ 449 Joe Pettini	.15	.05
❑ 450 Gary Carter	.25	.08
❑ 451 Bob Jones	.15	.05
❑ 452 Chuck Porter	.15	.05
❑ 453 Willie Upshaw	.15	.05
❑ 454 Joe Beckwith	.15	.05
❑ 455 Terry Kennedy	.15	.05
❑ 456 Cubs TL/F.Jenkins	.15	.05
❑ 457 Dave Rozema	.15	.05
❑ 458 Kiko Garcia	.15	.05
❑ 459 Kevin Hickey	.15	.05
❑ 460 Dave Winfield	.25	.08
❑ 461 Jim Maler	.15	.05
❑ 462 Lee Lacy	.15	.05
❑ 463 Dave Engle	.15	.05
❑ 464 Jeff A. Jones	.15	.05
❑ 465 Mookie Wilson	.25	.08
❑ 466 Gene Garber	.15	.05
❑ 467 Mike Ramsey	.15	.05
❑ 468 Geoff Zahn	.15	.05
❑ 469 Tom O'Malley	.15	.05
❑ 470 Nolan Ryan	3.00	1.25
❑ 471 Dick Howser MG	.15	.05
❑ 472 Mike G. Brown RC	.15	.05
❑ 473 Jim Dwyer	.15	.05
❑ 474 Greg Bargar	.15	.05
❑ 475 Gary Redus RC*	.40	.15
❑ 476 Tom Tellmann	.15	.05
❑ 477 Rafael Landestoy	.15	.05
❑ 478 Alan Bannister	.15	.05
❑ 479 Frank Tanana	.25	.08
❑ 480 Ron Kittle	.15	.05
❑ 481 Mark Thurmond	.15	.05
❑ 482 Enos Cabell	.15	.05
❑ 483 Fergie Jenkins	.25	.08
❑ 484 Ozzie Virgil	.15	.05
❑ 485 Rick Rhoden	.15	.05
❑ 486 D.Baylor/R.Guidry TL	.25	.08
❑ 487 Ricky Adams	.15	.05
❑ 488 Jesse Barfield	.25	.08
❑ 489 Dave Von Ohlen	.15	.05
❑ 490 Cal Ripken	4.00	1.50
❑ 491 Bobby Castillo	.15	.05
❑ 492 Tucker Ashford	.15	.05
❑ 493 Mike Norris	.15	.05
❑ 494 Chili Davis	.25	.08
❑ 495 Rollie Fingers	.25	.08
❑ 496 Terry Francona	.25	.08
❑ 497 Bud Anderson	.15	.05
❑ 498 Rich Gedman	.15	.05
❑ 499 Mike Witt	.15	.05
❑ 500 George Brett	1.50	.60
❑ 501 Steve Henderson	.15	.05
❑ 502 Joe Torre MG	.25	.08
❑ 503 Elias Sosa	.15	.05
❑ 504 Mickey Rivers	.15	.05
❑ 505 Pete Vuckovich	.15	.05
❑ 506 Ernie Whitt	.15	.05
❑ 507 Mike LaCoss	.15	.05
❑ 508 Mel Hall	.25	.08
❑ 509 Brad Havens	.15	.05
❑ 510 Alan Trammell	.25	.08
❑ 511 Marty Bystrom	.15	.05
❑ 512 Oscar Gamble	.15	.05
❑ 513 Dave Beard	.15	.05
❑ 514 Floyd Rayford	.15	.05
❑ 515 Gorman Thomas	.25	.08
❑ 516 Montreal Expos TL Al Oliver Charlie Lea (Checkl)	.25	.08
❑ 517 John Moses	.15	.05
❑ 518 Greg Walker	.40	.15
❑ 519 Ron Davis	.15	.05
❑ 520 Bob Boone	.25	.08
❑ 521 Pete Falcone	.15	.05
❑ 522 Dave Bergman	.15	.05
❑ 523 Glenn Hoffman	.15	.05
❑ 524 Carlos Diaz	.15	.05
❑ 525 Willie Wilson	.25	.08
❑ 526 Ron Oester	.15	.05
❑ 527 Checklist 397-528	.25	.08
❑ 528 Mark Brouhard	.15	.05
❑ 529 Keith Atherton	.15	.05
❑ 530 Dan Ford	.15	.05
❑ 531 Steve Boros MG	.15	.05
❑ 532 Eric Show	.15	.05
❑ 533 Ken Landreaux	.15	.05
❑ 534 Pete O'Brien RC*	.40	.15
❑ 535 Bo Diaz	.15	.05
❑ 536 Doug Bair	.15	.05
❑ 537 Johnny Ray	.15	.05
❑ 538 Kevin Bass	.15	.05
❑ 539 George Frazier	.15	.05
❑ 540 George Hendrick	.25	.08
❑ 541 Dennis Lamp	.15	.05
❑ 542 Duane Kuiper	.15	.05
❑ 543 Craig McMurtry	.15	.05
❑ 544 Cesar Geronimo	.15	.05
❑ 545 Bill Buckner	.25	.08
❑ 546 Indians TL Mike Hargrove Lary Sorensen (Checkli)	.25	.08
❑ 547 Mike Moore	.15	.05
❑ 548 Ron Jackson	.15	.05
❑ 549 Walt Terrell	.15	.05
❑ 550 Jim Rice	.25	.08
❑ 551 Scott Ullger	.15	.05
❑ 552 Ray Burris	.15	.05
❑ 553 Joe Nolan	.15	.05
❑ 554 Ted Power	.15	.05
❑ 555 Greg Brock	.15	.05
❑ 556 Joey McLaughlin	.15	.05
❑ 557 Wayne Tolleson	.15	.05
❑ 558 Mike Davis	.15	.05
❑ 559 Mike Scott	.25	.08
❑ 560 Carlton Fisk	.40	.15
❑ 561 Whitey Herzog MG	.25	.08
❑ 562 Manny Castillo	.15	.05
❑ 563 Glenn Wilson	.25	.08
❑ 564 Al Holland	.15	.05
❑ 565 Leon Durham	.15	.05
❑ 566 Jim Bibby	.15	.05
❑ 567 Mike Heath	.15	.05
❑ 568 Pete Filson	.15	.05
❑ 569 Bake McBride	.25	.08
❑ 570 Dan Quisenberry	.15	.05
❑ 571 Bruce Bochy	.15	.05
❑ 572 Jerry Royster	.15	.05
❑ 573 Dave Kingman	.25	.08
❑ 574 Brian Downing	.25	.08
❑ 575 Jim Clancy	.15	.05
❑ 576 Giants TL Jeff Leonard Atlee Hammaker (Checklis)	.25	.08
❑ 577 Mark Clear	.15	.05
❑ 578 Lenn Sakata	.15	.05
❑ 579 Bob James	.15	.05
❑ 580 Lonnie Smith	.15	.05
❑ 581 Jose DeLeon RC	.40	.15
❑ 582 Bob McClure	.15	.05
❑ 583 Derrel Thomas	.15	.05
❑ 584 Dave Schmidt	.15	.05
❑ 585 Dan Driessen	.15	.05
❑ 586 Joe Niekro	.15	.05
❑ 587 Von Hayes	.15	.05
❑ 588 Milt Wilcox	.15	.05
❑ 589 Mike Easler	.15	.05
❑ 590 Dave Stieb	.25	.08
❑ 591 Tony LaRussa MG	.25	.08
❑ 592 Andre Robertson	.15	.05
❑ 593 Jeff Lahti	.15	.05
❑ 594 Gene Richards	.15	.05
❑ 595 Jeff Reardon	.25	.08
❑ 596 Ryne Sandberg	2.50	1.00
❑ 597 Rick Camp	.15	.05
❑ 598 Rusty Kuntz	.15	.05
❑ 599 Doug Sisk	.15	.05
❑ 600 Rod Carew	.40	.15
❑ 601 John Tudor	.25	.08
❑ 602 John Wathan	.15	.05
❑ 603 Renie Martin	.15	.05
❑ 604 John Lowenstein	.15	.05
❑ 605 Mike Caldwell	.15	.05
❑ 606 Blue Jays TL Lloyd Moseby Dave Stieb (Checklist)	.25	.08
❑ 607 Tom Hume	.15	.05
❑ 608 Bobby Johnson	.15	.05
❑ 609 Dan Meyer	.15	.05
❑ 610 Steve Sax	.15	.05
❑ 611 Chet Lemon	.25	.08
❑ 612 Harry Spilman	.15	.05
❑ 613 Greg Gross	.15	.05
❑ 614 Len Barker	.15	.05
❑ 615 Garry Templeton	.25	.08
❑ 616 Don Robinson	.15	.05
❑ 617 Rick Cerone	.15	.05
❑ 618 Dickie Noles	.15	.05
❑ 619 Jerry Dybzinski	.15	.05
❑ 620 Al Oliver	.25	.08
❑ 621 Frank Howard MG	.25	.08
❑ 622 Al Cowens	.15	.05
❑ 623 Ron Washington	.15	.05

❑ 624 Terry Harper	.15	.05
❑ 625 Larry Gura	.15	.05
❑ 626 Bob Clark	.15	.05
❑ 627 Dave LaPoint	.15	.05
❑ 628 Ed Jurak	.15	.05
❑ 629 Rick Langford	.15	.05
❑ 630 Ted Simmons	.25	.08
❑ 631 Dennis Martinez	.25	.08
❑ 632 Tom Foley	.15	.05
❑ 633 Mike Krukow	.15	.05
❑ 634 Mike Marshall	.15	.05
❑ 635 Dave Righetti	.25	.08
❑ 636 Pat Putnam	.15	.05
❑ 637 Phillies TL		
Gary Matthews		
John Denny		
(Checklist)	.25	.08
❑ 638 George Vukovich	.15	.05
❑ 639 Rick Lysander	.15	.05
❑ 640 Lance Parrish	.40	.15
❑ 641 Mike Richardt	.15	.05
❑ 642 Tom Underwood	.15	.05
❑ 643 Mike C. Brown	.15	.05
❑ 644 Tim Lollar	.15	.05
❑ 645 Tony Pena	.15	.05
❑ 646 Checklist 529-660	.25	.08
❑ 647 Ron Roenicke	.15	.05
❑ 648 Len Whitehouse	.15	.05
❑ 649 Tom Herr	.15	.05
❑ 650 Phil Niekro	.25	.08
❑ 651 John McNamara MG	.15	.05
❑ 652 Rudy May	.15	.05
❑ 653 Dave Stapleton	.15	.05
❑ 654 Bob Bailor	.15	.05
❑ 655 Amos Otis	.25	.08
❑ 656 Bryn Smith	.15	.05
❑ 657 Thad Bosley	.15	.05
❑ 658 Jerry Augustine	.15	.05
❑ 659 Duane Walker	.15	.05
❑ 660 Ray Knight	.25	.08
❑ 661 Steve Yeager	.25	.08
❑ 662 Tom Brennan	.15	.05
❑ 663 Johnnie LeMaster	.15	.05
❑ 664 Dave Stegman	.15	.05
❑ 665 Buddy Bell	.25	.08
❑ 666 Tigers TL/Morris/Whitak	.25	.08
❑ 667 Vance Law	.15	.05
❑ 668 Larry McWilliams	.15	.05
❑ 669 Dave Lopes	.25	.08
❑ 670 Rich Gossage	.25	.08
❑ 671 Jamie Quirk	.15	.05
❑ 672 Ricky Nelson	.15	.05
❑ 673 Mike Walters	.15	.05
❑ 674 Tim Flannery	.15	.05
❑ 675 Pascual Perez	.15	.05
❑ 676 Brian Giles	.15	.05
❑ 677 Doyle Alexander	.15	.05
❑ 678 Chris Speier	.15	.05
❑ 679 Art Howe	.15	.05
❑ 680 Fred Lynn	.25	.08
❑ 681 Tom Lasorda MG	.40	.15
❑ 682 Dan Morogiello	.15	.05
❑ 683 Marty Barrett RC	.40	.15
❑ 684 Bob Shirley	.15	.05
❑ 685 Willie Aikens	.15	.05
❑ 686 Joe Price	.15	.05
❑ 687 Roy Howell	.15	.05
❑ 688 George Wright	.15	.05
❑ 689 Mike Fischlin	.15	.05
❑ 690 Jack Clark	.25	.08
❑ 691 Steve Lake	.15	.05
❑ 692 Dickie Thon	.15	.05
❑ 693 Alan Wiggins	.15	.05
❑ 694 Mike Stanton	.15	.05
❑ 695 Lou Whitaker	.25	.08
❑ 696 Pirates TL		
Bill Madlock		
Rick Rhoden		
(Checklist)	.25	.08
❑ 697 Dale Murray	.15	.05
❑ 698 Marc Hill	.15	.05
❑ 699 Dave Rucker	.15	.05
❑ 700 Mike Schmidt	1.50	.60
❑ 701 Madlock/Rose/Parker LL	.60	.25
❑ 702 Rose/Staub/Perez LL	.60	.25
❑ 703 Schmidt/Perez/Kingm LL	.60	.25
❑ 704 Tony Perez		
Rusty Staub		
Al Oliver LL	.25	.08
❑ 705 Morgan/Cedeno/Bowa LL	.40	.15
❑ 706 S.Carlton/Jenk/Seaver LL	.25	.08
❑ 707 N.Ryan/Seaver/Carlton LL	1.50	.60
❑ 708 Seaver/Carlton/Rog LL	.25	.08
❑ 709 NL Active Save		
Bruce Sutter		
Tug McGraw		
Gene Gar	.25	.08
❑ 710 Carew/Brett/Cooper LL	.40	.15
❑ 711 Carew/Camp/Reggie LL	.25	.08
❑ 712 Reggie/Nettles/Luz LL	.25	.08
❑ 713 Reggie/Simmons/Nett LL	.25	.08
❑ 714 AL Active Steals		
Bert Campaneris		
Dave Lopes		
Oma	.25	.08
❑ 715 Palmer/Sutton/John LL	.25	.08
❑ 716 AL Active Strikeout		
Don Sutton		
Bert Blyleven		
Je	.40	.15
❑ 717 Jim Palmer/Fingers LL	.25	.08
❑ 718 Fingers/Goose/Quis LL	.25	.08
❑ 719 Andy Hassler	.15	.05
❑ 720 Dwight Evans	.40	.15
❑ 721 Del Crandall MG	.15	.05
❑ 722 Bob Welch	.25	.08
❑ 723 Rich Dauer	.15	.05
❑ 724 Eric Rasmussen	.15	.05
❑ 725 Cesar Cedeno	.25	.08
❑ 726 Brewers TL		
Ted Simmons		
Moose Haas		
(Checklist on)	.25	.08
❑ 727 Joel Youngblood	.15	.05
❑ 728 Tug McGraw	.25	.08
❑ 729 Gene Tenace	.25	.08
❑ 730 Bruce Sutter	.40	.15
❑ 731 Lynn Jones	.15	.05
❑ 732 Terry Crowley	.15	.05
❑ 733 Dave Collins	.15	.05
❑ 734 Odell Jones	.15	.05
❑ 735 Rick Burleson	.15	.05
❑ 736 Dick Ruthven	.15	.05
❑ 737 Jim Essian	.15	.05
❑ 738 Bill Schroeder	.15	.05
❑ 739 Bob Watson	.15	.05
❑ 740 Tom Seaver	.60	.25
❑ 741 Wayne Gross	.15	.05
❑ 742 Dick Williams MG	.15	.05
❑ 743 Don Hood	.15	.05
❑ 744 Jamie Allen	.15	.05
❑ 745 Dennis Eckersley	.40	.15
❑ 746 Mickey Hatcher	.15	.05
❑ 747 Pat Zachry	.15	.05
❑ 748 Jeff Leonard	.15	.05
❑ 749 Doug Flynn	.15	.05
❑ 750 Jim Palmer	.25	.08
❑ 751 Charlie Moore	.15	.05
❑ 752 Phil Garner	.25	.08
❑ 753 Doug Gwosdz	.15	.05
❑ 754 Kent Tekulve	.15	.05
❑ 755 Garry Maddox	.15	.05
❑ 756 Reds TL		
Ron Oester		
Mario Soto		
(Checklist on bac)	.25	.08
❑ 757 Larry Bowa	.25	.08
❑ 758 Bill Stein	.15	.05
❑ 759 Richard Dotson	.15	.05
❑ 760 Bob Horner	.25	.08
❑ 761 John Montefusco	.15	.05
❑ 762 Rance Mulliniks	.15	.05
❑ 763 Craig Swan	.15	.05
❑ 764 Mike Hargrove	.15	.05
❑ 765 Ken Forsch	.15	.05
❑ 766 Mike Vail	.15	.05
❑ 767 Carney Lansford	.25	.08
❑ 768 Champ Summers	.15	.05
❑ 769 Bill Caudill	.15	.05
❑ 770 Ken Griffey	.25	.08
❑ 771 Billy Gardner MG	.15	.05
❑ 772 Jim Slaton	.15	.05
❑ 773 Todd Cruz	.15	.05
❑ 774 Tom Gorman	.15	.05
❑ 775 Dave Parker	.25	.08
❑ 776 Craig Reynolds	.15	.05
❑ 777 Tom Paciorek	.15	.05
❑ 778 Andy Hawkins	.15	.05
❑ 779 Jim Sundberg	.25	.08
❑ 780 Steve Carlton	.40	.15
❑ 781 Checklist 661-792	.25	.08
❑ 782 Steve Balboni	.15	.05
❑ 783 Luis Leal	.15	.05
❑ 784 Leon Roberts	.15	.05
❑ 785 Joaquin Andujar	.25	.08
❑ 786 Red Sox TL/Boggs/Ojeda	.40	.15
❑ 787 Bill Campbell	.15	.05
❑ 788 Milt May	.15	.05
❑ 789 Bert Blyleven	.25	.08
❑ 790 Doug DeCinces	.15	.05
❑ 791 Terry Forster	.25	.08
❑ 792 Bill Russell	.25	.08

1984 Topps Traded

❑ COMP.FACT.SET (132)	30.00	15.00
❑ 1T Willie Aikens	.40	.15
❑ 2T Luis Aponte	.40	.15
❑ 3T Mike Armstrong	.40	.15
❑ 4T Bob Bailor	.40	.15
❑ 5T Dusty Baker	.60	.25
❑ 6T Steve Balboni	.40	.15
❑ 7T Alan Bannister	.40	.15
❑ 8T Dave Beard	.40	.15
❑ 9T Joe Beckwith	.40	.15
❑ 10T Bruce Berenyi	.40	.15
❑ 11T Dave Bergman	.40	.15
❑ 12T Tony Bernazard	.40	.15
❑ 13T Yogi Berra MG	1.50	.60
❑ 14T Barry Bonnell	.40	.15
❑ 15T Phil Bradley	1.00	.40
❑ 16T Fred Breining	.40	.15
❑ 17T Bill Buckner	.60	.25
❑ 18T Ray Burris	.40	.15
❑ 19T John Butcher	.40	.15
❑ 20T Brett Butler	.60	.25
❑ 21T Enos Cabell	.40	.15
❑ 22T Bill Campbell	.40	.15
❑ 23T Bill Caudill	.40	.15
❑ 24T Bob Clark	.40	.15
❑ 25T Bryan Clark	.40	.15
❑ 26T Jaime Cocanower	.40	.15
❑ 27T Ron Darling XRC*	2.00	.75
❑ 28T Alvin Davis XRC	1.00	.40
❑ 29T Ken Dayley	.40	.15
❑ 30T Jeff Dedmon	.40	.15
❑ 31T Bob Dernier	.40	.15
❑ 32T Carlos Diaz	.40	.15
❑ 33T Mike Easler	.40	.15
❑ 34T Dennis Eckersley	1.00	.40
❑ 35T Jim Essian	.40	.15
❑ 36T Darrell Evans	.60	.25
❑ 37T Mike Fitzgerald	.40	.15
❑ 38T Tim Foli	.40	.15
❑ 39T George Frazier	.40	.15
❑ 40T Rich Gale	.40	.15
❑ 41T Barbaro Garbey	.40	.15
❑ 42T Dwight Gooden XRC	10.00	4.00
❑ 43T Rich Gossage	.60	.25
❑ 44T Wayne Gross	.40	.15
❑ 45T Mark Gubicza XRC	1.00	.40

❑ 46T	Jackie Gutierrez	.40	.15
❑ 47T	Mel Hall	.60	.25
❑ 48T	Toby Harrah	.60	.25
❑ 49T	Ron Hassey	.40	.15
❑ 50T	Rich Hebner	.40	.15
❑ 51T	Willie Hernandez	.40	.15
❑ 52T	Ricky Horton	.40	.15
❑ 53T	Art Howe	.40	.15
❑ 54T	Dane Iorg	.40	.15
❑ 55T	Brook Jacoby	1.00	.40
❑ 56T	Mike Jeffcoat XRC	.50	.20
❑ 57T	Dave Johnson MG	.40	.15
❑ 58T	Lynn Jones	.40	.15
❑ 59T	Ruppert Jones	.40	.15
❑ 60T	Mike Jorgensen	.40	.15
❑ 61T	Bob Kearney	.40	.15
❑ 62T	Jimmy Key XRC	2.00	.75
❑ 63T	Dave Kingman	.60	.25
❑ 64T	Jerry Koosman	.60	.25
❑ 65T	Wayne Krenchicki	.40	.15
❑ 66T	Rusty Kuntz	.40	.15
❑ 67T	Rene Lachemann MG	.40	.15
❑ 68T	Frank LaCorte	.40	.15
❑ 69T	Dennis Lamp	.40	.15
❑ 70T	Mark Langston XRC	2.00	.75
❑ 71T	Rick Leach	.40	.15
❑ 72T	Craig Lefferts	.50	.20
❑ 73T	Gary Lucas	.40	.15
❑ 74T	Jerry Martin	.40	.15
❑ 75T	Carmelo Martinez	.40	.15
❑ 76T	Mike Mason XRC	.50	.20
❑ 77T	Gary Matthews	.60	.25
❑ 78T	Andy McGaffigan	.40	.15
❑ 79T	Larry Milbourne	.40	.15
❑ 80T	Sid Monge	.40	.15
❑ 81T	Jackie Moore MG	.40	.15
❑ 82T	Joe Morgan	.60	.25
❑ 83T	Graig Nettles	.60	.25
❑ 84T	Phil Niekro	.60	.25
❑ 85T	Ken Oberkfell	.40	.15
❑ 86T	Mike O'Berry	.40	.15
❑ 87T	Al Oliver	.60	.25
❑ 88T	Jorge Orta	.40	.15
❑ 89T	Amos Otis	.60	.25
❑ 90T	Dave Parker	.60	.25
❑ 91T	Tony Perez	1.00	.40
❑ 92T	Gerald Perry	1.00	.40
❑ 93T	Gary Pettis	.40	.15
❑ 94T	Rob Picciolo	.40	.15
❑ 95T	Vern Rapp MG	.40	.15
❑ 96T	Floyd Rayford	.40	.15
❑ 97T	Randy Ready XRC	1.00	.40
❑ 98T	Ron Reed	.40	.15
❑ 99T	Gene Richards	.40	.15
❑ 100T	Jose Rijo XRC	2.00	.75
❑ 101T	Jeff D. Robinson	.40	.15
❑ 102T	Ron Romanick	.40	.15
❑ 103T	Pete Rose	5.00	2.00
❑ 104T	Bret Saberhagen XRC	4.00	1.50
❑ 105T	Juan Samuel XRC*	2.00	.75
❑ 106T	Scott Sanderson	.40	.15
❑ 107T	Dick Schofield XRC*	1.00	.40
❑ 108T	Tom Seaver	1.50	.60
❑ 109T	Jim Slaton	.40	.15
❑ 110T	Mike Smithson	.40	.15
❑ 111T	Lary Sorensen	.40	.15
❑ 112T	Tim Stoddard	.40	.15
❑ 113T	Champ Summers	.40	.15
❑ 114T	Jim Sundberg	.60	.25
❑ 115T	Rick Sutcliffe	.60	.25
❑ 116T	Craig Swan	.40	.15
❑ 117T	Tim Teufel XRC*	1.00	.40
❑ 118T	Derrel Thomas	.40	.15
❑ 119T	Gorman Thomas	.60	.25
❑ 120T	Alex Trevino	.40	.15
❑ 121T	Manny Trillo	.40	.15
❑ 122T	John Tudor	.60	.25
❑ 123T	Tom Underwood	.40	.15
❑ 124T	Mike Vail	.40	.15
❑ 125T	Tom Waddell	.40	.15
❑ 126T	Gary Ward	.40	.15
❑ 127T	Curt Wilkerson	.40	.15
❑ 128T	Frank Williams	.40	.15
❑ 129T	Glenn Wilson	.60	.25
❑ 130T	John Wockenfuss	.40	.15
❑ 131T	Ned Yost	.40	.15
❑ 132T	Checklist 1T-132T	.40	.15

1985 Topps

❑	COMPLETE SET (792)	80.00	40.00
❑	COMP.FACT.SET (792)	175.00	100.00
❑ 1	Carlton Fisk RB	.25	.08
❑ 2	Steve Garvey RB	.15	.05
❑ 3	Dwight Gooden RB	.60	.25
❑ 4	Cliff Johnson RB	.15	.05
❑ 5	Joe Morgan RB	.15	.05
❑ 6	Pete Rose RB	.40	.15
❑ 7	Nolan Ryan RB	1.50	.60
❑ 8	Juan Samuel RB	.15	.05
❑ 9	Bruce Sutter RB	.15	.05
❑ 10	Don Sutton RB	.15	.05
❑ 11	Ralph Houk MG	.15	.05
❑ 12	Dave Lopes	.25	.08
❑ 13	Tim Lollar	.15	.05
❑ 14	Chris Bando	.15	.05
❑ 15	Jerry Koosman	.25	.08
❑ 16	Bobby Meacham	.15	.05
❑ 17	Mike Scott	.25	.08
❑ 18	Mickey Hatcher	.15	.05
❑ 19	George Frazier	.15	.05
❑ 20	Chet Lemon	.25	.08
❑ 21	Lee Tunnell	.15	.05
❑ 22	Duane Kuiper	.15	.05
❑ 23	Bret Saberhagen RC	1.00	.40
❑ 24	Jesse Barfield	.25	.08
❑ 25	Steve Bedrosian	.15	.05
❑ 26	Roy Smalley	.15	.05
❑ 27	Bruce Berenyi	.15	.05
❑ 28	Dann Bilardello	.15	.05
❑ 29	Odell Jones	.15	.05
❑ 30	Cal Ripken	2.50	1.00
❑ 31	Terry Whitfield	.15	.05
❑ 32	Chuck Porter	.15	.05
❑ 33	Tito Landrum	.15	.05
❑ 34	Ed Nunez	.15	.05
❑ 35	Graig Nettles	.25	.08
❑ 36	Fred Breining	.15	.05
❑ 37	Reid Nichols	.15	.05
❑ 38	Jackie Moore MG	.15	.05
❑ 39	John Wockenfuss	.15	.05
❑ 40	Phil Niekro	.25	.08
❑ 41	Mike Fischlin	.15	.05
❑ 42	Luis Sanchez	.15	.05
❑ 43	Andre David	.15	.05
❑ 44	Dickie Thon	.15	.05
❑ 45	Greg Minton	.15	.05
❑ 46	Gary Woods	.15	.05
❑ 47	Dave Rozema	.15	.05
❑ 48	Tony Fernandez	.25	.08
❑ 49	Butch Davis	.15	.05
❑ 50	John Candelaria	.15	.05
❑ 51	Bob Watson	.15	.05
❑ 52	Jerry Dybzinski	.15	.05
❑ 53	Tom Gorman	.15	.05
❑ 54	Cesar Cedeno	.25	.08
❑ 55	Frank Tanana	.25	.08
❑ 56	Jim Dwyer	.15	.05
❑ 57	Pat Zachry	.15	.05
❑ 58	Orlando Mercado	.15	.05
❑ 59	Rick Waits	.15	.05
❑ 60	George Hendrick	.25	.08
❑ 61	Curt Kaufman	.15	.05
❑ 62	Mike Ramsey	.15	.05
❑ 63	Steve McCatty	.15	.05
❑ 64	Mark Bailey	.15	.05
❑ 65	Bill Buckner	.25	.08
❑ 66	Dick Williams MG	.15	.05
❑ 67	Rafael Santana	.15	.05
❑ 68	Von Hayes	.15	.05
❑ 69	Jim Winn	.15	.05
❑ 70	Don Baylor	.25	.08
❑ 71	Tim Laudner	.15	.05
❑ 72	Rick Sutcliffe	.25	.08
❑ 73	Rusty Kuntz	.15	.05
❑ 74	Mike Krukow	.15	.05
❑ 75	Willie Upshaw	.15	.05
❑ 76	Alan Bannister	.15	.05
❑ 77	Joe Beckwith	.15	.05
❑ 78	Scott Fletcher	.15	.05
❑ 79	Rick Mahler	.15	.05
❑ 80	Keith Hernandez	.25	.08
❑ 81	Lenn Sakata	.15	.05
❑ 82	Joe Price	.15	.05
❑ 83	Charlie Moore	.15	.05
❑ 84	Spike Owen	.15	.05
❑ 85	Mike Marshall	.15	.05
❑ 86	Don Aase	.15	.05
❑ 87	David Green	.15	.05
❑ 88	Bryn Smith	.15	.05
❑ 89	Jackie Gutierrez	.15	.05
❑ 90	Rich Gossage	.25	.08
❑ 91	Jeff Burroughs	.15	.05
❑ 92	Paul Owens MG	.15	.05
❑ 93	Don Schulze	.15	.05
❑ 94	Toby Harrah	.25	.08
❑ 95	Jose Cruz	.25	.08
❑ 96	Johnny Ray	.15	.05
❑ 97	Pete Filson	.15	.05
❑ 98	Steve Lake	.15	.05
❑ 99	Milt Wilcox	.15	.05
❑ 100	George Brett	1.50	.60
❑ 101	Jim Acker	.15	.05
❑ 102	Tommy Dunbar	.15	.05
❑ 103	Randy Lerch	.15	.05
❑ 104	Mike Fitzgerald	.15	.05
❑ 105	Ron Kittle	.15	.05
❑ 106	Pascual Perez	.15	.05
❑ 107	Tom Foley	.15	.05
❑ 108	Darnell Coles	.15	.05
❑ 109	Gary Roenicke	.15	.05
❑ 110	Alejandro Pena	.15	.05
❑ 111	Doug DeCinces	.15	.05
❑ 112	Tom Tellmann	.15	.05
❑ 113	Tom Herr	.15	.05
❑ 114	Bob James	.15	.05
❑ 115	Rickey Henderson	.75	.30
❑ 116	Dennis Boyd	.15	.05
❑ 117	Greg Gross	.15	.05
❑ 118	Eric Show	.15	.05
❑ 119	Pat Corrales MG	.15	.05
❑ 120	Steve Kemp	.15	.05
❑ 121	Checklist: 1-132	.15	.05
❑ 122	Tom Brunansky	.15	.05
❑ 123	Dave Smith	.15	.05
❑ 124	Rich Hebner	.15	.05
❑ 125	Kent Tekulve	.15	.05
❑ 126	Ruppert Jones	.15	.05
❑ 127	Mark Gubicza RC*	.40	.15
❑ 128	Ernie Whitt	.15	.05
❑ 129	Gene Garber	.15	.05
❑ 130	Al Oliver	.25	.08
❑ 131	Buddy/Gus Bell FS	.25	.08
❑ 132	Yogi/Dale Berra FS	.60	.25
❑ 133	Bob/Ray Boone FS	.15	.05
❑ 134	Terry/Tito Francona FS	.25	.08
❑ 135	Terry/Bob Kennedy FS	.15	.05
❑ 136	Jeff/Bill Kunkel FS	.15	.05
❑ 137	Vance/Vern Law FS	.25	.08
❑ 138	Dick/Dick Schofield FS	.15	.05
❑ 139	Joel/Bob Skinner FS	.15	.05
❑ 140	Roy/Roy Smalley FS	.15	.05
❑ 141	Mike/Dave Stenhouse FS	.15	.05
❑ 142	Steve/Dizzy Trout FS	.15	.05
❑ 143	Ozzie/Ossie Virgil FS	.15	.05
❑ 144	Ron Gardenhire	.15	.05
❑ 145	Alvin Davis RC*	.40	.15
❑ 146	Gary Redus	.15	.05
❑ 147	Bill Swaggerty	.15	.05
❑ 148	Steve Yeager	.25	.08

❑ 149 Dickie Noles .15 .05
❑ 150 Jim Rice .25 .08
❑ 151 Moose Haas .15 .05
❑ 152 Steve Braun .15 .05
❑ 153 Frank LaCorte .15 .05
❑ 154 Angel Salazar .15 .05
❑ 155 Yogi Berra MG/TC .60 .25
❑ 156 Craig Reynolds .15 .05
❑ 157 Tug McGraw .25 .08
❑ 158 Pat Tabler .15 .05
❑ 159 Carlos Diaz .15 .05
❑ 160 Lance Parrish .25 .08
❑ 161 Ken Schrom .15 .05
❑ 162 Benny Distefano .15 .05
❑ 163 Dennis Eckersley .40 .15
❑ 164 Jorge Orta .15 .05
❑ 165 Dusty Baker .25 .08
❑ 166 Keith Atherton .15 .05
❑ 167 Rufino Linares .15 .05
❑ 168 Garth Iorg .15 .05
❑ 169 Dan Spillner .15 .05
❑ 170 George Foster .25 .08
❑ 171 Bill Stein .15 .05
❑ 172 Jack Perconte .15 .05
❑ 173 Mike Young .15 .05
❑ 174 Rick Honeycutt .15 .05
❑ 175 Dave Parker .25 .08
❑ 176 Bill Schroeder .15 .05
❑ 177 Dave Von Ohlen .15 .05
❑ 178 Miguel Dilone .15 .05
❑ 179 Tommy John .25 .08
❑ 180 Dave Winfield .25 .08
❑ 181 Roger Clemens RC 25.00 10.00
❑ 182 Tim Flannery .15 .05
❑ 183 Larry McWilliams .15 .05
❑ 184 Carmen Castillo .15 .05
❑ 185 Al Holland .15 .05
❑ 186 Bob Lillis MG .15 .05
❑ 187 Mike Walters .15 .05
❑ 188 Greg Pryor .15 .05
❑ 189 Warren Brusstar .15 .05
❑ 190 Rusty Staub .25 .08
❑ 191 Steve Nicosia .15 .05
❑ 192 Howard Johnson .25 .08
❑ 193 Jimmy Key RC .75 .30
❑ 194 Dave Stegman .15 .05
❑ 195 Glenn Hubbard .15 .05
❑ 196 Pete O'Brien .15 .05
❑ 197 Mike Warren .15 .05
❑ 198 Eddie Milner .15 .05
❑ 199 Dennis Martinez .25 .08
❑ 200 Reggie Jackson .40 .15
❑ 201 Burt Hooton .15 .05
❑ 202 Gorman Thomas .25 .08
❑ 203 Bob McClure .15 .05
❑ 204 Art Howe .15 .05
❑ 205 Steve Rogers .25 .08
❑ 206 Phil Garner .25 .08
❑ 207 Mark Clear .15 .05
❑ 208 Champ Summers .15 .05
❑ 209 Bill Campbell .15 .05
❑ 210 Gary Matthews .25 .08
❑ 211 Clay Christiansen .15 .05
❑ 212 George Vukovich .15 .05
❑ 213 Billy Gardner MG .15 .05
❑ 214 John Tudor .25 .08
❑ 215 Bob Brenly .15 .05
❑ 216 Jerry Don Gleaton .15 .05
❑ 217 Leon Roberts .15 .05
❑ 218 Doyle Alexander .15 .05
❑ 219 Gerald Perry .15 .05
❑ 220 Fred Lynn .25 .08
❑ 221 Ron Reed .15 .05
❑ 222 Hubie Brooks .15 .05
❑ 223 Tom Hume .15 .05
❑ 224 Al Cowens .15 .05
❑ 225 Mike Boddicker .15 .05
❑ 226 Juan Beniquez .15 .05
❑ 227 Danny Darwin .15 .05
❑ 228 Dion James .15 .05
❑ 229 Dave LaPoint .15 .05
❑ 230 Gary Carter .25 .08
❑ 231 Dwayne Murphy .15 .05
❑ 232 Dave Beard .15 .05
❑ 233 Ed Jurak .15 .05
❑ 234 Jerry Narron .15 .05
❑ 235 Garry Maddox .15 .05
❑ 236 Mark Thurmond .15 .05
❑ 237 Julio Franco .25 .08
❑ 238 Jose Rijo RC .75 .30
❑ 239 Tim Teufel .15 .05
❑ 240 Dave Stieb .25 .08
❑ 241 Jim Frey MG .15 .05
❑ 242 Greg Harris .15 .05
❑ 243 Barbaro Garbey .15 .05
❑ 244 Mike Jones .15 .05
❑ 245 Chili Davis .25 .08
❑ 246 Mike Norris .15 .05
❑ 247 Wayne Tolleson .15 .05
❑ 248 Terry Forster .25 .08
❑ 249 Harold Baines .25 .08
❑ 250 Jesse Orosco .15 .05
❑ 251 Brad Gulden .15 .05
❑ 252 Dan Ford .15 .05
❑ 253 Sid Bream RC .40 .15
❑ 254 Pete Vuckovich .15 .05
❑ 255 Lonnie Smith .15 .05
❑ 256 Mike Stanton .15 .05
❑ 257 Bryan Little .15 .05
❑ 258 Mike C. Brown .15 .05
❑ 259 Gary Allenson .15 .05
❑ 260 Dave Righetti .25 .08
❑ 261 Checklist: 133-264 .15 .05
❑ 262 Greg Booker .15 .05
❑ 263 Mel Hall .15 .05
❑ 264 Joe Sambito .15 .05
❑ 265 Juan Samuel .15 .05
❑ 266 Frank Viola .25 .08
❑ 267 Henry Cotto RC .15 .05
❑ 268 Chuck Tanner MG .15 .05
❑ 269 Doug Baker .15 .05
❑ 270 Dan Quisenberry .15 .05
❑ 271 Tim Foli FDP .15 .05
❑ 272 Jeff Burroughs FDP .15 .05
❑ 273 Bill Almon FDP .15 .05
❑ 274 Floyd Bannister FDP .15 .05
❑ 275 Harold Baines FDP .15 .05
❑ 276 Bob Horner FDP .15 .05
❑ 277 Al Chambers FDP .15 .05
❑ 278 Darryl Strawberry FDP .40 .15
❑ 279 Mike Moore FDP .15 .05
❑ 280 Shawon Dunston FDP RC .75 .30
❑ 281 Tim Belcher FDP RC .40 .15
❑ 282 Shawn Abner FDP RC .15 .05
❑ 283 Fran Mullins .15 .05
❑ 284 Marty Bystrom .15 .05
❑ 285 Dan Driessen .15 .05
❑ 286 Rudy Law .15 .05
❑ 287 Walt Terrell .15 .05
❑ 288 Jeff Kunkel .15 .05
❑ 289 Tom Underwood .15 .05
❑ 290 Cecil Cooper .25 .08
❑ 291 Bob Welch .25 .08
❑ 292 Brad Komminsk .15 .05
❑ 293 Curt Young .15 .05
❑ 294 Tom Nieto .15 .05
❑ 295 Joe Niekro .15 .05
❑ 296 Ricky Nelson .15 .05
❑ 297 Gary Lucas .15 .05
❑ 298 Marty Barrett .15 .05
❑ 299 Andy Hawkins .15 .05
❑ 300 Rod Carew .40 .15
❑ 301 John Montefusco .15 .05
❑ 302 Tim Corcoran .15 .05
❑ 303 Mike Jeffcoat .15 .05
❑ 304 Gary Gaetti .25 .08
❑ 305 Dale Berra .15 .05
❑ 306 Rick Reuschel .25 .08
❑ 307 Sparky Anderson MG .25 .08
❑ 308 John Wathan .15 .05
❑ 309 Mike Witt .15 .05
❑ 310 Manny Trillo .15 .05
❑ 311 Jim Gott .15 .05
❑ 312 Marc Hill .15 .05
❑ 313 Dave Schmidt .15 .05
❑ 314 Ron Oester .15 .05
❑ 315 Doug Sisk .15 .05
❑ 316 John Lowenstein .15 .05
❑ 317 Jack Lazorko .15 .05
❑ 318 Ted Simmons .25 .08
❑ 319 Jeff Jones .15 .05
❑ 320 Dale Murphy .40 .15
❑ 321 Ricky Horton .15 .05
❑ 322 Dave Stapleton .15 .05
❑ 323 Andy McGaffigan .15 .05
❑ 324 Bruce Bochy .15 .05
❑ 325 John Denny .15 .05
❑ 326 Kevin Bass .15 .05
❑ 327 Brook Jacoby .15 .05
❑ 328 Bob Shirley .15 .05
❑ 329 Ron Washington .15 .05
❑ 330 Leon Durham .15 .05
❑ 331 Bill Laskey .15 .05
❑ 332 Brian Harper .15 .05
❑ 333 Willie Hernandez .15 .05
❑ 334 Dick Howser MG .15 .05
❑ 335 Bruce Benedict .15 .05
❑ 336 Rance Mulliniks .15 .05
❑ 337 Billy Sample .15 .05
❑ 338 Britt Burns .15 .05
❑ 339 Danny Heep .15 .05
❑ 340 Robin Yount 1.00 .40
❑ 341 Floyd Rayford .15 .05
❑ 342 Ted Power .15 .05
❑ 343 Bill Russell .25 .08
❑ 344 Dave Henderson .15 .05
❑ 345 Charlie Lea .15 .05
❑ 346 Terry Pendleton RC .75 .30
❑ 347 Rick Langford .15 .05
❑ 348 Bob Boone .25 .08
❑ 349 Domingo Ramos .15 .05
❑ 350 Wade Boggs .60 .25
❑ 351 Juan Agosto .15 .05
❑ 352 Joe Morgan .25 .08
❑ 353 Julio Solano .15 .05
❑ 354 Andre Robertson .15 .05
❑ 355 Bert Blyleven .25 .08
❑ 356 Dave Meier .15 .05
❑ 357 Rich Bordi .15 .05
❑ 358 Tony Pena .15 .05
❑ 359 Pat Sheridan .15 .05
❑ 360 Steve Carlton .25 .08
❑ 361 Alfredo Griffin .15 .05
❑ 362 Craig McMurtry .15 .05
❑ 363 Ron Hodges .15 .05
❑ 364 Richard Dotson .15 .05
❑ 365 Danny Ozark MG .15 .05
❑ 366 Todd Cruz .15 .05
❑ 367 Keefe Cato .15 .05
❑ 368 Dave Bergman .15 .05
❑ 369 R.J. Reynolds .15 .05
❑ 370 Bruce Sutter .25 .08
❑ 371 Mickey Rivers .15 .05
❑ 372 Roy Howell .15 .05
❑ 373 Mike Moore .15 .05
❑ 374 Brian Downing .25 .08
❑ 375 Jeff Reardon .25 .08
❑ 376 Jeff Newman .15 .05
❑ 377 Checklist: 265-396 .15 .05
❑ 378 Alan Wiggins .15 .05
❑ 379 Charles Hudson .15 .05
❑ 380 Ken Griffey .25 .08
❑ 381 Roy Smith .15 .05
❑ 382 Denny Walling .15 .05
❑ 383 Rick Lysander .15 .05
❑ 384 Jody Davis .15 .05
❑ 385 Jose DeLeon .15 .05
❑ 386 Dan Gladden RC .40 .15
❑ 387 Buddy Biancalana .15 .05
❑ 388 Bert Roberge .15 .05
❑ 389 Rod Dedeaux OLY CO RC .25 .08
❑ 390 Sid Akins OLY RC .15 .05
❑ 391 Flavio Alfaro OLY RC .15 .05
❑ 392 Don August OLY RC .15 .05
❑ 393 Scott Bankhead OLY RC .15 .05
❑ 394 Bob Caffrey OLY RC .15 .05
❑ 395 Mike Dunne OLY RC .15 .05
❑ 396 Gary Green OLY RC .15 .05
❑ 397 John Hoover OLY RC .15 .05
❑ 398 Shane Mack OLY RC .40 .15
❑ 399 John Marzano OLY RC .15 .05
❑ 400 Oddibe McDowell OLY RC .40 .15
❑ 401 Mark McGwire OLY RC 30.00 12.50
❑ 402 Pat Pacillo OLY RC .15 .05
❑ 403 Cory Snyder OLY RC .75 .30
❑ 404 Bill Swift OLY RC .40 .15
❑ 405 Tom Veryzer .15 .05
❑ 406 Len Whitehouse .15 .05

❑ 407 Bobby Ramos .15 .05
❑ 408 Sid Monge .15 .05
❑ 409 Brad Wellman .15 .05
❑ 410 Bob Horner .25 .08
❑ 411 Bobby Cox MG .25 .08
❑ 412 Bud Black .15 .05
❑ 413 Vance Law .15 .05
❑ 414 Gary Ward .15 .05
❑ 415 Ron Darling UER .25 .08
❑ 416 Wayne Gross .15 .05
❑ 417 John Franco RC .75 .30
❑ 418 Ken Landreaux .15 .05
❑ 419 Mike Caldwell .15 .05
❑ 420 Andre Dawson .25 .08
❑ 421 Dave Rucker .15 .05
❑ 422 Carney Lansford .25 .08
❑ 423 Barry Bonnell .15 .05
❑ 424 Al Nipper .15 .05
❑ 425 Mike Hargrove .15 .05
❑ 426 Vern Ruhle .15 .05
❑ 427 Mario Ramirez .15 .05
❑ 428 Larry Andersen .15 .05
❑ 429 Rick Cerone .15 .05
❑ 430 Ron Davis .15 .05
❑ 431 U.L. Washington .15 .05
❑ 432 Thad Bosley .15 .05
❑ 433 Jim Morrison .15 .05
❑ 434 Gene Richards .15 .05
❑ 435 Dan Petry .15 .05
❑ 436 Willie Aikens .15 .05
❑ 437 Al Jones .15 .05
❑ 438 Joe Torre MG .25 .08
❑ 439 Junior Ortiz .15 .05
❑ 440 Fernando Valenzuela .25 .08
❑ 441 Duane Walker .15 .05
❑ 442 Ken Forsch .15 .05
❑ 443 George Wright .15 .05
❑ 444 Tony Phillips .15 .05
❑ 445 Tippy Martinez .15 .05
❑ 446 Jim Sundberg .25 .08
❑ 447 Jeff Lahti .15 .05
❑ 448 Derrel Thomas .15 .05
❑ 449 Phil Bradley .40 .15
❑ 450 Steve Garvey .25 .08
❑ 451 Bruce Hurst .15 .05
❑ 452 John Castino .15 .05
❑ 453 Tom Waddell .15 .05
❑ 454 Glenn Wilson .15 .05
❑ 455 Bob Knepper .15 .05
❑ 456 Tim Foli .15 .05
❑ 457 Cecilio Guante .15 .05
❑ 458 Randy Johnson .15 .05
❑ 459 Charlie Leibrandt .15 .05
❑ 460 Ryne Sandberg 1.25 .50
❑ 461 Marty Castillo .15 .05
❑ 462 Gary Lavelle .15 .05
❑ 463 Dave Collins .15 .05
❑ 464 Mike Mason RC .15 .05
❑ 465 Bob Grich .25 .08
❑ 466 Tony LaRussa MG .25 .08
❑ 467 Ed Lynch .15 .05
❑ 468 Wayne Krenchicki .15 .05
❑ 469 Sammy Stewart .15 .05
❑ 470 Steve Sax .15 .05
❑ 471 Pete Ladd .15 .05
❑ 472 Jim Essian .15 .05
❑ 473 Tim Wallach .15 .05
❑ 474 Kurt Kepshire .15 .05
❑ 475 Andre Thornton .15 .05
❑ 476 Jeff Stone .15 .05
❑ 477 Bob Ojeda .15 .05
❑ 478 Kurt Bevacqua .15 .05
❑ 479 Mike Madden .15 .05
❑ 480 Lou Whitaker .25 .08
❑ 481 Dale Murray .15 .05
❑ 482 Harry Spilman .15 .05
❑ 483 Mike Smithson .15 .05
❑ 484 Larry Bowa .25 .08
❑ 485 Matt Young .15 .05
❑ 486 Steve Balboni .15 .05
❑ 487 Frank Williams .15 .05
❑ 488 Joel Skinner .15 .05
❑ 489 Bryan Clark .15 .05
❑ 490 Jason Thompson .15 .05
❑ 491 Rick Camp .15 .05
❑ 492 Dave Johnson MG .15 .05
❑ 493 Orel Hershiser RC 2.00 .75
❑ 494 Rich Dauer .15 .05
❑ 495 Mario Soto .25 .08
❑ 496 Donnie Scott .15 .05
❑ 497 Gary Pettis UER .15 .05
❑ 498 Ed Romero .15 .05
❑ 499 Danny Cox .15 .05
❑ 500 Mike Schmidt 1.50 .60
❑ 501 Dan Schatzeder .15 .05
❑ 502 Rick Miller .15 .05
❑ 503 Tim Conroy .15 .05
❑ 504 Jerry Willard .15 .05
❑ 505 Jim Beattie .15 .05
❑ 506 Franklin Stubbs .15 .05
❑ 507 Ray Fontenot .15 .05
❑ 508 John Shelby .15 .05
❑ 509 Milt May .15 .05
❑ 510 Kent Hrbek .25 .08
❑ 511 Lee Smith .25 .08
❑ 512 Tom Brookens .15 .05
❑ 513 Lynn Jones .15 .05
❑ 514 Jeff Cornell .15 .05
❑ 515 Dave Concepcion .25 .08
❑ 516 Roy Lee Jackson .15 .05
❑ 517 Jerry Martin .15 .05
❑ 518 Chris Chambliss .25 .08
❑ 519 Doug Rader MG .15 .05
❑ 520 LaMarr Hoyt .15 .05
❑ 521 Rick Dempsey .15 .05
❑ 522 Paul Molitor .25 .08
❑ 523 Candy Maldonado .15 .05
❑ 524 Rob Wilfong .15 .05
❑ 525 Darrell Porter .15 .05
❑ 526 David Palmer .15 .05
❑ 527 Checklist: 397-528 .15 .05
❑ 528 Bill Krueger .15 .05
❑ 529 Rich Gedman .15 .05
❑ 530 Dave Dravecky .15 .05
❑ 531 Joe Lefebvre .15 .05
❑ 532 Frank DiPino .15 .05
❑ 533 Tony Bernazard .15 .05
❑ 534 Brian Dayett .15 .05
❑ 535 Pat Putnam .15 .05
❑ 536 Kirby Puckett RC 10.00 4.00
❑ 537 Don Robinson .15 .05
❑ 538 Keith Moreland .15 .05
❑ 539 Aurelio Lopez .15 .05
❑ 540 Claudell Washington .15 .05
❑ 541 Mark Davis .15 .05
❑ 542 Don Slaught .15 .05
❑ 543 Mike Squires .15 .05
❑ 544 Bruce Kison .15 .05
❑ 545 Lloyd Moseby .15 .05
❑ 546 Brent Gaff .15 .05
❑ 547 Pete Rose MG/TC .40 .15
❑ 548 Larry Parrish .15 .05
❑ 549 Mike Scioscia .25 .08
❑ 550 Scott McGregor .15 .05
❑ 551 Andy Van Slyke .40 .15
❑ 552 Chris Codiroli .15 .05
❑ 553 Bob Clark .15 .05
❑ 554 Doug Flynn .15 .05
❑ 555 Bob Stanley .15 .05
❑ 556 Sixto Lezcano .15 .05
❑ 557 Len Barker .15 .05
❑ 558 Carmelo Martinez .15 .05
❑ 559 Jay Howell .15 .05
❑ 560 Bill Madlock .25 .08
❑ 561 Darryl Motley .15 .05
❑ 562 Houston Jimenez .15 .05
❑ 563 Dick Ruthven .15 .05
❑ 564 Alan Ashby .15 .05
❑ 565 Kirk Gibson .25 .08
❑ 566 Ed VandeBerg .15 .05
❑ 567 Joel Youngblood .15 .05
❑ 568 Cliff Johnson .15 .05
❑ 569 Ken Oberkfell .15 .05
❑ 570 Darryl Strawberry .60 .25
❑ 571 Charlie Hough .25 .08
❑ 572 Tom Paciorek .15 .05
❑ 573 Jay Tibbs .15 .05
❑ 574 Joe Altobelli MG .15 .05
❑ 575 Pedro Guerrero .25 .08
❑ 576 Jaime Cocanower .15 .05
❑ 577 Chris Speier .15 .05
❑ 578 Terry Francona .25 .08
❑ 579 Ron Romanick .15 .05
❑ 580 Dwight Evans .40 .15
❑ 581 Mark Wagner .15 .05
❑ 582 Ken Phelps .15 .05
❑ 583 Bobby Brown .15 .05
❑ 584 Kevin Gross .15 .05
❑ 585 Butch Wynegar .15 .05
❑ 586 Bill Scherrer .15 .05
❑ 587 Doug Frobel .15 .05
❑ 588 Bobby Castillo .15 .05
❑ 589 Bob Dernier .15 .05
❑ 590 Ray Knight .25 .08
❑ 591 Larry Herndon .15 .05
❑ 592 Jeff D. Robinson .15 .05
❑ 593 Rick Leach .15 .05
❑ 594 Curt Wilkerson .15 .05
❑ 595 Larry Gura .15 .05
❑ 596 Jerry Hairston .15 .05
❑ 597 Brad Lesley .15 .05
❑ 598 Jose Oquendo .15 .05
❑ 599 Storm Davis .15 .05
❑ 600 Pete Rose 1.50 .60
❑ 601 Tom Lasorda MG .40 .15
❑ 602 Jeff Dedmon .15 .05
❑ 603 Rick Manning .15 .05
❑ 604 Daryl Sconiers .15 .05
❑ 605 Ozzie Smith 1.00 .40
❑ 606 Rich Gale .15 .05
❑ 607 Bill Almon .15 .05
❑ 608 Craig Lefferts .15 .05
❑ 609 Broderick Perkins .15 .05
❑ 610 Jack Morris .25 .08
❑ 611 Ozzie Virgil .15 .05
❑ 612 Mike Armstrong .15 .05
❑ 613 Terry Puhl .15 .05
❑ 614 Al Williams .15 .05
❑ 615 Marvell Wynne .15 .05
❑ 616 Scott Sanderson .15 .05
❑ 617 Willie Wilson .25 .08
❑ 618 Pete Falcone .15 .05
❑ 619 Jeff Leonard .15 .05
❑ 620 Dwight Gooden RC 2.00 .75
❑ 621 Marvis Foley .15 .05
❑ 622 Luis Leal .15 .05
❑ 623 Greg Walker .15 .05
❑ 624 Benny Ayala .15 .05
❑ 625 Mark Langston RC .75 .30
❑ 626 German Rivera .15 .05
❑ 627 Eric Davis RC 2.00 .75
❑ 628 Rene Lachemann MG .15 .05
❑ 629 Dick Schofield .15 .05
❑ 630 Tim Raines .25 .08
❑ 631 Bob Forsch .15 .05
❑ 632 Bruce Bochte .15 .05
❑ 633 Glenn Hoffman .15 .05
❑ 634 Bill Dawley .15 .05
❑ 635 Terry Kennedy .15 .05
❑ 636 Shane Rawley .15 .05
❑ 637 Brett Butler .25 .08
❑ 638 Mike Pagliarulo .15 .05
❑ 639 Ed Hodge .15 .05
❑ 640 Steve Henderson .15 .05
❑ 641 Rod Scurry .15 .05
❑ 642 Dave Owen .15 .05
❑ 643 Johnny Grubb .15 .05
❑ 644 Mark Huismann .15 .05
❑ 645 Damaso Garcia .15 .05
❑ 646 Scot Thompson .15 .05
❑ 647 Rafael Ramirez .15 .05
❑ 648 Bob Jones .15 .05
❑ 649 Sid Fernandez .25 .08
❑ 650 Greg Luzinski .25 .08
❑ 651 Jeff Russell .15 .05
❑ 652 Joe Nolan .15 .05
❑ 653 Mark Brouhard .15 .05
❑ 654 Dave Anderson .15 .05
❑ 655 Joaquin Andujar .25 .08
❑ 656 Chuck Cottier MG .15 .05
❑ 657 Jim Slaton .15 .05
❑ 658 Mike Stenhouse .15 .05
❑ 659 Checklist: 529-660 .15 .05
❑ 660 Tony Gwynn 1.25 .50
❑ 661 Steve Crawford .15 .05
❑ 662 Mike Heath .15 .05
❑ 663 Luis Aguayo .15 .05
❑ 664 Steve Farr RC .40 .15

665	Don Mattingly	2.50	1.00
666	Mike LaCoss	.15	.05
667	Dave Engle	.15	.05
668	Steve Trout	.15	.05
669	Lee Lacy	.15	.05
670	Tom Seaver	.40	.15
671	Dane Iorg	.15	.05
672	Juan Berenguer	.15	.05
673	Buck Martinez	.15	.05
674	Atlee Hammaker	.15	.05
675	Tony Perez	.40	.15
676	Albert Hall	.15	.05
677	Wally Backman	.15	.05
678	Joey McLaughlin	.15	.05
679	Bob Kearney	.15	.05
680	Jerry Reuss	.15	.05
681	Ben Oglivie	.25	.08
682	Doug Corbett	.15	.05
683	Whitey Herzog MG	.25	.08
684	Bill Doran	.15	.05
685	Bill Caudill	.15	.05
686	Mike Easler	.15	.05
687	Bill Gullickson	.15	.05
688	Len Matuszek	.15	.05
689	Luis DeLeon	.15	.05
690	Alan Trammell	.25	.08
691	Dennis Rasmussen	.15	.05
692	Randy Bush	.15	.05
693	Tim Stoddard	.15	.05
694	Joe Carter	.60	.25
695	Rick Rhoden	.15	.05
696	John Rabb	.15	.05
697	Onix Concepcion	.15	.05
698	George Bell	.25	.08
699	Donnie Moore	.15	.05
700	Eddie Murray	.60	.25
701	Eddie Murray AS	.40	.15
702	Damaso Garcia AS	.15	.05
703	George Brett AS	.60	.25
704	Cal Ripken AS	1.50	.60
705	Dave Winfield AS	.15	.05
706	Rickey Henderson AS	.40	.15
707	Tony Armas AS	.15	.05
708	Lance Parrish AS	.15	.05
709	Mike Boddicker AS	.15	.05
710	Frank Viola AS	.15	.05
711	Dan Quisenberry AS	.15	.05
712	Keith Hernandez AS	.15	.05
713	Ryne Sandberg AS	.60	.25
714	Mike Schmidt AS	.60	.25
715	Ozzie Smith AS	.60	.25
716	Dale Murphy AS	.25	.08
717	Tony Gwynn AS	1.00	.40
718	Jeff Leonard AS	.15	.05
719	Gary Carter AS	.15	.05
720	Rick Sutcliffe AS	.15	.05
721	Bob Knepper AS	.15	.05
722	Bruce Sutter AS	.15	.05
723	Dave Stewart	.25	.08
724	Oscar Gamble	.15	.05
725	Floyd Bannister	.15	.05
726	Al Bumbry	.15	.05
727	Frank Pastore	.15	.05
728	Bob Bailor	.15	.05
729	Don Sutton	.25	.08
730	Dave Kingman	.25	.08
731	Neil Allen	.15	.05
732	John McNamara MG	.15	.05
733	Tony Scott	.15	.05
734	John Henry Johnson	.15	.05
735	Garry Templeton	.25	.08
736	Jerry Mumphrey	.15	.05
737	Bo Diaz	.15	.05
738	Omar Moreno	.15	.05
739	Ernie Camacho	.15	.05
740	Jack Clark	.25	.08
741	John Butcher	.15	.05
742	Ron Hassey	.15	.05
743	Frank White	.25	.08
744	Doug Bair	.15	.05
745	Buddy Bell	.25	.08
746	Jim Clancy	.15	.05
747	Alex Trevino	.15	.05
748	Lee Mazzilli	.25	.08
749	Julio Cruz	.15	.05
750	Rollie Fingers	.25	.08
751	Kelvin Chapman	.15	.05
752	Bob Owchinko	.15	.05
753	Greg Brock	.15	.05
754	Larry Milbourne	.15	.05
755	Ken Singleton	.25	.08
756	Rob Picciolo	.15	.05
757	Willie McGee	.25	.08
758	Ray Burris	.15	.05
759	Jim Fanning MG	.15	.05
760	Nolan Ryan	3.00	1.25
761	Jerry Remy	.15	.05
762	Eddie Whitson	.15	.05
763	Kiko Garcia	.15	.05
764	Jamie Easterly	.15	.05
765	Willie Randolph	.25	.08
766	Paul Mirabella	.15	.05
767	Darrell Brown	.15	.05
768	Ron Cey	.25	.08
769	Joe Cowley	.15	.05
770	Carlton Fisk	.40	.15
771	Geoff Zahn	.15	.05
772	Johnnie LeMaster	.15	.05
773	Hal McRae	.25	.08
774	Dennis Lamp	.15	.05
775	Mookie Wilson	.25	.08
776	Jerry Royster	.15	.05
777	Ned Yost	.15	.05
778	Mike Davis	.15	.05
779	Nick Esasky	.15	.05
780	Mike Flanagan	.15	.05
781	Jim Gantner	.15	.05
782	Tom Niedenfuer	.15	.05
783	Mike Jorgensen	.15	.05
784	Checklist: 661-792	.15	.05
785	Tony Armas	.25	.08
786	Enos Cabell	.15	.05
787	Jim Wohlford	.15	.05
788	Steve Comer	.15	.05
789	Luis Salazar	.15	.05
790	Ron Guidry	.25	.08
791	Ivan DeJesus	.15	.05
792	Darrell Evans	.25	.08

1985 Topps Traded

	COMP.FACT.SET (132)	8.00	3.00
1T	Don Aase	.15	.05
2T	Bill Almon	.15	.05
3T	Benny Ayala	.15	.05
4T	Dusty Baker	.40	.15
5T	George Bamberger MG	.15	.05
6T	Dale Berra	.15	.05
7T	Rich Bordi	.15	.05
8T	Daryl Boston XRC*	.25	.08
9T	Hubie Brooks	.15	.05
10T	Chris Brown XRC	.25	.08
11T	Tom Browning XRC*	.50	.20
12T	Al Bumbry	.15	.05
13T	Ray Burris	.15	.05
14T	Jeff Burroughs	.15	.05
15T	Bill Campbell	.15	.05
16T	Don Carman	.15	.05
17T	Gary Carter	.40	.15
18T	Bobby Castillo	.15	.05
19T	Bill Caudill	.15	.05
20T	Rick Cerone	.15	.05
21T	Bryan Clark	.15	.05
22T	Jack Clark	.40	.15
23T	Pat Clements	.15	.05
24T	Vince Coleman XRC	1.00	.40
25T	Dave Collins	.15	.05
26T	Danny Darwin	.15	.05
27T	Jim Davenport MG	.15	.05
28T	Jerry Davis	.15	.05
29T	Brian Dayett	.15	.05
30T	Ivan DeJesus	.15	.05
31T	Ken Dixon	.15	.05
32T	Mariano Duncan XRC	.50	.20
33T	John Felske MG	.15	.05
34T	Mike Fitzgerald	.15	.05
35T	Ray Fontenot	.15	.05
36T	Greg Gagne XRC*	.50	.20
37T	Oscar Gamble	.15	.05
38T	Scott Garrelts	.15	.05
39T	Bob L. Gibson	.15	.05
40T	Jim Gott	.15	.05
41T	David Green	.15	.05
42T	Alfredo Griffin	.15	.05
43T	Ozzie Guillen XRC	5.00	2.00
44T	Eddie Haas MG	.15	.05
45T	Terry Harper	.15	.05
46T	Toby Harrah	.40	.15
47T	Greg Harris	.15	.05
48T	Ron Hassey	.15	.05
49T	Rickey Henderson	2.50	1.00
50T	Steve Henderson	.15	.05
51T	George Hendrick	.40	.15
52T	Joe Hesketh	.15	.05
53T	Teddy Higuera XRC	.50	.20
54T	Donnie Hill	.15	.05
55T	Al Holland	.15	.05
56T	Burt Hooton	.15	.05
57T	Jay Howell	.15	.05
58T	Ken Howell	.15	.05
59T	LaMarr Hoyt	.15	.05
60T	Tim Hulett XRC*	.25	.08
61T	Bob James	.15	.05
62T	Steve Jeltz XRC	.25	.08
63T	Cliff Johnson	.15	.05
64T	Howard Johnson	.40	.15
65T	Ruppert Jones	.15	.05
66T	Steve Kemp	.15	.05
67T	Bruce Kison	.15	.05
68T	Alan Knicely	.15	.05
69T	Mike LaCoss	.15	.05
70T	Lee Lacy	.15	.05
71T	Dave LaPoint	.15	.05
72T	Gary Lavelle	.15	.05
73T	Vance Law	.15	.05
74T	Johnnie LeMaster	.15	.05
75T	Sixto Lezcano	.15	.05
76T	Tim Lollar	.15	.05
77T	Fred Lynn	.40	.15
78T	Billy Martin MG	.75	.30
79T	Ron Mathis	.15	.05
80T	Len Matuszek	.15	.05
81T	Gene Mauch MG	.15	.05
82T	Oddibe McDowell	.50	.20
83T	Roger McDowell XRC	.50	.20
84T	John McNamara MG	.15	.05
85T	Donnie Moore	.15	.05
86T	Gene Nelson	.15	.05
87T	Steve Nicosia	.15	.05
88T	Al Oliver	.40	.15
89T	Joe Orsulak XRC	.50	.20
90T	Rob Picciolo	.15	.05
91T	Chris Pittaro	.15	.05
92T	Jim Presley	.50	.20
93T	Rick Reuschel	.40	.15
94T	Bert Roberge	.15	.05
95T	Bob Rodgers MG	.15	.05
96T	Jerry Royster	.15	.05
97T	Dave Rozema	.15	.05
98T	Dave Rucker	.15	.05
99T	Vern Ruhle	.15	.05
100T	Paul Runge XRC	.25	.08
101T	Mark Salas	.15	.05
102T	Luis Salazar	.15	.05
103T	Joe Sambito	.15	.05
104T	Rick Schu	.15	.05
105T	Donnie Scott	.15	.05
106T	Larry Sheets XRC	.25	.08
107T	Don Slaught	.15	.05
108T	Roy Smalley	.15	.05
109T	Lonnie Smith	.15	.05

❑ 110T Nate Snell UER (Headings on back for a batter) .15 .05
❑ 111T Chris Speier .15 .05
❑ 112T Mike Stenhouse .15 .05
❑ 113T Tim Stoddard .15 .05
❑ 114T Jim Sundberg .40 .15
❑ 115T Bruce Sutter .40 .15
❑ 116T Don Sutton .40 .15
❑ 117T Kent Tekulve .15 .05
❑ 118T Tom Tellmann .15 .05
❑ 119T Walt Terrell .15 .05
❑ 120T Mickey Tettleton XRC .50 .20
❑ 121T Derrel Thomas .15 .05
❑ 122T Rich Thompson .15 .05
❑ 123T Alex Trevino .15 .05
❑ 124T John Tudor .40 .15
❑ 125T Jose Uribe .15 .05
❑ 126T Bobby Valentine MG .40 .15
❑ 127T Dave Von Ohlen .15 .05
❑ 128T U.L. Washington .15 .05
❑ 129T Earl Weaver MG .40 .15
❑ 130T Eddie Whitson .15 .05
❑ 131T Herm Winningham .15 .05
❑ 132T Checklist 1-132 .15 .05

1986 Topps

❑ COMPLETE SET (792) 25.00 10.00
❑ COMP.X-MAS.SET (792) 150.00 75.00
❑ 1 Pete Rose 2.00 .75
❑ 2 Rose Special: '63-'66 .25 .08
❑ 3 Rose Special: '67-'70 .25 .08
❑ 4 Rose Special: '71-'74 .25 .08
❑ 5 Rose Special: '75-'78 .25 .08
❑ 6 Rose Special: '79-'82 .25 .08
❑ 7 Rose Special: '83-'85 .25 .08
❑ 8 Dwayne Murphy .10 .02
❑ 9 Roy Smith .10 .02
❑ 10 Tony Gwynn .60 .25
❑ 11 Bob Ojeda .10 .02
❑ 12 Jose Uribe .10 .02
❑ 13 Bob Kearney .10 .02
❑ 14 Julio Cruz .10 .02
❑ 15 Eddie Whitson .10 .02
❑ 16 Rick Schu .10 .02
❑ 17 Mike Stenhouse .10 .02
❑ 18 Brent Gaff .10 .02
❑ 19 Rich Hebner .10 .02
❑ 20 Lou Whitaker .15 .05
❑ 21 George Bamberger MG .10 .02
❑ 22 Duane Walker .10 .02
❑ 23 Manuel Lee RC* .10 .02
❑ 24 Len Barker .10 .02
❑ 25 Willie Wilson .15 .05
❑ 26 Frank DiPino .10 .02
❑ 27 Ray Knight .15 .05
❑ 28 Eric Davis .40 .15
❑ 29 Tony Phillips .10 .02
❑ 30 Eddie Murray .40 .15
❑ 31 Jamie Easterly .10 .02
❑ 32 Steve Yeager .15 .05
❑ 33 Jeff Lahti .10 .02
❑ 34 Ken Phelps .10 .02
❑ 35 Jeff Reardon .15 .05
❑ 36 Tigers Leaders Lance Parrish .15 .05
❑ 37 Mark Thurmond .10 .02
❑ 38 Glenn Hoffman .10 .02
❑ 39 Dave Rucker .10 .02
❑ 40 Ken Griffey .15 .05
❑ 41 Brad Wellman .10 .02
❑ 42 Geoff Zahn .10 .02
❑ 43 Dave Engle .10 .02
❑ 44 Lance McCullers .10 .02
❑ 45 Damaso Garcia .10 .02
❑ 46 Billy Hatcher .10 .02
❑ 47 Juan Berenguer .10 .02
❑ 48 Bill Almon .10 .02
❑ 49 Rick Manning .10 .02
❑ 50 Dan Quisenberry .10 .02
❑ 51 Bobby Wine MG ERR (Checklist back) (Number of ca) .10 .02
❑ 52 Chris Welsh .10 .02
❑ 53 Len Dykstra RC .75 .30
❑ 54 John Franco .15 .05
❑ 55 Fred Lynn .15 .05
❑ 56 Tom Niedenfuer .10 .02
❑ 57 Bill Doran (See also 51) .10 .02
❑ 58 Bill Krueger .10 .02
❑ 59 Andre Thornton .10 .02
❑ 60 Dwight Evans .25 .08
❑ 61 Karl Best .10 .02
❑ 62 Bob Boone .15 .05
❑ 63 Ron Roenicke .10 .02
❑ 64 Floyd Bannister .10 .02
❑ 65 Dan Driessen .10 .02
❑ 66 Cardinals Leaders Bob Forsch .10 .02
❑ 67 Carmelo Martinez .10 .02
❑ 68 Ed Lynch .10 .02
❑ 69 Luis Aguayo .10 .02
❑ 70 Dave Winfield .15 .05
❑ 71 Ken Schrom .10 .02
❑ 72 Shawon Dunston .15 .05
❑ 73 Randy O'Neal .10 .02
❑ 74 Rance Mulliniks .10 .02
❑ 75 Jose DeLeon .10 .02
❑ 76 Dion James .10 .02
❑ 77 Charlie Leibrandt .10 .02
❑ 78 Bruce Benedict .10 .02
❑ 79 Dave Schmidt .10 .02
❑ 80 Darryl Strawberry .25 .08
❑ 81 Gene Mauch MG .10 .02
❑ 82 Tippy Martinez .10 .02
❑ 83 Phil Garner .15 .05
❑ 84 Curt Young .10 .02
❑ 85 Tony Perez w/E.Davis .15 .05
❑ 86 Tom Waddell .10 .02
❑ 87 Candy Maldonado .10 .02
❑ 88 Tom Nieto .10 .02
❑ 89 Randy St.Claire .10 .02
❑ 90 Garry Templeton .15 .05
❑ 91 Steve Crawford .10 .02
❑ 92 Al Cowens .10 .02
❑ 93 Scot Thompson .10 .02
❑ 94 Rich Bordi .10 .02
❑ 95 Ozzie Virgil .10 .02
❑ 96 Blue Jays Leaders Jim Clancy .10 .02
❑ 97 Gary Gaetti .15 .05
❑ 98 Dick Ruthven .10 .02
❑ 99 Buddy Biancalana .10 .02
❑ 100 Nolan Ryan 2.00 .75
❑ 101 Dave Bergman .10 .02
❑ 102 Joe Orsulak RC* .25 .08
❑ 103 Luis Salazar .10 .02
❑ 104 Sid Fernandez .10 .02
❑ 105 Gary Ward .10 .02
❑ 106 Ray Burris .10 .02
❑ 107 Rafael Ramirez .10 .02
❑ 108 Ted Power .10 .02
❑ 109 Len Matuszek .10 .02
❑ 110 Scott McGregor .10 .02
❑ 111 Roger Craig MG .15 .05
❑ 112 Bill Campbell .10 .02
❑ 113 U.L. Washington .10 .02
❑ 114 Mike C. Brown .10 .02
❑ 115 Jay Howell .10 .02
❑ 116 Brook Jacoby .10 .02
❑ 117 Bruce Kison .10 .02
❑ 118 Jerry Royster .10 .02
❑ 119 Barry Bonnell .10 .02
❑ 120 Steve Carlton .15 .05
❑ 121 Nelson Simmons .10 .02
❑ 122 Pete Filson .10 .02
❑ 123 Greg Walker .10 .02
❑ 124 Luis Sanchez .10 .02
❑ 125 Dave Lopes .15 .05
❑ 126 Mets Leaders Mookie Wilson .10 .02
❑ 127 Jack Howell .10 .02
❑ 128 John Wathan .10 .02
❑ 129 Jeff Dedmon .10 .02
❑ 130 Alan Trammell .15 .05
❑ 131 Checklist: 1-132 .15 .05
❑ 132 Razor Shines .10 .02
❑ 133 Andy McGaffigan .10 .02
❑ 134 Carney Lansford .15 .05
❑ 135 Joe Niekro .10 .02
❑ 136 Mike Hargrove .10 .02
❑ 137 Charlie Moore .10 .02
❑ 138 Mark Davis .10 .02
❑ 139 Daryl Boston .10 .02
❑ 140 John Candelaria .10 .02
❑ 141 Chuck Cottier MG See also 171 .10 .02
❑ 142 Bob Jones .10 .02
❑ 143 Dave Van Gorder .10 .02
❑ 144 Doug Sisk .10 .02
❑ 145 Pedro Guerrero .15 .05
❑ 146 Jack Perconte .10 .02
❑ 147 Larry Sheets .10 .02
❑ 148 Mike Heath .10 .02
❑ 149 Brett Butler .15 .05
❑ 150 Joaquin Andujar .15 .05
❑ 151 Dave Stapleton .10 .02
❑ 152 Mike Morgan .10 .02
❑ 153 Ricky Adams .10 .02
❑ 154 Bert Roberge .10 .02
❑ 155 Bob Grich .15 .05
❑ 156 White Sox Leaders Richard Dotson .10 .02
❑ 157 Ron Hassey .10 .02
❑ 158 Derrel Thomas .10 .02
❑ 159 Orel Hershiser UER .40 .15
❑ 160 Chet Lemon .15 .05
❑ 161 Lee Tunnell .10 .02
❑ 162 Greg Gagne .10 .02
❑ 163 Pete Ladd .10 .02
❑ 164 Steve Balboni .10 .02
❑ 165 Mike Davis .10 .02
❑ 166 Dickie Thon .10 .02
❑ 167 Zane Smith .10 .02
❑ 168 Jeff Burroughs .10 .02
❑ 169 George Wright .10 .02
❑ 170 Gary Carter .15 .05
❑ 171 Bob Rodgers MG ERR (Checklist back) (Number of c) .10 .02
❑ 172 Jerry Reed .10 .02
❑ 173 Wayne Gross .10 .02
❑ 174 Brian Snyder .10 .02
❑ 175 Steve Sax .10 .02
❑ 176 Jay Tibbs .10 .02
❑ 177 Joel Youngblood .10 .02
❑ 178 Ivan DeJesus .10 .02
❑ 179 Stu Cliburn .10 .02
❑ 180 Don Mattingly 1.25 .50
❑ 181 Al Nipper .10 .02
❑ 182 Bobby Brown .10 .02
❑ 183 Larry Andersen .10 .02
❑ 184 Tim Laudner .10 .02
❑ 185 Rollie Fingers .15 .05
❑ 186 Astros Leaders Jose Cruz .10 .02
❑ 187 Scott Fletcher .10 .02
❑ 188 Bob Dernier .10 .02
❑ 189 Mike Mason .10 .02
❑ 190 George Hendrick .15 .05
❑ 191 Wally Backman .10 .02
❑ 192 Milt Wilcox .10 .02
❑ 193 Daryl Sconiers .10 .02
❑ 194 Craig McMurtry .10 .02
❑ 195 Dave Concepcion .15 .05
❑ 196 Doyle Alexander .10 .02
❑ 197 Enos Cabell .10 .02
❑ 198 Ken Dixon .10 .02
❑ 199 Dick Howser MG .10 .02

❑ 200 Mike Schmidt 1.00 .40
❑ 201 Vince Coleman RB Most stolen bases& season& rook .15 .05
❑ 202 Dwight Gooden RB .25 .08
❑ 203 Keith Hernandez RB .10 .02
❑ 204 Phil Niekro RB (Oldest shutout pitcher) .15 .05
❑ 205 Tony Perez RB (Oldest grand slammer) .15 .05
❑ 206 Pete Rose RB .40 .15
❑ 207 Fernando Valenzuela RB (Most cons. innings& start) .10 .02
❑ 208 Ramon Romero .10 .02
❑ 209 Randy Ready .10 .02
❑ 210 Calvin Schiraldi .10 .02
❑ 211 Ed Wojna .10 .02
❑ 212 Chris Speier .10 .02
❑ 213 Bob Shirley .10 .02
❑ 214 Randy Bush .10 .02
❑ 215 Frank White .15 .05
❑ 216 A's Leaders Dwayne Murphy .10 .02
❑ 217 Bill Scherrer .10 .02
❑ 218 Randy Hunt .10 .02
❑ 219 Dennis Lamp .10 .02
❑ 220 Bob Horner .15 .05
❑ 221 Dave Henderson .10 .02
❑ 222 Craig Gerber .10 .02
❑ 223 Atlee Hammaker .10 .02
❑ 224 Cesar Cedeno .15 .05
❑ 225 Ron Darling .15 .05
❑ 226 Lee Lacy .10 .02
❑ 227 Al Jones .10 .02
❑ 228 Tom Lawless .10 .02
❑ 229 Bill Gullickson .10 .02
❑ 230 Terry Kennedy .10 .02
❑ 231 Jim Frey MG .10 .02
❑ 232 Rick Rhoden .10 .02
❑ 233 Steve Lyons .10 .02
❑ 234 Doug Corbett .10 .02
❑ 235 Butch Wynegar .10 .02
❑ 236 Frank Eufemia .10 .02
❑ 237 Ted Simmons .15 .05
❑ 238 Larry Parrish .10 .02
❑ 239 Joel Skinner .10 .02
❑ 240 Tommy John .15 .05
❑ 241 Tony Fernandez .10 .02
❑ 242 Rich Thompson .10 .02
❑ 243 Johnny Grubb .10 .02
❑ 244 Craig Lefferts .10 .02
❑ 245 Jim Sundberg .15 .05
❑ 246 Steve Carlton TL .10 .02
❑ 247 Terry Harper .10 .02
❑ 248 Spike Owen .10 .02
❑ 249 Rob Deer .10 .02
❑ 250 Dwight Gooden .40 .15
❑ 251 Rich Dauer .10 .02
❑ 252 Bobby Castillo .10 .02
❑ 253 Dann Bilardello .10 .02
❑ 254 Ozzie Guillen RC 1.50 .60
❑ 255 Tony Armas .15 .05
❑ 256 Kurt Kepshire .10 .02
❑ 257 Doug DeCinces .10 .02
❑ 258 Tim Burke .10 .02
❑ 259 Dan Pasqua .10 .02
❑ 260 Tony Pena .10 .02
❑ 261 Bobby Valentine MG .15 .05
❑ 262 Mario Ramirez .10 .02
❑ 263 Checklist: 133-264 .15 .05
❑ 264 Darren Daulton RC .50 .20
❑ 265 Ron Davis .10 .02
❑ 266 Keith Moreland .10 .02
❑ 267 Paul Molitor .15 .05
❑ 268 Mike Scott .15 .05
❑ 269 Dane Iorg .10 .02
❑ 270 Jack Morris .15 .05
❑ 271 Dave Collins .10 .02
❑ 272 Tim Tolman .10 .02
❑ 273 Jerry Willard .10 .02
❑ 274 Ron Gardenhire .10 .02
❑ 275 Charlie Hough .15 .05
❑ 276 Yankees Leaders Willie Randolph .15 .05
❑ 277 Jaime Cocanower .10 .02
❑ 278 Sixto Lezcano .10 .02
❑ 279 Al Pardo .10 .02
❑ 280 Tim Raines .15 .05
❑ 281 Steve Mura .10 .02
❑ 282 Jerry Mumphrey .10 .02
❑ 283 Mike Fischlin .10 .02
❑ 284 Brian Dayett .10 .02
❑ 285 Buddy Bell .15 .05
❑ 286 Luis DeLeon .10 .02
❑ 287 John Christensen .10 .02
❑ 288 Don Aase .10 .02
❑ 289 Johnnie LeMaster .10 .02
❑ 290 Carlton Fisk .25 .08
❑ 291 Tom Lasorda MG .25 .08
❑ 292 Chuck Porter .10 .02
❑ 293 Chris Chambliss .15 .05
❑ 294 Danny Cox .10 .02
❑ 295 Kirk Gibson .15 .05
❑ 296 Geno Petralli .10 .02
❑ 297 Tim Lollar .10 .02
❑ 298 Craig Reynolds .10 .02
❑ 299 Bryn Smith .10 .02
❑ 300 George Brett 1.00 .40
❑ 301 Dennis Rasmussen .10 .02
❑ 302 Greg Gross .10 .02
❑ 303 Curt Wardle .10 .02
❑ 304 Mike Gallego RC .10 .02
❑ 305 Phil Bradley .10 .02
❑ 306 Padres Leaders Terry Kennedy .10 .02
❑ 307 Dave Sax .10 .02
❑ 308 Ray Fontenot .10 .02
❑ 309 John Shelby .10 .02
❑ 310 Greg Minton .10 .02
❑ 311 Dick Schofield .10 .02
❑ 312 Tom Filer .10 .02
❑ 313 Joe DeSa .10 .02
❑ 314 Frank Pastore .10 .02
❑ 315 Mookie Wilson .15 .05
❑ 316 Sammy Khalifa .10 .02
❑ 317 Ed Romero .10 .02
❑ 318 Terry Whitfield .10 .02
❑ 319 Rick Camp .10 .02
❑ 320 Jim Rice .15 .05
❑ 321 Earl Weaver MG .15 .05
❑ 322 Bob Forsch .10 .02
❑ 323 Jerry Davis .10 .02
❑ 324 Dan Schatzeder .10 .02
❑ 325 Juan Beniquez .10 .02
❑ 326 Kent Tekulve .10 .02
❑ 327 Mike Pagliarulo .10 .02
❑ 328 Pete O'Brien .10 .02
❑ 329 Kirby Puckett 1.00 .40
❑ 330 Rick Sutcliffe .15 .05
❑ 331 Alan Ashby .10 .02
❑ 332 Darryl Motley .10 .02
❑ 333 Tom Henke .15 .05
❑ 334 Ken Oberkfell .10 .02
❑ 335 Don Sutton .15 .05
❑ 336 Indians Leaders Andre Thornton .15 .05
❑ 337 Darnell Coles .10 .02
❑ 338 Jorge Bell .15 .05
❑ 339 Bruce Berenyi .10 .02
❑ 340 Cal Ripken 1.50 .60
❑ 341 Frank Williams .10 .02
❑ 342 Gary Redus .10 .02
❑ 343 Carlos Diaz .10 .02
❑ 344 Jim Wohlford .10 .02
❑ 345 Donnie Moore .10 .02
❑ 346 Bryan Little .10 .02
❑ 347 Teddy Higuera RC* .25 .08
❑ 348 Cliff Johnson .10 .02
❑ 349 Mark Clear .10 .02
❑ 350 Jack Clark .15 .05
❑ 351 Chuck Tanner MG .10 .02
❑ 352 Harry Spilman .10 .02
❑ 353 Keith Atherton .10 .02
❑ 354 Tony Bernazard .10 .02
❑ 355 Lee Smith .15 .05
❑ 356 Mickey Hatcher .10 .02
❑ 357 Ed VandeBerg .10 .02
❑ 358 Rick Dempsey .10 .02
❑ 359 Mike LaCoss .10 .02
❑ 360 Lloyd Moseby .10 .02
❑ 361 Shane Rawley .10 .02
❑ 362 Tom Paciorek .10 .02
❑ 363 Terry Forster .15 .05
❑ 364 Reid Nichols .10 .02
❑ 365 Mike Flanagan .10 .02
❑ 366 Reds Leaders Dave Concepcion .15 .05
❑ 367 Aurelio Lopez .10 .02
❑ 368 Greg Brock .10 .02
❑ 369 Al Holland .10 .02
❑ 370 Vince Coleman RC .50 .20
❑ 371 Bill Stein .10 .02
❑ 372 Ben Oglivie .15 .05
❑ 373 Urbano Lugo .10 .02
❑ 374 Terry Francona .15 .05
❑ 375 Rich Gedman .10 .02
❑ 376 Bill Dawley .10 .02
❑ 377 Joe Carter .15 .05
❑ 378 Bruce Bochte .10 .02
❑ 379 Bobby Meacham .10 .02
❑ 380 LaMarr Hoyt .10 .02
❑ 381 Ray Miller MG .10 .02
❑ 382 Ivan Calderon RC* .25 .08
❑ 383 Chris Brown RC .10 .02
❑ 384 Steve Trout .10 .02
❑ 385 Cecil Cooper .15 .05
❑ 386 Cecil Fielder RC 1.00 .40
❑ 387 Steve Kemp .10 .02
❑ 388 Dickie Noles .10 .02
❑ 389 Glenn Davis .10 .02
❑ 390 Tom Seaver .25 .08
❑ 391 Julio Franco .15 .05
❑ 392 John Russell .10 .02
❑ 393 Chris Pittaro .10 .02
❑ 394 Checklist: 265-396 .15 .05
❑ 395 Scott Garrelts .10 .02
❑ 396 Red Sox Leaders Dwight Evans .25 .08
❑ 397 Steve Buechele RC .25 .08
❑ 398 Earnie Riles .10 .02
❑ 399 Bill Swift .10 .02
❑ 400 Rod Carew .25 .08
❑ 401 Fernando Valenzuela TBC '81 .10 .02
❑ 402 Tom Seaver TBC .15 .05
❑ 403 Willie Mays TBC .40 .15
❑ 404 Frank Robinson TBC .15 .05
❑ 405 Roger Maris TBC .40 .15
❑ 406 Scott Sanderson .10 .02
❑ 407 Sal Butera .10 .02
❑ 408 Dave Smith .10 .02
❑ 409 Paul Runge RC .10 .02
❑ 410 Dave Kingman .15 .05
❑ 411 Sparky Anderson MG .15 .05
❑ 412 Jim Clancy .10 .02
❑ 413 Tim Flannery .10 .02
❑ 414 Tom Gorman .10 .02
❑ 415 Hal McRae .15 .05
❑ 416 Dennis Martinez .15 .05
❑ 417 R.J. Reynolds .10 .02
❑ 418 Alan Knicely .10 .02
❑ 419 Frank Wills .10 .02
❑ 420 Von Hayes .10 .02
❑ 421 David Palmer .10 .02
❑ 422 Mike Jorgensen .10 .02
❑ 423 Dan Spillner .10 .02
❑ 424 Rick Miller .10 .02
❑ 425 Larry McWilliams .10 .02
❑ 426 Brewers Leaders Charlie Moore .10 .02
❑ 427 Joe Cowley .10 .02
❑ 428 Max Venable .10 .02
❑ 429 Greg Booker .10 .02
❑ 430 Kent Hrbek .15 .05
❑ 431 George Frazier .10 .02
❑ 432 Mark Bailey .10 .02
❑ 433 Chris Codiroli .10 .02
❑ 434 Curt Wilkerson .10 .02
❑ 435 Bill Caudill .10 .02
❑ 436 Doug Flynn .10 .02
❑ 437 Rick Mahler .10 .02
❑ 438 Clint Hurdle .10 .02
❑ 439 Rick Honeycutt .10 .02
❑ 440 Alvin Davis .10 .02
❑ 441 Whitey Herzog MG .25 .08
❑ 442 Ron Robinson .10 .02
❑ 443 Bill Buckner .15 .05

	No.	Card		
❑	444	Alex Trevino	.10	.02
❑	445	Bert Blyleven	.15	.05
❑	446	Lenn Sakata	.10	.02
❑	447	Jerry Don Gleaton	.10	.02
❑	448	Herm Winningham	.10	.02
❑	449	Rod Scurry	.10	.02
❑	450	Graig Nettles	.15	.05
❑	451	Mark Brown	.10	.02
❑	452	Bob Clark	.10	.02
❑	453	Steve Jeltz	.10	.02
❑	454	Burt Hooton	.10	.02
❑	455	Willie Randolph	.15	.05
❑	456	Braves Leaders Dale Murphy	.25	.08
❑	457	Mickey Tettleton RC	.25	.08
❑	458	Kevin Bass	.10	.02
❑	459	Luis Leal	.10	.02
❑	460	Leon Durham	.10	.02
❑	461	Walt Terrell	.10	.02
❑	462	Domingo Ramos	.10	.02
❑	463	Jim Gott	.10	.02
❑	464	Ruppert Jones	.10	.02
❑	465	Jesse Orosco	.10	.02
❑	466	Tom Foley	.10	.02
❑	467	Bob James	.10	.02
❑	468	Mike Scioscia	.15	.05
❑	469	Storm Davis	.10	.02
❑	470	Bill Madlock	.15	.05
❑	471	Bobby Cox MG	.15	.05
❑	472	Joe Hesketh	.10	.02
❑	473	Mark Brouhard	.10	.02
❑	474	John Tudor	.15	.05
❑	475	Juan Samuel	.10	.02
❑	476	Ron Mathis	.10	.02
❑	477	Mike Easler	.10	.02
❑	478	Andy Hawkins	.10	.02
❑	479	Bob Melvin	.10	.02
❑	480	Oddibe McDowell	.10	.02
❑	481	Scott Bradley	.10	.02
❑	482	Rick Lysander	.10	.02
❑	483	George Vukovich	.10	.02
❑	484	Donnie Hill	.10	.02
❑	485	Gary Matthews	.15	.05
❑	486	Angels Leaders Bobby Grich	.10	.02
❑	487	Bret Saberhagen	.15	.05
❑	488	Lou Thornton	.10	.02
❑	489	Jim Winn	.10	.02
❑	490	Jeff Leonard	.10	.02
❑	491	Pascual Perez	.10	.02
❑	492	Kelvin Chapman	.10	.02
❑	493	Gene Nelson	.10	.02
❑	494	Gary Roenicke	.10	.02
❑	495	Mark Langston	.15	.05
❑	496	Jay Johnstone	.10	.02
❑	497	John Stuper	.10	.02
❑	498	Tito Landrum	.10	.02
❑	499	Bob L. Gibson	.10	.02
❑	500	Rickey Henderson	.40	.15
❑	501	Dave Johnson MG	.10	.02
❑	502	Glen Cook	.10	.02
❑	503	Mike Fitzgerald	.10	.02
❑	504	Denny Walling	.10	.02
❑	505	Jerry Koosman	.15	.05
❑	506	Bill Russell	.15	.05
❑	507	Steve Ontiveros RC	.10	.02
❑	508	Alan Wiggins	.10	.02
❑	509	Ernie Camacho	.10	.02
❑	510	Wade Boggs	.25	.08
❑	511	Ed Nunez	.10	.02
❑	512	Thad Bosley	.10	.02
❑	513	Ron Washington	.10	.02
❑	514	Mike Jones	.10	.02
❑	515	Darrell Evans	.15	.05
❑	516	Giants Leaders Greg Minton	.10	.02
❑	517	Milt Thompson RC	.25	.08
❑	518	Buck Martinez	.10	.02
❑	519	Danny Darwin	.10	.02
❑	520	Keith Hernandez	.15	.05
❑	521	Nate Snell	.10	.02
❑	522	Bob Bailor	.10	.02
❑	523	Joe Price	.10	.02
❑	524	Darrell Miller	.10	.02
❑	525	Marvell Wynne	.10	.02
❑	526	Charlie Lea	.10	.02
❑	527	Checklist: 397-528	.15	.05
❑	528	Terry Pendleton	.15	.05
❑	529	Marc Sullivan	.10	.02
❑	530	Rich Gossage	.15	.05
❑	531	Tony LaRussa MG	.15	.05
❑	532	Don Carman	.10	.02
❑	533	Billy Sample	.10	.02
❑	534	Jeff Calhoun	.10	.02
❑	535	Toby Harrah	.15	.05
❑	536	Jose Rijo	.15	.05
❑	537	Mark Salas	.10	.02
❑	538	Dennis Eckersley	.25	.08
❑	539	Glenn Hubbard	.10	.02
❑	540	Dan Petry	.10	.02
❑	541	Jorge Orta	.10	.02
❑	542	Don Schulze	.10	.02
❑	543	Jerry Narron	.10	.02
❑	544	Eddie Milner	.10	.02
❑	545	Jimmy Key	.15	.05
❑	546	Mariners Leaders Dave Henderson	.10	.02
❑	547	Roger McDowell RC*	.25	.08
❑	548	Mike Young	.10	.02
❑	549	Bob Welch	.15	.05
❑	550	Tom Herr	.10	.02
❑	551	Dave LaPoint	.10	.02
❑	552	Marc Hill	.10	.02
❑	553	Jim Morrison	.10	.02
❑	554	Paul Householder	.10	.02
❑	555	Hubie Brooks	.10	.02
❑	556	John Denny	.10	.02
❑	557	Gerald Perry	.10	.02
❑	558	Tim Stoddard	.10	.02
❑	559	Tommy Dunbar	.10	.02
❑	560	Dave Righetti	.15	.05
❑	561	Bob Lillis MG	.10	.02
❑	562	Joe Beckwith	.10	.02
❑	563	Alejandro Sanchez	.10	.02
❑	564	Warren Brusstar	.10	.02
❑	565	Tom Brunansky	.10	.02
❑	566	Alfredo Griffin	.10	.02
❑	567	Jeff Barkley	.10	.02
❑	568	Donnie Scott	.10	.02
❑	569	Jim Acker	.10	.02
❑	570	Rusty Staub	.15	.05
❑	571	Mike Jeffcoat	.10	.02
❑	572	Paul Zuvella	.10	.02
❑	573	Tom Hume	.10	.02
❑	574	Ron Kittle	.10	.02
❑	575	Mike Boddicker	.10	.02
❑	576	Andre Dawson TL	.10	.02
❑	577	Jerry Reuss	.10	.02
❑	578	Lee Mazzilli	.15	.05
❑	579	Jim Slaton	.10	.02
❑	580	Willie McGee	.15	.05
❑	581	Bruce Hurst	.10	.02
❑	582	Jim Gantner	.10	.02
❑	583	Al Bumbry	.10	.02
❑	584	Brian Fisher RC	.10	.02
❑	585	Garry Maddox	.10	.02
❑	586	Greg Harris	.10	.02
❑	587	Rafael Santana	.10	.02
❑	588	Steve Lake	.10	.02
❑	589	Sid Bream	.10	.02
❑	590	Bob Knepper	.10	.02
❑	591	Jackie Moore MG	.10	.02
❑	592	Frank Tanana	.15	.05
❑	593	Jesse Barfield	.15	.05
❑	594	Chris Bando	.10	.02
❑	595	Dave Parker	.15	.05
❑	596	Onix Concepcion	.10	.02
❑	597	Sammy Stewart	.10	.02
❑	598	Jim Presley	.10	.02
❑	599	Rick Aguilera RC	.25	.08
❑	600	Dale Murphy	.25	.08
❑	601	Gary Lucas	.10	.02
❑	602	Mariano Duncan RC	.25	.08
❑	603	Bill Laskey	.10	.02
❑	604	Gary Pettis	.10	.02
❑	605	Dennis Boyd	.10	.02
❑	606	Royals Leaders Hal McRae	.15	.05
❑	607	Ken Dayley	.10	.02
❑	608	Bruce Bochy	.10	.02
❑	609	Barbaro Garbey	.10	.02
❑	610	Ron Guidry	.15	.05
❑	611	Gary Woods	.10	.02
❑	612	Richard Dotson	.10	.02
❑	613	Roy Smalley	.10	.02
❑	614	Rick Waits	.10	.02
❑	615	Johnny Ray	.10	.02
❑	616	Glenn Brummer	.10	.02
❑	617	Lonnie Smith	.10	.02
❑	618	Jim Pankovits	.10	.02
❑	619	Danny Heep	.10	.02
❑	620	Bruce Sutter	.15	.05
❑	621	John Felske MG	.10	.02
❑	622	Gary Lavelle	.10	.02
❑	623	Floyd Rayford	.10	.02
❑	624	Steve McCatty	.10	.02
❑	625	Bob Brenly	.10	.02
❑	626	Roy Thomas	.10	.02
❑	627	Ron Oester	.10	.02
❑	628	Kirk McCaskill RC	.25	.08
❑	629	Mitch Webster	.10	.02
❑	630	Fernando Valenzuela	.15	.05
❑	631	Steve Braun	.10	.02
❑	632	Dave Von Ohlen	.10	.02
❑	633	Jackie Gutierrez	.10	.02
❑	634	Roy Lee Jackson	.10	.02
❑	635	Jason Thompson	.10	.02
❑	636	Lee Smith TL	.10	.02
❑	637	Rudy Law	.10	.02
❑	638	John Butcher	.10	.02
❑	639	Bo Diaz	.10	.02
❑	640	Jose Cruz	.15	.05
❑	641	Wayne Tolleson	.10	.02
❑	642	Ray Searage	.10	.02
❑	643	Tom Brookens	.10	.02
❑	644	Mark Gubicza	.10	.02
❑	645	Dusty Baker	.15	.05
❑	646	Mike Moore	.10	.02
❑	647	Mel Hall	.10	.02
❑	648	Steve Bedrosian	.10	.02
❑	649	Ronn Reynolds	.10	.02
❑	650	Dave Stieb	.15	.05
❑	651	Billy Martin MG/TC	.25	.08
❑	652	Tom Browning	.10	.02
❑	653	Jim Dwyer	.10	.02
❑	654	Ken Howell	.10	.02
❑	655	Manny Trillo	.10	.02
❑	656	Brian Harper	.10	.02
❑	657	Juan Agosto	.10	.02
❑	658	Rob Wilfong	.10	.02
❑	659	Checklist: 529-660	.15	.05
❑	660	Steve Garvey	.15	.05
❑	661	Roger Clemens	4.00	1.50
❑	662	Bill Schroeder	.10	.02
❑	663	Neil Allen	.10	.02
❑	664	Tim Corcoran	.10	.02
❑	665	Alejandro Pena	.10	.02
❑	666	Rangers Leaders Charlie Hough	.15	.05
❑	667	Tim Teufel	.10	.02
❑	668	Cecilio Guante	.10	.02
❑	669	Ron Cey	.15	.05
❑	670	Willie Hernandez	.10	.02
❑	671	Lynn Jones	.10	.02
❑	672	Rob Picciolo	.10	.02
❑	673	Ernie Whitt	.10	.02
❑	674	Pat Tabler	.10	.02
❑	675	Claudell Washington	.10	.02
❑	676	Matt Young	.10	.02
❑	677	Nick Esasky	.10	.02
❑	678	Dan Gladden	.10	.02
❑	679	Britt Burns	.10	.02
❑	680	George Foster	.15	.05
❑	681	Dick Williams MG	.10	.02
❑	682	Junior Ortiz	.10	.02
❑	683	Andy Van Slyke	.25	.08
❑	684	Bob McClure	.10	.02
❑	685	Tim Wallach	.10	.02
❑	686	Jeff Stone	.10	.02
❑	687	Mike Trujillo	.10	.02
❑	688	Larry Herndon	.10	.02
❑	689	Dave Stewart	.15	.05
❑	690	Ryne Sandberg	.75	.30
❑	691	Mike Madden	.10	.02
❑	692	Dale Berra	.10	.02
❑	693	Tom Tellmann	.10	.02
❑	694	Garth Iorg	.10	.02
❑	695	Mike Smithson	.10	.02

❑ 696 Dodgers Leaders
Bill Russell .15 .05
❑ 697 Bud Black .10 .02
❑ 698 Brad Komminsk .10 .02
❑ 699 Pat Corrales MG .10 .02
❑ 700 Reggie Jackson .25 .08
❑ 701 Keith Hernandez AS .10 .02
❑ 702 Tom Herr AS .10 .02
❑ 703 Tim Wallach AS .10 .02
❑ 704 Ozzie Smith AS .40 .15
❑ 705 Dale Murphy AS .15 .05
❑ 706 Pedro Guerrero AS .10 .02
❑ 707 Willie McGee AS .10 .02
❑ 708 Gary Carter AS .10 .02
❑ 709 Dwight Gooden AS .25 .08
❑ 710 John Tudor AS .10 .02
❑ 711 Jeff Reardon AS .10 .02
❑ 712 Don Mattingly AS .60 .25
❑ 713 Damaso Garcia AS .10 .02
❑ 714 George Brett AS .40 .15
❑ 715 Cal Ripken AS .40 .15
❑ 716 Rickey Henderson AS .25 .08
❑ 717 Dave Winfield AS .10 .02
❑ 718 George Bell AS .10 .02
❑ 719 Carlton Fisk AS .15 .05
❑ 720 Bret Saberhagen AS .10 .02
❑ 721 Ron Guidry AS .10 .02
❑ 722 Dan Quisenberry AS .10 .02
❑ 723 Marty Bystrom .10 .02
❑ 724 Tim Hulett .10 .02
❑ 725 Mario Soto .15 .05
❑ 726 Orioles Leaders
Rick Dempsey .15 .05
❑ 727 David Green .10 .02
❑ 728 Mike Marshall .10 .02
❑ 729 Jim Beattie .10 .02
❑ 730 Ozzie Smith .60 .25
❑ 731 Don Robinson .10 .02
❑ 732 Floyd Youmans .10 .02
❑ 733 Ron Romanick .10 .02
❑ 734 Marty Barrett .10 .02
❑ 735 Dave Dravecky .10 .02
❑ 736 Glenn Wilson .10 .02
❑ 737 Pete Vuckovich .10 .02
❑ 738 Andre Robertson .10 .02
❑ 739 Dave Rozema .10 .02
❑ 740 Lance Parrish .15 .05
❑ 741 Pete Rose MG/TC .40 .15
❑ 742 Frank Viola .15 .05
❑ 743 Pat Sheridan .10 .02
❑ 744 Lary Sorensen .10 .02
❑ 745 Willie Upshaw .10 .02
❑ 746 Denny Gonzalez .10 .02
❑ 747 Rick Cerone .10 .02
❑ 748 Steve Henderson .10 .02
❑ 749 Ed Jurak .10 .02
❑ 750 Gorman Thomas .15 .05
❑ 751 Howard Johnson .15 .05
❑ 752 Mike Krukow .10 .02
❑ 753 Dan Ford .10 .02
❑ 754 Pat Clements .10 .02
❑ 755 Harold Baines .15 .05
❑ 756 Pirates Leaders
Rick Rhoden .10 .02
❑ 757 Darrell Porter .10 .02
❑ 758 Dave Anderson .10 .02
❑ 759 Moose Haas .10 .02
❑ 760 Andre Dawson .15 .05
❑ 761 Don Slaught .10 .02
❑ 762 Eric Show .10 .02
❑ 763 Terry Puhl .10 .02
❑ 764 Kevin Gross .10 .02
❑ 765 Don Baylor .15 .05
❑ 766 Rick Langford .10 .02
❑ 767 Jody Davis .10 .02
❑ 768 Vern Ruhle .10 .02
❑ 769 Harold Reynolds RC .75 .30
❑ 770 Vida Blue .15 .05
❑ 771 John McNamara MG .10 .02
❑ 772 Brian Downing .15 .05
❑ 773 Greg Pryor .10 .02
❑ 774 Terry Leach .10 .02
❑ 775 Al Oliver .15 .05
❑ 776 Gene Garber .10 .02
❑ 777 Wayne Krenchicki .10 .02
❑ 778 Jerry Hairston .10 .02
❑ 779 Rick Reuschel .15 .05
❑ 780 Robin Yount .60 .25
❑ 781 Joe Nolan .10 .02
❑ 782 Ken Landreaux .10 .02
❑ 783 Ricky Horton .10 .02
❑ 784 Alan Bannister .10 .02
❑ 785 Bob Stanley .10 .02
❑ 786 Twins Leaders
Mickey Hatcher .10 .02
❑ 787 Vance Law .10 .02
❑ 788 Marty Castillo .10 .02
❑ 789 Kurt Bevacqua .10 .02
❑ 790 Phil Niekro .15 .05
❑ 791 Checklist: 661-792 .15 .05
❑ 792 Charles Hudson .10 .02

1986 Topps Traded

❑ COMP.FACT.SET (132) 30.00 12.50
❑ 1T Andy Allanson XRC .10 .02
❑ 2T Neil Allen .10 .02
❑ 3T Joaquin Andujar .15 .05
❑ 4T Paul Assenmacher .40 .15
❑ 5T Scott Bailes .10 .02
❑ 6T Don Baylor .15 .05
❑ 7T Steve Bedrosian .10 .02
❑ 8T Juan Beniquez .10 .02
❑ 9T Juan Berenguer .10 .02
❑ 10T Mike Bielecki .10 .02
❑ 11T Barry Bonds XRC 20.00 8.00
❑ 12T Bobby Bonilla XRC .75 .30
❑ 13T Juan Bonilla .10 .02
❑ 14T Rich Bordi .10 .02
❑ 15T Steve Boros MG .10 .02
❑ 16T Rick Burleson .10 .02
❑ 17T Bill Campbell .10 .02
❑ 18T Tom Candiotti .10 .02
❑ 19T John Cangelosi .10 .02
❑ 20T Jose Canseco XRC 4.00 1.50
❑ 21T Carmen Castillo .10 .02
❑ 22T Rick Cerone .10 .02
❑ 23T John Cerutti .10 .02
❑ 24T Will Clark XRC 1.50 .60
❑ 25T Mark Clear .10 .02
❑ 26T Darnell Coles .10 .02
❑ 27T Dave Collins .10 .02
❑ 28T Tim Conroy .10 .02
❑ 29T Joe Cowley .10 .02
❑ 30T Joel Davis .10 .02
❑ 31T Rob Deer .10 .02
❑ 32T John Denny .10 .02
❑ 33T Mike Easler .10 .02
❑ 34T Mark Eichhorn .10 .02
❑ 35T Steve Farr .10 .02
❑ 36T Scott Fletcher .10 .02
❑ 37T Terry Forster .15 .05
❑ 38T Terry Francona .15 .05
❑ 39T Jim Fregosi MG .10 .02
❑ 40T Andres Galarraga XRC 1.00 .40
❑ 41T Ken Griffey .15 .05
❑ 42T Bill Gullickson .10 .02
❑ 43T Jose Guzman XRC .10 .02
❑ 44T Moose Haas .10 .02
❑ 45T Billy Hatcher .10 .02
❑ 46T Mike Heath .10 .02
❑ 47T Tom Hume .10 .02
❑ 48T Pete Incaviglia XRC .40 .15
❑ 49T Dane Iorg .10 .02
❑ 50T Bo Jackson XRC 5.00 2.00
❑ 51T Wally Joyner XRC .75 .30
❑ 52T Charlie Kerfeld .10 .02
❑ 53T Eric King .10 .02
❑ 54T Bob Kipper .10 .02
❑ 55T Wayne Krenchicki .10 .02
❑ 56T John Kruk XRC 1.00 .40
❑ 57T Mike LaCoss .10 .02
❑ 58T Pete Ladd .10 .02
❑ 59T Mike Laga .10 .02
❑ 60T Hal Lanier MG .10 .02
❑ 61T Dave LaPoint .10 .02
❑ 62T Rudy Law .10 .02
❑ 63T Rick Leach .10 .02
❑ 64T Tim Leary .10 .02
❑ 65T Dennis Leonard .10 .02
❑ 66T Jim Leyland MG XRC .50 .20
❑ 67T Steve Lyons .10 .02
❑ 68T Mickey Mahler .10 .02
❑ 69T Candy Maldonado .10 .02
❑ 70T Roger Mason XRC .10 .02
❑ 71T Bob McClure .10 .02
❑ 72T Andy McGaffigan .10 .02
❑ 73T Gene Michael MG .10 .02
❑ 74T Kevin Mitchell XRC .75 .30
❑ 75T Omar Moreno .10 .02
❑ 76T Jerry Mumphrey .10 .02
❑ 77T Phil Niekro .15 .05
❑ 78T Randy Niemann .10 .02
❑ 79T Juan Nieves .10 .02
❑ 80T Otis Nixon XRC .75 .30
❑ 81T Bob Ojeda .10 .02
❑ 82T Jose Oquendo .10 .02
❑ 83T Tom Paciorek .10 .02
❑ 84T David Palmer .10 .02
❑ 85T Frank Pastore .10 .02
❑ 86T Lou Piniella MG .15 .05
❑ 87T Dan Plesac .40 .15
❑ 88T Darrell Porter .10 .02
❑ 89T Rey Quinones .10 .02
❑ 90T Gary Redus .10 .02
❑ 91T Bip Roberts XRC .40 .15
❑ 92T Billy Joe Robidoux XRC .10 .02
❑ 93T Jeff D. Robinson .10 .02
❑ 94T Gary Roenicke .10 .02
❑ 95T Ed Romero .10 .02
❑ 96T Angel Salazar .10 .02
❑ 97T Joe Sambito .10 .02
❑ 98T Billy Sample .10 .02
❑ 99T Dave Schmidt .10 .02
❑ 100T Ken Schrom .10 .02
❑ 101T Tom Seaver .25 .08
❑ 102T Ted Simmons .15 .05
❑ 103T Sammy Stewart .10 .02
❑ 104T Kurt Stillwell .10 .02
❑ 105T Franklin Stubbs .10 .02
❑ 106T Dale Sveum .10 .02
❑ 107T Chuck Tanner MG .10 .02
❑ 108T Danny Tartabull .15 .05
❑ 109T Tim Teufel .10 .02
❑ 110T Bob Tewksbury XRC .40 .15
❑ 111T Andres Thomas .10 .02
❑ 112T Milt Thompson .40 .15
❑ 113T Robby Thompson XRC .40 .15
❑ 114T Jay Tibbs .10 .02
❑ 115T Wayne Tolleson .10 .02
❑ 116T Alex Trevino .10 .02
❑ 117T Manny Trillo .10 .02
❑ 118T Ed VandeBerg .10 .02
❑ 119T Ozzie Virgil .10 .02
❑ 120T Bob Walk .10 .02
❑ 121T Gene Walter .10 .02
❑ 122T Claudell Washington .10 .02
❑ 123T Bill Wegman XRC .10 .02
❑ 124T Dick Williams MG .10 .02
❑ 125T Mitch Williams XRC .40 .15
❑ 126T Bobby Witt XRC .40 .15
❑ 127T Todd Worrell XRC .40 .15
❑ 128T George Wright .10 .02
❑ 129T Ricky Wright .10 .02
❑ 130T Steve Yeager .15 .05
❑ 131T Paul Zuvella .10 .02
❑ 132T Checklist 1T-132T .10 .02

1987 Topps

❑ COMPLETE SET (792) 25.00 10.00
❑ COMP.FACT SET (792) 40.00 15.00

❑ COMP.HOBBY SET (792) 40.00 15.00
❑ COMP.X-MAS.SET (792) 40.00 15.00
❑ 1 Roger Clemens RB 1.00 .40
❑ 2 Jim Deshaies RB (Most cons. K's& start of game) .05 .01
❑ 3 Dwight Evans RB (Earliest home run& season) .15 .05
❑ 4 Davey Lopes RB (Most steals& season& 40-year-old) .05 .01
❑ 5 Dave Righetti RB (Most saves& season) .05 .01
❑ 6 Ruben Sierra RB .25 .08
❑ 7 Todd Worrell RB (Most saves& season& rookie) .05 .01
❑ 8 Terry Pendleton .10 .02
❑ 9 Jay Tibbs .05 .01
❑ 10 Cecil Cooper .10 .02
❑ 11 Indians Team (Mound conference) .05 .01
❑ 12 Jeff Sellers .05 .01
❑ 13 Nick Esasky .05 .01
❑ 14 Dave Stewart .10 .02
❑ 15 Claudell Washington .05 .01
❑ 16 Pat Clements .05 .01
❑ 17 Pete O'Brien .05 .01
❑ 18 Dick Howser MG .05 .01
❑ 19 Matt Young .05 .01
❑ 20 Gary Carter .10 .02
❑ 21 Mark Davis .05 .01
❑ 22 Doug DeCinces .05 .01
❑ 23 Lee Smith .10 .02
❑ 24 Tony Walker .05 .01
❑ 25 Bert Blyleven .10 .02
❑ 26 Greg Brock .05 .01
❑ 27 Joe Cowley .05 .01
❑ 28 Rick Dempsey .05 .01
❑ 29 Jimmy Key .10 .02
❑ 30 Tim Raines .10 .02
❑ 31 Braves Team (Glenn Hubbard and Rafael Ramirez) .05 .01
❑ 32 Tim Leary .05 .01
❑ 33 Andy Van Slyke .15 .05
❑ 34 Jose Rijo .10 .02
❑ 35 Sid Bream .05 .01
❑ 36 Eric King .05 .01
❑ 37 Marvell Wynne .05 .01
❑ 38 Dennis Leonard .05 .01
❑ 39 Marty Barrett .05 .01
❑ 40 Dave Righetti .10 .02
❑ 41 Bo Diaz .05 .01
❑ 42 Gary Redus .05 .01
❑ 43 Gene Michael MG .05 .01
❑ 44 Greg Harris .05 .01
❑ 45 Jim Presley .05 .01
❑ 46 Dan Gladden .05 .01
❑ 47 Dennis Powell .05 .01
❑ 48 Wally Backman .05 .01
❑ 49 Terry Harper .05 .01
❑ 50 Dave Smith .05 .01
❑ 51 Mel Hall .05 .01
❑ 52 Keith Atherton .05 .01
❑ 53 Ruppert Jones .05 .01
❑ 54 Bill Dawley .05 .01
❑ 55 Tim Wallach .05 .01
❑ 56 Brewers Team (Mound conference) .10 .02
❑ 57 Scott Nielsen .05 .01
❑ 58 Thad Bosley .05 .01
❑ 59 Ken Dayley .05 .01
❑ 60 Tony Pena .05 .01
❑ 61 Bobby Thigpen RC .25 .08
❑ 62 Bobby Meacham .05 .01
❑ 63 Fred Toliver .05 .01
❑ 64 Harry Spilman .05 .01
❑ 65 Tom Browning .05 .01
❑ 66 Marc Sullivan .05 .01
❑ 67 Bill Swift .05 .01
❑ 68 Tony LaRussa MG .10 .02
❑ 69 Lonnie Smith .05 .01
❑ 70 Charlie Hough .10 .02
❑ 71 Mike Aldrete .05 .01
❑ 72 Walt Terrell .05 .01
❑ 73 Dave Anderson .05 .01
❑ 74 Dan Pasqua .05 .01
❑ 75 Ron Darling .10 .02
❑ 76 Rafael Ramirez .05 .01
❑ 77 Bryan Oelkers .05 .01
❑ 78 Tom Foley .05 .01
❑ 79 Juan Nieves .05 .01
❑ 80 Wally Joyner RC .40 .15
❑ 81 Padres Team (Andy Hawkins and Terry Kennedy) .05 .01
❑ 82 Rob Murphy .05 .01
❑ 83 Mike Davis .05 .01
❑ 84 Steve Lake .05 .01
❑ 85 Kevin Bass .05 .01
❑ 86 Nate Snell .05 .01
❑ 87 Mark Salas .05 .01
❑ 88 Ed Wojna .05 .01
❑ 89 Ozzie Guillen .15 .05
❑ 90 Dave Stieb .10 .02
❑ 91 Harold Reynolds .10 .02
❑ 92A Urbano Lugo ERR (no trademark) .15 .05
❑ 92B Urbano Lugo COR .05 .01
❑ 93 Jim Leyland MG/TC RC * .25 .08
❑ 94 Calvin Schiraldi .05 .01
❑ 95 Oddibe McDowell .05 .01
❑ 96 Frank Williams .05 .01
❑ 97 Glenn Wilson .05 .01
❑ 98 Bill Scherrer .05 .01
❑ 99 Darryl Motley (Now with Braves on card front) .05 .01
❑ 100 Steve Garvey .10 .02
❑ 101 Carl Willis RC .10 .02
❑ 102 Paul Zuvella .05 .01
❑ 103 Rick Aguilera .05 .01
❑ 104 Billy Sample .05 .01
❑ 105 Floyd Youmans .05 .01
❑ 106 Blue Jays Team (George Bell and Jesse Barfield) .05 .01
❑ 107 John Butcher .05 .01
❑ 108 Jim Gantner UER (Brewers logo reversed) .05 .01
❑ 109 R.J. Reynolds .05 .01
❑ 110 John Tudor .10 .02
❑ 111 Alfredo Griffin .05 .01
❑ 112 Alan Ashby .05 .01
❑ 113 Neil Allen .05 .01
❑ 114 Billy Beane .10 .02
❑ 115 Donnie Moore .05 .01
❑ 116 Bill Russell .10 .02
❑ 117 Jim Beattie .05 .01
❑ 118 Bobby Valentine MG .10 .02
❑ 119 Ron Robinson .05 .01
❑ 120 Eddie Murray .25 .08
❑ 121 Kevin Romine .05 .01
❑ 122 Jim Clancy .05 .01
❑ 123 John Kruk RC .50 .20
❑ 124 Ray Fontenot .05 .01
❑ 125 Bob Brenly .05 .01
❑ 126 Mike Loynd RC .10 .02
❑ 127 Vance Law .05 .01
❑ 128 Checklist 1-132 .05 .01
❑ 129 Rick Cerone .05 .01
❑ 130 Dwight Gooden .15 .05
❑ 131 Pirates Team (Sid Bream and Tony Pena) .05 .01
❑ 132 Paul Assenmacher .25 .08
❑ 133 Jose Oquendo .05 .01
❑ 134 Rich Yett .05 .01
❑ 135 Mike Easler .05 .01
❑ 136 Ron Romanick .05 .01
❑ 137 Jerry Willard .05 .01
❑ 138 Roy Lee Jackson .05 .01
❑ 139 Devon White RC .40 .15
❑ 140 Bret Saberhagen .10 .02
❑ 141 Herm Winningham .05 .01
❑ 142 Rick Sutcliffe .10 .02
❑ 143 Steve Boros MG .05 .01
❑ 144 Mike Scioscia .10 .02
❑ 145 Charlie Kerfeld .05 .01
❑ 146 Tracy Jones .05 .01
❑ 147 Randy Niemann .05 .01
❑ 148 Dave Collins .05 .01
❑ 149 Ray Searage .05 .01
❑ 150 Wade Boggs .15 .05
❑ 151 Mike LaCoss .05 .01
❑ 152 Toby Harrah .10 .02
❑ 153 Duane Ward RC * .25 .08
❑ 154 Tom O'Malley .05 .01
❑ 155 Eddie Whitson .05 .01
❑ 156 Mariners Team (Mound conference) .05 .01
❑ 157 Danny Darwin .05 .01
❑ 158 Tim Teufel .05 .01
❑ 159 Ed Olwine .05 .01
❑ 160 Julio Franco .10 .02
❑ 161 Steve Ontiveros .05 .01
❑ 162 Mike LaValliere RC * .25 .08
❑ 163 Kevin Gross .05 .01
❑ 164 Sammy Khalifa .05 .01
❑ 165 Jeff Reardon .10 .02
❑ 166 Bob Boone .10 .02
❑ 167 Jim Deshaies RC * .10 .02
❑ 168 Lou Piniella MG .10 .02
❑ 169 Ron Washington .05 .01
❑ 170 Bo Jackson RC 3.00 1.25
❑ 171 Chuck Cary .05 .01
❑ 172 Ron Oester .05 .01
❑ 173 Alex Trevino .05 .01
❑ 174 Henry Cotto .05 .01
❑ 175 Bob Stanley .05 .01
❑ 176 Steve Buechele .05 .01
❑ 177 Keith Moreland .05 .01
❑ 178 Cecil Fielder .10 .02
❑ 179 Bill Wegman .05 .01
❑ 180 Chris Brown .05 .01
❑ 181 Cardinals Team (Mound conference) .05 .01
❑ 182 Lee Lacy .05 .01
❑ 183 Andy Hawkins .05 .01
❑ 184 Bobby Bonilla RC .40 .15
❑ 185 Roger McDowell .05 .01
❑ 186 Bruce Benedict .05 .01
❑ 187 Mark Huismann .05 .01
❑ 188 Tony Phillips .05 .01
❑ 189 Joe Hesketh .05 .01
❑ 190 Jim Sundberg .10 .02
❑ 191 Charles Hudson .05 .01
❑ 192 Cory Snyder .05 .01
❑ 193 Roger Craig MG .10 .02
❑ 194 Kirk McCaskill .05 .01
❑ 195 Mike Pagliarulo .05 .01
❑ 196 Randy O'Neal UER (Wrong ML career W-L totals) .05 .01
❑ 197 Mark Bailey .05 .01
❑ 198 Lee Mazzilli .10 .02
❑ 199 Mariano Duncan .05 .01
❑ 200 Pete Rose .60 .25
❑ 201 John Cangelosi .05 .01
❑ 202 Ricky Wright .05 .01
❑ 203 Mike Kingery RC .10 .02
❑ 204 Sammy Stewart .05 .01
❑ 205 Graig Nettles .10 .02
❑ 206 Twins Team (Frank Viola and Tim Laudner) .05 .01
❑ 207 George Frazier .05 .01

Card		
❑ 208 John Shelby	.05	.01
❑ 209 Rick Schu	.05	.01
❑ 210 Lloyd Moseby	.05	.01
❑ 211 John Morris	.05	.01
❑ 212 Mike Fitzgerald	.05	.01
❑ 213 Randy Myers RC	.40	.15
❑ 214 Omar Moreno	.05	.01
❑ 215 Mark Langston	.05	.01
❑ 216 B.J. Surhoff RC	.40	.15
❑ 217 Chris Codiroli	.05	.01
❑ 218 Sparky Anderson MG	.10	.02
❑ 219 Cecilio Guante	.05	.01
❑ 220 Joe Carter	.10	.02
❑ 221 Vern Ruhle	.05	.01
❑ 222 Denny Walling	.05	.01
❑ 223 Charlie Leibrandt	.05	.01
❑ 224 Wayne Tolleson	.05	.01
❑ 225 Mike Smithson	.05	.01
❑ 226 Max Venable	.05	.01
❑ 227 Jamie Moyer RC	.50	.20
❑ 228 Curt Wilkerson	.05	.01
❑ 229 Mike Birkbeck	.10	.02
❑ 230 Don Baylor	.10	.02
❑ 231 Giants Team (Bob Brenly and Jim Gott)	.05	.01
❑ 232 Reggie Williams	.05	.01
❑ 233 Russ Morman	.05	.01
❑ 234 Pat Sheridan	.05	.01
❑ 235 Alvin Davis	.05	.01
❑ 236 Tommy John	.10	.02
❑ 237 Jim Morrison	.05	.01
❑ 238 Bill Krueger	.05	.01
❑ 239 Juan Espino	.05	.01
❑ 240 Steve Balboni	.05	.01
❑ 241 Danny Heep	.05	.01
❑ 242 Rick Mahler	.05	.01
❑ 243 Whitey Herzog MG	.10	.02
❑ 244 Dickie Noles	.05	.01
❑ 245 Willie Upshaw	.05	.01
❑ 246 Jim Dwyer	.05	.01
❑ 247 Jeff Reed	.05	.01
❑ 248 Gene Walter	.05	.01
❑ 249 Jim Pankovits	.05	.01
❑ 250 Teddy Higuera	.05	.01
❑ 251 Rob Wilfong	.05	.01
❑ 252 Dennis Martinez	.10	.02
❑ 253 Eddie Milner	.05	.01
❑ 254 Bob Tewksbury RC *	.25	.08
❑ 255 Juan Samuel	.05	.01
❑ 256 Royals TL/George Brett	.15	.05
❑ 257 Bob Forsch	.05	.01
❑ 258 Steve Yeager	.10	.02
❑ 259 Mike Greenwell RC	.25	.08
❑ 260 Vida Blue	.10	.02
❑ 261 Ruben Sierra RC	.50	.20
❑ 262 Jim Winn	.05	.01
❑ 263 Stan Javier	.05	.01
❑ 264 Checklist 133-264	.05	.01
❑ 265 Darrell Evans	.10	.02
❑ 266 Jeff Hamilton	.05	.01
❑ 267 Howard Johnson	.10	.02
❑ 268 Pat Corrales MG	.05	.01
❑ 269 Cliff Speck	.05	.01
❑ 270 Jody Davis	.05	.01
❑ 271 Mike G. Brown	.05	.01
❑ 272 Andres Galarraga	.10	.02
❑ 273 Gene Nelson	.05	.01
❑ 274 Jeff Hearron UER (Duplicate 1986 stat line on ba)	.05	.01
❑ 275 LaMarr Hoyt	.05	.01
❑ 276 Jackie Gutierrez	.05	.01
❑ 277 Juan Agosto	.05	.01
❑ 278 Gary Pettis	.05	.01
❑ 279 Dan Plesac	.05	.01
❑ 280 Jeff Leonard	.05	.01
❑ 281 Reds TL/Rose	.25	.08
❑ 282 Jeff Calhoun	.05	.01
❑ 283 Doug Drabek RC	.40	.15
❑ 284 John Moses	.05	.01
❑ 285 Dennis Boyd	.05	.01
❑ 286 Mike Woodard	.05	.01
❑ 287 Dave Von Ohlen	.05	.01
❑ 288 Tito Landrum	.05	.01
❑ 289 Bob Kipper	.05	.01
❑ 290 Leon Durham	.05	.01
❑ 291 Mitch Williams RC *	.25	.08
❑ 292 Franklin Stubbs	.05	.01
❑ 293 Bob Rodgers MG (Checklist back& inconsistent des)	.05	.01
❑ 294 Steve Jeltz	.05	.01
❑ 295 Len Dykstra	.10	.02
❑ 296 Andres Thomas	.05	.01
❑ 297 Don Schulze	.05	.01
❑ 298 Larry Herndon	.05	.01
❑ 299 Joel Davis	.05	.01
❑ 300 Reggie Jackson	.15	.05
❑ 301 Luis Aquino UER (No trademark never corrected)	.05	.01
❑ 302 Bill Schroeder	.05	.01
❑ 303 Juan Berenguer	.05	.01
❑ 304 Phil Garner	.10	.02
❑ 305 John Franco	.10	.02
❑ 306 Red Sox TL/Seaver	.10	.02
❑ 307 Lee Guetterman	.05	.01
❑ 308 Don Slaught	.05	.01
❑ 309 Mike Young	.05	.01
❑ 310 Frank Viola	.10	.02
❑ 311 Rickey Henderson TBC	.15	.05
❑ 312 Reggie Jackson TBC	.10	.02
❑ 313 Roberto Clemente TBC	.25	.08
❑ 314 Carl Yastrzemski TBC	.25	.08
❑ 315 Maury Wills TBC '62	.10	.02
❑ 316 Brian Fisher	.05	.01
❑ 317 Clint Hurdle	.05	.01
❑ 318 Jim Fregosi MG	.05	.01
❑ 319 Greg Swindell RC	.25	.08
❑ 320 Barry Bonds RC	8.00	3.00
❑ 321 Mike Laga	.05	.01
❑ 322 Chris Bando	.05	.01
❑ 323 Al Newman RC	.05	.01
❑ 324 David Palmer	.05	.01
❑ 325 Garry Templeton	.10	.02
❑ 326 Mark Gubicza	.05	.01
❑ 327 Dale Sveum	.05	.01
❑ 328 Bob Welch	.10	.02
❑ 329 Ron Roenicke	.05	.01
❑ 330 Mike Scott	.10	.02
❑ 331 Mets TL/Carter/Straw	.10	.02
❑ 332 Joe Price	.05	.01
❑ 333 Ken Phelps	.05	.01
❑ 334 Ed Correa	.05	.01
❑ 335 Candy Maldonado	.05	.01
❑ 336 Allan Anderson RC	.05	.01
❑ 337 Darrell Miller	.05	.01
❑ 338 Tim Conroy	.05	.01
❑ 339 Donnie Hill	.05	.01
❑ 340 Roger Clemens	1.50	.60
❑ 341 Mike C. Brown	.05	.01
❑ 342 Bob James	.05	.01
❑ 343 Hal Lanier MG	.05	.01
❑ 344A Joe Niekro (Copyright inside righthand border)	.05	.01
❑ 344B Joe Niekro (Copyright outside righthand border)	.05	.01
❑ 345 Andre Dawson	.10	.02
❑ 346 Shawon Dunston	.05	.01
❑ 347 Mickey Brantley	.05	.01
❑ 348 Carmelo Martinez	.05	.01
❑ 349 Storm Davis	.05	.01
❑ 350 Keith Hernandez	.10	.02
❑ 351 Gene Garber	.05	.01
❑ 352 Mike Felder	.05	.01
❑ 353 Ernie Camacho	.05	.01
❑ 354 Jamie Quirk	.05	.01
❑ 355 Don Carman	.05	.01
❑ 356 White Sox Team (Mound conference)	.05	.01
❑ 357 Steve Fireovid	.05	.01
❑ 358 Sal Butera	.05	.01
❑ 359 Doug Corbett	.05	.01
❑ 360 Pedro Guerrero	.10	.02
❑ 361 Mark Thurmond	.05	.01
❑ 362 Luis Quinones	.05	.01
❑ 363 Jose Guzman	.05	.01
❑ 364 Randy Bush	.05	.01
❑ 365 Rick Rhoden	.05	.01
❑ 366 Mark McGwire	4.00	1.50
❑ 367 Jeff Lahti	.05	.01
❑ 368 John McNamara MG	.05	.01
❑ 369 Brian Dayett	.05	.01
❑ 370 Fred Lynn	.10	.02
❑ 371 Mark Eichhorn	.05	.01
❑ 372 Jerry Mumphrey	.05	.01
❑ 373 Jeff Dedmon	.05	.01
❑ 374 Glenn Hoffman	.05	.01
❑ 375 Ron Guidry	.10	.02
❑ 376 Scott Bradley	.05	.01
❑ 377 John Henry Johnson	.05	.01
❑ 378 Rafael Santana	.05	.01
❑ 379 John Russell	.05	.01
❑ 380 Rich Gossage	.10	.02
❑ 381 Expos Team (Mound conference)	.05	.01
❑ 382 Rudy Law	.05	.01
❑ 383 Ron Davis	.05	.01
❑ 384 Johnny Grubb	.05	.01
❑ 385 Orel Hershiser	.15	.05
❑ 386 Dickie Thon	.05	.01
❑ 387 T.R. Bryden	.05	.01
❑ 388 Geno Petralli	.05	.01
❑ 389 Jeff D. Robinson	.05	.01
❑ 390 Gary Matthews	.10	.02
❑ 391 Jay Howell	.05	.01
❑ 392 Checklist 265-396	.05	.01
❑ 393 Pete Rose MG/TC	.15	.05
❑ 394 Mike Bielecki	.05	.01
❑ 395 Damaso Garcia	.05	.01
❑ 396 Tim Lollar	.05	.01
❑ 397 Greg Walker	.05	.01
❑ 398 Brad Havens	.05	.01
❑ 399 Curt Ford	.05	.01
❑ 400 George Brett	.60	.25
❑ 401 Billy Joe Robidoux	.05	.01
❑ 402 Mike Trujillo	.05	.01
❑ 403 Jerry Royster	.05	.01
❑ 404 Doug Sisk	.05	.01
❑ 405 Brook Jacoby	.05	.01
❑ 406 Yankees TL/Hend/Matt	.50	.20
❑ 407 Jim Acker	.05	.01
❑ 408 John Mizerock	.05	.01
❑ 409 Milt Thompson	.05	.01
❑ 410 Fernando Valenzuela	.10	.02
❑ 411 Darnell Coles	.05	.01
❑ 412 Eric Davis	.15	.05
❑ 413 Moose Haas	.05	.01
❑ 414 Joe Orsulak	.05	.01
❑ 415 Bobby Witt RC	.25	.08
❑ 416 Tom Nieto	.05	.01
❑ 417 Pat Perry	.05	.01
❑ 418 Dick Williams MG	.05	.01
❑ 419 Mark Portugal RC *	.25	.08
❑ 420 Will Clark RC	1.00	.40
❑ 421 Jose DeLeon	.05	.01
❑ 422 Jack Howell	.05	.01
❑ 423 Jaime Cocanower	.05	.01
❑ 424 Chris Speier	.05	.01
❑ 425 Tom Seaver	.15	.05
❑ 426 Floyd Rayford	.05	.01
❑ 427 Edwin Nunez	.05	.01
❑ 428 Bruce Bochy	.05	.01
❑ 429 Tim Pyznarski	.05	.01
❑ 430 Mike Schmidt	.50	.20
❑ 431 Dodgers Team (Mound conference)	.05	.01
❑ 432 Jim Slaton	.05	.01
❑ 433 Ed Hearn	.05	.01
❑ 434 Mike Fischlin	.05	.01
❑ 435 Bruce Sutter	.10	.02
❑ 436 Andy Allanson RC	.05	.01
❑ 437 Ted Power	.05	.01
❑ 438 Kelly Downs RC	.10	.02
❑ 439 Karl Best	.05	.01
❑ 440 Willie McGee	.10	.02
❑ 441 Dave Leiper	.05	.01
❑ 442 Mitch Webster	.05	.01
❑ 443 John Felske MG	.05	.01
❑ 444 Jeff Russell	.05	.01
❑ 445 Dave Lopes	.10	.02
❑ 446 Chuck Finley RC	.40	.15
❑ 447 Bill Almon	.05	.01
❑ 448 Chris Bosio RC	.25	.08
❑ 449 Pat Dodson	.10	.02

❑ 450 Kirby Puckett .50 .20
❑ 451 Joe Sambito .05 .01
❑ 452 Dave Henderson .05 .01
❑ 453 Scott Terry RC .10 .02
❑ 454 Luis Salazar .05 .01
❑ 455 Mike Boddicker .05 .01
❑ 456 A's Team (Mound conference) .05 .01
❑ 457 Len Matuszek .05 .01
❑ 458 Kelly Gruber .05 .01
❑ 459 Dennis Eckersley .15 .05
❑ 460 Darryl Strawberry .10 .02
❑ 461 Craig McMurtry .05 .01
❑ 462 Scott Fletcher .05 .01
❑ 463 Tom Candiotti .05 .01
❑ 464 Butch Wynegar .05 .01
❑ 465 Todd Worrell .05 .01
❑ 466 Kal Daniels .05 .01
❑ 467 Randy St.Claire .05 .01
❑ 468 George Bamberger MG .05 .01
❑ 469 Mike Diaz .05 .01
❑ 470 Dave Dravecky .05 .01
❑ 471 Ronn Reynolds .05 .01
❑ 472 Bill Doran .05 .01
❑ 473 Steve Farr .05 .01
❑ 474 Jerry Narron .05 .01
❑ 475 Scott Garrelts .05 .01
❑ 476 Danny Tartabull .05 .01
❑ 477 Ken Howell .05 .01
❑ 478 Tim Laudner .05 .01
❑ 479 Bob Sebra .05 .01
❑ 480 Jim Rice .10 .02
❑ 481 Phillies Team (Glenn Wilson& Juan Samuel& and V) .05 .01
❑ 482 Daryl Boston .05 .01
❑ 483 Dwight Lowry .05 .01
❑ 484 Jim Traber .05 .01
❑ 485 Tony Fernandez .05 .01
❑ 486 Otis Nixon .05 .01
❑ 487 Dave Gumpert .05 .01
❑ 488 Ray Knight .10 .02
❑ 489 Bill Gullickson .05 .01
❑ 490 Dale Murphy .15 .05
❑ 491 Ron Karkovice RC .25 .08
❑ 492 Mike Heath .05 .01
❑ 493 Tom Lasorda MG .15 .05
❑ 494 Barry Jones .05 .01
❑ 495 Gorman Thomas .10 .02
❑ 496 Bruce Bochte .05 .01
❑ 497 Dale Mohorcic .05 .01
❑ 498 Bob Kearney .05 .01
❑ 499 Bruce Ruffin RC .10 .02
❑ 500 Don Mattingly .60 .25
❑ 501 Craig Lefferts .05 .01
❑ 502 Dick Schofield .05 .01
❑ 503 Larry Andersen .05 .01
❑ 504 Mickey Hatcher .05 .01
❑ 505 Bryn Smith .05 .01
❑ 506 Orioles Team (Mound conference) .05 .01
❑ 507 Dave L. Stapleton .05 .01
❑ 508 Scott Bankhead .05 .01
❑ 509 Enos Cabell .05 .01
❑ 510 Tom Henke .05 .01
❑ 511 Steve Lyons .05 .01
❑ 512 Dave Magadan RC .25 .08
❑ 513 Carmen Castillo .05 .01
❑ 514 Orlando Mercado .05 .01
❑ 515 Willie Hernandez .05 .01
❑ 516 Ted Simmons .10 .02
❑ 517 Mario Soto .10 .02
❑ 518 Gene Mauch MG .05 .01
❑ 519 Curt Young .05 .01
❑ 520 Jack Clark .10 .02
❑ 521 Rick Reuschel .10 .02
❑ 522 Checklist 397-528 .05 .01
❑ 523 Earnie Riles .05 .01
❑ 524 Bob Shirley .05 .01
❑ 525 Phil Bradley .05 .01
❑ 526 Roger Mason .05 .01
❑ 527 Jim Wohlford .05 .01
❑ 528 Ken Dixon .05 .01
❑ 529 Alvaro Espinoza RC .10 .02
❑ 530 Tony Gwynn .30 .10
❑ 531 Astros TL/Y.Berra .10 .02
❑ 532 Jeff Stone .05 .01
❑ 533 Angel Salazar .05 .01
❑ 534 Scott Sanderson .05 .01
❑ 535 Tony Armas .10 .02
❑ 536 Terry Mulholland RC .25 .08
❑ 537 Rance Mulliniks .05 .01
❑ 538 Tom Niedenfuer .05 .01
❑ 539 Reid Nichols .05 .01
❑ 540 Terry Kennedy .05 .01
❑ 541 Rafael Belliard RC .25 .08
❑ 542 Ricky Horton .05 .01
❑ 543 Dave Johnson MG .05 .01
❑ 544 Zane Smith .05 .01
❑ 545 Buddy Bell .10 .02
❑ 546 Mike Morgan .05 .01
❑ 547 Rob Deer .05 .01
❑ 548 Bill Mooneyham .05 .01
❑ 549 Bob Melvin .05 .01
❑ 550 Pete Incaviglia RC * .25 .08
❑ 551 Frank Wills .05 .01
❑ 552 Larry Sheets .05 .01
❑ 553 Mike Maddux .05 .01
❑ 554 Buddy Biancalana .05 .01
❑ 555 Dennis Rasmussen .05 .01
❑ 556 Angels Team (Rene Lachemann CO& Mike Witt& and) .05 .01
❑ 557 John Cerutti .05 .01
❑ 558 Greg Gagne .05 .01
❑ 559 Lance McCullers .05 .01
❑ 560 Glenn Davis .05 .01
❑ 561 Rey Quinones .05 .01
❑ 562 Bryan Clutterbuck .05 .01
❑ 563 John Stefero .05 .01
❑ 564 Larry McWilliams .05 .01
❑ 565 Dusty Baker .10 .02
❑ 566 Tim Hulett .05 .01
❑ 567 Greg Mathews .05 .01
❑ 568 Earl Weaver MG .10 .02
❑ 569 Wade Rowdon .05 .01
❑ 570 Sid Fernandez .05 .01
❑ 571 Ozzie Virgil .05 .01
❑ 572 Pete Ladd .05 .01
❑ 573 Hal McRae .10 .02
❑ 574 Manny Lee .05 .01
❑ 575 Pat Tabler .05 .01
❑ 576 Frank Pastore .05 .01
❑ 577 Dann Bilardello .05 .01
❑ 578 Billy Hatcher .05 .01
❑ 579 Rick Burleson .05 .01
❑ 580 Mike Krukow .05 .01
❑ 581 Cubs Team (Ron Cey and Steve Trout) .05 .01
❑ 582 Bruce Berenyi .05 .01
❑ 583 Junior Ortiz .05 .01
❑ 584 Ron Kittle .05 .01
❑ 585 Scott Bailes .05 .01
❑ 586 Ben Oglivie .10 .02
❑ 587 Eric Plunk .05 .01
❑ 588 Wallace Johnson .05 .01
❑ 589 Steve Crawford .05 .01
❑ 590 Vince Coleman .05 .01
❑ 591 Spike Owen .05 .01
❑ 592 Chris Welsh .05 .01
❑ 593 Chuck Tanner MG .05 .01
❑ 594 Rick Anderson .05 .01
❑ 595 Keith Hernandez AS .05 .01
❑ 596 Steve Sax AS .05 .01
❑ 597 Mike Schmidt AS .25 .08
❑ 598 Ozzie Smith AS .25 .08
❑ 599 Tony Gwynn AS .15 .05
❑ 600 Dave Parker AS .05 .01
❑ 601 Darryl Strawberry AS .05 .01
❑ 602 Gary Carter AS .05 .01
❑ 603A Dwight Gooden AS NoTM .10 .02
❑ 603B Dwight Gooden AS TM .10 .02
❑ 604 Fernando Valenzuela AS .05 .01
❑ 605 Todd Worrell AS .05 .01
❑ 606 Don Mattingly AS .30 .10
❑ 606A Don Mattingly AS NoTM 1.00 .40
❑ 607 Tony Bernazard AS .05 .01
❑ 608 Wade Boggs AS .10 .02
❑ 609 Cal Ripken AS .25 .08
❑ 610 Jim Rice AS .05 .01
❑ 611 Kirby Puckett AS .25 .08
❑ 612 George Bell AS .05 .01
❑ 613 Lance Parrish AS UER (Pitcher heading on back) .05 .01
❑ 614 Roger Clemens AS 1.00 .40
❑ 615 Teddy Higuera AS .05 .01
❑ 616 Dave Righetti AS .05 .01
❑ 617 Al Nipper .05 .01
❑ 618 Tom Kelly MG .05 .01
❑ 619 Jerry Reed .05 .01
❑ 620 Jose Canseco 1.00 .40
❑ 621 Danny Cox .05 .01
❑ 622 Glenn Braggs RC .10 .02
❑ 623 Kurt Stillwell .05 .01
❑ 624 Tim Burke .05 .01
❑ 625 Mookie Wilson .10 .02
❑ 626 Joel Skinner .05 .01
❑ 627 Ken Oberkfell .05 .01
❑ 628 Bob Walk .05 .01
❑ 629 Larry Parrish .05 .01
❑ 630 John Candelaria .05 .01
❑ 631 Tigers Team (Mound conference) .05 .01
❑ 632 Rob Woodward .05 .01
❑ 633 Jose Uribe .05 .01
❑ 634 Rafael Palmeiro RC 1.50 .60
❑ 635 Ken Schrom .05 .01
❑ 636 Darren Daulton .10 .02
❑ 637 Bip Roberts RC .25 .08
❑ 638 Rich Bordi .05 .01
❑ 639 Gerald Perry .05 .01
❑ 640 Mark Clear .05 .01
❑ 641 Domingo Ramos .05 .01
❑ 642 Al Pulido .05 .01
❑ 643 Ron Shepherd .05 .01
❑ 644 John Denny .05 .01
❑ 645 Dwight Evans .15 .05
❑ 646 Mike Mason .05 .01
❑ 647 Tom Lawless .05 .01
❑ 648 Barry Larkin RC 1.00 .40
❑ 649 Mickey Tettleton .05 .01
❑ 650 Hubie Brooks .05 .01
❑ 651 Benny Distefano .05 .01
❑ 652 Terry Forster .10 .02
❑ 653 Kevin Mitchell RC * .40 .15
❑ 654 Checklist 529-660 .10 .02
❑ 655 Jesse Barfield .10 .02
❑ 656 Rangers Team (Bobby Valentine MG and Ricky Wrigh) .05 .01
❑ 657 Tom Waddell .05 .01
❑ 658 Robby Thompson RC * .25 .08
❑ 659 Aurelio Lopez .05 .01
❑ 660 Bob Horner .10 .02
❑ 661 Lou Whitaker .10 .02
❑ 662 Frank DiPino .05 .01
❑ 663 Cliff Johnson .05 .01
❑ 664 Mike Marshall .05 .01
❑ 665 Rod Scurry .05 .01
❑ 666 Von Hayes .05 .01
❑ 667 Ron Hassey .05 .01
❑ 668 Juan Bonilla .05 .01
❑ 669 Bud Black .05 .01
❑ 670 Jose Cruz .10 .02
❑ 671A Ray Soff ERR (No D* before copyright line) .05 .01
❑ 671B Ray Soff COR (D* before copyright line) .05 .01
❑ 672 Chili Davis .10 .02
❑ 673 Don Sutton .10 .02
❑ 674 Bill Campbell .05 .01
❑ 675 Ed Romero .05 .01
❑ 676 Charlie Moore .05 .01
❑ 677 Bob Grich .10 .02
❑ 678 Carney Lansford .10 .02
❑ 679 Kent Hrbek .10 .02
❑ 680 Ryne Sandberg .40 .15
❑ 681 George Bell .10 .02
❑ 682 Jerry Reuss .05 .01
❑ 683 Gary Roenicke .05 .01
❑ 684 Kent Tekulve .05 .01
❑ 685 Jerry Hairston .05 .01

❑ 686 Doyle Alexander .05 .01
❑ 687 Alan Trammell .10 .02
❑ 688 Juan Beniquez .05 .01
❑ 689 Darrell Porter .05 .01
❑ 690 Dane Iorg .05 .01
❑ 691 Dave Parker .10 .02
❑ 692 Frank White .10 .02
❑ 693 Terry Puhl .05 .01
❑ 694 Phil Niekro .10 .02
❑ 695 Chico Walker .05 .01
❑ 696 Gary Lucas .05 .01
❑ 697 Ed Lynch .05 .01
❑ 698 Ernie Whitt .05 .01
❑ 699 Ken Landreaux .05 .01
❑ 700 Dave Bergman .05 .01
❑ 701 Willie Randolph .10 .02
❑ 702 Greg Gross .05 .01
❑ 703 Dave Schmidt .05 .01
❑ 704 Jesse Orosco .05 .01
❑ 705 Bruce Hurst .05 .01
❑ 706 Rick Manning .05 .01
❑ 707 Bob McClure .05 .01
❑ 708 Scott McGregor .05 .01
❑ 709 Dave Kingman .10 .02
❑ 710 Gary Gaetti .10 .02
❑ 711 Ken Griffey .10 .02
❑ 712 Don Robinson .05 .01
❑ 713 Tom Brookens .05 .01
❑ 714 Dan Quisenberry .05 .01
❑ 715 Bob Dernier .05 .01
❑ 716 Rick Leach .05 .01
❑ 717 Ed VandeBerg .05 .01
❑ 718 Steve Carlton .10 .02
❑ 719 Tom Hume .05 .01
❑ 720 Richard Dotson .05 .01
❑ 721 Tom Herr .05 .01
❑ 722 Bob Knepper .05 .01
❑ 723 Brett Butler .10 .02
❑ 724 Greg Minton .05 .01
❑ 725 George Hendrick .10 .02
❑ 726 Frank Tanana .10 .02
❑ 727 Mike Moore .05 .01
❑ 728 Tippy Martinez .05 .01
❑ 729 Tom Paciorek .05 .01
❑ 730 Eric Show .05 .01
❑ 731 Dave Concepcion .10 .02
❑ 732 Manny Trillo .05 .01
❑ 733 Bill Caudill .05 .01
❑ 734 Bill Madlock .10 .02
❑ 735 Rickey Henderson .25 .08
❑ 736 Steve Bedrosian .05 .01
❑ 737 Floyd Bannister .05 .01
❑ 738 Jorge Orta .05 .01
❑ 739 Chet Lemon .10 .02
❑ 740 Rich Gedman .05 .01
❑ 741 Paul Molitor .10 .02
❑ 742 Andy McGaffigan .05 .01
❑ 743 Dwayne Murphy .05 .01
❑ 744 Roy Smalley .05 .01
❑ 745 Glenn Hubbard .05 .01
❑ 746 Bob Ojeda .05 .01
❑ 747 Johnny Ray .05 .01
❑ 748 Mike Flanagan .05 .01
❑ 749 Ozzie Smith .40 .15
❑ 750 Steve Trout .05 .01
❑ 751 Garth Iorg .05 .01
❑ 752 Dan Petry .05 .01
❑ 753 Rick Honeycutt .05 .01
❑ 754 Dave LaPoint .05 .01
❑ 755 Luis Aguayo .05 .01
❑ 756 Carlton Fisk .15 .05
❑ 757 Nolan Ryan 1.00 .40
❑ 758 Tony Bernazard .05 .01
❑ 759 Joel Youngblood .05 .01
❑ 760 Mike Witt .05 .01
❑ 761 Greg Pryor .05 .01
❑ 762 Gary Ward .05 .01
❑ 763 Tim Flannery .05 .01
❑ 764 Bill Buckner .10 .02
❑ 765 Kirk Gibson .10 .02
❑ 766 Don Aase .05 .01
❑ 767 Ron Cey .10 .02
❑ 768 Dennis Lamp .05 .01
❑ 769 Steve Sax .05 .01
❑ 770 Dave Winfield .10 .02
❑ 771 Shane Rawley .05 .01
❑ 772 Harold Baines .10 .02
❑ 773 Robin Yount .40 .15
❑ 774 Wayne Krenchicki .05 .01
❑ 775 Joaquin Andujar .10 .02
❑ 776 Tom Brunansky .05 .01
❑ 777 Chris Chambliss .10 .02
❑ 778 Jack Morris .10 .02
❑ 779 Craig Reynolds .05 .01
❑ 780 Andre Thornton .05 .01
❑ 781 Atlee Hammaker .05 .01
❑ 782 Brian Downing .10 .02
❑ 783 Willie Wilson .10 .02
❑ 784 Cal Ripken .75 .30
❑ 785 Terry Francona .10 .02
❑ 786 Jimy Williams MG .05 .01
❑ 787 Alejandro Pena .05 .01
❑ 788 Tim Stoddard .05 .01
❑ 789 Dan Schatzeder .05 .01
❑ 790 Julio Cruz .05 .01
❑ 791 Lance Parrish UER
(No trademark&
never corrected) .10 .02
❑ 792 Checklist 661-792 .05 .01

1987 Topps Traded

❑ COMP.FACT.SET (132) 8.00 3.00
❑ 1T Bill Almon .05 .01
❑ 2T Scott Bankhead .05 .01
❑ 3T Eric Bell .10 .02
❑ 4T Juan Beniquez .05 .01
❑ 5T Juan Berenguer .05 .01
❑ 6T Greg Booker .05 .01
❑ 7T Thad Bosley .05 .01
❑ 8T Larry Bowa MG .10 .02
❑ 9T Greg Brock .05 .01
❑ 10T Bob Brower .05 .01
❑ 11T Jerry Browne .10 .02
❑ 12T Ralph Bryant .05 .01
❑ 13T DeWayne Buice .05 .01
❑ 14T Ellis Burks XRC .50 .20
❑ 15T Ivan Calderon .05 .01
❑ 16T Jeff Calhoun .05 .01
❑ 17T Casey Candaele .05 .01
❑ 18T John Cangelosi .05 .01
❑ 19T Steve Carlton .10 .02
❑ 20T Juan Castillo .10 .02
❑ 21T Rick Cerone .05 .01
❑ 22T Ron Cey .10 .02
❑ 23T John Christensen .05 .01
❑ 24T David Cone XRC .75 .30
❑ 25T Chuck Crim .05 .01
❑ 26T Storm Davis .05 .01
❑ 27T Andre Dawson .10 .02
❑ 28T Rick Dempsey .05 .01
❑ 29T Doug Drabek .50 .20
❑ 30T Mike Dunne .05 .01
❑ 31T Dennis Eckersley .15 .05
❑ 32T Lee Elia MG .05 .01
❑ 33T Brian Fisher .05 .01
❑ 34T Terry Francona .10 .02
❑ 35T Willie Fraser .10 .02
❑ 36T Billy Gardner MG .05 .01
❑ 37T Ken Gerhart .05 .01
❑ 38T Dan Gladden .05 .01
❑ 39T Jim Gott .05 .01
❑ 40T Cecilio Guante .05 .01
❑ 41T Albert Hall .05 .01
❑ 42T Terry Harper .05 .01
❑ 43T Mickey Hatcher .05 .01
❑ 44T Brad Havens .05 .01
❑ 45T Neal Heaton .05 .01
❑ 46T Mike Henneman XRC .25 .08
❑ 47T Donnie Hill .05 .01
❑ 48T Guy Hoffman .05 .01
❑ 49T Brian Holton .05 .01
❑ 50T Charles Hudson .05 .01
❑ 51T Danny Jackson .05 .01
❑ 52T Reggie Jackson .15 .05
❑ 53T Chris James XRC .10 .02
❑ 54T Dion James .05 .01
❑ 55T Stan Jefferson .05 .01
❑ 56T Joe Johnson .05 .01
❑ 57T Terry Kennedy .05 .01
❑ 58T Mike Kingery .10 .02
❑ 59T Ray Knight .10 .02
❑ 60T Gene Larkin XRC .25 .08
❑ 61T Mike LaValliere .25 .08
❑ 62T Jack Lazorko .05 .01
❑ 63T Terry Leach .05 .01
❑ 64T Tim Leary .05 .01
❑ 65T Jim Lindeman .10 .02
❑ 66T Steve Lombardozzi .05 .01
❑ 67T Bill Long .05 .01
❑ 68T Barry Lyons .05 .01
❑ 69T Shane Mack .05 .01
❑ 70T Greg Maddux XRC 5.00 2.00
❑ 71T Bill Madlock .10 .02
❑ 72T Joe Magrane XRC .10 .02
❑ 73T Dave Martinez XRC .25 .08
❑ 74T Fred McGriff .60 .25
❑ 75T Mark McLemore .10 .02
❑ 76T Kevin McReynolds .05 .01
❑ 77T Dave Meads .05 .01
❑ 78T Eddie Milner .05 .01
❑ 79T Greg Minton .05 .01
❑ 80T John Mitchell XRC .10 .02
❑ 81T Kevin Mitchell .15 .05
❑ 82T Charlie Moore .05 .01
❑ 83T Jeff Musselman .05 .01
❑ 84T Gene Nelson .05 .01
❑ 85T Graig Nettles .10 .02
❑ 86T Al Newman .05 .01
❑ 87T Reid Nichols .05 .01
❑ 88T Tom Niedenfuer .05 .01
❑ 89T Joe Niekro .05 .01
❑ 90T Tom Nieto .05 .01
❑ 91T Matt Nokes XRC .25 .08
❑ 92T Dickie Noles .05 .01
❑ 93T Pat Pacillo .05 .01
❑ 94T Lance Parrish .10 .02
❑ 95T Tony Pena .05 .01
❑ 96T Luis Polonia XRC .25 .08
❑ 97T Randy Ready .05 .01
❑ 98T Jeff Reardon .10 .02
❑ 99T Gary Redus .05 .01
❑ 100T Jeff Reed .05 .01
❑ 101T Rick Rhoden .05 .01
❑ 102T Cal Ripken Sr. MG .05 .01
❑ 103T Wally Ritchie .05 .01
❑ 104T Jeff M. Robinson .05 .01
❑ 105T Gary Roenicke .05 .01
❑ 106T Jerry Royster .05 .01
❑ 107T Mark Salas .05 .01
❑ 108T Luis Salazar .05 .01
❑ 109T Benito Santiago .10 .02
❑ 110T Dave Schmidt .05 .01
❑ 111T Kevin Seitzer XRC .25 .08
❑ 112T John Shelby .05 .01
❑ 113T Steve Shields .05 .01
❑ 114T John Smiley XRC .25 .08
❑ 115T Chris Speier .05 .01
❑ 116T Mike Stanley XRC .25 .08
❑ 117T Terry Steinbach XRC .50 .20
❑ 118T Les Straker .05 .01
❑ 119T Jim Sundberg .10 .02
❑ 120T Danny Tartabull .05 .01
❑ 121T Tom Trebelhorn MG .05 .01
❑ 122T Dave Valle XRC .10 .02
❑ 123T Ed VandeBerg .05 .01
❑ 124T Andy Van Slyke .15 .05
❑ 125T Gary Ward .05 .01
❑ 126T Alan Wiggins .05 .01
❑ 127T Bill Wilkinson .05 .01
❑ 128T Frank Williams .05 .01

❑ 129T Matt Williams XRC	1.00	.40
❑ 130T Jim Winn	.05	.01
❑ 131T Matt Young	.05	.01
❑ 132T Checklist 1T-132T	.05	.01

1988 Topps

❑ COMPLETE SET (792)	15.00	6.00
❑ COMP.FACT SET (792)	15.00	6.00
❑ COMP.X-MAS.SET (792)	40.00	15.00
❑ 1 Vince Coleman RB 100 Steals for Third Cons. Seas	.05	.01
❑ 2 Don Mattingly RB	.30	.10
❑ 3 Mark McGwire RB	.75	.30
❑ 3A Mark McGwire ERR RB	.75	.30
❑ 4 Eddie Murray RB	.15	.05
❑ 4A Eddie Murray ERR RB	.50	.20
❑ 5 Phil Niekro Joe Niekro RB Brothers Win Record	.10	.02
❑ 6 Nolan Ryan RB	.40	.15
❑ 7 Benito Santiago RB	.05	.01
❑ 8 Kevin Elster	.05	.01
❑ 9 Andy Hawkins	.05	.01
❑ 10 Ryne Sandberg	.40	.15
❑ 11 Mike Young	.05	.01
❑ 12 Bill Schroeder	.05	.01
❑ 13 Andres Thomas	.05	.01
❑ 14 Sparky Anderson MG	.10	.02
❑ 15 Chili Davis	.10	.02
❑ 16 Kirk McCaskill	.05	.01
❑ 17 Ron Oester	.05	.01
❑ 18A Al Leiter ERR RC	.50	.20
❑ 18B Al Leiter RC	.50	.20
❑ 19 Mark Davidson	.05	.01
❑ 20 Kevin Gross	.05	.01
❑ 21 Wade Boggs Spike Owen TL	.10	.02
❑ 22 Greg Swindell	.05	.01
❑ 23 Ken Landreaux	.05	.01
❑ 24 Jim Deshaies	.05	.01
❑ 25 Andres Galarraga	.10	.02
❑ 26 Mitch Williams	.05	.01
❑ 27 R.J. Reynolds	.05	.01
❑ 28 Jose Nunez	.05	.01
❑ 29 Angel Salazar	.05	.01
❑ 30 Sid Fernandez	.05	.01
❑ 31 Bruce Bochy	.05	.01
❑ 32 Mike Morgan	.05	.01
❑ 33 Rob Deer	.05	.01
❑ 34 Ricky Horton	.05	.01
❑ 35 Harold Baines	.10	.02
❑ 36 Jamie Moyer	.10	.02
❑ 37 Ed Romero	.05	.01
❑ 38 Jeff Calhoun	.05	.01
❑ 39 Gerald Perry	.05	.01
❑ 40 Orel Hershiser	.10	.02
❑ 41 Bob Melvin	.05	.01
❑ 42 Bill Landrum	.05	.01
❑ 43 Dick Schofield	.05	.01
❑ 44 Lou Piniella MG	.10	.02
❑ 45 Kent Hrbek	.10	.02
❑ 46 Darnell Coles	.05	.01
❑ 47 Joaquin Andujar	.10	.02
❑ 48 Alan Ashby	.05	.01
❑ 49 Dave Clark	.05	.01
❑ 50 Hubie Brooks	.05	.01
❑ 51 C.Ripken/E.Murray TL	.40	.15
❑ 52 Don Robinson	.05	.01
❑ 53 Curt Wilkerson	.05	.01
❑ 54 Jim Clancy	.05	.01
❑ 55 Phil Bradley	.05	.01
❑ 56 Ed Hearn	.05	.01
❑ 57 Tim Crews RC	.25	.08
❑ 58 Dave Magadan	.05	.01
❑ 59 Danny Cox	.05	.01
❑ 60 Rickey Henderson	.20	.07
❑ 61 Mark Knudson	.05	.01
❑ 62 Jeff Hamilton	.05	.01
❑ 63 Jimmy Jones	.05	.01
❑ 64 Ken Caminiti RC	2.00	.75
❑ 65 Leon Durham	.05	.01
❑ 66 Shane Rawley	.05	.01
❑ 67 Ken Oberkfell	.05	.01
❑ 68 Dave Dravecky	.05	.01
❑ 69 Mike Hart	.05	.01
❑ 70 Roger Clemens	1.00	.40
❑ 71 Gary Pettis	.05	.01
❑ 72 Dennis Eckersley	.15	.05
❑ 73 Randy Bush	.05	.01
❑ 74 Tom Lasorda MG	.15	.05
❑ 75 Joe Carter	.10	.02
❑ 76 Dennis Martinez	.10	.02
❑ 77 Tom O'Malley	.05	.01
❑ 78 Dan Petry	.05	.01
❑ 79 Ernie Whitt	.05	.01
❑ 80 Mark Langston	.05	.01
❑ 81 Ron Robinson John Franco TL	.05	.01
❑ 82 Darrel Akerfelds	.05	.01
❑ 83 Jose Oquendo	.05	.01
❑ 84 Cecilio Guante	.05	.01
❑ 85 Howard Johnson	.10	.02
❑ 86 Ron Karkovice	.05	.01
❑ 87 Mike Mason	.05	.01
❑ 88 Earnie Riles	.05	.01
❑ 89 Gary Thurman	.05	.01
❑ 90 Dale Murphy	.15	.05
❑ 91 Joey Cora RC	.25	.08
❑ 92 Len Matuszek	.05	.01
❑ 93 Bob Sebra	.05	.01
❑ 94 Chuck Jackson	.05	.01
❑ 95 Lance Parrish	.10	.02
❑ 96 Todd Benzinger RC*	.25	.08
❑ 97 Scott Garrelts	.05	.01
❑ 98 Rene Gonzales RC	.10	.02
❑ 99 Chuck Finley	.10	.02
❑ 100 Jack Clark	.10	.02
❑ 101 Allan Anderson	.05	.01
❑ 102 Barry Larkin	.15	.05
❑ 103 Curt Young	.05	.01
❑ 104 Dick Williams MG	.05	.01
❑ 105 Jesse Orosco	.05	.01
❑ 106 Jim Walewander	.05	.01
❑ 107 Scott Bailes	.05	.01
❑ 108 Steve Lyons	.05	.01
❑ 109 Joel Skinner	.05	.01
❑ 110 Teddy Higuera	.05	.01
❑ 111 Hubie Brooks Vance Law TL	.05	.01
❑ 112 Les Lancaster	.05	.01
❑ 113 Kelly Gruber	.05	.01
❑ 114 Jeff Russell	.05	.01
❑ 115 Johnny Ray	.05	.01
❑ 116 Jerry Don Gleaton	.05	.01
❑ 117 James Steels	.05	.01
❑ 118 Bob Welch	.10	.02
❑ 119 Robbie Wine	.05	.01
❑ 120 Kirby Puckett	.20	.07
❑ 121 Checklist 1-132	.05	.01
❑ 122 Tony Bernazard	.05	.01
❑ 123 Tom Candiotti	.05	.01
❑ 124 Ray Knight	.10	.02
❑ 125 Bruce Hurst	.05	.01
❑ 126 Steve Jeltz	.05	.01
❑ 127 Jim Gott	.05	.01
❑ 128 Johnny Grubb	.05	.01
❑ 129 Greg Minton	.05	.01
❑ 130 Buddy Bell	.10	.02
❑ 131 Don Schulze	.05	.01
❑ 132 Donnie Hill	.05	.01
❑ 133 Greg Mathews	.05	.01
❑ 134 Chuck Tanner MG	.05	.01
❑ 135 Dennis Rasmussen	.05	.01
❑ 136 Brian Dayett	.05	.01
❑ 137 Chris Bosio	.05	.01
❑ 138 Mitch Webster	.05	.01
❑ 139 Jerry Browne	.05	.01
❑ 140 Jesse Barfield	.10	.02
❑ 141 G.Brett/B.Saberhagen TL	.20	.07
❑ 142 Andy Van Slyke	.15	.05
❑ 143 Mickey Tettleton	.05	.01
❑ 144 Don Gordon	.05	.01
❑ 145 Bill Madlock	.10	.02
❑ 146 Donell Nixon	.05	.01
❑ 147 Bill Buckner	.10	.02
❑ 148 Carmelo Martinez	.05	.01
❑ 149 Ken Howell	.05	.01
❑ 150 Eric Davis	.10	.02
❑ 151 Bob Knepper	.05	.01
❑ 152 Jody Reed RC	.25	.08
❑ 153 John Habyan	.05	.01
❑ 154 Jeff Stone	.05	.01
❑ 155 Bruce Sutter	.10	.02
❑ 156 Gary Matthews	.10	.02
❑ 157 Atlee Hammaker	.05	.01
❑ 158 Tim Hulett	.05	.01
❑ 159 Brad Arnsberg	.05	.01
❑ 160 Willie McGee	.10	.02
❑ 161 Bryn Smith	.05	.01
❑ 162 Mark McLemore	.05	.01
❑ 163 Dale Mohorcic	.05	.01
❑ 164 Dave Johnson MG	.05	.01
❑ 165 Robin Yount	.30	.10
❑ 166 Rick Rodriquez	.05	.01
❑ 167 Rance Mulliniks	.05	.01
❑ 168 Barry Jones	.05	.01
❑ 169 Ross Jones	.05	.01
❑ 170 Rich Gossage	.10	.02
❑ 171 Shawon Dunston Manny Trillo TL	.05	.01
❑ 172 Lloyd McClendon RC	.25	.08
❑ 173 Eric Plunk	.05	.01
❑ 174 Phil Garner	.10	.02
❑ 175 Kevin Bass	.05	.01
❑ 176 Jeff Reed	.05	.01
❑ 177 Frank Tanana	.10	.02
❑ 178 Dwayne Henry	.05	.01
❑ 179 Charlie Puleo	.05	.01
❑ 180 Terry Kennedy	.05	.01
❑ 181 David Cone	.10	.02
❑ 182 Ken Phelps	.05	.01
❑ 183 Tom Lawless	.05	.01
❑ 184 Ivan Calderon	.05	.01
❑ 185 Rick Rhoden	.05	.01
❑ 186 Rafael Palmeiro	.40	.15
❑ 187 Steve Kiefer	.05	.01
❑ 188 John Russell	.05	.01
❑ 189 Wes Gardner	.05	.01
❑ 190 Candy Maldonado	.05	.01
❑ 191 John Cerutti	.05	.01
❑ 192 Devon White	.10	.02
❑ 193 Brian Fisher	.05	.01
❑ 194 Tom Kelly MG	.05	.01
❑ 195 Dan Quisenberry	.05	.01
❑ 196 Dave Engle	.05	.01
❑ 197 Lance McCullers	.05	.01
❑ 198 Franklin Stubbs	.05	.01
❑ 199 Dave Meads	.05	.01
❑ 200 Wade Boggs	.15	.05
❑ 201 Rangers TL Bobby Valentine MG& Pete O'Brien& Pe	.05	.01
❑ 202 Glenn Hoffman	.05	.01
❑ 203 Fred Toliver	.05	.01
❑ 204 Paul O'Neill	.15	.05
❑ 205 Nelson Liriano	.05	.01
❑ 206 Domingo Ramos	.05	.01
❑ 207 John Mitchell RC	.10	.02
❑ 208 Steve Lake	.05	.01
❑ 209 Richard Dotson	.05	.01
❑ 210 Willie Randolph	.10	.02
❑ 211 Frank DiPino	.05	.01
❑ 212 Greg Brock	.05	.01
❑ 213 Albert Hall	.05	.01
❑ 214 Dave Schmidt	.05	.01
❑ 215 Von Hayes	.05	.01
❑ 216 Jerry Reuss	.05	.01
❑ 217 Harry Spilman	.05	.01

Card		
❑ 218 Dan Schatzeder	.05	.01
❑ 219 Mike Stanley	.05	.01
❑ 220 Tom Henke	.05	.01
❑ 221 Rafael Belliard	.05	.01
❑ 222 Steve Farr	.05	.01
❑ 223 Stan Jefferson	.05	.01
❑ 224 Tom Trebelhorn MG	.05	.01
❑ 225 Mike Scioscia	.10	.02
❑ 226 Dave Lopes	.10	.02
❑ 227 Ed Correa	.05	.01
❑ 228 Wallace Johnson	.05	.01
❑ 229 Jeff Musselman	.05	.01
❑ 230 Pat Tabler	.05	.01
❑ 231 B.Bonds/B.Bonilla TL	1.00	.40
❑ 232 Bob James	.05	.01
❑ 233 Rafael Santana	.05	.01
❑ 234 Ken Dayley	.05	.01
❑ 235 Gary Ward	.05	.01
❑ 236 Ted Power	.05	.01
❑ 237 Mike Heath	.05	.01
❑ 238 Luis Polonia RC*	.25	.08
❑ 239 Roy Smalley	.05	.01
❑ 240 Lee Smith	.10	.02
❑ 241 Damaso Garcia	.05	.01
❑ 242 Tom Niedenfuer	.05	.01
❑ 243 Mark Ryal	.05	.01
❑ 244 Jeff D. Robinson	.05	.01
❑ 245 Rich Gedman	.05	.01
❑ 246 Mike Campbell	.05	.01
❑ 247 Thad Bosley	.05	.01
❑ 248 Storm Davis	.05	.01
❑ 249 Mike Marshall	.05	.01
❑ 250 Nolan Ryan	1.00	.40
❑ 251 Tom Foley	.05	.01
❑ 252 Bob Brower	.05	.01
❑ 253 Checklist 133-264	.05	.01
❑ 254 Lee Elia MG	.05	.01
❑ 255 Mookie Wilson	.10	.02
❑ 256 Ken Schrom	.05	.01
❑ 257 Jerry Royster	.05	.01
❑ 258 Ed Nunez	.05	.01
❑ 259 Ron Kittle	.05	.01
❑ 260 Vince Coleman	.05	.01
❑ 261 Giants TL (Five players)	.05	.01
❑ 262 Drew Hall	.05	.01
❑ 263 Glenn Braggs	.05	.01
❑ 264 Les Straker	.05	.01
❑ 265 Bo Diaz	.05	.01
❑ 266 Paul Assenmacher	.05	.01
❑ 267 Billy Bean RC	.10	.02
❑ 268 Bruce Ruffin	.05	.01
❑ 269 Ellis Burks RC	.40	.15
❑ 270 Mike Witt	.05	.01
❑ 271 Ken Gerhart	.05	.01
❑ 272 Steve Ontiveros	.05	.01
❑ 273 Garth Iorg	.05	.01
❑ 274 Junior Ortiz	.05	.01
❑ 275 Kevin Seitzer	.05	.01
❑ 276 Luis Salazar	.05	.01
❑ 277 Alejandro Pena	.05	.01
❑ 278 Jose Cruz	.10	.02
❑ 279 Randy St.Claire	.05	.01
❑ 280 Pete Incaviglia	.05	.01
❑ 281 Jerry Hairston	.05	.01
❑ 282 Pat Perry	.05	.01
❑ 283 Phil Lombardi	.05	.01
❑ 284 Larry Bowa MG	.10	.02
❑ 285 Jim Presley	.05	.01
❑ 286 Chuck Crim	.05	.01
❑ 287 Manny Trillo	.05	.01
❑ 288 Pat Pacillo	.05	.01
❑ 289 Dave Bergman	.05	.01
❑ 290 Tony Fernandez	.05	.01
❑ 291 Billy Hatcher Kevin Bass TL	.05	.01
❑ 292 Carney Lansford	.10	.02
❑ 293 Doug Jones RC	.25	.08
❑ 294 Al Pedrique	.05	.01
❑ 295 Bert Blyleven	.10	.02
❑ 296 Floyd Rayford	.05	.01
❑ 297 Zane Smith	.05	.01
❑ 298 Milt Thompson	.05	.01
❑ 299 Steve Crawford	.05	.01
❑ 300 Don Mattingly	.60	.25
❑ 301 Bud Black	.05	.01
❑ 302 Jose Uribe	.05	.01
❑ 303 Eric Show	.05	.01
❑ 304 George Hendrick	.10	.02
❑ 305 Steve Sax	.05	.01
❑ 306 Billy Hatcher	.05	.01
❑ 307 Mike Trujillo	.05	.01
❑ 308 Lee Mazzilli	.10	.02
❑ 309 Bill Long	.05	.01
❑ 310 Tom Herr	.05	.01
❑ 311 Scott Sanderson	.05	.01
❑ 312 Joey Meyer	.05	.01
❑ 313 Bob McClure	.05	.01
❑ 314 Jimy Williams MG	.05	.01
❑ 315 Dave Parker	.10	.02
❑ 316 Jose Rijo	.10	.02
❑ 317 Tom Nieto	.05	.01
❑ 318 Mel Hall	.05	.01
❑ 319 Mike Loynd	.05	.01
❑ 320 Alan Trammell	.10	.02
❑ 321 Harold Baines Carlton Fisk TL	.10	.02
❑ 322 Vicente Palacios	.05	.01
❑ 323 Rick Leach	.05	.01
❑ 324 Danny Jackson	.05	.01
❑ 325 Glenn Hubbard	.05	.01
❑ 326 Al Nipper	.05	.01
❑ 327 Larry Sheets	.05	.01
❑ 328 Greg Cadaret	.05	.01
❑ 329 Chris Speier	.05	.01
❑ 330 Eddie Whitson	.05	.01
❑ 331 Brian Downing	.10	.02
❑ 332 Jerry Reed	.05	.01
❑ 333 Wally Backman	.05	.01
❑ 334 Dave LaPoint	.05	.01
❑ 335 Claudell Washington	.05	.01
❑ 336 Ed Lynch	.05	.01
❑ 337 Jim Gantner	.05	.01
❑ 338 Brian Holton UER (1987 ERA .389& should be 3.89)	.05	.01
❑ 339 Kurt Stillwell	.05	.01
❑ 340 Jack Morris	.10	.02
❑ 341 Carmen Castillo	.05	.01
❑ 342 Larry Andersen	.05	.01
❑ 343 Greg Gagne	.05	.01
❑ 344 Tony LaRussa MG	.10	.02
❑ 345 Scott Fletcher	.05	.01
❑ 346 Vance Law	.05	.01
❑ 347 Joe Johnson	.05	.01
❑ 348 Jim Eisenreich	.05	.01
❑ 349 Bob Walk	.05	.01
❑ 350 Will Clark	.20	.07
❑ 351 Red Schoendienst CO Tony Pena TL	.10	.02
❑ 352 Bill Ripken RC*	.05	.01
❑ 353 Ed Olwine	.05	.01
❑ 354 Marc Sullivan	.05	.01
❑ 355 Roger McDowell	.05	.01
❑ 356 Luis Aguayo	.05	.01
❑ 357 Floyd Bannister	.05	.01
❑ 358 Rey Quinones	.05	.01
❑ 359 Tim Stoddard	.05	.01
❑ 360 Tony Gwynn	.30	.10
❑ 361 Greg Maddux	1.00	.40
❑ 362 Juan Castillo	.05	.01
❑ 363 Willie Fraser	.05	.01
❑ 364 Nick Esasky	.05	.01
❑ 365 Floyd Youmans	.05	.01
❑ 366 Chet Lemon	.10	.02
❑ 367 Tim Leary	.05	.01
❑ 368 Gerald Young	.05	.01
❑ 369 Greg Harris	.05	.01
❑ 370 Jose Canseco	.50	.20
❑ 371 Joe Hesketh	.05	.01
❑ 372 Matt Williams RC	.75	.30
❑ 373 Checklist 265-396	.05	.01
❑ 374 Doc Edwards MG	.05	.01
❑ 375 Tom Brunansky	.05	.01
❑ 376 Bill Wilkinson	.05	.01
❑ 377 Sam Horn RC	.10	.02
❑ 378 Todd Frohwirth	.05	.01
❑ 379 Rafael Ramirez	.05	.01
❑ 380 Joe Magrane RC*	.05	.01
❑ 381 Wally Joyner Jack Howell TL	.10	.02
❑ 382 Keith Miller RC	.25	.08
❑ 383 Eric Bell	.05	.01
❑ 384 Neil Allen	.05	.01
❑ 385 Carlton Fisk	.15	.05
❑ 386 Don Mattingly AS	.30	.10
❑ 387 Willie Randolph AS	.05	.01
❑ 388 Wade Boggs AS	.10	.02
❑ 389 Alan Trammell AS	.05	.01
❑ 390 George Bell AS	.05	.01
❑ 391 Kirby Puckett AS	.15	.05
❑ 392 Dave Winfield AS	.05	.01
❑ 393 Matt Nokes AS	.05	.01
❑ 394 Roger Clemens AS	.50	.20
❑ 395 Jimmy Key AS	.05	.01
❑ 396 Tom Henke AS	.05	.01
❑ 397 Jack Clark AS	.05	.01
❑ 398 Juan Samuel AS	.05	.01
❑ 399 Tim Wallach AS	.05	.01
❑ 400 Ozzie Smith AS	.20	.07
❑ 401 Andre Dawson AS	.05	.01
❑ 402 Tony Gwynn AS	.15	.05
❑ 403 Tim Raines AS	.05	.01
❑ 404 Benny Santiago AS	.05	.01
❑ 405 Dwight Gooden AS	.05	.01
❑ 406 Shane Rawley AS	.05	.01
❑ 407 Steve Bedrosian AS	.05	.01
❑ 408 Dion James	.05	.01
❑ 409 Joel McKeon	.05	.01
❑ 410 Tony Pena	.05	.01
❑ 411 Wayne Tolleson	.05	.01
❑ 412 Randy Myers	.10	.02
❑ 413 John Christensen	.05	.01
❑ 414 John McNamara MG	.05	.01
❑ 415 Don Carman	.05	.01
❑ 416 Keith Moreland	.05	.01
❑ 417 Mark Ciardi	.05	.01
❑ 418 Joel Youngblood	.05	.01
❑ 419 Scott McGregor	.05	.01
❑ 420 Wally Joyner	.10	.02
❑ 421 Ed VandeBerg	.05	.01
❑ 422 Dave Concepcion	.10	.02
❑ 423 John Smiley RC*	.25	.08
❑ 424 Dwayne Murphy	.05	.01
❑ 425 Jeff Reardon	.10	.02
❑ 426 Randy Ready	.05	.01
❑ 427 Paul Kilgus	.05	.01
❑ 428 John Shelby	.05	.01
❑ 429 A.Trammell/K.Gibson TL	.10	.02
❑ 430 Glenn Davis	.05	.01
❑ 431 Casey Candaele	.05	.01
❑ 432 Mike Moore	.05	.01
❑ 433 Bill Pecota RC*	.05	.01
❑ 434 Rick Aguilera	.05	.01
❑ 435 Mike Pagliarulo	.05	.01
❑ 436 Mike Bielecki	.05	.01
❑ 437 Fred Manrique	.05	.01
❑ 438 Rob Ducey	.05	.01
❑ 439 Dave Martinez	.05	.01
❑ 440 Steve Bedrosian	.05	.01
❑ 441 Rick Manning	.05	.01
❑ 442 Tom Bolton	.05	.01
❑ 443 Ken Griffey	.10	.02
❑ 444 Cal Ripken& Sr. MG (Checklist back) UER (two cop)	.05	.01
❑ 445 Mike Krukow	.05	.01
❑ 446 Doug DeCinces (Now with Cardinals on card front)	.05	.01
❑ 447 Jeff Montgomery RC	.25	.08
❑ 448 Mike Davis	.05	.01
❑ 449 Jeff M. Robinson	.05	.01
❑ 450 Barry Bonds	2.00	.75
❑ 451 Keith Atherton	.05	.01
❑ 452 Willie Wilson	.10	.02
❑ 453 Dennis Powell	.05	.01
❑ 454 Marvell Wynne	.05	.01
❑ 455 Shawn Hillegas	.05	.01
❑ 456 Dave Anderson	.05	.01
❑ 457 Terry Leach	.05	.01
❑ 458 Ron Hassey	.05	.01
❑ 459 Dave Winfield Willie Randolph TL	.05	.01
❑ 460 Ozzie Smith	.30	.10
❑ 461 Danny Darwin	.05	.01
❑ 462 Don Slaught	.05	.01
❑ 463 Fred McGriff	.20	.07

❑ 464 Jay Tibbs .05 .01
❑ 465 Paul Molitor .10 .02
❑ 466 Jerry Mumphrey .05 .01
❑ 467 Don Aase .05 .01
❑ 468 Darren Daulton .10 .02
❑ 469 Jeff Dedmon .05 .01
❑ 470 Dwight Evans .15 .05
❑ 471 Donnie Moore .05 .01
❑ 472 Robby Thompson .05 .01
❑ 473 Joe Niekro .05 .01
❑ 474 Tom Brookens .05 .01
❑ 475 Pete Rose MG/TC .50 .20
❑ 476 Dave Stewart .10 .02
❑ 477 Jamie Quirk .05 .01
❑ 478 Sid Bream .05 .01
❑ 479 Brett Butler .10 .02
❑ 480 Dwight Gooden .10 .02
❑ 481 Mariano Duncan .05 .01
❑ 482 Mark Davis .05 .01
❑ 483 Rod Booker .05 .01
❑ 484 Pat Clements .05 .01
❑ 485 Harold Reynolds .10 .02
❑ 486 Pat Keedy .05 .01
❑ 487 Jim Pankovits .05 .01
❑ 488 Andy McGaffigan .05 .01
❑ 489 Dodgers TL
Pedro Guerrero and
Fernando Valenzuel .05 .01
❑ 490 Larry Parrish .05 .01
❑ 491 B.J. Surhoff .10 .02
❑ 492 Doyle Alexander .05 .01
❑ 493 Mike Greenwell .05 .01
❑ 494 Wally Ritchie .05 .01
❑ 495 Eddie Murray .20 .07
❑ 496 Guy Hoffman .05 .01
❑ 497 Kevin Mitchell .10 .02
❑ 498 Bob Boone .10 .02
❑ 499 Eric King .05 .01
❑ 500 Andre Dawson .10 .02
❑ 501 Tim Birtsas .05 .01
❑ 502 Dan Gladden .05 .01
❑ 503 Junior Noboa .05 .01
❑ 504 Bob Rodgers MG .05 .01
❑ 505 Willie Upshaw .05 .01
❑ 506 John Cangelosi .05 .01
❑ 507 Mark Gubicza .05 .01
❑ 508 Tim Teufel .05 .01
❑ 509 Bill Dawley .05 .01
❑ 510 Dave Winfield .10 .02
❑ 511 Joel Davis .05 .01
❑ 512 Alex Trevino .05 .01
❑ 513 Tim Flannery .05 .01
❑ 514 Pat Sheridan .05 .01
❑ 515 Juan Nieves .05 .01
❑ 516 Jim Sundberg .10 .02
❑ 517 Ron Robinson .05 .01
❑ 518 Greg Gross .05 .01
❑ 519 Harold Reynolds
Phil Bradley TL .05 .01
❑ 520 Dave Smith .05 .01
❑ 521 Jim Dwyer .05 .01
❑ 522 Bob Patterson .05 .01
❑ 523 Gary Roenicke .05 .01
❑ 524 Gary Lucas .05 .01
❑ 525 Marty Barrett .05 .01
❑ 526 Juan Berenguer .05 .01
❑ 527 Steve Henderson .05 .01
❑ 528A Checklist 397-528
ERR (455 S. Carlton) .15 .05
❑ 528B Checklist 397-528
COR (455 S. Hillegas) .10 .02
❑ 529 Tim Burke .05 .01
❑ 530 Gary Carter .10 .02
❑ 531 Rich Yett .05 .01
❑ 532 Mike Kingery .05 .01
❑ 533 John Farrell RC .10 .02
❑ 534 John Wathan MG .05 .01
❑ 535 Ron Guidry .10 .02
❑ 536 John Morris .05 .01
❑ 537 Steve Buechele .05 .01
❑ 538 Bill Wegman .05 .01
❑ 539 Mike LaValliere .05 .01
❑ 540 Bret Saberhagen .10 .02
❑ 541 Juan Beniquez .05 .01
❑ 542 Paul Noce .05 .01
❑ 543 Kent Tekulve .05 .01
❑ 544 Jim Traber .05 .01
❑ 545 Don Baylor .10 .02
❑ 546 John Candelaria .05 .01
❑ 547 Felix Fermin .05 .01
❑ 548 Shane Mack .05 .01
❑ 549 Braves TL
Albert Hall&
Dale Murphy&
Ken Griffey .10 .02
❑ 550 Pedro Guerrero .10 .02
❑ 551 Terry Steinbach .10 .02
❑ 552 Mark Thurmond .05 .01
❑ 553 Tracy Jones .05 .01
❑ 554 Mike Smithson .05 .01
❑ 555 Brook Jacoby .05 .01
❑ 556 Stan Clarke .05 .01
❑ 557 Craig Reynolds .05 .01
❑ 558 Bob Ojeda .05 .01
❑ 559 Ken Williams .05 .01
❑ 560 Tim Wallach .05 .01
❑ 561 Rick Cerone .05 .01
❑ 562 Jim Lindeman .05 .01
❑ 563 Jose Guzman .05 .01
❑ 564 Frank Lucchesi MG .05 .01
❑ 565 Lloyd Moseby .05 .01
❑ 566 Charlie O'Brien .05 .01
❑ 567 Mike Diaz .05 .01
❑ 568 Chris Brown .05 .01
❑ 569 Charlie Leibrandt .05 .01
❑ 570 Jeffrey Leonard .05 .01
❑ 571 Mark Williamson .05 .01
❑ 572 Chris James .05 .01
❑ 573 Bob Stanley .05 .01
❑ 574 Graig Nettles .10 .02
❑ 575 Don Sutton .10 .02
❑ 576 Tommy Hinzo .05 .01
❑ 577 Tom Browning .05 .01
❑ 578 Gary Gaetti .10 .02
❑ 579 Gary Carter
Kevin McReynolds TL .05 .01
❑ 580 Mark McGwire 1.50 .60
❑ 581 Tito Landrum .05 .01
❑ 582 Mike Henneman RC* .25 .08
❑ 583 Dave Valle .05 .01
❑ 584 Steve Trout .05 .01
❑ 585 Ozzie Guillen .10 .02
❑ 586 Bob Forsch .05 .01
❑ 587 Terry Puhl .05 .01
❑ 588 Jeff Parrett .05 .01
❑ 589 Geno Petralli .05 .01
❑ 590 George Bell .10 .02
❑ 591 Doug Drabek .05 .01
❑ 592 Dale Sveum .05 .01
❑ 593 Bob Tewksbury .05 .01
❑ 594 Bobby Valentine MG .10 .02
❑ 595 Frank White .10 .02
❑ 596 John Kruk .10 .02
❑ 597 Gene Garber .05 .01
❑ 598 Lee Lacy .05 .01
❑ 599 Calvin Schiraldi .05 .01
❑ 600 Mike Schmidt .50 .20
❑ 601 Jack Lazorko .05 .01
❑ 602 Mike Aldrete .05 .01
❑ 603 Rob Murphy .05 .01
❑ 604 Chris Bando .05 .01
❑ 605 Kirk Gibson .20 .07
❑ 606 Moose Haas .05 .01
❑ 607 Mickey Hatcher .05 .01
❑ 608 Charlie Kerfeld .05 .01
❑ 609 Gary Gaetti
Kent Hrbek TL .10 .02
❑ 610 Keith Hernandez .10 .02
❑ 611 Tommy John .10 .02
❑ 612 Curt Ford .05 .01
❑ 613 Bobby Thigpen .05 .01
❑ 614 Herm Winningham .05 .01
❑ 615 Jody Davis .05 .01
❑ 616 Jay Aldrich .05 .01
❑ 617 Oddibe McDowell .05 .01
❑ 618 Cecil Fielder .10 .02
❑ 619 Mike Dunne
(Inconsistent design&
black name on f .05 .01
❑ 620 Cory Snyder .05 .01
❑ 621 Gene Nelson .05 .01
❑ 622 Kal Daniels .05 .01
❑ 623 Mike Flanagan .05 .01
❑ 624 Jim Leyland MG .10 .02
❑ 625 Frank Viola .10 .02
❑ 626 Glenn Wilson .05 .01
❑ 627 Joe Boever .05 .01
❑ 628 Dave Henderson .05 .01
❑ 629 Kelly Downs .05 .01
❑ 630 Darrell Evans .10 .02
❑ 631 Jack Howell .05 .01
❑ 632 Steve Shields .05 .01
❑ 633 Barry Lyons .05 .01
❑ 634 Jose DeLeon .05 .01
❑ 635 Terry Pendleton .10 .02
❑ 636 Charles Hudson .05 .01
❑ 637 Jay Bell RC .40 .15
❑ 638 Steve Balboni .05 .01
❑ 639 Glenn Braggs
Tony Muser CO TL .05 .01
❑ 640 Garry Templeton
(Inconsistent design&
green bord .10 .02
❑ 641 Rick Honeycutt .05 .01
❑ 642 Bob Dernier .05 .01
❑ 643 Rocky Childress .05 .01
❑ 644 Terry McGriff .05 .01
❑ 645 Matt Nokes RC* .25 .08
❑ 646 Checklist 529-660 .05 .01
❑ 647 Pascual Perez .05 .01
❑ 648 Al Newman .05 .01
❑ 649 DeWayne Buice .05 .01
❑ 650 Cal Ripken .75 .30
❑ 651 Mike Jackson RC* .25 .08
❑ 652 Bruce Benedict .05 .01
❑ 653 Jeff Sellers .05 .01
❑ 654 Roger Craig MG .10 .02
❑ 655 Len Dykstra .10 .02
❑ 656 Lee Guetterman .05 .01
❑ 657 Gary Redus .05 .01
❑ 658 Tim Conroy
(Inconsistent design,
name in white) .05 .01
❑ 659 Bobby Meacham .05 .01
❑ 660 Rick Reuschel .10 .02
❑ 661 Nolan Ryan TBC .50 .20
❑ 662 Jim Rice TBC .05 .01
❑ 663 Ron Blomberg TBC .05 .01
❑ 664 Bob Gibson TBC .25 .08
❑ 665 Stan Musial TBC .20 .07
❑ 666 Mario Soto .10 .02
❑ 667 Luis Quinones .05 .01
❑ 668 Walt Terrell .05 .01
❑ 669 Lance Parrish
Mike Ryan CO TL .05 .01
❑ 670 Dan Plesac .05 .01
❑ 671 Tim Laudner .05 .01
❑ 672 John Davis .05 .01
❑ 673 Tony Phillips .05 .01
❑ 674 Mike Fitzgerald .05 .01
❑ 675 Jim Rice .10 .02
❑ 676 Ken Dixon .05 .01
❑ 677 Eddie Milner .05 .01
❑ 678 Jim Acker .05 .01
❑ 679 Darrell Miller .05 .01
❑ 680 Charlie Hough .10 .02
❑ 681 Bobby Bonilla .10 .02
❑ 682 Jimmy Key .10 .02
❑ 683 Julio Franco .10 .02
❑ 684 Hal Lanier MG .05 .01
❑ 685 Ron Darling .10 .02
❑ 686 Terry Francona .10 .02
❑ 687 Mickey Brantley .05 .01
❑ 688 Jim Winn .05 .01
❑ 689 Tom Pagnozzi RC .10 .02
❑ 690 Jay Howell .05 .01
❑ 691 Dan Pasqua .05 .01
❑ 692 Mike Birkbeck .05 .01
❑ 693 Benito Santiago .10 .02
❑ 694 Eric Nolte .05 .01
❑ 695 Shawon Dunston .05 .01
❑ 696 Duane Ward .05 .01
❑ 697 Steve Lombardozzi .05 .01
❑ 698 Brad Havens .05 .01
❑ 699 B.Santiago/T.Gwynn TL .10 .02
❑ 700 George Brett .50 .20
❑ 701 Sammy Stewart .05 .01
❑ 702 Mike Gallego .05 .01

❑ 703 Bob Brenly .05 .01
❑ 704 Dennis Boyd .05 .01
❑ 705 Juan Samuel .05 .01
❑ 706 Rick Mahler .05 .01
❑ 707 Fred Lynn .10 .02
❑ 708 Gus Polidor .05 .01
❑ 709 George Frazier .05 .01
❑ 710 Darryl Strawberry .10 .02
❑ 711 Bill Gullickson .05 .01
❑ 712 John Moses .05 .01
❑ 713 Willie Hernandez .05 .01
❑ 714 Jim Fregosi MG .05 .01
❑ 715 Todd Worrell .05 .01
❑ 716 Lenn Sakata .05 .01
❑ 717 Jay Baller .05 .01
❑ 718 Mike Felder .05 .01
❑ 719 Denny Walling .05 .01
❑ 720 Tim Raines .10 .02
❑ 721 Pete O'Brien .05 .01
❑ 722 Manny Lee .05 .01
❑ 723 Bob Kipper .05 .01
❑ 724 Danny Tartabull .05 .01
❑ 725 Mike Boddicker .05 .01
❑ 726 Alfredo Griffin .05 .01
❑ 727 Greg Booker .05 .01
❑ 728 Andy Allanson .05 .01
❑ 729 G.Bell/F.McGriff TL .10 .02
❑ 730 John Franco .10 .02
❑ 731 Rick Schu .05 .01
❑ 732 David Palmer .05 .01
❑ 733 Spike Owen .05 .01
❑ 734 Craig Lefferts .05 .01
❑ 735 Kevin McReynolds .05 .01
❑ 736 Matt Young .05 .01
❑ 737 Butch Wynegar .05 .01
❑ 738 Scott Bankhead .05 .01
❑ 739 Daryl Boston .05 .01
❑ 740 Rick Sutcliffe .10 .02
❑ 741 Mike Easler .05 .01
❑ 742 Mark Clear .05 .01
❑ 743 Larry Herndon .05 .01
❑ 744 Whitey Herzog MG .10 .02
❑ 745 Bill Doran .05 .01
❑ 746 Gene Larkin RC* .25 .08
❑ 747 Bobby Witt .05 .01
❑ 748 Reid Nichols .05 .01
❑ 749 Mark Eichhorn .05 .01
❑ 750 Bo Jackson .20 .07
❑ 751 Jim Morrison .05 .01
❑ 752 Mark Grant .05 .01
❑ 753 Danny Heep .05 .01
❑ 754 Mike LaCoss .05 .01
❑ 755 Ozzie Virgil .05 .01
❑ 756 Mike Maddux .05 .01
❑ 757 John Marzano .05 .01
❑ 758 Eddie Williams RC .10 .02
❑ 759 M.McGwire/J.Canseco TL 1.00 .40
❑ 760 Mike Scott .10 .02
❑ 761 Tony Armas .10 .02
❑ 762 Scott Bradley .05 .01
❑ 763 Doug Sisk .05 .01
❑ 764 Greg Walker .05 .01
❑ 765 Neal Heaton .05 .01
❑ 766 Henry Cotto .05 .01
❑ 767 Jose Lind RC .25 .08
❑ 768 Dickie Noles
(Now with Tigers
on card front) .05 .01
❑ 769 Cecil Cooper .10 .02
❑ 770 Lou Whitaker .10 .02
❑ 771 Ruben Sierra .10 .02
❑ 772 Sal Butera .05 .01
❑ 773 Frank Williams .05 .01
❑ 774 Gene Mauch MG .05 .01
❑ 775 Dave Stieb .10 .02
❑ 776 Checklist 661-792 .05 .01
❑ 777 Lonnie Smith .05 .01
❑ 778A Keith Comstock ERR WL 2.00 .75
❑ 778B Keith Comstock COR
(Blue "Padres") .05 .01
❑ 779 Tom Glavine RC 2.50 1.00
❑ 780 Fernando Valenzuela .10 .02
❑ 781 Keith Hughes .05 .01
❑ 782 Jeff Ballard .05 .01
❑ 783 Ron Roenicke .05 .01
❑ 784 Joe Sambito .05 .01
❑ 785 Alvin Davis .05 .01
❑ 786 Joe Price
(Inconsistent design&
orange team name .05 .01
❑ 787 Bill Almon .05 .01
❑ 788 Ray Searage .05 .01
❑ 789 Joe Carter TL .05 .01
❑ 790 Dave Righetti .10 .02
❑ 791 Ted Simmons .10 .02
❑ 792 John Tudor .10 .02

1988 Topps Traded

❑ COMP.FACT.SET (132) 8.00 3.00
❑ 1T Jim Abbott OLY XRC 2.00 .75
❑ 2T Juan Agosto .10 .02
❑ 3T Luis Alicea XRC .50 .20
❑ 4T Roberto Alomar XRC 2.00 .75
❑ 5T Brady Anderson XRC .75 .30
❑ 6T Jack Armstrong XRC .50 .20
❑ 7T Don August .10 .02
❑ 8T Floyd Bannister .10 .02
❑ 9T Bret Barberie OLY XRC .25 .08
❑ 10T Jose Bautista XRC .25 .08
❑ 11T Don Baylor .20 .07
❑ 12T Tim Belcher .10 .02
❑ 13T Buddy Bell .20 .07
❑ 14T Andy Benes OLY XRC .75 .30
❑ 15T Damon Berryhill XRC* .50 .20
❑ 16T Bud Black .10 .02
❑ 17T Pat Borders XRC .50 .20
❑ 18T Phil Bradley .10 .02
❑ 19T Jeff Branson XRC OLY .50 .20
❑ 20T Tom Brunansky .10 .02
❑ 21T Jay Buhner XRC 1.00 .40
❑ 22T Brett Butler .20 .07
❑ 23T Jim Campanis OLY XRC .10 .02
❑ 24T Sil Campusano .10 .02
❑ 25T John Candelaria .10 .02
❑ 26T Jose Cecena .10 .02
❑ 27T Rick Cerone .10 .02
❑ 28T Jack Clark .20 .07
❑ 29T Kevin Coffman .10 .02
❑ 30T Pat Combs OLY XRC .25 .08
❑ 31T Henry Cotto .10 .02
❑ 32T Chili Davis .20 .07
❑ 33T Mike Davis .10 .02
❑ 34T Jose DeLeon .10 .02
❑ 35T Richard Dotson .10 .02
❑ 36T Cecil Espy .10 .02
❑ 37T Tom Filer .10 .02
❑ 38T Mike Fiore OLY .10 .02
❑ 39T Ron Gant XRC .75 .30
❑ 40T Kirk Gibson .50 .20
❑ 41T Rich Gossage .20 .07
❑ 42T Mark Grace XRC 2.00 .75
❑ 43T Alfredo Griffin .10 .02
❑ 44T Ty Griffin OLY .10 .02
❑ 45T Bryan Harvey XRC .50 .20
❑ 46T Ron Hassey .10 .02
❑ 47T Ray Hayward .10 .02
❑ 48T Dave Henderson .10 .02
❑ 49T Tom Herr .10 .02
❑ 50T Bob Horner .20 .07
❑ 51T Ricky Horton .10 .02
❑ 52T Jay Howell .10 .02
❑ 53T Glenn Hubbard .10 .02
❑ 54T Jeff Innis .10 .02
❑ 55T Danny Jackson .10 .02
❑ 56T Darrin Jackson XRC .25 .08
❑ 57T Roberto Kelly XRC .50 .20
❑ 58T Ron Kittle .10 .02
❑ 59T Ray Knight .20 .07
❑ 60T Vance Law .10 .02
❑ 61T Jeffrey Leonard .10 .02
❑ 62T Mike Macfarlane XRC .50 .20
❑ 63T Scotti Madison .10 .02
❑ 64T Kirt Manwaring .10 .02
❑ 65T Mark Marquess OLY CO .10 .02
❑ 66T Tino Martinez OLY XRC 3.00 1.25
❑ 67T Billy Masse OLY XRC .25 .08
❑ 68T Jack McDowell XRC .75 .30
❑ 69T Jack McKeon MG .20 .07
❑ 70T Larry McWilliams .10 .02
❑ 71T Mickey Morandini OLY XRC .50 .20
❑ 72T Keith Moreland .10 .02
❑ 73T Mike Morgan .10 .02
❑ 74T Charles Nagy OLY XRC .50 .20
❑ 75T Al Nipper .10 .02
❑ 76T Russ Nixon MG .10 .02
❑ 77T Jesse Orosco .10 .02
❑ 78T Joe Orsulak .10 .02
❑ 79T Dave Palmer .10 .02
❑ 80T Mark Parent .10 .02
❑ 81T Dave Parker .20 .07
❑ 82T Dan Pasqua .10 .02
❑ 83T Melido Perez XRC .50 .20
❑ 84T Steve Peters .10 .02
❑ 85T Dan Petry .10 .02
❑ 86T Gary Pettis .10 .02
❑ 87T Jeff Pico .10 .02
❑ 88T Jim Poole OLY XRC .25 .08
❑ 89T Ted Power .10 .02
❑ 90T Rafael Ramirez .10 .02
❑ 91T Dennis Rasmussen .10 .02
❑ 92T Jose Rijo .20 .07
❑ 93T Ernie Riles .10 .02
❑ 94T Luis Rivera .10 .02
❑ 95T Doug Robbins OLY XRC .25 .08
❑ 96T Frank Robinson MG .30 .10
❑ 97T Cookie Rojas MG .10 .02
❑ 98T Chris Sabo XRC .75 .30
❑ 99T Mark Salas .10 .02
❑ 100T Luis Salazar .10 .02
❑ 101T Rafael Santana .10 .02
❑ 102T Nelson Santovenia .10 .02
❑ 103T Mackey Sasser XRC .50 .20
❑ 104T Calvin Schiraldi .10 .02
❑ 105T Mike Schooler .10 .02
❑ 106T Scott Servais OLY XRC .50 .20
❑ 107T Dave Silvestri OLY XRC .25 .08
❑ 108T Don Slaught .10 .02
❑ 109T Joe Slusarski OLY XRC .25 .08
❑ 110T Lee Smith .20 .07
❑ 111T Pete Smith XRC .25 .08
❑ 112T Jim Snyder MG .10 .02
❑ 113T Ed Sprague OLY XRC .50 .20
❑ 114T Pete Stanicek .10 .02
❑ 115T Kurt Stillwell .10 .02
❑ 116T Todd Stottlemyre XRC .50 .20
❑ 117T Bill Swift .10 .02
❑ 118T Pat Tabler .10 .02
❑ 119T Scott Terry .10 .02
❑ 120T Mickey Tettleton .10 .02
❑ 121T Dickie Thon .10 .02
❑ 122T Jeff Treadway XRC .50 .20
❑ 123T Willie Upshaw .10 .02
❑ 124T Robin Ventura OLY XRC 1.50 .60
❑ 125T Ron Washington .10 .02
❑ 126T Walt Weiss XRC .75 .30
❑ 127T Bob Welch .20 .07
❑ 128T David Wells XRC 1.50 .60
❑ 129T Glenn Wilson .10 .02
❑ 130T Ted Wood OLY XRC .25 .08
❑ 131T Don Zimmer MG .20 .07
❑ 132T Checklist 1T-132T .10 .02

1989 Topps

❑ COMPLETE SET (792) 20.00 8.00
❑ COMP.FACT SET (792) 25.00 10.00
❑ COMP.X-MAS.SET (792) 25.00 10.00
❑ FS SUBSET VARIATIONS EXIST
❑ FS PHOTOS ARE PLACED
HIGHER/LOWER
❑ 1 George Bell RB .05 .01

❑ 2 Wade Boggs RB .10 .02
❑ 3 Gary Carter RB .05 .01
❑ 4 Andre Dawson RB .05 .01
❑ 5 Orel Hershiser RB .05 .01
❑ 6 Doug Jones RB UER .05 .01
❑ 7 Kevin McReynolds RB .05 .01
❑ 8 Dave Eiland .05 .01
❑ 9 Tim Teufel .05 .01
❑ 10 Andre Dawson .10 .02
❑ 11 Bruce Sutter .10 .02
❑ 12 Dale Sveum .05 .01
❑ 13 Doug Sisk .05 .01
❑ 14 Tom Kelly MG .05 .01
❑ 15 Robby Thompson .05 .01
❑ 16 Ron Robinson .05 .01
❑ 17 Brian Downing .10 .02
❑ 18 Rick Rhoden .05 .01
❑ 19 Greg Gagne .05 .01
❑ 20 Steve Bedrosian .05 .01
❑ 21 Greg Walker TL .05 .01
❑ 22 Tim Crews .05 .01
❑ 23 Mike Fitzgerald .05 .01
❑ 24 Larry Andersen .05 .01
❑ 25 Frank White .10 .02
❑ 26 Dale Mohorcic .05 .01
❑ 27A Orestes Destrade RC * .10 .02
❑ 27B Orestes Destrade VAR .10 .02
❑ 28 Mike Moore .05 .01
❑ 29 Kelly Gruber .05 .01
❑ 30 Dwight Gooden .10 .02
❑ 31 Terry Francona .10 .02
❑ 32 Dennis Rasmussen .05 .01
❑ 33 B.J. Surhoff .10 .02
❑ 34 Ken Williams .05 .01
❑ 35 John Tudor UER
(With Red Sox in '84,should be Pir) .10 .02
❑ 36 Mitch Webster .05 .01
❑ 37 Bob Stanley .05 .01
❑ 38 Paul Runge .05 .01
❑ 39 Mike Maddux .05 .01
❑ 40 Steve Sax .05 .01
❑ 41 Terry Mulholland .05 .01
❑ 42 Jim Eppard .05 .01
❑ 43 Guillermo Hernandez .05 .01
❑ 44 Jim Snyder MG .05 .01
❑ 45 Kal Daniels .05 .01
❑ 46 Mark Portugal .05 .01
❑ 47 Carney Lansford .10 .02
❑ 48 Tim Burke .05 .01
❑ 49 Craig Biggio RC 2.00 .75
❑ 50 George Bell .10 .02
❑ 51 Mark McLemore TL .05 .01
❑ 52 Bob Brenly .05 .01
❑ 53 Ruben Sierra .10 .02
❑ 54 Steve Trout .05 .01
❑ 55 Julio Franco .10 .02
❑ 56 Pat Tabler .05 .01
❑ 57 Alejandro Pena .05 .01
❑ 58 Lee Mazzilli .10 .02
❑ 59 Mark Davis .05 .01
❑ 60 Tom Brunansky .05 .01
❑ 61 Neil Allen .05 .01
❑ 62 Alfredo Griffin .05 .01
❑ 63 Mark Clear .05 .01
❑ 64 Alex Trevino .05 .01
❑ 65 Rick Reuschel .10 .02
❑ 66 Manny Trillo .05 .01
❑ 67 Dave Palmer .05 .01
❑ 68 Darrell Miller .05 .01
❑ 69 Jeff Ballard .05 .01
❑ 70 Mark McGwire 1.00 .40
❑ 71 Mike Boddicker .05 .01
❑ 72 John Moses .05 .01
❑ 73 Pascual Perez .05 .01
❑ 74 Nick Leyva MG .05 .01
❑ 75 Tom Henke .05 .01
❑ 76 Terry Blocker .05 .01
❑ 77 Doyle Alexander .05 .01
❑ 78 Jim Sundberg .10 .02
❑ 79 Scott Bankhead .05 .01
❑ 80 Cory Snyder .05 .01
❑ 81 Tim Raines TL .05 .01
❑ 82 Dave Leiper .05 .01
❑ 83 Jeff Blauser .05 .01
❑ 84 Bill Bene FDP .05 .01
❑ 85 Kevin McReynolds .05 .01
❑ 86 Al Nipper .05 .01
❑ 87 Larry Owen .05 .01
❑ 88 Darryl Hamilton RC * .25 .08
❑ 89 Dave LaPoint .05 .01
❑ 90 Vince Coleman UER
(Wrong birth year) .05 .01
❑ 91 Floyd Youmans .05 .01
❑ 92 Jeff Kunkel .05 .01
❑ 93 Ken Howell .05 .01
❑ 94 Chris Speier .05 .01
❑ 95 Gerald Young .05 .01
❑ 96 Rick Cerone .05 .01
❑ 97 Greg Mathews .05 .01
❑ 98 Larry Sheets .05 .01
❑ 99 Sherman Corbett .05 .01
❑ 100 Mike Schmidt .50 .20
❑ 101 Les Straker .05 .01
❑ 102 Mike Gallego .05 .01
❑ 103 Tim Birtsas .05 .01
❑ 104 Dallas Green MG .05 .01
❑ 105 Ron Darling .10 .02
❑ 106 Willie Upshaw .05 .01
❑ 107 Jose DeLeon .05 .01
❑ 108 Fred Manrique .05 .01
❑ 109 Hipolito Pena .05 .01
❑ 110 Paul Molitor .10 .02
❑ 111 Eric Davis TL .05 .01
❑ 112 Jim Presley .05 .01
❑ 113 Lloyd Moseby .05 .01
❑ 114 Bob Kipper .05 .01
❑ 115 Jody Davis .05 .01
❑ 116 Jeff Montgomery .05 .01
❑ 117 Dave Anderson .05 .01
❑ 118 Checklist 1-132 .05 .01
❑ 119 Terry Puhl .05 .01
❑ 120 Frank Viola .10 .02
❑ 121 Garry Templeton .10 .02
❑ 122 Lance Johnson .05 .01
❑ 123 Spike Owen .05 .01
❑ 124 Jim Traber .05 .01
❑ 125 Mike Krukow .05 .01
❑ 126 Sid Bream .05 .01
❑ 127 Walt Terrell .05 .01
❑ 128 Milt Thompson .05 .01
❑ 129 Terry Clark .05 .01
❑ 130 Gerald Perry .05 .01
❑ 131 Dave Otto .05 .01
❑ 132 Curt Ford .05 .01
❑ 133 Bill Long .05 .01
❑ 134 Don Zimmer MG .10 .02
❑ 135 Jose Rijo .10 .02
❑ 136 Joey Meyer .05 .01
❑ 137 Geno Petralli .05 .01
❑ 138 Wallace Johnson .05 .01
❑ 139 Mike Flanagan .05 .01
❑ 140 Shawon Dunston .05 .01
❑ 141 Brook Jacoby TL .05 .01
❑ 142 Mike Diaz .05 .01
❑ 143 Mike Campbell .05 .01
❑ 144 Jay Bell .10 .02
❑ 145 Dave Stewart .10 .02
❑ 146 Gary Pettis .05 .01
❑ 147 DeWayne Buice .05 .01
❑ 148 Bill Pecota .05 .01
❑ 149 Doug Dascenzo .05 .01
❑ 150 Fernando Valenzuela .10 .02
❑ 151 Terry McGriff .05 .01
❑ 152 Mark Thurmond .05 .01
❑ 153 Jim Pankovits .05 .01
❑ 154 Don Carman .05 .01
❑ 155 Marty Barrett .05 .01
❑ 156 Dave Gallagher .05 .01
❑ 157 Tom Glavine .25 .08
❑ 158 Mike Aldrete .05 .01
❑ 159 Pat Clements .05 .01
❑ 160 Jeffrey Leonard .05 .01
❑ 161 Gregg Olson UER RC .25 .08
❑ 162 John Davis .05 .01
❑ 163 Bob Forsch .05 .01
❑ 164 Hal Lanier MG .05 .01
❑ 165 Mike Dunne .05 .01
❑ 166 Doug Jennings .05 .01
❑ 167 Steve Searcy FS .05 .01
❑ 168 Willie Wilson .10 .02
❑ 169 Mike Jackson .05 .01
❑ 170 Tony Fernandez .05 .01
❑ 171 Andres Thomas TL .05 .01
❑ 172 Frank Williams .05 .01
❑ 173 Mel Hall .05 .01
❑ 174 Todd Burns .05 .01
❑ 175 John Shelby .05 .01
❑ 176 Jeff Parrett .05 .01
❑ 177 Monty Fariss FDP .05 .01
❑ 178 Mark Grant .05 .01
❑ 179 Ozzie Virgil .05 .01
❑ 180 Mike Scott .10 .02
❑ 181 Craig Worthington .05 .01
❑ 182 Bob McClure .05 .01
❑ 183 Oddibe McDowell .05 .01
❑ 184 John Costello .05 .01
❑ 185 Claudell Washington .05 .01
❑ 186 Pat Perry .05 .01
❑ 187 Darren Daulton .10 .02
❑ 188 Dennis Lamp .05 .01
❑ 189 Kevin Mitchell .10 .02
❑ 190 Mike Witt .05 .01
❑ 191 Sil Campusano .05 .01
❑ 192 Paul Mirabella .05 .01
❑ 193 Sparky Anderson MG
(Team checklist back)
UER (55) .10 .02
❑ 194 Greg W.Harris RC .10 .02
❑ 195 Ozzie Guillen .10 .02
❑ 196 Denny Walling .05 .01
❑ 197 Neal Heaton .05 .01
❑ 198 Danny Heep .05 .01
❑ 199 Mike Schooler RC * .10 .02
❑ 200 George Brett .60 .25
❑ 201 Kelly Gruber TL .05 .01
❑ 202 Brad Moore .05 .01
❑ 203 Rob Ducey .05 .01
❑ 204 Brad Havens .05 .01
❑ 205 Dwight Evans .15 .05
❑ 206 Roberto Alomar .25 .08
❑ 207 Terry Leach .05 .01
❑ 208 Tom Pagnozzi .05 .01
❑ 209 Jeff Bittiger .05 .01
❑ 210 Dale Murphy .15 .05
❑ 211 Mike Pagliarulo .05 .01
❑ 212 Scott Sanderson .05 .01
❑ 213 Rene Gonzales .05 .01
❑ 214 Charlie O'Brien .05 .01
❑ 215 Kevin Gross .05 .01
❑ 216 Jack Howell .05 .01
❑ 217 Joe Price .05 .01
❑ 218 Mike LaValliere .05 .01
❑ 219 Jim Clancy .05 .01
❑ 220 Gary Gaetti .10 .02
❑ 221 Cecil Espy .05 .01
❑ 222 Mark Lewis RC .25 .08
❑ 223 Jay Buhner .10 .02
❑ 224 Tony LaRussa MG .10 .02
❑ 225 Ramon Martinez RC .25 .08
❑ 226 Bill Doran .05 .01
❑ 227 John Farrell .05 .01
❑ 228 Nelson Santovenia .05 .01
❑ 229 Jimmy Key .10 .02
❑ 230 Ozzie Smith .40 .15
❑ 231 Padres TL/R.Alomar .25 .08
❑ 232 Ricky Horton .05 .01
❑ 233 Gregg Jefferies .05 .01
❑ 234 Tom Browning .05 .01
❑ 235 John Kruk .10 .02
❑ 236 Charles Hudson .05 .01

❑ 237	Glenn Hubbard	.05	.01
❑ 238	Eric King	.05	.01
❑ 239	Tim Laudner	.05	.01
❑ 240	Greg Maddux	.50	.20
❑ 241	Brett Butler	.10	.02
❑ 242	Ed VandeBerg	.05	.01
❑ 243	Bob Boone	.10	.02
❑ 244	Jim Acker	.05	.01
❑ 245	Jim Rice	.10	.02
❑ 246	Rey Quinones	.05	.01
❑ 247	Shawn Hillegas	.05	.01
❑ 248	Tony Phillips	.05	.01
❑ 249	Tim Leary	.05	.01
❑ 250	Cal Ripken	.75	.30
❑ 251	John Dopson	.05	.01
❑ 252	Billy Hatcher	.05	.01
❑ 253	Jose Alvarez RC	.10	.02
❑ 254	Tom Lasorda MG	.15	.05
❑ 255	Ron Guidry	.10	.02
❑ 256	Benny Santiago	.10	.02
❑ 257	Rick Aguilera	.05	.01
❑ 258	Checklist 133-264	.05	.01
❑ 259	Larry McWilliams	.05	.01
❑ 260	Dave Winfield	.10	.02
❑ 261	St.Louis Cardinals TL Tom Brunansky (With Luis A)	.05	.01
❑ 262	Jeff Pico	.05	.01
❑ 263	Mike Felder	.05	.01
❑ 264	Rob Dibble RC	.40	.15
❑ 265	Kent Hrbek	.10	.02
❑ 266	Luis Aquino	.05	.01
❑ 267	Jeff M. Robinson	.05	.01
❑ 268	Keith Miller RC	.25	.08
❑ 269	Tom Bolton	.05	.01
❑ 270	Wally Joyner	.10	.02
❑ 271	Jay Tibbs	.05	.01
❑ 272	Ron Hassey	.05	.01
❑ 273	Jose Lind	.05	.01
❑ 274	Mark Eichhorn	.05	.01
❑ 275	Danny Tartabull UER (Born San Juan& PR should be)	.05	.01
❑ 276	Paul Kilgus	.05	.01
❑ 277	Mike Davis	.05	.01
❑ 278	Andy McGaffigan	.05	.01
❑ 279	Scott Bradley	.05	.01
❑ 280	Bob Knepper	.05	.01
❑ 281	Gary Redus	.05	.01
❑ 282	Cris Carpenter RC *	.10	.02
❑ 283	Andy Allanson	.05	.01
❑ 284	Jim Leyland MG	.10	.02
❑ 285	John Candelaria	.05	.01
❑ 286	Darrin Jackson	.10	.02
❑ 287	Juan Nieves	.05	.01
❑ 288	Pat Sheridan	.05	.01
❑ 289	Ernie Whitt	.05	.01
❑ 290	John Franco	.10	.02
❑ 291	New York Mets TL Darryl Strawberry (With Keith H)	.05	.01
❑ 292	Jim Corsi	.05	.01
❑ 293	Glenn Wilson	.05	.01
❑ 294	Juan Berenguer	.05	.01
❑ 295	Scott Fletcher	.05	.01
❑ 296	Ron Gant	.10	.02
❑ 297	Oswald Peraza	.05	.01
❑ 298	Chris James	.05	.01
❑ 299	Steve Ellsworth	.05	.01
❑ 300	Darryl Strawberry	.10	.02
❑ 301	Charlie Leibrandt	.05	.01
❑ 302	Gary Ward	.05	.01
❑ 303	Felix Fermin	.05	.01
❑ 304	Joel Youngblood	.05	.01
❑ 305	Dave Smith	.05	.01
❑ 306	Tracy Woodson	.05	.01
❑ 307	Lance McCullers	.05	.01
❑ 308	Ron Karkovice	.05	.01
❑ 309	Mario Diaz	.05	.01
❑ 310	Rafael Palmeiro	.25	.08
❑ 311	Chris Bosio	.05	.01
❑ 312	Tom Lawless	.05	.01
❑ 313	Dennis Martinez	.10	.02
❑ 314	Bobby Valentine MG	.10	.02
❑ 315	Greg Swindell	.05	.01
❑ 316	Walt Weiss	.05	.01
❑ 317	Jack Armstrong RC *	.25	.08
❑ 318	Gene Larkin	.05	.01
❑ 319	Greg Booker	.05	.01
❑ 320	Lou Whitaker	.10	.02
❑ 321	Jody Reed TL	.05	.01
❑ 322	John Smiley	.05	.01
❑ 323	Gary Thurman	.05	.01
❑ 324	Bob Milacki	.05	.01
❑ 325	Jesse Barfield	.10	.02
❑ 326	Dennis Boyd	.05	.01
❑ 327	Mark Lemke RC	.40	.15
❑ 328	Rick Honeycutt	.05	.01
❑ 329	Bob Melvin	.05	.01
❑ 330	Eric Davis	.10	.02
❑ 331	Curt Wilkerson	.05	.01
❑ 332	Tony Armas	.10	.02
❑ 333	Bob Ojeda	.05	.01
❑ 334	Steve Lyons	.05	.01
❑ 335	Dave Righetti	.10	.02
❑ 336	Steve Balboni	.05	.01
❑ 337	Calvin Schiraldi	.05	.01
❑ 338	Jim Adduci	.05	.01
❑ 339	Scott Bailes	.05	.01
❑ 340	Kirk Gibson	.10	.02
❑ 341	Jim Deshaies	.05	.01
❑ 342	Tom Brookens	.05	.01
❑ 343	Gary Sheffield RC	1.50	.60
❑ 344	Tom Trebelhorn MG	.05	.01
❑ 345	Charlie Hough	.10	.02
❑ 346	Rex Hudler	.05	.01
❑ 347	John Cerutti	.05	.01
❑ 348	Ed Hearn	.05	.01
❑ 349	Ron Jones	.10	.02
❑ 350	Andy Van Slyke	.15	.05
❑ 351	San Fran. Giants TL Bob Melvin (With Bill Fahey)	.05	.01
❑ 352	Rick Schu	.05	.01
❑ 353	Marvell Wynne	.05	.01
❑ 354	Larry Parrish	.05	.01
❑ 355	Mark Langston	.05	.01
❑ 356	Kevin Elster	.05	.01
❑ 357	Jerry Reuss	.05	.01
❑ 358	Ricky Jordan RC *	.25	.08
❑ 359	Tommy John	.10	.02
❑ 360	Ryne Sandberg	.40	.15
❑ 361	Kelly Downs	.05	.01
❑ 362	Jack Lazorko	.05	.01
❑ 363	Rich Yett	.05	.01
❑ 364	Rob Deer	.05	.01
❑ 365	Mike Henneman	.05	.01
❑ 366	Herm Winningham	.05	.01
❑ 367	Johnny Paredes	.05	.01
❑ 368	Brian Holton	.05	.01
❑ 369	Ken Caminiti	.15	.05
❑ 370	Dennis Eckersley	.15	.05
❑ 371	Manny Lee	.05	.01
❑ 372	Craig Lefferts	.05	.01
❑ 373	Tracy Jones	.05	.01
❑ 374	John Wathan MG	.05	.01
❑ 375	Terry Pendleton	.10	.02
❑ 376	Steve Lombardozzi	.05	.01
❑ 377	Mike Smithson	.05	.01
❑ 378	Checklist 265-396	.05	.01
❑ 379	Tim Flannery	.05	.01
❑ 380	Rickey Henderson	.25	.08
❑ 381	Larry Sheets TL	.05	.01
❑ 382	John Smoltz RC	1.50	.60
❑ 383	Howard Johnson	.10	.02
❑ 384	Mark Salas	.05	.01
❑ 385	Von Hayes	.05	.01
❑ 386	Andres Galarraga AS	.05	.01
❑ 387	Ryne Sandberg AS	.25	.08
❑ 388	Bobby Bonilla AS	.05	.01
❑ 389	Ozzie Smith AS	.25	.08
❑ 390	Darryl Strawberry AS	.05	.01
❑ 391	Andre Dawson AS	.05	.01
❑ 392	Andy Van Slyke AS	.10	.02
❑ 393	Gary Carter AS	.05	.01
❑ 394	Orel Hershiser AS	.05	.01
❑ 395	Danny Jackson AS	.05	.01
❑ 396	Kirk Gibson AS	.10	.02
❑ 397	Don Mattingly AS	.30	.10
❑ 398	Julio Franco AS	.05	.01
❑ 399	Wade Boggs AS	.10	.02
❑ 400	Alan Trammell AS	.05	.01
❑ 401	Jose Canseco AS	.15	.05
❑ 402	Mike Greenwell AS	.05	.01
❑ 403	Kirby Puckett AS	.15	.05
❑ 404	Bob Boone AS	.05	.01
❑ 405	Roger Clemens AS	.50	.20
❑ 406	Frank Viola AS	.05	.01
❑ 407	Dave Winfield AS	.05	.01
❑ 408	Greg Walker	.05	.01
❑ 409	Ken Dayley	.05	.01
❑ 410	Jack Clark	.10	.02
❑ 411	Mitch Williams	.05	.01
❑ 412	Barry Lyons	.05	.01
❑ 413	Mike Kingery	.05	.01
❑ 414	Jim Fregosi MG	.05	.01
❑ 415	Rich Gossage	.10	.02
❑ 416	Fred Lynn	.10	.02
❑ 417	Mike LaCoss	.05	.01
❑ 418	Bob Dernier	.05	.01
❑ 419	Tom Filer	.05	.01
❑ 420	Joe Carter	.10	.02
❑ 421	Kirk McCaskill	.05	.01
❑ 422	Bo Diaz	.05	.01
❑ 423	Brian Fisher	.05	.01
❑ 424	Luis Polonia UER (Wrong birthdate)	.05	.01
❑ 425	Jay Howell	.05	.01
❑ 426	Dan Gladden	.05	.01
❑ 427	Eric Show	.05	.01
❑ 428	Craig Reynolds	.05	.01
❑ 429	Minnesota Twins TL Greg Gagne (Taking throw at 2)	.05	.01
❑ 430	Mark Gubicza	.05	.01
❑ 431	Luis Rivera	.05	.01
❑ 432	Chad Kreuter RC	.25	.08
❑ 433	Albert Hall	.05	.01
❑ 434	Ken Patterson	.05	.01
❑ 435	Len Dykstra	.10	.02
❑ 436	Bobby Meacham	.05	.01
❑ 437	Andy Benes RC *	.40	.15
❑ 438	Greg Gross	.05	.01
❑ 439	Frank DiPino	.05	.01
❑ 440	Bobby Bonilla	.10	.02
❑ 441	Jerry Reed	.05	.01
❑ 442	Jose Oquendo	.05	.01
❑ 443	Rod Nichols	.05	.01
❑ 444	Moose Stubing MG	.05	.01
❑ 445	Matt Nokes	.05	.01
❑ 446	Rob Murphy	.05	.01
❑ 447	Donell Nixon	.05	.01
❑ 448	Eric Plunk	.05	.01
❑ 449	Carmelo Martinez	.05	.01
❑ 450	Roger Clemens	1.00	.40
❑ 451	Mark Davidson	.05	.01
❑ 452	Israel Sanchez	.05	.01
❑ 453	Tom Prince	.05	.01
❑ 454	Paul Assenmacher	.05	.01
❑ 455	Johnny Ray	.05	.01
❑ 456	Tim Belcher	.05	.01
❑ 457	Mackey Sasser	.05	.01
❑ 458	Donn Pall	.05	.01
❑ 459	Dave Valle TL	.05	.01
❑ 460	Dave Stieb	.10	.02
❑ 461	Buddy Bell	.10	.02
❑ 462	Jose Guzman	.05	.01
❑ 463	Steve Lake	.05	.01
❑ 464	Bryn Smith	.05	.01
❑ 465	Mark Grace	.25	.08
❑ 466	Chuck Crim	.05	.01
❑ 467	Jim Walewander	.05	.01
❑ 468	Henry Cotto	.05	.01
❑ 469	Jose Bautista RC	.10	.02
❑ 470	Lance Parrish	.10	.02
❑ 471	Steve Curry	.05	.01
❑ 472	Brian Harper	.05	.01
❑ 473	Don Robinson	.05	.01
❑ 474	Bob Rodgers MG	.05	.01
❑ 475	Dave Parker	.10	.02
❑ 476	Jon Perlman	.05	.01
❑ 477	Dick Schofield	.05	.01
❑ 478	Doug Drabek	.05	.01
❑ 479	Mike Macfarlane RC *	.25	.08
❑ 480	Keith Hernandez	.10	.02
❑ 481	Chris Brown	.05	.01
❑ 482	Steve Peters	.05	.01
❑ 483	Mickey Hatcher	.05	.01

❑ 484 Steve Shields .05 .01
❑ 485 Hubie Brooks .05 .01
❑ 486 Jack McDowell .10 .02
❑ 487 Scott Lusader .05 .01
❑ 488 Kevin Coffman ('Now with Cubs') .05 .01
❑ 489 Phillies TL/M.Schmidt .15 .05
❑ 490 Chris Sabo RC * .40 .15
❑ 491 Mike Birkbeck .05 .01
❑ 492 Alan Ashby .05 .01
❑ 493 Todd Benzinger .05 .01
❑ 494 Shane Rawley .05 .01
❑ 495 Candy Maldonado .05 .01
❑ 496 Dwayne Henry .05 .01
❑ 497 Pete Stanicek .05 .01
❑ 498 Dave Valle .05 .01
❑ 499 Don Heinkel .05 .01
❑ 500 Jose Canseco .25 .08
❑ 501 Vance Law .05 .01
❑ 502 Duane Ward .05 .01
❑ 503 Al Newman .05 .01
❑ 504 Bob Walk .05 .01
❑ 505 Pete Rose MG/TC .50 .20
❑ 506 Kirt Manwaring .05 .01
❑ 507 Steve Farr .05 .01
❑ 508 Wally Backman .05 .01
❑ 509 Bud Black .05 .01
❑ 510 Bob Horner .10 .02
❑ 511 Richard Dotson .05 .01
❑ 512 Donnie Hill .05 .01
❑ 513 Jesse Orosco .05 .01
❑ 514 Chet Lemon .10 .02
❑ 515 Barry Larkin .15 .05
❑ 516 Eddie Whitson .05 .01
❑ 517 Greg Brock .05 .01
❑ 518 Bruce Ruffin .05 .01
❑ 519 Willie Randolph TL .05 .01
❑ 520 Rick Sutcliffe .10 .02
❑ 521 Mickey Tettleton .05 .01
❑ 522 Randy Kramer .05 .01
❑ 523 Andres Thomas .05 .01
❑ 524 Checklist 397-528 .05 .01
❑ 525 Chili Davis .10 .02
❑ 526 Wes Gardner .05 .01
❑ 527 Dave Henderson .05 .01
❑ 528 Luis Medina (Lower left front has white triangle) .05 .01
❑ 529 Tom Foley .05 .01
❑ 530 Nolan Ryan 1.00 .40
❑ 531 Dave Hengel .05 .01
❑ 532 Jerry Browne .05 .01
❑ 533 Andy Hawkins .05 .01
❑ 534 Doc Edwards MG .05 .01
❑ 535 Todd Worrell UER (4 wins in '88& should be 5) .05 .01
❑ 536 Joel Skinner .05 .01
❑ 537 Pete Smith .05 .01
❑ 538 Juan Castillo .05 .01
❑ 539 Barry Jones .05 .01
❑ 540 Bo Jackson .25 .08
❑ 541 Cecil Fielder .10 .02
❑ 542 Todd Frohwirth .05 .01
❑ 543 Damon Berryhill .05 .01
❑ 544 Jeff Sellers .05 .01
❑ 545 Mookie Wilson .10 .02
❑ 546 Mark Williamson .05 .01
❑ 547 Mark McLemore .05 .01
❑ 548 Bobby Witt .05 .01
❑ 549 Jamie Moyer TL .05 .01
❑ 550 Orel Hershiser .10 .02
❑ 551 Randy Ready .05 .01
❑ 552 Greg Cadaret .05 .01
❑ 553 Luis Salazar .05 .01
❑ 554 Nick Esasky .05 .01
❑ 555 Bert Blyleven .10 .02
❑ 556 Bruce Fields .05 .01
❑ 557 Keith A. Miller .05 .01
❑ 558 Dan Pasqua .05 .01
❑ 559 Juan Agosto .05 .01
❑ 560 Tim Raines .10 .02
❑ 561 Luis Aguayo .05 .01
❑ 562 Danny Cox .05 .01
❑ 563 Bill Schroeder .05 .01
❑ 564 Russ Nixon MG .05 .01
❑ 565 Jeff Russell .05 .01
❑ 566 Al Pedrique .05 .01
❑ 567 David Wells UER .10 .02
❑ 568 Mickey Brantley .05 .01
❑ 569 German Jimenez .05 .01
❑ 570 Tony Gwynn .30 .10
❑ 571 Billy Ripken .05 .01
❑ 572 Atlee Hammaker .05 .01
❑ 573 Jim Abbott RC 1.00 .40
❑ 574 Dave Clark .05 .01
❑ 575 Juan Samuel .05 .01
❑ 576 Greg Minton .05 .01
❑ 577 Randy Bush .05 .01
❑ 578 John Morris .05 .01
❑ 579 Glenn Davis TL .05 .01
❑ 580 Harold Reynolds .10 .02
❑ 581 Gene Nelson .05 .01
❑ 582 Mike Marshall .05 .01
❑ 583 Paul Gibson .05 .01
❑ 584 Randy Velarde UER (Signed 1935& should be 1985) .05 .01
❑ 585 Harold Baines .10 .02
❑ 586 Joe Boever .05 .01
❑ 587 Mike Stanley .05 .01
❑ 588 Luis Alicea RC * .25 .08
❑ 589 Dave Meads .05 .01
❑ 590 Andres Galarraga .10 .02
❑ 591 Jeff Musselman .05 .01
❑ 592 John Cangelosi .05 .01
❑ 593 Drew Hall .05 .01
❑ 594 Jimy Williams MG .05 .01
❑ 595 Teddy Higuera .05 .01
❑ 596 Kurt Stillwell .05 .01
❑ 597 Terry Taylor RC .10 .02
❑ 598 Ken Gerhart .05 .01
❑ 599 Tom Candiotti .05 .01
❑ 600 Wade Boggs .15 .05
❑ 601 Dave Dravecky .05 .01
❑ 602 Devon White .10 .02
❑ 603 Frank Tanana .10 .02
❑ 604 Paul O'Neill .15 .05
❑ 605A Bob Welch ML Line ERR 10.00 4.00
❑ 605B Bob Welch COR .10 .02
❑ 606 Rick Dempsey .05 .01
❑ 607 Willie Ansley RC .10 .02
❑ 608 Phil Bradley .05 .01
❑ 609 Detroit Tigers TL Frank Tanana (With Alan Tramme) .05 .01
❑ 610 Randy Myers .10 .02
❑ 611 Don Slaught .05 .01
❑ 612 Dan Quisenberry .05 .01
❑ 613 Gary Varsho .05 .01
❑ 614 Joe Hesketh .05 .01
❑ 615 Robin Yount .40 .15
❑ 616 Steve Rosenberg .05 .01
❑ 617 Mark Parent .05 .01
❑ 618 Rance Mulliniks .05 .01
❑ 619 Checklist 529-660 .05 .01
❑ 620 Barry Bonds 1.50 .60
❑ 621 Rick Mahler .05 .01
❑ 622 Stan Javier .05 .01
❑ 623 Fred Toliver .05 .01
❑ 624 Jack McKeon MG .10 .02
❑ 625 Eddie Murray .25 .08
❑ 626 Jeff Reed .05 .01
❑ 627 Greg A. Harris .05 .01
❑ 628 Matt Williams .25 .08
❑ 629 Pete O'Brien .05 .01
❑ 630 Mike Greenwell .05 .01
❑ 631 Dave Bergman .05 .01
❑ 632 Bryan Harvey RC * .25 .08
❑ 633 Daryl Boston .05 .01
❑ 634 Marvin Freeman .05 .01
❑ 635 Willie Randolph .10 .02
❑ 636 Bill Wilkinson .05 .01
❑ 637 Carmen Castillo .05 .01
❑ 638 Floyd Bannister .05 .01
❑ 639 Walt Weiss TL .05 .01
❑ 640 Willie McGee .10 .02
❑ 641 Curt Young .05 .01
❑ 642 Angel Salazar .05 .01
❑ 643 Louie Meadows .05 .01
❑ 644 Lloyd McClendon .05 .01
❑ 645 Jack Morris .10 .02
❑ 646 Kevin Bass .05 .01
❑ 647 Randy Johnson RC 2.50 1.00
❑ 648 Sandy Alomar Jr. RC .40 .15
❑ 649 Stu Cliburn .05 .01
❑ 650 Kirby Puckett .25 .08
❑ 651 Tom Niedenfuer .05 .01
❑ 652 Rich Gedman .05 .01
❑ 653 Tommy Barrett .05 .01
❑ 654 Whitey Herzog MG .10 .02
❑ 655 Dave Magadan .05 .01
❑ 656 Ivan Calderon .05 .01
❑ 657 Joe Magrane .05 .01
❑ 658 R.J. Reynolds .05 .01
❑ 659 Al Leiter .25 .08
❑ 660 Will Clark .15 .05
❑ 661 Dwight Gooden TBC 84 .05 .01
❑ 662 Lou Brock TBC .10 .02
❑ 663 Hank Aaron TBC .25 .08
❑ 664 Gil Hodges TBC 69 .10 .02
❑ 665A T.Oliva TBC Copyright ERR
❑ 665B Tony Oliva TBC 64 COR (fabricated card) .10 .02
❑ 666 Randy St.Claire .05 .01
❑ 667 Dwayne Murphy .05 .01
❑ 668 Mike Bielecki .05 .01
❑ 669 L.A. Dodgers TL Orel Hershiser (Mound conference) .10 .02
❑ 670 Kevin Seitzer .05 .01
❑ 671 Jim Gantner .05 .01
❑ 672 Allan Anderson .05 .01
❑ 673 Don Baylor .10 .02
❑ 674 Otis Nixon .05 .01
❑ 675 Bruce Hurst .05 .01
❑ 676 Ernie Riles .05 .01
❑ 677 Dave Schmidt .05 .01
❑ 678 Dion James .05 .01
❑ 679 Willie Fraser .05 .01
❑ 680 Gary Carter .10 .02
❑ 681 Jeff D. Robinson .05 .01
❑ 682 Rick Leach .05 .01
❑ 683 Jose Cecena .05 .01
❑ 684 Dave Johnson MG .05 .01
❑ 685 Jeff Treadway .05 .01
❑ 686 Scott Terry .05 .01
❑ 687 Alvin Davis .05 .01
❑ 688 Zane Smith .05 .01
❑ 689A Stan Jefferson Pink ERR 10.00 4.00
❑ 689B Stan Jefferson (Violet triangle on front bottom) .05 .01
❑ 690 Doug Jones .05 .01
❑ 691 Roberto Kelly UER .05 .01
❑ 692 Steve Ontiveros .05 .01
❑ 693 Pat Borders RC * .25 .08
❑ 694 Les Lancaster .05 .01
❑ 695 Carlton Fisk .15 .05
❑ 696 Don August .05 .01
❑ 697A Franklin Stubbs White ERR 10.004.00
❑ 697B Franklin Stubbs (Team name on front in gray) .05 .01
❑ 698 Keith Atherton .05 .01
❑ 699 Pittsburgh Pirates TL Al Pedrique (Tony Gwynn sl) .05 .01
❑ 700 Don Mattingly .60 .25
❑ 701 Storm Davis .05 .01
❑ 702 Jamie Quirk .05 .01
❑ 703 Scott Garrelts .05 .01
❑ 704 Carlos Quintana RC .10 .02
❑ 705 Terry Kennedy .05 .01
❑ 706 Pete Incaviglia .05 .01
❑ 707 Steve Jeltz .05 .01
❑ 708 Chuck Finley .10 .02
❑ 709 Tom Herr .05 .01
❑ 710 David Cone .10 .02
❑ 711 Candy Sierra .05 .01
❑ 712 Bill Swift .05 .01
❑ 713 Ty Griffin FDP .05 .01
❑ 714 Joe Morgan MG .10 .02
❑ 715 Tony Pena .05 .01
❑ 716 Wayne Tolleson .05 .01
❑ 717 Jamie Moyer .10 .02
❑ 718 Glenn Braggs .05 .01

❑	719 Danny Darwin	.05	.01
❑	720 Tim Wallach	.05	.01
❑	721 Ron Tingley	.05	.01
❑	722 Todd Stottlemyre	.05	.01
❑	723 Rafael Belliard	.05	.01
❑	724 Jerry Don Gleaton	.05	.01
❑	725 Terry Steinbach	.10	.02
❑	726 Dickie Thon	.05	.01
❑	727 Joe Orsulak	.05	.01
❑	728 Charlie Puleo	.05	.01
❑	729 Texas Rangers TL Steve Buechele (Inconsistent de)	.05	.01
❑	730 Danny Jackson	.05	.01
❑	731 Mike Young	.05	.01
❑	732 Steve Buechele	.05	.01
❑	733 Randy Bockus	.05	.01
❑	734 Jody Reed	.05	.01
❑	735 Roger McDowell	.05	.01
❑	736 Jeff Hamilton	.05	.01
❑	737 Norm Charlton RC	.25	.08
❑	738 Darnell Coles	.05	.01
❑	739 Brook Jacoby	.05	.01
❑	740 Dan Plesac	.05	.01
❑	741 Ken Phelps	.05	.01
❑	742 Mike Harkey RC	.10	.02
❑	743 Mike Heath	.05	.01
❑	744 Roger Craig MG	.10	.02
❑	745 Fred McGriff	.15	.05
❑	746 German Gonzalez UER (Wrong birthdate)	.05	.01
❑	747 Wil Tejada	.05	.01
❑	748 Jimmy Jones	.05	.01
❑	749 Rafael Ramirez	.05	.01
❑	750 Bret Saberhagen	.10	.02
❑	751 Ken Oberkfell	.05	.01
❑	752 Jim Gott	.05	.01
❑	753 Jose Uribe	.05	.01
❑	754 Bob Brower	.05	.01
❑	755 Mike Scioscia	.10	.02
❑	756 Scott Medvin	.05	.01
❑	757 Brady Anderson RC	.40	.15
❑	758 Gene Walter	.05	.01
❑	759 Milwaukee Brewers TL Rob Deer	.05	.01
❑	760 Lee Smith	.10	.02
❑	761 Dante Bichette RC	.40	.15
❑	762 Bobby Thigpen	.05	.01
❑	763 Dave Martinez	.05	.01
❑	764 Robin Ventura RC	.75	.30
❑	765 Glenn Davis	.05	.01
❑	766 Cecilio Guante	.05	.01
❑	767 Mike Capel	.05	.01
❑	768 Bill Wegman	.05	.01
❑	769 Junior Ortiz	.05	.01
❑	770 Alan Trammell	.10	.02
❑	771 Ron Kittle	.05	.01
❑	772 Ron Oester	.05	.01
❑	773 Keith Moreland	.05	.01
❑	774 Frank Robinson MG/TC	.15	.05
❑	775 Jeff Reardon	.10	.02
❑	776 Nelson Liriano	.05	.01
❑	777 Ted Power	.05	.01
❑	778 Bruce Benedict	.05	.01
❑	779 Craig McMurtry	.05	.01
❑	780 Pedro Guerrero	.10	.02
❑	781 Greg Briley	.10	.02
❑	782 Checklist 661-792	.05	.01
❑	783 Trevor Wilson RC	.10	.02
❑	784 Steve Avery RC	.25	.08
❑	785 Ellis Burks	.10	.02
❑	786 Melido Perez	.05	.01
❑	787 Dave West RC	.10	.02
❑	788 Mike Morgan	.05	.01
❑	789 Royals TL/Bo Jackson	.25	.08
❑	790 Sid Fernandez	.05	.01
❑	791 Jim Lindeman	.05	.01
❑	792 Rafael Santana	.05	.01

1989 Topps Traded

❑	COMP.FACT.SET (132)	10.00	4.00
❑	1T Don Aase	.05	.01
❑	2T Jim Abbott	.50	.20
❑	3T Kent Anderson	.05	.01
❑	4T Keith Atherton	.05	.01
❑	5T Wally Backman	.05	.01
❑	6T Steve Balboni	.05	.01
❑	7T Jesse Barfield	.10	.02
❑	8T Steve Bedrosian	.05	.01
❑	9T Todd Benzinger	.05	.01
❑	10T Geronimo Berroa	.05	.01
❑	11T Bert Blyleven	.10	.02
❑	12T Bob Boone	.10	.02
❑	13T Phil Bradley	.05	.01
❑	14T Jeff Brantley RC	.25	.08
❑	15T Kevin Brown	.25	.08
❑	16T Jerry Browne	.05	.01
❑	17T Chuck Cary	.05	.01
❑	18T Carmen Castillo	.05	.01
❑	19T Jim Clancy	.05	.01
❑	20T Jack Clark	.10	.02
❑	21T Bryan Clutterbuck	.05	.01
❑	22T Jody Davis	.05	.01
❑	23T Mike Devereaux	.05	.01
❑	24T Frank DiPino	.05	.01
❑	25T Benny Distefano	.05	.01
❑	26T John Dopson	.05	.01
❑	27T Len Dykstra	.10	.02
❑	28T Jim Eisenreich	.05	.01
❑	29T Nick Esasky	.05	.01
❑	30T Alvaro Espinoza	.05	.01
❑	31T Darrell Evans UER	.10	.02
❑	32T Junior Felix RC	.10	.02
❑	33T Felix Fermin	.05	.01
❑	34T Julio Franco	.10	.02
❑	35T Terry Francona	.10	.02
❑	36T Cito Gaston MG	.05	.01
❑	37T Bob Geren UER RC	.05	.01
❑	38T Tom Gordon RC	.50	.20
❑	39T Tommy Gregg	.05	.01
❑	40T Ken Griffey Sr.	.10	.02
❑	41T Ken Griffey Jr. RC	8.00	3.00
❑	42T Kevin Gross	.05	.01
❑	43T Lee Guetterman	.05	.01
❑	44T Mel Hall	.05	.01
❑	45T Erik Hanson RC	.25	.08
❑	46T Gene Harris RC	.10	.02
❑	47T Andy Hawkins	.05	.01
❑	48T Rickey Henderson	.25	.08
❑	49T Tom Herr	.05	.01
❑	50T Ken Hill RC	.25	.08
❑	51T Brian Holman RC	.10	.02
❑	52T Brian Holton	.05	.01
❑	53T Art Howe MG	.05	.01
❑	54T Ken Howell	.05	.01
❑	55T Bruce Hurst	.05	.01
❑	56T Chris James	.05	.01
❑	57T Randy Johnson	2.00	.75
❑	58T Jimmy Jones	.05	.01
❑	59T Terry Kennedy	.05	.01
❑	60T Paul Kilgus	.05	.01
❑	61T Eric King	.05	.01
❑	62T Ron Kittle	.05	.01
❑	63T John Kruk	.10	.02
❑	64T Randy Kutcher	.05	.01
❑	65T Steve Lake	.05	.01
❑	66T Mark Langston	.05	.01
❑	67T Dave LaPoint	.05	.01
❑	68T Rick Leach	.05	.01
❑	69T Terry Leach	.05	.01
❑	70T Jim Lefebvre MG	.05	.01
❑	71T Al Leiter	.25	.08
❑	72T Jeffrey Leonard	.05	.01
❑	73T Derek Lilliquist RC	.10	.02
❑	74T Rick Mahler	.05	.01
❑	75T Tom McCarthy	.05	.01
❑	76T Lloyd McClendon	.05	.01
❑	77T Lance McCullers	.05	.01
❑	78T Oddibe McDowell	.05	.01
❑	79T Roger McDowell	.05	.01
❑	80T Larry McWilliams	.05	.01
❑	81T Randy Milligan	.05	.01
❑	82T Mike Moore	.05	.01
❑	83T Keith Moreland	.05	.01
❑	84T Mike Morgan	.05	.01
❑	85T Jamie Moyer	.10	.02
❑	86T Rob Murphy	.05	.01
❑	87T Eddie Murray	.25	.08
❑	88T Pete O'Brien	.05	.01
❑	89T Gregg Olson	.25	.08
❑	90T Steve Ontiveros	.05	.01
❑	91T Jesse Orosco	.05	.01
❑	92T Spike Owen	.05	.01
❑	93T Rafael Palmeiro	.25	.08
❑	94T Clay Parker	.05	.01
❑	95T Jeff Parrett	.05	.01
❑	96T Lance Parrish	.10	.02
❑	97T Dennis Powell	.05	.01
❑	98T Rey Quinones	.05	.01
❑	99T Doug Rader MG	.05	.01
❑	100T Willie Randolph	.10	.02
❑	101T Shane Rawley	.05	.01
❑	102T Randy Ready	.05	.01
❑	103T Bip Roberts	.05	.01
❑	104T Kenny Rogers RC	2.00	.75
❑	105T Ed Romero	.05	.01
❑	106T Nolan Ryan	1.50	.60
❑	107T Luis Salazar	.05	.01
❑	108T Juan Samuel	.05	.01
❑	109T Alex Sanchez RC	.05	.01
❑	110T Deion Sanders RC	1.50	.60
❑	111T Steve Sax	.05	.01
❑	112T Rick Schu	.05	.01
❑	113T Dwight Smith RC	.25	.08
❑	114T Lonnie Smith	.05	.01
❑	115T Billy Spiers RC	.25	.08
❑	116T Kent Tekulve	.05	.01
❑	117T Walt Terrell	.05	.01
❑	118T Milt Thompson	.05	.01
❑	119T Dickie Thon	.05	.01
❑	120T Jeff Torborg MG	.05	.01
❑	121T Jeff Treadway	.05	.01
❑	122T Omar Vizquel RC	1.00	.40
❑	123T Jerome Walton RC	.25	.08
❑	124T Gary Ward	.05	.01
❑	125T Claudell Washington	.05	.01
❑	126T Curt Wilkerson	.05	.01
❑	127T Eddie Williams	.05	.01
❑	128T Frank Williams	.05	.01
❑	129T Ken Williams	.05	.01
❑	130T Mitch Williams	.05	.01
❑	131T Steve Wilson RC	.10	.02
❑	132T Checklist 1T-132T	.05	.01

1990 Topps

❑	COMPLETE SET (792)	20.00	8.00
❑	COMP.FACT.SET (792)	25.00	10.00
❑	COMP.X-MAS.SET (792)	40.00	15.00
❑	1 Nolan Ryan	1.00	.40
❑	2 Nolan Ryan Salute New York Mets	.50	.20
❑	3 Nolan Ryan Salute		

California Angels .50 .20
❑ 4 Nolan Ryan Salute Houston Astros .50 .20
❑ 5 Nolan Ryan Salute Texas Rangers UER (Says Texas) .50 .20
❑ 6 Vince Coleman RB (50 consecutive stolen bases) .05 .01
❑ 7 Rickey Henderson RB .15 .05
❑ 8 Cal Ripken RB .25 .08
❑ 9 Eric Plunk .05 .01
❑ 10 Barry Larkin .15 .05
❑ 11 Paul Gibson .05 .01
❑ 12 Joe Girardi .15 .05
❑ 13 Mark Williamson .05 .01
❑ 14 Mike Fetters RC .25 .08
❑ 15 Teddy Higuera .05 .01
❑ 16 Kent Anderson .05 .01
❑ 17 Kelly Downs .05 .01
❑ 18 Carlos Quintana .05 .01
❑ 19 Al Newman .05 .01
❑ 20 Mark Gubicza .05 .01
❑ 21 Jeff Torborg MG .05 .01
❑ 22 Bruce Ruffin .05 .01
❑ 23 Randy Velarde .05 .01
❑ 24 Joe Hesketh .05 .01
❑ 25 Willie Randolph .10 .02
❑ 26 Don Slaught .05 .01
❑ 27 Rick Leach .05 .01
❑ 28 Duane Ward .05 .01
❑ 29 John Cangelosi .05 .01
❑ 30 David Cone .10 .02
❑ 31 Henry Cotto .05 .01
❑ 32 John Farrell .05 .01
❑ 33 Greg Walker .05 .01
❑ 34 Tony Fossas RC .05 .01
❑ 35 Benito Santiago .10 .02
❑ 36 John Costello .05 .01
❑ 37 Domingo Ramos .05 .01
❑ 38 Wes Gardner .05 .01
❑ 39 Curt Ford .05 .01
❑ 40 Jay Howell .05 .01
❑ 41 Matt Williams .10 .02
❑ 42 Jeff M. Robinson .05 .01
❑ 43 Dante Bichette .10 .02
❑ 44 Roger Salkeld FDP RC .10 .02
❑ 45 Dave Parker UER .10 .02
❑ 46 Rob Dibble .10 .02
❑ 47 Brian Harper .05 .01
❑ 48 Zane Smith .05 .01
❑ 49 Tom Lawless .05 .01
❑ 50 Glenn Davis .05 .01
❑ 51 Doug Rader MG .05 .01
❑ 52 Jack Daugherty RC .05 .01
❑ 53 Mike LaCoss .05 .01
❑ 54 Joel Skinner .05 .01
❑ 55 Darrell Evans UER (HR total should be 414& not 4) .10 .02
❑ 56 Franklin Stubbs .05 .01
❑ 57 Greg Vaughn .05 .01
❑ 58 Keith Miller .05 .01
❑ 59 Ted Power .05 .01
❑ 60 George Brett .60 .25
❑ 61 Deion Sanders .25 .08
❑ 62 Ramon Martinez .05 .01
❑ 63 Mike Pagliarulo .05 .01
❑ 64 Danny Darwin .05 .01
❑ 65 Devon White .10 .02
❑ 66 Greg Litton .05 .01
❑ 67 Scott Sanderson .05 .01
❑ 68 Dave Henderson .05 .01
❑ 69 Todd Frohwirth .05 .01
❑ 70 Mike Greenwell .05 .01
❑ 71 Allan Anderson .05 .01
❑ 72 Jeff Huson RC .10 .02
❑ 73 Bob Milacki .05 .01
❑ 74 Jeff Jackson FDP RC .10 .02
❑ 75 Doug Jones .05 .01
❑ 76 Dave Valle .05 .01
❑ 77 Dave Bergman .05 .01
❑ 78 Mike Flanagan .05 .01
❑ 79 Ron Kittle .05 .01
❑ 80 Jeff Russell .05 .01
❑ 81 Bob Rodgers MG .05 .01
❑ 82 Scott Terry .05 .01
❑ 83 Hensley Meulens .05 .01
❑ 84 Ray Searage .05 .01
❑ 85 Juan Samuel .05 .01
❑ 86 Paul Kilgus .05 .01
❑ 87 Rick Luecken RC .05 .01
❑ 88 Glenn Braggs .05 .01
❑ 89 Clint Zavaras RC .05 .01
❑ 90 Jack Clark .10 .02
❑ 91 Steve Frey RC .05 .01
❑ 92 Mike Stanley .05 .01
❑ 93 Shawn Hillegas .05 .01
❑ 94 Herm Winningham .05 .01
❑ 95 Todd Worrell .05 .01
❑ 96 Jody Reed .05 .01
❑ 97 Curt Schilling 1.00 .40
❑ 98 Jose Gonzalez .05 .01
❑ 99 Rich Monteleone .05 .01
❑ 100 Will Clark .15 .05
❑ 101 Shane Rawley .05 .01
❑ 102 Stan Javier .05 .01
❑ 103 Marvin Freeman .05 .01
❑ 104 Bob Knepper .05 .01
❑ 105 Randy Myers .10 .02
❑ 106 Charlie O'Brien .05 .01
❑ 107 Fred Lynn .05 .01
❑ 108 Rod Nichols .05 .01
❑ 109 Roberto Kelly .05 .01
❑ 110 Tommy Helms MG .05 .01
❑ 111 Ed Whited RC .05 .01
❑ 112 Glenn Wilson .05 .01
❑ 113 Manny Lee .05 .01
❑ 114 Mike Bielecki .05 .01
❑ 115 Tony Pena .05 .01
❑ 116 Floyd Bannister .05 .01
❑ 117 Mike Sharperson .05 .01
❑ 118 Erik Hanson .05 .01
❑ 119 Billy Hatcher .05 .01
❑ 120 John Franco .10 .02
❑ 121 Robin Ventura .25 .08
❑ 122 Shawn Abner .05 .01
❑ 123 Rich Gedman .05 .01
❑ 124 Dave Dravecky .10 .02
❑ 125 Kent Hrbek .10 .02
❑ 126 Randy Kramer .05 .01
❑ 127 Mike Devereaux .05 .01
❑ 128 Checklist 1 .05 .01
❑ 129 Ron Jones .05 .01
❑ 130 Bert Blyleven .10 .02
❑ 131 Matt Nokes .05 .01
❑ 132 Lance Blankenship .05 .01
❑ 133 Ricky Horton .05 .01
❑ 134 Earl Cunningham FDP RC .10 .02
❑ 135 Dave Magadan .05 .01
❑ 136 Kevin Brown .10 .02
❑ 137 Marty Pevey RC .05 .01
❑ 138 Al Leiter .25 .08
❑ 139 Greg Brock .05 .01
❑ 140 Andre Dawson .10 .02
❑ 141 John Hart MG RC .05 .01
❑ 142 Jeff Wetherby RC .05 .01
❑ 143 Rafael Belliard .05 .01
❑ 144 Bud Black .05 .01
❑ 145 Terry Steinbach .05 .01
❑ 146 Rob Richie RC .05 .01
❑ 147 Chuck Finley .10 .02
❑ 148 Edgar Martinez .15 .05
❑ 149 Steve Farr .05 .01
❑ 150 Kirk Gibson .10 .02
❑ 151 Rick Mahler .05 .01
❑ 152 Lonnie Smith .05 .01
❑ 153 Randy Milligan .05 .01
❑ 154 Mike Maddux .05 .01
❑ 155 Ellis Burks .15 .05
❑ 156 Ken Patterson .05 .01
❑ 157 Craig Biggio .25 .08
❑ 158 Craig Lefferts .05 .01
❑ 159 Mike Felder .05 .01
❑ 160 Dave Righetti .05 .01
❑ 161 Harold Reynolds .10 .02
❑ 162 Todd Zeile .10 .02
❑ 163 Phil Bradley .05 .01
❑ 164 Jeff Juden FDP RC .10 .02
❑ 165 Walt Weiss .05 .01
❑ 166 Bobby Witt .05 .01
❑ 167 Kevin Appier .10 .02
❑ 168 Jose Lind .05 .01
❑ 169 Richard Dotson .05 .01
❑ 170 George Bell .05 .01
❑ 171 Russ Nixon MG .05 .01
❑ 172 Tom Lampkin .05 .01
❑ 173 Tim Belcher .05 .01
❑ 174 Jeff Kunkel .05 .01
❑ 175 Mike Moore .05 .01
❑ 176 Luis Quinones .05 .01
❑ 177 Mike Henneman .05 .01
❑ 178 Chris James .05 .01
❑ 179 Brian Holton .05 .01
❑ 180 Tim Raines .10 .02
❑ 181 Juan Agosto .05 .01
❑ 182 Mookie Wilson .10 .02
❑ 183 Steve Lake .05 .01
❑ 184 Danny Cox .05 .01
❑ 185 Ruben Sierra .10 .02
❑ 186 Dave LaPoint .05 .01
❑ 187 Rick Wrona .05 .01
❑ 188 Mike Smithson .05 .01
❑ 189 Dick Schofield .05 .01
❑ 190 Rick Reuschel .05 .01
❑ 191 Pat Borders .05 .01
❑ 192 Don August .05 .01
❑ 193 Andy Benes .10 .02
❑ 194 Glenallen Hill .05 .01
❑ 195 Tim Burke .05 .01
❑ 196 Gerald Young .05 .01
❑ 197 Doug Drabek .05 .01
❑ 198 Mike Marshall .05 .01
❑ 199 Sergio Valdez RC .05 .01
❑ 200 Don Mattingly .60 .25
❑ 201 Cito Gaston MG .05 .01
❑ 202 Mike Macfarlane .05 .01
❑ 203 Mike Roesler RC .05 .01
❑ 204 Bob Dernier .05 .01
❑ 205 Mark Davis .05 .01
❑ 206 Nick Esasky .05 .01
❑ 207 Bob Ojeda .05 .01
❑ 208 Brook Jacoby .05 .01
❑ 209 Greg Mathews .05 .01
❑ 210 Ryne Sandberg .40 .15
❑ 211 John Cerutti .05 .01
❑ 212 Joe Orsulak .05 .01
❑ 213 Scott Bankhead .05 .01
❑ 214 Terry Francona .10 .02
❑ 215 Kirk McCaskill .05 .01
❑ 216 Ricky Jordan .05 .01
❑ 217 Don Robinson .05 .01
❑ 218 Wally Backman .05 .01
❑ 219 Donn Pall .05 .01
❑ 220 Barry Bonds 1.00 .40
❑ 221 Gary Mielke RC .05 .01
❑ 222 Kurt Stillwell UER (Graduate misspelled as gradu) .05 .01
❑ 223 Tommy Gregg .05 .01
❑ 224 Delino DeShields RC .25 .08
❑ 225 Jim Deshaies .05 .01
❑ 226 Mickey Hatcher .05 .01
❑ 227 Kevin Tapani RC .25 .08
❑ 228 Dave Martinez .05 .01
❑ 229 David Wells .10 .02
❑ 230 Keith Hernandez .10 .02
❑ 231 Jack McKeon MG .05 .01
❑ 232 Darnell Coles .05 .01
❑ 233 Ken Hill .10 .02
❑ 234 Mariano Duncan .05 .01
❑ 235 Jeff Reardon .10 .02
❑ 236 Hal Morris .05 .01
❑ 237 Kevin Ritz RC .05 .01
❑ 238 Felix Jose .05 .01
❑ 239 Eric Show .05 .01
❑ 240 Mark Grace .15 .05
❑ 241 Mike Krukow .05 .01
❑ 242 Fred Manrique .05 .01
❑ 243 Barry Jones .05 .01
❑ 244 Bill Schroeder .05 .01
❑ 245 Roger Clemens 1.00 .40
❑ 246 Jim Eisenreich .05 .01
❑ 247 Jerry Reed .05 .01
❑ 248 Dave Anderson .05 .01
❑ 249 Mike (Texas) Smith RC .05 .01
❑ 250 Jose Canseco .15 .05
❑ 251 Jeff Blauser .05 .01

❑	252	Otis Nixon	.05	.01
❑	253	Mark Portugal	.05	.01
❑	254	Francisco Cabrera	.05	.01
❑	255	Bobby Thigpen	.05	.01
❑	256	Marvell Wynne	.05	.01
❑	257	Jose DeLeon	.05	.01
❑	258	Barry Lyons	.05	.01
❑	259	Lance McCullers	.05	.01
❑	260	Eric Davis	.10	.02
❑	261	Whitey Herzog MG	.10	.02
❑	262	Checklist 2	.05	.01
❑	263	Mel Stottlemyre Jr.	.05	.01
❑	264	Bryan Clutterbuck	.05	.01
❑	265	Pete O'Brien	.05	.01
❑	266	German Gonzalez	.05	.01
❑	267	Mark Davidson	.05	.01
❑	268	Rob Murphy	.05	.01
❑	269	Dickie Thon	.05	.01
❑	270	Dave Stewart	.10	.02
❑	271	Chet Lemon	.05	.01
❑	272	Bryan Harvey	.05	.01
❑	273	Bobby Bonilla	.10	.02
❑	274	Mauro Gozzo RC	.05	.01
❑	275	Mickey Tettleton	.05	.01
❑	276	Gary Thurman	.05	.01
❑	277	Lenny Harris	.05	.01
❑	278	Pascual Perez	.05	.01
❑	279	Steve Buechele	.05	.01
❑	280	Lou Whitaker	.10	.02
❑	281	Kevin Bass	.05	.01
❑	282	Derek Lilliquist	.05	.01
❑	283	Albert Belle	.25	.08
❑	284	Mark Gardner RC	.10	.02
❑	285	Willie McGee	.10	.02
❑	286	Lee Guetterman	.05	.01
❑	287	Vance Law	.05	.01
❑	288	Greg Briley	.05	.01
❑	289	Norm Charlton	.05	.01
❑	290	Robin Yount	.40	.15
❑	291	Dave Johnson MG	.10	.02
❑	292	Jim Gott	.05	.01
❑	293	Mike Gallego	.05	.01
❑	294	Craig McMurtry	.05	.01
❑	295	Fred McGriff	.25	.08
❑	296	Jeff Ballard	.05	.01
❑	297	Tommy Herr	.05	.01
❑	298	Dan Gladden	.05	.01
❑	299	Adam Peterson	.05	.01
❑	300	Bo Jackson	.25	.08
❑	301	Don Aase	.05	.01
❑	302	Marcus Lawton RC	.05	.01
❑	303	Rick Cerone	.05	.01
❑	304	Marty Clary	.05	.01
❑	305	Eddie Murray	.25	.08
❑	306	Tom Niedenfuer	.05	.01
❑	307	Bip Roberts	.05	.01
❑	308	Jose Guzman	.05	.01
❑	309	Eric Yelding RC	.05	.01
❑	310	Steve Bedrosian	.05	.01
❑	311	Dwight Smith	.05	.01
❑	312	Dan Quisenberry	.05	.01
❑	313	Gus Polidor	.05	.01
❑	314	Donald Harris FDP RC	.05	.01
❑	315	Bruce Hurst	.05	.01
❑	316	Carney Lansford	.10	.02
❑	317	Mark Guthrie RC	.05	.01
❑	318	Wallace Johnson	.05	.01
❑	319	Dion James	.05	.01
❑	320	Dave Stieb	.10	.02
❑	321	Joe Morgan MG	.05	.01
❑	322	Junior Ortiz	.05	.01
❑	323	Willie Wilson	.05	.01
❑	324	Pete Harnisch	.05	.01
❑	325	Robby Thompson	.05	.01
❑	326	Tom McCarthy	.05	.01
❑	327	Ken Williams	.05	.01
❑	328	Curt Young	.05	.01
❑	329	Oddibe McDowell	.05	.01
❑	330	Ron Darling	.05	.01
❑	331	Juan Gonzalez RC	1.00	.40
❑	332	Paul O'Neill	.15	.05
❑	333	Bill Wegman	.05	.01
❑	334	Johnny Ray	.05	.01
❑	335	Andy Hawkins	.05	.01
❑	336	Ken Griffey Jr.	.75	.30
❑	337	Lloyd McClendon	.05	.01
❑	338	Dennis Lamp	.05	.01
❑	339	Dave Clark	.05	.01
❑	340	Fernando Valenzuela	.10	.02
❑	341	Tom Foley	.05	.01
❑	342	Alex Trevino	.05	.01
❑	343	Frank Tanana	.05	.01
❑	344	George Canale RC	.05	.01
❑	345	Harold Baines	.10	.02
❑	346	Jim Presley	.05	.01
❑	347	Junior Felix	.05	.01
❑	348	Gary Wayne	.05	.01
❑	349	Steve Finley	.10	.02
❑	350	Bret Saberhagen	.10	.02
❑	351	Roger Craig MG	.05	.01
❑	352	Bryn Smith	.05	.01
❑	353	Sandy Alomar Jr. (Not listed as Jr. on card fron)	.10	.02
❑	354	Stan Belinda RC	.10	.02
❑	355	Marty Barrett	.05	.01
❑	356	Randy Ready	.05	.01
❑	357	Dave West	.05	.01
❑	358	Andres Thomas	.05	.01
❑	359	Jimmy Jones	.05	.01
❑	360	Paul Molitor	.10	.02
❑	361	Randy McCament RC	.05	.01
❑	362	Damon Berryhill	.05	.01
❑	363	Dan Petry	.05	.01
❑	364	Rolando Roomes	.05	.01
❑	365	Ozzie Guillen	.10	.02
❑	366	Mike Heath	.05	.01
❑	367	Mike Morgan	.05	.01
❑	368	Bill Doran	.05	.01
❑	369	Todd Burns	.05	.01
❑	370	Tim Wallach	.05	.01
❑	371	Jimmy Key	.10	.02
❑	372	Terry Kennedy	.05	.01
❑	373	Alvin Davis	.05	.01
❑	374	Steve Cummings RC	.05	.01
❑	375	Dwight Evans	.15	.05
❑	376	Checklist 3 UER (Higuera misalphabet-ized in Br)	.05	.01
❑	377	Mickey Weston RC	.05	.01
❑	378	Luis Salazar	.05	.01
❑	379	Steve Rosenberg	.05	.01
❑	380	Dave Winfield	.10	.02
❑	381	Frank Robinson MG	.15	.05
❑	382	Jeff Musselman	.05	.01
❑	383	John Morris	.05	.01
❑	384	Pat Combs	.05	.01
❑	385	Fred McGriff AS	.10	.02
❑	386	Julio Franco AS	.05	.01
❑	387	Wade Boggs AS	.10	.02
❑	388	Cal Ripken AS	.40	.15
❑	389	Robin Yount AS	.25	.08
❑	390	Ruben Sierra AS	.05	.01
❑	391	Kirby Puckett AS	.15	.05
❑	392	Carlton Fisk AS	.10	.02
❑	393	Bret Saberhagen AS	.05	.01
❑	394	Jeff Ballard AS	.05	.01
❑	395	Jeff Russell AS	.05	.01
❑	396	Bart Giamatti MEM	.25	.08
❑	397	Will Clark AS	.10	.02
❑	398	Ryne Sandberg AS	.25	.08
❑	399	Howard Johnson AS	.05	.01
❑	400	Ozzie Smith AS	.25	.08
❑	401	Kevin Mitchell AS	.05	.01
❑	402	Eric Davis AS	.05	.01
❑	403	Tony Gwynn AS	.15	.05
❑	404	Craig Biggio AS	.25	.08
❑	405	Mike Scott AS	.05	.01
❑	406	Joe Magrane AS	.05	.01
❑	407	Mark Davis AS	.05	.01
❑	408	Trevor Wilson	.05	.01
❑	409	Tom Brunansky	.05	.01
❑	410	Joe Boever	.05	.01
❑	411	Ken Phelps	.05	.01
❑	412	Jamie Moyer	.10	.02
❑	413	Brian DuBois RC	.05	.01
❑	414A	FrankThomas NNOF !	600.00	300.00
❑	414B	Frank Thomas RC	2.00	.75
❑	415	Shawon Dunston	.05	.01
❑	416	Dave Wayne Johnson RC	.05	.01
❑	417	Jim Gantner	.05	.01
❑	418	Tom Browning	.05	.01
❑	419	Beau Allred RC	.05	.01
❑	420	Carlton Fisk	.15	.05
❑	421	Greg Minton	.05	.01
❑	422	Pat Sheridan	.05	.01
❑	423	Fred Toliver	.05	.01
❑	424	Jerry Reuss	.05	.01
❑	425	Bill Landrum	.05	.01
❑	426	Jeff Hamilton UER (Stats say he fanned 197 times)	.05	.01
❑	427	Carmen Castillo	.05	.01
❑	428	Steve Davis RC	.05	.01
❑	429	Tom Kelly MG	.05	.01
❑	430	Pete Incaviglia	.05	.01
❑	431	Randy Johnson	.50	.20
❑	432	Damaso Garcia	.05	.01
❑	433	Steve Olin RC	.25	.08
❑	434	Mark Carreon	.05	.01
❑	435	Kevin Seitzer	.05	.01
❑	436	Mel Hall	.05	.01
❑	437	Les Lancaster	.05	.01
❑	438	Greg Myers	.05	.01
❑	439	Jeff Parrett	.05	.01
❑	440	Alan Trammell	.10	.02
❑	441	Bob Kipper	.05	.01
❑	442	Jerry Browne	.05	.01
❑	443	Cris Carpenter	.05	.01
❑	444	Kyle Abbott FDP RC	.05	.01
❑	445	Danny Jackson	.05	.01
❑	446	Dan Pasqua	.05	.01
❑	447	Atlee Hammaker	.05	.01
❑	448	Greg Gagne	.05	.01
❑	449	Dennis Rasmussen	.05	.01
❑	450	Rickey Henderson	.25	.08
❑	451	Mark Lemke	.05	.01
❑	452	Luis DeLosSantos	.05	.01
❑	453	Jody Davis	.05	.01
❑	454	Jeff King	.05	.01
❑	455	Jeffrey Leonard	.05	.01
❑	456	Chris Gwynn	.05	.01
❑	457	Gregg Jefferies	.10	.02
❑	458	Bob McClure	.05	.01
❑	459	Jim Lefebvre MG	.05	.01
❑	460	Mike Scott	.05	.01
❑	461	Carlos Martinez	.05	.01
❑	462	Denny Walling	.05	.01
❑	463	Drew Hall	.05	.01
❑	464	Jerome Walton	.05	.01
❑	465	Kevin Gross	.05	.01
❑	466	Rance Mulliniks	.05	.01
❑	467	Juan Nieves	.05	.01
❑	468	Bill Ripken	.05	.01
❑	469	John Kruk	.10	.02
❑	470	Frank Viola	.05	.01
❑	471	Mike Brumley	.05	.01
❑	472	Jose Uribe	.05	.01
❑	473	Joe Price	.05	.01
❑	474	Rich Thompson	.05	.01
❑	475	Bob Welch	.05	.01
❑	476	Brad Komminsk	.05	.01
❑	477	Willie Fraser	.05	.01
❑	478	Mike LaValliere	.05	.01
❑	479	Frank White	.10	.02
❑	480	Sid Fernandez	.05	.01
❑	481	Garry Templeton	.05	.01
❑	482	Steve Carter	.05	.01
❑	483	Alejandro Pena	.05	.01
❑	484	Mike Fitzgerald	.05	.01
❑	485	John Candelaria	.05	.01
❑	486	Jeff Treadway	.05	.01
❑	487	Steve Searcy	.05	.01
❑	488	Ken Oberkfell	.05	.01
❑	489	Nick Leyva MG	.05	.01
❑	490	Dan Plesac	.05	.01
❑	491	Dave Cochrane RC	.05	.01
❑	492	Ron Oester	.05	.01
❑	493	Jason Grimsley RC	.10	.02
❑	494	Terry Puhl	.05	.01
❑	495	Lee Smith	.10	.02
❑	496	Cecil Espy UER ('88 stats have 3 SB's& should be)	.05	.01
❑	497	Dave Schmidt	.05	.01
❑	498	Rick Schu	.05	.01
❑	499	Bill Long	.05	.01
❑	500	Kevin Mitchell	.05	.01

❑ 501 Matt Young .05 .01
❑ 502 Mitch Webster .05 .01
❑ 503 Randy St.Claire .05 .01
❑ 504 Tom O'Malley .05 .01
❑ 505 Kelly Gruber .05 .01
❑ 506 Tom Glavine .15 .05
❑ 507 Gary Redus .05 .01
❑ 508 Terry Leach .05 .01
❑ 509 Tom Pagnozzi .05 .01
❑ 510 Dwight Gooden .10 .02
❑ 511 Clay Parker .05 .01
❑ 512 Gary Pettis .05 .01
❑ 513 Mark Eichhorn .05 .01
❑ 514 Andy Allanson .05 .01
❑ 515 Len Dykstra .10 .02
❑ 516 Tim Leary .05 .01
❑ 517 Roberto Alomar .15 .05
❑ 518 Bill Krueger .05 .01
❑ 519 Bucky Dent MG .05 .01
❑ 520 Mitch Williams .05 .01
❑ 521 Craig Worthington .05 .01
❑ 522 Mike Dunne .05 .01
❑ 523 Jay Bell .10 .02
❑ 524 Daryl Boston .05 .01
❑ 525 Wally Joyner .10 .02
❑ 526 Checklist 4 .05 .01
❑ 527 Ron Hassey .05 .01
❑ 528 Kevin Wickander UER (Monthly scoreboard strikeou .05 .01
❑ 529 Greg A. Harris .05 .01
❑ 530 Mark Langston .05 .01
❑ 531 Ken Caminiti .10 .02
❑ 532 Cecilio Guante .05 .01
❑ 533 Tim Jones .05 .01
❑ 534 Louie Meadows .05 .01
❑ 535 John Smoltz .25 .08
❑ 536 Bob Geren .05 .01
❑ 537 Mark Grant .05 .01
❑ 538 Bill Spiers UER (Photo actually George Canale) .05 .01
❑ 539 Neal Heaton .05 .01
❑ 540 Danny Tartabull .05 .01
❑ 541 Pat Perry .05 .01
❑ 542 Darren Daulton .10 .02
❑ 543 Nelson Liriano .05 .01
❑ 544 Dennis Boyd .05 .01
❑ 545 Kevin McReynolds .05 .01
❑ 546 Kevin Hickey .05 .01
❑ 547 Jack Howell .05 .01
❑ 548 Pat Clements .05 .01
❑ 549 Don Zimmer MG .05 .01
❑ 550 Julio Franco .10 .02
❑ 551 Tim Crews .05 .01
❑ 552 Mike (Miss.) Smith RC .05 .01
❑ 553 Scott Scudder UER (Cedar Rap1ds) .05 .01
❑ 554 Jay Buhner .10 .02
❑ 555 Jack Morris .10 .02
❑ 556 Gene Larkin .05 .01
❑ 557 Jeff Innis RC .05 .01
❑ 558 Rafael Ramirez .05 .01
❑ 559 Andy McGaffigan .05 .01
❑ 560 Steve Sax .05 .01
❑ 561 Ken Dayley .05 .01
❑ 562 Chad Kreuter .05 .01
❑ 563 Alex Sanchez .05 .01
❑ 564 Tyler Houston FDP RC .25 .08
❑ 565 Scott Fletcher .05 .01
❑ 566 Mark Knudson .05 .01
❑ 567 Ron Gant .10 .02
❑ 568 John Smiley .05 .01
❑ 569 Ivan Calderon .05 .01
❑ 570 Cal Ripken .75 .30
❑ 571 Brett Butler .10 .02
❑ 572 Greg W. Harris .05 .01
❑ 573 Danny Heep .05 .01
❑ 574 Bill Swift .05 .01
❑ 575 Lance Parrish .05 .01
❑ 576 Mike Dyer RC .05 .01
❑ 577 Charlie Hayes .05 .01
❑ 578 Joe Magrane .05 .01
❑ 579 Art Howe MG .05 .01
❑ 580 Joe Carter .10 .02
❑ 581 Ken Griffey Sr. .10 .02
❑ 582 Rick Honeycutt .05 .01
❑ 583 Bruce Benedict .05 .01
❑ 584 Phil Stephenson .05 .01
❑ 585 Kal Daniels .05 .01
❑ 586 Edwin Nunez .05 .01
❑ 587 Lance Johnson .05 .01
❑ 588 Rick Rhoden .05 .01
❑ 589 Mike Aldrete .05 .01
❑ 590 Ozzie Smith .40 .15
❑ 591 Todd Stottlemyre .10 .02
❑ 592 R.J. Reynolds .05 .01
❑ 593 Scott Bradley .05 .01
❑ 594 Luis Sojo RC .05 .01
❑ 595 Greg Swindell .05 .01
❑ 596 Jose DeJesus .05 .01
❑ 597 Chris Bosio .05 .01
❑ 598 Brady Anderson .10 .02
❑ 599 Frank Williams .05 .01
❑ 600 Darryl Strawberry .10 .02
❑ 601 Luis Rivera .05 .01
❑ 602 Scott Garrelts .05 .01
❑ 603 Tony Armas .05 .01
❑ 604 Ron Robinson .05 .01
❑ 605 Mike Scioscia .05 .01
❑ 606 Storm Davis .05 .01
❑ 607 Steve Jeltz .05 .01
❑ 608 Eric Anthony RC .10 .02
❑ 609 Sparky Anderson MG .10 .02
❑ 610 Pedro Guerrero .05 .01
❑ 611 Walt Terrell .05 .01
❑ 612 Dave Gallagher .05 .01
❑ 613 Jeff Pico .05 .01
❑ 614 Nelson Santovenia .05 .01
❑ 615 Rob Deer .05 .01
❑ 616 Brian Holman .05 .01
❑ 617 Geronimo Berroa .05 .01
❑ 618 Ed Whitson .05 .01
❑ 619 Rob Ducey .05 .01
❑ 620 Tony Castillo .05 .01
❑ 621 Melido Perez .05 .01
❑ 622 Sid Bream .05 .01
❑ 623 Jim Corsi .05 .01
❑ 624 Darrin Jackson .05 .01
❑ 625 Roger McDowell .05 .01
❑ 626 Bob Melvin .05 .01
❑ 627 Jose Rijo .05 .01
❑ 628 Candy Maldonado .05 .01
❑ 629 Eric Hetzel .05 .01
❑ 630 Gary Gaetti .10 .02
❑ 631 John Wetteland .25 .08
❑ 632 Scott Lusader .05 .01
❑ 633 Dennis Cook .05 .01
❑ 634 Luis Polonia .05 .01
❑ 635 Brian Downing .05 .01
❑ 636 Jesse Orosco .05 .01
❑ 637 Craig Reynolds .05 .01
❑ 638 Jeff Montgomery .10 .02
❑ 639 Tony LaRussa MG .10 .02
❑ 640 Rick Sutcliffe .10 .02
❑ 641 Doug Strange RC .05 .01
❑ 642 Jack Armstrong .05 .01
❑ 643 Alfredo Griffin .05 .01
❑ 644 Paul Assenmacher .05 .01
❑ 645 Jose Oquendo .05 .01
❑ 646 Checklist 5 .05 .01
❑ 647 Rex Hudler .05 .01
❑ 648 Jim Clancy .05 .01
❑ 649 Dan Murphy RC .10 .02
❑ 650 Mike Witt .05 .01
❑ 651 Rafael Santana .05 .01
❑ 652 Mike Boddicker .05 .01
❑ 653 John Moses .05 .01
❑ 654 Paul Coleman FDP RC .10 .02
❑ 655 Gregg Olson .10 .02
❑ 656 Mackey Sasser .05 .01
❑ 657 Terry Mulholland .05 .01
❑ 658 Donell Nixon .05 .01
❑ 659 Greg Cadaret .05 .01
❑ 660 Vince Coleman .05 .01
❑ 661 Dick Howser TBC'85 UER (Seaver's 300th on 7/11/8 .05 .01
❑ 662 Mike Schmidt TBC .25 .08
❑ 663 Fred Lynn TBC'75 .05 .01
❑ 664 Johnny Bench TBC .15 .05
❑ 665 Sandy Koufax TBC .50 .20
❑ 666 Brian Fisher .05 .01
❑ 667 Curt Wilkerson .05 .01
❑ 668 Joe Oliver .05 .01
❑ 669 Tom Lasorda MG .25 .08
❑ 670 Dennis Eckersley .10 .02
❑ 671 Bob Boone .10 .02
❑ 672 Roy Smith .05 .01
❑ 673 Joey Meyer .05 .01
❑ 674 Spike Owen .05 .01
❑ 675 Jim Abbott .15 .05
❑ 676 Randy Kutcher .05 .01
❑ 677 Jay Tibbs .05 .01
❑ 678 Kirt Manwaring UER ('88 Phoenix stats repeated) .05 .01
❑ 679 Gary Ward .05 .01
❑ 680 Howard Johnson .05 .01
❑ 681 Mike Schooler .05 .01
❑ 682 Dann Bilardello .05 .01
❑ 683 Kenny Rogers .10 .02
❑ 684 Julio Machado RC .05 .01
❑ 685 Tony Fernandez .05 .01
❑ 686 Carmelo Martinez .05 .01
❑ 687 Tim Birtsas .05 .01
❑ 688 Milt Thompson .05 .01
❑ 689 Rich Yett .05 .01
❑ 690 Mark McGwire .60 .25
❑ 691 Chuck Cary .05 .01
❑ 692 Sammy Sosa RC 2.50 1.00
❑ 693 Calvin Schiraldi .05 .01
❑ 694 Mike Stanton RC .25 .08
❑ 695 Tom Henke .05 .01
❑ 696 B.J. Surhoff .10 .02
❑ 697 Mike Davis .05 .01
❑ 698 Omar Vizquel .25 .08
❑ 699 Jim Leyland MG .05 .01
❑ 700 Kirby Puckett .25 .08
❑ 701 Bernie Williams RC 1.50 .60
❑ 702 Tony Phillips .05 .01
❑ 703 Jeff Brantley .05 .01
❑ 704 Chip Hale RC .05 .01
❑ 705 Claudell Washington .05 .01
❑ 706 Geno Petralli .05 .01
❑ 707 Luis Aquino .05 .01
❑ 708 Larry Sheets .05 .01
❑ 709 Juan Berenguer .05 .01
❑ 710 Von Hayes .05 .01
❑ 711 Rick Aguilera .10 .02
❑ 712 Todd Benzinger .05 .01
❑ 713 Tim Drummond RC .05 .01
❑ 714 Marquis Grissom RC .40 .15
❑ 715 Greg Maddux .40 .15
❑ 716 Steve Balboni .05 .01
❑ 717 Ron Karkovice .05 .01
❑ 718 Gary Sheffield .25 .08
❑ 719 Wally Whitehurst .05 .01
❑ 720 Andres Galarraga .10 .02
❑ 721 Lee Mazzilli .05 .01
❑ 722 Felix Fermin .05 .01
❑ 723 Jeff D. Robinson .05 .01
❑ 724 Juan Bell .05 .01
❑ 725 Terry Pendleton .10 .02
❑ 726 Gene Nelson .05 .01
❑ 727 Pat Tabler .05 .01
❑ 728 Jim Acker .05 .01
❑ 729 Bobby Valentine MG .05 .01
❑ 730 Tony Gwynn .30 .10
❑ 731 Don Carman .05 .01
❑ 732 Ernest Riles .05 .01
❑ 733 John Dopson .05 .01
❑ 734 Kevin Elster .05 .01
❑ 735 Charlie Hough .10 .02
❑ 736 Rick Dempsey .05 .01
❑ 737 Chris Sabo .05 .01
❑ 738 Gene Harris .05 .01
❑ 739 Dale Sveum .05 .01
❑ 740 Jesse Barfield .05 .01
❑ 741 Steve Wilson .05 .01
❑ 742 Ernie Whitt .05 .01
❑ 743 Tom Candiotti .05 .01
❑ 744 Kelly Mann RC .05 .01
❑ 745 Hubie Brooks .05 .01
❑ 746 Dave Smith .05 .01
❑ 747 Randy Bush .05 .01
❑ 748 Doyle Alexander .05 .01
❑ 749 Mark Parent UER

('87 BA .80,
should be .080) .05 .01
❑ 750 Dale Murphy .15 .05
❑ 751 Steve Lyons .05 .01
❑ 752 Tom Gordon .10 .02
❑ 753 Chris Speier .05 .01
❑ 754 Bob Walk .05 .01
❑ 755 Rafael Palmeiro .15 .05
❑ 756 Ken Howell .05 .01
❑ 757 Larry Walker RC 1.00 .40
❑ 758 Mark Thurmond .05 .01
❑ 759 Tom Trebelhorn MG .05 .01
❑ 760 Wade Boggs .15 .05
❑ 761 Mike Jackson .05 .01
❑ 762 Doug Dascenzo .05 .01
❑ 763 Dennis Martinez .10 .02
❑ 764 Tim Teufel .05 .01
❑ 765 Chili Davis .10 .02
❑ 766 Brian Meyer .05 .01
❑ 767 Tracy Jones .05 .01
❑ 768 Chuck Crim .05 .01
❑ 769 Greg Hibbard RC .10 .02
❑ 770 Cory Snyder .05 .01
❑ 771 Pete Smith .05 .01
❑ 772 Jeff Reed .05 .01
❑ 773 Dave Leiper .05 .01
❑ 774 Ben McDonald RC .25 .08
❑ 775 Andy Van Slyke .15 .05
❑ 776 Charlie Leibrandt .05 .01
❑ 777 Tim Laudner .05 .01
❑ 778 Mike Jeffcoat .05 .01
❑ 779 Lloyd Moseby .05 .01
❑ 780 Orel Hershiser .10 .02
❑ 781 Mario Diaz .05 .01
❑ 782 Jose Alvarez .05 .01
❑ 783 Checklist 6 .05 .01
❑ 784 Scott Bailes .05 .01
❑ 785 Jim Rice .10 .02
❑ 786 Eric King .05 .01
❑ 787 Rene Gonzales .05 .01
❑ 788 Frank DiPino .05 .01
❑ 789 John Wathan MG .05 .01
❑ 790 Gary Carter .10 .02
❑ 791 Alvaro Espinoza .05 .01
❑ 792 Gerald Perry .05 .01
❑ XX George Bush PRES

1991 Topps

❑ COMPLETE SET (792) 20.00 8.00
❑ COMP.FACT.SET (792) 25.00 10.00
❑ 1 Nolan Ryan 1.50 .60
❑ 2 George Brett RB .30 .10
❑ 3 Carlton Fisk RB .10 .02
❑ 4 Kevin Maas RB .05 .01
❑ 5 Cal Ripken RB .40 .15
❑ 6 Nolan Ryan RB .50 .20
❑ 7 Ryne Sandberg RB .25 .08
❑ 8 Bobby Thigpen RB .05 .01
❑ 9 Darrin Fletcher .05 .01
❑ 10 Gregg Olson .05 .01
❑ 11 Roberto Kelly .05 .01
❑ 12 Paul Assenmacher .05 .01
❑ 13 Mariano Duncan .05 .01
❑ 14 Dennis Lamp .05 .01
❑ 15 Von Hayes .05 .01
❑ 16 Mike Heath .05 .01
❑ 17 Jeff Brantley .05 .01
❑ 18 Nelson Liriano .05 .01
❑ 19 Jeff D. Robinson .05 .01
❑ 20 Pedro Guerrero .10 .02
❑ 21 Joe Morgan MG .05 .01
❑ 22 Storm Davis .05 .01
❑ 23 Jim Gantner .05 .01
❑ 24 Dave Martinez .05 .01
❑ 25 Tim Belcher .05 .01
❑ 26 Luis Sojo UER
(Born in Barquisimento&
not Carqui .05 .01
❑ 27 Bobby Witt .05 .01
❑ 28 Alvaro Espinoza .05 .01
❑ 29 Bob Walk .05 .01
❑ 30 Gregg Jefferies .05 .01
❑ 31 Colby Ward RC .05 .01
❑ 32 Mike Simms RC .05 .01
❑ 33 Barry Jones .05 .01
❑ 34 Atlee Hammaker .05 .01
❑ 35 Greg Maddux .40 .15
❑ 36 Donnie Hill .05 .01
❑ 37 Tom Bolton .05 .01
❑ 38 Scott Bradley .05 .01
❑ 39 Jim Neidlinger RC .05 .01
❑ 40 Kevin Mitchell .05 .01
❑ 41 Ken Dayley .05 .01
❑ 42 Chris Hoiles .05 .01
❑ 43 Roger McDowell .05 .01
❑ 44 Mike Felder .05 .01
❑ 45 Chris Sabo .05 .01
❑ 46 Tim Drummond .05 .01
❑ 47 Brook Jacoby .05 .01
❑ 48 Dennis Boyd .05 .01
❑ 49A Pat Borders ERR
(40 steals at
Kinston in '86) .25 .08
❑ 49B Pat Borders COR
(0 steals at
Kinston in '86) .05 .01
❑ 50 Bob Welch .05 .01
❑ 51 Art Howe MG .05 .01
❑ 52 Francisco Oliveras .05 .01
❑ 53 Mike Sharperson UER
(Born in 1961, not 1960) .05 .01
❑ 54 Gary Mielke .05 .01
❑ 55 Jeffrey Leonard .05 .01
❑ 56 Jeff Parrett .05 .01
❑ 57 Jack Howell .05 .01
❑ 58 Mel Stottlemyre Jr. .05 .01
❑ 59 Eric Yelding .05 .01
❑ 60 Frank Viola .10 .02
❑ 61 Stan Javier .05 .01
❑ 62 Lee Guetterman .05 .01
❑ 63 Milt Thompson .05 .01
❑ 64 Tom Herr .05 .01
❑ 65 Bruce Hurst .05 .01
❑ 66 Terry Kennedy .05 .01
❑ 67 Rick Honeycutt .05 .01
❑ 68 Gary Sheffield .10 .02
❑ 69 Steve Wilson .05 .01
❑ 70 Ellis Burks .10 .02
❑ 71 Jim Acker .05 .01
❑ 72 Junior Ortiz .05 .01
❑ 73 Craig Worthington .05 .01
❑ 74 Shane Andrews RC .25 .08
❑ 75 Jack Morris .10 .02
❑ 76 Jerry Browne .05 .01
❑ 77 Drew Hall .05 .01
❑ 78 Geno Petralli .05 .01
❑ 79 Frank Thomas .25 .08
❑ 80A Fernando Valenzuela ERR .40 .15
❑ 80B Fernando Valenzuela COR .10 .02
❑ 81 Cito Gaston MG .05 .01
❑ 82 Tom Glavine .15 .05
❑ 83 Daryl Boston .05 .01
❑ 84 Bob McClure .05 .01
❑ 85 Jesse Barfield .05 .01
❑ 86 Les Lancaster .05 .01
❑ 87 Tracy Jones .05 .01
❑ 88 Bob Tewksbury .05 .01
❑ 89 Darren Daulton .10 .02
❑ 90 Danny Tartabull .05 .01
❑ 91 Greg Colbrunn RC .25 .08
❑ 92 Danny Jackson .05 .01
❑ 93 Ivan Calderon .05 .01
❑ 94 John Dopson .05 .01
❑ 95 Paul Molitor .10 .02
❑ 96 Trevor Wilson .05 .01
❑ 97A Brady Anderson ERR .40 .15
❑ 97B Brady Anderson COR .10 .02
❑ 98 Sergio Valdez .05 .01
❑ 99 Chris Gwynn .05 .01
❑ 100 Don Mattingly .60 .25
❑ 100A Don Mattingly ERR 2.00 .75
❑ 101 Rob Ducey .05 .01
❑ 102 Gene Larkin .05 .01
❑ 103 Tim Costo RC .05 .01
❑ 104 Don Robinson .05 .01
❑ 105 Kevin McReynolds .05 .01
❑ 106 Ed Nunez .05 .01
❑ 107 Luis Polonia .05 .01
❑ 108 Matt Young .05 .01
❑ 109 Greg Riddoch MG .05 .01
❑ 110 Tom Henke .05 .01
❑ 111 Andres Thomas .05 .01
❑ 112 Frank DiPino .05 .01
❑ 113 Carl Everett RC .50 .20
❑ 114 Lance Dickson RC .10 .02
❑ 115 Hubie Brooks .05 .01
❑ 116 Mark Davis .05 .01
❑ 117 Dion James .05 .01
❑ 118 Tom Edens RC .05 .01
❑ 119 Carl Nichols .05 .01
❑ 120 Joe Carter .10 .02
❑ 121 Eric King .05 .01
❑ 122 Paul O'Neill .15 .05
❑ 123 Greg A. Harris .05 .01
❑ 124 Randy Bush .05 .01
❑ 125 Steve Bedrosian .05 .01
❑ 126 Bernard Gilkey .05 .01
❑ 127 Joe Price .05 .01
❑ 128 Travis Fryman .10 .02
❑ 129 Mark Eichhorn .05 .01
❑ 130 Ozzie Smith .40 .15
❑ 131A Checklist 1 ERR
727 Phil Bradley .25 .08
❑ 131B Checklist 1 COR
717 Phil Bradley .05 .01
❑ 132 Jamie Quirk .05 .01
❑ 133 Greg Briley .05 .01
❑ 134 Kevin Elster .05 .01
❑ 135 Jerome Walton .05 .01
❑ 136 Dave Schmidt .05 .01
❑ 137 Randy Ready .05 .01
❑ 138 Jamie Moyer .10 .02
❑ 139 Jeff Treadway .05 .01
❑ 140 Fred McGriff .15 .05
❑ 141 Nick Leyva MG .05 .01
❑ 142 Curt Wilkerson .05 .01
❑ 143 John Smiley .05 .01
❑ 144 Dave Henderson .05 .01
❑ 145 Lou Whitaker .10 .02
❑ 146 Dan Plesac .05 .01
❑ 147 Carlos Baerga .05 .01
❑ 148 Rey Palacios .05 .01
❑ 149 Al Osuna UER RC .10 .02
❑ 150 Cal Ripken .75 .30
❑ 151 Tom Browning .05 .01
❑ 152 Mickey Hatcher .05 .01
❑ 153 Bryan Harvey .05 .01
❑ 154 Jay Buhner .10 .02
❑ 155A Dwight Evans ERR .50 .20
❑ 155B Dwight Evans COR .15 .05
❑ 156 Carlos Martinez .05 .01
❑ 157 John Smoltz .15 .05
❑ 158 Jose Uribe .05 .01
❑ 159 Joe Boever .05 .01
❑ 160 Vince Coleman UER
(Wrong birth year&
born 9/22/6 .05 .01
❑ 161 Tim Leary .05 .01
❑ 162 Ozzie Canseco .05 .01
❑ 163 Dave Johnson .05 .01
❑ 164 Edgar Diaz .05 .01
❑ 165 Sandy Alomar Jr. .05 .01
❑ 166 Harold Baines .10 .02
❑ 167A Randy Tomlin ERR .25 .08
❑ 167B Randy Tomlin COR RC .10 .02
❑ 168 John Olerud .10 .02
❑ 169 Luis Aquino .05 .01
❑ 170 Carlton Fisk .15 .05
❑ 171 Tony LaRussa MG .10 .02
❑ 172 Pete Incaviglia .05 .01

❑ 173 Jason Grimsley .05 .01
❑ 174 Ken Caminiti .10 .02
❑ 175 Jack Armstrong .05 .01
❑ 176 John Orton .05 .01
❑ 177 Reggie Harris .05 .01
❑ 178 Dave Valle .05 .01
❑ 179 Pete Harnisch .05 .01
❑ 180 Tony Gwynn .30 .10
❑ 181 Duane Ward .05 .01
❑ 182 Junior Noboa .05 .01
❑ 183 Clay Parker .05 .01
❑ 184 Gary Green .05 .01
❑ 185 Joe Magrane .05 .01
❑ 186 Rod Booker .05 .01
❑ 187 Greg Cadaret .05 .01
❑ 188 Damon Berryhill .05 .01
❑ 189 Daryl Irvine RC .05 .01
❑ 190 Matt Williams .10 .02
❑ 191 Willie Blair .05 .01
❑ 192 Rob Deer .05 .01
❑ 193 Felix Fermin .05 .01
❑ 194 Xavier Hernandez .05 .01
❑ 195 Wally Joyner .10 .02
❑ 196 Jim Vatcher RC .05 .01
❑ 197 Chris Nabholz .05 .01
❑ 198 R.J. Reynolds .05 .01
❑ 199 Mike Hartley .05 .01
❑ 200 Darryl Strawberry .10 .02
❑ 201 Tom Kelly MG .05 .01
❑ 202 Jim Leyritz .05 .01
❑ 203 Gene Harris .05 .01
❑ 204 Herm Winningham .05 .01
❑ 205 Mike Perez RC .10 .02
❑ 206 Carlos Quintana .05 .01
❑ 207 Gary Wayne .05 .01
❑ 208 Willie Wilson .05 .01
❑ 209 Ken Howell .05 .01
❑ 210 Lance Parrish .10 .02
❑ 211 Brian Barnes RC .05 .01
❑ 212 Steve Finley .10 .02
❑ 213 Frank Wills .05 .01
❑ 214 Joe Girardi .05 .01
❑ 215 Dave Smith .05 .01
❑ 216 Greg Gagne .05 .01
❑ 217 Chris Bosio .05 .01
❑ 218 Rick Parker .05 .01
❑ 219 Jack McDowell .05 .01
❑ 220 Tim Wallach .05 .01
❑ 221 Don Slaught .05 .01
❑ 222 Brian McRae RC .25 .08
❑ 223 Allan Anderson .05 .01
❑ 224 Juan Gonzalez .25 .08
❑ 225 Randy Johnson .30 .10
❑ 226 Alfredo Griffin .05 .01
❑ 227 Steve Avery UER .05 .01
❑ 228 Rex Hudler .05 .01
❑ 229 Rance Mulliniks .05 .01
❑ 230 Sid Fernandez .05 .01
❑ 231 Doug Rader MG .05 .01
❑ 232 Jose DeJesus .05 .01
❑ 233 Al Leiter .10 .02
❑ 234 Scott Erickson .05 .01
❑ 235 Dave Parker .10 .02
❑ 236A Frank Tanana ERR (Tied for lead with 269 K's in .25 .08
❑ 236B Frank Tanana COR (Led league with 269 K's in '75 .05 .01
❑ 237 Rick Cerone .05 .01
❑ 238 Mike Dunne .05 .01
❑ 239 Darren Lewis FTC .05 .01
❑ 240 Mike Scott .05 .01
❑ 241 Dave Clark UER (Career totals 19 HR and 5 3B& sh .05 .01
❑ 242 Mike LaCoss .05 .01
❑ 243 Lance Johnson .05 .01
❑ 244 Mike Jeffcoat .05 .01
❑ 245 Kal Daniels .05 .01
❑ 246 Kevin Wickander .05 .01
❑ 247 Jody Reed .05 .01
❑ 248 Tom Gordon .05 .01
❑ 249 Bob Melvin .05 .01
❑ 250 Dennis Eckersley .10 .02
❑ 251 Mark Lemke .05 .01
❑ 252 Mel Rojas .05 .01
❑ 253 Garry Templeton .05 .01
❑ 254 Shawn Boskie .05 .01
❑ 255 Brian Downing .05 .01
❑ 256 Greg Hibbard .05 .01
❑ 257 Tom O'Malley .05 .01
❑ 258 Chris Hammond FTC .05 .01
❑ 259 Hensley Meulens .05 .01
❑ 260 Harold Reynolds .10 .02
❑ 261 Bud Harrelson MG .05 .01
❑ 262 Tim Jones .05 .01
❑ 263 Checklist 2 .05 .01
❑ 264 Dave Hollins .05 .01
❑ 265 Mark Gubicza .05 .01
❑ 266 Carmelo Castillo .05 .01
❑ 267 Mark Knudson .05 .01
❑ 268 Tom Brookens .05 .01
❑ 269 Joe Hesketh .05 .01
❑ 270 Mark McGwire .75 .30
❑ 270A Mark McGwire ERR 2.00 .75
❑ 271 Omar Olivares RC .10 .02
❑ 272 Jeff King .05 .01
❑ 273 Johnny Ray .05 .01
❑ 274 Ken Williams .05 .01
❑ 275 Alan Trammell .10 .02
❑ 276 Bill Swift .05 .01
❑ 277 Scott Coolbaugh .05 .01
❑ 278 Alex Fernandez UER .05 .01
❑ 279A Jose Gonzalez ERR (Photo actually Billy Bean) .25 .08
❑ 279B Jose Gonzalez COR .05 .01
❑ 280 Bret Saberhagen .10 .02
❑ 281 Larry Sheets .05 .01
❑ 282 Don Carman .05 .01
❑ 283 Marquis Grissom .10 .02
❑ 284 Billy Spiers .05 .01
❑ 285 Jim Abbott .15 .05
❑ 286 Ken Oberkfell .05 .01
❑ 287 Mark Grant .05 .01
❑ 288 Derrick May .05 .01
❑ 289 Tim Birtsas .05 .01
❑ 290 Steve Sax .05 .01
❑ 291 John Wathan MG .05 .01
❑ 292 Bud Black .05 .01
❑ 293 Jay Bell .10 .02
❑ 294 Mike Moore .05 .01
❑ 295 Rafael Palmeiro .15 .05
❑ 296 Mark Williamson .05 .01
❑ 297 Manny Lee .05 .01
❑ 298 Omar Vizquel .15 .05
❑ 299 Scott Radinsky .05 .01
❑ 300 Kirby Puckett .25 .08
❑ 301 Steve Farr .05 .01
❑ 302 Tim Teufel .05 .01
❑ 303 Mike Boddicker .05 .01
❑ 304 Kevin Reimer .05 .01
❑ 305 Mike Scioscia .05 .01
❑ 306A Lonnie Smith ERR (136 games in '90) .40 .15
❑ 306B Lonnie Smith COR (135 games in '90) .05 .01
❑ 307 Andy Benes .05 .01
❑ 308 Tom Pagnozzi .05 .01
❑ 309 Norm Charlton .05 .01
❑ 310 Gary Carter .10 .02
❑ 311 Jeff Pico .05 .01
❑ 312 Charlie Hayes .05 .01
❑ 313 Ron Robinson .05 .01
❑ 314 Gary Pettis .05 .01
❑ 315 Roberto Alomar .15 .05
❑ 316 Gene Nelson .05 .01
❑ 317 Mike Fitzgerald .05 .01
❑ 318 Rick Aguilera .10 .02
❑ 319 Jeff McKnight .05 .01
❑ 320 Tony Fernandez .05 .01
❑ 321 Bob Rodgers MG .05 .01
❑ 322 Terry Shumpert .05 .01
❑ 323 Cory Snyder .05 .01
❑ 324A Ron Kittle ERR (Set another standard ...) .40 .15
❑ 324B Ron Kittle COR (Tied another standard ...) .05 .01
❑ 325 Brett Butler .10 .02
❑ 326 Ken Patterson .05 .01
❑ 327 Ron Hassey .05 .01
❑ 328 Walt Terrell .05 .01
❑ 329 David Justice UER .10 .02
❑ 330 Dwight Gooden .10 .02
❑ 331 Eric Anthony .05 .01
❑ 332 Kenny Rogers .10 .02
❑ 333 Chipper Jones RC 4.00 1.50
❑ 334 Todd Benzinger .05 .01
❑ 335 Mitch Williams .05 .01
❑ 336 Matt Nokes .05 .01
❑ 337A Keith Comstock ERR (Cubs logo on front) .25 .08
❑ 337B Keith Comstock COR (Mariners logo on front) .05 .01
❑ 338 Luis Rivera .05 .01
❑ 339 Larry Walker .25 .08
❑ 340 Ramon Martinez .05 .01
❑ 341 John Moses .05 .01
❑ 342 Mickey Morandini .05 .01
❑ 343 Jose Oquendo .05 .01
❑ 344 Jeff Russell .05 .01
❑ 345 Len Dykstra .10 .02
❑ 346 Jesse Orosco .05 .01
❑ 347 Greg Vaughn .05 .01
❑ 348 Todd Stottlemyre .05 .01
❑ 349 Dave Gallagher .05 .01
❑ 350 Glenn Davis .05 .01
❑ 351 Joe Torre MG .10 .02
❑ 352 Frank White .10 .02
❑ 353 Tony Castillo .05 .01
❑ 354 Sid Bream .05 .01
❑ 355 Chili Davis .10 .02
❑ 356 Mike Marshall .05 .01
❑ 357 Jack Savage .05 .01
❑ 358 Mark Parent .05 .01
❑ 359 Chuck Cary .05 .01
❑ 360 Tim Raines .10 .02
❑ 361 Scott Garrelts .05 .01
❑ 362 Hector Villenueva .05 .01
❑ 363 Rick Mahler .05 .01
❑ 364 Dan Pasqua .05 .01
❑ 365 Mike Schooler .05 .01
❑ 366A Checklist 3 ERR 19 Carl Nichols .25 .08
❑ 366B Checklist 3 COR 119 Carl Nichols .05 .01
❑ 367 Dave Walsh RC .05 .01
❑ 368 Felix Jose .05 .01
❑ 369 Steve Searcy .05 .01
❑ 370 Kelly Gruber .05 .01
❑ 371 Jeff Montgomery .05 .01
❑ 372 Spike Owen .05 .01
❑ 373 Darrin Jackson .05 .01
❑ 374 Larry Casian RC .05 .01
❑ 375 Tony Pena .05 .01
❑ 376 Mike Harkey .05 .01
❑ 377 Rene Gonzales .05 .01
❑ 378A Wilson Alvarez ERR .25 .08
❑ 378B Wilson Alvarez FTC COR .05 .01
❑ 379 Randy Velarde .05 .01
❑ 380 Willie McGee .10 .02
❑ 381 Jim Leyland MG .05 .01
❑ 382 Mackey Sasser .05 .01
❑ 383 Pete Smith .05 .01
❑ 384 Gerald Perry .05 .01
❑ 385 Mickey Tettleton .05 .01
❑ 386 Cecil Fielder AS .05 .01
❑ 387 Julio Franco AS .05 .01
❑ 388 Kelly Gruber AS .05 .01
❑ 389 Alan Trammell AS .10 .02
❑ 390 Jose Canseco AS .10 .02
❑ 391 Rickey Henderson AS .15 .05
❑ 392 Ken Griffey Jr. AS .40 .15
❑ 393 Carlton Fisk AS .10 .02
❑ 394 Bob Welch AS .05 .01
❑ 395 Chuck Finley AS .05 .01
❑ 396 Bobby Thigpen AS .05 .01
❑ 397 Eddie Murray AS .15 .05
❑ 398 Ryne Sandberg AS .25 .08
❑ 399 Matt Williams AS .05 .01
❑ 400 Barry Larkin AS .10 .02
❑ 401 Barry Bonds AS .50 .20
❑ 402 Darryl Strawbery AS .05 .01
❑ 403 Bobby Bonilla AS .05 .01
❑ 404 Mike Scioscia AS .05 .01

❑ 405 Doug Drabek AS .05 .01
❑ 406 Frank Viola AS .05 .01
❑ 407 John Franco AS .05 .01
❑ 408 Earnest Riles .05 .01
❑ 409 Mike Stanley .05 .01
❑ 410 Dave Righetti .10 .02
❑ 411 Lance Blankenship .05 .01
❑ 412 Dave Bergman .05 .01
❑ 413 Terry Mulholland .05 .01
❑ 414 Sammy Sosa .25 .08
❑ 415 Rick Sutcliffe .10 .02
❑ 416 Randy Milligan .05 .01
❑ 417 Bill Krueger .05 .01
❑ 418 Nick Esasky .05 .01
❑ 419 Jeff Reed .05 .01
❑ 420 Bobby Thigpen .05 .01
❑ 421 Alex Cole .05 .01
❑ 422 Rick Reuschel .05 .01
❑ 423 Rafael Ramirez UER
(Born 1959, not 1958) .05 .01
❑ 424 Calvin Schiraldi .05 .01
❑ 425 Andy Van Slyke .15 .05
❑ 426 Joe Grahe RC .10 .02
❑ 427 Rick Dempsey .05 .01
❑ 428 John Barfield .05 .01
❑ 429 Stump Merrill MG .05 .01
❑ 430 Gary Gaetti .10 .02
❑ 431 Paul Gibson .05 .01
❑ 432 Delino DeShields .10 .02
❑ 433 Pat Tabler .05 .01
❑ 434 Julio Machado .05 .01
❑ 435 Kevin Maas .05 .01
❑ 436 Scott Bankhead .05 .01
❑ 437 Doug Dascenzo .05 .01
❑ 438 Vicente Palacios .05 .01
❑ 439 Dickie Thon .05 .01
❑ 440 George Bell .05 .01
❑ 441 Zane Smith .05 .01
❑ 442 Charlie O'Brien .05 .01
❑ 443 Jeff Innis .05 .01
❑ 444 Glenn Braggs .05 .01
❑ 445 Greg Swindell .05 .01
❑ 446 Craig Grebeck .05 .01
❑ 447 John Burkett .05 .01
❑ 448 Craig Lefferts .05 .01
❑ 449 Juan Berenguer .05 .01
❑ 450 Wade Boggs .15 .05
❑ 451 Neal Heaton .05 .01
❑ 452 Bill Schroeder .05 .01
❑ 453 Lenny Harris .05 .01
❑ 454A Kevin Appier ERR .40 .15
❑ 454B Kevin Appier COR .10 .02
❑ 455 Walt Weiss .05 .01
❑ 456 Charlie Leibrandt .05 .01
❑ 457 Todd Hundley .05 .01
❑ 458 Brian Holman .05 .01
❑ 459 Tom Trebelhorn MG UER
(Pitching and batting
colu .05 .01
❑ 460 Dave Stieb .05 .01
❑ 461 Robin Ventura .10 .02
❑ 462 Steve Frey .05 .01
❑ 463 Dwight Smith .05 .01
❑ 464 Steve Buechele .05 .01
❑ 465 Ken Griffey Sr. .10 .02
❑ 466 Charles Nagy .05 .01
❑ 467 Dennis Cook .05 .01
❑ 468 Tim Hulett .05 .01
❑ 469 Chet Lemon .05 .01
❑ 470 Howard Johnson .05 .01
❑ 471 Mike Lieberthal RC .40 .15
❑ 472 Kirt Manwaring .05 .01
❑ 473 Curt Young .05 .01
❑ 474 Phil Plantier RC .10 .02
❑ 475 Ted Higuera .05 .01
❑ 476 Glenn Wilson .05 .01
❑ 477 Mike Fetters .05 .01
❑ 478 Kurt Stillwell .05 .01
❑ 479 Bob Patterson UER
(Has a decimal point
between 7 .05 .01
❑ 480 Dave Magadan .05 .01
❑ 481 Eddie Whitson .05 .01
❑ 482 Tino Martinez .25 .08
❑ 483 Mike Aldrete .05 .01
❑ 484 Dave LaPoint .05 .01
❑ 485 Terry Pendleton .10 .02
❑ 486 Tommy Greene .05 .01
❑ 487 Rafael Belliard .05 .01
❑ 488 Jeff Manto .05 .01
❑ 489 Bobby Valentine MG .05 .01
❑ 490 Kirk Gibson .10 .02
❑ 491 Kurt Miller RC .05 .01
❑ 492 Ernie Whitt .05 .01
❑ 493 Jose Rijo .05 .01
❑ 494 Chris James .05 .01
❑ 495 Charlie Hough .10 .02
❑ 496 Marty Barrett .05 .01
❑ 497 Ben McDonald .05 .01
❑ 498 Mark Salas .05 .01
❑ 499 Melido Perez .05 .01
❑ 500 Will Clark .15 .05
❑ 501 Mike Bielecki .05 .01
❑ 502 Carney Lansford .10 .02
❑ 503 Roy Smith .05 .01
❑ 504 Julio Valera .05 .01
❑ 505 Chuck Finley .10 .02
❑ 506 Darnell Coles .05 .01
❑ 507 Steve Jeltz .05 .01
❑ 508 Mike York RC .05 .01
❑ 509 Glenallen Hill .05 .01
❑ 510 John Franco .10 .02
❑ 511 Steve Balboni .05 .01
❑ 512 Jose Mesa .05 .01
❑ 513 Jerald Clark .05 .01
❑ 514 Mike Stanton .05 .01
❑ 515 Alvin Davis .05 .01
❑ 516 Karl Rhodes .05 .01
❑ 517 Joe Oliver .05 .01
❑ 518 Cris Carpenter .05 .01
❑ 519 Sparky Anderson MG .10 .02
❑ 520 Mark Grace .15 .05
❑ 521 Joe Orsulak .05 .01
❑ 522 Stan Belinda .05 .01
❑ 523 Rodney McCray RC .05 .01
❑ 524 Darrel Akerfelds .05 .01
❑ 525 Willie Randolph .10 .02
❑ 526A Moises Alou ERR .40 .15
❑ 526B Moises Alou COR .10 .02
❑ 527A Checklist 4 ERR
105 Keith Miller
719 Kevin McRey .25 .08
❑ 527B Checklist 4 COR
105 Kevin McReynolds
719 Keith M .05 .01
❑ 528 Dennis Martinez .10 .02
❑ 529 Marc Newfield RC .10 .02
❑ 530 Roger Clemens .75 .30
❑ 531 Dave Rohde .05 .01
❑ 532 Kirk McCaskill .05 .01
❑ 533 Oddibe McDowell .05 .01
❑ 534 Mike Jackson .05 .01
❑ 535 Ruben Sierra UER .10 .02
❑ 536 Mike Witt .05 .01
❑ 537 Jose Lind .05 .01
❑ 538 Bip Roberts .05 .01
❑ 539 Scott Terry .05 .01
❑ 540 George Brett .60 .25
❑ 541 Domingo Ramos .05 .01
❑ 542 Rob Murphy .05 .01
❑ 543 Junior Felix .05 .01
❑ 544 Alejandro Pena .05 .01
❑ 545 Dale Murphy .15 .05
❑ 546 Jeff Ballard .05 .01
❑ 547 Mike Pagliarulo .05 .01
❑ 548 Jaime Navarro .05 .01
❑ 549 John McNamara MG .05 .01
❑ 550 Eric Davis .10 .02
❑ 551 Bob Kipper .05 .01
❑ 552 Jeff Hamilton .05 .01
❑ 553 Joe Klink .05 .01
❑ 554 Brian Harper .05 .01
❑ 555 Turner Ward RC .10 .02
❑ 556 Gary Ward .05 .01
❑ 557 Wally Whitehurst .05 .01
❑ 558 Otis Nixon .05 .01
❑ 559 Adam Peterson .05 .01
❑ 560 Greg Smith .05 .01
❑ 561 Tim McIntosh .05 .01
❑ 562 Jeff Kunkel .05 .01
❑ 563 Brent Knackert .05 .01
❑ 564 Dante Bichette .10 .02
❑ 565 Craig Biggio .15 .05
❑ 566 Craig Wilson RC .05 .01
❑ 567 Dwayne Henry .05 .01
❑ 568 Ron Karkovice .05 .01
❑ 569 Curt Schilling .25 .08
❑ 570 Barry Bonds 1.00 .40
❑ 571 Pat Combs .05 .01
❑ 572 Dave Anderson .05 .01
❑ 573 Rich Rodriguez UER RC .05 .01
❑ 574 John Marzano .05 .01
❑ 575 Robin Yount .40 .15
❑ 576 Jeff Kaiser .05 .01
❑ 577 Bill Doran .05 .01
❑ 578 Dave West .05 .01
❑ 579 Roger Craig MG .05 .01
❑ 580 Dave Stewart .10 .02
❑ 581 Luis Quinones .05 .01
❑ 582 Marty Clary .05 .01
❑ 583 Tony Phillips .05 .01
❑ 584 Kevin Brown .10 .02
❑ 585 Pete O'Brien .05 .01
❑ 586 Fred Lynn .05 .01
❑ 587 Jose Offerman UER .05 .01
❑ 588 Mark Whiten FTC .05 .01
❑ 589 Scott Ruskin .05 .01
❑ 590 Eddie Murray .25 .08
❑ 591 Ken Hill .05 .01
❑ 592 B.J. Surhoff .10 .02
❑ 593A Mike Walker ERR
('90 Canton-Akron
stat line omit .25 .08
❑ 593B Mike Walker COR .05 .01
❑ 594 Rich Garces RC .10 .02
❑ 595 Bill Landrum .05 .01
❑ 596 Ronnie Walden RC .10 .02
❑ 597 Jerry Don Gleaton .05 .01
❑ 598 Sam Horn .05 .01
❑ 599A Greg Myers ERR
('90 Syracuse
stat line omitted) .25 .08
❑ 599B Greg Myers COR .05 .01
❑ 600 Bo Jackson .25 .08
❑ 601 Bob Ojeda .05 .01
❑ 602 Casey Candaele .05 .01
❑ 603A Wes Chamberlain ERR .40 .15
❑ 603B Wes Chamberlain COR RC .10 .02
❑ 604 Billy Hatcher .05 .01
❑ 605 Jeff Reardon .10 .02
❑ 606 Jim Gott .05 .01
❑ 607 Edgar Martinez .15 .05
❑ 608 Todd Burns .05 .01
❑ 609 Jeff Torborg MG .05 .01
❑ 610 Andres Galarraga .10 .02
❑ 611 Dave Eiland .05 .01
❑ 612 Steve Lyons .05 .01
❑ 613 Eric Show .05 .01
❑ 614 Luis Salazar .05 .01
❑ 615 Bert Blyleven .10 .02
❑ 616 Todd Zeile .05 .01
❑ 617 Bill Wegman .05 .01
❑ 618 Sil Campusano .05 .01
❑ 619 David Wells .10 .02
❑ 620 Ozzie Guillen .10 .02
❑ 621 Ted Power .05 .01
❑ 622 Jack Daugherty .05 .01
❑ 623 Jeff Blauser .05 .01
❑ 624 Tom Candiotti .05 .01
❑ 625 Terry Steinbach .05 .01
❑ 626 Gerald Young .05 .01
❑ 627 Tim Layana .05 .01
❑ 628 Greg Litton .05 .01
❑ 629 Wes Gardner .05 .01
❑ 630 Dave Winfield .10 .02
❑ 631 Mike Morgan .05 .01
❑ 632 Lloyd Moseby .05 .01
❑ 633 Kevin Tapani .05 .01
❑ 634 Henry Cotto .05 .01
❑ 635 Andy Hawkins .05 .01
❑ 636 Geronimo Pena .05 .01
❑ 637 Bruce Ruffin .05 .01
❑ 638 Mike Macfarlane .05 .01
❑ 639 Frank Robinson MG .15 .05
❑ 640 Andre Dawson .10 .02
❑ 641 Mike Henneman .05 .01
❑ 642 Hal Morris .05 .01
❑ 643 Jim Presley .05 .01

❑ 644 Chuck Crim .05 .01
❑ 645 Juan Samuel .05 .01
❑ 646 Andujar Cedeno .05 .01
❑ 647 Mark Portugal .05 .01
❑ 648 Lee Stevens .05 .01
❑ 649 Bill Sampen .05 .01
❑ 650 Jack Clark .10 .02
❑ 651 Alan Mills .05 .01
❑ 652 Kevin Romine .05 .01
❑ 653 Anthony Telford RC .05 .01
❑ 654 Paul Sorrento .05 .01
❑ 655 Erik Hanson .05 .01
❑ 656A Checklist 5 ERR
348 Vicente Palacios
381 Jose Li .25 .08
❑ 656B Checklist 5 ERR
433 Vicente Palacios
(Palacios s) .25 .08
❑ 656C Checklist 5 COR
438 Vicente Palacios
537 Jose Li .05 .01
❑ 657 Mike Kingery .05 .01
❑ 658 Scott Aldred .05 .01
❑ 659 Oscar Azocar .05 .01
❑ 660 Lee Smith .10 .02
❑ 661 Steve Lake .05 .01
❑ 662 Ron Dibble .10 .02
❑ 663 Greg Brock .05 .01
❑ 664 John Farrell .05 .01
❑ 665 Mike LaValliere .05 .01
❑ 666 Danny Darwin .05 .01
❑ 667 Kent Anderson .05 .01
❑ 668 Bill Long .05 .01
❑ 669 Lou Piniella MG .10 .02
❑ 670 Rickey Henderson .25 .08
❑ 671 Andy McGaffigan .05 .01
❑ 672 Shane Mack .05 .01
❑ 673 Greg Olson UER
(6 RBI in '88 at Tide-
water and) .05 .01
❑ 674A Kevin Gross ERR
(89 BB with Phillies
in '88 tied) .25 .08
❑ 674B Kevin Gross COR
(89 BB with Phillies
in '88 led) .05 .01
❑ 675 Tom Brunansky .05 .01
❑ 676 Scott Chiamparino .05 .01
❑ 677 Billy Ripken .05 .01
❑ 678 Mark Davidson .05 .01
❑ 679 Bill Bathe .05 .01
❑ 680 David Cone .10 .02
❑ 681 Jeff Schaefer .05 .01
❑ 682 Ray Lankford .10 .02
❑ 683 Derek Lilliquist .05 .01
❑ 684 Milt Cuyler .05 .01
❑ 685 Doug Drabek .05 .01
❑ 686 Mike Gallego .05 .01
❑ 687A John Cerutti ERR
(4.46 ERA in '90) .25 .08
❑ 687B John Cerutti COR
(4.76 ERA in '90) .05 .01
❑ 688 Rosario Rodriguez RC .05 .01
❑ 689 John Kruk .10 .02
❑ 690 Orel Hershiser .10 .02
❑ 691 Mike Blowers .05 .01
❑ 692A Efrain Valdez ERR .25 .08
❑ 692B Efrain Valdez COR RC .05 .01
❑ 693 Francisco Cabrera .05 .01
❑ 694 Randy Veres .05 .01
❑ 695 Kevin Seitzer .05 .01
❑ 696 Steve Olin .05 .01
❑ 697 Shawn Abner .05 .01
❑ 698 Mark Guthrie .05 .01
❑ 699 Jim Lefebvre MG .05 .01
❑ 700 Jose Canseco .15 .05
❑ 701 Pascual Perez .05 .01
❑ 702 Tim Naehring .05 .01
❑ 703 Juan Agosto .05 .01
❑ 704 Devon White .10 .02
❑ 705 Robby Thompson .05 .01
❑ 706A Brad Arnsberg ERR .25 .08
❑ 706B Brad Arnsberg COR .05 .01
❑ 707 Jim Eisenreich .05 .01
❑ 708 John Mitchell .05 .01
❑ 709 Matt Sinatro .05 .01
❑ 710 Kent Hrbek .10 .02
❑ 711 Jose DeLeon .05 .01
❑ 712 Ricky Jordan .05 .01
❑ 713 Scott Scudder .05 .01
❑ 714 Marvell Wynne .05 .01
❑ 715 Tim Burke .05 .01
❑ 716 Bob Geren .05 .01
❑ 717 Phil Bradley .05 .01
❑ 718 Steve Crawford .05 .01
❑ 719 Keith Miller .05 .01
❑ 720 Cecil Fielder .10 .02
❑ 721 Mark Lee RC .05 .01
❑ 722 Wally Backman .05 .01
❑ 723 Candy Maldonado .05 .01
❑ 724 David Segui .05 .01
❑ 725 Ron Gant .10 .02
❑ 726 Phil Stephenson .05 .01
❑ 727 Mookie Wilson .10 .02
❑ 728 Scott Sanderson .05 .01
❑ 729 Don Zimmer MG .10 .02
❑ 730 Barry Larkin .15 .05
❑ 731 Jeff Gray RC .05 .01
❑ 732 Franklin Stubbs .05 .01
❑ 733 Kelly Downs .05 .01
❑ 734 John Russell .05 .01
❑ 735 Ron Darling .05 .01
❑ 736 Dick Schofield .05 .01
❑ 737 Tim Crews .05 .01
❑ 738 Mel Hall .05 .01
❑ 739 Russ Swan .05 .01
❑ 740 Ryne Sandberg .40 .15
❑ 741 Jimmy Key .10 .02
❑ 742 Tommy Gregg .05 .01
❑ 743 Bryn Smith .05 .01
❑ 744 Nelson Santovenia .05 .01
❑ 745 Doug Jones .05 .01
❑ 746 John Shelby .05 .01
❑ 747 Tony Fossas .05 .01
❑ 748 Al Newman .05 .01
❑ 749 Greg W. Harris .05 .01
❑ 750 Bobby Bonilla .10 .02
❑ 751 Wayne Edwards .05 .01
❑ 752 Kevin Bass .05 .01
❑ 753 Paul Marak UER RC .05 .01
❑ 754 Bill Pecota .05 .01
❑ 755 Mark Langston .05 .01
❑ 756 Jeff Huson .05 .01
❑ 757 Mark Gardner .05 .01
❑ 758 Mike Devereaux .05 .01
❑ 759 Bobby Cox MG .05 .01
❑ 760 Benny Santiago .10 .02
❑ 761 Larry Andersen .05 .01
❑ 762 Mitch Webster .05 .01
❑ 763 Dana Kiecker .05 .01
❑ 764 Mark Carreon .05 .01
❑ 765 Shawon Dunston .05 .01
❑ 766 Jeff Robinson .05 .01
❑ 767 Dan Wilson RC .25 .08
❑ 768 Don Pall .05 .01
❑ 769 Tim Sherrill .05 .01
❑ 770 Jay Howell .05 .01
❑ 771 Gary Redus UER
(Born in Tanner&
should say Athen) .05 .01
❑ 772 Kent Mercker
(Born in Indianapolis&
should say D) .05 .01
❑ 773 Tom Foley .05 .01
❑ 774 Dennis Rasmussen .05 .01
❑ 775 Julio Franco .10 .02
❑ 776 Brent Mayne .05 .01
❑ 777 John Candelaria .05 .01
❑ 778 Dan Gladden .05 .01
❑ 779 Carmelo Martinez .05 .01
❑ 780A Randy Myers ERR
(15 career losses) .40 .15
❑ 780B Randy Myers COR
(19 career losses) .05 .01
❑ 781 Darryl Hamilton .05 .01
❑ 782 Jim Deshaies .05 .01
❑ 783 Joel Skinner .05 .01
❑ 784 Willie Fraser .05 .01
❑ 785 Scott Fletcher .05 .01
❑ 786 Eric Plunk .05 .01
❑ 787 Checklist 6 .05 .01
❑ 788 Bob Milacki .05 .01
❑ 789 Tom Lasorda MG .25 .08
❑ 790 Ken Griffey Jr. .75 .30
❑ 791 Mike Benjamin .05 .01
❑ 792 Mike Greenwell .05 .01

1991 Topps Traded

❑ COMPLETE SET (132) 10.00 4.00
❑ COMP.FACT.SET (132) 10.00 4.00
❑ 1T Juan Agosto .05 .01
❑ 2T Roberto Alomar .15 .05
❑ 3T Wally Backman .05 .01
❑ 4T Jeff Bagwell RC 2.00 .75
❑ 5T Skeeter Barnes .05 .01
❑ 6T Steve Bedrosian .05 .01
❑ 7T Derek Bell .10 .02
❑ 8T George Bell .05 .01
❑ 9T Rafael Belliard .05 .01
❑ 10T Dante Bichette .10 .02
❑ 11T Bud Black .05 .01
❑ 12T Mike Boddicker .05 .01
❑ 13T Sid Bream .05 .01
❑ 14T Hubie Brooks .05 .01
❑ 15T Brett Butler .10 .02
❑ 16T Ivan Calderon .05 .01
❑ 17T John Candelaria .05 .01
❑ 18T Tom Candiotti .05 .01
❑ 19T Gary Carter .10 .02
❑ 20T Joe Carter .10 .02
❑ 21T Rick Cerone .05 .01
❑ 22T Jack Clark .10 .02
❑ 23T Vince Coleman .05 .01
❑ 24T Scott Coolbaugh .05 .01
❑ 25T Danny Cox .05 .01
❑ 26T Danny Darwin .05 .01
❑ 27T Chili Davis .10 .02
❑ 28T Glenn Davis .05 .01
❑ 29T Steve Decker RC .05 .01
❑ 30T Rob Deer .05 .01
❑ 31T Rich DeLucia RC .05 .01
❑ 32T John Dettmer USA RC .25 .08
❑ 33T Brian Downing .05 .01
❑ 34T Darren Dreifort USA RC .25 .08
❑ 35T Kirk Dressendorfer RC .05 .01
❑ 36T Jim Essian MG .05 .01
❑ 37T Dwight Evans .15 .05
❑ 38T Steve Farr .05 .01
❑ 39T Jeff Fassero RC .25 .08
❑ 40T Junior Felix .05 .01
❑ 41T Tony Fernandez .05 .01
❑ 42T Steve Finley .10 .02
❑ 43T Jim Fregosi MG .05 .01
❑ 44T Gary Gaetti .10 .02
❑ 45T Jason Giambi USA RC 5.00 2.00
❑ 46T Kirk Gibson .10 .02
❑ 47T Leo Gomez .05 .01
❑ 48T Luis Gonzalez RC .50 .20
❑ 49T Jeff Granger USA RC .25 .08
❑ 50T Todd Greene USA RC .50 .20
❑ 51T Jeffrey Hammonds USA RC .50 .20
❑ 52T Mike Hargrove MG .05 .01
❑ 53T Pete Harnisch .05 .01
❑ 54T Rick Helling USA RC .50 .20
❑ 55T Glenallen Hill .05 .01
❑ 56T Charlie Hough .10 .02
❑ 57T Pete Incaviglia .05 .01
❑ 58T Bo Jackson .25 .08
❑ 59T Danny Jackson .05 .01
❑ 60T Reggie Jefferson .05 .01

❑	61T Charles Johnson USA RC	.75	.30
❑	62T Jeff Johnson RC	.05	.01
❑	63T Todd Johnson USA RC	.25	.08
❑	64T Barry Jones	.05	.01
❑	65T Chris Jones RC	.10	.02
❑	66T Scott Kamieniecki RC	.10	.02
❑	67T Pat Kelly RC	.10	.02
❑	68T Darryl Kile	.10	.02
❑	69T Chuck Knoblauch	.10	.02
❑	70T Bill Krueger	.05	.01
❑	71T Scott Leius	.05	.01
❑	72T Donnie Leshnock USA RC	.25	.08
❑	73T Mark Lewis	.05	.01
❑	74T Candy Maldonado	.05	.01
❑	75T Jason McDonald USA RC	.25	.08
❑	76T Willie McGee	.10	.02
❑	77T Fred McGriff	.15	.05
❑	78T Billy McMillon USA RC	.25	.08
❑	79T Hal McRae MG	.10	.02
❑	80T Dan Melendez USA RC	.25	.08
❑	81T Orlando Merced RC	.10	.02
❑	82T Jack Morris	.10	.02
❑	83T Phil Nevin USA RC	.75	.30
❑	84T Otis Nixon	.05	.01
❑	85T Johnny Oates MG	.05	.01
❑	86T Bob Ojeda	.05	.01
❑	87T Mike Pagliarulo	.05	.01
❑	88T Dean Palmer	.10	.02
❑	89T Dave Parker	.10	.02
❑	90T Terry Pendleton	.10	.02
❑	91T Tony Phillips (P) USA RC	.25	.08
❑	92T Doug Piatt RC	.05	.01
❑	93T Ron Polk USA CO	.25	.08
❑	94T Tim Raines	.10	.02
❑	95T Willie Randolph	.10	.02
❑	96T Dave Righetti	.10	.02
❑	97T Ernie Riles	.05	.01
❑	98T Chris Roberts USA RC	.25	.08
❑	99T Jeff D. Robinson	.05	.01
❑	100T Jeff M. Robinson	.05	.01
❑	101T Ivan Rodriguez RC	3.00	1.25
❑	102T Steve Rodriguez USA RC	.25	.08
❑	103T Tom Runnells MG	.05	.01
❑	104T Scott Sanderson	.05	.01
❑	105T Bob Scanlan RC	.05	.01
❑	106T Pete Schourek RC	.10	.02
❑	107T Gary Scott RC	.05	.01
❑	108T Paul Shuey USA RC	.50	.20
❑	109T Doug Simons RC	.05	.01
❑	110T Dave Smith	.05	.01
❑	111T Cory Snyder	.05	.01
❑	112T Luis Sojo	.05	.01
❑	113T Kennie Steenstra USA RC	.25	.08
❑	114T Darryl Strawberry	.10	.02
❑	115T Franklin Stubbs	.05	.01
❑	116T Todd Taylor USA RC	.25	.08
❑	117T Wade Taylor RC	.05	.01
❑	118T Garry Templeton	.05	.01
❑	119T Mickey Tettleton	.05	.01
❑	120T Tim Teufel	.05	.01
❑	121T Mike Timlin RC	.25	.08
❑	122T David Tuttle USA RC	.25	.08
❑	123T Mo Vaughn	.10	.02
❑	124T Jeff Ware USA RC	.25	.08
❑	125T Devon White	.10	.02
❑	126T Mark Whiten	.05	.01
❑	127T Mitch Williams	.05	.01
❑	128T Craig Wilson USA RC	.25	.08
❑	129T Willie Wilson	.05	.01
❑	130T Chris Wimmer USA RC	.25	.08
❑	131T Ivan Zweig USA RC	.25	.08
❑	132T Checklist 1T-132T	.05	.01

1992 Topps

❑	COMPLETE SET (792)	25.00	10.00
❑	COMP.FACT.SET (802)	25.00	10.00
❑	COMP.HOLIDAY SET (811)	40.00	15.00
❑	1 Nolan Ryan	1.00	.40
❑	2 Rickey Henderson RB	.15	.05
❑	3 Jeff Reardon RB	.05	.01
❑	4 Nolan Ryan RB	.50	.20
❑	5 Dave Winfield RB	.05	.01
❑	6 Brien Taylor RC	.25	.08
❑	7 Jim Olander	.05	.01
❑	8 Bryan Hickerson RC	.10	.02
❑	9 Jon Farrell RC	.10	.02

❑	10 Wade Boggs	.15	.05
❑	11 Jack McDowell	.05	.01
❑	12 Luis Gonzalez	.10	.02
❑	13 Mike Scioscia	.05	.01
❑	14 Wes Chamberlain	.05	.01
❑	15 Dennis Martinez	.10	.02
❑	16 Jeff Montgomery	.05	.01
❑	17 Randy Milligan	.05	.01
❑	18 Greg Cadaret	.05	.01
❑	19 Jamie Quirk	.05	.01
❑	20 Bip Roberts	.05	.01
❑	21 Buck Rodgers MG	.05	.01
❑	22 Bill Wegman	.05	.01
❑	23 Chuck Knoblauch	.10	.02
❑	24 Randy Myers	.05	.01
❑	25 Ron Gant	.10	.02
❑	26 Mike Bielecki	.05	.01
❑	27 Juan Gonzalez	.15	.05
❑	28 Mike Schooler	.05	.01
❑	29 Mickey Tettleton	.05	.01
❑	30 John Kruk	.10	.02
❑	31 Bryn Smith	.05	.01
❑	32 Chris Nabholz	.05	.01
❑	33 Carlos Baerga	.05	.01
❑	34 Jeff Juden	.05	.01
❑	35 Dave Righetti	.10	.02
❑	36 Scott Ruffcorn RC	.10	.02
❑	37 Luis Polonia	.05	.01
❑	38 Tom Candiotti	.05	.01
❑	39 Greg Olson	.05	.01
❑	40 Cal Ripken/Gehrig	2.00	.75
❑	41 Craig Lefferts	.05	.01
❑	42 Mike Macfarlane	.05	.01
❑	43 Jose Lind	.05	.01
❑	44 Rick Aguilera	.10	.02
❑	45 Gary Carter	.10	.02
❑	46 Steve Farr	.05	.01
❑	47 Rex Hudler	.05	.01
❑	48 Scott Scudder	.05	.01
❑	49 Damon Berryhill	.05	.01
❑	50 Ken Griffey Jr.	.40	.15
❑	51 Tom Runnells MG	.05	.01
❑	52 Juan Bell	.05	.01
❑	53 Tommy Gregg	.05	.01
❑	54 David Wells	.10	.02
❑	55 Rafael Palmeiro	.15	.05
❑	56 Charlie O'Brien	.05	.01
❑	57 Donn Pall	.05	.01
❑	58 Brad Ausmus RC	1.50	.60
❑	59 Mo Vaughn	.10	.02
❑	60 Tony Fernandez	.05	.01
❑	61 Paul O'Neill	.15	.05
❑	62 Gene Nelson	.05	.01
❑	63 Randy Ready	.05	.01
❑	64 Bob Kipper	.05	.01
❑	65 Willie McGee	.10	.02
❑	66 Scott Stahoviak RC	.10	.02
❑	67 Luis Salazar	.05	.01
❑	68 Marvin Freeman	.05	.01
❑	69 Kenny Lofton	.15	.05
❑	70 Gary Gaetti	.10	.02
❑	71 Erik Hanson	.05	.01
❑	72 Eddie Zosky	.05	.01
❑	73 Brian Barnes	.05	.01
❑	74 Scott Leius	.05	.01
❑	75 Bret Saberhagen	.10	.02
❑	76 Mike Gallego	.05	.01
❑	77 Jack Armstrong	.05	.01
❑	78 Ivan Rodriguez	.25	.08
❑	79 Jesse Orosco	.05	.01
❑	80 David Justice	.10	.02
❑	81 Ced Landrum	.05	.01
❑	82 Doug Simons	.05	.01
❑	83 Tommy Greene	.05	.01
❑	84 Leo Gomez	.05	.01
❑	85 Jose DeLeon	.05	.01
❑	86 Steve Finley	.10	.02
❑	87 Bob MacDonald	.05	.01
❑	88 Darrin Jackson	.05	.01
❑	89 Neal Heaton	.05	.01
❑	90 Robin Yount	.40	.15
❑	91 Jeff Reed	.05	.01
❑	92 Lenny Harris	.05	.01
❑	93 Reggie Jefferson	.05	.01
❑	94 Sammy Sosa	.25	.08
❑	95 Scott Bailes	.05	.01
❑	96 Tom McKinnon RC	.10	.02
❑	97 Luis Rivera	.05	.01
❑	98 Mike Harkey	.05	.01
❑	99 Jeff Treadway	.05	.01
❑	100 Jose Canseco	.15	.05
❑	101 Omar Vizquel	.15	.05
❑	102 Scott Kamieniecki	.05	.01
❑	103 Ricky Jordan	.05	.01
❑	104 Jeff Ballard	.05	.01
❑	105 Felix Jose	.05	.01
❑	106 Mike Boddicker	.05	.01
❑	107 Dan Pasqua	.05	.01
❑	108 Mike Timlin	.05	.01
❑	109 Roger Craig MG	.05	.01
❑	110 Ryne Sandberg	.40	.15
❑	111 Mark Carreon	.05	.01
❑	112 Oscar Azocar	.05	.01
❑	113 Mike Greenwell	.05	.01
❑	114 Mark Portugal	.05	.01
❑	115 Terry Pendleton	.10	.02
❑	116 Willie Randolph	.10	.02
❑	117 Scott Terry	.05	.01
❑	118 Chili Davis	.10	.02
❑	119 Mark Gardner	.05	.01
❑	120 Alan Trammell	.10	.02
❑	121 Derek Bell	.10	.02
❑	122 Gary Varsho	.05	.01
❑	123 Bob Ojeda	.05	.01
❑	124 Shawn Livsey RC	.10	.02
❑	125 Chris Hoiles	.05	.01
❑	126 Klesko/Jaha/Brogna/Staton	.25	.08
❑	127 Carlos Quintana	.05	.01
❑	128 Kurt Stillwell	.05	.01
❑	129 Melido Perez	.05	.01
❑	130 Alvin Davis	.05	.01
❑	131 Checklist 1-132	.05	.01
❑	132 Eric Show	.05	.01
❑	133 Rance Mulliniks	.05	.01
❑	134 Darryl Kile	.10	.02
❑	135 Von Hayes	.05	.01
❑	136 Bill Doran	.05	.01
❑	137 Jeff D. Robinson	.05	.01
❑	138 Monty Fariss	.05	.01
❑	139 Jeff Innis	.05	.01
❑	140 Mark Grace UER	.15	.05
❑	141 Jim Leyland MG UER (No closed parenthesis after)	.10	.02
❑	142 Todd Van Poppel	.05	.01
❑	143 Paul Gibson	.05	.01
❑	144 Bill Swift	.05	.01
❑	145 Danny Tartabull	.05	.01
❑	146 Al Newman	.05	.01
❑	147 Cris Carpenter	.05	.01
❑	148 Anthony Young	.05	.01
❑	149 Brian Bohanon	.05	.01
❑	150 Roger Clemens	.50	.20
❑	151 Jeff Hamilton	.05	.01
❑	152 Charlie Leibrandt	.05	.01
❑	153 Ron Karkovice	.05	.01
❑	154 Hensley Meulens	.05	.01
❑	155 Scott Bankhead	.05	.01
❑	156 Manny Ramirez RC	4.00	1.50
❑	157 Keith Miller	.05	.01
❑	158 Todd Frohwirth	.05	.01
❑	159 Darrin Fletcher	.05	.01
❑	160 Bobby Bonilla	.10	.02
❑	161 Casey Candaele	.05	.01

❑ 162 Paul Faries .05 .01
❑ 163 Dana Kiecker .05 .01
❑ 164 Shane Mack .05 .01
❑ 165 Mark Langston .05 .01
❑ 166 Geronimo Pena .05 .01
❑ 167 Andy Allanson .05 .01
❑ 168 Dwight Smith .05 .01
❑ 169 Chuck Crim .05 .01
❑ 170 Alex Cole .05 .01
❑ 171 Bill Plummer MG .05 .01
❑ 172 Juan Berenguer .05 .01
❑ 173 Brian Downing .05 .01
❑ 174 Steve Frey .05 .01
❑ 175 Orel Hershiser .10 .02
❑ 176 Ramon Garcia .05 .01
❑ 177 Dan Gladden .05 .01
❑ 178 Jim Acker .05 .01
❑ 179 DeJard/Bern/Moreno/Stank .05 .01
❑ 180 Kevin Mitchell .05 .01
❑ 181 Hector Villanueva .05 .01
❑ 182 Jeff Reardon .10 .02
❑ 183 Brent Mayne .05 .01
❑ 184 Jimmy Jones .05 .01
❑ 185 Benito Santiago .10 .02
❑ 186 Cliff Floyd RC .75 .30
❑ 187 Ernie Riles .05 .01
❑ 188 Jose Guzman .05 .01
❑ 189 Junior Felix .05 .01
❑ 190 Glenn Davis .05 .01
❑ 191 Charlie Hough .10 .02
❑ 192 Dave Fleming .05 .01
❑ 193 Omar Olivares .05 .01
❑ 194 Eric Karros .10 .02
❑ 195 David Cone .10 .02
❑ 196 Frank Castillo .05 .01
❑ 197 Glenn Braggs .05 .01
❑ 198 Scott Aldred .05 .01
❑ 199 Jeff Blauser .05 .01
❑ 200 Len Dykstra .10 .02
❑ 201 Buck Showalter MG RC .25 .08
❑ 202 Rick Honeycutt .05 .01
❑ 203 Greg Myers .05 .01
❑ 204 Trevor Wilson .05 .01
❑ 205 Jay Howell .05 .01
❑ 206 Luis Sojo .05 .01
❑ 207 Jack Clark .10 .02
❑ 208 Julio Machado .05 .01
❑ 209 Lloyd McClendon .05 .01
❑ 210 Ozzie Guillen .10 .02
❑ 211 Jeremy Hernandez RC .10 .02
❑ 212 Randy Velarde .05 .01
❑ 213 Les Lancaster .05 .01
❑ 214 Andy Mota .05 .01
❑ 215 Rich Gossage .10 .02
❑ 216 Brent Gates RC .10 .02
❑ 217 Brian Harper .05 .01
❑ 218 Mike Flanagan .05 .01
❑ 219 Jerry Browne .05 .01
❑ 220 Jose Rijo .05 .01
❑ 221 Skeeter Barnes .05 .01
❑ 222 Jaime Navarro .05 .01
❑ 223 Mel Hall .05 .01
❑ 224 Bret Barberie .05 .01
❑ 225 Roberto Alomar .15 .05
❑ 226 Pete Smith .05 .01
❑ 227 Daryl Boston .05 .01
❑ 228 Eddie Whitson .05 .01
❑ 229 Shawn Boskie .05 .01
❑ 230 Dick Schofield .05 .01
❑ 231 Brian Drahman .05 .01
❑ 232 John Smiley .05 .01
❑ 233 Mitch Webster .05 .01
❑ 234 Terry Steinbach .05 .01
❑ 235 Jack Morris .10 .02
❑ 236 Bill Pecota .05 .01
❑ 237 Jose Hernandez RC .25 .08
❑ 238 Greg Litton .05 .01
❑ 239 Brian Holman .05 .01
❑ 240 Andres Galarraga .10 .02
❑ 241 Gerald Young .05 .01
❑ 242 Mike Mussina .25 .08
❑ 243 Alvaro Espinoza .05 .01
❑ 244 Darren Daulton .10 .02
❑ 245 John Smoltz .15 .05
❑ 246 Jason Pruitt RC .10 .02
❑ 247 Chuck Finley .10 .02
❑ 248 Jim Gantner .05 .01
❑ 249 Tony Fossas .05 .01
❑ 250 Ken Griffey Sr. .10 .02
❑ 251 Kevin Elster .05 .01
❑ 252 Dennis Rasmussen .05 .01
❑ 253 Terry Kennedy .05 .01
❑ 254 Ryan Bowen .05 .01
❑ 255 Robin Ventura .10 .02
❑ 256 Mike Aldrete .05 .01
❑ 257 Jeff Russell .05 .01
❑ 258 Jim Lindeman .05 .01
❑ 259 Ron Darling .05 .01
❑ 260 Devon White .10 .02
❑ 261 Tom Lasorda MG .10 .02
❑ 262 Terry Lee .05 .01
❑ 263 Bob Patterson .05 .01
❑ 264 Checklist 133-264 .05 .01
❑ 265 Teddy Higuera .05 .01
❑ 266 Roberto Kelly .05 .01
❑ 267 Steve Bedrosian .05 .01
❑ 268 Brady Anderson .10 .02
❑ 269 Ruben Amaro .05 .01
❑ 270 Tony Gwynn .30 .10
❑ 271 Tracy Jones .05 .01
❑ 272 Jerry Don Gleaton .05 .01
❑ 273 Craig Grebeck .05 .01
❑ 274 Bob Scanlan .05 .01
❑ 275 Todd Zeile .05 .01
❑ 276 Shawn Green RC 1.00 .40
❑ 277 Scott Chiamparino .05 .01
❑ 278 Darryl Hamilton .05 .01
❑ 279 Jim Clancy .05 .01
❑ 280 Carlos Martinez .05 .01
❑ 281 Kevin Appier .10 .02
❑ 282 John Wehner .05 .01
❑ 283 Reggie Sanders .10 .02
❑ 284 Gene Larkin .05 .01
❑ 285 Bob Welch .05 .01
❑ 286 Gilberto Reyes .05 .01
❑ 287 Pete Schourek .05 .01
❑ 288 Andujar Cedeno .05 .01
❑ 289 Mike Morgan .05 .01
❑ 290 Bo Jackson .25 .08
❑ 291 Phil Garner MG .10 .02
❑ 292 Ray Lankford .10 .02
❑ 293 Mike Henneman .05 .01
❑ 294 Dave Valle .05 .01
❑ 295 Alonzo Powell .05 .01
❑ 296 Tom Brunansky .05 .01
❑ 297 Kevin Brown .10 .02
❑ 298 Kelly Gruber .05 .01
❑ 299 Charles Nagy .05 .01
❑ 300 Don Mattingly .60 .25
❑ 301 Kirk McCaskill .05 .01
❑ 302 Joey Cora .05 .01
❑ 303 Dan Plesac .05 .01
❑ 304 Joe Oliver .05 .01
❑ 305 Tom Glavine .15 .05
❑ 306 Al Shirley RC .10 .02
❑ 307 Bruce Ruffin .05 .01
❑ 308 Craig Shipley .05 .01
❑ 309 Dave Martinez .05 .01
❑ 310 Jose Mesa .05 .01
❑ 311 Henry Cotto .05 .01
❑ 312 Mike LaValliere .05 .01
❑ 313 Kevin Tapani .05 .01
❑ 314 Jeff Huson .05 .01
❑ 315 Juan Samuel .05 .01
❑ 316 Curt Schilling .15 .05
❑ 317 Mike Bordick .05 .01
❑ 318 Steve Howe .05 .01
❑ 319 Tony Phillips .05 .01
❑ 320 George Bell .05 .01
❑ 321 Lou Piniella MG .10 .02
❑ 322 Tim Burke .05 .01
❑ 323 Milt Thompson .05 .01
❑ 324 Danny Darwin .05 .01
❑ 325 Joe Orsulak .05 .01
❑ 326 Eric King .05 .01
❑ 327 Jay Buhner .10 .02
❑ 328 Joel Johnston .05 .01
❑ 329 Franklin Stubbs .05 .01
❑ 330 Will Clark .15 .05
❑ 331 Steve Lake .05 .01
❑ 332 Chris Jones .05 .01
❑ 333 Pat Tabler .05 .01
❑ 334 Kevin Gross .05 .01
❑ 335 Dave Henderson .05 .01
❑ 336 Greg Anthony RC .10 .02
❑ 337 Alejandro Pena .05 .01
❑ 338 Shawn Abner .05 .01
❑ 339 Tom Browning .05 .01
❑ 340 Otis Nixon .05 .01
❑ 341 Bob Geren .05 .01
❑ 342 Tim Spehr .05 .01
❑ 343 John Vander Wal .05 .01
❑ 344 Jack Daugherty .05 .01
❑ 345 Zane Smith .05 .01
❑ 346 Rheal Cormier .05 .01
❑ 347 Kent Hrbek .10 .02
❑ 348 Rick Wilkins .05 .01
❑ 349 Steve Lyons .05 .01
❑ 350 Gregg Olson .05 .01
❑ 351 Greg Riddoch MG .05 .01
❑ 352 Ed Nunez .05 .01
❑ 353 Braulio Castillo .05 .01
❑ 354 Dave Bergman .05 .01
❑ 355 Warren Newson .05 .01
❑ 356 Luis Quinones .05 .01
❑ 357 Mike Witt .05 .01
❑ 358 Ted Wood .05 .01
❑ 359 Mike Moore .05 .01
❑ 360 Lance Parrish .10 .02
❑ 361 Barry Jones .05 .01
❑ 362 Javier Ortiz .05 .01
❑ 363 John Candelaria .05 .01
❑ 364 Glenallen Hill .05 .01
❑ 365 Duane Ward .05 .01
❑ 366 Checklist 265-396 .05 .01
❑ 367 Rafael Belliard .05 .01
❑ 368 Bill Krueger .05 .01
❑ 369 Steve Whitaker RC .10 .02
❑ 370 Shawon Dunston .05 .01
❑ 371 Dante Bichette .10 .02
❑ 372 Kip Gross .05 .01
❑ 373 Don Robinson .05 .01
❑ 374 Bernie Williams .15 .05
❑ 375 Bert Blyleven .10 .02
❑ 376 Chris Donnels .05 .01
❑ 377 Bob Zupcic RC .10 .02
❑ 378 Joel Skinner .05 .01
❑ 379 Steve Chitren .05 .01
❑ 380 Barry Bonds 1.00 .40
❑ 381 Sparky Anderson MG .10 .02
❑ 382 Sid Fernandez .05 .01
❑ 383 Dave Hollins .05 .01
❑ 384 Mark Lee .05 .01
❑ 385 Tim Wallach .05 .01
❑ 386 Will Clark AS .10 .02
❑ 387 Ryne Sandberg AS .25 .08
❑ 388 Howard Johnson AS .05 .01
❑ 389 Barry Larkin AS .10 .02
❑ 390 Barry Bonds AS .50 .20
❑ 391 Ron Gant AS .05 .01
❑ 392 Bobby Bonilla AS .05 .01
❑ 393 Craig Biggio AS .10 .02
❑ 394 Dennis Martinez AS .05 .01
❑ 395 Tom Glavine AS .10 .02
❑ 396 Lee Smith AS .05 .01
❑ 397 Cecil Fielder AS .05 .01
❑ 398 Julio Franco AS .05 .01
❑ 399 Wade Boggs AS .10 .02
❑ 400 Cal Ripken AS .40 .15
❑ 401 Jose Canseco AS .15 .05
❑ 402 Joe Carter AS .05 .01
❑ 403 Ruben Sierra AS .05 .01
❑ 404 Matt Nokes AS .05 .01
❑ 405 Roger Clemens AS .25 .08
❑ 406 Jim Abbott AS .10 .02
❑ 407 Bryan Harvey AS .05 .01
❑ 408 Bob Milacki .05 .01
❑ 409 Geno Petralli .05 .01
❑ 410 Dave Stewart .10 .02
❑ 411 Mike Jackson .05 .01
❑ 412 Luis Aquino .05 .01
❑ 413 Tim Teufel .05 .01
❑ 414 Jeff Ware .05 .01
❑ 415 Jim Deshaies .05 .01
❑ 416 Ellis Burks .10 .02
❑ 417 Allan Anderson .05 .01
❑ 418 Alfredo Griffin .05 .01
❑ 419 Wally Whitehurst .05 .01

❑	420	Sandy Alomar Jr.	.05	.01
❑	421	Juan Agosto	.05	.01
❑	422	Sam Horn	.05	.01
❑	423	Jeff Fassero	.05	.01
❑	424	Paul McClellan	.05	.01
❑	425	Cecil Fielder	.10	.02
❑	426	Tim Raines	.10	.02
❑	427	Eddie Taubensee RC	.25	.08
❑	428	Dennis Boyd	.05	.01
❑	429	Tony LaRussa MG	.10	.02
❑	430	Steve Sax	.05	.01
❑	431	Tom Gordon	.05	.01
❑	432	Billy Hatcher	.05	.01
❑	433	Cal Eldred	.05	.01
❑	434	Wally Backman	.05	.01
❑	435	Mark Eichhorn	.05	.01
❑	436	Mookie Wilson	.10	.02
❑	437	Scott Servais	.05	.01
❑	438	Mike Maddux	.05	.01
❑	439	Chico Walker	.05	.01
❑	440	Doug Drabek	.05	.01
❑	441	Rob Deer	.05	.01
❑	442	Dave West	.05	.01
❑	443	Spike Owen	.05	.01
❑	444	Tyrone Hill RC	.10	.02
❑	445	Matt Williams	.10	.02
❑	446	Mark Lewis	.05	.01
❑	447	David Segui	.05	.01
❑	448	Tom Pagnozzi	.05	.01
❑	449	Jeff Johnson	.05	.01
❑	450	Mark McGwire	.60	.25
❑	451	Tom Henke	.05	.01
❑	452	Wilson Alvarez	.05	.01
❑	453	Gary Redus	.05	.01
❑	454	Darren Holmes	.05	.01
❑	455	Pete O'Brien	.05	.01
❑	456	Pat Combs	.05	.01
❑	457	Hubie Brooks	.05	.01
❑	458	Frank Tanana	.05	.01
❑	459	Tom Kelly MG	.05	.01
❑	460	Andre Dawson	.10	.02
❑	461	Doug Jones	.05	.01
❑	462	Rich Rodriguez	.05	.01
❑	463	Mike Simms	.05	.01
❑	464	Mike Jeffcoat	.05	.01
❑	465	Barry Larkin	.15	.05
❑	466	Stan Belinda	.05	.01
❑	467	Lonnie Smith	.05	.01
❑	468	Greg Harris	.05	.01
❑	469	Jim Eisenreich	.05	.01
❑	470	Pedro Guerrero	.10	.02
❑	471	Jose DeJesus	.05	.01
❑	472	Rich Rowland RC	.10	.02
❑	473	Bolick/Paquette/Red/Russo	.05	.01
❑	474	Mike Rossiter RC	.10	.02
❑	475	Robby Thompson	.05	.01
❑	476	Randy Bush	.05	.01
❑	477	Greg Hibbard	.05	.01
❑	478	Dale Sveum	.05	.01
❑	479	Chito Martinez	.05	.01
❑	480	Scott Sanderson	.05	.01
❑	481	Tino Martinez	.15	.05
❑	482	Jimmy Key	.10	.02
❑	483	Terry Shumpert	.05	.01
❑	484	Mike Hartley	.05	.01
❑	485	Chris Sabo	.05	.01
❑	486	Bob Walk	.05	.01
❑	487	John Cerutti	.05	.01
❑	488	Scott Cooper	.05	.01
❑	489	Bobby Cox MG	.10	.02
❑	490	Julio Franco	.10	.02
❑	491	Jeff Brantley	.05	.01
❑	492	Mike Devereaux	.05	.01
❑	493	Jose Offerman	.05	.01
❑	494	Gary Thurman	.05	.01
❑	495	Carney Lansford	.10	.02
❑	496	Joe Grahe	.05	.01
❑	497	Andy Ashby	.05	.01
❑	498	Gerald Perry	.05	.01
❑	499	Dave Otto	.05	.01
❑	500	Vince Coleman	.05	.01
❑	501	Rob Mallicoat	.05	.01
❑	502	Greg Briley	.05	.01
❑	503	Pascual Perez	.05	.01
❑	504	Aaron Sele RC	.25	.08
❑	505	Bobby Thigpen	.05	.01
❑	506	Todd Benzinger	.05	.01
❑	507	Candy Maldonado	.05	.01
❑	508	Bill Gullickson	.05	.01
❑	509	Doug Dascenzo	.05	.01
❑	510	Frank Viola	.10	.02
❑	511	Kenny Rogers	.10	.02
❑	512	Mike Heath	.05	.01
❑	513	Kevin Bass	.05	.01
❑	514	Kim Batiste	.05	.01
❑	515	Delino DeShields	.05	.01
❑	516	Ed Sprague	.05	.01
❑	517	Jim Gott	.05	.01
❑	518	Jose Melendez	.05	.01
❑	519	Hal McRae MG	.10	.02
❑	520	Jeff Bagwell	.25	.08
❑	521	Joe Hesketh	.05	.01
❑	522	Milt Cuyler	.05	.01
❑	523	Shawn Hillegas	.05	.01
❑	524	Don Slaught	.05	.01
❑	525	Randy Johnson	.25	.08
❑	526	Doug Piatt	.05	.01
❑	527	Checklist 397-528	.05	.01
❑	528	Steve Foster	.05	.01
❑	529	Joe Girardi	.05	.01
❑	530	Jim Abbott	.15	.05
❑	531	Larry Walker	.15	.05
❑	532	Mike Huff	.05	.01
❑	533	Mackey Sasser	.05	.01
❑	534	Benji Gil RC	.25	.08
❑	535	Dave Stieb	.05	.01
❑	536	Willie Wilson	.05	.01
❑	537	Mark Leiter	.05	.01
❑	538	Jose Uribe	.05	.01
❑	539	Thomas Howard	.05	.01
❑	540	Ben McDonald	.05	.01
❑	541	Jose Tolentino	.05	.01
❑	542	Keith Mitchell	.05	.01
❑	543	Jerome Walton	.05	.01
❑	544	Cliff Brantley	.05	.01
❑	545	Andy Van Slyke	.15	.05
❑	546	Paul Sorrento	.05	.01
❑	547	Herm Winningham	.05	.01
❑	548	Mark Guthrie	.05	.01
❑	549	Joe Torre MG	.10	.02
❑	550	Darryl Strawberry	.10	.02
❑	551	Chipper Jones	.25	.08
❑	552	Dave Gallagher	.05	.01
❑	553	Edgar Martinez	.15	.05
❑	554	Donald Harris	.05	.01
❑	555	Frank Thomas	.25	.08
❑	556	Storm Davis	.05	.01
❑	557	Dickie Thon	.05	.01
❑	558	Scott Garrelts	.05	.01
❑	559	Steve Olin	.05	.01
❑	560	Rickey Henderson	.25	.08
❑	561	Jose Vizcaino	.05	.01
❑	562	Wade Taylor	.05	.01
❑	563	Pat Borders	.05	.01
❑	564	Jimmy Gonzalez RC	.10	.02
❑	565	Lee Smith	.10	.02
❑	566	Bill Sampen	.05	.01
❑	567	Dean Palmer	.10	.02
❑	568	Bryan Harvey	.05	.01
❑	569	Tony Pena	.05	.01
❑	570	Lou Whitaker	.10	.02
❑	571	Randy Tomlin	.05	.01
❑	572	Greg Vaughn	.05	.01
❑	573	Kelly Downs	.05	.01
❑	574	Steve Avery UER	.05	.01
❑	575	Kirby Puckett	.25	.08
❑	576	Heathcliff Slocumb	.05	.01
❑	577	Kevin Seitzer	.05	.01
❑	578	Lee Guetterman	.05	.01
❑	579	Johnny Oates MG	.05	.01
❑	580	Greg Maddux	.40	.15
❑	581	Stan Javier	.05	.01
❑	582	Vicente Palacios	.05	.01
❑	583	Mel Rojas	.05	.01
❑	584	Wayne Rosenthal RC	.10	.02
❑	585	Lenny Webster	.05	.01
❑	586	Rod Nichols	.05	.01
❑	587	Mickey Morandini	.05	.01
❑	588	Russ Swan	.05	.01
❑	589	Mariano Duncan	.05	.01
❑	590	Howard Johnson	.05	.01
❑	591	Burnitz/Brum/Coc/Dozier	.10	.02
❑	592	Denny Neagle	.10	.02
❑	593	Steve Decker	.05	.01
❑	594	Brian Barber RC	.10	.02
❑	595	Bruce Hurst	.05	.01
❑	596	Kent Mercker	.05	.01
❑	597	Mike Magnante RC	.10	.02
❑	598	Jody Reed	.05	.01
❑	599	Steve Searcy	.05	.01
❑	600	Paul Molitor	.10	.02
❑	601	Dave Smith	.05	.01
❑	602	Mike Fetters	.05	.01
❑	603	Luis Mercedes	.05	.01
❑	604	Chris Gwynn	.05	.01
❑	605	Scott Erickson	.05	.01
❑	606	Brook Jacoby	.05	.01
❑	607	Todd Stottlemyre	.05	.01
❑	608	Scott Bradley	.05	.01
❑	609	Mike Hargrove MG	.10	.02
❑	610	Eric Davis	.10	.02
❑	611	Brian Hunter	.05	.01
❑	612	Pat Kelly	.05	.01
❑	613	Pedro Munoz	.05	.01
❑	614	Al Osuna	.05	.01
❑	615	Matt Merullo	.05	.01
❑	616	Larry Andersen	.05	.01
❑	617	Junior Ortiz	.05	.01
❑	618	Hern/Hosey/McNeely/Pelt	.05	.01
❑	619	Danny Jackson	.05	.01
❑	620	George Brett	.60	.25
❑	621	Dan Gakeler	.05	.01
❑	622	Steve Buechele	.05	.01
❑	623	Bob Tewksbury	.05	.01
❑	624	Shawn Estes RC	.25	.08
❑	625	Kevin McReynolds	.05	.01
❑	626	Chris Haney	.05	.01
❑	627	Mike Sharperson	.05	.01
❑	628	Mark Williamson	.05	.01
❑	629	Wally Joyner	.10	.02
❑	630	Carlton Fisk	.15	.05
❑	631	Armando Reynoso RC	.25	.08
❑	632	Felix Fermin	.05	.01
❑	633	Mitch Williams	.05	.01
❑	634	Manuel Lee	.05	.01
❑	635	Harold Baines	.10	.02
❑	636	Greg Harris	.05	.01
❑	637	Orlando Merced	.05	.01
❑	638	Chris Bosio	.05	.01
❑	639	Wayne Housie	.05	.01
❑	640	Xavier Hernandez	.05	.01
❑	641	David Howard	.05	.01
❑	642	Tim Crews	.05	.01
❑	643	Rick Cerone	.05	.01
❑	644	Terry Leach	.05	.01
❑	645	Deion Sanders	.15	.05
❑	646	Craig Wilson	.05	.01
❑	647	Marquis Grissom	.10	.02
❑	648	Scott Fletcher	.05	.01
❑	649	Norm Charlton	.05	.01
❑	650	Jesse Barfield	.05	.01
❑	651	Joe Slusarski	.05	.01
❑	652	Bobby Rose	.05	.01
❑	653	Dennis Lamp	.05	.01
❑	654	Allen Watson RC	.10	.02
❑	655	Brett Butler	.10	.02
❑	656	Pem/H.Rod/Tinsley/G.Will	.10	.02
❑	657	Dave Johnson	.05	.01
❑	658	Checklist 529-660	.05	.01
❑	659	Brian McRae	.05	.01
❑	660	Fred McGriff	.15	.05
❑	661	Bill Landrum	.05	.01
❑	662	Juan Guzman	.05	.01
❑	663	Greg Gagne	.05	.01
❑	664	Ken Hill	.05	.01
❑	665	Dave Haas	.05	.01
❑	666	Tom Foley	.05	.01
❑	667	Roberto Hernandez	.05	.01
❑	668	Dwayne Henry	.05	.01
❑	669	Jim Fregosi MG	.05	.01
❑	670	Harold Reynolds	.10	.02
❑	671	Mark Whiten	.05	.01
❑	672	Eric Plunk	.05	.01
❑	673	Todd Hundley	.05	.01
❑	674	Mo Sanford	.05	.01
❑	675	Bobby Witt	.05	.01
❑	676	Mil/Mahomes/Wendell/Salk	.25	.08
❑	677	John Marzano	.05	.01

678	Joe Klink	.05	.01
679	Pete Incaviglia	.05	.01
680	Dale Murphy	.15	.05
681	Rene Gonzales	.05	.01
682	Andy Benes	.05	.01
683	Jim Poole	.05	.01
684	Trever Miller RC	.10	.02
685	Scott Livingstone	.05	.01
686	Rich DeLucia	.05	.01
687	Harvey Pulliam	.05	.01
688	Tim Belcher	.05	.01
689	Mark Lemke	.05	.01
690	John Franco	.10	.02
691	Walt Weiss	.05	.01
692	Scott Ruskin	.05	.01
693	Jeff King	.05	.01
694	Mike Gardiner	.05	.01
695	Gary Sheffield	.10	.02
696	Joe Boever	.05	.01
697	Mike Felder	.05	.01
698	John Habyan	.05	.01
699	Cito Gaston MG	.05	.01
700	Ruben Sierra	.10	.02
701	Scott Radinsky	.05	.01
702	Lee Stevens	.05	.01
703	Mark Wohlers	.05	.01
704	Curt Young	.05	.01
705	Dwight Evans	.15	.05
706	Rob Murphy	.05	.01
707	Gregg Jefferies	.05	.01
708	Tom Bolton	.05	.01
709	Chris James	.05	.01
710	Kevin Maas	.05	.01
711	Ricky Bones	.05	.01
712	Curt Wilkerson	.05	.01
713	Roger McDowell	.05	.01
714	Pokey Reese RC	.25	.08
715	Craig Biggio	.15	.05
716	Kirk Dressendorfer	.05	.01
717	Ken Dayley	.05	.01
718	B.J. Surhoff	.10	.02
719	Terry Mulholland	.05	.01
720	Kirk Gibson	.10	.02
721	Mike Pagliarulo	.05	.01
722	Walt Terrell	.05	.01
723	Jose Oquendo	.05	.01
724	Kevin Morton	.05	.01
725	Dwight Gooden	.10	.02
726	Kirt Manwaring	.05	.01
727	Chuck McElroy	.05	.01
728	Dave Burba	.05	.01
729	Art Howe MG	.05	.01
730	Ramon Martinez	.05	.01
731	Donnie Hill	.05	.01
732	Nelson Santovenia	.05	.01
733	Bob Melvin	.05	.01
734	Scott Hatteberg RC	.25	.08
735	Greg Swindell	.05	.01
736	Lance Johnson	.05	.01
737	Kevin Reimer	.05	.01
738	Dennis Eckersley	.10	.02
739	Rob Ducey	.05	.01
740	Ken Caminiti	.10	.02
741	Mark Gubicza	.05	.01
742	Bill Spiers	.05	.01
743	Darren Lewis	.05	.01
744	Chris Hammond	.05	.01
745	Dave Magadan	.05	.01
746	Bernard Gilkey	.05	.01
747	Willie Banks	.05	.01
748	Matt Nokes	.05	.01
749	Jerald Clark	.05	.01
750	Travis Fryman	.10	.02
751	Steve Wilson	.05	.01
752	Billy Ripken	.05	.01
753	Paul Assenmacher	.05	.01
754	Charlie Hayes	.05	.01
755	Alex Fernandez	.05	.01
756	Gary Pettis	.05	.01
757	Rob Dibble	.10	.02
758	Tim Naehring	.05	.01
759	Jeff Torborg MG	.05	.01
760	Ozzie Smith	.40	.15
761	Mike Fitzgerald	.05	.01
762	John Burkett	.05	.01
763	Kyle Abbott	.05	.01
764	Tyler Green RC	.10	.02
765	Pete Harnisch	.05	.01
766	Mark Davis	.05	.01
767	Kal Daniels	.05	.01
768	Jim Thome	.25	.08
769	Jack Howell	.05	.01
770	Sid Bream	.05	.01
771	Arthur Rhodes	.05	.01
772	Garry Templeton UER (Stat heading in for pitchers	.05	.01
773	Hal Morris	.05	.01
774	Bud Black	.05	.01
775	Ivan Calderon	.05	.01
776	Doug Henry RC	.10	.02
777	John Olerud	.10	.02
778	Tim Leary	.05	.01
779	Jay Bell	.10	.02
780	Eddie Murray	.25	.08
781	Paul Abbott	.05	.01
782	Phil Plantier	.05	.01
783	Joe Magrane	.05	.01
784	Ken Patterson	.05	.01
785	Albert Belle	.10	.02
786	Royce Clayton	.05	.01
787	Checklist 661-792	.05	.01
788	Mike Stanton	.05	.01
789	Bobby Valentine MG	.05	.01
790	Joe Carter	.10	.02
791	Danny Cox	.05	.01
792	Dave Winfield	.10	.02

1992 Topps Traded

	COMP.FACT.SET (132)	50.00	20.00
1T	Willie Adams USA RC	.25	.08
2T	Jeff Alkire USA RC	.25	.08
3T	Felipe Alou MG	.20	.07
4T	Moises Alou	.20	.07
5T	Ruben Amaro	.10	.02
6T	Jack Armstrong	.10	.02
7T	Scott Bankhead	.10	.02
8T	Tim Belcher	.10	.02
9T	George Bell	.10	.02
10T	Freddie Benavides	.10	.02
11T	Todd Benzinger	.10	.02
12T	Joe Boever	.10	.02
13T	Ricky Bones	.10	.02
14T	Bobby Bonilla	.20	.07
15T	Hubie Brooks	.10	.02
16T	Jerry Browne	.10	.02
17T	Jim Bullinger	.10	.02
18T	Dave Burba	.10	.02
19T	Kevin Campbell	.10	.02
20T	Tom Candiotti	.10	.02
21T	Mark Carreon	.10	.02
22T	Gary Carter	.20	.07
23T	Archi Cianfrocco RC	.10	.02
24T	Phil Clark	.10	.02
25T	Chad Curtis RC	.40	.15
26T	Eric Davis	.20	.07
27T	Tim Davis USA RC	.25	.08
28T	Gary DiSarcina	.10	.02
29T	Darren Dreifort USA	.10	.02
30T	Mariano Duncan	.10	.02
31T	Mike Fitzgerald	.10	.02
32T	John Flaherty	.10	.02
33T	Darrin Fletcher	.10	.02
34T	Scott Fletcher	.10	.02
35T	Ron Fraser USA CO RC	.25	.08
36T	Andres Galarraga	.20	.07
37T	Dave Gallagher	.10	.02
38T	Mike Gallego	.10	.02
39T	Nomar Garciaparra USA RC	20.00	8.00
40T	Jason Giambi USA	1.00	.40
41T	Danny Gladden	.10	.02
42T	Rene Gonzales	.10	.02
43T	Jeff Granger USA	.10	.02
44T	Rick Greene USA RC	.25	.08
45T	Jeffrey Hammonds USA	.20	.07
46T	Charlie Hayes	.10	.02
47T	Von Hayes	.10	.02
48T	Rick Helling USA	.10	.02
49T	Butch Henry RC	.10	.02
50T	Carlos Hernandez	.10	.02
51T	Ken Hill	.10	.02
52T	Butch Hobson	.10	.02
53T	Vince Horsman	.10	.02
54T	Pete Incaviglia	.10	.02
55T	Gregg Jefferies	.10	.02
56T	Charles Johnson USA	.20	.07
57T	Doug Jones	.10	.02
58T	Brian Jordan RC	.75	.30
59T	Wally Joyner	.20	.07
60T	Daron Kirkreit USA RC	.25	.08
61T	Bill Krueger	.10	.02
62T	Gene Lamont MG	.10	.02
63T	Jim Lefebvre MG	.10	.02
64T	Danny Leon	.10	.02
65T	Pat Listach RC	.40	.15
66T	Kenny Lofton	.30	.10
67T	Dave Martinez	.10	.02
68T	Derrick May	.10	.02
69T	Kirk McCaskill	.10	.02
70T	Chad McConnell USA RC	.25	.08
71T	Kevin McReynolds	.10	.02
72T	Rusty Meacham	.10	.02
73T	Keith Miller	.10	.02
74T	Kevin Mitchell	.10	.02
75T	Jason Moler USA RC	.25	.08
76T	Mike Morgan	.10	.02
77T	Jack Morris	.20	.07
78T	Calvin Murray USA RC	.75	.30
79T	Eddie Murray	.50	.20
80T	Randy Myers	.10	.02
81T	Denny Neagle	.20	.07
82T	Phil Nevin USA	.20	.07
83T	Dave Nilsson	.10	.02
84T	Junior Ortiz	.10	.02
85T	Donovan Osborne	.10	.02
86T	Bill Pecota	.10	.02
87T	Melido Perez	.10	.02
88T	Mike Perez	.10	.02
89T	Hipolito Pichardo RC	.10	.02
90T	Willie Randolph	.20	.07
91T	Darren Reed	.10	.02
92T	Bip Roberts	.10	.02
93T	Chris Roberts USA	.10	.02
94T	Steve Rodriguez USA	.10	.02
95T	Bruce Ruffin	.10	.02
96T	Scott Ruskin	.10	.02
97T	Bret Saberhagen	.20	.07
98T	Rey Sanchez RC	.40	.15
99T	Steve Sax	.10	.02
100T	Curt Schilling	.30	.10
101T	Dick Schofield	.10	.02
102T	Gary Scott	.10	.02
103T	Kevin Seitzer	.10	.02
104T	Frank Seminara RC	.10	.02
105T	Gary Sheffield	.20	.07
106T	John Smiley	.10	.02
107T	Cory Snyder	.10	.02
108T	Paul Sorrento	.10	.02
109T	Sammy Sosa Cubs	1.50	.60
110T	Matt Stairs RC	.50	.20
111T	Andy Stankiewicz	.10	.02
112T	Kurt Stillwell	.10	.02
113T	Rick Sutcliffe	.20	.07
114T	Bill Swift	.10	.02
115T	Jeff Tackett	.10	.02
116T	Danny Tartabull	.10	.02
117T	Eddie Taubensee	.20	.07
118T	Dickie Thon	.10	.02
119T	Michael Tucker USA RC	.75	.30
120T	Scooter Tucker	.10	.02
121T	Marc Valdes USA RC	.25	.08

❑ 122T Julio Valera .10 .02
❑ 123T Jason Varitek USA RC 15.00 6.00
❑ 124T Ron Villone USA RC .25 .08
❑ 125T Frank Viola .20 .07
❑ 126T B.J.Wallace USA RC .25 .08
❑ 127T Dan Walters .10 .02
❑ 128T Craig Wilson USA .10 .02
❑ 129T Chris Wimmer USA .10 .02
❑ 130T Dave Winfield .20 .07
❑ 131T Herm Winningham .10 .02
❑ 132T Checklist 1T-132T .10 .02

1993 Topps

❑ COMPLETE SET (825) 50.00 20.00
❑ COMP.HOBBY.SET (847) 60.00 30.00
❑ COMP.RETAIL.SET (838) 50.00 20.00
❑ COMPLETE SERIES 1 (396) 25.00 10.00
❑ COMPLETE SERIES 2 (429) 25.00 10.00
❑ 1 Robin Yount .75 .30
❑ 2 Barry Bonds 1.50 .60
❑ 3 Ryne Sandberg .75 .30
❑ 4 Roger Clemens 1.00 .40
❑ 5 Tony Gwynn .60 .25
❑ 6 Jeff Tackett .10 .02
❑ 7 Pete Incaviglia .10 .02
❑ 8 Mark Wohlers .10 .02
❑ 9 Kent Hrbek .20 .07
❑ 10 Will Clark .30 .10
❑ 11 Eric Karros .20 .07
❑ 12 Lee Smith .20 .07
❑ 13 Esteban Beltre .10 .02
❑ 14 Greg Briley .10 .02
❑ 15 Marquis Grissom .20 .07
❑ 16 Dan Plesac .10 .02
❑ 17 Dave Hollins .10 .02
❑ 18 Terry Steinbach .10 .02
❑ 19 Ed Nunez .10 .02
❑ 20 Tim Salmon .30 .10
❑ 21 Luis Salazar .10 .02
❑ 22 Jim Eisenreich .10 .02
❑ 23 Todd Stottlemyre .10 .02
❑ 24 Tim Naehring .10 .02
❑ 25 John Franco .20 .07
❑ 26 Skeeter Barnes .10 .02
❑ 27 Carlos Garcia .10 .02
❑ 28 Joe Orsulak .10 .02
❑ 29 Dwayne Henry .10 .02
❑ 30 Fred McGriff .30 .10
❑ 31 Derek Lilliquist .10 .02
❑ 32 Don Mattingly 1.25 .50
❑ 33 B.J.Wallace .10 .02
❑ 34 Juan Gonzalez .20 .07
❑ 35 John Smoltz .30 .10
❑ 36 Scott Servais .10 .02
❑ 37 Lenny Webster .10 .02
❑ 38 Chris James .10 .02
❑ 39 Roger McDowell .10 .02
❑ 40 Ozzie Smith .75 .30
❑ 41 Alex Fernandez .10 .02
❑ 42 Spike Owen .10 .02
❑ 43 Ruben Amaro .10 .02
❑ 44 Kevin Seitzer .10 .02
❑ 45 Dave Fleming .10 .02
❑ 46 Eric Fox .10 .02
❑ 47 Bob Scanlan .10 .02
❑ 48 Bert Blyleven .20 .07
❑ 49 Brian McRae .10 .02
❑ 50 Roberto Alomar .30 .10
❑ 51 Mo Vaughn .20 .07
❑ 52 Bobby Bonilla .20 .07
❑ 53 Frank Tanana .10 .02
❑ 54 Mike LaValliere .10 .02
❑ 55 Mark McLemore .10 .02
❑ 56 Chad Mottola RC .10 .02
❑ 57 Norm Charlton .10 .02
❑ 58 Jose Melendez .10 .02
❑ 59 Carlos Martinez .10 .02
❑ 60 Roberto Kelly .10 .02
❑ 61 Gene Larkin .10 .02
❑ 62 Rafael Belliard .10 .02
❑ 63 Al Osuna .10 .02
❑ 64 Scott Chiamparino .10 .02
❑ 65 Brett Butler .20 .07
❑ 66 John Burkett .10 .02
❑ 67 Felix Jose .10 .02
❑ 68 Omar Vizquel .30 .10
❑ 69 John Vander Wal .10 .02
❑ 70 Roberto Hernandez .10 .02
❑ 71 Ricky Bones .10 .02
❑ 72 Jeff Grotewold .10 .02
❑ 73 Mike Moore .10 .02
❑ 74 Steve Buechele .10 .02
❑ 75 Juan Guzman .10 .02
❑ 76 Kevin Appier .20 .07
❑ 77 Junior Felix .10 .02
❑ 78 Greg W. Harris .10 .02
❑ 79 Dick Schofield .10 .02
❑ 80 Cecil Fielder .20 .07
❑ 81 Lloyd McClendon .10 .02
❑ 82 David Segui .10 .02
❑ 83 Reggie Sanders .20 .07
❑ 84 Kurt Stillwell .10 .02
❑ 85 Sandy Alomar Jr. .10 .02
❑ 86 John Habyan .10 .02
❑ 87 Kevin Reimer .10 .02
❑ 88 Mike Stanton .10 .02
❑ 89 Eric Anthony .10 .02
❑ 90 Scott Erickson .10 .02
❑ 91 Craig Colbert .10 .02
❑ 92 Tom Pagnozzi .10 .02
❑ 93 Pedro Astacio .10 .02
❑ 94 Lance Johnson .10 .02
❑ 95 Larry Walker .20 .07
❑ 96 Russ Swan .10 .02
❑ 97 Scott Fletcher .10 .02
❑ 98 Derek Jeter RC 10.00 4.00
❑ 99 Mike Williams .10 .02
❑ 100 Mark McGwire 1.25 .50
❑ 101 Jim Bullinger .10 .02
❑ 102 Brian Hunter .10 .02
❑ 103 Jody Reed .10 .02
❑ 104 Mike Butcher .10 .02
❑ 105 Gregg Jefferies .10 .02
❑ 106 Howard Johnson .10 .02
❑ 107 John Kiely .10 .02
❑ 108 Jose Lind .10 .02
❑ 109 Sam Horn .10 .02
❑ 110 Barry Larkin .30 .10
❑ 111 Bruce Hurst .10 .02
❑ 112 Brian Barnes .10 .02
❑ 113 Thomas Howard .10 .02
❑ 114 Mel Hall .10 .02
❑ 115 Robby Thompson .10 .02
❑ 116 Mark Lemke .10 .02
❑ 117 Eddie Taubensee .10 .02
❑ 118 David Hulse RC .10 .02
❑ 119 Pedro Munoz .10 .02
❑ 120 Ramon Martinez .10 .02
❑ 121 Todd Worrell .10 .02
❑ 122 Joey Cora .10 .02
❑ 123 Moises Alou .20 .07
❑ 124 Franklin Stubbs .10 .02
❑ 125 Pete O'Brien .10 .02
❑ 126 Bob Ayrault .10 .02
❑ 127 Carney Lansford .20 .07
❑ 128 Kal Daniels .10 .02
❑ 129 Joe Grahe .10 .02
❑ 130 Jeff Montgomery .10 .02
❑ 131 Dave Winfield .20 .07
❑ 132 Preston Wilson RC .75 .30
❑ 133 Steve Wilson .10 .02
❑ 134 Lee Guetterman .10 .02
❑ 135 Mickey Tettleton .10 .02
❑ 136 Jeff King .10 .02
❑ 137 Alan Mills .10 .02
❑ 138 Joe Oliver .10 .02
❑ 139 Gary Gaetti .20 .07
❑ 140 Gary Sheffield .20 .07
❑ 141 Dennis Cook .10 .02
❑ 142 Charlie Hayes .10 .02
❑ 143 Jeff Huson .10 .02
❑ 144 Kent Mercker .10 .02
❑ 145 Eric Young .10 .02
❑ 146 Scott Leius .10 .02
❑ 147 Bryan Hickerson .10 .02
❑ 148 Steve Finley .20 .07
❑ 149 Rheal Cormier .10 .02
❑ 150 Frank Thomas .50 .20
❑ 151 Archi Cianfrocco .10 .02
❑ 152 Rich DeLucia .10 .02
❑ 153 Greg Vaughn .10 .02
❑ 154 Wes Chamberlain .10 .02
❑ 155 Dennis Eckersley .20 .07
❑ 156 Sammy Sosa .50 .20
❑ 157 Gary DiSarcina .10 .02
❑ 158 Kevin Koslofski .10 .02
❑ 159 Doug Linton .10 .02
❑ 160 Lou Whitaker .20 .07
❑ 161 Chad McConnell .10 .02
❑ 162 Joe Hesketh .10 .02
❑ 163 Tim Wakefield .50 .20
❑ 164 Leo Gomez .10 .02
❑ 165 Jose Rijo .10 .02
❑ 166 Tim Scott .10 .02
❑ 167 Steve Olin UER .10 .02
❑ 168 Kevin Maas .10 .02
❑ 169 Kenny Rogers .20 .07
❑ 170 David Justice .20 .07
❑ 171 Doug Jones .10 .02
❑ 172 Jeff Reboulet .10 .02
❑ 173 Andres Galarraga .20 .07
❑ 174 Randy Velarde .10 .02
❑ 175 Kirk McCaskill .10 .02
❑ 176 Darren Lewis .10 .02
❑ 177 Lenny Harris .10 .02
❑ 178 Jeff Fassero .10 .02
❑ 179 Ken Griffey Jr. .75 .30
❑ 180 Darren Daulton .20 .07
❑ 181 John Jaha .10 .02
❑ 182 Ron Darling .10 .02
❑ 183 Greg Maddux .75 .30
❑ 184 Damion Easley .10 .02
❑ 185 Jack Morris .20 .07
❑ 186 Mike Magnante .10 .02
❑ 187 John Dopson .10 .02
❑ 188 Sid Fernandez .10 .02
❑ 189 Tony Phillips .10 .02
❑ 190 Doug Drabek .10 .02
❑ 191 Sean Lowe RC .10 .02
❑ 192 Bob Milacki .10 .02
❑ 193 Steve Foster .10 .02
❑ 194 Jerald Clark .10 .02
❑ 195 Pete Harnisch .10 .02
❑ 196 Pat Kelly .10 .02
❑ 197 Jeff Frye .10 .02
❑ 198 Alejandro Pena .10 .02
❑ 199 Junior Ortiz .10 .02
❑ 200 Kirby Puckett .50 .20
❑ 201 Jose Uribe .10 .02
❑ 202 Mike Scioscia .10 .02
❑ 203 Bernard Gilkey .10 .02
❑ 204 Dan Pasqua .10 .02
❑ 205 Gary Carter .20 .07
❑ 206 Henry Cotto .10 .02
❑ 207 Paul Molitor .20 .07
❑ 208 Mike Hartley .10 .02
❑ 209 Jeff Parrett .10 .02
❑ 210 Mark Langston .10 .02
❑ 211 Doug Dascenzo .10 .02
❑ 212 Rick Reed .10 .02
❑ 213 Candy Maldonado .10 .02
❑ 214 Danny Darwin .10 .02
❑ 215 Pat Howell .10 .02
❑ 216 Mark Leiter .10 .02
❑ 217 Kevin Mitchell .10 .02
❑ 218 Ben McDonald .10 .02
❑ 219 Bip Roberts .10 .02
❑ 220 Benny Santiago .20 .07
❑ 221 Carlos Baerga .10 .02
❑ 222 Bernie Williams .30 .10

❑ 223 Roger Pavlik .10 .02
❑ 224 Sid Bream .10 .02
❑ 225 Matt Williams .20 .07
❑ 226 Willie Banks .10 .02
❑ 227 Jeff Bagwell .30 .10
❑ 228 Tom Goodwin .10 .02
❑ 229 Mike Perez .10 .02
❑ 230 Carlton Fisk .30 .10
❑ 231 John Wetteland .20 .07
❑ 232 Tino Martinez .30 .10
❑ 233 Rick Greene .10 .02
❑ 234 Tim McIntosh .10 .02
❑ 235 Mitch Williams .10 .02
❑ 236 Kevin Campbell .10 .02
❑ 237 Jose Vizcaino .10 .02
❑ 238 Chris Donnels .10 .02
❑ 239 Mike Boddicker .10 .02
❑ 240 John Olerud .20 .07
❑ 241 Mike Gardiner .10 .02
❑ 242 Charlie O'Brien .10 .02
❑ 243 Rob Deer .10 .02
❑ 244 Denny Neagle .20 .07
❑ 245 Chris Sabo .10 .02
❑ 246 Gregg Olson .10 .02
❑ 247 Frank Seminara UER .10 .02
❑ 248 Scott Scudder .10 .02
❑ 249 Tim Burke .10 .02
❑ 250 Chuck Knoblauch .20 .07
❑ 251 Mike Bielecki .10 .02
❑ 252 Xavier Hernandez .10 .02
❑ 253 Jose Guzman .10 .02
❑ 254 Cory Snyder .10 .02
❑ 255 Orel Hershiser .20 .07
❑ 256 Wil Cordero .10 .02
❑ 257 Luis Alicea .10 .02
❑ 258 Mike Schooler .10 .02
❑ 259 Craig Grebeck .10 .02
❑ 260 Duane Ward .10 .02
❑ 261 Bill Wegman .10 .02
❑ 262 Mickey Morandini .10 .02
❑ 263 Vince Horsman .10 .02
❑ 264 Paul Sorrento .10 .02
❑ 265 Andre Dawson .20 .07
❑ 266 Rene Gonzales .10 .02
❑ 267 Keith Miller .10 .02
❑ 268 Derek Bell .10 .02
❑ 269 Todd Steverson RC .10 .02
❑ 270 Frank Viola .20 .07
❑ 271 Wally Whitehurst .10 .02
❑ 272 Kurt Knudsen .10 .02
❑ 273 Dan Walters .10 .02
❑ 274 Rick Sutcliffe .20 .07
❑ 275 Andy Van Slyke .30 .10
❑ 276 Paul O'Neill .30 .10
❑ 277 Mark Whiten .10 .02
❑ 278 Chris Nabholz .10 .02
❑ 279 Todd Burns .10 .02
❑ 280 Tom Glavine .30 .10
❑ 281 Butch Henry .10 .02
❑ 282 Shane Mack .10 .02
❑ 283 Mike Jackson .10 .02
❑ 284 Henry Rodriguez .10 .02
❑ 285 Bob Tewksbury .10 .02
❑ 286 Ron Karkovice .10 .02
❑ 287 Mike Gallego .10 .02
❑ 288 Dave Cochrane .10 .02
❑ 289 Jesse Orosco .10 .02
❑ 290 Dave Stewart .20 .07
❑ 291 Tommy Greene .10 .02
❑ 292 Rey Sanchez .10 .02
❑ 293 Rob Ducey .10 .02
❑ 294 Brent Mayne .10 .02
❑ 295 Dave Stieb .10 .02
❑ 296 Luis Rivera .10 .02
❑ 297 Jeff Innis .10 .02
❑ 298 Scott Livingstone .10 .02
❑ 299 Bob Patterson .10 .02
❑ 300 Cal Ripken 1.50 .60
❑ 301 Cesar Hernandez .10 .02
❑ 302 Randy Myers .10 .02
❑ 303 Brook Jacoby .10 .02
❑ 304 Melido Perez .10 .02
❑ 305 Rafael Palmeiro .30 .10
❑ 306 Damon Berryhill .10 .02
❑ 307 Dan Serafini RC .10 .02
❑ 308 Darryl Kile .20 .07
❑ 309 J.T. Bruett .10 .02
❑ 310 Dave Righetti .20 .07
❑ 311 Jay Howell .10 .02
❑ 312 Geronimo Pena .10 .02
❑ 313 Greg Hibbard .10 .02
❑ 314 Mark Gardner .10 .02
❑ 315 Edgar Martinez .30 .10
❑ 316 Dave Nilsson .10 .02
❑ 317 Kyle Abbott .10 .02
❑ 318 Willie Wilson .10 .02
❑ 319 Paul Assenmacher .10 .02
❑ 320 Tim Fortugno .10 .02
❑ 321 Rusty Meacham .10 .02
❑ 322 Pat Borders .10 .02
❑ 323 Mike Greenwell .10 .02
❑ 324 Willie Randolph .20 .07
❑ 325 Bill Gullickson .10 .02
❑ 326 Gary Varsho .10 .02
❑ 327 Tim Hulett .10 .02
❑ 328 Scott Ruskin .10 .02
❑ 329 Mike Maddux .10 .02
❑ 330 Danny Tartabull .10 .02
❑ 331 Kenny Lofton .20 .07
❑ 332 Geno Petralli .10 .02
❑ 333 Otis Nixon .10 .02
❑ 334 Jason Kendall RC 1.00 .40
❑ 335 Mark Portugal .10 .02
❑ 336 Mike Pagliarulo .10 .02
❑ 337 Kirt Manwaring .10 .02
❑ 338 Bob Ojeda .10 .02
❑ 339 Mark Clark .10 .02
❑ 340 John Kruk .20 .07
❑ 341 Mel Rojas .10 .02
❑ 342 Erik Hanson .10 .02
❑ 343 Doug Henry .10 .02
❑ 344 Jack McDowell .10 .02
❑ 345 Harold Baines .20 .07
❑ 346 Chuck McElroy .10 .02
❑ 347 Luis Sojo .10 .02
❑ 348 Andy Stankiewicz .10 .02
❑ 349 Hipolito Pichardo .10 .02
❑ 350 Joe Carter .20 .07
❑ 351 Ellis Burks .20 .07
❑ 352 Pete Schourek .10 .02
❑ 353 Buddy Groom .10 .02
❑ 354 Jay Bell .20 .07
❑ 355 Brady Anderson .20 .07
❑ 356 Freddie Benavides .10 .02
❑ 357 Phil Stephenson .10 .02
❑ 358 Kevin Wickander .10 .02
❑ 359 Mike Stanley .10 .02
❑ 360 Ivan Rodriguez .30 .10
❑ 361 Scott Bankhead .10 .02
❑ 362 Luis Gonzalez .20 .07
❑ 363 John Smiley .10 .02
❑ 364 Trevor Wilson .10 .02
❑ 365 Tom Candiotti .10 .02
❑ 366 Craig Wilson .10 .02
❑ 367 Steve Sax .10 .02
❑ 368 Delino DeShields .10 .02
❑ 369 Jaime Navarro .10 .02
❑ 370 Dave Valle .10 .02
❑ 371 Mariano Duncan .10 .02
❑ 372 Rod Nichols .10 .02
❑ 373 Mike Morgan .10 .02
❑ 374 Julio Valera .10 .02
❑ 375 Wally Joyner .20 .07
❑ 376 Tom Henke .10 .02
❑ 377 Herm Winningham .10 .02
❑ 378 Orlando Merced .10 .02
❑ 379 Mike Munoz .10 .02
❑ 380 Todd Hundley .10 .02
❑ 381 Mike Flanagan .10 .02
❑ 382 Tim Belcher .10 .02
❑ 383 Jerry Browne .10 .02
❑ 384 Mike Benjamin .10 .02
❑ 385 Jim Leyritz .10 .02
❑ 386 Ray Lankford .20 .07
❑ 387 Devon White .20 .07
❑ 388 Jeremy Hernandez .10 .02
❑ 389 Brian Harper .10 .02
❑ 390 Wade Boggs .30 .10
❑ 391 Derrick May .10 .02
❑ 392 Travis Fryman .20 .07
❑ 393 Ron Gant .20 .07
❑ 394 Checklist 1-132 .10 .02
❑ 395 Checklist 133-264 UER .10 .02
❑ 396 Checklist 265-396 .10 .02
❑ 397 George Brett 1.25 .50
❑ 398 Bobby Witt .10 .02
❑ 399 Daryl Boston .10 .02
❑ 400 Bo Jackson .50 .20
❑ 401 F.McGriff/F.Thomas AS .30 .10
❑ 402 R.Sandberg/C.Baerga AS .50 .20
❑ 403 G.Sheffield/E.Martinez AS .20 .07
❑ 404 B.Larkin/T.Fryman AS .20 .07
❑ 405 K.Griffey Jr./A.Van Slyke AS .50 .20
❑ 406 L.Walker/K.Puckett AS .30 .10
❑ 407 B.Bonds/J.Carter AS .75 .30
❑ 408 D.Daulton/B.Harper AS .20 .07
❑ 409 G.Maddux/R.Clemens AS .50 .20
❑ 410 T.Glavine/D.Fleming AS .20 .07
❑ 411 L.Smith/D.Eckersley AS .20 .07
❑ 412 Jamie McAndrew .10 .02
❑ 413 Pete Smith .10 .02
❑ 414 Juan Guerrero .10 .02
❑ 415 Todd Frohwirth .10 .02
❑ 416 Randy Tomlin .10 .02
❑ 417 B.J. Surhoff .20 .07
❑ 418 Jim Gott .10 .02
❑ 419 Mark Thompson RC .10 .02
❑ 420 Kevin Tapani .10 .02
❑ 421 Curt Schilling .20 .07
❑ 422 J.T.Snow RC .50 .20
❑ 423 Ryan Klesko .20 .07
❑ 424 John Valentin .10 .02
❑ 425 Joe Girardi .10 .02
❑ 426 Nigel Wilson .10 .02
❑ 427 Bob MacDonald .10 .02
❑ 428 Todd Zeile .10 .02
❑ 429 Milt Cuyler .10 .02
❑ 430 Eddie Murray .50 .20
❑ 431 Rich Amaral .10 .02
❑ 432 Pete Young .10 .02
❑ 433 Tom Schmidt RC .10 .02
❑ 434 Jack Armstrong .10 .02
❑ 435 Willie McGee .20 .07
❑ 436 Greg W. Harris .10 .02
❑ 437 Chris Hammond .10 .02
❑ 438 Ritchie Moody RC .10 .02
❑ 439 Bryan Harvey .10 .02
❑ 440 Ruben Sierra .20 .07
❑ 441 Todd Pridy RC .10 .02
❑ 442 Kevin McReynolds .10 .02
❑ 443 Terry Leach .10 .02
❑ 444 David Nied .10 .02
❑ 445 Dale Murphy .30 .10
❑ 446 Luis Mercedes .10 .02
❑ 447 Keith Shepherd RC .10 .02
❑ 448 Ken Caminiti .20 .07
❑ 449 Jim Austin .10 .02
❑ 450 Darryl Strawberry .20 .07
❑ 451 Quinton McCracken RC .25 .08
❑ 452 Bob Wickman .10 .02
❑ 453 Victor Cole .10 .02
❑ 454 John Johnstone RC .10 .02
❑ 455 Chili Davis .20 .07
❑ 456 Scott Taylor .10 .02
❑ 457 Tracy Woodson .10 .02
❑ 458 David Wells .20 .07
❑ 459 Derek Wallace RC .10 .02
❑ 460 Randy Johnson .50 .20
❑ 461 Steve Reed RC .10 .02
❑ 462 Felix Fermin .10 .02
❑ 463 Scott Aldred .10 .02
❑ 464 Greg Colbrunn .10 .02
❑ 465 Tony Fernandez .10 .02
❑ 466 Mike Felder .10 .02
❑ 467 Lee Stevens .10 .02
❑ 468 Matt Whiteside RC .10 .02
❑ 469 Dave Hansen .10 .02
❑ 470 Rob Dibble .20 .07
❑ 471 Dave Gallagher .10 .02
❑ 472 Chris Gwynn .10 .02
❑ 473 Dave Henderson .10 .02
❑ 474 Ozzie Guillen .20 .07
❑ 475 Jeff Reardon .20 .07
❑ 476 Will Scalzitti RC .10 .02
❑ 477 Jimmy Jones .10 .02
❑ 478 Greg Cadaret .10 .02
❑ 479 Todd Pratt RC .10 .02
❑ 480 Pat Listach .10 .02

❑ 481 Ryan Luzinski RC	.10	.02
❑ 482 Darren Reed	.10	.02
❑ 483 Brian Griffiths RC	.10	.02
❑ 484 John Wehner	.10	.02
❑ 485 Glenn Davis	.10	.02
❑ 486 Eric Wedge RC	.10	.02
❑ 487 Jesse Hollins	.10	.02
❑ 488 Manuel Lee	.10	.02
❑ 489 Scott Fredrickson RC	.10	.02
❑ 490 Omar Olivares	.10	.02
❑ 491 Shawn Hare	.10	.02
❑ 492 Tom Lampkin	.10	.02
❑ 493 Jeff Nelson	.10	.02
❑ 494 L.Lucca RC/E.Perez	.10	.02
❑ 495 Ken Hill	.10	.02
❑ 496 Reggie Jefferson	.10	.02
❑ 497 Willie Brown RC	.10	.02
❑ 498 Bud Black	.10	.02
❑ 499 Chuck Crim	.10	.02
❑ 500 Jose Canseco	.30	.10
❑ 501 Johnny Oates MG		
Bobby Cox MG	.20	.07
❑ 502 Butch Hobson MG		
Jim Lefebvre MG	.10	.02
❑ 503 Buck Rodgers MG		
Tony Perez MG	.20	.07
❑ 504 Gene Lamont MG		
Don Baylor MG	.20	.07
❑ 505 Mike Hargrove MG		
Rene Lachemann MG	.20	.07
❑ 506 Sparky Anderson MG		
Art Howe MG	.20	.07
❑ 507 Hal McRae MG		
Tom Lasorda MG	.20	.07
❑ 508 Phil Garner MG		
Felipe Alou MG	.20	.07
❑ 509 Tom Kelly MG		
Jeff Torborg MG	.10	.02
❑ 510 Buck Showalter MG		
Jim Fregosi MG	.20	.07
❑ 511 Tony LaRussa MG		
Jim Leyland MG	.20	.07
❑ 512 Lou Piniella MG		
Joe Torre MG	.20	.07
❑ 513 Kevin Kennedy MG		
Jim Riggleman MG	.10	.02
❑ 514 Cito Gaston MG		
Dusty Baker MG	.20	.07
❑ 515 Greg Swindell	.10	.02
❑ 516 Alex Arias	.10	.02
❑ 517 Bill Pecota	.10	.02
❑ 518 Benji Grigsby RC	.10	.02
❑ 519 David Howard	.10	.02
❑ 520 Charlie Hough	.20	.07
❑ 521 Kevin Flora	.10	.02
❑ 522 Shane Reynolds	.10	.02
❑ 523 Doug Bochtler RC	.10	.02
❑ 524 Chris Hoiles	.10	.02
❑ 525 Scott Sanderson	.10	.02
❑ 526 Mike Sharperson	.10	.02
❑ 527 Mike Fetters	.10	.02
❑ 528 Paul Quantrill	.10	.02
❑ 529 Chipper Jones	.50	.20
❑ 530 Sterling Hitchcock RC	.25	.08
❑ 531 Joe Millette	.10	.02
❑ 532 Tom Brunansky	.10	.02
❑ 533 Frank Castillo	.10	.02
❑ 534 Randy Knorr	.10	.02
❑ 535 Jose Oquendo	.10	.02
❑ 536 Dave Haas	.10	.02
❑ 537 Jason Hutchins RC	.10	.02
❑ 538 Jimmy Baron RC	.10	.02
❑ 539 Kerry Woodson	.10	.02
❑ 540 Ivan Calderon	.10	.02
❑ 541 Denis Boucher	.10	.02
❑ 542 Royce Clayton	.10	.02
❑ 543 Reggie Williams	.10	.02
❑ 544 Steve Decker	.10	.02
❑ 545 Dean Palmer	.20	.07
❑ 546 Hal Morris	.10	.02
❑ 547 Ryan Thompson	.10	.02
❑ 548 Lance Blankenship	.10	.02
❑ 549 Hensley Meulens	.10	.02
❑ 550 Scott Radinsky	.10	.02
❑ 551 Eric Young	.10	.02
❑ 552 Jeff Blauser	.10	.02

❑ 553 Andujar Cedeno	.10	.02
❑ 554 Arthur Rhodes	.10	.02
❑ 555 Terry Mulholland	.10	.02
❑ 556 Darryl Hamilton	.10	.02
❑ 557 Pedro Martinez	1.00	.40
❑ 558 Ryan Whitman RC	.10	.02
❑ 559 Jamie Arnold RC	.10	.02
❑ 560 Zane Smith	.10	.02
❑ 561 Matt Nokes	.10	.02
❑ 562 Bob Zupcic	.10	.02
❑ 563 Shawn Boskie	.10	.02
❑ 564 Mike Timlin	.10	.02
❑ 565 Jerald Clark	.10	.02
❑ 566 Rod Brewer	.10	.02
❑ 567 Mark Carreon	.10	.02
❑ 568 Andy Benes	.10	.02
❑ 569 Shawn Barton RC	.10	.02
❑ 570 Tim Wallach	.10	.02
❑ 571 Dave Mlicki	.10	.02
❑ 572 Trevor Hoffman	.50	.20
❑ 573 John Patterson	.10	.02
❑ 574 DeShawn Warren RC	.10	.02
❑ 575 Monty Fariss	.10	.02
❑ 576 Cliff Floyd	.20	.07
❑ 577 Tim Costo	.10	.02
❑ 578 Dave Magadan	.10	.02
❑ 579 Jason Bates RC	.10	.02
❑ 580 Walt Weiss	.10	.02
❑ 581 Chris Haney	.10	.02
❑ 582 Shawn Abner	.10	.02
❑ 583 Marvin Freeman	.10	.02
❑ 584 Casey Candaele	.10	.02
❑ 585 Ricky Jordan	.10	.02
❑ 586 Jeff Tabaka RC	.10	.02
❑ 587 Manny Alexander	.10	.02
❑ 588 Mike Trombley	.10	.02
❑ 589 Carlos Hernandez	.10	.02
❑ 590 Cal Eldred	.10	.02
❑ 591 Alex Cole	.10	.02
❑ 592 Phil Plantier	.10	.02
❑ 593 Brett Merriman RC	.10	.02
❑ 594 Jerry Nielsen	.10	.02
❑ 595 Shawon Dunston	.10	.02
❑ 596 Jimmy Key	.20	.07
❑ 597 Gerald Perry	.10	.02
❑ 598 Rico Brogna	.10	.02
❑ 599 Clemente Nunez	.10	.02
❑ 600 Bret Saberhagen	.20	.07
❑ 601 Craig Shipley	.10	.02
❑ 602 Henry Mercedes	.10	.02
❑ 603 Jim Thome	.30	.10
❑ 604 Rod Beck	.10	.02
❑ 605 Chuck Finley	.20	.07
❑ 606 Jayhawk Owens RC	.10	.02
❑ 607 Dan Smith	.10	.02
❑ 608 Bill Doran	.10	.02
❑ 609 Lance Parrish	.20	.07
❑ 610 Dennis Martinez	.20	.07
❑ 611 Tom Gordon	.10	.02
❑ 612 Byron Mathews RC	.10	.02
❑ 613 Joel Adamson RC	.10	.02
❑ 614 Brian Williams	.10	.02
❑ 615 Steve Avery	.10	.02
❑ 616 Midre Cummings RC	.10	.02
❑ 617 Craig Lefferts	.10	.02
❑ 618 Tony Pena	.10	.02
❑ 619 Billy Spiers	.10	.02
❑ 620 Todd Benzinger	.10	.02
❑ 621 Greg Boyd RC	.10	.02
❑ 622 Ben Rivera	.10	.02
❑ 623 Al Martin	.10	.02
❑ 624 Sam Militello UER	.10	.02
❑ 625 Rick Aguilera	.10	.02
❑ 626 Dan Gladden	.10	.02
❑ 627 Andres Berumen RC	.10	.02
❑ 628 Kelly Gruber	.10	.02
❑ 629 Cris Carpenter	.10	.02
❑ 630 Mark Grace	.30	.10
❑ 631 Jeff Brantley	.10	.02
❑ 632 Chris Widger RC	.25	.08
❑ 633 Three Russians	.10	.02
❑ 634 Mo Sanford	.10	.02
❑ 635 Albert Belle	.20	.07
❑ 636 Tim Teufel	.10	.02
❑ 637 Greg Myers	.10	.02
❑ 638 Brian Bohanon	.10	.02

❑ 639 Mike Bordick	.10	.02
❑ 640 Dwight Gooden	.20	.07
❑ 641 P.Leahy/G.Baugh RC	.10	.02
❑ 642 Milt Hill	.10	.02
❑ 643 Luis Aquino	.10	.02
❑ 644 Dante Bichette	.20	.07
❑ 645 Bobby Thigpen	.10	.02
❑ 646 Rich Scheid RC	.10	.02
❑ 647 Brian Sackinsky RC	.10	.02
❑ 648 Ryan Hawblitzel	.10	.02
❑ 649 Tom Marsh	.10	.02
❑ 650 Terry Pendleton	.20	.07
❑ 651 Rafael Bournigal	.10	.02
❑ 652 Dave West	.10	.02
❑ 653 Steve Hosey	.10	.02
❑ 654 Gerald Williams	.10	.02
❑ 655 Scott Cooper	.10	.02
❑ 656 Gary Scott	.10	.02
❑ 657 Mike Harkey	.10	.02
❑ 658 J.Burnitz/S.Walker RC	.20	.07
❑ 659 Ed Sprague	.10	.02
❑ 660 Alan Trammell	.20	.07
❑ 661 Garvin Alston RC	.10	.02
❑ 662 Donovan Osborne	.10	.02
❑ 663 Jeff Gardner	.10	.02
❑ 664 Calvin Jones	.10	.02
❑ 665 Darrin Fletcher	.10	.02
❑ 666 Glenallen Hill	.10	.02
❑ 667 Jim Rosenbohm RC	.10	.02
❑ 668 Scott Lewis	.10	.02
❑ 669 Kip Yaughn RC	.10	.02
❑ 670 Julio Franco	.20	.07
❑ 671 Dave Martinez	.10	.02
❑ 672 Kevin Bass	.10	.02
❑ 673 Todd Van Poppel	.10	.02
❑ 674 Mark Gubicza	.10	.02
❑ 675 Tim Raines	.20	.07
❑ 676 Rudy Seanez	.10	.02
❑ 677 Charlie Leibrandt	.10	.02
❑ 678 Randy Milligan	.10	.02
❑ 679 Kim Batiste	.10	.02
❑ 680 Craig Biggio	.30	.10
❑ 681 Darren Holmes	.10	.02
❑ 682 John Candelaria	.10	.02
❑ 683 Eddie Christian RC	.10	.02
❑ 684 Pat Mahomes	.10	.02
❑ 685 Bob Walk	.10	.02
❑ 686 Russ Springer	.10	.02
❑ 687 Tony Sheffield RC	.10	.02
❑ 688 Dwight Smith	.10	.02
❑ 689 Eddie Zosky	.10	.02
❑ 690 Bien Figueroa	.10	.02
❑ 691 Jim Tatum RC	.10	.02
❑ 692 Chad Kreuter	.10	.02
❑ 693 Rich Rodriguez	.10	.02
❑ 694 Shane Turner	.10	.02
❑ 695 Kent Bottenfield	.10	.02
❑ 696 Jose Mesa	.10	.02
❑ 697 Darrell Whitmore RC	.10	.02
❑ 698 Ted Wood	.10	.02
❑ 699 Chad Curtis	.10	.02
❑ 700 Nolan Ryan	2.00	.75
❑ 701 M.Piazza/C.Delgado	3.00	1.25
❑ 702 Tim Pugh RC	.10	.02
❑ 703 Jeff Kent	.50	.20
❑ 704 J.Goodrich/D.Figueroa RC	.10	.02
❑ 705 Bob Welch	.10	.02
❑ 706 Sherard Clinkscales RC	.10	.02
❑ 707 Donn Pall	.10	.02
❑ 708 Greg Olson	.10	.02
❑ 709 Jeff Juden	.10	.02
❑ 710 Mike Mussina	.30	.10
❑ 711 Scott Chiamparino	.10	.02
❑ 712 Stan Javier	.10	.02
❑ 713 John Doherty	.10	.02
❑ 714 Kevin Gross	.10	.02
❑ 715 Greg Gagne	.10	.02
❑ 716 Steve Cooke	.10	.02
❑ 717 Steve Farr	.10	.02
❑ 718 Jay Buhner	.20	.07
❑ 719 Butch Henry	.10	.02
❑ 720 David Cone	.20	.07
❑ 721 Rick Wilkins	.10	.02
❑ 722 Chuck Carr	.10	.02
❑ 723 Kenny Felder RC	.10	.02
❑ 724 Guillermo Velasquez	.10	.02

- ❑ 725 Billy Hatcher .10 .02
- ❑ 726 Mike Veneziale RC .10 .02
- ❑ 727 Jonathan Hurst .10 .02
- ❑ 728 Steve Frey .10 .02
- ❑ 729 Mark Leonard .10 .02
- ❑ 730 Charles Nagy .10 .02
- ❑ 731 Donald Harris .10 .02
- ❑ 732 Travis Buckley RC .10 .02
- ❑ 733 Tom Browning .10 .02
- ❑ 734 Anthony Young .10 .02
- ❑ 735 Steve Shifflett .10 .02
- ❑ 736 Jeff Russell .10 .02
- ❑ 737 Wilson Alvarez .10 .02
- ❑ 738 Lance Painter RC .10 .02
- ❑ 739 Dave Weathers .10 .02
- ❑ 740 Len Dykstra .20 .07
- ❑ 741 Mike Devereaux .10 .02
- ❑ 742 R.Arocha RC/A.Embree .25 .08
- ❑ 743 Dave Landaker RC .10 .02
- ❑ 744 Chris George .10 .02
- ❑ 745 Eric Davis .20 .07
- ❑ 746 Lamar Rogers RC .10 .02
- ❑ 747 Carl Willis .10 .02
- ❑ 748 Stan Belinda .10 .02
- ❑ 749 Scott Kamieniecki .10 .02
- ❑ 750 Rickey Henderson .50 .20
- ❑ 751 Eric Hillman .10 .02
- ❑ 752 Pat Hentgen .10 .02
- ❑ 753 Jim Corsi .10 .02
- ❑ 754 Brian Jordan .20 .07
- ❑ 755 Bill Swift .10 .02
- ❑ 756 Mike Henneman .10 .02
- ❑ 757 Harold Reynolds .20 .07
- ❑ 758 Sean Berry .10 .02
- ❑ 759 Charlie Hayes .10 .02
- ❑ 760 Luis Polonia .10 .02
- ❑ 761 Darrin Jackson .10 .02
- ❑ 762 Mark Lewis .10 .02
- ❑ 763 Rob Maurer .10 .02
- ❑ 764 Willie Greene .10 .02
- ❑ 765 Vince Coleman .10 .02
- ❑ 766 Todd Revenig .10 .02
- ❑ 767 Rich Ireland RC .10 .02
- ❑ 768 Mike Macfarlane .10 .02
- ❑ 769 Francisco Cabrera .10 .02
- ❑ 770 Robin Ventura .20 .07
- ❑ 771 Kevin Ritz .10 .02
- ❑ 772 Chito Martinez .10 .02
- ❑ 773 Cliff Brantley .10 .02
- ❑ 774 Curt Leskanic RC .25 .08
- ❑ 775 Chris Bosio .10 .02
- ❑ 776 Jose Offerman .10 .02
- ❑ 777 Mark Guthrie .10 .02
- ❑ 778 Don Slaught .10 .02
- ❑ 779 Rich Monteleone .10 .02
- ❑ 780 Jim Abbott .30 .10
- ❑ 781 Jack Clark .20 .07
- ❑ 782 R.Mendoza/D.Roman RC .10 .02
- ❑ 783 Heathcliff Slocumb .10 .02
- ❑ 784 Jeff Branson .10 .02
- ❑ 785 Kevin Brown .20 .07
- ❑ 786 K.Ryan/Gandarillas RC .10 .02
- ❑ 787 Mike Matthews RC .10 .02
- ❑ 788 Mackey Sasser .10 .02
- ❑ 789 Jeff Conine UER .20 .07
- ❑ 790 George Bell .10 .02
- ❑ 791 Pat Rapp .10 .02
- ❑ 792 Joe Boever .10 .02
- ❑ 793 Jim Poole .10 .02
- ❑ 794 Andy Ashby .10 .02
- ❑ 795 Deion Sanders .30 .10
- ❑ 796 Scott Brosius .20 .07
- ❑ 797 Brad Pennington .10 .02
- ❑ 798 Greg Blosser .10 .02
- ❑ 799 Jim Edmonds RC 2.00 .75
- ❑ 800 Shawn Jeter .10 .02
- ❑ 801 Jesse Levis .10 .02
- ❑ 802 Phil Clark UER .10 .02
- ❑ 803 Eddie Pierce RC .10 .02
- ❑ 804 Jose Valentin RC .25 .08
- ❑ 805 Terry Jorgensen .10 .02
- ❑ 806 Mark Hutton .10 .02
- ❑ 807 Troy Neel .10 .02
- ❑ 808 Bret Boone .20 .07
- ❑ 809 Cris Colon .10 .02
- ❑ 810 Domingo Martinez RC .10 .02
- ❑ 811 Javier Lopez .30 .10
- ❑ 812 Matt Walbeck RC .10 .02
- ❑ 813 Dan Wilson .20 .07
- ❑ 814 Scooter Tucker .10 .02
- ❑ 815 Billy Ashley .10 .02
- ❑ 816 Tim Laker RC .10 .02
- ❑ 817 Bobby Jones .20 .07
- ❑ 818 Brad Brink .10 .02
- ❑ 819 William Pennyfeather .10 .02
- ❑ 820 Stan Royer .10 .02
- ❑ 821 Doug Brocail .10 .02
- ❑ 822 Kevin Rogers .10 .02
- ❑ 823 Checklist 397-540 .10 .02
- ❑ 824 Checklist 541-691 .10 .02
- ❑ 825 Checklist 692-825 .10 .02

1993 Topps Traded

- ❑ COMP.FACT.SET (132) 25.00 10.00
- ❑ 1T Barry Bonds 1.50 .60
- ❑ 2T Rich Renteria .10 .02
- ❑ 3T Aaron Sele .10 .02
- ❑ 4T Carlton Loewer USA RC .25 .08
- ❑ 5T Erik Pappas .10 .02
- ❑ 6T Greg McMichael RC .25 .08
- ❑ 7T Freddie Benavides .10 .02
- ❑ 8T Kirk Gibson .20 .07
- ❑ 9T Tony Fernandez .10 .02
- ❑ 10T Jay Gainer RC .25 .08
- ❑ 11T Orestes Destrade .10 .02
- ❑ 12T A.J. Hinch USA RC .50 .20
- ❑ 13T Bobby Munoz .10 .02
- ❑ 14T Tom Henke .10 .02
- ❑ 15T Rob Butler .10 .02
- ❑ 16T Gary Wayne .10 .02
- ❑ 17T David McCarty .10 .02
- ❑ 18T Walt Weiss .10 .02
- ❑ 19T Todd Helton USA RC 15.00 6.00
- ❑ 20T Mark Whiten .10 .02
- ❑ 21T Ricky Gutierrez .10 .02
- ❑ 22T Dustin Hermanson USA RC 1.00 .40
- ❑ 23T Sherman Obando RC .25 .08
- ❑ 24T Mike Piazza 3.00 1.25
- ❑ 25T Jeff Russell .10 .02
- ❑ 26T Jason Bere .10 .02
- ❑ 27T Jack Voigt RC .25 .08
- ❑ 28T Chris Bosio .10 .02
- ❑ 29T Phil Hiatt .10 .02
- ❑ 30T Matt Beaumont USA RC .25 .08
- ❑ 31T Andres Galarraga .20 .07
- ❑ 32T Greg Swindell .10 .02
- ❑ 33T Vinny Castilla .50 .20
- ❑ 34T Pat Clougherty RC USA .25 .08
- ❑ 35T Greg Briley .10 .02
- ❑ 36T Dallas Green MG
Davey Johnson MG .10 .02
- ❑ 37T Tyler Green .10 .02
- ❑ 38T Craig Paquette .10 .02
- ❑ 39T Danny Sheaffer RC .25 .08
- ❑ 40T Jim Converse RC .25 .08
- ❑ 41T Terry Harvey USA RC .25 .08
- ❑ 42T Phil Plantier .10 .02
- ❑ 43T Doug Saunders RC .25 .08
- ❑ 44T Benny Santiago .20 .07
- ❑ 45T Dante Powell USA RC .25 .08
- ❑ 46T Jeff Parrett .10 .02
- ❑ 47T Wade Boggs .30 .10
- ❑ 48T Paul Molitor .20 .07
- ❑ 49T Turk Wendell .10 .02
- ❑ 50T David Wells .20 .07
- ❑ 51T Gary Sheffield .20 .07
- ❑ 52T Kevin Young .20 .07
- ❑ 53T Nelson Liriano .10 .02
- ❑ 54T Greg Maddux .75 .30
- ❑ 55T Derek Bell .10 .02
- ❑ 56T Matt Turner RC .25 .08
- ❑ 57T Charlie Nelson USA RC .25 .08
- ❑ 58T Mike Hampton .20 .07
- ❑ 59T Troy O'Leary RC .50 .20
- ❑ 60T Benji Gil .10 .02
- ❑ 61T Mitch Lyden RC .25 .08
- ❑ 62T J.T.Snow .30 .10
- ❑ 63T Damon Buford .10 .02
- ❑ 64T Gene Harris .10 .02
- ❑ 65T Randy Myers .10 .02
- ❑ 66T Felix Jose .10 .02
- ❑ 67T Todd Dunn USA RC .25 .08
- ❑ 68T Jimmy Key .20 .07
- ❑ 69T Pedro Castellano .10 .02
- ❑ 70T Mark Merila USA RC .25 .08
- ❑ 71T Rich Rodriguez .10 .02
- ❑ 72T Matt Mieske .10 .02
- ❑ 73T Pete Incaviglia .10 .02
- ❑ 74T Carl Everett .20 .07
- ❑ 75T Jim Abbott .30 .10
- ❑ 76T Luis Aquino .10 .02
- ❑ 77T Rene Arocha .20 .07
- ❑ 78T Jon Shave .10 .02
- ❑ 79T Todd Walker USA RC 1.00 .40
- ❑ 80T Jack Armstrong .10 .02
- ❑ 81T Jeff Richardson .10 .02
- ❑ 82T Blas Minor .10 .02
- ❑ 83T Dave Winfield .20 .07
- ❑ 84T Paul O'Neill .30 .10
- ❑ 85T Steve Reich USA RC .25 .08
- ❑ 86T Chris Hammond .10 .02
- ❑ 87T Hilly Hathaway RC .25 .08
- ❑ 88T Fred McGriff .30 .10
- ❑ 89T Dave Telgheder RC .25 .08
- ❑ 90T Richie Lewis RC .25 .08
- ❑ 91T Brent Gates .10 .02
- ❑ 92T Andre Dawson .20 .07
- ❑ 93T Andy Barkett USA RC .25 .08
- ❑ 94T Doug Drabek .10 .02
- ❑ 95T Joe Klink .10 .02
- ❑ 96T Willie Blair .10 .02
- ❑ 97T Danny Graves USA RC .50 .20
- ❑ 98T Pat Meares RC .50 .20
- ❑ 99T Mike Lansing RC .50 .20
- ❑ 100T Marcos Armas RC .25 .08
- ❑ 101T Darren Grass USA RC .25 .08
- ❑ 102T Chris Jones .10 .02
- ❑ 103T Ken Ryan RC .25 .08
- ❑ 104T Ellis Burks .20 .07
- ❑ 105T Roberto Kelly .10 .02
- ❑ 106T Dave Magadan .10 .02
- ❑ 107T Paul Wilson USA RC .50 .20
- ❑ 108T Rob Natal .10 .02
- ❑ 109T Paul Wagner .10 .02
- ❑ 110T Jeromy Burnitz .20 .07
- ❑ 111T Monty Fariss .10 .02
- ❑ 112T Kevin Mitchell .10 .02
- ❑ 113T Scott Pose RC .25 .08
- ❑ 114T Dave Stewart .20 .07
- ❑ 115T Russ Johnson USA RC .25 .08
- ❑ 116T Armando Reynoso .10 .02
- ❑ 117T Geronimo Berroa .10 .02
- ❑ 118T Woody Williams RC 1.00 .40
- ❑ 119T Tim Bogar RC .25 .08
- ❑ 120T Bob Scafa USA RC .25 .08
- ❑ 121T Henry Cotto .10 .02
- ❑ 122T Gregg Jefferies .10 .02
- ❑ 123T Norm Charlton .10 .02
- ❑ 124T Bret Wagner USA RC .25 .08
- ❑ 125T David Cone .20 .07
- ❑ 126T Daryl Boston .10 .02
- ❑ 127T Tim Wallach .10 .02
- ❑ 128T Mike Martin USA RC .25 .08
- ❑ 129T John Cummings RC .25 .08
- ❑ 130T Ryan Bowen .10 .02
- ❑ 131T John Powell USA RC .25 .08
- ❑ 132T Checklist 1-132 .10 .02

1994 Topps

Card		
COMPLETE SET (792)	50.00	20.00
COMP.FACT.SET (808)	80.00	40.00
COMP.BAKER SET (818)	80.00	40.00
COMPLETE SERIES 1 (396)	25.00	10.00
COMPLETE SERIES 2 (396)	25.00	10.00
1 Mike Piazza	1.00	.40
2 Bernie Williams	.30	.10
3 Kevin Rogers	.10	.02
4 Paul Carey	.10	.02
5 Ozzie Guillen	.20	.07
6 Derrick May	.10	.02
7 Jose Mesa	.10	.02
8 Todd Hundley	.10	.02
9 Chris Haney	.10	.02
10 John Olerud	.20	.07
11 Andujar Cedeno	.10	.02
12 John Smiley	.10	.02
13 Phil Plantier	.10	.02
14 Willie Banks	.10	.02
15 Jay Bell	.20	.07
16 Doug Henry	.10	.02
17 Lance Blankenship	.10	.02
18 Greg W. Harris	.10	.02
19 Scott Livingstone	.10	.02
20 Bryan Harvey	.10	.02
21 Wil Cordero	.10	.02
22 Roger Pavlik	.10	.02
23 Mark Lemke	.10	.02
24 Jeff Nelson	.10	.02
25 Todd Zeile	.10	.02
26 Billy Hatcher	.10	.02
27 Joe Magrane	.10	.02
28 Tony Longmire	.10	.02
29 Omar Daal	.10	.02
30 Kirt Manwaring	.10	.02
31 Melido Perez	.10	.02
32 Tim Hulett	.10	.02
33 Jeff Schwarz	.10	.02
34 Nolan Ryan	2.00	.75
35 Jose Guzman	.10	.02
36 Felix Fermin	.10	.02
37 Jeff Innis	.10	.02
38 Brett Mayne	.10	.02
39 Huck Flener RC	.10	.02
40 Jeff Bagwell	.30	.10
41 Kevin Wickander	.10	.02
42 Ricky Gutierrez	.10	.02
43 Pat Mahomes	.10	.02
44 Jeff King	.10	.02
45 Cal Eldred	.10	.02
46 Craig Paquette	.10	.02
47 Richie Lewis	.10	.02
48 Tony Phillips	.10	.02
49 Armando Reynoso	.10	.02
50 Moises Alou	.20	.07
51 Manuel Lee	.10	.02
52 Otis Nixon	.10	.02
53 Billy Ashley	.10	.02
54 Mark Whiten	.10	.02
55 Jeff Russell	.10	.02
56 Chad Curtis	.10	.02
57 Kevin Stocker	.10	.02
58 Mike Jackson	.10	.02
59 Matt Nokes	.10	.02
60 Chris Bosio	.10	.02
61 Damon Buford	.10	.02
62 Tim Belcher	.10	.02
63 Glenallen Hill	.10	.02
64 Bill Wertz	.10	.02
65 Eddie Murray	.50	.20
66 Tom Gordon	.10	.02
67 Alex Gonzalez	.10	.02
68 Eddie Taubensee	.10	.02
69 Jacob Brumfield	.10	.02
70 Andy Benes	.10	.02
71 Rich Becker	.10	.02
72 Steve Cooke	.10	.02
73 Billy Spiers	.10	.02
74 Scott Brosius	.20	.07
75 Alan Trammell	.20	.07
76 Luis Aquino	.10	.02
77 Jerald Clark	.10	.02
78 Mel Rojas	.10	.02
79 Craig McClure RC	.10	.02
80 Jose Canseco	.30	.10
81 Greg McMichael	.10	.02
82 Brian Turang RC	.10	.02
83 Tom Urbani	.10	.02
84 Garret Anderson	.50	.20
85 Tony Pena	.10	.02
86 Ricky Jordan	.10	.02
87 Jim Gott	.10	.02
88 Pat Kelly	.10	.02
89 Bud Black	.10	.02
90 Robin Ventura	.20	.07
91 Rick Sutcliffe	.20	.07
92 Jose Bautista	.10	.02
93 Bob Ojeda	.10	.02
94 Phil Hiatt	.10	.02
95 Tim Pugh	.10	.02
96 Randy Knorr	.10	.02
97 Todd Jones	.10	.02
98 Ryan Thompson	.10	.02
99 Tim Mauser	.10	.02
100 Kirby Puckett	.50	.20
101 Mark Dewey	.10	.02
102 B.J. Surhoff	.20	.07
103 Sterling Hitchcock	.10	.02
104 Alex Arias	.10	.02
105 David Wells	.20	.07
106 Daryl Boston	.10	.02
107 Mike Stanton	.10	.02
108 Gary Redus	.10	.02
109 Delino DeShields	.10	.02
110 Lee Smith	.20	.07
111 Greg Litton	.10	.02
112 Frankie Rodriguez	.10	.02
113 Russ Springer	.10	.02
114 Mitch Williams	.10	.02
115 Eric Karros	.20	.07
116 Jeff Brantley	.10	.02
117 Jack Voigt	.10	.02
118 Jason Bere	.10	.02
119 Kevin Roberson	.10	.02
120 Jimmy Key	.20	.07
121 Reggie Jefferson	.10	.02
122 Jeromy Burnitz	.20	.07
123 Billy Brewer	.10	.02
124 Willie Canate	.10	.02
125 Greg Swindell	.10	.02
126 Hal Morris	.10	.02
127 Brad Ausmus	.30	.10
128 George Tsamis	.10	.02
129 Denny Neagle	.20	.07
130 Pat Listach	.10	.02
131 Steve Karsay	.10	.02
132 Bret Barberie	.10	.02
133 Mark Leiter	.10	.02
134 Greg Colbrunn	.10	.02
135 David Nied	.10	.02
136 Dean Palmer	.20	.07
137 Steve Avery	.10	.02
138 Bill Haselman	.10	.02
139 Tripp Cromer	.10	.02
140 Frank Viola	.20	.07
141 Rene Gonzales	.10	.02
142 Curt Schilling	.20	.07
143 Tim Wallach	.10	.02
144 Bobby Munoz	.10	.02
145 Brady Anderson	.20	.07
146 Rod Beck	.10	.02
147 Mike LaValliere	.10	.02
148 Greg Hibbard	.10	.02
149 Kenny Lofton	.20	.07
150 Dwight Gooden	.20	.07
151 Greg Gagne	.10	.02
152 Ray McDavid	.10	.02
153 Chris Donnels	.10	.02
154 Dan Wilson	.10	.02
155 Todd Stottlemyre	.10	.02
156 David McCarty	.10	.02
157 Paul Wagner	.10	.02
158 Derek Jeter	1.50	.60
159 Mike Fetters	.10	.02
160 Scott Lydy	.10	.02
161 Darrell Whitmore	.10	.02
162 Bob MacDonald	.10	.02
163 Vinny Castilla	.20	.07
164 Denis Boucher	.10	.02
165 Ivan Rodriguez	.30	.10
166 Ron Gant	.20	.07
167 Tim Davis	.10	.02
168 Steve Dixon	.10	.02
169 Scott Fletcher	.10	.02
170 Terry Mulholland	.10	.02
171 Greg Myers	.10	.02
172 Brett Butler	.20	.07
173 Bob Wickman	.10	.02
174 Dave Martinez	.10	.02
175 Fernando Valenzuela	.20	.07
176 Craig Grebeck	.10	.02
177 Shawn Boskie	.10	.02
178 Albie Lopez	.10	.02
179 Butch Huskey	.10	.02
180 George Brett	1.25	.50
181 Juan Guzman	.10	.02
182 Eric Anthony	.10	.02
183 Rob Dibble	.20	.07
184 Craig Shipley	.10	.02
185 Kevin Tapani	.10	.02
186 Marcus Moore	.10	.02
187 Graeme Lloyd	.10	.02
188 Mike Bordick	.10	.02
189 Chris Hammond	.10	.02
190 Cecil Fielder	.20	.07
191 Curt Leskanic	.10	.02
192 Lou Frazier	.10	.02
193 Steve Dreyer RC	.10	.02
194 Javier Lopez	.20	.07
195 Edgar Martinez	.30	.10
196 Allen Watson	.10	.02
197 John Flaherty	.10	.02
198 Kurt Stillwell	.10	.02
199 Danny Jackson	.10	.02
200 Cal Ripken	1.50	.60
201 Mike Bell RC	.10	.02
202 Alan Benes RC	.25	.08
203 Matt Farner RC	.10	.02
204 Jeff Granger	.10	.02
205 Brooks Kieschnick RC	.10	.02
206 Jeremy Lee RC	.10	.02
207 Charles Peterson RC	.10	.02
208 Andy Rice RC	.10	.02
209 Billy Wagner RC	1.50	.60
210 Kelly Wunsch RC	.25	.08
211 Tom Candiotti	.10	.02
212 Domingo Jean	.10	.02
213 John Burkett	.10	.02
214 George Bell	.10	.02
215 Dan Plesac	.10	.02
216 Manny Ramirez	.50	.20
217 Mike Maddux	.10	.02
218 Kevin McReynolds	.10	.02
219 Pat Borders	.10	.02
220 Doug Drabek	.10	.02
221 Larry Luebbers RC	.10	.02
222 Trevor Hoffman	.30	.10
223 Pat Meares	.10	.02
224 Danny Miceli	.10	.02
225 Greg Vaughn	.10	.02
226 Scott Hemond	.10	.02
227 Pat Rapp	.10	.02
228 Kirk Gibson	.20	.07
229 Lance Painter	.10	.02
230 Larry Walker	.20	.07
231 Benji Gil	.10	.02
232 Mark Wohlers	.10	.02
233 Rich Amaral	.10	.02

	No.	Player		
❑	234	Eric Pappas	.10	.02
❑	235	Scott Cooper	.10	.02
❑	236	Mike Butcher	.10	.02
❑	237	Pride RC/Green/Sweeney RC	.50	.20
❑	238	Kim Batiste	.10	.02
❑	239	Paul Assenmacher	.10	.02
❑	240	Will Clark	.30	.10
❑	241	Jose Offerman	.10	.02
❑	242	Todd Frohwirth	.10	.02
❑	243	Tim Raines	.20	.07
❑	244	Rick Wilkins	.10	.02
❑	245	Bret Saberhagen	.20	.07
❑	246	Thomas Howard	.10	.02
❑	247	Stan Belinda	.10	.02
❑	248	Rickey Henderson	.50	.20
❑	249	Brian Williams	.10	.02
❑	250	Barry Larkin	.30	.10
❑	251	Jose Valentin	.10	.02
❑	252	Lenny Webster	.10	.02
❑	253	Blas Minor	.10	.02
❑	254	Tim Teufel	.10	.02
❑	255	Bobby Witt	.10	.02
❑	256	Walt Weiss	.10	.02
❑	257	Chad Kreuter	.10	.02
❑	258	Roberto Mejia	.10	.02
❑	259	Cliff Floyd	.20	.07
❑	260	Julio Franco	.20	.07
❑	261	Rafael Belliard	.10	.02
❑	262	Marc Newfield	.10	.02
❑	263	Gerald Perry	.10	.02
❑	264	Ken Ryan	.10	.02
❑	265	Chili Davis	.20	.07
❑	266	Dave West	.10	.02
❑	267	Royce Clayton	.10	.02
❑	268	Pedro Martinez	.50	.20
❑	269	Mark Hutton	.10	.02
❑	270	Frank Thomas	.50	.20
❑	271	Brad Pennington	.10	.02
❑	272	Mike Harkey	.10	.02
❑	273	Sandy Alomar Jr.	.10	.02
❑	274	Dave Gallagher	.10	.02
❑	275	Wally Joyner	.20	.07
❑	276	Ricky Trlicek	.10	.02
❑	277	Al Osuna	.10	.02
❑	278	Pokey Reese	.10	.02
❑	279	Kevin Higgins	.10	.02
❑	280	Rick Aguilera	.10	.02
❑	281	Orlando Merced	.10	.02
❑	282	Mike Mohler	.10	.02
❑	283	John Jaha	.10	.02
❑	284	Robb Nen	.20	.07
❑	285	Travis Fryman	.20	.07
❑	286	Mark Thompson	.10	.02
❑	287	Mike Lansing	.10	.02
❑	288	Craig Lefferts	.10	.02
❑	289	Damon Berryhill	.10	.02
❑	290	Randy Johnson	.50	.20
❑	291	Jeff Reed	.10	.02
❑	292	Danny Darwin	.10	.02
❑	293	J.T.Snow	.20	.07
❑	294	Tyler Green	.10	.02
❑	295	Chris Hoiles	.10	.02
❑	296	Roger McDowell	.10	.02
❑	297	Spike Owen	.10	.02
❑	298	Salomon Torres	.10	.02
❑	299	Wilson Alvarez	.10	.02
❑	300	Ryne Sandberg	.75	.30
❑	301	Derek Lilliquist	.10	.02
❑	302	Howard Johnson	.10	.02
❑	303	Greg Cadaret	.10	.02
❑	304	Pat Hentgen	.10	.02
❑	305	Craig Biggio	.30	.10
❑	306	Scott Service	.10	.02
❑	307	Melvin Nieves	.10	.02
❑	308	Mike Trombley	.10	.02
❑	309	Carlos Garcia	.10	.02
❑	310	Robin Yount	.75	.30
❑	311	Marcos Armas	.10	.02
❑	312	Rich Rodriguez	.10	.02
❑	313	Justin Thompson	.10	.02
❑	314	Danny Sheaffer	.10	.02
❑	315	Ken Hill	.10	.02
❑	316	Terrell Wade RC	.10	.02
❑	317	Cris Carpenter	.10	.02
❑	318	Jeff Blauser	.10	.02
❑	319	Ted Power	.10	.02
❑	320	Ozzie Smith	.75	.30
❑	321	John Dopson	.10	.02
❑	322	Chris Turner	.10	.02
❑	323	Pete Incaviglia	.10	.02
❑	324	Alan Mills	.10	.02
❑	325	Jody Reed	.10	.02
❑	326	Rich Monteleone	.10	.02
❑	327	Mark Carreon	.10	.02
❑	328	Donn Pall	.10	.02
❑	329	Matt Walbeck	.10	.02
❑	330	Charley Nagy	.10	.02
❑	331	Jeff McKnight	.10	.02
❑	332	Jose Lind	.10	.02
❑	333	Mike Timlin	.10	.02
❑	334	Doug Jones	.10	.02
❑	335	Kevin Mitchell	.10	.02
❑	336	Luis Lopez	.10	.02
❑	337	Shane Mack	.10	.02
❑	338	Randy Tomlin	.10	.02
❑	339	Matt Mieske	.10	.02
❑	340	Mark McGwire	1.25	.50
❑	341	Nigel Wilson	.10	.02
❑	342	Danny Gladden	.10	.02
❑	343	Mo Sanford	.10	.02
❑	344	Sean Berry	.10	.02
❑	345	Kevin Brown	.20	.07
❑	346	Greg Olson	.10	.02
❑	347	Dave Magadan	.10	.02
❑	348	Rene Arocha	.10	.02
❑	349	Carlos Quintana	.10	.02
❑	350	Jim Abbott	.30	.10
❑	351	Gary DiSarcina	.10	.02
❑	352	Ben Rivera	.10	.02
❑	353	Carlos Hernandez	.10	.02
❑	354	Darren Lewis	.10	.02
❑	355	Harold Reynolds	.20	.07
❑	356	Scott Ruffcorn	.10	.02
❑	357	Mark Gubicza	.10	.02
❑	358	Paul Sorrento	.10	.02
❑	359	Anthony Young	.10	.02
❑	360	Mark Grace	.30	.10
❑	361	Rob Butler	.10	.02
❑	362	Kevin Bass	.10	.02
❑	363	Eric Helfand	.10	.02
❑	364	Derek Bell	.10	.02
❑	365	Scott Erickson	.10	.02
❑	366	Al Martin	.10	.02
❑	367	Ricky Bones	.10	.02
❑	368	Jeff Branson	.10	.02
❑	369	J.Giambi/D.Bell RC	.50	.20
❑	370	Benito Santiago	.20	.07
❑	371	John Doherty	.10	.02
❑	372	Joe Girardi	.10	.02
❑	373	Tim Scott	.10	.02
❑	374	Marvin Freeman	.10	.02
❑	375	Deion Sanders	.30	.10
❑	376	Roger Salkeld	.10	.02
❑	377	Bernard Gilkey	.10	.02
❑	378	Tony Fossas	.10	.02
❑	379	Mark McLemore UER	.10	.02
❑	380	Darren Daulton	.20	.07
❑	381	Chuck Finley	.20	.07
❑	382	Mitch Webster	.10	.02
❑	383	Gerald Williams	.10	.02
❑	384	F.Thomas/F.McGriff AS	.30	.10
❑	385	R.Alomar/R.Thompson AS	.20	.07
❑	386	W.Boggs/M.Williams AS	.20	.07
❑	387	C.Ripken/J.Blauser AS	.50	.20
❑	388	K.Griffey/L.Dykstra AS	.50	.20
❑	389	J.Gonzalez/D.Justice AS	.20	.07
❑	390	A.Belle/B.Bonds AS	.75	.30
❑	391	M.Stanley/M.Piazza AS	.50	.20
❑	392	J.McDowell/G.Maddux AS	.30	.10
❑	393	J.Key/T.Glavine AS	.20	.07
❑	394	J.Montgomery/R.Myers AS	.10	.02
❑	395	Checklist 1-198	.10	.02
❑	396	Checklist 199-396	.10	.02
❑	397	Tim Salmon	.30	.10
❑	398	Todd Benzinger	.10	.02
❑	399	Frank Castillo	.10	.02
❑	400	Ken Griffey Jr.	.75	.30
❑	401	John Kruk	.20	.07
❑	402	Dave Telgheder	.10	.02
❑	403	Gary Gaetti	.20	.07
❑	404	Jim Edmonds	.50	.20
❑	405	Don Slaught	.10	.02
❑	406	Jose Oquendo	.10	.02
❑	407	Bruce Ruffin	.10	.02
❑	408	Phil Clark	.10	.02
❑	409	Joe Klink	.10	.02
❑	410	Lou Whitaker	.20	.07
❑	411	Kevin Seitzer	.10	.02
❑	412	Darrin Fletcher	.10	.02
❑	413	Kenny Rogers	.20	.07
❑	414	Bill Pecota	.10	.02
❑	415	Dave Fleming	.10	.02
❑	416	Luis Alicea	.10	.02
❑	417	Paul Quantrill	.10	.02
❑	418	Damion Easley	.10	.02
❑	419	Wes Chamberlain	.10	.02
❑	420	Harold Baines	.20	.07
❑	421	Scott Radinsky	.10	.02
❑	422	Rey Sanchez	.10	.02
❑	423	Junior Ortiz	.10	.02
❑	424	Jeff Kent	.30	.10
❑	425	Brian McRae	.10	.02
❑	426	Ed Sprague	.10	.02
❑	427	Tom Edens	.10	.02
❑	428	Willie Greene	.10	.02
❑	429	Bryan Hickerson	.10	.02
❑	430	Dave Winfield	.20	.07
❑	431	Pedro Astacio	.10	.02
❑	432	Mike Gallego	.10	.02
❑	433	Dave Burba	.10	.02
❑	434	Bob Walk	.10	.02
❑	435	Darryl Hamilton	.10	.02
❑	436	Vince Horsman	.10	.02
❑	437	Bob Natal	.10	.02
❑	438	Mike Henneman	.10	.02
❑	439	Willie Blair	.10	.02
❑	440	Dennis Martinez	.20	.07
❑	441	Dan Peltier	.10	.02
❑	442	Tony Tarasco	.10	.02
❑	443	John Cummings	.10	.02
❑	444	Geronimo Pena	.10	.02
❑	445	Aaron Sele	.10	.02
❑	446	Stan Javier	.10	.02
❑	447	Mike Williams	.10	.02
❑	448	D.J. Boston RC	.10	.02
❑	449	Jim Poole	.10	.02
❑	450	Carlos Baerga	.10	.02
❑	451	Bob Scanlan	.10	.02
❑	452	Lance Johnson	.10	.02
❑	453	Eric Hillman	.10	.02
❑	454	Keith Miller	.10	.02
❑	455	Dave Stewart	.20	.07
❑	456	Pete Harnisch	.10	.02
❑	457	Roberto Kelly	.10	.02
❑	458	Tim Worrell	.10	.02
❑	459	Pedro Munoz	.10	.02
❑	460	Orel Hershiser	.20	.07
❑	461	Randy Velarde	.10	.02
❑	462	Trevor Wilson	.10	.02
❑	463	Jerry Goff	.10	.02
❑	464	Bill Wegman	.10	.02
❑	465	Dennis Eckersley	.20	.07
❑	466	Jeff Conine	.20	.07
❑	467	Joe Boever	.10	.02
❑	468	Dante Bichette	.20	.07
❑	469	Jeff Shaw	.10	.02
❑	470	Rafael Palmeiro	.30	.10
❑	471	Phil Leftwich RC	.10	.02
❑	472	Jay Buhner	.20	.07
❑	473	Bob Tewksbury	.10	.02
❑	474	Tim Naehring	.10	.02
❑	475	Tom Glavine	.30	.10
❑	476	Dave Hollins	.10	.02
❑	477	Arthur Rhodes	.10	.02
❑	478	Joey Cora	.10	.02
❑	479	Mike Morgan	.10	.02
❑	480	Albert Belle	.20	.07
❑	481	John Franco	.20	.07
❑	482	Hipolito Pichardo	.10	.02
❑	483	Duane Ward	.10	.02
❑	484	Luis Gonzalez	.20	.07
❑	485	Joe Oliver	.10	.02
❑	486	Wally Whitehurst	.10	.02
❑	487	Mike Benjamin	.10	.02
❑	488	Eric Davis	.20	.07
❑	489	Scott Kamieniecki	.10	.02
❑	490	Kent Hrbek	.20	.07
❑	491	John Hope RC	.10	.02

Card	Player		
❑ 492	Jesse Orosco	.10	.02
❑ 493	Troy Neel	.10	.02
❑ 494	Ryan Bowen	.10	.02
❑ 495	Mickey Tettleton	.10	.02
❑ 496	Chris Jones	.10	.02
❑ 497	John Wetteland	.20	.07
❑ 498	David Hulse	.10	.02
❑ 499	Greg Maddux	.75	.30
❑ 500	Bo Jackson	.50	.20
❑ 501	Donovan Osborne	.10	.02
❑ 502	Mike Greenwell	.10	.02
❑ 503	Steve Frey	.10	.02
❑ 504	Jim Eisenreich	.10	.02
❑ 505	Robby Thompson	.10	.02
❑ 506	Leo Gomez	.10	.02
❑ 507	Dave Staton	.10	.02
❑ 508	Wayne Kirby	.10	.02
❑ 509	Tim Bogar	.10	.02
❑ 510	David Cone	.20	.07
❑ 511	Devon White	.20	.07
❑ 512	Xavier Hernandez	.10	.02
❑ 513	Tim Costo	.10	.02
❑ 514	Gene Harris	.10	.02
❑ 515	Jack McDowell	.10	.02
❑ 516	Kevin Gross	.10	.02
❑ 517	Scott Leius	.10	.02
❑ 518	Lloyd McClendon	.10	.02
❑ 519	Alex Diaz RC	.10	.02
❑ 520	Wade Boggs	.30	.10
❑ 521	Bob Welch	.10	.02
❑ 522	Henry Cotto	.10	.02
❑ 523	Mike Moore	.10	.02
❑ 524	Tim Laker	.10	.02
❑ 525	Andres Galarraga	.20	.07
❑ 526	Jamie Moyer	.20	.07
❑ 527	J.Hardtke RC/C.Sexton RC	.10	.02
❑ 528	Sid Bream	.10	.02
❑ 529	Erik Hanson	.10	.02
❑ 530	Ray Lankford	.20	.07
❑ 531	Rob Deer	.10	.02
❑ 532	Rod Correia	.10	.02
❑ 533	Roger Mason	.10	.02
❑ 534	Mike Devereaux	.10	.02
❑ 535	Jeff Montgomery	.10	.02
❑ 536	Dwight Smith	.10	.02
❑ 537	Jeremy Hernandez	.10	.02
❑ 538	Ellis Burks	.20	.07
❑ 539	Bobby Jones	.10	.02
❑ 540	Paul Molitor	.20	.07
❑ 541	Jeff Juden	.10	.02
❑ 542	Chris Sabo	.10	.02
❑ 543	Larry Casian	.10	.02
❑ 544	Jeff Gardner	.10	.02
❑ 545	Ramon Martinez	.10	.02
❑ 546	Paul O'Neill	.30	.10
❑ 547	Steve Hosey	.10	.02
❑ 548	Dave Nilsson	.10	.02
❑ 549	Ron Darling	.10	.02
❑ 550	Matt Williams	.20	.07
❑ 551	Jack Armstrong	.10	.02
❑ 552	Bill Krueger	.10	.02
❑ 553	Freddie Benavides	.10	.02
❑ 554	Jeff Fassero	.10	.02
❑ 555	Chuck Knoblauch	.20	.07
❑ 556	Guillermo Velasquez	.10	.02
❑ 557	Joel Johnston	.10	.02
❑ 558	Tom Lampkin	.10	.02
❑ 559	Todd Van Poppel	.10	.02
❑ 560	Gary Sheffield	.20	.07
❑ 561	Skeeter Barnes	.10	.02
❑ 562	Darren Holmes	.10	.02
❑ 563	John Vander Wal	.10	.02
❑ 564	Mike Ignasiak	.10	.02
❑ 565	Fred McGriff	.30	.10
❑ 566	Luis Polonia	.10	.02
❑ 567	Mike Perez	.10	.02
❑ 568	John Valentin	.10	.02
❑ 569	Mike Felder	.10	.02
❑ 570	Tommy Greene	.10	.02
❑ 571	David Segui	.10	.02
❑ 572	Roberto Hernandez	.10	.02
❑ 573	Steve Wilson	.10	.02
❑ 574	Willie McGee	.20	.07
❑ 575	Randy Myers	.10	.02
❑ 576	Darrin Jackson	.10	.02
❑ 577	Eric Plunk	.10	.02
❑ 578	Mike Macfarlane	.10	.02
❑ 579	Doug Brocail	.10	.02
❑ 580	Steve Finley	.20	.07
❑ 581	John Roper	.10	.02
❑ 582	Danny Cox	.10	.02
❑ 583	Chip Hale	.10	.02
❑ 584	Scott Bullett	.10	.02
❑ 585	Kevin Reimer	.10	.02
❑ 586	Brent Gates	.10	.02
❑ 587	Matt Turner	.10	.02
❑ 588	Rich Rowland	.10	.02
❑ 589	Kent Bottenfield	.10	.02
❑ 590	Marquis Grissom	.20	.07
❑ 591	Doug Strange	.10	.02
❑ 592	Jay Howell	.10	.02
❑ 593	Omar Vizquel	.30	.10
❑ 594	Rheal Cormier	.10	.02
❑ 595	Andre Dawson	.20	.07
❑ 596	Hilly Hathaway	.10	.02
❑ 597	Todd Pratt	.10	.02
❑ 598	Mike Mussina	.30	.10
❑ 599	Alex Fernandez	.10	.02
❑ 600	Don Mattingly	1.25	.50
❑ 601	Frank Thomas MOG	.30	.10
❑ 602	Ryne Sandberg MOG	.50	.20
❑ 603	Wade Boggs MOG	.20	.07
❑ 604	Cal Ripken MOG	.75	.30
❑ 605	Barry Bonds MOG	.75	.30
❑ 606	Ken Griffey Jr. MOG	.50	.20
❑ 607	Kirby Puckett MOG	.30	.10
❑ 608	Darren Daulton MOG	.10	.02
❑ 609	Paul Molitor MOG	.10	.02
❑ 610	Terry Steinbach	.10	.02
❑ 611	Todd Worrell	.10	.02
❑ 612	Jim Thome	.30	.10
❑ 613	Chuck McElroy	.10	.02
❑ 614	John Habyan	.10	.02
❑ 615	Sid Fernandez	.10	.02
❑ 616	Jermaine Allensworth RC	.10	.02
❑ 617	Steve Bedrosian	.10	.02
❑ 618	Rob Ducey	.10	.02
❑ 619	Tom Browning	.10	.02
❑ 620	Tony Gwynn	.60	.25
❑ 621	Carl Willis	.10	.02
❑ 622	Kevin Young	.10	.02
❑ 623	Rafael Novoa	.10	.02
❑ 624	Jerry Browne	.10	.02
❑ 625	Charlie Hough	.20	.07
❑ 626	Chris Gomez	.10	.02
❑ 627	Steve Reed	.10	.02
❑ 628	Kirk Rueter	.10	.02
❑ 629	Matt Whiteside	.10	.02
❑ 630	David Justice	.20	.07
❑ 631	Brad Holman	.10	.02
❑ 632	Brian Jordan	.20	.07
❑ 633	Scott Bankhead	.10	.02
❑ 634	Torey Lovullo	.10	.02
❑ 635	Len Dykstra	.20	.07
❑ 636	Ben McDonald	.10	.02
❑ 637	Steve Howe	.10	.02
❑ 638	Jose Vizcaino	.10	.02
❑ 639	Bill Swift	.10	.02
❑ 640	Darryl Strawberry	.20	.07
❑ 641	Steve Farr	.10	.02
❑ 642	Tom Kramer	.10	.02
❑ 643	Joe Orsulak	.10	.02
❑ 644	Tom Henke	.10	.02
❑ 645	Joe Carter	.20	.07
❑ 646	Ken Caminiti	.20	.07
❑ 647	Reggie Sanders	.20	.07
❑ 648	Andy Ashby	.10	.02
❑ 649	Derek Parks	.10	.02
❑ 650	Andy Van Slyke	.30	.10
❑ 651	Juan Bell	.10	.02
❑ 652	Roger Smithberg	.10	.02
❑ 653	Chuck Carr	.10	.02
❑ 654	Bill Gullickson	.10	.02
❑ 655	Charlie Hayes	.10	.02
❑ 656	Chris Nabholz	.10	.02
❑ 657	Karl Rhodes	.10	.02
❑ 658	Pete Smith	.10	.02
❑ 659	Bret Boone	.20	.07
❑ 660	Gregg Jefferies	.10	.02
❑ 661	Bob Zupcic	.10	.02
❑ 662	Steve Sax	.10	.02
❑ 663	Mariano Duncan	.10	.02
❑ 664	Jeff Tackett	.10	.02
❑ 665	Mark Langston	.10	.02
❑ 666	Steve Buechele	.10	.02
❑ 667	Candy Maldonado	.10	.02
❑ 668	Woody Williams	.20	.07
❑ 669	Tim Wakefield	.30	.10
❑ 670	Danny Tartabull	.10	.02
❑ 671	Charlie O'Brien	.10	.02
❑ 672	Felix Jose	.10	.02
❑ 673	Bobby Ayala	.10	.02
❑ 674	Scott Servais	.10	.02
❑ 675	Roberto Alomar	.30	.10
❑ 676	Pedro A.Martinez RC	.10	.02
❑ 677	Eddie Guardado	.20	.07
❑ 678	Mark Lewis	.10	.02
❑ 679	Jaime Navarro	.10	.02
❑ 680	Ruben Sierrra	.20	.07
❑ 681	Rick Renteria	.10	.02
❑ 682	Storm Davis	.10	.02
❑ 683	Cory Snyder	.10	.02
❑ 684	Ron Karkovice	.10	.02
❑ 685	Juan Gonzalez	.20	.07
❑ 686	Carlos Delgado	.30	.10
❑ 687	John Smoltz	.30	.10
❑ 688	Brian Dorsett	.10	.02
❑ 689	Omar Olivares	.10	.02
❑ 690	Mo Vaughn	.20	.07
❑ 691	Joe Grahe	.10	.02
❑ 692	Mickey Morandini	.10	.02
❑ 693	Tino Martinez	.30	.10
❑ 694	Brian Barnes	.10	.02
❑ 695	Mike Stanley	.10	.02
❑ 696	Mark Clark	.10	.02
❑ 697	Dave Hansen	.10	.02
❑ 698	Willie Wilson	.10	.02
❑ 699	Pete Schourek	.10	.02
❑ 700	Barry Bonds	1.50	.60
❑ 701	Kevin Appier	.20	.07
❑ 702	Tony Fernandez	.10	.02
❑ 703	Darryl Kile	.20	.07
❑ 704	Archi Cianfrocco	.10	.02
❑ 705	Jose Rijo	.10	.02
❑ 706	Brian Harper	.10	.02
❑ 707	Zane Smith	.10	.02
❑ 708	Dave Henderson	.10	.02
❑ 709	Angel Miranda UER	.10	.02
❑ 710	Orestes Destrade	.10	.02
❑ 711	Greg Gohr	.10	.02
❑ 712	Eric Young	.10	.02
❑ 713	Bullinger/Will/Wat/Welch	.10	.02
❑ 714	Tim Spehr	.10	.02
❑ 715	Hank Aaron 715 HR	.50	.20
❑ 716	Nate Minchey	.10	.02
❑ 717	Mike Blowers	.10	.02
❑ 718	Kent Mercker	.10	.02
❑ 719	Tom Pagnozzi	.10	.02
❑ 720	Roger Clemens	1.00	.40
❑ 721	Eduardo Perez	.10	.02
❑ 722	Milt Thompson	.10	.02
❑ 723	Gregg Olson	.10	.02
❑ 724	Kirk McCaskill	.10	.02
❑ 725	Sammy Sosa	.50	.20
❑ 726	Alvaro Espinoza	.10	.02
❑ 727	Henry Rodriguez	.10	.02
❑ 728	Jim Leyritz	.10	.02
❑ 729	Steve Scarsone	.10	.02
❑ 730	Bobby Bonilla	.20	.07
❑ 731	Chris Gwynn	.10	.02
❑ 732	Al Leiter	.20	.07
❑ 733	Bip Roberts	.10	.02
❑ 734	Mark Portugal	.10	.02
❑ 735	Terry Pendleton	.20	.07
❑ 736	Dave Valle	.10	.02
❑ 737	Paul Kilgus	.10	.02
❑ 738	Greg A. Harris	.10	.02
❑ 739	Jon Ratliff RC	.10	.02
❑ 740	Kirk Presley RC	.10	.02
❑ 741	Josue Estrada RC	.10	.02
❑ 742	Wayne Gomes RC	.10	.02
❑ 743	Pat Watkins RC	.10	.02
❑ 744	Jamey Wright RC	.25	.08
❑ 745	Jay Powell RC	.10	.02
❑ 746	Ryan McGuire RC	.10	.02
❑ 747	Marc Barcelo RC	.10	.02
❑ 748	Sloan Smith RC	.10	.02
❑ 749	John Wasdin RC	.10	.02

❑ 750	Marc Valdes	.10	.02
❑ 751	Dan Ehler RC	.10	.02
❑ 752	Andre King RC	.10	.02
❑ 753	Greg Keagle RC	.10	.02
❑ 754	Jason Myers RC	.10	.02
❑ 755	Dax Winslett RC	.10	.02
❑ 756	Casey Whitten RC	.10	.02
❑ 757	Tony Fuduric RC	.10	.02
❑ 758	Greg Norton RC	.25	.08
❑ 759	Jeff D'Amico RC	.10	.02
❑ 760	Ryan Hancock RC	.10	.02
❑ 761	David Cooper RC	.10	.02
❑ 762	Kevin Orie RC	.10	.02
❑ 763	J.O'Donoghue/M.Oquist	.10	.02
❑ 764	C.Bailey RC/S.Hatteberg	.10	.02
❑ 765	M.Holzemer/P.Swingle RC	.10	.02
❑ 766	J.Baldwin/R.Bolton	.10	.02
❑ 767	J.Tavarez RC/J.DiPoto	.25	.08
❑ 768	D.Bautista/S.Bergman	.10	.02
❑ 769	B.Hamelin/J.Vitiello	.10	.02
❑ 770	M.Kiefer/T.O'Leary	.10	.02
❑ 771	D.Hocking/O.Munoz RC	.10	.02
❑ 772	Russ Davis/B.Taylor	.10	.02
❑ 773	K.Abbott/M.Jimenez	.25	.08
❑ 774	K.King RC/Plantenberg RC	.10	.02
❑ 775	J.Shave/D.Wilson	.10	.02
❑ 776	D.Cedeno/P.Spoljaric	.10	.02
❑ 777	C.Jones/R.Klesko	.50	.20
❑ 778	S.Trachsel/T.Wendell	.10	.02
❑ 779	J.Spradlin RC/J.Ruffin	.10	.02
❑ 780	J.Bates/J.Burke	.10	.02
❑ 781	C.Everett/D.Weathers	.20	.07
❑ 782	J.Mouton/G.Mota	.10	.02
❑ 783	R.Mondesi/B.Van Ryn	.20	.07
❑ 784	R.White/G.White	.20	.07
❑ 785	B.Pulsipher/B.Fordyce	.20	.07
❑ 786	K.Foster RC/G.Schall	.10	.02
❑ 787	Rich Aude RC/M.Cummings	.10	.02
❑ 788	B.Barber/R.Batchelor	.10	.02
❑ 789	B.Johnson RC/S.Sanders	.10	.02
❑ 790	J.Phillips/R.Faneyte	.10	.02
❑ 791	Checklist 3	.10	.02
❑ 792	Checklist 4	.10	.02

1994 Topps Traded

❑	COMP.FACT.SET (140)	40.00	20.00
❑ 1T	Paul Wilson	.10	.02
❑ 2T	Bill Taylor RC	1.00	.40
❑ 3T	Dan Wilson	.10	.02
❑ 4T	Mark Smith	.10	.02
❑ 5T	Toby Borland RC	.25	.08
❑ 6T	Dave Clark	.10	.02
❑ 7T	Dennis Martinez	.20	.07
❑ 8T	Dave Gallagher	.10	.02
❑ 9T	Josias Manzanillo	.10	.02
❑ 10T	Brian Anderson RC	1.00	.40
❑ 11T	Damon Berryhill	.10	.02
❑ 12T	Alex Cole	.10	.02
❑ 13T	Jacob Shumate RC	.25	.08
❑ 14T	Oddibe McDowell	.10	.02
❑ 15T	Willie Banks	.10	.02
❑ 16T	Jerry Browne	.10	.02
❑ 17T	Donnie Elliott	.10	.02
❑ 18T	Ellis Burks	.20	.07
❑ 19T	Chuck McElroy	.10	.02
❑ 20T	Luis Polonia	.10	.02
❑ 21T	Brian Harper	.10	.02
❑ 22T	Mark Portugal	.10	.02
❑ 23T	Dave Henderson	.10	.02
❑ 24T	Mark Acre RC	.25	.08
❑ 25T	Julio Franco	.20	.07
❑ 26T	Darren Hall RC	.25	.08
❑ 27T	Eric Anthony	.10	.02
❑ 28T	Sid Fernandez	.10	.02
❑ 29T	Rusty Greer RC	1.50	.60
❑ 30T	Riccardo Ingram RC	.25	.08
❑ 31T	Gabe White	.10	.02
❑ 32T	Tim Belcher	.10	.02
❑ 33T	Terrence Long RC	1.00	.40
❑ 34T	Mark Dalesandro RC	.25	.08
❑ 35T	Mike Kelly	.10	.02
❑ 36T	Jack Morris	.20	.07
❑ 37T	Jeff Brantley	.10	.02
❑ 38T	Larry Barnes RC	.25	.08
❑ 39T	Brian R. Hunter	.10	.02
❑ 40T	Otis Nixon	.10	.02
❑ 41T	Bret Wagner	.10	.02
❑ 42T	P.Martinez/D.Deshields TR	.50	.20
❑ 43T	Heathcliff Slocumb	.10	.02
❑ 44T	Ben Grieve RC	1.00	.40
❑ 45T	John Hudek RC	.25	.08
❑ 46T	Shawon Dunston	.10	.02
❑ 47T	Greg Colbrunn	.10	.02
❑ 48T	Joey Hamilton	.10	.02
❑ 49T	Marvin Freeman	.10	.02
❑ 50T	Terry Mulholland	.10	.02
❑ 51T	Keith Mitchell	.10	.02
❑ 52T	Dwight Smith	.10	.02
❑ 53T	Shawn Boskie	.10	.02
❑ 54T	Kevin Witt RC	1.00	.40
❑ 55T	Ron Gant	.20	.07
❑ 56T	Jason Schmidt RC	10.00	4.00
❑ 57T	Jody Reed	.10	.02
❑ 58T	Rick Helling	.10	.02
❑ 59T	John Powell	.10	.02
❑ 60T	Eddie Murray	.50	.20
❑ 61T	Joe Hall RC	.25	.08
❑ 62T	Jorge Fabregas	.10	.02
❑ 63T	Mike Mordecai RC	.25	.08
❑ 64T	Ed Vosberg	.10	.02
❑ 65T	Rickey Henderson	.50	.20
❑ 66T	Tim Grieve RC	.25	.08
❑ 67T	Jon Lieber	.20	.07
❑ 68T	Chris Howard	.10	.02
❑ 69T	Matt Walbeck	.10	.02
❑ 70T	Chan Ho Park RC	1.50	.60
❑ 71T	Bryan Eversgerd RC	.25	.08
❑ 72T	John Dettmer	.10	.02
❑ 73T	Erik Hanson	.10	.02
❑ 74T	Mike Thurman RC	.25	.08
❑ 75T	Bobby Ayala	.10	.02
❑ 76T	Rafael Palmeiro	.30	.10
❑ 77T	Bret Boone	.20	.07
❑ 78T	Paul Shuey	.10	.02
❑ 79T	Kevin Foster RC	.25	.08
❑ 80T	Dave Magadan	.10	.02
❑ 81T	Bip Roberts	.10	.02
❑ 82T	Howard Johnson	.10	.02
❑ 83T	Xavier Hernandez	.10	.02
❑ 84T	Ross Powell RC	.25	.08
❑ 85T	Doug Million RC	.25	.08
❑ 86T	Geronimo Berroa	.10	.02
❑ 87T	Mark Farris RC	.25	.08
❑ 88T	Butch Henry	.10	.02
❑ 89T	Junior Felix	.10	.02
❑ 90T	Bo Jackson	.50	.20
❑ 91T	Hector Carrasco	.10	.02
❑ 92T	Charlie O'Brien	.10	.02
❑ 93T	Omar Vizquel	.30	.10
❑ 94T	David Segui	.10	.02
❑ 95T	Dustin Hermanson	.10	.02
❑ 96T	Gar Finnvold RC	.25	.08
❑ 97T	Dave Stevens	.10	.02
❑ 98T	Corey Pointer RC	.25	.08
❑ 99T	Felix Fermin	.10	.02
❑ 100T	Lee Smith	.20	.07
❑ 101T	Reid Ryan RC	1.00	.40
❑ 102T	Bobby Munoz	.10	.02
❑ 103T	D.Sanders/R.Kelly TR	.30	.10
❑ 104T	Turner Ward	.10	.02
❑ 105T	W.VanLandingham RC	.25	.08
❑ 106T	Vince Coleman	.10	.02
❑ 107T	Stan Javier	.10	.02
❑ 108T	Darrin Jackson	.10	.02
❑ 109T	C.J.Nitkowski RC	.25	.08
❑ 110T	Anthony Young	.10	.02
❑ 111T	Kurt Miller	.10	.02
❑ 112T	Paul Konerko RC	15.00	6.00
❑ 113T	Walt Weiss	.10	.02
❑ 114T	Daryl Boston	.10	.02
❑ 115T	Will Clark	.30	.10
❑ 116T	Matt Smith RC	.25	.08
❑ 117T	Mark Leiter	.10	.02
❑ 118T	Gregg Olson	.10	.02
❑ 119T	Tony Pena	.10	.02
❑ 120T	Jose Vizcaino	.10	.02
❑ 121T	Rick White RC	.25	.08
❑ 122T	Rich Rowland	.10	.02
❑ 123T	Jeff Reboulet	.10	.02
❑ 124T	Greg Hibbard	.10	.02
❑ 125T	Chris Sabo	.10	.02
❑ 126T	Doug Jones	.10	.02
❑ 127T	Tony Fernandez	.10	.02
❑ 128T	Carlos Reyes RC	.25	.08
❑ 129T	Kevin L.Brown RC	1.00	.40
❑ 130T	Ryne Sandberg HL	1.25	.50
❑ 131T	Ryne Sandberg HL	1.25	.50
❑ 132T	Checklist 1-132	.10	.02

1995 Topps

❑	COMPLETE SET (660)	80.00	50.00
❑	COMP.HOBBY SET (677)	120.00	60.00
❑	COMP.RETAIL SET (677)	120.00	60.00
❑	COMPLETE SERIES 1 (396)	40.00	25.00
❑	COMPLETE SERIES 2 (264)	40.00	25.00
❑ 1	Frank Thomas	.75	.30
❑ 2	Mickey Morandini	.15	.05
❑ 3	Babe Ruth 100th B-Day	2.00	.75
❑ 4	Scott Cooper	.15	.05
❑ 5	David Cone	.30	.10
❑ 6	Jacob Shumate	.15	.05
❑ 7	Trevor Hoffman	.30	.10
❑ 8	Shane Mack	.15	.05
❑ 9	Delino DeShields	.15	.05
❑ 10	Matt Williams	.30	.10
❑ 11	Sammy Sosa	.75	.30
❑ 12	Gary DiSarcina	.15	.05
❑ 13	Kenny Rogers	.30	.10
❑ 14	Jose Vizcaino	.15	.05
❑ 15	Lou Whitaker	.30	.10
❑ 16	Ron Darling	.15	.05
❑ 17	Dave Nilsson	.15	.05
❑ 18	Chris Hammond	.15	.05
❑ 19	Sid Bream	.15	.05
❑ 20	Denny Martinez	.30	.10
❑ 21	Orlando Merced	.15	.05
❑ 22	John Wetteland	.30	.10
❑ 23	Mike Devereaux	.15	.05
❑ 24	Rene Arocha	.15	.05
❑ 25	Jay Buhner	.30	.10
❑ 26	Darren Holmes	.15	.05
❑ 27	Hal Morris	.15	.05
❑ 28	Brian Buchanan RC	.15	.05
❑ 29	Keith Miller	.15	.05
❑ 30	Paul Molitor	.30	.10
❑ 31	Dave West	.15	.05
❑ 32	Tony Tarasco	.15	.05
❑ 33	Scott Sanders	.15	.05
❑ 34	Eddie Zambrano	.15	.05
❑ 35	Ricky Bones	.15	.05
❑ 36	John Valentin	.15	.05
❑ 37	Kevin Tapani	.15	.05

❑ 38	Tim Wallach	.15	.05
❑ 39	Darren Lewis	.15	.05
❑ 40	Travis Fryman	.30	.10
❑ 41	Mark Leiter	.15	.05
❑ 42	Jose Bautista	.15	.05
❑ 43	Pete Smith	.15	.05
❑ 44	Bret Barberie	.15	.05
❑ 45	Dennis Eckersley	.30	.10
❑ 46	Ken Hill	.15	.05
❑ 47	Chad Ogea	.15	.05
❑ 48	Pete Harnisch	.15	.05
❑ 49	James Baldwin	.15	.05
❑ 50	Mike Mussina	.50	.20
❑ 51	Al Martin	.15	.05
❑ 52	Mark Thompson	.15	.05
❑ 53	Matt Smith	.15	.05
❑ 54	Joey Hamilton	.15	.05
❑ 55	Edgar Martinez	.50	.20
❑ 56	John Smiley	.15	.05
❑ 57	Rey Sanchez	.15	.05
❑ 58	Mike Timlin	.15	.05
❑ 59	Ricky Bottalico	.15	.05
❑ 60	Jim Abbott	.50	.20
❑ 61	Mike Kelly	.15	.05
❑ 62	Brian Jordan	.30	.10
❑ 63	Ken Ryan	.15	.05
❑ 64	Matt Mieske	.15	.05
❑ 65	Rick Aguilera	.15	.05
❑ 66	Ismael Valdes	.15	.05
❑ 67	Royce Clayton	.15	.05
❑ 68	Junior Felix	.15	.05
❑ 69	Harold Reynolds	.30	.10
❑ 70	Juan Gonzalez	.30	.10
❑ 71	Kelly Stinnett	.15	.05
❑ 72	Carlos Reyes	.15	.05
❑ 73	Dave Weathers	.15	.05
❑ 74	Mel Rojas	.15	.05
❑ 75	Doug Drabek	.15	.05
❑ 76	Charles Nagy	.15	.05
❑ 77	Tim Raines	.30	.10
❑ 78	Midre Cummings	.15	.05
❑ 79	Ray Brown RC	.15	.05
❑ 80	Rafael Palmeiro	.50	.20
❑ 81	Charlie Hayes	.15	.05
❑ 82	Ray Lankford	.30	.10
❑ 83	Tim Davis	.15	.05
❑ 84	C.J. Nitkowski	.15	.05
❑ 85	Andy Ashby	.15	.05
❑ 86	Gerald Williams	.15	.05
❑ 87	Terry Shumpert	.15	.05
❑ 88	Heathcliff Slocumb	.15	.05
❑ 89	Domingo Cedeno	.15	.05
❑ 90	Mark Grace	.50	.20
❑ 91	Brad Woodall RC	.15	.05
❑ 92	Gar Finnvold	.15	.05
❑ 93	Jaime Navarro	.15	.05
❑ 94	Carlos Hernandez	.15	.05
❑ 95	Mark Langston	.15	.05
❑ 96	Chuck Carr	.15	.05
❑ 97	Mike Gardiner	.15	.05
❑ 98	Dave McCarty	.15	.05
❑ 99	Cris Carpenter	.15	.05
❑ 100	Barry Bonds	2.00	.75
❑ 101	David Segui	.15	.05
❑ 102	Scott Brosius	.30	.10
❑ 103	Mariano Duncan	.15	.05
❑ 104	Kenny Lofton	.30	.10
❑ 105	Ken Caminiti	.30	.10
❑ 106	Darrin Jackson	.15	.05
❑ 107	Jim Poole	.15	.05
❑ 108	Wil Cordero	.15	.05
❑ 109	Danny Miceli	.15	.05
❑ 110	Walt Weiss	.15	.05
❑ 111	Tom Pagnozzi	.15	.05
❑ 112	Terrence Long	.15	.05
❑ 113	Bret Boone	.30	.10
❑ 114	Daryl Boston	.15	.05
❑ 115	Wally Joyner	.30	.10
❑ 116	Rob Butler	.15	.05
❑ 117	Rafael Belliard	.15	.05
❑ 118	Luis Lopez	.15	.05
❑ 119	Tony Fossas	.15	.05
❑ 120	Len Dykstra	.30	.10
❑ 121	Mike Morgan	.15	.05
❑ 122	Denny Hocking	.15	.05
❑ 123	Kevin Gross	.15	.05
❑ 124	Todd Benzinger	.15	.05
❑ 125	John Doherty	.15	.05
❑ 126	Eduardo Perez	.15	.05
❑ 127	Dan Smith	.15	.05
❑ 128	Joe Orsulak	.15	.05
❑ 129	Brent Gates	.15	.05
❑ 130	Jeff Conine	.30	.10
❑ 131	Doug Henry	.15	.05
❑ 132	Paul Sorrento	.15	.05
❑ 133	Mike Hampton	.30	.10
❑ 134	Tim Spehr	.15	.05
❑ 135	Julio Franco	.30	.10
❑ 136	Mike Dyer	.15	.05
❑ 137	Chris Sabo	.15	.05
❑ 138	Rheal Cormier	.15	.05
❑ 139	Paul Konerko	1.00	.40
❑ 140	Dante Bichette	.30	.10
❑ 141	Chuck McElroy	.15	.05
❑ 142	Mike Stanley	.15	.05
❑ 143	Bob Hamelin	.15	.05
❑ 144	Tommy Greene	.15	.05
❑ 145	John Smoltz	.50	.20
❑ 146	Ed Sprague	.15	.05
❑ 147	Ray McDavid	.15	.05
❑ 148	Otis Nixon	.15	.05
❑ 149	Turk Wendell	.15	.05
❑ 150	Chris James	.15	.05
❑ 151	Derek Parks	.15	.05
❑ 152	Jose Offerman	.15	.05
❑ 153	Tony Clark	.15	.05
❑ 154	Chad Curtis	.15	.05
❑ 155	Mark Portugal	.15	.05
❑ 156	Bill Pulsipher	.15	.05
❑ 157	Troy Neel	.15	.05
❑ 158	Dave Winfield	.30	.10
❑ 159	Bill Wegman	.15	.05
❑ 160	Benito Santiago	.30	.10
❑ 161	Jose Mesa	.15	.05
❑ 162	Luis Gonzalez	.30	.10
❑ 163	Alex Fernandez	.15	.05
❑ 164	Freddie Benavides	.15	.05
❑ 165	Ben McDonald	.15	.05
❑ 166	Blas Minor	.15	.05
❑ 167	Bret Wagner	.15	.05
❑ 168	Mac Suzuki	.15	.05
❑ 169	Roberto Mejia	.15	.05
❑ 170	Wade Boggs	.50	.20
❑ 171	Pokey Reese	.15	.05
❑ 172	Hipolito Pichardo	.15	.05
❑ 173	Kim Batiste	.15	.05
❑ 174	Darren Hall	.15	.05
❑ 175	Tom Glavine	.50	.20
❑ 176	Phil Plantier	.15	.05
❑ 177	Chris Howard	.15	.05
❑ 178	Karl Rhodes	.15	.05
❑ 179	LaTroy Hawkins	.15	.05
❑ 180	Raul Mondesi	.30	.10
❑ 181	Jeff Reed	.15	.05
❑ 182	Milt Cuyler	.15	.05
❑ 183	Jim Edmonds	.50	.20
❑ 184	Hector Fajardo	.15	.05
❑ 185	Jeff Kent	.30	.10
❑ 186	Wilson Alvarez	.15	.05
❑ 187	Geronimo Berroa	.15	.05
❑ 188	Billy Spiers	.15	.05
❑ 189	Derek Lilliquist	.15	.05
❑ 190	Craig Biggio	.50	.20
❑ 191	Roberto Hernandez	.15	.05
❑ 192	Bob Natal	.15	.05
❑ 193	Bobby Ayala	.15	.05
❑ 194	Travis Miller RC	.15	.05
❑ 195	Bob Tewksbury	.15	.05
❑ 196	Rondell White	.30	.10
❑ 197	Steve Cooke	.15	.05
❑ 198	Jeff Branson	.15	.05
❑ 199	Derek Jeter	2.00	.75
❑ 200	Tim Salmon	.50	.20
❑ 201	Steve Frey	.15	.05
❑ 202	Kent Mercker	.15	.05
❑ 203	Randy Johnson	.75	.30
❑ 204	Todd Worrell	.15	.05
❑ 205	Mo Vaughn	.30	.10
❑ 206	Howard Johnson	.15	.05
❑ 207	John Wasdin	.15	.05
❑ 208	Eddie Williams	.15	.05
❑ 209	Tim Belcher	.15	.05
❑ 210	Jeff Montgomery	.15	.05
❑ 211	Kirt Manwaring	.15	.05
❑ 212	Ben Grieve	.15	.05
❑ 213	Pat Hentgen	.15	.05
❑ 214	Shawon Dunston	.15	.05
❑ 215	Mike Greenwell	.15	.05
❑ 216	Alex Diaz	.15	.05
❑ 217	Pat Mahomes	.15	.05
❑ 218	Dave Hansen	.15	.05
❑ 219	Kevin Rogers	.15	.05
❑ 220	Cecil Fielder	.30	.10
❑ 221	Andrew Lorraine	.15	.05
❑ 222	Jack Armstrong	.15	.05
❑ 223	Todd Hundley	.15	.05
❑ 224	Mark Acre	.15	.05
❑ 225	Darrell Whitmore	.15	.05
❑ 226	Randy Milligan	.15	.05
❑ 227	Wayne Kirby	.15	.05
❑ 228	Darryl Kile	.30	.10
❑ 229	Bob Zupcic	.15	.05
❑ 230	Jay Bell	.30	.10
❑ 231	Dustin Hermanson	.15	.05
❑ 232	Harold Baines	.30	.10
❑ 233	Alan Benes	.15	.05
❑ 234	Felix Fermin	.15	.05
❑ 235	Ellis Burks	.30	.10
❑ 236	Jeff Brantley	.15	.05
❑ 237	Karim Garcia RC	.15	.05
❑ 238	Matt Nokes	.15	.05
❑ 239	Ben Rivera	.15	.05
❑ 240	Joe Carter	.30	.10
❑ 241	Jeff Granger	.15	.05
❑ 242	Terry Pendleton	.30	.10
❑ 243	Melvin Nieves	.15	.05
❑ 244	Frankie Rodriguez	.15	.05
❑ 245	Darryl Hamilton	.15	.05
❑ 246	Brooks Kieschnick	.15	.05
❑ 247	Todd Hollandsworth	.15	.05
❑ 248	Joe Rosselli	.15	.05
❑ 249	Bill Gullickson	.15	.05
❑ 250	Chuck Knoblauch	.30	.10
❑ 251	Kurt Miller	.15	.05
❑ 252	Bobby Jones	.15	.05
❑ 253	Lance Blankenship	.15	.05
❑ 254	Matt Whiteside	.15	.05
❑ 255	Darrin Fletcher	.15	.05
❑ 256	Eric Plunk	.15	.05
❑ 257	Shane Reynolds	.15	.05
❑ 258	Norberto Martin	.15	.05
❑ 259	Mike Thurman	.15	.05
❑ 260	Andy Van Slyke	.50	.20
❑ 261	Dwight Smith	.15	.05
❑ 262	Allen Watson	.15	.05
❑ 263	Dan Wilson	.15	.05
❑ 264	Brent Mayne	.15	.05
❑ 265	Bip Roberts	.15	.05
❑ 266	Sterling Hitchcock	.15	.05
❑ 267	Alex Gonzalez	.15	.05
❑ 268	Greg Harris	.15	.05
❑ 269	Ricky Jordan	.15	.05
❑ 270	Johnny Ruffin	.15	.05
❑ 271	Mike Stanton	.15	.05
❑ 272	Rich Rowland	.15	.05
❑ 273	Steve Trachsel	.15	.05
❑ 274	Pedro Munoz	.15	.05
❑ 275	Ramon Martinez	.15	.05
❑ 276	Dave Henderson	.15	.05
❑ 277	Chris Gomez	.15	.05
❑ 278	Joe Grahe	.15	.05
❑ 279	Rusty Greer	.30	.10
❑ 280	John Franco	.30	.10
❑ 281	Mike Bordick	.15	.05
❑ 282	Jeff D'Amico	.15	.05
❑ 283	Dave Magadan	.15	.05
❑ 284	Tony Pena	.15	.05
❑ 285	Greg Swindell	.15	.05
❑ 286	Doug Million	.15	.05
❑ 287	Gabe White	.15	.05
❑ 288	Trey Beamon	.15	.05
❑ 289	Arthur Rhodes	.15	.05
❑ 290	Juan Guzman	.15	.05
❑ 291	Jose Oquendo	.15	.05
❑ 292	Willie Blair	.15	.05
❑ 293	Eddie Taubensee	.15	.05
❑ 294	Steve Howe	.15	.05
❑ 295	Greg Maddux	1.25	.50

296	Mike Macfarlane	.15	.05
297	Curt Schilling	.30	.10
298	Phil Clark	.15	.05
299	Woody Williams	.15	.05
300	Jose Canseco	.50	.20
301	Aaron Sele	.15	.05
302	Carl Willis	.15	.05
303	Steve Buechele	.15	.05
304	Dave Burba	.15	.05
305	Orel Hershiser	.30	.10
306	Damion Easley	.15	.05
307	Mike Henneman	.15	.05
308	Josias Manzanillo	.15	.05
309	Kevin Seitzer	.15	.05
310	Ruben Sierra	.30	.10
311	Bryan Harvey	.15	.05
312	Jim Thome	.50	.20
313	Ramon Castro RC	.40	.15
314	Lance Johnson	.15	.05
315	Marquis Grissom	.30	.10
316	Eddie Priest RC	.15	.05
317	Paul Wagner	.15	.05
318	Jamie Moyer	.30	.10
319	Todd Zeile	.15	.05
320	Chris Bosio	.15	.05
321	Steve Reed	.15	.05
322	Erik Hanson	.15	.05
323	Luis Polonia	.15	.05
324	Ryan Klesko	.30	.10
325	Kevin Appier	.30	.10
326	Jim Eisenreich	.15	.05
327	Randy Knorr	.15	.05
328	Craig Shipley	.15	.05
329	Tim Naehring	.15	.05
330	Randy Myers	.15	.05
331	Alex Cole	.15	.05
332	Jim Gott	.15	.05
333	Mike Jackson	.15	.05
334	John Flaherty	.15	.05
335	Chili Davis	.30	.10
336	Benji Gil	.15	.05
337	Jason Jacome	.15	.05
338	Stan Javier	.15	.05
339	Mike Fetters	.15	.05
340	Rich Renteria	.15	.05
341	Kevin Witt	.15	.05
342	Scott Servais	.15	.05
343	Craig Grebeck	.15	.05
344	Kirk Rueter	.15	.05
345	Don Slaught	.15	.05
346	Armando Benitez	.15	.05
347	Ozzie Smith	1.25	.50
348	Mike Blowers	.15	.05
349	Armando Reynoso	.15	.05
350	Barry Larkin	.50	.20
351	Mike Williams	.15	.05
352	Scott Kamieniecki	.15	.05
353	Gary Gaetti	.30	.10
354	Todd Stottlemyre	.15	.05
355	Fred McGriff	.50	.20
356	Tim Mauser	.15	.05
357	Chris Gwynn	.15	.05
358	Frank Castillo	.15	.05
359	Jeff Reboulet	.15	.05
360	Roger Clemens	1.50	.60
361	Mark Carreon	.15	.05
362	Chad Kreuter	.15	.05
363	Mark Farris	.15	.05
364	Bob Welch	.15	.05
365	Dean Palmer	.30	.10
366	Jeromy Burnitz	.30	.10
367	B.J. Surhoff	.30	.10
368	Mike Butcher	.15	.05
369	B.Buckles RC/B.Clontz	.15	.05
370	Eddie Murray	.75	.30
371	Orlando Miller	.15	.05
372	Ron Karkovice	.15	.05
373	Richie Lewis	.15	.05
374	Lenny Webster	.15	.05
375	Jeff Tackett	.15	.05
376	Tom Urbani	.15	.05
377	Tino Martinez	.50	.20
378	Mark Dewey	.15	.05
379	Charles O'Brien	.15	.05
380	Terry Mulholland	.15	.05
381	Thomas Howard	.15	.05
382	Chris Haney	.15	.05
383	Billy Hatcher	.15	.05
384	F.Thomas/J.Bagwell AS	.50	.20
385	B.Boone/C.Baerga AS	.30	.10
386	M.Williams/W.Boggs AS	.30	.10
387	C.Ripken/W.Cordero AS	.75	.30
388	K.Griffey Jr./B.Bonds AS	1.00	.40
389	T.Gwynn/A.Belle AS	.30	.10
390	D.Bichette/K.Puckett AS	.50	.20
391	M.Piazza/M.Stanley AS	.75	.30
392	G.Maddux/D.Cone AS	.75	.30
393	D.Jackson/J.Key AS	.15	.05
394	J.Franco/L.Smith AS	.15	.05
395	Checklist 1-198	.15	.05
396	Checklist 199-396	.15	.05
397	Ken Griffey Jr.	1.25	.50
398	Rick Heiserman RC	.15	.05
399	Don Mattingly	2.00	.75
400	Henry Rodriguez	.15	.05
401	Lenny Harris	.15	.05
402	Ryan Thompson	.15	.05
403	Darren Oliver	.15	.05
404	Omar Vizquel	.50	.20
405	Jeff Bagwell	.50	.20
406	Doug Webb RC	.15	.05
407	Todd Van Poppel	.15	.05
408	Leo Gomez	.15	.05
409	Mark Whiten	.15	.05
410	Pedro A.Martinez	.15	.05
411	Reggie Sanders	.30	.10
412	Kevin Foster	.15	.05
413	Danny Tartabull	.15	.05
414	Jeff Blauser	.15	.05
415	Mike Magnante	.15	.05
416	Tom Candiotti	.15	.05
417	Rod Beck	.15	.05
418	Jody Reed	.15	.05
419	Vince Coleman	.15	.05
420	Danny Jackson	.15	.05
421	Ryan Nye RC	.15	.05
422	Larry Walker	.30	.10
423	Russ Johnson DP	.15	.05
424	Pat Borders	.15	.05
425	Lee Smith	.30	.10
426	Paul O'Neill	.50	.20
427	Devon White	.30	.10
428	Jim Bullinger	.15	.05
429	Rob Welch RC	.15	.05
430	Steve Avery	.15	.05
431	Tony Gwynn	1.00	.40
432	Pat Meares	.15	.05
433	Bill Swift	.15	.05
434	David Wells	.30	.10
435	John Briscoe	.15	.05
436	Roger Pavlik	.15	.05
437	Jayson Peterson RC	.15	.05
438	Roberto Alomar	.50	.20
439	Billy Brewer	.15	.05
440	Gary Sheffield	.30	.10
441	Lou Frazier	.15	.05
442	Terry Steinbach	.15	.05
443	Jay Payton RC	.75	.30
444	Jason Bere	.15	.05
445	Denny Neagle	.30	.10
446	Andres Galarraga	.30	.10
447	Hector Carrasco	.15	.05
448	Bill Risley	.15	.05
449	Andy Benes	.15	.05
450	Jim Leyritz	.15	.05
451	Jose Oliva	.15	.05
452	Greg Vaughn	.15	.05
453	Rich Monteleone	.15	.05
454	Tony Eusebio	.15	.05
455	Chuck Finley	.30	.10
456	Kevin Brown	.30	.10
457	Joe Boever	.15	.05
458	Bobby Munoz	.15	.05
459	Bret Saberhagen	.30	.10
460	Kurt Abbott	.15	.05
461	Bobby Witt	.15	.05
462	Cliff Floyd	.30	.10
463	Mark Clark	.15	.05
464	Andujar Cedeno	.15	.05
465	Marvin Freeman	.15	.05
466	Mike Piazza	1.25	.50
467	Willie Greene	.15	.05
468	Pat Kelly	.15	.05
469	Carlos Delgado	.30	.10
470	Willie Banks	.15	.05
471	Matt Walbeck	.15	.05
472	Mark McGwire	2.00	.75
473	McKay Christensen RC	.15	.05
474	Alan Trammell	.30	.10
475	Tom Gordon	.15	.05
476	Greg Colbrunn	.15	.05
477	Darren Daulton	.30	.10
478	Albie Lopez	.15	.05
479	Robin Ventura	.30	.10
480	Eddie Perez RC	.40	.15
481	Bryan Eversgerd	.15	.05
482	Dave Fleming	.15	.05
483	Scott Livingstone	.15	.05
484	Pete Schourek	.15	.05
485	Bernie Williams	.50	.20
486	Mark Lemke	.15	.05
487	Eric Karros	.30	.10
488	Scott Ruffcorn	.15	.05
489	Billy Ashley	.15	.05
490	Rico Brogna	.15	.05
491	John Burkett	.15	.05
492	Cade Gaspar RC	.15	.05
493	Jorge Fabregas	.15	.05
494	Greg Gagne	.15	.05
495	Doug Jones	.15	.05
496	Troy O'Leary	.15	.05
497	Pat Rapp	.15	.05
498	Butch Henry	.15	.05
499	John Olerud	.30	.10
500	John Hudek	.15	.05
501	Jeff King	.15	.05
502	Bobby Bonilla	.30	.10
503	Albert Belle	.30	.10
504	Rick Wilkins	.15	.05
505	John Jaha	.15	.05
506	Nigel Wilson	.15	.05
507	Sid Fernandez	.15	.05
508	Deion Sanders	.50	.20
509	Gil Heredia	.15	.05
510	Scott Elarton RC	.40	.15
511	Melido Perez	.15	.05
512	Greg McMichael	.15	.05
513	Rusty Meacham	.15	.05
514	Shawn Green	.30	.10
515	Carlos Garcia	.15	.05
516	Dave Stevens	.15	.05
517	Eric Young	.15	.05
518	Omar Daal	.15	.05
519	Kirk Gibson	.30	.10
520	Spike Owen	.15	.05
521	Jacob Cruz RC	.30	.10
522	Sandy Alomar Jr.	.15	.05
523	Steve Bedrosian	.15	.05
524	Ricky Gutierrez	.15	.05
525	Dave Veres	.15	.05
526	Gregg Jefferies	.15	.05
527	Jose Valentin	.15	.05
528	Robb Nen	.30	.10
529	Jose Rijo	.15	.05
530	Sean Berry	.15	.05
531	Mike Gallego	.15	.05
532	Roberto Kelly	.15	.05
533	Kevin Stocker	.15	.05
534	Kirby Puckett	.75	.30
535	Chipper Jones	.75	.30
536	Russ Davis	.15	.05
537	Jon Lieber	.15	.05
538	Trey Moore RC	.15	.05
539	Joe Girardi	.15	.05
540	Miguel Cairo RC	.15	.05
541	Tony Phillips	.15	.05
542	Brian Anderson	.15	.05
543	Ivan Rodriguez	.50	.20
544	Jeff Cirillo	.15	.05
545	Joey Cora	.15	.05
546	Chris Hoiles	.15	.05
547	Bernard Gilkey	.15	.05
548	Mike Lansing	.15	.05
549	Jimmy Key	.30	.10
550	Mark Wohlers	.15	.05
551	Chris Clemons RC	.15	.05
552	Vinny Castilla	.30	.10
553	Mark Guthrie	.15	.05

❑ 554	Mike Lieberthal	.30	.10
❑ 555	Tommy Davis RC	.15	.05
❑ 556	Robby Thompson	.15	.05
❑ 557	Danny Bautista	.15	.05
❑ 558	Will Clark	.50	.20
❑ 559	Rickey Henderson	.75	.30
❑ 560	Todd Jones	.15	.05
❑ 561	Jack McDowell	.15	.05
❑ 562	Carlos Rodriguez	.15	.05
❑ 563	Mark Eichhorn	.15	.05
❑ 564	Jeff Nelson	.15	.05
❑ 565	Eric Anthony	.15	.05
❑ 566	Randy Velarde	.15	.05
❑ 567	Javier Lopez	.30	.10
❑ 568	Kevin Mitchell	.15	.05
❑ 569	Steve Karsay	.15	.05
❑ 570	Brian Meadows RC	.15	.05
❑ 571	Rey Ordonez RC	.75	.30
❑ 572	John Kruk	.30	.10
❑ 573	Scott Leius	.15	.05
❑ 574	John Patterson	.15	.05
❑ 575	Kevin Brown	.30	.10
❑ 576	Mike Moore	.15	.05
❑ 577	Manny Ramirez	.50	.20
❑ 578	Jose Lind	.15	.05
❑ 579	Derrick May	.15	.05
❑ 580	Cal Eldred	.15	.05
❑ 581	A.Boone RC/D.Bell	.75	.30
❑ 582	J.T. Snow	.30	.10
❑ 583	Luis Sojo	.15	.05
❑ 584	Moises Alou	.30	.10
❑ 585	Dave Clark	.15	.05
❑ 586	Dave Hollins	.15	.05
❑ 587	Nomar Garciaparra	2.00	.75
❑ 588	Cal Ripken	2.50	1.00
❑ 589	Pedro Astacio	.15	.05
❑ 590	J.R. Phillips	.15	.05
❑ 591	Jeff Frye	.15	.05
❑ 592	Bo Jackson	.75	.30
❑ 593	Steve Ontiveros	.15	.05
❑ 594	David Nied	.15	.05
❑ 595	Brad Ausmus	.30	.10
❑ 596	Carlos Baerga	.15	.05
❑ 597	James Mouton	.15	.05
❑ 598	Ozzie Guillen	.30	.10
❑ 599	Johnny Damon	.75	.30
❑ 600	Yorkis Perez	.15	.05
❑ 601	Rich Rodriguez	.15	.05
❑ 602	Mark McLemore	.15	.05
❑ 603	Jeff Fassero	.15	.05
❑ 604	John Roper	.15	.05
❑ 605	Mark Johnson RC	.40	.15
❑ 606	Wes Chamberlain	.15	.05
❑ 607	Felix Jose	.15	.05
❑ 608	Tony Longmire	.15	.05
❑ 609	Duane Ward	.15	.05
❑ 610	Brett Butler	.30	.10
❑ 611	William VanLandingham	.15	.05
❑ 612	Mickey Tettleton	.15	.05
❑ 613	Brady Anderson	.30	.10
❑ 614	Reggie Jefferson	.15	.05
❑ 615	Mike Kingery	.15	.05
❑ 616	Derek Bell	.15	.05
❑ 617	Scott Erickson	.15	.05
❑ 618	Bob Wickman	.15	.05
❑ 619	Phil Leftwich	.15	.05
❑ 620	David Justice	.30	.10
❑ 621	Paul Wilson	.15	.05
❑ 622	Pedro Martinez	.50	.20
❑ 623	Terry Mathews	.15	.05
❑ 624	Brian McRae	.15	.05
❑ 625	Bruce Ruffin	.15	.05
❑ 626	Steve Finley	.30	.10
❑ 627	Ron Gant	.30	.10
❑ 628	Rafael Bournigal	.15	.05
❑ 629	Darryl Strawberry	.30	.10
❑ 630	Luis Alicea	.15	.05
❑ 631	Mark Smith	.15	.05
❑ 632	C.Bailey/S.Hatteberg	.15	.05
❑ 633	Todd Greene	.30	.10
❑ 634	Rod Bolton	.15	.05
❑ 635	Herbert Perry	.15	.05
❑ 636	Sean Bergman	.15	.05
❑ 637	J.Randa/J.Vitiello	.30	.10
❑ 638	Jose Mercedes	.15	.05
❑ 639	Marty Cordova	.15	.05
❑ 640	R.Rivera/A.Pettitte	.30	.10
❑ 641	W.Adams/S.Spiezio	.15	.05
❑ 642	Eddy Diaz RC	.15	.05
❑ 643	Jon Shave	.15	.05
❑ 644	Paul Spoljaric	.15	.05
❑ 645	Damon Hollins	.15	.05
❑ 646	Doug Glanville	.15	.05
❑ 647	Tim Belk	.15	.05
❑ 648	Rod Pedraza	.15	.05
❑ 649	Marc Valdes	.15	.05
❑ 650	Rick Huisman	.15	.05
❑ 651	Ron Coomer RC	.15	.05
❑ 652	Carlos Perez RC	.40	.15
❑ 653	Jason Isringhausen	.30	.10
❑ 654	Kevin Jordan	.15	.05
❑ 655	Esteban Loaiza	.15	.05
❑ 656	John Frascatore	.15	.05
❑ 657	Bryce Florie	.15	.05
❑ 658	Keith Williams	.15	.05
❑ 659	Checklist	.15	.05
❑ 660	Checklist	.15	.05

1995 Topps Traded

❑	COMPLETE SET (165)	40.00	15.00
❑ 1T	Frank Thomas AB	.60	.25
❑ 2T	Ken Griffey Jr. AB	1.00	.40
❑ 3T	Barry Bonds AB	1.25	.50
❑ 4T	Albert Belle AB	.40	.15
❑ 5T	Cal Ripken AB	1.50	.60
❑ 6T	Mike Piazza AB	1.00	.40
❑ 7T	Tony Gwynn AB	.60	.25
❑ 8T	Jeff Bagwell AB	.40	.15
❑ 9T	Mo Vaughn AB	.20	.07
❑ 10T	Matt Williams AB	.20	.07
❑ 11T	Ray Durham	.40	.15
❑ 12T	J.LeBron RC UER Beltran	6.00	2.50
❑ 13T	Shawn Green	.40	.15
❑ 14T	Kevin Gross	.20	.07
❑ 15T	Jon Nunnally	.20	.07
❑ 16T	Brian Maxcy RC	.25	.08
❑ 17T	Mark Kiefer	.20	.07
❑ 18T	C.Beltran RC UER LeBron	20.00	8.00
❑ 19T	Michael Mimbs RC	.25	.08
❑ 20T	Larry Walker	.40	.15
❑ 21T	Chad Curtis	.20	.07
❑ 22T	Jeff Barry	.20	.07
❑ 23T	Joe Oliver	.20	.07
❑ 24T	Tomas Perez RC	.25	.08
❑ 25T	Michael Barrett RC	1.00	.40
❑ 26T	Brian McRae	.20	.07
❑ 27T	Derek Bell	.20	.07
❑ 28T	Ray Durham	.40	.15
❑ 29T	Todd Williams	.20	.07
❑ 30T	Ryan Jaroncyk RC	.25	.08
❑ 31T	Todd Steverson	.20	.07
❑ 32T	Mike Devereaux	.20	.07
❑ 33T	Rheal Cormier	.20	.07
❑ 34T	Benny Santiago	.40	.15
❑ 35T	Bob Higginson RC	1.00	.40
❑ 36T	Jack McDowell	.20	.07
❑ 37T	Mike MacFarlane	.20	.07
❑ 38T	Tony McKnight RC	.25	.08
❑ 39T	Brian L.Hunter	.20	.07
❑ 40T	Hideo Nomo RC	4.00	1.50
❑ 41T	Brett Butler	.40	.15
❑ 42T	Donovan Osborne	.20	.07
❑ 43T	Scott Karl	.20	.07
❑ 44T	Tony Phillips	.20	.07
❑ 45T	Marty Cordova	.20	.07
❑ 46T	Dave Mlicki	.20	.07
❑ 47T	Bronson Arroyo RC	8.00	3.00
❑ 48T	John Burkett	.20	.07
❑ 49T	J.D.Smart RC	.25	.08
❑ 50T	Mickey Tettleton	.20	.07
❑ 51T	Todd Stottlemyre	.20	.07
❑ 52T	Mike Perez	.20	.07
❑ 53T	Terry Mulholland	.20	.07
❑ 54T	Edgardo Alfonzo	.20	.07
❑ 55T	Zane Smith	.20	.07
❑ 56T	Jacob Brumfield	.20	.07
❑ 57T	Andujar Cedeno	.20	.07
❑ 58T	Jose Parra	.20	.07
❑ 59T	Manny Alexander	.20	.07
❑ 60T	Tony Tarasco	.20	.07
❑ 61T	Orel Hershiser	.40	.15
❑ 62T	Tim Scott	.20	.07
❑ 63T	Felix Rodriguez RC	.25	.08
❑ 64T	Ken Hill	.20	.07
❑ 65T	Marquis Grissom	.40	.15
❑ 66T	Lee Smith	.40	.15
❑ 67T	Jason Bates	.20	.07
❑ 68T	Felipe Lira	.20	.07
❑ 69T	Alex Hernandez RC	.25	.08
❑ 70T	Tony Fernandez	.20	.07
❑ 71T	Scott Radinsky	.20	.07
❑ 72T	Jose Canseco	.60	.25
❑ 73T	Mark Grudzielanek RC	1.00	.40
❑ 74T	Ben Davis RC	.25	.08
❑ 75T	Jim Abbott	.60	.25
❑ 76T	Roger Bailey	.20	.07
❑ 77T	Gregg Jefferies	.20	.07
❑ 78T	Erik Hanson	.20	.07
❑ 79T	Brad Radke RC	1.00	.40
❑ 80T	Jaime Navarro	.20	.07
❑ 81T	John Wetteland	.40	.15
❑ 82T	Chad Fonville RC	.25	.08
❑ 83T	John Mabry	.20	.07
❑ 84T	Glenallen Hill	.20	.07
❑ 85T	Ken Caminiti	.40	.15
❑ 86T	Tom Goodwin	.20	.07
❑ 87T	Darren Bragg	.20	.07
❑ 88T	Robbie Bell RC	.25	.08
❑ 89T	Jeff Russell	.20	.07
❑ 90T	Dave Gallagher	.20	.07
❑ 91T	Steve Finley	.40	.15
❑ 92T	Vaughn Eshelman	.20	.07
❑ 93T	Kevin Jarvis	.20	.07
❑ 94T	Mark Gubicza	.20	.07
❑ 95T	Tim Wakefield	.40	.15
❑ 96T	Bob Tewksbury	.20	.07
❑ 97T	Sid Roberson RC	.25	.08
❑ 98T	Tom Henke	.20	.07
❑ 99T	Michael Tucker	.20	.07
❑ 100T	Jason Bates	.20	.07
❑ 101T	Otis Nixon	.20	.07
❑ 102T	Mark Whiten	.20	.07
❑ 103T	Dilson Torres RC	.25	.08
❑ 104T	Melvin Bunch RC	.25	.08
❑ 105T	Terry Pendleton	.40	.15
❑ 106T	Corey Jenkins RC	.25	.08
❑ 107T	Glenn Dishman RC	.25	.08
❑ 108T	Reggie Taylor RC	.25	.08
❑ 109T	Curtis Goodwin	.20	.07
❑ 110T	David Cone	.40	.15
❑ 111T	Antonio Osuna	.20	.07
❑ 112T	Paul Shuey	.20	.07
❑ 113T	Doug Jones	.20	.07
❑ 114T	Mark McLemore	.20	.07
❑ 115T	Kevin Ritz	.20	.07
❑ 116T	John Kruk	.40	.15
❑ 117T	Trevor Wilson	.20	.07
❑ 118T	Jerald Clark	.20	.07
❑ 119T	Julian Tavarez	.20	.07
❑ 120T	Tim Pugh	.20	.07
❑ 121T	Todd Zeile	.20	.07
❑ 122T	R.Sexson/B.Schneider RC	4.00	1.50
❑ 123T	Bobby Witt	.20	.07
❑ 124T	Hideo Nomo ROY	1.50	.60
❑ 125T	Joey Cora	.20	.07
❑ 126T	Jim Scharrer RC	.25	.08
❑ 127T	Paul Quantrill	.20	.07
❑ 128T	Chipper Jones ROY	.60	.25
❑ 129T	Kenny James RC	.25	.08
❑ 130T	Mariano Rivera	1.25	.50

❑ 131T Tyler Green .20 .07
❑ 132T Brad Clontz .20 .07
❑ 133T Jon Nunnally .20 .07
❑ 134T Dave Magadan .20 .07
❑ 135T Al Leiter .40 .15
❑ 136T Bret Barberie .20 .07
❑ 137T Bill Swift .20 .07
❑ 138T Scott Cooper .20 .07
❑ 139T Roberto Kelly .20 .07
❑ 140T Charlie Hayes .20 .07
❑ 141T Pete Harnisch .20 .07
❑ 142T Rich Amaral .20 .07
❑ 143T Rudy Seanez .20 .07
❑ 144T Pat Listach .20 .07
❑ 145T Quilvio Veras .20 .07
❑ 146T Jose Olmeda RC .25 .08
❑ 147T Roberto Petagine .20 .07
❑ 148T Kevin Brown .40 .15
❑ 149T Phil Plantier .20 .07
❑ 150T Carlos Perez .40 .15
❑ 151T Pat Borders .20 .07
❑ 152T Tyler Green .20 .07
❑ 153T Stan Belinda .20 .07
❑ 154T Dave Stewart .40 .15
❑ 155T Andre Dawson .40 .15
❑ 156T F.Thomas/F.McGriff AS .60 .25
❑ 157T C.Baerga/C.Biggio AS .40 .15
❑ 158T W.Boggs/M.Williams AS .40 .15
❑ 159T C.Ripken/O.Smith AS 1.00 .40
❑ 160T K.Griffey/T.Gwynn AS 1.00 .40
❑ 161T A.Belle/B.Bonds AS 1.25 .50
❑ 162T K.Puckett/L.Dykstra AS .60 .25
❑ 163T I.Rodriguez/M.Piazza AS 1.00 .40
❑ 164T H.Nomo/R.Johnson AS 1.50 .60
❑ 165T Checklist .20 .07

1996 Topps

❑ COMPLETE SET (440) 40.00 15.00
❑ COMP.HOBBY SET (449) 40.00 15.00
❑ COMP.CEREAL SET (444) 50.00 25.00
❑ COMPLETE SERIES 1 (220) 20.00 8.00
❑ COMPLETE SERIES 2 (220) 20.00 8.00
❑ COMMON CARD (1-440) .20 .07
❑ COMMON RC .25 .08
❑ 1 Tony Gwynn STP .30 .10
❑ 2 Mike Piazza STP .50 .20
❑ 3 Greg Maddux STP .50 .20
❑ 4 Jeff Bagwell STP .20 .07
❑ 5 Larry Walker STP .20 .07
❑ 6 Barry Larkin STP .20 .07
❑ 7 Mickey Mantle 4.00 1.50
❑ 8 Tom Glavine STP .20 .07
❑ 9 Craig Biggio STP .20 .07
❑ 10 Barry Bonds STP .75 .30
❑ 11 Heathcliff Slocumb STP .20 .07
❑ 12 Matt Williams STP .20 .07
❑ 13 Todd Helton 1.00 .40
❑ 14 Mark Redman .25 .08
❑ 15 Michael Barrett .25 .08
❑ 16 Ben Davis .25 .08
❑ 17 Juan LeBron .25 .08
❑ 18 Tony McKnight .25 .08
❑ 19 Ryan Jaroncyk .25 .08
❑ 20 Corey Jenkins .25 .08
❑ 21 Jim Scharrer .25 .08
❑ 22 Mark Bellhorn RC 1.00 .40
❑ 23 Jarrod Washburn RC .75 .30
❑ 24 Geoff Jenkins RC .75 .30
❑ 25 Sean Casey RC 4.00 1.50
❑ 26 Brett Tomko RC .40 .15
❑ 27 Tony Fernandez .20 .07
❑ 28 Rich Becker .20 .07
❑ 29 Andujar Cedeno .20 .07
❑ 30 Paul Molitor .20 .07
❑ 31 Brent Gates .20 .07
❑ 32 Glenallen Hill .20 .07
❑ 33 Mike Macfarlane .20 .07
❑ 34 Manny Alexander .20 .07
❑ 35 Todd Zeile .20 .07
❑ 36 Joe Girardi .20 .07
❑ 37 Tony Tarasco .20 .07
❑ 38 Tim Belcher .20 .07
❑ 39 Tom Goodwin .20 .07
❑ 40 Orel Hershiser .20 .07
❑ 41 Tripp Cromer .20 .07
❑ 42 Sean Bergman .20 .07
❑ 43 Troy Percival .20 .07
❑ 44 Kevin Stocker .20 .07
❑ 45 Albert Belle .20 .07
❑ 46 Tony Eusebio .20 .07
❑ 47 Sid Roberson .20 .07
❑ 48 Todd Hollandsworth .20 .07
❑ 49 Mark Wohlers .20 .07
❑ 50 Kirby Puckett .50 .20
❑ 51 Darren Holmes .20 .07
❑ 52 Ron Karkovice .20 .07
❑ 53 Al Martin .20 .07
❑ 54 Pat Rapp .20 .07
❑ 55 Mark Grace .30 .10
❑ 56 Greg Gagne .20 .07
❑ 57 Stan Javier .20 .07
❑ 58 Scott Sanders .20 .07
❑ 59 J.T. Snow .20 .07
❑ 60 David Justice .20 .07
❑ 61 Royce Clayton .20 .07
❑ 62 Kevin Foster .20 .07
❑ 63 Tim Naehring .20 .07
❑ 64 Orlando Miller .20 .07
❑ 65 Mike Mussina .30 .10
❑ 66 Jim Eisenreich .20 .07
❑ 67 Felix Fermin .20 .07
❑ 68 Bernie Williams .30 .10
❑ 69 Robb Nen .20 .07
❑ 70 Ron Gant .20 .07
❑ 71 Felipe Lira .20 .07
❑ 72 Jacob Brumfield .20 .07
❑ 73 John Mabry .20 .07
❑ 74 Mark Carreon .20 .07
❑ 75 Carlos Baerga .20 .07
❑ 76 Jim Dougherty .20 .07
❑ 77 Ryan Thompson .20 .07
❑ 78 Scott Leius .20 .07
❑ 79 Roger Pavlik .20 .07
❑ 80 Gary Sheffield .20 .07
❑ 81 Julian Tavarez .20 .07
❑ 82 Andy Ashby .20 .07
❑ 83 Mark Lemke .20 .07
❑ 84 Omar Vizquel .30 .10
❑ 85 Darren Daulton .20 .07
❑ 86 Mike Lansing .20 .07
❑ 87 Rusty Greer .20 .07
❑ 88 Dave Stevens .20 .07
❑ 89 Jose Offerman .20 .07
❑ 90 Tom Henke .20 .07
❑ 91 Troy O'Leary .20 .07
❑ 92 Michael Tucker .20 .07
❑ 93 Marvin Freeman .20 .07
❑ 94 Alex Diaz .20 .07
❑ 95 John Wetteland .20 .07
❑ 96 Cal Ripken 2131 2.00 .75
❑ 97 Mike Mimbs .20 .07
❑ 98 Bobby Higginson .20 .07
❑ 99 Edgardo Alfonzo .20 .07
❑ 100 Frank Thomas .50 .20
❑ 101 Bob Abreu .50 .20
❑ 102 B.Givens/T.J.Mathews .25 .08
❑ 103 C.Pritchett/T.Hubbard .25 .08
❑ 104 E.Owens/B.Huskey .25 .08
❑ 105 Doug Drabek .20 .07
❑ 106 Tomas Perez .20 .07
❑ 107 Mark Leiter .20 .07
❑ 108 Joe Oliver .20 .07
❑ 109 Tony Castillo .20 .07
❑ 110 Checklist (1-110) .20 .07
❑ 111 Kevin Seitzer .20 .07
❑ 112 Pete Schourek .20 .07
❑ 113 Sean Berry .20 .07
❑ 114 Todd Stottlemyre .20 .07
❑ 115 Joe Carter .20 .07
❑ 116 Jeff King .20 .07
❑ 117 Dan Wilson .20 .07
❑ 118 Kurt Abbott .20 .07
❑ 119 Lyle Mouton .20 .07
❑ 120 Jose Rijo .20 .07
❑ 121 Curtis Goodwin .20 .07
❑ 122 Jose Valentin .20 .07
❑ 123 Ellis Burks .20 .07
❑ 124 David Cone .20 .07
❑ 125 Eddie Murray .50 .20
❑ 126 Brian Jordan .20 .07
❑ 127 Darrin Fletcher .20 .07
❑ 128 Curt Schilling .20 .07
❑ 129 Ozzie Guillen .20 .07
❑ 130 Kenny Rogers .20 .07
❑ 131 Tom Pagnozzi .20 .07
❑ 132 Garret Anderson .20 .07
❑ 133 Bobby Jones .20 .07
❑ 134 Chris Gomez .20 .07
❑ 135 Mike Stanley .20 .07
❑ 136 Hideo Nomo .50 .20
❑ 137 Jon Nunnally .20 .07
❑ 138 Tim Wakefield .20 .07
❑ 139 Steve Finley .20 .07
❑ 140 Ivan Rodriguez .30 .10
❑ 141 Quilvio Veras .20 .07
❑ 142 Mike Fetters .20 .07
❑ 143 Mike Greenwell .20 .07
❑ 144 Bill Pulsipher .20 .07
❑ 145 Mark McGwire 1.25 .50
❑ 146 Frank Castillo .20 .07
❑ 147 Greg Vaughn .20 .07
❑ 148 Pat Hentgen .20 .07
❑ 149 Walt Weiss .20 .07
❑ 150 Randy Johnson .50 .20
❑ 151 David Segui .20 .07
❑ 152 Benji Gil .20 .07
❑ 153 Tom Candiotti .20 .07
❑ 154 Geronimo Berroa .20 .07
❑ 155 John Franco .20 .07
❑ 156 Jay Bell .20 .07
❑ 157 Mark Gubicza .20 .07
❑ 158 Hal Morris .20 .07
❑ 159 Wilson Alvarez .20 .07
❑ 160 Derek Bell .20 .07
❑ 161 Ricky Bottalico .20 .07
❑ 162 Bret Boone .20 .07
❑ 163 Brad Radke .20 .07
❑ 164 John Valentin .20 .07
❑ 165 Steve Avery .20 .07
❑ 166 Mark McLemore .20 .07
❑ 167 Danny Jackson .20 .07
❑ 168 Tino Martinez .30 .10
❑ 169 Shane Reynolds .20 .07
❑ 170 Terry Pendleton .20 .07
❑ 171 Jim Edmonds .20 .07
❑ 172 Esteban Loaiza .20 .07
❑ 173 Ray Durham .20 .07
❑ 174 Carlos Perez .20 .07
❑ 175 Raul Mondesi .20 .07
❑ 176 Steve Ontiveros .20 .07
❑ 177 Chipper Jones .50 .20
❑ 178 Otis Nixon .20 .07
❑ 179 John Burkett .20 .07
❑ 180 Gregg Jefferies .20 .07
❑ 181 Denny Martinez .20 .07
❑ 182 Ken Caminiti .20 .07
❑ 183 Doug Jones .20 .07
❑ 184 Brian McRae .20 .07
❑ 185 Don Mattingly 1.25 .50
❑ 186 Mel Rojas .20 .07
❑ 187 Marty Cordova .20 .07
❑ 188 Vinny Castilla .20 .07
❑ 189 John Smoltz .30 .10
❑ 190 Travis Fryman .20 .07
❑ 191 Chris Hoiles .20 .07
❑ 192 Chuck Finley .20 .07
❑ 193 Ryan Klesko .20 .07
❑ 194 Alex Fernandez .20 .07
❑ 195 Dante Bichette .20 .07
❑ 196 Eric Karros .20 .07

	Player		
❑ 197	Roger Clemens	1.00	.40
❑ 198	Randy Myers	.20	.07
❑ 199	Tony Phillips	.20	.07
❑ 200	Cal Ripken	1.50	.60
❑ 201	Rod Beck	.20	.07
❑ 202	Chad Curtis	.20	.07
❑ 203	Jack McDowell	.20	.07
❑ 204	Gary Gaetti	.20	.07
❑ 205	Ken Griffey Jr.	.75	.30
❑ 206	Ramon Martinez	.20	.07
❑ 207	Jeff Kent	.20	.07
❑ 208	Brad Ausmus	.20	.07
❑ 209	Devon White	.20	.07
❑ 210	Jason Giambi	.20	.07
❑ 211	Nomar Garciaparra	.75	.30
❑ 212	Billy Wagner	.20	.07
❑ 213	Todd Greene	.20	.07
❑ 214	Paul Wilson	.20	.07
❑ 215	Johnny Damon	.30	.10
❑ 216	Alan Benes	.20	.07
❑ 217	Karim Garcia	.20	.07
❑ 218	Dustin Hermanson	.20	.07
❑ 219	Derek Jeter	1.25	.50
❑ 220	Checklist (111-220)	.20	.07
❑ 221	Kirby Puckett STP	.30	.10
❑ 222	Cal Ripken STP	.75	.30
❑ 223	Albert Belle STP	.20	.07
❑ 224	Randy Johnson STP	.30	.10
❑ 225	Wade Boggs STP	.20	.07
❑ 226	Carlos Baerga STP	.20	.07
❑ 227	Ivan Rodriguez STP	.20	.07
❑ 228	Mike Mussina STP	.20	.07
❑ 229	Frank Thomas STP	.30	.10
❑ 230	Ken Griffey Jr. STP	.50	.20
❑ 231	Jose Mesa STP	.20	.07
❑ 232	Matt Morris RC	1.50	.60
❑ 233	Craig Wilson RC	.75	.30
❑ 234	Alvie Shepherd	.25	.08
❑ 235	Randy Winn RC	.75	.30
❑ 236	David Yocum RC	.25	.08
❑ 237	Jason Brester RC	.25	.08
❑ 238	Shane Monahan RC	.25	.08
❑ 239	Brian McNichol RC	.25	.08
❑ 240	Reggie Taylor	.25	.08
❑ 241	Garrett Long	.25	.08
❑ 242	Jonathan Johnson	.25	.08
❑ 243	Jeff Liefer RC	.25	.08
❑ 244	Brian Powell	.25	.08
❑ 245	Brian Buchanan RC	.25	.08
❑ 246	Mike Piazza	.75	.30
❑ 247	Edgar Martinez	.30	.10
❑ 248	Chuck Knoblauch	.20	.07
❑ 249	Andres Galarraga	.20	.07
❑ 250	Tony Gwynn	.60	.25
❑ 251	Lee Smith	.20	.07
❑ 252	Sammy Sosa	.50	.20
❑ 253	Jim Thome	.30	.10
❑ 254	Frank Rodriguez	.20	.07
❑ 255	Charlie Hayes	.20	.07
❑ 256	Bernard Gilkey	.20	.07
❑ 257	John Smiley	.20	.07
❑ 258	Brady Anderson	.20	.07
❑ 259	Rico Brogna	.20	.07
❑ 260	Kirt Manwaring	.20	.07
❑ 261	Len Dykstra	.20	.07
❑ 262	Tom Glavine	.30	.10
❑ 263	Vince Coleman	.20	.07
❑ 264	John Olerud	.20	.07
❑ 265	Orlando Merced	.20	.07
❑ 266	Kent Mercker	.20	.07
❑ 267	Terry Steinbach	.20	.07
❑ 268	Brian L. Hunter	.20	.07
❑ 269	Jeff Fassero	.20	.07
❑ 270	Jay Buhner	.20	.07
❑ 271	Jeff Brantley	.20	.07
❑ 272	Tim Raines	.20	.07
❑ 273	Jimmy Key	.20	.07
❑ 274	Mo Vaughn	.20	.07
❑ 275	Andre Dawson	.20	.07
❑ 276	Jose Mesa	.20	.07
❑ 277	Brett Butler	.20	.07
❑ 278	Luis Gonzalez	.20	.07
❑ 279	Steve Sparks	.20	.07
❑ 280	Chili Davis	.20	.07
❑ 281	Carl Everett	.20	.07
❑ 282	Jeff Cirillo	.20	.07
❑ 283	Thomas Howard	.20	.07
❑ 284	Paul O'Neill	.30	.10
❑ 285	Pat Meares	.20	.07
❑ 286	Mickey Tettleton	.20	.07
❑ 287	Rey Sanchez	.20	.07
❑ 288	Bip Roberts	.20	.07
❑ 289	Roberto Alomar	.30	.10
❑ 290	Ruben Sierra	.20	.07
❑ 291	John Flaherty	.20	.07
❑ 292	Bret Saberhagen	.20	.07
❑ 293	Barry Larkin	.30	.10
❑ 294	Sandy Alomar Jr.	.20	.07
❑ 295	Ed Sprague	.20	.07
❑ 296	Gary DiSarcina	.20	.07
❑ 297	Marquis Grissom	.20	.07
❑ 298	John Frascatore	.20	.07
❑ 299	Will Clark	.30	.10
❑ 300	Barry Bonds	1.50	.60
❑ 301	Ozzie Smith	.75	.30
❑ 302	Dave Nilsson	.20	.07
❑ 303	Pedro Martinez	.30	.10
❑ 304	Joey Cora	.20	.07
❑ 305	Rick Aguilera	.20	.07
❑ 306	Craig Biggio	.30	.10
❑ 307	Jose Vizcaino	.20	.07
❑ 308	Jeff Montgomery	.20	.07
❑ 309	Moises Alou	.20	.07
❑ 310	Robin Ventura	.20	.07
❑ 311	David Wells	.20	.07
❑ 312	Delino DeShields	.20	.07
❑ 313	Trevor Hoffman	.20	.07
❑ 314	Andy Benes	.20	.07
❑ 315	Deion Sanders	.30	.10
❑ 316	Jim Bullinger	.20	.07
❑ 317	John Jaha	.20	.07
❑ 318	Greg Maddux	.75	.30
❑ 319	Tim Salmon	.30	.10
❑ 320	Ben McDonald	.20	.07
❑ 321	Sandy Martinez	.20	.07
❑ 322	Dan Miceli	.20	.07
❑ 323	Wade Boggs	.30	.10
❑ 324	Ismael Valdes	.20	.07
❑ 325	Juan Gonzalez	.20	.07
❑ 326	Charles Nagy	.20	.07
❑ 327	Ray Lankford	.20	.07
❑ 328	Mark Portugal	.20	.07
❑ 329	Bobby Bonilla	.20	.07
❑ 330	Reggie Sanders	.20	.07
❑ 331	Jamie Brewington RC	.25	.08
❑ 332	Aaron Sele	.20	.07
❑ 333	Pete Harnisch	.20	.07
❑ 334	Cliff Floyd	.20	.07
❑ 335	Cal Eldred	.20	.07
❑ 336	Jason Bates	.20	.07
❑ 337	Tony Clark	.20	.07
❑ 338	Jose Herrera	.20	.07
❑ 339	Alex Ochoa	.20	.07
❑ 340	Mark Loretta	.20	.07
❑ 341	Donne Wall	.20	.07
❑ 342	Jason Kendall	.20	.07
❑ 343	Shannon Stewart	.20	.07
❑ 344	Brooks Kieschnick	.20	.07
❑ 345	Chris Snopek	.20	.07
❑ 346	Ruben Rivera	.20	.07
❑ 347	Jeff Suppan	.20	.07
❑ 348	Phil Nevin	.20	.07
❑ 349	John Wasdin	.20	.07
❑ 350	Jay Payton	.20	.07
❑ 351	Tim Crabtree	.20	.07
❑ 352	Rick Krivda	.20	.07
❑ 353	Bob Wolcott	.20	.07
❑ 354	Jimmy Haynes	.20	.07
❑ 355	Herb Perry	.20	.07
❑ 356	Ryne Sandberg	.75	.30
❑ 357	Harold Baines	.20	.07
❑ 358	Chad Ogea	.20	.07
❑ 359	Lee Tinsley	.20	.07
❑ 360	Matt Williams	.20	.07
❑ 361	Randy Velarde	.20	.07
❑ 362	Jose Canseco	.30	.10
❑ 363	Larry Walker	.20	.07
❑ 364	Kevin Appier	.20	.07
❑ 365	Darryl Hamilton	.20	.07
❑ 366	Jose Lima	.20	.07
❑ 367	Javy Lopez	.20	.07
❑ 368	Dennis Eckersley	.20	.07
❑ 369	Jason Isringhausen	.20	.07
❑ 370	Mickey Morandini	.20	.07
❑ 371	Scott Cooper	.20	.07
❑ 372	Jim Abbott	.30	.10
❑ 373	Paul Sorrento	.20	.07
❑ 374	Chris Hammond	.20	.07
❑ 375	Lance Johnson	.20	.07
❑ 376	Kevin Brown	.20	.07
❑ 377	Luis Alicea	.20	.07
❑ 378	Andy Pettitte	.30	.10
❑ 379	Dean Palmer	.20	.07
❑ 380	Jeff Bagwell	.30	.10
❑ 381	Jaime Navarro	.20	.07
❑ 382	Rondell White	.20	.07
❑ 383	Erik Hanson	.20	.07
❑ 384	Pedro Munoz	.20	.07
❑ 385	Heathcliff Slocumb	.20	.07
❑ 386	Wally Joyner	.20	.07
❑ 387	Bob Tewksbury	.20	.07
❑ 388	David Bell	.20	.07
❑ 389	Fred McGriff	.30	.10
❑ 390	Mike Henneman	.20	.07
❑ 391	Robby Thompson	.20	.07
❑ 392	Norm Charlton	.20	.07
❑ 393	Cecil Fielder	.20	.07
❑ 394	Benito Santiago	.20	.07
❑ 395	Rafael Palmeiro	.30	.10
❑ 396	Ricky Bones	.20	.07
❑ 397	Rickey Henderson	.50	.20
❑ 398	C.J. Nitkowski	.20	.07
❑ 399	Shawon Dunston	.20	.07
❑ 400	Manny Ramirez	.30	.10
❑ 401	Bill Swift	.20	.07
❑ 402	Chad Fonville	.20	.07
❑ 403	Joey Hamilton	.20	.07
❑ 404	Alex Gonzalez	.20	.07
❑ 405	Roberto Hernandez	.20	.07
❑ 406	Jeff Blauser	.20	.07
❑ 407	LaTroy Hawkins	.20	.07
❑ 408	Greg Colbrunn	.20	.07
❑ 409	Todd Hundley	.20	.07
❑ 410	Glenn Dishman	.20	.07
❑ 411	Joe Vitiello	.20	.07
❑ 412	Todd Worrell	.20	.07
❑ 413	Wil Cordero	.20	.07
❑ 414	Ken Hill	.20	.07
❑ 415	Carlos Garcia	.20	.07
❑ 416	Bryan Rekar	.20	.07
❑ 417	Shawn Green	.20	.07
❑ 418	Tyler Green	.20	.07
❑ 419	Mike Blowers	.20	.07
❑ 420	Kenny Lofton	.20	.07
❑ 421	Denny Neagle	.20	.07
❑ 422	Jeff Conine	.20	.07
❑ 423	Mark Langston	.20	.07
❑ 424	Ron Wright RC/D.Lee	.75	.30
❑ 425	D.Ward RC/R.Sexson	1.00	.40
❑ 426	Adam Riggs RC	.25	.08
❑ 427	N.Perez/E.Wilson	.25	.08
❑ 428	Bartolo Colon	.50	.20
❑ 429	Marty Janzen RC	.25	.08
❑ 430	Rich Hunter RC	.25	.08
❑ 431	Dave Coggin RC	.25	.08
❑ 432	R.Ibanez RC/P.Konerko	1.50	.60
❑ 433	Marc Kroon	.20	.07
❑ 434	S.Rolen/S.Spiezio	.50	.20
❑ 435	V.Guerrero/A.Jones	2.50	1.00
❑ 436	Shane Spencer RC	.40	.15
❑ 437	A.French/D.Stovall RC	.25	.08
❑ 438	M.Coleman RC/R.Hidalgo	.25	.08
❑ 439	Jermaine Dye	.20	.07
❑ 440	Checklist	.20	.07
❑ F7	Mickey Mantle Last Day	5.00	2.00
❑ NNO	Mickey Mantle Tribute Card, promotes the Mantle F7	3.00	1.25

1997 Topps

	Player		
❑	COMPLETE SET (495)	80.00	40.00
❑	COMPLETE SERIES 1 (276)	40.00	20.00
❑	COMPLETE SERIES 2 (220)	40.00	20.00
❑ 1	Barry Bonds	1.50	.60
❑ 2	Tom Pagnozzi	.20	.07
❑ 3	Terrell Wade	.20	.07
❑ 4	Jose Valentin	.20	.07
❑ 5	Mark Clark	.20	.07
❑ 6	Brady Anderson	.20	.07

❑	8	Wade Boggs	.30	.10
❑	9	Scott Stahoviak	.20	.07
❑	10	Andres Galarraga	.20	.07
❑	11	Steve Avery	.20	.07
❑	12	Rusty Greer	.20	.07
❑	13	Derek Jeter	1.25	.50
❑	14	Ricky Bottalico	.20	.07
❑	15	Andy Ashby	.20	.07
❑	16	Paul Shuey	.20	.07
❑	17	F.P. Santangelo	.20	.07
❑	18	Royce Clayton	.20	.07
❑	19	Mike Mohler	.20	.07
❑	20	Mike Piazza	.75	.30
❑	21	Jaime Navarro	.20	.07
❑	22	Billy Wagner	.20	.07
❑	23	Mike Timlin	.20	.07
❑	24	Garret Anderson	.20	.07
❑	25	Ben McDonald	.20	.07
❑	26	Mel Rojas	.20	.07
❑	27	John Burkett	.20	.07
❑	28	Jeff King	.20	.07
❑	29	Reggie Jefferson	.20	.07
❑	30	Kevin Appier	.20	.07
❑	31	Felipe Lira	.20	.07
❑	32	Kevin Tapani	.20	.07
❑	33	Mark Portugal	.20	.07
❑	34	Carlos Garcia	.20	.07
❑	35	Joey Cora	.20	.07
❑	36	David Segui	.20	.07
❑	37	Mark Grace	.30	.10
❑	38	Erik Hanson	.20	.07
❑	39	Jeff D'Amico	.20	.07
❑	40	Jay Buhner	.20	.07
❑	41	B.J. Surhoff	.20	.07
❑	42	Jackie Robinson TRIB	.50	.20
❑	43	Roger Pavlik	.20	.07
❑	44	Hal Morris	.20	.07
❑	45	Mariano Duncan	.20	.07
❑	46	Harold Baines	.20	.07
❑	47	Jorge Fabregas	.20	.07
❑	48	Jose Herrera	.20	.07
❑	49	Jeff Cirillo	.20	.07
❑	50	Tom Glavine	.30	.10
❑	51	Pedro Astacio	.20	.07
❑	52	Mark Gardner	.20	.07
❑	53	Arthur Rhodes	.20	.07
❑	54	Troy O'Leary	.20	.07
❑	55	Bip Roberts	.20	.07
❑	56	Mike Lieberthal	.20	.07
❑	57	Shane Andrews	.20	.07
❑	58	Scott Karl	.20	.07
❑	59	Gary DiSarcina	.20	.07
❑	60	Andy Pettitte	.30	.10
❑	61	Kevin Elster	.20	.07
❑	61B	Mike Fetters UER	.20	.07
❑	62	Mark McGwire	1.25	.50
❑	63	Dan Wilson	.20	.07
❑	64	Mickey Morandini	.20	.07
❑	65	Chuck Knoblauch	.20	.07
❑	66	Tim Wakefield	.20	.07
❑	67	Raul Mondesi	.20	.07
❑	68	Todd Jones	.20	.07
❑	69	Albert Belle	.20	.07
❑	70	Trevor Hoffman	.20	.07
❑	71	Eric Young	.20	.07
❑	72	Robert Perez	.20	.07
❑	73	Butch Huskey	.20	.07
❑	74	Brian McRae	.20	.07
❑	75	Jim Edmonds	.20	.07
❑	76	Mike Henneman	.20	.07
❑	77	Frank Rodriguez	.20	.07
❑	78	Danny Tartabull	.20	.07
❑	79	Robb Nen	.20	.07
❑	80	Reggie Sanders	.20	.07
❑	81	Ron Karkovice	.20	.07
❑	82	Benito Santiago	.20	.07
❑	83	Mike Lansing	.20	.07
❑	85	Craig Biggio	.30	.10
❑	86	Mike Bordick	.20	.07
❑	87	Ray Lankford	.20	.07
❑	88	Charles Nagy	.20	.07
❑	89	Paul Wilson	.20	.07
❑	90	John Wetteland	.20	.07
❑	91	Tom Candiotti	.20	.07
❑	92	Carlos Delgado	.20	.07
❑	93	Derek Bell	.20	.07
❑	94	Mark Lemke	.20	.07
❑	95	Edgar Martinez	.30	.10
❑	96	Rickey Henderson	.50	.20
❑	97	Greg Myers	.20	.07
❑	98	Jim Leyritz	.20	.07
❑	99	Mark Johnson	.20	.07
❑	100	Dwight Gooden HL	.20	.07
❑	101	Al Leiter HL	.20	.07
❑	102	John Mabry HL	.20	.07
❑	103	Alex Ochoa HL	.20	.07
❑	104	Mike Piazza HL	.50	.20
❑	105	Jim Thome	.30	.10
❑	106	Ricky Otero	.20	.07
❑	107	Jamey Wright	.20	.07
❑	108	Frank Thomas	.50	.20
❑	109	Jody Reed	.20	.07
❑	110	Orel Hershiser	.20	.07
❑	111	Terry Steinbach	.20	.07
❑	112	Mark Loretta	.20	.07
❑	113	Turk Wendell	.20	.07
❑	114	Marvin Benard	.20	.07
❑	115	Kevin Brown	.20	.07
❑	116	Robert Person	.20	.07
❑	117	Joey Hamilton	.20	.07
❑	118	Francisco Cordova	.20	.07
❑	119	John Smiley	.20	.07
❑	120	Travis Fryman	.20	.07
❑	121	Jimmy Key	.20	.07
❑	122	Tom Goodwin	.20	.07
❑	123	Mike Greenwell	.20	.07
❑	124	Juan Gonzalez	.20	.07
❑	125	Pete Harnisch	.20	.07
❑	126	Roger Cedeno	.20	.07
❑	127	Ron Gant	.20	.07
❑	128	Mark Langston	.20	.07
❑	129	Tim Crabtree	.20	.07
❑	130	Greg Maddux	.75	.30
❑	131	William VanLandingham	.20	.07
❑	132	Wally Joyner	.20	.07
❑	133	Randy Myers	.20	.07
❑	134	John Valentin	.20	.07
❑	135	Bret Boone	.20	.07
❑	136	Bruce Ruffin	.20	.07
❑	137	Chris Snopek	.20	.07
❑	138	Paul Molitor	.20	.07
❑	139	Mark McLemore	.20	.07
❑	140	Rafael Palmeiro	.30	.10
❑	141	Herb Perry	.20	.07
❑	142	Luis Gonzalez	.20	.07
❑	143	Doug Drabek	.20	.07
❑	144	Ken Ryan	.20	.07
❑	145	Todd Hundley	.20	.07
❑	146	Ellis Burks	.20	.07
❑	147	Ozzie Guillen	.20	.07
❑	148	Rich Becker	.20	.07
❑	149	Sterling Hitchcock	.20	.07
❑	150	Bernie Williams	.30	.10
❑	151	Mike Stanley	.20	.07
❑	152	Roberto Alomar	.30	.10
❑	153	Jose Mesa	.20	.07
❑	154	Steve Trachsel	.20	.07
❑	155	Alex Gonzalez	.20	.07
❑	156	Troy Percival	.20	.07
❑	157	John Smoltz	.30	.10
❑	158	Pedro Martinez	.30	.10
❑	159	Jeff Conine	.20	.07
❑	160	Bernard Gilkey	.20	.07
❑	161	Jim Eisenreich	.20	.07
❑	162	Mickey Tettleton	.20	.07
❑	163	Justin Thompson	.20	.07
❑	164	Jose Offerman	.20	.07
❑	165	Tony Phillips	.20	.07
❑	166	Ismael Valdes	.20	.07
❑	167	Ryne Sandberg	.75	.30
❑	168	Matt Mieske	.20	.07
❑	169	Geronimo Berroa	.20	.07
❑	170	Otis Nixon	.20	.07
❑	171	John Mabry	.20	.07
❑	172	Shawon Dunston	.20	.07
❑	173	Omar Vizquel	.30	.10
❑	174	Chris Hoiles	.20	.07
❑	175	Dwight Gooden	.20	.07
❑	176	Wilson Alvarez	.20	.07
❑	177	Todd Hollandsworth	.20	.07
❑	178	Roger Salkeld	.20	.07
❑	179	Rey Sanchez	.20	.07
❑	180	Rey Ordonez	.20	.07
❑	181	Denny Martinez	.20	.07
❑	182	Ramon Martinez	.20	.07
❑	183	Dave Nilsson	.20	.07
❑	184	Marquis Grissom	.20	.07
❑	185	Randy Velarde	.20	.07
❑	186	Ron Coomer	.20	.07
❑	187	Tino Martinez	.30	.10
❑	188	Jeff Brantley	.20	.07
❑	189	Steve Finley	.20	.07
❑	190	Andy Benes	.20	.07
❑	191	Terry Adams	.20	.07
❑	192	Mike Blowers	.20	.07
❑	193	Russ Davis	.20	.07
❑	194	Darryl Hamilton	.20	.07
❑	195	Jason Kendall	.20	.07
❑	196	Johnny Damon	.30	.10
❑	197	Dave Martinez	.20	.07
❑	198	Mike Macfarlane	.20	.07
❑	199	Norm Charlton	.20	.07
❑	200	Damian Moss	.25	.08
❑	201	Jenkins/Ibanez/Cameron	.20	.07
❑	202	Sean Casey	.30	.10
❑	203	J.Hansen/H.Bush/F.Crespo	.20	.07
❑	204	K.Orie/G.Alvarez/A.Boone	.20	.07
❑	205	B.Davis/K.Brown/B.Estalella	.20	.07
❑	206	Bubba Trammell RC	.40	.15
❑	207	Jarrod Washburn	.20	.07
❑	208	Brian Hunter	.20	.07
❑	209	Jason Giambi	.20	.07
❑	210	Henry Rodriguez	.20	.07
❑	211	Edgar Renteria	.20	.07
❑	212	Edgardo Alfonzo	.20	.07
❑	213	Fernando Vina	.20	.07
❑	214	Shawn Green	.20	.07
❑	215	Ray Durham	.20	.07
❑	216	Joe Randa	.20	.07
❑	217	Armando Reynoso	.20	.07
❑	218	Eric Davis	.20	.07
❑	219	Bob Tewksbury	.20	.07
❑	220	Jacob Cruz	.20	.07
❑	221	Glenallen Hill	.20	.07
❑	222	Gary Gaetti	.20	.07
❑	223	Donne Wall	.20	.07
❑	224	Brad Clontz	.20	.07
❑	225	Marty Janzen	.20	.07
❑	226	Todd Worrell	.20	.07
❑	227	John Franco	.20	.07
❑	228	David Wells	.20	.07
❑	229	Gregg Jefferies	.20	.07
❑	230	Tim Naehring	.20	.07
❑	231	Thomas Howard	.20	.07
❑	232	Roberto Hernandez	.20	.07
❑	233	Kevin Ritz	.20	.07
❑	234	Julian Tavarez	.20	.07
❑	235	Ken Hill	.20	.07
❑	236	Greg Gagne	.20	.07
❑	237	Bobby Chouinard	.20	.07
❑	238	Joe Carter	.20	.07
❑	239	Jermaine Dye	.20	.07
❑	240	Antonio Osuna	.20	.07
❑	241	Julio Franco	.20	.07
❑	242	Mike Grace	.20	.07
❑	243	Aaron Sele	.20	.07
❑	244	David Justice	.20	.07
❑	245	Sandy Alomar Jr.	.20	.07
❑	246	Jose Canseco	.30	.10
❑	247	Paul O'Neill	.30	.10

❑ 248	Sean Berry	.20	.07
❑ 249	N.Bierbrodt/K.Sweeney RC	.25	.08
❑ 250	Vladimir Nunez RC	.25	.08
❑ 251	R.Hartman/D.Hayman RC	.25	.08
❑ 252	A.Sanchez/M.Quatraro RC	.40	.15
❑ 253	Ronni Seberino RC	.25	.08
❑ 254	Rex Hudler	.20	.07
❑ 255	Orlando Miller	.20	.07
❑ 256	Mariano Rivera	.50	.20
❑ 257	Brad Radke	.20	.07
❑ 258	Bobby Higginson	.20	.07
❑ 259	Jay Bell	.20	.07
❑ 260	Mark Grudzielanek	.20	.07
❑ 261	Lance Johnson	.20	.07
❑ 262	Ken Caminiti	.20	.07
❑ 263	J.T. Snow	.20	.07
❑ 264	Gary Sheffield	.20	.07
❑ 265	Darrin Fletcher	.20	.07
❑ 266	Eric Owens	.20	.07
❑ 267	Luis Castillo	.20	.07
❑ 268	Scott Rolen	.30	.10
❑ 269	T.Noel/J.Oliver RC	.25	.08
❑ 270	Robert Stratton RC	.40	.15
❑ 271	Gil Meche RC	1.00	.40
❑ 272	E.Milton RC/D.Brown RC	.40	.15
❑ 273	Chris Reitsma RC	.40	.15
❑ 274	J.Marquis/A.J.Zapp RC	.50	.20
❑ 275	Checklist	.20	.07
❑ 276	Checklist	.20	.07
❑ 277	Chipper Jones UER276	.50	.20
❑ 278	Orlando Merced	.20	.07
❑ 279	Ariel Prieto	.20	.07
❑ 280	Al Leiter	.20	.07
❑ 281	Pat Meares	.20	.07
❑ 282	Darryl Strawberry	.20	.07
❑ 283	Jamie Moyer	.20	.07
❑ 284	Scott Servais	.20	.07
❑ 285	Delino DeShields	.20	.07
❑ 286	Danny Graves	.20	.07
❑ 287	Gerald Williams	.20	.07
❑ 288	Todd Greene	.20	.07
❑ 289	Rico Brogna	.20	.07
❑ 290	Derrick Gibson	.20	.07
❑ 291	Joe Girardi	.20	.07
❑ 292	Darren Lewis	.20	.07
❑ 293	Nomar Garciaparra	.75	.30
❑ 294	Greg Colbrunn	.20	.07
❑ 295	Jeff Bagwell	.30	.10
❑ 296	Brent Gates	.20	.07
❑ 297	Jose Vizcaino	.20	.07
❑ 298	Alex Ochoa	.20	.07
❑ 299	Sid Fernandez	.20	.07
❑ 300	Ken Griffey Jr.	.75	.30
❑ 301	Chris Gomez	.20	.07
❑ 302	Wendell Magee	.20	.07
❑ 303	Darren Oliver	.20	.07
❑ 304	Mel Nieves	.20	.07
❑ 305	Sammy Sosa	.50	.20
❑ 306	George Arias	.20	.07
❑ 307	Jack McDowell	.20	.07
❑ 308	Stan Javier	.20	.07
❑ 309	Kimera Bartee	.20	.07
❑ 310	James Baldwin	.20	.07
❑ 311	Rocky Coppinger	.20	.07
❑ 312	Keith Lockhart	.20	.07
❑ 313	C.J. Nitkowski	.20	.07
❑ 314	Allen Watson	.20	.07
❑ 315	Darryl Kile	.20	.07
❑ 316	Amaury Telemaco	.20	.07
❑ 317	Jason Isringhausen	.20	.07
❑ 318	Manny Ramirez	.30	.10
❑ 319	Terry Pendleton	.20	.07
❑ 320	Tim Salmon	.30	.10
❑ 321	Eric Karros	.20	.07
❑ 322	Mark Whiten	.20	.07
❑ 323	Rick Krivda	.20	.07
❑ 324	Brett Butler	.20	.07
❑ 325	Randy Johnson	.50	.20
❑ 326	Eddie Taubensee	.20	.07
❑ 327	Mark Leiter	.20	.07
❑ 328	Kevin Gross	.20	.07
❑ 329	Ernie Young	.20	.07
❑ 330	Pat Hentgen	.20	.07
❑ 331	Rondell White	.20	.07
❑ 332	Bobby Witt	.20	.07
❑ 333	Eddie Murray	.50	.20
❑ 334	Tim Raines	.20	.07
❑ 335	Jeff Fassero	.20	.07
❑ 336	Chuck Finley	.20	.07
❑ 337	Willie Adams	.20	.07
❑ 338	Chan Ho Park	.20	.07
❑ 339	Jay Powell	.20	.07
❑ 340	Ivan Rodriguez	.30	.10
❑ 341	Jermaine Allensworth	.20	.07
❑ 342	Jay Payton	.20	.07
❑ 343	T.J. Mathews	.20	.07
❑ 344	Tony Batista	.20	.07
❑ 345	Ed Sprague	.20	.07
❑ 346	Jeff Kent	.20	.07
❑ 347	Scott Erickson	.20	.07
❑ 348	Jeff Suppan	.20	.07
❑ 349	Pete Schourek	.20	.07
❑ 350	Kenny Lofton	.20	.07
❑ 351	Alan Benes	.20	.07
❑ 352	Fred McGriff	.30	.10
❑ 353	Charlie O'Brien	.20	.07
❑ 354	Darren Bragg	.20	.07
❑ 355	Alex Fernandez	.20	.07
❑ 356	Al Martin	.20	.07
❑ 357	Bob Wells	.20	.07
❑ 358	Chad Mottola	.20	.07
❑ 359	Devon White	.20	.07
❑ 360	David Cone	.20	.07
❑ 361	Bobby Jones	.20	.07
❑ 362	Scott Sanders	.20	.07
❑ 363	Karim Garcia	.20	.07
❑ 364	Kirt Manwaring	.20	.07
❑ 365	Chili Davis	.20	.07
❑ 366	Mike Hampton	.20	.07
❑ 367	Chad Ogea	.20	.07
❑ 368	Curt Schilling	.20	.07
❑ 369	Phil Nevin	.20	.07
❑ 370	Roger Clemens	1.00	.40
❑ 371	Willie Greene	.20	.07
❑ 372	Kenny Rogers	.20	.07
❑ 373	Jose Rijo	.20	.07
❑ 374	Bobby Bonilla	.20	.07
❑ 375	Mike Mussina	.30	.10
❑ 376	Curtis Pride	.20	.07
❑ 377	Todd Walker	.20	.07
❑ 378	Jason Bere	.20	.07
❑ 379	Heathcliff Slocumb	.20	.07
❑ 380	Dante Bichette	.20	.07
❑ 381	Carlos Baerga	.20	.07
❑ 382	Livan Hernandez	.20	.07
❑ 383	Jason Schmidt	.20	.07
❑ 384	Kevin Stocker	.20	.07
❑ 385	Matt Williams	.20	.07
❑ 386	Bartolo Colon	.20	.07
❑ 387	Will Clark	.30	.10
❑ 388	Dennis Eckersley	.20	.07
❑ 389	Brooks Kieschnick	.20	.07
❑ 390	Ryan Klesko	.20	.07
❑ 391	Mark Carreon	.20	.07
❑ 392	Tim Worrell	.20	.07
❑ 393	Dean Palmer	.20	.07
❑ 394	Wil Cordero	.20	.07
❑ 395	Javy Lopez	.20	.07
❑ 396	Rich Aurilia	.20	.07
❑ 397	Greg Vaughn	.20	.07
❑ 398	Vinny Castilla	.20	.07
❑ 399	Jeff Montgomery	.20	.07
❑ 400	Cal Ripken	1.50	.60
❑ 401	Walt Weiss	.20	.07
❑ 402	Brad Ausmus	.20	.07
❑ 403	Ruben Rivera	.20	.07
❑ 404	Mark Wohlers	.20	.07
❑ 405	Rick Aguilera	.20	.07
❑ 406	Tony Clark	.20	.07
❑ 407	Lyle Mouton	.20	.07
❑ 408	Bill Pulsipher	.20	.07
❑ 409	Jose Rosado	.20	.07
❑ 410	Tony Gwynn	.60	.25
❑ 411	Cecil Fielder	.20	.07
❑ 412	John Flaherty	.20	.07
❑ 413	Lenny Dykstra	.20	.07
❑ 414	Ugueth Urbina	.20	.07
❑ 415	Brian Jordan	.20	.07
❑ 416	Bob Abreu	.30	.10
❑ 417	Craig Paquette	.20	.07
❑ 418	Sandy Martinez	.20	.07
❑ 419	Jeff Blauser	.20	.07
❑ 420	Barry Larkin	.30	.10
❑ 421	Kevin Seitzer	.20	.07
❑ 422	Tim Belcher	.20	.07
❑ 423	Paul Sorrento	.20	.07
❑ 424	Cal Eldred	.20	.07
❑ 425	Robin Ventura	.20	.07
❑ 426	John Olerud	.20	.07
❑ 427	Bob Wolcott	.20	.07
❑ 428	Matt Lawton	.20	.07
❑ 429	Rod Beck	.20	.07
❑ 430	Shane Reynolds	.20	.07
❑ 431	Mike James	.20	.07
❑ 432	Steve Wojciechowski	.20	.07
❑ 433	Vladimir Guerrero	.50	.20
❑ 434	Dustin Hermanson	.20	.07
❑ 435	Marty Cordova	.20	.07
❑ 436	Marc Newfield	.20	.07
❑ 437	Todd Stottlemyre	.20	.07
❑ 438	Jeffrey Hammonds	.20	.07
❑ 439	Dave Stevens	.20	.07
❑ 440	Hideo Nomo	.50	.20
❑ 441	Mark Thompson	.20	.07
❑ 442	Mark Lewis	.20	.07
❑ 443	Quinton McCracken	.20	.07
❑ 444	Cliff Floyd	.20	.07
❑ 445	Denny Neagle	.20	.07
❑ 446	John Jaha	.20	.07
❑ 447	Mike Sweeney	.20	.07
❑ 448	John Wasdin	.20	.07
❑ 449	Chad Curtis	.20	.07
❑ 450	Mo Vaughn	.20	.07
❑ 451	Donovan Osborne	.20	.07
❑ 452	Ruben Sierra	.20	.07
❑ 453	Michael Tucker	.20	.07
❑ 454	Kurt Abbott	.20	.07
❑ 455	Andruw Jones UER	.30	.10
❑ 456	Shannon Stewart	.20	.07
❑ 457	Scott Brosius	.20	.07
❑ 458	Juan Guzman	.20	.07
❑ 459	Ron Villone	.20	.07
❑ 460	Moises Alou	.20	.07
❑ 461	Larry Walker	.20	.07
❑ 462	Eddie Murray SH	.30	.10
❑ 463	Paul Molitor SH	.20	.07
❑ 464	Hideo Nomo SH	.20	.07
❑ 465	Barry Bonds SH	.75	.30
❑ 466	Todd Hundley SH	.20	.07
❑ 467	Rheal Cormier	.20	.07
❑ 468	J.Sandoval/J.Conti RC	.25	.08
❑ 469	R.Barajas/J.Rexrode RC	1.50	.60
❑ 470	Jared Sandberg RC	.25	.08
❑ 471	P.Wilder/C.Gunner RC	.25	.08
❑ 472	M.DeCelle/M.McCain RC	.25	.08
❑ 473	Todd Zeile	.20	.07
❑ 474	Neifi Perez	.20	.07
❑ 475	Jeromy Burnitz	.20	.07
❑ 476	Trey Beamon	.20	.07
❑ 477	J.Patterson/B.Looper RC	.75	.30
❑ 478	Jake Westbrook RC	.50	.20
❑ 479	E.Chavez/A.Eaton RC	2.00	.75
❑ 480	P.Tucci/J.Lawrence RC	.25	.08
❑ 481	K.Benson/B.Koch RC	.50	.20
❑ 482	J.Nicholson/A.Prater RC	.25	.08
❑ 483	M.Kotsay/M.Johnson RC	.75	.30
❑ 484	Armando Benitez	.20	.07
❑ 485	Mike Matheny	.20	.07
❑ 486	Jeff Reed	.20	.07
❑ 487	M.Bellhorn/R.Johnson/E.Wilson	.20	.07
❑ 488	R.Hidalgo/B.Grieve	.20	.07
❑ 489	Konerko/D.Lee/Wright	.30	.10
❑ 490	Bill Mueller RC	1.25	.50
❑ 491	J.Abbott/S.Monahan/E.Velazquez	.20	.07
❑ 492	Jimmy Anderson RC	.25	.08
❑ 493	Carl Pavano	.20	.07
❑ 494	Nelson Figueroa RC	.25	.08
❑ 495	Checklist (277-400)	.20	.07
❑ 496	Checklist (401-496)	.20	.07
❑ NNO	Derek Jeter AU	150.00	75.00

1998 Topps

❑	COMPLETE SET (503)	80.00	40.00
❑	COMP.HOBBY SET (511)	120.00	60.00
❑	COMP.RETAIL SET (511)	120.00	60.00
❑	COMPLETE SERIES 1 (282)	40.00	20.00
❑	COMPLETE SERIES 2 (221)	40.00	20.00
❑ 1	Tony Gwynn	.60	.25

❑ 2	Larry Walker	.20	.07
❑ 3	Billy Wagner	.20	.07
❑ 4	Denny Neagle	.20	.07
❑ 5	Vladimir Guerrero	.50	.20
❑ 6	Kevin Brown	.30	.10
❑ 8	Mariano Rivera	.50	.20
❑ 9	Tony Clark	.20	.07
❑ 10	Deion Sanders	.30	.10
❑ 11	Francisco Cordova	.20	.07
❑ 12	Matt Williams	.20	.07
❑ 13	Carlos Baerga	.20	.07
❑ 14	Mo Vaughn	.20	.07
❑ 15	Bobby Witt	.20	.07
❑ 16	Matt Stairs	.20	.07
❑ 17	Chan Ho Park	.20	.07
❑ 18	Mike Bordick	.20	.07
❑ 19	Michael Tucker	.20	.07
❑ 20	Frank Thomas	.50	.20
❑ 21	Roberto Clemente	1.00	.40
❑ 22	Dmitri Young	.20	.07
❑ 23	Steve Trachsel	.20	.07
❑ 24	Jeff Kent	.20	.07
❑ 25	Scott Rolen	.30	.10
❑ 26	John Thomson	.20	.07
❑ 27	Joe Vitiello	.20	.07
❑ 28	Eddie Guardado	.20	.07
❑ 29	Charlie Hayes	.20	.07
❑ 30	Juan Gonzalez	.20	.07
❑ 31	Garret Anderson	.20	.07
❑ 32	John Jaha	.20	.07
❑ 33	Omar Vizquel	.30	.10
❑ 34	Brian Hunter	.20	.07
❑ 35	Jeff Bagwell	.30	.10
❑ 36	Mark Lemke	.20	.07
❑ 37	Doug Glanville	.20	.07
❑ 38	Dan Wilson	.20	.07
❑ 39	Steve Cooke	.20	.07
❑ 40	Chili Davis	.20	.07
❑ 41	Mike Cameron	.20	.07
❑ 42	F.P. Santangelo	.20	.07
❑ 43	Brad Ausmus	.20	.07
❑ 44	Gary DiSarcina	.20	.07
❑ 45	Pat Hentgen	.20	.07
❑ 46	Wilton Guerrero	.20	.07
❑ 47	Devon White	.20	.07
❑ 48	Danny Patterson	.20	.07
❑ 49	Pat Meares	.20	.07
❑ 50	Rafael Palmeiro	.30	.10
❑ 51	Mark Gardner	.20	.07
❑ 52	Jeff Blauser	.20	.07
❑ 53	Dave Hollins	.20	.07
❑ 54	Carlos Garcia	.20	.07
❑ 55	Ben McDonald	.20	.07
❑ 56	John Mabry	.20	.07
❑ 57	Trevor Hoffman	.20	.07
❑ 58	Tony Fernandez	.20	.07
❑ 59	Rich Loiselle	.20	.07
❑ 60	Mark Lelter	.20	.07
❑ 61	Pat Kelly	.20	.07
❑ 62	John Flaherty	.20	.07
❑ 63	Roger Bailey	.20	.07
❑ 64	Tom Gordon	.20	.07
❑ 65	Ryan Klesko	.20	.07
❑ 66	Darryl Hamilton	.20	.07
❑ 67	Jim Eisenreich	.20	.07
❑ 68	Butch Huskey	.20	.07
❑ 69	Mark Grudzielanek	.20	.07
❑ 70	Marquis Grissom	.20	.07
❑ 71	Mark McLemore	.20	.07
❑ 72	Gary Gaetti	.20	.07
❑ 73	Greg Gagne	.20	.07
❑ 74	Lyle Mouton	.20	.07
❑ 75	Jim Edmonds	.20	.07
❑ 76	Shawn Green	.20	.07
❑ 77	Greg Vaughn	.20	.07
❑ 78	Terry Adams	.20	.07
❑ 79	Kevin Polcovich	.20	.07
❑ 80	Troy O'Leary	.20	.07
❑ 81	Jeff Shaw	.20	.07
❑ 82	Rich Becker	.20	.07
❑ 83	David Wells	.20	.07
❑ 84	Steve Karsay	.20	.07
❑ 85	Charles Nagy	.20	.07
❑ 86	B.J. Surhoff	.20	.07
❑ 87	Jamey Wright	.20	.07
❑ 88	James Baldwin	.20	.07
❑ 89	Edgardo Alfonzo	.20	.07
❑ 90	Jay Buhner	.20	.07
❑ 91	Brady Anderson	.20	.07
❑ 92	Scott Servais	.20	.07
❑ 93	Edgar Renteria	.20	.07
❑ 94	Mike Lieberthal	.20	.07
❑ 95	Rick Aguilera	.20	.07
❑ 96	Walt Weiss	.20	.07
❑ 97	Deivi Cruz	.20	.07
❑ 98	Kurt Abbott	.20	.07
❑ 99	Henry Rodriguez	.20	.07
❑ 100	Mike Piazza	.75	.30
❑ 101	Bill Taylor	.20	.07
❑ 102	Todd Zeile	.20	.07
❑ 103	Rey Ordonez	.20	.07
❑ 104	Willie Greene	.20	.07
❑ 105	Tony Womack	.20	.07
❑ 106	Mike Sweeney	.20	.07
❑ 107	Jeffrey Hammonds	.20	.07
❑ 108	Kevin Orie	.20	.07
❑ 109	Alex Gonzalez	.20	.07
❑ 110	Jose Canseco	.30	.10
❑ 111	Paul Sorrento	.20	.07
❑ 112	Joey Hamilton	.20	.07
❑ 113	Brad Radke	.20	.07
❑ 114	Steve Avery	.20	.07
❑ 115	Esteban Loaiza	.20	.07
❑ 116	Stan Javier	.20	.07
❑ 117	Chris Gomez	.20	.07
❑ 118	Royce Clayton	.20	.07
❑ 119	Orlando Merced	.20	.07
❑ 120	Kevin Appier	.20	.07
❑ 121	Mel Nieves	.20	.07
❑ 122	Joe Girardi	.20	.07
❑ 123	Rico Brogna	.20	.07
❑ 124	Kent Mercker	.20	.07
❑ 125	Manny Ramirez	.30	.10
❑ 126	Jeromy Burnitz	.20	.07
❑ 127	Kevin Foster	.20	.07
❑ 128	Matt Morris	.20	.07
❑ 129	Jason Dickson	.20	.07
❑ 130	Tom Glavine	.30	.10
❑ 131	Wally Joyner	.20	.07
❑ 132	Rick Reed	.20	.07
❑ 133	Todd Jones	.20	.07
❑ 134	Dave Martinez	.20	.07
❑ 135	Sandy Alomar Jr.	.20	.07
❑ 136	Mike Lansing	.20	.07
❑ 137	Sean Berry	.20	.07
❑ 138	Doug Jones	.20	.07
❑ 139	Todd Stottlemyre	.20	.07
❑ 140	Jay Bell	.20	.07
❑ 141	Jaime Navarro	.20	.07
❑ 142	Chris Hoiles	.20	.07
❑ 143	Joey Cora	.20	.07
❑ 144	Scott Spiezio	.20	.07
❑ 145	Joe Carter	.20	.07
❑ 146	Jose Guillen	.20	.07
❑ 147	Damion Easley	.20	.07
❑ 148	Lee Stevens	.20	.07
❑ 149	Alex Fernandez	.20	.07
❑ 150	Randy Johnson	.50	.20
❑ 151	J.T. Snow	.20	.07
❑ 152	Chuck Finley	.20	.07
❑ 153	Bernard Gilkey	.20	.07
❑ 154	David Segui	.20	.07
❑ 155	Dante Bichette	.20	.07
❑ 156	Kevin Stocker	.20	.07
❑ 157	Carl Everett	.20	.07
❑ 158	Jose Valentin	.20	.07
❑ 159	Pokey Reese	.20	.07
❑ 160	Derek Jeter	1.25	.50
❑ 161	Roger Pavlik	.20	.07
❑ 162	Mark Wohlers	.20	.07
❑ 163	Ricky Bottalico	.20	.07
❑ 164	Ozzie Guillen	.20	.07
❑ 165	Mike Mussina	.30	.10
❑ 166	Gary Sheffield	.20	.07
❑ 167	Hideo Nomo	.50	.20
❑ 168	Mark Grace	.30	.10
❑ 169	Aaron Sele	.20	.07
❑ 170	Darryl Kile	.20	.07
❑ 171	Shawn Estes	.20	.07
❑ 172	Vinny Castilla	.20	.07
❑ 173	Ron Coomer	.20	.07
❑ 174	Jose Rosado	.20	.07
❑ 175	Kenny Lofton	.20	.07
❑ 176	Jason Giambi	.20	.07
❑ 177	Hal Morris	.20	.07
❑ 178	Darren Bragg	.20	.07
❑ 179	Orel Hershiser	.20	.07
❑ 180	Ray Lankford	.20	.07
❑ 181	Hideki Irabu	.20	.07
❑ 182	Kevin Young	.20	.07
❑ 183	Javy Lopez	.20	.07
❑ 184	Jeff Montgomery	.20	.07
❑ 185	Mike Holtz	.20	.07
❑ 186	George Williams	.20	.07
❑ 187	Cal Eldred	.20	.07
❑ 188	Tom Candiotti	.20	.07
❑ 189	Glenallen Hill	.20	.07
❑ 190	Brian Giles	.20	.07
❑ 191	Dave Mlicki	.20	.07
❑ 192	Garrett Stephenson	.20	.07
❑ 193	Jeff Frye	.20	.07
❑ 194	Joe Oliver	.20	.07
❑ 195	Bob Hamelin	.20	.07
❑ 196	Luis Sojo	.20	.07
❑ 197	LaTroy Hawkins	.20	.07
❑ 198	Kevin Elster	.20	.07
❑ 199	Jeff Reed	.20	.07
❑ 200	Dennis Eckersley	.20	.07
❑ 201	Bill Mueller	.20	.07
❑ 202	Russ Davis	.20	.07
❑ 203	Armando Benitez	.20	.07
❑ 204	Quilvio Veras	.20	.07
❑ 205	Tim Naehring	.20	.07
❑ 206	Quinton McCracken	.20	.07
❑ 207	Raul Casanova	.20	.07
❑ 208	Matt Lawton	.20	.07
❑ 209	Luis Alicea	.20	.07
❑ 210	Luis Gonzalez	.20	.07
❑ 211	Allen Watson	.20	.07
❑ 212	Gerald Williams	.20	.07
❑ 213	David Bell	.20	.07
❑ 214	Todd Hollandsworth	.20	.07
❑ 215	Wade Boggs	.30	.10
❑ 216	Jose Mesa	.20	.07
❑ 217	Jamie Moyer	.20	.07
❑ 218	Darren Daulton	.20	.07
❑ 219	Mickey Morandini	.20	.07
❑ 220	Rusty Greer	.20	.07
❑ 221	Jim Bullinger	.20	.07
❑ 222	Jose Offerman	.20	.07
❑ 223	Matt Karchner	.20	.07
❑ 224	Woody Williams	.20	.07
❑ 225	Mark Loretta	.20	.07
❑ 226	Mike Hampton	.20	.07
❑ 227	Willie Adams	.20	.07
❑ 228	Scott Hatteberg	.20	.07
❑ 229	Rich Amaral	.20	.07
❑ 230	Terry Steinbach	.20	.07
❑ 231	Glendon Rusch	.20	.07
❑ 232	Bret Boone	.20	.07
❑ 233	Robert Person	.20	.07
❑ 234	Jose Hernandez	.20	.07
❑ 235	Doug Drabek	.20	.07
❑ 236	Jason McDonald	.20	.07
❑ 237	Chris Widger	.20	.07
❑ 238	Tom Martin	.20	.07
❑ 239	Dave Burba	.20	.07
❑ 240	Pete Rose Jr.	.20	.07
❑ 241	Bobby Ayala	.20	.07
❑ 242	Tim Wakefield	.20	.07

❑ 243 Dennis Springer .20 .07
❑ 244 Tim Belcher .20 .07
❑ 245 J.Garland/G.Goetz .30 .10
❑ 246 L.Berkman/G.Davis .30 .10
❑ 247 V.Wells/A.Akin .30 .10
❑ 248 A.Kennedy/J.Romano .20 .07
❑ 249 J.Dellaero/T.Cameron .20 .07
❑ 250 J.Sandberg/A.Sanchez .20 .07
❑ 251 P.Ortega/J.Manias .20 .07
❑ 252 Mike Stoner RC .20 .07
❑ 253 J.Patterson/L.Rodriguez .20 .07
❑ 254 R.Minor RC/A.Beltre .30 .10
❑ 255 B.Grieve/D.Brown .20 .07
❑ 256 Wood/Pavano/Meche .30 .10
❑ 257 D.Ortiz/Sexson/Ward 2.50 1.00
❑ 258 J.Encarn/Winn/Vessel .20 .07
❑ 259 Bens/T.Smith RC/C.Dunc RC .20 .07
❑ 260 Warren Morris RC .20 .07
❑ 261 R.Hernandez/B.Davis/E.Marrero .20 .07
❑ 262 E.Chavez/R.Branyan .30 .10
❑ 263 Ryan Jackson RC .20 .07
❑ 264 B.Fuentes RC/Clement/Halladay .30 .10
❑ 265 Randy Johnson SH .30 .10
❑ 266 Kevin Brown SH .20 .07
❑ 267 R.Rincon/F.Cordova SH .20 .07
❑ 268 Nomar Garciaparra SH .50 .20
❑ 269 Tino Martinez SH .20 .07
❑ 270 Chuck Knoblauch IL .20 .07
❑ 271 Pedro Martinez IL .30 .10
❑ 272 Denny Neagle IL .20 .07
❑ 273 Juan Gonzalez IL .20 .07
❑ 274 Andres Galarraga IL .20 .07
❑ 275 Checklist (1-195) .20 .07
❑ 276 Checklist (196-283/inserts) .20 .07
❑ 277 Moises Alou WS .20 .07
❑ 278 Sandy Alomar Jr. WS .20 .07
❑ 279 Gary Sheffield WS .20 .07
❑ 280 Matt Williams WS .20 .07
❑ 281 Livan Hernandez WS .20 .07
❑ 282 Chad Ogea WS .20 .07
❑ 283 Marlins Champs .20 .07
❑ 284 Tino Martinez .30 .10
❑ 285 Roberto Alomar .30 .10
❑ 286 Jeff King .20 .07
❑ 287 Brian Jordan .20 .07
❑ 288 Darin Erstad .20 .07
❑ 289 Ken Caminiti .20 .07
❑ 290 Jim Thome .30 .10
❑ 291 Paul Molitor .20 .07
❑ 292 Ivan Rodriguez .30 .10
❑ 293 Bernie Williams .30 .10
❑ 294 Todd Hundley .20 .07
❑ 295 Andres Galarraga .20 .07
❑ 296 Greg Maddux .75 .30
❑ 297 Edgar Martinez .30 .10
❑ 298 Ron Gant .20 .07
❑ 299 Derek Bell .20 .07
❑ 300 Roger Clemens 1.00 .40
❑ 301 Rondell White .20 .07
❑ 302 Barry Larkin .30 .10
❑ 303 Robin Ventura .20 .07
❑ 304 Jason Kendall .20 .07
❑ 305 Chipper Jones .50 .20
❑ 306 John Franco .20 .07
❑ 307 Sammy Sosa .50 .20
❑ 308 Troy Percival .20 .07
❑ 309 Chuck Knoblauch .20 .07
❑ 310 Ellis Burks .20 .07
❑ 311 Al Martin .20 .07
❑ 312 Tim Salmon .30 .10
❑ 313 Moises Alou .20 .07
❑ 314 Lance Johnson .20 .07
❑ 315 Justin Thompson .20 .07
❑ 316 Will Clark .30 .10
❑ 317 Barry Bonds 1.50 .60
❑ 318 Craig Biggio .30 .10
❑ 319 John Smoltz .30 .10
❑ 320 Cal Ripken 1.50 .60
❑ 321 Ken Griffey Jr. .75 .30
❑ 322 Paul O'Neill .30 .10
❑ 323 Todd Helton .30 .10
❑ 324 John Olerud .20 .07
❑ 325 Mark McGwire 1.25 .50
❑ 326 Jose Cruz Jr. .20 .07
❑ 327 Jeff Cirillo .20 .07
❑ 328 Dean Palmer .20 .07
❑ 329 John Wetteland .20 .07
❑ 330 Steve Finley .20 .07
❑ 331 Albert Belle .20 .07
❑ 332 Curt Schilling .20 .07
❑ 333 Raul Mondesi .20 .07
❑ 334 Andruw Jones .30 .10
❑ 335 Nomar Garciaparra .75 .30
❑ 336 David Justice .20 .07
❑ 337 Andy Pettitte .30 .10
❑ 338 Pedro Martinez .30 .10
❑ 339 Travis Miller .20 .07
❑ 340 Chris Stynes .20 .07
❑ 341 Gregg Jefferies .20 .07
❑ 342 Jeff Fassero .20 .07
❑ 343 Craig Counsell .20 .07
❑ 344 Wilson Alvarez .20 .07
❑ 345 Bip Roberts .20 .07
❑ 346 Kelvim Escobar .20 .07
❑ 347 Mark Bellhorn .20 .07
❑ 348 Cory Lidle RC 1.50 .60
❑ 349 Fred McGriff .30 .10
❑ 350 Chuck Carr .20 .07
❑ 351 Bob Abreu .20 .07
❑ 352 Juan Guzman .20 .07
❑ 353 Fernando Vina .20 .07
❑ 354 Andy Benes .20 .07
❑ 355 Dave Nilsson .20 .07
❑ 356 Bobby Bonilla .20 .07
❑ 357 Ismael Valdes .20 .07
❑ 358 Carlos Perez .20 .07
❑ 359 Kirk Rueter .20 .07
❑ 360 Bartolo Colon .20 .07
❑ 361 Mel Rojas .20 .07
❑ 362 Johnny Damon .30 .10
❑ 363 Geronimo Berroa .20 .07
❑ 364 Reggie Sanders .20 .07
❑ 365 Jermaine Allensworth .20 .07
❑ 366 Orlando Cabrera .20 .07
❑ 367 Jorge Fabregas .20 .07
❑ 368 Scott Stahoviak .20 .07
❑ 369 Ken Cloude .20 .07
❑ 370 Donovan Osborne .20 .07
❑ 371 Roger Cedeno .20 .07
❑ 372 Neifi Perez .20 .07
❑ 373 Chris Holt .20 .07
❑ 374 Cecil Fielder .20 .07
❑ 375 Marty Cordova .20 .07
❑ 376 Tom Goodwin .20 .07
❑ 377 Jeff Suppan .20 .07
❑ 378 Jeff Brantley .20 .07
❑ 379 Mark Langston .20 .07
❑ 380 Shane Reynolds .20 .07
❑ 381 Mike Fetters .20 .07
❑ 382 Todd Greene .20 .07
❑ 383 Ray Durham .20 .07
❑ 384 Carlos Delgado .20 .07
❑ 385 Jeff D'Amico .20 .07
❑ 386 Brian McRae .20 .07
❑ 387 Alan Benes .20 .07
❑ 388 Heathcliff Slocumb .20 .07
❑ 389 Eric Young .20 .07
❑ 390 Travis Fryman .20 .07
❑ 391 David Cone .20 .07
❑ 392 Otis Nixon .20 .07
❑ 393 Jeremi Gonzalez .20 .07
❑ 394 Jeff Juden .20 .07
❑ 395 Jose Vizcaino .20 .07
❑ 396 Ugueth Urbina .20 .07
❑ 397 Ramon Martinez .20 .07
❑ 398 Robb Nen .20 .07
❑ 399 Harold Baines .20 .07
❑ 400 Delino DeShields .20 .07
❑ 401 John Burkett .20 .07
❑ 402 Sterling Hitchcock .20 .07
❑ 403 Mark Clark .20 .07
❑ 404 Terrell Wade .20 .07
❑ 405 Scott Brosius .20 .07
❑ 406 Chad Curtis .20 .07
❑ 407 Brian Johnson .20 .07
❑ 408 Roberto Kelly .20 .07
❑ 409 Dave Dellucci RC .40 .15
❑ 410 Michael Tucker .20 .07
❑ 411 Mark Kotsay .20 .07
❑ 412 Mark Lewis .20 .07
❑ 413 Ryan McGuire .20 .07
❑ 414 Shawon Dunston .20 .07
❑ 415 Brad Rigby .20 .07
❑ 416 Scott Erickson .20 .07
❑ 417 Bobby Jones .20 .07
❑ 418 Darren Oliver .20 .07
❑ 419 John Smiley .20 .07
❑ 420 T.J. Mathews .20 .07
❑ 421 Dustin Hermanson .20 .07
❑ 422 Mike Timlin .20 .07
❑ 423 Willie Blair .20 .07
❑ 424 Manny Alexander .20 .07
❑ 425 Bob Tewksbury .20 .07
❑ 426 Pete Schourek .20 .07
❑ 427 Reggie Jefferson .20 .07
❑ 428 Ed Sprague .20 .07
❑ 429 Jeff Conine .20 .07
❑ 430 Roberto Hernandez .20 .07
❑ 431 Tom Pagnozzi .20 .07
❑ 432 Jaret Wright .20 .07
❑ 433 Livan Hernandez .20 .07
❑ 434 Andy Ashby .20 .07
❑ 435 Todd Dunn .20 .07
❑ 436 Bobby Higginson .20 .07
❑ 437 Rod Beck .20 .07
❑ 438 Jim Leyritz .20 .07
❑ 439 Matt Williams .20 .07
❑ 440 Brett Tomko .20 .07
❑ 441 Joe Randa .20 .07
❑ 442 Chris Carpenter .20 .07
❑ 443 Dennis Reyes .20 .07
❑ 444 Al Leiter .20 .07
❑ 445 Jason Schmidt .20 .07
❑ 446 Ken Hill .20 .07
❑ 447 Shannon Stewart .20 .07
❑ 448 Enrique Wilson .20 .07
❑ 449 Fernando Tatis .20 .07
❑ 450 Jimmy Key .20 .07
❑ 451 Darrin Fletcher .20 .07
❑ 452 John Valentin .20 .07
❑ 453 Kevin Tapani .20 .07
❑ 454 Eric Karros .20 .07
❑ 455 Jay Bell .20 .07
❑ 456 Walt Weiss .20 .07
❑ 457 Devon White .20 .07
❑ 458 Carl Pavano .20 .07
❑ 459 Mike Lansing .20 .07
❑ 460 John Flaherty .20 .07
❑ 461 Richard Hidalgo .20 .07
❑ 462 Quinton McCracken .20 .07
❑ 463 Karim Garcia .20 .07
❑ 464 Miguel Cairo .20 .07
❑ 465 Edwin Diaz .20 .07
❑ 466 Bobby Smith .20 .07
❑ 467 Yamil Benitez .20 .07
❑ 468 Rich Butler .20 .07
❑ 469 Ben Ford RC .20 .07
❑ 470 Bubba Trammell .20 .07
❑ 471 Brent Brede .20 .07
❑ 472 Brooks Kieschnick .20 .07
❑ 473 Carlos Castillo .20 .07
❑ 474 Brad Radke SH .20 .07
❑ 475 Roger Clemens SH .50 .20
❑ 476 Curt Schilling SH .20 .07
❑ 477 John Olerud SH .20 .07
❑ 478 Mark McGwire SH .60 .25
❑ 479 M.Piazza/K.Griffey Jr. IL .50 .20
❑ 480 J.Bagwell/F.Thomas IL .30 .10
❑ 481 C.Jones/N.Garciaparra IL .30 .10
❑ 482 L.Walker/J.Gonzalez IL .20 .07
❑ 483 G.Sheffield/T.Martinez IL .20 .07
❑ 484 D.Gib/M.Colem/Hutchins .20 .07
❑ 485 B.Rose/Looper/Politte .20 .07
❑ 486 E.Milton/Marquis/C.Lee .20 .07
❑ 487 Robert Fick RC .30 .10
❑ 488 A.Ramirez/A.Gonz/Casey .30 .10
❑ 489 D.Bridges/T.Drew RC .20 .07
❑ 490 D.McDonald/N.Ndungidi RC .20 .07
❑ 491 Ryan Anderson RC .20 .07
❑ 492 Troy Glaus RC 1.50 .60
❑ 493 J.Werth/D.Reichert RC .20 .07
❑ 494 Michael Cuddyer RC .75 .30
❑ 495 Jack Cust RC .20 .07
❑ 496 Brian Anderson .20 .07
❑ 497 Tony Saunders .20 .07
❑ 498 J.Sandoval/V.Nunez .20 .07
❑ 499 B.Penny/N.Bierbrodt .30 .10
❑ 500 D.Carr/L.Cruz RC .20 .07

❑ 501 C.Bowers/M.McCain .20 .07
❑ 502 Checklist .20 .07
❑ 503 Checklist .20 .07
❑ 504 Alex Rodriguez 2.00 .75

1999 Topps

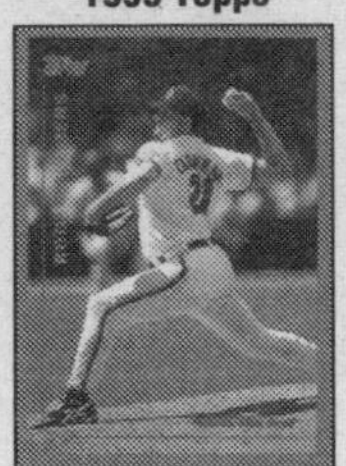

❑ COMPLETE SET (462) 80.00 30.00
❑ COMP.HOBBY SET (462) 80.00 40.00
❑ COMP.X-MAS SET (463) 80.00 40.00
❑ COMPLETE SERIES 1 (241) 40.00 15.00
❑ COMPLETE SERIES 2 (221) 40.00 15.00
❑ COMP.MAC HR SET (70) 500.00 250.00
❑ COMP.SOSA HR SET (66) 250.00 100.00
❑ 1 Roger Clemens 1.00 .40
❑ 2 Andres Galarraga .20 .07
❑ 3 Scott Brosius .20 .07
❑ 4 John Flaherty .20 .07
❑ 5 Jim Leyritz .20 .07
❑ 6 Ray Durham .20 .07
❑ 8 Jose Vizcaino .20 .07
❑ 9 Will Clark .30 .10
❑ 10 David Wells .20 .07
❑ 11 Jose Guillen .20 .07
❑ 12 Scott Hatteberg .20 .07
❑ 13 Edgardo Alfonzo .20 .07
❑ 14 Mike Bordick .20 .07
❑ 15 Manny Ramirez .30 .10
❑ 16 Greg Maddux .75 .30
❑ 17 David Segui .20 .07
❑ 18 Darryl Strawberry .20 .07
❑ 19 Brad Radke .20 .07
❑ 20 Kerry Wood .20 .07
❑ 21 Matt Anderson .20 .07
❑ 22 Derrek Lee .30 .10
❑ 23 Mickey Morandini .20 .07
❑ 24 Paul Konerko .20 .07
❑ 25 Travis Lee .20 .07
❑ 26 Ken Hill .20 .07
❑ 27 Kenny Rogers .20 .07
❑ 28 Paul Sorrento .20 .07
❑ 29 Quilvio Veras .20 .07
❑ 30 Todd Walker .20 .07
❑ 31 Ryan Jackson .20 .07
❑ 32 John Olerud .20 .07
❑ 33 Doug Glanville .20 .07
❑ 34 Nolan Ryan 2.00 .75
❑ 35 Ray Lankford .20 .07
❑ 36 Mark Loretta .20 .07
❑ 37 Jason Dickson .20 .07
❑ 38 Sean Bergman .20 .07
❑ 39 Quinton McCracken .20 .07
❑ 40 Bartolo Colon .20 .07
❑ 41 Brady Anderson .20 .07
❑ 42 Chris Stynes .20 .07
❑ 43 Jorge Posada .30 .10
❑ 44 Justin Thompson .20 .07
❑ 45 Johnny Damon .30 .10
❑ 46 Armando Benitez .20 .07
❑ 47 Brant Brown .20 .07
❑ 48 Charlie Hayes .20 .07
❑ 49 Darren Dreifort .20 .07
❑ 50 Juan Gonzalez .20 .07
❑ 51 Chuck Knoblauch .20 .07
❑ 52 Todd Helton .30 .10
❑ 53 Rick Reed .20 .07
❑ 54 Chris Gomez .20 .07
❑ 55 Gary Sheffield .20 .07
❑ 56 Rod Beck .20 .07
❑ 57 Rey Sanchez .20 .07
❑ 58 Garret Anderson .20 .07
❑ 59 Jimmy Haynes .20 .07
❑ 60 Steve Woodard .20 .07
❑ 61 Rondell White .20 .07
❑ 62 Vladimir Guerrero .50 .20
❑ 63 Eric Karros .20 .07
❑ 64 Russ Davis .20 .07
❑ 65 Mo Vaughn .20 .07
❑ 66 Sammy Sosa .50 .20
❑ 67 Troy Percival .20 .07
❑ 68 Kenny Lofton .20 .07
❑ 69 Bill Taylor .20 .07
❑ 70 Mark McGwire 1.25 .50
❑ 71 Roger Cedeno .20 .07
❑ 72 Javy Lopez .20 .07
❑ 73 Damion Easley .20 .07
❑ 74 Andy Pettitte .30 .10
❑ 75 Tony Gwynn .60 .25
❑ 76 Ricardo Rincon .20 .07
❑ 77 F.P. Santangelo .20 .07
❑ 78 Jay Bell .20 .07
❑ 79 Scott Servais .20 .07
❑ 80 Jose Canseco .30 .10
❑ 81 Roberto Hernandez .20 .07
❑ 82 Todd Dunwoody .20 .07
❑ 83 John Wetteland .20 .07
❑ 84 Mike Caruso .20 .07
❑ 85 Derek Jeter 1.25 .50
❑ 86 Aaron Sele .20 .07
❑ 87 Jose Lima .20 .07
❑ 88 Ryan Christenson .20 .07
❑ 89 Jeff Cirillo .20 .07
❑ 90 Jose Hernandez .20 .07
❑ 91 Mark Kotsay .20 .07
❑ 92 Darren Bragg .20 .07
❑ 93 Albert Belle .20 .07
❑ 94 Matt Lawton .20 .07
❑ 95 Pedro Martinez .30 .10
❑ 96 Greg Vaughn .20 .07
❑ 97 Neifi Perez .20 .07
❑ 98 Gerald Williams .20 .07
❑ 99 Derek Bell .20 .07
❑ 100 Ken Griffey Jr. .75 .30
❑ 101 David Cone .20 .07
❑ 102 Brian Johnson .20 .07
❑ 103 Dean Palmer .20 .07
❑ 104 Javier Valentin .20 .07
❑ 105 Trevor Hoffman .20 .07
❑ 106 Butch Huskey .20 .07
❑ 107 Dave Martinez .20 .07
❑ 108 Billy Wagner .20 .07
❑ 109 Shawn Green .20 .07
❑ 110 Ben Grieve .20 .07
❑ 111 Tom Goodwin .20 .07
❑ 112 Jaret Wright .20 .07
❑ 113 Aramis Ramirez .20 .07
❑ 114 Dmitri Young .20 .07
❑ 115 Hideki Irabu .20 .07
❑ 116 Roberto Kelly .20 .07
❑ 117 Jeff Fassero .20 .07
❑ 118 Mark Clark .20 .07
❑ 119 Jason McDonald .20 .07
❑ 120 Matt Williams .20 .07
❑ 121 Dave Burba .20 .07
❑ 122 Bret Saberhagen .20 .07
❑ 123 Deivi Cruz .20 .07
❑ 124 Chad Curtis .20 .07
❑ 125 Scott Rolen .30 .10
❑ 126 Lee Stevens .20 .07
❑ 127 J.T. Snow .20 .07
❑ 128 Rusty Greer .20 .07
❑ 129 Brian Meadows .20 .07
❑ 130 Jim Edmonds .20 .07
❑ 131 Ron Gant .20 .07
❑ 132 A.J. Hinch .20 .07
❑ 133 Shannon Stewart .20 .07
❑ 134 Brad Fullmer .20 .07
❑ 135 Cal Eldred .20 .07
❑ 136 Matt Walbeck .20 .07
❑ 137 Carl Everett .20 .07
❑ 138 Walt Weiss .20 .07
❑ 139 Fred McGriff .30 .10
❑ 140 Darin Erstad .20 .07
❑ 141 Dave Nilsson .20 .07
❑ 142 Eric Young .20 .07
❑ 143 Dan Wilson .20 .07
❑ 144 Jeff Reed .20 .07
❑ 145 Brett Tomko .20 .07
❑ 146 Terry Steinbach .20 .07
❑ 147 Seth Greisinger .20 .07
❑ 148 Pat Meares .20 .07
❑ 149 Livan Hernandez .20 .07
❑ 150 Jeff Bagwell .30 .10
❑ 151 Bob Wickman .20 .07
❑ 152 Omar Vizquel .30 .10
❑ 153 Eric Davis .20 .07
❑ 154 Larry Sutton .20 .07
❑ 155 Magglio Ordonez .20 .07
❑ 156 Eric Milton .20 .07
❑ 157 Darren Lewis .20 .07
❑ 158 Rick Aguilera .20 .07
❑ 159 Mike Lieberthal .20 .07
❑ 160 Robb Nen .20 .07
❑ 161 Brian Giles .20 .07
❑ 162 Jeff Brantley .20 .07
❑ 163 Gary DiSarcina .20 .07
❑ 164 John Valentin .20 .07
❑ 165 David Dellucci .20 .07
❑ 166 Chan Ho Park .20 .07
❑ 167 Masato Yoshii .20 .07
❑ 168 Jason Schmidt .20 .07
❑ 169 LaTroy Hawkins .20 .07
❑ 170 Bret Boone .20 .07
❑ 171 Jerry DiPoto .20 .07
❑ 172 Mariano Rivera .50 .20
❑ 173 Mike Cameron .20 .07
❑ 174 Scott Erickson .20 .07
❑ 175 Charles Johnson .20 .07
❑ 176 Bobby Jones .20 .07
❑ 177 Francisco Cordova .20 .07
❑ 178 Todd Jones .20 .07
❑ 179 Jeff Montgomery .20 .07
❑ 180 Mike Mussina .30 .10
❑ 181 Bob Abreu .20 .07
❑ 182 Ismael Valdes .20 .07
❑ 183 Andy Fox .20 .07
❑ 184 Woody Williams .20 .07
❑ 185 Denny Neagle .20 .07
❑ 186 Jose Valentin .20 .07
❑ 187 Darrin Fletcher .20 .07
❑ 188 Gabe Alvarez .20 .07
❑ 189 Eddie Taubensee .20 .07
❑ 190 Edgar Martinez .30 .10
❑ 191 Jason Kendall .20 .07
❑ 192 Darryl Kile .20 .07
❑ 193 Jeff King .20 .07
❑ 194 Rey Ordonez .20 .07
❑ 195 Andruw Jones .30 .10
❑ 196 Tony Fernandez .20 .07
❑ 197 Jamey Wright .20 .07
❑ 198 B.J. Surhoff .20 .07
❑ 199 Vinny Castilla .20 .07
❑ 200 David Wells HL .20 .07
❑ 201 Mark McGwire HL .60 .25
❑ 202 Sammy Sosa HL .30 .10
❑ 203 Roger Clemens HL .50 .20
❑ 204 Kerry Wood HL .20 .07
❑ 205 L.Berkman/G.Kapler .40 .15
❑ 206 Alex Escobar RC .40 .15
❑ 207 Peter Bergeron RC .25 .08
❑ 208 M.Barrett/B.Davis/R.Fick .25 .08
❑ 209 P.Cline/R.Hernandez/J.Werth .25 .08
❑ 210 R.Anderson/Chen/Enochs .25 .08
❑ 211 B.Penny/Dotel/Lincoln .25 .08
❑ 212 Chuck Abbott RC .25 .08
❑ 213 C.Jones/J.Urban RC .25 .08
❑ 214 T.Torcato/A.McDowell RC .25 .08
❑ 215 J.Tyner/J.McKinley RC .25 .08
❑ 216 M.Burch/S.Etherton RC .25 .08
❑ 217 R.Elder/M.Tucker RC .25 .08
❑ 218 J.M.Gold/R.Mills RC .25 .08
❑ 219 A.Brown/C.Freeman RC .25 .08
❑ 220A Mark McGwire HR 1 40.00 15.00
❑ 220B Mark McGwire HR 2 15.00 6.00
❑ 220C Mark McGwire HR 3 15.00 6.00
❑ 220D Mark McGwire HR 4 15.00 6.00
❑ 220E Mark McGwire HR 5 15.00 6.00
❑ 220F Mark McGwire HR 6 15.00 6.00
❑ 220G Mark McGwire HR 7 15.00 6.00
❑ 220H Mark McGwire HR 8 15.00 6.00
❑ 220I Mark McGwire HR 9 15.00 6.00

❑ 220J Mark McGwire HR 10 15.00 6.00
❑ 220K Mark McGwire HR 11 15.00 6.00
❑ 220L Mark McGwire HR 12 15.00 6.00
❑ 220M Mark McGwire HR 13 15.00 6.00
❑ 220N Mark McGwire HR 14 15.00 6.00
❑ 220O Mark McGwire HR 15 15.00 6.00
❑ 220P Mark McGwire HR 16 15.00 6.00
❑ 220Q Mark McGwire HR 17 15.00 6.00
❑ 220R Mark McGwire HR 18 15.00 6.00
❑ 220S Mark McGwire HR 19 15.00 6.00
❑ 220T Mark McGwire HR 20 15.00 6.00
❑ 220U Mark McGwire HR 21 15.00 6.00
❑ 220V Mark McGwire HR 22 15.00 6.00
❑ 220W Mark McGwire HR 23 15.00 6.00
❑ 220X Mark McGwire HR 24 15.00 6.00
❑ 220Y Mark McGwire HR 25 15.00 6.00
❑ 220Z Mark McGwire HR 26 15.00 6.00
❑ 220AA Mark McGwire HR 27 15.00 6.00
❑ 220AB Mark McGwire HR 28 15.00 6.00
❑ 220AC Mark McGwire HR 29 15.00 6.00
❑ 220AD Mark McGwire HR 30 15.00 6.00
❑ 220AE Mark McGwire HR 31 15.00 6.00
❑ 220AF Mark McGwire HR 32 15.00 6.00
❑ 220AG Mark McGwire HR 33 15.00 6.00
❑ 220AH Mark McGwire HR 34 15.00 6.00
❑ 220AI Mark McGwire HR 35 15.00 6.00
❑ 220AJ Mark McGwire HR 36 15.00 6.00
❑ 220AK Mark McGwire HR 37 15.00 6.00
❑ 220AL Mark McGwire HR 38 15.00 6.00
❑ 220AM Mark McGwire HR 39 15.00 6.00
❑ 220AN Mark McGwire HR 40 15.00 6.00
❑ 220AO Mark McGwire HR 41 15.00 6.00
❑ 220AP Mark McGwire HR 42 15.00 6.00
❑ 220AQ Mark McGwire HR 43 15.00 6.00
❑ 220AR Mark McGwire HR 44 15.00 6.00
❑ 220AS Mark McGwire HR 45 15.00 6.00
❑ 220AT Mark McGwire HR 46 15.00 6.00
❑ 220AU Mark McGwire HR 47 15.00 6.00
❑ 220AV Mark McGwire HR 48 15.00 6.00
❑ 220AW Mark McGwire HR 49 15.00 6.00
❑ 220AX Mark McGwire HR 50 15.00 6.00
❑ 220AY Mark McGwire HR 51 15.00 6.00
❑ 220AZ Mark McGwire HR 52 15.00 6.00
❑ 220BB Mark McGwire HR 53 15.00 6.00
❑ 220CC Mark McGwire HR 54 15.00 6.00
❑ 220DD Mark McGwire HR 55 15.00 6.00
❑ 220EE Mark McGwire HR 56 15.00 6.00
❑ 220FF Mark McGwire HR 57 15.00 6.00
❑ 220GG Mark McGwire HR 58 15.00 6.00
❑ 220HH Mark McGwire HR 59 15.00 6.00
❑ 220II Mark McGwire HR 60 15.00 6.00
❑ 220JJ Mark McGwire HR 61 30.00 12.50
❑ 220KK Mark McGwire HR 62 40.00 15.00
❑ 220LL Mark McGwire HR 63 15.00 6.00
❑ 220MM Mark McGwire HR 64 15.00 6.00
❑ 220NN Mark McGwire HR 65 15.00 6.00
❑ 220OO Mark McGwire HR 66 15.00 6.00
❑ 220PP Mark McGwire HR 67 15.00 6.00
❑ 220QQ Mark McGwire HR 68 15.00 6.00
❑ 220RR Mark McGwire HR 69 15.00 6.00
❑ 220SS Mark McGwire HR 70 100.00 50.00
❑ 221 Larry Walker LL .20 .07
❑ 222 Bernie Williams LL .20 .07
❑ 223 Mark McGwire LL .60 .25
❑ 224 Ken Griffey Jr. LL .50 .20
❑ 225 Sammy Sosa LL .30 .10
❑ 226 Juan Gonzalez LL .20 .07
❑ 227 Dante Bichette LL .20 .07
❑ 228 Alex Rodriguez LL .50 .20
❑ 229 Sammy Sosa LL .30 .10
❑ 230 Derek Jeter LL .60 .25
❑ 231 Greg Maddux LL .50 .20
❑ 232 Roger Clemens LL .50 .20
❑ 233 Ricky Ledee WS .20 .07
❑ 234 Chuck Knoblauch WS .20 .07
❑ 235 Bernie Williams WS .20 .07
❑ 236 Tino Martinez WS .20 .07
❑ 237 Orlando Hernandez WS .20 .07
❑ 238 Scott Brosius WS .20 .07
❑ 239 Andy Pettitte WS .20 .07
❑ 240 Mariano Rivera WS .30 .10
❑ 241 Checklist 1 .20 .07
❑ 242 Checklist 2 .20 .07
❑ 243 Tom Glavine .30 .10
❑ 244 Andy Benes .20 .07
❑ 245 Sandy Alomar Jr. .20 .07
❑ 246 Wilton Guerrero .20 .07
❑ 247 Alex Gonzalez .20 .07
❑ 248 Roberto Alomar .30 .10
❑ 249 Ruben Rivera .20 .07
❑ 250 Eric Chavez .20 .07
❑ 251 Ellis Burks .20 .07
❑ 252 Richie Sexson .20 .07
❑ 253 Steve Finley .20 .07
❑ 254 Dwight Gooden .20 .07
❑ 255 Dustin Hermanson .20 .07
❑ 256 Kirk Rueter .20 .07
❑ 257 Steve Trachsel .20 .07
❑ 258 Gregg Jefferies .20 .07
❑ 259 Matt Stairs .20 .07
❑ 260 Shane Reynolds .20 .07
❑ 261 Gregg Olson .20 .07
❑ 262 Kevin Tapani .20 .07
❑ 263 Matt Morris .20 .07
❑ 264 Carl Pavano .20 .07
❑ 265 Nomar Garciaparra .75 .30
❑ 266 Kevin Young .20 .07
❑ 267 Rick Helling .20 .07
❑ 268 Matt Franco .20 .07
❑ 269 Brian McRae .20 .07
❑ 270 Cal Ripken 1.50 .60
❑ 271 Jeff Abbott .20 .07
❑ 272 Tony Batista .20 .07
❑ 273 Bill Simas .20 .07
❑ 274 Brian Hunter .20 .07
❑ 275 John Franco .20 .07
❑ 276 Devon White .20 .07
❑ 277 Rickey Henderson .50 .20
❑ 278 Chuck Finley .20 .07
❑ 279 Mike Blowers .20 .07
❑ 280 Mark Grace .30 .10
❑ 281 Randy Winn .20 .07
❑ 282 Bobby Bonilla .20 .07
❑ 283 David Justice .20 .07
❑ 284 Shane Monahan .20 .07
❑ 285 Kevin Brown .30 .10
❑ 286 Todd Zeile .20 .07
❑ 287 Al Martin .20 .07
❑ 288 Troy O'Leary .20 .07
❑ 289 Darryl Hamilton .20 .07
❑ 290 Tino Martinez .30 .10
❑ 291 David Ortiz .50 .20
❑ 292 Tony Clark .20 .07
❑ 293 Ryan Minor .20 .07
❑ 294 Mark Leiter .20 .07
❑ 295 Wally Joyner .20 .07
❑ 296 Cliff Floyd .20 .07
❑ 297 Shawn Estes .20 .07
❑ 298 Pat Hentgen .20 .07
❑ 299 Scott Elarton .20 .07
❑ 300 Alex Rodriguez .75 .30
❑ 301 Ozzie Guillen .20 .07
❑ 302 Hideo Nomo .50 .20
❑ 303 Ryan McGuire .20 .07
❑ 304 Brad Ausmus .20 .07
❑ 305 Alex Gonzalez .20 .07
❑ 306 Brian Jordan .20 .07
❑ 307 John Jaha .20 .07
❑ 308 Mark Grudzielanek .20 .07
❑ 309 Juan Guzman .20 .07
❑ 310 Tony Womack .20 .07
❑ 311 Dennis Reyes .20 .07
❑ 312 Marty Cordova .20 .07
❑ 313 Ramiro Mendoza .20 .07
❑ 314 Robin Ventura .20 .07
❑ 315 Rafael Palmeiro .30 .10
❑ 316 Ramon Martinez .20 .07
❑ 317 Pedro Astacio .20 .07
❑ 318 Dave Hollins .20 .07
❑ 319 Tom Candiotti .20 .07
❑ 320 Al Leiter .20 .07
❑ 321 Rico Brogna .20 .07
❑ 322 Reggie Jefferson .20 .07
❑ 323 Bernard Gilkey .20 .07
❑ 324 Jason Giambi .20 .07
❑ 325 Craig Biggio .30 .10
❑ 326 Troy Glaus .30 .10
❑ 327 Delino DeShields .20 .07
❑ 328 Fernando Vina .20 .07
❑ 329 John Smoltz .30 .10
❑ 330 Jeff Kent .20 .07
❑ 331 Roy Halladay .20 .07
❑ 332 Andy Ashby .20 .07
❑ 333 Tim Wakefield .20 .07
❑ 334 Roger Clemens 1.00 .40
❑ 335 Bernie Williams .30 .10
❑ 336 Desi Relaford .20 .07
❑ 337 John Burkett .20 .07
❑ 338 Mike Hampton .20 .07
❑ 339 Royce Clayton .20 .07
❑ 340 Mike Piazza .75 .30
❑ 341 Jeremi Gonzalez .20 .07
❑ 342 Mike Lansing .20 .07
❑ 343 Jamie Moyer .20 .07
❑ 344 Ron Coomer .20 .07
❑ 345 Barry Larkin .30 .10
❑ 346 Fernando Tatis .20 .07
❑ 347 Chili Davis .20 .07
❑ 348 Bobby Higginson .20 .07
❑ 349 Hal Morris .20 .07
❑ 350 Larry Walker .20 .07
❑ 351 Carlos Guillen .20 .07
❑ 352 Miguel Tejada .20 .07
❑ 353 Travis Fryman .20 .07
❑ 354 Jarrod Washburn .20 .07
❑ 355 Chipper Jones .50 .20
❑ 356 Todd Stottlemyre .20 .07
❑ 357 Henry Rodriguez .20 .07
❑ 358 Eli Marrero .20 .07
❑ 359 Alan Benes .20 .07
❑ 360 Tim Salmon .30 .10
❑ 361 Luis Gonzalez .20 .07
❑ 362 Scott Spiezio .20 .07
❑ 363 Chris Carpenter .20 .07
❑ 364 Bobby Howry .20 .07
❑ 365 Raul Mondesi .20 .07
❑ 366 Ugueth Urbina .20 .07
❑ 367 Tom Evans .20 .07
❑ 368 Kerry Ligtenberg RC .25 .08
❑ 369 Adrian Beltre .20 .07
❑ 370 Ryan Klesko .20 .07
❑ 371 Wilson Alvarez .20 .07
❑ 372 John Thomson .20 .07
❑ 373 Tony Saunders .20 .07
❑ 374 Dave Mlicki .20 .07
❑ 375 Ken Caminiti .20 .07
❑ 376 Jay Buhner .20 .07
❑ 377 Bill Mueller .20 .07
❑ 378 Jeff Blauser .20 .07
❑ 379 Edgar Renteria .20 .07
❑ 380 Jim Thome .30 .10
❑ 381 Joey Hamilton .20 .07
❑ 382 Calvin Pickering .20 .07
❑ 383 Marquis Grissom .20 .07
❑ 384 Omar Daal .20 .07
❑ 385 Curt Schilling .20 .07
❑ 386 Jose Cruz Jr. .20 .07
❑ 387 Chris Widger .20 .07
❑ 388 Pete Harnisch .20 .07
❑ 389 Charles Nagy .20 .07
❑ 390 Tom Gordon .20 .07
❑ 391 Bobby Smith .20 .07
❑ 392 Derrick Gibson .20 .07
❑ 393 Jeff Conine .20 .07
❑ 394 Carlos Perez .20 .07
❑ 395 Barry Bonds 1.50 .60
❑ 396 Mark McLemore .20 .07
❑ 397 Juan Encarnacion .20 .07
❑ 398 Wade Boggs .30 .10
❑ 399 Ivan Rodriguez .30 .10
❑ 400 Moises Alou .20 .07
❑ 401 Jeromy Burnitz .20 .07
❑ 402 Sean Casey .20 .07
❑ 403 Jose Offerman .20 .07
❑ 404 Joe Fontenot .20 .07
❑ 405 Kevin Millwood .20 .07
❑ 406 Lance Johnson .20 .07
❑ 407 Richard Hidalgo .20 .07
❑ 408 Mike Jackson .20 .07
❑ 409 Brian Anderson .20 .07
❑ 410 Jeff Shaw .20 .07
❑ 411 Preston Wilson .20 .07
❑ 412 Todd Hundley .20 .07
❑ 413 Jim Parque .20 .07
❑ 414 Justin Baughman .20 .07
❑ 415 Dante Bichette .20 .07
❑ 416 Paul O'Neill .30 .10
❑ 417 Miguel Cairo .20 .07

	Card	Player	Price	Price
❑	418	Randy Johnson	.50	.20
❑	419	Jesus Sanchez	.20	.07
❑	420	Carlos Delgado	.20	.07
❑	421	Ricky Ledee	.20	.07
❑	422	Orlando Hernandez	.20	.07
❑	423	Frank Thomas	.50	.20
❑	424	Pokey Reese	.20	.07
❑	425	C.Lee/M.Lowell	.40	.15
❑	426	M.Cuddyer/DeRosa/Hairston	.25	.08
❑	427	M.Anderson/Belliard/Cabrera	.40	.15
❑	428	M.Bowie/P.Norton RC/Wolf	.25	.08
❑	429	J.Cressend RC/Rocker	.40	.15
❑	430	R.Mateo/M.Zywica RC	.25	.08
❑	431	J.LaRue/LeCroy/Meluskey	.25	.08
❑	432	Gabe Kapler	.40	.15
❑	433	A.Kennedy/M.Lopez RC	.25	.08
❑	434	Jose Fernandez RC/C.Truby	.25	.08
❑	435	Doug Mientkiewicz RC	.50	.20
❑	436	R.Brown RC/V.Wells	.25	.08
❑	437	A.J. Burnett RC	.75	.30
❑	438	M.Belisle/M.Roney RC	.25	.08
❑	439	A.Kearns/C.George RC	1.50	.60
❑	440	N.Cornejo/N.Bump RC	.25	.08
❑	441	B.Lidge/M.Nannini RC	1.50	.60
❑	442	M.Holliday/J.Winchester RC	1.50	.60
❑	443	A.Everett/C.Ambres RC	.50	.20
❑	444	P.Burrell/E.Valent RC	1.50	.60
❑	445	Roger Clemens SK	.50	.20
❑	446	Kerry Wood SK	.20	.07
❑	447	Curt Schilling SK	.20	.07
❑	448	Randy Johnson SK	.30	.10
❑	449	Pedro Martinez SK	.30	.10
❑	450	Bagwell/Galar/McGwire AT	.50	.20
❑	451	Olerud/Thome/Martinez AT	.20	.07
❑	452	ARod/Nomar/Jeter AT	.60	.25
❑	453	Castilla/Jones/Rolen AT	.30	.10
❑	454	Sosa/Griffey/Gonzalez AT	.50	.20
❑	455	Bonds/Ramirez/Walker AT	.75	.30
❑	456	Thomas/Salmon/Justice AT	.50	.20
❑	457	Lee/Helton/Grieve AT	.20	.07
❑	458	Guerrero/Vaughn/B.Will AT	.20	.07
❑	459	Piazza/IRod/Kendall AT	.50	.20
❑	460	Clemens/Wood/Maddux AT	.50	.20
❑	461A	Sammy Sosa HR 1	15.00	6.00
❑	461B	Sammy Sosa HR 2	6.00	2.50
❑	461C	Sammy Sosa HR 3	6.00	2.50
❑	461D	Sammy Sosa HR 4	6.00	2.50
❑	461E	Sammy Sosa HR 5	6.00	2.50
❑	461F	Sammy Sosa HR 6	6.00	2.50
❑	461G	Sammy Sosa HR 7	6.00	2.50
❑	461H	Sammy Sosa HR 8	6.00	2.50
❑	461I	Sammy Sosa HR 9	6.00	2.50
❑	461J	Sammy Sosa HR 10	6.00	2.50
❑	461K	Sammy Sosa HR 11	6.00	2.50
❑	461L	Sammy Sosa HR 12	6.00	2.50
❑	461M	Sammy Sosa HR 13	6.00	2.50
❑	461N	Sammy Sosa HR 14	6.00	2.50
❑	461O	Sammy Sosa HR 15	6.00	2.50
❑	461P	Sammy Sosa HR 16	6.00	2.50
❑	461Q	Sammy Sosa HR 17	6.00	2.50
❑	461R	Sammy Sosa HR 18	6.00	2.50
❑	461S	Sammy Sosa HR 19	6.00	2.50
❑	461T	Sammy Sosa HR 20	6.00	2.50
❑	461U	Sammy Sosa HR 21	6.00	2.50
❑	461V	Sammy Sosa HR 22	6.00	2.50
❑	461W	Sammy Sosa HR 23	6.00	2.50
❑	461X	Sammy Sosa HR 24	6.00	2.50
❑	461Y	Sammy Sosa HR 25	6.00	2.50
❑	461Z	Sammy Sosa HR 26	6.00	2.50
❑	461AA	Sammy Sosa HR 27	6.00	2.50
❑	461AB	Sammy Sosa HR 28	6.00	2.50
❑	461AC	Sammy Sosa HR 29	6.00	2.50
❑	461AD	Sammy Sosa HR 30	6.00	2.50
❑	461AE	Sammy Sosa HR 31	6.00	2.50
❑	461AF	Sammy Sosa HR 32	6.00	2.50
❑	461AG	Sammy Sosa HR 33	6.00	2.50
❑	461AH	Sammy Sosa HR 34	6.00	2.50
❑	461AI	Sammy Sosa HR 35	6.00	2.50
❑	461AJ	Sammy Sosa HR 36	6.00	2.50
❑	461AK	Sammy Sosa HR 37	6.00	2.50
❑	461AL	Sammy Sosa HR 38	6.00	2.50
❑	461AM	Sammy Sosa HR 39	6.00	2.50
❑	461AN	Sammy Sosa HR 40	6.00	2.50
❑	461AO	Sammy Sosa HR 41	6.00	2.50
❑	461AP	Sammy Sosa HR 42	6.00	2.50
❑	461AR	Sammy Sosa HR 43	6.00	2.50
❑	461AS	Sammy Sosa HR 44	6.00	2.50
❑	461AT	Sammy Sosa HR 45	6.00	2.50
❑	461AU	Sammy Sosa HR 46	6.00	2.50
❑	461AV	Sammy Sosa HR 47	6.00	2.50
❑	461AW	Sammy Sosa HR 48	6.00	2.50
❑	461AX	Sammy Sosa HR 49	6.00	2.50
❑	461AY	Sammy Sosa HR 50	6.00	2.50
❑	461AZ	Sammy Sosa HR 51	6.00	2.50
❑	461BB	Sammy Sosa HR 52	6.00	2.50
❑	461CC	Sammy Sosa HR 53	6.00	2.50
❑	461DD	Sammy Sosa HR 54	6.00	2.50
❑	461EE	Sammy Sosa HR 55	6.00	2.50
❑	461FF	Sammy Sosa HR 56	6.00	2.50
❑	461GG	Sammy Sosa HR 57	6.00	2.50
❑	461HH	Sammy Sosa HR 58	6.00	2.50
❑	461II	Sammy Sosa HR 59	6.00	2.50
❑	461JJ	Sammy Sosa HR 60	6.00	2.50
❑	461KK	Sammy Sosa HR 61	15.00	6.00
❑	461LL	Sammy Sosa HR 62	20.00	8.00
❑	461MM	Sammy Sosa HR 63	8.00	3.00
❑	461NN	Sammy Sosa HR 64	8.00	3.00
❑	461OO	Sammy Sosa HR 65	8.00	3.00
❑	461PP	Sammy Sosa HR 66	25.00	10.00
❑	462	Checklist	.20	.07
❑	463	Checklist	.20	.07

1999 Topps Traded

	Card	Player	Price	Price
❑		COMP.FACT.SET (122)	40.00	15.00
❑		COMPLETE SET (121)	25.00	10.00
❑	T1	Seth Etherton	.20	.07
❑	T2	Mark Harriger RC	.25	.08
❑	T3	Matt Wise RC	.25	.08
❑	T4	Carlos Eduardo Hernandez RC	.40	.15
❑	T5	Julio Lugo RC	.60	.25
❑	T6	Mike Nannini	.20	.07
❑	T7	Justin Bowles RC	.25	.08
❑	T8	Mark Mulder RC	1.50	.60
❑	T9	Roberto Vaz RC	.25	.08
❑	T10	Felipe Lopez RC	1.50	.60
❑	T11	Matt Belisle	.20	.07
❑	T12	Micah Bowie	.20	.07
❑	T13	Ruben Quevedo RC	.25	.08
❑	T14	Jose Garcia RC	.25	.08
❑	T15	David Kelton RC	.25	.08
❑	T16	Phil Norton	.20	.07
❑	T17	Corey Patterson RC	1.00	.40
❑	T18	Ron Walker RC	.25	.08
❑	T19	Paul Hoover RC	.25	.08
❑	T20	Ryan Rupe RC	.25	.08
❑	T21	J.D. Closser RC	.40	.15
❑	T22	Rob Ryan RC	.25	.08
❑	T23	Steve Colyer RC	.25	.08
❑	T24	Bubba Crosby RC	.60	.25
❑	T25	Luke Prokopec RC	.25	.08
❑	T26	Matt Blank RC	.25	.08
❑	T27	Josh McKinley	.20	.07
❑	T28	Nate Bump	.20	.07
❑	T29	Giuseppe Chiaramonte RC	.25	.08
❑	T30	Arturo McDowell	.20	.07
❑	T31	Tony Torcato	.20	.07
❑	T32	Dave Roberts RC	.60	.25
❑	T33	C.C. Sabathia RC	1.25	.50
❑	T34	Sean Spencer RC	.25	.08
❑	T35	Chip Ambres	.20	.07
❑	T36	A.J. Burnett	1.00	.40
❑	T37	Mo Bruce RC	.25	.08
❑	T38	Jason Tyner	.20	.07
❑	T39	Mamon Tucker	.20	.07
❑	T40	Sean Burroughs RC	.60	.25
❑	T41	Kevin Eberwein RC	.25	.08
❑	T42	Junior Herndon RC	.25	.08
❑	T43	Bryan Wolff RC	.25	.08
❑	T44	Pat Burrell	1.25	.50
❑	T45	Eric Valent	.20	.07
❑	T46	Carlos Pena RC	.40	.15
❑	T47	Mike Zywica	.20	.07
❑	T48	Adam Everett	.30	.10
❑	T49	Juan Pena RC	.40	.15
❑	T50	Adam Dunn RC	4.00	1.50
❑	T51	Austin Kearns	1.25	.50
❑	T52	Jacobo Sequea RC	.25	.08
❑	T53	Choo Freeman	.20	.07
❑	T54	Jeff Winchester	.20	.07
❑	T55	Matt Burch	.20	.07
❑	T56	Chris George	.20	.07
❑	T57	Scott Mullen RC	.25	.08
❑	T58	Kit Pellow	.20	.07
❑	T59	Mark Quinn RC	.25	.08
❑	T60	Nate Cornejo	.25	.08
❑	T61	Ryan Mills	.20	.07
❑	T62	Kevin Beirne RC	.25	.08
❑	T63	Kip Wells RC	.40	.15
❑	T64	Juan Rivera RC	1.00	.40
❑	T65	Alfonso Soriano RC	5.00	2.00
❑	T66	Josh Hamilton RC	.40	.15
❑	T67	Josh Girdley RC	.25	.08
❑	T68	Kyle Snyder RC	.25	.08
❑	T69	Mike Paradis RC	.25	.08
❑	T70	Jason Jennings RC	.60	.25
❑	T71	David Walling RC	.25	.08
❑	T72	Omar Ortiz RC	.25	.08
❑	T73	Jay Gehrke RC	.40	.15
❑	T74	Casey Burns RC	.40	.15
❑	T75	Carl Crawford RC	3.00	1.25
❑	T76	Reggie Sanders	.20	.07
❑	T77	Will Clark	.30	.10
❑	T78	David Wells	.20	.07
❑	T79	Paul Konerko	.20	.07
❑	T80	Armando Benitez	.20	.07
❑	T81	Brant Brown	.20	.07
❑	T82	Mo Vaughn	.20	.07
❑	T83	Jose Canseco	.30	.10
❑	T84	Albert Belle	.20	.07
❑	T85	Dean Palmer	.20	.07
❑	T86	Greg Vaughn	.20	.07
❑	T87	Mark Clark	.20	.07
❑	T88	Pat Meares	.20	.07
❑	T89	Eric Davis	.20	.07
❑	T90	Brian Giles	.20	.07
❑	T91	Jeff Brantley	.20	.07
❑	T92	Bret Boone	.20	.07
❑	T93	Ron Gant	.20	.07
❑	T94	Mike Cameron	.20	.07
❑	T95	Charles Johnson	.20	.07
❑	T96	Denny Neagle	.20	.07
❑	T97	Brian Hunter	.20	.07
❑	T98	Jose Hernandez	.20	.07
❑	T99	Rick Aguilera	.20	.07
❑	T100	Tony Batista	.20	.07
❑	T101	Roger Cedeno	.20	.07
❑	T102	Creighton Gubanich RC	.25	.08
❑	T103	Tim Belcher	.20	.07
❑	T104	Bruce Aven	.20	.07
❑	T105	Brian Daubach RC	.40	.15
❑	T106	Ed Sprague	.20	.07
❑	T107	Michael Tucker	.20	.07
❑	T108	Homer Bush	.20	.07
❑	T109	Armando Reynoso	.20	.07
❑	T110	Brook Fordyce	.20	.07
❑	T111	Matt Mantei	.20	.07
❑	T112	Dave Mlicki	.20	.07
❑	T113	Kenny Rogers	.20	.07
❑	T114	Livan Hernandez	.20	.07
❑	T115	Butch Huskey	.20	.07
❑	T116	David Segui	.20	.07
❑	T117	Darryl Hamilton	.20	.07
❑	T118	Terry Mulholland	.20	.07
❑	T119	Randy Velarde	.20	.07
❑	T120	Bill Taylor	.20	.07
❑	T121	Kevin Appier	.20	.07

2000 Topps

❑	COMPLETE SET (478)	50.00	20.00
❑	COMP.HOBBY SET (478)	60.00	30.00
❑	COMPLETE SERIES 1 (239)	25.00	10.00
❑	COMPLETE SERIES 2 (240)	25.00	10.00
❑	MCGWIRE MM SET (5)	12.00	5.00
❑	AARON MM SET (5)	10.00	4.00
❑	RIPKEN MM SET (5)	15.00	6.00
❑	BOGGS MM SET (5)	3.00	1.25
❑	GWYNN MM SET (5)	6.00	2.50
❑	GRIFFEY MM SET (5)	8.00	3.00
❑	BONDS MM SET (5)	12.00	5.00
❑	SOSA MM SET (5)	8.00	3.00
❑	JETER MM SET (5)	12.00	5.00
❑	A.ROD MM SET (5)	8.00	3.00
❑ 1	Mark McGwire	1.25	.50
❑ 2	Tony Gwynn	.60	.25
❑ 3	Wade Boggs	.30	.10
❑ 4	Cal Ripken	1.50	.60
❑ 5	Matt Williams	.20	.07
❑ 6	Jay Buhner	.20	.07
❑ 8	Jeff Conine	.20	.07
❑ 9	Todd Greene	.20	.07
❑ 10	Mike Lieberthal	.20	.07
❑ 11	Steve Avery	.20	.07
❑ 12	Bret Saberhagen	.20	.07
❑ 13	Magglio Ordonez	.20	.07
❑ 14	Brad Radke	.20	.07
❑ 15	Derek Jeter	1.25	.50
❑ 16	Javy Lopez	.20	.07
❑ 17	Russ Davis	.20	.07
❑ 18	Armando Benitez	.20	.07
❑ 19	B.J. Surhoff	.20	.07
❑ 20	Darryl Kile	.20	.07
❑ 21	Mark Lewis	.20	.07
❑ 22	Mike Williams	.20	.07
❑ 23	Mark McLemore	.20	.07
❑ 24	Sterling Hitchcock	.20	.07
❑ 25	Darin Erstad	.20	.07
❑ 26	Ricky Gutierrez	.20	.07
❑ 27	John Jaha	.20	.07
❑ 28	Homer Bush	.20	.07
❑ 29	Darrin Fletcher	.20	.07
❑ 30	Mark Grace	.30	.10
❑ 31	Fred McGriff	.30	.10
❑ 32	Omar Daal	.20	.07
❑ 33	Eric Karros	.20	.07
❑ 34	Orlando Cabrera	.20	.07
❑ 35	J.T. Snow	.20	.07
❑ 36	Luis Castillo	.20	.07
❑ 37	Rey Ordonez	.20	.07
❑ 38	Bob Abreu	.20	.07
❑ 39	Warren Morris	.20	.07
❑ 40	Juan Gonzalez	.20	.07
❑ 41	Mike Lansing	.20	.07
❑ 42	Chili Davis	.20	.07
❑ 43	Dean Palmer	.20	.07
❑ 44	Hank Aaron	.75	.30
❑ 45	Jeff Bagwell	.30	.10
❑ 46	Jose Valentin	.20	.07
❑ 47	Shannon Stewart	.20	.07
❑ 48	Kent Bottenfield	.20	.07
❑ 49	Jeff Shaw	.20	.07
❑ 50	Sammy Sosa	.50	.20
❑ 51	Randy Johnson	.50	.20
❑ 52	Benny Agbayani	.20	.07
❑ 53	Dante Bichette	.20	.07
❑ 54	Pete Harnisch	.20	.07
❑ 55	Frank Thomas	.50	.20
❑ 56	Jorge Posada	.30	.10
❑ 57	Todd Walker	.20	.07
❑ 58	Juan Encarnacion	.20	.07
❑ 59	Mike Sweeney	.20	.07
❑ 60	Pedro Martinez	.30	.10
❑ 61	Lee Stevens	.20	.07
❑ 62	Brian Giles	.20	.07
❑ 63	Chad Ogea	.20	.07
❑ 64	Ivan Rodriguez	.30	.10
❑ 65	Roger Cedeno	.20	.07
❑ 66	David Justice	.20	.07
❑ 67	Steve Trachsel	.20	.07
❑ 68	Eli Marrero	.20	.07
❑ 69	Dave Nilsson	.20	.07
❑ 70	Ken Caminiti	.20	.07
❑ 71	Tim Raines	.20	.07
❑ 72	Brian Jordan	.20	.07
❑ 73	Jeff Blauser	.20	.07
❑ 74	Bernard Gilkey	.20	.07
❑ 75	John Flaherty	.20	.07
❑ 76	Brent Mayne	.20	.07
❑ 77	Jose Vidro	.20	.07
❑ 78	David Bell	.20	.07
❑ 79	Bruce Aven	.20	.07
❑ 80	John Olerud	.20	.07
❑ 81	Pokey Reese	.20	.07
❑ 82	Woody Williams	.20	.07
❑ 83	Ed Sprague	.20	.07
❑ 84	Joe Girardi	.20	.07
❑ 85	Barry Larkin	.30	.10
❑ 86	Mike Caruso	.20	.07
❑ 87	Bobby Higginson	.20	.07
❑ 88	Roberto Kelly	.20	.07
❑ 89	Edgar Martinez	.30	.10
❑ 90	Mark Kotsay	.20	.07
❑ 91	Paul Sorrento	.20	.07
❑ 92	Eric Young	.20	.07
❑ 93	Carlos Delgado	.20	.07
❑ 94	Troy Glaus	.20	.07
❑ 95	Ben Grieve	.20	.07
❑ 96	Jose Lima	.20	.07
❑ 97	Garret Anderson	.20	.07
❑ 98	Luis Gonzalez	.20	.07
❑ 99	Carl Pavano	.20	.07
❑ 100	Alex Rodriguez	.75	.30
❑ 101	Preston Wilson	.20	.07
❑ 102	Ron Gant	.20	.07
❑ 103	Brady Anderson	.20	.07
❑ 104	Rickey Henderson	.50	.20
❑ 105	Gary Sheffield	.20	.07
❑ 106	Mickey Morandini	.20	.07
❑ 107	Jim Edmonds	.20	.07
❑ 108	Kris Benson	.20	.07
❑ 109	Adrian Beltre	.20	.07
❑ 110	Alex Fernandez	.20	.07
❑ 111	Dan Wilson	.20	.07
❑ 112	Mark Clark	.20	.07
❑ 113	Greg Vaughn	.20	.07
❑ 114	Neifi Perez	.20	.07
❑ 115	Paul O'Neill	.30	.10
❑ 116	Jermaine Dye	.20	.07
❑ 117	Todd Jones	.20	.07
❑ 118	Terry Steinbach	.20	.07
❑ 119	Greg Norton	.20	.07
❑ 120	Curt Schilling	.20	.07
❑ 121	Todd Zeile	.20	.07
❑ 122	Edgardo Alfonzo	.20	.07
❑ 123	Ryan McGuire	.20	.07
❑ 124	Rich Aurilia	.20	.07
❑ 125	John Smoltz	.30	.10
❑ 126	Bob Wickman	.20	.07
❑ 127	Richard Hidalgo	.20	.07
❑ 128	Chuck Finley	.20	.07
❑ 129	Billy Wagner	.20	.07
❑ 130	Todd Hundley	.20	.07
❑ 131	Dwight Gooden	.20	.07
❑ 132	Russ Ortiz	.20	.07
❑ 133	Mike Lowell	.20	.07
❑ 134	Reggie Sanders	.20	.07
❑ 135	John Valentin	.20	.07
❑ 136	Brad Ausmus	.20	.07
❑ 137	Chad Kreuter	.20	.07
❑ 138	David Cone	.20	.07
❑ 139	Brook Fordyce	.20	.07
❑ 140	Roberto Alomar	.30	.10
❑ 141	Charles Nagy	.20	.07
❑ 142	Brian Hunter	.20	.07
❑ 143	Mike Mussina	.30	.10
❑ 144	Robin Ventura	.30	.10
❑ 145	Kevin Brown	.30	.10
❑ 146	Pat Hentgen	.20	.07
❑ 147	Ryan Klesko	.20	.07
❑ 148	Derek Bell	.20	.07
❑ 149	Andy Sheets	.20	.07
❑ 150	Larry Walker	.20	.07
❑ 151	Scott Williamson	.20	.07
❑ 152	Jose Offerman	.20	.07
❑ 153	Doug Mientkiewicz	.20	.07
❑ 154	John Snyder RC	.40	.15
❑ 155	Sandy Alomar Jr.	.20	.07
❑ 156	Joe Nathan	.20	.07
❑ 157	Lance Johnson	.20	.07
❑ 158	Odalis Perez	.20	.07
❑ 159	Hideo Nomo	.50	.20
❑ 160	Steve Finley	.20	.07
❑ 161	Dave Martinez	.20	.07
❑ 162	Matt Walbeck	.20	.07
❑ 163	Bill Spiers	.20	.07
❑ 164	Fernando Tatis	.20	.07
❑ 165	Kenny Lofton	.20	.07
❑ 166	Paul Byrd	.20	.07
❑ 167	Aaron Sele	.20	.07
❑ 168	Eddie Taubensee	.20	.07
❑ 169	Reggie Jefferson	.20	.07
❑ 170	Roger Clemens	1.00	.40
❑ 171	Francisco Cordova	.20	.07
❑ 172	Mike Bordick	.20	.07
❑ 173	Wally Joyner	.20	.07
❑ 174	Marvin Benard	.20	.07
❑ 175	Jason Kendall	.20	.07
❑ 176	Mike Stanley	.20	.07
❑ 177	Chad Allen	.20	.07
❑ 178	Carlos Beltran	.20	.07
❑ 179	Deivi Cruz	.20	.07
❑ 180	Chipper Jones	.50	.20
❑ 181	Vladimir Guerrero	.50	.20
❑ 182	Dave Burba	.20	.07
❑ 183	Tom Goodwin	.20	.07
❑ 184	Brian Daubach	.20	.07
❑ 185	Jay Bell	.20	.07
❑ 186	Roy Halladay	.20	.07
❑ 187	Miguel Tejada	.20	.07
❑ 188	Armando Rios	.20	.07
❑ 189	Fernando Vina	.20	.07
❑ 190	Eric Davis	.20	.07
❑ 191	Henry Rodriguez	.20	.07
❑ 192	Joe McEwing	.20	.07
❑ 193	Jeff Kent	.20	.07
❑ 194	Mike Jackson	.20	.07
❑ 195	Mike Morgan	.20	.07
❑ 196	Jeff Montgomery	.20	.07
❑ 197	Jeff Zimmerman	.20	.07
❑ 198	Tony Fernandez	.20	.07
❑ 199	Jason Giambi	.20	.07
❑ 200	Jose Canseco	.30	.10
❑ 201	Alex Gonzalez	.20	.07
❑ 202	J.Cust/Colangelo/D.Brown	.40	.15
❑ 203	A.Soriano/F.Lopez	.50	.20
❑ 204	Durazo/Burrell/Johnson	.40	.15
❑ 205	John Sneed RC/K.Wells	.40	.15
❑ 206	Kalinowski/Tejera/Mears RC	.40	.15
❑ 207	L.Berkman/C.Patterson	.40	.15
❑ 208	K.Pellow/K.Barker/R.Branyan	.40	.15
❑ 209	B.Garbe/L.Bigbie RC	.50	.20
❑ 210	B.Bradley RC/E.Munson	.40	.15
❑ 211	J.Girdley/K.Snyder	.40	.15
❑ 212	Chance Caple RC/J.Jennings	.40	.15
❑ 213	B.Myers/R.Christianson RC	1.25	.50
❑ 214	J.Stumm/R.Purvis RC	.40	.15
❑ 215	D.Walling/M.Paradis	.40	.15
❑ 216	O.Ortiz/J.Gehrke	.40	.15
❑ 217	David Cone HL	.20	.07
❑ 218	Jose Jimenez HL	.20	.07
❑ 219	Chris Singleton HL	.20	.07
❑ 220	Fernando Tatis HL	.20	.07
❑ 221	Todd Helton HL	.20	.07
❑ 222	Kevin Millwood DIV	.20	.07
❑ 223	Todd Pratt DIV	.20	.07
❑ 224	Orlando Hernandez DIV	.20	.07
❑ 225	Pedro Martinez DIV	.30	.10

❑ 226	Tom Glavine LCS	.20	.07
❑ 227	Bernie Williams LCS	.20	.07
❑ 228	Mariano Rivera WS	.30	.10
❑ 229	Tony Gwynn 20CB	.60	.25
❑ 230	Wade Boggs 20CB	.30	.10
❑ 231	Lance Johnson CB	.20	.07
❑ 232	Mark McGwire 20CB	1.25	.50
❑ 233	Rickey Henderson 20CB	.50	.20
❑ 234	Rickey Henderson 20CB	.50	.20
❑ 235	Roger Clemens 20CB	1.00	.40
❑ 236A	M.McGwire MM 1st HR		
❑ 236B	M.McGwire MM 1987 ROY		
❑ 236C	M.McGwire MM 62nd HR		
❑ 236D	M.McGwire MM 70th HR		
❑ 236E	M.McGwire MM 500th HR		
❑ 237A	H.Aaron MM 1st Career HR	2.00	.75
❑ 237B	H.Aaron MM 1957 MVP	2.00	.75
❑ 237C	H.Aaron MM 3000th Hit	2.00	.75
❑ 237D	H.Aaron MM 715th HR	2.00	.75
❑ 237E	H.Aaron MM 755th HR	2.00	.75
❑ 238A	C.Ripken MM 1982 ROY	4.00	1.50
❑ 238B	C.Ripken MM 1991 MVP	4.00	1.50
❑ 238C	C.Ripken MM 2131 Game	4.00	1.50
❑ 238D	C.Ripken MM Streak Ends	4.00	1.50
❑ 238E	C.Ripken MM 400th HR	4.00	1.50
❑ 239A	W.Boggs MM 1983 Batting	.75	.30
❑ 239B	W.Boggs MM 1988 Batting	.75	.30
❑ 239C	W.Boggs MM 2000th Hit	.75	.30
❑ 239D	W.Boggs MM 1996 Champs	.75	.30
❑ 239E	W.Boggs MM 3000th Hit	.75	.30
❑ 240A	T.Gwynn MM 1984 Batting	1.50	.60
❑ 240B	T.Gwynn MM 1984 NLCS	1.50	.60
❑ 240C	T.Gwynn MM 1995 Batting	1.50	.60
❑ 240D	T.Gwynn MM 1998 NLCS	1.50	.60
❑ 240E	T.Gwynn MM 3000th Hit	1.50	.60
❑ 241	Tom Glavine	.30	.10
❑ 242	David Wells	.20	.07
❑ 243	Kevin Appier	.20	.07
❑ 244	Troy Percival	.20	.07
❑ 245	Ray Lankford	.20	.07
❑ 246	Marquis Grissom	.20	.07
❑ 247	Randy Winn	.20	.07
❑ 248	Miguel Batista	.20	.07
❑ 249	Darren Dreifort	.20	.07
❑ 250	Barry Bonds	1.50	.60
❑ 251	Harold Baines	.20	.07
❑ 252	Cliff Floyd	.20	.07
❑ 253	Freddy Garcia	.20	.07
❑ 254	Kenny Rogers	.20	.07
❑ 255	Ben Davis	.20	.07
❑ 256	Charles Johnson	.20	.07
❑ 257	Bubba Trammell	.20	.07
❑ 258	Desi Relaford	.20	.07
❑ 259	Al Martin	.20	.07
❑ 260	Andy Pettitte	.30	.10
❑ 261	Carlos Lee	.20	.07
❑ 262	Matt Lawton	.20	.07
❑ 263	Andy Fox	.20	.07
❑ 264	Chan Ho Park	.20	.07
❑ 265	Billy Koch	.20	.07
❑ 266	Dave Roberts	.20	.07
❑ 267	Carl Everett	.20	.07
❑ 268	Orel Hershiser	.20	.07
❑ 269	Trot Nixon	.20	.07
❑ 270	Rusty Greer	.20	.07
❑ 271	Will Clark	.30	.10
❑ 272	Quilvio Veras	.20	.07
❑ 273	Rico Brogna	.20	.07
❑ 274	Devon White	.20	.07
❑ 275	Tim Hudson	.20	.07
❑ 276	Mike Hampton	.20	.07
❑ 277	Miguel Cairo	.20	.07
❑ 278	Darren Oliver	.20	.07
❑ 279	Jeff Cirillo	.20	.07
❑ 280	Al Leiter	.20	.07
❑ 281	Shane Andrews	.20	.07
❑ 282	Carlos Febles	.20	.07
❑ 283	Pedro Astacio	.20	.07
❑ 284	Juan Guzman	.20	.07
❑ 285	Orlando Hernandez	.20	.07
❑ 286	Paul Konerko	.20	.07
❑ 287	Tony Clark	.20	.07
❑ 288	Aaron Boone	.20	.07
❑ 289	Ismael Valdes	.20	.07
❑ 290	Moises Alou	.20	.07
❑ 291	Kevin Tapani	.20	.07
❑ 292	John Franco	.20	.07
❑ 293	Todd Zeile	.20	.07
❑ 294	Jason Schmidt	.20	.07
❑ 295	Johnny Damon	.30	.10
❑ 296	Scott Brosius	.20	.07
❑ 297	Travis Fryman	.20	.07
❑ 298	Jose Vizcaino	.20	.07
❑ 299	Eric Chavez	.20	.07
❑ 300	Mike Piazza	.75	.30
❑ 301	Matt Clement	.20	.07
❑ 302	Cristian Guzman	.20	.07
❑ 303	C.J. Nitkowski	.20	.07
❑ 304	Michael Tucker	.20	.07
❑ 305	Brett Tomko	.20	.07
❑ 306	Mike Lansing	.20	.07
❑ 307	Eric Owens	.20	.07
❑ 308	Livan Hernandez	.20	.07
❑ 309	Rondell White	.20	.07
❑ 310	Todd Stottlemyre	.20	.07
❑ 311	Chris Carpenter	.20	.07
❑ 312	Ken Hill	.20	.07
❑ 313	Mark Loretta	.20	.07
❑ 314	John Rocker	.20	.07
❑ 315	Richie Sexson	.20	.07
❑ 316	Ruben Mateo	.20	.07
❑ 317	Joe Randa	.20	.07
❑ 318	Mike Sirotka	.20	.07
❑ 319	Jose Rosado	.20	.07
❑ 320	Matt Mantei	.20	.07
❑ 321	Kevin Millwood	.20	.07
❑ 322	Gary Disarcina	.20	.07
❑ 323	Dustin Hermanson	.20	.07
❑ 324	Mike Stanton	.20	.07
❑ 325	Kirk Rueter	.20	.07
❑ 326	Damian Miller RC	.40	.15
❑ 327	Doug Glanville	.20	.07
❑ 328	Scott Rolen	.30	.10
❑ 329	Ray Durham	.20	.07
❑ 330	Butch Huskey	.20	.07
❑ 331	Mariano Rivera	.50	.20
❑ 332	Darren Lewis	.20	.07
❑ 333	Mike Timlin	.20	.07
❑ 334	Mark Grudzielanek	.20	.07
❑ 335	Mike Cameron	.20	.07
❑ 336	Kelvim Escobar	.20	.07
❑ 337	Bret Boone	.20	.07
❑ 338	Mo Vaughn	.20	.07
❑ 339	Craig Biggio	.30	.10
❑ 340	Michael Barrett	.20	.07
❑ 341	Marlon Anderson	.20	.07
❑ 342	Bobby Jones	.20	.07
❑ 343	John Halama	.20	.07
❑ 344	Todd Ritchie	.20	.07
❑ 345	Chuck Knoblauch	.20	.07
❑ 346	Rick Reed	.20	.07
❑ 347	Kelly Stinnett	.20	.07
❑ 348	Tim Salmon	.30	.10
❑ 349	A.J. Hinch	.20	.07
❑ 350	Jose Cruz Jr.	.20	.07
❑ 351	Roberto Hernandez	.20	.07
❑ 352	Edgar Renteria	.20	.07
❑ 353	Jose Hernandez	.20	.07
❑ 354	Brad Fullmer	.20	.07
❑ 355	Trevor Hoffman	.20	.07
❑ 356	Troy O'Leary	.20	.07
❑ 357	Justin Thompson	.20	.07
❑ 358	Kevin Young	.20	.07
❑ 359	Hideki Irabu	.20	.07
❑ 360	Jim Thome	.30	.10
❑ 361	Steve Karsay	.20	.07
❑ 362	Octavio Dotel	.20	.07
❑ 363	Omar Vizquel	.30	.10
❑ 364	Raul Mondesi	.20	.07
❑ 365	Shane Reynolds	.20	.07
❑ 366	Bartolo Colon	.20	.07
❑ 367	Chris Widger	.20	.07
❑ 368	Gabe Kapler	.20	.07
❑ 369	Bill Simas	.20	.07
❑ 370	Tino Martinez	.30	.10
❑ 371	John Thomson	.20	.07
❑ 372	Delino Deshields	.20	.07
❑ 373	Carlos Perez	.20	.07
❑ 374	Eddie Perez	.20	.07
❑ 375	Jeromy Burnitz	.20	.07
❑ 376	Jimmy Haynes	.20	.07
❑ 377	Travis Lee	.20	.07
❑ 378	Darryl Hamilton	.20	.07
❑ 379	Jamie Moyer	.20	.07
❑ 380	Alex Gonzalez	.20	.07
❑ 381	John Wetteland	.20	.07
❑ 382	Vinny Castilla	.20	.07
❑ 383	Jeff Suppan	.20	.07
❑ 384	Jim Leyritz	.20	.07
❑ 385	Robb Nen	.20	.07
❑ 386	Wilson Alvarez	.20	.07
❑ 387	Andres Galarraga	.20	.07
❑ 388	Mike Remlinger	.20	.07
❑ 389	Geoff Jenkins	.20	.07
❑ 390	Matt Stairs	.20	.07
❑ 391	Bill Mueller	.20	.07
❑ 392	Mike Lowell	.20	.07
❑ 393	Andy Ashby	.20	.07
❑ 394	Ruben Rivera	.20	.07
❑ 395	Todd Helton	.30	.10
❑ 396	Bernie Williams	.30	.10
❑ 397	Royce Clayton	.20	.07
❑ 398	Manny Ramirez	.30	.10
❑ 399	Kerry Wood	.20	.07
❑ 400	Ken Griffey Jr.	.75	.30
❑ 401	Enrique Wilson	.20	.07
❑ 402	Joey Hamilton	.20	.07
❑ 403	Shawn Estes	.20	.07
❑ 404	Ugueth Urbina	.20	.07
❑ 405	Albert Belle	.20	.07
❑ 406	Rick Helling	.20	.07
❑ 407	Steve Parris	.20	.07
❑ 408	Eric Milton	.20	.07
❑ 409	Dave Mlicki	.20	.07
❑ 410	Shawn Green	.20	.07
❑ 411	Jaret Wright	.20	.07
❑ 412	Tony Womack	.20	.07
❑ 413	Vernon Wells	.20	.07
❑ 414	Ron Belliard	.20	.07
❑ 415	Ellis Burks	.20	.07
❑ 416	Scott Erickson	.20	.07
❑ 417	Rafael Palmeiro	.30	.10
❑ 418	Damion Easley	.20	.07
❑ 419	Jamey Wright	.20	.07
❑ 420	Corey Koskie	.20	.07
❑ 421	Bobby Howry	.20	.07
❑ 422	Ricky Ledee	.20	.07
❑ 423	Dmitri Young	.20	.07
❑ 424	Sidney Ponson	.20	.07
❑ 425	Greg Maddux	.75	.30
❑ 426	Jose Guillen	.20	.07
❑ 427	Jon Lieber	.20	.07
❑ 428	Andy Benes	.20	.07
❑ 429	Randy Velarde	.20	.07
❑ 430	Sean Casey	.20	.07
❑ 431	Torii Hunter	.20	.07
❑ 432	Ryan Rupe	.20	.07
❑ 433	David Segui	.20	.07
❑ 434	Todd Pratt	.20	.07
❑ 435	Nomar Garciaparra	.75	.30
❑ 436	Denny Neagle	.20	.07
❑ 437	Ron Coomer	.20	.07
❑ 438	Chris Singleton	.20	.07
❑ 439	Tony Batista	.20	.07
❑ 440	Andruw Jones	.30	.10
❑ 441	Burroughs/Piatt/Huff	.20	.07
❑ 442	Rafael Furcal	.40	.15
❑ 443	M.Lamb RC/J.Crede	1.00	.40
❑ 444	Julio Zuleta RC	.40	.15
❑ 445	Garry Maddox Jr. RC	.40	.15
❑ 446	Riley/Sabathia/Mulder	.40	.15
❑ 447	Scott Downs RC	.40	.15
❑ 448	D.Mirabelli/B.Petrick/J.Werth	.40	.15
❑ 449	C.Myers RC/J.Hamilton	.40	.15
❑ 450	B.Christensen/R.Stahl RC	.40	.15
❑ 451	B.Zito/B.Sheets RC	2.50	1.00
❑ 452	K.Ainsworth/Howington RC	.40	.15
❑ 453	R.Asadoorian/V.Faison RC	.40	.15
❑ 454	K.Reed/J.Heaverlo RC	.40	.15
❑ 455	M.MacDougal/B.Baker RC	.40	.15
❑ 456	Mark McGwire SH	.60	.25
❑ 457	Cal Ripken SH	.75	.30
❑ 458	Wade Boggs SH	.20	.07
❑ 459	Tony Gwynn SH	.30	.10
❑ 460	Jesse Orosco SH	.20	.07
❑ 461	L.Walker/N.Garciaparra LL	.30	.10
❑ 462	K.Griffey Jr./M.McGwire LL	.50	.20
❑ 463	M.Ramirez/M.McGwire LL	.50	.20

❑ 464 P.Martinez/R.Johnson LL .30 .10
❑ 465 P.Martinez/R.Johnson LL .30 .10
❑ 466 D.Jeter/L.Gonzalez LL .50 .20
❑ 467 L.Walker/M.Ramirez LL .30 .10
❑ 468 Tony Gwynn 20CB .60 .25
❑ 469 Mark McGwire 20CB 1.25 .50
❑ 470 Frank Thomas 20CB .30 .10
❑ 471 Harold Baines 20CB .20 .07
❑ 472 Roger Clemens 20CB 1.00 .40
❑ 473 John Franco 20CB .20 .07
❑ 474 John Franco 20CB .20 .07
❑ 475A K.Griffey Jr. MM 350th HR 2.00 .75
❑ 475B K.Griffey Jr. MM 1997 MVP 2.00 .75
❑ 475C K.Griffey Jr. MM HR Dad 2.00 .75
❑ 475D K.Griffey Jr. MM 1992 AS MVP 2.00 .75
❑ 475E K.Griffey Jr. MM 50 HR 1997 2.00 .75
❑ 476A B.Bonds MM 400HR/400SB 3.00 1.25
❑ 476B B.Bonds MM 40HR/40SB 3.00 1.25
❑ 476C B.Bonds MM 1993 MVP 3.00 1.25
❑ 476D B.Bonds MM 1990 MVP 3.00 1.25
❑ 476E B.Bonds MM 1992 MVP 3.00 1.25
❑ 477A S.Sosa MM 20 HR June 2.00 .75
❑ 477B S.Sosa MM 66 HR 1998 2.00 .75
❑ 477C S.Sosa MM 60 HR 1999 2.00 .75
❑ 477D S.Sosa MM 1998 MVP 2.00 .75
❑ 477E S.Sosa MM HR's 61/62 2.00 .75
❑ 478A D.Jeter MM 1996 ROY 3.00 1.25
❑ 478B D.Jeter MM Wins 1999 WS 3.00 1.25
❑ 478C D.Jeter MM Wins 1998 WS 3.00 1.25
❑ 478D D.Jeter MM Wins 1996 WS 3.00 1.25
❑ 478E D.Jeter MM 17 GM Hit Streak 3.00 1.25
❑ 479A A.Rodriguez MM 40HR/40SB 2.00 .75
❑ 479B A.Rodriguez MM 100th HR 2.00 .75
❑ 479C A.Rodriguez MM 1996 POY 2.00 .75
❑ 479D A.Rodriguez MM Wins 1 Million 2.00 .75
❑ 479E A.Rodriguez MM 1996 Batting Leader 2.00 .75
❑ NNO M.McGwire 85 Reprint 5.00 2.00

2000 Topps Traded

❑ COMP.FACT.SET (136) 50.00 30.00
❑ COMPLETE SET (135) 30.00 15.00
❑ FACT.SET PRICE IS FOR SEALED SETS
❑ T1 Mike MacDougal .30 .10
❑ T2 Andy Tracy RC .30 .10
❑ T3 Brandon Phillips RC 1.00 .40
❑ T4 Brandon Inge RC 2.00 .75
❑ T5 Robbie Morrison RC .30 .10
❑ T6 Josh Pressley RC .30 .10
❑ T7 Todd Moser RC .30 .10
❑ T8 Rob Purvis .30 .10
❑ T9 Chance Caple .20 .07
❑ T10 Ben Sheets 1.00 .40
❑ T11 Russ Jacobson RC .30 .10
❑ T12 Brian Cole RC .30 .10
❑ T13 Brad Baker .20 .07
❑ T14 Alex Cintron RC .30 .10
❑ T15 Lyle Overbay RC .75 .30
❑ T16 Mike Edwards RC .30 .10
❑ T17 Sean McGowan RC .30 .10
❑ T18 Jose Molina .20 .07
❑ T19 Marcos Castillo RC .30 .10
❑ T20 Josue Espada RC .30 .10
❑ T21 Alex Gordon RC .30 .10
❑ T22 Rob Pugmire RC .30 .10
❑ T23 Jason Stumm .20 .07
❑ T24 Ty Howington .20 .07
❑ T25 Brett Myers .75 .30
❑ T26 Maicer Izturis RC .30 .10
❑ T27 John McDonald .20 .07
❑ T28 Wilfredo Rodriguez RC .30 .10
❑ T29 Carlos Zambrano RC 4.00 1.50
❑ T30 Alejandro Diaz RC .30 .10
❑ T31 Geraldo Guzman RC .30 .10
❑ T32 J.R. House RC .30 .10
❑ T33 Elvin Nina RC .30 .10
❑ T34 Juan Pierre RC .75 .30
❑ T35 Ben Johnson RC 1.25 .50
❑ T36 Jeff Bailey RC .30 .10
❑ T37 Miguel Olivo RC .50 .20
❑ T38 Francisco Rodriguez RC 1.50 .60
❑ T39 Tony Pena Jr. RC .30 .10
❑ T40 Miguel Cabrera RC 20.00 8.00
❑ T41 Asdrubal Oropeza RC .30 .10
❑ T42 Junior Zamora RC .30 .10
❑ T43 Jovanny Cedeno RC .30 .10
❑ T44 John Sneed .30 .10
❑ T45 Josh Kalinowski .30 .10
❑ T46 Mike Young RC 5.00 2.00
❑ T47 Rico Washington RC .30 .10
❑ T48 Chad Durbin RC .30 .10
❑ T49 Junior Brignac RC .30 .10
❑ T50 Carlos Hernandez RC .30 .10
❑ T51 Cesar Izturis RC .50 .20
❑ T52 Oscar Salazar RC .30 .10
❑ T53 Pat Strange RC .30 .10
❑ T54 Rick Asadoorian .30 .10
❑ T55 Keith Reed .20 .07
❑ T56 Leo Estrella RC .30 .10
❑ T57 Wascar Serrano RC .30 .10
❑ T58 Richard Gomez RC .30 .10
❑ T59 Ramon Santiago RC .30 .10
❑ T60 Jovanny Sosa RC .30 .10
❑ T61 Aaron Rowand RC 1.25 .50
❑ T62 Junior Guerrero RC .30 .10
❑ T63 Luis Terrero RC .30 .10
❑ T64 Brian Sanches RC .30 .10
❑ T65 Scott Sobkowiak RC .30 .10
❑ T66 Gary Majewski RC .30 .10
❑ T67 Barry Zito 1.25 .50
❑ T68 Ryan Christianson .20 .07
❑ T69 Cristian Guerrero RC .30 .10
❑ T70 Tomas De La Rosa RC .30 .10
❑ T71 Andrew Beinbrink RC .30 .10
❑ T72 Ryan Knox RC .30 .10
❑ T73 Alex Graman RC .30 .10
❑ T74 Juan Guzman RC .30 .10
❑ T75 Ruben Salazar RC .30 .10
❑ T76 Luis Matos RC .30 .10
❑ T77 Tony Mota RC .30 .10
❑ T78 Doug Davis .30 .10
❑ T79 Ben Christensen .20 .07
❑ T80 Mike Lamb .50 .20
❑ T81 Adrian Gonzalez RC 2.50 1.00
❑ T82 Mike Stodolka RC .30 .10
❑ T83 Adam Johnson RC .30 .10
❑ T84 Matt Wheatland RC .30 .10
❑ T85 Corey Smith RC .30 .10
❑ T86 Rocco Baldelli RC 1.50 .60
❑ T87 Keith Bucktrot RC .30 .10
❑ T88 Adam Wainwright RC 1.00 .40
❑ T89 Scott Thorman RC .75 .30
❑ T90 Tripper Johnson RC .30 .10
❑ T91 Jim Edmonds Cards .30 .10
❑ T92 Masato Yoshii .20 .07
❑ T93 Adam Kennedy .20 .07
❑ T94 Darryl Kile .30 .10
❑ T95 Mark McLemore .20 .07
❑ T96 Ricky Gutierrez .20 .07
❑ T97 Juan Gonzalez .30 .10
❑ T98 Melvin Mora .30 .10
❑ T99 Dante Bichette .30 .10
❑ T100 Lee Stevens .20 .07
❑ T101 Roger Cedeno .20 .07
❑ T102 John Olerud .30 .10
❑ T103 Eric Young .20 .07
❑ T104 Mickey Morandini .20 .07
❑ T105 Travis Lee .20 .07
❑ T106 Greg Vaughn .20 .07
❑ T107 Todd Zeile .30 .10
❑ T108 Chuck Finley .30 .10
❑ T109 Ismael Valdes .20 .07
❑ T110 Reggie Sanders .30 .10
❑ T111 Pat Hentgen .20 .07
❑ T112 Ryan Klesko .30 .10
❑ T113 Derek Bell .20 .07
❑ T114 Hideo Nomo .75 .30
❑ T115 Aaron Sele .20 .07
❑ T116 Fernando Vina .20 .07
❑ T117 Wally Joyner .30 .10
❑ T118 Brian Hunter .20 .07
❑ T119 Joe Girardi .20 .07
❑ T120 Omar Daal .20 .07
❑ T121 Brook Fordyce .20 .07
❑ T122 Jose Valentin .20 .07
❑ T123 Curt Schilling .30 .10
❑ T124 B.J. Surhoff .30 .10
❑ T125 Henry Rodriguez .20 .07
❑ T126 Mike Bordick .20 .07
❑ T127 David Justice .30 .10
❑ T128 Charles Johnson .30 .10
❑ T129 Will Clark .50 .20
❑ T130 Dwight Gooden .30 .10
❑ T131 David Segui .20 .07
❑ T132 Denny Neagle .30 .10
❑ T133 Jose Canseco .50 .20
❑ T134 Bruce Chen .20 .07
❑ T135 Jason Bere .20 .07

2001 Topps

❑ COMPLETE SET (790) 80.00 40.00
❑ COMP.FACT.BLUE SET (795) 120.00 60.00
❑ COMPLETE SERIES 1 (405) 40.00 20.00
❑ COMPLETE SERIES 2 (385) 40.00 20.00
❑ COMMON CARD (1-6/8-791) .20 .07
❑ COMMON (352-376/727-751) .25 .08
❑ 1 Cal Ripken 1.50 .60
❑ 2 Chipper Jones .50 .20
❑ 3 Roger Cedeno .20 .07
❑ 4 Garret Anderson .20 .07
❑ 5 Robin Ventura .20 .07
❑ 6 Daryle Ward .20 .07
❑ 7 Does Not Exist
❑ 8 Craig Paquette .20 .07
❑ 9 Phil Nevin .20 .07
❑ 10 Jermaine Dye .20 .07
❑ 11 Chris Singleton .20 .07
❑ 12 Mike Stanton .20 .07
❑ 13 Brian Hunter .20 .07
❑ 14 Mike Redmond .20 .07
❑ 15 Jim Thome .30 .10
❑ 16 Brian Jordan .20 .07
❑ 17 Joe Girardi .20 .07
❑ 18 Steve Woodard .20 .07
❑ 19 Dustin Hermanson .20 .07
❑ 20 Shawn Green .20 .07
❑ 21 Todd Stottlemyre .20 .07
❑ 22 Dan Wilson .20 .07
❑ 23 Todd Pratt .20 .07
❑ 24 Derek Lowe .20 .07
❑ 25 Juan Gonzalez .20 .07
❑ 26 Clay Bellinger .20 .07
❑ 27 Jeff Fassero .20 .07
❑ 28 Pat Meares .20 .07
❑ 29 Eddie Taubensee .20 .07
❑ 30 Paul O'Neill .30 .10
❑ 31 Jeffrey Hammonds .20 .07
❑ 32 Pokey Reese .20 .07
❑ 33 Mike Mussina .30 .10
❑ 34 Rico Brogna .20 .07
❑ 35 Jay Buhner .20 .07
❑ 36 Steve Cox .20 .07

❑ 37 Quilvio Veras .20 .07
❑ 38 Marquis Grissom .20 .07
❑ 39 Shigetoshi Hasegawa .20 .07
❑ 40 Shane Reynolds .20 .07
❑ 41 Adam Piatt .20 .07
❑ 42 Luis Polonia .20 .07
❑ 43 Brook Fordyce .20 .07
❑ 44 Preston Wilson .20 .07
❑ 45 Ellis Burks .20 .07
❑ 46 Armando Rios .20 .07
❑ 47 Chuck Finley .20 .07
❑ 48 Dan Plesac .20 .07
❑ 49 Shannon Stewart .20 .07
❑ 50 Mark McGwire 1.25 .50
❑ 51 Mark Loretta .20 .07
❑ 52 Gerald Williams .20 .07
❑ 53 Eric Young .20 .07
❑ 54 Peter Bergeron .20 .07
❑ 55 Dave Hansen .20 .07
❑ 56 Arthur Rhodes .20 .07
❑ 57 Bobby Jones .20 .07
❑ 58 Matt Clement .20 .07
❑ 59 Mike Benjamin .20 .07
❑ 60 Pedro Martinez .30 .10
❑ 61 Jose Canseco .30 .10
❑ 62 Matt Anderson .20 .07
❑ 63 Torii Hunter .20 .07
❑ 64 Carlos Lee .20 .07
❑ 65 David Cone .20 .07
❑ 66 Rey Sanchez .20 .07
❑ 67 Eric Chavez .20 .07
❑ 68 Rick Helling .20 .07
❑ 69 Manny Alexander .20 .07
❑ 70 John Franco .20 .07
❑ 71 Mike Bordick .20 .07
❑ 72 Andres Galarraga .20 .07
❑ 73 Jose Cruz Jr. .20 .07
❑ 74 Mike Matheny .20 .07
❑ 75 Randy Johnson .50 .20
❑ 76 Richie Sexson .20 .07
❑ 77 Vladimir Nunez .20 .07
❑ 78 Harold Baines .20 .07
❑ 79 Aaron Boone .20 .07
❑ 80 Darin Erstad .20 .07
❑ 81 Alex Gonzalez .20 .07
❑ 82 Gil Heredia .20 .07
❑ 83 Shane Andrews .20 .07
❑ 84 Todd Hundley .20 .07
❑ 85 Bill Mueller .20 .07
❑ 86 Mark McLemore .20 .07
❑ 87 Scott Spiezio .20 .07
❑ 88 Kevin McGlinchy .20 .07
❑ 89 Bubba Trammell .20 .07
❑ 90 Manny Ramirez .30 .10
❑ 91 Mike Lamb .20 .07
❑ 92 Scott Karl .20 .07
❑ 93 Brian Buchanan .20 .07
❑ 94 Chris Turner .20 .07
❑ 95 Mike Sweeney .20 .07
❑ 96 John Wetteland .20 .07
❑ 97 Rob Bell .20 .07
❑ 98 Pat Rapp .20 .07
❑ 99 John Burkett .20 .07
❑ 100 Derek Jeter 1.25 .50
❑ 101 J.D. Drew .20 .07
❑ 102 Jose Offerman .20 .07
❑ 103 Rick Reed .20 .07
❑ 104 Will Clark .30 .10
❑ 105 Rickey Henderson .50 .20
❑ 106 Dave Berg .20 .07
❑ 107 Kirk Rueter .20 .07
❑ 108 Lee Stevens .20 .07
❑ 109 Jay Bell .20 .07
❑ 110 Fred McGriff .30 .10
❑ 111 Julio Zuleta .20 .07
❑ 112 Brian Anderson .20 .07
❑ 113 Orlando Cabrera .20 .07
❑ 114 Alex Fernandez .20 .07
❑ 115 Derek Bell .20 .07
❑ 116 Eric Owens .20 .07
❑ 117 Brian Bohanon .20 .07
❑ 118 Dennys Reyes .20 .07
❑ 119 Mike Stanley .20 .07
❑ 120 Jorge Posada .30 .10
❑ 121 Rich Becker .20 .07
❑ 122 Paul Konerko .20 .07
❑ 123 Mike Remlinger .20 .07
❑ 124 Travis Lee .20 .07
❑ 125 Ken Caminiti .20 .07
❑ 126 Kevin Barker .20 .07
❑ 127 Paul Quantrill .20 .07
❑ 128 Ozzie Guillen .20 .07
❑ 129 Kevin Tapani .20 .07
❑ 130 Mark Johnson .20 .07
❑ 131 Randy Wolf .20 .07
❑ 132 Michael Tucker .20 .07
❑ 133 Darren Lewis .20 .07
❑ 134 Joe Randa .20 .07
❑ 135 Jeff Cirillo .20 .07
❑ 136 David Ortiz .50 .20
❑ 137 Herb Perry .20 .07
❑ 138 Jeff Nelson .20 .07
❑ 139 Chris Stynes .20 .07
❑ 140 Johnny Damon .30 .10
❑ 141 Jeff Reboulet .20 .07
❑ 142 Jason Schmidt .20 .07
❑ 143 Charles Johnson .20 .07
❑ 144 Pat Burrell .20 .07
❑ 145 Gary Sheffield .20 .07
❑ 146 Tom Glavine .30 .10
❑ 147 Jason Isringhausen .20 .07
❑ 148 Chris Carpenter .20 .07
❑ 149 Jeff Suppan .20 .07
❑ 150 Ivan Rodriguez .30 .10
❑ 151 Luis Sojo .20 .07
❑ 152 Ron Villone .20 .07
❑ 153 Mike Sirotka .20 .07
❑ 154 Chuck Knoblauch .20 .07
❑ 155 Jason Kendall .20 .07
❑ 156 Dennis Cook .20 .07
❑ 157 Bobby Estalella .20 .07
❑ 158 Jose Guillen .20 .07
❑ 159 Thomas Howard .20 .07
❑ 160 Carlos Delgado .20 .07
❑ 161 Benji Gil .20 .07
❑ 162 Tim Bogar .20 .07
❑ 163 Kevin Elster .20 .07
❑ 164 Einar Diaz .20 .07
❑ 165 Andy Benes .20 .07
❑ 166 Adrian Beltre .20 .07
❑ 167 David Bell .20 .07
❑ 168 Turk Wendell .20 .07
❑ 169 Pete Harnisch .20 .07
❑ 170 Roger Clemens 1.00 .40
❑ 171 Scott Williamson .20 .07
❑ 172 Kevin Jordan .20 .07
❑ 173 Brad Penny .20 .07
❑ 174 John Flaherty .20 .07
❑ 175 Troy Glaus .20 .07
❑ 176 Kevin Appier .20 .07
❑ 177 Walt Weiss .20 .07
❑ 178 Tyler Houston .20 .07
❑ 179 Michael Barrett .20 .07
❑ 180 Mike Hampton .20 .07
❑ 181 Francisco Cordova .20 .07
❑ 182 Mike Jackson .20 .07
❑ 183 David Segui .20 .07
❑ 184 Carlos Febles .20 .07
❑ 185 Roy Halladay .20 .07
❑ 186 Seth Etherton .20 .07
❑ 187 Charlie Hayes .20 .07
❑ 188 Fernando Tatis .20 .07
❑ 189 Steve Trachsel .20 .07
❑ 190 Livan Hernandez .20 .07
❑ 191 Joe Oliver .20 .07
❑ 192 Stan Javier .20 .07
❑ 193 B.J. Surhoff .20 .07
❑ 194 Rob Ducey .20 .07
❑ 195 Barry Larkin .30 .10
❑ 196 Danny Patterson .20 .07
❑ 197 Bobby Howry .20 .07
❑ 198 Dmitri Young .20 .07
❑ 199 Brian Hunter .20 .07
❑ 200 Alex Rodriguez .75 .30
❑ 201 Hideo Nomo .50 .20
❑ 202 Luis Alicea .20 .07
❑ 203 Warren Morris .20 .07
❑ 204 Antonio Alfonseca .20 .07
❑ 205 Edgardo Alfonzo .20 .07
❑ 206 Mark Grudzielanek .20 .07
❑ 207 Fernando Vina .20 .07
❑ 208 Willie Greene .20 .07
❑ 209 Homer Bush .20 .07
❑ 210 Jason Giambi .20 .07
❑ 211 Mike Morgan .20 .07
❑ 212 Steve Karsay .20 .07
❑ 213 Matt Lawton .20 .07
❑ 214 Wendell Magee Jr. .20 .07
❑ 215 Rusty Greer .20 .07
❑ 216 Keith Lockhart .20 .07
❑ 217 Billy Koch .20 .07
❑ 218 Todd Hollandsworth .20 .07
❑ 219 Raul Ibanez .20 .07
❑ 220 Tony Gwynn .60 .25
❑ 221 Carl Everett .20 .07
❑ 222 Hector Carrasco .20 .07
❑ 223 Jose Valentin .20 .07
❑ 224 Deivi Cruz .20 .07
❑ 225 Bret Boone .20 .07
❑ 226 Kurt Abbott .20 .07
❑ 227 Melvin Mora .20 .07
❑ 228 Danny Graves .20 .07
❑ 229 Jose Jimenez .20 .07
❑ 230 James Baldwin .20 .07
❑ 231 C.J. Nitkowski .20 .07
❑ 232 Jeff Zimmerman .20 .07
❑ 233 Mike Lowell .20 .07
❑ 234 Hideki Irabu .20 .07
❑ 235 Greg Vaughn .20 .07
❑ 236 Omar Daal .20 .07
❑ 237 Darren Dreifort .20 .07
❑ 238 Gil Meche .20 .07
❑ 239 Damian Jackson .20 .07
❑ 240 Frank Thomas .50 .20
❑ 241 Travis Miller .20 .07
❑ 242 Jeff Frye .20 .07
❑ 243 Dave Magadan .20 .07
❑ 244 Luis Castillo .20 .07
❑ 245 Bartolo Colon .20 .07
❑ 246 Steve Kline .20 .07
❑ 247 Shawon Dunston .20 .07
❑ 248 Rick Aguilera .20 .07
❑ 249 Omar Olivares .20 .07
❑ 250 Craig Biggio .30 .10
❑ 251 Scott Schoeneweis .20 .07
❑ 252 Dave Veres .20 .07
❑ 253 Ramon Martinez .20 .07
❑ 254 Jose Vidro .20 .07
❑ 255 Todd Helton .30 .10
❑ 256 Greg Norton .20 .07
❑ 257 Jacque Jones .20 .07
❑ 258 Jason Grimsley .20 .07
❑ 259 Dan Reichert .20 .07
❑ 260 Robb Nen .20 .07
❑ 261 Mark Clark .20 .07
❑ 262 Scott Hatteberg .20 .07
❑ 263 Doug Brocail .20 .07
❑ 264 Mark Johnson .20 .07
❑ 265 Eric Davis .20 .07
❑ 266 Terry Shumpert .20 .07
❑ 267 Kevin Millar .20 .07
❑ 268 Ismael Valdes .20 .07
❑ 269 Richard Hidalgo .20 .07
❑ 270 Randy Velarde .20 .07
❑ 271 Bengie Molina .20 .07
❑ 272 Tony Womack .20 .07
❑ 273 Enrique Wilson .20 .07
❑ 274 Jeff Brantley .20 .07
❑ 275 Rick Ankiel .20 .07
❑ 276 Terry Mulholland .20 .07
❑ 277 Ron Belliard .20 .07
❑ 278 Terrence Long .20 .07
❑ 279 Alberto Castillo .20 .07
❑ 280 Royce Clayton .20 .07
❑ 281 Joe McEwing .20 .07
❑ 282 Jason McDonald .20 .07
❑ 283 Ricky Bottalico .20 .07
❑ 284 Keith Foulke .20 .07
❑ 285 Brad Radke .20 .07
❑ 286 Gabe Kapler .20 .07
❑ 287 Pedro Astacio .20 .07
❑ 288 Armando Reynoso .20 .07
❑ 289 Darryl Kile .20 .07
❑ 290 Reggie Sanders .20 .07
❑ 291 Esteban Yan .20 .07
❑ 292 Joe Nathan .20 .07
❑ 293 Jay Payton .20 .07
❑ 294 Francisco Cordero .20 .07

❑ 295	Gregg Jefferies	.20	.07
❑ 296	LaTroy Hawkins	.20	.07
❑ 297	Jeff Tam RC	.40	.15
❑ 298	Jacob Cruz	.20	.07
❑ 299	Chris Holt	.20	.07
❑ 300	Vladimir Guerrero	.50	.20
❑ 301	Marvin Benard	.20	.07
❑ 302	Alex Ramirez	.20	.07
❑ 303	Mike Williams	.20	.07
❑ 304	Sean Bergman	.20	.07
❑ 305	Juan Encarnacion	.20	.07
❑ 306	Russ Davis	.20	.07
❑ 307	Hanley Frias	.20	.07
❑ 308	Ramon Hernandez	.20	.07
❑ 309	Matt Walbeck	.20	.07
❑ 310	Bill Spiers	.20	.07
❑ 311	Bob Wickman	.20	.07
❑ 312	Sandy Alomar Jr.	.20	.07
❑ 313	Eddie Guardado	.20	.07
❑ 314	Shane Halter	.20	.07
❑ 315	Geoff Jenkins	.20	.07
❑ 316	Brian Meadows	.20	.07
❑ 317	Damian Miller	.20	.07
❑ 318	Darrin Fletcher	.20	.07
❑ 319	Rafael Furcal	.20	.07
❑ 320	Mark Grace	.30	.10
❑ 321	Mark Mulder	.20	.07
❑ 322	Joe Torre MG	.30	.10
❑ 323	Bobby Cox MG	.20	.07
❑ 324	Mike Scioscia MG	.20	.07
❑ 325	Mike Hargrove MG	.20	.07
❑ 326	Jimy Williams MG	.20	.07
❑ 327	Jerry Manuel MG	.20	.07
❑ 328	Buck Showalter MG	.20	.07
❑ 329	Charlie Manuel MG	.20	.07
❑ 330	Don Baylor MG	.20	.07
❑ 331	Phil Garner MG	.20	.07
❑ 332	Jack McKeon MG	.20	.07
❑ 333	Tony Muser MG	.20	.07
❑ 334	Buddy Bell MG	.20	.07
❑ 335	Tom Kelly MG	.20	.07
❑ 336	John Boles MG	.20	.07
❑ 337	Art Howe MG	.20	.07
❑ 338	Larry Dierker MG	.20	.07
❑ 339	Lou Piniella MG	.20	.07
❑ 340	Davey Johnson MG	.20	.07
❑ 341	Larry Rothschild MG	.20	.07
❑ 342	Davey Lopes MG	.20	.07
❑ 343	Johnny Oates MG	.20	.07
❑ 344	Felipe Alou MG	.20	.07
❑ 345	Jim Fregosi MG	.20	.07
❑ 346	Bobby Valentine MG	.20	.07
❑ 347	Terry Francona MG	.20	.07
❑ 348	Gene Lamont MG	.20	.07
❑ 349	Tony LaRussa MG	.20	.07
❑ 350	Bruce Bochy MG	.20	.07
❑ 351	Dusty Baker MG	.20	.07
❑ 352	A.Gonzalez/A.Johnson	.25	.08
❑ 353	M.Wheatland/B.Digby	.25	.08
❑ 354	T.Johnson/S.Thorman	.25	.08
❑ 355	P.Dumatrait/A.Wainwright	.25	.08
❑ 356	David Parrish RC	.25	.08
❑ 357	M.Folsom RC/R.Baldelli	.40	.15
❑ 358	Dominic Rich RC	.25	.08
❑ 359	M.Stodolka/S.Burnett	.25	.08
❑ 360	D.Thompson/C.Smith	.25	.08
❑ 361	D.Borrell RC/J.Bourgeois RC	.25	.08
❑ 362	Chen/Patterson/Hamilton	.25	.08
❑ 363	B.Zito/C.Sabathia	.50	.20
❑ 364	Ben Sheets	.50	.20
❑ 365	Howington/Kalinowski/Girdley	.25	.08
❑ 366	Hee Seop Choi RC	.50	.20
❑ 367	Bradley/Ainsworth/Tsao	.40	.15
❑ 368	Glendenning/Kelly/Silvestre	.25	.08
❑ 369	J.R. House	.25	.08
❑ 370	Rafael Soriano RC	.40	.15
❑ 371	T.Hafner RC/B.Jacobsen	4.00	1.50
❑ 372	Conti/Wakeland/Cole	.25	.08
❑ 373	Seabol/Huff/Crede	.75	.30
❑ 374	Everett/Ortiz/Ginter	.25	.08
❑ 375	Hernandez/Guzman/Eaton	.25	.08
❑ 376	Kielty/Bradley/J.Rivera	.40	.15
❑ 377	Mark McGwire GM	.60	.25
❑ 378	Don Larsen GM	.20	.07
❑ 379	Bobby Thomson GM	.20	.07
❑ 380	Bill Mazeroski GM	.20	.07
❑ 381	Reggie Jackson GM	.30	.10
❑ 382	Kirk Gibson GM	.20	.07
❑ 383	Roger Maris GM	.30	.10
❑ 384	Cal Ripken GM	.75	.30
❑ 385	Hank Aaron GM	.50	.20
❑ 386	Joe Carter GM	.20	.07
❑ 387	Cal Ripken SH	1.50	.60
❑ 388	Randy Johnson SH	.30	.10
❑ 389	Ken Griffey Jr. SH	.75	.30
❑ 390	Troy Glaus SH	.20	.07
❑ 391	Kazuhiro Sasaki SH	.20	.07
❑ 392	S.Sosa/T.Glaus LL	.30	.10
❑ 393	T.Helton/E.Martinez LL	.20	.07
❑ 394	T.Helton/N.Garicaparra LL	.50	.20
❑ 395	B.Bonds/J.Giambi LL	.75	.30
❑ 396	T.Helton/M.Ramirez LL	.20	.07
❑ 397	T.Helton/D.Erstad LL	.20	.07
❑ 398	K.Brown/P.Martinez LL	.30	.10
❑ 399	R.Johnson/P.Martinez LL	.30	.10
❑ 400	Will Clark HL	.30	.10
❑ 401	New York Mets HL	.50	.20
❑ 402	New York Yankees HL	.75	.30
❑ 403	Seattle Mariners HL	.20	.07
❑ 404	Mike Hampton HL	.20	.07
❑ 405	New York Yankees HL	1.00	.40
❑ 406	New York Yankees Champs	2.00	.75
❑ 407	Jeff Bagwell	.30	.10
❑ 408	Brant Brown	.20	.07
❑ 409	Brad Fullmer	.20	.07
❑ 410	Dean Palmer	.20	.07
❑ 411	Greg Zaun	.20	.07
❑ 412	Jose Vizcaino	.20	.07
❑ 413	Jeff Abbott	.20	.07
❑ 414	Travis Fryman	.20	.07
❑ 415	Mike Cameron	.20	.07
❑ 416	Matt Mantei	.20	.07
❑ 417	Alan Benes	.20	.07
❑ 418	Mickey Morandini	.20	.07
❑ 419	Troy Percival	.20	.07
❑ 420	Eddie Perez	.20	.07
❑ 421	Vernon Wells	.20	.07
❑ 422	Ricky Gutierrez	.20	.07
❑ 423	Carlos Hernandez	.20	.07
❑ 424	Chan Ho Park	.20	.07
❑ 425	Armando Benitez	.20	.07
❑ 426	Sidney Ponson	.20	.07
❑ 427	Adrian Brown	.20	.07
❑ 428	Ruben Mateo	.20	.07
❑ 429	Alex Ochoa	.20	.07
❑ 430	Jose Rosado	.20	.07
❑ 431	Masato Yoshii	.20	.07
❑ 432	Corey Koskie	.20	.07
❑ 433	Andy Pettitte	.30	.10
❑ 434	Brian Daubach	.20	.07
❑ 435	Sterling Hitchcock	.20	.07
❑ 436	Timo Perez	.20	.07
❑ 437	Shawn Estes	.20	.07
❑ 438	Tony Armas Jr.	.20	.07
❑ 439	Danny Bautista	.20	.07
❑ 440	Randy Winn	.20	.07
❑ 441	Wilson Alvarez	.20	.07
❑ 442	Rondell White	.20	.07
❑ 443	Jeromy Burnitz	.20	.07
❑ 444	Kelvim Escobar	.20	.07
❑ 445	Paul Bako	.20	.07
❑ 446	Javier Vazquez	.20	.07
❑ 447	Eric Gagne	.20	.07
❑ 448	Kenny Lofton	.20	.07
❑ 449	Mark Kotsay	.20	.07
❑ 450	Jamie Moyer	.20	.07
❑ 451	Delino DeShields	.20	.07
❑ 452	Rey Ordonez	.20	.07
❑ 453	Russ Ortiz	.20	.07
❑ 454	Dave Burba	.20	.07
❑ 455	Eric Karros	.20	.07
❑ 456	Felix Martinez	.20	.07
❑ 457	Tony Batista	.20	.07
❑ 458	Bobby Higginson	.20	.07
❑ 459	Jeff D'Amico	.20	.07
❑ 460	Shane Spencer	.20	.07
❑ 461	Brent Mayne	.20	.07
❑ 462	Glendon Rusch	.20	.07
❑ 463	Chris Gomez	.20	.07
❑ 464	Jeff Shaw	.20	.07
❑ 465	Damon Buford	.20	.07
❑ 466	Mike DiFelice	.20	.07
❑ 467	Jimmy Haynes	.20	.07
❑ 468	Billy Wagner	.20	.07
❑ 469	A.J. Hinch	.20	.07
❑ 470	Gary DiSarcina	.20	.07
❑ 471	Tom Lampkin	.20	.07
❑ 472	Adam Eaton	.20	.07
❑ 473	Brian Giles	.20	.07
❑ 474	John Thomson	.20	.07
❑ 475	Cal Eldred	.20	.07
❑ 476	Ramiro Mendoza	.20	.07
❑ 477	Scott Sullivan	.20	.07
❑ 478	Scott Rolen	.30	.10
❑ 479	Todd Ritchie	.20	.07
❑ 480	Pablo Ozuna	.20	.07
❑ 481	Carl Pavano	.20	.07
❑ 482	Matt Morris	.20	.07
❑ 483	Matt Stairs	.20	.07
❑ 484	Tim Belcher	.20	.07
❑ 485	Lance Berkman	.20	.07
❑ 486	Brian Meadows	.20	.07
❑ 487	Bob Abreu	.20	.07
❑ 488	John VanderWal	.20	.07
❑ 489	Donnie Sadler	.20	.07
❑ 490	Damion Easley	.20	.07
❑ 491	David Justice	.20	.07
❑ 492	Ray Durham	.20	.07
❑ 493	Todd Zeile	.20	.07
❑ 494	Desi Relaford	.20	.07
❑ 495	Cliff Floyd	.20	.07
❑ 496	Scott Downs	.20	.07
❑ 497	Barry Bonds	1.25	.50
❑ 498	Jeff D'Amico	.20	.07
❑ 499	Octavio Dotel	.20	.07
❑ 500	Kent Mercker	.20	.07
❑ 501	Craig Grebeck	.20	.07
❑ 502	Roberto Hernandez	.20	.07
❑ 503	Matt Williams	.20	.07
❑ 504	Bruce Aven	.20	.07
❑ 505	Brett Tomko	.20	.07
❑ 506	Kris Benson	.20	.07
❑ 507	Neifi Perez	.20	.07
❑ 508	Alfonso Soriano	.30	.10
❑ 509	Keith Osik	.20	.07
❑ 510	Matt Franco	.20	.07
❑ 511	Steve Finley	.20	.07
❑ 512	Olmedo Saenz	.20	.07
❑ 513	Esteban Loaiza	.20	.07
❑ 514	Adam Kennedy	.20	.07
❑ 515	Scott Elarton	.20	.07
❑ 516	Moises Alou	.20	.07
❑ 517	Bryan Rekar	.20	.07
❑ 518	Darryl Hamilton	.20	.07
❑ 519	Osvaldo Fernandez	.20	.07
❑ 520	Kip Wells	.20	.07
❑ 521	Bernie Williams	.30	.10
❑ 522	Mike Darr	.20	.07
❑ 523	Marlon Anderson	.20	.07
❑ 524	Derrek Lee	.30	.10
❑ 525	Ugueth Urbina	.20	.07
❑ 526	Vinny Castilla	.20	.07
❑ 527	David Wells	.20	.07
❑ 528	Jason Marquis	.20	.07
❑ 529	Orlando Palmeiro	.20	.07
❑ 530	Carlos Perez	.20	.07
❑ 531	J.T. Snow	.20	.07
❑ 532	Al Leiter	.20	.07
❑ 533	Jimmy Anderson	.20	.07
❑ 534	Brett Laxton	.20	.07
❑ 535	Dutch Huskey	.20	.07
❑ 536	Orlando Hernandez	.20	.07
❑ 537	Magglio Ordonez	.20	.07
❑ 538	Willie Blair	.20	.07
❑ 539	Kevin Sefcik	.20	.07
❑ 540	Chad Curtis	.20	.07
❑ 541	John Halama	.20	.07
❑ 542	Andy Fox	.20	.07
❑ 543	Juan Guzman	.20	.07
❑ 544	Frank Menechino RC	.20	.07
❑ 545	Raul Mondesi	.20	.07
❑ 546	Tim Salmon	.30	.10
❑ 547	Ryan Rupe	.20	.07
❑ 548	Jeff Reed	.20	.07
❑ 549	Mike Mordecai	.20	.07
❑ 550	Jeff Kent	.20	.07
❑ 551	Wiki Gonzalez	.20	.07
❑ 552	Kenny Rogers	.20	.07

❑ 553 Kevin Young .20 .07
❑ 554 Brian Johnson .20 .07
❑ 555 Tom Goodwin .20 .07
❑ 556 Tony Clark .20 .07
❑ 557 Mac Suzuki .20 .07
❑ 558 Brian Moehler .20 .07
❑ 559 Jim Parque .20 .07
❑ 560 Mariano Rivera .50 .20
❑ 561 Trot Nixon .20 .07
❑ 562 Mike Mussina .30 .10
❑ 563 Nelson Figueroa .20 .07
❑ 564 Alex Gonzalez .20 .07
❑ 565 Benny Agbayani .20 .07
❑ 566 Ed Sprague .20 .07
❑ 567 Scott Erickson .20 .07
❑ 568 Abraham Nunez .20 .07
❑ 569 Jerry DiPoto .20 .07
❑ 570 Sean Casey .20 .07
❑ 571 Wilton Veras .20 .07
❑ 572 Joe Mays .20 .07
❑ 573 Bill Simas .20 .07
❑ 574 Doug Glanville .20 .07
❑ 575 Scott Sauerbeck .20 .07
❑ 576 Ben Davis .20 .07
❑ 577 Jesus Sanchez .20 .07
❑ 578 Ricardo Rincon .20 .07
❑ 579 John Olerud .20 .07
❑ 580 Curt Schilling .20 .07
❑ 581 Alex Cora .20 .07
❑ 582 Pat Hentgen .20 .07
❑ 583 Javy Lopez .20 .07
❑ 584 Ben Grieve .20 .07
❑ 585 Frank Castillo .20 .07
❑ 586 Kevin Stocker .20 .07
❑ 587 Mark Sweeney .20 .07
❑ 588 Ray Lankford .20 .07
❑ 589 Turner Ward .20 .07
❑ 590 Felipe Crespo .20 .07
❑ 591 Omar Vizquel .30 .10
❑ 592 Mike Lieberthal .20 .07
❑ 593 Ken Griffey Jr. .75 .30
❑ 594 Troy O'Leary .20 .07
❑ 595 Dave Mlicki .20 .07
❑ 596 Manny Ramirez Sox .30 .10
❑ 597 Mike Lansing .20 .07
❑ 598 Rich Aurilia .20 .07
❑ 599 Russell Branyan .20 .07
❑ 600 Russ Johnson .20 .07
❑ 601 Greg Colbrunn .20 .07
❑ 602 Andruw Jones .30 .10
❑ 603 Henry Blanco .20 .07
❑ 604 Jarrod Washburn .20 .07
❑ 605 Tony Eusebio .20 .07
❑ 606 Aaron Sele .20 .07
❑ 607 Charles Nagy .20 .07
❑ 608 Ryan Klesko .20 .07
❑ 609 Dante Bichette .20 .07
❑ 610 Bill Haselman .20 .07
❑ 611 Jerry Spradlin .20 .07
❑ 612 Alex Rodriguez Rangers .75 .30
❑ 613 Jose Silva .20 .07
❑ 614 Darren Oliver .20 .07
❑ 615 Pat Mahomes .20 .07
❑ 616 Roberto Alomar .30 .10
❑ 617 Edgar Renteria .20 .07
❑ 618 Jon Lieber .20 .07
❑ 619 John Rocker .20 .07
❑ 620 Miguel Tejada .20 .07
❑ 621 Mo Vaughn .20 .07
❑ 622 Jose Lima .20 .07
❑ 623 Kerry Wood .20 .07
❑ 624 Mike Timlin .20 .07
❑ 625 Wil Cordero .20 .07
❑ 626 Albert Belle .20 .07
❑ 627 Bobby Jones .20 .07
❑ 628 Doug Mirabelli .20 .07
❑ 629 Jason Tyner .20 .07
❑ 630 Andy Ashby .20 .07
❑ 631 Jose Hernandez .20 .07
❑ 632 Devon White .20 .07
❑ 633 Ruben Rivera .20 .07
❑ 634 Steve Parris .20 .07
❑ 635 David McCarty .20 .07
❑ 636 Jose Canseco .30 .10
❑ 637 Todd Walker .20 .07
❑ 638 Stan Spencer .20 .07
❑ 639 Wayne Gomes .20 .07
❑ 640 Freddy Garcia .20 .07
❑ 641 Jeremy Giambi .20 .07
❑ 642 Luis Lopez .20 .07
❑ 643 John Smoltz .30 .10
❑ 644 Kelly Stinnett .20 .07
❑ 645 Kevin Brown .20 .07
❑ 646 Wilton Guerrero .20 .07
❑ 647 Al Martin .20 .07
❑ 648 Woody Williams .20 .07
❑ 649 Brian Rose .20 .07
❑ 650 Rafael Palmeiro .30 .10
❑ 651 Pete Schourek .20 .07
❑ 652 Kevin Jarvis .20 .07
❑ 653 Mark Redman .20 .07
❑ 654 Ricky Ledee .20 .07
❑ 655 Larry Walker .20 .07
❑ 656 Paul Byrd .20 .07
❑ 657 Jason Bere .20 .07
❑ 658 Rick White .20 .07
❑ 659 Calvin Murray .20 .07
❑ 660 Greg Maddux .75 .30
❑ 661 Ron Gant .20 .07
❑ 662 Eli Marrero .20 .07
❑ 663 Graeme Lloyd .20 .07
❑ 664 Trevor Hoffman .20 .07
❑ 665 Nomar Garciaparra .75 .30
❑ 666 Glenallen Hill .20 .07
❑ 667 Matt LeCroy .20 .07
❑ 668 Justin Thompson .20 .07
❑ 669 Brady Anderson .20 .07
❑ 670 Miguel Batista .20 .07
❑ 671 Erubiel Durazo .20 .07
❑ 672 Kevin Millwood .20 .07
❑ 673 Mitch Meluskey .20 .07
❑ 674 Luis Gonzalez .20 .07
❑ 675 Edgar Martinez .30 .10
❑ 676 Robert Person .20 .07
❑ 677 Benito Santiago .20 .07
❑ 678 Todd Jones .20 .07
❑ 679 Tino Martinez .30 .10
❑ 680 Carlos Beltran .20 .07
❑ 681 Gabe White .20 .07
❑ 682 Bret Saberhagen .20 .07
❑ 683 Jeff Conine .20 .07
❑ 684 Jaret Wright .20 .07
❑ 685 Bernard Gilkey .20 .07
❑ 686 Garrett Stephenson .20 .07
❑ 687 Jamey Wright .20 .07
❑ 688 Sammy Sosa .50 .20
❑ 689 John Jaha .20 .07
❑ 690 Ramon Martinez .20 .07
❑ 691 Robert Fick .20 .07
❑ 692 Eric Milton .20 .07
❑ 693 Denny Neagle .20 .07
❑ 694 Ron Coomer .20 .07
❑ 695 John Valentin .20 .07
❑ 696 Placido Polanco .20 .07
❑ 697 Tim Hudson .20 .07
❑ 698 Marty Cordova .20 .07
❑ 699 Chad Kreuter .20 .07
❑ 700 Frank Catalanotto .20 .07
❑ 701 Tim Wakefield .20 .07
❑ 702 Jim Edmonds .20 .07
❑ 703 Michael Tucker .20 .07
❑ 704 Cristian Guzman .20 .07
❑ 705 Joey Hamilton .20 .07
❑ 706 Mike Piazza .75 .30
❑ 707 Dave Martinez .20 .07
❑ 708 Mike Hampton .20 .07
❑ 709 Bobby Bonilla .20 .07
❑ 710 Juan Pierre .20 .07
❑ 711 John Parrish .20 .07
❑ 712 Kory DeHaan .20 .07
❑ 713 Brian Tollberg .20 .07
❑ 714 Chris Truby .20 .07
❑ 715 Emil Brown .20 .07
❑ 716 Ryan Dempster .20 .07
❑ 717 Rich Garces .20 .07
❑ 718 Mike Myers .20 .07
❑ 719 Luis Ordaz .20 .07
❑ 720 Kazuhiro Sasaki .20 .07
❑ 721 Mark Quinn .20 .07
❑ 722 Ramon Ortiz .20 .07
❑ 723 Kerry Ligtenberg .20 .07
❑ 724 Rolando Arrojo .20 .07
❑ 725 Tsuyoshi Shinjo RC .50 .20
❑ 726 Ichiro Suzuki RC 15.00 6.00
❑ 727 Oswalt/Strange/Rauch .75 .30
❑ 728 Jake Peavy RC 2.50 1.00
❑ 729 S.Smyth RC/Bynum/Haynes .25 .08
❑ 730 Cuddyer/Lawrence/Freeman .25 .08
❑ 731 C.Pena/Barnes/Wise .25 .08
❑ 732 E.Almonte RC/F.Lopez .25 .08
❑ 733 Escobar/Valent/Wilkerson .25 .08
❑ 734 Hall/Barajas/Goldbach .25 .08
❑ 735 Romano/Giles/Ozuna .40 .15
❑ 736 D.Brown/Cust/V.Wells .25 .08
❑ 737 L.Montanez RC/D.Espinosa .25 .08
❑ 738 J.Wayne RC/A.Pluta RC .25 .08
❑ 739 J.Axelson RC/C.Cali RC .25 .08
❑ 740 S.Boyd RC/C.Morris RC .25 .08
❑ 741 T.Arko RC/D.Moylan RC .25 .08
❑ 742 L.Cotto RC/L.Escobar .25 .08
❑ 743 B.Mims RC/B.Williams RC .25 .08
❑ 744 C.Russ RC/B.Edwards .25 .08
❑ 745 J.Torres/B.Diggins .25 .08
❑ 746 Edwin Encarnacion RC 3.00 1.25
❑ 747 B.Bass RC/O.Ayala RC .25 .08
❑ 748 M.Matthews RC/J.Kaanoi .25 .08
❑ 749 S.McFarland RC/A.Sterrett RC .25 .08
❑ 750 D.Krynzel/G.Sizemore 1.00 .40
❑ 751 K.Bucktrot/D.Sardinha .25 .08
❑ 752 Anaheim Angels TC .20 .07
❑ 753 Arizona Diamondbacks TC .20 .07
❑ 754 Atlanta Braves TC .20 .07
❑ 755 Baltimore Orioles TC .20 .07
❑ 756 Boston Red Sox TC .20 .07
❑ 757 Chicago Cubs TC .20 .07
❑ 758 Chicago White Sox TC .20 .07
❑ 759 Cincinnati Reds TC .20 .07
❑ 760 Cleveland Indians TC .20 .07
❑ 761 Colorado Rockies TC .20 .07
❑ 762 Detroit Tigers TC .20 .07
❑ 763 Florida Marlins TC .20 .07
❑ 764 Houston Astros TC .20 .07
❑ 765 Kansas City Royals TC .20 .07
❑ 766 Los Angeles Dodgers TC .20 .07
❑ 767 Milwaukee Brewers TC .20 .07
❑ 768 Minnesota Twins TC .20 .07
❑ 769 Montreal Expos TC .20 .07
❑ 770 New York Mets TC .20 .07
❑ 771 New York Yankees TC 1.00 .40
❑ 772 Oakland Athletics TC .20 .07
❑ 773 Philadelphia Phillies TC .20 .07
❑ 774 Pittsburgh Pirates TC .20 .07
❑ 775 San Diego Padres TC .20 .07
❑ 776 San Francisco Giants TC .20 .07
❑ 777 Seattle Mariners TC .20 .07
❑ 778 St. Louis Cardinals TC .20 .07
❑ 779 Tampa Bay Devil Rays TC .20 .07
❑ 780 Texas Rangers TC .20 .07
❑ 781 Toronto Blue Jays TC .20 .07
❑ 782 Bucky Dent GM .20 .07
❑ 783 Jackie Robinson GM .50 .20
❑ 784 Roberto Clemente GM .60 .25
❑ 785 Nolan Ryan GM .75 .30
❑ 786 Kerry Wood GM .20 .07
❑ 787 Rickey Henderson GM .20 .07
❑ 788 Lou Brock GM .30 .10
❑ 789 David Wells GM .20 .07
❑ 790 Andruw Jones GM .20 .07
❑ 791 Carlton Fisk GM .20 .07
❑ TK B.Jackson/D.Sanders Bat 120.00 60.00
❑ NNO B.Thomson/R.Branca AU 60.00 30.00

2001 Topps Traded

❑ COMPLETE SET (265) 175.00 100.00
❑ COMMON CARD (1-99/145-265) .40 .15
❑ COMMON REPRINT (100-144) 1.00 .40
❑ T1 Sandy Alomar Jr. .40 .15
❑ T2 Kevin Appier .50 .20
❑ T3 Brad Ausmus .50 .20
❑ T4 Derek Bell .40 .15
❑ T5 Bret Boone .50 .20
❑ T6 Rico Brogna .40 .15
❑ T7 Ellis Burks .50 .20
❑ T8 Ken Caminiti .50 .20
❑ T9 Roger Cedeno .40 .15
❑ T10 Royce Clayton .40 .15
❑ T11 Enrique Wilson .40 .15
❑ T12 Rheal Cormier .40 .15

	Card	Player	Hi	Lo
❑	T13	Eric Davis	.50	.20
❑	T14	Shawon Dunston	.40	.15
❑	T15	Andres Galarraga	.50	.20
❑	T16	Tom Gordon	.40	.15
❑	T17	Mark Grace	.75	.30
❑	T18	Jeffrey Hammonds	.40	.15
❑	T19	Dustin Hermanson	.40	.15
❑	T20	Quinton McCracken	.40	.15
❑	T21	Todd Hundley	.40	.15
❑	T22	Charles Johnson	.50	.20
❑	T23	Marquis Grissom	.50	.20
❑	T24	Jose Mesa	.40	.15
❑	T25	Brian Boehringer	.40	.15
❑	T26	John Rocker	.50	.20
❑	T27	Jeff Frye	.40	.15
❑	T28	Reggie Sanders	.50	.20
❑	T29	David Segui	.40	.15
❑	T30	Mike Sirotka	.40	.15
❑	T31	Fernando Tatis	.40	.15
❑	T32	Steve Trachsel	.40	.15
❑	T33	Ismael Valdes	.40	.15
❑	T34	Randy Velarde	.40	.15
❑	T35	Ryan Kohlmeier	.40	.15
❑	T36	Mike Bordick	.50	.20
❑	T37	Kent Bottenfield	.40	.15
❑	T38	Pat Rapp	.40	.15
❑	T39	Jeff Nelson	.40	.15
❑	T40	Ricky Bottalico	.40	.15
❑	T41	Luke Prokopec	.40	.15
❑	T42	Hideo Nomo	1.25	.50
❑	T43	Bill Mueller	.50	.20
❑	T44	Roberto Kelly	.40	.15
❑	T45	Chris Holt	.40	.15
❑	T46	Mike Jackson	.40	.15
❑	T47	Devon White	.50	.20
❑	T48	Gerald Williams	.40	.15
❑	T49	Eddie Taubensee	.40	.15
❑	T50	Brian Hunter	.40	.15
❑	T51	Nelson Cruz	.40	.15
❑	T52	Jeff Fassero	.40	.15
❑	T53	Bubba Trammell	.40	.15
❑	T54	Bo Porter	.40	.15
❑	T55	Greg Norton	.40	.15
❑	T56	Benito Santiago	.50	.20
❑	T57	Ruben Rivera	.40	.15
❑	T58	Dee Brown	.40	.15
❑	T59	Jose Canseco	.75	.30
❑	T60	Chris Michalak	.40	.15
❑	T61	Tim Worrell	.40	.15
❑	T62	Matt Clement	.50	.20
❑	T63	Bill Pulsipher	.40	.15
❑	T64	Troy Brohawn RC	.40	.15
❑	T65	Mark Kotsay	.50	.20
❑	T66	Jimmy Rollins	.50	.20
❑	T67	Shea Hillenbrand	.50	.20
❑	T68	Ted Lilly	.40	.15
❑	T69	Jermaine Dye	.50	.20
❑	T70	Jerry Hairston Jr.	.40	.15
❑	T71	John Mabry	.40	.15
❑	T72	Kurt Abbott	.40	.15
❑	T73	Eric Owens	.40	.15
❑	T74	Jeff Brantley	.40	.15
❑	T75	Roy Oswalt	1.25	.50
❑	T76	Doug Mientkiewicz	.50	.20
❑	T77	Rickey Henderson	1.25	.50
❑	T78	Jason Grimsley	.40	.15
❑	T79	Christian Parker RC	.40	.15
❑	T80	Donne Wall	.40	.15
❑	T81	Alex Arias	.40	.15
❑	T82	Willis Roberts	.40	.15
❑	T83	Ryan Minor	.40	.15
❑	T84	Jason LaRue	.40	.15
❑	T85	Ruben Sierra	.50	.20
❑	T86	Johnny Damon	.75	.30
❑	T87	Juan Gonzalez	.50	.20
❑	T88	C.C. Sabathia	.50	.20
❑	T89	Tony Batista	.40	.15
❑	T90	Jay Witasick	.40	.15
❑	T91	Brent Abernathy	.40	.15
❑	T92	Paul LoDuca	.50	.20
❑	T93	Wes Helms	.40	.15
❑	T94	Mark Wohlers	.40	.15
❑	T95	Rob Bell	.40	.15
❑	T96	Tim Redding	.40	.15
❑	T97	Bud Smith RC	.40	.15
❑	T98	Adam Dunn	.75	.30
❑	T99	I.Suzuki/A.Pujols ROY	15.00	6.00
❑	T100	Carlton Fisk 81	1.25	.50
❑	T101	Tim Raines 81	1.00	.40
❑	T102	Juan Marichal 74	1.00	.40
❑	T103	Dave Winfield 81	1.00	.40
❑	T104	Reggie Jackson 82	1.25	.50
❑	T105	Cal Ripken 82	6.00	2.50
❑	T106	Ozzie Smith 82	3.00	1.25
❑	T107	Tom Seaver 83	1.25	.50
❑	T108	Lou Piniella 74	1.00	.40
❑	T109	Dwight Gooden 84	1.00	.40
❑	T110	Bret Saberhagen 84	1.00	.40
❑	T111	Gary Carter 85	1.00	.40
❑	T112	Jack Clark 85	1.00	.40
❑	T113	Rickey Henderson 85	2.00	.75
❑	T114	Barry Bonds 86	5.00	2.00
❑	T115	Bobby Bonilla 86	1.00	.40
❑	T116	Jose Canseco 86	1.25	.50
❑	T117	Will Clark 86	1.25	.50
❑	T118	Andres Galarraga 86	1.00	.40
❑	T119	Bo Jackson 86	2.00	.75
❑	T120	Wally Joyner 86	1.00	.40
❑	T121	Ellis Burks 87	1.00	.40
❑	T122	David Cone 87	1.00	.40
❑	T123	Greg Maddux 87	3.00	1.25
❑	T124	Willie Randolph 76	1.00	.40
❑	T125	Dennis Eckersley 87	1.00	.40
❑	T126	Matt Williams 87	1.00	.40
❑	T127	Joe Morgan 81	1.00	.40
❑	T128	Fred McGriff 87	1.25	.50
❑	T129	Roberto Alomar 88	1.25	.50
❑	T130	Lee Smith 88	1.00	.40
❑	T131	David Wells 88	1.00	.40
❑	T132	Ken Griffey Jr. 89	3.00	1.25
❑	T133	Deion Sanders 89	1.25	.50
❑	T134	Nolan Ryan 89	4.00	1.50
❑	T135	David Justice 90	1.00	.40
❑	T136	Joe Carter 91	1.00	.40
❑	T137	Jack Morris 92	1.00	.40
❑	T138	Mike Piazza 93	3.00	1.25
❑	T139	Barry Bonds 93	5.00	2.00
❑	T140	Terrence Long 94	1.00	.40
❑	T141	Ben Grieve 94	1.00	.40
❑	T142	Richie Sexson 95	1.00	.40
❑	T143	Sean Burroughs 99	1.00	.40
❑	T144	Alfonso Soriano 99	1.25	.50
❑	T145	Bob Boone MG	.50	.20
❑	T146	Larry Bowa MG	.50	.20
❑	T147	Bob Brenly MG	.40	.15
❑	T148	Buck Martinez MG	.40	.15
❑	T149	Lloyd McClendon MG	.40	.15
❑	T150	Jim Tracy MG	.40	.15
❑	T151	Jared Abruzzo RC	.40	.15
❑	T152	Kurt Ainsworth	.40	.15
❑	T153	Willie Bloomquist	.50	.20
❑	T154	Ben Broussard	.40	.15
❑	T155	Bobby Bradley	.40	.15
❑	T156	Mike Bynum	.40	.15
❑	T157	A.J. Hinch	.40	.15
❑	T158	Ryan Christianson	.40	.15
❑	T159	Carlos Silva	.40	.15
❑	T160	Joe Crede	1.25	.50
❑	T161	Jack Cust	.40	.15
❑	T162	Ben Diggins	.40	.15
❑	T163	Phil Dumatrait	.40	.15
❑	T164	Alex Escobar	.40	.15
❑	T165	Miguel Olivo	.40	.15
❑	T166	Chris George	.40	.15
❑	T167	Marcus Giles	.50	.20
❑	T168	Keith Ginter	.40	.15
❑	T169	Josh Girdley	.40	.15
❑	T170	Tony Alvarez	.40	.15
❑	T171	Scott Seabol	.40	.15
❑	T172	Josh Hamilton	.40	.15
❑	T173	Jason Hart	.40	.15
❑	T174	Israel Alcantara	.40	.15
❑	T175	Jake Peavy	1.50	.60
❑	T176	Stubby Clapp RC	.40	.15
❑	T177	D'Angelo Jimenez	.40	.15
❑	T178	Nick Johnson	.50	.20
❑	T179	Ben Johnson	.50	.20
❑	T180	Larry Bigbie	.40	.15
❑	T181	Allen Levrault	.40	.15
❑	T182	Felipe Lopez	.50	.20
❑	T183	Sean Burnett	.40	.15
❑	T184	Nick Neugebauer	.40	.15
❑	T185	Austin Kearns	.50	.20
❑	T186	Corey Patterson	.40	.15
❑	T187	Carlos Pena	.40	.15
❑	T188	Ricardo Rodriguez RC	.40	.15
❑	T189	Juan Rivera	.40	.15
❑	T190	Grant Roberts	.40	.15
❑	T191	Adam Pettyjohn RC	.40	.15
❑	T192	Jared Sandberg	.40	.15
❑	T193	Xavier Nady	.40	.15
❑	T194	Dane Sardinha	.40	.15
❑	T195	Shawn Sonnier	.40	.15
❑	T196	Rafael Soriano	.40	.15
❑	T197	Brian Specht RC	.40	.15
❑	T198	Aaron Myette	.40	.15
❑	T199	Juan Uribe RC	.50	.20
❑	T200	Jayson Werth	.40	.15
❑	T201	Brad Wilkerson	.40	.15
❑	T202	Horacio Estrada	.40	.15
❑	T203	Joel Pineiro	.50	.20
❑	T204	Matt LeCroy	.40	.15
❑	T205	Michael Coleman	.40	.15
❑	T206	Ben Sheets	.75	.30
❑	T207	Eric Byrnes	.40	.15
❑	T208	Sean Burroughs	.40	.15
❑	T209	Ken Harvey	.40	.15
❑	T210	Travis Hafner	4.00	1.50
❑	T211	Erick Almonte	.40	.15
❑	T212	Jason Belcher RC	.40	.15
❑	T213	Wilson Betemit RC	1.50	.60
❑	T214	Hank Blalock RC	2.50	1.00
❑	T215	Danny Borrell	.40	.15
❑	T216	John Buck RC	.50	.20
❑	T217	Freddie Bynum RC	.40	.15
❑	T218	Noel Devarez RC	.40	.15
❑	T219	Juan Diaz RC	.40	.15
❑	T220	Felix Diaz RC	.40	.15
❑	T221	Josh Fogg RC	.40	.15
❑	T222	Matt Ford RC	.40	.15
❑	T223	Scott Heard	.40	.15
❑	T224	Ben Hendrickson RC	.40	.15
❑	T225	Cody Ross RC	.40	.15
❑	T226	Adrian Hernandez RC	.40	.15
❑	T227	Alfredo Amezaga RC	.40	.15
❑	T228	Bob Keppel RC	.40	.15
❑	T229	Ryan Madson RC	.75	.30
❑	T230	Octavio Martinez RC	.40	.15
❑	T231	Hee Seop Choi	.50	.20
❑	T232	Thomas Mitchell	.40	.15
❑	T233	Luis Montanez	.40	.15
❑	T234	Andy Morales RC	.40	.15
❑	T235	Justin Morneau RC	6.00	2.50
❑	T236	Toe Nash RC	.40	.15
❑	T237	Valentino Pascucci RC	.40	.15
❑	T238	Roy Smith RC	.40	.15
❑	T239	Antonio Perez RC	.50	.20
❑	T240	Chad Petty RC	.40	.15
❑	T241	Steve Smyth	.40	.15
❑	T242	Jose Reyes RC	10.00	4.00
❑	T243	Eric Reynolds RC	.40	.15
❑	T244	Dominic Rich	.40	.15
❑	T245	Jason Richardson RC	.40	.15
❑	T246	Ed Rogers RC	.40	.15
❑	T247	Albert Pujols RC	60.00	35.00
❑	T248	Esix Snead RC	.40	.15
❑	T249	Luis Torres RC	.40	.15
❑	T250	Matt White RC	.40	.15
❑	T251	Blake Williams	.40	.15
❑	T252	Chris Russ	.40	.15

❑ T253	Joe Kennedy RC	.50	.20
❑ T254	Jeff Randazzo RC	.40	.15
❑ T255	Beau Hale RC	.40	.15
❑ T256	Brad Hennessey RC	1.25	.50
❑ T257	Jake Gautreau RC	.40	.15
❑ T258	Jeff Mathis RC	.50	.20
❑ T259	Aaron Heilman RC	.50	.20
❑ T260	Bronson Sardinha RC	.40	.15
❑ T261	Irvin Guzman RC	4.00	1.50
❑ T262	Gabe Gross RC	.50	.20
❑ T263	J.D. Martin RC	.40	.15
❑ T264	Chris Smith RC	.40	.15
❑ T265	Kenny Baugh RC	.40	.15

2002 Topps

❑	COMPLETE SET (718)	80.00	30.00
❑	COMP.FACT.BROWN SET (723)	80.00	40.00
❑	COMP.FACT.GREEN SET (723)	80.00	40.00
❑	COMPLETE SERIES 1 (364)	40.00	15.00
❑	COMPLETE SERIES 2 (354)	40.00	15.00
❑	COMMON CARD (1-6/8-719)	.20	.07
❑	COMMON (307-331/671-695)	.50	.20
❑	COMMON CARD (332-364)	.50	.20
❑ 1	Pedro Martinez	.30	.10
❑ 2	Mike Stanton	.20	.07
❑ 3	Brad Penny	.20	.07
❑ 4	Mike Matheny	.20	.07
❑ 5	Johnny Damon	.30	.10
❑ 6	Bret Boone	.20	.07
❑ 7	Does Not Exist		
❑ 8	Chris Truby	.20	.07
❑ 9	B.J. Surhoff	.20	.07
❑ 10	Mike Hampton	.20	.07
❑ 11	Juan Pierre	.20	.07
❑ 12	Mark Buehrle	.20	.07
❑ 13	Bob Abreu	.20	.07
❑ 14	David Cone	.20	.07
❑ 15	Aaron Sele	.20	.07
❑ 16	Fernando Tatis	.20	.07
❑ 17	Bobby Jones	.20	.07
❑ 18	Rick Helling	.20	.07
❑ 19	Dmitri Young	.20	.07
❑ 20	Mike Mussina	.30	.10
❑ 21	Mike Sweeney	.20	.07
❑ 22	Cristian Guzman	.20	.07
❑ 23	Ryan Kohlmeier	.20	.07
❑ 24	Adam Kennedy	.20	.07
❑ 25	Larry Walker	.20	.07
❑ 26	Eric Davis	.20	.07
❑ 27	Jason Tyner	.20	.07
❑ 28	Eric Young	.20	.07
❑ 29	Jason Marquis	.20	.07
❑ 30	Luis Gonzalez	.20	.07
❑ 31	Kevin Tapani	.20	.07
❑ 32	Orlando Cabrera	.20	.07
❑ 33	Marty Cordova	.20	.07
❑ 34	Brad Ausmus	.20	.07
❑ 35	Livan Hernandez	.20	.07
❑ 36	Alex Gonzalez	.20	.07
❑ 37	Edgar Renteria	.20	.07
❑ 38	Bengie Molina	.20	.07
❑ 39	Frank Menechino	.20	.07
❑ 40	Rafael Palmeiro	.30	.10
❑ 41	Brad Fullmer	.20	.07
❑ 42	Julio Zuleta	.20	.07
❑ 43	Darren Dreifort	.20	.07
❑ 44	Trot Nixon	.20	.07
❑ 45	Trevor Hoffman	.20	.07
❑ 46	Vladimir Nunez	.20	.07
❑ 47	Mark Kotsay	.20	.07
❑ 48	Kenny Rogers	.20	.07
❑ 49	Ben Petrick	.20	.07
❑ 50	Jeff Bagwell	.30	.10
❑ 51	Juan Encarnacion	.20	.07
❑ 52	Ramiro Mendoza	.20	.07
❑ 53	Brian Meadows	.20	.07
❑ 54	Chad Curtis	.20	.07
❑ 55	Aramis Ramirez	.20	.07
❑ 56	Mark McLemore	.20	.07
❑ 57	Dante Bichette	.20	.07
❑ 58	Scott Schoeneweis	.20	.07
❑ 59	Jose Cruz Jr.	.20	.07
❑ 60	Roger Clemens	1.00	.40
❑ 61	Jose Guillen	.20	.07
❑ 62	Darren Oliver	.20	.07
❑ 63	Chris Reitsma	.20	.07
❑ 64	Jeff Abbott	.20	.07
❑ 65	Robin Ventura	.20	.07
❑ 66	Denny Neagle	.20	.07
❑ 67	Al Martin	.20	.07
❑ 68	Benito Santiago	.20	.07
❑ 69	Roy Oswalt	.20	.07
❑ 70	Juan Gonzalez	.20	.07
❑ 71	Garret Anderson	.20	.07
❑ 72	Bobby Bonilla	.20	.07
❑ 73	Danny Bautista	.20	.07
❑ 74	J.T. Snow	.20	.07
❑ 75	Derek Jeter	1.25	.50
❑ 76	John Olerud	.20	.07
❑ 77	Kevin Appier	.20	.07
❑ 78	Phil Nevin	.20	.07
❑ 79	Sean Casey	.20	.07
❑ 80	Troy Glaus	.20	.07
❑ 81	Joe Randa	.20	.07
❑ 82	Jose Valentin	.20	.07
❑ 83	Ricky Bottalico	.20	.07
❑ 84	Todd Zeile	.20	.07
❑ 85	Barry Larkin	.30	.10
❑ 86	Bob Wickman	.20	.07
❑ 87	Jeff Shaw	.20	.07
❑ 88	Greg Vaughn	.20	.07
❑ 89	Fernando Vina	.20	.07
❑ 90	Mark Mulder	.20	.07
❑ 91	Paul Bako	.20	.07
❑ 92	Aaron Boone	.20	.07
❑ 93	Esteban Loaiza	.20	.07
❑ 94	Richie Sexson	.20	.07
❑ 95	Alfonso Soriano	.20	.07
❑ 96	Tony Womack	.20	.07
❑ 97	Paul Shuey	.20	.07
❑ 98	Melvin Mora	.20	.07
❑ 99	Tony Gwynn	.60	.25
❑ 100	Vladimir Guerrero	.50	.20
❑ 101	Keith Osik	.20	.07
❑ 102	Bud Smith	.20	.07
❑ 103	Scott Williamson	.20	.07
❑ 104	Daryle Ward	.20	.07
❑ 105	Doug Mientkiewicz	.20	.07
❑ 106	Stan Javier	.20	.07
❑ 107	Russ Ortiz	.20	.07
❑ 108	Wade Miller	.20	.07
❑ 109	Luke Prokopec	.20	.07
❑ 110	Andruw Jones	.30	.10
❑ 111	Ron Coomer	.20	.07
❑ 112	Dan Wilson	.20	.07
❑ 113	Luis Castillo	.20	.07
❑ 114	Derek Bell	.20	.07
❑ 115	Gary Sheffield	.20	.07
❑ 116	Ruben Rivera	.20	.07
❑ 117	Paul O'Neill	.30	.10
❑ 118	Craig Paquette	.20	.07
❑ 119	Kelvin Escobar	.20	.07
❑ 120	Brad Radke	.20	.07
❑ 121	Jorge Fabregas	.20	.07
❑ 122	Randy Winn	.20	.07
❑ 123	Tom Goodwin	.20	.07
❑ 124	Jaret Wright	.20	.07
❑ 125	Manny Ramirez	.30	.10
❑ 126	Al Leiter	.20	.07
❑ 127	Ben Davis	.20	.07
❑ 128	Frank Catalanotto	.20	.07
❑ 129	Jose Cabrera	.20	.07
❑ 130	Magglio Ordonez	.20	.07
❑ 131	Jose Macias	.20	.07
❑ 132	Ted Lilly	.20	.07
❑ 133	Chris Holt	.20	.07
❑ 134	Eric Milton	.20	.07
❑ 135	Shannon Stewart	.20	.07
❑ 136	Omar Olivares	.20	.07
❑ 137	David Segui	.20	.07
❑ 138	Jeff Nelson	.20	.07
❑ 139	Matt Williams	.20	.07
❑ 140	Ellis Burks	.20	.07
❑ 141	Jason Bere	.20	.07
❑ 142	Jimmy Haynes	.20	.07
❑ 143	Ramon Hernandez	.20	.07
❑ 144	Craig Counsell	.20	.07
❑ 145	John Smoltz	.30	.10
❑ 146	Homer Bush	.20	.07
❑ 147	Quilvio Veras	.20	.07
❑ 148	Esteban Yan	.20	.07
❑ 149	Ramon Ortiz	.20	.07
❑ 150	Carlos Delgado	.20	.07
❑ 151	Lee Stevens	.20	.07
❑ 152	Wil Cordero	.20	.07
❑ 153	Mike Bordick	.20	.07
❑ 154	John Flaherty	.20	.07
❑ 155	Omar Daal	.20	.07
❑ 156	Todd Ritchie	.20	.07
❑ 157	Carl Everett	.20	.07
❑ 158	Scott Sullivan	.20	.07
❑ 159	Deivi Cruz	.20	.07
❑ 160	Albert Pujols	1.00	.40
❑ 160A	Albert Pujols COR		
❑ 161	Royce Clayton	.20	.07
❑ 162	Jeff Suppan	.20	.07
❑ 163	C.C. Sabathia	.20	.07
❑ 164	Jimmy Rollins	.20	.07
❑ 165	Rickey Henderson	.50	.20
❑ 166	Rey Ordonez	.20	.07
❑ 167	Shawn Estes	.20	.07
❑ 168	Reggie Sanders	.20	.07
❑ 169	Jon Lieber	.20	.07
❑ 170	Armando Benitez	.20	.07
❑ 171	Mike Remlinger	.20	.07
❑ 172	Billy Wagner	.20	.07
❑ 173	Troy Percival	.20	.07
❑ 174	Devon White	.20	.07
❑ 175	Ivan Rodriguez	.30	.10
❑ 176	Dustin Hermanson	.20	.07
❑ 177	Brian Anderson	.20	.07
❑ 178	Graeme Lloyd	.20	.07
❑ 179	Russell Branyan	.20	.07
❑ 180	Bobby Higginson	.20	.07
❑ 181	Alex Gonzalez	.20	.07
❑ 182	John Franco	.20	.07
❑ 183	Sidney Ponson	.20	.07
❑ 184	Jose Mesa	.20	.07
❑ 185	Todd Hollandsworth	.20	.07
❑ 186	Kevin Young	.20	.07
❑ 187	Tim Wakefield	.20	.07
❑ 188	Craig Biggio	.30	.10
❑ 189	Jason Isringhausen	.20	.07
❑ 190	Mark Quinn	.20	.07
❑ 191	Glendon Rusch	.20	.07
❑ 192	Damian Miller	.20	.07
❑ 193	Sandy Alomar Jr.	.20	.07
❑ 194	Scott Brosius	.20	.07
❑ 195	Dave Martinez	.20	.07
❑ 196	Danny Graves	.20	.07
❑ 197	Shea Hillenbrand	.20	.07
❑ 198	Jimmy Anderson	.20	.07
❑ 199	Travis Lee	.20	.07
❑ 200	Randy Johnson	.50	.20
❑ 201	Carlos Beltran	.20	.07
❑ 202	Jerry Hairston	.20	.07
❑ 203	Jesus Sanchez	.20	.07
❑ 204	Eddie Taubensee	.20	.07
❑ 205	David Wells	.20	.07
❑ 206	Russ Davis	.20	.07
❑ 207	Michael Barrett	.20	.07
❑ 208	Marquis Grissom	.20	.07
❑ 209	Byung-Hyun Kim	.20	.07
❑ 210	Hideo Nomo	.50	.20
❑ 211	Ryan Rupe	.20	.07
❑ 212	Ricky Gutierrez	.20	.07
❑ 213	Darryl Kile	.20	.07
❑ 214	Rico Brogna	.20	.07
❑ 215	Terrence Long	.20	.07
❑ 216	Mike Jackson	.20	.07

❑ 217 Jamey Wright .20 .07
❑ 218 Adrian Beltre .20 .07
❑ 219 Benny Agbayani .20 .07
❑ 220 Chuck Knoblauch .20 .07
❑ 221 Randy Wolf .20 .07
❑ 222 Andy Ashby .20 .07
❑ 223 Corey Koskie .20 .07
❑ 224 Roger Cedeno .20 .07
❑ 225 Ichiro Suzuki 1.00 .40
❑ 226 Keith Foulke .20 .07
❑ 227 Ryan Minor .20 .07
❑ 228 Shawon Dunston .20 .07
❑ 229 Alex Cora .20 .07
❑ 230 Jeromy Burnitz .20 .07
❑ 231 Mark Grace .30 .10
❑ 232 Aubrey Huff .20 .07
❑ 233 Jeffrey Hammonds .20 .07
❑ 234 Olmedo Saenz .20 .07
❑ 235 Brian Jordan .20 .07
❑ 236 Jeremy Giambi .20 .07
❑ 237 Joe Girardi .20 .07
❑ 238 Eric Gagne .20 .07
❑ 239 Masato Yoshii .20 .07
❑ 240 Greg Maddux .75 .30
❑ 241 Bryan Rekar .20 .07
❑ 242 Ray Durham .20 .07
❑ 243 Torii Hunter .20 .07
❑ 244 Derrek Lee .30 .10
❑ 245 Jim Edmonds .20 .07
❑ 246 Einar Diaz .20 .07
❑ 247 Brian Bohanon .20 .07
❑ 248 Ron Belliard .20 .07
❑ 249 Mike Lowell .20 .07
❑ 250 Sammy Sosa .50 .20
❑ 251 Richard Hidalgo .20 .07
❑ 252 Bartolo Colon .20 .07
❑ 253 Jorge Posada .30 .10
❑ 254 LaTroy Hawkins .20 .07
❑ 255 Paul LoDuca .20 .07
❑ 256 Carlos Febles .20 .07
❑ 257 Nelson Cruz .20 .07
❑ 258 Edgardo Alfonzo .20 .07
❑ 259 Joey Hamilton .20 .07
❑ 260 Cliff Floyd .20 .07
❑ 261 Wes Helms .20 .07
❑ 262 Jay Bell .20 .07
❑ 263 Mike Cameron .20 .07
❑ 264 Paul Konerko .20 .07
❑ 265 Jeff Kent .20 .07
❑ 266 Robert Fick .20 .07
❑ 267 Allen Levrault .20 .07
❑ 268 Placido Polanco .20 .07
❑ 269 Marlon Anderson .20 .07
❑ 270 Mariano Rivera .50 .20
❑ 271 Chan Ho Park .20 .07
❑ 272 Jose Vizcaino .20 .07
❑ 273 Jeff D'Amico .20 .07
❑ 274 Mark Gardner .20 .07
❑ 275 Travis Fryman .20 .07
❑ 276 Darren Lewis .20 .07
❑ 277 Bruce Bochy MG .20 .07
❑ 278 Jerry Manuel MG .20 .07
❑ 279 Bob Brenly MG .20 .07
❑ 280 Don Baylor MG .20 .07
❑ 281 Davey Lopes MG .20 .07
❑ 282 Jerry Narron MG .20 .07
❑ 283 Tony Muser MG .20 .07
❑ 284 Hal McRae MG .20 .07
❑ 285 Bobby Cox MG .20 .07
❑ 286 Larry Dierker MG .20 .07
❑ 287 Phil Garner MG .20 .07
❑ 288 Joe Kerrigan MG .20 .07
❑ 289 Bobby Valentine MG .20 .07
❑ 290 Dusty Baker MG .20 .07
❑ 291 Lloyd McClendon MG .20 .07
❑ 292 Mike Scioscia MG .20 .07
❑ 293 Buck Martinez MG .20 .07
❑ 294 Larry Bowa MG .20 .07
❑ 295 Tony LaRussa MG .20 .07
❑ 296 Jeff Torborg MG .20 .07
❑ 297 Tom Kelly MG .20 .07
❑ 298 Mike Hargrove MG .20 .07
❑ 299 Art Howe MG .20 .07
❑ 300 Lou Piniella MG .20 .07
❑ 301 Charlie Manuel MG .20 .07
❑ 302 Buddy Bell MG .20 .07
❑ 303 Tony Perez MG .20 .07
❑ 304 Bob Boone MG .20 .07
❑ 305 Joe Torre MG .30 .10
❑ 306 Jim Tracy MG .20 .07
❑ 307 Jason Lane PROS .50 .20
❑ 308 Chris George PROS .50 .20
❑ 309 Hank Blalock PROS 1.00 .40
❑ 310 Joe Borchard PROS .50 .20
❑ 311 Marlon Byrd PROS .50 .20
❑ 312 Raymond Cabrera PROS RC .50 .20
❑ 313 Freddy Sanchez PROS RC 2.00 .75
❑ 314 Scott Wiggins PROS RC .50 .20
❑ 315 Jason Maule PROS RC .50 .20
❑ 316 Dionys Cesar PROS RC .50 .20
❑ 317 Boof Bonser PROS .50 .20
❑ 318 Juan Tolentino PROS RC .50 .20
❑ 319 Earl Snyder PROS RC .50 .20
❑ 320 Travis Wade PROS RC .50 .20
❑ 321 Napoleon Calzado PROS RC .50 .20
❑ 322 Eric Glaser PROS RC .50 .20
❑ 323 Craig Kuzmic PROS RC .50 .20
❑ 324 Nic Jackson PROS RC .50 .20
❑ 325 Mike Rivera PROS .50 .20
❑ 326 Jason Bay PROS RC 3.00 1.25
❑ 327 Chris Smith DP .50 .20
❑ 328 Jake Gautreau DP .50 .20
❑ 329 Gabe Gross DP .50 .20
❑ 330 Kenny Baugh DP .50 .20
❑ 331 J.D. Martin DP .50 .20
❑ 332 Barry Bonds HL 1.25 .50
❑ 333 Rickey Henderson HL .50 .20
❑ 334 Bud Smith HL .50 .20
❑ 335 Rickey Henderson HL .50 .20
❑ 336 Barry Bonds HL 1.25 .50
❑ 337 Ichiro/Giambi/Alomar LL .50 .20
❑ 338 A.Rod/Ichiro/Boone LL .50 .20
❑ 339 A.Rod/Thome/Palmeiro LL .50 .20
❑ 340 Boone/J.Gonz/A.Rod LL .50 .20
❑ 341 Garcia/Mussina/Mays LL .50 .20
❑ 342 Nomo/Mussina/Clemens LL .50 .20
❑ 343 Walker/Helton/Alou/Berk LL .50 .20
❑ 344 Sosa/Helton/Bonds LL .75 .30
❑ 345 Bonds/Sosa/L.Gonz LL .75 .30
❑ 346 Sosa/Helton/L.Gonz LL .50 .20
❑ 347 R.John/Schilling/Burkett LL .50 .20
❑ 348 R.John/Schilling/Park LL .50 .20
❑ 349 Seattle Mariners PB .50 .20
❑ 350 Oakland Athletics PB .50 .20
❑ 351 New York Yankees PB .50 .20
❑ 352 Cleveland Indians PB .50 .20
❑ 353 Arizona Diamondbacks PB .50 .20
❑ 354 Atlanta Braves PB .50 .20
❑ 355 St. Louis Cardinals PB .50 .20
❑ 356 Houston Astros PB .50 .20
❑ 357 Diamondbacks-Astros UWS .50 .20
❑ 358 Mike Piazza UWS .50 .20
❑ 359 Braves-Phillies UWS .50 .20
❑ 360 Curt Schilling UWS .50 .20
❑ 361 R.Clemens/L.Mazzilli UWS .50 .20
❑ 362 Sammy Sosa UWS .30 .10
❑ 363 Lampkin/Ichiro/Boone UWS .50 .20
❑ 364 B.Bonds/J.Bagwell UWS .75 .30
❑ 365 Barry Bonds HR 1 15.00 6.00
❑ 365 Barry Bonds HR 2 10.00 4.00
❑ 365 Barry Bonds HR 3 10.00 4.00
❑ 365 Barry Bonds HR 4 10.00 4.00
❑ 365 Barry Bonds HR 5 10.00 4.00
❑ 365 Barry Bonds HR 6 10.00 4.00
❑ 365 Barry Bonds HR 7 10.00 4.00
❑ 365 Barry Bonds HR 8 10.00 4.00
❑ 365 Barry Bonds HR 9 10.00 4.00
❑ 365 Barry Bonds HR 10 10.00 4.00
❑ 365 Barry Bonds HR 11 10.00 4.00
❑ 365 Barry Bonds HR 12 10.00 4.00
❑ 365 Barry Bonds HR 13 10.00 4.00
❑ 365 Barry Bonds HR 14 10.00 4.00
❑ 365 Barry Bonds HR 15 10.00 4.00
❑ 365 Barry Bonds HR 16 10.00 4.00
❑ 365 Barry Bonds HR 17 10.00 4.00
❑ 365 Barry Bonds HR 18 10.00 4.00
❑ 365 Barry Bonds HR 19 10.00 4.00
❑ 365 Barry Bonds HR 20 10.00 4.00
❑ 365 Barry Bonds HR 21 10.00 4.00
❑ 365 Barry Bonds HR 22 10.00 4.00
❑ 365 Barry Bonds HR 23 10.00 4.00
❑ 365 Barry Bonds HR 24 10.00 4.00
❑ 365 Barry Bonds HR 25 10.00 4.00
❑ 365 Barry Bonds HR 26 10.00 4.00
❑ 365 Barry Bonds HR 27 10.00 4.00
❑ 365 Barry Bonds HR 28 10.00 4.00
❑ 365 Barry Bonds HR 29 10.00 4.00
❑ 365 Barry Bonds HR 30 10.00 4.00
❑ 365 Barry Bonds HR 31 10.00 4.00
❑ 365 Barry Bonds HR 32 10.00 4.00
❑ 365 Barry Bonds HR 33 10.00 4.00
❑ 365 Barry Bonds HR 34 10.00 4.00
❑ 365 Barry Bonds HR 35 10.00 4.00
❑ 365 Barry Bonds HR 36 10.00 4.00
❑ 365 Barry Bonds HR 37 10.00 4.00
❑ 365 Barry Bonds HR 38 10.00 4.00
❑ 365 Barry Bonds HR 39 10.00 4.00
❑ 365 Barry Bonds HR 40 10.00 4.00
❑ 365 Barry Bonds HR 41 10.00 4.00
❑ 365 Barry Bonds HR 42 10.00 4.00
❑ 365 Barry Bonds HR 43 10.00 4.00
❑ 365 Barry Bonds HR 44 10.00 4.00
❑ 365 Barry Bonds HR 45 10.00 4.00
❑ 365 Barry Bonds HR 46 10.00 4.00
❑ 365 Barry Bonds HR 47 10.00 4.00
❑ 365 Barry Bonds HR 48 10.00 4.00
❑ 365 Barry Bonds HR 49 10.00 4.00
❑ 365 Barry Bonds HR 50 10.00 4.00
❑ 365 Barry Bonds HR 51 10.00 4.00
❑ 365 Barry Bonds HR 52 10.00 4.00
❑ 365 Barry Bonds HR 53 10.00 4.00
❑ 365 Barry Bonds HR 54 10.00 4.00
❑ 365 Barry Bonds HR 55 10.00 4.00
❑ 365 Barry Bonds HR 56 10.00 4.00
❑ 365 Barry Bonds HR 57 10.00 4.00
❑ 365 Barry Bonds HR 58 10.00 4.00
❑ 365 Barry Bonds HR 59 10.00 4.00
❑ 365 Barry Bonds HR 60 10.00 4.00
❑ 365 Barry Bonds HR 61 15.00 6.00
❑ 365 Barry Bonds HR 62 10.00 4.00
❑ 365 Barry Bonds HR 63 10.00 4.00
❑ 365 Barry Bonds HR 64 10.00 4.00
❑ 365 Barry Bonds HR 65 10.00 4.00
❑ 365 Barry Bonds HR 66 10.00 4.00
❑ 365 Barry Bonds HR 67 10.00 4.00
❑ 365 Barry Bonds HR 68 10.00 4.00
❑ 365 Barry Bonds HR 69 10.00 4.00
❑ 365 Barry Bonds HR 70 15.00 6.00
❑ 365 Barry Bonds HR 71 10.00 4.00
❑ 365 Barry Bonds HR 72 10.00 4.00
❑ 365 Barry Bonds HR 73 50.00 20.00
❑ 366 Pat Meares .20 .07
❑ 367 Mike Lieberthal .20 .07
❑ 368 Larry Bigbie .20 .07
❑ 369 Ron Gant .20 .07
❑ 370 Moises Alou .20 .07
❑ 371 Chad Kreuter .20 .07
❑ 372 Willis Roberts .20 .07
❑ 373 Toby Hall .20 .07
❑ 374 Miguel Batista .20 .07
❑ 375 John Burkett .20 .07
❑ 376 Cory Lidle .20 .07
❑ 377 Nick Neugebauer .20 .07
❑ 378 Jay Payton .20 .07
❑ 379 Steve Karsay .20 .07
❑ 380 Eric Chavez .20 .07
❑ 381 Kelly Stinnett .20 .07
❑ 382 Jarrod Washburn .20 .07
❑ 383 Rick White .20 .07
❑ 384 Jeff Conine .20 .07
❑ 385 Fred McGriff .30 .10
❑ 386 Marvin Benard .20 .07
❑ 387 Joe Crede .20 .07
❑ 388 Dennis Cook .20 .07
❑ 389 Rick Reed .20 .07
❑ 390 Tom Glavine .30 .10
❑ 391 Rondell White .20 .07
❑ 392 Matt Morris .20 .07
❑ 393 Pat Rapp .20 .07
❑ 394 Robert Person .20 .07
❑ 395 Omar Vizquel .30 .10
❑ 396 Jeff Cirillo .20 .07
❑ 397 Dave Mlicki .20 .07
❑ 398 Jose Ortiz .20 .07
❑ 399 Ryan Dempster .20 .07
❑ 400 Curt Schilling .20 .07
❑ 401 Peter Bergeron .20 .07
❑ 402 Kyle Lohse .20 .07

❑ 403 Craig Wilson .20 .07
❑ 404 David Justice .20 .07
❑ 405 Darin Erstad .20 .07
❑ 406 Jose Mercedes .20 .07
❑ 407 Carl Pavano .20 .07
❑ 408 Albie Lopez .20 .07
❑ 409 Alex Ochoa .20 .07
❑ 410 Chipper Jones .50 .20
❑ 411 Tyler Houston .20 .07
❑ 412 Dean Palmer .20 .07
❑ 413 Damian Jackson .20 .07
❑ 414 Josh Towers .20 .07
❑ 415 Rafael Furcal .20 .07
❑ 416 Mike Morgan .20 .07
❑ 417 Herb Perry .20 .07
❑ 418 Mike Sirotka .20 .07
❑ 419 Mark Wohlers .20 .07
❑ 420 Nomar Garciaparra .75 .30
❑ 421 Felipe Lopez .20 .07
❑ 422 Joe McEwing .20 .07
❑ 423 Jacque Jones .20 .07
❑ 424 Julio Franco .20 .07
❑ 425 Frank Thomas .50 .20
❑ 426 So Taguchi RC .75 .30
❑ 427 Kazuhisa Ishii RC .50 .20
❑ 428 D'Angelo Jimenez .20 .07
❑ 429 Chris Stynes .20 .07
❑ 430 Kerry Wood .20 .07
❑ 431 Chris Singleton .20 .07
❑ 432 Erubiel Durazo .20 .07
❑ 433 Matt Lawton .20 .07
❑ 434 Bill Mueller .20 .07
❑ 435 Jose Canseco .30 .10
❑ 436 Ben Grieve .20 .07
❑ 437 Terry Mulholland .20 .07
❑ 438 David Bell .20 .07
❑ 439 A.J. Pierzynski .20 .07
❑ 440 Adam Dunn .20 .07
❑ 441 Jon Garland .20 .07
❑ 442 Jeff Fassero .20 .07
❑ 443 Julio Lugo .20 .07
❑ 444 Carlos Guillen .20 .07
❑ 445 Orlando Hernandez .20 .07
❑ 446 M.Loretta UER Leskanic .20 .07
❑ 447 Scott Spiezio .20 .07
❑ 448 Kevin Millwood .20 .07
❑ 449 Jamie Moyer .20 .07
❑ 450 Todd Helton .30 .10
❑ 451 Todd Walker .20 .07
❑ 452 Jose Lima .20 .07
❑ 453 Brook Fordyce .20 .07
❑ 454 Aaron Rowand .20 .07
❑ 455 Barry Zito .20 .07
❑ 456 Eric Owens .20 .07
❑ 457 Charles Nagy .20 .07
❑ 458 Raul Ibanez .20 .07
❑ 459 Joe Mays .20 .07
❑ 460 Jim Thome .30 .10
❑ 461 Adam Eaton .20 .07
❑ 462 Felix Martinez .20 .07
❑ 463 Vernon Wells .20 .07
❑ 464 Donnie Sadler .20 .07
❑ 465 Tony Clark .20 .07
❑ 466 Jose Hernandez .20 .07
❑ 467 Ramon Martinez .20 .07
❑ 468 Rusty Greer .20 .07
❑ 469 Rod Barajas .20 .07
❑ 470 Lance Berkman .20 .07
❑ 471 Brady Anderson .20 .07
❑ 472 Pedro Astacio .20 .07
❑ 473 Shane Halter .20 .07
❑ 474 Bret Prinz .20 .07
❑ 475 Edgar Martinez .30 .10
❑ 476 Steve Trachsel .20 .07
❑ 477 Gary Matthews Jr. .20 .07
❑ 478 Ismael Valdes .20 .07
❑ 479 Juan Uribe .20 .07
❑ 480 Shawn Green .20 .07
❑ 481 Kirk Rueter .20 .07
❑ 482 Damion Easley .20 .07
❑ 483 Chris Carpenter .20 .07
❑ 484 Kris Benson .20 .07
❑ 485 Antonio Alfonseca .20 .07
❑ 486 Kyle Farnsworth .20 .07
❑ 487 Brandon Lyon .20 .07
❑ 488 Hideki Irabu .20 .07
❑ 489 David Ortiz .50 .20
❑ 490 Mike Piazza .75 .30
❑ 491 Derek Lowe .20 .07
❑ 492 Chris Gomez .20 .07
❑ 493 Mark Johnson .20 .07
❑ 494 John Rocker .20 .07
❑ 495 Eric Karros .20 .07
❑ 496 Bill Haselman .20 .07
❑ 497 Dave Veres .20 .07
❑ 498 Pete Harnisch .20 .07
❑ 499 Tomokazu Ohka .20 .07
❑ 500 Barry Bonds 1.25 .50
❑ 501 David Dellucci .20 .07
❑ 502 Wendell Magee .20 .07
❑ 503 Tom Gordon .20 .07
❑ 504 Javier Vazquez .20 .07
❑ 505 Ben Sheets .20 .07
❑ 506 Wilton Guerrero .20 .07
❑ 507 John Halama .20 .07
❑ 508 Mark Redman .20 .07
❑ 509 Jack Wilson .20 .07
❑ 510 Bernie Williams .30 .10
❑ 511 Miguel Cairo .20 .07
❑ 512 Denny Hocking .20 .07
❑ 513 Tony Batista .20 .07
❑ 514 Mark Grudzielanek .20 .07
❑ 515 Jose Vidro .20 .07
❑ 516 Sterling Hitchcock .20 .07
❑ 517 Billy Koch .20 .07
❑ 518 Matt Clement .20 .07
❑ 519 Bruce Chen .20 .07
❑ 520 Roberto Alomar .30 .10
❑ 521 Orlando Palmeiro .20 .07
❑ 522 Steve Finley .20 .07
❑ 523 Danny Patterson .20 .07
❑ 524 Terry Adams .20 .07
❑ 525 Tino Martinez .30 .10
❑ 526 Tony Armas Jr. .20 .07
❑ 527 Geoff Jenkins .20 .07
❑ 528 Kerry Robinson .20 .07
❑ 529 Corey Patterson .20 .07
❑ 530 Brian Giles .20 .07
❑ 531 Jose Jimenez .20 .07
❑ 532 Joe Kennedy .20 .07
❑ 533 Armando Rios .20 .07
❑ 534 Osvaldo Fernandez .20 .07
❑ 535 Ruben Sierra .20 .07
❑ 536 Octavio Dotel .20 .07
❑ 537 Luis Sojo .20 .07
❑ 538 Brent Butler .20 .07
❑ 539 Pablo Ozuna .20 .07
❑ 540 Freddy Garcia .20 .07
❑ 541 Chad Durbin .20 .07
❑ 542 Orlando Merced .20 .07
❑ 543 Michael Tucker .20 .07
❑ 544 Roberto Hernandez .20 .07
❑ 545 Pat Burrell .20 .07
❑ 546 A.J. Burnett .20 .07
❑ 547 Bubba Trammell .20 .07
❑ 548 Scott Elarton .20 .07
❑ 549 Mike Darr .20 .07
❑ 550 Ken Griffey Jr. .75 .30
❑ 551 Ugueth Urbina .20 .07
❑ 552 Todd Jones .20 .07
❑ 553 Delino Deshields .20 .07
❑ 554 Adam Piatt .20 .07
❑ 555 Jason Kendall .20 .07
❑ 556 Hector Ortiz .20 .07
❑ 557 Turk Wendell .20 .07
❑ 558 Rob Bell .20 .07
❑ 559 Sun Woo Kim .20 .07
❑ 560 Raul Mondesi .20 .07
❑ 561 Brent Abernathy .20 .07
❑ 562 Seth Etherton .20 .07
❑ 563 Shawn Wooten .20 .07
❑ 564 Jay Buhner .20 .07
❑ 565 Andres Galarraga .20 .07
❑ 566 Shane Reynolds .20 .07
❑ 567 Rod Beck .20 .07
❑ 568 Dee Brown .20 .07
❑ 569 Pedro Feliz .20 .07
❑ 570 Ryan Klesko .20 .07
❑ 571 John Vander Wal .20 .07
❑ 572 Nick Bierbrodt .20 .07
❑ 573 Joe Nathan .20 .07
❑ 574 James Baldwin .20 .07
❑ 575 J.D. Drew .20 .07
❑ 576 Greg Colbrunn .20 .07
❑ 577 Doug Glanville .20 .07
❑ 578 Brandon Duckworth .20 .07
❑ 579 Shawn Chacon .20 .07
❑ 580 Rich Aurilia .20 .07
❑ 581 Chuck Finley .20 .07
❑ 582 Abraham Nunez .20 .07
❑ 583 Kenny Lofton .20 .07
❑ 584 Brian Daubach .20 .07
❑ 585 Miguel Tejada .20 .07
❑ 586 Nate Cornejo .20 .07
❑ 587 Kazuhiro Sasaki .20 .07
❑ 588 Chris Richard .20 .07
❑ 589 Armando Reynoso .20 .07
❑ 590 Tim Hudson .20 .07
❑ 591 Neifi Perez .20 .07
❑ 592 Steve Cox .20 .07
❑ 593 Henry Blanco .20 .07
❑ 594 Ricky Ledee .20 .07
❑ 595 Tim Salmon .30 .10
❑ 596 Luis Rivas .20 .07
❑ 597 Jeff Zimmerman .20 .07
❑ 598 Matt Stairs .20 .07
❑ 599 Preston Wilson .20 .07
❑ 600 Mark McGwire 1.25 .50
❑ 601 Timo Perez .20 .07
❑ 602 Matt Anderson .20 .07
❑ 603 Todd Hundley .20 .07
❑ 604 Rick Ankiel .20 .07
❑ 605 Tsuyoshi Shinjo .20 .07
❑ 606 Woody Williams .20 .07
❑ 607 Jason LaRue .20 .07
❑ 608 Carlos Lee .20 .07
❑ 609 Russ Johnson .20 .07
❑ 610 Scott Rolen .30 .10
❑ 611 Brent Mayne .20 .07
❑ 612 Darrin Fletcher .20 .07
❑ 613 Ray Lankford .20 .07
❑ 614 Troy O'Leary .20 .07
❑ 615 Javier Lopez .20 .07
❑ 616 Randy Velarde .20 .07
❑ 617 Vinny Castilla .20 .07
❑ 618 Milton Bradley .20 .07
❑ 619 Ruben Mateo .20 .07
❑ 620 Jason Giambi Yankees .20 .07
❑ 621 Andy Benes .20 .07
❑ 622 Joe Mauer RC 10.00 4.00
❑ 623 Andy Pettitte .30 .10
❑ 624 Jose Offerman .20 .07
❑ 625 Mo Vaughn .20 .07
❑ 626 Steve Sparks .20 .07
❑ 627 Mike Matthews .20 .07
❑ 628 Robb Nen .20 .07
❑ 629 Kip Wells .20 .07
❑ 630 Kevin Brown .20 .07
❑ 631 Arthur Rhodes .20 .07
❑ 632 Gabe Kapler .20 .07
❑ 633 Jermaine Dye .20 .07
❑ 634 Josh Beckett .20 .07
❑ 635 Pokey Reese .20 .07
❑ 636 Benji Gil .20 .07
❑ 637 Marcus Giles .20 .07
❑ 638 Julian Tavarez .20 .07
❑ 639 Jason Schmidt .20 .07
❑ 640 Alex Rodriguez .75 .30
❑ 641 Anaheim Angels TC .20 .07
❑ 642 Arizona Diamondbacks TC .30 .10
❑ 643 Atlanta Braves TC .20 .07
❑ 644 Baltimore Orioles TC .20 .07
❑ 645 Boston Red Sox TC .20 .07
❑ 646 Chicago Cubs TC .20 .07
❑ 647 Chicago White Sox TC .20 .07
❑ 648 Cincinnati Reds TC .20 .07
❑ 649 Cleveland Indians TC .20 .07
❑ 650 Colorado Rockies TC .20 .07
❑ 651 Detroit Tigers TC .20 .07
❑ 652 Florida Marlins TC .20 .07
❑ 653 Houston Astros TC .20 .07
❑ 654 Kansas City Royals TC .20 .07
❑ 655 Los Angeles Dodgers TC .20 .07
❑ 656 Milwaukee Brewers TC .20 .07
❑ 657 Minnesota Twins TC .20 .07
❑ 658 Montreal Expos TC .20 .07
❑ 659 New York Mets TC .20 .07
❑ 660 New York Yankees TC .50 .20

❑ 661 Oakland Athletics TC .20 .07
❑ 662 Philadelphia Phillies TC .20 .07
❑ 663 Pittsburgh Pirates TC .20 .07
❑ 664 San Diego Padres TC .20 .07
❑ 665 San Francisco Giants TC .20 .07
❑ 666 Seattle Mariners TC .30 .10
❑ 667 St. Louis Cardinals TC .20 .07
❑ 668 Tampa Bay Devil Rays TC .20 .07
❑ 669 Texas Rangers TC .20 .07
❑ 670 Toronto Blue Jays TC .20 .07
❑ 671 Juan Cruz PROS .50 .20
❑ 672 Kevin Cash PROS RC .50 .20
❑ 673 Jimmy Gobble PROS RC .50 .20
❑ 674 Mike Hill PROS RC .50 .20
❑ 675 Taylor Buchholz PROS RC .50 .20
❑ 676 Bill Hall PROS .50 .20
❑ 677 Brett Roneberg PROS RC .50 .20
❑ 678 Royce Huffman PROS RC .50 .20
❑ 679 Chris Tritle PROS RC .50 .20
❑ 680 Nate Espy PROS RC .50 .20
❑ 681 Nick Alvarez PROS RC .50 .20
❑ 682 Jason Botts PROS RC .50 .20
❑ 683 Ryan Gripp PROS RC .50 .20
❑ 684 Dan Phillips PROS RC .50 .20
❑ 685 Pablo Arias PROS RC .50 .20
❑ 686 John Rodriguez PROS RC .50 .20
❑ 687 Rich Harden PROS RC 3.00 1.25
❑ 688 Neal Frendling PROS RC .50 .20
❑ 689 Rich Thompson PROS RC .50 .20
❑ 690 Greg Montalbano PROS RC .50 .20
❑ 691 Len Dinardo DP RC .50 .20
❑ 692 Ryan Raburn DP RC .50 .20
❑ 693 Josh Barfield DP RC 2.50 1.00
❑ 694 David Bacani DP RC .50 .20
❑ 695 Dan Johnson DP RC 1.00 .40
❑ 696 Mike Mussina GG .20 .07
❑ 697 Ivan Rodriguez GG .30 .10
❑ 698 Doug Mientkiewicz GG .20 .07
❑ 699 Roberto Alomar GG .20 .07
❑ 700 Eric Chavez GG .20 .07
❑ 701 Omar Vizquel GG .20 .07
❑ 702 Mike Cameron GG .20 .07
❑ 703 Torii Hunter GG .20 .07
❑ 704 Ichiro Suzuki GG .50 .20
❑ 705 Greg Maddux GG .50 .20
❑ 706 Brad Ausmus GG .20 .07
❑ 707 Todd Helton GG .20 .07
❑ 708 Fernando Vina GG .20 .07
❑ 709 Scott Rolen GG .20 .07
❑ 710 Orlando Cabrera GG .20 .07
❑ 711 Andruw Jones GG .20 .07
❑ 712 Jim Edmonds GG .20 .07
❑ 713 Larry Walker GG .20 .07
❑ 714 Roger Clemens CY .50 .20
❑ 715 Randy Johnson CY .30 .10
❑ 716 Ichiro Suzuki MVP .50 .20
❑ 717 Barry Bonds MVP .75 .30
❑ 718 Ichiro Suzuki ROY .50 .20
❑ 719 Albert Pujols ROY .50 .20

2002 Topps Traded

❑ COMPLETE SET (275) 200.00 100.00
❑ COMMON CARD (T1-T110) 2.00 .75
❑ COMMON CARD (T111-T275) .40 .15
❑ T1 Jeff Weaver 2.00 .75
❑ T2 Jay Powell 2.00 .75
❑ T3 Alex Gonzalez 2.00 .75
❑ T4 Jason Isringhausen 2.00 .75
❑ T5 Tyler Houston 2.00 .75
❑ T6 Ben Broussard 2.00 .75
❑ T7 Chuck Knoblauch 2.00 .75
❑ T8 Brian L. Hunter 2.00 .75
❑ T9 Dustan Mohr 2.00 .75
❑ T10 Eric Hinske 2.00 .75
❑ T11 Roger Cedeno 2.00 .75
❑ T12 Eddie Perez 2.00 .75
❑ T13 Jeromy Burnitz 2.00 .75
❑ T14 Bartolo Colon 2.00 .75
❑ T15 Rick Helling 2.00 .75
❑ T16 Dan Plesac 2.00 .75
❑ T17 Scott Strickland 2.00 .75
❑ T18 Antonio Alfonseca 2.00 .75
❑ T19 Ricky Gutierrez 2.00 .75
❑ T20 John Valentin 2.00 .75
❑ T21 Raul Mondesi 2.00 .75
❑ T22 Ben Davis 2.00 .75
❑ T23 Nelson Figueroa 2.00 .75
❑ T24 Earl Snyder 2.00 .75
❑ T25 Robin Ventura 2.00 .75
❑ T26 Jimmy Haynes 2.00 .75
❑ T27 Kenny Kelly 2.00 .75
❑ T28 Morgan Ensberg 1.00 .40
❑ T29 Reggie Sanders 2.00 .75
❑ T30 Shigetoshi Hasegawa 2.00 .75
❑ T31 Mike Timlin 2.00 .75
❑ T32 Russell Branyan 2.00 .75
❑ T33 Alan Embree 2.00 .75
❑ T34 D'Angelo Jimenez 2.00 .75
❑ T35 Kent Mercker 2.00 .75
❑ T36 Jesse Orosco 2.00 .75
❑ T37 Gregg Zaun 2.00 .75
❑ T38 Reggie Taylor 2.00 .75
❑ T39 Andres Galarraga 2.00 .75
❑ T40 Chris Truby 2.00 .75
❑ T41 Bruce Chen 2.00 .75
❑ T42 Darren Lewis 2.00 .75
❑ T43 Ryan Kohlmeier 2.00 .75
❑ T44 John McDonald 2.00 .75
❑ T45 Omar Daal 2.00 .75
❑ T46 Matt Clement 2.00 .75
❑ T47 Glendon Rusch 2.00 .75
❑ T48 Chan Ho Park 2.00 .75
❑ T49 Benny Agbayani 2.00 .75
❑ T50 Juan Gonzalez 2.00 .75
❑ T51 Carlos Baerga 2.00 .75
❑ T52 Tim Raines 2.00 .75
❑ T53 Kevin Appier 2.00 .75
❑ T54 Marty Cordova 2.00 .75
❑ T55 Jeff D'Amico 2.00 .75
❑ T56 Dmitri Young 2.00 .75
❑ T57 Roosevelt Brown 2.00 .75
❑ T58 Dustin Hermanson 2.00 .75
❑ T59 Jose Hijo 2.00 .75
❑ T60 Todd Ritchie 2.00 .75
❑ T61 Lee Stevens 2.00 .75
❑ T62 Placido Polanco 2.00 .75
❑ T63 Eric Young 2.00 .75
❑ T64 Chuck Finley 2.00 .75
❑ T65 Dicky Gonzalez 2.00 .75
❑ T66 Jose Macias 2.00 .75
❑ T67 Gabe Kapler 2.00 .75
❑ T68 Sandy Alomar Jr. 2.00 .75
❑ T69 Henry Blanco 2.00 .75
❑ T70 Julian Tavarez 2.00 .75
❑ T71 Paul Bako 2.00 .75
❑ T72 Scott Rolen 3.00 1.25
❑ T73 Brian Jordan 2.00 .75
❑ T74 Rickey Henderson 4.00 1.50
❑ T75 Kevin Mench 2.00 .75
❑ T76 Hideo Nomo 4.00 1.50
❑ T77 Jeremy Giambi 2.00 .75
❑ T78 Brad Fullmer 2.00 .75
❑ T79 Carl Everett 2.00 .75
❑ T80 David Wells 2.00 .75
❑ T81 Aaron Sele 2.00 .75
❑ T82 Todd Hollandsworth 2.00 .75
❑ T83 Vicente Padilla 2.00 .75
❑ T84 Kenny Lofton 2.00 .75
❑ T85 Corky Miller 2.00 .75
❑ T86 Josh Fogg 2.00 .75
❑ T87 Cliff Floyd 2.00 .75
❑ T88 Craig Paquette 2.00 .75
❑ T89 Jay Payton 2.00 .75
❑ T90 Carlos Pena 2.00 .75
❑ T91 Juan Encarnacion 2.00 .75
❑ T92 Rey Sanchez 2.00 .75
❑ T93 Ryan Dempster 2.00 .75
❑ T94 Mario Encarnacion 2.00 .75
❑ T95 Jorge Julio 2.00 .75
❑ T96 John Mabry 2.00 .75
❑ T97 Todd Zeile 2.00 .75
❑ T98 Johnny Damon Sox 3.00 1.25
❑ T99 Deivi Cruz 2.00 .75
❑ T100 Gary Sheffield 2.00 .75
❑ T101 Ted Lilly 2.00 .75
❑ T102 Todd Van Poppel 2.00 .75
❑ T103 Shawn Estes 2.00 .75
❑ T104 Cesar Izturis 2.00 .75
❑ T105 Ron Coomer 2.00 .75
❑ T106 Grady Little MG RC 2.00 .75
❑ T107 Jimy Williams MG 2.00 .75
❑ T108 Tony Pena MG 2.00 .75
❑ T109 Frank Robinson MG 3.00 1.25
❑ T110 Ron Gardenhire MG 2.00 .75
❑ T111 Dennis Tankersley .40 .15
❑ T112 Alejandro Cadena RC .40 .15
❑ T113 Justin Reid RC .40 .15
❑ T114 Nate Field RC .40 .15
❑ T115 Rene Reyes RC .40 .15
❑ T116 Nelson Castro RC .40 .15
❑ T117 Miguel Olivo .40 .15
❑ T118 David Espinosa .40 .15
❑ T119 Chris Bootcheck RC .40 .15
❑ T120 Rob Henkel RC .40 .15
❑ T121 Steve Bechler RC .40 .15
❑ T122 Mark Outlaw RC .40 .15
❑ T123 Henry Pichardo RC .40 .15
❑ T124 Michael Floyd RC .40 .15
❑ T125 Richard Lane RC .40 .15
❑ T126 Pete Zamora RC .40 .15
❑ T127 Javier Colina .40 .15
❑ T128 Greg Sain RC .40 .15
❑ T129 Ronnie Merrill .40 .15
❑ T130 Gavin Floyd RC 1.00 .40
❑ T131 Josh Bonifay RC .40 .15
❑ T132 Tommy Marx RC .40 .15
❑ T133 Gary Cates Jr. RC .40 .15
❑ T134 Neal Cotts RC 1.00 .40
❑ T135 Angel Berroa .40 .15
❑ T136 Elio Serrano RC .40 .15
❑ T137 J.J. Putz RC .50 .20
❑ T138 Ruben Gotay RC .50 .20
❑ T139 Eddie Rogers .40 .15
❑ T140 Wily Mo Pena .40 .15
❑ T141 Tyler Yates RC .40 .15
❑ T142 Colin Young RC .40 .15
❑ T143 Chance Caple .40 .15
❑ T144 Ben Howard RC .40 .15
❑ T145 Ryan Bukvich RC .40 .15
❑ T146 Cliff Bartosh RC .40 .15
❑ T147 Brandon Claussen .40 .15
❑ T148 Cristian Guerrero .40 .15
❑ T149 Derrick Lewis .40 .15
❑ T150 Eric Miller RC .40 .15
❑ T151 Justin Huber RC .75 .30
❑ T152 Adrian Gonzalez .40 .15
❑ T153 Brian West RC .40 .15
❑ T154 Chris Baker RC .40 .15
❑ T155 Drew Henson .40 .15
❑ T156 Scott Hairston RC .50 .20
❑ T157 Jason Simontacchi RC .40 .15
❑ T158 Jason Arnold RC .40 .15
❑ T159 Brandon Phillips .40 .15
❑ T160 Adam Roller RC .40 .15
❑ T161 Scotty Layfield RC .40 .15
❑ T162 Freddie Money RC .40 .15
❑ T163 Noochie Varner RC .40 .15
❑ T164 Terrance Hill RC .40 .15
❑ T165 Jeremy Hill RC .40 .15
❑ T166 Carlos Cabrera RC .40 .15
❑ T167 Jose Morban RC .40 .15
❑ T168 Kevin Frederick RC .40 .15
❑ T169 Mark Teixeira 1.50 .60
❑ T170 Brian Rogers .40 .15
❑ T171 Anastacio Martinez RC .40 .15
❑ T172 Bobby Jenks RC 1.50 .60
❑ T173 David Gil RC .40 .15
❑ T174 Andres Torres .40 .15
❑ T175 James Barrett RC .40 .15
❑ T176 Jimmy Journell .40 .15

❑ T177 Brett Kay RC .40 .15
❑ T178 Jason Young RC .40 .15
❑ T179 Mark Hamilton RC .40 .15
❑ T180 Jose Bautista RC 1.00 .40
❑ T181 Blake McGinley RC .40 .15
❑ T182 Ryan Mottl RC .40 .15
❑ T183 Jeff Austin RC .40 .15
❑ T184 Xavier Nady .40 .15
❑ T185 Kyle Kane RC .40 .15
❑ T186 Travis Foley RC .40 .15
❑ T187 Nathan Kaup RC .40 .15
❑ T188 Eric Cyr .40 .15
❑ T189 Josh Cisneros RC .40 .15
❑ T190 Brad Nelson RC .40 .15
❑ T191 Clint Weibl RC .40 .15
❑ T192 Ron Calloway RC .40 .15
❑ T193 Jung Bong .40 .15
❑ T194 Rolando Viera RC .40 .15
❑ T195 Jason Bulger RC .40 .15
❑ T196 Chone Figgins RC 1.50 .60
❑ T197 Jimmy Alvarez RC .40 .15
❑ T198 Joel Crump RC .40 .15
❑ T199 Ryan Doumit RC .60 .25
❑ T200 Demetrius Heath RC .40 .15
❑ T201 John Ennis RC .40 .15
❑ T202 Doug Sessions RC .40 .15
❑ T203 Clinton Hosford RC .40 .15
❑ T204 Chris Narveson RC .40 .15
❑ T205 Ross Peeples RC .40 .15
❑ T206 Alex Requena RC .40 .15
❑ T207 Matt Erickson RC .40 .15
❑ T208 Brian Forystek RC .40 .15
❑ T209 Dewon Brazelton .40 .15
❑ T210 Nathan Haynes .40 .15
❑ T211 Jack Cust .40 .15
❑ T212 Jesse Foppert RC .50 .20
❑ T213 Jesus Cota RC .40 .15
❑ T214 Juan M. Gonzalez RC .40 .15
❑ T215 Tim Kalita RC .40 .15
❑ T216 Manny Delcarmen RC .50 .20
❑ T217 Jim Kavourias RC .40 .15
❑ T218 C.J. Wilson RC .40 .15
❑ T219 Edwin Yan RC .40 .15
❑ T220 Andy Van Hekken .40 .15
❑ T221 Michael Cuddyer .40 .15
❑ T222 Jeff Verplancke RC .40 .15
❑ T223 Mike Wilson RC .40 .15
❑ T224 Corwin Malone RC .40 .15
❑ T225 Chris Snelling RC .60 .25
❑ T226 Joe Rogers RC .40 .15
❑ T227 Jason Bay 4.00 1.50
❑ T228 Ezequiel Astacio RC .40 .15
❑ T229 Joey Hammond RC .40 .15
❑ T230 Chris Duffy RC 1.00 .40
❑ T231 Mark Prior 1.60 .60
❑ T232 Hansel Izquierdo RC .40 .15
❑ T233 Franklyn German RC .40 .15
❑ T234 Alexis Gomez .40 .15
❑ T235 Jorge Padilla RC .40 .15
❑ T236 Ryan Snare RC .40 .15
❑ T237 Deivis Santos .40 .15
❑ T238 Taggert Bozied RC .50 .20
❑ T239 Mike Peeples RC .40 .15
❑ T240 Ronald Acuna RC .40 .15
❑ T241 Koyie Hill .40 .15
❑ T242 Garrett Guzman RC .40 .15
❑ T243 Ryan Church RC 1.00 .40
❑ T244 Tony Fontana RC .40 .15
❑ T245 Keto Anderson RC .40 .15
❑ T246 Brad Bouras RC .40 .15
❑ T247 Jason Dubois RC .50 .20
❑ T248 Angel Guzman RC .75 .30
❑ T249 Joel Hanrahan RC .40 .15
❑ T250 Joe Jiannetti RC .40 .15
❑ T251 Sean Pierce RC .40 .15
❑ T252 Jake Mauer RC .40 .15
❑ T253 Marshall McDougall RC .40 .15
❑ T254 Edwin Almonte RC .40 .15
❑ T255 Shawn Riggans RC .40 .15
❑ T256 Steven Shell RC .40 .15
❑ T257 Kevin Hooper RC .40 .15
❑ T258 Michael Frick RC .40 .15
❑ T259 Travis Chapman RC .40 .15
❑ T260 Tim Hummel RC .40 .15
❑ T261 Adam Morrissey RC .40 .15
❑ T262 Dontrelle Willis RC 5.00 2.00
❑ T263 Justin Sherrod RC .40 .15
❑ T264 Gerald Smiley RC .40 .15
❑ T265 Tony Miller RC .40 .15
❑ T266 Nolan Ryan WW 2.50 1.00
❑ T267 Reggie Jackson WW .60 .25
❑ T268 Steve Garvey WW .40 .15
❑ T269 Wade Boggs WW .60 .25
❑ T270 Sammy Sosa WW 1.00 .40
❑ T271 Curt Schilling WW .40 .15
❑ T272 Mark Grace WW .60 .25
❑ T273 Jason Giambi WW .40 .15
❑ T274 Ken Griffey Jr. WW 1.50 .60
❑ T275 Roberto Alomar WW .60 .25

2003 Topps

❑ COMPLETE SET (720) 80.00 40.00
❑ COMPLETE SERIES 1 (366) 40.00 20.00
❑ COMPLETE SERIES 2 (354) 40.00 20.00
❑ COMMON CARD (1-6/8-721) .20 .07
❑ COMMON (292-331/660-684) .50 .20
❑ 1 Alex Rodriguez .75 .30
❑ 2 Dan Wilson .20 .07
❑ 3 Jimmy Rollins .20 .07
❑ 4 Jermaine Dye .20 .07
❑ 5 Steve Karsay .20 .07
❑ 6 Timo Perez .20 .07
❑ 8 Jose Vidro .20 .07
❑ 9 Eddie Guardado .20 .07
❑ 10 Mark Prior .30 .10
❑ 11 Curt Schilling .20 .07
❑ 12 Dennis Cook .20 .07
❑ 13 Andruw Jones .30 .10
❑ 14 David Segui .20 .07
❑ 15 Trot Nixon .20 .07
❑ 16 Kerry Wood .20 .07
❑ 17 Magglio Ordonez .20 .07
❑ 18 Jason LaRue .20 .07
❑ 19 Danys Baez .20 .07
❑ 20 Todd Helton .30 .10
❑ 21 Denny Neagle .20 .07
❑ 22 Dave Mlicki .20 .07
❑ 23 Roberto Hernandez .20 .07
❑ 24 Odalis Perez .20 .07
❑ 25 Nick Neugebauer .20 .07
❑ 26 David Ortiz .50 .20
❑ 27 Andres Galarraga .20 .07
❑ 28 Edgardo Alfonzo .20 .07
❑ 29 Chad Bradford .20 .07
❑ 30 Jason Giambi .20 .07
❑ 31 Brian Giles .20 .07
❑ 32 Deivi Cruz .20 .07
❑ 33 Robb Nen .20 .07
❑ 34 Jeff Nelson .20 .07
❑ 35 Edgar Renteria .20 .07
❑ 36 Aubrey Huff .20 .07
❑ 37 Brandon Duckworth .20 .07
❑ 38 Juan Gonzalez .20 .07
❑ 39 Sidney Ponson .20 .07
❑ 40 Eric Hinske .20 .07
❑ 41 Kevin Appier .20 .07
❑ 42 Danny Bautista .20 .07
❑ 43 Javier Lopez .20 .07
❑ 44 Jeff Conine .20 .07
❑ 45 Carlos Baerga .20 .07
❑ 46 Ugueth Urbina .20 .07
❑ 47 Mark Buehrle .20 .07
❑ 48 Aaron Boone .20 .07
❑ 49 Jason Simontacchi .20 .07
❑ 50 Sammy Sosa .50 .20
❑ 51 Jose Jimenez .20 .07
❑ 52 Bobby Higginson .20 .07
❑ 53 Luis Castillo .20 .07
❑ 54 Orlando Merced .20 .07
❑ 55 Brian Jordan .20 .07
❑ 56 Eric Young .20 .07
❑ 57 Bobby Kielty .20 .07
❑ 58 Luis Rivas .20 .07
❑ 59 Brad Wilkerson .20 .07
❑ 60 Roberto Alomar .30 .10
❑ 61 Roger Clemens 1.00 .40
❑ 62 Scott Hatteberg .20 .07
❑ 63 Andy Ashby .20 .07
❑ 64 Mike Williams .20 .07
❑ 65 Ron Gant .20 .07
❑ 66 Benito Santiago .20 .07
❑ 67 Bret Boone .20 .07
❑ 68 Matt Morris .20 .07
❑ 69 Troy Glaus .20 .07
❑ 70 Austin Kearns .20 .07
❑ 71 Jim Thome .30 .10
❑ 72 Rickey Henderson .50 .20
❑ 73 Luis Gonzalez .20 .07
❑ 74 Brad Fullmer .20 .07
❑ 75 Herbert Perry .20 .07
❑ 76 Randy Wolf .20 .07
❑ 77 Miguel Tejada .20 .07
❑ 78 Jimmy Anderson .20 .07
❑ 79 Ramon Martinez .20 .07
❑ 80 Ivan Rodriguez .30 .10
❑ 81 John Flaherty .20 .07
❑ 82 Shannon Stewart .20 .07
❑ 83 Orlando Palmeiro .20 .07
❑ 84 Rafael Furcal .20 .07
❑ 85 Kenny Rogers .20 .07
❑ 86 Terry Adams .20 .07
❑ 87 Mo Vaughn .20 .07
❑ 88 Jose Cruz Jr. .20 .07
❑ 89 Mike Matheny .20 .07
❑ 90 Alfonso Soriano .20 .07
❑ 91 Orlando Cabrera .20 .07
❑ 92 Jeffrey Hammonds .20 .07
❑ 93 Hideo Nomo .50 .20
❑ 94 Carlos Febles .20 .07
❑ 95 Billy Wagner .20 .07
❑ 96 Alex Gonzalez .20 .07
❑ 97 Todd Zeile .20 .07
❑ 98 Omar Vizquel .30 .10
❑ 99 Jose Rijo .20 .07
❑ 100 Ichiro Suzuki 1.00 .40
❑ 101 Steve Cox .20 .07
❑ 102 Hideki Irabu .20 .07
❑ 103 Roy Halladay .20 .07
❑ 104 David Eckstein .20 .07
❑ 105 Greg Maddux .75 .30
❑ 106 Jay Gibbons .20 .07
❑ 107 Travis Driskill .20 .07
❑ 108 Fred McGriff .30 .10
❑ 109 Frank Thomas .50 .20
❑ 110 Shawn Green .20 .07
❑ 111 Ruben Quevedo .20 .07
❑ 112 Jacque Jones .20 .07
❑ 113 Tomo Ohka .20 .07
❑ 114 Joe McEwing .20 .07
❑ 115 Ramiro Mendoza .20 .07
❑ 116 Mark Mulder .20 .07
❑ 117 Mike Lieberthal .20 .07
❑ 118 Jack Wilson .20 .07
❑ 119 Randall Simon .20 .07
❑ 120 Bernie Williams .30 .10
❑ 121 Marvin Benard .20 .07
❑ 122 Jamie Moyer .20 .07
❑ 123 Andy Benes .20 .07
❑ 124 Tino Martinez .30 .10
❑ 125 Esteban Yan .20 .07
❑ 126 Juan Uribe .20 .07
❑ 127 Jason Isringhausen .20 .07
❑ 128 Chris Carpenter .20 .07
❑ 129 Mike Cameron .20 .07
❑ 130 Gary Sheffield .20 .07
❑ 131 Geronimo Gil .20 .07
❑ 132 Brian Daubach .20 .07
❑ 133 Corey Patterson .20 .07
❑ 134 Aaron Rowand .20 .07
❑ 135 Chris Reitsma .20 .07

❑ 136	Bob Wickman	.20	.07
❑ 137	Cesar Izturis	.20	.07
❑ 138	Jason Jennings	.20	.07
❑ 139	Brandon Inge	.20	.07
❑ 140	Larry Walker	.20	.07
❑ 141	Ramon Santiago	.20	.07
❑ 142	Vladimir Nunez	.20	.07
❑ 143	Jose Vizcaino	.20	.07
❑ 144	Mark Quinn	.20	.07
❑ 145	Michael Tucker	.20	.07
❑ 146	Darren Dreifort	.20	.07
❑ 147	Ben Sheets	.20	.07
❑ 148	Corey Koskie	.20	.07
❑ 149	Tony Armas Jr.	.20	.07
❑ 150	Kazuhisa Ishii	.20	.07
❑ 151	Al Leiter	.20	.07
❑ 152	Steve Trachsel	.20	.07
❑ 153	Mike Stanton	.20	.07
❑ 154	David Justice	.20	.07
❑ 155	Marlon Anderson	.20	.07
❑ 156	Jason Kendall	.20	.07
❑ 157	Brian Lawrence	.20	.07
❑ 158	J.T. Snow	.20	.07
❑ 159	Edgar Martinez	.30	.10
❑ 160	Pat Burrell	.20	.07
❑ 161	Kerry Robinson	.20	.07
❑ 162	Greg Vaughn	.20	.07
❑ 163	Carl Everett	.20	.07
❑ 164	Vernon Wells	.20	.07
❑ 165	Jose Mesa	.20	.07
❑ 166	Troy Percival	.20	.07
❑ 167	Erubiel Durazo	.20	.07
❑ 168	Jason Marquis	.20	.07
❑ 169	Jerry Hairston Jr.	.20	.07
❑ 170	Vladimir Guerrero	.50	.20
❑ 171	Byung-Hyun Kim	.20	.07
❑ 172	Marcus Giles	.20	.07
❑ 173	Johnny Damon	.30	.10
❑ 174	Jon Lieber	.20	.07
❑ 175	Terrence Long	.20	.07
❑ 176	Sean Casey	.20	.07
❑ 177	Adam Dunn	.20	.07
❑ 178	Juan Pierre	.20	.07
❑ 179	Wendell Magee	.20	.07
❑ 180	Barry Zito	.20	.07
❑ 181	Aramis Ramirez	.20	.07
❑ 182	Pokey Reese	.20	.07
❑ 183	Jeff Kent	.20	.07
❑ 184	Russ Ortiz	.20	.07
❑ 185	Ruben Sierra	.20	.07
❑ 186	Brent Abernathy	.20	.07
❑ 187	Ismael Valdes	.20	.07
❑ 188	Tom Wilson	.20	.07
❑ 189	Craig Counsell	.20	.07
❑ 190	Mike Mussina	.30	.10
❑ 191	Ramon Hernandez	.20	.07
❑ 192	Adam Kennedy	.20	.07
❑ 193	Tony Womack	.20	.07
❑ 194	Wes Helms	.20	.07
❑ 195	Tony Batista	.20	.07
❑ 196	Rolando Arrojo	.20	.07
❑ 197	Kyle Farnsworth	.20	.07
❑ 198	Gary Bennett	.20	.07
❑ 199	Scott Sullivan	.20	.07
❑ 200	Albert Pujols	1.00	.40
❑ 201	Kirk Rueter	.20	.07
❑ 202	Phil Nevin	.20	.07
❑ 203	Kip Wells	.20	.07
❑ 204	Ron Coomer	.20	.07
❑ 205	Jeromy Burnitz	.20	.07
❑ 206	Kyle Lohse	.20	.07
❑ 207	Mike DeJean	.20	.07
❑ 208	Paul Lo Duca	.20	.07
❑ 209	Carlos Beltran	.20	.07
❑ 210	Roy Oswalt	.20	.07
❑ 211	Mike Lowell	.20	.07
❑ 212	Robert Fick	.20	.07
❑ 213	Todd Jones	.20	.07
❑ 214	C.C. Sabathia	.20	.07
❑ 215	Danny Graves	.20	.07
❑ 216	Todd Hundley	.20	.07
❑ 217	Tim Wakefield	.20	.07
❑ 218	Derek Lowe	.20	.07
❑ 219	Kevin Millwood	.20	.07
❑ 220	Jorge Posada	.30	.10
❑ 221	Bobby J. Jones	.20	.07
❑ 222	Carlos Guillen	.20	.07
❑ 223	Fernando Vina	.20	.07
❑ 224	Ryan Rupe	.20	.07
❑ 225	Kelvim Escobar	.20	.07
❑ 226	Ramon Ortiz	.20	.07
❑ 227	Junior Spivey	.20	.07
❑ 228	Juan Cruz	.20	.07
❑ 229	Melvin Mora	.20	.07
❑ 230	Lance Berkman	.20	.07
❑ 231	Brent Butler	.20	.07
❑ 232	Shane Halter	.20	.07
❑ 233	Derrek Lee	.30	.10
❑ 234	Matt Lawton	.20	.07
❑ 235	Chuck Knoblauch	.20	.07
❑ 236	Eric Gagne	.20	.07
❑ 237	Alex Sanchez	.20	.07
❑ 238	Denny Hocking	.20	.07
❑ 239	Eric Milton	.20	.07
❑ 240	Rey Ordonez	.20	.07
❑ 241	Orlando Hernandez	.20	.07
❑ 242	Robert Person	.20	.07
❑ 243	Sean Burroughs	.20	.07
❑ 244	Jeff Cirillo	.20	.07
❑ 245	Mike Lamb	.20	.07
❑ 246	Jose Valentin	.20	.07
❑ 247	Ellis Burks	.20	.07
❑ 248	Shawn Chacon	.20	.07
❑ 249	Josh Beckett	.20	.07
❑ 250	Nomar Garciaparra	.75	.30
❑ 251	Craig Biggio	.30	.10
❑ 252	Joe Randa	.20	.07
❑ 253	Mark Grudzielanek	.20	.07
❑ 254	Glendon Rusch	.20	.07
❑ 255	Michael Barrett	.20	.07
❑ 256	Omar Daal	.20	.07
❑ 257	Elmer Dessens	.20	.07
❑ 258	Wade Miller	.20	.07
❑ 259	Adrian Beltre	.20	.07
❑ 260	Vicente Padilla	.20	.07
❑ 261	Kazuhiro Sasaki	.20	.07
❑ 262	Mike Scioscia MG	.20	.07
❑ 263	Bobby Cox MG	.20	.07
❑ 264	Mike Hargrove MG	.20	.07
❑ 265	Grady Little MG RC	.20	.07
❑ 266	Alex Gonzalez	.20	.07
❑ 267	Jerry Manuel MG	.20	.07
❑ 268	Bob Boone MG	.20	.07
❑ 269	Joel Skinner MG	.20	.07
❑ 270	Clint Hurdle MG	.20	.07
❑ 271	Miguel Batista	.20	.07
❑ 272	Bob Brenly MG	.20	.07
❑ 273	Jeff Torborg MG	.20	.07
❑ 274	Jimy Williams MG	.20	.07
❑ 275	Tony Pena MG	.20	.07
❑ 276	Jim Tracy MG	.20	.07
❑ 277	Jerry Royster MG	.20	.07
❑ 278	Ron Gardenhire MG	.20	.07
❑ 279	Frank Robinson MG	.30	.10
❑ 280	John Halama	.20	.07
❑ 281	Joe Torre MG	.30	.10
❑ 282	Art Howe MG	.20	.07
❑ 283	Larry Bowa MG	.20	.07
❑ 284	Lloyd McClendon MG	.20	.07
❑ 285	Bruce Bochy MG	.20	.07
❑ 286	Dusty Baker MG	.20	.07
❑ 287	Lou Piniella MG	.20	.07
❑ 288	Tony LaRussa MG	.20	.07
❑ 289	Todd Walker	.20	.07
❑ 290	Jerry Narron MG	.20	.07
❑ 291	Carlos Tosca MG	.20	.07
❑ 292	Chris Duncan FY RC	4.00	1.50
❑ 293	Franklin Gutierrez FY RC	1.00	.40
❑ 294	Adam LaRoche FY	.50	.20
❑ 295	Manuel Ramirez FY RC	.50	.20
❑ 296	Il Kim FY RC	.50	.20
❑ 297	Wayne Lydon FY RC	.50	.20
❑ 298	Daryl Clark FY RC	.50	.20
❑ 299	Sean Pierce FY	.50	.20
❑ 300	Andy Marte FY RC	3.00	1.25
❑ 301	Matthew Peterson FY RC	.50	.20
❑ 302	Gonzalo Lopez FY RC	.50	.20
❑ 303	Bernie Castro FY RC	.50	.20
❑ 304	Cliff Lee FY	.50	.20
❑ 305	Jason Perry FY RC	.50	.20
❑ 306	Jaime Bubela FY RC	.50	.20
❑ 307	Alexis Rios FY	1.00	.40
❑ 308	Brendan Harris FY RC	.50	.20
❑ 309	Ramon Nivar-Martinez FY RC	.50	.20
❑ 310	Terry Tiffee FY RC	.50	.20
❑ 311	Kevin Youkilis FY RC	1.25	.50
❑ 312	Ruddy Lugo FY RC	.50	.20
❑ 313	C.J. Wilson FY	.50	.20
❑ 314	Mike McNutt FY RC	.50	.20
❑ 315	Jeff Clark FY RC	.50	.20
❑ 316	Mark Malaska FY RC	.50	.20
❑ 317	Doug Waechter FY RC	.50	.20
❑ 318	Derell McCall FY RC	.50	.20
❑ 319	Scott Tyler FY RC	.50	.20
❑ 320	Craig Brazell FY RC	.50	.20
❑ 321	Walter Young FY	.50	.20
❑ 322	M.Byrd/J.Padilla FS	.50	.20
❑ 323	C.Snelling/S.Choo FS	.50	.20
❑ 324	H.Blalock/M.Teixeira FS	.50	.20
❑ 325	J.Hamilton/C.Crawford FS	.50	.20
❑ 326	O.Hudson/J.Phelps FS	.50	.20
❑ 327	J.Cust/R.Reyes FS	.50	.20
❑ 328	A.Berroa/A.Gomez FS	.50	.20
❑ 329	M.Cuddyer/M.Restovich FS	.50	.20
❑ 330	J.Rivera/M.Thames FS	.50	.20
❑ 331	B.Puffer/J.Bong FS	.50	.20
❑ 332	Mike Cameron SH	.20	.07
❑ 333	Shawn Green SH	.20	.07
❑ 334	Oakland A's SH	.20	.07
❑ 335	Jason Giambi SH	.20	.07
❑ 336	Derek Lowe SH	.20	.07
❑ 337	AL Batting Average LL	.30	.10
❑ 338	AL Runs Scored LL	.20	.07
❑ 339	AL Home Runs LL	.30	.10
❑ 340	AL RBI's LL	.50	.20
❑ 341	AL ERA LL	.20	.07
❑ 342	AL Strikeouts LL	.30	.10
❑ 343	NL Batting Average LL	.50	.20
❑ 344	NL Runs Scored LL	.50	.20
❑ 345	NL Home Runs LL	.50	.20
❑ 346	NL RBI's LL	.20	.07
❑ 347	NL ERA LL	.30	.10
❑ 348	NL Strikeouts LL	.30	.10
❑ 349	AL Division Angels	.20	.07
❑ 350	AL/NL Division Twins/Cards	.30	.10
❑ 351	AL/NL Division Angels/Giants	.30	.10
❑ 352	NL Division Cardinals	.30	.10
❑ 353	Adam Kennedy ALCS	.20	.07
❑ 354	J.T. Snow WS	.30	.10
❑ 355	David Bell NLCS	.30	.10
❑ 356	Jason Giambi AS	.20	.07
❑ 357	Alfonso Soriano AS	.20	.07
❑ 358	Alex Rodriguez AS	.50	.20
❑ 359	Eric Chavez AS	.20	.07
❑ 360	Torii Hunter AS	.20	.07
❑ 361	Bernie Williams AS	.20	.07
❑ 362	Garret Anderson AS	.20	.07
❑ 363	Jorge Posada AS	.20	.07
❑ 364	Derek Lowe AS	.20	.07
❑ 365	Barry Zito AS	.20	.07
❑ 366	Manny Ramirez AS	.30	.10
❑ 367	Mike Scioscia AS	.20	.07
❑ 368	Francisco Rodriguez	.20	.07
❑ 369	Chris Hammond	.20	.07
❑ 370	Chipper Jones	.50	.20
❑ 371	Chris Singleton	.20	.07
❑ 372	Cliff Floyd	.20	.07
❑ 373	Bobby Hill	.20	.07
❑ 374	Antonio Osuna	.20	.07
❑ 375	Barry Larkin	.30	.10
❑ 376	Charles Nagy	.20	.07
❑ 377	Denny Stark	.20	.07
❑ 378	Dean Palmer	.20	.07
❑ 379	Eric Owens	.20	.07
❑ 380	Randy Johnson	.50	.20
❑ 381	Jeff Suppan	.20	.07
❑ 382	Eric Karros	.20	.07
❑ 383	Luis Vizcaino	.20	.07
❑ 384	Johan Santana	.75	.30
❑ 385	Javier Vazquez	.20	.07
❑ 386	John Thomson	.20	.07
❑ 387	Nick Johnson	.20	.07
❑ 388	Mark Ellis	.20	.07
❑ 389	Doug Glanville	.20	.07
❑ 390	Ken Griffey Jr.	.75	.30
❑ 391	Bubba Trammell	.20	.07
❑ 392	Livan Hernandez	.20	.07
❑ 393	Desi Relaford	.20	.07

❑	394	Eli Marrero	.20	.07
❑	395	Jared Sandberg	.20	.07
❑	396	Barry Bonds	1.25	.50
❑	397	Esteban Loaiza	.20	.07
❑	398	Aaron Sele	.20	.07
❑	399	Geoff Blum	.20	.07
❑	400	Derek Jeter	1.25	.50
❑	401	Eric Byrnes	.20	.07
❑	402	Mike Timlin	.20	.07
❑	403	Mark Kotsay	.20	.07
❑	404	Rich Aurilia	.20	.07
❑	405	Joel Pineiro	.20	.07
❑	406	Chuck Finley	.20	.07
❑	407	Bengie Molina	.20	.07
❑	408	Steve Finley	.20	.07
❑	409	Julio Franco	.20	.07
❑	410	Marty Cordova	.20	.07
❑	411	Shea Hillenbrand	.20	.07
❑	412	Mark Bellhorn	.20	.07
❑	413	Jon Garland	.20	.07
❑	414	Reggie Taylor	.20	.07
❑	415	Milton Bradley	.20	.07
❑	416	Carlos Pena	.20	.07
❑	417	Andy Fox	.20	.07
❑	418	Brad Ausmus	.20	.07
❑	419	Brent Mayne	.20	.07
❑	420	Paul Quantrill	.20	.07
❑	421	Carlos Delgado	.20	.07
❑	422	Kevin Mench	.20	.07
❑	423	Joe Kennedy	.20	.07
❑	424	Mike Crudale	.20	.07
❑	425	Mark McLemore	.20	.07
❑	426	Bill Mueller	.20	.07
❑	427	Rob Mackowiak	.20	.07
❑	428	Ricky Ledee	.20	.07
❑	429	Ted Lilly	.20	.07
❑	430	Sterling Hitchcock	.20	.07
❑	431	Scott Strickland	.20	.07
❑	432	Damion Easley	.20	.07
❑	433	Torii Hunter	.20	.07
❑	434	Brad Radke	.20	.07
❑	435	Geoff Jenkins	.20	.07
❑	436	Paul Byrd	.20	.07
❑	437	Morgan Ensberg	.20	.07
❑	438	Mike Maroth	.20	.07
❑	439	Mike Hampton	.20	.07
❑	440	Adam Hyzdu	.20	.07
❑	441	Vance Wilson	.20	.07
❑	442	Todd Ritchie	.20	.07
❑	443	Tom Gordon	.20	.07
❑	444	John Burkett	.20	.07
❑	445	Rodrigo Lopez	.20	.07
❑	446	Tim Spooneybarger	.20	.07
❑	447	Quinton Mccracken	.20	.07
❑	448	Tim Salmon	.30	.10
❑	449	Jarrod Washburn	.20	.07
❑	450	Pedro Martinez	.30	.10
❑	451	Dustan Mohr	.20	.07
❑	452	Julio Lugo	.20	.07
❑	453	Scott Stewart	.20	.07
❑	454	Armando Benitez	.20	.07
❑	455	Raul Mondesi	.20	.07
❑	456	Robin Ventura	.20	.07
❑	457	Bobby Abreu	.20	.07
❑	458	Josh Fogg	.20	.07
❑	459	Ryan Klesko	.20	.07
❑	460	Tsuyoshi Shinjo	.20	.07
❑	461	Jim Edmonds	.20	.07
❑	462	Cliff Politte	.20	.07
❑	463	Chan Ho Park	.20	.07
❑	464	John Mabry	.20	.07
❑	465	Woody Williams	.20	.07
❑	466	Jason Michaels	.20	.07
❑	467	Scott Schoeneweis	.20	.07
❑	468	Brian Anderson	.20	.07
❑	469	Brett Tomko	.20	.07
❑	470	Scott Erickson	.20	.07
❑	471	Kevin Millar Sox	.20	.07
❑	472	Danny Wright	.20	.07
❑	473	Jason Schmidt	.20	.07
❑	474	Scott Williamson	.20	.07
❑	475	Einar Diaz	.20	.07
❑	476	Jay Payton	.20	.07
❑	477	Juan Acevedo	.20	.07
❑	478	Ben Grieve	.20	.07
❑	479	Raul Ibanez	.20	.07
❑	480	Richie Sexson	.20	.07
❑	481	Rick Reed	.20	.07
❑	482	Pedro Astacio	.20	.07
❑	483	Adam Piatt	.20	.07
❑	484	Bud Smith	.20	.07
❑	485	Tomas Perez	.20	.07
❑	486	Adam Eaton	.20	.07
❑	487	Rafael Palmeiro	.30	.10
❑	488	Jason Tyner	.20	.07
❑	489	Scott Rolen	.30	.10
❑	490	Randy Winn	.20	.07
❑	491	Ryan Jensen	.20	.07
❑	492	Trevor Hoffman	.20	.07
❑	493	Craig Wilson	.20	.07
❑	494	Jeremy Giambi	.20	.07
❑	495	Daryle Ward	.20	.07
❑	496	Shane Spencer	.20	.07
❑	497	Andy Pettitte	.30	.10
❑	498	John Franco	.20	.07
❑	499	Felipe Lopez	.20	.07
❑	500	Mike Piazza	.75	.30
❑	501	Cristian Guzman	.20	.07
❑	502	Jose Hernandez	.20	.07
❑	503	Octavio Dotel	.20	.07
❑	504	Brad Penny	.20	.07
❑	505	Dave Veres	.20	.07
❑	506	Ryan Dempster	.20	.07
❑	507	Joe Crede	.20	.07
❑	508	Chad Hermansen	.20	.07
❑	509	Gary Matthews Jr.	.20	.07
❑	510	Matt Franco	.20	.07
❑	511	Ben Weber	.20	.07
❑	512	Dave Berg	.20	.07
❑	513	Michael Young	.30	.10
❑	514	Frank Catalanotto	.20	.07
❑	515	Darin Erstad	.20	.07
❑	516	Matt Williams	.20	.07
❑	517	B.J. Surhoff	.20	.07
❑	518	Kerry Ligtenberg	.20	.07
❑	519	Mike Bordick	.20	.07
❑	520	Arthur Rhodes	.20	.07
❑	521	Joe Girardi	.20	.07
❑	522	D'Angelo Jimenez	.20	.07
❑	523	Paul Konerko	.20	.07
❑	524	Jose Macias	.20	.07
❑	525	Joe Mays	.20	.07
❑	526	Marquis Grissom	.20	.07
❑	527	Neifi Perez	.20	.07
❑	528	Preston Wilson	.20	.07
❑	529	Jeff Weaver	.20	.07
❑	530	Eric Chavez	.20	.07
❑	531	Placido Polanco	.20	.07
❑	532	Matt Mantei	.20	.07
❑	533	James Baldwin	.20	.07
❑	534	Toby Hall	.20	.07
❑	535	Brendan Donnelly	.20	.07
❑	536	Benji Gil	.20	.07
❑	537	Damian Moss	.20	.07
❑	538	Jorge Julio	.20	.07
❑	539	Matt Clement	.20	.07
❑	540	Brian Moehler	.20	.07
❑	541	Lee Stevens	.20	.07
❑	542	Jimmy Haynes	.20	.07
❑	543	Terry Mulholland	.20	.07
❑	544	Dave Roberts	.20	.07
❑	545	J.C. Romero	.20	.07
❑	546	Bartolo Colon	.20	.07
❑	547	Roger Cedeno	.20	.07
❑	548	Mariano Rivera	.50	.20
❑	549	Billy Koch	.20	.07
❑	550	Manny Ramirez	.30	.10
❑	551	Travis Lee	.20	.07
❑	552	Oliver Perez	.20	.07
❑	553	Tim Worrell	.20	.07
❑	554	Rafael Soriano	.20	.07
❑	555	Damian Miller	.20	.07
❑	556	John Smoltz	.30	.10
❑	557	Willis Roberts	.20	.07
❑	558	Tim Hudson	.20	.07
❑	559	Moises Alou	.20	.07
❑	560	Gary Glover	.20	.07
❑	561	Corky Miller	.20	.07
❑	562	Ben Broussard	.20	.07
❑	563	Gabe Kapler	.20	.07
❑	564	Chris Woodward	.20	.07
❑	565	Paul Wilson	.20	.07
❑	566	Todd Hollandsworth	.20	.07
❑	567	So Taguchi	.20	.07
❑	568	John Olerud	.20	.07
❑	569	Reggie Sanders	.20	.07
❑	570	Jake Peavy	.20	.07
❑	571	Kris Benson	.20	.07
❑	572	Todd Pratt	.20	.07
❑	573	Ray Durham	.20	.07
❑	574	Boomer Wells	.20	.07
❑	575	Chris Widger	.20	.07
❑	576	Shawn Wooten	.20	.07
❑	577	Tom Glavine	.30	.10
❑	578	Antonio Alfonseca	.20	.07
❑	579	Keith Foulke	.20	.07
❑	580	Shawn Estes	.20	.07
❑	581	Mark Grace	.30	.10
❑	582	Dmitri Young	.20	.07
❑	583	A.J. Burnett	.20	.07
❑	584	Richard Hidalgo	.20	.07
❑	585	Mike Sweeney	.20	.07
❑	586	Alex Cora	.20	.07
❑	587	Matt Stairs	.20	.07
❑	588	Doug Mientkiewicz	.20	.07
❑	589	Fernando Tatis	.20	.07
❑	590	David Weathers	.20	.07
❑	591	Cory Lidle	.20	.07
❑	592	Dan Plesac	.20	.07
❑	593	Jeff Bagwell	.30	.10
❑	594	Steve Sparks	.20	.07
❑	595	Sandy Alomar Jr.	.20	.07
❑	596	John Lackey	.20	.07
❑	597	Rick Helling	.20	.07
❑	598	Mark DeRosa	.20	.07
❑	599	Carlos Lee	.20	.07
❑	600	Garret Anderson	.20	.07
❑	601	Vinny Castilla	.20	.07
❑	602	Ryan Drese	.20	.07
❑	603	LaTroy Hawkins	.20	.07
❑	604	David Bell	.20	.07
❑	605	Freddy Garcia	.20	.07
❑	606	Miguel Cairo	.20	.07
❑	607	Scott Spiezio	.20	.07
❑	608	Mike Remlinger	.20	.07
❑	609	Tony Graffanino	.20	.07
❑	610	Russell Branyan	.20	.07
❑	611	Chris Magruder	.20	.07
❑	612	Jose Contreras RC	1.00	.40
❑	613	Carl Pavano	.20	.07
❑	614	Kevin Brown	.20	.07
❑	615	Tyler Houston	.20	.07
❑	616	A.J. Pierzynski	.20	.07
❑	617	Tony Fiore	.20	.07
❑	618	Peter Bergeron	.20	.07
❑	619	Rondell White	.20	.07
❑	620	Brett Myers	.20	.07
❑	621	Kevin Young	.20	.07
❑	622	Kenny Lofton	.20	.07
❑	623	Ben Davis	.20	.07
❑	624	J.D. Drew	.20	.07
❑	625	Chris Gomez	.20	.07
❑	626	Karim Garcia	.20	.07
❑	627	Ricky Gutierrez	.20	.07
❑	628	Mark Redman	.20	.07
❑	629	Juan Encarnacion	.20	.07
❑	630	Anaheim Angels TC	.30	.10
❑	631	Arizona Diamondbacks TC	.20	.07
❑	632	Atlanta Braves TC	.20	.07
❑	633	Baltimore Orioles TC	.20	.07
❑	634	Boston Red Sox TC	.20	.07
❑	635	Chicago Cubs TC	.20	.07
❑	636	Chicago White Sox TC	.20	.07
❑	637	Cincinnati Reds TC	.20	.07
❑	638	Cleveland Indians TC	.20	.07
❑	639	Colorado Rockies TC	.20	.07
❑	640	Detroit Tigers TC	.20	.07
❑	641	Florida Marlins TC	.20	.07
❑	642	Houston Astros TC	.20	.07
❑	643	Kansas City Royals TC	.20	.07
❑	644	Los Angeles Dodgers TC	.20	.07
❑	645	Milwaukee Brewers TC	.20	.07
❑	646	Minnesota Twins TC	.20	.07
❑	647	Montreal Expos TC	.20	.07
❑	648	New York Mets TC	.20	.07
❑	649	New York Yankees TC	.30	.10
❑	650	Oakland Athletics TC	.20	.07
❑	651	Philadelphia Phillies TC	.20	.07

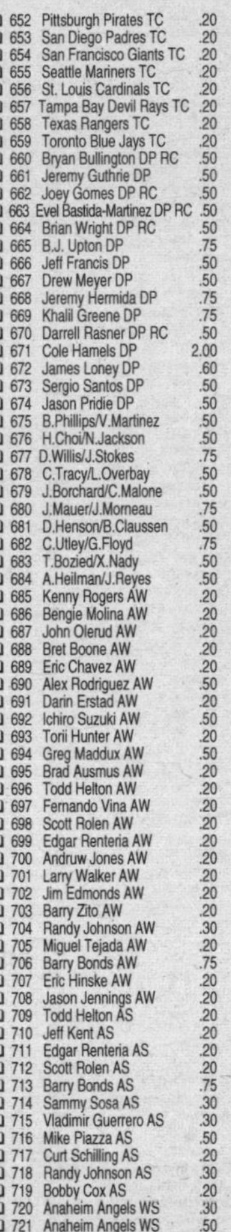

❑ 652	Pittsburgh Pirates TC	.20	.07
❑ 653	San Diego Padres TC	.20	.07
❑ 654	San Francisco Giants TC	.20	.07
❑ 655	Seattle Mariners TC	.20	.07
❑ 656	St. Louis Cardinals TC	.20	.07
❑ 657	Tampa Bay Devil Rays TC	.20	.07
❑ 658	Texas Rangers TC	.20	.07
❑ 659	Toronto Blue Jays TC	.20	.07
❑ 660	Bryan Bullington DP RC	.50	.20
❑ 661	Jeremy Guthrie DP	.50	.20
❑ 662	Joey Gomes DP RC	.50	.20
❑ 663	Evel Bastida-Martinez DP RC	.50	.20
❑ 664	Brian Wright DP RC	.50	.20
❑ 665	B.J. Upton DP	.75	.30
❑ 666	Jeff Francis DP	.50	.20
❑ 667	Drew Meyer DP	.50	.20
❑ 668	Jeremy Hermida DP	.75	.30
❑ 669	Khalil Greene DP	.75	.30
❑ 670	Darrell Rasner DP RC	.50	.20
❑ 671	Cole Hamels DP	2.00	.75
❑ 672	James Loney DP	.60	.25
❑ 673	Sergio Santos DP	.50	.20
❑ 674	Jason Pridie DP	.50	.20
❑ 675	B.Phillips/V.Martinez	.50	.20
❑ 676	H.Choi/N.Jackson	.50	.20
❑ 677	D.Willis/J.Stokes	.75	.30
❑ 678	C.Tracy/L.Overbay	.50	.20
❑ 679	J.Borchard/C.Malone	.50	.20
❑ 680	J.Mauer/J.Morneau	.75	.30
❑ 681	D.Henson/B.Claussen	.50	.20
❑ 682	C.Utley/G.Floyd	.75	.30
❑ 683	T.Bozied/X.Nady	.50	.20
❑ 684	A.Heilman/J.Reyes	.50	.20
❑ 685	Kenny Rogers AW	.20	.07
❑ 686	Bengie Molina AW	.20	.07
❑ 687	John Olerud AW	.20	.07
❑ 688	Bret Boone AW	.20	.07
❑ 689	Eric Chavez AW	.20	.07
❑ 690	Alex Rodriguez AW	.50	.20
❑ 691	Darin Erstad AW	.20	.07
❑ 692	Ichiro Suzuki AW	.50	.20
❑ 693	Torii Hunter AW	.20	.07
❑ 694	Greg Maddux AW	.50	.20
❑ 695	Brad Ausmus AW	.20	.07
❑ 696	Todd Helton AW	.20	.07
❑ 697	Fernando Vina AW	.20	.07
❑ 698	Scott Rolen AW	.20	.07
❑ 699	Edgar Renteria AW	.20	.07
❑ 700	Andruw Jones AW	.20	.07
❑ 701	Larry Walker AW	.20	.07
❑ 702	Jim Edmonds AW	.20	.07
❑ 703	Barry Zito AW	.20	.07
❑ 704	Randy Johnson AW	.30	.10
❑ 705	Miguel Tejada AW	.20	.07
❑ 706	Barry Bonds AW	.75	.30
❑ 707	Eric Hinske AW	.20	.07
❑ 708	Jason Jennings AW	.20	.07
❑ 709	Todd Helton AS	.20	.07
❑ 710	Jeff Kent AS	.20	.07
❑ 711	Edgar Renteria AS	.20	.07
❑ 712	Scott Rolen AS	.20	.07
❑ 713	Barry Bonds AS	.75	.30
❑ 714	Sammy Sosa AS	.30	.10
❑ 715	Vladimir Guerrero AS	.30	.10
❑ 716	Mike Piazza AS	.50	.20
❑ 717	Curt Schilling AS	.20	.07
❑ 718	Randy Johnson AS	.30	.10
❑ 719	Bobby Cox AS	.20	.07
❑ 720	Anaheim Angels WS	.30	.10
❑ 721	Anaheim Angels WS	.50	.20

2003 Topps Traded

❑	COMPLETE SET (275)	50.00	20.00
❑	COMMON CARD (T1-T120)	.20	.07
❑	COMMON CARD (121-165)	.40	.15
❑ T1	Juan Pierre	.20	.07
❑ T2	Mark Grudzielanek	.20	.07
❑ T3	Tanyon Sturtze	.20	.07
❑ T4	Greg Vaughn	.20	.07
❑ T5	Greg Myers	.20	.07
❑ T6	Randall Simon	.20	.07
❑ T7	Todd Hundley	.20	.07
❑ T8	Marlon Anderson	.20	.07
❑ T9	Jeff Reboulet	.20	.07
❑ T10	Alex Sanchez	.20	.07
❑ T11	Mike Rivera	.20	.07

❑ T12	Todd Walker	.20	.07
❑ T13	Ray King	.20	.07
❑ T14	Shawn Estes	.20	.07
❑ T15	Gary Matthews Jr.	.20	.07
❑ T16	Jaret Wright	.20	.07
❑ T17	Edgardo Alfonzo	.20	.07
❑ T18	Omar Daal	.20	.07
❑ T19	Ryan Rupe	.20	.07
❑ T20	Tony Clark	.20	.07
❑ T21	Jeff Suppan	.20	.07
❑ T22	Mike Stanton	.20	.07
❑ T23	Ramon Martinez	.20	.07
❑ T24	Armando Rios	.20	.07
❑ T25	Johnny Estrada	.20	.07
❑ T26	Joe Girardi	.20	.07
❑ T27	Ivan Rodriguez	.30	.10
❑ T28	Robert Fick	.20	.07
❑ T29	Rick White	.20	.07
❑ T30	Robert Person	.20	.07
❑ T31	Alan Benes	.20	.07
❑ T32	Chris Carpenter	.20	.07
❑ T33	Chris Widger	.20	.07
❑ T34	Travis Hafner	.20	.07
❑ T35	Mike Venafro	.20	.07
❑ T36	Jon Lieber	.20	.07
❑ T37	Orlando Hernandez	.20	.07
❑ T38	Aaron Myette	.20	.07
❑ T39	Paul Bako	.20	.07
❑ T40	Erubiel Durazo	.20	.07
❑ T41	Mark Guthrie	.20	.07
❑ T42	Steve Avery	.20	.07
❑ T43	Damian Jackson	.20	.07
❑ T44	Rey Ordonez	.20	.07
❑ T45	John Flaherty	.20	.07
❑ T46	Byung-Hyun Kim	.20	.07
❑ T47	Tom Goodwin	.20	.07
❑ T48	Elmer Dessens	.20	.07
❑ T49	Al Martin	.20	.07
❑ T50	Gene Kingsale	.20	.07
❑ T51	Lenny Harris	.20	.07
❑ T52	David Ortiz Sox	.50	.20
❑ T53	Jose Lima	.20	.07
❑ T54	Mike Difelice	.20	.07
❑ T55	Jose Hernandez	.20	.07
❑ T56	Todd Zeile	.20	.07
❑ T57	Roberto Hernandez	.20	.07
❑ T58	Albie Lopez	.20	.07
❑ T59	Roberto Alomar	.30	.10
❑ T60	Russ Ortiz	.20	.07
❑ T61	Brian Daubach	.20	.07
❑ T62	Carl Everett	.20	.07
❑ T63	Jeromy Burnitz	.20	.07
❑ T64	Mark Bellhorn	.20	.07
❑ T65	Ruben Sierra	.20	.07
❑ T66	Mike Fetters	.20	.07
❑ T67	Armando Benitez	.20	.07
❑ T68	Deivi Cruz	.20	.07
❑ T69	Jose Cruz Jr.	.20	.07
❑ T70	Jeremy Fikac	.20	.07
❑ T71	Jeff Kent	.20	.07
❑ T72	Andres Galarraga	.20	.07
❑ T73	Rickey Henderson	.50	.20
❑ T74	Royce Clayton	.20	.07
❑ T75	Troy O'Leary	.20	.07
❑ T76	Ron Coomer	.20	.07
❑ T77	Greg Colbrunn	.20	.07
❑ T78	Wes Helms	.20	.07
❑ T79	Kevin Millwood	.20	.07
❑ T80	Damion Easley	.20	.07
❑ T81	Bobby Kielty	.20	.07
❑ T82	Keith Osik	.20	.07
❑ T83	Ramiro Mendoza	.20	.07
❑ T84	Shea Hillenbrand	.20	.07
❑ T85	Shannon Stewart	.20	.07
❑ T86	Eddie Perez	.20	.07
❑ T87	Ugueth Urbina	.20	.07
❑ T88	Orlando Palmeiro	.20	.07
❑ T89	Graeme Lloyd	.20	.07
❑ T90	John Vander Wal	.20	.07
❑ T91	Gary Bennett	.20	.07
❑ T92	Shane Reynolds	.20	.07
❑ T93	Steve Parris	.20	.07
❑ T94	Julio Lugo	.20	.07
❑ T95	John Halama	.20	.07
❑ T96	Carlos Baerga	.20	.07
❑ T97	Jim Parque	.20	.07
❑ T98	Mike Williams	.20	.07
❑ T99	Fred McGriff	.30	.10
❑ T100	Kenny Rogers	.20	.07
❑ T101	Matt Herges	.20	.07
❑ T102	Jay Bell	.20	.07
❑ T103	Esteban Yan	.20	.07
❑ T104	Eric Owens	.20	.07
❑ T105	Aaron Fultz	.20	.07
❑ T106	Rey Sanchez	.20	.07
❑ T107	Jim Thome	.30	.10
❑ T108	Aaron Boone	.20	.07
❑ T109	Raul Mondesi	.20	.07
❑ T110	Kenny Lofton	.20	.07
❑ T111	Jose Guillen	.20	.07
❑ T112	Aramis Ramirez	.20	.07
❑ T113	Sidney Ponson	.20	.07
❑ T114	Scott Williamson	.20	.07
❑ T115	Robin Ventura	.20	.07
❑ T116	Dusty Baker MG	.20	.07
❑ T117	Felipe Alou MG	.20	.07
❑ T118	Buck Showalter MG	.20	.07
❑ T119	Jack McKeon MG	.20	.07
❑ T120	Art Howe MG	.20	.07
❑ T121	Bobby Crosby PROS	.40	.15
❑ T122	Adrian Gonzalez PROS	.40	.15
❑ T123	Kevin Cash PROS	.40	.15
❑ T124	Shin-Soo Choo PROS	.40	.15
❑ T125	Chin-Feng Chen PROS	1.00	.40
❑ T126	Miguel Cabrera PROS	1.00	.40
❑ T127	Jason Young PROS	.40	.15
❑ T128	Alex Herrera PROS	.40	.15
❑ T129	Jason Dubois PROS	.40	.15
❑ T130	Jeff Mathis PROS	.40	.15
❑ T131	Casey Kotchman PROS	.40	.15
❑ T132	Ed Rogers PROS	.40	.15
❑ T133	Wilson Betemit PROS	.40	.15
❑ T134	Jim Kavourias PROS	.40	.15
❑ T135	Taylor Buchholz PROS	.40	.15
❑ T136	Adam LaRoche PROS	.40	.15
❑ T137	Dallas McPherson PROS	.40	.15
❑ T138	Jesus Cota PROS	.40	.15
❑ T139	Clint Nageotte PROS	.40	.15
❑ T140	Boof Bonser PROS	.40	.15
❑ T141	Walter Young PROS	.40	.15
❑ T142	Joe Crede PROS	.40	.15
❑ T143	Denny Bautista PROS	.40	.15
❑ T144	Victor Diaz PROS	.40	.15
❑ T145	Chris Narveson PROS	.40	.15
❑ T146	Gabe Gross PROS	.40	.15
❑ T147	Jimmy Journell PROS	.40	.15
❑ T148	Rafael Soriano PROS	.40	.15
❑ T149	Jerome Williams PROS	.40	.15
❑ T150	Aaron Cook PROS	.40	.15
❑ T151	Anastacio Martinez PROS	.40	.15
❑ T152	Scott Hairston PROS	.40	.15
❑ T153	John Buck PROS	.40	.15
❑ T154	Ryan Ludwick PROS	.40	.15
❑ T155	Chris Bootcheck PROS	.40	.15
❑ T156	John Rheinecker PROS	.40	.15
❑ T157	Jason Lane PROS	.40	.15
❑ T158	Shelley Duncan PROS	.40	.15
❑ T159	Adam Wainwright PROS	.40	.15
❑ T160	Jason Arnold PROS	.40	.15
❑ T161	Jonny Gomes PROS	.60	.25
❑ T162	James Loney PROS	.50	.20
❑ T163	Mike Fontenot PROS	.40	.15
❑ T164	Khalil Greene PROS	1.00	.40
❑ T165	Sean Burnett PROS	.40	.15

❑ T166 David Martinez FY RC .40 .15
❑ T167 Felix Pie FY RC 4.00 1.50
❑ T168 Joe Valentine FY RC .40 .15
❑ T169 Brandon Webb FY RC 2.50 1.00
❑ T170 Matt Diaz FY RC .75 .30
❑ T171 Lew Ford FY RC .50 .20
❑ T172 Jeremy Griffiths FY RC .40 .15
❑ T173 Matt Hensley FY RC .40 .15
❑ T174 Charlie Manning FY RC .40 .15
❑ T175 Elizardo Ramirez FY RC .50 .20
❑ T176 Greg Aquino FY RC .40 .15
❑ T177 Felix Sanchez FY RC .40 .15
❑ T178 Kelly Shoppach FY RC .75 .30
❑ T179 Bubba Nelson FY RC .50 .20
❑ T180 Mike Oâ ™Keefe FY RC .40 .15
❑ T181 Hanley Ramirez FY RC 4.00 1.50
❑ T182 Todd Wellemeyer FY RC .40 .15
❑ T183 Dustin Moseley FY RC .40 .15
❑ T184 Eric Crozier FY RC .50 .20
❑ T185 Ryan Shealy FY RC 2.50 1.00
❑ T186 Jeremy Bonderman FY RC 3.00 1.25
❑ T187 T.Story-Harden FY RC .40 .15
❑ T188 Dusty Brown FY RC .40 .15
❑ T189 Rob Hammock FY RC .40 .15
❑ T190 Jorge Piedra FY RC .50 .20
❑ T191 Chris De La Cruz FY RC .40 .15
❑ T192 Eli Whiteside FY RC .40 .15
❑ T193 Jason Kubel FY RC 1.00 .40
❑ T194 Jon Schuerholz FY RC .40 .15
❑ T195 Stephen Randolph FY RC .40 .15
❑ T196 Andy Sisco FY RC .40 .15
❑ T197 Sean Smith FY RC .50 .20
❑ T198 Jon-Mark Sprowl FY RC .40 .15
❑ T199 Matt Kata FY RC .40 .15
❑ T200 Robinson Cano FY RC 8.00 3.00
❑ T201 Nook Logan FY RC .50 .20
❑ T202 Ben Francisco FY RC .40 .15
❑ T203 Arnie Munoz FY RC .40 .15
❑ T204 Ozzie Chavez FY RC .40 .15
❑ T205 Eric Riggs FY RC .50 .20
❑ T206 Beau Kemp FY RC .40 .15
❑ T207 Travis Wong FY RC .50 .20
❑ T208 Dustin Yount FY RC .50 .20
❑ T209 Brian McCann FY RC 4.00 1.50
❑ T210 Wilton Reynolds FY RC .50 .20
❑ T211 Matt Bruback FY RC .40 .15
❑ T212 Andrew Brown FY RC .50 .20
❑ T213 Edgar Gonzalez FY RC .40 .15
❑ T214 Eider Torres FY RC .40 .15
❑ T215 Aquilino Lopez FY RC .40 .15
❑ T216 Bobby Basham FY RC .40 .15
❑ T217 Tim Olson FY RC .40 .15
❑ T218 Nathan Panther FY RC .40 .15
❑ T219 Bryan Grace FY RC .40 .15
❑ T220 Dusty Gomon FY RC .50 .20
❑ T221 Wil Ledezma FY RC .40 .15
❑ T222 Josh Willingham FY RC 1.00 .40
❑ T223 David Cash FY RC .40 .15
❑ T224 Oscar Villarreal FY RC .40 .15
❑ T225 Jeff Duncan FY RC .40 .15
❑ T226 Kade Johnson FY RC .40 .15
❑ T227 Luke Steidlmayer FY RC .40 .15
❑ T228 Brandon Watson FY RC .40 .15
❑ T229 Jose Morales FY RC .40 .15
❑ T230 Mike Gallo FY RC .40 .15
❑ T231 Tyler Adamczyk FY RC .40 .15
❑ T232 Adam Stern FY RC .40 .15
❑ T233 Brennan King FY RC .40 .15
❑ T234 Dan Haren FY RC .75 .30
❑ T235 Michel Hernandez FY RC .40 .15
❑ T236 Ben Fritz FY RC .40 .15
❑ T237 Clay Hensley FY RC .40 .15
❑ T238 Tyler Johnson FY RC .40 .15
❑ T239 Pete LaForest FY RC .40 .15
❑ T240 Tyler Martin FY RC .40 .15
❑ T241 J.D. Durbin FY RC .40 .15
❑ T242 Shane Victorino FY RC .75 .30
❑ T243 Rajai Davis FY RC .40 .15
❑ T244 Ismael Castro FY RC .40 .15
❑ T245 Chien-Ming Wang FY RC 6.00 2.50
❑ T246 Travis Ishikawa FY RC .75 .30
❑ T247 Corey Shafer FY RC .40 .15
❑ T248 Gary Schneidmiller FY RC .40 .15
❑ T249 Dave Pember FY RC .40 .15
❑ T250 Keith Stamler FY RC .40 .15
❑ T251 Tyson Graham FY RC .40 .15
❑ T252 Ryan Cameron FY RC .40 .15
❑ T253 Eric Eckenstahler FY .40 .15
❑ T254 Matthew Peterson FY RC .40 .15
❑ T255 Dustin McGowan FY RC .50 .20
❑ T256 Prentice Redman FY RC .40 .15
❑ T257 Haj Turay FY RC .40 .15
❑ T258 Carlos Guzman FY RC .50 .20
❑ T259 Matt DeMarco FY RC .40 .15
❑ T260 Derek Michaelis FY RC .40 .15
❑ T261 Brian Burgamy FY RC .40 .15
❑ T262 Jay Sitzman FY RC .40 .15
❑ T263 Chris Fallon FY RC .40 .15
❑ T264 Mike Adams FY RC .40 .15
❑ T265 Clint Barmes FY RC 1.00 .40
❑ T266 Eric Reed FY RC .40 .15
❑ T267 Willie Eyre FY RC .40 .15
❑ T268 Carlos Duran FY RC .40 .15
❑ T269 Nick Trzesniak FY RC .40 .15
❑ T270 Ferdin Tejeda FY RC .40 .15
❑ T271 Michael Garciaparra FY RC .40 .15
❑ T272 Michael Hinckley FY RC .50 .20
❑ T273 Branden Florence FY RC .40 .15
❑ T274 Trent Oeltjen FY RC .50 .20
❑ T275 Mike Neu FY RC .40 .15

2004 Topps

❑ COMP.HOBBY SET (737) 80.00 40.00
❑ COMP.HOLIDAY SET (742) 80.00 40.00
❑ COMP.RETAIL SET (737) 80.00 40.00
❑ COMP.ASTROS SET (737) 80.00 40.00
❑ COMP.CUBS SET (737) 80.00 40.00
❑ COMP.RED SOX SET (737) 80.00 40.00
❑ COMP.YANKEES SET (737) 80.00 40.00
❑ COMPLETE SET (732) 80.00 30.00
❑ COMPLETE SERIES 1 (366) 40.00 15.00
❑ COMPLETE SERIES 2 (366) 40.00 15.00
❑ COMMON CARD (1-6/8-732) .20 .07
❑ COMMON (297-326/668-687) .50 .20
❑ COMMON (327-331/688-692) .50 .20
❑ 1 Jim Thome .30 .10
❑ 2 Reggie Sanders .20 .07
❑ 3 Mark Kotsay .20 .07
❑ 4 Edgardo Alfonzo .20 .07
❑ 5 Ben Davis .20 .07
❑ 6 Mike Matheny .20 .07
❑ 8 Marlon Anderson .20 .07
❑ 9 Chan Ho Park .20 .07
❑ 10 Ichiro Suzuki 1.00 .40
❑ 11 Kevin Millwood .20 .07
❑ 12 Bengie Molina .20 .07
❑ 13 Tom Glavine .30 .10
❑ 14 Junior Spivey .20 .07
❑ 15 Marcus Giles .20 .07
❑ 16 David Segui .20 .07
❑ 17 Kevin Millar .20 .07
❑ 18 Corey Patterson .20 .07
❑ 19 Aaron Rowand .20 .07
❑ 20 Derek Jeter 1.00 .40
❑ 21 Jason LaRue .20 .07
❑ 22 Chris Hammond .20 .07
❑ 23 Jay Payton .20 .07
❑ 24 Bobby Higginson .20 .07
❑ 25 Lance Berkman .20 .07
❑ 26 Juan Pierre .20 .07
❑ 27 Brent Mayne .20 .07
❑ 28 Fred McGriff .30 .10
❑ 29 Richie Sexson .20 .07
❑ 30 Tim Hudson .20 .07
❑ 31 Mike Piazza .75 .30
❑ 32 Brad Radke .20 .07
❑ 33 Jeff Weaver .20 .07
❑ 34 Ramon Hernandez .20 .07
❑ 35 David Bell .20 .07
❑ 36 Craig Wilson .20 .07
❑ 37 Jake Peavy .20 .07
❑ 38 Tim Worrell .20 .07
❑ 39 Gil Meche .20 .07
❑ 40 Albert Pujols 1.00 .40
❑ 41 Michael Young .20 .07
❑ 42 Josh Phelps .20 .07
❑ 43 Brendan Donnelly .20 .07
❑ 44 Steve Finley .20 .07
❑ 45 John Smoltz .30 .10
❑ 46 Jay Gibbons .20 .07
❑ 47 Trot Nixon .20 .07
❑ 48 Carl Pavano .20 .07
❑ 49 Frank Thomas .50 .20
❑ 50 Mark Prior .30 .10
❑ 51 Danny Graves .20 .07
❑ 52 Milton Bradley UER .20 .07
❑ 53 Jose Jimenez .20 .07
❑ 54 Shane Halter .20 .07
❑ 55 Mike Lowell .20 .07
❑ 56 Geoff Blum .20 .07
❑ 57 Michael Tucker UER .20 .07
❑ 58 Paul Lo Duca .20 .07
❑ 59 Vicente Padilla .20 .07
❑ 60 Jacque Jones .20 .07
❑ 61 Fernando Tatis .20 .07
❑ 62 Ty Wigginton .20 .07
❑ 63 Pedro Astacio .20 .07
❑ 64 Andy Pettitte .30 .10
❑ 65 Terrence Long .20 .07
❑ 66 Cliff Floyd .20 .07
❑ 67 Mariano Rivera .50 .20
❑ 68 Carlos Silva .20 .07
❑ 69 Marlon Byrd .20 .07
❑ 70 Mark Mulder .20 .07
❑ 71 Kerry Ligtenberg .20 .07
❑ 72 Carlos Guillen .20 .07
❑ 73 Fernando Vina .20 .07
❑ 74 Lance Carter .20 .07
❑ 75 Hank Blalock .20 .07
❑ 76 Jimmy Rollins .20 .07
❑ 77 Francisco Rodriguez .20 .07
❑ 78 Javy Lopez .20 .07
❑ 79 Jerry Hairston Jr. .20 .07
❑ 80 Andruw Jones .30 .10
❑ 81 Rodrigo Lopez .20 .07
❑ 82 Johnny Damon .30 .10
❑ 83 Hee Seop Choi .20 .07
❑ 84 Miguel Olivo .20 .07
❑ 85 Jon Garland .20 .07
❑ 86 Matt Lawton .20 .07
❑ 87 Juan Uribe .20 .07
❑ 88 Steve Sparks .20 .07
❑ 89 Tim Spooneybarger .20 .07
❑ 90 Jose Vidro .20 .07
❑ 91 Luis Rivas .20 .07
❑ 92 Hideo Nomo .50 .20
❑ 93 Javier Vazquez .20 .07
❑ 94 Al Leiter .20 .07
❑ 95 Darren Dreifort .20 .07
❑ 96 Alex Cintron .20 .07
❑ 97 Zach Day .20 .07
❑ 98 Jorge Posada .30 .10
❑ 99 John Halama .20 .07
❑ 100 Alex Rodriguez .75 .30
❑ 101 Orlando Palmeiro .20 .07
❑ 102 Dave Berg .20 .07
❑ 103 Brad Fullmer .20 .07
❑ 104 Mike Hampton .20 .07
❑ 105 Willis Roberts .20 .07
❑ 106 Ramiro Mendoza .20 .07
❑ 107 Juan Cruz .20 .07
❑ 108 Esteban Loaiza .20 .07
❑ 109 Russell Branyan .20 .07
❑ 110 Todd Helton .30 .10
❑ 111 Braden Looper .20 .07
❑ 112 Octavio Dotel .20 .07
❑ 113 Mike MacDougal .20 .07
❑ 114 Cesar Izturis .20 .07
❑ 115 Johan Santana .50 .20
❑ 116 Jose Contreras .20 .07

❑ 117	Placido Polanco	.20	.07
❑ 118	Jason Phillips	.20	.07
❑ 119	Adam Eaton	.20	.07
❑ 120	Vernon Wells	.20	.07
❑ 121	Ben Grieve	.20	.07
❑ 122	Randy Winn	.20	.07
❑ 123	Ismael Valdes	.20	.07
❑ 124	Eric Owens	.20	.07
❑ 125	Curt Schilling	.20	.07
❑ 126	Russ Ortiz	.20	.07
❑ 127	Mark Buehrle	.20	.07
❑ 128	Danys Baez	.20	.07
❑ 129	Dmitri Young	.20	.07
❑ 130	Kazuhisa Ishii	.20	.07
❑ 131	A.J. Pierzynski	.20	.07
❑ 132	Michael Barrett	.20	.07
❑ 133	Joe McEwing	.20	.07
❑ 134	Alex Cora	.20	.07
❑ 135	Tom Wilson	.20	.07
❑ 136	Carlos Zambrano	.20	.07
❑ 137	Brett Tomko	.20	.07
❑ 138	Shigetoshi Hasegawa	.20	.07
❑ 139	Jarrod Washburn	.20	.07
❑ 140	Greg Maddux	.75	.30
❑ 141	Craig Counsell	.20	.07
❑ 142	Reggie Taylor	.20	.07
❑ 143	Omar Vizquel	.30	.10
❑ 144	Alex Gonzalez	.20	.07
❑ 145	Billy Wagner	.20	.07
❑ 146	Brian Jordan	.20	.07
❑ 147	Wes Helms	.20	.07
❑ 148	Kyle Lohse	.20	.07
❑ 149	Timo Perez	.20	.07
❑ 150	Jason Giambi	.20	.07
❑ 151	Erubiel Durazo	.20	.07
❑ 152	Mike Lieberthal	.20	.07
❑ 153	Jason Kendall	.20	.07
❑ 154	Xavier Nady	.20	.07
❑ 155	Kirk Rueter	.20	.07
❑ 156	Mike Cameron	.20	.07
❑ 157	Miguel Cairo	.20	.07
❑ 158	Woody Williams	.20	.07
❑ 159	Toby Hall	.20	.07
❑ 160	Bernie Williams	.30	.10
❑ 161	Darin Erstad	.20	.07
❑ 162	Matt Mantei	.20	.07
❑ 163	Geronimo Gil	.20	.07
❑ 164	Bill Mueller	.20	.07
❑ 165	Damian Miller	.20	.07
❑ 166	Tony Graffanino	.20	.07
❑ 167	Sean Casey	.20	.07
❑ 168	Brandon Phillips	.20	.07
❑ 169	Mike Remlinger	.20	.07
❑ 170	Adam Dunn	.20	.07
❑ 171	Carlos Lee	.20	.07
❑ 172	Juan Encarnacion	.20	.07
❑ 173	Angel Berroa	.20	.07
❑ 174	Desi Relaford	.20	.07
❑ 175	Paul Quantrill	.20	.07
❑ 176	Ben Sheets	.20	.07
❑ 177	Eddie Guardado	.20	.07
❑ 178	Rocky Biddle	.20	.07
❑ 179	Mike Stanton	.20	.07
❑ 180	Eric Chavez	.20	.07
❑ 181	Jason Michaels	.20	.07
❑ 182	Terry Adams	.20	.07
❑ 183	Kip Wells	.20	.07
❑ 184	Brian Lawrence	.20	.07
❑ 185	Bret Boone	.20	.07
❑ 186	Tino Martinez	.30	.10
❑ 187	Aubrey Huff	.20	.07
❑ 188	Kevin Mench	.20	.07
❑ 189	Tim Salmon	.30	.10
❑ 190	Carlos Delgado	.20	.07
❑ 191	John Lackey	.20	.07
❑ 192	Oscar Villarreal	.20	.07
❑ 193	Luis Matos	.20	.07
❑ 194	Derek Lowe	.20	.07
❑ 195	Mark Grudzielanek	.20	.07
❑ 196	Tom Gordon	.20	.07
❑ 197	Matt Clement	.20	.07
❑ 198	Byung-Hyun Kim	.20	.07
❑ 199	Brandon Inge	.20	.07
❑ 200	Nomar Garciaparra	.75	.30
❑ 201	Antonio Osuna	.20	.07
❑ 202	Jose Mesa	.20	.07
❑ 203	Bo Hart	.20	.07
❑ 204	Jack Wilson	.20	.07
❑ 205	Ray Durham	.20	.07
❑ 206	Freddy Garcia	.20	.07
❑ 207	J.D. Drew	.20	.07
❑ 208	Einar Diaz	.20	.07
❑ 209	Roy Halladay	.20	.07
❑ 210	David Eckstein UER	.20	.07
❑ 211	Jason Marquis	.20	.07
❑ 212	Jorge Julio	.20	.07
❑ 213	Tim Wakefield	.20	.07
❑ 214	Moises Alou	.20	.07
❑ 215	Bartolo Colon	.20	.07
❑ 216	Jimmy Haynes	.20	.07
❑ 217	Preston Wilson	.20	.07
❑ 218	Luis Castillo	.20	.07
❑ 219	Richard Hidalgo	.20	.07
❑ 220	Manny Ramirez	.30	.10
❑ 221	Mike Mussina	.30	.10
❑ 222	Randy Wolf	.20	.07
❑ 223	Kris Benson	.20	.07
❑ 224	Ryan Klesko	.20	.07
❑ 225	Rich Aurilia	.20	.07
❑ 226	Kelvim Escobar	.20	.07
❑ 227	Francisco Cordero	.20	.07
❑ 228	Kazuhiro Sasaki	.20	.07
❑ 229	Danny Bautista	.20	.07
❑ 230	Rafael Furcal	.20	.07
❑ 231	Travis Driskill	.20	.07
❑ 232	Kyle Farnsworth	.20	.07
❑ 233	Jose Valentin	.20	.07
❑ 234	Felipe Lopez	.20	.07
❑ 235	C.C. Sabathia	.20	.07
❑ 236	Brad Penny	.20	.07
❑ 237	Brad Ausmus	.20	.07
❑ 238	Raul Ibanez	.20	.07
❑ 239	Adrian Beltre	.20	.07
❑ 240	Rocco Baldelli	.20	.07
❑ 241	Orlando Hudson	.20	.07
❑ 242	Dave Roberts	.20	.07
❑ 243	Doug Mientkiewicz	.20	.07
❑ 244	Brad Wilkerson	.20	.07
❑ 245	Scott Strickland	.20	.07
❑ 246	Ryan Franklin	.20	.07
❑ 247	Chad Bradford	.20	.07
❑ 248	Gary Bennett	.20	.07
❑ 249	Jose Cruz Jr.	.20	.07
❑ 250	Jeff Kent	.20	.07
❑ 251	Josh Beckett	.20	.07
❑ 252	Ramon Ortiz	.20	.07
❑ 253	Miguel Batista	.20	.07
❑ 254	Jung Bong	.20	.07
❑ 255	Deivi Cruz	.20	.07
❑ 256	Alex Gonzalez	.20	.07
❑ 257	Shawn Chacon	.20	.07
❑ 258	Runelvys Hernandez	.20	.07
❑ 259	Joe Mays	.20	.07
❑ 260	Eric Gagne	.20	.07
❑ 261	Dustan Mohr	.20	.07
❑ 262	Tomokazu Ohka	.20	.07
❑ 263	Eric Byrnes	.20	.07
❑ 264	Frank Catalanotto	.20	.07
❑ 265	Cristian Guzman	.20	.07
❑ 266	Orlando Cabrera	.20	.07
❑ 267A	Juan Castro	.20	.07
❑ 267B	Mike Scioscia MG UER 274	.20	.07
❑ 268	Bob Brenly MG	.20	.07
❑ 269	Bobby Cox MG	.20	.07
❑ 270	Mike Hargrove MG	.20	.07
❑ 271	Grady Little MG	.20	.07
❑ 272	Dusty Baker MG	.20	.07
❑ 273	Jerry Manuel MG	.20	.07
❑ 275	Eric Wedge MG	.20	.07
❑ 276	Clint Hurdle MG	.20	.07
❑ 277	Alan Trammell MG	.20	.07
❑ 278	Jack McKeon MG	.20	.07
❑ 279	Jimy Williams MG	.20	.07
❑ 280	Tony Pena MG	.20	.07
❑ 281	Jim Tracy MG	.20	.07
❑ 282	Ned Yost MG	.20	.07
❑ 283	Ron Gardenhire MG	.20	.07
❑ 284	Frank Robinson MG	.20	.07
❑ 285	Art Howe MG	.20	.07
❑ 286	Joe Torre MG	.30	.10
❑ 287	Ken Macha MG	.20	.07
❑ 288	Larry Bowa MG	.20	.07
❑ 289	Lloyd McClendon MG	.20	.07
❑ 290	Bruce Bochy MG	.20	.07
❑ 291	Felipe Alou MG	.20	.07
❑ 292	Bob Melvin MG	.20	.07
❑ 293	Tony LaRussa MG	.20	.07
❑ 294	Lou Piniella MG	.20	.07
❑ 295	Buck Showalter MG	.20	.07
❑ 296	Carlos Tosca MG	.20	.07
❑ 297	Anthony Acevedo FY RC	.50	.20
❑ 298	Anthony Lerew FY RC	.75	.30
❑ 299	Blake Hawksworth FY RC	.50	.20
❑ 300	Brayan Pena FY RC	.50	.20
❑ 301	Casey Myers FY RC	.50	.20
❑ 302	Craig Ansman FY RC	.50	.20
❑ 303	David Murphy FY RC	.75	.30
❑ 304	Dave Crouthers FY RC	.50	.20
❑ 305	Dioner Navarro FY RC	.75	.30
❑ 306	Donald Levinski FY RC	.50	.20
❑ 307	Jesse Roman FY RC	.50	.20
❑ 308	Sung Jung FY RC	.50	.20
❑ 309	Jon Knott FY RC	.50	.20
❑ 310	Josh Labandeira FY RC	.50	.20
❑ 311	Kenny Perez FY RC	.50	.20
❑ 312	Khalid Ballouli FY RC	.50	.20
❑ 313	Kyle Davies FY RC	2.50	1.00
❑ 314	Marcus McBeth FY RC	.50	.20
❑ 315	Matt Creighton FY RC	.50	.20
❑ 316	Chris O'Riordan FY RC	.50	.20
❑ 317	Mike Gosling FY RC	.50	.20
❑ 318	Nic Ungs FY RC	.50	.20
❑ 319	Omar Falcon FY RC	.50	.20
❑ 320	Rodney Choy Foo FY RC	.50	.20
❑ 321	Tim Frend FY RC	.50	.20
❑ 322	Todd Self FY RC	.50	.20
❑ 323	Tydus Meadows FY RC	.50	.20
❑ 324	Yadier Molina FY RC	2.00	.75
❑ 325	Zach Duke FY RC	2.00	.75
❑ 326	Zach Miner FY RC	1.25	.50
❑ 327	B.Castro/K.Greene FS	.50	.20
❑ 328	R.Madson/E.Ramirez FS	.50	.20
❑ 329	R.Harden/B.Crosby FS	.50	.20
❑ 330	Z.Greinke/J.Gobble FS	.50	.20
❑ 331	B.Jenks/C.Kotchman FS	.50	.20
❑ 332	Sammy Sosa HL	.30	.10
❑ 333	Kevin Millwood HL	.20	.07
❑ 334	Rafael Palmeiro HL	.20	.07
❑ 335	Roger Clemens HL	.50	.20
❑ 336	Eric Gagne HL	.20	.07
❑ 337	Mueller/Manny/Jeter LL	.30	.10
❑ 338	V.Wells/Ichiro/M.Young LL	.50	.20
❑ 339	A-Rod/Thomas/Delgado LL	.50	.20
❑ 340	Delgado/A-Rod/Boone LL	.50	.20
❑ 341	Pedro/Hudson/Loaiza LL	.30	.10
❑ 342	Loaiza/Pedro/Halladay LL	.30	.10
❑ 343	Pujols/Helton/Renteria LL	.50	.20
❑ 344	Pujols/Helton/Pierre LL	.50	.20
❑ 345	Thome/Sexson/J.Lopez LL	.20	.07
❑ 346	P.Wilson/Sheff/Thome LL	.20	.07
❑ 347	Schmidt/K.Brown/Prior LL	.30	.10
❑ 348	Wood/Prior/Vazquez LL	.30	.10
❑ 349	R.Clemens/D.Wells ALDS	.50	.20
❑ 350	K.Wood/M.Prior NLDS	.30	.10
❑ 351	Beckett/Cabrera/I.Rod NLCS	.50	.20
❑ 352	Giambi/Rivera/Boone ALCS	.50	.20
❑ 353	D.Lowe/I.Rod AL/NLDS	.50	.20
❑ 354	Pedro/Posa/Clemens ALCS	.50	.20
❑ 355	Juan Pierre WS	.20	.07
❑ 356	Carlos Delgado AS	.20	.07
❑ 357	Bret Boone AS	.20	.07
❑ 358	Alex Rodriguez AS	.50	.20
❑ 359	Bill Mueller AS	.20	.07
❑ 360	Vernon Wells AS	.20	.07
❑ 361	Garret Anderson AS	.20	.07
❑ 362	Magglio Ordonez AS	.20	.07
❑ 363	Jorge Posada AS	.20	.07
❑ 364	Roy Halladay AS	.20	.07
❑ 365	Andy Pettitte AS	.20	.07
❑ 366	Frank Thomas AS	.30	.10
❑ 367	Jody Gerut AS	.20	.07
❑ 368	Sammy Sosa	.50	.20
❑ 369	Joe Crede	.20	.07
❑ 370	Gary Sheffield	.20	.07
❑ 371	Coco Crisp	.20	.07
❑ 372	Torii Hunter	.20	.07
❑ 373	Derrek Lee	.30	.10
❑ 374	Adam Everett	.20	.07

❑ 375 Miguel Tejada .20 .07
❑ 376 Jeremy Affeldt .20 .07
❑ 377 Robin Ventura .20 .07
❑ 378 Scott Podsednik .20 .07
❑ 379 Matthew LeCroy .20 .07
❑ 380 Vladimir Guerrero .50 .20
❑ 381 Tike Redman .20 .07
❑ 382 Jeff Nelson .20 .07
❑ 383 Cliff Lee .20 .07
❑ 384 Bobby Abreu .20 .07
❑ 385 Josh Fogg .20 .07
❑ 386 Trevor Hoffman .20 .07
❑ 387 Jesse Foppert .20 .07
❑ 388 Edgar Martinez .30 .10
❑ 389 Edgar Renteria .20 .07
❑ 390 Chipper Jones .50 .20
❑ 391 Eric Munson .20 .07
❑ 392 Dewon Brazelton .20 .07
❑ 393 John Thomson .20 .07
❑ 394 Chris Woodward .20 .07
❑ 395 Adam LaRoche .20 .07
❑ 396 Elmer Dessens .20 .07
❑ 397 Johnny Estrada .20 .07
❑ 398 Damian Moss .20 .07
❑ 399 Gabe Kapler .20 .07
❑ 400 Dontrelle Willis .30 .10
❑ 401 Troy Glaus .20 .07
❑ 402 Raul Mondesi .20 .07
❑ 403 Shane Reynolds .20 .07
❑ 404 Kurt Ainsworth .20 .07
❑ 405 Pedro Martinez .30 .10
❑ 406 Eric Karros .20 .07
❑ 407 Billy Koch .20 .07
❑ 408 Scott Schoeneweis .20 .07
❑ 409 Paul Wilson .20 .07
❑ 410 Mike Sweeney .20 .07
❑ 411 Jason Bay .20 .07
❑ 412 Mark Redman .20 .07
❑ 413 Jason Jennings .20 .07
❑ 414 Rondell White .20 .07
❑ 415 Todd Hundley .20 .07
❑ 416 Shannon Stewart .20 .07
❑ 417 Jae Weong Seo .20 .07
❑ 418 Livan Hernandez .20 .07
❑ 419 Mark Ellis .20 .07
❑ 420 Pat Burrell .20 .07
❑ 421 Mark Loretta .20 .07
❑ 422 Robb Nen .20 .07
❑ 423 Joel Pineiro .20 .07
❑ 424 Jason Simontacchi .20 .07
❑ 425 Sterling Hitchcock .20 .07
❑ 426 Rey Ordonez .20 .07
❑ 427 Greg Myers .20 .07
❑ 428 Shane Spencer .20 .07
❑ 429 Carlos Baerga .20 .07
❑ 430 Garret Anderson .20 .07
❑ 431 Horacio Ramirez .20 .07
❑ 432 Brian Roberts .20 .07
❑ 433 Damian Jackson .20 .07
❑ 434 Doug Glanville .20 .07
❑ 435 Brian Daubach .20 .07
❑ 436 Alex Escobar .20 .07
❑ 437 Alex Sanchez .20 .07
❑ 438 Jeff Bagwell .30 .10
❑ 439 Darrell May .20 .07
❑ 440 Shawn Green .20 .07
❑ 441 Geoff Jenkins .20 .07
❑ 442 Endy Chavez .20 .07
❑ 443 Nick Johnson .20 .07
❑ 444 Jose Guillen .20 .07
❑ 445 Tomas Perez .20 .07
❑ 446 Phil Nevin .20 .07
❑ 447 Jason Schmidt .20 .07
❑ 448 Julio Mateo .20 .07
❑ 449 So Taguchi .20 .07
❑ 450 Randy Johnson .50 .20
❑ 451 Paul Byrd .20 .07
❑ 452 Chone Figgins .20 .07
❑ 453 Larry Bigbie .20 .07
❑ 454 Scott Williamson .20 .07
❑ 455 Ramon Martinez .20 .07
❑ 456 Roberto Alomar .30 .10
❑ 457 Ryan Dempster .20 .07
❑ 458 Ryan Ludwick .20 .07
❑ 459 Ramon Santiago .20 .07
❑ 460 Jeff Conine .20 .07
❑ 461 Brad Lidge .20 .07
❑ 462 Ken Harvey .20 .07
❑ 463 Guillermo Mota .20 .07
❑ 464 Rick Reed .20 .07
❑ 465 Joey Eischen .20 .07
❑ 466 Wade Miller .20 .07
❑ 467 Steve Karsay .20 .07
❑ 468 Chase Utley .30 .10
❑ 469 Matt Stairs .20 .07
❑ 470 Yorvit Torrealba .20 .07
❑ 471 Joe Kennedy .20 .07
❑ 472 Reed Johnson .20 .07
❑ 473 Victor Zambrano .20 .07
❑ 474 Jeff Davanon .20 .07
❑ 475 Luis Gonzalez .20 .07
❑ 476 Eli Marrero .20 .07
❑ 477 Ray King .20 .07
❑ 478 Jack Cust .20 .07
❑ 479 Omar Daal .20 .07
❑ 480 Todd Walker .20 .07
❑ 481 Shawn Estes .20 .07
❑ 482 Chris Reitsma .20 .07
❑ 483 Jake Westbrook .20 .07
❑ 484 Jeremy Bonderman .20 .70
❑ 485 A.J. Burnett .20 .07
❑ 486 Roy Oswalt .20 .07
❑ 487 Kevin Brown .20 .07
❑ 488 Eric Milton .20 .07
❑ 489 Claudio Vargas .20 .07
❑ 490 Roger Cedeno .20 .07
❑ 491 David Wells .20 .07
❑ 492 Scott Hatteberg .20 .07
❑ 493 Ricky Ledee .20 .07
❑ 494 Eric Young .20 .07
❑ 495 Armando Benitez .20 .07
❑ 496 Dan Haren .20 .07
❑ 497 Carl Crawford .20 .07
❑ 498 Laynce Nix .20 .07
❑ 499 Eric Hinske .20 .07
❑ 500 Ivan Rodriguez .30 .10
❑ 501 Scot Shields .20 .07
❑ 502 Brandon Webb .20 .07
❑ 503 Mark DeRosa .20 .07
❑ 504 Jhonny Peralta .20 .07
❑ 505 Adam Kennedy .20 .07
❑ 506 Tony Batista .20 .07
❑ 507 Jeff Suppan .20 .07
❑ 508 Kenny Lofton .20 .07
❑ 509 Scott Sullivan .20 .07
❑ 510 Ken Griffey Jr. .75 .30
❑ 511 Billy Traber .20 .07
❑ 512 Larry Walker .20 .07
❑ 513 Mike Maroth .20 .07
❑ 514 Todd Hollandsworth .20 .07
❑ 515 Kirk Saarloos .20 .07
❑ 516 Carlos Beltran .20 .07
❑ 517 Juan Rivera .20 .07
❑ 518 Roger Clemens 1.00 .40
❑ 519 Karim Garcia .20 .07
❑ 520 Jose Reyes .20 .07
❑ 521 Brandon Duckworth .20 .07
❑ 522 Brian Giles .20 .07
❑ 523 J.T. Snow .20 .07
❑ 524 Jamie Moyer .20 .07
❑ 525 Jason Isringhausen .20 .07
❑ 526 Julio Lugo .20 .07
❑ 527 Mark Teixeira .30 .10
❑ 528 Cory Lidle .20 .07
❑ 529 Lyle Overbay .20 .07
❑ 530 Troy Percival .20 .07
❑ 531 Robby Hammock .20 .07
❑ 532 Robert Fick .20 .07
❑ 533 Jason Johnson .20 .07
❑ 534 Brandon Lyon .20 .07
❑ 535 Antonio Alfonseca .20 .07
❑ 536 Tom Goodwin .20 .07
❑ 537 Paul Konerko .20 .07
❑ 538 D'Angelo Jimenez .20 .07
❑ 539 Ben Broussard .20 .07
❑ 540 Magglio Ordonez .20 .07
❑ 541 Ellis Burks .20 .07
❑ 542 Carlos Pena .20 .07
❑ 543 Chad Fox .20 .07
❑ 544 Jerome Robertson .20 .07
❑ 545 Travis Hafner .20 .07
❑ 546 Joe Randa .20 .07
❑ 547 Wil Cordero .20 .07
❑ 548 Brady Clark .20 .07
❑ 549 Ruben Sierra .20 .07
❑ 550 Barry Zito .20 .07
❑ 551 Brett Myers .20 .07
❑ 552 Oliver Perez .20 .07
❑ 553 Trey Hodges .20 .07
❑ 554 Benito Santiago .20 .07
❑ 555 David Ross .20 .07
❑ 556 Ramon Vazquez .20 .07
❑ 557 Joe Nathan .20 .07
❑ 558 Dan Wilson .20 .07
❑ 559 Joe Mauer .50 .20
❑ 560 Jim Edmonds .20 .07
❑ 561 Shawn Wooten .20 .07
❑ 562 Matt Kata .20 .07
❑ 563 Vinny Castilla .20 .07
❑ 564 Marty Cordova .20 .07
❑ 565 Aramis Ramirez .20 .07
❑ 566 Carl Everett .20 .07
❑ 567 Ryan Freel .20 .07
❑ 568 Jason Davis .20 .07
❑ 569 Mark Bellhorn Sox .20 .07
❑ 570 Craig Monroe .20 .07
❑ 571 Roberto Hernandez .20 .07
❑ 572 Tim Redding .20 .07
❑ 573 Kevin Appier .20 .07
❑ 574 Jeromy Burnitz .20 .07
❑ 575 Miguel Cabrera .30 .10
❑ 576 Ramon Nivar .20 .07
❑ 577 Casey Blake .20 .07
❑ 578 Aaron Boone .20 .07
❑ 579 Jermaine Dye .20 .07
❑ 580 Jerome Williams .20 .07
❑ 581 John Olerud .20 .07
❑ 582 Scott Rolen .30 .10
❑ 583 Bobby Kielty .20 .07
❑ 584 Travis Lee .20 .07
❑ 585 Jeff Cirillo .20 .07
❑ 586 Scott Spiezio .20 .07
❑ 587 Stephen Randolph .20 .07
❑ 588 Melvin Mora .20 .07
❑ 589 Mike Timlin .20 .07
❑ 590 Kerry Wood .20 .07
❑ 591 Tony Womack .20 .07
❑ 592 Jody Gerut .20 .07
❑ 593 Franklyn German .20 .07
❑ 594 Morgan Ensberg .20 .07
❑ 595 Odalis Perez .20 .07
❑ 596 Michael Cuddyer .20 .07
❑ 597 Jon Lieber .20 .07
❑ 598 Mike Williams .20 .07
❑ 599 Jose Hernandez .20 .07
❑ 600 Alfonso Soriano .20 .07
❑ 601 Marquis Grissom .20 .07
❑ 602 Matt Morris .20 .07
❑ 603 Damian Rolls .20 .07
❑ 604 Juan Gonzalez .20 .07
❑ 605 Aquilino Lopez .20 .07
❑ 606 Jose Valverde .20 .07
❑ 607 Kenny Rogers .20 .07
❑ 608 Joe Borowski .20 .07
❑ 609 Josh Bard .20 .07
❑ 610 Austin Kearns .20 .07
❑ 611 Chin-Hui Tsao .20 .07
❑ 612 Wil Ledezma .20 .07
❑ 613 Aaron Guiel .20 .07
❑ 614 LaTroy Hawkins .20 .07
❑ 615 Tony Armas Jr. .20 .07
❑ 616 Steve Trachsel .20 .07
❑ 617 Ted Lilly .20 .07
❑ 618 Todd Pratt .20 .07
❑ 619 Sean Burroughs .20 .07
❑ 620 Rafael Palmeiro .30 .10
❑ 621 Jeremi Gonzalez .20 .07
❑ 622 Quinton McCracken .20 .07
❑ 623 David Ortiz .50 .20
❑ 624 Randall Simon .20 .07
❑ 625 Wily Mo Pena .20 .07
❑ 626 Nate Cornejo .20 .07
❑ 627 Brian Anderson .20 .07
❑ 628 Corey Koskie .20 .07
❑ 629 Keith Foulke Sox .20 .07
❑ 630 Rheal Cormier .20 .07
❑ 631 Sidney Ponson .20 .07
❑ 632 Gary Matthews Jr. .20 .07

❑ 633 Herbert Perry .20 .07
❑ 634 Shea Hillenbrand .20 .07
❑ 635 Craig Biggio .30 .10
❑ 636 Barry Larkin .30 .10
❑ 637 Arthur Rhodes .20 .07
❑ 638 Anaheim Angels TC .20 .07
❑ 639 Arizona Diamondbacks TC .20 .07
❑ 640 Atlanta Braves TC .20 .07
❑ 641 Baltimore Orioles TC .20 .07
❑ 642 Boston Red Sox TC .30 .10
❑ 643 Chicago Cubs TC .20 .07
❑ 644 Chicago White Sox TC .20 .07
❑ 645 Cincinnati Reds TC .20 .07
❑ 646 Cleveland Indians TC .20 .07
❑ 647 Colorado Rockies TC .20 .07
❑ 648 Detroit Tigers TC .20 .07
❑ 649 Florida Marlins TC .20 .07
❑ 650 Houston Astros TC .20 .07
❑ 651 Kansas City Royals TC .20 .07
❑ 652 Los Angeles Dodgers TC .20 .07
❑ 653 Milwaukee Brewers TC .20 .07
❑ 654 Minnesota Twins TC .20 .07
❑ 655 Montreal Expos TC .20 .07
❑ 656 New York Mets TC .20 .07
❑ 657 New York Yankees TC .50 .20
❑ 658 Oakland Athletics TC .20 .07
❑ 659 Philadelphia Phillies TC .20 .07
❑ 660 Pittsburgh Pirates TC .20 .07
❑ 661 San Diego Padres TC .20 .07
❑ 662 San Francisco Giants TC .20 .07
❑ 663 Seattle Mariners TC .20 .07
❑ 664 St. Louis Cardinals TC .20 .07
❑ 665 Tampa Bay Devil Rays TC .20 .07
❑ 666 Texas Rangers TC .20 .07
❑ 667 Toronto Blue Jays TC .20 .07
❑ 668 Kyle Sleeth DP RC .50 .20
❑ 669 Bradley Sullivan DP RC .50 .20
❑ 670 Carlos Quentin DP RC 2.50 1.00
❑ 671 Conor Jackson DP RC 3.00 1.25
❑ 672 Jeffrey Allison DP RC .50 .20
❑ 673 Matthew Moses DP RC 1.00 .40
❑ 674 Tim Stauffer DP RC .75 .30
❑ 675 Estee Harris DP RC .50 .20
❑ 676 David Aardsma DP RC .50 .20
❑ 677 Omar Quintanilla DP RC .50 .20
❑ 678 Aaron Hill DP .50 .20
❑ 679 Tony Richie DP RC .50 .20
❑ 680 Lastings Milledge DP RC 4.00 1.50
❑ 681 Brad Snyder DP RC 1.00 .40
❑ 682 Jason Hirsh DP RC 1.50 .60
❑ 683 Logan Kensing DP RC .50 .20
❑ 684 Chris Lubanski DP .50 .20
❑ 685 Ryan Harvey DP .50 .20
❑ 686 Ryan Wagner DP .50 .20
❑ 687 Rickie Weeks DP .50 .20
❑ 688 G.Sizemore/J.Guthrie .50 .20
❑ 689 E.Jackson/G.Miller .50 .20
❑ 690 J.Reed/N.Cotts .50 .20
❑ 691 A.Loewen/N.Markakis .50 .20
❑ 692 B.Upton/D.Young .50 .20
❑ 693 A.Rodriguez/D.Jeter 1.50 .60
❑ 694 I.Suzuki/A.Pujols 1.00 .40
❑ 695 J.Thome/M.Schmidt 1.00 .40
❑ 696 Mike Mussina GG .20 .07
❑ 697 Bengie Molina GG .20 .07
❑ 698 John Olerud GG .20 .07
❑ 699 Bret Boone GG .20 .07
❑ 700 Eric Chavez GG .20 .07
❑ 701 Alex Rodriguez GG .50 .20
❑ 702 Mike Cameron GG .20 .07
❑ 703 Ichiro Suzuki GG .50 .20
❑ 704 Torii Hunter GG .20 .07
❑ 705 Mike Hampton GG .20 .07
❑ 706 Mike Matheny GG .20 .07
❑ 707 Derrek Lee GG .20 .07
❑ 708 Luis Castillo GG .20 .07
❑ 709 Scott Rolen GG .20 .07
❑ 710 Edgar Renteria GG .20 .07
❑ 711 Andruw Jones GG .20 .07
❑ 712 Jose Cruz Jr. GG .20 .07
❑ 713 Jim Edmonds GG .20 .07
❑ 714 Roy Halladay CY .20 .07
❑ 715 Eric Gagne CY .20 .07
❑ 716 Alex Rodriguez MVP .50 .20
❑ 717 Angel Berroa ROY .20 .07
❑ 718 Dontrelle Willis ROY .20 .07
❑ 719 Todd Helton AS .20 .07
❑ 720 Marcus Giles AS .20 .07
❑ 721 Edgar Renteria AS .20 .07
❑ 722 Scott Rolen AS .20 .07
❑ 723 Albert Pujols AS .50 .20
❑ 724 Gary Sheffield AS .20 .07
❑ 725 Javy Lopez AS .20 .07
❑ 726 Eric Gagne AS .20 .07
❑ 727 Randy Wolf AS .20 .07
❑ 728 Bobby Cox AS .20 .07
❑ 729 Scott Podsednik AS .20 .07
❑ 730 Alex Gonzalez WS .30 .10
❑ 731 Brad Penny WS .30 .10
❑ 732 Beckett/I.Rod/A.Gonz WS .30 .10
❑ 733 Josh Beckett WS MVP .30 .10

2004 Topps Traded

❑ COMPLETE SET (220) 50.00 20.00
❑ COMMON CARD (1-70) .20 .07
❑ COMMON CARD (71-90) .50 .20
❑ COMMON CARD (91-110) .40 .15
❑ COMMON CARD (111-220) .40 .15
❑ BONDS AVAIL VIA HTA SHOP EXCHANGE
❑ PLATE ODDS 1:1151 H, 1:1173 R, 1:327 HTA
❑ PLATE PRINT RUN 1 SET PER COLOR
❑ BLACK-CYAN-MAGENTA-YELLOW ISSUED
❑ NO PLATE PRICING DUE TO SCARCITY
❑ T1 Pokey Reese .20 .07
❑ T2 Tony Womack .20 .07
❑ T3 Richard Hidalgo .20 .07
❑ T4 Juan Uribe .20 .07
❑ T5 J.D. Drew .20 .07
❑ T6 Alex Gonzalez .20 .07
❑ T7 Carlos Guillen .20 .07
❑ T8 Doug Mientkiewicz .20 .07
❑ T9 Fernando Vina .20 .07
❑ T10 Milton Bradley .20 .07
❑ T11 Kelvim Escobar .20 .07
❑ T12 Ben Grieve .20 .07
❑ T13 Brian Jordan .20 .07
❑ T14 A.J. Pierzynski .20 .07
❑ T15 Billy Wagner .20 .07
❑ T16 Terrence Long .20 .07
❑ T17 Carlos Beltran .20 .07
❑ T18 Carl Everett .20 .07
❑ T19 Reggie Sanders .20 .07
❑ T20 Javy Lopez .20 .07
❑ T21 Jay Payton .20 .07
❑ T22 Octavio Dotel .20 .07
❑ T23 Eddie Guardado .20 .07
❑ T24 Andy Pettitte .30 .10
❑ T25 Richie Sexson .20 .07
❑ T26 Ronnie Belliard .20 .07
❑ T27 Michael Tucker .20 .07
❑ T28 Brad Fullmer .20 .07
❑ T29 Freddy Garcia .20 .07
❑ T30 Bartolo Colon .20 .07
❑ T31 Larry Walker Cards .30 .10
❑ T32 Mark Kotsay .20 .07
❑ T33 Jason Marquis .20 .07
❑ T34 Dustan Mohr .20 .07
❑ T35 Javier Vazquez .20 .07
❑ T36 Nomar Garciaparra .75 .30
❑ T37 Tino Martinez .30 .10
❑ T38 Hee Seop Choi .20 .07
❑ T39 Damian Miller .20 .07
❑ T40 Jose Lima .20 .07
❑ T41 Ty Wigginton .20 .07
❑ T42 Raul Ibanez .20 .07
❑ T43 Danys Baez .20 .07
❑ T44 Tony Clark .20 .07
❑ T45 Greg Maddux .75 .30
❑ T46 Victor Zambrano .20 .07
❑ T47 Orlando Cabrera Sox .20 .07
❑ T48 Jose Cruz Jr. .20 .07
❑ T49 Kris Benson .20 .07
❑ T50 Alex Rodriguez 1.00 .40
❑ T51 Steve Finley .20 .07
❑ T52 Ramon Hernandez .20 .07
❑ T53 Esteban Loaiza .20 .07
❑ T54 Ugueth Urbina .20 .07
❑ T55 Jeff Weaver .20 .07
❑ T56 Flash Gordon .20 .07
❑ T57 Jose Contreras .20 .07
❑ T58 Paul Lo Duca .20 .07
❑ T59 Junior Spivey .20 .07
❑ T60 Curt Schilling .30 .10
❑ T61 Brad Penny .20 .07
❑ T62 Braden Looper .20 .07
❑ T63 Miguel Cairo .20 .07
❑ T64 Juan Encarnacion .20 .07
❑ T65 Miguel Batista .20 .07
❑ T66 Terry Francona MG .20 .07
❑ T67 Lee Mazzilli MG .20 .07
❑ T68 Al Pedrique MG .20 .07
❑ T69 Ozzie Guillen MG .50 .20
❑ T70 Phil Garner MG .20 .07
❑ T71 Matt Bush DP RC 1.50 .60
❑ T72 Homer Bailey DP RC 3.00 1.25
❑ T73 Greg Golson DP RC 1.50 .60
❑ T74 Kyle Waldrop DP RC 1.25 .50
❑ T75 Richie Robnett DP RC 1.25 .50
❑ T76 Jay Rainville DP RC 1.50 .60
❑ T77 Bill Bray DP RC .50 .20
❑ T78 Philip Hughes DP RC 8.00 3.00
❑ T79 Scott Elbert DP RC 1.25 .50
❑ T80 Josh Fields DP RC 2.00 .75
❑ T81 Justin Orenduff DP RC .75 .30
❑ T82 Dan Putnam DP RC .75 .30
❑ T83 Chris Nelson DP RC 2.00 .75
❑ T84 Blake DeWitt DP RC 2.00 .75
❑ T85 J.P. Howell DP RC 1.25 .50
❑ T86 Huston Street DP RC 2.00 .75
❑ T87 Kurt Suzuki DP RC 1.25 .50
❑ T88 Erick San Pedro DP RC .50 .20
❑ T89 Matt Tuiasosopo DP RC 2.00 .75
❑ T90 Matt Macri DP RC 1.00 .40
❑ T91 Chad Tracy PROS .40 .15
❑ T92 Scott Hairston PROS .40 .15
❑ T93 Jonny Gomes PROS .40 .15
❑ T94 Chin-Feng Chen PROS .40 .15
❑ T95 Chien-Ming Wang PROS .75 .30
❑ T96 Dustin McGowan PROS .40 .15
❑ T97 Chris Burke PROS .40 .15
❑ T98 Denny Bautista PROS .40 .15
❑ T99 Preston Larrison PROS .40 .15
❑ T100 Kevin Youkilis PROS .40 .15
❑ T101 John Maine PROS .40 .15
❑ T102 Guillermo Quiroz PROS .40 .15
❑ T103 Dave Krynzel PROS .40 .15
❑ T104 David Kelton PROS .40 .15
❑ T105 Edwin Encarnacion PROS .40 .15
❑ T106 Chad Gaudin PROS .40 .15
❑ T107 Sergio Mitre PROS .40 .15
❑ T108 Laynce Nix PROS .40 .15
❑ T109 David Parrish PROS .40 .15
❑ T110 Brandon Claussen PROS .40 .15
❑ T111 Frank Francisco FY RC .40 .15
❑ T112 Brian Dallimore FY RC .40 .15
❑ T113 Jim Crowell FY RC .50 .20
❑ T114 Andres Blanco FY RC .40 .15
❑ T115 Eduardo Villacis FY RC .40 .15
❑ T116 Kazuhito Tadano FY RC .50 .20
❑ T117 Aarom Baldiris FY RC .50 .20
❑ T118 Justin Germano FY RC .40 .15
❑ T119 Joey Gathright FY RC 1.25 .50
❑ T120 Franklyn Gracesqui FY RC .40 .15
❑ T121 Chin-Lung Hu FY RC 1.25 .50
❑ T122 Scott Olsen FY RC 1.50 .60
❑ T123 Tyler Davidson FY RC .50 .20
❑ T124 Fausto Carmona FY RC 1.25 .50
❑ T125 Tim Hutting FY RC .40 .15
❑ T126 Ryan Meaux FY RC .40 .15
❑ T127 Jon Connolly FY RC 1.00 .40

	Card	Player	Price 1	Price 2
❑	T128	Hector Made FY RC	.75	.30
❑	T129	Jamie Brown FY RC	.40	.15
❑	T130	Paul McAnulty FY RC	.75	.30
❑	T131	Chris Saenz FY RC	.40	.15
❑	T132	Marland Williams FY RC	.50	.20
❑	T133	Mike Huggins FY RC	.40	.15
❑	T134	Jesse Crain FY RC	.75	.30
❑	T135	Chad Bentz FY RC	.40	.15
❑	T136	Kazuo Matsui FY RC	.75	.30
❑	T137	Paul Maholm FY RC	1.25	.50
❑	T138	Brock Jacobsen FY RC	.40	.15
❑	T139	Casey Daigle FY RC	.40	.15
❑	T140	Nyjer Morgan FY RC	.40	.15
❑	T141	Tom Mastny FY RC	.40	.15
❑	T142	Kody Kirkland FY RC	.50	.20
❑	T143	Jose Capellan FY RC	.50	.20
❑	T144	Felix Hernandez FY RC	6.00	2.50
❑	T145	Shawn Hill FY RC	.40	.15
❑	T146	Danny Gonzalez FY RC	.40	.15
❑	T147	Scott Dohmann FY RC	.40	.15
❑	T148	Tommy Murphy FY RC	.40	.15
❑	T149	Akinori Otsuka FY RC	.40	.15
❑	T150	Miguel Perez FY RC	.40	.15
❑	T151	Mike Rouse FY RC	.40	.15
❑	T152	Ramon Ramirez FY RC	.40	.15
❑	T153	Luke Hughes FY RC	.40	.15
❑	T154	Howie Kendrick FY RC	10.00	4.00
❑	T155	Ryan Budde FY RC	.40	.15
❑	T156	Charlie Zink FY RC	.40	.15
❑	T157	Warner Madrigal FY RC	.75	.30
❑	T158	Jason Szuminski FY RC	.40	.15
❑	T159	Chad Chop FY RC	.40	.15
❑	T160	Shingo Takatsu FY RC	.75	.30
❑	T161	Matt Lemanczyk FY RC	.40	.15
❑	T162	Wardell Starling FY RC	.40	.15
❑	T163	Nick Gorneault FY RC	.50	.20
❑	T164	Scott Proctor FY RC	.50	.20
❑	T165	Brooks Conrad FY RC	.50	.20
❑	T166	Hector Gimenez FY RC	.40	.15
❑	T167	Kevin Howard FY RC	.50	.20
❑	T168	Vince Perkins FY RC	.50	.20
❑	T169	Brock Peterson FY RC	.40	.15
❑	T170	Chris Shelton FY RC	1.25	.50
❑	T171	Erick Aybar FY RC	.75	.30
❑	T172	Paul Bacot FY RC	.50	.20
❑	T173	Matt Capps FY RC	.40	.15
❑	T174	Kory Casto FY RC	.50	.20
❑	T175	Juan Cedeno FY RC	.40	.15
❑	T176	Vito Chiaravalloti FY RC	.40	.15
❑	T177	Alec Zumwalt FY RC	.40	.15
❑	T178	J.J. Furmaniak FY RC	.75	.30
❑	T179	Lee Gwaltney FY RC	.40	.15
❑	T180	Donald Kelly FY RC	.40	.15
❑	T181	Benji DeQuin FY RC	.40	.15
❑	T182	Brant Colamarino FY RC	.75	.30
❑	T183	Juan Gutierrez FY RC	.40	.15
❑	T184	Carl Loadenthal FY RC	.50	.20
❑	T185	Ricky Nolasco FY RC	1.50	.60
❑	T186	Jeff Salazar FY RC	1.00	.40
❑	T187	Rob Tejeda FY RC	.75	.30
❑	T188	Alex Romero FY RC	.40	.15
❑	T189	Yoann Torrealba FY RC	.40	.15
❑	T190	Carlos Sosa FY RC	.40	.15
❑	T191	Tim Bittner FY RC	.40	.15
❑	T192	Chris Aguila FY RC	.40	.15
❑	T193	Jason Frasor FY RC	.40	.15
❑	T194	Reid Gorecki FY RC	.40	.15
❑	T195	Dustin Nippert FY RC	.50	.20
❑	T196	Javier Guzman FY RC	.50	.20
❑	T197	Harvey Garcia FY RC	.40	.15
❑	T198	Ivan Ochoa FY RC	.40	.15
❑	T199	David Wallace FY RC	.50	.20
❑	T200	Joel Zumaya FY RC	4.00	1.50
❑	T201	Casey Kopitzke FY RC	.40	.15
❑	T202	Lincoln Holdzkom FY RC	.40	.15
❑	T203	Chad Santos FY RC	.40	.15
❑	T204	Brian Pilkington FY RC	.40	.15
❑	T205	Terry Jones FY RC	.50	.20
❑	T206	Jerome Gamble FY RC	.40	.15
❑	T207	Brad Eldred FY RC	.50	.20
❑	T208	David Pauley FY RC	1.50	.60
❑	T209	Kevin Davidson FY RC	.40	.15
❑	T210	Damaso Espino FY RC	.40	.15
❑	T211	Tom Farmer FY RC	.40	.15
❑	T212	Michael Mooney FY RC	.40	.15
❑	T213	James Tomlin FY RC	.40	.15
❑	T214	Greg Thissen FY RC	.40	.15
❑	T215	Calvin Hayes FY RC	.50	.20
❑	T216	Fernando Cortez FY RC	.40	.15
❑	T217	Sergio Silva FY RC	.40	.15
❑	T218	Jon de Vries FY RC	.40	.15
❑	T219	Don Sutton FY RC	1.00	.40
❑	T220	Leo Nunez FY RC	.40	.15
❑	T221	Barry Bonds HTA EXCH	8.00	3.00

2005 Topps

	Item	Price 1	Price 2
❑	COMP.HOBBY SET (737)	80.00	40.00
❑	COMP.HOLIDAY SET (742)	80.00	40.00
❑	COMP.CUBS SET (737)	80.00	40.00
❑	COMP.GIANTS SET (737)	80.00	40.00
❑	COMP.NATIONALS SET (737)	80.00	40.00
❑	COMP.RED SOX SET (737)	80.00	40.00
❑	COMP.TIGERS SET (737)	80.00	40.00
❑	COMP.YANKEES SET (737)	80.00	40.00
❑	COMPLETE SET (732)	80.00	40.00
❑	COMPLETE SERIES 1 (366)	40.00	20.00
❑	COMPLETE SERIES 2 (366)	40.00	20.00
❑	COMMON CARD (1-6/8-734)	.20	.07
❑	COMMON (297-326/668-687)	.50	.20
❑	COMMON (327-331/688-692)	.50	.20
❑	COM (349-355/368/731-734)	1.00	.40
❑	CARD NUMBER 7 DOES NOT EXIST		
❑	OVERALL PLATE SER.1 ODDS 1:154 HTA		
❑	OVERALL PLATE SER.2 ODDS 1:112 HTA		
❑	PLATE PRINT RUN 1 SET PER COLOR		
❑	BLACK-CYAN-MAGENTA-YELLOW ISSUED		
❑	NO PLATE PRICING DUE TO SCARCITY		

	Card	Player	Price 1	Price 2
❑	1	Alex Rodriguez	1.00	.40
❑	2	Placido Polanco	.20	.07
❑	3	Torii Hunter	.20	.07
❑	4	Lyle Overbay	.20	.07
❑	5	Johnny Damon	.30	.10
❑	6	Johnny Estrada	.20	.07
❑	8	Francisco Rodriguez	.20	.07
❑	9	Jason LaRue	.20	.07
❑	10	Sammy Sosa	.50	.20
❑	11	Randy Wolf	.20	.07
❑	12	Jason Bay	.20	.07
❑	13	Tom Glavine	.30	.10
❑	14	Michael Tucker	.20	.07
❑	15	Brian Giles	.20	.07
❑	16	Dan Wilson	.20	.07
❑	17	Jim Edmonds	.20	.07
❑	18	Danys Baez	.20	.07
❑	19	Roy Halladay	.20	.07
❑	20	Hank Blalock	.20	.07
❑	21	Darin Erstad	.20	.07
❑	22	Robby Hammock	.20	.07
❑	23	Mike Hampton	.20	.07
❑	24	Mark Bellhorn	.20	.07
❑	25	Jim Thome	.30	.10
❑	26	Scott Schoeneweis	.20	.07
❑	27	Jody Gerut	.20	.07
❑	28	Vinny Castilla	.20	.07
❑	29	Luis Castillo	.20	.07
❑	30	Ivan Rodriguez	.30	.10
❑	31	Craig Biggio	.30	.10
❑	32	Joe Randa	.20	.07
❑	33	Adrian Beltre	.20	.07
❑	34	Scott Podsednik	.20	.07
❑	35	Cliff Floyd	.20	.07
❑	36	Livan Hernandez	.20	.07
❑	37	Eric Byrnes	.20	.07
❑	38	Gabe Kapler	.20	.07
❑	39	Jack Wilson	.20	.07
❑	40	Gary Sheffield	.20	.07
❑	41	Chan Ho Park	.20	.07
❑	42	Carl Crawford	.20	.07
❑	43	Miguel Batista	.20	.07
❑	44	David Bell	.20	.07
❑	45	Jeff DaVanon	.20	.07
❑	46	Brandon Webb	.20	.07
❑	47	Bronson Arroyo	.20	.07
❑	48	Melvin Mora	.20	.07
❑	49	David Ortiz	.50	.20
❑	50	Andruw Jones	.30	.10
❑	51	Chone Figgins	.20	.07
❑	52	Danny Graves	.20	.07
❑	53	Preston Wilson	.20	.07
❑	54	Jeremy Bonderman	.20	.07
❑	55	Chad Fox	.20	.07
❑	56	Dan Miceli	.20	.07
❑	57	Jimmy Gobble	.20	.07
❑	58	Darren Dreifort	.20	.07
❑	59	Matt LeCroy	.20	.07
❑	60	Jose Vidro	.20	.07
❑	61	Al Leiter	.20	.07
❑	62	Javier Vazquez	.20	.07
❑	63	Erubiel Durazo	.20	.07
❑	64	Doug Glanville	.20	.07
❑	65	Scot Shields	.20	.07
❑	66	Edgardo Alfonzo	.20	.07
❑	67	Ryan Franklin	.20	.07
❑	68	Francisco Cordero	.20	.07
❑	69	Brett Myers	.20	.07
❑	70	Curt Schilling	.30	.10
❑	71	Matt Kata	.20	.07
❑	72	Mark DeRosa	.20	.07
❑	73	Rodrigo Lopez	.20	.07
❑	74	Tim Wakefield	.30	.10
❑	75	Frank Thomas	.50	.20
❑	76	Jimmy Rollins	.20	.07
❑	77	Barry Zito	.20	.07
❑	78	Hideo Nomo	.50	.20
❑	79	Brad Wilkerson	.20	.07
❑	80	Adam Dunn	.20	.07
❑	81	Billy Traber	.20	.07
❑	82	Fernando Vina	.20	.07
❑	83	Nate Robertson	.20	.07
❑	84	Brad Ausmus	.20	.07
❑	85	Mike Sweeney	.20	.07
❑	86	Kip Wells	.20	.07
❑	87	Chris Reitsma	.20	.07
❑	88	Zach Day	.20	.07
❑	89	Tony Clark	.20	.07
❑	90	Bret Boone	.20	.07
❑	91	Mark Loretta	.20	.07
❑	92	Jerome Williams	.20	.07
❑	93	Randy Winn	.20	.07
❑	94	Marlon Anderson	.20	.07
❑	95	Aubrey Huff	.20	.07
❑	96	Kevin Mench	.20	.07
❑	97	Frank Catalanotto	.20	.07
❑	98	Flash Gordon	.20	.07
❑	99	Scott Hatteberg	.20	.07
❑	100	Albert Pujols	1.00	.40
❑	101	Jose/Bengie Molina	.50	.20
❑	102	Oscar Villarreal	.20	.07
❑	103	Jay Gibbons	.20	.07
❑	104	Byung-Hyun Kim	.20	.07
❑	105	Joe Borowski	.20	.07
❑	106	Mark Grudzielanek	.20	.07
❑	107	Mark Buehrle	.20	.07
❑	108	Paul Wilson	.20	.07
❑	109	Ronnie Belliard	.20	.07
❑	110	Reggie Sanders	.20	.07
❑	111	Tim Redding	.20	.07
❑	112	Brian Lawrence	.20	.07
❑	113	Darrell May	.20	.07
❑	114	Jose Hernandez	.20	.07
❑	115	Ben Sheets	.20	.07
❑	116	Johan Santana	.50	.20
❑	117	Billy Wagner	.20	.07
❑	118	Mariano Rivera	.50	.20
❑	119	Steve Trachsel	.20	.07
❑	120	Akinori Otsuka	.20	.07
❑	121	Bobby Kielty	.20	.07
❑	122	Orlando Hernandez	.20	.07
❑	123	Raul Ibanez	.20	.07
❑	124	Mike Matheny	.20	.07

	No.	Card		
❑	125	Vernon Wells	.20	.07
❑	126	Jason Isringhausen	.20	.07
❑	127	Jose Guillen	.20	.07
❑	128	Danny Bautista	.20	.07
❑	129	Marcus Giles	.20	.07
❑	130	Javy Lopez	.20	.07
❑	131	Kevin Millar	.20	.07
❑	132	Kyle Farnsworth	.20	.07
❑	133	Carl Pavano	.20	.07
❑	134	D'Angelo Jimenez	.20	.07
❑	135	Casey Blake	.20	.07
❑	136	Matt Holliday	.20	.07
❑	137	Bobby Higginson	.20	.07
❑	138	Nate Field	.20	.07
❑	139	Alex Gonzalez	.20	.07
❑	140	Jeff Kent	.20	.07
❑	141	Aaron Guiel	.20	.07
❑	142	Shawn Green	.20	.07
❑	143	Bill Hall	.20	.07
❑	144	Shannon Stewart	.20	.07
❑	145	Juan Rivera	.20	.07
❑	146	Coco Crisp	.20	.07
❑	147	Mike Mussina	.30	.10
❑	148	Eric Chavez	.20	.07
❑	149	Jon Lieber	.20	.07
❑	150	Vladimir Guerrero	.50	.20
❑	151	Alex Cintron	.20	.07
❑	152	Horacio Ramirez	.20	.07
❑	153	Sidney Ponson	.20	.07
❑	154	Trot Nixon	.30	.10
❑	155	Greg Maddux	.75	.30
❑	156	Edgar Renteria	.20	.07
❑	157	Ryan Freel	.20	.07
❑	158	Matt Lawton	.20	.07
❑	159	Shawn Chacon	.20	.07
❑	160	Josh Beckett	.20	.07
❑	161	Ken Harvey	.20	.07
❑	162	Juan Cruz	.20	.07
❑	163	Juan Encarnacion	.20	.07
❑	164	Wes Helms	.20	.07
❑	165	Brad Radke	.20	.07
❑	166	Claudio Vargas	.20	.07
❑	167	Mike Cameron	.20	.07
❑	168	Billy Koch	.20	.07
❑	169	Bobby Crosby	.20	.07
❑	170	Mike Lieberthal	.20	.07
❑	171	Rob Mackowiak	.20	.07
❑	172	Sean Burroughs	.20	.07
❑	173	J.T. Snow Jr.	.20	.07
❑	174	Paul Konerko	.20	.07
❑	175	Luis Gonzalez	.20	.07
❑	176	John Lackey	.20	.07
❑	177	Antonio Alfonseca	.20	.07
❑	178	Brian Roberts	.20	.07
❑	179	Bill Mueller	.20	.07
❑	180	Carlos Lee	.20	.07
❑	181	Corey Patterson	.20	.07
❑	182	Sean Casey	.20	.07
❑	183	Cliff Lee	.20	.07
❑	184	Jason Jennings	.20	.07
❑	185	Dmitri Young	.20	.07
❑	186	Juan Uribe	.20	.07
❑	187	Andy Pettitte	.30	.10
❑	188	Juan Gonzalez	.20	.07
❑	189	Pokey Reese	.20	.07
❑	190	Jason Phillips	.20	.07
❑	191	Rocky Biddle	.20	.07
❑	192	Lew Ford	.20	.07
❑	193	Mark Mulder	.20	.07
❑	194	Bobby Abreu	.20	.07
❑	195	Jason Kendall	.20	.07
❑	196	Terrence Long	.20	.07
❑	197	A.J. Pierzynski	.20	.07
❑	198	Eddie Guardado	.20	.07
❑	199	So Taguchi	.20	.07
❑	200	Jason Giambi	.20	.07
❑	201	Tony Batista	.20	.07
❑	202	Kyle Lohse	.20	.07
❑	203	Trevor Hoffman	.20	.07
❑	204	Tike Redman	.20	.07
❑	205	Matt Herges	.20	.07
❑	206	Gil Meche	.20	.07
❑	207	Chris Carpenter	.20	.07
❑	208	Ben Broussard	.20	.07
❑	209	Eric Young	.20	.07
❑	210	Doug Waechter	.20	.07
❑	211	Jarrod Washburn	.20	.07
❑	212	Chad Tracy	.20	.07
❑	213	John Smoltz	.30	.10
❑	214	Jorge Julio	.20	.07
❑	215	Todd Walker	.20	.07
❑	216	Shingo Takatsu	.20	.07
❑	217	Jose Acevedo	.20	.07
❑	218	David Riske	.20	.07
❑	219	Shawn Estes	.20	.07
❑	220	Lance Berkman	.20	.07
❑	221	Carlos Guillen	.20	.07
❑	222	Jeremy Affeldt	.20	.07
❑	223	Cesar Izturis	.20	.07
❑	224	Scott Sullivan	.20	.07
❑	225	Kazuo Matsui	.20	.07
❑	226	Josh Fogg	.20	.07
❑	227	Jason Schmidt	.20	.07
❑	228	Jason Marquis	.20	.07
❑	229	Scott Spiezio	.20	.07
❑	230	Miguel Tejada	.20	.07
❑	231	Bartolo Colon	.20	.07
❑	232	Jose Valverde	.20	.07
❑	233	Derrek Lee	.30	.10
❑	234	Scott Williamson	.20	.07
❑	235	Joe Crede	.20	.07
❑	236	John Thomson	.20	.07
❑	237	Mike MacDougal	.20	.07
❑	238	Eric Gagne	.20	.07
❑	239	Alex Sanchez	.20	.07
❑	240	Miguel Cabrera	.30	.10
❑	241	Luis Rivas	.20	.07
❑	242	Adam Everett	.20	.07
❑	243	Jason Johnson	.20	.07
❑	244	Travis Hafner	.20	.07
❑	245	Jose Valentin	.20	.07
❑	246	Stephen Randolph	.20	.07
❑	247	Rafael Furcal	.20	.07
❑	248	Adam Kennedy	.20	.07
❑	249	Luis Matos	.20	.07
❑	250	Mark Prior	.30	.10
❑	251	Angel Berroa	.20	.07
❑	252	Phil Nevin	.20	.07
❑	253	Oliver Perez	.20	.07
❑	254	Orlando Hudson	.20	.07
❑	255	Braden Looper	.20	.07
❑	256	Khalil Greene	.30	.10
❑	257	Tim Worrell	.20	.07
❑	258	Carlos Zambrano	.20	.07
❑	259	Odalis Perez	.20	.07
❑	260	Gerald Laird	.20	.07
❑	261	Jose Cruz Jr.	.20	.07
❑	262	Michael Barrett	.20	.07
❑	263	Michael Young UER	.20	.07
❑	264	Toby Hall	.20	.07
❑	265	Woody Williams	.20	.07
❑	266	Rich Harden	.20	.07
❑	267	Mike Scioscia MG	.20	.07
❑	268	Al Pedrique MG	.20	.07
❑	269	Bobby Cox MG	.20	.07
❑	270	Lee Mazzilli MG	.20	.07
❑	271	Terry Francona MG	.30	.10
❑	272	Dusty Baker MG	.20	.07
❑	273	Ozzie Guillen MG	.50	.20
❑	274	Dave Miley MG	.20	.07
❑	275	Eric Wedge MG	.20	.07
❑	276	Clint Hurdle MG	.20	.07
❑	277	Alan Trammell MG	.20	.07
❑	278	Jack McKeon MG	.20	.07
❑	279	Phil Garner MG	.20	.07
❑	280	Tony Pena MG	.20	.07
❑	281	Jim Tracy MG	.20	.07
❑	282	Ned Yost MG	.20	.07
❑	283	Ron Gardenhire MG	.20	.07
❑	284	Frank Robinson MG	.20	.07
❑	285	Art Howe MG	.20	.07
❑	286	Joe Torre MG	.30	.10
❑	287	Ken Macha MG	.20	.07
❑	288	Larry Bowa MG	.20	.07
❑	289	Lloyd McClendon MG	.20	.07
❑	290	Bruce Bochy MG	.20	.07
❑	291	Felipe Alou MG	.20	.07
❑	292	Bob Melvin MG	.20	.07
❑	293	Tony LaRussa MG	.20	.07
❑	294	Lou Piniella MG	.20	.07
❑	295	Buck Showalter MG	.20	.07
❑	296	John Gibbons MG	.20	.07
❑	297	Steve Doetsch FY RC	.75	.30
❑	298	Melky Cabrera FY RC	2.00	.75
❑	299	Luis Ramirez FY RC	.50	.20
❑	300	Chris Seddon FY RC	.50	.20
❑	301	Nate Schierholtz FY	.75	.30
❑	302	Ian Kinsler FY RC	2.00	.75
❑	303	Brandon Moss FY RC	1.50	.60
❑	304	Chadd Blasko FY RC	.75	.30
❑	305	Jeremy West FY RC	.75	.30
❑	306	Sean Marshall FY RC	1.50	.60
❑	307	Matt DeSalvo FY RC	.75	.30
❑	308	Ryan Sweeney FY RC	1.00	.40
❑	309	Matthew Lindstrom FY RC	.50	.20
❑	310	Ryan Goleski FY RC	.75	.30
❑	311	Brett Harper FY RC	.75	.30
❑	312	Chris Roberson FY RC	.50	.20
❑	313	Andre Ethier FY RC	5.00	2.00
❑	314	Chris Denorfia FY RC	1.00	.40
❑	315	Ian Bladergroen FY RC	.75	.30
❑	316	Darren Fenster FY RC	.50	.20
❑	317	Kevin West FY RC	.50	.20
❑	318	Chaz Lytle FY RC	.75	.30
❑	319	James Jurries FY RC	.75	.30
❑	320	Matt Rogelstad FY RC	.50	.20
❑	321	Wade Robinson FY RC	.50	.20
❑	322	Jake Dittler FY	.50	.20
❑	323	Brian Stavisky FY RC	.50	.20
❑	324	Kole Strayhorn FY RC	.50	.20
❑	325	Jose Vaquedano FY RC	.50	.20
❑	326	Elvys Quezada FY RC	.50	.20
❑	327	J.Maine/V.Majewski FS	.50	.20
❑	328	R.Weeks/J.Hardy FS	.50	.20
❑	329	G.Gross/G.Quiroz FS	.50	.20
❑	330	D.Wright/C.Brazell FS	3.00	1.25
❑	331	D.McPherson/J.Mathis FS	.50	.20
❑	332	Randy Johnson SH	.30	.10
❑	333	Randy Johnson SH	.30	.10
❑	334	Ichiro Suzuki SH	.50	.20
❑	335	Ken Griffey Jr. SH	.50	.20
❑	336	Greg Maddux SH	.50	.20
❑	337	Ichiro/Mora/Guerrero LL	.50	.20
❑	338	Ichiro/Young/Guerrero LL	.50	.20
❑	339	Manny/Konerko/Ortiz LL	.30	.10
❑	340	Tejada/Ortiz/Manny LL	.30	.10
❑	341	Johan/Schill/West LL	.30	.10
❑	342	Johan/Pedro/Schill LL	.30	.10
❑	343	Helton/Loretta/Beltre LL	.20	.07
❑	344	Pierre/Loretta/Wilson LL	.20	.07
❑	345	Beltre/Dunn/Pujols LL	.50	.20
❑	346	Castilla/Rolen/Pujols LL	.50	.20
❑	347	Peavy/Johnson/Sheets LL	.30	.10
❑	348	Johnson/Sheets/Schmidt LL	.30	.10
❑	349	A.Rodriguez/R.Sierra ALDS	1.00	.40
❑	350	L.Walker/A.Pujols NLDS	1.00	.40
❑	351	C.Schilling/D.Ortiz ALDS	1.00	.40
❑	352	Curt Schilling WS2	1.00	.40
❑	353	Sox Celeb/Ortiz-Schil ALCS	1.00	.40
❑	354	Cards Celeb/Puj-Edm NLCS	1.00	.40
❑	355	Mark Bellhorn WS1	1.00	.40
❑	356	Paul Konerko AS	.20	.07
❑	357	Alfonso Soriano AS	.20	.07
❑	358	Miguel Tejada AS	.20	.07
❑	359	Melvin Mora AS	.20	.07
❑	360	Vladimir Guerrero AS	.30	.10
❑	361	Ichiro Suzuki AS	.50	.20
❑	362	Manny Ramirez AS	.30	.10
❑	363	Ivan Rodriguez AS	.20	.07
❑	364	Johan Santana AS	.30	.10
❑	365	Paul Konerko AS	.20	.07
❑	366	David Ortiz AS	.30	.10
❑	367	Bobby Crosby AS	.20	.07
❑	368	Sox Celeb/Ram-Lowe WS4	1.50	.60
❑	369	Garret Anderson	.20	.07
❑	370	Randy Johnson	.50	.20
❑	371	Charles Thomas	.20	.07
❑	372	Rafael Palmeiro	.30	.10
❑	373	Kevin Youkilis	.20	.07
❑	374	Freddy Garcia	.20	.07
❑	375	Magglio Ordonez	.20	.07
❑	376	Aaron Harang	.20	.07
❑	377	Grady Sizemore	.30	.10
❑	378	Chin-Hui Tsao	.20	.07
❑	379	Eric Munson	.20	.07
❑	380	Juan Pierre	.20	.07
❑	381	Brad Lidge	.20	.07
❑	382	Brian Anderson	.20	.07

❑ 383	Alex Cora	.20	.07
❑ 384	Brady Clark	.20	.07
❑ 385	Todd Helton	.30	.10
❑ 386	Chad Cordero	.20	.07
❑ 387	Kris Benson	.20	.07
❑ 388	Brad Halsey	.20	.07
❑ 389	Jermaine Dye	.20	.07
❑ 390	Manny Ramirez	.30	.10
❑ 391	Daryle Ward	.20	.07
❑ 392	Adam Eaton	.20	.07
❑ 393	Brett Tomko	.20	.07
❑ 394	Bucky Jacobsen	.20	.07
❑ 395	Dontrelle Willis	.20	.07
❑ 396	B.J. Upton	.20	.07
❑ 397	Rocco Baldelli	.20	.07
❑ 398	Ted Lilly	.20	.07
❑ 399	Ryan Drese	.20	.07
❑ 400	Ichiro Suzuki	1.00	.40
❑ 401	Brendan Donnelly	.20	.07
❑ 402	Brandon Lyon	.20	.07
❑ 403	Nick Green	.20	.07
❑ 404	Jerry Hairston Jr.	.20	.07
❑ 405	Mike Lowell	.20	.07
❑ 406	Kerry Wood	.20	.07
❑ 407	Carl Everett	.20	.07
❑ 408	Hideki Matsui	.75	.30
❑ 409	Omar Vizquel	.30	.10
❑ 410	Joe Kennedy	.20	.07
❑ 411	Carlos Pena	.20	.07
❑ 412	Armando Benitez	.20	.07
❑ 413	Carlos Beltran	.20	.07
❑ 414	Kevin Appier	.20	.07
❑ 415	Jeff Weaver	.20	.07
❑ 416	Chad Moeller	.20	.07
❑ 417	Joe Mays	.20	.07
❑ 418	Termel Sledge	.20	.07
❑ 419	Richard Hidalgo	.20	.07
❑ 420	Kenny Lofton	.20	.07
❑ 421	Justin Duchscherer	.20	.07
❑ 422	Eric Milton	.20	.07
❑ 423	Jose Mesa	.20	.07
❑ 424	Ramon Hernandez	.20	.07
❑ 425	Jose Reyes	.20	.07
❑ 426	Joel Pineiro	.20	.07
❑ 427	Matt Morris	.20	.07
❑ 428	John Halama	.20	.07
❑ 429	Gary Matthews Jr.	.20	.07
❑ 430	Ryan Madson	.20	.07
❑ 431	Mark Kotsay	.20	.07
❑ 432	Carlos Delgado	.20	.07
❑ 433	Casey Kotchman	.20	.07
❑ 434	Greg Aquino	.20	.07
❑ 435	Eli Marrero	.20	.07
❑ 436	David Newhan	.20	.07
❑ 437	Mike Timlin	.20	.07
❑ 438	LaTroy Hawkins	.20	.07
❑ 439	Jose Contreras	.20	.07
❑ 440	Ken Griffey Jr.	.75	.30
❑ 441	C.C. Sabathia	.20	.07
❑ 442	Brandon Inge	.20	.07
❑ 443	Pete Munro	.20	.07
❑ 444	John Buck	.20	.07
❑ 445	Hee Seop Choi	.20	.07
❑ 446	Chris Capuano	.20	.07
❑ 447	Jesse Crain	.20	.07
❑ 448	Geoff Jenkins	.20	.07
❑ 449	Brian Schneider	.20	.07
❑ 450	Mike Piazza	.50	.20
❑ 451	Jorge Posada	.30	.10
❑ 452	Nick Swisher	.20	.07
❑ 453	Kevin Millwood	.20	.07
❑ 454	Mike Gonzalez	.20	.07
❑ 455	Jake Peavy	.20	.07
❑ 456	Dustin Hermanson	.20	.07
❑ 457	Jeremy Reed	.20	.07
❑ 458	Julian Tavarez	.20	.07
❑ 459	Geoff Blum	.20	.07
❑ 460	Alfonso Soriano	.20	.07
❑ 461	Alexis Rios	.20	.07
❑ 462	David Eckstein	.20	.07
❑ 463	Shea Hillenbrand	.20	.07
❑ 464	Russ Ortiz	.20	.07
❑ 465	Kurt Ainsworth	.20	.07
❑ 466	Orlando Cabrera	.20	.07
❑ 467	Carlos Silva	.20	.07
❑ 468	Ross Gload	.20	.07
❑ 469	Josh Phelps	.20	.07
❑ 470	Marquis Grissom	.20	.07
❑ 471	Mike Maroth	.20	.07
❑ 472	Guillermo Mota	.20	.07
❑ 473	Chris Burke	.20	.07
❑ 474	David DeJesus	.20	.07
❑ 475	Jose Lima	.20	.07
❑ 476	Cristian Guzman	.20	.07
❑ 477	Nick Johnson	.20	.07
❑ 478	Victor Zambrano	.20	.07
❑ 479	Rod Barajas	.20	.07
❑ 480	Damian Miller	.20	.07
❑ 481	Chase Utley	.30	.10
❑ 482	Todd Pratt	.20	.07
❑ 483	Sean Burnett	.20	.07
❑ 484	Boomer Wells	.20	.07
❑ 485	Dustan Mohr	.20	.07
❑ 486	Bobby Madritsch	.20	.07
❑ 487	Ray King	.20	.07
❑ 488	Reed Johnson	.20	.07
❑ 489	R.A. Dickey	.20	.07
❑ 490	Scott Kazmir	.20	.07
❑ 491	Tony Womack	.20	.07
❑ 492	Tomas Perez	.20	.07
❑ 493	Esteban Loaiza	.20	.07
❑ 494	Tomo Ohka	.20	.07
❑ 495	Mike Lamb	.20	.07
❑ 496	Ramon Ortiz	.20	.07
❑ 497	Richie Sexson	.20	.07
❑ 498	J.D. Drew	.20	.07
❑ 499	David Segui	.20	.07
❑ 500	Barry Bonds	2.00	.75
❑ 501	Aramis Ramirez	.20	.07
❑ 502	Wily Mo Pena	.20	.07
❑ 503	Jeromy Burnitz	.20	.07
❑ 504	Craig Monroe	.20	.07
❑ 505	Nomar Garciaparra	.50	.20
❑ 506	Brandon Backe	.20	.07
❑ 507	Marcus Thameş	.20	.07
❑ 508	Derek Lowe	.20	.07
❑ 509	Doug Davis	.20	.07
❑ 510	Joe Mauer	.50	.20
❑ 511	Endy Chavez	.20	.07
❑ 512	Bernie Williams	.30	.10
❑ 513	Mark Redman	.20	.07
❑ 514	Jason Michaels	.20	.07
❑ 515	Craig Wilson	.20	.07
❑ 516	Ryan Klesko	.20	.07
❑ 517	Ray Durham	.20	.07
❑ 518	Jose Lopez	.20	.07
❑ 519	Jeff Suppan	.20	.07
❑ 520	Julio Lugo	.20	.07
❑ 521	Mike Wood	.20	.07
❑ 522	David Bush	.20	.07
❑ 523	Juan Rincon	.20	.07
❑ 524	Paul Quantrill	.20	.07
❑ 525	Marlon Byrd	.20	.07
❑ 526	Roy Oswalt	.20	.07
❑ 527	Rondell White	.20	.07
❑ 528	Troy Glaus	.20	.07
❑ 529	Scott Hairston	.20	.07
❑ 530	Chipper Jones	.50	.20
❑ 531	Daniel Cabrera	.20	.07
❑ 532	Doug Mientkiewicz	.20	.07
❑ 533	Glendon Rusch	.20	.07
❑ 534	Jon Garland	.20	.07
❑ 535	Austin Kearns	.20	.07
❑ 536	Jake Westbrook	.20	.07
❑ 537	Aaron Miles	.20	.07
❑ 538	Omar Infante	.20	.07
❑ 539	Paul Lo Duca	.20	.07
❑ 540	Morgan Ensberg	.20	.07
❑ 541	Tony Graffanino	.20	.07
❑ 542	Milton Bradley	.20	.07
❑ 543	Keith Ginter	.20	.07
❑ 544	Justin Morneau	.20	.07
❑ 545	Tony Armas Jr.	.20	.07
❑ 546	Mike Stanton	.20	.07
❑ 547	Kevin Brown	.20	.07
❑ 548	Marco Scutaro	.20	.07
❑ 549	Tim Hudson	.20	.07
❑ 550	Pat Burrell	.20	.07
❑ 551	Ty Wigginton	.20	.07
❑ 552	Jeff Cirillo	.20	.07
❑ 553	Jim Brower	.20	.07
❑ 554	Jamie Moyer	.20	.07
❑ 555	Larry Walker	.30	.10
❑ 556	Dewon Brazelton	.20	.07
❑ 557	Brian Jordan	.20	.07
❑ 558	Josh Towers	.20	.07
❑ 559	Shigetoshi Hasegawa	.20	.07
❑ 560	Octavio Dotel	.20	.07
❑ 561	Travis Lee	.20	.07
❑ 562	Michael Cuddyer	.20	.07
❑ 563	Junior Spivey	.20	.07
❑ 564	Zack Greinke	.20	.07
❑ 565	Roger Clemens	.75	.30
❑ 566	Chris Shelton	.30	.10
❑ 567	Ugueth Urbina	.20	.07
❑ 568	Rafael Betancourt	.20	.07
❑ 569	Willie Harris	.20	.07
❑ 570	Todd Hollandsworth	.20	.07
❑ 571	Keith Foulke	.20	.07
❑ 572	Larry Bigbie	.20	.07
❑ 573	Paul Byrd	.20	.07
❑ 574	Troy Percival	.20	.07
❑ 575	Pedro Martinez	.30	.10
❑ 576	Matt Clement	.20	.07
❑ 577	Ryan Wagner	.20	.07
❑ 578	Jeff Francis	.20	.07
❑ 579	Jeff Conine	.20	.07
❑ 580	Wade Miller	.20	.07
❑ 581	Matt Stairs	.20	.07
❑ 582	Gavin Floyd	.20	.07
❑ 583	Kazuhisa Ishii	.20	.07
❑ 584	Victor Santos	.20	.07
❑ 585	Jacque Jones	.20	.07
❑ 586	Sunny Kim	.20	.07
❑ 587	Dan Kolb	.20	.07
❑ 588	Cory Lidle	.20	.07
❑ 589	Jose Castillo	.20	.07
❑ 590	Alex Gonzalez	.20	.07
❑ 591	Kirk Rueter	.20	.07
❑ 592	Jolbert Cabrera	.20	.07
❑ 593	Erik Bedard	.20	.07
❑ 594	Ben Grieve	.20	.07
❑ 595	Ricky Ledee	.20	.07
❑ 596	Mark Hendrickson	.20	.07
❑ 597	Laynce Nix	.20	.07
❑ 598	Jason Frasor	.20	.07
❑ 599	Kevin Gregg	.20	.07
❑ 600	Derek Jeter	1.00	.40
❑ 601	Luis Terrero	.20	.07
❑ 602	Jaret Wright	.20	.07
❑ 603	Edwin Jackson	.20	.07
❑ 604	Dave Roberts	.20	.07
❑ 605	Moises Alou	.20	.07
❑ 606	Aaron Rowand	.20	.07
❑ 607	Kazuhito Tadano	.20	.07
❑ 608	Luis A. Gonzalez	.20	.07
❑ 609	A.J. Burnett	.20	.07
❑ 610	Jeff Bagwell	.30	.10
❑ 611	Brad Penny	.20	.07
❑ 612	Craig Counsell	.20	.07
❑ 613	Corey Koskie	.20	.07
❑ 614	Mark Ellis	.20	.07
❑ 615	Felix Rodriguez	.20	.07
❑ 616	Jay Payton	.20	.07
❑ 617	Hector Luna	.20	.07
❑ 618	Miguel Olivo	.20	.07
❑ 619	Rob Bell	.20	.07
❑ 620	Scott Rolen	.30	.10
❑ 621	Ricardo Rodriguez	.20	.07
❑ 622	Eric Hinske	.20	.07
❑ 623	Tim Salmon	.30	.10
❑ 624	Adam LaRoche	.20	.07
❑ 625	B.J. Ryan	.20	.07
❑ 626	Roberto Alomar	.30	.10
❑ 627	Steve Finley	.20	.07
❑ 628	Joe Nathan	.20	.07
❑ 629	Scott Linebrink	.20	.07
❑ 630	Vicente Padilla	.20	.07
❑ 631	Raul Mondesi	.20	.07
❑ 632	Yadier Molina	.20	.07
❑ 633	Tino Martinez	.30	.10
❑ 634	Mark Teixeira	.30	.10
❑ 635	Kelvim Escobar	.20	.07
❑ 636	Pedro Feliz	.20	.07
❑ 637	Rich Aurilia	.20	.07
❑ 638	Los Angeles Angels TC	.20	.07
❑ 639	Arizona Diamondbacks TC	.20	.07
❑ 640	Atlanta Braves TC	.30	.10

❑ 641	Baltimore Orioles TC	.20	.07
❑ 642	Boston Red Sox TC	.50	.20
❑ 643	Chicago Cubs TC	.30	.10
❑ 644	Chicago White Sox TC	.20	.07
❑ 645	Cincinnati Reds TC	.20	.07
❑ 646	Cleveland Indians TC	.20	.07
❑ 647	Colorado Rockies TC	.20	.07
❑ 648	Detroit Tigers TC	.20	.07
❑ 649	Florida Marlins TC	.20	.07
❑ 650	Houston Astros TC	.20	.07
❑ 651	Kansas City Royals TC	.20	.07
❑ 652	Los Angeles Dodgers TC	.20	.07
❑ 653	Milwaukee Brewers TC	.20	.07
❑ 654	Minnesota Twins TC	.20	.07
❑ 655	Montreal Expos TC	.20	.07
❑ 656	New York Mets TC	.20	.07
❑ 657	New York Yankees TC	.50	.20
❑ 658	Oakland Athletics TC	.20	.07
❑ 659	Philadelphia Phillies TC	.20	.07
❑ 660	Pittsburgh Pirates TC	.20	.07
❑ 661	San Diego Padres TC	.20	.07
❑ 662	San Francisco Giants TC	.20	.07
❑ 663	Seattle Mariners TC	.20	.07
❑ 664	St. Louis Cardinals TC	.30	.10
❑ 665	Tampa Bay Devil Rays TC	.20	.07
❑ 666	Texas Rangers TC	.20	.07
❑ 667	Toronto Blue Jays TC	.20	.07
❑ 668	Billy Butler FY RC	4.00	1.50
❑ 669	Wes Swackhamer FY RC	.50	.20
❑ 670	Matt Campbell FY RC	.50	.20
❑ 671	Ryan Webb FY	.50	.20
❑ 672	Glen Perkins FY RC	.75	.30
❑ 673	Michael Rogers FY RC	.50	.20
❑ 674	Kevin Melillo FY RC	.75	.30
❑ 675	Erik Cordier FY RC	.50	.20
❑ 676	Landon Powell FY RC	.75	.30
❑ 677	Justin Verlander FY RC	4.00	1.50
❑ 678	Eric Nielsen FY RC	.50	.20
❑ 679	Alexander Smit FY RC	.50	.20
❑ 680	Ryan Garko FY RC	1.50	.60
❑ 681	Bobby Livingston FY RC	.50	.20
❑ 682	Jeff Niemann FY RC	.75	.30
❑ 683	Wladimir Balentien FY RC	.75	.30
❑ 684	Chip Cannon FY RC	.75	.30
❑ 685	Yorman Bazardo FY RC	.50	.20
❑ 686	Mike Bourn FY RC	.75	.30
❑ 687	Andy LaRoche FY RC	3.00	1.25
❑ 688	F.Hernandez/J.Leone	.50	.20
❑ 689	R.Howard/C.Hamels	5.00	2.00
❑ 690	M.Cain/M.Valdez	1.00	.40
❑ 691	A.Marte/J.Francoeur	2.00	.75
❑ 692	C.Billingsley/J.Guzman	.50	.20
❑ 693	J.Hairston Jr./S.Hairston	.20	.07
❑ 694	M.Tejada/L.Berkman	.30	.10
❑ 695	Kenny Rogers GG	.20	.07
❑ 696	Ivan Rodriguez GG	.20	.07
❑ 697	Darin Erstad GG	.20	.07
❑ 698	Bret Boone GG	.20	.07
❑ 699	Eric Chavez GG	.20	.07
❑ 700	Derek Jeter GG	.50	.20
❑ 701	Vernon Wells GG	.20	.07
❑ 702	Ichiro Suzuki GG	.50	.20
❑ 703	Torii Hunter GG	.20	.07
❑ 704	Greg Maddux GG	.50	.20
❑ 705	Mike Matheny GG	.20	.07
❑ 706	Todd Helton GG	.20	.07
❑ 707	Luis Castillo GG	.20	.07
❑ 708	Scott Rolen GG	.20	.07
❑ 709	Cesar Izturis GG	.20	.07
❑ 710	Jim Edmonds GG	.20	.07
❑ 711	Andruw Jones GG	.20	.07
❑ 712	Steve Finley GG	.20	.07
❑ 713	Johan Santana CY	.30	.10
❑ 714	Roger Clemens CY	.50	.20
❑ 715	Vladimir Guerrero MVP	.30	.10
❑ 716	Barry Bonds MVP	1.00	.40
❑ 717	Bobby Crosby ROY	.20	.07
❑ 718	Jason Bay ROY	.20	.07
❑ 719	Albert Pujols AS	.50	.20
❑ 720	Mark Loretta AS	.20	.07
❑ 721	Edgar Renteria AS	.20	.07
❑ 722	Scott Rolen AS	.20	.07
❑ 723	J.D. Drew AS	.20	.07
❑ 724	Jim Edmonds AS	.20	.07
❑ 725	Johnny Estrada AS	.20	.07
❑ 726	Jason Schmidt AS	.20	.07
❑ 727	Chris Carpenter AS	.20	.07
❑ 728	Eric Gagne AS	.20	.07
❑ 729	Jason Bay AS	.20	.07
❑ 730	Bobby Cox MG AS	.20	.07
❑ 731	D.Ortiz/M.Bellhorn WS1	1.00	.40
❑ 732	Curt Schilling WS2	1.00	.40
❑ 733	M.Ramirez/P.Martinez WS3	1.00	.40
❑ 734	Sox Win Damon/Lowe WS4	1.50	.60

2005 Topps Factory Set Draft Picks Bonus

❑	COMPLETE SET (5)	20.00	10.00
❑	ONE SET PER FACTORY SET		
❑ 1	Beau Jones	5.00	2.00
❑ 2	Cliff Pennington	4.00	1.50
❑ 3	Chris Volstad	5.00	2.00
❑ 4	Ricky Romero	5.00	2.00
❑ 5	Jay Bruce	10.00	4.00

2005 Topps Update

❑	COMPLETE SET (330)	40.00	15.00
❑	COMP.FACT.SET (330)	40.00	25.00
❑	COMMON CARD (1-330)	.20	.07
❑	COM (90-110/203-220)	.50	.20
❑	COMMON (116-134)	.50	.20
❑	COM (14/66/221-310)	.50	.20
❑	COMMON (311-330)	.50	.20
❑	PLATE ODDS 1:2009 H, 1:582 HTA, 1:2009 R		
❑	PLATE PRINT RUN 1 SET PER COLOR		
❑	BLACK-CYAN-MAGENTA-YELLOW ISSUED		
❑	NO PLATE PRICING DUE TO SCARCITY		
❑ 1	Sammy Sosa	.50	.20
❑ 2	Jeff Francoeur	1.50	.60
❑ 3	Tony Clark	.20	.07
❑ 4	Michael Tucker	.20	.07
❑ 5	Mike Matheny	.20	.07
❑ 6	Eric Young	.20	.07
❑ 7	Jose Valentin	.20	.07
❑ 8	Matt Lawton	.20	.07
❑ 9	Juan Rivera	.20	.07
❑ 10	Shawn Green	.20	.07
❑ 11	Aaron Boone	.20	.07
❑ 12	Woody Williams	.20	.07
❑ 13	Brad Wilkerson	.20	.07
❑ 14	Anthony Reyes RC	1.00	.40
❑ 15	Russ Adams	.20	.07
❑ 16	Gustavo Chacin	.20	.07
❑ 17	Michael Restovich	.20	.07
❑ 18	Humberto Quintero	.20	.07
❑ 19	Matt Ginter	.20	.07
❑ 20	Scott Podsednik	.20	.07
❑ 21	Byung-Hyun Kim	.20	.07
❑ 22	Orlando Hernandez	.20	.07
❑ 23	Mark Grudzielanek	.20	.07
❑ 24	Jody Gerut	.20	.07
❑ 25	Adrian Beltre	.20	.07
❑ 26	Scott Schoeneweis	.20	.07
❑ 27	Marlon Anderson	.20	.07
❑ 28	Jason Vargas	.20	.07
❑ 29	Claudio Vargas	.20	.07
❑ 30	Jason Kendall	.20	.07
❑ 31	Aaron Small	.20	.07
❑ 32	Juan Cruz	.20	.07
❑ 33	Placido Polanco	.20	.07
❑ 34	Jorge Sosa	.20	.07
❑ 35	John Olerud	.20	.07
❑ 36	Ryan Langerhans	.20	.07
❑ 37	Randy Winn	.20	.07
❑ 38	Zach Duke	.30	.10
❑ 39	Garrett Atkins	.20	.07
❑ 40	Al Leiter	.20	.07
❑ 41	Shawn Chacon	.20	.07
❑ 42	Mark DeRosa	.20	.07
❑ 43	Miguel Ojeda	.20	.07
❑ 44	A.J. Pierzynski	.20	.07
❑ 45	Carlos Lee	.20	.07
❑ 46	LaTroy Hawkins	.20	.07
❑ 47	Nick Green	.20	.07
❑ 48	Shawn Estes	.20	.07
❑ 49	Eli Marrero	.20	.07
❑ 50	Jeff Kent	.20	.07
❑ 51	Joe Randa	.20	.07
❑ 52	Jose Hernandez	.20	.07
❑ 53	Joe Blanton	.20	.07
❑ 54	Huston Street	.30	.10
❑ 55	Marlon Byrd	.20	.07
❑ 56	Alex Sanchez	.20	.07
❑ 57	Livan Hernandez	.20	.07
❑ 58	Chris Young	.20	.07
❑ 59	Brad Eldred	.20	.07
❑ 60	Terrence Long	.20	.07
❑ 61	Phil Nevin	.20	.07
❑ 62	Kyle Farnsworth	.20	.07
❑ 63	Jon Lieber	.20	.07
❑ 64	Antonio Alfonseca	.20	.07
❑ 65	Tony Graffanino	.20	.07
❑ 66	Tadahito Iguchi RC	1.50	.60
❑ 67	Brad Thompson	.20	.07
❑ 68	Jose Vidro	.20	.07
❑ 69	Jason Phillips	.20	.07
❑ 70	Carl Pavano	.20	.07
❑ 71	Pokey Reese	.20	.07
❑ 72	Jerome Williams	.20	.07
❑ 73	Kazuhisa Ishii	.20	.07
❑ 74	Zach Day	.20	.07
❑ 75	Edgar Renteria	.20	.07
❑ 76	Mike Myers	.20	.07
❑ 77	Jeff Cirillo	.20	.07
❑ 78	Endy Chavez	.20	.07
❑ 79	Jose Guillen	.20	.07
❑ 80	Ugueth Urbina	.20	.07
❑ 81	Vinny Castilla	.20	.07
❑ 82	Javier Vazquez	.20	.07
❑ 83	Willy Taveras	.20	.07
❑ 84	Mark Mulder	.20	.07
❑ 85	Mike Hargrove MG	.20	.07
❑ 86	Buddy Bell MG	.20	.07
❑ 87	Charlie Manuel MG	.20	.07
❑ 88	Willie Randolph MG	.20	.07
❑ 89	Bob Melvin MG	.20	.07
❑ 90	Chris Lambert PROS	.50	.20
❑ 91	Homer Bailey PROS	.50	.20
❑ 92	Ervin Santana PROS	.50	.20
❑ 93	Bill Bray PROS	.50	.20
❑ 94	Thomas Diamond PROS	.50	.20
❑ 95	Trevor Plouffe PROS	.50	.20
❑ 96	James Houser PROS	.50	.20
❑ 97	Jake Stevens PROS	.50	.20
❑ 98	Anthony Whittington PROS	.50	.20
❑ 99	Philip Hughes PROS	.50	.20
❑ 100	Greg Golson PROS	.50	.20
❑ 101	Paul Maholm PROS	.50	.20
❑ 102	Carlos Quentin PROS	.50	.20
❑ 103	Dan Johnson PROS	.50	.20
❑ 104	Mark Rogers PROS	.50	.20
❑ 105	Neil Walker PROS	.50	.20
❑ 106	Omar Quintanilla PROS	.50	.20
❑ 107	Blake DeWitt PROS	.50	.20
❑ 108	Taylor Tankersley PROS	.50	.20
❑ 109	David Murphy PROS	.50	.20
❑ 110	Felix Hernandez PROS	1.00	.40
❑ 111	Craig Biggio HL	.20	.07
❑ 112	Greg Maddux HL	.50	.20
❑ 113	Bobby Abreu HL	.20	.07
❑ 114	Alex Rodriguez HL	.50	.20
❑ 115	Trevor Hoffman HL	.20	.07
❑ 116	A.Pierzynski/T.Iguchi ALDS	.50	.20
❑ 117	Reggie Sanders NLDS	.50	.20
❑ 118	B.Molina/E.Santana ALDS	.50	.20
❑ 119	Burke/Berkman/LaR NLDS	.50	.20
❑ 120	Garret Anderson ALCS	.50	.20
❑ 121	A.J. Pierzynski ALCS	.50	.20
❑ 122	Paul Konerko ALCS	.50	.20

❑ 123 Joe Crede ALCS .50 .20
❑ 124 M.Buehrle/J.Garland ALCS .50 .20
❑ 125 F.Garcia/J.Contreras ALCS .50 .20
❑ 126 Reggie Sanders NLCS .50 .20
❑ 127 Roy Oswalt NLCS .50 .20
❑ 128 Roger Clemens NLCS 1.00 .40
❑ 129 Albert Pujols NLCS 1.00 .40
❑ 130 Roy Oswalt NLCS .50 .20
❑ 131 J.Crede/B.Jenks WS .75 .30
❑ 132 P.Konerko/S.Podsed WS .75 .30
❑ 133 Geoff Blum WS .50 .20
❑ 134 White Sox Sweep WS 1.00 .40
❑ 135 ARod/Ortiz/Manny AL HR .50 .20
❑ 136 Young/ARod/Vlad AL BA .30 .10
❑ 137 Ortiz/Teix/Manny AL RBI .30 .10
❑ 138 Colon/Garland/Lee AL W .20 .07
❑ 139 Mill/Johan/Buehrle AL ERA .30 .10
❑ 140 Johan/Randy/Lackey AL K .30 .10
❑ 141 Andruw/Lee/Pujols NL HR .50 .20
❑ 142 Lee/Pujols/Cabrera NL BA .50 .20
❑ 143 Andruw/Pujols/Burr NL RBI .50 .20
❑ 144 Willis/Carp/Oswalt NL W .20 .07
❑ 145 Roger/Andy/Willis NL ERA .50 .20
❑ 146 Peavy/Carp/Pedro NL K .20 .07
❑ 147 Mark Teixeira AS .20 .07
❑ 148 Brian Roberts AS .20 .07
❑ 149 Michael Young AS .20 .07
❑ 150 Alex Rodriguez AS .50 .20
❑ 151 Johnny Damon AS .20 .07
❑ 152 Vladimir Guerrero AS .30 .10
❑ 153 Manny Ramirez AS .20 .07
❑ 154 David Ortiz AS .30 .10
❑ 155 Mariano Rivera AS .30 .10
❑ 156 Joe Nathan AS .20 .07
❑ 157 Albert Pujols AS .50 .20
❑ 158 Jeff Kent AS .20 .07
❑ 159 Felipe Lopez AS .20 .07
❑ 160 Morgan Ensberg AS .20 .07
❑ 161 Miguel Cabrera AS .20 .07
❑ 162 Ken Griffey Jr. AS .50 .20
❑ 163 Andruw Jones AS .20 .07
❑ 164 Paul Lo Duca AS .20 .07
❑ 165 Chad Cordero AS .20 .07
❑ 166 Ken Griffey Jr. Comeback .50 .20
❑ 167 Jason Giambi Comeback .20 .07
❑ 168 Willy Taveras ROY .20 .07
❑ 169 Huston Street ROY .20 .07
❑ 170 Chris Carpenter AS .20 .07
❑ 171 Bartolo Colon AS .20 .07
❑ 172 Bobby Cox AS MG .20 .07
❑ 173 Ozzie Guillen AS MG .50 .20
❑ 174 Andruw Jones POY .20 .07
❑ 175 Johnny Damon AS .20 .07
❑ 176 Alex Rodriguez AS .50 .20
❑ 177 David Ortiz AS .30 .10
❑ 178 Manny Ramirez AS .20 .07
❑ 179 Miguel Tejada AS .20 .07
❑ 180 Vladimir Guerrero AS .30 .10
❑ 181 Mark Teixeira AS .20 .07
❑ 182 Ivan Rodriguez AS .20 .07
❑ 183 Brian Roberts AS .20 .07
❑ 184 Mark Buehrle AS .20 .07
❑ 185 Bobby Abreu AS .20 .07
❑ 186 Carlos Beltran AS .20 .07
❑ 187 Albert Pujols AS .50 .20
❑ 188 Derrek Lee AS .20 .07
❑ 189 Jim Edmonds AS .20 .07
❑ 190 Aramis Ramirez AS .20 .07
❑ 191 Mike Piazza AS .30 .10
❑ 192 Jeff Kent AS .20 .07
❑ 193 David Eckstein AS .20 .07
❑ 194 Chris Carpenter AS .20 .07
❑ 195 Bobby Abreu HR .20 .07
❑ 196 Ivan Rodriguez HR .20 .07
❑ 197 Carlos Lee HR .20 .07
❑ 198 David Ortiz HR .30 .10
❑ 199 Hee-Seop Choi HR .20 .07
❑ 200 Andruw Jones HR .20 .07
❑ 201 Mark Teixeira HR .20 .07
❑ 202 Jason Bay HR .20 .07
❑ 203 Hanley Ramirez FUT .50 .20
❑ 204 Shin-Soo Choo FUT .50 .20
❑ 205 Justin Huber FUT .50 .20
❑ 206 Nelson Cruz FUT RC 1.25 .50
❑ 207 Edwin Encarnacion FUT .50 .20
❑ 208 Miguel Montero FUT RC 1.25 .50
❑ 209 William Bergolla FUT .50 .20
❑ 210 Luis Montanez FUT .50 .20
❑ 211 Francisco Liriano FUT 1.50 .60
❑ 212 Kevin Thompson FUT .50 .20
❑ 213 B.J. Upton FUT .50 .20
❑ 214 Conor Jackson FUT .50 .20
❑ 215 Delmon Young FUT .50 .20
❑ 216 Andy LaRoche FUT 1.00 .40
❑ 217 Ryan Garko FUT 1.25 .50
❑ 218 Josh Barfield FUT .50 .20
❑ 219 Chris B.Young FUT .50 .20
❑ 220 Justin Verlander FUT 1.50 .60
❑ 221 Drew Anderson FY RC .50 .20
❑ 222 Luis Hernandez FY RC .50 .20
❑ 223 Jim Burt FY RC .50 .20
❑ 224 Mike Morse FY RC .50 .20
❑ 225 Elliot Johnson FY RC .50 .20
❑ 226 C.J. Smith FY RC .50 .20
❑ 227 Casey McGehee FY RC .50 .20
❑ 228 Brian Miller FY RC .50 .20
❑ 229 Chris Vines FY RC .50 .20
❑ 230 D.J. Houlton FY RC .50 .20
❑ 231 Chuck Tiffany FY RC 1.00 .40
❑ 232 Humberto Sanchez FY RC 2.00 .75
❑ 233 Baltazar Lopez FY RC .50 .20
❑ 234 Russ Martin FY RC 1.25 .50
❑ 235 Dana Eveland FY RC .50 .20
❑ 236 Johan Silva FY RC .50 .20
❑ 237 Adam Harben FY RC .75 .30
❑ 238 Brian Bannister FY RC 1.00 .40
❑ 239 Adam Boeve FY RC .50 .20
❑ 240 Thomas Oldham FY RC .50 .20
❑ 241 Cody Haerther FY RC .50 .20
❑ 242 Dan Santin FY RC .50 .20
❑ 243 Daniel Haigwood FY RC .75 .30
❑ 244 Craig Tatum FY RC .50 .20
❑ 245 Martin Prado FY RC .50 .20
❑ 246 Errol Simonitsch FY RC .75 .30
❑ 247 Lorenzo Scott FY RC .50 .20
❑ 248 Hayden Penn FY RC .75 .30
❑ 249 Heath Totten FY RC .50 .20
❑ 250 Nick Masset FY RC .50 .20
❑ 251 Pedro Lopez FY RC .50 .20
❑ 252 Ben Harrison FY .50 .20
❑ 253 Mike Spidale FY RC .50 .20
❑ 254 Jeremy Harts FY RC .50 .20
❑ 255 Danny Zell FY RC .50 .20
❑ 256 Kevin Collins FY RC .50 .20
❑ 257 Tony Americh FY RC .50 .20
❑ 258 Matt Albers FY RC 1.25 .50
❑ 259 Ricky Barrett FY RC .50 .20
❑ 260 Hernan Iribarren FY RC .75 .30
❑ 261 Sean Tracey FY RC .50 .20
❑ 262 Jerry Owens FY RC .75 .30
❑ 263 Steve Nelson FY RC .50 .20
❑ 264 Brandon McCarthy FY RC 1.00 .40
❑ 265 David Shepard FY RC .50 .20
❑ 266 Steven Bondurant FY RC .50 .20
❑ 267 Billy Sadler FY RC .50 .20
❑ 268 Ryan Feierabend FY RC .50 .20
❑ 269 Stuart Pomeranz FY RC .50 .20
❑ 270 Shaun Marcum FY .50 .20
❑ 271 Erik Schindewolf FY RC .50 .20
❑ 272 Stefan Bailie FY RC .50 .20
❑ 273 Mike Esposito FY RC .50 .20
❑ 274 Buck Coats FY RC .50 .20
❑ 275 Andy Sides FY RC .50 .20
❑ 276 Micah Schnurstein FY RC .50 .20
❑ 277 Jesse Gutierrez FY RC .50 .20
❑ 278 Jake Postlewait FY RC .50 .20
❑ 279 Willy Mota FY RC .50 .20
❑ 280 Ryan Speier FY RC .50 .20
❑ 281 Frank Mata FY RC .50 .20
❑ 282 Jair Jurrjens FY RC 1.25 .50
❑ 283 Nick Touchstone FY RC .50 .20
❑ 284 Matthew Kemp FY RC 3.00 1.25
❑ 285 Vinny Rottino FY RC .50 .20
❑ 286 J.B. Thurmond FY RC .50 .20
❑ 287 Kelvin Pichardo FY RC .50 .20
❑ 288 Scott Mitchinson FY RC .50 .20
❑ 289 Darwinson Salazar FY RC .50 .20
❑ 290 George Kottaras FY RC .75 .30
❑ 291 Kenny Durost FY RC .50 .20
❑ 292 Jonathan Sanchez FY RC 1.25 .50
❑ 293 Brandon Moorhead FY RC .50 .20
❑ 294 Kennard Bibbs FY RC .50 .20
❑ 295 David Gassner FY RC .50 .20
❑ 296 Micah Furtado FY RC .50 .20
❑ 297 Ismael Ramirez FY RC .50 .20
❑ 298 Carlos Gonzalez FY RC 2.00 .75
❑ 299 Brandon Sing FY RC .75 .30
❑ 300 Jason Motte FY RC .50 .20
❑ 301 Chuck James FY RC 1.25 .50
❑ 302 Andy Santana FY RC .50 .20
❑ 303 Manny Parra FY RC .50 .20
❑ 304 Chris B.Young FY RC 1.25 .50
❑ 305 Juan Senreiso FY RC .50 .20
❑ 306 Franklin Morales FY RC .75 .30
❑ 307 Jared Gothreaux FY RC .50 .20
❑ 308 Jayce Tingler FY RC .50 .20
❑ 309 Matt Brown FY RC .50 .20
❑ 310 Frank Diaz FY RC .50 .20
❑ 311 Stephen Drew DP RC 4.00 1.50
❑ 312 Jered Weaver DP RC 4.00 1.50
❑ 313 Ryan Braun DP RC 2.50 1.00
❑ 314 John Mayberry Jr. DP RC 1.00 .40
❑ 315 Aaron Thompson DP RC .75 .30
❑ 316 Cesar Carrillo DP RC 1.00 .40
❑ 317 Jacoby Ellsbury DP RC 1.50 .60
❑ 318 Matt Garza DP RC 2.00 .75
❑ 319 Cliff Pennington DP RC .75 .30
❑ 320 Colby Rasmus DP RC 2.00 .75
❑ 321 Chris Volstad DP RC 1.00 .40
❑ 322 Ricky Romero DP RC .75 .30
❑ 323 Ryan Zimmerman DP RC 5.00 2.00
❑ 324 C.J. Henry DP RC 1.50 .60
❑ 325 Jay Bruce DP RC 3.00 1.25
❑ 326 Beau Jones DP RC 1.00 .40
❑ 327 Mark McCormick DP RC .75 .30
❑ 328 Eli Iorg DP RC .75 .30
❑ 329 Andrew McCutchen DP RC 2.00 .75
❑ 330 Mike Costanzo DP RC 1.25 .50

2006 Topps

❑ COMP.HOBBY SET (664) 80.00 50.00
❑ COMP.HOLIDAY SET (659) 80.00 50.00
❑ COMP.CARDINALS SET (664) 80.00 50.00
❑ COMP.CUBS SET (664) 80.00 50.00
❑ COMP.PIRATES SET (664) 80.00 50.00
❑ COMP.RED SOX SET (664) 80.00 50.00
❑ COMP.YANKEES SET (664) 80.00 50.00
❑ COMPLETE SET (659) 80.00 30.00
❑ COMPLETE SERIES 1 (329) 40.00 15.00
❑ COMPLETE SERIES 2 (330) 40.00 15.00
❑ COMMON CARD (1-660) .20 .07
❑ COMP.SER.1 SET EXCLUDES CARD 297
❑ CARD 297 NOT INTENDED FOR RELEASE
❑ CARDS 287b AND 312b ISSUED IN FACT.SET
❑ 2 TICKETS EXCH.CARD RANDOM IN PACKS
❑ OVERALL PLATE SER.1 ODDS 1:246 HTA
❑ OVERALL PLATE SER.2 ODDS 1:193 HTA
❑ PLATE PRINT RUN 1 SET PER COLOR
❑ BLACK-CYAN-MAGENTA-YELLOW ISSUED
❑ NO PLATE PRICING DUE TO SCARCITY
❑ 1 Alex Rodriguez .75 .30
❑ 2 Jose Valentin .20 .07
❑ 3 Garrett Atkins .20 .07
❑ 4 Scott Hatteberg .20 .07
❑ 5 Carl Crawford .20 .07
❑ 6 Armando Benitez .20 .07
❑ 7 Mickey Mantle 8.00 3.00
❑ 8 Mike Morse .20 .07
❑ 9 Damian Miller .20 .07

❑ 10	Clint Barmes	.20	.07
❑ 11	Michael Barrett	.20	.07
❑ 12	Coco Crisp	.20	.07
❑ 13	Tadahito Iguchi	.20	.07
❑ 14	Chris Snyder	.20	.07
❑ 15	Brian Roberts	.20	.07
❑ 16	David Wright	.75	.30
❑ 17	Victor Santos	.20	.07
❑ 18	Trevor Hoffman	.20	.07
❑ 19	Jeremy Reed	.20	.07
❑ 20	Bobby Abreu	.20	.07
❑ 21	Lance Berkman	.20	.07
❑ 22	Zach Day	.20	.07
❑ 23	Jonny Gomes	.20	.07
❑ 24	Jason Marquis	.20	.07
❑ 25	Chipper Jones	.50	.20
❑ 26	Scott Hairston	.20	.07
❑ 27	Ryan Dempster	.20	.07
❑ 28	Brandon Inge	.20	.07
❑ 29	Aaron Harang	.20	.07
❑ 30	Jon Garland	.20	.07
❑ 31	Pokey Reese	.20	.07
❑ 32	Mike MacDougal	.20	.07
❑ 33	Mike Lieberthal	.20	.07
❑ 34	Cesar Izturis	.20	.07
❑ 35	Brad Wilkerson	.20	.07
❑ 36	Jeff Suppan	.20	.07
❑ 37	Adam Everett	.20	.07
❑ 38	Bengie Molina	.20	.07
❑ 39	Rickie Weeks	.20	.07
❑ 40	Jorge Posada	.30	.10
❑ 41	Rheal Cormier	.20	.07
❑ 42	Reed Johnson	.20	.07
❑ 43	Laynce Nix	.20	.07
❑ 44	Carl Everett	.20	.07
❑ 45	Greg Maddux	.75	.30
❑ 46	Jeff Francis	.20	.07
❑ 47	Felipe Lopez	.20	.07
❑ 48	Dan Johnson	.20	.07
❑ 49	Humberto Cota	.20	.07
❑ 50	Manny Ramirez	.30	.10
❑ 51	Juan Uribe	.20	.07
❑ 52	Jaret Wright	.20	.07
❑ 53	Tomo Ohka	.20	.07
❑ 54	Mike Matheny	.20	.07
❑ 55	Joe Mauer	.50	.20
❑ 56	Jarrod Washburn	.20	.07
❑ 57	Randy Winn	.20	.07
❑ 58	Pedro Feliz	.20	.07
❑ 59	Kenny Rogers	.20	.07
❑ 60	Rocco Baldelli	.20	.07
❑ 61	Eric Hinske	.20	.07
❑ 62	Damaso Marte	.20	.07
❑ 63	Desi Relaford	.20	.07
❑ 64	Juan Encarnacion	.20	.07
❑ 65	Nomar Garciaparra	.50	.20
❑ 66	Shawn Estes	.20	.07
❑ 67	Brian Jordan	.20	.07
❑ 68	Steve Kline	.20	.07
❑ 69	Braden Looper	.20	.07
❑ 70	Carlos Lee	.20	.07
❑ 71	Tom Glavine	.30	.10
❑ 72	Craig Biggio	.30	.10
❑ 73	Steve Finley	.20	.07
❑ 74	David Newhan	.20	.07
❑ 75	Eric Gagne	.20	.07
❑ 76	Tony Graffanino	.20	.07
❑ 77	Dallas McPherson	.20	.07
❑ 78	Nick Punto	.20	.07
❑ 79	Mark Kotsay	.20	.07
❑ 80	Kerry Wood	.20	.07
❑ 81	Kyle Farnsworth	.20	.07
❑ 82	Huston Street	.20	.07
❑ 83	Endy Chavez	.20	.07
❑ 84	So Taguchi	.20	.07
❑ 85	Hank Blalock	.20	.07
❑ 86	Brad Radke	.20	.07
❑ 87	Chien-Ming Wang	.75	.30
❑ 88	B.J. Surhoff	.20	.07
❑ 89	Glendon Rusch	.20	.07
❑ 90	Mark Buehrle	.20	.07
❑ 91	Rafael Betancourt	.20	.07
❑ 92	Lance Cormier	.20	.07
❑ 93	Alex Gonzalez	.20	.07
❑ 94	Matt Stairs	.20	.07
❑ 95	Andy Pettitte	.30	.10
❑ 96	Jesse Crain	.20	.07
❑ 97	Kenny Lofton	.20	.07
❑ 98	Geoff Blum	.20	.07
❑ 99	Mark Redman	.20	.07
❑ 100	Barry Bonds	1.00	.40
❑ 101	Chad Orvella	.20	.07
❑ 102	Xavier Nady	.20	.07
❑ 103	Junior Spivey	.20	.07
❑ 104	Bernie Williams	.30	.10
❑ 105	Victor Martinez	.20	.07
❑ 106	Nook Logan	.20	.07
❑ 107	Mark Teahen	.20	.07
❑ 108	Mike Lamb	.20	.07
❑ 109	Jayson Werth	.20	.07
❑ 110	Mariano Rivera	.50	.20
❑ 111	Erubiel Durazo	.20	.07
❑ 112	Ryan Vogelsong	.20	.07
❑ 113	Bobby Madritsch	.20	.07
❑ 114	Travis Lee	.20	.07
❑ 115	Adam Dunn	.20	.07
❑ 116	David Riske	.20	.07
❑ 117	Troy Percival	.20	.07
❑ 118	Chad Tracy	.20	.07
❑ 119	Andy Marte	.20	.07
❑ 120	Edgar Renteria	.20	.07
❑ 121	Jason Giambi	.20	.07
❑ 122	Justin Morneau	.20	.07
❑ 123	J.T. Snow	.20	.07
❑ 124	Danys Baez	.20	.07
❑ 125	Carlos Delgado	.20	.07
❑ 126	John Buck	.20	.07
❑ 127	Shannon Stewart	.20	.07
❑ 128	Mike Cameron	.20	.07
❑ 129	Joe McEwing	.20	.07
❑ 130	Richie Sexson	.20	.07
❑ 131	Rod Barajas	.20	.07
❑ 132	Russ Adams	.20	.07
❑ 133	J.D. Closser	.20	.07
❑ 134	Ramon Ortiz	.20	.07
❑ 135	Josh Beckett	.20	.07
❑ 136	Ryan Freel	.20	.07
❑ 137	Victor Zambrano	.20	.07
❑ 138	Ronnie Belliard	.20	.07
❑ 139	Jason Michaels	.20	.07
❑ 140	Brian Giles	.20	.07
❑ 141	Randy Wolf	.20	.07
❑ 142	Robinson Cano	.30	.10
❑ 143	Joe Blanton	.20	.07
❑ 144	Esteban Loaiza	.20	.07
❑ 145	Troy Glaus	.20	.07
❑ 146	Matt Clement	.20	.07
❑ 147	Geoff Jenkins	.20	.07
❑ 148	John Thomson	.20	.07
❑ 149	A.J. Pierzynski	.20	.07
❑ 150	Pedro Martinez	.30	.10
❑ 151	Roger Clemens	1.00	.40
❑ 152	Jack Wilson	.20	.07
❑ 153	Ray King	.20	.07
❑ 154	Ryan Church	.20	.07
❑ 155	Paul Lo Duca	.20	.07
❑ 156	Dan Wheeler	.20	.07
❑ 157	Carlos Zambrano	.20	.07
❑ 158	Mike Timlin	.20	.07
❑ 159	Brandon Claussen	.20	.07
❑ 160	Travis Hafner	.20	.07
❑ 161	Chris Shelton	.20	.07
❑ 162	Rafael Furcal	.20	.07
❑ 163	Tom Gordon	.20	.07
❑ 164	Noah Lowry	.20	.07
❑ 165	Larry Walker	.30	.10
❑ 166	Dave Roberts	.20	.07
❑ 167	Scott Schoeneweis	.20	.07
❑ 168	Julian Tavarez	.20	.07
❑ 169	Jhonny Peralta	.20	.07
❑ 170	Vernon Wells	.20	.07
❑ 171	Jorge Cantu	.20	.07
❑ 172	Todd Greene	.20	.07
❑ 173	Willy Taveras	.20	.07
❑ 174	Corey Patterson	.20	.07
❑ 175	Ivan Rodriguez	.30	.10
❑ 176	Bobby Kielty	.20	.07
❑ 177	Jose Reyes	.20	.07
❑ 178	Barry Zito	.20	.07
❑ 179	Deivi Cruz	.20	.07
❑ 180	Mark Teixeira	.30	.10
❑ 181	Chone Figgins	.20	.07
❑ 182	Aaron Rowand	.20	.07
❑ 183	Tim Wakefield	.20	.07
❑ 184	Mike Maroth	.20	.07
❑ 185	Johnny Damon	.30	.10
❑ 186	Vicente Padilla	.20	.07
❑ 187	Ryan Klesko	.20	.07
❑ 188	Gary Matthews	.20	.07
❑ 189	Jose Mesa	.20	.07
❑ 190	Nick Johnson	.20	.07
❑ 191	Freddy Garcia	.20	.07
❑ 192	Larry Bigbie	.20	.07
❑ 193	Chris Ray	.20	.07
❑ 194	Torii Hunter	.20	.07
❑ 195	Mike Sweeney	.20	.07
❑ 196	Brad Penny	.20	.07
❑ 197	Jason Frasor	.20	.07
❑ 198	Kevin Mench	.20	.07
❑ 199	Adam Kennedy	.20	.07
❑ 200	Albert Pujols	1.00	.40
❑ 201	Jody Gerut	.20	.07
❑ 202	Luis Gonzalez	.20	.07
❑ 203	Zack Greinke	.20	.07
❑ 204	Miguel Cairo	.20	.07
❑ 205	Jimmy Rollins	.20	.07
❑ 206	Edgardo Alfonzo	.20	.07
❑ 207	Billy Wagner	.20	.07
❑ 208	B.J. Ryan	.20	.07
❑ 209	Orlando Hudson	.20	.07
❑ 210	Preston Wilson	.20	.07
❑ 211	Melvin Mora	.20	.07
❑ 212	Bill Mueller	.20	.07
❑ 213	Javy Lopez	.20	.07
❑ 214	Wilson Betemit	.20	.07
❑ 215	Garret Anderson	.20	.07
❑ 216	Russell Branyan	.20	.07
❑ 217	Jeff Weaver	.20	.07
❑ 218	Doug Mientkiewicz	.20	.07
❑ 219	Mark Ellis	.20	.07
❑ 220	Jason Bay	.20	.07
❑ 221	Adam LaRoche	.20	.07
❑ 222	C.C. Sabathia	.20	.07
❑ 223	Humberto Quintero	.20	.07
❑ 224	Bartolo Colon	.20	.07
❑ 225	Ichiro Suzuki	.75	.30
❑ 226	Brett Tomko	.20	.07
❑ 227	Corey Koskie	.20	.07
❑ 228	David Eckstein	.20	.07
❑ 229	Cristian Guzman	.20	.07
❑ 230	Jeff Kent	.20	.07
❑ 231	Chris Capuano	.20	.07
❑ 232	Rodrigo Lopez	.20	.07
❑ 233	Jason Phillips	.20	.07
❑ 234	Luis Rivas	.20	.07
❑ 235	Cliff Floyd	.20	.07
❑ 236	Gil Meche	.20	.07
❑ 237	Adam Eaton	.20	.07
❑ 238	Matt Morris	.20	.07
❑ 239	Kyle Davies	.20	.07
❑ 240	David Wells	.20	.07
❑ 241	John Smoltz	.30	.10
❑ 242	Felix Hernandez	.50	.20
❑ 243	Kenny Rogers GG	.20	.07
❑ 244	Mark Teixeira GG	.20	.07
❑ 245	Orlando Hudson GG	.20	.07
❑ 246	Derek Jeter GG	.50	.20
❑ 247	Eric Chavez GG	.20	.07
❑ 248	Torii Hunter GG	.20	.07
❑ 249	Vernon Wells GG	.20	.07
❑ 250	Ichiro Suzuki GG	.50	.20
❑ 251	Greg Maddux GG	.50	.20
❑ 252	Mike Matheny GG	.20	.07
❑ 253	Derrek Lee GG	.20	.07
❑ 254	Luis Castillo GG	.20	.07
❑ 255	Omar Vizquel GG	.20	.07
❑ 256	Mike Lowell GG	.20	.07
❑ 257	Andruw Jones GG	.20	.07
❑ 258	Jim Edmonds GG	.20	.07
❑ 259	Bobby Abreu GG	.20	.07
❑ 260	Bartolo Colon CY	.20	.07
❑ 261	Chris Carpenter CY	.20	.07
❑ 262	Alex Rodriguez MVP	.50	.20
❑ 263	Albert Pujols MVP	.50	.20
❑ 264	Huston Street ROY	.20	.07
❑ 265	Ryan Howard ROY	.40	.15
❑ 266	Bob Melvin MG	.20	.07
❑ 267	Bobby Cox MG	.20	.07

❑ 268 Baltimore Orioles TC .20 .07
❑ 269 Boston Red Sox TC .50 .20
❑ 270 Chicago White Sox TC .50 .20
❑ 271 Dusty Baker MG .20 .07
❑ 272 Jerry Narron MG .20 .07
❑ 273 Cleveland Indians TC .20 .07
❑ 274 Clint Hurdle MG .20 .07
❑ 275 Detroit Tigers TC .20 .07
❑ 276 Jack McKeon MG .20 .07
❑ 277 Phil Garner MG .20 .07
❑ 278 Kansas City Royals TC .20 .07
❑ 279 Jim Tracy MG .20 .07
❑ 280 Los Angeles Angels TC .20 .07
❑ 281 Milwaukee Brewers TC .20 .07
❑ 282 Minnesota Twins TC .20 .07
❑ 283 Willie Randolph MG .20 .07
❑ 284 New York Yankees TC .50 .20
❑ 285 Oakland Athletics TC .20 .07
❑ 286 Charlie Manuel MG .20 .07
❑ 287a Pete Mackanin MG UER .20 .07
❑ 287b Pete Mackanin MG COR .20 .07
❑ 288 Bruce Bochy MG .20 .07
❑ 289 Felipe Alou MG .20 .07
❑ 290 Seattle Mariners TC .20 .07
❑ 291 Tony LaRussa MG .20 .07
❑ 292 Tampa Bay Devil Rays TC .20 .07
❑ 293 Texas Rangers TC .20 .07
❑ 294 Toronto Blue Jays TC .20 .07
❑ 295 Frank Robinson MG .30 .10
❑ 296 Anderson Hernandez (RC) .50 .20
❑ 297A Alex Gordon (RC) Full 1200.00 800.00
❑ 297B Alex Gordon Cut Out 120.00 60.00
❑ 297C Alex Gordon Blank Gold 400.00 250.00
❑ 297D Alex Gordon Blank Silver
❑ 298 Jason Botts (RC) .50 .20
❑ 299 Jeff Mathis (RC) .50 .20
❑ 300 Ryan Garko (RC) .50 .20
❑ 301 Charlton Jimerson (RC) .50 .20
❑ 302 Chris Denorfia (RC) .50 .20
❑ 303 Anthony Reyes (RC) .50 .20
❑ 304 Bryan Bullington (RC) .50 .20
❑ 305 Chuck James (RC) .50 .20
❑ 306 Danny Sandoval RC .50 .20
❑ 307 Walter Young (RC) .50 .20
❑ 308 Fausto Carmona (RC) .50 .20
❑ 309 Francisco Liriano (RC) 2.00 .75
❑ 310 Hong-Chih Kuo (RC) 1.00 .40
❑ 311 Joe Saunders (RC) .50 .20
❑ 312a John Koronka UER (RC) .50 .20
❑ 312b John Koronka COR (RC) .50 .20
❑ 313 Robert Andino RC .50 .20
❑ 314 Shaun Marcum (RC) .50 .20
❑ 315 Tom Gorzelanny (RC) .50 .20
❑ 316 Craig Breslow RC .50 .20
❑ 317 Chris DeMaria RC .50 .20
❑ 318 Brayan Pena (RC) .50 .20
❑ 319 Rich Hill (RC) .50 .20
❑ 320 Rick Short (RC) .50 .20
❑ 321 C.J. Wilson (RC) .50 .20
❑ 322 Marshall McDougall (RC) .50 .20
❑ 323 Darrell Rasner (RC) .50 .20
❑ 324 Brandon Watson (RC) .50 .20
❑ 325 Paul McAnulty (RC) .50 .20
❑ 326 D.Jeter/A.Rodriguez TS 1.00 .40
❑ 327 M.Tejada/M.Mora TS .20 .07
❑ 328 M.Giles/C.Jones TS .30 .10
❑ 329 M.Ramirez/D.Ortiz TS .50 .20
❑ 330 M.Barrett/G.Maddux TS .50 .20
❑ 331 Matt Holliday .20 .07
❑ 332 Orlando Cabrera .20 .07
❑ 333 Ryan Langerhans .20 .07
❑ 334 Lew Ford .20 .07
❑ 335 Mark Prior .30 .10
❑ 336 Ted Lilly .20 .07
❑ 337 Michael Young .20 .07
❑ 338 Livan Hernandez .20 .07
❑ 339 Yadier Molina .20 .07
❑ 340 Eric Chavez .20 .07
❑ 341 Miguel Batista .20 .07
❑ 342 Bruce Chen .20 .07
❑ 343 Sean Casey .20 .07
❑ 344 Doug Davis .20 .07
❑ 345 Andruw Jones .30 .10
❑ 346 Hideki Matsui .50 .20
❑ 347 Joe Randa .20 .07
❑ 348 Reggie Sanders .20 .07
❑ 349 Jason Jennings .20 .07
❑ 350 Joe Nathan .20 .07
❑ 351 Jose Lopez .20 .07
❑ 352 John Lackey .20 .07
❑ 353 Claudio Vargas .20 .07
❑ 354 Grady Sizemore .30 .10
❑ 355 Jon Papelbon (RC) 2.00 .75
❑ 356 Luis Matos .20 .07
❑ 357 Orlando Hernandez .20 .07
❑ 358 Jamie Moyer .20 .07
❑ 359 Chase Utley .50 .20
❑ 360 Moises Alou .20 .07
❑ 361 Chad Cordero .20 .07
❑ 362 Brian McCann .20 .07
❑ 363 Jermaine Dye .20 .07
❑ 364 Ryan Madson .20 .07
❑ 365 Aramis Ramirez .20 .07
❑ 366 Matt Treanor .20 .07
❑ 367 Ray Durham .20 .07
❑ 368 Khalil Greene .30 .10
❑ 369 Mike Hampton .20 .07
❑ 370 Mike Mussina .30 .10
❑ 371 Brad Hawpe .20 .07
❑ 372 Marlon Byrd .20 .07
❑ 373 Woody Williams .20 .07
❑ 374 Victor Diaz .20 .07
❑ 375 Brady Clark .20 .07
❑ 376 Luis Gonzalez .20 .07
❑ 377 Raul Ibanez .20 .07
❑ 378 Tony Clark .20 .07
❑ 379 Shawn Chacon .20 .07
❑ 380 Marcus Giles .20 .07
❑ 381 Odalis Perez .20 .07
❑ 382 Steve Trachsel .20 .07
❑ 383 Russ Ortiz .20 .07
❑ 384 Toby Hall .20 .07
❑ 385 Bill Hall .20 .07
❑ 386 Luke Hudson .20 .07
❑ 387 Ken Griffey Jr. .75 .30
❑ 388 Tim Hudson .20 .07
❑ 389 Brian Moehler .20 .07
❑ 390 Jake Peavy .20 .07
❑ 391 Casey Blake .20 .07
❑ 392 Sidney Ponson .20 .07
❑ 393 Brian Schneider .20 .07
❑ 394 J.J. Hardy .20 .07
❑ 395 Austin Kearns .20 .07
❑ 396 Pat Burrell .20 .07
❑ 397 Jason Vargas .20 .07
❑ 398 Ryan Howard .75 .30
❑ 399 Joe Crede .20 .07
❑ 400 Vladimir Guerrero .50 .20
❑ 401 Roy Halladay .20 .07
❑ 402 David Dellucci .20 .07
❑ 403 Brandon Webb .20 .07
❑ 404 Marlon Anderson .20 .07
❑ 405 Miguel Tejada .20 .07
❑ 406 Ryan Doumit .20 .07
❑ 407 Kevin Youkilis .20 .07
❑ 408 Jon Lieber .20 .07
❑ 409 Edwin Encarnacion .20 .07
❑ 410 Miguel Cabrera .30 .10
❑ 411 A.J. Burnett .20 .07
❑ 412 David Bell .20 .07
❑ 413 Gregg Zaun .20 .07
❑ 414 Lance Niekro .20 .07
❑ 415 Shawn Green .20 .07
❑ 416 Roberto Hernandez .20 .07
❑ 417 Jay Gibbons .20 .07
❑ 418 Johnny Estrada .20 .07
❑ 419 Omar Vizquel .30 .10
❑ 420 Gary Sheffield .20 .07
❑ 421 Brad Halsey .20 .07
❑ 422 Aaron Cook .20 .07
❑ 423 David Ortiz .50 .20
❑ 424 Tony Womack .20 .07
❑ 425 Joe Kennedy .20 .07
❑ 426 Dustin McGowan .20 .07
❑ 427 Carl Pavano .20 .07
❑ 428 Nick Green .20 .07
❑ 429 Francisco Cordero .20 .07
❑ 430 Octavio Dotel .20 .07
❑ 431 Julio Franco .20 .07
❑ 432 Brett Myers .20 .07
❑ 433 Casey Kotchman .20 .07
❑ 434 Frank Catalanotto .20 .07
❑ 435 Paul Konerko .20 .07
❑ 436 Keith Foulke .20 .07
❑ 437 Juan Rivera .20 .07
❑ 438 Todd Pratt .20 .07
❑ 439 Ben Broussard .20 .07
❑ 440 Scott Kazmir .30 .10
❑ 441 Rich Aurilia .20 .07
❑ 442 Craig Monroe .20 .07
❑ 443 Danny Kolb .20 .07
❑ 444 Curtis Granderson .20 .07
❑ 445 Jeff Francoeur .50 .20
❑ 446 Dustin Hermanson .20 .07
❑ 447 Jacque Jones .20 .07
❑ 448 Bobby Crosby .20 .07
❑ 449 Jason LaRue .20 .07
❑ 450 Derrek Lee .20 .07
❑ 451 Curt Schilling .30 .10
❑ 452 Jake Westbrook .20 .07
❑ 453 Daniel Cabrera .20 .07
❑ 454 Bobby Jenks .20 .07
❑ 455 Dontrelle Willis .20 .07
❑ 456 Brad Lidge .20 .07
❑ 457 Shea Hillenbrand .20 .07
❑ 458 Luis Castillo .20 .07
❑ 459 Mark Hendrickson .20 .07
❑ 460 Randy Johnson .50 .20
❑ 461 Placido Polanco .20 .07
❑ 462 Aaron Boone .20 .07
❑ 463 Todd Walker .20 .07
❑ 464 Nick Swisher .20 .07
❑ 465 Joel Pineiro .20 .07
❑ 466 Jay Payton .20 .07
❑ 467 Cliff Lee .20 .07
❑ 468 Johan Santana .30 .10
❑ 469 Josh Willingham .20 .07
❑ 470 Jeremy Bonderman .20 .07
❑ 471 Runelvys Hernandez .20 .07
❑ 472 Duaner Sanchez .20 .07
❑ 473 Jason Lane .20 .07
❑ 474 Trot Nixon .20 .07
❑ 475 Ramon Hernandez .20 .07
❑ 476 Mike Lowell .20 .07
❑ 477 Chan Ho Park .20 .07
❑ 478 Doug Waechter .20 .07
❑ 479 Carlos Silva .20 .07
❑ 480 Jose Contreras .20 .07
❑ 481 Vinny Castilla .20 .07
❑ 482 Chris Reitsma .20 .07
❑ 483 Jose Guillen .20 .07
❑ 484 Aaron Hill .20 .07
❑ 485 Kevin Millwood .20 .07
❑ 486 Wily Mo Pena .20 .07
❑ 487 Rich Harden .20 .07
❑ 488 Chris Carpenter .20 .07
❑ 489 Jason Bartlett .20 .07
❑ 490 Magglio Ordonez .20 .07
❑ 491 John Rodriguez .20 .07
❑ 492 Bob Wickman .20 .07
❑ 493 Eddie Guardado .20 .07
❑ 494 Kip Wells .20 .07
❑ 495 Adrian Beltre .20 .07
❑ 496 Jose Capellan (RC) .50 .20
❑ 497 Scott Podsednik .20 .07
❑ 498 Brad Thompson .20 .07
❑ 499 Aaron Heilman .20 .07
❑ 500 Derek Jeter 1.25 .50
❑ 501 Emil Brown .20 .07
❑ 502 Morgan Ensberg .20 .07
❑ 503 Nate Bump .20 .07
❑ 504 Phil Nevin .20 .07
❑ 505 Jason Schmidt .20 .07
❑ 506 Michael Cuddyer .20 .07
❑ 507 John Patterson .20 .07
❑ 508 Danny Haren .20 .07
❑ 509 Freddy Sanchez .20 .07
❑ 510 J.D. Drew .20 .07
❑ 511 Dmitri Young .20 .07
❑ 512 Eric Milton .20 .07
❑ 513 Ervin Santana .20 .07
❑ 514 Mark Loretta .20 .07
❑ 515 Mark Grudzielanek .20 .07
❑ 516 Derrick Turnbow .20 .07
❑ 517 Denny Bautista .20 .07
❑ 518 Lyle Overbay .20 .07
❑ 519 Julio Lugo .20 .07
❑ 520 Carlos Beltran .20 .07

No.	Card		
521	Jose Cruz Jr.	.20	.07
522	Jason Isringhausen	.20	.07
523	Bronson Arroyo	.20	.07
524	Ben Sheets	.20	.07
525	Zach Duke	.20	.07
526	Ryan Wagner	.20	.07
527	Jose Vidro	.20	.07
528	Doug Mirabelli	.20	.07
529	Kris Benson	.20	.07
530	Carlos Guillen	.20	.07
531	Juan Pierre	.20	.07
532	Scot Shields	.20	.07
533	Scott Hatteberg	.20	.07
534	Tim Stauffer	.20	.07
535	Jim Edmonds	.30	.10
536	Scot Eyre	.20	.07
537	Ben Johnson	.20	.07
538	Mark Mulder	.20	.07
539	Juan Rincon	.20	.07
540	Gustavo Chacin	.20	.07
541	Oliver Perez	.20	.07
542	Chris Young	.20	.07
543	Edinson Volquez	.20	.07
544	Mark Bellhorn	.20	.07
545	Kelvim Escobar	.20	.07
546	Andy Sisco	.20	.07
547	Derek Lowe	.20	.07
548	Sean Burroughs	.20	.07
549	Erik Bedard	.20	.07
550	Alfonso Soriano	.20	.07
551	Matt Murton	.20	.07
552	Eric Byrnes	.20	.07
553	Chris Duffy	.20	.07
554	Kazuo Matsui	.20	.07
555	Scott Rolen	.30	.10
556	Rob Mackowiak	.20	.07
557	Chris Burke	.20	.07
558	Jeromy Burnitz	.20	.07
559	Jerry Hairston Jr.	.20	.07
560	Jim Thome	.30	.10
561	Miguel Olivo	.20	.07
562	Jose Castillo	.20	.07
563	Brad Ausmus	.20	.07
564	Yorvit Torrealba	.20	.07
565	David DeJesus	.20	.07
566	Paul Byrd	.20	.07
567	Brandon Backe	.20	.07
568	Aubrey Huff	.20	.07
569	Mike Jacobs	.20	.07
570	Todd Helton	.30	.10
571	Angel Berroa	.20	.07
572	Todd Jones	.20	.07
573	Jeff Bagwell	.30	.10
574	Darin Erstad	.20	.07
575	Roy Oswalt	.20	.07
576	Rondell White	.20	.07
577	Alex Rios	.20	.07
578	Wes Helms	.20	.07
579	Javier Vazquez	.20	.07
580	Frank Thomas	.50	.20
581	Brian Fuentes	.20	.07
582	Francisco Rodriguez	.20	.07
583	Craig Counsell	.20	.07
584	Jorge Sosa	.20	.07
585	Mike Piazza	.50	.20
586	Mike Scioscia MG	.20	.07
587	Joe Torre MG	.30	.10
588	Ken Macha MG	.20	.07
589	John Gibbons MG	.20	.07
590	Joe Maddon MG	.20	.07
591	Eric Wedge MG	.20	.07
592	Mike Hargrove MG	.20	.07
593	Sam Perlozzo MG	.20	.07
594	Buck Showalter MG	.20	.07
595	Terry Francona MG	.20	.07
596	Buddy Bell MG	.20	.07
597	Jim Leyland MG	.20	.07
598	Ron Gardenhire MG	.20	.07
599	Ozzie Guillen MG	.20	.07
600	Ned Yost MG	.20	.07
601	Atlanta Braves TC	.30	.10
602	Philadelphia Phillies TC	.20	.07
603	New York Mets TC	.20	.07
604	Washington Nationals TC	.20	.07
605	Florida Marlins TC	.20	.07
606	Houston Astros TC	.20	.07
607	Chicago Cubs TC	.30	.10
608	St. Louis Cardinals TC	.30	.10
609	Pittsburgh Pirates TC	.20	.07
610	Cincinnati Reds TC	.20	.07
611	Colorado Rockies TC	.20	.07
612	Los Angeles Dodgers TC	.20	.07
613	San Francisco Giants TC	.20	.07
614	San Diego Padres TC	.20	.07
615	Arizona Diamondbacks TC	.20	.07
616	Kenji Johjima RC	2.00	.75
617	Ryan Zimmerman (RC)	2.50	1.00
618	Craig Hansen RC	1.50	.60
619	Joey Devine RC	.50	.20
620	Hanley Ramirez (RC)	.60	.25
621	Scott Olsen (RC)	.50	.20
622	Jason Bergmann RC	.50	.20
623	Geovany Soto (RC)	.50	.20
624	J.J. Furmaniak (RC)	.50	.20
625	Jeremy Accardo RC	.50	.20
626	Mark Woodyard (RC)	.50	.20
627	Matt Capps (RC)	.50	.20
628	Tim Corcoran RC	.50	.20
629	Ryan Jorgensen RC	.50	.20
630	Ronny Paulino (RC)	.50	.20
631	Dan Uggla (RC)	1.00	.40
632	Ian Kinsler (RC)	.60	.25
633	Josh Barfield (RC)	.50	.20
634	Reggie Abercrombie (RC)	.50	.20
635	Joel Zumaya (RC)	1.25	.50
636	Matt Cain (RC)	.75	.30
637	Conor Jackson (RC)	.75	.30
638	Brian Anderson (RC)	.50	.20
639	Prince Fielder (RC)	1.50	.60
640	Jeremy Hermida (RC)	.75	.30
641	Justin Verlander (RC)	1.50	.60
642	Brian Bannister (RC)	.50	.20
643	Willie Eyre (RC)	.50	.20
644	Ricky Nolasco (RC)	.50	.20
645	Paul Maholm (RC)	.50	.20
646	J.Damon/J.Giambi	.30	.10
647	R.White/L.Ford	.20	.07
648	O.Hernandez/O.Hudson	.20	.07
649	A.Dunn/K.Griffey Jr.	.75	.30
650	P.Burrell/M.Lieberthal	.20	.07
651	J.Reyes/K.Matsui	.20	.07
652	H.Blalock/M.Young	.20	.07
653	P.Fielder/R.Weeks	.75	.30
654	T.Lee/R.Baldelli	.20	.07
655	D.Lee/A.Ramirez	.20	.07
656	G.Sizemore/A.Boone	.30	.10
657	Gonzalez/Green/Hill	.20	.07
658	I.Rodriguez/C.Guillen	.30	.10
659	A.Rodriguez/G.Sheffield	.75	.30
660	E.Santana/F.Rodriguez	.20	.07
RC1	Alay Soler	150.00	90.00
NNO	2 Tickets EXCH	20.00	8.00

2003 Topps 205

COMPLETE SERIES 1 (165)	40.00	15.00
COMPLETE SERIES 2 (175)	125.00	75.00
COMP.SERIES 2 w/o SP's (155)	40.00	15.00
COM (1-130/161-169/193-315)	.50	.20
COMMON (131-145/170-192)	.50	.20
COMMON CARD (146-160)	1.00	.40
COMMON SP	2.50	1.00
SERIES 2 SP STATED ODDS 1:5		

No.	Card		
1A	Barry Bonds w/Cap	3.00	1.25
1B	Barry Bonds w/Helmet	3.00	1.25
2	Bret Boone	.50	.20
3A	Albert Pujols Clear Logo	2.50	1.00
3B	Albert Pujols White Logo	2.50	1.00
4	Carl Crawford	.50	.20
5	Bartolo Colon	.50	.20
6	Cliff Floyd	.50	.20
7	John Olerud	.50	.20
8A	Jason Giambi Full Jkt	.50	.20
8B	Jason Giambi Partial Jkt	.50	.20
9	Edgardo Alfonzo	.50	.20
10	Ivan Rodriguez	.75	.30
11	Jim Edmonds	.50	.20
12A	Mike Piazza Orange	2.00	.75
12B	Mike Piazza Yellow	2.00	.75
13	Greg Maddux	2.00	.75
14	Jose Vidro	.50	.20
15A	Vlad Guerrero Clear Logo	1.25	.50
15B	Vlad Guerrero White Logo	1.25	.50
16	Bernie Williams	.75	.30
17	Roger Clemens	2.50	1.00
18A	Miguel Tejada Blue	.50	.20
18B	Miguel Tejada Green	.50	.20
19	Carlos Delgado	.50	.20
20A	Alfonso Soriano w/Bat	.50	.20
20B	Alfonso Soriano Sunglasses	.50	.20
21	Bobby Cox MG	.50	.20
22	Mike Scioscia	.50	.20
23	John Smoltz	.75	.30
24	Luis Gonzalez	.50	.20
25	Shawn Green	.50	.20
26	Raul Ibanez	.50	.20
27	Andruw Jones	.75	.30
28	Josh Beckett	.50	.20
29	Derek Lowe	.50	.20
30	Todd Helton	.75	.30
31	Barry Larkin	.75	.30
32	Jason Jennings	.50	.20
33	Darin Erstad	.50	.20
34	Magglio Ordonez	.50	.20
35	Mike Sweeney	.50	.20
36	Kazuhisa Ishii	.50	.20
37	Ron Gardenhire MG	.50	.20
38	Tim Hudson	.50	.20
39	Tim Salmon	.75	.30
40A	Pat Burrell Black Bat	.50	.20
40B	Pat Burrell Brown Bat	.50	.20
41	Manny Ramirez	.75	.30
42	Nick Johnson	.50	.20
43	Tom Glavine	.75	.30
44	Mark Mulder	.50	.20
45	Brian Jordan	.50	.20
46	Rafael Palmeiro	.75	.30
47	Vernon Wells	.50	.20
48	Bob Brenly MG	.50	.20
49	C.C. Sabathia	.50	.20
50A	Alex Rodriguez Look Ahead	2.00	.75
50B	Alex Rodriguez Look Away	2.00	.75
51A	Sammy Sosa Head Duck	1.25	.50
51B	Sammy Sosa Head Left	1.25	.50
52	Paul Konerko	.50	.20
53	Craig Biggio	.75	.30
54	Moises Alou	.50	.20
55	Johnny Damon	.75	.30
56	Torii Hunter	.50	.20
57	Omar Vizquel	.75	.30
58	Orlando Hernandez	.50	.20
59	Barry Zito	.50	.20
60	Lance Berkman	.50	.20
61	Carlos Beltran	.50	.20
62	Edgar Renteria	.50	.20
63	Ben Sheets	.50	.20
64	Doug Mientkiewicz	.50	.20
65	Troy Glaus	.50	.20
66	Preston Wilson	.50	.20
67	Kerry Wood	.50	.20
68	Frank Thomas	1.25	.50
69	Jimmy Rollins	.50	.20
70	Brian Giles	.50	.20
71	Bobby Higginson	.50	.20
72	Larry Walker	.50	.20
73	Randy Johnson	1.25	.50
74	Tony LaRussa MG	.50	.20
75A	Derek Jeter w/Gold Trim	3.00	1.25
75B	Derek Jeter w/o Gold Trim	3.00	1.25
76	Bobby Abreu	.50	.20
77A	Adam Dunn Closed Mouth	.50	.20

❑ 77B Adam Dunn Open Mouth .50 .20
❑ 78 Ryan Klesko .50 .20
❑ 79 Francisco Rodriguez .50 .20
❑ 80 Scott Rolen .75 .30
❑ 81 Roberto Alomar .75 .30
❑ 82 Joe Torre MG .75 .30
❑ 83 Jim Thome .75 .30
❑ 84 Kevin Millwood .50 .20
❑ 85 J.T. Snow .50 .20
❑ 86 Trevor Hoffman .50 .20
❑ 87 Jay Gibbons .50 .20
❑ 88A Mark Prior New Logo .75 .30
❑ 88B Mark Prior Old Logo .75 .30
❑ 89 Rich Aurilia .50 .20
❑ 90 Chipper Jones 1.25 .50
❑ 91 Richie Sexson .50 .20
❑ 92 Gary Sheffield .50 .20
❑ 93 Pedro Martinez .75 .30
❑ 94 Rodrigo Lopez .50 .20
❑ 95 Al Leiter .50 .20
❑ 96 Jorge Posada .75 .30
❑ 97 Luis Castillo .50 .20
❑ 98 Aubrey Huff .50 .20
❑ 99 A.J. Pierzynski .50 .20
❑ 100A Ichiro Suzuki Look Ahead 2.50 1.00
❑ 100B Ichiro Suzuki Look Right 2.50 1.00
❑ 101 Eric Chavez .50 .20
❑ 102 Brett Myers .50 .20
❑ 103 Jason Kendall .50 .20
❑ 104 Jeff Kent .50 .20
❑ 105 Eric Hinske .50 .20
❑ 106 Jacque Jones .50 .20
❑ 107 Phil Nevin .50 .20
❑ 108 Roy Oswalt .50 .20
❑ 109 Curt Schilling .50 .20
❑ 110A N.Garciaparra w/Gold Trim 2.00 .75
❑ 110B N.Garciaparra w/o Gold Trim 2.00 .75
❑ 111 Garret Anderson .50 .20
❑ 112 Eric Gagne .50 .20
❑ 113 Javier Vazquez .50 .20
❑ 114 Jeff Bagwell .75 .30
❑ 115 Mike Lowell .50 .20
❑ 116 Carlos Pena .50 .20
❑ 117 Ken Griffey Jr. 2.00 .75
❑ 118 Tony Batista .50 .20
❑ 119 Edgar Martinez .75 .30
❑ 120 Austin Kearns .50 .20
❑ 121 Jason Stokes PROS .50 .20
❑ 122 Jose Reyes PROS .50 .20
❑ 123 Rocco Baldelli PROS .50 .20
❑ 124 Joe Borchard PROS .50 .20
❑ 125 Joe Mauer PROS 1.25 .50
❑ 126 Gavin Floyd PROS .50 .20
❑ 127 Mark Teixeira PROS .75 .30
❑ 128 Jeremy Guthrie PROS .50 .20
❑ 129 B.J. Upton PROS 1.25 .50
❑ 130 Khalil Greene PROS 1.25 .50
❑ 131 Hanley Ramirez FY RC 5.00 2.00
❑ 132 Andy Marte FY RC 4.00 1.50
❑ 133 J.D. Durbin FY RC .50 .20
❑ 134 Jason Kubel FY RC 1.25 .50
❑ 135 Craig Brazell FY RC .50 .20
❑ 136 Bryan Bullington FY RC .50 .20
❑ 137 Jose Contreras FY RC 1.00 .40
❑ 138 Brian Burgamy FY RC .50 .20
❑ 139 Evel Bastida-Martinez FY RC .50 .20
❑ 140 Joey Gomes FY RC .50 .20
❑ 141 Ismael Castro FY RC .60 .25
❑ 142 Travis Wong FY RC .60 .25
❑ 143 Michael Garciaparra FY RC .50 .20
❑ 144 Arnaldo Munoz FY RC .50 .20
❑ 145 Louis Sockalexis FY XRC .50 .20
❑ 146 Richard Hoblitzell REP 1.00 .40
❑ 147 George Graham REP 1.00 .40
❑ 148 Hal Chase REP 1.00 .40
❑ 149 John McGraw REP 1.50 .60
❑ 150 Bobby Wallace REP 1.00 .40
❑ 151 David Shean REP 1.00 .40
❑ 152 Richard Hoblitzell REP SP 2.50 1.00
❑ 153 Hal Chase REP 1.00 .40
❑ 154 Hooks Wiltse REP 1.00 .40
❑ 155 George Brett RET 3.00 1.25
❑ 156 Willie Mays RET 3.00 1.25
❑ 157 Honus Wagner RET SP 10.00 4.00
❑ 158 Nolan Ryan RET 4.00 1.50
❑ 159 Reggie Jackson RET 1.50 .60
❑ 160 Mike Schmidt RET 3.00 1.25
❑ 161 Josh Barfield PROS .50 .20
❑ 162 Grady Sizemore PROS 1.25 .50
❑ 163 Justin Morneau PROS .50 .20
❑ 164 Laynce Nix PROS .50 .20
❑ 165 Zack Greinke PROS .50 .20
❑ 166 Victor Martinez PROS .75 .30
❑ 167 Jeff Mathis PROS .50 .20
❑ 168 Casey Kotchman PROS .50 .20
❑ 169 Gabe Gross PROS .50 .20
❑ 170 Edwin Jackson FY RC .60 .25
❑ 171 Delmon Young FY SP RC 10.00 4.00
❑ 172 Eric Duncan FY SP RC 5.00 2.00
❑ 173 Brian Snyder FY SP RC 5.00 2.00
❑ 174 Chris Lubanski FY SP RC 5.00 2.00
❑ 175 Ryan Harvey FY SP RC 6.00 2.50
❑ 176 Nick Markakis FY SP RC 8.00 3.00
❑ 177 Chad Billingsley FY SP RC 8.00 3.00
❑ 178 Elizardo Ramirez FY RC .60 .25
❑ 179 Ben Francisco FY RC .50 .20
❑ 180 Franklin Gutierrez FY SP RC 5.00 2.00
❑ 181 Aaron Hill FY SP RC 5.00 2.00
❑ 182 Kevin Correia FY RC .50 .20
❑ 183 Kelly Shoppach FY RC 1.00 .40
❑ 184 Felix Pie FY SP RC 8.00 3.00
❑ 185 Adam Loewen FY SP RC 5.00 2.00
❑ 186 Danny Garcia FY RC .50 .20
❑ 187 Rickie Weeks FY SP RC 8.00 3.00
❑ 188 Robby Hammock FY SP RC 4.00 1.50
❑ 189 Ryan Wagner FY SP RC 4.00 1.50
❑ 190 Matt Kata FY SP RC 4.00 1.50
❑ 191 Bo Hart FY SP RC 4.00 1.50
❑ 192 Brandon Webb FY SP RC 6.00 2.50
❑ 193 Bengie Molina .50 .20
❑ 194 Junior Spivey .50 .20
❑ 195 Gary Sheffield .50 .20
❑ 196 Jason Johnson .50 .20
❑ 197 David Ortiz 1.25 .50
❑ 198 Roberto Alomar .75 .30
❑ 199 Wily Mo Pena .50 .20
❑ 200 Sammy Sosa 1.25 .50
❑ 201 Jay Payton .50 .20
❑ 202 Dmitri Young .50 .20
❑ 203 Derrek Lee .75 .30
❑ 204A Jeff Bagwell w/Hat .75 .30
❑ 204B Jeff Bagwell w/o Hat .75 .30
❑ 205 Runelvys Hernandez .50 .20
❑ 206 Kevin Brown .50 .20
❑ 207 Wes Helms .50 .20
❑ 208 Eddie Guardado .50 .20
❑ 209 Orlando Cabrera .50 .20
❑ 210 Alfonso Soriano .50 .20
❑ 211 Ty Wigginton .50 .20
❑ 212A Rich Harden Look Left .75 .30
❑ 212B Rich Harden Look Right .75 .30
❑ 213 Mike Lieberthal .50 .20
❑ 214 Brian Giles .50 .20
❑ 215 Jason Schmidt .50 .20
❑ 216 Jamie Moyer .50 .20
❑ 217 Matt Morris .50 .20
❑ 218 Victor Zambrano .50 .20
❑ 219 Roy Halladay .50 .20
❑ 220 Mike Hampton .50 .20
❑ 221 Kevin Millar Sox .50 .20
❑ 222 Hideo Nomo 1.25 .50
❑ 223 Milton Bradley .50 .20
❑ 224 Jose Guillen .50 .20
❑ 225 Derek Jeter 3.00 1.25
❑ 226 Rondell White .50 .20
❑ 227A Hank Blalock Blue Jsy .50 .20
❑ 227B Hank Blalock White Jsy .50 .20
❑ 228 Shigetoshi Hasegawa .50 .20
❑ 229 Mike Mussina .75 .30
❑ 230 Cristian Guzman .50 .20
❑ 231A Todd Helton Blue .75 .30
❑ 231B Todd Helton Green .75 .30
❑ 232 Kenny Lofton .50 .20
❑ 233 Carl Everett .50 .20
❑ 234 Shea Hillenbrand .50 .20
❑ 235 Brad Fullmer .50 .20
❑ 236 Bernie Williams .75 .30
❑ 237 Vicente Padilla .50 .20
❑ 238 Tim Worrell .50 .20
❑ 239 Juan Gonzalez .50 .20
❑ 240 Ichiro Suzuki 2.50 1.00
❑ 241 Aaron Boone .50 .20
❑ 242 Shannon Stewart .50 .20
❑ 243A Barry Zito Blue .50 .20
❑ 243B Barry Zito Green .50 .20
❑ 244 Reggie Sanders .50 .20
❑ 245 Scott Podsednik .50 .20
❑ 246 Miguel Cabrera 1.25 .50
❑ 247 Angel Berroa .50 .20
❑ 248 Carlos Zambrano .50 .20
❑ 249 Marlon Byrd .50 .20
❑ 250 Mark Prior .75 .30
❑ 251 Esteban Loaiza .50 .20
❑ 252 David Eckstein .50 .20
❑ 253 Alex Cintron .50 .20
❑ 254 Melvin Mora .50 .20
❑ 255 Russ Ortiz .50 .20
❑ 256 Carlos Lee .50 .20
❑ 257 Tino Martinez .75 .30
❑ 258 Randy Wolf .50 .20
❑ 259 Jason Phillips .50 .20
❑ 260 Vladimir Guerrero 1.25 .50
❑ 261 Brad Wilkerson .50 .20
❑ 262 Ivan Rodriguez .75 .30
❑ 263 Matt Lawton .50 .20
❑ 264 Adam Dunn .50 .20
❑ 265 Joe Borowski .50 .20
❑ 266 Jody Gerut .50 .20
❑ 267 Alex Rodriguez 2.00 .75
❑ 268 Brendan Donnelly .50 .20
❑ 269A Randy Johnson Grey 1.25 .50
❑ 269B Randy Johnson Pink 1.25 .50
❑ 270 Nomar Garciaparra 2.00 .75
❑ 271 Javy Lopez .50 .20
❑ 272 Travis Hafner .50 .20
❑ 273 Juan Pierre .50 .20
❑ 274 Morgan Ensberg .50 .20
❑ 275 Albert Pujols 2.50 1.00
❑ 276 Jason LaRue .50 .20
❑ 277 Paul Lo Duca .50 .20
❑ 278 Andy Pettitte .75 .30
❑ 279 Mike Piazza 2.00 .75
❑ 280A Jim Thome Blue .75 .30
❑ 280B Jim Thome Green .75 .30
❑ 281 Marquis Grissom .50 .20
❑ 282 Woody Williams .50 .20
❑ 283A Curt Schilling Look Ahead .50 .20
❑ 283B Curt Schilling Look Right .50 .20
❑ 284A Chipper Jones Blue 1.25 .50
❑ 284B Chipper Jones Yellow 1.25 .50
❑ 285 Deivi Cruz .50 .20
❑ 286 Johnny Damon .75 .30
❑ 287 Chin-Hui Tsao .50 .20
❑ 288 Alex Gonzalez .50 .20
❑ 289 Billy Wagner .50 .20
❑ 290 Jason Giambi .50 .20
❑ 291 Keith Foulke .50 .20
❑ 292 Jerome Williams .50 .20
❑ 293 Livan Hernandez .50 .20
❑ 294 Aaron Guiel .50 .20
❑ 295 Randall Simon .50 .20
❑ 296 Byung-Hyun Kim .50 .20
❑ 297 Jorge Julio .50 .20
❑ 298 Miguel Batista .50 .20
❑ 299 Rafael Furcal .50 .20
❑ 300A Dontrelle Willis No Smile 1.25 .50
❑ 300B Dontrelle Willis Smile SP 4.00 1.50
❑ 301 Alex Sanchez .50 .20
❑ 302 Shawn Chacon .50 .20
❑ 303 Matt Clement .50 .20
❑ 304 Luis Matos .50 .20
❑ 305 Steve Finley .50 .20
❑ 306 Marcus Giles .50 .20
❑ 307 Boomer Wells .50 .20
❑ 308 Jeromy Burnitz .50 .20
❑ 309 Mike MacDougal .50 .20
❑ 310 Mariano Rivera 1.25 .50
❑ 311 Adrian Beltre .50 .20
❑ 312 Mark Loretta .50 .20
❑ 313 Ugueth Urbina .50 .20
❑ 314 Bill Mueller .50 .20
❑ 315 Johan Santana .75 .30
❑ NNO Vintage Buyback

2002 Topps 206

❑ COMPLETE SET (525) 220.00 110.00
❑ COMPLETE SERIES 1 (180) 60.00 25.00
❑ COMPLETE SERIES 2 (180) 60.00 25.00

❑ COMPLETE SERIES 3 (165) 100.00 50.00
❑ COM(1-140/181-270/308-418) .50 .20
❑ COMMON (141-155/271-285) .50 .20
❑ COMMON RC (308-418) .50 .20
❑ COMMON SP (308-398) 2.00 .75
❑ COMMON FYP SP (419-432) 1.00 .40
❑ COMMON RET SP (433-447) 2.00 .75
❑ 1 Vladimir Guerrero 1.25 .50
❑ 2 Sammy Sosa 1.25 .50
❑ 3 Garret Anderson .50 .20
❑ 4 Rafael Palmeiro .75 .30
❑ 5 Juan Gonzalez .50 .20
❑ 6 John Smoltz .75 .30
❑ 7 Mark Mulder .50 .20
❑ 8 Jon Lieber .50 .20
❑ 9 Greg Maddux 2.00 .75
❑ 10 Moises Alou .50 .20
❑ 11 Joe Randa .50 .20
❑ 12 Bobby Abreu .50 .20
❑ 13 Juan Pierre .50 .20
❑ 14 Kerry Wood .50 .20
❑ 15 Craig Biggio .75 .30
❑ 16 Curt Schilling .50 .20
❑ 17 Brian Jordan .50 .20
❑ 18 Edgardo Alfonzo .50 .20
❑ 19 Darren Dreifort .50 .20
❑ 20 Todd Helton .75 .30
❑ 21 Ramon Ortiz .50 .20
❑ 22 Ichiro Suzuki 2.50 1.00
❑ 23 Jimmy Rollins .50 .20
❑ 24 Darin Erstad .50 .20
❑ 25 Shawn Green .50 .20
❑ 26 Tino Martinez .75 .30
❑ 27 Bret Boone .50 .20
❑ 28 Alfonso Soriano .50 .20
❑ 29 Chan Ho Park .50 .20
❑ 30 Roger Clemens 2.50 1.00
❑ 31 Cliff Floyd .50 .20
❑ 32 Johnny Damon .75 .30
❑ 33 Frank Thomas 1.25 .50
❑ 34 Barry Bonds 3.00 1.25
❑ 35 Luis Gonzalez .50 .20
❑ 36 Carlos Lee .50 .20
❑ 37 Roberto Alomar .75 .30
❑ 38 Carlos Delgado .50 .20
❑ 39 Nomar Garciaparra 2.00 .75
❑ 40 Jason Kendall .50 .20
❑ 41 Scott Rolen .75 .30
❑ 42 Tom Glavine .75 .30
❑ 43 Ryan Klesko .50 .20
❑ 44 Brian Giles .50 .20
❑ 45 Bud Smith .50 .20
❑ 46 Charles Nagy .50 .20
❑ 47 Tony Gwynn 1.50 .60
❑ 48 C.C. Sabathia .50 .20
❑ 49 Frank Catalanotto .50 .20
❑ 50 Jerry Hairston .50 .20
❑ 51 Jeromy Burnitz .50 .20
❑ 52 David Justice .50 .20
❑ 53 Bartolo Colon .50 .20
❑ 54 Andres Galarraga .50 .20
❑ 55 Jeff Weaver .50 .20
❑ 56 Terrence Long .50 .20
❑ 57 Tsuyoshi Shinjo .50 .20
❑ 58 Barry Zito .50 .20
❑ 59 Mariano Rivera 1.25 .50
❑ 60 John Olerud .50 .20
❑ 61 Randy Johnson 1.25 .50
❑ 62 Kenny Lofton .50 .20
❑ 63 Jermaine Dye .50 .20
❑ 64 Troy Glaus .50 .20
❑ 65 Larry Walker .50 .20
❑ 66 Hideo Nomo 1.25 .50
❑ 67 Mike Mussina .75 .30
❑ 68 Paul LoDuca .50 .20
❑ 69 Magglio Ordonez .50 .20
❑ 70 Paul O'Neill .75 .30
❑ 71 Sean Casey .50 .20
❑ 72 Lance Berkman .50 .20
❑ 73 Adam Dunn .50 .20
❑ 74 Aramis Ramirez .50 .20
❑ 75 Rafael Furcal .50 .20
❑ 76 Gary Sheffield .50 .20
❑ 77 Todd Hollandsworth .50 .20
❑ 78 Chipper Jones 1.25 .50
❑ 79 Bernie Williams .75 .30
❑ 80 Richard Hidalgo .50 .20
❑ 81 Eric Chavez .50 .20
❑ 82 Mike Piazza 2.00 .75
❑ 83 J.D. Drew .50 .20
❑ 84 Ken Griffey Jr. 2.00 .75
❑ 85 Joe Kennedy .50 .20
❑ 86 Joel Pineiro .50 .20
❑ 87 Josh Towers .50 .20
❑ 88 Andruw Jones .75 .30
❑ 89 Carlos Beltran .50 .20
❑ 90 Mike Cameron .50 .20
❑ 91 Albert Pujols 2.50 1.00
❑ 92 Alex Rodriguez 2.00 .75
❑ 93 Omar Vizquel .75 .30
❑ 94 Juan Encarnacion .50 .20
❑ 95 Jeff Bagwell .75 .30
❑ 96 Jose Canseco .75 .30
❑ 97 Ben Sheets .50 .20
❑ 98 Mark Grace .75 .30
❑ 99 Mike Sweeney .50 .20
❑ 100 Mark McGwire 3.00 1.25
❑ 101 Ivan Rodriguez .75 .30
❑ 102 Rich Aurilia .50 .20
❑ 103 Cristian Guzman .50 .20
❑ 104 Roy Oswalt .50 .20
❑ 105 Tim Hudson .50 .20
❑ 106 Brent Abernathy .50 .20
❑ 107 Mike Hampton .50 .20
❑ 108 Miguel Tejada .50 .20
❑ 109 Bobby Higginson .50 .20
❑ 110 Edgar Martinez .75 .30
❑ 111 Jorge Posada .75 .30
❑ 112 Jason Giambi Yankees .50 .20
❑ 113 Pedro Astacio .50 .20
❑ 114 Kazuhiro Sasaki .50 .20
❑ 115 Preston Wilson .50 .20
❑ 116 Jason Bere .50 .20
❑ 117 Mark Quinn .50 .20
❑ 118 Pokey Reese .50 .20
❑ 119 Derek Jeter 3.00 1.25
❑ 120 Shannon Stewart .50 .20
❑ 121 Jeff Kent .50 .20
❑ 122 Jeremy Giambi .50 .20
❑ 123 Pat Burrell .50 .20
❑ 124 Jim Edmonds .50 .20
❑ 125 Mark Buehrle .50 .20
❑ 126 Kevin Brown .50 .20
❑ 127 Raul Mondesi .50 .20
❑ 128 Pedro Martinez .75 .30
❑ 129 Jim Thome .75 .30
❑ 130 Russ Ortiz .50 .20
❑ 131 Brandon Duckworth PROS .50 .20
❑ 132 Ryan Jamison PROS .50 .20
❑ 133 Brandon Inge PROS .50 .20
❑ 134 Felipe Lopez PROS .50 .20
❑ 135 Jason Lane PROS .50 .20
❑ 136 Forrest Johnson PROS RC .50 .20
❑ 137 Greg Nash PROS .50 .20
❑ 138 Covelli Crisp PROS 2.00 .75
❑ 139 Nick Neugebauer PROS .50 .20
❑ 140 Dustan Mohr PROS .50 .20
❑ 141 Freddy Sanchez FYP RC 2.00 .75
❑ 142 Justin Backsmeyer FYP RC .50 .20
❑ 143 Jorge Julio FYP .50 .20
❑ 144 Ryan Mottl FYP RC .50 .20
❑ 145 Chris Tritle FYP RC .50 .20
❑ 146 Noochie Varner FYP RC .50 .20
❑ 147 Brian Rogers FYP .50 .20
❑ 148 Michael Hill FYP RC .50 .20
❑ 149 Luis Pineda FYP .50 .20
❑ 150 Rich Thompson FYP RC .50 .20
❑ 151 Bill Hall FYP .50 .20
❑ 152 Juan Dominguez FYP RC .50 .20
❑ 153 Justin Woodrow FYP .50 .20
❑ 154 Nic Jackson FYP RC .50 .20
❑ 155 Laynce Nix FYP RC 1.50 .60
❑ 156 Hank Aaron RET 5.00 2.00
❑ 157 Ernie Banks RET 2.50 1.00
❑ 158 Johnny Bench RET 2.50 1.00
❑ 159 George Brett RET 5.00 2.00
❑ 160 Carlton Fisk RET 1.50 .60
❑ 161 Bob Gibson RET 1.50 .60
❑ 162 Reggie Jackson RET 1.50 .60
❑ 163 Don Mattingly RET 5.00 2.00
❑ 164 Kirby Puckett RET 2.50 1.00
❑ 165 Frank Robinson RET 1.50 .60
❑ 166 Nolan Ryan RET 6.00 2.50
❑ 167 Tom Seaver RET 1.50 .60
❑ 168 Mike Schmidt RET 5.00 2.00
❑ 169 Dave Winfield RET 1.00 .40
❑ 170 Carl Yastrzemski RET 3.00 1.25
❑ 171 Frank Chance REP 1.00 .40
❑ 172 Ty Cobb REP 5.00 2.00
❑ 173 Sam Crawford REP 1.00 .40
❑ 174 Johnny Evers REP 1.00 .40
❑ 175 John McGraw REP 1.50 .60
❑ 176 Eddie Plank REP 2.50 1.00
❑ 177 Tris Speaker REP 2.50 1.00
❑ 178 Joe Tinker REP 1.00 .40
❑ 179 H.Wagner Orange REP 8.00 3.00
❑ 180 Cy Young REP 2.50 1.00
❑ 181 Javier Vazquez .50 .20
❑ 182A Mark Mulder Green Jsy .50 .20
❑ 182B Mark Mulder White Jsy .50 .20
❑ 183A Roger Clemens Blue Jsy 2.50 1.00
❑ 183B Roger Clemens Pinstripes 2.50 1.00
❑ 184 Kazuhisa Ishii RC .75 .30
❑ 185 Roberto Alomar .75 .30
❑ 186 Lance Berkman .50 .20
❑ 187A Adam Dunn Arms Folded .50 .20
❑ 187B Adam Dunn w/Bat .50 .20
❑ 188A Aramis Ramirez w/Bat .50 .20
❑ 188B Aramis Ramirez w/o Bat .50 .20
❑ 189 Chuck Knoblauch .50 .20
❑ 190 Nomar Garciaparra 2.00 .75
❑ 191 Brad Penny .50 .20
❑ 192A Gary Sheffield w/Bat .50 .20
❑ 192B Gary Sheffield w/o Bat .50 .20
❑ 193 Alfonso Soriano .50 .20
❑ 194 Andruw Jones .75 .30
❑ 195A Randy Johnson Black Jsy 1.25 .50
❑ 195B Randy Johnson Purple Jsy 1.25 .50
❑ 196A Corey Patterson Blue Jsy .50 .20
❑ 196B Corey Patterson Pinstripes .50 .20
❑ 197 Milton Bradley .50 .20
❑ 198A J.Damon Blue Jsy/Cap .75 .30
❑ 198B J.Damon Blue Jsy/Hlmt .75 .30
❑ 198C J.Damon White Jsy .75 .30
❑ 199A Paul Lo Duca Blue Jsy .50 .20
❑ 199B Paul Lo Duca White Jsy .50 .20
❑ 200A Albert Pujols Red Jsy 2.50 1.00
❑ 200B Albert Pujols Running 2.50 1.00
❑ 200C Albert Pujols w/Bat 2.50 1.00
❑ 201 Scott Rolen .75 .30
❑ 202A J.D. Drew Running .50 .20
❑ 202B J.D. Drew w/Bat .50 .20
❑ 202C J.D. Drew White Jsy .50 .20
❑ 203 Vladimir Guerrero 1.25 .50
❑ 204A Jason Giambi Blue Jsy .50 .20
❑ 204B Jason Giambi Grey Jsy .50 .20
❑ 204C Jason Giambi Pinstripes .50 .20
❑ 205A Moises Alou Grey Jsy .50 .20
❑ 205B Moises Alou Pinstripes .50 .20
❑ 206A Magglio Ordonez Signing .50 .20
❑ 206B Magglio Ordonez w/Bat .50 .20
❑ 207 Carlos Febles .50 .20
❑ 208 So Taguchi RC .75 .30
❑ 209A Rafael Palmeiro One Hand .75 .30
❑ 209B Rafael Palmeiro Two Hands .75 .30
❑ 210 David Wells .50 .20
❑ 211 Orlando Cabrera .50 .20
❑ 212 Sammy Sosa 1.25 .50
❑ 213 Armando Benitez .50 .20
❑ 214 Wes Helms .50 .20

❑ 215A Mariano Rivera Arms Folded 1.25 .50
❑ 215B Mariano Rivera Holding Ball 1.25 .50
❑ 216 Jimmy Rollins .50 .20
❑ 217 Matt Lawton .50 .20
❑ 218A Shawn Green w/Bat .50 .20
❑ 218B Shawn Green w/o Bat .50 .20
❑ 219A Bernie Williams w/Bat .75 .30
❑ 219B Bernie Williams w/o Bat .75 .30
❑ 220A Bret Boone Blue Jsy .50 .20
❑ 220B Bret Boone White Jsy .50 .20
❑ 221A Alex Rodriguez Blue Jsy 2.00 .75
❑ 221B Alex Rodriguez One Hand 2.00 .75
❑ 221C Alex Rodriguez Two Hands 2.00 .75
❑ 222 Roger Cedeno .50 .20
❑ 223 Marty Cordova .50 .20
❑ 224 Fred McGriff .75 .30
❑ 225A Chipper Jones Batting 1.25 .50
❑ 225B Chipper Jones Running 1.25 .50
❑ 226 Kerry Wood .50 .20
❑ 227A Larry Walker Grey Jsy .50 .20
❑ 227B Larry Walker Purple Jsy .50 .20
❑ 228 Robin Ventura .50 .20
❑ 229 Robert Fick .50 .20
❑ 230A Tino Martinez Black Glove .75 .30
❑ 230B Tino Martinez Throwing .75 .30
❑ 230C Tino Martinez w/Bat .75 .30
❑ 231 Ben Petrick .50 .20
❑ 232 Neifi Perez .50 .20
❑ 233 Pedro Martinez .75 .30
❑ 234A Brian Jordan Grey Jsy .50 .20
❑ 234B Brian Jordan White Jsy .50 .20
❑ 235 Freddy Garcia .50 .20
❑ 236A Derek Jeter Batting 3.00 1.25
❑ 236B Derek Jeter Blue Jsy 3.00 1.25
❑ 236C Derek Jeter Kneeling 3.00 1.25
❑ 237 Ben Grieve .50 .20
❑ 238A Barry Bonds Black Jsy 3.00 1.25
❑ 238B Barry Bonds w/Wrist Band 3.00 1.25
❑ 238C B.Bonds w/o Wrist Band 3.00 1.25
❑ 239 Luis Gonzalez .50 .20
❑ 240 Shane Halter .50 .20
❑ 241A Brian Giles Black Jsy .50 .20
❑ 241B Brian Giles Grey Jsy .50 .20
❑ 242 Bud Smith .50 .20
❑ 243 Richie Sexson .50 .20
❑ 244A Barry Zito Green Jsy .50 .20
❑ 244B Barry Zito White Jsy .50 .20
❑ 245 Eric Milton .50 .20
❑ 246A Ivan Rodriguez Blue Jsy .75 .30
❑ 246B Ivan Rodriguez Grey Jsy .75 .30
❑ 246C Ivan Rodriguez White Jsy .75 .30
❑ 247 Toby Hall .50 .20
❑ 248A Mike Piazza Black Jsy 2.00 .75
❑ 248B Mike Piazza Grey Jsy 2.00 .75
❑ 249 Ruben Sierra .50 .20
❑ 250A Tsuyoshi Shinjo Cap .50 .20
❑ 250B Tsuyoshi Shinjo Helmet .50 .20
❑ 251A Jermaine Dye Green Jsy .50 .20
❑ 251B Jermaine Dye White Jsy .50 .20
❑ 252 Roy Oswalt .50 .20
❑ 253 Todd Helton .75 .30
❑ 254 Adrian Beltre .50 .20
❑ 255 Doug Mientkiewicz .50 .20
❑ 256A Ichiro Suzuki Blue Jsy 2.50 1.00
❑ 256B Ichiro Suzuki w/Bat 2.50 1.00
❑ 256C Ichiro Suzuki White Jsy 2.50 1.00
❑ 257A C.C. Sabathia Blue Jsy .50 .20
❑ 257B C.C. Sabathia White Jsy .50 .20
❑ 258 Paul Konerko .50 .20
❑ 259 Ken Griffey Jr. 2.00 .75
❑ 260A Jeromy Burnitz w/Bat .50 .20
❑ 260B Jeromy Burnitz w/o Bat .50 .20
❑ 261 Hank Blalock PROS .75 .30
❑ 262 Mark Prior PROS .75 .30
❑ 263 Josh Beckett PROS .50 .20
❑ 264 Carlos Pena PROS .50 .20
❑ 265 Sean Burroughs PROS .50 .20
❑ 266 Austin Kearns PROS .50 .20
❑ 267 Chin-Hui Tsao PROS .50 .20
❑ 268 Dewon Brazelton PROS .50 .20
❑ 269 J.D. Martin PROS .50 .20
❑ 270 Marlon Byrd PROS .50 .20
❑ 271 Joe Mauer FYP RC 10.00 4.00
❑ 272 Jason Botts FYP RC .50 .20
❑ 273 Mauricio Lara FYP RC .50 .20
❑ 274 Jonny Gomes FYP RC 2.50 1.00
❑ 275 Gavin Floyd FYP RC 1.00 .40
❑ 276 Alex Requena FYP RC .50 .20
❑ 277 Jimmy Gobble FYP RC .50 .20
❑ 278 Chris Duffy FYP RC 1.00 .40
❑ 279 Colt Griffin FYP RC .50 .20
❑ 280 Ryan Church FYP RC 1.00 .40
❑ 281 Beltran Perez FYP RC .50 .20
❑ 282 Clint Nageotte FYP RC .75 .30
❑ 283 Justin Schuda FYP RC .50 .20
❑ 284 Scott Hairston FYP RC .75 .30
❑ 285 Mario Ramos FYP RC .50 .20
❑ 286B Tom Seaver Mets RET 1.50 .60
❑ 286A Tom Seaver White Sox RET 1.50 .60
❑ 287A Hank Aaron White Jsy RET 5.00 2.00
❑ 287B Hank Aaron Blue Jsy RET 5.00 2.00
❑ 288 Mike Schmidt RET 5.00 2.00
❑ 289A Robin Yount Blue Jsy RET 2.50 1.00
❑ 289B Robin Yount P'stripes RET 2.50 1.00
❑ 290 Joe Morgan RET 1.00 .40
❑ 291 Frank Robinson RET 1.50 .60
❑ 292A Reggie Jackson A's RET 1.50 .60
❑ 292B Reggie Jackson Yanks RET 1.50 .60
❑ 293A Nolan Ryan Astros RET 6.00 2.50
❑ 293B Nolan Ryan Rangers RET 6.00 2.50
❑ 294 Dave Winfield RET 1.00 .40
❑ 295 Willie Mays RET 5.00 2.00
❑ 296 Brooks Robinson RET 1.50 .60
❑ 297A Mark McGwire A's RET 6.00 2.50
❑ 297B Mark McGwire Cards RET 6.00 2.50
❑ 298 Honus Wagner RET 2.50 1.00
❑ 299A Sherry Magee REP 1.00 .40
❑ 299B Sherry Magie UER REP 1.00 .40
❑ 300 Frank Chance REP 1.00 .40
❑ 301A Joe Doyle NY REP 1.00 .40
❑ 301B Joe Doyle NY Nat'l REP 1.00 .40
❑ 302 John McGraw REP 1.50 .60
❑ 303 Jimmy Collins REP 1.00 .40
❑ 304 Buck Herzog REP 1.00 .40
❑ 305 Sam Crawford REP 1.00 .40
❑ 306 Cy Young REP 2.50 1.00
❑ 307 Honus Wagner Blue REP 8.00 3.00
❑ 308A A.Rodriguez Blue Jsy SP 4.00 1.50
❑ 308B A.Rodriguez White Jsy 2.00 .75
❑ 309 Vernon Wells .50 .20
❑ 310A B.Bonds w/Elbow Pad 3.00 1.25
❑ 310B B.Bonds w/o Elbow Pad SP 6.002.50
❑ 311 Vicente Padilla .50 .20
❑ 312A A.Soriano w/Wristband .50 .20
❑ 312B A.Soriano w/o Wristband SP 2.00 .75
❑ 313 Mike Piazza 2.00 .75
❑ 314 Jacque Jones .50 .20
❑ 315 Shawn Green SP 2.00 .75
❑ 316 Paul Byrd .50 .20
❑ 317 Lance Berkman .50 .20
❑ 318 Larry Walker .50 .20
❑ 319 Ken Griffey Jr. SP 4.00 1.50
❑ 320 Shea Hillenbrand .50 .20
❑ 321 Jay Gibbons .50 .20
❑ 322 Andruw Jones .75 .30
❑ 323 Luis Gonzalez SP 2.00 .75
❑ 324 Garret Anderson .50 .20
❑ 325 Roy Halladay .50 .20
❑ 326 Randy Winn .50 .20
❑ 327 Matt Morris .50 .20
❑ 328 Robb Nen .50 .20
❑ 329 Trevor Hoffman .50 .20
❑ 330 Kip Wells .50 .20
❑ 331 Orlando Hernandez .50 .20
❑ 332 Rey Ordonez .50 .20
❑ 333 Torii Hunter .50 .20
❑ 334 Geoff Jenkins .50 .20
❑ 335 Eric Karros .50 .20
❑ 336 Mike Lowell .50 .20
❑ 337 Nick Johnson .50 .20
❑ 338 Randall Simon .50 .20
❑ 339 Ellis Burks .50 .20
❑ 340A Sammy Sosa Blue Jsy SP 2.50 1.00
❑ 340B Sammy Sosa White Jsy 1.25 .50
❑ 341 Pedro Martinez .75 .30
❑ 342 Junior Spivey .50 .20
❑ 343 Vinny Castilla .50 .20
❑ 344 Randy Johnson SP 2.50 1.00
❑ 345 Chipper Jones SP 2.50 1.00
❑ 346 Orlando Hudson .50 .20
❑ 347 Albert Pujols SP 5.00 2.00
❑ 348 Rondell White .50 .20
❑ 349 Vladimir Guerrero 1.25 .50
❑ 350A Mark Prior Red SP 1.50 .60
❑ 350B Mark Prior Yellow .75 3.00
❑ 351 Eric Gagne .50 .20
❑ 352 Todd Zeile .50 .20
❑ 353 Manny Ramirez SP 2.00 .75
❑ 354 Kevin Millwood .50 .20
❑ 355 Troy Percival .50 .20
❑ 356A Jason Giambi Batting SP 2.00 .75
❑ 356B Jason Giambi Throwing .50 .20
❑ 357 Bartolo Colon .50 .20
❑ 358 Jeremy Giambi .50 .20
❑ 359 Jose Cruz Jr. .50 .20
❑ 360A I.Suzuki Blue Jsy SP 5.00 2.00
❑ 360B I.Suzuki White Jsy 2.50 1.00
❑ 361 Eddie Guardado .50 .20
❑ 362 Ivan Rodriguez .75 .30
❑ 363 Carl Crawford .50 .20
❑ 364 Jason Simontacchi RC .50 .20
❑ 365 Kenny Lofton .50 .20
❑ 366 Raul Mondesi .50 .20
❑ 367 A.J. Pierzynski .50 .20
❑ 368 Ugueth Urbina .50 .20
❑ 369 Rodrigo Lopez .50 .20
❑ 370A N.Garciaparra One Bat SP 4.00 1.50
❑ 370B N.Garciaparra Two Bats 2.00 .75
❑ 371 Craig Counsell .50 .20
❑ 372 Barry Larkin .75 .30
❑ 373 Carlos Pena .50 .20
❑ 374 Luis Castillo .50 .20
❑ 375 Raul Ibanez .50 .20
❑ 376 Kazuhisa Ishii SP 2.00 .75
❑ 377 Derek Lowe .50 .20
❑ 378 Curt Schilling .50 .20
❑ 379 Jim Thome Phillies .75 .30
❑ 380A Derek Jeter Blue SP 6.00 2.50
❑ 380B Derek Jeter Seats 3.00 1.25
❑ 381 Pat Burrell .50 .20
❑ 382 Jamie Moyer .50 .20
❑ 383 Eric Hinske .50 .20
❑ 384 Scott Rolen .75 .30
❑ 385 Miguel Tejada SP 2.00 .75
❑ 386 Andy Pettitte .75 .30
❑ 387 Mike Lieberthal .50 .20
❑ 388 Al Leiter .50 .20
❑ 389 Todd Helton SP 2.00 .75
❑ 390A Adam Dunn Bat SP 2.00 .75
❑ 390B Adam Dunn Glove .50 .20
❑ 391 Cliff Floyd .50 .20
❑ 392 Tim Salmon .75 .30
❑ 393 Joe Torre MG .75 .30
❑ 394 Bobby Cox MG .50 .20
❑ 395 Tony LaRussa MG .50 .20
❑ 396 Art Howe MG .50 .20
❑ 397 Bob Brenly MG .50 .20
❑ 398 Ron Gardenhire MG .50 .20
❑ 399 Mike Cuddyer PROS .50 .20
❑ 400 Joe Mauer PROS 10.00 4.00
❑ 401 Mark Teixeira PROS 1.25 .50
❑ 402 Hee Seop Choi PROS .50 .20
❑ 403 Angel Berroa PROS .50 .20
❑ 404 Jesse Foppert PROS RC .75 .30
❑ 405 Bobby Crosby PROS 1.25 .50
❑ 406 Jose Reyes PROS .75 .30
❑ 407 Casey Kotchman PROS RC 1.00 .40
❑ 408 Aaron Heilman PROS .50 .20
❑ 409 Adrian Gonzalez PROS .50 .20
❑ 410 Delwyn Young PROS RC 1.00 .40
❑ 411 Brett Myers PROS .50 .20
❑ 412 Justin Huber PROS RC .75 .30
❑ 413 Drew Henson PROS .50 .20
❑ 414 Taggert Bozied PROS RC .75 .30
❑ 415 Dontrelle Willis PROS RC 5.00 2.00
❑ 416 Rocco Baldelli PROS .50 .20
❑ 417 Jason Stokes PROS RC .50 .20
❑ 418 Brandon Phillips PROS .50 .20
❑ 419 Jake Blalock FYP RC .50 .20
❑ 420 Micah Schilling FYP RC 1.00 .40
❑ 421 Denard Span FYP RC 1.00 .40
❑ 422A J.Loney Red FYP RC 4.00 1.50
❑ 422B J.Loney w/Sky FYP RC 4.00 1.50
❑ 423A W.Bankston Blue FYP RC 2.00 .75
❑ 423B W.Bankston w/Sky FYP RC 2.00 .75
❑ 424 Jeremy Hermida FYP RC 5.00 2.00
❑ 425 Curtis Granderson FYP RC 3.00 1.25
❑ 426A J.Pridie Red FYP RC 1.00 .40

❑ 426B J.Pridie w/Sky FYP RC 1.00 .40
❑ 427 Larry Broadway FYP RC .50 .20
❑ 428A K.Greene Green FYP RC 8.00 3.00
❑ 428B K.Greene Red FYP RC 8.00 3.00
❑ 429 Joey Votto FYP RC 2.50 1.00
❑ 430A B.Upton Grey FYP RC 5.00 2.00
❑ 430B B.Upton w/People FYP RC 5.00 2.00
❑ 431A S.Santos Gold FYP RC 1.00 .40
❑ 431B S.Santos Grey FYP RC 1.00 .40
❑ 432 Brian Dopirak FYP RC 1.00 .40
❑ 433 Ozzie Smith RET SP 4.00 1.50
❑ 434 Wade Boggs RET SP 2.50 1.00
❑ 435 Yogi Berra RET SP 4.00 1.50
❑ 436 Al Kaline RET SP 4.00 1.50
❑ 437 Robin Roberts RET SP 2.00 .75
❑ 438 Roberto Clemente RET SP 8.00 3.00
❑ 439 Gary Carter RET SP 2.00 .75
❑ 440 Fergie Jenkins RET SP 2.00 .75
❑ 441 Orlando Cepeda RET SP 2.00 .75
❑ 442 Rod Carew RET SP 2.50 1.00
❑ 443 Harmon Killebrew RET SP 4.00 1.50
❑ 444 Duke Snider RET SP 2.50 1.00
❑ 445 Stan Musial RET SP 6.00 2.50
❑ 446 Hank Greenberg RET SP 4.00 1.50
❑ 447 Lou Brock RET SP 2.50 1.00
❑ 448 Jim Palmer RET 1.00 .40
❑ 449 John McGraw REP 1.50 .60
❑ 450 Mordecai Brown REP 1.00 .40
❑ 451 Christy Mathewson REP 1.50 .60
❑ 452 Sam Crawford REP 1.00 .40
❑ 453 Bill O'Hara REP 1.00 .40
❑ 454 Joe Tinker REP 1.00 .40
❑ 455 Nap Lajoie REP 1.50 .60
❑ 456 Honus Wagner Red REP 8.00 3.00
❑ NNO Repurchased Tobacco Card

2006 Topps Allen and Ginter

❑ COMPLETE SET (350) 120.00 60.00
❑ COMP.SET w/o SP's (300) 40.00 15.00
❑ COMMON SP 3.00 1.25
❑ SP STATED ODDS 1:2 HOBBY, 1:2 RETAIL
❑ SP CL: 5/15/25/35/45/50-59/65/85/105/115
❑ SP CL: 125/135/145/150-159/165/175/185
❑ SP CL: 205/215/235/245/251/255-256/265
❑ SP CL: 285/295/305/315/325/335/345
❑ FRAMED ORIGINALS ODDS 1:3227 H, 1:3227 R
❑ 1 Albert Pujols 1.00 .40
❑ 2 Aubrey Huff .20 .10
❑ 3 Mark Teixeira .30 .15
❑ 4 Vernon Wells .20 .10
❑ 5 Ken Griffey Jr. SP 5.00 2.00
❑ 6 Nick Swisher .20 .10
❑ 7 Jose Reyes .20 .10
❑ 8 David Wright .75 .30
❑ 9 Vladimir Guerrero .50 .20
❑ 10 Andruw Jones .30 .15
❑ 11 Ramon Hernandez .20 .10
❑ 12 Miguel Tejada .20 .10
❑ 13 Juan Pierre .20 .10
❑ 14 Jim Thome .30 .15
❑ 15 Austin Kearns SP 3.00 1.25
❑ 16 Jhonny Peralta .20 .10
❑ 17 Clint Barmes .20 .10
❑ 18 Angel Berroa .20 .10
❑ 19 Nomar Garciaparra .50 .20
❑ 20 Joe Nathan .20 .10
❑ 21 Brandon Webb .20 .10
❑ 22 Chad Tracy .20 .10
❑ 23 Derek Jeter 1.25 .50
❑ 24 Conor Jackson (RC) .30 .15
❑ 25 Jason Giambi SP 3.00 1.25
❑ 26 Johnny Estrada .20 .10
❑ 27 Luis Gonzalez .20 .10
❑ 28 Javier Vazquez .20 .10
❑ 29 Orlando Hudson .20 .10
❑ 30 Shawn Green .20 .10
❑ 31 Mark Buehrle .20 .10
❑ 32 Wily Mo Pena .20 .10
❑ 33 C.C. Sabathia .20 .10
❑ 34 Ronnie Belliard .20 .10
❑ 35 Travis Hafner SP 3.00 1.25
❑ 36 Mike Jacobs (RC) .20 .10
❑ 37 Roy Oswalt .20 .10
❑ 38 Zack Greinke .20 .10
❑ 39 J.D. Drew .20 .10
❑ 40 Jeff Kent .20 .10
❑ 41 Ben Sheets .20 .10
❑ 42 Luis Castillo .20 .10
❑ 43 Carlos Delgado .20 .10
❑ 44 Cliff Floyd .20 .10
❑ 45 Danny Haren SP 3.00 1.25
❑ 46 Bobby Abreu .20 .10
❑ 47 Jeromy Burnitz .20 .10
❑ 48 Khalil Greene .30 .15
❑ 49 Moises Alou .20 .10
❑ 50 Alex Rodriguez SP 5.00 2.00
❑ 51 Ervin Santana SP 3.00 1.25
❑ 52 Bartolo Colon SP 3.00 1.25
❑ 53 John Smoltz SP 3.00 1.25
❑ 54 David Ortiz SP 3.00 1.25
❑ 55 Hideki Matsui SP 3.00 1.25
❑ 56 Jermaine Dye SP 3.00 1.25
❑ 57 Victor Martinez SP 3.00 1.25
❑ 58 Willy Taveras SP 3.00 1.25
❑ 59 Brady Clark SP 3.00 1.25
❑ 60 Justin Morneau .20 .10
❑ 61 Xavier Nady .20 .10
❑ 62 Rich Harden .20 .10
❑ 63 Jack Wilson .20 .10
❑ 64 Brian Giles .20 .10
❑ 65 Jon Lieber SP 3.00 1.25
❑ 66 Dan Johnson .20 .10
❑ 67 Billy Wagner .20 .10
❑ 68 Rickie Weeks .20 .10
❑ 69 Chris Ray (RC) .20 .10
❑ 70 Chris Shelton .20 .10
❑ 71 Dmitri Young .20 .10
❑ 72 Ivan Rodriguez .30 .15
❑ 73 Jeremy Bonderman .20 .10
❑ 74 Justin Verlander (RC) .75 .30
❑ 75 Randy Johnson .50 .20
❑ 76 Magglio Ordonez .20 .10
❑ 77 Brandon Inge .20 .10
❑ 78 Placido Polanco .20 .10
❑ 79 Ryan Howard .75 .30
❑ 80 Jason Bay .20 .10
❑ 81 Sean Casey .20 .10
❑ 82 Jeremy Hermida (RC) .30 .15
❑ 83 Mike Cameron .20 .10
❑ 84 Trevor Hoffman .20 .10
❑ 85 Mike Matheny SP 3.00 1.25
❑ 86 Steve Finley .20 .10
❑ 87 Adam Everett .20 .10
❑ 88 Jason Isringhausen .20 .10
❑ 89 Jonny Gomes .20 .10
❑ 90 Barry Zito .20 .10
❑ 91 Bobby Crosby .20 .10
❑ 92 Eric Chavez .20 .10
❑ 93 Frank Thomas .50 .20
❑ 94 Huston Street .20 .10
❑ 95 Jorge Posada .30 .15
❑ 96 Casey Kotchman .20 .10
❑ 97 Darin Erstad .20 .10
❑ 98 Chipper Jones .50 .20
❑ 99 Jeff Francoeur .50 .20
❑ 100 Barry Bonds 1.00 .40
❑ 101 Alfonso Soriano .20 .10
❑ 102 Brandon Claussen .20 .10
❑ 103 Aaron Boone .20 .10
❑ 104 Roger Clemens 1.00 .40
❑ 105 Andy Pettitte SP 3.00 1.25
❑ 106 Nick Johnson .20 .10
❑ 107 Tom Gordon .20 .10
❑ 108 Orlando Hernandez .20 .10
❑ 109 Francisco Rodriguez .20 .10
❑ 110 Orlando Cabrera .20 .10
❑ 111 Edgar Renteria .20 .10
❑ 112 Tim Hudson .20 .10
❑ 113 Coco Crisp .20 .10
❑ 114 Matt Clement .20 .10
❑ 115 Greg Maddux SP 5.00 2.00
❑ 116 Paul Konerko .20 .10
❑ 117 Felipe Lopez .20 .10
❑ 118 Garrett Atkins .20 .10
❑ 119 Akinori Otsuka .20 .10
❑ 120 Craig Biggio .30 .15
❑ 121 Danys Baez .20 .10
❑ 122 Brad Penny .20 .10
❑ 123 Eric Gagne .20 .10
❑ 124 Lew Ford .20 .10
❑ 125 Mariano Rivera SP 3.00 1.25
❑ 126 Carlos Beltran .20 .10
❑ 127 Pedro Martinez .30 .15
❑ 128 Todd Helton .30 .15
❑ 129 Aaron Rowand .20 .10
❑ 130 Mike Lieberthal .20 .10
❑ 131 Oliver Perez .20 .10
❑ 132 Ryan Klesko .20 .10
❑ 133 Randy Winn .20 .10
❑ 134 Yuniesky Betancourt .20 .10
❑ 135 David Eckstein SP 3.00 1.25
❑ 136 Chad Orvella .20 .10
❑ 137 Toby Hall .20 .10
❑ 138 Hank Blalock .20 .10
❑ 139 B.J. Ryan .20 .10
❑ 140 Roy Halladay .20 .10
❑ 141 Livan Hernandez .20 .10
❑ 142 John Patterson .20 .10
❑ 143 Bengie Molina .20 .10
❑ 144 Brad Wilkerson .20 .10
❑ 145 Jorge Cantu SP 3.00 1.25
❑ 146 Mark Mulder .20 .10
❑ 147 Felix Hernandez .30 .15
❑ 148 Paul Lo Duca .20 .10
❑ 149 Prince Fielder (RC) .75 .30
❑ 150 Johnny Damon SP 3.00 1.25
❑ 151 Ryan Langerhans SP 3.00 1.25
❑ 152 Kris Benson SP 3.00 1.25
❑ 153 Curt Schilling SP 3.00 1.25
❑ 154 Manny Ramirez SP 3.00 1.25
❑ 155 Robinson Cano SP 3.00 1.25
❑ 156 Derrek Lee SP 3.00 1.25
❑ 157 A.J. Pierzynski SP 3.00 1.25
❑ 158 Adam Dunn SP 3.00 1.25
❑ 159 Cliff Lee SP 3.00 1.25
❑ 160 Grady Sizemore .30 .15
❑ 161 Jeff Francis .20 .10
❑ 162 Dontrelle Willis .20 .10
❑ 163 Brad Ausmus .20 .10
❑ 164 Preston Wilson .20 .10
❑ 165 Derek Lowe SP 3.00 1.25
❑ 166 Chris Capuano .20 .10
❑ 167 Joe Mauer .30 .15
❑ 168 Torii Hunter .20 .10
❑ 169 Chase Utley .50 .20
❑ 170 Zach Duke .20 .10
❑ 171 Jason Schmidt .20 .10
❑ 172 Adrian Beltre .20 .10
❑ 173 Eddie Guardado .20 .10
❑ 174 Richie Sexson .20 .10
❑ 175 Miguel Cabrera SP 3.00 1.25
❑ 176 Julio Lugo .20 .10
❑ 177 Francisco Cordero .20 .10
❑ 178 Kevin Millwood .20 .10
❑ 179 A.J. Burnett .20 .10
❑ 180 Jose Guillen .20 .10
❑ 181 Larry Bigbie .20 .10
❑ 182 Raul Ibanez .20 .10
❑ 183 Jake Peavy .20 .10
❑ 184 Pat Burrell .20 .10
❑ 185 Tom Glavine SP 3.00 1.25
❑ 186 J.J. Hardy .20 .10
❑ 187 Emil Brown .20 .10
❑ 188 Lance Berkman .20 .10
❑ 189 Marcus Giles .20 .10
❑ 190 Scott Podsednik .20 .10
❑ 191 Chone Figgins .20 .10
❑ 192 Melvin Mora .20 .10

❑ 193 Mark Loretta .20 .10
❑ 194 Carlos Zambrano .20 .10
❑ 195 Chien-Ming Wang .75 .30
❑ 196 Mark Prior .30 .15
❑ 197 Bobby Jenks .20 .10
❑ 198 Brian Fuentes .20 .10
❑ 199 Garret Anderson .30 .10
❑ 200 Ichiro Suzuki .75 .30
❑ 201 Brian Roberts .20 .10
❑ 202 Jason Kendall .20 .10
❑ 203 Milton Bradley .20 .10
❑ 204 Jimmy Rollins .20 .10
❑ 205 Brett Myers SP 3.00 1.25
❑ 206 Joe Randa .20 .10
❑ 207 Mike Piazza .50 .20
❑ 208 Matt Morris .20 .10
❑ 209 Omar Vizquel .30 .15
❑ 210 Jeremy Reed .20 .10
❑ 211 Chris Carpenter .20 .10
❑ 212 Jim Edmonds .30 .15
❑ 213 Scott Kazmir .30 .15
❑ 214 Travis Lee .20 .10
❑ 215 Michael Young SP 3.00 1.25
❑ 216 Rod Barajas .20 .10
❑ 217 Gustavo Chacin .20 .10
❑ 218 Lyle Overbay .20 .10
❑ 219 Troy Glaus .20 .10
❑ 220 Chad Cordero .20 .10
❑ 221 Jose Vidro .20 .10
❑ 222 Scott Rolen .30 .15
❑ 223 Carl Crawford .20 .10
❑ 224 Rocco Baldelli .20 .10
❑ 225 Mike Mussina .30 .15
❑ 226 Kelvim Escobar .20 .10
❑ 227 Corey Patterson .20 .10
❑ 228 Javy Lopez .20 .10
❑ 229 Jonathan Papelbon (RC) 1.00 .40
❑ 230 Aramis Ramirez .20 .10
❑ 231 Tadahito Iguchi .20 .10
❑ 232 Morgan Ensberg .20 .10
❑ 233 Mark Grudzielanek .20 .10
❑ 234 Mike Sweeney .20 .10
❑ 235 Shawn Chacon SP 3.00 1.25
❑ 236 Nick Punto .20 .10
❑ 237 Geoff Jenkins .20 .10
❑ 238 Carlos Lee .20 .10
❑ 239 David DeJesus .20 .10
❑ 240 Brad Lidge .20 .10
❑ 241 Bob Wickman .20 .10
❑ 242 Jon Garland .20 .10
❑ 243 Kerry Wood .20 .10
❑ 244 Bronson Arroyo .20 .10
❑ 245 Matt Holliday SP 3.00 1.25
❑ 246 Josh Beckett .20 .10
❑ 247 Johan Santana .30 .15
❑ 248 Rafael Furcal .20 .10
❑ 249 Shannon Stewart .20 .10
❑ 250 Gary Sheffield .20 .10
❑ 251 Josh Barfield SP (RC) 3.00 1.25
❑ 252 Kenji Johjima RC 1.00 .40
❑ 253 Ian Kinsler (RC) .30 .12
❑ 254 Brian Anderson (RC) .20 .10
❑ 255 Matt Cain SP (RC) 3.00 1.25
❑ 256 Josh Willingham SP (RC) 3.00 1.25
❑ 257 John Koronka (RC) .20 .10
❑ 258 Chris Duffy (RC) .20 .10
❑ 259 Brian McCann (RC) .20 .10
❑ 260 Hanley Ramirez (RC) .50 .20
❑ 261 Hong-Chih Kuo (RC) .50 .20
❑ 262 Francisco Liriano (RC) 1.00 .40
❑ 263 Anderson Hernandez (RC) .20 .10
❑ 264 Ryan Zimmerman (RC) 1.25 .50
❑ 265 Brian Bannister SP (RC) 3.00 1.25
❑ 266 Nolan Ryan 1.25 .50
❑ 267 Frank Robinson .20 .10
❑ 268 Roberto Clemente 1.50 .60
❑ 269 Hank Greenberg .50 .20
❑ 270 Napolean Lajoie .30 .10
❑ 271 Lloyd Waner .30 .10
❑ 272 Paul Waner .30 .10
❑ 273 Frankie Frisch .30 .10
❑ 274 Moose Skowron .20 .10
❑ 275 Mickey Mantle 2.50 1.00
❑ 276 Brooks Robinson .30 .15
❑ 277 Carl Yastrzemski .75 .30
❑ 278 Johnny Pesky .20 .10
❑ 279 Stan Musial .75 .30
❑ 280 Bill Mazeroski .30 .15
❑ 281 Harmon Killebrew .50 .20
❑ 282 Monte Irvin .20 .10
❑ 283 Bob Gibson .30 .15
❑ 284 Ted Williams 1.25 .50
❑ 285 Yogi Berra SP 3.00 1.25
❑ 286 Ernie Banks .50 .20
❑ 287 Bobby Doerr .20 .10
❑ 288 Josh Gibson .50 .20
❑ 289 Bob Feller .20 .10
❑ 290 Cal Ripken 2.00 .75
❑ 291 Bobby Cox MG .20 .10
❑ 292 Terry Francona MG .20 .10
❑ 293 Dusty Baker MG .20 .10
❑ 294 Ozzie Guillen MG .20 .10
❑ 295 Jim Leyland MG SP 3.00 1.25
❑ 296 Willie Randolph MG .20 .10
❑ 297 Joe Torre MG .30 .15
❑ 298 Felipe Alou MG .20 .10
❑ 299 Tony La Russa MG .20 .10
❑ 300 Frank Robinson MG .20 .10
❑ 301 Mike Tyson .75 .30
❑ 302 Duke Paoa Kahanamoku .20 .10
❑ 303 Jennie Finch .75 .30
❑ 304 Brandi Chastain .20 .10
❑ 305 Danica Patrick SP 8.00 3.00
❑ 306 Wendy Guey .20 .10
❑ 307 Hulk Hogan .60 .25
❑ 308 Carl Lewis .30 .10
❑ 309 John Wooden .30 .10
❑ 310 Randy Couture .20 .10
❑ 311 Andy Irons .20 .10
❑ 312 Takeru Kobayashi .60 .25
❑ 313 Leon Spinks .20 .10
❑ 314 Jim Thorpe .30 .10
❑ 315 Jerry Bailey SP 3.00 1.25
❑ 316 Adrian C. Anson REP .30 .15
❑ 317 John M. Ward REP .20 .10
❑ 318 Mike Kelly REP .30 .10
❑ 319 Capt. Jack Glasscock REP .20 .10
❑ 320 Aaron Hill .20 .10
❑ 321 Derrick Turnbow .20 .10
❑ 322 Nick Markakis (RC) .30 .15
❑ 323 Brad Hawpe .20 .10
❑ 324 Kevin Mench .20 .10
❑ 325 John Lackey SP 3.00 1.25
❑ 326 Chester A. Arthur .20 .10
❑ 327 Ulysses S. Grant .20 .10
❑ 328 Abraham Lincoln .30 .10
❑ 329 Grover Cleveland .20 .10
❑ 330 Benjamin Harrison .20 .10
❑ 331 Theodore Roosevelt .30 .10
❑ 332 Rutherford B. Hayes .20 .10
❑ 333 Chancellor Otto Von Bismarck .20 .10
❑ 334 Kaiser Wilhelm II .20 .10
❑ 335 Queen Victoria SP 3.00 1.25
❑ 336 Pope Leo XIII .20 .10
❑ 337 Thomas Edison .20 .10
❑ 338 Orville Wright .20 .10
❑ 339 Wilbur Wright .20 .10
❑ 340 Nathaniel Hawthorne .20 .10
❑ 341 Herman Melville .20 .10
❑ 342 Stonewall Jackson .20 .10
❑ 343 Robert E. Lee .20 .10
❑ 344 Andrew Carnegie .20 .10
❑ 345 John Rockefeller SP 3.00 1.25
❑ 346 Bob Fitzsimmons .20 .10
❑ 347 Billy The Kid .20 .10
❑ 348 Buffalo Bill .20 .10
❑ 349 Jesse James .20 .10
❑ 350 Statue Of Liberty .20 .10
❑ NNO Framed Originals 150.00 75.00

1998 Topps Chrome

❑ COMPLETE SET (503) 150.00 60.00
❑ COMPLETE SERIES 1 (282) 80.00 30.00
❑ COMPLETE SERIES 2 (221) 80.00 30.00
❑ 1 Tony Gwynn 2.50 1.00
❑ 2 Larry Walker .75 .30
❑ 3 Billy Wagner .75 .30
❑ 4 Denny Neagle .75 .30
❑ 5 Vladimir Guerrero 2.00 .75
❑ 6 Kevin Brown 1.25 .50
❑ 8 Mariano Rivera 2.00 .75
❑ 9 Tony Clark .75 .30

❑ 10 Deion Sanders 1.25 .50
❑ 11 Francisco Cordova .75 .30
❑ 12 Matt Williams .75 .30
❑ 13 Carlos Baerga .75 .30
❑ 14 Mo Vaughn .75 .30
❑ 15 Bobby Witt .75 .30
❑ 16 Matt Stairs .75 .30
❑ 17 Chan Ho Park .75 .30
❑ 18 Mike Bordick .75 .30
❑ 19 Michael Tucker .75 .30
❑ 20 Frank Thomas 2.00 .75
❑ 21 Roberto Clemente 5.00 2.00
❑ 22 Dmitri Young .75 .30
❑ 23 Steve Trachsel .75 .30
❑ 24 Jeff Kent .75 .30
❑ 25 Scott Rolen 1.25 .50
❑ 26 John Thomson .75 .30
❑ 27 Joe Vitiello .75 .30
❑ 28 Eddie Guardado .75 .30
❑ 29 Charlie Hayes .75 .30
❑ 30 Juan Gonzalez .75 .30
❑ 31 Garret Anderson .75 .30
❑ 32 John Jaha .75 .30
❑ 33 Omar Vizquel 1.25 .50
❑ 34 Brian Hunter .75 .30
❑ 35 Jeff Bagwell 1.25 .50
❑ 36 Mark Lemke .75 .30
❑ 37 Doug Glanville .75 .30
❑ 38 Dan Wilson .75 .30
❑ 39 Steve Cooke .75 .30
❑ 40 Chili Davis .75 .30
❑ 41 Mike Cameron .75 .30
❑ 42 F.P. Santangelo .75 .30
❑ 43 Brad Ausmus .75 .30
❑ 44 Gary DiSarcina .75 .30
❑ 45 Pat Hentgen .75 .30
❑ 46 Wilton Guerrero .75 .30
❑ 47 Devon White .75 .30
❑ 48 Danny Patterson .75 .30
❑ 49 Pat Meares .75 .30
❑ 50 Rafael Palmeiro 1.25 .50
❑ 51 Mark Gardner .75 .30
❑ 52 Jeff Blauser .75 .30
❑ 53 Dave Hollins .75 .30
❑ 54 Carlos Garcia .75 .30
❑ 55 Ben McDonald .75 .30
❑ 56 John Mabry .75 .30
❑ 57 Trevor Hoffman .75 .30
❑ 58 Tony Fernandez .75 .30
❑ 59 Rich Loiselle RC .75 .30
❑ 60 Mark Leiter .75 .30
❑ 61 Pat Kelly .75 .30
❑ 62 John Flaherty .75 .30
❑ 63 Roger Bailey .75 .30
❑ 64 Tom Gordon .75 .30
❑ 65 Ryan Klesko .75 .30
❑ 66 Darryl Hamilton .75 .30
❑ 67 Jim Eisenreich .75 .30
❑ 68 Butch Huskey .75 .30
❑ 69 Mark Grudzielanek .75 .30
❑ 70 Marquis Grissom .75 .30
❑ 71 Mark McLemore .75 .30
❑ 72 Gary Gaetti .75 .30
❑ 73 Greg Gagne .75 .30
❑ 74 Lyle Mouton .75 .30
❑ 75 Jim Edmonds .75 .30
❑ 76 Shawn Green .75 .30
❑ 77 Greg Vaughn .75 .30

❑ 78	Terry Adams	.75	.30
❑ 79	Kevin Polcovich	.75	.30
❑ 80	Troy O'Leary	.75	.30
❑ 81	Jeff Shaw	.75	.30
❑ 82	Rich Becker	.75	.30
❑ 83	David Wells	.75	.30
❑ 84	Steve Karsay	.75	.30
❑ 85	Charles Nagy	.75	.30
❑ 86	B.J. Surhoff	.75	.30
❑ 87	Jamey Wright	.75	.30
❑ 88	James Baldwin	.75	.30
❑ 89	Edgardo Alfonzo	.75	.30
❑ 90	Jay Buhner	.75	.30
❑ 91	Brady Anderson	.75	.30
❑ 92	Scott Servais	.75	.30
❑ 93	Edgar Renteria	.75	.30
❑ 94	Mike Lieberthal	.75	.30
❑ 95	Rick Aguilera	.75	.30
❑ 96	Walt Weiss	.75	.30
❑ 97	Deivi Cruz	.75	.30
❑ 98	Kurt Abbott	.75	.30
❑ 99	Henry Rodriguez	.75	.30
❑ 100	Mike Piazza	3.00	1.25
❑ 101	Billy Taylor	.75	.30
❑ 102	Todd Zeile	.75	.30
❑ 103	Rey Ordonez	.75	.30
❑ 104	Willie Greene	.75	.30
❑ 105	Tony Womack	.75	.30
❑ 106	Mike Sweeney	.75	.30
❑ 107	Jeffrey Hammonds	.75	.30
❑ 108	Kevin Orie	.75	.30
❑ 109	Alex Gonzalez	.75	.30
❑ 110	Jose Canseco	1.25	.50
❑ 111	Paul Sorrento	.75	.30
❑ 112	Joey Hamilton	.75	.30
❑ 113	Brad Radke	.75	.30
❑ 114	Steve Avery	.75	.30
❑ 115	Esteban Loaiza	.75	.30
❑ 116	Stan Javier	.75	.30
❑ 117	Chris Gomez	.75	.30
❑ 118	Royce Clayton	.75	.30
❑ 119	Orlando Merced	.75	.30
❑ 120	Kevin Appier	.75	.30
❑ 121	Mel Nieves	.75	.30
❑ 122	Joe Girardi	.75	.30
❑ 123	Rico Brogna	.75	.30
❑ 124	Kent Mercker	.75	.30
❑ 125	Manny Ramirez	1.25	.50
❑ 126	Jeromy Burnitz	.75	.30
❑ 127	Kevin Foster	.75	.30
❑ 128	Matt Morris	.75	.30
❑ 129	Jason Dickson	.75	.30
❑ 130	Tom Glavine	1.25	.50
❑ 131	Wally Joyner	.75	.30
❑ 132	Rick Reed	.75	.30
❑ 133	Todd Jones	.75	.30
❑ 134	Dave Martinez	.75	.30
❑ 135	Sandy Alomar Jr.	.75	.30
❑ 136	Mike Lansing	.75	.30
❑ 137	Sean Berry	.75	.30
❑ 138	Doug Jones	.75	.30
❑ 139	Todd Stottlemyre	.75	.30
❑ 140	Jay Bell	.75	.30
❑ 141	Jaime Navarro	.75	.30
❑ 142	Chris Hoiles	.75	.30
❑ 143	Joey Cora	.75	.30
❑ 144	Scott Spiezio	.75	.30
❑ 145	Joe Carter	.75	.30
❑ 146	Jose Guillen	.75	.30
❑ 147	Damion Easley	.75	.30
❑ 148	Lee Stevens	.75	.30
❑ 149	Alex Fernandez	.75	.30
❑ 150	Randy Johnson	2.00	.75
❑ 151	J.T. Snow	.75	.30
❑ 152	Chuck Finley	.75	.30
❑ 153	Bernard Gilkey	.75	.30
❑ 154	David Segui	.75	.30
❑ 155	Dante Bichette	.75	.30
❑ 156	Kevin Stocker	.75	.30
❑ 157	Carl Everett	.75	.30
❑ 158	Jose Valentin	.75	.30
❑ 159	Pokey Reese	.75	.30
❑ 160	Derek Jeter	5.00	2.00
❑ 161	Roger Pavlik	.75	.30
❑ 162	Mark Wohlers	.75	.30
❑ 163	Ricky Bottalico	.75	.30
❑ 164	Ozzie Guillen	.75	.30
❑ 165	Mike Mussina	1.25	.50
❑ 166	Gary Sheffield	.75	.30
❑ 167	Hideo Nomo	2.00	.75
❑ 168	Mark Grace	1.25	.50
❑ 169	Aaron Sele	.75	.30
❑ 170	Darryl Kile	.75	.30
❑ 171	Shawn Estes	.75	.30
❑ 172	Vinny Castilla	.75	.30
❑ 173	Ron Coomer	.75	.30
❑ 174	Jose Rosado	.75	.30
❑ 175	Kenny Lofton	.75	.30
❑ 176	Jason Giambi	.75	.30
❑ 177	Hal Morris	.75	.30
❑ 178	Darren Bragg	.75	.30
❑ 179	Orel Hershiser	.75	.30
❑ 180	Ray Lankford	.75	.30
❑ 181	Hideki Irabu	.75	.30
❑ 182	Kevin Young	.75	.30
❑ 183	Javy Lopez	.75	.30
❑ 184	Jeff Montgomery	.75	.30
❑ 185	Mike Holtz	.75	.30
❑ 186	George Williams	.75	.30
❑ 187	Cal Eldred	.75	.30
❑ 188	Tom Candiotti	.75	.30
❑ 189	Glenallen Hill	.75	.30
❑ 190	Brian Giles	.75	.30
❑ 191	Dave Mlicki	.75	.30
❑ 192	Garrett Stephenson	.75	.30
❑ 193	Jeff Frye	.75	.30
❑ 194	Joe Oliver	.75	.30
❑ 195	Bob Hamelin	.75	.30
❑ 196	Luis Sojo	.75	.30
❑ 197	LaTroy Hawkins	.75	.30
❑ 198	Kevin Elster	.75	.30
❑ 199	Jeff Reed	.75	.30
❑ 200	Dennis Eckersley	.75	.30
❑ 201	Bill Mueller	.75	.30
❑ 202	Russ Davis	.75	.30
❑ 203	Armando Benitez	.75	.30
❑ 204	Quilvio Veras	.75	.30
❑ 205	Tim Naehring	.75	.30
❑ 206	Quinton McCracken	.75	.30
❑ 207	Raul Casanova	.75	.30
❑ 208	Matt Lawton	.75	.30
❑ 209	Luis Alicea	.75	.30
❑ 210	Luis Gonzalez	.75	.30
❑ 211	Allen Watson	.75	.30
❑ 212	Gerald Williams	.75	.30
❑ 213	David Bell	.75	.30
❑ 214	Todd Hollandsworth	.75	.30
❑ 215	Wade Boggs	1.25	.50
❑ 216	Jose Mesa	.75	.30
❑ 217	Jamie Moyer	.75	.30
❑ 218	Darren Daulton	.75	.30
❑ 219	Mickey Morandini	.75	.30
❑ 220	Rusty Greer	.75	.30
❑ 221	Jim Bullinger	.75	.30
❑ 222	Jose Offerman	.75	.30
❑ 223	Matt Karchner	.75	.30
❑ 224	Woody Williams	.75	.30
❑ 225	Mark Loretta	.75	.30
❑ 226	Mike Hampton	.75	.30
❑ 227	Willie Adams	.75	.30
❑ 228	Scott Hatteberg	.75	.30
❑ 229	Rich Amaral	.75	.30
❑ 230	Terry Steinbach	.75	.30
❑ 231	Glendon Rusch	.75	.30
❑ 232	Bret Boone	.75	.30
❑ 233	Robert Person	.75	.30
❑ 234	Jose Hernandez	.75	.30
❑ 235	Doug Drabek	.75	.30
❑ 236	Jason McDonald	.75	.30
❑ 237	Chris Widger	.75	.30
❑ 238	Tom Martin	.75	.30
❑ 239	Dave Burba	.75	.30
❑ 240	Pete Rose Jr. RC	.75	.30
❑ 241	Bobby Ayala	.75	.30
❑ 242	Tim Wakefield	.75	.30
❑ 243	Dennis Springer	.75	.30
❑ 244	Tim Belcher	.75	.30
❑ 245	J.Garland/G.Goetz	1.00	.40
❑ 246	L.Berkman/G.Davis	1.00	.40
❑ 247	V.Wells/A.Akin	1.00	.40
❑ 248	A.Kennedy/J.Romano	1.00	.40
❑ 249	J.Dellaero/T.Cameron	1.00	.40
❑ 250	J.Sandberg/A.Sanchez	1.00	.40
❑ 251	P.Ortega/J.Manias	1.00	.40
❑ 252	Mike Stoner RC	1.00	.40
❑ 253	J.Patterson/L.Rodriguez	1.00	.40
❑ 254	R.Minor RC/A.Beltre	1.00	.40
❑ 255	B.Grieve/D.Brown	1.00	.40
❑ 256	Wood/Pavano/Meche	1.00	.40
❑ 257	D.Ortiz/Sexson/Ward	5.00	2.00
❑ 258	J.Encarnacion/Winn/Vess	1.00	.40
❑ 259	Bens/T.Smith RC/C.Dunc RC	1.00	.40
❑ 260	Warren Morris RC	1.00	.40
❑ 261	B.Davis/Marrero/R.Hern.	1.00	.40
❑ 262	E.Chavez/R.Branyan	1.00	.40
❑ 263	Ryan Jackson RC	1.00	.40
❑ 264	B.Fuentes RC/Clement/Halladay	1.00	.40
❑ 265	Randy Johnson SH	1.25	.50
❑ 266	Kevin Brown SH	.75	.30
❑ 267	Ricardo Rincon SH	.75	.30
❑ 268	Nomar Garciaparra SH	2.00	.75
❑ 269	Tino Martinez SH	.75	.30
❑ 270	Chuck Knoblauch IL	.75	.30
❑ 271	Pedro Martinez IL	1.25	.50
❑ 272	Denny Neagle IL	.75	.30
❑ 273	Juan Gonzalez IL	.75	.30
❑ 274	Andres Galarraga IL	.75	.30
❑ 275	Checklist	.75	.30
❑ 276	Checklist	.75	.30
❑ 277	Moises Alou WS	.75	.30
❑ 278	Sandy Alomar Jr. WS	.75	.30
❑ 279	Gary Sheffield WS	.75	.30
❑ 280	Matt Williams WS	.75	.30
❑ 281	Livan Hernandez WS	.75	.30
❑ 282	Chad Ogea WS	.75	.30
❑ 283	Marlins Champs	.75	.30
❑ 284	Tino Martinez	1.25	.50
❑ 285	Roberto Alomar	1.25	.50
❑ 286	Jeff King	.75	.30
❑ 287	Brian Jordan	.75	.30
❑ 288	Darin Erstad	.75	.30
❑ 289	Ken Caminiti	.75	.30
❑ 290	Jim Thome	1.25	.50
❑ 291	Paul Molitor	.75	.30
❑ 292	Ivan Rodriguez	1.25	.50
❑ 293	Bernie Williams	1.25	.50
❑ 294	Todd Hundley	.75	.30
❑ 295	Andres Galarraga	.75	.30
❑ 296	Greg Maddux	3.00	1.25
❑ 297	Edgar Martinez	1.25	.50
❑ 298	Ron Gant	.75	.30
❑ 299	Derek Bell	.75	.30
❑ 300	Roger Clemens	4.00	1.50
❑ 301	Rondell White	.75	.30
❑ 302	Barry Larkin	1.25	.50
❑ 303	Robin Ventura	.75	.30
❑ 304	Jason Kendall	.75	.30
❑ 305	Chipper Jones	2.00	.75
❑ 306	John Franco	.75	.30
❑ 307	Sammy Sosa	2.00	.75
❑ 308	Troy Percival	.75	.30
❑ 309	Chuck Knoblauch	.75	.30
❑ 310	Ellis Burks	.75	.30
❑ 311	Al Martin	.75	.30
❑ 312	Tim Salmon	1.25	.50
❑ 313	Moises Alou	.75	.30
❑ 314	Lance Johnson	.75	.30
❑ 315	Justin Thompson	.75	.30
❑ 316	Will Clark	1.25	.50
❑ 317	Barry Bonds	5.00	2.00
❑ 318	Craig Biggio	1.25	.50
❑ 319	John Smoltz	1.25	.50
❑ 320	Cal Ripken	6.00	2.50
❑ 321	Ken Griffey Jr.	3.00	1.25
❑ 322	Paul O'Neill	1.25	.50
❑ 323	Todd Helton	1.25	.50
❑ 324	John Olerud	.75	.30
❑ 325	Mark McGwire	5.00	2.00
❑ 326	Jose Cruz Jr.	.75	.30
❑ 327	Jeff Cirillo	.75	.30
❑ 328	Dean Palmer	.75	.30
❑ 329	John Wetteland	.75	.30
❑ 330	Steve Finley	.75	.30
❑ 331	Albert Belle	.75	.30
❑ 332	Curt Schilling	.75	.30
❑ 333	Raul Mondesi	.75	.30
❑ 334	Andruw Jones	1.25	.50
❑ 335	Nomar Garciaparra	3.00	1.25

No.	Player	Price 1	Price 2
336	David Justice	.75	.30
337	Andy Pettitte	1.25	.50
338	Pedro Martinez	1.25	.50
339	Travis Miller	.75	.30
340	Chris Stynes	.75	.30
341	Gregg Jefferies	.75	.30
342	Jeff Fassero	.75	.30
343	Craig Counsell	.75	.30
344	Wilson Alvarez	.75	.30
345	Bip Roberts	.75	.30
346	Kelvim Escobar	.75	.30
347	Mark Bellhorn	.75	.30
348	Cory Lidle RC	8.00	3.00
349	Fred McGriff	1.25	.50
350	Chuck Carr	.75	.30
351	Bob Abreu	.75	.30
352	Juan Guzman	.75	.30
353	Fernando Vina	.75	.30
354	Andy Benes	.75	.30
355	Dave Nilsson	.75	.30
356	Bobby Bonilla	.75	.30
357	Ismael Valdes	.75	.30
358	Carlos Perez	.75	.30
359	Kirk Rueter	.75	.30
360	Bartolo Colon	.75	.30
361	Mel Rojas	.75	.30
362	Johnny Damon	1.25	.50
363	Geronimo Berroa	.75	.30
364	Reggie Sanders	.75	.30
365	Jermaine Allensworth	.75	.30
366	Orlando Cabrera	.75	.30
367	Jorge Fabregas	.75	.30
368	Scott Stahoviak	.75	.30
369	Ken Cloude	.75	.30
370	Donovan Osborne	.75	.30
371	Roger Cedeno	.75	.30
372	Neifi Perez	.75	.30
373	Chris Holt	.75	.30
374	Cecil Fielder	.75	.30
375	Marty Cordova	.75	.30
376	Tom Goodwin	.75	.30
377	Jeff Suppan	.75	.30
378	Jeff Brantley	.75	.30
379	Mark Langston	.75	.30
380	Shane Reynolds	.75	.30
381	Mike Fetters	.75	.30
382	Todd Greene	.75	.30
383	Ray Durham	.75	.30
384	Carlos Delgado	.75	.30
385	Jeff D'Amico	.75	.30
386	Brian McRae	.75	.30
387	Alan Benes	.75	.30
388	Heathcliff Slocumb	.75	.30
389	Eric Young	.75	.30
390	Travis Fryman	.75	.30
391	David Cone	.75	.30
392	Otis Nixon	.75	.30
393	Jeremi Gonzalez	.75	.30
394	Jeff Juden	.75	.30
395	Jose Vizcaino	.75	.30
396	Ugueth Urbina	.75	.30
397	Ramon Martinez	.75	.30
398	Robb Nen	.75	.30
399	Harold Baines	.75	.30
400	Delino DeShields	.75	.30
401	John Burkett	.75	.30
402	Sterling Hitchcock	.75	.30
403	Mark Clark	.75	.30
404	Terrell Wade	.75	.30
405	Scott Brosius	.75	.30
406	Chad Curtis	.75	.30
407	Brian Johnson	.75	.30
408	Roberto Kelly	.75	.30
409	Dave Dellucci RC	1.25	.50
410	Michael Tucker	.75	.30
411	Mark Kotsay	.75	.30
412	Mark Lewis	.75	.30
413	Ryan McGuire	.75	.30
414	Shawon Dunston	.75	.30
415	Brad Rigby	.75	.30
416	Scott Erickson	.75	.30
417	Bobby Jones	.75	.30
418	Darren Oliver	.75	.30
419	John Smiley	.75	.30
420	T.J. Mathews	.75	.30
421	Dustin Hermanson	.75	.30
422	Mike Timlin	.75	.30
423	Willie Blair	.75	.30
424	Manny Alexander	.75	.30
425	Bob Tewksbury	.75	.30
426	Pete Schourek	.75	.30
427	Reggie Jefferson	.75	.30
428	Ed Sprague	.75	.30
429	Jeff Conine	.75	.30
430	Roberto Hernandez	.75	.30
431	Tom Pagnozzi	.75	.30
432	Jaret Wright	.75	.30
433	Livan Hernandez	.75	.30
434	Andy Ashby	.75	.30
435	Todd Dunn	.75	.30
436	Bobby Higginson	.75	.30
437	Rod Beck	.75	.30
438	Jim Leyritz	.75	.30
439	Matt Williams	.75	.30
440	Brett Tomko	.75	.30
441	Joe Randa	.75	.30
442	Chris Carpenter	.75	.30
443	Dennis Reyes	.75	.30
444	Al Leiter	.75	.30
445	Jason Schmidt	.75	.30
446	Ken Hill	.75	.30
447	Shannon Stewart	.75	.30
448	Enrique Wilson	.75	.30
449	Fernando Tatis	.75	.30
450	Jimmy Key	.75	.30
451	Darrin Fletcher	.75	.30
452	John Valentin	.75	.30
453	Kevin Tapani	.75	.30
454	Eric Karros	.75	.30
455	Jay Bell	.75	.30
456	Walt Weiss	.75	.30
457	Devon White	.75	.30
458	Carl Pavano	.75	.30
459	Mike Lansing	.75	.30
460	John Flaherty	.75	.30
461	Richard Hidalgo	.75	.30
462	Quinton McCracken	.75	.30
463	Karim Garcia	.75	.30
464	Miguel Cairo	.75	.30
465	Edwin Diaz	.75	.30
466	Bobby Smith	.75	.30
467	Yamil Benitez	.75	.30
468	Rich Butler RC	.75	.30
469	Ben Ford RC	.75	.30
470	Bubba Trammell	.75	.30
471	Brent Brede	.75	.30
472	Brooks Kieschnick	.75	.30
473	Carlos Castillo	.75	.30
474	Brad Radke SH	.75	.30
475	Roger Clemens SH	2.00	.75
476	Curt Schilling SH	.75	.30
477	John Olerud SH	.75	.30
478	Mark McGwire SH	2.50	1.00
479	M.Piazza/K.Griffey Jr. IL	2.00	.75
480	J.Bagwell/F.Thomas IL	1.25	.50
481	C.Jones/N.Garciaparra IL	1.25	.50
482	L.Walker/J.Gonzalez IL	.75	.30
483	G.Sheffield/T.Martinez IL	.75	.30
484	D.Gib/M.Colem/Hutchins	1.00	.40
485	B.Rose/Looper/Politte	1.00	.40
486	E.Milton/Marquis/C.Lee	1.00	.40
487	Rob Fick RC	1.00	.40
488	A.Ramirez/A.Gonz/Casey	1.00	.40
489	D.Bridges/T.Drew RC	1.00	.40
490	D.McDonald/N.Ndungidi RC	1.00	.40
491	Ryan Anderson RC	1.00	.40
492	Troy Glaus RC	5.00	2.00
493	Dan Reichert RC	1.00	.40
494	Michael Cuddyer RC	2.50	1.00
495	Jack Cust RC	1.00	.40
496	Brian Anderson	1.00	.40
497	Tony Saunders	1.00	.40
498	J.Sandoval/V.Nunez	1.00	.40
499	B.Penny/N.Bierbrodt	1.00	.40
500	D.Carr/L.Cruz RC	1.00	.40
501	C.Bowers/M.McCain	1.00	.40
502	Checklist	.75	.30
503	Checklist	.75	.30
504	Alex Rodriguez	4.00	1.50

1999 Topps Chrome

No.	Player	Price 1	Price 2
	COMPLETE SET (462)	120.00	50.00
	COMPLETE SERIES 1 (241)	60.00	25.00
	COMPLETE SERIES 2 (221)	60.00	25.00
	COMMON CARD (1-6/8-463)	.50	.20
	COMMON (205-212/425-437)	1.00	.40
1	Roger Clemens	4.00	1.50
2	Andres Galarraga	.75	.30
3	Scott Brosius	.75	.30
4	John Flaherty	.50	.20
5	Jim Leyritz	.50	.20
6	Ray Durham	.75	.30
8	Jose Vizcaino	.50	.20
9	Will Clark	1.25	.50
10	David Wells	.75	.30
11	Jose Guillen	.75	.30
12	Scott Hatteberg	.50	.20
13	Edgardo Alfonzo	.50	.20
14	Mike Bordick	.50	.20
15	Manny Ramirez	1.25	.50
16	Greg Maddux	3.00	1.25
17	David Segui	.50	.20
18	Darryl Strawberry	.75	.30
19	Brad Radke	.75	.30
20	Kerry Wood	.75	.30
21	Matt Anderson	.50	.20
22	Derrek Lee	1.25	.50
23	Mickey Morandini	.50	.20
24	Paul Konerko	.75	.30
25	Travis Lee	.50	.20
26	Ken Hill	.50	.20
27	Kenny Rogers	.75	.30
28	Paul Sorrento	.50	.20
29	Quilvio Veras	.50	.20
30	Todd Walker	.50	.20
31	Ryan Jackson	.50	.20
32	John Olerud	.75	.30
33	Doug Glanville	.50	.20
34	Nolan Ryan	6.00	2.50
35	Ray Lankford	.75	.30
36	Mark Loretta	.50	.20
37	Jason Dickson	.50	.20
38	Sean Bergman	.50	.20
39	Quinton McCracken	.50	.20
40	Bartolo Colon	.75	.30
41	Brady Anderson	.75	.30
42	Chris Stynes	.50	.20
43	Jorge Posada	1.25	.50
44	Justin Thompson	.50	.20
45	Johnny Damon	1.25	.50
46	Armando Benitez	.50	.20
47	Brant Brown	.50	.20
48	Charlie Hayes	.50	.20
49	Darren Dreifort	.50	.20
50	Juan Gonzalez	.75	.30
51	Chuck Knoblauch	.75	.30
52	Todd Helton	1.25	.50
53	Rick Reed	.50	.20
54	Chris Gomez	.50	.20
55	Gary Sheffield	.75	.30
56	Rod Beck	.50	.20
57	Rey Sanchez	.50	.20
58	Garret Anderson	.75	.30
59	Jimmy Haynes	.50	.20
60	Steve Woodard	.50	.20
61	Rondell White	.75	.30
62	Vladimir Guerrero	2.00	.75

❑	63	Eric Karros	.75	.30
❑	64	Russ Davis	.50	.20
❑	65	Mo Vaughn	.75	.30
❑	66	Sammy Sosa	2.00	.75
❑	67	Troy Percival	.75	.30
❑	68	Kenny Lofton	.75	.30
❑	69	Bill Taylor	.50	.20
❑	70	Mark McGwire	5.00	2.00
❑	71	Roger Cedeno	.50	.20
❑	72	Javy Lopez	.75	.30
❑	73	Damion Easley	.50	.20
❑	74	Andy Pettitte	1.25	.50
❑	75	Tony Gwynn	2.50	1.00
❑	76	Ricardo Rincon	.50	.20
❑	77	F.P. Santangelo	.50	.20
❑	78	Jay Bell	.75	.30
❑	79	Scott Servais	.50	.20
❑	80	Jose Canseco	1.25	.50
❑	81	Roberto Hernandez	.50	.20
❑	82	Todd Dunwoody	.50	.20
❑	83	John Wetteland	.75	.30
❑	84	Mike Caruso	.50	.20
❑	85	Derek Jeter	5.00	2.00
❑	86	Aaron Sele	.50	.20
❑	87	Jose Lima	.50	.20
❑	88	Ryan Christenson	.50	.20
❑	89	Jeff Cirillo	.50	.20
❑	90	Jose Hernandez	.50	.20
❑	91	Mark Kotsay	.75	.30
❑	92	Darren Bragg	.50	.20
❑	93	Albert Belle	.75	.30
❑	94	Matt Lawton	.50	.20
❑	95	Pedro Martinez	1.25	.50
❑	96	Greg Vaughn	.50	.20
❑	97	Neifi Perez	.50	.20
❑	98	Gerald Williams	.50	.20
❑	99	Derek Bell	.50	.20
❑	100	Ken Griffey Jr.	3.00	1.25
❑	101	David Cone	.75	.30
❑	102	Brian Johnson	.50	.20
❑	103	Dean Palmer	.75	.30
❑	104	Javier Valentin	.50	.20
❑	105	Trevor Hoffman	.75	.30
❑	106	Butch Huskey	.50	.20
❑	107	Dave Martinez	.50	.20
❑	108	Billy Wagner	.75	.30
❑	109	Shawn Green	.75	.30
❑	110	Ben Grieve	.50	.20
❑	111	Tom Goodwin	.50	.20
❑	112	Jaret Wright	.50	.20
❑	113	Aramis Ramirez	.75	.30
❑	114	Dmitri Young	.75	.30
❑	115	Hideki Irabu	.50	.20
❑	116	Roberto Kelly	.50	.20
❑	117	Jeff Fassero	.50	.20
❑	118	Mark Clark	.50	.20
❑	119	Jason McDonald	.50	.20
❑	120	Matt Williams	.75	.30
❑	121	Dave Burba	.50	.20
❑	122	Bret Saberhagen	.75	.30
❑	123	Deivi Cruz	.50	.20
❑	124	Chad Curtis	.50	.20
❑	125	Scott Rolen	1.25	.50
❑	126	Lee Stevens	.50	.20
❑	127	J.T. Snow	.75	.30
❑	128	Rusty Greer	.75	.30
❑	129	Brian Meadows	.50	.20
❑	130	Jim Edmonds	.75	.30
❑	131	Ron Gant	.75	.30
❑	132	A.J. Hinch	.50	.20
❑	133	Shannon Stewart	.75	.30
❑	134	Brad Fullmer	.50	.20
❑	135	Cal Eldred	.50	.20
❑	136	Matt Walbeck	.50	.20
❑	137	Carl Everett	.75	.30
❑	138	Walt Weiss	.50	.20
❑	139	Fred McGriff	1.25	.50
❑	140	Darin Erstad	.75	.30
❑	141	Dave Nilsson	.50	.20
❑	142	Eric Young	.50	.20
❑	143	Dan Wilson	.50	.20
❑	144	Jeff Reed	.50	.20
❑	145	Brett Tomko	.50	.20
❑	146	Terry Steinbach	.50	.20
❑	147	Seth Greisinger	.50	.20
❑	148	Pat Meares	.50	.20
❑	149	Livan Hernandez	.75	.30
❑	150	Jeff Bagwell	1.25	.50
❑	151	Bob Wickman	.50	.20
❑	152	Omar Vizquel	1.25	.50
❑	153	Eric Davis	.75	.30
❑	154	Larry Sutton	.50	.20
❑	155	Magglio Ordonez	.75	.30
❑	156	Eric Milton	.50	.20
❑	157	Darren Lewis	.50	.20
❑	158	Rick Aguilera	.50	.20
❑	159	Mike Lieberthal	.75	.30
❑	160	Robb Nen	.75	.30
❑	161	Brian Giles	.75	.30
❑	162	Jeff Brantley	.50	.20
❑	163	Gary DiSarcina	.50	.20
❑	164	John Valentin	.50	.20
❑	165	Dave Dellucci	.50	.20
❑	166	Chan Ho Park	.75	.30
❑	167	Masato Yoshii	.50	.20
❑	168	Jason Schmidt	.75	.30
❑	169	LaTroy Hawkins	.50	.20
❑	170	Bret Boone	.75	.30
❑	171	Jerry DiPoto	.50	.20
❑	172	Mariano Rivera	2.00	.75
❑	173	Mike Cameron	.50	.20
❑	174	Scott Erickson	.50	.20
❑	175	Charles Johnson	.75	.30
❑	176	Bobby Jones	.50	.20
❑	177	Francisco Cordova	.50	.20
❑	178	Todd Jones	.50	.20
❑	179	Jeff Montgomery	.50	.20
❑	180	Mike Mussina	1.25	.50
❑	181	Bob Abreu	.75	.30
❑	182	Ismael Valdes	.50	.20
❑	183	Andy Fox	.50	.20
❑	184	Woody Williams	.50	.20
❑	185	Denny Neagle	.50	.20
❑	186	Jose Valentin	.50	.20
❑	187	Darrin Fletcher	.50	.20
❑	188	Gabe Alvarez	.50	.20
❑	189	Eddie Taubensee	.50	.20
❑	190	Edgar Martinez	1.25	.50
❑	191	Jason Kendall	.75	.30
❑	192	Darryl Kile	.75	.30
❑	193	Jeff King	.50	.20
❑	194	Rey Ordonez	.50	.20
❑	195	Andruw Jones	1.25	.50
❑	196	Tony Fernandez	.50	.20
❑	197	Jamey Wright	.50	.20
❑	198	B.J. Surhoff	.75	.30
❑	199	Vinny Castilla	.75	.30
❑	200	David Wells HL	.50	.20
❑	201	Mark McGwire HL	2.50	1.00
❑	202	Sammy Sosa HL	1.25	.50
❑	203	Roger Clemens HL	2.00	.75
❑	204	Kerry Wood HL	.50	.20
❑	205	L.Berkman/G.Kapler	1.00	.40
❑	206	Alex Escobar RC	1.00	.40
❑	207	Peter Bergeron RC	1.00	.40
❑	208	M.Barrett/B.Davis/R.Fick	1.00	.40
❑	209	J.Werth/Hernandez/Cline	1.00	.40
❑	210	Ryan Anderson	1.00	.40
❑	211	B.Penny/Dotel/Lincoln	1.00	.40
❑	212	Chuck Abbott RC	1.00	.40
❑	213	C.Jones/J.Urban RC	1.00	.40
❑	214	T.Torcato/A.McDowell RC	1.00	.40
❑	215	J.Tyner/J.McKinley RC	1.00	.40
❑	216	M.Burch/S.Etherton RC	1.00	.40
❑	217	R.Elder/M.Tucker RC	1.00	.40
❑	218	J.M.Gold/R.Mills RC	1.00	.40
❑	219	A.Brown/C.Freeman RC	1.00	.40
❑	220A	Mark McGwire HR 1	50.00	20.00
❑	220B	Mark McGwire HR 2	30.00	12.50
❑	220C	Mark McGwire HR 3	30.00	12.50
❑	220D	Mark McGwire HR 4	30.00	12.50
❑	220E	Mark McGwire HR 5	30.00	12.50
❑	220F	Mark McGwire HR 6	30.00	12.50
❑	220G	Mark McGwire HR 7	30.00	12.50
❑	220H	Mark McGwire HR 8	30.00	12.50
❑	220I	Mark McGwire HR 9	30.00	12.50
❑	220J	Mark McGwire HR 10	30.00	12.50
❑	220K	Mark McGwire HR 11	30.00	12.50
❑	220L	Mark McGwire HR 12	30.00	12.50
❑	220M	Mark McGwire HR 13	30.00	12.50
❑	220N	Mark McGwire HR 14	30.00	12.50
❑	220O	Mark McGwire HR 15	30.00	12.50
❑	220P	Mark McGwire HR 16	30.00	12.50
❑	220Q	Mark McGwire HR 17	30.00	12.50
❑	220R	Mark McGwire HR 18	30.00	12.50
❑	220S	Mark McGwire HR 19	30.00	12.50
❑	220T	Mark McGwire HR 20	30.00	12.50
❑	220U	Mark McGwire HR 21	30.00	12.50
❑	220V	Mark McGwire HR 22	30.00	12.50
❑	220W	Mark McGwire HR 23	30.00	12.50
❑	220X	Mark McGwire HR 24	30.00	12.50
❑	220Y	Mark McGwire HR 25	30.00	12.50
❑	220Z	Mark McGwire HR 26	30.00	12.50
❑	220AA	Mark McGwire HR 27	30.00	12.50
❑	220AB	Mark McGwire HR 28	30.00	12.50
❑	220AC	Mark McGwire HR 29	30.00	12.50
❑	220AD	Mark McGwire HR 30	30.00	12.50
❑	220AE	Mark McGwire HR 31	30.00	12.50
❑	220AF	Mark McGwire HR 32	30.00	12.50
❑	220AG	Mark McGwire HR 33	30.00	12.50
❑	220AH	Mark McGwire HR 34	30.00	12.50
❑	220AI	Mark McGwire HR 35	30.00	12.50
❑	220AJ	Mark McGwire HR 36	30.00	12.50
❑	220AK	Mark McGwire HR 37	30.00	12.50
❑	220AL	Mark McGwire HR 38	30.00	12.50
❑	220AM	Mark McGwire HR 39	30.00	12.50
❑	220AN	Mark McGwire HR 40	30.00	12.50
❑	220AO	Mark McGwire HR 41	30.00	12.50
❑	220AP	Mark McGwire HR 42	30.00	12.50
❑	220AQ	Mark McGwire HR 43	30.00	12.50
❑	220AR	Mark McGwire HR 44	30.00	12.50
❑	220AS	Mark McGwire HR 45	30.00	12.50
❑	220AT	Mark McGwire HR 46	30.00	12.50
❑	220AU	Mark McGwire HR 47	30.00	12.50
❑	220AV	Mark McGwire HR 48	30.00	12.50
❑	220AW	Mark McGwire HR 49	30.00	12.50
❑	220AX	Mark McGwire HR 50	30.00	12.50
❑	220AY	Mark McGwire HR 51	30.00	12.50
❑	220AZ	Mark McGwire HR 52	30.00	12.50
❑	220BB	Mark McGwire HR 53	30.00	12.50
❑	220CC	Mark McGwire HR 54	30.00	12.50
❑	220DD	Mark McGwire HR 55	30.00	12.50
❑	220EE	Mark McGwire HR 56	30.00	12.50
❑	220FF	Mark McGwire HR 57	30.00	12.50
❑	220GG	Mark McGwire HR 58	30.00	12.50
❑	220HH	Mark McGwire HR 59	30.00	12.50
❑	220II	Mark McGwire HR 60	30.00	12.50
❑	220JJ	Mark McGwire HR 61	50.00	20.00
❑	220KK	Mark McGwire HR 62	80.00	40.00
❑	220LL	Mark McGwire HR 63	50.00	20.00
❑	220MM	Mark McGwire HR 64	50.00	20.00
❑	220NN	Mark McGwire HR 65	50.00	20.00
❑	220OO	Mark McGwire HR 66	50.00	20.00
❑	220PP	Mark McGwire HR 67	50.00	20.00
❑	220QQ	Mark McGwire HR 68	50.00	20.00
❑	220RR	Mark McGwire HR 69	50.00	20.00
❑	220SS	Mark McGwire HR 70	120.00	60.00
❑	221	Larry Walker LL	.50	.20
❑	222	Bernie Williams LL	.75	.30
❑	223	Mark McGwire LL	2.50	1.00
❑	224	Ken Griffey Jr. LL	2.00	.75
❑	225	Sammy Sosa LL	1.25	.50
❑	226	Juan Gonzalez LL	.50	.20
❑	227	Dante Bichette LL	.50	.20
❑	228	Alex Rodriguez LL	2.00	.75
❑	229	Sammy Sosa LL	1.25	.50
❑	230	Derek Jeter LL	2.50	1.00
❑	231	Greg Maddux LL	2.00	.75
❑	232	Roger Clemens LL	2.00	.75
❑	233	Ricky Ledee WS	.50	.20
❑	234	Chuck Knoblauch WS	.50	.20
❑	235	Bernie Williams WS	.75	.30
❑	236	Tino Martinez WS	.75	.30
❑	237	Orlando Hernandez WS	.75	.30
❑	238	Scott Brosius WS	.50	.20
❑	239	Andy Pettitte WS	.75	.30
❑	240	Mariano Rivera WS	1.25	.50
❑	241	Checklist	.50	.20
❑	242	Checklist	.50	.20
❑	243	Tom Glavine	1.25	.50
❑	244	Andy Benes	.50	.20
❑	245	Sandy Alomar Jr.	.50	.20
❑	246	Wilton Guerrero	.50	.20
❑	247	Alex Gonzalez	.50	.20
❑	248	Roberto Alomar	1.25	.50
❑	249	Ruben Rivera	.50	.20
❑	250	Eric Chavez	.75	.30
❑	251	Ellis Burks	.75	.30

❑	252	Richie Sexson	.75	.30
❑	253	Steve Finley	.75	.30
❑	254	Dwight Gooden	.75	.30
❑	255	Dustin Hermanson	.50	.20
❑	256	Kirk Rueter	.50	.20
❑	257	Steve Trachsel	.50	.20
❑	258	Gregg Jefferies	.50	.20
❑	259	Matt Stairs	.50	.20
❑	260	Shane Reynolds	.50	.20
❑	261	Gregg Olson	.50	.20
❑	262	Kevin Tapani	.50	.20
❑	263	Matt Morris	.75	.30
❑	264	Carl Pavano	.75	.30
❑	265	Nomar Garciaparra	3.00	1.25
❑	266	Kevin Young	.75	.30
❑	267	Rick Helling	.50	.20
❑	268	Matt Franco	.50	.20
❑	269	Brian McRae	.50	.20
❑	270	Cal Ripken	6.00	2.50
❑	271	Jeff Abbott	.50	.20
❑	272	Tony Batista	.50	.20
❑	273	Bill Simas	.50	.20
❑	274	Brian Hunter	.50	.20
❑	275	John Franco	.75	.30
❑	276	Devon White	.75	.30
❑	277	Rickey Henderson	2.00	.75
❑	278	Chuck Finley	.75	.30
❑	279	Mike Blowers	.50	.20
❑	280	Mark Grace	1.25	.50
❑	281	Randy Winn	.50	.20
❑	282	Bobby Bonilla	.75	.30
❑	283	David Justice	.75	.30
❑	284	Shane Monahan	.50	.20
❑	285	Kevin Brown	1.25	.50
❑	286	Todd Zeile	.75	.30
❑	287	Al Martin	.50	.20
❑	288	Troy O'Leary	.50	.20
❑	289	Darryl Hamilton	.50	.20
❑	290	Tino Martinez	1.25	.50
❑	291	David Ortiz	2.00	.75
❑	292	Tony Clark	.50	.20
❑	293	Ryan Minor	.50	.20
❑	294	Mark Leiter	.50	.20
❑	295	Wally Joyner	.75	.30
❑	296	Cliff Floyd	.75	.30
❑	297	Shawn Estes	.50	.20
❑	298	Pat Hentgen	.50	.20
❑	299	Scott Elarton	.50	.20
❑	300	Alex Rodriguez	3.00	1.25
❑	301	Ozzie Guillen	.75	.30
❑	302	Hideo Nomo	2.00	.75
❑	303	Ryan McGuire	.50	.20
❑	304	Brad Ausmus	.75	.30
❑	305	Alex Gonzalez	.50	.20
❑	306	Brian Jordan	.75	.30
❑	307	John Jaha	.50	.20
❑	308	Mark Grudzielanek	.50	.20
❑	309	Juan Guzman	.50	.20
❑	310	Tony Womack	.50	.20
❑	311	Dennis Reyes	.50	.20
❑	312	Marty Cordova	.50	.20
❑	313	Ramiro Mendoza	.50	.20
❑	314	Robin Ventura	.75	.30
❑	315	Rafael Palmeiro	1.25	.50
❑	316	Ramon Martinez	.50	.20
❑	317	Pedro Astacio	.50	.20
❑	318	Dave Hollins	.50	.20
❑	319	Tom Candiotti	.50	.20
❑	320	Al Leiter	.75	.30
❑	321	Rico Brogna	.50	.20
❑	322	Reggie Jefferson	.50	.20
❑	323	Bernard Gilkey	.50	.20
❑	324	Jason Giambi	.75	.30
❑	325	Craig Biggio	1.25	.50
❑	326	Troy Glaus	1.25	.50
❑	327	Delino DeShields	.50	.20
❑	328	Fernando Vina	.50	.20
❑	329	John Smoltz	1.25	.50
❑	330	Jeff Kent	.75	.30
❑	331	Roy Halladay	.75	.30
❑	332	Andy Ashby	.50	.20
❑	333	Tim Wakefield	.75	.30
❑	334	Roger Clemens	4.00	1.50
❑	335	Bernie Williams	1.25	.50
❑	336	Desi Relaford	.50	.20
❑	337	John Burkett	.50	.20
❑	338	Mike Hampton	.75	.30
❑	339	Royce Clayton	.50	.20
❑	340	Mike Piazza	3.00	1.25
❑	341	Jeremi Gonzalez	.50	.20
❑	342	Mike Lansing	.50	.20
❑	343	Jamie Moyer	.75	.30
❑	344	Ron Coomer	.50	.20
❑	345	Barry Larkin	1.25	.50
❑	346	Fernando Tatis	.50	.20
❑	347	Chili Davis	.75	.30
❑	348	Bobby Higginson	.75	.30
❑	349	Hal Morris	.50	.20
❑	350	Larry Walker	.75	.30
❑	351	Carlos Guillen	.75	.30
❑	352	Miguel Tejada	.75	.30
❑	353	Travis Fryman	.75	.30
❑	354	Jarrod Washburn	.50	.20
❑	355	Chipper Jones	2.00	.75
❑	356	Todd Stottlemyre	.50	.20
❑	357	Henry Rodriguez	.50	.20
❑	358	Eli Marrero	.50	.20
❑	359	Alan Benes	.50	.20
❑	360	Tim Salmon	1.25	.50
❑	361	Luis Gonzalez	.75	.30
❑	362	Scott Spiezio	.50	.20
❑	363	Chris Carpenter	.75	.30
❑	364	Bobby Howry	.50	.20
❑	365	Raul Mondesi	.75	.30
❑	366	Ugueth Urbina	.50	.20
❑	367	Tom Evans	.50	.20
❑	368	Kerry Ligtenberg RC	.75	.30
❑	369	Adrian Beltre	.75	.30
❑	370	Ryan Klesko	.75	.30
❑	371	Wilson Alvarez	.50	.20
❑	372	John Thomson	.50	.20
❑	373	Tony Saunders	.50	.20
❑	374	Dave Mlicki	.50	.20
❑	375	Ken Caminiti	.75	.30
❑	376	Jay Buhner	.75	.30
❑	377	Bill Mueller	.75	.30
❑	378	Jeff Blauser	.50	.20
❑	379	Edgar Renteria	.75	.30
❑	380	Jim Thome	1.25	.50
❑	381	Joey Hamilton	.50	.20
❑	382	Calvin Pickering	.50	.20
❑	383	Marquis Grissom	.75	.30
❑	384	Omar Daal	.50	.20
❑	385	Curt Schilling	.75	.30
❑	386	Jose Cruz Jr.	.50	.20
❑	387	Chris Widger	.50	.20
❑	388	Pete Harnisch	.50	.20
❑	389	Charles Nagy	.50	.20
❑	390	Tom Gordon	.50	.20
❑	391	Bobby Smith	.50	.20
❑	392	Derrick Gibson	.50	.20
❑	393	Jeff Conine	.75	.30
❑	394	Carlos Perez	.50	.20
❑	395	Barry Bonds	5.00	2.00
❑	396	Mark McLemore	.50	.20
❑	397	Juan Encarnacion	.50	.20
❑	398	Wade Boggs	1.25	.50
❑	399	Ivan Rodriguez	1.25	.50
❑	400	Moises Alou	.75	.30
❑	401	Jeromy Burnitz	.75	.30
❑	402	Sean Casey	.75	.30
❑	403	Jose Offerman	.50	.20
❑	404	Joe Fontenot	.50	.20
❑	405	Kevin Millwood	.75	.30
❑	406	Lance Johnson	.50	.20
❑	407	Richard Hidalgo	.50	.20
❑	408	Mike Jackson	.50	.20
❑	409	Brian Anderson	.50	.20
❑	410	Jeff Shaw	.50	.20
❑	411	Preston Wilson	.75	.30
❑	412	Todd Hundley	.50	.20
❑	413	Jim Parque	.50	.20
❑	414	Justin Baughman	.50	.20
❑	415	Dante Bichette	.75	.30
❑	416	Paul O'Neill	1.25	.50
❑	417	Miguel Cairo	.50	.20
❑	418	Randy Johnson	2.00	.75
❑	419	Jesus Sanchez	.50	.20
❑	420	Carlos Delgado	.75	.30
❑	421	Ricky Ledee	.50	.20
❑	422	Orlando Hernandez	.75	.30
❑	423	Frank Thomas	2.00	.75
❑	424	Pokey Reese	.50	.20
❑	425	C.Lee/M.Lowell	1.00	.40
❑	426	M.Cuddyer/DeRosa/Hairston	1.00	.40
❑	427	M.Anderson/Belliard/Cabrera	1.00	.40
❑	428	M.Bowie/P.Norton RC/Wolf	1.00	.40
❑	429	J.Cressend RC/Rocker	1.00	.40
❑	430	R.Mateo/M.Zywica RC	1.00	.40
❑	431	J.LaRue/LeCroy/Meluskey	1.00	.40
❑	432	Gabe Kapler	1.00	.40
❑	433	A.Kennedy/M.Lopez RC	1.00	.40
❑	434	Jose Fernandez RC/C.Truby	1.00	.40
❑	435	Doug Mientkiewicz RC	1.50	.60
❑	436	R.Brown RC/V.Wells	1.00	.40
❑	437	A.J. Burnett RC	2.00	.75
❑	438	M.Belisle/M.Roney RC	1.00	.40
❑	439	A.Kearns/C.George RC	4.00	1.50
❑	440	N.Cornejo/N.Bump RC	1.00	.40
❑	441	B.Lidge/M.Nannini RC	4.00	1.50
❑	442	M.Holliday/J.Winchester RC	4.00	1.50
❑	443	A.Everett/C.Ambres RC	1.50	.60
❑	444	P.Burrell/E.Valent RC	4.00	1.50
❑	445	Roger Clemens SK	2.00	.75
❑	446	Kerry Wood SK	.50	.20
❑	447	Curt Schilling SK	.50	.20
❑	448	Randy Johnson SK	1.25	.50
❑	449	Pedro Martinez SK	1.25	.50
❑	450	Bagwell/Galar/McGwire AT	2.00	.75
❑	451	Olerud/Thome/Martinez AT	.75	.30
❑	452	ARod/Nomar/Jeter AT	2.50	1.00
❑	453	Castilla/Jones/Rolen AT	1.25	.50
❑	454	Sosa/Griffey/Gonzalez AT	2.00	.75
❑	455	Bonds/Ramirez/Walker AT	2.50	1.00
❑	456	Thomas/Salmon/Justice AT	2.00	.75
❑	457	Lee/Helton/Grieve AT	.75	.30
❑	458	Guerrero/Vaughn/B.Will AT	.75	.30
❑	459	Piazza/IRod/Kendall AT	2.00	.75
❑	460	Clemens/Wood/Maddux AT	2.00	.75
❑	461A	Sammy Sosa HR 1	20.00	8.00
❑	461B	Sammy Sosa HR 2	12.00	5.00
❑	461C	Sammy Sosa HR 3	12.00	5.00
❑	461D	Sammy Sosa HR 4	12.00	5.00
❑	461E	Sammy Sosa HR 5	12.00	5.00
❑	461F	Sammy Sosa HR 6	12.00	5.00
❑	461G	Sammy Sosa HR 7	12.00	5.00
❑	461H	Sammy Sosa HR 8	12.00	5.00
❑	461I	Sammy Sosa HR 9	12.00	5.00
❑	461J	Sammy Sosa HR 10	12.00	5.00
❑	461K	Sammy Sosa HR 11	12.00	5.00
❑	461L	Sammy Sosa HR 12	12.00	5.00
❑	461M	Sammy Sosa HR 13	12.00	5.00
❑	461N	Sammy Sosa HR 14	12.00	5.00
❑	461O	Sammy Sosa HR 15	12.00	5.00
❑	461P	Sammy Sosa HR 16	12.00	5.00
❑	461Q	Sammy Sosa HR 17	12.00	5.00
❑	461R	Sammy Sosa HR 18	12.00	5.00
❑	461S	Sammy Sosa HR 19	12.00	5.00
❑	461T	Sammy Sosa HR 20	12.00	5.00
❑	461U	Sammy Sosa HR 21	12.00	5.00
❑	461V	Sammy Sosa HR 22	12.00	5.00
❑	461W	Sammy Sosa HR 23	12.00	5.00
❑	461X	Sammy Sosa HR 24	12.00	5.00
❑	461Y	Sammy Sosa HR 25	12.00	5.00
❑	461Z	Sammy Sosa HR 26	12.00	5.00
❑	461AA	Sammy Sosa HR 27	12.00	5.00
❑	461AB	Sammy Sosa HR 28	12.00	5.00
❑	461AC	Sammy Sosa HR 29	12.00	5.00
❑	461AD	Sammy Sosa HR 30	12.00	5.00
❑	461AE	Sammy Sosa HR 31	12.00	5.00
❑	461AF	Sammy Sosa HR 32	12.00	5.00
❑	461AG	Sammy Sosa HR 33	12.00	5.00
❑	461AH	Sammy Sosa HR 34	12.00	5.00
❑	461AI	Sammy Sosa HR 35	12.00	5.00
❑	461AJ	Sammy Sosa HR 36	12.00	5.00
❑	461AK	Sammy Sosa HR 37	12.00	5.00
❑	461AL	Sammy Sosa HR 38	12.00	5.00
❑	461AM	Sammy Sosa HR 39	12.00	5.00
❑	461AN	Sammy Sosa HR 40	12.00	5.00
❑	461AO	Sammy Sosa HR 41	12.00	5.00
❑	461AP	Sammy Sosa HR 42	12.00	5.00
❑	461AR	Sammy Sosa HR 43	12.00	5.00
❑	461AS	Sammy Sosa HR 44	12.00	5.00
❑	461AT	Sammy Sosa HR 45	12.00	5.00
❑	461AU	Sammy Sosa HR 46	12.00	5.00
❑	461AV	Sammy Sosa HR 47	12.00	5.00
❑	461AW	Sammy Sosa HR 48	12.00	5.00
❑	461AX	Sammy Sosa HR 49	12.00	5.00

Card	Player		
❑ 461AY	Sammy Sosa HR 50	12.00	5.00
❑ 461AZ	Sammy Sosa HR 51	12.00	5.00
❑ 461BB	Sammy Sosa HR 52	12.00	5.00
❑ 461CC	Sammy Sosa HR 53	12.00	5.00
❑ 461DD	Sammy Sosa HR 54	12.00	5.00
❑ 461EE	Sammy Sosa HR 55	12.00	5.00
❑ 461FF	Sammy Sosa HR 56	12.00	5.00
❑ 461GG	Sammy Sosa HR 57	12.00	5.00
❑ 461HH	Sammy Sosa HR 58	12.00	5.00
❑ 461II	Sammy Sosa HR 59	12.00	5.00
❑ 461JJ	Sammy Sosa HR 60	12.00	5.00
❑ 461KK	Sammy Sosa HR 61	20.00	8.00
❑ 461LL	Sammy Sosa HR 62	30.00	12.50
❑ 461MM	Sammy Sosa HR 63	20.00	8.00
❑ 461NN	Sammy Sosa HR 64	20.00	8.00
❑ 461OO	Sammy Sosa HR 65	20.00	8.00
❑ 461PP	Sammy Sosa HR 66	60.00	30.00
❑ 462	Checklist	.50	.20
❑ 463	Checklist	.50	.20

1999 Topps Chrome Traded

Card	Player		
❑	COMP.FACT SET (121)	80.00	40.00
❑ T1	Seth Etherton	.40	.15
❑ T2	Mark Harriger RC	.50	.20
❑ T3	Matt Wise RC	.50	.20
❑ T4	Carlos Eduardo Hernandez RC	.75	.30
❑ T5	Julio Lugo RC	1.25	.50
❑ T6	Mike Nannini	.40	.15
❑ T7	Justin Bowles RC	.50	.20
❑ T8	Mark Mulder RC	3.00	1.25
❑ T9	Roberto Vaz RC	.50	.20
❑ T10	Felipe Lopez RC	3.00	1.25
❑ T11	Matt Belisle	.40	.15
❑ T12	Micah Bowie	.40	.15
❑ T13	Ruben Quevedo RC	.50	.20
❑ T14	Jose Garcia RC	.50	.20
❑ T15	David Kelton RC	.50	.20
❑ T16	Phil Norton	.40	.15
❑ T17	Corey Patterson RC	2.00	.75
❑ T18	Ron Walker RC	.50	.20
❑ T19	Paul Hoover RC	.50	.20
❑ T20	Ryan Rupe RC	.50	.20
❑ T21	J.D. Closser RC	.75	.30
❑ T22	Rob Ryan RC	.50	.20
❑ T23	Steve Colyer RC	.50	.20
❑ T24	Bubba Crosby RC	1.25	.50
❑ T25	Luke Prokopec RC	.50	.20
❑ T26	Matt Blank RC	.50	.20
❑ T27	Josh McKinley	.40	.15
❑ T28	Nate Bump	.50	.20
❑ T29	Giuseppe Chiaramonte RC	.50	.20
❑ T30	Arturo McDowell	.40	.15
❑ T31	Tony Torcato	.40	.15
❑ T32	Dave Roberts RC	1.25	.50
❑ T33	C.C. Sabathia RC	2.50	1.00
❑ T34	Sean Spencer RC	.50	.20
❑ T35	Chip Ambres	.40	.15
❑ T36	A.J. Burnett	2.00	.75
❑ T37	Mo Bruce RC	.50	.20
❑ T38	Jason Tyner	.40	.15
❑ T39	Mamon Tucker	.40	.15
❑ T40	Sean Burroughs RC	1.25	.50
❑ T41	Kevin Eberwein RC	.50	.20
❑ T42	Junior Herndon RC	.50	.20
❑ T43	Bryan Wolff RC	.50	.20
❑ T44	Pat Burrell	3.00	1.25
❑ T45	Eric Valent	.75	.30
❑ T46	Carlos Pena RC	.75	.30
❑ T47	Mike Zywica	.40	.15
❑ T48	Adam Everett	1.00	.40
❑ T49	Juan Pena RC	.50	.20
❑ T50	Adam Dunn RC	8.00	3.00
❑ T51	Austin Kearns	3.00	1.25
❑ T52	Jacobo Sequea RC	.50	.20
❑ T53	Choo Freeman	.60	.25
❑ T54	Jeff Winchester	.40	.15
❑ T55	Matt Burch	.50	.20
❑ T56	Chris George	.40	.15
❑ T57	Scott Mullen RC	.50	.20
❑ T58	Kit Pellow	.50	.20
❑ T59	Mark Quinn RC	.50	.20
❑ T60	Nate Cornejo	.50	.20
❑ T61	Ryan Mills	.40	.15
❑ T62	Kevin Beirne RC	.50	.20
❑ T63	Kip Wells RC	.75	.30
❑ T64	Juan Rivera RC	2.00	.75
❑ T65	Alfonso Soriano RC	10.00	4.00
❑ T66	Josh Hamilton RC	.75	.30
❑ T67	Josh Girdley RC	.50	.20
❑ T68	Kyle Snyder RC	.50	.20
❑ T69	Mike Paradis RC	.50	.20
❑ T70	Jason Jennings RC	1.25	.50
❑ T71	David Walling RC	.50	.20
❑ T72	Omar Ortiz RC	.50	.20
❑ T73	Jay Gehrke RC	.50	.20
❑ T74	Casey Burns RC	.50	.20
❑ T75	Carl Crawford RC	6.00	2.50
❑ T76	Reggie Sanders	.60	.25
❑ T77	Will Clark	1.00	.40
❑ T78	David Wells	.60	.25
❑ T79	Paul Konerko	.60	.25
❑ T80	Armando Benitez	.40	.15
❑ T81	Brant Brown	.40	.15
❑ T82	Mo Vaughn	.60	.25
❑ T83	Jose Canseco	1.00	.40
❑ T84	Albert Belle	.60	.25
❑ T85	Dean Palmer	.60	.25
❑ T86	Greg Vaughn	.40	.15
❑ T87	Mark Clark	.40	.15
❑ T88	Pat Meares	.40	.15
❑ T89	Eric Davis	.60	.25
❑ T90	Brian Giles	.60	.25
❑ T91	Jeff Brantley	.40	.15
❑ T92	Bret Boone	.60	.25
❑ T93	Ron Gant	.60	.25
❑ T94	Mike Cameron	.40	.15
❑ T95	Charles Johnson	.60	.25
❑ T96	Denny Neagle	.40	.15
❑ T97	Brian Hunter	.40	.15
❑ T98	Jose Hernandez	.40	.15
❑ T99	Rick Aguilera	.40	.15
❑ T100	Tony Batista	.40	.15
❑ T101	Roger Cedeno	.40	.15
❑ T102	Creighton Gubanich RC	.50	.20
❑ T103	Tim Belcher	.40	.15
❑ T104	Bruce Aven	.40	.15
❑ T105	Brian Daubach RC	.75	.30
❑ T106	Ed Sprague	.40	.15
❑ T107	Michael Tucker	.40	.15
❑ T108	Homer Bush	.40	.15
❑ T109	Armando Reynoso	.40	.15
❑ T110	Brook Fordyce	.40	.15
❑ T111	Matt Mantei	.40	.15
❑ T112	Dave Mlicki	.40	.15
❑ T113	Kenny Rogers	.60	.25
❑ T114	Livan Hernandez	.60	.25
❑ T115	Butch Huskey	.40	.15
❑ T116	David Segui	.40	.15
❑ T117	Darryl Hamilton	.40	.15
❑ T118	Terry Mulholland	.40	.15
❑ T119	Randy Velarde	.40	.15
❑ T120	Bill Taylor	.40	.15
❑ T121	Kevin Appier	.60	.25

2000 Topps Chrome Traded

Card	Player		
❑	COMP.FACT.SET (135)	80.00	40.00
❑ T1	Mike MacDougal	.75	.30
❑ T2	Andy Tracy RC	.50	.20
❑ T3	Brandon Phillips RC	2.50	1.00
❑ T4	Brandon Inge RC	4.00	1.50
❑ T5	Robbie Morrison RC	.50	.20

Card	Player		
❑ T6	Josh Pressley RC	.50	.20
❑ T7	Todd Moser RC	.50	.20
❑ T8	Rob Purvis	.60	.25
❑ T9	Chance Caple	.40	.15
❑ T10	Ben Sheets	2.50	1.00
❑ T11	Russ Jacobson RC	.50	.20
❑ T12	Brian Cole RC	.50	.20
❑ T13	Brad Baker	.40	.15
❑ T14	Alex Cintron RC	.75	.30
❑ T15	Lyle Overbay RC	2.00	.75
❑ T16	Mike Edwards RC	.50	.20
❑ T17	Sean McGowan RC	.50	.20
❑ T18	Jose Molina	.40	.15
❑ T19	Marcos Castillo RC	.50	.20
❑ T20	Josue Espada RC	.50	.20
❑ T21	Alex Gordon RC	.50	.20
❑ T22	Rob Pugmire RC	.50	.20
❑ T23	Jason Stumm	.50	.20
❑ T24	Ty Howington	.40	.15
❑ T25	Brett Myers	2.00	.75
❑ T26	Maicer Izturis RC	.75	.30
❑ T27	John McDonald	.40	.15
❑ T28	Wilfredo Rodriguez RC	.50	.20
❑ T29	Carlos Zambrano RC	8.00	3.00
❑ T30	Alejandro Diaz RC	.50	.20
❑ T31	Geraldo Guzman RC	.50	.20
❑ T32	J.R. House RC	.50	.20
❑ T33	Elvin Nina RC	.50	.20
❑ T34	Juan Pierre RC	2.00	.75
❑ T35	Ben Johnson RC	3.00	1.25
❑ T36	Jeff Bailey RC	.50	.20
❑ T37	Miguel Olivo RC	1.25	.50
❑ T38	Francisco Rodriguez RC	4.00	1.50
❑ T39	Tony Pena Jr. RC	.50	.20
❑ T40	Miguel Cabrera RC	50.00	25.00
❑ T41	Asdrubal Oropeza RC	.50	.20
❑ T42	Junior Zamora RC	.75	.30
❑ T43	Jovanny Cedeno RC	.50	.20
❑ T44	John Sneed	.60	.25
❑ T45	Josh Kalinowski	.60	.25
❑ T46	Mike Young RC	10.00	4.00
❑ T47	Rico Washington RC	.50	.20
❑ T48	Chad Durbin RC	.50	.20
❑ T49	Junior Brignac RC	.50	.20
❑ T50	Carlos Hernandez RC	.75	.30
❑ T51	Cesar Izturis RC	1.25	.50
❑ T52	Oscar Salazar RC	.50	.20
❑ T53	Pat Strange RC	.50	.20
❑ T54	Rick Asadoorian	.75	.30
❑ T55	Keith Reed	.40	.15
❑ T56	Leo Estrella RC	.50	.20
❑ T57	Wascar Serrano RC	.50	.20
❑ T58	Richard Gomez RC	.50	.20
❑ T59	Ramon Santiago RC	.50	.20
❑ T60	Jovanny Sosa RC	.50	.20
❑ T61	Aaron Rowand RC	3.00	1.25
❑ T62	Junior Guerrero RC	.50	.20
❑ T63	Luis Terrero RC	.75	.30
❑ T64	Brian Sanches RC	.50	.20
❑ T65	Scott Sobkowiak RC	.50	.20
❑ T66	Gary Majewski RC	.75	.30
❑ T67	Barry Zito	3.00	1.25
❑ T68	Ryan Christianson	.50	.20
❑ T69	Cristian Guerrero RC	.50	.20
❑ T70	Tomas De La Rosa RC	.50	.20
❑ T71	Andrew Beinbrink RC	.50	.20
❑ T72	Ryan Knox RC	.50	.20
❑ T73	Alex Graman RC	.50	.20

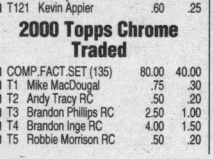

❑ T74 Juan Guzman RC .50 .20
❑ T75 Ruben Salazar RC .50 .20
❑ T76 Luis Matos RC .75 .30
❑ T77 Tony Mota RC .50 .20
❑ T78 Doug Davis .60 .25
❑ T79 Ben Christensen .40 .15
❑ T80 Mike Lamb 1.25 .50
❑ T81 Adrian Gonzalez RC 5.00 2.00
❑ T82 Mike Stodolka RC .50 .20
❑ T83 Adam Johnson RC .50 .20
❑ T84 Matt Wheatland RC .50 .20
❑ T85 Corey Smith RC .50 .20
❑ T86 Rocco Baldelli RC 4.00 1.50
❑ T87 Keith Bucktrot RC .50 .20
❑ T88 Adam Wainwright RC 2.00 .75
❑ T89 Scott Thorman RC 2.00 .75
❑ T90 Tripper Johnson RC .50 .20
❑ T91 Jim Edmonds Cards .60 .25
❑ T92 Masato Yoshii .40 .15
❑ T93 Adam Kennedy .40 .15
❑ T94 Darryl Kile .60 .25
❑ T95 Mark McLemore .40 .15
❑ T96 Ricky Gutierrez .40 .15
❑ T97 Juan Gonzalez .60 .25
❑ T98 Melvin Mora .60 .25
❑ T99 Dante Bichette .60 .25
❑ T100 Lee Stevens .40 .15
❑ T101 Roger Cedeno .40 .15
❑ T102 John Olerud .60 .25
❑ T103 Eric Young .40 .15
❑ T104 Mickey Morandini .40 .15
❑ T105 Travis Lee .40 .15
❑ T106 Greg Vaughn .40 .15
❑ T107 Todd Zeile .60 .25
❑ T108 Chuck Finley .60 .25
❑ T109 Ismael Valdes .40 .15
❑ T110 Reggie Sanders .60 .25
❑ T111 Pat Hentgen .40 .15
❑ T112 Ryan Klesko .60 .25
❑ T113 Derek Bell .40 .15
❑ T114 Hideo Nomo 1.50 .60
❑ T115 Aaron Sele .40 .15
❑ T116 Fernando Vina .40 .15
❑ T117 Wally Joyner .60 .25
❑ T118 Brian Hunter .40 .15
❑ T119 Joe Girardi .40 .15
❑ T120 Omar Daal .40 .15
❑ T121 Brook Fordyce .40 .15
❑ T122 Jose Valentin .40 .15
❑ T123 Curt Schilling .60 .25
❑ T124 B.J. Surhoff .60 .25
❑ T125 Henry Rodriguez .40 .15
❑ T126 Mike Bordick .40 .15
❑ T127 David Justice .60 .25
❑ T128 Charles Johnson .60 .25
❑ T129 Will Clark 1.00 .40
❑ T130 Dwight Gooden .60 .25
❑ T131 David Segui .40 .15
❑ T132 Denny Neagle .60 .25
❑ T133 Jose Canseco 1.00 .40
❑ T134 Bruce Chen .40 .15
❑ T135 Jason Bere .40 .15

2001 Topps Chrome

❑ COMPLETE SET (661) 300.00 150.00
❑ COMPLETE SERIES 1 (331) 150.00 75.00
❑ COMPLETE SERIES 2 (330) 150.00 75.00
❑ 1 Cal Ripken 6.00 2.50
❑ 2 Chipper Jones 2.00 .75
❑ 3 Roger Cedeno .50 .20
❑ 4 Garret Anderson .75 .30
❑ 5 Robin Ventura .75 .30
❑ 6 Daryle Ward .50 .20
❑ 7 Does Not Exist
❑ 8 Phil Nevin .75 .30
❑ 9 Jermaine Dye .75 .30
❑ 10 Chris Singleton .50 .20
❑ 11 Mike Redmond .50 .20
❑ 12 Jim Thome 1.25 .50
❑ 13 Brian Jordan .75 .30
❑ 14 Dustin Hermanson .50 .20
❑ 15 Shawn Green .75 .30
❑ 16 Todd Stottlemyre .50 .20
❑ 17 Dan Wilson .50 .20
❑ 18 Derek Lowe .75 .30
❑ 19 Juan Gonzalez .75 .30
❑ 20 Pat Meares .50 .20
❑ 21 Paul O'Neill 1.25 .50
❑ 22 Jeffrey Hammonds .50 .20
❑ 23 Pokey Reese .50 .20
❑ 24 Mike Mussina 1.25 .50
❑ 25 Rico Brogna .50 .20
❑ 26 Jay Buhner .75 .30
❑ 27 Steve Cox .50 .20
❑ 28 Quilvio Veras .50 .20
❑ 29 Marquis Grissom .75 .30
❑ 30 Shigetoshi Hasegawa .75 .30
❑ 31 Shane Reynolds .50 .20
❑ 32 Adam Piatt .50 .20
❑ 33 Preston Wilson .75 .30
❑ 34 Ellis Burks .75 .30
❑ 35 Armando Rios .50 .20
❑ 36 Chuck Finley .75 .30
❑ 37 Shannon Stewart .75 .30
❑ 38 Mark McGwire 5.00 2.00
❑ 39 Gerald Williams .50 .20
❑ 40 Eric Young .50 .20
❑ 41 Peter Bergeron .50 .20
❑ 42 Arthur Rhodes .50 .20
❑ 43 Bobby Jones .50 .20
❑ 44 Matt Clement .75 .30
❑ 45 Pedro Martinez 1.25 .50
❑ 46 Jose Canseco 1.25 .50
❑ 47 Matt Anderson .50 .20
❑ 48 Torii Hunter .75 .30
❑ 49 Carlos Lee .75 .30
❑ 50 Eric Chavez .75 .30
❑ 51 Rick Helling .50 .20
❑ 52 John Franco .75 .30
❑ 53 Mike Bordick .75 .30
❑ 54 Andres Galarraga .75 .30
❑ 55 Jose Cruz Jr. .50 .20
❑ 56 Mike Matheny .50 .20
❑ 57 Randy Johnson 2.00 .75
❑ 58 Richie Sexson .75 .30
❑ 59 Vladimir Nunez .50 .20
❑ 60 Aaron Boone .75 .30
❑ 61 Darin Erstad .75 .30
❑ 62 Alex Gonzalez .50 .20
❑ 63 Gil Heredia .50 .20
❑ 64 Shane Andrews .50 .20
❑ 65 Todd Hundley .50 .20
❑ 66 Bill Mueller .75 .30
❑ 67 Mark McLemore .50 .20
❑ 68 Scott Spiezio .50 .20
❑ 69 Kevin McGlinchy .50 .20
❑ 70 Manny Ramirez 1.25 .50
❑ 71 Mike Lamb .50 .20
❑ 72 Brian Buchanan .50 .20
❑ 73 Mike Sweeney .75 .30
❑ 74 John Wetteland .75 .30
❑ 75 Rob Bell .50 .20
❑ 76 John Burkett .50 .20
❑ 77 Derek Jeter 5.00 2.00
❑ 78 J.D. Drew .75 .30
❑ 79 Jose Offerman .50 .20
❑ 80 Rick Reed .50 .20
❑ 81 Will Clark 1.25 .50
❑ 82 Rickey Henderson 2.00 .75
❑ 83 Kirk Rueter .50 .20
❑ 84 Lee Stevens .50 .20
❑ 85 Jay Bell .75 .30
❑ 86 Fred McGriff 1.25 .50
❑ 87 Julio Zuleta .50 .20
❑ 88 Brian Anderson .50 .20
❑ 89 Orlando Cabrera .75 .30
❑ 90 Alex Fernandez .50 .20
❑ 91 Derek Bell .50 .20
❑ 92 Eric Owens .50 .20
93 Dennys Reyes .50 .20
❑ 94 Mike Stanley .50 .20
❑ 95 Jorge Posada 1.25 .50
❑ 96 Paul Konerko .75 .30
❑ 97 Mike Remlinger .50 .20
❑ 98 Travis Lee .50 .20
❑ 99 Ken Caminiti .75 .30
❑ 100 Kevin Barker .50 .20
❑ 101 Ozzie Guillen .75 .30
❑ 102 Randy Wolf .50 .20
❑ 103 Michael Tucker .50 .20
❑ 104 Darren Lewis .50 .20
❑ 105 Joe Randa .75 .30
❑ 106 Jeff Cirillo .50 .20
❑ 107 David Ortiz 2.00 .75
❑ 108 Herb Perry .50 .20
❑ 109 Jeff Nelson .50 .20
❑ 110 Chris Stynes .50 .20
❑ 111 Johnny Damon 1.25 .50
❑ 112 Jason Schmidt .75 .30
❑ 113 Charles Johnson .50 .20
❑ 114 Pat Burrell .75 .30
❑ 115 Gary Sheffield .75 .30
❑ 116 Tom Glavine 1.25 .50
❑ 117 Jason Isringhausen .75 .30
❑ 118 Chris Carpenter .75 .30
❑ 119 Jeff Suppan .50 .20
❑ 120 Ivan Rodriguez 1.25 .50
❑ 121 Luis Sojo .50 .20
❑ 122 Ron Villone .50 .20
❑ 123 Mike Sirotka .50 .20
❑ 124 Chuck Knoblauch .75 .30
❑ 125 Jason Kendall .75 .30
❑ 126 Bobby Estalella .50 .20
❑ 127 Jose Guillen .75 .30
❑ 128 Carlos Delgado .75 .30
❑ 129 Benji Gil .50 .20
❑ 130 Einar Diaz .50 .20
❑ 131 Andy Benes .50 .20
❑ 132 Adrian Beltre .75 .30
❑ 133 Roger Clemens 4.00 1.50
❑ 134 Scott Williamson .50 .20
❑ 135 Brad Penny .50 .20
❑ 136 Troy Glaus .75 .30
❑ 137 Kevin Appier .75 .30
❑ 138 Walt Weiss .50 .20
❑ 139 Michael Barrett .50 .20
❑ 140 Mike Hampton .75 .30
❑ 141 Francisco Cordova .50 .20
❑ 142 David Segui .50 .20
❑ 143 Carlos Febles .50 .20
❑ 144 Roy Halladay .75 .30
❑ 145 Seth Etherton .50 .20
❑ 146 Fernando Tatis .50 .20
❑ 147 Livan Hernandez .75 .30
❑ 148 B.J. Surhoff .75 .30
❑ 149 Barry Larkin 1.25 .50
❑ 150 Bobby Howry .50 .20
❑ 151 Dmitri Young .75 .30
❑ 152 Brian Hunter .50 .20
❑ 153 Alex Rodriguez Rangers 3.00 1.25
❑ 154 Hideo Nomo 2.00 .75
❑ 155 Warren Morris .50 .20
❑ 156 Antonio Alfonseca .50 .20
❑ 157 Edgardo Alfonzo .50 .20
❑ 158 Mark Grudzielanek .50 .20
❑ 159 Fernando Vina .50 .20
❑ 160 Homer Bush .50 .20
❑ 161 Jason Giambi .75 .30
❑ 162 Steve Karsay .50 .20
❑ 163 Matt Lawton .50 .20
❑ 164 Rusty Greer .75 .30
❑ 165 Billy Koch .50 .20
❑ 166 Todd Hollandsworth .50 .20
❑ 167 Raul Ibanez .50 .20
❑ 168 Tony Gwynn 2.50 1.00
❑ 169 Carl Everett .75 .30
❑ 170 Hector Carrasco .50 .20
❑ 171 Jose Valentin .50 .20
❑ 172 Deivi Cruz .50 .20
❑ 173 Bret Boone .75 .30

174	Melvin Mora	.75	.30
175	Danny Graves	.50	.20
176	Jose Jimenez	.50	.20
177	James Baldwin	.50	.20
178	C.J. Nitkowski	.50	.20
179	Jeff Zimmerman	.50	.20
180	Mike Lowell	.75	.30
181	Hideki Irabu	.50	.20
182	Greg Vaughn	.50	.20
183	Omar Daal	.50	.20
184	Darren Dreifort	.50	.20
185	Gil Meche	.50	.20
186	Damian Jackson	.50	.20
187	Frank Thomas	2.00	.75
188	Luis Castillo	.50	.20
189	Bartolo Colon	.75	.30
190	Craig Biggio	1.25	.50
191	Scott Schoeneweis	.50	.20
192	Dave Veres	.50	.20
193	Ramon Martinez	.50	.20
194	Jose Vidro	.50	.20
195	Todd Helton	1.25	.50
196	Greg Norton	.50	.20
197	Jacque Jones	.75	.30
198	Jason Grimsley	.50	.20
199	Dan Reichert	.50	.20
200	Robb Nen	.75	.30
201	Scott Hatteberg	.50	.20
202	Terry Shumpert	.50	.20
203	Kevin Millar	.75	.30
204	Ismael Valdes	.50	.20
205	Richard Hidalgo	.50	.20
206	Randy Velarde	.50	.20
207	Bengie Molina	.50	.20
208	Tony Womack	.50	.20
209	Enrique Wilson	.50	.20
210	Jeff Brantley	.50	.20
211	Rick Ankiel	.50	.20
212	Terry Mulholland	.50	.20
213	Ron Belliard	.50	.20
214	Terrence Long	.50	.20
215	Alberto Castillo	.50	.20
216	Royce Clayton	.50	.20
217	Joe McEwing	.50	.20
218	Jason McDonald	.50	.20
219	Ricky Bottalico	.50	.20
220	Keith Foulke	.75	.30
221	Brad Radke	.75	.30
222	Gabe Kapler	.75	.30
223	Pedro Astacio	.50	.20
224	Armando Reynoso	.50	.20
225	Darryl Kile	.75	.30
226	Reggie Sanders	.75	.30
227	Esteban Yan	.50	.20
228	Joe Nathan	.75	.30
229	Jay Payton	.50	.20
230	Francisco Cordero	.50	.20
231	Gregg Jefferies	.50	.20
232	LaTroy Hawkins	.50	.20
233	Jacob Cruz	.50	.20
234	Chris Holt	.50	.20
235	Vladimir Guerrero	2.00	.75
236	Marvin Benard	.50	.20
237	Alex Ramirez	.50	.20
238	Mike Williams	.50	.20
239	Sean Bergman	.50	.20
240	Juan Encarnacion	.50	.20
241	Russ Davis	.50	.20
242	Ramon Hernandez	.50	.20
243	Sandy Alomar Jr.	.50	.20
244	Eddie Guardado	.50	.20
245	Shane Halter	.50	.20
246	Geoff Jenkins	.50	.20
247	Brian Meadows	.50	.20
248	Damian Miller	.50	.20
249	Darrin Fletcher	.50	.20
250	Rafael Furcal	.75	.30
251	Mark Grace	1.25	.50
252	Mark Mulder	.75	.30
253	Joe Torre MG	1.25	.50
254	Bobby Cox MG	.50	.20
255	Mike Scioscia MG	.50	.20
256	Mike Hargrove MG	.50	.20
257	Jimy Williams MG	.50	.20
258	Jerry Manuel MG	.50	.20
259	Charlie Manuel MG	.50	.20
260	Don Baylor MG	.75	.30
261	Phil Garner MG	.75	.30
262	Tony Muser MG	.50	.20
263	Buddy Bell MG	.75	.30
264	Tom Kelly MG	.50	.20
265	John Boles MG	.50	.20
266	Art Howe MG	.50	.20
267	Larry Dierker MG	.50	.20
268	Lou Piniella MG	.75	.30
269	Larry Rothschild MG	.50	.20
270	Davey Lopes MG	.75	.30
271	Johnny Oates MG	.50	.20
272	Felipe Alou MG	.50	.20
273	Bobby Valentine MG	.50	.20
274	Tony LaRussa MG	.50	.20
275	Bruce Bochy MG	.50	.20
276	Dusty Baker MG	.75	.30
277	A.Gonzalez/A.Johnson	1.00	.40
278	M.Wheatland/B.Digby	1.00	.40
279	T.Johnson/S.Thorman	1.00	.40
280	P.Dumatrait/A.Wainwright	1.00	.40
281	David Parrish RC	1.00	.40
282	M.Folsom RC/R.Baldelli	1.50	.60
283	Dominic Rich RC	1.00	.40
284	M.Stodolka/S.Burnett	1.00	.40
285	D.Thompson/C.Smith	1.00	.40
286	D.Borrell RC/J.Bourgeois RC	1.00	.40
287	Chen/Patterson/Hamilton	1.00	.40
288	B.Zito/C.Sabathia	2.00	.75
289	Ben Sheets	2.00	.75
290	Howington/Kalinowski/Girdley	1.00	.40
291	Hee Seop Choi RC	2.00	.75
292	Bradley/Ainsworth/Tsao	1.50	.60
293	Glendenning/Kelly/Silvestre	1.00	.40
294	J.R. House	1.00	.40
295	Rafael Soriano RC	1.50	.60
296	T.Hafner RC/B.Jacobsen	10.00	4.00
297	Conti/Wakeland/Cole	1.00	.40
298	Seabol/Huff/Crede	2.50	1.00
299	Everett/Ortiz/Ginter	1.00	.40
300	Hernandez/Guzman/Eaton	1.00	.40
301	Kielty/Bradley/J.Rivera	1.50	.60
302	Mark McGwire GM	2.50	1.00
303	Don Larsen GM	.75	.30
304	Bobby Thomson GM	.75	.30
305	Bill Mazeroski GM	.75	.30
306	Reggie Jackson GM	1.25	.50
307	Kirk Gibson GM	.75	.30
308	Roger Maris GM	1.25	.50
309	Cal Ripken GM	3.00	1.25
310	Hank Aaron GM	2.00	.75
311	Joe Carter GM	.75	.30
312	Cal Ripken SH	3.00	1.25
313	Randy Johnson SH	1.25	.50
314	Ken Griffey Jr. SH	2.00	.75
315	Troy Glaus SH	.75	.30
316	Kazuhiro Sasaki SH	.75	.30
317	S.Sosa/T.Glaus LL	1.25	.50
318	T.Helton/E.Martinez LL	.75	.30
319	T.Helton/N.Garicaparra LL	2.00	.75
320	B.Bonds/J.Giambi LL	2.00	.75
321	T.Helton/M.Ramirez LL	.75	.30
322	T.Helton/D.Erstad LL	.75	.30
323	K.Brown/P.Martinez LL	1.25	.50
324	R.Johnson/P.Martinez LL	1.25	.50
325	Will Clark HL	1.25	.50
326	New York Mets HL	2.00	.75
327	New York Yankees HL	3.00	1.25
328	Seattle Mariners HL	.75	.30
329	Mike Hampton HL	.75	.30
330	New York Yankees HL	4.00	1.50
331	New York Yankees Champs	8.00	3.00
332	Jeff Bagwell	1.25	.50
333	Andy Pettitte	1.25	.50
334	Tony Armas Jr.	.50	.20
335	Jeromy Burnitz	.75	.30
336	Javier Vazquez	.75	.30
337	Eric Karros	.75	.30
338	Brian Giles	.75	.30
339	Scott Rolen	1.25	.50
340	David Justice	.75	.30
341	Ray Durham	.75	.30
342	Todd Zeile	.75	.30
343	Cliff Floyd	.75	.30
344	Barry Bonds	5.00	2.00
345	Matt Williams	.75	.30
346	Steve Finley	.75	.30
347	Scott Elarton	.50	.20
348	Bernie Williams	1.25	.50
349	David Wells	.75	.30
350	J.T. Snow	.75	.30
351	Al Leiter	.75	.30
352	Magglio Ordonez	.75	.30
353	Raul Mondesi	.75	.30
354	Tim Salmon	1.25	.50
355	Jeff Kent	.75	.30
356	Mariano Rivera	2.00	.75
357	John Olerud	.75	.30
358	Javy Lopez	.75	.30
359	Ben Grieve	.50	.20
360	Ray Lankford	.75	.30
361	Ken Griffey Jr.	3.00	1.25
362	Rich Aurilia	.50	.20
363	Andruw Jones	1.25	.50
364	Ryan Klesko	.75	.30
365	Roberto Alomar	1.25	.50
366	Miguel Tejada	.75	.30
367	Mo Vaughn	.75	.30
368	Albert Belle	.75	.30
369	Jose Canseco	1.25	.50
370	Kevin Brown	.75	.30
371	Rafael Palmeiro	1.25	.50
372	Mark Redman	.50	.20
373	Larry Walker	.75	.30
374	Greg Maddux	3.00	1.25
375	Nomar Garciaparra	3.00	1.25
376	Kevin Millwood	.75	.30
377	Edgar Martinez	1.25	.50
378	Sammy Sosa	2.00	.75
379	Tim Hudson	.75	.30
380	Jim Edmonds	.75	.30
381	Mike Piazza	3.00	1.25
382	Brant Brown	.50	.20
383	Brad Fullmer	.50	.20
384	Alan Benes	.50	.20
385	Mickey Morandini	.50	.20
386	Troy Percival	.75	.30
387	Eddie Perez	.50	.20
388	Vernon Wells	.75	.30
389	Ricky Gutierrez	.50	.20
390	Rondell White	.75	.30
391	Kelvim Escobar	.50	.20
392	Tony Batista	.50	.20
393	Jimmy Haynes	.50	.20
394	Billy Wagner	.75	.30
395	A.J. Hinch	.50	.20
396	Matt Morris	.75	.30
397	Lance Berkman	.75	.30
398	Jeff D'Amico	.50	.20
399	Octavio Dotel	.50	.20
400	Olmedo Saenz	.50	.20
401	Esteban Loaiza	.50	.20
402	Adam Kennedy	.50	.20
403	Moises Alou	.75	.30
404	Orlando Palmeiro	.50	.20
405	Kevin Young	.50	.20
406	Tom Goodwin	.50	.20
407	Mac Suzuki	.75	.30
408	Pat Hentgen	.50	.20
409	Kevin Stocker	.50	.20
410	Mark Sweeney	.50	.20
411	Tony Eusebio	.50	.20
412	Edgar Renteria	.75	.30
413	John Rocker	.75	.30
414	Jose Lima	.50	.20
415	Kerry Wood	.75	.30
416	Mike Timlin	.50	.20
417	Jose Hernandez	.50	.20
418	Jeremy Giambi	.50	.20
419	Luis Lopez	.50	.20
420	Mitch Meluskey	.50	.20
421	Garrett Stephenson	.50	.20
422	Jamey Wright	.50	.20
423	John Jaha	.50	.20
424	Placido Polanco	.50	.20
425	Marty Cordova	.50	.20
426	Joey Hamilton	.50	.20
427	Travis Fryman	.75	.30
428	Mike Cameron	.50	.20
429	Matt Mantei	.50	.20
430	Chan Ho Park	.75	.30
431	Shawn Estes	.50	.20

❑ 432 Danny Bautista .50 .20
❑ 433 Wilson Alvarez .50 .20
❑ 434 Kenny Lofton .75 .30
❑ 435 Russ Ortiz .50 .20
❑ 436 Dave Burba .50 .20
❑ 437 Felix Martinez .50 .20
❑ 438 Jeff Shaw .50 .20
❑ 439 Mike DiFelice .50 .20
❑ 440 Roberto Hernandez .50 .20
❑ 441 Bryan Rekar .50 .20
❑ 442 Ugueth Urbina .50 .20
❑ 443 Vinny Castilla .75 .30
❑ 444 Carlos Perez .50 .20
❑ 445 Juan Guzman .50 .20
❑ 446 Ryan Rupe .50 .20
❑ 447 Mike Mordecai .50 .20
❑ 448 Ricardo Rincon .50 .20
❑ 449 Curt Schilling .75 .30
❑ 450 Alex Cora .50 .20
❑ 451 Turner Ward .50 .20
❑ 452 Omar Vizquel 1.25 .50
❑ 453 Russ Branyan .50 .20
❑ 454 Russ Johnson .50 .20
❑ 455 Greg Colbrunn .50 .20
❑ 456 Charles Nagy .50 .20
❑ 457 Wil Cordero .50 .20
❑ 458 Jason Tyner .50 .20
❑ 459 Devon White .75 .30
❑ 460 Kelly Stinnett .50 .20
❑ 461 Wilton Guerrero .50 .20
❑ 462 Jason Bere .50 .20
❑ 463 Calvin Murray .50 .20
❑ 464 Miguel Batista .50 .20
❑ 466 Luis Gonzalez .75 .30
❑ 467 Jaret Wright .50 .20
❑ 468 Chad Kreuter .50 .20
❑ 469 Armando Benitez .50 .20
❑ 470 Erubiel Durazo .50 .20
❑ 470 Sidney Ponson .50 .20
❑ 471 Adrian Brown .50 .20
❑ 472 Sterling Hitchcock .50 .20
❑ 473 Timo Perez .50 .20
❑ 474 Jamie Moyer .75 .30
❑ 475 Delino DeShields .50 .20
❑ 476 Glendon Rusch .50 .20
❑ 477 Chris Gomez .50 .20
❑ 478 Adam Eaton .50 .20
❑ 479 Pablo Ozuna .50 .20
❑ 480 Bob Abreu .75 .30
❑ 481 Kris Benson .50 .20
❑ 482 Keith Osik .50 .20
❑ 483 Darryl Hamilton .50 .20
❑ 484 Marlon Anderson .50 .20
❑ 485 Jimmy Anderson .50 .20
❑ 486 John Halama .50 .20
❑ 487 Nelson Figueroa .50 .20
❑ 488 Alex Gonzalez .50 .20
❑ 489 Benny Agbayani .50 .20
❑ 490 Ed Sprague .50 .20
❑ 491 Scott Erickson .50 .20
❑ 492 Doug Glanville .50 .20
❑ 493 Jesus Sanchez .50 .20
❑ 494 Mike Lieberthal .75 .30
❑ 495 Aaron Sele .50 .20
❑ 496 Pat Mahomes .50 .20
❑ 497 Ruben Rivera .50 .20
❑ 498 Wayne Gomes .50 .20
❑ 499 Freddy Garcia .75 .30
❑ 500 Al Martin .50 .20
❑ 501 Woody Williams .50 .20
❑ 502 Paul Byrd .50 .20
❑ 503 Rick White .50 .20
❑ 504 Trevor Hoffman .75 .30
❑ 505 Brady Anderson .75 .30
❑ 506 Robert Person .50 .20
❑ 507 Jeff Conine .75 .30
❑ 508 Chris Truby .50 .20
❑ 509 Emil Brown .50 .20
❑ 510 Ryan Dempster .50 .20
❑ 511 Ruben Mateo .50 .20
❑ 512 Alex Ochoa .50 .20
❑ 513 Jose Rosado .50 .20
❑ 514 Masato Yoshii .50 .20
❑ 515 Brian Daubach .50 .20
❑ 516 Jeff D'Amico .50 .20
❑ 517 Brent Mayne .50 .20
❑ 518 John Thomson .50 .20
❑ 519 Todd Ritchie .50 .20
❑ 520 John VanderWal .50 .20
❑ 521 Neifi Perez .50 .20
❑ 522 Chad Curtis .50 .20
❑ 523 Kenny Rogers .75 .30
❑ 524 Trot Nixon .75 .30
❑ 525 Sean Casey .75 .30
❑ 526 Wilton Veras .50 .20
❑ 527 Troy O'Leary .50 .20
❑ 528 Dante Bichette .75 .30
❑ 529 Jose Silva .50 .20
❑ 530 Darren Oliver .50 .20
❑ 531 Steve Parris .50 .20
❑ 532 David McCarty .50 .20
❑ 533 Todd Walker .50 .20
❑ 534 Brian Rose .50 .20
❑ 535 Pete Schourek .50 .20
❑ 536 Ricky Ledee .50 .20
❑ 537 Justin Thompson .50 .20
❑ 538 Benito Santiago .75 .30
❑ 539 Carlos Beltran .75 .30
❑ 540 Gabe White .50 .20
❑ 541 Bret Saberhagen .75 .30
❑ 542 Ramon Martinez .50 .20
❑ 543 John Valentin .50 .20
❑ 544 Frank Catalanotto .50 .20
❑ 545 Tim Wakefield .75 .30
❑ 546 Michael Tucker .50 .20
❑ 547 Juan Pierre .75 .30
❑ 548 Rich Garces .50 .20
❑ 549 Luis Ordaz .50 .20
❑ 550 Jerry Spradlin .50 .20
❑ 551 Corey Koskie .50 .20
❑ 552 Cal Eldred .50 .20
❑ 553 Alfonso Soriano 1.25 .50
❑ 554 Kip Wells .50 .20
❑ 555 Orlando Hernandez .75 .30
❑ 556 Bill Simas .50 .20
❑ 557 Jim Parque .50 .20
❑ 558 Joe Mays .50 .20
❑ 559 Tim Belcher .50 .20
❑ 560 Shane Spencer .50 .20
❑ 561 Glenallen Hill .50 .20
❑ 562 Matt LeCroy .50 .20
❑ 563 Tino Martinez 1.25 .50
❑ 564 Eric Milton .50 .20
❑ 565 Ron Coomer .50 .20
❑ 566 Cristian Guzman .50 .20
❑ 567 Kazuhiro Sasaki .75 .30
❑ 568 Mark Quinn .50 .20
❑ 569 Eric Gagne .75 .30
❑ 570 Kerry Ligtenberg .50 .20
❑ 571 Rolando Arrojo .50 .20
❑ 572 Jon Lieber .50 .20
❑ 573 Jose Vizcaino .50 .20
❑ 574 Jeff Abbott .50 .20
❑ 575 Carlos Hernandez .50 .20
❑ 576 Scott Sullivan .50 .20
❑ 577 Matt Stairs .50 .20
❑ 578 Tom Lampkin .50 .20
❑ 579 Donnie Sadler .50 .20
❑ 580 Desi Relaford .50 .20
❑ 581 Scott Downs .50 .20
❑ 582 Mike Mussina 1.25 .50
❑ 583 Ramon Ortiz .50 .20
❑ 584 Mike Myers .50 .20
❑ 585 Frank Castillo .50 .20
❑ 586 Manny Ramirez Sox 1.25 .50
❑ 587 Alex Rodriguez 3.00 1.25
❑ 588 Andy Ashby .50 .20
❑ 589 Felipe Crespo .50 .20
❑ 590 Bobby Bonilla .75 .30
❑ 591 Denny Neagle .50 .20
❑ 592 Dave Martinez .50 .20
❑ 593 Mike Hampton .75 .30
❑ 594 Gary DiSarcina .50 .20
❑ 595 Tsuyoshi Shinjo RC 2.00 .75
❑ 596 Albert Pujols RC 80.00 50.00
❑ 597 Oswalt/Strange/Rauch 2.50 1.00
❑ 598 Jake Peavy RC 8.00 3.00
❑ 599 S.Smyth RC/Bynum/Haynes 1.00 .40
❑ 600 Cuddyer/Lawrence/Freeman 1.00 .40
❑ 601 C.Pena/Barnes/Wise 1.00 .40
❑ 602 E.Almonte RC/F.Lopez 1.00 .40
❑ 603 Escobar/Valent/Wilkerson 1.00 .40
❑ 604 Hall/Barajas/Goldbach 1.00 .40
❑ 605 Romano/Giles/Ozuna 1.50 .60
❑ 606 D.Brown/Cust/V.Wells 1.00 .40
❑ 607 L.Montanez RC/D.Espinosa 1.00 .40
❑ 608 J.Wayne RC/A.Pluta RC 1.00 .40
❑ 609 J.Axelson RC/C.Cali RC 1.00 .40
❑ 610 S.Boyd RC/C.Morris RC 1.00 .40
❑ 611 T.Arko RC/D.Moylan RC 1.00 .40
❑ 612 L.Cotto RC/L.Escobar 1.00 .40
❑ 613 B.Mims RC/B.Williams RC 1.00 .40
❑ 614 C.Russ RC/B.Edwards 1.00 .40
❑ 615 J.Torres/B.Diggins 1.00 .40
❑ 616 Edwin Encarnacion RC 10.00 4.00
❑ 617 B.Bass RC/O.Ayala RC 1.00 .40
❑ 618 M.Matthews RC/J.Kanooi 1.00 .40
❑ 619 S.McFarland RC/A.Sterrett RC 1.00 .40
❑ 620 D.Krynzel/G.Sizemore 3.00 1.25
❑ 621 K.Bucktrot/D.Sardinha 1.00 .40
❑ 622 Anaheim Angels TC .75 .30
❑ 623 Arizona Diamondbacks TC .75 .30
❑ 624 Atlanta Braves TC .75 .30
❑ 625 Baltimore Orioles TC .75 .30
❑ 626 Boston Red Sox TC .75 .30
❑ 627 Chicago Cubs TC .75 .30
❑ 628 Chicago White Sox TC .75 .30
❑ 629 Cincinnati Reds TC .75 .30
❑ 630 Cleveland Indians TC .75 .30
❑ 631 Colorado Rockies TC .75 .30
❑ 632 Detroit Tigers TC .75 .30
❑ 633 Florida Marlins TC .75 .30
❑ 634 Houston Astros TC .75 .30
❑ 635 Kansas City Royals TC .75 .30
❑ 636 Los Angeles Dodgers TC .75 .30
❑ 637 Milwaukee Brewers TC .75 .30
❑ 638 Minnesota Twins TC .75 .30
❑ 639 Montreal Expos TC .75 .30
❑ 640 New York Mets TC .75 .30
❑ 641 New York Yankees TC 4.00 1.50
❑ 642 Oakland Athletics TC .75 .30
❑ 643 Philadelphia Phillies TC .75 .30
❑ 644 Pittsburgh Pirates TC .75 .30
❑ 645 San Diego Padres TC .75 .30
❑ 646 San Francisco Giants TC .75 .30
❑ 647 Seattle Mariners TC .75 .30
❑ 648 St. Louis Cardinals TC .75 .30
❑ 649 Tampa Bay Devil Rays TC .75 .30
❑ 650 Texas Rangers TC .75 .30
❑ 651 Toronto Blue Jays TC .75 .30
❑ 652 Bucky Dent GM .50 .20
❑ 653 Jackie Robinson GM 2.00 .75
❑ 654 Roberto Clemente GM 2.50 1.00
❑ 655 Nolan Ryan GM 3.00 1.25
❑ 656 Kerry Wood GM .75 .30
❑ 657 Rickey Henderson GM 2.00 .75
❑ 658 Lou Brock GM 1.25 .50
❑ 659 David Wells GM .50 .20
❑ 660 Andruw Jones GM .75 .30
❑ 661 Carlton Fisk GM .75 .30

2001 Topps Chrome Traded

❑ COMPLETE SET (266) 150.00 75.00
❑ COMMON CARD (1-99/145-266) .75 .30
❑ COMMON REPRINT (100-144) 1.25 .50
❑ T1 Sandy Alomar Jr. .75 .30
❑ T2 Kevin Appier 1.25 .50
❑ T3 Brad Ausmus 1.25 .50
❑ T4 Derek Bell .75 .30

Card	Player		
❑ T5	Bret Boone	1.25	.50
❑ T6	Rico Brogna	.75	.30
❑ T7	Ellis Burks	1.25	.50
❑ T8	Ken Caminiti	1.25	.50
❑ T9	Roger Cedeno	.75	.30
❑ T10	Royce Clayton	.75	.30
❑ T11	Enrique Wilson	.75	.30
❑ T12	Rheal Cormier	.75	.30
❑ T13	Eric Davis	1.25	.50
❑ T14	Shawon Dunston	.75	.30
❑ T15	Andres Galarraga	1.25	.50
❑ T16	Tom Gordon	.75	.30
❑ T17	Mark Grace	2.00	.75
❑ T18	Jeffrey Hammonds	.75	.30
❑ T19	Dustin Hermanson	.75	.30
❑ T20	Quinton McCracken	.75	.30
❑ T21	Todd Hundley	.75	.30
❑ T22	Charles Johnson	1.25	.50
❑ T23	Marquis Grissom	1.25	.50
❑ T24	Jose Mesa	.75	.30
❑ T25	Brian Boehringer	.75	.30
❑ T26	John Rocker	1.25	.50
❑ T27	Jeff Frye	.75	.30
❑ T28	Reggie Sanders	1.25	.50
❑ T29	David Segui	.75	.30
❑ T30	Mike Sirotka	.75	.30
❑ T31	Fernando Tatis	.75	.30
❑ T32	Steve Trachsel	.75	.30
❑ T33	Ismael Valdes	.75	.30
❑ T34	Randy Velarde	.75	.30
❑ T35	Ryan Kohlmeier	.75	.30
❑ T36	Mike Bordick	1.25	.50
❑ T37	Kent Bottenfield	.75	.30
❑ T38	Pat Rapp	.75	.30
❑ T39	Jeff Nelson	.75	.30
❑ T40	Ricky Bottalico	.75	.30
❑ T41	Luke Prokopec	.75	.30
❑ T42	Hideo Nomo	3.00	1.25
❑ T43	Bill Mueller	1.25	.50
❑ T44	Roberto Kelly	.75	.30
❑ T45	Chris Holt	.75	.30
❑ T46	Mike Jackson	.75	.30
❑ T47	Devon White	1.25	.50
❑ T48	Gerald Williams	.75	.30
❑ T49	Eddie Taubensee	.75	.30
❑ T50	Brian Hunter	.75	.30
❑ T51	Nelson Cruz	.75	.30
❑ T52	Jeff Fassero	.75	.30
❑ T53	Bubba Trammell	.75	.30
❑ T54	Bo Porter	.75	.30
❑ T55	Greg Norton	.75	.30
❑ T56	Benito Santiago	1.25	.50
❑ T57	Ruben Rivera	.75	.30
❑ T58	Dee Brown	.75	.30
❑ T59	Jose Canseco	2.00	.75
❑ T60	Chris Michalak	.75	.30
❑ T61	Tim Worrell	.75	.30
❑ T62	Matt Clement	1.25	.50
❑ T63	Bill Pulsipher	.75	.30
❑ T64	Troy Brohawn RC	1.00	.40
❑ T65	Mark Kotsay	1.25	.50
❑ T66	Jimmy Rollins	1.25	.50
❑ T67	Shea Hillenbrand	1.25	.50
❑ T68	Ted Lilly	.75	.30
❑ T69	Jermaine Dye	1.25	.50
❑ T70	Jerry Hairston Jr.	.75	.30
❑ T71	John Mabry	.75	.30
❑ T72	Kurt Abbott	.75	.30
❑ T73	Eric Owens	.75	.30
❑ T74	Jeff Brantley	.75	.30
❑ T75	Roy Oswalt	3.00	1.25
❑ T76	Doug Mientkiewicz	1.25	.50
❑ T77	Rickey Henderson	3.00	1.25
❑ T78	Jason Grimsley	.75	.30
❑ T79	Christian Parker RC	1.00	.40
❑ T80	Donne Wall	.75	.30
❑ T81	Alex Arias	.75	.30
❑ T82	Willis Roberts	.75	.30
❑ T83	Ryan Minor	.75	.30
❑ T84	Jason LaRue	.75	.30
❑ T85	Ruben Sierra	1.25	.50
❑ T86	Johnny Damon	2.00	.75
❑ T87	Juan Gonzalez	1.25	.50
❑ T88	C.C. Sabathia	1.25	.50
❑ T89	Tony Batista	.75	.30
❑ T90	Jay Witasick	.75	.30
❑ T91	Brent Abernathy	.75	.30
❑ T92	Paul LoDuca	1.25	.50
❑ T93	Wes Helms	.75	.30
❑ T94	Mark Wohlers	.75	.30
❑ T95	Rob Bell	.75	.30
❑ T96	Tim Redding	.75	.30
❑ T97	Bud Smith RC	1.00	.40
❑ T98	Adam Dunn	2.00	.75
❑ T99	I.Suzuki/A.Pujols ROY	25.00	10.00
❑ T100	Carlton Fisk 81	2.00	.75
❑ T101	Tim Raines 81	1.25	.50
❑ T102	Juan Marichal 74	1.25	.50
❑ T103	Dave Winfield 81	1.25	.50
❑ T104	Reggie Jackson 82	2.00	.75
❑ T105	Cal Ripken 82	10.00	4.00
❑ T106	Ozzie Smith 82	5.00	2.00
❑ T107	Tom Seaver 83	2.00	.75
❑ T108	Lou Piniella 74	1.25	.50
❑ T109	Dwight Gooden 84	1.25	.50
❑ T110	Bret Saberhagen 84	1.25	.50
❑ T111	Gary Carter 85	1.25	.50
❑ T112	Jack Clark 85	1.25	.50
❑ T113	Rickey Henderson 85	3.00	1.25
❑ T114	Barry Bonds 86	8.00	3.00
❑ T115	Bobby Bonilla 86	1.25	.50
❑ T116	Jose Canseco 86	2.00	.75
❑ T117	Will Clark 86	2.00	.75
❑ T118	Andres Galarraga 86	1.25	.50
❑ T119	Bo Jackson 86	3.00	1.25
❑ T120	Wally Joyner 86	1.25	.50
❑ T121	Ellis Burks 87	1.25	.50
❑ T122	David Cone 87	1.25	.50
❑ T123	Greg Maddux 87	5.00	2.00
❑ T124	Willie Randolph 76	1.25	.50
❑ T125	Dennis Eckersley 87	1.25	.50
❑ T126	Matt Williams 87	1.25	.50
❑ T127	Joe Morgan 81	1.25	.50
❑ T128	Fred McGriff 87	2.00	.75
❑ T129	Roberto Alomar 88	2.00	.75
❑ T130	Lee Smith 88	1.25	.50
❑ T131	David Wells 88	1.25	.50
❑ T132	Ken Griffey Jr. 89	5.00	2.00
❑ T133	Deion Sanders 89	2.00	.75
❑ T134	Nolan Ryan 89	8.00	3.00
❑ T135	David Justice 90	1.25	.50
❑ T136	Joe Carter 91	1.25	.50
❑ T137	Jack Morris 92	1.25	.50
❑ T138	Mike Piazza 93	5.00	2.00
❑ T139	Barry Bonds 93	8.00	3.00
❑ T140	Terrence Long 94	1.25	.50
❑ T141	Ben Grieve 94	1.25	.50
❑ T142	Richie Sexson 95	1.25	.50
❑ T143	Sean Burroughs 99	1.25	.50
❑ T144	Alfonso Soriano 99	2.00	.75
❑ T145	Bob Boone MG	1.25	.50
❑ T146	Larry Bowa MG	1.25	.50
❑ T147	Bob Brenly MG	.75	.30
❑ T148	Buck Martinez MG	.75	.30
❑ T149	Lloyd McClendon MG	.75	.30
❑ T150	Jim Tracy MG	.75	.30
❑ T151	Jared Abruzzo RC	1.00	.40
❑ T152	Kurt Ainsworth	.75	.30
❑ T153	Willie Bloomquist	1.25	.50
❑ T154	Ben Broussard	.75	.30
❑ T155	Bobby Bradley	.75	.30
❑ T156	Mike Bynum	.75	.30
❑ T157	A.J. Hinch	.75	.30
❑ T158	Ryan Christianson	.75	.30
❑ T159	Carlos Silva	.75	.30
❑ T160	Joe Crede	3.00	1.25
❑ T161	Jack Cust	.75	.30
❑ T162	Ben Diggins	.75	.30
❑ T163	Phil Dumatrait	.75	.30
❑ T164	Alex Escobar	.75	.30
❑ T165	Miguel Olivo	.75	.30
❑ T166	Chris George	.75	.30
❑ T167	Marcus Giles	1.25	.50
❑ T168	Keith Ginter	.75	.30
❑ T169	Josh Girdley	.75	.30
❑ T170	Tony Alvarez	.75	.30
❑ T171	Scott Seabol	.75	.30
❑ T172	Josh Hamilton	.75	.30
❑ T173	Jason Hart	.75	.30
❑ T174	Israel Alcantara	.75	.30
❑ T175	Jake Peavy	4.00	1.50
❑ T176	Stubby Clapp RC	1.00	.40
❑ T177	D'Angelo Jimenez	.75	.30
❑ T178	Nick Johnson	1.25	.50
❑ T179	Ben Johnson	1.25	.50
❑ T180	Larry Bigbie	.75	.30
❑ T181	Allen Levrault	.75	.30
❑ T182	Felipe Lopez	1.25	.50
❑ T183	Sean Burnett	.75	.30
❑ T184	Nick Neugebauer	.75	.30
❑ T185	Austin Kearns	1.25	.50
❑ T186	Corey Patterson	.75	.30
❑ T187	Carlos Pena	.75	.30
❑ T188	Ricardo Rodriguez RC	1.00	.40
❑ T189	Juan Rivera	.75	.30
❑ T190	Grant Roberts	.75	.30
❑ T191	Adam Pettyjohn RC	1.00	.40
❑ T192	Jared Sandberg	.75	.30
❑ T193	Xavier Nady	.75	.30
❑ T194	Dane Sardinha	.75	.30
❑ T195	Shawn Sonnier	.75	.30
❑ T196	Rafael Soriano	1.00	.40
❑ T197	Brian Specht RC	1.00	.40
❑ T198	Aaron Myette	.75	.30
❑ T199	Juan Uribe RC	1.25	.50
❑ T200	Jayson Werth	.75	.30
❑ T201	Brad Wilkerson	.75	.30
❑ T202	Horacio Estrada	.75	.30
❑ T203	Joel Pineiro	1.25	.50
❑ T204	Matt LeCroy	.75	.30
❑ T205	Michael Coleman	.75	.30
❑ T206	Ben Sheets	2.00	.75
❑ T207	Eric Byrnes	.75	.30
❑ T208	Sean Burroughs	.75	.30
❑ T209	Ken Harvey	.75	.30
❑ T210	Travis Hafner	8.00	3.00
❑ T211	Erick Almonte	1.00	.40
❑ T212	Jason Belcher RC	1.00	.40
❑ T213	Wilson Betemit RC	4.00	1.50
❑ T214	Hank Blalock RC	6.00	2.50
❑ T215	Danny Borrell	1.00	.40
❑ T216	John Buck RC	1.25	.50
❑ T217	Freddie Bynum RC	1.00	.40
❑ T218	Noel Devarez RC	1.00	.40
❑ T219	Juan Diaz RC	1.00	.40
❑ T220	Felix Diaz RC	1.00	.40
❑ T221	Josh Fogg RC	1.00	.40
❑ T222	Matt Ford RC	1.00	.40
❑ T223	Scott Heard	.75	.30
❑ T224	Ben Hendrickson RC	1.00	.40
❑ T225	Cody Ross RC	1.00	.40
❑ T226	Adrian Hernandez RC	1.00	.40
❑ T227	Alfredo Amezaga RC	1.00	.40
❑ T228	Bob Keppel RC	1.00	.40
❑ T229	Ryan Madson RC	2.00	.75
❑ T230	Octavio Martinez RC	1.00	.40
❑ T231	Hee Seop Choi	1.25	.50
❑ T232	Thomas Mitchell	.75	.30
❑ T233	Luis Montanez	1.00	.40
❑ T234	Andy Morales RC	1.00	.40
❑ T235	Justin Morneau RC	12.00	5.00
❑ T236	Toe Nash RC	1.00	.40
❑ T237	Valentino Pascucci RC	1.00	.40
❑ T238	Roy Smith RC	1.00	.40
❑ T239	Antonio Perez RC	1.25	.50
❑ T240	Chad Petty RC	1.00	.40
❑ T241	Steve Smyth	1.00	.40
❑ T242	Jose Reyes RC	20.00	8.00
❑ T243	Eric Reynolds RC	1.00	.40
❑ T244	Dominic Rich	1.00	.40
❑ T245	Jason Richardson RC	1.00	.40
❑ T246	Ed Rogers RC	1.00	.40
❑ T247	Albert Pujols	80.00	50.00
❑ T248	Esix Snead RC	1.00	.40
❑ T249	Luis Torres RC	1.00	.40
❑ T250	Matt White RC	1.00	.40
❑ T251	Blake Williams	1.00	.40
❑ T252	Chris Russ	1.00	.40
❑ T253	Joe Kennedy RC	1.25	.50
❑ T254	Jeff Randazzo RC	1.00	.40
❑ T255	Beau Hale RC	1.00	.40
❑ T256	Brad Hennessey RC	2.00	.75
❑ T257	Jake Gautreau RC	1.00	.40
❑ T258	Jeff Mathis RC	1.25	.50
❑ T259	Aaron Heilman RC	1.25	.50
❑ T260	Bronson Sardinha RC	1.00	.40
❑ T261	Irvin Guzman RC	8.00	3.00
❑ T262	Gabe Gross RC	1.25	.50

❑	T263 J.D. Martin RC	1.00	.40
❑	T264 Chris Smith RC	1.00	.40
❑	T265 Kenny Baugh RC	1.00	.40
❑	T266 Ichiro Suzuki RC	25.00	10.00

2002 Topps Chrome

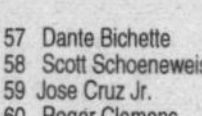

❑	COMPLETE SET (660)	250.00	100.00
❑	COMPLETE SERIES 1 (330)	125.00	50.00
❑	COMPLETE SERIES 2 (330)	125.00	50.00
❑	COMMON (1-331/366-695)	.50	.20
❑	COMMON (307-326/671-690)	1.50	.60
❑	COMMON (327-331/691-695)	1.50	.60
❑	1 Pedro Martinez	1.50	.60
❑	2 Mike Stanton	.50	.20
❑	3 Brad Penny	.50	.20
❑	4 Mike Matheny	.50	.20
❑	5 Johnny Damon	1.50	.60
❑	6 Bret Boone	1.00	.40
❑	7 Does Not Exist		
❑	8 Chris Truby	.50	.20
❑	9 B.J. Surhoff	1.00	.40
❑	10 Mike Hampton	1.00	.40
❑	11 Juan Pierre	1.00	.40
❑	12 Mark Buehrle	1.00	.40
❑	13 Bob Abreu	1.00	.40
❑	14 David Cone	1.00	.40
❑	15 Aaron Sele	.50	.20
❑	16 Fernando Tatis	.50	.20
❑	17 Bobby Jones	.50	.20
❑	18 Rick Helling	.50	.20
❑	19 Dmitri Young	1.00	.40
❑	20 Mike Mussina	1.50	.60
❑	21 Mike Sweeney	1.00	.40
❑	22 Cristian Guzman	.50	.20
❑	23 Ryan Kohlmeier	.50	.20
❑	24 Adam Kennedy	.50	.20
❑	25 Larry Walker	1.00	.40
❑	26 Eric Davis	1.00	.40
❑	27 Jason Tyner	.50	.20
❑	28 Eric Young	.50	.20
❑	29 Jason Marquis	.50	.20
❑	30 Luis Gonzalez	1.00	.40
❑	31 Kevin Tapani	.50	.20
❑	32 Orlando Cabrera	1.00	.40
❑	33 Marty Cordova	.50	.20
❑	34 Brad Ausmus	1.00	.40
❑	35 Livan Hernandez	1.00	.40
❑	36 Alex Gonzalez	.50	.20
❑	37 Edgar Renteria	1.00	.40
❑	38 Bengie Molina	.50	.20
❑	39 Frank Menechino	.50	.20
❑	40 Rafael Palmeiro	1.50	.60
❑	41 Brad Fullmer	.50	.20
❑	42 Julio Zuleta	.50	.20
❑	43 Darren Dreifort	.50	.20
❑	44 Trot Nixon	1.00	.40
❑	45 Trevor Hoffman	1.00	.40
❑	46 Vladimir Nunez	.50	.20
❑	47 Mark Kotsay	1.00	.40
❑	48 Kenny Rogers	1.00	.40
❑	49 Ben Petrick	.50	.20
❑	50 Jeff Bagwell	1.50	.60
❑	51 Juan Encarnacion	.50	.20
❑	52 Ramiro Mendoza	.50	.20
❑	53 Brian Meadows	.50	.20
❑	54 Chad Curtis	.50	.20
❑	55 Aramis Ramirez	1.00	.40
❑	56 Mark McLemore	.50	.20
❑	57 Dante Bichette	1.00	.40
❑	58 Scott Schoeneweis	.50	.20
❑	59 Jose Cruz Jr.	.50	.20
❑	60 Roger Clemens	5.00	2.00
❑	61 Jose Guillen	1.00	.40
❑	62 Darren Oliver	.50	.20
❑	63 Chris Reitsma	.50	.20
❑	64 Jeff Abbott	.50	.20
❑	65 Robin Ventura	1.00	.40
❑	66 Denny Neagle	.50	.20
❑	67 Al Martin	.50	.20
❑	68 Benito Santiago	1.00	.40
❑	69 Roy Oswalt	1.00	.40
❑	70 Juan Gonzalez	1.00	.40
❑	71 Garret Anderson	1.00	.40
❑	72 Bobby Bonilla	1.00	.40
❑	73 Danny Bautista	.50	.20
❑	74 J.T. Snow	1.00	.40
❑	75 Derek Jeter	6.00	2.50
❑	76 John Olerud	1.00	.40
❑	77 Kevin Appier	1.00	.40
❑	78 Phil Nevin	1.00	.40
❑	79 Sean Casey	1.00	.40
❑	80 Troy Glaus	1.00	.40
❑	81 Joe Randa	1.00	.40
❑	82 Jose Valentin	.50	.20
❑	83 Ricky Bottalico	.50	.20
❑	84 Todd Zeile	1.00	.40
❑	85 Barry Larkin	1.50	.60
❑	86 Bob Wickman	.50	.20
❑	87 Jeff Shaw	.50	.20
❑	88 Greg Vaughn	.50	.20
❑	89 Fernando Vina	.50	.20
❑	90 Mark Mulder	1.00	.40
❑	91 Paul Bako	.50	.20
❑	92 Aaron Boone	1.00	.40
❑	93 Esteban Loaiza	.50	.20
❑	94 Richie Sexson	1.00	.40
❑	95 Alfonso Soriano	1.00	.40
❑	96 Tony Womack	.50	.20
❑	97 Paul Shuey	.50	.20
❑	98 Melvin Mora	1.00	.40
❑	99 Tony Gwynn	3.00	1.25
❑	100 Vladimir Guerrero	2.50	1.00
❑	101 Keith Osik	.50	.20
❑	102 Bud Smith	.50	.20
❑	103 Scott Williamson	.50	.20
❑	104 Daryle Ward	.50	.20
❑	105 Doug Mientkiewicz	1.00	.40
❑	106 Stan Javier	.50	.20
❑	107 Russ Ortiz	.50	.20
❑	108 Wade Miller	.50	.20
❑	109 Luke Prokopec	.50	.20
❑	110 Andruw Jones	1.50	.60
❑	111 Ron Coomer	.50	.20
❑	112 Dan Wilson	.50	.20
❑	113 Luis Castillo	.50	.20
❑	114 Derek Bell	.50	.20
❑	115 Gary Sheffield	1.00	.40
❑	116 Ruben Rivera	.50	.20
❑	117 Paul O'Neill	1.50	.60
❑	118 Craig Paquette	.50	.20
❑	119 Kelvim Escobar	.50	.20
❑	120 Brad Radke	1.00	.40
❑	121 Jorge Fabregas	.50	.20
❑	122 Randy Winn	.50	.20
❑	123 Tom Goodwin	.50	.20
❑	124 Jaret Wright	.50	.20
❑	125 Barry Bonds HR 73	40.00	15.00
❑	126 Al Leiter	.50	.20
❑	127 Ben Davis	.50	.20
❑	128 Frank Catalanotto	.50	.20
❑	129 Jose Cabrera	.50	.20
❑	130 Magglio Ordonez	1.00	.40
❑	131 Jose Macias	.50	.20
❑	132 Ted Lilly	.50	.20
❑	133 Chris Holt	.50	.20
❑	134 Eric Milton	.50	.20
❑	135 Shannon Stewart	1.00	.40
❑	136 Omar Olivares	.50	.20
❑	137 David Segui	.50	.20
❑	138 Jeff Nelson	.50	.20
❑	139 Matt Williams	1.00	.40
❑	140 Ellis Burks	1.00	.40
❑	141 Jason Bere	.50	.20
❑	142 Jimmy Haynes	.50	.20
❑	143 Ramon Hernandez	.50	.20
❑	144 Craig Counsell	.50	.20
❑	145 John Smoltz	1.50	.60
❑	146 Homer Bush	.50	.20
❑	147 Quilvio Veras	.50	.20
❑	148 Esteban Yan	.50	.20
❑	149 Ramon Ortiz	.50	.20
❑	150 Carlos Delgado	1.00	.40
❑	151 Lee Stevens	.50	.20
❑	152 Wil Cordero	.50	.20
❑	153 Mike Bordick	1.00	.40
❑	154 John Flaherty	.50	.20
❑	155 Omar Daal	.50	.20
❑	156 Todd Ritchie	.50	.20
❑	157 Carl Everett	1.00	.40
❑	158 Scott Sullivan	.50	.20
❑	159 Deivi Cruz	.50	.20
❑	160 Albert Pujols	5.00	2.00
❑	161 Royce Clayton	.50	.20
❑	162 Jeff Suppan	.50	.20
❑	163 C.C. Sabathia	1.00	.40
❑	164 Jimmy Rollins	1.00	.40
❑	165 Rickey Henderson	2.50	1.00
❑	166 Rey Ordonez	.50	.20
❑	167 Shawn Estes	.50	.20
❑	168 Reggie Sanders	1.00	.40
❑	169 Jon Lieber	.50	.20
❑	170 Armando Benitez	.50	.20
❑	171 Mike Remlinger	.50	.20
❑	172 Billy Wagner	1.00	.40
❑	173 Troy Percival	1.00	.40
❑	174 Devon White	1.00	.40
❑	175 Ivan Rodriguez	1.50	.60
❑	176 Dustin Hermanson	.50	.20
❑	177 Brian Anderson	.50	.20
❑	178 Graeme Lloyd	.50	.20
❑	179 Russell Branyan	.50	.20
❑	180 Bobby Higginson	1.00	.40
❑	181 Alex Gonzalez	.50	.20
❑	182 John Franco	1.00	.40
❑	183 Sidney Ponson	.50	.20
❑	184 Jose Mesa	.50	.20
❑	185 Todd Hollandsworth	.50	.20
❑	186 Kevin Young	.50	.20
❑	187 Tim Wakefield	1.00	.40
❑	188 Craig Biggio	1.50	.60
❑	189 Jason Isringhausen	1.00	.40
❑	190 Mark Quinn	.50	.20
❑	191 Glendon Rusch	.50	.20
❑	192 Damian Miller	.50	.20
❑	193 Sandy Alomar Jr.	.50	.20
❑	194 Scott Brosius	1.00	.40
❑	195 Dave Martinez	.50	.20
❑	196 Danny Graves	.50	.20
❑	197 Shea Hillenbrand	1.00	.40
❑	198 Jimmy Anderson	.50	.20
❑	199 Travis Lee	.50	.20
❑	200 Randy Johnson	2.50	1.00
❑	201 Carlos Beltran	1.00	.40
❑	202 Jerry Hairston	.50	.20
❑	203 Jesus Sanchez	.50	.20
❑	204 Eddie Taubensee	.50	.20
❑	205 David Wells	1.00	.40
❑	206 Russ Davis	.50	.20
❑	207 Michael Barrett	.50	.20
❑	208 Marquis Grissom	1.00	.40
❑	209 Byung-Hyun Kim	1.00	.40
❑	210 Hideo Nomo	2.50	1.00
❑	211 Ryan Rupe	.50	.20
❑	212 Ricky Gutierrez	.50	.20
❑	213 Darryl Kile	1.00	.40
❑	214 Rico Brogna	.50	.20
❑	215 Terrence Long	.50	.20
❑	216 Mike Jackson	.50	.20
❑	217 Jamey Wright	.50	.20
❑	218 Adrian Beltre	1.00	.40
❑	219 Benny Agbayani	.50	.20
❑	220 Chuck Knoblauch	1.00	.40
❑	221 Randy Wolf	.50	.20
❑	222 Andy Ashby	.50	.20
❑	223 Corey Koskie	.50	.20
❑	224 Roger Cedeno	.50	.20
❑	225 Ichiro Suzuki	5.00	2.00
❑	226 Keith Foulke	1.00	.40
❑	227 Ryan Minor	.50	.20
❑	228 Shawon Dunston	.50	.20

❑	229	Alex Cora	.50	.20
❑	230	Jeromy Burnitz	1.00	.40
❑	231	Mark Grace	1.50	.60
❑	232	Aubrey Huff	1.00	.40
❑	233	Jeffrey Hammonds	.50	.20
❑	234	Olmedo Saenz	.50	.20
❑	235	Brian Jordan	1.00	.40
❑	236	Jeremy Giambi	.50	.20
❑	237	Joe Girardi	.50	.20
❑	238	Eric Gagne	1.00	.40
❑	239	Masato Yoshii	.50	.20
❑	240	Greg Maddux	4.00	1.50
❑	241	Bryan Rekar	.50	.20
❑	242	Ray Durham	1.00	.40
❑	243	Torii Hunter	1.00	.40
❑	244	Derrek Lee	1.50	.60
❑	245	Jim Edmonds	1.00	.40
❑	246	Einar Diaz	.50	.20
❑	247	Brian Bohanon	.50	.20
❑	248	Ron Belliard	.50	.20
❑	249	Mike Lowell	1.00	.40
❑	250	Sammy Sosa	2.50	1.00
❑	251	Richard Hidalgo	.50	.20
❑	252	Bartolo Colon	1.00	.40
❑	253	Jorge Posada	1.50	.60
❑	254	Latroy Hawkins	.50	.20
❑	255	Paul LoDuca	1.00	.40
❑	256	Carlos Febles	.50	.20
❑	257	Nelson Cruz	.50	.20
❑	258	Edgardo Alfonzo	.50	.20
❑	259	Joey Hamilton	.50	.20
❑	260	Cliff Floyd	1.00	.40
❑	261	Wes Helms	.50	.20
❑	262	Jay Bell	1.00	.40
❑	263	Mike Cameron	.50	.20
❑	264	Paul Konerko	1.00	.40
❑	265	Jeff Kent	1.00	.40
❑	266	Robert Fick	.50	.20
❑	267	Allen Levrault	.50	.20
❑	268	Placido Polanco	.50	.20
❑	269	Marlon Anderson	.50	.20
❑	270	Mariano Rivera	2.50	1.00
❑	271	Chan Ho Park	1.00	.40
❑	272	Jose Vizcaino	.50	.20
❑	273	Jeff D'Amico	.50	.20
❑	274	Mark Gardner	.50	.20
❑	275	Travis Fryman	1.00	.40
❑	276	Darren Lewis	.50	.20
❑	277	Bruce Bochy MG	.50	.20
❑	278	Jerry Manuel MG	.50	.20
❑	279	Bob Brenly MG	.50	.20
❑	280	Don Baylor MG	1.00	.40
❑	281	Davey Lopes MG	1.00	.40
❑	282	Jerry Narron MG	.50	.20
❑	283	Tony Muser MG	.50	.20
❑	284	Hal McRae MG	1.00	.40
❑	285	Bobby Cox MG	.50	.20
❑	286	Larry Dierker MG	.50	.20
❑	287	Phil Garner MG	1.00	.40
❑	288	Joe Kerrigan MG	.50	.20
❑	289	Bobby Valentine MG	.50	.20
❑	290	Dusty Baker MG	1.00	.40
❑	291	Lloyd McClendon MG	.50	.20
❑	292	Mike Scioscia MG	.50	.20
❑	293	Buck Martinez MG	.50	.20
❑	294	Larry Bowa MG	1.00	.40
❑	295	Tony LaRussa MG	1.00	.40
❑	296	Jeff Torborg MG	.50	.20
❑	297	Tom Kelly MG	.50	.20
❑	298	Mike Hargrove MG	.50	.20
❑	299	Art Howe MG	.50	.20
❑	300	Lou Piniella MG	1.00	.40
❑	301	Charlie Manuel MG	.50	.20
❑	302	Buddy Bell MG	1.00	.40
❑	303	Tony Perez MG	1.00	.40
❑	304	Bob Boone MG	1.00	.40
❑	305	Joe Torre MG	1.50	.60
❑	306	Jim Tracy MG	.50	.20
❑	307	Jason Lane PROS	1.50	.60
❑	308	Chris George PROS	1.50	.60
❑	309	Hank Blalock PROS	2.50	1.00
❑	310	Joe Borchard PROS	1.50	.60
❑	311	Marlon Byrd PROS	1.50	.60
❑	312	Raymond Cabrera PROS RC	1.50	.60
❑	313	Freddy Sanchez PROS RC	6.00	2.50
❑	314	Scott Wiggins PROS RC	1.50	.60
❑	315	Jason Maule PROS RC	1.50	.60
❑	316	Dionys Cesar PROS RC	1.50	.60
❑	317	Boof Bonser PROS	1.50	.60
❑	318	Juan Tolentino PROS RC	1.50	.60
❑	319	Earl Snyder PROS RC	1.50	.60
❑	320	Travis Wade PROS RC	1.50	.60
❑	321	Napolean Calzado PROS RC	1.50	.60
❑	322	Eric Glaser PROS RC	1.50	.60
❑	323	Craig Kuzmic PROS RC	1.50	.60
❑	324	Nic Jackson PROS RC	1.50	.60
❑	325	Mike Rivera PROS	1.50	.60
❑	326	Jason Bay PROS RC	8.00	3.00
❑	327	Chris Smith DP	1.50	.60
❑	328	Jake Gautreau DP	1.50	.60
❑	329	Gabe Gross DP	1.50	.60
❑	330	Kenny Baugh DP	1.50	.60
❑	331	J.D. Martin DP	1.50	.60
❑	366	Pat Meares	.50	.20
❑	367	Mike Lieberthal	1.00	.40
❑	368	Larry Bigbie	.50	.20
❑	369	Ron Gant	1.00	.40
❑	370	Moises Alou	1.00	.40
❑	371	Chad Kreuter	.50	.20
❑	372	Willis Roberts	.50	.20
❑	373	Toby Hall	.50	.20
❑	374	Miguel Batista	.50	.20
❑	375	John Burkett	.50	.20
❑	376	Cory Lidle	.50	.20
❑	377	Nick Neugebauer	.50	.20
❑	378	Jay Payton	.50	.20
❑	379	Steve Karsay	.50	.20
❑	380	Eric Chavez	1.00	.40
❑	381	Kelly Stinnett	.50	.20
❑	382	Jarrod Washburn	.50	.20
❑	383	Rick White	.50	.20
❑	384	Jeff Conine	1.00	.40
❑	385	Fred McGriff	1.50	.60
❑	386	Marvin Benard	.50	.20
❑	387	Joe Crede	1.00	.40
❑	388	Dennis Cook	.50	.20
❑	389	Rick Reed	.50	.20
❑	390	Tom Glavine	1.50	.60
❑	391	Rondell White	1.00	.40
❑	392	Matt Morris	1.00	.40
❑	393	Pat Rapp	.50	.20
❑	394	Robert Person	.50	.20
❑	395	Omar Vizquel	1.50	.60
❑	396	Jeff Cirillo	.50	.20
❑	397	Dave Mlicki	.50	.20
❑	398	Jose Ortiz	.50	.20
❑	399	Ryan Dempster	.50	.20
❑	400	Curt Schilling	1.00	.40
❑	401	Peter Bergeron	.50	.20
❑	402	Kyle Lohse	.50	.20
❑	403	Craig Wilson	.50	.20
❑	404	David Justice	1.00	.40
❑	405	Darin Erstad	1.00	.40
❑	406	Jose Mercedes	.50	.20
❑	407	Carl Pavano	1.00	.40
❑	408	Albie Lopez	.50	.20
❑	409	Alex Ochoa	.50	.20
❑	410	Chipper Jones	2.50	1.00
❑	411	Tyler Houston	.50	.20
❑	412	Dean Palmer	1.00	.40
❑	413	Damian Jackson	.50	.20
❑	414	Josh Towers	.50	.20
❑	415	Rafael Furcal	1.00	.40
❑	416	Mike Morgan	.50	.20
❑	417	Herb Perry	.50	.20
❑	418	Mike Sirotka	.50	.20
❑	419	Mark Wohlers	.50	.20
❑	420	Nomar Garciaparra	4.00	1.50
❑	421	Felipe Lopez	.50	.20
❑	422	Joe McEwing	.50	.20
❑	423	Jacque Jones	1.00	.40
❑	424	Julio Franco	1.00	.40
❑	425	Frank Thomas	2.50	1.00
❑	426	So Taguchi RC	2.50	1.00
❑	427	Kazuhisa Ishii RC	2.50	1.00
❑	428	D'Angelo Jimenez	.50	.20
❑	429	Chris Stynes	.50	.20
❑	430	Kerry Wood	1.00	.40
❑	431	Chris Singleton	.50	.20
❑	432	Erubiel Durazo	.50	.20
❑	433	Matt Lawton	.50	.20
❑	434	Bill Mueller	1.00	.40
❑	435	Jose Canseco	1.50	.60
❑	436	Ben Grieve	.50	.20
❑	437	Terry Mulholland	.50	.20
❑	438	David Bell	.50	.20
❑	439	A.J. Pierzynski	1.00	.40
❑	440	Adam Dunn	1.00	.40
❑	441	Jon Garland	1.00	.40
❑	442	Jeff Fassero	.50	.20
❑	443	Julio Lugo	.50	.20
❑	444	Carlos Guillen	1.00	.40
❑	445	Orlando Hernandez	1.00	.40
❑	446	Mark Loretta	.50	.20
❑	447	Scott Spiezio	.50	.20
❑	448	Kevin Millwood	1.00	.40
❑	449	Jamie Moyer	1.00	.40
❑	450	Todd Helton	1.50	.60
❑	451	Todd Walker	.50	.20
❑	452	Jose Lima	.50	.20
❑	453	Brook Fordyce	.50	.20
❑	454	Aaron Rowand	1.00	.40
❑	455	Barry Zito	1.00	.40
❑	456	Eric Owens	.50	.20
❑	457	Charles Nagy	.50	.20
❑	458	Raul Ibanez	.50	.20
❑	459	Joe Mays	.50	.20
❑	460	Jim Thome	1.50	.60
❑	461	Adam Eaton	.50	.20
❑	462	Felix Martinez	.50	.20
❑	463	Vernon Wells	1.00	.40
❑	464	Donnie Sadler	.50	.20
❑	465	Tony Clark	.50	.20
❑	466	Jose Hernandez	.50	.20
❑	467	Ramon Martinez	.50	.20
❑	468	Rusty Greer	1.00	.40
❑	469	Rod Barajas	.50	.20
❑	470	Lance Berkman	1.00	.40
❑	471	Brady Anderson	1.00	.40
❑	472	Pedro Astacio	.50	.20
❑	473	Shane Halter	.50	.20
❑	474	Bret Prinz	.50	.20
❑	475	Edgar Martinez	1.50	.60
❑	476	Steve Trachsel	.50	.20
❑	477	Gary Matthews Jr.	.50	.20
❑	478	Ismael Valdes	.50	.20
❑	479	Juan Uribe	.50	.20
❑	480	Shawn Green	1.00	.40
❑	481	Kirk Rueter	.50	.20
❑	482	Damion Easley	.50	.20
❑	483	Chris Carpenter	1.00	.40
❑	484	Kris Benson	.50	.20
❑	485	Antonio Alfonseca	.50	.20
❑	486	Kyle Farnsworth	.50	.20
❑	487	Brandon Lyon	.50	.20
❑	488	Hideki Irabu	.50	.20
❑	489	David Ortiz	2.50	1.00
❑	490	Mike Piazza	4.00	1.50
❑	491	Derek Lowe	1.00	.40
❑	492	Chris Gomez	.50	.20
❑	493	Mark Johnson	.50	.20
❑	494	John Rocker	1.00	.40
❑	495	Eric Karros	1.00	.40
❑	496	Bill Haselman	.50	.20
❑	497	Dave Veres	.50	.20
❑	498	Pete Harnisch	.50	.20
❑	499	Tomokazu Ohka	.50	.20
❑	500	Barry Bonds	6.00	2.50
❑	501	David Dellucci	.50	.20
❑	502	Wendell Magee	.50	.20
❑	503	Tom Gordon	.50	.20
❑	504	Javier Vazquez	1.00	.40
❑	505	Ben Sheets	1.00	.40
❑	506	Wilton Guerrero	.50	.20
❑	507	John Halama	.50	.20
❑	508	Mark Redman	.50	.20
❑	509	Jack Wilson	.50	.20
❑	510	Bernie Williams	1.50	.60
❑	511	Miguel Cairo	.50	.20
❑	512	Denny Hocking	.50	.20
❑	513	Tony Batista	.50	.20
❑	514	Mark Grudzielanek	.50	.20
❑	515	Jose Vidro	.50	.20
❑	516	Sterling Hitchcock	.50	.20
❑	517	Billy Koch	.50	.20
❑	518	Matt Clement	1.00	.40
❑	519	Bruce Chen	.50	.20
❑	520	Roberto Alomar	1.50	.60

❑ 521 Orlando Palmeiro .50 .20
❑ 522 Steve Finley 1.00 .40
❑ 523 Danny Patterson .50 .20
❑ 524 Terry Adams .50 .20
❑ 525 Tino Martinez 1.50 .60
❑ 526 Tony Armas Jr. .50 .20
❑ 527 Geoff Jenkins .50 .20
❑ 528 Kerry Robinson .50 .20
❑ 529 Corey Patterson .50 .20
❑ 530 Brian Giles 1.00 .40
❑ 531 Jose Jimenez .50 .20
❑ 532 Joe Kennedy .50 .20
❑ 533 Armando Rios .50 .20
❑ 534 Osvaldo Fernandez .50 .20
❑ 535 Ruben Sierra 1.00 .40
❑ 536 Octavio Dotel .50 .20
❑ 537 Luis Sojo .50 .20
❑ 538 Brent Butler .50 .20
❑ 539 Pablo Ozuna .50 .20
❑ 540 Freddy Garcia 1.00 .40
❑ 541 Chad Durbin .50 .20
❑ 542 Orlando Merced .50 .20
❑ 543 Michael Tucker .50 .20
❑ 544 Roberto Hernandez .50 .20
❑ 545 Pat Burrell 1.00 .40
❑ 546 A.J. Burnett 1.00 .40
❑ 547 Bubba Trammell .50 .20
❑ 548 Scott Elarton .50 .20
❑ 549 Mike Darr .50 .20
❑ 550 Ken Griffey Jr. 4.00 1.50
❑ 551 Ugueth Urbina .50 .20
❑ 552 Todd Jones .50 .20
❑ 553 Delino Deshields .50 .20
❑ 554 Adam Piatt .50 .20
❑ 555 Jason Kendall 1.00 .40
❑ 556 Hector Ortiz .50 .20
❑ 557 Turk Wendell .50 .20
❑ 558 Rob Bell .50 .20
❑ 559 Sun Woo Kim .50 .20
❑ 560 Raul Mondesi 1.00 .40
❑ 561 Brent Abernathy .50 .20
❑ 562 Seth Etherton .50 .20
❑ 563 Shawn Wooten .50 .20
❑ 564 Jay Buhner 1.00 .40
❑ 565 Andres Galarraga 1.00 .40
❑ 566 Shane Reynolds .50 .20
❑ 567 Rod Beck .50 .20
❑ 568 Dee Brown .50 .20
❑ 569 Pedro Feliz .50 .20
❑ 570 Ryan Klesko 1.00 .40
❑ 571 John Vander Wal .50 .20
❑ 572 Nick Bierbrodt .50 .20
❑ 573 Joe Nathan 1.00 .40
❑ 574 James Baldwin .50 .20
❑ 575 J.D. Drew 1.00 .40
❑ 576 Greg Colbrunn .50 .20
❑ 577 Doug Glanville .50 .20
❑ 578 Brandon Duckworth .50 .20
❑ 579 Shawn Chacon .50 .20
❑ 580 Rich Aurilia .50 .20
❑ 581 Chuck Finley 1.00 .40
❑ 582 Abraham Nunez .50 .20
❑ 583 Kenny Lofton 1.00 .40
❑ 584 Brian Daubach .50 .20
❑ 585 Miguel Tejada 1.00 .40
❑ 586 Nate Cornejo .50 .20
❑ 587 Kazuhiro Sasaki 1.00 .40
❑ 588 Chris Richard .50 .20
❑ 589 Armando Reynoso .50 .20
❑ 590 Tim Hudson 1.00 .40
❑ 591 Neifi Perez .50 .20
❑ 592 Steve Cox .50 .20
❑ 593 Henry Blanco .50 .20
❑ 594 Ricky Ledee .50 .20
❑ 595 Tim Salmon 1.50 .60
❑ 596 Luis Rivas .50 .20
❑ 597 Jeff Zimmerman .50 .20
❑ 598 Matt Stairs .50 .20
❑ 599 Preston Wilson 1.00 .40
❑ 600 Mark McGwire 6.00 2.50
❑ 601 Timo Perez .50 .20
❑ 602 Matt Anderson .50 .20
❑ 603 Todd Hundley .50 .20
❑ 604 Rick Ankiel .50 .20
❑ 605 Tsuyoshi Shinjo 1.00 .40
❑ 606 Woody Williams .50 .20
❑ 607 Jason LaRue .50 .20
❑ 608 Carlos Lee 1.00 .40
❑ 609 Russ Johnson .50 .20
❑ 610 Scott Rolen 1.50 .60
❑ 611 Brent Mayne .50 .20
❑ 612 Darrin Fletcher .50 .20
❑ 613 Ray Lankford 1.00 .40
❑ 614 Troy O'Leary .50 .20
❑ 615 Javier Lopez 1.00 .40
❑ 616 Randy Velarde .50 .20
❑ 617 Vinny Castilla 1.00 .40
❑ 618 Milton Bradley 1.00 .40
❑ 619 Ruben Mateo .50 .20
❑ 620 Jason Giambi Yankees 1.00 .40
❑ 621 Andy Benes .50 .20
❑ 622 Joe Mauer RC 15.00 6.00
❑ 623 Andy Pettitte 1.50 .60
❑ 624 Jose Offerman .50 .20
❑ 625 Mo Vaughn 1.00 .40
❑ 626 Steve Sparks .50 .20
❑ 627 Mike Matthews .50 .20
❑ 628 Robb Nen 1.00 .40
❑ 629 Kip Wells .50 .20
❑ 630 Kevin Brown 1.00 .40
❑ 631 Arthur Rhodes .50 .20
❑ 632 Gabe Kapler 1.00 .40
❑ 633 Jermaine Dye 1.00 .40
❑ 634 Josh Beckett 1.00 .40
❑ 635 Pokey Reese .50 .20
❑ 636 Benji Gil .50 .20
❑ 637 Marcus Giles 1.00 .40
❑ 638 Julian Tavarez .50 .20
❑ 639 Jason Schmidt 1.00 .40
❑ 640 Alex Rodriguez 4.00 1.50
❑ 641 Anaheim Angels TC 1.00 .40
❑ 642 Arizona Diamondbacks TC 1.50 .60
❑ 643 Atlanta Braves TC 1.00 .40
❑ 644 Baltimore Orioles TC 1.00 .40
❑ 645 Boston Red Sox TC 1.00 .40
❑ 646 Chicago Cubs TC 1.00 .40
❑ 647 Chicago White Sox TC 1.00 .40
❑ 648 Cincinnati Reds TC 1.00 .40
❑ 649 Cleveland Indians TC 1.00 .40
❑ 650 Colorado Rockies TC 1.00 .40
❑ 651 Detroit Tigers TC 1.00 .40
❑ 652 Florida Marlins TC 1.00 .40
❑ 653 Houston Astros TC 1.00 .40
❑ 654 Kansas City Royals TC 1.00 .40
❑ 655 Los Angeles Dodgers TC 1.00 .40
❑ 656 Milwaukee Brewers TC 1.00 .40
❑ 657 Minnesota Twins TC 1.00 .40
❑ 658 Montreal Expos TC 1.00 .40
❑ 659 New York Mets TC 1.00 .40
❑ 660 New York Yankees TC 2.50 1.00
❑ 661 Oakland Athletics TC 1.00 .40
❑ 662 Philadelphia Phillies TC 1.00 .40
❑ 663 Pittsburgh Pirates TC 1.00 .40
❑ 664 San Diego Padres TC 1.00 .40
❑ 665 San Francisco Giants TC 1.00 .40
❑ 666 Seattle Mariners TC 1.50 .60
❑ 667 St. Louis Cardinals TC 1.00 .40
❑ 668 Tampa Bay Devil Rays TC 1.00 .40
❑ 669 Texas Rangers TC 1.00 .40
❑ 670 Toronto Blue Jays TC 1.00 .40
❑ 671 Juan Cruz PROS 1.50 .60
❑ 672 Kevin Cash PROS RC 1.50 .60
❑ 673 Jimmy Gobble PROS RC 1.50 .60
❑ 674 Mike Hill PROS RC 1.50 .60
❑ 675 Taylor Buchholz PROS RC 1.50 .60
❑ 676 Bill Hall PROS 1.50 .60
❑ 677 Brett Roneberg PROS RC 1.50 .60
❑ 678 Royce Huffman PROS RC 1.50 .60
❑ 679 Chris Tritle PROS RC 1.50 .60
❑ 680 Nate Espy PROS 1.50 .60
❑ 681 Nick Alvarez PROS RC 1.50 .60
❑ 682 Jason Botts PROS RC 1.50 .60
❑ 683 Ryan Gripp PROS RC 1.50 .60
❑ 684 Dan Phillips PROS RC 1.50 .60
❑ 685 Pablo Arias PROS RC 1.50 .60
❑ 686 John Rodriguez PROS RC 2.50 1.00
❑ 687 Rich Harden PROS RC 8.00 3.00
❑ 688 Neal Frendling PROS RC 1.50 .60
❑ 689 Rich Thompson PROS RC 1.50 .60
❑ 690 Greg Montalbano PROS RC 1.50 .60
❑ 691 Len Dinardo DP RC 1.50 .60
❑ 692 Ryan Raburn DP RC 1.50 .60
❑ 693 Josh Barfield DP RC 5.00 2.00
❑ 694 David Bacani DP RC 1.50 .60
❑ 695 Dan Johnson DP RC 2.50 1.00

2002 Topps Chrome Traded

❑ COMPLETE SET (275) 120.00 60.00
❑ T1 Jeff Weaver .50 .20
❑ T2 Jay Powell .50 .20
❑ T3 Alex Gonzalez .50 .20
❑ T4 Jason Isringhausen .75 .30
❑ T5 Tyler Houston .50 .20
❑ T6 Ben Broussard .50 .20
❑ T7 Chuck Knoblauch .75 .30
❑ T8 Brian L. Hunter .50 .20
❑ T9 Dustan Mohr .50 .20
❑ T10 Eric Hinske .50 .20
❑ T11 Roger Cedeno .50 .20
❑ T12 Eddie Perez .50 .20
❑ T13 Jeromy Burnitz .75 .30
❑ T14 Bartolo Colon .75 .30
❑ T15 Rick Helling .50 .20
❑ T16 Dan Plesac .50 .20
❑ T17 Scott Strickland .50 .20
❑ T18 Antonio Alfonseca .50 .20
❑ T19 Ricky Gutierrez .50 .20
❑ T20 John Valentin .50 .20
❑ T21 Raul Mondesi .75 .30
❑ T22 Ben Davis .50 .20
❑ T23 Nelson Figueroa .50 .20
❑ T24 Earl Snyder .50 .20
❑ T25 Robin Ventura .75 .30
❑ T26 Jimmy Haynes .50 .20
❑ T27 Kenny Kelly .50 .20
❑ T28 Morgan Ensberg .75 .30
❑ T29 Reggie Sanders .75 .30
❑ T30 Shigetoshi Hasegawa .75 .30
❑ T31 Mike Timlin .50 .20
❑ T32 Russell Branyan .50 .20
❑ T33 Alan Embree .50 .20
❑ T34 D'Angelo Jimenez .50 .20
❑ T35 Kent Mercker .50 .20
❑ T36 Jesse Orosco .50 .20
❑ T37 Gregg Zaun .50 .20
❑ T38 Reggie Taylor .50 .20
❑ T39 Andres Galarraga .75 .30
❑ T40 Chris Truby .50 .20
❑ T41 Bruce Chen .50 .20
❑ T42 Darren Lewis .50 .20
❑ T43 Ryan Kohlmeier .50 .20
❑ T44 John McDonald .50 .20
❑ T45 Omar Daal .50 .20
❑ T46 Matt Clement .75 .30
❑ T47 Glendon Rusch .50 .20
❑ T48 Chan Ho Park .75 .30
❑ T49 Benny Agbayani .50 .20
❑ T50 Juan Gonzalez .75 .30
❑ T51 Carlos Baerga .50 .20
❑ T52 Tim Raines .75 .30
❑ T53 Kevin Appier .75 .30
❑ T54 Marty Cordova .50 .20
❑ T55 Jeff D'Amico .50 .20
❑ T56 Dmitri Young .75 .30
❑ T57 Roosevelt Brown .50 .20
❑ T58 Dustin Hermanson .50 .20
❑ T59 Jose Rijo .50 .20
❑ T60 Todd Ritchie .50 .20
❑ T61 Lee Stevens .50 .20

❑ T62 Placido Polanco .50 .20
❑ T63 Eric Young .50 .20
❑ T64 Chuck Finley .75 .30
❑ T65 Dicky Gonzalez .50 .20
❑ T66 Jose Macias .50 .20
❑ T67 Gabe Kapler .75 .30
❑ T68 Sandy Alomar Jr. .50 .20
❑ T69 Henry Blanco .50 .20
❑ T70 Julian Tavarez .50 .20
❑ T71 Paul Bako .50 .20
❑ T72 Scott Rolen 1.25 .50
❑ T73 Brian Jordan .75 .30
❑ T74 Rickey Henderson 2.00 .75
❑ T75 Kevin Mench .50 .20
❑ T76 Hideo Nomo 2.00 .75
❑ T77 Jeremy Giambi .50 .20
❑ T78 Brad Fullmer .50 .20
❑ T79 Carl Everett .75 .30
❑ T80 David Wells .75 .30
❑ T81 Aaron Sele .50 .20
❑ T82 Todd Hollandsworth .50 .20
❑ T83 Vicente Padilla .50 .20
❑ T84 Kenny Lofton .75 .30
❑ T85 Corky Miller .50 .20
❑ T86 Josh Fogg .50 .20
❑ T87 Cliff Floyd .75 .30
❑ T88 Craig Paquette .50 .20
❑ T89 Jay Payton .50 .20
❑ T90 Carlos Pena .50 .20
❑ T91 Juan Encarnacion .50 .20
❑ T92 Rey Sanchez .50 .20
❑ T93 Ryan Dempster .50 .20
❑ T94 Mario Encarnacion .50 .20
❑ T95 Jorge Julio .50 .20
❑ T96 John Mabry .50 .20
❑ T97 Todd Zeile .75 .30
❑ T98 Johnny Damon 1.25 .50
❑ T99 Deivi Cruz .50 .20
❑ T100 Gary Sheffield .75 .30
❑ T101 Ted Lilly .50 .20
❑ T102 Todd Van Poppel .50 .20
❑ T103 Shawn Estes .50 .20
❑ T104 Cesar Izturis .50 .20
❑ T105 Ron Coomer .50 .20
❑ T106 Grady Little MG RC .50 .20
❑ T107 Jimy Williams MGR .50 .20
❑ T108 Tony Pena MGR .50 .20
❑ T109 Frank Robinson MGR 1.25 .50
❑ T110 Ron Gardenhire MGR .50 .20
❑ T111 Dennis Tankersley .50 .20
❑ T112 Alejandro Cadena RC 1.00 .40
❑ T113 Justin Reid RC 1.00 .40
❑ T114 Nate Field RC 1.00 .40
❑ T115 Rene Reyes RC 1.00 .40
❑ T116 Nelson Castro RC 1.00 .40
❑ T117 Miguel Olivo .50 .20
❑ T118 David Espinosa .50 .20
❑ T119 Chris Bootcheck RC 1.00 .40
❑ T120 Rob Henkel RC 1.00 .40
❑ T121 Steve Bechler RC 1.00 .40
❑ T122 Mark Outlaw RC 1.00 .40
❑ T123 Henry Pichardo RC 1.00 .40
❑ T124 Michael Floyd RC 1.00 .40
❑ T125 Richard Lane RC 1.00 .40
❑ T126 Pete Zamora RC 1.00 .40
❑ T127 Javier Colina .50 .20
❑ T128 Greg Sain RC 1.00 .40
❑ T129 Ronnie Merrill .50 .20
❑ T130 Gavin Floyd RC 2.50 1.00
❑ T131 Josh Bonifay RC 1.00 .40
❑ T132 Tommy Marx RC 1.00 .40
❑ T133 Gary Cates Jr. RC 1.00 .40
❑ T134 Neal Cotts RC 2.50 1.00
❑ T135 Angel Berroa .50 .20
❑ T136 Elio Serrano RC 1.00 .40
❑ T137 J.J. Putz RC 1.25 .50
❑ T138 Ruben Gotay RC 1.25 .50
❑ T139 Eddie Rogers .50 .20
❑ T140 Wily Mo Pena .75 .30
❑ T141 Tyler Yates RC 1.00 .40
❑ T142 Colin Young RC .75 .30
❑ T143 Chance Caple .50 .20
❑ T144 Ben Howard RC 1.00 .40
❑ T145 Ryan Bukvich RC 1.00 .40
❑ T146 Cliff Bartosh RC 1.00 .40
❑ T147 Brandon Claussen .50 .20
❑ T148 Cristian Guerrero .50 .20
❑ T149 Derrick Lewis .50 .20
❑ T150 Eric Miller RC 1.00 .40
❑ T151 Justin Huber RC 2.00 .75
❑ T152 Adrian Gonzalez .50 .20
❑ T153 Brian West RC 1.00 .40
❑ T154 Chris Baker RC 1.00 .40
❑ T155 Drew Henson .50 .20
❑ T156 Scott Hairston RC 1.25 .50
❑ T157 Jason Simontacchi RC 1.00 .40
❑ T158 Jason Arnold RC 1.00 .40
❑ T159 Brandon Phillips .50 .20
❑ T160 Adam Roller RC 1.00 .40
❑ T161 Scotty Layfield RC 1.00 .40
❑ T162 Freddie Money RC 1.00 .40
❑ T163 Noochie Varner RC 1.00 .40
❑ T164 Terrance Hill RC 1.00 .40
❑ T165 Jeremy Hill RC 1.00 .40
❑ T166 Carlos Cabrera RC 1.00 .40
❑ T167 Jose Morban RC 1.00 .40
❑ T168 Kevin Frederick RC 1.00 .40
❑ T169 Mark Teixeira 4.00 1.50
❑ T170 Brian Rogers .50 .20
❑ T171 Anastacio Martinez RC 1.00 .40
❑ T172 Bobby Jenks RC 4.00 1.50
❑ T173 David Gil RC 1.00 .40
❑ T174 Andres Torres .50 .20
❑ T175 James Barrett RC 1.00 .40
❑ T176 Jimmy Journell .50 .20
❑ T177 Brett Kay RC 1.00 .40
❑ T178 Jason Young RC 1.00 .40
❑ T179 Mark Hamilton RC 1.00 .40
❑ T180 Jose Bautista RC 2.50 1.00
❑ T181 Blake McGinley RC 1.00 .40
❑ T182 Ryan Mottl RC 1.00 .40
❑ T183 Jeff Austin RC 1.00 .40
❑ T184 Xavier Nady .50 .20
❑ T185 Kyle Kane RC 1.00 .40
❑ T186 Travis Foley RC 1.00 .40
❑ T187 Nathan Kaup RC 1.00 .40
❑ T188 Eric Cyr .50 .20
❑ T189 Josh Cisneros RC 1.00 .40
❑ T190 Brad Nelson RC 1.00 .40
❑ T191 Clint Weibl RC 1.00 .40
❑ T192 Ron Calloway RC 1.00 .40
❑ T193 Jung Bong .50 .20
❑ T194 Rolando Viera RC 1.00 .40
❑ T195 Jason Bulger RC 1.00 .40
❑ T196 Chone Figgins RC 4.00 1.50
❑ T197 Jimmy Alvarez RC 1.00 .40
❑ T198 Joel Crump RC 1.00 .40
❑ T199 Ryan Doumit RC 1.50 .60
❑ T200 Demetrius Heath RC 1.00 .40
❑ T201 John Ennis RC 1.00 .40
❑ T202 Doug Sessions RC 1.00 .40
❑ T203 Clinton Hosford RC 1.00 .40
❑ T204 Chris Narveson RC 1.00 .40
❑ T205 Ross Peeples RC 1.00 .40
❑ T206 Alex Requena RC 1.00 .40
❑ T207 Matt Erickson RC 1.00 .40
❑ T208 Brian Forystek RC 1.00 .40
❑ T209 Dewon Brazelton .50 .20
❑ T210 Nathan Haynes .50 .20
❑ T211 Jack Cust .50 .20
❑ T212 Jesse Foppert RC 1.25 .50
❑ T213 Jesus Cota RC 1.00 .40
❑ T214 Juan M. Gonzalez RC 1.00 .40
❑ T215 Tim Kalita RC 1.00 .40
❑ T216 Manny Delcarmen RC 1.25 .50
❑ T217 Jim Kavourias RC 1.00 .40
❑ T218 C.J. Wilson RC 1.00 .40
❑ T219 Edwin Yan RC 1.00 .40
❑ T220 Andy Van Hekken .50 .20
❑ T221 Michael Cuddyer .50 .20
❑ T222 Jeff Verplancke RC 1.00 .40
❑ T223 Mike Wilson RC 1.00 .40
❑ T224 Corwin Malone RC 1.00 .40
❑ T225 Chris Snelling RC 1.50 .60
❑ T226 Joe Rogers RC 1.00 .40
❑ T227 Jason Bay 8.00 3.00
❑ T228 Ezequiel Astacio RC 1.00 .40
❑ T229 Joey Hammond RC 1.00 .40
❑ T230 Chris Duffy RC 2.00 .75
❑ T231 Mark Prior 1.25 .50
❑ T232 Hansel Izquierdo RC 1.00 .40
❑ T233 Franklyn German RC 1.00 .40
❑ T234 Alexis Gomez .50 .20
❑ T235 Jorge Padilla RC 1.00 .40
❑ T236 Ryan Snare RC 1.00 .40
❑ T237 Deivis Santos .50 .20
❑ T238 Taggert Bozied RC 1.25 .50
❑ T239 Mike Peeples RC 1.00 .40
❑ T240 Ronald Acuna RC 1.00 .40
❑ T241 Koyie Hill .50 .20
❑ T242 Garrett Guzman RC 1.00 .40
❑ T243 Ryan Church RC 2.50 1.00
❑ T244 Tony Fontana RC 1.00 .40
❑ T245 Keto Anderson RC 1.00 .40
❑ T246 Brad Bouras RC 1.00 .40
❑ T247 Jason Dubois RC 1.25 .50
❑ T248 Angel Guzman RC 2.00 .75
❑ T249 Joel Hanrahan RC 1.00 .40
❑ T250 Joe Jiannetti RC 1.00 .40
❑ T251 Sean Pierce RC 1.00 .40
❑ T252 Jake Mauer RC 1.00 .40
❑ T253 Marshall McDougall RC 1.00 .40
❑ T254 Edwin Almonte RC 1.00 .40
❑ T255 Shawn Riggans RC 1.00 .40
❑ T256 Steven Shell RC 1.00 .40
❑ T257 Kevin Hooper RC 1.00 .40
❑ T258 Michael Frick RC 1.00 .40
❑ T259 Travis Chapman RC 1.00 .40
❑ T260 Tim Hummel RC 1.00 .40
❑ T261 Adam Morrissey RC 1.00 .40
❑ T262 Dontrelle Willis RC 10.00 4.00
❑ T263 Justin Sherrod RC 1.00 .40
❑ T264 Gerald Smiley RC 1.00 .40
❑ T265 Tony Miller RC 1.00 .40
❑ T266 Nolan Ryan WW 5.00 2.00
❑ T267 Reggie Jackson WW 1.25 .50
❑ T268 Steve Garvey WW .75 .30
❑ T269 Wade Boggs WW 1.25 .50
❑ T270 Sammy Sosa WW 2.00 .75
❑ T271 Curt Schilling WW .75 .30
❑ T272 Mark Grace WW 1.25 .50
❑ T273 Jason Giambi WW .50 .20
❑ T274 Ken Griffey Jr. WW 3.00 1.25
❑ T275 Roberto Alomar WW 1.25 .50

2003 Topps Chrome

❑ COMPLETE SET (440) 200.00 80.00
❑ COMPLETE SERIES 1 (220) 100.00 40.00
❑ COMPLETE SERIES 2 (220) 100.00 40.00
❑ COMMON (1-200/221-420) 1.00 .40
❑ COMMON (201-220/421-440) 1.50 .60
❑ 1 Alex Rodriguez 4.00 1.50
❑ 2 Eddie Guardado 1.00 .40
❑ 3 Curt Schilling 1.00 .40
❑ 4 Andruw Jones 1.50 .60
❑ 5 Maggio Ordonez 1.00 .40
❑ 6 Todd Helton 1.50 .60
❑ 7 Odalis Perez 1.00 .40
❑ 8 Edgardo Alfonzo 1.00 .40
❑ 9 Eric Hinske 1.00 .40
❑ 10 Danny Bautista 1.00 .40
❑ 11 Sammy Sosa 2.50 1.00
❑ 12 Roberto Alomar 1.50 .60
❑ 13 Roger Clemens 5.00 2.00
❑ 14 Austin Kearns 1.00 .40
❑ 15 Luis Gonzalez 1.00 .40
❑ 16 Mo Vaughn 1.00 .40
❑ 17 Alfonso Soriano 1.00 .40
❑ 18 Orlando Cabrera 1.00 .40
❑ 19 Hideo Nomo 2.50 1.00

20	Omar Vizquel	1.50	.60
21	Greg Maddux	4.00	1.50
22	Fred McGriff	1.50	.60
23	Frank Thomas	2.50	1.00
24	Shawn Green	1.00	.40
25	Jacque Jones	1.00	.40
26	Bernie Williams	1.50	.60
27	Corey Patterson	1.00	.40
28	Cesar Izturis	1.00	.40
29	Larry Walker	1.00	.40
30	Darren Dreifort	1.00	.40
31	Al Leiter	1.00	.40
32	Jason Marquis	1.00	.40
33	Sean Casey	1.00	.40
34	Craig Counsell	1.00	.40
35	Albert Pujols	5.00	2.00
36	Kyle Lohse	1.00	.40
37	Paul Lo Duca	1.00	.40
38	Roy Oswalt	1.00	.40
39	Danny Graves	1.00	.40
40	Kevin Millwood	1.00	.40
41	Lance Berkman	1.00	.40
42	Denny Hocking	1.00	.40
43	Jose Valentin	1.00	.40
44	Josh Beckett	1.00	.40
45	Nomar Garciaparra	4.00	1.50
46	Craig Biggio	1.50	.60
47	Omar Daal	1.00	.40
48	Jimmy Rollins	1.00	.40
49	Jermaine Dye	1.00	.40
50	Edgar Renteria	1.00	.40
51	Brandon Duckworth	1.00	.40
52	Luis Castillo	1.00	.40
53	Andy Ashby	1.00	.40
54	Mike Williams	1.00	.40
55	Benito Santiago	1.00	.40
56	Bret Boone	1.00	.40
57	Randy Wolf	1.00	.40
58	Ivan Rodriguez	1.50	.60
59	Shannon Stewart	1.00	.40
60	Jose Cruz Jr.	1.00	.40
61	Billy Wagner	1.00	.40
62	Alex Gonzalez	1.00	.40
63	Ichiro Suzuki	5.00	2.00
64	Joe McEwing	1.00	.40
65	Mark Mulder	1.00	.40
66	Mike Cameron	1.00	.40
67	Corey Koskie	1.00	.40
68	Marlon Anderson	1.00	.40
69	Jason Kendall	1.00	.40
70	J.T. Snow	1.00	.40
71	Edgar Martinez	1.50	.60
72	Vernon Wells	1.00	.40
73	Vladimir Guerrero	2.50	1.00
74	Adam Dunn	1.00	.40
75	Barry Zito	1.00	.40
76	Jeff Kent	1.00	.40
77	Russ Ortiz	1.00	.40
78	Phil Nevin	1.00	.40
79	Carlos Beltran	1.00	.40
80	Mike Lowell	1.00	.40
81	Bob Wickman	1.00	.40
82	Junior Spivey	1.00	.40
83	Melvin Mora	1.00	.40
84	Derrek Lee	1.50	.60
85	Chuck Knoblauch	1.00	.40
86	Eric Gagne	1.00	.40
87	Orlando Hernandez	1.00	.40
88	Robert Person	1.00	.40
89	Elmer Dessens	1.00	.40
90	Wade Miller	1.00	.40
91	Adrian Beltre	1.00	.40
92	Kazuhiro Sasaki	1.00	.40
93	Timo Perez	1.00	.40
94	Jose Vidro	1.00	.40
95	Geronimo Gil	1.00	.40
96	Trot Nixon	1.00	.40
97	Denny Neagle	1.00	.40
98	Roberto Hernandez	1.00	.40
99	David Ortiz	2.50	1.00
100	Robb Nen	1.00	.40
101	Sidney Ponson	1.00	.40
102	Kevin Appier	1.00	.40
103	Javier Lopez	1.00	.40
104	Jeff Conine	1.00	.40
105	Mark Buehrle	1.00	.40
106	Jason Simontacchi	1.00	.40
107	Jose Jimenez	1.00	.40
108	Brian Jordan	1.00	.40
109	Brad Wilkerson	1.00	.40
110	Scott Hatteberg	1.00	.40
111	Matt Morris	1.00	.40
112	Miguel Tejada	1.00	.40
113	Rafael Furcal	1.00	.40
114	Steve Cox	1.00	.40
115	Roy Halladay	1.00	.40
116	David Eckstein	1.00	.40
117	Tomo Ohka	1.00	.40
118	Jack Wilson	1.00	.40
119	Randall Simon	1.00	.40
120	Jamie Moyer	1.00	.40
121	Andy Benes	1.00	.40
122	Tino Martinez	1.50	.60
123	Esteban Yan	1.00	.40
124	Jason Isringhausen	1.00	.40
125	Chris Carpenter	1.00	.40
126	Aaron Rowand	1.00	.40
127	Brandon Inge	1.00	.40
128	Jose Vizcaino	1.00	.40
129	Jose Mesa	1.00	.40
130	Troy Percival	1.00	.40
131	Jon Lieber	1.00	.40
132	Brian Giles	1.00	.40
133	Aaron Boone	1.00	.40
134	Bobby Higginson	1.00	.40
135	Luis Rivas	1.00	.40
136	Troy Glaus	1.00	.40
137	Jim Thome	1.50	.60
138	Ramon Martinez	1.00	.40
139	Jay Gibbons	1.00	.40
140	Mike Lieberthal	1.00	.40
141	Juan Uribe	1.00	.40
142	Gary Sheffield	1.00	.40
143	Ramon Santiago	1.00	.40
144	Ben Sheets	1.00	.40
145	Tony Armas Jr.	1.00	.40
146	Kazuhisa Ishii	1.00	.40
147	Erubiel Durazo	1.00	.40
148	Jerry Hairston Jr.	1.00	.40
149	Byung-Hyun Kim	1.00	.40
150	Marcus Giles	1.00	.40
151	Johnny Damon	1.50	.60
152	Terrence Long	1.00	.40
153	Juan Pierre	1.00	.40
154	Aramis Ramirez	1.00	.40
155	Brent Abernathy	1.00	.40
156	Ismael Valdes	1.00	.40
157	Mike Mussina	1.50	.60
158	Ramon Hernandez	1.00	.40
159	Adam Kennedy	1.00	.40
160	Tony Womack	1.00	.40
161	Tony Batista	1.00	.40
162	Kip Wells	1.00	.40
163	Jeromy Burnitz	1.00	.40
164	Todd Hundley	1.00	.40
165	Tim Wakefield	1.00	.40
166	Derek Lowe	1.00	.40
167	Jorge Posada	1.50	.60
168	Ramon Ortiz	1.00	.40
169	Brent Butler	1.00	.40
170	Shane Halter	1.00	.40
171	Matt Lawton	1.00	.40
172	Alex Sanchez	1.00	.40
173	Eric Milton	1.00	.40
174	Vicente Padilla	1.00	.40
175	Steve Karsay	1.00	.40
176	Mark Prior	1.50	.60
177	Kerry Wood	1.00	.40
178	Jason LaRue	1.00	.40
179	Danys Baez	1.00	.40
180	Nick Neugebauer	1.00	.40
181	Andres Galarraga	1.00	.40
182	Jason Giambi	1.00	.40
183	Aubrey Huff	1.00	.40
184	Juan Gonzalez	1.00	.40
185	Ugueth Urbina	1.00	.40
186	Rickey Henderson	2.50	1.00
187	Brad Fullmer	1.00	.40
188	Todd Zeile	1.00	.40
189	Jason Jennings	1.00	.40
190	Vladimir Nunez	1.00	.40
191	David Justice	1.00	.40
192	Brian Lawrence	1.00	.40
193	Pat Burrell	1.00	.40
194	Pokey Reese	1.00	.40
195	Robert Fick	1.00	.40
196	C.C. Sabathia	1.00	.40
197	Fernando Vina	1.00	.40
198	Sean Burroughs	1.00	.40
199	Ellis Burks	1.00	.40
200	Joe Randa	1.00	.40
201	Chris Duncan FY RC	6.00	2.50
202	Franklin Gutierrez FY RC	3.00	1.25
203	Adam LaRoche FY	1.50	.60
204	Manuel Ramirez FY RC	2.50	1.00
205	Il Kim FY RC	1.50	.60
206	Daryl Clark FY RC	1.50	.60
207	Sean Pierce FY	1.50	.60
208	Andy Marte FY RC	8.00	3.00
209	Bernie Castro FY RC	1.50	.60
210	Jason Perry FY RC	2.50	1.00
211	Jaime Bubela FY RC	1.50	.60
212	Alexis Rios FY	2.50	1.00
213	Brendan Harris FY RC	2.50	1.00
214	Ramon Nivar-Martinez FY RC	1.50	.60
215	Terry Tiffee FY RC	1.50	.60
216	Kevin Youkilis FY RC	4.00	1.50
217	Derell McCall FY RC	1.50	.60
218	Scott Tyler FY RC	2.50	1.00
219	Craig Brazell FY RC	1.50	.60
220	Walter Young FY	1.50	.60
221	Francisco Rodriguez	1.00	.40
222	Chipper Jones	2.50	1.00
223	Chris Singleton	1.00	.40
224	Cliff Floyd	1.00	.40
225	Bobby Hill	1.00	.40
226	Antonio Osuna	1.00	.40
227	Barry Larkin	1.50	.60
228	Dean Palmer	1.00	.40
229	Eric Owens	1.00	.40
230	Randy Johnson	2.50	1.00
231	Jeff Suppan	1.00	.40
232	Eric Karros	1.00	.40
233	Johan Santana	1.50	.60
234	Javier Vazquez	1.00	.40
235	John Thomson	1.00	.40
236	Nick Johnson	1.00	.40
237	Mark Ellis	1.00	.40
238	Doug Glanville	1.00	.40
239	Ken Griffey Jr.	4.00	1.50
240	Bubba Trammell	1.00	.40
241	Livan Hernandez	1.00	.40
242	Desi Relaford	1.00	.40
243	Eli Marrero	1.00	.40
244	Jared Sandberg	1.00	.40
245	Barry Bonds	6.00	2.50
246	Aaron Sele	1.00	.40
247	Derek Jeter	6.00	2.50
248	Eric Byrnes	1.00	.40
249	Rich Aurilia	1.00	.40
250	Joel Pineiro	1.00	.40
251	Chuck Finley	1.00	.40
252	Bengie Molina	1.00	.40
253	Steve Finley	1.00	.40
254	Marty Cordova	1.00	.40
255	Shea Hillenbrand	1.00	.40
256	Milton Bradley	1.00	.40
257	Carlos Pena	1.00	.40
258	Brad Ausmus	1.00	.40
259	Carlos Delgado	1.00	.40
260	Kevin Mench	1.00	.40
261	Joe Kennedy	1.00	.40
262	Mark McLemore	1.00	.40
263	Bill Mueller	1.00	.40
264	Ricky Ledee	1.00	.40
265	Ted Lilly	1.00	.40
266	Sterling Hitchcock	1.00	.40
267	Scott Strickland	1.00	.40
268	Damion Easley	1.00	.40
269	Torii Hunter	1.00	.40
270	Brad Radke	1.00	.40
271	Geoff Jenkins	1.00	.40
272	Paul Byrd	1.00	.40
273	Morgan Ensberg	1.00	.40
274	Mike Maroth	1.00	.40
275	Mike Hampton	1.00	.40
276	Flash Gordon	1.00	.40
277	John Burkett	1.00	.40

❑ 278 Rodrigo Lopez 1.00 .40
❑ 279 Tim Spooneybarger 1.00 .40
❑ 280 Quinton McCracken 1.00 .40
❑ 281 Tim Salmon 1.50 .60
❑ 282 Jarrod Washburn 1.00 .40
❑ 283 Pedro Martinez 1.50 .60
❑ 284 Julio Lugo 1.00 .40
❑ 285 Armando Benitez 1.00 .40
❑ 286 Raul Mondesi 1.00 .40
❑ 287 Robin Ventura 1.00 .40
❑ 288 Bobby Abreu 1.00 .40
❑ 289 Josh Fogg 1.00 .40
❑ 290 Ryan Klesko 1.00 .40
❑ 291 Tsuyoshi Shinjo 1.00 .40
❑ 292 Jim Edmonds 1.00 .40
❑ 293 Chan Ho Park 1.00 .40
❑ 294 John Mabry 1.00 .40
❑ 295 Woody Williams 1.00 .40
❑ 296 Scott Schoeneweis 1.00 .40
❑ 297 Brian Anderson 1.00 .40
❑ 298 Brett Tomko 1.00 .40
❑ 299 Scott Erickson 1.00 .40
❑ 300 Kevin Millar Sox 1.00 .40
❑ 301 Danny Wright 1.00 .40
❑ 302 Jason Schmidt 1.00 .40
❑ 303 Scott Williamson 1.00 .40
❑ 304 Einar Diaz 1.00 .40
❑ 305 Jay Payton 1.00 .40
❑ 306 Juan Acevedo 1.00 .40
❑ 307 Ben Grieve 1.00 .40
❑ 308 Raul Ibanez 1.00 .40
❑ 309 Richie Sexson 1.00 .40
❑ 310 Rick Reed 1.00 .40
❑ 311 Pedro Astacio 1.00 .40
❑ 312 Bud Smith 1.00 .40
❑ 313 Tomas Perez 1.00 .40
❑ 314 Rafael Palmeiro 1.50 .60
❑ 315 Jason Tyner 1.00 .40
❑ 316 Scott Rolen 1.50 .60
❑ 317 Randy Winn 1.00 .40
❑ 318 Ryan Jensen 1.00 .40
❑ 319 Trevor Hoffman 1.00 .40
❑ 320 Craig Wilson 1.00 .40
❑ 321 Jeremy Giambi 1.00 .40
❑ 322 Andy Pettitte 1.50 .60
❑ 323 John Franco 1.00 .40
❑ 324 Felipe Lopez 1.00 .40
❑ 325 Mike Piazza 4.00 1.50
❑ 326 Cristian Guzman 1.00 .40
❑ 327 Jose Hernandez 1.00 .40
❑ 328 Octavio Dotel 1.00 .40
❑ 329 Brad Penny 1.00 .40
❑ 330 Dave Veres 1.00 .40
❑ 331 Ryan Dempster 1.00 .40
❑ 332 Joe Crede 1.00 .40
❑ 333 Chad Hermansen 1.00 .40
❑ 334 Gary Matthews Jr. 1.00 .40
❑ 335 Frank Catalanotto 1.00 .40
❑ 336 Darin Erstad 1.00 .40
❑ 337 Matt Williams 1.00 .40
❑ 338 B.J. Surhoff 1.00 .40
❑ 339 Kerry Ligtenberg 1.00 .40
❑ 340 Mike Bordick 1.00 .40
❑ 341 Joe Girardi 1.00 .40
❑ 342 D'Angelo Jimenez 1.00 .40
❑ 343 Paul Konerko 1.00 .40
❑ 344 Joe Mays 1.00 .40
❑ 345 Marquis Grissom 1.00 .40
❑ 346 Neifi Perez 1.00 .40
❑ 347 Preston Wilson 1.00 .40
❑ 348 Jeff Weaver 1.00 .40
❑ 349 Eric Chavez 1.00 .40
❑ 350 Placido Polanco 1.00 .40
❑ 351 Matt Mantei 1.00 .40
❑ 352 James Baldwin 1.00 .40
❑ 353 Toby Hall 1.00 .40
❑ 354 Benji Gil 1.00 .40
❑ 355 Damian Moss 1.00 .40
❑ 356 Jorge Julio 1.00 .40
❑ 357 Matt Clement 1.00 .40
❑ 358 Lee Stevens 1.00 .40
❑ 359 Dave Roberts 1.00 .40
❑ 360 J.C. Romero 1.00 .40
❑ 361 Bartolo Colon 1.00 .40
❑ 362 Roger Cedeno 1.00 .40
❑ 363 Mariano Rivera 2.50 1.00
❑ 364 Billy Koch 1.00 .40
❑ 365 Manny Ramirez 1.50 .60
❑ 366 Travis Lee 1.00 .40
❑ 367 Oliver Perez 1.00 .40
❑ 368 Tim Worrell 1.00 .40
❑ 369 Damian Miller 1.00 .40
❑ 370 John Smoltz 1.50 .60
❑ 371 Willis Roberts 1.00 .40
❑ 372 Tim Hudson 1.00 .40
❑ 373 Moises Alou 1.00 .40
❑ 374 Corky Miller 1.00 .40
❑ 375 Ben Broussard 1.00 .40
❑ 376 Gabe Kapler 1.00 .40
❑ 377 Chris Woodward 1.00 .40
❑ 378 Todd Hollandsworth 1.00 .40
❑ 379 So Taguchi 1.00 .40
❑ 380 John Olerud 1.00 .40
❑ 381 Reggie Sanders 1.00 .40
❑ 382 Jake Peavy 1.00 .40
❑ 383 Kris Benson 1.00 .40
❑ 384 Ray Durham 1.00 .40
❑ 385 Boomer Wells 1.00 .40
❑ 386 Tom Glavine 1.50 .60
❑ 387 Antonio Alfonseca 1.00 .40
❑ 388 Keith Foulke 1.00 .40
❑ 389 Shawn Estes 1.00 .40
❑ 390 Mark Grace 1.50 .60
❑ 391 Dmitri Young 1.00 .40
❑ 392 A.J. Burnett 1.00 .40
❑ 393 Richard Hidalgo 1.00 .40
❑ 394 Mike Sweeney 1.00 .40
❑ 395 Doug Mientkiewicz 1.00 .40
❑ 396 Cory Lidle 1.00 .40
❑ 397 Jeff Bagwell 1.50 .60
❑ 398 Steve Sparks 1.00 .40
❑ 399 Sandy Alomar Jr. 1.00 .40
❑ 400 John Lackey 1.00 .40
❑ 401 Rick Helling 1.00 .40
❑ 402 Carlos Lee 1.00 .40
❑ 403 Garret Anderson 1.00 .40
❑ 404 Vinny Castilla 1.00 .40
❑ 405 David Bell 1.00 .40
❑ 406 Freddy Garcia 1.00 .40
❑ 407 Scott Spiezio 1.00 .40
❑ 408 Russell Branyan 1.00 .40
❑ 409 Jose Contreras RC 3.00 1.25
❑ 410 Kevin Brown 1.00 .40
❑ 411 Tyler Houston 1.00 .40
❑ 412 A.J. Pierzynski 1.00 .40
❑ 413 Peter Bergeron 1.00 .40
❑ 414 Brett Myers 1.00 .40
❑ 415 Kenny Lofton 1.00 .40
❑ 416 Ben Davis 1.00 .40
❑ 417 J.D. Drew 1.00 .40
❑ 418 Ricky Gutierrez 1.00 .40
❑ 419 Mark Redman 1.00 .40
❑ 420 Juan Encarnacion 1.00 .40
❑ 421 Bryan Bullington DP RC 1.50 .60
❑ 422 Jeremy Guthrie DP 1.50 .60
❑ 423 Joey Gomes DP RC 1.50 .60
❑ 424 Evel Bastida-Martinez DP RC 1.50 .60
❑ 425 Brian Wright DP RC 1.50 .60
❑ 426 B.J. Upton DP 2.50 1.00
❑ 427 Jeff Francis DP 1.50 .60
❑ 428 Jeremy Hermida DP 2.50 1.00
❑ 429 Khalil Greene DP 2.50 1.00
❑ 430 Darrell Rasner DP RC 1.50 .60
❑ 431 B.Phillips/V.Martinez 2.50 1.00
❑ 432 H.Choi/N.Jackson 1.50 .60
❑ 433 D.Willis/J.Stokes 2.50 1.00
❑ 434 C.Tracy/L.Overbay 1.50 .60
❑ 435 J.Borchard/C.Malone 1.50 .60
❑ 436 J.Mauer/J.Morneau 2.50 1.00
❑ 437 D.Henson/B.Claussen 1.50 .60
❑ 438 C.Utley/G.Floyd 2.50 1.00
❑ 439 T.Bozied/X.Nady 1.50 .60
❑ 440 A.Heilman/J.Reyes 1.50 .60

2003 Topps Chrome Traded

❑ COMPLETE SET (275) 120.00 60.00
❑ COMMON CARD (T1-T120) .75 .30
❑ COMMON CARD (121-165) 1.00 .40
❑ COMMON CARD (166-275) 1.00 .40
❑ 2 PER 2003 TOPPS TRADED HOBBY PACK
❑ 2 PER 2003 TOPPS TRADED HTA PACK
❑ 2 PER 2003 TOPPS TRADED RETAIL PACK
❑ T1 Juan Pierre .75 .30
❑ T2 Mark Grudzielanek .75 .30
❑ T3 Tanyon Sturtze .75 .30
❑ T4 Greg Vaughn .75 .30
❑ T5 Greg Myers .75 .30
❑ T6 Randall Simon .75 .30
❑ T7 Todd Hundley .75 .30
❑ T8 Marlon Anderson .75 .30
❑ T9 Jeff Reboulet .75 .30
❑ T10 Alex Sanchez .75 .30
❑ T11 Mike Rivera .75 .30
❑ T12 Todd Walker .75 .30
❑ T13 Ray King .75 .30
❑ T14 Shawn Estes .75 .30
❑ T15 Gary Matthews Jr. .75 .30
❑ T16 Jaret Wright .75 .30
❑ T17 Edgardo Alfonzo .75 .30
❑ T18 Omar Daal .75 .30
❑ T19 Ryan Rupe .75 .30
❑ T20 Tony Clark .75 .30
❑ T21 Jeff Suppan .75 .30
❑ T22 Mike Stanton .75 .30
❑ T23 Ramon Martinez .75 .30
❑ T24 Armando Rios .75 .30
❑ T25 Johnny Estrada .75 .30
❑ T26 Joe Girardi .75 .30
❑ T27 Ivan Rodriguez 1.25 .50
❑ T28 Robert Fick .75 .30
❑ T29 Rick White .75 .30
❑ T30 Robert Person .75 .30
❑ T31 Alan Benes .75 .30
❑ T32 Chris Carpenter .75 .30
❑ T33 Chris Widger .75 .30
❑ T34 Travis Hafner .75 .30
❑ T35 Mike Venafro .75 .30
❑ T36 Jon Lieber .75 .30
❑ T37 Orlando Hernandez .75 .30
❑ T38 Aaron Myette .75 .30
❑ T39 Paul Bako .75 .30
❑ T40 Erubiel Durazo .75 .30
❑ T41 Mark Guthrie .75 .30
❑ T42 Steve Avery .75 .30
❑ T43 Damian Jackson .75 .30
❑ T44 Rey Ordonez .75 .30
❑ T45 John Flaherty .75 .30
❑ T46 Byung-Hyun Kim .75 .30
❑ T47 Tom Goodwin .75 .30
❑ T48 Elmer Dessens .75 .30
❑ T49 Al Martin .75 .30
❑ T50 Gene Kingsale .75 .30
❑ T51 Lenny Harris .75 .30
❑ T52 David Ortiz Sox 2.00 .75
❑ T53 Jose Lima .75 .30
❑ T54 Mike Difelice .75 .30
❑ T55 Jose Hernandez .75 .30
❑ T56 Todd Zeile .75 .30
❑ T57 Roberto Hernandez .75 .30
❑ T58 Albie Lopez .75 .30
❑ T59 Roberto Alomar 1.25 .50
❑ T60 Russ Ortiz .75 .30
❑ T61 Brian Daubach .75 .30
❑ T62 Carl Everett .75 .30
❑ T63 Jeromy Burnitz .75 .30
❑ T64 Mark Bellhorn .75 .30
❑ T65 Ruben Sierra .75 .30
❑ T66 Mike Fetters .75 .30

	Card	Player		
❑	T67	Armando Benitez	.75	.30
❑	T68	Deivi Cruz	.75	.30
❑	T69	Jose Cruz Jr.	.75	.30
❑	T70	Jeremy Fikac	.75	.30
❑	T71	Jeff Kent	.75	.30
❑	T72	Andres Galarraga	.75	.30
❑	T73	Rickey Henderson	2.00	.75
❑	T74	Royce Clayton	.75	.30
❑	T75	Troy O'Leary	.75	.30
❑	T76	Ron Coomer	.75	.30
❑	T77	Greg Colbrunn	.75	.30
❑	T78	Wes Helms	.75	.30
❑	T79	Kevin Millwood	.75	.30
❑	T80	Damion Easley	.75	.30
❑	T81	Bobby Kielty	.75	.30
❑	T82	Keith Osik	.75	.30
❑	T83	Ramiro Mendoza	.75	.30
❑	T84	Shea Hillenbrand	.75	.30
❑	T85	Shannon Stewart	.75	.30
❑	T86	Eddie Perez	.75	.30
❑	T87	Ugueth Urbina	.75	.30
❑	T88	Orlando Palmeiro	.75	.30
❑	T89	Graeme Lloyd	.75	.30
❑	T90	John Vander Wal	.75	.30
❑	T91	Gary Bennett	.75	.30
❑	T92	Shane Reynolds	.75	.30
❑	T93	Steve Parris	.75	.30
❑	T94	Julio Lugo	.75	.30
❑	T95	John Halama	.75	.30
❑	T96	Carlos Baerga	.75	.30
❑	T97	Jim Parque	.75	.30
❑	T98	Mike Williams	.75	.30
❑	T99	Fred McGriff	1.25	.50
❑	T100	Kenny Rogers	.75	.30
❑	T101	Matt Herges	.75	.30
❑	T102	Jay Bell	.75	.30
❑	T103	Esteban Yan	.75	.30
❑	T104	Eric Owens	.75	.30
❑	T105	Aaron Fultz	.75	.30
❑	T106	Rey Sanchez	.75	.30
❑	T107	Jim Thome	1.25	.50
❑	T108	Aaron Boone	.75	.30
❑	T109	Raul Mondesi	.75	.30
❑	T110	Kenny Lofton	.75	.30
❑	T111	Jose Guillen	.75	.30
❑	T112	Aramis Ramirez	.75	.30
❑	T113	Sidney Ponson	.75	.30
❑	T114	Scott Williamson	.75	.30
❑	T115	Robin Ventura	.75	.30
❑	T116	Dusty Baker MG	.75	.30
❑	T117	Felipe Alou MG	.75	.30
❑	T118	Buck Showalter MG	.75	.30
❑	T119	Jack McKeon MG	.75	.30
❑	T120	Art Howe MG	.75	.30
❑	T121	Bobby Crosby PROS	1.00	.40
❑	T122	Adrian Gonzalez PROS	1.00	.40
❑	T123	Kevin Cash PROS	1.00	.40
❑	T124	Shin-Soo Choo PROS	1.00	.40
❑	T125	Chin-Feng Chen PROS	2.50	1.00
❑	T126	Miguel Cabrera PROS	2.50	1.00
❑	T127	Jason Young PROS	1.00	.40
❑	T128	Alex Herrera PROS	1.00	.40
❑	T129	Jason Dubois PROS	1.00	.40
❑	T130	Jeff Mathis PROS	1.00	.40
❑	T131	Casey Kotchman PROS	1.00	.40
❑	T132	Ed Rogers PROS	1.00	.40
❑	T133	Wilson Betemit PROS	1.00	.40
❑	T134	Jim Kavourias PROS	1.00	.40
❑	T135	Taylor Buchholz PROS	1.00	.40
❑	T136	Adam LaRoche PROS	1.00	.40
❑	T137	Dallas McPherson PROS	1.00	.40
❑	T138	Jesus Cota PROS	1.00	.40
❑	T139	Clint Nageotte PROS	1.00	.40
❑	T140	Boof Bonser PROS	1.00	.40
❑	T141	Walter Young PROS	1.00	.40
❑	T142	Joe Crede PROS	1.00	.40
❑	T143	Denny Bautista PROS	1.00	.40
❑	T144	Victor Diaz PROS	1.00	.40
❑	T145	Chris Narveson PROS	1.00	.40
❑	T146	Gabe Gross PROS	1.00	.40
❑	T147	Jimmy Journell PROS	1.00	.40
❑	T148	Rafael Soriano PROS	1.00	.40
❑	T149	Jerome Williams PROS	1.00	.40
❑	T150	Aaron Cook PROS	1.00	.40
❑	T151	Anastacio Martinez PROS	1.00	.40
❑	T152	Scott Hairston PROS	1.00	.40
❑	T153	John Buck PROS	1.00	.40
❑	T154	Ryan Ludwick PROS	1.00	.40
❑	T155	Chris Bootcheck PROS	1.00	.40
❑	T156	John Rheinecker PROS	1.00	.40
❑	T157	Jason Lane PROS	1.00	.40
❑	T158	Shelley Duncan PROS	1.00	.40
❑	T159	Adam Wainwright PROS	1.00	.40
❑	T160	Jason Arnold PROS	1.00	.40
❑	T161	Jonny Gomes PROS	1.50	.60
❑	T162	James Loney PROS	1.25	.50
❑	T163	Mike Fontenot PROS	1.00	.40
❑	T164	Khalil Greene PROS	2.50	1.00
❑	T165	Sean Burnett PROS	1.00	.40
❑	T166	David Martinez FY RC	1.00	.40
❑	T167	Felix Pie FY RC	10.00	4.00
❑	T168	Joe Valentine FY RC	1.00	.40
❑	T169	Brandon Webb FY RC	6.00	2.50
❑	T170	Matt Diaz FY RC	1.50	.60
❑	T171	Lew Ford FY RC	1.25	.50
❑	T172	Jeremy Griffiths FY RC	1.00	.40
❑	T173	Matt Hensley FY RC	1.00	.40
❑	T174	Charlie Manning FY RC	1.00	.40
❑	T175	Elizardo Ramirez FY RC	1.25	.50
❑	T176	Greg Aquino FY RC	1.00	.40
❑	T177	Felix Sanchez FY RC	1.00	.40
❑	T178	Kelly Shoppach FY RC	2.00	.75
❑	T179	Bubba Nelson FY RC	1.25	.50
❑	T180	Mike Oâ ™Keefe FY RC	1.00	.40
❑	T181	Hanley Ramirez FY RC	8.00	3.00
❑	T182	Todd Wellemeyer FY RC	1.00	.40
❑	T183	Dustin Moseley FY RC	1.00	.40
❑	T184	Eric Crozier FY RC	1.25	.50
❑	T185	Ryan Shealy FY RC	5.00	2.00
❑	T186	Jeremy Bonderman FY RC	8.00	3.00
❑	T187	T.Story-Harden FY RC	1.00	.40
❑	T188	Dusty Brown FY RC	1.00	.40
❑	T189	Rob Hammock FY RC	1.00	.40
❑	T190	Jorge Piedra FY RC	1.25	.50
❑	T191	Chris De La Cruz FY RC	1.00	.40
❑	T192	Eli Whiteside FY RC	1.00	.40
❑	T193	Jason Kubel FY RC	3.00	1.25
❑	T194	Jon Schuerholz FY RC	1.00	.40
❑	T195	Stephen Randolph FY RC	1.00	.40
❑	T196	Andy Sisco FY RC	1.00	.40
❑	T197	Sean Smith FY RC	1.25	.50
❑	T198	Jon-Mark Sprowl FY RC	1.00	.40
❑	T199	Matt Kata FY RC	1.00	.40
❑	T200	Robinson Cano FY RC	12.00	5.00
❑	T201	Nook Logan FY RC	1.25	.50
❑	T202	Ben Francisco FY RC	1.00	.40
❑	T203	Arnie Munoz FY RC	1.00	.40
❑	T204	Ozzie Chavez FY RC	1.00	.40
❑	T205	Eric Riggs FY RC	1.25	.50
❑	T206	Beau Kemp FY RC	1.00	.40
❑	T207	Travis Wong FY RC	1.25	.50
❑	T208	Dustin Yount FY RC	1.25	.50
❑	T209	Brian McCann FY RC	12.00	5.00
❑	T210	Wilton Reynolds FY RC	1.25	.50
❑	T211	Matt Bruback FY RC	1.00	.40
❑	T212	Andrew Brown FY RC	1.25	.50
❑	T213	Edgar Gonzalez FY RC	1.00	.40
❑	T214	Eider Torres FY RC	1.00	.40
❑	T215	Aquilino Lopez FY RC	1.00	.40
❑	T216	Bobby Basham FY RC	1.00	.40
❑	T217	Tim Olson FY RC	1.00	.40
❑	T218	Nathan Panther FY RC	1.00	.40
❑	T219	Bryan Grace FY RC	1.00	.40
❑	T220	Dusty Gomon FY RC	1.25	.50
❑	T221	Wil Ledezma FY RC	1.00	.40
❑	T222	Josh Willingham FY RC	2.50	1.00
❑	T223	David Cash FY RC	1.00	.40
❑	T224	Oscar Villarreal FY RC	1.00	.40
❑	T225	Jeff Duncan FY RC	1.00	.40
❑	T226	Kade Johnson FY RC	1.00	.40
❑	T227	Luke Steidlmayer FY RC	1.00	.40
❑	T228	Brandon Watson FY RC	1.00	.40
❑	T229	Jose Morales FY RC	1.00	.40
❑	T230	Mike Gallo FY RC	1.00	.40
❑	T231	Tyler Adamczyk FY RC	1.00	.40
❑	T232	Adam Stern FY RC	1.00	.40
❑	T233	Brennan King FY RC	1.00	.40
❑	T234	Dan Haren FY RC	2.00	.75
❑	T235	Michel Hernandez FY RC	1.00	.40
❑	T236	Ben Fritz FY RC	1.00	.40
❑	T237	Clay Hensley FY RC	1.00	.40
❑	T238	Tyler Johnson FY RC	1.00	.40
❑	T239	Pete LaForest FY RC	1.00	.40
❑	T240	Tyler Martin FY RC	1.00	.40
❑	T241	J.D. Durbin FY RC	1.00	.40
❑	T242	Shane Victorino FY RC	1.50	.60
❑	T243	Rajai Davis FY RC	1.00	.40
❑	T244	Ismael Castro FY RC	1.00	.40
❑	T245	Chien-Ming Wang FY RC	10.00	4.00
❑	T246	Travis Ishikawa FY RC	2.00	.75
❑	T247	Corey Shafer FY RC	1.00	.40
❑	T248	Gary Schneidmiller FY RC	1.00	.40
❑	T249	Dave Pember FY RC	1.00	.40
❑	T250	Keith Stamler FY RC	1.00	.40
❑	T251	Tyson Graham FY RC	1.00	.40
❑	T252	Ryan Cameron FY RC	1.00	.40
❑	T253	Eric Eckenstahler FY	1.00	.40
❑	T254	Matthew Peterson FY RC	1.00	.40
❑	T255	Dustin McGowan FY RC	1.25	.50
❑	T256	Prentice Redman FY RC	1.00	.40
❑	T257	Haj Turay FY RC	1.00	.40
❑	T258	Carlos Guzman FY RC	1.25	.50
❑	T259	Matt DeMarco FY RC	1.00	.40
❑	T260	Derek Michaelis FY RC	1.00	.40
❑	T261	Brian Burgamy FY RC	1.00	.40
❑	T262	Jay Sitzman FY RC	1.00	.40
❑	T263	Chris Fallon FY RC	1.00	.40
❑	T264	Mike Adams FY RC	1.00	.40
❑	T265	Clint Barmes FY RC	2.50	1.00
❑	T266	Eric Reed FY RC	1.00	.40
❑	T267	Willie Eyre FY RC	1.00	.40
❑	T268	Carlos Duran FY RC	1.00	.40
❑	T269	Nick Trzesniak FY RC	1.00	.40
❑	T270	Ferdin Tejeda FY RC	1.00	.40
❑	T271	Michael Garciaparra FY RC	1.00	.40
❑	T272	Michael Hinckley FY RC	1.25	.50
❑	T273	Branden Florence FY RC	1.00	.40
❑	T274	Trent Oeltjen FY RC	1.25	.50
❑	T275	Mike Neu FY RC	1.00	.40

2004 Topps Chrome

	Card	Player		
❑		COMP.SERIES 1 w/o SP's (220)	80.00	40.00
❑		COMP.SERIES 2 w/o SP's (220)	80.00	40.00
❑		COMMON (1-210/257-466)	1.00	.40
❑		COMMON (211-220/247-256)	2.00	.75
❑		COMMON AU (221-246)	10.00	4.00
❑	1	Jim Thome	1.50	.60
❑	2	Reggie Sanders	1.00	.40
❑	3	Mark Kotsay	1.00	.40
❑	4	Edgardo Alfonzo	1.00	.40
❑	5	Tim Wakefield	1.00	.40
❑	6	Moises Alou	1.00	.40
❑	7	Jorge Julio	1.00	.40
❑	8	Bartolo Colon	1.00	.40
❑	9	Chan Ho Park	1.00	.40
❑	10	Ichiro Suzuki	5.00	2.00
❑	11	Kevin Millwood	1.00	.40
❑	12	Preston Wilson	1.00	.40
❑	13	Tom Glavine	1.50	.60
❑	14	Junior Spivey	1.00	.40
❑	15	Marcus Giles	1.00	.40
❑	16	David Segui	1.00	.40
❑	17	Kevin Millar	1.00	.40
❑	18	Corey Patterson	1.00	.40
❑	19	Aaron Rowand	1.00	.40
❑	20	Derek Jeter	5.00	2.00
❑	21	Luis Castillo	1.00	.40
❑	22	Manny Ramirez	1.50	.60
❑	23	Jay Payton	1.00	.40
❑	24	Bobby Higginson	1.00	.40

❑	25	Lance Berkman	1.00	.40
❑	26	Juan Pierre	1.00	.40
❑	27	Mike Mussina	1.50	.60
❑	28	Fred McGriff	1.50	.60
❑	29	Richie Sexson	1.00	.40
❑	30	Tim Hudson	1.00	.40
❑	31	Mike Piazza	4.00	1.50
❑	32	Brad Radke	1.00	.40
❑	33	Jeff Weaver	1.00	.40
❑	34	Ramon Hernandez	1.00	.40
❑	35	David Bell	1.00	.40
❑	36	Randy Wolf	1.00	.40
❑	37	Jake Peavy	1.00	.40
❑	38	Tim Worrell	1.00	.40
❑	39	Gil Meche	1.00	.40
❑	40	Albert Pujols	5.00	2.00
❑	41	Michael Young	1.00	.40
❑	42	Josh Phelps	1.00	.40
❑	43	Brendan Donnelly	1.00	.40
❑	44	Steve Finley	1.00	.40
❑	45	John Smoltz	1.50	.60
❑	46	Jay Gibbons	1.00	.40
❑	47	Trot Nixon	1.00	.40
❑	48	Carl Pavano	1.00	.40
❑	49	Frank Thomas	2.50	1.00
❑	50	Mark Prior	1.50	.60
❑	51	Danny Graves	1.00	.40
❑	52	Milton Bradley	1.00	.40
❑	53	Kris Benson	1.00	.40
❑	54	Ryan Klesko	1.00	.40
❑	55	Mike Lowell	1.00	.40
❑	56	Geoff Blum	1.00	.40
❑	57	Michael Tucker	1.00	.40
❑	58	Paul Lo Duca	1.00	.40
❑	59	Vicente Padilla	1.00	.40
❑	60	Jacque Jones	1.00	.40
❑	61	Fernando Tatis	1.00	.40
❑	62	Ty Wigginton	1.00	.40
❑	63	Rich Aurilia	1.00	.40
❑	64	Andy Pettitte	1.50	.60
❑	65	Terrence Long	1.00	.40
❑	66	Cliff Floyd	1.00	.40
❑	67	Mariano Rivera	2.50	1.00
❑	68	Kelvim Escobar	1.00	.40
❑	69	Marlon Byrd	1.00	.40
❑	70	Mark Mulder	1.00	.40
❑	71	Francisco Cordero	1.00	.40
❑	72	Carlos Guillen	1.00	.40
❑	73	Fernando Vina	1.00	.40
❑	74	Lance Carter	1.00	.40
❑	75	Hank Blalock	1.00	.40
❑	76	Jimmy Rollins	1.00	.40
❑	77	Francisco Rodriguez	1.00	.40
❑	78	Javy Lopez	1.00	.40
❑	79	Jerry Hairston Jr.	1.00	.40
❑	80	Andruw Jones	1.50	.60
❑	81	Rodrigo Lopez	1.00	.40
❑	82	Johnny Damon	1.50	.60
❑	83	Hee Seop Choi	1.00	.40
❑	84	Kazuhiro Sasaki	1.00	.40
❑	85	Danny Bautista	1.00	.40
❑	86	Matt Lawton	1.00	.40
❑	87	Juan Uribe	1.00	.40
❑	88	Rafael Furcal	1.00	.40
❑	89	Kyle Farnsworth	1.00	.40
❑	90	Jose Vidro	1.00	.40
❑	91	Luis Rivas	1.00	.40
❑	92	Hideo Nomo	2.50	1.00
❑	93	Javier Vazquez	1.00	.40
❑	94	Al Leiter	1.00	.40
❑	95	Jose Valentin	1.00	.40
❑	96	Alex Cintron	1.00	.40
❑	97	Zach Day	1.00	.40
❑	98	Jorge Posada	1.50	.60
❑	99	C.C. Sabathia	1.00	.40
❑	100	Alex Rodriguez	4.00	1.50
❑	101	Brad Penny	1.00	.40
❑	102	Brad Ausmus	1.00	.40
❑	103	Raul Ibanez	1.00	.40
❑	104	Mike Hampton	1.00	.40
❑	105	Adrian Beltre	1.00	.40
❑	106	Ramiro Mendoza	1.00	.40
❑	107	Rocco Baldelli	1.00	.40
❑	108	Esteban Loaiza	1.00	.40
❑	109	Russell Branyan	1.00	.40
❑	110	Todd Helton	1.50	.60
❑	111	Braden Looper	1.00	.40
❑	112	Octavio Dotel	1.00	.40
❑	113	Mike MacDougal	1.00	.40
❑	114	Cesar Izturis	1.00	.40
❑	115	Johan Santana	2.50	1.00
❑	116	Jose Contreras	1.00	.40
❑	117	Placido Polanco	1.00	.40
❑	118	Jason Phillips	1.00	.40
❑	119	Orlando Hudson	1.00	.40
❑	120	Vernon Wells	1.00	.40
❑	121	Ben Grieve	1.00	.40
❑	122	Dave Roberts	1.00	.40
❑	123	Ismael Valdes	1.00	.40
❑	124	Eric Owens	1.00	.40
❑	125	Curt Schilling	1.00	.40
❑	126	Russ Ortiz	1.00	.40
❑	127	Mark Buehrle	1.00	.40
❑	128	Doug Mientkiewicz	1.00	.40
❑	129	Dmitri Young	1.00	.40
❑	130	Kazuhisa Ishii	1.00	.40
❑	131	A.J. Pierzynski	1.00	.40
❑	132	Brad Wilkerson	1.00	.40
❑	133	Joe McEwing	1.00	.40
❑	134	Alex Cora	1.00	.40
❑	135	Jose Cruz Jr.	1.00	.40
❑	136	Carlos Zambrano	1.00	.40
❑	137	Jeff Kent	1.00	.40
❑	138	Shigetoshi Hasegawa	1.00	.40
❑	139	Jarrod Washburn	1.00	.40
❑	140	Greg Maddux	4.00	1.50
❑	141	Josh Beckett	1.00	.40
❑	142	Miguel Batista	1.00	.40
❑	143	Omar Vizquel	1.50	.60
❑	144	Alex Gonzalez	1.00	.40
❑	145	Billy Wagner	1.00	.40
❑	146	Brian Jordan	1.00	.40
❑	147	Wes Helms	1.00	.40
❑	148	Deivi Cruz	1.00	.40
❑	149	Alex Gonzalez	1.00	.40
❑	150	Jason Giambi	1.00	.40
❑	151	Erubiel Durazo	1.00	.40
❑	152	Mike Lieberthal	1.00	.40
❑	153	Jason Kendall	1.00	.40
❑	154	Xavier Nady	1.00	.40
❑	155	Kirk Rueter	1.00	.40
❑	156	Mike Cameron	1.00	.40
❑	157	Miguel Cairo	1.00	.40
❑	158	Woody Williams	1.00	.40
❑	159	Toby Hall	1.00	.40
❑	160	Bernie Williams	1.50	.60
❑	161	Darin Erstad	1.00	.40
❑	162	Matt Mantei	1.00	.40
❑	163	Shawn Chacon	1.00	.40
❑	164	Bill Mueller	1.00	.40
❑	165	Damian Miller	1.00	.40
❑	166	Tony Graffanino	1.00	.40
❑	167	Sean Casey	1.00	.40
❑	168	Brandon Phillips	1.00	.40
❑	169	Runelvys Hernandez	1.00	.40
❑	170	Adam Dunn	1.00	.40
❑	171	Carlos Lee	1.00	.40
❑	172	Juan Encarnacion	1.00	.40
❑	173	Angel Berroa	1.00	.40
❑	174	Desi Relaford	1.00	.40
❑	175	Joe Mays	1.00	.40
❑	176	Ben Sheets	1.00	.40
❑	177	Eddie Guardado	1.00	.40
❑	178	Rocky Biddle	1.00	.40
❑	179	Eric Gagne	1.00	.40
❑	180	Eric Chavez	1.00	.40
❑	181	Jason Michaels	1.00	.40
❑	182	Dustan Mohr	1.00	.40
❑	183	Kip Wells	1.00	.40
❑	184	Brian Lawrence	1.00	.40
❑	185	Bret Boone	1.00	.40
❑	186	Tino Martinez	1.50	.60
❑	187	Aubrey Huff	1.00	.40
❑	188	Kevin Mench	1.00	.40
❑	189	Tim Salmon	1.50	.60
❑	190	Carlos Delgado	1.00	.40
❑	191	John Lackey	1.00	.40
❑	192	Eric Byrnes	1.00	.40
❑	193	Luis Matos	1.00	.40
❑	194	Derek Lowe	1.00	.40
❑	195	Mark Grudzielanek	1.00	.40
❑	196	Tom Gordon	1.00	.40
❑	197	Matt Clement	1.00	.40
❑	198	Byung-Hyun Kim	1.00	.40
❑	199	Brandon Inge	1.00	.40
❑	200	Nomar Garciaparra	4.00	1.50
❑	201	Frank Catalanotto	1.00	.40
❑	202	Cristian Guzman	1.00	.40
❑	203	Bo Hart	1.00	.40
❑	204	Jack Wilson	1.00	.40
❑	205	Ray Durham	1.00	.40
❑	206	Freddy Garcia	1.00	.40
❑	207	J.D. Drew	1.00	.40
❑	208	Orlando Cabrera	1.00	.40
❑	209	Roy Halladay	1.00	.40
❑	210	David Eckstein	1.00	.40
❑	211	Omar Falcon FY RC	2.00	.75
❑	212	Todd Self FY RC	3.00	1.25
❑	213	David Murphy FY RC	3.00	1.25
❑	214	Dioner Navarro FY RC	3.00	1.25
❑	215	Marcus McBeth FY RC	2.00	.75
❑	216	Chris O'Riordan FY RC	2.00	.75
❑	217	Rodney Choy Foo FY RC	2.00	.75
❑	218	Tim Frend FY RC	2.00	.75
❑	219	Yadier Molina FY RC	6.00	2.50
❑	220	Zach Duke FY RC	5.00	2.00
❑	221	Anthony Lerew FY AU RC	15.00	6.00
❑	222	B.Hawksworth FY AU RC	15.00	6.00
❑	223	Brayan Pena FY AU RC	10.00	4.00
❑	224	Craig Ansman FY AU RC	10.00	4.00
❑	225	Jon Knott FY AU RC	10.00	4.00
❑	226	Josh Labandeira FY AU RC	10.00	4.00
❑	227	Khalid Ballouli FY AU RC	10.00	4.00
❑	228	Kyle Davies FY AU RC	25.00	10.00
❑	229	Matt Creighton FY AU RC	10.00	4.00
❑	230	Mike Gosling FY AU RC	10.00	4.00
❑	231	Nic Ungs FY AU RC	10.00	4.00
❑	232	Zach Miner FY AU RC	25.00	10.00
❑	233	Donald Levinski FY AU RC	10.00	4.00
❑	234A	Bradley Sullivan FY AU RC	15.00	6.00
❑	234B	B.Sullivan FY AU ERR 345	25.00	10.00
❑	235	Carlos Quentin FY AU RC	40.00	20.00
❑	236	Conor Jackson FY AU RC	50.00	30.00
❑	237	Estee Harris FY AU RC	15.00	6.00
❑	238	Jeffrey Allison FY AU RC	10.00	4.00
❑	239	Kyle Sleeth FY AU RC	15.00	6.00
❑	240	Matthew Moses FY AU RC	15.00	6.00
❑	241	Tim Stauffer FY AU RC	10.00	4.00
❑	242	Brad Snyder FY AU RC	12.00	5.00
❑	243	Jason Hirsh FY AU RC	25.00	10.00
❑	244	L.Milledge FY AU RC	50.00	20.00
❑	245	Logan Kensing FY AU RC	10.00	4.00
❑	246	Kory Casto FY AU RC	15.00	6.00
❑	247	David Aardsma FY RC	3.00	1.25
❑	248	Omar Quintanilla FY RC	3.00	1.25
❑	249	Ervin Santana FY RC	5.00	2.00
❑	250	Merkin Valdez FY RC	2.00	.75
❑	251	Vito Chiaravalloti FY RC	2.00	.75
❑	252	Travis Blackley FY RC	2.00	.75
❑	253	Chris Shelton FY RC	3.00	1.25
❑	254	Rudy Guillen FY RC	3.00	1.25
❑	255	Bobby Brownlie FY RC	2.50	1.00
❑	256	Paul Maholm FY RC	4.00	1.50
❑	257	Roger Clemens	5.00	2.00
❑	258	Laynce Nix	1.00	.40
❑	259	Eric Hinske	1.00	.40
❑	260	Ivan Rodriguez	1.50	.60
❑	261	Brandon Webb	1.00	.40
❑	262	Jhonny Peralta	1.00	.40
❑	263	Adam Kennedy	1.00	.40
❑	264	Tony Batista	1.00	.40
❑	265	Jeff Suppan	1.00	.40
❑	266	Kenny Lofton	1.00	.40
❑	267	Scott Sullivan	1.00	.40
❑	268	Ken Griffey Jr.	4.00	1.50
❑	269	Juan Rivera	1.00	.40
❑	270	Larry Walker	1.00	.40
❑	271	Todd Hollandsworth	1.00	.40
❑	272	Carlos Beltran	1.00	.40
❑	273	Carl Crawford	1.00	.40
❑	274	Karim Garcia	1.00	.40
❑	275	Jose Reyes	1.00	.40
❑	276	Brandon Duckworth	1.00	.40
❑	277	Brian Giles	1.00	.40
❑	278	J.T. Snow	1.00	.40
❑	279	Jamie Moyer	1.00	.40
❑	280	Julio Lugo	1.00	.40
❑	281	Mark Teixeira	1.50	.60

❑	282	Cory Lidle	1.00	.40
❑	283	Lyle Overbay	1.00	.40
❑	284	Troy Percival	1.00	.40
❑	285	Robby Hammock	1.00	.40
❑	286	Jason Johnson	1.00	.40
❑	287	Damian Rolls	1.00	.40
❑	288	Antonio Alfonseca	1.00	.40
❑	289	Tom Goodwin	1.00	.40
❑	290	Paul Konerko	1.00	.40
❑	291	D'Angelo Jimenez	1.00	.40
❑	292	Ben Broussard	1.00	.40
❑	293	Maggio Ordonez	1.00	.40
❑	294	Carlos Pena	1.00	.40
❑	295	Chad Fox	1.00	.40
❑	296	Jeriome Robertson	1.00	.40
❑	297	Travis Hafner	1.00	.40
❑	298	Joe Randa	1.00	.40
❑	299	Brady Clark	1.00	.40
❑	300	Barry Zito	1.00	.40
❑	301	Ruben Sierra	1.00	.40
❑	302	Brett Myers	1.00	.40
❑	303	Oliver Perez	1.00	.40
❑	304	Benito Santiago	1.00	.40
❑	305	David Ross	1.00	.40
❑	306	Joe Nathan	1.00	.40
❑	307	Jim Edmonds	1.00	.40
❑	308	Matt Kata	1.00	.40
❑	309	Vinny Castilla	1.00	.40
❑	310	Marty Cordova	1.00	.40
❑	311	Aramis Ramirez	1.00	.40
❑	312	Carl Everett	1.00	.40
❑	313	Ryan Freel	1.00	.40
❑	314	Mark Bellhorn Sox	1.00	.40
❑	315	Joe Mauer	2.50	1.00
❑	316	Tim Redding	1.00	.40
❑	317	Jeromy Burnitz	1.00	.40
❑	318	Miguel Cabrera	1.50	.60
❑	319	Ramon Nivar	1.00	.40
❑	320	Casey Blake	1.00	.40
❑	321	Adam LaRoche	1.00	.40
❑	322	Jermaine Dye	1.00	.40
❑	323	Jerome Williams	1.00	.40
❑	324	John Olerud	1.00	.40
❑	325	Scott Rolen	1.50	.60
❑	326	Bobby Kielty	1.00	.40
❑	327	Travis Lee	1.00	.40
❑	328	Jeff Cirillo	1.00	.40
❑	329	Scott Spiezio	1.00	.40
❑	330	Melvin Mora	1.00	.40
❑	331	Mike Timlin	1.00	.40
❑	332	Kerry Wood	1.00	.40
❑	333	Tony Womack	1.00	.40
❑	334	Jody Gerut	1.00	.40
❑	335	Morgan Ensberg	1.00	.40
❑	336	Odalis Perez	1.00	.40
❑	337	Michael Cuddyer	1.00	.40
❑	338	Jose Hernandez	1.00	.40
❑	339	LaTroy Hawkins	1.00	.40
❑	340	Marquis Grissom	1.00	.40
❑	341	Matt Morris	1.00	.40
❑	342	Juan Gonzalez	1.00	.40
❑	343	Jose Valverde	1.00	.40
❑	344	Joe Borowski	1.00	.40
❑	345	Josh Bard	1.00	.40
❑	346	Austin Kearns	1.00	.40
❑	347	Chin-Hui Tsao	1.00	.40
❑	348	Wil Ledezma	1.00	.40
❑	349	Aaron Guiel	1.00	.40
❑	350	Alfonso Soriano	1.00	.40
❑	351	Ted Lilly	1.00	.40
❑	352	Sean Burroughs	1.00	.40
❑	353	Rafael Palmeiro	1.50	.60
❑	354	Quinton McCracken	1.00	.40
❑	355	David Ortiz	2.50	1.00
❑	356	Randall Simon	1.00	.40
❑	357	Wily Mo Pena	1.00	.40
❑	358	Brian Anderson	1.00	.40
❑	359	Corey Koskie	1.00	.40
❑	360	Keith Foulke Sox	1.00	.40
❑	361	Sidney Ponson	1.00	.40
❑	362	Gary Matthews Jr.	1.00	.40
❑	363	Herbert Perry	1.00	.40
❑	364	Shea Hillenbrand	1.00	.40
❑	365	Craig Biggio	1.50	.60
❑	366	Barry Larkin	1.50	.60
❑	367	Arthur Rhodes	1.00	.40
❑	368	Sammy Sosa	2.50	1.00
❑	369	Joe Crede	1.00	.40
❑	370	Gary Sheffield	1.00	.40
❑	371	Coco Crisp	1.00	.40
❑	372	Torii Hunter	1.00	.40
❑	373	Dorrek Lee	1.50	.60
❑	374	Adam Everett	1.00	.40
❑	375	Miguel Tejada	1.00	.40
❑	376	Jeremy Affeldt	1.00	.40
❑	377	Robin Ventura	1.00	.40
❑	378	Scott Podsednik	1.00	.40
❑	379	Matthew LeCroy	1.00	.40
❑	380	Vladimir Guerrero	2.50	1.00
❑	381	Steve Karsay	1.00	.40
❑	382	Jeff Nelson	1.00	.40
❑	383	Chase Utley	1.50	.60
❑	384	Bobby Abreu	1.00	.40
❑	385	Josh Fogg	1.00	.40
❑	386	Trevor Hoffman	1.00	.40
❑	387	Matt Stairs	1.00	.40
❑	388	Edgar Martinez	1.50	.60
❑	389	Edgar Renteria	1.00	.40
❑	390	Chipper Jones	2.50	1.00
❑	391	Eric Munson	1.00	.40
❑	392	Dewon Brazelton	1.00	.40
❑	393	John Thomson	1.00	.40
❑	394	Chris Woodward	1.00	.40
❑	395	Joe Kennedy	1.00	.40
❑	396	Reed Johnson	1.00	.40
❑	397	Johnny Estrada	1.00	.40
❑	398	Damian Moss	1.00	.40
❑	399	Victor Zambrano	1.00	.40
❑	400	Dontrelle Willis	1.50	.60
❑	401	Troy Glaus	1.00	.40
❑	402	Raul Mondesi	1.00	.40
❑	403	Jeff Davanon	1.00	.40
❑	404	Kurt Ainsworth	1.00	.40
❑	405	Pedro Martinez	1.50	.60
❑	406	Eric Karros	1.00	.40
❑	407	Billy Koch	1.00	.40
❑	408	Luis Gonzalez	1.00	.40
❑	409	Jack Cust	1.00	.40
❑	410	Mike Sweeney	1.00	.40
❑	411	Jason Bay	1.00	.40
❑	412	Mark Redman	1.00	.40
❑	413	Jason Jennings	1.00	.40
❑	414	Rondell White	1.00	.40
❑	415	Todd Hundley	1.00	.40
❑	416	Shannon Stewart	1.00	.40
❑	417	Jae Weong Seo	1.00	.40
❑	418	Livan Hernandez	1.00	.40
❑	419	Mark Ellis	1.00	.40
❑	420	Pat Burrell	1.00	.40
❑	421	Mark Loretta	1.00	.40
❑	422	Robb Nen	1.00	.40
❑	423	Joel Pineiro	1.00	.40
❑	424	Todd Walker	1.00	.40
❑	425	Jeremy Bonderman	1.00	.40
❑	426	A.J. Burnett	1.00	.40
❑	427	Greg Myers	1.00	.40
❑	428	Roy Oswalt	1.00	.40
❑	429	Carlos Baerga	1.00	.40
❑	430	Garret Anderson	1.00	.40
❑	431	Horacio Ramirez	1.00	.40
❑	432	Brian Roberts	1.00	.40
❑	433	Kevin Brown	1.00	.40
❑	434	Eric Milton	1.00	.40
❑	435	Ramon Vazquez	1.00	.40
❑	436	Alex Escobar	1.00	.40
❑	437	Alex Sanchez	1.00	.40
❑	438	Jeff Bagwell	1.50	.60
❑	439	Claudio Vargas	1.00	.40
❑	440	Shawn Green	1.00	.40
❑	441	Geoff Jenkins	1.00	.40
❑	442	David Wells	1.00	.40
❑	443	Nick Johnson	1.00	.40
❑	444	Jose Guillen	1.00	.40
❑	445	Scott Hatteberg	1.00	.40
❑	446	Phil Nevin	1.00	.40
❑	447	Jason Schmidt	1.00	.40
❑	448	Ricky Ledee	1.00	.40
❑	449	So Taguchi	1.00	.40
❑	450	Randy Johnson	2.50	1.00
❑	451	Eric Young	1.00	.40
❑	452	Chone Figgins	1.00	.40
❑	453	Larry Bigbie	1.00	.40
❑	454	Scott Williamson	1.00	.40
❑	455	Ramon Martinez	1.00	.40
❑	456	Roberto Alomar	1.50	.60
❑	457	Ryan Dempster	1.00	.40
❑	458	Ryan Ludwick	1.00	.40
❑	459	Ramon Santiago	1.00	.40
❑	460	Jeff Conine	1.00	.40
❑	461	Brad Lidge	1.00	.40
❑	462	Ken Harvey	1.00	.40
❑	463	Guillermo Mota	1.00	.40
❑	464	Rick Reed	1.00	.40
❑	465	Armando Benitez	1.00	.40
❑	466	Wade Miller	1.00	.40

2004 Topps Chrome Traded

❑	COMPLETE SET (220)	120.00	60.00
❑	COMMON CARD (1-70)	.75	.30
❑	COMMON CARD (71-90)	1.00	.40
❑	COMMON CARD (91-110)	1.00	.40
❑	COMMON CARD (111-220)	1.00	.40
❑	2 PER 2004 TOPPS TRADED HOBBY PACK		
❑	2 PER 2004 TOPPS TRADED HTA PACK		
❑	2 PER 2004 TOPPS TRADED RETAIL PACK		
❑	PLATE ODDS 1:1151 H, 1:1173 R, 1:327 HTA		
❑	PLATE PRINT RUN 1 SET PER COLOR		
❑	BLACK-CYAN-MAGENTA-YELLOW ISSUED		
❑	NO PLATE PRICING DUE TO SCARCITY		

❑	T1	Pokey Reese	.75	.30
❑	T2	Tony Womack	.75	.30
❑	T3	Richard Hidalgo	.75	.30
❑	T4	Juan Uribe	.75	.30
❑	T5	J.D. Drew	.75	.30
❑	T6	Alex Gonzalez	.75	.30
❑	T7	Carlos Guillen	.75	.30
❑	T8	Doug Mientkiewicz	.75	.30
❑	T9	Fernando Vina	.75	.30
❑	T10	Milton Bradley	.75	.30
❑	T11	Kelvim Escobar	.75	.30
❑	T12	Ben Grieve	.75	.30
❑	T13	Brian Jordan	.75	.30
❑	T14	A.J. Pierzynski	.75	.30
❑	T15	Billy Wagner	.75	.30
❑	T16	Terrence Long	.75	.30
❑	T17	Carlos Beltran	.75	.30
❑	T18	Carl Everett	.75	.30
❑	T19	Reggie Sanders	.75	.30
❑	T20	Javy Lopez	.75	.30
❑	T21	Jay Payton	.75	.30
❑	T22	Octavio Dotel	.75	.30
❑	T23	Eddie Guardado	.75	.30
❑	T24	Andy Pettitte	1.25	.50
❑	T25	Richie Sexson	.75	.30
❑	T26	Ronnie Belliard	.75	.30
❑	T27	Michael Tucker	.75	.30
❑	T28	Brad Fullmer	.75	.30
❑	T29	Freddy Garcia	.75	.30
❑	T30	Bartolo Colon	.75	.30
❑	T31	Larry Walker Cards	1.25	.50
❑	T32	Mark Kotsay	.75	.30
❑	T33	Jason Marquis	.75	.30
❑	T34	Dustan Mohr	.75	.30
❑	T35	Javier Vazquez	.75	.30
❑	T36	Nomar Garciaparra	3.00	1.25
❑	T37	Tino Martinez	1.25	.50
❑	T38	Hee Seop Choi	.75	.30
❑	T39	Damian Miller	.75	.30
❑	T40	Jose Lima	.75	.30

Card	Player	Price	Price
❑ T41	Ty Wigginton	.75	.30
❑ T42	Raul Ibanez	.75	.30
❑ T43	Danys Baez	.75	.30
❑ T44	Tony Clark	.75	.30
❑ T45	Greg Maddux	3.00	1.25
❑ T46	Victor Zambrano	.75	.30
❑ T47	Orlando Cabrera Sox	.75	.30
❑ T48	Jose Cruz Jr.	.75	.30
❑ T49	Kris Benson	.75	.30
❑ T50	Alex Rodriguez	4.00	1.50
❑ T51	Steve Finley	.75	.30
❑ T52	Ramon Hernandez	.75	.30
❑ T53	Esteban Loaiza	.75	.30
❑ T54	Ugueth Urbina	.75	.30
❑ T55	Jeff Weaver	.75	.30
❑ T56	Flash Gordon	.75	.30
❑ T57	Jose Contreras	.75	.30
❑ T58	Paul Lo Duca	.75	.30
❑ T59	Junior Spivey	.75	.30
❑ T60	Curt Schilling	1.25	.50
❑ T61	Brad Penny	.75	.30
❑ T62	Braden Looper	.75	.30
❑ T63	Miguel Cairo	.75	.30
❑ T64	Juan Encarnacion	.75	.30
❑ T65	Miguel Batista	.75	.30
❑ T66	Terry Francona MG	.75	.30
❑ T67	Lee Mazzilli MG	.75	.30
❑ T68	Al Pedrique MG	.75	.30
❑ T69	Ozzie Guillen MG	2.00	.75
❑ T70	Phil Garner MG	.75	.30
❑ T71	Matt Bush DP RC	4.00	1.50
❑ T72	Homer Bailey DP RC	6.00	2.50
❑ T73	Greg Golson DP RC	3.00	1.25
❑ T74	Kyle Waldrop DP RC	2.50	1.00
❑ T75	Richie Robnett DP RC	3.00	1.25
❑ T76	Jay Rainville DP RC	4.00	1.50
❑ T77	Bill Bray DP RC	1.00	.40
❑ T78	Philip Hughes DP RC	15.00	6.00
❑ T79	Scott Elbert DP RC	2.50	1.00
❑ T80	Josh Fields DP RC	5.00	2.00
❑ T81	Justin Orenduff DP RC	2.00	.75
❑ T82	Dan Putnam DP RC	2.00	.75
❑ T83	Chris Nelson DP RC	5.00	2.00
❑ T84	Blake DeWitt DP RC	4.00	1.50
❑ T85	J.P. Howell DP RC	2.50	1.00
❑ T86	Huston Street DP RC	6.00	2.50
❑ T87	Kurt Suzuki DP RC	3.00	1.25
❑ T88	Erick San Pedro DP RC	1.00	.40
❑ T89	Matt Tuiasosopo DP RC	5.00	2.00
❑ T90	Matt Macri DP RC	2.50	1.00
❑ T91	Chad Tracy PROS	1.00	.40
❑ T92	Scott Hairston PROS	1.00	.40
❑ T93	Jonny Gomes PROS	1.00	.40
❑ T94	Chin-Feng Chen PROS	1.00	.40
❑ T95	Chien-Ming Wang PROS	3.00	1.25
❑ T96	Dustin McGowan PROS	1.00	.40
❑ T97	Chris Burke PROS	1.00	.40
❑ T98	Denny Bautista PROS	1.00	.40
❑ T99	Preston Larrison PROS	1.00	.40
❑ T100	Kevin Youkilis PROS	1.00	.40
❑ T101	John Maine PROS	1.00	.40
❑ T102	Guillermo Quiroz PROS	1.00	.40
❑ T103	Dave Krynzel PROS	1.00	.40
❑ T104	David Kelton PROS	1.00	.40
❑ T105	Edwin Encarnacion PROS	1.00	.40
❑ T106	Chad Gaudin PROS	1.00	.40
❑ T107	Sergio Mitre PROS	1.00	.40
❑ T108	Laynce Nix PROS	1.00	.40
❑ T109	David Parrish PROS	1.00	.40
❑ T110	Brandon Claussen PROS	1.00	.40
❑ T111	Frank Francisco FY RC	1.00	.40
❑ T112	Brian Dallimore FY RC	1.00	.40
❑ T113	Jim Crowell FY RC	1.25	.50
❑ T114	Andres Blanco FY RC	1.00	.40
❑ T115	Eduardo Villacis FY RC	1.00	.40
❑ T116	Kazuhito Tadano FY RC	1.25	.50
❑ T117	Aarom Baldiris FY RC	1.25	.50
❑ T118	Justin Germano FY RC	1.00	.40
❑ T119	Joey Gathright FY RC	3.00	1.25
❑ T120	Franklyn Gracesqui FY RC	1.00	.40
❑ T121	Chin-Lung Hu FY RC	3.00	1.25
❑ T122	Scott Olsen FY RC	4.00	1.50
❑ T123	Tyler Davidson FY RC	1.25	.50
❑ T124	Fausto Carmona FY RC	3.00	1.25
❑ T125	Tim Hutting FY RC	1.00	.40
❑ T126	Ryan Meaux FY RC	1.00	.40
❑ T127	Jon Connolly FY RC	2.50	1.00
❑ T128	Hector Made FY RC	2.00	.75
❑ T129	Jamie Brown FY RC	1.00	.40
❑ T130	Paul McAnulty FY RC	2.00	.75
❑ T131	Chris Saenz FY RC	1.00	.40
❑ T132	Marland Williams FY RC	1.25	.50
❑ T133	Mike Huggins FY RC	1.00	.40
❑ T134	Jesse Crain FY RC	2.00	.75
❑ T135	Chad Bentz FY RC	1.00	.40
❑ T136	Kazuo Matsui FY RC	2.00	.75
❑ T137	Paul Maholm FY	2.50	1.00
❑ T138	Brock Jacobsen FY RC	1.00	.40
❑ T139	Casey Daigle FY RC	1.00	.40
❑ T140	Nyjer Morgan FY RC	1.00	.40
❑ T141	Tom Mastny FY RC	1.00	.40
❑ T142	Kody Kirkland FY RC	1.25	.50
❑ T143	Jose Capellan FY RC	1.25	.50
❑ T144	Felix Hernandez FY RC	15.00	6.00
❑ T145	Shawn Hill FY RC	1.00	.40
❑ T146	Danny Gonzalez FY RC	1.00	.40
❑ T147	Scott Dohmann FY RC	1.00	.40
❑ T148	Tommy Murphy FY RC	1.00	.40
❑ T149	Akinori Otsuka FY RC	1.00	.40
❑ T150	Miguel Perez FY RC	1.00	.40
❑ T151	Mike Rouse FY RC	1.00	.40
❑ T152	Ramon Ramirez FY RC	1.00	.40
❑ T153	Luke Hughes FY RC	1.00	.40
❑ T154	Howie Kendrick FY RC	30.00	20.00
❑ T155	Ryan Budde FY RC	1.00	.40
❑ T156	Charlie Zink FY RC	1.00	.40
❑ T157	Warner Madrigal FY RC	2.00	.75
❑ T158	Jason Szuminski FY RC	1.00	.40
❑ T159	Chad Chop FY RC	1.00	.40
❑ T160	Shingo Takatsu FY RC	2.00	.75
❑ T161	Matt Lemanczyk FY RC	1.00	.40
❑ T162	Wardell Starling FY RC	1.00	.40
❑ T163	Nick Gorneault FY RC	1.25	.50
❑ T164	Scott Proctor FY RC	1.25	.50
❑ T165	Brooks Conrad FY RC	1.25	.50
❑ T166	Hector Gimenez FY RC	1.00	.40
❑ T167	Kevin Howard FY RC	1.25	.50
❑ T168	Vince Perkins FY RC	1.25	.50
❑ T169	Brock Peterson FY RC	1.00	.40
❑ T170	Chris Shelton FY	2.00	.75
❑ T171	Erick Aybar FY RC	2.00	.75
❑ T172	Paul Bacot FY RC	1.25	.50
❑ T173	Matt Capps FY RC	1.00	.40
❑ T174	Kory Casto FY	1.25	.50
❑ T175	Juan Cedeno FY RC	1.00	.40
❑ T176	Vito Chiaravalloti FY	1.00	.40
❑ T177	Alec Zumwalt FY RC	1.00	.40
❑ T178	J.J. Furmaniak FY RC	2.00	.75
❑ T179	Lee Gwaltney FY RC	1.00	.40
❑ T180	Donald Kelly FY RC	1.00	.40
❑ T181	Benji DeQuin FY RC	1.00	.40
❑ T182	Brant Colamarino FY RC	2.00	.75
❑ T183	Juan Gutierrez FY RC	1.00	.40
❑ T184	Carl Loadenthal FY RC	1.25	.50
❑ T185	Ricky Nolasco FY RC	3.00	1.25
❑ T186	Jeff Salazar FY RC	2.50	1.00
❑ T187	Rob Tejeda FY RC	2.00	.75
❑ T188	Alex Romero FY RC	1.00	.40
❑ T189	Yoann Torrealba FY RC	1.00	.40
❑ T190	Carlos Sosa FY RC	1.00	.40
❑ T191	Tim Bittner FY RC	1.00	.40
❑ T192	Chris Aguila FY RC	1.00	.40
❑ T193	Jason Frasor FY RC	1.00	.40
❑ T194	Reid Gorecki FY RC	1.00	.40
❑ T195	Dustin Nippert FY RC	1.25	.50
❑ T196	Javier Guzman FY RC	1.25	.50
❑ T197	Harvey Garcia FY RC	1.00	.40
❑ T198	Ivan Ochoa FY RC	1.00	.40
❑ T199	David Wallace FY RC	1.25	.50
❑ T200	Joel Zumaya FY RC	8.00	3.00
❑ T201	Casey Kopitzke FY RC	1.00	.40
❑ T202	Lincoln Holdzkom FY RC	1.00	.40
❑ T203	Chad Santos FY RC	1.00	.40
❑ T204	Brian Pilkington FY RC	1.00	.40
❑ T205	Terry Jones FY RC	1.25	.50
❑ T206	Jerome Gamble FY RC	1.00	.40
❑ T207	Brad Eldred FY RC	1.25	.50
❑ T208	David Pauley FY RC	3.00	1.25
❑ T209	Kevin Davidson FY RC	1.00	.40
❑ T210	Damaso Espino FY RC	1.00	.40
❑ T211	Tom Farmer FY RC	1.00	.40
❑ T212	Michael Mooney FY RC	1.00	.40
❑ T213	James Tomlin FY RC	1.00	.40
❑ T214	Greg Thissen FY RC	1.00	.40
❑ T215	Calvin Hayes FY RC	1.25	.50
❑ T216	Fernando Cortez FY RC	1.00	.40
❑ T217	Sergio Silva FY RC	1.00	.40
❑ T218	Jon de Vries FY RC	1.00	.40
❑ T219	Don Sutton FY RC	2.50	1.00
❑ T220	Leo Nunez FY RC	1.00	.40

2005 Topps Chrome

Card	Player	Price	Price
❑	COMP.SET w/o AU'S (440)	160.00	80.00
❑	COMP.SERIES 1 w/o AU's (220)	80.00	40.00
❑	COMP.SERIES 2 w/o AU's (220)	80.00	40.00
❑	COMMON (1-210/253-467)	1.00	.40
❑	COMMON (211-220/468-472)	2.00	.75
❑	221-252 PRINT RUN PROVIDED BY TOPPS		
❑	EXCHANGE DEADLINE 05/31/07		
❑	1-234 PLATE ODDS 1:310 SER.1 HOBBY		
❑	235-252 PLATE ODDS 1:350 SER.2 MINI BOX		
❑	253-472 PLATE ODDS 1:29 SER.2 MINI BOX		
❑	PLATE PRINT RUN 1 SET PER COLOR		
❑	BLACK-CYAN-MAGENTA-YELLOW ISSUED		
❑	NO PLATE PRICING DUE TO SCARCITY		
❑ 1	Alex Rodriguez	4.00	1.50
❑ 2	Placido Polanco	1.00	.40
❑ 3	Torii Hunter	1.00	.40
❑ 4	Lyle Overbay	1.00	.40
❑ 5	Johnny Damon	1.50	.60
❑ 6	Johnny Estrada	1.00	.40
❑ 7	Rich Harden	1.00	.40
❑ 8	Francisco Rodriguez	1.00	.40
❑ 9	Jarrod Washburn	1.00	.40
❑ 10	Sammy Sosa	2.50	1.00
❑ 11	Randy Wolf	1.00	.40
❑ 12	Jason Bay	1.00	.40
❑ 13	Tom Glavine	1.50	.60
❑ 14	Michael Tucker	1.00	.40
❑ 15	Brian Giles	1.00	.40
❑ 16	Chad Tracy	1.00	.40
❑ 17	Jim Edmonds	1.00	.40
❑ 18	John Smoltz	1.50	.60
❑ 19	Roy Halladay	1.00	.40
❑ 20	Hank Blalock	1.00	.40
❑ 21	Darin Erstad	1.00	.40
❑ 22	Todd Walker	1.00	.40
❑ 23	Mike Hampton	1.00	.40
❑ 24	Mark Bellhorn	1.00	.40
❑ 25	Jim Thome	1.50	.60
❑ 26	Shingo Takatsu	1.00	.40
❑ 27	Jody Gerut	1.00	.40
❑ 28	Vinny Castilla	1.00	.40
❑ 29	Luis Castillo	1.00	.40
❑ 30	Ivan Rodriguez	1.50	.60
❑ 31	Craig Biggio	1.50	.60
❑ 32	Joe Randa	1.00	.40
❑ 33	Adrian Beltre	1.00	.40
❑ 34	Scott Podsednik	1.00	.40
❑ 35	Cliff Floyd	1.00	.40
❑ 36	Livan Hernandez	1.00	.40
❑ 37	Eric Byrnes	1.00	.40
❑ 38	Jose Acevedo	1.00	.40
❑ 39	Jack Wilson	1.00	.40
❑ 40	Gary Sheffield	1.00	.40
❑ 41	Chan Ho Park	1.00	.40
❑ 42	Carl Crawford	1.00	.40
❑ 43	Shawn Estes	1.00	.40
❑ 44	David Bell	1.00	.40
❑ 45	Jeff DaVanon	1.00	.40

46	Brandon Webb	1.00	.40
47	Lance Berkman	1.00	.40
48	Melvin Mora	1.00	.40
49	David Ortiz	2.50	1.00
50	Andruw Jones	1.50	.60
51	Chone Figgins	1.00	.40
52	Danny Graves	1.00	.40
53	Preston Wilson	1.00	.40
54	Jeremy Bonderman	1.00	.40
55	Carlos Guillen	1.00	.40
56	Cesar Izturis	1.00	.40
57	Kazuo Matsui	1.00	.40
58	Jason Schmidt	1.00	.40
59	Jason Marquis	1.00	.40
60	Jose Vidro	1.00	.40
61	Al Leiter	1.00	.40
62	Javier Vazquez	1.00	.40
63	Erubiel Durazo	1.00	.40
64	Scott Spiezio	1.00	.40
65	Scot Shields	1.00	.40
66	Edgardo Alfonzo	1.00	.40
67	Miguel Tejada	1.00	.40
68	Francisco Cordero	1.00	.40
69	Brett Myers	1.00	.40
70	Curt Schilling	1.50	.60
71	Matt Kata	1.00	.40
72	Bartolo Colon	1.00	.40
73	Rodrigo Lopez	1.00	.40
74	Tim Wakefield	1.00	.40
75	Frank Thomas	2.50	1.00
76	Jimmy Rollins	1.00	.40
77	Barry Zito	1.00	.40
78	Hideo Nomo	2.50	1.00
79	Brad Wilkerson	1.00	.40
80	Adam Dunn	1.00	.40
81	Derrek Lee	1.50	.60
82	Joe Crede	1.00	.40
83	Nate Robertson	1.00	.40
84	John Thomson	1.00	.40
85	Mike Sweeney	1.00	.40
86	Kip Wells	1.00	.40
87	Eric Gagne	1.00	.40
88	Zach Day	1.00	.40
89	Alex Sanchez	1.00	.40
90	Bret Boone	1.00	.40
91	Mark Loretta	1.00	.40
92	Miguel Cabrera	1.50	.60
93	Randy Winn	1.00	.40
94	Adam Everett	1.00	.40
95	Aubrey Huff	1.00	.40
96	Kevin Mench	1.00	.40
97	Frank Catalanotto	1.00	.40
98	Flash Gordon	1.00	.40
99	Scott Hatteberg	1.00	.40
100	Albert Pujols	5.00	2.00
101	J.Molina/B.Molina	1.00	.40
102	Jason Johnson	1.00	.40
103	Jay Gibbons	1.00	.40
104	Byung-Hyun Kim	1.00	.40
105	Joe Borowski	1.00	.40
106	Mark Grudzielanek	1.00	.40
107	Mark Buehrle	1.00	.40
108	Paul Wilson	1.00	.40
109	Ronnie Belliard	1.00	.40
110	Reggie Sanders	1.00	.40
111	Tim Redding	1.00	.40
112	Brian Lawrence	1.00	.40
113	Travis Hafner	1.00	.40
114	Jose Hernandez	1.00	.40
115	Ben Sheets	1.00	.40
116	Johan Santana	2.50	1.00
117	Billy Wagner	1.00	.40
118	Mariano Rivera	2.50	1.00
119	Steve Trachsel	1.00	.40
120	Akinori Otsuka	1.00	.40
121	Jose Valentin	1.00	.40
122	Orlando Hernandez	1.00	.40
123	Raul Ibanez	1.00	.40
124	Mike Matheny	1.00	.40
125	Vernon Wells	1.00	.40
126	Jason Isringhausen	1.00	.40
127	Jose Guillen	1.00	.40
128	Danny Bautista	1.00	.40
129	Marcus Giles	1.00	.40
130	Javy Lopez	1.00	.40
131	Kevin Millar	1.00	.40
132	Kyle Farnsworth	1.00	.40
133	Carl Pavano	1.00	.40
134	Rafael Furcal	1.00	.40
135	Casey Blake	1.00	.40
136	Matt Holliday	1.00	.40
137	Bobby Higginson	1.00	.40
138	Adam Kennedy	1.00	.40
139	Alex Gonzalez	1.00	.40
140	Jeff Kent	1.00	.40
141	Aaron Guiel	1.00	.40
142	Shawn Green	1.00	.40
143	Bill Hall	1.00	.40
144	Shannon Stewart	1.00	.40
145	Juan Rivera	1.00	.40
146	Coco Crisp	1.00	.40
147	Mike Mussina	1.50	.60
148	Eric Chavez	1.00	.40
149	Jon Lieber	1.00	.40
150	Vladimir Guerrero	2.50	1.00
151	Alex Cintron	1.00	.40
152	Luis Matos	1.00	.40
153	Sidney Ponson	1.00	.40
154	Trot Nixon	1.00	.40
155	Greg Maddux	4.00	1.50
156	Edgar Renteria	1.00	.40
157	Ryan Freel	1.00	.40
158	Matt Lawton	1.00	.40
159	Mark Prior	1.50	.60
160	Josh Beckett	1.00	.40
161	Ken Harvey	1.00	.40
162	Angel Berroa	1.00	.40
163	Juan Encarnacion	1.00	.40
164	Wes Helms	1.00	.40
165	Brad Radke	1.00	.40
166	Phil Nevin	1.00	.40
167	Mike Cameron	1.00	.40
168	Billy Koch	1.00	.40
169	Bobby Crosby	1.00	.40
170	Mike Lieberthal	1.00	.40
171	Rob Mackowiak	1.00	.40
172	Sean Burroughs	1.00	.40
173	J.T. Snow	1.00	.40
174	Paul Konerko	1.00	.40
175	Luis Gonzalez	1.00	.40
176	John Lackey	1.00	.40
177	Oliver Perez	1.00	.40
178	Brian Roberts	1.00	.40
179	Bill Mueller	1.00	.40
180	Carlos Lee	1.00	.40
181	Corey Patterson	1.00	.40
182	Sean Casey	1.00	.40
183	Cliff Lee	1.00	.40
184	Jason Jennings	1.00	.40
185	Dmitri Young	1.00	.40
186	Juan Uribe	1.00	.40
187	Andy Pettitte	1.50	.60
188	Juan Gonzalez	1.00	.40
189	Orlando Hudson	1.00	.40
190	Jason Phillips	1.00	.40
191	Braden Looper	1.00	.40
192	Lew Ford	1.00	.40
193	Mark Mulder	1.00	.40
194	Bobby Abreu	1.00	.40
195	Jason Kendall	1.00	.40
196	Khalil Greene	1.50	.60
197	A.J. Pierzynski	1.00	.40
198	Tim Worrell	1.00	.40
199	So Taguchi	1.00	.40
200	Jason Giambi	1.00	.40
201	Tony Batista	1.00	.40
202	Carlos Zambrano	1.00	.40
203	Trevor Hoffman	1.00	.40
204	Odalis Perez	1.00	.40
205	Jose Cruz Jr.	1.00	.40
206	Michael Barrett	1.00	.40
207	Chris Carpenter	1.00	.40
208	Michael Young UER	1.00	.40
209	Toby Hall	1.00	.40
210	Woody Williams	1.00	.40
211	Chris Denorfia FY RC	3.00	1.25
212	Darren Fenster FY RC	2.00	.75
213	Elvys Quezada FY RC	2.00	.75
214	Ian Kinsler FY RC	6.00	2.50
215	Matthew Lindstrom FY RC	2.00	.75
216	Ryan Goleski FY RC	3.00	1.25
217	Ryan Sweeney FY RC	4.00	1.50
218	Sean Marshall FY RC	5.00	2.00
219	Steve Doetsch FY RC	3.00	1.25
220	Wade Robinson FY RC	2.00	.75
221	Andre Ethier FY AU RC	80.00	40.00
222	Brandon Moss FY AU RC	25.00	12.50
223	Chadd Blasko FY AU RC	15.00	6.00
224	Chris Roberson FY AU RC	10.00	4.00
225	Chris Seddon FY AU RC	10.00	4.00
226	Ian Bladergroen FY AU RC	15.00	6.00
227	Jake Dittler FY AU	10.00	4.00
228	Jose Vaquedano FY AU RC	10.00	4.00
229	Jeremy West FY AU RC	15.00	6.00
230	Kole Strayhorn FY AU RC	10.00	4.00
231	Kevin West FY AU RC	10.00	4.00
232	Luis Ramirez FY AU RC	10.00	4.00
233	Melky Cabrera FY AU RC	40.00	20.00
234	Nate Schierholtz FY AU	10.00	4.00
235	Billy Butler FY AU RC	60.00	35.00
236	B.Szymanski FY AU EXCH	10.00	4.00
237	Chad Orvella FY AU RC	10.00	4.00
238	Chip Cannon FY AU RC	20.00	8.00
239	Eric Nielsen FY AU RC	10.00	4.00
240	Erik Cordier FY AU RC	10.00	4.00
241	Glen Perkins FY AU RC	20.00	8.00
242	Justin Verlander FY AU RC	50.00	30.00
243	Kevin Melillo FY AU RC	15.00	6.00
244	Landon Powell FY AU RC	15.00	6.00
245	Matt Campbell FY AU RC	10.00	4.00
246	Michael Rogers FY AU RC	10.00	4.00
247	Nate McLouth FY AU RC	15.00	6.00
248	Scott Mathieson FY AU RC	10.00	4.00
249	Shane Costa FY AU RC	10.00	4.00
250	Tony Giarratano FY AU RC	10.00	4.00
251	Tyler Pelland FY AU RC	15.00	6.00
252	Wes Swackhamer FY AU RC	10.00	4.00
253	Garret Anderson	1.00	.40
254	Randy Johnson	2.50	1.00
255	Charles Thomas	1.00	.40
256	Rafael Palmeiro	1.50	.60
257	Kevin Youkilis	1.00	.40
258	Freddy Garcia	1.00	.40
259	Magglio Ordonez	1.00	.40
260	Aaron Harang	1.00	.40
261	Grady Sizemore	1.50	.60
262	Chin-hui Tsao	1.00	.40
263	Eric Munson	1.00	.40
264	Juan Pierre	1.00	.40
265	Brad Lidge	1.00	.40
266	Brian Anderson	1.00	.40
267	Todd Helton	1.50	.60
268	Chad Cordero	1.00	.40
269	Kris Benson	1.00	.40
270	Brad Halsey	1.00	.40
271	Jermaine Dye	1.00	.40
272	Manny Ramirez	1.50	.60
273	Adam Eaton	1.00	.40
274	Brett Tomko	1.00	.40
275	Bucky Jacobsen	1.00	.40
276	Dontrelle Willis	1.00	.40
277	B.J. Upton	1.00	.40
278	Rocco Baldelli	1.00	.40
279	Ryan Drese	1.00	.40
280	Ichiro Suzuki	5.00	2.00
281	Brandon Lyon	1.00	.40
282	Nick Green	1.00	.40
283	Jerry Hairston Jr.	1.00	.40
284	Mike Lowell	1.00	.40
285	Kerry Wood	1.00	.40
286	Omar Vizquel	1.50	.60
287	Carlos Beltran	1.00	.40
288	Carlos Pena	1.00	.40
289	Jeff Weaver	1.00	.40
290	Chad Moeller	1.00	.40
291	Joe Mays	1.00	.40
292	Terrmel Sledge	1.00	.40
293	Richard Hidalgo	1.00	.40
294	Justin Duchscherer	1.00	.40
295	Eric Milton	1.00	.40
296	Ramon Hernandez	1.00	.40
297	Jose Reyes	1.00	.40
298	Joel Pineiro	1.00	.40
299	Matt Morris	1.00	.40
300	John Halama	1.00	.40
301	Gary Matthews Jr.	1.00	.40
302	Ryan Madson	1.00	.40
303	Mark Kotsay	1.00	.40

❑ 304	Carlos Delgado	1.00	.40
❑ 305	Casey Kotchman	1.00	.40
❑ 306	Greg Aquino	1.00	.40
❑ 307	LaTroy Hawkins	1.00	.40
❑ 308	Jose Contreras	1.00	.40
❑ 309	Ken Griffey Jr.	4.00	1.50
❑ 310	C.C. Sabathia	1.00	.40
❑ 311	Brandon Inge	1.00	.40
❑ 312	John Buck	1.00	.40
❑ 313	Hee Seop Choi	1.00	.40
❑ 314	Chris Capuano	1.00	.40
❑ 315	Jesse Crain	1.00	.40
❑ 316	Geoff Jenkins	1.00	.40
❑ 317	Mike Piazza	2.50	1.00
❑ 318	Jorge Posada	1.50	.60
❑ 319	Nick Swisher	1.00	.40
❑ 320	Kevin Millwood	1.00	.40
❑ 321	Mike Gonzalez	1.00	.40
❑ 322	Jake Peavy	1.00	.40
❑ 323	Dustin Hermanson	1.00	.40
❑ 324	Jeremy Reed	1.00	.40
❑ 325	Alfonso Soriano	1.00	.40
❑ 326	Alexis Rios	1.00	.40
❑ 327	David Eckstein	1.00	.40
❑ 328	Shea Hillenbrand	1.00	.40
❑ 329	Russ Ortiz	1.00	.40
❑ 330	Kurt Ainsworth	1.00	.40
❑ 331	Orlando Cabrera	1.00	.40
❑ 332	Carlos Silva	1.00	.40
❑ 333	Ross Gload	1.00	.40
❑ 334	Josh Phelps	1.00	.40
❑ 335	Mike Maroth	1.00	.40
❑ 336	Guillermo Mota	1.00	.40
❑ 337	Chris Burke	1.00	.40
❑ 338	David DeJesus	1.00	.40
❑ 339	Jose Lima	1.00	.40
❑ 340	Cristian Guzman	1.00	.40
❑ 341	Nick Johnson	1.00	.40
❑ 342	Victor Zambrano	1.00	.40
❑ 343	Rod Barajas	1.00	.40
❑ 344	Damian Miller	1.00	.40
❑ 345	Chase Utley	1.50	.60
❑ 346	Sean Burnett	1.00	.40
❑ 347	David Wells	1.00	.40
❑ 348	Dustan Mohr	1.00	.40
❑ 349	Bobby Madritsch	1.00	.40
❑ 350	Reed Johnson	1.00	.40
❑ 351	R.A. Dickey	1.00	.40
❑ 352	Scott Kazmir	1.00	.40
❑ 353	Tony Womack	1.00	.40
❑ 354	Tomas Perez	1.00	.40
❑ 355	Esteban Loaiza	1.00	.40
❑ 356	Tomokazu Ohka	1.00	.40
❑ 357	Ramon Ortiz	1.00	.40
❑ 358	Richie Sexson	1.00	.40
❑ 359	J.D. Drew	1.00	.40
❑ 360	Barry Bonds	6.00	2.50
❑ 361	Aramis Ramirez	1.00	.40
❑ 362	Wily Mo Pena	1.00	.40
❑ 363	Jeromy Burnitz	1.00	.40
❑ 364	Nomar Garciaparra	2.50	1.00
❑ 365	Brandon Backe	1.00	.40
❑ 366	Derek Lowe	1.00	.40
❑ 367	Doug Davis	1.00	.40
❑ 368	Joe Mauer	2.50	1.00
❑ 369	Endy Chavez	1.00	.40
❑ 370	Bernie Williams	1.50	.60
❑ 371	Jason Michaels	1.00	.40
❑ 372	Craig Wilson	1.00	.40
❑ 373	Ryan Klesko	1.00	.40
❑ 374	Ray Durham	1.00	.40
❑ 375	Jose Lopez	1.00	.40
❑ 376	Jeff Suppan	1.00	.40
❑ 377	David Bush	1.00	.40
❑ 378	Marlon Byrd	1.00	.40
❑ 379	Roy Oswalt	1.00	.40
❑ 380	Rondell White	1.00	.40
❑ 381	Troy Glaus	1.00	.40
❑ 382	Scott Hairston	1.00	.40
❑ 383	Chipper Jones	2.50	1.00
❑ 384	Daniel Cabrera	1.00	.40
❑ 385	Jon Garland	1.00	.40
❑ 386	Austin Kearns	1.00	.40
❑ 387	Jake Westbrook	1.00	.40
❑ 388	Aaron Miles	1.00	.40
❑ 389	Omar Infante	1.00	.40
❑ 390	Paul Lo Duca	1.00	.40
❑ 391	Morgan Ensberg	1.00	.40
❑ 392	Tony Graffanino	1.00	.40
❑ 393	Milton Bradley	1.00	.40
❑ 394	Keith Ginter	1.00	.40
❑ 395	Justin Morneau	1.00	.40
❑ 396	Tony Armas Jr.	1.00	.40
❑ 397	Kevin Brown	1.00	.40
❑ 398	Marco Scutaro	1.00	.40
❑ 399	Tim Hudson	1.00	.40
❑ 400	Pat Burrell	1.00	.40
❑ 401	Jeff Cirillo	1.00	.40
❑ 402	Larry Walker	1.50	.60
❑ 403	Dewon Brazelton	1.00	.40
❑ 404	Shigetoshi Hasegawa	1.00	.40
❑ 405	Octavio Dotel	1.00	.40
❑ 406	Michael Cuddyer	1.00	.40
❑ 407	Junior Spivey	1.00	.40
❑ 408	Zack Greinke	1.00	.40
❑ 409	Roger Clemens	4.00	1.50
❑ 410	Chris Shelton	1.50	.60
❑ 411	Ugueth Urbina	1.00	.40
❑ 412	Rafael Betancourt	1.00	.40
❑ 413	Willie Harris	1.00	.40
❑ 414	Keith Foulke	1.00	.40
❑ 415	Larry Bigbie	1.00	.40
❑ 416	Paul Byrd	1.00	.40
❑ 417	Troy Percival	1.00	.40
❑ 418	Pedro Martinez	1.50	.60
❑ 419	Matt Clement	1.00	.40
❑ 420	Ryan Wagner	1.00	.40
❑ 421	Jeff Francis	1.00	.40
❑ 422	Jeff Conine	1.00	.40
❑ 423	Wade Miller	1.00	.40
❑ 424	Gavin Floyd	1.00	.40
❑ 425	Kazuhisa Ishii	1.00	.40
❑ 426	Victor Santos	1.00	.40
❑ 427	Jacque Jones	1.00	.40
❑ 428	Hideki Matsui	4.00	1.50
❑ 429	Cory Lidle	1.00	.40
❑ 430	Jose Castillo	1.00	.40
❑ 431	Alex Gonzalez	1.00	.40
❑ 432	Kirk Rueter	1.00	.40
❑ 433	Jolbert Cabrera	1.00	.40
❑ 434	Erik Bedard	1.00	.40
❑ 435	Ricky Ledee	1.00	.40
❑ 436	Mark Hendrickson	1.00	.40
❑ 437	Laynce Nix	1.00	.40
❑ 438	Jason Frasor	1.00	.40
❑ 439	Kevin Gregg	1.00	.40
❑ 440	Derek Jeter	5.00	2.00
❑ 441	Jaret Wright	1.00	.40
❑ 442	Edwin Jackson	1.00	.40
❑ 443	Moises Alou	1.00	.40
❑ 444	Aaron Rowand	1.00	.40
❑ 445	Kazuhito Tadano	1.00	.40
❑ 446	Luis Gonzalez	1.00	.40
❑ 447	A.J. Burnett	1.00	.40
❑ 448	Jeff Bagwell	1.50	.60
❑ 449	Brad Penny	1.00	.40
❑ 450	Corey Koskie	1.00	.40
❑ 451	Mark Ellis	1.00	.40
❑ 452	Hector Luna	1.00	.40
❑ 453	Miguel Olivo	1.00	.40
❑ 454	Scott Rolen	1.50	.60
❑ 455	Ricardo Rodriguez	1.00	.40
❑ 456	Eric Hinske	1.00	.40
❑ 457	Tim Salmon	1.50	.60
❑ 458	Adam LaRoche	1.00	.40
❑ 459	B.J. Ryan	1.00	.40
❑ 460	Steve Finley	1.00	.40
❑ 461	Joe Nathan	1.00	.40
❑ 462	Vicente Padilla	1.00	.40
❑ 463	Yadier Molina	1.00	.40
❑ 464	Tino Martinez	1.50	.60
❑ 465	Mark Teixeira	1.50	.60
❑ 466	Kelvim Escobar	1.00	.40
❑ 467	Pedro Feliz	1.00	.40
❑ 468	Ryan Garko FY RC	5.00	2.00
❑ 469	Bobby Livingston FY RC	2.00	.75
❑ 470	Yorman Bazardo FY RC	2.00	.75
❑ 471	Mike Bourn FY RC	3.00	1.25
❑ 472	Andy LaRoche FY RC	8.00	3.00

2005 Topps Chrome Update

❑	COMPLETE SET (237)	300.00	200.00
❑	COMP.SET w/o SP's (220)	80.00	40.00
❑	COM (1-85/216-220)	.75	.30
❑	COMMON (86-105)	.75	.30
❑	COM (14/65/106-215)	1.00	.40
❑	221-237 GROUP A ODDS 1:25 H, 1:49 R		
❑	221-237 GROUP B ODDS 1:29 H, 1:57 R		
❑	1-220 PLATE ODDS 1:347 H		
❑	221-237 PLATE AU ODDS 1:4857 H		
❑	PLATE PRINT RUN 1 SET PER COLOR		
❑	BLACK-CYAN-MAGENTA-YELLOW ISSUED		
❑	NO PLATE PRICING DUE TO SCARCITY		
❑ 1	Sammy Sosa	2.00	.75
❑ 2	Jeff Francoeur	2.50	1.00
❑ 3	Tony Clark	.75	.30
❑ 4	Michael Tucker	.75	.30
❑ 5	Mike Matheny	.75	.30
❑ 6	Eric Young	.75	.30
❑ 7	Jose Valentin	.75	.30
❑ 8	Matt Lawton	.75	.30
❑ 9	Juan Rivera	.75	.30
❑ 10	Shawn Green	.75	.30
❑ 11	Aaron Boone	.75	.30
❑ 12	Woody Williams	.75	.30
❑ 13	Brad Wilkerson	.75	.30
❑ 14	Anthony Reyes RC	5.00	2.00
❑ 15	Gustavo Chacin	.75	.30
❑ 16	Michael Restovich	.75	.30
❑ 17	Humberto Quintero	.75	.30
❑ 18	Matt Ginter	.75	.30
❑ 19	Scott Podsednik	.75	.30
❑ 20	Byung-Hyun Kim	.75	.30
❑ 21	Orlando Hernandez	.75	.30
❑ 22	Mark Grudzielanek	.75	.30
❑ 23	Jody Gerut	.75	.30
❑ 24	Adrian Beltre	.75	.30
❑ 25	Scott Schoeneweis	.75	.30
❑ 26	Marlon Anderson	.75	.30
❑ 27	Jason Vargas	.75	.30
❑ 28	Claudio Vargas	.75	.30
❑ 29	Jason Kendall	.75	.30
❑ 30	Aaron Small	.75	.30
❑ 31	Juan Cruz	.75	.30
❑ 32	Placido Polanco	.75	.30
❑ 33	Jorge Sosa	.75	.30
❑ 34	John Olerud	.75	.30
❑ 35	Ryan Langerhans	.75	.30
❑ 36	Randy Winn	.75	.30
❑ 37	Zach Duke	2.00	.75
❑ 38	Garrett Atkins	.75	.30
❑ 39	Al Leiter	.75	.30
❑ 40	Shawn Chacon	.75	.30
❑ 41	Mark DeRosa	.75	.30
❑ 42	Miguel Ojeda	.75	.30
❑ 43	A.J. Pierzynski	.75	.30
❑ 44	Carlos Lee	.75	.30
❑ 45	LaTroy Hawkins	.75	.30
❑ 46	Nick Green	.75	.30
❑ 47	Shawn Estes	.75	.30
❑ 48	Eli Marrero	.75	.30
❑ 49	Jeff Kent	.75	.30
❑ 50	Joe Randa	.75	.30
❑ 51	Jose Hernandez	.75	.30
❑ 52	Joe Blanton	.75	.30
❑ 53	Huston Street	2.00	.75

❑ 54 Marlon Byrd .75 .30
❑ 55 Alex Sanchez .75 .30
❑ 56 Livan Hernandez .75 .30
❑ 57 Chris Young .75 .30
❑ 58 Brad Eldred .75 .30
❑ 59 Terrence Long .75 .30
❑ 60 Phil Nevin .75 .30
❑ 61 Kyle Farnsworth .75 .30
❑ 62 Jon Lieber .75 .30
❑ 63 Antonio Alfonseca .75 .30
❑ 64 Tony Graffanino .75 .30
❑ 65 Tadahito Iguchi RC 3.00 1.25
❑ 66 Brad Thompson .75 .30
❑ 67 Jose Vidro .75 .30
❑ 68 Jason Phillips .75 .30
❑ 69 Carl Pavano .75 .30
❑ 70 Pokey Reese .75 .30
❑ 71 Jerome Williams .75 .30
❑ 72 Kazuhisa Ishii .75 .30
❑ 73 Felix Hernandez 3.00 1.25
❑ 74 Edgar Renteria .75 .30
❑ 75 Mike Myers .75 .30
❑ 76 Jeff Cirillo .75 .30
❑ 77 Endy Chavez .75 .30
❑ 78 Jose Guillen .75 .30
❑ 79 Ugueth Urbina .75 .30
❑ 80 Zach Day .75 .30
❑ 81 Javier Vazquez .75 .30
❑ 82 Willy Taveras .75 .30
❑ 83 Mark Mulder .75 .30
❑ 84 Vinny Castilla .75 .30
❑ 85 Russ Adams .75 .30
❑ 86 Homer Bailey PROS .75 .30
❑ 87 Ervin Santana PROS .75 .30
❑ 88 Bill Bray PROS .75 .30
❑ 89 Thomas Diamond PROS .75 .30
❑ 90 Trevor Plouffe PROS .75 .30
❑ 91 James Houser PROS .75 .30
❑ 92 Jake Stevens PROS .75 .30
❑ 93 Anthony Whittington PROS .75 .30
❑ 94 Philip Hughes PROS .75 .30
❑ 95 Greg Golson PROS .75 .30
❑ 96 Paul Maholm PROS .75 .30
❑ 97 Carlos Quentin PROS .75 .30
❑ 98 Dan Johnson PROS .75 .30
❑ 99 Mark Rogers PROS .75 .30
❑ 100 Neil Walker PROS .75 .30
❑ 101 Omar Quintanilla PROS .75 .30
❑ 102 Blake DeWitt PROS .75 .30
❑ 103 Taylor Tankersley PROS .75 .30
❑ 104 David Murphy PROS .75 .30
❑ 105 Chris Lambert PROS .75 .30
❑ 106 Drew Anderson FY RC 1.00 .40
❑ 107 Luis Hernandez FY RC 1.00 .40
❑ 108 Jim Burt FY RC 1.00 .40
❑ 109 Mike Morse FY RC 2.00 .75
❑ 110 Elliot Johnson FY RC 1.00 .40
❑ 111 C.J. Smith FY RC 1.00 .40
❑ 112 Casey McGehee FY RC 1.00 .40
❑ 113 Brian Miller FY RC 1.00 .40
❑ 114 Chris Vines FY RC 1.00 .40
❑ 115 D.J. Houlton FY RC 1.00 .40
❑ 116 Chuck Tiffany FY RC 3.00 1.25
❑ 117 Humberto Sanchez FY RC 4.00 1.50
❑ 118 Baltazar Lopez FY RC 1.00 .40
❑ 119 Russ Martin FY RC 3.00 1.25
❑ 120 Dana Eveland FY RC 1.00 .40
❑ 121 Johan Silva FY RC 1.00 .40
❑ 122 Adam Harben FY RC 1.25 .50
❑ 123 Brian Bannister FY RC 2.50 1.00
❑ 124 Adam Boeve FY RC 1.00 .40
❑ 125 Thomas Oldham FY RC 1.00 .40
❑ 126 Cody Haerther FY RC 1.00 .40
❑ 127 Dan Santin FY RC 1.00 .40
❑ 128 Daniel Haigwood FY RC 2.00 .75
❑ 129 Craig Tatum FY RC 1.00 .40
❑ 130 Martin Prado FY RC 1.00 .40
❑ 131 Errol Simonitsch FY RC 1.25 .50
❑ 132 Lorenzo Scott FY RC 1.00 .40
❑ 133 Hayden Penn FY RC 2.00 .75
❑ 134 Heath Totten FY RC 1.00 .40
❑ 135 Nick Masset FY RC 1.00 .40
❑ 136 Pedro Lopez FY RC 1.00 .40
❑ 137 Ben Harrison FY 1.00 .40
❑ 138 Mike Spidale FY RC 1.00 .40
❑ 139 Jeremy Harts FY RC 1.00 .40
❑ 140 Danny Zell FY RC 1.00 .40
❑ 141 Kevin Collins FY RC 1.00 .40
❑ 142 Tony Arnerich FY RC 1.00 .40
❑ 143 Matt Albers FY RC 2.50 1.00
❑ 144 Ricky Barrett FY RC 1.00 .40
❑ 145 Hernan Iribarren FY RC 1.25 .50
❑ 146 Sean Tracey FY RC 1.00 .40
❑ 147 Jerry Owens FY RC 1.25 .50
❑ 148 Steve Nelson FY RC 1.00 .40
❑ 149 Brandon McCarthy FY RC 2.50 1.00
❑ 150 David Shepard FY RC 1.00 .40
❑ 151 Steven Bondurant FY RC 1.00 .40
❑ 152 Billy Sadler FY RC 1.00 .40
❑ 153 Ryan Feierabend FY RC 1.00 .40
❑ 154 Stuart Pomeranz FY RC 1.00 .40
❑ 155 Shaun Marcum FY 1.00 .40
❑ 156 Erik Schindewolf FY RC 1.00 .40
❑ 157 Stefan Bailie FY RC 1.00 .40
❑ 158 Mike Esposito FY RC 1.00 .40
❑ 159 Buck Coats FY RC 1.00 .40
❑ 160 Andy Sides FY RC 1.00 .40
❑ 161 Micah Schnurstein FY RC 1.00 .40
❑ 162 Jesse Gutierrez FY RC 1.00 .40
❑ 163 Jake Postlewait FY RC 1.00 .40
❑ 164 Willy Mota FY RC 1.00 .40
❑ 165 Ryan Speier FY RC 1.00 .40
❑ 166 Frank Mata FY RC 1.00 .40
❑ 167 Jair Jurrjens FY RC 2.00 .75
❑ 168 Nick Touchstone FY RC 1.00 .40
❑ 169 Matthew Kemp FY RC 8.00 3.00
❑ 170 Vinny Rottino FY RC 1.00 .40
❑ 171 J.B. Thurmond FY RC 1.00 .40
❑ 172 Kelvin Pichardo FY RC 1.00 .40
❑ 173 Scott Mitchinson FY RC 1.00 .40
❑ 174 Darwinson Salazar FY RC 1.00 .40
❑ 175 George Kottaras FY RC 2.00 .75
❑ 176 Kenny Durost FY RC 1.00 .40
❑ 177 Jonathan Sanchez FY RC 3.00 1.25
❑ 178 Brandon Moorhead FY RC 1.00 .40
❑ 179 Kennard Bibbs FY RC 1.00 .40
❑ 180 David Gassner FY RC 1.00 .40
❑ 181 Micah Furtado FY RC 1.00 .40
❑ 182 Ismael Ramirez FY RC 1.00 .40
❑ 183 Carlos Gonzalez FY RC 6.00 2.50
❑ 184 Brandon Sing FY RC 1.25 .50
❑ 185 Jason Motte FY RC 1.00 .40
❑ 186 Chuck James FY RC 5.00 2.00
❑ 187 Andy Santana FY RC 1.00 .40
❑ 188 Manny Parra FY RC 1.00 .40
❑ 189 Chris B.Young FY RC 4.00 1.50
❑ 190 Juan Senreiso FY RC 1.00 .40
❑ 191 Franklin Morales FY RC 2.00 .75
❑ 192 Jared Gothreaux FY RC 1.00 .40
❑ 193 Jayce Tingler FY RC 1.00 .40
❑ 194 Matt Brown FY RC 1.00 .40
❑ 195 Frank Diaz FY RC 1.00 .40
❑ 196 Stephen Drew FY RC 12.00 5.00
❑ 197 Jered Weaver FY RC 10.00 4.00
❑ 198 Ryan Braun FY RC 6.00 2.50
❑ 199 John Mayberry Jr. FY RC 2.50 1.00
❑ 200 Aaron Thompson FY RC 2.00 .75
❑ 201 Ben Copeland FY RC 4.00 1.50
❑ 202 Jacoby Ellsbury FY RC 4.00 1.50
❑ 203 Garrett Olson FY RC 2.00 .75
❑ 204 Cliff Pennington FY RC 2.00 .75
❑ 205 Colby Rasmus FY RC 5.00 2.00
❑ 206 Chris Volstad FY RC 2.50 1.00
❑ 207 Ricky Romero FY RC 2.00 .75
❑ 208 Ryan Zimmerman FY RC 15.00 6.00
❑ 209 C.J. Henry FY RC 4.00 1.50
❑ 210 Nelson Cruz FY RC 3.00 1.25
❑ 211 Josh Wall FY RC 1.25 .50
❑ 212 Nick Webber FY RC 1.00 .40
❑ 213 Paul Kelly FY RC 1.25 .50
❑ 214 Kyle Winters FY RC 1.25 .50
❑ 215 Mitch Boggs FY RC 1.00 .40
❑ 216 Craig Biggio HL .75 .30
❑ 217 Greg Maddux HL 2.00 .75
❑ 218 Bobby Abreu HL .75 .30
❑ 219 Alex Rodriguez HL 2.00 .75
❑ 220 Trevor Hoffman HL .75 .30
❑ 221 Trevor Bell FY AU A RC 15.00 6.00
❑ 222 Jay Bruce FY AU A RC 50.00 20.00
❑ 223 Travis Buck FY AU B RC 20.00 8.00
❑ 224 Cesar Carrillo FY AU B RC 15.00 6.00
❑ 225 Mike Costanzo FY AU A RC 20.008.00
❑ 226 Brent Cox FY AU A RC 10.00 4.00
❑ 227 Matt Garza FY AU A RC 30.00 15.00
❑ 228 Josh Geer FY AU A RC 10.00 4.00
❑ 229 Tyler Greene FY AU A RC 15.00 6.00
❑ 230 Eli Iorg FY AU A RC 10.00 4.00
❑ 231 Craig Italiano FY AU B RC 10.00 4.00
❑ 232 Beau Jones FY AU A RC 15.00 6.00
❑ 233 M.McCormick FY AU B RC 10.00 4.00
❑ 234 A.McCutchen FY AU B RC 40.0020.00
❑ 235 Micah Owings FY AU B RC 12.005.00
❑ 236 Cesar Ramos FY AU B RC 10.00 4.00
❑ 237 Chaz Roe FY AU A RC 10.00 4.00

2006 Topps Chrome

❑ COMP.SET w/o AU's (330) 80.00 40.00
❑ COMMON CARD (1-252) .60 .25
❑ COMMON CARD (253-275) .40 .15
❑ COMMON ROOKIE (276-330) 1.00 .40
❑ COMMON AUTO (285b/331-354) 10.004.00
❑ AU 331-354 ODDS 1:15 HOBBY
❑ JOHJIMA AU ODDS 1:1650 HOBBY
❑ 1-330 PLATES 1:25 HOBBY BOX LDR
❑ 331-354 AU PLATES 1:324 HOBBY BOX LDR
❑ PLATE PRINT RUN 1 SET PER COLOR
❑ BLACK-CYAN-MAGENTA-YELLOW ISSUED
❑ NO PLATE PRICING DUE TO SCARCITY
❑ 1 Alex Rodriguez 2.50 1.00
❑ 2 Garrett Atkins .60 .25
❑ 3 Carl Crawford .60 .25
❑ 4 Clint Barmes .60 .25
❑ 5 Tadahito Iguchi .60 .25
❑ 6 Brian Roberts .60 .25
❑ 7 Mickey Mantle 8.00 3.00
❑ 8 David Wright 2.50 1.00
❑ 9 Jeremy Reed .60 .25
❑ 10 Bobby Abreu .60 .25
❑ 11 Lance Berkman .60 .25
❑ 12 Jonny Gomes .60 .25
❑ 13 Jason Marquis .60 .25
❑ 14 Chipper Jones 1.50 .60
❑ 15 Jon Garland .60 .25
❑ 16 Brad Wilkerson .60 .25
❑ 17 Rickie Weeks .60 .25
❑ 18 Jorge Posada 1.00 .40
❑ 19 Greg Maddux 2.50 1.00
❑ 20 Jeff Francis .60 .25
❑ 21 Felipe Lopez .60 .25
❑ 22 Dan Johnson .60 .25
❑ 23 Manny Ramirez 1.00 .40
❑ 24 Joe Mauer 1.00 .40
❑ 25 Randy Winn .60 .25
❑ 26 Pedro Feliz .60 .25
❑ 27 Kenny Rogers .60 .25
❑ 28 Rocco Baldelli .60 .25
❑ 29 Nomar Garciaparra 1.50 .60
❑ 30 Carlos Lee .60 .25
❑ 31 Tom Glavine 1.00 .40
❑ 32 Craig Biggio 1.00 .40
❑ 33 Steve Finley .60 .25
❑ 34 Eric Gagne .60 .25
❑ 35 Dallas McPherson .60 .25
❑ 36 Mark Kotsay .60 .25
❑ 37 Kerry Wood .60 .25
❑ 38 Huston Street .60 .25
❑ 39 Hank Blalock .60 .25
❑ 40 Brad Radke .60 .25
❑ 41 Chien-Ming Wang 2.50 1.00
❑ 42 Mark Buehrle .60 .25

❑ 43 Andy Pettitte .60 .25
❑ 44 Bernie Williams 1.00 .40
❑ 45 Victor Martinez .60 .25
❑ 46 Darin Erstad .60 .25
❑ 47 Gustavo Chacin .60 .25
❑ 48 Carlos Guillen .60 .25
❑ 49 Lyle Overbay .60 .25
❑ 50 Barry Bonds 3.00 1.25
❑ 51 Nook Logan .60 .25
❑ 52 Mark Teahen .60 .25
❑ 53 Mike Lamb .60 .25
❑ 54 Jayson Werth .60 .25
❑ 55 Mariano Rivera 1.50 .60
❑ 56 Julio Lugo .60 .25
❑ 57 Adam Dunn .60 .25
❑ 58 Troy Percival .60 .25
❑ 59 Chad Tracy .60 .25
❑ 60 Edgar Renteria .60 .25
❑ 61 Jason Giambi .60 .25
❑ 62 Justin Morneau .60 .25
❑ 63 Carlos Delgado .60 .25
❑ 64 John Buck .60 .25
❑ 65 Shannon Stewart .60 .25
❑ 66 Mike Cameron .60 .25
❑ 67 Richie Sexson .60 .25
❑ 68 Russ Adams .60 .25
❑ 69 Josh Beckett .60 .25
❑ 70 Ryan Freel .60 .25
❑ 71 Victor Zambrano .60 .25
❑ 72 Ronnie Belliard .60 .25
❑ 73 Brian Giles .60 .25
❑ 74 Randy Wolf .60 .25
❑ 75 Robinson Cano 1.00 .40
❑ 76 Joe Blanton .60 .25
❑ 77 Esteban Loaiza .60 .25
❑ 78 Troy Glaus .60 .25
❑ 79 Matt Clement .60 .25
❑ 80 Geoff Jenkins .60 .25
❑ 81 Roy Oswalt .60 .25
❑ 82 A.J. Pierzynski .60 .25
❑ 83 Pedro Martinez 1.00 .40
❑ 84 Roger Clemens 3.00 1.25
❑ 85 Jack Wilson .60 .25
❑ 86 Mike Piazza 1.50 .60
❑ 87 Paul Lo Duca .60 .25
❑ 88 Jeff Bagwell 1.00 .40
❑ 89 Carlos Zambrano .60 .25
❑ 90 Brandon Claussen .60 .25
❑ 91 Travis Hafner .60 .25
❑ 92 Chris Shelton .60 .25
❑ 93 Rafael Furcal .60 .25
❑ 94 Frank Thomas 1.50 .60
❑ 95 Noah Lowry .60 .25
❑ 96 Jhonny Peralta .60 .25
❑ 97 Vernon Wells .60 .25
❑ 98 Jorge Cantu .60 .25
❑ 99 Willy Taveras .60 .25
❑ 100 Ivan Rodriguez 1.00 .40
❑ 101 Jose Reyes .60 .25
❑ 102 Barry Zito .60 .25
❑ 103 Mark Teixeira 1.00 .40
❑ 104 Chone Figgins .60 .25
❑ 105 Todd Helton 1.00 .40
❑ 106 Tim Wakefield .60 .25
❑ 107 Mike Maroth .60 .25
❑ 108 Johnny Damon 1.00 .40
❑ 109 David DeJesus .60 .25
❑ 110 Ryan Klesko .60 .25
❑ 111 Nick Johnson .60 .25
❑ 112 Freddy Garcia .60 .25
❑ 113 Torii Hunter .60 .25
❑ 114 Mike Sweeney .60 .25
❑ 115 Scott Rolen 1.00 .40
❑ 116 Jim Thome 1.00 .40
❑ 117 Adam Kennedy .60 .25
❑ 118 Albert Pujols 3.00 1.25
❑ 119 Kazuo Matsui .60 .25
❑ 120 Zack Greinke .60 .25
❑ 121 Jimmy Rollins .60 .25
❑ 122 Edgardo Alfonzo .60 .25
❑ 123 Billy Wagner .60 .25
❑ 124 B.J. Ryan .60 .25
❑ 125 Orlando Hudson .60 .25
❑ 126 Preston Wilson .60 .25
❑ 127 Melvin Mora .60 .25
❑ 128 Alfonso Soriano .60 .25
❑ 129 Javy Lopez .60 .25
❑ 130 Wilson Betemit .60 .25
❑ 131 Garret Anderson .60 .25
❑ 132 Jason Bay .60 .25
❑ 133 Adam LaRoche .60 .25
❑ 134 C.C. Sabathia .60 .25
❑ 135 Bartolo Colon .60 .25
❑ 136 Ichiro Suzuki 2.50 1.00
❑ 137 Jim Edmonds 1.00 .40
❑ 138 David Eckstein .60 .25
❑ 139 Cristian Guzman .60 .25
❑ 140 Jeff Kent .60 .25
❑ 141 Chris Capuano .60 .25
❑ 142 Cliff Floyd .60 .25
❑ 143 Zach Duke .60 .25
❑ 144 Matt Morris .60 .25
❑ 145 Jose Vidro .60 .25
❑ 146 David Wells .60 .25
❑ 147 John Smoltz 1.00 .40
❑ 148 Felix Hernandez 1.50 .60
❑ 149 Orlando Cabrera .60 .25
❑ 150 Mark Prior 1.00 .40
❑ 151 Ted Lilly .60 .25
❑ 152 Michael Young .60 .25
❑ 153 Livan Hernandez .60 .25
❑ 154 Yadier Molina .60 .25
❑ 155 Eric Chavez .60 .25
❑ 156 Miguel Batista .60 .25
❑ 157 Ben Sheets .60 .25
❑ 158 Oliver Perez .60 .25
❑ 159 Doug Davis .60 .25
❑ 160 Andruw Jones 1.00 .40
❑ 161 Hideki Matsui 1.50 .60
❑ 162 Reggie Sanders .60 .25
❑ 163 Joe Nathan .60 .25
❑ 164 John Lackey .60 .25
❑ 165 Matt Murton .60 .25
❑ 166 Grady Sizemore 1.00 .40
❑ 167 Brad Thompson .60 .25
❑ 168 Kevin Millwood .60 .25
❑ 169 Orlando Hernandez .60 .25
❑ 170 Mark Mulder .60 .25
❑ 171 Chase Utley 1.50 .60
❑ 172 Moises Alou .60 .25
❑ 173 Wily Mo Pena .60 .25
❑ 174 Brian McCann .60 .25
❑ 175 Jermaine Dye .60 .25
❑ 176 Ryan Madson .60 .25
❑ 177 Aramis Ramirez .60 .25
❑ 178 Khalil Greene 1.00 .40
❑ 179 Mike Hampton .60 .25
❑ 180 Mike Mussina 1.00 .40
❑ 181 Rich Harden .60 .25
❑ 182 Woody Williams .60 .25
❑ 183 Chris Carpenter .60 .25
❑ 184 Brady Clark .60 .25
❑ 185 Luis Gonzalez .60 .25
❑ 186 Raul Ibanez .60 .25
❑ 187 Magglio Ordonez .60 .25
❑ 188 Adrian Beltre .60 .25
❑ 189 Marcus Giles .60 .25
❑ 190 Odalis Perez .60 .25
❑ 191 Derek Jeter 4.00 1.50
❑ 192 Jason Schmidt .60 .25
❑ 193 Toby Hall .60 .25
❑ 194 Danny Haren .60 .25
❑ 195 Tim Hudson .60 .25
❑ 196 Jake Peavy .60 .25
❑ 197 Casey Blake .60 .25
❑ 198 J.D. Drew .60 .25
❑ 199 Ervin Santana .60 .25
❑ 200 J.J. Hardy .60 .25
❑ 201 Austin Kearns .60 .25
❑ 202 Pat Burrell .60 .25
❑ 203 Jason Vargas .60 .25
❑ 204 Ryan Howard 2.50 1.00
❑ 205 Joe Crede .60 .25
❑ 206 Vladimir Guerrero 1.50 .60
❑ 207 Roy Halladay .60 .25
❑ 208 David Dellucci .60 .25
❑ 209 Brandon Webb .60 .25
❑ 210 Ryan Church .60 .25
❑ 211 Miguel Tejada .60 .25
❑ 212 Mark Loretta .60 .25
❑ 213 Kevin Youkilis .60 .25
❑ 214 Jon Lieber .60 .25
❑ 215 Miguel Cabrera 1.00 .40
❑ 216 A.J. Burnett .60 .25
❑ 217 David Bell .60 .25
❑ 218 Eric Byrnes .60 .25
❑ 219 Lance Niekro .60 .25
❑ 220 Shawn Green .60 .25
❑ 221 Ken Griffey Jr. 2.50 1.00
❑ 222 Johnny Estrada .60 .25
❑ 223 Omar Vizquel 1.00 .40
❑ 224 Gary Sheffield .60 .25
❑ 225 Brad Halsey .60 .25
❑ 226 Aaron Cook .60 .25
❑ 227 David Ortiz 1.50 .60
❑ 228 Scott Kazmir 1.00 .40
❑ 229 Dustin McGowan .60 .25
❑ 230 Gregg Zaun .60 .25
❑ 231 Carlos Beltran .60 .25
❑ 232 Bob Wickman .60 .25
❑ 233 Brett Myers .60 .25
❑ 234 Casey Kotchman .60 .25
❑ 235 Jeff Francoeur 1.50 .60
❑ 236 Paul Konerko .60 .25
❑ 237 Juan Rivera .60 .25
❑ 238 Bobby Crosby .60 .25
❑ 239 Derrek Lee .60 .25
❑ 240 Curt Schilling 1.00 .40
❑ 241 Jake Westbrook .60 .25
❑ 242 Dontrelle Willis .60 .25
❑ 243 Brad Lidge .60 .25
❑ 244 Randy Johnson 1.50 .60
❑ 245 Nick Swisher .60 .25
❑ 246 Johan Santana 1.00 .40
❑ 247 Jeremy Bonderman .60 .25
❑ 248 Ramon Hernandez .60 .25
❑ 249 Mike Lowell .60 .25
❑ 250 Javier Vazquez .60 .25
❑ 251 Jose Contreras .60 .25
❑ 252 Aubrey Huff .60 .25
❑ 253 Kenny Rogers AW .40 .15
❑ 254 Mark Teixeira AW .60 .25
❑ 255 Orlando Hudson AW .40 .15
❑ 256 Derek Jeter AW 2.50 1.00
❑ 257 Eric Chavez AW .40 .15
❑ 258 Torii Hunter AW .40 .15
❑ 259 Vernon Wells AW .40 .15
❑ 260 Ichiro Suzuki AW 1.50 .60
❑ 261 Greg Maddux AW 1.50 .60
❑ 262 Mike Matheny AW .40 .15
❑ 263 Derrek Lee AW .40 .15
❑ 264 Luis Castillo AW .40 .15
❑ 265 Omar Vizquel AW .60 .25
❑ 266 Mike Lowell AW .40 .15
❑ 267 Andruw Jones AW .60 .25
❑ 268 Jim Edmonds AW .60 .25
❑ 269 Bobby Abreu AW .40 .15
❑ 270 Bartolo Colon AW .40 .15
❑ 271 Chris Carpenter AW .40 .15
❑ 272 Alex Rodriguez AW 1.50 .60
❑ 273 Albert Pujols AW 2.00 .75
❑ 274 Huston Street AW .40 .15
❑ 275 Ryan Howard AW 1.50 .60
❑ 276 Chris Denorfia (RC) 1.00 .40
❑ 277 John Van Benschoten (RC) 1.00 .40
❑ 278 Russ Martin (RC) 1.50 .60
❑ 279 Fausto Carmona (RC) 1.00 .40
❑ 280 Freddie Bynum (RC) 1.00 .40
❑ 281 Kelly Shoppach (RC) 1.00 .40
❑ 282 Chris Demaria RC 1.00 .40
❑ 283 Jordan Tata RC 1.00 .40
❑ 284 Ryan Zimmerman (RC) 6.00 2.50
❑ 285a Kenji Johjima RC 5.00 2.00
❑ 285b Kenji Johjima AU 100.00 50.00
❑ 286 Ruddy Lugo (RC) 1.00 .40
❑ 287 Tommy Murphy (RC) 1.00 .40
❑ 288 Bobby Livingston (RC) 1.00 .40
❑ 289 Anderson Hernandez (RC) 1.00 .40
❑ 290 Brian Slocum (RC) 1.00 .40
❑ 291 Sendy Rleal RC 1.00 .40
❑ 292 Ryan Spilborghs (RC) 1.50 .60
❑ 293 Brandon Fahey RC 1.00 .40
❑ 294 Jason Kubel (RC) 1.00 .40
❑ 295 James Loney (RC) 1.50 .60
❑ 296 Jeremy Accardo RC 1.00 .40
❑ 297 Fabio Castro RC 1.00 .40
❑ 298 Matt Capps (RC) 1.00 .40
❑ 299 Casey Janssen RC 1.00 .40

❑ 300 Martin Prado (RC) 1.00 .40
❑ 301 Ronny Paulino (RC) 1.00 .40
❑ 302 Josh Barfield (RC) 1.00 .40
❑ 303 Joel Zumaya (RC) 2.50 1.00
❑ 304 Matt Cain (RC) 1.50 .60
❑ 305 Conor Jackson (RC) 1.50 .60
❑ 306 Brian Anderson (RC) 1.00 .40
❑ 307 Prince Fielder (RC) 4.00 1.50
❑ 308 Jeremy Hermida (RC) 1.50 .60
❑ 309 Justin Verlander (RC) 4.00 1.50
❑ 310 Brian Bannister (RC) 1.00 .40
❑ 311 Josh Willingham (RC) 1.00 .40
❑ 312 John Rheinecker (RC) 1.00 .40
❑ 313 Nick Markakis (RC) 1.50 .60
❑ 314 Jonathan Papelbon (RC) 5.00 2.00
❑ 315 Mike Jacobs (RC) 1.00 .40
❑ 316 Jose Capellan (RC) 1.00 .40
❑ 317 Mike Napoli RC 5.00 2.00
❑ 318 Ricky Nolasco (RC) 1.00 .40
❑ 319 Ben Johnson (RC) 1.00 .40
❑ 320 Paul Maholm (RC) 1.00 .40
❑ 321 Drew Meyer (RC) 1.00 .40
❑ 322 Jeff Mathis (RC) 1.00 .40
❑ 323 Fernando Nieve (RC) 1.00 .40
❑ 324 John Koronka (RC) 1.00 .40
❑ 325 Wil Nieves (RC) 1.00 .40
❑ 326 Nate McLouth (RC) 1.00 .40
❑ 327 Howie Kendrick (RC) 5.00 2.00
❑ 328 Sean Marshall (RC) 1.00 .40
❑ 329 Brandon Watson (RC) 1.00 .40
❑ 330 Skip Schumaker (RC) 1.00 .40
❑ 331 Ryan Garko AU (RC) 10.00 4.00
❑ 332 Jason Bergmann AU RC 10.00 4.00
❑ 333 Chuck James AU (RC) 15.00 6.00
❑ 334 Adam Wainwright AU (RC) 10.00 4.00
❑ 335 Dan Ortmeier AU (RC) 10.00 4.00
❑ 336 Francisco Liriano AU (RC) 50.00 20.00
❑ 337 Craig Breslow AU RC 10.00 4.00
❑ 338 Darrell Rasner AU (RC) 10.00 4.00
❑ 339 Jason Botts AU (RC) 10.00 4.00
❑ 340 Ian Kinsler AU (RC) 15.00 6.00
❑ 341 Joey Devine AU RC 10.00 4.00
❑ 342 Miguel Perez AU (RC) 10.00 4.00
❑ 343 Scott Olsen AU (RC) 15.00 6.00
❑ 344 Tyler Johnson AU (RC) 10.00 4.00
❑ 345 Anthony Lerew AU (RC) 10.00 4.00
❑ 346 Nelson Cruz AU (RC) 10.00 4.00
❑ 347 Willie Eyre AU (RC) 10.00 4.00
❑ 348 Josh Johnson AU (RC) 20.00 8.00
❑ 349 Shaun Marcum AU (RC) 10.00 4.00
❑ 350 Dustin Nippert AU (RC) 10.00 4.00
❑ 351 Josh Wilson AU (RC) 10.00 4.00
❑ 352 Hanley Ramirez AU (RC) 25.00 10.00
❑ 353 Reggie Abercrombie AU (RC) 10.00 4.00
❑ 354 Dan Uggla AU (RC) 30.00 12.50

2006 Topps Co-Signers

❑ COMP.SET w/o AU's (100) 40.00 15.00
❑ COMMON CARD (1-100) .75 .30
❑ 101-120 GROUP A ODDS 1:2025
❑ 101-120 GROUP B ODDS 1:1625
❑ 101-120 GROUP C ODDS 1:920
❑ 101-120 GROUP D ODDS 1:81
❑ 101-120 GROUP E ODDS 1:270
❑ 101-120 GROUP F ODDS 1:68
❑ 101-120 GROUP G ODDS 1:12
❑ 101-120 GROUP A PRINT RUN 200 CARDS
❑ 101-120 GROUP B PRINT RUN 250 CARDS
❑ 101-120 GROUP C PRINT RUN 440 CARDS
❑ A-C CARDS ARE NOT SERIAL NUMBERED
❑ A-C PRINT RUNS PROVIDED BY TOPPS
❑ 1 Albert Pujols 4.00 1.50
❑ 2 Roger Clemens 4.00 1.50
❑ 3 Paul Konerko .75 .30
❑ 4 Jeff Francouer 2.00 .75
❑ 5 Miguel Tejada .75 .30
❑ 6 Curt Schilling 1.25 .50
❑ 7 Mickey Mantle 5.00 2.00
❑ 8 Miguel Cabrera 1.25 .50
❑ 9 Derrek Lee .75 .30
❑ 10 Jeff Kent .75 .30
❑ 11 Gary Sheffield .75 .30
❑ 12 Rich Harden .75 .30
❑ 13 Scott Rolen 1.25 .50
❑ 14 David Wright 3.00 1.25
❑ 15 Troy Glaus .75 .30
❑ 16 Torii Hunter .75 .30
❑ 17 Nolan Ryan 5.00 2.00
❑ 18 Alfonso Soriano .75 .30
❑ 19 Hank Blalock .75 .30
❑ 20 Chase Utley 2.00 .75
❑ 21 Ryan Howard 3.00 1.25
❑ 22 Robinson Cano 1.25 .50
❑ 23 Derek Jeter 5.00 2.00
❑ 24 Huston Street .75 .30
❑ 25 Jason Giambi .75 .30
❑ 26 Rafael Furcal .75 .30
❑ 27 Rickie Weeks .75 .30
❑ 28 Ivan Rodriguez 1.25 .50
❑ 29 Travis Hafner .75 .30
❑ 30 Greg Maddux 3.00 1.25
❑ 31 Andruw Jones 1.25 .50
❑ 32 Andy Pettitte .75 .30
❑ 33 Scott Podsednik .75 .30
❑ 34 Francisco Rodriguez .75 .30
❑ 35 Josh Beckett .75 .30
❑ 36 Lance Berkman .75 .30
❑ 37 Roy Oswalt .75 .30
❑ 38 Pedro Martinez 1.25 .50
❑ 39 Jimmy Rollins .75 .30
❑ 40 Johan Santana 1.25 .50
❑ 41 Randy Johnson 2.00 .75
❑ 42 Mariano Rivera 2.00 .75
❑ 43 Nick Johnson .75 .30
❑ 44 Josh Gibson 2.00 .75
❑ 45 Shawn Green .75 .30
❑ 46 Adrian Beltre .75 .30
❑ 47 Johnny Damon 1.25 .50
❑ 48 Joe Mauer 1.25 .50
❑ 49 Todd Helton 1.25 .50
❑ 50 Alex Rodriguez 3.00 1.25
❑ 51 Jake Peavy .75 .30
❑ 52 David Ortiz 2.00 .75
❑ 53 Mark Buehrle .75 .30
❑ 54 Eric Gagne .75 .30
❑ 55 Hideki Matsui 3.00 1.25
❑ 56 Bobby Abreu .75 .30
❑ 57 Victor Martinez .75 .30
❑ 58 Brian Roberts .75 .30
❑ 59 Chipper Jones 2.00 .75
❑ 60 Carlos Beltran .75 .30
❑ 61 Tim Hudson .75 .30
❑ 62 Carlos Lee .75 .30
❑ 63 Barry Zito .75 .30
❑ 64 Moises Alou .75 .30
❑ 65 Mark Teixeira 1.25 .50
❑ 66 Lyle Overbay .75 .30
❑ 67 Kerry Wood .75 .30
❑ 68 B.J. Ryan .75 .30
❑ 69 Jim Edmonds 1.25 .50
❑ 70 Carlos Delgado .75 .30
❑ 71 Magglio Ordonez .75 .30
❑ 72 Juan Pierre .75 .30
❑ 73 Manny Ramirez 1.25 .50
❑ 74 Dontrelle Willis .75 .30
❑ 75 Ichiro Suzuki 3.00 1.25
❑ 76 Nomar Garciaparra 2.00 .75
❑ 77 Zach Duke .75 .30
❑ 78 Chris Carpenter .75 .30
❑ 79 A.J. Burnett .75 .30
❑ 80 Scott Kazmir 1.25 .50
❑ 81 Carl Crawford .75 .30
❑ 82 Mark Prior 1.25 .50
❑ 83 Adam Dunn .75 .30
❑ 84 Justin Morneau .75 .30
❑ 85 Morgan Ensberg .75 .30
❑ 86 Pat Burrell .75 .30
❑ 87 Paul Lo Duca .75 .30
❑ 88 Jason Bay .75 .30
❑ 89 Aubrey Huff .75 .30
❑ 90 Kevin Millwood .75 .30
❑ 91 Vernon Wells .75 .30
❑ 92 Javy Lopez .75 .30
❑ 93 Michael Young .75 .30
❑ 94 Felix Hernandez 1.25 .50
❑ 95 Ken Griffey Jr. 3.00 1.25
❑ 96 Bartolo Colon .75 .30
❑ 97 Billy Wagner .75 .30
❑ 98 Vladimir Guerrero 2.00 .75
❑ 99 Jose Reyes .75 .30
❑ 100 Barry Bonds 5.00 2.00
❑ 101 Anthony LeRew AU G (RC) 10.00 4.00
❑ 102 R.Zimm AU C/440 (RC) * 50.00 20.00
❑ 103 C.Hansen AU B/250 RC * 50.00 20.00
❑ 104 F.Liriano AU G (RC) 40.00 15.00
❑ 105 Jason Botts AU G (RC) 10.00 4.00
❑ 106 Josh Johnson AU G (RC) 15.00 6.00
❑ 107 Hanley Ramirez AU G (RC) 20.00 8.00
❑ 108 A.Wainwright AU G (RC) 15.00 6.00
❑ 109 K.Johjima AU A/200 RC * 100.00 50.00
❑ 110 Dan Ortmeier AU G (RC) 10.00 4.00
❑ 111 Darrell Rasner AU G (RC) 10.00 4.00
❑ 112 Chuck James AU F (RC) 15.00 6.00
❑ 113 Nelson Cruz AU F (RC) 10.00 4.00
❑ 114 Hong-Chih Kuo AU E (RC) 40.00 15.00
❑ 115 Ryan Garko AU G (RC) 10.00 4.00
❑ 116 R.Abercrombie AU D (RC) 10.00 4.00
❑ 117 Ian Kinsler AU D (RC) 15.00 6.00
❑ 118 Joel Zumaya AU D (RC) 25.00 10.00
❑ 119 Willie Eyre AU D (RC) 10.00 4.00
❑ 120 Dan Uggla AU D (RC) 30.00 12.50

2001 Topps Heritage

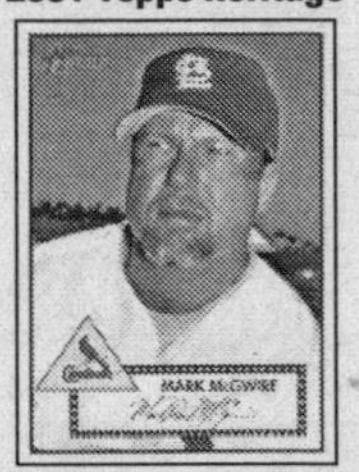

❑ COMP.MASTER SET (487) 500.00 350.00
❑ COMPLETE SET (407) 450.00 300.00
❑ COMP.BASIC SET (230) 80.00 40.00
❑ COMMON CARD (81-310) .50 .20
❑ COMMON CARD (1-80) 2.50 1.00
❑ COMMON CARD (311-407) 5.00 2.00
❑ 1 Kris Benson 2.50 1.00
❑ 1 Kris Benson Black 2.50 1.00
❑ 2 Brian Jordan 2.50 1.00
❑ 2 Brian Jordan Black 2.50 1.00
❑ 3 Fernando Vina 2.50 1.00
❑ 3 Fernando Vina Black 2.50 1.00
❑ 4 Mike Sweeney 2.50 1.00
❑ 4 Mike Sweeney Black 2.50 1.00
❑ 5 Rafael Palmeiro 2.50 1.00
❑ 5 Rafael Palmeiro Black 2.50 1.00
❑ 6 Paul O'Neill 2.50 1.00
❑ 6 Paul O'Neill Black 2.50 1.00
❑ 7 Todd Helton 2.50 1.00
❑ 7 Todd Helton Black 2.50 1.00
❑ 8 Ramiro Mendoza 2.50 1.00
❑ 8 Ramiro Mendoza Black 2.50 1.00
❑ 9 Kevin Millwood 2.50 1.00
❑ 9 Kevin Millwood Black 2.50 1.00
❑ 10 Chuck Knoblauch 2.50 1.00
❑ 10 Chuck Knoblauch Black 2.50 1.00
❑ 11 Derek Jeter 10.00 4.00
❑ 11 Derek Jeter Black 10.00 4.00

❑ 12	Alex Rodriguez Rangers	6.00	2.50
❑ 12	A.Rod Black Rangers	6.00	2.50
❑ 13	Geoff Jenkins	2.50	1.00
❑ 13	Geoff Jenkins Black	2.50	1.00
❑ 14	David Justice	2.50	1.00
❑ 14	David Justice Black	2.50	1.00
❑ 15	David Cone	2.50	1.00
❑ 15	David Cone Black	2.50	1.00
❑ 16	Andres Galarraga	2.50	1.00
❑ 16	Andres Galarraga Black	2.50	1.00
❑ 17	Garret Anderson	2.50	1.00
❑ 17	Garret Anderson Black	2.50	1.00
❑ 18	Roger Cedeno	2.50	1.00
❑ 18	Roger Cedeno Black	2.50	1.00
❑ 19	Randy Velarde	2.50	1.00
❑ 19	Randy Velarde Black	2.50	1.00
❑ 20	Carlos Delgado	2.50	1.00
❑ 20	Carlos Delgado Black	2.50	1.00
❑ 21	Quilvio Veras	2.50	1.00
❑ 21	Quilvio Veras Black	2.50	1.00
❑ 22	Jose Vidro	2.50	1.00
❑ 22	Jose Vidro Black	2.50	1.00
❑ 23	Corey Patterson	2.50	1.00
❑ 23	Corey Patterson Black	2.50	1.00
❑ 24	Jorge Posada	2.50	1.00
❑ 24	Jorge Posada Black	2.50	1.00
❑ 25	Eddie Perez	2.50	1.00
❑ 25	Eddie Perez Black	2.50	1.00
❑ 26	Jack Cust	2.50	1.00
❑ 26	Jack Cust Black	2.50	1.00
❑ 27	Sean Burroughs	2.50	1.00
❑ 27	Sean Burroughs Black	2.50	1.00
❑ 28	Randy Wolf	2.50	1.00
❑ 28	Randy Wolf Black	2.50	1.00
❑ 29	Mike Lamb	2.50	1.00
❑ 29	Mike Lamb Black	2.50	1.00
❑ 30	Rafael Furcal	2.50	1.00
❑ 30	Rafael Furcal Black	2.50	1.00
❑ 31	Barry Bonds	10.00	4.00
❑ 31	Barry Bonds Black	10.00	4.00
❑ 32	Tim Hudson	2.50	1.00
❑ 32	Tim Hudson Black	2.50	1.00
❑ 33	Tom Glavine	2.50	1.00
❑ 33	Tom Glavine Black	2.50	1.00
❑ 34	Javy Lopez	2.50	1.00
❑ 34	Javy Lopez Black	2.50	1.00
❑ 35	Aubrey Huff	2.50	1.00
❑ 35	Aubrey Huff Black	2.50	1.00
❑ 36	Wally Joyner	2.50	1.00
❑ 36	Wally Joyner Black	2.50	1.00
❑ 37	Magglio Ordonez	2.50	1.00
❑ 37	Magglio Ordonez Black	2.50	1.00
❑ 38	Matt Lawton	2.50	1.00
❑ 38	Matt Lawton Black	2.50	1.00
❑ 39	Mariano Rivera	4.00	1.50
❑ 39	Mariano Rivera Black	4.00	1.50
❑ 40	Andy Ashby	2.50	1.00
❑ 40	Andy Ashby Black	2.50	1.00
❑ 41	Mark Buehrle	2.50	1.00
❑ 41	Mark Buehrle Black	2.50	1.00
❑ 42	Esteban Loaiza	2.50	1.00
❑ 42	Esteban Loaiza Black	2.50	1.00
❑ 43	Mark Redman	2.50	1.00
❑ 43	Mark Redman Black	2.50	1.00
❑ 44	Mark Quinn	2.50	1.00
❑ 44	Mark Quinn Black	2.50	1.00
❑ 45	Tino Martinez	2.50	1.00
❑ 45	Tino Martinez Black	2.50	1.00
❑ 46	Joe Mays	2.50	1.00
❑ 46	Joe Mays Black	2.50	1.00
❑ 47	Walt Weiss	2.50	1.00
❑ 47	Walt Weiss Black	2.50	1.00
❑ 48	Roger Clemens	8.00	3.00
❑ 48	Roger Clemens Black	8.00	3.00
❑ 49	Greg Maddux	6.00	2.50
❑ 49	Greg Maddux Black	6.00	2.50
❑ 50	Richard Hidalgo	2.50	1.00
❑ 50	Richard Hidalgo Black	2.50	1.00
❑ 51	Orlando Hernandez	2.50	1.00
❑ 51	Orlando Hernandez Black	2.50	1.00
❑ 52	Chipper Jones	4.00	1.50
❑ 52	Chipper Jones Black	4.00	1.50
❑ 53	Ben Grieve	2.50	1.00
❑ 53	Ben Grieve Black	2.50	1.00
❑ 54	Jimmy Haynes	2.50	1.00
❑ 54	Jimmy Haynes Black	2.50	1.00
❑ 55	Ken Caminiti	2.50	1.00
❑ 55	Ken Caminiti Black	2.50	1.00
❑ 56	Tim Salmon	2.50	1.00
❑ 56	Tim Salmon Black	2.50	1.00
❑ 57	Andy Pettitte	2.50	1.00
❑ 57	Andy Pettitte Black	2.50	1.00
❑ 58	Darin Erstad	2.50	1.00
❑ 58	Darin Erstad Black	2.50	1.00
❑ 59	Marquis Grissom	2.50	1.00
❑ 59	Marquis Grissom Black	2.50	1.00
❑ 60	Raul Mondesi	2.50	1.00
❑ 60	Raul Mondesi Black	2.50	1.00
❑ 61	Bengie Molina	2.50	1.00
❑ 61	Bengie Molina Black	2.50	1.00
❑ 62	Miguel Tejada	2.50	1.00
❑ 62	Miguel Tejada Black	2.50	1.00
❑ 63	Jose Cruz Jr.	2.50	1.00
❑ 63	Jose Cruz Jr. Black	2.50	1.00
❑ 64	Billy Koch	2.50	1.00
❑ 64	Billy Koch Black	2.50	1.00
❑ 65	Troy Glaus	2.50	1.00
❑ 65	Troy Glaus Black	2.50	1.00
❑ 66	Cliff Floyd	2.50	1.00
❑ 66	Cliff Floyd Black	2.50	1.00
❑ 67	Tony Batista	2.50	1.00
❑ 67	Tony Batista Black	2.50	1.00
❑ 68	Jeff Bagwell	2.50	1.00
❑ 68	Jeff Bagwell Black	2.50	1.00
❑ 69	Billy Wagner	2.50	1.00
❑ 69	Billy Wagner Black	2.50	1.00
❑ 70	Eric Chavez	2.50	1.00
❑ 70	Eric Chavez Black	2.50	1.00
❑ 71	Troy Percival	2.50	1.00
❑ 71	Troy Percival Black	2.50	1.00
❑ 72	Andruw Jones	2.50	1.00
❑ 72	Andruw Jones Black	2.50	1.00
❑ 73	Shane Reynolds	2.50	1.00
❑ 73	Shane Reynolds Black	2.50	1.00
❑ 74	Barry Zito	2.50	1.00
❑ 74	Barry Zito Black	2.50	1.00
❑ 75	Roy Halladay	2.50	1.00
❑ 75	Roy Halladay Black	2.50	1.00
❑ 76	David Wells	2.50	1.00
❑ 76	David Wells Black	2.50	1.00
❑ 77	Jason Giambi	2.50	1.00
❑ 77	Jason Giambi Black	2.50	1.00
❑ 78	Scott Elarton	2.50	1.00
❑ 78	Scott Elarton Black	2.50	1.00
❑ 79	Moises Alou	2.50	1.00
❑ 79	Moises Alou Black	2.50	1.00
❑ 80	Adam Piatt	2.50	1.00
❑ 80	Adam Piatt Black	2.50	1.00
❑ 81	Wilton Veras	.50	.20
❑ 82	Darryl Kile	.60	.25
❑ 83	Johnny Damon	1.00	.40
❑ 84	Tony Armas Jr.	.50	.20
❑ 85	Ellis Burks	.60	.25
❑ 86	Jamey Wright	.50	.20
❑ 87	Jose Vizcaino	.50	.20
❑ 88	Bartolo Colon	.60	.25
❑ 89	Carmen Cali RC	.50	.20
❑ 90	Kevin Brown	.60	.25
❑ 91	Josh Hamilton	.50	.20
❑ 92	Jay Buhner	.60	.25
❑ 93	Scott Pratt RC	.60	.25
❑ 94	Alex Cora	.50	.20
❑ 95	Luis Montanez RC	.60	.25
❑ 96	Dmitri Young	.60	.25
❑ 97	J.T. Snow	.60	.25
❑ 98	Damion Easley	.50	.20
❑ 99	Greg Norton	.50	.20
❑ 100	Matt Wheatland	.50	.20
❑ 101	Chin-Feng Chen	.60	.25
❑ 102	Tony Womack	.50	.20
❑ 103	Adam Kennedy Black	.50	.20
❑ 104	J.D. Drew	.60	.25
❑ 105	Carlos Febles	.50	.20
❑ 106	Jim Thome	1.00	.40
❑ 107	Danny Graves	.50	.20
❑ 108	Dave Mlicki	.50	.20
❑ 109	Ron Coomer	.50	.20
❑ 110	James Baldwin	.50	.20
❑ 111	Shaun Boyd RC	.50	.20
❑ 112	Brian Bohanon	.50	.20
❑ 113	Jacque Jones	.60	.25
❑ 114	Alfonso Soriano	1.00	.40
❑ 115	Tony Clark	.50	.20
❑ 116	Terrence Long	.50	.20
❑ 117	Todd Hundley	.50	.20
❑ 118	Kazuhiro Sasaki	.60	.25
❑ 119	Brian Sellier RC	.50	.20
❑ 120	John Olerud	.60	.25
❑ 121	Javier Vazquez	.60	.25
❑ 122	Sean Burnett	.50	.20
❑ 123	Matt LeCroy	.50	.20
❑ 124	Erubiel Durazo	.50	.20
❑ 125	Juan Encarnacion	.50	.20
❑ 126	Pablo Ozuna	.50	.20
❑ 127	Russ Ortiz	.50	.20
❑ 128	David Segui	.50	.20
❑ 129	Mark McGwire	4.00	1.50
❑ 130	Mark Grace	1.00	.40
❑ 131	Fred McGriff	1.00	.40
❑ 132	Carl Pavano	.60	.25
❑ 133	Derek Thompson	.50	.20
❑ 134	Shawn Green	.60	.25
❑ 135	B.J. Surhoff	.60	.25
❑ 136	Michael Tucker	.50	.20
❑ 137	Jason Isringhausen	.60	.25
❑ 138	Eric Milton	.50	.20
❑ 139	Mike Stodolka	.50	.20
❑ 140	Milton Bradley	.60	.25
❑ 141	Curt Schilling	.60	.25
❑ 142	Sandy Alomar Jr.	.50	.20
❑ 143	Brent Mayne	.50	.20
❑ 144	Todd Jones	.50	.20
❑ 145	Charles Johnson	.60	.25
❑ 146	Dean Palmer	.60	.25
❑ 147	Masato Yoshii	.50	.20
❑ 148	Edgar Renteria	.60	.25
❑ 149	Joe Randa	.60	.25
❑ 150	Adam Johnson	.50	.20
❑ 151	Greg Vaughn	.50	.20
❑ 152	Adrian Beltre	.60	.25
❑ 153	Glenallen Hill	.50	.20
❑ 154	David Parrish RC	.50	.20
❑ 155	Neifi Perez	.50	.20
❑ 156	Pete Harnisch	.50	.20
❑ 157	Paul Konerko	.60	.25
❑ 158	Dennys Reyes	.50	.20
❑ 159	Jose Lima Black	.50	.20
❑ 160	Eddie Taubensee	.50	.20
❑ 161	Miguel Cairo	.50	.20
❑ 162	Jeff Kent	.60	.25
❑ 163	Dustin Hermanson	.50	.20
❑ 164	Alex Gonzalez	.50	.20
❑ 165	Hideo Nomo	1.50	.60
❑ 166	Sammy Sosa	1.50	.60
❑ 167	C.J. Nitkowski	.50	.20
❑ 168	Cal Eldred	.50	.20
❑ 169	Jeff Abbott	.50	.20
❑ 170	Jim Edmonds	.60	.25
❑ 171	Mark Mulder Black	.60	.25
❑ 172	Dominic Rich RC	.50	.20
❑ 173	Ray Lankford	.60	.25
❑ 174	Danny Borrell RC	.50	.20
❑ 175	Rick Aguilera	.50	.20
❑ 176	Shannon Stewart Black	.60	.25
❑ 177	Steve Finley	.60	.25
❑ 178	Jim Parque	.50	.20
❑ 179	Kevin Appier Black	.60	.25
❑ 180	Adrian Gonzalez	.50	.20
❑ 181	Tom Goodwin	.50	.20
❑ 182	Kevin Tapani	.50	.20
❑ 183	Fernando Tatis	.50	.20
❑ 184	Mark Grudzielanek	.50	.20
❑ 185	Ryan Anderson	.50	.20
❑ 186	Jeffrey Hammonds	.50	.20
❑ 187	Corey Koskie	.50	.20
❑ 188	Brad Fullmer Black	.50	.20
❑ 189	Rey Sanchez	.50	.20
❑ 190	Michael Barrett	.50	.20
❑ 191	Rickey Henderson	1.50	.60
❑ 192	Jermaine Dye	.60	.25
❑ 193	Scott Brosius	.60	.25
❑ 194	Matt Anderson	.50	.20
❑ 195	Brian Buchanan	.50	.20
❑ 196	Derrek Lee	1.00	.40
❑ 197	Larry Walker	.60	.25
❑ 198	Dan Moylan RC	.50	.20
❑ 199	Vinny Castilla	.60	.25
❑ 200	Ken Griffey Jr.	2.50	1.00

	Card	Player		
❑	201	Matt Stairs Black	.50	.20
❑	202	Ty Howington	.50	.20
❑	203	Andy Benes	.50	.20
❑	204	Luis Gonzalez	.60	.25
❑	205	Brian Moehler	.50	.20
❑	206	Harold Baines	.60	.25
❑	207	Pedro Astacio	.50	.20
❑	208	Cristian Guzman	.50	.20
❑	209	Kip Wells	.50	.20
❑	210	Frank Thomas	1.50	.60
❑	211	Jose Rosado	.50	.20
❑	212	Vernon Wells Black	.60	.25
❑	213	Bobby Higginson	.60	.25
❑	214	Juan Gonzalez	.60	.25
❑	215	Omar Vizquel	1.00	.40
❑	216	Bernie Williams	1.00	.40
❑	217	Aaron Sele	.50	.20
❑	218	Shawn Estes	.50	.20
❑	219	Roberto Alomar	1.00	.40
❑	220	Rick Ankiel	.50	.20
❑	221	Josh Kalinowski	.50	.20
❑	222	David Bell	.50	.20
❑	223	Keith Foulke	.60	.25
❑	224	Craig Biggio Black	1.00	.40
❑	225	Josh Axelson RC	.50	.20
❑	226	Scott Williamson	.50	.20
❑	227	Ron Belliard	.50	.20
❑	228	Chris Singleton	.50	.20
❑	229	Alex Serrano RC	.50	.20
❑	230	Deivi Cruz	.50	.20
❑	231	Eric Munson	.50	.20
❑	232	Luis Castillo	.50	.20
❑	233	Edgar Martinez	1.00	.40
❑	234	Jeff Shaw	.50	.20
❑	235	Jeromy Burnitz	.60	.25
❑	236	Richie Sexson	.60	.25
❑	237	Will Clark	1.00	.40
❑	238	Ron Villone	.50	.20
❑	239	Kerry Wood	.60	.25
❑	240	Rich Aurilia	.50	.20
❑	241	Mo Vaughn Black	.60	.25
❑	242	Travis Fryman	.60	.25
❑	243	Manny Ramirez Sox	1.00	.40
❑	244	Chris Stynes	.50	.20
❑	245	Ray Durham	.60	.25
❑	246	Juan Uribe RC	1.00	.40
❑	247	Juan Guzman	.50	.20
❑	248	Lee Stevens	.50	.20
❑	249	Devon White	.60	.25
❑	250	Kyle Lohse RC	1.00	.40
❑	251	Bryan Wolff	.50	.20
❑	252	Matt Galante RC	.60	.25
❑	253	Eric Young	.50	.20
❑	254	Freddy Garcia	.60	.25
❑	255	Jay Bell	.60	.25
❑	256	Steve Cox	.50	.20
❑	257	Torii Hunter	.60	.25
❑	258	Jose Canseco	1.00	.40
❑	259	Brad Ausmus	.60	.25
❑	260	Jeff Cirillo	.50	.20
❑	261	Brad Penny	.50	.20
❑	262	Antonio Alfonseca	.50	.20
❑	263	Russ Branyan	.50	.20
❑	264	Chris Morris RC	.50	.20
❑	265	John Lackey	.50	.20
❑	266	Justin Wayne RC	.60	.25
❑	267	Brad Radke	.60	.25
❑	268	Todd Stottlemyre	.50	.20
❑	269	Mark Loretta	.50	.20
❑	270	Matt Williams	.60	.25
❑	271	Kenny Lofton	.60	.25
❑	272	Jeff D'Amico	.50	.20
❑	273	Jamie Moyer	.60	.25
❑	274	Darren Dreifort	.50	.20
❑	275	Denny Neagle	.50	.20
❑	276	Orlando Cabrera	.60	.25
❑	277	Chuck Finley	.60	.25
❑	278	Miguel Batista	.60	.25
❑	279	Carlos Beltran	.60	.25
❑	280	Eric Karros	.60	.25
❑	281	Mark Kotsay	.60	.25
❑	282	Ryan Dempster	.50	.20
❑	283	Barry Larkin	1.00	.40
❑	284	Jeff Suppan	.50	.20
❑	285	Gary Sheffield	.60	.25
❑	286	Jose Valentin	.50	.20
❑	287	Robb Nen	.60	.25
❑	288	Chan Ho Park	.60	.25
❑	289	John Halama	.50	.20
❑	290	Steve Smyth RC	.60	.25
❑	291	Gerald Williams	.50	.20
❑	292	Preston Wilson	.60	.25
❑	293	Victor Hall RC	.60	.25
❑	294	Ben Sheets	1.00	.40
❑	295	Eric Davis	.60	.25
❑	296	Kirk Rueter	.50	.20
❑	297	Chad Petty RC	.50	.20
❑	298	Kevin Millar	.60	.25
❑	299	Marvin Benard	.50	.20
❑	300	Vladimir Guerrero	1.50	.60
❑	301	Livan Hernandez	.60	.25
❑	302	Travis Baptist RC	.50	.20
❑	303	Bill Mueller	.60	.25
❑	304	Mike Cameron	.50	.20
❑	305	Randy Johnson	1.50	.60
❑	306	Alan Mahaffey RC	.50	.20
❑	307	Timo Perez UER	.50	.20
❑	308	Pokey Reese	.50	.20
❑	309	Ryan Rupe	.50	.20
❑	310	Carlos Lee	.60	.25
❑	311	Doug Glanville SP	5.00	2.00
❑	312	Jay Payton SP	5.00	2.00
❑	313	Troy O'Leary SP	5.00	2.00
❑	314	Francisco Cordero SP	5.00	2.00
❑	315	Rusty Greer SP	5.00	2.00
❑	316	Cal Ripken SP	25.00	10.00
❑	317	Ricky Ledee SP	5.00	2.00
❑	318	Brian Daubach SP	5.00	2.00
❑	319	Robin Ventura SP	5.00	2.00
❑	320	Todd Zeile SP	5.00	2.00
❑	321	Francisco Cordova SP	5.00	2.00
❑	322	Henry Rodriguez SP	5.00	2.00
❑	323	Pat Meares SP	5.00	2.00
❑	324	Glendon Rusch SP	5.00	2.00
❑	325	Keith Osik SP	5.00	2.00
❑	326	Robert Keppel SP RC	5.00	2.00
❑	327	Bobby Jones SP	5.00	2.00
❑	328	Alex Ramirez SP	5.00	2.00
❑	329	Robert Person SP	5.00	2.00
❑	330	Ruben Mateo SP	5.00	2.00
❑	331	Rob Bell SP	5.00	2.00
❑	332	Carl Everett SP	5.00	2.00
❑	333	Jason Schmidt SP	5.00	2.00
❑	334	Scott Rolen SP	8.00	3.00
❑	335	Jimmy Anderson SP	5.00	2.00
❑	336	Bret Boone SP	5.00	2.00
❑	337	Delino DeShields SP	5.00	2.00
❑	338	Trevor Hoffman SP	5.00	2.00
❑	339	Bob Abreu SP	5.00	2.00
❑	340	Mike Williams SP	5.00	2.00
❑	341	Mike Hampton SP	5.00	2.00
❑	342	John Wetteland SP	5.00	2.00
❑	343	Scott Erickson SP	5.00	2.00
❑	344	Enrique Wilson SP	5.00	2.00
❑	345	Tim Wakefield SP	5.00	2.00
❑	346	Mike Lowell SP	5.00	2.00
❑	347	Todd Pratt SP	5.00	2.00
❑	348	Brook Fordyce SP	5.00	2.00
❑	349	Benny Agbayani SP	5.00	2.00
❑	350	Gabe Kapler SP	5.00	2.00
❑	351	Sean Casey SP	5.00	2.00
❑	352	Darren Oliver SP	5.00	2.00
❑	353	Todd Ritchie SP	5.00	2.00
❑	354	Kenny Rogers SP	5.00	2.00
❑	355	Jason Kendall SP	5.00	2.00
❑	356	John Vander Wal SP	5.00	2.00
❑	357	Ramon Martinez SP	5.00	2.00
❑	358	Edgardo Alfonzo SP	5.00	2.00
❑	359	Phil Nevin SP	5.00	2.00
❑	360	Albert Belle SP	5.00	2.00
❑	361	Ruben Rivera SP	5.00	2.00
❑	362	Pedro Martinez SP	8.00	3.00
❑	363	Derek Lowe SP	5.00	2.00
❑	364	Pat Burrell SP	5.00	2.00
❑	365	Mike Mussina SP	8.00	3.00
❑	366	Brady Anderson SP	5.00	2.00
❑	367	Darren Lewis SP	5.00	2.00
❑	368	Sidney Ponson SP	5.00	2.00
❑	369	Adam Eaton SP	5.00	2.00
❑	370	Eric Owens SP	5.00	2.00
❑	371	Aaron Boone SP	5.00	2.00
❑	372	Matt Clement SP	5.00	2.00
❑	373	Derek Bell SP	5.00	2.00
❑	374	Trot Nixon SP	5.00	2.00
❑	375	Travis Lee SP	5.00	2.00
❑	376	Mike Benjamin SP	5.00	2.00
❑	377	Jeff Zimmerman SP	5.00	2.00
❑	378	Mike Lieberthal SP	5.00	2.00
❑	379	Rick Reed SP	5.00	2.00
❑	380	Nomar Garciaparra SP	12.00	5.00
❑	381	Omar Daal SP	5.00	2.00
❑	382	Ryan Klesko SP	5.00	2.00
❑	383	Rey Ordonez SP	5.00	2.00
❑	384	Kevin Young SP	5.00	2.00
❑	385	Rick Helling SP	5.00	2.00
❑	386	Brian Giles SP	5.00	2.00
❑	387	Tony Gwynn SP	10.00	4.00
❑	388	Ed Sprague SP	5.00	2.00
❑	389	J.R. House SP	5.00	2.00
❑	390	Scott Hatteberg SP	5.00	2.00
❑	391	John Valentin SP	5.00	2.00
❑	392	Melvin Mora SP	5.00	2.00
❑	393	Royce Clayton SP	5.00	2.00
❑	394	Jeff Fassero SP	5.00	2.00
❑	395	Manny Alexander SP	5.00	2.00
❑	396	John Franco SP	5.00	2.00
❑	397	Luis Alicea SP	5.00	2.00
❑	398	Ivan Rodriguez SP	8.00	3.00
❑	399	Kevin Jordan SP	5.00	2.00
❑	400	Jose Offerman SP	5.00	2.00
❑	401	Jeff Conine SP	5.00	2.00
❑	402	Seth Etherton SP	5.00	2.00
❑	403	Mike Bordick SP	5.00	2.00
❑	404	Al Leiter SP	5.00	2.00
❑	405	Mike Piazza SP	12.00	5.00
❑	406	Armando Benitez SP	5.00	2.00
❑	407	Warren Morris SP	5.00	2.00
❑	NNO	1952 Card Redemption EXCH		
❑	NNO	Replica Hat-Jsy EXCH		

2002 Topps Heritage

	Card	Player		
❑		COMPLETE SET (440)	400.00	200.00
❑		COMP.SET w/o SP's (350)	80.00	40.00
❑		COMMON CARD (1-363)	.50	.20
❑		COMMON SP (364-446)	5.00	2.00
❑	1	Ichiro Suzuki SP	15.00	6.00
❑	2	Darin Erstad	.60	.25
❑	3	Rod Beck	.60	.25
❑	4	Doug Mientkiewicz	.60	.25
❑	5	Mike Sweeney	.60	.25
❑	6	Roger Clemens	3.00	1.25
❑	7	Jason Tyner	.50	.20
❑	8	Alex Gonzalez	.50	.20
❑	9	Eric Young	.50	.20
❑	10	Randy Johnson	1.50	.60
❑	10N	Randy Johnson Night SP	8.00	3.00
❑	11	Aaron Sele	.50	.20
❑	12	Tony Clark	.50	.20
❑	13	C.C. Sabathia	.60	.25
❑	14	Melvin Mora	.60	.25
❑	15	Tim Hudson	.60	.25
❑	16	Ben Petrick	.50	.20
❑	17	Tom Glavine	1.00	.40
❑	18	Jason Lane	.60	.25
❑	19	Larry Walker	.60	.25
❑	20	Mark Mulder	.60	.25
❑	21	Steve Finley	.60	.25
❑	22	Bengie Molina	.50	.20
❑	23	Rob Bell	.50	.20
❑	24	Nathan Haynes	.50	.20

25	Rafael Furcal	.60	.25
25N	Rafael Furcal Night SP	5.00	2.00
26	Mike Mussina	1.00	.40
27	Paul LoDuca	.60	.25
28	Torii Hunter	.60	.25
29	Carlos Lee	.60	.25
30	Jimmy Rollins	.60	.25
31	Arthur Rhodes	.50	.20
32	Ivan Rodriguez	1.00	.40
33	Wes Helms	.50	.20
34	Cliff Floyd	.60	.25
35	Julian Tavarez	.50	.20
36	Mark McGwire	4.00	1.50
37	Chipper Jones SP	8.00	3.00
38	Denny Neagle	.50	.20
39	Odalis Perez	.50	.20
40	Antonio Alfonseca	.50	.20
41	Edgar Renteria	.60	.25
42	Troy Glaus	.60	.25
43	Scott Brosius	.60	.25
44	Abraham Nunez	.50	.20
45	Jamey Wright	.50	.20
46	Bobby Bonilla	.60	.25
47	Ismael Valdes	.50	.20
48	Chris Reitsma	.50	.20
49	Neifi Perez	.50	.20
50	Juan Cruz	.50	.20
51	Kevin Brown	.60	.25
52	Ben Grieve	.50	.20
53	Alex Rodriguez SP	12.00	5.00
54	Charles Nagy	.50	.20
55	Reggie Sanders	.60	.25
56	Nelson Figueroa	.50	.20
57	Felipe Lopez	.50	.20
58	Bill Ortega	.50	.20
59	Jeffrey Hammonds	.60	.25
60	Johnny Estrada	.50	.20
61	Bob Wickman	.50	.20
62	Doug Glanville	.50	.20
63	Jeff Cirillo	.50	.20
63N	Jeff Cirillo Night SP	5.00	2.00
64	Corey Patterson	.50	.20
65	Aaron Myette	.50	.20
66	Magglio Ordonez	.60	.25
67	Ellis Burks	.60	.25
68	Miguel Tejada	.60	.25
69	John Olerud	.60	.25
69N	John Olerud Night SP	5.00	2.00
70	Greg Vaughn	.50	.20
71	Andy Pettitte	1.00	.40
72	Mike Matheny	.50	.20
73	Brandon Duckworth	.50	.20
74	Scott Schoeneweis	.50	.20
75	Mike Lowell	.60	.25
76	Einar Diaz	.50	.20
77	Tino Martinez	1.00	.40
78	Matt Williams	.60	.25
79	Jason Young RC	1.00	.40
80	Nate Cornejo	.50	.20
81	Andres Galarraga	.60	.25
82	Bernie Williams SP	8.00	3.00
83	Ryan Klesko	.60	.25
84	Dan Wilson	.50	.20
85	Henry Pichardo RC	1.00	.40
86	Ray Durham	.60	.25
87	Omar Daal	.50	.20
88	Derrek Lee	1.00	.40
89	Al Leiter	.60	.25
90	Darrin Fletcher	.50	.20
91	Josh Beckett	.60	.25
92	Johnny Damon	1.00	.40
92N	Johnny Damon Night SP	8.00	3.00
93	Abraham Nunez	.50	.20
94	Ricky Ledee	.50	.20
95	Richie Sexson	.60	.25
96	Adam Kennedy	.50	.20
97	Raul Mondesi	.60	.25
98	John Burkett	.60	.25
99	Ben Sheets	.60	.25
99N	Ben Sheets Night SP	5.00	2.00
100	Preston Wilson	.60	.25
100N	Preston Wilson Night SP	5.00	2.00
101	Boof Bonser	.50	.20
102	Shigetoshi Hasegawa	.60	.25
103	Carlos Febles	.50	.20
104	Jorge Posada SP	8.00	3.00
105	Michael Tucker	.50	.20
106	Roberto Hernandez	.60	.25
107	John Rodriguez RC	1.00	.40
108	Danny Graves	.50	.20
109	Rich Aurilia	.50	.20
110	Jon Lieber	.50	.20
111	Tim Hummel RC	1.00	.40
112	J.T. Snow	.60	.25
113	Kris Benson	.50	.20
114	Derek Jeter	4.00	1.50
115	John Franco	.60	.25
116	Matt Stairs	.50	.20
117	Ben Davis	.50	.20
118	Darryl Kile	.60	.25
119	Mike Peeples RC	1.00	.40
120	Kevin Tapani	.50	.20
121	Armando Benitez	.50	.20
122	Damian Miller	.50	.20
123	Jose Jimenez	.50	.20
124	Pedro Astacio	.50	.20
125	Marlyn Tisdale RC	1.00	.40
126	Deivi Cruz	.50	.20
127	Paul O'Neill	1.00	.40
128	Jermaine Dye	.60	.25
129	Marcus Giles	.60	.25
130	Mark Loretta	.50	.20
131	Garret Anderson	.60	.25
132	Todd Ritchie	.50	.20
133	Joe Crede	.60	.25
134	Kevin Millwood	.60	.25
135	Shane Reynolds	.50	.20
136	Mark Grace	1.00	.40
137	Shannon Stewart	.60	.25
138	Nick Neugebauer	.50	.20
139	Nic Jackson RC	1.00	.40
140	Robb Nen UER	.60	.25
141	Dmitri Young	.60	.25
142	Kevin Appier	.60	.25
143	Jack Cust	.50	.20
144	Andres Torres	.50	.20
145	Frank Thomas	1.50	.60
146	Jason Kendall	.60	.25
147	Greg Maddux	2.50	1.00
148	David Justice	.60	.25
149	Hideo Nomo	1.50	.60
150	Bret Boone	.60	.25
151	Wade Miller	.50	.20
152	Jeff Kent	.60	.25
153	Scott Williamson	.50	.20
154	Julio Lugo	.50	.20
155	Bobby Higginson	.60	.25
156	Geoff Jenkins	.50	.20
157	Darren Dreifort	.50	.20
158	Freddy Sanchez RC	3.00	1.25
159	Bud Smith	.50	.20
160	Phil Nevin	.60	.25
161	Cesar Izturis	.50	.20
162	Sean Casey	.60	.25
163	Jose Ortiz	.50	.20
164	Brent Abernathy	.50	.20
165	Kevin Young	.50	.20
166	Daryle Ward	.50	.20
167	Trevor Hoffman	.60	.25
168	Rondell White	.60	.25
169	Kip Wells	.50	.20
170	John Vander Wal	.50	.20
171	Jose Lima	.50	.20
172	Wilton Guerrero	.50	.20
173	Aaron Dean RC	1.00	.40
174	Rick Helling	.50	.20
175	Juan Pierre	.60	.25
176	Jay Bell	.60	.25
177	Craig House	.50	.20
178	David Bell	.50	.20
179	Pat Burrell	.60	.25
180	Eric Gagne	.60	.25
181	Adam Pettyjohn	.50	.20
182	Ugueth Urbina	.50	.20
183	Peter Bergeron	.50	.20
184	Adrian Gonzalez	.50	.20
184N	Adrian Gonzalez Night SP	5.00	2.00
185	Damion Easley	.50	.20
186	Gookie Dawkins	.50	.20
187	Matt Lawton	.50	.20
188	Frank Catalanotto	.50	.20
189	David Wells	.60	.25
190	Roger Cedeno	.50	.20
191	Brian Giles	.60	.25
192	Julio Zuleta	.50	.20
193	Timo Perez	.50	.20
194	Billy Wagner	.60	.25
195	Craig Counsell	.50	.20
196	Bart Miadich	.50	.20
197	Gary Sheffield	.60	.25
198	Richard Hidalgo	.50	.20
199	Juan Uribe	.50	.20
200	Curt Schilling	.60	.25
201	Javy Lopez	.60	.25
202	Jimmy Haynes	.50	.20
203	Jim Edmonds	.60	.25
204	Pokey Reese	.50	.20
204N	Pokey Reese Night SP	5.00	2.00
205	Matt Clement	.60	.25
206	Dean Palmer	.60	.25
207	Nick Johnson	.60	.25
208	Nate Espy RC	1.00	.40
209	Pedro Feliz	.50	.20
210	Aaron Rowand	.60	.25
211	Masato Yoshii	.50	.20
212	Jose Cruz Jr.	.50	.20
213	Paul Byrd	.50	.20
214	Mark Phillips RC	1.00	.40
215	Benny Agbayani	.50	.20
216	Frank Menechino	.50	.20
217	John Flaherty	.50	.20
218	Brian Boehringer	.50	.20
219	Todd Hollandsworth	.50	.20
220	Sammy Sosa SP	8.00	3.00
221	Steve Sparks	.50	.20
222	Homer Bush	.50	.20
223	Mike Hampton	.60	.25
224	Bobby Abreu	.60	.25
225	Barry Larkin	1.00	.40
226	Ryan Rupe	.50	.20
227	Bubba Trammell	.50	.20
228	Todd Zeile	.60	.25
229	Jeff Shaw	.50	.20
230	Alex Ochoa	.50	.20
231	Orlando Cabrera	.60	.25
232	Jeremy Giambi	.50	.20
233	Tomo Ohka	.50	.20
234	Luis Castillo	.50	.20
235	Chris Holt	.50	.20
236	Shawn Green	.60	.25
237	Sidney Ponson	.50	.20
238	Lee Stevens	.50	.20
239	Hank Blalock	1.00	.40
240	Randy Winn	.50	.20
241	Pedro Martinez	1.00	.40
242	Vinny Castilla	.60	.25
243	Steve Karsay	.50	.20
244	Barry Bonds SP	20.00	8.00
245	Jason Bere	.50	.20
246	Scott Rolen	1.00	.40
246N	Scott Rolen Night SP	8.00	3.00
247	Ryan Kohlmeier	.50	.20
248	Kerry Wood	.60	.25
249	Aramis Ramirez	.60	.25
250	Lance Berkman	.60	.25
251	Omar Vizquel	1.00	.40
252	Juan Encarnacion	.50	.20
253	Does Not Exist		
254	David Segui	.50	.20
255	Brian Anderson	.50	.20
256	Jay Payton	.50	.20
257	Mark Grudzielanek	.50	.20
258	Jimmy Anderson	.50	.20
259	Eric Valent	.50	.20
260	Chad Durbin	.50	.20
261	Does Not Exist		
262	Alex Gonzalez	.50	.20
263	Scott Dunn	.50	.20
264	Scott Elarton	.50	.20
265	Tom Gordon	.50	.20
266	Moises Alou	.60	.25
267	Does Not Exist		
268	Does Not Exist		
269	Mark Buehrle	.60	.25
270	Jerry Hairston	.50	.20
271	Does Not Exist		
272	Luke Prokopec	.50	.20
273	Graeme Lloyd	.50	.20

❑	274	Bret Prinz	.50	.20
❑	275	Does Not Exist		
❑	276	Chris Carpenter	.60	.25
❑	277	Ryan Minor	.50	.20
❑	278	Jeff D'Amico	.50	.20
❑	279	Raul Ibanez	.50	.20
❑	280	Joe Mays	.50	.20
❑	281	Livan Hernandez	.60	.25
❑	282	Robin Ventura	.60	.25
❑	283	Gabe Kapler	.60	.25
❑	284	Tony Batista	.50	.20
❑	285	Ramon Hernandez	.50	.20
❑	286	Craig Paquette	.50	.20
❑	287	Mark Kotsay	.60	.25
❑	288	Mike Lieberthal	.60	.25
❑	289	Joe Borchard	.50	.20
❑	290	Cristian Guzman	.50	.20
❑	291	Craig Biggio	1.00	.40
❑	292	Joaquin Benoit	.50	.20
❑	293	Ken Caminiti	.60	.25
❑	294	Sean Burroughs	.50	.20
❑	295	Eric Karros	.60	.25
❑	296	Eric Chavez	.60	.25
❑	297	LaTroy Hawkins	.50	.20
❑	298	Alfonso Soriano	.60	.25
❑	299	John Smoltz	1.00	.40
❑	300	Adam Dunn	.60	.25
❑	301	Ryan Dempster	.50	.20
❑	302	Travis Hafner	.60	.25
❑	303	Russell Branyan	.50	.20
❑	304	Dustin Hermanson	.50	.20
❑	305	Jim Thome	1.00	.40
❑	306	Carlos Beltran	.60	.25
❑	307	Jason Botts RC	.60	.25
❑	308	David Cone	.60	.25
❑	309	Ivanon Coffie	.50	.20
❑	310	Brian Jordan	.60	.25
❑	311	Todd Walker	.50	.20
❑	312	Jeromy Burnitz	.60	.25
❑	313	Tony Armas Jr.	.50	.20
❑	314	Jeff Conine	.60	.25
❑	315	Todd Jones	.50	.20
❑	316	Roy Oswalt	.60	.25
❑	317	Aubrey Huff	.60	.25
❑	318	Josh Fogg	.50	.20
❑	319	Jose Vidro	.50	.20
❑	320	Jace Brewer	.50	.20
❑	321	Mike Redmond	.50	.20
❑	322	Noochie Varner RC	1.00	.40
❑	323	Russ Ortiz	.50	.20
❑	324	Edgardo Alfonzo	.50	.20
❑	325	Ruben Sierra	.60	.25
❑	326	Calvin Murray	.50	.20
❑	327	Marlon Anderson	.50	.20
❑	328	Albie Lopez	.50	.20
❑	329	Chris Gomez	.50	.20
❑	330	Fernando Tatis	.50	.20
❑	331	Stubby Clapp	.50	.20
❑	332	Rickey Henderson	1.50	.60
❑	333	Brad Radke	.60	.25
❑	334	Brent Mayne	.50	.20
❑	335	Cory Lidle	.50	.20
❑	336	Edgar Martinez	1.00	.40
❑	337	Aaron Boone	.60	.25
❑	338	Jay Witasick	.50	.20
❑	339	Benito Santiago	.60	.25
❑	340	Jose Mercedes	.50	.20
❑	341	Fernando Vina	.50	.20
❑	342	A.J. Pierzynski	.60	.25
❑	343	Jeff Bagwell	1.00	.40
❑	344	Brian Bohanon	.50	.20
❑	345	Adrian Beltre	.60	.25
❑	346	Troy Percival	.60	.25
❑	347	Napoleon Calzado RC	1.00	.40
❑	348	Ruben Rivera	.50	.20
❑	349	Rafael Soriano	.50	.20
❑	350	Damian Jackson	.50	.20
❑	351	Joe Randa	.60	.25
❑	352	Chan Ho Park	.60	.25
❑	353	Dante Bichette	.60	.25
❑	354	Bartolo Colon	.60	.25
❑	355	Jason Bay RC	5.00	2.00
❑	356	Shea Hillenbrand	.60	.25
❑	357	Matt Morris	.60	.25
❑	358	Brad Penny	.50	.20
❑	359	Mark Quinn	.50	.20
❑	360	Marquis Grissom	.60	.25
❑	361	Henry Blanco	.50	.20
❑	362	Billy Koch	.50	.20
❑	363	Mike Cameron	.50	.20
❑	364	Albert Pujols SP	15.00	6.00
❑	365	Paul Konerko SP	5.00	2.00
❑	366	Eric Milton SP	5.00	2.00
❑	367	Nick Bierbrodt SP	5.00	2.00
❑	368	Rafael Palmeiro SP	8.00	3.00
❑	369	Jorge Padilla SP RC	5.00	2.00
❑	370	Jason Giambi Yankees SP	5.00	2.00
❑	371	Mike Piazza SP	12.00	5.00
❑	372	Alex Cora SP	5.00	2.00
❑	373	Todd Helton SP	8.00	3.00
❑	374	Juan Gonzalez SP	5.00	2.00
❑	375	Mariano Rivera SP	8.00	3.00
❑	376	Jason LaRue SP	5.00	2.00
❑	377	Tony Gwynn SP	10.00	4.00
❑	378	Wilson Betemit SP	5.00	2.00
❑	379	J.J. Trujillo SP RC	5.00	2.00
❑	380	Brad Ausmus SP	5.00	2.00
❑	381	Chris George SP	5.00	2.00
❑	382	Jose Canseco SP	8.00	3.00
❑	383	Ramon Ortiz SP	5.00	2.00
❑	384	John Rocker SP	5.00	2.00
❑	385	Rey Ordonez SP	5.00	2.00
❑	386	Ken Griffey Jr. SP	12.00	5.00
❑	387	Juan Pena SP	5.00	2.00
❑	388	Michael Barrett SP	5.00	2.00
❑	389	J.D. Drew SP	5.00	2.00
❑	390	Corey Koskie SP	5.00	2.00
❑	391	Vernon Wells SP	5.00	2.00
❑	392	Juan Tolentino SP RC	5.00	2.00
❑	393	Luis Gonzalez SP	5.00	2.00
❑	394	Terrence Long SP	5.00	2.00
❑	395	Travis Lee SP	5.00	2.00
❑	396	Earl Snyder SP RC	5.00	2.00
❑	397	Nomar Garciaparra SP	12.00	5.00
❑	398	Jason Schmidt SP	5.00	2.00
❑	399	David Espinosa SP	5.00	2.00
❑	400	Steve Green SP	5.00	2.00
❑	401	Jack Wilson SP	5.00	2.00
❑	402	Chris Tritle SP RC	5.00	2.00
❑	403	Angel Berroa SP	5.00	2.00
❑	404	Josh Towers SP	5.00	2.00
❑	405	Andruw Jones SP	8.00	3.00
❑	406	Brent Butler SP	5.00	2.00
❑	407	Craig Kuzmic SP	5.00	2.00
❑	408	Derek Bell SP	5.00	2.00
❑	409	Eric Glaser SP RC	5.00	2.00
❑	410	Joel Pineiro SP	5.00	2.00
❑	411	Alexis Gomez SP	5.00	2.00
❑	412	Mike Rivera SP	5.00	2.00
❑	413	Shawn Estes SP	5.00	2.00
❑	414	Milton Bradley SP	5.00	2.00
❑	415	Carl Everett SP	5.00	2.00
❑	416	Kazuhiro Sasaki SP	5.00	2.00
❑	417	Tony Fontana SP RC	5.00	2.00
❑	418	Josh Pearce SP	5.00	2.00
❑	419	Gary Matthews Jr. SP	5.00	2.00
❑	420	Raymond Cabrera SP RC	5.00	2.00
❑	421	Joe Kennedy SP	5.00	2.00
❑	422	Jason Maule SP RC	5.00	2.00
❑	423	Casey Fossum SP	5.00	2.00
❑	424	Christian Parker SP	5.00	2.00
❑	425	Laynce Nix SP RC	10.00	4.00
❑	426	Byung-Hyun Kim SP	5.00	2.00
❑	427	Freddy Garcia SP	5.00	2.00
❑	428	Herbert Perry SP	5.00	2.00
❑	429	Jason Marquis SP	5.00	2.00
❑	430	Sandy Alomar Jr. SP	5.00	2.00
❑	431	Roberto Alomar SP	8.00	3.00
❑	432	Tsuyoshi Shinjo SP	5.00	2.00
❑	433	Tim Wakefield SP	5.00	2.00
❑	434	Robert Fick SP	5.00	2.00
❑	435	Vladimir Guerrero SP	8.00	3.00
❑	436	Jose Mesa SP	5.00	2.00
❑	437	Scott Spiezio SP	5.00	2.00
❑	438	Jose Hernandez SP	5.00	2.00
❑	439	Jose Acevedo SP	5.00	2.00
❑	440	Brian West SP RC	5.00	2.00
❑	441	Barry Zito SP	5.00	2.00
❑	442	Luis Maza SP	5.00	2.00
❑	443	Marlon Byrd SP	5.00	2.00
❑	444	A.J. Burnett SP	5.00	2.00
❑	445	Dee Brown SP	5.00	2.00
❑	446	Carlos Delgado SP	5.00	2.00
❑	NNO	1953 Repurchased EXCH.		

2003 Topps Heritage

❑		COMPLETE SET (450)	300.00	175.00
❑		COMP.SET w/o SP's (350)	80.00	40.00
❑		COMMON CARD	.50	.20
❑		COMMON RC	1.00	.40
❑		COMMON SP	5.00	2.00
❑		COMMON SP RC	5.00	2.00
❑	1A	Alex Rodriguez Red	2.50	1.00
❑	1B	Alex Rodriguez Black SP	12.00	5.00
❑	2	Jose Cruz Jr.	.50	.20
❑	3	Ichiro Suzuki SP	15.00	6.00
❑	4	Rich Aurilia	.50	.20
❑	5	Trevor Hoffman	.60	.25
❑	6A	Brian Giles New Logo	.60	.25
❑	6B	Brian Giles Old Logo SP	5.00	2.00
❑	7A	Albert Pujols Orange	3.00	1.25
❑	7B	Albert Pujols Black SP	15.00	6.00
❑	8	Vicente Padilla	.50	.20
❑	9	Bobby Crosby	.60	.25
❑	10A	Derek Jeter New Logo	4.00	1.50
❑	10B	Derek Jeter Old Logo SP	15.00	6.00
❑	11A	Pat Burrell New Logo	.60	.25
❑	11B	Pat Burrell Old Logo SP	5.00	2.00
❑	12	Armando Benitez	.50	.20
❑	13	Javier Vazquez	.60	.25
❑	14	Justin Morneau	.60	.25
❑	15	Doug Mientkiewicz	.60	.25
❑	16	Kevin Brown	.60	.25
❑	17	Alexis Gomez	.50	.20
❑	18A	Lance Berkman Blue	.60	.25
❑	18B	Lance Berkman Black SP	5.00	2.00
❑	19	Adrian Gonzalez	.50	.20
❑	20A	Todd Helton Green	1.00	.40
❑	20B	Todd Helton Black SP	8.00	3.00
❑	21	Carlos Pena	.50	.20
❑	22	Matt Lawton	.50	.20
❑	23	Elmer Dessens	.50	.20
❑	24	Hee Seop Choi	.50	.20
❑	25	Chris Duncan SP RC	10.00	4.00
❑	26	Ugueth Urbina	.50	.20
❑	27A	Rodrigo Lopez New Logo	.50	.20
❑	27B	Rodrigo Lopez Old Logo SP	5.00	2.00
❑	28	Damian Moss	.50	.20
❑	29	Steve Finley	.60	.25
❑	30A	Sammy Sosa New Logo	1.50	.60
❑	30B	Sammy Sosa Old Logo SP	8.00	3.00
❑	31	Kevin Cash	.50	.20
❑	32	Kenny Rogers	.60	.25
❑	33	Ben Grieve	.50	.20
❑	34	Jason Simontacchi	.50	.20
❑	35	Shin-Soo Choo	.50	.20
❑	36	Freddy Garcia	.60	.25
❑	37	Jesse Foppert	.50	.20
❑	38	Tony LaRussa MG	.60	.25
❑	39	Mark Kotsay	.60	.25
❑	40	Barry Zito	.60	.25
❑	41	Josh Fogg	.50	.20
❑	42	Marlon Byrd	.50	.20
❑	43	Marcus Thames	.50	.20
❑	44	Al Leiter	.60	.25
❑	45	Michael Barrett	.50	.20
❑	46	Jake Peavy	.60	.25
❑	47	Dustan Mohr	.50	.20
❑	48	Alex Sanchez	.50	.20
❑	49	Chin-Feng Chen	.60	.25

❑ 50A Kazuhisa Ishii Blue .60 .25
❑ 50B Kazuhisa Ishii Black SP 5.00 2.00
❑ 51 Carlos Beltran .60 .25
❑ 52 Franklin Gutierrez RC 1.00 .40
❑ 53 Miguel Cabrera 1.50 .60
❑ 54 Roger Clemens 3.00 1.25
❑ 55 Juan Cruz .50 .20
❑ 56 Jason Young .50 .20
❑ 57 Alex Herrera .50 .20
❑ 58 Aaron Boone .60 .25
❑ 59 Mark Buehrle .60 .25
❑ 60 Larry Walker .60 .25
❑ 61 Morgan Ensberg .60 .25
❑ 62 Barry Larkin 1.00 .40
❑ 63 Joe Borchard .50 .20
❑ 64 Jason Dubois .50 .20
❑ 65 Shea Hillenbrand .60 .25
❑ 66 Jay Gibbons .50 .20
❑ 67 Vinny Castilla .60 .25
❑ 68 Jeff Mathis .50 .20
❑ 69 Curt Schilling .60 .25
❑ 70 Garret Anderson .60 .25
❑ 71 Josh Phelps .50 .20
❑ 72 Chan Ho Park .60 .25
❑ 73 Edgar Renteria .60 .25
❑ 74 Kazuhiro Sasaki .60 .25
❑ 75 Lloyd McClendon MG .50 .20
❑ 76 Jon Lieber .50 .20
❑ 77 Rolando Viera .50 .20
❑ 78 Jeff Conine .60 .25
❑ 79 Kevin Millwood .60 .25
❑ 80A Randy Johnson Green 1.50 .60
❑ 80B Randy Johnson Black SP 12.00 5.00
❑ 81 Troy Percival .60 .25
❑ 82 Cliff Floyd .60 .25
❑ 83 Tony Graffanino .50 .20
❑ 84 Austin Kearns .50 .20
❑ 85 Manuel Ramirez SP RC 8.00 3.00
❑ 86 Jim Tracy MG .50 .20
❑ 87 Rondell White .60 .25
❑ 88 Trot Nixon .60 .25
❑ 89 Carlos Lee .60 .25
❑ 90 Mike Lowell .60 .25
❑ 91 Raul Ibanez .50 .20
❑ 92 Ricardo Rodriguez .50 .20
❑ 93 Ben Sheets .60 .25
❑ 94 Jason Perry SP RC 8.00 3.00
❑ 95 Mark Teixeira 1.00 .40
❑ 96 Brad Fullmer .50 .20
❑ 97 Casey Kotchman .60 .25
❑ 98 Craig Counsell .50 .20
❑ 99 Jason Marquis .50 .20
❑ 100A N.Garciaparra New Logo 2.50 1.00
❑ 100B N.Garciaparra Old Logo SP 12.005.00
❑ 101 Ed Rogers .50 .20
❑ 102 Wilson Betemit .50 .20
❑ 103 Wayne Lydon RC 1.00 .40
❑ 104 Jack Cust .50 .20
❑ 105 Derrek Lee 1.00 .40
❑ 106 Jim Kavourias .50 .20
❑ 107 Joe Randa .60 .25
❑ 108 Taylor Buchholz .50 .20
❑ 109 Gabe Kapler .60 .25
❑ 110 Preston Wilson .60 .25
❑ 111 Craig Biggio 1.00 .40
❑ 112 Paul Lo Duca .60 .25
❑ 113 Eddie Guardado .50 .20
❑ 114 Andres Galarraga 1.00 .40
❑ 115 Edgardo Alfonzo .50 .20
❑ 116 Robin Ventura .60 .25
❑ 117 Jeremy Giambi .50 .20
❑ 118 Ray Durham .60 .25
❑ 119 Mariano Rivera 1.50 .60
❑ 120 Jimmy Rollins .60 .25
❑ 121 Dennis Tankersley .50 .20
❑ 122 Jason Schmidt .60 .25
❑ 123 Bret Boone .60 .25
❑ 124 Josh Hamilton .50 .20
❑ 125 Scott Rolen 1.00 .40
❑ 126 Steve Cox .50 .20
❑ 127 Larry Bowa MG .60 .25
❑ 128 Adam LaRoche SP 5.00 2.00
❑ 129 Ryan Klesko .60 .25
❑ 130 Tim Hudson .60 .25
❑ 131 Brandon Claussen .50 .20
❑ 132 Craig Brazell SP RC 5.00 2.00
❑ 133 Grady Little MG .50 .20
❑ 134 Jarrod Washburn .50 .20
❑ 135 Lyle Overbay .50 .20
❑ 136 John Burkett .50 .20
❑ 137 Daryl Clark RC 1.00 .40
❑ 138 Kirk Rueter .50 .20
❑ 139A Mauer Brothers Green 1.50 .60
❑ 139B Mauer Brothers Black SP 10.00 4.00
❑ 140 Troy Glaus .60 .25
❑ 141 Trey Hodges SP 5.00 2.00
❑ 142 Dallas McPherson .60 .25
❑ 143 Art Howe MG .50 .20
❑ 144 Jesus Cota .50 .20
❑ 145 J.R. House .50 .20
❑ 146 Reggie Sanders .60 .25
❑ 147 Clint Nageotte .50 .20
❑ 148 Jim Edmonds .60 .25
❑ 149 Carl Crawford .60 .25
❑ 150A Mike Piazza Blue 2.50 1.00
❑ 150B Mike Piazza Black SP 12.00 5.00
❑ 151 Seung Song .50 .20
❑ 152 Roberto Hernandez .60 .25
❑ 153 Marquis Grissom .60 .25
❑ 154 Billy Wagner .60 .25
❑ 155 Josh Beckett .60 .25
❑ 156A Randall Simon New Logo .50 .20
❑ 156B Randall Simon Old Logo SP 5.002.00
❑ 157 Ben Broussard .50 .20
❑ 158 Russell Branyan .50 .20
❑ 159 Frank Thomas 1.50 .60
❑ 160 Alex Escobar .50 .20
❑ 161 Mark Bellhorn .60 .25
❑ 162 Melvin Mora .60 .25
❑ 163 Andruw Jones 1.00 .40
❑ 164 Danny Bautista .50 .20
❑ 165 Ramon Ortiz .50 .20
❑ 166 Wily Mo Pena .60 .25
❑ 167 Jose Jimenez .50 .20
❑ 168 Mark Redman .50 .20
❑ 169 Angel Berroa .50 .20
❑ 170 Andy Marte SP RC 12.00 5.00
❑ 171 Juan Gonzalez .60 .25
❑ 172 Fernando Vina .50 .20
❑ 173 Joel Pineiro .50 .20
❑ 174 Boof Bonser .50 .20
❑ 175 Bernie Castro SP RC 5.00 2.00
❑ 176 Bobby Cox MG .50 .20
❑ 177 Jeff Kent .60 .25
❑ 178 Oliver Perez .60 .25
❑ 179 Chase Utley 1.50 .60
❑ 180 Mark Mulder .60 .25
❑ 181 Bobby Abreu .60 .25
❑ 182 Ramiro Mendoza .50 .20
❑ 183 Aaron Heilman .50 .20
❑ 184 A.J. Pierzynski .60 .25
❑ 185 Eric Gagne .60 .25
❑ 186 Kirk Saarloos .50 .20
❑ 187 Ron Gardenhire MG .50 .20
❑ 188 Dmitri Young .60 .25
❑ 189 Todd Zeile .60 .25
❑ 190A Jim Thome New Logo 1.00 .40
❑ 190B Jim Thome Old Logo SP 8.00 3.00
❑ 191 Cliff Lee .50 .20
❑ 192 Matt Morris .60 .25
❑ 193 Robert Fick .50 .20
❑ 194 C.C. Sabathia .60 .25
❑ 195 Alexis Rios .60 .25
❑ 196 D'Angelo Jimenez .50 .20
❑ 197 Edgar Martinez 1.00 .40
❑ 198 Robb Nen .60 .25
❑ 199 Taggert Bozied .50 .20
❑ 200 Vladimir Guerrero SP 8.00 3.00
❑ 201 Walter Young SP 5.00 2.00
❑ 202 Brendan Harris RC 1.00 .40
❑ 203 Mike Hargrove MG .50 .20
❑ 204 Vernon Wells .60 .25
❑ 205 Hank Blalock .60 .25
❑ 206 Mike Cameron .50 .20
❑ 207 Tony Batista .50 .20
❑ 208 Matt Williams .60 .25
❑ 209 Tony Womack .50 .20
❑ 210 Ramon Nivar-Martinez RC 1.00 .40
❑ 211 Aaron Sele .50 .20
❑ 212 Mark Grace 1.00 .40
❑ 213 Joe Crede .60 .25
❑ 214 Ryan Dempster .50 .20
❑ 215 Omar Vizquel 1.00 .40
❑ 216 Juan Pierre .60 .25
❑ 217 Denny Bautista .50 .20
❑ 218 Chuck Knoblauch .60 .25
❑ 219 Eric Karros .60 .25
❑ 220 Victor Diaz .60 .25
❑ 221 Jacque Jones .60 .25
❑ 222 Jose Vidro .50 .20
❑ 223 Joe McEwing .50 .20
❑ 224 Nick Johnson .60 .25
❑ 225 Eric Chavez .60 .25
❑ 226 Jose Mesa .50 .20
❑ 227 Aramis Ramirez .60 .25
❑ 228 John Lackey .50 .20
❑ 229 David Bell .50 .20
❑ 230 John Olerud .60 .25
❑ 231 Tino Martinez 1.00 .40
❑ 232 Randy Winn .50 .20
❑ 233 Todd Hollandsworth .50 .20
❑ 234 Ruddy Lugo RC 1.00 .40
❑ 235 Carlos Delgado .60 .25
❑ 236 Chris Narveson .50 .20
❑ 237 Tim Salmon 1.00 .40
❑ 238 Orlando Palmeiro .50 .20
❑ 239 Jeff Clark SP RC 5.00 2.00
❑ 240 Byung-Hyun Kim .60 .25
❑ 241 Mike Remlinger .50 .20
❑ 242 Johnny Damon 1.00 .40
❑ 243 Corey Patterson .50 .20
❑ 244 Paul Konerko .60 .25
❑ 245 Danny Graves .50 .20
❑ 246 Ellis Burks .60 .25
❑ 247 Gavin Floyd .50 .20
❑ 248 Jaime Bubela RC 1.00 .40
❑ 249 Sean Burroughs .50 .20
❑ 250 Alex Rodriguez SP 12.00 5.00
❑ 251 Gabe Gross .50 .20
❑ 252 Rafael Palmeiro 1.00 .40
❑ 253 Dewon Brazelton .50 .20
❑ 254 Jimmy Journell .50 .20
❑ 255 Rafael Soriano .50 .20
❑ 256 Jerome Williams .50 .20
❑ 257 Xavier Nady .50 .20
❑ 258 Mike Williams .50 .20
❑ 259 Randy Wolf .50 .20
❑ 260A Miguel Tejada Orange .60 .25
❑ 260B Miguel Tejada Black SP 5.00 2.00
❑ 261 Juan Rivera .50 .20
❑ 262 Rey Ordonez .50 .20
❑ 263 Bartolo Colon .60 .25
❑ 264 Eric Milton .50 .20
❑ 265 Jeffrey Hammonds .50 .20
❑ 266 Odalis Perez .50 .20
❑ 267 Mike Sweeney .60 .25
❑ 268 Richard Hidalgo .50 .20
❑ 269 Alex Gonzalez .50 .20
❑ 270 Aaron Cook .50 .20
❑ 271 Earl Snyder .50 .20
❑ 272 Todd Walker .50 .20
❑ 273 Aaron Rowand .60 .25
❑ 274 Matt Clement .60 .25
❑ 275 Anastacio Martinez .50 .20
❑ 276 Mike Bordick .60 .25
❑ 277 John Smoltz 1.00 .40
❑ 278 Scott Hairston .50 .20
❑ 279 David Eckstein .60 .25
❑ 280 Shannon Stewart .60 .25
❑ 281 Carl Everett .60 .25
❑ 282 Aubrey Huff .60 .25
❑ 283 Mike Mussina 1.00 .40
❑ 284 Ruben Sierra .60 .25
❑ 285 Russ Ortiz .50 .20
❑ 286 Brian Lawrence .50 .20
❑ 287 Kip Wells .50 .20
❑ 288 Placido Polanco .50 .20
❑ 289 Ted Lilly .50 .20
❑ 290 Andy Pettitte 1.00 .40
❑ 291 John Buck .50 .20
❑ 292 Orlando Cabrera .60 .25
❑ 293 Cristian Guzman .50 .20
❑ 294 Ruben Quevedo .50 .20
❑ 295 Cesar Izturis .50 .20
❑ 296 Ryan Ludwick .50 .20
❑ 297 Roy Oswalt .60 .25
❑ 298 Jason Stokes .50 .20
❑ 299 Mike Hampton .60 .25

- ❑ 300 Pedro Martinez 1.00 .40
- ❑ 301 Nic Jackson .50 .20
- ❑ 302A Magglio Ordonez New Logo .60 .25
- ❑ 302B Magglio Ordonez Old Logo SP 5.00 2.00
- ❑ 303 Manny Ramirez 1.00 .40
- ❑ 304 Jorge Julio .50 .20
- ❑ 305 Javy Lopez .60 .25
- ❑ 306 Roy Halladay .60 .25
- ❑ 307 Kevin Mench .50 .20
- ❑ 308 Jason Isringhausen .60 .25
- ❑ 309 Carlos Guillen .60 .25
- ❑ 310 Tsuyoshi Shinjo .60 .25
- ❑ 311 Phil Nevin .60 .25
- ❑ 312 Pokey Reese .50 .20
- ❑ 313 Jorge Padilla .50 .20
- ❑ 314 Jermaine Dye .60 .25
- ❑ 315 David Wells .60 .25
- ❑ 316 Mo Vaughn .60 .25
- ❑ 317 Bernie Williams 1.00 .40
- ❑ 318 Michael Restovich .50 .20
- ❑ 319 Jose Hernandez .50 .20
- ❑ 320 Richie Sexson .60 .25
- ❑ 321 Daryle Ward .50 .20
- ❑ 322 Luis Castillo .50 .20
- ❑ 323 Rene Reyes .50 .20
- ❑ 324 Victor Martinez 1.00 .40
- ❑ 325A Adam Dunn New Logo .60 .25
- ❑ 325B Adam Dunn Old Logo SP 5.00 2.00
- ❑ 326 Corwin Malone .50 .20
- ❑ 327 Kerry Wood .60 .25
- ❑ 328 Rickey Henderson 1.50 .60
- ❑ 329 Marty Cordova .50 .20
- ❑ 330 Greg Maddux 2.50 1.00
- ❑ 331 Miguel Batista .50 .20
- ❑ 332 Chris Bootcheck .50 .20
- ❑ 333 Carlos Baerga .50 .20
- ❑ 334 Antonio Alfonseca .50 .20
- ❑ 335 Shane Halter .50 .20
- ❑ 336 Juan Encarnacion .50 .20
- ❑ 337 Tom Gordon .50 .20
- ❑ 338 Hideo Nomo 1.50 .60
- ❑ 339 Torii Hunter .60 .25
- ❑ 340A Alfonso Soriano Yellow .60 .25
- ❑ 340B Alfonso Soriano Black SP 5.00 2.00
- ❑ 341 Roberto Alomar 1.00 .40
- ❑ 342 David Justice .60 .25
- ❑ 343 Mike Lieberthal .60 .25
- ❑ 344 Jeff Weaver .50 .20
- ❑ 345 Timo Perez .50 .20
- ❑ 346 Travis Lee .50 .20
- ❑ 347 Sean Casey .60 .25
- ❑ 348 Willie Harris .50 .20
- ❑ 349 Derek Lowe .60 .25
- ❑ 350 Tom Glavine 1.00 .40
- ❑ 351 Eric Hinske .50 .20
- ❑ 352 Rocco Baldelli .60 .25
- ❑ 353 J.D. Drew .60 .25
- ❑ 354 Jamie Moyer .60 .25
- ❑ 355 Todd Linden .50 .20
- ❑ 356 Benito Santiago .60 .25
- ❑ 357 Brad Baker .50 .20
- ❑ 358 Alex Gonzalez .50 .20
- ❑ 359 Brandon Duckworth .50 .20
- ❑ 360 John Rheinecker .50 .20
- ❑ 361 Orlando Hernandez .60 .25
- ❑ 362 Pedro Astacio .50 .20
- ❑ 363 Brad Wilkerson .50 .20
- ❑ 364 David Ortiz SP 8.00 3.00
- ❑ 365 Geoff Jenkins SP 5.00 2.00
- ❑ 366 Brian Jordan SP 5.00 2.00
- ❑ 367 Paul Byrd SP 5.00 2.00
- ❑ 368 Jason Lane SP 5.00 2.00
- ❑ 369 Jeff Bagwell SP 8.00 3.00
- ❑ 370 Bobby Higginson SP 5.00 2.00
- ❑ 371 Juan Uribe SP 5.00 2.00
- ❑ 372 Lee Stevens SP 5.00 2.00
- ❑ 373 Jimmy Haynes SP 5.00 2.00
- ❑ 374 Jose Valentin SP 5.00 2.00
- ❑ 375 Ken Griffey Jr. SP 12.00 5.00
- ❑ 376 Barry Bonds SP 20.00 8.00
- ❑ 377 Gary Matthews Jr. SP 5.00 2.00
- ❑ 378 Gary Sheffield SP 5.00 2.00
- ❑ 379 Rick Helling SP 5.00 2.00
- ❑ 380 Junior Spivey SP 5.00 2.00
- ❑ 381 Francisco Rodriguez SP 5.00 2.00
- ❑ 382 Chipper Jones SP 8.00 3.00
- ❑ 383 Orlando Hudson SP 5.00 2.00
- ❑ 384 Ivan Rodriguez SP 8.00 3.00
- ❑ 385 Chris Snelling SP 5.00 2.00
- ❑ 386 Kenny Lofton SP 5.00 2.00
- ❑ 387 Eric Cyr SP 5.00 2.00
- ❑ 388 Jason Kendall SP 5.00 2.00
- ❑ 389 Marlon Anderson SP 5.00 2.00
- ❑ 390 Billy Koch SP 5.00 2.00
- ❑ 391 Shelley Duncan SP 5.00 2.00
- ❑ 392 Jose Reyes SP 5.00 2.00
- ❑ 393 Fernando Tatis SP 5.00 2.00
- ❑ 394 Michael Cuddyer SP 5.00 2.00
- ❑ 395 Mark Prior SP 8.00 3.00
- ❑ 396 Dontrelle Willis SP 8.00 3.00
- ❑ 397 Jay Payton SP 5.00 2.00
- ❑ 398 Brandon Phillips SP 5.00 2.00
- ❑ 399 Dustin Moseley SP RC 5.00 2.00
- ❑ 400 Jason Giambi SP 5.00 2.00
- ❑ 401 John Mabry SP 5.00 2.00
- ❑ 402 Ron Gant SP 5.00 2.00
- ❑ 403 J.T. Snow SP 5.00 2.00
- ❑ 404 Jeff Cirillo SP 5.00 2.00
- ❑ 405 Darin Erstad SP 5.00 2.00
- ❑ 406 Luis Gonzalez SP 5.00 2.00
- ❑ 407 Marcus Giles SP 5.00 2.00
- ❑ 408 Brian Daubach SP 5.00 2.00
- ❑ 409 Moises Alou SP 5.00 2.00
- ❑ 410 Raul Mondesi SP 5.00 2.00
- ❑ 411 Adrian Beltre SP 5.00 2.00
- ❑ 412 A.J. Burnett SP 5.00 2.00
- ❑ 413 Jason Jennings SP 5.00 2.00
- ❑ 414 Edwin Almonte SP 5.00 2.00
- ❑ 415 Fred McGriff SP 8.00 3.00
- ❑ 416 Tim Raines Jr. SP 5.00 2.00
- ❑ 417 Rafael Furcal SP 5.00 2.00
- ❑ 418 Erubiel Durazo SP 5.00 2.00
- ❑ 419 Drew Henson SP 5.00 2.00
- ❑ 420 Kevin Appier SP 5.00 2.00
- ❑ 421 Chad Tracy SP 5.00 2.00
- ❑ 422 Adam Wainwright SP 5.00 2.00
- ❑ 423 Choo Freeman SP 5.00 2.00
- ❑ 424 Sandy Alomar Jr. SP 5.00 2.00
- ❑ 425 Corey Koskie SP 5.00 2.00
- ❑ 426 Jeromy Burnitz SP 5.00 2.00
- ❑ 427 Jorge Posada SP 8.00 3.00
- ❑ 428 Jason Arnold SP 5.00 2.00
- ❑ 429 Brett Myers SP 5.00 2.00
- ❑ 430 Shawn Green SP 5.00 2.00

2004 Topps Heritage

- ❑ COMPLETE SET (495) 350.00 200.00
- ❑ COMP.SET w/o SP's (385) 60.00 30.00
- ❑ 1A Jim Thome Fielding 1.00 .40
- ❑ 1B Jim Thome Hitting SP 8.00 3.00
- ❑ 2 Nomar Garciaparra SP 10.00 4.00
- ❑ 3 Aramis Ramirez .60 .25
- ❑ 4 Rafael Palmeiro SP 8.00 3.00
- ❑ 5 Danny Graves .50 .20
- ❑ 6 Casey Blake .50 .20
- ❑ 7 Juan Uribe .50 .20
- ❑ 8A Dmitri Young New Logo .60 .25
- ❑ 8B Dmitri Young Old Logo SP 5.00 2.00
- ❑ 9 Billy Wagner .60 .25
- ❑ 10A Jason Giambi Swinging .60 .25
- ❑ 10B Jason Giambi Btg Stance SP 5.00 2.00
- ❑ 11 Carlos Beltran .60 .25
- ❑ 12 Chad Hermansen .50 .20
- ❑ 13 B.J. Upton 1.00 .40
- ❑ 14 Dustan Mohr .50 .20
- ❑ 15 Endy Chavez .50 .20
- ❑ 16 Cliff Floyd .60 .25
- ❑ 17 Bernie Williams 1.00 .40
- ❑ 18 Eric Chavez .00 .25
- ❑ 19 Chase Utley 1.00 .40
- ❑ 20 Randy Johnson 1.50 .60
- ❑ 21 Vernon Wells .60 .25
- ❑ 22 Juan Gonzalez .60 .25
- ❑ 23 Joe Kennedy .50 .20
- ❑ 24 Bengie Molina .50 .20
- ❑ 25 Carlos Lee .60 .25
- ❑ 26 Horacio Ramirez .50 .20
- ❑ 27 Anthony Acevedo RC .75 .30
- ❑ 28 Sammy Sosa SP 8.00 3.00
- ❑ 29 Jon Garland .60 .25
- ❑ 30A Adam Dunn Fielding .60 .25
- ❑ 30B Adam Dunn Hitting SP 5.00 2.00
- ❑ 31 Aaron Rowand .60 .25
- ❑ 32 Jody Gerut .50 .20
- ❑ 33 Chin-Hui Tsao .60 .25
- ❑ 34 Alex Sanchez .50 .20
- ❑ 35 A.J. Burnett .60 .25
- ❑ 36 Brad Ausmus .60 .25
- ❑ 37 Blake Hawksworth RC 1.00 .40
- ❑ 38 Francisco Rodriguez .60 .25
- ❑ 39 Alex Cintron .50 .20
- ❑ 40A Chipper Jones Pointing 1.50 .60
- ❑ 40B Chipper Jones Fielding SP 8.00 3.00
- ❑ 41 Deivi Cruz .50 .20
- ❑ 42 Bill Mueller .60 .25
- ❑ 43 Joe Borowski .50 .20
- ❑ 44 Jimmy Haynes .50 .20
- ❑ 45 Mark Loretta .50 .20
- ❑ 46 Jerome Williams .50 .20
- ❑ 47 Gary Sheffield Yanks SP 8.00 3.00
- ❑ 48 Richard Hidalgo .50 .20
- ❑ 49A Jason Kendall New Logo .60 .25
- ❑ 49B Jason Kendall Old Logo SP 5.00 2.00
- ❑ 50 Ichiro Suzuki SP 12.00 5.00
- ❑ 51 Jim Edmonds .60 .25
- ❑ 52 Frank Catalanotto .50 .20
- ❑ 53 Jose Contreras .50 .20
- ❑ 54 Mo Vaughn .60 .25
- ❑ 55 Brendan Donnelly .50 .20
- ❑ 56 Luis Gonzalez .60 .25
- ❑ 57 Robert Fick .50 .20
- ❑ 58 Laynce Nix .50 .20
- ❑ 59 Johnny Damon 1.00 .40
- ❑ 60A Magglio Ordonez Running .60 .25
- ❑ 60B Magglio Ordonez Hitting SP 5.00 2.00
- ❑ 61 Matt Clement .60 .25
- ❑ 62 Ryan Ludwick .50 .20
- ❑ 63 Luis Castillo .50 .20
- ❑ 64 Dave Crouthers RC .75 .30
- ❑ 65 Dave Berg .50 .20
- ❑ 66 Kyle Davies RC 4.00 1.50
- ❑ 67 Tim Salmon 1.00 .40
- ❑ 68 Marcus Giles .60 .25
- ❑ 69 Marty Cordova .50 .20
- ❑ 70A Todd Helton White Jsy 1.00 .40
- ❑ 70B Todd Helton Purple Jsy SP 8.00 3.00
- ❑ 71 Jeff Kent .60 .25
- ❑ 72 Michael Tucker .50 .20
- ❑ 73 Cesar Izturis .50 .20
- ❑ 74 Paul Quantrill .50 .20
- ❑ 75 Conor Jackson RC 3.00 1.25
- ❑ 76 Placido Polanco .50 .20
- ❑ 77 Adam Eaton .50 .20
- ❑ 78 Ramon Hernandez .60 .25
- ❑ 79 Edgardo Alfonzo .50 .20
- ❑ 80 Dioner Navarro RC 1.00 .40
- ❑ 81 Woody Williams .50 .20
- ❑ 82 Rey Ordonez .50 .20
- ❑ 83 Randy Winn .50 .20
- ❑ 84 Casey Myers RC .75 .30
- ❑ 85A R.Choy Foo New Logo RC .75 .30
- ❑ 85B R.Choy Foo Old Logo SP 5.00 2.00
- ❑ 86 Ray Durham .60 .25
- ❑ 87 Sean Burroughs .50 .20
- ❑ 88 Tim Frend RC .75 .30
- ❑ 89 Shigetoshi Hasegawa .60 .25
- ❑ 90 Jeffrey Allison RC .75 .30
- ❑ 91 Orlando Hudson .50 .20
- ❑ 92 Matt Creighton SP RC 5.00 2.00
- ❑ 93 Tim Worrell .50 .20

Card	Player		
❑ 94	Kris Benson	.50	.20
❑ 95	Mike Lieberthal	.60	.25
❑ 96	David Wells	.60	.25
❑ 97	Jason Phillips	.50	.20
❑ 98	Bobby Cox MGR	.50	.20
❑ 99	Johan Santana	1.50	.60
❑ 100A	Alex Rodriguez Hitting	2.50	1.00
❑ 100B	Alex Rodriguez Throwing SP	10.00	4.00
❑ 101	John Vander Wal	.50	.20
❑ 102	Orlando Cabrera	.60	.25
❑ 103	Hideo Nomo	1.50	.60
❑ 104	Todd Walker	.50	.20
❑ 105	Jason Johnson	.50	.20
❑ 106	Matt Mantei	.50	.20
❑ 107	Jarrod Washburn	.50	.20
❑ 108	Preston Wilson	.60	.25
❑ 109	Carl Pavano	.60	.25
❑ 110	Geoff Blum	.50	.20
❑ 111	Eric Gagne	.60	.25
❑ 112	Geoff Jenkins	.50	.20
❑ 113	Joe Torre MG	1.00	.40
❑ 114	Jon Knott RC	.75	.30
❑ 115	Hank Blalock	.60	.25
❑ 116	John Olerud	.60	.25
❑ 117A	Pat Burrell New Logo	.60	.25
❑ 117B	Pat Burrell Old Logo SP	5.00	2.00
❑ 118	Aaron Boone	.60	.25
❑ 119	Zach Day	.50	.20
❑ 120A	Frank Thomas New Logo	1.50	.60
❑ 120B	Frank Thomas Old Logo SP	8.00	3.00
❑ 121	Kyle Farnsworth	.50	.20
❑ 122	Derek Lowe	.60	.25
❑ 123	Zach Miner SP RC	8.00	3.00
❑ 124	Matthew Moses SP RC	8.00	3.00
❑ 125	Jesse Roman RC	.75	.30
❑ 126	Josh Phelps	.50	.20
❑ 127	Nic Ungs RC	.75	.30
❑ 128	Dan Haren	.50	.20
❑ 129	Kirk Rueter	.50	.20
❑ 130	Jack McKeon MGR	.60	.25
❑ 131	Keith Foulke	.60	.25
❑ 132	Garrett Stephenson	.50	.20
❑ 133	Wes Helms	.50	.20
❑ 134	Raul Ibanez	.50	.20
❑ 135	Morgan Ensberg	.60	.25
❑ 136	Jay Payton	.60	.25
❑ 137	Billy Koch	.50	.20
❑ 138	Mark Grudzielanek	.50	.20
❑ 139	Rodrigo Lopez	.50	.20
❑ 140	Corey Patterson	.50	.20
❑ 141	Troy Percival	.60	.25
❑ 142	Shea Hillenbrand	.60	.25
❑ 143	Brad Fullmer	.60	.25
❑ 144	Ricky Nolasco RC	1.50	.60
❑ 145	Mark Teixeira	1.00	.40
❑ 146	Tydus Meadows RC	.75	.30
❑ 147	Toby Hall	.50	.20
❑ 148	Orlando Palmeiro	.50	.20
❑ 149	Khalid Ballouli RC	.75	.30
❑ 150	Grady Little MGR	.50	.20
❑ 151	David Eckstein	.60	.25
❑ 152	Kenny Perez RC	.75	.30
❑ 153	Ben Grieve	.50	.20
❑ 154	Ismael Valdes	.50	.20
❑ 155	Bret Boone	.60	.25
❑ 156	Jesse Foppert	.50	.20
❑ 157	Vicente Padilla	.50	.20
❑ 158	Bobby Abreu	.60	.25
❑ 159	Scott Hatteberg	.50	.20
❑ 160	Carlos Quentin RC	2.50	1.00
❑ 161	Anthony Lerew RC	1.00	.40
❑ 162	Lance Carter	.50	.20
❑ 163	Robb Nen	.60	.25
❑ 164	Zach Duke SP RC	10.00	4.00
❑ 165	Xavier Nady	.50	.20
❑ 166	Kip Wells	.50	.20
❑ 167	Kevin Millwood	.60	.25
❑ 168	Jon Lieber	.50	.20
❑ 169	Jose Reyes	.60	.25
❑ 170	Eric Byrnes	.50	.20
❑ 171	Paul Konerko	.60	.25
❑ 172	Chris Lubanski	.60	.25
❑ 173	Jae Weong Seo	.50	.20
❑ 174	Corey Koskie	.50	.20
❑ 175	Tim Stauffer RC	1.00	4.00
❑ 176	John Lackey	.50	.20
❑ 177	Danny Bautista	.50	.20
❑ 178	Shane Reynolds	.50	.20
❑ 179	Jorge Julio	.50	.20
❑ 180A	Manny Ramirez New Logo	1.00	.40
❑ 180B	Manny Ramirez Old Logo SP	8.00	3.00
❑ 181	Alex Gonzalez	.50	.20
❑ 182A	Moises Alou New Logo	.60	.25
❑ 182B	Moises Alou Old Logo SP	5.00	2.00
❑ 183	Mark Buehrle	.60	.25
❑ 184	Carlos Guillen	.60	.25
❑ 185	Nate Cornejo	.50	.20
❑ 186	Billy Traber	.50	.20
❑ 187	Jason Jennings	.50	.20
❑ 188	Eric Munson	.50	.20
❑ 189	Braden Looper	.50	.20
❑ 190	Juan Encarnacion	.50	.20
❑ 191	Dusty Baker MGR	.60	.25
❑ 192	Travis Lee	.50	.20
❑ 193	Miguel Cairo	.50	.20
❑ 194	Rich Aurilia SP	5.00	2.00
❑ 195	Tom Gordon	.50	.20
❑ 196	Freddy Garcia	.60	.25
❑ 197	Brian Lawrence	.50	.20
❑ 198	Jorge Posada SP	8.00	3.00
❑ 199	Javier Vazquez	.60	.25
❑ 200A	Albert Pujols New Logo	3.00	1.25
❑ 200B	Albert Pujols Old Logo SP	12.00	5.00
❑ 201	Victor Zambrano	.50	.20
❑ 202	Eli Marrero	.50	.20
❑ 203	Joel Pineiro	.50	.20
❑ 204	Rondell White	.60	.25
❑ 205	Craig Ansman RC	.75	.30
❑ 206	Michael Young	.60	.25
❑ 207	Carlos Baerga	.50	.20
❑ 208	Andruw Jones	1.00	.40
❑ 209	Jerry Hairston Jr.	.50	.20
❑ 210	Shawn Green SP	5.00	2.00
❑ 211	Ron Gardenhire MGR	.50	.20
❑ 212	Darin Erstad	.60	.25
❑ 213A	Brandon Webb Glove Chest	.50	.20
❑ 213B	Brandon Webb Glove Out SP	5.00	2.00
❑ 214	Greg Maddux	2.50	1.00
❑ 215	Reed Johnson	.50	.20
❑ 216	John Thomson	.50	.20
❑ 217	Tino Martinez	1.00	.40
❑ 218	Mike Cameron	.50	.20
❑ 219	Edgar Martinez	1.00	.40
❑ 220	Eric Young	.50	.20
❑ 221	Reggie Sanders	.60	.25
❑ 222	Randy Wolf	.50	.20
❑ 223	Erubiel Durazo	.50	.20
❑ 224	Mike Mussina	1.00	.40
❑ 225	Tom Glavine	1.00	.40
❑ 226	Troy Glaus	.60	.25
❑ 227	Oscar Villarreal	.50	.20
❑ 228	David Segui	.50	.20
❑ 229	Jeff Suppan	.50	.20
❑ 230	Kenny Lofton	.60	.25
❑ 231	Esteban Loaiza	.50	.20
❑ 232	Felipe Lopez	.50	.20
❑ 233	Matt Lawton	.50	.20
❑ 234	Mark Bellhorn	.60	.25
❑ 235	Wil Ledezma	.50	.20
❑ 236	Todd Hollandsworth	.50	.20
❑ 237	Octavio Dotel	.50	.20
❑ 238	Darren Dreifort	.50	.20
❑ 239	Paul Lo Duca	.60	.25
❑ 240	Richie Sexson	.60	.25
❑ 241	Doug Mientkiewicz	.60	.25
❑ 242	Luis Rivas	.50	.20
❑ 243	Claudio Vargas	.50	.20
❑ 244	Mark Ellis	.50	.20
❑ 245	Brett Myers	.60	.25
❑ 246	Jake Peavy	.60	.25
❑ 247	Marquis Grissom	.60	.25
❑ 248	Armando Benitez	.50	.20
❑ 249	Ryan Franklin	.50	.20
❑ 250A	Alfonso Soriano Throwing	.60	.25
❑ 250B	Alfonso Soriano Fielding SP	5.00	2.00
❑ 251	Tim Hudson	.60	.25
❑ 252	Shannon Stewart	.60	.25
❑ 253	A.J. Pierzynski	.60	.25
❑ 254	Runelvys Hernandez	.50	.20
❑ 255	Roy Oswalt	.60	.25
❑ 256	Shawn Chacon	.50	.20
❑ 257	Tony Graffanino	.50	.20
❑ 258	Tim Wakefield	.60	.25
❑ 259	Damian Miller	.50	.20
❑ 260	Joe Crede	.60	.25
❑ 261	Jason LaRue	.50	.20
❑ 262	Jose Jimenez	.50	.20
❑ 263	Juan Pierre	.60	.25
❑ 264	Wade Miller	.50	.20
❑ 265	Odalis Perez	.50	.20
❑ 266	Eddie Guardado	.50	.20
❑ 267	Rocky Biddle	.50	.20
❑ 268	Jeff Nelson	.50	.20
❑ 269	Terrence Long	.50	.20
❑ 270	Ramon Ortiz	.50	.20
❑ 271	Raul Mondesi	.60	.25
❑ 272	Ugueth Urbina	.50	.20
❑ 273	Jeromy Burnitz	.60	.25
❑ 274	Brad Radke	.60	.25
❑ 275	Jose Vidro	.50	.20
❑ 276	Bobby Jenks	.60	.25
❑ 277	Ty Wigginton	.50	.20
❑ 278	Jose Guillen	.60	.25
❑ 279	Delmon Young	1.00	.40
❑ 280	Brian Giles	.60	.25
❑ 281	Jason Schmidt	.60	.25
❑ 282	Nick Markakis	.60	.25
❑ 283	Felipe Alou MGR	.60	.25
❑ 284	Carl Crawford	.60	.25
❑ 285	Neifi Perez	.50	.20
❑ 286	Miguel Tejada	.60	.25
❑ 287	Victor Martinez	.60	.25
❑ 288	Adam Kennedy	.50	.20
❑ 289	Kerry Ligtenberg	.50	.20
❑ 290	Scott Williamson	.50	.20
❑ 291	Tony Womack	.50	.20
❑ 292	Travis Hafner	.60	.25
❑ 293	Bobby Crosby	.60	.25
❑ 294	Chad Billingsley	.60	.25
❑ 295	Russ Ortiz	.50	.20
❑ 296	John Burkett	.50	.20
❑ 297	Carlos Zambrano	.60	.25
❑ 298	Randall Simon	.50	.20
❑ 299	Juan Castro	.50	.20
❑ 300	Mike Lowell	.60	.25
❑ 301	Fred McGriff	1.00	.40
❑ 302	Glendon Rusch	.50	.20
❑ 303	Sung Jung RC	.75	.30
❑ 304	Rocco Baldelli	.60	.25
❑ 305	Fernando Vina	.50	.20
❑ 306	Gil Meche	.50	.20
❑ 307	Jose Cruz Jr.	.50	.20
❑ 308	Bernie Castro	.50	.20
❑ 309	Scott Spiezio	.50	.20
❑ 310	Paul Byrd	.50	.20
❑ 311A	Jay Gibbons New Logo	.50	.20
❑ 311B	Jay Gibbons Old Logo SP	5.00	2.00
❑ 312	Trot Nixon	.60	.25
❑ 313	Chris O'Riordan RC	.75	.30
❑ 314	Julio Lugo	.50	.20
❑ 315	Ben Davis	.50	.20
❑ 316	Mike Williams	.50	.20
❑ 317	Trevor Hoffman	.60	.25
❑ 318	Andy Pettitte	1.00	.40
❑ 319	Orlando Hernandez	.60	.25
❑ 320	Juan Rivera	.50	.20
❑ 321	Elizardo Ramirez	.50	.20
❑ 322	Junior Spivey	.50	.20
❑ 323	Tony Batista	.50	.20
❑ 324	Mike Remlinger	.50	.20
❑ 325	Alex Gonzalez	.50	.20
❑ 326	Aaron Hill	.50	.20
❑ 327	Steve Finley	.60	.25
❑ 328	Vinny Castilla	.60	.25
❑ 329	Eric Duncan	.60	.25
❑ 330	Mike Gosling RC	.75	.30
❑ 331	Eric Hinske	.50	.20
❑ 332	Scott Rolen	1.00	.40
❑ 333	Benito Santiago	.60	.25
❑ 334	Jimmy Gobble	.50	.20
❑ 335	Bobby Higginson	.60	.25
❑ 336	Kelvim Escobar	.50	.20
❑ 337	Mike DeJean	.50	.20
❑ 338	Sidney Ponson	.50	.20
❑ 339	Todd Self RC	1.00	.40
❑ 340	Jeff Cirillo	.50	.20
❑ 341	Jimmy Rollins	.60	.25
❑ 342A	Barry Zito White Jsy	.60	.25

❑ 342B Barry Zito Green Jsy SP 5.00 2.00
❑ 343 Felix Pie 1.00 .40
❑ 344 Matt Morris .60 .25
❑ 345 Kazuhiro Sasaki .60 .25
❑ 346 Jack Wilson .50 .20
❑ 347 Nick Johnson .60 .25
❑ 348 Wil Cordero .50 .20
❑ 349 Ryan Madson .50 .20
❑ 350 Torii Hunter .60 .25
❑ 351 Andy Ashby .50 .20
❑ 352 Aubrey Huff .60 .25
❑ 353 Brad Lidge .60 .25
❑ 354 Derrek Lee 1.00 .40
❑ 355 Yadier Molina RC 2.50 1.00
❑ 356 Paul Wilson .50 .20
❑ 357 Omar Vizquel 1.00 .40
❑ 358 Rene Reyes .50 .20
❑ 359 Marlon Anderson .50 .20
❑ 360 Bobby Kielty .50 .20
❑ 361A Ryan Wagner New Logo .50 .20
❑ 361B Ryan Wagner Old Logo SP 5.00 2.00
❑ 362 Justin Morneau .60 .25
❑ 363 Shane Spencer .50 .20
❑ 364 David Bell .50 .20
❑ 365 Matt Stairs .50 .20
❑ 366 Joe Borchard .50 .20
❑ 367 Mark Redman .50 .20
❑ 368 Dave Roberts .50 .20
❑ 369 Desi Relaford .50 .20
❑ 370 Rich Harden .60 .25
❑ 371 Fernando Tatis .50 .20
❑ 372 Eric Karros .60 .25
❑ 373 Eric Milton .50 .20
❑ 374 Mike Sweeney .60 .25
❑ 375 Brian Daubach .50 .20
❑ 376 Brian Snyder .50 .20
❑ 377 Chris Reitsma .50 .20
❑ 378 Kyle Lohse .50 .20
❑ 379 Livan Hernandez .60 .25
❑ 380 Robin Ventura .60 .25
❑ 381 Jacque Jones .60 .25
❑ 382 Danny Kolb .50 .20
❑ 383 Casey Kotchman .60 .25
❑ 384 Cristian Guzman .50 .20
❑ 385 Josh Beckett .60 .25
❑ 386 Khalil Greene 1.00 .40
❑ 387 Greg Myers .50 .20
❑ 388 Francisco Cordero .50 .20
❑ 389 Donald Levinski RC .75 .30
❑ 390 Roy Halladay .60 .25
❑ 391 J.D. Drew .60 .25
❑ 392 Jamie Moyer .60 .25
❑ 393 Ken Macha MGR .50 .20
❑ 394 Jeff Davanon .50 .20
❑ 395 Matt Kata .50 .20
❑ 396 Jack Cust .50 .20
❑ 397 Mike Timlin .50 .20
❑ 398 Zack Greinke SP 5.00 2.00
❑ 399 Byung-Hyun Kim SP 5.00 2.00
❑ 400 Kazuhisa Ishii SP 5.00 2.00
❑ 401 Brayan Pena SP RC 5.00 2.00
❑ 402 Garret Anderson SP 5.00 2.00
❑ 403 Kyle Sleeth SP RC 8.00 3.00
❑ 404 Javy Lopez SP 5.00 2.00
❑ 405 Damian Moss SP 5.00 2.00
❑ 406 David Ortiz SP 8.00 3.00
❑ 407 Pedro Martinez SP 8.00 3.00
❑ 408 Hee Seop Choi SP 5.00 2.00
❑ 409 Carl Everett SP 5.00 2.00
❑ 410 Dontrelle Willis SP 8.00 3.00
❑ 411 Ryan Harvey SP 5.00 2.00
❑ 412 Russell Branyan SP 5.00 2.00
❑ 413 Milton Bradley SP 5.00 2.00
❑ 414 Marcus McBeth SP RC 5.00 2.00
❑ 415 Carlos Pena SP 5.00 2.00
❑ 416 Ivan Rodriguez SP 8.00 3.00
❑ 417 Craig Biggio SP 8.00 3.00
❑ 418 Angel Berroa SP 5.00 2.00
❑ 419 Brian Jordan SP 5.00 2.00
❑ 420 Scott Podsednik SP 5.00 2.00
❑ 421 Omar Falcon SP RC 5.00 2.00
❑ 422 Joe Mays SP 5.00 2.00
❑ 423 Brad Wilkerson SP 5.00 2.00
❑ 424 Al Leiter SP 5.00 2.00
❑ 425 Derek Jeter SP 12.00 5.00
❑ 426 Mark Mulder SP 5.00 2.00
❑ 427 Marlon Byrd SP 5.00 2.00
❑ 428 David Murphy SP RC 8.00 3.00
❑ 429 Phil Nevin SP 5.00 2.00
❑ 430 J.T. Snow SP 5.00 2.00
❑ 431 Brad Sullivan SP RC 8.00 3.00
❑ 432 Bo Hart SP 5.00 2.00
❑ 433 Josh Labandeira SP RC 5.00 2.00
❑ 434 Chan Ho Park SP 5.00 2.00
❑ 435 Carlos Delgado SP 5.00 2.00
❑ 436 Curt Schilling Sox SP 8.00 3.00
❑ 437 John Smoltz SP 8.00 3.00
❑ 438 Luis Matos SP 5.00 2.00
❑ 439 Mark Prior SP 8.00 3.00
❑ 440 Roberto Alomar SP 8.00 3.00
❑ 441 Coco Crisp SP 5.00 2.00
❑ 442 Austin Kearns SP 5.00 2.00
❑ 443 Larry Walker SP 5.00 2.00
❑ 444 Neal Cotts SP 5.00 2.00
❑ 445 Jeff Bagwell SP 8.00 3.00
❑ 446 Adrian Beltre SP 5.00 2.00
❑ 447 Grady Sizemore SP 8.00 3.00
❑ 448 Keith Ginter SP 5.00 2.00
❑ 449 Vladimir Guerrero SP 8.00 3.00
❑ 450 Lyle Overbay SP 5.00 2.00
❑ 451 Rafael Furcal SP 5.00 2.00
❑ 452 Melvin Mora SP 5.00 2.00
❑ 453 Kerry Wood SP 5.00 2.00
❑ 454 Jose Valentin SP 5.00 2.00
❑ 455 Ken Griffey Jr. SP 10.00 4.00
❑ 456 Brandon Phillips SP 5.00 2.00
❑ 457 Miguel Cabrera SP 8.00 3.00
❑ 458 Edwin Jackson SP 5.00 2.00
❑ 459 Eric Owens SP 5.00 2.00
❑ 460 Miguel Batista SP 5.00 2.00
❑ 461 Mike Hampton SP 5.00 2.00
❑ 462 Kevin Millar SP 5.00 2.00
❑ 463 Bartolo Colon SP 5.00 2.00
❑ 464 Sean Casey SP 5.00 2.00
❑ 465 C.C. Sabathia SP 5.00 2.00
❑ 466 Rickie Weeks SP 5.00 2.00
❑ 467 Brad Penny SP 5.00 2.00
❑ 468 Mike MacDougal SP 5.00 2.00
❑ 469 Kevin Brown SP 5.00 2.00
❑ 470 Lance Berkman SP 5.00 2.00
❑ 471 Ben Sheets SP 5.00 2.00
❑ 472 Mariano Rivera SP 8.00 3.00
❑ 473 Mike Piazza SP 10.00 4.00
❑ 474 Ryan Klesko SP 5.00 2.00
❑ 475 Edgar Renteria SP 5.00 2.00

2005 Topps Heritage

❑ COMPLETE SET (495) 400.00 250.00
❑ COMP.SET w/o SP's (385) 60.00 30.00
❑ COMMON CARD .50 .20
❑ COMMON RC .50 .20
❑ COMMON TEAM CARD .50 .20
❑ COMMON SP 8.00 3.00
❑ COMMON SP RC 8.00 3.00
❑ SP STATED ODDS 1:2 HOBBY/RETAIL
❑ BASIC SP: 5/20/30/31/33/79/101/110/130
❑ BASIC SP: 135/260/292/398-475
❑ VARIATION SP: 3/6/7/31/50/69/78/82/118
❑ VARIATION SP: 125/135/155/261/273/286
❑ VARIATION SP: 296/300/312/353/389
❑ SEE BECKETT.COM FOR VAR.DESCRIPTIONS
❑ 1 Will Harridge .50 .20
❑ 2 Warren Giles .50 .20
❑ 3A Alfonso Soriano Fldg .50 .20
❑ 3B Alfonso Soriano Running SP 8.00 3.00
❑ 4 Mark Mulder .50 .20
❑ 5 Todd Helton SP 8.00 3.00
❑ 6A Jason Bay Black Cap .50 .20
❑ 6B Jason Bay Yellow Cap SP 8.00 3.00
❑ 7A Ichiro Suzuki Running 1.50 .60
❑ 7B Ichiro Suzuki Crouch SP 10.00 4.00
❑ 8 Jim Tracy MG .50 .20
❑ 9 Gavin Floyd .50 .20
❑ 10 John Smoltz .75 .30
❑ 11 Chicago Cubs TC .75 .30
❑ 12 Darin Erstad .50 .20
❑ 13 Chad Tracy .50 .20
❑ 14 Charles Thomas .50 .20
❑ 15 Miguel Tejada .50 .20
❑ 16 Andre Ethier RC 5.00 2.00
❑ 17 Jeff Francis .50 .20
❑ 18 Derrek Lee .75 .30
❑ 19 Juan Uribe .50 .20
❑ 20 Jim Edmonds SP 8.00 3.00
❑ 21 Kenny Lofton .50 .20
❑ 22 Brad Ausmus .50 .20
❑ 23 Jon Garland .50 .20
❑ 24 Edwin Jackson .50 .20
❑ 25 Joe Mauer 1.00 .40
❑ 26 Wes Helms .50 .20
❑ 27 Brian Schneider .50 .20
❑ 28 Kazuo Matsui .50 .20
❑ 29 Flash Gordon .50 .20
❑ 30 Hideo Nomo SP 8.00 3.00
❑ 31A Albert Pujols Red Hat SP 12.00 5.00
❑ 31B Albert Pujols Blue Hat SP 12.00 5.00
❑ 32 Carl Crawford .50 .20
❑ 33 Vladimir Guerrero SP 8.00 3.00
❑ 34 Nick Green .50 .20
❑ 35 Jay Gibbons .50 .20
❑ 36 Kevin Youkilis .50 .20
❑ 37 Billy Wagner .50 .20
❑ 38 Terrence Long .50 .20
❑ 39 Kevin Mench .50 .20
❑ 40 Garret Anderson .50 .20
❑ 41 Reed Johnson .50 .20
❑ 42 Reggie Sanders .50 .20
❑ 43 Kirk Rueter .50 .20
❑ 44 Jay Payton .50 .20
❑ 45 Tike Redman .50 .20
❑ 46 Mike Lieberthal .50 .20
❑ 47 Damian Miller .50 .20
❑ 48 Zach Day .50 .20
❑ 49 Juan Rincon .50 .20
❑ 50A Jim Thome At Bat .75 .30
❑ 50B Jim Thome Fldg SP 8.00 3.00
❑ 51 Jose Guillen .50 .20
❑ 52 Richie Sexson .50 .20
❑ 53 Juan Cruz .50 .20
❑ 54 Byung-Hyun Kim .50 .20
❑ 55 Carlos Zambrano .50 .20
❑ 56 Carlos Lee .50 .20
❑ 57 Adam Dunn .50 .20
❑ 58 David Riske .50 .20
❑ 59 Carlos Guillen .50 .20
❑ 60 Larry Bowa MG .50 .20
❑ 61 Barry Bonds 8.00 3.00
❑ 62 Chris Woodward .50 .20
❑ 63 Matt DeSalvo RC .75 .30
❑ 64 Brian Stavisky RC .50 .20
❑ 65 Scot Shields .50 .20
❑ 66 J.D. Drew .50 .20
❑ 67 Erik Bedard .50 .20
❑ 68 Scott Williamson .50 .20
❑ 69A M.Prior New C on Cap .75 .30
❑ 69B M.Prior Old C on Cap SP 8.00 3.00
❑ 70 Ken Griffey Jr. 1.50 .60
❑ 71 Kazuhito Tadano .50 .20
❑ 72 Philadelphia Phillies TC .50 .20
❑ 73 Jeremy Reed .50 .20
❑ 74 Ricardo Rodriguez .50 .20
❑ 75 Carlos Delgado .50 .20
❑ 76 Eric Milton .50 .20
❑ 77 Miguel Olivo .50 .20
❑ 78A E.Alfonzo No Socks .50 .20
❑ 78B E.Alfonzo Black Socks SP 8.00 3.00
❑ 79 Kazuhisa Ishii SP 8.00 3.00
❑ 80 Jason Giambi .50 .20
❑ 81 Cliff Floyd .50 .20
❑ 82A Torii Hunter Twins Cap .50 .20

❑ 82B Torii Hunter Wash Cap SP 8.00 3.00
❑ 83 Odalis Perez .50 .20
❑ 84 Scott Podsednik .50 .20
❑ 85 Cleveland Indians TC .50 .20
❑ 86 Jeff Suppan .50 .20
❑ 87 Ray Durham .50 .20
❑ 88 Tyler Clippard RC 12.00 5.00
❑ 89 Ryan Howard 2.50 1.00
❑ 90 Cincinnati Reds TC .50 .20
❑ 91 Bengie Molina .50 .20
❑ 92 Danny Bautista .50 .20
❑ 93 Eli Marrero .50 .20
❑ 94 Larry Bigbie .50 .20
❑ 95 Atlanta Braves TC .50 .20
❑ 96 Merkin Valdez .50 .20
❑ 97 Rocco Baldelli .50 .20
❑ 98 Woody Williams .50 .20
❑ 99 Jason Frasor .50 .20
❑ 100 Baltimore Orioles TC .50 .20
❑ 101 Ivan Rodriguez SP 8.00 3.00
❑ 102 Joe Kennedy .50 .20
❑ 103 Mike Lowell .50 .20
❑ 104 Armando Benitez .50 .20
❑ 105 Craig Biggio .75 .30
❑ 106 David DeJesus .50 .20
❑ 107 Adrian Beltre .50 .20
❑ 108 Phil Nevin .50 .20
❑ 109 Cristian Guzman .50 .20
❑ 110 Jorge Posada SP 8.00 3.00
❑ 111 Boston Red Sox TC 1.00 .40
❑ 112 Jeff Mathis .50 .20
❑ 113 Bartolo Colon .50 .20
❑ 114 Alex Cintron .50 .20
❑ 115 Russ Ortiz .50 .20
❑ 116 Doug Mientkiewicz .50 .20
❑ 117 Placido Polanco .50 .20
❑ 118A M.Ordonez Black Uni .50 .20
❑ 118B M.Ordonez White Uni SP 8.00 3.00
❑ 119 Chris Seddon RC .50 .20
❑ 120 Bobby Abreu .50 .20
❑ 121 Pittsburgh Pirates TC .50 .20
❑ 122 Dallas McPherson .50 .20
❑ 123 Rodrigo Lopez .50 .20
❑ 124 Mark Bellhorn .50 .20
❑ 125A N.Garciaparra Red Cap 1.00 .40
❑ 125B N.Garciaparra Blue Cap SP 8.00 3.00
❑ 126 Sean Casey .50 .20
❑ 127 Ronnie Belliard .50 .20
❑ 128 Tom Goodwin .50 .20
❑ 129 Preston Wilson .50 .20
❑ 130 Andruw Jones SP 8.00 3.00
❑ 131 Roberto Alomar .75 .30
❑ 132 John Buck .50 .20
❑ 133 Jason LaRue .50 .20
❑ 134 St. Louis Cardinals TC .75 .30
❑ 135A Alex Rodriguez Fldg SP 10.00 4.00
❑ 135B Alex Rodriguez At Bat SP 10.00 4.00
❑ 136 Nate Robertson .50 .20
❑ 137 Juan Pierre .50 .20
❑ 138 Morgan Ensberg .50 .20
❑ 139 Vinny Castilla .50 .20
❑ 140 Jake Dittler .50 .20
❑ 141 Chan Ho Park .50 .20
❑ 142 Felix Hernandez 3.00 1.25
❑ 143 Jason Isringhausen .50 .20
❑ 144 Dustan Mohr .50 .20
❑ 145 Khalil Greene .75 .30
❑ 146 Minnesota Twins TC .50 .20
❑ 147 Vicente Padilla .50 .20
❑ 148 Oliver Perez .50 .20
❑ 149 Brian Giles .50 .20
❑ 150 Shawn Green .50 .20
❑ 151 Matt Lawton .50 .20
❑ 152 Casey Blake .50 .20
❑ 153 Frank Thomas 1.00 .40
❑ 154 Orlando Hernandez .50 .20
❑ 155A Eric Chavez Green Cap .50 .20
❑ 155B Eric Chavez Blue Cap SP 8.00 3.00
❑ 156 Chase Utley .75 .30
❑ 157 John Olerud .50 .20
❑ 158 Adam Eaton .50 .20
❑ 159 Josh Fogg .50 .20
❑ 160 Michael Tucker .50 .20
❑ 161 Kevin Brown .50 .20
❑ 162 Bobby Crosby .50 .20
❑ 163 Jason Schmidt .50 .20
❑ 164 Shannon Stewart .50 .20
❑ 165 Tony Womack .50 .20
❑ 166 Los Angeles Dodgers TC .75 .30
❑ 167 Franklin Gutierrez .50 .20
❑ 168 Ted Lilly .50 .20
❑ 169 Mark Teixeira .75 .30
❑ 170 Matt Morris .50 .20
❑ 171 Bucky Jacobsen .50 .20
❑ 172 Steve Doetsch RC .75 .30
❑ 173 Jeff Weaver .50 .20
❑ 174 Tony Graffanino .50 .20
❑ 175 Jeff Bagwell .75 .30
❑ 176 Carl Pavano .50 .20
❑ 177 Junior Spivey .50 .20
❑ 178 Carlos Silva .50 .20
❑ 179 Tim Redding .50 .20
❑ 180 Brett Myers .50 .20
❑ 181 Mike Mussina .75 .30
❑ 182 Richard Hidalgo .50 .20
❑ 183 Nick Johnson .50 .20
❑ 184 Lew Ford .50 .20
❑ 185 Barry Zito .50 .20
❑ 186 Jimmy Rollins .50 .20
❑ 187 Jack Wilson .50 .20
❑ 188 Chicago White Sox TC .50 .20
❑ 189 Guillermo Quiroz .50 .20
❑ 190 Mark Hendrickson .50 .20
❑ 191 Jeremy Bonderman .50 .20
❑ 192 Jason Jennings .50 .20
❑ 193 Paul Lo Duca .50 .20
❑ 194 A.J. Burnett .50 .20
❑ 195 Ken Harvey .50 .20
❑ 196 Geoff Jenkins .50 .20
❑ 197 Joe Mays .50 .20
❑ 198 Jose Vidro .50 .20
❑ 199 David Wright 2.00 .75
❑ 200 Randy Johnson 1.00 .40
❑ 201 Jeff DaVanon .50 .20
❑ 202 Paul Byrd .50 .20
❑ 203 David Ortiz 1.00 .40
❑ 204 Kyle Farnsworth .50 .20
❑ 205 Keith Foulke .50 .20
❑ 206 Joe Crede .50 .20
❑ 207 Austin Kearns .50 .20
❑ 208 Jody Gerut .50 .20
❑ 209 Shawn Chacon .50 .20
❑ 210 Carlos Pena .50 .20
❑ 211 Luis Castillo .50 .20
❑ 212 Chris Denorfia RC 1.00 .40
❑ 213 Detroit Tigers TC .50 .20
❑ 214 Aubrey Huff .50 .20
❑ 215 Brad Fullmer .50 .20
❑ 216 Frank Catalanotto .50 .20
❑ 217 Raul Ibanez .50 .20
❑ 218 Ryan Klesko .50 .20
❑ 219 Octavio Dotel .50 .20
❑ 220 Rob Mackowiak .50 .20
❑ 221 Scott Hatteberg .50 .20
❑ 222 Pat Burrell .50 .20
❑ 223 Bernie Williams .75 .30
❑ 224 Kris Benson .50 .20
❑ 225 Eric Gagne .50 .20
❑ 226 San Francisco Giants TC .75 .30
❑ 227 Roy Oswalt .50 .20
❑ 228 Josh Beckett .50 .20
❑ 229 Lee Mazzilli MG .50 .20
❑ 230 Rickie Weeks .50 .20
❑ 231 Troy Glaus .50 .20
❑ 232 Chone Figgins .50 .20
❑ 233 John Thomson .50 .20
❑ 234 Trot Nixon .50 .20
❑ 235 Brad Penny .50 .20
❑ 236 Oakland A's TC .50 .20
❑ 237 Miguel Batista .50 .20
❑ 238 Ryan Drese .50 .20
❑ 239 Aaron Miles .50 .20
❑ 240 Randy Wolf .50 .20
❑ 241 Brian Lawrence .50 .20
❑ 242 A.J. Pierzynski .50 .20
❑ 243 Jamie Moyer .50 .20
❑ 244 Chris Carpenter .50 .20
❑ 245 So Taguchi .50 .20
❑ 246 Rob Bell .50 .20
❑ 247 Francisco Cordero .50 .20
❑ 248 Tom Glavine .75 .30
❑ 249 Jermaine Dye .50 .20
❑ 250 Cliff Lee .50 .20
❑ 251 New York Yankees TC 1.00 .40
❑ 252 Vernon Wells .50 .20
❑ 253 R.A. Dickey .50 .20
❑ 254 Larry Walker .75 .30
❑ 255 Randy Winn .50 .20
❑ 256 Pedro Feliz .50 .20
❑ 257 Mark Loretta .50 .20
❑ 258 Tim Worrell .50 .20
❑ 259 Kip Wells .50 .20
❑ 260 Cesar Izturis SP 8.00 3.00
❑ 261A Carlos Beltran Fldg .50 .20
❑ 261B Carlos Beltran At Bat SP 8.00 3.00
❑ 262 Juan Encarnacion .50 .20
❑ 263 Luis A. Gonzalez .50 .20
❑ 264 Grady Sizemore .75 .30
❑ 265 Paul Wilson .50 .20
❑ 266 Mark Buehrle .50 .20
❑ 267 Todd Hollandsworth .50 .20
❑ 268 Orlando Cabrera .50 .20
❑ 269 Sidney Ponson .50 .20
❑ 270 Mike Hampton .50 .20
❑ 271 Luis Gonzalez .50 .20
❑ 272 Brendan Donnelly .50 .20
❑ 273A Chipper Jones Slide 1.00 .40
❑ 273B Chipper Jones Fldg SP 8.00 3.00
❑ 274 Brandon Webb .50 .20
❑ 275 Marty Cordova .50 .20
❑ 276 Greg Maddux 1.50 .60
❑ 277 Jose Contreras .50 .20
❑ 278 Aaron Harang .50 .20
❑ 279 Coco Crisp .50 .20
❑ 280 Bobby Higginson .50 .20
❑ 281 Guillermo Mota .50 .20
❑ 282 Andy Pettitte .75 .30
❑ 283 Jeremy West RC .75 .30
❑ 284 Craig Brazell .50 .20
❑ 285 Eric Hinske .50 .20
❑ 286A Hank Blalock Hitting .50 .20
❑ 286B Hank Blalock Fldg SP 8.00 3.00
❑ 287 B.J. Upton .75 .30
❑ 288 Jason Marquis .50 .20
❑ 289 Matt Herges .50 .20
❑ 290 Ramon Hernandez .50 .20
❑ 291 Marlon Byrd .50 .20
❑ 292 Ryan Sweeney SP RC 8.00 3.00
❑ 293 Esteban Loaiza .50 .20
❑ 294 Al Leiter .50 .20
❑ 295 Alex Gonzalez .50 .20
❑ 296A J.Santana Twins Cap 1.00 .40
❑ 296B J.Santana Wash Cap SP 8.00 3.00
❑ 297 Milton Bradley .50 .20
❑ 298 Mike Sweeney .50 .20
❑ 299 Wade Miller .50 .20
❑ 300A Sammy Sosa Hitting 1.00 .40
❑ 300B Sammy Sosa Standing SP 8.00 3.00
❑ 301 Wily Mo Pena .50 .20
❑ 302 Tim Wakefield .50 .20
❑ 303 Rafael Palmeiro .75 .30
❑ 304 Rafael Furcal .50 .20
❑ 305 David Eckstein .50 .20
❑ 306 David Segui .50 .20
❑ 307 Kevin Millar .50 .20
❑ 308 Matt Clement .50 .20
❑ 309 Wade Robinson RC .50 .20
❑ 310 Brad Radke .50 .20
❑ 311 Steve Finley .50 .20
❑ 312A Lance Berkman Hitting .50 .20
❑ 312B Lance Berkman Fldg SP 8.00 3.00
❑ 313 Joe Randa .50 .20
❑ 314 Miguel Cabrera .75 .30
❑ 315 Billy Koch .50 .20
❑ 316 Alex Sanchez .50 .20
❑ 317 Chin-Hui Tsao .50 .20
❑ 318 Omar Vizquel .75 .30
❑ 319 Ryan Freel .50 .20
❑ 320 LaTroy Hawkins .50 .20
❑ 321 Aaron Rowand .50 .20
❑ 322 Paul Konerko .50 .20
❑ 323 Joe Borowski .50 .20
❑ 324 Jarrod Washburn .50 .20
❑ 325 Jaret Wright .50 .20
❑ 326 Johnny Damon .75 .30
❑ 327 Corey Patterson .50 .20
❑ 328 Travis Hafner .50 .20
❑ 329 Shingo Takatsu .50 .20

❑	330	Dmitri Young	.50	.20
❑	331	Matt Holliday	.50	.20
❑	332	Jeff Kent	.50	.20
❑	333	Desi Relaford	.50	.20
❑	334	Jose Hernandez	.50	.20
❑	335	Lyle Overbay	.50	.20
❑	336	Jacque Jones	.50	.20
❑	337	Termel Sledge	.50	.20
❑	338	Victor Zambrano	.50	.20
❑	339	Gary Sheffield	.50	.20
❑	340	Brad Wilkerson	.50	.20
❑	341	Ian Kinsler RC	2.50	1.00
❑	342	Jesse Crain	.50	.20
❑	343	Orlando Hudson	.50	.20
❑	344	Laynce Nix	.50	.20
❑	345	Jose Cruz Jr.	.50	.20
❑	346	Edgar Renteria	.50	.20
❑	347	Eddie Guardado	.50	.20
❑	348	Jerome Williams	.50	.20
❑	349	Trevor Hoffman	.50	.20
❑	350	Mike Piazza	1.00	.40
❑	351	Jason Kendall	.50	.20
❑	352	Kevin Millwood	.50	.20
❑	353A	Tim Hudson Atl Cap	.50	.20
❑	353B	Tim Hudson Milw Cap SP	8.00	3.00
❑	354	Paul Quantrill	.50	.20
❑	355	Jon Lieber	.50	.20
❑	356	Braden Looper	.50	.20
❑	357	Chad Cordero	.50	.20
❑	358	Joe Nathan	.50	.20
❑	359	Doug Davis	.50	.20
❑	360	Ian Bladergroen RC	.75	.30
❑	361	Val Majewski	.50	.20
❑	362	Francisco Rodriguez	.50	.20
❑	363	Kelvim Escobar	.50	.20
❑	364	Marcus Giles	.50	.20
❑	365	Darren Fenster RC	.50	.20
❑	366	David Bell	.50	.20
❑	367	Shea Hillenbrand	.50	.20
❑	368	Manny Ramirez	.75	.30
❑	369	Ben Broussard	.50	.20
❑	370	Luis Ramirez RC	.50	.20
❑	371	Dustin Hermanson	.50	.20
❑	372	Akinori Otsuka	.50	.20
❑	373	Chadd Blasko RC	.75	.30
❑	374	Delmon Young	.75	.30
❑	375	Michael Young	.50	.20
❑	376	Bret Boone	.50	.20
❑	377	Jake Peavy	.50	.20
❑	378	Matthew Lindstrom RC	.50	.20
❑	379	Sean Burroughs	.50	.20
❑	380	Rich Harden	.50	.20
❑	381	Chris Roberson RC	.50	.20
❑	382	John Lackey	.50	.20
❑	383	Johnny Estrada	.50	.20
❑	384	Matt Rogelstad RC	.50	.20
❑	385	Toby Hall	.50	.20
❑	386	Adam LaRoche	.50	.20
❑	387	Bill Hall	.50	.20
❑	388	Tim Salmon	.50	.20
❑	389A	Curt Schilling Throw	.75	.30
❑	389B	Curt Schilling Glove Up SP	8.00	3.00
❑	390	Michael Barrett	.50	.20
❑	391	Jose Acevedo	.50	.20
❑	392	Nate Schierholtz	.75	.30
❑	393	J.T. Snow Jr.	.50	.20
❑	394	Mark Redman	.50	.20
❑	395	Ryan Madson	.50	.20
❑	396	Kevin West RC	.50	.20
❑	397	Ramon Ortiz	.50	.20
❑	398	Derek Lowe SP	8.00	3.00
❑	399	Kerry Wood SP	8.00	3.00
❑	400	Derek Jeter SP	12.00	5.00
❑	401	Livan Hernandez SP	8.00	3.00
❑	402	Casey Kotchman SP	8.00	3.00
❑	403	Chaz Lytle SP RC	8.00	3.00
❑	404	Alexis Rios SP	8.00	3.00
❑	405	Scott Spiezio SP	8.00	3.00
❑	406	Craig Wilson SP	8.00	3.00
❑	407	Felix Rodriguez SP	8.00	3.00
❑	408	D'Angelo Jimenez SP	8.00	3.00
❑	409	Rondell White SP	8.00	3.00
❑	410	Shawn Estes SP	8.00	3.00
❑	411	Troy Percival SP	8.00	3.00
❑	412	Melvin Mora SP	8.00	3.00
❑	413	Aramis Ramirez SP	8.00	3.00
❑	414	Carl Everett SP	8.00	3.00
❑	415	Elvys Quezada SP RC	8.00	3.00
❑	416	Ben Sheets SP	8.00	3.00
❑	417	Matt Stairs SP	8.00	3.00
❑	418	Adam Everett SP	8.00	3.00
❑	419	Jason Johnson SP	8.00	3.00
❑	420	Billy Butler SP RC	10.00	4.00
❑	421	Justin Morneau SP	8.00	3.00
❑	422	Jose Reyes SP	8.00	3.00
❑	423	Mariano Rivera SP	8.00	3.00
❑	424	Jose Vaquedano SP RC	8.00	3.00
❑	425	Gabe Gross SP	8.00	3.00
❑	426	Scott Rolen SP	8.00	3.00
❑	427	Ty Wigginton SP	8.00	3.00
❑	428	James Jurries SP RC	8.00	3.00
❑	429	Pedro Martinez SP	8.00	3.00
❑	430	Mark Grudzielanek SP	8.00	3.00
❑	431	Josh Phelps SP	8.00	3.00
❑	432	Ryan Goleski SP RC	8.00	3.00
❑	433	Mike Matheny SP	8.00	3.00
❑	434	Bobby Kielty SP	8.00	3.00
❑	435	Tony Batista SP	8.00	3.00
❑	436	Corey Koskie SP	8.00	3.00
❑	437	Brad Lidge SP	8.00	3.00
❑	438	Dontrelle Willis SP	8.00	3.00
❑	439	Angel Berroa SP	8.00	3.00
❑	440	Jason Kubel SP	8.00	3.00
❑	441	Roy Halladay SP	8.00	3.00
❑	442	Brian Roberts SP	8.00	3.00
❑	443	Bill Mueller SP	8.00	3.00
❑	444	Adam Kennedy SP	8.00	3.00
❑	445	Brandon Moss SP RC	8.00	3.00
❑	446	Sean Burnett SP	8.00	3.00
❑	447	Eric Byrnes SP	8.00	3.00
❑	448	Matt Campbell SP RC	8.00	3.00
❑	449	Ryan Webb SP	8.00	3.00
❑	450	Jose Valentin SP	8.00	3.00
❑	451	Jake Westbrook SP	8.00	3.00
❑	452	Glen Perkins SP RC	8.00	3.00
❑	453	Alex Gonzalez SP	8.00	3.00
❑	454	Jeromy Burnitz SP	8.00	3.00
❑	455	Zack Greinke SP	8.00	3.00
❑	456	Sean Marshall SP RC	6.00	2.50
❑	457	Erubiel Durazo SP	8.00	3.00
❑	458	Michael Cuddyer SP	8.00	3.00
❑	459	Hee Seop Choi SP	8.00	3.00
❑	460	Melky Cabrera SP RC	10.00	4.00
❑	461	Jerry Hairston Jr. SP	8.00	3.00
❑	462	Moises Alou SP	8.00	3.00
❑	463	Michael Rogers SP RC	8.00	3.00
❑	464	Javy Lopez SP	8.00	3.00
❑	465	Freddy Garcia SP	8.00	3.00
❑	466	Brett Harper SP RC	8.00	3.00
❑	467	Juan Gonzalez SP	8.00	3.00
❑	468	Kevin Melillo SP RC	8.00	3.00
❑	469	Todd Walker SP	8.00	3.00
❑	470	C.C. Sabathia SP	8.00	3.00
❑	471	Kole Strayhorn SP RC	8.00	3.00
❑	472	Mark Kotsay SP	8.00	3.00
❑	473	Javier Vazquez SP	8.00	3.00
❑	474	Mike Cameron SP	8.00	3.00
❑	475	Wes Swackhamer SP RC	8.00	3.00

2006 Topps Heritage

❑	COMPLETE SET (494)	400.00	250.00
❑	COMP.SET w/o SP's (384)	60.00	30.00
❑	COMMON CARD	.50	.20
❑	COMMON RC	.50	.20
❑	COMMON TEAM CARD	.50	.20
❑	COMMON SP	8.00	3.00
❑	SP STATED ODDS 1:2 HOBBY/RETAIL		
❑	SP CL: 1/2/10/18/20B/23B/25/35/55		
❑	SP CL: 70/76/80B/91/95A/95B/99/106		
❑	SP CL: 123/127/165B/200B/212B/265-269		
❑	SP CL: 271-274/276-316/318-323/325A		
❑	SP CL: 325B/326-328/330-349/350A/350B		
❑	SP CL: 351-352/400/407/475B		
❑	VARIATION CL: 20/23/80/95/165/200		
❑	VARIATION CL: 212/325/350/475		
❑	TWO VERSIONS OF EACH VARIATION EXIST		
❑	SEE BECKETT.COM FOR VAR.DESCRIPTIONS		
❑	CARD 255 NOT INTENDED FOR RELEASE		
❑	COMP.SET EXCLUDES CARD 255 CUT OUT		

❑	1	David Ortiz SP	8.00	3.00
❑	2	Mike Piazza SP	10.00	4.00
❑	3	Daryle Ward	.50	.20
❑	4	Rafael Furcal	.50	.20
❑	5	Derek Lowe	.50	.20
❑	6	Eric Chavez	.50	.20
❑	7	Juan Uribe	.50	.20
❑	8	C.C. Sabathia	.50	.20
❑	9	Sean Casey	.50	.20
❑	10	Barry Bonds SP	12.00	5.00
❑	11	Gary Sheffield	.50	.20
❑	12	Ted Lilly	.50	.20
❑	13	Lew Ford	.50	.20
❑	14	Tom Gordon	.50	.20
❑	15	Curt Schilling	1.00	.40
❑	16	Jason Kendall	.50	.20
❑	17	Frank Catalanotto	.50	.20
❑	18	Pedro Martinez SP	8.00	3.00
❑	19	David Dellucci	.50	.20
❑	20A	A.Jones w/o Seats	1.00	.40
❑	20B	A.Jones w/Seats SP	8.00	3.00
❑	21	Brad Halsey	.50	.20
❑	22	Vernon Wells	.50	.20
❑	23A	D.Jeter Yellow/White Ltr	4.00	1.50
❑	23B	D.Jeter Blue Ltr SP	12.00	5.00
❑	24	Todd Helton	1.00	.40
❑	25	Randy Johnson SP	10.00	4.00
❑	26	Jay Gibbons	.50	.20
❑	27	Joe Mays	.50	.20
❑	28	Paul Konerko	.50	.20
❑	29	Lyle Overbay	.50	.20
❑	30	Jorge Posada	1.00	.40
❑	31	Brandon Webb	.50	.20
❑	32	Marcus Giles	.50	.20
❑	33	J.T. Snow	.50	.20
❑	34	Todd Walker	.50	.20
❑	35	Wily Mo Pena SP	8.00	3.00
❑	36	Carlos Delgado	.50	.20
❑	37	David Wright	1.50	.60
❑	38	Shea Hillenbrand	.50	.20
❑	39	Daniel Cabrera	.50	.20
❑	40	Trevor Hoffman	.50	.20
❑	41	Matt Morris	.50	.20
❑	42	Mariano Rivera	1.50	.60
❑	43	Jeff Bagwell	1.00	.40
❑	44	J.D. Drew	.50	.20
❑	45	Carl Pavano	.50	.20
❑	46	Placido Polanco	.50	.20
❑	47	Adrian Beltre	.50	.20
❑	48	J.D. Closser	.50	.20
❑	49	Paul Lo Duca	.50	.20
❑	50	Scott Rolen	.50	.20
❑	51	Bernie Williams	1.00	.40
❑	52	Jose Guillen	.50	.20
❑	53	Aubrey Huff	.50	.20
❑	54	Greg Maddux	2.50	1.00
❑	55	Derrek Lee SP	8.00	3.00
❑	56	Hideki Matsui	1.50	.60
❑	57	Jose Bautista	.50	.20
❑	58	Kyle Farnsworth	.50	.20
❑	59	Nate Robertson	.50	.20
❑	60	Sammy Sosa	1.50	.60
❑	61	Javier Vazquez	.50	.20
❑	62	Jeff Mathis	.50	.20
❑	63	Mark Buehrle	.50	.20
❑	64	Orlando Hernandez	.50	.20
❑	65	Brandon Claussen	.50	.20
❑	66	Miguel Batista	.50	.20
❑	67	Eddie Guardado	.50	.20
❑	68	Alex Gonzalez	.50	.20
❑	69	Kris Benson	.50	.20

❑ 70	Bobby Abreu SP	8.00	3.00
❑ 71	Vinny Castilla	.50	.20
❑ 72	Ben Broussard	.50	.20
❑ 73	Travis Hafner	.50	.20
❑ 74	Dmitri Young	.50	.20
❑ 75	Alex S. Gonzalez	.50	.20
❑ 76	Jason Bay SP	8.00	3.00
❑ 77	Charlton Jimerson	.50	.20
❑ 78	Ryan Garko	.50	.20
❑ 79	Lance Berkman	.50	.20
❑ 80A	T.Hudson Red/Blue Ltr	.50	.20
❑ 80B	T.Hudson Blue Ltr SP	8.00	3.00
❑ 81	Guillermo Mota	.50	.20
❑ 82	Chris B. Young	.50	.20
❑ 83	Brad Lidge	.50	.20
❑ 84	A.J. Pierzynski	.50	.20
❑ 85	Maicer Izturis	.50	.20
❑ 86	Vladimir Guerrero	1.50	.60
❑ 87	J.J. Hardy	.50	.20
❑ 88	Cesar Izturis	.50	.20
❑ 89	Mark Ellis	.50	.20
❑ 90	Chipper Jones	1.50	.60
❑ 91	Chris Snelling SP	8.00	3.00
❑ 92	Jose Reyes	.50	.20
❑ 93	Mike Lieberthal	.50	.20
❑ 94	Octavio Dotel	.50	.20
❑ 95A	A.Rodriguez Fielding SP	10.00	4.00
❑ 95B	A.Rodriguez w/Bat SP	10.00	4.00
❑ 96	Brett Myers	.50	.20
❑ 97	New York Yankees TC	1.00	.40
❑ 98	Ryan Klesko	.50	.20
❑ 99	Brian Jordan SP	8.00	3.00
❑ 100	W.Harridge/W.Giles	.50	.20
❑ 101	Adam Eaton	.50	.20
❑ 102	Aaron Boone	.50	.20
❑ 103	Alex Rios	.50	.20
❑ 104	Andy Pettitte	1.00	.40
❑ 105	Barry Zito	.50	.20
❑ 106	Bengie Molina SP	8.00	3.00
❑ 107	Austin Kearns	.50	.20
❑ 108	Adam Everett	.50	.20
❑ 109	A.J. Burnett	.50	.20
❑ 110	Mark Prior	1.00	.40
❑ 111	Russ Ortiz	.50	.20
❑ 112	Adam Dunn	.50	.20
❑ 113	Byung-Hyun Kim	.50	.20
❑ 114	Atlanta Braves TC	.50	.20
❑ 115	Carlos Silva	.50	.20
❑ 116	Chad Cordero	.50	.20
❑ 117	Chone Figgins	.50	.20
❑ 118	Chris Reitsma	.50	.20
❑ 119	Coco Crisp	.50	.20
❑ 120	David DeJesus	.50	.20
❑ 121	Chris Snyder	.50	.20
❑ 122	Brad Eldred	.50	.20
❑ 123	Humberto Cota SP	8.00	3.00
❑ 124	Erubiel Durazo	.50	.20
❑ 125	Josh Beckett	.50	.20
❑ 126	Kenny Lofton	.50	.20
❑ 127	Joe Nathan SP	8.00	3.00
❑ 128	Bryan Bullington	.50	.20
❑ 129	Jim Thome	1.00	.40
❑ 130	Shawn Green	.50	.20
❑ 131	LaTroy Hawkins	.50	.20
❑ 132	Mark Kotsay	.50	.20
❑ 133	Matt Lawton	.50	.20
❑ 134	Luis Castillo	.50	.20
❑ 135	Michael Barrett	.50	.20
❑ 136	Preston Wilson	.50	.20
❑ 137	Orlando Cabrera	.50	.20
❑ 138	Chuck James	.50	.20
❑ 139	Raul Ibanez	.50	.20
❑ 140	Frank Thomas	1.50	.60
❑ 141	Orlando Hudson	.50	.20
❑ 142	Scott Kazmir	.50	.20
❑ 143	Steve Finley	.50	.20
❑ 144	Danny Sandoval RC	.50	.20
❑ 145	Javy Lopez	.50	.20
❑ 146	Tony Giarratano	.50	.20
❑ 147	Terrence Long	.50	.20
❑ 148	Victor Martinez	.50	.20
❑ 149	Toby Hall	.50	.20
❑ 150	Fausto Carmona	.50	.20
❑ 151	Tim Wakefield	.50	.20
❑ 152	Troy Percival	.50	.20
❑ 153	Chris Denorfia	.50	.20
❑ 154	Junior Spivey	.50	.20
❑ 155	Desi Relaford	.50	.20
❑ 156	Francisco Liriano	3.00	1.25
❑ 157	Corey Koskie	.50	.20
❑ 158	Chris Carpenter	.50	.20
❑ 159	Robert Andino RC	.50	.20
❑ 160	Cliff Floyd	.50	.20
❑ 161	Pittsburgh Pirates TC	.50	.20
❑ 162	Anderson Hernandez	.50	.20
❑ 163	Mike Maroth	.50	.20
❑ 164	Aaron Rowand	.50	.20
❑ 165A	A.Pujols Grey Shirt	3.00	1.25
❑ 165B	A.Pujols Red Shirt SP	12.00	5.00
❑ 166	David Bell	.50	.20
❑ 167	Angel Berroa	.50	.20
❑ 168	B.J. Ryan	.50	.20
❑ 169	Bartolo Colon	.50	.20
❑ 170	Hong-Chih Kuo	1.50	.60
❑ 171	Cincinnati Reds TC	.50	.20
❑ 172	Bill Mueller	.50	.20
❑ 173	John Koronka	.50	.20
❑ 174	Billy Wagner	.50	.20
❑ 175	Zack Greinke	.50	.20
❑ 176	Rick Short	.50	.20
❑ 177	Yadier Molina	.50	.20
❑ 178	Willy Taveras	.50	.20
❑ 179	Wes Helms	.50	.20
❑ 180	Wade Miller	.50	.20
❑ 181	Luis Gonzalez	.50	.20
❑ 182	Victor Zambrano	.50	.20
❑ 183	Chicago Cubs TC	.50	.20
❑ 184	Victor Santos	.50	.20
❑ 185	Tyler Walker	.50	.20
❑ 186	Bobby Crosby	.50	.20
❑ 187	Trot Nixon	.50	.20
❑ 188	Nick Johnson	.50	.20
❑ 189	Nick Swisher	.50	.20
❑ 190	Brian Roberts	.50	.20
❑ 191	Nomar Garciaparra	1.50	.60
❑ 192	Oliver Perez	.50	.20
❑ 193	Ramon Hernandez	.50	.20
❑ 194	Randy Winn	.50	.20
❑ 195	Ryan Church	.50	.20
❑ 196	Ryan Wagner	.50	.20
❑ 197	Todd Hollandsworth	.50	.20
❑ 198	Detroit Tigers TC	.50	.20
❑ 199	Tino Martinez	1.00	.40
❑ 200A	R.Clemens On Mound	3.00	1.25
❑ 200B	R.Clemens Red Shirt SP	10.00	4.00
❑ 201	Shawn Estes	.50	.20
❑ 202	Justin Morneau	.50	.20
❑ 203	Jeff Francis	.50	.20
❑ 204	Oakland Athletics TC	.50	.20
❑ 205	Jeff Francoeur	1.50	.60
❑ 206	C.J. Wilson	.50	.20
❑ 207	Francisco Rodriguez	.50	.20
❑ 208	Edgardo Alfonzo	.50	.20
❑ 209	David Eckstein	.50	.20
❑ 210	Cory Lidle	.50	.20
❑ 211	Chase Utley	1.00	.40
❑ 212A	R.Baldelli Yellow/White Ltr	.50	.20
❑ 212B	R.Baldelli Blue Ltr SP	8.00	3.00
❑ 213	So Taguchi	.50	.20
❑ 214	Philadelphia Phillies TC	.50	.20
❑ 215	Brad Hawpe	.50	.20
❑ 216	Walter Young	.50	.20
❑ 217	Tom Gorzelanny	.50	.20
❑ 218	Shaun Marcum	.50	.20
❑ 219	Ryan Howard	2.50	1.00
❑ 220	Damian Jackson	.50	.20
❑ 221	Craig Counsell	.50	.20
❑ 222	Damian Miller	.50	.20
❑ 223	Derrick Turnbow	.50	.20
❑ 224	Hank Blalock	.50	.20
❑ 225	Brayan Pena	.50	.20
❑ 226	Grady Sizemore	1.00	.40
❑ 227	Ivan Rodriguez	1.00	.40
❑ 228	Jason Isringhausen	.50	.20
❑ 229	Brian Fuentes	.50	.20
❑ 230	Jason Phillips	.50	.20
❑ 231	Jason Schmidt	.50	.20
❑ 232	Javier Valentin	.50	.20
❑ 233	Jeff Kent	.50	.20
❑ 234	John Buck	.50	.20
❑ 235	Mike Matheny	.50	.20
❑ 236	Jorge Cantu	.50	.20
❑ 237	Jose Castillo	.50	.20
❑ 238	Kenny Rogers	.50	.20
❑ 239	Kerry Wood	.50	.20
❑ 240	Kevin Mench	.50	.20
❑ 241	Tim Stauffer	.50	.20
❑ 242	Eric Milton	.50	.20
❑ 243	St. Louis Cardinals TC	.50	.20
❑ 244	Shawn Chacon	.50	.20
❑ 245	Mike Jacobs	.50	.20
❑ 246	Ryan Dempster	.50	.20
❑ 247	Todd Jones	.50	.20
❑ 248	Tom Glavine	1.00	.40
❑ 249	Tony Graffanino	.50	.20
❑ 250	Ichiro Suzuki	2.50	1.00
❑ 251	Baltimore Orioles TC	.50	.20
❑ 252	Brad Radke	.50	.20
❑ 253	Brad Wilkerson	.50	.20
❑ 254	Carlos Lee	.50	.20
❑ 255	Alex Gordon Cut Out	250.00	175.00
❑ 256	Gustavo Chacin	.50	.20
❑ 257	Jermaine Dye	.50	.20
❑ 258	Jose Mesa	.50	.20
❑ 259	Julio Lugo	.50	.20
❑ 260	Mark Redman	.50	.20
❑ 261	Brandon Watson	.50	.20
❑ 262	Pedro Feliz	.50	.20
❑ 263	Esteban Loaiza	.50	.20
❑ 264	Anthony Reyes	1.00	.40
❑ 265	Jose Contreras SP	8.00	3.00
❑ 266	Tadahito Iguchi SP	8.00	3.00
❑ 267	Mark Loretta SP	8.00	3.00
❑ 268	Ray Durham SP	8.00	3.00
❑ 269	Neifi Perez SP	8.00	3.00
❑ 270	Washington Nationals TC	.50	.20
❑ 271	Troy Glaus SP	8.00	3.00
❑ 272	Matt Holliday SP	8.00	3.00
❑ 273	Kevin Millwood SP	8.00	3.00
❑ 274	Jon Lieber SP	8.00	3.00
❑ 275	Cleveland Indians TC	.50	.20
❑ 276	Jeremy Reed SP	8.00	3.00
❑ 277	Garrett Atkins SP	8.00	3.00
❑ 278	Geoff Jenkins SP	8.00	3.00
❑ 279	Joey Gathright SP	8.00	3.00
❑ 280	Ben Sheets SP	8.00	3.00
❑ 281	Melvin Mora SP	8.00	3.00
❑ 282	Jonathan Papelbon SP	10.00	4.00
❑ 283	John Smoltz SP	8.00	3.00
❑ 284	Jake Peavy SP	8.00	3.00
❑ 285	Felix Hernandez SP	8.00	3.00
❑ 286	Alfonso Soriano SP	8.00	3.00
❑ 287	Bronson Arroyo SP	8.00	3.00
❑ 288	Adam LaRoche SP	8.00	3.00
❑ 289	Aramis Ramirez SP	8.00	3.00
❑ 290	Brad Hennessey SP	8.00	3.00
❑ 291	Conor Jackson SP	8.00	3.00
❑ 292	Rod Barajas SP	8.00	3.00
❑ 293	Chris R. Young SP	8.00	3.00
❑ 294	Jeremy Bonderman SP	8.00	3.00
❑ 295	Jack Wilson SP	8.00	3.00
❑ 296	Jay Payton SP	8.00	3.00
❑ 297	Danys Baez SP	8.00	3.00
❑ 298	Jose Lima SP	8.00	3.00
❑ 299	Luis A. Gonzalez SP	8.00	3.00
❑ 300	Mike Sweeney SP	8.00	3.00
❑ 301	Nelson Cruz SP	8.00	3.00
❑ 302	Eric Gagne SP	8.00	3.00
❑ 303	Juan Castro SP	8.00	3.00
❑ 304	Joe Mauer SP	8.00	3.00
❑ 305	Richie Sexson SP	8.00	3.00
❑ 306	Roy Oswalt SP	8.00	3.00
❑ 307	Rickie Weeks SP	8.00	3.00
❑ 308	Pat Borders SP	8.00	3.00
❑ 309	Mike Morse SP	8.00	3.00
❑ 310	Matt Stairs SP	8.00	3.00
❑ 311	Chad Tracy SP	8.00	3.00
❑ 312	Matt Cain SP	8.00	3.00
❑ 313	Mark Mulder SP	8.00	3.00
❑ 314	Mark Grudzielanek SP	8.00	3.00
❑ 315	Johnny Damon Yanks SP	10.00	4.00
❑ 316	Casey Kotchman SP	8.00	3.00
❑ 317	San Francisco Giants TC	.50	.20
❑ 318	Chris Burke SP	8.00	3.00
❑ 319	Carl Crawford SP	8.00	3.00
❑ 320	Edgar Renteria SP	8.00	3.00
❑ 321	Chan Ho Park SP	8.00	3.00
❑ 322	Boston Red Sox TC SP	8.00	3.00

No.	Card		
❑ 323	Robinson Cano SP	8.00	3.00
❑ 324	Los Angeles Dodgers TC	.50	.20
❑ 325A	M.Tejada w/Bat SP	8.00	3.00
❑ 325B	M.Tejada Hand Up SP	8.00	3.00
❑ 326	Jimmy Rollins SP	8.00	3.00
❑ 327	Juan Pierre SP	8.00	3.00
❑ 328	Dan Johnson SP	8.00	3.00
❑ 329	Chicago White Sox TC	1.00	.40
❑ 330	Pat Burrell SP	8.00	3.00
❑ 331	Ramon Ortiz SP	8.00	3.00
❑ 332	Rondell White SP	8.00	3.00
❑ 333	David Wells SP	8.00	3.00
❑ 334	Michael Young SP	8.00	3.00
❑ 335	Mike Mussina SP	8.00	3.00
❑ 336	Moises Alou SP	8.00	3.00
❑ 337	Scott Podsednik SP	8.00	3.00
❑ 338	Rich Harden SP	8.00	3.00
❑ 339	Mark Teahen SP	8.00	3.00
❑ 340	Jacque Jones SP	8.00	3.00
❑ 341	Jason Giambi SP	8.00	3.00
❑ 342	Bill Hall SP	8.00	3.00
❑ 343	Jon Garland SP	8.00	3.00
❑ 344	Dontrelle Willis SP	8.00	3.00
❑ 345	Danny Haren SP	8.00	3.00
❑ 346	Brian Giles SP	8.00	3.00
❑ 347	Brad Penny SP	8.00	3.00
❑ 348	Brandon McCarthy SP	8.00	3.00
❑ 349	Chien-Ming Wang SP	10.00	4.00
❑ 350A	T.Hunter Red/Blue Ltr SP	8.00	3.00
❑ 350B	T.Hunter Blue Ltr SP	8.00	3.00
❑ 351	Yhency Brazoban SP	8.00	3.00
❑ 352	Rodrigo Lopez SP	8.00	3.00
❑ 353	Paul McAnulty	.50	.20
❑ 354	Francisco Cordero	.50	.20
❑ 355	Brandon Inge	.50	.20
❑ 356	Jason Lane	.50	.20
❑ 357	Brian Schneider	.50	.20
❑ 358	Dustin Hermanson	.50	.20
❑ 359	Eric Hinske	.50	.20
❑ 360	Jarrod Washburn	.50	.20
❑ 361	Jayson Werth	.50	.20
❑ 362	Craig Breslow RC	.50	.20
❑ 363	Jeff Weaver	.50	.20
❑ 364	Jeromy Burnitz	.50	.20
❑ 365	Jhonny Peralta	.50	.20
❑ 366	Joe Crede	.50	.20
❑ 367	Johan Santana	1.50	.60
❑ 368	Jose Valentin	.50	.20
❑ 369	Keith Foulke	.50	.20
❑ 370	Larry Bigbie	.50	.20
❑ 371	Manny Ramirez	1.00	.40
❑ 372	Jim Edmonds	.50	.20
❑ 373	Horacio Ramirez	.50	.20
❑ 374	Garret Anderson	.50	.20
❑ 375	Felipe Lopez	.50	.20
❑ 376	Eric Byrnes	.50	.20
❑ 377	Darin Erstad	.50	.20
❑ 378	Carlos Zambrano	.50	.20
❑ 379	Craig Biggio	1.00	.40
❑ 380	Darrell Rasner	.50	.20
❑ 381	Dave Roberts	.50	.20
❑ 382	Hanley Ramirez	.50	.20
❑ 383	Geoff Blum	.50	.20
❑ 384	Joel Pineiro	.50	.20
❑ 385	Kip Wells	.50	.20
❑ 386	Kelvim Escobar	.50	.20
❑ 387	John Patterson	.50	.20
❑ 388	Jody Gerut	.50	.20
❑ 389	Marshall McDougall	.50	.20
❑ 390	Mike MacDougal	.50	.20
❑ 391	Orlando Palmeiro	.50	.20
❑ 392	Rich Aurilia	.50	.20
❑ 393	Ronnie Belliard	.50	.20
❑ 394	Rich Hill	.50	.20
❑ 395	Scott Hatteberg	.50	.20
❑ 396	Ryan Langerhans	.50	.20
❑ 397	Richard Hidalgo	.50	.20
❑ 398	Omar Vizquel	1.00	.40
❑ 399	Mike Lowell	.50	.20
❑ 400	Astros Aces SP	8.00	3.00
❑ 401	Mike Cameron	.50	.20
❑ 402	Matt Clement	.50	.20
❑ 403	Miguel Cabrera	1.00	.40
❑ 404	Milton Bradley	.50	.20
❑ 405	Laynce Nix	.50	.20
❑ 406	Rob Mackowiak	.50	.20
❑ 407	White Sox Power Hitters SP	8.00	3.00
❑ 408	Mark Teixeira	1.00	.40
❑ 409	Brady Clark	.50	.20
❑ 410	Johnny Estrada	.50	.20
❑ 411	Juan Encarnacion	.50	.20
❑ 412	Morgan Ensberg	.50	.20
❑ 413	Nook Logan	.50	.20
❑ 414	Phil Nevin	.50	.20
❑ 415	Reggie Sanders	.50	.20
❑ 416	Roy Halladay	.50	.20
❑ 417	Livan Hernandez	.50	.20
❑ 418	Jose Vidro	.50	.20
❑ 419	Shannon Stewart	.50	.20
❑ 420	Brian Bruney	.50	.20
❑ 421	Royce Clayton	.50	.20
❑ 422	Chris Demaria RC	.50	.20
❑ 423	Eduardo Perez	.50	.20
❑ 424	Jeff Suppan	.50	.20
❑ 425	Jaret Wright	.50	.20
❑ 426	Joe Randa	.50	.20
❑ 427	Bobby Kielty	.50	.20
❑ 428	Jason Ellison	.50	.20
❑ 429	Gregg Zaun	.50	.20
❑ 430	Runelvys Hernandez	.50	.20
❑ 431	Joe McEwing	.50	.20
❑ 432	Jason LaRue	.50	.20
❑ 433	Aaron Miles	.50	.20
❑ 434	Adam Kennedy	.50	.20
❑ 435	Ambiorix Burgos	.50	.20
❑ 436	Armando Benitez	.50	.20
❑ 437	Brad Ausmus	.50	.20
❑ 438	Brandon Backe	.50	.20
❑ 439	Brian James Anderson	.50	.20
❑ 440	Bruce Chen	.50	.20
❑ 441	Carlos Guillen	.50	.20
❑ 442	Casey Blake	.50	.20
❑ 443	Chris Capuano	.50	.20
❑ 444	Chris Duffy	.50	.20
❑ 445	Chris Ray	.50	.20
❑ 446	Clint Barmes	.50	.20
❑ 447	Andrew Sisco	.50	.20
❑ 448	Dallas McPherson	.50	.20
❑ 449	Tanyon Sturtze	.50	.20
❑ 450	Carlos Beltran	.50	.20
❑ 451	Jason Vargas	.50	.20
❑ 452	Ervin Santana	.50	.20
❑ 453	Jason Marquis	.50	.20
❑ 454	Juan Rivera	.50	.20
❑ 455	Jake Westbrook	.50	.20
❑ 456	Jason Johnson	.50	.20
❑ 457	Joe Blanton	.50	.20
❑ 458	Kevin Millar	.50	.20
❑ 459	John Thomson	.50	.20
❑ 460	J.P. Howell	.50	.20
❑ 461	Justin Verlander	2.50	1.00
❑ 462	Kelly Johnson	.50	.20
❑ 463	Kyle Davies	.50	.20
❑ 464	Lance Niekro	.50	.20
❑ 465	Magglio Ordonez	.50	.20
❑ 466	Melky Cabrera	.50	.20
❑ 467	Nick Punto	.50	.20
❑ 468	Paul Byrd	.50	.20
❑ 469	Randy Wolf	.50	.20
❑ 470	Ruben Gotay	.50	.20
❑ 471	Ryan Madson	.50	.20
❑ 472	Victor Diaz	.50	.20
❑ 473	Xavier Nady	.50	.20
❑ 474	Zach Duke	.50	.20
❑ 475A	H.Street Yellow/White Ltr	.50	.20
❑ 475B	H.Street Blue Ltr SP	8.00	3.00
❑ 476	Brad Thompson	.50	.20
❑ 477	Jonny Gomes	.50	.20
❑ 478	B.J. Upton	.50	.20
❑ 479	Jamey Carroll	.50	.20
❑ 480	Mike Hampton	.50	.20
❑ 481	Tony Clark	.50	.20
❑ 482	Antonio Alfonseca	.50	.20
❑ 483	Justin Duchscherer	.50	.20
❑ 484	Mike Timlin	.50	.20
❑ 485	Joe Saunders	.50	.20

2005 Topps Opening Day

No.	Card		
❑	COMPLETE SET (165)	40.00	15.00
❑	COMMON CARD (1-165)	.40	.15
❑	ISSUED IN OPENING DAY PACKS		
❑ 1	Alex Rodriguez	1.50	.60

No.	Card		
❑ 2	Placido Polanco	.40	.15
❑ 3	Torii Hunter	.40	.15
❑ 4	Lyle Overbay	.40	.15
❑ 5	Johnny Damon	.60	.25
❑ 6	Mike Cameron	.40	.15
❑ 7	Ichiro Suzuki	2.00	.75
❑ 8	Francisco Rodriguez	.40	.15
❑ 9	Bobby Crosby	.40	.15
❑ 10	Sammy Sosa	1.00	.40
❑ 11	Randy Wolf	.40	.15
❑ 12	Jason Bay	.40	.15
❑ 13	Mike Lieberthal	.40	.15
❑ 14	Paul Konerko	.40	.15
❑ 15	Brian Giles	.40	.15
❑ 16	Luis Gonzalez	.40	.15
❑ 17	Jim Edmonds	.40	.15
❑ 18	Carlos Lee	.40	.15
❑ 19	Corey Patterson	.40	.15
❑ 20	Hank Blalock	.40	.15
❑ 21	Sean Casey	.40	.15
❑ 22	Dmitri Young	.40	.15
❑ 23	Mark Mulder	.40	.15
❑ 24	Bobby Abreu	.40	.15
❑ 25	Jim Thome	.60	.25
❑ 26	Jason Kendall	.40	.15
❑ 27	Jason Giambi	.40	.15
❑ 28	Vinny Castilla	.40	.15
❑ 29	Tony Batista	.40	.15
❑ 30	Ivan Rodriguez	.60	.25
❑ 31	Craig Biggio	.60	.25
❑ 32	Chris Carpenter	.40	.15
❑ 33	Adrian Beltre	.40	.15
❑ 34	Scott Podsednik	.40	.15
❑ 35	Cliff Floyd	.40	.15
❑ 36	Chad Tracy	.40	.15
❑ 37	John Smoltz	.60	.25
❑ 38	Shingo Takatsu	.40	.15
❑ 39	Jack Wilson	.40	.15
❑ 40	Gary Sheffield	.40	.15
❑ 41	Lance Berkman	.40	.15
❑ 42	Carl Crawford	.40	.15
❑ 43	Carlos Guillen	.40	.15
❑ 44	David Bell	.40	.15
❑ 45	Kazuo Matsui	.40	.15
❑ 46	Jason Schmidt	.40	.15
❑ 47	Jason Marquis	.40	.15
❑ 48	Melvin Mora	.40	.15
❑ 49	David Ortiz	1.00	.40
❑ 50	Andruw Jones	.60	.25
❑ 51	Miguel Tejada	.40	.15
❑ 52	Bartolo Colon	.40	.15
❑ 53	Derrek Lee	.60	.25
❑ 54	Eric Gagne	.40	.15
❑ 55	Miguel Cabrera	.60	.25
❑ 56	Travis Hafner	.40	.15
❑ 57	Jose Valentin	.40	.15
❑ 58	Mark Prior	.60	.25
❑ 59	Phil Nevin	.40	.15
❑ 60	Jose Vidro	.40	.15
❑ 61	Khalil Greene	.60	.25
❑ 62	Carlos Zambrano	.40	.15
❑ 63	Erubiel Durazo	.40	.15
❑ 64	Michael Young UER	.40	.15
❑ 65	Woody Williams	.40	.15
❑ 66	Edgardo Alfonzo	.40	.15
❑ 67	Troy Glaus	.40	.15
❑ 68	Garret Anderson	.40	.15
❑ 69	Richie Sexson	.40	.15

❑ 70 Curt Schilling .60 .25
❑ 71 Randy Johnson 1.00 .40
❑ 72 Chipper Jones 1.00 .40
❑ 73 J.D. Drew .40 .15
❑ 74 Russ Ortiz .40 .15
❑ 75 Frank Thomas 1.00 .40
❑ 76 Jimmy Rollins .40 .15
❑ 77 Barry Zito .40 .15
❑ 78 Rafael Palmeiro .60 .25
❑ 79 Brad Wilkerson .40 .15
❑ 80 Adam Dunn .40 .15
❑ 81 Doug Mientkiewicz .40 .15
❑ 82 Manny Ramirez .60 .25
❑ 83 Pedro Martinez .60 .25
❑ 84 Moises Alou .40 .15
❑ 85 Mike Sweeney .40 .15
❑ 86 Boston Red Sox WC 1.00 .40
❑ 87 Matt Clement .40 .15
❑ 88 Nomar Garciaparra 1.00 .40
❑ 89 Magglio Ordonez .40 .15
❑ 90 Bret Boone .40 .15
❑ 91 Mark Loretta .40 .15
❑ 92 Jose Contreras .40 .15
❑ 93 Randy Winn .40 .15
❑ 94 Austin Kearns .40 .15
❑ 95 Ken Griffey Jr. 1.50 .60
❑ 96 Jake Westbrook .40 .15
❑ 97 Kazuhito Tadano .40 .15
❑ 98 C.C. Sabathia .40 .15
❑ 99 Todd Helton .60 .25
❑ 100 Albert Pujols 2.00 .75
❑ 101 Jose Molina
Bengie Molina .40 .15
❑ 102 Aaron Miles .40 .15
❑ 103 Mike Lowell .40 .15
❑ 104 Paul Lo Duca .40 .15
❑ 105 Juan Pierre .40 .15
❑ 106 Dontrelle Willis .40 .15
❑ 107 Jeff Bagwell .60 .25
❑ 108 Carlos Beltran .40 .15
❑ 109 Ronnie Belliard .40 .15
❑ 110 Roy Oswalt .40 .15
❑ 111 Zack Greinke .40 .15
❑ 112 Steve Finley .40 .15
❑ 113 Kazuhisa Ishii .40 .15
❑ 114 Justin Morneau .40 .15
❑ 115 Ben Sheets .40 .15
❑ 116 Johan Santana 1.00 .40
❑ 117 Billy Wagner .40 .15
❑ 118 Mariano Rivera 1.00 .40
❑ 119 Corey Koskie .40 .15
❑ 120 Akinori Otsuka .40 .15
❑ 121 Joe Mauer 1.00 .40
❑ 122 Jacque Jones .40 .15
❑ 123 Joe Nathan .40 .15
❑ 124 Nick Johnson .40 .15
❑ 125 Vernon Wells .40 .15
❑ 126 Mike Piazza 1.00 .40
❑ 127 Jose Guillen .40 .15
❑ 128 Jose Reyes .40 .15
❑ 129 Marcus Giles .40 .15
❑ 130 Javy Lopez .40 .15
❑ 131 Kevin Millar .40 .15
❑ 132 Jorge Posada .60 .25
❑ 133 Carl Pavano .40 .15
❑ 134 Bernie Williams .60 .25
❑ 135 Kerry Wood .40 .15
❑ 136 Matt Holliday .40 .15
❑ 137 Kevin Brown .40 .15
❑ 138 Derek Jeter 2.00 .75
❑ 139 Barry Bonds 2.50 1.00
❑ 140 Jeff Kent .40 .15
❑ 141 Mark Kotsay .40 .15
❑ 142 Shawn Green .40 .15
❑ 143 Tim Hudson .40 .15
❑ 144 Shannon Stewart .40 .15
❑ 145 Pat Burrell .40 .15
❑ 146 Gavin Floyd .40 .15
❑ 147 Mike Mussina .60 .25
❑ 148 Eric Chavez .40 .15
❑ 149 Jon Lieber .40 .15
❑ 150 Vladimir Guerrero 1.00 .40
❑ 151 Vicente Padilla .40 .15
❑ 152 Ryan Klesko .40 .15
❑ 153 Jake Peavy .40 .15
❑ 154 Scott Rolen .60 .25
❑ 155 Greg Maddux 1.50 .60
❑ 156 Edgar Renteria .40 .15
❑ 157 Larry Walker .60 .25
❑ 158 Scott Kazmir .40 .15
❑ 159 B.J. Upton .60 .25
❑ 160 Mark Teixeira .60 .25
❑ 161 Ken Harvey .40 .15
❑ 162 Alfonso Soriano .40 .15
❑ 163 Carlos Delgado .40 .15
❑ 164 Alexis Rios .40 .15
❑ 165 Checklist .40 .15

2006 Topps Opening Day

❑ COMPLETE SET (165) 40.00 15.00
❑ COMMON CARD (1-165) .40 .15
❑ OVERALL PLATE SER.1 ODDS 1:246 HTA
❑ PLATE PRINT RUN 1 SET PER COLOR
❑ BLACK-CYAN-MAGENTA-YELLOW ISSUED
❑ NO PLATE PRICING DUE TO SCARCITY
❑ 1 Alex Rodriguez 1.50 .60
❑ 2 Jhonny Peralta .50 .20
❑ 3 Garrett Atkins .40 .15
❑ 4 Vernon Wells .40 .15
❑ 5 Carl Crawford .40 .15
❑ 6 Josh Beckett .40 .15
❑ 7 Mickey Mantle 8.00 3.00
❑ 8 Willy Taveras .40 .15
❑ 9 Ivan Rodriguez .60 .25
❑ 10 Clint Barmes .40 .15
❑ 11 Jose Reyes .40 .15
❑ 12 Travis Hafner .40 .15
❑ 13 Tadahito Iguchi .40 .15
❑ 14 Barry Zito .40 .15
❑ 15 Brian Roberts .40 .15
❑ 16 David Wright 1.50 .60
❑ 17 Mark Teixeira .60 .25
❑ 18 Roy Halladay .40 .15
❑ 19 Scott Rolen .60 .25
❑ 20 Bobby Abreu .40 .15
❑ 21 Lance Berkman .40 .15
❑ 22 Moises Alou .40 .15
❑ 23 Chone Figgins .40 .15
❑ 24 Aaron Rowand .40 .15
❑ 25 Chipper Jones 1.00 .40
❑ 26 Johnny Damon .60 .25
❑ 27 Matt Clement .40 .15
❑ 28 Nick Johnson .40 .15
❑ 29 Freddy Garcia .40 .15
❑ 30 Jon Garland .40 .15
❑ 31 Torii Hunter .40 .15
❑ 32 Mike Sweeney .40 .15
❑ 33 Mike Lieberthal .40 .15
❑ 34 Rafael Furcal .40 .15
❑ 35 Brad Wilkerson .40 .15
❑ 36 Brad Penny .40 .15
❑ 37 Jorge Cantu .40 .15
❑ 38 Paul Konerko .40 .15
❑ 39 Rickie Weeks .40 .15
❑ 40 Jorge Posada .60 .25
❑ 41 Albert Pujols 2.00 .75
❑ 42 Zack Greinke .40 .15
❑ 43 Jimmy Rollins .40 .15
❑ 44 Mark Prior .60 .25
❑ 45 Greg Maddux 1.50 .60
❑ 46 Jeff Francis .40 .15
❑ 47 Felipe Lopez .40 .15
❑ 48 Dan Johnson .40 .15
❑ 49 B.J. Ryan .40 .15
❑ 50 Manny Ramirez .60 .25
❑ 51 Melvin Mora .40 .15
❑ 52 Javy Lopez .40 .15
❑ 53 Garret Anderson .40 .15
❑ 54 Jason Bay .40 .15
❑ 55 Joe Mauer .60 .25
❑ 56 C.C. Sabathia .40 .15
❑ 57 Bartolo Colon .40 .15
❑ 58 Ichiro Suzuki 1.50 .60
❑ 59 Andruw Jones .60 .25
❑ 60 Rocco Baldelli .40 .15
❑ 61 Jeff Kent .40 .15
❑ 62 Cliff Floyd .40 .15
❑ 63 John Smoltz .60 .25
❑ 64 Shawn Green .40 .15
❑ 65 Nomar Garciaparra 1.00 .40
❑ 66 Miguel Cabrera .60 .25
❑ 67 Vladimir Guerrero 1.00 .40
❑ 68 Gary Sheffield .40 .15
❑ 69 Jake Peavy .40 .15
❑ 70 Carlos Lee .40 .15
❑ 71 Tom Glavine .60 .25
❑ 72 Craig Biggio .60 .25
❑ 73 Steve Finley .40 .15
❑ 74 Adrian Beltre .40 .15
❑ 75 Eric Gagne .40 .15
❑ 76 Aubrey Huff .40 .15
❑ 77 Livan Hernandez .40 .15
❑ 78 Scott Podsednik .40 .15
❑ 79 Todd Helton .60 .25
❑ 80 Kerry Wood .40 .15
❑ 81 Randy Johnson 1.00 .40
❑ 82 Huston Street .40 .15
❑ 83 Pedro Martinez .60 .25
❑ 84 Roger Clemens 2.00 .75
❑ 85 Hank Blalock .40 .15
❑ 86 Carlos Beltran .40 .15
❑ 87 Chien-Ming Wang 1.50 .60
❑ 88 Rich Harden .40 .15
❑ 89 Mike Mussina .60 .25
❑ 90 Mark Buehrle .40 .15
❑ 91 Michael Young .40 .15
❑ 92 Mark Mulder .40 .15
❑ 93 Khalil Greene .60 .25
❑ 94 Johan Santana .60 .25
❑ 95 Andy Pettitte .40 .15
❑ 96 Derek Jeter 2.50 1.00
❑ 97 Jack Wilson .40 .15
❑ 98 Ben Sheets .40 .15
❑ 99 Miguel Tejada .40 .15
❑ 100 Barry Bonds 2.50 1.00
❑ 101 Dontrelle Willis .40 .15
❑ 102 Curt Schilling .60 .25
❑ 103 Jose Contreras .40 .15
❑ 104 Jeremy Bonderman .40 .15
❑ 105 David Ortiz 1.00 .40
❑ 106 Lyle Overbay .40 .15
❑ 107 Robinson Cano .60 .25
❑ 108 Tim Hudson .40 .15
❑ 109 Paul Lo Duca .40 .15
❑ 110 Mariano Rivera .60 .25
❑ 111 Derrek Lee .40 .15
❑ 112 Morgan Ensberg .40 .15
❑ 113 Wily Mo Pena .40 .15
❑ 114 Roy Oswalt .40 .15
❑ 115 Adam Dunn .40 .15
❑ 116 Hideki Matsui 1.50 .60
❑ 117 Pat Burrell .40 .15
❑ 118 Jason Schmidt .40 .15
❑ 119 Alfonso Soriano .40 .15
❑ 120 Aramis Ramirez .40 .15
❑ 121 Jason Giambi .40 .15
❑ 122 Orlando Hernandez .40 .15
❑ 123 Magglio Ordonez .40 .15
❑ 124 Troy Glaus .40 .15
❑ 125 Carlos Delgado .40 .15
❑ 126 Kevin Millwood .40 .15
❑ 127 Shannon Stewart .40 .15
❑ 128 Luis Castillo .40 .15
❑ 129 Jim Edmonds .60 .25
❑ 130 Richie Sexson .40 .15
❑ 131 Dmitri Young .40 .15
❑ 132 Russ Adams .40 .15
❑ 133 Nick Swisher .40 .15
❑ 134 Jermaine Dye .40 .15
❑ 135 Anderson Hernandez (RC) .40 .15

Card		
136 Justin Huber (RC)	.40	.15
137 Jason Botts (RC)	.40	.15
138 Jeff Mathis (RC)	.40	.15
139 Ryan Garko (RC)	.40	.15
140 Charlton Jimerson (RC)	.40	.15
141 Chris Denorfia (RC)	.40	.15
142 Anthony Reyes (RC)	.40	.15
143 Bryan Bullington (RC)	.40	.15
144 Chuck James (RC)	.60	.25
145 Danny Sandoval RC	.40	.15
146 Walter Young (RC)	.40	.15
147 Fausto Carmona (RC)	.40	.15
148 Francisco Liriano (RC)	2.00	.75
149 Hong-Chih Kuo (RC)	1.00	.40
150 Joe Saunders (RC)	.40	.15
151 John Koronka (RC)	.40	.15
152 Robert Andino RC	.40	.15
153 Shaun Marcum (RC)	.40	.15
154 Tom Gorzelanny (RC)	.40	.15
155 Craig Breslow RC	.40	.15
156 Chris Demaria RC	.40	.15
157 Brayan Pena (RC)	.40	.15
158 Rich Hill (RC)	.40	.15
159 Rick Short (RC)	.40	.15
160 Darrell Rasner (RC)	.40	.15
161 C.J. Wilson (RC)	.40	.15
162 Brandon Watson (RC)	.40	.15
163 Paul McAnulty (RC)	.40	.15
164 Marshall McDougall (RC)	.40	.15
165 Checklist	.40	.15

2006 Topps Sterling

Card		
B.BONDS (1-19)	12.00	5.00
B.BONDS ODDS 1:10		
M.MANTLE (20-39)	25.00	10.00
M.MANTLE ODDS 1:10		
J.GIBSON (40-43)	30.00	12.50
J.GIBSON ODDS 1:191		
R.HENDERSON (44-53)	10.00	4.00
R.HENDERSON ODDS 1:22		
T.WILLIAMS (54-62)	12.00	5.00
T.WILLIAMS ODDS 1:27		
R.CLEMENTE (63-67)	25.00	10.00
R.CLEMENTE ODDS 1:40		
N.RYAN (68-77)	20.00	8.00
N.RYAN ODDS 1:20		
C.RIPKEN (78-96)	20.00	8.00
C.RIPKEN ODDS 1:10		
S.MUSIAL (97-101)	10.00	4.00
S.MUSIAL ODDS 1:40		
R.JACKSON (102-106)	10.00	4.00
R.JACKSON ODDS 1:40		
J.BENCH (107-111)	10.00	4.00
J.BENCH ODDS 1:43		
G.BRETT (112-121)	10.00	4.00
G.BRETT ODDS 1:20		
D.MATTINGLY (122-131)	12.00	5.00
D.MATTINGLY ODDS 1:20		
R.MARIS (132-136)	12.00	5.00
R.MARIS ODDS 1:40		
R.CAREW (137-146)	10.00	4.00
R.CAREW ODDS 1:20		
Y.BERRA (147-151)	10.00	4.00
Y.BERRA ODDS 1:40		
M.SCHMIDT (152-156)	10.00	4.00
M.SCHMIDT ODDS 1:40		
C.YASTRZEMSKI (157-175)	10.00	4.00
C.YASTRZEMSKI ODDS 1:10		
T.GWYNN (176-185)	10.00	4.00
T.GWYNN ODDS 1:20		
R.SANDBERG (186-190)	10.00	4.00
R.SANDBERG ODDS 1:40		
O.SMITH (191-200)	10.00	4.00
O.SMITH ODDS 1:20		
STATED PRINT RUN 250 SER.#'d SETS		

2002 Topps Total

Card		
COMPLETE SET (990)	150.00	75.00
1 Joe Mauer RC	10.00	4.00
2 Derek Jeter	2.00	.75
3 Shawn Green	.30	.10
4 Vladimir Guerrero	.75	.30
5 Mike Piazza	1.25	.50
6 Brandon Duckworth	.20	.07
7 Aramis Ramirez	.30	.10
8 Josh Barfield RC	2.50	1.00
9 Troy Glaus	.30	.10
10 Sammy Sosa	.75	.30
11 Rod Barajas	.20	.07
12 Tsuyoshi Shinjo	.30	.10
13 Larry Bigbie	.20	.07
14 Tino Martinez	.50	.20
15 Craig Biggio	.50	.20
16 Anastacio Martinez RC	.40	.15
17 John McDonald	.20	.07
18 Kyle Kane RC	.25	.08
19 Aubrey Huff	.30	.10
20 Juan Cruz	.20	.07
21 Doug Creek	.20	.07
22 Luther Hackman	.20	.07
23 Rafael Furcal	.30	.10
24 Andres Torres	.20	.07
25 Jason Giambi	.30	.10
26 Jose Paniagua	.20	.07
27 Jose Offerman	.20	.07
28 Alex Arias	.20	.07
29 J.M. Gold	.20	.07
30 Jeff Bagwell	.50	.20
31 Brent Cookson	.20	.07
32 Kelly Wunsch	.20	.07
33 Larry Walker	.30	.10
34 Luis Gonzalez	.30	.10
35 John Franco	.30	.10
36 Roy Oswalt	.30	.10
37 Tom Glavine	.50	.20
38 C.C. Sabathia	.30	.10
39 Jay Gibbons	.20	.07
40 Wilson Betemit	.20	.07
41 Tony Armas Jr.	.20	.07
42 Mo Vaughn	.30	.10
43 Gerard Oakes RC	.40	.15
44 Dmitri Young	.30	.10
45 Tim Salmon	.50	.20
46 Barry Zito	.30	.10
47 Adrian Gonzalez	.20	.07
48 Joe Davenport	.20	.07
49 Adrian Hernandez	.20	.07
50 Randy Johnson	.75	.30
52 Adam Pettyjohn	.20	.07
53 Alex Escobar	.20	.07
54 Stevenson Agosto RC	.25	.08
55 Omar Daal	.20	.07
56 Mike Buddie	.20	.07
57 Dave Williams	.20	.07
58 Marquis Grissom	.30	.10
59 Pat Burrell	.30	.10
60 Mark Prior	.50	.20
61 Mike Bynum	.20	.07
62 Mike Hill RC	.40	.15
63 Brandon Backe RC	.50	.20
64 Dan Wilson	.20	.07
65 Nick Johnson	.30	.10
66 Jason Grimsley	.20	.07
67 Russ Johnson	.20	.07
68 Todd Walker	.20	.07
69 Kyle Farnsworth	.20	.07
70 Ben Broussard	.20	.07
71 Garrett Guzman RC	.40	.15
72 Terry Mulholland	.20	.07
73 Tyler Houston	.20	.07
74 Jace Brewer	.20	.07
75 Chris Baker RC	.40	.15
76 Frank Catalanotto	.20	.07
77 Mike Redmond	.20	.07
78 Matt Wise	.20	.07
79 Fernando Vina	.20	.07
80 Kevin Brown	.30	.10
81 Grant Balfour	.20	.07
82 Clint Nageotte RC	.50	.20
83 Jeff Tam	.20	.07
84 Steve Trachsel	.20	.07
85 Tomo Ohka	.20	.07
86 Keith McDonald	.20	.07
87 Jose Ortiz	.20	.07
88 Rusty Greer	.30	.10
89 Jeff Suppan	.20	.07
90 Moises Alou	.30	.10
91 Juan Encarnacion	.20	.07
92 Tyler Yates RC	.40	.15
93 Scott Strickland	.20	.07
94 Brent Butler	.20	.07
95 Jon Rauch	.20	.07
96 Brian Mallette RC	.25	.08
97 Joe Randa	.30	.10
98 Cesar Crespo	.20	.07
99 Felix Rodriguez	.20	.07
100 Chipper Jones	.75	.30
101 Victor Martinez	.75	.30
102 Danny Graves	.20	.07
103 Brandon Berger	.20	.07
104 Carlos Garcia	.20	.07
105 Alfonso Soriano	.30	.10
106 Allan Simpson RC	.25	.08
107 Brad Thomas	.20	.07
108 Devon White	.30	.10
109 Scott Chiasson	.20	.07
110 Cliff Floyd	.30	.10
111 Scott Williamson	.20	.07
112 Julio Zuleta	.20	.07
113 Terry Adams	.20	.07
114 Zach Day	.20	.07
115 Ben Grieve	.20	.07
116 Mark Ellis	.20	.07
117 Bobby Jenks RC	1.50	.60
118 LaTroy Hawkins	.20	.07
119 Tim Raines Jr.	.20	.07
120 Juan Uribe	.20	.07
121 Bob Scanlan	.20	.07
122 Brad Nelson RC	.40	.15
123 Adam Johnson	.20	.07
124 Raul Casanova	.20	.07
125 Jeff D'Amico	.20	.07
126 Aaron Cook RC	.40	.15
127 Alan Benes	.20	.07
128 Mark Little	.20	.07
129 Randy Wolf	.20	.07
130 Phil Nevin	.30	.10
131 Guillermo Mota	.20	.07
132 Nick Neugebauer	.20	.07
133 Pedro Borbon Jr.	.20	.07
134 Doug Mientkiewicz	.30	.10
135 Edgardo Alfonzo	.20	.07
136 Dustan Mohr	.20	.07
137 Dan Reichert	.20	.07
138 Dewon Brazelton	.20	.07
139 Orlando Cabrera	.30	.10
140 Todd Hollandsworth	.20	.07
141 Darren Dreifort	.20	.07
142 Jose Valentin	.20	.07
143 Josh Kalinowski	.20	.07
144 Randy Keisler	.20	.07
145 Bret Boone	.30	.10

❑	146	Roosevelt Brown	.20	.07
❑	147	Brent Abernathy	.20	.07
❑	148	Jorge Julio	.20	.07
❑	149	Alex Gonzalez	.20	.07
❑	150	Juan Pierre	.30	.10
❑	151	Roger Cedeno	.20	.07
❑	152	Javier Vazquez	.30	.10
❑	153	Armando Benitez	.20	.07
❑	154	Dave Burba	.20	.07
❑	155	Brad Penny	.20	.07
❑	156	Ryan Jensen	.20	.07
❑	157	Jeromy Burnitz	.30	.10
❑	158	Matt Childers RC	.40	.15
❑	159	Wilmy Caceres	.20	.07
❑	160	Roger Clemens	1.50	.60
❑	161	Jamie Cerda RC	.40	.15
❑	162	Jason Christiansen	.20	.07
❑	163	Pokey Reese	.20	.07
❑	164	Ivanon Coffie	.20	.07
❑	165	Joaquin Benoit	.20	.07
❑	166	Mike Matheny	.20	.07
❑	167	Eric Cammack	.20	.07
❑	168	Alex Graman	.20	.07
❑	169	Brook Fordyce	.20	.07
❑	170	Mike Lieberthal	.30	.10
❑	171	Giovanni Carrara	.20	.07
❑	172	Antonio Perez	.20	.07
❑	173	Fernando Tatis	.20	.07
❑	174	Jason Bay RC	5.00	2.00
❑	175	Jason Botts RC	.50	.20
❑	176	Danys Baez	.20	.07
❑	177	Shea Hillenbrand	.30	.10
❑	178	Jack Cust	.20	.07
❑	179	Clay Bellinger	.20	.07
❑	180	Roberto Alomar	.50	.20
❑	181	Graeme Lloyd	.20	.07
❑	182	Clint Weibl RC	.25	.08
❑	183	Royce Clayton	.20	.07
❑	184	Ben Davis	.20	.07
❑	185	Brian Adams RC	.25	.08
❑	186	Jack Wilson	.20	.07
❑	187	David Coggin	.20	.07
❑	188	Derrick Turnbow	.20	.07
❑	189	Vladimir Nunez	.20	.07
❑	190	Mariano Rivera	.75	.30
❑	191	Wilson Guzman	.20	.07
❑	192	Michael Barrett	.20	.07
❑	193	Corey Patterson	.20	.07
❑	194	Luis Sojo	.20	.07
❑	195	Scott Elarton	.20	.07
❑	196	Charles Thomas RC	.40	.15
❑	197	Ricky Bottalico	.20	.07
❑	198	Wilfredo Rodriguez	.20	.07
❑	199	Ricardo Rincon	.20	.07
❑	200	John Smoltz	.50	.20
❑	201	Travis Miller	.20	.07
❑	202	Ben Weber	.20	.07
❑	203	T.J. Tucker	.20	.07
❑	204	Terry Shumpert	.20	.07
❑	205	Bernie Williams	.50	.20
❑	206	Russ Ortiz	.20	.07
❑	207	Nate Rolison	.20	.07
❑	208	Jose Cruz Jr.	.20	.07
❑	209	Bill Ortega	.20	.07
❑	210	Carl Everett	.30	.10
❑	211	Luis Lopez	.20	.07
❑	212	Brian Wolfe RC	.40	.15
❑	213	Doug Davis	.20	.07
❑	214	Troy Mattes	.20	.07
❑	215	Al Leiter	.30	.10
❑	216	Joe Mays	.20	.07
❑	217	Bobby Smith	.20	.07
❑	218	J.J. Trujillo RC	.40	.15
❑	219	Hideo Nomo	.75	.30
❑	220	Jimmy Rollins	.30	.10
❑	221	Bobby Seay	.20	.07
❑	222	Mike Thurman	.20	.07
❑	223	Bartolo Colon	.30	.10
❑	224	Jesus Sanchez	.20	.07
❑	225	Ray Durham	.30	.10
❑	226	Juan Diaz	.20	.07
❑	227	Lee Stevens	.20	.07
❑	228	Ben Howard RC	.40	.15
❑	229	James Mouton	.20	.07
❑	230	Paul Quantrill	.20	.07
❑	231	Randy Knorr	.20	.07
❑	232	Abraham Nunez	.20	.07
❑	233	Mike Fetters	.20	.07
❑	234	Mario Encarnacion	.20	.07
❑	235	Jeremy Fikac	.20	.07
❑	236	Travis Lee	.20	.07
❑	237	Bob File	.20	.07
❑	238	Pete Harnisch	.20	.07
❑	239	Randy Galvez RC	.40	.15
❑	240	Geoff Goetz	.20	.07
❑	241	Gary Glover	.20	.07
❑	242	Troy Percival	.30	.10
❑	243	Len Dinardo RC	.40	.15
❑	244	Jonny Gomes RC	2.50	1.00
❑	245	Jesus Medrano RC	.40	.15
❑	246	Rey Ordonez	.20	.07
❑	247	Juan Gonzalez	.30	.10
❑	248	Jose Guillen	.30	.10
❑	249	Franklyn German RC	.40	.15
❑	250	Mike Mussina	.50	.20
❑	251	Ugueth Urbina	.20	.07
❑	252	Melvin Mora	.30	.10
❑	253	Gerald Williams	.20	.07
❑	254	Jared Sandberg	.20	.07
❑	255	Darrin Fletcher	.20	.07
❑	256	A.J. Pierzynski	.30	.10
❑	257	Lenny Harris	.20	.07
❑	258	Blaine Neal	.20	.07
❑	259	Denny Neagle	.20	.07
❑	260	Jason Hart	.20	.07
❑	261	Henry Mateo	.20	.07
❑	262	Rheal Cormier	.20	.07
❑	263	Luis Terrero	.20	.07
❑	264	Shigetoshi Hasegawa	.30	.10
❑	265	Bill Haselman	.20	.07
❑	266	Scott Hatteberg	.20	.07
❑	267	Adam Hyzdu	.20	.07
❑	268	Mike Williams	.20	.07
❑	269	Marlon Anderson	.20	.07
❑	270	Bruce Chen	.20	.07
❑	271	Eli Marrero	.20	.07
❑	272	Jimmy Haynes	.20	.07
❑	273	Bronson Arroyo	.30	.10
❑	274	Kevin Jordan	.20	.07
❑	275	Rick Helling	.20	.07
❑	276	Mark Loretta	.20	.07
❑	277	Dustin Hermanson	.20	.07
❑	278	Pablo Ozuna	.20	.07
❑	279	Keto Anderson RC	.40	.15
❑	280	Jermaine Dye	.30	.10
❑	281	Will Smith	.20	.07
❑	282	Brian Daubach	.20	.07
❑	283	Eric Hinske	.20	.07
❑	284	Joe Jiannetti RC	.40	.15
❑	285	Chan Ho Park	.30	.10
❑	286	Curtis Legendre RC	.40	.15
❑	287	Jeff Reboulet	.20	.07
❑	288	Scott Rolen	.50	.20
❑	289	Chris Richard	.20	.07
❑	290	Eric Chavez	.30	.10
❑	291	Scot Shields	.20	.07
❑	292	Donnie Sadler	.20	.07
❑	293	Dave Veres	.20	.07
❑	294	Craig Counsell	.20	.07
❑	295	Armando Reynoso	.20	.07
❑	296	Kyle Lohse	.20	.07
❑	297	Arthur Rhodes	.20	.07
❑	298	Sidney Ponson	.20	.07
❑	299	Trevor Hoffman	.30	.10
❑	300	Kerry Wood	.30	.10
❑	301	Danny Bautista	.20	.07
❑	302	Scott Sauerbeck	.20	.07
❑	303	Johnny Estrada	.20	.07
❑	304	Mike Timlin	.20	.07
❑	305	Orlando Hernandez	.30	.10
❑	306	Tony Clark	.20	.07
❑	307	Tomas Perez	.20	.07
❑	308	Marcus Giles	.30	.10
❑	309	Mike Bordick	.30	.10
❑	310	Jorge Posada	.50	.20
❑	311	Jason Conti	.20	.07
❑	312	Kevin Millar	.30	.10
❑	313	Paul Shuey	.20	.07
❑	314	Jake Mauer RC	.40	.15
❑	315	Luke Hudson	.20	.07
❑	316	Angel Berroa	.20	.07
❑	317	Fred Bastardo RC	.40	.15
❑	318	Shawn Estes	.20	.07
❑	319	Andy Ashby	.20	.07
❑	320	Ryan Klesko	.30	.10
❑	321	Kevin Appier	.30	.10
❑	322	Juan Pena	.20	.07
❑	323	Alex Herrera	.20	.07
❑	324	Robb Nen	.30	.10
❑	325	Orlando Hudson	.20	.07
❑	326	Lyle Overbay	.20	.07
❑	327	Ben Sheets	.30	.10
❑	328	Mike DiFelice	.20	.07
❑	329	Pablo Arias RC	.40	.15
❑	330	Mike Sweeney	.30	.10
❑	331	Rick Ankiel	.20	.07
❑	332	Tomas De La Rosa	.20	.07
❑	333	Kazuhisa Ishii RC	.50	.20
❑	334	Jose Reyes	.50	.20
❑	335	Jeremy Giambi	.20	.07
❑	336	Jose Mesa	.20	.07
❑	337	Ralph Roberts RC	.40	.15
❑	338	Jose Nunez	.20	.07
❑	339	Curt Schilling	.30	.10
❑	340	Sean Casey	.30	.10
❑	341	Bob Wells	.20	.07
❑	342	Carlos Beltran	.30	.10
❑	343	Alexis Gomez	.20	.07
❑	344	Brandon Claussen	.20	.07
❑	345	Buddy Groom	.20	.07
❑	346	Mark Phillips RC	.40	.15
❑	347	Francisco Cordova	.20	.07
❑	348	Joe Oliver	.20	.07
❑	349	Danny Patterson	.20	.07
❑	350	Joel Pineiro	.20	.07
❑	351	J.R. House	.20	.07
❑	352	Benny Agbayani	.20	.07
❑	353	Jose Vidro	.20	.07
❑	354	Reed Johnson RC	1.00	.40
❑	355	Mike Lowell	.30	.10
❑	356	Scott Schoeneweis	.20	.07
❑	357	Brian Jordan	.30	.10
❑	358	Steve Finley	.30	.10
❑	359	Randy Choate	.20	.07
❑	360	Jose Lima	.20	.07
❑	361	Miguel Olivo	.20	.07
❑	362	Kenny Rogers	.30	.10
❑	363	David Justice	.30	.10
❑	364	Brandon Knight	.20	.07
❑	365	Joe Kennedy	.20	.07
❑	366	Eric Valent	.20	.07
❑	367	Nelson Cruz	.20	.07
❑	368	Brian Giles	.30	.10
❑	369	Charles Gipson RC	.25	.08
❑	370	Juan Pena	.20	.07
❑	371	Mark Redman	.20	.07
❑	372	Billy Koch	.20	.07
❑	373	Ted Lilly	.20	.07
❑	374	Craig Paquette	.20	.07
❑	375	Kevin Jarvis	.20	.07
❑	376	Scott Erickson	.20	.07
❑	377	Josh Paul	.20	.07
❑	378	Darwin Cubillan	.20	.07
❑	379	Nelson Figueroa	.20	.07
❑	380	Darin Erstad	.30	.10
❑	381	Jeremy Hill RC	.40	.15
❑	382	Elvin Nina	.20	.07
❑	383	David Wells	.30	.10
❑	384	Jay Caligiuri RC	.40	.15
❑	385	Freddy Garcia	.30	.10
❑	386	Damian Miller	.20	.07
❑	387	Bobby Higginson	.30	.10
❑	388	Alejandro Giron RC	.40	.15
❑	389	Ivan Rodriguez	.50	.20
❑	390	Ed Rogers	.20	.07
❑	391	Andy Benes	.20	.07
❑	392	Matt Blank	.20	.07
❑	393	Ryan Vogelsong	.20	.07
❑	394	Kelly Ramos RC	.25	.08
❑	395	Eric Karros	.30	.10
❑	396	Bobby J. Jones	.20	.07
❑	397	Omar Vizquel	.50	.20
❑	398	Matt Perisho	.20	.07
❑	399	Delino DeShields	.20	.07
❑	400	Carlos Hernandez	.20	.07
❑	401	Derrek Lee	.50	.20
❑	402	Kirk Rueter	.20	.07
❑	403	David Wright RC	30.00	12.50

❑	404	Paul LoDuca	.30	.10
❑	405	Brian Schneider	.20	.07
❑	406	Milton Bradley	.30	.10
❑	407	Daryle Ward	.20	.07
❑	408	Cody Ransom	.20	.07
❑	409	Fernando Rodney	.20	.07
❑	410	John Suomi RC	.40	.15
❑	411	Joe Girardi	.20	.07
❑	412	Demetrius Heath RC	.40	.15
❑	413	John Foster RC	.40	.15
❑	414	Doug Glanville	.20	.07
❑	415	Ryan Kohlmeier	.20	.07
❑	416	Mike Matthews	.20	.07
❑	417	Craig Wilson	.20	.07
❑	418	Jay Witasick	.20	.07
❑	419	Jay Payton	.20	.07
❑	420	Andruw Jones	.50	.20
❑	421	Benji Gil	.20	.07
❑	422	Jeff Liefer	.20	.07
❑	423	Kevin Young	.20	.07
❑	424	Richie Sexson	.30	.10
❑	425	Cory Lidle	.20	.07
❑	426	Shane Halter	.20	.07
❑	427	Jesse Foppert RC	.50	.20
❑	428	Jose Molina	.20	.07
❑	429	Nick Alvarez RC	.40	.15
❑	430	Brian L. Hunter	.20	.07
❑	431	Cliff Bartosh RC	.40	.15
❑	432	Junior Spivey	.20	.07
❑	433	Eric Good RC	.40	.15
❑	434	Chin-Feng Chen	.30	.10
❑	435	T.J. Mathews	.20	.07
❑	436	Rich Rodriguez	.20	.07
❑	437	Bobby Abreu	.30	.10
❑	438	Joe McEwing	.20	.07
❑	439	Michael Tucker	.20	.07
❑	440	Preston Wilson	.30	.10
❑	441	Mike MacDougal	.20	.07
❑	442	Shannon Stewart	.30	.10
❑	443	Bob Howry	.20	.07
❑	444	Mike Benjamin	.20	.07
❑	445	Erik Hiljus	.20	.07
❑	446	Ryan Gripp RC	.40	.15
❑	447	Jose Vizcaino	.20	.07
❑	448	Shawn Wooten	.20	.07
❑	449	Steve Kent RC	.40	.15
❑	450	Ramiro Mendoza	.20	.07
❑	451	Jake Westbrook	.20	.07
❑	452	Joe Lawrence	.20	.07
❑	453	Jae Seo	.20	.07
❑	454	Ryan Fry RC	.40	.15
❑	455	Darren Lewis	.20	.07
❑	456	Brad Wilkerson	.20	.07
❑	457	Gustavo Chacin RC	1.00	.40
❑	458	Adrian Brown	.20	.07
❑	459	Mike Cameron	.20	.07
❑	460	Bud Smith	.20	.07
❑	461	Derrick Lewis	.20	.07
❑	462	Derek Lowe	.30	.10
❑	463	Matt Williams	.30	.10
❑	464	Jason Jennings	.20	.07
❑	465	Albie Lopez	.20	.07
❑	466	Felipe Lopez	.20	.07
❑	467	Luke Allen	.20	.07
❑	468	Brian Anderson	.20	.07
❑	469	Matt Riley	.20	.07
❑	470	Ryan Dempster	.20	.07
❑	471	Matt Ginter	.20	.07
❑	472	David Ortiz	.75	.30
❑	473	Cole Barthel RC	.25	.08
❑	474	Damian Jackson	.20	.07
❑	475	Andy Van Hekken	.20	.07
❑	476	Doug Brocail	.20	.07
❑	477	Denny Hocking	.20	.07
❑	478	Sean Douglass	.20	.07
❑	479	Eric Owens	.20	.07
❑	480	Ryan Ludwick	.20	.07
❑	481	Todd Pratt	.20	.07
❑	482	Aaron Sele	.20	.07
❑	483	Edgar Renteria	.30	.10
❑	484	Raymond Cabrera RC	.40	.15
❑	485	Brandon Lyon	.20	.07
❑	486	Chase Utley	2.50	1.00
❑	487	Robert Fick	.20	.07
❑	488	Wilfredo Cordero	.20	.07
❑	489	Octavio Dotel	.20	.07
❑	490	Paul Abbott	.20	.07
❑	491	Jason Kendall	.30	.10
❑	492	Jarrod Washburn	.20	.07
❑	493	Dane Sardinha	.20	.07
❑	494	Jung Bong	.20	.07
❑	495	J.D. Drew	.30	.10
❑	496	Jason Schmidt	.30	.10
❑	497	Mike Magnante	.20	.07
❑	498	Jorge Padilla RC	.40	.15
❑	499	Eric Gagne	.30	.10
❑	500	Todd Helton	.50	.20
❑	501	Jeff Weaver	.20	.07
❑	502	Alex Sanchez	.20	.07
❑	503	Ken Griffey Jr.	1.25	.50
❑	504	Abraham Nunez	.20	.07
❑	505	Reggie Sanders	.30	.10
❑	506	Casey Kotchman RC	1.00	.40
❑	507	Jim Mann	.20	.07
❑	508	Matt LeCroy	.20	.07
❑	509	Frank Castillo	.20	.07
❑	510	Geoff Jenkins	.20	.07
❑	511	Jayson Durocher RC	.25	.08
❑	512	Ellis Burks	.30	.10
❑	513	Aaron Fultz	.20	.07
❑	514	Hiram Bocachica	.20	.07
❑	515	Nate Espy RC	.40	.15
❑	516	Placido Polanco	.20	.07
❑	517	Kerry Ligtenberg	.20	.07
❑	518	Doug Nickle	.20	.07
❑	519	Ramon Ortiz	.20	.07
❑	520	Greg Swindell	.20	.07
❑	521	J.J. Davis	.20	.07
❑	522	Sandy Alomar Jr.	.20	.07
❑	523	Chris Carpenter	.30	.10
❑	524	Vance Wilson	.20	.07
❑	525	Nomar Garciaparra	1.25	.50
❑	526	Jim Mecir	.20	.07
❑	527	Taylor Buchholz RC	.50	.20
❑	528	Brent Mayne	.20	.07
❑	529	John Rodriguez RC	.50	.20
❑	530	David Segui	.20	.07
❑	531	Nate Cornejo	.20	.07
❑	532	Gil Heredia	.20	.07
❑	533	Esteban Loaiza	.20	.07
❑	534	Pat Mahomes	.20	.07
❑	535	Matt Morris	.30	.10
❑	536	Todd Stottlemyre	.20	.07
❑	537	Brian Lesher	.20	.07
❑	538	Arturo McDowell	.20	.07
❑	539	Felix Diaz	.20	.07
❑	540	Mark Mulder	.30	.10
❑	541	Kevin Frederick RC	.40	.15
❑	542	Andy Fox	.20	.07
❑	543	Dionys Cesar RC	.25	.08
❑	544	Justin Miller	.20	.07
❑	545	Keith Osik	.20	.07
❑	546	Shane Reynolds	.20	.07
❑	547	Mike Myers	.20	.07
❑	548	Raul Chavez RC	.25	.08
❑	549	Joe Nathan	.30	.10
❑	550	Ryan Anderson	.20	.07
❑	551	Jason Marquis	.20	.07
❑	552	Marty Cordova	.20	.07
❑	553	Kevin Tapani	.20	.07
❑	554	Jimmy Anderson	.20	.07
❑	555	Pedro Martinez	.50	.20
❑	556	Rocky Biddle	.20	.07
❑	557	Alex Ochoa	.20	.07
❑	558	D'Angelo Jimenez	.20	.07
❑	559	Wilkin Ruan	.20	.07
❑	560	Terrence Long	.20	.07
❑	561	Mark Lukasiewicz	.20	.07
❑	562	Jose Santiago	.20	.07
❑	563	Brad Fullmer	.20	.07
❑	564	Corky Miller	.20	.07
❑	565	Matt White	.20	.07
❑	566	Mark Grace	.50	.20
❑	567	Raul Ibanez	.20	.07
❑	568	Josh Towers	.20	.07
❑	569	Juan M. Gonzalez RC	.40	.15
❑	570	Brian Buchanan	.20	.07
❑	571	Ken Harvey	.20	.07
❑	572	Jeffrey Hammonds	.20	.07
❑	573	Wade Miller	.20	.07
❑	574	Elpidio Guzman	.20	.07
❑	575	Kevin Olsen	.20	.07
❑	576	Austin Kearns	.20	.07
❑	577	Tim Kalita RC	.40	.15
❑	578	David Dellucci	.20	.07
❑	579	Alex Gonzalez	.20	.07
❑	580	Joe Orloski RC	.40	.15
❑	581	Gary Matthews Jr.	.20	.07
❑	582	Ryan Mills	.20	.07
❑	583	Erick Almonte	.20	.07
❑	584	Jeremy Affeldt	.20	.07
❑	585	Chris Tritle RC	.25	.08
❑	586	Michael Cuddyer	.20	.07
❑	587	Kris Foster	.20	.07
❑	588	Russell Branyan	.20	.07
❑	589	Darren Oliver	.20	.07
❑	590	Freddie Money RC	.40	.15
❑	591	Carlos Lee	.30	.10
❑	592	Tim Wakefield	.30	.10
❑	593	Bubba Trammell	.20	.07
❑	594	John Koronka RC	1.00	.40
❑	595	Geoff Blum	.20	.07
❑	596	Darryl Kile	.30	.10
❑	597	Neifi Perez	.20	.07
❑	598	Torii Hunter	.30	.10
❑	599	Luis Castillo	.20	.07
❑	600	Mark Buehrle	.30	.10
❑	601	Jeff Zimmerman	.20	.07
❑	602	Mike DeJean	.20	.07
❑	603	Julio Lugo	.20	.07
❑	604	Chad Hermansen	.20	.07
❑	605	Keith Foulke	.30	.10
❑	606	Lance Davis	.20	.07
❑	607	Jeff Austin RC	.40	.15
❑	608	Brandon Inge	.20	.07
❑	609	Orlando Merced	.20	.07
❑	610	Johnny Damon Sox	.50	.20
❑	611	Doug Henry	.20	.07
❑	612	Adam Kennedy	.20	.07
❑	613	Wiki Gonzalez	.20	.07
❑	614	Brian West RC	.40	.15
❑	615	Andy Pettitte	.50	.20
❑	616	Chone Figgins RC	1.50	.60
❑	617	Matt Lawton	.20	.07
❑	618	Paul Rigdon	.20	.07
❑	619	Keith Lockhart	.20	.07
❑	620	Tim Redding	.20	.07
❑	621	John Parrish	.20	.07
❑	622	Homer Bush	.20	.07
❑	623	Todd Greene	.20	.07
❑	624	David Eckstein	.30	.10
❑	625	Greg Montalbano RC	.40	.15
❑	626	Joe Beimel	.20	.07
❑	627	Adrian Beltre	.30	.10
❑	628	Charles Nagy	.20	.07
❑	629	Cristian Guzman	.20	.07
❑	630	Toby Hall	.20	.07
❑	631	Jose Hernandez	.20	.07
❑	632	Jose Macias	.30	.10
❑	633	Jaret Wright	.20	.07
❑	634	Steve Parris	.20	.07
❑	635	Gene Kingsale	.20	.07
❑	636	Tim Worrell	.20	.07
❑	637	Billy Martin	.20	.07
❑	638	Jovanny Cedeno	.20	.07
❑	639	Curtis Leskanic	.20	.07
❑	640	Tim Hudson	.30	.10
❑	641	Juan Castro	.20	.07
❑	642	Rafael Soriano	.20	.07
❑	643	Juan Rincon	.20	.07
❑	644	Mark DeRosa	.20	.07
❑	645	Carlos Pena	.20	.07
❑	646	Robin Ventura	.30	.10
❑	647	Odalis Perez	.20	.07
❑	648	Damion Easley	.20	.07
❑	649	Benito Santiago	.30	.10
❑	650	Alex Rodriguez	1.25	.50
❑	651	Aaron Rowand	.30	.10
❑	652	Alex Cora	.20	.07
❑	653	Bobby Kielty	.20	.07
❑	654	Jose Rodriguez RC	.40	.15
❑	655	Herbert Perry	.20	.07
❑	656	Jeff Urban	.20	.07
❑	657	Paul Bako	.20	.07
❑	658	Shane Spencer	.20	.07
❑	659	Pat Hentgen	.20	.07
❑	660	Jeff Kent	.30	.10
❑	661	Mark McLemore	.20	.07

❑ 662	Chuck Knoblauch	.30	.10
❑ 663	Blake Stein	.20	.07
❑ 664	Brett Roneberg RC	.40	.15
❑ 665	Josh Phelps	.20	.07
❑ 666	Byung-Hyun Kim	.30	.10
❑ 667	Dave Martinez	.20	.07
❑ 668	Mike Maroth	.20	.07
❑ 669	Shawn Chacon	.20	.07
❑ 670	Billy Wagner	.30	.10
❑ 671	Luis Alicea	.20	.07
❑ 672	Sterling Hitchcock	.20	.07
❑ 673	Adam Piatt	.20	.07
❑ 674	Ryan Franklin	.20	.07
❑ 675	Luke Prokopec	.20	.07
❑ 676	Alfredo Amezaga	.20	.07
❑ 677	Gookie Dawkins	.20	.07
❑ 678	Eric Byrnes	.20	.07
❑ 679	Barry Larkin	.50	.20
❑ 680	Albert Pujols	1.50	.60
❑ 681	Edwards Guzman	.20	.07
❑ 682	Jason Bere	.20	.07
❑ 683	Adam Everett	.20	.07
❑ 684	Greg Colbrunn	.20	.07
❑ 685	Brandon Puffer RC	.40	.15
❑ 686	Mark Kotsay	.30	.10
❑ 687	Willie Bloomquist	.30	.10
❑ 688	Hank Blalock	.50	.20
❑ 689	Travis Hafner	.30	.10
❑ 690	Lance Berkman	.30	.10
❑ 691	Joe Crede	.30	.10
❑ 692	Chuck Finley	.30	.10
❑ 693	John Grabow	.20	.07
❑ 694	Randy Winn	.20	.07
❑ 695	Mike James	.20	.07
❑ 696	Kris Benson	.20	.07
❑ 697	Bret Prinz	.20	.07
❑ 698	Jeff Williams	.20	.07
❑ 699	Eric Munson	.20	.07
❑ 700	Mike Hampton	.30	.10
❑ 701	Ramon E. Martinez	.20	.07
❑ 702	Hansel Izquierdo RC	.40	.15
❑ 703	Nathan Haynes	.20	.07
❑ 704	Eddie Taubensee	.20	.07
❑ 705	Esteban German	.20	.07
❑ 706	Ross Gload	.20	.07
❑ 707	Matt Merricks RC	.40	.15
❑ 708	Chris Piersoll RC	.25	.08
❑ 709	Seth Greisinger	.20	.07
❑ 710	Ichiro Suzuki	1.50	.60
❑ 711	Cesar Izturis	.20	.07
❑ 712	Brad Cresse	.20	.07
❑ 713	Carl Pavano	.30	.10
❑ 714	Steve Sparks	.20	.07
❑ 715	Dennis Tankersley	.20	.07
❑ 716	Kelvim Escobar	.20	.07
❑ 717	Jason LaRue	.20	.07
❑ 718	Corey Koskie	.20	.07
❑ 719	Vinny Castilla	.30	.10
❑ 720	Tim Drew	.20	.07
❑ 721	Chin-Hui Tsao	.30	.10
❑ 722	Paul Byrd	.20	.07
❑ 723	Alex Cintron	.20	.07
❑ 724	Orlando Palmeiro	.20	.07
❑ 725	Ramon Hernandez	.20	.07
❑ 726	Mark Johnson	.20	.07
❑ 727	B.J. Ryan	.20	.07
❑ 728	Wendell Magee	.20	.07
❑ 729	Michael Coleman	.20	.07
❑ 730	Mario Ramos RC	.40	.15
❑ 731	Mike Stanton	.20	.07
❑ 732	Dee Brown	.20	.07
❑ 733	Brad Ausmus	.30	.10
❑ 734	Napoleon Calzado RC	.40	.15
❑ 735	Woody Williams	.20	.07
❑ 736	Paxton Crawford	.20	.07
❑ 737	Jason Karnuth	.20	.07
❑ 738	Michael Restovich	.20	.07
❑ 739	Ramon Castro	.20	.07
❑ 740	Magglio Ordonez	.30	.10
❑ 741	Tom Gordon	.20	.07
❑ 742	Mark Grudzielanek	.20	.07
❑ 743	Jaime Moyer	.30	.10
❑ 744	Marlyn Tisdale RC	.40	.15
❑ 745	Steve Kline	.20	.07
❑ 746	Adam Eaton	.20	.07
❑ 747	Eric Glaser RC	.40	.15
❑ 748	Sean DePaula	.20	.07
❑ 749	Greg Norton	.20	.07
❑ 750	Steve Reed	.20	.07
❑ 751	Ricardo Aramboles	.20	.07
❑ 752	Matt Mantei	.20	.07
❑ 753	Gene Stechschulte	.20	.07
❑ 754	Chuck McElroy	.20	.07
❑ 755	Barry Bonds	2.00	.75
❑ 756	Matt Anderson	.20	.07
❑ 757	Yorvit Torrealba	.20	.07
❑ 758	Jason Standridge	.20	.07
❑ 759	Desi Relaford	.20	.07
❑ 760	Jolbert Cabrera	.20	.07
❑ 761	Chris George	.20	.07
❑ 762	Erubiel Durazo	.20	.07
❑ 763	Paul Konerko	.30	.10
❑ 764	Tike Redman	.20	.07
❑ 765	Chad Ricketts RC	.25	.08
❑ 766	Roberto Hernandez	.20	.07
❑ 767	Mark Lewis	.20	.07
❑ 768	Livan Hernandez	.30	.10
❑ 769	Carlos Brackley RC	.40	.15
❑ 770	Kazuhiro Sasaki	.30	.10
❑ 771	Bill Hall	.30	.10
❑ 772	Nelson Castro RC	.40	.15
❑ 773	Eric Milton	.20	.07
❑ 774	Tom Davey	.20	.07
❑ 775	Todd Ritchie	.20	.07
❑ 776	Seth Etherton	.20	.07
❑ 777	Chris Singleton	.20	.07
❑ 778	Robert Averette RC	.25	.08
❑ 779	Robert Person	.20	.07
❑ 780	Fred McGriff	.50	.20
❑ 781	Richard Hidalgo	.20	.07
❑ 782	Kris Wilson	.20	.07
❑ 783	John Rocker	.30	.10
❑ 784	Justin Kaye	.20	.07
❑ 785	Glendon Rusch	.20	.07
❑ 786	Greg Vaughn	.20	.07
❑ 787	Mike Lamb	.20	.07
❑ 788	Greg Myers	.20	.07
❑ 789	Nate Field RC	.40	.15
❑ 790	Jim Edmonds	.30	.10
❑ 791	Olmedo Saenz	.20	.07
❑ 792	Jason Johnson	.20	.07
❑ 793	Mike Lincoln	.20	.07
❑ 794	Todd Coffey RC	.40	.15
❑ 795	Jesus Sanchez	.20	.07
❑ 796	Aaron Myette	.20	.07
❑ 797	Tony Womack	.20	.07
❑ 798	Chad Kreuter	.20	.07
❑ 799	Brady Clark	.20	.07
❑ 800	Adam Dunn	.30	.10
❑ 801	Jacque Jones	.30	.10
❑ 802	Kevin Millwood	.30	.10
❑ 803	Mike Rivera	.20	.07
❑ 804	Jim Thome	.50	.20
❑ 805	Jeff Conine	.30	.10
❑ 806	Elmer Dessens	.20	.07
❑ 807	Randy Velarde	.20	.07
❑ 808	Carlos Delgado	.30	.10
❑ 809	Steve Karsay	.20	.07
❑ 810	Casey Fossum	.20	.07
❑ 811	J.C. Romero	.20	.07
❑ 812	Chris Truby	.20	.07
❑ 813	Tony Graffanino	.20	.07
❑ 814	Wascar Serrano	.20	.07
❑ 815	Delvin James	.20	.07
❑ 816	Pedro Feliz	.20	.07
❑ 817	Damian Rolls	.20	.07
❑ 818	Scott Linebrink	.20	.07
❑ 819	Rafael Palmeiro	.50	.20
❑ 820	Javy Lopez	.30	.10
❑ 821	Larry Barnes	.20	.07
❑ 822	Brian Lawrence	.20	.07
❑ 823	Scotty Layfield RC	.40	.15
❑ 824	Jeff Cirillo	.20	.07
❑ 825	Willis Roberts	.20	.07
❑ 826	Rich Harden RC	3.00	1.25
❑ 827	Chris Snelling RC	.60	.25
❑ 828	Gary Sheffield	.30	.10
❑ 829	Jeff Heaverlo	.20	.07
❑ 830	Matt Clement	.30	.10
❑ 831	Rich Garces	.20	.07
❑ 832	Rondell White	.30	.10
❑ 833	Henry Pichardo RC	.40	.15
❑ 834	Aaron Boone	.30	.10
❑ 835	Ruben Sierra	.30	.10
❑ 836	Deivis Santos	.20	.07
❑ 837	Tony Batista	.20	.07
❑ 838	Rob Bell	.20	.07
❑ 839	Frank Thomas	.75	.30
❑ 840	Jose Silva	.20	.07
❑ 841	Dan Johnson RC	1.00	.40
❑ 842	Steve Cox	.20	.07
❑ 843	Jose Acevedo	.20	.07
❑ 844	Jay Bell	.30	.10
❑ 845	Mike Sirotka	.20	.07
❑ 846	Garret Anderson	.30	.10
❑ 847	James Shanks RC	.40	.15
❑ 848	Trot Nixon	.30	.10
❑ 849	Keith Ginter	.20	.07
❑ 850	Tim Spooneybarger	.20	.07
❑ 851	Matt Stairs	.20	.07
❑ 852	Chris Stynes	.20	.07
❑ 853	Marvin Benard	.20	.07
❑ 854	Raul Mondesi	.30	.10
❑ 855	Jeremy Owens	.20	.07
❑ 856	Jon Garland	.30	.10
❑ 857	Mitch Meluskey	.20	.07
❑ 858	Chad Durbin	.20	.07
❑ 859	John Burkett	.20	.07
❑ 860	Jon Switzer RC	.40	.15
❑ 861	Peter Bergeron	.20	.07
❑ 862	Jesus Colome	.20	.07
❑ 863	Todd Hundley	.20	.07
❑ 864	Ben Petrick	.20	.07
❑ 865	So Taguchi RC	.50	.20
❑ 866	Ryan Drese	.20	.07
❑ 867	Mike Trombley	.20	.07
❑ 868	Rick Reed	.20	.07
❑ 869	Mark Teixeira	.75	.30
❑ 870	Corey Thurman RC	.40	.15
❑ 871	Brian Roberts	.30	.10
❑ 872	Mike Timlin	.20	.07
❑ 873	Chris Reitsma	.20	.07
❑ 874	Jeff Fassero	.20	.07
❑ 875	Carlos Valderrama	.20	.07
❑ 876	John Lackey	.20	.07
❑ 877	Travis Fryman	.30	.10
❑ 878	Ismael Valdes	.20	.07
❑ 879	Rick White	.20	.07
❑ 880	Edgar Martinez	.50	.20
❑ 881	Dean Palmer	.30	.10
❑ 882	Matt Allegra RC	.40	.15
❑ 883	Greg Sain RC	.40	.15
❑ 884	Carlos Silva	.20	.07
❑ 885	Jose Valverde RC	.40	.15
❑ 886	Dernell Stenson	.20	.07
❑ 887	Todd Van Poppel	.20	.07
❑ 888	Wes Anderson	.20	.07
❑ 889	Bill Mueller	.30	.10
❑ 890	Morgan Ensberg	.30	.10
❑ 891	Marcus Thames	.20	.07
❑ 892	Adam Walker RC	.40	.15
❑ 893	John Halama	.20	.07
❑ 894	Frank Menechino	.20	.07
❑ 895	Greg Maddux	1.25	.50
❑ 896	Gary Bennett	.20	.07
❑ 897	Mauricio Lara RC	.40	.15
❑ 898	Mike Young	.75	.30
❑ 899	Travis Phelps	.20	.07
❑ 900	Rich Aurilia	.20	.07
❑ 901	Henry Blanco	.20	.07
❑ 902	Carlos Febles	.20	.07
❑ 903	Scott MacRae	.20	.07
❑ 904	Lou Merloni	.20	.07
❑ 905	Dicky Gonzalez	.20	.07
❑ 906	Jeff DaVanon	.20	.07
❑ 907	A.J. Burnett	.30	.10
❑ 908	Einar Diaz	.20	.07
❑ 909	Julio Franco	.30	.10
❑ 910	John Olerud	.30	.10
❑ 911	Mark Hamilton RC	.40	.15
❑ 912	David Riske	.20	.07
❑ 913	Jason Tyner	.20	.07
❑ 914	Britt Reames	.20	.07
❑ 915	Vernon Wells	.30	.10
❑ 916	Eddie Perez	.20	.07
❑ 917	Edwin Almonte RC	.40	.15
❑ 918	Enrique Wilson	.20	.07
❑ 919	Chris Gomez	.20	.07

❑	920	Jayson Werth	.20	.07
❑	921	Jeff Nelson	.20	.07
❑	922	Freddy Sanchez RC	2.00	.75
❑	923	John Vander Wal	.20	.07
❑	924	Chad Qualls RC	.50	.20
❑	925	Gabe White	.20	.07
❑	926	Chad Harville	.20	.07
❑	927	Ricky Gutierrez	.20	.07
❑	928	Carlos Guillen	.30	.10
❑	929	B.J. Surhoff	.30	.10
❑	930	Chris Woodward	.20	.07
❑	931	Ricardo Rodriguez	.20	.07
❑	932	Jimmy Gobble RC	.40	.15
❑	933	Jon Lieber	.20	.07
❑	934	Craig Kuzmic RC	.40	.15
❑	935	Eric Young	.20	.07
❑	936	Greg Zaun	.20	.07
❑	937	Miguel Batista	.20	.07
❑	938	Danny Wright	.20	.07
❑	939	Todd Zeile	.30	.10
❑	940	Chad Zerbe	.20	.07
❑	941	Jason Young RC	.25	.08
❑	942	Ronnie Belliard	.20	.07
❑	943	John Ennis RC	.40	.15
❑	944	John Flaherty	.20	.07
❑	945	Jerry Hairston Jr.	.20	.07
❑	946	Al Levine	.20	.07
❑	947	Antonio Alfonseca	.20	.07
❑	948	Brian Moehler	.20	.07
❑	949	Calvin Murray	.20	.07
❑	950	Nick Bierbrodt	.20	.07
❑	951	Sun Woo Kim	.20	.07
❑	952	Noochie Varner RC	.40	.15
❑	953	Luis Rivas	.20	.07
❑	954	Donnie Bridges	.20	.07
❑	955	Ramon Vazquez	.20	.07
❑	956	Luis Garcia	.20	.07
❑	957	Mark Quinn	.20	.07
❑	958	Armando Rios	.20	.07
❑	959	Chad Fox	.20	.07
❑	960	Hee Seop Choi	.20	.07
❑	961	Turk Wendell	.20	.07
❑	962	Adam Roller RC	.40	.15
❑	963	Grant Roberts	.20	.07
❑	964	Ben Molina	.20	.07
❑	965	Juan Rivera	.20	.07
❑	966	Matt Kinney	.20	.07
❑	967	Rod Beck	.20	.07
❑	968	Xavier Nady	.20	.07
❑	969	Masato Yoshii	.20	.07
❑	970	Miguel Tejada	.30	.10
❑	971	Danny Kolb	.20	.07
❑	972	Mike Remlinger	.20	.07
❑	973	Ray Lankford	.30	.10
❑	974	Ryan Minor	.20	.07
❑	975	J.T. Snow	.30	.10
❑	976	Brad Radke	.30	.10
❑	977	Jason Lane	.30	.10
❑	978	Jamey Wright	.20	.07
❑	979	Tom Goodwin	.20	.07
❑	980	Erik Bedard	.30	.10
❑	981	Gabe Kapler	.30	.10
❑	982	Brian Reith	.20	.07
❑	983	Nic Jackson RC	.40	.15
❑	984	Kurt Ainsworth	.20	.07
❑	985	Jason Isringhausen	.30	.10
❑	986	Willie Harris	.20	.07
❑	987	David Cone	.30	.10
❑	988	Bob Wickman	.20	.07
❑	989	Wes Helms	.20	.07
❑	990	Josh Beckett	.30	.10

2003 Topps Total

❑		COMPLETE SET (990)	200.00	100.00
❑		COMMON CARD (1-990)	.20	.07
❑		COMMON RC	.25	.08
❑	1	Brent Abernathy	.20	.07
❑	2	Bobby Hill	.20	.07
❑	3	Victor Martinez	.50	.20
❑	4	Chip Ambres	.20	.07
❑	5	Matt Anderson	.20	.07
❑	6	Ricardo Aramboles	.20	.07
❑	7	Carlos Pena	.20	.07
❑	8	Aaron Guiel	.20	.07
❑	9	Luke Allen	.20	.07
❑	10	Francisco Rodriguez	.30	.10

❑	11	Jason Marquis	.20	.07
❑	12	Edwin Almonte	.20	.07
❑	13	Grant Balfour	.20	.07
❑	14	Adam Piatt	.20	.07
❑	15	Andy Phillips	.20	.07
❑	16	Adrian Beltre	.30	.10
❑	17	Brandon Backe	.20	.07
❑	18	Dave Berg	.20	.07
❑	19	Brett Myers	.30	.10
❑	20	Brian Meadows	.20	.07
❑	21	Chin-Feng Chen	.30	.10
❑	22	Blake Williams	.20	.07
❑	23	Josh Bard	.20	.07
❑	24	Josh Beckett	.30	.10
❑	25	Tommy Whiteman	.20	.07
❑	26	Matt Childers	.20	.07
❑	27	Adam Everett	.20	.07
❑	28	Mike Bordick	.30	.10
❑	29	Antonio Alfonseca	.20	.07
❑	30	Doug Creek	.20	.07
❑	31	J.D. Drew	.30	.10
❑	32	Milton Bradley	.30	.10
❑	33	David Wells	.30	.10
❑	34	Vance Wilson	.20	.07
❑	35	Jeff Fassero	.20	.07
❑	36	Sandy Alomar Jr.	.20	.07
❑	37	Ryan Vogelsong	.20	.07
❑	38	Roger Clemens	1.50	.60
❑	39	Juan Gonzalez	.30	.10
❑	40	Dustin Hermanson	.20	.07
❑	41	Andy Ashby	.20	.07
❑	42	Adam Hyzdu	.20	.07
❑	43	Ben Broussard	.20	.07
❑	44	Ryan Klesko	.30	.10
❑	45	Chris Buglovsky FY RC	.40	.15
❑	46	Bud Smith	.20	.07
❑	47	Aaron Boone	.30	.10
❑	48	Cliff Floyd	.30	.10
❑	49	Alex Cora	.20	.07
❑	50	Curt Schilling	.30	.10
❑	51	Michael Cuddyer	.20	.07
❑	52	Joe Valentine FY RC	.40	.15
❑	53	Carlos Guillen	.30	.10
❑	54	Angel Berroa	.20	.07
❑	55	Eli Marrero	.20	.07
❑	56	A.J. Burnett	.30	.10
❑	57	Oliver Perez	.30	.10
❑	58	Matt Morris	.30	.10
❑	59	Valerio De Los Santos	.20	.07
❑	60	Austin Kearns	.20	.07
❑	61	Darren Dreifort	.20	.07
❑	62	Jason Standridge	.20	.07
❑	63	Carlos Silva	.20	.07
❑	64	Moises Alou	.30	.10
❑	65	Jason Anderson	.20	.07
❑	66	Russell Branyan	.20	.07
❑	67	B.J. Ryan	.20	.07
❑	68	Cory Aldridge	.20	.07
❑	69	Ellis Burks	.30	.10
❑	70	Troy Glaus	.30	.10
❑	71	Kelly Wunsch	.20	.07
❑	72	Brad Wilkerson	.20	.07
❑	73	Jayson Durocher	.20	.07
❑	74	Tony Fiore	.20	.07
❑	75	Brian Giles	.30	.10
❑	76	Billy Wagner	.30	.10
❑	77	Neifi Perez	.20	.07
❑	78	Jose Valverde	.20	.07
❑	79	Brent Butler	.20	.07
❑	80	Mario Ramos	.20	.07
❑	81	Kerry Robinson	.20	.07
❑	82	Brent Mayne	.20	.07
❑	83	Sean Casey	.30	.10
❑	84	Danys Baez	.20	.07
❑	85	Chase Utley	.75	.30
❑	86	Jared Sandberg	.20	.07
❑	87	Terrence Long	.20	.07
❑	88	Kevin Walker	.20	.07
❑	89	Royce Clayton	.20	.07
❑	90	Shea Hillenbrand	.30	.10
❑	91	Brad Lidge	.30	.10
❑	92	Shawn Chacon	.20	.07
❑	93	Kenny Rogers	.30	.10
❑	94	Chris Snelling	.20	.07
❑	95	Omar Vizquel	.50	.20
❑	96	Joe Borchard	.20	.07
❑	97	Matt Belisle	.20	.07
❑	98	Steve Smyth	.20	.07
❑	99	Raul Mondesi	.30	.10
❑	100	Chipper Jones	.75	.30
❑	101	Victor Alvarez	.20	.07
❑	102	J.M. Gold	.20	.07
❑	103	Willis Roberts	.20	.07
❑	104	Eddie Guardado	.20	.07
❑	105	Brad Voyles	.20	.07
❑	106	Bronson Arroyo	.30	.10
❑	107	Juan Castro	.20	.07
❑	108	Dan Plesac	.20	.07
❑	109	Ramon Castro	.20	.07
❑	110	Tim Salmon	.50	.20
❑	111	Gene Kingsale	.20	.07
❑	112	J.D. Closser	.20	.07
❑	113	Mark Buehrle	.30	.10
❑	114	Steve Karsay	.20	.07
❑	115	Cristian Guerrero	.20	.07
❑	116	Brad Ausmus	.30	.10
❑	117	Cristian Guzman	.20	.07
❑	118	Dan Wilson	.20	.07
❑	119	Jake Westbrook	.20	.07
❑	120	Manny Ramirez	.50	.20
❑	121	Jason Giambi	.30	.10
❑	122	Bob Wickman	.20	.07
❑	123	Aaron Cook	.20	.07
❑	124	Alfredo Amezaga	.20	.07
❑	125	Corey Thurman	.20	.07
❑	126	Brandon Puffer	.20	.07
❑	127	Hee Seop Choi	.20	.07
❑	128	Javier Vazquez	.30	.10
❑	129	Carlos Valderrama	.20	.07
❑	130	Jerome Williams	.20	.07
❑	131	Wilson Betemit	.20	.07
❑	132	Luke Prokopec	.20	.07
❑	133	Esteban Yan	.20	.07
❑	134	Brandon Berger	.20	.07
❑	135	Bill Hall	.20	.07
❑	136	LaTroy Hawkins	.20	.07
❑	137	Nate Cornejo	.20	.07
❑	138	Jim Mecir	.20	.07
❑	139	Joe Crede	.30	.10
❑	140	Andres Galarraga	.30	.10
❑	141	Reggie Sanders	.30	.10
❑	142	Joey Eischen	.20	.07
❑	143	Mike Timlin	.20	.07
❑	144	Jose Cruz Jr.	.20	.07
❑	145	Wes Helms	.20	.07
❑	146	Brian Roberts	.30	.10
❑	147	Bret Prinz	.20	.07
❑	148	Brian Hunter	.20	.07
❑	149	Chad Hermansen	.20	.07
❑	150	Andruw Jones	.50	.20
❑	151	Kurt Ainsworth	.20	.07
❑	152	Cliff Bartosh	.20	.07
❑	153	Kyle Lohse	.20	.07
❑	154	Brian Jordan	.30	.10
❑	155	Coco Crisp	.50	.20
❑	156	Tomas Perez	.20	.07
❑	157	Keith Foulke	.30	.10
❑	158	Chris Carpenter	.30	.10
❑	159	Mike Remlinger	.20	.07
❑	160	Dewon Brazelton	.20	.07
❑	161	Brook Fordyce	.20	.07
❑	162	Rusty Greer	.30	.10
❑	163	Scott Downs	.20	.07
❑	164	Jason Dubois	.20	.07

❑ 165 David Coggin .20 .07
❑ 166 Mike DeJean .20 .07
❑ 167 Carlos Hernandez .20 .07
❑ 168 Matt Williams .30 .10
❑ 169 Rheal Cormier .20 .07
❑ 170 Duaner Sanchez .20 .07
❑ 171 Craig Counsell .20 .07
❑ 172 Edgar Martinez .50 .20
❑ 173 Zack Greinke .30 .10
❑ 174 Pedro Feliz .20 .07
❑ 175 Randy Choate .20 .07
❑ 176 Jon Garland .30 .10
❑ 177 Keith Ginter .20 .07
❑ 178 Carlos Febles .20 .07
❑ 179 Kerry Wood .30 .10
❑ 180 Jack Cust .20 .07
❑ 181 Koyie Hill .20 .07
❑ 182 Ricky Gutierrez .20 .07
❑ 183 Ben Grieve .20 .07
❑ 184 Scott Eyre .20 .07
❑ 185 Jason Isringhausen .30 .10
❑ 186 Gookie Dawkins .20 .07
❑ 187 Roberto Alomar .50 .20
❑ 188 Eric Junge .20 .07
❑ 189 Carlos Beltran .30 .10
❑ 190 Denny Hocking .20 .07
❑ 191 Jason Schmidt .30 .10
❑ 192 Cory Lidle .20 .07
❑ 193 Rob Mackowiak .20 .07
❑ 194 Charlton Jimerson RC .40 .15
❑ 195 Darin Erstad .30 .10
❑ 196 Jason Davis .20 .07
❑ 197 Luis Castillo .20 .07
❑ 198 Juan Encarnacion .20 .07
❑ 199 Jeffrey Hammonds .20 .07
❑ 200 Nomar Garciaparra 1.25 .50
❑ 201 Ryan Christianson .20 .07
❑ 202 Robert Person .20 .07
❑ 203 Damian Moss .20 .07
❑ 204 Chris Richard .20 .07
❑ 205 Todd Hundley .20 .07
❑ 206 Paul Bako .20 .07
❑ 207 Adam Kennedy .20 .07
❑ 208 Scott Hatteberg .20 .07
❑ 209 Andy Pratt .20 .07
❑ 210 Ken Griffey Jr. 1.25 .50
❑ 211 Chris George .20 .07
❑ 212 Lance Niekro .20 .07
❑ 213 Greg Colbrunn .20 .07
❑ 214 Herbert Perry .20 .07
❑ 215 Cody Ransom .20 .07
❑ 216 Craig Biggio .50 .20
❑ 217 Miguel Batista .20 .07
❑ 218 Alex Escobar .20 .07
❑ 219 Willie Harris .20 .07
❑ 220 Scott Strickland .20 .07
❑ 221 Felix Rodriguez .20 .07
❑ 222 Torii Hunter .30 .10
❑ 223 Tyler Houston .20 .07
❑ 224 Darrell May .20 .07
❑ 225 Benito Santiago .30 .10
❑ 226 Ryan Dempster .20 .07
❑ 227 Andy Fox .20 .07
❑ 228 Jung Bong .20 .07
❑ 229 Jose Macias .20 .07
❑ 230 Shannon Stewart .30 .10
❑ 231 Buddy Groom .20 .07
❑ 232 Eric Valent .20 .07
❑ 233 Scott Schoenweis .20 .07
❑ 234 Corey Hart .20 .07
❑ 235 Brett Tomko .20 .07
❑ 236 Shane Bazzell RC .40 .15
❑ 237 Tim Hummel .20 .07
❑ 238 Matt Stairs .20 .07
❑ 239 Pete Munro .20 .07
❑ 240 Ismael Valdes .20 .07
❑ 241 Brian Fuentes .20 .07
❑ 242 Cesar Izturis .20 .07
❑ 243 Mark Bellhorn .30 .10
❑ 244 Geoff Jenkins .20 .07
❑ 245 Derek Jeter 2.00 .75
❑ 246 Anderson Machado .20 .07
❑ 247 Dave Roberts .20 .07
❑ 248 Jaime Cerda .20 .07
❑ 249 Woody Williams .20 .07
❑ 250 Vernon Wells .30 .10
❑ 251 Jon Lieber .20 .07
❑ 252 Franklyn German .20 .07
❑ 253 David Segui .20 .07
❑ 254 Freddy Garcia .30 .10
❑ 255 James Baldwin .20 .07
❑ 256 Tony Alvarez .20 .07
❑ 257 Walter Young .20 .07
❑ 258 Alex Herrera .20 .07
❑ 259 Robert Fick .20 .07
❑ 260 Rob Bell .20 .07
❑ 261 Ben Petrick .20 .07
❑ 262 Dee Brown .20 .07
❑ 263 Mike Bacsik .20 .07
❑ 264 Corey Patterson .20 .07
❑ 265 Marvin Benard .20 .07
❑ 266 Eddie Rogers .20 .07
❑ 267 Elio Serrano .20 .07
❑ 268 D'Angelo Jimenez .20 .07
❑ 269 Adam Johnson .20 .07
❑ 270 Gregg Zaun .20 .07
❑ 271 Nick Johnson .30 .10
❑ 272 Geoff Goetz .20 .07
❑ 273 Ryan Drese .20 .07
❑ 274 Eric Dubose .20 .07
❑ 275 Barry Zito .30 .10
❑ 276 Mike Crudale .20 .07
❑ 277 Paul Byrd .20 .07
❑ 278 Eric Gagne .30 .10
❑ 279 Aramis Ramirez .30 .10
❑ 280 Ray Durham .30 .10
❑ 281 Tony Graffanino .20 .07
❑ 282 Jeremy Guthrie .20 .07
❑ 283 Erik Bedard .20 .07
❑ 284 Vince Faison .20 .07
❑ 285 Bobby Kielty .20 .07
❑ 286 Francis Beltran .20 .07
❑ 287 Alexis Gomez .20 .07
❑ 288 Vladimir Guerrero .75 .30
❑ 289 Kevin Appier .30 .10
❑ 290 Gil Meche .20 .07
❑ 291 Marquis Grissom .30 .10
❑ 292 John Burkett .20 .07
❑ 293 Vinny Castilla .30 .10
❑ 294 Tyler Walker .20 .07
❑ 295 Shane Halter .20 .07
❑ 296 Geronimo Gil .20 .07
❑ 297 Eric Hinske .20 .07
❑ 298 Adam Dunn .30 .10
❑ 299 Mike Kinkade .20 .07
❑ 300 Mark Prior .50 .20
❑ 301 Corey Koskie .20 .07
❑ 302 David Dellucci .20 .07
❑ 303 Todd Helton .50 .20
❑ 304 Greg Miller .20 .07
❑ 305 Delvin James .20 .07
❑ 306 Humberto Cota .20 .07
❑ 307 Aaron Harang .20 .07
❑ 308 Jeremy Hill .20 .07
❑ 309 Billy Koch .20 .07
❑ 310 Brandon Claussen .20 .07
❑ 311 Matt Ginter .20 .07
❑ 312 Jason Lane .20 .07
❑ 313 Ben Weber .20 .07
❑ 314 Alan Benes .20 .07
❑ 315 Matt Walbeck .20 .07
❑ 316 Danny Graves .20 .07
❑ 317 Jason Johnson .20 .07
❑ 318 Jason Grimsley .20 .07
❑ 319 Steve Kline .20 .07
❑ 320 Johnny Damon .50 .20
❑ 321 Jay Gibbons .20 .07
❑ 322 J.J. Putz .20 .07
❑ 323 Stephen Randolph RC .40 .15
❑ 324 Bobby Higginson .30 .10
❑ 325 Kazuhisa Ishii .30 .10
❑ 326 Carlos Lee .30 .10
❑ 327 J.R. House .20 .07
❑ 328 Mark Loretta .20 .07
❑ 329 Mike Matheny .20 .07
❑ 330 Ben Diggins .20 .07
❑ 331 Seth Etherton .20 .07
❑ 332 Eli Whiteside FY RC .40 .15
❑ 333 Juan Rivera .20 .07
❑ 334 Jeff Conine .30 .10
❑ 335 John McDonald .20 .07
❑ 336 Erik Hiljus .20 .07
❑ 337 David Eckstein .30 .10
❑ 338 Jeff Bagwell .50 .20
❑ 339 Matt Holliday .20 .07
❑ 340 Jeff Liefer .20 .07
❑ 341 Greg Myers .20 .07
❑ 342 Scott Sauerbeck .20 .07
❑ 343 Omar Infante .20 .07
❑ 344 Ryan Langerhans .30 .10
❑ 345 Abraham Nunez .20 .07
❑ 346 Mike MacDougal .20 .07
❑ 347 Travis Phelps .20 .07
❑ 348 Terry Shumpert .20 .07
❑ 349 Alex Rodriguez 1.25 .50
❑ 350 Bobby Seay .20 .07
❑ 351 Ichiro Suzuki 1.50 .60
❑ 352 Brandon Inge .20 .07
❑ 353 Jack Wilson .20 .07
❑ 354 John Ennis .20 .07
❑ 355 Jamal Strong .20 .07
❑ 356 Jason Jennings .20 .07
❑ 357 Jeff Kent .30 .10
❑ 358 Scott Chiasson .20 .07
❑ 359 Jeremy Griffiths RC .40 .15
❑ 360 Paul Konerko .30 .10
❑ 361 Jeff Austin .20 .07
❑ 362 Todd Van Poppel .20 .07
❑ 363 Sun Woo Kim .20 .07
❑ 364 Jerry Hairston Jr. .20 .07
❑ 365 Tony Torcato .20 .07
❑ 366 Arthur Rhodes .20 .07
❑ 367 Jose Jimenez .20 .07
❑ 368 Matt LeCroy .20 .07
❑ 369 Curtis Leskanic .20 .07
❑ 370 Ramon Vazquez .20 .07
❑ 371 Joe Randa .30 .10
❑ 372 John Franco .30 .10
❑ 373 Bobby Estalella .20 .07
❑ 374 Craig Wilson .20 .07
❑ 375 Michael Young .50 .20
❑ 376 Mark Ellis .20 .07
❑ 377 Joe Mauer .75 .30
❑ 378 Checklist 1 .20 .07
❑ 379 Jason Kendall .30 .10
❑ 380 Checklist 2 .20 .07
❑ 381 Alex Gonzalez .20 .07
❑ 382 Tom Gordon .20 .07
❑ 383 John Buck .20 .07
❑ 384 Shigetoshi Hasegawa .30 .10
❑ 385 Scott Stewart .20 .07
❑ 386 Luke Hudson .20 .07
❑ 387 Todd Jones .20 .07
❑ 388 Fred McGriff .50 .20
❑ 389 Mike Sweeney .30 .10
❑ 390 Marlon Anderson .20 .07
❑ 391 Terry Adams .20 .07
❑ 392 Mark DeRosa .20 .07
❑ 393 Doug Mientkiewicz .30 .10
❑ 394 Miguel Cairo .20 .07
❑ 395 Jamie Moyer .30 .10
❑ 396 Jose Leon .20 .07
❑ 397 Matt Clement .30 .10
❑ 398 Bengie Molina .20 .07
❑ 399 Marcus Thames .20 .07
❑ 400 Nick Bierbrodt .20 .07
❑ 401 Tim Kalita .20 .07
❑ 402 Corwin Malone .20 .07
❑ 403 Jesse Orosco .20 .07
❑ 404 Brandon Phillips .20 .07
❑ 405 Eric Cyr .20 .07
❑ 406 Jason Michaels .20 .07
❑ 407 Julio Lugo .20 .07
❑ 408 Gabe Kapler .30 .10
❑ 409 Mark Mulder .30 .10
❑ 410 Adam Eaton .20 .07
❑ 411 Ken Harvey .20 .07
❑ 412 Jolbert Cabrera .20 .07
❑ 413 Eric Milton .20 .07
❑ 414 Josh Hall RC .40 .15
❑ 415 Bob File .20 .07
❑ 416 Brett Evert .20 .07
❑ 417 Ron Chiavacci .20 .07
❑ 418 Jorge De La Rosa .20 .07
❑ 419 Quinton McCracken .20 .07
❑ 420 Luther Hackman .20 .07
❑ 421 Gary Knotts .20 .07
❑ 422 Kevin Brown .30 .10

	#	Player		
❑	423	Jeff Cirillo	.20	.07
❑	424	Damaso Marte	.20	.07
❑	425	Chan Ho Park	.30	.10
❑	426	Nathan Haynes	.20	.07
❑	427	Matt Lawton	.20	.07
❑	428	Mike Stanton	.20	.07
❑	429	Bernie Williams	.50	.20
❑	430	Kevin Jarvis	.20	.07
❑	431	Joe McEwing	.20	.07
❑	432	Mark Kotsay	.30	.10
❑	433	Juan Cruz	.20	.07
❑	434	Russ Ortiz	.20	.07
❑	435	Jeff Nelson	.20	.07
❑	436	Alan Embree	.20	.07
❑	437	Miguel Tejada	.30	.10
❑	438	Kirk Saarloos	.20	.07
❑	439	Cliff Lee	.20	.07
❑	440	Ryan Ludwick	.20	.07
❑	441	Derrek Lee	.50	.20
❑	442	Bobby Abreu	.30	.10
❑	443	Dustan Mohr	.20	.07
❑	444	Nook Logan RC	.50	.20
❑	445	Seth McClung	.20	.07
❑	446	Miguel Olivo	.20	.07
❑	447	Henry Blanco	.20	.07
❑	448	Seung Song	.20	.07
❑	449	Kris Wilson	.20	.07
❑	450	Xavier Nady	.20	.07
❑	451	Corky Miller	.20	.07
❑	452	Jim Thome	.50	.20
❑	453	George Lombard	.20	.07
❑	454	Rey Ordonez	.20	.07
❑	455	Deivis Santos	.20	.07
❑	456	Mike Myers	.20	.07
❑	457	Edgar Renteria	.30	.10
❑	458	Braden Looper	.20	.07
❑	459	Guillermo Mota	.20	.07
❑	460	Scott Rolen	.50	.20
❑	461	Lance Berkman	.30	.10
❑	462	Jeff Heaverlo	.20	.07
❑	463	Ramon Hernandez	.20	.07
❑	464	Jason Simontacchi	.20	.07
❑	465	So Taguchi	.30	.10
❑	466	Dave Veres	.20	.07
❑	467	Shane Loux	.20	.07
❑	468	Rodrigo Lopez	.20	.07
❑	469	Bubba Trammell	.20	.07
❑	470	Scott Sullivan	.20	.07
❑	471	Mike Mussina	.50	.20
❑	472	Ramon Ortiz	.20	.07
❑	473	Lyle Overbay	.20	.07
❑	474	Mike Lowell	.30	.10
❑	475	Al Martin	.20	.07
❑	476	Larry Bigbie	.20	.07
❑	477	Rey Sanchez	.20	.07
❑	478	Magglio Ordonez	.30	.10
❑	479	Rondell White	.30	.10
❑	480	Jay Witasick	.20	.07
❑	481	Jimmy Rollins	.30	.10
❑	482	Mike Maroth	.20	.07
❑	483	Alejandro Machado	.20	.07
❑	484	Nick Neugebauer	.20	.07
❑	485	Victor Zambrano	.20	.07
❑	486	Travis Lee	.20	.07
❑	487	Bobby Bradley	.20	.07
❑	488	Marcus Giles	.30	.10
❑	489	Steve Trachsel	.20	.07
❑	490	Derek Lowe	.30	.10
❑	491	Hideo Nomo	.75	.30
❑	492	Brad Hawpe	.30	.10
❑	493	Jesus Medrano	.20	.07
❑	494	Rick Ankiel	.20	.07
❑	495	Pasqual Coco	.20	.07
❑	496	Michael Barrett	.20	.07
❑	497	Joe Beimel	.20	.07
❑	498	Marty Cordova	.20	.07
❑	499	Aaron Sele	.20	.07
❑	500	Sammy Sosa	.75	.30
❑	501	Ivan Rodriguez	.50	.20
❑	502	Keith Osik	.20	.07
❑	503	Hank Blalock	.30	.10
❑	504	Hiram Bocachica	.20	.07
❑	505	Junior Spivey	.20	.07
❑	506	Edgardo Alfonzo	.20	.07
❑	507	Alex Graman	.20	.07
❑	508	J.J. Davis	.20	.07
❑	509	Roger Cedeno	.20	.07
❑	510	Joe Roa	.20	.07
❑	511	Wily Mo Pena	.30	.10
❑	512	Eric Munson	.20	.07
❑	513	Arnie Munoz RC	.40	.15
❑	514	Albie Lopez	.20	.07
❑	515	Andy Pettitte	.50	.20
❑	516	Jim Edmonds	.30	.10
❑	517	Jeff Davanon	.20	.07
❑	518	Aaron Myette	.20	.07
❑	519	C.C. Sabathia	.30	.10
❑	520	Gerardo Garcia	.20	.07
❑	521	Brian Schneider	.20	.07
❑	522	Wes Obermueller	.20	.07
❑	523	John Mabry	.20	.07
❑	524	Casey Fossum	.20	.07
❑	525	Toby Hall	.20	.07
❑	526	Denny Neagle	.20	.07
❑	527	Willie Bloomquist	.30	.10
❑	528	A.J. Pierzynski	.30	.10
❑	529	Bartolo Colon	.30	.10
❑	530	Chad Harville	.20	.07
❑	531	Blaine Neal	.20	.07
❑	532	Luis Terrero	.20	.07
❑	533	Reggie Taylor	.20	.07
❑	534	Melvin Mora	.30	.10
❑	535	Tino Martinez	.50	.20
❑	536	Peter Bergeron	.20	.07
❑	537	Jorge Padilla	.20	.07
❑	538	Oscar Villarreal RC	.40	.15
❑	539	David Weathers	.20	.07
❑	540	Mike Lamb	.20	.07
❑	541	Greg Norton	.20	.07
❑	542	Michael Tucker	.20	.07
❑	543	Ben Kozlowski	.20	.07
❑	544	Alex Sanchez	.20	.07
❑	545	Trey Lunsford	.20	.07
❑	546	Abraham Nunez	.20	.07
❑	547	Mike Lincoln	.20	.07
❑	548	Orlando Hernandez	.30	.10
❑	549	Kevin Mench	.20	.07
❑	550	Garret Anderson	.30	.10
❑	551	Kyle Farnsworth	.20	.07
❑	552	Kevin Olsen	.20	.07
❑	553	Joel Pineiro	.20	.07
❑	554	Jorge Julio	.20	.07
❑	555	Jose Mesa	.20	.07
❑	556	Jorge Posada	.50	.20
❑	557	Jose Ortiz	.20	.07
❑	558	Mike Tonis	.20	.07
❑	559	Gabe White	.20	.07
❑	560	Rafael Furcal	.30	.10
❑	561	Matt Franco	.20	.07
❑	562	Trey Hodges	.20	.07
❑	563	Esteban German	.20	.07
❑	564	Josh Fogg	.20	.07
❑	565	Fernando Tatis	.20	.07
❑	566	Alex Cintron	.20	.07
❑	567	Grant Roberts	.20	.07
❑	568	Gene Stechschulte	.20	.07
❑	569	Rafael Palmeiro	.50	.20
❑	570	Mike Hampton	.30	.10
❑	571	Ben Davis	.20	.07
❑	572	Dean Palmer	.30	.10
❑	573	Jerrod Riggan	.20	.07
❑	574	Nate Frese	.20	.07
❑	575	Josh Phelps	.20	.07
❑	576	Freddie Bynum	.20	.07
❑	577	Morgan Ensberg	.30	.10
❑	578	Juan Rincon	.20	.07
❑	579	Kazuhiro Sasaki	.30	.10
❑	580	Yorvit Torrealba	.20	.07
❑	581	Tim Wakefield	.30	.10
❑	582	Sterling Hitchcock	.20	.07
❑	583	Craig Paquette	.20	.07
❑	584	Kevin Millwood	.30	.10
❑	585	Damian Rolls	.20	.07
❑	586	Brad Baisley	.20	.07
❑	587	Kyle Snyder	.20	.07
❑	588	Paul Quantrill	.20	.07
❑	589	Trot Nixon	.30	.10
❑	590	J.T. Snow	.30	.10
❑	591	Kevin Young	.20	.07
❑	592	Tomo Ohka	.20	.07
❑	593	Brian Boehringer	.20	.07
❑	594	Danny Patterson	.20	.07
❑	595	Jeff Tam	.20	.07
❑	596	Anastacio Martinez	.20	.07
❑	597	Rod Barajas	.20	.07
❑	598	Octavio Dotel	.20	.07
❑	599	Jason Tyner	.20	.07
❑	600	Gary Sheffield	.30	.10
❑	601	Ruben Quevedo	.20	.07
❑	602	Jay Payton	.20	.07
❑	603	Mo Vaughn	.30	.10
❑	604	Pat Burrell	.30	.10
❑	605	Fernando Vina	.20	.07
❑	606	Wes Anderson	.20	.07
❑	607	Alex Gonzalez	.20	.07
❑	608	Ted Lilly	.20	.07
❑	609	Nick Punto	.20	.07
❑	610	Ryan Madson	.20	.07
❑	611	Odalis Perez	.20	.07
❑	612	Chris Woodward	.20	.07
❑	613	John Olerud	.30	.10
❑	614	Brad Cresse	.20	.07
❑	615	Chad Zerbe	.20	.07
❑	616	Brad Penny	.20	.07
❑	617	Barry Larkin	.50	.20
❑	618	Brandon Duckworth	.20	.07
❑	619	Brad Radke	.30	.10
❑	620	Troy Brohawn	.20	.07
❑	621	Juan Pierre	.30	.10
❑	622	Rick Reed	.20	.07
❑	623	Omar Daal	.20	.07
❑	624	Jose Hernandez	.20	.07
❑	625	Greg Maddux	1.25	.50
❑	626	Henry Mateo	.20	.07
❑	627	Kip Wells	.20	.07
❑	628	Kevin Cash	.20	.07
❑	629	Wil Ledezma FY RC	.40	.15
❑	630	Luis Gonzalez	.30	.10
❑	631	Jason Conti	.20	.07
❑	632	Ricardo Rincon	.20	.07
❑	633	Mike Bynum	.20	.07
❑	634	Mike Redmond	.20	.07
❑	635	Chance Caple	.20	.07
❑	636	Chris Widger	.20	.07
❑	637	Michael Restovich	.20	.07
❑	638	Mark Grudzielanek	.20	.07
❑	639	Brandon Larson	.20	.07
❑	640	Rocco Baldelli	.30	.10
❑	641	Javy Lopez	.30	.10
❑	642	Rene Reyes	.20	.07
❑	643	Orlando Merced	.20	.07
❑	644	Jason Phillips	.20	.07
❑	645	Luis Ugueto	.20	.07
❑	646	Ron Calloway	.20	.07
❑	647	Josh Paul	.20	.07
❑	648	Todd Greene	.20	.07
❑	649	Joe Girardi	.20	.07
❑	650	Todd Ritchie	.20	.07
❑	651	Kevin Millar Sox	.30	.10
❑	652	Shawn Wooten	.20	.07
❑	653	David Riske	.20	.07
❑	654	Luis Rivas	.20	.07
❑	655	Roy Halladay	.30	.10
❑	656	Travis Driskill	.20	.07
❑	657	Ricky Ledee	.20	.07
❑	658	Timo Perez	.20	.07
❑	659	Fernando Rodney	.20	.07
❑	660	Trevor Hoffman	.30	.10
❑	661	Pat Hentgen	.30	.10
❑	662	Bret Boone	.30	.10
❑	663	Ryan Jensen	.20	.07
❑	664	Ricardo Rodriguez	.20	.07
❑	665	Jeremy Lambert	.20	.07
❑	666	Troy Percival	.30	.10
❑	667	Jon Rauch	.20	.07
❑	668	Mariano Rivera	.75	.30
❑	669	Jason LaRue	.20	.07
❑	670	J.C. Romero	.20	.07
❑	671	Cody Ross	.20	.07
❑	672	Eric Byrnes	.20	.07
❑	673	Paul Lo Duca	.30	.10
❑	674	Brad Fullmer	.20	.07
❑	675	Cliff Politte	.20	.07
❑	676	Justin Miller	.20	.07
❑	677	Nic Jackson	.20	.07
❑	678	Kris Benson	.20	.07
❑	679	Carl Sadler	.20	.07
❑	680	Joe Nathan	.30	.10

❑ 681 Julio Santana .20 .07
❑ 682 Wade Miller .20 .07
❑ 683 Josh Pearce .20 .07
❑ 684 Tony Armas Jr. .20 .07
❑ 685 Al Leiter .30 .10
❑ 686 Raul Ibanez .20 .07
❑ 687 Danny Bautista .20 .07
❑ 688 Travis Hafner .30 .10
❑ 689 Carlos Zambrano .30 .10
❑ 690 Pedro Martinez .50 .20
❑ 691 Ramon Santiago .20 .07
❑ 692 Felipe Lopez .20 .07
❑ 693 David Ross .20 .07
❑ 694 Chone Figgins .20 .07
❑ 695 Antonio Osuna .20 .07
❑ 696 Jay Powell .20 .07
❑ 697 Ryan Church .30 .10
❑ 698 Alexis Rios .30 .10
❑ 699 Tanyon Sturtze .20 .07
❑ 700 Turk Wendell .20 .07
❑ 701 Richard Hidalgo .20 .07
❑ 702 Joe Mays .20 .07
❑ 703 Jorge Sosa .20 .07
❑ 704 Eric Karros .30 .10
❑ 705 Steve Finley .30 .10
❑ 706 Sean Smith FY RC .50 .20
❑ 707 Jeremy Giambi .20 .07
❑ 708 Scott Hodges .20 .07
❑ 709 Vicente Padilla .20 .07
❑ 710 Erubiel Durazo .20 .07
❑ 711 Aaron Rowand .30 .10
❑ 712 Dennis Tankersley .20 .07
❑ 713 Rick Bauer .20 .07
❑ 714 Tim Olson FY RC .40 .15
❑ 715 Jeff Urban .20 .07
❑ 716 Steve Sparks .20 .07
❑ 717 Glendon Rusch .20 .07
❑ 718 Ricky Stone .20 .07
❑ 719 Benji Gil .20 .07
❑ 720 Pete Walker .20 .07
❑ 721 Tim Worrell .20 .07
❑ 722 Michael Tejera .20 .07
❑ 723 David Kelton .20 .07
❑ 724 Britt Reames .20 .07
❑ 725 John Stephens .20 .07
❑ 726 Mark McLemore .20 .07
❑ 727 Jeff Zimmerman .20 .07
❑ 728 Checklist 3 .20 .07
❑ 729 Andres Torres .20 .07
❑ 730 Checklist 4 .20 .07
❑ 731 Johan Santana .50 .20
❑ 732 Dane Sardinha .20 .07
❑ 733 Rodrigo Rosario .20 .07
❑ 734 Frank Thomas .75 .30
❑ 735 Tom Glavine .50 .20
❑ 736 Doug Mirabelli .20 .07
❑ 737 Juan Uribe .20 .07
❑ 738 Ryan Anderson .20 .07
❑ 739 Sean Burroughs .20 .07
❑ 740 Eric Chavez .30 .10
❑ 741 Enrique Wilson .20 .07
❑ 742 Elmer Dessens .20 .07
❑ 743 Marlon Byrd .20 .07
❑ 744 Brendan Donnelly .20 .07
❑ 745 Gary Bennett .20 .07
❑ 746 Roy Oswalt .30 .10
❑ 747 Andy Van Hekken .20 .07
❑ 748 Jesus Colome .20 .07
❑ 749 Erick Almonte .20 .07
❑ 750 Frank Catalanotto .20 .07
❑ 751 Kenny Lofton .30 .10
❑ 752 Carlos Delgado .30 .10
❑ 753 Ryan Franklin .20 .07
❑ 754 Wilkin Ruan .20 .07
❑ 755 Kelvim Escobar .20 .07
❑ 756 Tim Drew .20 .07
❑ 757 Jarrod Washburn .20 .07
❑ 758 Runelvys Hernandez .20 .07
❑ 759 Cory Vance .20 .07
❑ 760 Doug Glanville .20 .07
❑ 761 Ryan Rupe .20 .07
❑ 762 Jermaine Dye .30 .10
❑ 763 Mike Cameron .20 .07
❑ 764 Scott Erickson .20 .07
❑ 765 Richie Sexson .30 .10
❑ 766 Jose Vidro .20 .07
❑ 767 Brian West .20 .07
❑ 768 Shawn Estes .20 .07
❑ 769 Brian Tallet .20 .07
❑ 770 Larry Walker .30 .10
❑ 771 Josh Hamilton .20 .07
❑ 772 Orlando Hudson .20 .07
❑ 773 Justin Morneau .30 .10
❑ 774 Ryan Bukvich .20 .07
❑ 775 Mike Gonzalez .20 .07
❑ 776 Tsuyoshi Shinjo .30 .10
❑ 777 Matt Mantei .20 .07
❑ 778 Jimmy Journell .20 .07
❑ 779 Brian Lawrence .20 .07
❑ 780 Mike Lieberthal .30 .10
❑ 781 Scott Mullen .20 .07
❑ 782 Zach Day .20 .07
❑ 783 John Thomson .20 .07
❑ 784 Ben Sheets .30 .10
❑ 785 Damon Minor .20 .07
❑ 786 Jose Valentin .20 .07
❑ 787 Armando Benitez .20 .07
❑ 788 Jamie Walker RC .25 .08
❑ 789 Preston Wilson .30 .10
❑ 790 Josh Wilson .20 .07
❑ 791 Phil Nevin .30 .10
❑ 792 Roberto Hernandez .20 .07
❑ 793 Mike Williams .20 .07
❑ 794 Jake Peavy .30 .10
❑ 795 Paul Shuey .20 .07
❑ 796 Chad Bradford .20 .07
❑ 797 Bobby Jenks .30 .10
❑ 798 Sean Douglass .20 .07
❑ 799 Damian Miller .20 .07
❑ 800 Mark Wohlers .20 .07
❑ 801 Ty Wigginton .20 .07
❑ 802 Alfonso Soriano .30 .10
❑ 803 Randy Johnson .75 .30
❑ 804 Placido Polanco .20 .07
❑ 805 Drew Henson .20 .07
❑ 806 Tony Womack .20 .07
❑ 807 Pokey Reese .20 .07
❑ 808 Albert Pujols 1.50 .60
❑ 809 Henri Stanley .20 .07
❑ 810 Mike Rivera .20 .07
❑ 811 John Lackey .20 .07
❑ 812 Brian Wright FY RC .40 .15
❑ 813 Eric Good .20 .07
❑ 814 Dernell Stenson .20 .07
❑ 815 Kirk Rueter .20 .07
❑ 816 Todd Zeile .20 .07
❑ 817 Brad Thomas .20 .07
❑ 818 Shawn Sedlacek .20 .07
❑ 819 Garrett Stephenson .20 .07
❑ 820 Mark Teixeira .50 .20
❑ 821 Tim Hudson .30 .10
❑ 822 Mike Koplove .20 .07
❑ 823 Chris Reitsma .20 .07
❑ 824 Rafael Soriano .20 .07
❑ 825 Ugueth Urbina .20 .07
❑ 826 Lance Carter .20 .07
❑ 827 Colin Young .20 .07
❑ 828 Pat Strange .20 .07
❑ 829 Juan Pena .20 .07
❑ 830 Joe Thurston .20 .07
❑ 831 Shawn Green .30 .10
❑ 832 Pedro Astacio .20 .07
❑ 833 Danny Wright .20 .07
❑ 834 Wes O'Brien FY RC .40 .15
❑ 835 Luis Lopez .20 .07
❑ 836 Randall Simon .20 .07
❑ 837 Jaret Wright .20 .07
❑ 838 Jayson Werth .20 .07
❑ 839 Endy Chavez .20 .07
❑ 840 Checklist 5 .20 .07
❑ 841 Chad Paronto .20 .07
❑ 842 Randy Winn .20 .07
❑ 843 Sidney Ponson .20 .07
❑ 844 Robin Ventura .30 .10
❑ 845 Rich Aurilia .20 .07
❑ 846 Joaquin Benoit .20 .07
❑ 847 Barry Bonds 2.00 .75
❑ 848 Carl Crawford .30 .10
❑ 849 Jeromy Burnitz .30 .10
❑ 850 Orlando Cabrera .30 .10
❑ 851 Luis Vizcaino .20 .07
❑ 852 Randy Wolf .20 .07
❑ 853 Todd Walker .20 .07
❑ 854 Jeremy Affeldt .20 .07
❑ 855 Einar Diaz .20 .07
❑ 856 Carl Everett .30 .10
❑ 857 Wiki Gonzalez .20 .07
❑ 858 Mike Paradis .20 .07
❑ 859 Travis Harper .20 .07
❑ 860 Mike Piazza 1.25 .50
❑ 861 Will Ohman .20 .07
❑ 862 Eric Young .20 .07
❑ 863 Jason Grabowski .20 .07
❑ 864 Rett Johnson RC .40 .15
❑ 865 Aubrey Huff .30 .10
❑ 866 John Smoltz .50 .20
❑ 867 Mickey Callaway .20 .07
❑ 868 Joe Kennedy .20 .07
❑ 869 Tim Redding .20 .07
❑ 870 Colby Lewis .20 .07
❑ 871 Salomon Torres .20 .07
❑ 872 Marco Scutaro .20 .07
❑ 873 Tony Batista .20 .07
❑ 874 Dmitri Young .30 .10
❑ 875 Scott Williamson .20 .07
❑ 876 Scott Spiezio .20 .07
❑ 877 John Webb .20 .07
❑ 878 Jose Acevedo .20 .07
❑ 879 Kevin Orie .20 .07
❑ 880 Jacque Jones .30 .10
❑ 881 Ben Francisco FY RC .40 .15
❑ 882 Bobby Basham FY RC .40 .15
❑ 883 Corey Shafer FY RC .40 .15
❑ 884 J.D. Durbin FY RC .40 .15
❑ 885 Chien-Ming Wang FY RC 8.00 3.00
❑ 886 Adam Stern FY RC .25 .08
❑ 887 Wayne Lydon FY RC .40 .15
❑ 888 Derell McCall FY RC .40 .15
❑ 889 Jon Nelson FY RC .50 .20
❑ 890 Willie Eyre FY RC .40 .15
❑ 891 Ramon Nivar-Martinez FY RC .40 .15
❑ 892 Adrian Myers FY RC .25 .08
❑ 893 Jamie Athas FY RC .40 .15
❑ 894 Ismael Castro FY RC .50 .20
❑ 895 David Martinez FY RC .40 .15
❑ 896 Terry Tiffee FY RC .40 .15
❑ 897 Nathan Panther FY RC .40 .15
❑ 898 Kyle Roat FY RC .40 .15
❑ 899 Kason Gabbard FY RC .40 .15
❑ 900 Hanley Ramirez FY RC 4.00 1.50
❑ 901 Bryan Grace FY RC .40 .15
❑ 902 B.J. Barns FY RC .40 .15
❑ 903 Greg Bruso FY RC .40 .15
❑ 904 Mike Neu FY RC .40 .15
❑ 905 Dustin Yount FY RC .50 .20
❑ 906 Shane Victorino FY RC .75 .30
❑ 907 Brian Burgamy FY RC .40 .15
❑ 908 Beau Kemp FY RC .40 .15
❑ 909 David Corrente FY RC .40 .15
❑ 910 Dexter Cooper FY RC .40 .15
❑ 911 Chris Colton FY RC .40 .15
❑ 912 David Cash FY RC .40 .15
❑ 913 Bernie Castro FY RC .40 .15
❑ 914 Luis Hodge FY RC .40 .15
❑ 915 Jeff Clark FY RC .40 .15
❑ 916 Jason Kubel FY RC 1.00 .40
❑ 917 T.J. Bohn FY RC .40 .15
❑ 918 Luke Steidlmayer FY RC .40 .15
❑ 919 Matthew Peterson FY RC .40 .15
❑ 920 Darrell Rasner FY RC .40 .15
❑ 921 Scott Tyler FY RC .50 .20
❑ 922 Gary Schneidmiller FY RC .40 .15
❑ 923 Gregor Blanco FY RC .40 .15
❑ 924 Ryan Cameron FY RC .40 .15
❑ 925 Wilfredo Rodriguez FY .20 .07
❑ 926 Rajai Davis FY RC .40 .15
❑ 927 Evel Bastida-Martinez FY RC .40 .15
❑ 928 Chris Duncan FY RC 4.00 1.50
❑ 929 Dave Pember FY RC .40 .15
❑ 930 Branden Florence FY RC .40 .15
❑ 931 Eric Eckenstahler FY .20 .07
❑ 932 Hong-Chih Kuo FY RC 5.00 2.00
❑ 933 Il Kim FY RC .40 .15
❑ 934 Michael Garciaparra FY RC .40 .15
❑ 935 Kip Bouknight FY RC .50 .20
❑ 936 Gary Harris FY RC .40 .15
❑ 937 Derry Hammond FY RC .40 .15
❑ 938 Joey Gomes FY RC .40 .15

❑ 939 Donnie Hood FY RC .50 .20
❑ 940 Clay Hensley FY RC .40 .15
❑ 941 David Pahucki FY RC .40 .15
❑ 942 Wilton Reynolds FY RC .40 .15
❑ 943 Michael Hinckley FY RC .50 .20
❑ 944 Josh Willingham FY RC 1.00 .40
❑ 945 Pete LaForest FY RC .40 .15
❑ 946 Pete Smart FY RC .40 .15
❑ 947 Jay Sitzman FY RC .40 .15
❑ 948 Mark Malaska FY RC .40 .15
❑ 949 Mike Gallo FY RC .40 .15
❑ 950 Matt Diaz FY RC .75 .30
❑ 951 Brennan King FY RC .40 .15
❑ 952 Ryan Howard FY RC 30.00 12.50
❑ 953 Daryl Clark FY RC .40 .15
❑ 954 Dayton Buller FY RC .40 .15
❑ 955 Rylan Reed FY RC .40 .15
❑ 956 Chris Booker FY .20 .07
❑ 957 Brandon Watson FY RC .40 .15
❑ 958 Matt DeMarco FY RC .40 .15
❑ 959 Doug Waechter FY RC .50 .20
❑ 960 Callix Crabbe FY RC .50 .20
❑ 961 Jairo Garcia FY RC .50 .20
❑ 962 Jason Perry FY RC .50 .20
❑ 963 Eric Riggs FY RC .50 .20
❑ 964 Travis Ishikawa FY RC .75 .30
❑ 965 Simon Pond FY RC .40 .15
❑ 966 Manuel Ramirez FY RC .50 .20
❑ 967 Tyler Johnson FY RC .40 .15
❑ 968 Jaime Bubela FY RC .40 .15
❑ 969 Haj Turay FY RC .25 .08
❑ 970 Tyson Graham FY RC .40 .15
❑ 971 David DeJesus FY RC .75 .30
❑ 972 Franklin Gutierrez FY RC 1.00 .40
❑ 973 Craig Brazell FY RC .40 .15
❑ 974 Keith Stamler FY RC .40 .15
❑ 975 Jemel Spearman FY RC .40 .15
❑ 976 Ozzie Chavez FY RC .40 .15
❑ 977 Nick Trzesniak FY RC .40 .15
❑ 978 Bill Simon FY RC .40 .15
❑ 979 Matthew Hagen FY RC .40 .15
❑ 980 Chris Kroski FY RC .40 .15
❑ 981 Prentice Redman FY RC .40 .15
❑ 982 Kevin Randel FY RC .40 .15
❑ 983 Thomari Story-Harden FY RC .40 .15
❑ 984 Brian Shackelford FY RC .40 .15
❑ 985 Mike Adams FY RC .40 .15
❑ 986 Brian McCann FY RC 4.00 1.50
❑ 987 Mike McNutt FY RC .40 .15
❑ 988 Aron Weston FY RC .40 .15
❑ 989 Dustin Moseley FY RC .40 .15
❑ 990 Bryan Bullington FY RC .40 .15

2004 Topps Total

❑ COMPLETE SET (880) 150.00 75.00
❑ OVERALL PRESS PLATES ODDS 1:159
❑ PLATES PRINT RUN 1 #'d SET PER COLOR
❑ PLATES: BLACK, CYAN, MAGENTA & YELLOW
❑ NO PLATES PRICING DUE TO SCARCITY
❑ 1 Kevin Brown .30 .10
❑ 2 Mike Mordecai .30 .10
❑ 3 Seung Song .30 .10
❑ 4 Mike Maroth .30 .10
❑ 5 Mike Lieberthal .30 .10
❑ 6 Billy Koch .30 .10
❑ 7 Mike Stanton .30 .10
❑ 8 Brad Penny .30 .10
❑ 9 Brooks Kieschnick .30 .10
❑ 10 Carlos Delgado .30 .10
❑ 11 Brady Clark .30 .10
❑ 12 Ramon Martinez .30 .10
❑ 13 Dan Wilson .30 .10
❑ 14 Guillermo Mota .30 .10
❑ 15 Trevor Hoffman .30 .10
❑ 16 Tony Batista .30 .10
❑ 17 Rusty Greer .30 .10
❑ 18 David Weathers .30 .10
❑ 19 Horacio Ramirez .30 .10
❑ 20 Aubrey Huff .30 .10
❑ 21 Casey Blake .30 .10
❑ 22 Ryan Bukvich .30 .10
❑ 23 Garrett Atkins .30 .10
❑ 24 Jose Contreras .30 .10
❑ 25 Chipper Jones .75 .30
❑ 26 Neifi Perez .30 .10
❑ 27 Scott Linebrink .30 .10
❑ 28 Matt Kinney .30 .10
❑ 29 Michael Restovich .30 .10
❑ 30 Scott Rolen .50 .20
❑ 31 John Franco .30 .10
❑ 32 Toby Hall .30 .10
❑ 33 Wily Mo Pena .30 .10
❑ 34 Dennis Tankersley .30 .10
❑ 35 Robb Nen .30 .10
❑ 36 Jose Valverde .30 .10
❑ 37 Chin-Feng Chen .30 .10
❑ 38 Gary Knotts .30 .10
❑ 39 Mark Sweeney .30 .10
❑ 40 Bret Boone .30 .10
❑ 41 Josh Phelps .30 .10
❑ 42 Jason LaRue .30 .10
❑ 43 Tim Redding .30 .10
❑ 44 Greg Myers .30 .10
❑ 45 Darin Erstad .30 .10
❑ 46 Kip Wells .30 .10
❑ 47 Matt Ford .30 .10
❑ 48 Jerome Williams .30 .10
❑ 49 Brian Meadows .30 .10
❑ 50 Albert Pujols 1.50 .60
❑ 51 Kirk Saarloos .30 .10
❑ 52 Scott Eyre .30 .10
❑ 53 John Flaherty .30 .10
❑ 54 Rafael Soriano .30 .10
❑ 55 Shea Hillenbrand .30 .10
❑ 56 Kyle Farnsworth .30 .10
❑ 57 Nate Cornejo .30 .10
❑ 58 Julian Tavarez .30 .10
❑ 59 Ryan Vogelsong .30 .10
❑ 60 Ryan Klesko .30 .10
❑ 61 Luke Hudson .30 .10
❑ 62 Justin Morneau .30 .10
❑ 63 Frank Catalanotto .30 .10
❑ 64 Derrick Turnbow .30 .10
❑ 65 Marcus Giles .30 .10
❑ 66 Mark Mulder .30 .10
❑ 67 Matt Anderson .30 .10
❑ 68 Mike Matheny .30 .10
❑ 69 Brian Lawrence .30 .10
❑ 70 Bobby Abreu .30 .10
❑ 71 Damian Moss .30 .10
❑ 72 Richard Hidalgo .30 .10
❑ 73 Mark Kotsay .30 .10
❑ 74 Mike Cameron .30 .10
❑ 75 Troy Glaus .30 .10
❑ 76 Matt Holliday .30 .10
❑ 77 Byung-Hyun Kim .30 .10
❑ 78 Aaron Sele .30 .10
❑ 79 Danny Graves .30 .10
❑ 80 Barry Zito .30 .10
❑ 81 Matt LeCroy .30 .10
❑ 82 Jason Isringhausen .30 .10
❑ 83 Colby Lewis .30 .10
❑ 84 Franklyn German .30 .10
❑ 85 Luis Matos .30 .10
❑ 86 Mike Timlin .30 .10
❑ 87 Miguel Batista .30 .10
❑ 88 John McDonald .30 .10
❑ 89 Joey Eischen .30 .10
❑ 90 Mike Mussina .50 .20
❑ 91 Jack Wilson .30 .10
❑ 92 Aaron Cook .30 .10
❑ 93 John Parrish .30 .10
❑ 94 Jose Valentin .30 .10
❑ 95 Johnny Damon .50 .20
❑ 96 Pat Burrell .30 .10
❑ 97 Brendan Donnelly .30 .10
❑ 98 Lance Carter .30 .10
❑ 99 Omar Daal .30 .10
❑ 100 Ichiro Suzuki 1.50 .60
❑ 101 Robin Ventura .30 .10
❑ 102 Brian Shouse .30 .10
❑ 103 Kevin Jarvis .30 .10
❑ 104 Jason Young .30 .10
❑ 105 Moises Alou .30 .10
❑ 106 Wes Obermueller .30 .10
❑ 107 David Segui .30 .10
❑ 108 Mike MacDougal .30 .10
❑ 109 John Buck .30 .10
❑ 110 Gary Sheffield .30 .10
❑ 111 Yorvit Torrealba .30 .10
❑ 112 Matt Kata .30 .10
❑ 113 David Bell .30 .10
❑ 114 Juan Gonzalez .30 .10
❑ 115 Kelvim Escobar .30 .10
❑ 116 Ruben Sierra .30 .10
❑ 117 Todd Wellemeyer .30 .10
❑ 118 Jamie Walker .30 .10
❑ 119 Will Cunnane .30 .10
❑ 120 Cliff Floyd .30 .10
❑ 121 Aramis Ramirez .30 .10
❑ 122 Damaso Marte .30 .10
❑ 123 Juan Castro .30 .10
❑ 124 Chris Woodward .30 .10
❑ 125 Andruw Jones .50 .20
❑ 126 Ben Weber .30 .10
❑ 127 Dee Brown .30 .10
❑ 128 Steve Reed .30 .10
❑ 129 Gabe Kapler .30 .10
❑ 130 Miguel Cabrera .50 .20
❑ 131 Billy McMillon .30 .10
❑ 132 Julio Mateo .30 .10
❑ 133 Preston Wilson .30 .10
❑ 134 Tony Clark .30 .10
❑ 135 Carlos Lee .30 .10
❑ 136 Carlos Baerga .30 .10
❑ 137 Mike Crudale .30 .10
❑ 138 David Ross .30 .10
❑ 139 Josh Fogg .30 .10
❑ 140 Dmitri Young .30 .10
❑ 141 Cliff Lee .30 .10
❑ 142 Mike Lowell .30 .10
❑ 143 Jason Lane .30 .10
❑ 144 Pedro Feliz .30 .10
❑ 145 Ken Griffey Jr. 1.25 .50
❑ 146 Dustin Hermanson .30 .10
❑ 147 Scott Hodges .30 .10
❑ 148 Aquilino Lopez .30 .10
❑ 149 Wes Helms .30 .10
❑ 150 Jason Giambi .30 .10
❑ 151 Erasmo Ramirez .30 .10
❑ 152 Sean Burroughs .30 .10
❑ 153 J.T. Snow .30 .10
❑ 154 Eddie Guardado .30 .10
❑ 155 C.C. Sabathia .30 .10
❑ 156 Kyle Lohse .30 .10
❑ 157 Roberto Hernandez .30 .10
❑ 158 Jason Simontacchi .30 .10
❑ 159 Tim Spooneybarger .30 .10
❑ 160 Alfonso Soriano .30 .10
❑ 161 Mike Gonzalez .30 .10
❑ 162 Alex Cora .30 .10
❑ 163 Kevin Gryboski .30 .10
❑ 164 Mike Lincoln .30 .10
❑ 165 Luis Castillo .30 .10
❑ 166 Odalis Perez .30 .10
❑ 167 Alex Sanchez .30 .10
❑ 168 Rob Mackowiak .30 .10
❑ 169 Francisco Rodriguez .30 .10
❑ 170 Roy Oswalt .30 .10
❑ 171 Omar Infante .30 .10
❑ 172 Ryan Jensen .30 .10
❑ 173 Ben Broussard .30 .10
❑ 174 Mark Hendrickson .30 .10
❑ 175 Manny Ramirez .50 .20
❑ 176 Rob Bell .30 .10
❑ 177 Adam Everett .30 .10
❑ 178 Chris George .30 .10
❑ 179 Ronnie Belliard .30 .10
❑ 180 Eric Gagne .30 .10
❑ 181 Scott Schoeneweis .30 .10

❑ 182 Kris Benson .30 .10
❑ 183 Amaury Telemaco .30 .10
❑ 184 John Riedling .30 .10
❑ 185 Juan Pierre .30 .10
❑ 186 Ramon Ortiz .30 .10
❑ 187 Luis Rivas .30 .10
❑ 188 Larry Bigbie .30 .10
❑ 189 Robby Hammock .30 .10
❑ 190 Geoff Jenkins .30 .10
❑ 191 Chad Cordero .30 .10
❑ 192 Mark Ellis .30 .10
❑ 193 Mark Loretta .30 .10
❑ 194 Ryan Drese .30 .10
❑ 195 Lance Berkman .30 .10
❑ 196 Kevin Appier .30 .10
❑ 197 Kiko Calero .30 .10
❑ 198 Mickey Callaway .30 .10
❑ 199 Chase Utley .50 .20
❑ 200 Nomar Garciaparra 1.25 .50
❑ 201 Kevin Cash .30 .10
❑ 202 Ramiro Mendoza .30 .10
❑ 203 Shane Reynolds .30 .10
❑ 204 Chris Spurling .30 .10
❑ 205 Aaron Guiel .30 .10
❑ 206 Mark DeRosa .30 .10
❑ 207 Adam Kennedy .30 .10
❑ 208 Andy Pettitte .50 .20
❑ 209 Rafael Palmeiro .50 .20
❑ 210 Luis Gonzalez .30 .10
❑ 211 Ryan Franklin .30 .10
❑ 212 Bob Wickman .30 .10
❑ 213 Ron Calloway .30 .10
❑ 214 Jae Weong Seo .30 .10
❑ 215 Kazuhisa Ishii .30 .10
❑ 216 Sterling Hitchcock .30 .10
❑ 217 Jimmy Gobble .30 .10
❑ 218 Chad Moeller .30 .10
❑ 219 Jake Peavy .30 .10
❑ 220 John Smoltz .50 .20
❑ 221 Donovan Osborne .30 .10
❑ 222 David Wells .30 .10
❑ 223 Brad Lidge .30 .10
❑ 224 Carlos Zambrano .30 .10
❑ 225 Kerry Wood .30 .10
❑ 226 Alex Cintron .30 .10
❑ 227 Javier A. Lopez .30 .10
❑ 228 Jeremy Griffiths .30 .10
❑ 229 Jon Garland .30 .10
❑ 230 Curt Schilling .50 .20
❑ 231 Alex Scott Gonzalez .30 .10
❑ 232 Jay Gibbons .30 .10
❑ 233 Aaron Miles .30 .10
❑ 234 Mike Gallo .30 .10
❑ 235 Johan Santana .75 .30
❑ 236 Jose Guillen .30 .10
❑ 237 Jeff Conine .30 .10
❑ 238 Matt Roney .30 .10
❑ 239 Desi Relaford .30 .10
❑ 240 Frank Thomas .75 .30
❑ 241 Danny Patterson .30 .10
❑ 242 Kevin Mench .30 .10
❑ 243 Mike Redmond .30 .10
❑ 244 Jeff Suppan .30 .10
❑ 245 Carl Everett .30 .10
❑ 246 Jack Cressend .30 .10
❑ 247 Matt Mantei .30 .10
❑ 248 Enrique Wilson .30 .10
❑ 249 Craig Counsell .30 .10
❑ 250 Mark Prior .50 .20
❑ 251 Jared Sandberg .30 .10
❑ 252 Scott Strickland .30 .10
❑ 253 Lew Ford .30 .10
❑ 254 Hee Seop Choi .30 .10
❑ 255 Jason Phillips .30 .10
❑ 256 Jason Jennings .30 .10
❑ 257 Todd Pratt .30 .10
❑ 258 Matt Herges .30 .10
❑ 259 Kerry Ligtenberg .30 .10
❑ 260 Austin Kearns .30 .10
❑ 261 Jay Witasick .30 .10
❑ 262 Tony Armas Jr. .30 .10
❑ 263 Tom Martin .30 .10
❑ 264 Oliver Perez .30 .10
❑ 265 Jorge Posada .50 .20
❑ 266 Jason Boyd .30 .10
❑ 267 Ben Hendrickson .30 .10
❑ 268 Reggie Sanders .30 .10
❑ 269 Julio Lugo .30 .10
❑ 270 Pedro Martinez .50 .20
❑ 271 Kyle Snyder .30 .10
❑ 272 Felipe Lopez .30 .10
❑ 273 Kevin Millar .30 .10
❑ 274 Travis Hafner .30 .10
❑ 275 Maggio Ordonez .30 .10
❑ 276 Marlon Byrd .30 .10
❑ 277 Scott Spiezio .30 .10
❑ 278 Mark Corey .30 .10
❑ 279 Tim Salmon .50 .20
❑ 280 Alex Gonzalez .30 .10
❑ 281 Marquis Grissom .30 .10
❑ 282 Miguel Olivo .30 .10
❑ 283 Orlando Hudson .30 .10
❑ 284 Rondell White .30 .10
❑ 285 Jermaine Dye .30 .10
❑ 286 Paul Shuey .30 .10
❑ 287 Brandon Inge .30 .10
❑ 288 B.J. Surhoff .30 .10
❑ 289 Edgar Gonzalez .30 .10
❑ 290 Angel Berroa .30 .10
❑ 291 Claudio Vargas .30 .10
❑ 292 Cesar Izturis .30 .10
❑ 293 Brandon Phillips .30 .10
❑ 294 Jeff Duncan .30 .10
❑ 295 Randy Wolf .30 .10
❑ 296 Barry Larkin .50 .20
❑ 297 Felix Rodriguez .30 .10
❑ 298 Robb Quinlan .30 .10
❑ 299 Brian Jordan .30 .10
❑ 300 Dontrelle Willis .50 .20
❑ 301 Doug Davis .30 .10
❑ 302 Ricky Stone .30 .10
❑ 303 Travis Harper .30 .10
❑ 304 Jaret Wright .30 .10
❑ 305 Edgardo Alfonzo .30 .10
❑ 306 Quinton McCracken .30 .10
❑ 307 Jason Bay .30 .10
❑ 308 Joe Randa .30 .10
❑ 309 Steve Sparks .30 .10
❑ 310 Roy Halladay .30 .10
❑ 311 Antonio Alfonseca .30 .10
❑ 312 Michael Cuddyer .30 .10
❑ 313 John Patterson .30 .10
❑ 314 Chris Widger .30 .10
❑ 315 Shigetoshi Hasegawa .30 .10
❑ 316 Tim Wakefield .30 .10
❑ 317 Scott Hatteberg .30 .10
❑ 318 Mike Remlinger .30 .10
❑ 319 Jose Vizcaino .30 .10
❑ 320 Rocco Baldelli .30 .10
❑ 321 David Riske .30 .10
❑ 322 Steve Karsay .30 .10
❑ 323 Peter Bergeron .30 .10
❑ 324 Jeff Weaver .30 .10
❑ 325 Larry Walker .30 .10
❑ 326 Jack Cust .30 .10
❑ 327 Bo Hart .30 .10
❑ 328 Rod Beck .30 .10
❑ 329 Jose Acevedo .30 .10
❑ 330 Hank Blalock .30 .10
❑ 331 Tom Gordon .30 .10
❑ 332 Brian Fuentes .30 .10
❑ 333 Tomas Perez .30 .10
❑ 334 Lenny Harris .30 .10
❑ 335 Matt Morris .30 .10
❑ 336 Jeremi Gonzalez .30 .10
❑ 337 David Eckstein .30 .10
❑ 338 Aaron Rowand .30 .10
❑ 339 Rick Bauer .30 .10
❑ 340 Jim Edmonds .30 .10
❑ 341 Joe Borowski .30 .10
❑ 342 Eric DuBose .30 .10
❑ 343 D'Angelo Jimenez .30 .10
❑ 344 Tomo Ohka .30 .10
❑ 345 Victor Zambrano .30 .10
❑ 346 Joe McEwing .30 .10
❑ 347 Jorge Sosa .30 .10
❑ 348 Keith Ginter .30 .10
❑ 349 A.J. Pierzynski .30 .10
❑ 350 Mike Sweeney .30 .10
❑ 351 Shawn Chacon .30 .10
❑ 352 Matt Clement .30 .10
❑ 353 Vance Wilson .30 .10
❑ 354 Benito Santiago .30 .10
❑ 355 Eric Hinske .30 .10
❑ 356 Vladimir Guerrero .75 .30
❑ 357 Kenny Rogers .30 .10
❑ 358 Travis Lee .30 .10
❑ 359 Jay Powell .30 .10
❑ 360 Phil Nevin .30 .10
❑ 361 Willie Harris .30 .10
❑ 362 Ty Wigginton .30 .10
❑ 363 Chad Fox .30 .10
❑ 364 Junior Spivey .30 .10
❑ 365 Brandon Webb .30 .10
❑ 366 Brett Myers .30 .10
❑ 367 Alexis Gomez .30 .10
❑ 368 Dave Roberts .30 .10
❑ 369 LaTroy Hawkins .30 .10
❑ 370 Kevin Millwood .30 .10
❑ 371 Brian Schneider .30 .10
❑ 372 Blaine Neal .30 .10
❑ 373 Jeromy Burnitz .30 .10
❑ 374 Ted Lilly .30 .10
❑ 375 Shawn Green .30 .10
❑ 376 Carlos Pena .30 .10
❑ 377 Gil Meche .30 .10
❑ 378 Jeff Bagwell .50 .20
❑ 379 Alex Escobar .30 .10
❑ 380 Erubiel Durazo .30 .10
❑ 381 Cristian Guzman .30 .10
❑ 382 Rocky Biddle .30 .10
❑ 383 Craig Wilson .30 .10
❑ 384 Rey Sanchez .30 .10
❑ 385 Russ Ortiz .30 .10
❑ 386 Freddy Garcia .30 .10
❑ 387 Luis Vizcaino .30 .10
❑ 388 David Ortiz .75 .30
❑ 389 Jose Molina .30 .10
❑ 390 Edgar Martinez .50 .20
❑ 391 Nate Bump .30 .10
❑ 392 Brent Mayne .30 .10
❑ 393 Ray King .30 .10
❑ 394 Paul Wilson .30 .10
❑ 395 Melvin Mora .30 .10
❑ 396 Morgan Ensberg .30 .10
❑ 397 Ramon Hernandez .30 .10
❑ 398 Juan Rincon .30 .10
❑ 399 Ron Mahay .30 .10
❑ 400 Jeff Kent .30 .10
❑ 401 Cal Eldred .30 .10
❑ 402 Mike Difelice .30 .10
❑ 403 Valerio De Los Santos .30 .10
❑ 404 Steve Finley .30 .10
❑ 405 Trot Nixon .30 .10
❑ 406 Akinori Otsuka RC .40 .15
❑ 407 Ryan Freel .30 .10
❑ 408 Ray Durham .30 .10
❑ 409 Aaron Heilman .30 .10
❑ 410 Edgar Renteria .30 .10
❑ 411 Mike Hampton .30 .10
❑ 412 Kirk Rueter .30 .10
❑ 413 Jim Mecir .30 .10
❑ 414 Brian Roberts .30 .10
❑ 415 Paul Konerko .30 .10
❑ 416 Reed Johnson .30 .10
❑ 417 Roger Clemens 1.50 .60
❑ 418 Coco Crisp .30 .10
❑ 419 Carlos Hernandez .30 .10
❑ 420 Scott Podsednik .30 .10
❑ 421 Miguel Cairo .30 .10
❑ 422 Abraham Nunez .30 .10
❑ 423 Endy Chavez .30 .10
❑ 424 Eric Munson .30 .10
❑ 425 Torii Hunter .30 .10
❑ 426 Ben Howard .30 .10
❑ 427 Chris Gomez .30 .10
❑ 428 Francisco Cordero .30 .10
❑ 429 Jeffrey Hammonds .30 .10
❑ 430 Shannon Stewart .30 .10
❑ 431 Einar Diaz .30 .10
❑ 432 Eric Byrnes .30 .10
❑ 433 Marty Cordova .30 .10
❑ 434 Matt Ginter .30 .10
❑ 435 Victor Martinez .30 .10
❑ 436 Geronimo Gil .30 .10
❑ 437 Grant Balfour .30 .10
❑ 438 Ramon Vazquez .30 .10
❑ 439 Jose Cruz Jr. .30 .10

❑	440	Orlando Cabrera	.30	.10
❑	441	Joe Kennedy	.30	.10
❑	442	Scott Williamson	.30	.10
❑	443	Troy Percival	.30	.10
❑	444	Derrek Lee	.50	.20
❑	445	Runelvys Hernandez	.30	.10
❑	446	Mark Grudzielanek	.30	.10
❑	447	Trey Hodges	.30	.10
❑	448	Jimmy Haynes	.30	.10
❑	449	Eric Milton	.30	.10
❑	450	Todd Helton	.50	.20
❑	451	Greg Zaun	.30	.10
❑	452	Woody Williams	.30	.10
❑	453	Todd Walker	.30	.10
❑	454	Juan Cruz	.30	.10
❑	455	Fernando Vina	.30	.10
❑	456	Omar Vizquel	.50	.20
❑	457	Roberto Alomar	.50	.20
❑	458	Bill Hall	.30	.10
❑	459	Juan Rivera	.30	.10
❑	460	Tom Glavine	.50	.20
❑	461	Ramon Castro	.30	.10
❑	462	Cory Vance	.30	.10
❑	463	Dan Miceli	.30	.10
❑	464	Lyle Overbay	.30	.10
❑	465	Craig Biggio	.50	.20
❑	466	Ricky Ledee	.30	.10
❑	467	Michael Barrett	.30	.10
❑	468	Jason Anderson	.30	.10
❑	469	Matt Stairs	.30	.10
❑	470	Jarrod Washburn	.30	.10
❑	471	Todd Hundley	.30	.10
❑	472	Grant Roberts	.30	.10
❑	473	Randy Winn	.30	.10
❑	474	Pat Hentgen	.30	.10
❑	475	Jose Vidro	.30	.10
❑	476	Tony Torcato	.30	.10
❑	477	Jeremy Affeldt	.30	.10
❑	478	Carlos Guillen	.30	.10
❑	479	Paul Quantrill	.30	.10
❑	480	Rafael Furcal	.30	.10
❑	481	Adam Melhuse	.30	.10
❑	482	Jerry Hairston Jr.	.30	.10
❑	483	Adam Bernero	.30	.10
❑	484	Terrence Long	.30	.10
❑	485	Paul Lo Duca	.30	.10
❑	486	Corey Koskie	.30	.10
❑	487	John Lackey	.30	.10
❑	488	Chad Zerbe	.30	.10
❑	489	Vinny Castilla	.30	.10
❑	490	Corey Patterson	.30	.10
❑	491	John Olerud	.30	.10
❑	492	Josh Bard	.30	.10
❑	493	Darren Dreifort	.30	.10
❑	494	Jason Standridge	.30	.10
❑	495	Ben Sheets	.30	.10
❑	496	Jose Castillo	.30	.10
❑	497	Jay Payton	.30	.10
❑	498	Rob Bowen	.30	.10
❑	499	Bobby Higginson	.30	.10
❑	500	Alex Rodriguez Yanks	1.25	.50
❑	501	Octavio Dotel	.30	.10
❑	502	Rheal Cormier	.30	.10
❑	503	Felix Heredia	.30	.10
❑	504	Dan Wright	.30	.10
❑	505	Michael Young	.30	.10
❑	506	Wilfredo Ledezma	.30	.10
❑	507	Sun Woo Kim	.30	.10
❑	508	Michael Tejera	.30	.10
❑	509	Herbert Perry	.30	.10
❑	510	Esteban Loaiza	.30	.10
❑	511	Alan Embree	.30	.10
❑	512	Ben Davis	.30	.10
❑	513	Greg Colbrunn	.30	.10
❑	514	Josh Hall	.30	.10
❑	515	Raul Ibanez	.30	.10
❑	516	Jason Kershner	.30	.10
❑	517	Corky Miller	.30	.10
❑	518	Jason Marquis	.30	.10
❑	519	Roger Cedeno	.30	.10
❑	520	Adam Dunn	.30	.10
❑	521	Paul Byrd	.30	.10
❑	522	Sandy Alomar Jr.	.30	.10
❑	523	Salomon Torres	.30	.10
❑	524	John Halama	.30	.10
❑	525	Mike Piazza	1.25	.50
❑	526	Buddy Groom	.30	.10
❑	527	Adrian Beltre	.30	.10
❑	528	Chad Harville	.30	.10
❑	529	Javier Vazquez	.30	.10
❑	530	Jody Gerut	.30	.10
❑	531	Elmer Dessens	.30	.10
❑	532	B.J. Ryan	.30	.10
❑	533	Chad Durbin	.30	.10
❑	534	Doug Mirabelli	.30	.10
❑	535	Bernie Williams	.50	.20
❑	536	Jeff DaVanon	.30	.10
❑	537	Dave Berg	.30	.10
❑	538	Geoff Blum	.30	.10
❑	539	John Thomson	.30	.10
❑	540	Jeremy Bonderman	.30	.10
❑	541	Jeff Zimmerman	.30	.10
❑	542	Derek Lowe	.30	.10
❑	543	Scot Shields	.30	.10
❑	544	Michael Tucker	.30	.10
❑	545	Tim Hudson	.30	.10
❑	546	Ryan Ludwick	.30	.10
❑	547	Rick Reed	.30	.10
❑	548	Placido Polanco	.30	.10
❑	549	Tony Graffanino	.30	.10
❑	550	Garret Anderson	.30	.10
❑	551	Timo Perez	.30	.10
❑	552	Jesus Colome	.30	.10
❑	553	R.A. Dickey	.30	.10
❑	554	Tim Worrell	.30	.10
❑	555	Jason Kendall	.30	.10
❑	556	Tom Goodwin	.30	.10
❑	557	Joaquin Benoit	.30	.10
❑	558	Stephen Randolph	.30	.10
❑	559	Miguel Tejada	.30	.10
❑	560	A.J. Burnett	.30	.10
❑	561	Ben Diggins	.30	.10
❑	562	Kent Mercker	.30	.10
❑	563	Zach Day	.30	.10
❑	564	Antonio Perez	.30	.10
❑	565	Jason Schmidt	.30	.10
❑	566	Armando Benitez	.30	.10
❑	567	Denny Neagle	.30	.10
❑	568	Eric Eckenstahler	.30	.10
❑	569	Chan Ho Park	.30	.10
❑	570	Carlos Beltran	.30	.10
❑	571	Brett Tomko	.30	.10
❑	572	Henry Mateo	.30	.10
❑	573	Ken Harvey	.30	.10
❑	574	Matt Lawton	.30	.10
❑	575	Mariano Rivera	.75	.30
❑	576	Darrell May	.30	.10
❑	577	Jamie Moyer	.30	.10
❑	578	Paul Bako	.30	.10
❑	579	Cory Lidle	.30	.10
❑	580	Jacque Jones	.30	.10
❑	581	Jolbert Cabrera	.30	.10
❑	582	Jason Grimsley	.30	.10
❑	583	Danny Kolb	.30	.10
❑	584	Billy Wagner	.30	.10
❑	585	Rich Aurilia	.30	.10
❑	586	Vicente Padilla	.30	.10
❑	587	Oscar Villarreal	.30	.10
❑	588	Rene Reyes	.30	.10
❑	589	Jon Lieber	.30	.10
❑	590	Nick Johnson	.30	.10
❑	591	Bobby Crosby	.30	.10
❑	592	Steve Trachsel	.30	.10
❑	593	Brian Boehringer	.30	.10
❑	594	Juan Uribe	.30	.10
❑	595	Bartolo Colon	.30	.10
❑	596	Bobby Hill	.30	.10
❑	597	Chris Shelton RC	1.00	.40
❑	598	Carl Pavano	.30	.10
❑	599	Kurt Ainsworth	.30	.10
❑	600	Derek Jeter	1.50	.60
❑	601	Doug Mientkiewicz	.30	.10
❑	602	Orlando Palmeiro	.30	.10
❑	603	J.C. Romero	.30	.10
❑	604	Scott Sullivan	.30	.10
❑	605	Brad Radke	.30	.10
❑	606	Fernando Rodney	.30	.10
❑	607	Jim Brower	.30	.10
❑	608	Josh Towers	.30	.10
❑	609	Brad Fullmer	.30	.10
❑	610	Jose Reyes	.30	.10
❑	611	Ryan Wagner	.30	.10
❑	612	Joe Mays	.30	.10
❑	613	Jung Bong	.30	.10
❑	614	Curtis Leskanic	.30	.10
❑	615	Al Leiter	.30	.10
❑	616	Wade Miller	.30	.10
❑	617	Keith Foulke Sox	.30	.10
❑	618	Casey Fossum	.30	.10
❑	619	Craig Monroe	.30	.10
❑	620	Hideo Nomo	.75	.30
❑	621	Bob File	.30	.10
❑	622	Steve Kline	.30	.10
❑	623	Bobby Kielty	.30	.10
❑	624	Dewon Brazelton	.30	.10
❑	625	Eric Chavez	.30	.10
❑	626	Chris Carpenter	.30	.10
❑	627	Alexis Rios	.30	.10
❑	628	Jason Davis	.30	.10
❑	629	Jose Jimenez	.30	.10
❑	630	Vernon Wells	.30	.10
❑	631	Kenny Lofton	.30	.10
❑	632	Chad Bradford	.30	.10
❑	633	Brad Wilkerson	.30	.10
❑	634	Pokey Reese	.30	.10
❑	635	Richie Sexson	.30	.10
❑	636	Chin-Hui Tsao	.30	.10
❑	637	Eli Marrero	.30	.10
❑	638	Chris Reitsma	.30	.10
❑	639	Daryle Ward	.30	.10
❑	640	Mark Teixeira	.50	.20
❑	641	Corwin Malone	.30	.10
❑	642	Adam Eaton	.30	.10
❑	643	Jimmy Rollins	.30	.10
❑	644	Brian Anderson	.30	.10
❑	645	Bill Mueller	.30	.10
❑	646	Jake Westbrook	.30	.10
❑	647	Bengie Molina	.30	.10
❑	648	Jorge Julio	.30	.10
❑	649	Billy Traber	.30	.10
❑	650	Randy Johnson	.75	.30
❑	651	Javy Lopez	.30	.10
❑	652	Doug Glanville	.30	.10
❑	653	Jeff Cirillo	.30	.10
❑	654	Tino Martinez	.50	.20
❑	655	Mark Buehrle	.30	.10
❑	656	Jason Michaels	.30	.10
❑	657	Damian Rolls	.30	.10
❑	658	Rosman Garcia	.30	.10
❑	659	Scott Hairston	.30	.10
❑	660	Carl Crawford	.30	.10
❑	661	Livan Hernandez	.30	.10
❑	662	Danny Bautista	.30	.10
❑	663	Brad Ausmus	.30	.10
❑	664	Juan Acevedo	.30	.10
❑	665	Sean Casey	.30	.10
❑	666	Josh Beckett	.30	.10
❑	667	Milton Bradley	.30	.10
❑	668	Braden Looper	.30	.10
❑	669	Paul Abbott	.30	.10
❑	670	Joel Pineiro	.30	.10
❑	671	Luis Terrero	.30	.10
❑	672	Rodrigo Lopez	.30	.10
❑	673	Joe Crede	.30	.10
❑	674	Mike Koplove	.30	.10
❑	675	Brian Giles	.30	.10
❑	676	Jeff Nelson	.30	.10
❑	677	Russell Branyan	.30	.10
❑	678	Mike DeJean	.30	.10
❑	679	Brian Daubach	.30	.10
❑	680	Ellis Burks	.30	.10
❑	681	Ryan Dempster	.30	.10
❑	682	Cliff Politte	.30	.10
❑	683	Brian Reith	.30	.10
❑	684	Scott Stewart	.30	.10
❑	685	Allan Simpson	.30	.10
❑	686	Shawn Estes	.30	.10
❑	687	Jason Johnson	.30	.10
❑	688	Wil Cordero	.30	.10
❑	689	Kelly Stinnett	.30	.10
❑	690	Jose Lima	.30	.10
❑	691	Gary Bennett	.30	.10
❑	692	T.J. Tucker	.30	.10
❑	693	Shane Spencer	.30	.10
❑	694	Chris Hammond	.30	.10
❑	695	Raul Mondesi	.30	.10
❑	696	Xavier Nady	.30	.10
❑	697	Cody Ransom	.30	.10

❑ 698 Ron Villone .30 .10
❑ 699 Brook Fordyce .30 .10
❑ 700 Sammy Sosa .75 .30
❑ 701 Terry Adams .30 .10
❑ 702 Ricardo Rincon .30 .10
❑ 703 Tike Redman .30 .10
❑ 704 Chris Stynes .30 .10
❑ 705 Mark Redman .30 .10
❑ 706 Juan Encarnacion .30 .10
❑ 707 Jhonny Peralta .30 .10
❑ 708 Denny Hocking .30 .10
❑ 709 Ivan Rodriguez .50 .20
❑ 710 Jose Hernandez .30 .10
❑ 711 Brandon Duckworth .30 .10
❑ 712 Dave Burba .30 .10
❑ 713 Joe Nathan .30 .10
❑ 714 Dan Smith .30 .10
❑ 715 Karim Garcia .30 .10
❑ 716 Arthur Rhodes .30 .10
❑ 717 Shawn Wooten .30 .10
❑ 718 Ramon Santiago .30 .10
❑ 719 Luis Ugueto .30 .10
❑ 720 Danys Baez .30 .10
❑ 721 Alfredo Amezaga PROS .30 .10
❑ 722 Sidney Ponson .30 .10
❑ 723 Joe Mauer PROS .75 .30
❑ 724 Jesse Foppert PROS .30 .10
❑ 725 Todd Greene .30 .10
❑ 726 Dan Haren PROS .30 .10
❑ 727 Brandon Larson PROS .30 .10
❑ 728 Bobby Jenks PROS .30 .10
❑ 729 Grady Sizemore PROS .75 .30
❑ 730 Ben Grieve .30 .10
❑ 731 Khalil Greene PROS .50 .20
❑ 732 Chad Gaudin PROS .30 .10
❑ 733 Johnny Estrada PROS .30 .10
❑ 734 Joe Valentine PROS .30 .10
❑ 735 Tim Raines Jr. PROS .30 .10
❑ 736 Brandon Claussen PROS .30 .10
❑ 737 Sam Marsonek PROS .30 .10
❑ 738 Delmon Young PROS .50 .20
❑ 739 David Dellucci .30 .10
❑ 740 Sergio Mitre PROS .30 .10
❑ 741 Nick Neugebauer PROS .30 .10
❑ 742 Laynce Nix PROS .30 .10
❑ 743 Joe Thurston PROS .30 .10
❑ 744 Ryan Langerhans PROS .30 .10
❑ 745 Pete LaForest PROS .30 .10
❑ 746 Arnie Munoz PROS .30 .10
❑ 747 Rickie Weeks PROS .30 .10
❑ 748 Neal Cotts PROS .30 .10
❑ 749 Jonny Gomes PROS .30 .10
❑ 750 Jim Thome .50 .20
❑ 751 Jon Rauch PROS .30 .10
❑ 752 Edwin Jackson PROS .30 .10
❑ 753 Ryan Madson PROS .30 .10
❑ 754 Andrew Good PROS .30 .10
❑ 755 Eddie Perez .30 .10
❑ 756 Joe Borchard PROS .30 .10
❑ 757 Jeremy Guthrie PROS .30 .10
❑ 758 Jose Mesa .30 .10
❑ 759 Doug Waechter PROS .30 .10
❑ 760 J.D. Drew .30 .10
❑ 761 Adam LaRoche PROS .30 .10
❑ 762 Rich Harden PROS .30 .10
❑ 763 Justin Speier .30 .10
❑ 764 Todd Zeile .30 .10
❑ 765 Turk Wendell .30 .10
❑ 766 Mark Bellhorn Sox .30 .10
❑ 767 Mike Jackson .30 .10
❑ 768 Chone Figgins .30 .10
❑ 769 Mike Neu .30 .10
❑ 770 Greg Maddux 1.25 .50
❑ 771 Frank Menechino .30 .10
❑ 772 Alec Zumwalt RC .30 .10
❑ 773 Eric Young .30 .10
❑ 774 Dustan Mohr .30 .10
❑ 775 Shane Halter .30 .10
❑ 776 Brian Buchanan .30 .10
❑ 777 So Taguchi .30 .10
❑ 778 Eric Karros .30 .10
❑ 779 Ramon Nivar .30 .10
❑ 780 Marlon Anderson .30 .10
❑ 781 Brayan Pena FY RC .40 .15
❑ 782 Chris O'Riordan FY RC .40 .15
❑ 783 Dioner Navarro FY RC .75 .30
❑ 784 Alberto Callaspo FY RC .75 .30
❑ 785 Hector Gimenez FY RC .30 .10
❑ 786 Yadier Molina FY RC 2.00 .75
❑ 787 Kevin Richardson FY RC .30 .10
❑ 788 Brian Pilkington FY RC .30 .10
❑ 789 Adam Greenberg FY RC .75 .30
❑ 790 Ervin Santana FY RC 2.00 .75
❑ 791 Brant Colamarino FY RC .75 .30
❑ 792 Ben Himes FY RC .30 .10
❑ 793 Todd Self FY RC .50 .20
❑ 794 Brad Vericker FY RC .40 .15
❑ 795 Donald Kelly FY RC .40 .15
❑ 796 Brock Jacobsen FY RC .30 .10
❑ 797 Brock Peterson FY RC .40 .15
❑ 798 Carlos Sosa FY RC .40 .15
❑ 799 Chad Chop FY RC .40 .15
❑ 800 Matt Moses FY RC 1.00 .40
❑ 801 Chris Aguila FY RC .40 .15
❑ 802 David Murphy FY RC .75 .30
❑ 803 Don Sutton FY RC 1.00 .40
❑ 804 Jereme Milons FY RC .50 .20
❑ 805 Jon Coutlangus FY RC .30 .10
❑ 806 Greg Thissen FY RC .40 .15
❑ 807 Jose Capellan FY RC .50 .20
❑ 808 Chad Santos FY RC .40 .15
❑ 809 Wardell Starling FY RC .40 .15
❑ 810 Kevin Kouzmanoff FY RC 2.00 .75
❑ 811 Kevin Davidson FY RC .30 .10
❑ 812 Michael Mooney FY RC .40 .15
❑ 813 Rodney Choy Foo FY RC .30 .10
❑ 814 Reid Gorecki FY RC .40 .15
❑ 815 Rudy Guillen FY RC .75 .30
❑ 816 Harvey Garcia FY RC .30 .10
❑ 817 Warner Madrigal FY RC .75 .30
❑ 818 Kenny Perez FY RC .40 .15
❑ 819 Joaquin Arias FY RC .75 .30
❑ 820 Benji DeQuin FY RC .30 .10
❑ 821 Lastings Milledge FY RC 5.00 2.00
❑ 822 Blake Hawksworth FY RC .50 .20
❑ 823 Estee Harris FY RC .50 .20
❑ 824 Bobby Brownlie FY RC 1.00 .40
❑ 825 Wanell Severino FY RC .30 .10
❑ 826 Bobby Madritsch FY .30 .10
❑ 827 Travis Hanson FY RC .50 .20
❑ 828 Brandon Medders FY RC .40 .15
❑ 829 Kevin Howard FY RC .50 .20
❑ 830 Brian Steffek FY RC .30 .10
❑ 831 Terry Jones FY RC .50 .20
❑ 832 Anthony Acevedo FY RC .40 .15
❑ 833 Kory Casto FY RC .50 .20
❑ 834 Brooks Conrad FY RC .40 .15
❑ 835 Juan Gutierrez FY RC .40 .15
❑ 836 Charlie Zink FY RC .30 .10
❑ 837 David Aardsma FY RC .50 .20
❑ 838 Carl Loadenthal FY RC .50 .20
❑ 839 Donald Levinski FY RC .30 .10
❑ 840 Dustin Nippert FY RC .50 .20
❑ 841 Calvin Hayes FY RC .50 .20
❑ 842 Felix Hernandez FY RC 8.00 3.00
❑ 843 Tyler Davidson FY RC .50 .20
❑ 844 George Sherrill FY RC .40 .15
❑ 845 Craig Ansman FY RC .40 .15
❑ 846 Jeff Allison FY RC .40 .15
❑ 847 Tommy Murphy FY RC .40 .15
❑ 848 Jerome Gamble FY RC .30 .10
❑ 849 Jesse English FY RC .40 .15
❑ 850 Alex Romero FY RC .40 .15
❑ 851 Joel Zumaya FY RC 3.00 1.25
❑ 852 Carlos Quentin FY RC 2.50 1.00
❑ 853 Jose Valdez FY RC .40 .15
❑ 854 J.J. Furmaniak FY RC .75 .30
❑ 855 Juan Cedeno FY RC .40 .15
❑ 856 Kyle Sleeth FY RC .50 .20
❑ 857 Josh Labandeira FY RC .40 .15
❑ 858 Lee Gwaltney FY RC .30 .10
❑ 859 Lincoln Holdzkom FY RC .40 .15
❑ 860 Ivan Ochoa FY RC .40 .15
❑ 861 Luke Anderson FY RC .30 .10
❑ 862 Conor Jackson FY RC 3.00 1.25
❑ 863 Matt Capps FY RC .40 .15
❑ 864 Merkin Valdez FY RC .50 .20
❑ 865 Paul Bacot FY RC .50 .20
❑ 866 Erick Aybar FY RC 1.00 .40
❑ 867 Scott Proctor FY RC .50 .20
❑ 868 Tim Stauffer FY RC 1.00 .40
❑ 869 Matt Creighton FY RC .40 .15
❑ 870 Zach Miner FY RC 1.25 .50
❑ 871 Danny Gonzalez FY RC .30 .10
❑ 872 Tom Farmer FY RC .40 .15
❑ 873 John Santor FY RC .30 .10
❑ 874 Logan Kensing FY RC .40 .15
❑ 875 Vito Chiaravalloti FY RC .40 .15
❑ 876 Checklist .30 .10
❑ 877 Checklist .30 .10
❑ 878 Checklist .30 .10
❑ 879 Checklist .30 .10
❑ 880 Checklist .30 .10

2005 Topps Total

❑ COMPLETE SET (770) 150.00 75.00
❑ COMMON (1-575/666) .30 .10
❑ COMMON CARD (576-690) .30 .10
❑ COM (269/588/691-765) .50 .20
❑ COMMON CL (766-770) .30 .10
❑ OVERALL PLATE ODDS 1:85 HOBBY
❑ PLATE PRINT RUN 1 SET PER COLOR
❑ BLACK-CYAN-MAGENTA-YELLOW ISSUED
❑ FRONT AND BACK PLATES PRODUCED
❑ NO PLATE PRICING DUE TO SCARCITY
❑ 1 Rafael Furcal .30 .10
❑ 2 Tony Clark .30 .10
❑ 3 Hideki Matsui 1.25 .50
❑ 4 Zach Day .30 .10
❑ 5 Garret Anderson .30 .10
❑ 6 B.J. Surhoff .30 .10
❑ 7 Trevor Hoffman .30 .10
❑ 8 Kenny Lofton .30 .10
❑ 9 Ross Gload .30 .10
❑ 10 Jorge Cantu .30 .10
❑ 11 Joel Pineiro .30 .10
❑ 12 Alex Cintron .30 .10
❑ 13 Mike Matheny .30 .10
❑ 14 Rod Barajas .30 .10
❑ 15 Ray Durham .30 .10
❑ 16 Danys Baez .30 .10
❑ 17 Brian Schneider .30 .10
❑ 18 Tike Redman .30 .10
❑ 19 Ricardo Rodriguez .30 .10
❑ 20 Mike Sweeney .30 .10
❑ 21 Greg Myers .30 .10
❑ 22 Chone Figgins .30 .10
❑ 23 Brian Lawrence .30 .10
❑ 24 Joe Nathan .30 .10
❑ 25 Placido Polanco .30 .10
❑ 26 Yadier Molina .30 .10
❑ 27 Gary Bennett .30 .10
❑ 28 Yorvit Torrealba .30 .10
❑ 29 Javier Valentin .30 .10
❑ 30 Jason Giambi .30 .10
❑ 31 Brandon Claussen .30 .10
❑ 32 Miguel Olivo .30 .10
❑ 33 Josh Bard .30 .10
❑ 34 Ramon Hernandez .30 .10
❑ 35 Geoff Jenkins .30 .10
❑ 36 Bobby Kielty .30 .10
❑ 37 Luis A. Gonzalez .30 .10
❑ 38 Benito Santiago .30 .10
❑ 39 Brandon Inge .30 .10
❑ 40 Mark Prior .50 .20
❑ 41 Mike Lieberthal .30 .10
❑ 42 Toby Hall .30 .10
❑ 43 Brad Ausmus .30 .10
❑ 44 Damian Miller .30 .10
❑ 45 Mark Kotsay .30 .10

❑ 46 John Buck .30 .10
❑ 47 Oliver Perez .30 .10
❑ 48 Matt Morris .30 .10
❑ 49 Raul Chavez .30 .10
❑ 50 Randy Johnson .75 .30
❑ 51 Dave Bush .30 .10
❑ 52 Jose Macias .30 .10
❑ 53 Paul Wilson .30 .10
❑ 54 Wilfredo Ledezma .30 .10
❑ 55 J.D. Drew .30 .10
❑ 56 Pedro Martinez .50 .20
❑ 57 Josh Towers .30 .10
❑ 58 Jamie Moyer .30 .10
❑ 59 Scott Elarton .30 .10
❑ 60 Ken Griffey Jr. 1.25 .50
❑ 61 Steve Trachsel .30 .10
❑ 62 Bubba Crosby .30 .10
❑ 63 Michael Barrett .30 .10
❑ 64 Odalis Perez .30 .10
❑ 65 B.J. Upton .30 .10
❑ 66 Eric Bruntlett .30 .10
❑ 67 Victor Zambrano .30 .10
❑ 68 Brandon League .30 .10
❑ 69 Carlos Silva .30 .10
❑ 70 Lyle Overbay .30 .10
❑ 71 Runelvys Hernandez .30 .10
❑ 72 Brad Penny .30 .10
❑ 73 Ty Wigginton .30 .10
❑ 74 Orlando Hudson .30 .10
❑ 75 Roy Oswalt .30 .10
❑ 76 Jason LaRue .30 .10
❑ 77 Ismael Valdez .30 .10
❑ 78 Calvin Pickering .30 .10
❑ 79 Bill Hall .30 .10
❑ 80 Carl Crawford .30 .10
❑ 81 Tomas Perez .30 .10
❑ 82 Joe Kennedy .30 .10
❑ 83 Chris Woodward .30 .10
❑ 84 Jason Lane .30 .10
❑ 85 Steve Finley .30 .10
❑ 86 Jeff Francis .30 .10
❑ 87 Felipe Lopez .30 .10
❑ 88 Chan Ho Park .30 .10
❑ 89 Joe Crede .30 .10
❑ 90 Jose Vidro .30 .10
❑ 91 Casey Kotchman .30 .10
❑ 92 Brandon Backe .30 .10
❑ 93 Mike Hampton .30 .10
❑ 94 Ryan Dempster .30 .10
❑ 95 Wily Mo Pena .30 .10
❑ 96 Matt Holliday .30 .10
❑ 97 A.J. Pierzynski .30 .10
❑ 98 Jason Jennings .30 .10
❑ 99 Eli Marrero .30 .10
❑ 100 Carlos Beltran .30 .10
❑ 101 Scott Kazmir .30 .10
❑ 102 Kenny Rogers .30 .10
❑ 103 Roy Halladay .30 .10
❑ 104 Alex Cora .30 .10
❑ 105 Richie Sexson .30 .10
❑ 106 Ben Sheets .30 .10
❑ 107 Bartolo Colon .30 .10
❑ 108 Eddie Perez .30 .10
❑ 109 Vicente Padilla .30 .10
❑ 110 Sammy Sosa .75 .30
❑ 111 Mark Ellis .30 .10
❑ 112 Woody Williams .30 .10
❑ 113 Todd Greene .30 .10
❑ 114 Nook Logan .30 .10
❑ 115 Francisco Rodriguez .30 .10
❑ 116 Miguel Batista .30 .10
❑ 117 Livan Hernandez .30 .10
❑ 118 Chris Aguila .30 .10
❑ 119 Coco Crisp .30 .10
❑ 120 Jose Reyes .30 .10
❑ 121 Ricky Ledee .30 .10
❑ 122 Brad Radke .30 .10
❑ 123 Carlos Guillen .30 .10
❑ 124 Paul Bako .30 .10
❑ 125 Tom Glavine .50 .20
❑ 126 Chad Moeller .30 .10
❑ 127 Mark Buehrle .30 .10
❑ 128 Casey Blake .30 .10
❑ 129 Juan Rivera .30 .10
❑ 130 Preston Wilson .30 .10
❑ 131 Nate Robertson .30 .10
❑ 132 Julio Franco .30 .10
❑ 133 Derek Lowe .30 .10
❑ 134 Rob Bell .30 .10
❑ 135 Javy Lopez .30 .10
❑ 136 Javier Vazquez .30 .10
❑ 137 Desi Relaford .30 .10
❑ 138 Danny Graves .30 .10
❑ 139 Josh Fogg .30 .10
❑ 140 Bobby Crosby .30 .10
❑ 141 Ramon Castro .30 .10
❑ 142 Jerry Hairston Jr. .30 .10
❑ 143 Morgan Ensberg .30 .10
❑ 144 Brandon Webb .30 .10
❑ 145 Jack Wilson .30 .10
❑ 146 Bill Mueller .30 .10
❑ 147 Troy Glaus .30 .10
❑ 148 Armando Benitez .30 .10
❑ 149 Adam LaRoche .30 .10
❑ 150 Hank Blalock .30 .10
❑ 151 Ryan Franklin .30 .10
❑ 152 Kevin Millwood .30 .10
❑ 153 Jason Marquis .30 .10
❑ 154 Dewon Brazelton .30 .10
❑ 155 Al Leiter .30 .10
❑ 156 Garrett Atkins .30 .10
❑ 157 Todd Walker .30 .10
❑ 158 Kris Benson .30 .10
❑ 159 Eric Milton .30 .10
❑ 160 Bret Boone .30 .10
❑ 161 Matt LeCroy .30 .10
❑ 162 Chris Widger .30 .10
❑ 163 Ruben Gotay .30 .10
❑ 164 Craig Monroe .30 .10
❑ 165 Travis Hafner .30 .10
❑ 166 Vance Wilson .30 .10
❑ 167 Jason Grabowski .30 .10
❑ 168 Tim Salmon .50 .20
❑ 169 Henry Blanco .30 .10
❑ 170 Josh Beckett .30 .10
❑ 171 Jake Westbrook .30 .10
❑ 172 Paul Lo Duca .30 .10
❑ 173 Julio Lugo .30 .10
❑ 174 Juan Cruz .30 .10
❑ 175 Mark Mulder .30 .10
❑ 176 Juan Castro .30 .10
❑ 177 Damion Easley .30 .10
❑ 178 LaTroy Hawkins .30 .10
❑ 179 Jon Lieber .30 .10
❑ 180 Vernon Wells .30 .10
❑ 181 Jeff DaVanon .30 .10
❑ 182 Dustan Mohr .30 .10
❑ 183 Ryan Freel .30 .10
❑ 184 Doug Davis .30 .10
❑ 185 Sean Casey .30 .10
❑ 186 Robb Quinlan .30 .10
❑ 187 J.D. Closser .30 .10
❑ 188 Tim Wakefield .30 .10
❑ 189 Brian Jordan .30 .10
❑ 190 Adam Dunn .30 .10
❑ 191 Antonio Perez .30 .10
❑ 192 Brett Tomko .30 .10
❑ 193 John Flaherty .30 .10
❑ 194 Michael Cuddyer .30 .10
❑ 195 Ronnie Belliard .30 .10
❑ 196 Tony Womack .30 .10
❑ 197 Jason Johnson .30 .10
❑ 198 Victor Santos .30 .10
❑ 199 Danny Haren .30 .10
❑ 200 Derek Jeter 1.50 .60
❑ 201 Brian Anderson .30 .10
❑ 202 Carlos Pena .30 .10
❑ 203 Jaret Wright .30 .10
❑ 204 Paul Byrd .30 .10
❑ 205 Shannon Stewart .30 .10
❑ 206 Chris Carpenter .30 .10
❑ 207 Matt Stairs .30 .10
❑ 208 Brad Hawpe .30 .10
❑ 209 Bobby Higginson .30 .10
❑ 210 Torii Hunter .30 .10
❑ 211 Shawn Green .30 .10
❑ 212 Todd Hollandsworth .30 .10
❑ 213 Scott Erickson .30 .10
❑ 214 C.C. Sabathia .30 .10
❑ 215 Mike Mussina .50 .20
❑ 216 Jason Kendall .30 .10
❑ 217 Todd Pratt .30 .10
❑ 218 Danny Kolb .30 .10
❑ 219 Tony Armas .30 .10
❑ 220 Edgar Renteria .30 .10
❑ 221 Dave Roberts .30 .10
❑ 222 Luis Rivas .30 .10
❑ 223 Adam Everett .30 .10
❑ 224 Jeff Cirillo .30 .10
❑ 225 Orlando Hernandez .30 .10
❑ 226 Ken Harvey .30 .10
❑ 227 Corey Patterson .30 .10
❑ 228 Humberto Cota .30 .10
❑ 229 A.J. Burnett .30 .10
❑ 230 Roger Clemens 1.25 .50
❑ 231 Joe Randa .30 .10
❑ 232 David Dellucci .30 .10
❑ 233 Troy Percival .30 .10
❑ 234 Dustin Hermanson .30 .10
❑ 235 Eric Gagne .30 .10
❑ 236 Terry Tiffee .30 .10
❑ 237 Tony Graffanino .30 .10
❑ 238 Jayson Werth .30 .10
❑ 239 Mark Sweeney .30 .10
❑ 240 Chipper Jones .75 .30
❑ 241 Aramis Ramirez .30 .10
❑ 242 Frank Catalanotto .30 .10
❑ 243 Mike Maroth .30 .10
❑ 244 Kelvim Escobar .30 .10
❑ 245 Bobby Abreu .30 .10
❑ 246 Kyle Lohse .30 .10
❑ 247 Jason Isringhausen .30 .10
❑ 248 Jose Lima .30 .10
❑ 249 Adrian Gonzalez .30 .10
❑ 250 Alex Rodriguez 1.25 .50
❑ 251 Ramon Ortiz .30 .10
❑ 252 Frank Menechino .30 .10
❑ 253 Keith Ginter .30 .10
❑ 254 Kip Wells .30 .10
❑ 255 Dmitri Young .30 .10
❑ 256 Craig Biggio .50 .20
❑ 257 Ramon E. Martinez .30 .10
❑ 258 Jason Bartlett .30 .10
❑ 259 Brad Lidge .30 .10
❑ 260 Brian Giles .30 .10
❑ 261 Luis Terrero .30 .10
❑ 262 Miguel Ojeda .30 .10
❑ 263 Rich Harden .30 .10
❑ 264 Jacque Jones .30 .10
❑ 265 Marcus Giles .30 .10
❑ 266 Carlos Zambrano .30 .10
❑ 267 Michael Tucker .30 .10
❑ 268 Wes Obermueller .30 .10
❑ 269 Pete Orr RC .50 .20
❑ 270 Jim Thome .50 .20
❑ 271 Omar Vizquel .50 .20
❑ 272 Jose Valentin .30 .10
❑ 273 Juan Uribe .30 .10
❑ 274 Doug Mirabelli .30 .10
❑ 275 Jeff Kent .30 .10
❑ 276 Brad Wilkerson .30 .10
❑ 277 Chris Burke .30 .10
❑ 278 Endy Chavez .30 .10
❑ 279 Richard Hidalgo .30 .10
❑ 280 John Smoltz .50 .20
❑ 281 Jarrod Washburn .30 .10
❑ 282 Larry Bigbie .30 .10
❑ 283 Edgardo Alfonzo .30 .10
❑ 284 Cliff Lee .30 .10
❑ 285 Carlos Lee .30 .10
❑ 286 Olmedo Saenz .30 .10
❑ 287 Tomo Ohka .30 .10
❑ 288 Ruben Sierra .30 .10
❑ 289 Nick Swisher .30 .10
❑ 290 Frank Thomas .75 .30
❑ 291 Aaron Cook .30 .10
❑ 292 Cody McKay .30 .10
❑ 293 Hee-Seop Choi .30 .10
❑ 294 Carl Pavano .30 .10
❑ 295 Scott Rolen .50 .20
❑ 296 Matt Kata .30 .10
❑ 297 Terrence Long .30 .10
❑ 298 Jimmy Gobble .30 .10
❑ 299 Jason Repko .30 .10
❑ 300 Manny Ramirez .50 .20
❑ 301 Dan Wilson .30 .10
❑ 302 Jhonny Peralta .30 .10
❑ 303 John Mabry .30 .10

❑ 304 Adam Melhuse	.30	.10
❑ 305 Kerry Wood	.30	.10
❑ 306 Ryan Langerhans	.30	.10
❑ 307 Antonio Alfonseca	.30	.10
❑ 308 Marco Scutaro	.30	.10
❑ 309 Jamey Carroll	.30	.10
❑ 310 Lance Berkman	.30	.10
❑ 311 Willie Harris	.30	.10
❑ 312 Phil Nevin	.30	.10
❑ 313 Gregg Zaun	.30	.10
❑ 314 Michael Ryan	.30	.10
❑ 315 Zack Greinke	.30	.10
❑ 316 Ted Lilly	.30	.10
❑ 317 David Eckstein	.30	.10
❑ 318 Tony Torcato	.30	.10
❑ 319 Rob Mackowiak	.30	.10
❑ 320 Mark Teixeira	.50	.20
❑ 321 Jason Phillips	.30	.10
❑ 322 Jeremy Reed	.30	.10
❑ 323 Bengie Molina	.30	.10
❑ 324 Terrmel Sledge	.30	.10
❑ 325 Justin Morneau	.30	.10
❑ 326 Sandy Alomar Jr.	.30	.10
❑ 327 Jon Garland	.30	.10
❑ 328 Jay Payton	.30	.10
❑ 329 Tino Martinez	.50	.20
❑ 330 Jason Bay	.30	.10
❑ 331 Jeff Conine	.30	.10
❑ 332 Shawn Chacon	.30	.10
❑ 333 Angel Berroa	.30	.10
❑ 334 Reggie Sanders	.30	.10
❑ 335 Kevin Brown	.30	.10
❑ 336 Brady Clark	.30	.10
❑ 337 Casey Fossum	.30	.10
❑ 338 Raul Ibanez	.30	.10
❑ 339 Derrek Lee	.50	.20
❑ 340 Victor Martinez	.30	.10
❑ 341 Kazuhisa Ishii	.30	.10
❑ 342 Royce Clayton	.30	.10
❑ 343 Trot Nixon	.30	.10
❑ 344 Eric Young	.30	.10
❑ 345 Aubrey Huff	.30	.10
❑ 346 Brett Myers	.30	.10
❑ 347 Joey Gathright	.30	.10
❑ 348 Mark Grudzielanek	.30	.10
❑ 349 Scott Spiezio	.30	.10
❑ 350 Eric Chavez	.30	.10
❑ 351 Einar Diaz	.30	.10
❑ 352 Dallas McPherson	.30	.10
❑ 353 John Thomson	.30	.10
❑ 354 Neifi Perez	.30	.10
❑ 355 Larry Walker	.50	.20
❑ 356 Billy Wagner	.30	.10
❑ 357 Mike Cameron	.30	.10
❑ 358 Jimmy Rollins	.30	.10
❑ 359 Kevin Mench	.30	.10
❑ 360 Joe Mauer	.75	.30
❑ 361 Jose Molina	.30	.10
❑ 362 Joe Borchard	.30	.10
❑ 363 Kevin Cash	.30	.10
❑ 364 Jay Gibbons	.30	.10
❑ 365 Khalil Greene	.50	.20
❑ 366 Justin Leone	.30	.10
❑ 367 Eddie Guardado	.30	.10
❑ 368 Mike Lamb	.30	.10
❑ 369 Matt Riley	.30	.10
❑ 370 Luis Gonzalez	.30	.10
❑ 371 Alfredo Amezaga	.30	.10
❑ 372 J.J. Hardy	.30	.10
❑ 373 Hector Luna	.30	.10
❑ 374 Greg Aquino	.30	.10
❑ 375 Jim Edmonds	.30	.10
❑ 376 Joe Blanton	.30	.10
❑ 377 Russell Branyan	.30	.10
❑ 378 J.T. Snow	.30	.10
❑ 379 Magglio Ordonez	.30	.10
❑ 380 Rafael Palmeiro	.50	.20
❑ 381 Andruw Jones	.50	.20
❑ 382 David DeJesus	.30	.10
❑ 383 Marquis Grissom	.30	.10
❑ 384 Bobby Hill	.30	.10
❑ 385 Kazuo Matsui	.30	.10
❑ 386 Mark Loretta	.30	.10
❑ 387 Chris Shelton	.40	.15
❑ 388 Johnny Estrada	.30	.10
❑ 389 Adam Hyzdu	.30	.10
❑ 390 Nomar Garciaparra	.75	.30
❑ 391 Mark Teahen	.30	.10
❑ 392 Chris Capuano	.30	.10
❑ 393 Ben Broussard	.30	.10
❑ 394 Daniel Cabrera	.30	.10
❑ 395 Jeremy Bonderman	.30	.10
❑ 396 Darin Erstad	.30	.10
❑ 397 Alex S. Gonzalez	.30	.10
❑ 398 Kevin Millar	.30	.10
❑ 399 Freddy Garcia	.30	.10
❑ 400 Alfonso Soriano	.30	.10
❑ 401 Koyie Hill	.30	.10
❑ 402 Omar Infante	.30	.10
❑ 403 Alex Gonzalez	.30	.10
❑ 404 Pat Burrell	.30	.10
❑ 405 Wes Helms	.30	.10
❑ 406 Júnior Spivey	.30	.10
❑ 407 Joe Mays	.30	.10
❑ 408 Jason Stanford	.30	.10
❑ 409 Gil Meche	.30	.10
❑ 410 Tim Hudson	.30	.10
❑ 411 Chase Utley	.50	.20
❑ 412 Matt Clement	.30	.10
❑ 413 Nick Green	.30	.10
❑ 414 Jose Vizcaino	.30	.10
❑ 415 Ryan Klesko	.30	.10
❑ 416 Vinny Castilla	.30	.10
❑ 417 Brian Roberts	.30	.10
❑ 418 Geronimo Gil	.30	.10
❑ 419 Gary Matthews	.30	.10
❑ 420 Jeff Weaver	.30	.10
❑ 421 Jerome Williams	.30	.10
❑ 422 Andy Pettitte	.50	.20
❑ 423 Randy Wolf	.30	.10
❑ 424 D'Angelo Jimenez	.30	.10
❑ 425 Moises Alou	.30	.10
❑ 426 Eric Byrnes	.30	.10
❑ 427 Mark Redman	.30	.10
❑ 428 Jermaine Dye	.30	.10
❑ 429 Cory Lidle	.30	.10
❑ 430 Jason Schmidt	.30	.10
❑ 431 Jason W. Smith	.30	.10
❑ 432 Jose Castillo	.30	.10
❑ 433 Pokey Reese	.30	.10
❑ 434 Matt Lawton	.30	.10
❑ 435 Jose Guillen	.30	.10
❑ 436 Craig Counsell	.30	.10
❑ 437 Jose Hernandez	.30	.10
❑ 438 Braden Looper	.30	.10
❑ 439 Scott Hatteberg	.30	.10
❑ 440 Gary Sheffield	.30	.10
❑ 441 Gabe Gross	.30	.10
❑ 442 Chris Gomez	.30	.10
❑ 443 Dontrelle Willis	.30	.10
❑ 444 Jamey Wright	.30	.10
❑ 445 Rocco Baldelli	.30	.10
❑ 446 Bernie Williams	.50	.20
❑ 447 Sean Burroughs	.30	.10
❑ 448 Willie Bloomquist	.30	.10
❑ 449 Luis Castillo	.30	.10
❑ 450 Mike Piazza	.75	.30
❑ 451 Ryan Drese	.30	.10
❑ 452 Pedro Feliz	.30	.10
❑ 453 Horacio Ramirez	.30	.10
❑ 454 Luis Matos	.30	.10
❑ 455 Craig Wilson	.30	.10
❑ 456 Russ Ortiz	.30	.10
❑ 457 Xavier Nady	.30	.10
❑ 458 Hideo Nomo	.75	.30
❑ 459 Miguel Cairo	.30	.10
❑ 460 Mike Lowell	.30	.10
❑ 461 Corky Miller	.30	.10
❑ 462 Bobby Madritsch	.30	.10
❑ 463 Jose Contreras	.30	.10
❑ 464 Johnny Damon	.50	.20
❑ 465 Miguel Cabrera	.50	.20
❑ 466 Eric Hinske	.30	.10
❑ 467 Marlon Byrd	.30	.10
❑ 468 Aaron Miles	.30	.10
❑ 469 Ramon Vazquez	.30	.10
❑ 470 Michael Young	.30	.10
❑ 471 Alex Sanchez	.30	.10
❑ 472 Shea Hillenbrand	.30	.10
❑ 473 Jeff Bagwell	.50	.20
❑ 474 Erik Bedard	.30	.10
❑ 475 Jake Peavy	.30	.10
❑ 476 Jody Gerut	.30	.10
❑ 477 Randy Winn	.30	.10
❑ 478 Kevin Youkilis	.30	.10
❑ 479 Eric Dubose	.30	.10
❑ 480 David Wright	1.25	.50
❑ 481 Wilson Valdez	.30	.10
❑ 482 Cliff Floyd	.30	.10
❑ 483 Jose Mesa	.30	.10
❑ 484 Doug Mientkiewicz	.30	.10
❑ 485 Jorge Posada	.50	.20
❑ 486 Sidney Ponson	.30	.10
❑ 487 Dave Krynzel	.30	.10
❑ 488 Octavio Dotel	.30	.10
❑ 489 Matt Treanor	.30	.10
❑ 490 Johan Santana	.75	.30
❑ 491 John Patterson	.30	.10
❑ 492 So Taguchi	.30	.10
❑ 493 Carl Everett	.30	.10
❑ 494 Jason Dubois	.30	.10
❑ 495 Albert Pujols	1.50	.60
❑ 496 Kirk Rueter	.30	.10
❑ 497 Geoff Blum	.30	.10
❑ 498 Juan Encarnacion	.30	.10
❑ 499 Mark Hendrickson	.30	.10
❑ 500 Barry Bonds	2.00	.75
❑ 501 Cesar Izturis	.30	.10
❑ 502 David Wells	.30	.10
❑ 503 Jorge Julio	.30	.10
❑ 504 Cristian Guzman	.30	.10
❑ 505 Juan Pierre	.30	.10
❑ 506 Adam Eaton	.30	.10
❑ 507 Nick Johnson	.30	.10
❑ 508 Mike Redmond	.30	.10
❑ 509 Daryle Ward	.30	.10
❑ 510 Adrian Beltre	.30	.10
❑ 511 Laynce Nix	.30	.10
❑ 512 Reed Johnson	.30	.10
❑ 513 Jeremy Affeldt	.30	.10
❑ 514 R.A. Dickey	.30	.10
❑ 515 Alex Rios	.30	.10
❑ 516 Orlando Palmeiro	.30	.10
❑ 517 Mark Bellhorn	.30	.10
❑ 518 Adam Kennedy	.30	.10
❑ 519 Curtis Granderson	.30	.10
❑ 520 Todd Helton	.50	.20
❑ 521 Aaron Boone	.30	.10
❑ 522 Milton Bradley	.30	.10
❑ 523 Timo Perez	.30	.10
❑ 524 Jeff Suppan	.30	.10
❑ 525 Austin Kearns	.30	.10
❑ 526 Charles Thomas	.30	.10
❑ 527 Bronson Arroyo	.30	.10
❑ 528 Roger Cedeno	.30	.10
❑ 529 Russ Adams	.30	.10
❑ 530 Barry Zito	.30	.10
❑ 531 Bob Wickman	.30	.10
❑ 532 Deivi Cruz	.30	.10
❑ 533 Mariano Rivera	.75	.30
❑ 534 J.J. Davis	.30	.10
❑ 535 Greg Maddux	1.25	.50
❑ 536 Ryan Vogelsong	.30	.10
❑ 537 Josh Phelps	.30	.10
❑ 538 Scott Hairston	.30	.10
❑ 539 Vladimir Guerrero	.75	.30
❑ 540 Ivan Rodriguez	.50	.20
❑ 541 David Newhan	.30	.10
❑ 542 David Bell	.30	.10
❑ 543 Lew Ford	.30	.10
❑ 544 Grady Sizemore	.50	.20
❑ 545 David Ortiz	.75	.30
❑ 546 Jose Cruz Jr.	.30	.10
❑ 547 Aaron Rowand	.30	.10
❑ 548 Marcus Thames	.30	.10
❑ 549 Scott Podsednik	.30	.10
❑ 550 Ichiro Suzuki	1.50	.60
❑ 551 Eduardo Perez	.30	.10
❑ 552 Chris Snyder	.30	.10
❑ 553 Corey Koskie	.30	.10
❑ 554 Miguel Tejada	.30	.10
❑ 555 Orlando Cabrera	.30	.10
❑ 556 Rondell White	.30	.10
❑ 557 Wade Miller	.30	.10
❑ 558 Rodrigo Lopez	.30	.10
❑ 559 Chad Tracy	.30	.10
❑ 560 Paul Konerko	.30	.10
❑ 561 Wil Cordero	.30	.10

❑ 562 John McDonald .30 .10
❑ 563 Jason Ellison .30 .10
❑ 564 Jason Michaels .30 .10
❑ 565 Melvin Mora .30 .10
❑ 566 Ryan Church .30 .10
❑ 567 Ryan Ludwick .30 .10
❑ 568 Erubiel Durazo .30 .10
❑ 569 Noah Lowry .30 .10
❑ 570 Curt Schilling .50 .20
❑ 571 Esteban Loaiza .30 .10
❑ 572 Freddy Sanchez .30 .10
❑ 573 Rich Aurilia .30 .10
❑ 574 Travis Lee .30 .10
❑ 575 Nick Punto .30 .10
❑ 576 J.Christiansen/K.Correia .30 .10
❑ 577 B.Baker/T.Redding .30 .10
❑ 578 T.Adams/G.Floyd .30 .10
❑ 579 S.Etherton/D.Meyer .30 .10
❑ 580 J.Lehr/D.Turnbow .30 .10
❑ 581 M.Gosling/B.Halsey .30 .10
❑ 582 J.Mecir/L.Kensing .30 .10
❑ 583 B.Hennessey/J.Fassero .30 .10
❑ 584 J.Adkins/F.Diaz .30 .10
❑ 585 J.Crain/J.Rincon .30 .10
❑ 586 J.Cerda/N.Field .30 .10
❑ 587 B.Fortunato/J.Seo .30 .10
❑ 588 S.Schmoll RC/Y.Brazoban .50 .20
❑ 589 U.Urbina/J.Walker .30 .10
❑ 590 J.De Paula/S.Proctor .30 .10
❑ 591 J.Davis/B.Howry .30 .10
❑ 592 T.Worrell/P.Liriano .30 .10
❑ 593 J.Acevedo/K.Mercker .30 .10
❑ 594 C.Hammond/S.Linebrink .30 .10
❑ 595 F.Nieve/J.Franco .30 .10
❑ 596 R.Flores/M.Lincoln .30 .10
❑ 597 J.Borowski/S.Mitre .30 .10
❑ 598 L.Carter/J.Colome .30 .10
❑ 599 J.Halama/L.DiNardo .30 .10
❑ 600 C.Bradford/K.Calero .30 .10
❑ 601 D.Aardsma/J.Brower .30 .10
❑ 602 G.Geary/R.Madson .30 .10
❑ 603 B.Moehler/N.Bump .30 .10
❑ 604 C.Tsao/R.Speier .30 .10
❑ 605 R.Wagner/A.Harang .30 .10
❑ 606 S.Kline/R.Bauer .30 .10
❑ 607 L.Cormier/R.Choate .30 .10
❑ 608 J.Leicester/T.Wellemeyer .30 .10
❑ 609 V.Chulk/J.Frasor .30 .10
❑ 610 S.Dohmann/B.Fuentes .30 .10
❑ 611 S.Colyer/R.Hernandez .30 .10
❑ 612 I.Snell/S.Torres .30 .10
❑ 613 C.Eldred/A.Wainwright .30 .10
❑ 614 R.Bukvich/D.Brocail .30 .10
❑ 615 J.Putz/A.Sele .30 .10
❑ 616 B.Chen/T.Williams .30 .10
❑ 617 D.Weathers/B.Weber .30 .10
❑ 618 D.Reyes/R.Seanez .30 .10
❑ 619 T.Harikkala/R.Rincon .30 .10
❑ 620 S.Camp/D.Bautista .30 .10
❑ 621 J.Lopez/A.Simpson .30 .10
❑ 622 M.Remlinger/G.Rusch .30 .10
❑ 623 R.Colon/K.Gryboski .30 .10
❑ 624 T.Martin/C.Reitsma .30 .10
❑ 625 C.Qualls/D.Wheeler .30 .10
❑ 626 T.Phelps/M.Wise .30 .10
❑ 627 S.Schoeneweis/J.Speier .30 .10
❑ 628 F.Cordero/F.Francisco .30 .10
❑ 629 R.Soriano/M.Thornton .30 .10
❑ 630 M.Stanton/S.Karsay .30 .10
❑ 631 M.MacDougal/S.Sullivan .30 .10
❑ 632 B.Bruney/O.Villarreal .30 .10
❑ 633 M.Adams/R.Bottalico .30 .10
❑ 634 E.Rodriguez/D.Borkowski .30 .10
❑ 635 R.Betancourt/D.Riske .30 .10
❑ 636 J.De La Rosa/G.Glover .30 .10
❑ 637 M.Perisho/B.Howard .30 .10
❑ 638 J.Bajenaru/L.Vizcaino .30 .10
❑ 639 R.Mahay/E.Ramirez .30 .10
❑ 640 J.Grabow/M.Gonzalez .30 .10
❑ 641 J.Romero/M.Guerrier .30 .10
❑ 642 C.Hernandez/B.Duckworth .30 .10
❑ 643 T.Harper/S.McClung .30 .10
❑ 644 M.Herges/T.Walker .30 .10
❑ 645 K.Wunsch/E.Dessens .30 .10
❑ 646 M.Malaska/M.Myers .30 .10
❑ 647 K.Farnsworth/G.Knotts .30 .10
❑ 648 J.Duchscherer/J.Garcia .30 .10
❑ 649 A.Rakers/S.Reed .30 .10
❑ 650 T.Gordon/P.Quantrill .30 .10
❑ 651 B.Lyon/S.Estes .30 .10
❑ 652 P.Walker/G.Chacin .30 .10
❑ 653 J.Lackey/S.Shields .30 .10
❑ 654 D.Waechter/T.Miller .30 .10
❑ 655 L.Ayala/C.Cordero .30 .10
❑ 656 R.Villone/J.Mateo .30 .10
❑ 657 M.Mantei/B.Neal .30 .10
❑ 658 D.Marte/C.Politte .30 .10
❑ 659 J.Valentine/L.Hudson .30 .10
❑ 660 T.Jones/J.Riedling .30 .10
❑ 661 H.Bell/A.Heilman .30 .10
❑ 662 D.May/A.Otsuka .30 .10
❑ 663 J.Eischen/J.Horgan .30 .10
❑ 664 A.Sisco/M.Wood .30 .10
❑ 665 A.Embree/M.Timlin .30 .10
❑ 666 Keith Foulke .30 .10
❑ 667 R.Cormier/A.Fultz .30 .10
❑ 668 J.Woods/K.Gregg .30 .10
❑ 669 M.Ginter/F.German .30 .10
❑ 670 S.Eyre/M.Valdez .30 .10
❑ 671 B.Meadows/R.White .30 .10
❑ 672 G.Mota/T.Spooneybarger .30 .10
❑ 673 J.Grimsley/B.Ryan .30 .10
❑ 674 N.Cotts/S.Takatsu .30 .10
❑ 675 M.DeJean/F.Heredia .30 .10
❑ 676 M.Belisle/J.Hancock .30 .10
❑ 677 J.Rauch/T.Tucker .30 .10
❑ 678 N.Regilio/B.Shouse .30 .10
❑ 679 J.Tavarez/R.King .30 .10
❑ 680 C.Fox/M.Wuertz .30 .10
❑ 681 J.Sosa/A.Bernero .30 .10
❑ 682 J.Valverde/M.Koplove .30 .10
❑ 683 A.Rhodes/S.Sauerbeck .30 .10
❑ 684 F.Rodriguez/T.Sturtze .30 .10
❑ 685 G.Carrara/D.Sanchez .30 .10
❑ 686 M.Gallo/C.Harville .30 .10
❑ 687 M.Johnston/S.Burnett .30 .10
❑ 688 J.Nelson/S.Hasegawa .30 .10
❑ 689 C.Vargas/A.Osuna .30 .10
❑ 690 B.Donnelly/E.Yan .30 .10
❑ 691 J.Mathis/E.Santana .50 .20
❑ 692 C.Everts/B.Bray .50 .20
❑ 693 J.Kubel/T.Plouffe .50 .20
❑ 694 J.Stevens/A.Marte .50 .20
❑ 695 A.Hill/C.Gaudin .50 .20
❑ 696 C.Quentin/J.Cota .50 .20
❑ 697 T.Diamond/C.Young .50 .20
❑ 698 O.Quintanilla/D.Johnson .50 .20
❑ 699 J.Maine/V.Majewski .50 .20
❑ 700 J.Houser/J.Gomes .50 .20
❑ 701 D.Murphy/H.Ramirez .50 .20
❑ 702 C.Lambert/R.Ankiel .50 .20
❑ 703 F.Pie/A.Guzman .50 .20
❑ 704 F.Lewis/N.Schierholtz .50 .20
❑ 705 A.Munoz/G.Gonzalez .50 .20
❑ 706 F.Hernandez/T.Blackley 1.50 .60
❑ 707 R.Olmedo/E.Encarnacion .50 .20
❑ 708 T.Stauffer/J.Germano .50 .20
❑ 709 J.Guthrie/J.Sowers .50 .20
❑ 710 J.Cortes/T.Gorzelanny .50 .20
❑ 711 T.Tankersley/E.Reed .50 .20
❑ 712 N.Walker/P.Maholm .50 .20
❑ 713 W.Taveras/L.Scott RC 1.50 .60
❑ 714 R.Howard/G.Golson 2.00 .75
❑ 715 B.DeWitt/E.Jackson .50 .20
❑ 716 H.Street/D.Putnam .50 .20
❑ 717 R.Weeks/M.Rogers .50 .20
❑ 718 R.Cano/P.Hughes .50 .20
❑ 719 K.Waldrop/J.Rainville .50 .20
❑ 720 C.Brazell/Y.Petit .50 .20
❑ 721 B.Lopez RC/M.Brown RC .50 .20
❑ 722 D.Thomp RC/E.Chavez RC .50 .20
❑ 723 D.Uggla RC/E.Sch'wolf RC 10.00 4.00
❑ 724 I.Ramirez RC/J.Tingler RC .50 .20
❑ 725 T.G'tano RC/E.de la Cruz RC .50 .20
❑ 726 M.Campbell RC/S.Costa RC .50 .20
❑ 727 M.Prado RC/Bi.McCarthy RC .50 .20
❑ 728 I.Kinsler RC/J.Senreiso RC 2.00 .75
❑ 729 L.Ramirez RC/Lo.Scott RC .50 .20
❑ 730 C.Seddon RC/E.Johnson RC .50 .20
❑ 731 C.Tatum RC/J.Moran RC .50 .20
❑ 732 S.Pomeranz RC/J.Motte RC .50 .20
❑ 733 J.Vaquedano RC/S.Bailie RC .50 .20
❑ 734 M.Albers RC/W.Robinson RC 1.25 .50
❑ 735 M.DeSalvo RC/Me.Cabr RC 2.00 .75
❑ 736 B.Stavisky RC/L.Powell RC .50 .20
❑ 737 S.Mathieson RC/S.Mitch RC .75 .30
❑ 738 S.Marshall RC/B.Bay RC 1.50 .60
❑ 739 B.McCarthy RC/P.Lopez RC 1.25 .50
❑ 740 A.Smit RC/R.Barrett RC .50 .20
❑ 741 M.R'stad RC/R.F'bend RC .50 .20
❑ 742 N.McLouth RC/A.Boeve RC .50 .20
❑ 743 K.Melillo RC/M.Rogers RC .75 .30
❑ 744 M.Kemp RC/H.Totten RC 4.00 1.50
❑ 745 J.Miller RC/T.Americh RC .50 .20
❑ 746 T.Pelland RC/J.Gutierrez RC .50 .20
❑ 747 J.West RC/W.Mota RC .50 .20
❑ 748 R.Goleski RC/R.Garko RC 1.50 .60
❑ 749 B.Triplett RC/J.Gothreaux RC .50 .20
❑ 750 K.West RC/G.Perkins RC .75 .30
❑ 751 M.Esposito RC/Z.Parker RC .50 .20
❑ 752 R.Sweeney RC/B.Miller RC 1.00 .40
❑ 753 C.McGehee RC/B.Coats RC .50 .20
❑ 754 M.Bourn RC/K.Pichardo RC .75 .30
❑ 755 M.Morse RC/B.Livingston RC .75 .30
❑ 756 W.Swack RC/B.Ryan RC .50 .20
❑ 757 M.Furtado RC/N.Masset RC .50 .20
❑ 758 P.Ramos RC/G.Kottaras RC .75 .30
❑ 759 E.Quezada RC/T.Beam RC .75 .30
❑ 760 D.Eveland RC/T.Hinton RC .50 .20
❑ 761 J.Jurries RC/C.Vines RC .50 .20
❑ 762 H.Sanch RC/J.Verlander RC 5.00 2.00
❑ 763 P.Humber RC/S.Bowman RC .75 .30
❑ 764 P.Misch RC/J.Thurmond RC .50 .20
❑ 765 C.Colonel RC/N.Wilson RC .50 .20
❑ 766 Checklist 1 .30 .10
❑ 767 Checklist 2 .30 .10
❑ 768 Checklist 3 .30 .10
❑ 769 Checklist 4 .30 .10
❑ 770 Checklist 5 .30 .10

2006 Topps Triple Threads

❑ COMMON CARD (1-100) 4.00 1.50
❑ 1-100 THREE PER PACK
❑ COMMON CARD (101-120) 15.00 6.00
❑ MINOR STARS 101-112 25.00 10.00
❑ SEMISTARS 101-112 40.00 15.00
❑ COMMON CARD (113-120) 15.00 6.00
❑ MINOR STARS 113-120 25.00 10.00
❑ SEMISTARS 113-120 40.00 15.00
❑ 101-120 ODDS 1:7 MINI
❑ 101-120 PRINT RUN 225 SERIAL #'d SETS
❑ OVERALL 1-100 PLATE ODDS 1:80 MINI
❑ PLATE PRINT RUN 1 SET PER COLOR
❑ BLACK-CYAN-MAGENTA-YELLOW ISSUED
❑ NO PLATE PRICING DUE TO SCARCITY
❑ 1 Hideki Matsui 5.00 2.00
❑ 2 Josh Gibson HOF 5.00 2.00
❑ 3 Roger Clemens 8.00 3.00
❑ 4 Paul Konerko 3.00 1.25
❑ 5 Brooks Robinson HOF 4.00 1.50
❑ 6 Stan Musial HOF 5.00 2.00
❑ 7 Dontrelle Willis 3.00 1.25
❑ 8 Yogi Berra HOF 5.00 2.00
❑ 9 John Smoltz 4.00 1.50
❑ 10 Brian Roberts 3.00 1.25
❑ 11 Gary Sheffield 3.00 1.25
❑ 12 Wade Boggs HOF 4.00 1.50
❑ 13 Alex Rodriguez 8.00 3.00
❑ 14 Ernie Banks HOF 5.00 2.00

❑ 15 Ichiro Suzuki 8.00 3.00
❑ 16 Whitey Ford HOF 4.00 1.50
❑ 17 Vladimir Guerrero 5.00 2.00
❑ 18 Tadahito Iguchi 3.00 1.25
❑ 19 Robin Yount HOF 5.00 2.00
❑ 20 Jason Schmidt 3.00 1.25
❑ 21 Roberto Clemente HOF 10.00 4.00
❑ 22 Andruw Jones 4.00 1.50
❑ 23 Don Mattingly HOF 10.00 4.00
❑ 24 Joe Mauer 4.00 1.50
❑ 25 Barry Bonds 12.00 5.00
❑ 26 Johnny Damon 4.00 1.50
❑ 27 Chris Carpenter 3.00 1.25
❑ 28 Garret Anderson 3.00 1.25
❑ 29 Scott Rolen 4.00 1.50
❑ 30 Tim Hudson 3.00 1.25
❑ 31 Dave Winfield HOF 3.00 1.25
❑ 32 Steve Carlton HOF 3.00 1.25
❑ 33 Miguel Tejada 3.00 1.25
❑ 34 Nolan Ryan HOF 10.00 4.00
❑ 35 Mark Buehrle 3.00 1.25
❑ 36 Travis Hafner 3.00 1.25
❑ 37 Rickie Weeks 3.00 1.25
❑ 38 Sammy Sosa 5.00 2.00
❑ 39 Carlos Beltran 3.00 1.25
❑ 40 Todd Helton 4.00 1.50
❑ 41 Tom Seaver HOF 4.00 1.50
❑ 42 Ted Williams HOF 6.00 2.50
❑ 43 Alfonso Soriano 3.00 1.25
❑ 44 Reggie Jackson HOF 4.00 1.50
❑ 45 Pedro Martinez 4.00 1.50
❑ 46 Randy Johnson 5.00 2.00
❑ 47 Ted Williams HOF 6.00 2.50
❑ 48 Torii Hunter 3.00 1.25
❑ 49 Manny Ramirez 4.00 1.50
❑ 50 George Brett HOF 6.00 2.50
❑ 51 Chipper Jones 5.00 2.00
❑ 52 Nomar Garciaparra 4.00 1.50
❑ 53 Richie Sexson 3.00 1.25
❑ 54 David Ortiz 5.00 2.00
❑ 55 Derek Jeter 15.00 6.00
❑ 56 Mickey Mantle HOF 15.00 6.00
❑ 57 Michael Young 3.00 1.25
❑ 58 Aramis Ramirez 3.00 1.25
❑ 59 Bartolo Colon 3.00 1.25
❑ 60 Troy Glaus 3.00 1.25
❑ 61 Carlos Delgado 3.00 1.25
❑ 62 Mike Sweeney 3.00 1.25
❑ 63 Jorge Cantu 3.00 1.25
❑ 64 Mike Mussina 4.00 1.50
❑ 65 Hank Blalock 3.00 1.25
❑ 66 Frank Robinson HOF 3.00 1.25
❑ 67 Carl Yastrzemski HOF 5.00 2.00
❑ 68 Adam Dunn 3.00 1.25
❑ 69 Eric Chavez 3.00 1.25
❑ 70 Curt Schilling 4.00 1.50
❑ 71 Jeff Francoeur 6.00 2.50
❑ 72 C.C. Sabathia 3.00 1.25
❑ 73 Roy Oswalt 3.00 1.25
❑ 74 Carlos Lee 3.00 1.25
❑ 75 Barry Zito 3.00 1.25
❑ 76 Derrek Lee 4.00 1.50
❑ 77 Greg Maddux 6.00 2.50
❑ 78 Ivan Rodriguez 4.00 1.50
❑ 79 Jeff Kent 3.00 1.25
❑ 80 Gary Carter HOF 3.00 1.25
❑ 81 Jose Reyes 3.00 1.25
❑ 82 Johan Santana 4.00 1.50
❑ 83 Magglio Ordonez 3.00 1.25
❑ 84 Mark Prior 4.00 1.50
❑ 85 Johnny Bench HOF 5.00 2.00
❑ 86 Vernon Wells 3.00 1.25
❑ 87 Mark Mulder 3.00 1.25
❑ 88 Cal Ripken 15.00 6.00
❑ 89 Mark Teixeira 4.00 1.50
❑ 90 Miguel Cabrera 4.00 1.50
❑ 91 Duke Snider HOF 4.00 1.50
❑ 92 Jason Giambi 3.00 1.25
❑ 93 Albert Pujols 8.00 3.00
❑ 94 Carl Crawford 3.00 1.25
❑ 95 Jim Edmonds 3.00 1.25
❑ 96 Jose Contreras 3.00 1.25
❑ 97 Victor Martinez 3.00 1.25
❑ 98 Jeremy Bonderman 3.00 1.25
❑ 99 Lance Berkman 3.00 1.25
❑ 100 Rocco Baldelli 3.00 1.25
❑ 101 Zach Duke AU J-J 25.00 10.00
❑ 102 Felix Hernandez AU J-J 40.00 15.00
❑ 103 Dan Johnson AU J-J 15.00 6.00
❑ 104 Brandon McCarthy AU J-J 25.00 10.00
❑ 105 Huston Street AU J-J 25.00 10.00
❑ 106 Robinson Cano AU J-J 50.00 20.00
❑ 107 Jason Bay AU J-J 25.00 10.00
❑ 108 Ryan Howard AU B-B 120.00 60.00
❑ 109 Ervin Santana AU J-J 15.00 6.00
❑ 110 Rich Harden AU J-J 15.00 6.00
❑ 111 Aaron Hill AU J-J 15.00 6.00
❑ 112 David Wright AU J-J 60.00 30.00
❑ 113 Rich Hill AU J-J (RC) 15.00 6.00
❑ 114 Nelson Cruz AU J-J (RC) 15.00 6.00
❑ 115 F.Liriano AU J-J (RC) 100.00 50.00
❑ 116 Hong-Chih Kuo AU J-J (RC) 120.00 60.00
❑ 117 Ryan Garko AU J-J (RC) 25.00 10.00
❑ 118 Craig Hansen AU J-J RC 50.00 20.00
❑ 119 Shin-Soo Choo AU J-J (RC) 15.00 6.00
❑ 120 Darrell Rasner AU J-J (RC) 15.00 6.00

2006 Topps Turkey Red

❑ COMPLETE SET (330) 250.00 150.00
❑ COMP.SET w/o SP's (275) 40.00 15.00
❑ COMMON CARD (316-580) .40 .15
❑ COMMON SP (316-580) 8.00 3.00
❑ SP UNLISTED 316-580 8.00 3.00
❑ SP STATED ODDS 1:4 HOBBY, 1:4 RETAIL
❑ SEE BECKETT.COM FOR SP CHECKLIST
❑ COMMON CL (571-580) .20 .07
❑ CL SEMIS 571-580 .30 .12
❑ COMMON RET (581-590) .75 .30
❑ COMMON RC (591-630) 1.00 .40
❑ OVERALL PLATE ODDS 1:477 H
❑ PLATE PRINT RUN 1 SET PER COLOR
❑ BLACK-CYAN-MAGENTA-YELLOW ISSUED
❑ NO PLATE PRICING DUE TO SCARCITY
❑ 316A A.Rodriguez Yanks 1.50 .60
❑ 316B A.Rodriguez Rangers SP 10.00 4.00
❑ 316C Alex Rodriguez M's SP 10.00 4.00
❑ 317 Jeff Francoeur SP 8.00 3.00
❑ 318 Shawn Green .40 .15
❑ 319 Daniel Cabrera .40 .15
❑ 320 Craig Biggio .60 .25
❑ 321 Jeremy Bonderman .40 .15
❑ 322 Mark Kotsay .40 .15
❑ 323 Cliff Floyd .40 .15
❑ 324 Jimmy Rollins .40 .15
❑ 325A M.Ordonez Tigers .40 .15
❑ 325B M.Ordonez W.Sox SP 8.00 3.00
❑ 326 C.C. Sabathia .40 .15
❑ 327 Oliver Perez .40 .15
❑ 328 Orlando Hudson .40 .15
❑ 329 Chris Ray .40 .15
❑ 330 Manny Ramirez .60 .25
❑ 331 Paul Konerko .40 .15
❑ 332 Joe Mauer SP 8.00 3.00
❑ 333 Jorge Posada .60 .25
❑ 334 Mark Ellis .40 .15
❑ 335 A.J. Burnett .40 .15
❑ 336 Mike Sweeney .40 .15
❑ 337 Shannon Stewart .40 .15
❑ 338 Jake Peavy SP 8.00 3.00
❑ 339A C.Delgado Mets SP 8.00 3.00
❑ 339B C.Delgado B.Jays SP 8.00 3.00
❑ 340 Brian Roberts .40 .15
❑ 341 Dontrelle Willis .40 .15
❑ 342 Aaron Rowand .40 .15
❑ 343A R.Sexson M's .40 .15
❑ 343B R.Sexson Brewers SP 8.00 3.00
❑ 344 Chris Carpenter .40 .15
❑ 345 Carlos Zambrano .40 .15
❑ 346 Nomar Garciaparra 1.00 .40
❑ 347 Carlos Lee .40 .15
❑ 348A P.Wilson Astros .40 .15
❑ 348B P.Wilson Marlins SP 8.00 3.00
❑ 349 Mariano Rivera 1.00 .40
❑ 350 Ichiro Suzuki SP 10.00 4.00
❑ 351A M.Piazza Padres 1.00 .40
❑ 351B Mike Piazza Mets SP 8.00 3.00
❑ 352 Jason Schmidt .40 .15
❑ 353 Jeff Weaver .40 .15
❑ 354 Rocco Baldelli .40 .15
❑ 355 Adam Dunn .40 .15
❑ 356 Jeromy Burnitz .40 .15
❑ 357 Chris Shelton SP 8.00 3.00
❑ 358 Chone Figgins SP 8.00 3.00
❑ 359 Javier Vazquez .40 .15
❑ 360 Chipper Jones 1.00 .40
❑ 361 Frank Thomas 1.00 .40
❑ 362 Mark Loretta .40 .15
❑ 363 Hideki Matsui 1.00 .40
❑ 364 J.J. Hardy SP 8.00 3.00
❑ 365 Todd Helton .60 .25
❑ 366 Reggie Sanders .40 .15
❑ 367 Jay Gibbons .40 .15
❑ 368 Johnny Estrada .40 .15
❑ 369 Grady Sizemore .60 .25
❑ 370 Jim Thome .60 .25
❑ 371 Ivan Rodriguez .60 .25
❑ 372 Jason Bay .40 .15
❑ 373 Carl Crawford .40 .15
❑ 374 Adrian Beltre .40 .15
❑ 375 Derrek Lee SP 8.00 3.00
❑ 376 Miguel Olivo .40 .15
❑ 377 Roy Oswalt .40 .15
❑ 378 Coco Crisp .40 .15
❑ 379 Moises Alou .40 .15
❑ 380 Kevin Millwood .40 .15
❑ 381 Mark Grudzielanek .40 .15
❑ 382 Justin Morneau .40 .15
❑ 383 Austin Kearns .40 .15
❑ 384 Brad Penny .40 .15
❑ 385 Troy Glaus .40 .15
❑ 386 Cliff Lee .40 .15
❑ 387 Armando Benitez .40 .15
❑ 388 Clint Barmes .40 .15
❑ 389 Orlando Cabrera .40 .15
❑ 390 Jim Edmonds SP 8.00 3.00
❑ 391 Jermaine Dye .40 .15
❑ 392 Morgan Ensberg SP 8.00 3.00
❑ 393 Paul LoDuca .40 .15
❑ 394 Eric Chavez .40 .15
❑ 395 Greg Maddux SP 10.00 4.00
❑ 396 Jack Wilson .40 .15
❑ 397 Omar Vizquel .60 .25
❑ 398 Joe Nathan .40 .15
❑ 399 Bobby Abreu .40 .15
❑ 400 Barry Bonds SP 15.00 6.00
❑ 401 Gary Sheffield .40 .15
❑ 402 John Patterson .40 .15
❑ 403 J.D. Drew .40 .15
❑ 404 Bruce Chen .40 .15
❑ 405 Johnny Damon SP 8.00 3.00
❑ 406 Aubrey Huff .40 .15
❑ 407 Mark Mulder .40 .15
❑ 408 Jamie Moyer .40 .15
❑ 409 Carlos Guillen .40 .15
❑ 410 Andruw Jones SP 8.00 3.00
❑ 411 Jhonny Peralta SP 8.00 3.00
❑ 412 Doug Davis .40 .15
❑ 413 Aaron Miles .40 .15
❑ 414 Jon Lieber .40 .15
❑ 415 Aaron Hill .40 .15
❑ 416 Josh Beckett SP 8.00 3.00
❑ 417 Bobby Crosby .40 .15
❑ 418 Noah Lowry SP 8.00 3.00
❑ 419 Sidney Ponson .40 .15
❑ 420 Luis Castillo .40 .15
❑ 421 Brad Wilkerson .40 .15
❑ 422 Felix Hernandez SP 8.00 3.00
❑ 423 Vinny Castilla .40 .15
❑ 424 Tom Glavine .60 .25
❑ 425 Vladimir Guerrero 1.00 .40

❑ 426 Javy Lopez .40 .15
❑ 427 Ronnie Belliard .40 .15
❑ 428 Dmitri Young .40 .15
❑ 429 Johan Santana .60 .25
❑ 430A D.Ortiz Red Sox SP 8.00 3.00
❑ 430B D.Ortiz Twins SP 8.00 3.00
❑ 431 Ben Sheets .40 .15
❑ 432 Matt Holliday .40 .15
❑ 433 Brian McCann .40 .15
❑ 434 Joe Blanton .40 .15
❑ 435 Sean Casey .40 .15
❑ 436 Brad Lidge .40 .15
❑ 437 Chad Tracy .40 .15
❑ 438 Brett Myers .40 .15
❑ 439 Matt Morris .40 .15
❑ 440 Brian Giles .40 .15
❑ 441 Zach Duke .40 .15
❑ 442 Jose Lopez .40 .15
❑ 443 Kris Benson .40 .15
❑ 444 Jose Reyes SP 8.00 3.00
❑ 445 Travis Hafner .40 .15
❑ 446 Orlando Hernandez .40 .15
❑ 447 Edgar Renteria .40 .15
❑ 448 Scott Podsednik .40 .15
❑ 449 Nick Swisher SP 8.00 3.00
❑ 450 Derek Jeter SP 15.00 6.00
❑ 451 Scott Kazmir SP 8.00 3.00
❑ 452 Hank Blalock .40 .15
❑ 453 Jake Westbrook .40 .15
❑ 454 Miguel Cabrera .60 .25
❑ 455A K.Griffey Jr. Reds 1.50 .60
❑ 455B K.Griffey Jr. M's SP 10.00 4.00
❑ 456 Rafael Furcal .40 .15
❑ 457 Lance Berkman .40 .15
❑ 458 Aramis Ramirez .40 .15
❑ 459A X.Nady Mets .40 .15
❑ 459B X.Nady Padres SP 8.00 3.00
❑ 460A R.Johnson Yanks 1.00 .40
❑ 460B R.Johnson Astros SP 8.00 3.00
❑ 461 Khalil Greene .60 .25
❑ 462 Bartolo Colon .40 .15
❑ 463 Mike Lowell .40 .15
❑ 464 David DeJesus .40 .15
❑ 465 Ryan Howard SP 10.00 4.00
❑ 466 Tim Salmon SP 8.00 3.00
❑ 467 Mark Buehrle SP 8.00 3.00
❑ 468 Curtis Granderson .40 .15
❑ 469 Kerry Wood .40 .15
❑ 470 Miguel Tejada .40 .15
❑ 471 Geoff Jenkins .40 .15
❑ 472 Jeremy Reed .40 .15
❑ 473 David Eckstein .40 .15
❑ 474 Lyle Overbay .40 .15
❑ 475 Michael Young .40 .15
❑ 476A N.Johnson Nats SP 8.00 3.00
❑ 476B N.Johnson Yanks SP 8.00 3.00
❑ 477 Carlos Beltran .40 .15
❑ 478 Huston Street .40 .15
❑ 479 Brandon Webb .40 .15
❑ 480 Phil Nevin .40 .15
❑ 481 Ryan Madson SP 8.00 3.00
❑ 482 Jason Giambi .40 .15
❑ 483 Angel Berroa .40 .15
❑ 484 Casey Blake .40 .15
❑ 485 Pat Burrell .40 .15
❑ 486 B.J. Ryan .40 .15
❑ 487 Torii Hunter .40 .15
❑ 488 Garret Anderson .40 .15
❑ 489 Chase Utley SP 8.00 3.00
❑ 490 Matt Murton .40 .15
❑ 491 Rich Harden .40 .15
❑ 492 Garrett Atkins .40 .15
❑ 493 Tadahito Iguchi SP 8.00 3.00
❑ 494 Jarrod Washburn .40 .15
❑ 495 Carl Everett .40 .15
❑ 496 Kameron Loe .40 .15
❑ 497 Jorge Cantu SP 8.00 3.00
❑ 498 Chris Young .40 .15
❑ 499 Marcus Giles .40 .15
❑ 500 Albert Pujols 2.00 .75
❑ 501A A.Soriano Nats SP 8.00 3.00
❑ 501B A.Soriano Yanks SP 8.00 3.00
❑ 502 Randy Winn .40 .15
❑ 503 Roy Halladay .40 .15
❑ 504 Victor Martinez .40 .15
❑ 505 Pedro Martinez .60 .25
❑ 506 Rickie Weeks .40 .15
❑ 507 Dan Johnson .40 .15
❑ 508A T.Hudson Braves .40 .15
❑ 508B T.Hudson A's SP 8.00 3.00
❑ 509 Mark Prior .60 .25
❑ 510 Melvin Mora .40 .15
❑ 511 Matt Clement .40 .15
❑ 512 Brandon Inge .40 .15
❑ 513 Mike Mussina .60 .25
❑ 514 Mike Cameron .40 .15
❑ 515 Barry Zito .40 .15
❑ 516 Luis Gonzalez .40 .15
❑ 517 Jose Castillo .40 .15
❑ 518 Andy Pettitte .40 .15
❑ 519 Wily Mo Pena .40 .15
❑ 520 Billy Wagner .40 .15
❑ 521 Ervin Santana SP 8.00 3.00
❑ 522 Juan Pierre .40 .15
❑ 523 Dan Haren .40 .15
❑ 524 Adrian Gonzalez SP 8.00 3.00
❑ 525 Robinson Cano .60 .25
❑ 526 Jeff Kent .40 .15
❑ 527 Cory Sullivan .40 .15
❑ 528 Joe Crede SP 8.00 3.00
❑ 529 John Smoltz .60 .25
❑ 530 David Wright 1.50 .60
❑ 531 Chad Cordero .40 .15
❑ 532 Scott Rolen SP 8.00 3.00
❑ 533 Edwin Jackson .40 .15
❑ 534 Doug Mientkiewicz .40 .15
❑ 535 Mark Teixeira SP 8.00 3.00
❑ 536 Kelvim Escobar .40 .15
❑ 537 Alex Rios .40 .15
❑ 538 Jose Vidro .40 .15
❑ 539 Alex Gonzalez .40 .15
❑ 540 Yadier Molina .40 .15
❑ 541 Ronny Cedeno SP 8.00 3.00
❑ 542 Mark Hendrickson .40 .15
❑ 543 Russ Adams .40 .15
❑ 544 Chris Capuano .40 .15
❑ 545 Raul Ibanez .40 .15
❑ 546 Vicente Padilla .40 .15
❑ 547 Chris Duffy .40 .15
❑ 548 Bengie Molina .40 .15
❑ 549 Chien-Ming Wang 1.50 .60
❑ 550 Curt Schilling .60 .25
❑ 551 Craig Wilson .40 .15
❑ 552 Mike Lieberthal .40 .15
❑ 553 Kazuo Matsui .40 .15
❑ 554 Jeff Francis .40 .15
❑ 555 Brady Clark .40 .15
❑ 556 Willy Taveras .40 .15
❑ 557 Mike Maroth .40 .15
❑ 558 Bernie Williams .60 .25
❑ 559 Edwin Encarnacion .40 .15
❑ 560 Vernon Wells .40 .15
❑ 561A L.Hernandez Nats .40 .15
❑ 561B L.Hernandez Giants SP 8.00 3.00
❑ 562 Kenny Rogers .40 .15
❑ 563 Steve Finley .40 .15
❑ 564 Trot Nixon .40 .15
❑ 565 Jonny Gomes SP 8.00 3.00
❑ 566 Brandon Phillips .40 .15
❑ 567 Shawn Chacon .40 .15
❑ 568 Dave Bush .40 .15
❑ 569 Jose Guillen .40 .15
❑ 570 Gustavo Chacin .40 .15
❑ 571 A.Rod Safe at the Plate CL .75 .30
❑ 572 Pujols At Bat CL 1.00 .40
❑ 573 Bonds On Deck CL 1.00 .40
❑ 574 Breaking Up Two CL .20 .07
❑ 575 Conference On The Mound CL .50 .20
❑ 576 Touch Em All CL .75 .30
❑ 577 Avoiding The Runner CL .20 .07
❑ 578 Bunting The Runner Over CL .20 .07
❑ 579 In The Hole CL .20 .07
❑ 580 Jeter Steals Third CL 1.25 .50
❑ 581 Nolan Ryan RET 5.00 2.00
❑ 582 Cal Ripken RET 8.00 3.00
❑ 583 Carl Yastrzemski RET 3.00 1.25
❑ 584 Duke Snider RET 1.25 .50
❑ 585 Tom Seaver RET 1.25 .50
❑ 586 Mickey Mantle RET 10.00 4.00
❑ 587 Jim Palmer RET .75 .30
❑ 588 Gary Carter RET .75 .30
❑ 589 Stan Musial RET 3.00 1.25
❑ 590 Luis Aparicio RET .75 .30
❑ 591 Prince Fielder (RC) 4.00 1.50
❑ 592 Conor Jackson (RC) 1.50 .60
❑ 593 Jeremy Hermida (RC) 1.50 .60
❑ 594 Jeff Mathis (RC) 1.00 .40
❑ 595 Alay Soler RC 1.00 .40
❑ 596 Ryan Spilborghs (RC) 1.50 .60
❑ 597 Chuck James (RC) 1.50 .60
❑ 598 Josh Barfield (RC) 1.00 .40
❑ 599 Ian Kinsler (RC) 1.50 .60
❑ 600 Val Majewski (RC) 1.00 .40
❑ 601 Brian Slocum (RC) 1.00 .40
❑ 602 Matt Kemp (RC) 1.50 .60
❑ 603 Nate McLouth (RC) 1.00 .40
❑ 604 Sean Marshall (RC) 1.00 .40
❑ 605 Brian Bannister (RC) 1.00 .40
❑ 606 Ryan Zimmerman (RC) 6.00 2.50
❑ 607 Kendry Morales (RC) 2.50 1.00
❑ 608 Jonathan Papelbon (RC) 5.00 2.00
❑ 609 Matt Cain (RC) 1.50 .60
❑ 610 Anderson Hernandez (RC) 1.00 .40
❑ 611 Jose Capellan (RC) 1.00 .40
❑ 612 Lastings Milledge (RC) 1.50 .60
❑ 613 Francisco Liriano (RC) 5.00 2.00
❑ 614 Hanley Ramirez (RC) 2.50 1.00
❑ 615 Brian Anderson (RC) 1.00 .40
❑ 616 Reggie Abercrombie (RC) 1.00 .40
❑ 617 Erick Aybar (RC) 1.00 .40
❑ 618 James Loney (RC) 1.50 .60
❑ 619 Joel Zumaya (RC) 2.50 1.00
❑ 620 Travis Ishikawa (RC) 1.00 .40
❑ 621 Jason Kubel (RC) 1.00 .40
❑ 622 Drew Meyer (RC) 1.00 .40
❑ 623 Kenji Johjima RC 5.00 2.00
❑ 624 Fausto Carmona (RC) 1.00 .40
❑ 625 Nick Markakis (RC) 1.50 .60
❑ 626 John Rheinecker (RC) 1.00 .40
❑ 627 Melky Cabrera (RC) 5.00 2.00
❑ 628 Michael Pelfrey RC 4.00 1.50
❑ 629 Dan Uggla (RC) 2.50 1.00
❑ 630 Justin Verlander (RC) 4.00 1.50

2006 Topps Update and Highlights

❑ COMPLETE SET (330) 50.00 20.00
❑ COMMON CARD (1-132) .20 .07
❑ SEMISTARS 1-132 .30 .12
❑ UNLISTED STARS 1-132 .50 .20
❑ COMMON ROOKIE (133-170) .50 .20
❑ RC SEMIS 133-170 .75 .30
❑ RC UNLISTED 133-170 1.25 .50
❑ COMMON CARD (171-330) .30 .12
❑ SEMISTARS 171-330 .50 .20
❑ UNLISTED STARS 171-330 .75 .30
❑ 1-330 PLATE ODDS 1:85 HTA
❑ PLATE PRINT RUN 1 SET PER COLOR
❑ BLACK-CYAN-MAGENTA-YELLOW ISSUED
❑ NO PLATE PRICING DUE TO SCARCITY
❑ 1 Austin Kearns .20 .07
❑ 2 Adam Eaton .20 .07
❑ 3 Juan Encarnacion .20 .07
❑ 4 Jarrod Washburn .20 .07
❑ 5 Alex Gonzalez .20 .07
❑ 6 Toby Hall .20 .07
❑ 7 Preston Wilson .20 .07
❑ 8 Ramon Ortiz .20 .07
❑ 9 Jason Michaels .20 .07
❑ 10 Jeff Weaver .20 .07

Card		
❑ 11 Russell Branyan	.20	.07
❑ 12 Brett Tomko	.20	.07
❑ 13 Doug Mientkiewicz	.20	.07
❑ 14 David Wells	.20	.07
❑ 15 Corey Koskie	.20	.07
❑ 16 Russ Ortiz	.20	.07
❑ 17 Carlos Pena	.20	.07
❑ 18 Mark Hendrickson	.20	.07
❑ 19 Julian Tavarez	.20	.07
❑ 20 Jeff Conine	.20	.07
❑ 21 Dioner Navarro	.20	.07
❑ 22 Bob Wickman	.20	.07
❑ 23 Felipe Lopez	.20	.07
❑ 24 Eddie Guardado	.20	.07
❑ 25 David Dellucci	.20	.07
❑ 26 Ryan Wagner	.20	.07
❑ 27 Nick Green	.20	.07
❑ 28 Gary Majewski	.20	.07
❑ 29 Shea Hillenbrand	.20	.07
❑ 30 Jae Seo	.20	.07
❑ 31 Royce Clayton	.20	.07
❑ 32 Dave Riske	.20	.07
❑ 33 Joey Gathright	.20	.07
❑ 34 Robinson Tejada	.20	.07
❑ 35 Edwin Jackson	.20	.07
❑ 36 Aubrey Huff	.20	.07
❑ 37 Akinori Otsuka	.20	.07
❑ 38 Juan Castro	.20	.07
❑ 39 Zach Day	.20	.07
❑ 40 Jeremy Accardo	.20	.07
❑ 41 Shawn Green	.20	.07
❑ 42 Kazuo Matsui	.20	.07
❑ 43 J.J. Putz	.20	.07
❑ 44 David Ross	.20	.07
❑ 45 Scott Williamson	.20	.07
❑ 46 Joe Borchard	.20	.07
❑ 47 Elmer Dessens	.20	.07
❑ 48 Odalis Perez	.20	.07
❑ 49 Kelly Shoppach	.20	.07
❑ 50 Brandon Phillips	.20	.07
❑ 51 Guillermo Mota	.20	.07
❑ 52 Alex Cintron	.20	.07
❑ 53 Denny Bautista	.20	.07
❑ 54 Josh Bard	.20	.07
❑ 55 Julio Lugo	.20	.07
❑ 56 Doug Mirabelli	.20	.07
❑ 57 Kip Wells	.20	.07
❑ 58 Adrian Gonzalez	.20	.07
❑ 59 Shawn Chacon	.20	.07
❑ 60 Marcus Thames	.20	.07
❑ 61 Craig Wilson	.20	.07
❑ 62 Cory Sullivan	.20	.07
❑ 63 Ben Broussard	.20	.07
❑ 64 Todd Walker	.20	.07
❑ 65 Greg Maddux	.75	.30
❑ 66 Xavier Nady	.20	.07
❑ 67 Oliver Perez	.20	.07
❑ 68 Sean Casey	.20	.07
❑ 69 Kyle Lohse	.20	.07
❑ 70 Carlos Lee	.20	.07
❑ 71 Rheal Cormier	.20	.07
❑ 72 Ronnie Belliard	.20	.07
❑ 73 Cory Lidle	4.00	1.50
❑ 74 David Bell	.20	.07
❑ 75 Wilson Betemit	.20	.07
❑ 76 Danys Baez	.20	.07
❑ 77 Mike Stanton	.20	.07
❑ 78 Kevin Mench	.20	.07
❑ 79 Sandy Alomar Jr.	.20	.07
❑ 80 Cesar Izturis	.20	.07
❑ 81 Jeremy Affeldt	.20	.07
❑ 82 Matt Stairs	.20	.07
❑ 83 Hector Luna	.20	.07
❑ 84 Tony Graffanino	.20	.07
❑ 85 J.P Howell	.20	.07
❑ 86 Bengie Molina	.20	.07
❑ 87 Maicer Izturis	.20	.07
❑ 88 Marco Scutaro	.20	.07
❑ 89 Daryle Ward	.20	.07
❑ 90 Sal Fasano	.20	.07
❑ 91 Oscar Villarreal	.20	.07
❑ 92 Gabe Gross	.20	.07
❑ 93 Phil Nevin	.20	.07
❑ 94 Damon Hollins	.20	.07
❑ 95 Juan Cruz	.20	.07
❑ 96 Marlon Anderson	.20	.07
❑ 97 Jason Davis	.20	.07
❑ 98 Ryan Shealy	.20	.07
❑ 99 Francisco Cordero	.20	.07
❑ 100 Bobby Abreu	.20	.07
❑ 101 Roberto Hernandez	.20	.07
❑ 102 Gary Bennett	.20	.07
❑ 103 Aaron Sele	.20	.07
❑ 104 Nook Logan	.20	.07
❑ 105 Alfredo Amezaga	.20	.07
❑ 106 Chris Woodward	.20	.07
❑ 107 Kevin Jarvis	.20	.07
❑ 108 B.J. Upton	.20	.07
❑ 109 Alan Embree	.20	.07
❑ 110 Milton Bradley	.20	.07
❑ 111 Pete Orr	.20	.07
❑ 112 Jeff Cirillo	.20	.07
❑ 113 Corey Patterson	.20	.07
❑ 114 Josh Paul	.20	.07
❑ 115 Fernando Rodney	.20	.07
❑ 116 Jerry Hairston Jr.	.20	.07
❑ 117 Scott Proctor	.20	.07
❑ 118 Ambiorix Burgos	.20	.07
❑ 119 Jose Bautista	.20	.07
❑ 120 Livan Hernandez	.20	.07
❑ 121 John Mcdonald	.20	.07
❑ 122 Ronny Cedeno	.20	.07
❑ 123 Nate Robertson	.20	.07
❑ 124 Jamey Carroll	.20	.07
❑ 125 Alex Escobar	.20	.07
❑ 126 Endy Chavez	.20	.07
❑ 127 Jorge Julio	.20	.07
❑ 128 Kenny Lofton	.20	.07
❑ 129 Matt Diaz	.20	.07
❑ 130 Dave Bush	.20	.07
❑ 131 Jose Molina	.20	.07
❑ 132 Mike MacDougal	.20	.07
❑ 133 Ben Zobrist (RC)	.75	.30
❑ 134 Shane Komine RC	.75	.30
❑ 135 Casey Janssen RC	.75	.30
❑ 136 Kevin Frandsen (RC)	.75	.30
❑ 137 John Rheinecker (RC)	.50	.20
❑ 138 Matt Kemp (RC)	.75	.30
❑ 139 Scott Mathieson (RC)	.50	.20
❑ 140 Jered Weaver (RC)	2.50	1.00
❑ 141 Joel Guzman (RC)	.50	.20
❑ 142 Anibal Sanchez (RC)	.50	.20
❑ 143 Melky Cabrera (RC)	2.50	1.00
❑ 144 Howie Kendrick (RC)	2.50	1.00
❑ 145 Cole Hamels (RC)	1.25	.50
❑ 146 Willy Aybar (RC)	.50	.20
❑ 147 Jamie Shields RC	.50	.20
❑ 148 Kevin Thompson (RC)	.50	.20
❑ 149 Jon Lester RC	4.00	1.50
❑ 150 Stephen Drew (RC)	1.25	.50
❑ 151 Andre Ethier (RC)	2.00	.75
❑ 152 Jordan Tata RC	.50	.20
❑ 153 Mike Napoli RC	2.50	1.00
❑ 154 Kason Gabbard (RC)	.50	.20
❑ 155 Lastings Milledge (RC)	.75	.30
❑ 156 Erick Aybar (RC)	.50	.20
❑ 157 Fausto Carmona (RC)	.50	.20
❑ 158 Russ Martin (RC)	.75	.30
❑ 159 David Pauley (RC)	.50	.20
❑ 160 Andy Marte (RC)	.50	.20
❑ 161 Carlos Quentin (RC)	.75	.30
❑ 162 Franklin Gutierrez (RC)	.50	.20
❑ 163 Taylor Buchholz (RC)	.75	.30
❑ 164 Josh Johnson (RC)	.75	.30
❑ 165 Chad Billingsley (RC)	.75	.30
❑ 166 Kendry Morales (RC)	1.25	.50
❑ 167 Adam Loewen (RC)	.75	.30
❑ 168 Yusmeiro Petit (RC)	.50	.20
❑ 169 Matt Albers (RC)	.50	.20
❑ 170 John Maine (RC)	.75	.30
❑ 171 Alex Rodriguez SH	1.25	.50
❑ 172 Mike Piazza SH	.75	.30
❑ 173 Cory Sullivan SH	.30	.12
❑ 174 Anibal Sanchez SH	.30	.12
❑ 175 Trevor Hoffman SH	.30	.12
❑ 176 Barry Bonds SH	1.50	.60
❑ 177 Derek Jeter SH	2.00	.75
❑ 178 Jose Reyes SH	.30	.12
❑ 179 Manny Ramirez SH	.50	.20
❑ 180 Vladimir Guerrero SH	.75	.30
❑ 181 Mariano Rivera SH	.75	.30
❑ 182 Mark Kotsay PH	.30	.12
❑ 183 Derek Jeter PH	2.00	.75
❑ 184 Carlos Delgado PH	.30	.12
❑ 185 Frank Thomas PH	.75	.30
❑ 186 Albert Pujols PH	1.50	.60
❑ 187 Magglio Ordonez PH	.30	.12
❑ 188 Carlos Delgado PH	.30	.12
❑ 189 Kenny Rogers PH	.30	.12
❑ 190 Tom Glavine PH	.50	.20
❑ 191 P.Polanco/J.Suppan PH	.30	.12
❑ 192 Jose Reyes PH	.30	.12
❑ 193 E.Chavez/Y.Molina PH	.30	.12
❑ 194 Craig Monroe PH	.30	.12
❑ 195 J.Verlander/J.Zumaya PH	1.25	.50
❑ 196 P.LoDuca/C.Beltran PH	.30	.12
❑ 197 A.Pujols/J.Edmonds/S.Rolen PH	1.50	.60
❑ 198 Anthony Reyes PH	.30	.12
❑ 199 Chris Carpenter PH	.30	.12
❑ 200 David Eckstein PH	.30	.12
❑ 201 Jered Weaver PH	1.50	.60
❑ 202 D.Ortiz/J.Dye/T.Hafner LL	.75	.30
❑ 203 J.Mauer/D.Jeter/R.Cano LL	2.00	.75
❑ 204 D.Ortiz/J.Morneau/R.Ibanez LL	.75	.30
❑ 205 C.Crawford/C.Figgins/I.Suzuki LL	1.25	.50
❑ 206 J.Santana/C.Wang/J.Garland LL	1.25	.50
❑ 207 J.Santana/R.Halladay/C.Sabathia LL	.50	.20
❑ 208 J.Santana/J.Bonderman/J.Lackey LL	.50	.20
❑ 209 F.Rodriguez/B.Jenks/B.Ryan LL	.30	.12
❑ 210 R.Howard/A.Pujols/A.Soriano LL	1.50	.60
❑ 211 F.Sanchez/M.Cabrera/A.Pujols LL	1.50	.60
❑ 212 R.Howard/A.Pujols/L.Berkman LL	1.50	.60
❑ 213 J.Reyes/J.Pierre/H.Ramirez LL	.75	.30
❑ 214 D.Lowe/B.Webb/C.Zambrano LL	.30	.12
❑ 215 R.Oswalt/C.Carpenter/B.Webb LL	.30	.12
❑ 216 A.Harang/J.Peavy/J.Smoltz LL	.50	.20
❑ 217 T.Hoffman/B.Wagner/J.Borowski LL	.30	.12
❑ 218 Ichiro Suzuki AS	1.25	.50
❑ 219 Derek Jeter AS	2.00	.75
❑ 220 Alex Rodriguez AS	1.25	.50
❑ 221 David Ortiz AS	.75	.30
❑ 222 Vladimir Guerrero AS	.75	.30
❑ 223 Ivan Rodriguez AS	.50	.20
❑ 224 Vernon Wells AS	.30	.12
❑ 225 Mark Loretta AS	.30	.12
❑ 226 Kenny Rogers AS	.30	.12
❑ 227 Alfonso Soriano AS	.30	.12
❑ 228 Carlos Beltran AS	.30	.12
❑ 229 Albert Pujols AS	1.50	.60
❑ 230 Jason Bay AS	.30	.12
❑ 231 Edgar Renteria AS	.30	.12
❑ 232 David Wright AS	1.25	.50
❑ 233 Chase Utley AS	.75	.30
❑ 234 Paul LoDuca AS	.30	.12
❑ 235 Brad Penny AS	.30	.12
❑ 236 Derrick Turnbow AS	.30	.12
❑ 237 Mark Redman AS	.30	.12
❑ 238 Francisco Liriano AS	1.50	.60
❑ 239 A.J. Pierzynski AS	.30	.12
❑ 240 Grady Sizemore AS	.50	.20
❑ 241 Jose Contreras AS	.30	.12
❑ 242 Jermaine Dye AS	.30	.12
❑ 243 Jason Schmidt AS	.30	.12
❑ 244 Nomar Garciaparra AS	.75	.30
❑ 245 Scott Kazmir AS	.50	.20
❑ 246 Johan Santana AS	.50	.20
❑ 247 Chris Capuano AS	.30	.12
❑ 248 Magglio Ordonez AS	.30	.12
❑ 249 Gary Matthews Jr. AS	.30	.12
❑ 250 Carlos Lee AS	.30	.12
❑ 251 David Eckstein AS	.30	.12
❑ 252 Michael Young AS	.30	.12
❑ 253 Matt Holliday AS	.30	.12
❑ 254 Lance Berkman AS	.30	.12
❑ 255 Scott Rolen AS	.50	.20
❑ 256 Bronson Arroyo AS	.30	.12
❑ 257 Barry Zito AS	.30	.12
❑ 258 Brian McCann AS	.30	.12
❑ 259 Jose Lopez AS	.30	.12
❑ 260 Chris Carpenter AS	.30	.12
❑ 261 Roy Halladay AS	.30	.12
❑ 262 Jim Thome AS	.50	.20
❑ 263 Dan Uggla AS	.75	.30
❑ 264 Mariano Rivera AS	.75	.30
❑ 265 Roy Oswalt AS	.30	.12
❑ 266 Tom Gordon AS	.30	.12
❑ 267 Troy Glaus AS	.30	.12
❑ 268 Bobby Jenks AS	.30	.12

- ❑ 269 Freddy Sanchez AS .30 .12
- ❑ 270 Paul Konerko AS .30 .12
- ❑ 271 Joe Mauer AS .50 .20
- ❑ 272 B.J. Ryan AS .30 .12
- ❑ 273 Ryan Howard AS 1.25 .50
- ❑ 274 Brian Fuentes AS .30 .12
- ❑ 275 Miguel Cabrera AS .50 .20
- ❑ 276 Brandon Webb AS .30 .12
- ❑ 277 Mark Buehrle AS .30 .12
- ❑ 278 Trevor Hoffman AS .30 .12
- ❑ 279 Jonathan Papelbon AS 1.50 .60
- ❑ 280 Andruw Jones AS .50 .20
- ❑ 281 Miguel Tejada AS .30 .12
- ❑ 282 Carlos Zambrano AS .30 .12
- ❑ 283 Ryan Howard HRD 1.25 .50
- ❑ 284 David Wright HRD 1.25 .50
- ❑ 285 Miguel Cabrera HRD .50 .20
- ❑ 286 David Ortiz HRD .75 .30
- ❑ 287 Jermaine Dye HRD .30 .12
- ❑ 288 Miguel Tejada HRD .30 .12
- ❑ 289 Lance Berkman HRD .30 .12
- ❑ 290 Troy Glaus HRD .30 .12
- ❑ 291 D.Wright/T.Glavine TL 1.25 .50
- ❑ 292 R.Howard/T.Gordon TL 1.25 .50
- ❑ 293 M.Cabrera/D.Willis TL .50 .20
- ❑ 294 A.Jones/J.Smoltz TL .50 .20
- ❑ 295 A.Soriano/A.Soriano TL .30 .12
- ❑ 296 A.Pujols/C.Carpenter TL 1.50 .60
- ❑ 297 A.Dunn/B.Arroyo TL .30 .12
- ❑ 298 L.Berkman/R.Oswalt TL .30 .12
- ❑ 299 C.Capuano/P.Fielder TL 1.25 .50
- ❑ 300 F.Sanchez/J.Bay TL .30 .12
- ❑ 301 C.Zambrano/J.Pierre TL .30 .12
- ❑ 302 A.Gonzalez/T.Hoffman TL .30 .12
- ❑ 303 D.Lowe/R.Furcal TL .30 .12
- ❑ 304 O.Vizquel/J.Schmidt TL .50 .20
- ❑ 305 B.Webb/C.Tracy TL .30 .12
- ❑ 306 M.Holliday/G.Atkins TL .30 .12
- ❑ 307 A.Rodriguez/C.Wang TL 1.25 .50
- ❑ 308 C.Schilling/D.Ortiz TL .75 .30
- ❑ 309 R.Halladay/V.Wells TL .30 .12
- ❑ 310 M.Tejada/E.Bedard TL .30 .12
- ❑ 311 C.Crawford/S.Kazmir TL .50 .20
- ❑ 312 J.Bonderman/M.Ordonez TL .30 .12
- ❑ 313 J.Morneau/J.Santana TL .50 .20
- ❑ 314 J.Garland/J.Dye TL .30 .12
- ❑ 315 T.Hafner/C.Sabathia TL .30 .12
- ❑ 316 E.Brown/M.Grudzielanek TL .30 .12
- ❑ 317 F.Thomas/B.Zito TL .75 .30
- ❑ 318 J.Weaver/V.Guerrero TL 1.50 .60
- ❑ 319 M.Young/G.Matthews TL .30 .12
- ❑ 320 I.Suzuki/J.Putz TL 1.25 .50
- ❑ 321 D.Jeter/R.Cano CD 2.00 .75
- ❑ 322 C.Carpenter/M.Mulder CD .30 .12
- ❑ 323 J.Schmidt/T.Hoffman CD .30 .12
- ❑ 324 D.Wright/P.LoDuca CD 1.25 .50
- ❑ 325 L.Berkman/R.Oswalt CD .30 .12
- ❑ 326 D.Jeter/J.Reyes CD 2.00 .75
- ❑ 327 C.Floyd/D.Wright CD 1.25 .50
- ❑ 328 F.Liriano/J.Santana CD 1.50 .60
- ❑ 329 J.Drew/S.Drew CD .75 .30
- ❑ 330 J.Weaver/J.Weaver CD 1.50 .60

2001 Ultimate Collection

- ❑ COMMON CARD (1-90) 4.00 1.50
- ❑ COMMON CARD (91-100) 10.00 4.00
- ❑ COMMON CARD (101-110) 10.00 4.00
- ❑ COMMON CARD (111-120) 15.00 6.00
- ❑ 1 Troy Glaus 4.00 1.50
- ❑ 2 Darin Erstad 4.00 1.50
- ❑ 3 Jason Giambi 4.00 1.50
- ❑ 4 Barry Zito 4.00 1.50
- ❑ 5 Tim Hudson 4.00 1.50
- ❑ 6 Miguel Tejada 4.00 1.50
- ❑ 7 Carlos Delgado 4.00 1.50
- ❑ 8 Shannon Stewart 4.00 1.50
- ❑ 9 Greg Vaughn 4.00 1.50
- ❑ 10 Toby Hall 4.00 1.50
- ❑ 11 Roberto Alomar 4.00 1.50
- ❑ 12 Juan Gonzalez 4.00 1.50
- ❑ 13 Jim Thome 4.00 1.50
- ❑ 14 Edgar Martinez 4.00 1.50
- ❑ 15 Freddy Garcia 4.00 1.50
- ❑ 16 Bret Boone 4.00 1.50
- ❑ 17 Kazuhiro Sasaki 4.00 1.50
- ❑ 18 Cal Ripken 20.00 8.00
- ❑ 19 Tim Raines Jr. 4.00 1.50
- ❑ 20 Alex Rodriguez 10.00 4.00
- ❑ 21 Ivan Rodriguez 4.00 1.50
- ❑ 22 Rafael Palmeiro 4.00 1.50
- ❑ 23 Pedro Martinez 4.00 1.50
- ❑ 24 Nomar Garciaparra 10.00 4.00
- ❑ 25 Manny Ramirez Sox 4.00 1.50
- ❑ 26 Hideo Nomo 6.00 2.50
- ❑ 27 Mike Sweeney 4.00 1.50
- ❑ 28 Carlos Beltran 4.00 1.50
- ❑ 29 Tony Clark 4.00 1.50
- ❑ 30 Dean Palmer 4.00 1.50
- ❑ 31 Doug Mientkiewicz 4.00 1.50
- ❑ 32 Cristian Guzman 4.00 1.50
- ❑ 33 Corey Koskie 4.00 1.50
- ❑ 34 Frank Thomas 6.00 2.50
- ❑ 35 Magglio Ordonez 4.00 1.50
- ❑ 36 Jose Canseco 4.00 1.50
- ❑ 37 Roger Clemens 12.00 5.00
- ❑ 38 Derek Jeter 15.00 6.00
- ❑ 39 Bernie Williams 4.00 1.50
- ❑ 40 Mike Mussina 4.00 1.50
- ❑ 41 Tino Martinez 4.00 1.50
- ❑ 42 Jeff Bagwell 4.00 1.50
- ❑ 43 Lance Berkman 4.00 1.50
- ❑ 44 Roy Oswalt 6.00 2.50
- ❑ 45 Chipper Jones 6.00 2.50
- ❑ 46 Greg Maddux 10.00 4.00
- ❑ 47 Andruw Jones 4.00 1.50
- ❑ 48 Tom Glavine 4.00 1.50
- ❑ 49 Richie Sexson 4.00 1.50
- ❑ 50 Jeromy Burnitz 4.00 1.50
- ❑ 51 Ben Sheets 4.00 1.50
- ❑ 52 Mark McGwire 15.00 6.00
- ❑ 53 Matt Morris 4.00 1.50
- ❑ 54 Jim Edmonds 4.00 1.50
- ❑ 55 J.D. Drew 4.00 1.50
- ❑ 56 Sammy Sosa 6.00 2.50
- ❑ 57 Fred McGriff 4.00 1.50
- ❑ 58 Kerry Wood 4.00 1.50
- ❑ 59 Randy Johnson 6.00 2.50
- ❑ 60 Luis Gonzalez 4.00 1.50
- ❑ 61 Curt Schilling 4.00 1.50
- ❑ 62 Shawn Green 4.00 1.50
- ❑ 63 Kevin Brown 4.00 1.50
- ❑ 64 Gary Sheffield 4.00 1.50
- ❑ 65 Vladimir Guerrero 6.00 2.50
- ❑ 66 Barry Bonds 15.00 6.00
- ❑ 67 Jeff Kent 4.00 1.50
- ❑ 68 Rich Aurilia 4.00 1.50
- ❑ 69 Cliff Floyd 4.00 1.50
- ❑ 70 Charles Johnson 4.00 1.50
- ❑ 71 Josh Beckett 4.00 1.50
- ❑ 72 Mike Piazza 10.00 4.00
- ❑ 73 Edgardo Alfonzo 4.00 1.50
- ❑ 74 Robin Ventura 4.00 1.50
- ❑ 75 Tony Gwynn 8.00 3.00
- ❑ 76 Ryan Klesko 4.00 1.50
- ❑ 77 Phil Nevin 4.00 1.50
- ❑ 78 Scott Rolen 4.00 1.50
- ❑ 79 Bobby Abreu 4.00 1.50
- ❑ 80 Jimmy Rollins 4.00 1.50
- ❑ 81 Brian Giles 4.00 1.50
- ❑ 82 Jason Kendall 4.00 1.50
- ❑ 83 Aramis Ramirez 4.00 1.50
- ❑ 84 Ken Griffey Jr. 10.00 4.00
- ❑ 85 Adam Dunn 4.00 1.50
- ❑ 86 Sean Casey 4.00 1.50
- ❑ 87 Barry Larkin 4.00 1.50
- ❑ 88 Larry Walker 4.00 1.50
- ❑ 89 Mike Hampton 4.00 1.50
- ❑ 90 Todd Helton 4.00 1.50
- ❑ 91 Ken Harvey T1 10.00 4.00
- ❑ 92 Bill Ortega T1 RC 10.00 4.00
- ❑ 93 Juan Diaz T1 RC 10.00 4.00
- ❑ 94 Greg Miller T1 RC 10.00 4.00
- ❑ 95 Brandon Berger T1 RC 10.00 4.00
- ❑ 96 Brandon Lyon T1 RC 10.00 4.00
- ❑ 97 Jay Gibbons T1 RC 15.00 6.00
- ❑ 98 Rob Mackowiak T1 RC 15.00 6.00
- ❑ 99 Erick Almonte T1 RC 10.00 4.00
- ❑ 100 Jason Middlebrook T1 RC 10.00 4.00
- ❑ 101 Johnny Estrada T2 RC 15.00 6.00
- ❑ 102 Juan Uribe T2 RC 15.00 6.00
- ❑ 103 Travis Hafner T2 RC 50.00 20.00
- ❑ 104 Morgan Ensberg T2 RC 15.00 6.00
- ❑ 105 Mike Rivera T2 RC 10.00 4.00
- ❑ 106 Josh Towers T2 RC 15.00 6.00
- ❑ 107 Adrian Hernandez T2 RC 10.00 4.00
- ❑ 108 Rafael Soriano T2 RC 10.00 4.00
- ❑ 109 Jackson Melian T2 RC 10.00 4.00
- ❑ 110 Wilkin Ruan T2 RC 10.00 4.00
- ❑ 111 Albert Pujols T3 RC 700.00 500.00
- ❑ 112 Tsuyoshi Shinjo T3 RC 25.00 10.00
- ❑ 113 Brandon Duckworth T3 RC 15.00 6.00
- ❑ 114 Juan Cruz T3 RC 15.00 6.00
- ❑ 115 Dewon Brazelton T3 RC 15.00 6.00
- ❑ 116 Mark Prior T3 AU RC 200.00 125.00
- ❑ 117 Mark Teixeira T3 AU RC 300.00200.00
- ❑ 118 Wilson Betemit T3 RC 25.00 10.00
- ❑ 119 Bud Smith T3 RC 15.00 6.00
- ❑ 120 Ichiro Suzuki T3 AU RC 1500.00 1000.00

2002 Ultimate Collection

- ❑ COMMON CARD (1-60) 4.00 1.50
- ❑ COMMON CARD (61-110) 10.00 4.00
- ❑ 61-110 PRINT RUN 550 SERIAL #'d SETS
- ❑ COMMON CARD (111-113) 15.00 6.00
- ❑ COMMON CARD (114-120) 15.00 6.00
- ❑ 1 Troy Glaus 4.00 1.50
- ❑ 2 Luis Gonzalez 4.00 1.50
- ❑ 3 Curt Schilling 4.00 1.50
- ❑ 4 Randy Johnson 6.00 2.50
- ❑ 5 Andruw Jones 4.00 1.50
- ❑ 6 Greg Maddux 10.00 4.00
- ❑ 7 Chipper Jones 6.00 2.50
- ❑ 8 Gary Sheffield 4.00 1.50
- ❑ 9 Cal Ripken 20.00 8.00
- ❑ 10 Manny Ramirez 4.00 1.50
- ❑ 11 Pedro Martinez 4.00 1.50
- ❑ 12 Nomar Garciaparra 10.00 4.00
- ❑ 13 Sammy Sosa 6.00 2.50
- ❑ 14 Kerry Wood 4.00 1.50
- ❑ 15 Mark Prior 6.00 2.50
- ❑ 16 Magglio Ordonez 4.00 1.50
- ❑ 17 Frank Thomas 6.00 2.50
- ❑ 18 Adam Dunn 4.00 1.50
- ❑ 19 Ken Griffey Jr. 10.00 4.00
- ❑ 20 Jim Thome 4.00 1.50
- ❑ 21 Larry Walker 4.00 1.50
- ❑ 22 Todd Helton 4.00 1.50
- ❑ 23 Nolan Ryan 15.00 6.00
- ❑ 24 Jeff Bagwell 4.00 1.50
- ❑ 25 Roy Oswalt 4.00 1.50
- ❑ 26 Lance Berkman 4.00 1.50
- ❑ 27 Mike Sweeney 4.00 1.50

❑ 28 Shawn Green 4.00 1.50
❑ 29 Hideo Nomo 6.00 2.50
❑ 30 Torii Hunter 4.00 1.50
❑ 31 Vladimir Guerrero 6.00 2.50
❑ 32 Tom Seaver 4.00 1.50
❑ 33 Mike Piazza 10.00 4.00
❑ 34 Roberto Alomar 4.00 1.50
❑ 35 Derek Jeter 15.00 6.00
❑ 36 Alfonso Soriano 4.00 1.50
❑ 37 Jason Giambi 4.00 1.50
❑ 38 Roger Clemens 12.00 5.00
❑ 39 Mike Mussina 4.00 1.50
❑ 40 Bernie Williams 4.00 1.50
❑ 41 Joe DiMaggio 12.00 5.00
❑ 42 Mickey Mantle 25.00 10.00
❑ 43 Miguel Tejada 4.00 1.50
❑ 44 Eric Chavez 4.00 1.50
❑ 45 Barry Zito 4.00 1.50
❑ 46 Pat Burrell 4.00 1.50
❑ 47 Jason Kendall 4.00 1.50
❑ 48 Brian Giles 4.00 1.50
❑ 49 Barry Bonds 15.00 6.00
❑ 50 Ichiro Suzuki 12.00 5.00
❑ 51 Stan Musial 10.00 4.00
❑ 52 J.D. Drew 4.00 1.50
❑ 53 Scott Rolen 4.00 1.50
❑ 54 Albert Pujols 12.00 5.00
❑ 55 Mark McGwire 15.00 6.00
❑ 56 Alex Rodriguez 10.00 4.00
❑ 57 Ivan Rodriguez 4.00 1.50
❑ 58 Juan Gonzalez 4.00 1.50
❑ 59 Rafael Palmeiro 4.00 1.50
❑ 60 Carlos Delgado 4.00 1.50
❑ 61 Jose Valverde UR RC 10.00 4.00
❑ 62 Doug Devore UR RC 10.00 4.00
❑ 63 John Ennis UR RC 10.00 4.00
❑ 64 Joey Dawley UR RC 10.00 4.00
❑ 65 Trey Hodges UR RC 10.00 4.00
❑ 66 Mike Mahoney UR 10.00 4.00
❑ 67 Aaron Cook UR RC 10.00 4.00
❑ 68 Rene Reyes UR RC 10.00 4.00
❑ 69 Mark Corey UR RC 10.00 4.00
❑ 70 Hansel Izquierdo UR RC 10.00 4.00
❑ 71 Brandon Puffer UR RC 10.00 4.00
❑ 72 Jeriome Robertson UR RC 10.00 4.00
❑ 73 Jose Diaz UR RC 10.00 4.00
❑ 74 David Ross UR RC 10.00 4.00
❑ 75 Jayson Durocher UR RC 10.00 4.00
❑ 76 Eric Good UR RC 10.00 4.00
❑ 77 Satoru Komiyama UR RC 10.00 4.00
❑ 78 Tyler Yates UR RC 10.00 4.00
❑ 79 Eric Junge UR RC 10.00 4.00
❑ 80 Anderson Machado UR RC 10.00 4.00
❑ 81 Adrian Burnside UR RC 10.00 4.00
❑ 82 Ben Howard UR RC 10.00 4.00
❑ 83 Clay Condrey UR RC 10.00 4.00
❑ 84 Nelson Castro UR RC 10.00 4.00
❑ 85 So Taguchi UR RC 15.00 6.00
❑ 86 Mike Crudale UR RC 10.00 4.00
❑ 87 Scotty Layfield UR RC 10.00 4.00
❑ 88 Steve Bechler UR RC 10.00 4.00
❑ 89 Travis Driskill UR RC 10.00 4.00
❑ 90 Howie Clark UR RC 10.00 4.00
❑ 91 Josh Hancock UR RC 10.00 4.00
❑ 92 Jorge De La Rosa UR RC 10.00 4.00
❑ 93 Anastacio Martinez UR RC 10.00 4.00
❑ 94 Brian Tallet UR RC 10.00 4.00
❑ 95 Carl Sadler UR RC 10.00 4.00
❑ 96 Cliff Lee UR RC 15.00 6.00
❑ 97 Josh Bard UR RC 10.00 4.00
❑ 98 Wes Obermueller UR RC 10.00 4.00
❑ 99 Juan Brito UR RC 10.00 4.00
❑ 100 Aaron Guiel UR RC 10.00 4.00
❑ 101 Jeremy Hill UR RC 10.00 4.00
❑ 102 Kevin Frederick UR RC 10.00 4.00
❑ 103 Nate Field UR RC 10.00 4.00
❑ 104 Julio Mateo UR RC 10.00 4.00
❑ 105 Chris Snelling UR RC 12.00 5.00
❑ 106 Felix Escalona UR RC 10.00 4.00
❑ 107 Reynaldo Garcia UR RC 10.00 4.00
❑ 108 Mike Smith UR RC 10.00 4.00
❑ 109 Ken Huckaby UR RC 10.00 4.00
❑ 110 Kevin Cash UR RC 10.00 4.00
❑ 111 Kazuhisa Ishii UR AU RC 40.00 15.00
❑ 112 Freddy Sanchez UR AU RC 50.00 25.00
❑ 113 Jas Simontacchi UR AU RC 15.00 6.00
❑ 114 Jorge Padilla UR AU RC 15.00 6.00
❑ 115 Kirk Saarloos UR AU RC 15.00 6.00
❑ 116 Rodrigo Rosario UR AU RC 15.00 6.00
❑ 117 Oliver Perez UR AU RC 30.00 12.50
❑ 118 Miguel Asencio UR AU RC 15.00 6.00
❑ 119 Franklyn German UR AU RC 15.00 6.00
❑ 120 Jaime Cerda UR AU RC 15.00 6.00
❑ MM M.McGwire Priority EXCH/100

2003 Ultimate Collection

❑ COMMON CARD (1-84) 3.00 1.25
❑ 1-84 STATED ODDS TWO PER PACK
❑ COMMON CARD (85-117) 5.00 2.00
❑ COMMON CARD (118-140) 5.00 2.00
❑ 118-140 PRINT RUN 399 SERIAL #'d SETS
❑ COMMON CARD (141-158) 6.00 2.50
❑ COMMON CARD (159-168) 12.00 5.00
❑ 159-168 PRINT RUN 100 SERIAL #'d SETS
❑ 85-168 STATED ODDS ONE PER PACK
❑ COMMON CARD (169-174) 15.00 6.00
❑ 169-174 & ULT.SIG.OVERALL ODDS 1:4
❑ COMMON CARD (175-180) 15.00 6.00
❑ 175-180 & BUYBACK OVERALL ODDS 1:8
❑ 169-180 PRINT RUN 250 SERIAL #'d SETS
❑ MATSUI PART LIVE/ PART EXCH
❑ EXCHANGE DEADLINE 12/17/06
❑ 1 Ichiro Suzuki 10.00 4.00
❑ 2 Ken Griffey Jr. 8.00 3.00
❑ 3 Sammy Sosa 5.00 2.00
❑ 4 Jason Giambi 3.00 1.25
❑ 5 Mike Piazza 8.00 3.00
❑ 6 Derek Jeter 10.00 4.00
❑ 7 Randy Johnson 5.00 2.00
❑ 8 Barry Bonds 12.00 5.00
❑ 9 Carlos Delgado 3.00 1.25
❑ 10 Mark Prior 5.00 2.00
❑ 11 Vladimir Guerrero 5.00 2.00
❑ 12 Alfonso Soriano 3.00 1.25
❑ 13 Jim Thome 5.00 2.00
❑ 14 Pedro Martinez 5.00 2.00
❑ 15 Nomar Garciaparra 8.00 3.00
❑ 16 Chipper Jones 5.00 2.00
❑ 17 Rocco Baldelli 3.00 1.25
❑ 18 Dontrelle Willis 5.00 2.00
❑ 19 Garret Anderson 3.00 1.25
❑ 20 Jeff Bagwell 5.00 2.00
❑ 21 Jim Edmonds 3.00 1.25
❑ 22 Rickey Henderson 5.00 2.00
❑ 23 Torii Hunter 3.00 1.25
❑ 24 Tom Glavine 5.00 2.00
❑ 25 Hideo Nomo 5.00 2.00
❑ 26 Luis Gonzalez 3.00 1.25
❑ 27 Alex Rodriguez 8.00 3.00
❑ 28 Albert Pujols 10.00 4.00
❑ 29 Manny Ramirez 5.00 2.00
❑ 30 Rafael Palmeiro 5.00 2.00
❑ 31 Bernie Williams 5.00 2.00
❑ 32 Curt Schilling 3.00 1.25
❑ 33 Roger Clemens 10.00 4.00
❑ 34 Andruw Jones 5.00 2.00
❑ 35 J.D. Drew 3.00 1.25
❑ 36 Kerry Wood 3.00 1.25
❑ 37 Scott Rolen 5.00 2.00
❑ 38 Darin Erstad 3.00 1.25
❑ 39 Joe DiMaggio 8.00 3.00
❑ 40 Magglio Ordonez 3.00 1.25
❑ 41 Todd Helton 5.00 2.00
❑ 42 Barry Zito 3.00 1.25
❑ 43 Mickey Mantle 15.00 6.00
❑ 44 Miguel Tejada 3.00 1.25
❑ 45 Troy Glaus 3.00 1.25
❑ 46 Kazuhisa Ishii 3.00 1.25
❑ 47 Adam Dunn 3.00 1.25
❑ 48 Ted Williams 10.00 4.00
❑ 49 Mike Mussina 5.00 2.00
❑ 50 Ivan Rodriguez 5.00 2.00
❑ 51 Jacque Jones 3.00 1.25
❑ 52 Stan Musial 8.00 3.00
❑ 53 Mariano Rivera 5.00 2.00
❑ 54 Larry Walker 3.00 1.25
❑ 55 Aaron Boone 3.00 1.25
❑ 56 Hank Blalock 3.00 1.25
❑ 57 Rich Harden 5.00 2.00
❑ 58 Lance Berkman 3.00 1.25
❑ 59 Eric Chavez 3.00 1.25
❑ 60 Carlos Beltran 3.00 1.25
❑ 61 Roy Oswalt 3.00 1.25
❑ 62 Moises Alou 3.00 1.25
❑ 63 Nolan Ryan 12.00 5.00
❑ 64 Jeff Kent 3.00 1.25
❑ 65 Roberto Alomar 5.00 2.00
❑ 66 Runelvys Hernandez 3.00 1.25
❑ 67 Roy Halladay 3.00 1.25
❑ 68 Tim Hudson 3.00 1.25
❑ 69 Tom Seaver 5.00 2.00
❑ 70 Edgardo Alfonzo 3.00 1.25
❑ 71 Andy Pettitte 5.00 2.00
❑ 72 Preston Wilson 3.00 1.25
❑ 73 Frank Thomas 5.00 2.00
❑ 74 Jerome Williams 3.00 1.25
❑ 75 Shawn Green 3.00 1.25
❑ 76 David Wells 3.00 1.25
❑ 77 John Smoltz 5.00 2.00
❑ 78 Jorge Posada 5.00 2.00
❑ 79 Marlon Byrd 3.00 1.25
❑ 80 Austin Kearns 3.00 1.25
❑ 81 Bret Boone 3.00 1.25
❑ 82 Rafael Furcal 3.00 1.25
❑ 83 Jay Gibbons 3.00 1.25
❑ 84 Shane Reynolds 3.00 1.25
❑ 85 Nate Bland UR T1 RC 5.00 2.00
❑ 86 Willie Eyre UR T1 RC 5.00 2.00
❑ 87 Jeremy Guthrie UR T1 5.00 2.00
❑ 88 Jeremy Wedel UR T1 RC 5.00 2.00
❑ 89 Jhonny Peralta UR T1 8.00 3.00
❑ 90 Luis Ayala UR T1 RC 5.00 2.00
❑ 91 Michael Hessman UR T1 RC 5.00 2.00
❑ 92 Michael Nakamura UR T1 RC 5.00 2.00
❑ 93 Nook Logan UR T1 RC 8.00 3.00
❑ 94 Rett Johnson UR T1 RC 5.00 2.00
❑ 95 Josh Hall UR T1 RC 5.00 2.00
❑ 96 Julio Manon UR T1 RC 5.00 2.00
❑ 97 Heath Bell UR T1 RC 5.00 2.00
❑ 98 Ian Ferguson UR T1 RC 5.00 2.00
❑ 99 Jason Gilfillan UR T1 RC 5.00 2.00
❑ 100 Jason Roach UR T1 RC 5.00 2.00
❑ 101 Jason Shiell UR T1 RC 5.00 2.00
❑ 102 Termel Sledge UR T1 RC 5.00 2.00
❑ 103 Phil Seibel UR T1 RC 5.00 2.00
❑ 104 Jeff Duncan UR T1 RC 5.00 2.00
❑ 105 Mike Neu UR T1 RC 5.00 2.00
❑ 106 Colin Porter UR T1 RC 5.00 2.00
❑ 107 David Matranga UR T1 RC 5.00 2.00
❑ 108 Aaron Looper UR T1 RC 5.00 2.00
❑ 109 Jeremy Bonderman UR T1 RC 20.00 8.00
❑ 110 Miguel Ojeda UR T1 RC 5.00 2.00
❑ 111 Chad Cordero UR T1 RC 10.00 4.00
❑ 112 Shane Bazzell UR T1 RC 5.00 2.00
❑ 113 Tim Olson UR T1 RC 5.00 2.00
❑ 114 Michel Hernandez UR T1 RC 5.00 2.00
❑ 115 Chien-Ming Wang UR T1 RC 50.00 20.00
❑ 116 Josh Stewart UR T1 RC 5.00 2.00
❑ 117 Clint Barmes UR T1 RC 5.00 2.00
❑ 118 Craig Brazell UR T2 RC 5.00 2.00
❑ 119 Josh Willingham UR T2 RC 10.00 4.00
❑ 120 Brent Hoard UR T2 RC 5.00 2.00
❑ 121 Francisco Rosario UR T2 RC 5.00 2.00
❑ 122 Rick Roberts UR T2 RC 5.00 2.00
❑ 123 Geoff Geary UR T2 RC 5.00 2.00
❑ 124 Edgar Gonzalez UR T2 RC 5.00 2.00
❑ 125 Kevin Correia UR T2 RC 5.00 2.00
❑ 126 Ryan Cameron UR T2 RC 5.00 2.00
❑ 127 Beau Kemp UR T2 RC 5.00 2.00
❑ 128 Tommy Phelps UR T2 5.00 2.00

❑ 129 Mark Malaska UR T2 RC 5.00 2.00
❑ 130 Kevin Ohme UR T2 RC 5.00 2.00
❑ 131 Humberto Quintero UR T2 RC 5.00 2.00
❑ 132 Aquilino Lopez UR T2 RC 5.00 2.00
❑ 133 Andrew Brown UR T2 RC 8.00 3.00
❑ 134 Wilfredo Ledezma UR T2 RC 5.00 2.00
❑ 135 Luis De Los Santos UR T2 5.00 2.00
❑ 136 Garrett Atkins UR T2 5.00 2.00
❑ 137 Fernando Cabrera UR T2 RC 5.00 2.00
❑ 138 D.J. Carrasco UR T2 RC 5.00 2.00
❑ 139 Alfredo Gonzalez UR T2 RC 5.00 2.00
❑ 140 Alex Prieto UR T2 RC 5.00 2.00
❑ 141 Matt Kata UR T3 RC 6.00 2.50
❑ 142 Chris Capuano UR T3 RC 15.00 6.00
❑ 143 Bobby Madritsch UR T3 RC 6.00 2.50
❑ 144 Greg Jones UR T3 RC 6.00 2.50
❑ 145 Pete Zoccolillo UR T3 RC 6.00 2.50
❑ 146 Chad Gaudin UR T3 RC 6.00 2.50
❑ 147 Rosman Garcia UR T3 RC 6.00 2.50
❑ 148 Gerald Laird UR T3 6.00 2.50
❑ 149 Danny Garcia UR T3 RC 6.00 2.50
❑ 150 Stephen Randolph UR T3 RC 6.00 2.50
❑ 151 Pete LaForest UR T3 RC 6.00 2.50
❑ 152 Brian Sweeney UR T3 RC 6.00 2.50
❑ 153 Aaron Miles UR T3 RC 10.00 4.00
❑ 154 Jorge DePaula UR T3 UER 6.00 2.50
❑ 155 Graham Koonce UR T3 RC 6.00 2.50
❑ 156 Tom Gregorio UR T3 RC 6.00 2.50
❑ 157 Javier A. Lopez UR T3 RC 6.00 2.50
❑ 158 Oscar Villarreal UR T3 RC 6.00 2.50
❑ 159 Prentice Redman UR T4 RC 12.00 5.00
❑ 160 Francisco Cruceta UR T4 RC 12.00 5.00
❑ 161 Guillermo Quiroz UR T4 RC 12.00 5.00
❑ 162 Jeremy Griffiths UR T4 RC 12.00 5.00
❑ 163 Lew Ford UR T4 RC 20.00 8.00
❑ 164 Rob Hammock UR T4 RC 12.00 5.00
❑ 165 Todd Wellemeyer UR T4 RC 12.00 5.00
❑ 166 Ryan Wagner UR T4 RC 12.00 5.00
❑ 167 Edwin Jackson UR T4 RC 20.00 8.00
❑ 168 Dan Haren UR T4 RC 20.00 8.00
❑ 169 Hideki Matsui AU RC 350.00 250.00
❑ 170 Jose Contreras AU RC 50.00 20.00
❑ 171 Delmon Young AU RC 325.00 225.00
❑ 172 Rickie Weeks AU RC 120.00 70.00
❑ 173 Brandon Webb AU RC 80.00 40.00
❑ 174 Bo Hart AU RC 15.00 6.00
❑ 175 Rocco Baldelli YS AU 25.00 10.00
❑ 176 Jose Reyes YS AU 25.00 10.00
❑ 177 Dontrelle Willis YS AU 50.00 20.00
❑ 178 Bobby Hill YS AU 15.00 6.00
❑ 179 Jae Weong Seo YS AU 25.00 10.00
❑ 180 Jesse Foppert YS AU 15.00 6.00

2004 Ultimate Collection

❑ COMMON CARD (1-42) 3.00 1.25
❑ COMMON CARD (43-126) 3.00 1.25
❑ 1-126 STATED ODDS TWO PER PACK
❑ 1-126 PRINT RUN 675 SERIAL #'d CARDS
❑ COMMON CARD (127-168) 5.00 2.00
❑ 127-209/222 STATED ODDS 3:4 PACKS
❑ 127-168 PRINT RUN 525 SERIAL #'d SETS
❑ COMMON CARD (169-194) 6.00 2.50
❑ 169-194 PRINT RUN 299 SERIAL #'d SETS
❑ COMMON (195-209/222) 8.00 3.00
❑ 195-209/222 PRINT RUN 199 SER.#'d SETS
❑ 210-221 STATED ODDS 1:10
❑ 210-221 PRINT RUN 75 SERIAL #'d SETS
❑ EXCHANGE DEADLINE 12/28/07

❑ 1 Al Kaline 5.00 2.00
❑ 2 Billy Williams 3.00 1.25
❑ 3 Bob Feller 3.00 1.25
❑ 4 Bob Gibson 5.00 2.00
❑ 5 Bob Lemon 3.00 1.25
❑ 6 Bobby Doerr 3.00 1.25
❑ 7 Brooks Robinson 5.00 2.00
❑ 8 Cal Ripken 15.00 6.00
❑ 9 Catfish Hunter 5.00 2.00
❑ 10 Eddie Mathews 5.00 2.00
❑ 11 Enos Slaughter 3.00 1.25
❑ 12 Ernie Banks 5.00 2.00
❑ 13 Fergie Jenkins 3.00 1.25
❑ 14 Gaylord Perry 3.00 1.25
❑ 15 Harmon Killebrew 5.00 2.00
❑ 16 Jim Bunning 3.00 1.25
❑ 17 Joe DiMaggio 8.00 3.00
❑ 18 Joe Morgan 3.00 1.25
❑ 19 Juan Marichal 3.00 1.25
❑ 20 Lou Brock 5.00 2.00
❑ 21 Luis Aparicio 3.00 1.25
❑ 22 Mickey Mantle 15.00 6.00
❑ 23 Mike Schmidt 10.00 4.00
❑ 24 Monte Irvin 3.00 1.25
❑ 25 Nolan Ryan 12.00 5.00
❑ 26 Pee Wee Reese 5.00 2.00
❑ 27 Phil Niekro 3.00 1.25
❑ 28 Phil Rizzuto 5.00 2.00
❑ 29 Ralph Kiner 5.00 2.00
❑ 30 Richie Ashburn 5.00 2.00
❑ 31 Robin Roberts 3.00 1.25
❑ 32 Robin Yount 5.00 2.00
❑ 33 Rod Carew 5.00 2.00
❑ 34 Rollie Fingers 3.00 1.25
❑ 35 Stan Musial 8.00 3.00
❑ 36 Ted Williams 10.00 4.00
❑ 37 Tom Seaver 5.00 2.00
❑ 38 Warren Spahn 5.00 2.00
❑ 39 Whitey Ford 5.00 2.00
❑ 40 Willie McCovey 5.00 2.00
❑ 41 Willie Stargell 5.00 2.00
❑ 42 Yogi Berra 5.00 2.00
❑ 43 Adrian Beltre 3.00 1.25
❑ 44 Albert Pujols 10.00 4.00
❑ 45 Alex Rodriguez 8.00 3.00
❑ 46 Alfonso Soriano 3.00 1.25
❑ 47 Andruw Jones 5.00 2.00
❑ 48 Andy Pettitte 5.00 2.00
❑ 49 Aubrey Huff 3.00 1.25
❑ 50 Barry Larkin 5.00 2.00
❑ 51 Ben Sheets 3.00 1.25
❑ 52 Bernie Williams 5.00 2.00
❑ 53 Bobby Abreu 3.00 1.25
❑ 54 Brad Penny 3.00 1.25
❑ 55 Bret Boone 3.00 1.25
❑ 56 Brian Giles 3.00 1.25
❑ 57 Carlos Beltran 3.00 1.25
❑ 58 Carlos Delgado 3.00 1.25
❑ 59 Carlos Guillen 3.00 1.25
❑ 60 Carlos Lee 3.00 1.25
❑ 61 Carlos Zambrano 3.00 1.25
❑ 62 Chipper Jones 5.00 2.00
❑ 63 Craig Biggio 5.00 2.00
❑ 64 Craig Wilson 3.00 1.25
❑ 65 Curt Schilling 5.00 2.00
❑ 66 David Ortiz 5.00 2.00
❑ 67 Derek Jeter 10.00 4.00
❑ 68 Eric Chavez 3.00 1.25
❑ 69 Eric Gagne 3.00 1.25
❑ 70 Frank Thomas 5.00 2.00
❑ 71 Garret Anderson 3.00 1.25
❑ 72 Gary Sheffield 3.00 1.25
❑ 73 Greg Maddux 8.00 3.00
❑ 74 Hank Blalock 3.00 1.25
❑ 75 Hideki Matsui 8.00 3.00
❑ 76 Ichiro Suzuki 10.00 4.00
❑ 77 Ivan Rodriguez 5.00 2.00
❑ 78 J.D. Drew 3.00 1.25
❑ 79 Jake Peavy 3.00 1.25
❑ 80 Jason Schmidt 3.00 1.25
❑ 81 Jeff Bagwell 5.00 2.00
❑ 82 Jeff Kent 3.00 1.25
❑ 83 Jim Thome 5.00 2.00
❑ 84 Joe Mauer 5.00 2.00
❑ 85 Johan Santana 5.00 2.00
❑ 86 Jose Reyes 3.00 1.25
❑ 87 Jose Vidro 3.00 1.25
❑ 88 Ken Griffey Jr. 8.00 3.00
❑ 89 Kerry Wood 3.00 1.25
❑ 90 Larry Walker Cards 5.00 2.00
❑ 91 Luis Gonzalez 3.00 1.25
❑ 92 Lyle Overbay 3.00 1.25
❑ 93 Magglio Ordonez 3.00 1.25
❑ 94 Manny Ramirez 5.00 2.00
❑ 95 Mark Mulder 3.00 1.25
❑ 96 Mark Prior 5.00 2.00
❑ 97 Mark Teixeira 5.00 2.00
❑ 98 Melvin Mora 3.00 1.25
❑ 99 Michael Young 3.00 1.25
❑ 100 Miguel Cabrera 5.00 2.00
❑ 101 Miguel Tejada 3.00 1.25
❑ 102 Mike Lowell 3.00 1.25
❑ 103 Mike Piazza 8.00 3.00
❑ 104 Mike Sweeney 3.00 1.25
❑ 105 Nomar Garciaparra 8.00 3.00
❑ 106 Oliver Perez 3.00 1.25
❑ 107 Pedro Martinez 5.00 2.00
❑ 108 Preston Wilson 3.00 1.25
❑ 109 Rafael Palmeiro 5.00 2.00
❑ 110 Randy Johnson 5.00 2.00
❑ 111 Roger Clemens 10.00 4.00
❑ 112 Roy Halladay 3.00 1.25
❑ 113 Roy Oswalt 3.00 1.25
❑ 114 Sammy Sosa 5.00 2.00
❑ 115 Scott Podsednik 3.00 1.25
❑ 116 Scott Rolen 5.00 2.00
❑ 117 Shawn Green 3.00 1.25
❑ 118 Tim Hudson 3.00 1.25
❑ 119 Todd Helton 5.00 2.00
❑ 120 Tom Glavine 5.00 2.00
❑ 121 Torii Hunter 3.00 1.25
❑ 122 Travis Hafner 3.00 1.25
❑ 123 Troy Glaus 3.00 1.25
❑ 124 Vernon Wells 3.00 1.25
❑ 125 Victor Martinez 3.00 1.25
❑ 126 Vladimir Guerrero 5.00 2.00
❑ 127 Aarom Baldiris UR T1 RC 8.00 3.00
❑ 128 Alfredo Simon UR T1 RC 5.00 2.00
❑ 129 Andres Blanco UR T1 RC 5.00 2.00
❑ 130 Jeff Bajenaru UR T1 RC 5.00 2.00
❑ 131 Bart Fortunato UR T1 RC 5.00 2.00
❑ 132 B.Medders UR T1 RC 5.00 2.00
❑ 133 Brian Dallimore UR T1 RC 5.00 2.00
❑ 134 Carlos Hines UR T1 RC 5.00 2.00
❑ 135 Carlos Vasquez UR T1 RC 8.00 3.00
❑ 136 Casey Daigle UR T1 RC 5.00 2.00
❑ 137 Chad Bentz UR T1 RC 5.00 2.00
❑ 138 Chris Aguila UR T1 RC 5.00 2.00
❑ 139 Chris Saenz UR T1 RC 5.00 2.00
❑ 140 Chris Shelton UR T1 RC 12.00 5.00
❑ 141 Colby Miller UR T1 RC 5.00 2.00
❑ 142 Dave Crouthers UR T1 RC 5.00 2.00
❑ 143 David Aardsma UR T1 RC 8.00 3.00
❑ 144 Dennis Sarfate UR T1 RC 5.00 2.00
❑ 145 Donnie Kelly UR T1 RC 5.00 2.00
❑ 146 Eddy Rodriguez UR T1 RC 8.00 3.00
❑ 147 Eduardo Villacis UR T1 RC 5.00 2.00
❑ 148 Edwardo Sierra UR T1 RC 8.00 3.00
❑ 149 Edwin Moreno UR T1 RC 8.00 3.00
❑ 150 Kyle Denney UR T1 RC 5.00 2.00
❑ 151 Evan Rust UR T1 RC 5.00 2.00
❑ 152 Fernando Nieve UR T1 RC 8.00 3.00
❑ 153 Frank Francisco UR T1 RC 5.00 2.00
❑ 154 Frank Gracesqui UR T1 RC 5.00 2.00
❑ 155 Freddy Guzman UR T1 RC 5.00 2.00
❑ 156 Greg Dobbs UR T1 RC 5.00 2.00
❑ 157 Hector Gimenez UR T1 RC 5.00 2.00
❑ 158 Jason Alfaro UR T1 RC 5.00 2.00
❑ 159 Jake Woods UR T1 RC 5.00 2.00
❑ 160 Andy Green UR T1 RC 5.00 2.00
❑ 161 Jason Bartlett UR T1 RC 8.00 3.00
❑ 162 Jason Frasor UR T1 RC 5.00 2.00
❑ 163 Jeff Bennett UR T1 RC 5.00 2.00
❑ 164 Jerome Gamble UR T1 RC 5.00 2.00
❑ 165 Jerry Gil UR T1 RC 5.00 2.00
❑ 166 Joe Hietpas UR T1 RC 5.00 2.00
❑ 167 Jorge Sequea UR T1 RC 5.00 2.00
❑ 168 Jorge Vasquez UR T1 RC 5.00 2.00
❑ 169 Josh Labandeira UR T2 RC 6.00 2.50
❑ 170 Justin Germano UR T2 RC 6.00 2.50
❑ 171 Justin Hampson UR T2 RC 6.00 2.50
❑ 172 Chris Young UR T2 RC 50.00 20.00

❑ 173 Justin Knoedler UR T2 RC 6.00 2.50
❑ 174 Justin Lehr UR T2 RC 6.00 2.50
❑ 175 Justin Leone UR T2 RC 10.00 4.00
❑ 176 Kaz Tadano UR T2 RC 10.00 4.00
❑ 177 Kevin Cave UR T2 RC 6.00 2.50
❑ 178 Linc Holdzkom UR T2 RC 6.00 2.50
❑ 179 Mike Rose UR T2 RC 6.00 2.50
❑ 180 Luis Gonzalez UR T2 RC 6.00 2.50
❑ 181 Mariano Gomez UR T2 RC 6.00 2.50
❑ 182 Rene Rivera UR T2 RC 6.00 2.50
❑ 183 Michael Wuertz UR T2 RC 10.00 4.00
❑ 184 Mike Gosling UR T2 RC 6.00 2.50
❑ 185 Mike Johnston UR T2 RC 6.00 2.50
❑ 186 Mike Rouse UR T2 RC 6.00 2.50
❑ 187 Nick Regilio UR T2 RC 6.00 2.50
❑ 188 Onil Joseph UR T2 RC 6.00 2.50
❑ 189 Orl Rodriguez UR T2 RC 6.00 2.50
❑ 190 Phil Stockman UR T2 RC 6.00 2.50
❑ 191 Renyel Pinto UR T2 RC 10.00 4.00
❑ 192 Roberto Novoa UR T2 RC 10.00 4.00
❑ 193 Roman Colon UR T2 RC 6.00 2.50
❑ 194 Ronald Belisario UR T2 RC 6.00 2.50
❑ 195 Ronny Cedeno UR T3 RC 10.00 4.00
❑ 196 Ryan Meaux UR T3 RC 8.00 3.00
❑ 197 Ryan Wing UR T3 RC 8.00 3.00
❑ 198 Scott Dohmann UR T3 RC 8.00 3.00
❑ 199 Joey Gathright UR T3 RC 12.00 5.00
❑ 200 Shawn Camp UR T3 RC 8.00 3.00
❑ 201 Shawn Hill UR T3 RC 8.00 3.00
❑ 202 Steve Andrade UR T3 RC 8.00 3.00
❑ 203 Tim Bausher UR T3 RC 8.00 3.00
❑ 204 Tim Bittner UR T3 RC 8.00 3.00
❑ 205 Brad Halsey UR T3 RC 12.00 5.00
❑ 206 William Bergolla UR T3 RC 8.00 3.00
❑ 207 Kameron Loe UR T3 RC 20.00 8.00
❑ 208 Jesse Crain UR T3 RC 12.00 5.00
❑ 209 Scott Kazmir UR T3 RC 30.00 12.50
❑ 210 Akinori Otsuka AU RC 50.00 20.00
❑ 211 Chris Oxspring AU RC 25.00 10.00
❑ 212 Ian Snell AU RC 40.00 15.00
❑ 213 John Gall AU RC 40.00 15.00
❑ 214 Jose Capellan AU RC 25.00 10.00
❑ 215 Yadier Molina AU RC 80.00 50.00
❑ 216 Merkin Valdez AU RC 25.00 10.00
❑ 217 R.Ramirez AU RC EXCH 25.00 10.00
❑ 218 Rusty Tucker AU RC 40.00 15.00
❑ 219 Scott Proctor AU RC 40.00 15.00
❑ 220 Sean Henn AU RC 25.00 10.00
❑ 221 Shingo Takatsu AU RC 40.00 15.00
❑ 222 Kazuo Matsui UR T3 RC 10.00 4.00

2005 Ultimate Collection

❑ COMMON CARD (1-100) 3.00 1.25
❑ 1-100 APPX ODDS 3:2 PACKS
❑ 1-100 PRINT RUN 475 SERIAL #'d SETS
❑ COMMON CARD (101-142) 5.00 2.00
❑ 101-142 APPX. ODDS 1:3
❑ 101-142 PRINT RUN 275 SERIAL #'d SETS
❑ COMMON CARD (143-237) 5.00 2.00
❑ COMMON RC (143-237) 5.00 2.00
❑ 143-237 STATED ODDS 3:4 PACKS
❑ 143-237 PRINT RUN 275 SERIAL #'d SETS
❑ 238-242 OVERALL AU ODDS 1:4
❑ 238-242 PRINT RUN 99 SERIAL #'d SETS
❑ 1 A.J. Burnett 3.00 1.25
❑ 2 Adam Dunn 3.00 1.25
❑ 3 Adrian Beltre 3.00 1.25
❑ 4 Albert Pujols 8.00 3.00
❑ 5 Alex Rodriguez 10.00 4.00
❑ 6 Alfonso Soriano 3.00 1.25
❑ 7 Andruw Jones 5.00 2.00
❑ 8 Andy Pettitte 5.00 2.00
❑ 9 Aramis Ramirez 3.00 1.25
❑ 10 Aubrey Huff 3.00 1.25
❑ 11 Ben Sheets 3.00 1.25
❑ 12 Bobby Abreu 3.00 1.25
❑ 13 Bobby Crosby 3.00 1.25
❑ 14 Chris Carpenter 3.00 1.25
❑ 15 Brian Giles 3.00 1.25
❑ 16 Brian Roberts 3.00 1.25
❑ 17 Carl Crawford 3.00 1.25
❑ 18 Carlos Beltran 3.00 1.25
❑ 19 Carlos Delgado 3.00 1.25
❑ 20 Carlos Zambrano 3.00 1.25
❑ 21 Chipper Jones 5.00 2.00
❑ 22 Corey Patterson 3.00 1.25
❑ 23 Craig Biggio 5.00 2.00
❑ 24 Curt Schilling 5.00 2.00
❑ 25 Dallas McPherson 3.00 1.25
❑ 26 David Ortiz 5.00 2.00
❑ 27 David Wright 8.00 3.00
❑ 28 Delmon Young 5.00 2.00
❑ 29 Derek Jeter 10.00 4.00
❑ 30 Derrek Lee 5.00 2.00
❑ 31 Dontrelle Willis 3.00 1.25
❑ 32 Eric Chavez 3.00 1.25
❑ 33 Eric Gagne 3.00 1.25
❑ 34 Francisco Rodriguez 3.00 1.25
❑ 35 Gary Sheffield 3.00 1.25
❑ 36 Greg Maddux 8.00 3.00
❑ 37 Hank Blalock 3.00 1.25
❑ 38 Hideki Matsui 6.00 2.50
❑ 39 Ichiro Suzuki 10.00 4.00
❑ 40 Ivan Rodriguez 5.00 2.00
❑ 41 J.D. Drew 3.00 1.25
❑ 42 Jake Peavy 3.00 1.25
❑ 43 Jason Bay 3.00 1.25
❑ 44 Jason Schmidt 3.00 1.25
❑ 45 Jeff Bagwell 5.00 2.00
❑ 46 Jeff Kent 3.00 1.25
❑ 47 Jeremy Bonderman 3.00 1.25
❑ 48 Jim Edmonds 3.00 1.25
❑ 49 Jim Thome 5.00 2.00
❑ 50 Joe Mauer 5.00 2.00
❑ 51 Johan Santana 5.00 2.00
❑ 52 John Smoltz 5.00 2.00
❑ 53 Johnny Damon 5.00 2.00
❑ 54 Jose Reyes 3.00 1.25
❑ 55 Jose Vidro 3.00 1.25
❑ 56 Josh Beckett 3.00 1.25
❑ 57 Justin Morneau 3.00 1.25
❑ 58 Ken Griffey Jr. 8.00 3.00
❑ 59 Kerry Wood 3.00 1.25
❑ 60 Khalil Greene 5.00 2.00
❑ 61 Lance Berkman 3.00 1.25
❑ 62 Larry Walker 5.00 2.00
❑ 63 Luis Gonzalez 3.00 1.25
❑ 64 Manny Ramirez 5.00 2.00
❑ 65 Mark Buehrle 3.00 1.25
❑ 66 Mark Mulder 3.00 1.25
❑ 67 Mark Prior 5.00 2.00
❑ 68 Mark Teixeira 5.00 2.00
❑ 69 Michael Young 3.00 1.25
❑ 70 Miguel Cabrera 5.00 2.00
❑ 71 Miguel Tejada 3.00 1.25
❑ 72 Mike Mussina 5.00 2.00
❑ 73 Mike Piazza 5.00 2.00
❑ 74 Moises Alou 3.00 1.25
❑ 75 Nomar Garciaparra 5.00 2.00
❑ 76 Oliver Perez 3.00 1.25
❑ 77 Pat Burrell 3.00 1.25
❑ 78 Paul Konerko 3.00 1.25
❑ 79 Pedro Feliz 3.00 1.25
❑ 80 Pedro Martinez 5.00 2.00
❑ 81 Randy Johnson 5.00 2.00
❑ 82 Richie Sexson 3.00 1.25
❑ 83 Rickie Weeks 3.00 1.25
❑ 84 Roger Clemens 8.00 3.00
❑ 85 Roy Halladay 3.00 1.25
❑ 86 Roy Oswalt 3.00 1.25
❑ 87 Sammy Sosa 5.00 2.00
❑ 88 Scott Kazmir 3.00 1.25
❑ 89 Scott Rolen 5.00 2.00
❑ 90 Shawn Green 3.00 1.25
❑ 91 Tim Hudson 3.00 1.25
❑ 92 Todd Helton 5.00 2.00
❑ 93 Tom Glavine 5.00 2.00
❑ 94 Torii Hunter 3.00 1.25
❑ 95 Travis Hafner 3.00 1.25
❑ 96 Troy Glaus 3.00 1.25
❑ 97 Vernon Wells 3.00 1.25
❑ 98 Victor Martinez 3.00 1.25
❑ 99 Vladimir Guerrero 5.00 2.00
❑ 100 Zack Greinke 3.00 1.25
❑ 101 Al Kaline RET 8.00 3.00
❑ 102 Babe Ruth RET 10.00 4.00
❑ 103 Bo Jackson RET 8.00 3.00
❑ 104 Bob Gibson RET 8.00 3.00
❑ 105 Brooks Robinson RET 8.00 3.00
❑ 106 Cal Ripken RET 20.00 8.00
❑ 107 Carl Yastrzemski RET 8.00 3.00
❑ 108 Carlton Fisk RET 8.00 3.00
❑ 109 Catfish Hunter RET 5.00 2.00
❑ 110 Christy Mathewson RET 8.00 3.00
❑ 111 Cy Young RET 8.00 3.00
❑ 112 Don Mattingly RET 10.00 4.00
❑ 113 Eddie Mathews RET 8.00 3.00
❑ 114 Eddie Murray RET 8.00 3.00
❑ 115 Gary Carter RET 5.00 2.00
❑ 116 Harmon Killebrew RET 8.00 3.00
❑ 117 Jim Palmer RET 5.00 2.00
❑ 118 Jimmie Foxx RET 8.00 3.00
❑ 119 Joe DiMaggio RET 8.00 3.00
❑ 120 Johnny Bench RET 8.00 3.00
❑ 121 Lefty Grove RET 8.00 3.00
❑ 122 Lou Gehrig RET 8.00 3.00
❑ 123 Mel Ott RET 8.00 3.00
❑ 124 Reggie Jackson RET 8.00 3.00
❑ 125 Mike Schmidt RET 10.00 4.00
❑ 126 Nolan Ryan RET 12.00 5.00
❑ 127 Ozzie Smith RET 8.00 3.00
❑ 128 Paul Molitor RET 5.00 2.00
❑ 129 Pee Wee Reese RET 8.00 3.00
❑ 130 Robin Yount RET 8.00 3.00
❑ 131 Ryne Sandberg RET 10.00 4.00
❑ 132 Ted Williams RET 8.00 3.00
❑ 133 Thurman Munson RET 8.00 3.00
❑ 134 Tom Seaver RET 8.00 3.00
❑ 135 Tony Gwynn RET 8.00 3.00
❑ 136 Wade Boggs RET 8.00 3.00
❑ 137 Walter Johnson RET 8.00 3.00
❑ 138 Warren Spahn RET 8.00 3.00
❑ 139 Will Clark RET 8.00 3.00
❑ 140 Willie McCovey RET 8.00 3.00
❑ 141 Willie Stargell RET 8.00 3.00
❑ 142 Yogi Berra RET 8.00 3.00
❑ 143 Ambiorix Burgos UP RC 5.00 2.00
❑ 144 Ambiorix Concepcion UP RC 5.002.00
❑ 145 Anibal Sanchez UP RC 15.00 6.00
❑ 146 Bill McCarthy UP RC 5.00 2.00
❑ 147 Brian Burres UP RC 5.00 2.00
❑ 148 Carlos Ruiz UP RC 5.00 2.00
❑ 149 Casey Rogowski UP RC 8.00 3.00
❑ 150 Chris Resop UP RC 5.00 2.00
❑ 151 Chris Roberson UP RC 5.00 2.00
❑ 152 Chris Seddon UP RC 5.00 2.00
❑ 153 Colter Bean UP RC 5.00 2.00
❑ 154 Dae-Sung Koo UP RC 5.00 2.00
❑ 155 Danny Rueckel UP RC 5.00 2.00
❑ 156 Dave Gassner UP RC 5.00 2.00
❑ 157 Ryan Howard UP 15.00 6.00
❑ 158 D.J. Houlton UP RC 5.00 2.00
❑ 159 Derek Wathan UP RC 5.00 2.00
❑ 160 Devon Lowery UP RC 5.00 2.00
❑ 161 Enrique Gonzalez UP RC 5.00 2.00
❑ 162 Erick Threets UP RC 5.00 2.00
❑ 163 Eude Brito UP RC 5.00 2.00
❑ 164 Francisco Butto UP RC 5.00 2.00
❑ 165 Franquelis Osoria UP RC 5.00 2.00
❑ 166 Garrett Jones UP RC 5.00 2.00
❑ 167 Geovany Soto UP RC 5.00 2.00
❑ 168 Ismael Ramirez UP RC 5.00 2.00
❑ 169 Jared Gothreaux UP RC 5.00 2.00
❑ 170 Jason Hammel UP RC 5.00 2.00
❑ 171 Jeff Housman UP RC 5.00 2.00
❑ 172 Jeff Miller UP RC 5.00 2.00
❑ 173 Jeff Francoeur UP 12.00 5.00
❑ 174 John Hattig UP RC 5.00 2.00
❑ 175 Jorge Campillo UP RC 5.00 2.00
❑ 176 Juan Morillo UP RC 5.00 2.00

❑ 177 Justin Wechsler UP RC 5.00 2.00
❑ 178 Keiichi Yabu UP RC 5.00 2.00
❑ 179 Kendry Morales UP RC 15.00 6.00
❑ 180 Luis Hernandez UP RC 5.00 2.00
❑ 181 Luis Mendoza UP RC 5.00 2.00
❑ 182 Luis Pena UP RC 5.00 2.00
❑ 183 Luis O.Rodriguez UP RC 5.00 2.00
❑ 184 Luke Scott UP RC 10.00 4.00
❑ 185 Marcos Carvajal UP RC 5.00 2.00
❑ 186 Mark Woodyard UP RC 5.00 2.00
❑ 187 Matt Smith UP RC 5.00 2.00
❑ 188 Matthew Lindstrom UP RC 5.00 2.00
❑ 189 Miguel Negron UP RC 8.00 3.00
❑ 190 Mike Morse UP RC 5.00 2.00
❑ 191 Nate McLouth UP RC 5.00 2.00
❑ 192 Nick Masset UP RC 5.00 2.00
❑ 193 Paulino Reynoso UP RC 5.00 2.00
❑ 194 Pedro Lopez UP RC 5.00 2.00
❑ 195 Pete Orr UP RC 5.00 2.00
❑ 196 Randy Messenger UP RC 5.00 2.00
❑ 197 Randy Williams UP RC 5.00 2.00
❑ 198 Raul Tablado UP RC 5.00 2.00
❑ 199 Ronny Paulino UP RC 6.00 2.50
❑ 200 Russ Rohlicek UP RC 5.00 2.00
❑ 201 Russell Martin UP RC 12.00 5.00
❑ 202 Scott Baker UP RC 8.00 3.00
❑ 203 Scott Munter UP RC 5.00 2.00
❑ 204 Sean Thompson UP RC 5.00 2.00
❑ 205 Sean Tracey UP RC 5.00 2.00
❑ 206 Steve Schmoll UP RC 5.00 2.00
❑ 207 Tony Pena UP RC 5.00 2.00
❑ 208 Travis Bowyer UP RC 5.00 2.00
❑ 209 Ubaldo Jimenez UP RC 5.00 2.00
❑ 210 Wladimir Balentien UP RC 10.00 4.00
❑ 211 Yorman Bazardo UP RC 5.00 2.00
❑ 212 Yuniesky Betancourt UP RC 10.00 4.00
❑ 213 Adam Shabala UP RC 5.00 2.00
❑ 214 Brandon McCarthy UP RC 10.00 4.00
❑ 215 Chad Orvella UP RC 5.00 2.00
❑ 216 Jermaine Van Buren UP 5.00 2.00
❑ 217 Anthony Reyes UP RC 25.00 10.00
❑ 218 Dana Eveland UP RC 5.00 2.00
❑ 219 Brian Anderson UP RC 8.00 3.00
❑ 220 Hayden Penn UP RC 8.00 3.00
❑ 221 Chris Denorfia UP RC 10.00 4.00
❑ 222 Joel Peralta UP RC 5.00 2.00
❑ 223 Ryan Garko UP RC 10.00 4.00
❑ 224 Felix Hernandez UP 10.00 4.00
❑ 225 Mark McLemore UP RC 5.00 2.00
❑ 226 Melky Cabrera UP RC 15.00 6.00
❑ 227 Nelson Cruz UP RC 10.00 4.00
❑ 228 Norihiro Nakamura UP RC 8.00 3.00
❑ 229 Oscar Robles UP RC 5.00 2.00
❑ 230 Rick Short UP RC 5.00 2.00
❑ 231 Ryan Zimmerman UP RC 30.00 12.50
❑ 232 Ryan Speier UP RC 5.00 2.00
❑ 233 Ryan Spilborghs UP RC 8.00 3.00
❑ 234 Shane Costa UP RC 5.00 2.00
❑ 235 Zach Duke UP 8.00 3.00
❑ 236 Tony Giarratano UP RC 5.00 2.00
❑ 237 Jeff Niemann UP RC 8.00 3.00
❑ 238 Stephen Drew AU RC 300.00 200.00
❑ 239 Justin Verlander AU RC 300.00 200.00
❑ 240 Prince Fielder AU RC 400.00 300.00
❑ 241 Philip Humber AU RC 60.00 30.00
❑ 242 Tadahito Iguchi AU RC 120.00 60.00

1991 Ultra Update

❑ COMP.FACT.SET (120) 25.00 10.00
❑ 1 Dwight Evans .75 .30
❑ 2 Chito Martinez RC .25 .08
❑ 3 Bob Melvin .25 .08
❑ 4 Mike Mussina RC 5.00 2.00
❑ 5 Jack Clark .50 .20
❑ 6 Dana Kiecker .25 .08
❑ 7 Steve Lyons .25 .08
❑ 8 Gary Gaetti .50 .20
❑ 9 Dave Gallagher .25 .08
❑ 10 Dave Parker .50 .20
❑ 11 Luis Polonia .25 .08
❑ 12 Luis Sojo .25 .08
❑ 13 Wilson Alvarez .25 .08
❑ 14 Alex Fernandez .25 .08
❑ 15 Craig Grebeck .25 .08
❑ 16 Ron Karkovice .25 .08
❑ 17 Warren Newson RC .25 .08
❑ 18 Scott Radinsky .25 .08
❑ 19 Glenallen Hill .25 .08
❑ 20 Charles Nagy .25 .08
❑ 21 Mark Whiten .25 .08
❑ 22 Milt Cuyler .25 .08
❑ 23 Paul Gibson .25 .08
❑ 24 Mickey Tettleton .25 .08
❑ 25 Todd Benzinger .25 .08
❑ 26 Storm Davis .25 .08
❑ 27 Kirk Gibson .50 .20
❑ 28 Bill Pecota .25 .08
❑ 29 Gary Thurman .25 .08
❑ 30 Darryl Hamilton .25 .08
❑ 31 Jaime Navarro .25 .08
❑ 32 Willie Randolph .50 .20
❑ 33 Bill Wegman .25 .08
❑ 34 Randy Bush .25 .08
❑ 35 Chili Davis .50 .20
❑ 36 Scott Erickson .25 .08
❑ 37 Chuck Knoblauch .50 .20
❑ 38 Scott Leius .25 .08
❑ 39 Jack Morris .50 .20
❑ 40 John Habyan .25 .08
❑ 41 Pat Kelly .25 .08
❑ 42 Matt Nokes .25 .08
❑ 43 Scott Sanderson .25 .08
❑ 44 Bernie Williams 2.00 .75
❑ 45 Harold Baines .50 .20
❑ 46 Brook Jacoby .25 .08
❑ 47 Earnest Riles .25 .08
❑ 48 Willie Wilson .25 .08
❑ 49 Jay Buhner .50 .20
❑ 50 Rich DeLucia RC .25 .08
❑ 51 Mike Jackson .25 .08
❑ 52 Bill Krueger .25 .08
❑ 53 Bill Swift .25 .08
❑ 54 Brian Downing .25 .08
❑ 55 Juan Gonzalez 1.50 .60
❑ 56 Dean Palmer .50 .20
❑ 57 Kevin Reimer .25 .08
❑ 58 Ivan Rodriguez RC 8.00 3.00
❑ 59 Tom Candiotti .25 .08
❑ 60 Juan Guzman RC .50 .20
❑ 61 Bob MacDonald RC .25 .08
❑ 62 Greg Myers .25 .08
❑ 63 Ed Sprague .25 .08
❑ 64 Devon White .50 .20
❑ 65 Rafael Belliard .25 .08
❑ 66 Juan Berenguer .25 .08
❑ 67 Brian R.Hunter RC .50 .20
❑ 68 Kent Mercker .25 .08
❑ 69 Otis Nixon .25 .08
❑ 70 Danny Jackson .25 .08
❑ 71 Chuck McElroy .25 .08
❑ 72 Gary Scott RC .25 .08
❑ 73 Heathcliff Slocumb RC .25 .08
❑ 74 Chico Walker .25 .08
❑ 75 Rick Wilkins RC .25 .08
❑ 76 Chris Hammond .25 .08
❑ 77 Luis Quinones .25 .08
❑ 78 Herm Winningham .25 .08
❑ 79 Jeff Bagwell RC 8.00 3.00
❑ 80 Jim Corsi .25 .08
❑ 81 Steve Finley .50 .20
❑ 82 Luis Gonzalez RC 1.50 .60
❑ 83 Pete Harnisch .25 .08
❑ 84 Darryl Kile .50 .20
❑ 85 Brett Butler .50 .20
❑ 86 Gary Carter .50 .20
❑ 87 Tim Crews .25 .08
❑ 88 Orel Hershiser .50 .20
❑ 89 Bob Ojeda .25 .08
❑ 90 Bret Barberie RC .25 .08
❑ 91 Barry Jones .25 .08
❑ 92 Gilberto Reyes .25 .08
❑ 93 Larry Walker 1.50 .60
❑ 94 Hubie Brooks .25 .08
❑ 95 Tim Burke .25 .08
❑ 96 Rick Cerone .25 .08
❑ 97 Jeff Innis .25 .08
❑ 98 Wally Backman .25 .08
❑ 99 Tommy Greene .25 .08
❑ 100 Ricky Jordan .25 .08
❑ 101 Mitch Williams .25 .08
❑ 102 John Smiley .25 .08
❑ 103 Randy Tomlin RC .25 .08
❑ 104 Gary Varsho .25 .08
❑ 105 Cris Carpenter .25 .08
❑ 106 Ken Hill .25 .08
❑ 107 Felix Jose .25 .08
❑ 108 Omar Olivares RC .25 .08
❑ 109 Gerald Perry .25 .08
❑ 110 Jerald Clark .25 .08
❑ 111 Tony Fernandez .25 .08
❑ 112 Darrin Jackson .25 .08
❑ 113 Mike Maddux .25 .08
❑ 114 Tim Teufel .25 .08
❑ 115 Bud Black .25 .08
❑ 116 Kelly Downs .25 .08
❑ 117 Mike Felder .25 .08
❑ 118 Willie McGee .50 .20
❑ 119 Trevor Wilson .25 .08
❑ 120 Checklist 1-120 .25 .08

1993 Ultra

❑ COMPLETE SET (650) 30.00 12.00
❑ COMPLETE SERIES 1 (300) 15.00 6.00
❑ COMPLETE SERIES 2 (350) 15.00 6.00
❑ 1 Steve Avery .15 .05
❑ 2 Rafael Belliard .15 .05
❑ 3 Damon Berryhill .15 .05
❑ 4 Sid Bream .15 .05
❑ 5 Ron Gant .30 .10
❑ 6 Tom Glavine .50 .20
❑ 7 Ryan Klesko .30 .10
❑ 8 Mark Lemke .15 .05
❑ 9 Javier Lopez .50 .20
❑ 10 Greg Olson .15 .05
❑ 11 Terry Pendleton .30 .10
❑ 12 Deion Sanders .50 .20
❑ 13 Mike Stanton .15 .05
❑ 14 Paul Assenmacher .15 .05
❑ 15 Steve Buechele .15 .05
❑ 16 Frank Castillo .15 .05
❑ 17 Shawon Dunston .15 .05
❑ 18 Mark Grace .50 .20
❑ 19 Derrick May .15 .05
❑ 20 Chuck McElroy .15 .05
❑ 21 Mike Morgan .15 .05
❑ 22 Bob Scanlan .15 .05
❑ 23 Dwight Smith .15 .05
❑ 24 Sammy Sosa .75 .30
❑ 25 Rick Wilkins .15 .05
❑ 26 Tim Belcher .15 .05
❑ 27 Jeff Branson .15 .05
❑ 28 Bill Doran .15 .05

❑	29	Chris Hammond	.15	.05
❑	30	Barry Larkin	.50	.20
❑	31	Hal Morris	.15	.05
❑	32	Joe Oliver	.15	.05
❑	33	Jose Rijo	.15	.05
❑	34	Bip Roberts	.15	.05
❑	35	Chris Sabo	.15	.05
❑	36	Reggie Sanders	.30	.10
❑	37	Craig Biggio	.50	.20
❑	38	Ken Caminiti	.30	.10
❑	39	Steve Finley	.30	.10
❑	40	Luis Gonzalez	.30	.10
❑	41	Juan Guerrero	.15	.05
❑	42	Pete Harnisch	.15	.05
❑	43	Xavier Hernandez	.15	.05
❑	44	Doug Jones	.15	.05
❑	45	Al Osuna	.15	.05
❑	46	Eddie Taubensee	.15	.05
❑	47	Scooter Tucker	.15	.05
❑	48	Brian Williams	.15	.05
❑	49	Pedro Astacio	.15	.05
❑	50	Rafael Bournigal	.15	.05
❑	51	Brett Butler	.30	.10
❑	52	Tom Candiotti	.15	.05
❑	53	Eric Davis	.30	.10
❑	54	Lenny Harris	.15	.05
❑	55	Orel Hershiser	.30	.10
❑	56	Eric Karros	.30	.10
❑	57	Pedro Martinez	1.50	.60
❑	58	Roger McDowell	.15	.05
❑	59	Jose Offerman	.15	.05
❑	60	Mike Piazza	3.00	1.25
❑	61	Moises Alou	.30	.10
❑	62	Kent Bottenfield	.15	.05
❑	63	Archi Cianfrocco	.15	.05
❑	64	Greg Colbrunn	.15	.05
❑	65	Wil Cordero	.15	.05
❑	66	Delino DeShields	.15	.05
❑	67	Darrin Fletcher	.15	.05
❑	68	Ken Hill	.15	.05
❑	69	Chris Nabholz	.15	.05
❑	70	Mel Rojas	.15	.05
❑	71	Larry Walker	.30	.10
❑	72	Sid Fernandez	.15	.05
❑	73	John Franco	.30	.10
❑	74	Dave Gallagher	.15	.05
❑	75	Todd Hundley	.15	.05
❑	76	Howard Johnson	.15	.05
❑	77	Jeff Kent	.75	.30
❑	78	Eddie Murray	.75	.30
❑	79	Bret Saberhagen	.30	.10
❑	80	Chico Walker	.15	.05
❑	81	Anthony Young	.15	.05
❑	82	Kyle Abbott	.15	.05
❑	83	Ruben Amaro	.15	.05
❑	84	Juan Bell	.15	.05
❑	85	Wes Chamberlain	.15	.05
❑	86	Darren Daulton	.30	.10
❑	87	Mariano Duncan	.15	.05
❑	88	Dave Hollins	.15	.05
❑	89	Ricky Jordan	.15	.05
❑	90	John Kruk	.30	.10
❑	91	Mickey Morandini	.15	.05
❑	92	Terry Mulholland	.15	.05
❑	93	Ben Rivera	.15	.05
❑	94	Mike Williams	.15	.05
❑	95	Stan Belinda	.15	.05
❑	96	Jay Bell	.30	.10
❑	97	Jeff King	.15	.05
❑	98	Mike LaValliere	.15	.05
❑	99	Lloyd McClendon	.15	.05
❑	100	Orlando Merced	.15	.05
❑	101	Zane Smith	.15	.05
❑	102	Randy Tomlin	.15	.05
❑	103	Andy Van Slyke	.50	.20
❑	104	Tim Wakefield	.75	.30
❑	105	John Wehner	.15	.05
❑	106	Bernard Gilkey	.15	.05
❑	107	Brian Jordan	.30	.10
❑	108	Ray Lankford	.30	.10
❑	109	Donovan Osborne	.15	.05
❑	110	Tom Pagnozzi	.15	.05
❑	111	Mike Perez	.15	.05
❑	112	Lee Smith	.30	.10
❑	113	Ozzie Smith	1.25	.50
❑	114	Bob Tewksbury	.15	.05
❑	115	Todd Zeile	.15	.05
❑	116	Andy Benes	.15	.05
❑	117	Greg W. Harris	.15	.05
❑	118	Darrin Jackson	.15	.05
❑	119	Fred McGriff	.50	.20
❑	120	Rich Rodriguez	.15	.05
❑	121	Frank Seminara	.15	.05
❑	122	Gary Sheffield	.30	.10
❑	123	Craig Shipley	.15	.05
❑	124	Kurt Stillwell	.15	.05
❑	125	Dan Walters	.15	.05
❑	126	Rod Beck	.15	.05
❑	127	Mike Benjamin	.15	.05
❑	128	Jeff Brantley	.15	.05
❑	129	John Burkett	.15	.05
❑	130	Will Clark	.50	.20
❑	131	Royce Clayton	.15	.05
❑	132	Steve Hosey	.15	.05
❑	133	Mike Jackson	.15	.05
❑	134	Darren Lewis	.15	.05
❑	135	Kirt Manwaring	.15	.05
❑	136	Bill Swift	.15	.05
❑	137	Robby Thompson	.15	.05
❑	138	Brady Anderson	.30	.10
❑	139	Glenn Davis	.15	.05
❑	140	Leo Gomez	.15	.05
❑	141	Chito Martinez	.15	.05
❑	142	Ben McDonald	.15	.05
❑	143	Alan Mills	.15	.05
❑	144	Mike Mussina	.50	.20
❑	145	Gregg Olson	.15	.05
❑	146	David Segui	.15	.05
❑	147	Jeff Tackett	.15	.05
❑	148	Jack Clark	.30	.10
❑	149	Scott Cooper	.15	.05
❑	150	Danny Darwin	.15	.05
❑	151	John Dopson	.15	.05
❑	152	Mike Greenwell	.15	.05
❑	153	Tim Naehring	.15	.05
❑	154	Tony Pena	.15	.05
❑	155	Paul Quantrill	.15	.05
❑	156	Mo Vaughn	.30	.10
❑	157	Frank Viola	.30	.10
❑	158	Bob Zupcic	.15	.05
❑	159	Chad Curtis	.15	.05
❑	160	Gary DiSarcina	.15	.05
❑	161	Damion Easley	.15	.05
❑	162	Chuck Finley	.30	.10
❑	163	Tim Fortugno	.15	.05
❑	164	Rene Gonzales	.15	.05
❑	165	Joe Grahe	.15	.05
❑	166	Mark Langston	.15	.05
❑	167	John Orton	.15	.05
❑	168	Luis Polonia	.15	.05
❑	169	Julio Valera	.15	.05
❑	170	Wilson Alvarez	.15	.05
❑	171	George Bell	.15	.05
❑	172	Joey Cora	.15	.05
❑	173	Alex Fernandez	.15	.05
❑	174	Lance Johnson	.15	.05
❑	175	Ron Karkovice	.15	.05
❑	176	Jack McDowell	.15	.05
❑	177	Scott Radinsky	.15	.05
❑	178	Tim Raines	.30	.10
❑	179	Steve Sax	.15	.05
❑	180	Bobby Thigpen	.15	.05
❑	181	Frank Thomas	.75	.30
❑	182	Sandy Alomar Jr.	.15	.05
❑	183	Carlos Baerga	.15	.05
❑	184	Felix Fermin	.15	.05
❑	185	Thomas Howard	.15	.05
❑	186	Mark Lewis	.15	.05
❑	187	Derek Lilliquist	.15	.05
❑	188	Carlos Martinez	.15	.05
❑	189	Charles Nagy	.15	.05
❑	190	Scott Scudder	.15	.05
❑	191	Paul Sorrento	.15	.05
❑	192	Jim Thome	.50	.20
❑	193	Mark Whiten	.15	.05
❑	194	Milt Cuyler UER	.15	.05
❑	195	Rob Deer	.15	.05
❑	196	John Doherty	.15	.05
❑	197	Travis Fryman	.30	.10
❑	198	Dan Gladden	.15	.05
❑	199	Mike Henneman	.15	.05
❑	200	John Kiely	.15	.05
❑	201	Chad Kreuter	.15	.05
❑	202	Scott Livingstone	.15	.05
❑	203	Tony Phillips	.15	.05
❑	204	Alan Trammell	.30	.10
❑	205	Mike Boddicker	.15	.05
❑	206	George Brett	2.00	.75
❑	207	Tom Gordon	.15	.05
❑	208	Mark Gubicza	.15	.05
❑	209	Gregg Jefferies	.15	.05
❑	210	Wally Joyner	.30	.10
❑	211	Kevin Koslofski	.15	.05
❑	212	Brent Mayne	.15	.05
❑	213	Brian McRae	.15	.05
❑	214	Kevin McReynolds	.15	.05
❑	215	Rusty Meacham	.15	.05
❑	216	Steve Shifflett	.15	.05
❑	217	Jim Austin	.15	.05
❑	218	Cal Eldred	.15	.05
❑	219	Darryl Hamilton	.15	.05
❑	220	Doug Henry	.15	.05
❑	221	John Jaha	.15	.05
❑	222	Dave Nilsson	.15	.05
❑	223	Jesse Orosco	.15	.05
❑	224	B.J. Surhoff	.30	.10
❑	225	Greg Vaughn	.15	.05
❑	226	Bill Wegman	.15	.05
❑	227	Robin Yount	1.25	.50
❑	228	Rick Aguilera	.15	.05
❑	229	J.T. Bruett	.15	.05
❑	230	Scott Erickson	.15	.05
❑	231	Kent Hrbek	.30	.10
❑	232	Terry Jorgensen	.15	.05
❑	233	Scott Leius	.15	.05
❑	234	Pat Mahomes	.15	.05
❑	235	Pedro Munoz	.15	.05
❑	236	Kirby Puckett	.75	.30
❑	237	Kevin Tapani	.15	.05
❑	238	Lenny Webster	.15	.05
❑	239	Carl Willis	.15	.05
❑	240	Mike Gallego	.15	.05
❑	241	John Habyan	.15	.05
❑	242	Pat Kelly	.15	.05
❑	243	Kevin Maas	.15	.05
❑	244	Don Mattingly	2.00	.75
❑	245	Hensley Meulens	.15	.05
❑	246	Sam Militello	.15	.05
❑	247	Matt Nokes	.15	.05
❑	248	Melido Perez	.15	.05
❑	249	Andy Stankiewicz	.15	.05
❑	250	Randy Velarde	.15	.05
❑	251	Bob Wickman	.15	.05
❑	252	Bernie Williams	.50	.20
❑	253	Lance Blankenship	.15	.05
❑	254	Mike Bordick	.15	.05
❑	255	Jerry Browne	.15	.05
❑	256	Ron Darling	.15	.05
❑	257	Dennis Eckersley	.30	.10
❑	258	Rickey Henderson	.75	.30
❑	259	Vince Horsman	.15	.05
❑	260	Troy Neel	.15	.05
❑	261	Jeff Parrett	.15	.05
❑	262	Terry Steinbach	.15	.05
❑	263	Bob Welch	.15	.05
❑	264	Bobby Witt	.15	.05
❑	265	Rich Amaral	.15	.05
❑	266	Bret Boone	.30	.10
❑	267	Jay Buhner	.30	.10
❑	268	Dave Fleming	.15	.05
❑	269	Randy Johnson	.75	.30
❑	270	Edgar Martinez	.50	.20
❑	271	Mike Schooler	.15	.05
❑	272	Russ Swan	.15	.05
❑	273	Dave Valle	.15	.05
❑	274	Omar Vizquel	.50	.20
❑	275	Kerry Woodson	.15	.05
❑	276	Kevin Brown	.30	.10
❑	277	Julio Franco	.30	.10
❑	278	Jeff Frye	.15	.05
❑	279	Juan Gonzalez	.30	.10
❑	280	Jeff Huson	.15	.05
❑	281	Rafael Palmeiro	.50	.20
❑	282	Dean Palmer	.30	.10
❑	283	Roger Pavlik	.15	.05
❑	284	Ivan Rodriguez	.50	.20
❑	285	Kenny Rogers	.30	.10
❑	286	Derek Bell	.15	.05

❑ 287 Pat Borders .15 .05
❑ 288 Joe Carter .30 .10
❑ 289 Bob MacDonald .15 .05
❑ 290 Jack Morris .30 .10
❑ 291 John Olerud .30 .10
❑ 292 Ed Sprague .15 .05
❑ 293 Todd Stottlemyre .15 .05
❑ 294 Mike Timlin .15 .05
❑ 295 Duane Ward .15 .05
❑ 296 David Wells .30 .10
❑ 297 Devon White .30 .10
❑ 298 Ray Lankford CL .15 .05
❑ 299 Bobby Witt CL .15 .05
❑ 300 Mike Piazza CL .75 .30
❑ 301 Steve Bedrosian .15 .05
❑ 302 Jeff Blauser .15 .05
❑ 303 Francisco Cabrera .15 .05
❑ 304 Marvin Freeman .15 .05
❑ 305 Brian Hunter .15 .05
❑ 306 David Justice .30 .10
❑ 307 Greg Maddux 1.25 .50
❑ 308 Greg McMichael RC .30 .10
❑ 309 Kent Mercker .15 .05
❑ 310 Otis Nixon .15 .05
❑ 311 Pete Smith .15 .05
❑ 312 John Smoltz .50 .20
❑ 313 Jose Guzman .15 .05
❑ 314 Mike Harkey .15 .05
❑ 315 Greg Hibbard .15 .05
❑ 316 Candy Maldonado .15 .05
❑ 317 Randy Myers .15 .05
❑ 318 Dan Plesac .15 .05
❑ 319 Rey Sanchez .15 .05
❑ 320 Ryne Sandberg 1.25 .50
❑ 321 Tommy Shields .15 .05
❑ 322 Jose Vizcaino .15 .05
❑ 323 Matt Walbeck RC .30 .10
❑ 324 Willie Wilson .15 .05
❑ 325 Tom Browning .15 .05
❑ 326 Tim Costo .15 .05
❑ 327 Rob Dibble .30 .10
❑ 328 Steve Foster .15 .05
❑ 329 Roberto Kelly .15 .05
❑ 330 Randy Milligan .15 .05
❑ 331 Kevin Mitchell .15 .05
❑ 332 Tim Pugh RC .30 .10
❑ 333 Jeff Reardon .30 .10
❑ 334 John Roper .15 .05
❑ 335 Juan Samuel .15 .05
❑ 336 John Smiley .15 .05
❑ 337 Dan Wilson .30 .10
❑ 338 Scott Aldred .15 .05
❑ 339 Andy Ashby .15 .05
❑ 340 Freddie Benavides .15 .05
❑ 341 Dante Bichette .30 .10
❑ 342 Willie Blair .15 .05
❑ 343 Daryl Boston .15 .05
❑ 344 Vinny Castilla .75 .30
❑ 345 Jerald Clark .15 .05
❑ 346 Alex Cole .15 .05
❑ 347 Andres Galarraga .30 .10
❑ 348 Joe Girardi .15 .05
❑ 349 Ryan Hawblitzel .15 .05
❑ 350 Charlie Hayes .15 .05
❑ 351 Butch Henry .15 .05
❑ 352 Darren Holmes .15 .05
❑ 353 Dale Murphy .50 .20
❑ 354 David Nied .15 .05
❑ 355 Jeff Parrett .15 .05
❑ 356 Steve Reed RC .30 .10
❑ 357 Bruce Ruffin .15 .05
❑ 358 Danny Sheaffer RC .30 .10
❑ 359 Bryn Smith .15 .05
❑ 360 Jim Tatum RC .30 .10
❑ 361 Eric Young .15 .05
❑ 362 Gerald Young .15 .05
❑ 363 Luis Aquino .15 .05
❑ 364 Alex Arias .15 .05
❑ 365 Jack Armstrong .15 .05
❑ 366 Bret Barberie .15 .05
❑ 367 Ryan Bowen .15 .05
❑ 368 Greg Briley .15 .05
❑ 369 Cris Carpenter .15 .05
❑ 370 Chuck Carr .15 .05
❑ 371 Jeff Conine .30 .10
❑ 372 Steve Decker .15 .05
❑ 373 Orestes Destrade .15 .05
❑ 374 Monty Fariss .15 .05
❑ 375 Junior Felix .15 .05
❑ 376 Chris Hammond .15 .05
❑ 377 Bryan Harvey .15 .05
❑ 378 Trevor Hoffman .75 .30
❑ 379 Charlie Hough .30 .10
❑ 380 Joe Klink .15 .05
❑ 381 Richie Lewis RC .30 .10
❑ 382 Dave Magadan .15 .05
❑ 383 Bob McClure .15 .05
❑ 384 Scott Pose RC .30 .10
❑ 385 Rich Renteria .15 .05
❑ 386 Benito Santiago .30 .10
❑ 387 Walt Weiss .15 .05
❑ 388 Nigel Wilson .15 .05
❑ 389 Eric Anthony .15 .05
❑ 390 Jeff Bagwell .50 .20
❑ 391 Andujar Cedeno .15 .05
❑ 392 Doug Drabek .15 .05
❑ 393 Darryl Kile .30 .10
❑ 394 Mark Portugal .15 .05
❑ 395 Karl Rhodes .15 .05
❑ 396 Scott Servais .15 .05
❑ 397 Greg Swindell .15 .05
❑ 398 Tom Goodwin .15 .05
❑ 399 Kevin Gross .15 .05
❑ 400 Carlos Hernandez .15 .05
❑ 401 Ramon Martinez .15 .05
❑ 402 Raul Mondesi .30 .10
❑ 403 Jody Reed .15 .05
❑ 404 Mike Sharperson .15 .05
❑ 405 Cory Snyder .15 .05
❑ 406 Darryl Strawberry .30 .10
❑ 407 Rick Trlicek .15 .05
❑ 408 Tim Wallach .15 .05
❑ 409 Todd Worrell .15 .05
❑ 410 Tavo Alvarez .15 .05
❑ 411 Sean Berry .15 .05
❑ 412 Frank Bolick .15 .05
❑ 413 Cliff Floyd .30 .10
❑ 414 Mike Gardiner .15 .05
❑ 415 Marquis Grissom .30 .10
❑ 416 Tim Laker RC .30 .10
❑ 417 Mike Lansing RC .50 .20
❑ 418 Dennis Martinez .30 .10
❑ 419 John Vander Wal .15 .05
❑ 420 John Wetteland .30 .10
❑ 421 Rondell White .30 .10
❑ 422 Bobby Bonilla .30 .10
❑ 423 Jeromy Burnitz .30 .10
❑ 424 Vince Coleman .15 .05
❑ 425 Mike Draper .15 .05
❑ 426 Tony Fernandez .15 .05
❑ 427 Dwight Gooden .30 .10
❑ 428 Jeff Innis .15 .05
❑ 429 Bobby Jones .30 .10
❑ 430 Mike Maddux .15 .05
❑ 431 Charlie O'Brien .15 .05
❑ 432 Joe Orsulak .15 .05
❑ 433 Pete Schourek .15 .05
❑ 434 Frank Tanana .15 .05
❑ 435 Ryan Thompson .15 .05
❑ 436 Kim Batiste .15 .05
❑ 437 Mark Davis .15 .05
❑ 438 Jose DeLeon .15 .05
❑ 439 Len Dykstra .30 .10
❑ 440 Jim Eisenreich .15 .05
❑ 441 Tommy Greene .15 .05
❑ 442 Pete Incaviglia .15 .05
❑ 443 Danny Jackson .15 .05
❑ 444 Todd Pratt RC .50 .20
❑ 445 Curt Schilling .30 .10
❑ 446 Milt Thompson .15 .05
❑ 447 David West .15 .05
❑ 448 Mitch Williams .15 .05
❑ 449 Steve Cooke .15 .05
❑ 450 Carlos Garcia .15 .05
❑ 451 Al Martin .15 .05
❑ 452 Blas Minor .15 .05
❑ 453 Dennis Moeller .15 .05
❑ 454 Denny Neagle .30 .10
❑ 455 Don Slaught .15 .05
❑ 456 Lonnie Smith .15 .05
❑ 457 Paul Wagner .15 .05
❑ 458 Bob Walk .15 .05
❑ 459 Kevin Young .30 .10
❑ 460 Rene Arocha RC .50 .20
❑ 461 Brian Barber .15 .05
❑ 462 Rheal Cormier .15 .05
❑ 463 Gregg Jefferies .15 .05
❑ 464 Joe Magrane .15 .05
❑ 465 Omar Olivares .15 .05
❑ 466 Geronimo Pena .15 .05
❑ 467 Allen Watson .15 .05
❑ 468 Mark Whiten .15 .05
❑ 469 Derek Bell .15 .05
❑ 470 Phil Clark .15 .05
❑ 471 Pat Gomez RC .30 .10
❑ 472 Tony Gwynn 1.00 .40
❑ 473 Jeremy Hernandez .15 .05
❑ 474 Bruce Hurst .15 .05
❑ 475 Phil Plantier .15 .05
❑ 476 Scott Sanders RC .30 .10
❑ 477 Tim Scott .15 .05
❑ 478 Darrell Sherman RC .30 .10
❑ 479 Guillermo Velasquez .15 .05
❑ 480 Tim Worrell RC .30 .10
❑ 481 Todd Benzinger .15 .05
❑ 482 Bud Black .15 .05
❑ 483 Barry Bonds 2.00 .75
❑ 484 Dave Burba .15 .05
❑ 485 Bryan Hickerson .15 .05
❑ 486 Dave Martinez .15 .05
❑ 487 Willie McGee .30 .10
❑ 488 Jeff Reed .15 .05
❑ 489 Kevin Rogers .15 .05
❑ 490 Matt Williams .30 .10
❑ 491 Trevor Wilson .15 .05
❑ 492 Harold Baines .30 .10
❑ 493 Mike Devereaux .15 .05
❑ 494 Todd Frohwirth .15 .05
❑ 495 Chris Hoiles .15 .05
❑ 496 Luis Mercedes .15 .05
❑ 497 Sherman Obando RC .30 .10
❑ 498 Brad Pennington .15 .05
❑ 499 Harold Reynolds .30 .10
❑ 500 Arthur Rhodes .15 .05
❑ 501 Cal Ripken 2.50 1.00
❑ 502 Rick Sutcliffe .30 .10
❑ 503 Fernando Valenzuela .30 .10
❑ 504 Mark Williamson .15 .05
❑ 505 Scott Bankhead .15 .05
❑ 506 Greg Blosser .15 .05
❑ 507 Ivan Calderon .15 .05
❑ 508 Roger Clemens 1.50 .60
❑ 509 Andre Dawson .30 .10
❑ 510 Scott Fletcher .15 .05
❑ 511 Greg A. Harris .15 .05
❑ 512 Billy Hatcher .15 .05
❑ 513 Bob Melvin .15 .05
❑ 514 Carlos Quintana .15 .05
❑ 515 Luis Rivera .15 .05
❑ 516 Jeff Russell .15 .05
❑ 517 Ken Ryan RC .30 .10
❑ 518 Chili Davis .30 .10
❑ 519 Jim Edmonds RC 5.00 2.00
❑ 520 Gary Gaetti .30 .10
❑ 521 Torey Lovullo .15 .05
❑ 522 Troy Percival .50 .20
❑ 523 Tim Salmon .50 .20
❑ 524 Scott Sanderson .15 .05
❑ 525 J.T.Snow RC .75 .30
❑ 526 Jerome Walton .15 .05
❑ 527 Jason Bere .15 .05
❑ 528 Rod Bolton .15 .05
❑ 529 Ellis Burks .30 .10
❑ 530 Carlton Fisk .50 .20
❑ 531 Craig Grebeck .15 .05
❑ 532 Ozzie Guillen .30 .10
❑ 533 Roberto Hernandez .15 .05
❑ 534 Bo Jackson .75 .30
❑ 535 Kirk McCaskill .15 .05
❑ 536 Dave Stieb .15 .05
❑ 537 Robin Ventura .30 .10
❑ 538 Albert Belle .30 .10
❑ 539 Mike Bielecki .15 .05
❑ 540 Glenallen Hill .15 .05
❑ 541 Reggie Jefferson .15 .05
❑ 542 Kenny Lofton .30 .10
❑ 543 Jeff Mutis .15 .05
❑ 544 Junior Ortiz .15 .05

❑ 545 Manny Ramirez 1.25 .50
❑ 546 Jeff Treadway .15 .05
❑ 547 Kevin Wickander .15 .05
❑ 548 Cecil Fielder .30 .10
❑ 549 Kirk Gibson .30 .10
❑ 550 Greg Gohr .15 .05
❑ 551 David Haas .15 .05
❑ 552 Bill Krueger .15 .05
❑ 553 Mike Moore .15 .05
❑ 554 Mickey Tettleton .15 .05
❑ 555 Lou Whitaker .30 .10
❑ 556 Kevin Appier .30 .10
❑ 557 Billy Brewer .15 .05
❑ 558 David Cone .30 .10
❑ 559 Greg Gagne .15 .05
❑ 560 Mark Gardner .15 .05
❑ 561 Phil Hiatt .15 .05
❑ 562 Felix Jose .15 .05
❑ 563 Jose Lind .15 .05
❑ 564 Mike Macfarlane .15 .05
❑ 565 Keith Miller .15 .05
❑ 566 Jeff Montgomery .15 .05
❑ 567 Hipolito Pichardo .15 .05
❑ 568 Ricky Bones .15 .05
❑ 569 Tom Brunansky .15 .05
❑ 570 Joe Kmak .15 .05
❑ 571 Pat Listach .15 .05
❑ 572 Graeme Lloyd RC .50 .20
❑ 573 Carlos Maldonado .15 .05
❑ 574 Josias Manzanillo .15 .05
❑ 575 Matt Mieske .15 .05
❑ 576 Kevin Reimer .15 .05
❑ 577 Bill Spiers .15 .05
❑ 578 Dickie Thon .15 .05
❑ 579 Willie Banks .15 .05
❑ 580 Jim Deshaies .15 .05
❑ 581 Mark Guthrie .15 .05
❑ 582 Brian Harper .15 .05
❑ 583 Chuck Knoblauch .30 .10
❑ 584 Gene Larkin .15 .05
❑ 585 Shane Mack .15 .05
❑ 586 David McCarty .15 .05
❑ 587 Mike Pagliarulo .15 .05
❑ 588 Mike Trombley .15 .05
❑ 589 Dave Winfield .30 .10
❑ 590 Jim Abbott .50 .20
❑ 591 Wade Boggs .50 .20
❑ 592 Russ Davis RC .30 .10
❑ 593 Steve Farr .15 .05
❑ 594 Steve Howe .15 .05
❑ 595 Mike Humphreys .15 .05
❑ 596 Jimmy Key .30 .10
❑ 597 Jim Leyritz .15 .05
❑ 598 Bobby Munoz .15 .05
❑ 599 Paul O'Neill .50 .20
❑ 600 Spike Owen .15 .05
❑ 601 Mike Stanley .15 .05
❑ 602 Danny Tartabull .15 .05
❑ 603 Scott Brosius .30 .10
❑ 604 Storm Davis .15 .05
❑ 605 Eric Fox .15 .05
❑ 606 Rich Gossage .30 .10
❑ 607 Scott Hemond .15 .05
❑ 608 Dave Henderson .15 .05
❑ 609 Mark McGwire 2.00 .75
❑ 610 Mike Mohler RC .30 .10
❑ 611 Edwin Nunez .15 .05
❑ 612 Kevin Seitzer .15 .05
❑ 613 Ruben Sierra .30 .10
❑ 614 Chris Bosio .15 .05
❑ 615 Norm Charlton .15 .05
❑ 616 Jim Converse RC .30 .10
❑ 617 John Cummings RC .30 .10
❑ 618 Mike Felder .15 .05
❑ 619 Ken Griffey Jr. 1.25 .50
❑ 620 Mike Hampton .30 .10
❑ 621 Erik Hanson .15 .05
❑ 622 Bill Haselman .15 .05
❑ 623 Tino Martinez .50 .20
❑ 624 Lee Tinsley .15 .05
❑ 625 Fernando Vina RC .50 .20
❑ 626 David Wainhouse .15 .05
❑ 627 Jose Canseco .50 .20
❑ 628 Benji Gil .15 .05
❑ 629 Tom Henke .15 .05
❑ 630 David Hulse RC .30 .10
❑ 631 Manuel Lee .15 .05
❑ 632 Craig Lefferts .15 .05
❑ 633 Robb Nen .30 .10
❑ 634 Gary Redus .15 .05
❑ 635 Bill Ripken .15 .05
❑ 636 Nolan Ryan 3.00 1.25
❑ 637 Dan Smith .15 .05
❑ 638 Matt Whiteside RC .30 .10
❑ 639 Roberto Alomar .50 .20
❑ 640 Juan Guzman .15 .05
❑ 641 Pat Hentgen .15 .05
❑ 642 Darrin Jackson .15 .05
❑ 643 Randy Knorr .15 .05
❑ 644 Domingo Martinez RC .30 .10
❑ 645 Paul Molitor .30 .10
❑ 646 Dick Schofield .15 .05
❑ 647 Dave Stewart .30 .10
❑ 648 Checklist 301-421
Rey Sanchez .15 .05
❑ 649 Jeremy Hernandez CL .15 .05
❑ 650 Junior Ortiz CL .15 .05

1997 Ultra

❑ COMPLETE SET (553) 110.00 55.00
❑ COMPLETE SERIES 1 (300) 30.00 15.00
❑ COMPLETE SERIES 2 (253) 80.00 40.00
❑ COMMON CARD (1-553) .30 .10
❑ COMMON RC .40 .15
❑ 1 Roberto Alomar .50 .20
❑ 2 Brady Anderson .30 .10
❑ 3 Rocky Coppinger .30 .10
❑ 4 Jeffrey Hammonds .30 .10
❑ 5 Chris Hoiles .30 .10
❑ 6 Eddie Murray .75 .30
❑ 7 Mike Mussina .50 .20
❑ 8 Jimmy Myers .30 .10
❑ 9 Randy Myers .30 .10
❑ 10 Arthur Rhodes .30 .10
❑ 11 Cal Ripken 2.50 1.00
❑ 12 Jose Canseco .50 .20
❑ 13 Roger Clemens 1.50 .60
❑ 14 Tom Gordon .30 .10
❑ 15 Jose Malave .30 .10
❑ 16 Tim Naehring .30 .10
❑ 17 Troy O'Leary .30 .10
❑ 18 Bill Selby .30 .10
❑ 19 Heathcliff Slocumb .30 .10
❑ 20 Mike Stanley .30 .10
❑ 21 Mo Vaughn .30 .10
❑ 22 Garret Anderson .30 .10
❑ 23 George Arias .30 .10
❑ 24 Chili Davis .30 .10
❑ 25 Jim Edmonds .30 .10
❑ 26 Darin Erstad .30 .10
❑ 27 Chuck Finley .30 .10
❑ 28 Todd Greene .30 .10
❑ 29 Troy Percival .30 .10
❑ 30 Tim Salmon .50 .20
❑ 31 Jeff Schmidt .30 .10
❑ 32 Randy Velarde .30 .10
❑ 33 Shad Williams .30 .10
❑ 34 Wilson Alvarez .30 .10
❑ 35 Harold Baines .30 .10
❑ 36 James Baldwin .30 .10
❑ 37 Mike Cameron .30 .10
❑ 38 Ray Durham .30 .10
❑ 39 Ozzie Guillen .30 .10
❑ 40 Roberto Hernandez .30 .10
❑ 41 Darren Lewis .30 .10
❑ 42 Jose Munoz .30 .10
❑ 43 Tony Phillips .30 .10
❑ 44 Frank Thomas .75 .30
❑ 45 Sandy Alomar Jr. .30 .10
❑ 46 Albert Belle .30 .10
❑ 47 Mark Carreon .30 .10
❑ 48 Julio Franco .30 .10
❑ 49 Orel Hershiser .30 .10
❑ 50 Kenny Lofton .30 .10
❑ 51 Jack McDowell .30 .10
❑ 52 Jose Mesa .30 .10
❑ 53 Charles Nagy .30 .10
❑ 54 Manny Ramirez .50 .20
❑ 55 Julian Tavarez .30 .10
❑ 56 Omar Vizquel .50 .20
❑ 57 Raul Casanova .30 .10
❑ 58 Tony Clark .30 .10
❑ 59 Travis Fryman .30 .10
❑ 60 Bob Higginson .30 .10
❑ 61 Melvin Nieves .30 .10
❑ 62 Curtis Pride .30 .10
❑ 63 Justin Thompson .30 .10
❑ 64 Alan Trammell .30 .10
❑ 65 Kevin Appier .30 .10
❑ 66 Johnny Damon .50 .20
❑ 67 Keith Lockhart .30 .10
❑ 68 Jeff Montgomery .30 .10
❑ 69 Jose Offerman .30 .10
❑ 70 Bip Roberts .30 .10
❑ 71 Jose Rosado .30 .10
❑ 72 Chris Stynes .30 .10
❑ 73 Mike Sweeney .30 .10
❑ 74 Jeff Cirillo .30 .10
❑ 75 Jeff D'Amico .30 .10
❑ 76 John Jaha .30 .10
❑ 77 Scott Karl .30 .10
❑ 78 Mike Matheny .30 .10
❑ 79 Ben McDonald .30 .10
❑ 80 Matt Mieske .30 .10
❑ 81 Marc Newfield .30 .10
❑ 82 Dave Nilsson .30 .10
❑ 83 Jose Valentin .30 .10
❑ 84 Fernando Vina .30 .10
❑ 85 Rick Aguilera .30 .10
❑ 86 Marty Cordova .30 .10
❑ 87 Chuck Knoblauch .30 .10
❑ 88 Matt Lawton .30 .10
❑ 89 Pat Meares .30 .10
❑ 90 Paul Molitor .30 .10
❑ 91 Greg Myers .30 .10
❑ 92 Dan Naulty .30 .10
❑ 93 Kirby Puckett .75 .30
❑ 94 Frank Rodriguez .30 .10
❑ 95 Wade Boggs .50 .20
❑ 96 Cecil Fielder .30 .10
❑ 97 Joe Girardi .30 .10
❑ 98 Dwight Gooden .30 .10
❑ 99 Derek Jeter 2.00 .75
❑ 100 Tino Martinez .50 .20
❑ 101 Ramiro Mendoza RC .30 .10
❑ 102 Andy Pettitte .50 .20
❑ 103 Mariano Rivera .75 .30
❑ 104 Ruben Rivera .30 .10
❑ 105 Kenny Rogers .30 .10
❑ 106 Darryl Strawberry .30 .10
❑ 107 Bernie Williams .50 .20
❑ 108 Tony Batista .30 .10
❑ 109 Geronimo Berroa .30 .10
❑ 110 Bobby Chouinard .30 .10
❑ 111 Brent Gates .30 .10
❑ 112 Jason Giambi .30 .10
❑ 113 Damon Mashore .30 .10
❑ 114 Mark McGwire 2.00 .75
❑ 115 Scott Spiezio .30 .10
❑ 116 John Wasdin .30 .10
❑ 117 Steve Wojciechowski .30 .10
❑ 118 Ernie Young .30 .10
❑ 119 Norm Charlton .30 .10
❑ 120 Joey Cora .30 .10
❑ 121 Ken Griffey Jr. 1.25 .50
❑ 122 Sterling Hitchcock .30 .10
❑ 123 Raul Ibanez .30 .10
❑ 124 Randy Johnson .75 .30
❑ 125 Edgar Martinez .50 .20
❑ 126 Alex Rodriguez 1.25 .50

❑	127	Matt Wagner	.30	.10
❑	128	Bob Wells	.30	.10
❑	129	Dan Wilson	.30	.10
❑	130	Will Clark	.50	.20
❑	131	Kevin Elster	.30	.10
❑	132	Juan Gonzalez	.30	.10
❑	133	Rusty Greer	.30	.10
❑	134	Darryl Hamilton	.30	.10
❑	135	Mike Henneman	.30	.10
❑	136	Ken Hill	.30	.10
❑	137	Mark McLemore	.30	.10
❑	138	Dean Palmer	.30	.10
❑	139	Roger Pavlik	.30	.10
❑	140	Ivan Rodriguez	.50	.20
❑	141	Joe Carter	.30	.10
❑	142	Carlos Delgado	.30	.10
❑	143	Alex Gonzalez	.30	.10
❑	144	Juan Guzman	.30	.10
❑	145	Pat Hentgen	.30	.10
❑	146	Marty Janzen	.30	.10
❑	147	Otis Nixon	.30	.10
❑	148	Charlie O'Brien	.30	.10
❑	149	John Olerud	.30	.10
❑	150	Robert Perez	.30	.10
❑	151	Jermaine Dye	.30	.10
❑	152	Tom Glavine	.50	.20
❑	153	Andruw Jones	.50	.20
❑	154	Chipper Jones	.75	.30
❑	155	Ryan Klesko	.30	.10
❑	156	Javier Lopez	.30	.10
❑	157	Greg Maddux	1.25	.50
❑	158	Fred McGriff	.50	.20
❑	159	Wonderful Monds	.30	.10
❑	160	John Smoltz	.50	.20
❑	161	Terrell Wade	.30	.10
❑	162	Mark Wohlers	.30	.10
❑	163	Brant Brown	.30	.10
❑	164	Mark Grace	.50	.20
❑	165	Tyler Houston	.30	.10
❑	166	Robin Jennings	.30	.10
❑	167	Jason Maxwell	.30	.10
❑	168	Ryne Sandberg	1.25	.50
❑	169	Sammy Sosa	.75	.30
❑	170	Amaury Telemaco	.30	.10
❑	171	Steve Trachsel	.30	.10
❑	172	Pedro Valdes RC	.30	.10
❑	173	Tim Belk	.30	.10
❑	174	Bret Boone	.30	.10
❑	175	Jeff Brantley	.30	.10
❑	176	Eric Davis	.30	.10
❑	177	Barry Larkin	.50	.20
❑	178	Chad Mottola	.30	.10
❑	179	Mark Portugal	.30	.10
❑	180	Reggie Sanders	.30	.10
❑	181	John Smiley	.30	.10
❑	182	Eddie Taubensee	.30	.10
❑	183	Dante Bichette	.30	.10
❑	184	Ellis Burks	.30	.10
❑	185	Andres Galarraga	.30	.10
❑	186	Curt Leskanic	.30	.10
❑	187	Quinton McCracken	.30	.10
❑	188	Jeff Reed	.30	.10
❑	189	Kevin Ritz	.30	.10
❑	190	Walt Weiss	.30	.10
❑	191	Jamey Wright	.30	.10
❑	192	Eric Young	.30	.10
❑	193	Kevin Brown	.30	.10
❑	194	Luis Castillo	.30	.10
❑	195	Jeff Conine	.30	.10
❑	196	Andre Dawson	.30	.10
❑	197	Charles Johnson	.30	.10
❑	198	Al Leiter	.30	.10
❑	199	Ralph Milliard	.30	.10
❑	200	Robb Nen	.30	.10
❑	201	Edgar Renteria	.30	.10
❑	202	Gary Sheffield	.30	.10
❑	203	Bob Abreu	.50	.20
❑	204	Jeff Bagwell	.50	.20
❑	205	Derek Bell	.30	.10
❑	206	Sean Berry	.30	.10
❑	207	Richard Hidalgo	.30	.10
❑	208	Todd Jones	.30	.10
❑	209	Darryl Kile	.30	.10
❑	210	Orlando Miller	.30	.10
❑	211	Shane Reynolds	.30	.10
❑	212	Billy Wagner	.30	.10
❑	213	Donne Wall	.30	.10
❑	214	Roger Cedeno	.30	.10
❑	215	Greg Gagne	.30	.10
❑	216	Karim Garcia	.30	.10
❑	217	Wilton Guerrero	.30	.10
❑	218	Todd Hollandsworth	.30	.10
❑	219	Ramon Martinez	.30	.10
❑	220	Raul Mondesi	.30	.10
❑	221	Hideo Nomo	.75	.30
❑	222	Chan Ho Park	.30	.10
❑	223	Mike Piazza	1.25	.50
❑	224	Ismael Valdes	.30	.10
❑	225	Moises Alou	.30	.10
❑	226	Derek Aucoin	.30	.10
❑	227	Yamil Benitez	.30	.10
❑	228	Jeff Fassero	.30	.10
❑	229	Darrin Fletcher	.30	.10
❑	230	Mark Grudzielanek	.30	.10
❑	231	Barry Manuel	.30	.10
❑	232	Pedro Martinez	.50	.20
❑	233	Henry Rodriguez	.30	.10
❑	234	Ugueth Urbina	.30	.10
❑	235	Rondell White	.30	.10
❑	236	Carlos Baerga	.30	.10
❑	237	John Franco	.30	.10
❑	238	Bernard Gilkey	.30	.10
❑	239	Todd Hundley	.30	.10
❑	240	Butch Huskey	.30	.10
❑	241	Jason Isringhausen	.30	.10
❑	242	Lance Johnson	.30	.10
❑	243	Bobby Jones	.30	.10
❑	244	Alex Ochoa	.30	.10
❑	245	Rey Ordonez	.30	.10
❑	246	Paul Wilson	.30	.10
❑	247	Ron Blazier	.30	.10
❑	248	David Doster	.30	.10
❑	249	Jim Eisenreich	.30	.10
❑	250	Mike Grace	.30	.10
❑	251	Mike Lieberthal	.30	.10
❑	252	Wendell Magee	.30	.10
❑	253	Mickey Morandini	.30	.10
❑	254	Ricky Otero	.30	.10
❑	255	Scott Rolen	.50	.20
❑	256	Curt Schilling	.30	.10
❑	257	Todd Zeile	.30	.10
❑	258	Jermaine Allensworth	.30	.10
❑	259	Trey Beamon	.30	.10
❑	260	Carlos Garcia	.30	.10
❑	261	Mark Johnson	.30	.10
❑	262	Jason Kendall	.30	.10
❑	263	Jeff King	.30	.10
❑	264	Al Martin	.30	.10
❑	265	Denny Neagle	.30	.10
❑	266	Matt Ruebel	.30	.10
❑	267	Marc Wilkins	.30	.10
❑	268	Alan Benes	.30	.10
❑	269	Dennis Eckersley	.30	.10
❑	270	Ron Gant	.30	.10
❑	271	Aaron Holbert	.30	.10
❑	272	Brian Jordan	.30	.10
❑	273	Ray Lankford	.30	.10
❑	274	John Mabry	.30	.10
❑	275	T.J. Mathews	.30	.10
❑	276	Ozzie Smith	1.25	.50
❑	277	Todd Stottlemyre	.30	.10
❑	278	Mark Sweeney	.30	.10
❑	279	Andy Ashby	.30	.10
❑	280	Steve Finley	.30	.10
❑	281	John Flaherty	.30	.10
❑	282	Chris Gomez	.30	.10
❑	283	Tony Gwynn	1.00	.40
❑	284	Joey Hamilton	.30	.10
❑	285	Rickey Henderson	.75	.30
❑	286	Trevor Hoffman	.30	.10
❑	287	Jason Thompson	.30	.10
❑	288	Fernando Valenzuela	.30	.10
❑	289	Greg Vaughn	.30	.10
❑	290	Barry Bonds	2.00	.75
❑	291	Jay Canizaro	.30	.10
❑	292	Jacob Cruz	.30	.10
❑	293	Shawon Dunston	.30	.10
❑	294	Shawn Estes	.30	.10
❑	295	Mark Gardner	.30	.10
❑	296	Marcus Jensen	.30	.10
❑	297	Bill Mueller RC	1.25	.50
❑	298	Chris Singleton	.30	.10
❑	299	Allen Watson	.30	.10
❑	300	Matt Williams	.30	.10
❑	301	Rod Beck	.30	.10
❑	302	Jay Bell	.30	.10
❑	303	Shawon Dunston	.30	.10
❑	304	Reggie Jefferson	.30	.10
❑	305	Darren Oliver	.30	.10
❑	306	Benito Santiago	.30	.10
❑	307	Gerald Williams	.30	.10
❑	308	Damon Buford	.30	.10
❑	309	Jeromy Burnitz	.30	.10
❑	310	Sterling Hitchcock	.30	.10
❑	311	Dave Hollins	.30	.10
❑	312	Mel Rojas	.30	.10
❑	313	Robin Ventura	.30	.10
❑	314	David Wells	.30	.10
❑	315	Cal Eldred	.30	.10
❑	316	Gary Gaetti	.30	.10
❑	317	John Hudek	.30	.10
❑	318	Brian Johnson	.30	.10
❑	319	Denny Neagle	.30	.10
❑	320	Larry Walker	.30	.10
❑	321	Russ Davis	.30	.10
❑	322	Delino DeShields	.30	.10
❑	323	Charlie Hayes	.30	.10
❑	324	Jermaine Dye	.30	.10
❑	325	John Ericks	.30	.10
❑	326	Jeff Fassero	.30	.10
❑	327	Nomar Garciaparra	1.25	.50
❑	328	Willie Greene	.30	.10
❑	329	Greg McMichael	.30	.10
❑	330	Damion Easley	.30	.10
❑	331	Ricky Bones	.30	.10
❑	332	John Burkett	.30	.10
❑	333	Royce Clayton	.30	.10
❑	334	Greg Colbrunn	.30	.10
❑	335	Tony Eusebio	.30	.10
❑	336	Gregg Jefferies	.30	.10
❑	337	Wally Joyner	.30	.10
❑	338	Jim Leyritz	.30	.10
❑	339	Paul O'Neill	.50	.20
❑	340	Bruce Ruffin	.30	.10
❑	341	Michael Tucker	.30	.10
❑	342	Andy Benes	.30	.10
❑	343	Craig Biggio	.50	.20
❑	344	Rex Hudler	.30	.10
❑	345	Brad Radke	.30	.10
❑	346	Deion Sanders	.50	.20
❑	347	Moises Alou	.30	.10
❑	348	Brad Ausmus	.30	.10
❑	349	Armando Benitez	.30	.10
❑	350	Mark Gubicza	.30	.10
❑	351	Terry Steinbach	.30	.10
❑	352	Mark Whiten	.30	.10
❑	353	Ricky Bottalico	.30	.10
❑	354	Brian Giles RC	1.50	.60
❑	355	Eric Karros	.30	.10
❑	356	Jimmy Key	.30	.10
❑	357	Carlos Perez	.30	.10
❑	358	Alex Fernandez	.30	.10
❑	359	J.T. Snow	.30	.10
❑	360	Bobby Bonilla	.30	.10
❑	361	Scott Brosius	.30	.10
❑	362	Greg Swindell	.30	.10
❑	363	Jose Vizcaino	.30	.10
❑	364	Matt Williams	.30	.10
❑	365	Darren Daulton	.30	.10
❑	366	Shane Andrews	.30	.10
❑	367	Jim Eisenreich	.30	.10
❑	368	Ariel Prieto	.30	.10
❑	369	Bob Tewksbury	.30	.10
❑	370	Mike Bordick	.30	.10
❑	371	Rheal Cormier	.30	.10
❑	372	Cliff Floyd	.30	.10
❑	373	David Justice	.30	.10
❑	374	John Wetteland	.30	.10
❑	375	Mike Blowers	.30	.10
❑	376	Jose Canseco	.50	.20
❑	377	Roger Clemens	1.50	.60
❑	378	Kevin Mitchell	.30	.10
❑	379	Todd Zeile	.30	.10
❑	380	Jim Thome	.50	.20
❑	381	Turk Wendell	.30	.10
❑	382	Rico Brogna	.30	.10
❑	383	Eric Davis	.30	.10
❑	384	Mike Lansing	.30	.10

❑ 385	Devon White	.30	.10
❑ 386	Marquis Grissom	.30	.10
❑ 387	Todd Worrell	.30	.10
❑ 388	Jeff Kent	.30	.10
❑ 389	Mickey Tettleton	.30	.10
❑ 390	Steve Avery	.30	.10
❑ 391	David Cone	.30	.10
❑ 392	Scott Cooper	.30	.10
❑ 393	Lee Stevens	.30	.10
❑ 394	Kevin Elster	.30	.10
❑ 395	Tom Goodwin	.30	.10
❑ 396	Shawn Green	.30	.10
❑ 397	Pete Harnisch	.30	.10
❑ 398	Eddie Murray	.75	.30
❑ 399	Joe Randa	.30	.10
❑ 400	Scott Sanders	.30	.10
❑ 401	John Valentin	.30	.10
❑ 402	Todd Jones	.30	.10
❑ 403	Terry Adams	.30	.10
❑ 404	Brian Hunter	.30	.10
❑ 405	Pat Listach	.30	.10
❑ 406	Kenny Lofton	.30	.10
❑ 407	Hal Morris	.30	.10
❑ 408	Ed Sprague	.30	.10
❑ 409	Rich Becker	.30	.10
❑ 410	Edgardo Alfonzo	.30	.10
❑ 411	Albert Belle	.30	.10
❑ 412	Jeff King	.30	.10
❑ 413	Kirt Manwaring	.30	.10
❑ 414	Jason Schmidt	.30	.10
❑ 415	Allen Watson	.30	.10
❑ 416	Lee Tinsley	.30	.10
❑ 417	Brett Butler	.30	.10
❑ 418	Carlos Garcia	.30	.10
❑ 419	Mark Lemke	.30	.10
❑ 420	Jaime Navarro	.30	.10
❑ 421	David Segui	.30	.10
❑ 422	Ruben Sierra	.30	.10
❑ 423	B.J. Surhoff	.30	.10
❑ 424	Julian Tavarez	.30	.10
❑ 425	Billy Taylor	.30	.10
❑ 426	Ken Caminiti	.30	.10
❑ 427	Chuck Carr	.30	.10
❑ 428	Benji Gil	.30	.10
❑ 429	Terry Mulholland	.30	.10
❑ 430	Mike Stanton	.30	.10
❑ 431	Wil Cordero	.30	.10
❑ 432	Chili Davis	.30	.10
❑ 433	Mariano Duncan	.30	.10
❑ 434	Orlando Merced	.30	.10
❑ 435	Kent Mercker	.30	.10
❑ 436	John Olerud	.30	.10
❑ 437	Quilvio Veras	.30	.10
❑ 438	Mike Fetters	.30	.10
❑ 439	Glenallen Hill	.30	.10
❑ 440	Bill Swift	.30	.10
❑ 441	Tim Wakefield	.30	.10
❑ 442	Pedro Astacio	.30	.10
❑ 443	Vinny Castilla	.30	.10
❑ 444	Doug Drabek	.30	.10
❑ 445	Alan Embree	.30	.10
❑ 446	Lee Smith	.30	.10
❑ 447	Darryl Hamilton	.30	.10
❑ 448	Brian McRae	.30	.10
❑ 449	Mike Timlin	.30	.10
❑ 450	Bob Wickman	.30	.10
❑ 451	Jason Dickson	.30	.10
❑ 452	Chad Curtis	.30	.10
❑ 453	Mark Leiter	.30	.10
❑ 454	Damon Berryhill	.30	.10
❑ 455	Kevin Orie	.30	.10
❑ 456	Dave Burba	.30	.10
❑ 457	Chris Holt	.30	.10
❑ 458	Ricky Ledee RC	.40	.15
❑ 459	Mike Devereaux	.30	.10
❑ 460	Pokey Reese	.30	.10
❑ 461	Tim Raines	.30	.10
❑ 462	Ryan Jones	.30	.10
❑ 463	Shane Mack	.30	.10
❑ 464	Darren Dreifort	.30	.10
❑ 465	Mark Parent	.30	.10
❑ 466	Mark Portugal	.30	.10
❑ 467	Dante Powell	.30	.10
❑ 468	Craig Grebeck	.30	.10
❑ 469	Ron Villone	.30	.10
❑ 470	Dmitri Young	.30	.10

❑ 471	Shannon Stewart	.30	.10
❑ 472	Rick Helling	.30	.10
❑ 473	Bill Haselman	.30	.10
❑ 474	Albie Lopez	.30	.10
❑ 475	Glendon Rusch	.30	.10
❑ 476	Derrick May	.30	.10
❑ 477	Chad Ogea	.30	.10
❑ 478	Kirk Rueter	.30	.10
❑ 479	Chris Hammond	.30	.10
❑ 480	Russ Johnson	.30	.10
❑ 481	James Mouton	.30	.10
❑ 482	Mike Macfarlane	.30	.10
❑ 483	Scott Ruffcorn	.30	.10
❑ 484	Jeff Frye	.30	.10
❑ 485	Richie Sexson	.30	.10
❑ 486	Emil Brown RC	.40	.15
❑ 487	Desi Wilson	.30	.10
❑ 488	Brent Gates	.30	.10
❑ 489	Tony Graffanino	.30	.10
❑ 490	Dan Miceli	.30	.10
❑ 491	Orlando Cabrera RC	1.00	.40
❑ 492	Tony Womack RC	.40	.15
❑ 493	Jerome Walton	.30	.10
❑ 494	Mark Thompson	.30	.10
❑ 495	Jose Guillen	.30	.10
❑ 496	Willie Blair	.30	.10
❑ 497	T.J. Staton RC	.40	.15
❑ 498	Scott Kamieniecki	.30	.10
❑ 499	Vince Coleman	.30	.10
❑ 500	Jeff Abbott	.30	.10
❑ 501	Chris Widger	.30	.10
❑ 502	Kevin Tapani	.30	.10
❑ 503	Carlos Castillo RC	.40	.15
❑ 504	Luis Gonzalez	.30	.10
❑ 505	Tim Belcher	.30	.10
❑ 506	Armando Reynoso	.30	.10
❑ 507	Jamie Moyer	.30	.10
❑ 508	Randall Simon RC	.40	.15
❑ 509	Vladimir Guerrero	.75	.30
❑ 510	Wady Almonte RC	.40	.15
❑ 511	Dustin Hermanson	.30	.10
❑ 512	Deivi Cruz RC	.40	.15
❑ 513	Luis Alicea	.30	.10
❑ 514	Felix Heredia RC	.40	.15
❑ 515	Don Slaught	.30	.10
❑ 516	Shigetoshi Hasegawa RC	.60	.25
❑ 517	Matt Walbeck	.30	.10
❑ 518	David Arias-Ortiz RC	70.00	40.00
❑ 519	Brady Raggio RC	.40	.15
❑ 520	Rudy Pemberton	.30	.10
❑ 521	Wayne Kirby	.30	.10
❑ 522	Calvin Maduro	.30	.10
❑ 523	Mark Lewis	.30	.10
❑ 524	Mike Jackson	.30	.10
❑ 525	Sid Fernandez	.30	.10
❑ 526	Mike Bielecki	.30	.10
❑ 527	Bubba Trammell RC	.40	.15
❑ 528	Brent Brede RC	.40	.15
❑ 529	Matt Morris	.30	.10
❑ 530	Joe Borowski RC	.40	.15
❑ 531	Orlando Miller	.30	.10
❑ 532	Jim Bullinger	.30	.10
❑ 533	Robert Person	.30	.10
❑ 534	Doug Glanville	.30	.10
❑ 535	Terry Pendleton	.30	.10
❑ 536	Jorge Posada	.50	.20
❑ 537	Marc Sagmoen RC	.40	.15
❑ 538	Fernando Tatis RC	.40	.15
❑ 539	Aaron Sele	.30	.10
❑ 540	Brian Banks	.30	.10
❑ 541	Derrek Lee	.50	.20
❑ 542	John Wasdin	.30	.10
❑ 543	Justin Towle RC	.40	.15
❑ 544	Pat Cline	.30	.10
❑ 545	Dave Magadan	.30	.10
❑ 546	Jeff Blauser	.30	.10
❑ 547	Phil Nevin	.30	.10
❑ 548	Todd Walker	.30	.10
❑ 549	Eli Marrero	.30	.10
❑ 550	Bartolo Colon	.30	.10
❑ 551	Jose Cruz Jr. RC	.40	.15
❑ 552	Todd Dunwoody	.30	.10
❑ 553	Hideki Irabu RC	.40	.15
❑ P11	C.Ripken Promo Strip	2.00	.75

1998 Ultra

❑	COMPLETE SET (501)	160.00	65.00
❑	COMPLETE SERIES 1 (250)	100.00	40.00
❑	COMPLETE SERIES 2 (251)	60.00	25.00
❑	COMP.SER.1 w/o SP's (210)	15.00	6.00
❑	COMP.SER.2 w/o SP's (226)	15.00	6.00
❑	COMMON 1 (1-220/246-250)	.30	.10
❑	COMMON 2 (251-475/501)	.30	.10
❑	COMMON SC (211-220)	2.00	.75
❑	COMMON PROS (221-245)	3.00	1.25
❑	COMMON PZ (476-500)	1.00	.40
❑ 1	Ken Griffey Jr.	1.25	.50
❑ 2	Matt Morris	.30	.10
❑ 3	Roger Clemens	1.50	.60
❑ 4	Matt Williams	.30	.10
❑ 5	Roberto Hernandez	.30	.10
❑ 6	Rondell White	.30	.10
❑ 7	Tim Salmon	.50	.20
❑ 8	Brad Radke	.30	.10
❑ 9	Brett Butler	.30	.10
❑ 10	Carl Everett	.30	.10
❑ 11	Chili Davis	.30	.10
❑ 12	Chuck Finley	.30	.10
❑ 13	Darryl Kile	.30	.10
❑ 14	Deivi Cruz	.30	.10
❑ 15	Gary Gaetti	.30	.10
❑ 16	Matt Stairs	.30	.10
❑ 17	Pat Meares	.30	.10
❑ 18	Will Cunnane	.30	.10
❑ 19	Steve Woodard	.30	.10
❑ 20	Andy Ashby	.30	.10
❑ 21	Bobby Higginson	.30	.10
❑ 22	Brian Jordan	.30	.10
❑ 23	Craig Biggio	.50	.20
❑ 24	Jim Edmonds	.30	.10
❑ 25	Ryan McGuire	.30	.10
❑ 26	Scott Hatteberg	.30	.10
❑ 27	Willie Greene	.30	.10
❑ 28	Albert Belle	.30	.10
❑ 29	Ellis Burks	.30	.10
❑ 30	Hideo Nomo	.75	.30
❑ 31	Jeff Bagwell	.50	.20
❑ 32	Kevin Brown	.50	.20
❑ 33	Nomar Garciaparra	1.25	.50
❑ 34	Pedro Martinez	.50	.20
❑ 35	Raul Mondesi	.30	.10
❑ 36	Ricky Bottalico	.30	.10
❑ 37	Shawn Estes	.30	.10
❑ 38	Otis Nixon	.30	.10
❑ 39	Terry Steinbach	.30	.10
❑ 40	Tom Glavine	.50	.20
❑ 41	Todd Dunwoody	.30	.10
❑ 42	Deion Sanders	.50	.20
❑ 43	Gary Sheffield	.30	.10
❑ 44	Mike Lansing	.30	.10
❑ 45	Mike Lieberthal	.30	.10
❑ 46	Paul Sorrento	.30	.10
❑ 47	Paul O'Neill	.50	.20
❑ 48	Tom Goodwin	.30	.10
❑ 49	Andruw Jones	.50	.20
❑ 50	Barry Bonds	2.00	.75
❑ 51	Bernie Williams	.50	.20
❑ 52	Jeremi Gonzalez	.30	.10
❑ 53	Mike Piazza	1.25	.50
❑ 54	Russ Davis	.30	.10
❑ 55	Vinny Castilla	.30	.10
❑ 56	Rod Beck	.30	.10

❑ 57 Andres Galarraga .30 .10
❑ 58 Ben McDonald .30 .10
❑ 59 Billy Wagner .30 .10
❑ 60 Charles Johnson .30 .10
❑ 61 Fred McGriff .50 .20
❑ 62 Dean Palmer .30 .10
❑ 63 Frank Thomas .75 .30
❑ 64 Ismael Valdes .30 .10
❑ 65 Mark Bellhorn .30 .10
❑ 66 Jeff King .30 .10
❑ 67 John Wetteland .30 .10
❑ 68 Mark Grace .50 .20
❑ 69 Mark Kotsay .30 .10
❑ 70 Scott Rolen .50 .20
❑ 71 Todd Hundley .30 .10
❑ 72 Todd Worrell .30 .10
❑ 73 Wilson Alvarez .30 .10
❑ 74 Bobby Jones .30 .10
❑ 75 Jose Canseco .50 .20
❑ 76 Kevin Appier .30 .10
❑ 77 Neifi Perez .30 .10
❑ 78 Paul Molitor .30 .10
❑ 79 Quilvio Veras .30 .10
❑ 80 Randy Johnson .75 .30
❑ 81 Glendon Rusch .30 .10
❑ 82 Curt Schilling .30 .10
❑ 83 Alex Rodriguez 1.25 .50
❑ 84 Rey Ordonez .30 .10
❑ 85 Jeff Juden .30 .10
❑ 86 Mike Cameron .30 .10
❑ 87 Ryan Klesko .30 .10
❑ 88 Trevor Hoffman .30 .10
❑ 89 Chuck Knoblauch .30 .10
❑ 90 Larry Walker .30 .10
❑ 91 Mark McLemore .30 .10
❑ 92 B.J. Surhoff .30 .10
❑ 93 Darren Daulton .30 .10
❑ 94 Ray Durham .30 .10
❑ 95 Sammy Sosa .75 .30
❑ 96 Eric Young .30 .10
❑ 97 Gerald Williams .30 .10
❑ 98 Javy Lopez .30 .10
❑ 99 John Smiley .30 .10
❑ 100 Juan Gonzalez .30 .10
❑ 101 Shawn Green .30 .10
❑ 102 Charles Nagy .30 .10
❑ 103 David Justice .30 .10
❑ 104 Joey Hamilton .30 .10
❑ 105 Pat Hentgen .30 .10
❑ 106 Raul Casanova .30 .10
❑ 107 Tony Phillips .30 .10
❑ 108 Tony Gwynn 1.00 .40
❑ 109 Will Clark .50 .20
❑ 110 Jason Giambi .30 .10
❑ 111 Jay Bell .30 .10
❑ 112 Johnny Damon .50 .20
❑ 113 Alan Benes .30 .10
❑ 114 Jeff Suppan .30 .10
❑ 115 Kevin Polcovich .30 .10
❑ 116 Shigetoshi Hasegawa .30 .10
❑ 117 Steve Finley .30 .10
❑ 118 Tony Clark .30 .10
❑ 119 David Cone .30 .10
❑ 120 Jose Guillen .30 .10
❑ 121 Kevin Millwood RC 1.00 .40
❑ 122 Greg Maddux 1.25 .50
❑ 123 Dave Nilsson .30 .10
❑ 124 Hideki Irabu .30 .10
❑ 125 Jason Kendall .30 .10
❑ 126 Jim Thome .50 .20
❑ 127 Delino DeShields .30 .10
❑ 128 Edgar Renteria .30 .10
❑ 129 Edgardo Alfonzo .30 .10
❑ 130 J.T. Snow .30 .10
❑ 131 Jeff Abbott .30 .10
❑ 132 Jeffrey Hammonds .30 .10
❑ 133 Todd Greene .30 .10
❑ 134 Vladimir Guerrero .75 .30
❑ 135 Jay Buhner .30 .10
❑ 136 Jeff Cirillo .30 .10
❑ 137 Jeromy Burnitz .30 .10
❑ 138 Mickey Morandini .30 .10
❑ 139 Tino Martinez .50 .20
❑ 140 Jeff Shaw .30 .10
❑ 141 Rafael Palmeiro .50 .20
❑ 142 Bobby Bonilla .30 .10
❑ 143 Cal Ripken 2.50 1.00
❑ 144 Chad Fox RC .30 .10
❑ 145 Dante Bichette .30 .10
❑ 146 Dennis Eckersley .30 .10
❑ 147 Mariano Rivera .75 .30
❑ 148 Mo Vaughn .30 .10
❑ 149 Reggie Sanders .30 .10
❑ 150 Derek Jeter 2.00 .75
❑ 151 Rusty Greer .30 .10
❑ 152 Brady Anderson .30 .10
❑ 153 Brett Tomko .30 .10
❑ 154 Jaime Navarro .30 .10
❑ 155 Kevin Orie .30 .10
❑ 156 Roberto Alomar .50 .20
❑ 157 Edgar Martinez .50 .20
❑ 158 John Olerud .30 .10
❑ 159 John Smoltz .50 .20
❑ 160 Ryne Sandberg 1.25 .50
❑ 161 Billy Taylor .30 .10
❑ 162 Chris Holt .30 .10
❑ 163 Damion Easley .30 .10
❑ 164 Darin Erstad .30 .10
❑ 165 Joe Carter .30 .10
❑ 166 Kelvim Escobar .30 .10
❑ 167 Ken Caminiti .30 .10
❑ 168 Pokey Reese .30 .10
❑ 169 Ray Lankford .30 .10
❑ 170 Livan Hernandez .30 .10
❑ 171 Steve Kline .30 .10
❑ 172 Tom Gordon .30 .10
❑ 173 Travis Fryman .30 .10
❑ 174 Al Martin .30 .10
❑ 175 Andy Pettitte .50 .20
❑ 176 Jeff Kent .30 .10
❑ 177 Jimmy Key .30 .10
❑ 178 Mark Grudzielanek .30 .10
❑ 179 Tony Saunders .30 .10
❑ 180 Barry Larkin .50 .20
❑ 181 Bubba Trammell .30 .10
❑ 182 Carlos Delgado .30 .10
❑ 183 Carlos Baerga .30 .10
❑ 184 Derek Bell .30 .10
❑ 185 Henry Rodriguez .30 .10
❑ 186 Jason Dickson .30 .10
❑ 187 Ron Gant .30 .10
❑ 188 Tony Womack .30 .10
❑ 189 Justin Thompson .30 .10
❑ 190 Fernando Tatis .30 .10
❑ 191 Mark Wohlers .30 .10
❑ 192 Takashi Kashiwada .30 .10
❑ 193 Garret Anderson .30 .10
❑ 194 Jose Cruz Jr. .30 .10
❑ 195 Ricardo Rincon .30 .10
❑ 196 Tim Naehring .30 .10
❑ 197 Moises Alou .30 .10
❑ 198 Eric Karros .30 .10
❑ 199 John Jaha .30 .10
❑ 200 Marty Cordova .30 .10
❑ 201 Ken Hill .30 .10
❑ 202 Chipper Jones .75 .30
❑ 203 Kenny Lofton .30 .10
❑ 204 Mike Mussina .50 .20
❑ 205 Manny Ramirez .50 .20
❑ 206 Todd Hollandsworth .30 .10
❑ 207 Cecil Fielder .30 .10
❑ 208 Mark McGwire 2.00 .75
❑ 209 Jim Leyritz .30 .10
❑ 210 Ivan Rodriguez .50 .20
❑ 211 Jeff Bagwell SC 2.00 .75
❑ 212 Barry Bonds SC 8.00 3.00
❑ 213 Roger Clemens SC 6.00 2.50
❑ 214 Nomar Garciaparra SC 5.00 2.00
❑ 215 Ken Griffey Jr. SC 5.00 2.00
❑ 216 Tony Gwynn SC 4.00 1.50
❑ 217 Randy Johnson SC 3.00 1.25
❑ 218 Mark McGwire SC 8.00 3.00
❑ 219 Scott Rolen SC 2.00 .75
❑ 220 Frank Thomas SC 3.00 1.25
❑ 221 Matt Perisho PROS 3.00 1.25
❑ 222 Wes Helms PROS 3.00 1.25
❑ 223 Dave Dellucci PROS RC 3.00 1.25
❑ 224 Todd Helton PROS 3.00 1.25
❑ 225 Brian Rose PROS 3.00 1.25
❑ 226 Aaron Boone PROS 3.00 1.25
❑ 227 Keith Foulke PROS 3.00 1.25
❑ 228 Homer Bush PROS 3.00 1.25
❑ 229 Shannon Stewart PROS 3.00 1.25
❑ 230 Richard Hidalgo PROS 3.00 1.25
❑ 231 Russ Johnson PROS 3.00 1.25
❑ 232 Henry Blanco PROS RC 3.00 1.25
❑ 233 Paul Konerko PROS 3.00 1.25
❑ 234 Antone Williamson PROS 3.00 1.25
❑ 235 Shane Bowers PROS RC 3.00 1.25
❑ 236 Jose Vidro PROS 3.00 1.25
❑ 237 Derek Wallace PROS 3.00 1.25
❑ 238 Ricky Ledee PROS SP 5.00 2.00
❑ 239 Ben Grieve PROS 3.00 1.25
❑ 240 Lou Collier PROS 3.00 1.25
❑ 241 Derrek Lee PROS 3.00 1.25
❑ 242 Ruben Rivera PROS 3.00 1.25
❑ 243 Jorge Velandia PROS SP 5.00 2.00
❑ 244 Andrew Vessel PROS 3.00 1.25
❑ 245 Chris Carpenter PROS 3.00 1.25
❑ 246 Ken Griffey Jr. CL .75 .30
❑ 247 Alex Rodriguez CL .75 .30
❑ 248 Diamond Ink CL .30 .10
❑ 249 Frank Thomas CL .50 .20
❑ 250 Cal Ripken CL 1.25 .50
❑ 251 Carlos Perez .30 .10
❑ 252 Larry Sutton .30 .10
❑ 253 Gary Sheffield .30 .10
❑ 254 Wally Joyner .30 .10
❑ 255 Todd Stottlemyre .30 .10
❑ 256 Nerio Rodriguez .30 .10
❑ 257 Charles Johnson .30 .10
❑ 258 Pedro Astacio .30 .10
❑ 259 Cal Eldred .30 .10
❑ 260 Chili Davis .30 .10
❑ 261 Freddy Garcia .30 .10
❑ 262 Bobby Witt .30 .10
❑ 263 Michael Coleman .30 .10
❑ 264 Mike Caruso .30 .10
❑ 265 Mike Lansing .30 .10
❑ 266 Dennis Reyes .30 .10
❑ 267 F.P. Santangelo .30 .10
❑ 268 Darryl Hamilton .30 .10
❑ 269 Mike Fetters .30 .10
❑ 270 Charlie Hayes .30 .10
❑ 271 Royce Clayton .30 .10
❑ 272 Doug Drabek .30 .10
❑ 273 James Baldwin .30 .10
❑ 274 Brian Hunter .30 .10
❑ 275 Chan Ho Park .30 .10
❑ 276 John Franco .30 .10
❑ 277 David Wells .30 .10
❑ 278 Eli Marrero .30 .10
❑ 279 Kerry Wood .40 .15
❑ 280 Donnie Sadler .30 .10
❑ 281 Scott Winchester RC .30 .10
❑ 282 Hal Morris .30 .10
❑ 283 Brad Fullmer .30 .10
❑ 284 Bernard Gilkey .30 .10
❑ 285 Ramiro Mendoza .30 .10
❑ 286 Kevin Brown .50 .20
❑ 287 David Segui .30 .10
❑ 288 Willie McGee .30 .10
❑ 289 Darren Oliver .30 .10
❑ 290 Antonio Alfonseca .30 .10
❑ 291 Eric Davis .30 .10
❑ 292 Mickey Morandini .30 .10
❑ 293 Frank Catalanotto RC .60 .25
❑ 294 Derrek Lee .50 .20
❑ 295 Todd Zeile .30 .10
❑ 296 Chuck Knoblauch .30 .10
❑ 297 Wilson Delgado .30 .10
❑ 298 Bobby Bonilla .30 .10
❑ 299 Orel Hershiser .30 .10
❑ 300 Ozzie Guillen .30 .10
❑ 301 Aaron Sele .30 .10
❑ 302 Joe Carter .30 .10
❑ 303 Darryl Kile .30 .10
❑ 304 Shane Reynolds .30 .10
❑ 305 Todd Dunn .30 .10
❑ 306 Bob Abreu .30 .10
❑ 307 Doug Strange .30 .10
❑ 308 Jose Canseco .50 .20
❑ 309 Lance Johnson .30 .10
❑ 310 Harold Baines .30 .10
❑ 311 Todd Pratt .30 .10
❑ 312 Greg Colbrunn .30 .10
❑ 313 Masato Yoshii RC .40 .15
❑ 314 Felix Heredia .30 .10

❑	315	Dennis Martinez	.30	.10
❑	316	Geronimo Berroa	.30	.10
❑	317	Darren Lewis	.30	.10
❑	318	Bill Ripken	.30	.10
❑	319	Enrique Wilson	.30	.10
❑	320	Alex Ochoa	.30	.10
❑	321	Doug Glanville	.30	.10
❑	322	Mike Stanley	.30	.10
❑	323	Gerald Williams	.30	.10
❑	324	Pedro Martinez	.50	.20
❑	325	Jaret Wright	.30	.10
❑	326	Terry Pendleton	.30	.10
❑	327	LaTroy Hawkins	.30	.10
❑	328	Emil Brown	.30	.10
❑	329	Walt Weiss	.30	.10
❑	330	Omar Vizquel	.50	.20
❑	331	Carl Everett	.30	.10
❑	332	Fernando Vina	.30	.10
❑	333	Mike Blowers	.30	.10
❑	334	Dwight Gooden	.30	.10
❑	335	Mark Lewis	.30	.10
❑	336	Jim Leyritz	.30	.10
❑	337	Kenny Lofton	.30	.10
❑	338	John Halama RC	.40	.15
❑	339	Jose Valentin	.30	.10
❑	340	Desi Relaford	.30	.10
❑	341	Dante Powell	.30	.10
❑	342	Ed Sprague	.30	.10
❑	343	Reggie Jefferson	.30	.10
❑	344	Mike Hampton	.30	.10
❑	345	Marquis Grissom	.30	.10
❑	346	Heathcliff Slocumb	.30	.10
❑	347	Francisco Cordova	.30	.10
❑	348	Ken Cloude	.30	.10
❑	349	Benito Santiago	.30	.10
❑	350	Denny Neagle	.30	.10
❑	351	Sean Casey	.30	.10
❑	352	Robb Nen	.30	.10
❑	353	Orlando Merced	.30	.10
❑	354	Adrian Brown	.30	.10
❑	355	Gregg Jefferies	.30	.10
❑	356	Otis Nixon	.30	.10
❑	357	Michael Tucker	.30	.10
❑	358	Eric Milton	.30	.10
❑	359	Travis Fryman	.30	.10
❑	360	Gary DiSarcina	.30	.10
❑	361	Mario Valdez	.30	.10
❑	362	Craig Counsell	.30	.10
❑	363	Jose Offerman	.30	.10
❑	364	Tony Fernandez	.30	.10
❑	365	Jason McDonald	.30	.10
❑	366	Sterling Hitchcock	.30	.10
❑	367	Donovan Osborne	.30	.10
❑	368	Troy Percival	.30	.10
❑	369	Henry Rodriguez	.30	.10
❑	370	Dmitri Young	.30	.10
❑	371	Jay Powell	.30	.10
❑	372	Jeff Conine	.30	.10
❑	373	Orlando Cabrera	.30	.10
❑	374	Butch Huskey	.30	.10
❑	375	Mike Lowell RC	1.25	.50
❑	376	Kevin Young	.30	.10
❑	377	Jamie Moyer	.30	.10
❑	378	Jeff D'Amico	.30	.10
❑	379	Scott Erickson	.30	.10
❑	380	Magglio Ordonez RC	2.50	1.00
❑	381	Melvin Nieves	.30	.10
❑	382	Ramon Martinez	.30	.10
❑	383	A.J. Hinch	.30	.10
❑	384	Jeff Brantley	.30	.10
❑	385	Kevin Elster	.30	.10
❑	386	Allen Watson	.30	.10
❑	387	Moises Alou	.30	.10
❑	388	Jeff Blauser	.30	.10
❑	389	Pete Harnisch	.30	.10
❑	390	Shane Andrews	.30	.10
❑	391	Rico Brogna	.30	.10
❑	392	Stan Javier	.30	.10
❑	393	David Howard	.30	.10
❑	394	Darryl Strawberry	.30	.10
❑	395	Kent Mercker	.30	.10
❑	396	Juan Encarnacion	.30	.10
❑	397	Sandy Alomar Jr.	.30	.10
❑	398	Al Leiter	.30	.10
❑	399	Tony Graffanino	.30	.10
❑	400	Terry Adams	.30	.10
❑	401	Bruce Aven	.30	.10
❑	402	Derrick Gibson	.30	.10
❑	403	Jose Cabrera RC	.30	.10
❑	404	Rich Becker	.30	.10
❑	405	David Ortiz	1.00	.40
❑	406	Brian McRae	.30	.10
❑	407	Bobby Estalella	.30	.10
❑	408	Bill Mueller	.30	.10
❑	409	Dennis Eckersley	.30	.10
❑	410	Sandy Martinez	.30	.10
❑	411	Jose Vizcaino	.30	.10
❑	412	Jermaine Allensworth	.30	.10
❑	413	Miguel Tejada	.75	.30
❑	414	Turner Ward	.30	.10
❑	415	Glenallen Hill	.30	.10
❑	416	Lee Stevens	.30	.10
❑	417	Cecil Fielder	.30	.10
❑	418	Ruben Sierra	.30	.10
❑	419	Jon Nunnally	.30	.10
❑	420	Rod Myers	.30	.10
❑	421	Dustin Hermanson	.30	.10
❑	422	James Mouton	.30	.10
❑	423	Dan Wilson	.30	.10
❑	424	Roberto Kelly	.30	.10
❑	425	Antonio Osuna	.30	.10
❑	426	Jacob Cruz	.30	.10
❑	427	Brent Mayne	.30	.10
❑	428	Matt Karchner	.30	.10
❑	429	Damian Jackson	.30	.10
❑	430	Roger Cedeno	.30	.10
❑	431	Rickey Henderson	.75	.30
❑	432	Joe Randa	.30	.10
❑	433	Greg Vaughn	.30	.10
❑	434	Andres Galarraga	.30	.10
❑	435	Rod Beck	.30	.10
❑	436	Curtis Goodwin	.30	.10
❑	437	Brad Ausmus	.30	.10
❑	438	Bob Hamelin	.30	.10
❑	439	Todd Walker	.30	.10
❑	440	Scott Brosius	.30	.10
❑	441	Len Dykstra	.30	.10
❑	442	Abraham Nunez	.30	.10
❑	443	Brian Johnson	.30	.10
❑	444	Randy Myers	.30	.10
❑	445	Bret Boone	.30	.10
❑	446	Oscar Henriquez	.30	.10
❑	447	Mike Sweeney	.30	.10
❑	448	Kenny Rogers	.30	.10
❑	449	Mark Langston	.30	.10
❑	450	Luis Gonzalez	.30	.10
❑	451	John Burkett	.30	.10
❑	452	Bip Roberts	.30	.10
❑	453	Travis Lee	.30	.10
❑	454	Felix Rodriguez	.30	.10
❑	455	Andy Benes	.30	.10
❑	456	Willie Blair	.30	.10
❑	457	Brian Anderson	.30	.10
❑	458	Jay Bell	.30	.10
❑	459	Matt Williams	.30	.10
❑	460	Devon White	.30	.10
❑	461	Karim Garcia	.30	.10
❑	462	Jorge Fabregas	.30	.10
❑	463	Wilson Alvarez	.30	.10
❑	464	Roberto Hernandez	.30	.10
❑	465	Tony Saunders	.30	.10
❑	466	Rolando Arrojo RC	.40	.15
❑	467	Wade Boggs	.75	.30
❑	468	Fred McGriff	.50	.20
❑	469	Paul Sorrento	.30	.10
❑	470	Kevin Stocker	.30	.10
❑	471	Bubba Trammell	.30	.10
❑	472	Quinton McCracken	.30	.10
❑	473	Ken Griffey Jr. CL	.75	.30
❑	474	Cal Ripken CL	1.25	.50
❑	475	Frank Thomas CL	.50	.20
❑	476	Ken Griffey Jr. PZ	4.00	1.50
❑	477	Cal Ripken PZ	8.00	3.00
❑	478	Frank Thomas PZ	2.50	1.00
❑	479	Alex Rodriguez PZ	4.00	1.50
❑	480	Nomar Garciaparra PZ	4.00	1.50
❑	481	Derek Jeter PZ	6.00	2.50
❑	482	Andruw Jones PZ	1.50	.60
❑	483	Chipper Jones PZ	2.50	1.00
❑	484	Greg Maddux PZ	4.00	1.50
❑	485	Mike Piazza PZ	4.00	1.50
❑	486	Juan Gonzalez PZ	1.00	.40
❑	487	Jose Cruz Jr. PZ	1.00	.40
❑	488	Jaret Wright PZ	1.00	.40
❑	489	Hideo Nomo PZ	2.50	1.00
❑	490	Scott Rolen PZ	1.50	.60
❑	491	Tony Gwynn PZ	3.00	1.25
❑	492	Roger Clemens PZ	5.00	2.00
❑	493	Darin Erstad PZ	1.00	.40
❑	494	Mark McGwire PZ	6.00	2.50
❑	495	Jeff Bagwell PZ	1.50	.60
❑	496	Mo Vaughn PZ	1.00	.40
❑	497	Albert Belle PZ	1.00	.40
❑	498	Kenny Lofton PZ	1.00	.40
❑	499	Ben Grieve PZ	1.00	.40
❑	500	Barry Bonds PZ	6.00	2.50
❑	501	Mike Piazza	1.25	.50
❑	S100	A.Rodriguez AU/750	120.00	60.00

2001 Ultra

❑		COMPLETE SET (275)	120.00	60.00
❑		COMP.SET w/o SP's (250)	25.00	10.00
❑		COMMON CARD (1-250)	.30	.10
❑		COMMON CARD (251-275)	3.00	1.25
❑		COMMON CARD (276-280)	5.00	2.00
❑	1	Pedro Martinez	.50	.20
❑	2	Derek Jeter	2.00	.75
❑	3	Cal Ripken	2.50	1.00
❑	4	Alex Rodriguez	1.25	.50
❑	5	Vladimir Guerrero	.75	.30
❑	6	Troy Glaus	.30	.10
❑	7	Sammy Sosa	.75	.30
❑	8	Mike Piazza	1.25	.50
❑	9	Tony Gwynn	1.00	.40
❑	10	Tim Hudson	.30	.10
❑	11	John Flaherty	.30	.10
❑	12	Jeff Cirillo	.30	.10
❑	13	Ellis Burks	.30	.10
❑	14	Carlos Lee	.30	.10
❑	15	Carlos Beltran	.30	.10
❑	16	Ruben Rivera	.30	.10
❑	17	Richard Hidalgo	.30	.10
❑	18	Omar Vizquel	.50	.20
❑	19	Michael Barrett	.30	.10
❑	20	Jose Canseco	.50	.20
❑	21	Jason Giambi	.30	.10
❑	22	Greg Maddux	1.25	.50
❑	23	Charles Johnson	.30	.10
❑	24	Sandy Alomar Jr.	.30	.10
❑	25	Rick Ankiel	.30	.10
❑	26	Richie Sexson	.30	.10
❑	27	Matt Williams	.30	.10
❑	28	Joe Girardi	.30	.10
❑	29	Jason Kendall	.30	.10
❑	30	Brad Fullmer	.30	.10
❑	31	Alex Gonzalez	.30	.10
❑	32	Rick Helling	.30	.10
❑	33	Mike Mussina	.50	.20
❑	34	Joe Randa	.30	.10
❑	35	J.T. Snow	.30	.10
❑	36	Edgardo Alfonzo	.30	.10
❑	37	Dante Bichette	.30	.10
❑	38	Brad Ausmus	.30	.10
❑	39	Bobby Abreu	.30	.10
❑	40	Warren Morris	.30	.10
❑	41	Tony Womack	.30	.10
❑	42	Russell Branyan	.30	.10
❑	43	Mike Lowell	.30	.10
❑	44	Mark Grace	.50	.20
❑	45	Jeromy Burnitz	.30	.10

❑ 46 J.D. Drew .30 .10
❑ 47 David Justice .30 .10
❑ 48 Alex Gonzalez .30 .10
❑ 49 Tino Martinez .50 .20
❑ 50 Raul Mondesi .30 .10
❑ 51 Rafael Furcal .30 .10
❑ 52 Marquis Grissom .30 .10
❑ 53 Kevin Young .30 .10
❑ 54 Jon Lieber .30 .10
❑ 55 Henry Rodriguez .30 .10
❑ 56 Dave Burba .30 .10
❑ 57 Shannon Stewart .30 .10
❑ 58 Preston Wilson .30 .10
❑ 59 Paul O'Neill .50 .20
❑ 60 Jimmy Haynes .30 .10
❑ 61 Darryl Kile .30 .10
❑ 62 Bret Boone .30 .10
❑ 63 Bartolo Colon .30 .10
❑ 64 Andres Galarraga .30 .10
❑ 65 Trot Nixon .30 .10
❑ 66 Steve Finley .30 .10
❑ 67 Shawn Green .30 .10
❑ 68 Robert Person .30 .10
❑ 69 Kenny Rogers .30 .10
❑ 70 Bobby Higginson .30 .10
❑ 71 Barry Larkin .50 .20
❑ 72 Al Martin .30 .10
❑ 73 Tom Glavine .50 .20
❑ 74 Rondell White .30 .10
❑ 75 Ray Lankford .30 .10
❑ 76 Moises Alou .30 .10
❑ 77 Matt Clement .30 .10
❑ 78 Geoff Jenkins .30 .10
❑ 79 David Wells .30 .10
❑ 80 Chuck Finley .30 .10
❑ 81 Andy Pettitte .50 .20
❑ 82 Travis Fryman .30 .10
❑ 83 Ron Coomer .30 .10
❑ 84 Mark McGwire 2.00 .75
❑ 85 Kerry Wood .30 .10
❑ 86 Jorge Posada .50 .20
❑ 87 Jeff Bagwell .50 .20
❑ 88 Andruw Jones .50 .20
❑ 89 Ryan Klesko .30 .10
❑ 90 Mariano Rivera .75 .30
❑ 91 Lance Berkman .30 .10
❑ 92 Kenny Lofton .30 .10
❑ 93 Jacque Jones .30 .10
❑ 94 Eric Young .30 .10
❑ 95 Edgar Renteria .30 .10
❑ 96 Chipper Jones .75 .30
❑ 97 Todd Helton .50 .20
❑ 98 Shawn Estes .30 .10
❑ 99 Mark Mulder .30 .10
❑ 100 Lee Stevens .30 .10
❑ 101 Jermaine Dye .30 .10
❑ 102 Greg Vaughn .30 .10
❑ 103 Chris Singleton .30 .10
❑ 104 Brady Anderson .30 .10
❑ 105 Terrence Long .30 .10
❑ 106 Quilvio Veras .30 .10
❑ 107 Magglio Ordonez .30 .10
❑ 108 Johnny Damon .50 .20
❑ 109 Jeffrey Hammonds .30 .10
❑ 110 Fred McGriff .50 .20
❑ 111 Carl Pavano .30 .10
❑ 112 Bobby Estalella .30 .10
❑ 113 Todd Hundley .30 .10
❑ 114 Scott Rolen .50 .20
❑ 115 Robin Ventura .30 .10
❑ 116 Pokey Reese .30 .10
❑ 117 Luis Gonzalez .30 .10
❑ 118 Jose Offerman .30 .10
❑ 119 Edgar Martinez .50 .20
❑ 120 Dean Palmer .30 .10
❑ 121 David Segui .30 .10
❑ 122 Troy O'Leary .30 .10
❑ 123 Tony Batista .30 .10
❑ 124 Todd Zeile .30 .10
❑ 125 Randy Johnson .75 .30
❑ 126 Luis Castillo .30 .10
❑ 127 Kris Benson .30 .10
❑ 128 John Olerud .30 .10
❑ 129 Eric Karros .30 .10
❑ 130 Eddie Taubensee .30 .10
❑ 131 Neifi Perez .30 .10
❑ 132 Matt Stairs .30 .10
❑ 133 Luis Alicea .30 .10
❑ 134 Jeff Kent .30 .10
❑ 135 Javier Vazquez .30 .10
❑ 136 Garret Anderson .30 .10
❑ 137 Frank Thomas .75 .30
❑ 138 Carlos Febles .30 .10
❑ 139 Albert Belle .30 .10
❑ 140 Tony Clark .30 .10
❑ 141 Pat Burrell .30 .10
❑ 142 Mike Sweeney .30 .10
❑ 143 Jay Buhner .30 .10
❑ 144 Gabe Kapler .30 .10
❑ 145 Derek Bell .30 .10
❑ 146 B.J. Surhoff .30 .10
❑ 147 Adam Kennedy .30 .10
❑ 148 Aaron Boone .30 .10
❑ 149 Todd Stottlemyre .30 .10
❑ 150 Roberto Alomar .50 .20
❑ 151 Orlando Hernandez .30 .10
❑ 152 Jason Varitek .75 .30
❑ 153 Gary Sheffield .30 .10
❑ 154 Cliff Floyd .30 .10
❑ 155 Chad Hermansen .30 .10
❑ 156 Carlos Delgado .30 .10
❑ 157 Aaron Sele .30 .10
❑ 158 Sean Casey .30 .10
❑ 159 Ruben Mateo .30 .10
❑ 160 Mike Bordick .30 .10
❑ 161 Mike Cameron .30 .10
❑ 162 Doug Glanville .30 .10
❑ 163 Damion Easley .30 .10
❑ 164 Carl Everett .30 .10
❑ 165 Bengie Molina .30 .10
❑ 166 Adrian Beltre .30 .10
❑ 167 Tom Goodwin .30 .10
❑ 168 Rickey Henderson .75 .30
❑ 169 Mo Vaughn .30 .10
❑ 170 Mike Lieberthal .30 .10
❑ 171 Ken Griffey Jr. 1.25 .50
❑ 172 Juan Gonzalez .30 .10
❑ 173 Ivan Rodriguez .50 .20
❑ 174 Al Leiter .30 .10
❑ 175 Vinny Castilla .30 .10
❑ 176 Peter Bergeron .30 .10
❑ 177 Pedro Astacio .30 .10
❑ 178 Paul Konerko .30 .10
❑ 179 Mitch Meluskey .30 .10
❑ 180 Kevin Millwood .30 .10
❑ 181 Ben Grieve .30 .10
❑ 182 Barry Bonds 2.00 .75
❑ 183 Rusty Greer .30 .10
❑ 184 Miguel Tejada .30 .10
❑ 185 Mark Quinn .30 .10
❑ 186 Larry Walker .30 .10
❑ 187 Jose Valentin .30 .10
❑ 188 Jose Vidro .30 .10
❑ 189 Delino DeShields .30 .10
❑ 190 Darin Erstad .30 .10
❑ 191 Bill Mueller .30 .10
❑ 192 Ray Durham .30 .10
❑ 193 Ken Caminiti .30 .10
❑ 194 Jim Thome .50 .20
❑ 195 Javy Lopez .30 .10
❑ 196 Fernando Vina .30 .10
❑ 197 Eric Chavez .30 .10
❑ 198 Eric Owens .30 .10
❑ 199 Brad Radke .30 .10
❑ 200 Travis Lee .30 .10
❑ 201 Tim Salmon .50 .20
❑ 202 Rafael Palmeiro .50 .20
❑ 203 Nomar Garciaparra 1.25 .50
❑ 204 Mike Hampton .30 .10
❑ 205 Kevin Brown .30 .10
❑ 206 Juan Encarnacion .30 .10
❑ 207 Danny Graves .30 .10
❑ 208 Carlos Guillen .30 .10
❑ 209 Phil Nevin .30 .10
❑ 210 Matt Lawton .30 .10
❑ 211 Manny Ramirez .50 .20
❑ 212 James Baldwin .30 .10
❑ 213 Fernando Tatis .30 .10
❑ 214 Craig Biggio .50 .20
❑ 215 Brian Jordan .30 .10
❑ 216 Bernie Williams .50 .20
❑ 217 Ryan Dempster .30 .10
❑ 218 Roger Clemens 1.50 .60
❑ 219 Jose Cruz Jr. .30 .10
❑ 220 John Valentin .30 .10
❑ 221 Dmitri Young .30 .10
❑ 222 Curt Schilling .30 .10
❑ 223 Jim Edmonds .30 .10
❑ 224 Chan Ho Park .30 .10
❑ 225 Brian Giles .30 .10
❑ 226 J.Anderson/T.Redman .30 .10
❑ 227 A.Piatt/J.Ortiz .30 .10
❑ 228 K.Kelly/A.Huff .30 .10
❑ 229 R.Choate/C.Dingman .30 .10
❑ 230 E.Cammack/G.Roberts .30 .10
❑ 231 Y.Lara/A.Tracy .30 .10
❑ 232 W.Franklin/S.Linebrink .30 .10
❑ 233 C.Cairncross/C.Perry .30 .10
❑ 234 J.Romero/M.LeCroy .30 .10
❑ 235 G.Guzman/J.Conti .30 .10
❑ 236 M.Burkhart/P.Crawford .30 .10
❑ 237 P.Coco/L.Estrella .30 .10
❑ 238 J.Parrish/F.Lunar .30 .10
❑ 239 K.McDonald/J.Brunette .30 .10
❑ 240 C.Casimiro/I.Coffie .30 .10
❑ 241 D.Garibay/R.Quevedo .30 .10
❑ 242 S.Lee/T.Ohka .30 .10
❑ 243 H.Ortiz/J.D'Amico .30 .10
❑ 244 J.Sparks/T.Harper .30 .10
❑ 245 J.Boyd/D.Coggin .30 .10
❑ 246 M.Buehrle/L.Barcelo .50 .20
❑ 247 A.Melhuse/B.Petrick .30 .10
❑ 248 K.Davis/P.Rigdon .30 .10
❑ 249 M.Darr/K.DeHaan .30 .10
❑ 250 V.Padilla/M.Brownson 3.00 1.25
❑ 251 Barry Zito PROS 5.00 2.00
❑ 252 Tim Drew PROS 3.00 1.25
❑ 253 Luis Matos PROS 3.00 1.25
❑ 254 Alex Cabrera PROS 3.00 1.25
❑ 255 Jon Garland PROS 3.00 1.25
❑ 256 Milton Bradley PROS 3.00 1.25
❑ 257 Juan Pierre PROS 3.00 1.25
❑ 258 Ismael Villegas PROS 3.00 1.25
❑ 259 Eric Munson PROS 3.00 1.25
❑ 260 Tomas De la Rosa PROS 3.00 1.25
❑ 261 Chris Richard PROS 3.00 1.25
❑ 262 Jason Tyner PROS 3.00 1.25
❑ 263 B.J. Waszgis PROS 3.00 1.25
❑ 264 Jason Marquis PROS 3.00 1.25
❑ 265 Dusty Allen PROS 3.00 1.25
❑ 266 Corey Patterson PROS 3.00 1.25
❑ 267 Eric Byrnes PROS 3.00 1.25
❑ 268 Xavier Nady PROS 3.00 1.25
❑ 269 George Lombard PROS 3.00 1.25
❑ 270 Timo Perez PROS 3.00 1.25
❑ 271 Gary Matthews Jr. PROS 3.00 1.25
❑ 272 Chad Durbin PROS 3.00 1.25
❑ 273 Tony Armas Jr. PROS 3.00 1.25
❑ 274 Francisco Cordero PROS 3.00 1.25
❑ 275 Alfonso Soriano PROS 5.00 2.00
❑ 276 J.Spivey RC/J.Uribe RC 8.00 3.00
❑ 277 A.Pujols RC/B.Smith RC 80.00 40.00
❑ 278 I.Suzuki RC/T.Shinjo RC 30.00 12.50
❑ 279 D.Henson RC/J.Melian RC 8.00 3.00
❑ 280 M.White RC/A.Hernandez RC 5.002.00

2003 Ultra

❑ COMP.LO SET (250) 100.00 40.00
❑ COMP.LO SET w/o SP's (200) 25.00 10.00
❑ COMMON CARD (201-220) 1.50 .60

Card		
❑ COMMON CARD (221-250)	2.00	.75
❑ COMMON CARD (251-265)	3.00	1.25
❑ 1 Barry Bonds	2.00	.75
❑ 2 Derek Jeter	2.00	.75
❑ 3 Ichiro Suzuki	1.50	.60
❑ 4 Mike Lowell	.30	.10
❑ 5 Hideo Nomo	.75	.30
❑ 6 Javier Vazquez	.30	.10
❑ 7 Jeremy Giambi	.30	.10
❑ 8 Jamie Moyer	.30	.10
❑ 9 Rafael Palmeiro	.50	.20
❑ 10 Magglio Ordonez	.30	.10
❑ 11 Trot Nixon	.30	.10
❑ 12 Luis Castillo	.30	.10
❑ 13 Paul Byrd	.30	.10
❑ 14 Adam Kennedy	.30	.10
❑ 15 Trevor Hoffman	.30	.10
❑ 16 Matt Morris	.30	.10
❑ 17 Nomar Garciaparra	1.25	.50
❑ 18 Matt Lawton	.30	.10
❑ 19 Carlos Beltran	.30	.10
❑ 20 Jason Giambi	.30	.10
❑ 21 Brian Giles	.30	.10
❑ 22 Jim Edmonds	.30	.10
❑ 23 Garret Anderson	.30	.10
❑ 24 Tony Batista	.30	.10
❑ 25 Aaron Boone	.30	.10
❑ 26 Mike Hampton	.30	.10
❑ 27 Billy Wagner	.30	.10
❑ 28 Kazuhisa Ishii	.30	.10
❑ 29 Al Leiter	.30	.10
❑ 30 Pat Burrell	.30	.10
❑ 31 Jeff Kent	.30	.10
❑ 32 Randy Johnson	.75	.30
❑ 33 Ray Durham	.30	.10
❑ 34 Josh Beckett	.30	.10
❑ 35 Cristian Guzman	.30	.10
❑ 36 Roger Clemens	1.50	.60
❑ 37 Freddy Garcia	.30	.10
❑ 38 Roy Halladay	.30	.10
❑ 39 David Eckstein	.30	.10
❑ 40 Jerry Hairston	.30	.10
❑ 41 Barry Larkin	.50	.20
❑ 42 Larry Walker	.30	.10
❑ 43 Craig Biggio	.50	.20
❑ 44 Edgardo Alfonzo	.30	.10
❑ 45 Marlon Byrd	.30	.10
❑ 46 J.T. Snow	.30	.10
❑ 47 Juan Gonzalez	.30	.10
❑ 48 Ramon Ortiz	.30	.10
❑ 49 Jay Gibbons	.30	.10
❑ 50 Adam Dunn	.30	.10
❑ 51 Juan Pierre	.30	.10
❑ 52 Jeff Bagwell	.50	.20
❑ 53 Kevin Brown	.30	.10
❑ 54 Pedro Astacio	.30	.10
❑ 55 Mike Lieberthal	.30	.10
❑ 56 Johnny Damon	.50	.20
❑ 57 Tim Salmon	.50	.20
❑ 58 Mike Bordick	.30	.10
❑ 59 Ken Griffey Jr.	1.25	.50
❑ 60 Jason Jennings	.30	.10
❑ 61 Lance Berkman	.30	.10
❑ 62 Jeromy Burnitz	.30	.10
❑ 63 Jimmy Rollins	.30	.10
❑ 64 Tsuyoshi Shinjo	.30	.10
❑ 65 Alex Rodriguez	1.25	.50
❑ 66 Greg Maddux	1.25	.50
❑ 67 Mark Prior	.50	.20
❑ 68 Mike Maroth	.30	.10
❑ 69 Geoff Jenkins	.30	.10
❑ 70 Tony Armas Jr.	.30	.10
❑ 71 Jermaine Dye	.30	.10
❑ 72 Albert Pujols	1.50	.60
❑ 73 Shannon Stewart	.30	.10
❑ 74 Troy Glaus	.30	.10
❑ 75 Brook Fordyce	.30	.10
❑ 76 Juan Encarnacion	.30	.10
❑ 77 Todd Hollandsworth	.30	.10
❑ 78 Roy Oswalt	.30	.10
❑ 79 Paul Lo Duca	.30	.10
❑ 80 Mike Piazza	1.25	.50
❑ 81 Bobby Abreu	.30	.10
❑ 82 Sean Burroughs	.30	.10
❑ 83 Randy Winn	.30	.10
❑ 84 Curt Schilling	.30	.10
❑ 85 Chris Singleton	.30	.10
❑ 86 Sean Casey	.30	.10
❑ 87 Todd Zeile	.30	.10
❑ 88 Richard Hidalgo	.30	.10
❑ 89 Roberto Alomar	.50	.20
❑ 90 Tim Hudson	.30	.10
❑ 91 Ryan Klesko	.30	.10
❑ 92 Greg Vaughn	.30	.10
❑ 93 Tony Womack	.30	.10
❑ 94 Fred McGriff	.50	.20
❑ 95 Tom Glavine	.50	.20
❑ 96 Todd Walker	.30	.10
❑ 97 Travis Fryman	.30	.10
❑ 98 Shane Reynolds	.30	.10
❑ 99 Shawn Green	.30	.10
❑ 100 Mo Vaughn	.30	.10
❑ 101 Adam Piatt	.30	.10
❑ 102 Deivi Cruz	.30	.10
❑ 103 Steve Cox	.30	.10
❑ 104 Luis Gonzalez	.30	.10
❑ 105 Russell Branyan	.30	.10
❑ 106 Daryle Ward	.30	.10
❑ 107 Mariano Rivera	.75	.30
❑ 108 Phil Nevin	.30	.10
❑ 109 Ben Grieve	.30	.10
❑ 110 Moises Alou	.30	.10
❑ 111 Omar Vizquel	.50	.20
❑ 112 Joe Randa	.30	.10
❑ 113 Jorge Posada	.50	.20
❑ 114 Mark Kotsay	.30	.10
❑ 115 Ryan Rupe	.30	.10
❑ 116 Javy Lopez	.30	.10
❑ 117 Corey Patterson	.30	.10
❑ 118 Bobby Higginson	.30	.10
❑ 119 Jose Vidro	.30	.10
❑ 120 Barry Zito	.30	.10
❑ 121 Scott Rolen	.50	.20
❑ 122 Gary Sheffield	.30	.10
❑ 123 Kerry Wood	.30	.10
❑ 124 Brandon Ingé	.30	.10
❑ 125 Jose Hernandez	.30	.10
❑ 126 Michael Barrett	.30	.10
❑ 127 Miguel Tejada	.30	.10
❑ 128 Edgar Renteria	.30	.10
❑ 129 Junior Spivey	.30	.10
❑ 130 Jose Valentin	.30	.10
❑ 131 Derrek Lee	.50	.20
❑ 132 A.J. Pierzynski	.30	.10
❑ 133 Mike Mussina	.50	.20
❑ 134 Bret Boone	.30	.10
❑ 135 Chan Ho Park	.30	.10
❑ 136 Steve Finley	.30	.10
❑ 137 Mark Buehrle	.30	.10
❑ 138 A.J. Burnett	.30	.10
❑ 139 Ben Sheets	.30	.10
❑ 140 David Ortiz	.75	.30
❑ 141 Nick Johnson	.30	.10
❑ 142 Randall Simon	.30	.10
❑ 143 Carlos Delgado	.30	.10
❑ 144 Darin Erstad	.30	.10
❑ 145 Shea Hillenbrand	.30	.10
❑ 146 Todd Helton	.50	.20
❑ 147 Preston Wilson	.30	.10
❑ 148 Eric Gagne	.30	.10
❑ 149 Vladimir Guerrero	.75	.30
❑ 150 Brandon Duckworth	.30	.10
❑ 151 Rich Aurilia	.30	.10
❑ 152 Ivan Rodriguez	.50	.20
❑ 153 Andruw Jones	.50	.20
❑ 154 Carlos Lee	.30	.10
❑ 155 Robert Fick	.30	.10
❑ 156 Jacque Jones	.30	.10
❑ 157 Bernie Williams	.50	.20
❑ 158 John Olerud	.30	.10
❑ 159 Eric Hinske	.30	.10
❑ 160 Matt Clement	.30	.10
❑ 161 Dmitri Young	.30	.10
❑ 162 Torii Hunter	.30	.10
❑ 163 Carlos Pena	.30	.10
❑ 164 Mike Cameron	.30	.10
❑ 165 Raul Mondesi	.30	.10
❑ 166 Pedro Martinez	.50	.20
❑ 167 Bob Wickman	.30	.10
❑ 168 Mike Sweeney	.30	.10
❑ 169 David Wells	.30	.10
❑ 170 Jason Kendall	.30	.10
❑ 171 Tino Martinez	.50	.20
❑ 172 Matt Williams	.30	.10
❑ 173 Frank Thomas	.75	.30
❑ 174 Cliff Floyd	.30	.10
❑ 175 Corey Koskie	.30	.10
❑ 176 Orlando Hernandez	.30	.10
❑ 177 Edgar Martinez	.50	.20
❑ 178 Richie Sexson	.30	.10
❑ 179 Manny Ramirez	.50	.20
❑ 180 Jim Thome	.50	.20
❑ 181 Andy Pettitte	.50	.20
❑ 182 Aramis Ramirez	.30	.10
❑ 183 J.D. Drew	.30	.10
❑ 184 Brian Jordan	.30	.10
❑ 185 Sammy Sosa	.75	.30
❑ 186 Jeff Weaver	.30	.10
❑ 187 Jeffrey Hammonds	.30	.10
❑ 188 Eric Milton	.30	.10
❑ 189 Eric Chavez	.30	.10
❑ 190 Kazuhiro Sasaki	.30	.10
❑ 191 Jose Cruz Jr.	.30	.10
❑ 192 Derek Lowe	.30	.10
❑ 193 C.C. Sabathia	.30	.10
❑ 194 Adrian Beltre	.30	.10
❑ 195 Alfonso Soriano	.30	.10
❑ 196 Jack Wilson	.30	.10
❑ 197 Fernando Vina	.30	.10
❑ 198 Chipper Jones	.75	.30
❑ 199 Paul Konerko	.30	.10
❑ 200 Rusty Greer	.30	.10
❑ 201 Jason Giambi AS	1.50	.60
❑ 202 Alfonso Soriano AS	1.50	.60
❑ 203 Shea Hillenbrand AS	1.50	.60
❑ 204 Alex Rodriguez AS	2.50	1.00
❑ 205 Jorge Posada AS	1.50	.60
❑ 206 Ichiro Suzuki AS	3.00	1.25
❑ 207 Manny Ramirez AS	1.50	.60
❑ 208 Torii Hunter AS	1.50	.60
❑ 209 Todd Helton AS	1.50	.60
❑ 210 Jose Vidro AS	1.50	.60
❑ 211 Scott Rolen AS	1.50	.60
❑ 212 Jimmy Rollins AS	1.50	.60
❑ 213 Mike Piazza AS	2.50	1.00
❑ 214 Barry Bonds AS	4.00	1.50
❑ 215 Sammy Sosa AS	1.50	.60
❑ 216 Vladimir Guerrero AS	1.50	.60
❑ 217 Lance Berkman AS	1.50	.60
❑ 218 Derek Jeter AS	4.00	1.50
❑ 219 Nomar Garciaparra AS	2.50	1.00
❑ 220 Luis Gonzalez AS	1.50	.60
❑ 221 Kazuhisa Ishii 02R	2.00	.75
❑ 222 Satoru Komiyama 02R	2.00	.75
❑ 223 So Taguchi 02R	2.00	.75
❑ 224 Jorge Padilla 02R	2.00	.75
❑ 225 Ben Howard 02R	2.00	.75
❑ 226 Jason Simontacchi 02R	2.00	.75
❑ 227 Barry Wesson 02R	2.00	.75
❑ 228 Howie Clark 02R	2.00	.75
❑ 229 Aaron Guiel 02R	2.00	.75
❑ 230 Oliver Perez 02R	2.00	.75
❑ 231 David Ross 02R	2.00	.75
❑ 232 Julius Matos 02R	2.00	.75
❑ 233 Chris Snelling 02R	2.00	.75
❑ 234 Rodrigo Lopez 02R	2.00	.75
❑ 235 Will Nieves 02R	2.00	.75
❑ 236 Joe Borchard 02R	2.00	.75
❑ 237 Aaron Cook 02R	2.00	.75
❑ 238 Anderson Machado 02R	2.00	.75
❑ 239 Corey Thurman 02R	2.00	.75
❑ 240 Tyler Yates 02R	2.00	.75
❑ 241 Coco Crisp 03R	3.00	1.25
❑ 242 Andy Van Hekken 03R	2.00	.75
❑ 243 Jim Rushford 03R	2.00	.75
❑ 244 Jeriome Robertson 03R	2.00	.75
❑ 245 Shane Nance 03R	2.00	.75
❑ 246 Kevin Cash 03R	2.00	.75
❑ 247 Kirk Saarloos 03R	2.00	.75
❑ 248 Josh Bard 03R	2.00	.75
❑ 249 Dave Pember 03R RC	2.00	.75
❑ 250 Freddy Sanchez 03R	2.00	.75
❑ 251 Chien-Ming Wang PROS RC	20.00	8.00
❑ 252 Rickie Weeks PROS RC	6.00	2.50
❑ 253 Brandon Webb PROS RC	8.00	3.00
❑ 254 Hideki Matsui PROS RC	10.00	4.00
❑ 255 Michael Hessman PROS RC	3.00	1.25
❑ 256 Ryan Wagner PROS RC	3.00	1.25

❑	257	Matt Kata PROS RC	3.00	1.25
❑	258	Edwin Jackson PROS RC	4.00	1.50
❑	259	Jose Contreras PROS RC	4.00	1.50
❑	260	Delmon Young PROS RC	10.00	4.00
❑	261	Bo Hart PROS RC	3.00	1.25
❑	262	Jeff Duncan PROS RC	3.00	1.25
❑	263	Robby Hammock PROS RC	3.00	1.25
❑	264	Jeremy Bonderman PROS RC	10.00	4.00
❑	265	Clint Barmes PROS RC	2.50	1.00

2004 Ultra

❑	COMPLETE SERIES 1 (220)	60.00	30.00
❑	COMP.SERIES 1 w/o SP's (200)	25.00	10.00
❑	COMP.SERIES 2 w/o SP's (75)	25.00	10.00
❑	COMP.SERIES 2 w/o L13 (162)	100.00	50.00
❑	COMMON CARD (1-200)	.30	.10
❑	COMMON CARD (201-220)	1.25	.50
❑	201-220 APPROXIMATE ODDS 1:2 HOBBY		
❑	201-220 RANDOM IN RETAIL PACKS		
❑	COMMON CARD (296-382)	2.00	.75
❑	296-382 ODDS TWO PER HOBBY/RETAIL		
❑	COMMON CARD (383-395)	12.00	5.00
❑	383-395 ODDS 1:28 HOBBY, 1:2000 RETAIL		
❑	383-395 PRINT RUN 500 SERIAL #'d SETS		

❑	1	Magglio Ordonez	.30	.10
❑	2	Bobby Abreu	.30	.10
❑	3	Eric Munson	.30	.10
❑	4	Eric Byrnes	.30	.10
❑	5	Bartolo Colon	.30	.10
❑	6	Juan Encarnacion	.30	.10
❑	7	Jody Gerut	.30	.10
❑	8	Eddie Guardado	.30	.10
❑	9	Shea Hillenbrand	.30	.10
❑	10	Andruw Jones	.50	.20
❑	11	Carlos Lee	.30	.10
❑	12	Pedro Martinez	.50	.20
❑	13	Barry Larkin	.50	.20
❑	14	Angel Berroa	.30	.10
❑	15	Edgar Martinez	.50	.20
❑	16	Sidney Ponson	.30	.10
❑	17	Mariano Rivera	.75	.30
❑	18	Richie Sexson	.30	.10
❑	19	Frank Thomas	.75	.30
❑	20	Jerome Williams	.30	.10
❑	21	Barry Zito	.30	.10
❑	22	Roberto Alomar	.50	.20
❑	23	Rocky Biddle	.30	.10
❑	24	Orlando Cabrera	.30	.10
❑	25	Placido Polanco	.30	.10
❑	26	Morgan Ensberg	.30	.10
❑	27	Jason Giambi	.30	.10
❑	28	Jim Thome	.50	.20
❑	29	Vladimir Guerrero	.75	.30
❑	30	Tim Hudson	.30	.10
❑	31	Jacque Jones	.30	.10
❑	32	Derrek Lee	.50	.20
❑	33	Rafael Palmeiro	.50	.20
❑	34	Mike Mussina	.50	.20
❑	35	Corey Patterson	.30	.10
❑	36	Mike Cameron	.30	.10
❑	37	Ivan Rodriguez	.50	.20
❑	38	Ben Sheets	.30	.10
❑	39	Woody Williams	.30	.10
❑	40	Ichiro Suzuki	1.50	.60
❑	41	Moises Alou	.30	.10
❑	42	Craig Biggio	.50	.20
❑	43	Jorge Posada	.50	.20
❑	44	Craig Monroe	.30	.10
❑	45	Darin Erstad	.30	.10
❑	46	Jay Gibbons	.30	.10
❑	47	Aaron Guiel	.30	.10
❑	48	Travis Lee	.30	.10
❑	49	Jorge Julio	.30	.10
❑	50	Torii Hunter	.30	.10
❑	51	Luis Matos	.30	.10
❑	52	Brett Myers	.30	.10
❑	53	Sean Casey	.30	.10
❑	54	Mark Prior	.50	.20
❑	55	Alex Rodriguez	1.25	.50
❑	56	Gary Sheffield	.30	.10
❑	57	Jason Varitek	.75	.30
❑	58	Dontrelle Willis	.50	.20
❑	59	Garret Anderson	.30	.10
❑	60	Casey Blake	.30	.10
❑	61	Jay Payton	.30	.10
❑	62	Carl Crawford	.30	.10
❑	63	Carl Everett	.30	.10
❑	64	Marcus Giles	.30	.10
❑	65	Jose Guillen	.30	.10
❑	66	Eric Karros	.30	.10
❑	67	Mike Lieberthal	.30	.10
❑	68	Hideki Matsui	1.25	.50
❑	69	Xavier Nady	.30	.10
❑	70	Hank Blalock	.30	.10
❑	71	Albert Pujols	1.50	.60
❑	72	Jose Cruz Jr.	.30	.10
❑	73	Randall Simon	.30	.10
❑	74	Javier Vazquez	.30	.10
❑	75	Preston Wilson	.30	.10
❑	76	Danys Baez	.30	.10
❑	77	Alex Cintron	.30	.10
❑	78	Jake Peavy	.30	.10
❑	79	Scott Rolen	.50	.20
❑	80	Robert Fick	.30	.10
❑	81	Brian Giles	.30	.10
❑	82	Roy Halladay	.30	.10
❑	83	Kazuhisa Ishii	.30	.10
❑	84	Austin Kearns	.30	.10
❑	85	Paul Lo Duca	.30	.10
❑	86	Darrell May	.30	.10
❑	87	Phil Nevin	.30	.10
❑	88	Carlos Pena	.30	.10
❑	89	Manny Ramirez	.50	.20
❑	90	C.C. Sabathia	.30	.10
❑	91	John Smoltz	.50	.20
❑	92	Jose Vidro	.30	.10
❑	93	Randy Wolf	.30	.10
❑	94	Jeff Bagwell	.50	.20
❑	95	Barry Bonds	2.00	.75
❑	96	Frank Catalanotto	.30	.10
❑	97	Zach Day	.30	.10
❑	98	David Ortiz	.75	.30
❑	99	Troy Glaus	.30	.10
❑	100	Bo Hart	.30	.10
❑	101	Geoff Jenkins	.30	.10
❑	102	Jason Kendall	.30	.10
❑	103	Esteban Loaiza	.30	.10
❑	104	Doug Mientkiewicz	.30	.10
❑	105	Trot Nixon	.30	.10
❑	106	Troy Percival	.30	.10
❑	107	Aramis Ramirez	.30	.10
❑	108	Alex Sanchez	.30	.10
❑	109	Alfonso Soriano	.30	.10
❑	110	Omar Vizquel	.50	.20
❑	111	Kerry Wood	.30	.10
❑	112	Rocco Baldelli	.30	.10
❑	113	Bret Boone	.30	.10
❑	114	Shawn Chacon	.30	.10
❑	115	Carlos Delgado	.30	.10
❑	116	Shawn Green	.30	.10
❑	117	Tim Worrell	.30	.10
❑	118	Tom Glavine	.50	.20
❑	119	Shigetoshi Hasegawa	.30	.10
❑	120	Derek Jeter	1.50	.60
❑	121	Jeff Kent	.30	.10
❑	122	Braden Looper	.30	.10
❑	123	Kevin Millwood	.30	.10
❑	124	Hideo Nomo	.75	.30
❑	125	Jason Phillips	.30	.10
❑	126	Tim Redding	.30	.10
❑	127	Reggie Sanders	.30	.10
❑	128	Sammy Sosa	.75	.30
❑	129	Billy Wagner	.30	.10
❑	130	Miguel Batista	.30	.10
❑	131	Milton Bradley	.30	.10
❑	132	Eric Chavez	.30	.10
❑	133	J.D. Drew	.30	.10
❑	134	Keith Foulke	.30	.10
❑	135	Luis Gonzalez	.30	.10
❑	136	LaTroy Hawkins	.30	.10
❑	137	Randy Johnson	.75	.30
❑	138	Byung-Hyun Kim	.30	.10
❑	139	Javy Lopez	.30	.10
❑	140	Melvin Mora	.30	.10
❑	141	Aubrey Huff	.30	.10
❑	142	Mike Piazza	1.25	.50
❑	143	Mark Redman	.30	.10
❑	144	Kazuhiro Sasaki	.30	.10
❑	145	Shannon Stewart	.30	.10
❑	146	Larry Walker	.30	.10
❑	147	Dmitri Young	.30	.10
❑	148	Josh Beckett	.30	.10
❑	149	Jae Weong Seo	.30	.10
❑	150	Hee Seop Choi	.30	.10
❑	151	Adam Dunn	.30	.10
❑	152	Rafael Furcal	.30	.10
❑	153	Juan Gonzalez	.30	.10
❑	154	Todd Helton	.50	.20
❑	155	Carlos Zambrano	.30	.10
❑	156	Ryan Klesko	.30	.10
❑	157	Mike Lowell	.30	.10
❑	158	Jamie Moyer	.30	.10
❑	159	Russ Ortiz	.30	.10
❑	160	Juan Pierre	.30	.10
❑	161	Edgar Renteria	.30	.10
❑	162	Curt Schilling	.30	.10
❑	163	Mike Sweeney	.30	.10
❑	164	Brandon Webb	.30	.10
❑	165	Michael Young	.30	.10
❑	166	Carlos Beltran	.30	.10
❑	167	Sean Burroughs	.30	.10
❑	168	Luis Castillo	.30	.10
❑	169	David Eckstein	.30	.10
❑	170	Eric Gagne	.30	.10
❑	171	Chipper Jones	.75	.30
❑	172	Livan Hernandez	.30	.10
❑	173	Nick Johnson	.30	.10
❑	174	Corey Koskie	.30	.10
❑	175	Jason Schmidt	.30	.10
❑	176	Bill Mueller	.30	.10
❑	177	Steve Finley	.30	.10
❑	178	A.J. Pierzynski	.30	.10
❑	179	Rene Reyes	.30	.10
❑	180	Jason Johnson	.30	.10
❑	181	Mark Teixeira	.50	.20
❑	182	Kip Wells	.30	.10
❑	183	Mike MacDougal	.30	.10
❑	184	Lance Berkman	.30	.10
❑	185	Victor Zambrano	.30	.10
❑	186	Roger Clemens	1.50	.60
❑	187	Jim Edmonds	.30	.10
❑	188	Nomar Garciaparra	1.25	.50
❑	189	Ken Griffey Jr.	1.25	.50
❑	190	Richard Hidalgo	.30	.10
❑	191	Cliff Floyd	.30	.10
❑	192	Greg Maddux	1.25	.50
❑	193	Mark Mulder	.30	.10
❑	194	Roy Oswalt	.30	.10
❑	195	Marlon Byrd	.30	.10
❑	196	Jose Reyes	.30	.10
❑	197	Kevin Brown	.30	.10
❑	198	Miguel Tejada	.30	.10
❑	199	Vernon Wells	.30	.10
❑	200	Joel Pineiro	.30	.10
❑	201	Rickie Weeks AR	2.00	.75
❑	202	Chad Gaudin AR	1.25	.50
❑	203	Ryan Wagner AR	1.25	.50
❑	204	Chris Bootcheck AR	1.25	.50
❑	205	Koyie Hill AR	1.25	.50
❑	206	Jeff Duncan AR	1.25	.50
❑	207	Rich Harden AR	2.00	.75
❑	208	Edwin Jackson AR	1.25	.50
❑	209	Robby Hammock AR	1.25	.50
❑	210	Khalil Greene AR	3.00	1.25
❑	211	Chien-Ming Wang AR	5.00	2.00
❑	212	Prentice Redman AR	1.25	.50
❑	213	Todd Wellemeyer AR	1.25	.50
❑	214	Clint Barmes AR	2.00	.75
❑	215	Matt Kata AR	1.25	.50
❑	216	Jon Leicester AR	1.25	.50

❑	217	Jeremy Guthrie AR	1.25	.50
❑	218	Chin-Hui Tsao AR	2.00	.75
❑	219	Dan Haren AR	1.25	.50
❑	220	Delmon Young AR	3.00	1.25
❑	221	Vladimir Guerrero	1.25	.50
❑	222	Andy Pettitte	.75	.30
❑	223	Gary Sheffield	.50	.20
❑	224	Javier Vazquez	.50	.20
❑	225	Alex Rodriguez	2.00	.75
❑	226	Billy Wagner	.50	.20
❑	227	Miguel Tejada	.50	.20
❑	228	Greg Maddux	2.00	.75
❑	229	Ivan Rodriguez	.75	.30
❑	230	Roger Clemens	2.50	1.00
❑	231	Alfonso Soriano	.50	.20
❑	232	Miguel Cabrera	.75	.30
❑	233	Javy Lopez	.50	.20
❑	234	David Wells	.50	.20
❑	235	Eric Milton	.50	.20
❑	236	Armando Benitez	.50	.20
❑	237	Mike Cameron	.50	.20
❑	238	J.D. Drew	.50	.20
❑	239	Carlos Beltran	.50	.20
❑	240	Bartolo Colon	.50	.20
❑	241	Jose Guillen	.50	.20
❑	242	Kevin Brown	.50	.20
❑	243	Carlos Guillen	.50	.20
❑	244	Kenny Lofton	.50	.20
❑	245	Pokey Reese	.50	.20
❑	246	Rafael Palmeiro	.75	.30
❑	247	Nomar Garciaparra	2.00	.75
❑	248	Hee Seop Choi	.50	.20
❑	249	Juan Uribe	.50	.20
❑	250	Nick Johnson	.50	.20
❑	251	Scott Podsednik	.50	.20
❑	252	Richie Sexson	.50	.20
❑	253	Keith Foulke Sox	.50	.20
❑	254	Jaret Wright	.50	.20
❑	255	Johnny Estrada	.50	.20
❑	256	Michael Barrett	.50	.20
❑	257	Bernie Williams	.75	.30
❑	258	Octavio Dotel	.50	.20
❑	259	Jeromy Burnitz	.50	.20
❑	260	Kevin Youkilis	.50	.20
❑	261	Derrek Lee	.75	.30
❑	262	Jack Wilson	.50	.20
❑	263	Craig Wilson	.50	.20
❑	264	Richard Hidalgo	.50	.20
❑	265	Royce Clayton	.50	.20
❑	266	Curt Schilling	.75	.30
❑	267	Joe Mauer	.75	.30
❑	268	Bobby Crosby	.50	.20
❑	269	Zack Greinke	.50	.20
❑	270	Victor Martinez	.50	.20
❑	271	Pedro Feliz	.50	.20
❑	272	Tony Batista	.50	.20
❑	273	Casey Kotchman	.50	.20
❑	274	Freddy Garcia	.50	.20
❑	275	Adam Everett	.50	.20
❑	276	Alexis Rios	.50	.20
❑	277	Lew Ford	.50	.20
❑	278	Adam LaRoche	.50	.20
❑	279	Lyle Overbay	.50	.20
❑	280	Juan Gonzalez	.50	.20
❑	281	A.J. Pierzynski	.50	.20
❑	282	Scott Hairston	.50	.20
❑	283	Danny Bautista	.50	.20
❑	284	Brad Penny	.50	.20
❑	285	Paul Konorko	.50	.20
❑	286	Matt Lawton	.50	.20
❑	287	Carl Pavano	.50	.20
❑	288	Pat Burrell	.50	.20
❑	289	Kenny Rogers	.50	.20
❑	290	Laynce Nix	.50	.20
❑	291	Johnny Damon	.75	.30
❑	292	Paul Wilson	.50	.20
❑	293	Vinny Castilla	.50	.20
❑	294	Aaron Miles	.50	.20
❑	295	Ken Harvey	.50	.20
❑	296	Onil Joseph RC	2.00	.75
❑	297	Kazuhito Tadano RC	3.00	1.25
❑	298	Jeff Bennett RC	2.00	.75
❑	299	Chad Bentz RC	2.00	.75
❑	300	Akinori Otsuka RC	2.00	.75
❑	301	Jon Knott RC	2.00	.75
❑	302	Ian Snell RC	3.00	1.25
❑	303	Fernando Nieve RC	3.00	1.25
❑	304	Mike Rouse RC	2.00	.75
❑	305	Dennis Sarfate RC	2.00	.75
❑	306	Josh Labandeira RC	2.00	.75
❑	307	Chris Oxspring RC	2.00	.75
❑	308	Alfredo Simon RC	2.00	.75
❑	309	Rusty Tucker RC	3.00	1.25
❑	310	Lincoln Holdzkom RC	2.00	.75
❑	311	Justin Leone RC	3.00	1.25
❑	312	Jorge Sequea RC	2.00	.75
❑	313	Brian Dallimore RC	2.00	.75
❑	314	Tim Bittner RC	2.00	.75
❑	315	Ronny Cedeno RC	3.00	1.25
❑	316	Justin Hampson RC	2.00	.75
❑	317	Ryan Wing RC	2.00	.75
❑	318	Mariano Gomez RC	2.00	.75
❑	319	Carlos Vasquez RC	3.00	1.25
❑	320	Casey Daigle RC	2.00	.75
❑	321	Renyel Pinto RC	3.00	1.25
❑	322	Chris Shelton RC	3.00	1.25
❑	323	Mike Gosling RC	2.00	.75
❑	324	Aarom Baldiris RC	3.00	1.25
❑	325	Ramon Ramirez RC	2.00	.75
❑	326	Roberto Novoa RC	3.00	1.25
❑	327	Sean Henn RC	2.00	.75
❑	328	Nick Regilio RC	2.00	.75
❑	329	Dave Crouthers RC	2.00	.75
❑	330	Greg Dobbs RC	2.00	.75
❑	331	Angel Chavez RC	2.00	.75
❑	332	Luis A. Gonzalez RC	2.00	.75
❑	333	Justin Knoedler RC	2.00	.75
❑	334	Jason Frasor RC	2.00	.75
❑	335	Jerry Gil RC	2.00	.75
❑	336	Carlos Hines RC	2.00	.75
❑	337	Ivan Ochoa RC	2.00	.75
❑	338	Jose Capellan RC	3.00	1.25
❑	339	Hector Gimenez RC	2.00	.75
❑	340	Shawn Hill RC	2.00	.75
❑	341	Freddy Guzman RC	2.00	.75
❑	342	Scott Proctor RC	3.00	1.25
❑	343	Frank Francisco RC	2.00	.75
❑	344	Brandon Medders RC	2.00	.75
❑	345	Andy Green RC	2.00	.75
❑	346	Eddy Rodriguez RC	3.00	1.25
❑	347	Tim Hamulack RC	2.00	.75
❑	348	Michael Wuertz RC	3.00	1.25
❑	349	Arnie Munoz	2.00	.75
❑	350	Enemencio Pacheco RC	2.00	.75
❑	351	Dusty Bergman RC	2.00	.75
❑	352	Charles Thomas RC	2.00	.75
❑	353	William Bergolla RC	2.00	.75
❑	354	Ramon Castro RC	2.00	.75
❑	355	Justin Lehr RC	2.00	.75
❑	356	Lino Urdaneta RC	2.00	.75
❑	357	Donnie Kelly RC	2.00	.75
❑	358	Kevin Cave RC	2.00	.75
❑	359	Franklyn Gracesqui RC	2.00	.75
❑	360	Chris Aguila RC	2.00	.75
❑	361	Jorge Vasquez RC	2.00	.75
❑	362	Andres Blanco RC	2.00	.75
❑	363	Orlando Rodriguez RC	2.00	.75
❑	364	Colby Miller RC	2.00	.75
❑	365	Shawn Camp RC	2.00	.75
❑	366	Jake Woods RC	2.00	.75
❑	367	George Sherrill RC	2.00	.75
❑	368	Justin Huisman RC	2.00	.75
❑	369	Jimmy Serrano RC	2.00	.75
❑	370	Mike Johnston RC	2.00	.75
❑	371	Ryan Meaux RC	2.00	.75
❑	372	Scott Dohmann RC	2.00	.75
❑	373	Brad Halsey RC	3.00	1.25
❑	374	Joey Gathright RC	4.00	1.50
❑	375	Yadier Molina RC	5.00	2.00
❑	376	Travis Blackley RC	2.00	.75
❑	377	Steve Andrade RC	2.00	.75
❑	378	Phil Stockman RC	2.00	.75
❑	379	Roman Colon RC	2.00	.75
❑	380	Jesse Crain RC	3.00	1.25
❑	381	Edwardo Sierra RC	3.00	1.25
❑	382	Justin Germano RC	2.00	.75
❑	383	Kaz Matsui L13 RC	10.00	4.00
❑	384	Shingo Takatsu L13 RC	10.00	4.00
❑	385	John Gall L13 RC	12.00	5.00
❑	386	Chris Saenz L13 RC	12.00	5.00
❑	387	Merkin Valdez L13 RC	10.00	4.00
❑	388	Jamie Brown L13 RC	12.00	5.00
❑	389	Jason Bartlett L13 RC	12.00	5.00
❑	390	David Aardsma L13 RC	12.00	5.00
❑	391	Scott Kazmir L13 RC	30.00	12.50
❑	392	David Wright L13	30.00	12.50
❑	393	Dioner Navarro L13 RC	10.00	4.00
❑	394	B.J. Upton L13	12.00	5.00
❑	395	Gavin Floyd L13	12.00	5.00

2005 Ultra

❑	COMPLETE SET (220)	100.00	40.00
❑	COMP.SET w/o SP's (200)	40.00	15.00
❑	COMMON CARD (1-200)	.30	.10
❑	COMMON CARD (201-220)	2.00	.75
❑	201-220 ODDS 1:4 HOBBY, 1:5 RETAIL		

❑	1	Andy Pettitte	.50	.20
❑	2	Jose Cruz Jr.	.30	.10
❑	3	Cliff Floyd	.30	.10
❑	4	Paul Konerko	.30	.10
❑	5	Joe Mauer	.75	.30
❑	6	Scott Spiezio	.30	.10
❑	7	Ben Sheets	.30	.10
❑	8	Kerry Wood	.30	.10
❑	9	Carl Pavano	.30	.10
❑	10	Matt Morris	.30	.10
❑	11	Kaz Matsui	.30	.10
❑	12	Ivan Rodriguez	.50	.20
❑	13	Victor Martinez	.30	.10
❑	14	Justin Morneau	.30	.10
❑	15	Adam Everett	.30	.10
❑	16	Carl Crawford	.30	.10
❑	17	David Ortiz	.75	.30
❑	18	Jason Giambi	.30	.10
❑	19	Derrek Lee	.50	.20
❑	20	Magglio Ordonez	.30	.10
❑	21	Bobby Abreu	.30	.10
❑	22	Milton Bradley	.30	.10
❑	23	Jeff Bagwell	.50	.20
❑	24	Jim Edmonds	.30	.10
❑	25	Garret Anderson	.30	.10
❑	26	Jacque Jones	.30	.10
❑	27	Ted Lilly	.30	.10
❑	28	Greg Maddux	1.25	.50
❑	29	Jermaine Dye	.30	.10
❑	30	Bill Mueller	.30	.10
❑	31	Roy Oswalt	.30	.10
❑	32	Tony Womack	.30	.10
❑	33	Andruw Jones	.50	.20
❑	34	Tom Glavine	.50	.20
❑	35	Mariano Rivera	.75	.30
❑	36	Sean Casey	.30	.10
❑	37	Edgardo Alfonzo	.30	.10
❑	38	Brad Penny	.30	.10
❑	39	Johan Santana	.75	.30
❑	40	Mark Teixeira	.50	.20
❑	41	Manny Ramirez	.50	.20
❑	42	Gary Sheffield	.30	.10
❑	43	Matt Lawton	.30	.10
❑	44	Troy Percival	.30	.10
❑	45	Rocco Baldelli	.30	.10
❑	46	Doug Mientkiewicz	.30	.10
❑	47	Corey Patterson	.30	.10
❑	48	Austin Kearns	.30	.10
❑	49	Edgar Martinez	.50	.20
❑	50	Brad Radke	.30	.10
❑	51	Barry Larkin	.50	.20
❑	52	Chone Figgins	.30	.10
❑	53	Alexis Rios	.30	.10
❑	54	Alex Rodriguez	1.25	.50

❑ 55	Vinny Castilla	.30	.10
❑ 56	Javier Vazquez	.30	.10
❑ 57	Javy Lopez	.30	.10
❑ 58	Mike Cameron	.30	.10
❑ 59	Brian Giles	.30	.10
❑ 60	Dontrelle Willis	.30	.10
❑ 61	Rafael Furcal	.30	.10
❑ 62	Trot Nixon	.30	.10
❑ 63	Mark Mulder	.30	.10
❑ 64	Josh Beckett	.30	.10
❑ 65	J.D. Drew	.30	.10
❑ 66	Brandon Webb	.30	.10
❑ 67	Wade Miller	.30	.10
❑ 68	Lyle Overbay	.30	.10
❑ 69	Pedro Martinez	.50	.20
❑ 70	Rich Harden	.30	.10
❑ 71	Al Leiter	.30	.10
❑ 72	Adam Eaton	.30	.10
❑ 73	Mike Sweeney	.30	.10
❑ 74	Steve Finley	.30	.10
❑ 75	Kris Benson	.30	.10
❑ 76	Jim Thome	.50	.20
❑ 77	Juan Pierre	.30	.10
❑ 78	Bartolo Colon	.30	.10
❑ 79	Carlos Delgado	.30	.10
❑ 80	Jack Wilson	.30	.10
❑ 81	Ken Harvey	.30	.10
❑ 82	Nomar Garciaparra	.75	.30
❑ 83	Paul Lo Duca	.30	.10
❑ 84	Cesar Izturis	.30	.10
❑ 85	Adrian Beltre	.30	.10
❑ 86	Brian Roberts	.30	.10
❑ 87	David Eckstein	.30	.10
❑ 88	Jimmy Rollins	.30	.10
❑ 89	Roger Clemens	1.25	.50
❑ 90	Randy Johnson	.75	.30
❑ 91	Orlando Hudson	.30	.10
❑ 92	Tim Hudson	.30	.10
❑ 93	Dmitri Young	.30	.10
❑ 94	Chipper Jones	.75	.30
❑ 95	John Smoltz	.50	.20
❑ 96	Billy Wagner	.30	.10
❑ 97	Hideo Nomo	.75	.30
❑ 98	Sammy Sosa	.75	.30
❑ 99	Darin Erstad	.30	.10
❑ 100	Todd Helton	.50	.20
❑ 101	Aubrey Huff	.30	.10
❑ 102	Alfonso Soriano	.30	.10
❑ 103	Jose Vidro	.30	.10
❑ 104	Carlos Lee	.30	.10
❑ 105	Corey Koskie	.30	.10
❑ 106	Bret Boone	.30	.10
❑ 107	Torii Hunter	.30	.10
❑ 108	Aramis Ramirez	.30	.10
❑ 109	Chase Utley	.50	.20
❑ 110	Reggie Sanders	.30	.10
❑ 111	Livan Hernandez	.30	.10
❑ 112	Jeromy Burnitz	.30	.10
❑ 113	Carlos Zambrano	.30	.10
❑ 114	Hank Blalock	.30	.10
❑ 115	Sidney Ponson	.30	.10
❑ 116	Zack Greinke	.30	.10
❑ 117	Trevor Hoffman	.30	.10
❑ 118	Jeff Kent	.30	.10
❑ 119	Richie Sexson	.30	.10
❑ 120	Melvin Mora	.30	.10
❑ 121	Eric Chavez	.30	.10
❑ 122	Miguel Cabrera	.50	.20
❑ 123	Ryan Freel	.30	.10
❑ 124	Russ Ortiz	.30	.10
❑ 125	Craig Wilson	.30	.10
❑ 126	Craig Biggio	.50	.20
❑ 127	Curt Schilling	.50	.20
❑ 128	Kaz Ishii	.30	.10
❑ 129	Marquis Grissom	.30	.10
❑ 130	Bernie Williams	.50	.20
❑ 131	Travis Hafner	.30	.10
❑ 132	Hee Seop Choi	.30	.10
❑ 133	Scott Rolen	.50	.20
❑ 134	Tony Batista	.30	.10
❑ 135	Frank Thomas	.75	.30
❑ 136	Jason Varitek	.75	.30
❑ 137	Ichiro Suzuki	1.50	.60
❑ 138	Junior Spivey	.30	.10
❑ 139	Adam Dunn	.30	.10
❑ 140	Jorge Posada	.50	.20
❑ 141	Edgar Renteria	.30	.10
❑ 142	Hideki Matsui	1.25	.50
❑ 143	Carlos Guillen	.30	.10
❑ 144	Jody Gerut	.30	.10
❑ 145	Wily Mo Pena	.30	.10
❑ 146	Derek Jeter	1.50	.60
❑ 147	C.C. Sabathia	.30	.10
❑ 148	Geoff Jenkins	.30	.10
❑ 149	Albert Pujols	1.50	.60
❑ 150	Eric Munson	.30	.10
❑ 151	Moises Alou	.30	.10
❑ 152	Jerry Hairston	.30	.10
❑ 153	Ray Durham	.30	.10
❑ 154	Mike Piazza	.75	.30
❑ 155	Omar Vizquel	.30	.10
❑ 156	A.J. Pierzynski	.30	.10
❑ 157	Michael Young	.30	.10
❑ 158	Jason Bay	.30	.10
❑ 159	Mark Loretta	.30	.10
❑ 160	Shawn Green	.30	.10
❑ 161	Luis Gonzalez	.30	.10
❑ 162	Johnny Damon	.50	.20
❑ 163	Eric Milton	.30	.10
❑ 164	Mike Lowell	.30	.10
❑ 165	Jose Guillen	.30	.10
❑ 166	Eric Hinske	.30	.10
❑ 167	Jason Kendall	.30	.10
❑ 168	Carlos Beltran	.30	.10
❑ 169	Johnny Estrada	.30	.10
❑ 170	Scott Hatteberg	.30	.10
❑ 171	Laynce Nix	.30	.10
❑ 172	Eric Gagne	.30	.10
❑ 173	Richard Hidalgo	.30	.10
❑ 174	Bobby Crosby	.30	.10
❑ 175	Woody Williams	.30	.10
❑ 176	Justin Leone	.30	.10
❑ 177	Orlando Cabrera	.30	.10
❑ 178	Mark Prior	.50	.20
❑ 179	Jorge Julio	.30	.10
❑ 180	Jamie Moyer	.30	.10
❑ 181	Jose Reyes	.30	.10
❑ 182	Ken Griffey Jr.	1.25	.50
❑ 183	Mike Lieberthal	.30	.10
❑ 184	Kenny Rogers	.30	.10
❑ 185	Mike Mussina	.50	.20
❑ 186	Preston Wilson	.30	.10
❑ 187	Khalil Greene	.50	.20
❑ 188	Angel Berroa	.30	.10
❑ 189	Miguel Tejada	.30	.10
❑ 190	Freddy Garcia	.30	.10
❑ 191	Pat Burrell	.30	.10
❑ 192	Luis Castillo	.30	.10
❑ 193	Vladimir Guerrero	.75	.30
❑ 194	Roy Halladay	.30	.10
❑ 195	Barry Zito	.30	.10
❑ 196	Lance Berkman	.30	.10
❑ 197	Rafael Palmeiro	.50	.20
❑ 198	Nate Robertson	.30	.10
❑ 199	Jason Schmidt	.30	.10
❑ 200	Scott Podsednik	.30	.10
❑ 201	Casey Kotchman AR	3.00	1.25
❑ 202	Scott Kazmir AR	5.00	2.00
❑ 203	Bucky Jacobsen AR	2.00	.75
❑ 204	Jeff Keppinger AR	2.00	.75
❑ 205	Dave Bush AR	2.00	.75
❑ 206	Gavin Floyd AR	2.00	.75
❑ 207	David Wright AR	8.00	3.00
❑ 208	B.J. Upton AR	5.00	2.00
❑ 209	David Aardsma AR	2.00	.75
❑ 210	Jason Bartlett AR	2.00	.75
❑ 211	Dioner Navarro AR	3.00	1.25
❑ 212	Jason Kubel AR	2.00	.75
❑ 213	Ryan Howard AR	8.00	3.00
❑ 214	Charles Thomas AR	2.00	.75
❑ 215	Freddy Guzman AR	2.00	.75
❑ 216	Brad Halsey AR	2.00	.75
❑ 217	Joey Gathright AR	3.00	1.25
❑ 218	Jeff Francis AR	2.00	.75
❑ 219	Terry Tiffee AR	2.00	.75
❑ 220	Nick Swisher AR	5.00	2.00

2006 Ultra

❑ COMP.SET w/o RL13 (200) 40.00 15.00
❑ COMMON CARD (1-180) .40 .15
❑ RL13 201-250 ODDS 1:4 HOBBY, 1:4 RETAIL
❑ 251 PRINT RUN 5000 CARDS
❑ 251 JOHJIMA IS NOT SERIAL NUMBERED
❑ 251 PRINT RUN INFO PROVIDED BY UD
❑ 251 JOHJIMA EXCH. DEADLINE 05/25/08

❑ 1	Vladimir Guerrero	1.00	.40
❑ 2	Bartolo Colon	.40	.15
❑ 3	Francisco Rodriguez	.40	.15
❑ 4	Darin Erstad	.40	.15
❑ 5	Chone Figgins	.40	.15
❑ 6	Bengie Molina	.40	.15
❑ 7	Roger Clemens	2.00	.75
❑ 8	Lance Berkman	.40	.15
❑ 9	Morgan Ensberg	.40	.15
❑ 10	Roy Oswalt	.40	.15
❑ 11	Andy Pettitte	.40	.15
❑ 12	Craig Biggio	.60	.25
❑ 13	Eric Chavez	.40	.15
❑ 14	Barry Zito	.40	.15
❑ 15	Huston Street	.40	.15
❑ 16	Bobby Crosby	.40	.15
❑ 17	Nick Swisher	.40	.15
❑ 18	Rich Harden	.40	.15
❑ 19	Vernon Wells	.40	.15
❑ 20	Roy Halladay	.40	.15
❑ 21	Alex Rios	.40	.15
❑ 22	Orlando Hudson	.40	.15
❑ 23	Shea Hillenbrand	.40	.15
❑ 24	Gustavo Chacin	.40	.15
❑ 25	Chipper Jones	1.00	.40
❑ 26	Andruw Jones	.60	.25
❑ 27	Jeff Francoeur	1.00	.40
❑ 28	John Smoltz	.60	.25
❑ 29	Tim Hudson	.40	.15
❑ 30	Marcus Giles	.40	.15
❑ 31	Carlos Lee	.40	.15
❑ 32	Ben Sheets	.40	.15
❑ 33	Rickie Weeks	.40	.15
❑ 34	Chris Capuano	.40	.15
❑ 35	Geoff Jenkins	.40	.15
❑ 36	Brady Clark	.40	.15
❑ 37	Albert Pujols	2.00	.75
❑ 38	Jim Edmonds	.60	.25
❑ 39	Chris Carpenter	.40	.15
❑ 40	Mark Mulder	.40	.15
❑ 41	Yadier Molina	.40	.15
❑ 42	Scott Rolen	.60	.25
❑ 43	Derrek Lee	.40	.15
❑ 44	Mark Prior	.60	.25
❑ 45	Aramis Ramirez	.40	.15
❑ 46	Carlos Zambrano	.40	.15
❑ 47	Greg Maddux	1.50	.60
❑ 48	Nomar Garciaparra	1.00	.40
❑ 49	Jonny Gomes	.40	.15
❑ 50	Carl Crawford	.40	.15
❑ 51	Scott Kazmir	.60	.25
❑ 52	Jorge Cantu	.40	.15
❑ 53	Julio Lugo	.40	.15
❑ 54	Aubrey Huff	.40	.15
❑ 55	Luis Gonzalez	.40	.15
❑ 56	Brandon Webb	.40	.15
❑ 57	Troy Glaus	.40	.15
❑ 58	Shawn Green	.40	.15
❑ 59	Craig Counsell	.40	.15
❑ 60	Conor Jackson (RC)	1.50	.60
❑ 61	Jeff Kent	.40	.15
❑ 62	Eric Gagne	.40	.15
❑ 63	J.D. Drew	.40	.15
❑ 64	Milton Bradley	.40	.15
❑ 65	Jeff Weaver	.40	.15

❑ 66 Cesar Izturis .40 .15
❑ 67 Jason Schmidt .40 .15
❑ 68 Moises Alou .40 .15
❑ 69 Pedro Feliz .40 .15
❑ 70 Randy Winn .40 .15
❑ 71 Omar Vizquel .60 .25
❑ 72 Noah Lowry .40 .15
❑ 73 Travis Hafner .40 .15
❑ 74 Victor Martinez .40 .15
❑ 75 C.C. Sabathia .40 .15
❑ 76 Grady Sizemore .60 .25
❑ 77 Coco Crisp .40 .15
❑ 78 Cliff Lee .40 .15
❑ 79 Raul IbaÃ±ez .40 .15
❑ 80 Ichiro Suzuki 1.50 .60
❑ 81 Richie Sexson .40 .15
❑ 82 Felix Hernandez .60 .25
❑ 83 Adrian Beltre .40 .15
❑ 84 Jamie Moyer .40 .15
❑ 85 Miguel Cabrera .60 .25
❑ 86 A.J. Burnett .40 .15
❑ 87 Juan Pierre .40 .15
❑ 88 Carlos Delgado .40 .15
❑ 89 Dontrelle Willis .40 .15
❑ 90 Juan Encarnacion .40 .15
❑ 91 Carlos Beltran .40 .15
❑ 92 Jose Reyes .40 .15
❑ 93 David Wright 1.50 .60
❑ 94 Tom Glavine .60 .25
❑ 95 Mike Piazza 1.00 .40
❑ 96 Pedro Martinez .60 .25
❑ 97 Ryan Zimmerman (RC) 3.00 1.25
❑ 98 Nick Johnson .40 .15
❑ 99 Jose Vidro .40 .15
❑ 100 Jose Guillen .40 .15
❑ 101 Livan Hernandez .40 .15
❑ 102 John Patterson .40 .15
❑ 103 Miguel Tejada .40 .15
❑ 104 Melvin Mora .40 .15
❑ 105 Brian Roberts .40 .15
❑ 106 Erik Bedard .40 .15
❑ 107 Javy Lopez .40 .15
❑ 108 Rodrigo Lopez .40 .15
❑ 109 Jake Peavy .40 .15
❑ 110 Mike Cameron .40 .15
❑ 111 Mark Loretta .40 .15
❑ 112 Brian Giles .40 .15
❑ 113 Trevor Hoffman .40 .15
❑ 114 Ramon Hernandez .40 .15
❑ 115 Bobby Abreu .40 .15
❑ 116 Chase Utley 1.00 .40
❑ 117 Pat Burrell .40 .15
❑ 118 Jimmy Rollins .40 .15
❑ 119 Ryan Howard 1.50 .60
❑ 120 Billy Wagner .40 .15
❑ 121 Jason Bay .40 .15
❑ 122 Oliver Perez .40 .15
❑ 123 Jack Wilson .40 .15
❑ 124 Zach Duke .40 .15
❑ 125 Rob Mackowiak .40 .15
❑ 126 Freddy Sanchez .40 .15
❑ 127 Mark Teixeira .60 .25
❑ 128 Michael Young .40 .15
❑ 129 Alfonso Soriano .40 .15
❑ 130 Hank Blalock .40 .15
❑ 131 Kenny Rogers .40 .15
❑ 132 Kevin Mench .40 .15
❑ 133 Manny Ramirez .60 .25
❑ 134 Josh Beckett .40 .15
❑ 135 David Ortiz 1.00 .40
❑ 136 Johnny Damon .60 .25
❑ 137 Edgar Renteria .40 .15
❑ 138 Curt Schilling .60 .25
❑ 139 Ken Griffey Jr. 1.50 .60
❑ 140 Adam Dunn .40 .15
❑ 141 Felipe Lopez .40 .15
❑ 142 Wily Mo Pena .40 .15
❑ 143 Aaron Harang .40 .15
❑ 144 Sean Casey .40 .15
❑ 145 Todd Helton .60 .25
❑ 146 Garrett Atkins .40 .15
❑ 147 Matt Holliday .40 .15
❑ 148 Jeff Francis .40 .15
❑ 149 Clint Barmes .40 .15
❑ 150 Luis Gonzalez .40 .15
❑ 151 Mike Sweeney .40 .15
❑ 152 Zack Greinke .40 .15
❑ 153 Angel Berroa .40 .15
❑ 154 Emil Brown .40 .15
❑ 155 David DeJesus .40 .15
❑ 156 Ivan Rodriguez .60 .25
❑ 157 Jeremy Bonderman .40 .15
❑ 158 Brandon Inge .40 .15
❑ 159 Craig Monroe .40 .15
❑ 160 Chris Shelton .40 .15
❑ 161 Dmitri Young .40 .15
❑ 162 Johan Santana .60 .25
❑ 163 Joe Mauer .60 .25
❑ 164 Torii Hunter .40 .15
❑ 165 Shannon Stewart .40 .15
❑ 166 Scott Baker .40 .15
❑ 167 Brad Radke .40 .15
❑ 168 Jon Garland .40 .15
❑ 169 Tadahito Iguchi .40 .15
❑ 170 Paul Konerko .40 .15
❑ 171 Scott Podsednik .40 .15
❑ 172 Mark Buehrle .40 .15
❑ 173 Joe Crede .40 .15
❑ 174 Derek Jeter 2.50 1.00
❑ 175 Alex Rodriguez 1.50 .60
❑ 176 Hideki Matsui 1.50 .60
❑ 177 Randy Johnson 1.00 .40
❑ 178 Gary Sheffield .40 .15
❑ 179 Mariano Rivera 1.00 .40
❑ 180 Jason Giambi .40 .15
❑ 181 Joey Devine RC 1.00 .40
❑ 182 Alejandro Freire RC 1.00 .40
❑ 183 Craig Hansen RC 2.00 .75
❑ 184 Robert Andino RC 1.00 .40
❑ 185 Ryan Jorgensen RC 1.00 .40
❑ 186 Chris Demaria RC 1.00 .40
❑ 187 Jonah Bayliss RC 1.00 .40
❑ 188 Ryan Theriot RC 1.00 .40
❑ 189 Steve Stemle RC 1.00 .40
❑ 190 Brian Myrow RC 1.00 .40
❑ 191 Chris Heintz RC 1.00 .40
❑ 192 Ron Flores RC 1.00 .40
❑ 193 Danny Sandoval RC 1.00 .40
❑ 194 Craig Breslow RC 1.00 .40
❑ 195 Jeremy Accardo RC 1.00 .40
❑ 196 Jeff Harris RC 1.00 .40
❑ 197 Tim Corcoran RC 1.00 .40
❑ 198 Scott Feldman RC 1.00 .40
❑ 199 Robinson Cano .60 .25
❑ 200 Jason Bergmann RC 2.00 .75
❑ 201 Ken Griffey Jr. RL13 8.00 3.00
❑ 202 Frank Thomas RL13 5.00 2.00
❑ 203 Chipper Jones RL13 5.00 2.00
❑ 204 Tony Clark RL13 2.00 .75
❑ 205 Mike Lieberthal RL13 2.00 .75
❑ 206 Manny Ramirez RL13 3.00 1.25
❑ 207 Phil Nevin RL13 2.00 .75
❑ 208 Derek Jeter RL13 10.00 4.00
❑ 209 Preston Wilson RL13 2.00 .75
❑ 210 Billy Wagner RL13 2.00 .75
❑ 211 Alex Rodriguez RL13 8.00 3.00
❑ 212 Trot Nixon RL13 2.00 .75
❑ 213 Jaret Wright RL13 2.00 .75
❑ 214 Nomar Garciaparra RL13 5.00 2.00
❑ 215 Paul Konerko RL13 2.00 .75
❑ 216 Paul Wilson RL13 2.00 .75
❑ 217 Dustin Hermanson RL13 2.00 .75
❑ 218 Todd Walker RL13 2.00 .75
❑ 219 Matt Morris RL13 2.00 .75
❑ 220 Darin Erstad RL13 2.00 .75
❑ 221 Todd Helton RL13 3.00 1.25
❑ 222 Geoff Jenkins RL13 2.00 .75
❑ 223 Eric Chavez RL13 2.00 .75
❑ 224 Kris Benson RL13 2.00 .75
❑ 225 Jon Garland RL13 2.00 .75
❑ 226 Troy Glaus RL13 2.00 .75
❑ 227 Vernon Wells RL13 2.00 .75
❑ 228 Michael Cuddyer RL13 2.00 .75
❑ 229 Justin Verlander RL13 8.00 3.00
❑ 230 Pat Burrell RL13 2.00 .75
❑ 231 Mark Mulder RL13 2.00 .75
❑ 232 Corey Patterson RL13 2.00 .75
❑ 233 J.D. Drew RL13 2.00 .75
❑ 234 Austin Kearns RL13 2.00 .75
❑ 235 Felipe Lopez RL13 2.00 .75
❑ 236 Sean Burroughs RL13 2.00 .75
❑ 237 Ben Sheets RL13 2.00 .75
❑ 238 Brett Myers RL13 2.00 .75
❑ 239 Josh Beckett RL13 2.00 .75
❑ 240 Barry Zito RL13 2.00 .75
❑ 241 Adrian Gonzalez RL13 2.00 .75
❑ 242 Rocco Baldelli RL13 2.00 .75
❑ 243 Chris Burke RL13 2.00 .75
❑ 244 Joe Mauer RL13 3.00 1.25
❑ 245 Mark Prior RL13 3.00 1.25
❑ 246 Mark Teixiera RL13 3.00 1.25
❑ 247 Khalil Greene RL13 3.00 1.25
❑ 248 Zack Greinke RL13 2.00 .75
❑ 249 Prince Fielder RL13 8.00 3.00
❑ 250 Rickie Weeks RL13 2.00 .75
❑ 251 Kenji Johjima 15.00 6.00

1989 Upper Deck

❑ COMPLETE SET (800) 80.00 40.00
❑ COMP.FACT.SET (800) 100.00 50.00
❑ COMP.HI FACT.SET (100) 10.00 4.00
❑ 1 Ken Griffey Jr. RC 50.00 20.00
❑ 2 Luis Medina RC .25 .08
❑ 3 Tony Chance RC .25 .08
❑ 4 Dave Otto .25 .08
❑ 5 Sandy Alomar Jr. RC 1.00 .40
❑ 6 Rolando Roomes RC .25 .08
❑ 7 Dave West RC .25 .08
❑ 8 Cris Carpenter RC * .25 .08
❑ 9 Gregg Jefferies .25 .08
❑ 10 Doug Dascenzo RC .25 .08
❑ 11 Ron Jones RC .25 .08
❑ 12 Luis DeLosSantos RC .25 .08
❑ 13 Gary Sheffield RC 5.00 2.00
❑ 13A Gary Sheffield ERR 5.00 2.00
❑ 14 Mike Harkey RC .25 .08
❑ 15 Lance Blankenship RC .25 .08
❑ 16 William Brennan RC .25 .08
❑ 17 John Smoltz RC 5.00 2.00
❑ 18 Ramon Martinez RC .50 .20
❑ 19 Mark Lemke RC 1.00 .40
❑ 20 Juan Bell RC .25 .08
❑ 21 Rey Palacios RC .25 .08
❑ 22 Felix Jose RC .25 .08
❑ 23 Van Snider RC .25 .08
❑ 24 Dante Bichette RC 1.00 .40
❑ 25 Randy Johnson RC 10.00 4.00
❑ 26 Carlos Quintana RC .25 .08
❑ 27 Star Rookie CL .25 .08
❑ 28 Mike Schooler .25 .08
❑ 29 Randy St.Claire .25 .08
❑ 30 Jerald Clark RC .25 .08
❑ 31 Kevin Gross .25 .08
❑ 32 Dan Firova .25 .08
❑ 33 Jeff Calhoun .25 .08
❑ 34 Tommy Hinzo .25 .08
❑ 35 Ricky Jordan RC * .50 .20
❑ 36 Larry Parrish .25 .08
❑ 37 Bret Saberhagen UER (Hit total 931& should be 10 .40 .15
❑ 38 Mike Smithson .25 .08
❑ 39 Dave Dravecky .25 .08
❑ 40 Ed Romero .25 .08
❑ 41 Jeff Musselman .25 .08
❑ 42 Ed Hearn .25 .08
❑ 43 Rance Mulliniks .25 .08
❑ 44 Jim Eisenreich .25 .08
❑ 45 Sil Campusano .25 .08
❑ 46 Mike Krukow .25 .08

❑	47	Paul Gibson	.25	.08
❑	48	Mike LaCoss	.25	.08
❑	49	Larry Herndon	.25	.08
❑	50	Scott Garrelts	.25	.08
❑	51	Dwayne Henry	.25	.08
❑	52	Jim Acker	.25	.08
❑	53	Steve Sax	.25	.08
❑	54	Pete O'Brien	.25	.08
❑	55	Paul Runge	.25	.08
❑	56	Rick Rhoden	.25	.08
❑	57	John Dopson	.25	.08
❑	58	Casey Candaele UER (No stats for Astros for '88)	.25	.08
❑	59	Dave Righetti	.40	.15
❑	60	Joe Hesketh	.25	.08
❑	61	Frank DiPino	.25	.08
❑	62	Tim Laudner	.25	.08
❑	63	Jamie Moyer	.40	.15
❑	64	Fred Toliver	.25	.08
❑	65	Mitch Webster	.25	.08
❑	66	John Tudor	.40	.15
❑	67	John Cangelosi	.25	.08
❑	68	Mike Devereaux	.25	.08
❑	69	Brian Fisher	.25	.08
❑	70	Mike Marshall	.25	.08
❑	71	Zane Smith	.25	.08
❑	72A	Brian Holton ERR	1.00	.40
❑	72B	Brian Holton COR	.40	.15
❑	73	Jose Guzman	.25	.08
❑	74	Rick Mahler	.25	.08
❑	75	John Shelby	.25	.08
❑	76	Jim Deshaies	.25	.08
❑	77	Bobby Meacham	.25	.08
❑	78	Bryn Smith	.25	.08
❑	79	Joaquin Andujar	.40	.15
❑	80	Richard Dotson	.25	.08
❑	81	Charlie Lea	.25	.08
❑	82	Calvin Schiraldi	.25	.08
❑	83	Les Straker	.25	.08
❑	84	Les Lancaster	.25	.08
❑	85	Allan Anderson	.25	.08
❑	86	Junior Ortiz	.25	.08
❑	87	Jesse Orosco	.25	.08
❑	88	Felix Fermin	.25	.08
❑	89	Dave Anderson	.25	.08
❑	90	Rafael Belliard UER (Born '61& not '51)	.25	.08
❑	91	Franklin Stubbs	.25	.08
❑	92	Cecil Espy	.25	.08
❑	93	Albert Hall	.25	.08
❑	94	Tim Leary	.25	.08
❑	95	Mitch Williams	.25	.08
❑	96	Tracy Jones	.25	.08
❑	97	Danny Darwin	.25	.08
❑	98	Gary Ward	.25	.08
❑	99	Neal Heaton	.25	.08
❑	100	Jim Pankovits	.25	.08
❑	101	Bill Doran	.25	.08
❑	102	Tim Wallach	.25	.08
❑	103	Joe Magrane	.25	.08
❑	104	Ozzie Virgil	.25	.08
❑	105	Alvin Davis	.25	.08
❑	106	Tom Brookens	.25	.08
❑	107	Shawon Dunston	.25	.08
❑	108	Tracy Woodson	.25	.08
❑	109	Nelson Liriano	.25	.08
❑	110	Devon White	.40	.15
❑	111	Steve Balboni	.25	.08
❑	112	Buddy Bell	.40	.15
❑	113	German Jimenez	.25	.08
❑	114	Ken Dayley	.25	.08
❑	115	Andres Galarraga	.40	.15
❑	116	Mike Scioscia	.40	.15
❑	117	Gary Pettis	.25	.08
❑	118	Ernie Whitt	.25	.08
❑	119	Bob Boone	.40	.15
❑	120	Ryne Sandberg	1.50	.60
❑	121	Bruce Benedict	.25	.08
❑	122	Hubie Brooks	.25	.08
❑	123	Mike Moore	.25	.08
❑	124	Wallace Johnson	.25	.08
❑	125	Bob Horner	.40	.15
❑	126	Chili Davis	.40	.15
❑	127	Manny Trillo	.25	.08
❑	128	Chet Lemon	.40	.15
❑	129	John Cerutti	.25	.08
❑	130	Orel Hershiser	.40	.15
❑	131	Terry Pendleton	.40	.15
❑	132	Jeff Blauser	.25	.08
❑	133	Mike Fitzgerald	.25	.08
❑	134	Henry Cotto	.25	.08
❑	135	Gerald Young	.25	.08
❑	136	Luis Salazar	.25	.08
❑	137	Alejandro Pena	.25	.08
❑	138	Jack Howell	.25	.08
❑	139	Tony Fernandez	.25	.08
❑	140	Mark Grace	1.00	.40
❑	141	Ken Caminiti	.60	.25
❑	142	Mike Jackson	.25	.08
❑	143	Larry McWilliams	.25	.08
❑	144	Andres Thomas	.25	.08
❑	145	Nolan Ryan 3X	4.00	1.50
❑	146	Mike Davis	.25	.08
❑	147	DeWayne Buice	.25	.08
❑	148	Jody Davis	.25	.08
❑	149	Jesse Barfield	.40	.15
❑	150	Matt Nokes	.25	.08
❑	151	Jerry Reuss	.25	.08
❑	152	Rick Cerone	.25	.08
❑	153	Storm Davis	.25	.08
❑	154	Marvell Wynne	.25	.08
❑	155	Will Clark	.60	.25
❑	156	Luis Aguayo	.25	.08
❑	157	Willie Upshaw	.25	.08
❑	158	Randy Bush	.25	.08
❑	159	Ron Darling	.40	.15
❑	160	Kal Daniels	.25	.08
❑	161	Spike Owen	.25	.08
❑	162	Luis Polonia	.25	.08
❑	163	Kevin Mitchell UER	.40	.15
❑	164	Dave Gallagher	.25	.08
❑	165	Benito Santiago	.40	.15
❑	166	Greg Gagne	.25	.08
❑	167	Ken Phelps	.25	.08
❑	168	Sid Fernandez	.25	.08
❑	169	Bo Diaz	.25	.08
❑	170	Cory Snyder	.25	.08
❑	171	Eric Show	.25	.08
❑	172	Robby Thompson	.25	.08
❑	173	Marty Barrett	.25	.08
❑	174	Dave Henderson	.25	.08
❑	175	Ozzie Guillen	.40	.15
❑	176	Barry Lyons	.25	.08
❑	177	Kelvin Torve	.25	.08
❑	178	Don Slaught	.25	.08
❑	179	Steve Lombardozzi	.25	.08
❑	180	Chris Sabo RC *	1.00	.40
❑	181	Jose Uribe	.25	.08
❑	182	Shane Mack	.25	.08
❑	183	Ron Karkovice	.25	.08
❑	184	Todd Benzinger	.25	.08
❑	185	Dave Stewart	.40	.15
❑	186	Julio Franco	.40	.15
❑	187	Ron Robinson	.25	.08
❑	188	Wally Backman	.25	.08
❑	189	Randy Velarde	.25	.08
❑	190	Joe Carter	.40	.15
❑	191	Bob Welch	.40	.15
❑	192	Kelly Paris	.25	.08
❑	193	Chris Brown	.25	.08
❑	194	Rick Reuschel	.40	.15
❑	195	Roger Clemens	2.00	.75
❑	196	Dave Concepcion	.40	.15
❑	197	Al Newman	.25	.08
❑	198	Brook Jacoby	.25	.08
❑	199	Mookie Wilson	.40	.15
❑	200	Don Mattingly	2.50	1.00
❑	201	Dick Schofield	.25	.08
❑	202	Mark Gubicza	.25	.08
❑	203	Gary Gaetti	.40	.15
❑	204	Dan Pasqua	.25	.08
❑	205	Andre Dawson	.40	.15
❑	206	Chris Speier	.25	.08
❑	207	Kent Tekulve	.25	.08
❑	208	Rod Scurry	.25	.08
❑	209	Scott Bailes	.25	.08
❑	210	Rickey Henderson	1.00	.40
❑	211	Harold Baines	.40	.15
❑	212	Tony Armas	.40	.15
❑	213	Kent Hrbek	.40	.15
❑	214	Darrin Jackson	.25	.08
❑	215	George Brett	2.50	1.00
❑	216	Rafael Santana	.25	.08
❑	217	Andy Allanson	.25	.08
❑	218	Brett Butler	.40	.15
❑	219	Steve Jeltz	.25	.08
❑	220	Jay Buhner	.40	.15
❑	221	Bo Jackson	1.00	.40
❑	222	Angel Salazar	.25	.08
❑	223	Kirk McCaskill	.25	.08
❑	224	Steve Lyons	.25	.08
❑	225	Bert Blyleven	.40	.15
❑	226	Scott Bradley	.25	.08
❑	227	Bob Melvin	.25	.08
❑	228	Ron Kittle	.25	.08
❑	229	Phil Bradley	.25	.08
❑	230	Tommy John	.40	.15
❑	231	Greg Walker	.25	.08
❑	232	Juan Berenguer	.25	.08
❑	233	Pat Tabler	.25	.08
❑	234	Terry Clark	.25	.08
❑	235	Rafael Palmeiro	1.00	.40
❑	236	Paul Zuvella	.25	.08
❑	237	Willie Randolph	.40	.15
❑	238	Bruce Fields	.25	.08
❑	239	Mike Aldrete	.25	.08
❑	240	Lance Parrish	.40	.15
❑	241	Greg Maddux	2.50	1.00
❑	242	John Moses	.25	.08
❑	243	Melido Perez	.25	.08
❑	244	Willie Wilson	.40	.15
❑	245	Mark McLemore	.25	.08
❑	246	Von Hayes	.25	.08
❑	247	Matt Williams	1.00	.40
❑	248	John Candelaria UER (Listed as Yankee for part o)	.25	.08
❑	249	Harold Reynolds	.40	.15
❑	250	Greg Swindell	.25	.08
❑	251	Juan Agosto	.25	.08
❑	252	Mike Felder	.25	.08
❑	253	Vince Coleman	.25	.08
❑	254	Larry Sheets	.25	.08
❑	255	George Bell	.40	.15
❑	256	Terry Steinbach	.40	.15
❑	257	Jack Armstrong RC *	.50	.20
❑	258	Dickie Thon	.25	.08
❑	259	Ray Knight	.40	.15
❑	260	Darryl Strawberry	.40	.15
❑	261	Doug Sisk	.25	.08
❑	262	Alex Trevino	.25	.08
❑	263	Jeffrey Leonard	.25	.08
❑	264	Tom Henke	.25	.08
❑	265	Ozzie Smith	1.50	.60
❑	266	Dave Bergman	.25	.08
❑	267	Tony Phillips	.25	.08
❑	268	Mark Davis	.25	.08
❑	269	Kevin Elster	.25	.08
❑	270	Barry Larkin	.60	.25
❑	271	Manny Lee	.25	.08
❑	272	Tom Brunansky	.25	.08
❑	273	Craig Biggio RC	5.00	2.00
❑	274	Jim Gantner	.25	.08
❑	275	Eddie Murray	1.00	.40
❑	276	Jeff Reed	.25	.08
❑	277	Tim Teufel	.25	.08
❑	278	Rick Honeycutt	.25	.08
❑	279	Guillermo Hernandez	.25	.08
❑	280	John Kruk	.40	.15
❑	281	Luis Alicea RC *	.50	.20
❑	282	Jim Clancy	.25	.08
❑	283	Billy Ripken	.25	.08
❑	284	Craig Reynolds	.25	.08
❑	285	Robin Yount	1.50	.60
❑	286	Jimmy Jones	.25	.08
❑	287	Ron Oester	.25	.08
❑	288	Terry Leach	.25	.08
❑	289	Dennis Eckersley	.60	.25
❑	290	Alan Trammell	.40	.15
❑	291	Jimmy Key	.40	.15
❑	292	Chris Bosio	.25	.08
❑	293	Jose DeLeon	.25	.08
❑	294	Jim Traber	.25	.08
❑	295	Mike Scott	.40	.15
❑	296	Roger McDowell	.25	.08
❑	297	Garry Templeton	.40	.15
❑	298	Doyle Alexander	.25	.08

❑ 299 Nick Esasky .25 .08
❑ 300 Mark McGwire 5.00 2.00
❑ 301 Darryl Hamilton RC * .50 .20
❑ 302 Dave Smith .25 .08
❑ 303 Rick Sutcliffe .40 .15
❑ 304 Dave Stapleton .25 .08
❑ 305 Alan Ashby .25 .08
❑ 306 Pedro Guerrero .40 .15
❑ 307 Ron Guidry .40 .15
❑ 308 Steve Farr .25 .08
❑ 309 Curt Ford .25 .08
❑ 310 Claudell Washington .25 .08
❑ 311 Tom Prince .25 .08
❑ 312 Chad Kreuter RC .50 .20
❑ 313 Ken Oberkfell .25 .08
❑ 314 Jerry Browne .25 .08
❑ 315 R.J. Reynolds .25 .08
❑ 316 Scott Bankhead .25 .08
❑ 317 Milt Thompson .25 .08
❑ 318 Mario Diaz .25 .08
❑ 319 Bruce Ruffin .25 .08
❑ 320 Dave Valle .25 .08
❑ 321A Gary Varsho ERR 2.00 .75
❑ 321B Gary Varsho COR
(In road uniform) .25 .08
❑ 322 Paul Mirabella .25 .08
❑ 323 Chuck Jackson .25 .08
❑ 324 Drew Hall .25 .08
❑ 325 Don August .25 .08
❑ 326 Israel Sanchez .25 .08
❑ 327 Denny Walling .25 .08
❑ 328 Joel Skinner .25 .08
❑ 329 Danny Tartabull .25 .08
❑ 330 Tony Pena .25 .08
❑ 331 Jim Sundberg .40 .15
❑ 332 Jeff D. Robinson .25 .08
❑ 333 Oddibe McDowell .25 .08
❑ 334 Jose Lind .25 .08
❑ 335 Paul Kilgus .25 .08
❑ 336 Juan Samuel .25 .08
❑ 337 Mike Campbell .25 .08
❑ 338 Mike Maddux .25 .08
❑ 339 Darnell Coles .25 .08
❑ 340 Bob Dernier .25 .08
❑ 341 Rafael Ramirez .25 .08
❑ 342 Scott Sanderson .25 .08
❑ 343 B.J. Surhoff .40 .15
❑ 344 Billy Hatcher .25 .08
❑ 345 Pat Perry .25 .08
❑ 346 Jack Clark .40 .15
❑ 347 Gary Thurman .25 .08
❑ 348 Tim Jones .25 .08
❑ 349 Dave Winfield .40 .15
❑ 350 Frank White .40 .15
❑ 351 Dave Collins .25 .08
❑ 352 Jack Morris .40 .15
❑ 353 Eric Plunk .25 .08
❑ 354 Leon Durham .25 .08
❑ 355 Ivan DeJesus .25 .08
❑ 356 Brian Holman RC * .25 .08
❑ 357A Dale Murphy RevNeg 30.00 12.50
❑ 357B Dale Murphy COR .60 .25
❑ 358 Mark Portugal .25 .08
❑ 359 Andy McGaffigan .25 .08
❑ 360 Tom Glavine 1.00 .40
❑ 361 Keith Moreland .25 .08
❑ 362 Todd Stottlemyre .25 .08
❑ 363 Dave Leiper .25 .08
❑ 364 Cecil Fielder .40 .15
❑ 365 Carmelo Martinez .25 .08
❑ 366 Dwight Evans .60 .25
❑ 367 Kevin McReynolds .25 .08
❑ 368 Rich Gedman .25 .08
❑ 369 Len Dykstra .40 .15
❑ 370 Jody Reed .25 .08
❑ 371 Jose Canseco 1.00 .40
❑ 372 Rob Murphy .25 .08
❑ 373 Mike Henneman .25 .08
❑ 374 Walt Weiss .25 .08
❑ 375 Rob Dibble RC 1.00 .40
❑ 376 Kirby Puckett 1.00 .40
❑ 377 Dennis Martinez .40 .15
❑ 378 Ron Gant .40 .15
❑ 379 Brian Harper .25 .08
❑ 380 Nelson Santovenia .25 .08
❑ 381 Lloyd Moseby .25 .08
❑ 382 Lance McCullers .25 .08
❑ 383 Dave Stieb .40 .15
❑ 384 Tony Gwynn 1.25 .50
❑ 385 Mike Flanagan .25 .08
❑ 386 Bob Ojeda .25 .08
❑ 387 Bruce Hurst .25 .08
❑ 388 Dave Magadan .25 .08
❑ 389 Wade Boggs .60 .25
❑ 390 Gary Carter .40 .15
❑ 391 Frank Tanana .40 .15
❑ 392 Curt Young .25 .08
❑ 393 Jeff Treadway .25 .08
❑ 394 Darrell Evans .40 .15
❑ 395 Glenn Hubbard .25 .08
❑ 396 Chuck Cary .25 .08
❑ 397 Frank Viola .40 .15
❑ 398 Jeff Parrett .25 .08
❑ 399 Terry Blocker .25 .08
❑ 400 Dan Gladden .25 .08
❑ 401 Louie Meadows .25 .08
❑ 402 Tim Raines .40 .15
❑ 403 Joey Meyer .25 .08
❑ 404 Larry Andersen .25 .08
❑ 405 Rex Hudler .25 .08
❑ 406 Mike Schmidt 2.00 .75
❑ 407 John Franco .40 .15
❑ 408 Brady Anderson RC 1.00 .40
❑ 409 Don Carman .25 .08
❑ 410 Eric Davis .40 .15
❑ 411 Bob Stanley .25 .08
❑ 412 Pete Smith .25 .08
❑ 413 Jim Rice .40 .15
❑ 414 Bruce Sutter .40 .15
❑ 415 Oil Can Boyd .25 .08
❑ 416 Ruben Sierra .40 .15
❑ 417 Mike LaValliere .25 .08
❑ 418 Steve Buechele .25 .08
❑ 419 Gary Redus .25 .08
❑ 420 Scott Fletcher .25 .08
❑ 421 Dale Sveum .25 .08
❑ 422 Bob Knepper .25 .08
❑ 423 Luis Rivera .25 .08
❑ 424 Ted Higuera .25 .08
❑ 425 Kevin Bass .25 .08
❑ 426 Ken Gerhart .25 .08
❑ 427 Shane Rawley .25 .08
❑ 428 Paul O'Neill .60 .25
❑ 429 Joe Orsulak .25 .08
❑ 430 Jackie Gutierrez .25 .08
❑ 431 Gerald Perry .25 .08
❑ 432 Mike Greenwell .25 .08
❑ 433 Jerry Royster .25 .08
❑ 434 Ellis Burks .40 .15
❑ 435 Ed Olwine .25 .08
❑ 436 Dave Rucker .25 .08
❑ 437 Charlie Hough .40 .15
❑ 438 Bob Walk .25 .08
❑ 439 Bob Brower .25 .08
❑ 440 Barry Bonds 5.00 2.00
❑ 441 Tom Foley .25 .08
❑ 442 Rob Deer .25 .08
❑ 443 Glenn Davis .25 .08
❑ 444 Dave Martinez .25 .08
❑ 445 Bill Wegman .25 .08
❑ 446 Lloyd McClendon .25 .08
❑ 447 Dave Schmidt .25 .08
❑ 448 Darren Daulton .40 .15
❑ 449 Frank Williams .25 .08
❑ 450 Don Aase .25 .08
❑ 451 Lou Whitaker .40 .15
❑ 452 Rich Gossage .40 .15
❑ 453 Ed Whitson .25 .08
❑ 454 Jim Walewander .25 .08
❑ 455 Damon Berryhill .25 .08
❑ 456 Tim Burke .25 .08
❑ 457 Barry Jones .25 .08
❑ 458 Joel Youngblood .25 .08
❑ 459 Floyd Youmans .25 .08
❑ 460 Mark Salas .25 .08
❑ 461 Jeff Russell .25 .08
❑ 462 Darrell Miller .25 .08
❑ 463 Jeff Kunkel .25 .08
❑ 464 Sherman Corbett .25 .08
❑ 465 Curtis Wilkerson .25 .08
❑ 466 Bud Black .25 .08
❑ 467 Cal Ripken 3.00 1.25
❑ 468 John Farrell .25 .08
❑ 469 Terry Kennedy .25 .08
❑ 470 Tom Candiotti .25 .08
❑ 471 Roberto Alomar 1.00 .40
❑ 472 Jeff M. Robinson .25 .08
❑ 473 Vance Law .25 .08
❑ 474 Randy Ready UER
(Strikeout total 136&
should be) .25 .08
❑ 475 Walt Terrell .25 .08
❑ 476 Kelly Downs .25 .08
❑ 477 Johnny Paredes .25 .08
❑ 478 Shawn Hillegas .25 .08
❑ 479 Bob Brenly .25 .08
❑ 480 Otis Nixon .25 .08
❑ 481 Johnny Ray .25 .08
❑ 482 Geno Petralli .25 .08
❑ 483 Stu Cliburn .25 .08
❑ 484 Pete Incaviglia .25 .08
❑ 485 Brian Downing .40 .15
❑ 486 Jeff Stone .25 .08
❑ 487 Carmen Castillo .25 .08
❑ 488 Tom Niedenfuer .25 .08
❑ 489 Jay Bell .40 .15
❑ 490 Rick Schu .25 .08
❑ 491 Jeff Pico .25 .08
❑ 492 Mark Parent .25 .08
❑ 493 Eric King .25 .08
❑ 494 Al Nipper .25 .08
❑ 495 Andy Hawkins .25 .08
❑ 496 Daryl Boston .25 .08
❑ 497 Ernie Riles .25 .08
❑ 498 Pascual Perez .25 .08
❑ 499 Bill Long UER
(Games started total
70& should be) .25 .08
❑ 500 Kirt Manwaring .25 .08
❑ 501 Chuck Crim .25 .08
❑ 502 Candy Maldonado .25 .08
❑ 503 Dennis Lamp .25 .08
❑ 504 Glenn Braggs .25 .08
❑ 505 Joe Price .25 .08
❑ 506 Ken Williams .25 .08
❑ 507 Bill Pecota .25 .08
❑ 508 Rey Quinones .25 .08
❑ 509 Jeff Bittiger .25 .08
❑ 510 Kevin Seitzer .25 .08
❑ 511 Steve Bedrosian .25 .08
❑ 512 Todd Worrell .25 .08
❑ 513 Chris James .25 .08
❑ 514 Jose Oquendo .25 .08
❑ 515 David Palmer .25 .08
❑ 516 John Smiley .25 .08
❑ 517 Dave Clark .25 .08
❑ 518 Mike Dunne .25 .08
❑ 519 Ron Washington .25 .08
❑ 520 Bob Kipper .25 .08
❑ 521 Lee Smith .40 .15
❑ 522 Juan Castillo .25 .08
❑ 523 Don Robinson .25 .08
❑ 524 Kevin Romine .25 .08
❑ 525 Paul Molitor .40 .15
❑ 526 Mark Langston .25 .08
❑ 527 Donnie Hill .25 .08
❑ 528 Larry Owen .25 .08
❑ 529 Jerry Reed .25 .08
❑ 530 Jack McDowell .40 .15
❑ 531 Greg Mathews .25 .08
❑ 532 John Russell .25 .08
❑ 533 Dan Quisenberry .25 .08
❑ 534 Greg Gross .25 .08
❑ 535 Danny Cox .25 .08
❑ 536 Terry Francona .40 .15
❑ 537 Andy Van Slyke .60 .25
❑ 538 Mel Hall .25 .08
❑ 539 Jim Gott .25 .08
❑ 540 Doug Jones .25 .08
❑ 541 Craig Lefferts .25 .08
❑ 542 Mike Boddicker .25 .08
❑ 543 Greg Brock .25 .08
❑ 544 Atlee Hammaker .25 .08
❑ 545 Tom Bolton .25 .08
❑ 546 Mike Macfarlane RC * .50 .20
❑ 547 Rich Renteria .25 .08
❑ 548 John Davis .25 .08
❑ 549 Floyd Bannister .25 .08

❑ 550 Mickey Brantley .25 .08
❑ 551 Duane Ward .25 .08
❑ 552 Dan Petry .25 .08
❑ 553 Mickey Tettleton .25 .08
❑ 554 Rick Leach .25 .08
❑ 555 Mike Witt .25 .08
❑ 556 Sid Bream .25 .08
❑ 557 Bobby Witt .25 .08
❑ 558 Tommy Herr .25 .08
❑ 559 Randy Milligan .25 .08
❑ 560 Jose Cecena .25 .08
❑ 561 Mackey Sasser .25 .08
❑ 562 Carney Lansford .40 .15
❑ 563 Rick Aguilera .25 .08
❑ 564 Ron Hassey .25 .08
❑ 565 Dwight Gooden .40 .15
❑ 566 Paul Assenmacher .25 .08
❑ 567 Neil Allen .25 .08
❑ 568 Jim Morrison .25 .08
❑ 569 Mike Pagliarulo .25 .08
❑ 570 Ted Simmons .40 .15
❑ 571 Mark Thurmond .25 .08
❑ 572 Fred McGriff .60 .25
❑ 573 Wally Joyner .40 .15
❑ 574 Jose Bautista RC .25 .08
❑ 575 Kelly Gruber .25 .08
❑ 576 Cecilio Guante .25 .08
❑ 577 Mark Davidson .25 .08
❑ 578 Bobby Bonilla UER .40 .15
❑ 579 Mike Stanley .25 .08
❑ 580 Gene Larkin .25 .08
❑ 581 Stan Javier .25 .08
❑ 582 Howard Johnson .40 .15
❑ 583A Mike Gallego Rev Ng 1.00 .40
❑ 583B Mike Gallego COR 1.00 .40
❑ 584 David Cone .40 .15
❑ 585 Doug Jennings .25 .08
❑ 586 Charles Hudson .25 .08
❑ 587 Dion James .25 .08
❑ 588 Al Leiter 1.00 .40
❑ 589 Charlie Puleo .25 .08
❑ 590 Roberto Kelly .25 .08
❑ 591 Thad Bosley .25 .08
❑ 592 Pete Stanicek .25 .08
❑ 593 Pat Borders RC * .50 .20
❑ 594 Bryan Harvey RC * .50 .20
❑ 595 Jeff Ballard .25 .08
❑ 596 Jeff Reardon .40 .15
❑ 597 Doug Drabek .25 .08
❑ 598 Edwin Correa .25 .08
❑ 599 Keith Atherton .25 .08
❑ 600 Dave LaPoint .25 .08
❑ 601 Don Baylor .40 .15
❑ 602 Tom Pagnozzi .25 .08
❑ 603 Tim Flannery .25 .08
❑ 604 Gene Walter .25 .08
❑ 605 Dave Parker .40 .15
❑ 606 Mike Diaz .25 .08
❑ 607 Chris Gwynn .25 .08
❑ 608 Odell Jones .25 .08
❑ 609 Carlton Fisk .60 .25
❑ 610 Jay Howell .25 .08
❑ 611 Tim Crews .25 .08
❑ 612 Keith Hernandez .40 .15
❑ 613 Willie Fraser .25 .08
❑ 614 Jim Eppard .25 .08
❑ 615 Jeff Hamilton .25 .08
❑ 616 Kurt Stillwell .25 .08
❑ 617 Tom Browning .25 .08
❑ 618 Jeff Montgomery .25 .08
❑ 619 Jose Rijo .40 .15
❑ 620 Jamie Quirk .25 .08
❑ 621 Willie McGee .40 .15
❑ 622 Mark Grant UER (Glove on wrong hand) .25 .08
❑ 623 Bill Swift .25 .08
❑ 624 Orlando Mercado .25 .08
❑ 625 John Costello .25 .08
❑ 626 Jose Gonzalez .25 .08
❑ 627A Bill Schroeder ERR .60 .25
❑ 627B Bill Schroeder COR .60 .25
❑ 628A Fred Manrique ERR Guillen .60 .25
❑ 628B Fred Manrique COR (Swinging bat on back) .25 .08
❑ 629 Ricky Horton .25 .08
❑ 630 Dan Plesac .25 .08
❑ 631 Alfredo Griffin .25 .08
❑ 632 Chuck Finley .40 .15
❑ 633 Kirk Gibson .40 .15
❑ 634 Randy Myers .40 .15
❑ 635 Greg Minton .25 .08
❑ 636A Herm Winningham ERR (W1nningham on back) 1.00 .40
❑ 636B Herm Winningham COR .25 .08
❑ 637 Charlie Leibrandt .25 .08
❑ 638 Tim Birtsas .25 .08
❑ 639 Bill Buckner .40 .15
❑ 640 Danny Jackson .25 .08
❑ 641 Greg Booker .25 .08
❑ 642 Jim Presley .25 .08
❑ 643 Gene Nelson .25 .08
❑ 644 Rod Booker .25 .08
❑ 645 Dennis Rasmussen .25 .08
❑ 646 Juan Nieves .25 .08
❑ 647 Bobby Thigpen .25 .08
❑ 648 Tim Belcher .25 .08
❑ 649 Mike Young .25 .08
❑ 650 Ivan Calderon .25 .08
❑ 651 Oswald Peraza .25 .08
❑ 652A Pat Sheridan ERR NPO 15.00 6.00
❑ 652B Pat Sheridan COR .25 .08
❑ 653 Mike Morgan .25 .08
❑ 654 Mike Heath .25 .08
❑ 655 Jay Tibbs .25 .08
❑ 656 Fernando Valenzuela .40 .15
❑ 657 Lee Mazzilli .40 .15
❑ 658 Frank Viola AL CY .25 .08
❑ 659A Jose Canseco MVP .60 .25
❑ 659B Jose Canseco MVP .60 .25
❑ 660 Walt Weiss AL ROY .25 .08
❑ 661 Orel Hershiser NL CY .25 .08
❑ 662 Kirk Gibson NL MVP .40 .15
❑ 663 Chris Sabo NL ROY .40 .15
❑ 664 D.Eckersley ALCS MVP .40 .15
❑ 665 O.Hershiser NLCS MVP .40 .15
❑ 666 Kirk Gibson WS 1.00 .40
❑ 667 Orel Hershiser WS MVP .25 .08
❑ 668 Wally Joyner TC California Angels .25 .08
❑ 669 Nolan Ryan TC 1.25 .50
❑ 670 Jose Canseco TC .60 .25
❑ 671 Fred McGriff TC .40 .15
❑ 672 Dale Murphy TC Atlanta Braves .40 .15
❑ 673 Paul Molitor TC .25 .08
❑ 674 Ozzie Smith TC 1.00 .40
❑ 675 Ryne Sandberg TC 1.00 .40
❑ 676 Kirk Gibson TC .40 .15
❑ 677 Andres Galarraga TC .25 .08
❑ 678 Will Clark TC .40 .15
❑ 679 Cory Snyder TC Cleveland Indians .25 .08
❑ 680 Alvin Davis TC Seattle Mariners .25 .08
❑ 681 Darryl Strawberry TC New York Mets .25 .08
❑ 682 Cal Ripken TC 1.00 .40
❑ 683 Tony Gwynn TC .60 .25
❑ 684 Mike Schmidt TC 1.00 .40
❑ 685 Andy Van Slyke TC Pittsburgh Pirates UER (96 Jun) .40 .15
❑ 686 Ruben Sierra TC .25 .08
❑ 687 Wade Boggs TC .40 .15
❑ 688 Eric Davis TC Cincinnati Reds .25 .08
❑ 689 George Brett TC 1.00 .40
❑ 690 Alan Trammell TC Detroit Tigers .25 .08
❑ 691 Frank Viola TC Minnesota Twins .25 .08
❑ 692 Harold Baines TC Chicago White Sox .25 .08
❑ 693 Don Mattingly TC 1.00 .40
❑ 694 Checklist 1-100 .25 .08
❑ 695 Checklist 101-200 .25 .08
❑ 696 Checklist 201-300 .25 .08
❑ 697 Checklist 301-400 .25 .08
❑ 698 Checklist UER .25 .08
❑ 699 Checklist 501-600 UER (543 Greg Booker) .25 .08
❑ 700 Checklist 601-700 .25 .08
❑ 701 Checklist 701-800 .25 .08
❑ 702 Jesse Barfield .40 .15
❑ 703 Walt Terrell .25 .08
❑ 704 Dickie Thon .25 .08
❑ 705 Al Leiter 1.00 .40
❑ 706 Dave LaPoint .25 .08
❑ 707 Charlie Hayes RC .50 .20
❑ 708 Andy Hawkins .25 .08
❑ 709 Mickey Hatcher .25 .08
❑ 710 Lance McCullers .25 .08
❑ 711 Ron Kittle .25 .08
❑ 712 Bert Blyleven .40 .15
❑ 713 Rick Dempsey .25 .08
❑ 714 Ken Williams .25 .08
❑ 715 Steve Rosenberg .25 .08
❑ 716 Joe Skalski .25 .08
❑ 717 Spike Owen .25 .08
❑ 718 Todd Burns .25 .08
❑ 719 Kevin Gross .25 .08
❑ 720 Tommy Herr .25 .08
❑ 721 Rob Ducey .25 .08
❑ 722 Gary Green .25 .08
❑ 723 Gregg Olson RC .50 .20
❑ 724 Greg W.Harris RC .25 .08
❑ 725 Craig Worthington .25 .08
❑ 726 Thomas Howard RC .25 .08
❑ 727 Dale Mohorcic .25 .08
❑ 728 Rich Yett .25 .08
❑ 729 Mel Hall .25 .08
❑ 730 Floyd Youmans .25 .08
❑ 731 Lonnie Smith .25 .08
❑ 732 Wally Backman .25 .08
❑ 733 Trevor Wilson RC .25 .08
❑ 734 Jose Alvarez RC .25 .08
❑ 735 Bob Milacki .25 .08
❑ 736 Tom Gordon RC 1.50 .60
❑ 737 Wally Whitehurst RC .25 .08
❑ 738 Mike Aldrete .25 .08
❑ 739 Keith Miller .25 .08
❑ 740 Randy Milligan .25 .08
❑ 741 Jeff Parrett .25 .08
❑ 742 Steve Finley RC 2.00 .75
❑ 743 Junior Felix RC .25 .08
❑ 744 Pete Harnisch RC .50 .20
❑ 745 Billy Spiers RC .50 .20
❑ 746 Hensley Meulens RC .25 .08
❑ 747 Juan Bell RC .25 .08
❑ 748 Steve Sax .25 .08
❑ 749 Phil Bradley .25 .08
❑ 750 Rey Quinones .25 .08
❑ 751 Tommy Gregg .25 .08
❑ 752 Kevin Brown 1.00 .40
❑ 753 Derek Lilliquist RC .25 .08
❑ 754 Todd Zeile RC 1.00 .40
❑ 755 Jim Abbott RC 2.00 .75
❑ 756 Ozzie Canseco .25 .08
❑ 757 Nick Esasky .25 .08
❑ 758 Mike Moore .25 .08
❑ 759 Rob Murphy .25 .08
❑ 760 Rick Mahler .25 .08
❑ 761 Fred Lynn .40 .15
❑ 762 Kevin Blankenship .25 .08
❑ 763 Eddie Murray 1.00 .40
❑ 764 Steve Searcy .25 .08
❑ 765 Jerome Walton RC .50 .20
❑ 766 Erik Hanson RC .50 .20
❑ 767 Bob Boone .40 .15
❑ 768 Edgar Martinez 1.00 .40
❑ 769 Jose DeJesus .25 .08
❑ 770 Greg Briley .25 .08
❑ 771 Steve Peters .25 .08
❑ 772 Rafael Palmeiro 1.00 .40
❑ 773 Jack Clark .40 .15
❑ 774 Nolan Ryan w/FB 4.00 1.50
❑ 775 Lance Parrish .40 .15
❑ 776 Joe Girardi RC 1.00 .40
❑ 777 Willie Randolph .40 .15
❑ 778 Mitch Williams .25 .08
❑ 779 Dennis Cook RC .50 .20
❑ 780 Dwight Smith RC .50 .20
❑ 781 Lenny Harris RC .50 .20
❑ 782 Torey Lovullo RC .25 .08
❑ 783 Norm Charlton RC .50 .20
❑ 784 Chris Brown .25 .08
❑ 785 Todd Benzinger .25 .08

❑ 786 Shane Rawley .25 .08
❑ 787 Omar Vizquel RC 3.00 1.25
❑ 788 LaVel Freeman .25 .08
❑ 789 Jeffrey Leonard .25 .08
❑ 790 Eddie Williams .25 .08
❑ 791 Jamie Moyer .40 .15
❑ 792 Bruce Hurst UER
(Workd Series) .25 .08
❑ 793 Julio Franco .40 .15
❑ 794 Claudell Washington .25 .08
❑ 795 Jody Davis .25 .08
❑ 796 Oddibe McDowell .25 .08
❑ 797 Paul Kilgus .25 .08
❑ 798 Tracy Jones .25 .08
❑ 799 Steve Wilson .25 .08
❑ 800 Pete O'Brien .25 .08

1990 Upper Deck

❑ COMPLETE SET (800) 25.00 10.00
❑ COMP.FACT.SET (800) 25.00 10.00
❑ COMPLETE LO SET (700) 25.00 15.00
❑ COMPLETE HI SET (100) 5.00 2.00
❑ COMP.HI FACT.SET (100) 4.00 2.00
❑ 1 Star Rookie Checklist .10 .02
❑ 2 Randy Nosek RC .10 .02
❑ 3 Tom Drees RC .10 .02
❑ 4 Curt Young .10 .02
❑ 5 Devon White TC .10 .02
❑ 6 Luis Salazar .10 .02
❑ 7 Von Hayes TC .10 .02
❑ 8 Jose Bautista .10 .02
❑ 9 Marquis Grissom RC .50 .20
❑ 10 Orel Hershiser TC .10 .02
❑ 11 Rick Aguilera .20 .07
❑ 12 Benito Santiago TC .10 .02
❑ 13 Deion Sanders .50 .20
❑ 14 Marvell Wynne .10 .02
❑ 15 Dave West .10 .02
❑ 16 Bobby Bonilla TC .10 .02
❑ 17 Sammy Sosa RC 3.00 1.25
❑ 18 Steve Sax TC .10 .02
❑ 19 Jack Howell .10 .02
❑ 20 Mike Schmidt SPEC 1.00 .40
❑ 21 Robin Ventura .50 .20
❑ 22 Brian Meyer .10 .02
❑ 23 Blaine Beatty RC .10 .02
❑ 24 Ken Griffey Jr. TC .60 .25
❑ 25 Greg Vaughn .10 .02
❑ 26 Xavier Hernandez RC .10 .02
❑ 27 Jason Grimsley RC .10 .02
❑ 28 Eric Anthony RC .10 .02
❑ 29 Tim Raines TC UER .10 .02
❑ 30 David Wells .20 .07
❑ 31 Hal Morris .10 .02
❑ 32 Bo Jackson TC .20 .07
❑ 33 Kelly Mann RC .10 .02
❑ 34 Nolan Ryan SPEC 1.00 .40
❑ 35 Scott Service UER
(Born Cincinatti on
7/27/67& s) .10 .02
❑ 36 Mark McGwire TC .75 .30
❑ 37 Tino Martinez 1.00 .40
❑ 38 Chili Davis .20 .07
❑ 39 Scott Sanderson .10 .02
❑ 40 Kevin Mitchell TC .10 .02
❑ 41 Lou Whitaker TC .10 .02
❑ 42 Scott Coolbaugh RC .10 .02
❑ 43 Jose Cano RC .10 .02
❑ 44 Jose Vizcaino RC .25 .08
❑ 45 Bob Hamelin RC .25 .08
❑ 46 Jose Offerman RC .25 .08
❑ 47 Kevin Blankenship .10 .02
❑ 48 Kirby Puckett TC .30 .10
❑ 49 Tommy Greene UER RC .10 .02
❑ 50 Will Clark SPEC .20 .07
❑ 51 Rob Nelson .10 .02
❑ 52 Chris Hammond UER RC .10 .02
❑ 53 Joe Carter TC .10 .02
❑ 54A Ben McDonald ERR 2.00 .75
❑ 54B Ben McDonald COR RC .25 .08
❑ 55 Andy Benes UER .20 .07
❑ 56 John Olerud RC .75 .30
❑ 57 Roger Clemens TC .75 .30
❑ 58 Tony Armas .10 .02
❑ 59 George Canale RC .10 .02
❑ 60A Mickey Tettleton TC ERR 2.00 .75
❑ 60B Mickey Tettleton TC COR .10 .02
❑ 61 Mike Stanton RC .25 .08
❑ 62 Dwight Gooden TC .10 .02
❑ 63 Kent Mercker RC .25 .08
❑ 64 Francisco Cabrera .10 .02
❑ 65 Steve Avery .10 .02
❑ 66 Jose Canseco .30 .10
❑ 67 Matt Merullo .10 .02
❑ 68 Vince Coleman TC UER .10 .02
❑ 69 Ron Karkovice .10 .02
❑ 70 Kevin Maas RC .25 .08
❑ 71 Dennis Cook UER
(Shown with righty
glove on card) .10 .02
❑ 72 Juan Gonzalez RC 1.50 .60
❑ 73 Andre Dawson TC .10 .02
❑ 74 Dean Palmer RC .25 .08
❑ 75 Bo Jackson SPEC .20 .07
❑ 76 Rob Richie RC .10 .02
❑ 77 Bobby Rose UER
(Pickin& should
be pick in) .10 .02
❑ 78 Brian DuBois UER RC .10 .02
❑ 79 Ozzie Guillen TC .10 .02
❑ 80 Gene Nelson .10 .02
❑ 81 Bob McClure .10 .02
❑ 82 Julio Franco TC .10 .02
❑ 83 Greg Minton .10 .02
❑ 84 John Smoltz TC UER .30 .10
❑ 85 Willie Fraser .10 .02
❑ 86 Neal Heaton .10 .02
❑ 87 Kevin Tapani RC .25 .08
❑ 88 Mike Scott TC .10 .02
❑ 89A Jim Gott ERR 2.00 .75
❑ 89B Jim Gott COR .10 .02
❑ 90 Lance Johnson .10 .02
❑ 91 Robin Yount TC UER .50 .20
❑ 92 Jeff Parrett .10 .02
❑ 93 Julio Machado RC .10 .02
❑ 94 Ron Jones .10 .02
❑ 95 George Bell TC .10 .02
❑ 96 Jerry Reuss .10 .02
❑ 97 Brian Fisher .10 .02
❑ 98 Kevin Ritz RC .10 .02
❑ 99 Barry Larkin TC .20 .07
❑ 100 Checklist 1-100 .10 .02
❑ 101 Gerald Perry .10 .02
❑ 102 Kevin Appier .20 .07
❑ 103 Julio Franco .20 .07
❑ 104 Craig Biggio .50 .20
❑ 105 Bo Jackson UER .50 .20
❑ 106 Junior Felix .10 .02
❑ 107 Mike Harkey .10 .02
❑ 108 Fred McGriff .50 .20
❑ 109 Rick Sutcliffe .20 .07
❑ 110 Pete O'Brien .10 .02
❑ 111 Kelly Gruber .10 .02
❑ 112 Dwight Evans .30 .10
❑ 113 Pat Borders .10 .02
❑ 114 Dwight Gooden .20 .07
❑ 115 Kevin Batiste RC .10 .02
❑ 116 Eric Davis .20 .07
❑ 117 Kevin Mitchell UER
(Career HR total 99&
should b) .10 .02
❑ 118 Ron Oester .10 .02
❑ 119 Brett Butler .20 .07
❑ 120 Danny Jackson .10 .02
❑ 121 Tommy Gregg .10 .02
❑ 122 Ken Caminiti .20 .07
❑ 123 Kevin Brown .20 .07
❑ 124 George Brett 1.25 .50
❑ 125 Mike Scott .10 .02
❑ 126 Cory Snyder .10 .02
❑ 127 George Bell .10 .02
❑ 128 Mark Grace .30 .10
❑ 129 Devon White .20 .07
❑ 130 Tony Fernandez .10 .02
❑ 131 Don Aase .10 .02
❑ 132 Rance Mulliniks .10 .02
❑ 133 Marty Barrett .10 .02
❑ 134 Nelson Liriano .10 .02
❑ 135 Mark Carreon .10 .02
❑ 136 Candy Maldonado .10 .02
❑ 137 Tim Birtsas .10 .02
❑ 138 Tom Brookens .10 .02
❑ 139 John Franco .20 .07
❑ 140 Mike LaCoss .10 .02
❑ 141 Jeff Treadway .10 .02
❑ 142 Pat Tabler .10 .02
❑ 143 Darrell Evans .20 .07
❑ 144 Rafael Ramirez .10 .02
❑ 145 Oddibe McDowell UER
(Misspelled Odibbe) .10 .02
❑ 146 Brian Downing .10 .02
❑ 147 Curt Wilkerson .10 .02
❑ 148 Ernie Whitt .10 .02
❑ 149 Bill Schroeder .10 .02
❑ 150 Domingo Ramos UER
(Says throws right&
but shows) .10 .02
❑ 151 Rick Honeycutt .10 .02
❑ 152 Don Slaught .10 .02
❑ 153 Mitch Webster .10 .02
❑ 154 Tony Phillips .10 .02
❑ 155 Paul Kilgus .10 .02
❑ 156 Ken Griffey Jr. 1.50 .60
❑ 157 Gary Sheffield .50 .20
❑ 158 Wally Backman .10 .02
❑ 159 B.J. Surhoff .20 .07
❑ 160 Louie Meadows .10 .02
❑ 161 Paul O'Neill .30 .10
❑ 162 Jeff McKnight RC .10 .02
❑ 163 Alvaro Espinoza .10 .02
❑ 164 Scott Scudder .10 .02
❑ 165 Jeff Reed .10 .02
❑ 166 Gregg Jefferies .20 .07
❑ 167 Barry Larkin .30 .10
❑ 168 Gary Carter .20 .07
❑ 169 Robby Thompson .10 .02
❑ 170 Rolando Roomes .10 .02
❑ 171 Mark McGwire 1.50 .60
❑ 172 Steve Sax .10 .02
❑ 173 Mark Williamson .10 .02
❑ 174 Mitch Williams .10 .02
❑ 175 Brian Holton .10 .02
❑ 176 Rob Deer .10 .02
❑ 177 Tim Raines .20 .07
❑ 178 Mike Felder .10 .02
❑ 179 Harold Reynolds .20 .07
❑ 180 Terry Francona .20 .07
❑ 181 Chris Sabo .10 .02
❑ 182 Darryl Strawberry .20 .07
❑ 183 Willie Randolph .20 .07
❑ 184 Bill Ripken .10 .02
❑ 185 Mackey Sasser .10 .02
❑ 186 Todd Benzinger .10 .02
❑ 187 Kevin Elster UER
(16 homers in 1989&
should be 1) .10 .02
❑ 188 Jose Uribe .10 .02
❑ 189 Tom Browning .10 .02
❑ 190 Keith Miller .10 .02
❑ 191 Don Mattingly 1.25 .50
❑ 192 Dave Parker .20 .07
❑ 193 Roberto Kelly UER .10 .02
❑ 194 Phil Bradley .10 .02
❑ 195 Ron Hassey .10 .02
❑ 196 Gerald Young .10 .02
❑ 197 Hubie Brooks .10 .02
❑ 198 Bill Doran .10 .02
❑ 199 Al Newman .10 .02
❑ 200 Checklist 101-200 .10 .02
❑ 201 Terry Puhl .10 .02

- ❑ 202 Frank DiPino .10 .02
- ❑ 203 Jim Clancy .10 .02
- ❑ 204 Bob Ojeda .10 .02
- ❑ 205 Alex Trevino .10 .02
- ❑ 206 Dave Henderson .10 .02
- ❑ 207 Henry Cotto .10 .02
- ❑ 208 Rafael Belliard UER (Born 1961& not 1951) .10 .02
- ❑ 209 Stan Javier .10 .02
- ❑ 210 Jerry Reed .10 .02
- ❑ 211 Doug Dascenzo .10 .02
- ❑ 212 Andres Thomas .10 .02
- ❑ 213 Greg Maddux .75 .30
- ❑ 214 Mike Schooler .10 .02
- ❑ 215 Lonnie Smith .10 .02
- ❑ 216 Jose Rijo .10 .02
- ❑ 217 Greg Gagne .10 .02
- ❑ 218 Jim Gantner .10 .02
- ❑ 219 Allan Anderson .10 .02
- ❑ 220 Rick Mahler .10 .02
- ❑ 221 Jim Deshaies .10 .02
- ❑ 222 Keith Hernandez .20 .07
- ❑ 223 Vince Coleman .10 .02
- ❑ 224 David Cone .20 .07
- ❑ 225 Ozzie Smith .75 .30
- ❑ 226 Matt Nokes .10 .02
- ❑ 227 Barry Bonds 1.50 .60
- ❑ 228 Felix Jose .10 .02
- ❑ 229 Dennis Powell .10 .02
- ❑ 230 Mike Gallego .10 .02
- ❑ 231 Shawon Dunston UER ('89 stats are Andre Dawson's) .10 .02
- ❑ 232 Ron Gant .20 .07
- ❑ 233 Omar Vizquel .50 .20
- ❑ 234 Derek Lilliquist .10 .02
- ❑ 235 Erik Hanson .10 .02
- ❑ 236 Kirby Puckett .50 .20
- ❑ 237 Bill Spiers .10 .02
- ❑ 238 Dan Gladden .10 .02
- ❑ 239 Bryan Clutterbuck .10 .02
- ❑ 240 John Moses .10 .02
- ❑ 241 Ron Darling .10 .02
- ❑ 242 Joe Magrane .10 .02
- ❑ 243 Dave Magadan .10 .02
- ❑ 244 Pedro Guerrero UER (Misspelled Guererro) .10 .02
- ❑ 245 Glenn Davis .10 .02
- ❑ 246 Terry Steinbach .10 .02
- ❑ 247 Fred Lynn .10 .02
- ❑ 248 Gary Redus .10 .02
- ❑ 249 Ken Williams .10 .02
- ❑ 250 Sid Bream .10 .02
- ❑ 251 Bob Welch UER (2587 career strike-outs& should) .10 .02
- ❑ 252 Bill Buckner .10 .02
- ❑ 253 Carney Lansford .20 .07
- ❑ 254 Paul Molitor .20 .07
- ❑ 255 Jose DeJesus .10 .02
- ❑ 256 Orel Hershiser .20 .07
- ❑ 257 Tom Brunansky .10 .02
- ❑ 258 Mike Davis .10 .02
- ❑ 259 Jeff Ballard .10 .02
- ❑ 260 Scott Terry .10 .02
- ❑ 261 Sid Fernandez .10 .02
- ❑ 262 Mike Marshall .10 .02
- ❑ 263 Howard Johnson UER (192 SO& should be 592) .10 .02
- ❑ 264 Kirk Gibson UER .20 .07
- ❑ 265 Kevin McReynolds .10 .02
- ❑ 266 Cal Ripken 1.50 .60
- ❑ 267 Ozzie Guillen UER .20 .07
- ❑ 268 Jim Traber .10 .02
- ❑ 269 Bobby Thigpen UER (31 saves in 1989& should be 3) .10 .02
- ❑ 270 Joe Orsulak .10 .02
- ❑ 271 Bob Boone .20 .07
- ❑ 272 Dave Stewart UER .20 .07
- ❑ 273 Tim Wallach .10 .02
- ❑ 274 Luis Aquino UER (Says throws lefty& but shows hi) .10 .02
- ❑ 275 Mike Moore .10 .02
- ❑ 276 Tony Pena .10 .02
- ❑ 277 Eddie Murray .50 .20
- ❑ 278 Milt Thompson .10 .02
- ❑ 279 Alejandro Pena .10 .02
- ❑ 280 Ken Dayley .10 .02
- ❑ 281 Carmelo Castillo .10 .02
- ❑ 282 Tom Henke .10 .02
- ❑ 283 Mickey Hatcher .10 .02
- ❑ 284 Roy Smith .10 .02
- ❑ 285 Manny Lee .10 .02
- ❑ 286 Dan Pasqua .10 .02
- ❑ 287 Larry Sheets .10 .02
- ❑ 288 Garry Templeton .10 .02
- ❑ 289 Eddie Williams .10 .02
- ❑ 290 Brady Anderson .20 .07
- ❑ 291 Spike Owen .10 .02
- ❑ 292 Storm Davis .10 .02
- ❑ 293 Chris Bosio .10 .02
- ❑ 294 Jim Eisenreich .10 .02
- ❑ 295 Don August .10 .02
- ❑ 296 Jeff Hamilton .10 .02
- ❑ 297 Mickey Tettleton .10 .02
- ❑ 298 Mike Scioscia .10 .02
- ❑ 299 Kevin Hickey .10 .02
- ❑ 300 Checklist 201-300 .10 .02
- ❑ 301 Shawn Abner .10 .02
- ❑ 302 Kevin Bass .10 .02
- ❑ 303 Bip Roberts .10 .02
- ❑ 304 Joe Girardi .30 .10
- ❑ 305 Danny Darwin .10 .02
- ❑ 306 Mike Heath .10 .02
- ❑ 307 Mike Macfarlane .10 .02
- ❑ 308 Ed Whitson .10 .02
- ❑ 309 Tracy Jones .10 .02
- ❑ 310 Scott Fletcher .10 .02
- ❑ 311 Darnell Coles .10 .02
- ❑ 312 Mike Brumley .10 .02
- ❑ 313 Bill Swift .10 .02
- ❑ 314 Charlie Hough .20 .07
- ❑ 315 Jim Presley .10 .02
- ❑ 316 Luis Polonia .10 .02
- ❑ 317 Mike Morgan .10 .02
- ❑ 318 Lee Guetterman .10 .02
- ❑ 319 Jose Oquendo .10 .02
- ❑ 320 Wayne Tolleson .10 .02
- ❑ 321 Jody Reed .10 .02
- ❑ 322 Damon Berryhill .10 .02
- ❑ 323 Roger Clemens 1.50 .60
- ❑ 324 Ryne Sandberg .75 .30
- ❑ 325 Benito Santiago UER .20 .07
- ❑ 326 Bret Saberhagen UER (1140 hits& should be 1240;) .20 .07
- ❑ 327 Lou Whitaker .20 .07
- ❑ 328 Dave Gallagher .10 .02
- ❑ 329 Mike Pagliarulo .10 .02
- ❑ 330 Doyle Alexander .10 .02
- ❑ 331 Jeffrey Leonard .10 .02
- ❑ 332 Torey Lovullo .10 .02
- ❑ 333 Pete Incaviglia .10 .02
- ❑ 334 Rickey Henderson .50 .20
- ❑ 335 Rafael Palmeiro .30 .10
- ❑ 336 Ken Hill .20 .07
- ❑ 337 Dave Winfield UER .20 .07
- ❑ 338 Alfredo Griffin .10 .02
- ❑ 339 Andy Hawkins .10 .02
- ❑ 340 Ted Power .10 .02
- ❑ 341 Steve Wilson .10 .02
- ❑ 342 Jack Clark UER (916 BB& should be 1006; 1142 SO&) .20 .07
- ❑ 343 Ellis Burks .30 .10
- ❑ 344 Tony Gwynn .60 .25
- ❑ 345 Jerome Walton UER (Total At Bats 476& should be) .10 .02
- ❑ 346 Roberto Alomar .30 .10
- ❑ 347 Carlos Martinez UER (Born 8/11/64& should be 8/1) .10 .02
- ❑ 348 Chet Lemon .10 .02
- ❑ 349 Willie Wilson .10 .02
- ❑ 350 Greg Walker .10 .02
- ❑ 351 Tom Bolton .10 .02
- ❑ 352 German Gonzalez .10 .02
- ❑ 353 Harold Baines .20 .07
- ❑ 354 Mike Greenwell .10 .02
- ❑ 355 Ruben Sierra .20 .07
- ❑ 356 Andres Galarraga .20 .07
- ❑ 357 Andre Dawson .20 .07
- ❑ 358 Jeff Brantley .10 .02
- ❑ 359 Mike Bielecki .10 .02
- ❑ 360 Ken Oberkfell .10 .02
- ❑ 361 Kurt Stillwell .10 .02
- ❑ 362 Brian Holman .10 .02
- ❑ 363 Kevin Seitzer UER (Career triples total does not) .10 .02
- ❑ 364 Alvin Davis .10 .02
- ❑ 365 Tom Gordon .20 .07
- ❑ 366 Bobby Bonilla UER (Two steals in 1987& should be) .20 .07
- ❑ 367 Carlton Fisk .30 .10
- ❑ 368 Steve Carter UER (Charlotesville) .10 .02
- ❑ 369 Joel Skinner .10 .02
- ❑ 370 John Cangelosi .10 .02
- ❑ 371 Cecil Espy .10 .02
- ❑ 372 Gary Wayne .10 .02
- ❑ 373 Jim Rice .20 .07
- ❑ 374 Mike Dyer RC .10 .02
- ❑ 375 Joe Carter .20 .07
- ❑ 376 Dwight Smith .10 .02
- ❑ 377 John Wetteland .50 .20
- ❑ 378 Earnie Riles .10 .02
- ❑ 379 Otis Nixon .10 .02
- ❑ 380 Vance Law .10 .02
- ❑ 381 Dave Bergman .10 .02
- ❑ 382 Frank White .20 .07
- ❑ 383 Scott Bradley .10 .02
- ❑ 384 Israel Sanchez UER (Totals don't include '89 s) .10 .02
- ❑ 385 Gary Pettis .10 .02
- ❑ 386 Donn Pall .10 .02
- ❑ 387 John Smiley .10 .02
- ❑ 388 Tom Candiotti .10 .02
- ❑ 389 Junior Ortiz .10 .02
- ❑ 390 Steve Lyons .10 .02
- ❑ 391 Brian Harper .10 .02
- ❑ 392 Fred Manrique .10 .02
- ❑ 393 Lee Smith .20 .07
- ❑ 394 Jeff Kunkel .10 .02
- ❑ 395 Claudell Washington .10 .02
- ❑ 396 John Tudor .10 .02
- ❑ 397 Terry Kennedy UER (Career totals all wrong) .10 .02
- ❑ 398 Lloyd McClendon .10 .02
- ❑ 399 Craig Lefferts .10 .02
- ❑ 400 Checklist 301-400 .10 .02
- ❑ 401 Keith Moreland .10 .02
- ❑ 402 Rich Gedman .10 .02
- ❑ 403 Jeff D. Robinson .10 .02
- ❑ 404 Randy Ready .10 .02
- ❑ 405 Rick Cerone .10 .02
- ❑ 406 Jeff Blauser .10 .02
- ❑ 407 Larry Andersen .10 .02
- ❑ 408 Joe Boever .10 .02
- ❑ 409 Felix Fermin .10 .02
- ❑ 410 Glenn Wilson .10 .02
- ❑ 411 Rex Hudler .10 .02
- ❑ 412 Mark Grant .10 .02
- ❑ 413 Dennis Martinez .20 .07
- ❑ 414 Darrin Jackson .10 .02
- ❑ 415 Mike Aldrete .10 .02
- ❑ 416 Roger McDowell .10 .02
- ❑ 417 Jeff Reardon .20 .07
- ❑ 418 Darren Daulton .20 .07
- ❑ 419 Tim Laudner .10 .02
- ❑ 420 Don Carman .10 .02
- ❑ 421 Lloyd Moseby .10 .02
- ❑ 422 Doug Drabek .10 .02
- ❑ 423 Lenny Harris UER (Walks 2 in '89& should be 20) .10 .02
- ❑ 424 Jose Lind .10 .02
- ❑ 425 Dave Wayne Johnson RC .10 .02
- ❑ 426 Jerry Browne .10 .02
- ❑ 427 Eric Yelding RC .10 .02
- ❑ 428 Brad Komminsk .10 .02
- ❑ 429 Jody Davis .10 .02

❑ 430 Mariano Duncan .10 .02
❑ 431 Mark Davis .10 .02
❑ 432 Nelson Santovenia .10 .02
❑ 433 Bruce Hurst .10 .02
❑ 434 Jeff Huson RC .10 .02
❑ 435 Chris James .10 .02
❑ 436 Mark Guthrie RC .10 .02
❑ 437 Charlie Hayes .10 .02
❑ 438 Shane Rawley .10 .02
❑ 439 Dickie Thon .10 .02
❑ 440 Juan Berenguer .10 .02
❑ 441 Kevin Romine .10 .02
❑ 442 Bill Landrum .10 .02
❑ 443 Todd Frohwirth .10 .02
❑ 444 Craig Worthington .10 .02
❑ 445 Fernando Valenzuela .20 .07
❑ 446 Albert Belle .50 .20
❑ 447 Ed Whited UER RC .10 .02
❑ 448 Dave Smith .10 .02
❑ 449 Dave Clark .10 .02
❑ 450 Juan Agosto .10 .02
❑ 451 Dave Valle .10 .02
❑ 452 Kent Hrbek .20 .07
❑ 453 Von Hayes .10 .02
❑ 454 Gary Gaetti .20 .07
❑ 455 Greg Briley .10 .02
❑ 456 Glenn Braggs .10 .02
❑ 457 Kirt Manwaring .10 .02
❑ 458 Mel Hall .10 .02
❑ 459 Brook Jacoby .10 .02
❑ 460 Pat Sheridan .10 .02
❑ 461 Rob Murphy .10 .02
❑ 462 Jimmy Key .20 .07
❑ 463 Nick Esasky .10 .02
❑ 464 Rob Ducey .10 .02
❑ 465 Carlos Quintana UER
(Internatinoal) .10 .02
❑ 466 Larry Walker RC 1.50 .60
❑ 467 Todd Worrell .10 .02
❑ 468 Kevin Gross .10 .02
❑ 469 Terry Pendleton .20 .07
❑ 470 Dave Martinez .10 .02
❑ 471 Gene Larkin .10 .02
❑ 472 Len Dykstra UER .20 .07
❑ 473 Barry Lyons .10 .02
❑ 474 Terry Mulholland .10 .02
❑ 475 Chip Hale RC .10 .02
❑ 476 Jesse Barfield .10 .02
❑ 477 Dan Plesac .10 .02
❑ 478A Scott Garrelts ERR 2.00 .75
❑ 478B Scott Garrelts COR .10 .02
❑ 479 Dave Righetti .10 .02
❑ 480 Gus Polidor UER
(Wearing 14 on front&
but 10 on) .10 .02
❑ 481 Mookie Wilson .20 .07
❑ 482 Luis Rivera .10 .02
❑ 483 Mike Flanagan .10 .02
❑ 484 Dennis Boyd .10 .02
❑ 485 John Cerutti .10 .02
❑ 486 John Costello .10 .02
❑ 487 Pascual Perez .10 .02
❑ 488 Tommy Herr .10 .02
❑ 489 Tom Foley .10 .02
❑ 490 Curt Ford .10 .02
❑ 491 Steve Lake .10 .02
❑ 492 Tim Teufel .10 .02
❑ 493 Randy Bush .10 .02
❑ 494 Mike Jackson .10 .02
❑ 495 Steve Jeltz .10 .02
❑ 496 Paul Gibson .10 .02
❑ 497 Steve Balboni .10 .02
❑ 498 Bud Black .10 .02
❑ 499 Dale Sveum .10 .02
❑ 500 Checklist 401-500 .10 .02
❑ 501 Tim Jones .10 .02
❑ 502 Mark Portugal .10 .02
❑ 503 Ivan Calderon .10 .02
❑ 504 Rick Rhoden .10 .02
❑ 505 Willie McGee .20 .07
❑ 506 Kirk McCaskill .10 .02
❑ 507 Dave LaPoint .10 .02
❑ 508 Jay Howell .10 .02
❑ 509 Johnny Ray .10 .02
❑ 510 Dave Anderson .10 .02
❑ 511 Chuck Crim .10 .02
❑ 512 Joe Hesketh .10 .02
❑ 513 Dennis Eckersley .20 .07
❑ 514 Greg Brock .10 .02
❑ 515 Tim Burke .10 .02
❑ 516 Frank Tanana .10 .02
❑ 517 Jay Bell .20 .07
❑ 518 Guillermo Hernandez .10 .02
❑ 519 Randy Kramer UER
(Codiroli misspelled
as Codorol) .10 .02
❑ 520 Charles Hudson .10 .02
❑ 521 Jim Corsi
(Word 'originally' is
misspelled on b) .10 .02
❑ 522 Steve Rosenberg .10 .02
❑ 523 Cris Carpenter .10 .02
❑ 524 Matt Winters RC .10 .02
❑ 525 Melido Perez .10 .02
❑ 526 Chris Gwynn UER
(Albeguergue) .10 .02
❑ 527 Bert Blyleven UER
(Games career total is
wrong&) .20 .07
❑ 528 Chuck Cary .10 .02
❑ 529 Daryl Boston .10 .02
❑ 530 Dale Mohorcic .10 .02
❑ 531 Geronimo Berroa .10 .02
❑ 532 Edgar Martinez .30 .10
❑ 533 Dale Murphy .30 .10
❑ 534 Jay Buhner .20 .07
❑ 535 John Smoltz .50 .20
❑ 536 Andy Van Slyke .30 .10
❑ 537 Mike Henneman .10 .02
❑ 538 Miguel Garcia .10 .02
❑ 539 Frank Williams .10 .02
❑ 540 R.J. Reynolds .10 .02
❑ 541 Shawn Hillegas .10 .02
❑ 542 Walt Weiss .10 .02
❑ 543 Greg Hibbard RC .10 .02
❑ 544 Nolan Ryan 2.00 .75
❑ 545 Todd Zeile .20 .07
❑ 546 Hensley Meulens .10 .02
❑ 547 Tim Belcher .10 .02
❑ 548 Mike Witt .10 .02
❑ 549 Greg Cadaret UER
(Aquiring& should
be Acquiring) .10 .02
❑ 550 Franklin Stubbs .10 .02
❑ 551 Tony Castillo .10 .02
❑ 552 Jeff M. Robinson .10 .02
❑ 553 Steve Olin RC .25 .08
❑ 554 Alan Trammell .20 .07
❑ 555 Wade Boggs 4X .30 .10
❑ 556 Will Clark .30 .10
❑ 557 Jeff King .10 .02
❑ 558 Mike Fitzgerald .10 .02
❑ 559 Ken Howell .10 .02
❑ 560 Bob Kipper .10 .02
❑ 561 Scott Bankhead .10 .02
❑ 562A Jeff Innis ERR 2.00 .75
❑ 562B Jeff Innis COR RC .10 .02
❑ 563 Randy Johnson 1.00 .40
❑ 564 Wally Whitehurst .10 .02
❑ 565 Gene Harris .10 .02
❑ 566 Norm Charlton .10 .02
❑ 567 Robin Yount UER .75 .30
❑ 568 Joe Oliver .10 .02
❑ 569 Mark Parent .10 .02
❑ 570 John Farrell UER
(Loss total added wrong) .10 .02
❑ 571 Tom Glavine .30 .10
❑ 572 Rod Nichols .10 .02
❑ 573 Jack Morris .20 .07
❑ 574 Greg Swindell .10 .02
❑ 575 Steve Searcy .10 .02
❑ 576 Ricky Jordan .10 .02
❑ 577 Matt Williams .20 .07
❑ 578 Mike LaValliere .10 .02
❑ 579 Bryn Smith .10 .02
❑ 580 Bruce Ruffin .10 .02
❑ 581 Randy Myers .20 .07
❑ 582 Rick Wrona .10 .02
❑ 583 Juan Samuel .10 .02
❑ 584 Les Lancaster .10 .02
❑ 585 Jeff Musselman .10 .02
❑ 586 Rob Dibble .20 .07
❑ 587 Eric Show .10 .02
❑ 588 Jesse Orosco .10 .02
❑ 589 Herm Winningham .10 .02
❑ 590 Andy Allanson .10 .02
❑ 591 Dion James .10 .02
❑ 592 Carmelo Martinez .10 .02
❑ 593 Luis Quinones .10 .02
❑ 594 Dennis Rasmussen .10 .02
❑ 595 Rich Yett .10 .02
❑ 596 Bob Walk .10 .02
❑ 597A Andy McGaffigan ERR
(Photo actually
Rich Thompso) 2.00 .75
❑ 597B Andy McGaffigan COR .10 .02
❑ 598 Billy Hatcher .10 .02
❑ 599 Bob Knepper .10 .02
❑ 600 Checklist 501-600 UER
(599 Bob Kneppers) .10 .02
❑ 601 Joey Cora .20 .07
❑ 602 Steve Finley .20 .07
❑ 603 Kal Daniels UER
(12 hits in '87& should
be 123;) .10 .02
❑ 604 Gregg Olson .20 .07
❑ 605 Dave Stieb .20 .07
❑ 606 Kenny Rogers .20 .07
❑ 607 Zane Smith .10 .02
❑ 608 Bob Geren UER
(Origionally) .10 .02
❑ 609 Chad Kreuter .10 .02
❑ 610 Mike Smithson .10 .02
❑ 611 Jeff Wetherby RC .10 .02
❑ 612 Gary Mielke RC .10 .02
❑ 613 Pete Smith .10 .02
❑ 614 Jack Daugherty RC .10 .02
❑ 615 Lance McCullers .10 .02
❑ 616 Don Robinson .10 .02
❑ 617 Jose Guzman .10 .02
❑ 618 Steve Bedrosian .10 .02
❑ 619 Jamie Moyer .20 .07
❑ 620 Atlee Hammaker .10 .02
❑ 621 Rick Luecken RC .10 .02
❑ 622 Greg W. Harris .10 .02
❑ 623 Pete Harnisch .10 .02
❑ 624 Jerald Clark .10 .02
❑ 625 Jack McDowell .10 .02
❑ 626 Frank Viola .10 .02
❑ 627 Teddy Higuera .10 .02
❑ 628 Marty Pevey RC .10 .02
❑ 629 Bill Wegman .10 .02
❑ 630 Eric Plunk .10 .02
❑ 631 Drew Hall .10 .02
❑ 632 Doug Jones .10 .02
❑ 633 Geno Petralli UER
(Sacremento) .10 .02
❑ 634 Jose Alvarez .10 .02
❑ 635 Bob Milacki .10 .02
❑ 636 Bobby Witt .10 .02
❑ 637 Trevor Wilson .10 .02
❑ 638 Jeff Russell UER
(Shutout stats wrong) .10 .02
❑ 639 Mike Krukow .10 .02
❑ 640 Rick Leach .10 .02
❑ 641 Dave Schmidt .10 .02
❑ 642 Terry Leach .10 .02
❑ 643 Calvin Schiraldi .10 .02
❑ 644 Bob Melvin .10 .02
❑ 645 Jim Abbott .30 .10
❑ 646 Jaime Navarro .10 .02
❑ 647 Mark Langston UER
(Several errors in
stats total) .10 .02
❑ 648 Juan Nieves .10 .02
❑ 649 Damaso Garcia .10 .02
❑ 650 Charlie O'Brien .10 .02
❑ 651 Eric King .10 .02
❑ 652 Mike Boddicker .10 .02
❑ 653 Duane Ward .10 .02
❑ 654 Bob Stanley .10 .02
❑ 655 Sandy Alomar Jr. .20 .07
❑ 656 Danny Tartabull UER .10 .02
❑ 657 Randy McCament RC .10 .02
❑ 658 Charlie Leibrandt .10 .02
❑ 659 Dan Quisenberry .10 .02
❑ 660 Paul Assenmacher .10 .02
❑ 661 Walt Terrell .10 .02

❑ 662	Tim Leary	.10	.02
❑ 663	Randy Milligan	.10	.02
❑ 664	Bo Diaz	.10	.02
❑ 665	Mark Lemke UER (Richmond misspelled as Richomond)	.10	.02
❑ 666	Jose Gonzalez	.10	.02
❑ 667	Chuck Finley UER (Born 11/16/62& should be 11/26)	.20	.07
❑ 668	John Kruk	.20	.07
❑ 669	Dick Schofield	.10	.02
❑ 670	Tim Crews	.10	.02
❑ 671	John Dopson	.10	.02
❑ 672	John Orton RC	.10	.02
❑ 673	Eric Hetzel	.10	.02
❑ 674	Lance Parrish	.10	.02
❑ 675	Ramon Martinez	.10	.02
❑ 676	Mark Gubicza	.10	.02
❑ 677	Greg Litton	.10	.02
❑ 678	Greg Mathews	.10	.02
❑ 679	Dave Dravecky	.20	.07
❑ 680	Steve Farr	.10	.02
❑ 681	Mike Devereaux	.10	.02
❑ 682	Ken Griffey Sr.	.20	.07
❑ 683A	Jamie Weston ERR	2.00	.75
❑ 683B	Mickey Weston COR RC	.10	.02
❑ 684	Jack Armstrong	.10	.02
❑ 685	Steve Buechele	.10	.02
❑ 686	Bryan Harvey	.10	.02
❑ 687	Lance Blankenship	.10	.02
❑ 688	Dante Bichette	.20	.07
❑ 689	Todd Burns	.10	.02
❑ 690	Dan Petry	.10	.02
❑ 691	Kent Anderson	.10	.02
❑ 692	Todd Stottlemyre	.20	.07
❑ 693	Wally Joyner UER (Several stats errors)	.20	.07
❑ 694	Mike Rochford	.10	.02
❑ 695	Floyd Bannister	.10	.02
❑ 696	Rick Reuschel	.10	.02
❑ 697	Jose DeLeon	.10	.02
❑ 698	Jeff Montgomery	.20	.07
❑ 699	Kelly Downs	.10	.02
❑ 700A	CL 601-700 ERR	2.00	.75
❑ 700B	Checklist 601-700 (683 Mickey Weston)	.10	.02
❑ 701	Jim Gott	.10	.02
❑ 702	L.Walker/Grissom/DeSh	.50	.20
❑ 702A	Mike Witt Black	10.00	5.00
❑ 703	Alejandro Pena	.10	.02
❑ 704	Willie Randolph	.20	.07
❑ 705	Tim Leary	.10	.02
❑ 706	Chuck McElroy RC	.10	.02
❑ 707	Gerald Perry	.10	.02
❑ 708	Tom Brunansky	.10	.02
❑ 709	John Franco	.20	.07
❑ 710	Mark Davis	.10	.02
❑ 711	David Justice RC	.75	.30
❑ 712	Storm Davis	.10	.02
❑ 713	Scott Ruskin RC	.10	.02
❑ 714	Glenn Braggs	.10	.02
❑ 715	Kevin Bearse RC	.10	.02
❑ 716	Jose Nunez	.10	.02
❑ 717	Tim Layana RC	.10	.02
❑ 718	Greg Myers	.10	.02
❑ 719	Pete O'Brien	.10	.02
❑ 720	John Candelaria	.10	.02
❑ 721	Craig Grebeck RC	.10	.02
❑ 722	Shawn Boskie RC	.10	.02
❑ 723	Jim Leyritz RC	.25	.08
❑ 724	Bill Sampen RC	.10	.02
❑ 725	Scott Radinsky RC	.10	.02
❑ 726	Todd Hundley RC	.25	.08
❑ 727	Scott Hemond RC	.10	.02
❑ 728	Lenny Webster RC	.10	.02
❑ 729	Jeff Reardon	.20	.07
❑ 730	Mitch Webster	.10	.02
❑ 731	Brian Bohanon RC	.10	.02
❑ 732	Rick Parker RC	.10	.02
❑ 733	Terry Shumpert RC	.10	.02
❑ 734A	Nolan Ryan 6th	3.00	1.25
❑ 734B	Nolan Ryan 6th/300	1.00	.40
❑ 735	John Burkett	.10	.02
❑ 736	Derrick May RC	.10	.02
❑ 737	Carlos Baerga RC	.25	.08
❑ 738	Greg Smith RC	.10	.02
❑ 739	Scott Sanderson	.10	.02
❑ 740	Joe Kraemer RC	.10	.02
❑ 741	Hector Villanueva RC	.10	.02
❑ 742	Mike Fetters RC	.25	.08
❑ 743	Mark Gardner RC	.10	.02
❑ 744	Matt Nokes	.10	.02
❑ 745	Dave Winfield	.20	.07
❑ 746	Delino DeShields RC	.25	.08
❑ 747	Dann Howitt RC	.10	.02
❑ 748	Tony Pena	.10	.02
❑ 749	Oil Can Boyd	.10	.02
❑ 750	Mike Benjamin RC	.10	.02
❑ 751	Alex Cole RC	.10	.02
❑ 752	Eric Gunderson RC	.10	.02
❑ 753	Howard Farmer RC	.10	.02
❑ 754	Joe Carter	.20	.07
❑ 755	Ray Lankford RC	.50	.20
❑ 756	Sandy Alomar Jr.	.20	.07
❑ 757	Alex Sanchez	.10	.02
❑ 758	Nick Esasky	.10	.02
❑ 759	Stan Belinda RC	.10	.02
❑ 760	Jim Presley	.10	.02
❑ 761	Gary DiSarcina RC	.25	.08
❑ 762	Wayne Edwards RC	.10	.02
❑ 763	Pat Combs	.10	.02
❑ 764	Mickey Pina RC	.10	.02
❑ 765	Wilson Alvarez RC	.25	.08
❑ 766	Dave Parker	.20	.07
❑ 767	Mike Blowers RC	.10	.02
❑ 768	Tony Phillips	.10	.02
❑ 769	Pascual Perez	.10	.02
❑ 770	Gary Pettis	.10	.02
❑ 771	Fred Lynn	.10	.02
❑ 772	Mel Rojas RC	.10	.02
❑ 773	David Segui RC	.50	.20
❑ 774	Gary Carter	.20	.07
❑ 775	Rafael Valdez RC	.10	.02
❑ 776	Glenallen Hill	.10	.02
❑ 777	Keith Hernandez	.20	.07
❑ 778	Billy Hatcher	.10	.02
❑ 779	Marty Clary	.10	.02
❑ 780	Candy Maldonado	.10	.02
❑ 781	Mike Marshall	.10	.02
❑ 782	Billy Joe Robidoux	.10	.02
❑ 783	Mark Langston	.10	.02
❑ 784	Paul Sorrento RC	.25	.08
❑ 785	Dave Hollins RC	.25	.08
❑ 786	Cecil Fielder	.20	.07
❑ 787	Matt Young	.10	.02
❑ 788	Jeff Huson	.10	.02
❑ 789	Lloyd Moseby	.10	.02
❑ 790	Ron Kittle	.10	.02
❑ 791	Hubie Brooks	.10	.02
❑ 792	Craig Lefferts	.10	.02
❑ 793	Kevin Bass	.10	.02
❑ 794	Bryn Smith	.10	.02
❑ 795	Juan Samuel	.10	.02
❑ 796	Sam Horn	.10	.02
❑ 797	Randy Myers	.20	.07
❑ 798	Chris James	.10	.02
❑ 799	Bill Gullickson	.10	.02
❑ 800	Checklist 701-800	.10	.02

1991 Upper Deck

❑ COMPLETE SET (800)	15.00	6.00
❑ COMP.FACT.SET (800)	20.00	8.00
❑ COMPLETE LO SET (700)	15.00	6.00
❑ COMPLETE HI SET (100)	5.00	2.00

❑ 1	Star Rookie Checklist	.05	.01
❑ 2	Phil Plantier RC	.10	.02
❑ 3	D.J. Dozier	.05	.01
❑ 4	Dave Hansen	.05	.01
❑ 5	Mo Vaughn	.10	.02
❑ 6	Leo Gomez	.05	.01
❑ 7	Scott Aldred	.05	.01
❑ 8	Scott Chiamparino	.05	.01
❑ 9	Lance Dickson RC	.10	.02
❑ 10	Sean Berry RC	.10	.02
❑ 11	Bernie Williams	.25	.08
❑ 12	Brian Barnes UER RC	.10	.02
❑ 13	Narciso Elvira RC	.05	.01
❑ 14	Mike Gardiner RC	.05	.01
❑ 15	Greg Colbrunn RC	.25	.08
❑ 16	Bernard Gilkey	.05	.01
❑ 17	Mark Lewis	.05	.01
❑ 18	Mickey Morandini	.05	.01
❑ 19	Charles Nagy	.05	.01
❑ 20	Geronimo Pena	.05	.01
❑ 21	Henry Rodriguez RC	.25	.08
❑ 22	Scott Cooper FUDC	.05	.01
❑ 23	Andujar Cedeno UER	.05	.01
❑ 24	Eric Karros RC	.75	.30
❑ 25	Steve Decker UER RC	.05	.01
❑ 26	Kevin Belcher RC	.05	.01
❑ 27	Jeff Conine RC	.50	.20
❑ 28	Dave Stewart TC	.05	.01
❑ 29	Carlton Fisk TC	.10	.02
❑ 30	Rafael Palmeiro TC	.10	.02
❑ 31	Chuck Finley TC	.05	.01
❑ 32	Harold Reynolds TC	.05	.01
❑ 33	Bret Saberhagen TC	.05	.01
❑ 34	Gary Gaetti TC	.05	.01
❑ 35	Scott Leius	.05	.01
❑ 36	Neal Heaton	.05	.01
❑ 37	Terry Lee RC	.05	.01
❑ 38	Gary Redus	.05	.01
❑ 39	Barry Jones	.05	.01
❑ 40	Chuck Knoblauch	.10	.02
❑ 41	Larry Andersen	.05	.01
❑ 42	Darryl Hamilton	.05	.01
❑ 43	Mike Greenwell TC	.05	.01
❑ 44	Kelly Gruber TC	.05	.01
❑ 45	Jack Morris TC	.05	.01
❑ 46	Sandy Alomar Jr. TC	.05	.01
❑ 47	Gregg Olson TC	.05	.01
❑ 48	Dave Parker TC	.05	.01
❑ 49	Roberto Kelly TC	.05	.01
❑ 50	Top Prospect Checklist	.05	.01
❑ 51	Kyle Abbott	.05	.01
❑ 52	Jeff Juden	.05	.01
❑ 53	Todd Van Poppel UER RC	.25	.08
❑ 54	Steve Karsay RC	.25	.08
❑ 55	Chipper Jones RC	4.00	1.50
❑ 56	Chris Johnson UER RC	.10	.02
❑ 57	John Ericks	.05	.01
❑ 58	Gary Scott RC	.05	.01
❑ 59	Kiki Jones	.05	.01
❑ 60	Wil Cordero RC	.10	.02
❑ 61	Royce Clayton	.05	.01
❑ 62	Tim Costo RC	.10	.02
❑ 63	Roger Salkeld FUDC	.05	.01
❑ 64	Brook Fordyce RC	.25	.08
❑ 65	Mike Mussina RC	2.00	.75
❑ 66	Dave Staton RC	.10	.02
❑ 67	Mike Lieberthal RC	.50	.20
❑ 68	Kurt Miller RC	.05	.01
❑ 69	Dan Peltier RC	.10	.02
❑ 70	Greg Blosser FUDC	.05	.01
❑ 71	Reggie Sanders RC	.75	.30
❑ 72	Brent Mayne	.05	.01
❑ 73	Rico Brogna	.05	.01
❑ 74	Willie Banks	.05	.01
❑ 75	Len Dutcher RC	.05	.01
❑ 76	Pat Kelly RC	.10	.02
❑ 77	Chris Sabo TC	.05	.01
❑ 78	Ramon Martinez TC	.05	.01
❑ 79	Matt Williams TC	.05	.01
❑ 80	Roberto Alomar TC	.10	.02
❑ 81	Glenn Davis TC	.05	.01
❑ 82	Ron Gant TC	.05	.01
❑ 83	Cecil Fielder's Feat	.05	.01
❑ 84	Orlando Merced RC	.10	.02
❑ 85	Domingo Ramos	.05	.01

Card		
❑ 86 Tom Bolton	.05	.01
❑ 87 Andres Santana	.05	.01
❑ 88 John Dopson	.05	.01
❑ 89 Kenny Williams	.05	.01
❑ 90 Marty Barrett	.05	.01
❑ 91 Tom Pagnozzi	.05	.01
❑ 92 Carmelo Martinez	.05	.01
❑ 93 Bobby Thigpen SAVE	.05	.01
❑ 94 Barry Bonds TC	.50	.20
❑ 95 Gregg Jefferies TC	.05	.01
❑ 96 Tim Wallach TC	.05	.01
❑ 97 Len Dykstra TC	.05	.01
❑ 98 Pedro Guerrero TC	.05	.01
❑ 99 Mark Grace TC	.10	.02
❑ 100 Checklist 1-100	.05	.01
❑ 101 Kevin Elster	.05	.01
❑ 102 Tom Brookens	.05	.01
❑ 103 Mackey Sasser	.05	.01
❑ 104 Felix Fermin	.05	.01
❑ 105 Kevin McReynolds	.05	.01
❑ 106 Dave Stieb	.05	.01
❑ 107 Jeffrey Leonard	.05	.01
❑ 108 Dave Henderson	.05	.01
❑ 109 Sid Bream	.05	.01
❑ 110 Henry Cotto	.05	.01
❑ 111 Shawon Dunston	.05	.01
❑ 112 Mariano Duncan	.05	.01
❑ 113 Joe Girardi	.05	.01
❑ 114 Billy Hatcher	.05	.01
❑ 115 Greg Maddux	.40	.15
❑ 116 Jerry Browne	.05	.01
❑ 117 Juan Samuel	.05	.01
❑ 118 Steve Olin	.05	.01
❑ 119 Alfredo Griffin	.05	.01
❑ 120 Mitch Webster	.05	.01
❑ 121 Joel Skinner	.05	.01
❑ 122 Frank Viola	.10	.02
❑ 123 Cory Snyder	.05	.01
❑ 124 Howard Johnson	.05	.01
❑ 125 Carlos Baerga	.05	.01
❑ 126 Tony Fernandez	.05	.01
❑ 127 Dave Stewart	.10	.02
❑ 128 Jay Buhner	.10	.02
❑ 129 Mike LaValliere	.05	.01
❑ 130 Scott Bradley	.05	.01
❑ 131 Tony Phillips	.05	.01
❑ 132 Ryne Sandberg	.40	.15
❑ 133 Paul O'Neill	.15	.05
❑ 134 Mark Grace	.15	.05
❑ 135 Chris Sabo	.05	.01
❑ 136 Ramon Martinez	.05	.01
❑ 137 Brook Jacoby	.05	.01
❑ 138 Candy Maldonado	.05	.01
❑ 139 Mike Scioscia	.05	.01
❑ 140 Chris James	.05	.01
❑ 141 Craig Worthington	.05	.01
❑ 142 Manny Lee	.05	.01
❑ 143 Tim Raines	.10	.02
❑ 144 Sandy Alomar Jr.	.05	.01
❑ 145 John Olerud	.10	.02
❑ 146 Ozzie Canseco w/Jose	.10	.02
❑ 147 Pat Borders	.05	.01
❑ 148 Harold Reynolds	.10	.02
❑ 149 Tom Henke	.05	.01
❑ 150 R.J. Reynolds	.05	.01
❑ 151 Mike Gallego	.05	.01
❑ 152 Bobby Bonilla	.10	.02
❑ 153 Terry Steinbach	.05	.01
❑ 154 Barry Bonds	1.00	.40
❑ 155 Jose Canseco	.15	.05
❑ 156 Gregg Jefferies	.05	.01
❑ 157 Matt Williams	.10	.02
❑ 158 Craig Biggio	.15	.05
❑ 159 Daryl Boston	.05	.01
❑ 160 Ricky Jordan	.05	.01
❑ 161 Stan Belinda	.05	.01
❑ 162 Ozzie Smith	.40	.15
❑ 163 Tom Brunansky	.05	.01
❑ 164 Todd Zeile	.05	.01
❑ 165 Mike Greenwell	.05	.01
❑ 166 Kal Daniels	.05	.01
❑ 167 Kent Hrbek	.10	.02
❑ 168 Franklin Stubbs	.05	.01
❑ 169 Dick Schofield	.05	.01
❑ 170 Junior Ortiz	.05	.01
❑ 171 Hector Villanueva	.05	.01
❑ 172 Dennis Eckersley	.10	.02
❑ 173 Mitch Williams	.05	.01
❑ 174 Mark McGwire	.75	.30
❑ 175 Fernando Valenzuela 3X	.10	.02
❑ 176 Gary Carter	.10	.02
❑ 177 Dave Magadan	.05	.01
❑ 178 Robby Thompson	.05	.01
❑ 179 Bob Ojeda	.05	.01
❑ 180 Ken Caminiti	.10	.02
❑ 181 Don Slaught	.05	.01
❑ 182 Luis Rivera	.05	.01
❑ 183 Jay Bell	.10	.02
❑ 184 Jody Reed	.05	.01
❑ 185 Wally Backman	.05	.01
❑ 186 Dave Martinez	.05	.01
❑ 187 Luis Polonia	.05	.01
❑ 188 Shane Mack	.05	.01
❑ 189 Spike Owen	.05	.01
❑ 190 Scott Bailes	.05	.01
❑ 191 John Russell	.05	.01
❑ 192 Walt Weiss	.05	.01
❑ 193 Jose Oquendo	.05	.01
❑ 194 Carney Lansford	.10	.02
❑ 195 Jeff Huson	.05	.01
❑ 196 Keith Miller	.05	.01
❑ 197 Eric Yelding	.05	.01
❑ 198 Ron Darling	.05	.01
❑ 199 John Kruk	.10	.02
❑ 200 Checklist 101-200	.05	.01
❑ 201 John Shelby	.05	.01
❑ 202 Bob Geren	.05	.01
❑ 203 Lance McCullers	.05	.01
❑ 204 Alvaro Espinoza	.05	.01
❑ 205 Mark Salas	.05	.01
❑ 206 Mike Pagliarulo	.05	.01
❑ 207 Jose Uribe	.05	.01
❑ 208 Jim Deshaies	.05	.01
❑ 209 Ron Karkovice	.05	.01
❑ 210 Rafael Ramirez	.05	.01
❑ 211 Donnie Hill	.05	.01
❑ 212 Brian Harper	.05	.01
❑ 213 Jack Howell	.05	.01
❑ 214 Wes Gardner	.05	.01
❑ 215 Tim Burke	.05	.01
❑ 216 Doug Jones	.05	.01
❑ 217 Hubie Brooks	.05	.01
❑ 218 Tom Candiotti	.05	.01
❑ 219 Gerald Perry	.05	.01
❑ 220 Jose DeLeon	.05	.01
❑ 221 Wally Whitehurst	.05	.01
❑ 222 Alan Mills	.05	.01
❑ 223 Alan Trammell	.10	.02
❑ 224 Dwight Gooden	.10	.02
❑ 225 Travis Fryman	.10	.02
❑ 226 Joe Carter	.10	.02
❑ 227 Julio Franco	.10	.02
❑ 228 Craig Lefferts	.05	.01
❑ 229 Gary Pettis	.05	.01
❑ 230 Dennis Rasmussen	.05	.01
❑ 231A Brian Downing ERR	.05	.01
❑ 231B Brian Downing COR	.25	.08
❑ 232 Carlos Quintana	.05	.01
❑ 233 Gary Gaetti	.10	.02
❑ 234 Mark Langston	.05	.01
❑ 235 Tim Wallach	.05	.01
❑ 236 Greg Swindell	.05	.01
❑ 237 Eddie Murray	.25	.08
❑ 238 Jeff Manto	.05	.01
❑ 239 Lenny Harris	.05	.01
❑ 240 Jesse Orosco	.05	.01
❑ 241 Scott Lusader	.05	.01
❑ 242 Sid Fernandez	.05	.01
❑ 243 Jim Leyritz	.05	.01
❑ 244 Cecil Fielder	.10	.02
❑ 245 Darryl Strawberry	.10	.02
❑ 246 Frank Thomas	.25	.08
❑ 247 Kevin Mitchell	.05	.01
❑ 248 Lance Johnson	.05	.01
❑ 249 Rick Reuschel	.05	.01
❑ 250 Mark Portugal	.05	.01
❑ 251 Derek Lilliquist	.05	.01
❑ 252 Brian Holman	.05	.01
❑ 253 Rafael Valdez UER	.05	.01
❑ 254 B.J. Surhoff	.10	.02
❑ 255 Tony Gwynn	.30	.10
❑ 256 Andy Van Slyke	.15	.05
❑ 257 Todd Stottlemyre	.05	.01
❑ 258 Jose Lind	.05	.01
❑ 259 Greg Myers	.05	.01
❑ 260 Jeff Ballard	.05	.01
❑ 261 Bobby Thigpen	.05	.01
❑ 262 Jimmy Kremers	.05	.01
❑ 263 Robin Ventura	.10	.02
❑ 264 John Smoltz	.15	.05
❑ 265 Sammy Sosa	.25	.08
❑ 266 Gary Sheffield	.10	.02
❑ 267 Len Dykstra	.10	.02
❑ 268 Bill Spiers	.05	.01
❑ 269 Charlie Hayes	.05	.01
❑ 270 Brett Butler	.10	.02
❑ 271 Bip Roberts	.05	.01
❑ 272 Rob Deer	.05	.01
❑ 273 Fred Lynn	.05	.01
❑ 274 Dave Parker	.10	.02
❑ 275 Andy Benes	.05	.01
❑ 276 Glenallen Hill	.05	.01
❑ 277 Steve Howard	.05	.01
❑ 278 Doug Drabek	.05	.01
❑ 279 Joe Oliver	.05	.01
❑ 280 Todd Benzinger	.05	.01
❑ 281 Eric King	.05	.01
❑ 282 Jim Presley	.05	.01
❑ 283 Ken Patterson	.05	.01
❑ 284 Jack Daugherty	.05	.01
❑ 285 Ivan Calderon	.05	.01
❑ 286 Edgar Diaz	.05	.01
❑ 287 Kevin Bass	.05	.01
❑ 288 Don Carman	.05	.01
❑ 289 Greg Brock	.05	.01
❑ 290 John Franco	.10	.02
❑ 291 Joey Cora	.05	.01
❑ 292 Bill Wegman	.05	.01
❑ 293 Eric Show	.05	.01
❑ 294 Scott Bankhead	.05	.01
❑ 295 Garry Templeton	.05	.01
❑ 296 Mickey Tettleton	.05	.01
❑ 297 Luis Sojo	.05	.01
❑ 298 Jose Rijo	.05	.01
❑ 299 Dave Johnson	.05	.01
❑ 300 Checklist 201-300	.05	.01
❑ 301 Mark Grant	.05	.01
❑ 302 Pete Harnisch	.05	.01
❑ 303 Greg Olson	.05	.01
❑ 304 Anthony Telford RC	.05	.01
❑ 305 Lonnie Smith	.05	.01
❑ 306 Chris Hoiles FUDC	.05	.01
❑ 307 Bryn Smith	.05	.01
❑ 308 Mike Devereaux	.05	.01
❑ 309A Milt Thompson ERR	.25	.08
❑ 309B Milt Thompson COR	.05	.01
❑ 310 Bob Melvin	.05	.01
❑ 311 Luis Salazar	.05	.01
❑ 312 Ed Whitson	.05	.01
❑ 313 Charlie Hough	.10	.02
❑ 314 Dave Clark	.05	.01
❑ 315 Eric Gunderson	.05	.01
❑ 316 Dan Petry	.05	.01
❑ 317 Dante Bichette	.10	.02
❑ 318 Mike Heath	.05	.01
❑ 319 Damon Berryhill	.05	.01
❑ 320 Walt Terrell	.05	.01
❑ 321 Scott Fletcher	.05	.01
❑ 322 Dan Plesac	.05	.01
❑ 323 Jack McDowell	.05	.01
❑ 324 Paul Molitor	.10	.02
❑ 325 Ozzie Guillen	.10	.02
❑ 326 Gregg Olson	.05	.01
❑ 327 Pedro Guerrero	.10	.02
❑ 328 Bob Milacki	.05	.01
❑ 329 John Tudor UER	.05	.01
❑ 330 Steve Finley UER	.10	.02
❑ 331 Jack Clark	.10	.02
❑ 332 Jerome Walton	.05	.01
❑ 333 Andy Hawkins	.05	.01
❑ 334 Derrick May	.05	.01
❑ 335 Roberto Alomar	.15	.05
❑ 336 Jack Morris	.10	.02
❑ 337 Dave Winfield	.10	.02
❑ 338 Steve Searcy	.05	.01
❑ 339 Chili Davis	.10	.02
❑ 340 Larry Sheets	.05	.01
❑ 341 Ted Higuera	.05	.01

❑ 342 David Segui .05 .01
❑ 343 Greg Cadaret .05 .01
❑ 344 Robin Yount .40 .15
❑ 345 Nolan Ryan 1.00 .40
❑ 346 Ray Lankford .10 .02
❑ 347 Cal Ripken .75 .30
❑ 348 Lee Smith .10 .02
❑ 349 Brady Anderson .10 .02
❑ 350 Frank DiPino .05 .01
❑ 351 Hal Morris .05 .01
❑ 352 Deion Sanders .15 .05
❑ 353 Barry Larkin .15 .05
❑ 354 Don Mattingly .60 .25
❑ 355 Eric Davis .10 .02
❑ 356 Jose Offerman .05 .01
❑ 357 Mel Rojas .05 .01
❑ 358 Rudy Seanez .05 .01
❑ 359 Oil Can Boyd .05 .01
❑ 360 Nelson Liriano .05 .01
❑ 361 Ron Gant .10 .02
❑ 362 Howard Farmer .05 .01
❑ 363 David Justice .10 .02
❑ 364 Delino DeShields .10 .02
❑ 365 Steve Avery .05 .01
❑ 366 David Cone .10 .02
❑ 367 Lou Whitaker .10 .02
❑ 368 Von Hayes .05 .01
❑ 369 Frank Tanana .05 .01
❑ 370 Tim Teufel .05 .01
❑ 371 Randy Myers .05 .01
❑ 372 Roberto Kelly .05 .01
❑ 373 Jack Armstrong .05 .01
❑ 374 Kelly Gruber .05 .01
❑ 375 Kevin Maas .05 .01
❑ 376 Randy Johnson .30 .10
❑ 377 David West .05 .01
❑ 378 Brent Knackert .05 .01
❑ 379 Rick Honeycutt .05 .01
❑ 380 Kevin Gross .05 .01
❑ 381 Tom Foley .05 .01
❑ 382 Jeff Blauser .05 .01
❑ 383 Scott Ruskin .05 .01
❑ 384 Andres Thomas .05 .01
❑ 385 Dennis Martinez .10 .02
❑ 386 Mike Henneman .05 .01
❑ 387 Felix Jose .05 .01
❑ 388 Alejandro Pena .05 .01
❑ 389 Chet Lemon .05 .01
❑ 390 Craig Wilson RC .05 .01
❑ 391 Chuck Crim .05 .01
❑ 392 Mel Hall .05 .01
❑ 393 Mark Knudson .05 .01
❑ 394 Norm Charlton .05 .01
❑ 395 Mike Felder .05 .01
❑ 396 Tim Layana .05 .01
❑ 397 Steve Frey .05 .01
❑ 398 Bill Doran .05 .01
❑ 399 Dion James .05 .01
❑ 400 Checklist 301-400 .05 .01
❑ 401 Ron Hassey .05 .01
❑ 402 Don Robinson .05 .01
❑ 403 Gene Nelson .05 .01
❑ 404 Terry Kennedy .05 .01
❑ 405 Todd Burns .05 .01
❑ 406 Roger McDowell .05 .01
❑ 407 Bob Kipper .05 .01
❑ 408 Darren Daulton .10 .02
❑ 409 Chuck Cary .05 .01
❑ 410 Bruce Ruffin .05 .01
❑ 411 Juan Berenguer .05 .01
❑ 412 Gary Ward .05 .01
❑ 413 Al Newman .05 .01
❑ 414 Danny Jackson .05 .01
❑ 415 Greg Gagne .05 .01
❑ 416 Tom Herr .05 .01
❑ 417 Jeff Parrett .05 .01
❑ 418 Jeff Reardon .10 .02
❑ 419 Mark Lemke .05 .01
❑ 420 Charlie O'Brien .05 .01
❑ 421 Willie Randolph .10 .02
❑ 422 Steve Bedrosian .05 .01
❑ 423 Mike Moore .05 .01
❑ 424 Jeff Brantley .05 .01
❑ 425 Bob Welch .05 .01
❑ 426 Terry Mulholland .05 .01
❑ 427 Willie Blair .05 .01
❑ 428 Darrin Fletcher .05 .01
❑ 429 Mike Witt .05 .01
❑ 430 Joe Boever .05 .01
❑ 431 Tom Gordon .05 .01
❑ 432 Pedro Munoz RC .10 .02
❑ 433 Kevin Seitzer .05 .01
❑ 434 Kevin Tapani .05 .01
❑ 435 Bret Saberhagen .10 .02
❑ 436 Ellis Burks .10 .02
❑ 437 Chuck Finley .10 .02
❑ 438 Mike Boddicker .05 .01
❑ 439 Francisco Cabrera .05 .01
❑ 440 Todd Hundley .05 .01
❑ 441 Kelly Downs .05 .01
❑ 442 Dann Howitt .05 .01
❑ 443 Scott Garrelts .05 .01
❑ 444 Rickey Henderson .25 .08
❑ 445 Will Clark .15 .05
❑ 446 Ben McDonald .05 .01
❑ 447 Dale Murphy .15 .05
❑ 448 Dave Righetti .10 .02
❑ 449 Dickie Thon .05 .01
❑ 450 Ted Power .05 .01
❑ 451 Scott Coolbaugh .05 .01
❑ 452 Dwight Smith .05 .01
❑ 453 Pete Incaviglia .05 .01
❑ 454 Andre Dawson .10 .02
❑ 455 Ruben Sierra .10 .02
❑ 456 Andres Galarraga .10 .02
❑ 457 Alvin Davis .05 .01
❑ 458 Tony Castillo .05 .01
❑ 459 Pete O'Brien .05 .01
❑ 460 Charlie Leibrandt .05 .01
❑ 461 Vince Coleman .05 .01
❑ 462 Steve Sax .05 .01
❑ 463 Omar Olivares RC .10 .02
❑ 464 Oscar Azocar .05 .01
❑ 465 Joe Magrane .05 .01
❑ 466 Karl Rhodes .05 .01
❑ 467 Benito Santiago .10 .02
❑ 468 Joe Klink .05 .01
❑ 469 Sil Campusano .05 .01
❑ 470 Mark Parent .05 .01
❑ 471 Shawn Boskie UER .05 .01
❑ 472 Kevin Brown .10 .02
❑ 473 Rick Sutcliffe .10 .02
❑ 474 Rafael Palmeiro .15 .05
❑ 475 Mike Harkey .05 .01
❑ 476 Jaime Navarro .05 .01
❑ 477 Marquis Grissom .10 .02
❑ 478 Marty Clary .05 .01
❑ 479 Greg Briley .05 .01
❑ 480 Tom Glavine .15 .05
❑ 481 Lee Guetterman .05 .01
❑ 482 Rex Hudler .05 .01
❑ 483 Dave LaPoint .05 .01
❑ 484 Terry Pendleton .10 .02
❑ 485 Jesse Barfield .05 .01
❑ 486 Jose DeJesus .05 .01
❑ 487 Paul Abbott RC .10 .02
❑ 488 Ken Howell .05 .01
❑ 489 Greg W. Harris .05 .01
❑ 490 Roy Smith .05 .01
❑ 491 Paul Assenmacher .05 .01
❑ 492 Geno Petralli .05 .01
❑ 493 Steve Wilson .05 .01
❑ 494 Kevin Reimer .05 .01
❑ 495 Bill Long .05 .01
❑ 496 Mike Jackson .05 .01
❑ 497 Oddibe McDowell .05 .01
❑ 498 Bill Swift .05 .01
❑ 499 Jeff Treadway .05 .01
❑ 500 Checklist 401-500 .05 .01
❑ 501 Gene Larkin .05 .01
❑ 502 Bob Boone .10 .02
❑ 503 Allan Anderson .05 .01
❑ 504 Luis Aquino .05 .01
❑ 505 Mark Guthrie .05 .01
❑ 506 Joe Orsulak .05 .01
❑ 507 Dana Kiecker .05 .01
❑ 508 Dave Gallagher .05 .01
❑ 509 Greg A. Harris .05 .01
❑ 510 Mark Williamson .05 .01
❑ 511 Casey Candaele .05 .01
❑ 512 Mookie Wilson .10 .02
❑ 513 Dave Smith .05 .01
❑ 514 Chuck Carr FUDC .05 .01
❑ 515 Glenn Wilson .05 .01
❑ 516 Mike Fitzgerald .05 .01
❑ 517 Devon White .10 .02
❑ 518 Dave Hollins .05 .01
❑ 519 Mark Eichhorn .05 .01
❑ 520 Otis Nixon .05 .01
❑ 521 Terry Shumpert .05 .01
❑ 522 Scott Erickson .05 .01
❑ 523 Danny Tartabull .05 .01
❑ 524 Orel Hershiser .10 .02
❑ 525 George Brett .60 .25
❑ 526 Greg Vaughn .05 .01
❑ 527 Tim Naehring FUDC .05 .01
❑ 528 Curt Schilling .25 .08
❑ 529 Chris Bosio .05 .01
❑ 530 Sam Horn .05 .01
❑ 531 Mike Scott .05 .01
❑ 532 George Bell .05 .01
❑ 533 Eric Anthony .05 .01
❑ 534 Julio Valera .05 .01
❑ 535 Glenn Davis .05 .01
❑ 536 Larry Walker .25 .08
❑ 537 Pat Combs .05 .01
❑ 538 Chris Nabholz .05 .01
❑ 539 Kirk McCaskill .05 .01
❑ 540 Randy Ready .05 .01
❑ 541 Mark Gubicza .05 .01
❑ 542 Rick Aguilera .10 .02
❑ 543 Brian McRae RC .25 .08
❑ 544 Kirby Puckett .25 .08
❑ 545 Bo Jackson .25 .08
❑ 546 Wade Boggs .15 .05
❑ 547 Tim McIntosh .05 .01
❑ 548 Randy Milligan .05 .01
❑ 549 Dwight Evans .15 .05
❑ 550 Billy Ripken .05 .01
❑ 551 Erik Hanson .05 .01
❑ 552 Lance Parrish .10 .02
❑ 553 Tino Martinez .25 .08
❑ 554 Jim Abbott .15 .05
❑ 555 Ken Griffey Jr. .50 .20
❑ 556 Milt Cuyler .05 .01
❑ 557 Mark Leonard RC .05 .01
❑ 558 Jay Howell .05 .01
❑ 559 Lloyd Moseby .05 .01
❑ 560 Chris Gwynn .05 .01
❑ 561 Mark Whiten FUDC .05 .01
❑ 562 Harold Baines .10 .02
❑ 563 Junior Felix .05 .01
❑ 564 Darren Lewis FUDC .05 .01
❑ 565 Fred McGriff .15 .05
❑ 566 Kevin Appier .10 .02
❑ 567 Luis Gonzalez RC .75 .30
❑ 568 Frank White .10 .02
❑ 560 Juan Agosto .05 .01
❑ 570 Mike Macfarlane .05 .01
❑ 571 Bert Blyleven .10 .02
❑ 572 Ken Griffey Sr./Jr. .25 .08
❑ 573 Lee Stevens .05 .01
❑ 574 Edgar Martinez .15 .05
❑ 575 Wally Joyner .10 .02
❑ 576 Tim Belcher .05 .01
❑ 577 John Burkett .05 .01
❑ 578 Mike Morgan .05 .01
❑ 579 Paul Gibson .05 .01
❑ 580 Jose Vizcaino .05 .01
❑ 581 Duane Ward .05 .01
❑ 582 Scott Sanderson .05 .01
❑ 583 David Wells .10 .02
❑ 584 Willie McGee .10 .02
❑ 585 John Cerutti .05 .01
❑ 586 Danny Darwin .05 .01
❑ 587 Kurt Stillwell .05 .01
❑ 588 Rich Gedman .05 .01
❑ 589 Mark Davis .05 .01
❑ 590 Bill Gullickson .05 .01
❑ 591 Matt Young .05 .01
❑ 592 Bryan Harvey .05 .01
❑ 593 Omar Vizquel .15 .05
❑ 594 Scott Lewis RC .10 .02
❑ 595 Dave Valle .05 .01
❑ 596 Tim Crews .05 .01
❑ 597 Mike Bielecki .05 .01
❑ 598 Mike Sharperson .05 .01
❑ 599 Dave Bergman .05 .01

❑ 600 Checklist 501-600 .05 .01
❑ 601 Steve Lyons .05 .01
❑ 602 Bruce Hurst .05 .01
❑ 603 Donn Pall .05 .01
❑ 604 Jim Vatcher RC .05 .01
❑ 605 Dan Pasqua .05 .01
❑ 606 Kenny Rogers .10 .02
❑ 607 Jeff Schulz RC .05 .01
❑ 608 Brad Arnsberg .05 .01
❑ 609 Willie Wilson .05 .01
❑ 610 Jamie Moyer .10 .02
❑ 611 Ron Oester .05 .01
❑ 612 Dennis Cook .05 .01
❑ 613 Rick Mahler .05 .01
❑ 614 Bill Landrum .05 .01
❑ 615 Scott Scudder .05 .01
❑ 616 Tom Edens RC .05 .01
❑ 617 1917 Revisited .10 .02
❑ 618 Jim Gantner .05 .01
❑ 619 Darrel Akerfelds .05 .01
❑ 620 Ron Robinson .05 .01
❑ 621 Scott Radinsky .05 .01
❑ 622 Pete Smith .05 .01
❑ 623 Melido Perez .05 .01
❑ 624 Jerald Clark .05 .01
❑ 625 Carlos Martinez .05 .01
❑ 626 Wes Chamberlain RC .25 .08
❑ 627 Bobby Witt .05 .01
❑ 628 Ken Dayley .05 .01
❑ 629 John Barfield .05 .01
❑ 630 Bob Tewksbury .05 .01
❑ 631 Glenn Braggs .05 .01
❑ 632 Jim Neidlinger RC .05 .01
❑ 633 Tom Browning .05 .01
❑ 634 Kirk Gibson .10 .02
❑ 635 Rob Dibble .10 .02
❑ 636 R.Henderson/L.Brock .25 .08
❑ 636A R.Henderson/L.Brock .25 .08
❑ 637 Jeff Montgomery .05 .01
❑ 638 Mike Schooler .05 .01
❑ 639 Storm Davis .05 .01
❑ 640 Rich Rodriguez RC .05 .01
❑ 641 Phil Bradley .05 .01
❑ 642 Kent Mercker .05 .01
❑ 643 Carlton Fisk .15 .05
❑ 644 Mike Bell RC .05 .01
❑ 645 Alex Fernandez .05 .01
❑ 646 Juan Gonzalez .25 .08
❑ 647 Ken Hill .05 .01
❑ 648 Jeff Russell .05 .01
❑ 649 Chuck Malone .05 .01
❑ 650 Steve Buechele .05 .01
❑ 651 Mike Benjamin .05 .01
❑ 652 Tony Pena .05 .01
❑ 653 Trevor Wilson .05 .01
❑ 654 Alex Cole .05 .01
❑ 655 Roger Clemens .75 .30
❑ 656 Mark McGwire BASH .40 .15
❑ 657 Joe Grahe RC .10 .02
❑ 658 Jim Eisenreich .05 .01
❑ 659 Dan Gladden .05 .01
❑ 660 Steve Farr .05 .01
❑ 661 Bill Sampen .05 .01
❑ 662 Dave Rohde .05 .01
❑ 663 Mark Gardner .05 .01
❑ 664 Mike Simms RC .05 .01
❑ 665 Moises Alou .10 .02
❑ 666 Mickey Hatcher .05 .01
❑ 667 Jimmy Key .10 .02
❑ 668 John Wetteland .10 .02
❑ 669 John Smiley .05 .01
❑ 670 Jim Acker .05 .01
❑ 671 Pascual Perez .05 .01
❑ 672 Reggie Harris UER .05 .01
❑ 673 Matt Nokes .05 .01
❑ 674 Rafael Novoa RC .05 .01
❑ 675 Hensley Meulens .05 .01
❑ 676 Jeff M. Robinson .05 .01
❑ 677 C.Fisk/R.Ventura .10 .02
❑ 678 Johnny Ray .05 .01
❑ 679 Greg Hibbard .05 .01
❑ 680 Paul Sorrento .05 .01
❑ 681 Mike Marshall .05 .01
❑ 682 Jim Clancy .05 .01
❑ 683 Rob Murphy .05 .01
❑ 684 Dave Schmidt .05 .01
❑ 685 Jeff Gray RC .05 .01
❑ 686 Mike Hartley .05 .01
❑ 687 Jeff King .05 .01
❑ 688 Stan Javier .05 .01
❑ 689 Bob Walk .05 .01
❑ 690 Jim Gott .05 .01
❑ 691 Mike LaCoss .05 .01
❑ 692 John Farrell .05 .01
❑ 693 Tim Leary .05 .01
❑ 694 Mike Walker .05 .01
❑ 695 Eric Plunk .05 .01
❑ 696 Mike Fetters .05 .01
❑ 697 Wayne Edwards .05 .01
❑ 698 Tim Drummond .05 .01
❑ 699 Willie Fraser .05 .01
❑ 700 Checklist 601-700 .05 .01
❑ 701 Mike Heath .05 .01
❑ 702 J.Bagwell/L.Gonz/K.Rhodes 1.00 .40
❑ 703 Jose Mesa .05 .01
❑ 704 Dave Smith .05 .01
❑ 705 Danny Darwin .05 .01
❑ 706 Rafael Belliard .05 .01
❑ 707 Rob Murphy .05 .01
❑ 708 Terry Pendleton .10 .02
❑ 709 Mike Pagliarulo .05 .01
❑ 710 Sid Bream .05 .01
❑ 711 Junior Felix .05 .01
❑ 712 Dante Bichette .10 .02
❑ 713 Kevin Gross .05 .01
❑ 714 Luis Sojo .05 .01
❑ 715 Bob Ojeda .05 .01
❑ 716 Julio Machado .05 .01
❑ 717 Steve Farr .05 .01
❑ 718 Franklin Stubbs .05 .01
❑ 719 Mike Boddicker .05 .01
❑ 720 Willie Randolph .10 .02
❑ 721 Willie McGee .10 .02
❑ 722 Chili Davis .10 .02
❑ 723 Danny Jackson .05 .01
❑ 724 Cory Snyder .05 .01
❑ 725 Dawson/Bell/Sandberg .25 .08
❑ 726 Rob Deer .05 .01
❑ 727 Rich DeLucia RC .05 .01
❑ 728 Mike Perez RC .10 .02
❑ 729 Mickey Tettleton .05 .01
❑ 730 Mike Blowers .05 .01
❑ 731 Gary Gaetti .10 .02
❑ 732 Brett Butler .10 .02
❑ 733 Dave Parker .10 .02
❑ 734 Eddie Zosky .05 .01
❑ 735 Jack Clark .10 .02
❑ 736 Jack Morris .10 .02
❑ 737 Kirk Gibson .10 .02
❑ 738 Steve Bedrosian .05 .01
❑ 739 Candy Maldonado .05 .01
❑ 740 Matt Young .05 .01
❑ 741 Rich Garces RC .10 .02
❑ 742 George Bell .05 .01
❑ 743 Deion Sanders .15 .05
❑ 744 Bo Jackson .25 .08
❑ 745 Luis Mercedes RC .10 .02
❑ 746 Reggie Jefferson .05 .01
❑ 747 Pete Incaviglia .05 .01
❑ 748 Chris Hammond .05 .01
❑ 749 Mike Stanton .05 .01
❑ 750 Scott Sanderson .05 .01
❑ 751 Paul Faries RC .05 .01
❑ 752 Al Osuna RC .05 .01
❑ 753 Steve Chitren RC .05 .01
❑ 754 Tony Fernandez .05 .01
❑ 755 Jeff Bagwell UER RC 2.00 .75
❑ 756 Kirk Dressendorfer RC .10 .02
❑ 757 Glenn Davis .05 .01
❑ 758 Gary Carter .10 .02
❑ 759 Zane Smith .05 .01
❑ 760 Vance Law .05 .01
❑ 761 Denis Boucher RC .10 .02
❑ 762 Turner Ward RC .10 .02
❑ 763 Roberto Alomar .15 .05
❑ 764 Albert Belle .10 .02
❑ 765 Joe Carter .10 .02
❑ 766 Pete Schourek RC .10 .02
❑ 767 Heathcliff Slocumb RC .10 .02
❑ 768 Vince Coleman .05 .01
❑ 769 Mitch Williams .05 .01
❑ 770 Brian Downing .05 .01
❑ 771 Dana Allison RC .05 .01
❑ 772 Pete Harnisch .05 .01
❑ 773 Tim Raines .10 .02
❑ 774 Darryl Kile .10 .02
❑ 775 Fred McGriff .15 .05
❑ 776 Dwight Evans .15 .05
❑ 777 Joe Slusarski RC .05 .01
❑ 778 Dave Righetti .10 .02
❑ 779 Jeff Hamilton .05 .01
❑ 780 Ernest Riles .05 .01
❑ 781 Ken Dayley .05 .01
❑ 782 Eric King .05 .01
❑ 783 Devon White .10 .02
❑ 784 Beau Allred .05 .01
❑ 785 Mike Timlin RC .25 .08
❑ 786 Ivan Calderon .05 .01
❑ 787 Hubie Brooks .05 .01
❑ 788 Juan Agosto .05 .01
❑ 789 Barry Jones .05 .01
❑ 790 Wally Backman .05 .01
❑ 791 Jim Presley .05 .01
❑ 792 Charlie Hough .10 .02
❑ 793 Larry Andersen .05 .01
❑ 794 Steve Finley .10 .02
❑ 795 Shawn Abner .05 .01
❑ 796 Jeff M. Robinson .05 .01
❑ 797 Joe Bitker RC .05 .01
❑ 798 Eric Show .05 .01
❑ 799 Bud Black .05 .01
❑ 800 Checklist 701-800 .05 .01
❑ HH1 Hank Aaron Hologram 1.50 .60
❑ SP1 Michael Jordan 8.00 3.00
❑ SP2 N.Ryan/R.Henderson 2.00 .75

1991 Upper Deck Final Edition

❑ COMP.FACT.SET (100) 10.00 4.00
❑ 1F R.Klesko/R.Sanders CL .25 .08
❑ 2F Pedro Martinez RC 8.00 3.00
❑ 3F Lance Dickson .05 .01
❑ 4F Royce Clayton .05 .01
❑ 5F Scott Bryant .05 .01
❑ 6F Dan Wilson RC .25 .08
❑ 7F Dmitri Young RC .75 .30
❑ 8F Ryan Klesko RC .50 .20
❑ 9F Tom Goodwin .05 .01
❑ 10F Rondell White RC .50 .20
❑ 11F Reggie Sanders .50 .20
❑ 12F Todd Van Poppel .05 .01
❑ 13F Arthur Rhodes RC .25 .08
❑ 14F Eddie Zosky .05 .01
❑ 15F Gerald Williams RC .25 .08
❑ 16F Robert Eenhoorn RC .10 .02
❑ 17F Jim Thome RC 4.00 1.50
❑ 18F Marc Newfield RC .10 .02
❑ 19F Kerwin Moore RC .10 .02
❑ 20F Jeff McNeely RC .10 .02
❑ 21F Frank Rodriguez RC .10 .02
❑ 22F Andy Mota RC .05 .01
❑ 23F Chris Haney RC .10 .02
❑ 24F Kenny Lofton RC .75 .30
❑ 25F Dave Nilsson RC .25 .08
❑ 26F Derek Bell .10 .02
❑ 27F Frank Castillo RC .25 .08
❑ 28F Candy Maldonado .05 .01
❑ 29F Chuck McElroy .05 .01
❑ 30F Chito Martinez RC .05 .01
❑ 31F Steve Howe .05 .01

❑ 32F Freddie Benavides RC .05 .01
❑ 33F Scott Kamieniecki RC .10 .02
❑ 34F Denny Neagle RC .25 .08
❑ 35F Mike Humphreys RC .10 .02
❑ 36F Mike Remlinger .05 .01
❑ 37F Scott Coolbaugh .05 .01
❑ 38F Darren Lewis .05 .01
❑ 39F Thomas Howard .05 .01
❑ 40F John Candelaria .05 .01
❑ 41F Todd Benzinger .05 .01
❑ 42F Wilson Alvarez .05 .01
❑ 43F Patrick Lennon RC .10 .02
❑ 44F Rusty Meacham RC .10 .02
❑ 45F Ryan Bowen RC .10 .02
❑ 46F Rick Wilkins RC .10 .02
❑ 47F Ed Sprague .05 .01
❑ 48F Bob Scanlan RC .05 .01
❑ 49F Tom Candiotti .05 .01
❑ 50F Dennis Martinez Perfect .10 .02
❑ 51F Oil Can Boyd .05 .01
❑ 52F Glenallen Hill .05 .01
❑ 53F Scott Livingstone RC .10 .02
❑ 54F Brian R.Hunter RC .25 .08
❑ 55F Ivan Rodriguez RC 2.00 .75
❑ 56F Keith Mitchell RC .10 .02
❑ 57F Roger McDowell .05 .01
❑ 58F Otis Nixon .05 .01
❑ 59F Juan Bell .05 .01
❑ 60F Bill Krueger .05 .01
❑ 61F Chris Donnels RC .05 .01
❑ 62F Tommy Greene .05 .01
❑ 63F Doug Simons RC .05 .01
❑ 64F Andy Ashby RC .25 .08
❑ 65F Anthony Young RC .10 .02
❑ 66F Kevin Morton RC .05 .01
❑ 67F Bret Barberie RC .10 .02
❑ 68F Scott Servais RC .25 .08
❑ 69F Ron Darling .05 .01
❑ 70F Tim Burke .05 .01
❑ 71F Vicente Palacios .05 .01
❑ 72F Gerald Alexander RC .05 .01
❑ 73F Reggie Jefferson .05 .01
❑ 74F Dean Palmer .10 .02
❑ 75F Mark Whiten .05 .01
❑ 76F Randy Tomlin RC .10 .02
❑ 77F Mark Wohlers RC .25 .08
❑ 78F Brook Jacoby .05 .01
❑ 79F K.Griffey Jr./R.Sandberg CL .40 .15
❑ 80F Jack Morris AS .05 .01
❑ 81F Sandy Alomar Jr. AS .05 .01
❑ 82F Cecil Fielder AS .05 .01
❑ 83F Roberto Alomar AS .10 .02
❑ 84F Wade Boggs AS .10 .02
❑ 85F Cal Ripken AS .40 .15
❑ 86F Rickey Henderson AS .15 .05
❑ 87F Ken Griffey Jr. AS .25 .08
❑ 88F Dave Henderson AS .05 .01
❑ 89F Danny Tartabull AS .05 .01
❑ 90F Tom Glavine AS .10 .02
❑ 91F Benito Santiago AS .05 .01
❑ 92F Will Clark AS .10 .02
❑ 93F Ryne Sandberg AS .25 .08
❑ 94F Chris Sabo AS .05 .01
❑ 95F Ozzie Smith AS .25 .08
❑ 96F Ivan Calderon AS .05 .01
❑ 97F Tony Gwynn AS .15 .05
❑ 98F Andre Dawson AS .05 .01
❑ 99F Bobby Bonilla AS .05 .01
❑ 100F Checklist 1-100 .05 .01

1992 Upper Deck

❑ COMPLETE SET (800) 25.00 10.00
❑ COMPLETE LO SET (700) 20.00 8.00
❑ COMPLETE HI SET (100) 5.00 2.00
❑ 1 J.Thome/R.Klesko CL .25 .08
❑ 2 Royce Clayton SR .05 .01
❑ 3 Brian Jordan RC .50 .20
❑ 4 Dave Fleming .05 .01
❑ 5 Jim Thome .25 .08
❑ 6 Jeff Juden SR .05 .01
❑ 7 Roberto Hernandez SR .05 .01
❑ 8 Kyle Abbott SR .05 .01
❑ 9 Chris George SR .05 .01
❑ 10 Rob Maurer SR .05 .01
❑ 11 Donald Harris SR .05 .01
❑ 12 Ted Wood SR .05 .01
❑ 13 Patrick Lennon SR .05 .01
❑ 14 Willie Banks SR .05 .01
❑ 15 Roger Salkeld SR UER
(Bill was his grand-
father .05 .01
❑ 16 Wil Cordero .05 .01
❑ 17 Arthur Rhodes SR .05 .01
❑ 18 Pedro Martinez 1.00 .40
❑ 19 Andy Ashby SR .05 .01
❑ 20 Tom Goodwin SR .05 .01
❑ 21 Braulio Castillo SR .05 .01
❑ 22 Todd Van Poppel .05 .01
❑ 23 Brian Williams RC .05 .01
❑ 24 Ryan Klesko .10 .02
❑ 25 Kenny Lofton .15 .05
❑ 26 Derek Bell .10 .02
❑ 27 Reggie Sanders .10 .02
❑ 28 Dave Winfield's 400th .05 .01
❑ 29 David Justice TC .05 .01
❑ 30 Rob Dibble TC
Cincinnati Reds .05 .01
❑ 31 Craig Biggio TC .10 .02
❑ 32 Eddie Murray TC .15 .05
❑ 33 Fred McGriff TC .10 .02
❑ 34 Willie McGee TC
San Francisco Giants .05 .01
❑ 35 Shawon Dunston TC
Chicago Cubs .05 .01
❑ 36 Delino DeShields TC .05 .01
❑ 37 Howard Johnson TC
New York Mets .05 .01
❑ 38 John Kruk TC .05 .01
❑ 39 Doug Drabek TC
Pittsburgh Pirates .05 .01
❑ 40 Todd Zeile TC .05 .01
❑ 41 Steve Avery Playoff .05 .01
❑ 42 Jeremy Hernandez RC .05 .01
❑ 43 Doug Henry RC .10 .02
❑ 44 Chris Donnels .05 .01
❑ 45 Mo Sanford .05 .01
❑ 46 Scott Kamieniecki .05 .01
❑ 47 Mark Lemke .05 .01
❑ 48 Steve Farr .05 .01
❑ 49 Francisco Oliveras .05 .01
❑ 50 Ced Landrum .05 .01
❑ 51 R.White/M.Newfield CL .10 .02
❑ 52 Eduardo Perez RC .25 .08
❑ 53 Tom Nevers TP .05 .01
❑ 54 David Zancanaro TP .05 .01
❑ 55 Shawn Green RC 1.00 .40
❑ 56 Mark Wohlers TP .05 .01
❑ 57 Dave Nilsson .05 .01
❑ 58 Dmitri Young .10 .02
❑ 59 Ryan Hawblitzel RC .10 .02
❑ 60 Raul Mondesi .10 .02
❑ 61 Rondell White .10 .02
❑ 62 Steve Hosey .05 .01
❑ 63 Manny Ramirez RC 4.00 1.50
❑ 64 Marc Newfield .05 .01
❑ 65 Jeromy Burnitz .10 .02
❑ 66 Mark Smith RC .10 .02
❑ 67 Joey Hamilton RC .10 .02
❑ 68 Tyler Green RC .10 .02
❑ 69 Jon Farrell RC .10 .02
❑ 70 Kurt Miller TP .05 .01
❑ 71 Jeff Plympton TP .05 .01
❑ 72 Dan Wilson TP .05 .01
❑ 73 Joe Vitiello RC .10 .02
❑ 74 Rico Brogna TP .05 .01
❑ 75 David McCarty RC .25 .08
❑ 76 Bob Wickman .25 .08
❑ 77 Carlos Rodriguez TP .05 .01
❑ 78 Jim Abbott
Stay In School .10 .02
❑ 79 P.Martinez/R.Martinez .25 .08
❑ 80 Kevin Mitchell
Keith Mitchell .05 .01
❑ 81 Sandy/Roberto Alomar .10 .02
❑ 82 Ripken Brothers .50 .20
❑ 83 Tony/Chris Gwynn .15 .05
❑ 84 D.Gooden/G.Sheffield .10 .02
❑ 85 K.Griffey Jr. w/Family .25 .08
❑ 86 Jim Abbott TC
California Angels .10 .02
❑ 87 Frank Thomas TC .15 .05
❑ 88 Danny Tartabull TC
Kansas City Royals .05 .01
❑ 89 Scott Erickson TC
Minnesota Twins .05 .01
❑ 90 Rickey Henderson TC .15 .05
❑ 91 Edgar Martinez TC .10 .02
❑ 92 Nolan Ryan TC .50 .20
❑ 93 Ben McDonald TC
Baltimore Orioles .05 .01
❑ 94 Ellis Burks TC
Boston Red Sox .05 .01
❑ 95 Greg Swindell TC
Cleveland Indians .05 .01
❑ 96 Cecil Fielder TC .05 .01
❑ 97 Greg Vaughn TC .05 .01
❑ 98 Kevin Maas TC
New York Yankees .05 .01
❑ 99 Dave Stieb TC
Toronto Blue Jays .05 .01
❑ 100 Checklist 1-100 .05 .01
❑ 101 Joe Oliver .05 .01
❑ 102 Hector Villanueva .05 .01
❑ 103 Ed Whitson .05 .01
❑ 104 Danny Jackson .05 .01
❑ 105 Chris Hammond .05 .01
❑ 106 Ricky Jordan .05 .01
❑ 107 Kevin Bass .05 .01
❑ 108 Darrin Fletcher .05 .01
❑ 109 Junior Ortiz .05 .01
❑ 110 Tom Bolton .05 .01
❑ 111 Jeff King .05 .01
❑ 112 Dave Magadan .05 .01
❑ 113 Mike LaValliere .05 .01
❑ 114 Hubie Brooks .05 .01
❑ 115 Jay Bell .10 .02
❑ 116 David Wells .10 .02
❑ 117 Jim Leyritz .05 .01
❑ 118 Manuel Lee .05 .01
❑ 119 Alvaro Espinoza .05 .01
❑ 120 B.J. Surhoff .10 .02
❑ 121 Hal Morris .05 .01
❑ 122 Shawon Dawson .05 .01
❑ 123 Chris Sabo .05 .01
❑ 124 Andre Dawson .10 .02
❑ 125 Eric Davis .10 .02
❑ 126 Chili Davis .10 .02
❑ 127 Dale Murphy .15 .05
❑ 128 Kirk McCaskill .05 .01
❑ 129 Terry Mulholland .05 .01
❑ 130 Rick Aguilera .10 .02
❑ 131 Vince Coleman .05 .01
❑ 132 Andy Van Slyke .15 .05
❑ 133 Gregg Jefferies .05 .01
❑ 134 Barry Bonds 1.00 .40
❑ 135 Dwight Gooden .10 .02
❑ 136 Dave Stieb .05 .01
❑ 137 Albert Belle .10 .02
❑ 138 Teddy Higuera .05 .01
❑ 139 Jesse Barfield .05 .01
❑ 140 Pat Borders .05 .01
❑ 141 Bip Roberts .05 .01
❑ 142 Rob Dibble .10 .02
❑ 143 Mark Grace .15 .05
❑ 144 Barry Larkin .15 .05
❑ 145 Ryne Sandberg .40 .15
❑ 146 Scott Erickson .05 .01
❑ 147 Luis Polonia .05 .01
❑ 148 John Burkett .05 .01

❑	149	Luis Sojo	.05	.01
❑	150	Dickie Thon	.05	.01
❑	151	Walt Weiss	.05	.01
❑	152	Mike Scioscia	.05	.01
❑	153	Mark McGwire	.60	.25
❑	154	Matt Williams	.10	.02
❑	155	Rickey Henderson	.25	.08
❑	156	Sandy Alomar Jr.	.05	.01
❑	157	Brian McRae	.05	.01
❑	158	Harold Baines	.10	.02
❑	159	Kevin Appier	.10	.02
❑	160	Felix Fermin	.05	.01
❑	161	Leo Gomez	.05	.01
❑	162	Craig Biggio	.15	.05
❑	163	Ben McDonald	.05	.01
❑	164	Randy Johnson	.25	.08
❑	165	Cal Ripken	.75	.30
❑	166	Frank Thomas	.25	.08
❑	167	Delino DeShields	.05	.01
❑	168	Greg Gagne	.05	.01
❑	169	Ron Karkovice	.05	.01
❑	170	Charlie Leibrandt	.05	.01
❑	171	Dave Righetti	.10	.02
❑	172	Dave Henderson	.05	.01
❑	173	Steve Decker	.05	.01
❑	174	Darryl Strawberry	.10	.02
❑	175	Will Clark	.15	.05
❑	176	Ruben Sierra	.10	.02
❑	177	Ozzie Smith	.40	.15
❑	178	Charles Nagy	.05	.01
❑	179	Gary Pettis	.05	.01
❑	180	Kirk Gibson	.10	.02
❑	181	Randy Milligan	.05	.01
❑	182	Dave Valle	.05	.01
❑	183	Chris Hoiles	.05	.01
❑	184	Tony Phillips	.05	.01
❑	185	Brady Anderson	.10	.02
❑	186	Scott Fletcher	.05	.01
❑	187	Gene Larkin	.05	.01
❑	188	Lance Johnson	.05	.01
❑	189	Greg Olson	.05	.01
❑	190	Melido Perez	.05	.01
❑	191	Lenny Harris	.05	.01
❑	192	Terry Kennedy	.05	.01
❑	193	Mike Gallego	.05	.01
❑	194	Willie McGee	.10	.02
❑	195	Juan Samuel	.05	.01
❑	196	Jeff Huson	.10	.02
❑	197	Alex Cole	.05	.01
❑	198	Ron Robinson	.05	.01
❑	199	Joel Skinner	.05	.01
❑	200	Checklist 101-200	.05	.01
❑	201	Kevin Reimer	.05	.01
❑	202	Stan Belinda	.05	.01
❑	203	Pat Tabler	.05	.01
❑	204	Jose Guzman	.05	.01
❑	205	Jose Lind	.05	.01
❑	206	Spike Owen	.05	.01
❑	207	Joe Orsulak	.05	.01
❑	208	Charlie Hayes	.05	.01
❑	209	Mike Devereaux	.05	.01
❑	210	Mike Fitzgerald	.05	.01
❑	211	Willie Randolph	.10	.02
❑	212	Rod Nichols	.05	.01
❑	213	Mike Boddicker	.05	.01
❑	214	Bill Spiers	.05	.01
❑	215	Steve Olin	.05	.01
❑	216	David Howard	.05	.01
❑	217	Gary Varsho	.05	.01
❑	218	Mike Harkey	.05	.01
❑	219	Luis Aquino	.05	.01
❑	220	Chuck McElroy	.05	.01
❑	221	Doug Drabek	.05	.01
❑	222	Dave Winfield	.10	.02
❑	223	Rafael Palmeiro	.15	.05
❑	224	Joe Carter	.10	.02
❑	225	Bobby Bonilla	.10	.02
❑	226	Ivan Calderon	.05	.01
❑	227	Gregg Olson	.05	.01
❑	228	Tim Wallach	.05	.01
❑	229	Terry Pendleton	.10	.02
❑	230	Gilberto Reyes	.05	.01
❑	231	Carlos Baerga	.05	.01
❑	232	Greg Vaughn	.05	.01
❑	233	Bret Saberhagen	.10	.02
❑	234	Gary Sheffield	.10	.02
❑	235	Mark Lewis	.05	.01
❑	236	George Bell	.05	.01
❑	237	Danny Tartabull	.05	.01
❑	238	Willie Wilson	.05	.01
❑	239	Doug Dascenzo	.05	.01
❑	240	Bill Pecota	.05	.01
❑	241	Julio Franco	.10	.02
❑	242	Ed Sprague	.05	.01
❑	243	Juan Gonzalez	.15	.05
❑	244	Chuck Finley	.10	.02
❑	245	Ivan Rodriguez	.25	.08
❑	246	Len Dykstra	.10	.02
❑	247	Deion Sanders	.15	.05
❑	248	Dwight Evans	.15	.05
❑	249	Larry Walker	.15	.05
❑	250	Billy Ripken	.05	.01
❑	251	Mickey Tettleton	.05	.01
❑	252	Tony Pena	.05	.01
❑	253	Benito Santiago	.10	.02
❑	254	Kirby Puckett	.25	.08
❑	255	Cecil Fielder	.10	.02
❑	256	Howard Johnson	.05	.01
❑	257	Andujar Cedeno	.05	.01
❑	258	Jose Rijo	.05	.01
❑	259	Al Osuna	.05	.01
❑	260	Todd Hundley	.05	.01
❑	261	Orel Hershiser	.10	.02
❑	262	Ray Lankford	.10	.02
❑	263	Robin Ventura	.10	.02
❑	264	Felix Jose	.05	.01
❑	265	Eddie Murray	.25	.08
❑	266	Kevin Mitchell	.05	.01
❑	267	Gary Carter	.10	.02
❑	268	Mike Benjamin	.05	.01
❑	269	Dick Schofield	.05	.01
❑	270	Jose Uribe	.05	.01
❑	271	Pete Incaviglia	.05	.01
❑	272	Tony Fernandez	.05	.01
❑	273	Alan Trammell	.10	.02
❑	274	Tony Gwynn	.30	.10
❑	275	Mike Greenwell	.05	.01
❑	276	Jeff Bagwell	.25	.08
❑	277	Frank Viola	.10	.02
❑	278	Randy Myers	.05	.01
❑	279	Ken Caminiti	.10	.02
❑	280	Bill Doran	.05	.01
❑	281	Dan Pasqua	.05	.01
❑	282	Alfredo Griffin	.05	.01
❑	283	Jose Oquendo	.05	.01
❑	284	Kal Daniels	.05	.01
❑	285	Bobby Thigpen	.05	.01
❑	286	Robby Thompson	.05	.01
❑	287	Mark Eichhorn	.05	.01
❑	288	Mike Felder	.05	.01
❑	289	Dave Gallagher	.05	.01
❑	290	Dave Anderson	.05	.01
❑	291	Mel Hall	.05	.01
❑	292	Jerald Clark	.05	.01
❑	293	Al Newman	.05	.01
❑	294	Rob Deer	.05	.01
❑	295	Matt Nokes	.05	.01
❑	296	Jack Armstrong	.05	.01
❑	297	Jim Deshaies	.05	.01
❑	298	Jeff Innis	.05	.01
❑	299	Jeff Reed	.05	.01
❑	300	Checklist 201-300	.05	.01
❑	301	Lonnie Smith	.05	.01
❑	302	Jimmy Key	.10	.02
❑	303	Junior Felix	.05	.01
❑	304	Mike Heath	.05	.01
❑	305	Mark Langston	.05	.01
❑	306	Greg W. Harris	.05	.01
❑	307	Brett Butler	.10	.02
❑	308	Luis Rivera	.05	.01
❑	309	Bruce Ruffin	.05	.01
❑	310	Paul Faries	.05	.01
❑	311	Terry Leach	.05	.01
❑	312	Scott Brosius RC	.50	.20
❑	313	Scott Leius	.05	.01
❑	314	Harold Reynolds	.10	.02
❑	315	Jack Morris	.10	.02
❑	316	David Segui	.05	.01
❑	317	Bill Gullickson	.05	.01
❑	318	Todd Frohwirth	.05	.01
❑	319	Mark Leiter	.05	.01
❑	320	Jeff M. Robinson	.05	.01
❑	321	Gary Gaetti	.10	.02
❑	322	John Smoltz	.15	.05
❑	323	Andy Benes	.05	.01
❑	324	Kelly Gruber	.05	.01
❑	325	Jim Abbott	.15	.05
❑	326	John Kruk	.10	.02
❑	327	Kevin Seitzer	.05	.01
❑	328	Darrin Jackson	.05	.01
❑	329	Kurt Stillwell	.05	.01
❑	330	Mike Maddux	.05	.01
❑	331	Dennis Eckersley	.10	.02
❑	332	Dan Gladden	.05	.01
❑	333	Jose Canseco	.15	.05
❑	334	Kent Hrbek	.10	.02
❑	335	Ken Griffey Sr.	.10	.02
❑	336	Greg Swindell	.05	.01
❑	337	Trevor Wilson	.05	.01
❑	338	Sam Horn	.05	.01
❑	339	Mike Henneman	.05	.01
❑	340	Jerry Browne	.05	.01
❑	341	Glenn Braggs	.05	.01
❑	342	Tom Glavine	.15	.05
❑	343	Wally Joyner	.10	.02
❑	344	Fred McGriff	.15	.05
❑	345	Ron Gant	.10	.02
❑	346	Ramon Martinez	.05	.01
❑	347	Wes Chamberlain	.05	.01
❑	348	Terry Shumpert	.05	.01
❑	349	Tim Teufel	.05	.01
❑	350	Wally Backman	.05	.01
❑	351	Joe Girardi	.05	.01
❑	352	Devon White	.10	.02
❑	353	Greg Maddux	.40	.15
❑	354	Ryan Bowen	.05	.01
❑	355	Roberto Alomar	.15	.05
❑	356	Don Mattingly	.60	.25
❑	357	Pedro Guerrero	.10	.02
❑	358	Steve Sax	.05	.01
❑	359	Joey Cora	.05	.01
❑	360	Jim Gantner	.05	.01
❑	361	Brian Barnes	.05	.01
❑	362	Kevin McReynolds	.05	.01
❑	363	Bret Barberie	.05	.01
❑	364	David Cone	.10	.02
❑	365	Dennis Martinez	.10	.02
❑	366	Brian Hunter	.05	.01
❑	367	Edgar Martinez	.15	.05
❑	368	Steve Finley	.10	.02
❑	369	Greg Briley	.05	.01
❑	370	Jeff Blauser	.05	.01
❑	371	Todd Stottlemyre	.05	.01
❑	372	Luis Gonzalez	.10	.02
❑	373	Rick Wilkins	.05	.01
❑	374	Darryl Kile	.10	.02
❑	375	John Olerud	.10	.02
❑	376	Lee Smith	.10	.02
❑	377	Kevin Maas	.05	.01
❑	378	Dante Bichette	.10	.02
❑	379	Tom Pagnozzi	.05	.01
❑	380	Mike Flanagan	.05	.01
❑	381	Charlie O'Brien	.05	.01
❑	382	Dave Martinez	.05	.01
❑	383	Keith Miller	.05	.01
❑	384	Scott Ruskin	.05	.01
❑	385	Kevin Elster	.05	.01
❑	386	Alvin Davis	.05	.01
❑	387	Casey Candaele	.05	.01
❑	388	Pete O'Brien	.05	.01
❑	389	Jeff Treadway	.05	.01
❑	390	Scott Bradley	.05	.01
❑	391	Mookie Wilson	.10	.02
❑	392	Jimmy Jones	.05	.01
❑	393	Candy Maldonado	.05	.01
❑	394	Eric Yelding	.05	.01
❑	395	Tom Henke	.05	.01
❑	396	Franklin Stubbs	.05	.01
❑	397	Milt Thompson	.05	.01
❑	398	Mark Carreon	.05	.01
❑	399	Randy Velarde	.05	.01
❑	400	Checklist 301-400	.05	.01
❑	401	Omar Vizquel	.15	.05
❑	402	Joe Boever	.05	.01
❑	403	Bill Krueger	.05	.01
❑	404	Jody Reed	.05	.01
❑	405	Mike Schooler	.05	.01
❑	406	Jason Grimsley	.05	.01

❑ 407 Greg Myers .05 .01
❑ 408 Randy Ready .05 .01
❑ 409 Mike Timlin .05 .01
❑ 410 Mitch Williams .05 .01
❑ 411 Garry Templeton .05 .01
❑ 412 Greg Cadaret .05 .01
❑ 413 Donnie Hill .05 .01
❑ 414 Wally Whitehurst .05 .01
❑ 415 Scott Sanderson .05 .01
❑ 416 Thomas Howard .05 .01
❑ 417 Neal Heaton .05 .01
❑ 418 Charlie Hough .10 .02
❑ 419 Jack Howell .05 .01
❑ 420 Greg Hibbard .05 .01
❑ 421 Carlos Quintana .05 .01
❑ 422 Kim Batiste .05 .01
❑ 423 Paul Molitor .10 .02
❑ 424 Ken Griffey Jr. .40 .15
❑ 425 Phil Plantier .05 .01
❑ 426 Denny Neagle .10 .02
❑ 427 Von Hayes .05 .01
❑ 428 Shane Mack .05 .01
❑ 429 Darren Daulton .10 .02
❑ 430 Dwayne Henry .05 .01
❑ 431 Lance Parrish .10 .02
❑ 432 Mike Humphreys .05 .01
❑ 433 Tim Burke .05 .01
❑ 434 Bryan Harvey .05 .01
❑ 435 Pat Kelly .05 .01
❑ 436 Ozzie Guillen .10 .02
❑ 437 Bruce Hurst .05 .01
❑ 438 Sammy Sosa .25 .08
❑ 439 Dennis Rasmussen .05 .01
❑ 440 Ken Patterson .05 .01
❑ 441 Jay Buhner .10 .02
❑ 442 Pat Combs .05 .01
❑ 443 Wade Boggs .15 .05
❑ 444 George Brett .60 .25
❑ 445 Mo Vaughn .10 .02
❑ 446 Chuck Knoblauch .10 .02
❑ 447 Tom Candiotti .05 .01
❑ 448 Mark Portugal .05 .01
❑ 449 Mickey Morandini .05 .01
❑ 450 Duane Ward .05 .01
❑ 451 Otis Nixon .05 .01
❑ 452 Bob Welch .05 .01
❑ 453 Rusty Meacham .05 .01
❑ 454 Keith Mitchell .05 .01
❑ 455 Marquis Grissom .10 .02
❑ 456 Robin Yount .40 .15
❑ 457 Harvey Pulliam .05 .01
❑ 458 Jose DeLeon .05 .01
❑ 459 Mark Gubicza .05 .01
❑ 460 Darryl Hamilton .05 .01
❑ 461 Tom Browning .05 .01
❑ 462 Monty Fariss .05 .01
❑ 463 Jerome Walton .05 .01
❑ 464 Paul O'Neill .15 .05
❑ 465 Dean Palmer .10 .02
❑ 466 Travis Fryman .10 .02
❑ 467 John Smiley .05 .01
❑ 468 Lloyd Moseby .05 .01
❑ 469 John Wehner .05 .01
❑ 470 Skeeter Barnes .05 .01
❑ 471 Steve Chitren .05 .01
❑ 472 Kent Mercker .05 .01
❑ 473 Terry Steinbach .05 .01
❑ 474 Andres Galarraga .10 .02
❑ 475 Steve Avery .05 .01
❑ 476 Tom Gordon .05 .01
❑ 477 Cal Eldred .05 .01
❑ 478 Omar Olivares .05 .01
❑ 479 Julio Machado .05 .01
❑ 480 Bob Milacki .05 .01
❑ 481 Les Lancaster .05 .01
❑ 482 John Candelaria .05 .01
❑ 483 Brian Downing .05 .01
❑ 484 Roger McDowell .05 .01
❑ 485 Scott Scudder .05 .01
❑ 486 Zane Smith .05 .01
❑ 487 John Cerutti .05 .01
❑ 488 Steve Buechele .05 .01
❑ 489 Paul Gibson .05 .01
❑ 490 Curtis Wilkerson .05 .01
❑ 491 Marvin Freeman .05 .01
❑ 492 Tom Foley .05 .01
❑ 493 Juan Berenguer .05 .01
❑ 494 Ernest Riles .05 .01
❑ 495 Sid Bream .05 .01
❑ 496 Chuck Crim .05 .01
❑ 497 Mike Macfarlane .05 .01
❑ 498 Dale Sveum .05 .01
❑ 499 Storm Davis .05 .01
❑ 500 Checklist 401-500 .05 .01
❑ 501 Jeff Reardon .10 .02
❑ 502 Shawn Abner .05 .01
❑ 503 Tony Fossas .05 .01
❑ 504 Cory Snyder .05 .01
❑ 505 Matt Young .05 .01
❑ 506 Allan Anderson .05 .01
❑ 507 Mark Lee .05 .01
❑ 508 Gene Nelson .05 .01
❑ 509 Mike Pagliarulo .05 .01
❑ 510 Rafael Belliard .05 .01
❑ 511 Jay Howell .05 .01
❑ 512 Bob Tewksbury .05 .01
❑ 513 Mike Morgan .05 .01
❑ 514 John Franco .10 .02
❑ 515 Kevin Gross .05 .01
❑ 516 Lou Whitaker .10 .02
❑ 517 Orlando Merced .05 .01
❑ 518 Todd Benzinger .05 .01
❑ 519 Gary Redus .05 .01
❑ 520 Walt Terrell .05 .01
❑ 521 Jack Clark .10 .02
❑ 522 Dave Parker .10 .02
❑ 523 Tim Naehring .05 .01
❑ 524 Mark Whiten .05 .01
❑ 525 Ellis Burks .10 .02
❑ 526 Frank Castillo .05 .01
❑ 527 Brian Harper .05 .01
❑ 528 Brook Jacoby .05 .01
❑ 529 Rick Sutcliffe .10 .02
❑ 530 Joe Klink .05 .01
❑ 531 Terry Bross .05 .01
❑ 532 Jose Offerman .05 .01
❑ 533 Todd Zeile .05 .01
❑ 534 Eric Karros .10 .02
❑ 535 Anthony Young .05 .01
❑ 536 Milt Cuyler .05 .01
❑ 537 Randy Tomlin .05 .01
❑ 538 Scott Livingstone .05 .01
❑ 539 Jim Eisenreich .05 .01
❑ 540 Don Slaught .05 .01
❑ 541 Scott Cooper .05 .01
❑ 542 Joe Grahe .05 .01
❑ 543 Tom Brunansky .05 .01
❑ 544 Eddie Zosky .05 .01
❑ 545 Roger Clemens .50 .20
❑ 546 David Justice .10 .02
❑ 547 Dave Stewart .10 .02
❑ 548 David West .05 .01
❑ 549 Dave Smith .05 .01
❑ 550 Dan Plesac .05 .01
❑ 551 Alex Fernandez .05 .01
❑ 552 Bernard Gilkey .05 .01
❑ 553 Jack McDowell .05 .01
❑ 554 Tino Martinez .15 .05
❑ 555 Bo Jackson .25 .08
❑ 556 Bernie Williams .15 .05
❑ 557 Mark Gardner .05 .01
❑ 558 Glenallen Hill .05 .01
❑ 559 Oil Can Boyd .05 .01
❑ 560 Chris James .05 .01
❑ 561 Scott Servais .05 .01
❑ 562 Rey Sanchez RC .25 .08
❑ 563 Paul McClellan .05 .01
❑ 564 Andy Mota .05 .01
❑ 565 Darren Lewis .05 .01
❑ 566 Jose Melendez .05 .01
❑ 567 Tommy Greene .05 .01
❑ 568 Rich Rodriguez .05 .01
❑ 569 Heathcliff Slocumb .05 .01
❑ 570 Joe Hesketh .05 .01
❑ 571 Carlton Fisk .15 .05
❑ 572 Erik Hanson .05 .01
❑ 573 Wilson Alvarez .05 .01
❑ 574 Rheal Cormier .05 .01
❑ 575 Tim Raines .10 .02
❑ 576 Bobby Witt .05 .01
❑ 577 Roberto Kelly .05 .01
❑ 578 Kevin Brown .10 .02
❑ 579 Chris Nabholz .05 .01
❑ 580 Jesse Orosco .05 .01
❑ 581 Jeff Brantley .05 .01
❑ 582 Rafael Ramirez .05 .01
❑ 583 Kelly Downs .05 .01
❑ 584 Mike Simms .05 .01
❑ 585 Mike Remlinger .05 .01
❑ 586 Dave Hollins .05 .01
❑ 587 Larry Andersen .05 .01
❑ 588 Mike Gardiner .05 .01
❑ 589 Craig Lefferts .05 .01
❑ 590 Paul Assenmacher .05 .01
❑ 591 Bryn Smith .05 .01
❑ 592 Donn Pall .05 .01
❑ 593 Mike Jackson .05 .01
❑ 594 Scott Radinsky .05 .01
❑ 595 Brian Holman .05 .01
❑ 596 Geronimo Pena .05 .01
❑ 597 Mike Jeffcoat .05 .01
❑ 598 Carlos Martinez .05 .01
❑ 599 Geno Petralli .05 .01
❑ 600 Checklist 501-600 .05 .01
❑ 601 Jerry Don Gleaton .05 .01
❑ 602 Adam Peterson .05 .01
❑ 603 Craig Grebeck .05 .01
❑ 604 Mark Guthrie .05 .01
❑ 605 Frank Tanana .05 .01
❑ 606 Hensley Meulens .05 .01
❑ 607 Mark Davis .05 .01
❑ 608 Eric Plunk .05 .01
❑ 609 Mark Williamson .05 .01
❑ 610 Lee Guetterman .05 .01
❑ 611 Bobby Rose .05 .01
❑ 612 Bill Wegman .05 .01
❑ 613 Mike Hartley .05 .01
❑ 614 Chris Beasley .05 .01
❑ 615 Chris Bosio .05 .01
❑ 616 Henry Cotto .05 .01
❑ 617 Chico Walker .05 .01
❑ 618 Russ Swan .05 .01
❑ 619 Bob Walk .05 .01
❑ 620 Bill Swift .05 .01
❑ 621 Warren Newson .05 .01
❑ 622 Steve Bedrosian .05 .01
❑ 623 Ricky Bones .05 .01
❑ 624 Kevin Tapani .05 .01
❑ 625 Juan Guzman .05 .01
❑ 626 Jeff Johnson .05 .01
❑ 627 Jeff Montgomery .05 .01
❑ 628 Ken Hill .05 .01
❑ 629 Gary Thurman .05 .01
❑ 630 Steve Howe .05 .01
❑ 631 Jose DeJesus .05 .01
❑ 632 Kirk Dressendorfer .05 .01
❑ 633 Jaime Navarro .05 .01
❑ 634 Lee Stevens .05 .01
❑ 635 Pete Harnisch .05 .01
❑ 636 Bill Landrum .05 .01
❑ 637 Rich DeLucia .05 .01
❑ 638 Luis Salazar .05 .01
❑ 639 Rob Murphy .05 .01
❑ 640 J.Canseco/R.Henderson CL .15 .05
❑ 641 Roger Clemens DS .25 .08
❑ 642 Jim Abbott DS .10 .02
❑ 643 Travis Fryman DS .05 .01
❑ 644 Jesse Barfield DS .05 .01
❑ 645 Cal Ripken DS .40 .15
❑ 646 Wade Boggs DS .10 .02
❑ 647 Cecil Fielder DS .05 .01
❑ 648 Rickey Henderson DS .15 .05
❑ 649 Jose Canseco DS .10 .02
❑ 650 Ken Griffey Jr. DS .25 .08
❑ 651 Kenny Rogers .10 .02
❑ 652 Luis Mercedes .05 .01
❑ 653 Mike Stanton .05 .01
❑ 654 Glenn Davis .05 .01
❑ 655 Nolan Ryan 1.00 .40
❑ 656 Reggie Jefferson .05 .01
❑ 657 Javier Ortiz .05 .01
❑ 658 Greg A. Harris .05 .01
❑ 659 Mariano Duncan .05 .01
❑ 660 Jeff Shaw .05 .01
❑ 661 Mike Moore .05 .01
❑ 662 Chris Haney .05 .01
❑ 663 Joe Slusarski .05 .01
❑ 664 Wayne Housie .05 .01

❑ 665 Carlos Garcia .05 .01
❑ 666 Bob Ojeda .05 .01
❑ 667 Bryan Hickerson RC .10 .02
❑ 668 Tim Belcher .05 .01
❑ 669 Ron Darling .05 .01
❑ 670 Rex Hudler .05 .01
❑ 671 Sid Fernandez .05 .01
❑ 672 Chito Martinez .05 .01
❑ 673 Pete Schourek .05 .01
❑ 674 Armando Reynoso RC .25 .08
❑ 675 Mike Mussina .25 .08
❑ 676 Kevin Morton .05 .01
❑ 677 Norm Charlton .05 .01
❑ 678 Danny Darwin .05 .01
❑ 679 Eric King .05 .01
❑ 680 Ted Power .05 .01
❑ 681 Barry Jones .05 .01
❑ 682 Carney Lansford .10 .02
❑ 683 Mel Rojas .05 .01
❑ 684 Rick Honeycutt .05 .01
❑ 685 Jeff Fassero .05 .01
❑ 686 Cris Carpenter .05 .01
❑ 687 Tim Crews .05 .01
❑ 688 Scott Terry .05 .01
❑ 689 Chris Gwynn .05 .01
❑ 690 Gerald Perry .05 .01
❑ 691 John Barfield .05 .01
❑ 692 Bob Melvin .05 .01
❑ 693 Juan Agosto .05 .01
❑ 694 Alejandro Pena .05 .01
❑ 695 Jeff Russell .05 .01
❑ 696 Carmelo Martinez .05 .01
❑ 697 Bud Black .05 .01
❑ 698 Dave Otto .05 .01
❑ 699 Billy Hatcher .05 .01
❑ 700 Checklist 601-700 .05 .01
❑ 701 Clemente Nunez RC .05 .01
❑ 702 M.Clark/Osborne/Jordan .05 .01
❑ 703 Mike Morgan .05 .01
❑ 704 Keith Miller .05 .01
❑ 705 Kurt Stillwell .05 .01
❑ 706 Damon Berryhill .05 .01
❑ 707 Von Hayes .05 .01
❑ 708 Rick Sutcliffe .10 .02
❑ 709 Hubie Brooks .05 .01
❑ 710 Ryan Turner RC .10 .02
❑ 711 B.Bonds/A.Van Slyke CL .50 .20
❑ 712 Jose Rijo DS .05 .01
❑ 713 Tom Glavine DS .10 .02
❑ 714 Shawon Dunston DS .05 .01
❑ 715 Andy Van Slyke DS .10 .02
❑ 716 Ozzie Smith DS .25 .08
❑ 717 Tony Gwynn DS .15 .05
❑ 718 Will Clark DS .10 .02
❑ 719 Marquis Grissom DS .05 .01
❑ 720 Howard Johnson DS .05 .01
❑ 721 Barry Bonds DS .50 .20
❑ 722 Kirk McCaskill .05 .01
❑ 723 Sammy Sosa Cubs .75 .30
❑ 724 George Bell .05 .01
❑ 725 Gregg Jefferies .05 .01
❑ 726 Gary DiSarcina .05 .01
❑ 727 Mike Bordick .05 .01
❑ 728 Eddie Murray 400 HR .15 .05
❑ 729 Rene Gonzales .05 .01
❑ 730 Mike Bielecki .05 .01
❑ 731 Calvin Jones .05 .01
❑ 732 Jack Morris .10 .02
❑ 733 Frank Viola .10 .02
❑ 734 Dave Winfield .10 .02
❑ 735 Kevin Mitchell .05 .01
❑ 736 Bill Swift .05 .01
❑ 737 Dan Gladden .05 .01
❑ 738 Mike Jackson .05 .01
❑ 739 Mark Carreon .05 .01
❑ 740 Kirt Manwaring .05 .01
❑ 741 Randy Myers .05 .01
❑ 742 Kevin McReynolds .05 .01
❑ 743 Steve Sax .05 .01
❑ 744 Wally Joyner .10 .02
❑ 745 Gary Sheffield .10 .02
❑ 746 Danny Tartabull .05 .01
❑ 747 Julio Valera .05 .01
❑ 748 Denny Neagle .10 .02
❑ 749 Lance Blankenship .05 .01
❑ 750 Mike Gallego .05 .01

❑ 751 Bret Saberhagen .10 .02
❑ 752 Ruben Amaro .05 .01
❑ 753 Eddie Murray .25 .08
❑ 754 Kyle Abbott .05 .01
❑ 755 Bobby Bonilla .10 .02
❑ 756 Eric Davis .10 .02
❑ 757 Eddie Taubensee RC .25 .08
❑ 758 Andres Galarraga .10 .02
❑ 759 Pete Incaviglia .05 .01
❑ 760 Tom Candiotti .05 .01
❑ 761 Tim Belcher .05 .01
❑ 762 Ricky Bones .05 .01
❑ 763 Bip Roberts .05 .01
❑ 764 Pedro Munoz .05 .01
❑ 765 Greg Swindell .05 .01
❑ 766 Kenny Lofton .15 .05
❑ 767 Gary Carter .10 .02
❑ 768 Charlie Hayes .05 .01
❑ 769 Dickie Thon .05 .01
❑ 770 Donovan Osborne DD CL .05 .01
❑ 771 Bret Boone .15 .05
❑ 772 Archi Cianfrocco RC .10 .02
❑ 773 Mark Clark RC .10 .02
❑ 774 Chad Curtis RC .25 .08
❑ 775 Pat Listach RC .25 .08
❑ 776 Pat Mahomes RC .25 .08
❑ 777 Donovan Osborne .05 .01
❑ 778 John Patterson RC .10 .02
❑ 779 Andy Stankiewicz DD .05 .01
❑ 780 Turk Wendell RC .25 .08
❑ 781 Bill Krueger .05 .01
❑ 782 Rickey Henderson 1000 .15 .05
❑ 783 Kevin Seitzer .05 .01
❑ 784 Dave Martinez .05 .01
❑ 785 John Smiley .05 .01
❑ 786 Matt Stairs RC .25 .08
❑ 787 Scott Scudder .05 .01
❑ 788 John Wetteland .10 .02
❑ 789 Jack Armstrong .05 .01
❑ 790 Ken Hill .05 .01
❑ 791 Dick Schofield .05 .01
❑ 792 Mariano Duncan .05 .01
❑ 793 Bill Pecota .05 .01
❑ 794 Mike Kelly RC .10 .02
❑ 795 Willie Randolph .10 .02
❑ 796 Butch Henry .05 .01
❑ 797 Carlos Hernandez .05 .01
❑ 798 Doug Jones .05 .01
❑ 799 Melido Perez .05 .01
❑ 800 Checklist 701-800 .05 .01
❑ HH2 Ted Williams Holo 2.00 .75
❑ SP3 Deion Sanders FB/BB 1.00 .40
❑ SP4 F.Thomas/T.Selleck 1.00 .40

1993 Upper Deck

❑ COMPLETE SET (840) 40.00 15.00
❑ COMP.FACT.SET (840) 50.00 20.00
❑ COMPLETE SERIES 1 (420) 15.00 6.00
❑ COMPLETE SERIES 2 (420) 25.00 10.00
❑ 1 Tim Salmon CL .20 .07
❑ 2 Mike Piazza 3.00 1.25
❑ 3 Rene Arocha RC .50 .20
❑ 4 Willie Greene .10 .02
❑ 5 Manny Alexander .10 .02
❑ 6 Dan Wilson .20 .07
❑ 7 Dan Smith .10 .02
❑ 8 Kevin Rogers .10 .02
❑ 9 Nigel Wilson .10 .02

❑ 10 Joe Vitko .10 .02
❑ 11 Tim Costo .10 .02
❑ 12 Alan Embree .10 .02
❑ 13 Jim Tatum RC .15 .05
❑ 14 Cris Colon .10 .02
❑ 15 Steve Hosey .10 .02
❑ 16 Sterling Hitchcock RC .50 .20
❑ 17 Dave Mlicki .10 .02
❑ 18 Jessie Hollins .10 .02
❑ 19 Bobby Jones .20 .07
❑ 20 Kurt Miller .10 .02
❑ 21 Melvin Nieves .10 .02
❑ 22 Billy Ashley .10 .02
❑ 23 J.T.Snow RC .75 .30
❑ 24 Chipper Jones .50 .20
❑ 25 Tim Salmon .30 .10
❑ 26 Tim Pugh RC .15 .05
❑ 27 David Nied .10 .02
❑ 28 Mike Trombley .10 .02
❑ 29 Javier Lopez .30 .10
❑ 30 Jim Abbott CH CL .20 .07
❑ 31 Jim Abbott CH .10 .02
❑ 32 Dale Murphy CH .30 .10
❑ 33 Tony Pena CH .10 .02
❑ 34 Kirby Puckett CH .30 .10
❑ 35 Harold Reynolds CH .10 .02
❑ 36 Cal Ripken CH .75 .30
❑ 37 Nolan Ryan CH 1.00 .40
❑ 38 Ryne Sandberg CH .50 .20
❑ 39 Dave Stewart CH .10 .02
❑ 40 Dave Winfield CH .10 .02
❑ 41 M.McGwire/J.Carter CL .50 .20
❑ 42 R.Alomar/J.Carter .20 .07
❑ 43 Molitor/Listach/Yount .50 .20
❑ 44 C.Ripken/B.Anderson .50 .20
❑ 45 Belle/Baerga/Thome/Lofton .20 .07
❑ 46 C.Fielder/M.Tettleton .10 .02
❑ 47 R.Kelly/D.Mattingly .60 .25
❑ 48 R.Clemens/F.Viola .50 .20
❑ 49 R.Sierra/M.McGwire .50 .20
❑ 50 K.Puckett/K.Hrbek .30 .10
❑ 51 F.Thomas/R.Ventura .30 .10
❑ 52 Cans/IRod/Gonz/Palmeiro .30 .10
❑ 53 Lethal Lefties
Mark Langston
Jim Abbott
Chuck F .20 .07
❑ 54 Joyner/Jefferies/Brett .50 .20
❑ 55 K.Griffey/Buhner/Mitchell .50 .20
❑ 56 George Brett 1.25 .50
❑ 57 Scott Cooper .10 .02
❑ 58 Mike Maddux .10 .02
❑ 59 Rusty Meacham .10 .02
❑ 60 Wil Cordero .10 .02
❑ 61 Tim Teufel .10 .02
❑ 62 Jeff Montgomery .10 .02
❑ 63 Scott Livingstone .10 .02
❑ 64 Doug Dascenzo .10 .02
❑ 65 Bret Boone .20 .07
❑ 66 Tim Wakefield .50 .20
❑ 67 Curt Schilling .20 .07
❑ 68 Frank Tanana .10 .02
❑ 69 Len Dykstra .20 .07
❑ 70 Derek Lilliquist .10 .02
❑ 71 Anthony Young .10 .02
❑ 72 Hipolito Pichardo .10 .02
❑ 73 Rod Beck .10 .02
❑ 74 Kent Hrbek .20 .07
❑ 75 Tom Glavine .30 .10
❑ 76 Kevin Brown .20 .07
❑ 77 Chuck Finley .20 .07
❑ 78 Bob Walk .10 .02
❑ 79 Rheal Cormier UER .10 .02
❑ 80 Rick Sutcliffe .20 .07
❑ 81 Harold Baines .20 .07
❑ 82 Lee Smith .20 .07
❑ 83 Geno Petralli .10 .02
❑ 84 Jose Oquendo .10 .02
❑ 85 Mark Gubicza .10 .02
❑ 86 Mickey Tettleton .10 .02
❑ 87 Bobby Witt .10 .02
❑ 88 Mark Lewis .10 .02
❑ 89 Kevin Appier .20 .07
❑ 90 Mike Stanton .10 .02
❑ 91 Rafael Belliard .10 .02
❑ 92 Kenny Rogers .20 .07

❑	93	Randy Velarde	.10	.02
❑	94	Luis Sojo	.10	.02
❑	95	Mark Leiter	.10	.02
❑	96	Jody Reed	.10	.02
❑	97	Pete Harnisch	.10	.02
❑	98	Tom Candiotti	.10	.02
❑	99	Mark Portugal	.10	.02
❑	100	Dave Valle	.10	.02
❑	101	Shawon Dunston	.10	.02
❑	102	B.J. Surhoff	.20	.07
❑	103	Jay Bell	.20	.07
❑	104	Sid Bream	.10	.02
❑	105	Frank Thomas CL	.30	.10
❑	106	Mike Morgan	.10	.02
❑	107	Bill Doran	.10	.02
❑	108	Lance Blankenship	.10	.02
❑	109	Mark Lemke	.10	.02
❑	110	Brian Harper	.10	.02
❑	111	Brady Anderson	.20	.07
❑	112	Bip Roberts	.10	.02
❑	113	Mitch Williams	.10	.02
❑	114	Craig Biggio	.30	.10
❑	115	Eddie Murray	.50	.20
❑	116	Matt Nokes	.10	.02
❑	117	Lance Parrish	.20	.07
❑	118	Bill Swift	.10	.02
❑	119	Jeff Innis	.10	.02
❑	120	Mike LaValliere	.10	.02
❑	121	Hal Morris	.10	.02
❑	122	Walt Weiss	.10	.02
❑	123	Ivan Rodriguez	.30	.10
❑	124	Andy Van Slyke	.30	.10
❑	125	Roberto Alomar	.30	.10
❑	126	Robby Thompson	.10	.02
❑	127	Sammy Sosa	.50	.20
❑	128	Mark Langston	.10	.02
❑	129	Jerry Browne	.10	.02
❑	130	Chuck McElroy	.10	.02
❑	131	Frank Viola	.20	.07
❑	132	Leo Gomez	.10	.02
❑	133	Ramon Martinez	.10	.02
❑	134	Don Mattingly	1.25	.50
❑	135	Roger Clemens	1.00	.40
❑	136	Rickey Henderson	.50	.20
❑	137	Darren Daulton	.20	.07
❑	138	Ken Hill	.10	.02
❑	139	Ozzie Guillen	.20	.07
❑	140	Jerald Clark	.10	.02
❑	141	Dave Fleming	.10	.02
❑	142	Delino DeShields	.10	.02
❑	143	Matt Williams	.20	.07
❑	144	Larry Walker	.20	.07
❑	145	Ruben Sierra	.20	.07
❑	146	Ozzie Smith	.75	.30
❑	147	Chris Sabo	.10	.02
❑	148	Carlos Hernandez	.10	.02
❑	149	Pat Borders	.10	.02
❑	150	Orlando Merced	.10	.02
❑	151	Royce Clayton	.10	.02
❑	152	Kurt Stillwell	.10	.02
❑	153	Dave Hollins	.10	.02
❑	154	Mike Greenwell	.10	.02
❑	155	Nolan Ryan	2.00	.75
❑	156	Felix Jose	.10	.02
❑	157	Junior Felix	.10	.02
❑	158	Derek Bell	.10	.02
❑	159	Steve Buechele	.10	.02
❑	160	John Burkett	.10	.02
❑	161	Pat Howell	.10	.02
❑	162	Milt Cuyler	.10	.02
❑	163	Terry Pendleton	.20	.07
❑	164	Jack Morris	.20	.07
❑	165	Tony Gwynn	.60	.25
❑	166	Deion Sanders	.30	.10
❑	167	Mike Devereaux	.10	.02
❑	168	Ron Darling	.10	.02
❑	169	Orel Hershiser	.20	.07
❑	170	Mike Jackson	.10	.02
❑	171	Doug Jones	.10	.02
❑	172	Dan Walters	.10	.02
❑	173	Darren Lewis	.10	.02
❑	174	Carlos Baerga	.10	.02
❑	175	Ryne Sandberg	.75	.30
❑	176	Gregg Jefferies	.10	.02
❑	177	John Jaha	.10	.02
❑	178	Luis Polonia	.10	.02
❑	179	Kirt Manwaring	.10	.02
❑	180	Mike Magnante	.10	.02
❑	181	Billy Ripken	.10	.02
❑	182	Mike Moore	.10	.02
❑	183	Eric Anthony	.10	.02
❑	184	Lenny Harris	.10	.02
❑	185	Tony Pena	.10	.02
❑	186	Mike Felder	.10	.02
❑	187	Greg Olson	.10	.02
❑	188	Rene Gonzales	.10	.02
❑	189	Mike Bordick	.10	.02
❑	190	Mel Rojas	.10	.02
❑	191	Todd Frohwirth	.10	.02
❑	192	Darryl Hamilton	.10	.02
❑	193	Mike Fetters	.10	.02
❑	194	Omar Olivares	.10	.02
❑	195	Tony Phillips	.10	.02
❑	196	Paul Sorrento	.10	.02
❑	197	Trevor Wilson	.10	.02
❑	198	Kevin Gross	.10	.02
❑	199	Ron Karkovice	.10	.02
❑	200	Brook Jacoby	.10	.02
❑	201	Mariano Duncan	.10	.02
❑	202	Dennis Cook	.10	.02
❑	203	Daryl Boston	.10	.02
❑	204	Mike Perez	.10	.02
❑	205	Manuel Lee	.10	.02
❑	206	Steve Olin	.10	.02
❑	207	Charlie Hough	.20	.07
❑	208	Scott Scudder	.10	.02
❑	209	Charlie O'Brien	.10	.02
❑	210	Barry Bonds CL	.75	.30
❑	211	Jose Vizcaino	.10	.02
❑	212	Scott Leius	.10	.02
❑	213	Kevin Mitchell	.10	.02
❑	214	Brian Barnes	.10	.02
❑	215	Pat Kelly	.10	.02
❑	216	Chris Hammond	.10	.02
❑	217	Rob Deer	.10	.02
❑	218	Cory Snyder	.10	.02
❑	219	Gary Carter	.20	.07
❑	220	Danny Darwin	.10	.02
❑	221	Tom Gordon	.10	.02
❑	222	Gary Sheffield 2X	.20	.07
❑	223	Joe Carter	.20	.07
❑	224	Jay Buhner	.20	.07
❑	225	Jose Offerman	.10	.02
❑	226	Jose Rijo	.10	.02
❑	227	Mark Whiten	.10	.02
❑	228	Randy Milligan	.10	.02
❑	229	Bud Black	.10	.02
❑	230	Gary DiSarcina	.10	.02
❑	231	Steve Finley	.20	.07
❑	232	Dennis Martinez	.20	.07
❑	233	Mike Mussina	.30	.10
❑	234	Joe Oliver	.10	.02
❑	235	Chad Curtis	.10	.02
❑	236	Shane Mack	.10	.02
❑	237	Jaime Navarro	.10	.02
❑	238	Brian McRae	.10	.02
❑	239	Chili Davis	.20	.07
❑	240	Jeff King	.10	.02
❑	241	Dean Palmer	.20	.07
❑	242	Danny Tartabull	.10	.02
❑	243	Charles Nagy	.10	.02
❑	244	Ray Lankford	.20	.07
❑	245	Barry Larkin	.30	.10
❑	246	Steve Avery	.10	.02
❑	247	John Kruk	.20	.07
❑	248	Derrick May	.10	.02
❑	249	Stan Javier	.10	.02
❑	250	Roger McDowell	.10	.02
❑	251	Dan Gladden	.10	.02
❑	252	Wally Joyner	.20	.07
❑	253	Pat Listach	.10	.02
❑	254	Chuck Knoblauch	.20	.07
❑	255	Sandy Alomar Jr.	.10	.02
❑	256	Jeff Bagwell	.30	.10
❑	257	Andy Stankiewicz	.10	.02
❑	258	Darrin Jackson	.10	.02
❑	259	Brett Butler	.20	.07
❑	260	Joe Orsulak	.10	.02
❑	261	Andy Benes	.10	.02
❑	262	Kenny Lofton	.20	.07
❑	263	Robin Ventura	.20	.07
❑	264	Ron Gant	.20	.07
❑	265	Ellis Burks	.20	.07
❑	266	Juan Guzman	.10	.02
❑	267	Wes Chamberlain	.10	.02
❑	268	John Smiley	.10	.02
❑	269	Franklin Stubbs	.10	.02
❑	270	Tom Browning	.10	.02
❑	271	Dennis Eckersley	.20	.07
❑	272	Carlton Fisk	.30	.10
❑	273	Lou Whitaker	.20	.07
❑	274	Phil Plantier	.10	.02
❑	275	Bobby Bonilla	.20	.07
❑	276	Ben McDonald	.10	.02
❑	277	Bob Zupcic	.10	.02
❑	278	Terry Steinbach	.10	.02
❑	279	Terry Mulholland	.10	.02
❑	280	Lance Johnson	.10	.02
❑	281	Willie McGee	.20	.07
❑	282	Bret Saberhagen	.20	.07
❑	283	Randy Myers	.10	.02
❑	284	Randy Tomlin	.10	.02
❑	285	Mickey Morandini	.10	.02
❑	286	Brian Williams	.10	.02
❑	287	Tino Martinez	.30	.10
❑	288	Jose Melendez	.10	.02
❑	289	Jeff Huson	.10	.02
❑	290	Joe Grahe	.10	.02
❑	291	Mel Hall	.10	.02
❑	292	Otis Nixon	.10	.02
❑	293	Todd Hundley	.10	.02
❑	294	Casey Candaele	.10	.02
❑	295	Kevin Seitzer	.10	.02
❑	296	Eddie Taubensee	.10	.02
❑	297	Moises Alou	.20	.07
❑	298	Scott Radinsky	.10	.02
❑	299	Thomas Howard	.10	.02
❑	300	Kyle Abbott	.10	.02
❑	301	Omar Vizquel	.30	.10
❑	302	Keith Miller	.10	.02
❑	303	Rick Aguilera	.10	.02
❑	304	Bruce Hurst	.10	.02
❑	305	Ken Caminiti	.20	.07
❑	306	Mike Pagliarulo	.10	.02
❑	307	Frank Seminara	.10	.02
❑	308	Andre Dawson	.20	.07
❑	309	Jose Lind	.10	.02
❑	310	Joe Boever	.10	.02
❑	311	Jeff Parrett	.10	.02
❑	312	Alan Mills	.10	.02
❑	313	Kevin Tapani	.10	.02
❑	314	Darryl Kile	.20	.07
❑	315	Checklist 211-315 Will Clark	.20	.07
❑	316	Mike Sharperson	.10	.02
❑	317	John Orton	.10	.02
❑	318	Bob Tewksbury	.10	.02
❑	319	Xavier Hernandez	.10	.02
❑	320	Paul Assenmacher	.10	.02
❑	321	John Franco	.20	.07
❑	322	Mike Timlin	.10	.02
❑	323	Jose Guzman	.10	.02
❑	324	Pedro Martinez	1.00	.40
❑	325	Bill Spiers	.10	.02
❑	326	Melido Perez	.10	.02
❑	327	Mike Macfarlane	.10	.02
❑	328	Ricky Bones	.10	.02
❑	329	Scott Bankhead	.10	.02
❑	330	Rich Rodriguez	.10	.02
❑	331	Geronimo Pena	.10	.02
❑	332	Bernie Williams	.30	.10
❑	333	Paul Molitor	.20	.07
❑	334	Carlos Garcia	.10	.02
❑	335	David Cone	.20	.07
❑	336	Randy Johnson	.50	.20
❑	337	Pat Mahomes	.10	.02
❑	338	Erik Hanson	.10	.02
❑	339	Duane Ward	.10	.02
❑	340	Al Martin	.10	.02
❑	341	Pedro Munoz	.10	.02
❑	342	Greg Colbrunn	.10	.02
❑	343	Julio Valera	.10	.02
❑	344	John Olerud	.20	.07
❑	345	George Bell	.10	.02
❑	346	Devon White	.20	.07
❑	347	Donovan Osborne	.10	.02
❑	348	Mark Gardner	.10	.02
❑	349	Zane Smith	.10	.02

❑ 350 Wilson Alvarez .10 .02
❑ 351 Kevin Koslofski .10 .02
❑ 352 Roberto Hernandez .10 .02
❑ 353 Glenn Davis .10 .02
❑ 354 Reggie Sanders .20 .07
❑ 355 Ken Griffey Jr. .75 .30
❑ 356 Marquis Grissom .20 .07
❑ 357 Jack McDowell .10 .02
❑ 358 Jimmy Key .20 .07
❑ 359 Stan Belinda .10 .02
❑ 360 Gerald Williams .10 .02
❑ 361 Sid Fernandez .10 .02
❑ 362 Alex Fernandez .10 .02
❑ 363 John Smoltz .30 .10
❑ 364 Travis Fryman .20 .07
❑ 365 Jose Canseco .30 .10
❑ 366 David Justice .20 .07
❑ 367 Pedro Astacio .10 .02
❑ 368 Tim Belcher .10 .02
❑ 369 Steve Sax .10 .02
❑ 370 Gary Gaetti .20 .07
❑ 371 Jeff Frye .10 .02
❑ 372 Bob Wickman .10 .02
❑ 373 Ryan Thompson .10 .02
❑ 374 David Hulse RC .15 .05
❑ 375 Cal Eldred .10 .02
❑ 376 Ryan Klesko .20 .07
❑ 377 Damion Easley .10 .02
❑ 378 John Kiely .10 .02
❑ 379 Jim Bullinger .10 .02
❑ 380 Brian Bohanon .10 .02
❑ 381 Rod Brewer .10 .02
❑ 382 Fernando Ramsey RC .15 .05
❑ 383 Sam Militello .10 .02
❑ 384 Arthur Rhodes .10 .02
❑ 385 Eric Karros .20 .07
❑ 386 Rico Brogna .10 .02
❑ 387 John Valentin .10 .02
❑ 388 Kerry Woodson .10 .02
❑ 389 Ben Rivera .10 .02
❑ 390 Matt Whiteside RC .15 .05
❑ 391 Henry Rodriguez .10 .02
❑ 392 John Wetteland .20 .07
❑ 393 Kent Mercker .10 .02
❑ 394 Bernard Gilkey .10 .02
❑ 395 Doug Henry .10 .02
❑ 396 Mo Vaughn .20 .07
❑ 397 Scott Erickson .10 .02
❑ 398 Bill Gullickson .10 .02
❑ 399 Mark Guthrie .10 .02
❑ 400 Dave Martinez .10 .02
❑ 401 Jeff Kent .50 .20
❑ 402 Chris Hoiles .10 .02
❑ 403 Mike Henneman .10 .02
❑ 404 Chris Nabholz .10 .02
❑ 405 Tom Pagnozzi .10 .02
❑ 406 Kelly Gruber .10 .02
❑ 407 Bob Welch .10 .02
❑ 408 Frank Castillo .10 .02
❑ 409 John Dopson .10 .02
❑ 410 Steve Farr .10 .02
❑ 411 Henry Cotto .10 .02
❑ 412 Bob Patterson .10 .02
❑ 413 Todd Stottlemyre .10 .02
❑ 414 Greg A. Harris .10 .02
❑ 415 Denny Neagle .20 .07
❑ 416 Bill Wegman .10 .02
❑ 417 Willie Wilson .10 .02
❑ 418 Terry Leach .10 .02
❑ 419 Willie Randolph .20 .07
❑ 420 Checklist 316-420 McGwire .30 .10
❑ 421 Calvin Murray CL .10 .02
❑ 422 Pete Janicki RC .15 .05
❑ 423 Todd Jones TP .20 .07
❑ 424 Mike Neill .10 .02
❑ 425 Carlos Delgado .50 .20
❑ 426 Jose Oliva .10 .02
❑ 427 Tyrone Hill .10 .02
❑ 428 Dmitri Young .20 .07
❑ 429 Derek Wallace RC .15 .05
❑ 430 Michael Moore RC .15 .05
❑ 431 Cliff Floyd .20 .07
❑ 432 Calvin Murray .10 .02
❑ 433 Manny Ramirez .75 .30
❑ 434 Marc Newfield .10 .02
❑ 435 Charles Johnson .20 .07
❑ 436 Butch Huskey .10 .02
❑ 437 Brad Pennington TP .10 .02
❑ 438 Ray McDavid RC .15 .05
❑ 439 Chad McConnell .10 .02
❑ 440 Midre Cummings RC .15 .05
❑ 441 Benji Gil .10 .02
❑ 442 Frankie Rodriguez .10 .02
❑ 443 Chad Mottola RC .15 .05
❑ 444 John Burke RC .15 .05
❑ 445 Michael Tucker .10 .02
❑ 446 Rick Greene .10 .02
❑ 447 Rich Becker .10 .02
❑ 448 Mike Robertson TP .10 .02
❑ 449 Derek Jeter RC ! 10.00 4.00
❑ 450 I.Rodriguez/D.McCarty CL .30 .10
❑ 451 Jim Abbott IN .20 .07
❑ 452 Jeff Bagwell IN .20 .07
❑ 453 Jason Bere IN .10 .02
❑ 454 Delino DeShields IN .10 .02
❑ 455 Travis Fryman IN .10 .02
❑ 456 Alex Gonzalez IN .10 .02
❑ 457 Phil Hiatt IN .10 .02
❑ 458 Dave Hollins IN .10 .02
❑ 459 Chipper Jones IN .30 .10
❑ 460 David Justice IN .10 .02
❑ 461 Ray Lankford IN .10 .02
❑ 462 David McCarty IN .10 .02
❑ 463 Mike Mussina IN .20 .07
❑ 464 Jose Offerman IN .10 .02
❑ 465 Dean Palmer IN .10 .02
❑ 466 Geronimo Pena IN .10 .02
❑ 467 Eduardo Perez IN .10 .02
❑ 468 Ivan Rodriguez IN .20 .07
❑ 469 Reggie Sanders IN .10 .02
❑ 470 Bernie Williams IN .20 .07
❑ 471 Bonds/Williams/Clark CL .75 .30
❑ 472 Madd/Avery/Smolt/Glav .50 .20
❑ 473 Red October
Jose Rijo
Rob Dibble
Roberto Kelly# .20 .07
❑ 474 Sheff/Plant/Gwynn/McGrif .20 .07
❑ 475 Biggio/Drabek/Bagwell .20 .07
❑ 476 Clark/Bonds/Williams .75 .30
❑ 477 Eric Davis
Darryl Strawberry .20 .07
❑ 478 Bich/Nied/Galarraga .20 .07
❑ 479 Maga/Destr/Barbe/Conine .10 .02
❑ 480 Wakefield/Van Slyke/Bell .20 .07
❑ 481 Griss/DeSh/Mart/Walker .30 .10
❑ 482 O.Smith/Redbirds .50 .20
❑ 483 Myers/Sandberg/Grace .50 .20
❑ 484 Big Apple Power Switch .30 .10
❑ 485 Kruk/Holl/Dault/Dyks .10 .02
❑ 486 Barry Bonds AW .75 .30
❑ 487 Dennis Eckersley AW .20 .07
❑ 488 Greg Maddux AW .50 .20
❑ 489 Dennis Eckersley AW .20 .07
❑ 490 Eric Karros AW .10 .02
❑ 491 Pat Listach AW .10 .02
❑ 492 Gary Sheffield AW .10 .02
❑ 493 Mark McGwire AW .60 .25
❑ 494 Gary Sheffield AW .10 .02
❑ 495 Edgar Martinez AW .20 .07
❑ 496 Fred McGriff AW .20 .07
❑ 497 Juan Gonzalez AW .10 .02
❑ 498 Darren Daulton AW .10 .02
❑ 499 Cecil Fielder AW .10 .02
❑ 500 Brent Gates CL .10 .02
❑ 501 Tavo Alvarez .10 .02
❑ 502 Rod Bolton .10 .02
❑ 503 John Cummings RC .15 .05
❑ 504 Brent Gates .10 .02
❑ 505 Tyler Green .10 .02
❑ 506 Jose Martinez RC .15 .05
❑ 507 Troy Percival .30 .10
❑ 508 Kevin Stocker .10 .02
❑ 509 Matt Walbeck RC .15 .05
❑ 510 Rondell White .20 .07
❑ 511 Billy Ripken .10 .02
❑ 512 Mike Moore .10 .02
❑ 513 Jose Lind .10 .02
❑ 514 Chito Martinez .10 .02
❑ 515 Jose Guzman .10 .02
❑ 516 Kim Batiste .10 .02
❑ 517 Jeff Tackett .10 .02
❑ 518 Charlie Hough .20 .07
❑ 519 Marvin Freeman .10 .02
❑ 520 Carlos Martinez .10 .02
❑ 521 Eric Young .10 .02
❑ 522 Pete Incaviglia .10 .02
❑ 523 Scott Fletcher .10 .02
❑ 524 Orestes Destrade .10 .02
❑ 525 Ken Griffey Jr. CL .50 .20
❑ 526 Ellis Burks .20 .07
❑ 527 Juan Samuel .10 .02
❑ 528 Dave Magadan .10 .02
❑ 529 Jeff Parrett .10 .02
❑ 530 Bill Krueger .10 .02
❑ 531 Frank Bolick .10 .02
❑ 532 Alan Trammell .20 .07
❑ 533 Walt Weiss .10 .02
❑ 534 David Cone .20 .07
❑ 535 Greg Maddux .75 .30
❑ 536 Kevin Young .20 .07
❑ 537 Dave Hansen .10 .02
❑ 538 Alex Cole .10 .02
❑ 539 Greg Hibbard .10 .02
❑ 540 Gene Larkin .10 .02
❑ 541 Jeff Reardon .20 .07
❑ 542 Felix Jose .10 .02
❑ 543 Jimmy Key .20 .07
❑ 544 Reggie Jefferson .10 .02
❑ 545 Gregg Jefferies .10 .02
❑ 546 Dave Stewart .20 .07
❑ 547 Tim Wallach .10 .02
❑ 548 Spike Owen .10 .02
❑ 549 Tommy Greene .10 .02
❑ 550 Fernando Valenzuela .20 .07
❑ 551 Rich Amaral .10 .02
❑ 552 Bret Barberie .10 .02
❑ 553 Edgar Martinez .30 .10
❑ 554 Jim Abbott .30 .10
❑ 555 Frank Thomas .50 .20
❑ 556 Wade Boggs .30 .10
❑ 557 Tom Henke .10 .02
❑ 558 Milt Thompson .10 .02
❑ 559 Lloyd McClendon .10 .02
❑ 560 Vinny Castilla .50 .20
❑ 561 Ricky Jordan .10 .02
❑ 562 Andujar Cedeno .10 .02
❑ 563 Greg Vaughn .10 .02
❑ 564 Cecil Fielder .20 .07
❑ 565 Kirby Puckett .50 .20
❑ 566 Mark McGwire 1.25 .50
❑ 567 Barry Bonds 1.50 .60
❑ 568 Jody Reed .10 .02
❑ 569 Todd Zeile .10 .02
❑ 570 Mark Carreon .10 .02
❑ 571 Joe Girardi .10 .02
❑ 572 Luis Gonzalez .20 .07
❑ 573 Mark Grace .30 .10
❑ 574 Rafael Palmeiro .30 .10
❑ 575 Darryl Strawberry .20 .07
❑ 576 Will Clark .30 .10
❑ 577 Fred McGriff .30 .10
❑ 578 Kevin Reimer .10 .02
❑ 579 Dave Righetti .20 .07
❑ 580 Juan Bell .10 .02
❑ 581 Jeff Brantley .10 .02
❑ 582 Brian Hunter .10 .02
❑ 583 Tim Naehring .10 .02
❑ 584 Glenallen Hill .10 .02
❑ 585 Cal Ripken 1.50 .60
❑ 586 Albert Belle .20 .07
❑ 587 Robin Yount .75 .30
❑ 588 Chris Bosio .10 .02
❑ 589 Pete Smith .10 .02
❑ 590 Chuck Carr .10 .02
❑ 591 Jeff Blauser .10 .02
❑ 592 Kevin McReynolds .10 .02
❑ 593 Andres Galarraga .20 .07
❑ 594 Kevin Maas .10 .02
❑ 595 Eric Davis .20 .07
❑ 596 Brian Jordan .20 .07
❑ 597 Tim Raines .20 .07
❑ 598 Rick Wilkins .10 .02
❑ 599 Steve Cooke .10 .02
❑ 600 Mike Gallego .10 .02
❑ 601 Mike Munoz .10 .02
❑ 602 Luis Rivera .10 .02
❑ 603 Junior Ortiz .10 .02

604	Brent Mayne	.10	.02
605	Luis Alicea	.10	.02
606	Damon Berryhill	.10	.02
607	Dave Henderson	.10	.02
608	Kirk McCaskill	.10	.02
609	Jeff Fassero	.10	.02
610	Mike Harkey	.10	.02
611	Francisco Cabrera	.10	.02
612	Rey Sanchez	.10	.02
613	Scott Servais	.10	.02
614	Darrin Fletcher	.10	.02
615	Felix Fermin	.10	.02
616	Kevin Seitzer	.10	.02
617	Bob Scanlan	.10	.02
618	Billy Hatcher	.10	.02
619	John Vander Wal	.10	.02
620	Joe Hesketh	.10	.02
621	Hector Villanueva	.10	.02
622	Randy Milligan	.10	.02
623	Tony Tarasco RC	.15	.05
624	Russ Swan	.10	.02
625	Willie Wilson	.10	.02
626	Frank Tanana	.10	.02
627	Pete O'Brien	.10	.02
628	Lenny Webster	.10	.02
629	Mark Clark	.10	.02
630	Roger Clemens CL	.50	.20
631	Alex Arias	.10	.02
632	Chris Gwynn	.10	.02
633	Tom Bolton	.10	.02
634	Greg Briley	.10	.02
635	Kent Bottenfield	.10	.02
636	Kelly Downs	.10	.02
637	Manuel Lee	.10	.02
638	Al Leiter	.20	.07
639	Jeff Gardner	.10	.02
640	Mike Gardiner	.10	.02
641	Mark Gardner	.10	.02
642	Jeff Branson	.10	.02
643	Paul Wagner	.10	.02
644	Sean Berry	.10	.02
645	Phil Hiatt	.10	.02
646	Kevin Mitchell	.10	.02
647	Charlie Hayes	.10	.02
648	Jim Deshaies	.10	.02
649	Dan Pasqua	.10	.02
650	Mike Maddux	.10	.02
651	Domingo Martinez RC	.15	.05
652	Greg McMichael RC	.15	.05
653	Eric Wedge RC	.50	.20
654	Mark Whiten	.10	.02
655	Roberto Kelly	.10	.02
656	Julio Franco	.20	.07
657	Gene Harris	.10	.02
658	Pete Schourek	.10	.02
659	Mike Bielecki	.10	.02
660	Ricky Gutierrez	.10	.02
661	Chris Hammond	.10	.02
662	Tim Scott	.10	.02
663	Norm Charlton	.10	.02
664	Doug Drabek	.10	.02
665	Dwight Gooden	.20	.07
666	Jim Gott	.10	.02
667	Randy Myers	.10	.02
668	Darren Holmes	.10	.02
669	Tim Spehr	.10	.02
670	Bruce Ruffin	.10	.02
671	Bobby Thigpen	.10	.02
672	Tony Fernandez	.10	.02
673	Darrin Jackson	.10	.02
674	Gregg Olson	.10	.02
675	Rob Dibble	.20	.07
676	Howard Johnson	.10	.02
677	Mike Lansing RC	.50	.20
678	Charlie Leibrandt	.10	.02
679	Kevin Bass	.10	.02
680	Hubie Brooks	.10	.02
681	Scott Brosius	.20	.07
682	Randy Knorr	.10	.02
683	Dante Bichette	.20	.07
684	Bryan Harvey	.10	.02
685	Greg Gohr	.10	.02
686	Willie Banks	.10	.02
687	Robb Nen	.20	.07
688	Mike Scioscia	.10	.02
689	John Farrell	.10	.02
690	John Candelaria	.10	.02
691	Damon Buford	.10	.02
692	Todd Worrell	.10	.02
693	Pat Hentgen	.10	.02
694	John Smiley	.10	.02
695	Greg Swindell	.10	.02
696	Derek Bell	.10	.02
697	Terry Jorgensen	.10	.02
698	Jimmy Jones	.10	.02
699	David Wells	.20	.07
700	Dave Martinez	.10	.02
701	Steve Bedrosian	.10	.02
702	Jeff Russell	.10	.02
703	Joe Magrane	.10	.02
704	Matt Mieske	.10	.02
705	Paul Molitor	.20	.07
706	Dale Murphy	.30	.10
707	Steve Howe	.10	.02
708	Greg Gagne	.10	.02
709	Dave Eiland	.10	.02
710	David West	.10	.02
711	Luis Aquino	.10	.02
712	Joe Orsulak	.10	.02
713	Eric Plunk	.10	.02
714	Mike Felder	.10	.02
715	Joe Klink	.10	.02
716	Lonnie Smith	.10	.02
717	Monty Fariss	.10	.02
718	Craig Lefferts	.10	.02
719	John Habyan	.10	.02
720	Willie Blair	.10	.02
721	Darnell Coles	.10	.02
722	Mark Williamson	.10	.02
723	Bryn Smith	.10	.02
724	Greg W. Harris	.10	.02
725	Graeme Lloyd RC	.50	.20
726	Cris Carpenter	.10	.02
727	Chico Walker	.10	.02
728	Tracy Woodson	.10	.02
729	Jose Uribe	.10	.02
730	Stan Javier	.10	.02
731	Jay Howell	.10	.02
732	Freddie Benavides	.10	.02
733	Jeff Reboulet	.10	.02
734	Scott Sanderson	.10	.02
735	Ryne Sandberg CL	.50	.20
736	Archi Cianfrocco	.10	.02
737	Daryl Boston	.10	.02
738	Craig Grebeck	.10	.02
739	Doug Dascenzo	.10	.02
740	Gerald Young	.10	.02
741	Candy Maldonado	.10	.02
742	Joey Cora	.10	.02
743	Don Slaught	.10	.02
744	Steve Decker	.10	.02
745	Blas Minor	.10	.02
746	Storm Davis	.10	.02
747	Carlos Quintana	.10	.02
748	Vince Coleman	.10	.02
749	Todd Burns	.10	.02
750	Steve Frey	.10	.02
751	Ivan Calderon	.10	.02
752	Steve Reed RC	.15	.05
753	Danny Jackson	.10	.02
754	Jeff Conine	.20	.07
755	Juan Gonzalez	.20	.07
756	Mike Kelly	.10	.02
757	John Doherty	.10	.02
758	Jack Armstrong	.10	.02
759	John Wehner	.10	.02
760	Scott Bankhead	.10	.02
761	Jim Tatum	.10	.02
762	Scott Pose RC	.15	.05
763	Andy Ashby	.10	.02
764	Ed Sprague	.10	.02
765	Harold Baines	.20	.07
766	Kirk Gibson	.20	.07
767	Troy Neel	.10	.02
768	Dick Schofield	.10	.02
769	Dickie Thon	.10	.02
770	Butch Henry	.10	.02
771	Junior Felix	.10	.02
772	Ken Ryan RC	.15	.05
773	Trevor Hoffman	.50	.20
774	Phil Plantier	.10	.02
775	Bo Jackson	.50	.20
776	Benito Santiago	.20	.07
777	Andre Dawson	.20	.07
778	Bryan Hickerson	.10	.02
779	Dennis Moeller	.10	.02
780	Ryan Bowen	.10	.02
781	Eric Fox	.10	.02
782	Joe Kmak	.10	.02
783	Mike Hampton	.20	.07
784	Darrell Sherman RC	.15	.05
785	J.T.Snow	.30	.10
786	Dave Winfield	.20	.07
787	Jim Austin	.10	.02
788	Craig Shipley	.10	.02
789	Greg Myers	.10	.02
790	Todd Benzinger	.10	.02
791	Cory Snyder	.10	.02
792	David Segui	.10	.02
793	Armando Reynoso	.10	.02
794	Chili Davis	.20	.07
795	Dave Nilsson	.10	.02
796	Paul O'Neill	.30	.10
797	Jerald Clark	.10	.02
798	Jose Mesa	.10	.02
799	Brain Holman	.10	.02
800	Jim Eisenreich	.10	.02
801	Mark McLemore	.10	.02
802	Luis Sojo	.10	.02
803	Harold Reynolds	.20	.07
804	Dan Plesac	.10	.02
805	Dave Stieb	.10	.02
806	Tom Brunansky	.10	.02
807	Kelly Gruber	.10	.02
808	Bob Ojeda	.10	.02
809	Dave Burba	.10	.02
810	Joe Boever	.10	.02
811	Jeremy Hernandez	.10	.02
812	Tim Salmon TC	.20	.07
813	Jeff Bagwell TC	.20	.07
814	Dennis Eckersley TC	.20	.07
815	Roberto Alomar TC	.20	.07
816	Steve Avery TC	.10	.02
817	Pat Listach TC	.10	.02
818	Gregg Jefferies TC	.10	.02
819	Sammy Sosa TC	.50	.20
820	Darryl Strawberry TC	.10	.02
821	Dennis Martinez TC	.10	.02
822	Robby Thompson TC	.10	.02
823	Albert Belle TC	.20	.07
824	Randy Johnson TC	.30	.10
825	Nigel Wilson TC	.10	.02
826	Bobby Bonilla TC	.10	.02
827	Glenn Davis TC	.10	.02
828	Gary Sheffield TC	.10	.02
829	Darren Daulton TC	.10	.02
830	Jay Bell TC	.10	.02
831	Juan Gonzalez TC	.10	.02
832	Andre Dawson TC	.10	.02
833	Hal Morris TC	.10	.02
834	David Nied TC	.10	.02
835	Felix Jose TC	.10	.02
836	Travis Fryman TC	.10	.02
837	Shane Mack TC	.10	.02
838	Robin Ventura TC	.10	.02
839	Danny Tartabull TC	.10	.02
840	Roberto Alomar CL	.20	.07
SP5	G.Brett/R.Yount	1.00	.40
SP6	Nolan Ryan	2.00	.75

1994 Upper Deck

	COMPLETE SET (550)	50.00	25.00
	COMPLETE SERIES 1 (280)	30.00	15.00
	COMPLETE SERIES 2 (270)	20.00	10.00
1	Brian Anderson RC	.40	.15
2	Shane Andrews	.15	.05
3	James Baldwin	.15	.05
4	Rich Becker	.15	.05
5	Greg Blosser	.15	.05
6	Ricky Bottalico RC	.15	.05
7	Midre Cummings	.15	.05
8	Carlos Delgado	.50	.20
9	Steve Dreyer RC	.15	.05
10	Joey Eischen	.15	.05
11	Carl Everett	.30	.10
12	Cliff Floyd	.30	.10
13	Alex Gonzalez	.15	.05
14	Jeff Granger	.15	.05

15	Shawn Green	.75	.30
16	Brian L.Hunter	.15	.05
17	Butch Huskey	.15	.05
18	Mark Hutton	.15	.05
19	Michael Jordan RC	8.00	3.00
20	Steve Karsay	.15	.05
21	Jeff McNeely	.15	.05
22	Marc Newfield	.15	.05
23	Manny Ramirez	.75	.30
24	Alex Rodriguez RC	15.00	6.00
25	Scott Ruffcorn UER	.15	.05
26	Paul Spoljaric UER	.15	.05
27	Salomon Torres	.15	.05
28	Steve Trachsel	.15	.05
29	Chris Turner	.15	.05
30	Gabe White	.15	.05
31	Randy Johnson FT	.50	.20
32	John Wetteland FT	.15	.05
33	Mike Piazza FT	.75	.30
34	Rafael Palmeiro FT	.30	.10
35	Roberto Alomar FT	.30	.10
36	Matt Williams FT	.15	.05
37	Travis Fryman FT	.15	.05
38	Barry Bonds FT	1.00	.40
39	Marquis Grissom FT	.15	.05
40	Albert Belle FT	.30	.10
41	Steve Avery FUT	.15	.05
42	Jason Bere FUT	.15	.05
43	Alex Fernandez FUT	.15	.05
44	Mike Mussina FUT	.30	.10
45	Aaron Sele FUT	.15	.05
46	Rod Beck FUT	.15	.05
47	Mike Piazza FUT	.75	.30
48	John Olerud FUT	.15	.05
49	Carlos Baerga FUT	.15	.05
50	Gary Sheffield FUT	.15	.05
51	Travis Fryman FUT	.15	.05
52	Juan Gonzalez FUT	.15	.05
53	Ken Griffey Jr. FUT	.75	.30
54	Tim Salmon FUT	.30	.10
55	Frank Thomas FUT	.50	.20
56	Tony Phillips	.15	.05
57	Julio Franco	.30	.10
58	Kevin Mitchell	.15	.05
59	Raul Mondesi	.30	.10
60	Rickey Henderson	.75	.30
61	Jay Buhner	.30	.10
62	Bill Swift	.15	.05
63	Brady Anderson	.30	.10
64	Ryan Klesko	.30	.10
65	Darren Daulton	.30	.10
66	Damion Easley	.15	.05
67	Mark McGwire	2.00	.75
68	John Roper	.15	.05
69	Dave Telgheder	.15	.05
70	David Nied	.15	.05
71	Mo Vaughn	.30	.10
72	Tyler Green	.15	.05
73	Dave Magadan	.15	.05
74	Chili Davis	.30	.10
75	Archi Cianfrocco	.15	.05
76	Joe Girardi	.15	.05
77	Chris Hoiles	.15	.05
78	Ryan Bowen	.15	.05
79	Greg Gagne	.15	.05
80	Aaron Sele	.15	.05
81	Dave Winfield	.30	.10
82	Chad Curtis	.15	.05
83	Andy Van Slyke	.50	.20
84	Kevin Stocker	.15	.05
85	Deion Sanders	.50	.20
86	Bernie Williams	.50	.20
87	John Smoltz	.50	.20
88	Ruben Santana	.15	.05
89	Dave Stewart	.30	.10
90	Don Mattingly	2.00	.75
91	Joe Carter	.30	.10
92	Ryne Sandberg	1.25	.50
93	Chris Gomez	.15	.05
94	Tino Martinez	.50	.20
95	Terry Pendleton	.30	.10
96	Andre Dawson	.30	.10
97	Wil Cordero	.15	.05
98	Kent Hrbek	.30	.10
99	John Olerud	.30	.10
100	Kirt Manwaring	.15	.05
101	Tim Bogar	.15	.05
102	Mike Mussina	.50	.20
103	Nigel Wilson	.15	.05
104	Ricky Gutierrez	.15	.05
105	Roberto Mejia	.15	.05
106	Tom Pagnozzi	.15	.05
107	Mike Macfarlane	.15	.05
108	Jose Bautista	.15	.05
109	Luis Ortiz	.15	.05
110	Brent Gates	.15	.05
111	Tim Salmon	.50	.20
112	Wade Boggs	.50	.20
113	Tripp Cromer	.15	.05
114	Denny Hocking	.15	.05
115	Carlos Baerga	.15	.05
116	J.R. Phillips	.15	.05
117	Bo Jackson	.75	.30
118	Lance Johnson	.15	.05
119	Bobby Jones	.15	.05
120	Bobby Witt	.15	.05
121	Ron Karkovice	.15	.05
122	Jose Vizcaino	.15	.05
123	Danny Darwin	.15	.05
124	Eduardo Perez	.15	.05
125	Brian Looney RC	.15	.05
126	Pat Hentgen	.15	.05
127	Frank Viola	.30	.10
128	Darren Holmes	.15	.05
129	Wally Whitehurst	.15	.05
130	Matt Walbeck	.15	.05
131	Albert Belle	.30	.10
132	Steve Cooke	.15	.05
133	Kevin Appier	.30	.10
134	Joe Oliver	.15	.05
135	Benji Gil	.15	.05
136	Steve Buechele	.15	.05
137	Devon White	.30	.10
138	Sterling Hitchcock UER	.15	.05
139	Phil Leftwich RC	.15	.05
140	Jose Canseco	.50	.20
141	Rick Aguilera	.15	.05
142	Rod Beck	.15	.05
143	Jose Rijo	.15	.05
144	Tom Glavine	.50	.20
145	Phil Plantier	.15	.05
146	Jason Bere	.15	.05
147	Jamie Moyer	.30	.10
148	Wes Chamberlain	.15	.05
149	Glenallen Hill	.15	.05
150	Mark Whiten	.15	.05
151	Bret Barberie	.15	.05
152	Chuck Knoblauch	.30	.10
153	Trevor Hoffman	.50	.20
154	Rick Wilkins	.15	.05
155	Juan Gonzalez	.30	.10
156	Ozzie Guillen	.30	.10
157	Jim Eisenreich	.15	.05
158	Pedro Astacio	.15	.05
159	Joe Magrane	.15	.05
160	Ryan Thompson	.15	.05
161	Jose Lind	.15	.05
162	Jeff Conine	.30	.10
163	Todd Benzinger	.15	.05
164	Roger Salkeld	.15	.05
165	Gary DiSarcina	.15	.05
166	Kevin Gross	.15	.05
167	Charlie Hayes	.15	.05
168	Tim Costo	.15	.05
169	Wally Joyner	.30	.10
170	Johnny Ruffin	.15	.05
171	Kirk Rueter	.15	.05
172	Lenny Dykstra	.30	.10
173	Ken Hill	.15	.05
174	Mike Bordick	.15	.05
175	Billy Hall	.15	.05
176	Rob Butler	.15	.05
177	Jay Bell	.30	.10
178	Jeff Kent	.50	.20
179	David Wells	.30	.10
180	Dean Palmer	.30	.10
181	Mariano Duncan	.15	.05
182	Orlando Merced	.15	.05
183	Brett Butler	.30	.10
184	Milt Thompson	.15	.05
185	Chipper Jones	.75	.30
186	Paul O'Neill	.50	.20
187	Mike Greenwell	.15	.05
188	Harold Baines	.30	.10
189	Todd Stottlemyre	.15	.05
190	Jeromy Burnitz	.30	.10
191	Rene Arocha	.15	.05
192	Jeff Fassero	.15	.05
193	Robby Thompson	.15	.05
194	Greg W. Harris	.15	.05
195	Todd Van Poppel	.15	.05
196	Jose Guzman	.15	.05
197	Shane Mack	.15	.05
198	Carlos Garcia	.15	.05
199	Kevin Roberson	.15	.05
200	David McCarty	.15	.05
201	Alan Trammell	.30	.10
202	Chuck Carr	.15	.05
203	Tommy Greene	.15	.05
204	Wilson Alvarez	.15	.05
205	Dwight Gooden	.30	.10
206	Tony Tarasco	.15	.05
207	Darren Lewis	.15	.05
208	Eric Karros	.30	.10
209	Chris Hammond	.15	.05
210	Jeffrey Hammonds	.15	.05
211	Rich Amaral	.15	.05
212	Danny Tartabull	.15	.05
213	Jeff Russell	.15	.05
214	Dave Staton	.15	.05
215	Kenny Lofton	.30	.10
216	Manuel Lee	.15	.05
217	Brian Koelling	.15	.05
218	Scott Lydy	.15	.05
219	Tony Gwynn	1.00	.40
220	Cecil Fielder	.30	.10
221	Royce Clayton	.15	.05
222	Reggie Sanders	.30	.10
223	Brian Jordan	.30	.10
224	Ken Griffey Jr.	1.25	.50
225	Fred McGriff	.50	.20
226	Felix Jose	.15	.05
227	Brad Pennington	.15	.05
228	Chris Bosio	.15	.05
229	Mike Stanley	.15	.05
230	Willie Greene	.15	.05
231	Alex Fernandez	.15	.05
232	Brad Ausmus	.50	.20
233	Darrell Whitmore	.15	.05
234	Marcus Moore	.15	.05
235	Allen Watson	.15	.05
236	Jose Offerman	.15	.05
237	Rondell White	.30	.10
238	Jeff King	.15	.05
239	Luis Alicea	.15	.05
240	Dan Wilson	.15	.05
241	Ed Sprague	.15	.05
242	Todd Hundley	.15	.05
243	Al Martin	.15	.05
244	Mike Lansing	.15	.05
245	Ivan Rodriguez	.50	.20
246	Dave Fleming	.15	.05
247	John Doherty	.15	.05
248	Mark McLemore	.15	.05
249	Bob Hamelin	.15	.05
250	Curtis Pride RC	.40	.15
251	Zane Smith	.15	.05
252	Eric Young	.15	.05
253	Brian McRae	.15	.05
254	Tim Raines	.30	.10

❑ 255 Javier Lopez .30 .10
❑ 256 Melvin Nieves .15 .05
❑ 257 Randy Myers .15 .05
❑ 258 Willie McGee .30 .10
❑ 259 Jimmy Key UER .30 .10
❑ 260 Tom Candiotti .15 .05
❑ 261 Eric Davis .30 .10
❑ 262 Craig Paquette .15 .05
❑ 263 Robin Ventura .30 .10
❑ 264 Pat Kelly .15 .05
❑ 265 Gregg Jefferies .15 .05
❑ 266 Cory Snyder .15 .05
❑ 267 David Justice HFA .15 .05
❑ 268 Sammy Sosa HFA .75 .30
❑ 269 Barry Larkin HFA .30 .10
❑ 270 Andres Galarraga HFA .15 .05
❑ 271 Gary Sheffield HFA .15 .05
❑ 272 Jeff Bagwell HFA .30 .10
❑ 273 Mike Piazza HFA .75 .30
❑ 274 Larry Walker HFA .15 .05
❑ 275 Bobby Bonilla HFA .15 .05
❑ 276 John Kruk HFA .15 .05
❑ 277 Jay Bell HFA .15 .05
❑ 278 Ozzie Smith HFA .75 .30
❑ 279 Tony Gwynn HFA .50 .20
❑ 280 Barry Bonds HFA 1.00 .40
❑ 281 Cal Ripken HFA 1.25 .50
❑ 282 Mo Vaughn HFA .15 .05
❑ 283 Tim Salmon HFA .30 .10
❑ 284 Frank Thomas HFA .50 .20
❑ 285 Albert Belle HFA .30 .10
❑ 286 Cecil Fielder HFA .15 .05
❑ 287 Wally Joyner HFA .15 .05
❑ 288 Greg Vaughn HFA .15 .05
❑ 289 Kirby Puckett HFA .50 .20
❑ 290 Don Mattingly HFA 1.00 .40
❑ 291 Terry Steinbach HFA .15 .05
❑ 292 Ken Griffey Jr. HFA .75 .30
❑ 293 Juan Gonzalez HFA .15 .05
❑ 294 Paul Molitor HFA .15 .05
❑ 295 Tavo Alvarez UDCA .15 .05
❑ 296 Matt Brunson UDCA .15 .05
❑ 297 Shawn Green UDCA .30 .10
❑ 298 Alex Rodriguez UDCA 5.00 2.00
❑ 299 Shannon Stewart UDCA .75 .30
❑ 300 Frank Thomas .75 .30
❑ 301 Mickey Tettleton .15 .05
❑ 302 Pedro Munoz .15 .05
❑ 303 Jose Valentin .15 .05
❑ 304 Orestes Destrade .15 .05
❑ 305 Pat Listach .15 .05
❑ 306 Scott Brosius .30 .10
❑ 307 Kurt Miller .15 .05
❑ 308 Rob Dibble .30 .10
❑ 309 Mike Blowers .15 .05
❑ 310 Jim Abbott .50 .20
❑ 311 Mike Jackson .15 .05
❑ 312 Craig Biggio .50 .20
❑ 313 Kurt Abbott RC .15 .05
❑ 314 Chuck Finley .30 .10
❑ 315 Andres Galarraga .30 .10
❑ 316 Mike Moore .15 .05
❑ 317 Doug Strange .15 .05
❑ 318 Pedro Martinez .75 .30
❑ 319 Kevin McReynolds .15 .05
❑ 320 Greg Maddux 1.25 .50
❑ 321 Mike Henneman .15 .05
❑ 322 Scott Leius .15 .05
❑ 323 John Franco .30 .10
❑ 324 Jeff Blauser .15 .05
❑ 325 Kirby Puckett .75 .30
❑ 326 Darryl Hamilton .15 .05
❑ 327 John Smiley .15 .05
❑ 328 Derrick May .15 .05
❑ 329 Jose Vizcaino .15 .05
❑ 330 Randy Johnson .75 .30
❑ 331 Jack Morris .30 .10
❑ 332 Graeme Lloyd .15 .05
❑ 333 Dave Valle .15 .05
❑ 334 Greg Myers .15 .05
❑ 335 John Wetteland .30 .10
❑ 336 Jim Gott .15 .05
❑ 337 Tim Naehring .15 .05
❑ 338 Mike Kelly .15 .05
❑ 339 Jeff Montgomery .15 .05
❑ 340 Rafael Palmeiro .50 .20
❑ 341 Eddie Murray .75 .30
❑ 342 Xavier Hernandez .15 .05
❑ 343 Bobby Munoz .15 .05
❑ 344 Bobby Bonilla .30 .10
❑ 345 Travis Fryman .30 .10
❑ 346 Steve Finley .30 .10
❑ 347 Chris Sabo .15 .05
❑ 348 Armando Reynoso .15 .05
❑ 349 Ramon Martinez .15 .05
❑ 350 Will Clark .50 .20
❑ 351 Moises Alou .30 .10
❑ 352 Jim Thome .50 .20
❑ 353 Bob Tewksbury .15 .05
❑ 354 Andujar Cedeno .15 .05
❑ 355 Orel Hershiser .30 .10
❑ 356 Mike Devereaux .15 .05
❑ 357 Mike Perez .15 .05
❑ 358 Dennis Martinez .30 .10
❑ 359 Dave Nilsson .15 .05
❑ 360 Ozzie Smith 1.25 .50
❑ 361 Eric Anthony .15 .05
❑ 362 Scott Sanders .15 .05
❑ 363 Paul Sorrento .15 .05
❑ 364 Tim Belcher .15 .05
❑ 365 Dennis Eckersley .30 .10
❑ 366 Mel Rojas .15 .05
❑ 367 Tom Henke .15 .05
❑ 368 Randy Tomlin .15 .05
❑ 369 B.J. Surhoff .30 .10
❑ 370 Larry Walker .30 .10
❑ 371 Joey Cora .15 .05
❑ 372 Mike Harkey .15 .05
❑ 373 John Valentin .15 .05
❑ 374 Doug Jones .15 .05
❑ 375 David Justice .30 .10
❑ 376 Vince Coleman .15 .05
❑ 377 David Hulse .15 .05
❑ 378 Kevin Seitzer .15 .05
❑ 379 Pete Harnisch .15 .05
❑ 380 Ruben Sierra .30 .10
❑ 381 Mark Lewis .15 .05
❑ 382 Bip Roberts .15 .05
❑ 383 Paul Wagner .15 .05
❑ 384 Stan Javier .15 .05
❑ 385 Barry Larkin .50 .20
❑ 386 Mark Portugal .15 .05
❑ 387 Roberto Kelly .15 .05
❑ 388 Andy Benes .15 .05
❑ 389 Felix Fermin .15 .05
❑ 390 Marquis Grissom .30 .10
❑ 391 Troy Neel .15 .05
❑ 392 Chad Kreuter .15 .05
❑ 393 Gregg Olson .15 .05
❑ 394 Charles Nagy .15 .05
❑ 395 Jack McDowell .15 .05
❑ 396 Luis Gonzalez .30 .10
❑ 397 Benito Santiago .30 .10
❑ 398 Chris James .15 .05
❑ 399 Terry Mulholland .15 .05
❑ 400 Barry Bonds 2.00 .75
❑ 401 Joe Grahe .15 .05
❑ 402 Duane Ward .15 .05
❑ 403 John Burkett .15 .05
❑ 404 Scott Servais .15 .05
❑ 405 Bryan Harvey .15 .05
❑ 406 Bernard Gilkey .15 .05
❑ 407 Greg McMichael .15 .05
❑ 408 Tim Wallach .15 .05
❑ 409 Ken Caminiti .30 .10
❑ 410 John Kruk .30 .10
❑ 411 Darrin Jackson .15 .05
❑ 412 Mike Gallego .15 .05
❑ 413 David Cone .30 .10
❑ 414 Lou Whitaker .30 .10
❑ 415 Sandy Alomar Jr. .15 .05
❑ 416 Bill Wegman .15 .05
❑ 417 Pat Borders .15 .05
❑ 418 Roger Pavlik .15 .05
❑ 419 Pete Smith .15 .05
❑ 420 Steve Avery .15 .05
❑ 421 David Segui .15 .05
❑ 422 Rheal Cormier .15 .05
❑ 423 Harold Reynolds .30 .10
❑ 424 Edgar Martinez .50 .20
❑ 425 Cal Ripken 2.50 1.00
❑ 426 Jaime Navarro .15 .05
❑ 427 Sean Berry .15 .05
❑ 428 Bret Saberhagen .30 .10
❑ 429 Bob Welch .15 .05
❑ 430 Juan Guzman .15 .05
❑ 431 Cal Eldred .15 .05
❑ 432 Dave Hollins .15 .05
❑ 433 Sid Fernandez .15 .05
❑ 434 Willie Banks .15 .05
❑ 435 Darryl Kile .30 .10
❑ 436 Henry Rodriguez .15 .05
❑ 437 Tony Fernandez .15 .05
❑ 438 Walt Weiss .15 .05
❑ 439 Kevin Tapani .15 .05
❑ 440 Mark Grace .50 .20
❑ 441 Brian Harper .15 .05
❑ 442 Kent Mercker .15 .05
❑ 443 Anthony Young .15 .05
❑ 444 Todd Zeile .15 .05
❑ 445 Greg Vaughn .15 .05
❑ 446 Ray Lankford .30 .10
❑ 447 Dave Weathers .15 .05
❑ 448 Bret Boone .30 .10
❑ 449 Charlie Hough .30 .10
❑ 450 Roger Clemens 1.50 .60
❑ 451 Mike Morgan .15 .05
❑ 452 Doug Drabek .15 .05
❑ 453 Danny Jackson .15 .05
❑ 454 Dante Bichette .30 .10
❑ 455 Roberto Alomar .50 .20
❑ 456 Ben McDonald .15 .05
❑ 457 Kenny Rogers .30 .10
❑ 458 Bill Gullickson .15 .05
❑ 459 Darrin Fletcher .15 .05
❑ 460 Curt Schilling .30 .10
❑ 461 Billy Hatcher .15 .05
❑ 462 Howard Johnson .15 .05
❑ 463 Mickey Morandini .15 .05
❑ 464 Frank Castillo .15 .05
❑ 465 Delino DeShields .15 .05
❑ 466 Gary Gaetti .30 .10
❑ 467 Steve Farr .15 .05
❑ 468 Roberto Hernandez .15 .05
❑ 469 Jack Armstrong .15 .05
❑ 470 Paul Molitor .30 .10
❑ 471 Melido Perez .15 .05
❑ 472 Greg Hibbard .15 .05
❑ 473 Jody Reed .15 .05
❑ 474 Tom Gordon .15 .05
❑ 475 Gary Sheffield .30 .10
❑ 476 John Jaha .15 .05
❑ 477 Shawon Dunston .15 .05
❑ 478 Reggie Jefferson .15 .05
❑ 479 Don Slaught .15 .05
❑ 480 Jeff Bagwell .50 .20
❑ 481 Tim Pugh .15 .05
❑ 482 Kevin Young .15 .05
❑ 483 Ellis Burks .30 .10
❑ 484 Greg Swindell .15 .05
❑ 485 Mark Langston .15 .05
❑ 486 Omar Vizquel .50 .20
❑ 487 Kevin Brown .30 .10
❑ 488 Terry Steinbach .15 .05
❑ 489 Mark Lemke .15 .05
❑ 490 Matt Williams .30 .10
❑ 491 Pete Incaviglia .15 .05
❑ 492 Karl Rhodes .15 .05
❑ 493 Shawn Green .75 .30
❑ 494 Hal Morris .15 .05
❑ 495 Derek Bell .15 .05
❑ 496 Luis Polonia .15 .05
❑ 497 Otis Nixon .15 .05
❑ 498 Ron Darling .15 .05
❑ 499 Mitch Williams .15 .05
❑ 500 Mike Piazza 1.50 .60
❑ 501 Pat Meares .15 .05
❑ 502 Scott Cooper .15 .05
❑ 503 Scott Erickson .15 .05
❑ 504 Jeff Juden .15 .05
❑ 505 Lee Smith .30 .10
❑ 506 Bobby Ayala .15 .05
❑ 507 Dave Henderson .15 .05
❑ 508 Erik Hanson .15 .05
❑ 509 Bob Wickman .15 .05
❑ 510 Sammy Sosa .75 .30
❑ 511 Hector Carrasco .15 .05
❑ 512 Tim Davis .15 .05

❑ 513 Joey Hamilton .15 .05
❑ 514 Robert Eenhoorn .15 .05
❑ 515 Jorge Fabregas .15 .05
❑ 516 Tim Hyers RC .15 .05
❑ 517 John Hudek RC .15 .05
❑ 518 James Mouton .15 .05
❑ 519 Herbert Perry RC .15 .05
❑ 520 Chan Ho Park RC .75 .30
❑ 521 W.VanLandingham RC .15 .05
❑ 522 Paul Shuey DD .15 .05
❑ 523 Ryan Hancock RC .15 .05
❑ 524 Billy Wagner RC 2.00 .75
❑ 525 Jason Giambi .75 .30
❑ 526 Jose Silva RC .15 .05
❑ 527 Terrell Wade RC .15 .05
❑ 528 Todd Dunn .15 .05
❑ 529 Alan Benes RC .40 .15
❑ 530 Brooks Kieschnick RC .15 .05
❑ 531 Todd Hollandsworth .15 .05
❑ 532 Brad Fullmer RC .40 .15
❑ 533 Steve Soderstrom RC .15 .05
❑ 534 Daron Kirkreit .15 .05
❑ 535 Arquimedez Pozo RC .15 .05
❑ 536 Charles Johnson .30 .10
❑ 537 Preston Wilson .30 .10
❑ 538 Alex Ochoa .15 .05
❑ 539 Derrek Lee RC 4.00 1.50
❑ 540 Wayne Gomes RC .15 .05
❑ 541 Jermaine Allensworth RC .15 .05
❑ 542 Mike Bell RC .15 .05
❑ 543 Trot Nixon RC 2.00 .75
❑ 544 Pokey Reese .15 .05
❑ 545 Neifi Perez RC .40 .15
❑ 546 Johnny Damon .75 .30
❑ 547 Matt Brunson RC .15 .05
❑ 548 LaTroy Hawkins RC .40 .15
❑ 549 Eddie Pearson RC .15 .05
❑ 550 Derek Jeter 2.50 1.00
❑ A298 Alex Rodriguez AU 400.00 250.00
❑ P224 Ken Griffey Jr. Promo 2.00 .75
❑ GM1 Griffey/Mantle AU/1000 1200.00 800.00
❑ KG1 K.Griffey Jr. AU/1000 250.00 150.00
❑ MM1 M.Mantle AU/1000 750.00 450.00

1995 Upper Deck

❑ COMP.MASTER SET (495) 110.00 55.00
❑ COMPLETE SET (450) 50.00 20.00
❑ COMPLETE SERIES 1 (225) 25.00 10.00
❑ COMPLETE SERIES 2 (225) 25.00 10.00
❑ COMMON CARD (1-450) .15 .05
❑ COMP.TRADE SET (45) 60.00 30.00
❑ COMMON TRADE (451T-495T) 1.00 .40
❑ 1 Ruben Rivera .15 .05
❑ 2 Bill Pulsipher .15 .05
❑ 3 Ben Grieve .15 .05
❑ 4 Curtis Goodwin .15 .05
❑ 5 Damon Hollins .15 .05
❑ 6 Todd Greene .15 .05
❑ 7 Glenn Williams .15 .05
❑ 8 Bret Wagner .15 .05
❑ 9 Karim Garcia RC .15 .05
❑ 10 Nomar Garciaparra 2.00 .75
❑ 11 Raul Casanova RC .15 .05
❑ 12 Matt Smith .15 .05
❑ 13 Paul Wilson .15 .05
❑ 14 Jason Isringhausen .30 .10
❑ 15 Reid Ryan .30 .10
❑ 16 Lee Smith .30 .10
❑ 17 Chili Davis .30 .10
❑ 18 Brian Anderson .15 .05
❑ 19 Gary DiSarcina .15 .05
❑ 20 Bo Jackson .75 .30
❑ 21 Chuck Finley .30 .10
❑ 22 Darryl Kile .30 .10
❑ 23 Shane Reynolds .15 .05
❑ 24 Tony Eusebio .15 .05
❑ 25 Craig Biggio .50 .20
❑ 26 Doug Drabek .15 .05
❑ 27 Brian L.Hunter .15 .05
❑ 28 James Mouton .15 .05
❑ 29 Geronimo Berroa .15 .05
❑ 30 Rickey Henderson .75 .30
❑ 31 Steve Karsay .15 .05
❑ 32 Steve Ontiveros .15 .05
❑ 33 Ernie Young .15 .05
❑ 34 Dennis Eckersley .30 .10
❑ 35 Mark McGwire 2.00 .75
❑ 36 Dave Stewart .30 .10
❑ 37 Pat Hentgen .15 .05
❑ 38 Carlos Delgado .30 .10
❑ 39 Joe Carter .30 .10
❑ 40 Roberto Alomar .50 .20
❑ 41 John Olerud .30 .10
❑ 42 Devon White .30 .10
❑ 43 Roberto Kelly .15 .05
❑ 44 Jeff Blauser .15 .05
❑ 45 Fred McGriff .50 .20
❑ 46 Tom Glavine .50 .20
❑ 47 Mike Kelly .15 .05
❑ 48 Javier Lopez .30 .10
❑ 49 Greg Maddux 1.25 .50
❑ 50 Matt Mieske .15 .05
❑ 51 Troy O'Leary .15 .05
❑ 52 Jeff Cirillo .15 .05
❑ 53 Cal Eldred .15 .05
❑ 54 Pat Listach .15 .05
❑ 55 Jose Valentin .15 .05
❑ 56 John Mabry .15 .05
❑ 57 Bob Tewksbury .15 .05
❑ 58 Brian Jordan .30 .10
❑ 59 Gregg Jefferies .15 .05
❑ 60 Ozzie Smith 1.25 .50
❑ 61 Geronimo Pena .15 .05
❑ 62 Mark Whiten .15 .05
❑ 63 Rey Sanchez .15 .05
❑ 64 Willie Banks .15 .05
❑ 65 Mark Grace .50 .20
❑ 66 Randy Myers .15 .05
❑ 67 Steve Trachsel .15 .05
❑ 68 Derrick May .15 .05
❑ 69 Brett Butler .30 .10
❑ 70 Eric Karros .30 .10
❑ 71 Tim Wallach .15 .05
❑ 72 Delino DeShields .15 .05
❑ 73 Darren Dreifort .15 .05
❑ 74 Orel Hershiser .30 .10
❑ 75 Billy Ashley .15 .05
❑ 76 Sean Berry .15 .05
❑ 77 Ken Hill .15 .05
❑ 78 John Wetteland .30 .10
❑ 79 Moises Alou .30 .10
❑ 80 Cliff Floyd .30 .10
❑ 81 Marquis Grissom .30 .10
❑ 82 Larry Walker .30 .10
❑ 83 Rondell White .30 .10
❑ 84 William VanLandingham .15 .05
❑ 85 Matt Williams .30 .10
❑ 86 Rod Beck .15 .05
❑ 87 Darren Lewis .15 .05
❑ 88 Robby Thompson .15 .05
❑ 89 Darryl Strawberry .30 .10
❑ 90 Kenny Lofton .30 .10
❑ 91 Charles Nagy .15 .05
❑ 92 Sandy Alomar Jr. .15 .05
❑ 93 Mark Clark .15 .05
❑ 94 Dennis Martinez .30 .10
❑ 95 Dave Winfield .30 .10
❑ 96 Jim Thome .50 .20
❑ 97 Manny Ramirez .50 .20
❑ 98 Goose Gossage .30 .10
❑ 99 Tino Martinez .50 .20
❑ 100 Ken Griffey Jr. 1.25 .50
❑ 101 Greg Maddux ANA .75 .30
❑ 102 Randy Johnson ANA .50 .20
❑ 103 Barry Bonds ANA 1.00 .40
❑ 104 Juan Gonzalez ANA .15 .05
❑ 105 Frank Thomas ANA .50 .20
❑ 106 Matt Williams ANA .15 .05
❑ 107 Paul Molitor ANA .15 .05
❑ 108 Fred McGriff ANA .30 .10
❑ 109 Carlos Baerga ANA .15 .05
❑ 110 Ken Griffey Jr. ANA .75 .30
❑ 111 Reggie Jefferson .15 .05
❑ 112 Randy Johnson .75 .30
❑ 113 Marc Newfield .15 .05
❑ 114 Robb Nen .30 .10
❑ 115 Jeff Conine .30 .10
❑ 116 Kurt Abbott .15 .05
❑ 117 Charlie Hough .30 .10
❑ 118 Dave Weathers .15 .05
❑ 119 Juan Castillo .15 .05
❑ 120 Bret Saberhagen .30 .10
❑ 121 Rico Brogna .15 .05
❑ 122 John Franco .30 .10
❑ 123 Todd Hundley .15 .05
❑ 124 Jason Jacome .15 .05
❑ 125 Bobby Jones .15 .05
❑ 126 Bret Barberie .15 .05
❑ 127 Ben McDonald .15 .05
❑ 128 Harold Baines .30 .10
❑ 129 Jeffrey Hammonds .15 .05
❑ 130 Mike Mussina .50 .20
❑ 131 Chris Hoiles .15 .05
❑ 132 Brady Anderson .30 .10
❑ 133 Eddie Williams .15 .05
❑ 134 Andy Benes .15 .05
❑ 135 Tony Gwynn 1.00 .40
❑ 136 Bip Roberts .15 .05
❑ 137 Joey Hamilton .15 .05
❑ 138 Luis Lopez .15 .05
❑ 139 Ray McDavid .15 .05
❑ 140 Lenny Dykstra .30 .10
❑ 141 Mariano Duncan .15 .05
❑ 142 Fernando Valenzuela .30 .10
❑ 143 Bobby Munoz .15 .05
❑ 144 Kevin Stocker .15 .05
❑ 145 John Kruk .30 .10
❑ 146 Jon Lieber .15 .05
❑ 147 Zane Smith .15 .05
❑ 148 Steve Cooke .15 .05
❑ 149 Andy Van Slyke .50 .20
❑ 150 Jay Bell .30 .10
❑ 151 Carlos Garcia .15 .05
❑ 152 John Dettmer .15 .05
❑ 153 Darren Oliver .15 .05
❑ 154 Dean Palmer .30 .10
❑ 155 Otis Nixon .15 .05
❑ 156 Rusty Greer .30 .10
❑ 157 Rick Helling .15 .05
❑ 158 Jose Canseco .50 .20
❑ 159 Roger Clemens 1.50 .60
❑ 160 Andre Dawson .30 .10
❑ 161 Mo Vaughn .30 .10
❑ 162 Aaron Sele .15 .05
❑ 163 John Valentin .15 .05
❑ 164 Brian R. Hunter .15 .05
❑ 165 Bret Boone .30 .10
❑ 166 Hector Carrasco .15 .05
❑ 167 Pete Schourek .15 .05
❑ 168 Willie Greene .15 .05
❑ 169 Kevin Mitchell .15 .05
❑ 170 Deion Sanders .50 .20
❑ 171 John Roper .15 .05
❑ 172 Charlie Hayes .15 .05
❑ 173 David Nied .15 .05
❑ 174 Ellis Burks .30 .10
❑ 175 Dante Bichette .30 .10
❑ 176 Marvin Freeman .15 .05
❑ 177 Eric Young .15 .05
❑ 178 David Cone .30 .10
❑ 179 Greg Gagne .15 .05
❑ 180 Bob Hamelin .15 .05
❑ 181 Wally Joyner .30 .10
❑ 182 Jeff Montgomery .15 .05
❑ 183 Jose Lind .15 .05
❑ 184 Chris Gomez .15 .05
❑ 185 Travis Fryman .30 .10
❑ 186 Kirk Gibson .30 .10
❑ 187 Mike Moore .15 .05
❑ 188 Lou Whitaker .30 .10

❑ 189 Sean Bergman .15 .05
❑ 190 Shane Mack .15 .05
❑ 191 Rick Aguilera .15 .05
❑ 192 Denny Hocking .15 .05
❑ 193 Chuck Knoblauch .30 .10
❑ 194 Kevin Tapani .15 .05
❑ 195 Kent Hrbek .30 .10
❑ 196 Ozzie Guillen .30 .10
❑ 197 Wilson Alvarez .15 .05
❑ 198 Tim Raines .30 .10
❑ 199 Scott Ruffcorn .15 .05
❑ 200 Michael Jordan 2.50 1.00
❑ 201 Robin Ventura .30 .10
❑ 202 Jason Bere .15 .05
❑ 203 Darrin Jackson .15 .05
❑ 204 Russ Davis .15 .05
❑ 205 Jimmy Key .30 .10
❑ 206 Jack McDowell .15 .05
❑ 207 Jim Abbott .50 .20
❑ 208 Paul O'Neill .50 .20
❑ 209 Bernie Williams .50 .20
❑ 210 Don Mattingly 2.00 .75
❑ 211 Orlando Miller .15 .05
❑ 212 Alex Gonzalez .15 .05
❑ 213 Terrell Wade .15 .05
❑ 214 Jose Oliva .15 .05
❑ 215 Alex Rodriguez 2.00 .75
❑ 216 Garret Anderson .30 .10
❑ 217 Alan Benes .15 .05
❑ 218 Armando Benitez .15 .05
❑ 219 Dustin Hermanson .15 .05
❑ 220 Charles Johnson .30 .10
❑ 221 Julian Tavarez .15 .05
❑ 222 Jason Giambi .50 .20
❑ 223 LaTroy Hawkins .15 .05
❑ 224 Todd Hollandsworth .15 .05
❑ 225 Derek Jeter 2.00 .75
❑ 226 Hideo Nomo RC 2.50 1.00
❑ 227 Tony Clark .15 .05
❑ 228 Roger Cedeno .15 .05
❑ 229 Scott Stahoviak .15 .05
❑ 230 Michael Tucker .15 .05
❑ 231 Joe Rosselli .15 .05
❑ 232 Antonio Osuna .15 .05
❑ 233 Bob Higginson RC .75 .30
❑ 234 Mark Grudzielanek RC .75 .30
❑ 235 Ray Durham .30 .10
❑ 236 Frank Rodriguez .15 .05
❑ 237 Quilvio Veras .15 .05
❑ 238 Darren Bragg .15 .05
❑ 239 Ugueth Urbina .15 .05
❑ 240 Jason Bates .15 .05
❑ 241 David Bell .15 .05
❑ 242 Ron Villone .15 .05
❑ 243 Joe Randa .30 .10
❑ 244 Carlos Perez RC .40 .15
❑ 245 Brad Clontz .15 .05
❑ 246 Steve Rodriguez .15 .05
❑ 247 Joe Vitiello .15 .05
❑ 248 Ozzie Timmons .15 .05
❑ 249 Rudy Pemberton .15 .05
❑ 250 Marty Cordova .15 .05
❑ 251 Tony Graffanino .15 .05
❑ 252 Mark Johnson RC .40 .15
❑ 253 Tomas Perez RC .15 .05
❑ 254 Jimmy Hurst .15 .05
❑ 255 Edgardo Alfonzo .15 .05
❑ 256 Jose Malave .15 .05
❑ 257 Brad Radke RC .75 .30
❑ 258 Jon Nunnally .15 .05
❑ 259 Dilson Torres RC .15 .05
❑ 260 Esteban Loaiza .15 .05
❑ 261 Freddy Adrian Garcia RC .15 .05
❑ 262 Don Wengert .15 .05
❑ 263 Robert Person RC .40 .15
❑ 264 Tim Unroe RC .15 .05
❑ 265 Juan Acevedo RC .15 .05
❑ 266 Eduardo Perez .15 .05
❑ 267 Tony Phillips .15 .05
❑ 268 Jim Edmonds .50 .20
❑ 269 Jorge Fabregas .15 .05
❑ 270 Tim Salmon .50 .20
❑ 271 Mark Langston .15 .05
❑ 272 J.T. Snow .30 .10
❑ 273 Phil Plantier .15 .05
❑ 274 Derek Bell .15 .05
❑ 275 Jeff Bagwell .50 .20
❑ 276 Luis Gonzalez .30 .10
❑ 277 John Hudek .15 .05
❑ 278 Todd Stottlemyre .15 .05
❑ 279 Mark Acre .15 .05
❑ 280 Ruben Sierra .30 .10
❑ 281 Mike Bordick .15 .05
❑ 282 Ron Darling .15 .05
❑ 283 Brent Gates .15 .05
❑ 284 Todd Van Poppel .15 .05
❑ 285 Paul Molitor .30 .10
❑ 286 Ed Sprague .15 .05
❑ 287 Juan Guzman .15 .05
❑ 288 David Cone .30 .10
❑ 289 Shawn Green .30 .10
❑ 290 Marquis Grissom .30 .10
❑ 291 Kent Mercker .15 .05
❑ 292 Steve Avery .15 .05
❑ 293 Chipper Jones .75 .30
❑ 294 John Smoltz .50 .20
❑ 295 David Justice .30 .10
❑ 296 Ryan Klesko .30 .10
❑ 297 Joe Oliver .15 .05
❑ 298 Ricky Bones .15 .05
❑ 299 John Jaha .15 .05
❑ 300 Greg Vaughn .15 .05
❑ 301 Dave Nilsson .15 .05
❑ 302 Kevin Seitzer .15 .05
❑ 303 Bernard Gilkey .15 .05
❑ 304 Allen Battle .15 .05
❑ 305 Ray Lankford .30 .10
❑ 306 Tom Pagnozzi .15 .05
❑ 307 Allen Watson .15 .05
❑ 308 Danny Jackson .15 .05
❑ 309 Ken Hill .15 .05
❑ 310 Todd Zeile .15 .05
❑ 311 Kevin Roberson .15 .05
❑ 312 Steve Buechele .15 .05
❑ 313 Rick Wilkins .15 .05
❑ 314 Kevin Foster .15 .05
❑ 315 Sammy Sosa .75 .30
❑ 316 Howard Johnson .15 .05
❑ 317 Greg Hansell .15 .05
❑ 318 Pedro Astacio .15 .05
❑ 319 Rafael Bournigal .15 .05
❑ 320 Mike Piazza 1.25 .50
❑ 321 Ramon Martinez .15 .05
❑ 322 Raul Mondesi .30 .10
❑ 323 Ismael Valdes .15 .05
❑ 324 Wil Cordero .15 .05
❑ 325 Tony Tarasco .15 .05
❑ 326 Roberto Kelly .15 .05
❑ 327 Jeff Fassero .15 .05
❑ 328 Mike Lansing .15 .05
❑ 329 Pedro Martinez .50 .20
❑ 330 Kirk Rueter .15 .05
❑ 331 Glenallen Hill .15 .05
❑ 332 Kirt Manwaring .15 .05
❑ 333 Royce Clayton .15 .05
❑ 334 J.R. Phillips .15 .05
❑ 335 Barry Bonds 2.00 .75
❑ 336 Mark Portugal .15 .05
❑ 337 Terry Mulholland .15 .05
❑ 338 Omar Vizquel .50 .20
❑ 339 Carlos Baerga .15 .05
❑ 340 Albert Belle .30 .10
❑ 341 Eddie Murray .75 .30
❑ 342 Wayne Kirby .15 .05
❑ 343 Chad Ogea .15 .05
❑ 344 Tim Davis .15 .05
❑ 345 Jay Buhner .30 .10
❑ 346 Bobby Ayala .15 .05
❑ 347 Mike Blowers .15 .05
❑ 348 Dave Fleming .15 .05
❑ 349 Edgar Martinez .50 .20
❑ 350 Andre Dawson .30 .10
❑ 351 Darrell Whitmore .15 .05
❑ 352 Chuck Carr .15 .05
❑ 353 John Burkett .15 .05
❑ 354 Chris Hammond .15 .05
❑ 355 Gary Sheffield .30 .10
❑ 356 Pat Rapp .15 .05
❑ 357 Greg Colbrunn .15 .05
❑ 358 David Segui .15 .05
❑ 359 Jeff Kent .30 .10
❑ 360 Bobby Bonilla .30 .10
❑ 361 Pete Harnisch .15 .05
❑ 362 Ryan Thompson .15 .05
❑ 363 Jose Vizcaino .15 .05
❑ 364 Brett Butler .30 .10
❑ 365 Cal Ripken 2.50 1.00
❑ 366 Rafael Palmeiro .50 .20
❑ 367 Leo Gomez .15 .05
❑ 368 Andy Van Slyke .50 .20
❑ 369 Arthur Rhodes .15 .05
❑ 370 Ken Caminiti .30 .10
❑ 371 Steve Finley .30 .10
❑ 372 Melvin Nieves .15 .05
❑ 373 Andujar Cedeno .15 .05
❑ 374 Trevor Hoffman .30 .10
❑ 375 Fernando Valenzuela .30 .10
❑ 376 Ricky Bottalico .15 .05
❑ 377 Dave Hollins .15 .05
❑ 378 Charlie Hayes .15 .05
❑ 379 Tommy Greene .15 .05
❑ 380 Darren Daulton .30 .10
❑ 381 Curt Schilling .30 .10
❑ 382 Midre Cummings .15 .05
❑ 383 Al Martin .15 .05
❑ 384 Jeff King .15 .05
❑ 385 Orlando Merced .15 .05
❑ 386 Denny Neagle .30 .10
❑ 387 Don Slaught .15 .05
❑ 388 Dave Clark .15 .05
❑ 389 Kevin Gross .15 .05
❑ 390 Will Clark .50 .20
❑ 391 Ivan Rodriguez .50 .20
❑ 392 Benji Gil .15 .05
❑ 393 Jeff Frye .15 .05
❑ 394 Kenny Rogers .30 .10
❑ 395 Juan Gonzalez .30 .10
❑ 396 Mike Macfarlane .15 .05
❑ 397 Lee Tinsley .15 .05
❑ 398 Tim Naehring .15 .05
❑ 399 Tim Vanegmond .15 .05
❑ 400 Mike Greenwell .15 .05
❑ 401 Ken Ryan .15 .05
❑ 402 John Smiley .15 .05
❑ 403 Tim Pugh .15 .05
❑ 404 Reggie Sanders .30 .10
❑ 405 Barry Larkin .50 .20
❑ 406 Hal Morris .15 .05
❑ 407 Jose Rijo .15 .05
❑ 408 Lance Painter .15 .05
❑ 409 Joe Girardi .15 .05
❑ 410 Andres Galarraga .30 .10
❑ 411 Mike Kingery .15 .05
❑ 412 Roberto Mejia .15 .05
❑ 413 Walt Weiss .15 .05
❑ 414 Bill Swift .15 .05
❑ 415 Larry Walker .30 .10
❑ 416 Billy Brewer .15 .05
❑ 417 Pat Borders .15 .05
❑ 418 Tom Gordon .15 .05
❑ 419 Kevin Appier .30 .10
❑ 420 Gary Gaetti .30 .10
❑ 421 Greg Gohr .15 .05
❑ 422 Felipe Lira .15 .05
❑ 423 John Doherty .15 .05
❑ 424 Chad Curtis .15 .05
❑ 425 Cecil Fielder .30 .10
❑ 426 Alan Trammell .30 .10
❑ 427 David McCarty .15 .05
❑ 428 Scott Erickson .15 .05
❑ 429 Pat Mahomes .15 .05
❑ 430 Kirby Puckett .75 .30
❑ 431 Dave Stevens .15 .05
❑ 432 Pedro Munoz .15 .05
❑ 433 Chris Sabo .15 .05
❑ 434 Alex Fernandez .15 .05
❑ 435 Frank Thomas .75 .30
❑ 436 Roberto Hernandez .15 .05
❑ 437 Lance Johnson .15 .05
❑ 438 Jim Abbott .50 .20
❑ 439 John Wetteland .30 .10
❑ 440 Melido Perez .15 .05
❑ 441 Tony Fernandez .15 .05
❑ 442 Pat Kelly .15 .05
❑ 443 Mike Stanley .15 .05
❑ 444 Danny Tartabull .15 .05
❑ 445 Wade Boggs .50 .20
❑ 446 Robin Yount TRIB 1.25 .50

❑ 447 Ryne Sandberg TRIB 1.25 .50
❑ 448 Nolan Ryan TRIB 3.00 1.25
❑ 449 George Brett TRIB 2.00 .75
❑ 450 Mike Schmidt TRIB 1.25 .50
❑ 451 Jim Abbott TRADE 2.00 .75
❑ 452 Danny Tartabull TRADE 1.00 .40
❑ 453 Ariel Prieto TRADE 1.00 .40
❑ 454 Scott Cooper TRADE 1.00 .40
❑ 455 Tom Henke TRADE 1.00 .40
❑ 456 Todd Zeile TRADE 1.00 .40
❑ 457 Brian McRae TRADE 1.00 .40
❑ 458 Luis Gonzalez TRADE 1.50 .60
❑ 459 Jaime Navarro TRADE 1.00 .40
❑ 460 Todd Worrell TRADE 1.00 .40
❑ 461 Roberto Kelly TRADE 1.00 .40
❑ 462 Chad Fonville TRADE 1.00 .40
❑ 463 Shane Andrews TRADE 1.00 .40
❑ 464 David Segui TRADE 1.00 .40
❑ 465 Deion Sanders TRADE 2.00 .75
❑ 466 Orel Hershiser TRADE 1.50 .60
❑ 467 Ken Hill TRADE 1.00 .40
❑ 468 Andy Benes TRADE 1.00 .40
❑ 469 Terry Pendleton TRADE 1.50 .60
❑ 470 Bobby Bonilla TRADE 1.50 .60
❑ 471 Scott Erickson TRADE 1.00 .40
❑ 472 Kevin Brown TRADE 1.50 .60
❑ 473 Glenn Dishman TRADE 1.00 .40
❑ 474 Phil Plantier TRADE 1.00 .40
❑ 475 Gregg Jefferies TRADE 1.00 .40
❑ 476 Tyler Green TRADE 1.00 .40
❑ 477 Heathcliff Slocumb TRADE 1.00 .40
❑ 478 Mark Whiten TRADE 1.00 .40
❑ 479 Mickey Tettleton TRADE 1.00 .40
❑ 480 Tim Wakefield TRADE 1.50 .60
❑ 481 Vaughn Eshelman TRADE 1.00 .40
❑ 482 Rick Aguilera TRADE 1.00 .40
❑ 483 Erik Hanson TRADE 1.00 .40
❑ 484 Willie McGee TRADE 1.50 .60
❑ 485 Troy O'Leary TRADE 1.00 .40
❑ 486 Benito Santiago TRADE 1.50 .60
❑ 487 Darren Lewis TRADE 1.00 .40
❑ 488 Dave Burba TRADE 1.00 .40
❑ 489 Ron Gant TRADE 1.50 .60
❑ 490 Bret Saberhagen TRADE 1.50 .60
❑ 491 Vinny Castilla TRADE 1.50 .60
❑ 492 Frank Rodriguez TRADE 1.00 .40
❑ 493 Andy Pettitte TRADE 2.00 .75
❑ 494 Ruben Sierra TRADE 1.50 .60
❑ 495 David Cone TRADE 1.50 .60
❑ J159 R.Clemens Jumbo AU 100.00 50.00
❑ J215 A.Rodriguez Jumbo AU 120.00 60.00
❑ P100 Ken Griffey Jr. Promo 2.00 .75

1996 Upper Deck

❑ COMPLETE SET (480) 50.00 20.00
❑ COMP.FACT.SET (510) 100.00 50.00
❑ COMPLETE SERIES 1 (240) 25.00 10.00
❑ COMPLETE SERIES 2 (240) 25.00 10.00
❑ COMMON CARD (1-480) .30 .10
❑ COMP.UPDATE SET (30) 20.00 10.00
❑ COMMON UPDATE (481U-510U) .50 .20
❑ 1 Cal Ripken 2131 4.00 1.50
❑ 2 Eddie Murray 3000 Hits .50 .20
❑ 3 Mark Wohlers .30 .10
❑ 4 David Justice .30 .10
❑ 5 Chipper Jones .75 .30
❑ 6 Javier Lopez .30 .10
❑ 7 Mark Lemke .30 .10
❑ 8 Marquis Grissom .30 .10
❑ 9 Tom Glavine .50 .20
❑ 10 Greg Maddux 1.25 .50
❑ 11 Manny Alexander .30 .10
❑ 12 Curtis Goodwin .30 .10
❑ 13 Scott Erickson .30 .10
❑ 14 Chris Hoiles .30 .10
❑ 15 Rafael Palmeiro .50 .20
❑ 16 Rick Krivda .30 .10
❑ 17 Jeff Manto .30 .10
❑ 18 Mo Vaughn .30 .10
❑ 19 Tim Wakefield .30 .10
❑ 20 Roger Clemens 1.50 .60
❑ 21 Tim Naehring .30 .10
❑ 22 Troy O'Leary .30 .10
❑ 23 Mike Greenwell .30 .10
❑ 24 Stan Belinda .30 .10
❑ 25 John Valentin .30 .10
❑ 26 J.T. Snow .30 .10
❑ 27 Gary DiSarcina .30 .10
❑ 28 Mark Langston .30 .10
❑ 29 Brian Anderson .30 .10
❑ 30 Jim Edmonds .30 .10
❑ 31 Garret Anderson .30 .10
❑ 32 Orlando Palmeiro .30 .10
❑ 33 Brian McRae .30 .10
❑ 34 Kevin Foster .30 .10
❑ 35 Sammy Sosa .75 .30
❑ 36 Todd Zeile .30 .10
❑ 37 Jim Bullinger .30 .10
❑ 38 Luis Gonzalez .30 .10
❑ 39 Lyle Mouton .30 .10
❑ 40 Ray Durham .30 .10
❑ 41 Ozzie Guillen .30 .10
❑ 42 Alex Fernandez .30 .10
❑ 43 Brian Keyser .30 .10
❑ 44 Robin Ventura .30 .10
❑ 45 Reggie Sanders .30 .10
❑ 46 Pete Schourek .30 .10
❑ 47 John Smiley .30 .10
❑ 48 Jeff Brantley .30 .10
❑ 49 Thomas Howard .30 .10
❑ 50 Bret Boone .30 .10
❑ 51 Kevin Jarvis .30 .10
❑ 52 Jeff Branson .30 .10
❑ 53 Carlos Baerga .30 .10
❑ 54 Jim Thome .50 .20
❑ 55 Manny Ramirez .50 .20
❑ 56 Omar Vizquel .50 .20
❑ 57 Jose Mesa .30 .10
❑ 58 Julian Tavarez UER .30 .10
❑ 59 Orel Hershiser .30 .10
❑ 60 Larry Walker .30 .10
❑ 61 Bret Saberhagen .30 .10
❑ 62 Vinny Castilla .30 .10
❑ 63 Eric Young .30 .10
❑ 64 Bryan Rekar .30 .10
❑ 65 Andres Galarraga .30 .10
❑ 66 Steve Reed .30 .10
❑ 67 Chad Curtis .30 .10
❑ 68 Bobby Higginson .30 .10
❑ 69 Phil Nevin .30 .10
❑ 70 Cecil Fielder .30 .10
❑ 71 Felipe Lira .30 .10
❑ 72 Chris Gomez .30 .10
❑ 73 Charles Johnson .30 .10
❑ 74 Quilvio Veras .30 .10
❑ 75 Jeff Conine .30 .10
❑ 76 John Burkett .30 .10
❑ 77 Greg Colbrunn .30 .10
❑ 78 Terry Pendleton .30 .10
❑ 79 Shane Reynolds .30 .10
❑ 80 Jeff Bagwell .50 .20
❑ 81 Orlando Miller .30 .10
❑ 82 Mike Hampton .30 .10
❑ 83 James Mouton .30 .10
❑ 84 Brian L. Hunter .30 .10
❑ 85 Derek Bell .30 .10
❑ 86 Kevin Appier .30 .10
❑ 87 Joe Vitiello .30 .10
❑ 88 Wally Joyner .30 .10
❑ 89 Michael Tucker .30 .10
❑ 90 Johnny Damon .50 .20
❑ 91 Jon Nunnally .30 .10
❑ 92 Jason Jacome .30 .10
❑ 93 Chad Fonville .30 .10
❑ 94 Chan Ho Park .30 .10
❑ 95 Hideo Nomo .75 .30
❑ 96 Ismael Valdes .30 .10
❑ 97 Greg Gagne .30 .10
❑ 98 Diamondbacks-Devil Rays .75 .30
❑ 99 Raul Mondesi .30 .10
❑ 100 Dave Winfield YH .30 .10
❑ 101 Dennis Eckersley YH .30 .10
❑ 102 Andre Dawson YH .30 .10
❑ 103 Dennis Martinez YH .30 .10
❑ 104 Lance Parrish YH .30 .10
❑ 105 Eddie Murray YH .50 .20
❑ 106 Alan Trammell YH .30 .10
❑ 107 Lou Whitaker YH .30 .10
❑ 108 Ozzie Smith YH .75 .30
❑ 109 Paul Molitor YH .30 .10
❑ 110 Rickey Henderson YH .50 .20
❑ 111 Tim Raines YH .30 .10
❑ 112 Harold Baines YH .30 .10
❑ 113 Lee Smith YH .30 .10
❑ 114 Fernando Valenzuela YH .30 .10
❑ 115 Cal Ripken YH 1.25 .50
❑ 116 Tony Gwynn YH .50 .20
❑ 117 Wade Boggs .50 .20
❑ 118 Todd Hollandsworth .30 .10
❑ 119 Dave Nilsson .30 .10
❑ 120 Jose Valentin .30 .10
❑ 121 Steve Sparks .30 .10
❑ 122 Chuck Carr .30 .10
❑ 123 John Jaha .30 .10
❑ 124 Scott Karl .30 .10
❑ 125 Chuck Knoblauch .30 .10
❑ 126 Brad Radke .30 .10
❑ 127 Pat Meares .30 .10
❑ 128 Ron Coomer .30 .10
❑ 129 Pedro Munoz .30 .10
❑ 130 Kirby Puckett .75 .30
❑ 131 David Segui .30 .10
❑ 132 Mark Grudzielanek .30 .10
❑ 133 Mike Lansing .30 .10
❑ 134 Sean Berry .30 .10
❑ 135 Rondell White .30 .10
❑ 136 Pedro Martinez .50 .20
❑ 137 Carl Everett .30 .10
❑ 138 Dave Mlicki .30 .10
❑ 139 Bill Pulsipher .30 .10
❑ 140 Jason Isringhausen .30 .10
❑ 141 Rico Brogna .30 .10
❑ 142 Edgardo Alfonzo .30 .10
❑ 143 Jeff Kent .30 .10
❑ 144 Andy Pettitte .50 .20
❑ 145 Mike Piazza BO .75 .30
❑ 146 Cliff Floyd BO .30 .10
❑ 147 Jason Isringhausen BO .30 .10
❑ 148 Tim Wakefield BO .30 .10
❑ 149 Chipper Jones BO .50 .20
❑ 150 Hideo Nomo BO .50 .20
❑ 151 Mark McGwire BO 1.00 .40
❑ 152 Ron Gant BO .30 .10
❑ 153 Gary Gaetti BO .30 .10
❑ 154 Don Mattingly 2.00 .75
❑ 155 Paul O'Neill .50 .20
❑ 156 Derek Jeter 2.00 .75
❑ 157 Joe Girardi .30 .10
❑ 158 Ruben Sierra .30 .10
❑ 159 Jorge Posada .50 .20
❑ 160 Geronimo Berroa .30 .10
❑ 161 Steve Ontiveros .30 .10
❑ 162 George Williams .30 .10
❑ 163 Doug Johns .30 .10
❑ 164 Ariel Prieto .30 .10
❑ 165 Scott Brosius .30 .10
❑ 166 Mike Bordick .30 .10
❑ 167 Tyler Green .30 .10
❑ 168 Mickey Morandini .30 .10
❑ 169 Darren Daulton .30 .10
❑ 170 Gregg Jefferies .30 .10
❑ 171 Jim Eisenreich .30 .10
❑ 172 Heathcliff Slocumb .30 .10
❑ 173 Kevin Stocker .30 .10
❑ 174 Esteban Loaiza .30 .10
❑ 175 Jeff King .30 .10
❑ 176 Mark Johnson .30 .10
❑ 177 Denny Neagle .30 .10
❑ 178 Orlando Merced .30 .10
❑ 179 Carlos Garcia .30 .10

❑	180	Brian Jordan	.30	.10
❑	181	Mike Morgan	.30	.10
❑	182	Mark Petkovsek	.30	.10
❑	183	Bernard Gilkey	.30	.10
❑	184	John Mabry	.30	.10
❑	185	Tom Henke	.30	.10
❑	186	Glenn Dishman	.30	.10
❑	187	Andy Ashby	.30	.10
❑	188	Bip Roberts	.30	.10
❑	189	Melvin Nieves	.30	.10
❑	190	Ken Caminiti	.30	.10
❑	191	Brad Ausmus	.30	.10
❑	192	Deion Sanders	.50	.20
❑	193	Jamie Brewington RC	.30	.10
❑	194	Glenallen Hill	.30	.10
❑	195	Barry Bonds	2.00	.75
❑	196	Wm. Van Landingham	.30	.10
❑	197	Mark Carreon	.30	.10
❑	198	Royce Clayton	.30	.10
❑	199	Joey Cora	.30	.10
❑	200	Ken Griffey Jr.	1.25	.50
❑	201	Jay Buhner	.30	.10
❑	202	Alex Rodriguez	1.50	.60
❑	203	Norm Charlton	.30	.10
❑	204	Andy Benes	.30	.10
❑	205	Edgar Martinez	.50	.20
❑	206	Juan Gonzalez	.30	.10
❑	207	Will Clark	.50	.20
❑	208	Kevin Gross	.30	.10
❑	209	Roger Pavlik	.30	.10
❑	210	Ivan Rodriguez	.50	.20
❑	211	Rusty Greer	.30	.10
❑	212	Angel Martinez	.30	.10
❑	213	Tomas Perez	.30	.10
❑	214	Alex Gonzalez	.30	.10
❑	215	Joe Carter	.30	.10
❑	216	Shawn Green	.30	.10
❑	217	Edwin Hurtado	.30	.10
❑	218	E.Martinez/T.Pena CL	.30	.10
❑	219	C.Jones/B.Larkin CL	.50	.20
❑	220	Orel Hershiser CL	.30	.10
❑	221	Mike Devereaux CL	.30	.10
❑	222	Tom Glavine CL	.30	.10
❑	223	Karim Garcia	.30	.10
❑	224	Arquimedez Pozo	.30	.10
❑	225	Billy Wagner	.30	.10
❑	226	John Wasdin	.30	.10
❑	227	Jeff Suppan	.30	.10
❑	228	Steve Gibralter	.30	.10
❑	229	Jimmy Haynes	.30	.10
❑	230	Ruben Rivera	.30	.10
❑	231	Chris Snopek	.30	.10
❑	232	Alex Ochoa	.30	.10
❑	233	Shannon Stewart	.30	.10
❑	234	Quinton McCracken	.30	.10
❑	235	Trey Beamon	.30	.10
❑	236	Billy McMillon	.30	.10
❑	237	Steve Cox	.30	.10
❑	238	George Arias	.30	.10
❑	239	Yamil Benitez	.30	.10
❑	240	Todd Greene	.30	.10
❑	241	Jason Kendall	.30	.10
❑	242	Brooks Kieschnick	.30	.10
❑	243	Osvaldo Fernandez RC	.30	.10
❑	244	Livan Hernandez RC	1.00	.40
❑	245	Rey Ordonez	.30	.10
❑	246	Mike Grace RC	.30	.10
❑	247	Jay Canizaro	.30	.10
❑	248	Bob Wolcott	.30	.10
❑	249	Jermaine Dye	.30	.10
❑	250	Jason Schmidt	.50	.20
❑	251	Mike Sweeney RC	1.00	.40
❑	252	Marcus Jensen	.30	.10
❑	253	Mendy Lopez	.30	.10
❑	254	Wilton Guerrero RC	.30	.10
❑	255	Paul Wilson	.30	.10
❑	256	Edgar Renteria	.30	.10
❑	257	Richard Hidalgo	.30	.10
❑	258	Bob Abreu	.75	.30
❑	259	Robert Smith RC	.30	.10
❑	260	Sal Fasano	.30	.10
❑	261	Enrique Wilson	.30	.10
❑	262	Rich Hunter RC	.30	.10
❑	263	Sergio Nunez	.30	.10
❑	264	Dan Serafini	.30	.10
❑	265	David Doster	.30	.10
❑	266	Ryan McGuire	.30	.10
❑	267	Scott Spiezio	.30	.10
❑	268	Rafael Orellano	.30	.10
❑	269	Steve Avery	.30	.10
❑	270	Fred McGriff	.50	.20
❑	271	John Smoltz	.50	.20
❑	272	Ryan Klesko	.30	.10
❑	273	Jeff Blauser	.30	.10
❑	274	Brad Clontz	.30	.10
❑	275	Roberto Alomar	.50	.20
❑	276	B.J. Surhoff	.30	.10
❑	277	Jeffrey Hammonds	.30	.10
❑	278	Brady Anderson	.30	.10
❑	279	Bobby Bonilla	.30	.10
❑	280	Cal Ripken	2.50	1.00
❑	281	Mike Mussina	.50	.20
❑	282	Wil Cordero	.30	.10
❑	283	Mike Stanley	.30	.10
❑	284	Aaron Sele	.30	.10
❑	285	Jose Canseco	.50	.20
❑	286	Tom Gordon	.30	.10
❑	287	Heathcliff Slocumb	.30	.10
❑	288	Lee Smith	.30	.10
❑	289	Troy Percival	.30	.10
❑	290	Tim Salmon	.50	.20
❑	291	Chuck Finley	.30	.10
❑	292	Jim Abbott	.50	.20
❑	293	Chili Davis	.30	.10
❑	294	Steve Trachsel	.30	.10
❑	295	Mark Grace	.50	.20
❑	296	Rey Sanchez	.30	.10
❑	297	Scott Servais	.30	.10
❑	298	Jaime Navarro	.30	.10
❑	299	Frank Castillo	.30	.10
❑	300	Frank Thomas	.75	.30
❑	301	Jason Bere	.30	.10
❑	302	Danny Tartabull	.30	.10
❑	303	Darren Lewis	.30	.10
❑	304	Roberto Hernandez	.30	.10
❑	305	Tony Phillips	.30	.10
❑	306	Wilson Alvarez	.30	.10
❑	307	Jose Rijo	.30	.10
❑	308	Hal Morris	.30	.10
❑	309	Mark Portugal	.30	.10
❑	310	Barry Larkin	.50	.20
❑	311	Dave Burba	.30	.10
❑	312	Eddie Taubensee	.30	.10
❑	313	Sandy Alomar Jr.	.30	.10
❑	314	Dennis Martinez	.30	.10
❑	315	Albert Belle	.30	.10
❑	316	Eddie Murray	.75	.30
❑	317	Charles Nagy	.30	.10
❑	318	Chad Ogea	.30	.10
❑	319	Kenny Lofton	.30	.10
❑	320	Dante Bichette	.30	.10
❑	321	Armando Reynoso	.30	.10
❑	322	Walt Weiss	.30	.10
❑	323	Ellis Burks	.30	.10
❑	324	Kevin Ritz	.30	.10
❑	325	Bill Swift	.30	.10
❑	326	Jason Bates	.30	.10
❑	327	Tony Clark	.30	.10
❑	328	Travis Fryman	.30	.10
❑	329	Mark Parent	.30	.10
❑	330	Alan Trammell	.30	.10
❑	331	C.J. Nitkowski	.30	.10
❑	332	Jose Lima	.30	.10
❑	333	Phil Plantier	.30	.10
❑	334	Kurt Abbott	.30	.10
❑	335	Andre Dawson	.30	.10
❑	336	Chris Hammond	.30	.10
❑	337	Robb Nen	.30	.10
❑	338	Pat Rapp	.30	.10
❑	339	Al Leiter	.30	.10
❑	340	Gary Sheffield	.30	.10
❑	341	Todd Jones	.30	.10
❑	342	Doug Drabek	.30	.10
❑	343	Greg Swindell	.30	.10
❑	344	Tony Eusebio	.30	.10
❑	345	Craig Biggio	.50	.20
❑	346	Darryl Kile	.30	.10
❑	347	Mike Macfarlane	.30	.10
❑	348	Jeff Montgomery	.30	.10
❑	349	Chris Haney	.30	.10
❑	350	Bip Roberts	.30	.10
❑	351	Tom Goodwin	.30	.10
❑	352	Mark Gubicza	.30	.10
❑	353	Joe Randa	.30	.10
❑	354	Ramon Martinez	.30	.10
❑	355	Eric Karros	.30	.10
❑	356	Delino DeShields	.30	.10
❑	357	Brett Butler	.30	.10
❑	358	Todd Worrell	.30	.10
❑	359	Mike Blowers	.30	.10
❑	360	Mike Piazza	1.25	.50
❑	361	Ben McDonald	.30	.10
❑	362	Ricky Bones	.30	.10
❑	363	Greg Vaughn	.30	.10
❑	364	Matt Mieske	.30	.10
❑	365	Kevin Seitzer	.30	.10
❑	366	Jeff Cirillo	.30	.10
❑	367	LaTroy Hawkins	.30	.10
❑	368	Frank Rodriguez	.30	.10
❑	369	Rick Aguilera	.30	.10
❑	370	Roberto Alomar BG	.30	.10
❑	371	Albert Belle BG	.30	.10
❑	372	Wade Boggs BG	.30	.10
❑	373	Barry Bonds BG	1.00	.40
❑	374	Roger Clemens BG	.75	.30
❑	375	Dennis Eckersley BG	.30	.10
❑	376	Ken Griffey Jr. BG	.75	.30
❑	377	Tony Gwynn BG	.50	.20
❑	378	Rickey Henderson BG	.50	.20
❑	379	Greg Maddux BG	.75	.30
❑	380	Fred McGriff BG	.30	.10
❑	381	Paul Molitor BG	.30	.10
❑	382	Eddie Murray BG	.50	.20
❑	383	Mike Piazza BG	.75	.30
❑	384	Kirby Puckett BG	.50	.20
❑	385	Cal Ripken BG	1.25	.50
❑	386	Ozzie Smith BG	.75	.30
❑	387	Frank Thomas BG	.50	.20
❑	388	Matt Walbeck	.30	.10
❑	389	Dave Stevens	.30	.10
❑	390	Marty Cordova	.30	.10
❑	391	Darrin Fletcher	.30	.10
❑	392	Cliff Floyd	.30	.10
❑	393	Mel Rojas	.30	.10
❑	394	Shane Andrews	.30	.10
❑	395	Moises Alou	.30	.10
❑	396	Carlos Perez	.30	.10
❑	397	Jeff Fassero	.30	.10
❑	398	Bobby Jones	.30	.10
❑	399	Todd Hundley	.30	.10
❑	400	John Franco	.30	.10
❑	401	Jose Vizcaino	.30	.10
❑	402	Bernard Gilkey	.30	.10
❑	403	Pete Harnisch	.30	.10
❑	404	Pat Kelly	.30	.10
❑	405	David Cone	.30	.10
❑	406	Bernie Williams	.50	.20
❑	407	John Wetteland	.30	.10
❑	408	Scott Kamieniecki	.30	.10
❑	409	Tim Raines	.30	.10
❑	410	Wade Boggs	.50	.20
❑	411	Terry Steinbach	.30	.10
❑	412	Jason Giambi	.30	.10
❑	413	Todd Van Poppel	.30	.10
❑	414	Pedro Munoz	.30	.10
❑	415	Eddie Murray SBT	.50	.20
❑	416	Dennis Eckersley SBT	.30	.10
❑	417	Bip Roberts SBT	.30	.10
❑	418	Glenallen Hill SBT	.30	.10
❑	419	John Hudek SBT	.30	.10
❑	420	Derek Bell SBT	.30	.10
❑	421	Larry Walker SBT	.30	.10
❑	422	Greg Maddux SBT	.75	.30
❑	423	Ken Caminiti SBT	.30	.10
❑	424	Brent Gates	.30	.10
❑	425	Mark McGwire	2.00	.75
❑	426	Mark Whiten	.30	.10
❑	427	Sid Fernandez	.30	.10
❑	428	Ricky Bottalico	.30	.10
❑	429	Mike Mimbs	.30	.10
❑	430	Lenny Dykstra	.30	.10
❑	431	Todd Zeile	.30	.10
❑	432	Benito Santiago	.30	.10
❑	433	Danny Miceli	.30	.10
❑	434	Al Martin	.30	.10
❑	435	Jay Bell	.30	.10
❑	436	Charlie Hayes	.30	.10
❑	437	Mike Kingery	.30	.10

❑ 438	Paul Wagner	.30	.10
❑ 439	Tom Pagnozzi	.30	.10
❑ 440	Ozzie Smith	1.25	.50
❑ 441	Ray Lankford	.30	.10
❑ 442	Dennis Eckersley	.30	.10
❑ 443	Ron Gant	.30	.10
❑ 444	Alan Benes	.30	.10
❑ 445	Rickey Henderson	.75	.30
❑ 446	Jody Reed	.30	.10
❑ 447	Trevor Hoffman	.30	.10
❑ 448	Andujar Cedeno	.30	.10
❑ 449	Steve Finley	.30	.10
❑ 450	Tony Gwynn	1.00	.40
❑ 451	Joey Hamilton	.30	.10
❑ 452	Mark Leiter	.30	.10
❑ 453	Rod Beck	.30	.10
❑ 454	Kirt Manwaring	.30	.10
❑ 455	Matt Williams	.30	.10
❑ 456	Robby Thompson	.30	.10
❑ 457	Shawon Dunston	.30	.10
❑ 458	Russ Davis	.30	.10
❑ 459	Paul Sorrento	.30	.10
❑ 460	Randy Johnson	.75	.30
❑ 461	Chris Bosio	.30	.10
❑ 462	Luis Sojo	.30	.10
❑ 463	Sterling Hitchcock	.30	.10
❑ 464	Benji Gil	.30	.10
❑ 465	Mickey Tettleton	.30	.10
❑ 466	Mark McLemore	.30	.10
❑ 467	Darryl Hamilton	.30	.10
❑ 468	Ken Hill	.30	.10
❑ 469	Dean Palmer	.30	.10
❑ 470	Carlos Delgado	.30	.10
❑ 471	Ed Sprague	.30	.10
❑ 472	Otis Nixon	.30	.10
❑ 473	Pat Hentgen	.30	.10
❑ 474	Juan Guzman	.30	.10
❑ 475	John Olerud	.30	.10
❑ 476	Buck Showalter CL	.30	.10
❑ 477	Bobby Cox CL	.30	.10
❑ 478	Tommy Lasorda CL	.30	.10
❑ 479	Buck Showalter CL	.30	.10
❑ 480	Sparky Anderson CL	.30	.10
❑ 481U	Randy Myers	.50	.20
❑ 482U	Kent Mercker	.50	.20
❑ 483U	David Wells	.75	.30
❑ 484U	Kevin Mitchell	.50	.20
❑ 485U	Randy Velarde	.50	.20
❑ 486U	Ryne Sandberg	4.00	1.50
❑ 487U	Doug Jones	.50	.20
❑ 488U	Terry Adams	.50	.20
❑ 489U	Kevin Tapani	.50	.20
❑ 490U	Harold Baines	.75	.30
❑ 491U	Eric Davis	.75	.30
❑ 492U	Julio Franco	.75	.30
❑ 493U	Jack McDowell	.50	.20
❑ 494U	Devon White	.75	.30
❑ 495U	Kevin Brown	.75	.30
❑ 496U	Rick Wilkins	.50	.20
❑ 497U	Sean Berry	.50	.20
❑ 498U	Keith Lockhart	.50	.20
❑ 499U	Mark Loretta	.50	.20
❑ 500U	Paul Molitor	.75	.30
❑ 501U	Roberto Kelly	.50	.20
❑ 502U	Lance Johnson	.50	.20
❑ 503U	Tino Martinez	1.25	.50
❑ 504U	Kenny Rogers	.75	.30
❑ 505U	Todd Stottlemyre	.50	.20
❑ 506U	Gary Gaetti	.75	.30
❑ 507U	Royce Clayton	.50	.20
❑ 508U	Andy Benes	.50	.20
❑ 509U	Wally Joyner	.75	.30
❑ 510U	Erik Hanson	.50	.20
❑ P100	Ken Griffey Jr Promo	3.00	1.25

1997 Upper Deck

❑ COMP.MASTER SET (550)	200.00	80.00
❑ COMPLETE SET (490)	100.00	50.00
❑ COMPLETE SERIES 1 (240)	40.00	20.00
❑ COMPLETE SERIES 2 (250)	60.00	30.00
❑ COMP.SER.2 w/o GHL (240)	25.00	10.00
❑ COMMON (1-240/271-520)	.30	.10
❑ COMP.UPDATE SET (30)	80.00	40.00
❑ COMMON UPDATE (241-270)	1.00	.40
❑ 1 UPD.SET VIA MAIL PER 10 SER.1 WRAPS		
❑ COMMON GHL (415-424)	1.50	.60

❑ COMP.TRADE SET (30)	20.00	8.00
❑ COMMON TRADE (521-550)	.50	.20

❑ 1	Jackie Robinson	.50	.20
❑ 2	Jackie Robinson	.50	.20
❑ 3	Jackie Robinson	.50	.20
❑ 4	Jackie Robinson	.50	.20
❑ 5	Jackie Robinson	.50	.20
❑ 6	Jackie Robinson	.50	.20
❑ 7	Jackie Robinson	.50	.20
❑ 8	Jackie Robinson	.50	.20
❑ 9	Jackie Robinson	.50	.20
❑ 10	Chipper Jones	.75	.30
❑ 11	Marquis Grissom	.30	.10
❑ 12	Jermaine Dye	.30	.10
❑ 13	Mark Lemke	.30	.10
❑ 14	Terrell Wade	.30	.10
❑ 15	Fred McGriff	.50	.20
❑ 16	Tom Glavine	.50	.20
❑ 17	Mark Wohlers	.30	.10
❑ 18	Randy Myers	.30	.10
❑ 19	Roberto Alomar	.50	.20
❑ 20	Cal Ripken	2.50	1.00
❑ 21	Rafael Palmeiro	.50	.20
❑ 22	Mike Mussina	.50	.20
❑ 23	Brady Anderson	.30	.10
❑ 24	Jose Canseco	.50	.20
❑ 25	Mo Vaughn	.30	.10
❑ 26	Roger Clemens	1.50	.60
❑ 27	Tim Naehring	.30	.10
❑ 28	Jeff Suppan	.30	.10
❑ 29	Troy Percival	.30	.10
❑ 30	Sammy Sosa	.75	.30
❑ 31	Amaury Telemaco	.30	.10
❑ 32	Rey Sanchez	.30	.10
❑ 33	Scott Servais	.30	.10
❑ 34	Steve Trachsel	.30	.10
❑ 35	Mark Grace	.50	.20
❑ 36	Wilson Alvarez	.30	.10
❑ 37	Harold Baines	.30	.10
❑ 38	Tony Phillips	.30	.10
❑ 39	James Baldwin	.30	.10
❑ 40	Frank Thomas UER	.75	.30
❑ 41	Lyle Mouton	.30	.10
❑ 42	Chris Snopek	.30	.10
❑ 43	Hal Morris	.30	.10
❑ 44	Eric Davis	.30	.10
❑ 45	Barry Larkin	.50	.20
❑ 46	Reggie Sanders	.30	.10
❑ 47	Pete Schourek	.30	.10
❑ 48	Lee Smith	.30	.10
❑ 49	Charles Nagy	.30	.10
❑ 50	Albert Belle	.30	.10
❑ 51	Julio Franco	.30	.10
❑ 52	Kenny Lofton	.30	.10
❑ 53	Orel Hershiser	.30	.10
❑ 54	Omar Vizquel	.50	.20
❑ 55	Eric Young	.30	.10
❑ 56	Curtis Leskanic	.30	.10
❑ 57	Quinton McCracken	.30	.10
❑ 58	Kevin Ritz	.30	.10
❑ 59	Walt Weiss	.30	.10
❑ 60	Dante Bichette	.30	.10
❑ 61	Mark Lewis	.30	.10
❑ 62	Tony Clark	.30	.10
❑ 63	Travis Fryman	.30	.10
❑ 64	John Smoltz SF	.30	.10
❑ 65	Greg Maddux SF	.75	.30
❑ 66	Tom Glavine SF	.30	.10
❑ 67	Mike Mussina SF	.30	.10
❑ 68	Andy Pettitte SF	.30	.10
❑ 69	Mariano Rivera SF	.50	.20
❑ 70	Hideo Nomo SF	.30	.10
❑ 71	Kevin Brown SF	.30	.10
❑ 72	Randy Johnson SF	.50	.20
❑ 73	Felipe Lira	.30	.10
❑ 74	Kimera Bartee	.30	.10
❑ 75	Alan Trammell	.30	.10
❑ 76	Kevin Brown	.30	.10
❑ 77	Edgar Renteria	.30	.10
❑ 78	Al Leiter	.30	.10
❑ 79	Charles Johnson	.30	.10
❑ 80	Andre Dawson	.30	.10
❑ 81	Billy Wagner	.30	.10
❑ 82	Donne Wall	.30	.10
❑ 83	Jeff Bagwell	.50	.20
❑ 84	Keith Lockhart	.30	.10
❑ 85	Jeff Montgomery	.30	.10
❑ 86	Tom Goodwin	.30	.10
❑ 87	Tim Belcher	.30	.10
❑ 88	Mike Macfarlane	.30	.10
❑ 89	Joe Randa	.30	.10
❑ 90	Brett Butler	.30	.10
❑ 91	Todd Worrell	.30	.10
❑ 92	Todd Hollandsworth	.30	.10
❑ 93	Ismael Valdes	.30	.10
❑ 94	Hideo Nomo	.75	.30
❑ 95	Mike Piazza	1.25	.50
❑ 96	Jeff Cirillo	.30	.10
❑ 97	Ricky Bones	.30	.10
❑ 98	Fernando Vina	.30	.10
❑ 99	Ben McDonald	.30	.10
❑ 100	John Jaha	.30	.10
❑ 101	Mark Loretta	.30	.10
❑ 102	Paul Molitor	.30	.10
❑ 103	Rick Aguilera	.30	.10
❑ 104	Marty Cordova	.30	.10
❑ 105	Kirby Puckett	.75	.30
❑ 106	Dan Naulty	.30	.10
❑ 107	Frank Rodriguez	.30	.10
❑ 108	Shane Andrews	.30	.10
❑ 109	Henry Rodriguez	.30	.10
❑ 110	Mark Grudzielanek	.30	.10
❑ 111	Pedro Martinez	.50	.20
❑ 112	Ugueth Urbina	.30	.10
❑ 113	David Segui	.30	.10
❑ 114	Rey Ordonez	.30	.10
❑ 115	Bernard Gilkey	.30	.10
❑ 116	Butch Huskey	.30	.10
❑ 117	Paul Wilson	.30	.10
❑ 118	Alex Ochoa	.30	.10
❑ 119	John Franco	.30	.10
❑ 120	Dwight Gooden	.30	.10
❑ 121	Ruben Rivera	.30	.10
❑ 122	Andy Pettitte	.50	.20
❑ 123	Tino Martinez	.50	.20
❑ 124	Bernie Williams	.50	.20
❑ 125	Wade Boggs	.50	.20
❑ 126	Paul O'Neill	.50	.20
❑ 127	Scott Brosius	.30	.10
❑ 128	Ernie Young	.30	.10
❑ 129	Doug Johns	.30	.10
❑ 130	Geronimo Berroa	.30	.10
❑ 131	Jason Giambi	.30	.10
❑ 132	John Wasdin	.30	.10
❑ 133	Jim Eisenreich	.30	.10
❑ 134	Ricky Otero	.30	.10
❑ 135	Ricky Bottalico	.30	.10
❑ 136	Mark Langston DG	.30	.10
❑ 137	Greg Maddux DG	.75	.30
❑ 138	Ivan Rodriguez DG	.30	.10
❑ 139	Charles Johnson DG	.30	.10
❑ 140	J.T. Snow DG	.30	.10
❑ 141	Mark Grace DG	.30	.10
❑ 142	Roberto Alomar DG	.30	.10
❑ 143	Craig Biggio DG	.30	.10
❑ 144	Ken Caminiti DG	.30	.10
❑ 145	Matt Williams DG	.30	.10
❑ 146	Omar Vizquel DG	.30	.10
❑ 147	Cal Ripken DG	1.25	.50
❑ 148	Ozzie Smith DG	.75	.30
❑ 149	Rey Ordonez DG	.30	.10
❑ 150	Ken Griffey Jr. DG	.75	.30
❑ 151	Devon White DG	.30	.10
❑ 152	Barry Bonds DG	1.00	.40

❑ 153	Kenny Lofton DG	.30	.10
❑ 154	Mickey Morandini	.30	.10
❑ 155	Gregg Jefferies	.30	.10
❑ 156	Curt Schilling	.30	.10
❑ 157	Jason Kendall	.30	.10
❑ 158	Francisco Cordova	.30	.10
❑ 159	Dennis Eckersley	.30	.10
❑ 160	Ron Gant	.30	.10
❑ 161	Ozzie Smith	1.25	.50
❑ 162	Brian Jordan	.30	.10
❑ 163	John Mabry	.30	.10
❑ 164	Andy Ashby	.30	.10
❑ 165	Steve Finley	.30	.10
❑ 166	Fernando Valenzuela	.30	.10
❑ 167	Archi Cianfrocco	.30	.10
❑ 168	Wally Joyner	.30	.10
❑ 169	Greg Vaughn	.30	.10
❑ 170	Barry Bonds	2.00	.75
❑ 171	William VanLandingham	.30	.10
❑ 172	Marvin Benard	.30	.10
❑ 173	Rich Aurilia	.30	.10
❑ 174	Jay Canizaro	.30	.10
❑ 175	Ken Griffey Jr.	1.25	.50
❑ 176	Bob Wells	.30	.10
❑ 177	Jay Buhner	.30	.10
❑ 178	Sterling Hitchcock	.30	.10
❑ 179	Edgar Martinez	.50	.20
❑ 180	Rusty Greer	.30	.10
❑ 181	Dave Nilsson GI	.30	.10
❑ 182	Larry Walker GI	.30	.10
❑ 183	Edgar Renteria GI	.30	.10
❑ 184	Rey Ordonez GI	.30	.10
❑ 185	Rafael Palmeiro GI	.30	.10
❑ 186	Osvaldo Fernandez GI	.30	.10
❑ 187	Raul Mondesi GI	.30	.10
❑ 188	Manny Ramirez GI	.30	.10
❑ 189	Sammy Sosa GI	.50	.20
❑ 190	Robert Eenhoorn GI	.30	.10
❑ 191	Devon White GI	.30	.10
❑ 192	Hideo Nomo GI	.30	.10
❑ 193	Mac Suzuki GI	.30	.10
❑ 194	Chan Ho Park GI	.30	.10
❑ 195	Fernando Valenzuela GI	.30	.10
❑ 196	Andruw Jones GI	.30	.10
❑ 197	Vinny Castilla GI	.30	.10
❑ 198	Dennis Martinez GI	.30	.10
❑ 199	Ruben Rivera GI	.30	.10
❑ 200	Juan Gonzalez GI	.30	.10
❑ 201	Roberto Alomar GI	.30	.10
❑ 202	Edgar Martinez GI	.30	.10
❑ 203	Ivan Rodriguez GI	.30	.10
❑ 204	Carlos Delgado GI	.30	.10
❑ 205	Andres Galarraga GI	.30	.10
❑ 206	Ozzie Guillen GI	.30	.10
❑ 207	Midre Cummings GI	.30	.10
❑ 208	Roger Pavlik	.30	.10
❑ 209	Darron Oliver	.30	.10
❑ 210	Dean Palmer	.30	.10
❑ 211	Ivan Rodriguez	.50	.20
❑ 212	Otis Nixon	.30	.10
❑ 213	Pat Hentgen	.30	.10
❑ 214	Ozzie/Dawson/Puckett HL/CL	.50	.20
❑ 215	Bonds/Sheff/Brady HL/CL	1.00	.40
❑ 216	Ken Caminiti SH CL	.30	.10
❑ 217	John Smoltz SH CL	.30	.10
❑ 218	Eric Young SH CL	.30	.10
❑ 219	Juan Gonzalez SH CL	.30	.10
❑ 220	Eddie Murray SH CL	.50	.20
❑ 221	Tommy Lasorda SH CL	.30	.10
❑ 222	Paul Molitor SH CL	.30	.10
❑ 223	Luis Castillo	.30	.10
❑ 224	Justin Thompson	.30	.10
❑ 225	Rocky Coppinger	.30	.10
❑ 226	Jermaine Allensworth	.30	.10
❑ 227	Jeff D'Amico	.30	.10
❑ 228	Jamey Wright	.30	.10
❑ 229	Scott Rolen	.50	.20
❑ 230	Darin Erstad	.30	.10
❑ 231	Marty Janzen	.30	.10
❑ 232	Jacob Cruz	.30	.10
❑ 233	Raul Ibanez	.30	.10
❑ 234	Nomar Garciaparra	1.25	.50
❑ 235	Todd Walker	.30	.10
❑ 236	Brian Giles RC	1.50	.60
❑ 237	Matt Beech	.30	.10
❑ 238	Mike Cameron	.30	.10
❑ 239	Jose Paniagua	.30	.10
❑ 240	Andruw Jones	.50	.20
❑ 241	Brant Brown UPD	1.00	.40
❑ 242	Robin Jennings UPD	1.00	.40
❑ 243	Willie Adams UPD	1.00	.40
❑ 244	Ken Caminiti UPD	1.50	.60
❑ 245	Brian Jordan UPD	1.50	.60
❑ 246	Chipper Jones UPD	4.00	1.50
❑ 247	Juan Gonzalez UPD	1.50	.60
❑ 248	Bernie Williams UPD	2.50	1.00
❑ 249	Roberto Alomar UPD	2.50	1.00
❑ 250	Bernie Williams UPD	2.50	1.00
❑ 251	David Wells UPD	1.50	.60
❑ 252	Cecil Fielder UPD	1.50	.60
❑ 253	Darryl Strawberry UPD	1.50	.60
❑ 254	Andy Pettitte UPD	2.50	1.00
❑ 255	Javier Lopez UPD	1.50	.60
❑ 256	Gary Gaetti UPD	1.50	.60
❑ 257	Ron Gant UPD	1.50	.60
❑ 258	Brian Jordan UPD	1.50	.60
❑ 259	John Smoltz UPD	2.50	1.00
❑ 260	Greg Maddux UPD	8.00	3.00
❑ 261	Tom Glavine UPD	2.50	1.00
❑ 262	Andruw Jones UPD	2.50	1.00
❑ 263	Greg Maddux UPD	8.00	3.00
❑ 264	David Cone UPD	1.50	.60
❑ 265	Jim Leyritz UPD	1.00	.40
❑ 266	Andy Pettitte UPD	2.50	1.00
❑ 267	John Wetteland UPD	1.50	.60
❑ 268	Dario Veras UPD	1.00	.40
❑ 269	Neifi Perez UPD	1.00	.40
❑ 270	Bill Mueller UPD	4.00	1.50
❑ 271	Vladimir Guerrero	.75	.30
❑ 272	Dmitri Young	.30	.10
❑ 273	Nerio Rodriguez RC	.30	.10
❑ 274	Kevin Orie	.30	.10
❑ 275	Felipe Crespo	.30	.10
❑ 276	Danny Graves	.30	.10
❑ 277	Rod Myers	.30	.10
❑ 278	Felix Heredia RC	.30	.10
❑ 279	Ralph Milliard	.30	.10
❑ 280	Greg Norton	.30	.10
❑ 281	Derek Wallace	.30	.10
❑ 282	Trot Nixon	.30	.10
❑ 283	Bobby Chouinard	.30	.10
❑ 284	Jay Witasick	.30	.10
❑ 285	Travis Miller	.30	.10
❑ 286	Brian Bevil	.30	.10
❑ 287	Bobby Estalella	.30	.10
❑ 288	Steve Soderstrom	.30	.10
❑ 289	Mark Langston	.30	.10
❑ 290	Tim Salmon	.50	.20
❑ 291	Jim Edmonds	.30	.10
❑ 292	Garret Anderson	.30	.10
❑ 293	George Arias	.30	.10
❑ 294	Gary DiSarcina	.30	.10
❑ 295	Chuck Finley	.30	.10
❑ 296	Todd Greene	.30	.10
❑ 297	Randy Velarde	.30	.10
❑ 298	David Justice	.30	.10
❑ 299	Ryan Klesko	.30	.10
❑ 300	John Smoltz	.50	.20
❑ 301	Javier Lopez	.30	.10
❑ 302	Greg Maddux	1.25	.50
❑ 303	Denny Neagle	.30	.10
❑ 304	B.J. Surhoff	.30	.10
❑ 305	Chris Hoiles	.30	.10
❑ 306	Eric Davis	.30	.10
❑ 307	Scott Erickson	.30	.10
❑ 308	Mike Bordick	.30	.10
❑ 309	John Valentin	.30	.10
❑ 310	Heathcliff Slocumb	.30	.10
❑ 311	Tom Gordon	.30	.10
❑ 312	Mike Stanley	.30	.10
❑ 313	Reggie Jefferson	.30	.10
❑ 314	Darren Bragg	.30	.10
❑ 315	Troy O'Leary	.30	.10
❑ 316	John Mabry SH CL	.30	.10
❑ 317	Mark Whiten SH CL	.30	.10
❑ 318	Edgar Martinez SH CL	.30	.10
❑ 319	Alex Rodriguez SH CL	.75	.30
❑ 320	Mark McGwire SH CL	1.00	.40
❑ 321	Hideo Nomo SH CL	.30	.10
❑ 322	Todd Hundley SH CL	.30	.10
❑ 323	Barry Bonds SH CL	1.00	.40
❑ 324	Andruw Jones SH CL	.30	.10
❑ 325	Ryne Sandberg	1.25	.50
❑ 326	Brian McRae	.30	.10
❑ 327	Frank Castillo	.30	.10
❑ 328	Shawon Dunston	.30	.10
❑ 329	Ray Durham	.30	.10
❑ 330	Robin Ventura	.30	.10
❑ 331	Ozzie Guillen	.30	.10
❑ 332	Roberto Hernandez	.30	.10
❑ 333	Albert Belle	.30	.10
❑ 334	Dave Martinez	.30	.10
❑ 335	Willie Greene	.30	.10
❑ 336	Jeff Brantley	.30	.10
❑ 337	Kevin Jarvis	.30	.10
❑ 338	John Smiley	.30	.10
❑ 339	Eddie Taubensee	.30	.10
❑ 340	Bret Boone	.30	.10
❑ 341	Kevin Seitzer	.30	.10
❑ 342	Jack McDowell	.30	.10
❑ 343	Sandy Alomar Jr.	.30	.10
❑ 344	Chad Curtis	.30	.10
❑ 345	Manny Ramirez	.50	.20
❑ 346	Chad Ogea	.30	.10
❑ 347	Jim Thome	.50	.20
❑ 348	Mark Thompson	.30	.10
❑ 349	Ellis Burks	.30	.10
❑ 350	Andres Galarraga	.30	.10
❑ 351	Vinny Castilla	.30	.10
❑ 352	Kirt Manwaring	.30	.10
❑ 353	Larry Walker	.30	.10
❑ 354	Omar Olivares	.30	.10
❑ 355	Bobby Higginson	.30	.10
❑ 356	Melvin Nieves	.30	.10
❑ 357	Brian Johnson	.30	.10
❑ 358	Devon White	.30	.10
❑ 359	Jeff Conine	.30	.10
❑ 360	Gary Sheffield	.30	.10
❑ 361	Robb Nen	.30	.10
❑ 362	Mike Hampton	.30	.10
❑ 363	Bob Abreu	.50	.20
❑ 364	Luis Gonzalez	.30	.10
❑ 365	Derek Bell	.30	.10
❑ 366	Sean Berry	.30	.10
❑ 367	Craig Biggio	.50	.20
❑ 368	Darryl Kile	.30	.10
❑ 369	Shane Reynolds	.30	.10
❑ 370	Jeff Bagwell CF	.30	.10
❑ 371	Ron Gant CF	.30	.10
❑ 372	Andy Benes CF	.30	.10
❑ 373	Gary Gaetti CF	.30	.10
❑ 374	Ramon Martinez CF	.30	.10
❑ 375	Raul Mondesi CF	.30	.10
❑ 376	Steve Finley CF	.30	.10
❑ 377	Ken Caminiti CF	.30	.10
❑ 378	Tony Gwynn CF	.50	.20
❑ 379	Dario Veras RC	.30	.10
❑ 380	Andy Pettitte CF	.30	.10
❑ 381	Ruben Rivera CF	.30	.10
❑ 382	David Cone CF	.30	.10
❑ 383	Roberto Alomar CF	.30	.10
❑ 384	Edgar Martinez CF	.30	.10
❑ 385	Ken Griffey Jr. CF	.75	.30
❑ 386	Mark McGwire CF	1.00	.40
❑ 387	Rusty Greer CF	.30	.10
❑ 388	Jose Rosado	.30	.10
❑ 389	Kevin Appier	.30	.10
❑ 390	Johnny Damon	.50	.20
❑ 391	Jose Offerman	.30	.10
❑ 392	Michael Tucker	.30	.10
❑ 393	Craig Paquette	.30	.10
❑ 394	Bip Roberts	.30	.10
❑ 395	Ramon Martinez	.30	.10
❑ 396	Greg Gagne	.30	.10
❑ 397	Chan Ho Park	.30	.10
❑ 398	Karim Garcia	.30	.10
❑ 399	Wilton Guerrero	.30	.10
❑ 400	Eric Karros	.30	.10
❑ 401	Raul Mondesi	.30	.10
❑ 402	Matt Mieske	.30	.10
❑ 403	Mike Fetters	.30	.10
❑ 404	Dave Nilsson	.30	.10
❑ 405	Jose Valentin	.30	.10
❑ 406	Scott Karl	.30	.10
❑ 407	Marc Newfield	.30	.10
❑ 408	Cal Eldred	.30	.10
❑ 409	Rich Becker	.30	.10
❑ 410	Terry Steinbach	.30	.10

❑ 411 Chuck Knoblauch .30 .10
❑ 412 Pat Meares .30 .10
❑ 413 Brad Radke .30 .10
❑ 414 Kirby Puckett UER .75 .30
❑ 415 Andruw Jones GHL SP 1.50 .60
❑ 416 Chipper Jones GHL SP 2.50 1.00
❑ 417 Mo Vaughn GHL SP 1.50 .60
❑ 418 Frank Thomas GHL SP 2.50 1.00
❑ 419 Albert Belle GHL SP 1.50 .60
❑ 420 Mark McGwire GHL SP 8.00 3.00
❑ 421 Derek Jeter GHL SP 8.00 3.00
❑ 422 Alex Rodriguez GHL SP 5.00 2.00
❑ 423 Juan Gonzalez GHL SP 1.50 .60
❑ 424 Ken Griffey Jr. GHL SP 5.00 2.00
❑ 425 Rondell White .30 .10
❑ 426 Darrin Fletcher .30 .10
❑ 427 Cliff Floyd .30 .10
❑ 428 Mike Lansing .30 .10
❑ 429 F.P. Santangelo .30 .10
❑ 430 Todd Hundley .30 .10
❑ 431 Mark Clark .30 .10
❑ 432 Pete Harnisch .30 .10
❑ 433 Jason Isringhausen .30 .10
❑ 434 Bobby Jones .30 .10
❑ 435 Lance Johnson .30 .10
❑ 436 Carlos Baerga .30 .10
❑ 437 Mariano Duncan .30 .10
❑ 438 David Cone .30 .10
❑ 439 Mariano Rivera .75 .30
❑ 440 Derek Jeter 2.00 .75
❑ 441 Joe Girardi .30 .10
❑ 442 Charlie Hayes .30 .10
❑ 443 Tim Raines .30 .10
❑ 444 Darryl Strawberry .30 .10
❑ 445 Cecil Fielder .30 .10
❑ 446 Ariel Prieto .30 .10
❑ 447 Tony Batista .30 .10
❑ 448 Brent Gates .30 .10
❑ 449 Scott Spiezio .30 .10
❑ 450 Mark McGwire 2.00 .75
❑ 451 Don Wengert .30 .10
❑ 452 Mike Lieberthal .30 .10
❑ 453 Lenny Dykstra .30 .10
❑ 454 Rex Hudler .30 .10
❑ 455 Darren Daulton .30 .10
❑ 456 Kevin Stocker .30 .10
❑ 457 Trey Beamon .30 .10
❑ 458 Midre Cummings .30 .10
❑ 459 Mark Johnson .30 .10
❑ 460 Al Martin .30 .10
❑ 461 Kevin Elster .30 .10
❑ 462 Jon Lieber .30 .10
❑ 463 Jason Schmidt .30 .10
❑ 464 Paul Wagner .30 .10
❑ 465 Andy Benes .30 .10
❑ 466 Alan Benes .30 .10
❑ 467 Royce Clayton .30 .10
❑ 468 Gary Gaetti .30 .10
❑ 469 Curt Lyons RC .30 .10
❑ 470 Eugene Kingsale DD .30 .10
❑ 471 Damian Jackson DD .30 .10
❑ 472 Wendell Magee DD .30 .10
❑ 473 Kevin L. Brown DD .30 .10
❑ 474 Raul Casanova DD .30 .10
❑ 475 Ramiro Mendoza RC .30 .10
❑ 476 Todd Dunn DD .30 .10
❑ 477 Chad Mottola DD .30 .10
❑ 478 Andy Larkin DD .30 .10
❑ 479 Jaime Bluma DD .30 .10
❑ 480 Mac Suzuki DD .30 .10
❑ 481 Brian Banks DD .30 .10
❑ 482 Desi Wilson DD .30 .10
❑ 483 Einar Diaz DD .30 .10
❑ 484 Tom Pagnozzi .30 .10
❑ 485 Ray Lankford .30 .10
❑ 486 Todd Stottlemyre .30 .10
❑ 487 Donovan Osborne .30 .10
❑ 488 Trevor Hoffman .30 .10
❑ 489 Chris Gomez .30 .10
❑ 490 Ken Caminiti .30 .10
❑ 491 John Flaherty .30 .10
❑ 492 Tony Gwynn 1.00 .40
❑ 493 Joey Hamilton .30 .10
❑ 494 Rickey Henderson .75 .30
❑ 495 Glenallen Hill .30 .10
❑ 496 Rod Beck .30 .10
❑ 497 Osvaldo Fernandez .30 .10
❑ 498 Rick Wilkins .30 .10
❑ 499 Joey Cora .30 .10
❑ 500 Alex Rodriguez 1.25 .50
❑ 501 Randy Johnson .75 .30
❑ 502 Paul Sorrento .30 .10
❑ 503 Dan Wilson .30 .10
❑ 504 Jamie Moyer .30 .10
❑ 505 Will Clark .50 .20
❑ 506 Mickey Tettleton .30 .10
❑ 507 John Burkett .30 .10
❑ 508 Ken Hill .30 .10
❑ 509 Mark McLemore .30 .10
❑ 510 Juan Gonzalez .30 .10
❑ 511 Bobby Witt .30 .10
❑ 512 Carlos Delgado .30 .10
❑ 513 Alex Gonzalez .30 .10
❑ 514 Shawn Green .30 .10
❑ 515 Joe Carter .30 .10
❑ 516 Juan Guzman .30 .10
❑ 517 Charlie O'Brien .30 .10
❑ 518 Ed Sprague .30 .10
❑ 519 Mike Timlin .30 .10
❑ 520 Roger Clemens 1.50 .60
❑ 521 Eddie Murray TRADE 2.00 .75
❑ 522 Jason Dickson TRADE .50 .20
❑ 523 Jim Leyritz TRADE .50 .20
❑ 524 Michael Tucker TRADE .50 .20
❑ 525 Kenny Lofton TRADE .75 .30
❑ 526 Jimmy Key TRADE .75 .30
❑ 527 Mel Rojas TRADE .50 .20
❑ 528 Deion Sanders TRADE 1.25 .50
❑ 529 Bartolo Colon TRADE .75 .30
❑ 530 Matt Williams TRADE .75 .30
❑ 531 Marquis Grissom TRADE .75 .30
❑ 532 David Justice TRADE .75 .30
❑ 533 Bubba Trammell TRADE .75 .30
❑ 534 Moises Alou TRADE .75 .30
❑ 535 Bobby Bonilla TRADE .75 .30
❑ 536 Alex Fernandez TRADE .50 .20
❑ 537 Jay Bell TRADE .75 .30
❑ 538 Chili Davis TRADE .75 .30
❑ 539 Jeff King TRADE .50 .20
❑ 540 Todd Zeile TRADE .50 .20
❑ 541 John Olerud TRADE .75 .30
❑ 542 Jose Guillen TRADE .75 .30
❑ 543 Derrek Lee TRADE 1.25 .50
❑ 544 Dante Powell TRADE .50 .20
❑ 545 J.T. Snow TRADE .75 .30
❑ 546 Jeff Kent TRADE .75 .30
❑ 547 Jose Cruz Jr. TRADE .75 .30
❑ 548 John Wetteland TRADE .75 .30
❑ 549 Orlando Merced TRADE .50 .20
❑ 550 Hideki Irabu TRADE .75 .30

1998 Upper Deck

❑ COMPLETE SET (751) 200.00 80.00
❑ COMPLETE SERIES 1 (270) 40.00 15.00
❑ COMPLETE SERIES 2 (270) 40.00 15.00
❑ COMPLETE SERIES 3 (211) 120.00 50.00
❑ COMMON (1-600/631-750) .30 .10
❑ COMMON EP (601-630) 2.00 .75
❑ EP SER.2 ODDS APPROXIMATELY 1:4
❑ 1 Tino Martinez HIST .30 .10
❑ 2 Jimmy Key HIST .30 .10
❑ 3 Jay Buhner HIST .30 .10
❑ 4 Mark Gardner HIST .30 .10
❑ 5 Greg Maddux HIST .75 .30
❑ 6 Pedro Martinez HIST .50 .20
❑ 7 Hideo Nomo HIST .50 .20
❑ 8 Sammy Sosa HIST .50 .20
❑ 9 Mark McGwire GHL 1.00 .40
❑ 10 Ken Griffey Jr. GHL .75 .30
❑ 11 Larry Walker GHL .30 .10
❑ 12 Tino Martinez GHL .30 .10
❑ 13 Mike Piazza GHL .75 .30
❑ 14 Jose Cruz Jr. GHL .30 .10
❑ 15 Tony Gwynn GHL .50 .20
❑ 16 Greg Maddux GHL .75 .30
❑ 17 Roger Clemens GHL .75 .30
❑ 18 Alex Rodriguez GHL .75 .30
❑ 19 Shigetoshi Hasegawa .30 .10
❑ 20 Eddie Murray .75 .30
❑ 21 Jason Dickson .30 .10
❑ 22 Darin Erstad .30 .10
❑ 23 Chuck Finley .30 .10
❑ 24 Dave Hollins .30 .10
❑ 25 Garret Anderson .30 .10
❑ 26 Michael Tucker .30 .10
❑ 27 Kenny Lofton .30 .10
❑ 28 Javier Lopez .30 .10
❑ 29 Fred McGriff .50 .20
❑ 30 Greg Maddux 1.25 .50
❑ 31 Jeff Blauser .30 .10
❑ 32 John Smoltz .50 .20
❑ 33 Mark Wohlers .30 .10
❑ 34 Scott Erickson .30 .10
❑ 35 Jimmy Key .30 .10
❑ 36 Harold Baines .30 .10
❑ 37 Randy Myers .30 .10
❑ 38 B.J. Surhoff .30 .10
❑ 39 Eric Davis .30 .10
❑ 40 Rafael Palmeiro .50 .20
❑ 41 Jeffrey Hammonds .30 .10
❑ 42 Mo Vaughn .30 .10
❑ 43 Tom Gordon .30 .10
❑ 44 Tim Naehring .30 .10
❑ 45 Darren Bragg .30 .10
❑ 46 Aaron Sele .30 .10
❑ 47 Troy O'Leary .30 .10
❑ 48 John Valentin .30 .10
❑ 49 Doug Glanville .30 .10
❑ 50 Ryne Sandberg 1.25 .50
❑ 51 Steve Trachsel .30 .10
❑ 52 Mark Grace .50 .20
❑ 53 Kevin Foster .30 .10
❑ 54 Kevin Tapani .30 .10
❑ 55 Kevin Orie .30 .10
❑ 56 Lyle Mouton .30 .10
❑ 57 Ray Durham .30 .10
❑ 58 Jaime Navarro .30 .10
❑ 59 Mike Cameron .30 .10
❑ 60 Albert Belle .30 .10
❑ 61 Doug Drabek .30 .10
❑ 62 Chris Snopek .30 .10
❑ 63 Eddie Taubensee .30 .10
❑ 64 Terry Pendleton .30 .10
❑ 65 Barry Larkin .50 .20
❑ 66 Willie Greene .30 .10
❑ 67 Deion Sanders .50 .20
❑ 68 Pokey Reese .30 .10
❑ 69 Jeff Shaw .30 .10
❑ 70 Jim Thome .50 .20
❑ 71 Orel Hershiser .30 .10
❑ 72 Omar Vizquel .50 .20
❑ 73 Brian Giles .30 .10
❑ 74 David Justice .30 .10
❑ 75 Bartolo Colon .30 .10
❑ 76 Sandy Alomar Jr. .30 .10
❑ 77 Neifi Perez .30 .10
❑ 78 Dante Bichette .30 .10
❑ 79 Vinny Castilla .30 .10
❑ 80 Eric Young .30 .10
❑ 81 Quinton McCracken .30 .10
❑ 82 Jamey Wright .30 .10
❑ 83 John Thomson .30 .10
❑ 84 Damion Easley .30 .10
❑ 85 Justin Thompson .30 .10
❑ 86 Willie Blair .30 .10
❑ 87 Raul Casanova .30 .10
❑ 88 Bobby Higginson .30 .10
❑ 89 Bubba Trammell .30 .10
❑ 90 Tony Clark .30 .10
❑ 91 Livan Hernandez .30 .10

❑ 92 Charles Johnson .30 .10
❑ 93 Edgar Renteria .30 .10
❑ 94 Alex Fernandez .30 .10
❑ 95 Gary Sheffield .30 .10
❑ 96 Moises Alou .30 .10
❑ 97 Tony Saunders .30 .10
❑ 98 Robb Nen .30 .10
❑ 99 Darryl Kile .30 .10
❑ 100 Craig Biggio .50 .20
❑ 101 Chris Holt .30 .10
❑ 102 Bob Abreu .30 .10
❑ 103 Luis Gonzalez .30 .10
❑ 104 Billy Wagner .30 .10
❑ 105 Brad Ausmus .30 .10
❑ 106 Chili Davis .30 .10
❑ 107 Tim Belcher .30 .10
❑ 108 Dean Palmer .30 .10
❑ 109 Jeff King .30 .10
❑ 110 Jose Rosado .30 .10
❑ 111 Mike Macfarlane .30 .10
❑ 112 Jay Bell .30 .10
❑ 113 Todd Worrell .30 .10
❑ 114 Chan Ho Park .30 .10
❑ 115 Raul Mondesi .30 .10
❑ 116 Brett Butler .30 .10
❑ 117 Greg Gagne .30 .10
❑ 118 Hideo Nomo .75 .30
❑ 119 Todd Zeile .30 .10
❑ 120 Eric Karros .30 .10
❑ 121 Cal Eldred .30 .10
❑ 122 Jeff D'Amico .30 .10
❑ 123 Antone Williamson .30 .10
❑ 124 Doug Jones .30 .10
❑ 125 Dave Nilsson .30 .10
❑ 126 Gerald Williams .30 .10
❑ 127 Fernando Vina .30 .10
❑ 128 Ron Coomer .30 .10
❑ 129 Matt Lawton .30 .10
❑ 130 Paul Molitor .30 .10
❑ 131 Todd Walker .30 .10
❑ 132 Rick Aguilera .30 .10
❑ 133 Brad Radke .30 .10
❑ 134 Bob Tewksbury .30 .10
❑ 135 Vladimir Guerrero .75 .30
❑ 136 Tony Gwynn DG .50 .20
❑ 137 Roger Clemens DG .75 .30
❑ 138 Dennis Eckersley DG .30 .10
❑ 139 Brady Anderson DG .30 .10
❑ 140 Ken Griffey Jr. DG .75 .30
❑ 141 Derek Jeter DG 1.00 .40
❑ 142 Ken Caminiti DG .30 .10
❑ 143 Frank Thomas DG .50 .20
❑ 144 Barry Bonds DG 1.00 .40
❑ 145 Cal Ripken DG 1.25 .50
❑ 146 Alex Rodriguez DG .75 .30
❑ 147 Greg Maddux DG .75 .30
❑ 148 Kenny Lofton DG .30 .10
❑ 149 Mike Piazza DG .75 .30
❑ 150 Mark McGwire DG 1.00 .40
❑ 151 Andruw Jones DG .30 .10
❑ 152 Rusty Greer DG .30 .10
❑ 153 F.P. Santangelo DG .30 .10
❑ 154 Mike Lansing .30 .10
❑ 155 Lee Smith .30 .10
❑ 156 Carlos Perez .30 .10
❑ 157 Pedro Martinez .50 .20
❑ 158 Ryan McGuire .30 .10
❑ 159 F.P. Santangelo .30 .10
❑ 160 Rondell White .30 .10
❑ 161 Takashi Kashiwada RC .40 .15
❑ 162 Butch Huskey .30 .10
❑ 163 Edgardo Alfonzo .30 .10
❑ 164 John Franco .30 .10
❑ 165 Todd Hundley .30 .10
❑ 166 Rey Ordonez .30 .10
❑ 167 Armando Reynoso .30 .10
❑ 168 John Olerud .30 .10
❑ 169 Bernie Williams .50 .20
❑ 170 Andy Pettitte .50 .20
❑ 171 Wade Boggs .50 .20
❑ 172 Paul O'Neill .50 .20
❑ 173 Cecil Fielder .30 .10
❑ 174 Charlie Hayes .30 .10
❑ 175 David Cone .30 .10
❑ 176 Hideki Irabu .30 .10
❑ 177 Mark Bellhorn .30 .10
❑ 178 Steve Karsay .30 .10
❑ 179 Damon Mashore .30 .10
❑ 180 Jason McDonald .30 .10
❑ 181 Scott Spiezio .30 .10
❑ 182 Ariel Prieto .30 .10
❑ 183 Jason Giambi .30 .10
❑ 184 Wendell Magee .30 .10
❑ 185 Rico Brogna .30 .10
❑ 186 Garrett Stephenson .30 .10
❑ 187 Wayne Gomes .30 .10
❑ 188 Ricky Bottalico .30 .10
❑ 189 Mickey Morandini .30 .10
❑ 190 Mike Lieberthal .30 .10
❑ 191 Kevin Polcovich .30 .10
❑ 192 Francisco Cordova .30 .10
❑ 193 Kevin Young .30 .10
❑ 194 Jon Lieber .30 .10
❑ 195 Kevin Elster .30 .10
❑ 196 Tony Womack .30 .10
❑ 197 Lou Collier .30 .10
❑ 198 Mike Difelice RC .40 .15
❑ 199 Gary Gaetti .30 .10
❑ 200 Dennis Eckersley .30 .10
❑ 201 Alan Benes .30 .10
❑ 202 Willie McGee .30 .10
❑ 203 Ron Gant .30 .10
❑ 204 Fernando Valenzuela .30 .10
❑ 205 Mark McGwire 2.00 .75
❑ 206 Archi Cianfrocco .30 .10
❑ 207 Andy Ashby .30 .10
❑ 208 Steve Finley .30 .10
❑ 209 Quilvio Veras .30 .10
❑ 210 Ken Caminiti .30 .10
❑ 211 Rickey Henderson .75 .30
❑ 212 Joey Hamilton .30 .10
❑ 213 Derrek Lee .50 .20
❑ 214 Bill Mueller .30 .10
❑ 215 Shawn Estes .30 .10
❑ 216 J.T. Snow .30 .10
❑ 217 Mark Gardner .30 .10
❑ 218 Terry Mulholland .30 .10
❑ 219 Dante Powell .30 .10
❑ 220 Jeff Kent .30 .10
❑ 221 Jamie Moyer .30 .10
❑ 222 Joey Cora .30 .10
❑ 223 Jeff Fassero .30 .10
❑ 224 Dennis Martinez .30 .10
❑ 225 Ken Griffey Jr. 1.25 .50
❑ 226 Edgar Martinez .50 .20
❑ 227 Russ Davis .30 .10
❑ 228 Dan Wilson .30 .10
❑ 229 Will Clark .50 .20
❑ 230 Ivan Rodriguez .50 .20
❑ 231 Benji Gil .30 .10
❑ 232 Lee Stevens .30 .10
❑ 233 Mickey Tettleton .30 .10
❑ 234 Julio Santana .30 .10
❑ 235 Rusty Greer .30 .10
❑ 236 Bobby Witt .30 .10
❑ 237 Ed Sprague .30 .10
❑ 238 Pat Hentgen .30 .10
❑ 239 Kelvim Escobar .30 .10
❑ 240 Joe Carter .30 .10
❑ 241 Carlos Delgado .30 .10
❑ 242 Shannon Stewart .30 .10
❑ 243 Benito Santiago .30 .10
❑ 244 Tino Martinez SH .30 .10
❑ 245 Ken Griffey Jr. SH .75 .30
❑ 246 Kevin Brown SH .30 .10
❑ 247 Ryne Sandberg SH .50 .20
❑ 248 Mo Vaughn SH .30 .10
❑ 249 Darryl Hamilton SH .30 .10
❑ 250 Randy Johnson SH .50 .20
❑ 251 Steve Finley SH .30 .10
❑ 252 Bobby Higginson SH .30 .10
❑ 253 Brett Tomko .30 .10
❑ 254 Mark Kotsay .30 .10
❑ 255 Jose Guillen .30 .10
❑ 256 Eli Marrero .30 .10
❑ 257 Dennis Reyes .30 .10
❑ 258 Richie Sexson .30 .10
❑ 259 Pat Cline .30 .10
❑ 260 Todd Helton .50 .20
❑ 261 Juan Melo .30 .10
❑ 262 Matt Morris .30 .10
❑ 263 Jeremi Gonzalez .30 .10
❑ 264 Jeff Abbott .30 .10
❑ 265 Aaron Boone .30 .10
❑ 266 Todd Dunwoody .30 .10
❑ 267 Jaret Wright .30 .10
❑ 268 Derrick Gibson .30 .10
❑ 269 Mario Valdez .30 .10
❑ 270 Fernando Tatis .30 .10
❑ 271 Craig Counsell .30 .10
❑ 272 Brad Rigby .30 .10
❑ 273 Danny Clyburn .30 .10
❑ 274 Brian Rose .30 .10
❑ 275 Miguel Tejada .75 .30
❑ 276 Jason Varitek .75 .30
❑ 277 Dave Dellucci RC .60 .25
❑ 278 Michael Coleman .30 .10
❑ 279 Adam Riggs .30 .10
❑ 280 Ben Grieve .30 .10
❑ 281 Brad Fullmer .30 .10
❑ 282 Ken Cloude .30 .10
❑ 283 Tom Evans .30 .10
❑ 284 Kevin Millwood RC 1.00 .40
❑ 285 Paul Konerko .30 .10
❑ 286 Juan Encarnacion .30 .10
❑ 287 Chris Carpenter .30 .10
❑ 288 Tom Fordham .30 .10
❑ 289 Gary DiSarcina .30 .10
❑ 290 Tim Salmon .50 .20
❑ 291 Troy Percival .30 .10
❑ 292 Todd Greene .30 .10
❑ 293 Ken Hill .30 .10
❑ 294 Dennis Springer .30 .10
❑ 295 Jim Edmonds .30 .10
❑ 296 Allen Watson .30 .10
❑ 297 Brian Anderson .30 .10
❑ 298 Keith Lockhart .30 .10
❑ 299 Tom Glavine .50 .20
❑ 300 Chipper Jones .75 .30
❑ 301 Randall Simon .30 .10
❑ 302 Mark Lemke .30 .10
❑ 303 Ryan Klesko .30 .10
❑ 304 Denny Neagle .30 .10
❑ 305 Andruw Jones .50 .20
❑ 306 Mike Mussina .50 .20
❑ 307 Brady Anderson .30 .10
❑ 308 Chris Hoiles .30 .10
❑ 309 Mike Bordick .30 .10
❑ 310 Cal Ripken 2.50 1.00
❑ 311 Geronimo Berroa .30 .10
❑ 312 Armando Benitez .30 .10
❑ 313 Roberto Alomar .50 .20
❑ 314 Tim Wakefield .30 .10
❑ 315 Reggie Jefferson .30 .10
❑ 316 Jeff Frye .30 .10
❑ 317 Scott Hatteberg .30 .10
❑ 318 Steve Avery .30 .10
❑ 319 Robinson Checo .30 .10
❑ 320 Nomar Garciaparra 1.25 .50
❑ 321 Lance Johnson .30 .10
❑ 322 Tyler Houston .30 .10
❑ 323 Mark Clark .30 .10
❑ 324 Terry Adams .30 .10
❑ 325 Sammy Sosa .75 .30
❑ 326 Scott Servais .30 .10
❑ 327 Manny Alexander .30 .10
❑ 328 Norberto Martin .30 .10
❑ 329 Scott Eyre .30 .10
❑ 330 Frank Thomas .75 .30
❑ 331 Robin Ventura .30 .10
❑ 332 Matt Karchner .30 .10
❑ 333 Keith Foulke .30 .10
❑ 334 James Baldwin .30 .10
❑ 335 Chris Stynes .30 .10
❑ 336 Bret Boone .30 .10
❑ 337 Jon Nunnally .30 .10
❑ 338 Dave Burba .30 .10
❑ 339 Eduardo Perez .30 .10
❑ 340 Reggie Sanders .30 .10
❑ 341 Mike Remlinger .30 .10
❑ 342 Pat Watkins .30 .10
❑ 343 Chad Ogea .30 .10
❑ 344 John Smiley .30 .10
❑ 345 Kenny Lofton .30 .10
❑ 346 Jose Mesa .30 .10
❑ 347 Charles Nagy .30 .10
❑ 348 Enrique Wilson .30 .10
❑ 349 Bruce Aven .30 .10

No.	Player		
350	Manny Ramirez	.50	.20
351	Jerry DiPoto	.30	.10
352	Ellis Burks	.30	.10
353	Kirt Manwaring	.30	.10
354	Vinny Castilla	.30	.10
355	Larry Walker	.30	.10
356	Kevin Ritz	.30	.10
357	Pedro Astacio	.30	.10
358	Scott Sanders	.30	.10
359	Deivi Cruz	.30	.10
360	Brian L. Hunter	.30	.10
361	Pedro Martinez HM	.50	.20
362	Tom Glavine HM	.30	.10
363	Willie McGee HM	.30	.10
364	J.T. Snow HM	.30	.10
365	Rusty Greer HM	.30	.10
366	Mike Grace HM	.30	.10
367	Tony Clark HM	.30	.10
368	Ben Grieve HM	.30	.10
369	Gary Sheffield HM	.30	.10
370	Joe Oliver	.30	.10
371	Todd Jones	.30	.10
372	Frank Catalanotto RC	.60	.25
373	Brian Moehler	.30	.10
374	Cliff Floyd	.30	.10
375	Bobby Bonilla	.30	.10
376	Al Leiter	.30	.10
377	Josh Booty	.30	.10
378	Darren Daulton	.30	.10
379	Jay Powell	.30	.10
380	Felix Heredia	.30	.10
381	Jim Eisenreich	.30	.10
382	Richard Hidalgo	.30	.10
383	Mike Hampton	.30	.10
384	Shane Reynolds	.30	.10
385	Jeff Bagwell	.50	.20
386	Derek Bell	.30	.10
387	Ricky Gutierrez	.30	.10
388	Bill Spiers	.30	.10
389	Jose Offerman	.30	.10
390	Johnny Damon	.50	.20
391	Jermaine Dye	.30	.10
392	Jeff Montgomery	.30	.10
393	Glendon Rusch	.30	.10
394	Mike Sweeney	.30	.10
395	Kevin Appier	.30	.10
396	Joe Vitiello	.30	.10
397	Ramon Martinez	.30	.10
398	Darren Dreifort	.30	.10
399	Wilton Guerrero	.30	.10
400	Mike Piazza	1.25	.50
401	Eddie Murray	.75	.30
402	Ismael Valdes	.30	.10
403	Todd Hollandsworth	.30	.10
404	Mark Loretta	.30	.10
405	Jeromy Burnitz	.30	.10
406	Jeff Cirillo	.30	.10
407	Scott Karl	.30	.10
408	Mike Matheny	.30	.10
409	Jose Valentin	.30	.10
410	John Jaha	.30	.10
411	Terry Steinbach	.30	.10
412	Torii Hunter	.30	.10
413	Pat Meares	.30	.10
414	Marty Cordova	.30	.10
415	Jaret Wright PH	.30	.10
416	Mike Mussina PH	.30	.10
417	John Smoltz PH	.30	.10
418	Devon White PH	.30	.10
419	Denny Neagle PH	.30	.10
420	Livan Hernandez PH	.30	.10
421	Kevin Brown PH	.30	.10
422	Marquis Grissom PH	.30	.10
423	Mike Mussina PH	.30	.10
424	Eric Davis PH	.30	.10
425	Tony Fernandez PH	.30	.10
426	Moises Alou PH	.30	.10
427	Sandy Alomar Jr. PH	.30	.10
428	Gary Sheffield PH	.30	.10
429	Jaret Wright PH	.30	.10
430	Livan Hernandez PH	.30	.10
431	Chad Ogea PH	.30	.10
432	Edgar Renteria PH	.30	.10
433	LaTroy Hawkins	.30	.10
434	Rich Robertson	.30	.10
435	Chuck Knoblauch	.30	.10
436	Jose Vidro	.30	.10
437	Dustin Hermanson	.30	.10
438	Jim Bullinger	.30	.10
439	Orlando Cabrera	.30	.10
440	Vladimir Guerrero	.75	.30
441	Ugueth Urbina	.30	.10
442	Brian McRae	.30	.10
443	Matt Franco	.30	.10
444	Bobby Jones	.30	.10
445	Bernard Gilkey	.30	.10
446	Dave Mlicki	.30	.10
447	Brian Bohanon	.30	.10
448	Mel Rojas	.30	.10
449	Tim Raines	.30	.10
450	Derek Jeter	2.00	.75
451	Roger Clemens UE	.75	.30
452	Nomar Garciaparra UE	.75	.30
453	Mike Piazza UE	.75	.30
454	Mark McGwire UE	1.00	.40
455	Ken Griffey Jr. UE	.75	.30
456	Larry Walker UE	.30	.10
457	Alex Rodriguez UE	.75	.30
458	Tony Gwynn UE	.50	.20
459	Frank Thomas UE	.50	.20
460	Tino Martinez	.50	.20
461	Chad Curtis	.30	.10
462	Ramiro Mendoza	.30	.10
463	Joe Girardi	.30	.10
464	David Wells	.30	.10
465	Mariano Rivera	.75	.30
466	Willie Adams	.30	.10
467	George Williams	.30	.10
468	Dave Telgheder	.30	.10
469	Dave Magadan	.30	.10
470	Matt Stairs	.30	.10
471	Bill Taylor	.30	.10
472	Jimmy Haynes	.30	.10
473	Gregg Jefferies	.30	.10
474	Midre Cummings	.30	.10
475	Curt Schilling	.30	.10
476	Mike Grace	.30	.10
477	Mark Leiter	.30	.10
478	Matt Beech	.30	.10
479	Scott Rolen	.50	.20
480	Jason Kendall	.30	.10
481	Esteban Loaiza	.30	.10
482	Jermaine Allensworth	.30	.10
483	Mark Smith	.30	.10
484	Jason Schmidt	.30	.10
485	Jose Guillen	.30	.10
486	Al Martin	.30	.10
487	Delino DeShields	.30	.10
488	Todd Stottlemyre	.30	.10
489	Brian Jordan	.30	.10
490	Ray Lankford	.30	.10
491	Matt Morris	.30	.10
492	Royce Clayton	.30	.10
493	John Mabry	.30	.10
494	Wally Joyner	.30	.10
495	Trevor Hoffman	.30	.10
496	Chris Gomez	.30	.10
497	Sterling Hitchcock	.30	.10
498	Pete Smith	.30	.10
499	Greg Vaughn	.30	.10
500	Tony Gwynn	1.00	.40
501	Will Cunnane	.30	.10
502	Darryl Hamilton	.30	.10
503	Brian Johnson	.30	.10
504	Kirk Rueter	.30	.10
505	Barry Bonds	2.00	.75
506	Osvaldo Fernandez	.30	.10
507	Stan Javier	.30	.10
508	Julian Tavarez	.30	.10
509	Rich Aurilia	.30	.10
510	Alex Rodriguez	1.25	.50
511	David Segui	.30	.10
512	Rich Amaral	.30	.10
513	Raul Ibanez	.30	.10
514	Jay Buhner	.30	.10
515	Randy Johnson	.75	.30
516	Heathcliff Slocumb	.30	.10
517	Tony Saunders	.30	.10
518	Kevin Elster	.30	.10
519	John Burkett	.30	.10
520	Juan Gonzalez	.30	.10
521	John Wetteland	.30	.10
522	Domingo Cedeno	.30	.10
523	Darren Oliver	.30	.10
524	Roger Pavlik	.30	.10
525	Jose Cruz Jr.	.30	.10
526	Woody Williams	.30	.10
527	Alex Gonzalez	.30	.10
528	Robert Person	.30	.10
529	Juan Guzman	.30	.10
530	Roger Clemens	1.50	.60
531	Shawn Green	.30	.10
532	F.Cordova/R.Rincon/M.Smith SH	.30	.10
533	Nomar Garciaparra SH	.75	.30
534	Roger Clemens SH	.75	.30
535	Mark McGwire SH	1.00	.40
536	Larry Walker SH	.30	.10
537	Mike Piazza SH	.75	.30
538	Curt Schilling SH	.30	.10
539	Tony Gwynn SH	.50	.20
540	Ken Griffey Jr. SH	.75	.30
541	Carl Pavano	.30	.10
542	Shane Monahan	.30	.10
543	Gabe Kapler RC	.60	.25
544	Eric Milton	.30	.10
545	Gary Matthews Jr. RC	.60	.25
546	Mike Kinkade RC	.30	.10
547	Ryan Christenson RC	.30	.10
548	Corey Koskie RC	.60	.25
549	Norm Hutchins	.30	.10
550	Russell Branyan	.30	.10
551	Masato Yoshii RC	.40	.15
552	Jesus Sanchez RC	.30	.10
553	Anthony Sanders	.30	.10
554	Edwin Diaz	.30	.10
555	Gabe Alvarez	.30	.10
556	Carlos Lee RC	2.00	.75
557	Mike Darr	.30	.10
558	Kerry Wood	.40	.15
559	Carlos Guillen	.30	.10
560	Sean Casey	.30	.10
561	Manny Aybar RC	.30	.10
562	Octavio Dotel	.30	.10
563	Jarrod Washburn	.30	.10
564	Mark L. Johnson	.30	.10
565	Ramon Hernandez	.30	.10
566	Rich Butler RC	.30	.10
567	Mike Caruso	.30	.10
568	Cliff Politte	.30	.10
569	Scott Elarton	.30	.10
570	Magglio Ordonez RC	2.50	1.00
571	Adam Butler RC	.30	.10
572	Marlon Anderson	.30	.10
573	Julio Ramirez RC	.30	.10
574	Darron Ingram RC	.30	.10
575	Bruce Chen	.30	.10
576	Steve Woodard	.30	.10
577	Hiram Bocachica	.30	.10
578	Kevin Witt	.30	.10
579	Javier Vazquez	.30	.10
580	Alex Gonzalez	.30	.10
581	Brian Powell	.30	.10
582	Wes Helms	.30	.10
583	Ron Wright	.30	.10
584	Rafael Medina	.30	.10
585	Daryle Ward	.30	.10
586	Geoff Jenkins	.30	.10
587	Preston Wilson	.30	.10
588	Jim Chamblee RC	.30	.10
589	Mike Lowell RC	1.25	.50
590	A.J. Hinch	.30	.10
591	Francisco Cordero RC	.60	.25
592	Rolando Arrojo RC	.40	.15
593	Braden Looper	.30	.10
594	Sidney Ponson	.30	.10
595	Matt Clement	.30	.10
596	Carlton Loewer	.30	.10
597	Brian Meadows	.30	.10
598	Danny Klassen	.30	.10
599	Larry Sutton	.30	.10
600	Travis Lee	.30	.10
601	Randy Johnson EP	2.50	1.00
602	Greg Maddux EP	4.00	1.50
603	Roger Clemens EP	5.00	2.00
604	Jaret Wright EP	2.00	.75
605	Mike Piazza EP	4.00	1.50
606	Tino Martinez EP	2.00	.75
607	Frank Thomas EP	2.50	1.00

608	Mo Vaughn EP	2.00	.75
609	Todd Helton EP	2.00	.75
610	Mark McGwire EP	6.00	3.00
611	Jeff Bagwell EP	2.00	.75
612	Travis Lee EP	2.00	.75
613	Scott Rolen EP	2.00	.75
614	Cal Ripken EP	8.00	3.00
615	Chipper Jones EP	2.50	1.00
616	Nomar Garciaparra EP	4.00	1.50
617	Alex Rodriguez EP	4.00	1.50
618	Derek Jeter EP	6.00	2.50
619	Tony Gwynn EP	3.00	1.25
620	Ken Griffey Jr. EP	4.00	1.50
621	Kenny Lofton EP	2.00	.75
622	Juan Gonzalez EP	2.00	.75
623	Jose Cruz Jr. EP	2.00	.75
624	Larry Walker EP	2.00	.75
625	Barry Bonds EP	6.00	2.50
626	Ben Grieve EP	2.00	.75
627	Andruw Jones EP	2.00	.75
628	Vladimir Guerrero EP	2.50	1.00
629	Paul Konerko EP	2.00	.75
630	Paul Molitor EP	2.00	.75
631	Cecil Fielder	.30	.10
632	Jack McDowell	.30	.10
633	Mike James	.30	.10
634	Brian Anderson	.30	.10
635	Jay Bell	.30	.10
636	Devon White	.30	.10
637	Andy Stankiewicz	.30	.10
638	Tony Batista	.30	.10
639	Omar Daal	.30	.10
640	Matt Williams	.30	.10
641	Brent Brede	.30	.10
642	Jorge Fabregas	.30	.10
643	Karim Garcia	.30	.10
644	Felix Rodriguez	.30	.10
645	Andy Benes	.30	.10
646	Willie Blair	.30	.10
647	Jeff Suppan	.30	.10
648	Yamil Benitez	.30	.10
649	Walt Weiss	.30	.10
650	Andres Galarraga	.30	.10
651	Doug Drabek	.30	.10
652	Ozzie Guillen	.30	.10
653	Joe Carter	.30	.10
654	Dennis Eckersley	.30	.10
655	Pedro Martinez	.50	.20
656	Jim Leyritz	.30	.10
657	Henry Rodriguez	.30	.10
658	Rod Beck	.30	.10
659	Mickey Morandini	.30	.10
660	Jeff Blauser	.30	.10
661	Ruben Sierra	.30	.10
662	Mike Sirotka	.30	.10
663	Pete Harnisch	.30	.10
664	Damian Jackson	.30	.10
665	Dmitri Young	.30	.10
666	Steve Cooke	.30	.10
667	Geronimo Berroa	.30	.10
668	Shawon Dunston	.30	.10
669	Mike Jackson	.30	.10
670	Travis Fryman	.30	.10
671	Dwight Gooden	.30	.10
672	Paul Assenmacher	.30	.10
673	Eric Plunk	.30	.10
674	Mike Lansing	.30	.10
675	Darryl Kile	.30	.10
676	Luis Gonzalez	.30	.10
677	Frank Castillo	.30	.10
678	Joe Randa	.30	.10
679	Bip Roberts	.30	.10
680	Derrek Lee	.50	.20
681	M.Piazza Mets SP	3.00	1.25
681A	M.Piazza Marlins SP	3.00	1.25
682	Sean Berry	.30	.10
683	Ramon Garcia	.30	.10
684	Carl Everett	.30	.10
685	Moises Alou	.30	.10
686	Hal Morris	.30	.10
687	Jeff Conine	.30	.10
688	Gary Sheffield	.30	.10
689	Jose Vizcaino	.30	.10
690	Charles Johnson	.30	.10
691	Bobby Bonilla	.30	.10
692	Marquis Grissom	.30	.10
693	Alex Ochoa	.30	.10
694	Mike Morgan	.30	.10
695	Orlando Merced	.30	.10
696	David Ortiz	1.00	.40
697	Brent Gates	.30	.10
698	Otis Nixon	.30	.10
699	Trey Moore	.30	.10
700	Derrick May	.30	.10
701	Rich Becker	.30	.10
702	Al Leiter	.30	.10
703	Chili Davis	.30	.10
704	Scott Brosius	.30	.10
705	Chuck Knoblauch	.30	.10
706	Kenny Rogers	.30	.10
707	Mike Blowers	.30	.10
708	Mike Fetters	.30	.10
709	Tom Candiotti	.30	.10
710	Rickey Henderson	.75	.30
711	Bob Abreu	.30	.10
712	Mark Lewis	.30	.10
713	Doug Glanville	.30	.10
714	Desi Relaford	.30	.10
715	Kent Mercker	.30	.10
716	Kevin Brown	.50	.20
717	James Mouton	.30	.10
718	Mark Langston	.30	.10
719	Greg Myers	.30	.10
720	Orel Hershiser	.30	.10
721	Charlie Hayes	.30	.10
722	Robb Nen	.30	.10
723	Glenallen Hill	.30	.10
724	Tony Saunders	.30	.10
725	Wade Boggs	.50	.20
726	Kevin Stocker	.30	.10
727	Wilson Alvarez	.30	.10
728	Albie Lopez	.30	.10
729	Dave Martinez	.30	.10
730	Fred McGriff	.50	.20
731	Quinton McCracken	.30	.10
732	Bryan Rekar	.30	.10
733	Paul Sorrento	.30	.10
734	Roberto Hernandez	.30	.10
735	Bubba Trammell	.30	.10
736	Miguel Cairo	.30	.10
737	John Flaherty	.30	.10
738	Terrell Wade	.30	.10
739	Roberto Kelly	.30	.10
740	Mark McLemore	.30	.10
741	Danny Patterson	.30	.10
742	Aaron Sele	.30	.10
743	Tony Fernandez	.30	.10
744	Randy Myers	.30	.10
745	Jose Canseco	.50	.20
746	Darrin Fletcher	.30	.10
747	Mike Stanley	.30	.10
748	Marquis Grissom SH CL	.30	.10
749	Fred McGriff SH CL	.30	.10
750	Travis Lee SH CL	.30	.10

1999 Upper Deck

	COMPLETE SET (525)	100.00	50.00
	COMPLETE SERIES 1 (255)	60.00	30.00
	COMPLETE SERIES 2 (270)	40.00	20.00
	COMMON (19-255/293-535)	.30	.10
	COMMON SER.1 SR (1-18)	.50	.20
	COMMON SER.2 SR (266-292)	.50	.20
1	Troy Glaus SR	1.00	.40
2	Adrian Beltre SR	.60	.25
3	Matt Anderson SR	.50	.20
4	Eric Chavez SR	.60	.25
5	Jin Ho Cho SR	.50	.20
6	Robert Smith SR	.50	.20
7	George Lombard SR	.50	.20
8	Mike Kinkade SR	.50	.20
9	Seth Greisinger SR	.50	.20
10	J.D. Drew SR	.60	.25
11	Aramis Ramirez SR	.60	.25
12	Carlos Guillen SR	.60	.25
13	Justin Baughman SR	.50	.20
14	Jim Parque SR	.50	.20
15	Ryan Jackson SR	.50	.20
16	Ramon E.Martinez SR RC	.50	.20
17	Orlando Hernandez SR	.60	.25
18	Jeremy Giambi SR	.50	.20
19	Gary DiSarcina	.30	.10
20	Darin Erstad	.30	.10
21	Troy Glaus	.50	.20
22	Chuck Finley	.30	.10
23	Dave Hollins	.30	.10
24	Troy Percival	.30	.10
25	Tim Salmon	.50	.20
26	Brian Anderson	.30	.10
27	Jay Bell	.30	.10
28	Andy Benes	.30	.10
29	Brent Brede	.30	.10
30	David Dellucci	.30	.10
31	Karim Garcia	.30	.10
32	Travis Lee	.30	.10
33	Andres Galarraga	.30	.10
34	Ryan Klesko	.30	.10
35	Keith Lockhart	.30	.10
36	Kevin Millwood	.30	.10
37	Denny Neagle	.30	.10
38	John Smoltz	.50	.20
39	Michael Tucker	.30	.10
40	Walt Weiss	.30	.10
41	Dennis Martinez	.30	.10
42	Javy Lopez	.30	.10
43	Brady Anderson	.30	.10
44	Harold Baines	.30	.10
45	Mike Bordick	.30	.10
46	Roberto Alomar	.50	.20
47	Scott Erickson	.30	.10
48	Mike Mussina	.50	.20
49	Cal Ripken	2.50	1.00
50	Darren Bragg	.30	.10
51	Dennis Eckersley	.30	.10
52	Nomar Garciaparra	1.25	.50
53	Scott Hatteberg	.30	.10
54	Troy O'Leary	.30	.10
55	Bret Saberhagen	.30	.10
56	John Valentin	.30	.10
57	Rod Beck	.30	.10
58	Jeff Blauser	.30	.10
59	Brant Brown	.30	.10
60	Mark Clark	.30	.10
61	Mark Grace	.50	.20
62	Kevin Tapani	.30	.10
63	Henry Rodriguez	.30	.10
64	Mike Cameron	.30	.10
65	Mike Caruso	.30	.10
66	Ray Durham	.30	.10
67	Jaime Navarro	.30	.10
68	Magglio Ordonez	.30	.10
69	Mike Sirotka	.30	.10
70	Sean Casey	.30	.10
71	Barry Larkin	.50	.20
72	Jon Nunnally	.30	.10
73	Paul Konerko	.30	.10
74	Chris Stynes	.30	.10
75	Brett Tomko	.30	.10
76	Dmitri Young	.30	.10
77	Sandy Alomar Jr.	.30	.10
78	Bartolo Colon	.30	.10
79	Travis Fryman	.30	.10
80	Brian Giles	.30	.10
81	David Justice	.30	.10
82	Omar Vizquel	.50	.20
83	Jaret Wright	.30	.10
84	Jim Thome	.50	.20
85	Charles Nagy	.30	.10
86	Pedro Astacio	.30	.10
87	Todd Helton	.50	.20
88	Darryl Kile	.30	.10

❑ 89	Mike Lansing	.30	.10
❑ 90	Neifi Perez	.30	.10
❑ 91	John Thomson	.30	.10
❑ 92	Larry Walker	.30	.10
❑ 93	Tony Clark	.30	.10
❑ 94	Deivi Cruz	.30	.10
❑ 95	Damion Easley	.30	.10
❑ 96	Brian L.Hunter	.30	.10
❑ 97	Todd Jones	.30	.10
❑ 98	Brian Moehler	.30	.10
❑ 99	Gabe Alvarez	.30	.10
❑ 100	Craig Counsell	.30	.10
❑ 101	Cliff Floyd	.30	.10
❑ 102	Livan Hernandez	.30	.10
❑ 103	Andy Larkin	.30	.10
❑ 104	Derrek Lee	.50	.20
❑ 105	Brian Meadows	.30	.10
❑ 106	Moises Alou	.30	.10
❑ 107	Sean Berry	.30	.10
❑ 108	Craig Biggio	.50	.20
❑ 109	Ricky Gutierrez	.30	.10
❑ 110	Mike Hampton	.30	.10
❑ 111	Jose Lima	.30	.10
❑ 112	Billy Wagner	.30	.10
❑ 113	Hal Morris	.30	.10
❑ 114	Johnny Damon	.50	.20
❑ 115	Jeff King	.30	.10
❑ 116	Jeff Montgomery	.30	.10
❑ 117	Glendon Rusch	.30	.10
❑ 118	Larry Sutton	.30	.10
❑ 119	Bobby Bonilla	.30	.10
❑ 120	Jim Eisenreich	.30	.10
❑ 121	Eric Karros	.30	.10
❑ 122	Matt Luke	.30	.10
❑ 123	Ramon Martinez	.30	.10
❑ 124	Gary Sheffield	.30	.10
❑ 125	Eric Young	.30	.10
❑ 126	Charles Johnson	.30	.10
❑ 127	Jeff Cirillo	.30	.10
❑ 128	Marquis Grissom	.30	.10
❑ 129	Jeromy Burnitz	.30	.10
❑ 130	Bob Wickman	.30	.10
❑ 131	Scott Karl	.30	.10
❑ 132	Mark Loretta	.30	.10
❑ 133	Fernando Vina	.30	.10
❑ 134	Matt Lawton	.30	.10
❑ 135	Pat Meares	.30	.10
❑ 136	Eric Milton	.30	.10
❑ 137	Paul Molitor	.30	.10
❑ 138	David Ortiz	.75	.30
❑ 139	Todd Walker	.30	.10
❑ 140	Shane Andrews	.30	.10
❑ 141	Brad Fullmer	.30	.10
❑ 142	Vladimir Guerrero	.75	.30
❑ 143	Dustin Hermanson	.30	.10
❑ 144	Ryan McGuire	.30	.10
❑ 145	Ugueth Urbina	.30	.10
❑ 146	John Franco	.30	.10
❑ 147	Butch Huskey	.30	.10
❑ 148	Bobby Jones	.30	.10
❑ 149	John Olerud	.30	.10
❑ 150	Rey Ordonez	.30	.10
❑ 151	Mike Piazza	1.25	.50
❑ 152	Hideo Nomo	.75	.30
❑ 153	Masato Yoshii	.30	.10
❑ 154	Derek Jeter	2.00	.75
❑ 155	Chuck Knoblauch	.30	.10
❑ 156	Paul O'Neill	.50	.20
❑ 157	Andy Pettitte	.50	.20
❑ 158	Mariano Rivera	.75	.30
❑ 159	Darryl Strawberry	.30	.10
❑ 160	David Wells	.30	.10
❑ 161	Jorge Posada	.50	.20
❑ 162	Ramiro Mendoza	.30	.10
❑ 163	Miguel Tejada	.30	.10
❑ 164	Ryan Christenson	.30	.10
❑ 165	Rickey Henderson	.75	.30
❑ 166	A.J. Hinch	.30	.10
❑ 167	Ben Grieve	.30	.10
❑ 168	Kenny Rogers	.30	.10
❑ 169	Matt Stairs	.30	.10
❑ 170	Bob Abreu	.30	.10
❑ 171	Rico Brogna	.30	.10
❑ 172	Doug Glanville	.30	.10
❑ 173	Mike Grace	.30	.10
❑ 174	Desi Relaford	.30	.10
❑ 175	Scott Rolen	.50	.20
❑ 176	Jose Guillen	.30	.10
❑ 177	Francisco Cordova	.30	.10
❑ 178	Al Martin	.30	.10
❑ 179	Jason Schmidt	.30	.10
❑ 180	Turner Ward	.30	.10
❑ 181	Kevin Young	.30	.10
❑ 182	Mark McGwire	2.00	.75
❑ 183	Delino DeShields	.30	.10
❑ 184	Eli Marrero	.30	.10
❑ 185	Tom Lampkin	.30	.10
❑ 186	Ray Lankford	.30	.10
❑ 187	Willie McGee	.30	.10
❑ 188	Matt Morris	.30	.10
❑ 189	Andy Ashby	.30	.10
❑ 190	Kevin Brown	.50	.20
❑ 191	Ken Caminiti	.30	.10
❑ 192	Trevor Hoffman	.30	.10
❑ 193	Wally Joyner	.30	.10
❑ 194	Greg Vaughn	.30	.10
❑ 195	Danny Darwin	.30	.10
❑ 196	Shawn Estes	.30	.10
❑ 197	Orel Hershiser	.30	.10
❑ 198	Jeff Kent	.30	.10
❑ 199	Bill Mueller	.30	.10
❑ 200	Robb Nen	.30	.10
❑ 201	J.T. Snow	.30	.10
❑ 202	Ken Cloude	.30	.10
❑ 203	Russ Davis	.30	.10
❑ 204	Jeff Fassero	.30	.10
❑ 205	Ken Griffey Jr.	1.25	.50
❑ 206	Shane Monahan	.30	.10
❑ 207	David Segui	.30	.10
❑ 208	Dan Wilson	.30	.10
❑ 209	Wilson Alvarez	.30	.10
❑ 210	Wade Boggs	.50	.20
❑ 211	Miguel Cairo	.30	.10
❑ 212	Bubba Trammell	.30	.10
❑ 213	Quinton McCracken	.30	.10
❑ 214	Paul Sorrento	.30	.10
❑ 215	Kevin Stocker	.30	.10
❑ 216	Will Clark	.50	.20
❑ 217	Rusty Greer	.30	.10
❑ 218	Rick Helling	.30	.10
❑ 219	Mark McLemore	.30	.10
❑ 220	Ivan Rodriguez	.50	.20
❑ 221	John Wetteland	.30	.10
❑ 222	Jose Canseco	.50	.20
❑ 223	Roger Clemens	1.50	.60
❑ 224	Carlos Delgado	.30	.10
❑ 225	Darrin Fletcher	.30	.10
❑ 226	Alex Gonzalez	.30	.10
❑ 227	Jose Cruz Jr.	.30	.10
❑ 228	Shannon Stewart	.30	.10
❑ 229	Rolando Arrojo FF	.30	.10
❑ 230	Livan Hernandez FF	.30	.10
❑ 231	Orlando Hernandez FF	.30	.10
❑ 232	Raul Mondesi FF	.30	.10
❑ 233	Moises Alou FF	.30	.10
❑ 234	Pedro Martinez FF	.50	.20
❑ 235	Sammy Sosa FF	.50	.20
❑ 236	Vladimir Guerrero FF	.75	.30
❑ 237	Bartolo Colon FF	.30	.10
❑ 238	Miguel Tejada FF	.30	.10
❑ 239	Ismael Valdes FF	.30	.10
❑ 240	Mariano Rivera FF	.50	.20
❑ 241	Jose Cruz Jr. FF	.30	.10
❑ 242	Juan Gonzalez FF	.30	.10
❑ 243	Ivan Rodriguez FF	.50	.20
❑ 244	Sandy Alomar Jr. FF	.30	.10
❑ 245	Roberto Alomar FF	.50	.20
❑ 246	Magglio Ordonez FF	.30	.10
❑ 247	Kerry Wood SH CL	.30	.10
❑ 248	Mark McGwire SH CL	2.00	.75
❑ 249	David Wells SH CL	.30	.10
❑ 250	Rolando Arrojo SH CL	.30	.10
❑ 251	Ken Griffey Jr. SH CL	1.25	.50
❑ 252	Trevor Hoffman SH CL	.30	.10
❑ 253	Travis Lee SH CL	.30	.10
❑ 254	Roberto Alomar SH CL	.30	.10
❑ 255	Sammy Sosa SH CL	.50	.20
❑ 266	Pat Burrell SR RC	3.00	1.25
❑ 267	Shea Hillenbrand SR RC	1.50	.60
❑ 268	Robert Fick SR	.50	.20
❑ 269	Roy Halladay SR	.60	.25
❑ 270	Ruben Mateo SR	.50	.20
❑ 271	Bruce Chen SR	.50	.20
❑ 272	Angel Pena SR	.50	.20
❑ 273	Michael Barrett SR	.50	.20
❑ 274	Kevin Witt SR	.50	.20
❑ 275	Damon Minor SR	.50	.20
❑ 276	Ryan Minor SR	.50	.20
❑ 277	A.J. Pierzynski SR	.60	.25
❑ 278	A.J. Burnett SR RC	1.50	.60
❑ 279	Dermal Brown SR	.50	.20
❑ 280	Joe Lawrence SR	.50	.20
❑ 281	Derrick Gibson SR	.50	.20
❑ 282	Carlos Febles SR	.50	.20
❑ 283	Chris Haas SR	.50	.20
❑ 284	Cesar King SR	.50	.20
❑ 285	Calvin Pickering SR	.50	.20
❑ 286	Mitch Meluskey SR	.50	.20
❑ 287	Carlos Beltran SR	1.00	.40
❑ 288	Ron Belliard SR	.50	.20
❑ 289	Jerry Hairston Jr. SR	.50	.20
❑ 290	Fernando Seguignol SR	.50	.20
❑ 291	Kris Benson SR	.50	.20
❑ 292	Chad Hutchinson SR RC	.60	.25
❑ 293	Jarrod Washburn	.30	.10
❑ 294	Jason Dickson	.30	.10
❑ 295	Mo Vaughn	.30	.10
❑ 296	Garret Anderson	.30	.10
❑ 297	Jim Edmonds	.30	.10
❑ 298	Ken Hill	.30	.10
❑ 299	Shigetoshi Hasegawa	.30	.10
❑ 300	Todd Stottlemyre	.30	.10
❑ 301	Randy Johnson	.75	.30
❑ 302	Omar Daal	.30	.10
❑ 303	Steve Finley	.30	.10
❑ 304	Matt Williams	.30	.10
❑ 305	Danny Klassen	.30	.10
❑ 306	Tony Batista	.30	.10
❑ 307	Brian Jordan	.30	.10
❑ 308	Greg Maddux	1.25	.50
❑ 309	Chipper Jones	.75	.30
❑ 310	Bret Boone	.30	.10
❑ 311	Ozzie Guillen	.30	.10
❑ 312	John Rocker	.30	.10
❑ 313	Tom Glavine	.50	.20
❑ 314	Andruw Jones	.50	.20
❑ 315	Albert Belle	.30	.10
❑ 316	Charles Johnson	.30	.10
❑ 317	Will Clark	.50	.20
❑ 318	B.J. Surhoff	.30	.10
❑ 319	Delino DeShields	.30	.10
❑ 320	Heathcliff Slocumb	.30	.10
❑ 321	Sidney Ponson	.30	.10
❑ 322	Juan Guzman	.30	.10
❑ 323	Reggie Jefferson	.30	.10
❑ 324	Mark Portugal	.30	.10
❑ 325	Tim Wakefield	.30	.10
❑ 326	Jason Varitek	.75	.30
❑ 327	Jose Offerman	.30	.10
❑ 328	Pedro Martinez	.50	.20
❑ 329	Trot Nixon	.30	.10
❑ 330	Kerry Wood	.30	.10
❑ 331	Sammy Sosa	.75	.30
❑ 332	Glenallen Hill	.30	.10
❑ 333	Gary Gaetti	.30	.10
❑ 334	Mickey Morandini	.30	.10
❑ 335	Benito Santiago	.30	.10
❑ 336	Jeff Blauser	.30	.10
❑ 337	Frank Thomas	.75	.30
❑ 338	Paul Konerko	.30	.10
❑ 339	Jaime Navarro	.30	.10
❑ 340	Carlos Lee	.30	.10
❑ 341	Brian Simmons	.30	.10
❑ 342	Mark Johnson	.30	.10
❑ 343	Jeff Abbott	.30	.10
❑ 344	Steve Avery	.30	.10
❑ 345	Mike Cameron	.30	.10
❑ 346	Michael Tucker	.30	.10
❑ 347	Greg Vaughn	.30	.10
❑ 348	Hal Morris	.30	.10
❑ 349	Pete Harnisch	.30	.10
❑ 350	Denny Neagle	.30	.10
❑ 351	Manny Ramirez	.50	.20
❑ 352	Roberto Alomar	.50	.20
❑ 353	Dwight Gooden	.30	.10
❑ 354	Kenny Lofton	.30	.10
❑ 355	Mike Jackson	.30	.10
❑ 356	Charles Nagy	.30	.10

❑ 357	Enrique Wilson	.30	.10
❑ 358	Russ Branyan	.30	.10
❑ 359	Richie Sexson	.30	.10
❑ 360	Vinny Castilla	.30	.10
❑ 361	Dante Bichette	.30	.10
❑ 362	Kirt Manwaring	.30	.10
❑ 363	Darryl Hamilton	.30	.10
❑ 364	Jamey Wright	.30	.10
❑ 365	Curtis Leskanic	.30	.10
❑ 366	Jeff Reed	.30	.10
❑ 367	Bobby Higginson	.30	.10
❑ 368	Justin Thompson	.30	.10
❑ 369	Brad Ausmus	.30	.10
❑ 370	Dean Palmer	.30	.10
❑ 371	Gabe Kapler	.30	.10
❑ 372	Juan Encarnacion	.30	.10
❑ 373	Karim Garcia	.30	.10
❑ 374	Alex Gonzalez	.30	.10
❑ 375	Braden Looper	.30	.10
❑ 376	Preston Wilson	.30	.10
❑ 377	Todd Dunwoody	.30	.10
❑ 378	Alex Fernandez	.30	.10
❑ 379	Mark Kotsay	.30	.10
❑ 380	Matt Mantei	.30	.10
❑ 381	Ken Caminiti	.30	.10
❑ 382	Scott Elarton	.30	.10
❑ 383	Jeff Bagwell	.50	.20
❑ 384	Derek Bell	.30	.10
❑ 385	Ricky Gutierrez	.30	.10
❑ 386	Richard Hidalgo	.30	.10
❑ 387	Shane Reynolds	.30	.10
❑ 388	Carl Everett	.30	.10
❑ 389	Scott Service	.30	.10
❑ 390	Jeff Suppan	.30	.10
❑ 391	Joe Randa	.30	.10
❑ 392	Kevin Appier	.30	.10
❑ 393	Shane Halter	.30	.10
❑ 394	Chad Kreuter	.30	.10
❑ 395	Mike Sweeney	.30	.10
❑ 396	Kevin Brown	.50	.20
❑ 397	Devon White	.30	.10
❑ 398	Todd Hollandsworth	.30	.10
❑ 399	Todd Hundley	.30	.10
❑ 400	Chan Ho Park	.30	.10
❑ 401	Mark Grudzielanek	.30	.10
❑ 402	Raul Mondesi	.30	.10
❑ 403	Ismael Valdes	.30	.10
❑ 404	Rafael Roque RC	.30	.10
❑ 405	Sean Berry	.30	.10
❑ 406	Kevin Barker	.30	.10
❑ 407	Dave Nilsson	.30	.10
❑ 408	Geoff Jenkins	.30	.10
❑ 409	Jim Abbott	.50	.20
❑ 410	Bobby Hughes	.30	.10
❑ 411	Corey Koskie	.30	.10
❑ 412	Rick Aguilera	.30	.10
❑ 413	LaTroy Hawkins	.30	.10
❑ 414	Ron Coomer	.30	.10
❑ 415	Denny Hocking	.30	.10
❑ 416	Marty Cordova	.30	.10
❑ 417	Terry Steinbach	.30	.10
❑ 418	Rondell White	.30	.10
❑ 419	Wilton Guerrero	.30	.10
❑ 420	Shane Andrews	.30	.10
❑ 421	Orlando Cabrera	.30	.10
❑ 422	Carl Pavano	.30	.10
❑ 423	Javier Vazquez	.30	.10
❑ 424	Chris Widger	.30	.10
❑ 425	Robin Ventura	.30	.10
❑ 426	Rickey Henderson	.75	.30
❑ 427	Al Leiter	.30	.10
❑ 428	Bobby Jones	.30	.10
❑ 429	Brian McRae	.30	.10
❑ 430	Roger Cedeno	.30	.10
❑ 431	Bobby Bonilla	.30	.10
❑ 432	Edgardo Alfonzo	.30	.10
❑ 433	Bernie Williams	.50	.20
❑ 434	Ricky Ledee	.30	.10
❑ 435	Chili Davis	.30	.10
❑ 436	Tino Martinez	.50	.20
❑ 437	Scott Brosius	.30	.10
❑ 438	David Cone	.30	.10
❑ 439	Joe Girardi	.30	.10
❑ 440	Roger Clemens	1.50	.60
❑ 441	Chad Curtis	.30	.10
❑ 442	Hideki Irabu	.30	.10

❑ 443	Jason Giambi	.30	.10
❑ 444	Scott Spiezio	.30	.10
❑ 445	Tony Phillips	.30	.10
❑ 446	Ramon Hernandez	.30	.10
❑ 447	Mike Macfarlane	.30	.10
❑ 448	Tom Candiotti	.30	.10
❑ 449	Billy Taylor	.30	.10
❑ 450	Bobby Estalella	.30	.10
❑ 451	Curt Schilling	.30	.10
❑ 452	Carlton Loewer	.30	.10
❑ 453	Marlon Anderson	.30	.10
❑ 454	Kevin Jordan	.30	.10
❑ 455	Ron Gant	.30	.10
❑ 456	Chad Ogea	.30	.10
❑ 457	Abraham Nunez	.30	.10
❑ 458	Jason Kendall	.30	.10
❑ 459	Pat Meares	.30	.10
❑ 460	Brant Brown	.30	.10
❑ 461	Brian Giles	.30	.10
❑ 462	Chad Hermansen	.30	.10
❑ 463	Freddy Adrian Garcia	.30	.10
❑ 464	Edgar Renteria	.30	.10
❑ 465	Fernando Tatis	.30	.10
❑ 466	Eric Davis	.30	.10
❑ 467	Darren Bragg	.30	.10
❑ 468	Donovan Osborne	.30	.10
❑ 469	Manny Aybar	.30	.10
❑ 470	Jose Jimenez	.30	.10
❑ 471	Kent Mercker	.30	.10
❑ 472	Reggie Sanders	.30	.10
❑ 473	Ruben Rivera	.30	.10
❑ 474	Tony Gwynn	1.00	.40
❑ 475	Jim Leyritz	.30	.10
❑ 476	Chris Gomez	.30	.10
❑ 477	Matt Clement	.30	.10
❑ 478	Carlos Hernandez	.30	.10
❑ 479	Sterling Hitchcock	.30	.10
❑ 480	Ellis Burks	.30	.10
❑ 481	Barry Bonds	2.00	.75
❑ 482	Marvin Benard	.30	.10
❑ 483	Kirk Rueter	.30	.10
❑ 484	F.P. Santangelo	.30	.10
❑ 485	Stan Javier	.30	.10
❑ 486	Jeff Kent	.30	.10
❑ 487	Alex Rodriguez	1.25	.50
❑ 488	Tom Lampkin	.30	.10
❑ 489	Jose Mesa	.30	.10
❑ 490	Jay Buhner	.30	.10
❑ 491	Edgar Martinez	.50	.20
❑ 492	Butch Huskey	.30	.10
❑ 493	John Mabry	.30	.10
❑ 494	Jamie Moyer	.30	.10
❑ 495	Roberto Hernandez	.30	.10
❑ 496	Tony Saunders	.30	.10
❑ 497	Fred McGriff	.50	.20
❑ 498	Dave Martinez	.30	.10
❑ 499	Jose Canseco	.50	.20
❑ 500	Rolando Arrojo	.30	.10
❑ 501	Esteban Yan	.30	.10
❑ 502	Juan Gonzalez	.30	.10
❑ 503	Rafael Palmeiro	.50	.20
❑ 504	Aaron Sele	.30	.10
❑ 505	Royce Clayton	.30	.10
❑ 506	Todd Zeile	.30	.10
❑ 507	Tom Goodwin	.30	.10
❑ 508	Lee Stevens	.30	.10
❑ 509	Esteban Loaiza	.30	.10
❑ 510	Joey Hamilton	.30	.10
❑ 511	Homer Bush	.30	.10
❑ 512	Willie Greene	.30	.10
❑ 513	Shawn Green	.30	.10
❑ 514	David Wells	.30	.10
❑ 515	Kelvim Escobar	.30	.10
❑ 516	Tony Fernandez	.30	.10
❑ 517	Pat Hentgen	.30	.10
❑ 518	Mark McGwire AR	1.00	.40
❑ 519	Ken Griffey Jr. AR	.75	.30
❑ 520	Sammy Sosa AR	.50	.20
❑ 521	Juan Gonzalez AR	.30	.10
❑ 522	J.D. Drew AR	.30	.10
❑ 523	Chipper Jones AR	.50	.20
❑ 524	Alex Rodriguez AR	.75	.30
❑ 525	Mike Piazza AR	.75	.30
❑ 526	Nomar Garciaparra AR	.75	.30
❑ 527	Mark McGwire SH CL	1.00	.40
❑ 528	Sammy Sosa SH CL	.50	.20

❑ 529	Scott Brosius SH CL	.30	.10
❑ 530	Cal Ripken SH CL	1.25	.50
❑ 531	Barry Bonds SH CL	1.00	.40
❑ 532	Roger Clemens SH CL	.75	.30
❑ 533	Ken Griffey Jr. SH CL	.75	.30
❑ 534	Alex Rodriguez SH CL	.75	.30
❑ 535	Curt Schilling SH CL	.30	.10
❑ NNO	K.Griffey Jr. '89 AU/100	1250.00	1000.00

2000 Upper Deck

❑	COMPLETE SET (540)	100.00	40.00
❑	COMPLETE SERIES 1 (270)	50.00	20.00
❑	COMPLETE SERIES 2 (270)	50.00	20.00
❑	COMMON CARD (1-540)	.30	.10
❑	COMMON SR (1-28/271-297)	.50	.20
❑ 1	Rick Ankiel SR	.50	.20
❑ 2	Vernon Wells SR	.75	.30
❑ 3	Ryan Anderson SR	.50	.20
❑ 4	Ed Yarnall SR	.50	.20
❑ 5	Brian McNichol SR	.50	.20
❑ 6	Ben Petrick SR	.50	.20
❑ 7	Kip Wells SR	.50	.20
❑ 8	Eric Munson SR	.50	.20
❑ 9	Matt Riley SR	.50	.20
❑ 10	Peter Bergeron SR	.50	.20
❑ 11	Eric Gagne SR	2.00	.75
❑ 12	Ramon Ortiz SR	.50	.20
❑ 13	Josh Beckett SR	2.00	.75
❑ 14	Alfonso Soriano SR	2.00	.75
❑ 15	Jorge Toca SR	.50	.20
❑ 16	Buddy Carlyle SR	.50	.20
❑ 17	Chad Hermansen SR	.50	.20
❑ 18	Matt Perisho SR	.50	.20
❑ 19	Tomokazu Ohka SR RC	.75	.30
❑ 20	Jacque Jones SR	.75	.30
❑ 21	Josh Paul SR	.50	.20
❑ 22	Dermal Brown SR	.50	.20
❑ 23	Adam Kennedy SR	.50	.20
❑ 24	Chad Harville SR	.50	.20
❑ 25	Calvin Murray SR	.50	.20
❑ 26	Chad Meyers SR	.50	.20
❑ 27	Brian Cooper SR	.50	.20
❑ 28	Troy Glaus	.30	.10
❑ 29	Ben Molina	.30	.10
❑ 30	Troy Percival	.30	.10
❑ 31	Ken Hill	.30	.10
❑ 32	Chuck Finley	.30	.10
❑ 33	Todd Greene	.30	.10
❑ 34	Tim Salmon	.50	.20
❑ 35	Gary DiSarcina	.30	.10
❑ 36	Luis Gonzalez	.30	.10
❑ 37	Tony Womack	.30	.10
❑ 38	Omar Daal	.30	.10
❑ 39	Randy Johnson	.75	.30
❑ 40	Erubiel Durazo	.30	.10
❑ 41	Jay Bell	.30	.10
❑ 42	Steve Finley	.30	.10
❑ 43	Travis Lee	.30	.10
❑ 44	Greg Maddux	1.25	.50
❑ 45	Bret Boone	.30	.10
❑ 46	Brian Jordan	.30	.10
❑ 47	Kevin Millwood	.30	.10
❑ 48	Odalis Perez	.30	.10
❑ 49	Javy Lopez	.30	.10
❑ 50	John Smoltz	.50	.20
❑ 51	Bruce Chen	.30	.10
❑ 52	Albert Belle	.30	.10
❑ 53	Jerry Hairston Jr.	.30	.10

❑ 54 Will Clark .50 .20
❑ 55 Sidney Ponson .30 .10
❑ 56 Charles Johnson .30 .10
❑ 57 Cal Ripken 2.50 1.00
❑ 58 Ryan Minor .30 .10
❑ 59 Mike Mussina .50 .20
❑ 60 Tom Gordon .30 .10
❑ 61 Jose Offerman .30 .10
❑ 62 Trot Nixon .30 .10
❑ 63 Pedro Martinez .50 .20
❑ 64 John Valentin .30 .10
❑ 65 Jason Varitek .75 .30
❑ 66 Juan Pena .30 .10
❑ 67 Troy O'Leary .30 .10
❑ 68 Sammy Sosa .75 .30
❑ 69 Henry Rodriguez .30 .10
❑ 70 Kyle Farnsworth .30 .10
❑ 71 Glenallen Hill .30 .10
❑ 72 Lance Johnson .30 .10
❑ 73 Mickey Morandini .30 .10
❑ 74 Jon Lieber .30 .10
❑ 75 Kevin Tapani .30 .10
❑ 76 Carlos Lee .30 .10
❑ 77 Ray Durham .30 .10
❑ 78 Jim Parque .30 .10
❑ 79 Bob Howry .30 .10
❑ 80 Magglio Ordonez .30 .10
❑ 81 Paul Konerko .30 .10
❑ 82 Mike Caruso .30 .10
❑ 83 Chris Singleton .30 .10
❑ 84 Sean Casey .30 .10
❑ 85 Barry Larkin .50 .20
❑ 86 Pokey Reese .30 .10
❑ 87 Eddie Taubensee .30 .10
❑ 88 Scott Williamson .30 .10
❑ 89 Jason LaRue .30 .10
❑ 90 Aaron Boone .30 .10
❑ 91 Jeffrey Hammonds .30 .10
❑ 92 Omar Vizquel .50 .20
❑ 93 Manny Ramirez .50 .20
❑ 94 Kenny Lofton .30 .10
❑ 95 Jaret Wright .30 .10
❑ 96 Einar Diaz .30 .10
❑ 97 Charles Nagy .30 .10
❑ 98 David Justice .30 .10
❑ 99 Richie Sexson .30 .10
❑ 100 Steve Karsay .30 .10
❑ 101 Todd Helton .50 .20
❑ 102 Dante Bichette .30 .10
❑ 103 Larry Walker .30 .10
❑ 104 Pedro Astacio .30 .10
❑ 105 Neifi Perez .30 .10
❑ 106 Brian Bohanon .30 .10
❑ 107 Edgard Clemente .30 .10
❑ 108 Dave Veres .30 .10
❑ 109 Gabe Kapler .30 .10
❑ 110 Juan Encarnacion .30 .10
❑ 111 Jeff Weaver .30 .10
❑ 112 Damion Easley .30 .10
❑ 113 Justin Thompson .30 .10
❑ 114 Brad Ausmus .30 .10
❑ 115 Frank Catalanotto .30 .10
❑ 116 Todd Jones .30 .10
❑ 117 Preston Wilson .30 .10
❑ 118 Cliff Floyd .30 .10
❑ 119 Mike Lowell .30 .10
❑ 120 Antonio Alfonseca .30 .10
❑ 121 Alex Gonzalez .30 .10
❑ 122 Braden Looper .30 .10
❑ 123 Bruce Aven .30 .10
❑ 124 Richard Hidalgo .30 .10
❑ 125 Mitch Meluskey .30 .10
❑ 126 Jeff Bagwell .50 .20
❑ 127 Jose Lima .30 .10
❑ 128 Derek Bell .30 .10
❑ 129 Billy Wagner .30 .10
❑ 130 Shane Reynolds .30 .10
❑ 131 Moises Alou .30 .10
❑ 132 Carlos Beltran .30 .10
❑ 133 Carlos Febles .30 .10
❑ 134 Jermaine Dye .30 .10
❑ 135 Jeremy Giambi .30 .10
❑ 136 Joe Randa .30 .10
❑ 137 Jose Rosado .30 .10
❑ 138 Chad Kreuter .30 .10
❑ 139 Jose Vizcaino .30 .10
❑ 140 Adrian Beltre .30 .10
❑ 141 Kevin Brown .50 .20
❑ 142 Ismael Valdes .30 .10
❑ 143 Angel Pena .30 .10
❑ 144 Chan Ho Park .30 .10
❑ 145 Mark Grudzielanek .30 .10
❑ 146 Jeff Shaw .30 .10
❑ 147 Geoff Jenkins .30 .10
❑ 148 Jeromy Burnitz .30 .10
❑ 149 Hideo Nomo .75 .30
❑ 150 Ron Belliard .30 .10
❑ 151 Sean Berry .30 .10
❑ 152 Mark Loretta .30 .10
❑ 153 Steve Woodard .30 .10
❑ 154 Joe Mays .30 .10
❑ 155 Eric Milton .30 .10
❑ 156 Corey Koskie .30 .10
❑ 157 Ron Coomer .30 .10
❑ 158 Brad Radke .30 .10
❑ 159 Terry Steinbach .30 .10
❑ 160 Cristian Guzman .30 .10
❑ 161 Vladimir Guerrero .75 .30
❑ 162 Wilton Guerrero .30 .10
❑ 163 Michael Barrett .30 .10
❑ 164 Chris Widger .30 .10
❑ 165 Fernando Seguignol .30 .10
❑ 166 Ugueth Urbina .30 .10
❑ 167 Dustin Hermanson .30 .10
❑ 168 Kenny Rogers .30 .10
❑ 169 Edgardo Alfonzo .30 .10
❑ 170 Orel Hershiser .30 .10
❑ 171 Robin Ventura .30 .10
❑ 172 Octavio Dotel .30 .10
❑ 173 Rickey Henderson .75 .30
❑ 174 Roger Cedeno .30 .10
❑ 175 John Olerud .30 .10
❑ 176 Derek Jeter 2.00 .75
❑ 177 Tino Martinez .50 .20
❑ 178 Orlando Hernandez .30 .10
❑ 179 Chuck Knoblauch .30 .10
❑ 180 Bernie Williams .50 .20
❑ 181 Chili Davis .30 .10
❑ 182 David Cone .30 .10
❑ 183 Ricky Ledee .30 .10
❑ 184 Paul O'Neill .50 .20
❑ 185 Jason Giambi .30 .10
❑ 186 Eric Chavez .30 .10
❑ 187 Matt Stairs .30 .10
❑ 188 Miguel Tejada .30 .10
❑ 189 Olmedo Saenz .30 .10
❑ 190 Tim Hudson .30 .10
❑ 191 John Jaha .30 .10
❑ 192 Randy Velarde .30 .10
❑ 193 Rico Brogna .30 .10
❑ 194 Mike Lieberthal .30 .10
❑ 195 Marlon Anderson .30 .10
❑ 196 Bob Abreu .30 .10
❑ 197 Ron Gant .30 .10
❑ 198 Randy Wolf .30 .10
❑ 199 Desi Relaford .30 .10
❑ 200 Doug Glanville .30 .10
❑ 201 Warren Morris .30 .10
❑ 202 Kris Benson .30 .10
❑ 203 Kevin Young .30 .10
❑ 204 Brian Giles .30 .10
❑ 205 Jason Schmidt .30 .10
❑ 206 Ed Sprague .30 .10
❑ 207 Francisco Cordova .30 .10
❑ 208 Mark McGwire 2.00 .75
❑ 209 Jose Jimenez .30 .10
❑ 210 Fernando Tatis .30 .10
❑ 211 Kent Bottenfield .30 .10
❑ 212 Eli Marrero .30 .10
❑ 213 Edgar Renteria .30 .10
❑ 214 Joe McEwing .30 .10
❑ 215 J.D. Drew .30 .10
❑ 216 Tony Gwynn 1.00 .40
❑ 217 Gary Matthews Jr. .30 .10
❑ 218 Eric Owens .30 .10
❑ 219 Damian Jackson .30 .10
❑ 220 Reggie Sanders .30 .10
❑ 221 Trevor Hoffman .30 .10
❑ 222 Ben Davis .30 .10
❑ 223 Shawn Estes .30 .10
❑ 224 F.P. Santangelo .30 .10
❑ 225 Livan Hernandez .30 .10
❑ 226 Ellis Burks .30 .10
❑ 227 J.T. Snow .30 .10
❑ 228 Jeff Kent .30 .10
❑ 229 Robb Nen .30 .10
❑ 230 Marvin Benard .30 .10
❑ 231 Ken Griffey Jr. 1.25 .50
❑ 232 John Halama .30 .10
❑ 233 Gil Meche .30 .10
❑ 234 David Bell .30 .10
❑ 235 Brian Hunter .30 .10
❑ 236 Jay Buhner .30 .10
❑ 237 Edgar Martinez .50 .20
❑ 238 Jose Mesa .30 .10
❑ 239 Wilson Alvarez .30 .10
❑ 240 Wade Boggs .50 .20
❑ 241 Fred McGriff .50 .20
❑ 242 Jose Canseco .50 .20
❑ 243 Kevin Stocker .30 .10
❑ 244 Roberto Hernandez .30 .10
❑ 245 Bubba Trammell .30 .10
❑ 246 John Flaherty .30 .10
❑ 247 Ivan Rodriguez .50 .20
❑ 248 Rusty Greer .30 .10
❑ 249 Rafael Palmeiro .50 .20
❑ 250 Jeff Zimmerman .30 .10
❑ 251 Royce Clayton .30 .10
❑ 252 Todd Zeile .30 .10
❑ 253 John Wetteland .30 .10
❑ 254 Ruben Mateo .30 .10
❑ 255 Kelvim Escobar .30 .10
❑ 256 David Wells .30 .10
❑ 257 Shawn Green .30 .10
❑ 258 Homer Bush .30 .10
❑ 259 Shannon Stewart .30 .10
❑ 260 Carlos Delgado .30 .10
❑ 261 Roy Halladay .30 .10
❑ 262 Fernando Tatis SH CL .30 .10
❑ 263 Jose Jimenez SH CL .30 .10
❑ 264 Tony Gwynn SH CL .50 .20
❑ 265 Wade Boggs SH CL .30 .10
❑ 266 Cal Ripken SH CL 1.25 .50
❑ 267 David Cone SH CL .30 .10
❑ 268 Mark McGwire SH CL 1.25 .50
❑ 269 Pedro Martinez SH CL .50 .20
❑ 270 Nomar Garciaparra SH CL .75 .30
❑ 271 Nick Johnson SR .75 .30
❑ 272 Mark Quinn SR .50 .20
❑ 273 Roosevelt Brown SR .50 .20
❑ 274 Terrence Long SR .50 .20
❑ 275 Jason Marquis SR .50 .20
❑ 276 Kazuhiro Sasaki SR RC 1.25 .50
❑ 277 Aaron Myette SR .50 .20
❑ 278 Danys Baez SR RC .75 .30
❑ 279 Travis Dawkins SR .50 .20
❑ 280 Mark Mulder SR .75 .30
❑ 281 Chris Haas SR .50 .20
❑ 282 Milton Bradley SR .75 .30
❑ 283 Brad Penny SR .50 .20
❑ 284 Rafael Furcal SR .75 .30
❑ 285 Luis Matos SR RC .75 .30
❑ 286 Victor Santos SR RC .75 .30
❑ 287 Rico Washington SR RC .50 .20
❑ 288 Rob Bell SR .50 .20
❑ 289 Joe Crede SR 2.50 1.00
❑ 290 Pablo Ozuna SR .50 .20
❑ 291 Wascar Serrano SR RC .50 .20
❑ 292 Sang-Hoon Lee SR RC .50 .20
❑ 293 Chris Wakeland SR RC .50 .20
❑ 294 Luis Rivera SR RC .50 .20
❑ 295 Mike Lamb SR RC 1.25 .50
❑ 296 Wily Mo Pena SR .75 .30
❑ 297 Mike Meyers SR RC .75 .30
❑ 298 Mo Vaughn .30 .10
❑ 299 Darin Erstad .30 .10
❑ 300 Garret Anderson .30 .10
❑ 301 Tim Belcher .30 .10
❑ 302 Scott Spiezio .30 .10
❑ 303 Kent Bottenfield .30 .10
❑ 304 Orlando Palmeiro .30 .10
❑ 305 Jason Dickson .30 .10
❑ 306 Matt Williams .30 .10
❑ 307 Brian Anderson .30 .10
❑ 308 Hanley Frias .30 .10
❑ 309 Todd Stottlemyre .30 .10
❑ 310 Matt Mantei .30 .10
❑ 311 David Dellucci .30 .10

❑ 312 Armando Reynoso .30 .10
❑ 313 Bernard Gilkey .30 .10
❑ 314 Chipper Jones .75 .30
❑ 315 Tom Glavine .50 .20
❑ 316 Quilvio Veras .30 .10
❑ 317 Andruw Jones .50 .20
❑ 318 Bobby Bonilla .30 .10
❑ 319 Reggie Sanders .30 .10
❑ 320 Andres Galarraga .30 .10
❑ 321 George Lombard .30 .10
❑ 322 John Rocker .30 .10
❑ 323 Wally Joyner .30 .10
❑ 324 B.J. Surhoff .30 .10
❑ 325 Scott Erickson .30 .10
❑ 326 Delino DeShields .30 .10
❑ 327 Jeff Conine .30 .10
❑ 328 Mike Timlin .30 .10
❑ 329 Brady Anderson .30 .10
❑ 330 Mike Bordick .30 .10
❑ 331 Harold Baines .30 .10
❑ 332 Nomar Garciaparra 1.25 .50
❑ 333 Bret Saberhagen .30 .10
❑ 334 Ramon Martinez .30 .10
❑ 335 Donnie Sadler .30 .10
❑ 336 Wilton Veras .30 .10
❑ 337 Mike Stanley .30 .10
❑ 338 Brian Rose .30 .10
❑ 339 Carl Everett .30 .10
❑ 340 Tim Wakefield .30 .10
❑ 341 Mark Grace .50 .20
❑ 342 Kerry Wood .30 .10
❑ 343 Eric Young .30 .10
❑ 344 Jose Nieves .30 .10
❑ 345 Ismael Valdes .30 .10
❑ 346 Joe Girardi .30 .10
❑ 347 Damon Buford .30 .10
❑ 348 Ricky Gutierrez .30 .10
❑ 349 Frank Thomas .75 .30
❑ 350 Brian Simmons .30 .10
❑ 351 James Baldwin .30 .10
❑ 352 Brook Fordyce .30 .10
❑ 353 Jose Valentin .30 .10
❑ 354 Mike Sirotka .30 .10
❑ 355 Greg Norton .30 .10
❑ 356 Dante Bichette .30 .10
❑ 357 Deion Sanders .50 .20
❑ 358 Ken Griffey Jr. 1.25 .50
❑ 359 Denny Neagle .30 .10
❑ 360 Dmitri Young .30 .10
❑ 361 Pete Harnisch .30 .10
❑ 362 Michael Tucker .30 .10
❑ 363 Roberto Alomar .50 .20
❑ 364 Dave Roberts .30 .10
❑ 365 Jim Thome .50 .20
❑ 366 Bartolo Colon .30 .10
❑ 367 Travis Fryman .30 .10
❑ 368 Chuck Finley .30 .10
❑ 369 Russell Branyan .30 .10
❑ 370 Alex Ramirez .30 .10
❑ 371 Jeff Cirillo .30 .10
❑ 372 Jeffrey Hammonds .30 .10
❑ 373 Scott Karl .30 .10
❑ 374 Brent Mayne .30 .10
❑ 375 Tom Goodwin .30 .10
❑ 376 Jose Jimenez .30 .10
❑ 377 Rolando Arrojo .30 .10
❑ 378 Terry Shumpert .30 .10
❑ 379 Juan Gonzalez .30 .10
❑ 380 Bobby Higginson .30 .10
❑ 381 Tony Clark .30 .10
❑ 382 Dave Mlicki .30 .10
❑ 383 Deivi Cruz .30 .10
❑ 384 Brian Moehler .30 .10
❑ 385 Dean Palmer .30 .10
❑ 386 Luis Castillo .30 .10
❑ 387 Mike Redmond .30 .10
❑ 388 Alex Fernandez .30 .10
❑ 389 Brant Brown .30 .10
❑ 390 Dave Berg .30 .10
❑ 391 A.J. Burnett .30 .10
❑ 392 Mark Kotsay .30 .10
❑ 393 Craig Biggio .50 .20
❑ 394 Daryle Ward .30 .10
❑ 395 Lance Berkman .30 .10
❑ 396 Roger Cedeno .30 .10
❑ 397 Scott Elarton .30 .10
❑ 398 Octavio Dotel .30 .10
❑ 399 Ken Caminiti .30 .10
❑ 400 Johnny Damon .50 .20
❑ 401 Mike Sweeney .30 .10
❑ 402 Jeff Suppan .30 .10
❑ 403 Rey Sanchez .30 .10
❑ 404 Blake Stein .30 .10
❑ 405 Ricky Bottalico .30 .10
❑ 406 Jay Witasick .30 .10
❑ 407 Shawn Green .30 .10
❑ 408 Orel Hershiser .30 .10
❑ 409 Gary Sheffield .30 .10
❑ 410 Todd Hollandsworth .30 .10
❑ 411 Terry Adams .30 .10
❑ 412 Todd Hundley .30 .10
❑ 413 Eric Karros .30 .10
❑ 414 F.P. Santangelo .30 .10
❑ 415 Alex Cora .30 .10
❑ 416 Marquis Grissom .30 .10
❑ 417 Henry Blanco .30 .10
❑ 418 Jose Hernandez .30 .10
❑ 419 Kyle Peterson .30 .10
❑ 420 John Snyder RC .30 .10
❑ 421 Bob Wickman .30 .10
❑ 422 Jamey Wright .30 .10
❑ 423 Chad Allen .30 .10
❑ 424 Todd Walker .30 .10
❑ 425 J.C. Romero RC .30 .10
❑ 426 Butch Huskey .30 .10
❑ 427 Jacque Jones .30 .10
❑ 428 Matt Lawton .30 .10
❑ 429 Rondell White .30 .10
❑ 430 Jose Vidro .30 .10
❑ 431 Hideki Irabu .30 .10
❑ 432 Javier Vazquez .30 .10
❑ 433 Lee Stevens .30 .10
❑ 434 Mike Thurman .30 .10
❑ 435 Geoff Blum .30 .10
❑ 436 Mike Hampton .30 .10
❑ 437 Mike Piazza 1.25 .50
❑ 438 Al Leiter .30 .10
❑ 439 Derek Bell .30 .10
❑ 440 Armando Benitez .30 .10
❑ 441 Rey Ordonez .30 .10
❑ 442 Todd Zeile .30 .10
❑ 443 Roger Clemens 1.50 .60
❑ 444 Ramiro Mendoza .30 .10
❑ 445 Andy Pettitte .50 .20
❑ 446 Scott Brosius .30 .10
❑ 447 Mariano Rivera .75 .30
❑ 448 Jim Leyritz .30 .10
❑ 449 Jorge Posada .50 .20
❑ 450 Omar Olivares .30 .10
❑ 451 Ben Grieve .30 .10
❑ 452 A.J. Hinch .30 .10
❑ 453 Gil Heredia .30 .10
❑ 454 Kevin Appier .30 .10
❑ 455 Ryan Christenson .30 .10
❑ 456 Ramon Hernandez .30 .10
❑ 457 Scott Rolen .50 .20
❑ 458 Alex Arias .30 .10
❑ 459 Andy Ashby .30 .10
❑ 460 Kevin Jordan UER 474 .30 .10
❑ 461 Robert Person .30 .10
❑ 462 Paul Byrd .30 .10
❑ 463 Curt Schilling .30 .10
❑ 464 Mike Jackson .30 .10
❑ 465 Jason Kendall .30 .10
❑ 466 Pat Meares .30 .10
❑ 467 Bruce Aven .30 .10
❑ 468 Todd Ritchie .30 .10
❑ 469 Wil Cordero .30 .10
❑ 470 Aramis Ramirez .30 .10
❑ 471 Andy Benes .30 .10
❑ 472 Ray Lankford .30 .10
❑ 473 Fernando Vina .30 .10
❑ 474 Jim Edmonds .30 .10
❑ 475 Craig Paquette .30 .10
❑ 476 Pat Hentgen .30 .10
❑ 477 Darryl Kile .30 .10
❑ 478 Sterling Hitchcock .30 .10
❑ 479 Ruben Rivera .30 .10
❑ 480 Ryan Klesko .30 .10
❑ 481 Phil Nevin .30 .10
❑ 482 Woody Williams .30 .10
❑ 483 Carlos Hernandez .30 .10
❑ 484 Brian Meadows .30 .10
❑ 485 Bret Boone .30 .10
❑ 486 Barry Bonds 2.00 .75
❑ 487 Russ Ortiz .30 .10
❑ 488 Bobby Estalella .30 .10
❑ 489 Rich Aurilia .30 .10
❑ 490 Bill Mueller .30 .10
❑ 491 Joe Nathan .30 .10
❑ 492 Russ Davis .30 .10
❑ 493 John Olerud .30 .10
❑ 494 Alex Rodriguez 1.25 .50
❑ 495 Freddy Garcia .30 .10
❑ 496 Carlos Guillen .30 .10
❑ 497 Aaron Sele .30 .10
❑ 498 Brett Tomko .30 .10
❑ 499 Jamie Moyer .30 .10
❑ 500 Mike Cameron .30 .10
❑ 501 Vinny Castilla .30 .10
❑ 502 Gerald Williams .30 .10
❑ 503 Mike DiFelice .30 .10
❑ 504 Ryan Rupe .30 .10
❑ 505 Greg Vaughn .30 .10
❑ 506 Miguel Cairo .30 .10
❑ 507 Juan Guzman .30 .10
❑ 508 Jose Guillen .30 .10
❑ 509 Gabe Kapler .30 .10
❑ 510 Rick Helling .30 .10
❑ 511 David Segui .30 .10
❑ 512 Doug Davis .30 .10
❑ 513 Justin Thompson .30 .10
❑ 514 Chad Curtis .30 .10
❑ 515 Tony Batista .30 .10
❑ 516 Billy Koch .30 .10
❑ 517 Raul Mondesi .30 .10
❑ 518 Joey Hamilton .30 .10
❑ 519 Darrin Fletcher .30 .10
❑ 520 Brad Fullmer .30 .10
❑ 521 Jose Cruz Jr. .30 .10
❑ 522 Kevin Witt .30 .10
❑ 523 Mark McGwire AUT 1.00 .40
❑ 524 Roberto Alomar AUT .30 .10
❑ 525 Chipper Jones AUT .50 .20
❑ 526 Derek Jeter AUT 1.00 .40
❑ 527 Ken Griffey Jr. AUT .75 .30
❑ 528 Sammy Sosa AUT .50 .20
❑ 529 Manny Ramirez AUT .50 .20
❑ 530 Ivan Rodriguez AUT .30 .10
❑ 531 Pedro Martinez AUT .50 .20
❑ 532 Mariano Rivera CL .50 .20
❑ 533 Sammy Sosa CL .50 .20
❑ 534 Cal Ripken CL 1.25 .50
❑ 535 Vladimir Guerrero CL .50 .20
❑ 536 Tony Gwynn CL .50 .20
❑ 537 Mark McGwire CL 1.00 .40
❑ 538 Bernie Williams CL .30 .10
❑ 539 Pedro Martinez CL .50 .20
❑ 540 Ken Griffey Jr. CL .75 .30

2001 Upper Deck

❑ COMPLETE SET (450) 150.00 90.00
❑ COMPLETE SERIES 1 (270) 40.00 20.00
❑ COMPLETE SERIES 2 (180) 100.00 60.00
❑ COMMON (46-270/300-450) .30 .10
❑ COMMON SR (1-45/271-300) .50 .20
❑ 1 Jeff DaVanon SR .50 .20
❑ 2 Aubrey Huff SR .50 .20
❑ 3 Pasqual Coco SR .50 .20
❑ 4 Barry Zito SR .60 .25

❑ 5 Augie Ojeda SR .50 .20
❑ 6 Chris Richard SR .50 .20
❑ 7 Josh Phelps SR .50 .20
❑ 8 Kevin Nicholson SR .50 .20
❑ 9 Juan Guzman SR .50 .20
❑ 10 Brandon Kolb SR .50 .20
❑ 11 Johan Santana SR 5.00 2.00
❑ 12 Josh Kalinowski SR .50 .20
❑ 13 Tike Redman SR .50 .20
❑ 14 Ivanon Coffie SR .50 .20
❑ 15 Chad Durbin SR .50 .20
❑ 16 Derrick Turnbow SR .50 .20
❑ 17 Scott Downs SR .50 .20
❑ 18 Jason Grilli SR .50 .20
❑ 19 Mark Buehrle SR .60 .25
❑ 20 Paxton Crawford SR .50 .20
❑ 21 Bronson Arroyo SR 1.00 .40
❑ 22 Tomas De la Rosa SR .50 .20
❑ 23 Paul Rigdon SR .50 .20
❑ 24 Rob Ramsay SR .50 .20
❑ 25 Damian Rolls SR .50 .20
❑ 26 Jason Conti SR .50 .20
❑ 27 John Parrish SR .50 .20
❑ 28 Geraldo Guzman SR .50 .20
❑ 29 Tony Mota SR .50 .20
❑ 30 Luis Rivas SR .50 .20
❑ 31 Brian Tollberg SR .50 .20
❑ 32 Adam Bernero SR .50 .20
❑ 33 Michael Cuddyer SR .50 .20
❑ 34 Josue Espada SR .50 .20
❑ 35 Joe Lawrence SR .50 .20
❑ 36 Chad Moeller SR .50 .20
❑ 37 Nick Bierbrodt SR .50 .20
❑ 38 DeWayne Wise SR .50 .20
❑ 39 Javier Cardona SR .50 .20
❑ 40 Hiram Bocachica SR .50 .20
❑ 41 Giuseppe Chiaramonte SR .50 .20
❑ 42 Alex Cabrera SR .50 .20
❑ 43 Jimmy Rollins SR .50 .20
❑ 44 Pat Flury SR RC .50 .20
❑ 45 Leo Estrella SR .50 .20
❑ 46 Darin Erstad .30 .10
❑ 47 Seth Etherton .30 .10
❑ 48 Troy Glaus .30 .10
❑ 49 Brian Cooper .30 .10
❑ 50 Tim Salmon .50 .20
❑ 51 Adam Kennedy .30 .10
❑ 52 Bengie Molina .30 .10
❑ 53 Jason Giambi .30 .10
❑ 54 Miguel Tejada .30 .10
❑ 55 Tim Hudson .30 .10
❑ 56 Eric Chavez .30 .10
❑ 57 Terrence Long .30 .10
❑ 58 Jason Isringhausen .30 .10
❑ 59 Ramon Hernandez .30 .10
❑ 60 Raul Mondesi .30 .10
❑ 61 David Wells .30 .10
❑ 62 Shannon Stewart .30 .10
❑ 63 Tony Batista .30 .10
❑ 64 Brad Fullmer .30 .10
❑ 65 Chris Carpenter .30 .10
❑ 66 Homer Bush .30 .10
❑ 67 Gerald Williams .30 .10
❑ 68 Miguel Cairo .30 .10
❑ 69 Ryan Rupe .30 .10
❑ 70 Greg Vaughn .30 .10
❑ 71 John Flaherty .30 .10
❑ 72 Dan Wheeler .30 .10
❑ 73 Fred McGriff .50 .20
❑ 74 Roberto Alomar .50 .20
❑ 75 Bartolo Colon .30 .10
❑ 76 Kenny Lofton .30 .10
❑ 77 David Segui .30 .10
❑ 78 Omar Vizquel .50 .20
❑ 79 Russ Branyan .30 .10
❑ 80 Chuck Finley .30 .10
❑ 81 Manny Ramirez UER .50 .20
❑ 82 Alex Rodriguez 1.25 .50
❑ 83 John Halama .30 .10
❑ 84 Mike Cameron .30 .10
❑ 85 David Bell .30 .10
❑ 86 Jay Buhner .30 .10
❑ 87 Aaron Sele .30 .10
❑ 88 Rickey Henderson .75 .30
❑ 89 Brook Fordyce .30 .10
❑ 90 Cal Ripken 2.50 1.00
❑ 91 Mike Mussina .50 .20
❑ 92 Delino DeShields .30 .10
❑ 93 Melvin Mora .30 .10
❑ 94 Sidney Ponson .30 .10
❑ 95 Brady Anderson .30 .10
❑ 96 Ivan Rodriguez .50 .20
❑ 97 Ricky Ledee .30 .10
❑ 98 Rick Helling .30 .10
❑ 99 Ruben Mateo .30 .10
❑ 100 Luis Alicea .30 .10
❑ 101 John Wetteland .30 .10
❑ 102 Mike Lamb .30 .10
❑ 103 Carl Everett .30 .10
❑ 104 Troy O'Leary .30 .10
❑ 105 Wilton Veras .30 .10
❑ 106 Pedro Martinez .50 .20
❑ 107 Rolando Arrojo .30 .10
❑ 108 Scott Hatteberg .30 .10
❑ 109 Jason Varitek .75 .30
❑ 110 Jose Offerman .30 .10
❑ 111 Carlos Beltran .30 .10
❑ 112 Johnny Damon .50 .20
❑ 113 Mark Quinn .30 .10
❑ 114 Rey Sanchez .30 .10
❑ 115 Mac Suzuki .30 .10
❑ 116 Jermaine Dye .30 .10
❑ 117 Chris Fussell .30 .10
❑ 118 Jeff Weaver .30 .10
❑ 119 Dean Palmer .30 .10
❑ 120 Robert Fick .30 .10
❑ 121 Brian Moehler .30 .10
❑ 122 Damion Easley .30 .10
❑ 123 Juan Encarnacion .30 .10
❑ 124 Tony Clark .30 .10
❑ 125 Cristian Guzman .30 .10
❑ 126 Matt LeCroy .30 .10
❑ 127 Eric Milton .30 .10
❑ 128 Jay Canizaro .30 .10
❑ 129 David Ortiz .75 .30
❑ 130 Brad Radke .30 .10
❑ 131 Jacque Jones .30 .10
❑ 132 Magglio Ordonez .30 .10
❑ 133 Carlos Lee .30 .10
❑ 134 Mike Sirotka .30 .10
❑ 135 Ray Durham .30 .10
❑ 136 Paul Konerko .30 .10
❑ 137 Charles Johnson .30 .10
❑ 138 James Baldwin .30 .10
❑ 139 Jeff Abbott .30 .10
❑ 140 Roger Clemens 1.50 .60
❑ 141 Derek Jeter 2.00 .75
❑ 142 David Justice .30 .10
❑ 143 Ramiro Mendoza .30 .10
❑ 144 Chuck Knoblauch .30 .10
❑ 145 Orlando Hernandez .30 .10
❑ 146 Alfonso Soriano .50 .20
❑ 147 Jeff Bagwell .50 .20
❑ 148 Julio Lugo .30 .10
❑ 149 Mitch Meluskey .30 .10
❑ 150 Jose Lima .30 .10
❑ 151 Richard Hidalgo .30 .10
❑ 152 Moises Alou .30 .10
❑ 153 Scott Elarton .30 .10
❑ 154 Andruw Jones .50 .20
❑ 155 Quilvio Veras .30 .10
❑ 156 Greg Maddux 1.25 .50
❑ 157 Brian Jordan .30 .10
❑ 158 Andres Galarraga .30 .10
❑ 159 Kevin Millwood .30 .10
❑ 160 Rafael Furcal .30 .10
❑ 161 Jeromy Burnitz .30 .10
❑ 162 Jimmy Haynes .30 .10
❑ 163 Mark Loretta .30 .10
❑ 164 Ron Belliard .30 .10
❑ 165 Richie Sexson .30 .10
❑ 166 Kevin Barker .30 .10
❑ 167 Jeff D'Amico .30 .10
❑ 168 Rick Ankiel .30 .10
❑ 169 Mark McGwire 2.00 .75
❑ 170 J.D. Drew .30 .10
❑ 171 Eli Marrero .30 .10
❑ 172 Darryl Kile .30 .10
❑ 173 Edgar Renteria .30 .10
❑ 174 Will Clark .50 .20
❑ 175 Eric Young .30 .10
❑ 176 Mark Grace .50 .20
❑ 177 Jon Lieber .30 .10
❑ 178 Damon Buford .30 .10
❑ 179 Kerry Wood .30 .10
❑ 180 Rondell White .30 .10
❑ 181 Joe Girardi .30 .10
❑ 182 Curt Schilling .30 .10
❑ 183 Randy Johnson .75 .30
❑ 184 Steve Finley .30 .10
❑ 185 Kelly Stinnett .30 .10
❑ 186 Jay Bell .30 .10
❑ 187 Matt Mantei .30 .10
❑ 188 Luis Gonzalez .30 .10
❑ 189 Shawn Green .30 .10
❑ 190 Todd Hundley .30 .10
❑ 191 Chan Ho Park .30 .10
❑ 192 Adrian Beltre .30 .10
❑ 193 Mark Grudzielanek .30 .10
❑ 194 Gary Sheffield .30 .10
❑ 195 Tom Goodwin .30 .10
❑ 196 Lee Stevens .30 .10
❑ 197 Javier Vazquez .30 .10
❑ 198 Milton Bradley .30 .10
❑ 199 Vladimir Guerrero .75 .30
❑ 200 Carl Pavano .30 .10
❑ 201 Orlando Cabrera .30 .10
❑ 202 Tony Armas Jr. .30 .10
❑ 203 Jeff Kent .30 .10
❑ 204 Calvin Murray .30 .10
❑ 205 Ellis Burks .30 .10
❑ 206 Barry Bonds 2.00 .75
❑ 207 Russ Ortiz .30 .10
❑ 208 Marvin Benard .30 .10
❑ 209 Joe Nathan .30 .10
❑ 210 Preston Wilson .30 .10
❑ 211 Cliff Floyd .30 .10
❑ 212 Mike Lowell .30 .10
❑ 213 Ryan Dempster .30 .10
❑ 214 Brad Penny .30 .10
❑ 215 Mike Redmond .30 .10
❑ 216 Luis Castillo .30 .10
❑ 217 Derek Bell .30 .10
❑ 218 Mike Hampton .30 .10
❑ 219 Todd Zeile .30 .10
❑ 220 Robin Ventura .30 .10
❑ 221 Mike Piazza 1.25 .50
❑ 222 Al Leiter .30 .10
❑ 223 Edgardo Alfonzo .30 .10
❑ 224 Mike Bordick .30 .10
❑ 225 Phil Nevin .30 .10
❑ 226 Ryan Klesko .30 .10
❑ 227 Adam Eaton .30 .10
❑ 228 Eric Owens .30 .10
❑ 229 Tony Gwynn 1.00 .40
❑ 230 Matt Clement .30 .10
❑ 231 Wiki Gonzalez .30 .10
❑ 232 Robert Person .30 .10
❑ 233 Doug Glanville .30 .10
❑ 234 Scott Rolen .50 .20
❑ 235 Mike Lieberthal .30 .10
❑ 236 Randy Wolf .30 .10
❑ 237 Bob Abreu .30 .10
❑ 238 Pat Burrell .30 .10
❑ 239 Bruce Chen .30 .10
❑ 240 Kevin Young .30 .10
❑ 241 Todd Ritchie .30 .10
❑ 242 Adrian Brown .30 .10
❑ 243 Chad Hermansen .30 .10
❑ 244 Warren Morris .30 .10
❑ 245 Kris Benson .30 .10
❑ 246 Jason Kendall .30 .10
❑ 247 Pokey Reese .30 .10
❑ 248 Rob Bell .30 .10
❑ 249 Ken Griffey Jr. 1.25 .50
❑ 250 Sean Casey .30 .10
❑ 251 Aaron Boone .30 .10
❑ 252 Pete Harnisch .30 .10
❑ 253 Barry Larkin .50 .20
❑ 254 Dmitri Young .30 .10
❑ 255 Todd Hollandsworth .30 .10
❑ 256 Pedro Astacio .30 .10
❑ 257 Todd Helton .50 .20
❑ 258 Terry Shumpert .30 .10
❑ 259 Neifi Perez .30 .10
❑ 260 Jeffrey Hammonds .30 .10
❑ 261 Ben Petrick .30 .10
❑ 262 Mark McGwire SH 1.00 .40

❑ 263	Derek Jeter SH	1.00	.40
❑ 264	Sammy Sosa SH	.50	.20
❑ 265	Cal Ripken SH	1.25	.50
❑ 266	Pedro Martinez SH	.50	.20
❑ 267	Barry Bonds SH	1.00	.40
❑ 268	Fred McGriff SH	.30	.10
❑ 269	Randy Johnson SH	.50	.20
❑ 270	Darin Erstad SH	.30	.10
❑ 271	Ichiro Suzuki SR RC	15.00	6.00
❑ 272	Wilson Betemit SR RC	2.00	.75
❑ 273	Corey Patterson SR	.50	.20
❑ 274	Sean Douglass SR RC	.50	.20
❑ 275	Mike Penney SR RC	.50	.20
❑ 276	Nate Teut SR RC	.50	.20
❑ 277	Ricardo Rodriguez SR RC	.50	.20
❑ 278	Brandon Duckworth SR RC	.50	.20
❑ 279	Rafael Soriano SR RC	.50	.20
❑ 280	Juan Diaz SR RC	.50	.20
❑ 281	Horacio Ramirez SR RC	.60	.25
❑ 282	Tsuyoshi Shinjo SR RC	.60	.25
❑ 283	Keith Ginter SR	.50	.20
❑ 284	Esix Snead SR RC	.50	.20
❑ 285	Erick Almonte SR RC	.50	.20
❑ 286	Travis Hafner SR RC	5.00	2.00
❑ 287	Jason Smith SR RC	.50	.20
❑ 288	Jackson Melian SR RC	.50	.20
❑ 289	Tyler Walker SR RC	.50	.20
❑ 290	Jason Standridge SR	.50	.20
❑ 291	Juan Uribe SR RC	.60	.25
❑ 292	Adrian Hernandez SR RC	.50	.20
❑ 293	Jason Michaels SR RC	.50	.20
❑ 294	Jason Hart SR	.50	.20
❑ 295	Albert Pujols SR RC	80.00	40.00
❑ 296	Morgan Ensberg SR RC	2.00	.75
❑ 297	Brandon Inge SR	.50	.20
❑ 298	Jesus Colome SR	.50	.20
❑ 299	Kyle Kessel SR RC	.50	.20
❑ 300	Timo Perez SR	.50	.20
❑ 301	Mo Vaughn	.30	.10
❑ 302	Ismael Valdes	.30	.10
❑ 303	Glenallen Hill	.30	.10
❑ 304	Garret Anderson	.30	.10
❑ 305	Johnny Damon	.50	.20
❑ 306	Jose Ortiz	.30	.10
❑ 307	Mark Mulder	.30	.10
❑ 308	Adam Piatt	.30	.10
❑ 309	Gil Heredia	.30	.10
❑ 310	Mike Sirotka	.30	.10
❑ 311	Carlos Delgado	.30	.10
❑ 312	Alex Gonzalez	.30	.10
❑ 313	Jose Cruz Jr.	.30	.10
❑ 314	Darrin Fletcher	.30	.10
❑ 315	Ben Grieve	.30	.10
❑ 316	Vinny Castilla	.30	.10
❑ 317	Wilson Alvarez	.30	.10
❑ 318	Brent Abernathy	.30	.10
❑ 319	Ellis Burks	.30	.10
❑ 320	Jim Thome	.50	.20
❑ 321	Juan Gonzalez	.30	.10
❑ 322	Ed Taubensee	.30	.10
❑ 323	Travis Fryman	.30	.10
❑ 324	John Olerud	.30	.10
❑ 325	Edgar Martinez	.50	.20
❑ 326	Freddy Garcia	.30	.10
❑ 327	Bret Boone	.50	.20
❑ 328	Kazuhiro Sasaki	.30	.10
❑ 329	Albert Belle	.30	.10
❑ 330	Mike Bordick	.30	.10
❑ 331	David Segui	.30	.10
❑ 332	Pat Hentgen	.30	.10
❑ 333	Alex Rodriguez	1.25	.50
❑ 334	Andres Galarraga	.30	.10
❑ 335	Gabe Kapler	.30	.10
❑ 336	Ken Caminiti	.30	.10
❑ 337	Rafael Palmeiro	.50	.20
❑ 338	Manny Ramirez Sox	.50	.20
❑ 339	David Cone	.30	.10
❑ 340	Nomar Garciaparra	1.25	.50
❑ 341	Trot Nixon	.30	.10
❑ 342	Derek Lowe	.30	.10
❑ 343	Roberto Hernandez	.30	.10
❑ 344	Mike Sweeney	.30	.10
❑ 345	Carlos Febles	.30	.10
❑ 346	Jeff Suppan	.30	.10
❑ 347	Roger Cedeno	.30	.10
❑ 348	Bobby Higginson	.30	.10
❑ 349	Deivi Cruz	.30	.10
❑ 350	Mitch Meluskey	.30	.10
❑ 351	Matt Lawton	.30	.10
❑ 352	Mark Redman	.30	.10
❑ 353	Jay Canizaro	.30	.10
❑ 354	Corey Koskie	.30	.10
❑ 355	Matt Kinney	.30	.10
❑ 356	Frank Thomas	.75	.30
❑ 357	Sandy Alomar Jr.	.30	.10
❑ 358	David Wells	.30	.10
❑ 359	Jim Parque	.30	.10
❑ 360	Chris Singleton	.30	.10
❑ 361	Tino Martinez	.50	.20
❑ 362	Paul O'Neill	.50	.20
❑ 363	Mike Mussina	.50	.20
❑ 364	Bernie Williams	.50	.20
❑ 365	Andy Pettite	.50	.20
❑ 366	Mariano Rivera	.75	.30
❑ 367	Brad Ausmus	.30	.10
❑ 368	Craig Biggio	.50	.20
❑ 369	Lance Berkman	.30	.10
❑ 370	Shane Reynolds	.30	.10
❑ 371	Chipper Jones	.75	.30
❑ 372	Tom Glavine	.50	.20
❑ 373	B.J. Surhoff	.30	.10
❑ 374	John Smoltz	.50	.20
❑ 375	Rico Brogna	.30	.10
❑ 376	Geoff Jenkins	.30	.10
❑ 377	Jose Hernandez	.30	.10
❑ 378	Tyler Houston	.30	.10
❑ 379	Henry Blanco	.30	.10
❑ 380	Jeffrey Hammonds	.30	.10
❑ 381	Jim Edmonds	.30	.10
❑ 382	Fernando Vina	.30	.10
❑ 383	Andy Benes	.30	.10
❑ 384	Ray Lankford	.30	.10
❑ 385	Dustin Hermanson	.30	.10
❑ 386	Todd Hundley	.30	.10
❑ 387	Sammy Sosa	.75	.30
❑ 388	Tom Gordon	.30	.10
❑ 389	Bill Mueller	.30	.10
❑ 390	Ron Coomer	.30	.10
❑ 391	Matt Stairs	.30	.10
❑ 392	Mark Grace	.50	.20
❑ 393	Matt Williams	.30	.10
❑ 394	Todd Stottlemyre	.30	.10
❑ 395	Tony Womack	.30	.10
❑ 396	Erubiel Durazo	.30	.10
❑ 397	Reggie Sanders	.30	.10
❑ 398	Andy Ashby	.30	.10
❑ 399	Eric Karros	.30	.10
❑ 400	Kevin Brown	.30	.10
❑ 401	Darren Dreifort	.30	.10
❑ 402	Fernando Tatis	.30	.10
❑ 403	Jose Vidro	.30	.10
❑ 404	Peter Bergeron	.30	.10
❑ 405	Geoff Blum	.30	.10
❑ 406	J.T. Snow	.30	.10
❑ 407	Livan Hernandez	.30	.10
❑ 408	Robb Nen	.30	.10
❑ 409	Bobby Estalella	.30	.10
❑ 410	Rich Aurilia	.30	.10
❑ 411	Eric Davis	.30	.10
❑ 412	Charles Johnson	.30	.10
❑ 413	Alex Gonzalez	.30	.10
❑ 414	A.J. Burnett	.30	.10
❑ 415	Antonio Alfonseca	.30	.10
❑ 416	Derrek Lee	.50	.20
❑ 417	Jay Payton	.30	.10
❑ 418	Kevin Appier	.30	.10
❑ 419	Steve Trachsel	.30	.10
❑ 420	Rey Ordonez	.30	.10
❑ 421	Darryl Hamilton	.30	.10
❑ 422	Ben Davis	.30	.10
❑ 423	Damian Jackson	.30	.10
❑ 424	Mark Kotsay	.30	.10
❑ 425	Trevor Hoffman	.30	.10
❑ 426	Travis Lee	.30	.10
❑ 427	Omar Daal	.30	.10
❑ 428	Paul Byrd	.30	.10
❑ 429	Reggie Taylor	.30	.10
❑ 430	Brian Giles	.30	.10
❑ 431	Derek Bell	.30	.10
❑ 432	Francisco Cordova	.30	.10
❑ 433	Pat Meares	.30	.10
❑ 434	Scott Williamson	.30	.10
❑ 435	Jason LaRue	.30	.10
❑ 436	Michael Tucker	.30	.10
❑ 437	Wilton Guerrero	.30	.10
❑ 438	Mike Hampton	.30	.10
❑ 439	Ron Gant	.30	.10
❑ 440	Jeff Cirillo	.30	.10
❑ 441	Denny Neagle	.30	.10
❑ 442	Larry Walker	.30	.10
❑ 443	Juan Pierre	.30	.10
❑ 444	Todd Walker	.30	.10
❑ 445	Jason Giambi SH CL	.30	.10
❑ 446	Jeff Kent SH CL	.30	.10
❑ 447	Mariano Rivera SH CL	.50	.20
❑ 448	Edgar Martinez SH CL	.30	.10
❑ 449	Troy Glaus SH CL	.30	.10
❑ 450	Alex Rodriguez SH CL	.75	.30

2002 Upper Deck

❑ COMPLETE SET (745)	160.00	85.00
❑ COMPLETE SERIES 1 (500)	110.00	60.00
❑ COMPLETE SERIES 2 (245)	50.00	25.00
❑ COMMON (51-500/546-745)	.30	.10
❑ COMMON SR (1-50/501-545)	1.00	.40
❑ 1 Mark Prior SR	2.00	.75
❑ 2 Mark Teixeira SR	5.00	2.00
❑ 3 Brian Roberts SR	2.00	.75
❑ 4 Jason Romano SR	1.00	.40
❑ 5 Dennis Stark SR	1.00	.40
❑ 6 Oscar Salazar SR	1.00	.40
❑ 7 John Patterson SR	1.00	.40
❑ 8 Shane Loux SR	1.00	.40
❑ 9 Marcus Giles SR	1.00	.40
❑ 10 Juan Cruz SR	1.00	.40
❑ 11 Jorge Julio SR	1.00	.40
❑ 12 Adam Dunn SR	1.00	.40
❑ 13 Delvin James SR	1.00	.40
❑ 14 Jeremy Affeldt SR	1.00	.40
❑ 15 Tim Raines Jr. SR	1.00	.40
❑ 16 Luke Hudson SR	1.00	.40
❑ 17 Todd Sears SR	1.00	.40
❑ 18 George Perez SR	1.00	.40
❑ 19 Wilmy Caceres SR	1.00	.40
❑ 20 Abraham Nunez SR	1.00	.40
❑ 21 Mike Amrhein SR RC	1.00	.40
❑ 22 Carlos Hernandez SR	1.00	.40
❑ 23 Scott Hodges SR	1.00	.40
❑ 24 Brandon Knight SR	1.00	.40
❑ 25 Geoff Goetz SR	1.00	.40
❑ 26 Carlos Garcia SR	1.00	.40
❑ 27 Luis Pineda SR	1.00	.40
❑ 28 Chris Gissell SR	1.00	.40
❑ 29 Jae Weong Seo SR	1.00	.40
❑ 30 Paul Phillips SR	1.00	.40
❑ 31 Cory Aldridge SR	1.00	.40
❑ 32 Aaron Cook SR RC	1.00	.40
❑ 33 Rendy Espina SR RC	1.00	.40
❑ 34 Jason Phillips SR	1.00	.40
❑ 35 Carlos Silva SR	1.00	.40
❑ 36 Ryan Mills SR	1.00	.40
❑ 37 Pedro Santana SR	1.00	.40
❑ 38 John Grabow SR	1.00	.40
❑ 39 Cody Ransom SR	1.00	.40
❑ 40 Orlando Woodards SR	1.00	.40
❑ 41 Bud Smith SR	1.00	.40
❑ 42 Junior Guerrero SR	1.00	.40
❑ 43 David Brous SR	1.00	.40
❑ 44 Steve Green SR	1.00	.40
❑ 45 Brian Rogers SR	1.00	.40

❑	46	Juan Figueroa SR RC	1.00	.40
❑	47	Nick Punto SR	1.00	.40
❑	48	Junior Herndon SR	1.00	.40
❑	49	Justin Kaye SR	1.00	.40
❑	50	Jason Karnuth SR	1.00	.40
❑	51	Troy Glaus	.30	.10
❑	52	Bengie Molina	.30	.10
❑	53	Ramon Ortiz	.30	.10
❑	54	Adam Kennedy	.30	.10
❑	55	Jarrod Washburn	.30	.10
❑	56	Troy Percival	.30	.10
❑	57	David Eckstein	.30	.10
❑	58	Ben Weber	.30	.10
❑	59	Larry Barnes	.30	.10
❑	60	Ismael Valdes	.30	.10
❑	61	Benji Gil	.30	.10
❑	62	Scott Schoeneweis	.30	.10
❑	63	Pat Rapp	.30	.10
❑	64	Jason Giambi	.30	.10
❑	65	Mark Mulder	.30	.10
❑	66	Ron Gant	.30	.10
❑	67	Johnny Damon	.50	.20
❑	68	Adam Piatt	.30	.10
❑	69	Jermaine Dye	.30	.10
❑	70	Jason Hart	.30	.10
❑	71	Eric Chavez	.30	.10
❑	72	Jim Mecir	.30	.10
❑	73	Barry Zito	.30	.10
❑	74	Jason Isringhausen	.30	.10
❑	75	Jeremy Giambi	.30	.10
❑	76	Olmedo Saenz	.30	.10
❑	77	Terrence Long	.30	.10
❑	78	Ramon Hernandez	.30	.10
❑	79	Chris Carpenter	.30	.10
❑	80	Raul Mondesi	.30	.10
❑	81	Carlos Delgado	.30	.10
❑	82	Billy Koch	.30	.10
❑	83	Vernon Wells	.30	.10
❑	84	Darrin Fletcher	.30	.10
❑	85	Homer Bush	.30	.10
❑	86	Pasqual Coco	.30	.10
❑	87	Shannon Stewart	.30	.10
❑	88	Chris Woodward	.30	.10
❑	89	Joe Lawrence	.30	.10
❑	90	Esteban Loaiza	.30	.10
❑	91	Cesar Izturis	.30	.10
❑	92	Kelvim Escobar	.30	.10
❑	93	Greg Vaughn	.30	.10
❑	94	Brent Abernathy	.30	.10
❑	95	Tanyon Sturtze	.30	.10
❑	96	Steve Cox	.30	.10
❑	97	Aubrey Huff	.30	.10
❑	98	Jesus Colome	.30	.10
❑	99	Ben Grieve	.30	.10
❑	100	Esteban Yan	.30	.10
❑	101	Joe Kennedy	.30	.10
❑	102	Felix Martinez	.30	.10
❑	103	Nick Bierbrodt	.30	.10
❑	104	Damian Rolls	.30	.10
❑	105	Russ Johnson	.30	.10
❑	106	Toby Hall	.30	.10
❑	107	Roberto Alomar	.50	.20
❑	108	Bartolo Colon	.30	.10
❑	109	John Rocker	.30	.10
❑	110	Juan Gonzalez	.30	.10
❑	111	Einar Diaz	.30	.10
❑	112	Chuck Finley	.30	.10
❑	113	Kenny Lofton	.30	.10
❑	114	Danys Baez	.30	.10
❑	115	Travis Fryman	.30	.10
❑	116	C.C. Sabathia	.30	.10
❑	117	Paul Shuey	.30	.10
❑	118	Marty Cordova	.30	.10
❑	119	Ellis Burks	.30	.10
❑	120	Bob Wickman	.30	.10
❑	121	Edgar Martinez	.50	.20
❑	122	Freddy Garcia	.30	.10
❑	123	Ichiro Suzuki	1.50	.60
❑	124	John Olerud	.30	.10
❑	125	Gil Meche	.30	.10
❑	126	Dan Wilson	.30	.10
❑	127	Aaron Sele	.30	.10
❑	128	Kazuhiro Sasaki	.30	.10
❑	129	Mark McLemore	.30	.10
❑	130	Carlos Guillen	.30	.10
❑	131	Al Martin	.30	.10
❑	132	David Bell	.30	.10
❑	133	Jay Buhner	.30	.10
❑	134	Stan Javier	.30	.10
❑	135	Tony Batista	.30	.10
❑	136	Jason Johnson	.30	.10
❑	137	Brook Fordyce	.30	.10
❑	138	Mike Kinkade	.30	.10
❑	139	Willis Roberts	.30	.10
❑	140	David Segui	.30	.10
❑	141	Josh Towers	.30	.10
❑	142	Jeff Conine	.30	.10
❑	143	Chris Richard	.30	.10
❑	144	Pat Hentgen	.30	.10
❑	145	Melvin Mora	.30	.10
❑	146	Jerry Hairston Jr.	.30	.10
❑	147	Calvin Maduro	.30	.10
❑	148	Brady Anderson	.30	.10
❑	149	Alex Rodriguez	1.25	.50
❑	150	Kenny Rogers	.30	.10
❑	151	Chad Curtis	.30	.10
❑	152	Ricky Ledee	.30	.10
❑	153	Rafael Palmeiro	.50	.20
❑	154	Rob Bell	.30	.10
❑	155	Rick Helling	.30	.10
❑	156	Doug Davis	.30	.10
❑	157	Mike Lamb	.30	.10
❑	158	Gabe Kapler	.30	.10
❑	159	Jeff Zimmerman	.30	.10
❑	160	Bill Haselman	.30	.10
❑	161	Tim Crabtree	.30	.10
❑	162	Carlos Pena	.30	.10
❑	163	Nomar Garciaparra	1.25	.50
❑	164	Shea Hillenbrand	.30	.10
❑	165	Hideo Nomo	.75	.30
❑	166	Manny Ramirez	.50	.20
❑	167	Jose Offerman	.30	.10
❑	168	Scott Hatteberg	.30	.10
❑	169	Trot Nixon	.30	.10
❑	170	Darren Lewis	.30	.10
❑	171	Derek Lowe	.30	.10
❑	172	Troy O'Leary	.30	.10
❑	173	Tim Wakefield	.30	.10
❑	174	Chris Stynes	.30	.10
❑	175	John Valentin	.30	.10
❑	176	David Cone	.30	.10
❑	177	Neifi Perez	.30	.10
❑	178	Brent Mayne	.30	.10
❑	179	Dan Reichert	.30	.10
❑	180	A.J. Hinch	.30	.10
❑	181	Chris George	.30	.10
❑	182	Mike Sweeney	.30	.10
❑	183	Jeff Suppan	.30	.10
❑	184	Roberto Hernandez	.30	.10
❑	185	Joe Randa	.30	.10
❑	186	Paul Byrd	.30	.10
❑	187	Luis Ordaz	.30	.10
❑	188	Kris Wilson	.30	.10
❑	189	Dee Brown	.30	.10
❑	190	Tony Clark	.30	.10
❑	191	Matt Anderson	.30	.10
❑	192	Robert Fick	.30	.10
❑	193	Juan Encarnacion	.30	.10
❑	194	Dean Palmer	.30	.10
❑	195	Victor Santos	.30	.10
❑	196	Damion Easley	.30	.10
❑	197	Jose Lima	.30	.10
❑	198	Deivi Cruz	.30	.10
❑	199	Roger Cedeno	.30	.10
❑	200	Jose Macias	.30	.10
❑	201	Jeff Weaver	.30	.10
❑	202	Brandon Inge	.30	.10
❑	203	Brian Moehler	.30	.10
❑	204	Brad Radke	.30	.10
❑	205	Doug Mientkiewicz	.30	.10
❑	206	Cristian Guzman	.30	.10
❑	207	Corey Koskie	.30	.10
❑	208	LaTroy Hawkins	.30	.10
❑	209	J.C. Romero	.30	.10
❑	210	Chad Allen	.30	.10
❑	211	Torii Hunter	.30	.10
❑	212	Travis Miller	.30	.10
❑	213	Joe Mays	.30	.10
❑	214	Todd Jones	.30	.10
❑	215	David Ortiz	.75	.30
❑	216	Brian Buchanan	.30	.10
❑	217	A.J. Pierzynski	.30	.10
❑	218	Carlos Lee	.30	.10
❑	219	Gary Glover	.30	.10
❑	220	Jose Valentin	.30	.10
❑	221	Aaron Rowand	.30	.10
❑	222	Sandy Alomar Jr.	.30	.10
❑	223	Herbert Perry	.30	.10
❑	224	Jon Garland	.30	.10
❑	225	Mark Buehrle	.30	.10
❑	226	Chris Singleton	.30	.10
❑	227	Kip Wells	.30	.10
❑	228	Ray Durham	.30	.10
❑	229	Joe Crede	.30	.10
❑	230	Keith Foulke	.30	.10
❑	231	Royce Clayton	.30	.10
❑	232	Andy Pettitte	.50	.20
❑	233	Derek Jeter	2.00	.75
❑	234	Jorge Posada	.50	.20
❑	235	Roger Clemens	1.50	.60
❑	236	Paul O'Neill	.50	.20
❑	237	Nick Johnson	.30	.10
❑	238	Gerald Williams	.30	.10
❑	239	Mariano Rivera	.75	.30
❑	240	Alfonso Soriano	.30	.10
❑	241	Ramiro Mendoza	.30	.10
❑	242	Mike Mussina	.50	.20
❑	243	Luis Sojo	.30	.10
❑	244	Scott Brosius	.30	.10
❑	245	David Justice	.30	.10
❑	246	Wade Miller	.30	.10
❑	247	Brad Ausmus	.30	.10
❑	248	Jeff Bagwell	.50	.20
❑	249	Daryle Ward	.30	.10
❑	250	Shane Reynolds	.30	.10
❑	251	Chris Truby	.30	.10
❑	252	Billy Wagner	.30	.10
❑	253	Craig Biggio	.50	.20
❑	254	Moises Alou	.30	.10
❑	255	Vinny Castilla	.30	.10
❑	256	Tim Redding	.30	.10
❑	257	Roy Oswalt	.30	.10
❑	258	Julio Lugo	.30	.10
❑	259	Chipper Jones	.75	.30
❑	260	Greg Maddux	1.25	.50
❑	261	Ken Caminiti	.30	.10
❑	262	Kevin Millwood	.30	.10
❑	263	Keith Lockhart	.30	.10
❑	264	Rey Sanchez	.30	.10
❑	265	Jason Marquis	.30	.10
❑	266	Brian Jordan	.30	.10
❑	267	Steve Karsay	.30	.10
❑	268	Wes Helms	.30	.10
❑	269	B.J. Surhoff	.30	.10
❑	270	Wilson Betemit	.30	.10
❑	271	John Smoltz	.50	.20
❑	272	Rafael Furcal	.30	.10
❑	273	Jeromy Burnitz	.30	.10
❑	274	Jimmy Haynes	.30	.10
❑	275	Mark Loretta	.30	.10
❑	276	Jose Hernandez	.30	.10
❑	277	Paul Rigdon	.30	.10
❑	278	Alex Sanchez	.30	.10
❑	279	Chad Fox	.30	.10
❑	280	Devon White	.30	.10
❑	281	Tyler Houston	.30	.10
❑	282	Ronnie Belliard	.30	.10
❑	283	Luis Lopez	.30	.10
❑	284	Ben Sheets	.30	.10
❑	285	Curtis Leskanic	.30	.10
❑	286	Henry Blanco	.30	.10
❑	287	Mark McGwire	2.00	.75
❑	288	Edgar Renteria	.30	.10
❑	289	Matt Morris	.30	.10
❑	290	Gene Stechschulte	.30	.10
❑	291	Dustin Hermanson	.30	.10
❑	292	Eli Marrero	.30	.10
❑	293	Albert Pujols	1.50	.60
❑	294	Luis Saturria	.30	.10
❑	295	Bobby Bonilla	.30	.10
❑	296	Garrett Stephenson	.30	.10
❑	297	Jim Edmonds	.30	.10
❑	298	Rick Ankiel	.30	.10
❑	299	Placido Polanco	.30	.10
❑	300	Dave Veres	.30	.10
❑	301	Sammy Sosa	.75	.30
❑	302	Eric Young	.30	.10
❑	303	Kerry Wood	.30	.10

❑ 304 Jon Lieber .30 .10
❑ 305 Joe Girardi .30 .10
❑ 306 Fred McGriff .50 .20
❑ 307 Jeff Fassero .30 .10
❑ 308 Julio Zuleta .30 .10
❑ 309 Kevin Tapani .30 .10
❑ 310 Rondell White .30 .10
❑ 311 Julian Tavarez .30 .10
❑ 312 Tom Gordon .30 .10
❑ 313 Corey Patterson .30 .10
❑ 314 Bill Mueller .30 .10
❑ 315 Randy Johnson .75 .30
❑ 316 Chad Moeller .30 .10
❑ 317 Tony Womack .30 .10
❑ 318 Erubiel Durazo .30 .10
❑ 319 Luis Gonzalez .30 .10
❑ 320 Brian Anderson .30 .10
❑ 321 Reggie Sanders .30 .10
❑ 322 Greg Colbrunn .30 .10
❑ 323 Robert Ellis .30 .10
❑ 324 Jack Cust .30 .10
❑ 325 Bret Prinz .30 .10
❑ 326 Steve Finley .30 .10
❑ 327 Byung-Hyun Kim .30 .10
❑ 328 Albie Lopez .30 .10
❑ 329 Gary Sheffield .30 .10
❑ 330 Mark Grudzielanek .30 .10
❑ 331 Paul LoDuca .30 .10
❑ 332 Tom Goodwin .30 .10
❑ 333 Andy Ashby .30 .10
❑ 334 Hiram Bocachica .30 .10
❑ 335 Dave Hansen .30 .10
❑ 336 Kevin Brown .30 .10
❑ 337 Marquis Grissom .30 .10
❑ 338 Terry Adams .30 .10
❑ 339 Chan Ho Park .30 .10
❑ 340 Adrian Beltre .30 .10
❑ 341 Luke Prokopec .30 .10
❑ 342 Jeff Shaw .30 .10
❑ 343 Vladimir Guerrero .75 .30
❑ 344 Orlando Cabrera .30 .10
❑ 345 Tony Armas Jr. .30 .10
❑ 346 Michael Barrett .30 .10
❑ 347 Geoff Blum .30 .10
❑ 348 Ryan Minor .30 .10
❑ 349 Peter Bergeron .30 .10
❑ 350 Graeme Lloyd .30 .10
❑ 351 Jose Vidro .30 .10
❑ 352 Javier Vazquez .30 .10
❑ 353 Matt Blank .30 .10
❑ 354 Masato Yoshii .30 .10
❑ 355 Carl Pavano .30 .10
❑ 356 Barry Bonds 2.00 .75
❑ 357 Shawon Dunston .30 .10
❑ 358 Livan Hernandez .30 .10
❑ 359 Felix Rodriguez .30 .10
❑ 360 Pedro Feliz .30 .10
❑ 361 Calvin Murray .30 .10
❑ 362 Robb Nen .30 .10
❑ 363 Marvin Benard .30 .10
❑ 364 Russ Ortiz .30 .10
❑ 365 Jason Schmidt .30 .10
❑ 366 Rich Aurilia .30 .10
❑ 367 John Vander Wal .30 .10
❑ 368 Benito Santiago .30 .10
❑ 369 Ryan Dempster .30 .10
❑ 370 Charles Johnson .30 .10
❑ 371 Alex Gonzalez .30 .10
❑ 372 Luis Castillo .30 .10
❑ 373 Mike Lowell .30 .10
❑ 374 Antonio Alfonseca .30 .10
❑ 375 A.J. Burnett .30 .10
❑ 376 Brad Penny .30 .10
❑ 377 Jason Grilli .30 .10
❑ 378 Derrek Lee .50 .20
❑ 379 Matt Clement .30 .10
❑ 380 Eric Owens .30 .10
❑ 381 Vladimir Nunez .30 .10
❑ 382 Cliff Floyd .30 .10
❑ 383 Mike Piazza 1.25 .50
❑ 384 Lenny Harris .30 .10
❑ 385 Glendon Rusch .30 .10
❑ 386 Todd Zeile .30 .10
❑ 387 Al Leiter .30 .10
❑ 388 Armando Benitez .30 .10
❑ 389 Alex Escobar .30 .10
❑ 390 Kevin Appier .30 .10
❑ 391 Matt Lawton .30 .10
❑ 392 Bruce Chen .30 .10
❑ 393 John Franco .30 .10
❑ 394 Tsuyoshi Shinjo .30 .10
❑ 395 Rey Ordonez .30 .10
❑ 396 Joe McEwing .30 .10
❑ 397 Ryan Klesko .30 .10
❑ 398 Brian Lawrence .30 .10
❑ 399 Kevin Walker .30 .10
❑ 400 Phil Nevin .30 .10
❑ 401 Bubba Trammell .30 .10
❑ 402 Wiki Gonzalez .30 .10
❑ 403 D'Angelo Jimenez .30 .10
❑ 404 Rickey Henderson .75 .30
❑ 405 Mike Darr .30 .10
❑ 406 Trevor Hoffman .30 .10
❑ 407 Damian Jackson .30 .10
❑ 408 Santiago Perez .30 .10
❑ 409 Cesar Crespo .30 .10
❑ 410 Robert Person .30 .10
❑ 411 Travis Lee .30 .10
❑ 412 Scott Rolen .50 .20
❑ 413 Turk Wendell .30 .10
❑ 414 Randy Wolf .30 .10
❑ 415 Kevin Jordan .30 .10
❑ 416 Jose Mesa .30 .10
❑ 417 Mike Lieberthal .30 .10
❑ 418 Bobby Abreu .30 .10
❑ 419 Tomas Perez .30 .10
❑ 420 Doug Glanville .30 .10
❑ 421 Reggie Taylor .30 .10
❑ 422 Jimmy Rollins .30 .10
❑ 423 Brian Giles .30 .10
❑ 424 Rob Mackowiak .30 .10
❑ 425 Bronson Arroyo .30 .10
❑ 426 Kevin Young .30 .10
❑ 427 Jack Wilson .30 .10
❑ 428 Adrian Brown .30 .10
❑ 429 Chad Hermansen .30 .10
❑ 430 Jimmy Anderson .30 .10
❑ 431 Aramis Ramirez .30 .10
❑ 432 Todd Ritchie .30 .10
❑ 433 Pat Meares .30 .10
❑ 434 Warren Morris .30 .10
❑ 435 Derek Bell .30 .10
❑ 436 Ken Griffey Jr. 1.25 .50
❑ 437 Elmer Dessens .30 .10
❑ 438 Ruben Rivera .30 .10
❑ 439 Jason LaRue .30 .10
❑ 440 Sean Casey .30 .10
❑ 441 Pete Harnisch .30 .10
❑ 442 Danny Graves .30 .10
❑ 443 Aaron Boone .30 .10
❑ 444 Dmitri Young .30 .10
❑ 445 Brandon Larson .30 .10
❑ 446 Pokey Reese .30 .10
❑ 447 Todd Walker .30 .10
❑ 448 Juan Castro .30 .10
❑ 449 Todd Helton .50 .20
❑ 450 Ben Petrick .30 .10
❑ 451 Juan Pierre .30 .10
❑ 452 Jeff Cirillo .30 .10
❑ 453 Juan Uribe .30 .10
❑ 454 Brian Bohanon .30 .10
❑ 455 Terry Shumpert .30 .10
❑ 456 Mike Hampton .30 .10
❑ 457 Shawn Chacon .30 .10
❑ 458 Adam Melhuse .30 .10
❑ 459 Greg Norton .30 .10
❑ 460 Gabe White .30 .10
❑ 461 Ichiro Suzuki WS .75 .30
❑ 462 Carlos Delgado WS .30 .10
❑ 463 Manny Ramirez WS .50 .20
❑ 464 Miguel Tejada WS .30 .10
❑ 465 Tsuyoshi Shinjo WS .30 .10
❑ 466 Bernie Williams WS .30 .10
❑ 467 Juan Gonzalez WS .30 .10
❑ 468 Andruw Jones WS .30 .10
❑ 469 Ivan Rodriguez WS .30 .10
❑ 470 Larry Walker WS .30 .10
❑ 471 Hideo Nomo WS .30 .10
❑ 472 Albert Pujols WS .75 .30
❑ 473 Pedro Martinez WS .50 .20
❑ 474 Vladimir Guerrero WS .50 .20
❑ 475 Tony Batista WS .30 .10
❑ 476 Kazuhiro Sasaki WS .30 .10
❑ 477 Richard Hidalgo WS .30 .10
❑ 478 Carlos Lee WS .30 .10
❑ 479 Roberto Alomar WS .30 .10
❑ 480 Rafael Palmeiro WS .30 .10
❑ 481 Ken Griffey Jr. GG .75 .30
❑ 482 Ken Griffey Jr. GG .75 .30
❑ 483 Ken Griffey Jr. GG .75 .30
❑ 484 Ken Griffey Jr. GG .75 .30
❑ 485 Ken Griffey Jr. GG .75 .30
❑ 486 Ken Griffey Jr. GG .75 .30
❑ 487 Ken Griffey Jr. GG .75 .30
❑ 488 Ken Griffey Jr. GG .75 .30
❑ 489 Ken Griffey Jr. GG .75 .30
❑ 490 Ken Griffey Jr. GG .75 .30
❑ 491 Barry Bonds CL 1.00 .40
❑ 492 Hideo Nomo CL .30 .10
❑ 493 Ichiro Suzuki CL .75 .30
❑ 494 Cal Ripken CL 1.25 .50
❑ 495 Tony Gwynn CL .50 .20
❑ 496 Randy Johnson CL .50 .20
❑ 497 A.J. Burnett CL .30 .10
❑ 498 Rickey Henderson CL .50 .20
❑ 499 Albert Pujols CL .75 .30
❑ 500 Luis Gonzalez CL .30 .10
❑ 501 Brandon Puffer SR RC 1.00 .40
❑ 502 Rodrigo Rosario SR RC 1.00 .40
❑ 503 Tom Shearn SR RC 1.00 .40
❑ 504 Reed Johnson SR RC 1.50 .60
❑ 505 Chris Baker SR RC 1.00 .40
❑ 506 John Ennis SR RC 1.00 .40
❑ 507 Luis Martinez SR RC 1.00 .40
❑ 508 So Taguchi SR RC 1.50 .60
❑ 509 Scotty Layfield SR RC 1.00 .40
❑ 510 Francis Beltran SR RC 1.00 .40
❑ 511 Brandon Backe SR RC 1.50 .60
❑ 512 Doug Devore SR RC 1.00 .40
❑ 513 Jeremy Ward SR RC 1.00 .40
❑ 514 Jose Valverde SR RC 1.00 .40
❑ 515 P.J. Bevis SR RC 1.00 .40
❑ 516 Victor Alvarez SR RC 1.00 .40
❑ 517 Kazuhisa Ishii SR RC 1.50 .60
❑ 518 Jorge Nunez SR RC 1.00 .40
❑ 519 Eric Good SR RC 1.00 .40
❑ 520 Ron Calloway SR RC 1.00 .40
❑ 521 Val Pascucci SR 1.00 .40
❑ 522 Nelson Castro SR RC 1.00 .40
❑ 523 Deivis Santos SR 1.00 .40
❑ 524 Luis Ugueto SR RC 1.00 .40
❑ 525 Matt Thornton SR RC 1.00 .40
❑ 526 Hansel Izquierdo SR RC 1.00 .40
❑ 527 Tyler Yates SR RC 1.00 .40
❑ 528 Mark Corey SR RC 1.00 .40
❑ 529 Jaime Cerda SR RC 1.00 .40
❑ 530 Satoru Komiyama SR RC 1.00 .40
❑ 531 Steve Bechler SR RC 1.00 .40
❑ 532 Ben Howard SR RC 1.00 .40
❑ 533 Anderson Machado SR RC 1.00 .40
❑ 534 Jorge Padilla SR RC 1.00 .40
❑ 535 Eric Junge SR RC 1.00 .40
❑ 536 Adrian Burnside SR RC 1.00 .40
❑ 537 Mike Gonzalez SR RC 1.00 .40
❑ 538 Josh Hancock SR RC 1.00 .40
❑ 539 Colin Young SR RC 1.00 .40
❑ 540 Rene Reyes SR RC 1.00 .40
❑ 541 Cam Esslinger SR RC 1.00 .40
❑ 542 Tim Kalita SR RC 1.00 .40
❑ 543 Kevin Frederick SR RC 1.00 .40
❑ 544 Kyle Kane SR RC 1.00 .40
❑ 545 Edwin Almonte SR RC 1.00 .40
❑ 546 Aaron Sele .30 .10
❑ 547 Garret Anderson .30 .10
❑ 548 Darin Erstad .30 .10
❑ 549 Brad Fullmer .30 .10
❑ 550 Kevin Appier .30 .10
❑ 551 Tim Salmon .50 .20
❑ 552 David Justice .30 .10
❑ 553 Billy Koch .30 .10
❑ 554 Scott Hatteberg .30 .10
❑ 555 Tim Hudson .30 .10
❑ 556 Miguel Tejada .30 .10
❑ 557 Carlos Pena .30 .10
❑ 558 Mike Sirotka .30 .10
❑ 559 Jose Cruz Jr. .30 .10
❑ 560 Josh Phelps .30 .10
❑ 561 Brandon Lyon .30 .10

- ❑ 562 Luke Prokopec .30 .10
- ❑ 563 Felipe Lopez .30 .10
- ❑ 564 Jason Standridge .30 .10
- ❑ 565 Chris Gomez .30 .10
- ❑ 566 John Flaherty .30 .10
- ❑ 567 Jason Tyner .30 .10
- ❑ 568 Bobby Smith .30 .10
- ❑ 569 Wilson Alvarez .30 .10
- ❑ 570 Matt Lawton .30 .10
- ❑ 571 Omar Vizquel .50 .20
- ❑ 572 Jim Thome .50 .20
- ❑ 573 Brady Anderson .30 .10
- ❑ 574 Alex Escobar .30 .10
- ❑ 575 Russell Branyan .30 .10
- ❑ 576 Bret Boone .30 .10
- ❑ 577 Ben Davis .30 .10
- ❑ 578 Mike Cameron .30 .10
- ❑ 579 Jamie Moyer .30 .10
- ❑ 580 Ruben Sierra .30 .10
- ❑ 581 Jeff Cirillo .30 .10
- ❑ 582 Marty Cordova .30 .10
- ❑ 583 Mike Bordick .30 .10
- ❑ 584 Brian Roberts .30 .10
- ❑ 585 Luis Matos .30 .10
- ❑ 586 Geronimo Gil .30 .10
- ❑ 587 Jay Gibbons .30 .10
- ❑ 588 Carl Everett .30 .10
- ❑ 589 Ivan Rodriguez .50 .20
- ❑ 590 Chan Ho Park .30 .10
- ❑ 591 Juan Gonzalez .30 .10
- ❑ 592 Hank Blalock .50 .20
- ❑ 593 Todd Van Poppel .30 .10
- ❑ 594 Pedro Martinez .50 .20
- ❑ 595 Jason Varitek .75 .30
- ❑ 596 Tony Clark .30 .10
- ❑ 597 Johnny Damon Sox .50 .20
- ❑ 598 Dustin Hermanson .30 .10
- ❑ 599 John Burkett .30 .10
- ❑ 600 Carlos Beltran .30 .10
- ❑ 601 Mark Quinn .30 .10
- ❑ 602 Chuck Knoblauch .30 .10
- ❑ 603 Michael Tucker .30 .10
- ❑ 604 Carlos Febles .30 .10
- ❑ 605 Jose Rosado .30 .10
- ❑ 606 Dmitri Young .30 .10
- ❑ 607 Bobby Higginson .30 .10
- ❑ 608 Craig Paquette .30 .10
- ❑ 609 Mitch Meluskey .30 .10
- ❑ 610 Wendell Magee .30 .10
- ❑ 611 Mike Rivera .30 .10
- ❑ 612 Jacque Jones .30 .10
- ❑ 613 Luis Rivas .30 .10
- ❑ 614 Eric Milton .30 .10
- ❑ 615 Eddie Guardado .30 .10
- ❑ 616 Matt LeCroy .30 .10
- ❑ 617 Mike Jackson .30 .10
- ❑ 618 Magglio Ordonez .30 .10
- ❑ 619 Frank Thomas .75 .30
- ❑ 620 Rocky Biddle .30 .10
- ❑ 621 Paul Konerko .30 .10
- ❑ 622 Todd Ritchie .30 .10
- ❑ 623 Jon Rauch .30 .10
- ❑ 624 John Vander Wal .30 .10
- ❑ 625 Rondell White .30 .10
- ❑ 626 Jason Giambi .30 .10
- ❑ 627 Robin Ventura .30 .10
- ❑ 628 David Wells .30 .10
- ❑ 629 Bernie Williams .50 .20
- ❑ 630 Lance Berkman .30 .10
- ❑ 631 Richard Hidalgo .30 .10
- ❑ 632 Greg Zaun .30 .10
- ❑ 633 Jose Vizcaino .30 .10
- ❑ 634 Octavio Dotel .30 .10
- ❑ 635 Morgan Ensberg .30 .10
- ❑ 636 Andruw Jones .50 .20
- ❑ 637 Tom Glavine .50 .20
- ❑ 638 Gary Sheffield .30 .10
- ❑ 639 Vinny Castilla .30 .10
- ❑ 640 Javy Lopez .30 .10
- ❑ 641 Albie Lopez .30 .10
- ❑ 642 Geoff Jenkins .30 .10
- ❑ 643 Jeffrey Hammonds .30 .10
- ❑ 644 Alex Ochoa .30 .10
- ❑ 645 Richie Sexson .30 .10
- ❑ 646 Eric Young .30 .10
- ❑ 647 Glendon Rusch .30 .10
- ❑ 648 Tino Martinez .50 .20
- ❑ 649 Fernando Vina .30 .10
- ❑ 650 J.D. Drew .30 .10
- ❑ 651 Woody Williams .30 .10
- ❑ 652 Darryl Kile .30 .10
- ❑ 653 Jason Isringhausen .30 .10
- ❑ 654 Moises Alou .30 .10
- ❑ 655 Alex Gonzalez .30 .10
- ❑ 656 Delino DeShields .30 .10
- ❑ 657 Todd Hundley .30 .10
- ❑ 658 Chris Stynes .30 .10
- ❑ 659 Jason Bere .30 .10
- ❑ 660 Curt Schilling .30 .10
- ❑ 661 Craig Counsell .30 .10
- ❑ 662 Mark Grace .50 .20
- ❑ 663 Matt Williams .30 .10
- ❑ 664 Jay Bell .30 .10
- ❑ 665 Rick Helling .30 .10
- ❑ 666 Shawn Green .30 .10
- ❑ 667 Eric Karros .30 .10
- ❑ 668 Hideo Nomo .75 .30
- ❑ 669 Omar Daal .30 .10
- ❑ 670 Brian Jordan .30 .10
- ❑ 671 Cesar Izturis .30 .10
- ❑ 672 Fernando Tatis .30 .10
- ❑ 673 Lee Stevens .30 .10
- ❑ 674 Tomo Ohka .30 .10
- ❑ 675 Brian Schneider .30 .10
- ❑ 676 Brad Wilkerson .30 .10
- ❑ 677 Bruce Chen .30 .10
- ❑ 678 Tsuyoshi Shinjo .30 .10
- ❑ 679 Jeff Kent .30 .10
- ❑ 680 Kirk Rueter .30 .10
- ❑ 681 J.T. Snow .30 .10
- ❑ 682 David Bell .30 .10
- ❑ 683 Reggie Sanders .30 .10
- ❑ 684 Preston Wilson .30 .10
- ❑ 685 Vic Darensbourg .30 .10
- ❑ 686 Josh Beckett .30 .10
- ❑ 687 Pablo Ozuna .30 .10
- ❑ 688 Mike Redmond .30 .10
- ❑ 689 Scott Strickland .30 .10
- ❑ 690 Mo Vaughn .30 .10
- ❑ 691 Roberto Alomar .50 .20
- ❑ 692 Edgardo Alfonzo .30 .10
- ❑ 693 Shawn Estes .30 .10
- ❑ 694 Roger Cedeno .30 .10
- ❑ 695 Jeromy Burnitz .30 .10
- ❑ 696 Ray Lankford .30 .10
- ❑ 697 Mark Kotsay .30 .10
- ❑ 698 Kevin Jarvis .30 .10
- ❑ 699 Bobby Jones .30 .10
- ❑ 700 Sean Burroughs .30 .10
- ❑ 701 Ramon Vazquez .30 .10
- ❑ 702 Pat Burrell .30 .10
- ❑ 703 Marlon Byrd .30 .10
- ❑ 704 Brandon Duckworth .30 .10
- ❑ 705 Marlon Anderson .30 .10
- ❑ 706 Vicente Padilla .30 .10
- ❑ 707 Kip Wells .30 .10
- ❑ 708 Jason Kendall .30 .10
- ❑ 709 Pokey Reese .30 .10
- ❑ 710 Pat Meares .30 .10
- ❑ 711 Kris Benson .30 .10
- ❑ 712 Armando Rios .30 .10
- ❑ 713 Mike Williams .30 .10
- ❑ 714 Barry Larkin .50 .20
- ❑ 715 Adam Dunn .30 .10
- ❑ 716 Juan Encarnacion .30 .10
- ❑ 717 Scott Williamson .30 .10
- ❑ 718 Wilton Guerrero .30 .10
- ❑ 719 Chris Reitsma .30 .10
- ❑ 720 Larry Walker .30 .10
- ❑ 721 Denny Neagle .30 .10
- ❑ 722 Todd Zeile .30 .10
- ❑ 723 Jose Ortiz .30 .10
- ❑ 724 Jason Jennings .30 .10
- ❑ 725 Tony Eusebio .30 .10
- ❑ 726 Ichiro Suzuki YR .75 .30
- ❑ 727 Barry Bonds YR 1.00 .40
- ❑ 728 Randy Johnson YR .50 .20
- ❑ 729 Albert Pujols YR .75 .30
- ❑ 730 Roger Clemens YR .75 .30
- ❑ 731 Sammy Sosa YR .50 .20
- ❑ 732 Alex Rodriguez YR .75 .30
- ❑ 733 Chipper Jones YR .50 .20
- ❑ 734 Rickey Henderson YR .50 .20
- ❑ 735 Ichiro Suzuki YR .75 .30
- ❑ 736 Luis Gonzalez SH CL .30 .10
- ❑ 737 Derek Jeter SH CL 1.00 .40
- ❑ 738 Ichiro Suzuki SH CL .75 .30
- ❑ 739 Barry Bonds SH CL 1.00 .40
- ❑ 740 Curt Schilling SH CL .30 .10
- ❑ 741 Shawn Green SH CL .30 .10
- ❑ 742 Jason Giambi SH CL .30 .10
- ❑ 743 Roberto Alomar SH CL .30 .10
- ❑ 744 Larry Walker SH CL .30 .10
- ❑ 745 Mark McGwire SH CL 1.00 .40

2003 Upper Deck

- ❑ COMPLETE SERIES 1 (270) 50.00 20.00
- ❑ COMPLETE SERIES 2 (270) 50.00 20.00
- ❑ COMP.UPDATE SET (60) 20.00 10.00
- ❑ COMMON (31-500/531-600) .30 .10
- ❑ COMMON (1-30/501-530) 1.00 .40
- ❑ COMMON RC (541-600) .50 .20
- ❑ SR 1-30/501-530 ARE NOT SHORT PRINTS
- ❑ CARD 19 DOES NOT EXIST
- ❑ SCUTARO/NOMAR ARE BOTH CARD 96
- ❑ 541-600 ISSUED IN 04 UD1 HOBBY BOXES
- ❑ UPDATE SET EXCH 1:240 '04 UD1 RETAIL
- ❑ UPDATE SET EXCH.DEADLINE 11/10/06
- ❑ 1 John Lackey SR 1.00 .40
- ❑ 2 Alex Cintron SR 1.00 .40
- ❑ 3 Jose Leon SR 1.00 .40
- ❑ 4 Bobby Hill SR 1.00 .40
- ❑ 5 Brandon Larson SR 1.00 .40
- ❑ 6 Raul Gonzalez SR 1.00 .40
- ❑ 7 Ben Broussard SR 1.00 .40
- ❑ 8 Earl Snyder SR 1.00 .40
- ❑ 9 Ramon Santiago SR 1.00 .40
- ❑ 10 Jason Lane SR 1.00 .40
- ❑ 11 Keith Ginter SR 1.00 .40
- ❑ 12 Kirk Saarloos SR 1.00 .40
- ❑ 13 Juan Brito SR 1.00 .40
- ❑ 14 Runelvys Hernandez SR 1.00 .40
- ❑ 15 Shawn Sedlacek SR 1.00 .40
- ❑ 16 Jayson Durocher SR 1.00 .40
- ❑ 17 Kevin Frederick SR 1.00 .40
- ❑ 18 Zach Day SR 1.00 .40
- ❑ 19 Marcos Scutaro SR 1.00 .40
- ❑ 20 Marcus Thames SR 1.00 .40
- ❑ 21 Esteban German SR 1.00 .40
- ❑ 22 Brett Myers SR 1.00 .40
- ❑ 23 Oliver Perez SR 1.00 .40
- ❑ 24 Dennis Tankersley SR 1.00 .40
- ❑ 25 Julius Matos SR 1.00 .40
- ❑ 26 Jake Peavy SR 1.00 .40
- ❑ 27 Eric Cyr SR 1.00 .40
- ❑ 28 Mike Crudale SR 1.00 .40
- ❑ 29 Josh Pearce SR 1.00 .40
- ❑ 30 Carl Crawford SR 1.00 .40
- ❑ 31 Tim Salmon .50 .20
- ❑ 32 Troy Glaus .30 .10
- ❑ 33 Adam Kennedy .30 .10
- ❑ 34 David Eckstein .30 .10
- ❑ 35 Ben Molina .30 .10
- ❑ 36 Jarrod Washburn .30 .10
- ❑ 37 Ramon Ortiz .30 .10
- ❑ 38 Eric Chavez .30 .10
- ❑ 39 Miguel Tejada .30 .10
- ❑ 40 Adam Piatt .30 .10
- ❑ 41 Jermaine Dye .30 .10
- ❑ 42 Olmedo Saenz .30 .10

❑ 43 Tim Hudson .30 .10
❑ 44 Barry Zito .30 .10
❑ 45 Billy Koch .30 .10
❑ 46 Shannon Stewart .30 .10
❑ 47 Kelvim Escobar .30 .10
❑ 48 Jose Cruz Jr. .30 .10
❑ 49 Vernon Wells .30 .10
❑ 50 Roy Halladay .30 .10
❑ 51 Esteban Loaiza .30 .10
❑ 52 Eric Hinske .30 .10
❑ 53 Steve Cox .30 .10
❑ 54 Brent Abernathy .30 .10
❑ 55 Ben Grieve .30 .10
❑ 56 Aubrey Huff .30 .10
❑ 57 Jared Sandberg .30 .10
❑ 58 Paul Wilson .30 .10
❑ 59 Tanyon Sturtze .30 .10
❑ 60 Jim Thome .50 .20
❑ 61 Omar Vizquel .50 .20
❑ 62 C.C. Sabathia .30 .10
❑ 63 Chris Magruder .30 .10
❑ 64 Ricky Gutierrez .30 .10
❑ 65 Einar Diaz .30 .10
❑ 66 Danys Baez .30 .10
❑ 67 Ichiro Suzuki 1.50 .60
❑ 68 Ruben Sierra .30 .10
❑ 69 Carlos Guillen .30 .10
❑ 70 Mark McLemore .30 .10
❑ 71 Dan Wilson .30 .10
❑ 72 Jamie Moyer .30 .10
❑ 73 Joel Pineiro .30 .10
❑ 74 Edgar Martinez .50 .20
❑ 75 Tony Batista .30 .10
❑ 76 Jay Gibbons .30 .10
❑ 77 Chris Singleton .30 .10
❑ 78 Melvin Mora .30 .10
❑ 79 Geronimo Gil .30 .10
❑ 80 Rodrigo Lopez .30 .10
❑ 81 Jorge Julio .30 .10
❑ 82 Rafael Palmeiro .50 .20
❑ 83 Juan Gonzalez .30 .10
❑ 84 Mike Young .50 .20
❑ 85 Hideki Irabu .30 .10
❑ 86 Chan Ho Park .30 .10
❑ 87 Kevin Mench .30 .10
❑ 88 Doug Davis .30 .10
❑ 89 Pedro Martinez .50 .20
❑ 90 Shea Hillenbrand .30 .10
❑ 91 Derek Lowe .30 .10
❑ 92 Jason Varitek .75 .30
❑ 93 Tony Clark .30 .10
❑ 94 John Burkett .30 .10
❑ 95 Frank Castillo .30 .10
❑ 96 Nomar Garciaparra 1.25 .50
❑ 97 Rickey Henderson .75 .30
❑ 98 Mike Sweeney .30 .10
❑ 99 Carlos Febles .30 .10
❑ 100 Mark Quinn .30 .10
❑ 101 Raul Ibanez .30 .10
❑ 102 A.J. Hinch .30 .10
❑ 103 Paul Byrd .30 .10
❑ 104 Chuck Knoblauch .30 .10
❑ 105 Dmitri Young .30 .10
❑ 106 Randall Simon .30 .10
❑ 107 Brandon Inge .30 .10
❑ 108 Damion Easley .30 .10
❑ 109 Carlos Pena .30 .10
❑ 110 George Lombard .30 .10
❑ 111 Juan Acevedo .30 .10
❑ 112 Torii Hunter .30 .10
❑ 113 Doug Mientkiewicz .30 .10
❑ 114 David Ortiz .50 .20
❑ 115 Eric Milton .30 .10
❑ 116 Eddie Guardado .30 .10
❑ 117 Cristian Guzman .30 .10
❑ 118 Corey Koskie .30 .10
❑ 119 Magglio Ordonez .30 .10
❑ 120 Mark Buehrle .30 .10
❑ 121 Todd Ritchie .30 .10
❑ 122 Jose Valentin .30 .10
❑ 123 Paul Konerko .30 .10
❑ 124 Carlos Lee .30 .10
❑ 125 Jon Garland .30 .10
❑ 126 Jason Giambi .30 .10
❑ 127 Derek Jeter 2.00 .75
❑ 128 Roger Clemens 1.50 .60
❑ 129 Raul Mondesi .30 .10
❑ 130 Jorge Posada .50 .20
❑ 131 Rondell White .30 .10
❑ 132 Robin Ventura .30 .10
❑ 133 Mike Mussina .50 .20
❑ 134 Jeff Bagwell .50 .20
❑ 135 Craig Biggio .50 .20
❑ 136 Morgan Ensberg .30 .10
❑ 137 Richard Hidalgo .30 .10
❑ 138 Brad Ausmus .30 .10
❑ 139 Roy Oswalt .30 .10
❑ 140 Carlos Hernandez .30 .10
❑ 141 Shane Reynolds .30 .10
❑ 142 Gary Sheffield .30 .10
❑ 143 Andruw Jones .50 .20
❑ 144 Tom Glavine .50 .20
❑ 145 Rafael Furcal .30 .10
❑ 146 Javy Lopez .30 .10
❑ 147 Vinny Castilla .30 .10
❑ 148 Marcus Giles .30 .10
❑ 149 Kevin Millwood .30 .10
❑ 150 Jason Marquis .30 .10
❑ 151 Ruben Quevedo .30 .10
❑ 152 Ben Sheets .30 .10
❑ 153 Geoff Jenkins .30 .10
❑ 154 Jose Hernandez .30 .10
❑ 155 Glendon Rusch .30 .10
❑ 156 Jeffrey Hammonds .30 .10
❑ 157 Alex Sanchez .30 .10
❑ 158 Jim Edmonds .30 .10
❑ 159 Tino Martinez .50 .20
❑ 160 Albert Pujols 1.50 .60
❑ 161 Eli Marrero .30 .10
❑ 162 Woody Williams .30 .10
❑ 163 Fernando Vina .30 .10
❑ 164 Jason Isringhausen .30 .10
❑ 165 Jason Simontacchi .30 .10
❑ 166 Kerry Robinson .30 .10
❑ 167 Sammy Sosa .75 .30
❑ 168 Juan Cruz .30 .10
❑ 169 Fred McGriff .50 .20
❑ 170 Antonio Alfonseca .30 .10
❑ 171 Jon Lieber .30 .10
❑ 172 Mark Prior .50 .20
❑ 173 Moises Alou .30 .10
❑ 174 Matt Clement .30 .10
❑ 175 Mark Bellhorn .30 .10
❑ 176 Randy Johnson .75 .30
❑ 177 Luis Gonzalez .30 .10
❑ 178 Tony Womack .30 .10
❑ 179 Mark Grace .50 .20
❑ 180 Junior Spivey .30 .10
❑ 181 Byung Hyun Kim .30 .10
❑ 182 Danny Bautista .30 .10
❑ 183 Brian Anderson .30 .10
❑ 184 Shawn Green .30 .10
❑ 185 Brian Jordan .30 .10
❑ 186 Eric Karros .30 .10
❑ 187 Andy Ashby .30 .10
❑ 188 Cesar Izturis .30 .10
❑ 189 Dave Roberts .30 .10
❑ 190 Eric Gagne .30 .10
❑ 191 Kazuhisa Ishii .30 .10
❑ 192 Adrian Beltre .30 .10
❑ 193 Vladimir Guerrero .75 .30
❑ 194 Tony Armas Jr. .30 .10
❑ 195 Bartolo Colon .30 .10
❑ 196 Troy O'Leary .30 .10
❑ 197 Tomo Ohka .30 .10
❑ 198 Brad Wilkerson .30 .10
❑ 199 Orlando Cabrera .30 .10
❑ 200 Barry Bonds 2.00 .75
❑ 201 David Bell .30 .10
❑ 202 Tsuyoshi Shinjo .30 .10
❑ 203 Benito Santiago .30 .10
❑ 204 Livan Hernandez .30 .10
❑ 205 Jason Schmidt .30 .10
❑ 206 Kirk Rueter .30 .10
❑ 207 Ramon E. Martinez .30 .10
❑ 208 Mike Lowell .30 .10
❑ 209 Luis Castillo .30 .10
❑ 210 Derrek Lee .50 .20
❑ 211 Andy Fox .30 .10
❑ 212 Eric Owens .30 .10
❑ 213 Charles Johnson .30 .10
❑ 214 Brad Penny .30 .10
❑ 215 A.J. Burnett .30 .10
❑ 216 Edgardo Alfonzo .30 .10
❑ 217 Roberto Alomar .50 .20
❑ 218 Rey Ordonez .30 .10
❑ 219 Al Leiter .30 .10
❑ 220 Roger Cedeno .30 .10
❑ 221 Timo Perez .30 .10
❑ 222 Jeromy Burnitz .30 .10
❑ 223 Pedro Astacio .30 .10
❑ 224 Joe McEwing .30 .10
❑ 225 Ryan Klesko .30 .10
❑ 226 Ramon Vazquez .30 .10
❑ 227 Mark Kotsay .30 .10
❑ 228 Bubba Trammell .30 .10
❑ 229 Wiki Gonzalez .30 .10
❑ 230 Trevor Hoffman .30 .10
❑ 231 Ron Gant .30 .10
❑ 232 Bob Abreu .30 .10
❑ 233 Marlon Anderson .30 .10
❑ 234 Jeremy Giambi .30 .10
❑ 235 Jimmy Rollins .30 .10
❑ 236 Mike Lieberthal .30 .10
❑ 237 Vicente Padilla .30 .10
❑ 238 Randy Wolf .30 .10
❑ 239 Pokey Reese .30 .10
❑ 240 Brian Giles .30 .10
❑ 241 Jack Wilson .30 .10
❑ 242 Mike Williams .30 .10
❑ 243 Kip Wells .30 .10
❑ 244 Rob Mackowiak .30 .10
❑ 245 Craig Wilson .30 .10
❑ 246 Adam Dunn .30 .10
❑ 247 Sean Casey .30 .10
❑ 248 Todd Walker .30 .10
❑ 249 Corky Miller .30 .10
❑ 250 Ryan Dempster .30 .10
❑ 251 Reggie Taylor .30 .10
❑ 252 Aaron Boone .30 .10
❑ 253 Larry Walker .30 .10
❑ 254 Jose Ortiz .30 .10
❑ 255 Todd Zeile .30 .10
❑ 256 Bobby Estalella .30 .10
❑ 257 Juan Pierre .30 .10
❑ 258 Terry Shumpert .30 .10
❑ 259 Mike Hampton .30 .10
❑ 260 Denny Stark .30 .10
❑ 261 Shawn Green SH CL .30 .10
❑ 262 Derek Lowe SH CL .30 .10
❑ 263 Barry Bonds SH CL 1.00 .40
❑ 264 Mike Cameron SH CL .30 .10
❑ 265 Luis Castillo SH CL .30 .10
❑ 266 Vladimir Guerrero SH CL .50 .20
❑ 267 Jason Giambi SH CL .30 .10
❑ 268 Eric Gagne SH CL .30 .10
❑ 269 Magglio Ordonez SH CL .30 .10
❑ 270 Jim Thome SH CL .30 .10
❑ 271 Garret Anderson .30 .10
❑ 272 Troy Percival .30 .10
❑ 273 Brad Fullmer .30 .10
❑ 274 Scott Spiezio .30 .10
❑ 275 Darin Erstad .30 .10
❑ 276 Francisco Rodriguez .30 .10
❑ 277 Kevin Appier .30 .10
❑ 278 Shawn Wooten .30 .10
❑ 279 Eric Owens .30 .10
❑ 280 Scott Hatteberg .30 .10
❑ 281 Terrence Long .30 .10
❑ 282 Mark Mulder .30 .10
❑ 283 Ramon Hernandez .30 .10
❑ 284 Ted Lilly .30 .10
❑ 285 Erubiel Durazo .30 .10
❑ 286 Mark Ellis .30 .10
❑ 287 Carlos Delgado .30 .10
❑ 288 Orlando Hudson .30 .10
❑ 289 Chris Woodward .30 .10
❑ 290 Mark Hendrickson .30 .10
❑ 291 Josh Phelps .30 .10
❑ 292 Ken Huckaby .30 .10
❑ 293 Justin Miller .30 .10
❑ 294 Travis Lee .30 .10
❑ 295 Jorge Sosa .30 .10
❑ 296 Joe Kennedy .30 .10
❑ 297 Carl Crawford .30 .10
❑ 298 Toby Hall .30 .10
❑ 299 Rey Ordonez .30 .10
❑ 300 Brandon Phillips .30 .10

❑ 301	Matt Lawton	.30	.10
❑ 302	Ellis Burks	.30	.10
❑ 303	Bill Selby	.30	.10
❑ 304	Travis Hafner	.30	.10
❑ 305	Milton Bradley	.30	.10
❑ 306	Karim Garcia	.30	.10
❑ 307	Cliff Lee	.30	.10
❑ 308	Jeff Cirillo	.30	.10
❑ 309	John Olerud	.30	.10
❑ 310	Kazuhiro Sasaki	.30	.10
❑ 311	Freddy Garcia	.30	.10
❑ 312	Bret Boone	.30	.10
❑ 313	Mike Cameron	.30	.10
❑ 314	Ben Davis	.30	.10
❑ 315	Randy Winn	.30	.10
❑ 316	Gary Matthews Jr.	.30	.10
❑ 317	Jeff Conine	.30	.10
❑ 318	Sidney Ponson	.30	.10
❑ 319	Jerry Hairston	.30	.10
❑ 320	David Segui	.30	.10
❑ 321	Scott Erickson	.30	.10
❑ 322	Marty Cordova	.30	.10
❑ 323	Hank Blalock	.30	.10
❑ 324	Herbert Perry	.30	.10
❑ 325	Alex Rodriguez	1.25	.50
❑ 326	Carl Everett	.30	.10
❑ 327	Einar Diaz	.30	.10
❑ 328	Ugueth Urbina	.30	.10
❑ 329	Mark Teixeira	.50	.20
❑ 330	Manny Ramirez	.50	.20
❑ 331	Johnny Damon	.50	.20
❑ 332	Trot Nixon	.30	.10
❑ 333	Tim Wakefield	.30	.10
❑ 334	Casey Fossum	.30	.10
❑ 335	Todd Walker	.30	.10
❑ 336	Jeremy Giambi	.30	.10
❑ 337	Bill Mueller	.30	.10
❑ 338	Ramiro Mendoza	.30	.10
❑ 339	Carlos Beltran	.30	.10
❑ 340	Jason Grimsley	.30	.10
❑ 341	Brent Mayne	.30	.10
❑ 342	Angel Berroa	.30	.10
❑ 343	Albie Lopez	.30	.10
❑ 344	Michael Tucker	.30	.10
❑ 345	Bobby Higginson	.30	.10
❑ 346	Shane Halter	.30	.10
❑ 347	Jeremy Bonderman RC	4.00	1.50
❑ 348	Eric Munson	.30	.10
❑ 349	Andy Van Hekken	.30	.10
❑ 350	Matt Anderson	.30	.10
❑ 351	Jacque Jones	.30	.10
❑ 352	A.J. Pierzynski	.30	.10
❑ 353	Joe Mays	.30	.10
❑ 354	Brad Radke	.30	.10
❑ 355	Dustan Mohr	.30	.10
❑ 356	Bobby Kielty	.30	.10
❑ 357	Michael Cuddyer	.30	.10
❑ 358	Luis Rivas	.30	.10
❑ 359	Frank Thomas	.75	.30
❑ 360	Joe Borchard	.30	.10
❑ 361	D'Angelo Jimenez	.30	.10
❑ 362	Bartolo Colon	.30	.10
❑ 363	Joe Crede	.30	.10
❑ 364	Miguel Olivo	.30	.10
❑ 365	Billy Koch	.30	.10
❑ 366	Bernie Williams	.50	.20
❑ 367	Nick Johnson	.30	.10
❑ 368	Andy Pettitte	.50	.20
❑ 369	Mariano Rivera	.75	.30
❑ 370	Alfonso Soriano	.30	.10
❑ 371	David Wells	.30	.10
❑ 372	Drew Henson	.30	.10
❑ 373	Juan Rivera	.30	.10
❑ 374	Steve Karsay	.30	.10
❑ 375	Jeff Kent	.30	.10
❑ 376	Lance Berkman	.30	.10
❑ 377	Octavio Dotel	.30	.10
❑ 378	Julio Lugo	.30	.10
❑ 379	Jason Lane	.30	.10
❑ 380	Wade Miller	.30	.10
❑ 381	Billy Wagner	.30	.10
❑ 382	Brad Ausmus	.30	.10
❑ 383	Mike Hampton	.30	.10
❑ 384	Chipper Jones	.75	.30
❑ 385	John Smoltz	.50	.20
❑ 386	Greg Maddux	1.25	.50
❑ 387	Javy Lopez	.30	.10
❑ 388	Robert Fick	.30	.10
❑ 389	Mark DeRosa	.30	.10
❑ 390	Russ Ortiz	.30	.10
❑ 391	Julio Franco	.30	.10
❑ 392	Richie Sexson	.30	.10
❑ 393	Eric Young	.30	.10
❑ 394	Robert Machado	.30	.10
❑ 395	Mike DeJean	.30	.10
❑ 396	Todd Ritchie	.30	.10
❑ 397	Royce Clayton	.30	.10
❑ 398	Nick Neugebauer	.30	.10
❑ 399	J.D. Drew	.30	.10
❑ 400	Edgar Renteria	.30	.10
❑ 401	Scott Rolen	.50	.20
❑ 402	Matt Morris	.30	.10
❑ 403	Garrett Stephenson	.30	.10
❑ 404	Eduardo Perez	.30	.10
❑ 405	Mike Matheny	.30	.10
❑ 406	Miguel Cairo	.30	.10
❑ 407	Brett Tomko	.30	.10
❑ 408	Bobby Hill	.30	.10
❑ 409	Troy O'Leary	.30	.10
❑ 410	Corey Patterson	.30	.10
❑ 411	Kerry Wood	.30	.10
❑ 412	Eric Karros	.30	.10
❑ 413	Hee Seop Choi	.30	.10
❑ 414	Alex Gonzalez	.30	.10
❑ 415	Matt Clement	.30	.10
❑ 416	Mark Grudzielanek	.30	.10
❑ 417	Curt Schilling	.30	.10
❑ 418	Steve Finley	.30	.10
❑ 419	Craig Counsell	.30	.10
❑ 420	Matt Williams	.30	.10
❑ 421	Quinton McCracken	.30	.10
❑ 422	Chad Moeller	.30	.10
❑ 423	Lyle Overbay	.30	.10
❑ 424	Miguel Batista	.30	.10
❑ 425	Paul Lo Duca	.30	.10
❑ 426	Kevin Brown	.30	.10
❑ 427	Hideo Nomo	.75	.30
❑ 428	Fred McGriff	.50	.20
❑ 429	Joe Thurston	.30	.10
❑ 430	Odalis Perez	.30	.10
❑ 431	Darren Dreifort	.30	.10
❑ 432	Todd Hundley	.30	.10
❑ 433	Dave Roberts	.30	.10
❑ 434	Jose Vidro	.30	.10
❑ 435	Javier Vazquez	.30	.10
❑ 436	Michael Barrett	.30	.10
❑ 437	Fernando Tatis	.30	.10
❑ 438	Peter Bergeron	.30	.10
❑ 439	Endy Chavez	.30	.10
❑ 440	Orlando Hernandez	.30	.10
❑ 441	Marvin Benard	.30	.10
❑ 442	Rich Aurilia	.30	.10
❑ 443	Pedro Feliz	.30	.10
❑ 444	Robb Nen	.30	.10
❑ 445	Ray Durham	.30	.10
❑ 446	Marquis Grissom	.30	.10
❑ 447	Damian Moss	.30	.10
❑ 448	Edgardo Alfonzo	.30	.10
❑ 449	Juan Pierre	.30	.10
❑ 450	Braden Looper	.30	.10
❑ 451	Alex Gonzalez	.30	.10
❑ 452	Justin Wayne	.30	.10
❑ 453	Josh Beckett	.30	.10
❑ 454	Juan Encarnacion	.30	.10
❑ 455	Ivan Rodriguez	.50	.20
❑ 456	Todd Hollandsworth	.30	.10
❑ 457	Cliff Floyd	.30	.10
❑ 458	Rey Sanchez	.30	.10
❑ 459	Mike Piazza	1.25	.50
❑ 460	Mo Vaughn	.30	.10
❑ 461	Armando Benitez	.30	.10
❑ 462	Tsuyoshi Shinjo	.30	.10
❑ 463	Tom Glavine	.50	.20
❑ 464	David Cone	.30	.10
❑ 465	Phil Nevin	.30	.10
❑ 466	Sean Burroughs	.30	.10
❑ 467	Jake Peavy	.30	.10
❑ 468	Brian Lawrence	.30	.10
❑ 469	Mark Loretta	.30	.10
❑ 470	Dennis Tankersley	.30	.10
❑ 471	Jesse Orosco	.30	.10
❑ 472	Jim Thome	.50	.20
❑ 473	Kevin Millwood	.30	.10
❑ 474	David Bell	.30	.10
❑ 475	Pat Burrell	.30	.10
❑ 476	Brandon Duckworth	.30	.10
❑ 477	Jose Mesa	.30	.10
❑ 478	Marlon Byrd	.30	.10
❑ 479	Reggie Sanders	.30	.10
❑ 480	Jason Kendall	.30	.10
❑ 481	Aramis Ramirez	.30	.10
❑ 482	Kris Benson	.30	.10
❑ 483	Matt Stairs	.30	.10
❑ 484	Kevin Young	.30	.10
❑ 485	Kenny Lofton	.30	.10
❑ 486	Austin Kearns	.30	.10
❑ 487	Barry Larkin	.50	.20
❑ 488	Jason LaRue	.30	.10
❑ 489	Ken Griffey Jr.	1.25	.50
❑ 490	Danny Graves	.30	.10
❑ 491	Russell Branyan	.30	.10
❑ 492	Reggie Taylor	.30	.10
❑ 493	Jimmy Haynes	.30	.10
❑ 494	Charles Johnson	.30	.10
❑ 495	Todd Helton	.50	.20
❑ 496	Juan Uribe	.30	.10
❑ 497	Preston Wilson	.30	.10
❑ 498	Chris Stynes	.30	.10
❑ 499	Jason Jennings	.30	.10
❑ 500	Jay Payton	.30	.10
❑ 501	Hideki Matsui SR RC	5.00	2.00
❑ 502	Jose Contreras SR RC	1.50	.60
❑ 503	Brandon Webb SR RC	3.00	1.25
❑ 504	Robby Hammock SR RC	1.00	.40
❑ 505	Matt Kata SR RC	1.00	.40
❑ 506	Tim Olson SR RC	1.00	.40
❑ 507	Michael Hessman SR RC	1.00	.40
❑ 508	Jon Leicester SR RC	1.00	.40
❑ 509	Todd Wellemeyer SR RC	1.00	.40
❑ 510	David Sanders SR RC	1.00	.40
❑ 511	Josh Stewart SR RC	1.00	.40
❑ 512	Luis Ayala SR RC	1.00	.40
❑ 513	Clint Barmes SR RC	1.25	.50
❑ 514	Josh Willingham SR RC	2.00	.75
❑ 515	Alejandro Machado SR RC	1.00	.40
❑ 516	Felix Sanchez SR RC	1.00	.40
❑ 517	Willie Eyre SR RC	1.00	.40
❑ 518	Brent Hoard SR RC	1.00	.40
❑ 519	Lew Ford SR RC	1.50	.60
❑ 520	Terrmel Sledge SR RC	1.00	.40
❑ 521	Jeremy Griffiths SR RC	1.00	.40
❑ 522	Phil Seibel SR RC	1.00	.40
❑ 523	Craig Brazell SR RC	1.00	.40
❑ 524	Prentice Redman SR RC	1.00	.40
❑ 525	Jeff Duncan SR RC	1.00	.40
❑ 526	Shane Bazzell SR RC	1.00	.40
❑ 527	Bernie Castro SR RC	1.00	.40
❑ 528	Rett Johnson SR RC	1.00	.40
❑ 529	Bobby Madritsch SR RC	1.00	.40
❑ 530	Rocco Baldelli SR	1.00	.40
❑ 531	Alex Rodriguez SH CL	.75	.30
❑ 532	Eric Chavez SH CL	.30	.10
❑ 533	Miguel Tejada SH CL	.30	.10
❑ 534	Ichiro Suzuki SH CL	.75	.30
❑ 535	Sammy Sosa SH CL	.50	.20
❑ 536	Barry Zito SH CL	.30	.10
❑ 537	Darin Erstad SH CL	.30	.10
❑ 538	Alfonso Soriano SH CL	.30	.10
❑ 539	Troy Glaus SH CL	.30	.10
❑ 540	Nomar Garciaparra SH CL	.75	.30
❑ 541	Bo Hart RC	.50	.20
❑ 542	Dan Haren RC	.75	.30
❑ 543	Ryan Wagner RC	.50	.20
❑ 544	Rich Harden	.50	.20
❑ 545	Dontrelle Willis	.75	.30
❑ 546	Jerome Williams	.30	.10
❑ 547	Bobby Crosby	.30	.10
❑ 548	Greg Jones RC	.50	.20
❑ 549	Todd Linden	.30	.10
❑ 550	Byung-Hyun Kim	.30	.10
❑ 551	Rickie Weeks RC	3.00	1.25
❑ 552	Jason Roach RC	.50	.20
❑ 553	Oscar Villarreal RC	.50	.20
❑ 554	Justin Duchscherer	.30	.10
❑ 555	Chris Capuano RC	1.50	.60
❑ 556	Josh Hall RC	.50	.20
❑ 557	Luis Matos	.30	.10
❑ 558	Miguel Ojeda RC	.50	.20

❑ 559 Kevin Ohme RC .50 .20
❑ 560 Julio Manon RC .50 .20
❑ 561 Kevin Correia RC .50 .20
❑ 562 Delmon Young RC 5.00 2.00
❑ 563 Aaron Boone .30 .10
❑ 564 Aaron Looper RC .50 .20
❑ 565 Mike Neu RC .50 .20
❑ 566 Aquilino Lopez RC .50 .20
❑ 567 Jhonny Peralta .75 .30
❑ 568 Duaner Sanchez .30 .10
❑ 569 Stephen Randolph RC .50 .20
❑ 570 Nate Bland RC .50 .20
❑ 571 Chin-Hui Tsao .30 .10
❑ 572 Michel Hernandez RC .50 .20
❑ 573 Rocco Baldelli .30 .10
❑ 574 Robb Quinlan .30 .10
❑ 575 Aaron Heilman .30 .10
❑ 576 Jae Weong Seo .30 .10
❑ 577 Joe Borowski .30 .10
❑ 578 Chris Bootcheck .30 .10
❑ 579 Michael Ryan RC .50 .20
❑ 580 Mark Malaska RC .50 .20
❑ 581 Jose Guillen .30 .10
❑ 582 Josh Towers .30 .10
❑ 583 Tom Gregorio RC .50 .20
❑ 584 Edwin Jackson RC .50 .20
❑ 585 Jason Anderson .30 .10
❑ 586 Jose Reyes .30 .10
❑ 587 Miguel Cabrera .75 .30
❑ 588 Nate Bump .30 .10
❑ 589 Jeromy Burnitz .30 .10
❑ 590 David Ross .30 .10
❑ 591 Chase Utley .75 .30
❑ 592 Brandon Webb 1.50 .60
❑ 593 Masao Kida .30 .10
❑ 594 Jimmy Journell .30 .10
❑ 595 Eric Young .30 .10
❑ 596 Tony Womack .30 .10
❑ 597 Amaury Telemaco .30 .10
❑ 598 Rickey Henderson .75 .30
❑ 599 Esteban Loaiza .30 .10
❑ 600 Sidney Ponson .30 .10
❑ NNO Update Set Exchange Card

2004 Upper Deck

❑ COMPLETE SERIES 1 (270) 50.00 20.00
❑ COMPLETE SERIES 2 (270) 50.00 20.00
❑ COMP.UPDATE SET (50) 15.00 7.50
❑ COMMON (31-480/541-565) .30 .10
❑ COMMON (1-30/481-540) 1.00 .40
❑ COMMON CARD (566-590) .50 .20
❑ 541-590 ONE SET PER '05 UD1 HOBBY BOX
❑ UPDATE SET EXCH 1:480 '05 UD1 RETAIL
❑ UPDATE SET EXCH.DEADLINE TBD
❑ 1 Dontrelle Willis SR 1.50 .60
❑ 2 Edgar Gonzalez SR 1.00 .40
❑ 3 Jose Reyes SR 1.00 .40
❑ 4 Jae Weong Seo SR 1.00 .40
❑ 5 Miguel Cabrera SR 1.50 .60
❑ 6 Jesse Foppert SR 1.00 .40
❑ 7 Mike Neu SR 1.00 .40
❑ 8 Michael Nakamura SR 1.00 .40
❑ 9 Luis Ayala SR 1.00 .40
❑ 10 Jared Sandberg SR 1.00 .40
❑ 11 Jhonny Peralta SR 1.00 .40
❑ 12 Wil Ledezma SR 1.00 .40
❑ 13 Jason Roach SR 1.00 .40
❑ 14 Kirk Saarloos SR 1.00 .40
❑ 15 Cliff Lee SR 1.00 .40
❑ 16 Bobby Hill SR 1.00 .40
❑ 17 Lyle Overbay SR 1.00 .40
❑ 18 Josh Hall SR 1.00 .40
❑ 19 Joe Thurston SR 1.00 .40
❑ 20 Matt Kata SR 1.00 .40
❑ 21 Jeremy Bonderman SR 1.00 .40
❑ 22 Julio Manon SR 1.00 .40
❑ 23 Rodrigo Rosario SR 1.00 .40
❑ 24 Robby Hammock SR 1.00 .40
❑ 25 David Sanders SR 1.00 .40
❑ 26 Miguel Ojeda SR 1.00 .40
❑ 27 Mark Teixeira SR 1.50 .60
❑ 28 Franklyn German SR 1.00 .40
❑ 29 Ken Harvey SR 1.00 .40
❑ 30 Xavier Nady SR 1.00 .40
❑ 31 Tim Salmon .50 .20
❑ 32 Troy Glaus .30 .10
❑ 33 Adam Kennedy .30 .10
❑ 34 David Eckstein .30 .10
❑ 35 Ben Molina .30 .10
❑ 36 Jarrod Washburn .30 .10
❑ 37 Ramon Ortiz .30 .10
❑ 38 Eric Chavez .30 .10
❑ 39 Miguel Tejada .30 .10
❑ 40 Chris Singleton .30 .10
❑ 41 Jermaine Dye .30 .10
❑ 42 John Halama .30 .10
❑ 43 Tim Hudson .30 .10
❑ 44 Barry Zito .30 .10
❑ 45 Ted Lilly .30 .10
❑ 46 Bobby Kielty .30 .10
❑ 47 Kelvim Escobar .30 .10
❑ 48 Josh Phelps .30 .10
❑ 49 Vernon Wells .30 .10
❑ 50 Roy Halladay .30 .10
❑ 51 Orlando Hudson .30 .10
❑ 52 Eric Hinske .30 .10
❑ 53 Brandon Backe .30 .10
❑ 54 Dewon Brazelton .30 .10
❑ 55 Ben Grieve .30 .10
❑ 56 Aubrey Huff .30 .10
❑ 57 Toby Hall .30 .10
❑ 58 Rocco Baldelli .30 .10
❑ 59 Al Martin .30 .10
❑ 60 Brandon Phillips .30 .10
❑ 61 Omar Vizquel .50 .20
❑ 62 C.C. Sabathia .30 .10
❑ 63 Milton Bradley .30 .10
❑ 64 Ricky Gutierrez .30 .10
❑ 65 Matt Lawton .30 .10
❑ 66 Danys Baez .30 .10
❑ 67 Ichiro Suzuki 1.50 .60
❑ 68 Randy Winn .30 .10
❑ 69 Carlos Guillen .30 .10
❑ 70 Mark McLemore .30 .10
❑ 71 Dan Wilson .30 .10
❑ 72 Jamie Moyer .30 .10
❑ 73 Joel Pineiro .30 .10
❑ 74 Edgar Martinez .50 .20
❑ 75 Tony Batista .30 .10
❑ 76 Jay Gibbons .30 .10
❑ 77 Jeff Conine .30 .10
❑ 78 Melvin Mora .30 .10
❑ 79 Geronimo Gil .30 .10
❑ 80 Rodrigo Lopez .30 .10
❑ 81 Jorge Julio .30 .10
❑ 82 Rafael Palmeiro .50 .20
❑ 83 Juan Gonzalez .30 .10
❑ 84 Mike Young .30 .10
❑ 85 Alex Rodriguez 1.25 .50
❑ 86 Einar Diaz .30 .10
❑ 87 Kevin Mench .30 .10
❑ 88 Hank Blalock .30 .10
❑ 89 Pedro Martinez .50 .20
❑ 90 Byung-Hyun Kim .30 .10
❑ 91 Derek Lowe .30 .10
❑ 92 Jason Varitek .75 .30
❑ 93 Manny Ramirez .50 .20
❑ 94 John Burkett .30 .10
❑ 95 Todd Walker .30 .10
❑ 96 Nomar Garciaparra 1.25 .50
❑ 97 Trot Nixon .30 .10
❑ 98 Mike Sweeney .30 .10
❑ 99 Carlos Febles .30 .10
❑ 100 Mike MacDougal .30 .10
❑ 101 Raul Ibanez .30 .10
❑ 102 Jason Grimsley .30 .10
❑ 103 Chris George .30 .10
❑ 104 Brent Mayne .30 .10
❑ 105 Dmitri Young .30 .10
❑ 106 Eric Munson .30 .10
❑ 107 A.J. Hinch .30 .10
❑ 108 Andres Torres .30 .10
❑ 109 Bobby Higginson .30 .10
❑ 110 Shane Halter .30 .10
❑ 111 Matt Walbeck .30 .10
❑ 112 Torii Hunter .30 .10
❑ 113 Doug Mientkiewicz .30 .10
❑ 114 Lew Ford .30 .10
❑ 115 Eric Milton .30 .10
❑ 116 Eddie Guardado .30 .10
❑ 117 Cristian Guzman .30 .10
❑ 118 Corey Koskie .30 .10
❑ 119 Magglio Ordonez .30 .10
❑ 120 Mark Buehrle .30 .10
❑ 121 Billy Koch .30 .10
❑ 122 Jose Valentin .30 .10
❑ 123 Paul Konerko .30 .10
❑ 124 Carlos Lee .30 .10
❑ 125 Jon Garland .30 .10
❑ 126 Jason Giambi .30 .10
❑ 127 Derek Jeter 1.50 .60
❑ 128 Roger Clemens 1.50 .60
❑ 129 Andy Pettitte .50 .20
❑ 130 Jorge Posada .50 .20
❑ 131 David Wells .30 .10
❑ 132 Hideki Matsui 1.25 .50
❑ 133 Mike Mussina .50 .20
❑ 134 Jeff Bagwell .50 .20
❑ 135 Craig Biggio .50 .20
❑ 136 Morgan Ensberg .30 .10
❑ 137 Richard Hidalgo .30 .10
❑ 138 Brad Ausmus .30 .10
❑ 139 Roy Oswalt .30 .10
❑ 140 Billy Wagner .30 .10
❑ 141 Octavio Dotel .30 .10
❑ 142 Gary Sheffield .30 .10
❑ 143 Andruw Jones .50 .20
❑ 144 John Smoltz .50 .20
❑ 145 Rafael Furcal .30 .10
❑ 146 Javy Lopez .30 .10
❑ 147 Shane Reynolds .30 .10
❑ 148 Horacio Ramirez .30 .10
❑ 149 Mike Hampton .30 .10
❑ 150 Jung Bong .30 .10
❑ 151 Ruben Quevedo .30 .10
❑ 152 Ben Sheets .30 .10
❑ 153 Geoff Jenkins .30 .10
❑ 154 Royce Clayton .30 .10
❑ 155 Glendon Rusch .30 .10
❑ 156 John Vander Wal .30 .10
❑ 157 Scott Podsednik .30 .10
❑ 158 Jim Edmonds .30 .10
❑ 159 Tino Martinez .50 .20
❑ 160 Albert Pujols 1.50 .60
❑ 161 Matt Morris .30 .10
❑ 162 Woody Williams .30 .10
❑ 163 Edgar Renteria .30 .10
❑ 164 Jason Isringhausen .30 .10
❑ 165 Jason Simontacchi .30 .10
❑ 166 Kerry Robinson .30 .10
❑ 167 Sammy Sosa .75 .30
❑ 168 Joe Borowski .30 .10
❑ 169 Tony Womack .30 .10
❑ 170 Antonio Alfonseca .30 .10
❑ 171 Corey Patterson .30 .10
❑ 172 Mark Prior .50 .20
❑ 173 Moises Alou .30 .10
❑ 174 Matt Clement .30 .10
❑ 175 Randall Simon .30 .10
❑ 176 Randy Johnson .75 .30
❑ 177 Luis Gonzalez .30 .10
❑ 178 Craig Counsell .30 .10
❑ 179 Miguel Batista .30 .10
❑ 180 Steve Finley .30 .10
❑ 181 Brandon Webb .30 .10
❑ 182 Danny Bautista .30 .10
❑ 183 Oscar Villarreal .30 .10
❑ 184 Shawn Green .30 .10
❑ 185 Brian Jordan .30 .10
❑ 186 Fred McGriff .50 .20

❑ 187 Andy Ashby .30 .10
❑ 188 Rickey Henderson .75 .30
❑ 189 Dave Roberts .30 .10
❑ 190 Eric Gagne .30 .10
❑ 191 Kazuhisa Ishii .30 .10
❑ 192 Adrian Beltre .30 .10
❑ 193 Vladimir Guerrero .75 .30
❑ 194 Livan Hernandez .30 .10
❑ 195 Ron Calloway .30 .10
❑ 196 Sun Woo Kim .30 .10
❑ 197 Wil Cordero .30 .10
❑ 198 Brad Wilkerson .30 .10
❑ 199 Orlando Cabrera .30 .10
❑ 200 Barry Bonds 2.00 .75
❑ 201 Ray Durham .30 .10
❑ 202 Andres Galarraga .30 .10
❑ 203 Benito Santiago .30 .10
❑ 204 Jose Cruz Jr. .30 .10
❑ 205 Jason Schmidt .30 .10
❑ 206 Kirk Rueter .30 .10
❑ 207 Felix Rodriguez .30 .10
❑ 208 Mike Lowell .30 .10
❑ 209 Luis Castillo .30 .10
❑ 210 Derrek Lee .50 .20
❑ 211 Andy Fox .30 .10
❑ 212 Tommy Phelps .30 .10
❑ 213 Todd Hollandsworth .30 .10
❑ 214 Brad Penny .30 .10
❑ 215 Juan Pierre .30 .10
❑ 216 Mike Piazza 1.25 .50
❑ 217 Jae Weong Seo .30 .10
❑ 218 Ty Wigginton .30 .10
❑ 219 Al Leiter .30 .10
❑ 220 Roger Cedeno .30 .10
❑ 221 Timo Perez .30 .10
❑ 222 Aaron Heilman .30 .10
❑ 223 Pedro Astacio .30 .10
❑ 224 Joe McEwing .30 .10
❑ 225 Ryan Klesko .30 .10
❑ 226 Brian Giles .30 .10
❑ 227 Mark Kotsay .30 .10
❑ 228 Brian Lawrence .30 .10
❑ 229 Rod Beck .30 .10
❑ 230 Trevor Hoffman .30 .10
❑ 231 Sean Burroughs .30 .10
❑ 232 Bob Abreu .30 .10
❑ 233 Jim Thome .50 .20
❑ 234 David Bell .30 .10
❑ 235 Jimmy Rollins .30 .10
❑ 236 Mike Lieberthal .30 .10
❑ 237 Vicente Padilla .30 .10
❑ 238 Randy Wolf .30 .10
❑ 239 Reggie Sanders .30 .10
❑ 240 Jason Kendall .30 .10
❑ 241 Jack Wilson .30 .10
❑ 242 Jose Hernandez .30 .10
❑ 243 Kip Wells .30 .10
❑ 244 Carlos Rivera .30 .10
❑ 245 Craig Wilson .30 .10
❑ 246 Adam Dunn .30 .10
❑ 247 Sean Casey .30 .10
❑ 248 Danny Graves .30 .10
❑ 249 Ryan Dempster .30 .10
❑ 250 Barry Larkin .50 .20
❑ 251 Reggie Taylor .30 .10
❑ 252 Wily Mo Pena .30 .10
❑ 253 Larry Walker .30 .10
❑ 254 Mark Sweeney .30 .10
❑ 255 Preston Wilson .30 .10
❑ 256 Jason Jennings .30 .10
❑ 257 Charles Johnson .30 .10
❑ 258 Jay Payton .30 .10
❑ 259 Chris Stynes .30 .10
❑ 260 Juan Uribe .30 .10
❑ 261 Hideki Matsui SH CL .75 .30
❑ 262 Barry Bonds SH CL 1.00 .40
❑ 263 Dontrelle Willis SH CL .30 .10
❑ 264 Kevin Millwood SH CL .30 .10
❑ 265 Billy Wagner SH CL .30 .10
❑ 266 Rocco Baldelli SH CL .30 .10
❑ 267 Roger Clemens SH CL .75 .30
❑ 268 Rafael Palmeiro SH CL .30 .10
❑ 269 Miguel Cabrera SH CL .50 .20
❑ 270 Jose Contreras SH CL .30 .10
❑ 271 Aaron Sele .30 .10
❑ 272 Bartolo Colon .30 .10
❑ 273 Darin Erstad .30 .10
❑ 274 Francisco Rodriguez .30 .10
❑ 275 Garret Anderson .30 .10
❑ 276 Jose Guillen .30 .10
❑ 277 Troy Percival .30 .10
❑ 278 Alex Cintron .30 .10
❑ 279 Casey Fossum .30 .10
❑ 280 Elmer Dessens .30 .10
❑ 281 Jose Valverde .30 .10
❑ 282 Matt Mantei .30 .10
❑ 283 Richie Sexson .30 .10
❑ 284 Roberto Alomar .50 .20
❑ 285 Shea Hillenbrand .30 .10
❑ 286 Chipper Jones .75 .30
❑ 287 Greg Maddux 1.25 .50
❑ 288 J.D. Drew .30 .10
❑ 289 Marcus Giles .30 .10
❑ 290 Mike Hessman .30 .10
❑ 291 John Thomson .30 .10
❑ 292 Russ Ortiz .30 .10
❑ 293 Adam Loewen .30 .10
❑ 294 Jack Cust .30 .10
❑ 295 Jerry Hairston Jr. .30 .10
❑ 296 Kurt Ainsworth .30 .10
❑ 297 Luis Matos .30 .10
❑ 298 Marty Cordova .30 .10
❑ 299 Sidney Ponson .30 .10
❑ 300 Bill Mueller .30 .10
❑ 301 Curt Schilling .30 .10
❑ 302 David Ortiz .50 .20
❑ 303 Johnny Damon .50 .20
❑ 304 Keith Foulke Sox .30 .10
❑ 305 Pokey Reese .30 .10
❑ 306 Scott Williamson .30 .10
❑ 307 Tim Wakefield .30 .10
❑ 308 Alex S. Gonzalez .30 .10
❑ 309 Aramis Ramirez .30 .10
❑ 310 Carlos Zambrano .30 .10
❑ 311 Juan Cruz .30 .10
❑ 312 Kerry Wood .30 .10
❑ 313 Kyle Farnsworth .30 .10
❑ 314 Aaron Rowand .30 .10
❑ 315 Esteban Loaiza .30 .10
❑ 316 Frank Thomas .75 .30
❑ 317 Joe Borchard .30 .10
❑ 318 Joe Crede .30 .10
❑ 319 Miguel Olivo .30 .10
❑ 320 Willie Harris .30 .10
❑ 321 Aaron Harang .30 .10
❑ 322 Austin Kearns .30 .10
❑ 323 Brandon Claussen .30 .10
❑ 324 Brandon Larson .30 .10
❑ 325 Ryan Freel .30 .10
❑ 326 Ken Griffey Jr. 1.25 .50
❑ 327 Ryan Wagner .30 .10
❑ 328 Alex Escobar .30 .10
❑ 329 Coco Crisp .30 .10
❑ 330 David Riske .30 .10
❑ 331 Jody Gerut .30 .10
❑ 332 Josh Bard .30 .10
❑ 333 Travis Hafner .30 .10
❑ 334 Chin-Hui Tsao .30 .10
❑ 335 Denny Stark .30 .10
❑ 336 Jeromy Burnitz .30 .10
❑ 337 Shawn Chacon .30 .10
❑ 338 Todd Helton .50 .20
❑ 339 Vinny Castilla .30 .10
❑ 340 Alex Sanchez .30 .10
❑ 341 Carlos Pena .30 .10
❑ 342 Fernando Vina .30 .10
❑ 343 Jason Johnson .30 .10
❑ 344 Matt Anderson .30 .10
❑ 345 Mike Maroth .30 .10
❑ 346 Rondell White .30 .10
❑ 347 A.J. Burnett .30 .10
❑ 348 Alex Gonzalez .30 .10
❑ 349 Armando Benitez .30 .10
❑ 350 Carl Pavano .30 .10
❑ 351 Hee Seop Choi .30 .10
❑ 352 Ivan Rodriguez .50 .20
❑ 353 Josh Beckett .30 .10
❑ 354 Josh Willingham .30 .10
❑ 355 Adam Everett .30 .10
❑ 356 Brandon Duckworth .30 .10
❑ 357 Jason Lane .30 .10
❑ 358 Jeff Kent .30 .10
❑ 359 Jeriome Robertson .30 .10
❑ 360 Lance Berkman .30 .10
❑ 361 Wade Miller .30 .10
❑ 362 Aaron Guiel .30 .10
❑ 363 Angel Berroa .30 .10
❑ 364 Carlos Beltran .30 .10
❑ 365 David DeJesus .30 .10
❑ 366 Desi Relaford .30 .10
❑ 367 Joe Randa .30 .10
❑ 368 Runelvys Hernandez .30 .10
❑ 369 Edwin Jackson .30 .10
❑ 370 Hideo Nomo .75 .30
❑ 371 Jeff Weaver .30 .10
❑ 372 Juan Encarnacion .30 .10
❑ 373 Odalis Perez .30 .10
❑ 374 Paul Lo Duca .30 .10
❑ 375 Robin Ventura .30 .10
❑ 376 Bill Hall .30 .10
❑ 377 Chad Moeller .30 .10
❑ 378 Chris Capuano .30 .10
❑ 379 Junior Spivey .30 .10
❑ 380 Rickie Weeks .30 .10
❑ 381 Wes Helms .30 .10
❑ 382 Brad Radke .30 .10
❑ 383 Jacque Jones .30 .10
❑ 384 Joe Mays .30 .10
❑ 385 Joe Nathan .30 .10
❑ 386 Johan Santana .75 .30
❑ 387 Nick Punto .30 .10
❑ 388 Shannon Stewart .30 .10
❑ 389 Carl Everett .30 .10
❑ 390 Claudio Vargas .30 .10
❑ 391 Jose Vidro .30 .10
❑ 392 Nick Johnson .30 .10
❑ 393 Rocky Biddle .30 .10
❑ 394 Tony Armas Jr. .30 .10
❑ 395 Braden Looper .30 .10
❑ 396 Cliff Floyd .30 .10
❑ 397 Jason Phillips .30 .10
❑ 398 Mike Cameron .30 .10
❑ 399 Tom Glavine .50 .20
❑ 400 Kenny Lofton .30 .10
❑ 401 Alfonso Soriano .30 .10
❑ 402 Bernie Williams .50 .20
❑ 403 Javier Vazquez .30 .10
❑ 404 Jon Lieber .30 .10
❑ 405 Jose Contreras .30 .10
❑ 406 Kevin Brown .30 .10
❑ 407 Mariano Rivera .75 .30
❑ 408 Arthur Rhodes .30 .10
❑ 409 Eric Byrnes .30 .10
❑ 410 Erubiel Durazo .30 .10
❑ 411 Graham Koonce .30 .10
❑ 412 Marco Scutaro .30 .10
❑ 413 Mark Mulder .30 .10
❑ 414 Mark Redman .30 .10
❑ 415 Rich Harden .30 .10
❑ 416 Brett Myers .30 .10
❑ 417 Chase Utley .50 .20
❑ 418 Kevin Millwood .30 .10
❑ 419 Marlon Byrd .30 .10
❑ 420 Pat Burrell .30 .10
❑ 421 Placido Polanco .30 .10
❑ 422 Tim Worrell .30 .10
❑ 423 Jason Bay .30 .10
❑ 424 Josh Fogg .30 .10
❑ 425 Kris Benson .30 .10
❑ 426 Mike Gonzalez .30 .10
❑ 427 Oliver Perez .30 .10
❑ 428 Tike Redman .30 .10
❑ 429 Adam Eaton .30 .10
❑ 430 Ismael Valdes .30 .10
❑ 431 Jake Peavy .30 .10
❑ 432 Khalil Greene .50 .20
❑ 433 Mark Loretta .30 .10
❑ 434 Phil Nevin .30 .10
❑ 435 Ramon Hernandez .30 .10
❑ 436 A.J. Pierzynski .30 .10
❑ 437 Edgardo Alfonzo .30 .10
❑ 438 J.T. Snow .30 .10
❑ 439 Jerome Williams .30 .10
❑ 440 Marquis Grissom .30 .10
❑ 441 Robb Nen .30 .10
❑ 442 Bret Boone .30 .10
❑ 443 Freddy Garcia .30 .10
❑ 444 Gil Meche .30 .10

❑ 445 John Olerud .30 .10
❑ 446 Rich Aurilia .30 .10
❑ 447 Shigetoshi Hasegawa .30 .10
❑ 448 Bo Hart .30 .10
❑ 449 Danny Haren .30 .10
❑ 450 Jason Marquis .30 .10
❑ 451 Marlon Anderson .30 .10
❑ 452 Scott Rolen .50 .20
❑ 453 So Taguchi .30 .10
❑ 454 Carl Crawford .30 .10
❑ 455 Delmon Young .50 .20
❑ 456 Geoff Blum .30 .10
❑ 457 Jesus Colome .30 .10
❑ 458 Jonny Gomes .30 .10
❑ 459 Lance Carter .30 .10
❑ 460 Robert Fick .30 .10
❑ 461 Chan Ho Park .30 .10
❑ 462 Francisco Cordero .30 .10
❑ 463 Jeff Nelson .30 .10
❑ 464 Jeff Zimmerman .30 .10
❑ 465 Kenny Rogers .30 .10
❑ 466 Aquilino Lopez .30 .10
❑ 467 Carlos Delgado .30 .10
❑ 468 Frank Catalanotto .30 .10
❑ 469 Reed Johnson .30 .10
❑ 470 Pat Hentgen .30 .10
❑ 471 Curt Schilling SH CL .30 .10
❑ 472 Gary Sheffield SH CL .30 .10
❑ 473 Javier Vazquez SH CL .30 .10
❑ 474 Kazuo Matsui SH CL .50 .20
❑ 475 Kevin Brown SH CL .30 .10
❑ 476 Rafael Palmeiro SH CL .30 .10
❑ 477 Richie Sexson SH CL .30 .10
❑ 478 Roger Clemens SH CL .75 .30
❑ 479 Vladimir Guerrero SH CL .50 .20
❑ 480 Alex Rodriguez SH CL .75 .30
❑ 481 Jake Woods SR RC 1.00 .40
❑ 482 Tim Bittner SR RC 1.00 .40
❑ 483 Brandon Medders SR RC 1.00 .40
❑ 484 Casey Daigle SR RC 1.00 .40
❑ 485 Jerry Gil SR RC 1.00 .40
❑ 486 Mike Gosling SR RC 1.00 .40
❑ 487 Jose Capellan SR RC 1.50 .60
❑ 488 Onil Joseph SR RC 1.00 .40
❑ 489 Roman Colon SR RC 1.00 .40
❑ 490 Dave Crouthers SR RC 1.00 .40
❑ 491 Eddy Rodriguez SR RC 1.50 .60
❑ 492 Franklyn Gracesqui SR RC 1.00 .40
❑ 493 Jamie Brown SR RC 1.00 .40
❑ 494 Jerome Gamble SR RC 1.00 .40
❑ 495 Tim Hamulack SR RC 1.00 .40
❑ 496 Carlos Vasquez SR RC 1.50 .60
❑ 497 Renyel Pinto SR RC 1.50 .60
❑ 498 Ronny Cedeno SR RC 2.00 .75
❑ 499 Enemencio Pacheco SR RC 1.00 .40
❑ 500 Ryan Meaux SR RC 1.00 .40
❑ 501 Ryan Wing SR RC 1.00 .40
❑ 502 Shingo Takatsu SR RC 1.50 .60
❑ 503 William Bergolla SR RC 1.00 .40
❑ 504 Ivan Ochoa SR RC 1.00 .40
❑ 505 Mariano Gomez SR RC 1.00 .40
❑ 506 Justin Hampson SR RC 1.00 .40
❑ 507 Justin Huisman SR RC 1.00 .40
❑ 508 Scott Dohmann SR RC 1.00 .40
❑ 509 Donnie Kelly SR RC 1.00 .40
❑ 510 Chris Aguila SR RC 1.00 .40
❑ 511 Lincoln Holdzkom SR RC 1.00 .40
❑ 512 Freddy Guzman SR RC 1.00 .40
❑ 513 Hector Gimenez SR RC 1.00 .40
❑ 514 Jorge Vasquez SR RC 1.00 .40
❑ 515 Jason Frasor SR RC 1.00 .40
❑ 516 Chris Saenz SR RC 1.00 .40
❑ 517 Dennis Sarfate SR RC 1.00 .40
❑ 518 Colby Miller SR RC 1.00 .40
❑ 519 Jason Bartlett SR RC 1.50 .60
❑ 520 Chad Bentz SR RC 1.00 .40
❑ 521 Josh Labandeira SR RC 1.00 .40
❑ 522 Shawn Hill SR RC 1.00 .40
❑ 523 Kazuo Matsui SR RC 1.50 .60
❑ 524 Carlos Hines SR RC 1.00 .40
❑ 525 Mike Vento SR RC 1.50 .60
❑ 526 Scott Proctor SR RC 1.50 .60
❑ 527 Sean Henn SR RC 1.00 .40
❑ 528 David Aardsma SR RC 1.50 .60
❑ 529 Ian Snell SR RC 2.00 .75
❑ 530 Mike Johnston SR RC 1.00 .40
❑ 531 Akinori Otsuka SR RC 1.00 .40
❑ 532 Rusty Tucker SR RC 1.50 .60
❑ 533 Justin Knoedler SR RC 1.00 .40
❑ 534 Merkin Valdez SR RC 1.50 .60
❑ 535 Greg Dobbs SR RC 1.00 .40
❑ 536 Justin Leone SR RC 1.50 .60
❑ 537 Shawn Camp SR RC 1.00 .40
❑ 538 Edwin Moreno SR RC 1.00 .40
❑ 539 Angel Chavez SR RC 1.00 .40
❑ 540 Jesse Harper SR RC 1.00 .40
❑ 541 Alex Rodriguez 1.25 .50
❑ 542 Roger Clemens 1.50 .60
❑ 543 Andy Pettitte .50 .20
❑ 544 Vladimir Guerrero .75 .30
❑ 545 David Wells .30 .10
❑ 546 Derrek Lee .50 .20
❑ 547 Carlos Beltran .30 .10
❑ 548 Orlando Cabrera Sox .30 .10
❑ 549 Paul Lo Duca .30 .10
❑ 550 Dave Roberts .30 .10
❑ 551 Guillermo Mota .30 .10
❑ 552 Steve Finley .30 .10
❑ 553 Juan Encarnacion .30 .10
❑ 554 Larry Walker .30 .10
❑ 555 Ty Wigginton .30 .10
❑ 556 Doug Mientkiewicz .30 .10
❑ 557 Roberto Alomar .50 .20
❑ 558 B.J. Upton .50 .20
❑ 559 Brad Penny .30 .10
❑ 560 Hee Seop Choi .30 .10
❑ 561 David Wright 3.00 1.25
❑ 562 Nomar Garciaparra 1.25 .50
❑ 563 Felix Rodriguez .30 .10
❑ 564 Victor Zambrano .30 .10
❑ 565 Kris Benson .30 .10
❑ 566 Aarom Baldiris SR RC .50 .20
❑ 567 Joey Gathright SR RC 1.00 .40
❑ 568 Charles Thomas SR RC .50 .20
❑ 569 Brian Dallimore SR RC .50 .20
❑ 570 Chris Oxspring SR RC .50 .20
❑ 571 Chris Shelton SR RC 2.00 .75
❑ 572 Dioner Navarro SR RC 1.25 .50
❑ 573 Edwardo Sierra SR RC .50 .20
❑ 574 Fernando Nieve SR RC .75 .30
❑ 575 Frank Francisco SR RC .50 .20
❑ 576 Jeff Bennett SR RC .50 .20
❑ 577 Justin Lehr SR RC .50 .20
❑ 578 John Gall SR RC .50 .20
❑ 579 Jorge Sequea SR RC .50 .20
❑ 580 Justin Germano SR RC .50 .20
❑ 581 Kazuhito Tadano SR RC .50 .20
❑ 582 Kevin Cave SR RC .50 .20
❑ 583 Jesse Crain SR RC .75 .30
❑ 584 Luis A. Gonzalez SR RC .50 .20
❑ 585 Michael Wuertz SR RC .50 .20
❑ 586 Orlando Rodriguez SR RC .50 .20
❑ 587 Phil Stockman SR RC .50 .20
❑ 588 Ramon Ramirez SR RC .50 .20
❑ 589 Roberto Novoa SR RC .50 .20
❑ 590 Scott Kazmir SR RC 4.00 1.50
❑ NNO Update Set Exchange Card

2005 Upper Deck

❑ COMPLETE SERIES 1 (300) 50.00 30.00
❑ COMMON CARD (1-500) .30 .10
❑ COMMON (211-250/426-450) 1.00 .40
❑ OVERALL PLATES SER.1 ODDS 1:1080 H
❑ PLATES PRINT RUN 1 #'d SET PER COLOR
❑ BLACK-CYAN-MAGENTA-YELLOW ISSUED
❑ NO PLATES PRICING DUE TO SCARCITY
❑ 1 Casey Kotchman .30 .10
❑ 2 Chone Figgins .30 .10
❑ 3 David Eckstein .30 .10
❑ 4 Jarrod Washburn .30 .10
❑ 5 Robb Quinlan .30 .10
❑ 6 Troy Glaus .30 .10
❑ 7 Vladimir Guerrero .75 .30
❑ 8 Brandon Webb .30 .10
❑ 9 Danny Bautista .30 .10
❑ 10 Luis Gonzalez .30 .10
❑ 11 Matt Kata .30 .10
❑ 12 Randy Johnson .75 .30
❑ 13 Robby Hammock .30 .10
❑ 14 Shea Hillenbrand .30 .10
❑ 15 Adam LaRoche .30 .10
❑ 16 Andruw Jones .50 .20
❑ 17 Horacio Ramirez .30 .10
❑ 18 John Smoltz .50 .20
❑ 19 Johnny Estrada .30 .10
❑ 20 Mike Hampton .30 .10
❑ 21 Rafael Furcal .30 .10
❑ 22 Brian Roberts .30 .10
❑ 23 Javy Lopez .30 .10
❑ 24 Jay Gibbons .30 .10
❑ 25 Jorge Julio .30 .10
❑ 26 Melvin Mora .30 .10
❑ 27 Miguel Tejada .30 .10
❑ 28 Rafael Palmeiro .50 .20
❑ 29 Derek Lowe .30 .10
❑ 30 Jason Varitek .75 .30
❑ 31 Kevin Youkilis .30 .10
❑ 32 Manny Ramirez .50 .20
❑ 33 Curt Schilling .50 .20
❑ 34 Pedro Martinez .50 .20
❑ 35 Trot Nixon .30 .10
❑ 36 Corey Patterson .30 .10
❑ 37 Derrek Lee .50 .20
❑ 38 LaTroy Hawkins .30 .10
❑ 39 Mark Prior .50 .20
❑ 40 Matt Clement .30 .10
❑ 41 Moises Alou .30 .10
❑ 42 Sammy Sosa .75 .30
❑ 43 Aaron Rowand .30 .10
❑ 44 Carlos Lee .30 .10
❑ 45 Jose Valentin .30 .10
❑ 46 Juan Uribe .30 .10
❑ 47 Magglio Ordonez .30 .10
❑ 48 Mark Buehrle .30 .10
❑ 49 Paul Konerko .30 .10
❑ 50 Adam Dunn .30 .10
❑ 51 Barry Larkin .50 .20
❑ 52 D'Angelo Jimenez .30 .10
❑ 53 Danny Graves .30 .10
❑ 54 Paul Wilson .30 .10
❑ 55 Sean Casey .30 .10
❑ 56 Wily Mo Pena .30 .10
❑ 57 Ben Broussard .30 .10
❑ 58 C.C. Sabathia .30 .10
❑ 59 Casey Blake .30 .10
❑ 60 Cliff Lee .30 .10
❑ 61 Matt Lawton .30 .10
❑ 62 Omar Vizquel .30 .10
❑ 63 Victor Martinez .30 .10
❑ 64 Charles Johnson .30 .10
❑ 65 Joe Kennedy .30 .10
❑ 66 Jeromy Burnitz .30 .10
❑ 67 Matt Holliday .30 .10
❑ 68 Preston Wilson .30 .10
❑ 69 Royce Clayton .30 .10
❑ 70 Shawn Estes .30 .10
❑ 71 Bobby Higginson .30 .10
❑ 72 Brandon Inge .30 .10
❑ 73 Carlos Guillen .30 .10
❑ 74 Dmitri Young .30 .10
❑ 75 Eric Munson .30 .10
❑ 76 Jeremy Bonderman .30 .10
❑ 77 Ugueth Urbina .30 .10
❑ 78 Josh Beckett .30 .10
❑ 79 Dontrelle Willis .30 .10
❑ 80 Jeff Conine .30 .10
❑ 81 Juan Pierre .30 .10
❑ 82 Luis Castillo .30 .10
❑ 83 Miguel Cabrera .50 .20
❑ 84 Mike Lowell .30 .10

❑ 85 Andy Pettitte .50 .20
❑ 86 Brad Lidge .30 .10
❑ 87 Carlos Beltran .30 .10
❑ 88 Craig Biggio .50 .20
❑ 89 Jeff Bagwell .50 .20
❑ 90 Roger Clemens 1.25 .50
❑ 91 Roy Oswalt .30 .10
❑ 92 Benito Santiago .30 .10
❑ 93 Jeremy Affeldt .30 .10
❑ 94 Juan Gonzalez .30 .10
❑ 95 Ken Harvey .30 .10
❑ 96 Mike MacDougal .30 .10
❑ 97 Mike Sweeney .30 .10
❑ 98 Zack Greinke .30 .10
❑ 99 Adrian Beltre .30 .10
❑ 100 Alex Cora .30 .10
❑ 101 Cesar Izturis .30 .10
❑ 102 Eric Gagne .30 .10
❑ 103 Kazuhisa Ishii .30 .10
❑ 104 Milton Bradley .30 .10
❑ 105 Shawn Green .30 .10
❑ 106 Danny Kolb .30 .10
❑ 107 Ben Sheets .30 .10
❑ 108 Brooks Kieschnick .30 .10
❑ 109 Craig Counsell .30 .10
❑ 110 Geoff Jenkins .30 .10
❑ 111 Lyle Overbay .30 .10
❑ 112 Scott Podsednik .30 .10
❑ 113 Corey Koskie .30 .10
❑ 114 Johan Santana .75 .30
❑ 115 Joe Mauer .75 .30
❑ 116 Justin Morneau .30 .10
❑ 117 Lew Ford .30 .10
❑ 118 Matt LeCroy .30 .10
❑ 119 Torii Hunter .30 .10
❑ 120 Brad Wilkerson .30 .10
❑ 121 Chad Cordero .30 .10
❑ 122 Livan Hernandez .30 .10
❑ 123 Jose Vidro .30 .10
❑ 124 Termel Sledge .30 .10
❑ 125 Tony Batista .30 .10
❑ 126 Zach Day .30 .10
❑ 127 Al Leiter .30 .10
❑ 128 Jae Weong Seo .30 .10
❑ 129 Jose Reyes .30 .10
❑ 130 Kazuo Matsui .30 .10
❑ 131 Mike Piazza .75 .30
❑ 132 Todd Zeile .30 .10
❑ 133 Cliff Floyd .30 .10
❑ 134 Alex Rodriguez 1.25 .50
❑ 135 Derek Jeter 1.50 .60
❑ 136 Gary Sheffield .30 .10
❑ 137 Hideki Matsui 1.25 .50
❑ 138 Jason Giambi .30 .10
❑ 139 Jorge Posada .50 .20
❑ 140 Mike Mussina .50 .20
❑ 141 Barry Zito .30 .10
❑ 142 Bobby Crosby .30 .10
❑ 143 Octavio Dotel .30 .10
❑ 144 Eric Chavez .30 .10
❑ 145 Jermaine Dye .30 .10
❑ 146 Mark Kotsay .30 .10
❑ 147 Tim Hudson .30 .10
❑ 148 Billy Wagner .30 .10
❑ 149 Bobby Abreu .30 .10
❑ 150 David Bell .30 .10
❑ 151 Jim Thome .50 .20
❑ 152 Jimmy Rollins .30 .10
❑ 153 Mike Lieberthal .30 .10
❑ 154 Randy Wolf .30 .10
❑ 155 Craig Wilson .30 .10
❑ 156 Daryle Ward .30 .10
❑ 157 Jack Wilson .30 .10
❑ 158 Jason Kendall .30 .10
❑ 159 Kip Wells .30 .10
❑ 160 Oliver Perez .30 .10
❑ 161 Rob Mackowiak .30 .10
❑ 162 Brian Giles .30 .10
❑ 163 Brian Lawrence .30 .10
❑ 164 David Wells .30 .10
❑ 165 Jay Payton .30 .10
❑ 166 Ryan Klesko .30 .10
❑ 167 Sean Burroughs .30 .10
❑ 168 Trevor Hoffman .30 .10
❑ 169 Brett Tomko .30 .10
❑ 170 J.T. Snow .30 .10
❑ 171 Jason Schmidt .30 .10
❑ 172 Kirk Rueter .30 .10
❑ 173 A.J. Pierzynski .30 .10
❑ 174 Pedro Feliz .30 .10
❑ 175 Ray Durham .30 .10
❑ 176 Eddie Guardado .30 .10
❑ 177 Edgar Martinez .50 .20
❑ 178 Ichiro Suzuki 1.50 .60
❑ 179 Jamie Moyer .30 .10
❑ 180 Joel Pineiro .30 .10
❑ 181 Randy Winn .30 .10
❑ 182 Raul Ibanez .30 .10
❑ 183 Albert Pujols 1.50 .60
❑ 184 Edgar Renteria .30 .10
❑ 185 Jason Isringhausen .30 .10
❑ 186 Jim Edmonds .30 .10
❑ 187 Matt Morris .30 .10
❑ 188 Reggie Sanders .30 .10
❑ 189 Tony Womack .30 .10
❑ 190 Aubrey Huff .30 .10
❑ 191 Danys Baez .30 .10
❑ 192 Carl Crawford .30 .10
❑ 193 Jose Cruz Jr. .30 .10
❑ 194 Rocco Baldelli .30 .10
❑ 195 Tino Martinez .50 .20
❑ 196 Dewon Brazelton .30 .10
❑ 197 Alfonso Soriano .30 .10
❑ 198 Brad Fullmer .30 .10
❑ 199 Gerald Laird .30 .10
❑ 200 Hank Blalock .30 .10
❑ 201 Laynce Nix .30 .10
❑ 202 Mark Teixeira .50 .20
❑ 203 Michael Young .30 .10
❑ 204 Alexis Rios .30 .10
❑ 205 Eric Hinske .30 .10
❑ 206 Miguel Batista .30 .10
❑ 207 Orlando Hudson .30 .10
❑ 208 Roy Halladay .30 .10
❑ 209 Ted Lilly .30 .10
❑ 210 Vernon Wells .30 .10
❑ 211 Aarom Baldiris SR 1.00 .40
❑ 212 B.J. Upton SR 1.00 .40
❑ 213 Dallas McPherson SR 1.00 .40
❑ 214 Brian Dallimore SR 1.00 .40
❑ 215 Chris Oxspring SR 1.00 .40
❑ 216 Chris Shelton SR 1.50 .60
❑ 217 David Wright SR 2.00 .75
❑ 218 Edwardo Sierra SR 1.00 .40
❑ 219 Fernando Nieve SR 1.00 .40
❑ 220 Frank Francisco SR 1.00 .40
❑ 221 Jeff Bennett SR 1.00 .40
❑ 222 Justin Lehr SR 1.00 .40
❑ 223 John Gall SR 1.00 .40
❑ 224 Jorge Sequea SR 1.00 .40
❑ 225 Justin Germano SR 1.00 .40
❑ 226 Kazuhito Tadano SR 1.00 .40
❑ 227 Kevin Cave SR 1.00 .40
❑ 228 Joe Blanton SR 1.00 .40
❑ 229 Luis A. Gonzalez SR 1.00 .40
❑ 230 Michael Wuertz SR 1.00 .40
❑ 231 Mike Rouse SR 1.00 .40
❑ 232 Nick Regilio SR 1.00 .40
❑ 233 Orlando Rodriguez SR 1.00 .40
❑ 234 Phil Stockman SR 1.00 .40
❑ 235 Ramon Ramirez SR 1.00 .40
❑ 236 Roberto Novoa SR 1.00 .40
❑ 237 Dioner Navarro SR 1.00 .40
❑ 238 Tim Bausher SR 1.00 .40
❑ 239 Logan Kensing SR 1.00 .40
❑ 240 Andy Green SR 1.00 .40
❑ 241 Brad Halsey SR 1.00 .40
❑ 242 Charles Thomas SR 1.00 .40
❑ 243 George Sherrill SR 1.00 .40
❑ 244 Jesse Crain SR 1.00 .40
❑ 245 Jimmy Serrano SR 1.00 .40
❑ 246 Joe Horgan SR 1.00 .40
❑ 247 Chris Young SR 1.00 .40
❑ 248 Joey Gathright SR 1.00 .40
❑ 249 Gavin Floyd SR 1.00 .40
❑ 250 Ryan Howard SR 5.00 2.00
❑ 251 Lance Cormier SR 1.00 .40
❑ 252 Matt Treanor SR 1.00 .40
❑ 253 Jeff Francis SR 1.00 .40
❑ 254 Nick Swisher SR 1.00 .40
❑ 255 Scott Atchison SR 1.00 .40
❑ 256 Travis Blackley SR 1.00 .40
❑ 257 Travis Smith SR 1.00 .40
❑ 258 Yadier Molina SR 1.00 .40
❑ 259 Jeff Keppinger SR 1.00 .40
❑ 260 Scott Kazmir SR 1.00 .40
❑ 261 G.Anderson/V.Guerrero TL .50 .20
❑ 262 L.Gonzalez/R.Johnson TL .50 .20
❑ 263 A.Jones/C.Jones TL .50 .20
❑ 264 M.Tejada/R.Palmeiro TL .30 .10
❑ 265 C.Schilling/M.Ramirez TL .50 .20
❑ 266 M.Prior/S.Sosa TL .50 .20
❑ 267 F.Thomas/M.Ordonez TL .50 .20
❑ 268 B.Larkin/K.Griffey Jr. TL .75 .30
❑ 269 C.Sabathia/V.Martinez TL .30 .10
❑ 270 J.Burnitz/T.Helton TL .30 .10
❑ 271 D.Young/I.Rodriguez TL .30 .10
❑ 272 J.Beckett/M.Cabrera TL .30 .10
❑ 273 J.Bagwell/R.Clemens TL .75 .30
❑ 274 K.Harvey/M.Sweeney TL .30 .10
❑ 275 A.Beltre/E.Gagne TL .30 .10
❑ 276 B.Sheets/G.Jenkins TL .30 .10
❑ 277 J.Mauer/T.Hunter TL .50 .20
❑ 278 J.Vidro/L.Hernandez TL .30 .10
❑ 279 K.Matsui/M.Piazza TL .50 .20
❑ 280 A.Rodriguez/D.Jeter TL 1.50 .60
❑ 281 E.Chavez/T.Hudson TL .30 .10
❑ 282 B.Abreu/J.Thome TL .30 .10
❑ 283 C.Wilson/J.Kendall TL .30 .10
❑ 284 B.Giles/P.Nevin TL .30 .10
❑ 285 A.Pierzynski/J.Schmidt TL .30 .10
❑ 286 B.Boone/I.Suzuki TL .75 .30
❑ 287 A.Pujols/S.Rolen TL .75 .30
❑ 288 A.Huff/T.Martinez TL .30 .10
❑ 289 H.Blalock/M.Teixeira TL .30 .10
❑ 290 C.Delgado/R.Halladay TL .30 .10
❑ 291 Vladimir Guerrero PR .50 .20
❑ 292 Curt Schilling PR .30 .10
❑ 293 Mark Prior PR .50 .20
❑ 294 Josh Beckett PR .30 .10
❑ 295 Roger Clemens PR .75 .30
❑ 296 Derek Jeter PR .75 .30
❑ 297 Eric Chavez PR .30 .10
❑ 298 Jim Thome PR .30 .10
❑ 299 Albert Pujols PR .75 .30
❑ 300 Hank Blalock PR .30 .10
❑ 301 Bartolo Colon .30 .10
❑ 302 Darin Erstad .30 .10
❑ 303 Garret Anderson .30 .10
❑ 304 Orlando Cabrera .30 .10
❑ 305 Steve Finley .30 .10
❑ 306 Javier Vazquez .30 .10
❑ 307 Russ Ortiz .30 .10
❑ 308 Chipper Jones .75 .30
❑ 309 Marcus Giles .30 .10
❑ 310 Raul Mondesi .30 .10
❑ 311 B.J. Ryan .30 .10
❑ 312 Luis Matos .30 .10
❑ 313 Sidney Ponson .30 .10
❑ 314 Bill Mueller .30 .10
❑ 315 David Ortiz .75 .30
❑ 316 Johnny Damon .50 .20
❑ 317 Keith Foulke .30 .10
❑ 318 Mark Bellhorn .30 .10
❑ 319 Wade Miller .30 .10
❑ 320 Aramis Ramirez .30 .10
❑ 321 Carlos Zambrano .30 .10
❑ 322 Greg Maddux 1.25 .50
❑ 323 Kerry Wood .30 .10
❑ 324 Nomar Garciaparra .75 .30
❑ 325 Todd Walker .30 .10
❑ 326 Frank Thomas .75 .30
❑ 327 Freddy Garcia .30 .10
❑ 328 Joe Crede .30 .10
❑ 329 Jose Contreras .30 .10
❑ 330 Orlando Hernandez .30 .10
❑ 331 Shingo Takatsu .30 .10
❑ 332 Austin Kearns .30 .10
❑ 333 Eric Milton .30 .10
❑ 334 Ken Griffey Jr. 1.25 .50
❑ 335 Aaron Boone .30 .10
❑ 336 David Riske .30 .10
❑ 337 Jake Westbrook .30 .10
❑ 338 Kevin Millwood .30 .10
❑ 339 Travis Hafner .30 .10
❑ 340 Aaron Miles .30 .10
❑ 341 Jeff Baker .30 .10
❑ 342 Todd Helton .50 .20

❑	343	Garrett Atkins	.30	.10
❑	344	Carlos Pena	.30	.10
❑	345	Ivan Rodriguez	.50	.20
❑	346	Rondell White	.30	.10
❑	347	Troy Percival	.30	.10
❑	348	A.J. Burnett	.30	.10
❑	349	Carlos Delgado	.30	.10
❑	350	Guillermo Mota	.30	.10
❑	351	Paul Lo Duca	.30	.10
❑	352	Jason Lane	.30	.10
❑	353	Lance Berkman	.30	.10
❑	354	Angel Berroa	.30	.10
❑	355	David DeJesus	.30	.10
❑	356	Ruben Gotay	.30	.10
❑	357	Jose Lima	.30	.10
❑	358	Brad Penny	.30	.10
❑	359	J.D. Drew	.30	.10
❑	360	Jayson Werth	.30	.10
❑	361	Jeff Kent	.30	.10
❑	362	Odalis Perez	.30	.10
❑	363	Brady Clark	.30	.10
❑	364	Junior Spivey	.30	.10
❑	365	Rickie Weeks	.30	.10
❑	366	Jacque Jones	.30	.10
❑	367	Joe Nathan	.30	.10
❑	368	Nick Punto	.30	.10
❑	369	Shannon Stewart	.30	.10
❑	370	Doug Mientkiewicz	.30	.10
❑	371	Kris Benson	.30	.10
❑	372	Tom Glavine	.50	.20
❑	373	Victor Zambrano	.30	.10
❑	374	Bernie Williams	.50	.20
❑	375	Carl Pavano	.30	.10
❑	376	Jaret Wright	.30	.10
❑	377	Kevin Brown	.30	.10
❑	378	Mariano Rivera	.75	.30
❑	379	Danny Haren	.30	.10
❑	380	Eric Byrnes	.30	.10
❑	381	Erubiel Durazo	.30	.10
❑	382	Rich Harden	.30	.10
❑	383	Brett Myers	.30	.10
❑	384	Chase Utley	.50	.20
❑	385	Marlon Byrd	.30	.10
❑	386	Pat Burrell	.30	.10
❑	387	Placido Polanco	.30	.10
❑	388	Freddy Sanchez	.30	.10
❑	389	Jason Bay	.30	.10
❑	390	Josh Fogg	.30	.10
❑	391	Adam Eaton	.30	.10
❑	392	Jake Peavy	.30	.10
❑	393	Khalil Greene	.50	.20
❑	394	Mark Loretta	.30	.10
❑	395	Phil Nevin	.30	.10
❑	396	Ramon Hernandez	.30	.10
❑	397	Woody Williams	.30	.10
❑	398	Armando Benitez	.30	.10
❑	399	Edgardo Alfonzo	.30	.10
❑	400	Marquis Grissom	.30	.10
❑	401	Mike Matheny	.30	.10
❑	402	Richie Sexson	.30	.10
❑	403	Bret Boone	.30	.10
❑	404	Gil Meche	.30	.10
❑	405	Chris Carpenter	.30	.10
❑	406	Jeff Suppan	.30	.10
❑	407	Larry Walker	.50	.20
❑	408	Mark Grudzielanek	.30	.10
❑	409	Mark Mulder	.30	.10
❑	410	Scott Rolen	.50	.20
❑	411	Josh Phelps	.30	.10
❑	412	Jonny Gomes	.30	.10
❑	413	Francisco Cordero	.30	.10
❑	414	Kenny Rogers	.30	.10
❑	415	Richard Hidalgo	.30	.10
❑	416	Dave Bush	.30	.10
❑	417	Frank Catalanotto	.30	.10
❑	418	Gabe Gross	.30	.10
❑	419	Guillermo Quiroz	.30	.10
❑	420	Reed Johnson	.30	.10
❑	421	Cristian Guzman	.30	.10
❑	422	Esteban Loaiza	.30	.10
❑	423	Jose Guillen	.30	.10
❑	424	Nick Johnson	.30	.10
❑	425	Vinny Castilla	.30	.10
❑	426	Pete Orr SR RC	1.00	.40
❑	427	Tadahito Iguchi SR RC	2.50	1.00
❑	428	Jeff Baker SR	1.00	.40
❑	429	Marcos Carvajal SR RC	1.00	.40
❑	430	Justin Verlander SR RC	5.00	2.00
❑	431	Luke Scott SR RC	3.00	1.25
❑	432	Willy Taveras SR	1.00	.40
❑	433	Ambiorix Burgos SR RC	1.00	.40
❑	434	Andy Sisco SR	1.00	.40
❑	435	Denny Bautista SR	1.00	.40
❑	436	Mark Teahen SR	1.00	.40
❑	437	Ervin Santana SR	1.00	.40
❑	438	Dennis Houlton SR RC	1.00	.40
❑	439	Philip Humber SR RC	1.50	.60
❑	440	Steve Schmoll SR RC	1.00	.40
❑	441	J.J. Hardy SR	1.00	.40
❑	442	Ambiorix Concepcion SR RC	1.00	.40
❑	443	Dae-Sung Koo SR RC	1.00	.40
❑	444	Andy Phillips SR	1.00	.40
❑	445	Dan Meyer SR	1.00	.40
❑	446	Huston Street SR	1.50	.60
❑	447	Keiichi Yabu SR RC	1.00	.40
❑	448	Jeff Niemann SR RC	1.50	.60
❑	449	Jeremy Reed SR	1.00	.40
❑	450	Tony Blanco SR	1.00	.40
❑	451	Albert Pujols BG	.75	.30
❑	452	Alex Rodriguez BG	.75	.30
❑	453	Curt Schilling BG	.30	.10
❑	454	Derek Jeter BG	.75	.30
❑	455	Greg Maddux BG	.75	.30
❑	456	Ichiro Suzuki BG	.75	.30
❑	457	Ivan Rodriguez BG	.30	.10
❑	458	Jeff Bagwell BG	.30	.10
❑	459	Jim Thome BG	.30	.10
❑	460	Ken Griffey Jr. BG	.75	.30
❑	461	Manny Ramirez BG	.50	.20
❑	462	Mike Mussina BG	.30	.10
❑	463	Mike Piazza BG	.50	.20
❑	464	Pedro Martinez BG	.30	.10
❑	465	Rafael Palmeiro BG	.30	.10
❑	466	Randy Johnson BG	.50	.20
❑	467	Roger Clemens BG	.75	.30
❑	468	Sammy Sosa BG	.50	.20
❑	469	Todd Helton BG	.30	.10
❑	470	Vladimir Guerrero BG	.50	.20
❑	471	Vladimir Guerrero TC	.50	.20
❑	472	Shawn Green TC	.30	.10
❑	473	John Smoltz TC	.30	.10
❑	474	Miguel Tejada TC	.30	.10
❑	475	Curt Schilling TC	.30	.10
❑	476	Mark Prior TC	.30	.10
❑	477	Frank Thomas TC	.50	.20
❑	478	Ken Griffey Jr. TC	.75	.30
❑	479	C.C. Sabathia TC	.30	.10
❑	480	Todd Helton TC	.30	.10
❑	481	Ivan Rodriguez TC	.30	.10
❑	482	Miguel Cabrera TC	.30	.10
❑	483	Roger Clemens TC	.75	.30
❑	484	Mike Sweeney TC	.30	.10
❑	485	Eric Gagne TC	.30	.10
❑	486	Ben Sheets TC	.30	.10
❑	487	Johan Santana TC	.30	.10
❑	488	Mike Piazza TC	.50	.20
❑	489	Derek Jeter TC	.75	.30
❑	490	Eric Chavez TC	.30	.10
❑	491	Jim Thome TC	.30	.10
❑	492	Craig Wilson TC	.30	.10
❑	493	Jake Peavy TC	.30	.10
❑	494	Jason Schmidt TC	.30	.10
❑	495	Ichiro Suzuki TC	.75	.30
❑	496	Albert Pujols TC	.75	.30
❑	497	Carl Crawford TC	.30	.10
❑	498	Mark Teixeira TC	.30	.10
❑	499	Vernon Wells TC	.30	.10
❑	500	Jose Vidro TC	.30	.10

2006 Upper Deck

❑	COMPLETE SET (1250)	450.00	275.00
❑	COMPLETE SERIES 1 (500)	250.00	150.00
❑	COMPLETE SERIES 2 (500)	200.00	125.00
❑	COMPLETE UPDATE (250)		
❑	COMP.UPDATE w/o SP's (50)		
❑	COMMON CARD (1-1250)	.40	.15
❑	1-500 ISSUED IN SERIES 1 PACKS		
❑	501-1000 ISSUED IN SERIES 2 PACKS		
❑	1001-1250 ISSUED IN UPDATE PACKS		
❑	CARD 245 DOES NOT EXIST		
❑	BAKER & REPKO BOTH CARD 283		
❑	1001-1250 SP STATED ODDS 1:2		

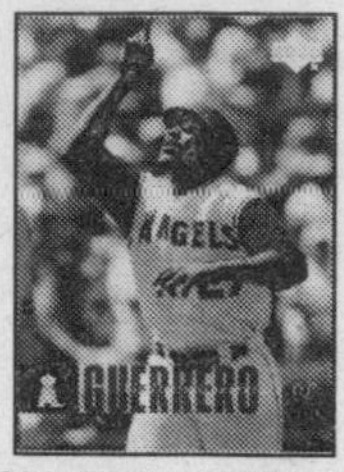

❑ SP CL: 1005/1013/1021/1037/1045/1061/1069
❑ SP CL: 1077/1093/1101/1117/1125/1133/1149
❑ SP CL: 1157/1173/1181/1189/1205/1213
❑ SP CL: 1221-1250
❑ 4 MATCHED PLATES 1:2 SER.2 HOBBY CASES
❑ PLATE PRINT RUN 1 SET PER COLOR
❑ BLACK-CYAN-MAGENTA-YELLOW ISSUED
❑ NO PLATE PRICING DUE TO SCARCITY
❑ EXQUISITE EXCH 1 PER SER.2 HOBBY CASE
❑ EXQUISITE EXCH RANDOM IN UPD.CASES
❑ EXQUISITE EXCH DEADLINE 07/27/07

❑	1	Adam Kennedy	.40	.15
❑	2	Bartolo Colon	.40	.15
❑	3	Bengie Molina	.40	.15
❑	4	Casey Kotchman	.40	.15
❑	5	Chone Figgins	.40	.15
❑	6	Dallas McPherson	.40	.15
❑	7	Darin Erstad	.40	.15
❑	8	Ervin Santana	.40	.15
❑	9	Francisco Rodriguez	.40	.15
❑	10	Garret Anderson	.40	.15
❑	11	Jarrod Washburn	.40	.15
❑	12	John Lackey	.40	.15
❑	13	Juan Rivera	.40	.15
❑	14	Orlando Cabrera	.40	.15
❑	15	Paul Byrd	.40	.15
❑	16	Steve Finley	.40	.15
❑	17	Vladimir Guerrero	1.00	.40
❑	18	Alex Cintron	.40	.15
❑	19	Brandon Lyon	.40	.15
❑	20	Brandon Webb	.40	.15
❑	21	Chad Tracy	.40	.15
❑	22	Chris Snyder	.40	.15
❑	23	Claudio Vargas	.40	.15
❑	24	Conor Jackson	.60	.25
❑	25	Craig Counsell	.40	.15
❑	26	Javier Vazquez	.40	.15
❑	27	Jose Valverde	.40	.15
❑	28	Luis Gonzalez	.40	.15
❑	29	Royce Clayton	.40	.15
❑	30	Russ Ortiz	.40	.15
❑	31	Shawn Green	.40	.15
❑	32	Dustin Nippert (RC)	.75	.30
❑	33	Tony Clark	.40	.15
❑	34	Troy Glaus	.40	.15
❑	35	Adam LaRoche	.40	.15
❑	36	Andruw Jones	.60	.25
❑	37	Craig Hansen RC	3.00	1.25
❑	38	Chipper Jones	1.00	.40
❑	39	Horacio Ramirez	.40	.15
❑	40	Jeff Francoeur	1.00	.40
❑	41	John Smoltz	.60	.25
❑	42	Joey Devine RC	.75	.30
❑	43	Johnny Estrada	.40	.15
❑	44	Anthony Lerew (RC)	.75	.30
❑	45	Julio Franco	.40	.15
❑	46	Kyle Farnsworth	.40	.15
❑	47	Marcus Giles	.40	.15
❑	48	Mike Hampton	.40	.15
❑	49	Rafael Furcal	.40	.15
❑	50	Chuck James (RC)	1.25	.50
❑	51	Tim Hudson	.40	.15
❑	52	B.J. Ryan	.40	.15
❑	53	Bernie Castro (RC)	.75	.30
❑	54	Brian Roberts	.40	.15
❑	55	Walter Young (RC)	.75	.30
❑	56	Daniel Cabrera	.40	.15
❑	57	Eric Byrnes	.40	.15

❑ 58	Alejandro Freire RC	.75	.30
❑ 59	Erik Bedard	.40	.15
❑ 60	Javy Lopez	.40	.15
❑ 61	Jay Gibbons	.40	.15
❑ 62	Jorge Julio	.40	.15
❑ 63	Luis Matos	.40	.15
❑ 64	Melvin Mora	.40	.15
❑ 65	Miguel Tejada	.40	.15
❑ 66	Rafael Palmeiro	.60	.25
❑ 67	Rodrigo Lopez	.40	.15
❑ 68	Sammy Sosa	1.00	.40
❑ 69	Alejandro Machado (RC)	.75	.30
❑ 70	Bill Mueller	.40	.15
❑ 71	Bronson Arroyo	.40	.15
❑ 72	Curt Schilling	.60	.25
❑ 73	David Ortiz	1.00	.40
❑ 74	David Wells	.40	.15
❑ 75	Edgar Renteria	.40	.15
❑ 76	Ryan Jorgensen RC	.75	.30
❑ 77	Jason Varitek	1.00	.40
❑ 78	Johnny Damon	.60	.25
❑ 79	Keith Foulke	.40	.15
❑ 80	Kevin Youkilis	.40	.15
❑ 81	Manny Ramirez	.60	.25
❑ 82	Matt Clement	.40	.15
❑ 83	Hanley Ramirez (RC)	2.00	.75
❑ 84	Tim Wakefield	.40	.15
❑ 85	Trot Nixon	.40	.15
❑ 86	Wade Miller	.40	.15
❑ 87	Aramis Ramirez	.40	.15
❑ 88	Carlos Zambrano	.40	.15
❑ 89	Corey Patterson	.40	.15
❑ 90	Derrek Lee	.40	.15
❑ 91	Geovany Soto (RC)	.75	.30
❑ 92	Greg Maddux	1.50	.60
❑ 93	Jeromy Burnitz	.40	.15
❑ 94	Jerry Hairston	.40	.15
❑ 95	Kerry Wood	.40	.15
❑ 96	Mark Prior	.60	.25
❑ 97	Matt Murton	.40	.15
❑ 98	Michael Barrett	.40	.15
❑ 99	Neifi Perez	.40	.15
❑ 100	Nomar Garciaparra	1.00	.40
❑ 101	Rich Hill	.40	.15
❑ 102	Ryan Dempster	.40	.15
❑ 103	Todd Walker	.40	.15
❑ 104	A.J. Pierzynski	.40	.15
❑ 105	Aaron Rowand	.40	.15
❑ 106	Bobby Jenks	.40	.15
❑ 107	Carl Everett	.40	.15
❑ 108	Dustin Hermanson	.40	.15
❑ 109	Frank Thomas	1.00	.40
❑ 110	Freddy Garcia	.40	.15
❑ 111	Jermaine Dye	.40	.15
❑ 112	Joe Crede	.40	.15
❑ 113	Jon Garland	.40	.15
❑ 114	Jose Contreras	.40	.15
❑ 115	Juan Uribe	.40	.15
❑ 116	Mark Buehrle	.40	.15
❑ 117	Orlando Hernandez	.40	.15
❑ 118	Paul Konerko	.40	.15
❑ 119	Scott Podsednik	.40	.15
❑ 120	Tadahito Iguchi	.40	.15
❑ 121	Aaron Harang	.40	.15
❑ 122	Adam Dunn	.40	.15
❑ 123	Austin Kearns	.40	.15
❑ 124	Brandon Claussen	.40	.15
❑ 125	Chris Denorfia (RC)	.75	.30
❑ 126	Edwin Encarnacion	.40	.15
❑ 127	Miguel Perez (RC)	.75	.30
❑ 128	Felipe Lopez	.40	.15
❑ 129	Jason LaRue	.40	.15
❑ 130	Ken Griffey Jr.	1.50	.60
❑ 131	Chris Booker (RC)	.75	.30
❑ 132	Luke Hudson	.40	.15
❑ 133	Jason Bergmann RC	.75	.30
❑ 134	Ryan Freel	.40	.15
❑ 135	Sean Casey	.40	.15
❑ 136	Wily Mo Pena	.40	.15
❑ 137	Aaron Boone	.40	.15
❑ 138	Ben Broussard	.40	.15
❑ 139	Ryan Garko (RC)	.75	.30
❑ 140	C.C. Sabathia	.40	.15
❑ 141	Casey Blake	.40	.15
❑ 142	Cliff Lee	.40	.15
❑ 143	Coco Crisp	.40	.15
❑ 144	David Riske	.40	.15
❑ 145	Grady Sizemore	.60	.25
❑ 146	Jake Westbrook	.40	.15
❑ 147	Jhonny Peralta	.40	.15
❑ 148	Josh Bard	.40	.15
❑ 149	Kevin Millwood	.40	.15
❑ 150	Ronnie Belliard	.40	.15
❑ 151	Scott Elarton	.40	.15
❑ 152	Travis Hafner	.40	.15
❑ 153	Victor Martinez	.40	.15
❑ 154	Aaron Cook	.40	.15
❑ 155	Aaron Miles	.40	.15
❑ 156	Brad Hawpe	.40	.15
❑ 157	Mike Esposito (RC)	.75	.30
❑ 158	Chin-Hui Tsao	.40	.15
❑ 159	Clint Barmes	.40	.15
❑ 160	Cory Sullivan	.40	.15
❑ 161	Garrett Atkins	.40	.15
❑ 162	J.D. Closser	.40	.15
❑ 163	Jason Jennings	.40	.15
❑ 164	Jeff Baker	.40	.15
❑ 165	Jeff Francis	.40	.15
❑ 166	Luis A. Gonzalez	.40	.15
❑ 167	Matt Holliday	.40	.15
❑ 168	Todd Helton	.60	.25
❑ 169	Bradon Inge	.40	.15
❑ 170	Carlos Guillen	.40	.15
❑ 171	Carlos Pena	.40	.15
❑ 172	Chris Shelton	.40	.15
❑ 173	Craig Monroe	.40	.15
❑ 174	Curtis Granderson	.40	.15
❑ 175	Dmitri Young	.40	.15
❑ 176	Ivan Rodriguez	.60	.25
❑ 177	Jason Johnson	.40	.15
❑ 178	Jeremy Bonderman	.40	.15
❑ 179	Magglio Ordonez	.40	.15
❑ 180	Mark Woodyard (RC)	.75	.30
❑ 181	Nook Logan	.40	.15
❑ 182	Omar Infante	.40	.15
❑ 183	Placido Polanco	.40	.15
❑ 184	Chris Heintz RC	.75	.30
❑ 185	A.J. Burnett	.40	.15
❑ 186	Alex Gonzalez	.40	.15
❑ 187	Josh Johnson (RC)	.75	.30
❑ 188	Carlos Delgado	.40	.15
❑ 189	Dontrelle Willis	.40	.15
❑ 190	Josh Wilson (RC)	.75	.30
❑ 191	Jason Vargas	.40	.15
❑ 192	Jeff Conine	.40	.15
❑ 193	Jeremy Hermida	.60	.25
❑ 194	Josh Beckett	.40	.15
❑ 195	Juan Encarnacion	.40	.15
❑ 196	Juan Pierre	.40	.15
❑ 197	Luis Castillo	.40	.15
❑ 198	Miguel Cabrera	.60	.25
❑ 199	Mike Lowell	.40	.15
❑ 200	Paul Lo Duca	.40	.15
❑ 201	Todd Jones	.40	.15
❑ 202	Adam Everett	.40	.15
❑ 203	Andy Pettitte	.40	.15
❑ 204	Brad Ausmus	.40	.15
❑ 205	Brad Lidge	.40	.15
❑ 206	Brandon Backe	.40	.15
❑ 207	Charlton Jimerson (RC)	.75	.30
❑ 208	Chris Burke	.40	.15
❑ 209	Craig Biggio	.60	.25
❑ 210	Dan Wheeler	.40	.15
❑ 211	Jason Lane	.40	.15
❑ 212	Jeff Bagwell	.60	.25
❑ 213	Lance Berkman	.40	.15
❑ 214	Luke Scott	.40	.15
❑ 215	Morgan Ensberg	.40	.15
❑ 216	Roger Clemens	2.00	.75
❑ 217	Roy Oswalt	.40	.15
❑ 218	Willy Taveras	.40	.15
❑ 219	Andres Blanco	.40	.15
❑ 220	Angel Berroa	.40	.15
❑ 221	Ruben Gotay	.40	.15
❑ 222	David DeJesus	.40	.15
❑ 223	Emil Brown	.40	.15
❑ 224	J.P. Howell	.40	.15
❑ 225	Jeremy Affeldt	.40	.15
❑ 226	Jimmy Gobble	.40	.15
❑ 227	John Buck	.40	.15
❑ 228	Jose Lima	.40	.15
❑ 229	Mark Teahen	.40	.15
❑ 230	Matt Stairs	.40	.15
❑ 231	Mike MacDougal	.40	.15
❑ 232	Mike Sweeney	.40	.15
❑ 233	Runelvys Hernandez	.40	.15
❑ 234	Terrence Long	.40	.15
❑ 235	Zack Greinke	.40	.15
❑ 236	Ron Flores RC	.75	.30
❑ 237	Brad Penny	.40	.15
❑ 238	Cesar Izturis	.40	.15
❑ 239	D.J. Houlton	.40	.15
❑ 240	Derek Lowe	.40	.15
❑ 241	Eric Gagne	.40	.15
❑ 242	Hee Seop Choi	.40	.15
❑ 243	J.D. Drew	.40	.15
❑ 244	Jason Phillips	.40	.15
❑ 246	Jayson Werth	.40	.15
❑ 247	Jeff Kent	.40	.15
❑ 248	Jeff Weaver	.40	.15
❑ 249	Milton Bradley	.40	.15
❑ 250	Odalis Perez	.40	.15
❑ 251	Hong-Chih Kuo (RC)	2.00	.75
❑ 252	Oscar Robles	.40	.15
❑ 253	Ben Sheets	.40	.15
❑ 254	Bill Hall	.40	.15
❑ 255	Brady Clark	.40	.15
❑ 256	Carlos Lee	.40	.15
❑ 257	Chris Capuano	.40	.15
❑ 258	Nelson Cruz (RC)	.75	.30
❑ 259	Derrick Turnbow	.40	.15
❑ 260	Doug Davis	.40	.15
❑ 261	Geoff Jenkins	.40	.15
❑ 262	J.J. Hardy	.40	.15
❑ 263	Lyle Overbay	.40	.15
❑ 264	Prince Fielder	1.50	.60
❑ 265	Rickie Weeks	.40	.15
❑ 266	Russell Branyan	.40	.15
❑ 267	Tomo Ohka	.40	.15
❑ 268	Jonah Bayliss (RC)	.75	.30
❑ 269	Brad Radke	.40	.15
❑ 270	Carlos Silva	.40	.15
❑ 271	Francisco Liriano (RC)	4.00	1.50
❑ 272	Jacque Jones	.40	.15
❑ 273	Joe Mauer	.60	.25
❑ 274	Travis Bowyer (RC)	.75	.30
❑ 275	Joe Nathan	.40	.15
❑ 276	Johan Santana	.60	.25
❑ 277	Justin Morneau	.40	.15
❑ 278	Kyle Lohse	.40	.15
❑ 279	Lew Ford	.40	.15
❑ 280	Matt LeCroy	.40	.15
❑ 281	Michael Cuddyer	.40	.15
❑ 282	Nick Punto	.40	.15
❑ 283a	Scott Baker	.40	.15
❑ 283b	Jason Repko UER	.40	.15
❑ 284	Shannon Stewart	.40	.15
❑ 285	Torii Hunter	.40	.15
❑ 286	Braden Looper	.40	.15
❑ 287	Carlos Beltran	.40	.15
❑ 288	Cliff Floyd	.40	.15
❑ 289	David Wright	1.50	.60
❑ 290	Doug Mientkiewicz	.40	.15
❑ 291	Anderson Hernandez (RC)	.75	.30
❑ 292	Jose Reyes	.40	.15
❑ 293	Kazuo Matsui	.40	.15
❑ 294	Kris Benson	.40	.15
❑ 295	Miguel Cairo	.40	.15
❑ 296	Mike Cameron	.40	.15
❑ 297	Robert Andino RC	.75	.30
❑ 298	Mike Piazza	1.00	.40
❑ 299	Pedro Martinez	.60	.25
❑ 300	Tom Glavine	.60	.25
❑ 301	Victor Diaz	.40	.15
❑ 302	Tim Hamulack (RC)	.75	.30
❑ 303	Alex Rodriguez	1.50	.60
❑ 304	Bernie Williams	.60	.25
❑ 305	Carl Pavano	.40	.15
❑ 306	Chien-Ming Wang	1.50	.60
❑ 307	Derek Jeter	2.50	1.00
❑ 308	Gary Sheffield	.40	.15
❑ 309	Hideki Matsui	1.00	.40
❑ 310	Jason Giambi	.40	.15
❑ 311	Jorge Posada	.60	.25
❑ 312	Kevin Brown	.40	.15
❑ 313	Mariano Rivera	1.00	.40
❑ 314	Matt Lawton	.40	.15
❑ 315	Mike Mussina	.60	.25

❑ 316	Randy Johnson	1.00	.40
❑ 317	Robinson Cano	.60	.25
❑ 318	Mike Vento (RC)	.75	.30
❑ 319	Tino Martinez	.40	.15
❑ 320	Tony Womack	.40	.15
❑ 321	Barry Zito	.40	.15
❑ 322	Bobby Crosby	.40	.15
❑ 323	Bobby Kielty	.40	.15
❑ 324	Dan Johnson	.40	.15
❑ 325	Danny Haren	.40	.15
❑ 326	Eric Chavez	.40	.15
❑ 327	Erubiel Durazo	.40	.15
❑ 328	Huston Street	.40	.15
❑ 329	Jason Kendall	.40	.15
❑ 330	Jay Payton	.40	.15
❑ 331	Joe Blanton	.40	.15
❑ 332	Joe Kennedy	.40	.15
❑ 333	Kirk Saarloos	.40	.15
❑ 334	Mark Kotsay	.40	.15
❑ 335	Nick Swisher	.40	.15
❑ 336	Rich Harden	.40	.15
❑ 337	Scott Hatteberg	.40	.15
❑ 338	Billy Wagner	.40	.15
❑ 339	Bobby Abreu	.40	.15
❑ 340	Brett Myers	.40	.15
❑ 341	Chase Utley	1.00	.40
❑ 342	Danny Sandoval RC	.75	.30
❑ 343	David Bell	.40	.15
❑ 344	Gavin Floyd	.40	.15
❑ 345	Jim Thome	.60	.25
❑ 346	Jimmy Rollins	.40	.15
❑ 347	Jon Lieber	.40	.15
❑ 348	Kenny Lofton	.40	.15
❑ 349	Mike Lieberthal	.40	.15
❑ 350	Pat Burrell	.40	.15
❑ 351	Randy Wolf	.40	.15
❑ 352	Ryan Howard	1.50	.60
❑ 353	Vicente Padilla	.40	.15
❑ 354	Bryan Bullington (RC)	.75	.30
❑ 355	J.J. Furmaniak (RC)	.75	.30
❑ 356	Craig Wilson	.40	.15
❑ 357	Matt Capps (RC)	.75	.30
❑ 358	Tom Gorzelanny (RC)	.75	.30
❑ 359	Jack Wilson	.40	.15
❑ 360	Jason Bay	.40	.15
❑ 361	Jose Mesa	.40	.15
❑ 362	Josh Fogg	.40	.15
❑ 363	Kip Wells	.40	.15
❑ 364	Steve Stemle RC	.75	.30
❑ 365	Oliver Perez	.40	.15
❑ 366	Rob Mackowiak	.40	.15
❑ 367	Ronny Paulino (RC)	.75	.30
❑ 368	Tike Redman	.40	.15
❑ 369	Zach Duke	.40	.15
❑ 370	Adam Eaton	.40	.15
❑ 371	Scott Feldman RC	.75	.30
❑ 372	Brian Giles	.40	.15
❑ 373	Brian Lawrence	.40	.15
❑ 374	Damian Jackson	.40	.15
❑ 375	Dave Roberts	.40	.15
❑ 376	Jake Peavy	.40	.15
❑ 377	Joe Randa	.40	.15
❑ 378	Khalil Greene	.60	.25
❑ 379	Mark Loretta	.40	.15
❑ 380	Ramon Hernandez	.40	.15
❑ 381	Robert Fick	.40	.15
❑ 382	Ryan Klesko	.40	.15
❑ 383	Trevor Hoffman	.40	.15
❑ 384	Woody Williams	.40	.15
❑ 385	Xavier Nady	.40	.15
❑ 386	Armando Benitez	.40	.15
❑ 387	Brad Hennessey	.40	.15
❑ 388	Brian Myrow RC	.75	.30
❑ 389	Edgardo Alfonzo	.40	.15
❑ 390	J.T. Snow	.40	.15
❑ 391	Jeremy Accardo RC	.75	.30
❑ 392	Jason Schmidt	.40	.15
❑ 393	Lance Niekro	.40	.15
❑ 394	Matt Cain	.60	.25
❑ 395	Dan Ortmeier (RC)	.75	.30
❑ 396	Moises Alou	.40	.15
❑ 397	Doug Clark (RC)	.75	.30
❑ 398	Omar Vizquel	.60	.25
❑ 399	Pedro Feliz	.40	.15
❑ 400	Randy Winn	.40	.15
❑ 401	Ray Durham	.40	.15
❑ 402	Adrian Beltre	.40	.15
❑ 403	Eddie Guardado	.40	.15
❑ 404	Felix Hernandez	.60	.25
❑ 405	Gil Meche	.40	.15
❑ 406	Ichiro Suzuki	1.50	.60
❑ 407	Jamie Moyer	.40	.15
❑ 408	Jeff Nelson	.40	.15
❑ 409	Jeremy Reed	.40	.15
❑ 410	Joel Pineiro	.40	.15
❑ 411	Jaime Bubela (RC)	.75	.30
❑ 412	Raul Ibanez	.40	.15
❑ 413	Rickie Sexson	.40	.15
❑ 414	Ryan Franklin	.40	.15
❑ 415	Willie Bloomquist	.40	.15
❑ 416	Yorvit Torrealba	.40	.15
❑ 417	Yuniesky Betancourt	.40	.15
❑ 418	Jeff Harris RC	.75	.30
❑ 419	Albert Pujols	2.00	.75
❑ 420	Chris Carpenter	.40	.15
❑ 421	David Eckstein	.40	.15
❑ 422	Jason Isringhausen	.40	.15
❑ 423	Jason Marquis	.40	.15
❑ 424	Adam Wainwright (RC)	.75	.30
❑ 425	Jim Edmonds	.60	.25
❑ 426	Ryan Theriot RC	.75	.30
❑ 427	Chris Duncan (RC)	.75	.30
❑ 428	Mark Grudzielanek	.40	.15
❑ 429	Mark Mulder	.40	.15
❑ 430	Matt Morris	.40	.15
❑ 431	Reggie Sanders	.40	.15
❑ 432	Scott Rolen	.60	.25
❑ 433	Tyler Johnson (RC)	.75	.30
❑ 434	Yadier Molina	.40	.15
❑ 435	Alex S. Gonzalez	.40	.15
❑ 436	Aubrey Huff	.40	.15
❑ 437	Tim Corcoran RC	.75	.30
❑ 438	Carl Crawford	.40	.15
❑ 439	Casey Fossum	.40	.15
❑ 440	Danys Baez	.40	.15
❑ 441	Edwin Jackson	.40	.15
❑ 442	Joey Gathright	.40	.15
❑ 443	Jonny Gomes	.40	.15
❑ 444	Jorge Cantu	.40	.15
❑ 445	Julio Lugo	.40	.15
❑ 446	Nick Green	.40	.15
❑ 447	Rocco Baldelli	.40	.15
❑ 448	Scott Kazmir	.60	.25
❑ 449	Seth McClung	.40	.15
❑ 450	Toby Hall	.40	.15
❑ 451	Travis Lee	.40	.15
❑ 452	Craig Breslow RC	.75	.30
❑ 453	Alfonso Soriano	.40	.15
❑ 454	Chris R. Young	.40	.15
❑ 455	David Dellucci	.40	.15
❑ 456	Francisco Cordero	.40	.15
❑ 457	Gary Matthews	.40	.15
❑ 458	Hank Blalock	.40	.15
❑ 459	Juan Dominguez	.40	.15
❑ 460	Josh Rupe (RC)	.75	.30
❑ 461	Kenny Rogers	.40	.15
❑ 462	Kevin Mench	.40	.15
❑ 463	Laynce Nix	.40	.15
❑ 464	Mark Teixeira	.60	.25
❑ 465	Michael Young	.40	.15
❑ 466	Richard Hidalgo	.40	.15
❑ 467	Jason Botts (RC)	.75	.30
❑ 468	Aaron Hill	.40	.15
❑ 469	Alex Rios	.40	.15
❑ 470	Corey Koskie	.40	.15
❑ 471	Chris Demaria RC	.75	.30
❑ 472	Eric Hinske	.40	.15
❑ 473	Frank Catalanotto	.40	.15
❑ 474	John-Ford Griffin (RC)	.75	.30
❑ 475	Gustavo Chacin	.40	.15
❑ 476	Josh Towers	.40	.15
❑ 477	Miguel Batista	.40	.15
❑ 478	Orlando Hudson	.40	.15
❑ 479	Reed Johnson	.40	.15
❑ 480	Roy Halladay	.40	.15
❑ 481	Shaun Marcum (RC)	.75	.30
❑ 482	Shea Hillenbrand	.40	.15
❑ 483	Ted Lilly	.40	.15
❑ 484	Vernon Wells	.40	.15
❑ 485	Brad Wilkerson	.40	.15
❑ 486	Darrell Rasner (RC)	.75	.30
❑ 487	Chad Cordero	.40	.15
❑ 488	Cristian Guzman	.40	.15
❑ 489	Esteban Loaiza	.40	.15
❑ 490	John Patterson	.40	.15
❑ 491	Jose Guillen	.40	.15
❑ 492	Jose Vidro	.40	.15
❑ 493	Livan Hernandez	.40	.15
❑ 494	Marlon Byrd	.40	.15
❑ 495	Nick Johnson	.40	.15
❑ 496	Preston Wilson	.40	.15
❑ 497	Ryan Church	.40	.15
❑ 498	Ryan Zimmerman (RC)	5.00	2.00
❑ 499	Tony Armas Jr.	.40	.15
❑ 500	Vinny Castilla	.40	.15
❑ 501	Andy Green	.40	.15
❑ 502	Damion Easley	.40	.15
❑ 503	Eric Byrnes	.40	.15
❑ 504	Jason Grimsley	.40	.15
❑ 505	Jeff DaVanon	.40	.15
❑ 506	Johnny Estrada	.40	.15
❑ 507	Luis Vizcaino	.40	.15
❑ 508	Miguel Batista	.40	.15
❑ 509	Orlando Hernandez	.40	.15
❑ 510	Orlando Hudson	.40	.15
❑ 511	Terry Mulholland	.40	.15
❑ 512	Chris Reitsma	.40	.15
❑ 513	Edgar Renteria	.40	.15
❑ 514	John Thomson	.40	.15
❑ 515	Jorge Sosa	.40	.15
❑ 516	Oscar Villarreal	.40	.15
❑ 517	Pete Orr	.40	.15
❑ 518	Ryan Langerhans	.40	.15
❑ 519	Todd Pratt	.40	.15
❑ 520	Wilson Betemit	.40	.15
❑ 521	Brian Jordan	.40	.15
❑ 522	Lance Cormier	.40	.15
❑ 523	Matt Diaz	.40	.15
❑ 524	Mike Remlinger	.40	.15
❑ 525	Bruce Chen	.40	.15
❑ 526	Chris Gomez	.40	.15
❑ 527	Chris Ray	.40	.15
❑ 528	Corey Patterson	.40	.15
❑ 529	David Newhan	.40	.15
❑ 530	Ed Rogers (RC)	.75	.30
❑ 531	John Halama	.40	.15
❑ 532	Kris Benson	.40	.15
❑ 533	LaTroy Hawkins	.40	.15
❑ 534	Raul Chavez	.40	.15
❑ 535	Alex Cora	.40	.15
❑ 536	Alex Gonzalez	.40	.15
❑ 537	Coco Crisp	.40	.15
❑ 538	David Riske	.40	.15
❑ 539	Doug Mirabelli	.40	.15
❑ 540	Josh Beckett	.40	.15
❑ 541	J.T. Snow	.40	.15
❑ 542	Mike Timlin	.40	.15
❑ 543	Julian Tavarez	.40	.15
❑ 544	Rudy Seanez	.40	.15
❑ 545	Wily Mo Pena	.40	.15
❑ 546	Bob Howry	.40	.15
❑ 547	Glendon Rusch	.40	.15
❑ 548	Henry Blanco	.40	.15
❑ 549	Jacque Jones	.40	.15
❑ 550	Jerome Williams	.40	.15
❑ 551	John Mabry	.40	.15
❑ 552	Juan Pierre	.40	.15
❑ 553	Scott Eyre	.40	.15
❑ 554	Scott Williamson	.40	.15
❑ 555	Wade Miller	.40	.15
❑ 556	Will Ohman	.40	.15
❑ 557	Alex Cintron	.40	.15
❑ 558	Rob Mackowiak	.40	.15
❑ 559	Brandon McCarthy	.40	.15
❑ 560	Chris Widger	.40	.15
❑ 561	Cliff Politte	.40	.15
❑ 562	Javier Vazquez	.40	.15
❑ 563	Jim Thome	.60	.25
❑ 564	Matt Thornton	.40	.15
❑ 565	Neal Cotts	.40	.15
❑ 566	Pablo Ozuna	.40	.15
❑ 567	Ross Gload	.40	.15
❑ 568	Brandon Phillips	.40	.15
❑ 569	Bronson Arroyo	.40	.15
❑ 570	Dave Williams	.40	.15
❑ 571	David Ross	.40	.15
❑ 572	David Weathers	.40	.15
❑ 573	Eric Milton	.40	.15

❑ 574 Javier Valentin	.40	.15
❑ 575 Kent Mercker	.40	.15
❑ 576 Matt Belisle	.40	.15
❑ 577 Paul Wilson	.40	.15
❑ 578 Rich Aurilia	.40	.15
❑ 579 Rick White	.40	.15
❑ 580 Scott Hatteberg	.40	.15
❑ 581 Todd Coffey	.40	.15
❑ 582 Bob Wickman	.40	.15
❑ 583 Danny Graves	.40	.15
❑ 584 Eduardo Perez	.40	.15
❑ 585 Guillermo Mota	.40	.15
❑ 586 Jason Davis	.40	.15
❑ 587 Jason Johnson	.40	.15
❑ 588 Jason Michaels	.40	.15
❑ 589 Rafael Betancourt	.40	.15
❑ 590 Ramon Vazquez	.40	.15
❑ 591 Scott Sauerbeck	.40	.15
❑ 592 Todd Hollandsworth	.40	.15
❑ 593 Brian Fuentes	.40	.15
❑ 594 Danny Ardoin	.40	.15
❑ 595 David Cortes	.40	.15
❑ 596 Eli Marrero	.40	.15
❑ 597 Jamey Carroll	.40	.15
❑ 598 Jason Smith	.40	.15
❑ 599 Josh Fogg	.40	.15
❑ 600 Miguel Ojeda	.40	.15
❑ 601 Mike DeJean	.40	.15
❑ 602 Ray King	.40	.15
❑ 603 Omar Quintanilla (RC)	.75	.30
❑ 604 Zach Day	.40	.15
❑ 605 Fernando Rodney	.40	.15
❑ 606 Kenny Rogers	.40	.15
❑ 607 Mike Maroth	.40	.15
❑ 608 Nate Robertson	.40	.15
❑ 609 Todd Jones	.40	.15
❑ 610 Vance Wilson	.40	.15
❑ 611 Bobby Seay	.40	.15
❑ 612 Chris Spurling	.40	.15
❑ 613 Roman Colon	.40	.15
❑ 614 Jason Grilli	.40	.15
❑ 615 Marcus Thames	.40	.15
❑ 616 Ramon Santiago	.40	.15
❑ 617 Alfredo Amezaga	.40	.15
❑ 618 Brian Moehler	.40	.15
❑ 619 Chris Aguila	.40	.15
❑ 620 Franklyn German	.40	.15
❑ 621 Joe Borowski	.40	.15
❑ 622 Logan Kensing (RC)	.75	.30
❑ 623 Matt Treanor	.40	.15
❑ 624 Miguel Olivo	.40	.15
❑ 625 Sergio Mitre	.40	.15
❑ 626 Todd Wellemeyer	.40	.15
❑ 627 Wes Helms	.40	.15
❑ 628 Chad Qualls	.40	.15
❑ 629 Eric Bruntlett	.40	.15
❑ 630 Mike Gallo	.40	.15
❑ 631 Mike Lamb	.40	.15
❑ 632 Orlando Palmeiro	.40	.15
❑ 633 Russ Springer	.40	.15
❑ 634 Dan Wheeler	.40	.15
❑ 635 Eric Munson	.40	.15
❑ 636 Preston Wilson	.40	.15
❑ 637 Trever Miller	.40	.15
❑ 638 Ambiorix Burgos	.40	.15
❑ 639 Andy Sisco	.40	.15
❑ 640 Denny Bautista	.40	.15
❑ 641 Doug Mientkiewicz	.40	.15
❑ 642 Elmer Dessens	.40	.15
❑ 643 Esteban German	.40	.15
❑ 644 Joe Nelson (RC)	.75	.30
❑ 645 Mark Grudzielanek	.40	.15
❑ 646 Mark Redman	.40	.15
❑ 647 Mike Wood	.40	.15
❑ 648 Paul Bako	.40	.15
❑ 649 Reggie Sanders	.40	.15
❑ 650 Scott Elarton	.40	.15
❑ 651 Shane Costa	.40	.15
❑ 652 Tony Graffanino	.40	.15
❑ 653 Jason Bulger (RC)	.75	.30
❑ 654 Chris Bootcheck (RC)	.75	.30
❑ 655 Esteban Yan	.40	.15
❑ 656 Hector Carrasco	.40	.15
❑ 657 J.C. Romero	.40	.15
❑ 658 Jeff Weaver	.40	.15
❑ 659 Jose Molina	.40	.15
❑ 660 Kelvim Escobar	.40	.15
❑ 661 Maicer Izturis	.40	.15
❑ 662 Robb Quinlan	.40	.15
❑ 663 Scot Shields	.40	.15
❑ 664 Tim Salmon	.40	.15
❑ 665 Bill Mueller	.40	.15
❑ 666 Brett Tomko	.40	.15
❑ 667 Dioner Navarro	.40	.15
❑ 668 Jae Seo	.40	.15
❑ 669 Jose Cruz Jr.	.40	.15
❑ 670 Kenny Lofton	.40	.15
❑ 671 Lance Carter	.40	.15
❑ 672 Nomar Garciaparra	1.00	.40
❑ 673 Olmedo Saenz	.40	.15
❑ 674 Rafael Furcal	.40	.15
❑ 675 Ramon Martinez	.40	.15
❑ 676 Ricky Ledee	.40	.15
❑ 677 Sandy Alomar Jr.	.40	.15
❑ 678 Yhency Brazoban	.40	.15
❑ 679 Corey Koskie	.40	.15
❑ 680 Dan Kolb	.40	.15
❑ 681 Gabe Gross	.40	.15
❑ 682 Jeff Cirillo	.40	.15
❑ 683 Matt Wise	.40	.15
❑ 684 Rick Helling	.40	.15
❑ 685 Chad Moeller	.40	.15
❑ 686 Dave Bush	.40	.15
❑ 687 Jorge De La Rosa	.40	.15
❑ 688 Justin Lehr	.40	.15
❑ 689 Jason Bartlett	.40	.15
❑ 690 Jesse Crain	.40	.15
❑ 691 Juan Rincon	.40	.15
❑ 692 Luis Castillo	.40	.15
❑ 693 Mike Redmond	.40	.15
❑ 694 Rondell White	.40	.15
❑ 695 Tony Batista	.40	.15
❑ 696 Juan Castro	.40	.15
❑ 697 Luis Rodriguez	.40	.15
❑ 698 Matt Guerrier	.40	.15
❑ 699 Willie Eyre (RC)	.75	.30
❑ 700 Aaron Heilman	.40	.15
❑ 701 Billy Wagner	.40	.15
❑ 702 Carlos Delgado	.40	.15
❑ 703 Chad Bradford	.40	.15
❑ 704 Chris Woodward	.40	.15
❑ 705 Darren Oliver	.40	.15
❑ 706 Duaner Sanchez	.40	.15
❑ 707 Endy Chavez	.40	.15
❑ 708 Jorge Julio	.40	.15
❑ 709 Jose Valentin	.40	.15
❑ 710 Julio Franco	.40	.15
❑ 711 Paul Lo Duca	.40	.15
❑ 712 Ramon Castro	.40	.15
❑ 713 Steve Trachsel	.40	.15
❑ 714 Victor Zambrano	.40	.15
❑ 715 Xavier Nady	.40	.15
❑ 716 Andy Phillips	.40	.15
❑ 717 Bubba Crosby	.40	.15
❑ 718 Jaret Wright	.40	.15
❑ 719 Kelly Stinnett	.40	.15
❑ 720 Kyle Farnsworth	.40	.15
❑ 721 Mike Meyers	.40	.15
❑ 722 Octavio Dotel	.40	.15
❑ 723 Ron Villone	.40	.15
❑ 724 Scott Proctor	.40	.15
❑ 725 Shawn Chacon	.40	.15
❑ 726 Tanyon Sturtze	.40	.15
❑ 727 Adam Melhuse	.40	.15
❑ 728 Brad Halsey	.40	.15
❑ 729 Esteban Loaiza	.40	.15
❑ 730 Frank Thomas	1.00	.40
❑ 731 Jay Witasick	.40	.15
❑ 732 Justin Duchscherer	.40	.15
❑ 733 Kiko Calero	.40	.15
❑ 734 Marco Scutaro	.40	.15
❑ 735 Mark Ellis	.40	.15
❑ 736 Milton Bradley	.40	.15
❑ 737 Aaron Fultz	.40	.15
❑ 738 Aaron Rowand	.40	.15
❑ 739 Geoff Geary	.40	.15
❑ 740 Arthur Rhodes	.40	.15
❑ 741 Chris Coste RC	.75	.30
❑ 742 Rheal Cormier	.40	.15
❑ 743 Ryan Franklin	.40	.15
❑ 744 Ryan Madson	.40	.15
❑ 745 Sal Fasano	.40	.15
❑ 746 Tom Gordon	.40	.15
❑ 747 Abraham Nunez	.40	.15
❑ 748 David Dellucci	.40	.15
❑ 749 Julio Santana	.40	.15
❑ 750 Shane Victorino	.40	.15
❑ 751 Damaso Marte	.40	.15
❑ 752 Freddy Sanchez	.40	.15
❑ 753 Humberto Cota	.40	.15
❑ 754 Jeromy Burnitz	.40	.15
❑ 755 Joe Randa	.40	.15
❑ 756 Jose Castillo	.40	.15
❑ 757 Mike Gonzalez	.40	.15
❑ 758 Ryan Doumit	.40	.15
❑ 759 Sean Burnett	.40	.15
❑ 760 Sean Casey	.40	.15
❑ 761 Ian Snell	.40	.15
❑ 762 John Grabow	.40	.15
❑ 763 Jose Hernandez	.40	.15
❑ 764 Roberto Hernandez	.40	.15
❑ 765 Ryan Vogelsong	.40	.15
❑ 766 Victor Santos	.40	.15
❑ 767 Adrian Gonzalez	.40	.15
❑ 768 Alan Embree	.40	.15
❑ 769 Brian Sweeney (RC)	.75	.30
❑ 770 Chan Ho Park	.40	.15
❑ 771 Clay Hensley	.40	.15
❑ 772 Dewon Brazelton	.40	.15
❑ 773 Doug Brocail	.40	.15
❑ 774 Eric Young	.40	.15
❑ 775 Geoff Blum	.40	.15
❑ 776 Josh Bard	.40	.15
❑ 777 Mark Bellhorn	.40	.15
❑ 778 Mike Cameron	.40	.15
❑ 779 Mike Piazza	1.00	.40
❑ 780 Rob Bowen	.40	.15
❑ 781 Scott Cassidy	.40	.15
❑ 782 Scott Linebrink	.40	.15
❑ 783 Shawn Estes	.40	.15
❑ 784 Termel Sledge	.40	.15
❑ 785 Vinny Castilla	.40	.15
❑ 786 Jeff Fassero	.40	.15
❑ 787 Jose Vizcaino	.40	.15
❑ 788 Mark Sweeney	.40	.15
❑ 789 Matt Morris	.40	.15
❑ 790 Steve Finley	.40	.15
❑ 791 Tim Worrell	.40	.15
❑ 792 Jamey Wright	.40	.15
❑ 793 Jason Ellison	.40	.15
❑ 794 Noah Lowry	.40	.15
❑ 795 Steve Kline	.40	.15
❑ 796 Todd Greene	.40	.15
❑ 797 Carl Everett	.40	.15
❑ 798 George Sherrill	.40	.15
❑ 799 J.J. Putz	.40	.15
❑ 800 Jake Woods	.40	.15
❑ 801 Jose Lopez	.40	.15
❑ 802 Julio Mateo	.40	.15
❑ 803 Mike Morse	.40	.15
❑ 804 Rafael Soriano	.40	.15

- ❑ 805 Roberto Petagine .40 .15
- ❑ 806 Aaron Miles .40 .15
- ❑ 807 Braden Looper .40 .15
- ❑ 808 Gary Bennett .40 .15
- ❑ 809 Hector Luna .40 .15
- ❑ 810 Jeff Suppan .40 .15
- ❑ 811 John Rodriguez .40 .15
- ❑ 812 Josh Hancock .40 .15
- ❑ 813 Juan Encarnacion .40 .15
- ❑ 814 Larry Bigbie .40 .15
- ❑ 815 Scott Spiezio .40 .15
- ❑ 816 Sidney Ponson .40 .15
- ❑ 817 So Taguchi .40 .15
- ❑ 818 Brian Meadows .40 .15
- ❑ 819 Damon Hollins .40 .15
- ❑ 820 Dan Miceli .40 .15
- ❑ 821 Doug Waechter .40 .15
- ❑ 822 Jason Childers RC .75 .30
- ❑ 823 Josh Paul .40 .15
- ❑ 824 Julio Lugo .40 .15
- ❑ 825 Mark Hendrickson .40 .15
- ❑ 826 Sean Burroughs .40 .15
- ❑ 827 Shawn Camp .40 .15
- ❑ 828 Travis Harper .40 .15
- ❑ 829 Ty Wigginton .40 .15
- ❑ 830 Adam Eaton .40 .15
- ❑ 831 Adrian Brown .40 .15
- ❑ 832 Akinori Otsuka .40 .15
- ❑ 833 Antonio Alfonseca .40 .15
- ❑ 834 Brad Wilkerson .40 .15
- ❑ 835 D'Angelo Jimenez .40 .15
- ❑ 836 Gerald Laird .40 .15
- ❑ 837 Joaquin Benoit .40 .15
- ❑ 838 Kameron Loe .40 .15
- ❑ 839 Kevin Millwood .40 .15
- ❑ 840 Mark DeRosa .40 .15
- ❑ 841 Phil Nevin .40 .15
- ❑ 842 Rod Barajas .40 .15
- ❑ 843 Vicente Padilla .40 .15
- ❑ 844 A.J. Burnett .40 .15
- ❑ 845 Bengie Molina .40 .15
- ❑ 846 Gregg Zaun .40 .15
- ❑ 847 John McDonald .40 .15
- ❑ 848 Lyle Overbay .40 .15
- ❑ 849 Russ Adams .40 .15
- ❑ 850 Troy Glaus .40 .15
- ❑ 851 Vinny Chulk .40 .15
- ❑ 852 B.J. Ryan .40 .15
- ❑ 853 Justin Speier .40 .15
- ❑ 854 Pete Walker .40 .15
- ❑ 855 Scott Downs .40 .15
- ❑ 856 Scott Schoeneweis .40 .15
- ❑ 857 Alfonso Soriano .40 .15
- ❑ 858 Brian Schneider .40 .15
- ❑ 859 Daryle Ward .40 .15
- ❑ 860 Felix Rodriguez .40 .15
- ❑ 861 Gary Majewski .40 .15
- ❑ 862 Joey Eischen .40 .15
- ❑ 863 Jon Rauch .40 .15
- ❑ 864 Marlon Anderson .40 .15
- ❑ 865 Matt LeCroy .40 .15
- ❑ 866 Mike Stanton .40 .15
- ❑ 867 Ramon Ortiz .40 .15
- ❑ 868 Robert Fick .40 .15
- ❑ 869 Royce Clayton .40 .15
- ❑ 870 Ryan Drese .40 .15
- ❑ 871 Vladimir Guerrero CL 1.00 .40
- ❑ 872 Craig Biggio CL .60 .25
- ❑ 873 Barry Zito CL .40 .15
- ❑ 874 Vernon Wells CL .40 .15
- ❑ 875 Chipper Jones CL 1.00 .40
- ❑ 876 Prince Fielder CL 1.50 .60
- ❑ 877 Albert Pujols CL 2.00 .75
- ❑ 878 Greg Maddux CL 1.50 .60
- ❑ 879 Carl Crawford CL .40 .15
- ❑ 880 Brandon Webb CL .40 .15
- ❑ 881 J.D. Drew CL .40 .15
- ❑ 882 Jason Schmidt CL .40 .15
- ❑ 883 Victor Martinez CL .40 .15
- ❑ 884 Ichiro Suzuki CL 1.50 .60
- ❑ 885 Miguel Cabrera CL .60 .25
- ❑ 886 David Wright CL 1.50 .60
- ❑ 887 Alfonso Soriano CL .40 .15
- ❑ 888 Miguel Tejada CL .40 .15
- ❑ 889 Khalil Greene CL .60 .25
- ❑ 890 Ryan Howard CL 1.50 .60
- ❑ 891 Jason Bay CL .40 .15
- ❑ 892 Mark Teixeira CL .60 .25
- ❑ 893 Manny Ramirez CL .60 .25
- ❑ 894 Ken Griffey Jr. CL 1.50 .60
- ❑ 895 Todd Helton CL .60 .25
- ❑ 896 Angel Berroa CL .40 .15
- ❑ 897 Ivan Rodriguez CL .60 .25
- ❑ 898 Johan Santana CL .60 .25
- ❑ 899 Paul Konerko CL .40 .15
- ❑ 900 Derek Jeter CL 2.50 1.00
- ❑ 901 Macay McBride (RC) .75 .30
- ❑ 902 Tony Pena (RC) .75 .30
- ❑ 903 Peter Moylan RC .75 .30
- ❑ 904 Aaron Rakers (RC) .75 .30
- ❑ 905 Chris Britton RC .75 .30
- ❑ 906 Nick Markakis (RC) 1.25 .50
- ❑ 907 Sendy Rleal RC .75 .30
- ❑ 908 Val Majewski (RC) .75 .30
- ❑ 909 Jermaine Van Buren (RC) .75 .30
- ❑ 910 Jonathan Papelbon (RC) 4.00 1.50
- ❑ 911 Angel Pagan (RC) .75 .30
- ❑ 912 David Aardsma (RC) .75 .30
- ❑ 913 Sean Marshall (RC) .75 .30
- ❑ 914 Brian Anderson (RC) .75 .30
- ❑ 915 Freddie Bynum (RC) .75 .30
- ❑ 916 Fausto Carmona (RC) .75 .30
- ❑ 917 Kelly Shoppach (RC) .75 .30
- ❑ 918 Choo Freeman (RC) .75 .30
- ❑ 919 Ryan Shealy (RC) .75 .30
- ❑ 920 Joel Zumaya (RC) 2.00 .75
- ❑ 921 Jordan Tata RC .75 .30
- ❑ 922 Justin Verlander (RC) 3.00 1.25
- ❑ 923 Carlos Martinez RC .75 .30
- ❑ 924 Chris Resop (RC) .75 .30
- ❑ 925 Dan Uggla (RC) 2.00 .75
- ❑ 926 Eric Reed (RC) .75 .30
- ❑ 927 Hanley Ramirez (RC) 2.00 .75
- ❑ 928 Yusmeiro Petit (RC) .75 .30
- ❑ 929 Josh Willingham (RC) .75 .30
- ❑ 930 Mike Jacobs (RC) .75 .30
- ❑ 931 Reggie Abercrombie (RC) .75 .30
- ❑ 932 Ricky Nolasco (RC) .75 .30
- ❑ 933 Scott Olsen (RC) .75 .30
- ❑ 934 Fernando Nieve (RC) .75 .30
- ❑ 935 Taylor Buchholz (RC) 1.25 .50
- ❑ 936 Cody Ross (RC) .75 .30
- ❑ 937 James Loney (RC) 1.25 .50
- ❑ 938 Takashi Saito RC .75 .30
- ❑ 939 Tim Hamulack (RC) .75 .30
- ❑ 940 Chris Demaria RC .75 .30
- ❑ 941 Jose Capellan (RC) .75 .30
- ❑ 942 David Gassner (RC) .75 .30
- ❑ 943 Jason Kubel (RC) .75 .30
- ❑ 944 Brian Bannister (RC) .75 .30
- ❑ 945 Mike Thompson RC .75 .30
- ❑ 946 Cole Hamels (RC) 2.00 .75
- ❑ 947 Paul Maholm (RC) .75 .30
- ❑ 948 John Van Benschoten (RC) .75 .30
- ❑ 949 Nate McLouth (RC) .75 .30
- ❑ 950 Ben Johnson (RC) .75 .30
- ❑ 951 Josh Barfield (RC) .75 .30
- ❑ 952 Travis Ishikawa (RC) .75 .30
- ❑ 953 Jack Taschner (RC) .75 .30
- ❑ 954 Kenji Johjima RC 4.00 1.50
- ❑ 955 Skip Schumaker (RC) .75 .30
- ❑ 956 Ruddy Lugo (RC) .75 .30
- ❑ 957 Jason Hammel (RC) .75 .30
- ❑ 958 Chris Roberson (RC) .75 .30
- ❑ 959 Fabio Castro RC .75 .30
- ❑ 960 Ian Kinsler (RC) 1.25 .50
- ❑ 961 John Koronka (RC) .75 .30
- ❑ 962 Brandon Watson (RC) .75 .30
- ❑ 963 Jon Lester RC 6.00 2.50
- ❑ 964 Ben Hendrickson (RC) .75 .30
- ❑ 965 Martin Prado (RC) .75 .30
- ❑ 966 Erick Aybar (RC) .75 .30
- ❑ 967 Bobby Livingston (RC) .75 .30
- ❑ 968 Ryan Spilborghs (RC) 1.25 .50
- ❑ 969 Tommy Murphy (RC) .75 .30
- ❑ 970 Howie Kendrick (RC) 4.00 1.50
- ❑ 971 Casey Janssen RC .75 .30
- ❑ 972 Michael O'Connor RC .75 .30
- ❑ 973 Conor Jackson (RC) 1.25 .50
- ❑ 974 Jeremy Hermida (RC) 1.25 .50
- ❑ 975 Renyel Pinto (RC) .75 .30
- ❑ 976 Prince Fielder (RC) 3.00 1.25
- ❑ 977 Kevin Frandsen (RC) 1.25 .50
- ❑ 978 Ty Taubenheim RC .75 .30
- ❑ 979 Rich Hill (RC) .75 .30
- ❑ 980 Jonathan Broxton (RC) .75 .30
- ❑ 981 Jamie Shields RC .75 .30
- ❑ 982 Carlos Villanueva RC .75 .30
- ❑ 983 Boone Logan RC .75 .30
- ❑ 984 Brian Wilson RC .75 .30
- ❑ 985 Andre Ethier (RC) 3.00 1.25
- ❑ 986 Mike Napoli RC 4.00 1.50
- ❑ 987 Agustin Montero (RC) .75 .30
- ❑ 988 Jack Hannahan RC .75 .30
- ❑ 989 Boof Bonser (RC) .75 .30
- ❑ 990 Carlos Ruiz (RC) .75 .30
- ❑ 991 Jason Botts (RC) .75 .30
- ❑ 992 Kendry Morales (RC) 2.00 .75
- ❑ 993 Alay Soler RC .75 .30
- ❑ 994 Santiago Ramirez (RC) .75 .30
- ❑ 995 Saul Rivera (RC) .75 .30
- ❑ 996 Anthony Reyes (RC) .75 .30
- ❑ 997 Matt Kemp (RC) 1.25 .50
- ❑ 998 Jae Kuk Ryu RC .75 .30
- ❑ 999 Lastings Milledge (RC) 1.25 .50
- ❑ 1000 Jered Weaver (RC) 4.00 1.50
- ❑ NNO Exquisite Redemption 200.00 125.00

2006 Upper Deck Epic

- ❑ COMMON CARD (1-300) 5.00 2.00
- ❑ COMMON ROOKIE 5.00 2.00
- ❑ STATED PRINT RUN 450 SERIAL #'d SETS
- ❑ 1 Conor Jackson (RC) 8.00 3.00
- ❑ 2 Brandon Webb 5.00 2.00
- ❑ 3 Craig Counsell 5.00 2.00
- ❑ 4 Luis Gonzalez 5.00 2.00
- ❑ 5 Miguel Batista 5.00 2.00
- ❑ 6 Orlando Hudson 5.00 2.00
- ❑ 7 Russ Ortiz 5.00 2.00
- ❑ 8 Shawn Green 5.00 2.00
- ❑ 9 Andruw Jones 8.00 3.00
- ❑ 10 Chipper Jones 8.00 3.00
- ❑ 11 Edgar Renteria 5.00 2.00
- ❑ 12 Jeff Francoeur 8.00 3.00
- ❑ 13 John Smoltz 8.00 3.00

❑ 14 Marcus Giles 5.00 2.00
❑ 15 Mike Hampton 5.00 2.00
❑ 16 Tim Hudson 5.00 2.00
❑ 17 Erik Bedard 5.00 2.00
❑ 18 Brian Roberts 5.00 2.00
❑ 19 Javy Lopez 5.00 2.00
❑ 20 Jay Gibbons 5.00 2.00
❑ 21 Jeff Conine 5.00 2.00
❑ 22 Melvin Mora 5.00 2.00
❑ 23 Miguel Tejada 5.00 2.00
❑ 24 Daniel Cabrera 5.00 2.00
❑ 25 Rodrigo Lopez 5.00 2.00
❑ 26 Ramon Hernandez 5.00 2.00
❑ 27 Bronson Arroyo 5.00 2.00
❑ 28 Curt Schilling 8.00 3.00
❑ 29 David Ortiz 8.00 3.00
❑ 30 David Wells 5.00 2.00
❑ 31 Jason Varitek 8.00 3.00
❑ 32 Josh Beckett 5.00 2.00
❑ 33 Kevin Youkilis 5.00 2.00
❑ 34 Manny Ramirez 8.00 3.00
❑ 35 Matt Clement 5.00 2.00
❑ 36 Mike Lowell 5.00 2.00
❑ 37 Tim Wakefield 5.00 2.00
❑ 38 Trot Nixon 5.00 2.00
❑ 39 Aramis Ramirez 5.00 2.00
❑ 40 Carlos Zambrano 5.00 2.00
❑ 41 Derrek Lee 5.00 2.00
❑ 42 Greg Maddux 12.00 5.00
❑ 43 Juan Pierre 5.00 2.00
❑ 44 Kerry Wood 5.00 2.00
❑ 45 Mark Prior 8.00 3.00
❑ 46 Michael Barrett 5.00 2.00
❑ 47 Ryan Dempster 5.00 2.00
❑ 48 Todd Walker 5.00 2.00
❑ 49 Wade Miller 5.00 2.00
❑ 50 A.J. Pierzynski 5.00 2.00
❑ 51 Brian Anderson (RC) 5.00 2.00
❑ 52 Frank Thomas 8.00 3.00
❑ 53 Javier Vazquez 5.00 2.00
❑ 54 Jim Thome 8.00 3.00
❑ 55 Joe Crede 5.00 2.00
❑ 56 Jon Garland 5.00 2.00
❑ 57 Juan Uribe 5.00 2.00
❑ 58 Mark Buehrle 5.00 2.00
❑ 59 Paul Konerko 5.00 2.00
❑ 60 Scott Podsednik 5.00 2.00
❑ 61 Tadahito Iguchi 5.00 2.00
❑ 62 Aaron Harang 5.00 2.00
❑ 63 Adam Dunn 5.00 2.00
❑ 64 Austin Kearns 5.00 2.00
❑ 65 Edwin Encarnacion 5.00 2.00
❑ 66 Eric Milton 5.00 2.00
❑ 67 Felipe Lopez 5.00 2.00
❑ 68 Jason LaRue 5.00 2.00
❑ 69 Ken Griffey Jr. 12.00 5.00
❑ 70 Wily Mo Pena 5.00 2.00
❑ 71 Aaron Boone 5.00 2.00
❑ 72 Ben Broussard 5.00 2.00
❑ 73 C.C. Sabathia 5.00 2.00
❑ 74 Casey Blake 5.00 2.00
❑ 75 Cliff Lee 5.00 2.00
❑ 76 Grady Sizemore 8.00 3.00
❑ 77 Jake Westbrook 5.00 2.00
❑ 78 Josh Bard 5.00 2.00
❑ 79 Travis Hafner 5.00 2.00
❑ 80 Victor Martinez 5.00 2.00
❑ 81 Chin-hui Tsao 5.00 2.00
❑ 82 Clint Barmes 5.00 2.00
❑ 83 Garrett Atkins 5.00 2.00
❑ 84 Josh Wilson (RC) 5.00 2.00
❑ 85 Luis Gonzalez 5.00 2.00
❑ 86 Matt Holliday 5.00 2.00
❑ 87 Todd Helton 8.00 3.00
❑ 88 Brandon Inge 5.00 2.00
❑ 89 Carlos Guillen 5.00 2.00
❑ 90 Chris Shelton 5.00 2.00
❑ 91 Craig Monroe 5.00 2.00
❑ 92 Dmitri Young 5.00 2.00
❑ 93 Ivan Rodriguez 8.00 3.00
❑ 94 Jeremy Bonderman 5.00 2.00
❑ 95 Magglio Ordonez 5.00 2.00
❑ 96 Alex Gonzalez 5.00 2.00
❑ 97 Brian Moehler 5.00 2.00
❑ 98 Dontrelle Willis 5.00 2.00
❑ 99 Jeremy Hermida (RC) 8.00 3.00
❑ 100 Jason Vargas 5.00 2.00
❑ 101 Miguel Cabrera 8.00 3.00
❑ 102 Adam Everett 5.00 2.00
❑ 103 Andy Pettitte 5.00 2.00
❑ 104 Brad Ausmus 5.00 2.00
❑ 105 Brad Lidge 5.00 2.00
❑ 106 Craig Biggio 8.00 3.00
❑ 107 Dan Wheeler 5.00 2.00
❑ 108 Jeff Bagwell 8.00 3.00
❑ 109 Lance Berkman 5.00 2.00
❑ 110 Morgan Ensberg 5.00 2.00
❑ 111 Preston Wilson 5.00 2.00
❑ 112 Roger Clemens 15.00 6.00
❑ 113 Roy Oswalt 5.00 2.00
❑ 114 Dave Gassner (RC) 5.00 2.00
❑ 115 Angel Berroa 5.00 2.00
❑ 116 Doug Mientkiewicz 5.00 2.00
❑ 117 Joe Mays 5.00 2.00
❑ 118 Mark Grudzielanek 5.00 2.00
❑ 119 Mike Sweeney 5.00 2.00
❑ 120 Reggie Sanders 5.00 2.00
❑ 121 Runelvys Hernandez 5.00 2.00
❑ 122 Scott Elarton 5.00 2.00
❑ 123 Brandon Watson (RC) 5.00 2.00
❑ 124 Zack Greinke 5.00 2.00
❑ 125 Brad Penny 5.00 2.00
❑ 126 Derek Lowe 5.00 2.00
❑ 127 Eric Gagne 5.00 2.00
❑ 128 J.D. Drew 5.00 2.00
❑ 129 Jayson Werth 5.00 2.00
❑ 130 Jeff Kent 5.00 2.00
❑ 131 Nomar Garciaparra 8.00 3.00
❑ 132 Olmedo Saenz 5.00 2.00
❑ 133 Rafael Furcal 5.00 2.00
❑ 134 Ben Sheets 5.00 2.00
❑ 135 Bill Hall 5.00 2.00
❑ 136 Carlos Lee 5.00 2.00
❑ 137 Geoff Jenkins 5.00 2.00
❑ 138 Prince Fielder (RC) 15.00 6.00
❑ 139 Rickie Weeks 5.00 2.00
❑ 140 Jose Capellan (RC) 5.00 2.00
❑ 141 Brad Radke 5.00 2.00
❑ 142 Joe Mauer 8.00 3.00
❑ 143 Joe Nathan 5.00 2.00
❑ 144 Johan Santana 8.00 3.00
❑ 145 Justin Morneau 5.00 2.00
❑ 146 Kyle Lohse 5.00 2.00
❑ 147 Lew Ford 5.00 2.00
❑ 148 Luis Castillo 5.00 2.00
❑ 149 Matt LeCroy 5.00 2.00
❑ 150 Michael Cuddyer 5.00 2.00
❑ 151 Shannon Stewart 5.00 2.00
❑ 152 Torii Hunter 5.00 2.00
❑ 153 Billy Wagner 5.00 2.00
❑ 154 Carlos Beltran 5.00 2.00
❑ 155 Carlos Delgado 5.00 2.00
❑ 156 Cliff Floyd 5.00 2.00
❑ 157 David Wright 12.00 5.00
❑ 158 Jose Reyes 5.00 2.00
❑ 159 Kazuo Matsui 5.00 2.00
❑ 160 Mike Piazza 8.00 3.00
❑ 161 Paul Lo Duca 5.00 2.00
❑ 162 Pedro Martinez 8.00 3.00
❑ 163 Tom Glavine 8.00 3.00
❑ 164 Victor Diaz 5.00 2.00
❑ 165 Alex Rodriguez 12.00 5.00
❑ 166 Bernie Williams 8.00 3.00
❑ 167 Carl Pavano 5.00 2.00
❑ 168 Chien-Ming Wang 12.00 5.00
❑ 169 Derek Jeter 20.00 8.00
❑ 170 Gary Sheffield 5.00 2.00
❑ 171 Hideki Matsui 8.00 3.00
❑ 172 Jason Giambi 5.00 2.00
❑ 173 Johnny Damon 8.00 3.00
❑ 174 Jorge Posada 8.00 3.00
❑ 175 Robinson Cano 8.00 3.00
❑ 176 Mariano Rivera 8.00 3.00
❑ 177 Mike Mussina 8.00 3.00
❑ 178 Randy Johnson 8.00 3.00
❑ 179 Miguel Cairo 5.00 2.00
❑ 180 Barry Zito 5.00 2.00
❑ 181 Bobby Crosby 5.00 2.00
❑ 182 Bobby Kielty 5.00 2.00
❑ 183 Eric Chavez 5.00 2.00
❑ 184 Josh Barfield (RC) 5.00 2.00
❑ 185 Esteban Loaiza 5.00 2.00
❑ 186 Huston Street 5.00 2.00
❑ 187 Jason Kendall 5.00 2.00
❑ 188 Nick Swisher 5.00 2.00
❑ 189 Aaron Rowand 5.00 2.00
❑ 190 Bobby Abreu 5.00 2.00
❑ 191 Chase Utley 8.00 3.00
❑ 192 Gavin Floyd 5.00 2.00
❑ 193 Jimmy Rollins 5.00 2.00
❑ 194 Mike Lieberthal 5.00 2.00
❑ 195 Pat Burrell 5.00 2.00
❑ 196 Ryan Howard 10.00 4.00
❑ 197 Craig Wilson 5.00 2.00
❑ 198 Jack Wilson 5.00 2.00
❑ 199 Jason Bay 5.00 2.00
❑ 200 Joe Randa 5.00 2.00
❑ 201 Josh Fogg 5.00 2.00
❑ 202 Kip Wells 5.00 2.00
❑ 203 Sean Casey 5.00 2.00
❑ 204 Zach Duke 5.00 2.00
❑ 205 Brian Giles 5.00 2.00
❑ 206 Dave Roberts 5.00 2.00
❑ 207 Jake Peavy 5.00 2.00
❑ 208 Khalil Greene 8.00 3.00
❑ 209 Mike Cameron 5.00 2.00
❑ 210 Ryan Klesko 5.00 2.00
❑ 211 Trevor Hoffman 5.00 2.00
❑ 212 Vinny Castilla 5.00 2.00
❑ 213 Armando Benitez 5.00 2.00
❑ 214 Jason Schmidt 5.00 2.00
❑ 215 Matt Morris 5.00 2.00
❑ 216 Moises Alou 5.00 2.00
❑ 217 Omar Vizquel 8.00 3.00
❑ 218 Ray Durham 5.00 2.00
❑ 219 Adrian Beltre 5.00 2.00
❑ 220 Carl Everett 5.00 2.00
❑ 221 Kenji Johjima RC 15.00 6.00
❑ 222 Felix Hernandez 8.00 3.00
❑ 223 Ichiro Suzuki 12.00 5.00
❑ 224 Jamie Moyer 5.00 2.00
❑ 225 Jeremy Reed 5.00 2.00
❑ 226 Joel Pineiro 5.00 2.00
❑ 227 Raul Ibanez 5.00 2.00
❑ 228 Richie Sexson 5.00 2.00
❑ 229 Albert Pujols 15.00 6.00
❑ 230 Chris Carpenter 5.00 2.00
❑ 231 David Eckstein 5.00 2.00
❑ 232 Jason Marquis 5.00 2.00
❑ 233 Jeff Suppan 5.00 2.00
❑ 234 Jim Edmonds 8.00 3.00
❑ 235 Yadier Molina 5.00 2.00
❑ 236 Mark Mulder 5.00 2.00
❑ 237 Scott Rolen 8.00 3.00
❑ 238 Alex Scott Gonzalez 5.00 2.00
❑ 239 Aubrey Huff 5.00 2.00
❑ 240 Carl Crawford 5.00 2.00
❑ 241 Casey Fossum 5.00 2.00
❑ 242 Joey Gathright 5.00 2.00
❑ 243 Scott Kazmir 5.00 2.00
❑ 244 Toby Hall 5.00 2.00

- ❑ 245 Travis Lee 5.00 2.00
- ❑ 246 Adam Eaton 5.00 2.00
- ❑ 247 Francisco Cordero 5.00 2.00
- ❑ 248 Hank Blalock 5.00 2.00
- ❑ 249 Kevin Mench 5.00 2.00
- ❑ 250 Kevin Millwood 5.00 2.00
- ❑ 251 Laynce Nix 5.00 2.00
- ❑ 252 Mark Teixeira 8.00 3.00
- ❑ 253 Michael Young 5.00 2.00
- ❑ 254 A.J. Burnett 5.00 2.00
- ❑ 255 Alex Rios 5.00 2.00
- ❑ 256 B.J. Ryan 5.00 2.00
- ❑ 257 Corey Koskie 5.00 2.00
- ❑ 258 Josh Towers 5.00 2.00
- ❑ 259 Lyle Overbay 5.00 2.00
- ❑ 260 Reed Johnson 5.00 2.00
- ❑ 261 Roy Halladay 5.00 2.00
- ❑ 262 Russ Adams 5.00 2.00
- ❑ 263 Troy Glaus 5.00 2.00
- ❑ 264 Vernon Wells 5.00 2.00
- ❑ 265 Alfonso Soriano 5.00 2.00
- ❑ 266 John Patterson 5.00 2.00
- ❑ 267 Damian Jackson 5.00 2.00
- ❑ 268 Jose Guillen 5.00 2.00
- ❑ 269 Jose Vidro 5.00 2.00
- ❑ 270 Livan Hernandez 5.00 2.00
- ❑ 271 Adam Kennedy 5.00 2.00
- ❑ 272 Bartolo Colon 5.00 2.00
- ❑ 273 Bengie Molina 5.00 2.00
- ❑ 274 Casey Kotchman 5.00 2.00
- ❑ 275 Chone Figgins 5.00 2.00
- ❑ 276 Matt Cain (RC) 8.00 3.00
- ❑ 277 Darin Erstad 5.00 2.00
- ❑ 278 Edgardo Alfonzo 5.00 2.00
- ❑ 279 Francisco Rodriguez 5.00 2.00
- ❑ 280 Garret Anderson 5.00 2.00
- ❑ 281 Vladimir Guerrero 8.00 3.00
- ❑ 282 Chris Denorfia (RC) 5.00 2.00
- ❑ 283 Joey Devine RC 5.00 2.00
- ❑ 284 Justin Verlander (RC) 15.00 6.00
- ❑ 285 Scott Feldman RC 5.00 2.00
- ❑ 286 Jason Bergmann RC 5.00 2.00
- ❑ 287 Jeremy Accardo RC 5.00 2.00
- ❑ 288 Adam Wainwright (RC) 8.00 3.00
- ❑ 289 Hanley Ramirez (RC) 6.00 2.50
- ❑ 290 Josh Johnson (RC) 8.00 3.00
- ❑ 291 Ryan Zimmerman (RC) 25.00 10.00
- ❑ 292 Anderson Hernandez (RC) 5.00 2.00
- ❑ 293 Francisco Liriano (RC) 20.00 8.00
- ❑ 294 Josh Willingham (RC) 5.00 2.00
- ❑ 295 Hong-Chih Kuo (RC) 10.00 4.00
- ❑ 296 Steve Stemle RC 5.00 2.00
- ❑ 297 Jeff Harris RC 5.00 2.00
- ❑ 298 John Van Benschoten (RC) 5.00 2.00
- ❑ 299 Jonathan Papelbon (RC) 20.00 8.00
- ❑ 300 Jason Kubel (RC) 5.00 2.00

2006 Upper Deck First Pitch

- ❑ COMPLETE SET (220) 50.00 20.00
- ❑ 1 Chad Tracy .30 .10
- ❑ 2 Conor Jackson .30 .10
- ❑ 3 Craig Counsell .30 .10
- ❑ 4 Javier Vazquez .30 .10
- ❑ 5 Luis Gonzalez .30 .10
- ❑ 6 Shawn Green .30 .10
- ❑ 7 Troy Glaus .30 .10
- ❑ 8 Joey Devine RC .50 .20
- ❑ 9 Andruw Jones .50 .20
- ❑ 10 Chipper Jones .75 .30
- ❑ 11 John Smoltz .50 .20
- ❑ 12 Marcus Giles .30 .10
- ❑ 13 Jeff Francoeur .75 .30
- ❑ 14 Tim Hudson .30 .10
- ❑ 15 Brian Roberts .30 .10
- ❑ 16 Erik Bedard .30 .10
- ❑ 17 Javy Lopez .30 .10
- ❑ 18 Melvin Mora .30 .10
- ❑ 19 Miguel Tejada .30 .10
- ❑ 20 Alejandro Freire RC .50 .20
- ❑ 21 Sammy Sosa .75 .30
- ❑ 22 Craig Hansen RC 3.00 1.25
- ❑ 23 Curt Schilling .50 .20
- ❑ 24 David Ortiz .75 .30
- ❑ 25 Edgar Renteria .30 .10
- ❑ 26 Johnny Damon .50 .20
- ❑ 27 Manny Ramirez .50 .20
- ❑ 28 Matt Clement .30 .10
- ❑ 29 Trot Nixon .30 .10
- ❑ 30 Aramis Ramirez .30 .10
- ❑ 31 Carlos Zambrano .30 .10
- ❑ 32 Derrek Lee .50 .20
- ❑ 33 Greg Maddux 1.25 .50
- ❑ 34 Jeromy Burnitz .30 .10
- ❑ 35 Kerry Wood .30 .10
- ❑ 36 Mark Prior .50 .20
- ❑ 37 Nomar Garciaparra .75 .30
- ❑ 38 Aaron Rowand .30 .10
- ❑ 39 Chris DeMaria RC .50 .20
- ❑ 40 Jon Garland .30 .10
- ❑ 41 Mark Buehrle .30 .10
- ❑ 42 Paul Konerko .30 .10
- ❑ 43 Scott Podsednik .30 .10
- ❑ 44 Tadahito Iguchi .30 .10
- ❑ 45 Adam Dunn .30 .10
- ❑ 46 Austin Kearns .30 .10
- ❑ 47 Felipe Lopez .30 .10
- ❑ 48 Ken Griffey Jr. 1.25 .50
- ❑ 49 Ryan Freel .30 .10
- ❑ 50 Sean Casey .30 .10
- ❑ 51 Wily Mo Pena .30 .10
- ❑ 52 C.C. Sabathia .30 .10
- ❑ 53 Cliff Lee .30 .10
- ❑ 54 Coco Crisp .30 .10
- ❑ 55 Grady Sizemore .50 .20
- ❑ 56 Jake Westbrook .30 .10
- ❑ 57 Travis Hafner .30 .10
- ❑ 58 Victor Martinez .30 .10
- ❑ 59 Aaron Miles .30 .10
- ❑ 60 Clint Barmes .30 .10
- ❑ 61 Garrett Atkins .30 .10
- ❑ 62 Jeff Baker .30 .10
- ❑ 63 Jeff Francis .30 .10
- ❑ 64 Matt Holliday .30 .10
- ❑ 65 Todd Helton .50 .20
- ❑ 66 Carlos Guillen .30 .10
- ❑ 67 Chris Shelton .30 .10
- ❑ 68 Dmitri Young .30 .10
- ❑ 69 Ivan Rodriguez .50 .20
- ❑ 70 Jeremy Bonderman .30 .10
- ❑ 71 Magglio Ordonez .30 .10
- ❑ 72 Placido Polanco .30 .10
- ❑ 73 A.J. Burnett .30 .10
- ❑ 74 Carlos Delgado .30 .10
- ❑ 75 Dontrelle Willis .30 .10
- ❑ 76 Josh Beckett .30 .10
- ❑ 77 Juan Pierre .30 .10
- ❑ 78 Ryan Jorgensen RC .50 .20
- ❑ 79 Miguel Cabrera .50 .20
- ❑ 80 Robert Andino RC .50 .20
- ❑ 81 Andy Pettitte .50 .20
- ❑ 82 Brad Lidge .30 .10
- ❑ 83 Craig Biggio .50 .20
- ❑ 84 Jeff Bagwell .50 .20
- ❑ 85 Lance Berkman .30 .10
- ❑ 86 Morgan Ensberg .30 .10
- ❑ 87 Roger Clemens 1.50 .60
- ❑ 88 Roy Oswalt .30 .10
- ❑ 89 Angel Berroa .30 .10
- ❑ 90 David DeJesus .30 .10
- ❑ 91 Steve Stemle RC .30 .10
- ❑ 92 Jonah Bayliss RC .30 .10
- ❑ 93 Mike Sweeney .30 .10
- ❑ 94 Ryan Theriot RC .50 .20
- ❑ 95 Zack Greinke .30 .10
- ❑ 96 Brad Penny .30 .10
- ❑ 97 Cesar Izturis .30 .10
- ❑ 98 Brian Myrow RC .30 .10
- ❑ 99 Eric Gagne .30 .10
- ❑ 100 J.D. Drew .30 .10
- ❑ 101 Jeff Kent .30 .10
- ❑ 102 Milton Bradley .30 .10
- ❑ 103 Odalis Perez .30 .10
- ❑ 104 Ben Sheets .30 .10
- ❑ 105 Brady Clark .30 .10
- ❑ 106 Carlos Lee .30 .10
- ❑ 107 Geoff Jenkins .30 .10
- ❑ 108 Lyle Overbay .30 .10
- ❑ 109 Prince Fielder .75 .30
- ❑ 110 Rickie Weeks .30 .10
- ❑ 111 Jacque Jones .30 .10
- ❑ 112 Joe Mauer .75 .30
- ❑ 113 Joe Nathan .30 .10
- ❑ 114 Johan Santana .75 .30
- ❑ 115 Justin Morneau .30 .10
- ❑ 116 Chris Heintz RC .30 .10
- ❑ 117 Torii Hunter .30 .10
- ❑ 118 Carlos Beltran .30 .10
- ❑ 119 Cliff Floyd .30 .10
- ❑ 120 David Wright .75 .30
- ❑ 121 Jose Reyes .30 .10
- ❑ 122 Mike Cameron .30 .10
- ❑ 123 Mike Piazza .75 .30
- ❑ 124 Pedro Martinez .50 .20
- ❑ 125 Tom Glavine .50 .20
- ❑ 126 Alex Rodriguez 1.25 .50
- ❑ 127 Derek Jeter 2.00 .75
- ❑ 128 Gary Sheffield .30 .10
- ❑ 129 Hideki Matsui .75 .30
- ❑ 130 Jason Giambi .30 .10
- ❑ 131 Jorge Posada .50 .20
- ❑ 132 Mariano Rivera .75 .30
- ❑ 133 Mike Mussina .50 .20
- ❑ 134 Randy Johnson .75 .30
- ❑ 135 Barry Zito .30 .10
- ❑ 136 Bobby Crosby .30 .10
- ❑ 137 Danny Haren .30 .10
- ❑ 138 Eric Chavez .30 .10
- ❑ 139 Huston Street .30 .10
- ❑ 140 Ron Flores RC .50 .20
- ❑ 141 Nick Swisher .30 .10
- ❑ 142 Rich Harden .30 .10
- ❑ 143 Bobby Abreu .30 .10
- ❑ 144 Danny Sandoval RC .50 .20
- ❑ 145 Chase Utley .50 .20
- ❑ 146 Jim Thome .50 .20
- ❑ 147 Jimmy Rollins .30 .10
- ❑ 148 Pat Burrell .30 .10
- ❑ 149 Ryan Howard 1.25 .50
- ❑ 150 Craig Wilson .30 .10
- ❑ 151 Jack Wilson .30 .10
- ❑ 152 Jason Bay .30 .10
- ❑ 153 Matt Lawton .30 .10
- ❑ 154 Oliver Perez .30 .10
- ❑ 155 Rob Mackowiak .30 .10

- ❑ 156 Zach Duke .50 .20
- ❑ 157 Brian Giles .30 .10
- ❑ 158 Jake Peavy .30 .10
- ❑ 159 Craig Breslow RC .50 .20
- ❑ 160 Khalil Greene .50 .20
- ❑ 161 Mark Loretta .30 .10
- ❑ 162 Ryan Klesko .30 .10
- ❑ 163 Trevor Hoffman .30 .10
- ❑ 164 J.T. Snow .30 .10
- ❑ 165 Jason Schmidt .30 .10
- ❑ 166 Marquis Grissom .30 .10
- ❑ 167 Moises Alou .30 .10
- ❑ 168 Omar Vizquel .50 .20
- ❑ 169 Pedro Feliz .30 .10
- ❑ 170 Jeremy Accardo RC .50 .20
- ❑ 171 Adrian Beltre .30 .10
- ❑ 172 Ichiro Suzuki 1.25 .50
- ❑ 173 Felix Hernandez .50 .20
- ❑ 174 Jeff Harris RC .30 .10
- ❑ 175 Randy Winn .30 .10
- ❑ 176 Raul Ibanez .30 .10
- ❑ 177 Richie Sexson .30 .10
- ❑ 178 Albert Pujols 1.50 .60
- ❑ 179 Chris Carpenter .30 .10
- ❑ 180 David Eckstein .30 .10
- ❑ 181 Jim Edmonds .30 .10
- ❑ 182 Larry Walker .50 .20
- ❑ 183 Matt Morris .30 .10
- ❑ 184 Reggie Sanders .30 .10
- ❑ 185 Scott Rolen .50 .20
- ❑ 186 Aubrey Huff .30 .10
- ❑ 187 Jonny Gomes .30 .10
- ❑ 188 Carl Crawford .30 .10
- ❑ 189 Tim Corcoran RC .50 .20
- ❑ 190 Julio Lugo .30 .10
- ❑ 191 Rocco Baldelli .30 .10
- ❑ 192 Scott Kazmir .30 .10
- ❑ 193 Alfonso Soriano .30 .10
- ❑ 194 Hank Blalock .30 .10
- ❑ 195 Kenny Rogers .30 .10
- ❑ 196 Scott Feldman RC .30 .10
- ❑ 197 Laynce Nix .30 .10
- ❑ 198 Mark Teixeira .50 .20
- ❑ 199 Michael Young .30 .10
- ❑ 200 Aaron Hill .30 .10
- ❑ 201 Alex Rios .30 .10
- ❑ 202 Eric Hinske .30 .10
- ❑ 203 Gustavo Chacin .30 .10
- ❑ 204 Roy Halladay .30 .10
- ❑ 205 Shea Hillenbrand .30 .10
- ❑ 206 Vernon Wells .30 .10
- ❑ 207 Brad Wilkerson .30 .10
- ❑ 208 Chad Cordero .30 .10
- ❑ 209 Jose Guillen .30 .10
- ❑ 210 Jose Vidro .30 .10
- ❑ 211 Livan Hernandez .30 .10
- ❑ 212 Preston Wilson .30 .10
- ❑ 213 Jason Bergmann RC .30 .10
- ❑ 214 Bartolo Colon .30 .10
- ❑ 215 Chone Figgins .30 .10
- ❑ 216 Darin Erstad .30 .10
- ❑ 217 Francisco Rodriguez .30 .10
- ❑ 218 Garret Anderson .30 .10
- ❑ 219 Steve Finley .30 .10
- ❑ 220 Vladimir Guerrero .75 .30

2001 Upper Deck Ovation

- ❑ COMP.SET w/o SP'S (60) 20.00 8.00
- ❑ COMMON CARD (1-60) .40 .15
- ❑ COMMON WP (61-90) 5.00 2.00
- ❑ 1 Troy Glaus .40 .15
- ❑ 2 Darin Erstad .40 .15
- ❑ 3 Jason Giambi .40 .15
- ❑ 4 Tim Hudson .40 .15
- ❑ 5 Eric Chavez .40 .15
- ❑ 6 Carlos Delgado .40 .15
- ❑ 7 David Wells .40 .15

- ❑ 8 Greg Vaughn .40 .15
- ❑ 9 Omar Vizquel UER .60 .25
- ❑ 10 Jim Thome .60 .25
- ❑ 11 Roberto Alomar .60 .25
- ❑ 12 John Olerud .40 .15
- ❑ 13 Edgar Martinez .60 .25
- ❑ 14 Cal Ripken 3.00 1.25
- ❑ 15 Alex Rodriguez 1.50 .60
- ❑ 16 Ivan Rodriguez .60 .25
- ❑ 17 Manny Ramirez Sox .60 .25
- ❑ 18 Nomar Garciaparra 1.50 .60
- ❑ 19 Pedro Martinez .60 .25
- ❑ 20 Jermaine Dye .40 .15
- ❑ 21 Juan Gonzalez .40 .15
- ❑ 22 Matt Lawton .40 .15
- ❑ 23 Frank Thomas 1.00 .40
- ❑ 24 Magglio Ordonez .40 .15
- ❑ 25 Bernie Williams .60 .25
- ❑ 26 Derek Jeter 2.50 1.00
- ❑ 27 Roger Clemens 2.00 .75
- ❑ 28 Jeff Bagwell .60 .25
- ❑ 29 Richard Hidalgo .40 .15
- ❑ 30 Chipper Jones 1.00 .40
- ❑ 31 Greg Maddux 1.50 .60
- ❑ 32 Andruw Jones .60 .25
- ❑ 33 Jeromy Burnitz .40 .15
- ❑ 34 Mark McGwire 2.50 1.00
- ❑ 35 Jim Edmonds .40 .15
- ❑ 36 Sammy Sosa 1.00 .40
- ❑ 37 Kerry Wood .40 .15
- ❑ 38 Randy Johnson 1.00 .40
- ❑ 39 Steve Finley .40 .15
- ❑ 40 Gary Sheffield .40 .15
- ❑ 41 Kevin Brown .40 .15
- ❑ 42 Shawn Green .40 .15
- ❑ 43 Vladimir Guerrero 1.00 .40
- ❑ 44 Jose Vidro .40 .15
- ❑ 45 Barry Bonds 2.50 1.00
- ❑ 46 Jeff Kent .40 .15
- ❑ 47 Preston Wilson .40 .15
- ❑ 48 Luis Castillo .40 .15
- ❑ 49 Mike Piazza 1.50 .60
- ❑ 50 Edgardo Alfonzo .40 .15
- ❑ 51 Tony Gwynn 1.25 .50
- ❑ 52 Ryan Klesko .40 .15
- ❑ 53 Scott Rolen .60 .25
- ❑ 54 Bob Abreu .40 .15
- ❑ 55 Jason Kendall .40 .15
- ❑ 56 Brian Giles .40 .15
- ❑ 57 Ken Griffey Jr. 1.50 .60
- ❑ 58 Barry Larkin .60 .25
- ❑ 59 Todd Helton .60 .25
- ❑ 60 Mike Hampton .40 .15
- ❑ 61 Corey Patterson WP 5.00 2.00
- ❑ 62 Timo Perez WP 5.00 2.00
- ❑ 63 Toby Hall WP 5.00 2.00
- ❑ 64 Brandon Inge WP 5.00 2.00
- ❑ 65 Joe Crede WP 8.00 3.00
- ❑ 66 Xavier Nady WP 5.00 2.00
- ❑ 67 Adam Pettyjohn WP RC 5.00 2.00
- ❑ 68 Keith Ginter WP 5.00 2.00
- ❑ 69 Brian Cole WP 5.00 2.00
- ❑ 70 Tyler Walker WP RC 5.00 2.00
- ❑ 71 Juan Uribe WP RC 5.00 2.00
- ❑ 72 Alex Hernandez WP 5.00 2.00
- ❑ 73 Leo Estrella WP 5.00 2.00
- ❑ 74 Joey Nation WP 5.00 2.00
- ❑ 75 Aubrey Huff WP 5.00 2.00
- ❑ 76 Ichiro Suzuki WP RC 50.00 25.00
- ❑ 77 Jay Spurgeon WP 5.00 2.00
- ❑ 78 Sun Woo Kim WP 5.00 2.00
- ❑ 79 Pedro Feliz WP 5.00 2.00
- ❑ 80 Pablo Ozuna WP 5.00 2.00
- ❑ 81 Hiram Bocachica WP 5.00 2.00
- ❑ 82 Brad Wilkerson WP 5.00 2.00
- ❑ 83 Rocky Biddle WP 5.00 2.00
- ❑ 84 Aaron McNeal WP 5.00 2.00
- ❑ 85 Adam Bernero WP 5.00 2.00
- ❑ 86 Danys Baez WP 5.00 2.00
- ❑ 87 Dee Brown WP 5.00 2.00
- ❑ 88 Jimmy Rollins WP 5.00 2.00
- ❑ 89 Jason Hart WP 5.00 2.00
- ❑ 90 Ross Gload WP 5.00 2.00

2006 Upper Deck Ovation

- ❑ COMP.SET w/o RC's (84) 25.00 10.00
- ❑ COMMON CARD (1-84) .50 .20
- ❑ COMMON ROOKIE (85-126) 5.00 2.00
- ❑ 85-126 STATED ODDS 1:18
- ❑ 85-126 PRINT RUN 999 SERIAL #'d SETS
- ❑ EXQUISITE EXCH ODDS 1:144
- ❑ EXQUISITE EXCH DEADLINE 07/27/07
- ❑ 1 Vladimir Guerrero 1.25 .50
- ❑ 2 Bartolo Colon .50 .20
- ❑ 3 Chone Figgins .50 .20
- ❑ 4 Lance Berkman .50 .20
- ❑ 5 Roy Oswalt .50 .20
- ❑ 6 Craig Biggio .75 .30
- ❑ 7 Rich Harden .50 .20
- ❑ 8 Eric Chavez .50 .20
- ❑ 9 Huston Street .50 .20
- ❑ 10 Vernon Wells .50 .20
- ❑ 11 Roy Halladay .50 .20
- ❑ 12 Troy Glaus .50 .20
- ❑ 13 Andruw Jones .75 .30
- ❑ 14 Chipper Jones 1.25 .50
- ❑ 15 John Smoltz .75 .30
- ❑ 16 Carlos Lee .50 .20
- ❑ 17 Rickie Weeks .50 .20
- ❑ 18 J.J. Hardy .50 .20
- ❑ 19 Albert Pujols 2.50 1.00
- ❑ 20 Chris Carpenter .50 .20
- ❑ 21 Scott Rolen .75 .30
- ❑ 22 Derrek Lee .50 .20
- ❑ 23 Mark Prior .75 .30
- ❑ 24 Aramis Ramirez .50 .20
- ❑ 25 Carl Crawford .50 .20
- ❑ 26 Scott Kazmir .75 .30
- ❑ 27 Luis Gonzalez .50 .20
- ❑ 28 Brandon Webb .50 .20
- ❑ 29 Chad Tracy .50 .20
- ❑ 30 Jeff Kent .50 .20

Card		
❑ 31 J.D. Drew	.50	.20
❑ 32 Jason Schmidt	.50	.20
❑ 33 Randy Winn	.50	.20
❑ 34 Travis Hafner	.50	.20
❑ 35 Victor Martinez	.50	.20
❑ 36 Grady Sizemore	.75	.30
❑ 37 Ichiro Suzuki	2.00	.75
❑ 38 Felix Hernandez	.75	.30
❑ 39 Adrian Beltre	.50	.20
❑ 40 Miguel Cabrera	.75	.30
❑ 41 Dontrelle Willis	.50	.20
❑ 42 David Wright	2.00	.75
❑ 43 Jose Reyes	.50	.20
❑ 44 Pedro Martinez	.75	.30
❑ 45 Carlos Beltran	.50	.20
❑ 46 Alfonso Soriano	.50	.20
❑ 47 Livan Hernandez	.50	.20
❑ 48 Jose Guillen	.50	.20
❑ 49 Miguel Tejada	.50	.20
❑ 50 Brian Roberts	.50	.20
❑ 51 Melvin Mora	.50	.20
❑ 52 Jake Peavy	.50	.20
❑ 53 Brian Giles	.50	.20
❑ 54 Khalil Greene	.75	.30
❑ 55 Bobby Abreu	.50	.20
❑ 56 Ryan Howard	2.00	.75
❑ 57 Chase Utley	1.25	.50
❑ 58 Jason Bay	.50	.20
❑ 59 Sean Casey	.50	.20
❑ 60 Mark Teixeira	.75	.30
❑ 61 Michael Young	.50	.20
❑ 62 Hank Blalock	.50	.20
❑ 63 Manny Ramirez	.75	.30
❑ 64 David Ortiz	1.25	.50
❑ 65 Josh Beckett	.50	.20
❑ 66 Jason Varitek	1.25	.50
❑ 67 Ken Griffey Jr.	2.00	.75
❑ 68 Adam Dunn	.50	.20
❑ 69 Todd Helton	.75	.30
❑ 70 Garrett Atkins	.50	.20
❑ 71 Reggie Sanders	.50	.20
❑ 72 Mike Sweeney	.50	.20
❑ 73 Chris Shelton	.50	.20
❑ 74 Ivan Rodriguez	.75	.30
❑ 75 Johan Santana	.75	.30
❑ 76 Torii Hunter	.50	.20
❑ 77 Justin Morneau	.50	.20
❑ 78 Jim Thome	.75	.30
❑ 79 Paul Konerko	.50	.20
❑ 80 Scott Podsednik	.50	.20
❑ 81 Derek Jeter	3.00	1.25
❑ 82 Hideki Matsui	1.25	.50
❑ 83 Johnny Damon	.75	.30
❑ 84 Alex Rodriguez	2.00	.75
❑ 85 Conor Jackson (RC)	8.00	3.00
❑ 86 Joey Devine RC	5.00	2.00
❑ 87 Jonathan Papelbon (RC)	15.00	6.00
❑ 88 Freddie Bynum (RC)	5.00	2.00
❑ 89 Chris Denorfia (RC)	5.00	2.00
❑ 90 Ryan Shealy (RC)	5.00	2.00
❑ 91 Josh Wilson (RC)	8.00	3.00
❑ 92 Brian Anderson (RC)	5.00	2.00
❑ 93 Justin Verlander (RC)	12.00	5.00
❑ 94 Jeremy Hermida (RC)	8.00	3.00
❑ 95 Mike Jacobs (RC)	5.00	2.00
❑ 96 Josh Johnson (RC)	8.00	3.00
❑ 97 Hanley Ramirez (RC)	10.00	4.00
❑ 98 Josh Willingham (RC)	5.00	2.00
❑ 99 Cole Hamels (RC)	10.00	4.00
❑ 100 Hong-Chih Kuo (RC)	15.00	6.00
❑ 101 Cody Ross (RC)	5.00	2.00
❑ 102 Jose Capellan (RC)	5.00	2.00
❑ 103 Prince Fielder (RC)	12.00	5.00
❑ 104 David Gassner (RC)	5.00	2.00
❑ 105 Jason Kubel (RC)	5.00	2.00
❑ 106 Francisco Liriano (RC)	15.00	6.00
❑ 107 Anderson Hernandez (RC)	5.00	2.00
❑ 108 Boof Bonser (RC)	5.00	2.00
❑ 109 Jered Weaver (RC)	15.00	6.00
❑ 110 Ben Johnson (RC)	5.00	2.00
❑ 111 Jeff Harris RC	5.00	2.00
❑ 112 Stephen Drew (RC)	10.00	4.00
❑ 113 Matt Cain (RC)	8.00	3.00
❑ 114 Skip Schumaker (RC)	5.00	2.00
❑ 115 Adam Wainwright (RC)	8.00	3.00
❑ 116 Jeremy Sowers (RC)	5.00	2.00
❑ 117 Jason Bergmann RC	5.00	2.00
❑ 118 Chad Billingsley (RC)	15.00	6.00
❑ 119 Ryan Zimmerman (RC)	20.00	8.00
❑ 120 Macay McBride (RC)	5.00	2.00
❑ 121 Aaron Rakers (RC)	5.00	2.00
❑ 122 Alay Soler RC	5.00	2.00
❑ 123 Melky Cabrera (RC)	15.00	6.00
❑ 124 Tim Hamulack (RC)	5.00	2.00
❑ 125 Andre Ethier (RC)	12.00	5.00
❑ 126 Kenji Johjima RC	15.00	6.00
❑ NNO Exquisite Redemption	200.00	125.00

2001 Upper Deck Prospect Premieres

Card		
❑ COMP.SET w/o SP's (90)	80.00	50.00
❑ COMMON CARD (1-90)	.40	.15
❑ COMMON AUTO (91-102)	15.00	6.00
❑ 1 Jeff Mathis XRC	.50	.20
❑ 2 Jake Woods XRC	.40	.15
❑ 3 Dallas McPherson XRC	1.00	.40
❑ 4 Steven Shell XRC	.40	.15
❑ 5 Ryan Budde XRC	.40	.15
❑ 6 Kirk Saarloos XRC	.40	.15
❑ 7 Ryan Stegall XRC	.40	.15
❑ 8 Bobby Crosby XRC	3.00	1.25
❑ 9 J.T. Stotts XRC	.40	.15
❑ 10 Neal Cotts XRC	1.00	.40
❑ 11 Jeremy Bonderman XRC	5.00	2.00
❑ 12 Brandon League XRC	.40	.15
❑ 13 Tyrell Godwin XRC	.40	.15
❑ 14 Gabe Gross XRC	.50	.20
❑ 15 Chris Neylan XRC	.40	.15
❑ 16 Macay McBride XRC	.75	.30
❑ 17 Josh Burrus XRC	.40	.15
❑ 18 Adam Stern XRC	.40	.15
❑ 19 Richard Lewis XRC	.40	.15
❑ 20 Cole Barthel XRC	.40	.15
❑ 21 Mike Jones XRC	.50	.20
❑ 22 J.J. Hardy XRC	2.00	.75
❑ 23 Jon Steitz XRC	.40	.15
❑ 24 Brad Nelson XRC	.40	.15
❑ 25 Justin Pope XRC	.40	.15
❑ 26 Dan Haren XRC	2.00	.75
❑ 27 Andy Sisco XRC	.40	.15
❑ 28 Ryan Theriot XRC	.40	.15
❑ 29 Ricky Nolasco XRC	2.00	.75
❑ 30 Jon Switzer XRC	.40	.15
❑ 31 Justin Wechsler XRC	.40	.15
❑ 32 Mike Gosling XRC	.40	.15
❑ 33 Scott Hairston XRC	.50	.20
❑ 34 Brian Pilkington XRC	.40	.15
❑ 35 Kole Strayhorn XRC	.40	.15
❑ 36 David Taylor XRC	.40	.15
❑ 37 Donald Levinski XRC	.40	.15
❑ 38 Mike Hinckley XRC	.50	.20
❑ 39 Nick Long XRC	.40	.15
❑ 40 Brad Hennessey XRC	.50	.20
❑ 41 Noah Lowry XRC	2.00	.75
❑ 42 Josh Cram XRC	.40	.15
❑ 43 Jesse Foppert XRC	.50	.20
❑ 44 Julian Benavidez XRC	.40	.15
❑ 45 Dan Denham XRC	.40	.15
❑ 46 Travis Foley XRC	.40	.15
❑ 47 Mike Conroy XRC	.40	.15
❑ 48 Jake Dittler XRC	.40	.15
❑ 49 Rene Rivera XRC	.40	.15
❑ 50 John Cole XRC	.40	.15
❑ 51 Lazaro Abreu XRC	.40	.15
❑ 52 David Wright XRC	40.00	20.00
❑ 53 Aaron Heilman XRC	.50	.20
❑ 54 Len DiNardo XRC	.40	.15
❑ 55 Alhaji Turay XRC	.40	.15
❑ 56 Chris Smith XRC	.40	.15
❑ 57 Rommie Lewis XRC	.40	.15
❑ 58 Bryan Bass XRC	.40	.15
❑ 59 David Crouthers XRC	.40	.15
❑ 60 Josh Barfield XRC	3.00	1.25
❑ 61 Jake Peavy XRC	3.00	1.25
❑ 62 Ryan Howard XRC	60.00	30.00
❑ 63 Gavin Floyd XRC	1.00	.40
❑ 64 Michael Floyd XRC	.40	.15
❑ 65 Stefan Bailie XRC	.40	.15
❑ 66 Jon DeVries XRC	.40	.15
❑ 67 Steve Kelly XRC	.40	.15
❑ 68 Alan Moye XRC	.40	.15
❑ 69 Justin Gillman XRC	.40	.15
❑ 70 Jayson Nix XRC	.40	.15
❑ 71 John Draper XRC	.40	.15
❑ 72 Kenny Baugh XRC	.40	.15
❑ 73 Michael Woods XRC	.40	.15
❑ 74 Preston Larrison XRC	.50	.20
❑ 75 Matt Coenen XRC	.40	.15
❑ 76 Scott Tyler XRC	.50	.20
❑ 77 Jose Morales XRC	.40	.15
❑ 78 Corwin Malone XRC	.40	.15
❑ 79 Dennis Ulacia XRC	.40	.15
❑ 80 Andy Gonzalez XRC	.40	.15
❑ 81 Kris Honel XRC	.40	.15
❑ 82 Wyatt Allen XRC	.40	.15
❑ 83 Ryan Wing XRC	.40	.15
❑ 84 Sean Henn XRC	.40	.15
❑ 85 John-Ford Griffin XRC	.40	.15
❑ 86 Bronson Sardinha XRC	.40	.15
❑ 87 Jon Skaggs XRC	.40	.15
❑ 88 Shelley Duncan XRC	.40	.15
❑ 89 Jason Arnold XRC	.40	.15
❑ 90 Aaron Rifkin XRC	.40	.15
❑ 91 Colt Griffin AU XRC	15.00	6.00
❑ 92 J.D. Martin AU XRC	15.00	6.00
❑ 93 Justin Wayne AU XRC	15.00	6.00
❑ 94 J.VanBenschoten AU XRC	15.00	6.00
❑ 95 Chris Burke AU XRC	25.00	10.00
❑ 96 Casey Kotchman AU XRC	30.00	12.50
❑ 97 Michael Garciaparra AU XRC	15.00	6.00
❑ 98 Jake Gautreau AU XRC	15.00	6.00
❑ 99 Jerome Williams AU XRC	15.00	6.00
❑ 100 Toe Nash AU XRC	15.00	6.00
❑ 101 Joe Borchard AU XRC	15.00	6.00
❑ 102 Mark Prior AU XRC	60.00	35.00

2002 Upper Deck Prospect Premieres

Card		
❑ COMP.SET w/o SP's (72)	40.00	25.00
❑ COMMON CARD (1-60)	.40	.15
❑ COMMON CARD (61-85)	5.00	2.00
❑ COMMON CARD (86-97)	8.00	3.00
❑ COMMON RIPKEN (98-99)	2.00	.75

❑ COMMON MCGWIRE (100-105) 2.00 .75
❑ COMMON DIMAGGIO (106-109) 1.50 .60
❑ PENDER COR AVAIL.VIA MAIL EXCHANGE
❑ 1 Josh Rupe XRC .40 .15
❑ 2 Blair Johnson XRC .40 .15
❑ 3 Jason Pridie XRC .40 .15
❑ 4 Tim Gilhooly XRC .40 .15
❑ 5 Kennard Jones XRC .40 .15
❑ 6 Darrell Rasner XRC .40 .15
❑ 7 Adam Donachie XRC .40 .15
❑ 8 Josh Murray XRC .40 .15
❑ 9 Brian Dopirak XRC 1.00 .40
❑ 10 Jason Cooper XRC .40 .15
❑ 11 Zach Hammes XRC .40 .15
❑ 12 Jon Lester XRC 15.00 6.00
❑ 13 Kevin Jepsen XRC .50 .20
❑ 14 Curtis Granderson XRC 4.00 1.50
❑ 15 David Bush XRC 1.00 .40
❑ 16 Joel Guzman .75 .30
❑ 17A M.Pender UER Granderson 1.50 .60
❑ 17B Matt Pender COR
❑ 18 Derick Grigsby XRC .40 .15
❑ 19 Jeremy Reed XRC 1.00 .40
❑ 20 Jonathan Broxton XRC 1.00 .40
❑ 21 Jesse Crain XRC .75 .30
❑ 22 Justin Jones XRC .50 .20
❑ 23 Brian Slocum XRC .40 .15
❑ 24 Brian McCann XRC 6.00 2.50
❑ 25 Francisco Liriano XRC 10.00 4.00
❑ 26 Fred Lewis XRC .40 .15
❑ 27 Steve Stanley XRC .40 .15
❑ 28 Chris Snyder XRC .50 .20
❑ 29 Dan Cevette XRC .40 .15
❑ 30 Kiel Fisher XRC .50 .20
❑ 31 Brandon Weeden XRC .40 .15
❑ 32 Pat Osborn XRC .40 .15
❑ 33 Taber Lee XRC .40 .15
❑ 34 Dan Ortmeier XRC .50 .20
❑ 35 Josh Johnson XRC 4.00 1.50
❑ 36 Val Majewski XRC .40 .15
❑ 37 Larry Broadway XRC .40 .15
❑ 38 Joey Gomes XRC .40 .15
❑ 39 Eric Thomas XRC .40 .15
❑ 40 James Loney XRC 5.00 2.00
❑ 41 Charlie Morton XRC .40 .15
❑ 42 Mark McLemore XRC .40 .15
❑ 43 Matt Craig XRC .50 .20
❑ 44 Ryan Rodriguez XRC .40 .15
❑ 45 Rich Hill XRC 2.50 1.00
❑ 46 Bob Malek XRC .40 .15
❑ 47 Justin Maureau XRC .40 .15
❑ 48 Randy Braun XRC .40 .15
❑ 49 Brian Grant XRC .40 .15
❑ 50 Tyler Davidson XRC .50 .20
❑ 51 Travis Hanson XRC .50 .20
❑ 52 Kyle Boyer XRC .40 .15
❑ 53 James Holcomb XRC .40 .15
❑ 54 Ryan Williams XRC .40 .15
❑ 55 Ben Crockett XRC .40 .15
❑ 56 Adam Greenberg XRC .75 .30
❑ 57 John Baker XRC .40 .15
❑ 58 Matt Carson XRC .40 .15
❑ 59 Jonathan George XRC .40 .15
❑ 60 David Jensen XRC .40 .15
❑ 61 Nick Swisher JSY XRC 15.00 6.00
❑ 62 Brent Clevlen JSY UER XRC 12.00 5.00
❑ 63 Royce Ring JSY XRC 5.00 2.00
❑ 64 Mike Nixon JSY XRC 5.00 2.00
❑ 65 Ricky Barrett JSY XRC 5.00 2.00
❑ 66 Russ Adams JSY XRC 5.00 2.00
❑ 67 Joe Mauer JSY XRC 25.00 10.00
❑ 68 Jeff Francoeur JSY XRC 30.00 15.00
❑ 69 Joe Blanton JSY XRC 10.00 4.00
❑ 70 Micah Schilling JSY XRC 5.00 2.00
❑ 71 John McCurdy JSY XRC 5.00 2.00
❑ 72 Sergio Santos JSY XRC 8.00 3.00
❑ 73 Josh Womack JSY XRC 5.00 2.00
❑ 74 Jared Doyle JSY XRC 5.00 2.00
❑ 75 Ben Fritz JSY XRC 5.00 2.00
❑ 76 Greg Miller JSY XRC 5.00 2.00
❑ 77 Luke Hagerty JSY XRC 5.00 2.00
❑ 78 Matt Whitney JSY XRC 5.00 2.00
❑ 79 Dan Meyer JSY XRC 8.00 3.00
❑ 80 Bill Murphy JSY XRC 5.00 2.00
❑ 81 Zach Segovia JSY XRC 5.00 2.00
❑ 82 Steve Obenchain JSY XRC 5.00 2.00
❑ 83 Matt Clanton JSY XRC 5.00 2.00
❑ 84 Mark Teahen JSY XRC 8.00 3.00
❑ 85 Kyle Pawelczyk JSY XRC 5.00 2.00
❑ 86 Khalil Greene AU XRC 40.00 20.00
❑ 87 Joe Saunders AU XRC 15.00 6.00
❑ 88 Jeremy Hermida AU XRC 50.00 30.00
❑ 89 Drew Meyer AU XRC 8.00 3.00
❑ 90 Jeff Francis AU XRC 15.00 6.00
❑ 91 Scott Moore AU XRC 8.00 3.00
❑ 92 Prince Fielder AU XRC 120.00 70.00
❑ 93 Zack Greinke AU XRC 25.00 10.00
❑ 94 Chris Gruler AU XRC 8.00 3.00
❑ 95 Scott Kazmir AU XRC 80.00 50.00
❑ 96 B.J. Upton AU XRC 50.00 30.00
❑ 97 Clint Everts AU XRC 8.00 3.00
❑ 98 Cal Ripken TRIB 2.00 .75
❑ 99 Cal Ripken TRIB 2.00 .75
❑ 100 Mark McGwire TRIB 2.00 .75
❑ 101 Mark McGwire TRIB 2.00 .75
❑ 102 Mark McGwire TRIB 2.00 .75
❑ 103 Mark McGwire TRIB 2.00 .75
❑ 104 Mark McGwire TRIB 2.00 .75
❑ 105 Joe DiMaggio TRIB 1.50 .60
❑ 106 Joe DiMaggio TRIB 1.50 .60
❑ 107 Joe DiMaggio TRIB 1.50 .60
❑ 108 Joe DiMaggio TRIB 1.50 .60
❑ 109 Joe DiMaggio TRIB 1.50 .60

2003 Upper Deck Prospect Premieres

❑ COMPLETE SET (90) 40.00 20.00
❑ 1 Bryan Opdyke XRC .40 .15
❑ 2 Gabriel Sosa XRC .40 .15
❑ 3 Tila Reynolds XRC .40 .15
❑ 4 Aaron Hill XRC .75 .30
❑ 5 Aaron Marsden XRC .50 .20
❑ 6 Abe Alvarez XRC .50 .20
❑ 7 Adam Jones XRC 5.00 2.00
❑ 8 Adam Miller XRC 2.50 1.00
❑ 9 Andre Ethier XRC 8.00 3.00
❑ 10 Anthony Gwynn XRC 1.25 .50
❑ 11 Brad Snyder XRC .75 .30
❑ 12 Brad Sullivan XRC .50 .20
❑ 13 Brian Anderson XRC 2.00 .75
❑ 14 Brian Buscher XRC .40 .15
❑ 15 Brian Snyder XRC .50 .20
❑ 16 Carlos Quentin XRC 4.00 1.50
❑ 17 Chad Billingsley XRC 4.00 1.50
❑ 18 Fraser Dizard XRC .40 .15
❑ 19 Chris Durbin XRC .40 .15
❑ 20 Chris Ray XRC 1.00 .40
❑ 21 Conor Jackson XRC 4.00 1.50
❑ 22 Kory Casto XRC .50 .20
❑ 23 Craig Whitaker XRC .50 .20
❑ 24 Daniel Moore XRC .40 .15
❑ 25 Daric Barton XRC 3.00 1.25
❑ 26 Darin Downs XRC .50 .20
❑ 27 David Murphy XRC .75 .30
❑ 28 Dustin Majewski XRC .50 .20
❑ 29 Edgardo Baez XRC .50 .20
❑ 30 Jake Fox XRC .75 .30
❑ 31 Jake Stevens XRC .50 .20
❑ 32 Jamie D'Antona XRC .75 .30
❑ 33 James Houser XRC .50 .20
❑ 34 Jarrod Saltalamacchia XRC 4.00 1.50
❑ 35 Jason Hirsh XRC 2.00 .75
❑ 36 Javi Herrera XRC .50 .20
❑ 37 Jeff Allison XRC .40 .15
❑ 38 John Hudgins XRC .40 .15
❑ 39 Jo Jo Reyes XRC 1.25 .50
❑ 40 Justin James XRC .40 .15
❑ 41 Kurt Isenberg XRC .40 .15
❑ 42 Kyle Boyer XRC .40 .15
❑ 43 Lastings Milledge XRC 5.00 2.00
❑ 44 Luis Atilano XRC .40 .15
❑ 45 Matt Murton XRC 2.00 .75
❑ 46 Matt Moses XRC .75 .30
❑ 47 Matt Harrison XRC .75 .30
❑ 48 Michael Bourn XRC .75 .30
❑ 49 Miguel Vega XRC .40 .15
❑ 50 Mitch Maier XRC .50 .20
❑ 51 Omar Quintanilla XRC .50 .20
❑ 52 Ryan Sweeney XRC 2.00 .75
❑ 53 Scott Baker XRC 1.00 .40
❑ 54 Sean Rodriguez XRC 1.50 .60
❑ 55 Steve Lerud XRC .50 .20
❑ 56 Thomas Pauly XRC .40 .15
❑ 57 Tom Gorzelanny XRC 1.25 .50
❑ 58 Tim Moss XRC .40 .15
❑ 59 Robbie Wooley XRC .50 .20
❑ 60 Trey Webb XRC .40 .15
❑ 61 Wes Littleton XRC .50 .20
❑ 62 Beau Vaughan XRC .50 .20
❑ 63 Willy Jo Ronda XRC .50 .20
❑ 64 Chris Lubanski XRC 1.00 .40
❑ 65 Ian Stewart XRC 8.00 3.00
❑ 66 John Danks XRC 1.50 .60
❑ 67 Kyle Sleeth XRC .50 .20
❑ 68 Michael Aubrey XRC .75 .30
❑ 69 Kevin Kouzmanoff XRC 4.00 1.50
❑ 70 Ryan Harvey XRC 2.00 .75
❑ 71 Tim Stauffer XRC .75 .30
❑ 72 Tony Richie XRC .40 .15
❑ 73 Brandon Wood XRC 8.00 3.00
❑ 74 David Aardsma XRC .50 .20
❑ 75 David Shinskie XRC .40 .15
❑ 76 Dennis Dove XRC .50 .20
❑ 77 Eric Sultemeier XRC .40 .15
❑ 78 Jay Sborz XRC .40 .15
❑ 79 Jimmy Barthmaier XRC .40 .15
❑ 80 Josh Whitesell XRC .40 .15
❑ 81 Josh Anderson XRC .50 .20

❑ 82 Kenny Lewis XRC .50 .20
❑ 83 Mateo Miramontes XRC .40 .15
❑ 84 Nick Markakis XRC 4.00 1.50
❑ 85 Paul Bacot XRC .50 .20
❑ 86 Peter Stonard XRC .40 .15
❑ 87 Reggie Willits XRC .40 .15
❑ 88 Shane Costa XRC .40 .15
❑ 89 Billy Sadler XRC .40 .15
❑ 90 Delmon Young XRC 8.00 3.00

2005 Upper Deck Update

❑ COMP.SET w/o SP's (100) 20.00 8.00
❑ COMMON CARD (1-100) .30 .10
❑ 1-100 ONE PER PACK
❑ COMMON CARD (101-177) 3.00 1.25
❑ 101-177: ONE #'d CARD OR AU PER PACK
❑ 101-177 PRINT RUN 599 SERIAL #'d SETS
❑ 178-186: OVERALL AU ODDS APPX 1:8
❑ 178-186 PRINT RUN 75 SERIAL #'d SETS
❑ 1 A.J. Burnett .30 .10
❑ 2 Adam Dunn .30 .10
❑ 3 Adrian Beltre .30 .10
❑ 4 Albert Pujols 1.50 .60
❑ 5 Alex Rodriguez 1.25 .50
❑ 6 Alfonso Soriano .30 .10
❑ 7 Andruw Jones .50 .20
❑ 8 Aramis Ramirez .30 .10
❑ 9 Barry Zito .30 .10
❑ 10 Bartolo Colon .30 .10
❑ 11 Ben Sheets .30 .10
❑ 12 Bobby Abreu .30 .10
❑ 13 Bobby Crosby .30 .10
❑ 14 Bret Boone .30 .10
❑ 15 Brian Giles .30 .10
❑ 16 Brian Roberts .30 .10
❑ 17 Carl Crawford .30 .10
❑ 18 Carlos Beltran .30 .10
❑ 19 Carlos Delgado .30 .10
❑ 20 Carlos Lee .30 .10
❑ 21 Carlos Zambrano .30 .10
❑ 22 Chase Utley .50 .20
❑ 23 Chipper Jones .75 .30
❑ 24 Chris Carpenter .30 .10
❑ 25 Craig Biggio .50 .20
❑ 26 Curt Schilling .50 .20
❑ 27 David Ortiz 1.00 .40
❑ 28 David Wright 1.25 .50
❑ 29 Derek Jeter 2.00 .75
❑ 30 Derrek Lee .50 .20
❑ 31 Dontrelle Willis .30 .10
❑ 32 Eric Chavez .30 .10
❑ 33 Eric Gagne .30 .10
❑ 34 Francisco Rodriguez .30 .10
❑ 35 Gary Sheffield .30 .10
❑ 36 Greg Maddux 1.25 .50
❑ 37 Hank Blalock .30 .10
❑ 38 Hideki Matsui 1.00 .40
❑ 39 Ichiro Suzuki 1.25 .50
❑ 40 Ivan Rodriguez .50 .20
❑ 41 J.D. Drew .30 .10
❑ 42 Jake Peavy .30 .10
❑ 43 Jason Bay .30 .10
❑ 44 Jason Schmidt .30 .10
❑ 45 Jeff Bagwell .50 .20
❑ 46 Jeff Kent .30 .10
❑ 47 Jeremy Bonderman .30 .10
❑ 48 Jim Edmonds .30 .10
❑ 49 Jim Thome .50 .20
❑ 50 Joe Mauer .75 .30
❑ 51 Johan Santana .75 .30
❑ 52 John Smoltz .50 .20
❑ 53 Johnny Damon .50 .20
❑ 54 Jose Reyes .30 .10
❑ 55 Jose Vidro .30 .10
❑ 56 Josh Beckett .30 .10
❑ 57 Justin Morneau .30 .10
❑ 58 Ken Griffey Jr. 1.25 .50
❑ 59 Kenny Rogers .30 .10
❑ 60 Kerry Wood .30 .10
❑ 61 Khalil Greene .50 .20
❑ 62 Lance Berkman .30 .10
❑ 63 Livan Hernandez .30 .10
❑ 64 Luis Gonzalez .30 .10
❑ 65 Manny Ramirez .50 .20
❑ 66 Mark Buehrle .30 .10
❑ 67 Mark Mulder .30 .10
❑ 68 Mark Prior .50 .20
❑ 69 Mark Teixeira .50 .20
❑ 70 Michael Young .30 .10
❑ 71 Miguel Cabrera .50 .20
❑ 72 Miguel Tejada .30 .10
❑ 73 Mike Mussina .50 .20
❑ 74 Mike Piazza .75 .30
❑ 75 Moises Alou .30 .10
❑ 76 Morgan Ensberg .30 .10
❑ 77 Nomar Garciaparra .75 .30
❑ 78 Pat Burrell .30 .10
❑ 79 Paul Konerko .30 .10
❑ 80 Pedro Martinez .50 .20
❑ 81 Randy Johnson .75 .30
❑ 82 Rich Harden .30 .10
❑ 83 Richie Sexson .30 .10
❑ 84 Rickie Weeks .30 .10
❑ 85 Robinson Cano .50 .20
❑ 86 Roger Clemens 1.25 .50
❑ 87 Roy Halladay .30 .10
❑ 88 Roy Oswalt .30 .10
❑ 89 Sammy Sosa .75 .30
❑ 90 Scott Kazmir .30 .10
❑ 91 Scott Rolen .50 .20
❑ 92 Shawn Green .30 .10
❑ 93 Tim Hudson .30 .10
❑ 94 Todd Helton .50 .20
❑ 95 Tom Glavine .50 .20
❑ 96 Torii Hunter .30 .10
❑ 97 Travis Hafner .30 .10
❑ 98 Troy Glaus .30 .10
❑ 99 Vernon Wells .30 .10
❑ 100 Vladimir Guerrero .75 .30
❑ 101 Adam Shabala PR RC 3.00 1.25
❑ 102 Ambiorix Burgos PR RC 3.00 1.25
❑ 103 Anibal Sanchez PR RC 8.00 3.00
❑ 104 Bill McCarthy PR RC 3.00 1.25
❑ 105 Brandon McCarthy PR RC 4.00 1.50
❑ 106 Brian Burres PR RC 3.00 1.25
❑ 107 Carlos Ruiz PR RC 3.00 1.25
❑ 108 Casey Rogowski PR RC 4.00 1.50
❑ 109 Chad Orvella PR RC 3.00 1.25
❑ 110 Chris Resop PR RC 3.00 1.25
❑ 111 Chris Roberson PR RC 3.00 1.25
❑ 112 Chris Seddon PR RC 3.00 1.25
❑ 113 Colter Bean PR RC 3.00 1.25
❑ 114 Dae-Sung Koo PR RC 3.00 1.25
❑ 115 Dave Gassner PR RC 3.00 1.25
❑ 116 Brian Anderson PR RC 4.00 1.50
❑ 117 D.J. Houlton PR RC 3.00 1.25
❑ 118 Derek Wathan PR RC 3.00 1.25
❑ 119 Devon Lowery PR RC 3.00 1.25
❑ 120 Enrique Gonzalez PR RC 3.00 1.25
❑ 121 Eude Brito PR RC 3.00 1.25
❑ 122 Francisco Butto PR RC 3.00 1.25
❑ 123 Franquelis Osoria PR RC 3.00 1.25
❑ 124 Garrett Jones PR RC 3.00 1.25
❑ 125 Geovany Soto PR RC 3.00 1.25
❑ 126 Hayden Penn PR RC 4.00 1.50
❑ 127 Ismael Ramirez PR RC 3.00 1.25
❑ 128 Jared Gothreaux PR RC 3.00 1.25
❑ 129 Jason Hammel PR RC 3.00 1.25
❑ 130 Jeff Miller PR RC 3.00 1.25
❑ 131 Joel Peralta PR RC 3.00 1.25
❑ 132 John Hattig PR RC 3.00 1.25
❑ 133 Jorge Campillo PR RC 3.00 1.25
❑ 134 Juan Morillo PR RC 3.00 1.25
❑ 135 Ryan Garko PR RC 5.00 2.00
❑ 136 Keiichi Yabu PR RC 3.00 1.25
❑ 137 Luis Hernandez PR RC 3.00 1.25
❑ 138 Luis Pena PR RC 3.00 1.25
❑ 139 Luis O.Rodriguez PR RC 3.00 1.25
❑ 140 Luke Scott PR RC 5.00 2.00
❑ 141 Marcos Carvajal PR RC 3.00 1.25
❑ 142 Mark Woodyard PR RC 3.00 1.25
❑ 143 Matt A.Smith PR RC 3.00 1.25
❑ 144 Matthew Lindstrom PR RC 3.00 1.25
❑ 145 Miguel Negron PR RC 4.00 1.50
❑ 146 Mike Morse PR RC 3.00 1.25
❑ 147 Nate McLouth PR RC 4.00 1.50
❑ 148 Nelson Cruz PR RC 5.00 2.00
❑ 149 Nick Masset PR RC 3.00 1.25
❑ 150 Oscar Robles PR RC 3.00 1.25
❑ 151 Paulino Reynoso PR RC 3.00 1.25
❑ 152 Pedro Lopez PR RC 3.00 1.25
❑ 153 Pete Orr PR RC 3.00 1.25
❑ 154 Randy Messenger PR RC 3.00 1.25
❑ 155 Randy Williams PR RC 3.00 1.25
❑ 156 Raul Tablado PR RC 3.00 1.25
❑ 157 Ronny Paulino PR RC 4.00 1.50
❑ 158 Russ Rohlicek PR RC 3.00 1.25
❑ 159 Russell Martin PR RC 6.00 2.50
❑ 160 Scott Baker PR RC 4.00 1.50
❑ 161 Scott Munter PR RC 3.00 1.25
❑ 162 Sean Thompson PR RC 3.00 1.25
❑ 163 Sean Tracey PR RC 3.00 1.25
❑ 164 Shane Costa PR RC 3.00 1.25
❑ 165 Steve Schmoll PR RC 3.00 1.25
❑ 166 Tony Giarratano PR RC 3.00 1.25
❑ 167 Tony Pena PR RC 3.00 1.25
❑ 168 Travis Bowyer PR RC 3.00 1.25
❑ 169 Ubaldo Jimenez PR RC 3.00 1.25
❑ 170 Wladimir Balentien PR RC 4.00 1.50
❑ 171 Yorman Bazardo PR RC 3.00 1.25
❑ 172 Yuniesky Betancourt PR RC 5.00 2.00
❑ 173 Chris Denorfia PR RC 4.00 1.50
❑ 174 Dana Eveland PR RC 3.00 1.25
❑ 175 Jermaine Van Buren PR 3.00 1.25
❑ 176 Mark McLemore PR RC 3.00 1.25
❑ 177 Ryan Spilborghs PR RC 4.00 1.50
❑ 178 Ambiorix Concepcion AU RC 15.00 6.00
❑ 179 Jeff Niemann AU RC 20.00 8.00
❑ 180 Justin Verlander AU RC 100.00 60.00
❑ 181 Kendry Morales AU RC 60.00 30.00
❑ 182 Philip Humber AU RC 20.00 8.00
❑ 183 Prince Fielder AU RC 100.00 60.00
❑ 184 Stephen Drew AU RC 150.00 75.00
❑ 185 Tadahito Iguchi AU RC 80.00 40.00
❑ 186 Ryan Zimmerman AU RC 175.00 100.00

619 / Acknowledgments

Each year we refine the process of developing the most accurate and up-to-date information for this book. I believe this year's Price Guide is our best yet. Thanks again to all the contributors nationwide (listed below) as well as our staff here in Dallas.

Those who have worked closely with us on this and many other books have again proven themselves invaluable: Ed Allan, Frank and Vivian Barning, Levi Bleam and Jim Fleck (707 Sportscards), T. Scott Brandon, Peter Brennan, Ray Bright, Card Collectors Co., Dwight Chapin, Theo Chen, Barry Colla, Bill and Diane Dodge, Brett Domue, Dan Even, David Festberg, Fleer/SkyBox (Josh Perlman), Steve Freedman, Gervise Ford, Larry and Jeff Fritsch, Tony Galovich, Georgia Music and Sports (Dick DeCourcey), Dick Gilkeson, Steve Gold (AU Sports), Bill Goodwin (St. Louis Baseball Cards), Mike and Howard Gordon, George Grauer, Steve Green (STB Sports), John Greenwald, Bill Henderson, Jerry and Etta Hersh, Mike Hersh, Neil Hoppenworth, Hunt Auction, Mike Jaspersen, Jay and Mary Kasper (Jay's Emporium), Jerry Katz, Pete Kennedy, David Kohler (SportsCards Plus), Terry Knouse (Tik and Tik), Tom Leon, Lew Lipset (Four Base Hits), Mike Livingston (U-Trading Cards), Mark Macrae, Bill Madden, Bill Mastro, Dr.William McAvoy, Michael McDonald, Mid-Atlantic Sports Cards (Bill Bossert), Gary Mills, Ernie Montella, Brian Morris, Mike Mosier (Columbia City Collectibles Co.), B.A. Murry, Ralph Nozaki, Mike O'Brien, Oldies and Goodies (Nigel Spill), Oregon Trail Auctions, Pacific Trading Cards (Mike Cramer and Mike Monson), Playoff Trading Cards (Ben Ecklar, Steve Judd, and Tracy Hackler), Jack Pollard, Jeff Prillaman, Pat Quinn, Jerald Reichstein (Fabulous Cardboard), Tom Reid, Gavin Riley, Clifton Rouse, John Rumierz, Pat Blandford, Lonn Passon and Kevin Savage (Sports Gallery), Gary Sawatski and Jim Justus (The Wizards of Odd), Mike Schechter, Bill and Darlene Shafer, Barry Sloate, John E. Spalding, Phil Spector, Murvin Sterling, Ted Taylor, Lee Temanson, Topps (Marty Appel), Treat (Harold Anderson), Ed Twombly, Upper Deck (Justin Kanoya), Wayne Varner, Rob Veres, Bill Vizas, Waukesha Sportscards, Bill Wesslund (Portland Sports Card Co.), Kit Young, Rick Young, Ted Zanidakis, Robert Zanze (Z-Cards and Sports), Bill Zimpleman, and Dean Zindler. Finally we give a special acknowledgment to the late Dennis W. Eckes, "Mr. Sport Americana." The success of the Beckett Price Guides has always been the result of a team effort.

It is very difficult to be "accurate" — one can only do one's best. But this job is especially difficult since we're shooting at a moving target: Prices are fluctuating all the time. Having several full-time pricing experts has definitely proven to be better than just one, and I thank all of them for working together to provide you, our readers, with the most accurate prices possible.

Many people have provided price input, illustrative material, checklist verifications, errata, and/or background information. We should like to individually thank AbD Cards (Dale Wesolewski), Action Card Sales, Jerry Adamic, Johnny and Sandy Adams, Mehdi Ahlei, Alex's MVP Cards & Comics, Doug Allen, Will Allison, Dennis Anderson, Ed Anderson, Shane Anderson, Ellis Anmuth, Alan Applegate, Ric Apter, Clyde Archer, Randy Archer, Burl Armstrong, Neil Armstrong, Carlos Ayala, B and J Sportscards, Jeremy Bachman, Dave Bailey, Ball Four Cards (Frank and Steve Pemper), Bob Bartosz, Bubba Bennett, Carl Berg, Beulah Sports (Jeff Blatt), B.J. Sportscollectables, David Boedicker (The Wild Pitch Inc.), Louis Bollman, Tim Bond, Andrew Bosarge, Terry Boyd, Dan Brandenberry, Jeff Breitenfield, Scott Brockleman, John Broggi, Virgil Burns, Greg Bussineau, David Byer, California Card Co., Capital Cards, Danny Cariseo, Carl Carlson (C.T.S.), Jim Carr, Ira Cetron, Sandy Chan, Ric Chandgie, Ray Cherry, Bigg Wayne Christian, Josh Chidester, Michael and Abe Citron, Dr. Jeffrey Clair, Michael Cohen, Tom Cohoon (Cardboard Dreams), Gary Collett, Rick Cosmen (RC Card Co.), Lou Costanzo (Champion Sports), Mike Coyne, Tony Craig (T.C. Card Co.), Solomon Cramer, Kevin Crane, Taylor Crane, Chad Cripe, Scott Crump, Allen Custer, Dave Dame, Scott Dantio, Dee's Baseball Cards (Dee Robinson), Joe Delgrippo, Mike DeLuca, Ken Dinerman (California Cruizers), Rob DiSalvatore, Cliff Dolgins, Discount Dorothy, Richard Dolloff (Dolloff Coin Center), Joe Donato, Jerry Dong, Pat Dorsey, Double Play Baseball Cards, Joe Drelich, Richard Duglin (Baseball Cards-N-More), The Dugout, Ken Edick (Home Plate of Utah), Brad Englehardt, Doak Ewing, Terry Falkner, Mike and Chris Fanning, Linda Ferrigno and Mark Mezzardi, Jay Finglass, Bob Flitter, Fremont Fong, Paul Franzetti, Ron Frasier, Tom Freeman, Bob Frye, Bill Fusaro, Chris Gala, Richard Galasso, David Garza, David Gaumer, Georgetown Card Exchange, David Giove, Dick Goddard, Jeff Goldstein, Ron Gomez, Rich Gove, Jay and Jan Grinsby, Bob Grissett, Gerry Guenther, Neil Gubitz (What-A-Card), Hall's Nostalgia, Hershell Hanks, Gregg Hara, Todd Harrell, Robert Harrison, Steve Hart, Floyd Haynes (H and H Baseball Cards), Kevin Heffner, Joel Hellman, Hit and Run Cards (Jon, David, and Kirk Peterson), Vinny Ho, Johnny Hustle Card Co., John Inouye, Vern Isenberg, Dale Jackson, Marshall Jackson, Mike Jardina, Paul Jastrzembski, Jeff's Sports Cards, Donn Jennings Cards, George Johnson, Craig Jones, Chuck Juliana, Nick Kardoulias, Scott Kashner, Frank and Rose Katen, Kevin's Kards, Kingdom Collectibles, Inc., John Klassnik, Steve Kluback,Don Knutsen, Gregg Kohn,

Mike Kohlhas, Bob & Bryan Kornfield, Carl and Maryanne Laron, Howard Lau, Richard S. Lawrence, William Lawrence, Brent Lee, Morley Leeking, Irv Lerner, Larry and Sally Levine, Larry Loeschen (A and J Sportscards), Neil Lopez, Kendall Loyd (Orlando Sportscards South), Steve Lowe, Jim Macie, Peter Maltin, Paul Marchant, Brian Marcy, Scott Martinez, James S. Maxwell Jr., McDag Productions Inc., Bob McDonald, Steve McHenry, Tony McLaughlin, Mendal Mearkle, Carlos Medina, Ken Melanson, William Mendel, Blake Meyer (Lone Star Sportscards), Tim Meyer, Joe Michalowicz, Lee Milazzo, Cary S. Miller, George Miller, Wayne Miller, Dick Millerd, Frank Mineo, Mitchell's Baseball Cards, John Morales, William Munn, Mark Murphy, Robert Nappe, National Sportscard Exchange, Roger Neufeldt, Steve Novella, Bud Obermeyer, John O'Hara, Glenn Olson, Scott Olson, Ron Oser, Luther Owen, Earle Parrish, Clay Pasternack, Michael Perrotta, Tom Pfirrmann, Don Phlong, Loran Pulver, Bob Ragonese, Bryan Rappaport, Don and Tom Ras, Robert M. Ray, Phil Regli, Rob Resnick, Dave Reynolds, Carson Ritchey, Bill Rodman, Craig Roehrig, Mike Sablow, Terry Sack, Thomas Salem, Barry Sanders, Jon Sands, Tony Scarpa, John Schad, Dave Schau (Baseball Cards), Masa Shinohara, Eddie Silard, Mike Slepcevic, Sam Sliheet, Art Smith, Lynn and Todd Solt, Jerry Sorice, Don Spagnolo, Sports Card Fan-Attic, The Sport Hobbyist, Norm Stapleton, Bill Steinberg, Lisa Stellato (Never Enough Cards), Rob Stenzel, Jason Stern, Andy Stoltz, Rob Stenzel, Bill Stone, Ted Straka, Tim Strandberg (East Texas Sports Cards), Edward Strauss, Strike Three, Richard Strobino, Kevin Struss, Superior Sport Card, Dr. Richard Swales, George Tahinos, Brent Thorton, Ian Taylor, The The Thirdhand Shoppe, Brent Thornton, Paul Thornton, Jim and Sally Thurtell, Bud Tompkins (Minnesota Connection), Philip J. Tremont, Ralph Triplette, Umpire's Choice Inc., Eric Unglaub, Hoyt Vanderpool, Steven Wagman, T. Wall, Gary A. Walter, Joe and John Weisenburger (The Wise Guys), Brian and Mike Wentz (BMW Sportscards), Richard West, Mike Wheat, Richard Wiercinski, Don Williams (Robin's Nest of Dolls), Jeff Williams, John Williams, Kent and Louise Williams, Craig Williamson, Rich Wojtasick, John Wolf Jr., Jay Wolt (Cavalcade of Sports), Joe Yanello, Peter Yee, Tom Zocco, Mark Zubrensky, and Tim Zwick.

Every year we make active solicitations for expert input. We are particularly appreciative of help (however extensive or cursory) provided for this volume. We receive many inquiries, comments, and questions regarding material within this book. In fact, each and every one is read and digested. Time constraints, however, prevent us from personally replying. But keep sharing your knowledge. Your letters and input are part of the "big picture" of hobby information we can pass along to readers in our books and magazines. Even though we cannot respond to each letter, you are making significant contributions to the hobby through your interest and comments.

The effort to continually refine and improve this book also involves a growing number of people and types of expertise on our home team. Our company boasts a substantial Sports Data Publishing team, which strengthens our ability to provide comprehensive analysis of the marketplace. SDP capably handled numerous technical details and provided able assistance in the preparation of this edition.

Our baseball analysts played a major part in compiling this year's book, traveling thousands of miles during the past year to attend sports card shows and visit card shops around the United States and Canada. The Beckett baseball specialists are: Gabe Harro, Rich Klein, Dave Porter, and Grant Sandground (Senior Price Guide Editor). Their pricing analysis and careful proofreading were key contributions to the accuracy of this annual.

Grant Sandground's coordination and reconciling of prices as Beckett Baseball Card Monthly Price Guide Editor helped immeasurably. Rich Klein, as research analyst, contributed detailed pricing analysis and hours of proofing.

The effort was led by Dan Hitt, the Senior Manager of Sports Data Publishing. He was ably assisted by the rest of the Price Guide analysts: Clint Hall, Keith Hower, Tony Joseph, Beverly Mills, Bill Sutherland, Tim Trout, and Joe White.

The price gathering and analytical talents of this fine group of hobbyists have helped make our Beckett team stronger, while making this guide and its companion monthly Price Guide more widely recognized as the hobby's most reliable and relied upon sources of pricing information.

The Beckett Interactive Division played a critical role in technology. They spent countless hours programming, testing, and implementing it to simplify the handling of thousands of prices that must be checked and updated for each edition.

In the years since this guide debuted, Beckett Publications has grown beyond any rational expectation. A great many talented and hard working individuals have been instrumental in this growth and success. Our whole team is to be congratulated for what we together have accomplished.

The whole Beckett Publications team has my thanks for jobs well done. Thank you, everyone.